# Collins

BESTSELLING BILINGUAL DICTIONARIES

# Polish Dictionary & Grammar

SŁOWNIK Z GRAMATYKĄ
POLSKO-ANGIELSKI
ANGIELSKO-POLSKI

**HarperCollins Publishers**
Westerhill Road
Bishopbriggs
Glasgow
G64 2QT
Great Britain

First Edition 2011

Reprint 10 9 8 7 6 5 4 3 2 1 0



ISBN 978-0-00-729845-7



www.collinslanguage.com

A catalogue record for this book is Available from the British Library

Typeset by Davidson Publishing Solutions, Glasgow

Printed in Great Britain by Clays Ltd, St Ives plc

**Acknowledgements**
We would like to thank those authors and publishers who kindly gave permission for copyright material to be used in the Collins Word Web. We would also like to thank Times Newspapers Ltd for providing valuable data.



**Contributors (1996 edition):**

**Editor-in-chief**
Jacek Fisiak

**Deputy Editor-in-chief**
Michał Jankowski

**Editor of the English-Polish Dictionary Text**
Arleta Adamska-Sałaciak

**Editor of the Polish-English Dictionary Text**
Mariusz Idzikowski

**Lexicographers**
Marek Daroszewski
Przemysław Kaszubski
Janusz Kaźmierczak
Agnieszka Kiełkiewicz-Janowiak
Tadeusz W. Lange
Robert Lew
Tomasz Lisowski
Magdalena Małaczyńska
Agnieszka Mielczarek
Danuta Romanowska
Liliana Sikorska
Grzegorz Skommer
Jacek Witkoś

**Consultants**
Ewa Dąbrowska
Alex Earle
Karol Janicki
Graham Knox-Crawford
Martin Parker
Magdalena Pieczka
Tadeusz Piotrowski
Geoffrey Shaw
Tadeusz Zgółka

**For the publisher (2011 edition):**
Gaëlle Amiot-Cadey
Susie Beattie
Magdalena Herok
Dorota Hołowiak
Rob Scriven

# Wstęp

Cieszymy się, że wybraliście Państwo słownik wydany na licencji Collinsa – renomowanego wydawcy brytyjskiego. Mamy nadzieję, że polubicie go i będziecie się nim chętnie posługiwać w domu, na wakacjach i w pracy. We wstępie znajdziecie Państwo szereg wskazówek wyjaśniających, jak najlepiej wykorzystać słownik – nie tylko jako listę wyrazów, ale również jako zbiór informacji zawartych w każdym artykule hasłowym. Pomoże to Państwu w czytaniu i rozumieniu współczesnych tekstów angielskich, a także ułatwi porozumiewanie się w tym języku.

# Introduction

We are delighted that you have chosen the Collins Polish Dictionary and hope that you will enjoy it and benefit from using it at home, on holiday or at work. This introduction gives you a few tips on how to get the most out of your dictionary – not simply from its comprehensive word list but also from the information provided in each entry. This will help you to read and understand modern Polish, as well as communicate and express yourself in the language.

# Spis treści



# Contents

# Jak korzystać ze słownika

## Wyrazy hasłowe

Wyraz hasłowy to wyraz, pod którym zamieszczony jest artykuł hasłowy. Wyrazy hasłowe są uporządkowane alfabetycznie i wyróżnione **wytłuszczonym drukiem**. Mogą one być częścią zwrotu lub wyrazu złożonego. U góry każdej strony umieszczono pierwszy i ostatni wyraz hasłowy występujący na danej stronie.

## Znaczenia

Znaczenia wyrazów hasłowych wydrukowane są zwykłą czcionką. Te, które oddzielone są przecinkiem, mogą najczęściej być używane wymiennie. Znaczenia oddzielone średnikiem nie są wymienne. Różnice znaczeń zaznaczone są zazwyczaj przez *kwalifikatory znaczeniowe* (zob. niżej) umieszczone w nawiasach i wydrukowane kursywą. Nie każdy termin występujący w jednym z języków ma swój odpowiednik znaczeniowy w drugim. Kiedy np. wyraz angielski określa przedmiot lub instytucję nieistniejącą w Polsce, słownik podaje albo przybliżony odpowiednik poprzedzony symbolem ≈, jeśli w języku polskim takowy występuje, albo opis danego przedmiotu czy instytucji, jeśli brak ekwiwalentu w polszczyźnie.

## Kwalifikatory

Kwalifikator to informacja w języku hasła umieszczona w nawiasach i wydrukowana kursywą. Ułatwia ona wybranie odpowiedniego znaczenia wyrazu hasłowego w zależności od kontekstu, w którym wyraz ów występuje, lub podaje jego synonim. Potoczne użycie wyrazów zaznaczone jest przy pomocy skrótu *inf* bezpośrednio po wyrazie hasłowym. Znaczenia polskie i angielskie wyrazów hasłowych są również odpowiednikami stylistycznymi, np. wulgarne wyrazy angielskie mają wulgarne odpowiedniki polskie. Aby uniknąć drastycznych nieporozumień wynikających z używania nieodpowiedniego tłumaczenia, wyrazy obraźliwe i wulgarne oznaczone zostały skrótem *inf!*.

## Wymowa

W części angielsko-polskiej słownika po wyrazie hasłowym podana jest wymowa w transkrypcji fonetycznej. Jeśli w pozycji wyrazu hasłowego znajduje się zestawienie lub zwrot składający się z dwóch lub więcej wyrazów, wymowy ich należy szukać tam, gdzie występują jako wyrazy hasłowe. Np. w przypadku **bank rate** wymowa jest zamieszczona w odpowiednich miejscach przy **bank** i **rate**. Lista symboli fonetycznych znajduje się na stronie XV–XVI. W części polsko-angielskiej słownik nie podaje wymowy. Informacje na temat reguł wymowy polskiej umieszczone są na stronach XVII–XIX.

## Słowa kluczowe

Nowością w naszym słowniku jest szczególne potraktowanie tzw. *słów kluczowych* zarówno w części polskiej, jak i angielskiej. *Słowa kluczowe* to wyrazy o wielu znaczeniach i szerokim zakresie użycia. W słowniku zostały one wyraźnie wyróżnione (w specjalnej ramce z nagłówkiem KEYWORD lub *SŁOWO KLUCZOWE*), aby ułatwić użytkownikowi ich czynne i bierne opanowanie.

## Skróty i nazwy własne
Akronimy i inne skróty oraz nazwy własne zostały w słowniku potraktowane jako wyrazy hasłowe i umieszczone w porządku alfabetycznym.

## Użycie *or/lub*, ukośnej kreski (/) i nawiasów
Wyrazy *or* w części angielsko-polskiej i *lub* w części polsko-angielskiej używane są między wymiennymi (synonimicznymi) znaczeniami wyrazu hasłowego lub zwrotu występującego pod hasłem. Ukośna kreska (/) oddziela różne znaczenia, niesynonimiczne i niewymienne. Nawiasy okrągłe oznaczają elementy, które można opuścić.

## Amerykanizmy
Warianty pisowni amerykańskiej w tych samych wyrazach znajdują się po wyrazie hasłowym, np. **colour**, (*US*) **color**. W wyrazach odległych alfabetycznie warianty amerykańskie podane są samodzielnie według porządku alfabetycznego, np. wyrazy **trousers** i **pants** wystepują oddzielnie.

## Polskie czasowniki zwrotne
Polskie czasowniki zwrotne nie są wyróżnione w słowniku jako osobne hasła. Należy ich szukać pod formami niezwrotnymi, np. **myć się** umieszczono pod hasłem **myć**.

# Using the dictionary

## Headwords

The headword is the word you look up in a dictionary. Headwords are listed in alphabetical order, and printed in **bold type** so that they stand out on the page. Each headword may contain other references such as phrases and compounds. The two headwords appearing at the top of each page indicate the first and last word dealt with on the page in question.

## Translations

The translations of the headword are printed in ordinary roman type. As a rule, translations separated by a comma can be regarded as interchangeable for the meaning indicated. Translations separated by a semicolon are not interchangeable, though the different meaning splits are generally marked by an indicator (see below). It is not always possible to give an exact translation equivalent, for instance when the English word denotes an object or institution which does not exist or exists in a different form in Polish. If an approximate equivalent exists, it is given preceded by ≈. If there is no cultural equivalent, a *gloss* is given to explain the source item.

## Indicators

An *indicator* is a piece of information in the source language about the usage of the headword to guide you to the most appropriate translation. Indicators give some idea of the contexts in which the headword might appear, or they provide synonyms for the headword. They are printed in italic type and shown in brackets. Colloquial and informal language in the dictionary is marked at the headword. You should assume that the translation will match the source language in register, and rude or offensive translations are also marked with *(inf!)*.

## Pronunciation

On the English-Polish side of the dictionary you will find the phonetic spelling of the word in square brackets after the headword. Where the entry is composed of two or more unhyphenated words, each of which is given elsewhere in the dictionary, you will find the pronunciation of each word in its alphabetical position. A list of symbols is given on pages XV–XVI. On the Polish-English side the pronunciation of Polish headwords is not provided. Information on Polish pronunciation is given on pages XVII–XIX.

## Keywords

In this dictionary we have given special status to "key" English and Polish words. As these words can be grammatically complex and often have many different usages, they have been given special attention in the dictionary, and are labelled **KEYWORD** and **SŁOWO KLUCZOWE**.

## Abbreviations and proper names

Abbreviations, acronyms and proper names have been included in the word list in alphabetical order.

## Use of *or/lub*, oblique and brackets

The words *or* on the English-Polish side and *lub* on the Polish-English side are used between interchangeable parts of a translation or source phrase. The oblique (/) is used between non-interchangeable alternatives in the translation or source phrase. Round brackets are used to show optional parts of the translation or source phrase.

## American variants

American spelling variants are generally shown at the British headword, eg. **colour**, (*US*) **color** and also as a separate entry if they are not alphabetically adjacent to the British form. Variant forms are generally shown as headwords in their own right, eg. **trousers** and **pants**, unless the British and American forms are alphabetically adjacent, in which case the American form is only shown separately if phonetics are required.

## Polish reflexive verbs

Polish reflexive verbs are listed under the basic verb, eg. **myć się** is listed under **myć**.

# Informacje gramatyczne w słowniku angielsko-polskim

## RZECZOWNIKI

### Rodzaj gramatyczny

W słowniku podano informację o rodzaju gramatycznym wszystkich rzeczowników w języku polskim stanowiących odpowiedniki haseł angielskich. Rzeczowniki, które posiadają dwa rodzaje, np. zrzęda, mają oznaczenie *m/f*. Rzeczowniki nieodmienne oznaczane są informacją o rodzaju i skrótem *inv*. W tych przypadkach, gdzie jako odpowiednik oprócz męskiej podana jest też forma żeńska, rodzaj formy żeńskiej podaje się w następujący sposób: *nauczyciel(ka) m(f)*. Odpowiedniki w liczbie mnogiej oznaczane są zawsze skrótem *pl*, np. *wakacje pl*.

### Formy żeńskie

Przy oznaczaniu form żeńskich używa się następujących konwencji:

- Jeśli formę żeńską tworzy się przez dodanie końcówki do formy męskiej, to końcówka ta podawana jest w nawiasie po formie męskiej, np. nauczyciel(ka) *m(f)*.
- Jeśli dodanie końcówki żeńskiej powoduje zmiany w formie męskiej, to po formie męskiej w nawiasie wraz z końcówką formy żeńskiej podaje się z myślnikiem ostatnią literę wspólną dla obu form, np. mieszkaniec (-nka).
- Jeśli formę żeńską podaje się w całości bezpośrednio po męskiej, to jest ona oddzielona od męskiej kreską ukośną, np. Czech/Czeszka.

## PRZYMIOTNIKI

Polskie odpowiedniki przymiotników podawane są zawsze w formie męskiej.

## CZASOWNIKI

Jako odpowiedniki wyrazów hasłowych podaje się czasowniki w pełnej formie w aspekcie niedokonanym i dokonanym wtedy, gdy oba aspekty mają zastosowanie, np. **beat** bić (zbić *perf*). Jeśli podany jest tylko jeden aspekt czasownika, to oznacza to, że dla tego znaczenia ma zastosowanie tylko ten jeden aspekt.

W tych przypadkach, gdzie fraza w języku angielskim zawiera formę czasu przeszłego czasownika w pierwszej osobie liczby pojedynczej, to polski odpowiednik może być podany albo w formie męskiej albo żeńskiej.

# Grammatical information in the English-Polish dictionary

## NOUNS

### Gender

The gender of Polish nouns given as translations is always shown in the dictionary. Nouns which have a common gender, eg. zrzęda, are labelled *m/f*. Indeclinable nouns are labelled with gender followed by the abbreviation *inv*. Where the feminine form of a masculine noun is also given a translation, the gender of the feminine is shown as follows: nauczyciel(ka) *m(f)*. Plural noun translations are always labelled with the abbreviation *pl*, eg. wakacje *pl*.

### Feminine forms

The following conventions are used in this dictionary to show feminine forms of masculine nouns:

- If the feminine ending adds on to the masculine form, the feminine ending is bracketed, eg. nauczyciel(ka).
- If the feminine ending substitutes part of the masculine form, the last common letter of the masculine and feminine form is shown before the feminine ending, preceded by a dash and enclosed in brackets, eg. mieszkaniec (-nka).
- If the feminine form is given in full it appears next to the masculine form and is separated by an oblique (/), eg. Czech/Czeszka.

## Adjectives

Polish translations of adjectives are always given in the masculine.

## Verbs

In translation of the headword, imperfective and perfective aspects are shown in full where they both apply, eg. **beat** bić (zbić *perf*).

If only one aspect is shown, it means that only one aspect works for this sense. In infinitive phrases, if the two aspects apply they are shown and labelled, eg. **to buy sth** kupować (kupić *perf*) coś.

Where the English phrase contains the past tense of a verb in the 1st person singular, the Polish translation gives either the masculine or the feminine form, eg. **I did** 'zrobiłem'/**I sang** 'śpiewałam'.

# Informacje gramatyczne w słowniku polsko-angielskim

## Końcówki fleksyjne i informacje gramatyczne

Końcówki fleksyjne podawane są w nawiasie bezpośrednio po wyrazie hasłowym przed skrótem części mowy, jeśli dotyczą one całego hasła, np. **motyl** (**-a**, **-e**) (*gen pl* **-i**) m. Jeśli końcówki dotyczą jedynie jednego ze znaczeń, to podane są one w dalszej części hasła. Informacje gramatyczne podawane są po symbolu literowym części mowy, np. **arty|sta** (**-sty**, **-ści**) (*dat sg* **-ście**) *m decl like f in sg*. Jeśli informacje gramatyczne podane są wewnątrz hasła, to dotyczą wszystkich pozostałych znaczeń.

## Użycie kreski pionowej ( | )

Kreska pionowa pokazuje, w którym miejscu dodaje się końcówki fleksyjne.

## Rzeczowniki

Aby ułatwić określenie deklinacji rzeczownika, w słowniku podaje się końcówkę dopełniacza liczby pojedynczej (lub mnogiej dla rzeczowników nieposiadających liczby pojedynczej) oraz końcówkę mianownika liczby mnogiej (dla rzeczowników policzalnych), np.

**szy|ja** (**-i**, **-je**) *f* oznacza *gen. sg.* = **szyi**, *nom. pl.* = **szyje**
**drzwi** (**-**) *pl* oznacza *gen. pl.* = **drzwi** (*brak l.p.*)
**wo|la** (**-i**) *f* oznacza *gen. sg.* = **woli** (*brak l.m.*)

Ewentualne dalsze nieregularne końcówki deklinacyjne podawano w drugim nawiasie wraz z odpowiednimi objaśnieniami, np.

**tema|t** (**-tu**, **-ty**) (*loc sg* **-cie**) *m*

## Przymiotniki

Przymiotniki jako wyrazy hasłowe podawane są w formie męskiej w liczbie pojedynczej. Po wyrazie hasłowym czasem podaje się nieregularne formy stopnia wyższego, np.

**wy|soki** (*comp* **-ższy**) *adj*...

## Czasowniki

Większość czasowników podana jest z uwzględnieniem aspektu dokonanego i niedokonanego, a odpowiedniki podawane są zwykle przy czasowniku w aspekcie niedokonanym. Formy dokonane zaopatrzone są w odwołania do swoich niedokonanych odpowiedników, chyba że mają inne znaczenie. W tych przypadkach, gdzie czasownik z odwołaniem znajduje się w bezpośrednim sąsiedztwie czasownika, do którego się odwołuje, nie jest on wyłączany do osobnego hasła, chyba że w jego odmianie jest jakaś nieregularność. Czasowniki, które nie występują w parach ze względu na aspekt, posiadają swoje osobne hasła. W wyrażeniach pokazano oba aspekty czasownika, jeśli oba istnieją dla danego znaczenia. Aby ułatwić tworzenie form czasownika, bezpośrednio po wyrazie hasłowym podano informacje o końcówkach koniugacyjnych według następujących reguł:

- dla większości czasowników podano formy 1. i 2. osoby liczby pojedynczej, np. **prac|ować (-uję, -ujesz)**
- dla czasowników, które nie posiadają form 1. i 2. osoby liczby pojedynczej, podana jest 3. osoba liczby pojedynczej, np. **bo|leć (-i)**
- dla wszystkich wyrazów hasłowych, które są czasownikami niedokonanymi występującymi w parze ze swoimi dokonanymi odpowiednikami, końcówka lub przedrostek formy dokonanej podane są zaraz za wyrazem hasłowym lub, jeśli dotyczą jedynie jednego ze znaczeń, w dalszej części hasła, np. **przepis|ywać (-uję, -ujesz)** (*perf* **-ać**) ...
- podaje się nieregularne formy 2. osoby l.p. trybu rozkazującego, np. **nieść (niosę, niesiesz)** (*imp* **nieś**)
- nieregularne formy czasu przeszłego podawane są w następującej kolejności:
  *3. osoba liczby pojedynczej rodzaju męskiego*
  *3. osoba liczby pojedynczej rodzaju żeńskiego*
  *3. osoba liczby mnogiej rodzaju męskoosobowego*

Jeśli tylko jedna z tych form jest nieregularna, to podaje się jedynie tę formę.

## Formy fleksyjne jako osobne hasła

Nieregularne formy fleksyjne, które nie występują w bezpośredniej bliskości form podstawowych, podane są w odpowiednim porządku alfabetycznym jako osobne hasła wraz z odwołaniem do hasła głównego. Jeśli po takim haśle podano skrót itd., oznacza to, że istnieją inne, podobnie tworzone, formy fleksyjne tego samego hasła podstawowego, np. **psa** itd. dotyczy **psa**, **psem**, **psami** itp., i wszystkie te formy odwołują się do **pies**.

# Grammatical information in the Polish-English dictionary

## Inflectional and grammatical information

Inflectional information is shown in the dictionary in brackets immediately after the headword and before the part of speech if it refers to the whole entry eg. **motyl** (**-a**, **-e**) (*gen pl* **-i**) *m*. If a particular inflection is restricted to one sense only, it is given in the middle of the entry.

Grammatical information is shown after the part of speech and refers to the whole entry eg. **arty|sta** (**-sty**, **-ści**) (*dat sg* **-ście**) *m decl like f in sg*. Where grammatical information is given in the middle of the entry, it then governs all the following senses.

## Use of hairline ( | )

The hairline is -used in headwords to show where the inflection adds on, eg. **dr|oga** (**-ogi**, **-ogi**) (*dat sg* **-odze**, *gen pl* **-óg**) *f* … .

## Nouns

In order to help you determine the declension of nouns, we have shown the genitive singular (or plural for plural-only nouns), and nominative plural (for countable nouns only), eg.

**szy|ja** (**-i**, **-je**) *f* means *gen. sg.* = **szyi**, *nom. pl.* = **szyje**
**drzwi** (**-**) *pl* means *gen. pl.* = **drzwi** (*no singular*)
**wo|la** (**-i**) *f* means *gen. sg.* = **woli** (*no plural*)

Where the noun has further irregularities in declension, these are shown in smaller print and appropriately labelled, eg.

**tema|t** (**-tu**, **-ty**) (*loc sg* **-cie**) *m*

## Adjectives

Adjective headwords have the form of nominative singular masculine. Some irregular comparative forms are given after the headword, eg.

**wy|soki** (*comp* **-ższy**) *adj*…

## Verbs

The majority of verbs are dealt with in aspectual pairs, but the translation is usually shown at the imperfective form of the pair. Perfective forms are cross-referred to their imperfective counterparts unless they have a specific meaning of their own. Where the aspect to be cross-referred is alphabetically adjacent to the other aspect, it is not shown separately unless there is some irregularity in its declension. Verbs which do not occur in aspectual pairs are dealt with at their individual headwords. In phrases both aspects are shown if both work in the context.

To help you see how a verb conjugates, inflections are shown immediately after the verb headword for all verbs according to the following rules:

- for most verbs the 1st and 2nd person singular are shown, eg. **prac|ować (-uję, -ujesz)**
- for verbs which are not used in the 1st and 2nd person, the 3rd person singular is shown, eg. **bo|leć** (**-i**)
- for all imperfective verb headwords constituting one element of an aspectual pair, the perfective ending or prefix is shown in smaller print right after the headword or, where it is restricted to a specific sense, in the middle of the entry, eg. **przepis|ywać (-uję, -ujesz)** (*perf* **-ać**) ...
- irregular 2nd person imperative forms are shown, eg. **nieść (niosę, niesiesz)** (*imp* **-nieś**)
- irregular past tense forms are shown in the following order:
  *3rd person singular masculine*
  *3rd person singular feminine*
  *3rd person plural virile*

If only the one of these forms is irregular, only one form is shown.

## Inflections given as separate entries

Irregular inflected forms which are distant alphabetically from their base forms are also shown at their alphabetical position and cross-referred to the base headword. In places an inflected form appears as a separate entry and is followed by *itd.*, meaning that there are other inflected forms of the same headword which follow the same pattern eg. **psa** *itd.* covers **psa**, **psem**, **psami** etc., which are all cross-referred to **pies**.

| Skróty | | Abbreviations |
|---|---|---|
| skrót | *abbr* | abbreviation |
| biernik | *acc* | accusative |
| przymiotnik | *adj* | adjective |
| administracja | *Admin* | administration |
| przysłówek | *adv* | adverb |
| rolnictwo | *Agr* | agriculture |
| anatomia | *Anat* | anatomy |
| architektura | *Archit* | architecture |
| astronomia | *Astron* | astronomy |
| przydawka | *attr* | attributive |
| motoryzacja | *Aut* | automobiles |
| lotnictwo | *Aviat* | aviation |
| biologia | *Bio* | biology |
| botanika | *Bot* | botany |
| angielszczyzna brytyjska | *Brit* | British English |
| budownictwo | *Bud* | construction |
| chemia | *Chem* | chemistry |
| handel | *Comm* | commerce |
| stopień wyższy | *comp* | comparative |
| informatyka i komputery | *Comput* | computer |
| spójnik | *conj* | conjunction |
| budownictwo | *Constr* | construction |
| wyraz złożony | *cpd* | compound |
| kulinarny | *Culin* | culinary |
| celownik | *dat* | dative |
| odmienny | *decl* | declinable |
| przedimek określony | *def art* | definite article |
| zdrobnienie | *dimin* | diminutive |
| dosłowny | *dosł* | literal |
| poligrafia | *Druk* | printing |
| ekonomia | *Ekon, Econ* | economics |
| elektronika, elektryczność | *Elektr, Elec* | electronics, electricity |
| szczególnie | *esp* | especially |
| itd. | *etc* | et cetera |
| wykrzyknik | *excl* | exclamation |
| rodzaj żeński | *f* | feminine |
| przenośny | *fig* | figurative |
| finanse | *Fin* | finance |
| formalny | *fml* | formal |
| fizyka | *Fiz* | physics |
| fotografia | *Fot* | photography |
| dopełniacz | *gen* | genitive |
| geografia | *Geog* | geography |
| geologia | *Geol* | geology |
| geometria | *Geom* | geometry |
| historia | *Hist* | history |
| tryb rozkazujący | *imp* | imperative |
| bezosobowy | *impers* | impersonal |
| czasownik niedokonany | *imperf* | imperfective verb |
| przedimek nieokreślony | *indef art* | indefinite article |

| | | |
|---|---|---|
| potoczny | *inf* | informal |
| obraźliwy, wulgarny | *inf!* | offensive |
| bezokolicznik | *infin* | infinitive |
| narzędnik | *instr* | instrumental |
| nieodmienny | *inv* | invariable |
| nieregularny | *irreg* | irregular |
| i tak dalej | *itd.* | etc (et cetera) |
| i tym podobne | *itp.* | and the like |
| językoznawstwo | *Jęz* | linguistics |
| prawo | *Jur* | law |
| informatyka i komputery | *Komput* | computer |
| użycie literackie | *książk* | formal |
| kulinarny | *Kulin* | culinary |
| językoznawstwo | *Ling* | linguistics |
| dosłowny | *lit* | literal |
| literatura | *Lit* | literature |
| miejscownik | *loc* | locative |
| lotnictwo | *Lot* | aviation |
| rodzaj męski | *m* | masculine |
| matematyka | *Mat(h)* | mathematics |
| medycyna | *Med* | medicine |
| meteorologia | *Meteo(r)* | meteorology |
| wojskowość | *Mil* | military |
| motoryzacja | *Mot* | automobiles |
| muzyka | *Muz, Mus* | music |
| mitologia | *Myth* | mythology |
| rzeczownik | *n* | noun |
| żegluga | *Naut* | nautical |
| mianownik | *nom* | nominative |
| rodzaj niemęskoosobowy | *nonvir* | non-virile |
| rzeczownik w liczbie mnogiej | *npl* | plural noun |
| rodzaj nijaki | *nt* | neuter |
| liczebnik | *num* | numeral |
| siebie, się | *o.s.* | oneself |
| parlament | *Parl* | parliament |
| dopełniacz cząstkowy | *part* | partitive |
| pejoratywny | *pej* | pejorative |
| czasownik dokonany | *perf* | perfective verb |
| fotografia | *Phot* | photography |
| fizyka | *Phys* | physics |
| fizjologia | *Physiol* | physiology |
| liczba mnoga | *pl* | plural |
| polityka | *Pol* | politics |
| nie występuje bezpośrednio przed rzeczownikiem | *post* | postpositive (does not immediately precede a noun) |
| potoczny | *pot* | informal |
| obraźliwy, wulgarny | *pot!* | offensive |
| imiesłów bierny | *pp* | past participle |
| orzecznik | *pred* | predicative |
| przedrostek | *pref* | prefix |
| przyimek | *prep* | preposition |
| zaimek | *pron* | pronoun |

| | | |
|---|---|---|
| przenośny | *przen* | figurative |
| psychologia | *Psych* | psychology |
| czas przeszły | *pt* | past tense |
| radio | *Radio* | radio |
| kolej | *Rail* | railways |
| religia | *Rel* | religion |
| rolnictwo | *Rol* | agriculture |
| ktoś | *sb* | somebody |
| liczba pojedyncza | *sg* | singular |
| coś | *sth* | something |
| stopień najwyższy | *superl* | superlative |
| szkoła | *Szkol, Scol* | school |
| technika i technologia | *Tech* | technology |
| telekomunikacja | *Tel* | telecommunication |
| teatr | *Theat* | theatre |
| telewizja | TV | television |
| poligrafia | *Typ* | printing |
| uniwersytet | *Uniw, Univ* | university |
| angielszczyzna amerykańska | *US* | American English |
| zwykle | *usu* | usually |
| czasownik | *vb* | verb |
| czasownik nieprzechodni | *vi* | intransitive verb |
| męskoosobowy | *vir* | virile |
| wołacz | *voc* | vocative |
| czasownik zwrotny | *vr* | reflexive verb |
| czasownik przechodni | *vt* | transitive verb |
| czasownik nierozdzielny | *vt fus* | inseparable verb |
| wojskowość | *Wojsk* | military |
| zoologia | *Zool* | zoology |
| żegluga | *żegl* | nautical |
| znak zastrzeżony | ® | registered trademark |
| poprzedza odpowiednik kulturowy | ≈ | introduces a cultural equivalent |
| zmiana osoby mówiącej | – | change of speaker |

# Wymowa angielska

## Samogłoski i dyftongi

| *Symbol fonetyczny* | *Przykład angielski* | *Przybliżony odpowiednik polski lub opis* |
|---|---|---|
| [iː] | tea, feet | kij, pij |
| [ɪ] | it, big | samogłoska podobna do polskiej „y" |
| [ɛ] | dress, egg | bez |
| [æ] | man, cat | bardzo otwarte „e" |
| [uː] | too, you | długie „u" |
| [u] | put, book | but |
| [ɔː] | saw, all | długie „o" |
| [ɔ] | hot, wash | pod |
| [ɑː] | part, father | tata |
| [ʌ] | but, come | agresja |
| [əː] | bird, heard | samogłoska centralna długa |
| [ə] | ago, potential | samogłoska centralna nieakcentowana |
| [ɑɪ] | fly, high | kraj |
| [au] | how, house | miał, miau |
| [eɪ] | day, obey | klej |
| [əu] | go, note | kombinacja [ə] i [u] |
| [ɔɪ] | boy, oil | kojec |
| [ɪə] | hear, here | kombinacja [ɪ] i centralnej samogłoski [ə] |
| [ɛə] | there, bear | kombinacja [e] i [ə] |
| [uə] | poor, sure | kombinacja [u] i [ə] |
| [ɔːʳ, ɑːʳ, əʳ itd] | more, far, father | końcowe [r] wymawia się, kiedy następny wyraz zaczyna się od samogłoski, np. *far away* |

## Spółgłoski

| *Symbol fonetyczny* | *Przykład angielski* | *Przybliżony odpowiednik polski lub opis* |
|---|---|---|
| [p] | pat, pop | papka |
| [b] | but, tub | but |
| [t] | take, hat | tak, kat |
| [d] | deck, mad | dom, bieda |
| [k] | come, rock | kamień, bok |
| [g] | go, big | góra, biegać |
| [tʃ] | chin, rich | czyn, ryczeć |
| [dʒ] | gin, judge | dżuma |
| [f] | face | fakt |
| [v] | valley | wał |
| [θ] | think | wymawia się jak „s" z językiem dotykającym górnych zębów |
| [ð] | this | wymawia się jak „z" z językiem dotykającym górnych zębów |

| | | |
|---|---|---|
| [s] | sand, city | sad, rysa |
| [z] | rose, zebra | baza, zebra |
| [ʃ] | she, machine | szyna, maszerować |
| [ʒ] | vision | ważny |
| [m] | must | musieć |
| [n] | nut | nuta |
| [ŋ] | sing | bank w wymowie, gdzie nie słychać „k” |
| [h] | house, he | słabsze polskie „ch” |
| [l] | lake | lekcja |
| [r] | red, tread | trące „r” nieprzerywane |
| [j] | young | jest |
| [w] | water, which | łotr |

# Polish pronunciation

## Vowels

1. Polish vowels are inherently short, whereas in English some vowels are inherently long (eg. beat) while others are inherently short (eg. bit). Polish stressed vowels, however, tend to be slightly longer than unstressed ones.

2. Polish, unlike English, has two nasal vowels, ie. [õ] and [ẽ], as in dąć and gęś. In informal speech ą is pronounced [õ] only before [s z ʃ ʒ ɕ ʑ f v x], eg. dąs, brązowy, gąszcz, dążyć, siąść, są źli, są filmy, wąwóz, wąchać. [õ] changes into [on] in front of [t d ts dz tʃ dʒ], eg. kąt, mądry, trącać, żądza, pączek, mądrze. ą is pronounced [oŋ] before [k g], eg. bąk, drągi. [õ] changes into [om] before [p b], eg. kąpać, trąba. [ẽ], like [õ], is pronounced in informal speech before [s z ʃ ʒ ɕ ʑ], eg. kęs, więzy, węszyć, wytężyć, gęś, więzi. [ẽ] changes into [en] in front of [t d ts tʃ dz], eg. pętla, gawęda, ręce, ręcznik, pędzel. [ẽ] changes into [e[ng]] before [k g], eg. lęk, tęgi and into [em] before [p b], eg. tępy, bęben. In word-final position [ẽ] appears as [e], eg. chcę, wezmę.

3. Polish has no diphthongs.

## Consonants

1. Polish has palatal and palatalized consonants. [ɲ], as in koń, is a palatal nasal consonant. 'Hard' consonants [p b k g m l f v x] have 'soft' or 'palatalised' counterparts which are indicated by the 'softening' vowel letter i, eg. piegi, bieg, kiedy, biegiem, miał, liana, fiasko, wiedzieć, hiena. The 'soft' consonants are pronounced like their 'hard' counterparts with simultaneous [j] as in the English word yet.

2. There are seven pairs of voiced and voiceless consonants:

| | | | | | | | |
|---|---|---|---|---|---|---|---|
| voiced: | b | d | g | v | z | ʒ | ʑ |
| voiceless: | p | t | k | f | s | ʃ | ɕ |

   a) At the end of a word a voiced consonant is replaced by the corresponding voiceless consonant, eg. *gen pl* bud [but] (cf *nom sg* buda [buda]).

   b) When a voiced consonant occurs before a voiceless consonant it is replaced by the corresponding voiceless consonant, eg. kłódka [kwutka], z katalogu [skatalogu] (cf z góry [zgurɪ]).

3. The consonants [p t k], eg. pod [pot], tak [tak], kot [kot] are pronounced without the slight puff of air which follows them in English before stressed vowels.

## Vowels

| *Symbol* | *Spelling* | *Polish example* | *English example/explanation* |
|---|---|---|---|
| [a] | a | kat | pronounced like the beginning of the diphthong in 'eye' |
| [i] | i | nit | neat |
| [ɪ] | y | byt | bit |
| [e] | e | ten | ten |
| [o] | o | kot | caught (but shorter) |
| [u] | u | but | boot |
| [ẽ] | ę | węch | *see note 2 under Vowels* |
| [õ] | ą | wąs | *see note 2 under Vowels* |

## Consonants

| *Symbol* | *Spelling* | *Polish example* | *English example/explanation* |
|---|---|---|---|
| [b] | b | byk | bit |
| [bʼ] | bi | biały | *see note 1 under Consonants* |
| [p] | p, b | pas, chleb | put (*see note 3 under Consonants*) |
| [pʼ] | pi | piasek | *see note 1 under Consonants* |
| [d] | d | dom | day |
| [t] | t, d | ton, pod | tone (*see note 3 under Consonants*) |
| [g] | g | góra | go |
| [gʼ] | gi | biegiem | *see note 1 under Consonants* |
| [k] | k, g | kot, róg | cat (*see note 3 under Consonants*) |
| [kʼ] | ki | kiedy | *see note 1 under Consonants* |
| [v] | w | woda | vat |
| [vʼ] | wi | wiadro | *see note 1 under Consonants* |
| [f] | f, w | fala, rów | foam |
| [fʼ] | fi | fiasko | *see note 1 under Consonants* |
| [s] | s, z | sól, raz | sea |
| [z] | z | za, mazać | zebra, housing |
| [ʃ] | sz, ż, rz | szum, już, malarz | shot |
| [ʒ] | ż, rz | żuk, rzecz | measure, decision |
| [ɕ] | si, ś, ź | się, wieś, wieź | pronounced 'softer' than English [ʃ] in *shield* |
| [ʑ] | zi, ź | zima, kuźnia | pronounced 'softer' than English [ʒ] in *regime* |
| [ts] | c, dz | cegła, widz | tsetse |
| [dz] | dz | dzban, sadza | needs |
| [tʃ] | cz, dż | czy, gwiżdż | chat, patch |
| [dʒ] | dż, drz | dżuma | jam, wedge |
| [tɕ] | ci, ć, dź | cichy, śmierć, jedź | pronounced 'softer' than English [tʃ] in *cheese* |
| [dʑ] | dzi, dź | dzień, dźwięk | pronounced 'softer' than English [dʒ] in *gene* |
| [r] | r | rok, bór | pronounced like rolled Scots "r" in all positions |
| [l] | l | lato | like |

| | | | |
|---|---|---|---|
| [l′] | li | liana | *see note 1 under Consonants* |
| [m] | m | mama | mother |
| [m′] | mi | miał | *see note 1 under Consonants* |
| [n] | n | noga | note |
| [ɲ] | ni, ń | nie, pień | 'soft' [n], as in *need* |
| [w] | ł | łodź | wood |
| [j] | j | jak | yet |
| [x] | h, ch | hak, chemia | hood |
| [x′] | hi, chi | hiena, Chiny | *see note 1 under Consonants* |

# Angielskie czasowniki nieregularne

| present | pt | pp |
|---|---|---|
| **arise** | arose | arisen |
| **awake** | awoke | awoken |
| **be** (**am, is, are; being**) | was, were | been |
| **bear** | bore | born(e) |
| **beat** | beat | beaten |
| **become** | became | become |
| **befall** | befell | befallen |
| **begin** | began | begun |
| **behold** | beheld | beheld |
| **bend** | bent | bent |
| **beset** | beset | beset |
| **bet** | bet, betted | bet, betted |
| **bid** (*at auction, cards*) | bid | bid |
| **bid** (*say*) | bade | bidden |
| **bind** | bound | bound |
| **bite** | bit | bitten |
| **bleed** | bled | bled |
| **blow** | blew | blown |
| **break** | broke | broken |
| **breed** | bred | bred |
| **bring** | brought | brought |
| **build** | built | built |
| **burn** | burnt, burned | burnt, burned |
| **burst** | burst | burst |
| **buy** | bought | bought |
| **can** | could | (been able) |
| **cast** | cast | cast |
| **catch** | caught | caught |
| **choose** | chose | chosen |
| **cling** | clung | clung |
| **come** | came | come |
| **cost** | cost | cost |
| **cost** (*work out price of*) | costed | costed |
| **creep** | crept | crept |
| **cut** | cut | cut |
| **deal** | dealt | dealt |
| **dig** | dug | dug |
| **do** (*3rd person: he/she/it* ***does***) | did | done |
| **draw** | drew | drawn |
| **dream** | dreamed, dreamt | dreamed, dreamt |
| **drink** | drank | drunk |
| **drive** | drove | driven |
| **dwell** | dwelt | dwelt |
| **eat** | ate | eaten |
| **fall** | fell | fallen |
| **feed** | fed | fed |
| **feel** | felt | felt |
| **fight** | fought | fought |
| **find** | found | found |
| **flee** | fled | fled |
| **fling** | flung | flung |
| **fly (flies)** | flew | flown |
| **forbid** | forbad(e) | forbidden |
| **forecast** | forecast | forecast |
| **forget** | forgot | forgotten |
| **forgive** | forgave | forgiven |
| **forsake** | forsook | forsaken |
| **freeze** | froze | frozen |
| **get** | got | got, (*US*) gotten |
| **give** | gave | given |
| **go** (**goes**) | went | gone |
| **grind** | ground | ground |
| **grow** | grew | grown |
| **hang** | hung | hung |
| **hang** (*execute*) | hanged | hanged |
| **have** (**has; having**) | had | had |
| **hear** | heard | heard |
| **hide** | hid | hidden |
| **hit** | hit | hit |
| **hold** | held | held |
| **hurt** | hurt | hurt |
| **keep** | kept | kept |
| **kneel** | knelt, kneeled | knelt, kneeled |
| **know** | knew | known |
| **lay** | laid | laid |
| **lead** | led | led |
| **lean** | leant, leaned | leant, leaned |
| **leap** | leapt, leaped | leapt, leaped |
| **learn** | learnt, learned | learnt, learned |
| **leave** | left | left |

| present | pt | pp |
|---|---|---|
| **lend** | lent | lent |
| **let** | let | let |
| **lie** (**lying**) | lay | lain |
| **light** | lit, lighted | lit, lighted |
| **lose** | lost | lost |
| **make** | made | made |
| **may** | might | – |
| **mean** | meant | meant |
| **meet** | met | met |
| **mistake** | mistook | mistaken |
| **mow** | mowed | mown, mowed |
| **must** | (had to) | (had to) |
| **pay** | paid | paid |
| **put** | put | put |
| **quit** | quit, quitted | quit, quitted |
| **read** | read | read |
| **rid** | rid | rid |
| **ride** | rode | ridden |
| **ring** | rang | rung |
| **rise** | rose | risen |
| **run** | ran | run |
| **saw** | sawed | sawed, sawn |
| **say** | said | said |
| **see** | saw | seen |
| **seek** | sought | sought |
| **sell** | sold | sold |
| **send** | sent | sent |
| **set** | set | set |
| **sew** | sewed | sewn |
| **shake** | shook | shaken |
| **shall** | should | – |
| **shear** | sheared | shorn, sheared |
| **shed** | shed | shed |
| **shine** | shone | shone |
| **shoot** | shot | shot |
| **show** | showed | shown |
| **shrink** | shrank | shrunk |
| **shut** | shut | shut |
| **sing** | sang | sung |
| **sink** | sank | sunk |
| **sit** | sat | sat |
| **slay** | slew | slain |
| **sleep** | slept | slept |
| **slide** | slid | slid |
| **sling** | slung | slung |
| **slit** | slit | slit |

| present | pt | pp |
|---|---|---|
| **smell** | smelt, smelled | smelt, smelled |
| **sow** | sowed | sown, sowed |
| **speak** | spoke | spoken |
| **speed** | sped, speeded | sped, speeded |
| **spell** | spelt, spelled | spelt, spelled |
| **spend** | spent | spent |
| **spill** | spilt, spilled | spilt, spilled |
| **spin** | spun | spun |
| **spit** | spat | spat |
| **spoil** | spoiled, spoilt | spoiled, spoilt |
| **spread** | spread | spread |
| **spring** | sprang | sprung |
| **stand** | stood | stood |
| **steal** | stole | stolen |
| **stick** | stuck | stuck |
| **sting** | stung | stung |
| **stink** | stank | stunk |
| **stride** | strode | stridden |
| **strike** | struck | struck |
| **strive** | strove | striven |
| **swear** | swore | sworn |
| **sweep** | swept | swept |
| **swell** | swelled | swollen, swelled |
| **swim** | swam | swum |
| **swing** | swung | swung |
| **take** | took | taken |
| **teach** | taught | taught |
| **tear** | tore | torn |
| **tell** | told | told |
| **think** | thought | thought |
| **throw** | threw | thrown |
| **thrust** | thrust | thrust |
| **tread** | trod | trodden |
| **wake** | woke, waked | woken, waked |
| **wear** | wore | worn |
| **weave** | wove | woven |
| **weave** (*wind*) | weaved | weaved |
| **wed** | wedded, wed | wedded, wed |
| **weep** | wept | wept |
| **win** | won | won |
| **wind** | wound | wound |
| **wring** | wrung | wrung |
| **write** | wrote | written |

# Liczby

# Numbers

## Liczebniki główne

## Cardinal numbers

| | | |
|---|---|---|
| jeden | **1** | one |
| dwa | **2** | two |
| trzy | **3** | three |
| cztery | **4** | four |
| pięć | **5** | five |
| sześć | **6** | six |
| siedem | **7** | seven |
| osiem | **8** | eight |
| dziewięć | **9** | nine |
| dziesięć | **10** | ten |
| jedenaście | **11** | eleven |
| dwanaście | **12** | twelve |
| trzynaście | **13** | thirteen |
| czternaście | **14** | fourteen |
| piętnaście | **15** | fifteen |
| szesnaście | **16** | sixteen |
| siedemnaście | **17** | seventeen |
| osiemnaście | **18** | eighteen |
| dziewiętnaście | **19** | nineteen |
| dwadzieścia | **20** | twenty |
| dwadzieścia jeden | **21** | twenty-one |
| dwadzieścia dwa | **22** | twenty-two |
| trzydzieści | **30** | thirty |
| czterdzieści | **40** | forty |
| pięćdziesiąt | **50** | fifty |
| sześćdziesiąt | **60** | sixty |
| siedemdziesiąt | **70** | seventy |
| osiemdziesiąt | **80** | eighty |
| dziewięćdziesiąt | **90** | ninety |
| sto | **100** | a hundred |
| sto jeden | **101** | a hundred and one |
| dwieście | **200** | two hundred |
| trzysta | **300** | three hundred |
| czterysta | **400** | four hundred |
| pięćset | **500** | five hundred |
| tysiąc | **1000** | a thousand |
| milion | **1000000** | a million |

## Liczebniki zbiorowe / Collective numerals

| Liczebniki zbiorowe | | Collective numerals |
|---|---|---|
| dwoje | **2** | two |
| troje | **3** | three |
| czworo | **4** | four |
| pięcioro | **5** | five |
| sześcioro | **6** | six |
| siedmioro | **7** | seven |

## Liczebniki porządkowe / Ordinal numbers

| Liczebniki porządkowe | | Ordinal numbers | |
|---|---|---|---|
| 1. | pierwszy | 1st | first |
| 2. | drugi | 2nd | second |
| 3. | trzeci | 3rd | third |
| 4. | czwarty | 4th | fourth |
| 5. | piąty | 5th | fifth |
| 6. | szósty | 6th | sixth |
| 7. | siódmy | 7th | seventh |
| 8. | ósmy | 8th | eighth |
| 9. | dziewiąty | 9th | ninth |
| 10. | dziesiąty | 10th | tenth |
| 11. | jedenasty | 11th | eleventh |
| 12. | dwunasty | 12th | twelfth |
| 13. | trzynasty | 13th | thirteenth |
| 14. | czternasty | 14th | fourteenth |
| 15. | piętnasty | 15th | fifteenth |
| 16. | szesnasty | 16th | sixteenth |
| 17. | siedemnasty | 17th | seventeenth |
| 18. | osiemnasty | 18th | eighteenth |
| 19. | dziewiętnasty | 19th | nineteenth |
| 20. | dwudziesty | 20th | twentieth |
| 21. | dwudziesty pierwszy | 21st | twenty-first |
| 30. | trzydziesty | 30th | thirtieth |
| 40. | czterdziesty | 40th | fortieth |
| 50. | pięćdziesiąty | 50th | fiftieth |
| 60. | sześćdziesiąty | 60th | sixtieth |
| 70. | siedemdziesiąty | 70th | seventieth |
| 80. | osiemdziesiąty | 80th | eightieth |
| 90. | dziewięćdziesiąty | 90th | ninetieth |
| 100. | setny | 100th | one hundredth |
| 101. | sto pierwszy | 101st | one hundred-and-first |
| 1.000. | tysiączny | 1 000th | thousandth |
| 1.000.000. | milionowy | 1 000 000th | millionth |

## Ułamki

| | |
|---|---|
| pół, połowa | 1/2 |
| jedna trzecia | 1/3 |
| jedna czwarta | 1/4 |
| jedna piąta | 1/5 |
| trzy czwarte | 3/4 |
| dwie trzecie | 2/3 |
| półtora | 1 1/2 |
| pięć dziesiątych | 0,5 |
| trzy przecinek cztery | 3,4 |
| sześć przecinek osiemdziesiąt dziewięć | 6,89 |
| dziesięć procent | 10% |
| sto procent | 100% |

## Fractions

| | |
|---|---|
| a half | 1/2 |
| a third | 1/3 |
| a quarter | 1/4 |
| a fifth | 1/5 |
| three quarters | 3/4 |
| two thirds | 2/3 |
| one and a half | 1 1/2 |
| (nought) point five | 0·5 |
| three point four | 3·4 |
| six point eight nine | 6.89 |
| ten per cent | 10% |
| a hundred per cent | 100% |

# Godziny i daty — Time and date

## Godzina — Time

| | | |
|---|---|---|
| | ***Która (jest) godzina?*** | ***What time is it?*** |
| | ***Jest (godzina) piąta.*** | ***It is** or **it's 5 o'clock.*** |
| 00.00 | północ | midnight |
| 01.00 | pierwsza (w nocy) | one o'clock (in the morning), 1 am |
| 01.05 | pięć (minut) po (godzinie) pierwszej | five (minutes) past one |
| 01.10 | dziesięć (minut) po pierwszej | ten (minutes) past one |
| 01.15 | kwadrans lub piętnaście po pierwszej | a quarter past one, fifteen minutes past one, one fifteen |
| 01.20 | dwadzieścia po pierwszej | twenty (minutes) past one |
| 01.30 | (w)pół do drugiej, pierwsza trzydzieści | half (past) one, one thirty |
| 01.35 | pięć po (w)pół do drugiej, za dwadzieścia pięć druga | twenty-five (minutes) to two, one thirty-five |
| 01.40 | za dwadzieścia (minut) druga, pierwsza czterdzieści | twenty (minutes) to two, one forty |
| 01.45 | za kwadrans druga, za piętnaście druga, pierwsza czterdzieści pięć | a quarter to two, fifteen minutes to two, one forty-five |
| 01.50 | dwunasta (w południe) | ten minutes to two, one fifty |
| 12.00 | za dziesięć druga, pierwsza pięćdziesiąt | twelve (o'clock) noon, midday |
| 12.30 | (w)pół do pierwszej, dwunasta trzydzieści | half (past) twelve or twelve thirty (in the afternoon), 12.30pm |
| 14.00 | druga (po południu), czternasta | two o'clock (in the afternoon), 2pm |
| 19.00 | siódma (wieczorem), dziewiętnasta | 7 o'clock (in the evening), 7pm |

| | |
|---|---|
| ***O której godzinie? O (godzinie) +loc.*** | ***At what time? At … (o'clock).*** |
| ***o (godzinie) siódmej*** | ***at 7 (o'clock)*** |
| o północy | at midnight |
| o zmierzchu | at dawn, at nightfall |
| o świcie | at dusk, at sunrise |
| o zachodzie słońca | at sunset |
| za dwadzieścia minut | in or within twenty minutes |
| (od teraz) za godzinę | in an hour, in an hour's time, in an hour from now |
| w ciągu dwudziestu minut | in the next twenty minutes |
| dziesięć minut temu | ten minutes ago |
| dwie godziny temu | two hours ago |
| pół godziny | half an hour |
| kwadrans, piętnaście minut | a quarter of an hour |
| półtorej godziny | an hour and a half |
| co godzinę | every hour |
| o pełnej godzinie | on the hour |
| co godzinę | hourly |

| **Daty** | **Date** |
|---|---|
| dzisiaj, dziś | today |
| jutro | tomorrow |
| pojutrze | the day after tomorrow |
| wczoraj | yesterday |
| przedwczoraj | the day before yesterday |
| w przeddzień | the day before |
| dzień po | the day after |
| rano | in the morning |
| wieczorem | in the evening |
| dziś rano | this morning |
| dziś wieczorem | tonight, this evening |
| dziś po południu | this afternoon |
| wczoraj rano | yesterday morning |
| wczoraj wieczorem | last night, yesterday evening |
| jutro rano | tomorrow morning |
| jutro wieczorem | tomorrow evening |
| w sobotę wieczorem | on Saturday night |
| w niedzielę rano | on Sunday morning |
| on przyjdzie w czwartek | he's coming on Thursday |
| w soboty, w sobotę | on Saturdays, on Saturday |
| w każdą sobotę, co sobotę | every Saturday |
| w ostatnią sobotę | last Saturday |
| w następną sobotę | next Saturday |
| od (tej) soboty za tydzień | a week on Saturday |
| od (tej) soboty za dwa tygodnie | two weeks on Saturday |
| od poniedziałku do soboty | from Monday to Saturday |
| codziennie, co dzień | every day |
| raz w tygodniu | once a week |
| dwa razy w tygodniu | twice a week |
| raz w miesiącu | once a month |
| tydzień temu | a week or seven days ago |
| dwa tygodnie temu | two weeks *or* a fortnight ago |
| w zeszłym roku | last year |
| za dwa dni | in two days' time |
| za tydzień | in seven days *or* one week or a week |
| za dwa tygodnie | in a fortnight *or* two weeks |
| w przyszłym miesiącu | next month |
| w przyszłym roku | next year |
| który dzisiaj jest? | what is today's date?, what date is it today? |
| pierwszego *lub* 1 października 2011 r. | the first *or* 1st October 2011 |
| urodziłem się piątego czerwca 1981 r. | I was born on the 5th of June 1981 |
| w 1995 r. | in 1995 |

| | |
|---|---|
| w tysiąc dziewięćset dziewięćdziesiątym piątym | in nineteen (hundred and) ninety-five |
| 44 p.n.e. | 44 B.C. |
| 14 n.e. | 14 A.D. |
| w XIX wieku | in the 19th century |
| w latach trzydziestych, w latach 30. (XX wieku) | in the (nineteen) thirties, in the 1930s |
| pewnego razu | once upon a time |
| dawno, dawno temu | a long, long time ago |

# Aa

**A[1], a[1]** *nt inv (litera)* A, a; **od A do Z** from A to Z; **A jak Adam** ≈ A for Andrew *(Brit)*, ≈ A for Able (US); **A-dur** A major; **a-moll** A minor
**A[2]** *abbr (= amper)* A, amp
**a[2]** *conj* and ▷ *part*: **a nie mówiłem?** (I) told you so!; **dzisiaj, a nie jutro** today, (and) not tomorrow; **ja skończyłem, a ty?** I'm done, and how about you?; **między szafą a biurkiem** between the wardrobe and the desk; **a to co?** now, what would that be?; **taki a taki** *(pot)* so-and-so *(pot)*
**abażu|r (-ru, -ry)** *(loc sg* **-rze***)* *m* lampshade
**ABC** *nt inv* ABC; **ABC dziennikarstwa** the ABC of journalism
**abdyk|ować (-uję, -ujesz)** *vi (im)perf* to abdicate
**abecad|ło (-ła, -ła)** *(loc sg* **-le**, *gen pl* **-eł***)* *nt* alphabet; *(przen: podstawy)* the ABC *sg*
**abonamen|t (-tu, -ty)** *(loc sg* **-cie***)* *m* *(telewizyjny)* licence fee *(Brit)*, ≈ service fee (US); *(telefoniczny)* standing charges *pl*; **~ na coś** subscription to sth
**abonen|t (-ta, -ci)** *(loc sg* **-cie***)* *m* subscriber
**abonent|ka (-ki, -ki)** *(dat sg* **-ce**, *gen pl* **-ek***)* *f* subscriber
**aborcj|a (-i, -e)** *(gen pl* **-i***)* *f* abortion; **dokonywać (dokonać** *perf***) aborcji** to have *lub* get an abortion
**absencj|a (-i, -e)** *(gen pl* **-i***)* *f (nieobecność: jednorazowa)* absence; *(: wielokrotna)* absenteeism
**absolu|t (-tu, -ty)** *(loc sg* **-cie***)* *m (Filozofia)* absolute
**absolutnie** *adv* absolutely
**absolutny** *adj* absolute; *(racja, cisza)* complete; **zero absolutne** *(Fiz)* absolute zero
**absolutori|um (-um, -a)** *nt inv in sg (Uniw)* certificate of completion; *(Pol)* vote of approval
**absolutyz|m (-mu)** *(loc sg* **-mie***)* *m* absolutism
**absolwen|t (-ta, -ci)** *(loc sg* **-cie***)* *m* graduate
**absolwent|ka (-ki, -ki)** *(dat sg* **-ce**, *gen pl* **-ek***)* *f* graduate
**absorb|ować (-uję, -ujesz)** *(perf* **za-***)* *vt* to absorb
**abstrah|ować (-uję, -ujesz)** *vi (im)perf*: **~ (od** *+gen***)** to disregard; **abstrahując od** *+gen* aside *lub* apart from
**abstrakcj|a (-i, -e)** *(gen pl* **-i***)* *f* abstraction
**abstrakcyjny** *adj* abstract
**abstynencj|a (-i)** *f (od napojów alkoholowych)* abstinence, teetotalism; *(płciowa)* abstinence
**abstynen|t (-ta, -ci)** *(loc sg* **-cie***)* *m* teetotaller *(Brit)*, teetotaler (US)
**abstynent|ka (-ki, -ki)** *(dat sg* **-ce**, *gen pl* **-ek***)* *f* teetotaller *(Brit)*, teetotaler (US)
**absur|d (-du, -dy)** *(loc sg* **-dzie***)* *m* nonsense, absurdity
**absurdalny** *adj* absurd
**aby** *conj* (in order) to, so that ▷ *part*: **czy on aby przyjdzie?** will he really come?; **ona pojechała do Anglii, aby uczyć się angielskiego** she went to England to learn English; **aby nie przestraszyć dziecka** so as not to frighten the child; **aby tylko** let's just hope (that)
**AC** *abbr (= autocasco)* ≈ comprehensive (motor) insurance
**ach** *excl* oh
**achillesowy** *adj*: **pięta achillesowa** Achilles' heel
**aczkolwiek** *conj* although, albeit
**adamasz|ek (-ku, -ki)** *(instr sg* **-kiem***)* *m* damask
**adaptacj|a (-i, -e)** *(gen pl* **-i***)* *f* adaptation; *(utworu muzycznego)* arrangement
**adapte|r (-ra, -ry)** *(loc sg* **-rze***)* *m* record player
**adapt|ować (-uję, -ujesz)** *(perf* **za-***)* *vt* to adapt; *(utwór muzyczny)* to arrange; **adaptować się** *vr* to adapt
**adekwatny** *adj*: **~ (do** *+gen***)** commensurate (with), adequate (to *lub* for)
**adidas|y (-ów)** *pl* trainers *pl (Brit)*, training shoes *pl (Brit)*, sneakers *pl* (US), tennis shoes *pl* (US)
**adiunk|t (-ta, -ci)** *(loc sg* **-cie***)* *m* ≈ (senior) lecturer
**adiust|ować (-uję, -ujesz)** *(perf* **z-***)* *vt* to edit
**adiutan|t (-ta, -ci)** *(loc sg* **-cie***)* *m* aide-de-camp

**adm.** *abbr (= administracja)* admin, Admin; *(= admirał)* Adm.
**administracj|a** (**-i, -e**) (*gen pl* **-i**) *f* (*zarządzanie*) administration, management; (*zarząd*) management, board of directors; (*władza*) administration
**administracyjny** *adj* administrative, managing
**administrato|r** (**-ra, -rzy**) (*loc sg* **-rze**) *m* administrator, manager
**administr|ować (-uję, -ujesz)** *vt* to administer, to manage
**admiralicj|a** (**-i**) *f* Admiralty
**admira|ł** (**-ła, -łowie**) (*loc sg* **-le**) *m* admiral
**adnotacj|a** (**-i, -e**) (*gen pl* **-i**) *f* (*w książce, artykule*) note, annotation; (*na dokumencie*) endorsement
**adopcj|a** (**-i, -e**) (*gen pl* **-i**) *f* adoption
**adopt|ować (-uję, -ujesz)** (*perf* **za-**) *vt* to adopt
**adoptowany** *adj* adopted
**adoracj|a** (**-i, -e**) (*gen pl* **-i**) *f* (*książk: podziw*) admiration; (*Rel*) adoration; **towarzystwo wzajemnej adoracji** mutual admiration society
**adorato|r** (**-ra, -rzy**) (*loc sg* **-rze**) *m* admirer
**ador|ować (-uję, -ujesz)** *vt* (*wielbić*) to adore
**adre|s** (**-su, -sy**) (*loc sg* **-sie**) *m* address; **~ elektroniczny** *lub* **emailowy** *lub* **e-maila** (*Komput*) email address; **~ zwrotny** return address; **trafić** (*perf*) **pod zły ~** (*przen*) to (have) come to the wrong place; **czy to było pod moim ~em?** are you talking to me?
**adresa|t** (**-ta, -ci**) (*loc sg* **-cie**) *m* (*odbiorca listu*) addressee; (*odbiorca dzieła*) audience
**adres|ować (-uję, -ujesz)** (*perf* **za-**) *vt* to address
**Adriaty|k** (**-ku**) (*instr sg* **-kiem**) *m* the Adriatic (Sea)
**adwen|t** (**-tu, -ty**) (*loc sg* **-cie**) *m* (*Rel*) Advent
**adwenty|sta** (**-sty, -ści**) (*loc sg* **-ście**) *m decl like f in sg* (*Rel*) Adventist
**adwoka|t** (**-ta, -ci**) (*loc sg* **-cie**) *m* barrister (*Brit*), attorney (*US*)
**aerobi|k** (**-ku**) (*instr pl* **-kiem**) *m* aerobics
**aerodynamiczny** *adj* (*kształt*) streamlined; (*siła*) aerodynamic
**aerozo|l** (**-lu, -le**) (*gen pl* **-li**) *m* aerosol
**afek|t** (**-tu, -ty**) (*loc sg* **-cie**) *m*: **popełnić zbrodnię w afekcie** to commit a crime of passion
**afektacj|a** (**-i**) *f* affectation
**afektowany** *adj* affected, artificial
**afe|ra** (**-ry, -ry**) (*dat sg* **-rze**) *f* scandal; **ale ~!** (*pot*) what a mess!
**aferzy|sta** (**-sty, -ści**) (*loc sg* **-ście**) *m decl like f in sg* swindler
**Afganista|n** (**-nu**) (*loc sg* **-nie**) *m* Afghanistan
**Afgan|ka** (**-ki, -ki**) (*dat sg* **-ce**, *gen pl* **-ek**) *f* Afghan
**Afgańczy|k** (**-ka, -cy**) (*instr sg* **-kiem**) *m* Afghan
**afgański** *adj* Afghan
**afisz** (**-a, -e**) *m* poster, bill
**afisz|ować się (-uję, -ujesz)** *vr*: **afiszować się (z) czymś** to parade sth
**aforyz|m** (**-mu, -my**) (*loc sg* **-mie**) *m* aphorism
**afrodyzja|k** (**-ku, -ki**) (*instr sg* **-kiem**) *m* aphrodisiac
**afron|t** (**-tu, -ty**) (*loc sg* **-cie**) *m* affront, insult; **zrobić** (*perf*) **komuś ~** to affront *lub* insult sb
**Afry|ka** (**-ki**) (*dat sg* **-ce**) *f* Africa
**Afryka|nin** (**-nina, -nie**) (*loc sg* **-ninie**, *gen pl* **-nów**) *m* African
**Afrykan|ka** (**-ki, -ki**) (*dat sg* **-ce**, *gen pl* **-ek**) *f* African
**Afrykańczy|k** (**-ka, -cy**) (*instr sg* **-kiem**) *m* African
**afrykański** *adj* African
**agencj|a** (**-i, -e**) (*gen pl* **-i**) *f* (*przedstawicielstwo*) agent(s) (*pl*); (*fotograficzna, prasowa*) agency
**agencyjny** *adj*: **wiadomości agencyjne** (world) news
**agen|da** (**-dy, -dy**) (*dat sg* **-dzie**) *f* (*filia*) branch; (*harmonogram*) agenda
**agen|t** (**-ta, -ci**) (*loc sg* **-cie**) *m* (*przedstawiciel*) agent, rep(resentative); (*szpieg*) agent, spy
**agitacj|a** (**-i**) *f* canvassing, campaigning
**agitato|r** (**-ra, -rzy**) (*loc sg* **-rze**) *m* canvasser, campaigner
**agit|ować (-uję, -ujesz)** *vi* to canvass, to campaign
**aglomeracj|a** (**-i, -e**) (*gen pl* **-i**) *f* (*skupisko*) agglomeration; (*miasto*) urban area
**agoni|a** (**-i**) *f* agony
**agraf|ka** (**-ki, -ki**) (*dat sg* **-ce**, *gen pl* **-ek**) *f* safety pin
**agrarny** *adj* agrarian
**agrega|t** (**-tu, -ty**) (*loc sg* **-cie**) *m* (*Tech*) unit, engine
**agresj|a** (**-i, -e**) (*gen pl* **-i**) *f* aggression
**agreso|r** (**-ra, -rzy**) (*loc sg* **-rze**) *m* aggressor
**agre|st** (**-stu, -sty**) (*loc sg* **-ście**) *m* gooseberry
**agresywnoś|ć** (**-ci**) *f* aggressiveness
**agresywny** *adj* aggressive
**agronomi|a** (**-i**) *f* agronomy
**agrotechni|ka** (**-ki**) (*dat sg* **-ce**) *f* agricultural science
**aha** *excl* oh
**AIDS** *abbr* AIDS (= *acquired immune deficiency syndrome*); **chory na ~** an AIDS victim
**aj** *excl* oh, ouch
**ajencj|a** (**-i, -e**) (*gen pl* **-i**) *f* branch; **oddawać (oddać** *perf*) **coś w ajencję** to franchise sth;

**brać (wziąć** *perf*) **coś w ajencję** to obtain *lub* be granted a franchise on sth
**ajen|t** (**-ta, -ci**) (*loc sg* **-cie**) *m* franchise holder
**ajerkonia|k** (**-ku, -ki**) (*instr sg* **-kiem**) *m* advocaat
**AK** *abbr* (= *Armia Krajowa*) Home Army (*Polish underground military organization active during* WW II)
**akacj|a** (**-i, -e**) (*gen pl* **-i**) *f* acacia
**akademi|a** (**-i, -e**) (*gen pl* **-i**) *f* academy; (*uroczystość*) ceremony; **A~ Nauk** Academy of Sciences; **A~ Sztuk Pięknych** Academy of Fine Arts
**akademicki** *adj* academic; **dom ~** hall of residence (*Brit*), dormitory (*US*); **rok ~** academic year
**akademi|k** (**-ka, -ki**) (*instr sg* **-kiem**) *m* (*pot*) dorm (*pot*)
**akapi|t** (**-tu, -ty**) (*loc sg* **-cie**) *m* paragraph
**akcen|t** (**-tu, -ty**) (*loc sg* **-cie**) *m* (*Jęz*) stress; (*wymowa*) accent; (*znak*) accent (mark); (*nacisk*) stress, emphasis; (*Muz*) emphasis; **kłaść (położyć** *perf*) **na coś ~** to lay *lub* put emphasis on sth
**akcent|ować (-uję, -ujesz)** (*perf* **za-**) *vt* (*Jęz*) to stress; (*przen*) to stress, to emphasize
**akceptacj|a** (**-i, -e**) (*gen pl* **-i**) *f* (*przyjęcie*) acceptance; (*aprobata*) approval
**akcept|ować (-uję, -ujesz)** (*perf* **za-**) *vt* (*przyjmować*) to accept; (*aprobować*) to approve of
**akcesori|a** (**-ów**) *pl* accessories *pl*
**akcie** *n patrz* **akt**
**akcj|a** (**-i, -e**) (*gen pl* **-i**) *f* (*kampania*) campaign, operation; (*działalność*) action; (*fabuła*) plot; (*Fin*) share; (*Sport*) breakaway
**akcjonariusz** (**-a, -e**) (*gen pl* **-y**) *m* shareholder, stockholder
**akcyjny** *adj* share *attr*, stock *attr*; **spółka akcyjna** joint-stock company
**akcy|za** (**-zy, -zy**) (*dat sg* **-zie**) *f* excise
**aklamacj|a** (**-i**) *f* acclamation; **przez aklamację** by acclamation
**aklimatyzacj|a** (**-i**) *f* (re)adjustment
**aklimatyz|ować się (-uję, -ujesz)** (*perf* **za-**) *vr* to (re)adjust
**akompaniamen|t** (**-tu**) (*loc sg* **-cie**) *m* accompaniment
**akompaniato|r** (**-ra, -rzy**) (*loc sg* **-rze**) *m* accompanist
**akompani|ować (-uję, -ujesz)** *vi* to accompany
**akon|to** (**-ta, -ta**) (*loc sg* **-cie**) *nt* (*zaliczka*) advance
**akor|d** (**-du, -dy**) (*loc sg* **-dzie**) *m* (*Muz*) chord; (*Ekon*) piece-work; **pracować na ~** to do piece-work
**akordeo|n** (**-nu, -ny**) (*loc sg* **-nie**) *m* accordion
**akordowy** *adj*: **praca akordowa** piece-work
**ak|r** (**-ra, -ry**) (*loc sg* **-rze**) *m* acre
**akredytacj|a** (**-i**) *f* accreditation
**akredyt|ować (-uję, -ujesz)** *vt* (*im*)*perf* to accredit
**akredytowany** *adj* accredited
**akrobacj|a** (**-i, -e**) (*gen pl* **-i**) *f* acrobatics; (*Film*) stunt(s) (*pl*); **~ lotnicza** aerial stunt(s) (*pl*), aerobatics
**akroba|ta** (**-ty, -ci**) (*dat sg* **-cie**) *m decl like f in sg* acrobat
**akrobat|ka** (**-ki, -ki**) (*dat sg* **-ce**, *gen pl* **-ek**) *f* acrobat
**akrobatyczny** *adj* acrobatic
**akrobaty|ka** (**-ki**) (*dat sg* **-ce**) *f* acrobatics
**aksami|t** (**-tu, -ty**) (*loc sg* **-cie**) *m* velvet
**aksamitny** *adj* velvet *attr*; (*mech, głos*) velvety
**ak|t** (**-tu, -ty**) (*loc sg* **-cie**) *m* act; (*ceremonia*) ceremony; (*Sztuka*) nude; (*dokument*) (*nom pl* **-ta** *lub* **-ty**) certificate; **akta** (*gen pl* **akt**) *pl* (*dokumenty*) record(s) (*pl*), file(s) (*pl*); (*dotyczące osoby, sprawy*) dossier; **akt przemocy/rozpaczy** an act of violence/despair; **akt notarialny** notarial deed *lub* act; **akt oskarżenia** indictment; **akt płciowy** sexual act; **akt ślubu/urodzenia/zgonu** marriage/birth/death certificate; **odkładać (odłożyć** *perf*) **coś do akt** to file sth away
**akto|r** (**-ra, -rzy**) (*loc sg* **-rze**) *m* actor
**aktor|ka** (**-ki, -ki**) (*dat sg* **-ce**, *gen pl* **-ek**) *f* actress
**aktorst|wo** (**-wa**) (*loc sg* **-wie**) *nt* acting
**aktów|ka** (**-ki, -ki**) (*dat sg* **-ce**, *gen pl* **-ek**) *f* briefcase, attaché case
**aktualiz|ować (-uję, -ujesz)** (*perf* **z-**) *vt* to update
**aktualnie** *adv* currently, at present
**aktualnoś|ć** (**-ci**) *f* topicality; **aktualności** *pl* news; **tracić (stracić** (*perf*)) **na aktualności** to go out of date
**aktualny** *adj* (*obecny*) current, present; (*będący na czasie*) up-to-date, current; **aktualne problemy** current *lub* topical issues
**aktywi|sta** (**-sty, -ści**) (*dat sg* **-ście**) *m decl like f in sg* activist
**aktywnie** *adv* actively
**aktywnoś|ć** (**-ci**) *f* activity
**aktywny** *adj* active
**akumulacj|a** (**-i**) *f* accumulation, accretion
**akumulato|r** (**-ra, -ry**) (*loc sg* **-rze**) *m* (*Elektr*) accumulator; (*Mot*) battery
**akumul|ować (-uję, -ujesz)** (*perf* **z-**) (*książk*) *vt* to accumulate; **akumulować się** *vr* to accumulate
**akupunktu|ra** (**-ry**) (*dat sg* **-rze**) *f* acupuncture

**akurat** *adv* (*dokładnie*) exactly; (*w tej chwili*) at this *lub* that very moment; **~!** (*pot*) tell me another! (*pot*)
**akustyczny** *adj* acoustic
**akusty|ka** (**-ki**) (*dat sg* **-ce**) *f* (*pomieszczenia*) acoustics *pl*; (*dziedzina fizyki*) acoustics *sg*
**akuszer|ka** (**-ki, -ki**) (*dat sg* **-ce**, *gen pl* **-ek**) *f* midwife
**akwarel|a** (**-i, -e**) *f* watercolour (*Brit*), watercolor (*US*)
**akwari|um** (**-um, -a**) (*gen pl* **-ów**) *nt inv in sg* (fish) tank, aquarium
**akweduk|t** (**-tu, -ty**) (*loc sg* **-cie**) *m* aqueduct
**akwe|n** (**-nu, -ny**) (*loc sg* **-nie**) *m* reservoir, body of water
**akwizycj|a** (**-i**) *f* canvassing
**akwizyto|r** (**-ra, -rzy**) (*loc sg* **-rze**) *m* canvasser
**alar|m** (**-mu, -my**) (*loc sg* **-mie**) *m* (*sygnał*) alarm; (*stan gotowości*) alert; (*pot: urządzenie*) alarm system; (*: w bibliotece, sklepie*) anti-theft system; (*: przeciwwłamaniowy*) burglar alarm; **podnosić (podnieść** *perf*) **~** to raise *lub* give the alarm; **bić na ~** (*przen*) to raise the alarm
**alarm|ować (-uję, -ujesz)** (*perf* **za-**) *vt* (*ostrzegać*) to alert; (*niepokoić*) to alarm, to startle
**alarmowy** *adj* alarm *attr*
**Alas|ka** (**-ki**) (*dat sg* **-ce**) *f* Alaska
**Albani|a** (**-i**) *f* Albania
**Alban|ka** (**-ki, -ki**) (*dat sg* **-ce**, *gen pl* **-ek**) *f* Albanian
**Albańczy|k** (**-ka, -cy**) (*instr sg* **-kiem**) *m* Albanian
**albański** *adj* Albanian
**albino|s** (**-sa, -si**) (*loc sg* **-sie**) *m* albino
**albo** *conj* or; **~ ... ~ ...** either ... or ...
**albowiem** *conj* for, because
**albu|m** (**-mu, -my**) (*loc sg* **-mie**) *m* album
**alchemi|a** (**-i**) *f* alchemy
**alchemi|k** (**-ka, -cy**) (*instr sg* **-kiem**) *m* alchemist
**alcie** *n patrz* **alt**
**ale** *conj* but ▹ *part*: **ale pogoda!** what weather!; **ale głupiec ze mnie!** what a fool I am!; **ale piękna!** what a beauty!
**alegori|a** (**-i, -e**) (*gen pl* **-i**) *f* allegory
**alegoryczny** *adj* allegorical
**ale|ja** (**-i, -je**) (*gen pl* **-i**) *f* (*uliczka, przejście*) alley; (*droga*) avenue
**alergi|a** (**-i, -e**) (*gen pl* **-i**) *f* allergy
**alergiczny** *adj* (*reakcja*) allergic; (*poradnia*) allergy *attr*
**ależ** *excl* but; **~ oczywiście!** but of course!; **~ skąd!** not at all!
**alfabe|t** (**-tu, -ty**) (*loc sg* **-cie**) *m* alphabet; **~ Braille'a** Braille; **~ Morse'a** Morse (code)
**alfabetyczny** *adj* alphabetical; **w porządku ~m** in alphabetical order
**alfon|s** (**-sa, -si** *lub* **-sy**) (*loc sg* **-sie**) *m* (*pot*) pimp
**algeb|ra** (**-ry**) (*dat sg* **-rze**) *f* algebra
**Algie|r** (**-ru**) (*loc sg* **-rze**) *m* Algiers
**Algierczy|k** (**-ka, -cy**) (*instr sg* **-kiem**) *m* Algerian
**Algieri|a** (**-i**) *f* Algeria
**Algier|ka** (**-ki, -ki**) (*dat sg* **-ce**, *gen pl* **-ek**) *f* Algerian
**algierski** *adj* Algerian
**algoryt|m** (**-mu, -my**) (*loc sg* **-mie**) *m* algorithm
**alian|t** (**-ta, -ci**) (*loc sg* **-cie**) *m* ally; **alianci** *pl* (*Hist*) the Allies *pl*, the allied forces *lub* nations *pl*
**alibi** *nt inv* alibi; **mieć ~** to have an alibi
**alienacj|a** (**-i**) (*gen pl* **-i**) *f* alienation
**aligato|r** (**-ra, -ry**) (*loc sg* **-rze**) *m* alligator
**aliment|y** (*gen pl* **-ów**) *pl* alimony
**alkohol** (**-u, -e**) (*gen pl* **-i** *lub* **-ów**) *m* (*Chem*) alcohol; (*napój alkoholowy*) alcohol, alcoholic drink *lub* beverage
**alkoholicz|ka** (**-ki, -ki**) (*dat sg* **-ce**, *gen pl* **-ek**) *f* alcoholic
**alkoholi|k** (**-ka, -cy**) (*instr sg* **-kiem**) *m* alcoholic
**alkoholiz|m** (**-mu**) (*loc sg* **-mie**) *m* alcoholism
**alkoholowy** *adj* (*choroba, napój*) alcoholic; (*roztwór*) of alcohol
**alkoma|t** (**-tu, -ty**) (*loc sg* **-cie**) *m* breathalyser (*Brit*), breathalyzer (*US*)
**alleluja** *nt inv* (*Rel*) hallelujah; **wesołego ~!** Happy Easter!
**aloe|s** (**-su, -sy**) (*loc sg* **-sie**) *m* aloe
**alpejski** *adj* Alpine; **fiołek ~** cyclamen; **kombinacja alpejska** Alpine combined
**alpini|sta** (**-sty, -ści**) (*dat sg* **-ście**) *m decl like f in sg* climber, mountaineer
**alpiniz|m** (**-mu**) (*loc sg* **-mie**) *m* climbing, mountaineering
**Alp|y** (**-**) *pl* the Alps
**al|t** (**-tu, -ty**) (*loc sg* **-cie**) *m* (*Muz*) alto; (*śpiewaczka*) (*gen sg* **-ta**) alto; **śpiewać altem** to sing alto *lub* in alt
**alta|na** (**-ny, -ny**) (*dat sg* **-nie**) *f* (*domek na działce*) garden shed; (*ażurowa konstrukcja*) arbour (*Brit*), arbor (*US*)
**altan|ka** (**-ki, -ki**) (*dat sg* **-ce**, *gen pl* **-ek**) *f* arbour (*Brit*), arbor (*US*)
**alternato|r** (**-ra, -ry**) (*loc sg* **-rze**) *m* (*Mot*) alternator
**alternaty|wa** (**-wy, -wy**) (*dat sg* **-wie**) *f* alternative
**alternatywny** *adj* alternative

a

**altów|ka** (**-ki, -ki**) (*dat sg* **-ce**, *gen pl* **-ek**) *f* (*Muz*) viola
**altrui|sta** (**-sty, -ści**) (*dat sg* **-ście**) *m decl like f in sg* altruist
**altruistyczny** *adj* altruistic, unselfish
**altruiz|m** (**-mu**) (*loc sg* **-mie**) *m* altruism
**aluminiowy** *adj* aluminium *attr* (*Brit*), aluminum *attr* (*US*); **folia aluminiowa** tinfoil
**aluminium** *nt inv* aluminium (*Brit*), aluminum (*US*)
**aluzj|a** (**-i, -e**) (*gen pl* **-i**) *f* hint, allusion; **robić (zrobić** *perf*) **aluzję do czegoś** to hint at sth, to allude to sth
**Alzheimera** *inv*: **choroba ~** Alzheimer's disease
**AM** *abbr* (= *Akademia Medyczna*) Medical School *lub* University
**aman|t** (**-ta, -ci**) (*loc sg* **-cie**) *m* (*kochanek*) beau, lover; **~ filmowy** screen lover
**amato|r** (**-ra, -rzy**) (*loc sg* **-rze**) *m* (*niefachowiec*) amateur, layman; (*miłośnik, chętny*) lover; (*Sport*) amateur
**amatorski** *adj* (*niedoskonały*) amateurish; (*niezawodowy*) amateur *attr*
**amazon|ka** (**-ki, -ki**) (*dat sg* **-ce**, *gen pl* **-ek**) *f* (*kobieta jeździec*) horsewoman; **Amazonka** (*Geog*) Amazon
**ambasa|da** (**-dy, -dy**) (*dat sg* **-dzie**) *f* embassy
**ambasado|r** (**-ra, -rzy** *lub* **-rowie**) (*loc sg* **-rze**) *m* ambassador; (*rzecznik*) champion, advocate
**ambicj|a** (**-i, -e**) (*gen pl* **-i**) *f* (*honor, pragnienie*) ambition; (*pycha*) pride
**ambitny** *adj* ambitious
**ambo|na** (**-ny, -ny**) (*dat sg* **-nie**) *f* (*w kościele*) pulpit; (*w lesie*) look-out
**ambulatori|um** (**-um, -a**) (*gen pl* **-ów**) *nt inv in sg* out-patients' clinic
**ame|ba** (**-by, -by**) (*dat sg* **-bie**) *f* amoeba (*Brit*), ameba (*US*)
**amen** *nt inv* amen; **jak ~ w pacierzu** (*pot*) as sure as eggs is eggs (*pot*); **na ~** (*pot*) for good
**Amery|ka** (**-ki, -ki**) (*dat sg* **-ce**) *f* America; **~ Łacińska** Latin America; **~ Południowa/ Północna** South/North America
**Ameryka|nin** (**-nina, -nie**) (*loc sg* **-ninie**, *gen pl* **-nów**) *m* American
**Amerykan|ka** (**-ki, -ki**) (*dat sg* **-ce**, *gen pl* **-ek**) *f* American; **amerykanka** (*mebel*) sofa bed
**amerykański** *adj* American
**amety|st** (**-stu, -sty**) (*loc sg* **-ście**) *m* amethyst
**amfetamin|a** (**-ny, -ny**) (*dat sg* **-nie**) *f* amphetamine
**amfibi|a** (**-i, -e**) (*gen pl* **-i**) *f* amphibious vehicle
**amfiteat|r** (**-ru, -ry**) (*loc sg* **-rze**) *m* amphitheatre (*Brit*), amphitheater (*US*)
**aminokwa|s** (**-su, -sy**) (*loc sg* **-sie**) *m* amino acid
**amnesti|a** (**-i, -e**) (*gen pl* **-i**) *f* amnesty, pardon; **~ powszechna** general pardon; **udzielać (udzielić** *perf*) **komuś amnestii** to grant a pardon *lub* an amnesty to sb; **na mocy amnestii** on pardon
**amonia|k** (**-ku**) (*instr sg* **-kiem**) *m* (*gaz*) ammonia; (*roztwór*) ammonia water
**Amo|r** (**-ra**) (*loc sg* **-rze**) *m* (*bóg*) Cupid; (*amorek*) cupid; **amory** *pl* romance
**amoralny** *adj* amoral
**amortyzacj|a** (**-i**) *f* (*Ekon*) depreciation; (*Tech*) shock absorption
**amortyzato|r** (**-ra, -ry**) (*loc sg* **-rze**) *m* (*Mot*) shock absorber
**amortyz|ować (-uję, -ujesz)** (*perf* **z-**) *vt* (*Ekon*) to allow for the depreciation of; (*Tech*) to cushion
**ampe|r** (**-ra, -ry**) (*loc sg* **-rze**) *m* (*Elektr*) ampère, amp (*pot*)
**amperomie|rz** (**-rza, -rze**) (*gen pl* **-rzy**) *m* (*Elektr*) ammeter
**amplitu|da** (**-dy, -dy**) (*dat sg* **-dzie**) *f* amplitude
**ampuł|ka** (**-ki, -ki**) (*dat sg* **-ce**, *gen pl* **-ek**) *f* ampoule
**amputacj|a** (**-i, -e**) (*gen pl* **-i**) *f* amputation
**amput|ować (-uję, -ujesz)** *vt* (*im*)*perf* to amputate
**amule|t** (**-tu, -ty**) (*loc sg* **-cie**) *m* amulet
**amunicj|a** (**-i**) *f* ammunition
**anachroniczny** *adj* (out)dated, anachronistic
**anachroniz|m** (**-mu, -my**) (*loc sg* **-mie**) *m* anachronism
**analfabe|ta** (**-ty, -ci**) (*dat sg* **-cie**) *m decl like f in sg* illiterate
**analfabetyz|m** (**-mu**) (*loc sg* **-mie**) *m* illiteracy
**analityczny** *adj* analytic(al)
**anali|za** (**-zy, -zy**) (*dat sg* **-zie**) *f* (*Chem, Fiz*) analysis; (*Med*) test
**analiz|ować (-uję, -ujesz)** (*perf* **z-**) *vt* to analyse (*Brit*), to analyze (*US*)
**analogi|a** (**-i, -e**) (*gen pl* **-i**) *f* analogy, parallel; **przez analogię** by analogy
**analogicznie** *adv* similarly
**analogiczny** *adj* analogous, parallel; **~ do** *+gen* analogous to
**analogowy** *adj* analog(ue)
**anana|s** (**-sa, -sy**) (*loc sg* **-sie**) *m* pineapple
**anarchi|a** (**-i**) *f* anarchy
**anarchi|sta** (**-sty, -ści**) (*dat sg* **-ście**) *m decl like f in sg* anarchist
**anarchistyczny** *adj* anarchist
**anatomi|a** (**-i**) *f* anatomy
**anatomiczny** *adj* anatomical
**anchois** *nt inv* anchovy

**andrzej|ki** (**-ek**) *pl St Andrew's Day (30th November)*
**And|y** (**-ów**) *pl* the Andes
**anegdo|ta** (**-ty, -ty**) (*loc sg* **-cie**) *f* anecdote
**anek|s** (**-su, -sy**) (*loc sg* **-sie**) *m* annexe (*Brit*), annex (*US*)
**aneksj|a** (**-i, -e**) (*gen pl* **-i**) *f* annexation
**anekt|ować (-uję, -ujesz)** (*perf* **za-**) *vt* to annex
**anemi|a** (**-i**) *f* anaemia (*Brit*), anemia (*US*)
**anemiczny** *adj* anaemic (*Brit*), anemic (*US*)
**anestezjolo|g** (**-ga, -dzy** *lub* **-gowie**) (*instr sg* **-giem**) *m* anaesthetist (*Brit*), anesthetist (*US*)
**anestezjologi|a** (**-i**) *f* (*Med*) anaesthesiology (*Brit*), anesthesiology (*US*)
**angaż|ować (-uję, -ujesz)** (*perf* **za-**) *vt* (*zatrudniać*) to hire, to employ; (*wciągać*) to engage, to involve; **angażować się** *vr* (*zatrudniać się*) to take up a job; (*wciągać się*) to become involved
**Angiel|ka** (**-ki, -ki**) (*dat sg* **-ce**, *gen pl* **-ek**) *f* Englishwoman
**angielski** *adj* English ▷ *m decl like adj* (*język*) English; **ziele ~e** (*całe*) pimento; (*mielone*) allspice; **mówić/czytać/rozumieć po angielsku** to speak/read/understand English; **tłumaczyć na ~** to translate into English
**angielszczy|zna** (**-zny**) (*dat sg* **-źnie**) *f*: **mówić łamaną angielszczyzną** to speak in broken English
**angi|na** (**-ny**) (*loc sg* **-nie**) *f* strep throat
**Angli|a** (**-i**) *f* England; (*pot: Wielka Brytania*) Britain, UK
**Angli|k** (**-ka, -cy**) (*instr sg* **-kiem**) *m* Englishman
**anglikański** *adj* Anglican; **Kościół A~** the Church of England
**Angol|a** (**-i**) *f* Angola
**ani** *conj* nor, neither; (*z innym wyrazem przeczącym*) or, either; **ani ... ani ...** neither ... nor ...; (*z innym wyrazem przeczącym*) either ... or ... ▷ *part* not a (single); (*z innym wyrazem przeczącym*) a (single); **ani chybi** most certainly, without fail; **ani jeden** not a single one, none; **ani mi się śni!** (*pot*) no way! (*pot*); **ani mi się waż!** (*pot*) don't you dare! (*pot*); **ani słowa!** button your lip!; **ani trochę** not a bit
**aniele** *itd. n patrz* **anioł**
**anielski** *adj* angelic
**animacj|a** (**-i**) *f* animation
**animowany** *adj*: **film ~** cartoon
**animusz** (**-u**) *m* (*zapał*) spirit, mettle; (*odwaga*) courage
**ani|oł** (**-oła, -ołowie** *lub* **-oły**) (*loc sg* **-ele**) *m* angel; **~ stróż** guardian angel
**ankie|ta** (**-ty, -ty**) (*dat sg* **-cie**) *f* (*badanie opinii*) poll; (*formularz*) questionnaire; **~ personalna** (a form for) personal details
**ano|da** (**-dy, -dy**) (*dat sg* **-dzie**) *f* anode
**anomali|a** (**-i, -e**) (*gen pl* **-i**) *f* anomaly
**anoni|m** (**-mu, -my**) (*loc sg* **-mie**) *m* (*człowiek*) anonymous person; (*list*) anonymous letter
**anonimowy** *adj* anonymous
**anon|s** (**-su, -sy** *lub* **-se**) (*loc sg* **-sie**) *m* (classified) advertisement
**anons|ować (-uję, -ujesz)** (*perf* **za-**) *vt* to announce
**anormalny** *adj* abnormal
**antagoni|sta** (**-sty, -ści**) (*dat sg* **-ście**) *m decl like f in sg* antagonist
**antagonistyczny** *adj* antagonistic
**antagoniz|m** (**-mu, -my**) (*loc sg* **-mie**) *m* antagonism
**antarktyczny** *adj* Antarctic
**Antarkty|da** (**-dy**) (*dat sg* **-dzie**) *f* Antarctica
**Antarkty|ka** (**-ki**) (*dat sg* **-ce**) *f* the Antarctic
**ante|na** (**-ny, -ny**) (*dat sg* **-nie**) *f* aerial (*Brit*), antenna (*US*); **~ satelitarna** satellite dish; **być na antenie** to be on the air
**antenowy** *adj*: **maszt ~** antenna mast; **czas ~** air time
**antidot|um** (**-um, -a**) *nt inv in sg* antidote
**antologi|a** (**-i, -e**) (*gen pl* **-i**) *f* anthology
**antoni|m** (**-mu, -my**) (*loc sg* **-mie**) *m* antonym
**antrak|t** (**-tu, -ty**) (*loc sg* **-cie**) *m* intermission
**antropolo|g** (**-ga, -dzy** *lub* **-gowie**) (*instr sg* **-giem**) *m* anthropologist
**antropologi|a** (**-i**) *f* anthropology
**anty...** *pref* anti...
**antybioty|k** (**-ku, -ki**) (*instr sg* **-kiem**) *m* antibiotic
**antyczny** *adj* (*epoka, świat*) ancient; (*literatura*) classical; (*mebel*) antique
**antydat|ować (-uję, -ujesz)** *vt* to backdate
**anty|k** (**-ku, -ki**) (*instr sg* **-kiem**) *m* (*okres, kultura*) antiquity; (*przedmiot*) antique
**antykoncepcj|a** (**-i**) *f* contraception
**antykoncepcyjny** *adj*: **środek ~** contraceptive
**antykwaria|t** (**-tu, -ty**) (*loc sg* **-cie**) *m* (*księgarnia*) second-hand bookshop (*Brit*) *lub* bookstore (*US*); (*sklep z antykami*) antique shop
**antykwariusz** (**-a, -e**) (*gen pl* **-y**) *m* antiquarian
**antylo|pa** (**-py, -py**) (*dat sg* **-pie**) *f* antelope
**antypati|a** (**-i, -e**) (*gen pl* **-i**) *f* antipathy
**antypatyczny** *adj* unsympathetic
**antypod|y** (**-ów**) *pl* the Antipodes
**antysemicki** *adj* anti-Semitic
**antysemi|ta** (**-ty, -ci**) (*dat sg* **-cie**) *m decl like f in sg* anti-Semite

**antysemityz|m (-mu)** (*loc sg* **-mie**) *m* anti-Semitism
**anul|ować (-uję, -ujesz)** *vt (im)perf* to annul
**anyż (-u, -e)** *m* aniseed
**aor|ta (-ty, -ty)** (*loc sg* **-cie**) *f* aorta
**apara|t (-tu, -ty)** (*loc sg* **-cie**) *m* (*urządzenie*) apparatus; **~ fotograficzny** camera; **~ słuchowy** hearing aid; **~ telefoniczny** telephone; **~ państwowy** state machinery *lub* apparatus
**aparatu|ra (-ry, -ry)** (*dat sg* **-rze**) *f* apparatus
**apartamen|t (-tu, -ty)** (*loc sg* **-cie**) *m* (*luksusowe mieszkanie*) apartment; (*w hotelu*) suite
**aparycj|a (-i)** *f* looks *pl*
**apasz|ka (-ki, -ki)** (*dat sg* **-ce**, *gen pl* **-ek**) *f* neckerchief; (*męska*) cravat
**apati|a (-i)** *f* apathy
**apatyczny** *adj* apathetic
**apel (-u, -e)** (*gen pl* **-i** *lub* **-ów**) *m* (*odezwa*) appeal; (*zbiórka*) assembly; **zwracać się (zwrócić się** *perf*) **z ~em do kogoś** to make an appeal to sb
**apelacj|a (-i, -e)** (*gen pl* **-i**) *f* (*Prawo*) appeal; **wnosić (wnieść** *perf*) **apelację** to lodge an appeal
**apelacyjny** *adj*: **sąd ~** court of appeal
**apel|ować (-uję, -ujesz)** *vi* (*Prawo*) to appeal; (*zwracać się*): **~ do** *+gen* (*perf* **za-**) to appeal to
**Apenin|y (-)** *pl* the Apennines
**aperiti|f (-fu, -fy)** (*loc sg* **-fie**) *m* aperitif
**apetyczny** *adj* appetizing
**apety|t (-tu, -ty)** (*loc sg* **-cie**) *m* appetite
**aplau|z (-zu, -zy)** (*loc sg* **-zie**) *m* applause; **przyjmować (przyjąć** *perf*) **coś z ~em** to applaud sth
**aplikacj|a (-i, -e)** (*gen pl* **-i**) *f* (*Prawo*) ≈ articles *pl* (*Brit*); (*Komput*) application
**aplikan|t (-ta, -ci)** (*loc sg* **-cie**) *m* articled clerk (*Brit*)
**aplik|ować (-uję, -ujesz)** *vt* (*perf* **za-**) (*lek*) to administer; (*odbywać aplikację*) to serve one's articles
**apodyktyczny** *adj* domineering
**apoge|um (-um, -a)** (*gen pl* **-ów**) *nt inv in sg* (*książk*) apogee
**apokalip|sa (-sy)** (*dat sg* **-sie**) *f* apocalypse
**apolityczny** *adj* apolitical
**aport|ować (-uje)** *vt* to fetch; **aport!** fetch!
**apostolski** *adj* (*praca*) apostolic; **list ~** epistle; **Stolica Apostolska** the Holy See
**aposto|ł (-ła, -łowie)** (*loc sg* **-le**) *m* apostle
**apostro|f (-fu, -fy)** (*loc sg* **-fie**) *m* apostrophe
**aproba|ta (-ty)** (*dat sg* **-cie**) *f* approval; **uzyskać** (*perf*) **aprobatę** to meet with approval; **wyrażać (wyrazić** *perf*) **swoją aprobatę** to give one's assent
**aprob|ować (-uję, -ujesz)** (*perf* **za-**) *vt* to approve of
**aprowizacj|a (-i)** *f* (*zaopatrzenie*) food supply
**aptecz|ka (-ki, -ki)** (*dat sg* **-ce**, *gen pl* **-ek**) *f* medicine cabinet *lub* chest; **~ samochodowa** first-aid kit
**apte|ka (-ki, -ki)** (*dat sg* **-ce**) *f* pharmacy, (dispensing) chemist('s) (*Brit*), drugstore (*US*)
**apteka|rz (-rza, -rze)** (*gen pl* **-rzy**) *m* pharmacist, chemist (*Brit*), druggist (*US*)
**Ara|b (-ba, -bowie)** (*loc sg* **-bie**) *m* Arab
**ara|b (-ba, -by)** (*loc sg* **-bie**) *m* (*koń*) Arab, Arabian (*US*)
**Arabi|a (-i)** *f*: **~ Saudyjska** Saudi Arabia
**Arab|ka (-ki, -ki)** (*dat sg* **-ce**, *gen pl* **-ek**) *f* Arab
**arabski** *adj* (*kraje, kultura*) Arab; (*pustynia, półwysep*) Arabian; (*język, cyfra*) Arabic ▷ *m decl like adj* (*język*) Arabic
**aranżacj|a (-i, -e)** (*gen pl* **-i**) *f* arrangement
**aranż|ować (-uję, -ujesz)** (*perf* **za-**) *vt* to arrange
**arbit|er (-ra, -rzy)** (*loc sg* **-rze**) *m* (*znawca, rozjemca*) arbiter; (*w tenisie, pływaniu, baseballu*) umpire; (*w koszykówce, piłce nożnej, hokeju*) referee
**arbitralny** *adj* arbitrary
**arbitraż (-u, -e)** (*gen pl* **-y**) *m* arbitration
**arbu|z (-za, -zy)** (*loc sg* **-zie**) *m* watermelon
**arce** *n patrz* **arka**
**archaiczny** *adj* archaic
**archaiz|m (-mu, -my)** (*loc sg* **-mie**) *m* archaism
**archani|oł (-oła, -ołowie** *lub* **-oły)** (*loc sg* **-ele**) *m* archangel
**archeolo|g (-ga, -dzy** *lub* **-gowie)** (*instr sg* **-giem**) *m* archaeologist (*Brit*), archeologist (*US*)
**archeologi|a (-i)** *f* archaeology (*Brit*), archeology (*US*)
**archeologiczny** *adj* archaeological (*Brit*), archeological (*US*)
**archipela|g (-gu, -gi)** (*instr sg* **-giem**) *m* archipelago
**architek|t (-ta, -ci)** (*loc sg* **-cie**) *m* architect; **~ wnętrz** interior designer
**architektoniczny** *adj* architectural
**architektu|ra (-ry)** (*dat sg* **-rze**) *f* architecture; **~ wnętrz** interior design
**archiwalny** *adj* archival
**archiw|um (-um, -a)** (*gen pl* **-ów**) *nt inv in sg* archive
**arcy...** *pref* (*z rzeczownikiem*) arch...; (*z przymiotnikiem*) super...
**arcybisku|p (-pa, -pi)** (*loc sg* **-pie**) *m* archbishop
**arcydzie|ło (-ła, -ła)** (*loc sg* **-le**) *nt* masterpiece

**arcyksi|ążę** (**-ęcia, -ążęta**) (*gen pl* **-ążąt**) *m* archduke
**arcymistrz** (**-a, -owie** *lub* **-e**) *m* grand master
**area|ł** (**-łu, -ły**) (*loc sg* **-le**) *m* acreage
**are|na** (**-ny, -ny**) (*loc sg* **-nie**) *f* arena
**aresz|t** (**-tu, -ty**) (*loc sg* **-cie**) *m* (*aresztowanie*) arrest; (*pomieszczenie*) detention house; **w areszcie** in custody; **~ domowy** house arrest; **~ tymczasowy** detention awaiting trial
**aresz|ować** (**-uję, -ujesz**) (*perf also* **za-**) *vt* (*im)perf* to arrest, to take into custody; **jest Pan aresztowany** you're under arrest
**aresztowa|nie** (**-nia, -nia**) (*gen pl* **-ń**) *nt* arrest; **nakaz aresztowania** warrant of arrest
**aresztowa|ny** (**-nego, -ni**) *m decl like adj* detainee
**Argenty|na** (**-ny**) (*dat sg* **-nie**) *f* Argentina
**Argentyn|ka** (**-ki, -ki**) (*dat sg* **-ce**, *gen pl* **-ek**) *f* Argentinian
**Argentyńczy|k** (**-ka, -cy**) (*instr sg* **-kiem**) *m* Argentinian
**argentyński** *adj* Argentinian
**argumen|t** (**-tu, -ty**) (*loc sg* **-cie**) *m* argument
**argumentacj|a** (**-i, -e**) (*gen pl* **-i**) *f* argumentation
**argument|ować** (**-uję, -ujesz**) (*perf* **u-**) *vi* to argue
**ari|a** (**-i, -e**) (*gen pl* **-i**) *f* aria
**ar|ka** (**-ki, -ki**) (*dat sg* **-ce**, *gen pl* **-k**) *f* ark; **A~ Noego** Noah's Ark; **A~ Przymierza** Ark of the Covenant
**arka|da** (**-dy, -dy**) (*dat sg* **-dzie**) *f* arcade
**arktyczny** *adj* Arctic
**Arkty|ka** (**-ki**) (*dat sg* **-ce**) *f* the Arctic
**arkusz** (**-a, -e**) (*gen pl* **-y**) *m* sheet; (*Druk*) quire, gathering (*16 pages*); **~ kalkulacyjny** (*Komput*) spreadsheet
**arma|ta** (**-ty, -ty**) (*dat sg* **-cie**) *f* cannon
**armatni** *adj*: **pocisk ~** cannonball; **mięso ~e** cannon fodder
**armato|r** (**-ra, -rzy**) (*loc sg* **-rze**) *m* shipowner
**armatu|ra** (**-ry, -ry**) (*dat sg* **-rze**) *f* (*zbrojenie*) reinforcement; (*wyposażenie*) fittings *pl*
**armi|a** (**-i, -e**) (*gen pl* **-i**) *f* army; **A~ Zbawienia** Salvation Army
**arogancj|a** (**-i**) *f* arrogance
**arogancki** *adj* arrogant
**aroma|t** (**-tu, -ty**) (*loc sg* **-cie**) *m* (*zapach*) aroma; (*substancja*) flavouring (*Brit*), flavoring (*US*)
**aromatyczny** *adj* aromatic
**arsena|ł** (**-łu, -ły**) (*loc sg* **-le**) *m* arsenal
**arszeni|k** (**-ku**) (*instr sg* **-kiem**) *m* arsenic
**arteri|a** (**-i, -e**) (*gen pl* **-i**) *f* artery
**artretyz|m** (**-mu**) (*loc sg* **-mie**) *m* arthritis
**artyku|ł** (**-łu, -ły**) (*loc sg* **-le**) *m* article; **~y spożywcze** groceries; **~y pierwszej potrzeby** necessities
**artyleri|a** (**-i**) *f* artillery
**artyleryjski** *adj*: **ogień ~** artillery fire
**artylerzy|sta** (**-sty, -ści**) (*dat sg* **-ście**) *m decl like f in sg* artilleryman, artillerist
**arty|sta** (**-sty, -ści**) (*dat sg* **-ście**) *m decl like f in sg* artist; (*pot*: *aktor*) actor; **~ malarz** painter
**artyst|ka** (**-ki, -ki**) (*dat sg* **-ce**, *gen pl* **-ek**) *f* artist; (*aktorka*) actress
**artystyczny** *adj* artistic
**artyz|m** (**-mu**) (*loc sg* **-mie**) *m* artistry
**arystokracj|a** (**-i**) *f* aristocracy
**arystokra|ta** (**-ty, -ci**) (*loc sg* **-cie**) *m decl like f in sg* aristocrat
**arystokratyczny** *adj* aristocratic, upper-class; (*przen*) aristocratic
**arytmetyczny** *adj* arithmetical
**arytmety|ka** (**-ki**) (*dat sg* **-ce**) *f* arithmetic
**as** (**asa, asy**) (*loc sg* **asie**) *m* ace; **as karo** the ace of diamonds
**asce|ta** (**-ty, -ci**) (*dat sg* **-cie**) *m decl like f in sg* ascetic
**ascetyczny** *adj* ascetic
**asce|za** (**-zy**) (*dat sg* **-zie**) *f* asceticism
**asekuracj|a** (**-i**) *f* (*ubezpieczenie*) insurance; (*zabezpieczenie*) security *lub* safety measures *pl*
**asekur|ować** (**-uję, -ujesz**) *vt* to protect, to safeguard; **asekurować się** *vr* to play safe, to cover o.s.
**aseptyczny** *adj* aseptic
**asertywnoś|ć** (**-ci**) *f* assertiveness
**asfal|t** (**-tu**) (*loc sg* **-cie**) *m* asphalt
**asortymen|t** (**-tu, -ty**) (*loc sg* **-cie**) *m* assortment, range
**ASP** *abbr* (= *Akademia Sztuk Pięknych*) School of Fine Arts
**aspek|t** (**-tu, -ty**) (*loc sg* **-cie**) *m* aspect, facet; (*Jęz*) aspect
**aspiracj|a** (**-i, -e**) (*gen pl* **-i**) *f* (*Jęz*) aspiration; **aspiracje** *pl* ambitions, aspirations
**aspiry|na** (**-ny, -ny**) (*loc sg* **-nie**) *f* aspirin
**aspołeczny** *adj* antisocial
**ast|er** (**-ra, -ry**) (*loc sg* **-rze**) *m* aster
**ast|ma** (**-my**) (*dat sg* **-mie**) *f* asthma
**astmaty|k** (**-ka, -cy**) (*instr sg* **-kiem**) *m* asthmatic
**astrofizy|ka** (**-ki**) (*dat sg* **-ce**) *f* astrophysics
**astrolo|g** (**-ga, -dzy** *lub* **-gowie**) (*instr sg* **-giem**) *m* astrologer
**astrologi|a** (**-i**) *f* astrology
**astronau|ta** (**-ty, -ci**) (*loc sg* **-cie**) *m* astronaut
**astrono|m** (**-ma, -mowie**) (*loc sg* **-mie**) *m* astronomer
**astronomi|a** (**-i**) *f* astronomy
**astronomiczny** *adj* astronomical
**asygn|ować** (**-uję, -ujesz**) (*perf* **wy-**) *vt* to appropriate
**asymetri|a** (**-i**) *f* asymmetry

**asymetryczny** *adj* asymmetrical
**asymilacj|a** (**-i**) *f* assimilation; (*wchłonięcie*) absorption
**asymil|ować (-uję, -ujesz)** (*perf* **z-**) *vt* to assimilate; **asymilować się** *vr* to adapt, to assimilate
**asy|sta** (**-sty, -sty**) (*dat sg* **-ście**) *f* company, escort; **w asyście ...** accompanied by ...
**asysten|t** (**-ta, -ci**) (*loc sg* **-cie**) *m* assistant
**asystent|ka** (**-ki, -ki**) (*dat sg* **-ce**, *gen pl* **-ek**) *f* assistant
**asyst|ować (-uję, -ujesz)** *vi*: **~ komuś** (*towarzyszyć*) to accompany sb; (*pomagać*) to assist sb; **~ przy operacji** to assist at an operation
**ata|k** (**-ku, -ki**) (*instr sg* **-kiem**) *m* attack; (*Med*) fit, attack; (*Sport*) the forwards; **~ serca** heart attack
**atak|ować (-uję, -ujesz)** (*perf* **za-**) *vt* to attack, to assault
**atei|sta** (**-sty, -ści**) (*dat sg* **-ście**) *m decl like f in sg* atheist
**ateistyczny** *adj* atheistic
**ateiz|m** (**-mu**) (*loc sg* **-mie**) *m* atheism
**atelier** *nt inv* studio
**Aten|y** (**-**) *pl* Athens
**ate|st** (**-stu, -sty**) (*loc sg* **-ście**) *m* certificate
**atest|ować (-uję, -ujesz)** *vt* to certify
**atlantycki** *adj* Atlantic; **Ocean A~** the Atlantic (Ocean)
**Atlanty|k** (**-ku**) (*instr sg* **-kiem**) *m* the Atlantic
**atla|s** (**-su, -sy**) (*loc sg* **-sie**) *m* atlas; **~ geograficzny/samochodowy** geographical/road atlas
**atle|ta** (**-ty, -ci**) (*dat sg* **-cie**) *m decl like f in sg* strongman
**atletyczny** *adj* athletic
**atlety|ka** (**-ki**) (*dat sg* **-ce**) *f*: **lekka ~** athletics *pl* (*Brit*), track and field sports *pl* (US)
**atła|s** (**-su, -sy**) (*loc sg* **-sie**) *m* satin
**atmosfe|ra** (**-ry, -ry**) (*loc sg* **-rze**) *f* atmosphere; (*przen*) atmosphere, climate
**atmosferyczny** *adj* atmospheric
**ato|m** (**-mu, -my**) (*loc sg* **-mie**) *m* atom
**atomize|r** (**-ra, -ry**) (*loc sg* **-rze**) *m* atomizer; **perfumy z ~em** perfume spray
**atomowy** *adj* nuclear; **bomba atomowa** atom(ic) bomb; **ciężar ~** atomic mass; **energia atomowa** atomic *lub* nuclear energy
**atrakcj|a** (**-i, -e**) (*gen pl* **-i**) *f* attraction; **główna ~** highlight, main feature; **atrakcje turystyczne** sights *pl*
**atrakcyjny** *adj* attractive
**atramen|t** (**-tu, -ty**) (*loc sg* **-cie**) *m* ink
**atramentowy** *adj*: **drukarka atramentowa** ink-jet printer
**atra|pa** (**-py, -py**) (*dat sg* **-pie**) *f* dummy
**atrybu|t** (**-tu, -ty**) (*loc sg* **-cie**) *m* attribute
**attaché** *m inv* attaché
**atu** *nt inv*; **bez atu** (*Karty*) no trump
**atu|t** (**-tu, -ty**) (*loc sg* **-cie**) *m* trump (card); **mieć wszystkie ~y w ręku** (*przen*) to have all the trumps in one's hand
**aucie** *n patrz* **aut, auto**
**audiencj|a** (**-i, -e**) (*gen pl* **-i**) *f* audience
**audiowizualny** *adj* audio-visual; **środki audiowizualne** audio-visual aids
**audycj|a** (**-i, -e**) (*gen pl* **-i**) *f* (radio) broadcast
**audytori|um** (**-um, -a**) (*gen pl* **-ów**) *nt inv in sg* (*sala*) auditorium; (*słuchacze*) audience
**aukcj|a** (**-i, -e**) (*gen pl* **-i**) *f* auction
**aul|a** (**-i, -e**) (*gen pl* **-i**) *f* hall
**au|ra** (**-ry**) (*dat sg* **-rze**) *f* (*pogoda*) weather; (*nastrój*) aura, atmosphere
**aureol|a** (**-i, -e**) (*gen pl* **-i**) *f* halo
**auspicj|e** (**-i**) *pl*: **pod auspicjami** *+gen* under the auspices of
**Australi|a** (**-i**) *f* Australia
**Australijczy|k** (**-ka, -cy**) (*instr sg* **-kiem**) *m* Australian
**Australij|ka** (**-ki, -ki**) (*dat sg* **-ce**, *gen pl* **-ek**) *f* Australian
**australijski** *adj* Australian
**Austri|a** (**-i**) *f* Austria
**austriacki** *adj* Austrian
**Austriacz|ka** (**-ki, -ki**) (*dat sg* **-ce**, *gen pl* **-ek**) *f* Austrian
**Austria|k** (**-ka, -cy**) (*instr sg* **-kiem**) *m* Austrian
**au|t** (**-tu, -ty**) (*loc sg* **-cie**) *m* (*Sport*) out
**autentyczny** *adj* authentic, genuine
**autenty|k** (**-ku, -ki**) (*instr sg* **-kiem**) *m* original
**au|to** (**-ta, -ta**) (*loc sg* **-cie**) *nt* car, automobile (US)
**autoalar|m** (**-mu, -my**) (*loc sg* **-mie**) *m* car alarm
**autobiografi|a** (**-i, -e**) (*gen pl* **-i**) *f* autobiography
**autobiograficzny** *adj* autobiographic
**autobu|s** (**-su, -sy**) (*loc sg* **-sie**) *m* (*miejski*) bus; (*międzymiastowy*) coach
**autobusowy** *adj* bus *attr*; **przystanek ~** bus stop
**autocasco** *nt inv* ≈ comprehensive (motor) insurance
**autogra|f** (**-fu, -fy**) (*loc sg* **-fie**) *m* autograph; **łowca ~ów** autograph hunter
**autoka|r** (**-ru, -ry**) (*loc sg* **-rze**) *m* coach
**autokratyczny** *adj* autocratic
**automa|t** (**-tu, -ty**) (*loc sg* **-cie**) *m* (*robot*) automaton; (*telefoniczny*) pay phone, public telephone; (*do sprzedaży*) vending machine, slot-machine; (*pralka*) automatic washing machine; (*pot: pistolet maszynowy*) automatic (gun)

**automatycznie** *adv* automatically
**automatyczny** *adj* automatic; **sekretarka automatyczna** answering machine; **ołówek ~** propelling pencil
**automatyzacj|a** (**-i**) *f* automation
**automatyz|ować (-uję, -ujesz)** (*perf* **z-**) *vt* to automate
**automyj|nia** (**-ni, -nie**) *f* car wash
**autonapra|wa** (**-wie, -wy**) *f* car service
**autonomi|a** (**-i**) *f* autonomy
**autonomiczny** *adj* autonomous
**autopilo|t** (**-ta, -ty**) (*loc sg* **-cie**) *m* automatic pilot, autopilot
**autoportre|t** (**-tu, -ty**) (*loc sg* **-cie**) *m* self-portrait
**autopsj|a** (**-i**) *f* autopsy; (*Med*) post-mortem examination; **znać coś z autopsji** to know sth from experience
**auto|r** (**-ra, -rzy**) (*loc sg* **-rze**) *m* author; (*pisarz*) writer
**autorekla|ma** (**-my, -my**) (*loc sg* **-mie**) *f* self-advertisement
**autor|ka** (**-ki, -ki**) (*dat sg* **-ce**, *gen pl* **-ek**) *f* author, authoress; (*pisarka*) writer
**autorski** *adj*: **prawa ~e** copyright; **honorarium ~e** royalty
**autorst|wo** (**-wa**) *nt* authorship
**autorytatywny** *adj* authoritative, reliable
**autoryte|t** (**-tu, -ty**) (*loc sg* **-cie**) *m* authority; (*poważanie*) prestige; **cieszyć się ~em** to enjoy respect; **być ~em w czymś** to be an authority on sth
**autoryz|ować (-uję, -ujesz)** *vt (im)perf* to authorize
**autoryzowany** *adj* authorized
**autosto|p** (**-pu**) (*loc sg* **-pie**) *m* hitch-hiking; **jechać ~em** to hitch-hike
**autostopowicz** (**-a, -e**) *m* hitch-hiker
**autostra|da** (**-dy, -dy**) (*dat sg* **-dzie**) *f* motorway (*Brit*), superhighway (*US*), freeway (*US*)
**awangar|da** (**-dy, -dy**) (*loc sg* **-dzie**) *f* avant-garde
**awangardowy** *adj* avant-garde
**awan|s** (**-su, -se** *lub* **-sy**) (*loc sg* **-sie**) *m* promotion; **dostać** (*perf*) **~** to get a promotion; **dać** (*perf*) **komuś ~** to promote sb
**awans|ować (-uję, -ujesz)** *vt (im)perf* to promote ▹ *vi* to be promoted
**awantu|ra** (**-ry, -ry**) (*dat sg* **-rze**) *f* row, disturbance; **zrobić** (*perf*) **komuś awanturę** to give sb a row
**awanturni|k** (**-ka, -cy**) (*instr sg* **-kiem**) *m* rowdy, trouble-maker
**awantur|ować się (-uję, -ujesz)** *vr* to make a fuss *lub* row
**awari|a** (**-i, -e**) (*gen pl* **-i**) *f* breakdown; **~ silnika** engine failure
**awaryjny** *adj* emergency *attr*, stand-by *attr*; **wyjście awaryjne** emergency exit; **lądowanie awaryjne** crash *lub* emergency landing; **światła awaryjne** hazard (warning) lights
**awersj|a** (**-i**) *f* aversion
**AWF** *abbr* (= *Akademia Wychowania Fizycznego*) School of Physical Education
**awista** *inv*: **płatny ~** payable at sight
**awitamino|za** (**-zy**) (*dat sg* **-zie**) *f* vitamin deficiency
**awi|zo** (**-za, -za**) (*loc sg* **-zie**, *gen pl* **-zów**) *nt* advice note
**awiz|ować (-uję, -ujesz)** (*perf* **za-**) *vt* to advise, to notify
**awokado** *nt inv* avocado
**azali|a** (**-i, -e**) (*gen pl* **-i**) *f* azalea
**azbe|st** (**-stu, -sty**) (*loc sg* **-ście**) *m* asbestos
**Azj|a** (**-i**) *f* Asia; **~ Mniejsza** Asia Minor
**Azja|ta** (**-ty, -ci**) (*dat sg* **-cie**) *m decl like f in sg* Asian
**Azjat|ka** (**-ki, -ki**) (*dat sg* **-ce**, *gen pl* **-ek**) *f* Asian
**azjatycki** *adj* Asian
**azo|t** (**-tu**) (*loc sg* **-cie**) *m* nitrogen
**azyl** (**-u, -e**) *m* (political) asylum; **prosić** (**poprosić** *perf*) **o ~** to ask for political asylum; **otrzymać** (*perf*) **~** to be granted political asylum
**azymu|t** (**-tu, -ty**) (*loc sg* **-cie**) *m* azimuth
**aż** *conj* till, until; **poczekaj, aż przyjdę** wait till I come; **poczekała, aż wyszedł** she waited until he had gone ▹ *part*: **to kosztuje aż 100 złotych** it costs as much as 100 zloty; **aż 10 błędów** as many as 10 errors; **aż do Berlina** all the way to Berlin; **aż tak dużo pieniędzy?** this *lub* that much money?; **aż za dużo** more than enough; **aż strach pomyśleć** one shudders to think; **posunął się aż do złożenia rezygnacji** he went so far as to resign; **idź aż do płotu** go as far as the fence; **nie mogę aż tyle pracować** I can't work that much; **to nie jest aż takie trudne** it's not as hard as all that
**ażeby** *conj* in order to, so that
**ażurowy** *adj* open-work *attr*

# Bb



**B, b** *nt inv (litera)* B, b; **B jak Barbara** ≈ B for Benjamin (US), ≈ B for Baker (Brit); **B-dur** B flat major; **b-moll** B flat minor

**b.** *abbr (= bardzo)* v. *(= very)*; *(= były)* ex-, former

**ba|ba** (**-by, -by**) *(dat sg* **-bie**) *f (pot: pej: kobieta)* woman; *(wieśniaczka)* countrywoman; *(tchórz)* coward

**bab|cia** (**-ci, -cie**) *(gen pl* **-ci** *lub* **-ć**) *f* grandma, granny; *(pot: staruszka)* old woman

**babi** *adj*: **~e lato** *(pajęczyna)* gossamer; *(pora roku)* Indian Summer

**babiarz** (**-a, -e**) *(gen pl* **-y**) *m (pot)* ladies' man, Don Juan

**bab|ka** (**-ki, -ki**) *(dat sg* **-ce**, *gen pl* **-ek**) *f (babcia)* grandmother; *(pot: dziewczyna)* chick *(pot)*; *(Kulin)* pound cake; *(z piasku)* mud pie

**bac|a** (**-y, -owie**) *m decl like f in sg senior shepherd in the Tatra mountains*

**bacho|r** (**-ra, -ry**) *(loc sg* **-rze**) *m* brat

**bacie** *n patrz* **bat**

**bacz|ki** (**-ków**) *pl* whiskers *pl*

**bacznie** *adv (obserwować)* intently

**baczność|ć** (**-ci**) *f*: **mieć się na baczności przed** *+instr* to beware, to be on one's guard against; **~!** *(Wojsk)* attention!; **stać na ~** to stand at attention

**baczny** *adj (uwaga)* close; *(spojrzenie)* intent; *(widz)* attentive

**bacz|yć** (**-ę, -ysz**) *vi*: **~ na** *+acc* to watch out for, to heed; **nie bacząc na** *+gen* heedless of

**bać się (boję, boisz)** *(imp* **bój**) *vr* to be afraid; **bać się kogoś/czegoś** to be afraid of sb/sth; **bać się o** *+acc* to be worried *lub* concerned about; **bój się Boga!** *(pot)* good heavens!; **nie bój się, on na pewno przyjdzie** never fear, I'm sure he'll come

**badacz** (**-a, -e**) *(gen pl* **-y**) *m (naukowiec)* researcher; *(odkrywca)* explorer

**bad|ać** (**-am, -asz**) *(perf* **z-**) *vt (zjawisko, język)* to study; *(krew, strukturę)* to test; *(dokumenty, pacjenta)* to examine

**bada|nie** (**-nia, -nia**) *(gen pl* **-ń**) *nt* examination, test; *(lekarskie)* examination; **~ krwi** blood count; **~ opinii publicznej** public opinion poll; **badania** *pl* research

**badawczy** *adj (metoda, instytut)* research *attr*; *(spojrzenie, wzrok)* scrutinizing

**badminto|n** (**-na**) *(loc sg* **-nie**) *m* badminton

**badyl** (**-a, -e**) *(gen pl* **-i**) *m* stalk

**bagateliz|ować (-uję, -ujesz)** *(perf* **z-**) *vt (pomniejszać znaczenie)* to belittle; *(lekceważyć)* to underestimate

**bagaż** (**-u, -e**) *(gen pl* **-y**) *m* luggage, baggage (US); **~ ręczny** carry-on luggage, hand luggage; **~ wiedzy** *(przen)* body of knowledge

**bagażni|k** (**-ka, -ki**) *(instr sg* **-kiem**) *m (samochodowy)* boot *(Brit)*, trunk *(US)*; *(: na dachu)* roof rack; *(rowerowy)* carrier

**bagażowy** *adj (kwit, wagon)* luggage *attr*, baggage *attr* ▷ *m decl like adj (tragarz)* porter

**Bagda|d** (**-du**) *(loc sg* **-dzie**) *m* Baghdad

**bagiet|ka** (**-ki, -ki**) *(dat sg* **-ce**, *gen pl* **-ek**) *f* baguette

**bagne|t** (**-tu, -ty**) *(loc sg* **-cie**) *m* bayonet

**bagnisty** *adj* boggy, marshy

**ba|gno** (**-gna, -gna**) *(loc sg* **-gnie**, *gen pl* **-gien**) *nt* bog, swamp; *(przen: pot)* morass; **bagna** *pl* swamps

**Bahama** *inv*: **Wyspy ~** the Bahamas *pl*

**Bahraj|n** (**-nu**) *(loc sg* **-nie**) *m* Bahrain

**bajeczny** *adj* fabulous

**baje|r** (**-ru, -ry**) *(loc sg* **-rze**) *m*: **wstawić** *(perf)* **komuś ~** give sb a (cock and bull) story; **bajery** *pl* frills, bells and whistles (US); **bez żadnych ~ów** with no *lub* without frills

**bajer|ować (-uję, -ujesz)** *vi (pot)* to pile it on (thick) *(pot)*

**baj|ka** (**-ki, -ki**) *(dat sg* **-ce**, *gen pl* **-ek**) *f* fairy tale; *(Lit)* fable; **jak z bajki** of dazzling beauty

**bajkopisarz** (**-a, -e**) *(gen pl* **-y**) *m* fable writer

**bajkowy** *adj (piękny)* fabulous

**bajoński** *adj*: **~e sumy** mind-boggling sums (of money)

**bajo|ro** (**-ra, -ra**) *(loc sg* **-rze**) *nt* puddle

**ba|k** (**-ku, -ki**) *(instr sg* **-kiem**) *m* (fuel) tank; **pełen bak proszę!** fill her up!

**bakali|e** (**-i**) *pl* nuts and raisins *pl*

**bakcyl** (**-a, -e**) *(gen pl* **-i**) *m* bacillus; *(przen)* bug

**ba|ki** (**-ków**) *pl* sideburns *pl*

**bakier** *inv*: **na** ~ (*krzywo*) aslant; **być na ~ z czymś** to have no idea about sth
**bakłaża|n** (**-na** *lub* **-nu, -ny**) (*loc sg* **-nie**) *m* aubergine (*Brit*), eggplant (*US*)
**bakteri|a** (**-i, -e**) (*gen pl* **-i**) *f* germ, bacterium; **bakterie** *pl* bacteria *pl*
**bakteriobójczy** *adj* germicidal, antiseptic
**bakteryjny** *adj* bacterial
**bal**[1] (**-u, -e**) (*gen pl* **-ów**) *m* (*zabawa*) ball; **bal kostiumowy** fancy-dress ball (*Brit*), costume ball (*US*)
**bal**[2] (**-a, -e**) (*gen pl* **-i**) *m* (*kłoda*) log
**balans|ować (-uję, -ujesz)** *vi* to balance
**bala|st** (**-stu**) (*loc sg* **-ście**) *m* ballast
**baldachi|m** (**-mu, -my**) (*loc sg* **-mie**) *m* canopy
**balero|n** (**-nu, -ny**) (*loc sg* **-nie**) *m* smoked ham
**bale|t** (**-tu, -ty**) (*loc sg* **-cie**) *m* ballet
**baletmistrz** (**-a, -e**) *m* ballet master
**baletnic|a** (**-y, -e**) *f* ballet dancer
**bali|a** (**-i, -e**) (*gen pl* **-i**) *f* (wash) tub
**balistyczny** *adj* ballistic
**balko|n** (**-nu, -ny**) (*loc sg* **-nie**) *m* balcony; (*w teatrze*) gallery, balcony
**balla|da** (**-dy, -dy**) (*dat sg* **-dzie**) *f* ballad
**balo|n** (**-nu, -ny**) (*loc sg* **-nie**) *m* balloon; **robić (zrobić** *perf***) z kogoś ~a** (*pot*) to take sb for a ride (*pot*)
**baloni|k** (**-ka, -ki**) (*instr sg* **-kiem**) *m* balloon
**balonowy** *adj* (*pilot*) balloon *attr*; **guma balonowa** bubble gum
**bal|ować (-uję, -ujesz)** *vi* to party
**balowy** *adj* (*strój, sala*) ball *attr*
**balsa|m** (**-mu, -my**) (*loc sg* **-mie**) *m* balm, balsam; (*przen*) balm
**balsam|ować (-uję, -ujesz)** (*perf* **za-**) *vt* to embalm
**balustra|da** (**-dy, -dy**) (*dat sg* **-dzie**) *f* (*zabezpieczenie*) balustrade, banister(s) (*pl*); (*poręcz*) rail(ing)
**bałaga|n** (**-nu**) (*loc sg* **-nie**) *m* mess
**bałaga|nić (-nię, -nisz)** (*imp* **-ń**, *perf* **na-**) *vi* to mess things up
**bałamu|cić (-cę, -cisz)** (*imp* **-ć**, *perf* **z-**) *vt* to flirt with
**Bałkan|y** (**-ów**) *pl* the Balkans
**bałkański** *adj* Balkan
**bałtycki** *adj* (*kraj, język*) Baltic; **Morze B~e** the Baltic (Sea)
**Bałty|k** (**-ku**) (*instr sg* **-kiem**) *m* the Baltic (Sea)
**bałwa|n** (**-na, -ny**) (*loc sg* **-nie**) *m* (*ze śniegu*) snowman; (*fala*) roller; (*głupiec*) moron; (*bożek*) idol
**bałwochwalczy** *adj* idolatrous; (*przen: bezkrytyczny*) blind
**bambosz** (**-a, -e**) (*gen pl* **-y**) *m* carpet slipper
**bambu|s** (**-sa, -sy**) (*loc sg* **-sie**) *m* bamboo
**banalny** *adj* (*prostacki*) corny, banal; (*trywialny*) trivial
**bana|ł** (**-łu, -ły**) (*loc sg* **-le**) *m* banality
**bana|n** (**-na, -ny**) (*loc sg* **-nie**) *m* banana
**bananowy** *adj* banana *attr*
**ban|da** (**-dy, -dy**) (*dat sg* **-dzie**) *f* gang; (*Hokej*) board
**bandaż** (**-a, -e**) (*gen pl* **-y**) *m* bandage; **~ elastyczny** elastic bandage
**bandaż|ować (-uję, -ujesz)** (*perf* **o-** *lub* **za-**) *vt* to bandage
**bande|ra** (**-ry, -ry**) (*dat sg* **-rze**) *f* banner, flag
**banderol|a** (**-i, -e**) (*gen pl* **-i**) *f* excise band
**bandycki** *adj* criminal
**bandy|ta** (**-ty, -ci**) (*dat sg* **-cie**) *m decl like f in sg* bandit
**bandżo** *nt inv* banjo
**Bangko|k** (**-ku**) (*instr sg* **-kiem**) *m* Bangkok
**Bangladesz** (**-u**) *m* Bangladesh
**ba|nia** (**-ni, -nie**) (*gen pl* **-ni** *lub* **-ń**) *f* (*naczynie*) flagon; **to jest do bani** (*pot*) it sucks (*pot*); **być na bani** (*pot*) to be stoned (*pot*)
**banicj|a** (**-i**) *f* exile
**ban|k** (**-ku, -ki**) (*instr sg* **-kiem**) *m* bank; **~ danych** data bank; **masz to jak w ~u!** it's in the bag!, you've got it! (*US*); **rozbić** (*perf*) **~** to break the bank
**bankie|r** (**-ra, -rzy**) (*loc sg* **-rze**) *m* banker
**bankie|t** (**-tu, -ty**) (*loc sg* **-cie**) *m* banquet
**bankno|t** (**-tu, -ty**) (*loc sg* **-cie**) *m* (bank)note (*Brit*), bill (*US*); **~ stuzłotowy** a hundred-zloty note *lub* bill
**bankoma|t** (**-tu, -ty**) (*loc sg* **-cie**) *m* cash machine, cash point *lub* dispenser (*Brit*), ATM (*US*)
**bankowoś|ć** (**-ci**) *f* banking
**bankowy** *adj* bank *attr*
**bankruct|wo** (**-wa, -wa**) (*loc sg* **-wie**) *nt* bankruptcy
**bankru|t** (**-ta, -ci**) (*loc sg* **-cie**) *m* bankrupt
**bankrut|ować (-uję, -ujesz)** (*perf* **z-**) *vi* to go bankrupt *lub* broke
**ba|ńka** (**-ńki, -ńki**) (*dat sg* **-ńce**, *gen pl* **-niek**) *f* (*blaszana*) can; (*szklana*) flagon; (*pęcherzyk*) bubble; (*Med*) cupping glass; **bańki mydlane** soap bubbles; **stawiać (postawić** *perf***) komuś bańki** to cup sb
**baoba|b** (**-bu, -by**) (*loc sg* **-bie**) *m* (*Bot*) baobab
**bapty|sta** (**-sty, -ści**) (*dat sg* **-ście**) *m decl like f in sg* Baptist
**ba|r** (**-ru, -ry**) (*loc sg* **-rze**) *m* bar; (*bufet*) cafeteria; **bar kawowy** coffee bar; **bar mleczny** *self-service restaurant serving cheap meals*; **bar szybkiej obsługi** fast food restaurant
**bara|k** (**-ku, -ki**) (*instr sg* **-kiem**) *m* barrack

**bara|n** (**-na, -ny**) (*loc sg* **-nie**) *m* ram; (*głupiec*) idiot; **B~** (*Astrologia*) Aries; **brać (wziąć** *perf*) **kogoś na ~a** to give sb a piggyback ride
**baran|ek** (**-ka, -ki**) (*instr sg* **-kiem**) *m* lamb; (*futro*) sheepskin; **baranki** *pl* (*chmury*) (fleecy) clouds *pl*; **B~ Boży** (*Rel*) the Lamb of God
**barani** *adj* (*czapka, kożuch*) sheepskin *attr*; (*mięso*) mutton *attr*; (*przen*: *wzrok*) dumb
**barani|na** (**-ny**) (*dat sg* **-nie**) *f* mutton
**baraszk|ować (-uję, -ujesz)** *vi* to frolic
**Barbados** *nt inv* Barbados
**barbaka|n** (**-nu, -ny**) (*loc sg* **-nie**) *m* barbican
**barbarzyńc|a** (**-y, -y**) *m decl like f in sg* barbarian
**barbarzyński** *adj* barbaric, barbarous
**barbarzyńst|wo** (**-wa**) (*loc sg* **-wie**) *nt* savagery
**Barbór|ka** (**-ki, -ki**) (*dat sg* **-ce**) *f* Miners' Day (*St. Barbara's day, 4th December*)
**Barcelo|na** (**-ny**) (*dat sg* **-nie**) *f* Barcelona
**barczysty** *adj* broad-shouldered
**bardziej** *adv comp od* **bardzo** more; **~ uważny/niebezpieczny** more careful/dangerous; **tym ~, że ...** especially as ..., the more so because ...; **coraz ~** more and more
**bar|dzo** (*comp* **-dziej**) *adv* (*z przymiotnikami*) very; (*z czasownikami*) very much; **~ mały** very small; **~ możliwe** very likely; **~ to lubię** I like it very much; **~ dobry** very good, ≈ A (*school grade*); **jak ~?** how much?; **tak ~** so much; **za ~** too much; **~ dziękuję** thank you very much; **~ proszę** I insist; **~ przepraszam** I'm very *lub* so sorry; **proszę ~** (*nie ma za co*) not at all, you're welcome; **nie ~** not much, not really
**bar|ek** (**-ku, -ki**) (*instr sg* **-kiem**) *m* cocktail cabinet
**baret|ka** (**-ki, -ki**) (*dat sg* **-ce**, *gen pl* **-ek**) *f* medal ribbon
**barie|ra** (**-ry, -ry**) (*dat sg* **-rze**) *f* (*przeszkoda, granica*) barrier; (*zapora*) gate; **~ dźwięku** sound barrier
**bar|k** (**-ku, -ki**) (*instr sg* **-kiem**) *m* shoulder; **brać (wziąć** *perf*) **coś na swoje ~i** to take sth on one's shoulders; **coś jest nie na czyjeś ~i** sth is too heavy for sb's shoulders; **składać (złożyć** *perf*) **coś na czyjeś ~i** to burden sb with sth
**bar|ka** (**-ki, -ki**) (*dat sg* **-ce**, *gen pl* **-ek**) *f* barge
**barma|n** (**-na, -ni**) (*loc sg* **-nie**) *m* barman, bartender (US)
**barman|ka** (**-ki, -ki**) (*dat sg* **-ce**, *gen pl* **-ek**) *f* barmaid
**baro|k** (**-ku**) (*instr sg* **-kiem**) *m* baroque
**barokowy** *adj* baroque
**baromet|r** (**-ru, -ry**) (*loc sg* **-rze**) *m* barometer; **~ idzie do góry/spada** the glass is rising/falling
**baro|n** (**-na, -nowie**) (*loc sg* **-nie**) *m* baron
**baronow|a** (**-ej, -e**) *f decl like adj* baroness
**barszcz** (**-u, -e**) (*gen pl* **-y**) *m*: **~ (czerwony)** beetroot soup; **~ ukraiński** borsch; **tani jak ~** (*przen*: *pot*) dirt-cheap (*pot*)
**barte|r** (**-ru**) (*loc sg* **-rze**) *m* (*Handel*) barter
**bar|wa** (**-wy, -wy**) (*dat sg* **-wie**) *f* (*kolor*) colour (*Brit*), color (US); (*brzmienie*) timbre; **~ ochronna** (*Zool*) protective colo(u)ring; **barwy państwowe** national colo(u)rs
**bar|wić (-wię, -wisz)** *vt* to dye
**barwnie** *adv* (*kolorowo*) colourfully (*Brit*), colorfully (US); (*obrazowo*) vividly
**barwni|k** (**-ka, -ki**) (*instr sg* **-kiem**) *m* dye; **~ spożywczy** food colo(u)ring dye
**barwny** *adj* (*wielobarwny*) colourful (*Brit*), colorful (US); (*nie czarno-biały*) colour *attr* (*Brit*), color *attr* (US); (*urozmaicony*) variegated
**bar|y** (**-ów**) *pl* (*ramiona*) shoulders *pl*; **brać (wziąć** *perf*) **się z kimś za ~** to wrestle with sb (*przen*)
**baryka|da** (**-dy, -dy**) (*gen pl* **-dzie**) *f* barricade
**barykad|ować (-uję, -ujesz)** (*perf* **za-**) *vt* to barricade; **barykadować się** *vr* to barricade o.s.
**baryto|n** (**-nu, -ny**) (*loc sg* **-nie**) *m* (*głos*) baritone; (*śpiewak*) (*gen sg* **-na**) baritone
**barze** *n patrz* **bar**
**ba|s** (**-su, -sy**) (*loc sg* **-sie**) *m* (*instrument, głos*) bass; (*śpiewak*) (*gen sg* **-sa**) bass
**baseball, bejsbol** (**-u**) *m* (*Sport*) baseball
**base|n** (**-nu, -ny**) (*loc sg* **-nie**) *m* (*zbiornik wodny*) basin; (*pływacki*) (swimming) pool; (*naczynie*) bedpan
**basi|sta** (**-sty, -ści**) (*dat sg* **-ście**) *m decl like f in sg* bass player
**Bas|k** (**-ka, -kowie**) (*instr sg* **-kiem**) *m* Basque
**Baskij|ka** (**-ki, -ki**) (*dat sg* **-ce**, *gen pl* **-ek**) *f* Basque
**baskijski** *adj* Basque
**basowy** *adj* (*gitara, partia*) bass *attr*; **klucz ~** (*Muz*) bass clef
**bastio|n** (**-nu, -ny**) (*loc sg* **-nie**) *m* bastion
**basz|ta** (**-ty, -ty**) (*dat sg* **-cie**) *f* keep, donjon
**baśniowy** *adj* fairy *attr*, fairylike
**baś|ń** (**-ni, -nie**) (*gen pl* **-ni**) *f* fairy tale
**ba|t** (**-ta, -ty**) (*loc sg* **-cie**) *m* whip; **baty** *pl* (*chłosta*) whipping
**batali|a** (**-i, -e**) (*gen pl* **-i**) *f* (*Wojsk*) campaign
**batalio|n** (**-nu, -ny**) (*loc sg* **-nie**) *m* (*Wojsk*) battalion
**batalistyczny** *adj* (*scena, malarstwo*) battle *attr*
**bateri|a** (**-i, -e**) (*gen pl* **-i**) *f* battery
**bateryj|ka** (**-ki, -ki**) (*dat sg* **-ce**, *gen pl* **-ek**) *f* battery
**bato|n** (**-nu, -ny**) (*loc sg* **-nie**) *m* bar (*of chocolate*)

**batoni|k** (**-ka, -ki**) (*instr sg* **-kiem**) *m dimin od* **baton**
**batu|ta** (**-ty, -ty**) (*dat sg* **-cie**) *f* baton; **pod batutą** *+gen* conducted by
**Bawari|a** (**-i**) *f* Bavaria
**baweł|na** (**-ny**) (*dat sg* **-nie**) *f* cotton; **owijać w bawełnę** (*przen*) to beat about the bush; **nie owijając w bawełnę** straight from the shoulder
**bawełniany** *adj* cotton *attr*
**ba|wić (-wię, -wisz)** *vt* (*zajmować: gościa*) to entertain; (*rozweselać, ciekawić*) (*perf* **u-**) to entertain, to amuse ▷ *vi* (*książk: gościć*) to stay; **to mnie nie bawi** I'm not amused; **~ na wczasach** to be (away) on holiday; **~ kogoś rozmową** to entertain sb with a conversation; **bawić się** *vr* (*o dziecku*) to play; (*hulać*) to have a good time; (*mieć uciechę*) (*perf* **u-**) to have fun; **~ się w coś** to play (at) sth; **~ się czymś** to play with sth; **~ się czyimś kosztem** to have fun at sb's expense; **~ się z kimś** (*zwodzić*) to mess sb about *lub* around; **baw się dobrze!** enjoy yourself!, have a good time!
**baw|ół** (**-ołu, -oły**) (*loc sg* **-ole**) *m* buffalo
**ba|za** (**-zy, -zy**) (*dat sg* **-zie**) *f* base; **~ danych** (*Komput*) database
**baza|r** (**-ru, -ry**) (*loc sg* **-rze**) *m* bazaar
**bazg|rać (-rzę, -rzesz)** (*imp* **-rz** *lub* **-raj**) *vi* to scribble
**ba|zie** (**-zi**) *pl* catkins *pl*
**baz|ować (-uję, -ujesz)** *vi*: **~ w** *+loc* to be based at *lub* in; **~ na** *+loc* to rely (up)on
**Bazyle|a** (**-i**) *f* Basle, Basel
**bazyli|a** (**-i, -e**) (*gen pl* **-i**) *f* basil
**bazyli|ka** (**-ki, -ki**) (*dat sg* **-ce**) *f* basilica
**bażan|t** (**-ta, -ty**) (*loc sg* **-cie**) *m* pheasant
**bąb|el** (**-la, -le**) (*gen pl* **-li**) *m* (*na ciele*) blister; (*na wodzie*) bubble
**bąbel|ek** (**-ka, -ki**) (*instr sg* **-kiem**) *m* bubble
**bądź** *vb patrz* **być**; **~ tak dobry i ...** would you be so kind and ... ▷ *conj*: **~ to... ~ to...** either ... or ... ▷ *part*: **co ~** anything; **kto ~** anybody; **gdzie ~** anywhere; **~ co ~** after all
**bą|k** (**-ka, -ki**) (*instr sg* **-kiem**) *m* (*owad*) gadfly; (*zabawka*) (spinning) top; (*pot: dziecko*) tot; **puścić** (*perf*) **bąka** (*pot*) to blow a fart (*pot*); **zbijać bąki** (*pot*) to mess about *lub* around (*pot*)
**bąk|ać (-am, -asz)** (*perf* **-nąć**) *vi* (*mówić niewyraźnie*) to mumble; (*napomykać*) to remark (*shyly or casually*)
**bąk|nąć (-nę, -niesz)** (*imp* **-nij**) *vb perf od* **bąkać**
**b-cia** *abbr* (= *bracia*) Bros.
**bdb** *abbr* (= *bardzo dobry*) (*Szkol*) ≈ A
**beatyfikacj|a** (**-i, -e**) (*gen pl* **-i**) *f* beatification
**bebech|y** (**-ów**) *pl* (*pot*) guts *pl* (*pot*)
**becz|eć (-ę, -ysz)** *vi* (*o owcy, kozie*) (*perf* **beknąć**) to bleat; (*pot: o dziecku*) to blubber
**becz|ka** (**-ki, -ki**) (*dat sg* **-ce**, *gen pl* **-ek**) *f* barrel; (*Lot*) roll; **zacząć** (*perf*) **z innej beczki** to shift *lub* change ground
**beczkowy** *adj*: **piwo beczkowe** draught (*Brit*) *lub* draft (*US*) beer
**befszty|k** (**-ka** *lub* **-ku, -ki**) (*instr sg* **-kiem**) *m* (beef)steak
**begoni|a** (**-i, -e**) (*gen pl* **-i**) *f* begonia
**bejc|a** (**-y, -e**) (*gen pl* **-y**) *f* stain (*colouring*)
**bejc|ować (-uję, -ujesz)** *vt* to stain (*wood*)
**Bejru|t** (**-tu**) (*loc sg* **-cie**) *m* Beirut
**be|k** (**-ku, -ki**) (*instr sg* **-kiem**) *m* (*owcy, kozy*) bleat; (*płacz*) blubbering
**bek|ać (-am, -asz)** (*perf* **-nąć**) *vi* (*pot*) to burp
**bekhen|d** (**-du, -dy**) (*loc sg* **-dzie**) *m* backhand
**bek|nąć (-nę, -niesz)** (*imp* **-nij**) *vb perf od* **beczeć, bekać**
**beko|n** (**-nu, -ny**) (*loc sg* **-nie**) *m* bacon
**bek|sa** (**-sy, -sy**) (*dat sg* **-sie**) *f* (*pot*) cry-baby
**bel|a** (**-i, -e**) (*gen pl* **-** *lub* **-i**) *f* (*materiału, papieru*) bale; **pijany jak ~** (*pot*) blind drunk
**beletrysty|ka** (**-ki**) (*dat sg* **-ce**) *f* fiction
**Belfa|st** (**-stu**) (*loc sg* **-ście**) *m* Belfast
**belf|er** (**-ra, -rowie** *lub* **-rzy**) (*loc sg* **-rze**) *m* (*pot*) teacher
**Bel|g** (**-ga, -gowie**) (*instr sg* **-giem**) *m* Belgian
**Belgi|a** (**-i**) *f* Belgium
**Belgij|ka** (**-ki, -ki**) (*dat sg* **-ce**, *gen pl* **-ek**) *f* Belgian
**belgijski** *adj* Belgian
**Belgra|d** (**-du**) (*log sg* **-dzie**) *m* Belgrade
**bel|ka** (**-ki, -ki**) (*dat sg* **-ce**, *gen pl* **-ek**) *f* beam; (*pot: naszywka*) stripe
**bełko|t** (**-tu, -ty**) (*loc sg* **-cie**) *m* gibberish
**bełko|tać (-czę, -czesz)** *vi* to gibber
**bemol** (**-a, -e**) (*gen pl* **-i**) *m* (*Muz*) flat
**Beneluk|s** (**-su**) (*loc sg* **-sie**) *m* Benelux
**benzy|na** (**-ny**) (*dat sg* **-nie**) *f* petrol (*Brit*), gas(oline) (*US*); (*do czyszczenia*) petroleum spirits
**benzynowy** *adj*: **stacja benzynowa** filling station, petrol (*Brit*) *lub* gas (*US*) station
**ber|ek** (**-ka**) (*instr sg* **-kiem**) *m* tag; **grać w berka** to play tag
**bere|t** (**-tu, -ty**) (*loc sg* **-cie**) *m* beret
**Berli|n** (**-na**) (*loc sg* **-nie**) *m* Berlin
**ber|ło** (**-ła, -ła**) (*loc sg* **-le**, *gen pl* **-eł**) *nt* sceptre (*Brit*), scepter (*US*)
**Bermud|y** (**-ów**) *pl* Bermuda; **bermudy** (*spodnie*) Bermuda shorts *pl*
**bernardy|n** (**-na, -ni**) (*loc sg* **-nie**) *m* (*zakonnik*) Bernardine; (*pies*) (*nom pl* **-ny**) Saint Bernard (dog)
**Ber|no** (**-na**) (*loc sg* **-nie**) *nt* Bern

**besti|a** (**-i, -e**) (*gen pl* **-i**) *f* beast
**bestialski** *adj* bestial
**bestialst|wo** (**-wa**) (*loc sg* **-wie**) *nt* bestiality
**bestselle|r** (**-ra, -ry**) (*loc sg* **-rze**) *m* bestseller
**beszt|ać (-am, -asz)** (*perf* **z-**) *vt* to scold, to chide
**Betlejem** *nt inv* Bethlehem
**beto|n** (**-nu, -ny**) (*loc sg* **-nie**) *m* concrete
**betoniar|ka** (**-ki, -ki**) (*dat sg* **-ce**, *gen pl* **-ek**) *f* concrete mixer
**beton|ować (-uję, -ujesz)** *vt* to concrete
**bez**[1] (**bzu, bzy**) (*loc sg* **bzie**) *m* lilac
**bez**[2] *prep* without; **bez wątpienia** undoubtedly; **bez końca** (*dyskusja*) endless, interminable; (*dyskutować*) endlessly, interminably; **wyszedł bez słowa** he left without (saying) a word; **siedzieliśmy bez słowa** we sat in silence; **bez ustanku** incessantly
**be|za** (**-zy, -zy**) (*dat sg* **-zie**) *f* meringue
**bezalkoholowy** *adj* (*wino, piwo*) non-alcoholic; (*kosmetyk*) alcohol-free; **napoje bezalkoholowe** soft drinks
**bezapelacyjny** *adj* (*zwycięstwo*) undisputed; (*wyrok*) final
**bezbarwny** *adj* colourless (*Brit*), colorless (*US*); (*przen*) pallid
**bezbłędny** *adj* faultless; (*pot*) super (*pot*)
**bezbolesny** *adj* painless
**bezbożny** *adj* ungodly
**bezbramkowy** *adj*: **wynik ~** goalless draw
**bezbronny** *adj* (*bezradny*) helpless; (*nie uzbrojony*) defenceless
**bezcelowy** *adj* pointless
**bezcen** *inv*: **za ~** for nothing
**bezcenny** *adj* (*wiadomość, pracownik*) invaluable; (*klejnot*) priceless
**bezceremonialny** *adj* unceremonious
**bezchmurny** *adj* cloudless
**bezcłowy** *adj* duty-free
**bezczelnoś|ć** (**-ci, -ci**) (*gen pl* **-ci**) *f* insolence
**bezczelny** *adj* insolent
**bezcze|ścić (-szczę, -ścisz)** (*imp* **-ść**, *perf* **z-**) *vt* to desecrate
**bezczynnoś|ć** (**-ci**) *f* idleness, inactivity
**bezczynny** *adj* idle, inactive
**bezdenny** *adj* bottomless; (*przen: głupota*) abysmal
**bezdętkowy** *adj*: **opona bezdętkowa** tubeless tyre
**bezdomny** *adj* homeless ▷ *m decl like adj*; **bezdomni** *pl* the homeless *pl*
**bezdroż|a** (**-y**) *pl* (*książk*) wilderness
**bezduszny** *adj* unfeeling, callous
**bezdyskusyjny** *adj* undisputed
**bezdzietny** *adj* childless
**bezdźwięczny** *adj* (*głos*) dull; (*Jęz*) voiceless
**beze** *prep* = **bez**; **~ mnie** without me
**bezgraniczny** *adj* endless; (*przen*) boundless, limitless
**bezgrzeszny** *adj* sinless
**bezimienny** *adj* (*bohater*) nameless; (*autor*) anonymous
**bezinteresowny** *adj* disinterested
**bezkarnie** *adv* with impunity; **to ci nie ujdzie ~!** you won't get away with it!
**bezkarnoś|ć** (**-ci**) *f* impunity
**bezkofeinowy** *adj* decaffeinated
**bezkompromisowy** *adj* uncompromising
**bezkonfliktowy** *adj* (*człowiek*) peaceful, peaceable
**bezkonkurencyjny** *adj* unbeatable
**bezkrwawy** *adj* bloodless
**bezkrytyczny** *adj* uncritical
**bezkształtny** *adj* shapeless
**bezlitosny** *adj* merciless, pitiless
**bezludny** *adj* uninhabited; **bezludna wyspa** desert island
**bezła|d** (**-du**) (*loc sg* **-dzie**) *m* disorder
**bezładny** *adj* disordered
**bezmięsny** *adj*: **dania bezmięsne** vegetarian dishes
**bezmyślnoś|ć** (**-ci**) *f* thoughtlessness
**bezmyślny** *adj* (*człowiek*) thoughtless; (*czyn*) mindless; (*wyraz twarzy*) blank
**beznadziejny** *adj* hopeless
**beznamiętny** *adj* (*spokojny*) dispassionate; (*nie wyrażający emocji*) impassive
**beznikotynowy** *adj* nicotine-free
**bezokoliczni|k** (**-ka, -ki**) (*instr sg* **-kiem**) *m* infinitive
**bezołowiowy** *adj*: **benzyna bezołowiowa** unleaded *lub* lead-free petrol (*Brit*) *lub* gasoline (*US*)
**bezosobowy** *adj* impersonal
**bezowocny** *adj* fruitless
**bezpański** *adj* (*pies, kot*) stray
**bezpaństwowy** *adj* stateless
**bezpardonowy** *adj* ruthless
**bezpartyjny** *adj* (*poseł itp.*) independent
**bezpieczeńst|wo** (**-wa**) (*loc sg* **-wie**) *nt* safety, security; **służba** *lub* **aparat bezpieczeństwa** secret police; **kaftan bezpieczeństwa** straitjacket
**bezpieczni|k** (**-ka, -ki**) (*instr sg* **-kiem**) *m* (*Elektr*) fuse; (*u broni*) safety catch
**bezpieczny** *adj* (*nie zagrożony*) safe, secure; (*nie zagrażający*) safe
**bezpłatnie** *adv* free of charge
**bezpłatny** *adj* (*bilet, porada*) free; (*urlop*) unpaid
**bezpłciowy** *adj* (*Bio*) asexual; (*przen: nijaki*) insipid
**bezpłodnoś|ć** (**-ci**) *f* infertility, sterility; (*przen*) sterility

**bezpłodny** *adj* infertile, sterile; (*przen*) sterile
**bezpodstawny** *adj* groundless, unfounded
**bezpośredni** *adj* direct
**bezpośrednio** *adv* directly
**bezpowrotny** *adj* (*chwila*) irretrievable; (*strata*) irreparable
**bezprawi|e** (**-a**) *nt* lawlessness
**bezprawnie** *adv* unlawfully
**bezprawny** *adj* unlawful
**bezprecedensowy** *adj* unprecedented
**bezpretensjonalny** *adj* unpretentious
**bezproblemowy** *adj* trouble-free
**bezproduktywny** *adj* unproductive
**bezprzedmiotowy** *adj* (*spór*) groundless; (*sztuka*) abstract
**bezprzewodowy** *adj* cordless; (*Komput*) wireless; **połączenie** *nt* **bezprzewodowe** wireless connection
**bezprzykładny** *adj* unparalleled
**bezradnoś|ć** (**-ci**) *f* helplessness
**bezradny** *adj*: **~ (wobec** *+gen***)** helpless (in the face of)
**bezrękawni|k** (**-ka, -ki**) (*instr sg* **-kiem**) *m* pinafore (dress)
**bezroboci|e** (**-a**) *nt* unemployment
**bezrobotny** *adj* unemployed, jobless ▷ *m decl like adj* unemployed person; **bezrobotni** *pl* the unemployed
**bezruch** (**-u**) *m* stillness; **zastygł w ~u** he stopped short
**bezsennoś|ć** (**-ci**) *f* sleeplessness, insomnia
**bezsenny** *adj* sleepless
**bezsen|s** (**-su, -sy**) (*loc sg* **-sie**) *m* (*czynu*) senselessness; (*brednia*) nonsense
**bezsensowny** *adj* (*czyn*) senseless; (*argument*) nonsensical
**bezsilnoś|ć** (**-ci**) *f* powerlessness
**bezsilny** *adj* (*bezradny*) powerless; (*płacz, złość*) helpless
**bezskuteczny** *adj* ineffective
**bezsporny** *adj* unquestionable, indisputable
**bezsprzeczny** *adj* unquestionable, indisputable
**bezstronny** *adj* impartial
**beztłuszczowy** *adj* fat-free
**beztros|ka** (**-ki**) (*dat sg* **-ce**) *f* (*brak trosk*) carefreeness; (*niefrasobliwość*) carelessness
**beztroski** *adj* (*dzieciństwo*) carefree; (*postępowanie*) careless
**bezustannie** *adv* incessantly
**bezustanny** *adj* incessant
**bezużyteczny** *adj* useless
**bezwartościowy** *adj* worthless
**bezwarunkowy** *adj* unconditional; **odruch ~** unconditional reflex
**bezwiedny** *adj* unintentional
**bezwietrzny** *adj* quiet
**bezwła|d** (**-du**) (*loc sg* **-dzie**) *m* (*ociężałość*) inertia; (*apatia*) inertia, inertness; (*Med*) palsy
**bezwładnoś|ć** (**-ci**) *f* inertia
**bezwładny** *adj* inert; (*ręka, noga*) numb
**bezwonny** *adj* odourless (*Brit*), odorless (*US*)
**bezwstydny** *adj* (*dowcip, zachowanie*) lewd; (*człowiek*) shameless; (*kłamstwo*) brazen
**bezwzględnie** *adv* (*traktować*) ruthlessly; (*przestrzegać*) strictly; (*ufać*) unreservedly; (*koniecznie*) definitely
**bezwzględnoś|ć** (**-ci**) *f* ruthlessness
**bezwzględny** *adj* (*człowiek, postępowanie*) ruthless; (*posłuszeństwo, zakaz*) strict; (*szacunek*) total; (*zero, skala, wysokość*) absolute
**bezzasadny** *adj* unjustified, unfounded
**bezzwłocznie** *adv* without delay, promptly
**bezzwłoczny** *adj* prompt
**bezzwrotny** *adj* non-returnable
**beż** (**-u, -e**) (*gen pl* **-ów**) *m* beige
**beżowy** *adj* beige
**bęb|en** (**-na, -ny**) (*loc sg* **-nie**) *m* drum
**bęben|ek** (**-ka, -ki**) (*instr sg* **-kiem**) *m* drum; (*pot*: *błona bębenkowa*) eardrum; **bębenki mi pękają** this noise is hurting my eardrums
**bębenkowy** *adj*: **błona bębenkowa** eardrum
**bęb|nić (-nię, -nisz)** (*imp* **-nij**) *vi* to drum
**będę, będzie** *itd. vb patrz* **być**
**bękar|t** (**-ta, -ty**) (*loc sg* **-cie**) *m* bastard
**BHP, bhp** *abbr* (*= bezpieczeństwo i higiena pracy*) health and safety-at-work legislation
**białacz|ka** (**-ki, -ki**) (*dat sg* **-ce**) *f* leukaemia (*Brit*), leukemia (*US*)
**biał|ko** (**-ka, -ka**) (*instr sg* **-kiem**, *gen pl* **-ek**) *nt* (*w jajku*) (egg)white; (*Chem, Bio*) protein; (*oka*) white
**Białorusi|n** (**-na, -ni**) (*loc sg* **-nie**) *m* Belorussian
**Białorusin|ka** (**-ki, -ki**) (*dat sg* **-ce**, *gen pl* **-ek**) *f* Belarussian
**białoruski** *adj* Belarussian
**Białoru|ś** (**-si**) *f* Belarus
**biały** (*comp* **bielszy**) *adj* white; **~ jak śnieg** (as) white as snow; **~ barszcz** white borsch; **B~ Dom** the White House; **~ kruk** (*przen*) collector's item; **białe szaleństwo** skiing; **doprowadzać kogoś do białej gorączki** to infuriate sb; **~ jak kreda/ściana** (as) white as a sheet/ghost; **do białego rana** till dawn; **malować (pomalować** *perf***) coś na biało** to paint sth white; **ubrany na biało** dressed in white; **w ~ dzień** in broad daylight ▷ *m decl like adj* white person; **biali** *pl* the whites *pl*
**biatlo|n** (**-nu**) (*loc sg* **-nie**) *m* biathlon
**bibelo|t** (**-tu, -ty**) (*loc sg* **-cie**) *m* trinket, knick-knack
**Bibli|a** (**-i, -e**) (*gen pl* **-i**) *f* the Bible

**biblijny** *adj* biblical
**bibliografi|a** (**-i, -e**) (*gen pl* **-i**) *f* bibliography
**biblioteczk|ka** (**-ki, -ki**) (*dat sg* **-ce**, *gen pl* **-ek**) *f* bookcase
**bibliote|ka** (**-ki, -ki**) (*dat sg* **-ce**) *f* library; (*szafa*) bookcase
**bibliotekar|ka** (**-ki, -ki**) (*dat sg* **-ce**, *gen pl* **-ek**) *f* librarian
**bibliotekarz** (**-a, -e**) (*gen pl* **-y**) *m* librarian
**bibu|ła** (**-ły, -ły**) (*dat sg* **-le**) *f* (*do atramentu*) blotting paper
**bibuł|ka** (**-ki, -ki**) (*dat sg* **-ce**, *gen pl* **-ek**) *f* (*cienki papier*) tissue paper; (*papierosowa*) cigarette paper
**bicep|s** (**-su, -sy**) (*loc sg* **-sie**) *m* biceps
**bicie**[1] *n patrz* **bit**
**bici|e**[2] (**-a**) *nt* (*dzwonu*) ringing; (*serca*) beating; (*zegara*) chiming; **z ~m serca** with a pounding heart
**bicz** (**-a, -e**) (*gen pl* **-ów**) *m* whip; **jak z ~a strzelił** *lub* **trzasnął** in no time, in next to no time; **kręcić (ukręcić** *perf*) **~ na siebie** to make a rod for one's own back
**bi|ć (-ję, -jesz)** *vt* (*człowieka*) to beat, to hit; (*monety*) (*perf* **wy-**) to mint; (*rekord*) (*perf* **po-**) to beat; (*zabijać: zwierzęta*) (*perf* **u-**) to slaughter; (*o zegarze*) (*perf* **wy-**) to strike ▷ *vi* (*o człowieku: uderzać*) to hit; (*o źródle*) to gush; (*o dzwonach*) to ring; (*o sercu*) to beat, to pound; **bić brawo** to applaud; **bić głową w mur** (*przen*) to bang one's head against a brick wall; **bić się** *vr* to fight; **bić się z myślami** to wrestle with one's thoughts; **bić się w piersi** to beat one's chest
**bide|t** (**-tu, -ty**) (*loc sg* **-cie**) *m* bidet
**bie|c, bie|gnąć (-gnę, -gniesz)** (*imp* **-gnij**, *pt* **-gł**) *vi* to run; (*o czasie*) to pass
**bie|da** (**-dy**) (*dat sg* **-dzie**) *f* (*ubóstwo*) poverty; (*pot: kłopot*) trouble; **od biedy** (*pot*) it will just do; **pół biedy** it's not that bad
**biedact|wo** (**-wa, -wa**) (*loc sg* **-wie**) *nt* poor thing
**bieda|k** (**-ka, -cy** *lub* **-ki**) (*instr sg* **-kiem**) *m* (*nędzarz*) poor person; (*przen: nieszczęśnik*) poor fellow
**biedny** *adj* poor
**biedo|ta** (**-ty**) (*dat sg* **-cie**) *f* the poor *pl*
**biedron|ka** (**-ki, -ki**) (*dat sg* **-ce**, *gen pl* **-ek**) *f* ladybird (*Brit*), ladybug (*US*)
**bie|g** (**-gu, -gi**) (*instr sg* **-giem**) *m* run; (*zdarzeń, rzeki*) course; (*Mot, Tech*) gear; **~ przez płotki** (*Sport*) hurdles *pl*; **~ z przeszkodami** steeplechase; **~ zjazdowy** downhill race; **być ciągle w ~u** to be always on the run; **z ~iem czasu** in the course of time, in time; **pierwszy/wsteczny ~** first/reverse gear; **zmieniać ~i** to change gears
**biegacz** (**-a, -e**) (*gen pl* **-y**) *m* runner
**biegacz|ka** (**-ki, -ki**) (*dat sg* **-ce**, *gen pl* **-ek**) *f* runner
**bieg|ać (-am, -asz)** *vi* to run; (*rekreacyjnie*) to jog; **~ za** *+instr* (*przen*) to chase
**biegle** *adv* (*mówić*) fluently; (*pisać na maszynie*) proficiently; **mówić ~ po angielsku** to speak English fluently
**biegł** *itd. vb patrz* **biec**
**biegłoś|ć** (**-ci**) *f* (*w mówieniu*) fluency; (*w pisaniu na maszynie*) proficiency
**biegły** *adj* (*w mówieniu*) fluent; (*w pisaniu na maszynie, liczeniu*) proficient ▷ *m decl like adj* expert
**bieg|nąć (-nę, -niesz)** (*pt* **-ł**) *vb* = **biec**
**biegu|n** (**-na, -ny**) (*loc sg* **-nie**) *m* pole; (*kołyski*) rocker; **fotel na ~ach** rocking chair, rocker; **koń na ~ach** rocking horse
**biegun|ka** (**-ki, -ki**) (*dat sg* **-ce**, *gen pl* **-ek**) *f* diarrhoea (*Brit*), diarrhea (*US*)
**biel** (**-i**) (*gen pl* **-i**) *f* whiteness; **w ~i** in white
**biel|ić (-ę, -isz)** *vt* (*ścianę*) to whitewash; (*pranie*) to bleach
**bieli|zna** (**-zny**) (*dat sg* **-źnie**) *f* (*pościelowa*) (bed) linen; (*osobista*) underwear, underclothes *pl*
**biel|mo** (**-ma, -ma**) (*loc sg* **-mie**) *nt* leucoma; **mieć ~ na oczach** (*przen*) to be blind to what's going on around one
**bielszy** *adj comp od* **biały**
**biennale** *nt inv* biennial exhibition
**bier|ki** (**-ek**) *pl* (*gra*) pick-a-stick
**biernie** *adv* passively
**bierni|k** (**-ka, -ki**) (*instr sg* **-kiem**) *m* accusative
**biernoś|ć** (**-ci**) *f* inaction, passivity
**bierny** *adj* passive; **strona bierna** the passive (voice); **~ opór** passive resistance; **bierne prawo wyborcze** *the right to stand for election*
**bierz** *itd. vb patrz* **brać**
**bierzmowa|nie** (**-nia, -nia**) (*gen pl* **-ń**) *nt* confirmation
**bież.** *abbr* = **bieżący**
**bieżąco** *adv*: **załatwiać sprawy na ~** to deal with matters as they come; **być z czymś na ~** to be up-to-date with sth, to keep abreast of *lub* with sth
**bieżący** *adj* (*rachunek*) current; (*rok, miesiąc*) current, this; (*numer sprawy*) current; (*woda, metr*) running; **list z 7-ego bieżącego miesiąca** a letter of the 7th instant
**bież|nia** (**-ni, -nie**) (*gen pl* **-ni**) *f* (race) track
**bieżni|k** (**-ka, -ki**) (*instr sg* **-kiem**) *m* (*Mot*) tread; (*serweta*) table runner
**bigami|a** (**-i**) *f* bigamy
**bigamiczny** *adj* bigamous
**bigami|sta** (**-sty, -ści**) (*dat sg* **-ście**) *m decl like f in sg* bigamist

**bigo|s** (**-su, -sy**) (*loc sg* **-sie**) *m Polish dish made of sauerkraut, sausage and mushrooms*; **narobić** (*perf*) **~u** (*przen*) to make a mess
**bigo|t** (**-ta, -ci**) (*loc sg* **-cie**) *m* bigot
**bigot|ka** (**-ka, -ki**) (*dat sg* **-ce**, *gen pl* **-ek**) *f* bigot
**bij** *itd. vb patrz* **bić**
**bijaty|ka** (**-ki, -ki**) (*dat sg* **-ce**) *f* brawl
**bikini** *nt inv* bikini
**bil|a** (**-i, -e**) *f* billiard ball
**bilan|s** (**-su, -se** *lub* **-sy**) (*loc sg* **-sie**) *m* (*Fin, Ekon*) balance; (*przen*) total effect; **~ handlowy** balance of trade; **~ płatniczy** balance of payments
**bilar|d** (**-du, -dy**) (*loc sg* **-dzie**) *m* billiards *sg*
**bile|t** (**-tu, -ty**) (*loc sg* **-cie**) *m* ticket; **~ wizytowy** visiting card (*Brit*), calling card (*US*)
**bilete|r** (**-ra, -rzy**) (*loc sg* **-rze**) *m* usher
**bileter|ka** (**-ki, -ki**) (*dat sg* **-ce**, *gen pl* **-ek**) *f* usherette
**biletowy** *adj*: **kasa biletowa** (*na dworcu*) ticket office; (*w kinie, teatrze*) box office
**bilio|n** (**-na, -ny**) (*loc sg* **-nie**) *m* trillion
**bilo|n** (**-nu**) (*loc sg* **-nie**) *m* (loose) change
**bimb|er** (**-ru**) (*loc sg* **-rze**) *m* (*pot*) bootleg vodka, ≈ moonshine (*US*)
**binarny** *adj* binary
**biochemi|a** (**-i**) *f* biochemistry
**biochemiczny** *adj* biochemical
**biod|ro** (**-ra, -ra**) (*loc sg* **-rze**, *gen pl* **-er**) *nt* hip
**biodrowy** *adj* pelvic
**biografi|a** (**-i, -e**) (*gen pl* **-i**) *f* biography
**biograficzny** *adj* biographical
**biolo|g** (**-ga, -gowie** *lub* **-dzy**) (*instr sg* **-giem**) *m* biologist
**biologi|a** (**-i**) *f* biology
**biologiczny** *adj* biological
**biorc|a** (**-y, -y**) *m decl like f in sg* recipient
**biorę** *itd. vb patrz* **brać**
**biosfe|ra** (**-ry, -ry**) (*dat sg* **-rze**) *f* biosphere
**Bir|ma** (**-my**) (*dat sg* **-mie**) *f* Burma
**birmański** *adj* Burmese
**bi|s** (**-su, -sy**) (*loc sg* **-sie**) *m* encore; **bis!** encore!; **grać/śpiewać na bis** to play/sing as an encore
**bisku|p** (**-pa, -pi**) (*loc sg* **-pie**) *m* bishop
**biskupst|wo** (**-wa, -wa**) (*loc sg* **-wie**) *nt* bishopric
**bis|ować** (**-uję, -ujesz**) *vi* to perform an encore
**bist|ro** (**-ra, -ra**) (*loc sg* **-rze**) *nt* (*also inv*) bistro, snack bar
**biszkop|t** (**-tu, -ty**) (*loc sg* **-cie**) *m* (*ciasto*) sponge cake; (*ciastko*) biscuit
**bi|t** (**-tu, -ty**) (*loc sg* **-cie**) *m* bit
**bit|ki** (**-ek**) *pl* cutlets *pl*
**bit|wa** (**-wy, -wy**) (*dat sg* **-wie**) *f* (*walka*) battle; (*pot*: *bójka*) fight
**bity** *adj* (*pot*: *cały*) full; **bita śmietana** whipped cream; **przez bite dwa dni** for two days on end; **nie w ciemię ~** (*pot*) as sharp as a razor
**biulety|n** (**-nu, -ny**) (*loc sg* **-nie**) *m* bulletin, newsletter
**biur|ko** (**-ka, -ka**) (*instr sg* **-kiem**, *gen pl* **-ek**) *nt* desk
**biu|ro** (**-ra, -ra**) (*loc sg* **-rze**) *nt* (*pomieszczenie*) office; (*instytucja*) office, bureau; **~ podróży** travel agency; **~ rzeczy znalezionych** lost property (office) (*Brit*), lost-and-found (office) (*US*); **~ matrymonialne** marriage bureau
**biurokracj|a** (**-i**) *f* bureaucracy
**biurokra|ta** (**-ty, -ci**) (*dat sg* **-cie**) *m decl like f in sg* bureaucrat
**biurokratyczny** *adj* bureaucratic
**biuro|wiec** (**-wca, -wce**) *m* office building
**biurowy** *adj* (*praca*) clerical; (*maszyna, lokal*) office *attr*
**biu|st** (**-stu, -sty**) (*loc sg* **-ście**) *m* (*piersi kobiece*) breasts *pl*, bosom; (*rzeźba*) bust
**biustonosz** (**-a, -e**) (*gen pl* **-y**) *m* bra
**biwa|k** (**-ku, -ki**) (*instr sg* **-kiem**) *m* bivouac
**biwak|ować** (**-uję, -ujesz**) *vi* to bivouac
**biwakowy** *adj*: **pole biwakowe** campsite, camping site
**bizne|s** (**-su, -sy**) (*loc sg* **-sie**) *m* business; **kobieta ~u** businesswoman
**biznesme|n** (**-na, -ni**) (*loc sg* **-nie**) *m* businessman
**bizo|n** (**-na, -ny**) (*loc sg* **-nie**) *m* buffalo, bison
**biżuteri|a** (**-i**) (*gen pl* **-i**) *f* jewellery (*Brit*), jewelry (*US*)
**bla|cha** (**-chy, -chy**) (*dat sg* **-sze**) *f* (*płyta metalowa*) sheet metal; (*forma do ciasta*) baking tray *lub* sheet; (*pot*): **wykuć** (*perf*) **coś na blachę** (*przen*) to learn sth by rote
**bl|ady** (*comp* **-edszy**) *adj* pale; **~ jak ściana/kreda** (as) white as a sheet/ghost; **blada twarz** (*przen*) paleface
**blak|nąć** (**-nie**) *vi* to fade
**blanco** *inv*: **czek in ~** blank cheque
**blankie|t** (**-tu, -ty**) (*loc sg* **-cie**) *m* blank form
**blas|k** (**-ku, -ki**) (*instr sg* **-kiem**) *m* (*klejnotów*) glitter; (*słońca*) glare; (*księżyca*) glow; **~i i cienie** pros and cons
**blaszany** *adj* tin; **instrumenty blaszane** the brass
**blasz|ka** (**-ki, -ki**) (*dat sg* **-ce**, *gen pl* **-ek**) *f* metal strip; (*Bot*) blade
**bla|t** (**-tu, -ty**) (*loc sg* **-cie**) *m* table top
**bled|nąć** (**-nę, -niesz**) (*imp* **-nij**, *perf* **z-**) *vi* to go pale *lub* white
**bledszy** *adj comp od* **blady**
**ble|f** (**-fu**) (*loc sg* **-fie**) *m* bluff

**blef|ować (-uję, -ujesz)** *vt* to bluff
**bli|ski** (*comp* **-ższy**) *adj* (*sąsiedni*) near; (*przyjaciel*) close; (*krewny*) close, near; (*związek, przyjaźń*) close; (*przyszłość*) near; **~ płaczu** close to tears; **być ~m śmierci** to be about to die; **z bliska** at close range; **B~ Wschód** the Middle East, the Near East ▷ *m decl like adj* relative; **bliscy** *pl* relatives *pl*
**bli|sko** (*comp* **-żej**) *adv* (*w przestrzeni*) close, near; (*w czasie*) near; (*prawie*) almost; (*w zażyłych stosunkach*) close ▷ *prep +gen* close to, near (to); **oni są ~ spokrewnieni** they are closely related; **zima już ~** winter is near; **on ma ~ 50 lat** he is almost 50
**bliskoś|ć** (**-ci**) *f* (*zażyłość*) closeness, intimacy; (*sąsiedztwo*) nearness
**bliskoznaczny** *adj*: **wyraz ~** synonym
**bli|zna** (**-zny, -zny**) (*dat sg* **-źnie**) *f* scar
**bliź|ni** (**-niego, -ni**) *m decl like adj* neighbour (*Brit*), neighbor (*US*), fellowman
**bliźniacz|ka** (**-ki, -ki**) (*dat sg* **-ce**, *gen pl* **-ek**) *f* twin (sister)
**bliźniaczy** *adj* (*jednakowy*) twin *attr*, sister *attr*; **dom ~** semidetached house
**bliźnia|k** (**-ka, -ki**) (*instr sg* **-kiem**) *m* (**-ki** *lub* **-cy**) (*bliźnię*) twin; (*domek*) semidetached house
**bliźni|ę** (**-ęcia, -ęta**) (*gen pl* **-ąt**) *nt* twin; **Bliźnięta** *pl* (*Astrologia*) Gemini
**bliżej** *adv comp od* **blisko**; **~ nieznany** little known
**bliższy** *adj comp od* **bliski**; (*dokładny*) specific; **dopełnienie bliższe** (*Jęz*) direct object
**blocz|ek** (**-ka, -ki**) (*instr sg* **-kiem**) *m* (*notes*) notepad; (*Tech*) (small) pulley
**blog|ować (-uję, -ujesz)** *vi* (*Komput*) to blog
**blo|k** (**-ku, -ki**) (*instr sg* **-kiem**) *m* (*bryła*) block; (*budynek*) block of flats, apartment house (*US*); (*zeszyt*) writing-pad; (*Pol*) bloc; (*Tech*) pulley; (*Sport*) starting block
**bloka|da** (**-dy, -dy**) (*dat sg* **-dzie**) *f* blockade
**blok|ować (-uję, -ujesz)** (*perf* **za-**) *vt* (*drogę, przejazd*) to block, to obstruct; (*miejsce, magazyn*) to take up; (*stosować blokadę*) to blockade
**blond** *adj*: **włosy ~** blonde *lub* fair hair
**blondy|n** (**-na, -ni**) (*loc sg* **-nie**) *m* blond, blonde (*esp Brit*)
**blondyn|ka** (**-ki, -ki**) (*dat sg* **-ce**, *dat pl* **-ek**) *f* blonde
**bluszcz** (**-u, -e**) (*gen pl* **-y** *lub* **-ów**) *m* ivy
**blu|za** (**-zy, -zy**) (*dat sg* **-zie**) *f* (*sportowa*) sweatshirt; (*część munduru*) tunic
**bluz|ka** (**-ki, -ki**) (*dat sg* **-ce**, *gen pl* **-ek**) *f* blouse
**bluź|nić (-nię, -nisz)** (*imp* **-nij**) *vi* to blaspheme
**bluźnierczy** *adj* blasphemous
**bluźnierst|wo** (**-wa, -wa**) (*loc sg* **-wie**) *nt* blasphemy
**błag|ać (-am, -asz)** *vi*: **~ (o coś)** to beg (for sth) ▷ *vt*: **~ kogoś (o coś)** to beg sb (for sth); **~, żeby ktoś coś zrobił** to beg sb to do sth
**błagalny** *adj* (*spojrzenie, modlitwa*) imploring; **błagalna prośba** plea
**błahost|ka** (**-ki, -ki**) (*dat sg* **-ce**, *gen pl* **-ek**) *f* trifle
**błahy** *adj* insignificant, trifling
**bła|zen** (**-zna, -zny** *lub* **-źni**) (*loc sg* **-źnie**) *m* clown; (*dworski*) jester; **robić (zrobić** *perf*) **z siebie błazna** to make a clown of o.s.
**błazn|ować (-uję, -ujesz)** *vi* to clown (around)
**bł|ąd** (**-ędu, -ędy**) (*loc sg* **-ędzie**) *m* (*pomyłka*) error, mistake; (*wada*) fault; **~ ortograficzny** spelling error; **~ maszynowy** typing error, typo; **być w błędzie** to be wrong; **popełniać (popełnić** *perf*) **~** to make a mistake; **wprowadzać (wprowadzić** *perf*) **kogoś w ~** to mislead sb; **wyprowadzić** (*perf*) **kogoś z błędu** to put sb right *lub* straight; **naprawić** (*perf*) **swój ~** to correct one's mistake
**błą|dzić (-dzę, -dzisz)** (*imp* **-dź**) *vi* (*szukać drogi*) to wander about *lub* around, to go round in circles; (*mylić się*) to err
**błąk|ać się (-am, -asz)** *vr* to wander (about)
**błędni|k** (**-ka, -ki**) (*instr sg* **-kiem**) *m* (*Anat*) labyrinth
**błędny** *adj* (*odpowiedź*) wrong; (*pogląd, założenie*) false; (*wzrok*) wild; **błędne koło** vicious circle; **~ ognik** will-o'-the-wisp; **~ rycerz** knight-errant
**błędu** *itp. n patrz* **błąd**
**błęki|t** (**-tu, -ty**) (*loc sg* **-cie**) *m* blue; (*przen: niebo*) the blue
**błękitny** *adj* blue; **błękitna krew** blue blood
**bło|cić (-cę, -cisz)** (*imp* **-ć**, *perf* **za-**) *vt* to soil with mud
**błogi** *adj* blissful
**błogosła|wić (-wię, -wisz)** *vt* (*Rel*) (*perf* **po-**) to bless
**błogosławieńst|wo** (**-wa, -wa**) (*loc sg* **-wie**) *nt* blessing
**błogosławiony** *adj* blessed; **być w ~m stanie** to be pregnant
**bło|na** (**-ny, -ny**) (*dat sg* **-nie**) *f* membrane; **~ fotograficzna** film; **~ śluzowa** mucous membrane; **~ dziewicza** hymen
**błonic|a** (**-y**) *f* (*Med*) diphtheria
**błotni|k** (**-ka, -ki**) (*instr sg* **-kiem**) *m* (*Mot*) wing (*Brit*), fender (*US*); (*roweru*) mudguard, fender (*US*)
**błotnisty** *adj* muddy
**bło|to** (**-ta, -ta**) (*loc sg* **-cie**) *nt* mud; **wyrzucać pieniądze w ~** (*przen*) to throw money down

the drain; **zmieszać** *(perf)* **kogoś z błotem** to sling mud at sb; **błota** *pl* *(bagno)* marsh *sg*
**błys|k** (**-ku, -ki**) *(instr sg* **-kiem**) *m* flash
**błys|kać (-kam, -kasz)** *(perf* **-nąć**) *vi* *(o świetle)* to flash; **~ latarką** to flash one's torch *(Brit)* *lub* flashlight *(US)*; **błyskać się** *vr*: **błyska się** there's lightning
**błyskawic|a** (**-y, -e**) *f* lightning; **szybki jak ~** (as) quick as lightning *lub* a flash; **plotka rozeszła się lotem błyskawicy** the rumour spread like wildfire
**błyskawicznie** *adv* *(szybko)* with lightning speed, in a flash; *(natychmiast)* instantly
**błyskawiczny** *adj* instant; **zamek ~** zip (fastener) *(Brit)*, zipper *(US)*; **zupa błyskawiczna** instant soup
**błyskot|ka** (**-ki, -ki**) *(dat sg* **-ce**, *gen pl* **-ek**) *f* trinket
**błyskotliwy** *adj* witty
**błyskowy** *adj*: **lampa błyskowa** flash
**bły|snąć (-snę, -śniesz)** *(imp* **-śnij**, *pt* **-snął, -snęła** *lub* **-sła, -snęli**) *vb perf od* **błyskać**
**błyst|ka** (**-ki, -ki**) *(dat sg* **-ce**, *gen pl* **-ek**) *f* *(Wędkarstwo)* spoon bait
**błyszczący** *adj* shiny, shining
**błyszcz|eć (-ę, -ysz)** *vi* *(o gwiazdach)* to shine, to glitter; *(o biżuterii)* to glitter; *(o oczach)* to glisten, to glitter; **błyszczeć się** *vr* to shine
**bm.** *abbr (= bieżącego miesiąca) (of) the current month*
**bo** *conj* *(ponieważ)* because; *(w przeciwnym razie)* or (else); **pospiesz się, bo się spóźnimy** hurry up, or we'll be late; **a bo ja wiem?** how should I know?
**boa** *m inv* *(Zool)* boa (constrictor) ▷ *nt inv* *(szal)* (feather) boa
**boazeri|a** (**-i, -e**) *(gen pl* **-i**) *f* panelling *(Brit)*, paneling *(US)*
**boba|s** (**-sa, -sy**) *(loc sg* **-sie**) *m* *(pot)* baby
**bobem** *itd. n patrz* **bób**
**bobkowy** *adj*: **liść ~** bay leaf
**bobra** *itd. n patrz* **bóbr**
**bobsle|j** (**-ja, -je**) *(gen pl* **-jów** *lub* **-i**) *m* *(Sport)* bobsleigh
**bochen|ek** (**-ka, -ki**) *(instr sg* **-kiem**) *m* loaf
**bocia|n** (**-na, -ny**) *(loc sg* **-nie**) *m* stork
**bociani** *adj*: **~e gniazdo** *(Żegl)* crow's nest
**bocz|ek** (**-ku, -ki**) *(instr sg* **-kiem**) *m* bacon
**bocznic|a** (**-y, -e**) *f* *(ulica)* side street; *(kolejowa)* siding
**boczny** *adj* *(droga, drzwi, kieszeń)* side *attr*; **~ wiatr** crosswind; **boczna droga** byway, back road
**bocz|yć się (-ę, -ysz)** *vr*: **boczyć się (na kogoś)** to be cross (with sb)
**boćwi|na** (**-ny, -ny**) *f* *(liście buraków)* beet greens *pl*; *(zupa)* beet greens soup
**bodaj, bodajże** *part* *(chyba)* probably; *(chociaż)* at least, just; **to było ~ w sobotę** it was on Saturday, I think; **żeby ~ mógł zadzwonić** if he could at least phone; **~byś tu nigdy nie wrócił** may you never come back here again
**bodę, bodzie** *itd. vb patrz* **bóść**
**bo|dziec** (**-dźca, -dźce**) *m* *(czynnik)* stimulus; *(zachęta)* spur, incentive
**boga** *itd. n patrz* **bóg**
**boga|cić się (-cę, -cisz)** *(imp* **-ć**, *perf* **wz-**) *vr* to grow *lub* become rich
**bogact|wo** (**-wa, -wa**) *(loc sg* **-wie**) *nt* *(dobrobyt)* wealth, affluence; *(obfitość)* abundance; **bogactwa naturalne** natural resources; **~ kolorów** richness of colour *(Brit)* *lub* color *(US)*
**bogacz** (**-a, -e**) *(gen pl* **-y**) *m* person of substance, wealthy person
**bogaty** *adj* rich; *(zamożny)* wealthy, rich; **~ w rudę/witaminy** rich in ore/vitamins ▷ *m decl like adj*; **bogaci** *pl* the rich *lub* wealthy
**bogi|ni** (**-ni, -nie**) *(gen pl* **-ń**) *f* goddess
**bogobojny** *adj* pious
**bohate|r** (**-ra, -rowie** *lub* **-rzy**) *(loc sg* **-rze**) *m* hero
**bohater|ka** (**-ki, -ki**) *(dat sg* **-ce**, *gen pl* **-ek**) *f* heroine
**bohaterski** *adj* heroic
**bohaterst|wo** (**-wa**) *(loc sg* **-wie**) *nt* heroism
**bohe|ma** (**-my**) *(dat sg* **-mie**) *f* bohemians *pl*
**boi**[1] *n patrz* **boja**
**boi** *itd.*[2] *vb patrz* **bać się**
**bois|ko** (**-ka, -ka**) *(instr sg* **-kiem**) *nt* sports field *lub* ground
**bo|ja** (**-i, -je**) *(gen pl* **-i**) *f* buoy
**bojaźliwy** *adj* fearful
**boje|r** (**-ra, -ry**) *(loc sg* **-rze**) *m* *(Sport)* iceboat
**boję** *itd. vb patrz* **bać się**
**bojko|t** (**-tu, -ty**) *(loc sg* **-cie**) *m* boycott
**bojkot|ować (-uję, -ujesz)** *(perf* **z-**) *vt* to boycott
**bojle|r** (**-ra, -ry**) *(loc sg* **-rze**) *m* boiler
**bojowni|k** (**-ka, -cy**) *(instr sg* **-kiem**) *m* fighter, militant
**bojowy** *adj* *(zawodnik)* combative; *(postawa)* militant; *(akcja)* combat *attr*; *(głowica, samolot, środek)* war *attr*; *(organizacja)* military; **oddział ~** task force
**bojów|ka** (**-ki, -ki**) *(dat sg* **-ce**, *gen pl* **-ek**) *f* raiding party
**boju** *itd. n patrz* **bój**
**bo|k** (**-ku, -ki**) *(instr sg* **-kiem**) *m* side; **omijać bokiem** to dodge sideways; **patrzeć na kogoś bokiem** to look askance at sb; **odsuwać na bok** to move aside; **u czyjegoś boku** at sb's side; **pod bokiem** at hand; **z boku na bok** from side to side; **to mi**

**wychodzi bokiem** (*przen*) I'm fed up with it; **odkładać (odłożyć** *perf*) **coś na bok** to put *lub* lay sth aside; **trzymać się na** *lub* **z boku** (*przen*) to keep *lub* stay away; **zrywać boki (ze śmiechu)** to split one's sides

**bok|s** (**-su**) (*loc sg* **-sie**) *m* (*Sport*) boxing

**bokse|r** (**-ra**) (*loc sg* **-rze**) *m* (*pięściarz*) (*nom pl* **-rzy**) boxer; (*pies*) (*nom pl* **-ry**) bulldog

**boks|ować (-uję, -ujesz)** *vi/vt* to box

**bolącz|ka** (**-ki, -ki**) (*dat sg* **-ce**, *gen pl* **-ek**) *f* problem

**bol|ec** (**-ca, -ce**) *m* (*Tech*) pin; (*z gwintem*) bolt

**bole|ć**[1] **(-ję, -jesz)** *vi*: **~ nad** *+instr* to be troubled by

**bol|eć**[2] **(-i)** *vi* to ache, to hurt; **boli mnie głowa** I have a headache; **co cię boli?** where does it hurt?

**bolesny** *adj* painful; (*miejsce, rana*) sore

**boleś|ć** (**-ci**) *f* (*smutek*) sorrow, grief; **boleści** *pl* (*bóle*) aches, pains; **od siedmiu boleści** (*pot*) poor, worthless

**Boliwi|a** (**-i**) *f* Bolivia

**boliwijski** *adj* Bolivian

**bom|ba** (**-by, -by**) (*dat sg* **-bie**) *f* (*pocisk*) bomb; (*sensacja*) sensation; **~ atomowa** atom(ic) bomb; **~ zegarowa** time bomb

**bombard|ować (-uję, -ujesz)** (*perf* **z-**) *vt* to bomb

**bomb|ka** (**-ki, -ki**) (*dat sg* **-ce**, *gen pl* **-ek**) *f* (*ozdoba choinkowa*) glass ball (*Christmas tree ornament*)

**bombonier|ka** (**-ki, -ki**) (*dat sg* **-ce**, *gen pl* **-ek**) *f* chocolate box

**bombo|wiec** (**-wca, -wca**) *m* bomber (*aircraft*)

**bombowy** *adj* (*nalot, samolot*) bomb *attr*; (*pot: efektowny*) smashing; **nalot ~** air raid

**bo|n** (**-nu, -ny**) (*loc sg* **-nie**) *m* (gift) token, voucher

**bonifika|ta** (**-ty, -ty**) (*dat sg* **-cie**) *f* (*Handel*) discount, rebate; (*Sport*) bonus

**BOR** *abbr* (*= Biuro Ochrony Rządu*) *government security office*

**bordowy** *adj* maroon

**bor|ować (-uję, -ujesz)** *vt* to drill

**borowi|k** (**-ka, -ki**) (*instr sg* **-kiem**) *m* (*Bot*) boletus (*edible fungus*)

**borów|ka** (**-ki, -ki**) (*dat sg* **-ce**, *gen pl* **-ek**) *f*: **~ brusznica** cowberry, mountain cranberry; **~ czarna** bilberry, whortleberry; **~ amerykańska** blueberry

**borsu|k** (**-ka, -ki**) (*instr sg* **-kiem**) *m* badger

**boru** *itd. n patrz* **bór**

**boryk|ać się (-am, -asz)** *vr*: **borykać się z czymś** to wrestle with sth, to contend with sth

**borze** *n patrz* **bór**

**bosa|k** (**-ka, -ki**) (*instr sg* **-kiem**) *m* (*drąg*) boathook; **na ~a** (*boso*) barefoot

**boski** *adj* divine; (*pot: cudowny*) heavenly

**boskoś|ć** (**-ci**) *f* divinity

**bosma|n** (**-na, -ni**) (*loc sg* **-nie**) *m* boatswain

**boso** *adv* barefoot

**bosy** *adj* barefoot

**Boś|nia** (**-ni**) *f* Bosnia

**bośniacki** *adj* Bosnian

**Bośniacz|ka** (**-ki, -ki**) (*dat sg* **-ce**, *gen pl* **-ek**) *f* Bosnian

**Bośnia|k** (**-ka, -cy**) (*instr sg* **-kiem**) *m* Bosnian

**botaniczny** *adj* botanical

**botani|k** (**-ka, -cy**) (*instr sg* **-kiem**) *m* botanist

**botani|ka** (**-ki**) (*dat sg* **-ce**) *f* botany

**bowiem** *conj* as, since

**boże** *n patrz* **bóg**

**boż|ek** (**-ka, -ki**) (*instr sg* **-kiem**) *m* god, idol

**boży** *adj* God's; **Boże Ciało** Corpus Christi; **Boże Narodzenie** Christmas; **boża krówka** (*Zool: biedronka*) ladybird (*Brit*), ladybug (*US*)

**bożyszcz|e** (**-a, -a**) (*gen pl* **-y**) *nt* (*ulubieniec*) idol; (*bożek*) god, idol

**bób** (**bobu**) (*dat sg* **bobu**, *loc sg* **bobie**) *m* broad bean; **dać** (*perf*) **komuś bobu** (*przen*) to teach sb a lesson

**bóbr** (**bobra, bobry**) (*loc sg* **bobrze**) *m* beaver; **płakać jak ~** to cry one's eyes out

**bóg** (**boga, bogowie**) (*dat sg* **bogu**, *voc sg* **boże**) *m* god; **(Pan) Bóg** God, Lord; **Bóg Ojciec** God the Father; **Bóg wie** God knows; **Bóg zapłać** God bless you; **broń Boże!** God forbid, Heaven forbid; **dzięki Bogu** thank God, thank heavens; **mój Boże!** my God!, goodness gracious; **na Boga!** for God's sake!, for heaven's sake!; **szczęść Boże!** God bless (you); **między Bogiem a prawdą** to tell the truth; **Bogu ducha winien** innocent (as a lamb)

**bój**[1] (**boju, boje**) *m* combat

**bój**[2] *vb patrz* **bać się**

**bój|ka** (**-ki, -ki**) (*dat sg* **-ce**, *gen pl* **-ek**) *f* fight, brawl

**ból** (**-u, -e**) (*dat sg* **-owi**) *m* (*fizyczny*) pain, ache; (*przen: zmartwienie*) pain, distress; **ból głowy** headache; **ból zęba** toothache; **ból gardła** sore throat; **ból brzucha** stomach *lub* belly ache; **z bólem serca** with a heavy heart

**bór** (**boru, bory**) (*loc sg* **borze**) *m* forest

**bóst|wo** (**-wa, -wa**) (*loc sg* **-wie**) *nt* deity; **robić (zrobić** *perf*) **się na ~** (*o kobiecie*) to doll o.s. up

**bóść (bodę, bodziesz)** (*imp* **bódź**, *pt* **bódł, bodła, bodli**, *perf* **u-**) *vt* to butt, to gore ▷ *vi* to butt

**bóżnic|a** (**-y, -e**) *f* (*synagoga*) synagogue

**br.** *abbr* (*= bieżącego roku*) of the current year; (*= brat*) brother

**bracie** *itd. n patrz* **brat**

**bracisz|ek (-ka, -kowie)** (*instr sg* **-kiem**) *m* (*młodszy brat*) little *lub* kid brother

**bract|wo (-wa, -wa)** (*loc sg* **-wie**) *nt* (*Hist*) guild; (*pot: towarzystwo*) company

**brać (biorę, bierzesz)** (*perf* **wziąć**) *vt* to take; (*wynagrodzenie*) to receive; (*kąpiel*) to take, to have; (*przykład*) to follow, to copy; (*posadę*) to take, to assume; (*obowiązek*) to take on ▷ *vi* (*o rybie*) to bite; **~ do niewoli** to take prisoner; **skąd on bierze pieniądze?** where does he get his money?; **śmiech mnie bierze** I can't help laughing; **bierze mnie ochota na ...** I feel like ...; **ryba mi bierze** I've got a bite; **mróz bierze** it's getting frosty; **~ (wziąć** *perf***) coś do siebie** to take sth personally; **~ (wziąć** *perf***) coś dosłownie/poważnie** to take sth literally/seriously; **~ (wziąć** *perf***) kogoś za kogoś innego** to take sb for sb else; **brać się** *vr* (*powstawać*) to arise; **~ się za głowę** to put one's head in one's hands; **~ się do czegoś** to set about doing sth; **skąd się to bierze?** where does it come from?

**brajl (-a)** *m* Braille

**bra|k¹ (-ku)** (*instr sg* **-kiem**) *m* (*czasu, dowodów*) lack; (*pieniędzy, pożywienia*) lack, shortage; (*produkt wybrakowany*) defective product, dud (*pot*); **z ~u czegoś** for *lub* through lack of sth; **cierpieć na ~ czegoś** to suffer for *lub* from the want of sth; **odczuwać ~ czegoś** to lack sth; **braki** *pl* (*niedociągnięcia*) defects

**brak²** *inv*: **~ mi 100 złotych** I'm short of 100 zloty; **~ mi ciebie** I miss you; **~ mi słów** I'm lost for words

**brakoróbst|wo (-wa)** (*loc sg* **-wie**) *nt* defective production

**brak|ować (-uje)** *vi* to lack; **brakuje mi ciebie** I miss you; **kogo brakuje?** who is missing?; **tego jeszcze brakowało!** that was all I needed!; **nie brakuje mu odwagi** he doesn't lack courage; **niewiele** *lub* **mało brakowało!** that was a close shave!

**bra|ma (-my, -my)** (*dat sg* **-mie**) *f* gate(way)

**bram|ka (-ki, -ki)** (*dat sg* **-ce**, *gen pl* **-ek**) *f* (*furtka*) gate; (*piłkarska*) goal; (*gol*) goal; (*slalomowa*) gate

**bramkarz (-a, -e)** (*gen pl* **-y**) *m* (*Sport*) goalkeeper; (*w klubie*) bouncer

**bransole|ta (-ty, -ty)** (*dat sg* **-cie**) *f* bracelet, bangle

**branż|a (-y, -e)** *f* line, trade

**branżowy** *adj* trade *attr*

**bra|t (-ta, -cia)** (*dat sg* **-tu**, *loc sg* **-cie**, *gen pl* **-ci**, *dat pl* **-ciom**, *instr pl* **-ćmi**, *loc pl* **-ciach**) *m* brother; (*zakonnik*) friar; **~ przyrodni** stepbrother, half-brother; **~ cioteczny** *lub* **stryjeczny** (first) cousin; **być z kimś za pan ~** to be on familiar terms with sb

**brat|ać się (-am, -asz)** (*perf* **z-**) *vr* to fraternize

**bratan|ek (-ka, -kowie)** (*instr sg* **-kiem**) *m* nephew (*brother's son*)

**bratanic|a (-y, -e)** *f* niece (*brother's daughter*)

**brat|ek (-ka, -ki)** (*instr sg* **-kiem**) *m* (*Bot*) pansy

**braterski** *adj* brotherly, fraternal

**braterst|wo (-wa)** (*loc sg* **-wie**) *nt* brotherhood, fraternity; **~ broni** brotherhood in arms

**bratni** *adj*: **~a dusza** kindred spirit; **~a dłoń** helping hand

**bratobójst|wo (-wa, -wa)** (*loc sg* **-wie**) *nt* fratricide

**bratow|a (-ej, -e)** *f decl like adj* sister-in-law

**bra|wo (-wa, -wa)** (*loc sg* **-wie**) *nt* applause; **~!** bravo!; **bić ~** to applaud

**brawu|ra (-ry)** (*dat sg* **-rze**) *f* (*werwa*) verve, enthusiasm; (*ryzykanctwo*) bravado

**brawurowy** *adj* (*śmiały*) daring

**Brazyli|a (-i)** *f* Brazil

**Brazylijczy|k (-ka, -cy)** (*instr sg* **-kiem**) *m* Brazilian

**Brazylij|ka (-ki, -ki)** (*dat sg* **-ce**, *gen pl* **-ek**) *f* Brazilian

**brazylijski** *adj* Brazilian

**brą|z (-zu, -zy)** (*loc sg* **-zie**) *m* (*kolor*) brown; (*metal*) bronze

**brązowy** *adj* brown; (*z brązu*) bronze; **~ medal** bronze (medal)

**bred|nie (-ni)** *pl* nonsense, rubbish (*pot*)

**bre|dzić (-dzę, -dzisz)** (*imp* **-dź**) *vi* to rave; (*przen*) to talk rubbish

**brelocz|ek, brelo|k (-ka, -ki)** (*instr sg* **-kiem**) *m* pendant; (*do klucza*) key ring

**Bretani|a (-i)** *f* Brittany

**br|ew (-wi, -wi)** (*gen pl* **-wi**) *f* eyebrow

**brezen|t (-tu, -ty)** (*loc sg* **-cie**) *m* tarpaulin

**br|nąć (-nę, -niesz)** (*imp* **-nij**, *perf* **za-**) *vi* (*iść z trudem*) to wade, to struggle; **~ w długi** to get *lub* go into debt

**brocz|yć (-ę, -ysz)** *vi* (*o krwi*) to flow; (*o ranie*): **~ krwią** to bleed

**br|oda (-ody, -ody)** (*dat sg* **-odzie**, *gen pl* **-ód**) *f* (*część twarzy*) chin; (*zarost*) beard; **kawał z brodą** an old chestnut

**brodacz (-a, -e)** (*gen pl* **-y**) *m* bearded man

**brodaty** *adj* bearded

**brodaw|ka (-ki, -ki)** (*dat sg* **-ce**, *gen pl* **-ek**) *f* (*sutek*) nipple; (*narośl*) wart

**bro|dzić (-dzę, -dzisz)** (*imp* **-dź**) *vi* to paddle (*in shallow water*)

**brodzi|k (-ka** *lub* **-ku, -ki)** (*instr sg* **-kiem**) *m* paddling pool

**br|oić (-oję, -oisz)** (*imp* **-ój**, *perf* **na-** *lub* **z-**) *vi* (*figlować*) to frolic, to romp; (*psocić*) to be up to mischief

**brojle|r** (**-ra, -ry**) (*loc sg* **-rze**) *m* broiler
**broka|t** (**-tu, -ty**) (*loc sg* **-cie**) *m* brocade
**brokuł|y** (**-ów**) *pl* broccoli
**bro|na** (**-ny, -ny**) (*dat sg* **-nie**) *f* harrow
**bronchi|t** (**-tu, -ty**) (*loc sg* **-cie**) *m* (*Med*) bronchitis
**bro|nić** (**-nię, -nisz**) (*imp* **-ń**) *vt* (*perf* **o-**) to defend; (*osłaniać, strzec*) to guard; (*zabraniać*) (*perf* **za-**) to forbid; **broń Boże!** God forbid!, heaven forbid!; **~ dostępu do kogoś/czegoś** to bar the way to sb/sth; **~ pracy doktorskiej** to defend one's PhD thesis *lub* dissertation; **bronić się** *vr* to defend o.s.
**bro|ń** (**-ni**) *f* weapon; (*zbiorowo*) arms *pl*; (*przen: środek*) weapon; **~ atomowa/chemiczna** nuclear/chemical weapons *pl*; **~ palna** firearms *pl*; **chwycić** (*perf*) **za ~** to take up arms
**brosz|ka** (**-ki, -ki**) (*dat sg* **-ce**, *gen pl* **-ek**) *f* brooch
**broszu|ra** (**-ry, -ry**) (*dat sg* **-rze**) *f* brochure, pamphlet
**browa|r** (**-ru, -ry**) (*loc sg* **-rze**) *m* brewery
**br|ód** (**-odu, -ody**) (*loc sg* **-odzie**) *m* ford; **przejść rzekę w ~** to ford a river; **jest czegoś w ~** sth is in profusion
**bru|d** (**-du, -dy**) (*loc sg* **-dzie**) *m* dirt, filth; **brudy** *pl* (*brudna bielizna*) laundry; (*przen*) filth; **prać swoje ~y publicznie** to wash one's dirty linen in public
**bruda|s** (**-sa, -sy**) (*loc sg* **-sie**) (*pot*) *m* sloven, pig (*pot*)
**bruderszaf|t** (**-tu, -ty**) (*loc sg* **-cie**) *m*: **wypić** (*perf*) **z kimś ~** to agree to use the familiar "ty" (*over a drink*)
**brudno** *adv*: **jest tu ~** it's dirty here; **pisać coś na ~** to write a rough copy of sth
**brudnopi|s** (**-su, -sy**) (*loc sg* **-sie**) *m* (*tekst*) first draft
**brudny** *adj* dirty, filthy
**bru|dzić** (**-dzę, -dzisz**) (*imp* **-dź**, *perf* **po-** *lub* **za-**) *vt* to dirty, to soil; **brudzić się** *vr* to get dirty
**bru|k** (**-ku, -ki**) (*instr sg* **-kiem**) *m* paving, pavement (US); **wyrzucić** (*perf*) **kogoś na ~** (*przen*) to throw sb on the street; **znaleźć się** (*perf*) **na ~u** (*przen*) to be down and out
**bru|kiew** (**-kwi, -kwie**) (*gen pl* **-kwi**) *f* swede, rutabaga (US)
**bruko|wiec** (**-wca, -wce**) *m* (*pot: czasopismo*) tabloid
**brukowy** *adj*: **gazeta brukowa** tabloid; **literatura brukowa** pulp fiction
**Bruksel|a** (**-i**) *f* Brussels
**bruksel|ka** (**-ki, -ki**) (*dat sg* **-ce**, *gen pl* **-ek**) *f* Brussels sprouts *pl*
**brulio|n** (**-nu, -ny**) (*loc sg* **-nie**) *m* (*zeszyt*) exercise book
**brunatny** *adj* dark brown; **węgiel ~** lignite, brown coal; **niedźwiedź ~** brown bear
**brune|t** (**-ta, -ci**) (*loc sg* **-cie**) *m* dark-haired man
**brunet|ka** (**-ki, -ki**) (*dat sg* **-ce**, *gen pl* **-ek**) *f* brunette
**brutalnoś|ć** (**-ci**) *f* brutality
**brutalny** *adj* brutal
**brutto** *inv* gross; **waga/zysk ~** gross weight/profit
**bru|zda** (**-zdy, -zdy**) (*dat sg* **-ździe**) *f* furrow
**bru|ździć** (**-żdżę, -ździsz**) (*imp* **-źdź**, *perf* **na-**) *vi*: **~ komuś** to put a spoke in sb's wheel
**brwi** *itd. n patrz* **brew**
**brydż** (**-a**) *m* bridge (*card game*)
**bryga|da** (**-dy, -dy**) (*dat sg* **-dzie**) *f* (*Wojsk*) brigade; (*robotników*) gang
**brygadzi|sta** (**-sty, -ści**) (*dat sg* **-ście**) *m* foreman
**bryk|ać** (**-am, -asz**) (*perf* **-nąć**) *vi* (*o koniu, cielaku*) to buck; (*o dzieciach*) to gambol, to frisk
**bryk|nąć** (**-nę, -niesz**) (*imp* **-nij**) *vb perf od* **brykać** ▷ *vi perf* (*pot: uciec*) to turn tail
**brylan|t** (**-tu, -ty**) (*loc sg* **-cie**) *m* diamond
**brylantowy** *adj*: **brylantowe gody** *lub* **wesele** diamond wedding
**brylanty|na** (**-ny**) (*dat sg* **-nie**) *f* brilliantine, Brylcreem®
**bry|ła** (**-ły, -ły**) (*dat sg* **-le**) *f* lump; (*ziemi*) clod; (*Mat, Fiz*) solid
**brystol** (**-u, -e**) (*gen pl* **-i**) *m* Bristol board
**brytfan|na** (**-ny, -ny**) (*dat sg* **-nie**) *f* baking pan
**Brytyjczy|k** (**-ka, -cy**) (*loc sg* **-kiem**) *m* Briton, Britisher (US); **Brytyjczycy** *pl* the British
**Brytyj|ka** (**-ki, -ki**) (*dat sg* **-ce**, *gen pl* **-ek**) *f* Briton, Britisher (US)
**brytyjski** *adj* British
**bry|za** (**-zy, -zy**) (*dat sg* **-zie**) *f* sea breeze
**bryz|gać** (**-gam, -gasz**) (*perf* **-nąć**) *vi* to splash
**bry|znąć** (**-znę, -źniesz**) (*imp* **-źnij**) *vb perf od* **bryzgać**
**bryzol** (**-u, -e**) (*gen pl* **-i** *lub* **-ów**) *m* (*thinly sliced fried*) steak
**brzas|k** (**-ku, -ki**) (*instr sg* **-kiem**) *m* dawn, daybreak
**brzdąk|ać** (**-am, -asz**) (*perf* **-nąć**) *vi* (*na gitarze*) to strum, to thrum; (*na pianinie*) to thump the keyboard
**brzdąk|nąć** (**-nę, -niesz**) (*imp* **-nij**) *vb perf od* **brzdąkać**
**brze|g** (**-gu, -gi**) (*instr sg* **-giem**) *m* (*rzeki*) bank, riverside; (*jeziora*) shore; (*morza*) shore, coast;

(*przepaści*) brink; (*plaża*) beach; (*naczynia, kapelusza*) brim; (*krawędź*) edge; **pierwszy z ~u** (*osoba*) anyone; (*przedmiot*) any
**brzemienny** *adj* (*kobieta*) pregnant; **to zdarzenie było brzemienne w skutki** this event had innumerable consequences
**brzemi|ę** (**-enia, -ona**) (*gen pl* **-on**) *nt* burden
**brzęcz|eć (-ę, -ysz)** *vi* (*o kluczach, monetach*) to clink; (*o owadzie*) to buzz, to hum; (*o szkle*) to clink, to clatter; (*o strunie*) to twang
**brzę|k** (**-ku, -ki**) (*instr sg* **-kiem**) *m* (*owadów*) buzz, hum; (*kluczy, monet*) clink; (*szkła*) clink, clatter
**brz|mieć (-mię, -misz)** (*imp* **-mij**) *vi* to sound, to ring; **list brzmi jak następuje ...** the letter reads as follows ...; **rozkaz brzmiał: nie strzelać!** the order was not to shoot; **to brzmi okropnie** that sounds awful
**brzmie|nie** (**-nia, -nia**) (*gen pl* **-ń**) *nt* tone
**brzoskwi|nia** (**-ni, -nie**) (*gen pl* **-ń**) *f* peach
**brz|oza** (**-ozy, -ozy**) (*dat sg* **-ozie**, *gen pl* **-óz**) *f* birch
**brzuch** (**-a, -y**) *m* stomach, belly (*pot*); **leżeć do góry ~em** (*pot*) to laze about
**brzuchomówc|a** (**-y, -y**) *m* ventriloquist
**brzuszny** *adj* abdominal
**brzyd|ki** (*comp* **-szy**) *adj* (*nieładny*) ugly; (*czyn, słowo*) dirty
**brzy|dko** (*comp* **-dziej**) *adv* (*wyglądać*) ugly; (*śpiewać, pisać*) terribly; (*postępować*) meanly; **na dworze jest ~** the weather is ugly
**brzyd|nąć (-nę, -niesz)** (*imp* **-nij**) *vi* (*stawać się brzydkim*) to grow *lub* become ugly; **życie mi brzydnie** I'm getting sick of life
**brzydo|ta** (**-ty**) (*dat sg* **-cie**) *f* ugliness
**brzy|dzić się (-dzę, -dzisz)** (*imp* **-dź**) *vr*: **brzydzić się kimś/czymś** to find sb/sth repulsive
**brzyt|wa** (**-wy, -wy**) (*dat sg* **-wie**) *f* razor
**bub|el** (**-la, -le**) (*gen pl* **-li**) *m* (*pot*) trash (*pot*)
**buch|ać (-am, -asz)** (*perf* **-nąć**) *vi*: **~ ogniem/dymem** to belch (out) fire/smoke
**buch|nąć (-nę, -niesz)** (*imp* **-nij**) *vb perf od* **buchać** ▷ *vt perf* (*pot*: *ukraść*) to filch (*pot*)
**bucie** *n patrz* **but**
**buci|k** (**-ka, -ki**) (*instr sg* **-kiem**) *m dimin od* **but**
**bucz|eć (-ę, -ysz)** *vi* (*o syrenie*) to sound; (*o owadzie*) to hum; (*pot*: *o dziecku*) to blubber
**bu|da** (**-dy, -dy**) (*dat sg* **-dzie**) *f* (*szopa*) shed; (*psia*) kennel; (*jarmarczna*) stall, booth; (*pot*) school
**Budapesz|t** (**-tu**) (*loc sg* **-cie**) *m* Budapest
**buddyjski** *adj* Buddhist
**buddyz|m** (**-mu**) (*loc sg* **-mie**) *m* Buddhism
**bud|ka** (**-ki, -ki**) (*dat sg* **-ce**, *gen pl* **-ek**) *f* (*z gazetami*) kiosk; (*dla ptaków*) nesting box; **~ suflera** prompt box; **~ telefoniczna** call *lub* (tele)phone box (*Brit*), (tele)phone booth (*US*); **~ wartownicza** sentry box
**budo|wa** (**-wy, -wy**) (*dat sg* **-wie**) *f* (*budowanie*: *domu itp.*) building; (: *silnika itp.*) construction; (*atomu, utworu, wyrazu*) structure; (*człowieka*) build, physique; (*teren budowy*) building site; **w budowie** under construction
**bud|ować (-uję, -ujesz)** (*perf* **z-** *lub* **wy-**) *vt* (*dom, państwo, szczęście*) to build; (*silnik*) to construct; **~ na czymś** (*przen*) to pin hope (up) on sth; **budować się** *vr*: **buduje się nowa szkoła** a new school is being built; **budujemy się** we're having a new house built
**budowl|a** (**-i, -e**) (*gen pl* **-i**) *f* (*budynek*) building; (*most, wieża*) structure
**budowlany** *adj* building *attr*; **przedsiębiorca ~** (building) contractor
**budownict|wo** (**-wa**) (*loc sg* **-wie**) *nt* building *lub* construction industry
**budownicz|y** (**-ego, -owie**) *m decl like adj* builder
**budujący** *adj* edifying
**budul|ec** (**-ca**) *m* building material
**budyn|ek** (**-ku, -ki**) (*instr sg* **-kiem**) *m* building
**budy|ń** (**-niu, -nie**) (*gen pl* **-ni** *lub* **-niów**) *m a kind of dessert made from milk, sugar and starch*
**budze|nie** (**-nia, -nia**) (*gen pl* **-ń**) *nt* alarm call
**bu|dzić (-dzę, -dzisz)** (*imp* **-dź**) *vt* (*perf* **z-** *lub* **o-**) (*człowieka*) to wake (up), to awake; (*zachwyt, lęk*) (*perf* **wz-**) to arouse, to awake; **budzić się** (*perf* **o-**) *vr* to wake (up), to awake; (*o nadziei*) to arise
**budzi|k** (**-ka, -ki**) (*instr sg* **-kiem**) *m* alarm clock
**budże|t** (**-tu, -ty**) (*dat sg* **-cie**) *m* budget; **~ państwa** national budget
**bufe|t** (**-tu, -ty**) (*loc sg* **-cie**) *m* buffet
**bufo|r** (**-ra, -ry**) (*loc sg* **-rze**) *m* buffer
**buj|ać (-am, -asz)** *vi* (*w powietrzu*) to float; (*pot*: *kłamać*) to tell fibs (*pot*) ▷ *vt* (*oszukiwać*) to cheat; (*kołysać*) to rock; **~ w obłokach** (*przen*) to have one's head in the clouds (*przen*); **bujać się** *vr* (*huśtać się*) to swing, to rock
**buj|da** (**-dy, -dy**) (*dat sg* **-dzie**) *f* (*pot*) fib (*pot*)
**bujny** *adj* (*roślinność*) lush, luxuriant; (*włosy*) luxuriant; (*wyobraźnia*) vivid; (*życie*) eventful
**bu|k** (**-ku** *lub* **-ka, -ki**) (*instr sg* **-kiem**) *m* beech
**Bukaresz|t** (**-tu**) (*loc sg* **-cie**) *m* Bucharest
**bukie|t** (**-tu, -ty**) (*loc sg* **-cie**) *m* bouquet; **~ z jarzyn** assorted vegetables
**bukmache|r** (**-ra, -rzy**) (*loc sg* **-rze**) *m* bookmaker
**buldo|g** (**-ga, -gi**) (*instr sg* **-giem**) *m* bulldog
**buldoże|r** (**-ra, -ry**) (*loc sg* **-rze**) *m* bulldozer
**bulgo|tać (-cze)** *vi* to gurgle
**bul|ić (-ę, -isz)** (*perf* **wy-** *lub* **za-**) *vi/vt* (*pot*) to fork *lub* shell out (*pot*)

**bulio|n** (**-nu, -ny**) (*loc sg* **-nie**) *m* consommé
**bulwa|r** (**-ru, -ry**) (*loc sg* **-rze**) *m* (*ulica*) boulevard; (*obmurowanie brzegu*) embankment
**bulwers|ować (-uję, -ujesz)** (*perf* **z-**) *vt* (*książk*) to shock
**Bułga|r** (**-ra, -rzy**) (*loc sg* **-rze**) *m* Bulgarian
**Bułgari|a** (**-i**) *f* Bulgaria
**Bułgar|ka** (**-ki, -ki**) (*dat sg* **-ce**, *gen pl* **-ek**) *f* Bulgarian
**bułgarski** *adj* Bulgarian
**buł|ka** (**-ki, -ki**) (*dat sg* **-ce**, *gen pl* **-ek**) *f* roll; (*słodka*) bun; **~ paryska** French stick, French loaf (*Brit*); **tarta ~** breadcrumbs; **~ z masłem** (*przen*) piece of cake
**bumelan|t** (**-ta, -ci**) (*loc sg* **-cie**) *m* (*pot*) layabout, loafer
**bumeran|g** (**-gu** *lub* **-ga, -gi**) (*instr sg* **-giem**) *m* boomerang
**bun|kier** (**-kra, -kry**) (*loc sg* **-krze**) *m* bunker
**bun|t** (**-tu, -ty**) (*loc sg* **-cie**) *m* rebellion, revolt
**bunt|ować (-uję, -ujesz)** (*perf* **z-**) *vt* to incite to protest; **buntował dziecko przeciwko rodzicom** he turned the child against his parents; **buntować się** *vr*: **~ się przeciw** *+dat* to rebel *lub* revolt against
**buntowniczy** *adj* rebellious
**buntowni|k** (**-ka, -cy**) (*instr sg* **-kiem**) *m* rebel
**buracz|ki** (**-ków**) *pl* (*Kulin*) beetroot salad
**bura|k** (**-ka, -ki**) (*instr sg* **-kiem**) *m* beet; **~ ćwikłowy** (red)beet, beetroot; **~ cukrowy** sugar beet
**burcz|eć (-ę, -ysz)** *vi*: **burczy mi w brzuchu** my stomach is rumbling
**bur|da** (**-dy, -dy**) (*dat sg* **-dzie**) *f* brawl
**burdel** (**-u, -e**) (*gen pl* **-i** *lub* **-ów**) (*pot!*) *m* (*dom publiczny*) brothel; (*bałagan*) mess
**burk|nąć (-nę, -niesz)** (*imp* **-nij**) *vi* to grunt
**burmistrz** (**-a, -e** *lub* **-owie**) *m* mayor
**bur|sa** (**-sy, -sy**) (*dat sg* **-sie**) *f* dormitory
**bursztyn|n** (**-nu, -ny**) (*loc sg* **-nie**) *m* amber
**bur|ta** (**-ty, -ty**) (*dat sg* **-cie**) *f* (*Żegl*) board; **prawa ~** starboard; **lewa ~** port; **człowiek za burtą!** man overboard!
**burz|a** (**-y, -e**) *f* (*z piorunami*) (thunder)storm; **~ piaskowa** sandstorm; **~ oklasków** a storm of applause; **~ w szklance wody** a storm in a teacup
**burzliwy** *adj* (*pogoda, dyskusja*) stormy; (*owacja*) thunderous; (*czas, dzieje*) tumultuous, turbulent
**burz|yć (-ę, -ysz)** *vt* (*dom, mur*) (*perf* **z-** *lub* **wy-**) to demolish, to knock down; (*spokój*) (*perf* **z-**) to destroy; (*włosy, wodę*) (*perf* **wz-**) to ruffle; **burzyć się** *vr* (*o wodzie*) (*perf* **wz-**) to surge; (*denerwować się*) (*perf* **wz-**) to seethe with anger; (*buntować się*) to riot
**burżuazj|a** (**-i**) *f* bourgeoisie
**busol|a** (**-i, -e**) *f* compass
**busz** (**-u**) *m* the bush
**busz|ować (-uję, -ujesz)** *vi*: **~ po** *+loc* (*po mieście, lesie*) to scour; (*po szufladzie*) to rummage through
**bu|t** (**-ta, -ty**) (*loc sg* **-cie**) *m* shoe; (*wysoki*) boot; **but narciarski** ski boot; **głupi jak but** (*pot*) as thick as two (short) planks
**buta|n** (**-nu**) (*loc sg* **-nie**) *m* butane
**butel|ka** (**-ki, -ki**) (*dat sg* **-ce**, *gen pl* **-ek**) *f* bottle; **nabić** (*perf*) **kogoś w butelkę** (*pot*) to take sb in; **zaglądać do butelki** (*przen*) to take to *lub* hit the bottle
**buti|k** (**-ku, -ki**) (*instr sg* **-kiem**) *m* boutique
**butl|a** (**-i, -e**) (*gen pl* **-i**) *f* (*do tlenu, gazu*) cylinder
**butonier|ka** (**-ki, -ki**) (*dat sg* **-ce**, *gen pl* **-ek**) *f*: **kwiat w butonierce** buttonhole (*Brit*), boutonniere (*US*)
**butwie|ć (-je)** (*perf* **z-**) *vi* to rot
**bu|zia** (**-zi, -zie**) (*gen pl* **-zi** *lub* **-ź**) (*pot*) *f* (*usta*) mouth; (*twarz*) face; **dać** (*perf*) **komuś buzi** to give sb a kiss; **zamknij buzię** shut your mouth
**buzia|k** (**-ka, -ki**) (*instr sg* **-kiem**) *m* (*pot*) kiss
**by** *part*: **on by tego nie zrobił** he wouldn't do that ▷ *conj* (in order) to
**bycie** *n patrz* **byt**
**bycz|yć się (-ę, -ysz)** *vr* (*pot*) to loaf about *lub* around (*pot*)
**być (jestem, jesteś)** (*1 pl* **jesteśmy**, *2 pl* **jesteście**, *3 pl* **są**, *imp* **bądź**, *pt* **był, była, byli**, *1 sg fut* **będę**, *2 sg fut* **będziesz**) *vi* to be; **jestem!** present!, here!; **jestem samochodem** I've come by car; **jesteśmy po obiedzie** we've already had dinner; **czy byłeś w partii?** were you a party member?; **jest ciepło/zimno** it's warm/cold; **jest mi zimno/przykro** I'm cold/sorry; **co ci jest?** what's the matter with you?; **będę pamiętać** *lub* **pamiętał** I will remember; **ten dom był zbudowany w 1874** this house was built in 1874; **co będzie, jeśli nie przyjdą?** what will happen if they don't come?; **być może** maybe; **nie może być!** this *lub* it can't be!; **tak jest!** yes, sir!; **to jest** that is; **jestem za** *+instr*/**przeciw** *+dat* I am for/against
**bydl|ę** (**-ęcia, -ęta**) (*gen pl* **-ąt**) *nt cow, bull, ox or calf*; (*pot*: *zwierzę, człowiek*) animal
**byd|ło** (**-ła**) (*loc sg* **-le**) *nt* cattle
**by|k** (**-ka, -ki**) (*instr sg* **-kiem**) *m* bull; (*pot*) spelling mistake; **palnąć byka** to blunder, to boob (*Brit*); **Byk** (*Astrologia*) Taurus; **silny jak byk** (as) strong as an ox; **brać byka za rogi** to take the bull by the horns; **z byka spadłeś?** (*pot*) are you out of your mind?
**byle** *conj*: **~ nie to** anything but that ▷ *part* any; **~ tylko nie padało** let's hope it

doesn't rain; **~ co** any old thing; **~ gdzie** anywhere; **to nie ~ kto** he's not just anybody; **~ jaki** (*jakikolwiek*) any; (*podłej jakości*) trashy; **zrobili to ~ jak** they did it just anyhow

**byleby** *conj* (*byle tylko*) as long as; **~ tylko wyzdrowiała!** if only she would get better!

**byli** *vb patrz* **być**

**byli|na** (**-ny, -ny**) (*dat sg* **-nie**) *f* perennial

**był** *itd. vb patrz* **być**

**były** *adj* former; **była żona** ex-wife; **~ premier** the former *lub* ex-Prime Minister; **w byłej Jugosławii** in the former Yugoslavia

**bynajmniej** *adv*: **~ nie** not in the least; **~!** far from it!

**bystroś|ć** (**-ci**) *f* (*szybkość*) swiftness; (*inteligencja*) brightness

**bystry** *adj* (*nurt, rzeka*) swift; (*wzrok*) sharp; (*człowiek*) bright, quick- *lub* sharp-witted

**by|t** (**-tu, -ty**) (*loc sg* **-cie**) *m* (*istnienie*) existence; (*Filozofia*) being; **zapewnić byt rodzinie** to provide for the family

**bytnoś|ć** (**-ci**) *f* stay

**bytowy** *adj*: **warunki bytowe** living conditions

**byw|ać (-am, -asz)** *vi* (*w restauracji, galerii*) to frequent; (*udzielać się towarzysko*) to mingle, to socialize; (*zdarzać się*) to happen; **on często u nas bywa** he often visits us; **tak bywa** this happens

**bywal|ec** (**-ca, -cy**) (*voc sg* **-cze**) *m*: **stały ~** frequent visitor

**b.z.** *abbr* (= *bez zmian*) no change(s); (*Med*) NAD (= *no abnormalities detected*)

**bzdu|ra** (**-ry, -ry**) (*dat sg* **-rze**) *f* nonsense, rubbish

**bzdurny** *adj* nonsensical

**bzi|k** (**-ka**) (*instr sg* **-kiem**) *m* (*pot*): **mieć ~a (na punkcie** *+gen*) to be crazy (about); **dostać** (*perf*) **~a** to go crazy

**bzu** *itd. n patrz* **bez**

**bzycz|eć (-ę, -ysz)** *vi* to hum, to drone

# Cc



**C¹, c** *nt inv (litera)* C, c; **C jak Cecylia** ≈ C for Charlie; **C-dur** C major; **c-moll** C minor

**C²** *abbr (= Celsjusza)* C (= *Celsius, centigrade*)

**ca** *abbr (= circa)* c, ca. (= *circa*)

**cack|ać się (-am, -asz)** *vr (pot)*: **cackać się z kimś/czymś** to handle *lub* treat sb/sth with kid gloves

**cac|ko (-ka, -ka)** *(instr sg* **-kiem**, *gen pl* **-ek**) *nt (przen)* gem

**ca|l (-la, -le)** *(gen pl* **-li**) *m* inch; **dżentelmen w każdym calu** every inch a gentleman

**cal.** *abbr (= kaloria)* cal. (= *calorie*)

**calów|ka (-ki, -ki)** *(dat sg* **-ce**, *gen pl* **-ek**) *f* (folding) rule

**cał|ka (-ki, -ki)** *(dat sg* **-ce**, *gen pl* **-ek**) *f (Mat)* integral

**całkiem** *adv (zupełnie)* entirely; *(dosyć)* quite, pretty

**całkowicie** *adv* entirely, completely

**całkowity** *adj (mrok, cisza)* complete, total; *(kwota)* total; *(Mat: liczba)* integer

**cało** *adv* safely; **wyjść** *(perf)* **~ z wypadku/choroby** to make it through an accident/illness

**całodobowy** *adj* twenty-four-hour *attr*

**całodzienny** *adj* daylong

**całokształ|t (-tu)** *(loc sg* **-cie**) *m* the whole (of), entirety

**całonocny** *adj* all-night *attr*

**całoroczny** *adj* yearlong

**całoś|ć (-ci, -ci)** *f (wszystko)* whole, the lot; *(nienaruszalność)* integrity; **iść (pójść** *perf*) **na ~** *(pot)* to go the whole hog, to go all the way; **w całości** entirely

**cał|ować (-uję, -ujesz)** *(perf* **po-**) *vt* to kiss; **~ kogoś w rękę** to kiss sb's hand; **~ kogoś w usta** to kiss sb's mouth, to kiss sb on the mouth; **~ kogoś na pożegnanie** to kiss sb goodbye; **całować się** *vr* to kiss; *(pieścić się)* to neck

**cału|n (-nu, -ny)** *(loc sg* **-nie**) *m* shroud

**cału|s (-sa, -sy)** *(loc sg* **-sie**) *m* kiss; **posyłać (posłać** *perf*) **komuś ~a** to blow sb a kiss

**cały** *adj* whole; **~ czas** all the time; **~ dzień** all day (long), the whole day; **całe miasto** the whole town; **cała nuta** *(Muz)* semibreve *(Brit)*, whole note *(US)*; **to cała moja pociecha** that's my only comfort; **cała naprzód/wstecz** full ahead/astern; **~mi godzinami/dniami** for hours/days on end; **~ i zdrów** *lub* **zdrowy** safe and sound; **iść (pójść** *perf*) **na całego** *(pot)* to go the whole hog, to go all the way

**campin|g, kempin|g (-gu, -gi)** *(instr sg* **-giem**) *m (obozowisko)* camp(ing) site, campground *(US)*; *(pot: domek)* chalet *(Brit)*, cabin *(US)*

**ca|p (-pa, -py)** *(loc sg* **-pie**) *m* billy goat

**cap|nąć (-nę, -niesz)** *(imp* **-nij**) *vt perf (pot: złapać)* to grab; *(: aresztować)* to nab

**ca|r (-ra, -rowie)** *(loc sg* **-rze**) *m* tsar, czar *(US)*

**cargo** *nt inv* cargo

**carski** *adj* tsarist, czarist *(US)*

**caryc|a (-y, -e)** *f* tsarina, czarina *(US)*

**cąż|ki (-ków)** *pl* clippers

**CD** *abbr (= Corps Diplomatique (Korpus Dyplomatyczny))* CD; *(= compact disk)* CD

**cd.** *abbr (= ciąg dalszy)* cont(d)

**cdn.** *abbr (= ciąg dalszy nastąpi)* to be continued

**CD-ROM (CD-ROM-u, CD-ROM-y)** *(loc sg* **~-ie**) *m* CD-ROM

**ceb|er (-ra, -ry)** *(loc sg* **-rze**) *m*: **leje jak z cebra** *(przen: pot)* the rain's *lub* it's pouring down

**cebu|la (-li, -le)** *f* onion

**cebul|ka (-ki, -ki)** *(dat sg* **-ce**, *gen pl* **-ek**) *f (Bot)* bulb; *(włosa)* root; **zielona ~** scallion, green onion

**cech (-u, -y)** *m* guild

**ce|cha (-chy, -chy)** *(dat sg* **-sze**) *f* feature; **~ szczególna** characteristic; **to jest ~ rodzinna** it runs in the family

**cech|ować (-uję, -ujesz)** *vt* to characterize, to mark; **cechować się** *vr*: **~ się czymś** to be characterized *lub* marked by sth

**ced|ować (-uję, -ujesz)** *(perf* **s-**) *vt* to cede

**ced|r (-ru, -ry)** *(loc sg* **-rze**) *m* cedar

**cedza|k (-ka, -ki)** *(instr sg* **-kiem**) *m* colander, strainer

**ce|dzić (-dzę, -dzisz)** *(imp* **-dź**) *vt (perf* **prze-**) to strain; *(słowa)* *(perf* **wy-**) to drawl

**cegiel|nia (-ni, -nie)** *(gen pl* **-ni**) *f* brickyard

**cegieł|ka** (**-ki, -ki**) (*dat sg* **-ce**, *gen pl* **-ek**) *f dimin od* **cegła**; (*przen*: *udział*) share, contribution
**ce|gła** (**-gły, -gły**) (*dat sg* **-gle**, *gen pl* **-gieł**) *f* brick
**Cejlo|n** (**-nu**) (*loc sg* **-nie**) *m* Ceylon
**cekae|m** (**-mu, -my**) (*loc sg* **-mie**) *m* (*Wojsk*) heavy machine gun
**ceki|n** (**-na** *lub* **-nu, -ny**) (*loc sg* **-nie**) *m* sequin
**cel** (**-u, -e**) *m* (*dążeń, życia*) aim, goal; (*podróży*) destination; (*tarcza*) target; **na cel charytatywny** for charity; **bez celu** aimlessly; **przekazać** (*perf*) **sumę na cel ...** to give *lub* donate money to ...; **w celu** *lub* **celem zrobienia czegoś** (in order) to do sth; **w tym celu** to this end, with this end in view; **mijać się z celem** to be purposeless *lub* pointless
**ce|la** (**-li, -le**) *f* cell
**celebr|ować** (**-uję, -ujesz**) *vt* (*mszę, zwyczaj*) to celebrate; (*czynność*) to make a ritual (out) of
**celiba|t** (**-tu**) (*loc sg* **-cie**) *m* celibacy
**celni|k** (**-ka, -cy**) (*instr sg* **-kiem**) *m* customs officer
**celnoś|ć** (**-ci**) *f* (*strzału, działania*) accuracy; (*uwagi*) relevance, pertinence
**celny** *adj* (*cios, strzał*) accurate; (*dowcip, uwaga*) relevant; (*urząd, opłata, kontrola*) customs *attr*
**celofa|n** (**-nu**) (*loc sg* **-nie**) *m* cellophane®
**cel|ować** (**-uję, -ujesz**) *vi* (*perf* **wy-**) to take aim; **~ do kogoś/w coś** to aim at sb/sth; **~ w czymś** to excel at sth
**celowni|k** (**-ka, -ki**) (*instr sg* **-kiem**) *m* (*karabinu*) sight; (*aparatu*) viewfinder; (*Jęz*) dative
**celowo** *adv* intentionally, on purpose
**celowoś|ć** (**-ci**) *f* (*przydatność*) usefulness, purposefulness; (*stosowność*) advisability
**celowy** *adj* intentional, purposeful
**Celsjusz** (**-a**) *m*: **5 stopni ~a** 5 degrees Celsius *lub* centigrade
**Cel|t** (**-ta, -towie**) (*loc sg* **-cie**) *m* Celt
**celtycki** *adj* Celtic
**celujący** *adj* (*stopień*) excellent; (*uczeń*) exceptional
**celuloi|d** (**-du**) (*loc sg* **-dzie**) *m* celluloid
**celulo|za** (**-zy**) (*dat sg* **-zie**) *f* cellulose
**cel** *n patrz* **cło**
**cemen|t** (**-tu, -ty**) (*loc sg* **-cie**) *m* cement
**cement|ować** (**-uję, -ujesz**) *vt* (*zalewać cementem*) (*perf* **za-**) to cement (over); (*przen*: *umacniać*) (*perf* **s-**) to cement
**cementowy** *adj* cement *attr*
**ce|na** (**-ny, -ny**) (*dat sg* **-nie**) *f* price; **~ detaliczna/hurtowa/fabryczna** retail/ wholesale/manufacturer's price; **za wszelką cenę** (*przen*) at all costs, at any price; **za żadną cenę** (*przen*) (not) at any price; **być w cenie** (*przen*) to be of value
**ce|nić** (**-nię, -nisz**) (*imp* **-ń**) *vt* (*szanować*) to value; **~ sobie kogoś/coś** to think highly of sb/sth; **cenić się** *vr* to have self-esteem
**ceniony** *adj* prized, highly valued
**cenni|k** (**-ka, -ki**) (*instr sg* **-kiem**) *m* price list
**cenny** *adj* valuable, precious
**cen|t** (**-ta, -ty**) (*loc sg* **-cie**) *m* cent
**cent|ra** (**-ry, -ry**) (*dat sg* **-rze**, *gen pl* **-r**) *f* (*Futbol*) cross; *patrz też* **centrum**
**centra|la** (**-li, -le**) (*gen pl* **-li** *lub* **-l**) *f* (*Tel*: *też*: **centrala telefoniczna**) (telephone) exchange, switchboard; (*w hotelu*) switchboard; (*instytucja nadrzędna*) headquarters, head office
**centralizacj|a** (**-i**) *f* centralization
**centraliz|ować** (**-uję, -ujesz**) (*perf* **s-**) *vt* to centralize
**centralny** *adj* central; **centralne ogrzewanie** central heating
**centr|um** (**-um, -a**) (*gen pl* **-ów**) *nt inv in sg* centre (*Brit*), center (*US*); **~ miasta** town *lub* city centre (*Brit*), downtown (*US*); **~ handlowe** shopping centre (*Brit*) *lub* center (*US*), mall; **telefoniczne ~ obsługi klienta** call centre (*Brit*) *lub* center (*US*); **być w ~ zainteresowania** to be in the limelight; **być w ~ uwagi** to be in the public eye
**centymet|r** (**-ra, -ry**) (*loc sg* **-rze**) *m* centimetre (*Brit*), centimeter (*US*); **~ krawiecki** tape measure
**cenzo|r** (**-ra, -rzy**) (*loc sg* **-rze**) *m* censor
**cenzu|ra** (**-ry**) (*dat sg* **-rze**) *f* censorship
**cenzur|ować** (**-uję, -ujesz**) (*perf* **o-**) *vt* to censor
**cenzu|s** (**-su, -sy**) (*loc sg* **-sie**) *m* qualification
**ceń** *vb patrz* **cenić**
**ce|p** (**-pa, -py**) (*loc sg* **-pie**) *m* (*narzędzie*) flail; (*pot!*: *głupiec*) blockhead
**ce|ra** (**-ry**) (*dat sg* **-rze**) *f* (*skóra twarzy*) complexion; (*na ubraniu*) darn
**ceramiczny** *adj* ceramic
**cerami|ka** (**-ki**) (*dat sg* **-ce**) *f* (*sztuka*) ceramics; (*przedmioty*) pottery, ceramics *pl*
**cera|ta** (**-ty, -ty**) (*dat sg* **-cie**) *f* (*materiał*) oilcloth; (*obrus*) plastic tablecloth
**cerat|ka** (**-ki, -ki**) (*dat sg* **-ce**, *gen pl* **-ek**) *f* nappy liner
**ceregie|le** (**-li**) *pl* (*pot*): **bez ceregieli** without ceremony; **robić ~** to make a fuss; **nie robić z czymś ceregieli** to make no bones about sth
**ceremoni|a** (**-i, -e**) (*gen pl* **-i**) *f* ceremony; **robić ceremonie** (*pot*) to make a fuss
**ceremonia|ł** (**-łu, -ły**) (*loc sg* **-le**) *m* ceremonial, etiquette
**cer|kiew** (**-kwi, -kwie**) (*gen pl* **-kwi**) *f* Orthodox church
**cerkiewny** *adj* Orthodox Church *attr*; **język ~** Church Slavonic

**cer|ować (-uję, -ujesz)** (*perf* **za-**) *vt* to darn
**certyfika|t (-tu, -ty)** (*loc sg* **-cie**) *m* certificate
**cesarski** *adj* imperial; **~e cięcie** (*Med*) Caesarean (*Brit*) *lub* Cesarean (*US*) section
**cesarst|wo (-wa, -wa)** (*loc sg* **-wie**) *nt* empire
**cesarz (-a, -e)** (*gen pl* **-y**) *m* emperor
**cesarzow|a (-ej, -e)** *f decl like adj* empress
**cesj|a (-i, -e)** (*gen pl* **-i**) *f* (*Prawo*) transfer; (*terytorialna*) cession
**cesze** *n patrz* **cecha**
**cew|ka (-ki, -ki)** (*dat sg* **-ce**, *gen pl* **-ek**) *f* (*Elektr*) coil; **~ moczowa** urethra; **~ zapłonowa** (*Mot*) coil
**cewni|k (-ka, -ki)** (*instr sg* **-kiem**) *m* (*Med*) catheter
**cezu|ra (-ry, -ry)** (*dat sg* **-rze**) *f* (*granica*) dividing line; (*moment przełomowy*) turning point; (*Muz, Lit*) c(a)esura
**cę|gi (-gów)** *pl* (*Tech*) pincers
**cęt|ka (-ki, -ki)** (*dat sg* **-ce**, *gen pl* **-ek**) *f* spot; **w cętki** spotted
**cętkowany** *adj* spotted
**chab|er (-ra** *lub* **-ru, -ry)** (*loc sg* **-rze**) *m* cornflower
**chacie** *n patrz* **chata**
**chadz|ać (-am, -asz)** *vi* (*chodzić czasami*) to go (*from time to time*); **~ w czymś** to wear sth (*habitually*)
**cha|ła (-ły, -ły)** (*dat sg* **-le**) *f* (*pot: film, książka*) trash
**chał|ka (-ki, -ki)** (*dat sg* **-ce**, *gen pl* **-ek**) *f* (*bułka*) *a kind of sweetened and braided white bread*
**chałtu|ra (-ry, -ry)** (*dat sg* **-rze**) *f* (*pot: źle wykonana praca*) slipshod work; (*dodatkowe zajęcie*) second job
**chałupnict|wo (-wa)** (*loc sg* **-wie**) *nt* cottage industry
**chał|wa (-wy, -wy)** (*dat sg* **-wie**) *f* halvah
**cha|m (-ma, -my)** (*loc sg* **-mie**) *m* (*pot!*) brute (*pot*)
**champio|n (-na, -ny)** (*loc sg* **-nie**) *m* champion
**chamski** *adj* (*pej*) boorish
**chamst|wo (-wa)** (*loc sg* **-wie**) *nt* (*pej*) boorishness
**chand|ra (-ry, -ry)** (*dat sg* **-rze**) *f*: **mieć chandrę** to have the blues
**chao|s (-su)** (*loc sg* **-sie**) *m* chaos
**chaotyczny** *adj* chaotic
**cha|pać (-pię, -piesz)** *vi* (*pot*) to sweat one's guts out
**chap|nąć (-nę, -niesz)** (*imp* **-nij**) *vt perf* (*pot*) to snap
**charakte|r (-ru, -ry)** (*loc sg* **-rze**) *m* (*człowieka*) character; (*zjawiska, przedmiotu*) character, nature; **w ~ze** *+gen* in the capacity of; **silny/słaby ~** strong/weak personality; **człowiek z ~em** a person of character; **czarny ~** (*przen*) villain; **~ pisma** handwriting
**charakterystyczny** *adj*: **~ (dla** *+gen*) characteristic (of)
**charakterysty|ka (-ki, -ki)** (*dat sg* **-ce**) *f* profile
**charakteryzacj|a (-i, -e)** (*gen pl* **-i**) *f* make-up
**charakteryzato|r (-ra, -rzy)** (*loc sg* **-rze**) *m* make-up man
**charakteryzator|ka (-ki, -ki)** (*dat sg* **-ce**, *gen pl* **-ek**) *f* make-up woman
**charakteryz|ować (-uję, -ujesz)** *vt* (*opisywać*) (*perf* **s-**) to characterize, to describe; (*o cechach, przymiotach*) to characterize; (*Teatr, Film*) (*perf* **u-**) to make up; **charakteryzować się** *vr*: **~ się czymś** to be characterized by sth
**charcz|eć (-ę, -ysz)** (*perf* **za-**) *vi* to wheeze
**char|t (-ta, -ty)** (*loc sg* **-cie**) *m* greyhound
**charytatywny** *adj* charitable; **na cele charytatywne** for charity
**charyz|ma (-my, -my)** (*dat sg* **-mie**) *f* charisma
**charyzmatyczny** *adj* charismatic
**chaszcz|e (-y** *lub* **-ów)** *pl* thicket
**cha|ta (-ty, -ty)** (*dat sg* **-cie**) *f* cabin, hut; (*pot: mieszkanie*) place
**chcieć (chcę, chcesz)** (*imp* **chciej**) *vt* to want; **~ coś zrobić** to want to do sth; **chcę, żeby on tam pojechał** I want him to go there; **chce mi się spać/pić** I feel sleepy/thirsty; **chce mi się tańczyć** I feel like dancing; **chciałbym …** I would like …; **czy chciałbyś …?** would you like …?; **jak chcesz** (*pot*) as you wish; **drzwi nie chcą się otworzyć** the door won't open; **chcąc nie chcąc** willy-nilly; **chce mi się siusiu** (*pot*) I must have a pee
**chci|wiec (-wca, -wcy)** (*voc sg* **-wcze**) *m* greedy person
**chciwoś|ć (-ci)** *f* greed
**chciwy** *adj* greedy
**cheł|pić się (-pię, -pisz)** *vr*: **chełpić się (czymś)** to boast (about sth)
**chełpliwy** *adj* boastful
**chemi|a (-i)** *f* chemistry
**chemicz|ka (-ki, -ki)** (*dat sg* **-ce**, *gen pl* **-ek**) *f* (*pot: nauczycielka*) chemistry teacher
**chemiczny** *adj* chemical
**chemi|k (-ka, -cy)** (*instr sg* **-kiem**) *m* (*naukowiec*) chemist; (*nauczyciel*) chemistry teacher
**chemikali|a (-ów)** *pl* chemicals
**chemoterapi|a (-i)** *f* chemotherapy
**cherla|k (-ka, -ki** *lub* **-cy)** (*instr sg* **-kiem**) *m* (*pot*) weakling
**cherlawy** *adj* sickly
**cherubi|n (-na, -ny** *lub* **-ni)** (*loc sg* **-nie**) *m* cherub
**chę|ć (-ci, -ci)** *f* desire; **~ do życia/pracy** a will to live/work; **z chęcią** willingly, with pleasure; **mam ~ wyjechać** I feel like going away; **dobre chęci** good intentions

**chęt|ka** (**-ki, -ki**) (*dat sg* **-ce**, *gen pl* **-ek**) *f* (*pot*): **mieć chętkę na coś** to fancy sth
**chętnie** *adv* willingly, eagerly
**chętny** *adj* willing, eager; **~ do pracy/pomocy** willing to work/help
**chicho|t** (**-tu, -ty**) (*loc sg* **-cie**) *m* giggle
**chicho|tać (-czę, -czesz)** (*perf* **za-**, *imp* **-cz**) *vi* to giggle
**Chile** *nt inv* Chile
**chilijski** *adj* Chilean
**chime|ra** (**-ry, -ry**) (*dat sg* **-rze**) *f* (*Mitologia*) chimera; **mieć chimery** to be moody *lub* whimsical
**Chin|ka** (**-ki, -ki**) (*dat sg* **-ce**, *gen pl* **-ek**) *f* Chinese
**Chi|ny** (**-n**) *pl* China
**Chińczy|k** (**-ka, -cy**) (*instr sg* **-kiem**) *m* Chinese
**chiński** *adj* Chinese; **Chińska Republika Ludowa** the People's Republic of China
**chińszczy|zna** (**-zny**) (*dat sg* **-źnie**) *f* (*pot*): **to dla mnie ~** it's all Greek to me
**chips|y** (**-ów**) *pl* crisps (*Brit*), chips (*US*)
**chiromancj|a** (**-i**) *f* palmistry
**chirur|g** (**-ga, -dzy**) (*instr sg* **-giem**) *m* surgeon
**chirurgi|a** (**-i**) *f* surgery
**chirurgiczny** *adj* surgical
**chl|ać (-eję, -ejesz)** (*imp* **-ej**, *perf* **wy-**) *vt* (*pot*) to booze
**chla|pa** (**-py, -py**) (*dat sg* **-pie**) *f* (*pot*) slush
**chla|pać (-pię, -piesz)** (*perf* **-pnąć**) *vt/vi* to splash; (*pot: pleść głupstwa*) to blab
**chlap|nąć (-nę, -niesz)** (*imp* **-nij**) *vb perf od* **chlapać**
**chle|b** (**-ba, -by**) (*loc sg* **-bie**) *m* bread; **zarabiać na ~** to earn one's daily bread
**chleba|k** (**-ka, -ki**) (*instr sg* **-kiem**) *m* haversack
**chlebodawc|a** (**-y, -y**) *m decl like f in sg* employer
**chle|w** (**-wa** *lub* **-wu, -wy**) (*loc sg* **-wie**) *m* pigsty (*Brit*), pigpen (*US*)
**chlewny** *adj*: **trzoda chlewna** swine *pl*, pigs *pl*
**chli|pać (-pię, -piesz)** *vi* (*płakać*) to sob
**chlo|r** (**-ru**) (*loc sg* **-rze**) *m* (*Chem*) chlorine
**chlor|ek** (**-ku, -ki**) (*instr sg* **-kiem**) *m* chloride
**chlorofor|m** (**-mu**) (*loc sg* **-mie**) *m* chloroform
**chlor|ować (-uję, -ujesz)** *vt* to chlorinate
**chlu|ba** (**-by, -by**) (*dat sg* **-bie**) *f* (*osoba, rzecz*) pride; (*sława*) glory; **być chlubą rodziców** to be the pride of one's parents; **przynosić komuś chlubę** to do sb credit
**chlu|bić się (-bię, -bisz)** *vr*: **chlubić się czymś** to take pride in sth
**chlubny** *adj* glorious
**chlu|pać (-pię, -piesz)** (*perf* **-pnąć**) *vi* to splash; (*bulgotać*) to squelch
**chlup|nąć (-nę, -niesz)** (*imp* **-nij**) *vb perf od* **chlupać**
**chlupo|t** (**-tu, -ty**) (*loc sg* **-cie**) *m* lap, squelch
**chlupo|tać (-cze)** (*perf* **za-**) *vi* to squelch
**chlu|snąć (-snę, -śniesz)** (*imp* **-śnij**) *vb perf od* **chlustać**
**chlu|stać (-stam, -stasz** *lub* **-szczę, -szczesz)** (*perf* **-snąć**) *vi* (*o płynie*) to spurt; **chlusnąć** (*perf*) **wodą** to spurt water
**chłep|tać (-czę, -czesz)** (*imp* **-cz**, *perf* **wy-**) *vt* to lap
**chłod|nia** (**-ni, -nie**) (*gen pl* **-ni**) *f* refrigerator; **samochód/statek ~** refrigeration truck/ship
**chłodnic|a** (**-y, -e**) *f* (*Mot*) radiator
**chłodni|k** (**-ka, -ki**) (*instr sg* **-kiem**) *m vegetable or fruit soup usually served cold*
**chłodno** *adv* (*witać, przyjmować*) coolly; **jest ~** it is cold *lub* chilly; **robi się ~** it is getting cold *lub* chilly
**chłodny** *adj* cool
**chłodzeni|e** (**-a**) *nt* cooling
**chłodziar|ka** (**-ki, -ki**) (*dat sg* **-ce**, *gen pl* **-ek**) *f* refrigerator
**chło|dzić (-dzę, -dzisz)** (*imp* **-dź**) *vt* to cool, to chill; (*zamrażać*) to refrigerate ▷ *vi* (*o wietrze, napoju*) to be cooling; **napoje chłodzące** cold drinks; **chłodzić się** *vr* to cool
**chło|nąć (-nę, -niesz)** (*imp* **-ń**) *vt* (*absorbować*) to absorb; (*przen: widoki, słowa*) to drink in
**chłonnoś|ć** (**-ci**) *f* (*przen: rynku*) absorptive power; (*umysłu*) receptivity
**chłonny** *adj* (*przen*) absorptive; (*umysł*) receptive; **węzły chłonne** lymph glands *lub* nodes
**chło|p** (**-pa**) (*loc sg* **-pie**) *m* (*nom pl* **-pi**) peasant; (*pot: mężczyzna*) (*nom pl* **-py**) fellow, chap
**chłopa|k** (**-ka, -cy**) (*instr sg* **-kiem**) *m* boy; (*sympatia*) boyfriend
**chłopczy|k** (**-ka, -ki**) (*instr sg* **-kiem**) *m* little boy
**chło|piec** (**-pca, -pcy**) (*dat sg* **-pcu**) *m* boy; (*sympatia*) boyfriend; **~ na posyłki** (*przen*) errand boy
**chłopięcy** *adj* boyish
**chłop|ka** (**-ki, -ki**) (*dat sg* **-ce**, *gen pl* **-ek**) *f* peasant woman, countrywoman
**chłopski** *adj* peasant *attr*; **~ rozum** (*pot*) common sense
**chłopst|wo** (**-wa**) (*loc sg* **-wie**) *nt* peasantry
**chło|sta** (**-sty, -sty**) (*dat sg* **-ście**) *f* flogging
**chło|stać (-szczę, -szczesz)** *vt* (*perf* **wy-**) to flog; (*o deszczu*) to lash
**chł|ód** (**-odu, -ody**) (*loc sg* **-odzie**) *m* chill; (*przen*) coldness
**chma|ra** (**-ry, -ry**) (*dat sg* **-rze**) *f* (*owadów*) swarm; **~ ludzi** hordes of people
**chmiel** (**-u**) *m* hop
**chmu|ra** (**-ry, -ry**) (*dat sg* **-rze**) *f* cloud
**chmurny** *adj* (*dzień, niebo*) cloudy; (*przen: czoło*) frowned; **~ wzrok** disconsolate look

**chmurz|yć (-ę, -ysz)** *(perf* **za-***) vt:* **~ czoło** to frown; **chmurzyć się** *vr* to cloud over

**choch|la** (**-li, -le**) *(gen pl* **-li***) f* ladle

**chochli|k** (**-ka, -ki**) *(instr sg* **-kiem***) m (duszek)* imp; **~ drukarski** misprint, typo *(pot)*

**chociaż, choć** *conj* though, although ▷ *part (przynajmniej)* at least; **mogłeś ~ zadzwonić** you could have called at least

**chociażby, choćby** *conj* even if ▷ *part (nawet)* even; **~ to było niemożliwe** even if it were impossible

**choć** *conj* = **chociaż**

**choćby** *conj* = **chociażby**

**choda|k** (**-ka, -ki**) *(instr sg* **-kiem***) m* clog

**chodliwy** *adj (pot: towar)* fast-selling

**chodni|k** (**-ka, -ki**) *(instr sg* **-kiem***) m (część ulicy)* pavement *(Brit)*, sidewalk *(US)*; *(dywan)* runner; *(w kopalni)* gallery

**cho|dzić (-dzę, -dzisz)** *(imp* **-dź***) vi (spacerować)* to walk; *(uczęszczać)* to go; *(funkcjonować)* to work; *(pot: kursować)* to run; *(poruszać się)* to move; **~ z kimś** *(pot)* to go out with sb; **o co chodzi?** what's the problem?; **chodzi o to, że…** the thing is that…; **o co mu chodzi?** what's his problem?; **chodzi mi to po głowie** *(pot)* it is on my mind; **chodź na spacer!** let's go for a walk

**choin|ka** (**-ki, -ki**) *(dat sg* **-ce**, *gen pl* **-ek***) f (w lesie)* spruce; *(świąteczna)* Christmas tree

**choinkowy** *adj* Christmas *attr*

**chole|ra** (**-ry**) *(dat sg* **-rze***) f (Med)* cholera; *(pot!: wyzwisko) (nom pl* **-ry***)* asshole *(pot!)*; *(: przekleństwo)*: **~!** shit! *(pot!)*, damn! *(pot!)*; **idź do cholery!** *(pot!)* go to hell! *(pot!)*; **zimno jak ~!** *(pot)* it is so damn cold! *(pot!)*

**cholernie** *adv (pot!)* damn(ed) *(pot!)*, bloody *(pot!) (Brit)*

**cholerny** *adj (pot!)* damn *(pot!)*, bloody *(pot!) (Brit)*

**cholerycz|ka** (**-ki, -ki**) *(dat sg* **-ce**, *gen pl* **-ek***) f* hot-tempered woman

**choleryk** (**-ka, -cy**) *(instr sg* **-kiem***) m* hot-tempered man

**cholestero|l** (**-lu**) *m* cholesterol

**chole|wa** (**-wy, -wy**) *(dat sg* **-wie***) f* leg *(part of a boot)*

**chomi|k** (**-ka, -ki**) *(instr sg* **-kiem***) m* hamster

**chomik|ować (-uję, -ujesz)** *vt (pot)* to hoard, to squirrel away

**cho|ra** (**-rej, -re**) *f decl like adj (chora kobieta)* ill *lub* sick woman; *(pacjentka)* (woman) patient

**chorą|giew** (**-gwi, -gwie**) *(gen pl* **-gwi***) f (flaga)* flag; *(sztandar)* standard; *(harcerska)* regiment

**chorągiew|ka** (**-ki, -ki**) *(gen pl* **-ce**, *gen pl* **-ek***) f dimin od* **chorągiew**; **~ na wietrze** *lub* **dachu** *(przen)* a changeable person

**chorąż|y** (**-ego, -owie**) *m decl like adj in sg* warrant officer

**choreogra|f** (**-fa, -fowie**) *(loc sg* **-fie***) m* choreographer

**choreografi|a** (**-i**) *f* choreography

**chor|oba** (**-oby, -oby**) *(dat sg* **-obie**, *gen pl* **-ób***) f (schorzenie)* disease; *(stan)* illness; **~ morska** seasickness; **~ popromienna** radiation sickness; **z powodu choroby** due to illness

**chorobliwy** *adj (niezdrowy)* unhealthy; *(nienormalny)* abnormal, pathological

**chorobotwórczy** *adj* pathogenic

**chorobow|e** (**-ego, -e**) *nt decl like adj in sg*; **być na chorobowym** to be off sick; **iść (pójść** *perf***) na ~** to go on a sick leave

**chorobowy** *adj* pathological; **karta chorobowa** progress report

**chor|ować (-uję, -ujesz)** *vi* to be ill, to be sick *(US)*; **~ na grypę** to have *lub* suffer from flu; **~ na serce** to have a bad heart, to have a heart condition *lub* problem; **~ na coś** *(pot: przen)* to be dying for sth

**chorowity** *adj* sickly

**Chorwacj|a** (**-i**) *f* Croatia

**chorwacki** *adj* Croatian

**Chorwa|t** (**-ta, -ci**) *(loc sg* **-cie***) m* Croat

**chory** *adj (człowiek, zwierzę)* ill, sick; *(gardło, noga)* sore; *(ząb, serce)* bad; *(drzewo, roślina)* sick ▷ *m decl like adj (chory człowiek)* sick person; *(pacjent)* patient; **być ~m na grypę/serce** to have flu/a bad heart; **śmiertelnie** *lub* **nieuleczalnie ~** fatally ill; **~ z miłości** *(przen)* lovesick

**chow|ać (-am, -asz)** *vt (wkładać) (perf* **s-***)* to put *(somewhere)*; *(odkładać) (perf* **s-***)* to put away; *(ukrywać) (perf* **s-***)* to hide; *(trzymać)* to keep; *(składać do grobu) (perf* **po-***)* to bury; *(wychowywać)* to bring up; *(hodować)* to raise, to breed; **~ głowę w piasek** *(przen)* to bury one's head in the sand; **chować się** *vr (kryć się) (perf* **s-***)* to hide; *(pot: wychowywać się) (perf* **wy-***)* to be brought up

**chowan|y** (**-ego**) *m decl like adj*; **bawić się w chowanego** to play hide and seek

**chód** (**chodu**) *(loc sg* **chodzie***) m* walk, gait; *(Sport: też:* **chód sportowy***)* (race) walking; **chody** *pl (pot)*: **mieć chody** to have connections, to know the ropes; **(być) na chodzie** *(pot)* (to be) in running order

**chó|r** (**-ry, -ry**) *(loc sg* **-rze***) m (zespół)* choir, chorus; *(utwór)* chorus; *(galeria: w kościele)* choir; **śpiewać ~em** to sing in chorus

**chóralny** *adj (Muz)* choral

**chór|ek** (**-ku, -ki**) *(instr sg* **-kiem***) m (pot)* backing singers

**chórzy|sta** (**-sty, -ści**) *(dat sg* **-ście***) m decl like f in sg* choir singer

**chórzyst|ka** (**-ki, -ki**) *(dat sg* **-ce**, *gen pl* **-ek***) f* choir singer

**chów** (**chowu**) (*dat sg* **chowu**, *loc sg* **chowie**) *m* (*bydła, drobiu*) raising, breeding
**chrabąszcz** (**-a, -e**) (*gen pl* **-y** *lub* **-ów**) *m* cockchafer, may-bug
**chra|pać (-pię, -piesz)** *vi* (*perf* **-pnąć**) to snore
**chrapliwy** *adj* hoarse
**chrap|nąć (-nę, -niesz)** (*imp* **-nij**) *vb perf od* **chrapać**
**ChRL** *abbr* (= *Chińska Republika Ludowa*) the People's Republic of China
**chro|m** (**-mu**) (*loc sg* **-mie**) *m* chrome; (*Chem*) chromium
**chromoso|m** (**-mu, -my**) (*loc sg* **-mie**) *m* chromosome
**chromowany** *adj* chromium-plated
**chromowy** *adj*: **taśma chromowa** chrome tape
**chroniczny** *adj* chronic
**chro|nić (-nię, -nisz)** (*imp* **-ń**) *vt* to protect; **~ kogoś/coś przed** *+instr* to protect sb/sth against; **chronić się** *vr* (*szukać schronienia*) (*perf* **s-**) to take shelter; (*strzec się*) (*perf* **u-**) to protect o.s.
**chroniony** *adj* (*zwierzęta, rośliny*) (legally) protected
**chronologi|a** (**-i**) *f* chronology
**chronologiczny** *adj* chronological
**chropowaty** *adj* rough
**chru|pać (-pię, -piesz)** *vt* (*gryźć*) to crunch
**chrupiący** *adj* crunchy, crispy
**chrup|ki** *adj* crispy ▹ *pl* (*gen pl* **-ek**) crisps *pl*; **pieczywo ~e** crisp bread
**chru|st** (**-stu**) (*loc sg* **-ście**) *m* brushwood
**chruści|k** (**-ku** *lub* **-ka, -ki**) (*instr sg* **-kiem**) *m* (*Kulin*) *a kind of crisp cake fried in oil*
**chry|pieć (-pię, -pisz)** (*perf* **za-**) *vi* (*o człowieku*) to have a hoarse *lub* husky voice
**chryp|ka** (**-ki, -ki**) (*dat sg* **-ce**, *gen pl* **-ek**) *f* hoarseness; **mieć chrypkę** to be hoarse
**chrystianizacj|a** (**-i**) *f* Christianization
**Chrystu|s** (**-sa**) (*loc sg* **-sie**) *m* Christ; **Jezus ~** Jesus Christ
**chryzante|ma** (**-my, -my**) (*dat sg* **-mie**) *f* chrysanthemum
**chrza|n** (**-nu**) (*loc sg* **-nie**) *m* horseradish
**chrza|nić (-nię, -nisz)** (*imp* **-ń**) *vt* (*pot: partaczyć*) (*perf* **s-**) to mess up, to screw up (*pot*) ▹ *vi* (*pot: gadać bzdury*) to talk rubbish
**chrząk|ać (-am, -asz)** (*perf* **-nąć**) *vi* (*o człowieku*) to clear one's throat; (*o świni*) to grunt
**chrząk|nąć (-nę, -niesz)** (*imp* **-nij**) *vb perf od* **chrząkać**
**chrząst|ka** (**-ki, -ki**) (*dat sg* **-ce**, *gen pl* **-ek**) *f* (*Anat*) cartilage, gristle; (*Kulin*) gristle
**chrząszcz** (**-a, -e**) (*gen pl* **-y**) *m* beetle
**chrz|cić (-czę, -cisz)** (*imp* **-cij**, *perf* **o-**) *vt* (*dziecko*) to baptize; (*nadawać imię*) to baptize, to christen; (*statek*) to christen
**chrzcielnic|a** (**-y, -e**) *f* (baptismal) font
**chrzci|ny** (**-n**) *pl party given by parents on the day of their child's baptism*
**chrz|est** (**-tu, -ty**) (*loc sg* **-cie**) *m* (*dziecka*) baptism; (*statku*) christening; **świadectwo chrztu** certificate of baptism; **~ bojowy** baptism of fire
**chrzestn|a** (**-ej, -e**) *f decl like adj* (*też*: **matka chrzestna**) godmother
**chrzestny** *adj* (*imię*) Christian ▹ *m decl like adj* (*też*: **ojciec chrzestny**) godfather
**chrześcija|nin** (**-nina, -nie**) (*loc sg* **-ninie**) *m* Christian
**chrześcijański** *adj* Christian; **chrześcijańska demokracja** Christian Democratic Party
**chrześcijańst|wo** (**-wa**) (*loc sg* **-wie**) *nt* Christianity
**chrześniacz|ka** (**-ki, -ki**) (*dat sg* **-ce**, *gen pl* **-ek**) *f* goddaughter
**chrześnia|k** (**-ka, -cy**) (*instr sg* **-kiem**) *m* godson
**chrzę|ścić (-szczę, -ścisz)** (*imp* **-ść**) *vi* (*o żwirze*) to crunch; (*o mechanizmie*) to grind
**chuch|ać (-am, -asz)** (*perf* **-nąć**) *vi*: **~ na** *+acc* (*zmarznięte ręce*) to blow on; (*przen*) to nurse
**chuch|nąć (-nę, -niesz)** (*imp* **-nij**) *vb perf od* **chuchać**
**chuch|ro** (**-ra, -ra**) (*loc sg* **-rze**, *gen pl* **-er**) *nt* (*pot*) weakling
**chu|ć** (**-ci, -ci** *lub* **-cie**) (*gen pl* **-ci**) *f* lust
**chud|nąć (-nę, -niesz)** (*imp* **-nij**, *perf* **s-**, *pt* **chudł** *lub* **chudnął, chudła, chudli**) *vi* to lose weight
**chudy** *adj* (*człowiek, zwierzę*) thin, skinny; (*mięso, ser*) lean; **~ jak szczapa** (*pot*) as thin as a lath *lub* rake
**chudziel|ec** (**-ca, -cy** *lub* **-ce**) (*voc sg* **-cze**) *m* (*pot*) scrag, a bag of bones
**chuj** (**-a, -e**) *m* (*pot!*) dick (*pot!*), prick (*pot!*)
**chuliga|n** (**-na, -ni**) (*loc sg* **-nie**) *m* hooligan
**chuligańst|wo** (**-wa**) (*loc sg* **-wie**) *nt* hooliganism
**chu|sta** (**-sty, -sty**) (*dat sg* **-ście**) *f* scarf
**chustecz|ka** (**-ki, -ki**) (*dat sg* **-ce**, *gen pl* **-ek**) *f* (*też*: **chusteczka do nosa**) handkerchief; (*też*: **chusteczka higieniczna**) tissue, Kleenex®
**chust|ka** (**-ki, -ki**) (*dat sg* **-ce**, *gen pl* **-ek**) *f* scarf; **~ do nosa** handkerchief
**chwalebny** *adj* praiseworthy
**chwa|lić (-lę, -lisz)** (*perf* **po-**) *vt* (*mówić z uznaniem*) to praise; (*wielbić*) to glorify; **~ sobie coś** to be satisfied with sth; **chwalić się** *vr*: **~ się (czymś)** to brag *lub* to boast (about sth)
**chwa|ła** (**-ły**) (*loc sg* **-le**) *f* glory; **poległy na polu chwały** killed in action; **~ Bogu!** thank God!

**chwa|st** (**-stu, -sty**) (*loc sg* **-ście**) *m* weed
**chwi|ać (-eję, -ejesz)** (*perf* **za-**) *vt*: **~ czymś** to shake sth; **chwiać się** *vr* (*o człowieku*) to sway; (*o płomieniu*) to flicker; (*o zębie*) to wobble; (*wahać się*) to waver, to falter
**chwiejnoś|ć** (**-ci**) *f* (*ruchów*) staggering; (*przen*: *poglądów, uczuć*) instability
**chwiejny** *adj* shaky; (*przen*) wavering
**chwi|la** (**-li, -le**) *f* moment, instant; **poczekaj chwilę!** wait a minute!, just a moment!; **~mi** now and then; **co ~** every now and then; **w każdej chwili** (*lada moment*) any minute now; **w tej chwili** (*teraz*) at the moment; (*obecnie*) at present; (*pot*: *natychmiast*) right now; **w ostatniej chwili** at the last moment; **za chwilę** in a minute
**chwilecz|ka** (**-ki, -ki**) (*dat sg* **-ce**, *gen pl* **-ek**) *f*: **chwileczkę!** just a minute!
**chwilowo** *adv* (*obecnie*) at the moment, for the time being; (*nieczynny, zamknięty*) temporarily
**chwilowy** *adj* temporary
**chwy|cić (-cę, -cisz)** (*imp* **-ć**) *vb perf od* **chwytać**
**chwy|t** (**-tu, -ty**) (*loc sg* **-cie**) *m* hold, grip; (*przen*: *fortel*) trick, catch
**chwyt|ać (-am, -asz)** (*perf* **chwycić**) *vt* (*łapać*: *piłkę itp.*) to catch; (*przen*: *życie, chwilę*) to seize; (: *pojmować*) to grasp ▷ *vi* (*pot*: *o pomyśle, reklamie*) to catch on; (: *o farbie, barwniku*) to hold; **chwycić kogoś za rękę** to grab *lub* to seize sb by the hand; **~ za broń** (*przen*) to take up arms; **mróz chwycił** it suddenly froze; **chwytać się** *vr*: **~ się czegoś** *lub* **za coś** to seize sth; **~ się za głowę** to take one's head in one's hands; **~ się na czymś** (*przen*) to catch o.s. doing sth
**chwytliwy** *adj* (*melodia, tytuł*) catchy
**chwytny** *adj* prehensile
**chyba** *part* probably ▷ *conj*: **~ że** unless; **~ wiesz o tym** you must know about it; **~ tak/~ nie** I think so/I don't think so
**chy|biać (-biam, -biasz)** (*perf* **-bić**) *vi* to miss; **chybić** (*perf*) **celu** to miss one's aim; **na chybił trafił** (*strzelać*) at random; (*strzał*) hit-or-miss
**chybiony** *adj* (*strzał*) missed; (*plan*) abortive; (*uwaga*) pointless
**chybo|tać się (-czę, -czesz)** *vr* to shake, to wobble
**chybotliwy** *adj* wobbling
**chy|lić (-lę, -lisz)** *vt* (*książk*): **~ czoło** *lub* **głowę przed kimś** to pay homage to sb; **chylić się** *vr* (*przen*): **~ się ku upadkowi** to be on the decline
**chyłkiem** *adv* stealthily
**chytroś|ć** (**-ci**) *f* (*przebiegłość*) cunningness, slyness; (*chciwość*) greed
**chytry** *adj* (*przebiegły*) cunning, sly; (*pot*: *urządzenie*) artful, ingenious; (: *chciwy*) greedy; **~ lis** (*przen*) cunning fox
**chyży** *adj* swift
**ci** *pron nom pl od* **ten** these ▷ *pron dat od* **ty** (to) you; **ci chłopcy** these boys; **powiedział ci?** has he told you? ▷ *part*: **a to ci głupiec/historia!** what a fool/story!
**ciał|ko** (**-ka, -ka**) (*instr sg* **-kiem**, *gen pl* **-ek**) *nt*: **białe/czerwone ciałka krwi** white/red blood cells
**ci|ało** (**-ała, -ała**) (*loc sg* **-ele**) *nt* body; **~ niebieskie** heavenly body; **~ stałe** solid; **Boże C~** Corpus Christi
**ciar|ki** (**-ek**) *pl*: **~ mnie przeszły na myśl o ...** the thought of ... sent shivers down my spine
**ciasno** *adv* tightly
**ciasno|ta** (**-ty**) (*dat sg* **-cie**) *f* lack of space
**cia|sny** (*comp* **-śniejszy**) *adj* tight; (*kąt, pokój*) small
**ciastkar|nia** (**-ni, -nie**) (*gen pl* **-ni** *lub* **-ń**) *f* (*sklep*) patisserie; (*wytwórnia*) bakery
**ciast|ko** (**-ka, -ka**) (*instr sg* **-kiem**, *gen pl* **-ek**) *nt* cake, pastry
**ci|asto** (**-asta, -asta**) (*loc sg* **-eście**) *nt* (*masa*) dough; (*wypiek*) cake
**ciąć (tnę, tniesz)** (*imp* **tnij**) *vt* (*nożem, nożyczkami*) to cut; (*o komarach, osach*) to sting; (*powietrze, fale*) to cut through; (*szablą*) to hack; (*batem*) to lash
**cią|g** (**-gu, -gi**) (*instr sg* **-giem**) *m* (*komunikacyjny*) route; (*myśli*) train; (*Lot*) thrust; (*powietrza*) draught (*Brit*), draft (*US*); (*Mat*) sequence; **~ technologiczny** *lub* **produkcyjny** production process; **w ~u dnia** by day; **w ~u trzech dni** within three days; **dalszy ~** sequel; **~ dalszy nastąpi** to be continued
**ciągle** *adv* (*nadal*) still; (*nieustannie*) continuously, continually; (*w sposób powtarzający się*) continually, constantly; **on ~ jeszcze jest bez pracy** he is still jobless
**ciągłoś|ć** (**-ci**) *f* continuity
**ciągły** *adj* continuous; (*strach, ból*) constant; (*ruch*) continual
**ciąg|nąć (-nę, -niesz)** (*imp* **-nij**) *vt* (*wlec*) (*perf* **po-**) to pull; (*losy*) to draw, to cast ▷ *vi* (*mówić dalej*) to continue, to go on; (*o wojsku*) to proceed, to move; **~ kogoś za włosy** to pull sb's hair; **~ kogoś za język** (*przen*) to cross-question sb; **~ zyski z czegoś** to derive profits from sth; **~ przewody** (*w ziemi*) to lay cables; (*w powietrzu*) to string cables; **ciągnie od okna** (*pot*) there is a draught (*Brit*) *lub* draft (*US*) from the window; **ciągnąć się** *vr* (*o drodze, lesie, plaży*) to extend, to stretch; (*o*

*dyskusji, procesie*) to drag on; (*pot: o cukierkach, gumie do żucia*) to be chewy
**ciągni|k** (**-ka, -ki**) (*instr sg* **-kiem**) *m* tractor
**ciągot|y** (-) *pl* (*pot*): **~ do** *+gen* inclination to
**ciąż|a** (**-y, -e**) *f* pregnancy; **być w ciąży** to be pregnant; **zajść** (*perf*) **w ciążę** to get pregnant
**ciążeni|e** (**-a**) *nt* (*też*: **ciążenie powszechne**) gravitation
**ciążowy** *adj* (*suknia, pas*) maternity *attr*; **próba ciążowa** pregnancy test
**ciąż|yć (-ę, -ysz)** *vi*: **~ komuś** (*być ciężarem*) to weigh sb down; (*być uciążliwym*) to be a burden for sb; **ciąży na nim obowiązek** duty weighs on him; **ciąży na nim odpowiedzialność** responsibility rests with him
**cichaczem** *adv* (*pot*) on the q.t. (*pot*)
**cich|nąć (-nę, -niesz)** (*imp* **-nij**, *perf* **u-**) *vi* (*o hałasie*) to die away, to fade; (*o miejscu*) to become quieter; (*o burzy*) to subside
**ci|cho** (*comp* **-szej**) *adv* quietly; (*bez żadnego dźwięku*) silently; (*mówić*) in a soft voice; **być** *lub* **siedzieć ~** to be quiet; **~!** quiet!
**cichy** *adj* (*dom, noc*) quiet, silent; (*głos, szept*) low; **po cichu** (*bezgłośnie*) quietly, silently; (*potajemnie*) on the quiet, secretly; **cicha woda** (*pot*) still waters *pl*; **~ wielbiciel** secret admirer
**ciebie** *pron gen, acc sg od* **ty** you; **telefon do ~** a call for you; **kocham tylko ~** I love only you
**cie|c, cie|knąć (-knie)** *vi* (*o wodzie*) (*perf* **po-**) to drip, to trickle; (*o kranie*) to leak
**ciecz** (**-y, -e**) (*gen pl* **-y**) *f* liquid
**ciecz|ka** (**-ki, -ki**) (*dat sg* **-ce**, *gen pl* **-ek**) *f*: **ta suka ma cieczkę** this bitch is on *lub* in heat
**ciekaw** *adj* = **ciekawy**
**cieka|wić (-wi)** *vt* to interest
**ciekawie** *adv* (*przypatrywać się*) curiously; (*opowiadać*) in an interesting way
**ciekawost|ka** (**-ki, -ki**) (*dat sg* **-ce**, *gen pl* **-ek**) *f* (*przedmiot*) curiosity; (*nowinka*) interesting fact
**ciekawoś|ć** (**-ci**) *f* curiosity
**ciekawski** *adj* (*pot*) prying, nosy (*pot*) ▷ *m decl like adj*; **tłumy ~ch** crowds of curious onlookers
**ciekawy** *adj* (*interesujący*) interesting; (*dociekliwy*) curious; **~ czegoś** curious about sth
**ciekły** *adj* liquid
**ciek|nąć (-nie)** *vi* = **ciec**
**ciela|k** (**-ka, -ki**) (*instr sg* **-kiem**) *m* calf
**ciele** *n patrz* **ciało**
**cielesny** *adj* (*miłość*) physical; (*żądza*) carnal; (*kara*) corporal
**ciel|ę** (**-ęcia, -ęta**) (*gen pl* **-ąt**) *nt* calf; (*przen*) oaf
**cielęci|na** (**-ny**) (*dat sg* **-nie**) *f* veal
**cielęcy** *adj*: **mięso cielęce** veal; **cielęca skóra** calf(skin)
**cie|lić się (-li)** (*perf* **o-**) *vr* to calve
**ciem** *n patrz* **ćma**
**ciemi|ę** (**-enia, -ona**) (*gen pl* **-on**) *nt* crown (of the head)
**ciemiężycie|l** (**-la, -le**) (*gen pl* **-li**) *m* (*książk*) oppressor
**ciemięż|yć (-ę, -ysz)** *vt* (*książk*) to oppress
**ciemku** *inv*: **po ~** in the dark
**ciem|nia** (**-ni, -nie**) (*gen pl* **-ni**) *f* darkroom
**ciemni|eć (-eje)** *vi* (*perf* **ś-** *lub* **po-**) to darken
**ciem|no** (**-na**) (*loc sg* **-nie**) *nt*: **w ~** on spec; **randka w ~** blind date; **strzał w ~** a shot in the dark ▷ *adv* darkly; **robi się ~** it's getting dark
**ciemno...** *pref* dark; **~bieski** dark blue; **~sy** dark-haired
**ciemnoś|ć** (**-ci, -ci**) (*dat sg* **-ci**) *f* darkness; **w ciemności** in the dark
**ciemno|ta** (**-ty**) (*dat sg* **-cie**) *f* (*pot*) ignorance
**ciemny** *adj* (*włosy, chmura, odcień*) dark; (*pokój*) dim; (*chleb*) brown; (*głupi*) dumb; (*podejrzany*) shady
**cieni|ować (-uję, -ujesz)** (*perf* **wy-**) *vt* (*Sztuka*) to shade; (*włosy*) to layer
**cienisty** *adj* shady, shadowy
**cie|nki** (*comp* **-ńszy**) *adj* thin
**cie|nko** (*comp* **-niej**) *adv* thinly
**cienkopi|s** (**-su, -sy**) (*loc sg* **-sie**) *m a fine-tip felt pen*
**cie|ń** (**-nia, -nie**) (*gen pl* **-ni**) *m* (*odbicie*) shadow; (*miejsce*) shade; **~ wątpliwości** a shadow of doubt; **~ nadziei** faint hope; **~ do powiek** eyeshadow; **~ drzewa/domu** shadow of a tree/house; **w cieniu** in the shade; **w cieniu kogoś** (*przen*) overshadowed by sb (*przen*)
**cieplar|nia** (**-ni, -nie**) (*gen pl* **-ni** *lub* **-ń**) *f* greenhouse
**cieplarniany** *adj* (*kwiaty, rośliny*) greenhouse *attr*; (*warunki*) favourable (*Brit*), favorable (*US*); **efekt ~** greenhouse effect
**cieplny** *adj* thermal
**ciep|ło** (**-ła**) (*loc sg* **-le**) *nt* warmth; (*Fiz*) heat ▷ *adv* (*comp* **-lej**) (*serdecznie*) warmly; **jest ~** it's warm; **było mi ~** I was warm
**ciep|ły** (*comp* **-lejszy**) *adj* warm; **ptaki odlatują do ~ch krajów** birds fly south
**cierniowy** *adj*: **korona cierniowa** crown of thorns
**ciernisty** *adj* thorny
**cier|ń** (**-nia, -nie**) (*gen pl* **-ni**) *m* thorn
**cier|pieć (-pię, -pisz)** *vt* (*nędzę, głód*) to suffer ▷ *vi* (*znosić ból*) to suffer, to be in pain; **nie ~ kogoś/czegoś** to hate sb/sth, to detest sb/sth; **~ na** *+acc* to suffer from
**cierpie|nie** (**-nia, -nia**) (*gen pl* **-ń**) *nt* suffering

C

**cierpki** *adj* tart
**cierpliwie** *adv* patiently
**cierpliwoś|ć** (**-ci**) *f* patience
**cierpliwy** *adj* patient
**cierp|nąć (-nę, -niesz)** (*perf* **ś-**) *vi* (*o kończynie*) to become *lub* grow numb; **skóra mi cierpnie na myśl o tym** it makes my flesh creep
**ciesz|yć (-ę, -ysz)** (*perf* **u-**) *vt* to delight, to gladden; **bardzo mnie to cieszy** I'm very pleased with it, I'm delighted with it; **cieszyć się** *vr*: **~ się (z czegoś)** to be pleased *lub* delighted (with sth); **~ się na coś** to look forward to sth; **~ się życiem/dobrym zdrowiem** to enjoy life/good health
**cieście** *n patrz* **ciasto**
**cieś|la** (**-li, -le**) (*gen pl* **-li**) *m decl like f in sg* carpenter
**cieśni|na** (**-ny, -ny**) (*dat sg* **-nie**) *f* strait
**cietrze|w** (**-wia, -wie**) (*gen pl* **-wi**) *m* black grouse *lub* game
**cię** *pron gen, acc sg od* **ty** you
**cię|cie** (**-cia, -cia**) (*gen pl* **-ć**) *nt* cut; **cięcia budżetowe** budget cuts
**cięci|wa** (**-wy, -wy**) (*dat sg* **-wie**) *f* (*łuku, kuszy*) bowstring; (*Geom*) chord
**cię|gi** (**-gów**) *pl* spanking *sg*
**cięła** *itd. vb patrz* **ciąć**
**cięty** *adj* (*pióro, język*) biting; (*uwaga*) cutting; **być ~m na** *+acc* to be tough on *lub* with; **kwiaty cięte** cut flowers
**cięża|r** (**-ru, -ry**) (*loc sg* **-rze**) *m* (*waga*) weight; (*ładunek*) load; (*przen*) burden; **być komuś ~em** to be a burden on *lub* to sb; **~ spadł mi z serca** it's taken a load off my mind; **podnoszenie ~ów** weight lifting
**ciężar|ek** (**-ka, -ki**) (*instr sg* **-kiem**) *m* weight
**ciężarna** *adj* pregnant ▷ *f decl like adj* pregnant woman
**ciężarowy** *adj*: **samochód ~** lorry (*Brit*), truck (*US*)
**ciężarów|ka** (**-ki, -ki**) (*dat sg* **-ce**, *gen pl* **-ek**) *f* lorry (*Brit*), truck (*US*)
**cięż|ki** (*comp* **-szy**) *adj* heavy; (*praca*) hard; (*problem*) tough; (*zarzut, choroba, wypadek*) serious; **przemysł ~** heavy industry; **waga ciężka** heavyweight; **z ~m sercem** with a heavy heart
**cięż|ko** (*comp* **-ej**) *adv* (*pracować*) hard; (*oddychać*) heavily; (*chory*) seriously; (*ranny*) badly; (*obrazić, zgrzeszyć*) gravely; **~ strawny** indigestible
**ciężkoś|ć** (**-ci**) *f*: **środek ciężkości** centre (*Brit*) *lub* center (*US*) of gravity; **siła ciężkości** (*Fiz*) gravity
**cinkciarz** (**-a, -e**) (*gen pl* **-y**) *m* (*pot*) (illegal) money changer
**cio|cia** (**-ci, -cie**) (*gen pl* **-ć**) *f* (*pot*) aunt, auntie (*pot*)
**cio|s** (**-su, -sy**) (*loc sg* **-sie**) *m* blow; **~ poniżej pasa** a low blow
**cios|ać (-am, -asz)** *vt* (*drewno, kamień*) to hew; (*figurę, posąg*) to carve
**cio|ta** (**-ty, -ty**) (*dat sg* **-cie**) *f* (*pej: homoseksualista*) fag(got) (*pej*)
**ciot|ka** (**-ki, -ki**) (*dat sg* **-ce**, *gen pl* **-ek**) *f* aunt
**circa** *adv* circa
**ci|s¹** (**-su, -sy**) (*loc sg* **-sie**) *m* (*Bot*) yew (tree)
**cis²** *inv* (*Muz*) C sharp; **cis-moll** C sharp minor
**cis|kać (-kam, -kasz)** (*imp* **-kaj**, *perf* **-nąć**) *vt* (*przedmiot*) to fling; (*wyzwiska, obelgi*) to hurl
**ci|snąć (-snę, -śniesz)** (*imp* **-śnij**) *vb perf od* **ciskać** ▷ *vt* (*o butach*) to pinch; **cisnąć się** *vr* (*o tłumie*) to swarm
**cisz|a** (**-y**) *f* silence; **~ na morzu** calm sea, lull; **~ przed burzą** lull before the storm; **~!** silence!
**ciszej** *adv comp od* **cicho**
**ciśnie|nie** (**-nia, -nia**) (*gen pl* **-ń**) *nt* pressure; **~ krwi** blood pressure
**ciśnieniomierz** (**-a, -e**) (*gen pl* **-y**) *m* manometer
**ciuch** (**-a, -y**) *m* (*pot*) garment; **ciuchy** *pl* (*pot*) clothes, togs (*pot*)
**ciuch|cia** (**-ci, -cie**) (*gen pl* **-ci**) *f* (*pot*) puffer train
**ciuciubab|ka** (**-ki**) (*dat sg* **-ce**) *f*: **bawić się w ciuciubabkę** to play blind man's buff
**ciułacz** (**-a, -e**) (*gen pl* **-y**) *m* (*pot*): **drobny ~** petty saver
**ciuł|ać (-am, -asz)** *vt* to put aside for a rainy day
**ciu|pa** (**-py, -py**) (*dat sg* **-pie**) *f* (*pot: więzienie*) clink (*pot*), can (*pot*)
**ciurkiem** *adv* (*pot*) nonstop; **płynąć** *lub* **lać się ~** to trickle
**ciut** *part* a bit
**ci|zia** (**-zi, -zie**) (*gen pl* **-ź**) *f* (*pot*) chick (*pot*)
**ckliwy** *adj* sentimental
**cle** *n patrz* **cło**
**clić (clę, clisz)** (*imp* **clij**, *perf* **o-**) *vt* to clear (*through customs*)
**cło** (**cła, cła**) (*loc sg* **cle**, *gen pl* **ceł**) *nt* duty; **wolny od cła** duty-free; **cło przywozowe** entrance duty; **nakładać (nałożyć** *perf***) cło na** *+acc* to impose *lub* lay duty on
**cm** *abbr* (*= centymetr*) cm
**cmentarz** (**-a, -e**) (*gen pl* **-y**) *m* cemetery; (*przy kościele*) churchyard, graveyard
**cmentarzys|ko** (**-ka, -ka**) (*instr sg* **-kiem**) *nt*: **~ samochodów** graveyard for old cars
**cmok|ać (-am, -asz)** (*perf* **-nąć**) *vt* (*fajkę*) to suck; (*pot: całować*) to peck (*pot*) ▷ *vi* (*z podziwu, zadowolenia*) to smack one's lips; **cmokać się** *vr* (*pot*) to kiss

**cmok|nąć (-nę, -niesz)** (*imp* **-nij**) *vb perf od* **cmokać**
**cn|ota** (**-oty**) (*gen sg* **-ocie**) *f* (*moralność*) virtue; (*zaleta*) (*nom pl* **-oty**, *gen pl* **-ót**) virtue; (*dziewictwo*) virginity
**cnotliwy** *adj* (*życie, kobieta*) virtuous; (*myśli*) virtuous, chaste
**c.o.** *abbr* (= *centralne ogrzewanie*) central heating

SŁOWO KLUCZOWE

**co** *pron* **1** (*w pytaniach*) what; **co to jest?** what is this?; **co to za książka?** what book is that?; **co powiedziałeś?** what did you say?; **co z tobą?** what's the matter with you?; **co Pan nie powie?** you don't say!
**2** (*w zdaniach względnych*): **to drzewo, co rośnie koło domu** the tree that grows by the house; **wspominał tych, co odeszli** he remembered those who had left; **zdałem egzamin, co wszystkich zaskoczyło** I passed the exam, which surprised everybody; **co się stało, to się nie odstanie** what's done cannot be undone
**3** (*w równoważnikach zdań*): **rób, co chcesz** do what you want; **nie ma co tu czekać** there's no point in waiting here; **Bóg wie co** God knows what
**4** (*w zdaniach wykrzyknikowych*): **co za niespodzianka!** what a surprise!
**5** (*tyle ile*): **krzyczała co sił** she shouted with all her might; **co niemiara** in abundance
**6** (*pot*: *cokolwiek*) anything; **jeśli co, daj mi znać** get in touch at the slightest thing
▷ *part* **1** (*wzmacniająco*): **co najwyżej** at (the) most; **co najmniej** at least; **co nieco** a little; **co prawda** as a matter of fact; **co gorsza** what's worse, worse still; **co więcej** what's more, furthermore
**2**: **co chwila/krok** every *lub* each minute/step; **co drugi/trzeci** *itd.* every second/third *itd.*
**3**: **co do** *+gen* (*odnośnie do*) as to, as for; **co do mnie** as far as I am concerned
**4** (*dokładnie*) (exact) to; **wszyscy co do jednego** all to a man; **co do sekundy** exactly on time
▷ *conj* (*pot*): **co strzelił, to chybił** every time he shot he missed
▷ *adv* (*pot*: *dlaczego*) why; **co się boisz?** why are you scared?

**codziennie** *adv* every day, daily
**codziennoś|ć** (**-ci**) *f* everyday life
**codzienny** *adj* daily, everyday
**cof|ać (-am, -asz)** (*perf* **-nąć**) *vt* (*rękę*) to take back; (*samochód*) to reverse; (*zegarek*) to put back; (*słowo, obietnicę*) to withdraw; **cofać się** *vr* (*ustępować miejsca*) to move back; (*uciekać*) to retreat, to pull back
**cof|nąć (-nę, -niesz)** (*imp* **-nij**) *vb perf od* **cofać**
**cokolwiek** (*jak*: **co**) *pron* anything ▷ *adv* (*trochę*) a little
**cok|ół** (**-ołu, -oły**) (*loc sg* **-ole**) *m* (*Archit*) pedestal
**co|la** (**-li, -le**) (*gen pl* **-li**) *f* Coke®
**comb|er** (**-ra, -ry**) (*loc sg* **-rze**) *m* (*Kulin*) saddle (*a meat cut*)
**comiesięczny** *adj* monthly
**consensu|s** (**-su, -sy**) (*loc sg* **-sie**) *m* consensus
**coraz** *adv*: **~ lepiej** better and better; **~ większy** bigger and bigger
**coroczny** *adj* yearly, annual
**corri|da** (**-dy, -dy**) (*loc sg* **-dzie**) *f* corrida, bullfight
**cosinu|s** (**-sa, -sy**) (*loc sg* **-sie**) *m* (*Mat*) cosine
**coś** *pron* (*w zdaniach twierdzących*) something; (*w zdaniach pytajnych*) anything; **coś innego** something else; **coś do picia/jedzenia** something to drink/eat; **coś do pisania** something to write with
**cotygodniowy** *adj* weekly
**country** *nt inv* (*też*: **muzyka country**) country music
**cór|ka** (**-ki, -ki**) (*dat sg* **-ce**, *gen pl* **-ek**) *f* daughter
**cóż** *pron* what(ever) ▷ *part* well; **cóż, trzeba będzie coś z tym zrobić** well, we'll have to do something about it
**cuchnący** *adj* stinking
**cuch|nąć (-nę, -niesz)** (*imp* **-nij**) *vi* to stink
**cu|cić (-cę, -cisz)** (*imp* **-ć**, *perf* **o-**) *vt* to bring round *lub* to, to revive
**cu|d** (**-du, -da**) (*loc sg* **-dzie**) *m* (*Rel*) miracle; (*zjawisko*) wonder; **cud architektury** a miracle of architecture; **cud piękności** a marvel of beauty; **czynić cuda** to work wonders; **ocaleć cudem** to be saved by a miracle; **jakim cudem?** (*pot*) how come?
**cudaczny** *adj* (*pot*) bizarre, weird
**cuda|k** (**-ka, -ki** *lub* **-cy**) (*instr sg* **-kiem**) *m* (*pot*) weirdo (*pot*)
**cudny** *adj* marvellous (*Brit*), marvelous (*US*)
**cu|do** (**-da, -da**) (*loc sg* **-dzie**) *nt* (*pot*: *przedmiot*) beauty; (*osoba*) stunner
**cudotwórc|a** (**-y, -y**) *m decl like f in sg* wonder-worker
**cudownie** *adv* wonderfully
**cudowny** *adj* (*nadprzyrodzony*) miraculous; (*wspaniały*) wonderful; **cudowne dziecko** child prodigy
**cudzołóst|wo** (**-wa, -wa**) (*loc sg* **-wie**) *nt* adultery
**cudzozie|miec** (**-mca, -mcy**) *m* foreigner, alien

**cudzoziem|ka** (**-ki, -ki**) (*dat sg* **-ce**, *gen pl* **-ek**) *f* foreigner, alien
**cudzoziemski** *adj* foreign
**cudzy** *adj* somebody else's
**cudzysł|ów** (**-owu, -owy**) (*loc sg* **-owie**) *m* quotation marks *pl*
**cug|le** (**-li**) *pl* reins
**cu|kier** (**-kru**) (*loc sg* **-krze**) *m* sugar; **~ puder** icing sugar
**cukier|ek** (**-ka, -ki**) (*instr sg* **-kiem**) *m* sweet (*Brit*), candy (*US*)
**cukier|nia** (**-ni, -nie**) (*gen pl* **-ni** *lub* **-ń**) *f* cake shop
**cukiernicz|ka** (**-ki, -ki**) (*dat sg* **-ce**, *gen pl* **-ek**) *f* sugar bowl
**cukierni|k** (**-ka, -cy**) (*instr sg* **-kiem**) *m* confectioner
**cuki|nia** (**-ni, -nie**) (*gen pl* **-ni**) *f* courgette (*Brit*), zucchini (*US*)
**cukrowni|a** (**-, -e**) (*gen pl* **-**) *f* sugar factory
**cukrowy** *adj*: **burak ~** sugar beet; **trzcina cukrowa** sugar cane; **wata cukrowa** candy(-)floss (*Brit*), cotton candy (*US*)
**cukrzyc|a** (**-y**) *f* (*Med*) diabetes
**cukrzy|k** (**-ka, -cy**) (*instr sg* **-kiem**) *m* diabetic
**cu|ma** (**-my, -my**) (*dat sg* **-mie**) *f* (*Żegl*) mooring rope
**cum|ować (-uję, -ujesz)** (*perf* **za-**) *vt/vi* to moor
**cwa|ł** (**-łu**) (*loc sg* **-le**) *m* gallop
**cwał|ować (-uję, -ujesz)** (*perf* **po-**) *vi* to gallop
**cwania|k** (**-ka, -cy** *lub* **-ki**) (*instr sg* **-kiem**) *m* (*pot*) smart ass (*pot*), sly fellow (*pot*)
**cwany** *adj* (*pot*) shrewd, canny
**cybernety|ka** (**-ki**) (*dat sg* **-ce**) *f* cybernetics
**cyc|ek** (**-ka, -ki**) (*instr sg* **-kiem**) *m* (*pot!*) boob (*pot*), tit (*pot*)
**cyf|ra** (**-ry, -ry**) (*dat sg* **-rze**) *f* digit, figure; **cyfry arabskie/rzymskie** Arabic/Roman numerals
**cyfrowy** *adj* (*maszyna*) digital; (*kod*) numeric(al)
**Cyga|n** (**-na, -nie**) (*loc sg* **-nie**) *m* Gypsy
**cyganeri|a** (**-i, -e**) (*gen pl* **-i**) *f* bohemians *pl*
**Cygan|ka** (**-ki, -ki**) (*dat sg* **-ce**, *gen pl* **-ek**) *f* Gypsy
**cygański** *adj* Gypsy *attr*
**cyga|ro** (**-ra, -ra**) (*loc sg* **-rze**) *nt* cigar
**cyjan|ek** (**-ku, -ki**) (*instr sg* **-kiem**) *m* cyanide
**cyk|ać (-a)** *vi* (*o zegarze*) to tick; (*o świerszczu*) to chirp
**cyka|da** (**-dy, -dy**) (*dat sg* **-dzie**) *f* (*Zool*) cicada
**cyk|l** (**-lu, -le**) (*gen pl* **-li** *lub* **-lów**) *m* cycle; (*wykładów, koncertów*) series
**cykliczny** *adj* serial
**cyklin|ować (-uję, -ujesz)** (*perf* **wy-**) *vt* to scrape (*floor, wood*)
**cyklo|n** (**-nu, -ny**) (*loc sg* **-nie**) *m* cyclone
**cykori|a** (**-i, -e**) (*gen pl* **-i**) *f* chicory
**cylind|er** (**-ra, -ry**) (*loc sg* **-rze**) *m* (*Tech*) cylinder; (*kapelusz*) top hat
**cylindryczny** *adj* cylindrical
**cymba|ł** (**-ła, -ły**) (*loc sg* **-le**) *m* (*pot: niezdara*) blockhead (*pot*); **cymbały** *pl* (*Muz*) dulcimer
**cymbał|ki** (**-ków**) *pl* glockenspiel, xylophone
**cy|na** (**-ny**) (*dat sg* **-nie**) *f* tin
**cynader|ki** (**-ek**) *pl* (*Kulin*) kidney stew
**cynamo|n** (**-nu**) (*loc sg* **-nie**) *m* cinnamon
**cyn|giel** (**-gla, -gle**) (*gen pl* **-gli** *lub* **-glów**) *m* trigger
**cyniczny** *adj* cynical
**cyni|k** (**-ka, -cy**) (*instr sg* **-kiem**) *m* cynic; (*Filozofia*) Cynic
**cyniz|m** (**-mu**) (*loc sg* **-mie**) *m* cynicism
**cyn|k** (**-ku**) (*instr sg* **-kiem**) *m* (*Chem*) zinc; **dać komuś ~** (*pot*) to tip sb off
**cynkowany** *adj* zinc-plated
**cyp|el** (**-la, -le**) (*gen pl* **-li** *lub* **-lów**) *m* cape, headland
**Cyp|r** (**-ru**) (*loc sg* **-rze**) *m* Cyprus
**Cypryjczy|k** (**-ka, -cy**) (*instr sg* **-kiem**) *m* Cypriot
**cypryjski** *adj* Cypriot
**cypry|s** (**-sa** *lub* **-su, -sy**) (*loc sg* **-sie**) *m* (*Bot*) cypress
**cyr|k** (**-ku, -ki**) (*instr sg* **-kiem**) *m* circus; **ale ~!** (*pot: przen*) what a lark *lub* farce!
**cyr|kiel** (**-kla, -kle**) (*gen pl* **-kli**) *m* compasses *pl*
**cyrkoni|a** (**-i, -e**) (*gen pl* **-i**) *f* (*kamień*) zircon
**cyrko|wiec** (**-wca, -wcy**) *m* circus artist
**cyrkowy** *adj* circus *attr*
**cyrkulacj|a** (**-i, -e**) (*gen pl* **-i**) *f* circulation
**cyrogra|f** (**-fu, -fy**) (*loc sg* **-fie**) *m*: **podpisać** (*perf*) **~** to sign a pact with the devil
**cy|sta** (**-sty, -sty**) (*dat sg* **-ście**) *f* (*Med*) cyst
**cyster|na** (**-ny, -ny**) (*dat sg* **-nie**) *f* (*pojazd*) tanker, tank truck (*US*)
**cytade|la** (**-li, -le**) (*gen pl* **-li**) *f* citadel
**cyta|t** (**-tu, -ty**) (*loc sg* **-cie**) *m* citation, quotation
**cyt|ować (-uję, -ujesz)** (*perf* **za-**) *vt* to quote, to cite
**cyt|ra** (**-ry, -ry**) (*dat sg* **-rze**) *f* (*Muz*) zither
**cytru|s** (**-sa, -sy**) (*dat sg* **-sie**) *m* citrus (fruit)
**cytrusowy** *adj* citrus *attr*
**cytry|na** (**-ny, -ny**) (*dat sg* **-nie**) *f* lemon; **herbata z cytryną** tea with lemon
**cytrynowy** *adj* lemon *attr*
**cywil** (**-a, -e**) *m* (*Wojsk*) civilian; **iść do ~a** to be discharged from the army
**cywilizacj|a** (**-i, -e**) (*gen pl* **-i**) *f* civilization
**cywiliz|ować (-uję, -ujesz)** (*perf* **u-**) *vt* to civilize
**cywilizowany** *adj* civilized

**cywilny** *adj* (*ludność, lotnictwo, ślub*) civil; (*ubranie*) ordinary, plain; **stan ~** marital status
**cz.** *abbr* (= *część*) part
**cza|d** (**-du, -dy**) (*loc sg* **-dzie**) *m* (*tlenek węgla*) carbon monoxide; **więcej ~u!** (*pot*) pump up the volume! (*pot*)
**czadowy** *adj* (*pot*) funky
**cza|ić się (-ję, -isz)** *vr*: **czaić się na** *+acc* to lie in wait for
**czaj|ka** (**-ki, -ki**) (*dat sg* **-ce**, *gen pl* **-ek**) *f* (*Zool*) lapwing, pe(e)wit
**czajnicz|ek** (**-ka, -ki**) (*instr sg* **-kiem**) *m* teapot
**czajni|k** (**-ka, -ki**) (*instr sg* **-kiem**) *m* kettle
**czap|ka** (**-ki, -ki**) (*dat sg* **-ce**, *gen pl* **-ek**) *f* hat; (*z daszkiem*) cap
**czap|la** (**-li, -le**) (*gen pl* **-li**) *f* (*Zool*) heron
**cza|r** (**-ru, -ry**) (*loc sg* **-rze**) *m* (*wdzięk*) charm; **czary** *pl* magic *sg*
**cza|ra** (**-ry, -ry**) (*dat sg* **-rze**) *f* goblet
**czarno-biały** *adj* black and white *attr*
**Czarnogó|ra** (**-ry**) (*dat sg* **-rze**) *f* (*Geog*) Montenegro
**czarnoksiężni|k** (**-ka, -cy**) (*instr sg* **-kiem**) *m* wizard
**czarnorynkowy** *adj* (*cena*) black market *attr*
**czarnoskóry** *adj* black
**czarnowidz** (**-a, -e**) *m* prophet of doom
**czarnozie|m** (**-mu, -my**) (*loc sg* **-mie**) *m* black earth, chernozem
**czarnuch** (**-a, -y**) *m* (*pej*) Nigger (*pej*)
**czarny** *adj* (*kolor, oczy*) black; (*pot*: *brudny*) black, dirty; (*pesymistyczny*: *wizja, humor, myśli*) dark, gloomy ▷ *m decl like adj* (*Murzyn*) Black; **~ chleb** brown bread; **czarna kawa** black coffee; **~ charakter** villain; **~ rynek** black market; **czarna porzeczka** blackcurrant; **czarna skrzynka** black box; **czarna owca** black sheep; **~ koń** (*przen*) dark horse; **czarna magia** black magic; **czarno na białym** (*przen*) down in black and white; **pracować na czarno** to work illegally
**czarodzie|j** (**-ja, -je**) (*gen pl* **-i** *lub* **-jów**) *m* wizard, sorcerer
**czarodziejski** *adj* magic
**czar|ować (-uję, -ujesz)** *vt* (*perf* **za-**) (*pot*) to charm, to bewitch, to hex (US); (*pot*: *zwodzić*) to lead up the garden path ▷ *vi* (*uprawiać czary*) to work charms
**czarownic|a** (**-y, -e**) *f* witch
**czarowni|k** (**-ka, -cy**) (*instr sg* **-kiem**) *m* medicine man
**czarte|r** (**-ru, -ry**) (*loc sg* **-rze**) *m* charter
**czarterowy** *adj* charter *attr*
**czarujący** *adj* charming, enchanting
**cza|s** (**-su**) (*loc sg* **-sie**) *m* time; (*okres*) (*nom pl* **-sy**) period; (*Jęz*) (*nom pl* **-sy**) tense; **dobre/złe/dawne ~y** good/bad/old times; **mieć mało ~u** to have little time; **nie ma (na to) ~u** there is no time (for that); **najwyższy ~** it is high time; **w swoim ~ie** in due time *lub* course; **być na ~ie** to be up to date; **na ~** in *lub* on time, on schedule; **po ~ie** too late; **przed ~em** ahead of time; **z ~em** with time; **od ~u** *+gen* since (the time of); **w ~ie** *+gen* during; **od ~u do ~u** from time to time, (every) now and then; **od pewnego ~u** for some time now
**czasami** *adv* sometimes
**czasem** *adv* (*czasami*) sometimes; (*pot*: *może*) by any chance
**czasochłonny** *adj* time-consuming
**czasopi|smo** (**-sma, -sma**) (*loc sg* **-śmie**) *nt* periodical
**czasowni|k** (**-ka, -ki**) (*instr sg* **-kiem**) *m* (*Jęz*) verb
**czasowy** *adj* (*chwilowy*) temporary; (*odnoszący się do czasu*) temporal
**czasz|ka** (**-ki, -ki**) (*dat sg* **-ce**, *gen pl* **-ek**) *f* skull
**cza|t** (**-tu**) (*loc sg* **-cie**) *m* (*Komput*) chat
**cza|ta** (**-ty, -ty**) (*dat sg* **-cie**) *f*: **stać na ~ch** to be on the watch *lub* look-out
**czat|ować (-uję, -ujesz)** *vi*: **~ (na** *+acc***)** to be on the lookout (for)
**cząb|er** (**-ra** *lub* **-ru, -ry**) (*loc sg* **-rze**) *m* (*Bot, Kulin*) savory
**cząstecz|ka** (**-ki, -ki**) (*dat sg* **-ce**, *gen pl* **-ek**) *f* (*Chem, Fiz*) particle, molecule
**cząst|ka** (**-ki, -ki**) (*dat sg* **-ce**, *gen pl* **-ek**) *f* (*drobna część*) particle
**czci** *n patrz* **cześć**
**czcicie|l** (**-la, -le**) (*gen pl* **-li**) *m* worshipper
**czcić (czczę, czcisz)** (*imp* **czcij**) *vt* (*Boga, bóstwo*) to worship; (*rocznicę*) (*perf* **u-**) to celebrate; **~ (u~** *perf***) pamięć** *+gen* to commemorate
**czcigodny** *adj* venerable, hono(u)rable
**czcion|ka** (**-ki, -ki**) (*dat sg* **-ce**, *gen pl* **-ek**) *f* type; (*Druk, Komput*) font
**czczo** *adv*: **na ~** on an empty stomach
**czczy** *adj* (*słowa, gadanina*) idle; **na ~ żołądek** on an empty stomach
**Cze|ch** (**-cha, -si**) *m* Czech
**Czechosłowacj|a** (**-i**) *f* (*Hist*) Czechoslovakia
**Czech|y** (**-**) *pl* (*region*) Bohemia; (*państwo*) the Czech Republic
**czego** *pron gen od* **co** what; **~ Pan sobie życzy?** can I help you, sir?; **jeszcze ~!** (*pot*) not likely!
**czegokolwiek** *pron gen od* **cokolwiek** anything
**czegoś** *pron gen od* **coś** something; **~ tu brakuje** there's something missing here
**cze|k** (**-ku, -ki**) (*instr sg* **-kiem**) *m* cheque (*Brit*), check (US); **płacić ~iem** to pay by cheque

(*Brit*) *lub* check (*US*); **~ na sumę ...** cheque (*Brit*) *lub* check (*US*) for ...
**czek|ać (-am, -asz)** *vt* (*o przyszłości*): **~ kogoś** to await sb; **~ czegoś** (*oczekiwać*) to expect sth ▷ *vi* (*oczekiwać*) (*perf* **po-** *lub* **za-**); **~ (na** *+acc*) to wait (for)
**czeka|n (-na, -ny)** (*loc sg* **-nie**) *m* alpenstock
**czekani|e (-a)** *nt* waiting
**czekola|da (-dy, -dy)** (*dat sg* **-dzie**) *f* chocolate; **tabliczka czekolady** a bar of chocolate
**czekolad|ka (-ki, -ki)** (*dat sg* **-ce**, *gen pl* **-ek**) *f* chocolate
**czekoladowy** *adj* chocolate *attr*
**czekowy** *adj*: **książeczka czekowa** chequebook (*Brit*), checkbook (*US*); **konto czekowe** current (*Brit*) *lub* checking (*US*) account
**czeladni|k (-ka, -cy)** (*instr sg* **-kiem**) *m* journeyman
**czele** *n patrz* **czoło**
**czelnoś|ć (-ci)** *f*: **mieć ~ coś zrobić** to have the audacity *lub* the cheek to do sth
**czempio|n (-na)** (*loc sg* **-nie**) *m* (*pies*) (*nom pl* **-ny**) champion; (*sportowiec*) (*nom pl* **-ni**) champion
**czemu** *pron dat od* **co**; **~?** (*pot*) how come? (*pot*)
**czep|ek (-ka, -ki)** (*instr sg* **-kiem**) *m* bonnet; **~ kąpielowy** bathing cap; **w czepku urodzony** (*przen*) born with a silver spoon in his mouth
**czepi|ać się (-am, -asz)** *vr*: **czepiać się** *+gen* (*chwytać się*) to stick to, to cling to; (*przen: krytykować*) to pick on
**czerem|cha (-chy, -chy)** (*dat sg* **-sze**) *f* (*Bot*) bird cherry
**czereś|nia (-ni, -nie)** (*gen pl* **-ni**) *f* (*owoc*) (sweet) cherry; (*drzewo*) cherry tree
**czer|ń (-ni, -nie)** (*gen pl* **-ni**) *f* (*kolor*) black; **kobieta w czerni** a woman in black
**czer|pać (-pię, -piesz)** *vt* (*wodę*) to draw; (*korzyści, przyjemność*) to derive, to draw
**czerpany** *adj*: **papier ~** wove paper
**czerstwy** *adj* (*pieczywo*) stale; (*przen: staruszek*) hale and hearty
**czerwcowy** *adj* June *attr*
**czer|wiec (-wca, -wce)** *m* June
**czerwie|nić się (-nię, -nisz)** (*imp* **-ń**, *perf* **za-**) *vr* (*stawać się czerwonym*) to redden, to turn red; (*rumienić się*) to blush
**czerwie|ń (-ni, -nie)** (*gen pl* **-ni**) *f* (*kolor*) red
**czerwon|ka (-ki)** (*dat sg* **-ce**) *f* (*Med*) dysentery
**czerwonoskó|ry (-rego, -rzy)** *m decl like adj* (*pej*) Redskin (*pej*)
**czer|wony** (*comp* **-wieńszy**) *adj* red; **~ jak burak** (as) red as a beetroot; **C~ Krzyż** Red Cross ▷ *m decl like adj* (*pot, pej: komunista*) Red
**cze|sać (-szę, -szesz)** *vt* (*włosy*) (*perf* **u-**) (*samemu*) to comb, to brush; (*o fryzjerze*) to do;
**czesać się** *vr* (*grzebieniem, szczotką*) to comb *lub* to brush one's hair; **~ się z przedziałkiem** to part one's hair
**czeski** *adj* Czech ▷ *m decl like adj* (*język*) Czech
**czesn|e (-ego)** *nt decl like adj* (*Szkol*) tuition (fee)
**Czesz|ka (-ki, -ki)** (*dat sg* **-ce**, *gen pl* **-ek**) *f* Czech
**cześć (czci)** *f* (*kult, uwielbienie*) reverence; (*pot*): **~!** (*na powitanie*) hi!, hello!; (*na pożegnanie*) see you!; **oddawać** *lub* **składać komuś ~** *+dat* to worship sb; **ku czci** *+gen* in memory of; **na ~ kogoś/czegoś** (*bankiet*) in hono(u)r of sb/sth
**czę|sto** (*comp* **-ściej**) *adv* often, frequently
**częstoś|ć (-ci)** *f* frequency
**częstotliwoś|ć (-ci)** *f* frequency
**częst|ować (-uję, -ujesz)** (*perf* **po-**) *vt*: **~ kogoś czymś** to treat sb to sth; **częstować się** *vr* to help oneself; **częstuj się, proszę!** help yourself, please!
**częsty** *adj* common, frequent
**częściowo** *adv* partially, partly
**częściowy** *adj* partial
**częś|ć (-ci, -ci)** (*gen pl* **-ci**) *f* part; **części zamienne** *lub* **zapasowe** spare parts; **~ mowy** (*Jęz*) part of speech; **rozebrać** (*perf*) **na części** to take apart (piece by piece), to take into pieces
**czk|ać (-am, -asz)** (*perf* **-nąć**) *vi* to hiccup *lub* hiccough
**czkaw|ka (-ki)** (*dat sg* **-ce**) *f* hiccup *lub* hiccough
**czk|nąć (-nę, -niesz)** *vb perf od* **czkać**
**czła|pać (-pię, -piesz)** *vi* (*pot*) to drag one's feet
**człekokształtny** *adj*: **małpa człekokształtna** ape
**czło|n (-nu, -ny)** (*loc sg* **-nie**) *m* (*statku kosmicznego*) module; (*zdania*) clause
**człon|ek (-ka)** (*instr sg* **-kiem**) *m* (*organizacji, klubu*) (*nom pl* **-kowie**) member; (*nom pl* **-ki**) (*część ciała*) limb; (*też*: **członek męski**) penis
**członki|ni (-ni, -nie)** (*gen pl* **-ń**) *f* member
**członkost|wo (-wa)** (*loc sg* **-wie**) *nt* membership
**członkowski** *adj* membership *attr*
**człowieczeńst|wo (-wa)** (*loc sg* **-wie**) *nt* humanity
**człowie|k (-ka, ludzie)** (*instr sg* **-kiem**, *gen pl* **ludzi**, *dat pl* **ludziom**, *instr pl* **ludźmi**, *loc pl* **ludziach**) *m* human being; (*mężczyzna*) man; (*bezosobowo*): **~ nie wie, co robić** one doesn't *lub* you don't know what to do; **szary ~** (*przen*) man in the street, ordinary man; **~ interesu** businessman; *patrz też* **ludzie**
**czmych|nąć (-nę, -niesz)** (*imp* **-nij**) *vi perf* (*pot*) to make off
**czoł|g (-gu, -gi)** (*instr sg* **-giem**) *m* tank

**czołg|ać się (-am, -asz)** *vr* (*pełzać*) to crawl; (*przen*): **czołgać się przed kimś** to grovel to *lub* before sb
**cz|oło** (**-oła, -oła**) (*dat sg* **-ołu**, *loc sg* **-ole**, *gen pl* **-ół**) *nt* forehead; (*przód*) (*loc sg* **-ele**) front; **chmurzyć ~** to frown; **stawić** (*perf*) **~** *+dat* to face, to oppose; **na czele** (*+gen*) in the front (of); **czołem, panie generale!** (*Wojsk*) good morning *lub* afternoon, General!
**czołowy** *adj* (*przedni*) front *attr*; (*przen*: *wybitny*) leading; **zderzenie czołowe** head-on collision
**czołów|ka** (**-ki, -ki**) (*dat sg* **-ce**, *gen pl* **-ek**) *f* (*front, czoło*) forefront; (*w gazecie*) front page; (*Film*) the credits (*at the beginning of a film*); (*Sport*) lead, top; **w czołówce** in the lead, at the head *lub* top
**czop|ek** (**-ka, -ki**) (*instr sg* **-kiem**) *m* (*Med*) suppository
**czor|t** (**-ta, -ty**) (*loc sg* **-cie**) *m* (*pot*) devil; **~ wie** devil only knows
**czosn|ek** (**-ku, -ki**) (*instr sg* **-kiem**) *m* garlic
**czółen|ka** (**-ek**) *pl* (*obuwie*) pumps *pl*
**czół|no** (**-na, -na**) (*loc sg* **-nie**) *nt* boat, canoe
**czterdziest|ka** (**-ki, -ki**) (*dat sg* **-ce**, *gen pl* **-ek**) *f* forty; **on jest po czterdziestce** he is in his forties
**czterdziestoletni** *adj* forty-year-old
**czterdziesty** *num* fortieth; **~ pierwszy** forty-first
**czterdzieści** (*jak*: **dwadzieścia**) *num* forty
**czterej** (*jak*: **trzej**) *num* four
**czternastoletni** *adj* fourteen-year-old
**czternasty** *num* fourteenth
**czternaście** (*jak*: **jedenaście**) *num* fourteen
**czterokrotny** *adj* four-times *attr*
**czteroosobowy** *adj* for four persons; **samochód ~** four-seater
**czteropiętrowy** *adj* (*budynek*) five-storey(ed) (*Brit*), five-storied (*US*)
**czterosuwowy** *adj* (*silnik*) four-stroke *attr*, four-cycle *attr*
**cztery** (*jak*: **trzy**) *num* four; **(rozmowa) w ~ oczy** tête-à-tête
**czterysta** (*jak*: **dwadzieścia**) *num* four hundred
**czu|b** (**-ba, -by**) (*loc sg* **-bie**) *m* (*u ptaka*) crest; **mieć w ~ie** (*przen*: *pot*) to be tipsy
**czubaty** *adj* (*łyżka, talerz*) heaped; (*ptak*) crested
**czub|ek** (**-ka, -ki**) (*instr sg* **-kiem**) *m* tip; (*głowy, drzewa*) top; (*pot*: *idiota*) nut (*pot*); **chodzić na czubkach palców** to tiptoe; **mam to na czubku języka** (*przen*) it's on the tip of my tongue
**czuci|e** (**-a**) *nt* sense, feeling
**czu|ć (-ję, -jesz)** (*perf* **po-**) *vt* to feel; (*zapach*) to smell; **czuję, że ...** I feel that ...; **czułem, jak ...** I could feel ...; **nie czuję nóg** *lub* **rąk** I'm dead tired; **~ pismo nosem** (*pot*) to smell a rat; **~ spaleniznę!** I can smell something burning!; **czuć się** *vr*: **~ się dobrze/źle** to feel well/unwell; **jak się czujesz?** how are you feeling?; **~ się jak u siebie w domu** to feel at home
**czujni|k** (**-ka, -ki**) (*instr sg* **-kiem**) *m* sensor
**czujnoś|ć** (**-ci**) *f* vigilance
**czujny** *adj* vigilant, wary
**czule** *adv* affectionately, tenderly
**czuł|ek** (**-ka, -ki**) (*instr sg* **-kiem**) *m* (*Zool*) antenna, feeler
**czułoś|ć** (**-ci**) *f* (*tkliwość*) affection, tenderness; (*filmu*) sensitivity, speed; (*przyrządu*) sensitivity; (*zmysłu*) acuteness; **czułości** *pl* caresses *pl*
**czu|ły** (*comp* **-lszy**) *adj* (*tkliwy*) affectionate, tender; (*wrażliwy*): **~ (na** *+acc*) sensitive (to); (*przyrząd, film*) sensitive; **czułe miejsce** sore spot; **~ punkt** sore point; **być ~m na punkcie** *+gen* to be sensitive about
**czupry|na** (**-ny, -ny**) (*dat sg* **-nie**) *f* (*pot*) mop (*mass of hair*)
**czupurny** *adj* quarrelsome
**czuw|ać (-am, -asz)** *vi* (*być czujnym*) to be on the alert; (*o strażnikach*) to keep watch; (*nie spać*) to keep vigil; **~ nad** *+instr* to watch over
**czuwani|e** (**-a**) *nt* vigil
**czwart|ek** (**-ku, -ki**) (*instr sg* **-kiem**) *m* Thursday; **Wielki C~** (*Rel*) Maundy Thursday; **tłusty ~** *the last Thursday before Lent*
**czwartoklasi|sta** (**-sty, -ści**) (*loc sg* **-ście**) *m* fourth-former (*Brit*), fourth-grader (*US*)
**czwarty** *num* fourth; **o czwartej** at four (o'clock); **jedna czwarta** one fourth, a quarter
**czworacz|ki** (**-ków**) *pl* quadruplets *pl*
**czwora|ki** (**-ków**) *pl*: **(chodzić) na czworakach** (to walk) on all fours ▷ *adj* (*w czterech rodzajach*) in four kinds *lub* types
**czworo** *num* four
**czworobo|k** (**-ku, -ki**) (*instr sg* **-kiem**) *m* quadrilateral
**czworoką|t** (**-ta, -ty**) (*loc sg* **-cie**) *m* quadrangle
**czworokątny** *adj* quadrangular
**czworonożny** *adj* four-footed
**czworon|óg** (**-oga, -ogi**) (*instr sg* **-ogiem**) *m* quadruped
**czwór|ka** (**-ki, -ki**) (*dat sg* **-ce**, *gen pl* **-ek**) *f* (*cyfra, numer*) four; (*grupa*) foursome; (*pot*: *autobus, pokój*) number four; (*Sport*: *obsada łodzi*): **wyścigi czwórek** (rowing) fours race; **robić coś w czwórkę** to do sth in a group of four; **maszerować ~mi** to march in fours
**czwórnasób** *adv*: **w ~** four times

SŁOWO KLUCZOWE

**czy** *part* **1** (*w pytaniach*): **czy znasz tę książkę?** do you know this book?; **czy byłeś kiedyś za granicą?** have you ever been abroad?; **czy mogę wstać?** can I stand up?; **czy ja wiem?** (*pot*) I don't know
**2** (*w zdaniach podrzędnych*) if, whether; **nie wiem, czy to jest prawda** I don't know if it's true; **zapytaj ją, czy przyjdzie** ask her if she's coming
▷ *conj* or; **kawa czy herbata?** coffee or tea?; **prędzej czy później** sooner or later; **tak czy inaczej** one way or another

**czyh|ać (-am, -asz)** *vi*: **~ na** *+acc* to lurk waiting for; (*przen*: *o niebezpieczeństwie*) to lurk
**czyj** *pron* whose; **~e to dziecko?** whose child is it?
**czyjkolwiek** *pron* anybody's, anyone's
**czyjś** (*jak*: **czyj**) *pron* someone's, somebody's
**czyli** *part* that is, i.e.
**czym** *pron instr, loc od* **co** what; **~ to zrobiłeś?** what did you do it with?; **~ się pan zajmuje?** what do you do?; **o ~ jest ta książka?** what is this book about?; **~ prędzej** as soon as possible
**czymkolwiek** *pron instr, loc od* **cokolwiek** anything; **przykryj to ~** cover it with anything; **napisz o ~** write about anything
**czymś** *pron instr, loc od* **coś** something; **uderzył mnie ~** he hit me with something; **rozmawiają o ~** they are talking about something
**czy|n (-nu, -ny)** (*loc sg* **-nie**) *m* (*postępek*) act, deed; **~ karalny** (*Prawo*) punishable offence; **przejść** (*perf*) **od słów do ~ów** to put the words into action
**czy|nić (-nię, -nisz)** (*imp* **-ń**, *perf* **u-**) *vt* (*wykonywać*) to do ▷ *vi* (*postępować*) to act; **~ cuda** to do *lub* work miracles *lub* wonders; **~ starania** *lub* **zabiegi** to take steps; **~ wszystko, co możliwe** to do one's best; **~ zadość czemuś** to satisfy sth
**czynieni|e (-a)** *nt*: **mieć z kimś do czynienia** to deal with sb
**czynnie** *adv* actively
**czynni|k (-ka, -ki)** (*instr sg* **-kiem**) *m* factor
**czynnoś|ć (-ci, -ci)** *f* (*akt działania*) action, activity; **czynności** *pl* (*urzędowe, sądowe*) actions; **zawiesić** (*perf*) **kogoś w czynnościach** to suspend sb from their duties
**czynny** *adj* active; (*sklep*) open; (*urządzenie*) in working order; **czynna służba** (*Wojsk*) active service; **strona czynna** (*Jęz*) the active (voice); **imiesłów ~** (*Jęz*) present participle; **czynna zniewaga** assault and battery
**czynsz (-u, -e)** (*gen pl* **-ów**) *m* rent
**czyra|k (-ka, -ki)** (*instr sg* **-kiem**) *m* boil
**czyst|a (-ej, -e)** *f decl like adj* (*pot*) vodka; *patrz też* **czysty**
**czyst|ka (-ki, -ki)** (*dat sg* **-ce**, *gen pl* **-ek**) *f* purge
**czy|sto** (*comp* **-ściej**) *adv* (*porządnie*) clean(ly); (*przejrzyście*) clear(ly); (*śpiewać, brzmieć*) in tune; (*tylko*: *ekonomiczny, formalny*) purely; **przepisywać (przepisać** *perf*) **coś na ~** to make a final copy of sth; **wyjść** (*perf*) **na ~** (*pot*) to break even
**czystopi|s (-su, -sy)** (*loc sg* **-sie**) *m* final draft
**czystoś|ć (-ci)** *f* (*porządek*) cleanliness; (*brak brudu*) cleanness; (*przejrzystość*: *powietrza, wody*) clarity; (*dźwięku*) purity, clarity; (*dziewiczość*) chastity; **~ serca/intencji** (*przen*) purity of heart/intention
**czy|sty** *adj* (*ręce, bielizna*) clean; (*powietrze, woda, niebo*) clear; (*tlen, wełna*) pure; (*pot*: *szaleństwo, przypadek*) sheer; (*pot*: *niewinny*) clean (*pot*); **czysta wódka** pure vodka; **~ jak łza** as pure as the driven snow; **czystej krwi** pure-blood; **z ~m sumieniem** with a clear conscience
**czyszczący** *adj*: **środek ~** cleaner; **płyn ~** liquid cleaner
**czyszczeni|e (-a)** *nt* (*dywanów, odzieży*) (dry-) cleaning; **proszek do czyszczenia** powder cleaner
**czy|ścić (-szczę, -ścisz)** (*imp* **-ść**, *perf* **wy-**) *vt* to clean; **~ chemicznie** to dry-clean; **~ szczotką** to brush
**czyś|ciec (-ćca, -ćce)** *m* (*Rel*) purgatory
**czyt|ać (-am, -asz)** (*perf* **prze-**) *vt/vi* to read; **~ w czyichś myślach** to read sb's thoughts
**czytani|e (-a)** *nt* (*czynność*) reading; (*w parlamencie, kościele*) (*nom pl* **-a**) reading
**czytan|ka (-ki, -ki)** (*dat sg* **-ce**, *gen pl* **-ek**) *f* (*Szkol*) text (*in a reader*)
**czytel|nia (-ni, -nie)** (*gen pl* **-ni**) *f* reading room
**czytelnicz|ka (-ki, -ki)** (*dat sg* **-ce**, *gen pl* **-ek**) *f* reader
**czytelnie** *adv* legibly
**czytelni|k (-ka, -cy)** (*instr sg* **-kiem**) *m* reader
**czytelnoś|ć (-ci)** *f* legibility
**czytelny** *adj* legible
**czytni|k (-ka, -ki)** (*instr sg* **-kiem**) *m* scanner
**czyt|ywać (-uję, -ujesz)** *vt* to read occasionally
**czyż** *part* = **czy**
**czyżby** *part*: **~ zapomniał?** could he have forgotten?; **~?** really?
**czyży|k (-ka, -ki)** (*instr sg* **-kiem**) *m* (*Zool*) siskin

C

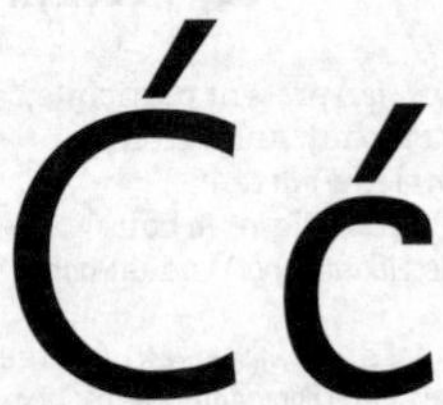

**Ć, ć** *nt inv* (*litera*) Ć, ć
**ćma** (**ćmy, ćmy**) (*dat sg* **ćmie**, *gen pl* **ciem**) *f* moth
**ćmić (ćmię, ćmisz)** (*imp* **ćmij**) *vt* (*pot: cygaro, papierosa*) to puff (on/at)
**ćp|ać (-am, -asz)** *vi* (*pot*) to do drugs (*pot*)
**ćpu|n** (**-na, -ny**) (*loc sg* **-nie**) *m* (*pot*) junkie (*pot*)
**ćwiart|ka** (**-ki, -ki**) (*dat sg* **-ce**, *gen pl* **-ek**) *f* a quarter
**ćwiart|ować (-uję, -ujesz)** (*perf* **po-**) *vt* to quarter
**ćwiczebny** *adj* training *attr*
**ćwicze|nie** (**-nia, -nia**) (*gen pl* **-ń**) *nt* (*czynność*) practice; (*Szkol, Sport*) exercise; **ćwiczenia** *pl* (*Uniw*) classes *pl*; (*Wojsk*) exercises *pl*
**ćwicz|yć (-ę, -ysz)** *vt* (*powtarzać*) to practise (*Brit*), to practice (*US*); (*doskonalić: człowieka*) (*perf* **wy-**) to train; (*: mięśnie, umysł*) (*perf* **wy-**) to exercise ▷ *vi* to practise (*Brit*), to practice (*US*); (*uprawiać sport*) to exercise
**ćwie|k** (**-ka, -ki**) (*instr sg* **-kiem**) *m* hobnail; **zabić** (*perf*) **komuś ~a** (*przen*) to baffle sb
**ćwier|ć** (**-ci, -ci**) *f* a quarter
**ćwierćfina|ł** (**-łu, -ły**) (*loc sg* **-le**) *m* quarterfinal
**ćwierćnu|ta** (**-ty, -ty**) (*dat sg* **-cie**) *f* (*Muz*) crotchet (*Brit*), quarter note (*US*)
**ćwierk|ać (-am, -asz)** (*perf* **za-**) *vi* to chirp
**ćwik|ła** (**-ły**) (*dat sg* **-le**) *f beetroot and horseradish salad*
**ćwikłowy** *adj*: **burak ~** (red) beet, beetroot

# Dd

d

**D, d** *nt inv (litera)* D, d; **D jak Dorota** ≈ D for David *(Brit)*, ≈ D for Dog *(US)*; **D-dur** D major; **d-moll** D minor
**d.** *abbr (= dawny)* former; *(= dawniej)* formerly
**dach** (**-u, -y**) *m* roof; **mieć ~ nad głową** to have a roof over one's head
**dachów|ka** (**-ki, -ki**) *(dat sg* **-ce**, *gen pl* **-ek**) *f* (roof) tile
**dacie** *n patrz* **data**
**dacz|a** (**-y, -e**) *f* dacha
**dać (dam, dasz)** *(3 pl* **dadzą**) *vb perf od* **dawać**
**dag** *abbr (= dekagram)* dag *(= decagram)*
**daktyl** (**-a, -e**) *(gen pl* **-i**) *m (Bot)* date
**dal** (**-i**) *(gen pl* **-i**) *f* distance; **skok w dal** long jump; **w dali** in the distance; **z dala/daleka** from afar; **z dala od domu** away from home; **trzymać się z dala od** *+gen* to stay *lub* keep away from
**dalece** *adv*: **jak ~?** how far?; **tak ~, że ...** so far that ...
**dalej** *adv comp od* **daleko**; *(w przestrzeni)* farther; *(w czasie)* further; **i tak ~** and so on; **mów ~!** go on!; **~!** go ahead!
**dal|eki** *(comp* **-szy**) *adj (kraj)* far-away; *(krewny, podobieństwo, czasy, cel)* distant; *(podróż, zasięg)* long; **D~ Wschód** the Far East; **to jest ~e od prawdy** this is far from the truth
**daleko** *(comp* **dalej**) *adv* far; **jak ~ (jest) do dworca?** how far is it to the station?; **~ lepiej/więcej** far better/more; **posuwać (posunąć** *perf***) się za ~** to go too far
**dalekobieżny** *adj* long-distance
**dalekopi|s** (**-su, -sy**) *(loc sg* **-sie**) *m* teleprinter, teletypewriter *(US)*
**dalekosiężny** *adj* far-reaching
**dalekowidz** (**-a, -e**) *m*: **być ~em** to be long-sighted
**dalekowzrocznoś|ć** (**-ci**) *f (Med)* long-sightedness; *(przen)* far-sightedness
**dalekowzroczny** *adj (Med)* long-sighted; *(przen)* far-sighted
**dali|a** (**-i, -e**) *(gen pl* **-i**) *f* dahlia
**dalmierz** (**-a, -e**) *(gen pl* **-y**) *m* rangefinder
**dalszy** *adj comp od* **daleki**; *(przyszły)* further; **dopełnienie dalsze** *(Jęz)* indirect object; **~ ciąg nastąpi** to be continued; **na dalszą metę** in the long run; **zejść na ~ plan** to fade into the background
**daltoni|sta** (**-sty, -ści**) *(dat sg* **-ście**) *m decl like f in sg*; **być daltonistą** to be colour-blind *(Brit) lub* color-blind *(US)*
**daltoniz|m** (**-mu**) *(loc sg* **-mie**) *m* colour-blindness *(Brit)*, color-blindness *(US)*
**da|ma** (**-my, -my**) *(dat sg* **-mie**) *f* lady; *(Karty)* queen; **~ dworu** lady-in-waiting
**Damasz|ek** (**-ku**) *(instr sg* **-kiem**) *m* Damascus
**dam|ka** (**-ki, -ki**) *(dat sg* **-ce**, *gen pl* **-ek**) *f (Warcaby)* king; *(pot: rower)* lady's bike
**damski** *adj* lady's; *(towarzystwo)* female
**dancin|g, dansin|g** (**-gu, -gi**) *(instr sg* **-giem**) *m* dance
**dan|e** (**-ych**) *pl* data; **~ personalne** personal details; **przetwarzanie danych** data processing
**Dani|a** (**-i**) *f* Denmark
**da|nie** (**-nia, -nia**) *(gen pl* **-ń**) *nt (potrawa)* dish; *(część posiłku)* course; **drugie ~** main course
**daniel** (**-a, -e**) *(gen pl* **-i**) *m* fallow deer
**dansin|g** (**-gu, -gi**) *(instr sg* **-giem**) *m* = **dancing**
**dany** *adj* given; **w danej chwili** at a given moment; **w danej sytuacji** in a given situation
**da|r** (**-ru, -ry**) *(loc sg* **-rze**) *m (upominek, talent)* gift; **w darze** as a gift
**daremnie** *adv* in vain
**daremny** *adj* futile
**darł** *itd. vb patrz* **drzeć**
**darmo** *adv*: **za ~** (for) free; **na ~** in vain
**darmowy** *adj* free
**darmozja|d** (**-da, -dy**) *(loc sg* **-dzie**) *m* sponger
**dar|ń** (**-ni, -nie**) *(gen pl* **-ni**) *f* turf
**dar|ować (-uję, -ujesz)** *vt perf (upominek)* to give; *(karę)* to pardon; *(życie)* to spare; *(dług)* to remit; *(urazę, winę)* to forgive; **nie mogę sobie tego ~** I could kick myself for that
**darowi|zna** (**-zny, -zny**) *(dat sg* **-źnie**) *f (dar)* donation; *(umowa)* deed of gift
**darz|yć (-ę, -ysz)** *vt*: **~ kogoś szacunkiem** to hold sb in high esteem; **~ kogoś sympatią** to feel affinity with *lub* for sb; **~ kogoś**

**zaufaniem** to have confidence in sb; **~ kogoś miłością** *lub* **uczuciem** to feel affection for sb

**dasz|ek** (**-ku, -ki**) (*instr sg* **-kiem**) *m* (*mały dach*) canopy; (*czapki*) peak, visor; **czapka z daszkiem** a peaked cap

**da|ta** (**-ty, -ty**) (*dat sg* **-cie**) *f* date; **człowiek starej daty** an old-fashioned person

**dat|ek** (**-ku, -ki**) (*instr sg* **-kiem**) *m* (*ofiara*) offering; **datki** *pl* (*jałmużna*) alms *pl*

**dat|ować (-uję, -ujesz)** *vt* to date; **datować się** *vr*: **~ się od** *+gen* to date back to; **~ się z** *+gen* to date from

**daw.** *abbr* = **dawny**

**da|wać (-ję, -jesz)** (*perf* **dać**) *vt* to give; **dajmy na to** let's say; **daj mi spokój** leave me alone; **dać komuś coś zrobić** to let sb do sth; **~ komuś łapówkę** to bribe sb; **~ komuś w łapę** (*pot*) to grease sb's palm (*pot*); **~ koncert** to give a concert; **~ słowo** to give one's word; **~ sobie radę z** *+instr* to manage; **dać** (*perf*) **komuś w twarz** to slap sb in the face; **~ komuś do zrozumienia, że ...** to give sb to understand that ...; **~ znać o sobie** to signal one's presence; **daj, ja to zrobię** let me do that; **daj spokój!** come off it! (*pot*); **~ za wygraną** to give up; **dawać się** *vr*: **nie daj się** don't give in; **to się da zrobić** it can be done; **tego się nie da zrobić** it can't be done; **ile się da** as much as possible

**dawc|a** (**-y, -y**) *m decl like f in sg* donor

**daw|ka** (**-ki, -ki**) (*dat sg* **-ce**, *gen pl* **-ek**) *f* dose

**dawk|ować (-uję, -ujesz)** *vt* to dose

**dawkowani|e** (**-a**) *nt* dosage

**dawniej** *adv comp od* **dawno**; (*przedtem*) formerly; **jak ~** as before

**dawno** *adv*: **~ (temu)** long ago; **już ~ go nie widziałem** I haven't seen him for a (long) while; **jak ~ (temu)?** how long ago?; **już ~ powinien tu być** he should have been here a long time ago

**dawny** *adj* former; (*starożytny*) ancient; **od dawna** for a long time

**dąb** (**dębu, dęby**) (*loc sg* **dębie**) *m* oak; **chłop jak dąb** a strapping fellow; **włosy stanęły mu dęba** his hair stood on end; **stawać (stanąć** *perf*) **dęba** (*o koniu*) to rear

**dąć (dmę, dmiesz)** (*imp* **dmij**, *perf* **za-**, *pt* **dął, dęła, dęli**) *vi* (*o wietrze*) to blow; **dąć (w trąbkę)** to blow on a trumpet

**dąs|ać się (-am, -asz)** *vr* to sulk

**dąże|nie** (**-niu, -nia**) (*gen pl* **-ń**) *nt*: **~ (do czegoś)** (*zmierzanie*) aspiration(s) (*pl*) (for *lub* after sth); (*pragnienie*) desire (for sth)

**dąż|yć (-ę, -ysz)** *vi*: **~ do** *+gen* to aim at; **~ do celu** to pursue a goal; **~ do doskonałości/władzy** to strive for perfection/power; **~ do tego, żeby ktoś coś zrobił** to try to make sb do sth

**dB** *abbr* (= *decybel*) dB

**db** *abbr* (= *dobry*) ≈ B (*grade at school*)

**db|ać (-am, -asz)** (*perf* **za-**) *vi*: **~ o kogoś/coś** to take care of sb/sth; **nie ~ o coś** not to care (a bit) about sth

**dbałoś|ć** (**-ci**) *f*: **~ (o coś)** care (of sth)

**dbały** *adj* (*troskliwy*) caring; (*staranny*) conscientious; **~ o** *+acc* careful of

**deale|r** (**-ra, -rzy**) (*loc sg* **-rze**) *m* dealer

**deba|ta** (**-ty, -ty**) (*dat sg* **-cie**) *f* debate

**debat|ować (-uję, -ujesz)** *vi*: **~ (nad czymś)** to debate sth

**deb|el** (**-la, -le**) (*gen pl* **-li** *lub* **-lów**) *m* (*Sport*) doubles *pl*

**debe|t** (**-tu**) (*loc sg* **-cie**) *m* debit

**debil** (**-a, -e**) (*gen pl* **-i**) *m* (*pot*) moron (*pot*)

**debiu|t** (**-tu, -ty**) (*loc sg* **-cie**) *m* debut

**debiut|ować (-uję, -ujesz)** (*perf* **za-**) *vi* to make one's debut

**decentralizacj|a** (**-i**) *f* decentralization

**dech** (**tchu**) *m* (*oddech*) breath; **~ mi zaparło** it took my breath away; **bez tchu** out of breath; **z zapartym tchem** with bated breath; **jednym tchem** at once; (*duszkiem*) at one gulp; **nabrać** (*perf*) **tchu** to draw breath; **ostatnim tchem** with one's last breath

**de|cha** (**-chy, -chy**) (*dat sg* **-sze**) *f* (*pot*) board, plank; **wieś zabita ~mi** (*pot*) whistle stop; **pijany w dechę** (*pot*) (as) drunk as a newt (*pot*); **naciskać (nacisnąć** *perf*) **gaz do dechy** to step on it (*pot*)

**decybel** (**-a, -e**) (*gen pl* **-i**) *m* decibel

**decyden|t** (**-ta, -ci**) (*loc sg* **-cie**) *m* decision-maker

**decyd|ować (-uję, -ujesz)** *vi*: **~ (o czymś)** (*podejmować decyzję*) (*perf* **z-**) to decide (on sth); (*mieć decydujące znaczenie*) (*perf* **za-**) to determine (sth); **decydować się** (*perf* **z-**) *vr* (*podejmować decyzję*) to make up one's mind; (*o losie: rozstrzygać się*) to be determined; **~ się na coś** to opt for sth; **~ się coś zrobić** to decide on doing sth

**decydujący** *adj* decisive; **w ~m momencie** at a crucial moment

**decymet|r** (**-ra, -ry**) (*loc sg* **-rze**) *m* decimetre (*Brit*), decimeter (*US*)

**decyzj|a** (**-i, -e**) (*gen pl* **-i**) *f* decision; **podjąć** *lub* **powziąć** (*perf*) **decyzję** to take *lub* make a decision

**dedykacj|a** (**-i, -e**) (*gen pl* **-i**) *f* (*tekst, napis*) inscription; (*fakt zadedykowania*) dedication

**dedyk|ować (-uję, -ujesz)** (*perf* **za-**) *vt* to dedicate

**defek|t** (**-tu, -ty**) (*loc sg* **-cie**) *m* (*usterka*) defect; (*wada fizyczna*) handicap

**defensy|wa** (**-wy, -wy**) (*dat sg* **-wie**) *f* defence (*Brit*), defense (*US*); **być w defensywie** to be on the defensive; **przejść** (*perf*) **do defensywy** to become defensive
**defetyz|m** (**-mu**) (*loc sg* **-mie**) *m* defeatism
**deficy|t** (**-tu**) (*loc sg* **-cie**) *m* (*Fin*) deficit; (*niedobór*) shortage; **~ budżetowy** budget deficit
**deficytowy** *adj* (*gospodarka, zakład*) loss-making; (*towar*) in short supply
**defila|da** (**-dy, -dy**) (*dat sg* **-dzie**) *f* military parade; (*przed trybuną*) march past
**defil|ować (-uję, -ujesz)** (*perf* **prze-**) *vi* to parade
**definicj|a** (**-i, -e**) (*gen pl* **-i**) *f* definition
**defini|ować (-uję, -ujesz)** (*perf* **z-**) *vt* to define
**definitywnie** *adv* finally
**definitywny** *adj* final
**deform|ować (-uję, -ujesz)** (*perf* **z-**) *vt* to deform; **deformować się** *vr* to become deformed
**defraudacj|a** (**-i, -e**) (*gen pl* **-i**) *f* embezzlement
**defraud|ować (-uję, -ujesz)** (*perf* **z-**) *vt* to embezzle
**degeneracj|a** (**-i**) *f* (*zwyrodnienie moralne*) degeneracy; (*Med, Bio*) degeneration, degeneracy
**degenera|t** (**-ta, -ci**) (*loc sg* **-cie**) *m* degenerate
**degradacj|a** (**-i**) (*gen pl* **-i**) *f* (*pracownika, oficera*) demotion; (*upadek*) degradation; (*środowiska naturalnego*) deterioration
**degrad|ować (-uję, -ujesz)** (*perf* **z-**) *vt* to demote
**degustacj|a** (**-i, -e**) *f* tasting
**degust|ować (-uję, -ujesz)** (*perf* **z-**) *vt* to taste
**deka** *nt* (*pot*: *dekagram*): **10 ~ kawy** 100 grams of coffee
**deka|da** (**-dy, -dy**) (*dat sg* **-dzie**) *f* ten days; **w trzeciej dekadzie lipca** towards the end of July
**dekadencj|a** (**-i**) *f* decadence
**dekadencki** *adj* decadent
**dekagra|m** (**-ma, -my**) (*loc sg* **-mie**) *m* dekagram, decagram (*10 grams*)
**dekalo|g** (**-gu, -gi**) (*instr sg* **-giem**) *m* (*Rel*) Decalogue
**dekapitalizacj|a** (**-i**) *f* decapitalization
**dekarz** (**-a, -e**) (*gen pl* **-y**) *m* roofer
**dekatyzowany** *adj* (*materiał*) pre-shrunk
**deklam|ować (-uję, -ujesz)** (*perf* **za-**) *vt* (*wiersz*) to recite
**deklaracj|a** (**-i, -e**) (*gen pl* **-i**) *f* declaration; (*zobowiązanie*) pledge; **~ celna** customs declaration; **~ podatkowa** tax return
**deklar|ować (-uję, -ujesz)** (*perf* **za-**) *vt* (*ogłaszać*) to declare; (*przyrzekać*) to pledge; **~ pomoc** to offer help; **~ chęć zrobienia czegoś** to declare one's readiness to do sth; **deklarować się** (*perf* **z-**) *vr*: **~ się za czymś** to declare for sth; **~ się przeciw czemuś** to declare against sth
**deklinacj|a** (**-i, -e**) (*gen pl* **-i**) *f* (*Jęz*) declension
**deklin|ować (-uję, -ujesz)** *vt* (*Jęz*) to decline
**dekode|r** (**-ra, -ry**) (*loc sg* **-rze**) *m* decoder
**dekod|ować (-uję, -ujesz)** (*perf* **z-**) *vt* to decode
**dekol|t** (**-tu, -ty**) (*loc sg* **-cie**) *m* (*krój przy szyi*) neckline; (*część ciała*) cleavage; **suknia z ~em** low-cut dress
**dekomunizacj|a** (**-i**) *f* decommunization (*in former communist countries*)
**dekomuniz|ować (-uję, -ujesz)** (*perf* **z-**) *vt* to decommunize
**dekoracj|a** (**-i, -e**) (*gen pl* **-i**) *f* decoration; (*Teatr, Film*) set
**dekoracyjny** *adj* (*sztuka, tkanina, roślina*) decorative
**dekorato|r** (**-ra, -rzy**) (*loc sg* **-rze**) *m*: **~ wnętrz** interior decorator
**dekor|ować (-uję, -ujesz)** (*perf* **u-**) *vt* to decorate
**dekre|t** (**-tu, -ty**) (*loc sg* **-cie**) *m* decree
**delegacj|a** (**-i, -e**) (*gen pl* **-i**) *f* (*grupa delegatów*) delegation; (*wyjazd służbowy*) business trip; (*zaświadczenie*) expense report
**delegaliz|ować (-uję, -ujesz)** (*perf* **z-**) *vt* to ban, to make illegal
**delega|t** (**-ta, -ci**) (*loc sg* **-cie**) *m* delegate
**deleg|ować (-uję, -ujesz)** (*perf* **wy-**) *vt* to delegate
**delekt|ować się (-uję, -ujesz)** *vr*: **delektować się czymś** to savour (*Brit*) *lub* savor (*US*) sth
**delfi|n** (**-na, -ny**) (*loc sg* **-nie**) *m* dolphin
**delicj|e** (**-i**) *pl* delicacies *pl*
**delikates|y** (**-ów**) *pl* (*przysmaki*) delicacies *pl*; (*sklep*) deli(catessen)
**delikatnie** *adv* (*dotykać, krytykować*) gently; (*dźwięczeć, pachnieć*) softly; **~ mówiąc** to put it mildly
**delikatnoś|ć** (**-ci**) *f* (*subtelność*) gentleness; (*zapachu*) mildness; (*barwy*) softness; (*wrażliwość*) fragility; (*drażliwość*) sensitivity
**delikatny** *adj* (*subtelny*) gentle; (*drobny*) delicate; (*kolor*) soft; (*zapach*) mild; (*chorowity*) delicate, fragile; (*sprawa, misja*) sensitive
**del|ta** (**-ty, -ty**) (*gen sg* **-cie**) *f* delta
**demago|g** (**-ga, -dzy** *lub* **-gowie**) (*instr sg* **-giem**) *m* demagogue
**demagogi|a** (**-i**) *f* demagoguery
**demagogiczny** *adj* demagogic
**demask|ować (-uję, -ujesz)** (*perf* **z-**) *vt* to expose, to debunk; **demaskować się** *vr* to throw off the mask

**dement|ować (-uję, -ujesz)** *(perf* **z-**) *vt* to deny
**demobilizacj|a** (**-i**) *f* demobilization
**demobiliz|ować (-uję, -ujesz)** *(perf* **z-**) *vt* (*Wojsk*) to demobilize; (*przen*) to discourage
**demografi|a** (**-i**) *f* demography
**demograficzny** *adj* demographic
**demokracj|a** (**-i, -e**) (*gen pl* **-i**) *f* democracy
**demokra|ta** (**-ty, -ci**) (*dat sg* **-cie**) *m decl like f in sg* democrat
**demokratyczny** *adj* democratic
**demol|ować (-uję, -ujesz)** *(perf* **z-**) *vt* to vandalize
**demo|n** (**-na, -ny**) (*loc sg* **-nie**) *m* demon
**demoniczny** *adj* demoniac(al)
**demonstracj|a** (**-i, -e**) (*gen pl* **-i**) *f* demonstration
**demonstracyjny** *adj* (*zachowanie*) ostentatious
**demonstr|ować (-uję, -ujesz)** *(perf* **za-**) *vt* (*pokazywać*) to demonstrate ▷ *vi* (*manifestować*) to demonstrate
**demontaż** (**-u, -e**) (*gen pl* **-y** *lub* **-ów**) *m* disassembly, dismantling
**demont|ować (-uję, -ujesz)** *(perf* **z-**) *vt* to disassemble, to take apart
**demoralizacj|a** (**-i**) *f* depravity
**demoraliz|ować (-uję, -ujesz)** *(perf* **z-**) *vt* to deprave; **demoralizować się** *vr* to become depraved
**den** *n patrz* **dno**
**dena|t** (**-ta, -ci**) (*loc sg* **-cie**) *m* (*Prawo*) the deceased
**denatura|t** (**-tu**) (*loc sg* **-cie**) *m* methylated spirits
**denerw|ować (-uję, -ujesz)** *(perf* **z-**) *vt* (*drażnić*) to irritate; (*złościć*) to annoy; **to mnie denerwuje** it gets on my nerves; **denerwować się** *vr* (*niepokoić się*) to be nervous; (*złościć się*) to be irritated; **~ się czymś** to be nervous about sth; **nie denerwuj się!** take it easy!
**denerwujący** *adj* irritating, annoying
**denominacj|a** (**-i**) *f* (*Fin*) redenomination
**denty|sta** (**-sty, -ści**) (*dat sg* **-ście**) *m decl like f in sg* dentist
**dentyst|ka** (**-ki, -ki**) (*dat sg* **-ce**, *gen pl* **-ek**) *f* dentist
**dentystyczny** *adj* (*gabinet, fotel*) dentist's *attr*; (*technik*) dental *attr*
**denuncj|ować (-uję, -ujesz)** *(perf* **za-**) *vt* to denounce
**departamen|t** (**-tu, -ty**) (*loc sg* **-cie**) *m* (*dział ministerstwa*) department; **~ stanu** Department of State; **dyrektor ~u** head of department
**depesz|a** (**-y, -e**) *f* (*telegram*) telegram, cable; (*wiadomość*) dispatch
**depilacj|a** (**-i**) *f* depilation
**depilato|r** (**-ra, -ry**) (*loc sg* **-rze**) *m* depilatory; (*urządzenie*) hair remover
**depon|ować (-uję, -ujesz)** *(perf* **z-**) *vt* to deposit
**deportacj|a** (**-i, -e**) (*gen pl* **-i**) *f* deportation
**deport|ować (-uję, -ujesz)** *vt* to deport
**depozy|t** (**-tu, -ty**) (*loc sg* **-cie**) *m* deposit; **oddawać (oddać** *perf*) **coś do ~u** to deposit sth
**deprawacj|a** (**-i**) *f* depravity; **~ nieletnich** (*Prawo*) corruption of minors
**depraw|ować (-uję, -ujesz)** *(perf* **z-**) *vt* to deprave; **deprawować się** *vr* to become depraved
**depresj|a** (**-i, -e**) (*gen pl* **-i**) *f* depression
**deprymujący** *adj* discouraging
**dep|tać (-czę, -czesz)** *(perf* **po-**) *vt* to tread, to trample (on); **„nie ~ trawnika"** "keep off the grass"; **~ komuś po piętach** (*przen*) to be hot on sb's heels, to tread hard on sb's heels
**depta|k** (**-ka, -ki**) (*instr sg* **-kiem**) *m* (*promenada*) promenade, walk; (*obszar*) pedestrian zone
**deputa|t** (**-tu, -ty**) (*loc sg* **-cie**) *m* allowance
**deputowa|ny** (**-nego, -ni**) *m decl like adj* deputy
**dermatolo|g** (**-ga, -dzy** *lub* **-gowie**) (*instr sg* **-giem**) *m* dermatologist
**dermatologi|a** (**-i**) *f* dermatology
**dermatologiczny** *adj* dermatological
**desan|t** (**-tu, -ty**) (*loc sg* **-cie**) *m* landing (operation)
**desantowy** *adj*: **wojska desantowe** landing troops *pl*
**dese|ń** (**-nia, -nie**) (*gen pl* **-ni**) *m* pattern, design
**dese|r** (**-ru, -ry**) (*loc sg* **-rze**) *m* dessert, afters *pl* (*pot*); **na ~** for dessert *lub* afters (*pot*)
**deserowy** *adj* dessert *attr*
**des|ka** (**-ki, -ki**) (*dat sg* **-ce**, *gen pl* **-ek**) *f* (*gruba*) board; (*cienka*) plank; **deski** *pl* (*pot: narty*) skis *pl*; **~ do prasowania** ironing board; **~ surfingowa** surfboard; **deski sceniczne** the stage; **ostatnia ~ ratunku** the last resort; **wieś zabita ~mi** whistle stop (*pot*); **od deski do deski** from cover to cover; **do grobowej deski** to the very end
**deskorol|ka** (**-ki, -ki**) (*dat sg* **-ce**, *gen pl* **-ek**) *f* skateboard
**desperacki** *adj* (*mina, krok, decyzja*) desperate
**despo|ta** (**-ty, -ci**) (*dat sg* **-cie**) *m decl like f in sg* despot
**despotyczny** *adj* (*władca, rządy*) authoritarian; (*człowiek*) despotic, bossy

**destabiliz|ować (-uję, -ujesz)** (*perf* **z-**) *vt* to destabilize
**destrukcj|a** (**-i, -e**) (*gen pl* **-i**) *f* destruction
**destrukcyjny, destruktywny** *adj* destructive
**destylacj|a** (**-i**) *f* distillation
**destyl|ować (-uję, -ujesz)** (*perf* **prze-**) *vt* to distil
**desygn|ować (-uję, -ujesz)** *vt* to designate, to appoint
**deszcz** (**-u, -e**) *m* rain; (*przen*) shower; **pada ~** it is raining; **kwaśny ~** acid rain; **z ~u pod rynnę** out of the frying pan into the fire
**deszczowy** *adj* rainy
**deszczy|k** (**-ku, -ki**) (*instr sg* **-kiem**) *m* drizzle
**detal** (**-u, -e**) (*gen pl* **-i** *lub* **-ów**) *m* (*szczegół*) detail; (*Handel*) retail
**detaliczny** *adj* (*Handel*) retail *attr*
**detekty|w** (**-wa, -wi**) (*loc sg* **-wie**) *m* detective; **prywatny ~** private detective *lub* investigator
**detektywistyczny** *adj* (*film, powieść*) detective *attr*
**detergen|t** (**-tu, -ty**) (*loc sg* **-cie**) *m* detergent
**determinacj|a** (**-i**) *f* determination
**determin|ować (-uję, -ujesz)** (*perf* **z-**) *vt* to determine
**detonacj|a** (**-i, -e**) (*gen pl* **-i**) *f* explosion
**detroniz|ować (-uję, -ujesz)** (*perf* **z-**) *vt* to depose, to dethrone
**dewaluacj|a** (**-i, -e**) (*gen pl* **-i**) *f* devaluation
**dewalu|ować (-uję, -ujesz)** (*perf* **z-**) *vt* to devalue; **dewaluować się** *vr* (*tracić wartość*) to be devalued; (*tracić znaczenie*) to lose its value
**dewastacj|a** (**-i, -e**) (*gen pl* **-i**) *f* vandalism
**dewast|ować (-uję, -ujesz)** (*perf* **z-**) *vt* to vandalize
**dewiacj|a** (**-i, -e**) (*gen pl* **-i**) *f* aberration
**dewi|za** (**-zy, -zy**) (*dat sg* **-zie**) *f* motto; **dewizy** *pl* foreign currency
**dewizowy** *adj* foreign exchange *attr*, currency *attr*
**dewocj|a** (**-i**) *f* bigotry
**dewot|ka** (**-ki, -ki**) (*dat sg* **-ce**, *gen pl* **-ek**) *f* bigot
**dezaktualiz|ować się (-uje)** (*perf* **z-**) *vr* to expire, to become outdated
**dezaproba|ta** (**-ty**) (*dat sg* **-cie**) *f* disapproval
**dezercj|a** (**-i, -e**) (*gen pl* **-i**) *f* desertion
**dezerte|r** (**-ra, -rzy**) (*loc sg* **-rze**) *m* deserter
**dezerter|ować (-uję, -ujesz)** (*perf* **z-**) *vi* to desert
**dezintegracj|a** (**-i**) *f* disintegration
**dezodoran|t** (**-tu, -ty**) (*loc sg* **-cie**) *m* deodorant
**dezorganizacj|a** (**-i**) *f* disorganization
**dezorganiz|ować (-uję, -ujesz)** (*perf* **z-**) *vt* to disorganize
**dezorient|ować (-uję, -ujesz)** (*perf* **z-**) *vt* to confuse
**dezynfekcj|a** (**-i**) *f* disinfection
**dezynfek|ować (-uję, -ujesz)** (*perf* **z-**) *vt* to disinfect
**dezynfekujący** *adj*: **środek ~** disinfectant
**dębowy** *adj* oak *attr*
**dębu** *itd. n patrz* **dąb**
**dęła** *itd. vb patrz* **dąć**
**dęt|ka** (**-ki, -ki**) (*dat sg* **-ce**, *gen pl* **-ek**) *f* (*w oponie*) (inner) tube; (*w piłce*) bladder
**dęty** *adj* (*instrument, orkiestra*) wind *attr*
**diabelski** *adj* devilish; **~ młyn** big *lub* Ferris wheel
**diab|eł** (**-ła, -ły** *lub* **-li**) (*dat sg* **-łu**, *loc sg* **-le**) *m* devil; **idź do diabła!** go to hell!; **do diabła!** damn it!; **co/kto u diabła ...** what/who the hell ...; **a niech to/cię diabli wezmą** to hell with it/you; **boli jak diabli** it hurts like hell
**diagno|za** (**-zy, -zy**) (*dat sg* **-zie**) *f* diagnosis; **stawiać (postawić** *perf*) **diagnozę** to diagnose
**diakrytyczny** *adj*: **znak ~** diacritic
**dialek|t** (**-tu, -ty**) (*loc sg* **-cie**) *m* dialect
**dialektyczny** *adj* (*Filozofia*) dialectical; (*Jęz*) dialectal
**dialekty|ka** (**-ki**) (*dat sg* **-ce**) *f* dialectics
**dialo|g** (**-gu, -gi**) (*instr sg* **-giem**) *m* dialogue (*Brit*), dialog (*US*)
**diamen|t** (**-tu, -ty**) (*loc sg* **-cie**) *m* diamond
**diamentowy** *adj* diamond *attr*; **diamentowe gody** diamond wedding
**diametralnie** *adv* (*całkowicie*) radically
**didaskali|a** (**-ów**) *pl* stage directions *pl*
**diecezj|a** (**-i, -e**) (*gen pl* **-i**) *f* diocese
**dieslowski** *adj* (*silnik*) diesel *attr*
**die|ta** (**-ty, -ty**) (*dat sg* **-cie**) *f* diet; **diety** *pl* (*zwrot kosztów utrzymania w podróży*) travelling allowance (*Brit*), traveling allowance (*US*); **być na diecie** to be on a diet; **diety poselskie** MP's salary
**dietetyczny** *adj* diet *attr*
**dinozau|r** (**-ra, -ry**) (*loc sg* **-rze**) *m* dinosaur
**dio|da** (**-dy, -dy**) (*loc sg* **-dzie**) *f* diode; **~ świecąca** LED
**dis** *inv* (*Muz*) D sharp
**disco** *nt inv* disco; **muzyka ~** disco music
**dla** *prep +gen* (*dla oznaczenia przeznaczenia*) for; (*wobec*) to, towards; **ta książka jest dla ciebie** this book is for you; **był to dla niej wielki cios** it was a great shock for her; **dla zrobienia czegoś** (in order) to do sth; **dla przyjemności** for pleasure; **życzliwy dla starszych** kind to the elderly
**dlaczego** *adv, conj* why; **~ nie?** why not?
**dlatego** *conj* (*więc*) so, therefore; (*z tego powodu*) that's why; **padał deszcz, ~ wziął parasol** it

was raining, so he took an umbrella; **~, że** because

**dł.** *abbr* (*= długość*) l., L (*= length*)

**dła|wić (-wię, -wisz)** *vt* (*dusić*) to choke; (*tłumić*) (*perf* **z-**) to stifle; **dławić się** (*perf* **u-**) *vr* to choke

**dło|ń** (**-ni, -nie**) (*gen pl* **-ni**, *instr pl* **-niami** *lub* **-ńmi**) *f* (*wewnętrzna część ręki*) palm; (*ręka*) hand; **jak na dłoni** (*przen*) very clearly; (*przen*): **mieć serce na dłoni** to wear one's heart on one's sleeve; **pomocna ~** helping hand

**dłu|bać (-bię, -biesz)** *vi*: **~ (w czymś)** (*drążyć*) to hollow (sth) out; (*pot*): **~ (przy czymś)** (*majstrować*) to tinker (with/at sth); **~ w nosie/zębach** to pick one's nose/teeth

**dłucie** *n patrz* **dłuto**

**dłu|g** (**-gu, -gi**) (*instr sg* **-giem**) *m* debt; **mieć ~i** to be in debt

**dłu|gi** (*comp* **-ższy**) *adj* long; **~ na dwa metry** two metres long; **upaść jak ~** to fall flat on the ground

**dłu|go** (*comp* **-żej**) *adv* long; **jak ~?** how long?; **tak ~ jak ...** as long as ...

**długodystanso|wiec** (**-wca, -wcy**) *m* long-distance runner

**długodystansowy** *adj*: **biegi długodystansowe** long-distance races

**długofalowy** *adj* long-range, long-term

**długogrający** *adj*: **płyta długogrająca** long-playing record

**długoletni** *adj* of long standing

**długometrażowy** *adj*: **film ~** feature (film)

**długopi|s** (**-su, -sy**) (*loc sg* **-sie**) *m* pen, ballpoint (pen)

**długoś|ć** (**-ci, -ci**) (*gen pl* **-ci**) *f* length; **~ fali** (*Fiz*) wavelength; **wąż długości sześciu metrów** a snake 6 metres long; **~ geograficzna** longitude; **wygrać o dwie długości** to win by two lengths

**długoterminowy** *adj* long-term

**długotrwały** *adj* long-lasting

**długowiecznoś|ć** (**-ci**) *f* longevity

**długowieczny** *adj* long-lived

**długowłosy** *adj* long-haired

**dłu|to** (**-ta, -ta**) (*loc sg* **-cie**) *nt* chisel

**dłużej** *adv comp od* **długo**

**dłużni|k** (**-ka, -cy**) (*instr sg* **-kiem**) *m* debtor

**dłużny** *adj*: **być komuś coś ~m** to owe sb sth, to owe sth to sb; **być komuś ~m (za coś)** to owe a debt to sb (for sth)

**dłuższy** *adj comp od* **długi**; **na dłuższą metę** in the long run

**dłuż|yć się (-y)** *vr* (*o czasie, koncercie*) to drag

**dłuży|zna** (**-zny, -zny**) (*dat sg* **-źnie**) *f* (*w filmie, opowiadaniu*) longueur

**dm** *abbr* (*= decymetr*) dm

**dmę** *itd. vb patrz* **dać**

**dmuch|ać (-am, -asz)** (*perf* **-nąć**) *vi* to blow; **~ na zimne** to be extra cautious

**dmuch|nąć (-nę, -niesz)** (*imp* **-nij**) *vb perf od* **dmuchać**

**dn.** *abbr*: **dn. 12 grudnia 1996** on 12th December 1996 (*Brit*), on December 12th 1996 (*US*)

**dnia** *itd. n patrz* **dzień**

**dnie|ć (-je)** *vi*: **dnieje** it's dawning

**dniów|ka** (**-ki, -ki**) (*dat sg* **-ce**, *gen pl* **-ek**) *f* (*dzień pracy*) working day; (*wynagrodzenie*) daily wage

**dno** (**dna, dna**) (*loc sg* **dnie**, *gen pl* **den**) *nt* (*naczynia*) bottom; (*oceanu, jeziora*) bed, bottom; (*przen: najniższy poziom*) bottom; **iść (pójść** *perf***) na dno** to go under *lub* down; **bez dna** bottomless; **pić (wypić** *perf***) do dna** to drink up; **do dna!** bottoms up! (*pot*)

**SŁOWO KLUCZOWE**

**do** *prep +gen* **1** (*w kierunku*) to; **jadę do Warszawy** I'm going to Warsaw; **idę do pracy/kina** I'm going to work/the cinema; **chodzić do szkoły** to go to school; **jadę do rodziców** I'm going to my parents' (place)
**2** (*do wnętrza*) into; **do szafy/szuflady/kieszeni** into a wardrobe/drawer/pocket; **wejść do pokoju** to enter a room
**3** (*nie dalej niż*) to; **odprowadź ją do drzwi** see her to the door; **podejdź do mnie** come up to me; **z** *lub* **od A do B** from A to B
**4** (*nie dłużej niż*) till, until; **zostanę do piątku** I'll stay till *lub* until Friday; **zrobię to do piątku** I'll do it by Friday; **(w)pół do drugiej** half past one; **do jutra!** see you tomorrow!; **do widzenia/zobaczenia!** good bye!, see you!
**5** (*nie więcej niż*) up to; **kara wynosi do 100 złotych** the fine is up to 100 zloty
**6** (*o przeznaczeniu*): **krem do rąk** hand cream; **coś do jedzenia/picia** something to eat/drink; **do czego to jest?** what is it for?
**7** (*o intensywności*) to; **była wzruszona do łez** she was moved to tears

**doba** (**doby, doby**) (*dat sg* **dobie**, *gen pl* **dób**) *f* (*dzień i noc*) day (and night), twenty four hours; (*przen: epoka*) age; **(przez) całą dobę** day and night; **24 godziny na dobę** round the clock

**do|bić (-biję, -bijesz)** (*imp* **-bij**) *vb perf od* **dobijać**

**dobie|c (-gnę, -gniesz)** (*imp* **-gnij**, *pt* **-gł**) *vb perf od* **dobiegać**

**dobi|egać (-egam, -egasz)** (*perf* **-ec**) *vi* (*o dźwięku, hałasie*) to come; (*o czasie*) to draw on; (*o ścieżce*) to run, to lead; **dobiegła trzecia** it turned three o'clock; **dobiega trzecia** it's almost three o'clock; **~ do mety** to run to the finish; **~ końca** to draw to a close *lub* an end; **dobiegał sześćdziesiątki** he was getting on for sixty

**do|bierać (-bieram, -bierasz)** (*perf* **-brać**) *vt* (*słowa, przyjaciół*) to select; **~ coś do czegoś** to match sth (up) with sth; **dobierać się** *vr*: **dobrze się dobrać** to make a good match; **~ się do czegoś** to tamper with sth; **~ się do kogoś** (*pot*) to make a pass at sb; **dobrali mu się do skóry** he got his comeuppance

**do|bijać (-bijam, -bijasz)** (*perf* **-bić**) *vt*: **dobić kogoś** (*zabić*) to finish sb off; (*skrócić cierpienia*) to put sb out of his misery ▷ *vi*: **dobić do brzegu/celu** to reach the shore/one's destination; **dobić targu** to strike *lub* make a bargain; **ta wiadomość go dobiła** he was devastated by this news; **dobijać się** *vr*: **~ się do drzwi** to bang on the door

**dobitny** *adj* (*głos, argument*) forcible

**doborowy** *adj* select, exclusive

**dobosz** (**-a, -e**) (*gen pl* **-y** *lub* **-ów**) *m* (*army*) drummer

**dob|ór** (**-oru**) (*loc sg* **-orze**) *m* selection; **~ naturalny** natural selection

**do|brać (-biorę, -bierzesz)** (*imp* **-bierz**) *vb perf od* **dobierać**

**dobranoc** *inv*: **~!** good night!; **pocałować kogoś na ~** to kiss sb good night

**dobranoc|ka** (**-ki, -ki**) (*dat sg* **-ce**, *gen pl* **-ek**) *f bedtime TV cartoon*

**dobrany** *adj* well matched

**dobr|nąć (-nę, -niesz)** (*imp* **-nij**) *vb perf*; **~ do domu/celu** to reach one's house/ destination

**dob|ro** (**-ra, -ra**) (*loc sg* **-ru**, *gen pl* **dóbr**) *nt* good; **dla czyjegoś dobra** for sb's (own) good, for sb's sake *lub* the sake of sb; **dobra** *pl* (*towary*) goods *pl*; (*majątek*) property

**dobroby|t** (**-tu**) (*loc sg* **-cie**) *m* prosperity, well-being

**dobroczynnoś|ć** (**-ci**) *f* charity

**dobroczynny** *adj* charitable; **działalność dobroczynna** charity; **na cele dobroczynne** for charity; **impreza dobroczynna** benefit

**dobroczyńc|a** (**-y, -y**) *m decl like f in sg* benefactor

**dobro|ć** (**-ci**) *f* goodness, kindness

**dobroduszny** *adj* good-natured

**dobrowolnie** *adv* voluntarily

**dobrowolny** *adj* voluntary

**dobry** (*comp* **lepszy**) *adj* good; (*uprzejmy*) good, kind; **ona jest dobra z matematyki** she's good at maths; **~ wieczór!** good evening!; **być dobrej myśli** to hope for the best; **dobra wola** goodwill; **bądź tak ~ i zrób to** would you be so kind as to do it?; **dostać** (*perf*) **się w dobre ręce** to end up in good hands; **czekam już dobrą godzinę** I've been waiting for a good hour; **wszystkiego dobrego!** all the best!; **przedstawić** (*perf*) **kogoś/coś w ~m świetle** to show sb/sth in a favourable (*Brit*) *lub* favorable (*US*) light; **na dobrą sprawę** actually; **na dobre** for good; **na dobre i złe** for better or for worse; **dobra!** (*pot*) O.K.! ▷ *m decl like adj* (*Szkol: ocena*) ≈ B

**dobrze** (*comp* **lepiej**) *adv* well; (*przyjmować*) warmly; (*sprzedać, kupić*) at a profit; **on się ~ uczy** he is a good student; **~ postąpiłeś** you did the right thing; **~ kogoś przedstawić** to show sb in a favourable (*Brit*) *lub* favorable (*US*) light; **~ się czuć** to feel good; **~ się bawić** to have a good time; **~!** O.K.!, all right!; **mieć się ~** to be well; **znać się ~** to know each other well; **znać się na czymś ~** to have a good grasp of sth; **~ ci w tym kapeluszu** this hat suits you; **~ poinformowany** well-informed; **~ znany** well-known; **coś komuś ~ robi** sth is good for sb; **~ mu z oczu patrzy** he looks like a good person; **~ komuś życzyć** to wish sb well; **jak ~ pójdzie** if everything goes well; **~ się komuś powodzi** sb is well off; **~ ci tak!** it serves you right!

**dobudow|ywać (-uję, -ujesz)** (*perf* **-ać**) *vt* to build an annexe (*Brit*) *lub* annex (*US*)

**dobyt|ek** (**-ku**) (*instr sg* **-kiem**) *m* belongings *pl*; (*Prawo*) goods and chattels *pl*

**doc.** *abbr* = **docent**

**docelowy** *adj* target *attr*

**doce|niać (-niam, -niasz)** (*perf* **-nić**) *vt* to appreciate; **nie ~** to underestimate

**doce|nić (-nię, -nisz)** (*imp* **-ń**) *vb perf od* **doceniać**

**docen|t** (**-ta, -ci**) (*loc sg* **-cie**) *m* (*Uniw*) reader (*Brit*), assistant professor (*US*)

**dochodowy** *adj* (*przedsięwzięcie*) profitable, profit-making; **podatek ~** income tax

**dochodze|nie** (**-nia, -nia**) (*gen pl* **-ń**) *nt* investigation

**do|chodzić (-chodzę, -chodzisz)** (*imp* **-chodź**, *perf* **-jść**) *vi*: **~** (**do** *+gen*) to reach; (*o liście*) to arrive; (*sięgać*) to reach (as far as); (*o dźwięku, zapachu*) to come; **dochodzi pierwsza/północ** it's almost one o'clock/ midnight; **~ do siebie (po chorobie)** to recover; (*odzyskiwać przytomność*) to come round; **~ do władzy** to rise to power; **doszło do bójki/wypadku** there was a fight/ an accident; **jak do tego doszło?** how did it happen?; **doszło do tego, że ...** things came to such a point that ...; **~ swoich praw** to assert *lub* claim one's rights; **~ prawdy** to seek *lub* search for the truth

d

**dochow|ywać (-uję, -ujesz)** (*perf* **-ać**) *vt*: ~ **tajemnicy/przysięgi** to keep a secret/ promise; **dochować zobowiązania** to keep to *lub* meet an obligation; ~ **wiary** to remain faithful

**doch|ód** (**-odu, -ody**) (*loc sg* **-odzie**) *m* (*zarobki*) income; (*zysk*) profit; **dochody** *pl* earnings *pl*; (*wpływy do budżetu*) revenue

**do|ciąć (-tnę, -tniesz)** (*imp* **-tnij**) *vb perf od* **docinać**

**do|ciec (-cieknę, -ciekniesz)** (*imp* **-cieknij**, *pt* **-ciekł**) *vb perf od* **dociekać**

**do|ciekać (-ciekam, -ciekasz)** (*perf* **-ciec**) *vt*: ~ **prawdy** to search for the truth; ~ **przyczyn** to investigate the causes

**dociekliwy** *adj* inquiring

**do|cierać (-cieram, -cierasz)** (*perf* **-trzeć**) *vt* (*samochód*) to run in ▷ *vi*: ~ **(do** *+gen*) to reach; **dotrzeć gdzieś** to arrive somewhere

**doci|nać (-nam, -nasz)** (*perf* **-ąć**) *vi*: ~ **komuś** to make cutting remarks at sb

**docin|ek** (**-ka, -ki**) (*instr sg* **-kiem**) *m* cutting remark, taunt

**docis|kać (-kam, -kasz)** (*perf* **-nąć**) *vt* (*pokrywę, drzwi*) to close tight; (*śrubę*) to tighten; ~ **pasa** (*przen*) to tighten one's belt

**doci|snąć (-snę, -śniesz)** (*imp* **-śnij**) *vb perf od* **dociskać**

**doczek|ać (-am, -asz)** *vi perf*: ~ *+gen* (*dotrwać czekając*) to wait till *lub* until; (*dożyć*) to live to; ~ **późnej starości** to live to an old age; **nie doczekał rana** he died before the morning; **doczekać się** *vr perf*: **nie mogę się ciebie ~** I can't wait to see you

**docze|piać (-piam, -piasz)** (*perf* **-pić**) *vt* (*wagon, przyczepę*) to couple on

**doczesny** *adj* (*świat, sprawy*) earthly; (*dobra*) worldly

**dod|ać (-am, -asz)** (*imp* **-aj**) *vb perf od* **dodawać**

**dodat|ek** (**-ku, -ki**) (*instr sg* **-kiem**) *m* (*do gazety, czasopisma*) supplement; (*do wynagrodzenia*) bonus; (*do potrawy*) additive; **na ~** *lub* **w dodatku** further, in addition; **z dodatkiem czegoś** with the addition of sth; ~ **rodzinny** child benefit (*Brit*), family allowance (*US*); ~ **nadzwyczajny** special supplement

**dodatkowo** *adv* additionally; (*płacić*) extra

**dodatkowy** *adj* additional, supplementary; **opłata dodatkowa** surcharge

**dodatni** *adj* positive

**dodatnio** *adv* positively

**doda|wać (-ję, -jesz)** (*perf* **dodać**) *vt* (*dokładać*) to add; (*sumować*) to add (up); ~ **gazu** to step on it, to step on the gas (*US*); ~ **komuś odwagi/otuchy** to boost sb's courage/morale

**dodawani|e** (**-a**) *nt* addition; **znak dodawania** plus sign

**dodzwo|nić się (-nię, -nisz)** (*imp* **-ń**) *vr perf*: **dodzwonić się (do** *+gen*) to get through (to)

**do|g** (**-ga, -gi**) (*instr sg* **-giem**) *m* (*pies*) great Dane

**dogad|ać (-am, -asz)** *vb perf od* **dogadywać**; **dogadać się** *vr perf* (*dojść do porozumienia*) to reach an agreement

**dogad|ywać (-uję, -ujesz)** (*perf* **-ać**) *vi*: ~ **komuś** to make *lub* pass nasty remarks about sb; **dogadywać się** *vr* (*w obcym języku*) to make o.s. understood

**dogadz|ać (-am, -asz)** (*perf* **dogodzić**) *vi*: ~ **komuś** to please *lub* pamper sb; ~ **sobie** to indulge *lub* pamper o.s.

**dogani|ać (-am, -asz)** (*perf* **dogonić**) *vt* to catch (up with)

**dogląd|ać (-am, -asz)** (*perf* **dojrzeć**) *vt* (*pielęgnować*) to tend; (*pilnować*) to mind

**dogłębny** *adj*: **dogłębna wiedza/analiza** in-depth knowledge/analysis

**dogma|t** (**-tu, -ty**) (*loc sg* **-cie**) *m* dogma

**dogmatyczny** *adj* dogmatic

**dogod|ny** (*comp* **-niejszy**) *adj* (*moment, położenie*) convenient; (*warunki*) favourable (*Brit*), favorable (*US*); (*cena, propozycja*) attractive; **na ~ch warunkach** on easy terms

**dog|odzić (-odzę, -odzisz)** (*imp* **-ódź**) *vb perf od* **dogadzać**

**dogo|nić (-nię, -nisz)** (*imp* **-ń**) *vb perf od* **doganiać**

**dogryw|ka** (**-ki, -ki**) (*dat sg* **-ce**, *gen pl* **-ek**) *f* (*Sport*) extra time (*Brit*), overtime (*US*); (*Giełda*) extra-time trading

**doić (doję, doisz)** (*imp* **dój**, *perf* **wy-**) *vt* to milk

**doigr|ać się (-am, -asz)** *vr perf* to come to a bad end; **doigrasz się!** you'll get yours!, you'll get your comeuppance!

**dojar|ka** (**-ki, -ki**) (*dat sg* **-ce**, *gen pl* **-ek**) *f* (*kobieta*) milkmaid; (*urządzenie*) milking-machine

**doj|azd** (**-azdu, -azdy**) (*loc sg* **-eździe**) *m* (*do budynku itp.*) drive, approach *lub* access road; (*dostęp*) access, approach

**doj|echać (-adę, -edziesz)** (*imp* **-edź**) *vb perf od* **dojeżdżać**

**dojeżdż|ać (-am, -asz)** (*perf* **dojechać**) *vi* to approach; ~ **do pracy** to commute

**dojrzałoś|ć** (**-ci**) *f* maturity; (*owocu*) ripeness; ~ **płciowa** sexual maturity; **świadectwo dojrzałości** *certificate of secondary education*, ≈ GCSE (*Brit*), ≈ High School Diploma (*US*)

**dojrza|ły** (*comp* **-lszy**) *adj* (*człowiek, wino, postępowanie*) mature; (*zboże, owoc*) ripe; (*ser*) ripe, mature

**dojrz|eć**[1] **(-ę, -ysz)** (*imp* **-yj**) *vb perf od* **doglądać** ▷ *vt perf* to catch sight of, to spot

**dojrz|eć²** **(-eję, -ejesz)** *vb perf od* **dojrzewać**
**dojrzew|ać (-am, -asz)** (*perf* **dojrzeć**) *vi* (*o człowieku, winie, planach*) to mature; (*o zbożu, owocach*) to ripen; (*o serze*) to ripen, to mature
**dojrzewani|e** (**-a**) *nt*: **okres dojrzewania** adolescence; **~ płciowe** puberty
**dojś|cie** (**-cia, -cia**) (*gen pl* **-ć**) *nt* approach, access; **dojścia** *pl* (*pot: znajomości*) connections
**dojść (dojdę, dojdziesz)** (*imp* **dojdź**, *pt* **doszedł, doszła, doszli**) *vb perf od* **dochodzić**
**do|k** (**-ku, -ki**) (*instr sg* **-kiem**) *m* dock; **suchy dok** dry dock
**dokańcz|ać (-am, -asz)** (*perf* **dokończyć**) *vt* to finish
**dokaz|ywać (-uję, -ujesz)** (*perf* **-ać**) *vi* to romp, to frolic
**dokąd** *pron*: **~?** where (to)?; **nie wiem, ~ poszła** I don't know where she went; **nie miał ~ pójść** he had nowhere to go
**dokądkolwiek** *pron* wherever
**dokądś** *pron* somewhere; (*w pytaniach*) anywhere
**doke|r** (**-ra, -rzy**) (*loc sg* **-rze**) *m* docker
**dokład|ać (-am, -asz)** (*perf* **dołożyć**) *vt* to add; **~ starań, żeby coś zrobić** to make an effort to do sth; **~ do interesu** to run a losing business
**dokład|ka** (**-ki, -ki**) (*dat sg* **-ce**, *gen pl* **-ek**) *f* (*pot*) seconds *pl*, second helping; **na dokładkę** (*pot*) on top of that
**dokładnie** *adv* exactly, precisely
**dokładnoś|ć** (**-ci**) *f* accuracy, precision; **z dokładnością do 1 mm** exact to a millimetre (*Brit*) *lub* millimeter (*US*)
**dokładny** *adj* (*plan, obliczenia*) accurate, exact; (*tłumaczenie*) close; (*czas*) exact, precise; (*pracownik*) thorough
**dokoła** *adv* (all) (a)round ▷ *prep +gen* (a)round
**dokon|ać (-am, -asz)** *vb perf od* **dokonywać**
**dokona|nie** (**-nia, -nia**) (*gen pl* **-ń**) *nt* accomplishment
**dokonany** *adj* (*czasownik*) perfective
**dokon|ywać (-uję, -ujesz)** (*perf* **-ać**) *vt +gen* (*odkrycia*) to make; (*wynalazku*) to come up with; (*morderstwa, przestępstwa*) to commit; **~ cudów** to work *lub* do wonders; **dokonywać się** *vr* (*o reformach, przemianach*) to take place
**dokończe|nie** (**-nia, -nia**) (*gen pl* **-ń**) *nt* conclusion
**dokoń|czyć (-czę, -czysz)** *vb perf od* **dokańczać** ▷ *vt perf*: **nie ~ czegoś** to leave sth unfinished
**dokształ|cać się (-cam, -casz)** (*perf* **-cić**) *vr* to supplement one's education
**dokto|r** (**-ra, -rzy**) (*loc sg* **-rze**) *m* doctor; **~ habilitowany** ≈ reader (*Brit*), ≈ assistant-professor (*US*); **~ honoris causa** honorary doctor
**doktora|t** (**-tu, -ty**) (*loc sg* **-cie**) *m* (*stopień*) doctorate; (*praca*) doctoral *lub* PhD dissertation *lub* thesis; **~ honoris causa** honorary doctorate
**doktorski** *adj*: **rozprawa doktorska** doctoral dissertation *lub* thesis; **obrona pracy ~ej** (doctoral) dissertation defence
**doktry|na** (**-ny, -ny**) (*dat sg* **-nie**) *f* doctrine
**dokucz|ać (-am, -asz)** (*perf* **-yć**) *vi*: **~ komuś** to tease sb; **cały dzień dokuczał mi ból/głód** pain/hunger was nagging me all day
**dokuczliwy** *adj* (*człowiek, komar*) bothersome; (*głód, ból*) nagging; (*wiatr, mróz*) gnawing
**dokucz|yć (-ę, -ysz)** *vb perf od* **dokuczać**
**dokumen|t** (**-tu, -ty**) (*loc sg* **-cie**) *m* document; **dokumenty** *pl* (*dowód tożsamości*) identification, I.D.
**dokumentacj|a** (**-i, -e**) (*gen pl* **-i**) *f* documentation
**dokumentalny** *adj*: **film ~** documentary
**dol|a** (**-i**) *f* (*los*) lot; (*pot: część łupu*) share
**dol|ać (-eję, -ejesz)** *vb perf od* **dolewać**
**dola|r** (**-ra, -ry**) (*loc sg* **-rze**) *m* dollar
**dolat|ywać (-uję, -ujesz)** (*perf* **dolecieć**) *vi* (*o samolocie*) to reach its destination; (*o dźwięku, zapachu*) to come
**dole** *n patrz* **dół**
**dole|cieć (-cę, -cisz)** (*imp* **-ć**) *vb perf od* **dolatywać**
**doleg|ać (-a)** *vi* (*o bólu, chłodzie*) to bother; (*o nodze, żołądku*) to give trouble; **co Panu/Pani dolega?** what seems to be the trouble?; **nic mi nie dolega** I'm all right
**dolegliwoś|ć** (**-ci, -ci**) (*gen pl* **-ci**) *f* ailment
**dolew|ać (-am, -asz)** (*perf* **dolać**) *vt*: **~ komuś** to top up sb's drink *lub* glass; **~ oliwy do ognia** to pour oil on the flames, to add fuel to the flame
**dolicz|ać (-am, -asz)** (*perf* **doliczyć**) *vt*: **~ coś do czegoś** to add sth to sth
**dolicz|yć (-ę, -ysz)** *vb perf od* **doliczać**; **~ do stu** to count (up) to a hundred; **doliczyć się** *vr perf* (*ustalić liczbę*) to count (up); **nie ~ się trzech książek** to have one's count three books short
**doli|na** (**-ny, -ny**) (*dat sg* **-nie**) *f* valley
**dolny** *adj* (*warga, kończyna*) lower; (*szuflada, półka, pokład*) bottom; (*granica*) minimum; **dolna Wisła** the lower Vistula; **D~ Śląsk** Lower Silesia
**doładow|ywać (-uję, -ujesz)** (*pf* **-ać**) *vt*: **doładować telefon** to top up one's phone
**dołącz|ać (-am, -asz)** (*perf* **dołączyć**) *vt* (*do listu, dokumentu*) to enclose ▷ *vi*: **~ do** *+gen* to

d

join; **dołączać się** *vr* (*do dyskusji, śpiewu*) to join in; **~ się do grupy** to join the group
**doł|ek** (**-ka, -ki**) (*instr sg* **-kiem**) *m* (*w ziemi*) hole; (*na policzku, brodzie*) dimple; **kopać pod kimś dołki** (*przen*) to undermine sb; **być w dołku (psychicznym)** (*pot*) to be down in the dumps (*pot*)
**doł|ożyć (-ożę, -ożysz)** (*imp* **-óż**) *vb perf od* **dokładać** ▷ *vi perf*: **~ komuś** (*pot*) to duff sb up (*pot*)
**dołu** *itd. n patrz* **dół**
**dom** (**-u, -y**) *m* (*budynek*) house; (*mieszkanie, rodzina*) home; (*gospodarstwo domowe*) household; **dom akademicki** *lub* **studencki** hall of residence (*Brit*), dormitory (*US*); **dom dziecka** orphanage; **dom kultury** ≈ community centre (*Brit*) *lub* center (*US*); **dom poprawczy** borstal (*Brit*), reformatory (*US*); **dom publiczny** brothel; **dom starców** old people's home; **dom towarowy** department store; **dom wariatów** (*pot*) madhouse (*pot*); **iść do domu** to go home; **w domu** at home; **czuć się jak u siebie w domu** to feel at home; **czuj się jak u siebie w domu** make yourself at home; **pan domu** host; **pani domu** hostess; **z domu Kowalska** née Kowalska
**domaciczny** *adj*: **wkładka domaciczna** intra-uterine device
**domag|ać się (-am, -asz)** *vr*: **domagać się czegoś** to demand sth
**domato|r** (**-ra, -rzy**) (*loc sg* **-rze**) *m* stay-at-home (*Brit*), homebody (*US*)
**dom|ek** (**-ku, -ki**) (*instr sg* **-kiem**) *m dimin od* **dom**; **~ dla ptaków** birdhouse; **~ z kart** house of cards; **~ kempingowy** (holiday) cabin *lub* chalet; **~ letniskowy** summer house
**dome|na** (**-ny**) (*dat sg* **-nie**) *f* domain
**domia|r** (**-ru, -ry**) (*loc sg* **-rze**) *m* (*podatek*) supertax; **na ~ złego** to make matters worse
**domiesz|ka** (**-ki, -ki**) (*dat sg* **-ce**, *gen pl* **-ek**) *f* admixture; (*przen*) tinge
**domięśniowy** *adj*: **zastrzyk ~** intramuscular injection
**dominacj|a** (**-i**) *f* domination
**Dominika|na** (**-ny**) (*dat sg* **-nie**) *f* the Dominican Republic
**dominika|nin** (**-nina, -nie**) (*loc sg* **-ninie**, *gen pl* **-nów**) *m* Dominican
**domi|no** (**-na, -na**) (*loc sg* **-nie**) *nt* (*gra*) dominoes *sg*; (*kostka*) domino
**domin|ować (-uję, -ujesz)** *vi* (*przeważać*) to predominate; **~ (nad** *+instr*) to dominate
**dominujący** *adj* dominant, predominant
**domniemany** *adj* alleged
**domofo|n** (**-nu, -ny**) (*loc sg* **-nie**) *m* intercom, entry phone (*Brit*)
**domokrążc|a** (**-y, -y**) *m decl like f in sg* door-to-door salesman, peddler
**domorosły** *adj* self-taught
**domost|wo** (**-wa, -wa**) (*loc sg* **-wie**) *nt* homestead
**domowni|k** (**-ka, -cy**) (*instr sg* **-kiem**) *m* household member
**domowy** *adj* (*adres, telefon*) home *attr*; (*jedzenie*) home-made; (*zwierzę*) domestic; **areszt ~** house arrest; **pomoc domowa** domestic (help); **praca domowa** homework; **prace domowe** housework; **wojna domowa** civil war; **zadanie domowe** homework (assignment); **domowego wyrobu** home-made
**domy|sł** (**-słu, -sły**) (*loc sg* **-śle**) *m* guess, conjecture; **domysły** *pl* guesswork
**domyśl|ać się (-am, -asz)** (*perf* **-ić**) *vr*: **domyślać się (czegoś)** to guess (at sth)
**donicz|ka** (**-ki, -ki**) (*dat sg* **-ce**, *gen pl* **-ek**) *f* flowerpot
**doniczkowy** *adj*: **kwiat ~** houseplant
**doniesie|nie** (**-nia, -nia**) (*gen pl* **-ń**) *nt* report
**doni|eść (-osę, -esiesz)** (*imp* **-eś**, *pt* **-ósł, -osła, -eśli**) *vb perf od* **donosić**
**donikąd** *adv* nowhere
**doniosłoś|ć** (**-ci**) *f* importance
**doniosły** *adj* momentous
**dono|s** (**-su, -sy**) (*loc sg* **-sie**) *m* denunciation
**donosiciel** (**-a, -e**) (*gen pl* **-i**) *m* informer
**dono|sić (-szę, -sisz)** (*imp* **-ś**, *perf* **donieść**) *vt* (*dostarczać*) to deliver; (*przynosić więcej*) to bring more (of) ▷ *vi*: **~ (o czymś)** to report (on sth); **~ (na kogoś)** to inform (on *lub* against sb)
**donośny** *adj* loud
**dookoła** *adv, prep* = **dokoła**
**dop.** *abbr* (= *dopełniacz*) gen (= *genitive*)
**dopas|ować (-uję, -ujesz)** *vb perf od* **dopasowywać**
**dopasow|ywać (-uję, -ujesz)** (*perf* **-ać**) *vt*: **dopasować coś do czegoś** (*dobrać kształt*) to fit sth into sth; (*dobrać kolor, styl*) to match sth with sth; **dopasowywać się** *vr*: **~ się (do** *+gen*) to adapt (o.s.) (to), to adjust (o.s.) (to)
**dopatr|ywać się (-uję, -ujesz)** (*perf* **dopatrzyć**) *vr*: **dopatrywać się czegoś** to suspect sth
**dopatrz|yć się (-ę, -ysz)** *vb perf od* **dopatrywać się** ▷ *vr perf*: **dopatrzyć się czegoś** (*zauważyć*) to detect sth
**dopełniacz** (**-a, -e**) (*gen pl* **-y**) *m* (*Jęz*) genitive
**dopeł|niać (-niam, -niasz)** (*perf* **-nić**) *vt*: **dopełnić obowiązku** to fulfil (*Brit*) *lub* fulfill (*US*) an obligation; **dopełnić formalności** to complete a formality

**dopeł|nić (-nię, -nisz)** (*imp* **-nij**) *vb perf od* **dopełniać**
**dopełnie|nie** (**-nia, -nia**) (*gen pl* **-ń**) *nt* (*Jęz*) object; **~ bliższe/dalsze** direct/indirect object
**dopę|dzać (-dzam, -dzasz)** (*perf* **-dzić**) *vt* to catch up with
**dopę|dzić (-dzę, -dzisz)** (*imp* **-dź**) *vb perf od* **dopędzać**
**do|piąć (-pnę, -pniesz)** (*imp* **-pnij**) *vt perf*: **~ celu** to achieve one's objective; **~ swego** to get *lub* have one's own way
**dopieprz|yć (-ę, -ysz)** *vi perf*: **~ komuś** (*pot*) to bash sb (*pot*), to knock the shit out of sb (*pot*)
**dopiero** *adv* (*tylko*) just, only; (*nie wcześniej niż*) only; **ona ma ~ dwa lata** she's only two years old; **~ co** (*przed chwilą*) only just; **~ wczoraj** only yesterday; **wyjeżdżam ~ jutro** I'm not leaving until tomorrow; **a co ~** let alone
**dopiln|ować (-uję, -ujesz)** *vi perf*: **~ czegoś** to see to sth; **~, żeby ktoś coś zrobił** to see *lub* make sure that sb does sth
**dopin|g** (**-gu**) (*instr sg* **-giem**) *m* (*Sport*) doping, use of steroids; (*publiczności*) cheers *pl*, cheering; (*przen*: *zachęta*) encouragement
**doping|ować (-uję, -ujesz)** (*perf* **z-**) *vt* (*zachęcać*) to encourage; (*o publiczności*) to cheer
**dopingujący** *adj*: **środek ~** (*Sport*) steroid
**dopi|sać (-szę, -szesz)** *vb perf od* **dopisywać**
**dopis|ek (-ku, -ki)** (*instr sg* **-kiem**) *m* postscript
**dopis|ywać (-uję, -ujesz)** (*perf* **-ać**) *vt* (*dodawać do tekstu*) to add ▷ *vi*: **pogoda dopisała** the weather was good; **zdrowie mu dopisuje** he is in good health
**dopła|cać (-cam, -casz)** (*perf* **-cić**) *vt* to pay extra; **~ do interesu** to sink money into a business
**dopła|ta (-ty, -ty)** (*dat sg* **-cie**) *f* extra (charge); (*do biletu*) excess fare
**dopły|nąć (-nę, -niesz)** (*imp* **-ń**) *vb perf od* **dopływać**
**dopły|w** (**-wu**) (*loc sg* **-wie**) *m* (*prądu, informacji*) supply; (*rzeka*) (*nom pl* **-wy**) tributary
**dopływ|ać (-am, -asz)** (*perf* **dopłynąć**) *vi*: **~ do** *+gen* (*o człowieku, rybie*) to swim up to; (*o wodzie, prądzie*) to flow to; **~ do portu** (*o statku, łodzi*) to make *lub* reach port
**dopomin|ać się (-am, -asz)** *vr*: **dopominać (dopomnieć** *perf*) **się o coś** to claim, to demand; **dopominać się czegoś** (*odczuwać brak*) to be in need *lub* want of sth
**dopom|nieć się (-nę, -nisz)** (*imp* **-nij**) *vb perf od* **dopominać się**
**dopóki** *adv* as long as; **~ nie będzie padać** as long as it doesn't rain; **zaczekaj ~ nie przyjdę** wait until I come; **~ ..., dopóty ...** (*książk*) as long as
**doprawdy** *adv* truly, really; **~?** really?
**dopra|wiać (-wiam, -wiasz)** (*perf* **-wić**) *vt* to season
**doprowa|dzać (-dzam, -dzasz)** (*perf* **-dzić**) *vt* (*więźnia*) to escort; (*gaz, prąd*) to supply ▷ *vi*: **~ do** *+gen* to lead to, to result in; **doprowadzić coś do końca** to carry sth through; **~ coś do porządku** to straighten sth out, to put *lub* set sth right; **doprowadzić kogoś do ostateczności** to drive sb into a frenzy; **~ kogoś do rozpaczy** to drive sb to despair; **~ kogoś do szału** *lub* **wściekłości** to drive sb mad
**doprowa|dzić (-dzę, -dzisz)** (*imp* **-dź**) *vb perf od* **doprowadzać**
**dopuszcz|ać (-am, -asz)** (*perf* **dopuścić**) *vt* to admit ▷ *vi*: **nie dopuszczę do tego** I won't let it happen; **~ kogoś do siebie** to let sb near one; **dopuścić kogoś do głosu** to let sb speak; **dopuścić kogoś do egzaminu** to admit sb to an examination; **dopuścić kogoś do tajemnicy** to let sb into a secret; **~ możliwość** to allow for a possibility; **dopuszczać się** *vr*: **~ się przestępstwa** to commit a crime
**dopuszczalny** *adj* permissible, acceptable
**dopu|ścić (-szczę, -ścisz)** (*imp* **-ść**) *vb perf od* **dopuszczać**
**dorabi|ać (-am, -asz)** (*perf* **dorobić**) *vt*: **~ klucz** to make a duplicate key ▷ *vi* (*pot*: *zarabiać dodatkowo*) to have a second job, to moonlight (*pot*); **dorabiać się** *vr* (*bogacić się*) to grow rich; **dorobić się autorytetu** to establish one's authority; **dorobić się szacunku** to earn *lub* win respect
**doradc|a** (**-y, -y**) *m decl like f in sg* adviser (*Brit*), advisor (*US*); **~ finansowy/inwestycyjny** financial/investments adviser (*Brit*) *lub* advisor (*US*)
**doradczy** *adj* advisory
**dora|dzać (-dzam, -dzasz)** (*perf* **-dzić**) *vt* to advise, to counsel
**dora|dzić (-dzę, -dzisz)** (*imp* **-dź**) *vb perf od* **doradzać**
**dorast|ać (-am, -asz)** (*perf* **dorosnąć**) *vi* (*o dziecku*) to grow up; **nie ~ komuś do pięt** to be no match for sb
**dorastający** *adj* adolescent
**doraźny** *adj* (*cel, korzyść*) short-term; (*środek*) temporary; (*prawo, sąd, kara*) summary; **doraźna pomoc** relief; (*pierwsza pomoc*) first aid
**doręcz|ać (-am, -asz)** (*perf* **-yć**) *vt* to deliver
**doręczyciel** (**-a, -e**) (*gen pl* **-i**) *m* (*też*: **doręczyciel pocztowy**) postman (*Brit*), mailman (*US*)

**dorę|czyć (-czę, -czysz)** *vb perf od* **doręczać**
**dorob|ek** (**-ku**) (*instr sg* **-kiem**) *m* (*majątek*) property; (*twórczość*) output; **być na dorobku** to feather one's nest
**dor|obić (-obię, -obisz)** (*imp* **-ób**) *vb perf od* **dorabiać**
**dorobkiewicz** (**-a, -e**) *m* nouveau riche
**doroczny** *adj* annual, yearly
**dorodny** *adj* (*człowiek, roślina*) robust; (*owoc*) ripe
**dorosły** *adj* (*człowiek*) adult, grown-up; (*zwierzę*) adult ▷ *m decl like adj* (*dorosły człowiek*) adult, grown-up (*pot*); **dorośli** *pl* adults *pl*, grown-ups *pl* (*pot*); **film tylko dla ~ch** adult *lub* X-rated film (*Brit*) *lub* movie (*US*)
**doro|snąć (-snę, -śniesz)** (*imp* **-śnij**) *vb perf od* **dorastać**
**doroż|ka** (**-ki, -ki**) (*dat sg* **-ce**, *gen pl* **-ek**) *f* hackney carriage
**dorówn|ywać (-uję, -ujesz)** (*perf* **-ać**) *vt*: **~ komuś (w czymś)** to equal sb (in sth); **~ czemuś** to match *lub* come up to sth
**dorsz** (**-a, -e**) (*gen pl* **-y**) *m* cod
**dorywczy** *adj*: **praca dorywcza** odd jobs *pl*
**dorzecz|e** (**-a, -a**) (*gen pl* **-y**) *nt* (river) basin
**dorzu|cać (-cam, -casz)** (*perf* **-cić**) *vt +gen* (*dokładać rzucając*) to throw in more ▷ *vt +acc* (*dopowiadać*) to throw in, to add
**dorzu|cić (-cę, -cisz)** (*imp* **-ć**) *vb perf od* **dorzucać**
**dosadny** *adj* (*wymowny*) plain, blunt; (*wulgarny*) crude
**dosiad|ać (-am, -asz)** (*perf* **dosiąść**) *vt* (*konia*) to mount; **dosiadać się** *vr*: **~ się do kogoś** to sit (down) next to sb; **czy można się dosiąść?** may I join you?
**dosięg|ać (-am, -asz)** (*perf* **-nąć**) *vt*: **~ kogoś/czegoś** to reach sb/sth; **dosięgnie cię kara/śmierć** you won't escape punishment/death
**doskonale** *adv* (*znakomicie*) perfectly; (*całkowicie*) absolutely; **~!** (*pot*) excellent!, fine!
**doskonal|ić (-ę, -isz)** (*perf* **u-**) *vt* to perfect, to improve; **doskonalić się (w czymś)** *vr* to improve o.s. (in sth)
**doskonałoś|ć** (**-ci**) *f* perfection
**doskonały** *adj* (*najlepszy*) perfect; (*świetny*) splendid; (*absolutny*) absolute
**doskwier|ać (-a)** *vi*: **~ komuś** to trouble *lub* annoy sb
**dosł.** *abbr* = **dosłownie**
**dosłownie** *adv* literally; (*tłumaczyć*) word for word; (*cytować*) verbatim
**dosłowny** *adj* literal; (*tłumaczenie*) word-for-word
**dosłysz|eć (-ę, -ysz)** *vt perf* to catch, to hear; **przepraszam, nie dosłyszałem** (I'm) sorry, I didn't catch you
**dosta|ć (-nę, -niesz)** (*imp* **-ń**) *vb perf od* **dostawać** ▷ *vt perf* (*pot*: *kupić*) to get; **gdzie to dostałaś?** where did you get it?
**dostarcz|ać (-am, -asz)** (*perf* **-yć**) *vt* (*towar, list*) to deliver; **~ coś komuś** to deliver sth to sb; **~ komuś czegoś** to supply *lub* provide sb with sth
**dostatecznie** *adv* (*wystarczająco*) sufficiently; (*zadowalająco*) satisfactorily, adequately
**dostateczny** *adj* (*wystarczający*) sufficient; (*zadowalający*) satisfactory, adequate ▷ *m decl like adj* (*Szkol*) ≈ C (*grade*)
**dostat|ek** (**-ku**) *n* (*dobrobyt*) affluence; (*obfitość*) abundance; **żyć w dostatku** to be well off; **pod dostatkiem** in abundance
**dostatni** *adj* affluent
**dosta|wa** (**-wy, -wy**) (*dat sg* **-wie**) *f* delivery
**dost|awać (-aję, -ajesz)** (*imp* **-awaj**, *perf* **-ać**) *vt* to get; (*zastrzyk*) to have ▷ *vi* (*otrzymywać ciosy*) to be beaten; **dostać wypieków** to blush; **nie można tego dostać** you can't get it in the shops (*Brit*) *lub* stores (*US*); **dostać za swoje** to be rightly served; **dostawać się** *vr*: **dostać się w czyjeś ręce** to fall into sb's hands; **dostać się na studia** to be admitted to a university *lub* college; **dostać się do niewoli** to be taken prisoner; **dostać się do więzienia** to be imprisoned; **dostać się do środka** to get inside; **dostać się pod koła samochodu** to get run over by a car; **dostało mu się** he got a scolding; **dostała mu się nagroda** he got a prize
**dostawc|a** (**-y, -y**) *m decl like f in sg* deliverer
**dostawczy** *adj*: **samochód ~** delivery van
**dosta|wiać (-wiam, -wiasz)** (*perf* **-wić**) *vt* (*dostarczać*) to deliver; **~ krzesło** to put in an extra chair; **dostawiać się** *vr*: **~ się do kogoś** (*pot*) to chase (after) sb
**dostą|pić (-pię, -pisz)** *vb perf od* **dostępować**
**dostę|p** (**-pu**) (*loc sg* **-pie**) *m* access; **mieć ~ do** *+gen* to have access to; **pamięć o ~ie swobodnym** (*Komput*) random access memory
**dostępny** *adj* (*miejsce*) easy to reach, accessible; (*osoba*) accessible, approachable; (*towar*) accessible, available; (*cena*) reasonable; (*zrozumiały*) accessible, comprehensible; **łatwo/trudno ~** (*towar*) easy/hard to get; (*szczyt*) easy/difficult to reach; **ogólnie ~** freely available
**dostęp|ować (-uję, -ujesz)** (*perf* **dostąpić**) *vt* (*osiągać*): **~ czegoś** (*łaski*) to obtain sth, to win sth; (*zaszczytu*) to be granted sth; (*szczęścia*) to gain sth
**dostojni|k** (**-ka, -cy**) (*instr sg* **-kiem**) *m* dignitary

**dostojny** *adj* (*starzec, mina*) dignified; (*gość*) distinguished
**dostos|ować (-uję, -ujesz)** *vb perf od* **dostosowywać**
**dostosow|ywać (-uję, -ujesz)** (*perf* **-ać**) *vt*: **~ coś do czegoś** to adjust sth to sth, to adapt sth to sth; **dostosowywać się** *vr*: **~ się do** *+gen* to adjust (o.s.) to, to adapt (o.s.) to; (*do przepisów*) to conform to
**dostrze|c (-gę, -żesz)** (*imp* **-ż**, *pt* **-gł**) *vb perf od* **dostrzegać** ▷ *vt perf* (*zobaczyć*) to spot
**dostrzeg|ać (-am, -asz)** (*perf* **dostrzec**) *vt* (*zauważać*) to perceive; **nie ~ kogoś/czegoś** to disregard sb/sth
**dostrzegalny** *adj* (*kształt*) discernible; (*różnica*) perceptible
**dosyć** *adv* (*wystarczająco dużo*) enough; (*bogaty, ładny*) fairly; (*biedny, brzydki*) rather; **mieć czegoś ~** to be tired *lub* sick of sth, to be fed up with sth; **mam tego ~!** I've had enough!; **nie ~, że ... to jeszcze ...** not only ... but also ...; **~ (tego)!** enough (of that)!
**doszczętnie** *adv* completely; **~ spalony** burnt to the ground
**doszedł** *itd. vb patrz* **dojść**
**doszkal|ać (-am, -asz)** (*perf* **doszkolić**) *vt* to give supplementary training; **doszkalać się** *vr* to improve *lub* raise one's qualifications
**doszuk|ać się (-am, -asz)** *vb perf od* **doszukiwać się** ▷ *vr perf*: **doszukać się czegoś** to detect sth
**doszu|kiwać się (-kuję, -kujesz)** (*perf* **-kać**) *vr*: **doszukiwać się czegoś** to suspect sth
**dościg|ać (-am, -asz)** (*perf* **-nąć**) *vt* (*dorównywać*) to equal sb
**dościg|nąć (-nę, -niesz)** (*imp* **-nij**) *vb perf od* **dościgać** ▷ *vt perf*: **~ kogoś** (*dogonić*) to catch up with sb
**dość** *adv* = **dosyć**
**dośrodk|ować (-uję, -ujesz)** *vb perf od* **dośrodkowywać**
**dośrodkowy** *adj*: **siła dośrodkowa** (*Fiz*) centripetal force
**dośrodkow|ywać (-uję, -ujesz)** (*perf* **-ać**) (*Sport*) *vt/vi*: **~ (piłkę)** to cross the ball to the centre (*Brit*) *lub* center (*US*)
**doświadcz|ać (-am, -asz)** (*perf* **-yć**) *vt*: **~ czegoś** to experience sth; (*głodu, przykrości*) to suffer from sth; **życie ciężko go doświadczyło** his life was full of tribulations
**doświadczalny** *adj* experimental; (*metoda*) experimental; (*badania*) empirical; **jazda doświadczalna** test drive; **pilot ~** test pilot; **królik ~** (*przen*) guinea pig
**doświadcze|nie (-nia, -nia)** (*gen pl* **-ń**) *nt* experience; (*eksperyment*) experiment; **brak doświadczenia** inexperience; **mieć ~ w czymś** to be experienced in sth; **nie mieć w czymś doświadczenia** to be inexperienced in sth; **robić doświadczenia** to make experiments
**doświadczony** *adj* experienced
**doświad|czyć (-czę, -czysz)** *vb perf od* **doświadczać**
**dot.** *abbr* (= *dotyczy*) re
**dotacj|a (-i, -e)** (*gen pl* **-i**) *f* subsidy
**dotarł** *itd. vb patrz* **dotrzeć**
**dotarty** *adj* (*Mot: silnik*) run-in; **nie ~** running-in
**dotąd** *adv* (*do tego miejsca: blisko*) this far; (*daleko*) that far; (*do tego czasu*) so far, until now
**dotkliwy** *adj* (*ból, strata*) severe; (*chłód, wiatr*) biting, bitter
**dotk|nąć (-nę, -niesz)** (*imp* **-nij**) *vb perf od* **dotykać** ▷ *vt perf*: **~ kogoś/czegoś** to touch sb/sth; **~ czegoś ręką** to feel sth; **~ kogoś** (*przen*) to hurt sb; **~ kogoś do żywego** to cut sb to the quick; **dotknąć się** *vr perf*: **~ się czegoś** (*przen*) to start doing sth
**dotknię|cie (-cia, -cia)** (*gen pl* **-ć**) *nt* touch; (*pędzla*) stroke
**dotknięty** *adj* (*obrażony*) aggrieved, sore (*US*); **poczuć się ~m** to feel aggrieved *lub* offended, to feel sore (*US*); **~ chorobą/kłopotami** afflicted with an illness/problems
**dot|ować (-uję, -ujesz)** *vt* to subsidize
**dotrw|ać (-am, -asz)** *vi perf* (*przetrwać*) to survive; (*wytrzymać*) to last out
**dot|rzeć (-rę, -rzesz)** (*imp* **-rzyj**, *pt* **-arł**) *vb perf od* **docierać**
**dotrzym|ywać (-uję, -ujesz)** (*perf* **dotrzymać**) *vt*: **~ słowa/obietnicy/tajemnicy** to keep one's word/a promise/a secret; **~ umowy/warunków** to keep to an agreement/conditions; **nie ~ umowy** to go back on an agreement; **~ komuś kroku** to keep pace with sb; **~ komuś towarzystwa** to keep sb company
**dotychczas** *adv* so far, until now
**dotychczasowy** *adj*: **jego dotychczasowa praca** the work he has been doing so far
**dotycz|yć (-y)** *vi*: **~ kogoś/czegoś** to concern sb/sth; (*mieć zastosowanie*) to apply to sb/sth
**doty|k (-ku)** (*instr sg* **-kiem**) *m* (*dotknięcie*) touch; (*zmysł*) (sense of) touch; **miękki/przyjemny w ~u** soft/nice to the touch
**dotyk|ać (-am, -asz)** (*perf* **dotknąć**) *vt*: **~ kogoś/czegoś** (*stykać się*) to touch sb/sth; (*badać dotykiem*) to feel sb/sth; **~ czegoś** (*podłogi, pedałów*) to reach sth; (*tematu, sprawy*) to touch on *lub* upon sth; **~ kogoś** (*o chorobie, nieszczęściu*) to afflict sb; **kto dotykał mojego**

d

radia? who has tampered with my radio?; **dotykać się** *vr* to touch
**doustny** *adj* oral
**dowci|p** (**-pu, -py**) (*loc sg* **-pie**) *m* (*żart*) joke; (*cecha umysłu*) wit; **opowiadać ~y** to tell jokes
**dowcipk|ować (-uję, -ujesz)** *vi* to joke
**dowcipni|ś** (**-sia, -sie**) *m* joker
**dowcipny** *adj* witty
**dowiad|ywać się (-uję, -ujesz)** (*perf* **dowiedzieć**) *vr*: **dowiadywać się o kogoś/coś** to inquire after sb/sth
**dowi|edzieć się (-em, -esz)** (*3 pl* **-edzą**) *vb perf od* **dowiadywać się** ▷ *vr perf*: **dowiedzieć się (o czymś)** to learn about *lub* of sth, to find sth out
**dowierz|ać (-am, -asz)** *vi*: **nie ~ komuś/czemuś** to distrust *lub* mistrust sb/sth
**dowi|eść (-odę, -edziesz)** (*imp* **-edź**, *pt* **-ódł, -odła, -edli**) *vb perf od* **dowodzić¹**
**dowi|eźć (-ozę, -eziesz)** (*imp* **-eź**, *pt* **-ózł, -ozła, -eźli**) *vb perf od* **dowozić**
**dowodowy** *adj*: **materiał ~** (*Prawo*) the evidence
**dow|odzić¹ (-odzę, -odzisz)** (*imp* **-ódź**, *perf* **dowieść**) *vt*: **~ czegoś** (*udowadniać*) to prove sth; (*ukazywać*) to show; (*być dowodem*) to prove ▷ *vi* to argue; **dowieść, że ...** to prove that ...
**dow|odzić² (-odzę, -odzisz)** (*imp* **-ódź**) *vi* (*sprawować dowództwo*): **~** (*+instr*) to command, to be in command (of)
**dowolnie** *adv* freely
**dowolny** *adj* (*jakikolwiek*) any; (*nieobowiązkowy*) discretionary; **przekład ~** free translation; **styl ~** (*Sport*) free style; **w ~m kierunku** in whichever direction
**dow|ozić (-ożę, -ozisz)** (*imp* **-oź** *lub* **-óź**, *perf* **dowieźć**) *vt* to drive, to bring
**dow|ód** (**-odu, -ody**) (*loc sg* **-odzie**) *m* (*okoliczność dowodząca czegoś*) evidence, proof; (*oznaka*) evidence; (*rozumowanie*) argument; **być dowodem** *lub* **stanowić ~ czegoś** to constitute a proof of sth; **na ~ czegoś** to prove sth; **w ~ przyjaźni/wdzięczności** as a mark of friendship/gratitude; **dać** (*perf*) **~ odwagi** to show o.s. courageous; **~ odbioru** delivery receipt; **~ osobisty** *lub* **tożsamości** identity card, (means of) identification; **~ rzeczowy** (*Prawo*) exhibit
**dowódc|a** (**-y, -y**) *m decl like f in sg* (*wódz*) commander; (*oficer dowodzący*) commanding officer; (*komendant*) commandant; **naczelny ~** commander-in-chief
**dowództ|wo** (**-wa**) (*loc sg* **-wie**) *nt* command; (*siedziba*) headquarters; **obejmować ~** to take command; **~ naczelne** command-in-chief
**doza** (**dozy, dozy**) (*dat sg* **dozie**, *gen pl* **dóz**) *f* dose; **z dużą dozą prawdopodobieństwa** in all probability
**dozgonny** *adj* (*przyjaźń*) undying, lifelong; (*wdzięczność*) undying
**dozn|ać (-am, -asz)** *vb perf od* **doznawać**
**dozna|nie** (**-nia, -nia**) (*gen pl* **-ń**) *nt* (*odczucie*) experience; (*też*: **doznanie zmysłowe**) sensation
**dozn|awać (-aję, -ajesz)** (*imp* **-awaj**, *perf* **-ać**) *vt*: **~** *+gen* to experience; (*obrażeń*) to sustain; (*cierpienia, bólu*) to suffer from; (*życzliwości, nieuprzejmości*) to meet with
**dozorc|a** (**-y, -y**) *m decl like f in sg* caretaker, janitor (US); (*strażnik*) guard
**dozor|ować (-uję, -ujesz)** *vt* to supervise
**doz|ór** (**-oru**) (*loc sg* **-orze**) *m* supervision
**dozwolony** *adj* (*prędkość*) permitted; **film ~ od lat 18** an X-rated film
**doży|ć (-ję, -jesz)** *vt perf*: **~ osiemdziesiątki** to live to be 80; **on nie dożyje do jutra** he won't live *lub* last through the night
**dożylny** *adj* intravenous
**dożyn|ki** (**-ek**) *pl* harvest home
**dożywoci|e** (**-a, -a**) *nt* (*pot*: *kara więzienia*) life imprisonment *lub* sentence
**dożywotni** *adj* life *attr*, lifelong; **kara ~ego więzienia** life imprisonment *lub* sentence
**dób** *n patrz* **doba**
**dóbr** *n patrz* **dobro**
**dój** *vb patrz* **doić**
**dół** (**dołu, doły**) (*loc sg* **dole**) *m* (*otwór w ziemi*) pit; (*najniższa część*) bottom; **na dole** at the bottom; (*na niższym piętrze*) downstairs; **na dół** down; (*na niższe piętro*) downstairs; **w dole** (down) below; **w dół** down; **w dół rzeki** downstream; **z dołu** from below
**dr** *abbr* = **doktor**
**drabi|na** (**-ny, -ny**) (*dat sg* **-nie**) *f* ladder; (*pokojowa*) stepladder
**dra|ka** (**-ki, -ki**) (*dat sg* **-ce**) *f* (*pot*: *awantura*) row (*pot*)
**drakoński** *adj* draconian
**drama|t** (**-tu, -ty**) (*loc sg* **-cie**) *m* drama; (*przen*) tragedy
**dramatopisarz** (**-a, -e**) (*gen pl* **-y**) *m* playwright, dramatist
**dramatur|g** (**-ga, -gowie** *lub* **-dzy**) (*instr sg* **-giem**) *m* playwright, dramatist
**dramaturgi|a** (**-i**) *f* drama
**dramatyczny** *adj* (*teatralny*) dramatic; (*przen*: *tragiczny*) tragic; (: *wstrząsający*) dramatic
**dramatyz|ować (-uję, -ujesz)** (*perf* **u-**) *vt* to dramatize
**dra|ń** (**-nia, -nie**) (*gen pl* **-ni**) *m* (*pot*) bastard (*pot*)
**drapacz** (**-a, -e**) (*gen pl* **-y**) *m*: **~ chmur** skyscraper

**dra|pać (-pię, -piesz)** *vt* (*perf* **po-**) (*skrobać*) to scratch ▷ *vi* (*o dymie*) to irritate; (*o ubraniu*) to be itchy; **drapie mnie w gardle** I have an itchy throat; **drapać się** *vr* (*skrobać się*) (*perf* **po-**) to scratch (o.s.); (*wspinać się*) (*perf* **w-**) to scramble; **~ się w głowę** to scratch one's head

**drapieżni|k (-ka, -ki)** (*instr sg* **-kiem**) *m* predator

**drapieżny** *adj* predatory; **ptaki drapieżne** birds of prey; **zwierzęta drapieżne** beasts of prey

**dra|snąć (-snę, -śniesz)** (*imp* **-śnij**) *vt perf* to graze

**drastycznie** *adv* drastically

**drastyczny** *adj* (*metoda, środki*) drastic; (*scena*) shocking

**draśnię|cie (-cia, -cia)** (*gen pl* **-ć**) *nt* graze

**drażet|ka (-ki, -ki)** (*dat sg* **-ce**, *gen pl* **-ek**) *f* (*pigułka*) coated tablet; (*cukierek*) sugar-coated sweet

**drażliwy** *adj* sensitive, touchy

**draż|nić (-nię, -nisz)** (*imp* **-nij**) *vt* (*zmysły*) to irritate; (*denerwować*) to irritate, to annoy; (*dokuczać*) to tease; **drażnić się** *vr*: **~ się z kimś** to tease sb

**drą|g (-ga, -gi)** (*instr sg* **-giem**) *m* pole

**drąż|ek (-ka, -ki)** (*instr sg* **-kiem**) *m* (*dźwignia*) lever; **~ sterowy** control stick, joystick (*pot*); **~ gimnastyczny** horizontal bar

**drąż|yć (-ę, -ysz)** (*perf* **wy-**) *vt* (*tunel, kanał*) to bore; (*owoce*) to pit, to core; (*przen*: *niepokoić*) to trouble; (*temat*) to dwell (up)on

**drelich (-u, -y)** *m* denim

**dre|n (-nu, -ny)** (*loc sg* **-nie**) *m* drain

**drenaż (-u, -e)** (*gen pl* **-y**) *m* drainage; **~ mózgów** brain drain

**dren|ować (-uję, -ujesz)** *vt* to drain

**drep|tać (-czę, -czesz)** *vi* (*o dziecku*) to toddle; (*o dorosłym*) to mince

**dre|s (-su, -sy)** (*loc sg* **-sie**) *m* tracksuit

**dreszcz (-u, -e)** (*gen pl* **-y**) *m* shiver, shudder; **dreszcze** *pl* the shivers; **mieć ~e** to be shivering

**dreszczo|wiec (-wca, -wce)** *m* thriller

**dreszczy|k (-ku, -ki)** (*instr sg* **-kiem**) *m* thrill

**drewnia|k (-ka, -ki)** (*instr sg* **-kiem**) *m* clog

**drewniany** *adj* wooden; **instrumenty drewniane** (*Muz*) woodwind instruments

**dre|wno (-wna, -wna)** (*loc sg* **-wnie**, *gen pl* **-wien**) *nt* (*materiał*) wood, timber; (*odrąbany kawałek*) piece of wood, log

**drę** *vb patrz* **drzeć**

**dręcz|yć (-ę, -ysz)** *vt* to torment

**drętwi|eć (-eję, -ejesz)** (*perf* **z-**) *vi* (*o człowieku*) to stiffen; (*o kończynie*) to go numb

**drętwy** *adj* (*kończyna*) numb; (*przemówienie*) dry

**drg|ać (-am, -asz)** (*perf* **-nąć**) *vi* (*o strunie*) to vibrate; (*o powiece, mięśniu*) to twitch; (*o głosie, dźwięku*) to tremble; (*o świetle*) to flicker

**drga|nie (-nia, -nia)** (*gen pl* **-ń**) *nt* vibration; **drgania** *pl* (*Fiz*) vibration; (*Elektr*) oscillation

**drgaw|ki (-ek)** *pl* convulsions *pl*

**drg|nąć (-nę, -niesz)** (*imp* **-nij**) *vb perf od* **drgać** ▷ *vi perf* (*poruszyć się*) to stir; (*: z przeczeniem*) to budge; (*ożywić się*) to liven up; **ani (nie) drgnął** he didn't turn a hair

**drin|k (-ka, -ki)** (*instr sg* **-kiem**) *m* (*pot*) drink

**drobiaz|g (-gu, -gi)** (*instr sg* **-giem**) *m* (*drobny przedmiot*) trinket, knick-knack; (*błahostka*) trifle; **drobiazgi** *pl* odds and ends *pl*; **to ~!** never mind!

**drobiazgowy** *adj* (*opis, badania*) detailed; (*człowiek*) meticulous

**dr|obić (-obię, -obisz)** (*imp* **-ób**) *vt* (*chleb*) to crumble ▷ *vi* (*o dziecku*) to toddle; (*o dorosłym*) to mince

**drobi|na (-ny, -ny)** (*dat sg* **-nie**) *f* particle

**drobiowy** *adj* chicken *attr*

**drobn|e (-ych)** *pl* small change; **rozmienić** (*perf*) **na ~** to change; **nie mam drobnych** I've no small change

**drobnomieszczański** *adj* ≈ lower middle class *attr*, petit-bourgeois

**drobnomieszczańst|wo (-wa)** (*loc sg* **-wie**) *nt* (*grupa*) ≈ lower middle class; (*postawa*) narrow-mindedness

**drobnost|ka (-ki, -ki)** (*dat sg* **-ce**, *gen pl* **-ek**) *f* trifle

**drobnoustr|ój (-oju, -oje)** *m* microorganism

**drobny** *adj* small; (*błahy*) petty; (*wątły*) frail; (*ziarno, deszcz, proszek*) fine

**drocz|yć się (-ę, -ysz)** *vr*: **droczyć się z kimś** to banter with sb

**dr|oga (-ogi, -ogi)** (*dat sg* **-odze**, *gen pl* **-óg**) *f* (*pas terenu*) road; (*trasa*) way; (*właściwy kierunek*) way; (*podróż*) journey; (*odległość między dwoma punktami*) distance; (*przen*) way; **~ boczna** side road; **~ dojazdowa** access road; **~ główna** main road; **D~ Krzyżowa** (*Rel*) the Way of the Cross; **D~ Mleczna** the Milky Way; **~ okrężna** bypass; **~ polna** dirt road; **w drodze powrotnej** on the way back; **~ wolna!** the coast is clear!; **drogą lotniczą/morską** by air/sea; **drogą służbową/urzędową** through official channels; **drogi oddechowe/moczowe** respiratory/urinary tract; **na drogę** for the road; **na drodze sądowej** in court; **być na drodze do czegoś** to be on the road to sth; **być na dobrej/złej drodze** to be on the right/wrong track; **stawać (stanąć** *perf*) **komuś na drodze** to stand *lub* be in sb's way; **po drodze** on the way, en route; **swoją drogą ...** still, ...; **w drodze wyjątku** by way of exception, as an exception; **coś jest w drodze** sth is in the pipeline; **w drodze do domu** on the way home; **w połowie** *lub* **pół drogi** half way there; **z drogi!** get out of my way!; **zejść** *(perf)* **komuś z drogi** to get out of sb's way; **pięć minut drogi (stąd)** *(piechotą)* five minutes' walk (from here); *(samochodem)* five minutes' drive (from here); **sprowadzać (sprowadzić** *perf*) **kogoś na złą drogę** to lead sb astray; **szczęśliwej drogi!** have a safe trip!

**drogeri|a** (**-i, -e**) (*gen pl* **-i**) *f* ≈ chemist('s) (*Brit*), ≈ drugstore (*US*)

**dro|gi** (*comp* **-ższy**) *adj* (*kosztowny*) expensive; (*kochany*) dear; **D~ Janku!** (*nagłówek listu*) Dear Janek; **~ kamień** precious stone; **mój ~/moja droga** my dear

**dro|go** (*comp* **-żej**) *adv* (*sprzedać*) at a high price; (*kosztować, zapłacić*) a lot; **~ za coś zapłacić** (*przen*) to pay dearly for sth

**drogocenny** *adj* (*pierścień, czas*) precious; (*wskazówka, rada*) valuable

**drogowska|z** (**-zu, -zy**) (*loc sg* **-zie**) *m* signpost

**drogowy** *adj* road *attr*; **kodeks ~** rules of the road, ≈ Highway Code (*Brit*); **kontrola drogowa** traffic patrol; **podatek ~** vehicle tax; **policja drogowa** traffic police; **przepisy drogowe** traffic regulations; **roboty drogowe** road works *pl* (*Brit*), roadwork (*US*); **wypadek ~** traffic accident; **znak ~** traffic *lub* road sign

**drogów|ka** (**-ki, -ki**) (*dat sg* **-ce**, *gen pl* **-ek**) *f* (*pot*) traffic police

**dromade|r** (**-ra, -ry**) (*loc sg* **-rze**) *m* dromedary

**drop|s** (**-sa, -sy**) (*loc sg* **-sie**) *m* drop (*sweet*)

**dro|zd** (**-zda, -zdy**) (*loc sg* **-ździe**) *m* thrush

**drożdż|e** (**-y**) *pl* yeast; **rosnąć jak na drożdżach** to shoot up

**drożdżowy** *adj* leavened

**drożdżów|ka** (**-ki, -ki**) (*dat sg* **-ce**, *gen pl* **-ek**) *f a kind of sweet bun*

**droż|eć (-eje)** (*perf* **z-** *lub* **po-**) *vi* to go up (*in price*)

**drożej** *adv comp od* **drogo**

**droższy** *adj comp od* **drogi**

**droży|zna** (**-zny**) (*dat sg* **-źnie**) *f* inflated prices

**dr|ób** (**-obiu**) *m* poultry

**dróż|ka** (**-ki, -ki**) (*dat sg* **-ce**, *gen pl* **-ek**) *f* path

**dróżni|k** (**-ka, -cy**) (*instr sg* **-kiem**) *m* gateman (*at railway crossing*)

**druciany** *adj* wire *attr*

**drucie** *n patrz* **drut**

**druci|k** (**-ka, -ki**) (*instr sg* **-kiem**) *m dimin od* **drut**

**drugi** *num decl like adj* second; (*jeden z dwóch*) (the) other; (*inny*) another; **druga klasa** (*w pociągu*) second class; (*w szkole*) second form (*Brit*) *lub* grade (*US*); **druga liga** second division; **~ maja** the second of May, May the second; **po ~e, ...** second(ly), ...; **~ gatunek** seconds *pl*; **~ obieg** underground printing; **~ plan** (*przen*) secondary importance; **~e śniadanie** (*posiłek*) elevenses (*Brit*), midmorning snack (*US*); (*kanapki*) packed lunch (*Brit*), box *lub* bag lunch (*US*); **druga wojna światowa** the Second World War, World War Two; **~ od góry** second from the top, second highest; **co ~ dzień** every other day; **zajął ~e miejsce** he took second place, he came in second; **numer ~** number two; **jest godzina druga** it's two (o'clock); **program ~** channel two; **~ od końca** last but one, next to the last (*US*); **na ~ dzień** (on) the following day; **po ~ej stronie ulicy** across the street; **z ~ej strony ...** on the other hand ...; **z ~ej ręki** second hand; **jeden ~ego** one another; **jeden za ~m** one after another, one by one; **pierwszy... ~...** the former... the latter...

**drugoplanowy** *adj* (*rola, postać*) supporting; (*sprawa*) minor

**drugorzędny** *adj* (*mniej ważny*) minor; (*podrzędny*) second-rate

**druh** (**-a, -owie**) *m* (boy) scout

**druh|na** (**-ny, -ny**) (*dat sg* **-nie**, *gen pl* **-en**) *f* (*harcerka*) (girl) scout, girl guide (*Brit*); (*na ślubie*) bridesmaid

**dru|k** (**-ku**) (*instr sg* **-kiem**) *m* (*drukowanie*) printing; (*krój liter*) type; (*tekst*) print; (*blankiet*) form; **druki** *pl* (*wydawnictwa drukowane*) printed matter; **błąd w ~u** misprint; **być w ~u** to be in press; **tłustym/pochyłym ~iem** in bold/italic type; **ukazać** (*perf*) **się ~iem** *lub* **w ~u** to appear in print

**drukar|ka** (**-ki, -ki**) (*dat sg* **-ce**, *gen pl* **-ek**) *f* printer; **~ igłowa** dot-matrix printer; **~ atramentowa** ink-jet printer; **~ laserowa** laser printer; **~ rozetkowa** daisy-wheel printer

**drukar|nia** (**-ni, -nie**) (*gen pl* **-ni**) *f* printing house

**drukarski** *adj* printing *attr*; **błąd ~** misprint

**drukarz** (**-a, -e**) (*gen pl* **-y**) *m* printer

**druk|ować (-uję, -ujesz)** (*perf* **wy-**) *vt* to print; (*publikować*) to publish

**drukowany** *adj* printed; **pisać ~mi literami** to print; **obwód ~** (*Elektr*) printed circuit

**dru|t** (**-tu, -ty**) (*loc sg* **-cie**) *m* wire; (*do robótek*) (knitting) needle; **~ kolczasty** barbed wire; **robić na ~ach** to knit

**druzgocący** *adj* crushing

**druzgo|tać (-czę, -czesz)** (*perf* **z-**) *vt* to crush

**druż|ba** (**-by, -bowie**) (*dat sg* **-bie**) *m decl like f in sg* (*na ślubie*) best man

**druży|na** (**-ny, -ny**) (*dat sg* **-nie**) *f* (*Sport*) team; (*Wojsk*) squad; **~ harcerska** scouting troop
**drużyno|wy** (**-wego, -wi**) *m decl like adj* scoutmaster
**drwal** (**-a, -e**) (*gen pl* **-i**) *m* woodcutter, lumberjack (US)
**dr|wić** (**-wię, -wisz**) (*imp* **-wij**, *perf* **za-**) *vi*: **~ (z** *+gen*) (*wyśmiewać się*) to mock (at); (*lekceważyć*) to sneer (at), to jeer (at)
**drwi|na** (**-ny, -ny**) (*dat sg* **-nie**) *f* derision, mockery
**drybl|ować** (**-uję, -ujesz**) *vt* (*Sport*) to dribble
**dry|f** (**-fu**) (*loc sg* **-fie**) *m* (*Geol, Żegl*) drift
**dryf|ować** (**-uję, -ujesz**) (*perf* **z-**) *vi* (*Żegl*) to drift
**dry|g** (**-gu**) (*instr sg* **-giem**) *m*: **mieć ~ do czegoś** to have a knack for sth
**dryl** (**-u**) *m* drill
**dryl|ować** (**-uję, -ujesz**) *vt* (*owoce*) to stone (*fruit*)
**drzaz|ga** (**-gi, -gi**) (*dat sg* **-dze**) *f* splinter
**drzeć** (**drę, drzesz**) (*imp* **drzyj**, *pt* **darł**) *vt* (*rozrywać*) (*perf* **po-**) to tear, to rip; (*zużywać: ubranie, buty*) (*perf* **ze-**) to wear out; **~ coś na kawałki/strzępy** to tear sth to pieces/shreds; **~ gardło** (*pot*) to holler (*pot*); **~ z kimś koty** to be at loggerheads with sb; **drzeć się** *vr* (*rozdzierać się*) (*perf* **po-**) to tear, to rip; (*zużywać się*) (*perf* **ze-**) to wear out; (*wrzeszczeć: pot*) to bawl (*pot*)
**drze|mać** (**-mię, -miesz**) *vi* to doze; (*przen: nie ujawniać się*) to lurk
**drzem|ka** (**-ki, -ki**) (*dat sg* **-ce**, *gen pl* **-ek**) *f* nap; **uciąć** (*perf*) **sobie drzemkę** (*pot*) to have a nap
**drzewc|e** (**-a, -e**) *nt* (*sztandaru*) staff; (*włóczni*) shaft
**drzew|ko** (**-ka, -ka**) (*instr sg* **-kiem**, *gen pl* **-ek**) *nt dimin od* **drzewo**; **~ wigilijne** Christmas tree
**drzewny** *adj* wood *attr*; **węgiel ~** charcoal
**drze|wo** (**-wa**) (*loc sg* **-wie**) *nt* (*roślina*) (*nom pl* **-wa**) tree; (*budulec*) timber, wood; (*opał*) wood; **~ genealogiczne** family tree
**drzewory|t** (**-tu, -ty**) (*loc sg* **-cie**) *m* woodcut
**drzwi** (**-**) *pl* door; **~ obrotowe/rozsuwane** a revolving/sliding door; **~ wejściowe/kuchenne** the main/back door; **wyrzucać** (**wyrzucić** *perf*) **kogoś za ~** to throw sb out; **przy ~ach otwartych/zamkniętych** in open court/in camera; **pokazać** *lub* **wskazać** (*perf*) **komuś ~** to show sb the door; **~ stoją przed kimś otworem** the door is open to sb; **~ się u nich nie zamykają** (*przen*) they keep an open house
**drzwicz|ki** (**-ek**) *pl dimin od* **drzwi** door

**drżący** *adj* shaking, trembling; **~m głosem** shakily
**drż|eć** (**-ę, -ysz**) (*imp* **-yj**) *vi* to tremble, to shake; **~ ze strachu/zimna/złości** to shudder with fear/cold/anger; **drżę na samą myśl o tym** I shudder to think of it
**dubbin|g** (**-gi**) (*instr sg* **-giem**) *m* dubbing
**dubeltów|ka** (**-ki, -ki**) (*dat sg* **-ce**, *gen pl* **-ek**) *f* double-barrelled gun (*Brit*), double-barreled gun (*US*)
**duble|r** (**-ra, -rzy**) (*loc sg* **-rze**) *m* (*Film: kaskader*) (stunt) double; (*: w scenach nie kaskaderskich*) body double; (*Teatr*) understudy
**dubl|ować** (**-uję, -ujesz**) *vt* (*Film*) to double; (*Teatr*) to understudy; (*Sport*) (*perf* **z-**) to lap
**duch** (**-a**) *m* spirit; (*zjawa*) (*nom pl* **-y**) ghost; **w ~u** inwardly; **ani żywego ~a** not a living soul; **~ czasów** the spirit of the times; **D~ Święty** (*Rel*) Holy Spirit *lub* Ghost; **wyzionąć** (*perf*) **~a** to give up the ghost; **iść z ~em czasu** to keep up with the times; **zły ~** jinx, gremlin; (*osoba*) evil genius; **upadać na ~u** to lose heart; **podnosić** (**podnieść** *perf*) **kogoś na ~u** to cheer sb up, to raise sb's spirit
**duchowieńst|wo** (**-wa**) (*loc sg* **-wie**) *nt* the clergy
**duchowny** *adj* (*stan, osoba*) clerical ▷ *m decl like adj* minister
**duchowy** *adj* spiritual; **pociecha duchowa** spiritual comfort; **przywódca ~** spiritual leader
**dud|ek** (**-ka, -ki**) (*instr sg* **-kiem**) *m* hoopoe (*bird*); **wystrychnąć** (*perf*) **kogoś na dudka** to make a fool of sb
**dud|nić** (**-nię, -nisz**) (*imp* **-nij**) *vi* to rumble
**dud|y** (**-**) *pl* (*Muz*) bagpipes *pl*
**due|t** (**-tu, -ty**) (*loc sg* **-cie**) *m* (*Muz: utwór*) duet; (*zespół*) duo
**dul|ka** (**-ki, -ki**) (*dat sg* **-ce**, *gen pl* **-ek**) *f* rowlock (*Brit*), oarlock (*US*)
**du|ma** (**-my**) (*dat sg* **-mie**) *f* pride
**dum|ać** (**-am, -asz**) *vi* to muse
**dumny** *adj*: **~ (z** *+gen*) proud (of); **~ jak paw** (as) proud as a peacock
**Dunaj** (**-u**) *m* the Danube
**Dun|ka** (**-ki, -ki**) (*dat sg* **-ce**, *gen pl* **-ek**) *f* Dane
**Dunkier|ka** (**-ki**) (*dat sg* **-ce**) *f* Dunkirk
**Duńczy|k** (**-ka, -cy**) (*instr sg* **-kiem**) *m* Dane
**duński** *adj* Danish
**du|pa** (**-py, -py**) (*dat sg* **-pie**) *f* (*pot!: pośladki*) arse (*Brit*) (*pot!*), ass (*US*) (*pot!*); (*pot!: oferma*) arsehole (*Brit*) (*pot!*), asshole (*US*) (*pot!*)
**duplika|t** (**-tu, -ty**) (*loc sg* **-cie**) *m* duplicate
**du|r**[1] (**-ru, -ry**) (*loc sg* **-rze**) *m* (*Med*): **dur brzuszny** typhoid (fever)
**dur**[2] *inv* (*Muz*) major; **C-dur** C major

**dur|eń** (**-nia, -nie**) (*gen pl* **-niów** *lub* **-ni**) *m* (*pot!*) idiot (*pot!*); **robić z kogoś durnia** to make a fool of sb

**durny** *adj* (*pot: głupi*) dumb (*pot*)

**durszla|k** (**-ka, -ki**) (*instr sg* **-kiem**) *m* strainer

**durz|yć się (-ę, -ysz)** *vr*: **durzyć się w kimś** to be infatuated with sb

**dusiciel** (**-a, -e**) (*gen pl* **-i**) *m* (*człowiek*) strangler; (*wąż*) constrictor

**du|sić (-szę, -sisz)** (*imp* **-ś**) *vt* (*ściskać za gardło*) (*perf* **u-**) to strangle; (*o gazie, dymie*) to choke; (*ściskać*) (*perf* **z-**) to squeeze; (*płacz, żal, tęsknotę*) (*perf* **z-**) to suppress; (*mięso, warzywa*) (*perf* **u-**) to stew; **dusić się** *vr* (*nie móc oddychać*) to suffocate; (*o mięsie, warzywach*) to stew

**dusigrosz** (**-a, -e**) (*gen pl* **-y**) *m* (*pot*) penny-pincher (*pot*)

**dusz|a** (**-y, -e**) *f* soul; **w (głębi) duszy** deep down; **z całej duszy** with all one's heart; **ani żywej duszy** not a living soul; **duszą i ciałem** body and soul; **ile ~ zapragnie** to one's heart content; **być duszą towarzystwa** to be the life and soul of a party; **mieć duszę na ramieniu** to have one's heart in one's mouth; **jest mu ciężko/lekko na duszy** he has a heavy/light heart; **bratnia ~** kindred spirit

**dusz|ek** (**-ka, -ki**) (*instr sg* **-kiem**) *m* elf

**duszkiem** *adv*: **wypić** (*perf*) **coś ~** to drink sth in *lub* at one gulp

**dusznic|a** (**-y**) *f*: **~ bolesna** (*Med*) angina pectoris

**duszno** *adv*: **jest ~** it's stuffy; **jest mi ~** I can't breathe

**dusznoś|ć** (**-ci, -ci**) *f* shortness of breath; **mieć duszności** to be short of breath

**duszny** *adj* (*powietrze, dzień*) stuffy; (*zapach*) sickly

**duszony** *adj* (*mięso, warzywa*) stewed

**duszpasterst|wo** (**-wa**) (*loc sg* **-wie**) *nt* priesthood

**duszpasterz** (**-a, -e**) (*gen pl* **-y**) *m* priest

**dużo** (*comp* **więcej**) *adv* (*ludzi, jabłek*) many, a lot of; (*mleka, pieniędzy*) much, a lot of; (*bez rzeczownika*) a lot; **za ~** too many/much; **dość ~** quite a lot (of); **~ więcej/mniej** far more/less, a lot more/less; **~ czytam** I read a lot

**duży** (*comp* **większy**) *adj* (*znacznych rozmiarów*) big, large; (*wybitny*) great; (*dorosły*) big; **duże litery** capital letters; **~ palec** (*u nogi*) big toe; (*u ręki*) thumb; **duże pieniądze** big money; **duża gorączka** high fever

**DVD** *nt inv* DVD; **płyta DVD** DVD disc; **odtwarzacz DVD** DVD player

**dwa** *num* two; **dwa koty/obrazy/jabłka** two cats/pictures/apples; **dwa razy** twice; **co dwa dni/miesiące/lata** every other day/month/year; **(gra w) dwa ognie** British bulldog (*Brit*), prison dodge ball (*US*); **w dwóch słowach** in a word, in short *lub* brief; **dwa kroki stąd** round the corner; **bez dwóch zdań** no doubt about it

**dwadzieścia** *num* twenty

**dwaj** *num* two; **idą ~ mężczyźni** *lub* **idzie dwóch mężczyzn** two men are coming

**dwanaście** (*jak*: **jedenaście**) *num* twelve

**dwie** *num* two; **~ kobiety/książki/owce** two women/books/sheep

**dwieście** (*jak*: **jedenaście**) *num* two hundred

**dw|oić się (-oję, -oisz)** (*imp* **-ój**, *perf* **z-**) *vr*: **dwoić się i troić** to go out of one's way

**dwojacz|ki** (**-ków**) *pl* twins *pl*

**dwojaki** *adj* twofold

**dwoje** *num* two; **~ ludzi/dzieci/drzwi** two people/children/doors; **jedno z dwojga** one or the other; **z dwojga złego** of (the) two evils

**dworcowy** *adj* station *attr*; **poczekalnia dworcowa** waiting-room

**dwor|ek** (**-ku, -ki**) (*instr sg* **-kiem**) *m* country manor

**dworu** *itd. n patrz* **dwór**

**dworza|nin** (**-nina, -nie**) (*loc sg* **-ninie**, *gen pl* **-n**) *m* courtier

**dwo|rzec** (**-rca, -rce**) *m*: **~ kolejowy** railway (*Brit*) *lub* railroad (*US*) station; **~ autobusowy** bus station; **~ lotniczy** airport

**dwóch** *num patrz* **dwa, dwaj, dwie**

**dwój|ka** (**-ki, -ki**) (*dat sg* **-ce**, *gen pl* **-ek**) *f* two; (*para*) twosome; **~mi** two by two

**dwójkowy** *adj* (*Mat*) binary

**dwójnasób** *adv*: **w ~** doubly; **powiększyć w ~** to double

**dwóm** *num patrz* **dwa, dwaj, dwie**

**dw|ór** (**-oru, -ory**) (*loc sg* **-orze**) *m* (*królewski*) court; (*ziemiański*) manor; **bawić się na dworze** to play outside; **wyjść na ~** to go out

**dwu** *num patrz* **dwa, dwaj, dwie**

**dwub|ój** (**-oju**) *m* biathlon; (*też*: **dwubój klasyczny**) Nordic combined

**dwucyfrowy** *adj* two-digit *attr*

**dwuczęściowy** *adj* (*kostium, suknia*) two-piece *attr*; (*film*) in two parts

**dwudniowy** *adj* two-day *attr*

**dwudrzwiowy** *adj* two-door *attr*

**dwudziest|ka** (**-ki, -ki**) (*dat sg* **-ce**, *gen pl* **-ek**) *f* twenty; (*opakowanie zawierające 20 sztuk*) twenty-pack

**dwudziestole|cie** (**-cia, -cia**) (*gen pl* **-ci**) *nt* (*okres*) two decades; (*jubileusz*) twentieth anniversary

**dwudziestoletni** *adj* (*okres*) twenty-year *attr*; (*osoba*) twenty-year-old *attr*

**dwudziestowieczny** *adj* twentieth-century *attr*
**dwudziestu** *itd. num patrz* **dwadzieścia**
**dwudziesty** *num* twentieth; ~ **pierwszy** twenty-first
**dwugodzinny** *adj* two-hour *attr*
**dwujęzyczny** *adj* bilingual
**dwukasetowy** *adj*: **magnetofon** ~ twin-tape player *lub* deck
**dwukierunkowy** *adj* (*ruch*) two-way
**dwukrop|ek** (**-ka, -ki**) (*instr sg* **-kiem**) *m* colon
**dwukrotnie** *adv* twice; ~ **większy** twice as big
**dwukrotny** *adj* (*mistrz, porażka*) two-time; (*wzrost*) double, twofold
**dwuletni** *adj* (*okres*) two-year *attr*; (*dziecko*) two-year-old *attr*; **roślina ~a** biennial (plant)
**dwulicowoś|ć** (**-ci**) *f* duplicity
**dwulicowy** *adj* hypocritical, duplicitous
**dwumia|n** (**-nu, -ny**) (*loc sg* **-nie**) *m* (*Mat*) binomial
**dwunast|ka** (**-ki, -ki**) (*dat sg* **-ce**, *gen pl* **-ek**) *f* twelve
**dwunastnic|a** (**-y, -e**) *f* (*Med*) duodenum
**dwunastoletni** *adj* (*rzecz, okres*) twelve-year *attr*; (*osoba, zwierzę*) twelve-year-old *attr*
**dwunastu** *itd. num patrz* **dwanaście**
**dwunasty** *num* twelfth; **jest dwunasta** it's twelve (o'clock); **o dwunastej** at twelve (o'clock)
**dwunożny** *adj* biped(al)
**dwuogniskowy** *adj*: **okulary dwuogniskowe** bifocals *pl*
**dwuosobowy** *adj* (*pokój, przedział, łóżko*) double; (*zespół, grupa*) two-person
**dwupartyjny** *adj* bipartisan
**dwupasmowy** *adj*: **droga dwupasmowa** dual carriageway (*Brit*), divided highway (*US*)
**dwupiętrowy** *adj* three-storey(ed) *attr* (*Brit*), three-storied *attr* (*US*)
**dwupłato|wiec** (**-wca, -wce**) *m* (*Lot*) biplane
**dwupokojowy** *adj* two-room *attr*
**dwupoziomowy** *adj*: **mieszkanie dwupoziomowe** bi-level flat (*Brit*) *lub* apartment (*US*)
**dwurzędowy** *adj* (*garnitur*) double-breasted
**dwusetny** *adj* two-hundredth
**dwustronny** *adj* (*materiał*) reversible; (*umowa*) bilateral
**dwustu** *itd. num patrz* **dwieście**
**dwusuwowy** *adj* (*silnik*) two-stroke *attr*, two-cycle *attr*
**dwutlen|ek** (**-ku, -ki**) (*instr sg* **-kiem**) *m* (*Chem*) dioxide; ~ **węgla** carbon dioxide
**dwutomowy** *adj* two-volume *attr*
**dwutorowy** *adj* double-track *attr*
**dwutygodni|k** (**-ka, -ki**) (*instr sg* **-kiem**) *m* biweekly
**dwutysięczny** *adj* two-thousandth
**dwuwarstwowy** *adj* two-ply *attr*
**dwuwiersz** (**-a, -e**) (*gen pl* **-y**) *m* couplet
**dwuwymiarowy** *adj* two-dimensional
**dwuznacznoś|ć** (**-ci**) *f* ambiguity
**dwuznaczny** *adj* ambiguous; (*komplement*) backhanded; (*uśmiech*) equivocal
**dyb|y** (**-ów**) *pl* stocks
**dy|cha** (**-chy, -chy**) (*dat sg* **-sze**) *f* (*pot*) tenner (*pot*)
**dydaktyczny** *adj* teaching *attr*
**dydakty|ka** (**-ki**) (*dat sg* **-ce**) *f* teaching
**dyfton|g** (**-gu, -gi**) (*instr sg* **-giem**) *m* diphthong
**dyg|ać (-am, -asz)** (*perf* **-nąć**) *vi* to curts(e)y
**dyg|nąć (-nę, -niesz)** (*imp* **-nij**) *vb perf od* **dygać**
**dygnitarz** (**-a, -e**) (*gen pl* **-y**) *m* dignitary
**dygo|tać (-czę, -czesz)** *vi* (*ze strachu*) to quake, to shudder; ~ **z zimna** to shiver with cold
**dygresj|a** (**-i, -e**) (*gen pl* **-i**) *f* digression
**dykcj|a** (**-i**) *f* diction
**dyk|ta** (**-ty, -ty**) (*dat sg* **-cie**) *f* plywood
**dyktafo|n** (**-nu, -ny**) (*loc sg* **-nie**) *m* Dictaphone®
**dyktan|do** (**-da, -da**) (*loc sg* **-dzie**) *nt* dictation; **pisać coś pod (czyjeś)** ~ to take dictation (from sb); **robić coś pod czyjeś** ~ to do what one is told by sb
**dyktato|r** (**-ra, -rzy**) (*loc sg* **-rze**) *m* dictator
**dyktatorski** *adj* dictatorial
**dyktatu|ra** (**-ry**) (*dat sg* **-rze**) *f* dictatorship
**dykt|ować (-uję, -ujesz)** (*perf* **po-**) *vt* to dictate; (*przen: o sercu, umyśle*) to tell
**dylema|t** (**-tu, -ty**) (*loc sg* **-cie**) *m* dilemma
**dyletancki** *adj* dilettantish, amateurish
**dyletan|t** (**-ta, -ci**) (*loc sg* **-cie**) *m* dilettante, dabbler
**dyliżan|s** (**-su, -se**) (*loc sg* **-sie**) *m* stagecoach
**dy|m** (**-mu, -my**) (*loc sg* **-mie**) *m* smoke; **pójść** (*perf*) **z dymem** to go up in smoke; **puścić** (*perf*) **coś z dymem** to burn sth
**dy|mić (-mię, -misz)** (*perf* **za-**) *vi* to be smoking; **dymić się** *vr*: **dymi się z komina** smoke is coming out of the chimney
**dymisj|a** (**-i, -e**) (*gen pl* **-i**) *f* (*zwolnienie*) dismissal; (*ustąpienie*) resignation; **podać się** (*perf*) **do dymisji** to resign; **udzielić** (*perf*) **komuś dymisji** to dismiss sb
**dymisjon|ować (-uję, -ujesz)** (*perf* **z-**) *vt* to depose
**dymny** *adj*: **zasłona dymna** smokescreen
**dynamiczny** *adj* dynamic
**dynami|ka** (**-ki**) (*dat sg* **-ce**) *f* dynamism; (Fiz) dynamics
**dynami|t** (**-tu**) (*loc sg* **-cie**) *m* dynamite

**dyna|mo** (**-ma, -ma**) (*loc sg* **-mie**) *nt* dynamo
**dynasti|a** (**-i, -e**) (*gen pl* **-i**) *f* dynasty; **~ Tudorów** the house of Tudor; **~ Ming** the Ming dynasty
**dynd|ać (-am, -asz)** (*perf* **za-**) *vi* (*pot*) to dangle
**dy|nia** (**-ni, -nie**) (*gen pl* **-ń**) *f* pumpkin
**dyplo|m** (**-mu, -my**) (*loc sg* **-mie**) *m* diploma; **~ uniwersytecki** university degree; **zdobyć** (*perf*) *lub* **uzyskać** (*perf*) **~ (z czegoś)** to obtain *lub* get a degree (in sth)
**dyplomacj|a** (**-i, -e**) (*gen pl* **-i**) *f* diplomacy; (*instytucja*) diplomatic service
**dyploma|ta** (**-ty, -ci**) (*dat sg* **-cie**) *m decl like f in sg* diplomat
**dyplomatyczny** *adj* diplomatic; **korpus ~** diplomatic corps; **stosunki dyplomatyczne** diplomatic relations; **placówka dyplomatyczna** *embassy or consulate*
**dyplomowany** *adj* (*pielęgniarka*) registered; (*księgowy*) chartered (*Brit*), certified (*US*)
**dyplomowy** *adj*: **praca dyplomowa** (*magisterska*) M.A thesis; **egzamin ~** (*magisterski*) M.A. defence; (*zawodowy*) final exam
**dyr.** *abbr* (= *dyrektor*) Mgr (= *manager*)
**dyrekcj|a** (**-i, -e**) (*gen pl* **-i**) *f* (*kierownictwo*) management; **pod dyrekcją ...** (*o orkiestrze*) conducted by ...
**dyrekto|r** (**-ra, -rzy** *lub* **-rowie**) (*loc sg* **-rze**) *m* (*przedsiębiorstwa, firmy*) manager, director; (*szkoły*) headmaster (*Brit*), principal (*US*)
**dyrektor|ka** (**-ki, -ki**) (*dat sg* **-ce**, *gen pl* **-ek**) *f* (*pot: szkoły*) headmistress (*Brit*), principal (*US*)
**dyrekty|wa** (**-wy, -wy**) (*dat sg* **-wie**) *f* directive
**dyrygen|t** (**-ta, -ci**) (*loc sg* **-cie**) *m* conductor
**dyryg|ować (-uję, -ujesz)** *vi* (*vt*): **~ (orkiestrą)** to conduct (an orchestra); **~ kimś** to order sb about *lub* around
**dyscypli|na** (**-ny, -ny**) (*dat sg* **-nie**) *f* discipline
**dyscyplinarny** *adj* disciplinary
**dys|k** (**-ku, -ki**) (*instr sg* **-kiem**) *m* (*Sport*) discus; (*Komput*) disk; (*Med*) disc (*Brit*), disk (*US*); **rzut ~iem** the discus; **twardy ~** hard disk; **stacja ~ów** disk drive
**dyskiet|ka** (**-ki, -ki**) (*dat sg* **-ce**, *gen pl* **-ek**) *f* (floppy) disk, diskette
**dyskografi|a** (**-i**) *f* recording history
**dyskontowy** *adj*: **stopa dyskontowa** discount rate; **bank ~** discount house
**dyskot|eka** (**-eki, -eki**) (*dat sg* **-ece**, *gen pl* **-ek**) *f* disco(theque)
**dyskotekowy** *adj* disco *attr*
**dyskrecj|a** (**-i**) *f* discretion
**dyskredyt|ować (-uję, -ujesz)** (*perf* **z-**) *vt* to discredit
**dyskretnie** *adv* discreetly
**dyskretny** *adj* discreet; (*światło, muzyka*) soft
**dyskryminacj|a** (**-i, -e**) (*gen pl* **-i**) *f* discrimination; **~ rasowa** racial discrimination
**dyskrymin|ować (-uję, -ujesz)** *vt* to discriminate against
**dyskusj|a** (**-i, -e**) (*gen pl* **-i**) *f* discussion; **poddawać (poddać** *perf***) coś pod dyskusję** to bring sth up for discussion; **to nie podlega dyskusji** this is indisputable
**dyskusyjny** *adj* debatable; **klub ~** debating society
**dyskutan|t** (**-ta, -ci**) (*loc sg* **-cie**) *m* debater
**dyskut|ować (-uję, -ujesz)** *vt* (*perf* **prze-**) to discuss ▷ *vi* to debate; **~ nad** *lub* **o czymś** to discuss sth
**dyskwalifikacj|a** (**-i**) *f* disqualification
**dyskwalifik|ować (-uję, -ujesz)** (*perf* **z-**) *vt* to disqualify
**dysleksj|a** (**-i**) *f* dyslexia
**dysonan|s** (**-su, -se**) (*loc sg* **-sie**) *m* discord
**dyspen|sa** (**-sy**) (*dat sg* **-sie**) *f* dispensation
**dyspon|ować (-uję, -ujesz)** (*imp* **-uj**, *perf* **za-**) *vt* (*majątkiem*) to administer; **~ gotówką** to have ready cash; **~ czasem** to have time to spare
**dyspozycj|a** (**-i, -e**) (*gen pl* **-i**) *f* order, instruction; **być do czyjejś dyspozycji** to be at sb's disposal; **mieć coś do swojej dyspozycji** to have sth at one's disposal; **wydawać (wydać** *perf***) dyspozycje** to give orders *lub* instructions
**dyspozycyjny** *adj* (*pracownik*) prepared to work flexible hours; **fundusz ~** discretional fund
**dysproporcj|a** (**-i, -e**) (*gen pl* **-i**) *f* disproportion
**dystan|s** (**-su, -se**) (*loc sg* **-sie**) *m* distance; **zachowywać (zachować** *perf***) ~** to keep o.s. at a distance; **trzymać się na ~** to keep one's distance; **trzymać kogoś na ~** to keep sb at a distance
**dystans|ować się (-uję, -ujesz)** (*perf* **z-**) *vr*: **dystansować się od** *+gen* to distance o.s. from
**dystrybucj|a** (**-i**) *f* distribution
**dystrybuto|r** (**-ra, -ry**) (*loc sg* **-rze**) *m* (*Handel*) distributor; (*paliwa*) pump; (*napojów*) dispenser
**dystyngowany** *adj* dignified, distinguished (*in appearance*)
**dystynkcj|e** (**-i**) *pl* insignia (of rank)
**dysyden|t** (**-ta, -ci**) (*loc sg* **-cie**) *m* dissident
**dysz|eć (-ę, -ysz)** *vi* (*ze zmęczenia*) to pant; (*o chorym*) to wheeze
**dysz|el** (**-la, -le**) (*gen pl* **-li**) *m* shafts *pl*
**dywa|n** (**-nu, -ny**) (*loc sg* **-nie**) *m* carpet

**dywani|k** (**-ka, -ki**) (*instr sg* **-kiem**) *m* rug, mat; (*przen*): **wzywać (wezwać** *perf***) kogoś na ~** to carpet sb (*pot*)
**dywanowy** *adj*: **wykładzina dywanowa** fitted carpet, carpeting
**dywersan|t** (**-ta, -ci**) (*loc sg* **-cie**) *m* saboteur
**dywersj|a** (**-i**) *f* sabotage
**dywiden|da** (**-dy, -dy**) (*dat sg* **-dzie**) *f* dividend
**dywizj|a** (**-i, -e**) (*gen pl* **-i**) *f* division; **generał dywizji** Major-General
**dywizjo|n** (**-nu, -ny**) (*loc sg* **-nie**) *m* (*Wojsk*) command; (*Lot*) squadron
**dyżu|r** (**-ru, -ry**) (*loc sg* **-rze**) *m* duty hours *pl*; **być na ~ze** (*o lekarzu, pielęgniarce*) to be on call; **ostry ~** *emergency service offered by a clinic*
**dyżurny** *adj*: **lekarz/oficer ~** doctor/officer on duty ▷ *m decl like adj* (*Szkol*) ≈ monitor
**dyżur|ować (-uję, -ujesz)** *vi* to be on duty
**dzba|n** (**-na, -ny**) (*loc sg* **-nie**) *m* pitcher (*Brit*), ewer
**dzban|ek** (**-ka, -ki**) (*instr sg* **-kiem**) *m* jug (*Brit*), pitcher (*US*); **~ do kawy** coffee pot; **~ do herbaty** teapot; **~ do mleka** milk jug
**dziać się (dzieje)** *vr*: **co tu się dzieje?** what's going on here?; **co się z tobą dzieje?** what's the matter with you?; **niech się dzieje co chce** come what may
**dzia|d** (**-da, -dy**) (*loc sg* **-dzie**, *voc sg* **-dzie**) *m* (*starzec*) old man; (*żebrak*) pauper; (*dziadek*) grandfather; **z ~a pra~a** for generations
**dziad|ek** (**-ka, -kowie**) (*instr sg* **-kiem**) *m* grandfather, grandpa (*pot*); (*starzec*) old man; **~ do orzechów** nutcracker(s *pl*); **dziadkowie** *pl* grandparents *pl*
**dziadost|wo** (**-wa**) (*loc sg* **-wie**) *nt* (*tandeta*) trash; (*nędza*) slum
**dziadowski** *adj* (*tandetny*) trashy; (*nędzny*) poor; **on jest rozpuszczony jak ~ bicz** (*przen*) he's a spoiled *lub* spoilt brat
**dzia|ł** (**-łu, -ły**) (*loc sg* **-le**) *m* (*gałąź*) branch; (*czasopisma*) section; (*instytucji*) department; **~ wodny** watershed
**działacz** (**-a, -e**) (*gen pl* **-y**) *m* activist; **~ związkowy** trade unionist
**dział|ać (-am, -asz)** *vt*: **~ cuda** to work *lub* do wonders *lub* miracles ▷ *vi* (*pracować*) to act; (*oddziaływać*) to have an effect; (*obowiązywać*) to operate; (*funkcjonować*) to work, to operate; **~ na własną rękę** to act on one's own; **~ w czyimś imieniu** to act for sb, to act on behalf of sb; **~ komuś na nerwy** to get on sb's nerves; **~ w dobrej wierze** to act in good faith; **~ wstecz** (*Prawo*) to retroact; **to nie działa** it isn't working; **to działa na baterie** it runs off batteries
**działalnoś|ć** (**-ci**) *f* activity; **prowadzić ~ gospodarczą** to run a business
**działa|nie** (**-nia, -nia**) (*gen pl* **-ń**) *nt* (*akcja*) action; (*funkcjonowanie*) operation, working; (*oddziaływanie*) effect; (*Mat*) operation; **działania wojenne** warfare; **~ uboczne** side effect
**dział|ka** (**-ki, -ki**) (*dat sg* **-ce**, *gen pl* **-ek**) *f* (*kawałek gruntu*) plot; (*ogródek działkowy*) allotment; **~ budowlana** building plot
**działkowy** *adj*: **ogródek ~** allotment
**dzia|ło** (**-ła, -ła**) (*loc sg* **-le**) *nt* cannon
**działowy** *adj*: **ścianka działowa** partition (*wall*)
**dziani|na** (**-ny, -ny**) (*loc sg* **-nie**) *f* knitwear
**dziarski** *adj* sprightly, spry
**dzią|sło** (**-sła, -sła**) (*loc sg* **-śle**, *gen pl* **-seł**) *nt* gum; **zapalenie dziąseł** gingivitis
**dzicz|eć (-eję, -ejesz)** (*perf* **z-**) *vi* to run wild
**dziczy|zna** (**-zny**) (*dat sg* **-źnie**) *f* game
**dzi|da** (**-dy, -dy**) (*dat sg* **-dzie**) *f* spear
**dzieci** *n patrz* **dziecko**
**dziecia|k** (**-ka, -ki**) (*instr sg* **-kiem**) *m* kid
**dziecięcy** *adj* children's *attr*, baby *attr*; (*głos*) child's *attr*
**dziecinny** *adj* (*naiwny*) childish, infantile; **pokój ~** nursery; **wózek ~** perambulator *lub* pram (*Brit*), baby carriage (*US*)
**dziecińst|wo** (**-wa**) (*loc sg* **-wie**) *nt* childhood
**dzie|cko** (**-cka, -ci**) (*instr sg* **-ckiem**, *gen pl* **-ci**) *nt* child; **dzieci** *pl* children; **dom dziecka** orphanage; **od dziecka** from *lub* since childhood; **~ z probówki** test-tube baby
**dziedzic** (**-a, -e**) *m* (*spadkobierca*) successor, heir; (*ziemianin*) squire
**dziedzict|wo** (**-wa, -wa**) (*loc sg* **-wie**) *nt* (*spadek*) inheritance; (*spuścizna*) heritage
**dziedziczeni|e** (**-a**) *nt* inheritance
**dziedzicznoś|ć** (**-ci**) *f* (*Bio*) heredity; (*tronu, urzędu*) succession
**dziedziczny** *adj* hereditary
**dziedzicz|yć (-ę, -ysz)** (*perf* **o-**) *vt* to inherit; **~ coś po kimś** to inherit sth from sb
**dziedzi|na** (**-ny, -ny**) (*dat sg* **-nie**) *f* (*nauki, literatury*) discipline, domain; (*działalności*) field
**dziedzi|niec** (**-ńca, -ńce**) *m* courtyard; (*kościoła*) churchyard
**dziej|e** (**-ów**) *pl* history; **od zarania dziejów** from the dawn of history
**dziejowy** *adj* historic
**dzieka|n** (**-na, -ni**) (*loc sg* **-nie**) *m* dean
**dziekana|t** (**-tu, -ty**) (*loc sg* **-cie**) *m* dean's office
**dzieleni|e** (**-a**) *nt* (*Mat*) division; **znak dzielenia** division sign
**dziel|ić (-ę, -isz)** (*perf* **po-**) *vt* to divide; (*rozdawać*) (*perf* **roz-**) to share out; (*różnić*) to differ; (*rozgraniczać*) to differentiate; (*korzystać*

*wspólnie)* to share; **~ coś na części/kawałki** to split sth into parts/pieces; **~ coś między** *+acc* to divide sth between *lub* among; **~ 6 przez 2** to divide six by two; **12 dzielone przez 3 równa się 4** twelve divided by three equals *lub* is four; **od świąt dzieli nas tydzień** there is a week to go to the holidays; **dzielić się** *vr* to divide; **~ się czymś z kimś** to share sth with sb; **ludzie dzielą się na dobrych i złych** there are good and bad people; **6 dzieli się przez 2** six is divisible by two

**dzielnic|a** (**-y, -e**) *f* (*część miasta*) district, quarter; (*prowincja*) province, region

**dzielnicowy** *adj* (*urząd, komisariat*) district *attr*, precinct *attr* (*US*) ▷ *m decl like adj* (*policjant*) constable

**dzielny** *adj* (*waleczny*) brave; (*zaradny*) resourceful

**dzie|ło** (**-ła, -ła**) (*loc sg* **-le**) *nt* (*praca*) work; (*utwór*) work, composition; (*wynik*) result; **~ sztuki** work of art; **brać się (wziąć się** *perf***) do dzieła** to get *lub* set to work

**dzienni cz|ek** (**-ka, -ki**) (*instr sg* **-kiem**) *m* (*pamiętnik*) diary; (*też*: **dzienniczek ucznia**) parent-teacher correspondence note-book

**dziennie** *adv* daily; **osiem godzin ~** eight hours per *lub* a day; **cztery razy ~** four times a day

**dzienni|k** (**-ka, -ki**) (*instr sg* **-kiem**) *m* (*gazeta*) daily (newspaper); (*pot: wiadomości*) daily news; (*pamiętnik*) diary; **~ lekcyjny** *lub* **klasowy** school *lub* class register; **~ okrętowy/pokładowy** log-book

**dziennikar|ka** (**-ki, -ki**) (*dat sg* **-ce**, *gen pl* **-ek**) *f* journalist

**dziennikarski** *adj* journalist *attr*

**dziennikarst|wo** (**-wa**) (*loc sg* **-wie**) *nt* journalism

**dziennikarz** (**-a, -e**) (*gen pl* **-y**) *m* journalist

**dzienny** *adj* day *attr*; (*połączenie*) daytime *attr*; (*zwierzę, ptak*) diurnal; (*przydział, utarg*) daily; (*nakład*) day's *attr*; **porządek ~** agenda; **światło dzienne** daylight; **pokój ~** living room; **rozkaz ~** order of the day; **przejść** (*perf*) **nad czymś do porządku dziennego** to pass sth off lightly, to pass over sth lightly; **ujrzeć** (*perf*) **światło dzienne** to see the light of day

**dzień** (**dnia, dni** *lub* **dnie**) *m* day; (*doba*) day and night; (*termin*) date; **~ dobry!** (*przed południem*) good morning; (*po południu*) good afternoon; **co ~** every day; **~ otwarty** open day; **~ powszedni** weekday; **~ pracy** *lub* **roboczy** weekday; **~ świąteczny** holiday; **~ wolny (od pracy)** day off; **D~ Matki** Mother's Day; **cały ~** all day (long), the whole day; **dnia** *lub* **w dniu drugiego czerwca** on the second day of June; **~ w ~** day in day out, every day; **w biały ~** in broad daylight; **w ~** *lub* **za dnia** in the daytime; **z dnia na ~** (*stopniowo*) from day to day; (*nagle*) overnight; **żyć z dnia na ~** to live from hand to mouth

**dzierża|wa** (**-wy, -wy**) (*dat sg* **-wie**) *f* lease, tenancy; **oddawać (oddać** *perf***) coś w dzierżawę** to lease sth, to rent sth; **brać (wziąć** *perf***) coś w dzierżawę** to take out a lease on sth, to rent sth

**dzierżawc|a** (**-y, -y**) *m* leaseholder, lessee

**dzierżawczy** *adj* (*Jęz*) possessive

**dzierża|wić (-wię, -wisz)** *vt* to rent

**dzierż|yć (-ę, -ysz)** *vt* (*książk*) to hold

**dziesiąt|ka** (**-ki, -ki**) (*dat sg* **-ce**, *gen pl* **-ek**) *f* ten; **trafić w dziesiątkę** to hit the bull's-eye; (*przen*) to be spot-on; **dziesiątki samochodów** dozens *lub* scores of cars

**dziesiątk|ować (-uję, -ujesz)** (*perf* **z-**) *vt* to decimate

**dziesiąty** *num decl like adj* tenth

**dziesięciob|ój** (**-oju, -oje**) (*gen pl* **-ojów**) *m* (*Sport*) decathlon

**dziesięciokrotny** *adj* tenfold, ten times *attr*

**dziesięcioleci|e** (**-a, -a**) *nt* (*okres*) decade; (*jubileusz*) tenth anniversary

**dziesięcioletni** *adj* (*dziecko, whisky*) ten-year-old; (*przerwa*) ten-year; (*praktyka*) ten years' *attr*

**dziesięcioro** (*jak*: **czworo**) *num* ten

**dziesięć** *num* ten

**dziesiętny** *adj* decimal

**dziewczęcy** *adj* girlish

**dziewcz|ęta** (**-ąt**) *pl* (*pot*) girls

**dziewczy|na** (**-ny, -ny**) (*dat sg* **-nie**) *f* (*młoda kobieta*) young woman; (*sympatia*) girlfriend

**dziewczyn|ka** (**-ki, -ki**) (*dat sg* **-ce**, *gen pl* **-ek**) *f* girl

**dziewiarst|wo** (**-wa**) (*loc sg* **-wie**) *nt* knitting

**dziewiąt|ka** (**-ki, -ki**) (*dat sg* **-ce**, *gen pl* **-ek**) *f* nine

**dziewiąty** *num decl like adj* ninth

**dziewic|a** (**-y, -e**) *f* virgin

**dziewict|wo** (**-wa**) (*loc sg* **-wie**) *nt* virginity

**dziewiczy** *adj* virgin *attr*; **błona dziewicza** hymen; **~ rejs** maiden voyage

**dziewięcioletni** *adj* (*dziecko*) nine-year-old; (*przerwa*) nine-year; (*praktyka*) nine years' *attr*

**dziewięcioro** (*jak*: **czworo**) *num* nine

**dziewięć** (*jak*: **pięć**) *num* nine

**dziewięćdziesiąt** (*jak*: **dziesięć**) *num* ninety

**dziewięćdziesiąty** *num decl like adj* ninetieth

**dziewięćset** (*jak*: **pięćset**) *num* nine hundred

**dziewięćsetny** *num decl like adj* nine hundredth

**dziewiętnast|ka** (**-ki, -ki**) (*dat sg* **-ce**, *gen pl* **-ek**) *f* nineteen

**dziewiętnasty** *num decl like adj* nineteenth; **dziewiętnasta** *f decl like adj* (*godzina*) seven (o'clock) p.m.
**dziewiętnaście** (*jak*: **jedenaście**) *num* nineteen
**dzięcio|ł** (**-ła, -ły**) (*loc sg* **-le**) *m* woodpecker
**dziękczynie|nie** (**-nia**) *nt*: **Święto Dziękczynienia** Thanksgiving (Day)
**dziękczynny** *adj* thankful
**dzięki** *prep*: **~ komuś/czemuś** thanks to sb/ sth; **~ Bogu!** thank God!; **~!** thanks!, ta! (*Brit*) (*pot*)
**dzięk|ować (-uję, -ujesz)** (*perf* **po-**) *vt*: **~ komuś (za coś)** to thank sb (for sth) ▷ *vi* to thank; **dziękuję (bardzo)!** thank you (very much)!
**dzi|k** (**-ka, -ki**) (*instr sg* **-kiem**) *m* wild boar
**dziki** *adj* wild; (*człowiek, plemię*) savage; (*okrutny*) fierce, ferocious; (*nietowarzyski*) anti-social; **~ strajk** wildcat strike; **~ lokator** squatter
**dzikoś|ć** (**-ci**) *f* wildness; (*człowieka*) savagery
**dziku|s** (**-sa, -sy**) (*loc sg* **-sie**) *m* savage, barbarian
**dzio|bać (-bię, -biesz)** (*perf* **-bnąć**) *vt* to peck; (*pot*: *jedzenie*) to pick *lub* peck at
**dziobaty** *adj* pock-marked
**dziob|nąć (-nę, -niesz)** (*imp* **-nij**) *vb perf od* **dziobać**
**dzi|ób** (**-obu, -oby**) (*loc sg* **-obie**) *m* (*ptaka*) beak, bill; (*statku*) bow; (*samolotu*) nose; (*pot*: *usta*) mouth
**dziób|ek** (**-ka, -ki**) (*instr sg* **-kiem**) *m* (*ptaka*) beak, bill; (*dzbanka, czajnika*) spout
**dzisiaj, dziś** *adv* today; (*obecnie*) nowadays, presently; **~ rano/wieczorem** this morning/ evening; **~ w nocy** tonight; **od ~** as of today, from now on; **którego ~ mamy?** what date is it today?
**dzisiejszy** *adj* today's *attr*; (*współczesny*) contemporary, present-day *attr*; **dzień ~** today; **dzisiejsza młodzież** the young people of today
**dziś** *adv* = **dzisiaj**; **po ~ dzień** up to this day; **od ~** from now on
**dziupl|a** (**-i, -e**) (*gen pl* **-i**) *f* hollow (*in a tree*)
**dziu|ra** (**-ry, -ry**) (*dat sg* **-rze**) *f* hole; (*w zębie*) cavity; (*pot*: *mała miejscowość*) hole; **wiercić komuś dziurę w brzuchu** to badger sb, to pester sb; **ona zawsze szuka dziury w całym** she's a nitpicker
**dziura|wić (-wię, -wisz)** (*perf* **prze-**) *vt* to perforate
**dziurawy** *adj* (*but, płaszcz*) full of holes; (*garnek*) leaky; (*ząb*) decayed
**dziur|ka** (**-ki, -ki**) (*dat sg* **-ce**, *gen pl* **-ek**) *f dimin od* **dziura**; **~ od guzika** buttonhole; **~ od klucza** keyhole; **mieć czegoś po dziurki w nosie** to be fed up with sth
**dziurkacz** (**-a, -e**) (*gen pl* **-y**) *m* punch
**dziurk|ować (-uję, -ujesz)** (*perf* **prze-**) *vt* to punch
**dzi|w** (**-wu, -wy**) (*loc sg* **-wie**) *m*: **aż ~ bierze, że ...** it is a wonder that ...; **nie ~, że ...** it is no wonder that ...; **dziwy** *pl* strange things
**dziwact|wo** (**-wa, -wa**) (*loc sg* **-wie**) *nt* eccentricity
**dziwaczny** *adj* (*nietypowy*) bizarre, odd; (*śmieszny*) funny
**dziwa|k** (**-ka, -cy**) (*instr sg* **-kiem**) *m* eccentric, freak
**dzi|wić (-wię, -wisz)** (*perf* **z-**) *vt* to surprise; **dziwić się** *vr* to be surprised
**dziw|ka** (**-ki, -ki**) (*dat sg* **-ce**, *gen pl* **-ek**) *f* (*pot!*) whore (*pot!*)
**dziwny** *adj* (*osobliwy*) strange, weird; (*niezrozumiały*) odd; **nic dziwnego, że ...** (it is) no wonder that ...
**dzi|wo** (**-wa, -wa**) (*loc sg* **-wie**) *nt*: **o ~!** fancy that!, would you believe it!
**dziwolą|g** (**-ga, -gi**) (*instr sg* **-giem**) *m* freak
**dzwo|n** (**-nu, -ny**) (*loc sg* **-nie**) *m* bell; (*dzwonienie*) ringing; **dzwony** *pl* (*spodnie*) bell-bottoms *pl*
**dzwon|ek** (**-ka, -ki**) (*instr sg* **-kiem**) *m* (*urządzenie*) bell; (*Tel*) ringtone; (*dzwonienie*) ringing; (*Bot*) bluebell; **~ do drzwi/roweru** door/bicycle bell; **~ do telefonu/komórki** ringtone for phone/mobile; **ostatni ~** the eleventh hour
**dzwo|nić (-nię, -nisz)** (*imp* **-ń**, *perf* **za-**) *vi* to ring the bell; (*kluczami*) to jangle, to clink; (*szklankami*) to clink; (*pot*: *telefonować*) to call, to ring (up); **~ do kogoś** to call sb, to ring sb (up); **dzwoniła zębami** (*przen*) her teeth were chattering; **dzwoni mi w uszach** my ears are ringing
**dzwon|ko** (**-ka, -ka**) (*instr sg* **-kiem**) *nt* slice (*of fish*)
**dzwonnic|a** (**-y, -e**) *f* belfry
**dzwonni|k** (**-ka, -cy**) (*instr sg* **-kiem**) *m* bell-ringer
**dźg|ać (-am, -asz)** (*perf* **-nąć**) *vt* (*łokciem*) to jab; (*ostrym narzędziem*) to pierce
**dźg|nąć (-nę, -niesz)** (*imp* **-nij**) *vb perf od* **dźgać**
**dźwięcz|eć (-y)** *vi* to ring
**dźwięczny** *adj* (*głos*) resonant; (*Jęz*) voiced
**dźwię|k** (**-ku, -ki**) (*instr sg* **-kiem**) *m* sound; (*Muz*) tone
**dźwiękonaśladowczy** *adj* onomatopoeic
**dźwiękoszczelny** *adj* soundproof
**dźwiękowy** *adj* sound *attr*; **ścieżka dźwiękowa** soundtrack; **efekty dźwiękowe** sound effects

**dźwi|g** (**-gu, -gi**) (*instr sg* **-giem**) *m* (*Tech*: *żuraw*) crane; (*winda*) lift (*Brit*), elevator (*US*)
**dźwig|ać** (**-am, -asz**) *vt* (*podnosić*) (*perf* **-nąć**) to lift; (*przenosić*) to carry
**dźwiga|r** (**-ra, -ry**) (*loc sg* **-rze**) *m* (*Tech*) (supporting) beam; (*stalowy*) girder
**dźwig|nąć** (**-nę, -niesz**) (*imp* **-nij**) *vb perf od* **dźwigać**; **dźwignąć się** *vr* (*podnieść się*) to lift o.s. up
**dźwig|nia** (**-ni, -nie**) (*gen pl* **-ni**) *f* lever; (*przen*) mainspring; **~ zmiany biegów** gear lever
**dźwigo|wy** (**-wego, -wi**) *m decl like adj* crane operator
**Dżakar|ta** (**-ty**) (*dat sg* **-cie**) *f* Djakarta
**dżdżownic|a** (**-y, -e**) *f* earthworm
**dżdżysty** *adj* rainy
**dże|m** (**-mu, -my**) (*loc sg* **-mie**) *m* jam
**dżentelme|n** (**-na, -ni**) (*loc sg* **-nie**) *m* gentleman
**dżentelmeński** *adj* gentlemanly; **umowa dżentelmeńska** gentleman's *lub* gentlemen's agreement
**dżersej** (**-u, -e**) (*gen pl* **-ów**) *m* jersey (*fabric*)
**dże|z** (**-zu**) (*loc sg* **-zie**) *m* = **jazz**
**dżin|s** (**-su**) (*loc sg* **-sie**) *m* (*materiał*) denim; **dżinsy** *pl* denims *pl*, jeans *pl*
**dżinsowy** *adj* denim *attr*, jeans *attr*
**dżokej** (**-a, -e**) (*gen pl* **-ów**) *m* jockey
**dżoke|r** (**-ra, -ry**) (*loc sg* **-rze**) *m* (*Karty*) joker
**dżudo** *nt inv* judo
**dżu|ma** (**-my**) (*dat sg* **-mie**) *f* plague
**dżungl|a** (**-i, -e**) (*gen pl* **-i**) *f* jungle

# Ee

**E, e** *nt inv (litera)* E, e; **E jak Ewa** ≈ E for Edward, ≈ E for Easy (*US*); **E-dur** E major; **e-moll** E minor

**ech|o** (**-a, -a**) *nt* echo; (*oddźwięk*) response; **odbijać się (odbić się** *perf*) **(głośnym) echem** to have (far-reaching) repercussions; **pozostawać (pozostać** *perf*) **bez echa** to meet with no response

**ecu** *nt inv (jednostka monetarna)* ECU

**edamski** *adj*: **ser ~** Edam (cheese)

**edukacj|a** (**-i**) *f* education

**edukacyjny** *adj* educational

**edycj|a** (**-i, -e**) (*gen pl* **-i**) *f* edition

**edyk|t** (**-tu, -ty**) (*loc sg* **-cie**) *m* edict

**Edynbur|g** (**-ga**) (*instr sg* **-giem**) *m* Edinburgh

**edyto|r** (**-ra**) (*loc sg* **-rze**) *m* (*redaktor*) (*nom pl* **-rzy**) editor; (*Komput*: *też*: **edytor tekstu**) (*nom pl* **-ry**) word processor

**edytorski** *adj* editorial; **szata edytorska** layout

**edyt|ować (-uję, -ujesz)** *vt* to edit; (*przeprowadzać korektę*) to copy-edit, to subedit (*Brit*)

**EEG** *abbr (= elektroencefalogram)* EEG

**efekciarski** *adj* (*chwyt*) flashy; (*gest*) grandiose; (*zachowanie*) show-offish; (*zwrot*) fancy

**efekciarz** (**-a, -e**) (*gen pl* **-y**) *m* show-off

**efek|t** (**-tu, -ty**) (*loc sg* **-cie**) *m* (*rezultat*) effect; (*wrażenie*) impression, effect; **~ cieplarniany** greenhouse effect; **~y specjalne** (*Film*) special effects

**efektownie** *adv* flashily, showily

**efektownoś|ć** (**-ci**) *f* flashiness, showiness

**efektowny** *adj* (*wygląd, strój*) showy; (*kobieta*) glamorous; (*gest*) show-offish

**efektywnoś|ć** (**-ci**) *f* efficiency

**efektywny** *adj* effective, efficient

**efemeryczny** *adj* ephemeral, transitory

**egalitarny** *adj* egalitarian

**egalitaryz|m** (**-mu**) (*loc sg* **-mie**) *m* egalitarianism

**egi|da** (**-dy**) (*dat sg* **-dzie**) *f*: **pod egidą kogoś/czegoś** under the aegis of sb/sth

**Egipcja|nin** (**-nina, -nie**) (*loc sg* **-ninie**, *gen pl* **-n**) *m* Egyptian

**Egipcjan|ka** (**-ki, -ki**) (*dat sg* **-ce**, *gen pl* **-ek**) *f* Egyptian

**egipski** *adj* Egyptian; **~e ciemności** (*przen*) Cimmerian darkness

**Egip|t** (**-tu**) (*loc sg* **-cie**) *m* Egypt

**egocentryczny** *adj* egocentric, self-centred

**egocentry|k** (**-ka, -cy**) (*instr sg* **-kiem**) *m* egocentric

**egoi|sta** (**-sty, -ści**) (*dat sg* **-ście**) *m decl like f in sg* egoist, egotist

**egoist|ka** (**-ki, -ki**) (*dat sg* **-ce**, *gen pl* **-ek**) *f* egoist, egotist

**egoistyczny** *adj* egoistic, selfish

**egoiz|m** (**-mu**) (*loc sg* **-mie**) *m* selfishness, egoism

**egz.** *abbr (= egzemplarz)* copy

**egzaltowany** *adj* pretentious, condescending

**egzami|n** (**-nu, -ny**) (*loc sg* **-nie**) *m* examination, exam (*pot*); **~ ustny/pisemny** oral/written exam(ination); **~ dojrzałości** *secondary school leaving exam*, ≈ A-levels *pl* (*Brit*); **~ wstępny/końcowy** entrance/final exam(ination); **~ poprawkowy** repeat *lub* resit examination; **~ na prawo jazdy** driving test; **~ z matematyki** an exam in mathematics; **zdawać** (*imperf*) **~** to take an exam(ination), to sit an examination (*Brit*); **zdać** (*perf*) **~** to pass an exam(ination); **nie zdać** (*perf*) **~u** to fail an exam(ination)

**egzaminacyjny** *adj* examination *attr*

**egzaminato|r** (**-ra, -rzy**) (*loc sg* **-rze**) *m* examiner

**egzamin|ować (-uję, -ujesz)** (*perf* **prze-**) *vt*: **~ kogoś (z czegoś)** to examine *lub* test sb (in sth)

**egzekucj|a** (**-i, -e**) (*gen pl* **-i**) *f* execution

**egzekucyjny** *adj*: **pluton ~** firing squad

**egzekw|ować (-uję, -ujesz)** (*perf* **wy-**) *vt* (*prawo, przepisy*) to enforce; (*podatki, zobowiązania*) to exact

**egze|ma** (**-my**) (*dat sg* **-mie**) *f* (*Med*) eczema

**egzemplarz** (**-a, -e**) (*gen pl* **-y**) *m* (*książki, pisma*) copy; (*okaz*) specimen; **w dwóch/trzech ~ach** in duplicate/triplicate

**egzorcy|sta** (**-sty, -ści**) (*dat sg* **-ście**) *m decl like f in sg* exorcist
**egzorcyz|m** (**-mu, -my**) (*loc sg* **-mie**) *m* exorcism
**egzotyczny** *adj* (*kraj, roślina*) exotic; (*uroda, zainteresowania*) rare, singular
**egzoty|ka** (**-ka**) (*dat sg* **-ce**) *f* exotism; (*przedmioty egzotyczne*) exotica *pl*
**egzystencj|a** (**-i, -e**) (*gen pl* **-i**) *f* existence
**egzystencjaliz|m** (**-mu**) (*loc sg* **-mie**) *m* existentialism
**egzyst|ować (-uję, -ujesz)** *vi* to subsist, to make (both) ends meet
**EKG, ekg** *abbr* (*= elektrokardiogram*) ECG
**ekier|ka** (**-ki, -ki**) (*dat sg* **-ce**, *gen pl* **-ek**) *f* set square
**eki|pa** (**-py, -py**) (*dat sg* **-pie**) *f* (*sportowców, naukowców*) team; (*ratowników, poszukiwaczy*) party; (*robotników*) (work) gang
**eklektyczny** *adj* eclectic
**ekle|r** (**-ra, -ry**) (*loc sg* **-rze**) *m* (*zamek błyskawiczny*) zip (fastener) (*Brit*), zipper (*US*); (*ciastko*) éclair
**ekolo|g** (**-ga, -dzy** *lub* **-gowie**) (*instr sg* **-giem**) *m* (*specjalista*) ecologist; (*pot: orędownik*) conservationist, environmentalist
**ekologi|a** (**-i**) *f* ecology, environmentalism
**ekologiczny** *adj* (*badania, warunki*) ecological; (*samochód, technologia*) environmentally friendly, green (*pot*)
**ekonomi|a** (**-i**) *f* (*nauka*) economics; (*gospodarka*) economy
**ekonomiczny** *adj* (*kryzys, polityka*) economic; (*samochód*) economical
**ekonomi|ka** (**-ki**) (*dat sg* **-ce**) *f* (*nauka*) economics
**ekonomi|sta** (**-sty, -ści**) (*dat sg* **-ście**) *m decl like f in sg* economist
**ekosyste|m** (**-mu, -my**) (*loc sg* **-mie**) *m* ecosystem
**ekra|n** (**-nu, -ny**) (*loc sg* **-nie**) *m* screen; **mały** *lub* **szklany ~** (*telewizja*) the small screen; **srebrny ~** the big *lub* silver screen; **wchodzić (wejść** *perf*) **na ~y** to be released *lub* screened
**ekranizacj|a** (**-i, -e**) (*gen pl* **-i**) *f* (*filmowanie*) filming; (*wersja filmowa*) screen version
**eks...** *pref* ex-
**ekscelencj|a** (**-i, -e**) (*gen pl* **-i**) *m decl like f*; **Wasza/Jego/Jej E~** Your/His/Her Excellency
**ekscentrycznoś|ć** (**-ci, -ci**) (*gen pl* **-ci**) *f* eccentricity
**ekscentryczny** *adj* eccentric
**ekscentry|k** (**-ka, -cy**) (*instr sg* **-kiem**) *m* eccentric
**eksces|y** (**-ów**) *pl* (*wybryki*) excesses; (*zamieszki*) riots, disturbances
**ekscyt|ować (-uję, -ujesz)** (*perf* **pod-**) *vt* to excite, to thrill; **ekscytować się** *vr*: **~ się (czymś)** to be excited (by sth), to rave (about sth)
**ekscytujący** *adj* thrilling, exciting
**ekshibicjoni|sta** (**-sty, -ści**) (*dat sg* **-ście**) *m decl like f in sg* exhibitionist
**ekshibicjoniz|m** (**-mu**) (*loc sg* **-mie**) *m* exhibitionism
**ekshumacj|a** (**-i, -e**) (*gen pl* **-i**) *f* exhumation
**ekskluzywny** *adj* exclusive
**ekskomuni|ka** (**-ki, -ki**) (*dat sg* **-ce**) *f* (*Rel*) excommunication
**ekskrement|y** (**-ów**) *pl* excrement
**ekslibri|s** (**-su, -sy**) (*loc sg* **-sie**) *m* book-plate, ex libris
**eksmisj|a** (**-i, -e**) (*gen pl* **-i**) *f* eviction; **nakaz eksmisji** eviction notice
**eksmit|ować (-uję, -ujesz)** (*perf* **wy-**) *vt* to evict
**ekspansj|a** (**-i**) *f* expansion
**ekspansywny** *adj* (*polityka*) expansionist; (*człowiek*) pushy
**ekspedien|t** (**-ta, -ci**) (*loc sg* **-cie**) *m* shop assistant, salesclerk (*US*)
**ekspedient|ka** (**-ki, -ki**) (*dat sg* **-ce**, *gen pl* **-ek**) *f* shop assistant, salesclerk (*US*)
**ekspedi|ować (-uję, -ujesz)** (*perf* **wy-**) *vt* to dispatch, to ship
**ekspedycj|a** (**-i, -e**) (*gen pl* **-i**) *f* (*wyprawa*) expedition; (*towaru, bagażu*) shipment; (*dział instytucji*) dispatch (department)
**eksper|t** (**-ta, -ci**) (*loc sg* **-cie**) *m* expert, authority
**eksperty|za** (**-zy, -zy**) (*dat sg* **-zie**) *f* (*lekarska*) medical assessment; (*prawna*) legal evaluation
**eksperymen|t** (**-tu, -ty**) (*loc sg* **-cie**) *m* experiment; **przeprowadzać ~y na** *+loc* to carry out experiments on
**eksperymentalny** *adj* experimental
**eksperyment|ować (-uję, -ujesz)** *vi*: **~ (na** *+instr*) to experiment (on)
**eksploatacj|a** (**-i**) *f* (*człowieka, bogactw*) exploitation; (*maszyny, kopalni*) utilization; (*samochodu*) operation
**eksploat|ować (-uję, -ujesz)** (*perf* **wy-**) *vt* (*wykorzystywać: złoża, robotników*) to exploit; (*maszynę*) to utilize; (*samochód*) to operate
**eksplod|ować (-uję, -ujesz)** *vi* to explode
**eksploracj|a** (**-i, -e**) (*gen pl* **-i**) *f* (*książk*) exploration
**eksplor|ować (-uję, -ujesz)** *vt* (*książk*) to explore
**eksplozj|a** (**-i, -e**) (*gen pl* **-i**) *f* explosion; (*przen*) outburst; **~ demograficzna** population explosion

**ekspona|t** (**-tu, -ty**) (*loc sg* **-cie**) *m* exhibit
**ekspon|ować (-uję, -ujesz)** (*perf* **wy-**) *vt* (*prezentować*) to display, to exhibit; (*wysuwać na pierwszy plan*) to feature, to give prominence to
**eksponowany** *adj* (*miejsce, stanowisko*) prominent
**ekspor|t** (**-tu**) (*loc sg* **-cie**) *m* export
**eksporte|r** (**-ra, -rzy**) (*loc sg* **-rze**) *m* exporter
**eksport|ować (-uję, -ujesz)** (*perf* **wy-**) *vt* to export
**eksportowy** *adj* export *attr*
**ekspozycj|a** (**-i, -e**) *f* (*wystawa*) display, exhibition
**ekspozytu|ra** (**-ry, -ry**) (*dat sg* **-rze**) *f* branch (office)
**ekspre|s** (**-su, -sy**) (*loc sg* **-sie**) *m* (*pociąg*) express (train); (*list*) express letter; (*do kawy*) espresso coffee maker; **kawa z ~u** espresso
**ekspresj|a** (**-i**) *f* expression
**ekspresjoniz|m** (**-mu**) (*loc sg* **-mie**) *m* expressionism
**ekspresowy** *adj* (*przesyłka, pociąg*) express *attr*; **herbata ekspresowa** tea bags *pl*
**ekstatyczny** *adj* ecstatic
**eksta|za** (**-zy**) (*dat sg* **-zie**) *f* ecstasy; **wpadać (wpaść** *perf*) **w ekstazę** to become ecstatic
**ekstensywny** *adj* extensive
**eksterminacj|a** (**-i, -e**) (*gen pl* **-i**) *f* extermination
**eksternistyczny** *adj* (*studia*) extramural; **egzamin ~** *an exam taken without attending a course*
**ekstra** *adv* (*dodatkowo*) extra, in addition; (*nadzwyczaj*) extremely ▷ *adj* (*pot: nadzwyczajny*) super
**ekstradycj|a** (**-i, -e**) (*gen pl* **-i**) *f* (*Prawo*) extradition
**ekstrakla|sa** (**-sy, -sy**) (*dat sg* **-sie**) *f* (*Sport*) Premier League
**ekstrak|t** (**-tu, -ty**) (*loc sg* **-cie**) *m* extract
**ekstrawagancj|a** (**-i, -e**) (*gen pl* **-i**) *f* eccentricity
**ekstrawagancki** *adj* eccentric
**ekstrawerty|k** (**-ka, -cy**) (*instr sg* **-kiem**) *m* extrovert
**ekstremalny** *adj* (*sytuacja, warunki*) extreme
**ekstremi|sta** (**-sty, -ści**) (*dat sg* **-ście**) *m decl like f in sg* extremist
**ekstremistyczny** *adj* extremist
**ekumeniczny** *adj* ecumenical
**Ekwado|r** (**-ru**) (*loc sg* **-rze**) *m* Ecuador
**ekwilibrysty|ka** (**-ki**) (*dat sg* **-ce**) *f* acrobatics; (*przen*) balancing
**ekwipun|ek** (**-ku**) (*instr sg* **-kiem**) *m* gear, equipment
**ekwiwalen|t** (**-tu, -ty**) (*loc sg* **-cie**) *m* equivalent
**elastycznoś|ć** (**-ci**) *f* (*sprężystość*) elasticity; (*przen*) flexibility
**elastyczny** *adj* (*sprężysty: guma, krok*) elastic; (*przen: człowiek, natura*) flexible; **bandaż ~** elastic bandage
**elegancj|a** (**-i**) *f* elegance
**elegancki** *adj* (*człowiek*) elegant, smart (*Brit*)
**elegan|t** (**-ta, -ci**) (*loc sg* **-cie**) *m* man of fashion
**elegant|ka** (**-ki, -ki**) (*dat sg* **-ce**, *gen pl* **-ek**) *f* snappy dresser
**elek|t** (**-ta, -ci**) (*loc sg* **-cie**) *m*: **prezydent ~** the President elect
**elektora|t** (**-tu**) (*loc sg* **-cie**) *m* electorate
**elektrociepłow|nia** (**-ni, -nie**) (*gen pl* **-ni**) *f* heat and power plant
**elektro|da** (**-dy, -dy**) (*loc sg* **-dzie**) *f* electrode
**elektrokardiogra|m** (**-mu, -my**) (*loc sg* **-mie**) *m* (*Med*) electrocardiogram
**elektroli|t** (**-tu, -ty**) (*loc sg* **-cie**) *m* electrolyte
**elektroli|za** (**-zy, -za**) (*dat sg* **-zie**) *f* (*Chem*) electrolysis
**elektroluk|s** (**-su, -sy**) (*loc sg* **-sie**) *m* vacuum cleaner, hoover® (*Brit*)
**elektromagne|s** (**-su, -sy**) (*loc sg* **-sie**) *m* electromagnet
**elektromagnetyczny** *adj* electromagnetic
**elektromechani|k** (**-ka, -cy**) (*instr sg* **-kiem**) *m* electrical engineer
**elektro|n** (**-nu, -ny**) (*loc sg* **-nie**) *m* (*Fiz*) electron
**elektroniczny** *adj* electronic; (*zegarek*) digital
**elektroni|k** (**-ka, -cy**) (*instr sg* **-kiem**) *m* electronic engineer
**elektroni|ka** (**-ki**) (*dat sg* **-ce**) *f* electronics
**elektronowy** *adj* electron *attr*
**elektrotechniczny** *adj* electrotechnical
**elektrotechni|k** (**-ka, -cy**) (*instr sg* **-kiem**) *m* electrician
**elektrotechni|ka** (**-ki**) (*dat sg* **-ce**) *f* electrical engineering
**elektrow|nia** (**-ni, -nie**) (*gen pl* **-ni**) *f* power plant *lub* station; **~ atomowa** *lub* **jądrowa** nuclear power station; **~ wodna** hydroelectric power station
**elektrow|óz** (**-ozu, -ozy**) (*loc sg* **-ozie**) *m* electric locomotive *lub* engine
**elektrowstrząs|y** (**-ów**) *pl* (*Med*) electroshock therapy
**elektrycznoś|ć** (**-ci**) *f* electricity
**elektryczny** *adj* (*prąd, urządzenie, światło*) electric; (*usterka*) electrical; **krzesło elektryczne** electric chair
**elektry|k** (**-ka, -cy**) (*instr sg* **-kiem**) *m* electrician
**elektryz|ować (-uję, -ujesz)** *vt* (*perf* **na-**) to electrify; (*przen: widzów*) (*perf* **z-**) to thrill,

e

to electrify; **elektryzować się** *vr* (*o materiale*) to pick up static
**elemen|t** (**-tu, -ty**) (*loc sg* **-cie**) *m* (*część*) element, component; (*grupa ludzi*) circle; **elementy** *pl* (*podstawy*) elements
**elementarny** *adj* elementary
**elementarz** (**-a, -e**) (*gen pl* **-y**) *m* reading primer
**elewacj|a** (**-i, -e**) (*gen pl* **-i**) *f* (*Archit*) elevation
**elewato|r** (**-ra, -ry**) (*loc sg* **-rze**) *m* elevator
**eliksi|r** (**-ru, -ry**) (*loc sg* **-rze**) *m* elixir
**eliminacj|a** (**-i, -e**) (*gen pl* **-i**) *f* elimination; **eliminacje** *pl* (*Sport*) qualifying round
**eliminacyjny** *adj* qualifying
**elimin|ować (-uję, -ujesz)** (*perf* **wy-**) *vt* to eliminate
**elip|sa** (**-sy, -sy**) (*dat sg* **-sie**) *f* (*Geom*) ellipse; (*Lit, Jęz*) ellipsis
**eli|ta** (**-ty, -ty**) (*dat sg* **-cie**) *f* elite
**elitarny** *adj* elitist
**elokwencj|a** (**-i**) *f* eloquence
**elokwentny** *adj* eloquent
**elżbietański** *adj* Elizabethan
**emali|a** (**-i, -e**) (*gen pl* **-i**) *f* enamel
**emaliowany** *adj* enamelled (*Brit*), enameled (*US*)
**emancypacj|a** (**-i**) *f* emancipation; **~ kobiet** the emancipation of women
**emancyp|ować się (-uję, -ujesz)** (*perf* **wy-**) *vr* to emancipate o.s.
**eman|ować (-uję, -ujesz)** *vt* to emit ▷ *vi* to emanate
**embar|go** (**-ga**) (*instr sg* **-giem**) *nt* embargo; **nakładać (nałożyć** *perf*) **~ na** *+acc* to impose an embargo on; **znosić (znieść** *perf*) **~** to lift an embargo
**emblema|t** (**-tu, -ty**) (*loc sg* **-cie**) *m* emblem
**embrio|n** (**-nu, -ny**) (*loc sg* **-nie**) *m* embryo
**embrionalny** *adj*: **w stanie ~m** (*przen*) in embryo
**emery|t** (**-ta, -ci**) (*loc sg* **-cie**) *m* (old age) pensioner
**emerytalny** *adj* (*wiek*) pensionable; **fundusz ~** pension fund
**emeryt|ka** (**-ki, -ki**) (*dat sg* **-ce**, *gen pl* **-ek**) *f* (old age) pensioner
**emerytowany** *adj* retired
**emerytu|ra** (**-ry, -ry**) (*dat sg* **-rze**) *f* (*świadczenie*) (old age) pension; (*okres*) retirement; **być na emeryturze** to be retired; **przechodzić (przejść** *perf*) **na emeryturę** to retire; **iść (pójść** *perf*) **na wcześniejszą emeryturę** to take early retirement
**emigracj|a** (**-i, -e**) (*gen pl* **-i**) *f* emigration; **przebywają na emigracji** they have emigrated; (*z powodów politycznych*) they are in exile
**emigracyjny** *adj*: **rząd ~** government in exile; **urząd ~** emigration office
**emigran|t** (**-ta, -ci**) (*loc sg* **-cie**) *m* emigrant; (*polityczny*) émigré
**emigrant|ka** (**-ki, -ki**) (*dat sg* **-ce**, *gen pl* **-ek**) *f* emigrant; (*polityczna*) émigré
**emigr|ować (-uję, -ujesz)** (*perf* **wy-**) *vi* to emigrate
**eminencj|a** (**-i, -e**) (*gen pl* **-i**) *m decl like f*; **Eminencjo!** Your Eminence!; **Jego E~** His Eminence; **szara ~** éminence grise
**emi|r** (**-ra, -rowie**) (*loc sg* **-rze**) *m* emir
**emira|t** (**-tu, -ty**) (*loc sg* **-cie**) *m* emirate
**emisj|a** (**-i, -e**) (*gen pl* **-i**) *f* (*pieniędzy, akcji*) issue; (*zanieczyszczeń*) emission, discharge; (*TV*) screening; (*Radio*) broadcasting; (*Fiz*) emission
**emisyjny** *adj*: **bank/kurs ~** bank/rate of issue; **prospekt ~** prospectus
**emit|ować (-uję, -ujesz)** (*perf* **wy-**) *vt* (*pieniądze, akcje*) to issue; (*zanieczyszczenia*) to emit, to discharge; (*TV*) to screen; (*Radio*) to broadcast; (*Fiz*) to emit
**emocj|a** (**-i, -e**) (*gen pl* **-i**) *f* emotion; **emocje** *pl* emotions *pl*
**emocjonalny** *adj* emotional
**emocjon|ować (-uję, -ujesz)** *vt*: **~ kogoś** to excite *lub* thrill sb; **emocjonować się** *vr*: **~ się czymś** to be excited about sth
**emocjonujący** *adj* exciting
**empiryczny** *adj* empirical
**emu** *m inv* emu
**emulsj|a** (**-i, -e**) (*gen pl* **-i**) *f* (*też*: **farba emulsyjna**) emulsion (paint); **~ do opalania** suntan lotion; **~ fotograficzna** photographic emulsion
**encykli|ka** (**-ki, -ki**) (*dat sg* **-ce**) *f* encyclical
**encyklopedi|a** (**-i, -e**) (*gen pl* **-i**) *f* encyclop(a)edia; **on jest chodzącą encyklopedią** he's a walking encyclop(a)edia
**encyklopedyczny** *adj* encyclop(a)edic
**energetyczny** *adj*: **przemysł ~** power industry; **surowiec ~** source of energy; **kryzys ~** energy crisis
**energety|ka** (**-ki**) (*dat sg* **-ce**) *f* (*przemysł*) power industry; (*Fiz*) energetics
**energi|a** (**-i**) *f* energy; **~ atomowa/słoneczna** atomic/solar energy; **~ życiowa** vigour (*Brit*), vigor (*US*)
**energiczny** *adj* energetic
**energochłonny** *adj* energy-consuming
**energooszczędny** *adj* energy-saving
**enigmatyczny** *adj* (*książk*) enigmatic
**enkla|wa** (**-wy, -wy**) (*dat sg* **-wie**) *f* enclave
**entuzja|sta** (**-sty, -ści**) (*dat sg* **-ście**) *m decl like f in sg* enthusiast; **być entuzjastą futbolu** to be a soccer enthusiast

**entuzjastyczny** *adj* enthusiastic
**entuzjaz|m** (**-mu**) (*loc sg* **-mie**) *m* enthusiasm; **pełen ~u** enthusiastic; **robić coś bez ~u** to do sth half-heartedly
**entuzjazm|ować się (-uję, -ujesz)** *vr*: **entuzjazmować się czymś** to be enthusiastic about sth
**enty** *adj*: **po raz ~** for the umpteenth time
**enzy|m** (**-mu, -my**) (*loc sg* **-mie**) *m* enzyme
**epicentr|um** (**-um, -a**) (*gen pl* **-ów**) *nt inv in sg* epicentre (*Brit*), epicenter (*US*)
**epicki** *adj* epic
**epidemi|a** (**-i, -e**) (*gen pl* **-i**) *f* epidemic
**epi|ka** (**-ki**) (*dat sg* **-ce**) *f* narrative literature
**epilepsj|a** (**-i**) *f* epilepsy
**epilepty|k** (**-ka, -cy**) (*instr sg* **-kiem**) *m* epileptic
**epilo|g** (**-gu, -gi**) (*instr sg* **-giem**) *m* epilogue
**episkopa|t** (**-tu, -ty**) (*loc sg* **-cie**) *m* episcopate
**epitafi|um** (**-um, -a**) (*gen pl* **-ów**) *nt inv in sg* epitaph
**epite|t** (**-tu, -ty**) (*loc sg* **-cie**) *m* epithet; **obrzucać (obrzucić** *perf***) kogoś ~ami** to call sb names
**epizo|d** (**-du, -dy**) (*loc sg* **-dzie**) *m* episode; (*Teatr, Film*) bit part
**epizodyczny** *adj* (*zdarzenie*) episodic; (*wątek, postać*) minor; (*rola*) small
**epo|ka** (**-ki, -ki**) (*dat sg* **-ce**) *f* epoch; (*Geol*) age; **stanowić epokę** to mark an epoch; **~ brązu/żelaza** Bronze/Iron Age; **~ lodowa** *lub* **lodowcowa** Ice Age
**epokowy** *adj* epoch-making
**epolet|y** (**-ów**) *pl* epaulet(te)s *pl*
**epope|ja** (**-i, -je**) (*gen pl* **-i**) *f* epic
**era** (**ery, ery**) (*dat sg* **erze**) *f* era; **naszej ery** A.D.; **przed naszą erą** B.C.
**erekcj|a** (**-i, -e**) (*gen pl* **-i**) *f* erection
**ergonomiczny** *adj* ergonomic
**erogenny** *adj* erogenous
**erotoma|n** (**-na, -ni**) (*loc sg* **-nie**) *m* sex maniac
**erotyczny** *adj* erotic
**eroty|ka** (**-ki**) (*dat sg* **-ce**) *f* (*erotyzm*) eroticism; (*sztuka*) erotica *sg/pl*
**erotyz|m** (**-mu**) (*loc sg* **-mie**) *m* eroticism
**erozj|a** (**-i, -e**) (*gen pl* **-i**) *f* erosion
**erra|ta** (**-ty, -ty**) (*dat sg* **-cie**) *f* erratum
**erudycj|a** (**-i**) *f* erudition
**erudy|ta** (**-ty, -ci**) (*dat sg* **-cie**) *m decl like f in sg* erudite person
**erupcj|a** (**-i, -e**) (*gen pl* **-i**) *f* eruption
**es** *inv* (*Muz*) E flat
**esej** (**-u, -e**) *m* essay
**esencj|a** (**-i, -e**) (*gen pl* **-i**) *f* essence; (*herbaciana*) *strong tea brew to which fresh boiling water is added before serving*
**esesma|n** (**-na, -ni**) (*loc sg* **-nie**) *m* (*Hist*) member of the S.S.
**eskad|ra** (**-ry, -ry**) (*dat sg* **-rze**) *f* flight
**eskalacj|a** (**-i, -e**) (*gen pl* **-i**) *f* escalation
**eskapa|da** (**-dy, -dy**) (*dat sg* **-dzie**) *f* escapade
**Eskimo|s** (**-sa, -si**) (*loc sg* **-sie**) *m* Eskimo
**Eskimos|ka** (**-ki, -ki**) (*dat sg* **-ce**, *gen pl* **-ek**) *f* Eskimo
**eskor|ta** (**-ty, -ty**) (*dat sg* **-cie**) *f* escort; **pod eskortą** under escort
**eskort|ować (-uję, -ujesz)** *vi* to escort
**esperan|to** (**-ta**) (*loc sg* **-cie**) *nt* Esperanto
**estaka|da** (**-dy, -dy**) (*dat sg* **-dzie**) *f* flyover (*Brit*), overpass (*US*)
**este|ta** (**-ty, -ci**) (*dat sg* **-cie**) *m decl like f in sg* aesthete (*Brit*), esthete (*US*)
**estetyczny** *adj* (*zmysł, doznania*) aesthetic (*Brit*), esthetic (*US*); (*gustowny*) tasteful
**estety|ka** (**-ki**) (*dat sg* **-ce**) *f* (*nauka*) aesthetics (*Brit*), esthetics (*US*); (*piękno*) beauty
**Estoni|a** (**-i**) *f* Estonia
**Eston|ka** (**-ki, -ki**) (*dat sg* **-ce**, *gen pl* **-ek**) *f* Estonian
**Estończy|k** (**-ka, -cy**) (*instr sg* **-kiem**) *m* Estonian
**estoński** *adj* Estonian
**estra|da** (**-dy, -dy**) (*loc sg* **-dzie**) *f* stage; (*na wolnym powietrzu*) bandstand
**estradowy** *adj*: **występ ~** stage performance; **artysta ~** entertainer
**eta|p** (**-pu, -py**) (*loc sg* **-pie**) *m* stage
**eta|t** (**-tu, -ty**) (*loc sg* **-cie**) *m*: **(wolny) ~** (job) vacancy; **na pełen ~** full-time; **na pół ~u** part-time
**etatowy** *adj*: **pracownik ~** full-time employee
**etc.** *abbr* (= *et cetera*) etc., and so on
**ete|r** (**-ru, -ry**) (*loc sg* **-rze**) *m* ether; **na falach ~u** on the air
**eteryczny** *adj* (*olejek*) aromatic; (*wygląd, postać*) ethereal
**Etiopi|a** (**-i**) *f* Ethiopia
**etiopski** *adj* Ethiopian
**etiu|da** (**-dy, -dy**) (*dat sg* **-dzie**) *f* étude
**etniczny** *adj* ethnic
**etnograficzny** *adj* ethnographic
**etnologi|a** (**-i**) *f* ethnology
**eto|s** (**-su**) (*loc sg* **-sie**) *m* ethos
**etui** *nt inv* case
**etyczny** *adj* ethical
**ety|ka** (**-ki**) (*dat sg* **-ce**) *f* (*zbiór norm*) ethics *pl*; (*nauka*) ethics
**etykie|ta** (**-ty**) (*dat sg* **-cie**) *f* (*nalepka*) (*nom pl* **-ty**) label; (*zachowanie*) etiquette
**etykiet|ować (-uję, -ujesz)** *vt* to label
**etyli|na** (**-ny**) (*dat sg* **-nie**) *f* high-octane petrol (*Brit*), premium gasoline (*US*)

**etymologi|a** (**-i**) *f* etymology
**etymologiczny** *adj* etymological
**eucharysti|a** (**-i**) *f* the Eucharist
**eufemistyczny** *adj* euphemistic
**eufemiz|m** (**-mu, -my**) (*loc sg* **-mie**) *m* euphemism
**eufori|a** (**-i**) *f* euphoria
**eukaliptu|s** (**-sa, -sy**) (*loc sg* **-sie**) *m* eucalyptus
**eunuch** (**-a, -owie** *lub* **-y**) *m* eunuch
**Eurazj|a** (**-i**) *f* Eurasia
**euro** *nt inv* (*waluta*) Euro
**euroczе|k** (**-ku, -ki**) (*instr sg* **-kiem**) *m* Eurocheque
**eurodola|r** (**-ra, -ry**) (*loc sg* **-rze**) *m* Eurodollar
**eurokra|ta** (**-ty, -ci**) (*loc sg* **-cie**) *m decl like f in sg* Eurocrat
**Euro|pa** (**-py**) (*dat sg* **-pie**) *f* Europe
**europeiz|ować (-uję, -ujesz)** (*perf* **z-**) *vt* to Europeanize
**Europejczy|k** (**-ka, -cy**) (*instr sg* **-kiem**) *m* European
**Europej|ka** (**-ki, -ki**) (*dat sg* **-ce**, *gen pl* **-ek**) *f* European
**europejski** *adj* European
**eutanazj|a** (**-i**) *f* euthanasia
**ew.** *abbr* (= *ewentualnie*) alternatively
**ewakuacj|a** (**-i, -e**) (*gen pl* **-i**) *f* evacuation
**ewakuacyjny** *adj*: **droga ewakuacyjna** escape route; **plan** ~ evacuation plan
**ewaku|ować (-uję, -ujesz)** *vt* to evacuate; **ewakuować się** *vr* to evacuate
**ewangeli|a** (**-i, -e**) (*gen pl* **-i**) *f* Gospel; ~ **według św. Łukasza** the Gospel according to St Luke
**ewangelicki** *adj* evangelical
**ewangeliczny** *adj* evangelical
**ewenemen|t** (**-tu, -ty**) (*loc sg* **-cie**) *m* sensation
**ewentualnie** *adv* (*w razie czego*) if need be; (*albo*) alternatively
**ewentualnoś|ć** (**-ci, -ci**) (*gen pl* **-ci**) *f* eventuality
**ewentualny** *adj* possible
**EWG** *abbr* (= *Europejska Wspólnota Gospodarcza*) E.E.C.
**ewidencj|a** (**-i, -e**) (*gen pl* **-i**) *f* record
**ewidencjon|ować (-uję, -ujesz)** *vt* (*perf* **za-**) to record
**ewidentnie** *adv* evidently
**ewidentny** *adj* evident
**ewolucj|a** (**-i, -e**) (*gen pl* **-i**) *f* evolution; **teoria ewolucji** the theory of evolution; **ewolucje** *pl* (*lotnicze*) aerobatics *pl*; (*baletowe*) acrobatics *pl*
**ewolucyjny** *adj* evolutionary
**ewolu|ować (-uję, -ujesz)** *vi* to evolve
**ex aequo** *inv*: **X i Y wygrali** ~ X and Y were joint winners
**exodu|s** (**-su**) (*loc sg* **-sie**) *m* exodus

**F, f** *nt inv (litera)* F, f; **F jak Franciszek** ≈ F for Frederick (*Brit*), ≈ F for Fox (*US*); **F-dur** F major; **f-moll** F minor
**fabryczny** *adj* factory *attr*; **znak ~** trademark
**fabry|ka** (**-ki, -ki**) (*dat sg* **-ce**) *f* factory
**fabryk|ować (-uję, -ujesz)** *vt* (*dokumenty, dowody*) (*perf* **s-**) to fabricate
**fabularny** *adj*: **film ~** feature film
**fabu|ła** (**-ły, -ły**) (*dat sg* **-le**) *f* plot
**face|t** (**-ta, -ci**) (*loc sg* **-cie**) *m* (*pot*) fellow (*pot*), guy (*pot*)
**fach** (**-u, -y**) *m* trade; **kolega po ~u** professional colleague
**facho|wiec** (**-wca, -wcy**) *m* (*specjalista*) specialist, expert; (*pot: rzemieślnik*) repairman
**fachowo** *adv* professionally
**fachowy** *adj* (*czasopismo, terminologia*) specialist; (*porada*) professional, expert; (*pracownik*) skilled
**fago|t** (**-tu, -ty**) (*loc sg* **-cie**) *m* (*Muz*) bassoon
**fair** *adj inv*; **to nie jest ~** it's not fair ▷ *adv*: **postępować (postąpić** *perf***) (nie) ~** (not) to play fair
**fair-play** *adj inv*; **zasady ~** principles of fair play; **walka ~** clean fight
**fajan|s** (**-su, -se**) (*loc sg* **-sie**) *m* (*tworzywo*) faience; (*naczynia*) pottery
**fajansowy** *adj* faience *attr*
**fajerwer|ki** (**-ków**) *pl* fireworks *pl*
**faj|ka** (**-ki, -ki**) (*dat sg* **-ce**, *gen pl* **-ek**) *f* pipe; (*pot: papieros*) fag (*pot*); **~ pokoju** pipe of peace, peace pipe
**fajnie** *adv* (*pot*) great (*pot*)
**fajny** *adj* (*pot*) great (*pot*)
**fajran|t** (**-tu, -ty**) (*loc sg* **-cie**) *m* (*pot*) knock-off time (*pot*)
**fajtła|pa** (**-py, -py**) (*dat sg* **-pie**) *m/f decl like f in sg* (*pot*) butterfingers (*pot*)
**faki|r** (**-ra, -rzy** *lub* **-rowie**) (*loc sg* **-rze**) *m* fakir
**fak|s** (**-su, -sy**) (*loc sg* **-sie**) *m* (*urządzenie*) fax (machine); (*wiadomość*) fax (message)
**faks|ować (-uję, -ujesz)** (*perf* **prze-**) *vt/vi* to fax
**fak|t** (**-tu, -ty**) (*loc sg* **-cie**) *m* fact; **literatura ~u** non-fiction; **suche ~y** dry *lub* plain facts; **~, że ...** (*pot*) true enough, ...; **stać się** (*perf*) **~em** to become fact; **stawiać (postawić** *perf***) kogoś przed ~em dokonanym** (*pot*) to present sb with a fait accompli
**faktu|ra** (**-ry, -ry**) (*dat sg* **-rze**) *f* (*Handel*) invoice; (*ściany, powierzchni*) texture
**faktycznie** *adv* actually, in fact
**faktyczny** *adj* actual
**fakultatywny** *adj* optional
**fakulte|t** (**-tu, -ty**) (*loc sg* **-cie**) *m* (*Uniw: wydział*) faculty; **robić drugi ~** (*pot*) to do a second degree
**fa|la** (**-li, -le**) *f* wave; (*przen*) surge; **być na fali** (*pot*) to be on top (of the heap) (*pot*)
**falban|ka** (**-ki, -ki**) (*dat sg* **-ce**, *gen pl* **-ek**) *f* frill
**falisty** *adj* wavy; **blacha falista** corrugated iron
**Falkland|y** (**-ów**) *pl* the Falkland Islands
**falliczny** *adj* phallic
**falochro|n** (**-nu, -ny**) (*loc sg* **-nie**) *m* breakwater
**fal|ować (-uje)** *vi* to roll
**false|t** (**-tu, -ty**) (*loc sg* **-cie**) *m* falsetto
**falstar|t** (**-tu, -ty**) (*loc sg* **-cie**) *m* (*Sport*) false start
**falsyfika|t** (**-tu, -ty**) (*loc sg* **-cie**) *m* forgery
**fał|d** (**-du, -dy**) (*loc sg* **-dzie**) *m* (*Anat, Geol*) fold
**fał|da** (**-dy, -dy**) (*dat sg* **-dzie**) *f, m* fold
**fałsz** (**-u, -e**) *m* falsity, falsehood
**fałszerst|wo** (**-wa, -wa**) (*loc sg* **-wie**) *nt* forgery
**fałszerz** (**-a, -e**) (*gen pl* **-y**) *m* forger
**fałsz|ować (-uję, -ujesz)** (*perf* **s-**) *vt* (*pieniądze, obrazy*) to forge; (*dane, dokumenty*) to fabricate, to cook up (*pot*); (*przen: prawdę, fakty*) to falsify ▷ *vi* (*grać nieczysto*) to play *lub* be out of tune; (*śpiewać nieczysto*) to sing *lub* be out of tune
**fałszywie** *adv* (*nieprawdziwie*) falsely; (*obłudnie*) insincerely
**fałszywoś|ć** (**-ci**) *f* (*nieprawdziwość*) falsity; (*obłuda*) insincerity
**fałszywy** *adj* (*podrobiony*) counterfeit; (*niezgodny z prawdą*) false; (*obłudny*) insincere; (*ton, dźwięk, nuta*) off-key; (*niewłaściwy: krok, ruch*) false; **~ trop** *lub* **ślad** wrong lead *lub* track; **~ świadek** (*Prawo*) false witness
**fa|ma** (**-my**) (*dat sg* **-mie**) *f*: **~ niesie** *lub* **głosi, że ...** rumour (*Brit*)/rumor (*US*) has it that ...

**fa|n** (**-na, -ni**) (*loc sg* **-nie**) *m* (*pot*) fan
**fanaberi|e** (**-i**) *pl* whims *pl*
**fanatyczny** *adj* fanatical
**fanaty|k** (**-ka, -cy**) (*instr sg* **-kiem**) *m* fanatic
**fanatyz|m** (**-mu**) (*loc sg* **-mie**) *m* fanaticism
**fan-clu|b** (**-bu, -by**) (*loc sg* **-bie**) *m* fan club
**fanfa|ra** (**-ry, -ry**) (*dat sg* **-rze**) *f* fanfare
**fan|t** (**-tu, -ty**) (*loc sg* **-cie**) *m* (*na loterii*) prize; (*w grze towarzyskiej*) forfeit; **co z tym ~em zrobić?** what shall I do now?
**fantastyczny** *adj* fantastic; **powieść fantastyczna** a science-fiction novel
**fantasty|ka** (**-ki**) (*dat sg* **-ce**) *f* (*Sztuka*) the fantastic; ~ **naukowa** science fiction
**fantazj|a** (**-i, -e**) (*gen pl* **-i**) *f* (*wyobraźnia*) imagination; (*wymysł*) fantasy; (*Muz*) fantasia
**fantazyjny** *adj* (*wzór, kapelusz*) fancy; (*pomysł*) fanciful
**farao|n** (**-na, -nowie**) (*loc sg* **-nie**) *m* pharaoh
**far|ba** (**-by, -by**) (*dat sg* **-bie**) *f* paint; (*drukarska*) ink; (*do włosów*) tint, dye; **puszczać (puścić** *perf*) **farbę** (*pot*: *zdradzić*) to blow the whistle (*pot*), to squeal (*pot*)
**farb|ować (-uję, -ujesz)** *vt* (*odzież, włosy*: *barwić*) (*perf* **u-** *lub* **po-**) to dye ▷ *vi* (*puszczać kolor*) to bleed, to run; **u~ włosy na rudo** to dye one's hair red
**far|ma** (**-my, -my**) (*dat sg* **-mie**) *f* farm; ~ **wiatrowa** wind farm
**farmaceu|ta** (**-ty, -ci**) (*dat sg* **-cie**) *m decl like f in sg* pharmacist
**farmaceutyczny** *adj* pharmaceutical
**farmacj|a** (**-i**) *f* pharmacy
**farmakolo|g** (**-ga, -dzy** *lub* **-gowie**) (*instr sg* **-giem**) *m* pharmacologist
**farmakologi|a** (**-i**) *f* pharmacology
**farmakologiczny** *adj* (*środek*) pharmacological
**farme|r** (**-ra, -rzy**) (*loc sg* **-rze**) *m* farmer
**far|sa** (**-sy, -sy**) (*dat sg* **-sie**) *f* (*Teatr*) farce; (*przen*) travesty
**farsz** (**-u, -e**) *m* stuffing
**far|t** (**-ta**) (*loc sg* **-cie**) *m* (*pot*) lucky streak
**fartuch** (**-a, -y**) *m* (*kuchenny*) apron; (*lekarski*) (doctor's) gown; (*Tech*) overalls *pl*
**fartusz|ek** (**-ka, -ki**) (*instr sg* **-kiem**) *m* (*dziecięcy*) pinafore
**faryzeusz** (**-a, -e**) *m* pharisee
**fasa|da** (**-dy, -dy**) (*dat sg* **-dzie**) *f* (*Archit*) facade
**fascynacj|a** (**-i, -e**) (*gen pl* **-i**) *f* fascination
**fascyn|ować (-uję, -ujesz)** *vt* (*perf* **za-**) to fascinate
**fascynujący** *adj* fascinating
**faso|la** (**-li, -le**) (*gen pl* **-li**) *f* bean; ~ **szparagowa** string bean
**fasol|ka** (**-ki, -ki**) (*dat sg* **-ce**, *gen pl* **-ek**) *f*: **~ po bretońsku** (baked) beans in tomato sauce
**faso|n** (**-nu, -ny**) (*loc sg* **-nie**) *m* (*krój*) cut; **trzymać/tracić** ~ (*przen*) to keep up/lose one's spirit; **robić coś z ~em** to do sth with aplomb
**fastryg|ować (-uję, -ujesz)** (*perf* **s-**) *vt* to baste
**faszer|ować (-uję, -ujesz)** (*perf* **na-**) *vt* to stuff
**faszy|sta** (**-sty, -ści**) (*dat sg* **-ście**) *m decl like f in sg* fascist
**faszystowski** *adj* fascist
**faszyz|m** (**-mu**) (*loc sg* **-mie**) *m* fascism
**fatali|sta** (**-sty, -ści**) (*dat sg* **-ście**) *m decl like f in sg* fatalist
**fatalnie** *adv* (*mówić, pisać*) awfully; **~ się składa** this is very *lub* most unfortunate; **czuć się** ~ to feel awful
**fatalny** *adj* (*błąd, skutek*) disastrous; (*liczba, numer*) unlucky; (*stan, pogoda, opinia*) appalling
**fatamorga|na** (**-ny**) (*dat sg* **-nie**) *f* mirage; (*przen*) mirage, illusion
**fat|um** (**-um, -a**) (*gen pl* **-ów**) *nt inv in sg* doom
**faty|ga** (**-gi**) (*dat sg* **-dze**) *f* trouble; **zadawać (zadać** *perf*) **sobie fatygę** to take the trouble
**fatyg|ować (-uję, -ujesz)** *vt* to trouble, to put out; **fatygować się** (*perf* **po-**) *vr* to take the trouble; **proszę się nie** ~ please don't trouble yourself/yourselves
**fau|l** (**-lu, -le**) (*gen pl* **-li** *lub* **-lów**) *m* (*Sport*) foul
**faul|ować (-uję, -ujesz)** (*perf* **s-**) *vt* (*Sport*) to foul
**fau|na** (**-ny**) (*dat sg* **-nie**) *f* fauna
**fawory|t** (**-ta, -ci**) (*loc sg* **-cie**) *m* front-runner, favourite (*Brit*), favorite (*US*)
**faworyz|ować (-uję, -ujesz)** *vt* to favour (*Brit*), to favor (*US*)
**fax** (**-u, -y**) *m* = **faks**
**fa|za** (**-zy, -zy**) (*dat sg* **-zie**) *f* stage, phase; (*Elektr*) phase; ~ **Księżyca** phase of the moon
**feb|ra** (**-ry**) (*dat sg* **-rze**) *f* (*gorączka*) fever
**federacj|a** (**-i, -e**) (*gen pl* **-i**) *f* federation
**federalny** *adj* federal; **Republika Federalna Niemiec** the Federal Republic of Germany
**fele|r** (**-ru, -ry**) (*loc sg* **-rze**) *m* (*pot*) flaw, snag (*pot*)
**fel|ga** (**-gi, -gi**) (*dat sg* **-dze**) *f* (*pot*) rim (*of a wheel*)
**felieto|n** (**-nu, -ny**) (*loc sg* **-nie**) *m* feature article
**feminist|ka** (**-ki, -ki**) (*dat sg* **-ce**, *gen pl* **-ek**) *f* feminist
**feministyczny** *adj* feminist
**feminiz|m** (**-mu**) (*loc sg* **-mie**) *m* feminism
**fenicki** *adj* Phoenician
**feni|g** (**-ga, -gi**) (*instr sg* **-giem**) *m* (*moneta*) pfennig
**fenik|s** (**-sa**) (*loc sg* **-sie**) *m* phoenix; **odrodzić się** (*perf*) *lub* **powstać** (*perf*) **jak ~ z popiołów**

to rise phoenix-like from the ashes (of defeat)

**fenome|n** (**-nu, -ny**) (*loc sg* **-nie**) *m* (*zjawisko*) wonder; (*człowiek*) (*gen sg* **-na**) prodigy

**fenomenalny** *adj* phenomenal

**feralny** *adj* unlucky

**feri|e** (**-i**) *pl* (*krótkie*) break; (*długie*) holiday(s) (*pl*) (*Brit*), vacation (*US*)

**fer|ma** (**-my, -my**) (*dat sg* **-mie**) *f* poultry *lub* chicken farm

**fermen|t** (**-tu, -ty**) (*loc sg* **-cie**) *m* (*przen: wrzenie*) ferment

**fermentacj|a** (**-i, -e**) (*gen pl* **-i**) *f* fermentation

**ferment|ować (-uje)** (*perf* **s-**) *vi* to ferment

**ferwo|r** (**-ru**) (*loc sg* **-rze**) *m*: **w ~ze walki** in the heat of the battle

**festiwa|l** (**-lu, -le**) (*gen pl* **-li** *lub* **-lów**) *m* festival

**festy|n** (**-nu, -ny**) (*loc sg* **-nie**) *m* gala

**fe|ta** (**-ty, -ty**) (*dat sg* **-cie**) *f* fete

**feto|r** (**-ru, -ry**) (*loc sg* **-rze**) *m* stench

**fet|ować (-uję, -ujesz)** *vt* to celebrate

**fetysz** (**-a, -e**) (*gen pl* **-y** *lub* **-ów**) *m* fetish

**feudaliz|m** (**-mu**) (*loc sg* **-mie**) *m* feudalism

**feudalny** *adj* feudal

**feuda|ł** (**-ła, -łowie**) (*loc sg* **-le**) *m* feudal lord

**fias|ko** (**-ka, -ka**) (*instr sg* **-kiem**) *nt* fiasco; **zakończyć się** (*perf*) **fiaskiem** to come to grief

**fie|sta** (**-sty, -sty**) (*dat sg* **-ście**) *f* fiesta

**fi|ga** (**-gi, -gi**) (*loc sg* **-dze**) *f* (*owoc, drzewo*) fig; (*pot: nic*) zero, nothing; **figi** *pl* (*majtki*) briefs *pl*, panties *pl*; **~ z makiem!** (*pot*) forget it! (*pot*), no way! (*pot*)

**fi|giel** (**-gla, -gle**) (*gen pl* **-glów**) *m* prank; **płatać figle** to play tricks; **spłatać** (*perf*) **komuś figla** to play a trick on sb

**figlarny** *adj* mischievous

**figlarz** (**-a, -e**) (*gen pl* **-y**) *m* prankster

**figo|wiec** (**-wca, -wce**) *m* fig (tree)

**figowy** *adj*: **listek ~** fig leaf

**figu|ra** (**-ry, -ry**) (*dat sg* **-rze**) *f* figure; (*szachowa*) piece; (*karciana*) court *lub* picture card

**figuran|t** (**-ta, -ci**) (*dat sg* **-cie**) *m decl like f in sg* figurehead

**figur|ka** (**-ki, -ki**) (*dat sg* **-ce**, *gen pl* **-ek**) *f* (*posążek*) figurine

**figur|ować (-uję, -ujesz)** *vi*: **~ w spisie/na liście** to be *lub* appear in a register/on a list

**figurowy** *adj*: **łyżwiarstwo figurowe** *lub* **jazda figurowa na lodzie** figure skating

**fik|ać (-am, -asz)** (*perf* **-nąć**) *vi* (*skakać*) to frolic, to gambol; **~ nogami** to kick; **~ koziołki** to turn somersaults

**fikcj|a** (**-i, -e**) (*gen pl* **-i**) *f* fiction; **~ literacka** literary fiction

**fikcyjny** *adj* (*postać, świat*) fictitious, fictional; (*nazwisko*) fictitious

**fik|nąć (-nę, -niesz)** (*imp* **-nij**) *vb perf od* **fikać**

**fikoł|ek** (**-ka, -ki**) (*instr sg* **-kiem**) *m* (*pot*) somersault

**fiku|s** (**-sa, -sy**) (*loc sg* **-sie**) *m* (*Bot*) rubber plant

**Filadelfi|a** (**-i**) *f* Philadelphia

**filantro|p** (**-pa, -pi**) (*loc sg* **-pie**) *m* philanthropist

**filantropi|a** (**-i**) *f* charity

**fila|r** (**-ru** *lub* **-ra, -ry**) (*loc sg* **-rze**) *m* pillar

**filateli|sta** (**-sty, -ści**) (*dat sg* **-ście**) *m decl like f in sg* stamp collector

**filatelisty|ka** (**-ki**) (*dat sg* **-ce**) *f* stamp collecting

**filc** (**-u, -e**) *m* felt

**file|t** (**-ta** *lub* **-tu, -ty**) (*loc sg* **-cie**) *m* fillet

**filet|ować (-uję, -ujesz)** (*perf* **s-**) *vt* to fillet

**filharmoni|a** (**-i, -e**) (*gen pl* **-i**) *f* (*instytucja*) philharmonic (society); (*budynek*) concert hall

**fili|a** (**-i, -e**) (*gen pl* **-i**) *f* branch

**filigranowy** *adj* dainty

**Filipin|ka** (**-ki, -ki**) (*dat sg* **-ce**, *gen pl* **-ek**) *f* Filipino (woman)

**Filipin|y** (**-**) *pl* the Philippines

**Filipińczy|k** (**-ka, -cy**) (*instr sg* **-kiem**) *m* Filipino (man)

**filiżan|ka** (**-ki, -ki**) (*dat sg* **-ce**, *gen pl* **-ek**) *f* (*naczynie*) cup; (*zawartość*) cupful; **~ kawy/herbaty** a cup of coffee/tea

**fil|m** (**-mu, -my**) (*loc sg* **-mie**) *m* film; (*fabularny*) (feature) film; (*dokumentalny*) documentary (film); (*kinematografia*) film (*Brit*) *lub* movie (*US*) industry; **~ animowany** *lub* **rysunkowy** (animated) cartoon; **~ reklamowy** infomercial; **nakręcić** (*perf*) **~** to shoot *lub* make a film

**film|ować (-uję, -ujesz)** (*perf* **s-**) *vt* (*scenę, krajobraz*) to film; (*powieść*) to make into a film

**filmo|wiec** (**-wca, -wcy**) (*loc sg* **-wcu**) *m* filmmaker

**filmowy** *adj* film *attr* (*Brit*), movie *attr* (*US*)

**filodendro|n** (**-nu, -ny**) (*loc sg* **-nie**) *m* (*Bot*) monstera

**filolo|g** (**-ga, -dzy** *lub* **-gowie**) (*instr sg* **-giem**) *m* philologist

**filologi|a** (**-i, -e**) (*gen pl* **-i**) *f* philology; **student filologii angielskiej** a student of English (studies); **student filologii klasycznej** a student of classics

**filologiczny** *adj* philological

**filozo|f** (**-fa, -fowie**) (*loc sg* **-fie**) *m* philosopher

**filozofi|a** (**-i, -e**) (*gen pl* **-i**) *f* philosophy; **to żadna ~** (*pot*) there's nothing to it (*pot*)

**filozoficzny** *adj* philosophical

**filozof|ować (-uję, -ujesz)** *vi* to philosophize

**filt|r** (**-ru** *lub* **-ra, -ry**) (*loc sg* **-rze**) *m* filter; (*papierosowy*) filter tip

**filtr|ować (-uję, -ujesz)** *vt* (*wodę*) (*perf* **prze-**) to filter; (*osad*) (*perf* **od-**) to filter out
**filuterny** *adj* playful
**Fi|n (-na, -nowie)** (*loc sg* **-nie**) *m* Finn
**finali|sta (-sty, -ści)** (*dat sg* **-ście**) *m decl like f in sg* finalist
**finalist|ka (-ki, -ki)** (*dat sg* **-ce**, *gen pl* **-ek**) *f* finalist
**finaliz|ować (-uję, -ujesz)** (*perf* **s-**) *vt* to finalize
**finalny** *adj* (*produkt*) finished
**fina|ł (-łu, -ły)** (*loc sg* **-le**) *m* (*zakończenie*) ending; (*Sport*) final; (*Muz*) finale
**finałowy** *adj* final; **scena finałowa** finale
**finans|e (-ów)** *pl* finance(s *pl*); **ministerstwo finansów** Ministry of Finance, ≈ the Treasury (*Brit*), ≈ the Exchequer (*Brit*), ≈ the Department of the Treasury (*US*)
**finansi|sta (-sty, -ści)** (*dat sg* **-ście**) *m decl like f in sg* banker, financier
**finansje|ra (-ry)** (*dat sg* **-rze**) *f* (high) finance
**finans|ować (-uję, -ujesz)** (*perf* **s-**) *vt* to fund, to finance
**finansowy** *adj* financial
**finezj|a (-i, -e)** (*gen pl* **-i**) *f* finesse
**finezyjny** *adj* fine
**finisz (-u, -e)** (*gen pl* **-ów**) *m* (*Sport*) finish
**finisz|ować (-uję, -ujesz)** *vi* to spurt (*in a race*)
**fin|ka (-ki, -ki)** (*dat sg* **-ce**, *gen pl* **-ek**) *f* (*nóż*) sheath knife; **Finka** (*mieszkanka Finlandii*) Finn
**Finlandi|a (-i)** *f* Finland
**fiński** *adj* Finnish ▷ *m decl like adj* (*język*) Finnish
**fiole|t (-tu, -ty)** (*loc sg* **-cie**) *m* purple
**fioletowy** *adj* purple
**fiol|ka (-ki, -ki)** (*dat sg* **-ce**, *gen pl* **-ek**) *f* phial
**fioł|ek (-ka, -ki)** (*instr sg* **-kiem**) *m* (*Bot*) violet; **~ alpejski** cyclamen
**fiołkowy** *adj* violet
**fior|d (-du, -dy)** (*loc sg* **-dzie**) *m* fjord, fiord
**fira|na (-ny, -ny)** (*loc sg* **-nie**) *f* net curtain
**firan|ka (-ki, -ki)** (*dat sg* **-ce**, *gen pl* **-ek**) *f* net curtain
**fir|ma (-my, -my)** (*dat sg* **-mie**) *f* (*małe przedsiębiorstwo*) firm, business; (*duże przedsiębiorstwo*) company
**firmowy** *adj* (*papier, samochód*) company *attr*; **danie firmowe** speciality (*Brit*), specialty (*US*); **znak ~** trademark
**fis** *inv* (*Muz*) F sharp
**fiskalny** *adj* fiscal
**fisku|s (-sa)** (*loc sg* **-sie**) *m* (*skarb państwa*) ≈ Inland Revenue (*Brit*), ≈ IRS (*US*)
**fistasz|ek (-ka, -ki)** (*instr sg* **-kiem**) *m* peanut
**fisz|ka (-ki, -ki)** (*dat sg* **-ce**, *gen pl* **-ek**) *f* index card
**fizjologi|a (-i)** *f* physiology
**fizjologiczny** *adj* physiological
**fizjonomi|a (-i, -e)** (*gen pl* **-i**) *f* physiognomy
**fizjoterapi|a (-i)** *f* physiotherapy
**fizyczny** *adj* physical; (*laboratorium*) physics *attr*; (*praca, pracownik*) manual; **wychowanie fizyczne** (*Szkol*) physical education
**fizy|k (-ka, -cy)** (*instr sg* **-kiem**) *m* physicist; (*nauczyciel*) physics teacher
**fizy|ka (-ki)** (*dat sg* **-ce**) *f* physics
**fizykoterapi|a (-i)** *f* physiotherapy
**f-ka** *abbr* = **fabryka**
**flacz|ki (-ków)** *pl* (*Kulin*) tripe
**fla|ga (-gi, -gi)** (*dat sg* **-dze**) *f* flag
**flago|wiec (-wca, -wce)** *m* (*Żegl*) flagship
**flagowy** *adj* (*okręt, sygnał*) flag *attr*
**fla|k (-ka, -ki)** (*instr sg* **-kiem**) *m* (*na kiełbasie*) skin; **flaki** *pl* (*pot*: *wnętrzności*) guts *pl* (*pot*); (*Kulin*) tripe; **nudny jak ~i z olejem** (*pot*) (as) dull as ditch-water (*pot*)
**flako|n (-nu, -ny)** (*loc sg* **-nie**) *m* (*do perfum*) bottle; (*do kwiatów*) vase
**Flaman|d (-da, -dowie)** (*loc sg* **-dzie**) *m* Fleming
**Flamand|ka (-ki, -ki)** (*dat sg* **-ce**, *gen pl* **-ek**) *f* Fleming
**flamandzki** *adj* Flemish
**flamast|er (-ra, -ry)** (*loc sg* **-rze**) *m* felt-tip pen
**flamin|g (-ga, -gi)** (*instr sg* **-giem**) *m* flamingo
**Flandri|a (-i)** *f* Flanders
**flane|la (-li, -le)** (*gen pl* **-li**) *f* flannel
**flanelowy** *adj* flannel *attr*
**flan|ka (-ki, -ki)** (*dat sg* **-ce**) *f* (*Wojsk*) flank
**flasz|ka (-ki, -ki)** (*dat sg* **-ce**, *gen pl* **-ek**) *f* (*pot*) bottle
**fląd|ra (-ry, -ry)** (*dat sg* **-rze**) *f* flounder
**fleci|sta (-sty, -ści)** (*dat sg* **-ście**) *m* flutist
**fleg|ma (-my)** (*dat sg* **-mie**) *f* phlegm
**flegmatyczny** *adj* phlegmatic
**flegmaty|k (-ka, -cy)** (*instr sg* **-kiem**) *m* phlegmatic person
**flejtuch (-a, -y)** *m* (*pot*) slob (*pot*)
**fleksj|a (-i)** *f* (*Jęz*) inflection
**fleksyjny** *adj* (*końcówka*) inflectional; (*język*) inflected
**flesz (-a** *lub* **-u, -e)** (*gen pl* **-ów**) *m* (*Fot*) flash
**fle|t (-tu, -ty)** (*loc sg* **-cie**) *m* flute; **~ prosty** recorder
**flir|t (-tu, -ty)** (*loc sg* **-cie**) *m* flirtation
**flirt|ować (-uję, -ujesz)** *vi*: **~ (z kimś)** to flirt (with sb)
**flisa|k (-ka, -cy)** (*instr sg* **-kiem**) *m* raftsman
**flo|ra (-ry)** (*dat sg* **-rze**) *f* flora
**Florencj|a (-i)** *f* Florence
**flore|t (-tu, -ty)** (*loc sg* **-cie**) *m* foil
**flo|ta (-ty, -ty)** (*dat sg* **-cie**) *f* fleet; **~ handlowa** merchant marine *lub* navy; **~ wojenna** navy
**fluktuacj|a (-i, -e)** (*gen pl* **-i**) *f* fluctuation
**fluo|r (-ru)** (*loc sg* **-rze**) *m* fluorine; **pasta z ~em** fluoride toothpaste

**fluor|ek** (**-ku, -ki**) (*instr sg* **-kiem**) *m* fluoride
**fluorescencyjny** *adj* fluorescent
**fobi|a** (**-i, -e**) (*gen pl* **-i**) *f* phobia
**fo|ka** (**-ki, -ki**) (*dat sg* **-ce**) *f* seal
**foksterie|r** (**-ra, -ry**) (*loc sg* **-rze**) *m* fox terrier
**fokstro|t** (**-ta, -ty**) (*loc sg* **-cie**) *m* foxtrot
**folde|r** (**-ru** *lub* **-ra, -ry**) (*loc sg* **-rze**) *m* brochure
**foli|a** (**-i, -e**) (*gen pl* **-i**) *f* foil
**folklo|r** (**-ru**) (*loc sg* **-rze**) *m* folklore
**fone|m** (**-mu, -my**) (*loc sg* **-mie**) *m* (*Jęz*) phoneme
**fonetyczny** *adj* phonetic
**fonety|ka** (**-ki**) (*dat sg* **-ce**) *f* phonetics
**foni|a** (**-i**) *f* sound
**fonologi|a** (**-i**) *f* phonology
**fontan|na** (**-ny, -ny**) (*dat sg* **-nie**) *f* fountain
**forem|ka** (**-ki, -ki**) (*dat sg* **-ce**, *gen pl* **-ek**) *f* (*do piasku*) mould (*Brit*), mold (*US*); (*do ciasta*) baking tin
**foremny** *adj* regular
**forhen|d** (**-du, -dy**) (*loc sg* **-dzie**) *m* forehand
**for|ma** (**-my, -my**) (*dat sg* **-mie**) *f* form; (*do ciasta*) baking tin; (*Tech*) mould (*Brit*), mold (*US*); **być w dobrej/złej formie** to be in good/bad shape *lub* form
**formacj|a** (**-i, -e**) (*gen pl* **-i**) *f* formation
**formali|sta** (**-sty, -ści**) (*dat sg* **-ście**) *m decl like f in sg* stickler for rules
**formalistyczny** *adj* formalistic
**formalnie** *adv* formally
**formalnoś|ć** (**-ci, -ci**) (*gen pl* **-ci**) *f* formality
**formalny** *adj* formal
**forma|t** (**-tu, -ty**) (*loc sg* **-cie**) *m* format
**format|ować** (**-uję, -ujesz**) (*perf* **s-**) *vt* (*Komput*) to format
**form|ować** (**-uję, -ujesz**) (*perf* **u-**) *vt* (*tworzyć*) to form; (*kształtować*) to shape; **formować się** *vr* (*tworzyć się*) to form; (*kształtować się*) to be shaped
**formularz** (**-a, -e**) (*gen pl* **-y**) *m* form; **~ wizowy** visa application form; **wypełniać ~** to fill in (*Brit*) *lub* out (*US*) a form
**formu|ła** (**-ły, -ły**) (*dat sg* **-le**) *f* formula
**formuł|ować** (**-uję, -ujesz**) (*perf* **s-**) *vt* to formulate
**forni|r** (**-ru, -ry**) (*loc sg* **-rze**) *m* veneer
**for|sa** (**-sy**) (*dat sg* **-sie**) *f* (*pot*) dough (*pot*)
**fors|ować** (**-uję, -ujesz**) *vt* (*kandydata, pomysł*) (*perf* **prze-**) to push, to press; (*wąwóz, rzekę*) (*perf* **s-**) to clear; **forsować się** (*perf* **prze-**) *vr* to overexert o.s.
**forsowny** *adj* strenuous
**forsycj|a** (**-i, -e**) (*gen pl* **-i**) *f* (*Bot*) forsythia
**for|t** (**-tu, -ty**) (*loc sg* **-cie**) *m* fort
**forte|ca** (**-cy, -ce**) *f* fortress
**forte|l** (**-lu, -le**) (*gen pl* **-li** *lub* **-lów**) *m* stratagem
**fortepia|n** (**-nu, -ny**) (*loc sg* **-nie**) *m* (grand) piano
**fortepianowy** *adj* piano *attr*
**fortu|na** (**-ny**) (*dat sg* **-nie**) *f* fortune
**fortyfikacj|a** (**-i, -e**) (*gen pl* **-i**) *f* fortification
**for|um** (**-um, -a**) (*gen pl* **-ów**) *nt inv in sg* forum; **na ~ publicznym** in public
**for|y** (**-ów**) *pl*: **mieć ~ u kogoś** to enjoy sb's favour (*Brit*) *lub* favor (*US*)
**fo|sa** (**-sy, -sy**) (*dat sg* **-sie**) *f* moat
**fosfo|r** (**-ru**) (*loc sg* **-rze**) *m* phosphorus
**fosforyzujący** *adj* luminous, phosphorescent
**fot.** *abbr* (= *fotografia*) phot.
**fotel** (**-a** *lub* **-u, -e**) (*gen pl* **-i**) *m* armchair; (*urząd*) office; **~ na biegunach** rocking chair, rocker
**fot|ka** (**-ki, -ki**) (*dat sg* **-ce**, *gen pl* **-ek**) *f* snap, snapshot
**fotoamato|r** (**-ra, -rzy**) (*loc sg* **-rze**) *m* (amateur) photographer
**fotogeniczny** *adj* photogenic
**fotogra|f** (**-fa, -fowie**) (*loc sg* **-fie**) *m* photographer
**fotografi|a** (**-i**) *f* (*rzemiosło, sztuka*) photography; (*zdjęcie*) (*nom pl* **-e**, *gen pl* **-i**) photo(graph)
**fotograficzny** *adj* photographic; **aparat ~** camera
**fotografi|k** (**-ka, -cy**) (*instr sg* **-kiem**) *m* (fine-art) photographer
**fotografi|ka** (**-ki**) (*dat sg* **-ce**) *f* (fine-art) photography
**fotograf|ować** (**-uję, -ujesz**) (*perf* **s-**) *vt* to photograph
**fotokomór|ka** (**-ki, -ki**) (*dat sg* **-ce**, *gen pl* **-ek**) *f* photocell, electric eye
**fotokopi|a** (**-i, -e**) (*gen pl* **-i**) *f* photocopy
**fotokopiar|ka** (**-ki, -ki**) (*dat sg* **-ce**, *gen pl* **-ek**) *f* photocopier
**fotomodel|ka** (**-ki, -ki**) (*dat sg* **-ce**, *gen pl* **-ek**) *f* model
**fotomontaż** (**-u, -e**) (*gen pl* **-y**) *m* trick photo(graph)
**fotoreportaż** (**-u, -e**) (*gen pl* **-y**) *m* photo essay
**fotoreporte|r** (**-ra, -rzy**) (*loc sg* **-rze**) *m* press *lub* news photographer
**foto|s** (**-su, -sy**) (*loc sg* **-sie**) *m* (*Film*) still
**fotosynte|za** (**-zy, -zy**) (*dat sg* **-zie**) *f* photosynthesis
**foyer** *nt inv* foyer
**frach|t** (**-tu, -ty**) (*loc sg* **-cie**) *m* freight
**frachto|wiec** (**-wca, -wce**) (*loc sg* **-wcu**) *m* freighter
**fragmen|t** (**-tu, -ty**) (*loc sg* **-cie**) *m* fragment
**fragmentaryczny** *adj* fragmentary
**fraj|da** (**-dy, -dy**) (*dat sg* **-dzie**) *f* (*pot*) fun, thrill (*pot*); **sprawić** (*perf*) **komuś frajdę** to tickle sb (pink) (*pot*)
**fraje|r** (**-ra, -rzy**) (*loc sg* **-rze**) *m* (*pej*) sucker (*pej*)
**fra|k** (**-ka, -ki**) (*instr sg* **-kiem**) *m* tail coat, tails *pl*

**frakcj|a** (**-i, -e**) (*gen pl* **-i**) *f* faction
**framu|ga** (**-gi, -gi**) (*dat sg* **-dze**) *f* frame
**franciszka|nin** (**-nina, -nie**) (*loc sg* **-ninie**, *gen pl* **-ów**) *m* Franciscan
**franciszkański** *adj* Franciscan
**Francj|a** (**-i**) *f* France
**francuski** *adj* French ▷ *m decl like adj* (*język*) French; **ciasto ~e** puff pastry; **klucz ~** monkey wrench
**Francu|z** (**-za, -zi**) (*loc sg* **-zie**) *m* Frenchman
**Francuz|ka** (**-ki, -ki**) (*dat sg* **-ce**, *gen pl* **-ek**) *f* Frenchwoman
**fran|k** (**-ka, -ki**) (*instr sg* **-kiem**) *m* franc
**frap|ować (-uję, -ujesz)** (*perf* **za-**) *vt* to fascinate
**frapujący** *adj* fascinating
**frasz|ka** (**-ki, -ki**) (*dat sg* **-ce**, *gen pl* **-ek**) *f* (*Lit*) epigram; (*błahostka*) trifle
**fra|za** (**-zy, -zy**) (*dat sg* **-zie**) *f* phrase
**frazeologi|a** (**-i**) *f* phraseology
**frazeologiczny** *adj* phraseological
**fraze|s** (**-su, -sy**) (*loc sg* **-sie**) *m* platitude
**frega|ta** (**-ty, -ty**) (*dat sg* **-cie**) *f* frigate
**frekwencj|a** (**-i**) *f* (*w szkole*) attendance; (*wyborcza*) turnout
**fres|k** (**-ku, -ki**) (*instr sg* **-kiem**) *m* fresco
**frezar|ka** (**-ki, -ki**) (*dat sg* **-ce**, *gen pl* **-ek**) *f* milling machine
**frezj|a** (**-i, -e**) (*gen pl* **-i**) *f* (*Bot*) freesia
**frędz|el** (**-la, -le**) (*gen pl* **-li**) *m* tassel; **frędzle** *pl* fringe
**fron|t** (**-tu, -ty**) (*loc sg* **-cie**) *m* front; **~em do** *+gen* facing; **zmienić** (*perf*) **~** to change front
**frontalny** *adj* frontal
**fronto|n** (**-nu, -ny**) (*loc sg* **-nie**) *m* frontage
**frontowy** *adj* front *attr*; (*żołnierz*) front-line *attr*
**froter|ka** (**-ki, -ki**) (*dat sg* **-ce**, *gen pl* **-ek**) *f* floor polisher
**froter|ować (-uję, -ujesz)** (*perf* **wy-**) *vt* to polish
**frotowy** *adj* terry(-cloth) *attr*
**frotte** *adj inv*; **ręcznik ~** terry towel
**frustracj|a** (**-i, -e**) (*gen pl* **-i**) *f* frustration
**frustr|ować (-uję, -ujesz)** (*perf* **s-**) *vt* to frustrate
**fruw|ać (-am, -asz)** *vi* to fly
**fryka|s** (**-sa, -sy**) (*loc sg* **-sie**) *m* delicacy
**fryt|ki** (**-ek**) *pl* (potato) chips *pl* (*Brit*), (French) fries *pl* (*US*)
**frywolny** *adj* frivolous
**fryzje|r** (**-ra, -rzy**) (*loc sg* **-rze**) *m* hairdresser; (*męski*) barber
**fryzjer|ka** (**-ki, -ki**) (*dat sg* **-ce**, *gen pl* **-ek**) *f* hairdresser
**fryzjerski** *adj*: **zakład ~** hairdresser's; (*męski*) barber's; **salon ~** hair(dressing) salon
**fryzu|ra** (**-ry, -ry**) (*dat sg* **-rze**) *f* hair style, haircut
**fu|cha** (**-chy, -chy**) (*dat sg* **-sze**) *f* (*pot*) sideline, odd job
**fu|ga** (**-gi, -gi**) (*dat sg* **-dze**) *f* (*Muz*) fugue; (*Tech*) joint
**fujar|ka** (**-ki, -ki**) (*dat sg* **-ce**, *gen pl* **-ek**) *f* pipe
**fuk|s** (**-sa, -sy**) (*loc sg* **-sie**) *m* (*pot: szczęśliwy traf*) fluke (*pot*); **~em** by a fluke
**fundacj|a** (**-i, -e**) (*gen pl* **-i**) *f* foundation
**fundamen|t** (**-tu, -ty**) (*loc sg* **-cie**) *m* (*budynku*) foundation(s *pl*); (*przen*) foundation
**fundamentali|sta** (**-sty, -ści**) (*dat sg* **-ście**) *m decl like f in sg* fundamentalist
**fundamentaliz|m** (**-mu**) (*loc sg* **-mie**) *m* fundamentalism
**fundamentalny** *adj* fundamental
**fundato|r** (**-ra, -rzy**) (*loc sg* **-rze**) *m* (*darczyńca*) benefactor; (*założyciel*) founder
**fund|ować (-uję, -ujesz)** *vt* (*perf* **za-**); **~ komuś coś** to treat sb to sth; (*stypendium*) (*perf* **u-**) to found, to establish
**fundusz** (**-u, -e**) (*gen pl* **-ów** *lub* **-y**) *m* fund; **~ płac** wages budget; **fundusze** *pl* funds *pl*
**funkcj|a** (**-i, -e**) (*gen pl* **-i**) *f* function; (*stanowisko*) function, position
**funkcjonalny** *adj* functional, practical
**funkcjonariusz** (**-a, -e**) (*gen pl* **-y**) *m* officer
**funkcjon|ować (-uję, -ujesz)** *vi* to function
**fun|t** (**-ta, -ty**) (*loc sg* **-cie**) *m* pound; **~ szterling** (pound) sterling
**funtowy** *adj* one-pound *attr*
**fu|ra** (**-ry, -ry**) (*dat sg* **-rze**) *f* (*wóz*) cart; (*pot: mnóstwo*) heaps *pl* (*pot*)
**furgonet|ka** (**-ki, -ki**) (*dat sg* **-ce**, *gen pl* **-ek**) *f* van
**furi|a** (**-i**) *f* fury
**furko|tać (-czę, -czesz)** (*perf* **za-**) *vi* to whirr (*Brit*), to whir (*US*)
**furo|ra** (**-ry**) (*dat sg* **-rze**) *f*: **robić (zrobić** *perf*) **furorę** to make it big
**furt|ka** (**-ki, -ki**) (*dat sg* **-ce**, *gen pl* **-ek**) *f* gate
**fus|y** (**-ów**) *pl* (*kawowe*) dregs; (*herbaciane*) tea leaves
**fuszer|ka** (**-ki, -ki**) (*dat sg* **-ce**, *gen pl* **-ek**) *f* (*pot*) botch-up (*pot*)
**futbol** (**-u**) *m* (association) football, soccer; **~ amerykański** (American) football
**futera|ł** (**-łu, -ły**) (*loc sg* **-le**) *m* holder, case
**futerkowy** *adj* fur *attr*
**fut|ro** (**-ra, -ra**) (*loc sg* **-rze**, *gen pl* **-er**) *nt* (*sierść*) fur; (*płaszcz*) fur coat
**futry|na** (**-ny, -ny**) (*dat sg* **-nie**) *f* frame
**futrzany** *adj* fur *attr*
**futurystyczny** *adj* futuristic
**fuzj|a** (**-i, -e**) (*gen pl* **-i**) *f* (*Ekon*) merger, amalgamation; (*strzelba*) rifle

# Gg

**G, g**[1] *nt inv (litera)* G, g; **G jak Genowefa** ≈ G for George; **G-dur** G major; **g-moll** G minor
**g**[2] *abbr (= godzina)* h (= *hour*); (= *gram*) g (= *gram*)
**gabardy|na (-ny, -ny)** (*dat sg* **-nie**) *f* gaberdine
**gabary|ty (-tów)** *pl* dimensions
**gabine|t (-tu, -ty)** (*loc sg* **-cie**) *m* (*w domu*) study; (*w pracy*) office; (*lekarski*) surgery (*Brit*), office (*US*); (*Pol*) Cabinet; **~ kosmetyczny** beauty salon *lub* parlor (*US*)
**gablo|ta (-ty, -ty)** (*dat sg* **-cie**) *f* showcase
**gablot|ka (-ki, -ki)** (*dat sg* **-ce**, *gen pl* **-ek**) *f* (small) showcase
**ga|cie (-ci)** *pl* (*pot*) underpants
**ga|d (-da, -dy)** (*loc sg* **-dzie**) *m* (*Zool*) reptile
**gad|ać (-am, -asz)** *vi* (*pot*) to talk, to chatter; **szkoda ~** (*pot*) it's no use talking
**gadani|e (-a)** *nt* (*pot*) idle talk, chatter; **bez gadania!** (*pot*) I want none of your backchat!
**gadatliwy** *adj* loquacious, garrulous
**gadu-gadu** *inv*: **my tu ~, a ...** here we are chit-chating while ...
**gadu|ła (-ły, -ły)** (*dat sg* **-le**) *m/f decl like f* (*pot*) chatterbox
**gadże|t (-tu, -ty)** (*loc sg* **-cie**) *m* (*pot*) gadget
**ga|fa (-fy, -fy)** (*dat sg* **-fie**) *f* gaffe; **popełnić** (*perf*) **gafę** to make a gaffe
**ga|g (-gu, -gi)** (*instr sg* **-giem**) *m* (*Film, Teatr*) gag
**ga|j (-ju, -je)** (*gen pl* **-i**) *m* grove
**gajo|wy (-wego, -wi)** *m decl like adj* forester
**ga|la (-li, -le)** *f* (*uroczystość*) gala, festivity; (*strój*) gala dress *lub* attire
**galakty|ka (-ki, -ki)** (*dat sg* **-ce**) *f* (*Astron*) galaxy
**galanteri|a (-i)** *f* (*wyroby*) haberdashery (*Brit*), notions *pl* (*US*)
**galare|ta (-ty, -ty)** (*dat sg* **-cie**) *f*: **trząść się jak ~** to shake *lub* tremble like a jelly *lub* leaf
**galaret|ka (-ki, -ki)** (*dat sg* **-ce**, *gen pl* **-ek**) *f* jelly
**galaretowaty** *adj* gelatinous, jelly-like
**gale|ra (-ry, -ry)** (*dat sg* **-rze**) *f* (*Hist*) galley
**galeri|a (-i, -e)** (*gen pl* **-i**) *f* gallery; **~ sztuki** art gallery
**galimatia|s (-su)** (*loc sg* **-sie**) *m* (*pot*) mess
**galo|n (-nu, -ny)** (*loc sg* **-nie**) *m* (*miara objętości*) gallon
**galo|p (-pu, -py)** (*loc sg* **-pie**) *m* gallop; **~em** at full gallop *lub* speed
**galop|ować (-uję, -ujesz)** *vi* to gallop
**galowy** *adj* gala *attr*; **ubiór ~** full dress
**galwanizowany** *adj* galvanized
**gałąz|ka (-ki, -ki)** (*dat sg* **-ce**, *gen pl* **-ek**) *f* twig, sprig; **~ oliwna** olive branch
**gał|ąź (-ęzi, -ęzie)** (*gen pl* **-ęzi**, *instr pl* **-ęziami** *lub* **-ęźmi**) *f* branch
**gał|ka (-ki, -ki)** (*dat sg* **-ce**, *gen pl* **-ek**) *f* (*na drzwiach, przy radiu*) knob; (*lodów*) scoop; **~ oczna** eyeball; **~ muszkatołowa** nutmeg
**ga|ma (-my, -my)** (*loc sg* **-mie**) *f* (*Muz*) scale; (*przen*) range
**gambi|t (-tu, -ty)** (*loc sg* **-cie**) *m* (*Szachy*) gambit
**gan|ek (-ku, -ki)** (*instr sg* **-kiem**) *m* (*przybudówka*) porch; (*przejście*) gallery
**gan|g (-gu, -gi)** (*instr sg* **-giem**) *m* gang, mob (*pot*)
**gangre|na (-ny)** (*dat sg* **-nie**) *f* (*Med*) gangrene
**gangste|r (-ra, -rzy)** (*loc sg* **-rze**) *m* gangster, mobster (*pot*)
**gangsterski** *adj* gangster *attr*
**gani|ać (-am, -asz)** *vi* to run; **~ za czymś** (*zabiegać*) to run after sth; **ganiać się** *vr* (*gonić się*) *vr* to chase one another
**ga|nić (-nię, -nisz)** (*imp* **-ń**, *perf* **z-**) *vt* to rebuke, to reprimand
**ga|p (-pia, -pie)** *m* onlooker
**ga|pa (-py, -py)** (*dat sg* **-pie**) *m/f decl like f* (*pot*) dope (*pot*) (*slow-witted person*); **pasażer na gapę** fare dodger; (*na statku, w samolocie*) stowaway; **jechać na gapę** (*pot*) to steal a ride, to dodge paying one's fare
**ga|pić się (-pię, -pisz)** *vr* (*pot*): **gapić się (na** *+acc*) to stare (at), to gape (at)
**garaż (-u, -e)** (*gen pl* **-y** *lub* **-ów**) *m* garage
**gar|b (-bu, -by)** (*loc sg* **-bie**) *m* hump
**garbar|nia (-ni, -nie)** (*gen pl* **-ni**) *f* tannery
**garbaty** *adj* (*człowiek*) hunchbacked; (*nos*) hooked
**gar|bić się (-bię, -bisz)** (*perf* **z-**) *vr* to stoop

**garb|ować (-uję, -ujesz)** (*perf* **wy-**) *vt* to tan; **~ komuś skórę** (*przen*) to tan sb's hide
**garbu|s** (**-sa, -sy**) (*loc sg* **-sie**) *m* (*pot: człowiek*) hunchback
**gar|da** (**-dy, -dy**) (*dat sg* **-dzie**) *f* (*Boks*) guard
**gardeni|a** (**-i, -e**) (*gen pl* **-i**) *f* (*Bot*) gardenia
**gardero|ba** (**-by, -by**) (*loc sg* **-bie**) *f* (*ubrania*) wardrobe, clothing; (*Teatr*) dressing room; (*szatnia*) cloakroom
**gard|ło** (**-ła, -ła**) (*loc sg* **-le**, *gen pl* **-eł**) *nt* throat; **jak psu z gardła (wyciągnięty)** (*pot*) crumpled; **wąskie ~** (*przen*) bottleneck; **mieć nóż na gardle** to be in a tight corner; **na całe ~** at the top of one's voice
**gardłowy** *adj* (*głos*) husky; **gardłowa sprawa** matter of life and death
**gar|dzić (-dzę, -dzisz)** (*imp* **-dź**, *perf* **wz-**) *vt*: **~ kimś/czymś** to despise sb/sth
**garmażer|ka** (**-ki, -ki**) (*dat sg* **-ce**, *gen pl* **-ek**) *f* (*pot*) cold foods *pl*
**gar|nąć się (-nę, -niesz)** (*imp* **-nij**) *vr*: **garnąć się do kogoś** to feel attracted to sb; **garnąć się do pracy/nauki** (*przen*) to crave for work/ education
**garncarst|wo** (**-wa**) (*loc sg* **-wie**) *nt* pottery
**garncarz** (**-a, -e**) (*gen pl* **-y**) *m* potter
**garn|ek** (**-ka, -ki**) (*instr sg* **-kiem**) *m* pot
**garnitu|r** (**-ru, -ry**) (*loc sg* **-rze**) *m* (*ubranie*) suit
**garnizo|n** (**-nu, -ny**) (*loc sg* **-nie**) *m* (*Wojsk*) garrison
**garnusz|ek** (**-ka, -ki**) (*instr sg* **-kiem**) *m* (*kubek*) little mug; (*garnek*) little pot; **być u kogoś na garnuszku** (*pot*) to live off sb
**garson|ka** (**-ki, -ki**) (*dat sg* **-ce**, *gen pl* **-ek**) *f* (woman's) suit
**garst|ka** (**-ki, -ki**) (*dat sg* **-ce**, *gen pl* **-ek**) *f* (*niewielka ilość*) handful
**garś|ć** (**-ci, -cie** *lub* **-ci**) (*gen pl* **-ci**) *f* (*dłoń*) cupped hand; (*pieniędzy, informacji*) handful; **brać się (wziąć się** *perf*) **w ~** to pull o.s. together; **mieć** *lub* **trzymać kogoś w garści** (*pot*) to have sb on toast
**ga|sić (-szę, -sisz)** (*imp* **-ś**, *perf* **z-**) *vt* (*ogień*) to put out, to extinguish; (*papierosa, świecę*) to put out; (*światło, radio, silnik*) to turn *lub* switch off; (*zapał, dobry humor*) to kill; (*pragnienie*) (*perf* **u-**) to quench
**ga|snąć (-snę, -śniesz)** (*imp* **-śnij**, *perf* **z-**) *vi* (*o ogniu, latarni*) to go out; (*o silniku*) to stall; (*o nadziei, zapale*) to fade; (*przen: o człowieku: umierać*) to be dying
**gastronomi|a** (**-i**) *f* (*sztuka kulinarna*) gastronomy; (*dział usług*) catering industry
**gastryczny** *adj* gastric
**gaśnic|a** (**-y, -e**) *f* fire-extinguisher
**gaśniczy** *adj* (*sprzęt, akcja*) fire-fighting *attr*
**gat.** *abbr* (= *gatunek*) quality
**gatun|ek** (**-ku, -ki**) (*instr sg* **-kiem**) *m* (*rodzaj, typ*) kind, sort; (*Bio*) species; (*jakość*) quality; **~ pierwszy/drugi** first(s)/second(s); **~ literacki** literary genre
**gatunkowy** *adj* choice, select
**gawę|da** (**-dy, -dy**) (*dat sg* **-dzie**) *f* (*rozmowa*) chat; (*opowiadanie*) tale
**gawędziarz** (**-a, -e**) (*gen pl* **-y**) *m* story-teller
**gawę|dzić (-dzę, -dzisz)** (*imp* **-dź**) *vi* to chat
**gawo|rzyć (-rzę, -rzysz)** *vi* (*o niemowlęciu*) to babble; (*rozmawiać*) to chat
**gawro|n** (**-na, -ny**) (*loc sg* **-nie**) *m* (*Zool*) rook
**ga|z** (**-zu, -zy**) (*loc sg* **-zie**) *m* (*Fiz, Chem*) gas; (*Mot*) gas pedal, accelerator; (*pot: instalacja gazowa*) gas fittings *pl*; **gazy** *pl* (*wiatry*) wind *sg*, flatus *sg*; **gaz łzawiący** tear gas; **gaz ziemny** natural gas; **włączyć/wyłączyć** (*perf*) **gaz** to turn the gas on/off; **dodawać (dodać** *perf*) **gazu** to step on it, to step on the gas (US); **na gazie** (*pot: podpity*) tipsy
**ga|za** (**-zy, -zy**) (*dat sg* **-zie**) *f* gauze
**ga|zda** (**-zdy, -zdowie**) (*dat sg* **-ździe**) *m decl like f in sg a farmer in the Tatra Mountains region*
**gazeciarz** (**-a, -e**) (*gen pl* **-y**) *m* newsboy
**gaze|la** (**-li, -le**) (*gen pl* **-l** *lub* **-li**) *f* gazelle
**gaze|ta** (**-ty, -ty**) (*dat sg* **-cie**) *f* newspaper
**gazet|ka** (**-ki, -ki**) (*dat sg* **-ce**, *gen pl* **-ek**) *f* (*ścienna*) board bulletin; (*szkolna*) school newspaper; (*ulotka*) pamphlet
**gazi|k** (**-ka, -ki**) (*instr sg* **-kiem**) *m* (*pot: samochód*) jeep
**gazocią|g** (**-gu, -gi**) (*instr sg* **-giem**) *m* gas pipeline
**gazomierz** (**-a, -e**) (*gen pl* **-y**) *m* gas-meter
**gaz|ować (-uję, -ujesz)** *vt* (*pot: prędko jechać*) to speed; (*truć gazem*) (*perf* **za-**) to gas
**gazowany** *adj* (*napój, woda*) carbonated, sparkling
**gazow|nia** (**-ni, -nie**) (*gen pl* **-ni**) *f* gas-works
**gazowy** *adj* (*kuchenka, maska*) gas *attr*; (*opatrunek*) gauze *attr*; **komora gazowa** (*Hist*) gas chamber
**gaźni|k** (**-ka, -ki**) (*instr sg* **-kiem**) *m* (*Mot*) carburettor (*Brit*), carburetor (*US*)
**gaż|a** (**-y, -e**) (*gen pl* **-** *lub* **-y**) *f* salary
**gąb** *n patrz* **gęba**
**gąbczasty** *adj* spongy
**gąb|ka** (**-ki, -ki**) (*dat sg* **-ce**, *gen pl* **-ek**) *f* sponge
**gąsienic|a** (**-y, -e**) *f* caterpillar; (*w ciągniku*) caterpillar tread
**gąsio|r** (**-ra, -ry**) (*loc sg* **-rze**) *m* (*Zool*) gander
**gąs|ka** (**-ki, -ki**) (*dat sg* **-ce**, *gen pl* **-ek**) *f dimin od* **gęś**
**gąszcz** (**-u, -e**) (*gen pl* **-ów** *lub* **-y**) *m* (*krzaków, lasu*) thicket; (*myśli, informacji*) tangle
**gbu|r** (**-ra, -ry**) (*loc sg* **-rze**) *m* (*pej*) boor
**gburowaty** *adj* boorish

**gda|kać (-cze)** *vi* (*o kurze*) to cackle
**gdakani|e** (**-a**) *nt* (*kury*) cackle
**gder|ać (-am, -asz)** *vi* (*pot*) to grumble; **~ na kogoś** to nag at sb

 **SŁOWO KLUCZOWE**

**gdy** *conj* **1** (*kiedy*) when, as; **spała już, gdy wróciłem** she was asleep when I returned; **podczas gdy** ((*wtedy*) *kiedy*) while; (*natomiast*) whereas; **gdy tylko** as soon as; **teraz, gdy ...** now that ...
**2** (*jeżeli*) when; **gdy raz zaczniesz, nie wolno ci przerwać** once you start you mustn't stop

**gdyby** *conj* if; **~ś tam (teraz) poszedł, przyjęliby cię** if you went there (now), they would accept you; **~ście tam (wtedy) poszli, przyjęliby was** if you had gone there (then), they would have accepted you; **~ żyła moja matka** I wish my mother were *lub* was still alive
**gdyż** *conj* because, for

 **SŁOWO KLUCZOWE**

**gdzie** *pron* **1** (*w zdaniach pytających*) where; **gdzie ona jest?** where is she?
**2** (*w zdaniach podrzędnych*) where; **nie wiem, gdzie ona jest** I don't know where she is
**3** (*w zdaniach względnych*) where; **wszedł do pokoju, gdzie stał duży stół** he entered the room where there was a big table
**4**: **nie miał gdzie spać** he didn't have anywhere to sleep, he had nowhere to sleep; **gdzie bądź** anywhere
▷ *part* (*w znaczeniu wzmacniającym*) how; **gdzie mi mierzyć się z tobą** how could I measure up to you; **gdzie tam!** (*pot*) nothing of the kind!

**gdziekolwiek** *pron* anywhere; **~ wszedł, odmawiano mu** he was turned away from every door
**gdzieniegdzie** *adv* here and there
**gdzieś** *adv* somewhere; **mam to ~!** (*pot*) I don't give a damn *lub* shit (about it)! (*pot*)
**gdzież** *pron, part* where on earth; *patrz też* **gdzie**
**gehen|na** (**-ny**) (*loc sg* **-nie**) *f* (*przen*) ordeal
**gej** (**-a, -e**) *m* (*homoseksualista*) homosexual, gay
**gejsz|a** (**-y, -e**) (*gen pl* **-y**) *f* geisha
**gejze|r** (**-ru, -ry**) (*loc sg* **-rze**) *m* geyser
**ge|m** (**-ma, -my**) (*loc sg* **-mie**) *m* (*Sport*) game
**ge|n** (**-nu, -ny**) (*loc sg* **-nie**) *m* (*Bio*) gene
**gen.** *abbr* (= *generał*) Gen.
**genealogi|a** (**-i, -e**) (*gen pl* **-i**) *f* genealogy
**genealogiczny** *adj*: **drzewo genealogiczne** family tree
**generacj|a** (**-i, -e**) (*gen pl* **-i**) *f* generation
**generalicj|a** (**-i**) *f* (*Wojsk*) body of generals
**generalizacj|a** (**-i, -e**) *f* generalization
**generaliz|ować (-uję, -ujesz)** *vt* to generalize
**generalny** *adj* general; **próba generalna** dress rehearsal; **Sekretarz G~** Secretary General; **generalne porządki** spring-clean; **sztab ~** chief headquarters
**genera|ł** (**-ła, -łowie**) (*loc sg* **-le**) *m* general; **~ broni** Lieutenant-General; **~ dywizji** Major-General; **~ brygady** ≈ Brigadier General (*US*)
**generato|r** (**-ra, -ry**) (*loc sg* **-rze**) *m* generator
**gener|ować (-uję, -ujesz)** (*perf* **wy-**) *vt* to generate
**genetyczny** *adj* genetic
**genety|ka** (**-ki**) (*dat sg* **-ce**) *f* (*Med*) genetics
**Gene|wa** (**-wy**) (*dat sg* **-wie**) *f* Geneva
**gene|za** (**-zy**) (*dat sg* **-zie**) *f* origin
**genialny** *adj* (*człowiek*) brilliant
**genitali|a** (**-ów**) *pl* genitals
**geniusz** (**-a, -e**) (*gen pl* **-y** *lub* **-ów**) *m* (*człowiek*) (man of) genius; (*talent, zdolności*) (*gen sg* **-u**) genius
**geode|ta** (**-ty, -ci**) (*dat sg* **-cie**) *m decl like f in sg* geodesist
**geodezj|a** (**-i**) *f* geodesy
**geogra|f** (**-fa, -fowie**) (*loc sg* **-fie**) *m* geographer
**geografi|a** (**-i**) *f* geography
**geograficzny** *adj* geographic(al); **atlas ~** geographical atlas
**geolo|g** (**-ga, -gowie** *lub* **-dzy**) (*instr sg* **-giem**) *m* geologist
**geologi|a** (**-i**) *f* geology
**geologiczny** *adj* geologic(al)
**geometri|a** (**-i**) *f* geometry
**geometryczny** *adj* geometrical
**geopolityczny** *adj* (*układ*) geopolitical
**gepar|d** (**-da, -dy**) (*loc sg* **-dzie**) *m* (*Zool*) cheetah
**geranium** *nt inv* (*Bot*) geranium
**gerbe|ra** (**-ry, -ry**) (*dat sg* **-rze**) *f* (*Bot*) gerbera
**geriatri|a** (**-i**) *f* (*Med*) geriatrics
**germani|sta** (**-sty, -ści**) (*dat sg* **-ście**) *m decl like f in sg* (*specjalista*) Germanist; (*student*) Germanist, student of German
**germanist|ka** (**-ki, -ki**) (*dat sg* **-ce**, *gen pl* **-ek**) *f* (*specjalistka*) Germanist; (*studentka*) Germanist, student of German
**germanisty|ka** (**-ki**) (*dat sg* **-ce**) *f* German studies
**germanizacj|a** (**-i**) *f* (*Hist*) Germanization

g

**germaniz|m** (**-mu, -my**) (*loc sg* **-mie**) *m* (*Jęz*) Germanism
**germaniz|ować (-uję, -ujesz)** (*perf* **z-**) *vt* to Germanize
**germański** *adj* (*Hist*) Germanic, Teutonic
**gerontologi|a** (**-i**) *f* gerontology
**ge|st** (**-stu, -sty**) (*loc sg* **-ście**) *m* gesture; **mieć (szeroki)** ~ (*przen*) to be free with money; **przywołać/zaprosić** (*perf*) **~em** to beckon; **teatralny** ~ (*przen*) theatrical gesture
**gestapo** *nt inv* (*Hist*) Gestapo
**gesti|a** (**-i**) *f*: **leżeć w czyjejś gestii** to be *lub* to lie in sb's hands
**gestykul|ować (-uję, -ujesz)** *vi* to gesticulate
**get|to** (**-ta, -ta**) (*loc sg* **-cie**) *nt* ghetto
**gęba** (**gęby, gęby**) (*dat sg* **gębie**, *gen pl* **gąb**) *f* (*pot*) mug (*pot*); **być mocnym w gębie** (*pot*) to have a ready tongue; **mieć niewyparzoną gębę** (*pot*) to have a big mouth; **zapomnieć** (*perf*) **języka w gębie** (*pot*) to be flabbergasted
**gęg|ać (-a)** *vi* (*o gęsi*) to gaggle
**gęsi** *adj* (*jajo, pióro*) goose *attr*; **~a skórka** gooseflesh, goose pimples; **iść ~ego** to walk (in) Indian *lub* single file
**gęstni|eć (-eje)** (*perf* **z-**) *vi* to thicken
**gęstoś|ć** (**-ci**) *f* density
**gęstwi|na** (**-ny**) (*dat sg* **-nie**) *f* thicket
**gęsty** *adj* (*las, mgła*) thick, dense; (*włosy, zupa*) thick
**gę|ś** (**-si, -si**) *f* goose; **rządzić się jak szara gęś** to boss around
**giąć (gnę, gniesz)** (*imp* **gnij**, *perf* **z-**) *vt* to bend; **giąć się** *vr* to bend
**gibki** *adj* supple, flexible
**Gibralta|r** (**-ru**) (*loc sg* **-rze**) *m* Gibraltar
**gieł|da** (**-dy, -dy**) (*dat sg* **-dzie**) *f* (*Ekon*) exchange; ~ **papierów wartościowych** stock exchange; ~ **samochodowa** car auction; ~ **pracy** employment exchange; ~ **towarowa** commodity exchange *lub* market
**giełdowy** *adj*: **makler** ~ stockbroker; **kurs** ~ exchange quotation
**gier** *n patrz* **gra**
**gierm|ek** (**-ka, -kowie**) (*instr sg* **-kiem**) *m* squire
**giętki** *adj* flexible
**giętkoś|ć** (**-ci**) *f* flexibility
**gigabaj|t** *nm* (**-ta, -ty**) (*loc sg* **-cie**) *m* (*Komput*) gigabyte
**gigan|t** (**-ta**) (*loc sg* **-cie**) *m* (*olbrzym*) (*nom pl* **-ci** *lub* **-ty**) giant; (*Sport*) (*nom pl* **-ty**) (*też*: **slalom gigant**) giant slalom
**gigantyczny** *adj* gigantic
**gi|l** (**-la, -le**) (*gen pl* **-li** *lub* **-lów**) *m* bullfinch
**giloty|na** (**-ny, -ny**) (*dat sg* **-nie**) *f* guillotine
**gimnastycz|ka** (**-ki, -ki**) (*dat sg* **-ce**, *gen pl* **-ek**) *f* gymnast
**gimnastyczny** *adj* (*ćwiczenia*) gymnastic; (*koszulka, obuwie*) gym *attr*; **sala gimnastyczna** gymnasium, gym (*pot*)
**gimnasty|k** (**-ka, -cy**) (*instr sg* **-kiem**) *m* gymnast
**gimnasty|ka** (**-ki**) (*dat sg* **-ce**) *f* gymnastics; **poranna** ~ morning exercises; **~ artystyczna** rhythmic gymnastics
**gimnastyk|ować (-uję, -ujesz)** *vt* to exercise; **gimnastykować się** *vr* to exercise; (*przen*: *głowić się*) to rack one's brain
**gimnazj|um** (**-um, -a**) (*gen pl* **-ów**) *nt inv in sg* grammar *lub* high school
**gi|n, dżi|n** (**-nu, -ny**) (*loc sg* **-nie**) *m* gin
**gi|nąć (-nę, -niesz)** (*imp* **-ń**, *perf* **z-**) *vi* (*tracić życie*) to perish; (*zanikać*) to disappear; (*zapodziewać się*) to get lost; **zginęły mi okulary** my glasses got lost, I lost my glasses
**ginekolo|g** (**-ga, -dzy** *lub* **-gowie**) (*instr sg* **-giem**) *m* gynaecologist (*Brit*), gynecologist (*US*)
**ginekologi|a** (**-i**) *f* gynaecology (*Brit*), gynecology (*US*)
**ginekologiczny** *adj* gynaecological (*Brit*), gynecological (*US*)
**gip|s** (**-su**) (*loc sg* **-sie**) *m* (*materiał*) plaster; (*opatrunek*) plaster cast; **w ~ie** in plaster
**gips|ować (-uję, -ujesz)** (*perf* **za-**) *vt* to plaster
**girlan|da** (**-dy, -dy**) (*dat sg* **-dzie**) *f* garland
**gita|ra** (**-ry, -ry**) (*dat sg* **-rze**) *f* guitar; ~ **elektryczna/basowa** electric/bass guitar; **grać na gitarze** to play the guitar; **zawracać komuś gitarę** (*pot*) to bother sb
**gitarzy|sta** (**-sty, -ści**) (*dat sg* **-ście**) *m decl like f in sg* guitarist, guitar player
**gladiato|r** (**-ra, -rzy** *lub* **-rowie**) (*loc sg* **-rze**) *m* gladiator
**glazu|ra** (**-ry, -ry**) (*loc sg* **-rze**) *f* (*płytki*) tiles *pl* (*on wall*); (*powłoka*) glazing
**gle|ba** (**-by, -by**) (*dat sg* **-bie**) *f* soil
**glę|dzić (-dzę, -dzisz)** (*imp* **-dź**) *vi* (*pot*) to chatter, to gab (*pot*)
**glicery|na** (**-ny**) (*dat sg* **-nie**) *f* glycerine
**gli|n** (**-nu**) (*loc sg* **-nie**) *m* aluminium (*Brit*), aluminum (*US*)
**gli|na** (**-ny, -ny**) (*dat sg* **-nie**) *f* clay ▷ *m decl like adj* (*pot*: *policjant*) cop
**gliniany** *adj* clay *attr*; **gliniane naczynia** pottery
**gliniarz** (**-a, -e**) (*gen pl* **-y**) *m* (*pot*: *policjant*) cop
**glo|b** (**-bu, -by**) (*loc sg* **-bie**) *m* globe
**globalizacj|a** (**-i**) (*dat sg* **-i**) *f* globalization
**globalny** *adj* global
**globu|s** (**-sa, -sy**) (*loc sg* **-sie**) *m* globe

**glo|n** (**-nu, -ny**) (*loc sg* **-nie**) *m* algae
**glori|a** (**-i, -e**) (*gen pl* **-i**) *f* glory
**gloryfik|ować (-uję, -ujesz)** *vt* to glorify
**gluko|za** (**-zy**) (*dat sg* **-zie**) *f* glucose
**glutaminia|n** (**-nu**) (*loc sg* **-nie**) *m*: **~ sodu** monosodium glutamate
**gł.** *abbr* (= *główny*) main
**gładki** *adj* (*skóra, morze*) smooth; (*droga*) smooth, even; (*włosy, fryzura*) sleek; (*materiał, bluzka*) plain; (*zeszyt*) unlined, unruled
**gładko** *adv* smoothly; (*ogolony*) clean *attr*; **była ~ uczesana** her hair was combed flat; **wszystko poszło ~** everything went smoothly
**gła|dzić (-dzę, -dzisz)** (*imp* **-dź**, *perf* **po-**) *vt* to stroke; **~ kogoś po głowie** to stroke sb's head
**gła|skać (-szczę, -szczesz)** (*perf* **po-**) *vt* to stroke; **po~ kogoś po ręce** to stroke sb's hand
**gła|z** (**-zu, -zy**) (*loc sg* **-zie**) *m* boulder; **on jest zimny jak ~** (*przen*) he is stone cold; **milczeć jak ~** to be silent as a tomb
**gł|ąb**[1] (**-ąba, -ąby**) (*loc sg* **-ąbie**) *m* (*w kapuście*) heart; (*przen*) idiot
**gł|ąb**[2] (**-ębi, -ębie**) (*gen pl* **-ębi**) *f*: **w ~ czegoś** deep *lub* far into sth
**głę|bia** (**-bi, -bie**) (*gen pl* **-bi**) *f* depth; **w głębi obrazu** in the (deep) background of the picture; **w głębi duszy** *lub* **serca** in the depth of one's soul *lub* heart
**głęboki** *adj* deep; (*ukłon, skłon*) low; (*dekolt*) low(-cut); (*umysł, cisza, zmiana*) profound; (*wiara*) strong; **~ talerz** soup plate
**głęboko** *adv* (*nurkować*) deep; (*zranić*) deeply
**głębokoś|ć** (**-ci, -ci**) (*gen pl* **-ci**) *f* depth
**głodny** *adj* hungry
**głod|ować (-uję, -ujesz)** *vi* to starve, to go hungry
**głodowy** *adj* (*strajk*) hunger *attr*; (*śmierć*) of hunger *lub* starvation; (*porcja, pensja*) meager, skimpy
**głodów|ka** (**-ki, -ki**) (*dat sg* **-ce**, *gen pl* **-ek**) *f* hunger strike
**głodu** *itd. n patrz* **głód**
**gł|odzić (-odzę, -odzisz)** (*imp* **-ódź**, *perf* **za-**) *vt* to starve
**głogu** *itd. n patrz* **głóg**
**gło|s** (**-su, -sy**) (*loc sg* **-sie**) *m* voice; (*prawo przemawiania*) voice, say; (*w wyborach*) vote; **śpiewać na ~y** to sing in harmony; **~ sumienia** voice of one's conscience; **na ~** aloud *lub* out loud; **na cały ~** at the top of one's voice; **dojść** (*perf*) **do ~u** (*w dyskusji*) to be allowed to speak; (*uzewnętrznić się*) to find expression; **podnosić (podnieść** *perf*) **~ na kogoś** to raise one's voice to sb; **udzielać (udzielić** *perf*) **komuś ~u** to grant *lub* give the floor to sb; **~ wstrzymujący się** abstention; **zabrać** (*perf*) **~** to take the floor; **odebrać** (*perf*) **komuś ~** to rule sb out of order; **oddać** (*perf*) **~ (na kogoś)** to cast one's vote (on sb)
**głosiciel|l** (**-la, -le**) (*gen pl* **-li**) *m* exponent, advocate
**gło|sić (-szę, -sisz)** (*imp* **-ś**) *vt* to advocate, to propagate; **wieść głosi, że ...** the rumour (*Brit*) *lub* rumor (*US*) is that ...
**głos|ka** (**-ki, -ki**) (*dat sg* **-ce**, *gen pl* **-ek**) *f* (*Jęz*) sound
**głos|ować (-uję, -ujesz)** (*perf* **za-**) *vi* to vote; **~ na kogoś/za czymś** to vote on sb/for sth
**głosowa|nie** (**-nia, -nia**) (*gen pl* **-ń**) *nt* vote, voting; **~ powszechne** general election
**głosowy** *adj*: **struny głosowe** vocal cords
**głośni|k** (**-ka, -ki**) (*instr sg* **-kiem**) *m* loudspeaker
**głośno** *adv* loudly; **~ myśleć** to think aloud *lub* think out loud; **mówić ~ (o czymś)** (*przen*) to speak one's mind (about sth), to speak up *lub* out (about sth); **~ o nim** (*przen*) his name is on everybody's lips
**głośny** *adj* (*słyszalny*) loud; (*hałaśliwy*) noisy; (*sławny*) famous
**gł|owa** (**-owy, -owy**) (*dat sg* **-owie**, *gen pl* **-ów**) *f* head; (*pot: umysł*) brain, mind; **na głowę** per capita; **~ państwa** head of state; **~ do góry!** chin up!; **mieć głowę na karku** to have one's head screwed on; **stracić** (*perf*) **głowę** to lose one's head; **z głowy** (*przen*) off the cuff *lub* the top of one's head; **całkiem mi to wyleciało z głowy** it completely slipped my mind; **koniak/sukces uderzył mu do głowy** the brandy/success went to his head; **nie zawracaj sobie głowy** don't bother; **przyszło mi do głowy, że ...** it (has) just occurred to me, that ...; **mieć coś/kogoś na (swojej) głowie** (*przen*) to have sth/sb on one's hands
**głowic|a** (**-y, -e**) *f* (*Tech*) head; (*Archit*) capital; **~ bojowa** warhead
**gł|owić się (-owię, -owisz)** (*imp* **-ów**) *vr*: **głowić się (nad czymś)** to rack one's brains (about sth)
**gł|ód** (**-odu**) (*loc sg* **-odzie**) *m* (*uczucie*) hunger; (*klęska głodu*) famine; **~ wiedzy** hunger for knowledge; **~ narkotyczny** *drug-related withdrawal symptoms*
**gł|óg** (**-ogu, -ogi**) (*instr sg* **-ogiem**) *m* hawthorn
**głów|ka** (**-ki, -ki**) (*dat sg* **-ce**, *gen pl* **-ek**) *f* head; (*Futbol*) header
**główk|ować (-uję, -ujesz)** *vi* (*Futbol*) to head; (*pot: myśleć*) to rack one's brain
**głównie** *adv* mainly, chiefly

g

**głównodowodząc|y** (**-ego, -y**) *m decl like adj* commander-in-chief
**główny** *adj* (*wejście, nagroda*) main; (*księgowy*) chief, head; (*rola*) lead; **liczebnik ~** cardinal number; **Poznań/Szczecin G~** Poznań/ Szczecin Central
**głuch|nąć (-nę, -niesz)** (*imp* **-nij**, *perf* **o-**) *vi* to grow *lub* become deaf
**głuchonie|my** (**-mego, -mi**) *m decl like adj* deaf-mute
**głucho|ta** (**-ty**) (*dat sg* **-cie**) *f* deafness
**głuchy** *adj* (*człowiek*) deaf; (*dźwięk*) hollow; **~ jak pień** (as) deaf as a post, stone-deaf; **głucha cisza** dead silence; **~ na coś** (*przen*) deaf to sth
**głup|ek** (**-ka, -ki**) (*instr sg* **-kiem**) *m* (*pej*) fool
**głupi** *adj* (*pot: niemądry*) foolish, stupid; (*błahy*) silly; (*kłopotliwy*) awkward ▷ *m decl like adj* fool
**głu|piec** (**-pca, -pcy**) *m* fool
**głupi|eć (-eję, -ejesz)** (*perf* **o-** *lub* **z-**) *vi* (*pot: stawać się głupim*) to become *lub* get silly; (*tracić głowę*) to lose one's head
**głupio** *adv* (*pot*) foolishly; **jest mi ~** I feel stupid
**głupo|ta** (**-ty**) (*dat sg* **-cie**) *f* foolishness, stupidity
**głupst|wo** (**-wa, -wa**) (*loc sg* **-wie**) *nt* foolish *lub* stupid thing; (*bzdura*) nonsense; (*błahostka*) trifle; **zrobić ~** to do something foolish; **palnąć** (*perf*) **~** (*pot: popełnić gafę*) to put one's foot in(to) it; (*powiedzieć coś niedorzecznego*) to say sth foolish
**głusz|ec** (**-ca, -ce**) *m* (*Zool*) capercaillie
**gmach** (**-u, -y**) *m* edifice, building
**gmatw|ać (-am, -asz)** (*perf* **za-**) *vt* to complicate; **gmatwać się** *vr* to get complicated
**gmatwani|na** (**-ny**) (*dat sg* **-nie**) *f* tangle
**gmi|na** (**-ny, -ny**) (*dat sg* **-nie**) *f* commune; **Izba Gmin** House of Commons
**gminny** *adj* communal
**gn|ać (-am, -asz)** (*perf* **po-**) *vi* to rush
**gna|t** (**-ta, -ty**) (*loc sg* **-cie**) *m* (*pot*) bone
**gnę** *itd. vb patrz* **giąć**
**gnę|bić (-bię, -bisz)** *vt* (*uciskać*) to oppress; (*trapić*) to worry, to bother
**gniady** *adj* bay
**gniazd|ko** (**-ka, -ka**) (*instr sg* **-kiem**, *gen pl* **-ek**) *nt* (*Elektr*) socket, outlet (*US*); (*przen*) nest
**gni|azdo** (**-azda, -azda**) (*loc sg* **-eździe**) *nt* nest
**gnić (gniję, gnijesz)** (*imp* **gnij**, *perf* **z-**) *vi* to rot, to decay
**gnie** *itd. vb patrz* **giąć**
**gnieść (gniotę, gnieciesz)** (*imp* **gnieć**, *perf* **po-** *lub* **wy-**) *vt* to crumple; **~ (u~** *perf*) **ciasto** to knead dough; **gnieść się** *vr* to crumple, to crease
**gnie|w** (**-wu**) (*loc sg* **-wie**) *m* anger, wrath; **wpadać (wpaść** *perf*) **w ~** to fly into a rage, to flare up
**gniew|ać (-am, -asz)** (*perf* **roz-**) *vt* to anger; **gniewać się** *vr* to be angry; **~ się na** *+acc* to be angry at *lub* with
**gniewny** *adj* angry
**gnie|ździć się (-żdżę, -ździsz)** (*imp* **-źdź**) *vr* (*o ptakach*) to nest; (*o ludziach*) to coop up
**gnoj|ek** (**-ka, -ki**) (*instr sg* **-kiem**) *m* (*pot!*) shithead (*pot!*)
**gnojów|ka** (**-ki, -ki**) (*dat sg* **-ce**, *gen pl* **-ek**) *f* liquid manure
**gn|ój** *m* (*nawóz*) (*gen sg* **-oju**) manure, dung; (*pot!: o człowieku*) (*gen sg* **-oja**, *nom pl* **-oje**) shitface (*pot!*)
**gnuśny** *adj* shiftless
**go** *pron acc od* **on**; (*o osobie*) him; (*o przedmiocie, zwierzęciu*) it
**gobeli|n** (**-nu, -ny**) (*loc sg* **-nie**) *m* Gobelin tapestry
**god|ło** (**-ła, -ła**) (*loc sg* **-le**, *gen pl* **-eł**) *nt* emblem
**godnoś|ć** (**-ci**) *f* (*duma, honor*) dignity, self-respect; (*urząd, funkcja*) (*nom pl* **-ci**) status; **jak Pana/Pani ~?** what's your name, please?
**godny** *adj* (*zachowanie, postawa*) stately; **~ zaufania** trustworthy; **~ wzmianki** worth mentioning; **~ podziwu** admirable
**god|y** (**-ów**) *pl* (*Zool*) mating; **złote ~** golden wedding
**godz.** *abbr* (*= godzina*) h. *lub* hr.
**godzić (godzę, godzisz)** (*imp* **gódź**, *perf* **po-**) *vt* (*doprowadzać do zgody*) to reconcile; **~ coś z czymś** to reconcile sth with sth ▷ *vi*: **~ w czyjeś prawa/interesy** to threaten sb's rights/interests; **godzić się** *vr* (*jednać się*) (*perf* **po-**) to become reconciled; **~ się z czymś** to come to terms with sth; **~ się (z~ się** *perf*) **na coś** to agree *lub* consent to sth
**godzi|na** (**-ny, -ny**) (*dat sg* **-nie**) *f* hour; **jest ~ czwarta** it's four o'clock; **pół godziny** half an hour; **~ lekcyjna** period; **~ policyjna** curfew; **godziny otwarcia/urzędowania/ pracy** opening/office/working hours; **~ odjazdu/przyjazdu** time of departure/ arrival, departure/arrival time; **(całymi) ~mi** for hours (on end); **z godziny na godzinę** hour by hour; **godzinę drogi stąd** an hour away from here; **na czarną godzinę** for the rainy day; **która (jest) ~?** what time is it?
**godzin|ka** (**-ki, -ki**) (*dat sg* **-ce**, *gen pl* **-ek**) *f* (*pot*) hour
**godzinny** *adj* hourlong
**godzinowy** *adj* (*stawka*) hourly; **wskazówka godzinowa** hour hand
**godziwy** *adj* decent
**gof|r** (**-ra, -ry**) (*loc sg* **-rze**) *m* waffle

**gog|le** (**-li**) *pl* goggles
**goić się (goi)** (*imp* **gój**, *perf* **za-**) *vr* to heal
**gokar|t** (**-ta, -ty**) (*loc sg* **-cie**) *m* go-kart
**go|l** (**-la, -le**) (*gen pl* **-li**) *m* goal; **strzelić** *lub* **zdobyć** (*perf*) **gola** to score a goal
**golar|ka** (**-ki, -ki**) (*dat sg* **-ce**, *gen pl* **-ek**) *f* shaver, (electrical) razor
**gola|s** (**-sa, -sy**) (*loc sg* **-sie**) *m* (*pot*) naked person; **na ~a** (*pot*) in the nude
**goleni|e** (**-a**) *nt* shaving; **krem do golenia** shaving cream
**gole|ń** (**-ni, -nie**) (*gen pl* **-ni**) *f* shin
**gol|f** (*loc sg* **-fie**) *m* (*Sport*) (*gen sg* **-fa**) golf; (*sweter*) (*gen sg* **-fu**, *nom pl* **-fy**) (*z luźno wywiniętym kołnierzem*) polo-necked sweater; (*z obcisłym kołnierzem*) turtle-necked sweater
**golić (golę, golisz)** (*imp* **gol**, *perf* **o-**) *vt* to shave; **golić się** *vr* to shave
**goli|zna** (**-zny, -zny**) (*dat sg* **-źnie**) *f* nakedness
**golon|ka** (**-ki, -ki**) (*dat sg* **-ce**, *gen pl* **-ek**) *f* (*Kulin*) knuckle of pork
**goł|ąb** (**-ębia, -ębie**) (*gen pl* **-ębi**) *m* pigeon; **~ pocztowy** carrier pigeon
**gołąb|ek** (**-ka, -ki**) (*instr sg* **-kiem**) *m* (*ptak*) dove; **~ pokoju** dove of peace; **gołąbki** *pl* (*Kulin*) stuffed cabbage
**gołole|dź** (**-dzi**) *f* glazed frost
**gołosłowny** *adj* groundless
**goły** *adj* (*nagi*) naked; (*pusty*) bare; (*pot: bez pieniędzy*) penniless, broke; **z gołą głową** bareheaded; **~mi rękami** with bare hands; **~m okiem** with the naked eye; **pod ~m niebem** in the open air
**gondo|la** (**-li, -le**) (*gen pl* **-li**) *f* gondola
**gon|g** (**-gu, -gi**) (*instr sg* **-giem**) *m* gong
**go|nić (-nię, -nisz)** (*imp* **-ń**) *vt* (*ścigać*) to chase; (*poganiać*) to drive; **~ za czymś** to chase (after) sth; **gonić się** *vr* to chase one another
**go|niec** (**-ńca**) *m* (*w biurze*) (*nom pl* **-ńcy**) office junior, office boy; (*Szachy*) (*nom pl* **-ńce**) bishop
**gonit|wa** (**-wy, -wy**) (*dat sg* **-wie**) *f* (*pościg*) chase; (*Sport*) race, run
**gończy** *adj*: **list ~** (arrest) warrant; **pies ~** hound
**googl|ować (-uję, -ujesz)** *vt* (*Komput*) to Google®
**GOPR** *abbr* (*= Górskie Ochotnicze Pogotowie Ratunkowe*) *mountain rescue team*
**gor|ąco** (**-ąca**) *nt* (*upał*) heat ▷ *adv* (*comp* **-ęcej**) (*ciepło*) hot; (*przen: oklaskiwać, pozdrawiać*) warmly; **~ mi** I'm hot; **na ~** served hot; **wiadomości na ~** live news; **było ~** (*przen*) it was hot work
**gor|ący** (*comp* **-ętszy**) *adj* hot; (*prośba*) urgent; (*wielbiciel, patriota*) fervent; **~ czas/okres** hectic *lub* hot time/period; **złapać** (*perf*) **kogoś na ~m uczynku** to catch sb red-handed *lub* in the act; **w gorącej wodzie kąpany** (*pot*) hot-headed
**gorącz|ka** (**-ki, -ki**) (*dat sg* **-ce**) *f* fever; **mieć gorączkę** to have a fever *lub* to run a temperature; **~ złota** gold rush
**gorączk|ować (-uję, -ujesz)** *vi* (*Med*) to run *lub* have a temperature; **gorączkować się** *vr* to get excited *lub* frantic
**gorączkowy** *adj* frantic, hectic
**gorczyc|a** (**-y**) *f* (*Bot*) white mustard
**gorliwoś|ć** (**-ci**) *f* zeal, ardour (*Brit*), ardor (*US*)
**gorliwy** *adj* zealous, ardent
**gorse|t** (**-tu, -ty**) (*loc sg* **-cie**) *m* corset
**gorszy** *adj comp od* **zły** worse; **nie ma nic gorszego niż ...** there's nothing worse than ...; **coraz ~** worse and worse; **co gorsza** what's worse, worse still; **zmiana na gorsze** a change for the worse
**gor|szyć (-szę, -szysz)** (*perf* **z-**) *vt* to scandalize, to shock; **gorszyć się** *vr* to be scandalized *lub* shocked
**gorycz** (**-y**) *f* bitterness
**gory|l** (**-la, -le**) (*gen pl* **-li**) *m* (*Zool*) gorilla; (*pot: obstawa*) bodyguard
**gorza|ła** (**-ły, -ły**) (*dat sg* **-le**) *f* (*pot*) booze (*pot*)
**gorzej** *adv comp od* **źle** worse
**gorzel|nia** (**-ni, -nie**) (*gen pl* **-ni**) *f* distillery
**gorzki** *adj* (*lekarstwo, prawda*) bitter; (*herbata*) unsweetened
**gorzknie|ć (-ję, -jesz)** (*perf* **z-**) *vi* to grow *lub* become embittered
**gorzko** *adv* bitterly
**gosp|oda** (**-ody, -ody**) (*dat sg* **-odzie**, *gen pl* **-ód**) *f* inn
**gospodarczy** *adj* economic; (*wiejski*) farm *attr*
**gospodar|ka** (**-ki, -ki**) (*dat sg* **-ce**, *gen pl* **-ek**) *f* economy; (*zarządzanie*) management, administration; **~ planowa/rynkowa** planned/market economy
**gospodarnoś|ć** (**-ci**) *f* thrift, economy
**gospodarny** *adj* thrifty, economical
**gospodar|ować (-uję, -ujesz)** *vt* (*zarządzać*) to husband; (*pieniędzmi*) to manage ▷ *vi* (*prowadzić gospodarstwo*) to farm
**gospodarski** *adj* farm *attr*
**gospodarst|wo** (**-wa, -wa**) (*loc sg* **-wie**) *nt* (*domowe*) household; (*rolne*) farm
**gospodarz** (**-a, -e**) (*gen pl* **-y**) *m* (*rolnik*) farmer; (*pan domu*) host; (*właściciel kamienicy*) landlord
**gospody|ni** (**-ni, -nie**) (*gen pl* **-ń**) *f* (*pani domu*) hostess; (*właścicielka domu*) landlady; (*żona rolnika*) farmer's wife
**gospo|sia** (**-si, -sie**) (*gen pl* **-ś**) *f* housekeeper
**go|ścić (-szczę, -ścisz)** (*imp* **-ść**) *vt* (*podejmować*) (*perf* **u-**) to entertain, to have as

g

a guest; (*o hotelu*) to house, to accommodate ▷ *vi*: **~ (u kogoś)** to stay (at sb's place)
**goś|ciec** (**-ćca**) *m* (*Med*) rheumatism
**gości|na** (**-ny**) (*dat sg* **-nie**) *f*: **być u kogoś w gościnie** to stay with sb; **podziękować** (*perf*) **(komuś) za gościnę** to thank sb for (their *itp.*) hospitality
**gościnnie** *adv* (*przyjmować, podejmować*) hospitably; **wykładać ~** to be a guest lecturer *lub* visiting professor
**gościnnoś|ć** (**-ci**) *f* hospitality
**gościnny** *adj* (*człowiek*) hospitable; (*pokój, występ*) guest *attr*
**goś|ć** (**-cia, -cie**) (*gen pl* **-ci**, *instr pl* **-ćmi**) *m* (*odwiedzający*) guest, visitor; (*klient*) guest; (*pot*: *mężczyzna*) fellow, guy, bloke (*Brit*)
**got|ować (-uję, -ujesz)** *vt* (*perf* **u-**) (*posiłek*) to cook; (*kartofle*) (*perf* **u-**) to boil; (*wodę, mleko*) (*perf* **za-**) to boil; **gotować się** *vr* (*o posiłku*) (*perf* **u-**) to cook; (*o kartoflach*) (*perf* **u-**) to boil; (*o wodzie, mleku*) (*perf* **za-**) to boil
**gotowany** *adj* boiled
**gotowoś|ć** (**-ci**) *f* (*przygotowanie*) readiness; (*chęć*) willingness; **w stanie gotowości** in readiness, on standby
**gotowy** *adj* (*skończony*) finished; (*przygotowany*) ready; (*kupiony w sklepie*) ready-made; (: *ubranie, suknia*) off the peg, ready-to-wear; **być ~m na wszystko** to be ready for anything
**gotów|ka** (**-ki**) (*dat sg* **-ce**) *f* cash, ready money (*pot*); **płacić (zapłacić** *perf*) **gotówką** to pay (in) cash; **kupować (kupić** *perf*) **coś za gotówkę** to buy sth for cash
**gotówkowy** *adj* cash; **rezerwy gotówkowe** cash reserves; **wpłata gotówkowa** cash deposit
**gotycki** *adj* Gothic
**goty|k** (**-ku**) (*instr sg* **-kiem**) *m* (*Archit*) Gothic
**goździ|k** (**-ka, -ki**) (*instr sg* **-kiem**) *m* (*kwiat*) carnation, pink; (*przyprawa*) clove
**gódź** *itd. vb patrz* **godzić**
**gój** *itd. vb patrz* **goić**
**gól** *itd. vb patrz* **golić**
**gó|ra** (**-ry, -ry**) (*dat sg* **-rze**) *f* mountain; (*ubrania*) top; (*domu*) upstairs; (*śmieci, książek*) heap; **~ lodowa** iceberg; **w ~ch** in the mountains; **jechać (pojechać** *perf*) **w góry** to go to the mountains; **mieszkać na górze** to live upstairs; **iść na górę** to go upstairs; **iść pod górę** to walk uphill; **spojrzeć** (*perf*) **do góry** to look up(wards); **do góry nogami** upside down; **iść (pójść** *perf*) **w górę** (*o cenach, akcjach*) to go up; **głowa do góry!** cheer up!; **traktować kogoś z góry** to patronize sb; **płacić/dziękować z góry** to pay/thank in advance; **to kosztuje ~ 10 funtów** it costs 10 pounds at (the) most!
**góra|l** (**-la, -le**) (*gen pl* **-li**) *m* highlander
**góral|ka** (**-ki, -ki**) (*dat sg* **-ce**, *gen pl* **-ek**) *f* highlander
**góralski** *adj* highlander *attr*
**gór|ka** (**-ki, -ki**) (*dat sg* **-ce**, *gen pl* **-ek**) *f* hill; **pod górkę** uphill
**górnict|wo** (**-wa**) (*loc sg* **-wie**) *nt* mining
**górniczy** *adj* (*sprzęt, przemysł*) mining *attr*; (*mundur, czapka*) miner's
**górni|k** (**-ka, -cy**) (*instr sg* **-kiem**) *m* miner
**górnolotny** *adj* high-flown, pompous
**górny** *adj* (*warga, piętro*) upper; (*półka*) top
**gór|ować (-uję, -ujesz)** *vi*: **~ nad kimś/czymś** (*być wyższym*) to tower over sb/sth; (*być lepszym*) to be head and shoulders above sb/sth
**górski** *adj* mountain *attr*
**górzysty** *adj* mountainous, hilly
**gówniarz** (**-a, -e**) (*gen pl* **-y**) *m* (*pot!*) squirt (*pot!*), punk (*pot!*)
**gó|wno** (**-wna, -wna**) (*loc sg* **-wnie**, *gen pl* **-wien**) *nt* (*pot!*) shit (*pot!*), crap (*pot!*)
**GPS** (**GPSa, GPSy**) (*loc sg* **GPSie**) *m abbr* (*Aut*) satnav
**gr** *abbr* = **grosz(y)**
**gra** (**gry, gry**) (*dat sg* **grze**, *gen pl* **gier**) *f* game; (*aktorska*) acting; (*przen*: *udawanie*) act, pretense; (*kolorów, świateł*) play; **gra w karty** card game; **gra podwójna/mieszana** (*w tenisie itp.*) doubles/mixed doubles; **gra słów** pun, play on words; **gra na giełdzie** speculation (on the stock exchange); **to nie wchodzi w grę** it's out of the question
**gra|b** (**-bu, -by**) (*loc sg* **-bie**) *m* (*Bot*) hornbeam (tree)
**grabarz** (**-a, -e**) (*gen pl* **-y**) *m* gravedigger
**gra|bić (-bię, -bisz)** *vt* (*liście*) to rake (*perf* **o-**) (*łupić*) to plunder, to loot; (*ludność*) to plunder
**gra|bie** (**-bi**) *pl* rake
**gra|bieć (-bieje)** (*perf* **z-**) *vi* to grow numb (with cold)
**grabież** (**-y, -e**) (*gen pl* **-y**) *f* plunder, pillage
**grabieżc|a** (**-y, -y**) *m decl like f in sg* plunderer
**gracj|a** (**-i**) *f* (*wdzięk*) grace
**gracz** (**-a, -e**) (*gen pl* **-y**) *m* player
**gr|ać (-am, -asz)** (*perf* **za-**) *vt/vi* to play; **~ na skrzypcach** to play the violin; **~ w piłkę/brydża** to play ball/bridge; **~ na wyścigach** to gamble on the horses, to play the horses; **~ w totalizator** to do the pools (*Brit*); **~ na zwłokę** to play for time; **~ na giełdzie** to play the stock exchange; **~ komuś na nerwach** to get on sb's nerves; **to nie gra roli** it doesn't matter; **coś dziś grają w kinie/teatrze?** what's on at the cinema/theatre?
**gra|d** (**-du**) (*loc sg* **-dzie**) *m* hail; (*przen*) hail, volley
**gradobici|e** (**-a**) *nt* hailstorm

**graffiti** *nt inv* graffiti
**graficzny** *adj* graphic
**grafi|k** (**-ka, -cy**) (*instr sg* **-kiem**) *m* graphic artist
**grafi|ka** (**-ki**) (*dat sg* **-ce**) *f* (*sztuka*) graphic arts *pl*; (*dzieło*) (*nom pl* **-ki**) print; **~ komputerowa** (*Komput*) computer graphics *pl*
**grafi|t** (**-tu, -ty**) (*loc sg* **-cie**) *m* (*minerał*) graphite; (*w ołówku*) lead
**grafolo|g** (**-ga, -gowie** *lub* **-dzy**) (*instr sg* **-giem**) *m* graphologist
**grafoma|n** (**-na, -ni**) (*loc sg* **-nie**) *m* third-rate writer, scribbler
**gra|m** (**-ma, -my**) (*loc sg* **-mie**) *m* gram(me)
**gramatyczny** *adj* grammatical
**gramaty|ka** (**-ki, -ki**) (*dat sg* **-ce**) *f* (*nauka*) grammar; (*podręcznik*) grammar (book)
**gramofo|n** (**-nu, -ny**) (*loc sg* **-nie**) *m* record player
**gramofonowy** *adj* (*płyta, igła*) gramophone *attr*
**grana|t** (**-tu, -ty**) (*loc sg* **-cie**) *m* (*pocisk*) grenade; (*kolor*) navy (blue); (*minerał*) garnet; (*Bot*) pomegranate
**granatowy** *adj* navy (blue)
**graniastosłu|p** (**-pa, -py**) (*loc sg* **-pie**) *m* (*Geom*) prism
**granic|a** (**-y, -e**) *f* (*państwa*) border; (*miasta*) boundary, limit(s) (*pl*) (*US*); (*kres, miara*) limit; **za granicą** (*mieszkać, studiować*) abroad; **za granicę** (*jechać, wysyłać*) abroad; **miłość bez granic** boundless love; **górna/dolna ~** upper/lower limit; **to przechodzi wszelkie granice** that's the limit; **wszystko ma swoje granice** there's a limit to everything
**graniczny** *adj* border *attr*
**granicz|yć** (**-ę, -ysz**) *vi*: **~ z** *+instr* (*mieć wspólną granicę*) to border on; (*być podobnym*) to verge on
**grani|t** (**-tu, -ty**) (*loc sg* **-cie**) *m* granite
**granitowy** *adj* granite *attr*
**granulowany** *adj* granulated
**grapefrui|t** (**-ta, -ty**) (*loc sg* **-cie**) *m* = **grejpfrut**
**gras|ować** (**-uję, -ujesz**) *vi* (*o chorobie*) to be rampant; (*o bandzie*) to prowl
**gra|t** (**-ta, -ty**) (*loc sg* **-cie**) *m* (*stary mebel, urządzenie*) piece of junk; (*pot: stary samochód*) jalopy
**gratis** *adv inv* free (of charge)
**gratisowy** *adj* free
**gratulacj|e** (**-i**) *pl* congratulations *pl*; **składać** (**złożyć** *perf*) **komuś ~** to offer sb one's congratulations; **moje ~!** congratulations!
**gratulacyjny** *adj* (*list, telegram*) congratulatory
**gratul|ować** (**-uję, -ujesz**) (*perf* **po-**) *vi*: **~ (komuś czegoś)** to congratulate (sb on sth)
**grawer|ować** (**-uję, -ujesz**) (*perf* **wy-**) *vt* to engrave
**grawitacj|a** (**-i, -e**) (*gen pl* **-i**) *f* gravitation
**grawitacyjny** *adj* gravitational
**grdy|ka** (**-ki, -ki**) (*dat sg* **-ce**) *f* Adam's apple
**Grecj|a** (**-i**) *f* Greece
**grecki** *adj* Greek; (*styl, sztuka*) Grecian; **ryba po grecku** fish à la grecque
**greckokatolicki** *adj* Greek Catholic
**Greczyn|ka** (**-ki, -ki**) (*dat sg* **-ce**, *gen pl* **-ek**) *f* Greek
**grejpfru|t** (**-ta** *lub* **-tu, -ty**) (*loc sg* **-cie**) *m* grapefruit
**Gre|k** (**-ka, -cy**) (*instr sg* **-kiem**) *m* Greek; **udawać ~a** to play dumb; **nie udawaj ~a!** don't act the idiot!
**gremialnie** *adv* in a body
**gremi|um** (**-um, -a**) (*gen pl* **-ów**) *nt inv in sg* body, assembly
**Grenlandczy|k** (**-ka, -cy**) *m* Greenlander
**Grenlandi|a** (**-i**) *f* Greenland
**grenlandzki** *adj* Greenlandic
**grill** (**-a, -e**) (*gen pl* **-ów**) *m* barbecue
**grobie** *itd. n patrz* **grób**
**grob|la** (**-li, -le**) (*gen pl* **-li** *lub* **-el**) *f* dike *lub* dyke, dam
**grobo|wiec** (**-wca, -wce**) *m* tomb; **~ rodzinny** family vault
**grobowy** *adj* grave *attr*, tomb *attr*; (*nastrój, głos*) sepulchral; (*mina*) gloomy; **grobowa cisza** dead silence
**groch** (**-u**) *m* (*Bot*) pea; (*zbiorowo*) peas *pl*; **grochy** *pl* (*deseń*) polka dots; **rzucać ~em o ścianę** (*przen*) to waste one's breath; **~ z kapustą** (*przen*) hotchpotch, hodgepodge (*US*)
**grochowy** *adj* pea *attr*
**grochów|ka** (**-ki, -ki**) (*dat sg* **-ce**, *gen pl* **-ek**) *f* pea soup
**gr|odzić** (**-odzę, -odzisz**) (*imp* **-odź** *lub* **-ódź**, *perf* **o-**) *vt* to fence
**gro|m** (**-mu, -my**) (*loc sg* **-mie**) *m* (a clap of) thunder; **jak ~ z jasnego nieba** like a bolt from the blue
**groma|da** (**-dy, -dy**) (*dat sg* **-dzie**) *f* group; (*Bio*) class
**groma|dzić** (**-dzę, -dzisz**) (*imp* **-dź**, *perf* **z-**) *vt* to accumulate; **gromadzić się** *vr* (*o ludziach, chmurach*) to gather
**gro|mić** (**-mię, -misz**) (*perf* **z-**) *vt* to scold
**gromki** *adj* (*brawa*) rapturous; (*głos*) booming; (*krzyk*) loud
**gromnic|a** (**-y, -e**) *f candle traditionally lit during storms and for dying people*
**gronko|wiec** (**-wca, -wce**) *m* (*Med*) staphylococcus
**gro|no** (**-na, -na**) (*loc sg* **-nie**) *nt* (*grupa ludzi*) team; (*winne*) bunch (of grapes);

~ **nauczycielskie** teaching staff; ~ **rodzinne** family (circle)
**gronowy** *adj* grape *attr*
**gros** *nt inv* the majority
**grosz** (**-a, -e**) (*gen pl* **-y**) *m* grosz (*Polish monetary unit equal to 1/100 zloty*); **nie dać** *perf* **ani ~a** not to give a penny; **zapłacić** *perf* **(wszystko) co do ~a** to pay (everything) to the last penny; **być bez ~a** to be penniless; **kupić** (*perf*) **coś za ~e** to buy something dirt-cheap; **nie mieć za ~ czegoś** not to have an ounce of sth
**grosz|ek** (**-ku, -ki**) (*instr sg* **-kiem**) *m* (*zielony*) green peas *pl*; (*Bot: pachnący*) sweet pea; (*deseń*): **w groszki** spotted, polka-dotted
**gro|t** (**-tu, -ty**) (*loc sg* **-cie**) *m* (*strzały*) arrowhead; (*włóczni itp.*) spearhead; (*Żegl: maszt*) mainmast; (*: żagiel*) mainsail
**gro|ta** (**-ty, -ty**) (*dat sg* **-cie**) *f* grotto, cave
**grotes|ka** (**-ki, -ki**) (*dat sg* **-ce**, *gen pl* **-ek**) *f* (*Lit*) burlesque; (*Sztuka*) grotesque
**groteskowy** *adj* grotesque
**gro|za** (**-zy**) (*dat sg* **-zie**) *f* (*niebezpieczeństwo*) peril; (*lęk*) terror, awe
**gr|ozić (-ożę, -ozisz)** (*imp* **-oź**) *vi* (*straszyć*) to threaten; (*zagrażać*) to be imminent
**gr|oźba** (**-oźby, -oźby**) (*dat sg* **-oźbie**, *gen pl* **-óźb**) *f* (*pogróżka*) threat; (*niebezpieczeństwo*) threat, menace; **pod groźbą kary** under threat
**groźny** *adj* (*przeciwnik*) dangerous, formidable; (*sytuacja*) dangerous, threatening; (*mina, głos*) menacing
**gr|ób** (**-obu, -oby**) (*loc sg* **-obie**) *m* grave; **milczeć jak ~** to be (as) silent as the grave; **stać nad grobem** (*przen*) to be at death's door; **wpędzić** (*perf*) **kogoś do grobu** to send sb to an early grave
**gr|ód** (**-odu, -ody**) (*loc sg* **-odzie**) *m* (*Hist: miasto*) city; (*obronny*) castle
**gruba|s** (**-sa, -sy**) (*loc sg* **-sie**) *m* (*pot*) fatty, fatso (*pot!*)
**grubia|nin** (**-nina, -nie**) (*loc sg* **-ninie**) *m* boor
**grubiański** *adj* boorish
**grubi|eć (-eję, -ejesz)** (*perf* **z-**) *vi* (*przybierać na wadze*) to put on weight; (*o warstwie*) to grow thicker
**grubo** *adv* (*mielić*) coarsely; (*smarować*) thickly; (*ubierać się*) warmly; ~ **się mylić** to be gravely mistaken; ~ **więcej** much more
**gruboskórny** *adj* inconsiderate, tactless
**gruboś|ć** (**-ci**) *f* thickness; **mieć 3 cm grubości** to be 3 cm thick
**gruboziarnisty** *adj* coarse-grained
**grubszy** *adj comp od* **gruby**; **z grubsza** roughly
**gruby** *adj* (*ołówek, książka*) thick; (*człowiek*) fat; ~ **błąd** grave mistake; **gruba ryba** (*przen*) bigwig (*pot*), big shot (*pot*)
**gruch|ać (-am, -asz)** *vi* (*o gołębiu*) to coo; (*przen*) to bill and coo
**grucho|t** (**-tu**) (*loc sg* **-cie**) *m* (*łoskot*) rattle; (*pot: stary samochód*) (*nom pl* **-ty**, *gen pl* **-tów**) jalopy
**grucho|tać (-czę, -czesz)** *vt* (*perf* **po-** *lub* **z-**) (*miażdżyć*) to crush
**gruczo|ł** (**-łu, -ły**) (*loc sg* **-le**) *m* (*Anat*) gland
**gru|da** (**-dy, -dy**) (*dat sg* **-dzie**) *f* lump; **robota idzie jak po grudzie** (*pot*) it is uphill work
**grud|ka** (**-ki, -ki**) (*dat sg* **-ce**, *gen pl* **-ek**) *f* lump
**grudkowaty** *adj* lumpy
**grudniowy** *adj* December *attr*
**gru|dzień** (**-dnia, -dnie**) (*gen pl* **-dni**) *m* December
**grun|t** (**-tu, -ty** *lub* **-ta**) (*loc sg* **-cie**) *m* (*gleba*) soil; (*teren*) land; (*dno*) bottom; **stać na twardym/pewnym gruncie** to be on firm ground; **tracić (stracić** *perf*) ~ **pod nogami** to be out of one's depth; **w gruncie rzeczy** in fact, essentially
**gruntowny** *adj* thorough
**gru|pa** (**-py, -py**) (*dat sg* **-pie**) *f* group; (*drzew*) cluster; ~ **krwi** blood group
**grup|ka** (**-ki, -ki**) (*dat sg* **-ce**, *gen pl* **-ek**) *f* (small) group
**grup|ować (-uję, -ujesz)** *vt* (*klasyfikować: fakty*) (*perf* **po-**) to group; (*gromadzić: słuchaczy, widzów*) (*perf* **z-**) to bring in; **grupować się** *vr* (*o ludziach*) to assemble
**grupowo** *adv* collectively
**grupowy** *adj* (*praca*) team *attr*; (*ubezpieczenie, zdjęcie*) group *attr*
**grusz|a** (**-y, -e**) *f* pear tree
**grusz|ka** (**-ki, -ki**) (*dat sg* **-ce**, *gen pl* **-ek**) *f* (*owoc*) pear; (*drzewo*) pear tree
**gru|z** (**-zu, -zy**) (*loc sg* **-zie**) *m* rubble; **gruzy** *pl* (*ruiny*) ruins *pl*; **leżeć (lec** *lub* **legnąć** *perf*) **w ~ach** to crumble into ruin
**Gruzi|n** (**-na, -ni**) (*loc sg* **-nie**) *m* Georgian
**Gruzin|ka** (**-ki, -ki**) (*dat sg* **-ce**, *gen pl* **-ek**) *f* Georgian
**gruziński** *adj* Georgian
**Gruzj|a** (**-i**) *f* Georgia
**gruźlic|a** (**-y**) *f* (*Med*) tuberculosis, TB (*pot*)
**gryczany** *adj*: **kasza gryczana** buckwheat groats *pl*
**gry|f** (*loc sg* **-fie**, *nom pl* **-fy**) *m* (*w instrumencie*) (*gen sg* **-fu**) neck; (*Mitologia*) (*gen sg* **-fa**) griffin, griffon
**gry|ka** (**-ki**) (*dat sg* **-ce**) *f* buckwheat
**gryma|s** (**-su, -sy**) (*loc sg* **-sie**) *m* (*mina*) grimace; **grymasy** *pl* (*kaprysy*) whims *pl*
**gryma|sić (-szę, -sisz)** (*imp* **-ś**, *perf* **po-**) *vi* (*wybredzać*) to be fussy *lub* choosy; (*o dziecku*) to be fretful
**grymaśny** *adj* (*dziecko*) fretful; (*usposobienie*) capricious

**gry|pa** (**-py**) (*dat sg* **-pie**) *f* influenza, flu (*pot*)
**gryzący** *adj* (*dym*) acrid, pungent; (*wełna*) scratchy; (*ironia*) biting
**gryzmol|ić (-ę, -isz)** *vt* (*słowo, zdanie*) (*perf* **na-**) to scrawl, to scribble; (*książkę, kartkę*) (*perf* **po-**) to scribble all over
**gryzmoł|y** (**-ów**) *pl* scribble
**gryzo|ń** (**-nia, -nie**) (*gen pl* **-ni**) *m* rodent
**gry|źć (-zę, -ziesz)** (*imp* **-ź**, *pt* **-zł, -zła, -źli**) *vt* to bite; (*rzuć*) to chew, to munch; (*kość*) to gnaw ▷ *vi* (*o dymie*) to sting; (*o wełnie*) to itch; (*o tęsknocie, sumieniu*) to gnaw (at); **co cię gryzie?** what's the matter with you?; **gryźć się** *vr* (*o psach*) to fight; (*o kolorach*) to clash
**grz|ać (-eję, -ejesz)** *vt* (*wodę*) (*perf* **za-**) to heat; (*ręce*) (*perf* **o-**) to warm ▷ *vi* (*o słońcu*) to beat down; (*o piecu*) to be hot, to give off heat; **grzać się** *vr* (*na słońcu*) to bask (in the sun); (*przy piecu*) to warm o.s.; (*o żelazku, wodzie*) to heat up
**grzał|ka** (**-ki, -ki**) (*dat sg* **-ce**, *gen pl* **-ek**) *f* (water) heater; (*do herbaty*) travel heater
**grzan|ka** (**-ki, -ki**) (*dat sg* **-ce**, *gen pl* **-ek**) *f* (a slice of) toast; **grzanki** *pl* toast
**grząd|ka** (**-ki, -ki**) (*dat sg* **-ce**, *gen pl* **-ek**) *f dimin od* **grzęda**; (*w ogrodzie*) bed
**grząski** *adj* (*teren*) boggy; (*błoto*) sticky
**grzbie|t** (**-tu, -ty**) (*loc sg* **-cie**) *m* back, spine; (*góry*) ridge; (*dłoni, książki*) back
**grzbietowy** *adj* dorsal; **styl ~** (*Sport*) backstroke
**grze|bać (-bię, -biesz)** *vt* (*chować zmarłego*) (*perf* **po-**) to bury ▷ *vi* (*szukać*) to rummage; **grzebać się** *vr* (*guzdrać się*) to dawdle
**grzebie|ń** (**-nia, -nie**) (*gen pl* **-ni**) *m* comb; (*u zwierząt*) crest
**grzech** (**-u, -y**) *m* sin; **~ śmiertelny** mortal sin; **~ pierworodny** the original sin; **popełniać (popełnić** *perf***) ~** to sin, to commit a sin
**grzecho|t** (**-tu**) (*loc sg* **-cie**) *m* rattle
**grzecho|tać (-czę, -czesz)** *vi* to rattle
**grzechot|ka** (**-ki, -ki**) (*dat sg* **-ce**, *gen pl* **-ek**) *f* rattle
**grzechotni|k** (**-ka, -ki**) (*instr sg* **-kiem**) *m* rattlesnake
**grzecznościowy** *adj* (*zwrot, formułka*) polite
**grzecznoś|ć** (**-ci**) *f* (*uprzejmość*) politeness; (*przysługa*) kindness, favour (Brit), favor (US); **wyświadczać (wyświadczyć** *perf***) komuś ~** to do sb a favo(u)r; **grzeczności** *pl* (*komplementy*) attentions; **prawić grzeczności** to pay compliments; **wymieniać (wymienić** *perf***) grzeczności** to exchange courtesies
**grzeczny** *adj* (*obsługa, ukłon*) polite; (*dziecko*) good
**grzejni|k** (**-ka, -ki**) (*instr sg* **-kiem**) *m* (*kaloryfer*) radiator; **~ elektryczny** (electric) heater
**grzejny** *adj* (*instalacja, urządzenie*) heating *attr*
**grzesznic|a** (**-y, -e**) *f* sinner
**grzeszni|k** (**-ka, -cy**) (*instr sg* **-kiem**) *m* sinner
**grzeszny** *adj* sinful
**grzesz|yć (-ę, -ysz)** (*perf* **z-**) *vi* to sin; **nie ~ mądrością** to be a bit soft in the head; **nie ~ urodą** not to be exactly a stunner
**grzę|da** (**-dy, -dy**) (*dat sg* **-dzie**) *f* (*dla ptaków*) perch, roost; (*w ogrodzie*) patch; *patrz też* **grządka**
**grzęzawis|ko** (**-ka, -ka**) (*instr sg* **-kiem**) *nt* bog
**grz|ęznąć (-ęznę, -ęźniesz)** (*imp* **-ęźnij**, *pt* **-ązł, -ęzła, -ęźli**, *perf* **u-**) *vi* to get stuck; (*o pojeździe*) to get bogged down; **~ w długach** to be up to one's ears in debt
**grz|mieć (-mię, -misz)** (*imp* **-mij**, *perf* **za-**) *vi* (*o oklaskach, o człowieku*) to thunder; (*o głosie, o działach*) to boom; **grzmi** (*w czasie burzy*) it's thundering
**grzmo|t** (**-tu, -ty**) (*loc sg* **-cie**) *m* (*wyładowanie atmosferyczne*) (a clap of) thunder; (*huk*) boom
**grzy|b** (**-ba, -by**) (*acc sg* **-ba** *lub* **-b**, *loc sg* **-bie**) *m* (*Bio*) fungus; (*jadalny*) mushroom; (*trujący*) toadstool; (*na ścianie*) mould; **iść na ~y** to go mushrooming; **wyrastać (wyrosnąć** *perf***) jak ~y po deszczu** to mushroom
**grzybic|a** (**-y, -e**) *f* (*Med*) mycosis; **~ stóp** athlete's foot
**grzybobójczy** *adj*: **środek ~** fungicide
**grzybobra|nie** (**-nia, -nia**) (*gen pl* **-ń**) *nt* mushroom picking
**grzybowy** *adj* mushroom *attr*
**grzy|wa** (**-wy, -wy**) (*dat sg* **-wie**) *f* (*końska, lwia*) mane
**grzyw|ka** (**-ki, -ki**) (*dat sg* **-ce**, *gen pl* **-ek**) *f* fringe
**grzy|wna** (**-wny, -wny**) (*dat sg* **-wnie**, *gen pl* **-wien**) *f* fine; **wymierzyć** (*perf*) **komuś grzywnę** to fine sb
**gubernato|r** (**-ra, -rzy** *lub* **-rowie**) (*loc sg* **-rze**) *m* governor
**gu|bić (-bię, -bisz)** (*perf* **z-**) *vt* to lose; **~ wątek/myśl** to lose the thread; **gubić się** *vr* (*w lesie*) to lose one's way; (*o przedmiotach*) to get lost, to be mislaid; **~ się w domysłach** to speculate blindly; **~ się w szczegółach** to get bogged down in details
**GUC** *abbr* (= *Główny Urząd Ceł*) Main Customs Office
**gulasz** (**-u, -e**) (*gen pl* **-ów**) *m* goulash
**gulde|n** (**-na, -ny**) (*loc sg* **-nie**) *m* guilder
**gulgo|tać (-cze)** *vi* (*o płynie*) to gurgle; (*o indyku*) to gobble
**guła|g** (**-gu, -gi**) (*instr sg* **-giem**) *m* Gulag

**gu|ma** (**-my, -my**) (*dat sg* **-mie**) *f* (*surowiec*) rubber; **~ do żucia** chewing gum; **złapać gumę** (*pot*) to have a flat tyre
**gumia|k** (**-ka, -ki**) (*instr sg* **-kiem**) *m* (*pot: kalosz*) rubber boot, wellington (boot)
**gum|ka** (**-ki, -ki**) (*dat sg* **-ce**, *gen pl* **-ek**) *f* (*do mazania*) rubber (*Brit*), eraser (*US*); (*do pakowania*) rubber band; (*do bielizny*) elastic
**gumowy** *adj* rubber *attr*
**guru** *m inv* guru
**GUS** *abbr* (= *Główny Urząd Statystyczny*) Central Office of Statistics
**gu|st** (**-stu, -sty** *lub* **-sta**) (*loc sg* **-ście**) *m* taste; **w dobrym/złym guście** in good/bad taste; **rzecz ~u** a matter of taste; **on przypadł mi do ~u** I took a fancy *lub* liking to him
**gust|ować (-uję, -ujesz)** *vi*: **~ w czymś** to have a liking for sth
**gustowny** *adj* tasteful
**guwernant|ka** (**-ki, -ki**) (*dat sg* **-ce**, *gen pl* **-ek**) *f* governess
**gu|z** (**-za, -zy**) (*loc sg* **-zie**) *m* (*stłuczenie*) bump; (*Med*) tumour (*Brit*), tumor (*US*); **nabijać (nabić** *perf*) **sobie guza** to bump one's head *lub* forehead; **szukać guza** to look for trouble
**guzd|rać się (-rzę, -rzesz** *lub* **-ram, -rasz)** (*imp* **-rz** *lub* **-raj**) *vr* (*pot*) to dawdle
**guz|ek** (**-ka, -ki**) (*instr sg* **-kiem**) *m* lump
**guzi|k** (**-ka, -ki**) (*instr sg* **-kiem**) *m* button; **zapięty na ostatni ~** all set (to go); **~ cię to obchodzi** (*pot*) it's none of your business
**gwałcicie|l** (**-la, -le**) (*gen pl* **-li**) *m* rapist; (*prawa*) law-breaker
**gwał|cić (-cę, -cisz)** (*imp* **-ć**) *vt* (*kobietę*) (*perf* **z-**) to rape; (*prawo*) (*perf* **po-**) to violate
**gwał|t** (**-tu, -ty**) (*dat sg* **-cie**) *m* (*przemoc*) violence; (*na kobiecie*) rape
**gwałtownoś|ć** (**-ci**) *f* (*porywczość*) impetuosity; (*nagłość*) suddenness
**gwałtowny** *adj* (*charakter, usposobienie*) violent; (*ulewa*) torrential; (*śmierć*) violent; (*zmiana*) sudden
**gwa|r** (**-ru**) (*loc sg* **-rze**) *m* din
**gwa|ra** (**-ry, -ry**) (*dat sg* **-rze**) *f* local dialect
**gwarancj|a** (**-i, -e**) (*gen pl* **-i**) *f* guarantee, warranty; **roczna ~** a year's guarantee *lub* warranty
**gwarancyjny** *adj* guarantee *attr*
**gwarant|ować (-uję, -ujesz)** (*perf* **za-**) *vt* to guarantee
**gwardi|a** (**-i, -e**) (*gen pl* **-i**) *f* (*Wojsk*) guard; **~ honorowa** guard of honour (*Brit*) *lub* honor (*US*); **stara ~** the Old Guard
**gwarny** *adj* bustling
**gwarowy** *adj* dialectal
**gwarz|yć (-ę, -ysz)** *vi* to chat
**gwi|azda** (**-azdy, -azdy**) (*dat sg* **-eździe**) *f* star; (*przen: sławny człowiek*) celebrity; **~ filmowa** film star
**gwiazd|ka** (**-ki, -ki**) (*dat sg* **-ce**, *gen pl* **-ek**) *f* (small) star; (*Boże Narodzenie*) Christmas; (*filmowa*) starlet; (*znak*) asterisk
**gwiazdkowy** *adj* Christmas *attr*
**gwiazdo|r** (**-ra, -rzy**) (*loc sg* **-rze**) *m* (*filmowy*) film star
**gwiazdozbi|ór** (**-oru, -ory**) (*loc sg* **-orze**) *m* constellation
**gwiaździsty** *adj* (*niebo*) starry; (*kształt*) star-shaped
**gwiezdny** *adj* star *attr*
**Gwine|a** (**-i**) *f* Guinea
**gwin|t** (**-tu, -ty**) (*loc sg* **-cie**) *m* thread (*of a screw*); **jasny ~!** (*pot*) oh gosh!
**gwint|ować (-uję, -ujesz)** (*perf* **na-**) *vt* to thread
**gwi|zd** (**-zdu, -zdy**) (*loc sg* **-ździe**) *m* (*człowieka, lokomotywy*) whistle; (*syreny*) whine; (*wiatru*) howling; (*pocisku*) whiz(z); **gwizdy** *pl* catcall, boos *pl*
**gwi|zdać (-żdżę, -żdżesz)** (*perf* **-zdnąć**) *vi* to whistle; (*o syrenie*) to whine; (*o publiczności*) to boo
**gwizd|ek** (**-ka, -ki**) (*instr sg* **-kiem**) *m* whistle
**gwizd|nąć (-nę, -niesz)** (*imp* **-nij**) *vb perf od* **gwizdać** ▷ *vt perf* (*pot: ukraść*) to pinch, to nick
**gw|óźdź** (**-oździa, -oździe**) (*gen pl* **-oździ**, *instr pl* **-oździami** *lub* **-oźdźmi**) *m* nail; (*pot*): **~ programu** highlight, main feature
**gzym|s** (**-su, -sy**) (*loc sg* **-sie**) *m* (*Archit, Bud*) cornice; (*występ skalny*) ledge

**H, h¹** *nt inv (litera)* H, h; **H jak Henryk** ≈ H for Harry *(Brit)*, ≈ H for How *(US)*; **H-dur** B major; **h-moll** B minor
**h²** *abbr (= godzina)* h *(= hour)*
**ha** *abbr (= hektar)* ha *(= hectare)*
**hab.** *abbr (= habilitowany)* habilitated *(officially qualified as a university lecturer)*
**habilitacj|a** (**-i, -e**) *(gen pl* **-i**) *f (Uniw) postdoctoral lecturing qualification*
**habilitowany** *adj*: **doktor ~** ≈ reader *(Brit)*, ≈ assistant professor *(US)*
**habi|t** (**-tu, -ty**) *(loc sg* **-cie**) *m* habit *(of monk or nun)*
**haczy|k** (**-ka, -ki**) *(instr sg* **-kiem**) *m* hook; *(u drzwi)* catch; *(na ryby)* (fish) hook; *(przen: szczegół)* catch; **połknąć** *(perf)* **~** *(przen)* to swallow the hook
**haf|t** (**-tu, -ty**) *(loc sg* **-cie**) *m* embroidery
**haft|ka** (**-ki, -ki**) *(dat sg* **-ce**, *gen pl* **-ek**) *f* hook and eye
**haft|ować (-uję, -ujesz)** *vt/vi (perf* **wy-**) to embroider ▷ *vi (pot: wymiotować)* to puke *(pot)*
**Ha|ga** (**-gi**) *(dat sg* **-dze**) *f* the Hague
**Haitan|ka** (**-ki, -ki**) *(dat sg* **-ce**, *gen pl* **-ek**) *f* Haitian
**Haitańczy|k** (**-ka, -cy**) *(instr sg* **-kiem**) *m* Haitian
**Haiti** *nt inv* Haiti
**ha|k** (**-ka, -ki**) *(instr sg* **-kiem**) *m* hook
**hake|r** (**-ra, -rzy**) *(loc sg* **-rze**) *m* hacker
**ha|la** (**-li, -le**) *f (duża sala)* hall; *(pastwisko w górach) meadow or pasture land in the mountains*; **~ przylotów/odlotów** arrivals/departures lounge; **~ sportowa** sports hall; **~ targowa** market; **~ fabryczna** workshop
**halibu|t** (**-ta, -ty**) *(loc sg* **-cie**) *m* halibut
**hal|ka** (**-ki, -ki**) *(dat sg* **-ce**, *gen pl* **-ek**) *f* slip
**hall, hol** (**-u, -e**) *(gen pl* **-i** *lub* **-ów**) *m (w mieszkaniu)* hall(way); *(w hotelu, teatrze)* foyer, lobby
**halny** *m decl like adj strong warm wind in the Tatra mountains*
**halo** *excl* hello
**haloge|n** (**-na, -ny**) *(loc sg* **-nie**) *m (Mot)* halogen *lub* fog headlamp
**halowy** *adj (rekord, zawody)* indoor *attr*
**halucynacj|a** (**-i, -e**) *(gen pl* **-i**) *f* hallucination
**hała|s** (**-su, -sy**) *(loc sg* **-sie**) *m* noise; **narobić** *perf* **~u** *(przen)* to make a fuss; **wiele ~u o nic** *(przen)* much ado about nothing
**hałas|ować (-uję, -ujesz)** *vi* to make noise
**hałaśliwy** *adj* noisy
**hał|da** (**-dy, -dy**) *(dat sg* **-dzie**) *f* slag heap
**hama|k** (**-ka, -ki**) *(instr sg* **-kiem**) *m* hammock
**hamburge|r** (**-ra, -ry**) *(dat sg* **-rze**) *m* hamburger
**ham|ować (-uję, -ujesz)** *vt (rozwój, wzrost)* to slow down, to restrain; *(łzy, płacz) (perf* **po-**) to hold back ▷ *vi* to brake; **hamować się** *vr (perf* **po-**) to hold back, to control o.s.; *patrz też* **zahamować**
**hamulcowy** *adj*: **płyn ~** brake fluid
**hamul|ec** (**-ca, -ce**) *m (Tech)* brake; **~ bezpieczeństwa** communication cord *(Brit)*, emergency brake *(US)*; **~ ręczny** handbrake *(Brit)*, parking brake *(US)*
**hand|el** (**-lu**) *m* trade, commerce; **~ detaliczny/hurtowy** retail/wholesale trade; **~ krajowy/zagraniczny** home/foreign trade
**handlarz** (**-a, -e**) *(gen pl* **-y**) *m* salesman, dealer; **~ obrazami/złotem** dealer in paintings/gold; **~ uliczny** street pedlar
**handl|ować (-uję, -ujesz)** *vi* to trade; **~ czymś** to trade *lub* deal in sth
**handlo|wiec** (**-wca, -wcy**) *m* tradesman, dealer
**handlowy** *adj* trade *attr*; **szkoła handlowa** business school *lub* college; **dzielnica handlowa** shopping district; **statek ~** merchantman; **korespondencja handlowa** business correspondence; **izba handlowa** chamber of commerce *lub* trade
**hanga|r** (**-ru, -ry**) *(loc sg* **-rze**) *m* hangar
**haniebny** *adj (czyn)* dishonourable *(Brit)*, dishonorable *(US)*
**hant|le** (**-li**) *pl* dumbbells *pl*
**hań|ba** (**-by**) *(dat sg* **-bie**) *f* dishonour *(Brit)*, dishonor *(US)*; **przynosić komuś hańbę** to bring disgrace on sb

**hańbiący** *adj* disgraceful
**hań|bić (-bię, -bisz)** (*perf* **z-**) *vt* to disgrace, to dishonour (*Brit*), to dishonor (*US*); **hańbić się** *vr* to disgrace o.s.
**happenin|g** (**-gu, -gi**) (*instr sg* **-giem**) *m* happening
**harcer|ka** (**-ki, -ki**) (*dat sg* **-ce**, *gen pl* **-ek**) *f* scout, girl guide (*Brit*), girl scout (*US*)
**harcerski** *adj* scout *attr*
**harcerst|wo** (**-wa**) (*loc sg* **-wie**) *nt* scout movement, scouting
**harcerz** (**-a, -e**) (*gen pl* **-y**) *m* scout, boy scout (*US*)
**hardwa|re** (**-re'u**) (*loc sg* **-rze**) *m* (*Komput*) hardware
**hardy** *adj* (*dumny*) proud; (*nieposłuszny*) defiant
**hare|m** (**-mu, -my**) (*loc sg* **-mie**) *m* harem
**har|fa** (**-fy, -fy**) (*dat sg* **-fie**) *f* harp
**harmoni|a** (**-i**) *f* harmony; (*instrument*) (*nom pl* **-e**, *gen pl* **-i**) concertina
**harmonij|ka** (**-ki, -ki**) (*dat sg* **-ce**, *gen pl* **-ek**) *f*: **~ ustna** harmonica, mouth organ
**harmonijny** *adj* harmonious
**harmoniz|ować (-uję, -ujesz)** (*perf* **z-**) *vt/vi* to harmonize
**harmonogra|m** (**-mu, -my**) (*loc sg* **-mie**) *m* schedule
**har|ować (-uję, -ujesz)** *vi* (*pot*) to slave, to work one's finger to the bone
**harpu|n** (**-na, -ny**) (*loc sg* **-nie**) *m* harpoon
**har|t** (**-tu**) (*loc sg* **-cie**) *m*: **~ ducha** toughness
**hart|ować (-uję, -ujesz)** *vt* (*Tech*: *stal*) to temper; (*dziecko*) to toughen; **hartować się** *vr* to toughen o.s.
**ha|sło** (**-sła, -sła**) (*loc sg* **-śle**, *gen pl* **-seł**) *nt* (*slogan*) watchword; (*sygnał*) signal; (*umożliwiające rozpoznanie*) password; (*w słowniku*) entry; **pod hasłem równouprawnienia** under the banner of equality; **dawać (dać** *perf*) **~ do działania** to give the go ahead
**haszysz** (**-u**) *m* hashish
**hau|st** (**-stu, -sty**) (*loc sg* **-ście**) *m* (*płynu*) gulp; **wypić** (*perf*) **coś jednym ~em** to drink sth in *lub* at one gulp
**Hawajczy|k** (**-ka, -cy**) (*instr sg* **-kiem**) *m* Hawaiian
**Hawaj|e** (**-ów**) *pl* Hawaii
**Hawaj|ka** (**-ki, -ki**) (*dat sg* **-ce**, *gen pl* **-ek**) *f* Hawaiian
**hawajski** *adj* Hawaiian; **gitara hawajska** Hawaiian *lub* steel guitar
**Hawa|na** (**-ny**) (*dat sg* **-nie**) *f* Havana
**hazar|d** (**-du, -dy**) (*loc sg* **-dzie**) *m* gambling
**hazardzi|sta** (**-sty, -ści**) (*dat sg* **-ście**) *m decl like f in sg* gambler
**heba|n** (**-nu**) (*loc sg* **-nie**) *m* ebony
**heb|el** (**-la, -le**) (*gen pl* **-li**) *m* plane
**hebl|ować (-uję, -ujesz)** (*perf* **z-**) *vt* to plane
**hebrajski** *adj* Hebrew ▷ *m decl like adj* (*język*) Hebrew
**Hebryd|y** (**-ów**) *pl* the Hebrides
**hec|a** (**-y, -e**) *f*: **robić (zrobić** *perf*) **coś dla hecy** to do sth for kicks; **ale ~!** what a farce!
**hegemoni|a** (**-i**) *f* hegemony
**hej** *excl* (*przywołując kogoś*) hey!; (*pozdrowienie*) hi!
**hejna|ł** (**-łu, -ły**) (*loc sg* **-le**) *m* bugle-call
**hekta|r** (**-ra, -ry**) (*loc sg* **-rze**) *m* hectare
**hel** (**-u**) *m* helium
**helikopte|r** (**-ra, -ry**) (*loc sg* **-rze**) *m* helicopter
**Helsin|ki** (**-ek**) *pl* Helsinki
**heł|m** (**-mu, -my**) (*loc sg* **-mie**) *m* helmet
**hemofili|a** (**-i**) *f* (*Med*) haemophilia (*Brit*), hemophilia (*US*)
**hemoglobi|na** (**-ny**) (*dat sg* **-nie**) *f* (*Med*) haemoglobin (*Brit*), hemoglobin (*US*)
**hemoroid|y** (**-ów**) *pl* haemorrhoids (*Brit*), hemorrhoids (*US*)
**heraldy|ka** (**-ki**) (*dat sg* **-ce**) *f* heraldry
**her|b** (**-bu, -by**) (*loc sg* **-bie**) *m* (*znak dziedziczny*) coat of arms; (*godło*: *miasta*) crest; (*: państwa*) emblem
**herbaciar|nia** (**-ni, -nie**) (*gen pl* **-ni** *lub* **-ń**) *f* tea shop
**herba|ta** (**-ty, -ty**) (*dat sg* **-cie**) *f* tea; **~ ziołowa** herbal tea
**herbat|ka** (**-ki, -ki**) (*dat sg* **-ce**, *gen pl* **-ek**) *f dimin od* **herbata**
**herbatni|k** (**-ka, -ki**) (*instr sg* **-kiem**) *m* biscuit
**herbicy|d** (**-du, -dy**) (*loc sg* **-dzie**) *m* herbicide
**Hercegowi|na** (**-ny**) (*dat sg* **-nie**) *f* Hercegovina
**herety|k** (**-ka, -cy**) (*instr sg* **-kiem**) *m* heretic
**herezj|a** (**-i, -e**) (*gen pl* **-i**) *f* heresy
**hermetyczny** *adj* hermetic, airtight; (*środowisko*) closed
**heroiczny** *adj* heroic
**heroi|na** (**-ny**) (*dat sg* **-nie**) *f* heroin
**heroiz|m** (**-mu**) (*loc sg* **-mie**) *m* heroism
**heteroseksualny** *adj* heterosexual
**hetma|n** (**-na**) (*loc sg* **-nie**) *m* (*Szachy*) (*nom pl* **-ny**) queen; (*Hist*) (*nom pl* **-ni**) hetman (*a commander-in-chief of the Polish army in 16-18th c.*)
**hiacyn|t** (**-tu** *lub* **-ta, -ty**) (*loc sg* **-cie**) *m* hyacinth
**hie|na** (**-ny, -ny**) (*dat sg* **-nie**) *f* (*Zool*) hyena
**hierarchi|a** (**-i, -e**) (*gen pl* **-i**) *f* hierarchy
**hierogli|f** (**-fu, -fy**) (*loc sg* **-fie**) *m* hieroglyph(ic)
**hi-fi** *adj inv*; **sprzęt ~** hi-fi equipment
**higie|na** (**-ny**) (*dat sg* **-nie**) *f* (*zachowanie czystości*) hygiene; **~ osobista** personal hygiene

**higieniczny** *adj* hygienic; **chusteczka higieniczna** paper tissue, Kleenex® (*US*)
**Himalaj|e** (**-ów**) *pl* the Himalayas
**hinduiz|m** (**-mu**) (*loc sg* **-mie**) *m* Hinduism
**Hindu|s** (**-sa, -si**) (*loc sg* **-sie**) *m* Indian (*male from India*)
**Hindus|ka** (**-ki, -ki**) (*dat sg* **-ce**, *gen pl* **-ek**) *f* Indian (*female from India*)
**hinduski** *adj* Hindu
**hiperinflacj|a** (**-i**) *f* hyperinflation
**hipermarke|t** (**-tu, -ty**) (*loc sg* **-cie**) *m* hypermarket
**hipi|s, hippi|s** (**-sa, -si**) (*loc sg* **-sie**) *m* hippie
**hipnotyze|r** (**-ra, -rzy**) (*loc sg* **-rze**) *m* hypnotist
**hipnotyz|ować (-uję, -ujesz)** (*perf* **za-**) *vt* to hypnotize
**hipno|za** (**-zy**) (*dat sg* **-zie**) *f* hypnosis
**hipochondry|k** (**-ka, -cy**) (*instr sg* **-kiem**) *m* hypochondriac
**hipokry|ta** (**-ty, -ci**) (*dat sg* **-cie**) *m decl like f in sg* hypocrite
**hipokryzj|a** (**-i**) *f* hypocrisy
**hipopota|m** (**-ma, -my**) (*loc sg* **-mie**) *m* hippopotamus
**hipoteczny** *adj*: **kredyt ~** mortgage
**hipote|ka** (**-ki, -ki**) (*dat sg* **-ce**) *f* (*zabezpieczenie*) collateral; (*księga*) mortgage deed
**hipotetyczny** *adj* hypothetical
**hipote|za** (**-zy, -zy**) (*dat sg* **-zie**) *f* hypothesis; **stawiać (postawić** *perf***) hipotezę** to advance a hypothesis
**histeri|a** (**-i**) *f* hysteria
**histerycz|ka** (**-ki, -ki**) (*dat sg* **-ce**, *gen pl* **-ek**) *f* hysteric
**histeryczny** *adj* hysterical
**histery|k** (**-ka, -cy**) (*instr sg* **-kiem**) *m* hysteric
**histeryz|ować (-uję, -ujesz)** *vi* to be hysterical
**histologi|a** (**-i**) *f* histology
**histori|a** (**-i, -e**) (*gen pl* **-i**) *f* history; (*opowieść*) story; **ładna** *lub* **przykra ~** a fine mess (*pot*); **~ literatury/sztuki/Polski** history of literature/art/Poland; **~ choroby** (*Med*) case history; **przejść** (*perf*) **do historii** to go down in history
**historyczny** *adj* historical; (*ważny*) historic; (*zabytkowy*) historic
**historyj|ka** (**-ki, -ki**) (*dat sg* **-ce**, *gen pl* **-ek**) *f* (*wymyślona historia*) story; **~ obrazkowa** strip cartoon
**history|k** (**-ka, -cy**) (*instr sg* **-kiem**) *m* historian; (*nauczyciel*) history teacher
**Hiszpa|n** (**-na, -nie**) (*loc sg* **-nie**) *m* Spaniard
**Hiszpani|a** (**-i**) *f* Spain
**Hiszpan|ka** (**-ki, -ki**) (*dat sg* **-ce**, *gen pl* **-ek**) *f* Spaniard
**hiszpański** *adj* Spanish ▷ *m decl like adj* (*język*) Spanish
**hi|t** (**-tu, -ty**) (*loc sg* **-cie**) *m* (*przebój*) hit
**hitlero|wiec** (**-wca, -wcy**) *m* Hitlerite, Nazi
**hitlerowski** *adj* Hitlerite, Nazi
**HIV** *abbr*: **(wirus) HIV** HIV
**hobbi|sta** (**-sty, -ści**) (*dat sg* **-ście**) *m decl like f in sg* hobbyist
**hobby** *nt inv* hobby
**hod|ować (-uję, -ujesz)** (*perf* **wy-**) *vt* (*rośliny, kwiaty*) to grow, to breed; (*zwierzęta*) to raise, to breed
**hodowc|a** (**-y, -y**) *m decl like f in sg* (*zwierząt*) raiser, breeder; (*kwiatów, warzyw*) grower
**hodowl|a** (**-i, -e**) (*gen pl* **-i**) *f* (*hodowanie*) raising, breeding; (*miejsce*) animal farm
**hodowlany** *adj*: **gospodarstwo hodowlane** animal farm; **zwierzęta hodowlane** farm animals
**hojnoś|ć** (**-ci**) *f* generosity
**hojny** *adj* generous
**hokei|sta** (**-sty, -ści**) (*dat sg* **-ście**) *m decl like f in sg* hockey player
**hokej** (**-a**) *m* (*też*: **hokej na lodzie**) (ice) hockey; **~ na trawie** field hockey
**hol** (**-u, -e**) *m* (*lina*) (*gen pl* **-ów**) towrope, towline; (*pomieszczenie*) (*gen pl* **-ów** *lub* **-i**) hall(way); **brać (wziąć** *perf***) kogoś na hol** to give sb a tow
**Holandi|a** (**-i**) *f* Holland, the Netherlands
**holdin|g** (**-gu, -gi**) (*instr sg* **-giem**) *m* holding company
**Holend|er** (**-ra, -rzy**) (*loc sg* **-rze**) *m* Dutchman
**Holender|ka** (**-ki, -ki**) (*dat sg* **-ce**, *gen pl* **-ek**) *f* Dutchwoman
**holenderski** *adj* Dutch ▷ *m decl like adj* (*język*) Dutch
**holocaus|t** (**-tu, -ty**) *m* (*Hist*) the Holocaust
**hologra|m** (**-mu, -my**) (*loc sg* **-mie**) *m* (*Tech*) hologram
**hol|ować (-uję, -ujesz)** *vt* to tow
**holowni|k** (**-ka, -ki**) (*instr sg* **-kiem**) *m* tug(boat)
**hoł|d** (**-du, -dy**) (*loc sg* **-dzie**) *m* homage; **oddawać (oddać** *perf***) komuś ~** to pay homage to sb
**hołd|ować (-uję, -ujesz)** *vi*: **~ czemuś** to adhere to sth
**hoło|ta** (**-ty**) (*dat sg* **-cie**) *f* (*pej*) the riffraff, the rabble
**homa|r** (**-ra, -ry**) (*loc sg* **-rze**) *m* lobster
**homeopati|a** (**-i**) *f* homeopathy
**homeopatyczny** *adj* homeopathic
**homili|a** (**-i, -e**) (*gen pl* **-i**) *f* homily
**homogenizowany** *adj* homogenized; **serek ~** cream cheese

h

**homologacj|a** (**-i, -e**) (*gen pl* **-i**) *f* certification of approval
**homoni|m** (**-mu, -my**) (*loc sg* **-mie**) *m* homonym
**homoseksuali|sta** (**-sty, -ści**) (*dat sg* **-ście**) *m decl like f in sg* homosexual, gay
**homoseksualny** *adj* homosexual
**hon.** *abbr* (= *honorowy*) hon. (= *honorary*)
**hono|r** (**-ru**) (*loc sg* **-rze**) *m* honour (*Brit*), honor (*US*); **honory** *pl*: **oddawać ~y** to salute; **słowo ~u** word of hono(u)r; **człowiek ~u** man of hono(u)r; **punkt ~u** point of hono(u)r; **pełnić ~y domu** to do the hono(u)rs
**honorari|um** (**-um, -a**) (*gen pl* **-ów**) *nt inv in sg* fee; (*też*: **honorarium autorskie**) royalty
**honor|ować** (**-uję, -ujesz**) *vt* (*czek, kartę rabatową*) to accept; (*wizę, zaświadczenie*) to recognize; (*człowieka: okazywać szacunek*) (*perf* **u-**) to honour (*Brit*) *lub* honor (*US*)
**honorowy** *adj* (*człowiek: mający poczucie honoru*) honourable (*Brit*), honorable (*US*); (*członek, konsul, gość*) honorary; (*bramka, punkt: Sport*) face-saving; **honorowe miejsce** seat of honour (*Brit*) *lub* honor (*US*); **kompania honorowa** guard of honour (*Brit*) *lub* honor (*US*); **runda honorowa** lap of honour (*Brit*) *lub* honor (*US*)
**hormo|n** (**-nu, -ny**) (*loc sg* **-nie**) *m* hormone
**hormonalny** *adj* hormonal
**horosko|p** (**-pu, -py**) (*loc sg* **-pie**) *m* horoscope
**horro|r** (**-ru, -ry**) (*loc sg* **-rze**) *m* (*film grozy*) horror (film *lub* movie); (*pot: dramat*) horror
**horyzon|t** (**-tu, -ty**) (*loc sg* **-cie**) *m* horizon; **mieć szerokie/wąskie ~y** (*przen*) to be broad-/narrow-minded
**hospicj|um** (**-um, -a**) (*gen pl* **-ów**) *nt inv in sg* hospice
**hospitacj|a** (**-i, -e**) (*gen pl* **-i**) *f* (*Szkol*) inspection
**hospitalizacj|a** (**-i**) *f* (*Med*) hospitalization, admission (*to a hospital*)
**hos|sa** (**-sy, -sy**) (*dat sg* **-sie**) *f* (*Fin*) bull market
**hostes|sa** (**-sy, -sy**) (*dat sg* **-sie**) *f* hostess
**hosti|a** (**-i, -e**) (*gen pl* **-i**) *f* (*Rel*) Host
**hot do|g** (**-ga, -gi**) (*instr sg* **-giem**) *m* hot dog
**hotel** (**-u, -e**) (*gen pl* **-i**) *m* hotel; **mieszkać w ~u** to stay at a hotel; **~ robotniczy** workers hostel
**hotelarst|wo** (**-wa**) (*loc sg* **-wie**) *nt* hotel industry
**hotelowy** *adj* (*restauracja, bufet*) hotel *attr*; **doba hotelowa kończy się o 12.00** the check-out time is 12 o'clock
**hr.** *abbr* = **hrabia**
**hra|bia** (**-biego, -biowie**) (*dat sg* **-biemu**, *instr sg* **-bią**, *loc sg* **-bi**, *voc sg* **-bio**, *gen pl* **-biów**) *m* count
**hrabi|na** (**-ny, -ny**) (*dat sg* **-nie**) *f* countess
**hrabst|wo** (**-wa, -wa**) (*loc sg* **-wie**) *nt* (*w Anglii*) county
**hu|ba** (**-by, -by**) (*dat sg* **-bie**) *f* bracket fungus
**hucie** *n patrz* **huta**
**hu|czeć** (**-czy**) *vi* (*o wodospadzie, falach*) (*perf* **za-**) to rumble; (*o strzałach, armatach*) (*perf* **-knąć**) to boom
**huczny** *adj* (*brawa*) loud; (*zabawa, wesele*) grand
**hu|fiec** (**-fca, -fce**) *m* (*Wojsk, Hist*) regiment; (*w harcerstwie*) regiment
**huj** (*pot!*) *m* = **chuj**
**hu|k** (**-ku, -ki**) (*instr sg* **-kiem**) *m* (*armat, dział, eksplozji*) bang; (*wodospadu, fal*) rumble; (*pioruna*) roll; **z hukiem** (*spaść, otworzyć się*) with a bang
**huk|nąć** (**-nę, -niesz**) (*imp* **-nij**) *vb perf od* **huczeć** ▷ *vt perf* (*pot: uderzyć*) to bash (*pot*)
**hul|ać** (**-am, -asz**) (*perf* **po-**) *vi* (*pot*) to party, to carouse
**hulajn|oga** (**-ogi, -ogi**) (*dat sg* **-odze**, *gen pl* **-óg**) *f* scooter
**humani|sta** (**-sty, -ści**) (*dat sg* **-ście**) *m decl like f in sg* humanist
**humanistyczny** *adj* (*wartości, ideały*) humanistic; (*przedmiot, studia*) arts *attr*; **nauki humanistyczne** the humanities
**humanitarny** *adj* humane; **pomoc humanitarna** humanitarian aid
**humo|r** (**-ru**) (*loc sg* **-rze**) *m* (*komizm*) humour (*Brit*), humor (*US*); (*nastrój*) mood; **humory** *pl* (*kaprysy*) whims; **poczucie ~u** sense of humo(u)r; **być w dobrym/złym ~ze** to be in a good/bad mood
**humores|ka** (**-ki, -ki**) (*dat sg* **-ce**, *gen pl* **-ek**) *f* (*Muz*) humoresque; (*Lit*) comic piece
**humorystyczny** *adj* humorous
**hura!, hurra!** *excl* hurray!, hurrah!; **hip, hip, ~** hip, hip, hurray!
**huraga|n** (**-nu, -ny**) (*loc sg* **-nie**) *m* hurricane; (*przen: oklasków, braw*) burst
**hur|t** (**-tu**) (*loc sg* **-cie**) *m* (*sprzedaż*) wholesale; **~em** (*pot: wszystko razem*) across the board
**hurtow|nia** (**-ni, -nie**) (*gen pl* **-ni**) *f* (*przedsiębiorstwo*) wholesalers *pl*; (*magazyn*) (wholesale) warehouse
**hurtowni|k** (**-ka, -cy**) (*instr sg* **-kiem**) *m* wholesaler
**hurtowy** *adj* (*sprzedaż*) wholesale *attr*
**husarz** (**-a, -e**) (*gen pl* **-y**) *m* (*Hist*) hussar
**huśt|ać** (**-am, -asz**) *vt* to swing; **~ łódką/statkiem** to rock a boat/ship; **huśtać się** *vr* to swing
**huśtaw|ka** (**-ki, -ki**) (*dat sg* **-ce**, *gen pl* **-ek**) *f* (*wisząca*) swing; (*pozioma*) seesaw; **~ nastrojów** (*przen*) swinging moods
**hu|ta** (**-ty, -ty**) (*dat sg* **-cie**) *f* (*też*: **huta żelaza**) steelworks; **~ szkła** glassworks

**hutnict|wo** (**-wa**) (*loc sg* **-wie**) *nt* (*przemysł*) steel industry
**hutniczy** *adj* metallurgical
**hutni|k** (**-ka, -cy**) (*instr sg* **-kiem**) *m* steelworker
**huza|r** (**-ra, -rzy** *lub* **-ry**) (*loc sg* **-rze**) *m* (*Hist*) hussar
**hybry|da** (**-dy, -dy**) (*dat sg* **-dzie**) *f* hybrid
**hydran|t** (**-tu, -ty**) (*loc sg* **-cie**) *m* hydrant
**hydrauliczny** *adj* hydraulic
**hydrauli|k** (**-ka, -cy**) (*instr sg* **-kiem**) *m* plumber
**hydroelektrow|nia** (**-ni, -nie**) (*gen pl* **-ni**) *f* hydro-electric power plant
**hydrofo|r** (**-ru, -ry**) (*loc sg* **-rze**) *m* (*Tech*) water supply pump
**hydropla|n** (**-nu, -ny**) (*loc sg* **-nie**) *m* seaplane
**hym|n** (**-nu, -ny**) (*loc sg* **-nie**) *m* (*kościelny*) hymn; **~ państwowy** national anthem

# Ii

**I, i**[1] *nt inv* (*litera*) I, i; **I jak Irena** ≈ I for Isaac, ≈ I for item (*US*)
**i**[2] *conj* and; **i ja, i on** both me and him; **czekałem i czekałem** I waited and waited, I waited forever
**Iberyjski** *adj*: **Półwysep** ~ the Iberian Peninsula
**iberysty|ka** (**-ki**) (*dat sg* **-ce**) *f* Spanish and Portuguese Studies
**ich** *pron gen pl od* **oni, one**; **nie było ich** they were not there; **zobaczyłem ich** I saw them ▷ *possessive pron* (*z rzeczownikiem*) their; (*bez rzeczownika*) theirs; **to jest ich samochód** this is their car; **ich przyjaciel** a friend of theirs
**ide|a** (**-i, -e**) (*gen pl* **-i**) *f* idea
**ideali|sta** (**-sty, -ści**) (*dat sg* **-ście**) *m decl like f in sg* idealist
**idealist|ka** (**-ki, -ki**) (*dat sg* **-ce**, *gen pl* **-ek**) *f* idealist
**idealistyczny** *adj* idealistic
**idealiz|m** (**-mu**) (*loc sg* **-mie**) *m* idealism
**idealiz|ować (-uję, -ujesz)** (*perf* **wy-**) *vt* to idealize
**idealnie** *adv* (*doskonale*) perfectly; (*nierealnie*) ideally
**idealny** *adj* (*doskonały*) perfect; (*nierealny*) ideal
**idea|ł** (**-łu, -ły**) (*loc sg* **-le**) *m* ideal; ~ **piękna** a paragon of beauty; ~ **męża** the ideal husband
**identyczny** *adj* identical
**identyfikacj|a** (**-i**) *f* identification
**identyfikato|r** (**-ra, -ry**) (*loc sg* **-rze**) *m* name tag
**identyfik|ować (-uję, -ujesz)** (*perf* **z-**) *vt* to identify; **identyfikować się** *vr*: ~ **się z kimś** to identify o.s. with sb
**ideologi|a** (**-i, -e**) (*gen pl* **-i**) *f* ideology
**ideologiczny** *adj* ideological
**ideowy** *adj* ideological
**idę** *itd. vb patrz* **iść**
**idio|m** (**-mu, -my**) (*loc sg* **-mie**) *m* (*Jęz*) idiom
**idiomatyczny** *adj* idiomatic
**idio|ta** (**-ty, -ci**) (*dat sg* **-cie**) *m decl like f in sg* (*pot*) idiot, moron (*pot*)
**idiot|ka** (**-ki, -ki**) (*dat sg* **-ce**, *gen pl* **-ek**) *f* (*pot*) idiot, moron (*pot*)
**idiotyczny** *adj* idiotic, stupid
**idiotyz|m** (**-mu**) (*loc sg* **-mie**) (*pot*) *m* (*głupota*) idiocy; (*bzdura, niedorzeczność*) (*nom pl* **-my**) stupidity, nonsense
**idol** (**-a, -e**) (*gen pl* **-i**) *m* idol
**idyll|a** (**-i**) *f* idyll
**idziesz** *itd. vb patrz* **iść**
**iglasty** *adj* coniferous; **drzewo iglaste** conifer, evergreen
**iglic|a** (**-y, -e**) *f* (*Archit*) spire; (*część broni*) firing pin
**igliwi|e** (**-a**) *nt* needles (*of a conifer*)
**igloo** *nt inv* igloo
**igła** (**igły, igły**) (*dat sg* **igle**, *gen pl* **igieł**) *f* needle; ~ **gramofonowa** stylus; **robić z igły widły** to make a mountain out of a molehill; **szukać igły w stogu siana** (*przen*) to look *lub* search for a needle in a haystack
**ignorancj|a** (**-i**) *f* ignorance
**ignorancki** *adj* ignorant
**ignoran|t** (**-ta, -ci**) (*loc sg* **-cie**) *m* (*pej*) ignoramus
**ignor|ować (-uję, -ujesz)** (*perf* **z-**) *vt* to ignore, to disregard
**igr|ać (-am, -asz)** *vi*: ~ **ze śmiercią/z niebezpieczeństwem** to court death/danger; ~ **z ogniem** (*przen*) to play with fire
**igrasz|ka** (**-ki, -ki**) (*dat sg* **-ce**, *gen pl* **-ek**) *f*: **być igraszką w czyichś rękach** to be sb's toy; **igraszki losu** twist of fate *sg*; **dziecinne igraszki** child's play
**igre|k** (**-ka, -ki**) (*instr sg* **-kiem**) *m* (letter) Y
**igrzysk|a** (**-**) *pl* (*Sport*): **I~ Olimpijskie** the Olympics, the Olympic Games; **letnie/zimowe** ~ summer/winter olympics
**iko|na** (**-ny, -ny**) (*dat sg* **-nie**) *f* icon
**ikon|ka** (**-ki, -ki**) (*dat sg* **-ce**) *f* (*Komput*) icon
**ik|ra** (**-ry**) (*dat sg* **-rze**) *f* (*w wodzie*) spawn; (*w ciele ryby*) (hard) roe; **chłopak z ikrą** (*przen*) a guy with guts
**ik|s** (**-sa, -sy**) (*loc sg* **-sie**) *m* (letter) X; **iksy** *pl* (*krzywe nogi*) knock-knees

SŁOWO KLUCZOWE

**ile** *pron +gen* **1** *(z rzeczownikami policzalnymi)* how many; **ile kwiatów/ludzi?** how many flowers/people?; **ilu mężczyzn/studentów?** how many men/students?; **ile masz lat?** how old are you?; **ile razy?** how many times?; **ile ich było?** how many of them were there?
**2** *(z rzeczownikami niepoliczalnymi)* how much; **ile masła/wody/pieniędzy?** how much butter/water/money?; **ile czasu?** how long?; **ile to kosztuje?** how much is it?
**3** *(w zdaniach względnych: z rzeczownikami policzalnymi)* as many; *(: z rzeczownikami niepoliczalnymi)* as much; **bierz ile chcesz** take as many/much as you want
**4**: **ile ludzi!** what a lot of people!; **ile wody!** what a lot of water!
**5**: **ile sił** as hard as you can; **ile tchu** as fast as you can
**6**: **o ile** if; **o ile nie** unless, if not; **o ile wiem/pamiętam** as far as I know/remember; **o tyle o ile** *(pot)* not too bad
**7**: **nie tyle mądry, ile sprytny** not so much wise as clever; *patrz też* **ił**

**ilekroć** *conj* whenever, every time
**ileś** *pron +gen* some, a number of; **~ lat temu** some years ago
**iloczy|n** (-nu, -ny) *(loc sg* **-nie**) *m (Mat)* product
**ilora|z** (-zu, -zy) *(loc sg* **-zie**) *m (Mat)* quotient; **~ inteligencji** intelligence quotient
**ilościowy** *adj* quantitative
**iloś|ć** (-ci, -ci) *(gen pl* **-ci**) *f* amount, quantity
**ilu** *pron patrz* **ile**
**iluminacj|a** (-i, -e) *(gen pl* **-i**) *f (książk)* illumination
**iluminato|r** (-ra, -ry) *(loc sg* **-rze**) *m (Żegl)* porthole
**ilustr.** *abbr (= ilustracja)* illustration
**ilustracj|a** (-i, -e) *(gen pl* **-i**) *f* illustration
**ilustrato|r** (-ra, -rzy) *(loc sg* **-rze**) *m* illustrator
**ilustr|ować (-uję, -ujesz)** *(perf* **z-**) *vt (książkę)* to illustrate; *(unaoczniać)* to illustrate, to exemplify
**ilustrowany** *adj* illustrated; **wykład ~ przezroczami** a lecture illustrated with slides
**iluś** *pron +gen* some, a number of
**iluzj|a** (-i, -e) *(gen pl* **-i**) *f* illusion
**iluzjoni|sta** (-sty, -ści) *(dat sg* **-ście**) *m decl like f in sg* conjurer
**iluzoryczny** *adj* illusory
**ił** (iłu, iły) *(loc sg* **ile**) *m* loam
**im** *pron dat pl od* **oni, one** (to) them; **nie wierzę im** I don't believe them; **daj im te pieniądze** give them the money; **daj im to** give it to them ▷ *adv*: **im prędzej, tym lepiej** the sooner the better
**im.** *abbr (= imienia)*: **Uniwersytet im. Adama Mickiewicza** Adam Mickiewicz University
**im|ać się (-am, -asz)** *vr (książk)*: **imał się różnych zajęć** he took (up) various jobs
**imad|ło** (-ła, -ła) *(loc sg* **-le**, *gen pl* **-eł**) *nt* vice, vise *(US)*
**image** (-'u) *m inv* image
**imaginacj|a** (-i) *f (książk)* imagination
**imbecyl** (-a, -e) *(gen pl* **-i** *lub* **-ów**) *m (pot)* imbecile *(pot)*
**imbi|r** (-ru) *(loc sg* **-rze**) *m* ginger
**imbrycz|ek** (-ka, -ki) *(instr sg* **-kiem**) *m* teapot
**imbry|k** (-ka, -ki) *(instr sg* **-kiem**) *m* kettle
**imieninowy** *adj*: **życzenia imieninowe** saint's-day greetings
**imienin|y** (-) *pl* saint's day, name day
**imiennicz|ka** (-ki, -ki) *(dat sg* **-ce**, *gen pl* **-ek**) *f* namesake
**imienni|k** (-ka, -cy) *(instr sg* **-kiem**) *m* namesake
**imiesł|ów** (-owu, -owy) *(loc sg* **-owie**) *m (Jęz)* participle; **~ czynny/bierny** active/passive participle
**imi|ę** (-enia, -ona) *nt* name; *(człowieka)* first name; *(reputacja)* reputation; **jak masz** *lub* **ci na ~?** *(pot)* what's your name?; **szkoła imienia Tadeusza Kościuszki** Tadeusz Kosciuszko School; **w czyimś imieniu** on behalf of sb; **w ~ czegoś** in the name of sth; **mówić sobie po imieniu** to be on first name terms with each other; **nazywać rzeczy po imieniu** *(przen)* to call a spade a spade
**imigracj|a** (-i, -e) *(gen pl* **-i**) *f* immigration
**imigran|t** (-ta, -ci) *(loc sg* **-cie**) *m* immigrant
**imitacj|a** (-i, -e) *(gen pl* **-i**) *f* imitation; **~ skóry/kryształu** imitation *lub* sham leather/crystal
**imit|ować (-uję, -ujesz)** *vt* to imitate, to mimic
**immatrykulacj|a** (-i) *f* matriculation
**immunite|t** (-tu, -ty) *(loc sg* **-cie**) *m* immunity
**immunologiczny** *adj* immunological
**impa|s** (-su) *(loc sg* **-sie**) *m (zastój)* deadlock, impasse; *(Karty) (nom pl* **-sy**) finesse
**imperato|r** (-ra, -rzy) *(loc sg* **-rze**) *m* emperor
**imperaty|w** (-wu, -wy) *(loc sg* **-wie**) *m* imperative
**imperialistyczny** *adj* imperialist
**imperializ|m** (-mu) *(loc sg* **-mie**) *m* imperialism
**imperialny** *adj* imperial
**imperi|um** (-um, -a) *(gen pl* **-ów**) *nt inv in sg* empire

i

**impertynencj|a** (**-i, -e**) (*gen pl* **-i**) *f* impertinence
**impertynencki** *adj* impertinent
**impertynen|t** (**-ta, -ci**) (*loc sg* **-cie**) *m* impertinent
**impe|t** (**-tu**) (*loc sg* **-cie**) *m* impetus, momentum; **z ~em** vehemently, vigorously; **nabierać (nabrać** *perf*) **~u** to gather momentum
**implikacj|a** (**-i, -e**) (*gen pl* **-i**) *f* implication; **implikacje** *pl* ramifications *pl*
**impon|ować (-uję, -ujesz)** (*perf* **za-**) *vi*: **~ (czymś) komuś** to impress sb (with sth)
**imponujący** *adj* (*godny podziwu*) impressive; (*ogromny*) grand, imposing
**impor|t** (**-tu**) (*loc sg* **-cie**) *m* importation; **towary z ~u** imports, imported goods
**importe|r** (**-ra, -rzy**) (*loc sg* **-rze**) *m* importer
**import|ować (-uję, -ujesz)** *vt* to import
**importowany** *adj* imported
**impotencj|a** (**-i**) *f* impotence
**impoten|t** (**-ta, -ci**) (*loc sg* **-cie**) *m* impotent
**impregnowany** *adj* waterproofed
**impresari|o** (**-a, -owie**) (*dat sg* **-owi**) *m decl like nt in sg* impresario
**impresj|a** (**-i, -e**) (*gen pl* **-i**) *f* impression
**impresjoni|sta** (**-sty, -ści**) (*dat sg* **-ście**) *m decl like f in sg* impressionist
**impresjoniz|m** (**-mu**) (*loc sg* **-mie**) *m* impressionism
**impre|za** (**-zy, -zy**) (*dat sg* **-zie**) *f* (*teatralna, sportowa*) event; (*pot: przyjęcie*) do; **kosztowna ~** (*pot*) costly venture
**imprez|ować (-uję, -ujesz)** *vi* to party
**improwizacj|a** (**-i, -e**) (*gen pl* **-i**) *f* improvisation
**improwiz|ować (-uję, -ujesz)** (*perf* **za-**) *vt/vi* to improvise
**improwizowany** *adj* (*utwór*) improvised; (*mowa, przyjęcie*) impromptu
**impul|s** (**-su, -sy**) (*loc sg* **-sie**) *m* impulse; **pod wpływem ~u** on impulse
**impulsywny** *adj* impulsive
**in.** *abbr* (= *inaczej*) that is; **i in.** (*i inni/inne*) and others, et al.
**inaczej** *adv* (*w inny sposób*) differently; (*w przeciwnym razie*) otherwise, or (else); **~ mówiąc** in other words; **tak czy ~** one way or another
**inauguracj|a** (**-i, -e**) (*gen pl* **-i**) *f* (*sezonu*) opening; (*roku szkolnego*) inauguration
**inauguracyjny** *adj* (*mowa, uroczystość, mecz*) inaugural; (*przedstawienie*) opening
**inaugur|ować (-uję, -ujesz)** (*perf* **za-**) *vt* (*sezon piłkarski*) to open; (*uroczystość, rok szkolny*) to inaugurate
**in blanco** *adv*: **czek ~** blank cheque
**incognito** *adv* incognito ▷ *nt inv*; **zachować** (*perf*) **~** to preserve one's incognito
**incyden|t** (**-tu, -ty**) (*loc sg* **-cie**) *m* incident
**indek|s** (**-su, -sy**) (*loc sg* **-sie**) *m* (*spis*) index; (*studencki*) ≈ credit book
**indeksacj|a** (**-i**) *f* indexation
**India|nin** (**-nina, -nie**) (*loc sg* **-ninie**, *gen pl* **-n**) *m* (American) Indian
**indiański** *adj* (American) Indian
**Indi|e** (**-i**) *pl* India
**Indochin|y** (-) *pl* Indo-China
**indoeuropejski** *adj* Indo-European
**indoktrynacj|a** (**-i**) *f* indoctrination
**indoktryn|ować (-uję, -ujesz)** *vt* to indoctrinate
**Indonezj|a** (**-i**) *f* Indonesia
**Indonezyjczy|k** (**-ka, -cy**) (*instr sg* **-kiem**) *m* Indonesian
**Indonezyj|ka** (**-ki, -ki**) (*dat sg* **-ce**, *gen pl* **-ek**) *f* Indonesian
**indonezyjski** *adj* Indonesian
**indukcj|a** (**-i, -e**) (*gen pl* **-i**) *f* induction
**indukcyjny** *adj* inductive
**indygo** *nt inv*; **kolor ~** indigo
**indyjski** *adj*: **Ocean I~** the Indian Ocean; **Półwysep I~** the Indian subcontinent
**indy|k** (**-ka, -ki**) (*instr sg* **-kiem**) *m* turkey
**indywiduali|sta** (**-sty, -ści**) (*dat sg* **-ście**) *m decl like f in sg* individualist
**indywidualist|ka** (**-ki, -ki**) (*dat sg* **-ce**, *gen pl* **-ek**) *f* individualist
**indywidualiz|m** (**-mu**) (*loc sg* **-mie**) *m* individualism
**indywidualnoś|ć** (**-ci**) *f* (*osoba*) (*nom pl* **-ci**, *gen pl* **-ci**) (*osobowość*) personality; (*odrębność*) individuality; **on jest wielką indywidualnością** he's a prominent personality
**indywidualny** *adj* individual; **turysta ~** freelance tourist
**indywidu|um** (**-um, -a**) (*gen pl* **-ów**) *nt inv in sg* (*pej*) a suspicious character
**indziej** *adv*: **gdzie ~** elsewhere, somewhere else; **kiedy ~** some other time
**infantylny** *adj* infantile
**infekcj|a** (**-i, -e**) (*gen pl* **-i**) *f* infection
**inflacj|a** (**-i, -e**) (*gen pl* **-i**) *f* inflation; **20-procentowa ~** twenty per cent inflation
**infolini|a** (**-i, -e**) (*dat sg* **-i**) *f* helpline
**informacj|a** (**-i, -e**) (*gen pl* **-i**) *f* (*wiadomość*) piece of information; (*dane*) information; (*biuro, okienko*) information office (*Brit*), information bureau (*US*); **~ turystyczna** tourist information centre (*Brit*) *lub* center (*US*); **~ o** *+loc* information about *lub* on; **zasięgnąć** (*perf*) **informacji o czymś** to inquire about sth; **zadzwonić** (*perf*) **do**

**informacji** to ring directory enquiries (Brit), to call information (US)
**informacyjny** *adj*: **serwis** ~ news bulletin; **polityka informacyjna** public relations policy; **punkt** ~ inquiry desk; **sieć informacyjna** communications network
**informato|r** (**-ra**) (*loc sg* **-rze**) *m* (*publikacja*) (*nom pl* **-ry**) brochure; (*osoba*) (*nom pl* **-rzy**) informer, informant
**informaty|k** (**-ka, -cy**) (*instr sg* **-kiem**) *m* computer scientist
**informaty|ka** (**-ki**) (*dat sg* **-ce**) *f* computing; (*nauka*) information *lub* computer science
**inform|ować (-uję, -ujesz)** *vt* (*perf* **po-**); ~ **kogoś o czymś** to inform sb of sth; **informować się** *vr*: ~ **się o czymś** to inquire about sth
**infrastruktu|ra** (**-ry, -ry**) (*dat sg* **-rze**) *f* infrastructure
**ingerencj|a** (**-i, -e**) (*gen pl* **-i**) *f* interference
**inger|ować (-uję, -ujesz)** *vi*: ~ (**w** +*acc*) to interfere (in)
**inhalacj|a** (**-i, -e**) (*gen pl* **-i**) *f* inhalation
**inicjacj|a** (**-i, -e**) (*gen pl* **-i**) *f* (*książk*) initiation
**inicja|ł** (**-łu, -ły**) (*loc sg* **-le**) *m* initial
**inicjato|r** (**-ra, -rzy**) (*loc sg* **-rze**) *m* originator, initiator
**inicjaty|wa** (**-wy**) (*dat sg* **-wie**) *f* (*nom pl* **-wy**) initiative; **z czyjejś/własnej inicjatywy** on sb's/one's own initiative; ~ **ustawodawcza** legislative initiative
**inicj|ować (-uję, -ujesz)** (*perf* **za-**) *vt* to initiate
**inkasen|t** (**-ta, -ci**) (*loc sg* **-cie**) *m* collector
**inkas|ować (-uję, -ujesz)** (*perf* **za-**) *vt* to collect
**inklinacj|e** (**-i**) *pl* inclinations *pl*
**inkubacj|a** (**-i**) *f* incubation
**inkubato|r** (**-ra, -ry**) (*loc sg* **-rze**) *m* incubator
**inkwizycj|a** (**-i**) *f* the Inquisition
**innowacj|a** (**-i, -e**) (*gen pl* **-i**) *f* innovation
**innowierc|a** (**-y, -y**) *m decl like f in sg* infidel
**inny** *pron* (*nie ten*) another; (*odmienny*) other, different ▷ *m decl like adj* (*pot*) another man; **inni** *pl* (the) others *pl*; **coś innego** something else; **ktoś** ~ somebody *lub* someone else; **między ~mi** among other things; **~m razem** some other time; **~mi słowy** in other words
**inscenizacj|a** (**-i, -e**) (*gen pl* **-i**) *f* staging
**insceniz|ować (-uję, -ujesz)** (*perf* **za-**) *vt* (*Teatr*) to stage
**insek|t** (**-ta, -ty**) (*loc sg* **-cie**) *m* insect
**inseminacj|a** (**-i**) *f* artificial insemination
**inspekcj|a** (**-i, -e**) (*gen pl* **-i**) *f* inspection; **przeprowadzić** (*perf*) **inspekcję** to inspect
**inspekto|r** (**-ra, -rzy** *lub* **-rowie**) (*loc sg* **-rze**) *m* inspector
**inspiracj|a** (**-i, -e**) (*gen pl* **-i**) *f* (*natchnienie*) inspiration; **z czyjejś inspiracji** at sb's suggestion
**inspir|ować (-uję, -ujesz)** (*perf* **za-**) *vt* to inspire; **inspirować się** *vr*: ~ **się czymś** to draw inspiration from sth
**Inst.** *abbr* (= *Instytut*) Institute
**instalacj|a** (**-i, -e**) (*gen pl* **-i**) *f* (*montaż*) installation; ~ **elektryczna** wiring; ~ **wodno-kanalizacyjna** plumbing
**instalato|r** (**-ra, -rzy**) (*loc sg* **-rze**) *m* (*hydraulik*) plumber; (*elektryk*) electrician; (*monter z gazowni*) gas fitter (Brit), pipe fitter (US)
**instal|ować (-uję, -ujesz)** (*perf* **za-**) *vt* to install, to put in
**instancj|a** (**-i, -e**) (*gen pl* **-i**) *f*: **sąd pierwszej instancji** court of first instance; **najwyższa** *lub* **ostatnia** ~ the last instance
**instant** *adj inv*; **kawa** ~ instant coffee; **mleko** ~ powdered milk
**instrukcj|a** (**-i, -e**) (*gen pl* **-i**) *f* (*rozkaz*) instruction; ~ **przeciwpożarowa** fire regulations *pl*; ~ **obsługi** instructions *pl* (for use)
**instruktaż** (**-u**) *m* briefing, instruction
**instrukto|r** (**-ra, -rzy**) (*loc sg* **-rze**) *m* instructor
**instrumen|t** (**-tu, -ty**) (*loc sg* **-cie**) *m* instrument
**instrumentali|sta** (**-sty, -ści**) (*dat sg* **-ście**) *m decl like f in sg* instrumentalist
**instrumentalny** *adj* (*muzyka*) instrumental; (*traktowanie*) manipulative
**instru|ować (-uję, -ujesz)** (*perf* **po-**) *vt* to instruct
**instynk|t** (**-tu, -ty**) (*loc sg* **-cie**) *m* instinct; ~ **macierzyński** maternal instinct; ~ **samozachowawczy** the instinct of *lub* for self-preservation
**instynktownie** *adv* instinctively
**instynktowny** *adj* instinctive
**instytucj|a** (**-i, -e**) (*gen pl* **-i**) *f* institution; ~ **małżeństwa** the institution of marriage
**instytu|t** (**-tu, -ty**) (*loc sg* **-cie**) *m* institute
**insuli|na** (**-ny**) (*dat sg* **-nie**) *f* insulin
**insygni|a** (**-ów**) *pl* insignia; ~ **królewskie** royal insignia, regalia
**insynuacj|a** (**-i, -e**) (*gen pl* **-i**) *f* insinuation, innuendo
**insynu|ować (-uję, -ujesz)** *vt* to insinuate
**integracj|a** (**-i**) *f* integration
**integralnoś|ć** (**-ci**) *f* integrity
**integralny** *adj* integral
**integr|ować (-uję, -ujesz)** (*perf* **z-**) *vt* to integrate; **integrować się** *vr* to integrate
**intelek|t** (**-tu**) (*loc sg* **-cie**) *m* intellect
**intelektuali|sta** (**-sty, -ści**) (*dat sg* **-ście**) *m decl like f in sg* intellectual

i

**intelektualist|ka** (**-ki, -ki**) (*dat sg* **-ce**, *gen pl* **-ek**) *f* intellectual
**intelektualny** *adj* intellectual
**inteligencj|a** (**-i**) *f* (*zdolność*) intelligence; (*warstwa społeczna*) intelligentsia
**inteligen|t** (**-ta, -ci**) (*loc sg* **-cie**) *m* (*pej*) highbrow
**inteligentny** *adj* intelligent
**intencj|a** (**-i, -e**) (*gen pl* **-i**) *f* intention, intent; **mieć dobre intencje** to mean well
**intendentu|ra** (**-ry, -ry**) (*dat sg* **-rze**) *f* (*Wojsk*) commissariat
**intensyfik|ować (-uję, -ujesz)** (*perf* **z-**) *vt* to intensify
**intensywnoś|ć** (**-ci**) *f* intensity
**intensywny** *adj* (*praca, poszukiwania*) intensive; (*barwy*) intense
**interdyscyplinarny** *adj* interdisciplinary
**intere|s** (**-su, -sy**) (*loc sg* **-sie**) *m* (*korzyść*) interest; (*sprawa, firma, sklep*) business; (*transakcja*) deal; **w czyimś/swoim ~ie** in sb's/one's (best) interest; **mam do ciebie ~** (*pot*) I want a word with you (*pot*); **(to) nie twój ~!** it's none of your business!; **zrobić** (*perf*) **dobry/kiepski ~ na** *+loc* to make a good/poor deal in; **człowiek ~u** businessman
**interesan|t** (**-ta, -ci**) (*loc sg* **-cie**) *m* client
**interes|ować (-uję, -ujesz)** (*perf* **za-**) *vt* to interest; **interesować się** *vr*: **~ się kimś/czymś** to be interested in sb/sth
**interesowny** *adj* mercenary
**interesujący** *adj* interesting
**interfej|s** (**-su, -sy**) (*loc sg* **-sie**) *m* interface
**interlini|a** (**-i, -e**) (*gen pl* **-i**) *f* (*Druk*) spacing
**interna|t** (**-tu, -ty**) (*loc sg* **-cie**) *m* (school) dormitory; **szkoła z ~em** boarding school
**interni|sta** (**-sty, -ści**) (*dat sg* **-ście**) *m decl like f in sg* (*Med*) internist
**intern|ować (-uję, -ujesz)** *vt* to intern
**interpelacj|a** (**-i, -e**) (*gen pl* **-i**) *f* interpellation; **interpelacje poselskie** (*Pol*) ≈ question time
**interpel|ować (-uję, -ujesz)** *vi* to interpellate
**interpretacj|a** (**-i, -e**) (*gen pl* **-i**) *f* interpretation
**interpret|ować (-uję, -ujesz)** (*perf* **z-**) *vt* (*wyjaśniać*) to interpret; (*odbierać, rozumieć*) to interpret, to construe; (*odtwarzać*) to interpret, to render
**interpunkcj|a** (**-i**) *f* punctuation
**interpunkcyjny** *adj*: **znak/błąd ~** punctuation mark/error
**interwa|ł** (**-łu, -ły**) (*loc sg* **-le**) *m* (*Muz*) interval
**interwencj|a** (**-i, -e**) (*gen pl* **-i**) *f* intervention; **~ zbrojna** armed intervention
**interweni|ować (-uję, -ujesz)** *vi* to intervene
**intonacj|a** (**-i, -e**) (*gen pl* **-i**) *f* intonation
**inton|ować (-uję, -ujesz)** (*perf* **za-**) *vt*: **~ pieśń** to strike up a song
**intratny** *adj* lucrative
**introligato|r** (**-ra, -rzy**) (*loc sg* **-rze**) *m* bookbinder
**introligator|nia** (**-ni, -nie**) (*gen pl* **-ni**) *f* bookbindery
**introspekcj|a** (**-i, -e**) (*gen pl* **-i**) *f* introspection
**introwerty|k** (**-ka, -cy**) (*instr sg* **-kiem**) *m* introvert
**intru|z** (**-za, -zy** *lub* **-zi**) (*loc sg* **-zie**) *m* intruder
**intry|ga** (**-gi, -gi**) (*dat sg* **-dze**) *f* (*podstępne działanie*) intrigue, plot; (*Teatr, Lit*) plot
**intrygan|t** (**-ta, -ci**) (*loc sg* **-cie**) *m* intriguer, plotter
**intryg|ować (-uję, -ujesz)** *vt* (*zaciekawiać*) (*perf* **za-**) to intrigue
**intuicj|a** (**-i**) *f* intuition
**intuicyjny** *adj* intuitive
**intymnoś|ć** (**-ci**) *f*: **nastrój intymności** an atmosphere of intimacy; **naruszać czyjąś ~** to invade sb's privacy
**intymny** *adj* intimate
**inwali|da** (**-dy, -dzi**) (*dat sg* **-dzie**) *m decl like f in sg* invalid, disabled person; **~ wojenny** disabled war veteran
**inwalidzki** *adj*: **renta inwalidzka** disability pension; **wózek ~** wheelchair
**inwazj|a** (**-i, -e**) (*gen pl* **-i**) *f*: **~ (na** *+acc*) invasion (of)
**inwencj|a** (**-i**) *f* (*pomysłowość*) inventiveness; (*Muz*) invention; **~ twórcza** creativity
**inwentaryzacj|a** (**-i, -e**) (*gen pl* **-i**) *f* (*towarów*) stocktaking; (*zabytków*) cataloguing
**inwentarz** (**-a, -e**) (*gen pl* **-y**) *m* (*spis majątku*) inventory; **żywy ~** livestock
**inwersj|a** (**-i, -e**) (*gen pl* **-i**) *f* (*Jęz*) inversion
**inwesto|r** (**-ra, -rzy**) (*loc sg* **-rze**) *m* investor
**inwest|ować (-uję, -ujesz)** (*perf* **za-**) *vi* (*vi*): **~ (w** *+acc*) to invest (in)
**inwestycj|a** (**-i, -e**) (*gen pl* **-i**) *f* (*przedsięwzięcie*) investment; (*obiekt*) construction
**inwestycyjny** *adj*: **spółka inwestycyjna** investment trust; **wydatki inwestycyjne** capital expenditure
**inwigilacj|a** (**-i, -e**) (*gen pl* **-i**) *f* surveillance
**inwokacj|a** (**-i, -e**) (*gen pl* **-i**) *f* invocation
**inż.** *abbr* (= *inżynier*) engineer
**inżynie|r** (**-ra, -rowie**) (*loc sg* **-rze**) *m* engineer; **~ budowlany** *lub* **budownictwa** civil engineer; **~ mechanik/elektronik** mechanical/electronic engineer
**inżynieri|a** (**-i**) *f* engineering
**iracki** *adj* Iraqi
**Ira|k** (**-ku**) (*instr sg* **-kiem**) *m* Iraq
**Irakijczy|k** (**-ka, -cy**) (*instr sg* **-kiem**) *m* Iraqi
**Ira|n** (**-nu**) (*loc sg* **-nie**) *m* Iran
**Irańczy|k** (**-ka, -cy**) (*instr sg* **-kiem**) *m* Iranian
**irański** *adj* Iranian

**ir|cha** (**-chy**) (*dat sg* **-sze**) *f* chamois
**Irlandczy|k** (**-ka, -cy**) (*instr sg* **-kiem**) *m* Irishman
**Irlandi|a** (**-i**) *f* Ireland; **~ Północna** Northern Ireland
**Irland|ka** (**-ki, -ki**) (*dat sg* **-ce**, *gen pl* **-ek**) *f* Irishwoman
**irlandzki** *adj* Irish
**ironi|a** (**-i**) *f* irony; **jak na ironię** to make things worse; **~ losu** (*przen*) an ironic twist of fate
**ironiczny** *adj* ironic
**ironiz|ować (-uję, -ujesz)** *vi* to be ironic
**irracjonalny** *adj* irrational
**iry|d** (**-du**) (*loc sg* **-dzie**) *m* (*Chem*) iridium
**irygacj|a** (**-i, -e**) (*gen pl* **-i**) *f* irrigation
**irygacyjny** *adj* irrigational
**iry|s** (**-sa, -sy**) (*loc sg* **-sie**) *m* (*Bot*) iris; (*cukierek*) toffee
**irytacj|a** (**-i**) *f* irritation, annoyance
**iryt|ować (-uję, -ujesz)** (*perf* **z-**) *vt* to annoy, to irritate; **irytować się** *vr*: **~ się (o coś)** to get annoyed (at sth), to get irritated (by sth)
**irytujący** *adj* irritating, annoying
**iskier|ka** (**-ki, -ki**) (*dat sg* **-ce**, *gen pl* **-ek**) *f dimin od* **iskra**; **~ nadziei** a flicker of hope
**is|kra** (**-kry, -kry**) (*dat sg* **-krze**, *gen pl* **-kier**) *f* spark
**iskrz|yć (-y)** (*perf* **za-**) *vi* to sparkle; **iskrzyć się** *vr* to sparkle
**isla|m** (**-mu**) (*loc sg* **-mie**) *m* Islam
**islamski** *adj* Islamic
**Islandczy|k** (**-ka, -cy**) (*instr sg* **-kiem**) *m* Icelander
**Islandi|a** (**-i**) *f* Iceland
**Island|ka** (**-ki, -ki**) (*dat sg* **-ce**, *gen pl* **-ek**) *f* Icelander
**islandzki** *adj* Icelandic ▷ *m decl like adj* (*język*) Icelandic
**Istambu|ł** (**-łu**) (*loc sg* **-le**) *m* Istanbul
**ist|nieć (-nieję, -niejesz)** *vi* to be, to exist; **~ od ...** to be in existence since ...
**istniejący** *adj* existing
**istnie|nie** (**-nia**) *nt* (*bycie, trwanie*) existence; (*książk*: *istota ludzka*) (*nom pl* **-nia**, *gen pl* **-ń**) human being
**istny** *adj*: **istne szaleństwo** real madness
**isto|ta** (**-ty, -ty**) (*dat sg* **-cie**) *f* (*stworzenie*) creature; (*sedno*) essence; **w istocie** in fact, in reality; **~ ludzka** human being; **żywa ~** living being
**istotnie** *adv* (*rzeczywiście*) indeed; (*zasadniczo*) essentially, fundamentally
**istotny** *adj* essential, crucial; (*różnica*) significant
**iść (idę, idziesz)** (*imp* **idź**, *pt* **szedł, szła, szli**, *perf* **pójść**) *vi* to go; (*pieszo*) to walk; (*o towarze*) to sell; **iść (do** *+gen*/**na** *+acc*) to go (to); **idę!** (I'm) coming!; **idziesz ze mną?** are you coming with me?; **iść dalej** to go on; **iść do domu** to go home; **iść ulicą** to walk down *lub* along the street; **iść na grzyby** to go mushrooming; **iść na sanki/zabawę** to go sledging/dancing; **iść na spacer** to go for a walk; **iść spać/do łóżka** to go to sleep/bed; **pójść po coś** to (go) fetch sth, to get sth; **iść za** *+instr* to follow; **pójść sobie** (*pot*: *odejść*) to leave; **idzie deszcz** it's going to rain; **idzie zima** winter is coming; **idzie burza** there is a storm coming; **wszystko idzie dobrze/źle** everything goes fine/wrong; **dobrze/fatalnie mi poszło** it went fine/terrible; **jak ci idzie?** (*pot*) how are you doing?, how is it going?; **idzie o pieniądze** we're talking about money; **iść na medycynę/prawo** (*pot*: *Uniw*) to go to Medical School/Law School; **iść na** *+acc* (*zgadzać się na*) to go along with, to go for; **o co mu idzie?** what's he on about?; **iść w górę** (*o cenach*) to go up; **co za tym idzie ...** and what follows ...
**itd.** *abbr* (*= i tak dalej*) etc
**itp.** *abbr* (*= i tym podobne lub podobnie*) etc.
**iz|ba** (**-by, -by**) (*loc sg* **-bie**) *f* (*pomieszczenie*) room; (*w parlamencie*) house; (*urząd państwowy*) chamber; **I~ Gmin/Lordów** the House of Commons/Lords; **I~ Reprezentantów** the House of Representatives; **Najwyższa I~ Kontroli** the Supreme Control Chamber
**izolacj|a** (**-i**) *f* (*odosobnienie*) isolation; (*Tech*) insulation
**izolacjoniz|m** (**-mu**) (*loc sg* **-mie**) *m* (*Pol*) isolationism
**izolacyjny** *adj* (*taśma, warstwa*) insulating
**izolat|ka** (**-ki, -ki**) (*dat sg* **-ce**, *gen pl* **-ek**) *f* (*w szpitalu*) isolation ward
**izolato|r** (**-ra, -ry**) (*loc sg* **-rze**) *m* (*materiał*) insulator
**izol|ować (-uję, -ujesz)** *vt* (*chorych, państwo*) (*perf* **od-**) to isolate; (*Tech*) (*perf* **za-**) to insulate; **izolować się** *vr* (*perf* **od-**); **~ się (od kogoś)** to isolate o.s. (from sb)
**izoto|p** (**-pu, -py**) (*loc sg* **-pie**) *m* (*Chem*) isotope
**Izrael** (**-a**) *m* Israel
**Izraelczy|k** (**-ka, -cy**) (*instr sg* **-kiem**) *m* Israeli
**izraelski** *adj* Israeli
**iż** *conj* (*książk*) that

i

**J, j** *nt inv (litera)* J, j; **J jak Jadwiga** ≈ J for Jack (*Brit*), ≈ J for Jig (*US*)

**j.** *abbr (= jezioro)* l. (*= lake*); (*= język*) language

**ja** *pron* I ▷ *nt inv (własna osoba)* self; **to tylko ja** it's only me; **wyższy niż ja** taller than I *lub* me; **moje drugie ja** my other self; **ja sam** I myself

**jabłeczni|k** (**-ka, -ki**) (*instr sg* **-kiem**) *m* (*ciasto*) apple cake; (*wino*) cider

**jabł|ko** (**-ka, -ka**) (*instr sg* **-kiem**, *gen pl* **-ek**) *nt* apple; **~ Adama** Adam's apple; **zbić** (*perf*) **kogoś na kwaśne ~** to beat sb to a pulp

**jabło|ń** (**-ni, -nie**) (*gen pl* **-ni**) *f* apple tree

**jabłusz|ko** (**-ka, -ka**) (*instr sg* **-kiem**, *gen pl* **-ek**) *nt dimin od* **jabłko**

**jach|t** (**-tu, -ty**) (*loc sg* **-cie**) *m* yacht

**jachtin|g** (**-gu**) (*instr sg* **-giem**) *m* yachting, boating

**jachtklu|b** (**-bu, -by**) (*loc sg* **-bie**) *m* yacht club

**ja|d** (**-du, -dy**) (*loc sg* **-dzie**) *m* venom, poison; (*przen*) venom

**jad|ać (-am, -asz)** *vt/vi* to eat; **gdzie jadasz obiady?** where do you usually have lunch/dinner?; **nie jadam zbyt wiele** I am not a heavy eater

**jadal|nia** (**-ni, -nie**) (*gen pl* **-ni**) *f* dining room

**jadalny** *adj* (*grzyb, roślina*) edible; **pokój ~** dining room ▷ *m decl like adj* (*pokój jadalny*) dining room

**jadę** *itd. vb patrz* **jechać**

**jadł** *itd. vb patrz* **jeść**

**jadłospi|s** (**-su, -sy**) (*loc sg* **-sie**) *m* menu

**jadłowstrę|t** (**-tu**) (*loc sg* **-cie**) *m* (*Med*) anorexia

**jadowity** *adj* poisonous, venomous

**jaglany** *adj*: **kasza jaglana** millet groats *pl*

**jagni|ę** (**-ęcia, -ęta**) (*gen pl* **-ąt**) *nt* lamb

**jagnięci|na** (**-ny**) (*dat sg* **-nie**) *f* lamb

**jagnięcy** *adj* lamb *attr*

**jag|oda** (**-ody, -ody**) (*dat sg* **-odzie**, *gen pl* **-ód**) *f* (*rodzaj owocu*) berry; (*też*: **czarna jagoda**) bilberry, whortleberry

**jagodowy** *adj* (*zupa*) bilberry *attr*, whortleberry *attr*

**jagua|r** (**-ra, -ry**) (*loc sg* **-rze**) *m* (*Zool*) jaguar

**jajecz|ko** (**-ka, -ka**) (*instr sg* **-kiem**, *gen pl* **-ek**) *nt dimin od* **jajo, jajko**

**jajeczkowani|e** (**-a**) *nt* (*Bio*) ovulation

**jajecznic|a** (**-y, -e**) *f* scrambled eggs *pl*; **smażyć (usmażyć** *perf*) **jajecznicę** to scramble eggs

**jaj|ko** (**-ka, -ka**) (*instr sg* **-kiem**, *gen pl* **-ek**) *nt* egg; **~ na miękko/twardo** soft-/hard-boiled egg; **~ sadzone** fried egg; **~ święcone** Easter egg; **obchodzić się z kimś/czymś jak z jajkiem** to handle sb/sth with kid gloves

**jajni|k** (**-ka, -ki**) (*instr sg* **-kiem**) *m* (*Anat*) ovary

**jaj|o** (**-a, -a**) *nt* egg; (*Bio*) ovum, egg; **jaja** *pl* (*pot!*: *jądra*) balls (*pot!*)

**jajowaty** *adj* (*owalny*) egg-shaped, oval

**jajow|ód** (**-odu, -ody**) (*loc sg* **-odzie**) *m* (*Anat*) fallopian tube

**jajowy** *adj*: **komórka jajowa** egg cell, ovum

 SŁOWO KLUCZOWE

**jak**[1] *pron* **1** (*w pytaniach*) how; **jak dużo?** how much/many?; **jak długo?** how long?; **jak się masz?** how are you? (*Brit*), how are you doing? (*US*); **jak wyglądam? — świetnie!** how do I look? — great!; **jak ona wygląda?** what does she look like?; **jak się robi omlet?** how do you *lub* how does one make an omelette?; **jak mu tam?** what-d'you-call-him?, what's-his-name?

**2** (*w zdaniach względnych*): **zrobiłem, jak chciałeś** I did as you wanted; **nie wiem, jak to zrobić** I don't know how to do it; **nie wiem, jak ona wygląda** I don't know what she looks like

**3** (*w jakim stopniu*): **jak szybko!** how quickly!

▷ *conj* **1** (*w porównaniach*) as; **biały jak śnieg** (as) white as snow; **za wysoki jak na dżokeja** too tall for a jockey; **tak jak ...** (just) like ...; **takie zwierzęta jak wilki i lisy** such animals as wolves and foxes

**2** (*kiedy*): **jak go zobaczysz, pozdrów go** when you see him, say hello from me; **widziałem (ją), jak wychodziła z biura** I saw her leave *lub* leaving the office; **minęły**

**już dwa lata, jak wyjechał** two years have passed since he left
**3** (*jeśli*) if, when; **jak nie chcesz jechać, możesz zostać z nami** you can stay with us if you don't want to go; **jak nie dziś, to jutro** if not today then tomorrow; **kto jak nie on?** who if not him?
▷ *part* **1: jak najlepiej/najszybciej** as well/soon as possible
**2: jak tylko** as soon as; **jak i** *lub* **również** as well as; **jak to?** what *lub* how do you mean?; **jak gdyby** as if, as though; **jak bądź** whichever way

**ja|k²** (**-ka, -ki**) (*instr sg* **-kiem**) *m* (*Zool*) yak
**jakby** *conj* (*gdyby*) if; (*w porównaniach*) as if
▷ *part*: **czuł ~ dreszcze** he felt sort of shivery; **~ś miała czas** if you have the time; **zachowywał się, ~ nic się nie stało** he behaved as if nothing had happened; **tak ~** almost

SŁOWO KLUCZOWE

**jaki** *pron decl like adj* **1** (*w pytaniach*) what; **jaki lubisz kolor?** what colo(u)r do you like?; **jaka dzisiaj jest pogoda?** what's the weather like today?
**2** (*który*) which; **jaki wybierasz: biały czy czarny?** which one do you choose: white or black?
**3** (*z przymiotnikami*) how; **jaka ona jest dobra!** how kind she is!
**4** (*z rzeczownikami*) what; **jaki piękny samochód!** what a beautiful car!

**jakikolwiek** (*f* **jakakolwiek**, *nt* **jakiekolwiek**) *pron* any
**jakiś** (*f* **jakaś**, *nt* **jakieś**) *pron* some; **dzwonił ~ Pan Kowalski** a Mr Kowalski called; **to jest jakieś 6 km stąd** it's about 6 km from here; **był ~ przygnębiony** he was kind of depressed
**jakkolwiek** *conj* (*chociaż*) although; (*obojętnie jak*) no matter how
**jako** *conj* as; **ja ~ były premier ...** as a former prime minister, I ...; **~ że** (*ponieważ*) since, as; **~ tako** (*nieźle*) quite well; (*tak sobie*) so-so
**jakoby** *conj*: **mówiono, ~ zamierzał odejść na emeryturę** he was presumably to retire
**jakoś** *adv* somehow; **czuł się ~ niewyraźnie** he was feeling kind of funny
**jakościowy** *adj* qualitative
**jakoś|ć** (**-ci**) *f* quality; **kontrola jakości** quality control; **znak jakości** ≈ British Standard mark (*Brit*); **produkt wysokiej jakości** high-quality product

**jakże** *pron* (*jak*): **~ tak można!** how can you!; **~ się cieszę!** I'm so happy!; **a ~!** you bet!
**jałmuż|na** (**-ny**) (*dat sg* **-nie**) *f* alms *pl*, charity
**jało|wiec** (**-wca, -wce**) *m* (*Bot*) juniper
**jałowy** *adj* (*ziemia*) barren; (*dyskusja*) idle; (*opatrunek*) sterile
**jałów|ka** (**-ki, -ki**) (*dat sg* **-ce**, *gen pl* **-ek**) *f* heifer
**ja|ma** (**-my, -my**) (*dat sg* **-mie**) *f* (*dół*) pit; (*jaskinia*) cave; (*nora*) hole; (*Anat*) cavity
**Jamajczy|k** (**-ka, -cy**) (*instr sg* **-kiem**) *m* Jamaican
**Jamaj|ka** (**-ki**) (*dat sg* **-ce**) *f* (*Geog*) Jamaica; (*mieszkanka Jamajki*) (*nom pl* **-ki**, *gen pl* **-ek**) Jamaican
**jamajski** *adj* Jamaican
**jamni|k** (**-ka, -ki**) (*instr sg* **-kiem**) *m* dachshund
**janke|s** (**-sa, -si**) (*loc sg* **-sie**) *m* (*pot: Amerykanin*) Yank (*pot*); (*Hist*) Yankee
**Japoni|a** (**-i**) *f* Japan
**Japon|ka** (**-ki, -ki**) (*dat sg* **-ce**, *gen pl* **-ek**) *f* Japanese *inv*
**Japończy|k** (**-ka, -cy**) (*instr sg* **-kiem**) *m* Japanese *inv*
**japoński** *adj* Japanese
**ja|r** (**-ru, -ry**) (*loc sg* **-rze**) *m* gorge
**jar|d** (**-da, -dy**) (*loc sg* **-dzie**) *m* yard
**jarmarczny** *adj* (*dzień*) market *attr*; (*literatura, ozdoba*) trashy
**jarmar|k** (**-ku, -ki**) (*instr sg* **-kiem**) *m* fair
**jarmuż** (**-u**) *m* (*Bot, Kulin*) kale, collard
**jarosz** (**-a, -e**) (*gen pl* **-ów** *lub* **-y**) *m* vegetarian
**jarski** *adj* vegetarian
**jary** *adj* (*zboże*) spring *attr*; **stary ale ~** (*przen*) old but strong, still going strong
**jarzeniów|ka** (**-ki, -ki**) (*dat sg* **-ce**, *gen pl* **-ek**) *f* arc lamp *lub* light; (*pot: świetlówka*) fluorescent lamp
**jarzębi|na** (**-ny, -ny**) (*dat sg* **-nie**) *f* (*Bot*) rowan, (European) mountain ash; (*owoc*) rowan(-berry)
**jarz|mo** (**-ma, -ma**) (*loc sg* **-mie**, *gen pl* **-m** *lub* **-em**) *nt* yoke
**jarz|yć się** (**-y**) *vr* to glow
**jarzy|na** (**-ny, -ny**) (*dat sg* **-nie**) *f* vegetable
**jarzynowy** *adj* vegetable *attr*
**jaseł|ka** (**-ek**) *pl* nativity play
**ja|siek** (**-śka, -śki**) (*instr sg* **-śkiem**) *m* small pillow
**jas|kier** (**-kra, -kry**) (*loc sg* **-krze**) *m* (*Bot*) buttercup
**jaski|nia** (**-ni, -nie**) (*gen pl* **-ń**) *f* cave; **~ zła** (*przen*) seat of evil
**jaskinio|wiec** (**-wca, -wcy**) *m* caveman
**jaskiniowy** *adj* cave *attr*
**jaskółczy** *adj*: **jaskółcze ziele** (*Bot*) celandine
**jaskół|ka** (**-ki, -ki**) (*dat sg* **-ce**, *gen pl* **-ek**) *f* swallow

j

**jask|ra** (**-ry**) (*dat sg* **-rze**) *f* (*Med*) glaucoma
**jaskrawo...** *pref* bright ...; **~rwony** bright red
**jaskrawy** *adj* (*kolor*) garish; (*przykład*) glaring
**ja|sno** (*comp* **-śniej**) *adv* (*mówić, tłumaczyć*) clearly; (*świecić*) brightly
**jasno...** *pref* light ...; **~bieski** light blue
**jasnoś|ć** (**-ci**) *f* (*światło*) brightness; (*bladość*) paleness; (*zrozumiałość*) clarity
**jasnowidz** (**-a, -e**) *m* clairvoyant
**jasnowłosy** *adj* fair-haired
**ja|sny** (*comp* **-śniejszy**) *adj* (*światło, dzień, uśmiech*) bright; (*kolor*) light; (*cera*) pale; (*język*) clear; **to jasne** that much is clear, that's for sure; **jasne, że wiem** of course I know; **to jasne jak słońce!** (that's as) clear as crystal!
**jastrz|ąb** (**-ębia, -ębie**) (*gen pl* **-ębi**) *m* hawk
**jaszczur|ka** (**-ki, -ki**) (*dat sg* **-ce**, *gen pl* **-ek**) *f* lizard
**jaśmi|n** (**-nu, -ny**) (*loc sg* **-nie**) *m* (*Bot*) jasmine
**jaśniej** *adv comp od* **jasno**
**jaśniejszy** *adj comp od* **jasny**
**jaw** *inv*: **wyjść** (*perf*) **na jaw** to come to light
**Ja|wa** (**-wy**) (*dat sg* **-wie**) *f* (*Geog*) Java
**ja|wa** (**-wy**) (*dat sg* **-wie**) *f* reality; **śnić na jawie** to daydream
**jawnie** *adv* (*głosować, obradować*) publicly; (*gardzić*) openly
**jawnoś|ć** (**-ci**) *f* publicness
**jawny** *adj* (*głosowanie, obrady*) public; (*niechęć, wzgarda*) open; (*sprzeczność*) evident
**jawo|r** (**-ru, -ry**) (*loc sg* **-rze**) *m* (*Bot*) sycamore maple
**jaz|da** (**-dy, -dy**) (*dat sg* **jeździe**) *f* (*podróż: samochodem*) drive; (*: pociągiem*) journey; (*: na motocyklu, rowerze, koniu*) ride; (*prowadzenie: samochodu*) driving; (*: motocykla, roweru*) riding; (*lekcja prowadzenia pojazdu*) driving lesson; **~ na łyżwach** skating; **~ na nartach** skiing; **~ konna** horse riding; **~ figurowa/szybka na lodzie** figure/speed skating; **nauka jazdy** (*kurs*) driving school; (*kierowca*) learner *lub* student driver; **prawo jazdy** driving licence (*Brit*), driver's license (*US*); **rozkład jazdy** timetable (*Brit*), schedule (*US*); **~ stąd!** get out (of here)!
**jazgo|tać** (**-czę, -czesz**) *vi* to yap
**jazz** (**jazzu**) (*loc sg* **~ie**) *m* jazz
**jazzma|n** (**-na, -ni**) (*loc sg* **-nie**) *m* jazzman
**jazzowy** *adj* jazz *attr*
**jaź|ń** (**-ni, -nie**) (*gen pl* **-ni**) *f* ego; **rozdwojenie jaźni** split personality
**ją** *pron acc od* **ona** her
**jąd|ro** (**-ra, -ra**) (*loc sg* **-rze**, *gen pl* **-er**) *nt* (*Anat*) testicle; (*orzecha*) kernel; (*Ziemi*) core; (*Bio: też:* **jądro komórkowe**) nucleus; (*Fiz: też:* **jądro atomowe**) (atomic) nucleus
**jądrowy** *adj* nuclear
**jąk|ać się** (**-am, -asz**) *vr* to stammer, to stutter; **on się lekko jąka** he has a slight stammer
**jąkani|e** (**się**) (**-a**) *nt* stammer, stutter
**jąt|rzyć** (**-rzę, -rzysz**) *vt* (*podburzać*) to incite; **jątrzyć się** *vr* (*o ranie*) to fester
**je** *pron acc sg od* **ono** it ▷ *pron acc pl od* **one** them
**je|bać** (**-bię, -biesz**) *vt* (*perf* **wy-**) (*pot!*) to fuck (*pot!*)
**jechać** (**jadę, jedziesz**) (*imp* **jedź**, *perf* **po-**) *vi* (*podróżować*) to go; (*motocyklem, rowerem, konno*) to ride; (*samochodem: jako kierowca*) to drive; (*: jako pasażer*) to ride; (*o samochodzie, pociągu*) to go; **~ na nartach** to ski; **~ na łyżwach** to skate; **~ samochodem** (*jako kierowca*) to drive a car; (*jako pasażer*) to ride in a car; **~ za granicę/na urlop** to go abroad/on holiday
**jeden** *num* one ▷ *adj* (*wspólny*) one; (*pewien*) a; **jedna druga** (one) half; **jeszcze ~** one more, (yet) another; **ani ~** not a single one, none; **~ za** *lub* **po drugim** one by one; **z jednej strony ... z drugiej strony ...** one (the) one hand ... on the other hand ...
**jedenast|ka** (**-ki, -ki**) (*dat sg* **-ce**, *gen pl* **-ek**) *f* eleven; (*drużyna piłkarska*) team; (*rzut karny*) penalty kick
**jedenastoletni** *adj* (*chłopiec*) eleven-year-old; (*okres*) eleven-year *attr*
**jedenasty** *num* eleventh; **godzina jedenasta** eleven (o'clock)
**jedenaście** *num* eleven
**jedli** *itd. vb patrz* **jeść**
**jedn.** *abbr* (= *jednostka*) unit
**jedn|ać** (**-am, -asz**) (*perf* **z-**) *vt*: **~ sobie kogoś** to win sb over; **jednać się** (*perf* **po-**) *vr*: **~ się (z kimś)** to become reconciled (with sb)
**jednak** *conj* but, (and) yet; **zwyciężył, ~ nie był zadowolony** he had won, and yet he wasn't pleased
**jednakowo** *adv* alike, equally
**jednakowy** *adj* equal; **w ~m stopniu** in *lub* to an equal degree *lub* extent
**jednakże** *conj* = **jednak**
**jedno** *pron* (*jedna rzecz*) one thing; (*całość*) one (whole); (*to samo*) one (and the same); **~ jest pewne** one thing's for sure; **~ z dwojga** one or the other; **zlewać się w ~** to become one; **wychodzi na ~** same difference; *patrz też* **jeden**
**jednoaktów|ka** (**-ki, -ki**) (*dat sg* **-ce**, *gen pl* **-ek**) *f* one-act play
**jednobarwny** *adj* monochromatic
**jednocyfrowy** *adj*: **numer ~** single-digit number
**jednoczesny** *adj* simultaneous
**jednocześnie** *adv* at the same time, simultaneously

**jedno|czyć (-czę, -czysz)** *(perf* **z-**) *vt* to unite; **jednoczyć się** *vr* to unite
**jednodniowy** *adj (strajk)* one-day; *(niemowlę)* one-day-old
**jednogłośnie** *adv* unanimously
**jednogłośny** *adj* unanimous
**jednojajowy** *adj*: **bliźnięta jednojajowe** identical twins
**jednojęzyczny** *adj* monolingual
**jednokierunkowy** *adj (ruch, ulica)* one-way
**jednokomórkowy** *adj (Bio)* unicellular
**jednokrotny** *adj* single-time *attr*
**jednolity** *adj* uniform
**jednomyślnie** *adv* unanimously
**jednomyślnoś|ć (-ci)** *f* unanimity
**jednomyślny** *adj* unanimous
**jednooki** *adj* one-eyed *attr*
**jednoosobowy** *adj (kierownictwo)* one-man *attr*; *(pokój)* single
**jednopartyjny** *adj* single-party *attr*
**jednopiętrowy** *adj* two-storey(ed) *attr (Brit)*, two-storied *attr (US)*
**jednopokojowy** *adj*: **mieszkanie jednopokojowe** studio (flat) *(Brit)*, efficiency (apartment) *(US)*
**jednorazowy** *adj (wysiłek, opłata)* single; **jednorazowego użytku** disposable
**jednoręki** *adj* one-handed; **~ bandyta** *(automat do gry)* one-armed bandit, fruit machine
**jednorodny** *adj* homogeneous
**jednorodzinny** *adj*: **domek ~** detached house
**jednoroż|ec (-ca, -ce)** *m* unicorn
**jednorzędowy** *adj*: **marynarka jednorzędowa** single-breasted jacket
**jednosilnikowy** *adj* single-engine *attr*
**jednostajnoś|ć (-ci)** *f* monotony
**jednostajny** *adj* monotonous
**jednost|ka (-ki, -ki)** *(dat sg* **-ce**, *gen pl* **-ek**) *f (człowiek)* individual; *(też:* **jednostka miary**) unit (of measure); **~ wojskowa** military unit
**jednostkowy** *adj (przypadek)* isolated; **cena jednostkowa** unit price
**jednostronny** *adj (rozwój, produkcja)* one-sided; *(druk)* one-side *attr*; *(Prawo, Pol)* unilateral; *(ruch)* one-way
**jednosylabowy** *adj* monosyllabic
**jednoszynowy** *adj*: **kolej jednoszynowa** monorail
**jednoś|ć (-ci)** *f (państwa, opinii)* unity; *(oddzielna całość)* whole
**jednośla|d (-du, -dy)** *(loc sg* **-dzie**) *m* single-track vehicle *(motorcycle or bicycle)*
**jednośladowy** *adj (pojazd)* two-wheeled
**jednotomowy** *adj* single-volume *attr*, one-volume *attr*
**jednotorowy** *adj (kolej)* single-track *attr*; *(myślenie)* one-track *attr*
**jednotygodniowy** *adj* one-week *attr*
**jednoznaczny** *adj* clear-cut, unambiguous
**jedwa|b (-biu, -bie)** *m* silk
**jedwabisty** *adj* silky
**jedwabni|k (-ka, -ki)** *(instr sg* **-kiem**) *m* silkworm
**jedwabny** *adj* silk *attr*
**jedynacz|ka (-ki, -ki)** *(dat sg* **-ce**, *gen pl* **-ek**) *f* only child
**jedyna|k (-ka, -cy)** *(instr sg* **-kiem**) *m* only child
**jedynie** *adv* only, merely; **~ on może to zrobić** no-one but him can do it
**jedyn|ka (-ki, -ki)** *(dat sg* **-ce**, *gen pl* **-ek**) *f* one; *(Szkol)* ≈ F *(grade)*; *(Mot)* first (gear)
**jedyny** *adj* only; *(ukochany)* dearest; **~ w swoim rodzaju** unique; **jedyne, co mnie pociesza, to ...** my only comfort is that ...
**jedz** *itd. vb patrz* **jeść**
**jedzeni|e (-a)** *nt (żywność)* food; *(spożywanie)* eating; **~ i picie** food and drink; **coś do jedzenia** something to eat; **nadający się do jedzenia** eatable
**jedzie** *itd. vb patrz* **jechać**
**jee|p (-pa, -py)** *(loc sg* **-pie**) *m* jeep
**jego** *pron gen od* **on, ono** ▷ *possessive pron inv (o osobie)* his; *(o przedmiocie, zwierzęciu)* its
**jegomoś|ć (-cia, -cie)** *m* gentleman
**Jeho|wa (-wy)** *(dat sg* **-wie**) *m decl like f* Jehovah; **świadek Jehowy** Jehovah's witness
**jej** *pron gen od* **ona** ▷ *possessive pron inv (o osobie: przed rzeczownikiem)* her; *(: bez rzeczownika)* hers; *(o przedmiocie, zwierzęciu)* its; **nie ma jej** she's not here; **nie widzę jej** I can't see her; **to jest jej klucz** it's her key
**jele|ń (-nia, -nie)** *(gen pl* **-ni**) *m (Zool)* (red) deer; *(przen)* sucker
**jeli|to (-ta, -ta)** *(loc sg* **-cie**) *nt* intestine; **~ cienkie/grube** small/large intestine
**jem** *itd. vb patrz* **jeść**
**jemio|ła (-ły, -ły)** *(dat sg* **-le**) *f* mistletoe
**jemu** *pron dat od* **on** (to) him ▷ *pron dat od* **ono** (to) it
**je|n (-na, -ny)** *(loc sg* **-nie**) *m* yen
**je|niec (-ńca, -ńcy)** *m* prisoner, captive; **~ wojenny** prisoner-of-war camp, PoW camp
**jeniecki** *adj*: **obóz ~** prison camp
**Jerozoli|ma (-my)** *(dat sg* **-mie**) *f* Jerusalem
**jerzy|k (-ka, -ki)** *(instr sg* **-kiem**) *m (Zool)* swift
**jesienny** *adj* autumn *attr*, fall *attr (US)*
**jesie|ń (-ni, -nie)** *(gen pl* **-ni**) *f (pora roku)* autumn, fall *(US)*; **jesienią** in autumn *lub* fall *(US)*; **~ życia** autumn of life
**jesio|n (-nu, -ny)** *(loc sg* **-nie**) *m* ash

**jesiot|r** (**-ra, -ry**) (*loc sg* **-rze**) *m* sturgeon
**jest** *itd. vb patrz* **być**
**jeszcze** *part* (*wciąż*) still; (*z przeczeniem*) yet; (*ze stopniem wyższym*) even; **~ przed wojną** already before the war; **mamy ~ dwie godziny** we still have two hours; **~ nie** not yet; **~ nie skończyłem** I haven't finished yet; **~ lepszy/gorszy** even better/worse; **kto/co ~?** who/what else?; **czy ktoś/coś ~?** anybody/anything else?; **~ raz** one more time, once again; **~ jak!** and how!
**jeść (jem, jesz)** (*3 pl* **jedzą**, *imp* **jedz**, *pt* **jadł, jedli**, *perf* **z-**) *vt* to eat; **~ śniadanie/kolację** to have breakfast/supper; **chce mi się ~** I'm hungry; **co jadłeś na śniadanie?** what did you have for breakfast?
**jeśli** *conj* if; **~ nie** if not, unless; **~ będziesz grzeczny, opowiem ci bajkę** if you behave, I'll tell you a story; **~ dobrze pamiętam ...** if I remember rightly ...; **~ nie on, to kto?** if not he *lub* him, then who?; **~ idzie o ...** as regards ...; **~ nawet** even if; **a ~ się nie zgodzi?** what if he says no?; **~ o mnie chodzi** as far as I am concerned
**jeśliby** *conj* if
**jez.** *abbr* (*= jezioro*) l. (*= lake*)
**jezd|nia** (**-ni, -nie**) (*gen pl* **-ni**) *f* road(way)
**jezio|ro** (**-ra, -ra**) (*loc sg* **-rze**) *nt* lake
**jezui|ta** (**-ty, -ci**) (*dat sg* **-cie**) *m decl like f in sg* Jesuit
**Jezu|s** (**-sa**) (*loc sg* **-sie**) *m* Jesus
**je|ździć (-żdżę, -ździsz)** (*imp* **-ździj**) *vi* to go; (*podróżować*) to travel; (*o pociągu, autobusie: kursować*) to run, to go; **~ za granicę/na urlop** to go abroad/on holiday; **~ konno** to ride (a horse); **~ samochodem** to drive (a car); **~ na łyżwach** to skate; **~ na nartach** to ski; **~ na rowerze** to cycle
**jeździe** *n patrz* **jazda**
**jeź|dziec** (**-dźca, -dźcy**) *m* rider
**jeździect|wo** (**-wa**) (*loc sg* **-wie**) *nt* horse-riding
**jeż** (**-a, -e**) (*gen pl* **-y**) *m* hedgehog; **fryzura na jeża** crew-cut
**jeżeli** *conj* if; **~ nie** if not, unless; *patrz też* **jeśli**
**jeżo|wiec** (**-wca, -wce**) *m* sea urchin
**jeżozwierz** (**-a, -e**) (*gen pl* **-y**) *m* (*Zool*) porcupine
**jeż|yć (-y)** *vt* (*grzywę, sierść*) (*perf* **z-**) to bristle (up); **jeżyć się** *vr* (*przen: o człowieku*) (*perf* **na-**) to bristle; (*: o przeszkodach*) to spring up
**jeży|k** (**-ka, -ki**) (*instr sg* **-kiem**) *m dimin od* **jeż**; (*fryzura*) crew-cut
**jeży|na** (**-ny, -ny**) (*dat sg* **-nie**) *f* blackberry, bramble
**ję|czeć (-czę, -czysz)** (*perf* **-knąć**) *vi* to groan, to moan
**jęczmie|ń** (**-nia, -nie**) (*gen pl* **-ni**) *m* (*Bot*) barley; (*Med*) sty(e)
**jędrny** *adj* firm
**jędz|a** (**-y, -e**) *f* (*w bajce*) witch; (*przen*) shrew
**ję|k** (**-ku, -ki**) (*instr sg* **-kiem**) *m* groan, moan
**jęk|nąć (-nę, -niesz)** (*imp* **-nij**) *vb perf od* **jęczeć**
**jęz.** *abbr* (*= język*) language
**języcz|ek** (**-ka, -ki**) (*instr sg* **-kiem**) *m dimin od* **język**; (*Anat*) uvula; **być języczkiem u wagi** (*przen*) to tip the balance
**języ|k** (**-ka, -ki**) (*instr sg* **-kiem**) *m* language; (*Anat*) tongue; **pokazywać (pokazać** *perf*) **komuś ~** to stick out one's tongue at sb; **mieć coś na końcu ~a** (*przen*) to have sth on the tip of one's tongue; **trzymać ~ za zębami** (*przen*) to keep one's tongue (between one's teeth); **z wywieszonym ~iem** breathless; **~ angielski** English, the English language; **~ ojczysty** mother tongue
**językowy** *adj* (*norma*) linguistic; (*laboratorium*) language *attr*
**językoznawc|a** (**-y, -y**) *m decl like f in sg* linguist
**językoznawst|wo** (**-wa**) (*loc sg* **-wie**) *nt* linguistics
**jidysz** *m inv* Yiddish
**jo|d** (**-du**) (*loc sg* **-dzie**) *m* iodine
**jodeł|ka** (**-ki, -ki**) (*dat sg* **-ce**, *gen pl* **-ek**) *f* (*wzór*) herring-bone
**jod|ła** (**-ły, -ły**) (*dat sg* **-le**, *gen pl* **-eł**) *f* fir (tree)
**jodł|ować (-uję, -ujesz)** *vi* to yodel
**jodowany** *adj*: **sól jodowana** iodized salt
**jody|na** (**-ny**) (*dat sg* **-nie**) *f* iodine (solution)
**jo|ga** (**-gi**) (*dat sg* **-dze**) *f* yoga
**joggin|g** (**-gu**) (*instr sg* **-giem**) *m* jogging
**jogur|t** (**-tu, -ty**) (*loc sg* **-cie**) *m* yoghurt
**jo|n** (**-nu, -ny**) (*loc sg* **-nie**) *m* ion
**joński** *adj* (*kolumna*) Ionic; **Morze J~e** the Ionian Sea
**Jordani|a** (**-i**) *f* Jordan
**Jordan|ka** (**-ki, -ki**) (*dat sg* **-ce**, *gen pl* **-ek**) *f* Jordanian
**Jordańczy|k** (**-ka, -cy**) (*instr sg* **-kiem**) *m* Jordanian
**jo|ta** (**-ty, -ty**) (*dat sg* **-cie**, *gen pl* **-t**) *f* iota; **ani na jotę** not a bit; **co do joty** to a T
**jowialny** *adj* jovial, genial
**Jowisz** (**-a**) *m* Jupiter
**jub|el** (**-la** *lub* **-lu, -le**) (*gen pl* **-li**) *m* (*pot*) booze-up (*pot*)
**jubila|t** (**-ta, -ci**) (*loc sg* **-cie**) *m man celebrating a birthday or an anniversary*
**jubilat|ka** (**-ki, -ki**) (*gen pl* **-ek**) *f woman celebrating a birthday or an anniversary*
**jubile|r** (**-ra, -rzy**) (*loc sg* **-rze**) *m* jeweller (*Brit*), jeweler (*US*)

**jubilerski** *adj*: **sklep** ~ jeweller's (shop) (*Brit*), jeweler's (shop) (*US*); **wyroby ~e** jewellery (*Brit*), jewelry (*US*)
**jubileusz** (**-u, -e**) (*gen pl* **-y** *lub* **-ów**) *m* jubilee
**juczny** *adj*: **zwierzę juczne** pack animal
**judaiz|m** (**-mu**) (*loc sg* **-mie**) *m* Judaism
**judasz** (**-a, -e**) (*gen pl* **-y** *lub* **-ów**) *m* (*zdrajca*) a Judas; (*wizjer*) peephole
**judo** *n patrz* **dżudo**
**Jugosławi|a** (**-i**) *f* Yugoslavia; **dawna** ~ the former Yugoslavia
**Jugosłowia|nin** (**-nina, -nie**) (*loc sg* **-ninie**, *gen pl* **-n**) *m* Yugoslav
**Jugosłowian|ka** (**-ki, -ki**) (*dat sg* **-ce**, *gen pl* **-ek**) *f* Yugoslav
**jugosłowiański** *adj* Yugoslav(ian)
**juha|s** (**-sa, -si**) (*loc sg* **-sie**) *m shepherd in the Tatra Mountains*
**junio|r** (**-ra, -rzy**) (*loc sg* **-rze**) *m* junior; **Mistrzostwa J~ów w Piłce Nożnej** Football Championship for Under-21's
**jun|ta** (**-ty, -ty**) (*dat sg* **-cie**) *f* junta
**jupite|r** (**-ra, -ry**) (*loc sg* **-rze**) *m* spotlight
**jurajski** *adj* Jurassic
**juro|r** (**-ra, -rzy**) (*loc sg* **-rze**) *m* juror; (*w piłce nożnej*) referee
**jury** *nt inv* jury
**jurysdykcj|a** (**-i, -e**) (*gen pl* **-i**) *f* jurisdiction
**just|ować** (**-uję, -ujesz**) (*perf* **wy-**) *vt* to justify
**Jutlandi|a** (**-i**) *f* Jutland
**jut|ro** (**-ra**) (*loc sg* **-rze**) *nt* tomorrow ▷ *adv* tomorrow; **do jutra!** see you tomorrow!; **~ wieczorem** tomorrow evening *lub* night
**jutrzejszy** *adj* tomorrow's *attr*
**jutrzen|ka** (**-ki**) (*dat sg* **-ce**) *f* (*książk: świt*) dawn; (*gwiazda*) morning star
**już** *adv* (*w zdaniach twierdzących*) already; (*w pytaniach*) yet; **już to widziałem** I've already seen it, I've seen it before; **czy widziałeś już ten film?** have you seen that film yet?; **pisano o tym już w osiemnastym wieku** it was mentioned as early as the 18th century; **już miał zrezygnować** he was on the verge of giving up; **już tutaj nie przychodzi** he no longer comes here; **powinienem już iść** I should go now; **już nie** no longer; **już nigdy** never again
**jw.** *abbr* (= *jak wyżej*) do. (= *ditto*)

J

**K, k** *nt inv (litera)* K, k; **K jak Karol** ≈ K for King
**k.** *abbr (= koło)* near
**kabacz|ek (-ka, -ki)** *(instr sg* **-kiem**) *m (Bot)* marrow *(Brit)*, squash *(US)*
**kabano|s (-sa, -sy)** *(loc sg* **-sie**) *m thin smoked pork sausage*
**kabare|t (-tu, -ty)** *(loc sg* **-cie**) *m* cabaret
**kabaretowy** *adj* cabaret *attr*
**kab|el (-la, -le)** *(gen pl* **-li**) *m* cable
**kabesta|n (-nu, -ny)** *(loc sg* **-nie**) *m* capstan
**kabi|na (-ny, -ny)** *(dat sg* **-nie**) *f (pilota, kierowcy, pasażerska)* cabin; *(w toalecie)* cubicle; *(do głosowania)* (polling *lub* voting) booth; *(przymierzalnia)* fitting room; **~ telefoniczna** (tele)phone booth
**kabinowy** *adj*: **tłumacz ~** simultaneous interpreter
**kablowy** *adj*: **telewizja kablowa** cable television
**kabłą|k (-ka, -ki)** *(instr sg* **-kiem**) *m (Tech)* bow; **zgiąć się** *(perf)* **w ~** to arch one's back
**kabriole|t (-tu, -ty)** *(loc sg* **-cie**) *m* convertible
**kabu|ra (-ry, -ry)** *(loc sg* **-rze**) *f* holster
**kac (-a)** *m* hangover
**kaczą|t|ko (-ka, -ka)** *(instr sg* **-kiem**, *gen pl* **-ek**) *nt* duckling; **brzydkie ~** *(przen)* ugly duckling
**kacze|niec (-ńca, -ńce)** *m* cowslip *(Brit)*, marsh marigold *(US)*
**kacz|ka (-ki, -ki)** *(dat sg* **-ce**, *gen pl* **-ek**) *f* duck; **~ dziennikarska** *(przen)* canard; **puszczać kaczki** to play ducks and drakes
**kaczo|r (-ra, -ry)** *(loc sg* **-rze**) *m* drake
**kaczy** *adj*: **~ chód** waddle
**kadencj|a (-i, -e)** *(gen pl* **-i**) *f* tenure, term (of office); *(Muz)* cadence
**kade|t (-ta, -ci)** *(loc sg* **-cie**) *m* cadet
**kadłu|b (-ba, -by)** *(loc sg* **-bie**) *m (samolotu)* fuselage; *(statku)* hull
**kadm.** *abbr (= kontradmirał)* R.A.
**kad|r (-ru, -ry)** *(loc sg* **-rze**) *m* frame
**kad|ra (-ry, -ry)** *(dat sg* **-rze**) *f* personnel, staff; *(Wojsk)* cadre; **biuro/dział kadr** personnel (department); **~ narodowa** *(Sport)* national team; **kadry** *pl (pot: biuro kadr)* personnel
**kadr|ować (-uję, -ujesz)** *(perf* **s-**) *vt* to frame
**kadrowy** *adj*: **rezerwy kadrowe** staff reserves; **polityka kadrowa** employment policy
**ka|dzić (-dzę, -dzisz)** *(imp* **-dź**) *vi (przen: pot)*: **~ komuś** to butter sb up
**kadzideł|ko (-ka, -ka)** *(instr sg* **-kiem**) *nt* joss stick
**kadzid|ło (-ła, -ła)** *(loc sg* **-le**, *gen pl* **-eł**) *nt* incense
**kafej|ka (-ki, -ki)** *(dat sg* **-ce**, *gen pl* **-ek**) *f (pot)* café
**kafel|ek (-ka, -ki)** *(instr sg* **-kiem**) *m* tile
**kaflowy** *adj*: **piec ~** tiled stove
**kafta|n (-na, -ny)** *(loc sg* **-nie**) *m (arabski)* kaftan; *(roboczy)* smock; **~ bezpieczeństwa** straitjacket
**kaftani|k (-ka, -ki)** *(instr sg* **-kiem**) *m (dziecięcy)* (wrapover) vest
**kaga|niec (-ńca, -ńce)** *m* muzzle
**Kai|r (-ru)** *(loc sg* **-rze**) *m* Cairo
**kaja|k (-ku, -ki)** *m* kayak, canoe
**kajakarst|wo (-wa)** *(loc sg* **-wie**) *nt* canoeing
**kajakarz (-a, -e)** *(gen pl* **-y**) *m* kayaker, canoeist
**kajdan|ki (-ek)** *pl* handcuffs *pl*; **zakładać (założyć** *perf***) komuś ~** to handcuff sb
**kajdan|y (-)** *pl* irons *pl*; *(przen)* shackles *pl*, fetters *pl*; **zakuwać (zakuć** *perf***) kogoś w ~** to clap sb in irons
**kaju|ta (-ty, -ty)** *(dat sg* **-cie**) *f* cabin
**kakao** *nt inv* cocoa
**kakaowy** *adj* cocoa *attr*
**kakofoni|a (-i, -e)** *(gen pl* **-i**) *f* cacophony
**kaktu|s (-sa, -sy)** *(loc sg* **-sie**) *m* cactus
**kalafio|r (-ra, -ry)** *(loc sg* **-rze**) *m* cauliflower
**kalambu|r (-ru, -ry)** *(loc sg* **-rze**) *m* pun
**kalare|pa (-py, -py)** *(dat sg* **-pie**) *f* kohlrabi
**kale** *n patrz* **kał**
**kalect|wo (-wa, -wa)** *(loc sg* **-wie**) *nt* disability
**kalecz|yć (-ę, -ysz)** *vt (perf* **s-**) to cut; *(przen: język)* to murder; **kaleczyć się** *vr* to cut o.s.; **s~** *(perf)* **się w palec** to cut one's finger
**kalejdosko|p (-pu, -py)** *(loc sg* **-pie**) *m* kaleidoscope
**kale|ka (-ki, -ki)** *(dat sg* **-ce**) *m/f decl like f* cripple

**kaleki** *adj* crippled, disabled
**kalendarz** (**-a, -e**) (*gen pl* **-y**) *m* calendar
**kalendarzowy** *adj*: **rok/miesiąc ~** calendar month/year; **wiosna kalendarzowa** *the period from 21st March to 23rd June*
**kalendarzy|k** (**-ka, -ki**) (*instr sg* **-kiem**) *m* (pocket) diary (*Brit*), calendar (*US*)
**kaleson|y** (**-ów**) *pl* long johns *pl* (*pot*)
**kalib|er** (**-ru, -ry**) (*loc sg* **-rze**) *m* calibre (*Brit*), caliber (*US*); **człowiek wielkiego kalibru** high calibre person
**Kaliforni|a** (**-i**) *f* California
**kaligrafi|a** (**-i**) *f* calligraphy
**kal|ka** (**-ki, -ki**) (*dat sg* **-ce**, *gen pl* **-k**) *f* (*maszynowa, ołówkowa*) carbon paper; (*też*: **kalka techniczna**) tracing paper; (*Jęz*) calque
**kalkomani|a** (**-i, -e**) (*gen pl* **-i**) *f* transfer (*Brit*), decal(comania) (*US*)
**kalkulacj|a** (**-i, -e**) (*gen pl* **-i**) *f* calculation
**kalkulacyjny** *adj*: **arkusz ~** spreadsheet
**kalkulato|r** (**-ra, -ry**) (*loc sg* **-rze**) *m* calculator
**kalkul|ować (-uję, -ujesz)** *vt* (*perf* **s-**) to calculate; **kalkulować się** *vr* (*pot*): **to mi się nie kalkuluje** it's not worth my while
**kalma|r** (**-ra, -ry**) (*loc sg* **-rze**) *m* = **kałamarnica**
**kalori|a** (**-i, -e**) (*gen pl* **-i**) *f* calorie
**kaloryczny** *adj* caloric
**kaloryfe|r** (**-ra, -ry**) (*loc sg* **-rze**) *m* radiator
**kalosz|e** (*gen* **-y**) *pl* wellingtons; (*nakładane na buty*) galoshes; **to inna para kaloszy** (*przen*) that's a different cup of tea
**ka|ł** (**-łu**) (*loc sg* **-le**) *m* faeces (*Brit*), feces (*US*)
**kałamarnic|a** (**-y, -e**) *f* squid
**kałamarz** (**-a, -e**) (*gen pl* **-y**) *m* ink-bottle
**kałuż|a** (**-y, -e**) (*dat sg* **-y**) *f* puddle
**Kambodż|a** (**-y**) *f* Cambodia
**kambu|z** (**-za, -zy**) (*loc sg* **-zie**) *m* galley
**kameleo|n** (**-na, -ny**) (*loc sg* **-nie**) *m* chameleon
**kame|ra** (**-ry, -ry**) (*loc sg* **-rze**) *f* camera; **~ telewizji przemysłowej** CCTV camera; **~ wideo** camcorder
**kameralny** *adj* (*nastrój*) intimate, cosy; **muzyka/orkiestra kameralna** chamber music/orchestra
**kamerdyne|r** (**-ra, -rzy**) (*loc sg* **-rze**) *m* butler
**kamerto|n** (**-nu, -ny**) (*loc sg* **-nie**) *m* tuning fork
**Kameru|n** (**-nu**) (*loc sg* **-nie**) *m* Cameroon
**kamerzy|sta** (**-sty, -ści**) (*dat sg* **-ście**) *m decl like f in sg* cameraman
**kamfo|ra** (**-ry**) (*dat sg* **-rze**) *f* camphor; **zniknąć** (*perf*) **jak ~** to disappear into thin air
**kamic|a** (**-y**) *f*: **~ nerkowa** nephrolithiasis; **~ pęcherzyka żółciowego** cholelithiasis
**kamieniarz** (**-a, -e**) (*gen pl* **-y**) *m* (stone)mason
**kamienic|a** (**-y, -e**) *f* tenement (house)
**kamienie|ć (-ję, -jesz)** (*perf* **s-**) *vi* to petrify; (*przen*) to become petrified
**kamienioło|m** (**-mu, -my**) (*loc sg* **-mie**) *m* quarry
**kamienisty** *adj* stony
**kamienny** *adj* (*most, posadzka*) stone *attr*; (*twarz, wzrok*) stony; (*sen*) heavy; **epoka kamienna** the Stone Age; **węgiel ~** hard coal
**kamien|ować (-uję, -ujesz)** (*perf* **u-**) *vt* to stone
**kamie|ń** (**-nia, -nie**) (*gen pl* **-ni**) *m* stone; (*w zegarku*) jewel; (*do zapalniczki*) flint; **~ szlachetny** gem(stone), precious stone; **~ nazębny** tartar; **~ żółciowy** gallstone; **~ nerkowy** kidney stone; **~ grobowy** *lub* **nagrobny** gravestone, tombstone; **~ kotłowy** fur; **~ młyński** millstone; **~ milowy** (*przen*) milestone; **~ węgielny** cornerstone; (*przen*) cornerstone, keystone; **~ spadł mi z serca** (*przen*) it's a weight *lub* load off my mind; **przepaść** (*perf*) **jak ~ w wodę** *lub* **w wodzie** to disappear into thin air
**kamikadze** *m inv* kamikaze
**kamion|ka** (**-ki, -ki**) (*dat sg* **-ce**, *gen pl* **-ek**) *f* (*materiał*) stoneware clay
**kamionkowy** *adj*: **naczynia kamionkowe** stone pottery, stoneware
**kamizel|ka** (**-ki, -ki**) (*dat sg* **-ce**, *gen pl* **-ek**) *f* waistcoat (*Brit*), vest (*US*); **~ kuloodporna** bullet-proof vest; **~ ratunkowa** life jacket
**kampani|a** (**-i, -e**) (*gen pl* **-i**) *f* campaign; **prowadzić kampanię na rzecz czegoś/przeciwko czemuś** to campaign for/against sth
**kamuflaż** (**-u, -e**) (*gen pl* **-y**) *m* camouflage
**kamy|k** (**-ka, -ki**) (*instr sg* **-kiem**) *m* pebble
**Kana|da** (**-dy**) (*loc sg* **-dzie**) *f* Canada
**Kanadyjczy|k** (**-ka, -cy**) (*instr sg* **-kiem**) *m* Canadian
**Kanadyj|ka** (**-ki, -ki**) (*dat sg* **-ce**, *gen pl* **-ek**) *f* Canadian; **kanadyjka** *f* (*łódź*) Canadian canoe
**kanadyjski** *adj* Canadian
**kanali|a** (**-i, -e**) (*gen pl* **-i**) *f* (*pej*) skunk (*pej*)
**kanalizacj|a** (**-i**) *f* sewage system
**kanalizacyjny** *adj*: **rura kanalizacyjna** sewage pipe; **instalacja wodno-kanalizacyjna** plumbing
**kana|ł** (**-łu, -ły**) (*loc sg* **-le**) *m* (*rów*) ditch; (*ściek*) sewer; (*morski, telewizyjny*) channel; (*sztuczna droga morska*) canal; (*dla orkiestry*) orchestra pit; (*w warsztacie samochodowym*) inspection pit; **~ La Manche** the English Channel; **K~ Sueski/Panamski** the Suez/Panama Canal
**kana|pa** (**-py, -py**) (*dat sg* **-pie**) *f* couch, sofa
**kanap|ka** (**-ki, -ki**) (*dat sg* **-ce**, *gen pl* **-ek**) *f* sandwich
**kanar|ek** (**-ka, -ki**) (*instr sg* **-kiem**) *m* canary

k

**kanarkowy** *adj* canary (yellow)
**kanaryjski** *adj*: **Wyspy K~e** the Canary Islands *pl*, the Canaries *pl*
**kancelari|a** (**-i, -e**) (*gen pl* **-i**) *f* office; **~ adwokacka** chambers *pl* (*Brit*)
**kanciarz** (**-a, -e**) (*gen pl* **-y**) *m* (*pot*) swindler
**kanciasty** *adj* (*kształt*) angular; (*ruchy*) awkward
**kanclerz** (**-a, -e**) (*gen pl* **-y**) *m* chancellor
**kandyda|t** (**-ta, -ci**) (*loc sg* **-cie**) *m* candidate
**kandydat|ka** (**-ki, -ki**) (*loc sg* **-ce**, *gen pl* **-ek**) *f* candidate
**kandydatu|ra** (**-ry, -ry**) (*dat sg* **-rze**) *f* candidacy, candidature (*Brit*); **wysunąć** (*perf*) **czyjąś kandydaturę** to nominate sb, to put sb forward
**kandyd|ować (-uję, -ujesz)** *vi*: **~ (do parlamentu)** to stand (for Parliament) (*Brit*), to run (for Congress) (*US*)
**kandyzowany** *adj*: **owoce kandyzowane** candied fruits
**kangu|r** (**-ra, -ry**) (*loc sg* **-rze**) *m* kangaroo
**kanibal** (**-a, -e**) (*gen pl* **-i**) *m* cannibal
**kanibaliz|m** (**-mu**) (*loc sg* **-mie**) *m* cannibalism
**kanio|n** (**-nu, -ny**) (*loc sg* **-nie**) *m* canyon
**kanist|er** (**-ra, -ry**) (*loc sg* **-rze**) *m* jerry can
**kano|n** (**-nu, -ny**) (*loc sg* **-nie**) *m* canon
**kanoniczny** *adj* (*Rel*) canonical; **prawo kanoniczne** canon law
**kanonier|ka** (**-ki, -ki**) (*dat sg* **-ce**, *gen pl* **-ek**) *f* gunboat
**kanoni|k** (**-ka, -cy**) *m* canon
**kanonizacj|a** (**-i, -e**) (*gen pl* **-i**) *f* canonization
**kanoniz|ować (-uję, -ujesz)** *vt* to canonize
**kan|t** (**-tu, -ty**) (*loc sg* **-cie**) *m* (*stołu, biurka*) edge; (*u spodni*) crease; (*oszustwo*) swindle; **puścić kogoś ~em** (*pot*) to ditch sb (*pot*)
**kanto|r** (**-ra, -ry**) (*loc sg* **-rze**) *m* (*też*: **kantor wymiany walut**) exchange office
**kant|ować (-uję, -ujesz)** (*perf* **o-**) *vt* (*pot*) to swindle
**kanty|na** (**-ny, -ny**) (*dat sg* **-nie**) *f* (*Wojsk*) canteen (*store*)
**ka|pać (-pie)** (*perf* **-pnąć**) *vi* to drip, to trickle
**kapa|r** (**-ra, -ry**) (*loc sg* **-rze**) *m* caper
**kap|eć** (**-cia, -cie**) (*gen pl* **-ci**) *m* (*miękki pantofel*) slipper
**kapel|a** (**-i, -e**) (*gen pl* **-** *lub* **-i**) *f* (*zespół ludowy*) folk group; (*pot: zespół młodzieżowy*) band
**kapela|n** (**-na, -ni**) (*loc sg* **-nie**) *m* chaplain
**kapelusz** (**-a, -e**) (*gen pl* **-y**) *m* hat; (*grzyba*) cap
**kapitali|sta** (**-sty, -ści**) (*dat sg* **-ście**) *m decl like f in sg* capitalist
**kapitalistyczny** *adj* capitalist, capitalistic (*pej*)
**kapitaliz|m** (**-mu**) (*loc sg* **-mie**) *m* capitalism
**kapitalny** *adj* (*zasadniczy, istotny*) cardinal, fundamental; (*świetny*) brilliant; **remont ~** major overhaul
**kapita|ł** (**-łu, -ły**) (*loc sg* **-le**) *m* capital; **~ zakładowy** initial capital; **lokata ~u** capital investment
**kapitałochłonny** *adj* capital-intensive
**kapitałowy** *adj*: **zyski kapitałowe** capital gains; **wkłady kapitałowe** assets
**kapita|n** (**-na, -nowie**) (*loc sg* **-nie**) *m* captain
**kapitana|t** (**-tu, -ty**) (*loc sg* **-cie**) *m* port authority
**kapitański** *adj*: **mostek ~** the bridge
**kapitulacj|a** (**-i**) *f* capitulation
**kapitul|ować (-uję, -ujesz)** (*perf* **s-**) *vi* to capitulate; (*przen: dawać za wygraną*) to give in *lub* up; **~ przed kimś/czymś** to capitulate to sb/sth
**kap|ka** (**-ki, -ki**) (*dat sg* **-ce**, *gen pl* **-ek**) *f*: **~ mleka** *itp.* a droplet of milk *itp.*
**kaplic|a** (**-y, -e**) *f* chapel
**kaplicz|ka** (**-ki, -ki**) (*dat sg* **-ce**, *gen pl* **-ek**) *f* wayside shrine
**kapła|n** (**-na, -ni**) (*loc sg* **-nie**) *m* (*Rel*) priest
**kapłan|ka** (**-ki, -ki**) (*dat sg* **-ce**, *gen pl* **-ek**) *f* priestess
**kapłański** *adj* priestly; **święcenia ~e** ordination
**kapłańst|wo** (**-wa**) (*loc sg* **-wie**) *nt* priesthood
**kap|nąć (-nę, -niesz)** (*imp* **-nij**) *vb perf od* **kapać**; **kapnąć się** *vr perf* (*pot: zorientować się*) to twig (*pot*) (*Brit*)
**kapo|k** (**-ka, -ki**) (*instr sg* **-kiem**) *m* life jacket
**kap|ować (-uję, -ujesz)** (*perf* **za-**) (*pot*) *vi* (*rozumieć*) to twig (*pot*) (*Brit*), to dig (*pot*) (*US*); (*donosić*) to grass (*pot*)
**kapral** (**-a, -e**) (*gen pl* **-i**) *m* corporal
**kapry|s** (**-su, -sy**) (*loc sg* **-sie**) *m* (*zachcianka*) caprice, whim; (*pogody, losu*) quirk, caprice
**kapry|sić (-szę, -sisz)** (*imp* **-ś**) *vi* to be capricious
**kapryśny** *adj* capricious
**kaps|el** (**-la, -le**) (*gen pl* **-li**) *m* crown cap
**kapsu|ła** (**-ły, -ły**) (*loc sg* **-le**, *gen pl* **-ł**) *f* (*space*) capsule
**kapsuł|ka** (**-ki, -ki**) (*dat sg* **-ce**, *gen pl* **-ek**) *f* capsule
**Kapszta|d** (**-du**) (*loc sg* **-dzie**) *m* Cape Town
**kaptu|r** (**-ra, -ry**) (*loc sg* **-rze**) *m* hood; **kurtka z ~em** hooded coat
**kaptur|ek** (**-ka, -ki**) (*instr sg* **-kiem**) *m* (small) hood; **Czerwony K~** Little Red Riding Hood; **~ dopochwowy** (Dutch) cap
**kapu|sta** (**-sty**) (*dat sg* **-ście**) *f* cabbage; **~ kiszona** *lub* **kwaszona** sauerkraut; **~ włoska** savoy (cabbage); **~ czerwona** red cabbage; **groch z kapustą** (*przen*) hotchpotch, hodgepodge (*US*)

**kapu|ś** (**-sia, -sie**) *m* (*pot*) grass (*pot*)
**kapuściany** *adj* cabbage *attr*; **kapuściana głowa** (*przen*) blockhead (*pot*)
**kapuśniacz|ek** (**-ka, -ki**) (*instr sg* **-kiem**) *m* (*deszcz*) drizzle
**kapuśnia|k**[1] (**-ku, -ki**) *m* cabbage soup
**kapuśnia|k**[2] (**-ka, -ki**) (*instr sg* **-kiem**) *m* (*deszcz*) drizzle
**ka|ra** (**-ry, -ry**) (*dat sg* **-rze**) *f* punishment; (*administracyjna, sądowa*) penalty; **~ cielesna** corporal punishment; **~ pieniężna** financial penalty; **~ grzywny** fine; **~ więzienia** imprisonment; **~ śmierci** capital punishment, the death penalty; **pod karą grzywny/więzienia** punishable by fine/ prison; **robić coś za karę** to do something as a punishment
**karabi|n** (**-nu, -ny**) (*loc sg* **-nie**) *m* rifle; **~ maszynowy** machine gun
**ka|rać (-rzę, -rzesz)** (*perf* **u-**) *vt* to punish; (*administracyjnie, sądownie*) to penalize; **~ kogoś za coś** to punish *lub* penalize sb for sth; **~ kogoś grzywną** to fine sb
**karaf|ka** (**-ki, -ki**) (*dat sg* **-ce**, *gen pl* **-ek**) *f* decanter
**karaibski** *adj* Caribbean; **Morze K~e** the Caribbean (Sea)
**karaku|ł** (**-ła, -ły**) (*loc sg* **-le**) *m* Persian lamb; **karakuły** *pl* astrakhan *lub* Persian lamb coat
**karalny** *adj* (*czyn*) punishable
**karaluch** (**-a, -y**) *m* cockroach
**karambol** (**-u, -e**) (*gen pl* **-i**) *m* multiple crash, pile-up
**karany** *adj* previously convicted; **nie ~** with no previous convictions, without criminal record
**kara|ś** (**-sia, -sie**) (*gen pl* **-si**) *m* (*Zool*) crucian (carp)
**kara|t** (**-ta, -ty**) (*loc sg* **-cie**) *m* (*jednostka masy*) carat; (*jednostka zawartości*) carat, karat (US)
**karate** *nt inv* karate
**karate|ka** (**-ki, -cy**) (*dat sg* **-ce**) *m decl like f in sg* karate fighter
**karawa|n** (**-nu, -ny**) (*loc sg* **-nie**) *m* hearse
**karawa|na** (**-ny, -ny**) (*dat sg* **-nie**) *f* caravan
**karawanin|g** (**-gu**) (*instr sg* **-giem**) *m* caravanning
**kar|b** (**-bu, -by**) (*loc sg* **-bie**) *m* (*nacięcie*) notch; **kłaść (złożyć** *perf*) **coś na ~ młodości/ niedoświadczenia** to put sth down to one's youth/inexperience; **wziąć** (*perf*) **kogoś/coś w ~y** to bring sb/sth under control
**karcący** *adj* (*ton, spojrzenie*) reproachful
**karciarz** (**-a, -e**) (*gen pl* **-y**) *m* card-player
**kar|cić (-cę, -cisz)** (*imp* **-ć**, *perf* **s-**) *vt* to scold, to rebuke
**karcz|ma** (**-my, -my**) (*loc sg* **-mie**, *gen pl* **-em**) *f* inn
**karczoch** (**-a, -y**) *m* artichoke
**karcz|ować (-uję, -ujesz)** (*perf* **wy-**) *vt* to grub out
**kard.** *abbr* (= *kardynał*) Card.
**kardiochirur|g** (**-ga, -dzy** *lub* **-gowie**) (*instr sg* **-giem**) *m* cardiac *lub* open-heart surgeon
**kardiochirurgi|a** (**-i**) *f* cardiosurgery, open-heart surgery
**kardiogra|m** (**-mu, -my**) (*loc sg* **-mie**) *m* cardiogram
**kardiolo|g** (**-ga, -dzy** *lub* **-gowie**) (*instr sg* **-giem**) *m* heart specialist, cardiologist
**kardiologi|a** (**-i**) *f* cardiology
**kardiologiczny** *adj* cardiological
**kardynalny** *adj* (*błąd*) fundamental; **kardynalna zasada** cardinal rule
**kardyna|ł** (**-ła, -łowie**) (*loc sg* **-le**) *m* cardinal
**kare|ta** (**-ty, -ty**) (*dat sg* **-cie**) *f* carriage; (*Karty*) four of a kind
**karet|ka** (**-ki, -ki**) (*dat sg* **-ce**, *gen pl* **-ek**) *f*: **~ pogotowia** ambulance; **~ więzienna** Black Maria
**karie|ra** (**-ry, -ry**) (*dat sg* **-rze**) *f* career; **robić karierę** to work one's way up; **zrobić** (*perf*) **karierę** to make a career for o.s., to make the big time (*pot*)
**karierowicz** (**-a, -e**) *m* (*pej*) careerist
**karima|ta** (**-ty, -ty**) (*loc sg* **-cie**) *f* carrimat
**kar|k** (**-ku, -ki**) (*instr sg* **-kiem**) *m* nape of the neck; **mieć głowę na ~u** to have one's head screwed on; **nadstawiać ~u (za kogoś)** to risk one's neck (for sb); **pędzić na złamanie ~u** to run *lub* rush headlong; **skręcić** (*perf*) **~** to break one's neck
**karkołomny** *adj* (*szybkość, tempo*) breakneck *attr*; (*ewolucja, wyczyn*) daredevil *attr*; (*hipoteza*) far-fetched
**karków|ka** (**-ki, -ki**) (*dat sg* **-ce**, *gen pl* **-ek**) *f* neck; (*wieprzowa*) shoulder
**karła** *itd. n patrz* **karzeł**
**karłowaty** *adj* dwarf *attr*
**kar|ma** (**-my**) (*dat sg* **-mie**) *f* fodder, feed
**karmazynowy** *adj* crimson
**karmel** (**-u**) *m* caramel
**karmel|ek** (**-ka, -ki**) (*instr sg* **-kiem**) *m* caramel
**kar|mić (-mię, -misz)** *vt* (*żywić*) (*perf* **na-**) to feed; (*piersią*) to breast-feed, to suckle; (*butelką*) to bottle-feed; **karmić się (czymś)** *vr* to feed (on sth)
**karmni|k** (**-ka, -ki**) (*instr sg* **-kiem**) *m* bird table
**karnacj|a** (**-i, -e**) (*gen pl* **-i**) *f* complexion
**karnawa|ł** (**-łu, -ły**) (*loc sg* **-le**) *m* carnival
**karne|t** (**-tu, -ty**) (*loc sg* **-cie**) *m* (*na przedstawienia, koncerty*) subscription card; (*: na autobus, tramwaj*) book of tickets
**karnisz** (**-a, -e**) (*gen pl* **-y** *lub* **-ów**) *m* (*szyna*) curtain rail; (*ozdobny*) cornice
**karnoś|ć** (**-ci**) *f* discipline

**karny** *adj* (*prawo, kodeks*) criminal; (*kolonia*) penal; (*Sport*) penalty *attr*; (*żołnierz, pies*) disciplined; **mandat ~** fine; **mandat ~ za parkowanie** parking ticket; **odpowiedzialność karna** criminal responsibility; **rzut ~** penalty kick; **punkt ~** (*Sport*) penalty ▷ *m decl like adj* (*Sport: rzut karny*) penalty (kick)

**ka|ro** (**-ra, -ra**) (*loc sg* **-rze**) *nt* (*Karty*) diamond(s) (*pl*); **dama ~** queen of diamonds

**karoseri|a** (**-i, -e**) (*gen pl* **-i**) *f* (*Mot*) body (*of a car*)

**kar|p** (**-pia, -pie**) (*gen pl* **-pi**) *m* carp

**Karpat|y** (-) *pl* the Carpathian Mountains, the Carpathians

**kar|ta** (**-ty, -ty**) (*dat sg* **-cie**) *f* (*do pisania, rysowania*) sheet (of paper); (*w książce*) leaf; (*do gry*) (playing) card; (*do głosowania*) ballot sheet; (*jadłospis*) menu; **~ kredytowa** credit card; **~ pocztowa** postcard; **~ bankowa** cash card; **~ gwarancyjna** warranty; **~ biblioteczna** library card; **~ rowerowa** *card authorizing use of bicycle on public roads*; **~ pływacka** *card authorizing use of sailing facilities*; **~ telefoniczna** phonecard; **~ wstępu** admission card; **grać w karty** to play cards; **grać w otwarte karty** (*przen*) to play with one's cards on the table; **stawiać (postawić** *perf*) **wszystko na jedną kartę** (*przen*) to stake everything on one roll of the dice

**kartel** (**-u, -e**) (*gen pl* **-i**) *m* (*Ekon*) cartel

**kart|ka** (**-ki, -ki**) (*dat sg* **-ce**, *gen pl* **-ek**) *f* (*do pisania, rysowania*) sheet (of paper); (*w książce*) leaf; **~ pocztowa** postcard; **~ świąteczna** Christmas card

**kartk|ować (-uję, -ujesz)** (*perf* **prze-**) *vt* to leaf through, to flick through

**kartof|el** (**-la, -le**) (*gen pl* **-li**) *m* potato

**kartogra|f** (**-fa, -fowie**) (*loc sg* **-fie**) *m* cartographer

**kartografi|a** (**-i**) *f* cartography

**karto|n** (**-nu, -ny**) (*loc sg* **-nie**) *m* (*papier*) cardboard; (*pudełko*) carton, cardboard box

**kartot|eka** (**-eki, -eki**) (*dat sg* **-ece**, *gen pl* **-ek**) *f* (*zbiór fiszek*) card index; (*zbiór danych*) files *pl*

**karuzel|a** (**-i, -e**) (*gen pl* **-i**) *f* merry-go-round, roundabout (*Brit*), carousel (*US*)

**kary** *adj* (*koń*) black

**karygodny** *adj* (*postępek*) reprehensible; (*zaniedbanie*) criminal

**karykatu|ra** (**-ry, -ry**) (*dat sg* **-rze**) *f* (*rysunek*) caricature; (*przen*): **~ człowieka** travesty of a human being

**karykaturzy|sta** (**-sty, -ści**) (*dat sg* **-ści**) *m decl like f in sg* cartoonist

**ka|rzeł** (**-rła, -rły**) (*loc sg* **-rle**) *m* dwarf

**ka|sa** (**-sy, -sy**) (*dat sg* **-sie**) *f* (*w sklepie*) cash desk; (*w supermarkecie*) check-out; (*w domu towarowym*) till; (*w kinie, teatrze*) box office; (*na dworcu*) ticket office; (*pieniądze organizacji*) treasury; **~ pancerna** strongbox, safe; **~ fiskalna** cash register

**kasacj|a** (**-i, -e**) (*gen pl* **-i**) *f*: **iść do kasacji** to be written off *lub* scrapped

**kase|ta** (**-ty, -ty**) (*dat sg* **-cie**) *f* (*magnetofonowa, video*) cassette; (*Fot*) cartridge

**kaset|ka** (**-ki, -ki**) (*dat sg* **-ce**, *gen pl* **-ek**) *f* casket (*Brit*), jewel box

**kaseto|n** (**-nu, -ny**) (*loc sg* **-nie**) *m* (*Archit*) coffer, caisson

**kasetowy** *adj* cassette *attr*

**kasje|r** (**-ra, -rzy**) (*loc sg* **-rze**) *m* (*w sklepie*) cashier; (*w kinie, teatrze*) box-office clerk; (*w banku*) cashier, teller; (*na dworcu*) booking clerk

**kasjer|ka** (**-ki, -ki**) (*dat sg* **-ce**, *gen pl* **-ek**) *f* (*w sklepie*) cashier; (*w kinie, teatrze*) box-office clerk; (*w banku*) cashier, teller; (*na dworcu*) ticket clerk

**kas|k** (**-ku, -ki**) (*instr sg* **-kiem**) *m* crash helmet

**kaska|da** (**-dy, -dy**) (*dat sg* **-dzie**) *f* cascade; (*dźwięków*) ripple

**kaskade|r** (**-ra, -rzy**) *m* (*loc sg* **-rze**) stuntman

**kas|ować (-uję, -ujesz)** (*perf* **s-**) *vt* (*bilet*) to punch; (*nagranie, plik*) to erase

**kasowni|k** (**-ka, -ki**) (*instr sg* **-kiem**) *m* (*do biletów*) ticket puncher; (*Muz*) natural; (*Poczta*) postmark

**kasowy** *adj* (*obrót, wpływy*) cash *attr*; (*sukces*) box-office *attr*; **~ film** box-office success *lub* hit

**kaspijski** *adj*: **Morze K~e** the Caspian Sea

**ka|sta** (**-sty, -sty**) (*dat sg* **-ście**) *f* caste

**kastaniet|y** (**-ów**) *pl* castanets *pl*

**kaste|t** (**-tu, -ty**) (*loc sg* **-cie**) *m* knuckle-duster (*Brit*), brass knuckles *pl* (*US*)

**kastr|ować (-uję, -ujesz)** (*perf* **wy-**) *vt* to castrate

**kasy|no** (**-na, -na**) (*loc sg* **-nie**) *nt* (*dom gry*) casino; (*Wojsk*) mess

**kasz|a** (**-y, -e**) *f* (*produkt*) groats *pl*; (*potrawa*) porridge; **~ gryczana** buckwheat groats *pl*; **~ jaglana** millet groats *pl*; **~ jęczmienna** pearl barley groats *pl*; **~ manna** semolina; **nie dać** (*perf*) **sobie w kaszę dmuchać** (*przen*) to know how to stick up for o.s.

**kaszalo|t** (**-ta, -ty**) (*loc sg* **-cie**) *m* (*Zool*) sperm whale

**kaszan|ka** (**-ki, -ki**) (*dat sg* **-ce**, *gen pl* **-ek**) *f* black *lub* blood pudding (*Brit*), blood sausage (*US*)

**kasz|el** (**-lu**) *m* cough

**kasz|ka** (**-ki, -ki**) (*dat sg* **-ce**, *gen pl* **-ek**) *f dimin od* **kasza**

**kaszl|eć (-ę, -esz)** (*perf* **-nąć**) *vi* to cough

**kaszl|nąć (-nę, -niesz)** (*imp* **-nij**) *vb perf od* **kaszleć**
**kaszmi|r** (**-ru**) (*loc sg* **-rze**) *m* cashmere
**kaszta|n** (**-na, -ny**) (*loc sg* **-nie**) *m* chestnut; (*niejadalny*) horse chestnut, conker
**kasztano|wiec** (**-wca, -wce**) *m* (*Bot*) horse chestnut
**kasztanowy** *adj* chestnut *attr*
**ka|t** (**-ta, -ci**) (*dat sg* **-towi** *lub* **-tu**, *loc sg* **-cie**) *m* executioner
**katafal|k** (**-ku, -ki**) (*instr sg* **-kiem**) *m* catafalque
**katakliz|m** (**-mu, -my**) (*loc sg* **-mie**) *m* disaster, calamity
**katakumb|y** (-) *pl* catacombs
**katalizato|r** (**-ra, -ry**) (*loc sg* **-rze**) *m* (*Mot*) catalytic converter; (*Chem*) catalyst
**katalo|g** (**-gu, -gi**) (*instr sg* **-giem**) *m* catalogue (*Brit*), catalog (*US*)
**katalog|ować (-uję, -ujesz)** (*perf* **s-**) *vt* to catalogue (*Brit*), to catalog (*US*)
**katamara|n** (**-nu, -ny**) (*loc sg* **-nie**) *m* (*Żegl*) catamaran
**katapul|ta** (**-ty, -ty**) (*loc sg* **-cie**) *f* (*Lot*) ejection *lub* ejector seat; (*Hist*) catapult
**katapult|ować się (-uję, -ujesz)** *vr* (*im*)*perf* to eject
**kata|r** (**-ru, -ry**) (*loc sg* **-rze**) *m* catarrh, runny nose (*pot*); ~ **sienny** hay fever; **mam** ~ my nose is running
**katarak|ta** (**-ty, -ty**) (*dat sg* **-cie**) *f* cataract
**kataryniarz** (**-a, -e**) (*gen pl* **-y**) *m* organ-grinder
**kataryn|ka** (**-ki, -ki**) (*dat sg* **-ce**, *gen pl* **-ek**) *f* barrel organ; **mówić jak** ~ to chatter
**katastro|fa** (**-fy, -fy**) (*dat sg* **-fie**) *f* (*drogowa, kolejowa*) accident; (*samolotowa*) (plane) crash; (*wielkie nieszczęście*) disaster, catastrophe
**katastrofalny** *adj* (*skutek, susza*) catastrophic, disastrous
**katastroficzny** *adj* (*wizja*) catastrophic; (*ton*) ominous
**kateche|ta** (**-ty, -ci**) (*loc sg* **-cie**) *m decl like f in sg* catechist, catechizer
**katechet|ka** (**-ki, -ki**) (*dat sg* **-ce**, *gen pl* **-ek**) *f* catechist, catechizer
**katechiz|m** (**-mu, -my**) (*loc sg* **-mie**) *m* (*Rel*) catechism
**kated|ra** (**-ry, -ry**) (*dat sg* **-rze**) *f* (*kościół*) cathedral; (*pulpit*) teacher's desk; (*w szkole wyższej: jednostka administracyjna*) department; (*: stanowisko*) chair
**kategori|a** (**-i, -e**) (*gen pl* **-i**) *f* category; **w ~ch ...** in terms of ...
**kategoryczny** *adj* (*ton*) emphatic; (*żądanie*) categorical
**kato|da** (**-dy, -dy**) (*dat sg* **-dzie**) *f* (*Fiz*) cathode
**katolicki** *adj* Catholic; **Kościół K~** the (Roman) Catholic Church
**katolicyz|m** (**-mu**) (*loc sg* **-mie**) *m* (Roman) Catholicism
**katolicz|ka** (**-ki, -ki**) (*loc sg* **-ce**, *gen pl* **-ek**) *f* (Roman) Catholic
**katoli|k** (**-ka, -cy**) (*instr sg* **-kiem**) *m* (Roman) Catholic
**kator|ga** (**-gi, -gi**) (*dat sg* **-dze**) *f* (*przen*) ordeal
**kat|ować (-uję, -ujesz)** (*perf* **s-**) *vt* to torture, to torment
**katusz|e** (**-y**) *pl* agony; **cierpieć** ~ to suffer agony
**kaucj|a** (**-i, -e**) (*gen pl* **-i**) *f* (*Prawo*) bail; (*za butelkę*) deposit; **zwolnić kogoś za kaucją** to release sb on bail
**kauczu|k** (**-ku, -ki**) (*instr sg* **-kiem**) *m* (India) rubber, caoutchouc
**Kauka|z** (**-zu**) (*loc sg* **-zie**) *m* the Caucasus
**ka|wa** (**-wy**) (*dat sg* **-wie**) *f* (*roślina*) coffee (tree); (*ziarna*) coffee (beans *pl*); (*napój*) coffee; (*porcja napoju*) (*nom pl* **-wy**) a (cup of) coffee; **biała/czarna** ~ white/black coffee; ~ **po turecku** Turkish coffee; ~ **na ławę!** (*pot*) out with it!, don't mince words with me!; **wyłożyć kawę na ławę** not to mince words
**kawalarz** (**-a, -e**) (*gen pl* **-y**) *m* joker, prankster
**kawale|r** (**-ra, -rowie** *lub* **-rzy**) (*loc sg* **-rze**) *m* (*nieżonaty mężczyzna*) bachelor; (*młodzieniec*) youth; (*orderu*) knight; **stary** ~ confirmed bachelor
**kawaleri|a** (**-i**) *f* cavalry
**kawaler|ka** (**-ki, -ki**) (*dat sg* **-ce**, *gen pl* **-ek**) *f* bachelor flat (*Brit*) *lub* apartment (*US*)
**kawalerski** *adj* (*stan*) unmarried; **wieczór** ~ stag (*Brit*) *lub* bachelor (*US*) party
**kawalerzy|sta** (**-sty, -ści**) (*dat sg* **-ście**) *m decl like f in sg* cavalryman, trooper
**kawalka|da** (**-dy, -dy**) (*dat sg* **-dzie**) *f* cavalcade; (*samochodów*) motorcade
**kawa|ł** (**-łu, -ły**) (*loc sg* **-le**) *m* (*duża część*) chunk; (*dowcip*) joke; (*psota*) trick, practical joke; ~ **czasu** ages *pl*; ~ **chłopa** (*pot*) strapping fellow; **opowiedzieć** (*perf*) ~ to tell a joke; **zrobić** (*perf*) **komuś** ~ to play a joke *lub* trick on sb; **zrobić** (*perf*) **coś dla ~u** to do sth in *lub* out of fun
**kawał|ek** (**-ka, -ki**) (*instr sg* **-kiem**) *m* bit, piece; (*pot: utwór muzyczny*) piece; **rozlecieć się** (*perf*) **na kawałki** to fall to pieces
**kawiaren|ka** (**-ki, -ki**) (*dat sg* **-ce**, *gen pl* **-ek**) *f* (small) café; ~ **internetowa** (*Komput*) Internet café
**kawiar|nia** (**-ni, -nie**) (*gen pl* **-ni**) *f* café
**kawio|r** (**-ru**) (*loc sg* **-rze**) *m* caviar
**kaw|ka** (**-ki, -ki**) (*dat sg* **-ce**, *gen pl* **-ek**) *f* (*Zool*) jackdaw
**kawowy** *adj* coffee *attr*

k

**ka|zać (-żę, -żesz)** *vi (im)perf*: **~ komuś coś zrobić** to tell sb to do sth; **rób, co ci każę** do as you are told; **~ komuś na siebie czekać** to keep sb waiting
**kaza|nie** (**-nia, -nia**) (*gen pl* **-ń**) *nt* sermon; (*przen*) talking-to; **wygłaszać (wygłosić** *perf*) **~** to preach (a sermon); **prawić komuś ~** (*przen*) to preach at sb
**kazirodzt|wo** (**-wa**) (*loc sg* **-wie**) *nt* incest
**kaznodzie|ja** (**-i, -je**) *m decl like f in sg* preacher
**każdorazowo** *adv* each *lub* every time
**każdy** *pron decl like adj* every; (*z określonych*) each; (*każdy człowiek*) everybody; **każdego dnia/roku** every day/year; **o każdej porze** any time of the day; **na ~m kroku** every step of the way; **za ~m razem** each *lub* every time; **w ~m razie** in any case, at any rate; **w każdej chwili** (*lada moment*) any time now; **~ z nas** each of us; **mam coś dla każdego z was** I have something for each of you
**każę** *itd. vb patrz* **kazać**
**kącie** *n patrz* **kąt**
**kąci|k** (**-ka, -ki**) (*instr sg* **-kiem**) *m* (*róg pokoju*) corner; (*pot*: *mieszkanie*) pad (*pot*); (*schronienie*) nook, cubbyhole; (*dział w gazecie*) column
**kądziel** (**-i, -e**) (*gen pl* **-i**) *f*: **po ~i** on the distaff side
**ką|pać (-pię, -piesz)** (*perf* **wy-**) *vt* to bath (*Brit*), to bathe (*US*); **w gorącej wodzie kąpany** (*przen*) hot-headed; **kąpać się** *vr* (*w łazience*) to take a bath, to bathe (*US*); (*w rzece*) to bathe, to swim
**kąpiel** (**-i, -e**) (*gen pl* **-i**) *f* (*w łazience*) bath; (*w rzece*) bathe, swim; **~ słoneczna** sun bath; **brać (wziąć** *perf*) **~** to take a bath
**kąpielis|ko** (**-ka, -ka**) (*instr sg* **-kiem**) *nt* (*miejscowość*) seaside resort; (*plaża*) bathing beach; (*basen*) swimming pool
**kąpielowy** *adj*: **czepek ~** bathing cap; **spodenki kąpielowe** swimming trunks; **kostium ~** swimming costume, bathing suit (*US*); **ręcznik ~** bath towel
**kąpielów|ki** (**-ek**) *pl* swimming trunks
**kąs|ać (-am, -asz)** (*perf* **ukąsić**) *vt* to bite
**kąs|ek** (**-ka, -ki**) (*instr sg* **-kiem**) *m* (*kawałek*) bite, morsel; **łakomy ~** (*przen*) titbit (*Brit*), tidbit (*US*)
**kąśliwy** *adj* (*uwaga*) cutting; (*ton*) withering
**ką|t** (**-ta, -ty**) (*loc sg* **-cie**) *m* (*Geom*) angle; (*róg*) corner; (*pot*: *mieszkanie*) pad; **kąt widzenia** (*przen*) point of view; **zapadły kąt** the backwoods, the back of beyond; **obserwować kogoś/coś kątem oka** to watch sb/sth out of the corner of one's eye; **chodzić z kąta w kąt** to walk back and forth; **postawić** (*perf*) **dziecko do kąta** to send a child to the corner; **mieszkać kątem u kogoś** to put up at sb's place
**kątomierz** (**-a, -e**) (*gen pl* **-y**) *m* protractor
**kątowni|k** (**-ka, -ki**) (*instr sg* **-kiem**) *m* (*Tech*) angle (iron)
**KBN** *abbr* (*= Komitet Badań Naukowych*) Committee for Research Projects
**KBWE** *abbr* (*= Konferencja Bezpieczeństwa i Współpracy w Europie*) CSCE (*= Conference for Security and Cooperation in Europe*)
**kciu|k** (**-ka, -ki**) (*instr sg* **-kiem**) *m* thumb; **trzymać ~i (za kogoś/coś)** (*przen*) to keep one's fingers crossed (for sb/sth)
**keba|b** (**-bu, -by**) (*loc sg* **-bie**) *m* (shish) kebab
**keczu|p** (**-pu**) (*loc sg* **-pie**) *m* ketchup
**kefi|r** (**-ru**) (*loc sg* **-rze**) *m* kefir
**kek|s** (**-su, -sy**) (*loc sg* **-sie**) *m* fruit cake
**kelne|r** (**-ra, -rzy**) (*loc sg* **-rze**) *m* waiter
**kelner|ka** (**-ki, -ki**) (*dat sg* **-ce**, *gen pl* **-ek**) *f* waitress
**kempin|g** (**-gu, -gi**) (*instr sg* **-giem**) *m* camp(ing) site, camping ground
**kempingowy** *adj* (*sprzęt*) camping *attr*; **przyczepa kempingowa** caravan (*Brit*), trailer (*US*); **domek ~** (holiday) cabin *lub* chalet
**Keni|a** (**-i**) *f* Kenya
**Kenijczy|k** (**-ka, -cy**) (*instr sg* **-kiem**) *m* Kenyan
**Kenij|ka** (**-ki, -ki**) (*dat sg* **-ce**, *gen pl* **-ek**) *f* Kenyan
**kenijski** *adj* Kenyan
**KERM** *abbr* (*= Komitet Ekonomiczny Rady Ministrów*) Economic Committee of the Cabinet
**kędzierzawy** *adj* curly
**kę|pa** (**-py, -py**) (*dat sg* **-pie**) *f* cluster
**kęp|ka** (**-ki, -ki**) (*loc sg* **-ce**, *gen pl* **-ek**) *f dimin od* **kępa**; (*przen*: *włosów*) tuft
**kę|s** (**-sa, -sy**) (*loc sg* **-sie**) *m* bite
**KG** *abbr* (*= Komenda Główna*) HQ, h.q.
**kg** *abbr* (*= kilogram*) kg
**khaki** *adj inv*; **koszula koloru ~** a khaki shirt
**kib|el** (**-la, -le**) (*gen pl* **-li**) *m* (*pot*: *ubikacja*) loo (*pot*) (*Brit*), bogs (*pot*) (*Brit*), john (*pot*) (*US*)
**kibic** (**-a, -e**) *m* looker-on; (*Sport*) supporter, fan
**kibic|ować (-uję, -ujesz)** *vi* to look on; **~ komuś** to support sb, to cheer sb on
**kibi|ć** (**-ci, -cie**) (*gen pl* **-ci**) *f* (*książk*) waist
**kich|ać (-am, -asz)** (*perf* **-nąć**) *vi* to sneeze; **~ na coś** (*przen*: *lekceważyć*) not to give a hoot about sth
**kich|nąć (-nę, -niesz)** (*imp* **-nij**) *vb perf od* **kichać**
**kicie** *n patrz* **kit**; **kita**
**kicz** (**-u, -e**) *m* kitsch
**kiczowaty** *adj* kitschy
**ki|ć** (**-cia, -cie**) *m* (*pot*: *więzienie*) clink (*Brit*), cooler (*US*); **pójść** (*perf*) **do kicia** to be put in clink (*Brit*), to be sent to the cooler (*US*);

**siedzieć w kiciu** to be in clink (*Brit*), to be in the cooler (*US*)
**kidnape|r** (**-ra, -rzy**) (*loc sg* **-rze**) *m* kidnapper
**kidnaperst|wo** (**-wa**) (*loc sg* **-wie**) *nt* kidnapping
**kiedy** *pron* when ▷ *conj* when, as; (*podczas gdy*) while; **~ wrócisz?** when will you be back?; **od ~?** since when?; **~ bądź** any time; **~ indziej** some other time; **~ tylko miałem okazję** whenever I had a chance; **~ tylko wstałem, on usiadł** as soon as I stood up, he sat down; **teraz, ~ jesteśmy razem ...** now that we are together ...; **czytała ~ wszedłem** she was reading when I came in; **nie wiem, ~ to się stało** I don't know when it happened
**kiedykolwiek** *adv* (*obojętnie kiedy*) at any time, whenever; (*w pytaniach*) ever; **czy byłaś ~ w Paryżu?** have you ever been to Paris?
**kiedyś** *adv* (*w przeszłości*) once, sometime; (*w przyszłości*) one *lub* some day, sometime
**kielich** (**-a, -y**) *m* goblet; (*kwiatu*) calyx; **~ mszalny** chalice
**kielisz|ek** (**-ka, -ki**) (*instr sg* **-kiem**) *m* (*do wina, wódki*) glass; (*do jaj*) (egg) cup; **zaglądać do kieliszka** (*pot*) to hit the bottle
**kiel|nia** (**-ni, -nie**) (*gen pl* **-ni**) *f* trowel
**kieł** (**kła, kły**) (*loc sg* **kle**) *m* (*Anat*) canine (tooth), eye tooth; (*u psa, wilka*) fang; (*u słonia, dzika*) tusk
**kiełba|sa** (**-sy, -sy**) (*loc sg* **-sie**) *f* sausage
**kiełbasiany** *adj*: **jad ~** botulin
**kieł|ek** (**-ka, -ki**) (*instr sg* **-kiem**) *m* shoot, sprout; **kiełki pszeniczne** wheatgerm
**kiełk|ować (-uje)** *vi* (*o roślinie*) (*perf* **wy-**) to sprout; (*o planie, pomyśle*) (*perf* **za-**) to germinate
**kiepski** *adj* lousy
**kiepsko** *adv* (*wyglądać, czuć się*) under the weather
**kie|r** (**-ra, -ry**) (*loc sg* **-rze**) *m* (*Karty*) heart(s) (*pl*); **król ~** king of hearts
**kiermasz** (**-u, -e**) *m* fair
**kier|ować (-uję, -ujesz)** *vt +acc* (*wysyłać*) (*perf* **s-**) to refer; (*krytykę, oskarżenie*) to direct, to level; (*broń, cios, wysiłki*) to aim; (*spojrzenie*) to direct; (*pretensje, skargi*) to file ▷ *vt +instr* (*samochodem*) to drive; (*samolotem, statkiem*) to steer, to navigate; (*firmą, pracą*) to manage; **kierować się** *vr*: **~ się do** (*perf* **s-**) to make one's way towards, to head *lub* make for; **~ się uczuciem/rozsądkiem** to be governed *lub* guided by emotions/(common) sense
**kierowc|a** (**-y, -y**) *m decl like f in sg* driver; (*osobisty*) chauffeur; **~ wyścigowy** racing driver
**kierownic|a** (**-y, -e**) *f* (*samochodu*) (steering) wheel; (*roweru*) handlebar(s *pl*)
**kierownict|wo** (**-wa**) (*loc sg* **-wie**) *nt* (*przywództwo*) leadership; (*zarząd, dyrekcja*) (*nom pl* **-wa**) management; **pracować pod czyimś kierownictwem** to work under sb's leadership
**kierownicz|ka** (**-ki, -ki**) (*dat sg* **-ce**, *gen pl* **-ek**) *f* (*działu, sklepu*) manageress
**kierowniczy** *adj* managerial; **układ ~** (*Tech*) steering (mechanism); **układ ~ prawostronny/lewostronny** right-/left-hand drive
**kierowni|k** (**-ka, -cy**) (*instr sg* **-kiem**) *m* manager
**kierun|ek** (**-ku, -ki**) *m* (*drogi, marszu*) direction; (*w sztuce*) trend; (*studiów*) ≈ major; **w kierunku Lublina** towards Lublin; **w przeciwnym kierunku** in the other direction; **pracować pod czyimś kierunkiem** to work under sb's guidance; **mieć zdolności w kierunku** *+gen* to have a gift for
**kierunkowska|z** (**-zu, -zy**) (*loc sg* **-zie**) *m* indicator (*Brit*), turn signal (*US*); **włączyć** (*perf*) **~** to signal a turn
**kierunkowy** *m decl like adj* (*też*: **numer kierunkowy**) area code
**kiesze|ń** (**-ni, -nie**) (*gen pl* **-ni**) *f* pocket; (*magnetofonu*) cassette compartment; **tylna/wewnętrzna ~** back/inside pocket; **mieć (już) coś w kieszeni** (*przen*) to have sth in one's pocket; **znać coś jak własną ~** (*przen*) to know sth inside out; **płacić z własnej kieszeni** to pay out of one's own pocket; **to nie na moją ~** I can't afford it
**kieszonko|wiec** (**-wca, -wcy**) *m* pickpocket
**kieszonkowy** *adj* pocket *attr*; **złodziej ~** pickpocket; **kieszonkowe** *pl* pocket money; (*dawane dziecku*) allowance, pocket money (*Brit*)
**ki|j** (**-ja, -je**) (*gen pl* **-jów**) *m* stick; **kij bilardowy** cue; **kij golfowy** (golf) club; **prosto jakby kij połknął** bolt upright; *patrz też* **kijek**
**kijan|ka** (**-ki, -ki**) (*dat sg* **-ce**, *gen pl* **-ek**) *f* tadpole
**kij|ek** (**-ka, -ki**) (*instr sg* **-kiem**) *m* stick; **~ narciarski** ski pole *lub* stick
**kiku|t** (**-ta, -ty**) (*loc sg* **-cie**) *m* stump
**kil** (**-u** *lub* **-a, -e**) *m* keel
**kilka** (*jak*: **ile**) *num* a few, several, some; **~ razy** a few times; **~ dni temu** several days ago; **przyniosę ~, dobrze?** let me bring some, OK?
**kilkadziesiąt** (*jak*: **dziesięć**) *num* a few dozen
**kilkakrotnie** *adv* several times, on several occasions
**kilkakrotny** *adj* multiple

K

**kilkanaście** (*jak*: **jedenaście**) *num* a dozen or so
**kilkaset** (*jak*: **pięćset**) *num* a few hundred
**kilkoro** (*jak*: **czworo**) *num* a few, several, some
**kilku** *itd. num patrz* **kilka**
**kilkudniowy** *adj*: ~ **pobyt** a few days' stay
**kilkugodzinny** *adj*: **kilkugodzinna jazda** a few hours' drive
**kilkuletni** *adj* (*pobyt*) of several years, a few years' *attr*; (*chłopiec*) small
**kilkunastoletni** *adj*: ~ **pobyt** a stay of over ten years; ~ **chłopiec** teenage boy
**kilo** *nt inv* kilo
**kilobaj|t** (**-ta, -ty**) (*loc sg* **-cie**) *m* kilobyte
**kilo|f** (**-fa, -fy**) (*loc sg* **-fie**) *m* pick(axe) (*Brit*), pick(ax) (*US*)
**kilogra|m** (**-ma, -my**) (*loc sg* **-mie**) *m* kilogram(me), kilo; **8 złotych za** ~ 8 zloty a *lub* per kilo
**kilogramowy** *adj* one-kilo *attr*
**kiloherc** (**-a, -e**) *m* kilohertz
**kilomet|r** (**-ra, -ry**) (*loc sg* **-rze**) *m* kilometre (*Brit*), kilometer (*US*); **100 ~ów na godzinę** a hundred kilometres (*Brit*) *lub* kilometers (*US*) an hour; **w odległości dwóch ~ów** two kilometres (*Brit*) *lub* kilometers (*US*) away
**kilometrowy** *adj* one-kilometre *attr* (*Brit*), one-kilometer *attr* (*US*)
**kilowa|t** (**-ta, -ty**) (*loc sg* **-cie**) *m* kilowatt
**kilowy** *adj*: **kilowa paczka** a one-kilo packet
**ki|ła** (**-ły**) (*dat sg* **-le**) *f* syphilis
**kim** *pron instr, loc od* **kto** who; **z kim rozmawiałeś?** who were you talking to?
**kim|ać (-am, -asz)** (*perf* **-nąć**) *vi* (*pot*) to kip (*pot*)
**kimkolwiek** *pron instr, loc od* **ktokolwiek**
**kim|nąć (-nę, -niesz)** (*imp* **-nij**) *vb perf od* **kimać**
**kimo|no** (**-na, -na**) (*loc sg* **-nie**) *nt* kimono; **uderzyć** (*perf*) **w** ~ (*pot*) to hit the sack (*pot*)
**kimś** *pron instr, loc od* **ktoś**
**kimże** *pron instr, loc od* **któż**
**kinematografi|a** (**-i, -e**) (*gen pl* **-i**) *f* (*produkcja*) filmmaking; (*sztuka, technika*) cinematography
**kinesko|p** (**-pu, -py**) (*loc sg* **-pie**) *m* picture tube
**kinetyczny** *adj* kinetic
**kinkie|t** (**-tu, -ty**) (*loc sg* **-cie**) *m* wall light *lub* lamp
**ki|no** (**-na, -na**) (*loc sg* **-nie**) *nt* (*budynek*) cinema (*Brit*), (movie) theater (*US*); (*sztuka*) the cinema (*Brit*), the movies *pl* (*US*); **iść (pójść** *perf*) **do kina** to go to the pictures (*Brit*) *lub* movies (*US*); **co grają w kinie?** what's on *lub* playing (at the cinema (*Brit*) *lub* movies (*US*))?
**kinoma|n** (**-na, -ni**) (*loc sg* **-nie**) *m* filmgoer (*Brit*), moviegoer (*US*)
**kinooperato|r** (**-ra, -rzy**) (*loc sg* **-rze**) *m* projectionist
**kinowy** *adj* (*sala*) cinema *attr* (*Brit*), theater *attr* (*US*); **kasa kinowa** box office
**kios|k** (**-ku, -ki**) (*instr sg* **-kiem**) *m* kiosk
**kioskar|ka** (**-ki, -ki**) (*dat sg* **-ce**, *gen pl* **-ek**) *f* newsagent
**kioskarz** (**-a, -e**) (*gen pl* **-y**) *m* newsagent
**ki|pieć (-pię, -pisz)** *vi* (*o mleku, wodzie*) (*perf* **wy-**) to boil over; ~ **ze złości** to boil with anger
**ki|sić (-szę, -sisz)** (*imp* **-ś**, *perf* **u-**) *vt* to pickle; **kisić się** *vr* to pickle
**kisiel** (**-u, -e**) (*gen pl* **-i**) *m jelly-type dessert made with potato starch*
**ki|snąć (-snę, -śniesz)** (*imp* **-śnij**, *pt* **-snął** *lub* **-sł, -sła, -śli**, *perf* **s-**) *vi* (*o mleku*) to turn sour
**kisz|ka** (**-ki, -ki**) (*dat sg* **-ce**, *gen pl* **-ek**) *f* (*pot*) gut; **ślepa** ~ (*Anat: pot*) (vermiform) appendix; **kiszki mi marsza grają** (*pot*) I'm starving (*pot*)
**kiszon|ka** (**-ki, -ki**) (*dat sg* **-ce**, *gen pl* **-ek**) *f* silage
**kiszony** *adj* (*ogórek*) pickled; **kiszona kapusta** sauerkraut
**kiś|ć** (**-ci, -cie**) (*gen pl* **-ci**) *f* bunch
**ki|t** (**-tu, -ty**) (*loc sg* **-cie**) *m* putty; **do kitu** (*pot*) crummy (*pot*); **wciskać komuś kit** (*pot*) to feed sb a line (*pot*)
**ki|ta** (**-ty, -ty**) (*dat sg* **-cie**) *f* (*pęk piór*) crest; (*ogon*) brush; **odwalić** (*perf*) **kitę** (*pot*) to snuff it (*pot*)
**kit|el** (**-la, -le**) (*gen pl* **-li** *lub* **-lów**) *m* overall
**kit|ka** (**-ki, -ki**) (*loc sg* **-ce**) *f dimin od* **kita**; (*koński ogon*) ponytail; **kitki** *pl* bunches *pl*
**kiw|ać (-am, -asz)** *vt* (*pot: nabierać*) (*perf* **wy-**) to double-cross ▷ *vi* (*perf* **-nąć**); ~ **głową** to nod; ~ **ręką** to wave one's hand; ~ **nogami** to swing one's legs; **pies kiwał ogonem** the dog was wagging its tail; **kiwać się** *vr* (*perf* **-nąć**) (*o głowie, człowieku*) to swing; (*o meblu*) to be rickety
**kiwi** *m inv* (*Zool*) kiwi; (*Bot*) kiwi (fruit)
**kiw|nąć (-nę, -niesz)** (*imp* **-nij**) *vb perf od* **kiwać**; ~ **do kogoś (głową)** to give sb a nod; **nie ~ palcem** (*przen*) not to lift a finger; **kiwnąć się** *vb perf od* **kiwać się**
**kiwnięci|e** (**-a, -a**) *nt* (*głową*) nod; (*ręką*) wave
**k.k., kk** *abbr* (= *kodeks karny*) criminal code
**klacz** (**-y, -e**) (*gen pl* **-y**) *f* mare
**klakso|n** (**-nu, -ny**) (*loc sg* **-nie**) *m* horn, hoot
**klamer|ka** (**-ki, -ki**) (*dat sg* **-ce**, *gen pl* **-ek**) *f* (*zapinka*) clasp; (*do bielizny*) (clothes) peg
**klam|ka** (**-ki, -ki**) (*dat sg* **-ce**, *gen pl* **-ek**) *f* (*podłużna*) handle; (*okrągła*) knob; ~ **zapadła** (*przen*) it's too late now, it's past the point of no return

**klam|ra** (**-ry, -ry**) (*dat sg* **-rze**, *gen pl* **-er**) *f* (*zapięcie*) buckle; (*umocowanie*) clamp; (*nawias*) brace, curly bracket
**klamrowy** *adj*: **nawias ~** brace, curly bracket
**kla|n** (**-nu, -ny**) (*loc sg* **-nie**) *m* clan
**kla|pa** (**-py, -py**) (*dat sg* **-pie**) *f* (*ciężarówki*) tailgate; (*toalety*) cover; (*kołnierza*) lapel; (*pot: fiasko*) flop (*pot*); **zrobić** (*perf*) **klapę** (*pot*) to flop (*pot*)
**klap|ki** (**-ek**) *pl* (*obuwie*) flip-flops *pl*
**klap|s** (**-sa, -sy**) (*loc sg* **-sie**) *m* smack, slap; (*Film*) take; **dać** (*perf*) **dziecku ~a** to smack *lub* slap a child
**klarne|t** (**-tu, -ty**) (*loc sg* **-cie**) *m* clarinet
**klar|ować** (**-uję, -ujesz**) (*perf* **wy-**) *vt* (*oczyszczać*) to clear; (*pot: tłumaczyć*) to clear up; **klarować się** *vr* (*o pogodzie*) to clear up
**klarownoś|ć** (**-ci**) *f* clarity
**klarowny** *adj* clear
**kla|sa** (**-sy, -sy**) (*dat sg* **-sie**) *f* class; (*Szkol: grupa uczniów*) class; (*: sala*) classroom; (*: rocznik nauczania*) form (*Brit*), grade (*US*); **z klasą** (*człowiek, miejsce*) classy; **jechać pierwszą/drugą klasą** to travel *lub* go first/second class; **~ turystyczna** tourist *lub* economy class; **mój syn chodzi do pierwszej klasy** my son is in the first form (*Brit*) *lub* grade (*US*); **klasy** *pl*: **grać w klasy** to play hopscotch
**klase|r** (**-ra, -ry**) (*loc sg* **-rze**) *m* stamp album
**kla|skać** (**-szczę, -szczesz**) (*perf* **-snąć**) *vi* to clap (one's hands)
**kla|snąć** (**-snę, -śniesz**) (*imp* **-śnij**) *vb perf od* **klaskać**
**klasowy** *adj*: **społeczeństwo klasowe** class society; **świadomość klasowa** class-consciousness; **dziennik ~** class *lub* attendance register; **praca klasowa** (classroom) test, test paper
**klasów|ka** (**-ki, -ki**) (*dat sg* **-ce**, *gen pl* **-ek**) *f* (classroom) test
**klasycyz|m** (**-mu**) (*loc sg* **-mie**) *m* classicism
**klasyczny** *adj* (*antyczny*) classic(al); (*typowy, doskonały*) classic; **styl ~** (*w pływaniu*) breast-stroke; **taniec/balet ~** classical dance/ballet; **filologia klasyczna** the Classics *pl*
**klasyfikacj|a** (**-i, -e**) (*gen pl* **-i**) *f* classification
**klasyfik|ować** (**-uję, -ujesz**) (*perf* **s-**) *vt* to classify
**klasy|k** (**-ka, -cy**) (*instr sg* **-kiem**) *m* classic
**klasy|ka** (**-ki**) (*dat sg* **-ce**) *f* classic(s *pl*)
**klaszto|r** (**-ru, -ry**) (*loc sg* **-rze**) *m* (*męski*) monastery; (*żeński*) convent; **wstąpić** (*perf*) **do ~u** to join a monastery/convent
**klasztorny** *adj* monastic
**klat|ka** (**-ki, -ki**) (*dat sg* **-ce**, *gen pl* **-ek**) *f* cage; (*Film*) frame; **~ schodowa** staircase; **~ piersiowa** chest; (*Anat*) ribcage

**klau|n** (**-na, -ni** *lub* **-ny**) (*loc sg* **-nie**) *m* clown
**klaustrofobi|a** (**-i**) *f* claustrophobia
**klauzul|a** (**-i, -e**) *f* clause
**klawesy|n** (**-nu, -ny**) (*loc sg* **-nie**) *m* harpsichord
**klawiatu|ra** (**-ry, -ry**) (*dat sg* **-rze**) *f* keyboard
**klawisz** (**-a, -e**) (*gen pl* **-y**) *m* key; (*pot: strażnik więzienny*) (*gen pl* **-y** *lub* **-ów**) screw (*pot*)
**kl|ąć** (**-nę, -niesz**) (*imp* **-nij**, *perf* **za-**) *vi* to swear, to curse; **~ na czym świat stoi** to swear like a trooper; **kląć się** *vr* (*zaklinać się*) to swear
**kląt|wa** (**-wy, -wy**) (*loc sg* **-wie**) *f* curse; **rzucić** (*perf*) **na kogoś klątwę** to put a curse on sb
**kle** *n patrz* **kieł**
**kle|ić** (**-ję, -isz**) (*imp* **-j**, *perf* **s-**) *vt* to glue (together); **kleić się** *vr* to stick; **powieki mu się kleją** (*przen*) his eyelids are drooping; **rozmowa się nie kleiła** the conversation was heavy going
**klei|k** (**-ku, -ki**) (*instr sg* **-kiem**) *m* gruel
**kleisty** *adj* glutinous
**klej** (**-u, -e**) *m* glue
**klejno|t** (**-tu, -ty**) (*loc sg* **-cie**) *m* jewel, gem
**kleko|t** (**-tu, -ty**) (*loc sg* **-cie**) *m* clatter
**kleko|tać** (**-czę, -czesz**) *vi* to clatter
**klek|s** (**-sa, -sy**) (*loc sg* **-sie**) *m* blot
**kle|pać** (**-pię, -piesz**) (*perf* **-pnąć**) *vt* to tap, to pat ▷ *vi* (*pot: paplać*) to prattle (on); **~ kogoś po plecach/ramieniu** to tap *lub* pat sb on the back/shoulder; **~ biedę** (*przen*) to be hard up
**klep|ka** (**-ki, -ki**) (*dat sg* **-ce**, *gen pl* **-ek**) *f* (*podłogowa*) floorboard; (*w beczce*) stave; **brak mu piątej klepki** (*pot*) he has a screw loose (*pot*)
**klep|nąć** (**-nę, -niesz**) (*imp* **-nij**) *vb perf od* **klepać**
**klepsyd|ra** (**-ry, -ry**) (*dat sg* **-rze**) *f* (*zegar*) hourglass; (*nekrolog*) obituary
**kleptoma|n** (**-na, -ni**) (*loc sg* **-nie**) *m* kleptomaniac
**kleptomani|a** (**-i**) *f* kleptomania
**kle|r** (**-ru**) (*loc sg* **-rze**) *m* clergy
**klery|k** (**-ka, -cy**) (*instr sg* **-kiem**) *m* clergyman
**klerykalny** *adj* clerical (*not secular*)
**kleszcz** (**-a, -e**) (*gen pl* **-y**) *m* (*Zool*) tick
**kleszcz|e** (**-y**) *pl* (*Tech*) pliers *pl*; (*Med*) forceps *pl*
**klęcz|eć** (**-ę, -ysz**) *vi* to kneel
**klęcz|ki** (**-ek**) *pl*: **na klęczkach** on one's knees
**klęczni|k** (**-ka, -ki**) (*instr sg* **-kiem**) *m* kneeler
**klęk|ać** (**-am, -asz**) (*perf* **-nąć** *lub* **uklęknąć**) *vi* to kneel (down)
**klęk|nąć** (**-nę, -niesz**) (*imp* **-nij**, *pt* **-nął, -ła, -li**) *vb perf od* **klękać**
**klęs|ka** (**-ki, -ki**) (*dat sg* **-ce**) *f* (*porażka*) defeat; (*nieszczęście*) disaster; **ponieść** (*perf*) **klęskę** to suffer defeat; **~ żywiołowa** natural disaster

k

**klien|t** (**-ta, -ci**) (*loc sg* **-cie**) *m* (*w sklepie*) customer; (*w banku, u adwokata*) client; **stały ~** regular customer, patron
**klientel|a** (**-i**) *f* clientele
**klient|ka** (**-ki, -ki**) (*dat sg* **-ce**, *gen pl* **-ek**) *f* (*w sklepie*) customer; (*w banku, u adwokata*) client
**kli|f** (**-fu, -fy**) (*loc sg* **-fie**) *m* cliff
**kli|ka** (**-ki, -ki**) (*dat sg* **-ce**) *f* clique
**kliknię|cie** (**-cia, -cia**) (*gen pl* **-ć**) *nt* (*Komput*) click; **podwójne ~** double click
**klimakterium** *nt inv* the menopause
**klima|t** (**-tu**) (*loc sg* **-cie**) *m* (*nom pl* **-ty**) climate
**klimatyczny** *adj* climatic
**klimatyzacj|a** (**-i**) *f* air conditioning
**klimatyzowany** *adj* air-conditioned
**kli|n** (**-na, -ny**) (*loc sg* **-nie**) *m* (*z drewna, metalu*) wedge; (*w rajstopach itp.*) gusset; **~ niskiego ciśnienia** a trough of low pressure; **zabić** (*perf*) **komuś ~a** to put sb on the spot
**klin|ga** (**-gi, -gi**) (*dat sg* **-dze**) *f* blade
**kliniczny** *adj* clinical; **śmierć kliniczna** clinical death
**klini|ka** (**-ki, -ki**) (*dat sg* **-ce**) *f* clinic
**klinowy** *adj*: **pasek ~** (*Mot*) fan belt; **pismo klinowe** cuneiform writing
**kli|p** (**-pu, -py**) (*loc sg* **-pie**) *m* (video) clip
**klip|s** (**-sa, -sy**) (*loc sg* **-sie**) *m* clip earring
**klisz|a** (**-y, -e**) *f* (*Fot*) film; (*Druk*) plate
**kloaczny** *adj*: **dół ~** cesspit
**kloc** (**-a, -e**) *m* (*kłoda*) log
**kloc|ek** (**-ka, -ki**) (*instr sg* **-kiem**) *m dimin od* **kloc**; (*do zabawy*) block; **~ hamulcowy** (*w hamulcu bębnowym*) brake shoe; (*w hamulcu tarczowym*) brake pad
**klom|b** (**-bu, -by**) (*loc sg* **-bie**) *m* (flower) bed
**klo|n** (**-nu, -ny**) (*loc sg* **-nie**) *m* (*Bot*) maple; (*Bio, Komput*) clone
**klon|ować** (**-uję, -ujesz**) *vt* to clone
**klop|s** (**-sa, -sy**) (*loc sg* **-sie**) *m* (*Kulin*) meatball; (*pot: niepowodzenie*) flop (*pot*); **no to ~** (*pot*) now we've had it (*pot*)
**klosz** (**-a, -e**) *m* (lamp)shade
**klow|n** (**-na, -ni** *lub* **-ny**) (*loc sg* **-nie**) *m* clown
**klozetowy** *adj*: **muszla klozetowa** toilet bowl
**klu|b** (**-bu, -by**) (*loc sg* **-bie**) *m* club; **~ sportowy/poselski** athletic/parliamentary club; **~ studencki** students' union
**klubowy** *adj* club *attr*
**klucz** (**-a, -e**) (*gen pl* **-y**) *m* (*do zamka, testu, szczęścia*) key; (*Muz*) clef; (*Tech*) spanner (*Brit*), wrench (*US*); (*ptaków, samolotów*) vee formation; **zamknąć** (*perf*) **coś na ~** to lock sth; **trzymać kogoś/coś pod ~em** to keep sb/sth under lock and key; **~ francuski** monkey wrench
**kluczowy** *adj* key *attr*; **~ dla** *+gen* crucial to
**klucz|yć** (**-ę, -ysz**) *vi* to weave (one's way)
**kluczy|k** (**-ka, -ki**) (*instr sg* **-kiem**) *m* key
**klus|ka** (**-ki, -ki**) (*dat sg* **-ce**, *gen pl* **-ek**) *f* dumpling
**kła** *itd. n patrz* **kieł**
**kład|ka** (**-ki, -ki**) (*dat sg* **-ce**, *gen pl* **-ek**) *f* footbridge
**kłam** *inv*: **zadawać (zadać** *perf*) **czemuś ~** to belie sth, to give the lie to sth
**kła|mać** (**-mię, -miesz**) (*perf* **s-**) *vi* to lie; **~ jak najęty** *lub* **jak z nut** to lie blatantly *lub* flatly; **~ w żywe oczy** to lie through one's teeth
**kłamc|a** (**-y, -y**) *m decl like f in sg* liar
**kłamczuch** (**-a, -y**) *m* (*pot*) liar
**kłamczuch|a** (**-y, -y**) *f* (*pot*) liar
**kłamliwy** *adj* (*człowiek*) lying; (*plotka*) untrue
**kłamst|wo** (**-wa, -wa**) (*loc sg* **-wie**) *nt* lie
**kłani|ać się** (**-am, -asz**) (*perf* **ukłonić**) *vr* (*pochylać tułów*) to bow; (*pochylać głowę*) to nod; (*przen*) to say hello; **kłaniam się** (*przy powitaniu*) good morning/afternoon/evening; (*przy pożegnaniu*) goodbye
**kła|pać** (**-pię, -piesz**) (*perf* **-pnąć**) *vt*: **~ zębami** to snap
**kłap|nąć** (**-nę, -niesz**) (*imp* **-nij**) *vb perf od* **kłapać**
**kła|ść** (**-dę, -dziesz**) (*imp* **-dź**, *pt* **-dł**, *perf* **położyć**) *vt* (*na stole, na stół*) to put, to lay; (*go garnka, torebki*) to put; (*fundamenty*) to lay; **~ kogoś spać** to put sb to bed; **położyć czemuś kres** to put an end to sth; **~ (wielki) nacisk na coś** to lay *lub* place (great) emphasis on sth; **kłaść się** *vr* (*na łóżku, podłodze*) to lie down; (*iść spać*) to go to bed; (*przen: o mgle, cieniu*) to fall; **nie ~ się spać** to stay *lub* sit up
**kł|ąb** (**-ębu, -ęby**) (*loc sg* **-ębie**) *m* (*kurzu, dymu*) cloud
**kłącz|e** (**-a, -a**) (*gen pl* **-y**) *nt* rhizome
**kłęb|ek** (**-ka, -ki**) (*instr sg* **-kiem**) *m* (*włóczki*) ball; **~ nerwów** (*przen*) a bundle of nerves; **dojść** (*perf*) **po nitce do kłębka** to follow the thread to the (bitter) end; **zwinąć się** (*perf*) **w ~** to roll o.s. up into a ball, to curl up (into a ball)
**kłębu** *itd. n patrz* **kłąb**
**kł|oda** (**-ody, -ody**) (*dat sg* **-odzie**, *gen pl* **-ód**) *f* log; **rzucać komuś kłody pod nogi** (*przen*) to put a spoke in sb's wheel
**kłopo|t** (**-tu, -ty**) (*loc sg* **-cie**) *m* problem; **mieć ~ z czymś** to have a problem with sth; **w czym ~?** what seems to be the problem *lub* trouble?; **sprawiać (sprawić** *perf*) **komuś ~** to inconvenience sb; **nie rób sobie ~u** don't put yourself out; **kłopoty** *pl* trouble; **mieć ~y** to be in trouble; **wpaść** (*perf*) **w ~y** to get into trouble
**kłopo|tać** (**-czę, -czesz**) *vt*: **~ kogoś czymś** to bother sb about *lub* with sth; **kłopotać się** *vr*:

~ **się (o coś)** to worry (about sth); **nie kłopocz się** don't bother
**kłopotliwy** *adj* (*sprawiający kłopot*) inconvenient; (*wprawiający w zakłopotanie*) embarrassing
**kło|s** (**-sa, -sy**) (*loc sg* **-sie**) *m* ear (*of a cereal plant*)
**kłó|cić się (-cę, -cisz)** (*imp* **-ć**) *vr* (*sprzeczać się*) (*perf* **po-**) to quarrel, to argue; (*nie pasować*): **kłócić się z czymś** to clash with sth
**kłód** *n patrz* **kłoda**
**kłód|ka** (**-ki, -ki**) (*dat sg* **-ce**, *gen pl* **-ek**) *f* padlock
**kłótliwy** *adj* quarrelsome, argumentative
**kłót|nia** (**-ni, -nie**) (*gen pl* **-ni**) *f* quarrel, argument; **wywoływać (wywołać** *perf*) **kłótnię (z kimś)** to pick a quarrel (with sb)
**kłu|ć (-ję, -jesz)** *vt* (*perf* **u-**) to prick; **kłuje mnie w boku** I have a stabbing pain in my side
**kłujący** *adj* (*roślina*) prickly; (*ból*) stabbing
**kłu|s** (**-sa**) (*loc sg* **-sie**) *m* trot
**kłus|ować (-uję, -ujesz)** *vi* (*o koniu, jeźdźcu*) to trot; (*o kłusowniku*) to poach
**kłusownict|wo** (**-wa**) (*loc sg* **-wie**) *nt* poaching
**kłusowni|k** (**-ka, -cy**) (*instr sg* **-kiem**) *m* poacher
**KM** *abbr* (= *koń mechaniczny*) hp., HP (= *horsepower*)
**km** *abbr* (= *kilometr*) km; (= *karabin maszynowy*) machine gun
**kmin|ek** (**-ku**) (*instr sg* **-kiem**) *m* caraway (seed)
**knaj|pa** (**-py, -py**) (*dat sg* **-pie**) *f* (*pot*) joint (*pot*)
**kneb|el** (**-la, -le**) (*gen pl* **-li**) *m* gag
**knebl|ować (-uję, -ujesz)** (*perf* **za-**) *vt* to gag
**kned|el** (**-la, -le**) (*gen pl* **-li**) *m fruit-filled dumpling*
**kno|cić (-cę, -cisz)** (*imp* **-ć**, *perf* **s-**) *vt* (*pot*) to botch (*pot*)
**kno|t** (**-ta, -ty**) (*loc sg* **-cie**) *m* wick
**knu|ć (-ję, -jesz)** (*perf* **u-**) *vt* to plot
**knu|r** (**-ra, -ry**) (*loc sg* **-rze**) *m* boar
**koal|a** (**-i, -e**) (*gen pl* **-i**) *m* koala
**koalicj|a** (**-i, -e**) (*gen pl* **-i**) *f* coalition
**koalicjan|t** (**-ta, -ci**) (*loc sg* **-cie**) *m* coalition partner
**koalicyjny** *adj*: **rząd** ~ coalition government
**kobal|t** (**-tu**) (*loc sg* **-cie**) *m* cobalt
**kobieciarz** (**-a, -e**) (*gen pl* **-y**) *m* (*pej*) womanizer (*pej*)
**kobiecoś|ć** (**-ci**) *f* femininity
**kobiecy** *adj* (*pismo, wdzięk, wrażliwość*) feminine; (*narządy*) female; (*literatura, choroby*) women's *attr*
**kobie|rzec** (**-rca, -rce**) *m* carpet; **stanąć na ślubnym kobiercu** (*przen*) to tie the knot
**kobie|ta** (**-ty, -ty**) (*dat sg* **-cie**) *f* woman
**kob|ra** (**-ry, -ry**) (*dat sg* **-rze**) *f* cobra
**kob|za** (**-zy, -zy**) (*dat sg* **-zie**) *f a short-necked lute*

**koc** (**-a, -e**) (*gen pl* **-ów**) *m* blanket
**koch|ać (-am, -asz)** *vt* to love; **kochać się** *vr* to love each other; ~ **się (z kimś)** to make love (to sb); ~ **się w kimś** to be in love with sb
**kochan|ek** (**-ka, -kowie**) (*instr sg* **-kiem**) *m* lover
**kochani|e** (**-a**) *nt*: **~!** darling!
**kochan|ka** (**-ki, -ki**) (*dat sg* **-ce**, *gen pl* **-ek**) *f* lover, mistress
**kochany** *adj* dear ▷ *m decl like adj*; **mój** ~ my love *lub* dear
**koci** *adj* feline; **~e łby** cobblestones *pl*
**kocia|k** (**-ka, -ki**) (*instr sg* **-kiem**) *m* (*mały kot*) kitten; (*pot: ładna dziewczyna*) chick (*pot*)
**ko|cić się (-ci)** (*perf* **o-**) *vr* (*o kotce*) to have kittens
**kocie** *n patrz* **kot**
**ko|cioł** (**-tła, -tły**) (*loc sg* **-tle**) *m* (*Tech*) boiler; **kotły** *pl* (*Muz*) kettledrums *pl*
**kocz|ować (-uję, -ujesz)** *vi* to migrate; (*pot: przebywać chwilowo*) to hang around (*pot*), to crash-pad (*pot*)
**koczowniczy** *adj* nomadic
**ko|d** (**-du, -dy**) (*loc sg* **-dzie**) *m* code; **kod pocztowy** postcode (*Brit*), zip code (*US*)
**kodek|s** (**-su, -sy**) (*loc sg* **-sie**) *m* code; ~ **drogowy** rules of the road, ≈ Highway Code (*Brit*); ~ **cywilny/karny** civil/criminal code; ~ **handlowy** commercial code
**kod|ować (-uję, -ujesz)** (*perf* **za-**) *vt* to (en)code
**koedukacyjny** *adj* coed(ucational)
**kofei|na** (**-ny**) (*dat sg* **-nie**) *f* caffeine; **kawa bez kofeiny** decaffeinated coffee, decaf
**kogo** *pron gen, acc od* **kto** who; ~ **nie ma?** who's absent?; ~ **spotkałeś?** who(m) did you meet?; **ktoś,** ~ **nie znam** someone I don't know
**kogokolwiek** *pron gen, acc od* **ktokolwiek**
**kogoś** *pron gen, acc od* **ktoś** somebody, someone
**kogoż, kogóż** *pron gen od* **któż**
**koguci** *adj*: **waga ~a** (*Sport*) bantam weight
**kogu|t** (**-ta, -ty**) (*loc sg* **-cie**) *m* cock (*Brit*), rooster (*US*)
**ko|ić (-ję, -isz)** (*imp* **kój**, *perf* **u-**) *vt* (*ból, cierpienie*) to soothe; (*nerwy*) to calm
**ko|ja** (**-i, -je**) (*gen pl* **-i**) *f* berth
**kojarz|yć (-ę, -ysz)** (*perf* **s-**) *vt* (*fakty*) to associate; (*pary, małżeństwa*) to join; **nie kojarzę** (*pot*) I don't get it (*pot*); **kojarzyć się** *vr*: **to się kojarzy z** *+instr* it makes me think of
**kojący** *adj* soothing
**koj|ec** (**-ca, -ce**) *m* (*dla dziecka*) playpen
**kojo|t** (**-ta, -ty**) (*loc sg* **-cie**) *m* coyote
**ko|k** (**-ka, -ki**) (*instr sg* **-kiem**) *m* bun (*hairstyle*)
**kokai|na** (**-ny**) (*dat sg* **-nie**) *f* cocaine

**kokar|da** (**-dy, -dy**) (*dat sg* **-dzie**) *f* bow
**kokard|ka** (**-ki, -ki**) (*dat sg* **-ce**, *gen pl* **-ek**) *f dimin od* **kokarda**; **zawiązać** *(perf)* **coś na kokardkę** to tie sth in a bow
**kokieteri|a** (**-i**) *f* coquetry
**kokieteryjny** *adj* coquettish
**kokiet|ka** (**-ki, -ki**) (*dat sg* **-ce**, *gen pl* **-ek**) *f* coquette
**koklusz** (**-u**) *m* whooping cough
**koko|n** (**-nu, -ny**) (*loc sg* **-nie**) *m* cocoon
**koko|s** (**-su** *lub* **-sa, -sy**) (*loc sg* **-sie**) *m* coconut; **robić** *lub* **zarabiać ~y** (*pot: przen*) to rake it in (*pot*)
**kokosowy** *adj* coconut *attr*; **wiórki kokosowe** desiccated coconut; **~ interes** (*pot: przen*) gold mine (*przen*)
**kokpi|t** (**-tu, -ty**) (*loc sg* **-cie**) *m* cockpit
**kok|s** (**-su**) (*loc sg* **-sie**) *m* coke
**koksow|nia** (**-ni, -nie**) (*gen pl* **-ni**) *f* coking plant
**koktajl** (**-u, -e**) (*gen pl* **-i**) *m* (*napój*) cocktail; (*przyjęcie*) cocktail party; (*mleczny*) milkshake; **~ bar** cocktail lounge
**kol.** *abbr* (*= kolega, koleżanka*): **~ J. Malinowski/~ M. Kowalska** *sometimes attached to names of employees on written memos by managerial staff; also used in letter addresses to and by teenagers*
**kolaboracj|a** (**-i**) *f* collaboration (*with an enemy*)
**kolaboran|t** (**-ta, -ci**) (*loc sg* **-cie**) *m* (*pej*) collaborator
**kolabor|ować** (**-uję, -ujesz**) *vi* (*pej*) to collaborate (*with an enemy*)
**kolacj|a** (**-i, -e**) (*gen pl* **-i**) *f* supper; (*wczesna i obfita*) dinner
**kolage|n** (**-nu**) (*loc sg* **-nie**) *m* collagen
**kolan|ko** (**-ka, -ka**) (*instr sg* **-kiem**, *gen pl* **-ek**) *nt dimin od* **kolano**; (*Tech*) elbow
**kola|no** (**-na, -na**) (*loc sg* **-nie**) *nt* knee; **na kolanach** on one's knees; **siedzieć u kogoś na kolanach** to sit in sb's lap; **po kolana** (*w śniegu, wodzie, błocie*) knee-deep; **do kolan** (*trawa, skarpetki*) knee-high; **robić (zrobić** *perf*) **coś na kolanie** (*przen*) to dash sth off (*pot*)
**kolarski** *adj* cycle *attr*
**kolarst|wo** (**-wa**) (*loc sg* **-wie**) *nt* cycling
**kolarz** (**-a, -e**) (*gen pl* **-y**) *m* cyclist
**kol|ba** (**-by, -by**) (*loc sg* **-bie**) *f* (*karabinu*) butt; (*kukurydzy*) cob; (*Chem*) flask
**kolce** *n patrz* **kolec, kolka**
**kolczasty** *adj* (*krzew*) prickly; **drut ~** barbed wire
**kolczy|k** (**-ka, -ki**) (*instr sg* **-kiem**) *m* earring
**kole** *n patrz* **koło**
**koleb|ka** (**-ki, -ki**) (*dat sg* **-ce**, *gen pl* **-ek**) *f* (*przen*) cradle
**kol|ec** (**-ca, -ce**) *m* (*u roślin*) spike, thorn; (*u zwierząt*) spine; **kolce** *pl* (*buty sportowe*) spikes *pl*
**kole|ga** (**-gi, -dzy**) (*dat sg* **-dze**) *m decl like f in sg* friend; **~ ze szkoły** school friend, schoolmate; **~ z pracy** colleague, fellow worker
**kolegi|um** (**-um, -a**) (*gen pl* **-ów**) *nt inv in sg* (*redakcyjne*) board; (*sędziowskie*) jury; (*orzekające*) *a court handling minor civil offences*; (*uczelnia*) college
**koleg|ować się** (**-uję, -ujesz**) *vr*: **kolegować się (z kimś)** to be friends (with sb)
**kolei|na** (**-ny, -ny**) (*dat sg* **-nie**) *f* rut
**kole|j** (**-i, -je**) (*gen pl* **-i**) *f* (*środek transportu*) railway (*Brit*), railroad (*US*); (*instytucja*) rail; (*kolejność*) turn; (*bieg rzeczy*) course of events; **jechać ~ą** to take a train, to go *lub* travel by rail; **moja ~** *lub* **~ na mnie** (it's) my turn; **po kolei** in turn; **nie po kolei** in the wrong order; **z kolei** (*następnie*) next; (*z rzędu*) in a row; **(zmienne) ~e losu** vicissitudes
**kolejarz** (**-a, -e**) (*gen pl* **-y**) *m* railwayman (*Brit*), railroader (*US*)
**kolej|ka** (**-ki, -ki**) (*dat sg* **-ce**, *gen pl* **-ek**) *f* (*środek transportu*) commuter train; (*zabawka*) model railway (*Brit*) *lub* railroad (*US*); (*następstwo*) turn; (*rząd czekających ludzi*) queue (*Brit*), line (*US*); **~ górska** (*w wesołym miasteczku*) roller coaster, big dipper; **~ linowa** (*system transportu*) cable railway; (*wagonik*) cable car; **~ wąskotorowa** narrow-gauge railway (*Brit*), narrow-gage railroad (*US*); **zamówić/postawić** *(perf)* **kolejkę** (*pot*) to order/buy a round (of drinks); **stać w kolejce po bilety** to queue *lub* line up (*US*) for tickets; **poza kolejką** without waiting for one's turn
**kolejno** *adv* in turn
**kolejnoś|ć** (**-ci**) *f* order, sequence; **poza kolejnością** without waiting for one's turn; **w kolejności alfabetycznej** in alphabetical order
**kolejny** *adj* (*następny*) next; (*sąsiedni*) consecutive; (*jeszcze jeden*) another
**kolejowy** *adj* (*dworzec, linia*) railway *attr* (*Brit*), railroad *attr* (*US*); (*bilet, połączenie, katastrofa*) train *attr*; (*transport*) rail *attr*
**kolekcj|a** (**-i, -e**) (*gen pl* **-i**) *f* collection
**kolekcjone|r** (**-ra, -rzy**) (*loc sg* **-rze**) *m* collector
**kolekcjon|ować** (**-uję, -ujesz**) *vt* to collect
**kolend|ra** (**-ry, -ry**) (*dat sg* **-rze**) *f* coriander
**koleżan|ka** (**-ki, -ki**) (*dat sg* **-ce**, *gen pl* **-ek**) *f* friend; **~ ze szkoły** school friend, schoolmate; **~ z pracy** colleague, fellow worker
**koleżeński** *adj* (*człowiek, przysługa*) friendly; (*spotkanie*) of friends; **zachować się** *(perf)* **po koleżeńsku** to act like a friend
**kolę|da** (**-dy, -dy**) (*dat sg* **-dzie**) *f* (Christmas) carol

**koli|a** (**-i, -e**) (*gen pl* **-i**) *f* necklace
**kolib|er** (**-ra, -ry**) (*loc sg* **-rze**) *m* hummingbird
**kolid|ować (-uje)** *vi*: **~ z czymś** to clash with sth; **~ z prawem** to be against the law
**kolizj|a** (**-i, -e**) (*gen pl* **-i**) *f* (*zderzenie*) collision; (*sprzeczność*) conflict
**kol|ka** (**-ki, -ki**) (*dat sg* **-ce**, *gen pl* **-ek**) *f* (*kłucie w boku*) stitch; (*Med*) colic
**kolokwialny** *adj* colloquial, informal
**kolokwi|um** (**-um, -a**) (*gen pl* **-ów**) *nt inv in sg* (*Uniw*) test
**koloni|a** (**-i, -e**) (*gen pl* **-i**) *f* colony; **Kolonia** (*Geog*) Cologne; **kolonie** *pl* (*wakacje*) holiday camp
**kolonializ|m** (**-mu**) (*loc sg* **-mie**) *m* colonialism
**kolonialny** *adj* colonial
**kolonizacj|a** (**-i**) *f* colonization
**koloniz|ować (-uję, -ujesz)** (*perf* **s-**) *vt* to colonize
**koloński** *adj*: **woda kolońska** (eau de) cologne
**kolo|r** (**-ru, -ry**) (*loc sg* **-rze**) *m* (*barwa*) colour (*Brit*), color (*US*); (*w kartach*) suit; **jaki ~ ma ...?** what colo(u)r is ...?; **jakiego ~u jest ...?** what colo(u)r is ...?
**kolorat|ka** (**-ki, -ki**) (*dat sg* **-ce**, *gen pl* **-ek**) *f* clerical collar, dog collar (*pot*)
**kolor|ować (-uję, -ujesz)** (*perf* **po-**) *vt* to colour (in) (*Brit*), to color (in) (*US*)
**kolorowy** *adj* (*nie czarno-biały*) colour *attr* (*Brit*), color *attr* (*US*); (*wielobarwny*) colourful (*Brit*), colorful (*US*); (*ludność, rasa*) coloured (*Brit*), colored (*US*) ▷ *m decl like adj* coloured person; **metale kolorowe** non-ferrous metals
**kolorystycznie** *adv*: **pasować do czegoś ~** to match sth for colour (*Brit*) *lub* color (*US*)
**kolorysty|ka** (**-ki**) (*dat sg* **-ce**) *f* colouring (*Brit*), coloring (*US*)
**kolory|t** (**-tu**) (*loc sg* **-cie**) *m* colour (*Brit*), color (*US*)
**koloryz|ować (-uję, -ujesz)** *vt* (*opowieść*) to embellish
**koloryzujący** *adj*: **szampon ~** shampooing colourant (*Brit*) *lub* colorant (*US*)
**kolo|s** (**-sa, -sy**) (*loc sg* **-sie**) *m* giant
**kolosalny** *adj* colossal
**kolportaż** (**-u**) *m* distribution
**kolporte|r** (**-ra, -rzy**) (*loc sg* **-rze**) *m* distributor
**Kolumbi|a** (**-i**) *f* Colombia
**Kolumbijczy|k** (**-ka, -cy**) (*instr sg* **-kiem**) *m* Colombian
**Kolumbij|ka** (**-ki, -ki**) (*dat sg* **-ce**, *gen pl* **-ek**) *f* Colombian
**kolumbijski** *adj* Colombian
**kolum|na** (**-ny, -ny**) (*dat sg* **-nie**) *f* column; (*też*: **kolumna głośnikowa**) speaker
**kołat|ka** (**-ki, -ki**) (*dat sg* **-ce**, *gen pl* **-ek**) *f* (*na drzwiach*) knocker; (*instrument*) rattle
**kołcza|n** (**-nu, -ny**) (*loc sg* **-nie**) *m* quiver
**kołd|ra** (**-ry, -ry**) (*dat sg* **-rze**, *gen pl* **-er**) *f* quilt
**koł|ek** (**-ka, -ki**) (*instr sg* **-kiem**) *m* (*bolec*) pin; (*do wbijania*) peg
**kołnierz** (**-a, -e**) (*gen pl* **-y**) *m* (*koszuli, płaszcza*) collar; (*krój przy szyi*) neck; (*Tech*) flange
**kołnierzy|k** (**-ka, -ki**) (*instr sg* **-kiem**) *m dimin od* **kołnierz**
**ko|ło** (**-ła, -ła**) (*loc sg* **-le**, *gen pl* **kół**) *nt* (*okrąg*) circle, ring; (*Mat, Geom*: *figura płaska*) circle; (*pojazdu, w maszynie*) wheel; (*grupa ludzi, grono*) circle ▷ *prep +gen* (*w pobliżu*) by, next to; (*w przybliżeniu, około*) about; **kołem** (*stać, siedzieć*) in a circle; **w ~** (*chodzić*) round (in circles); **~ podbiegunowe** *lub* **polarne** polar circle; **~ zapasowe** spare wheel; **~ zamachowe** flywheel; **~ zębate** cog(wheel); **~ ratunkowe** lifebelt; **koła polityczne/artystyczne** political/artistic circles; **błędne ~** (*przen*) vicious circle; **coś ~ tego** (*pot*) something like that (*pot*)
**koł|ować (-uje)** *vi* (*o samolocie*) to taxi
**kołowrot|ek** (**-ka, -ki**) (*instr sg* **-kiem**) *m* (*wędkarski*) fishing reel; (*do przędzenia*) spinning wheel; (*przy wejściu*) turnstile
**kołowy** *adj* (*tor, orbita*) circular; (*pojazd*) wheeled *attr*; **ruch ~** road traffic; **diagram ~** pie chart
**kołpa|k** (**-ka, -ki**) (*instr sg* **-kiem**) *m* (*Mot*) hub cap
**koły|sać (-szę, -szesz)** *vt +acc* (*wózek*) to rock ▷ *vt +instr* (*drzewami*) to sway, to swing ▷ *vi* (*o statku*) to roll; **~ (u~ *perf*) dziecko (do snu)** to lull *lub* rock a baby (to sleep); **kołysać się** *vr* (*w fotelu*) to rock; (*na falach*) to roll; (*o drzewie*) to sway
**kołysan|ka** (**-ki, -ki**) (*dat sg* **-ce**, *gen pl* **-ek**) *f* lullaby
**kołys|ka** (**-ki, -ki**) (*dat sg* **-ce**, *gen pl* **-ek**) *f* cradle
**komando|r** (**-ra, -rzy**) (*loc sg* **-rze**) *m* (*Wojsk*) captain
**komando|s** (**-sa, -si**) (*loc sg* **-sie**) *m* commando
**koma|r** (**-ra, -ry**) (*loc sg* **-rze**) *m* mosquito
**kombaj|n** (**-nu, -ny**) (*loc sg* **-nie**) *m* (combine) harvester
**kombatan|t** (**-ta, -ci**) (*loc sg* **-cie**) *m* veteran
**kombi** *nt inv* estate car (*Brit*), station wagon (*US*)
**kombinacj|a** (**-i, -e**) (*gen pl* **-i**) *f* combination; **~ alpejska** Alpine combined; **~ klasyczna** *lub* **norweska** Nordic combined
**kombina|t** (**-tu, -ty**) (*loc sg* **-cie**) *m* plant, factory
**kombiner|ki** (**-ek**) *pl* combination pliers *pl* (*Brit*), lineman's pliers *pl* (*US*)

k

**kombinezo|n** (**-nu, -ny**) (*loc sg* **-nie**) *m* (*roboczy*) overalls *pl*; (*narciarski*) ski suit; (*lotnika*) flying suit; (*astronauty*) spacesuit; (*dziecięcy zimowy*) snow suit, quilted suit; (*ogrodniczki*) dungarees *pl*

**kombin|ować (-uję, -ujesz)** *vt* (*zestawiać*) (*perf* **s-**) to put together ▷ *vi* (*pot*: *postępować nieuczciwie*) to wangle (*pot*); **on coś kombinuje** (*pot*) he's up to something (*pot*)

**komedi|a** (**-i, -e**) (*gen pl* **-i**) *f* (*Film, Teatr*) comedy; (*przen*: *udawanie*) game

**komediowy** *adj* comedy *attr*

**komen|da** (**-dy, -dy**) (*dat sg* **-dzie**) *f* command; (*siedziba*: *policji, straży pożarnej*) headquarters; **pod komendą** *+gen* under the command of; **obejmować (objąć** *perf*) **komendę (nad** *+instr*) to take command (of)

**komendan|t** (**-ta, -ci**) (*loc sg* **-cie**) *m* (*w wojsku, policji*) commanding officer; (*straży pożarnej*) fire chief; (*w harcerstwie*) scoutmaster

**komender|ować (-uję, -ujesz)** *vt +instr* (*dowodzić*) to command; (*pot*: *przen*) to push around (*pot*)

**komentarz** (**-a, -e**) (*gen pl* **-y**) *m* commentary; (*uwaga*) comment; **komentarze** *pl* (*pot*) gossip; **bez ~a** no comment

**komentato|r** (**-ra, -rzy**) (*loc sg* **-rze**) *m* commentator

**koment|ować (-uję, -ujesz)** (*perf* **s-**) *vt* to comment on; (*Sport*) to commentate on

**komercyjny** *adj* commercial

**kome|ta** (**-ty, -ty**) (*dat sg* **-cie**) *f* comet

**komet|ka** (**-ki, -ki**) (*dat sg* **-ce**, *gen pl* **-ek**) *f* (*pot*) badminton

**komfor|t** (**-tu**) (*loc sg* **-cie**) *m* comfort

**komfortowy** *adj* (*fotel, warunki*) comfortable; (*hotel, samochód*) luxury *attr*

**komiczny** *adj* (*zachowanie, sytuacja*) comical; (*mina, ubiór*) comic

**komi|k** (**-ka, -cy**) (*instr sg* **-kiem**) *m* (*aktor*) comedy actor; (*satyryk*) comedian, comic

**komik|s** (**-su, -sy**) (*loc sg* **-sie**) *m* (*rubryka w gazecie*) comic strip, (strip) cartoon; (*zeszyt*) comic book

**komi|n** (**-na, -ny**) (*loc sg* **-nie**) *m* chimney; (*fabryczny*) chimney, smokestack; (*na statku*) funnel

**komin|ek** (**-ka, -ki**) (*instr sg* **-kiem**) *m* fireplace

**kominiar|ka** (**-ki, -ki**) (*dat sg* **-ce**, *gen pl* **-ek**) *f* balaclava

**kominiarz** (**-a, -e**) (*gen pl* **-y**) *m* chimney sweep

**komi|s** (**-su, -sy**) (*loc sg* **-sie**) *m* (*Handel*) consignment; (*pot*) junk shop (*pot*); **oddawać (oddać** *perf*) **towar w ~** to consign goods

**komisaria|t** (**-tu, -ty**) (*loc sg* **-cie**) *m* (*też*: **komisariat policji**) police station

**komisarz** (**-a, -e**) (*gen pl* **-y**) *m* (*też*: **komisarz policji**) ≈ superintendent (*Brit*); (*wysoki urzędnik do specjalnych zadań*) commissioner

**komisj|a** (**-i, -e**) (*gen pl* **-i**) *f* (*sejmowa, kwalifikacyjna*) committee; (*egzaminacyjna, lekarska*) board; **(wspólna) ~ do spraw ...** a (joint) commission on ...

**komisyjny** *adj* (*egzamin*) *conducted before an examination board*; (*zbadanie, otwarcie*) *done in the presence of a committee*

**komite|t** (**-tu, -ty**) (*loc sg* **-cie**) *m* committee; **~ rodzicielski** ≈ parent-teacher association, ≈ PTA

**komiwojaże|r** (**-ra, -rowie** *lub* **-rzy**) (*loc sg* **-rze**) *m* travelling (*Brit*) *lub* traveling (*US*) salesman

**komiz|m** (**-mu**) (*loc sg* **-mie**) *m* comedy

**komna|ta** (**-ty, -ty**) (*dat sg* **-cie**) *f* (*Hist*) chamber

**komo|da** (**-dy, -dy**) (*dat sg* **-dzie**) *f* chest of drawers

**kom|ora** (**-ory, -ory**) (*dat sg* **-orze**, *gen pl* **-ór**) *f* (*Anat*) ventricle; (*Tech*) chamber; **~ gazowa** gas chamber

**komorn|e** (**-ego**) *nt decl like adj* (*pot*) rent

**komorni|k** (**-ka, -cy**) (*instr sg* **-kiem**) *m* (debt) collector

**komór|ka** (**-ki, -ki**) (*dat sg* **-ce**, *gen pl* **-ek**) *f* (*Bio*) cell; (*pomieszczenie*) closet; (*organizacyjna*) unit; **~ jajowa** egg cell, ovum

**komórkowy** *adj* cellular

**kompak|t** (**-tu, -ty**) (*loc sg* **-cie**) *m* (*pot*: *płyta kompaktowa*) CD; (*pot*: *odtwarzacz kompaktowy*) CD player

**kompaktowy** *adj*: **odtwarzacz ~** compact disc player; **płyta kompaktowa** compact disc

**kompa|n** (**-na, -ni**) (*loc sg* **-nie**) *m* (*pot*) buddy (*pot*)

**kompani|a** (**-i, -e**) (*gen pl* **-i**) *f* company; **~ honorowa** guard of honour (*Brit*) *lub* honor (*US*)

**kompa|s** (**-su, -sy**) (*loc sg* **-sie**) *m* compass

**kompatybilny** *adj* compatible

**kompens|ować (-uję, -ujesz)** (*perf* **s-**) *vt* to compensate for

**kompetencj|a** (**-i, -e**) (*gen pl* **-i**) *f* competence; **kompetencje** *pl* authority; **to nie leży w jego ~ch** it falls *lub* comes outside his jurisdiction

**kompetentny** *adj* (*organ*) pertinent; (*pracownik, opinia*) competent

**kompilacj|a** (**-i, -e**) (*gen pl* **-i**) *f* compilation

**komplek|s** (**-su, -sy**) (*loc sg* **-sie**) *m* complex; **~ niższości** inferiority complex

**kompleksowy** *adj* comprehensive

**komplemen|t** (**-tu, -ty**) (*loc sg* **-cie**) *m* compliment; **prawić komuś ~y** to pay compliments to sb

**komple|t** (**-tu, -ty**) (*loc sg* **-cie**) *m* (*sztućców, narzędzi*) set; (*ubraniowy*) suit; (*widzów*) full house; (*pasażerów w samolocie*) full flight; **być/ stawić się w komplecie** to be/come in full force
**kompletnie** *adv* completely
**kompletny** *adj* (*pełny*) complete; (*zupełny*) total
**komplet|ować (-uję, -ujesz)** (*perf* **s-**) *vt* (*listę*) to compile; (*załogę*) to assemble
**komplikacj|a** (**-i, -e**) (*gen pl* **-i**) *f* complication
**komplik|ować (-uję, -ujesz)** (*perf* **s-**) *vt* to complicate; **komplikować się** *vr* to become more complicated
**komponen|t** (**-tu, -ty**) (*loc sg* **-cie**) *m* component
**kompon|ować (-uję, -ujesz)** (*perf* **s-**) *vt* to compose
**kompo|st** (**-stu, -sty**) (*loc sg* **-ście**) *m* compost
**kompo|t** (**-tu, -ty**) (*loc sg* **-cie**) *m* (*napój*) stewed fruit; (*narkotyk*) *Polish home-made drug*
**kompozycj|a** (**-i, -e**) (*gen pl* **-i**) *f* (*Muz*) composition, piece; (*układ*) layout; (*budowa*) composition
**kompozyto|r** (**-ra, -rzy**) (*loc sg* **-rze**) *m* composer
**kompre|s** (**-su, -sy**) (*loc sg* **-sie**) *m* compress
**kompromi|s** (**-su, -sy**) (*loc sg* **-sie**) *m* compromise; **pójść** (*perf*) **na ~** to agree to a compromise
**kompromisowy** *adj* compromise *attr*
**kompromitacj|a** (**-i**) *f* embarrassment
**kompromit|ować (-uję, -ujesz)** (*perf* **s-**) *vt* to discredit; **kompromitować się** *vr* to compromise o.s.
**kompute|r** (**-ra, -ry**) (*loc sg* **-rze**) *m* computer; **~ osobisty** personal computer; **praca z ~em** computing
**komputero|wiec** (**-wca, -wcy**) *m* (*pot*) computer expert
**komputerowy** *adj* computer *attr*
**komputeryzacj|a** (**-i**) *f* computerization
**komputeryz|ować (-uję, -ujesz)** (*perf* **s-**) *vt* to computerize
**komu** *pron dat od* **kto** who, (to) whom; **~ to dałeś?** who did you give it to?
**komukolwiek** *pron dat od* **ktokolwiek** anybody, anyone; **daj to ~** give it to anyone
**komu|na** (**-ny, -ny**) (*dat sg* **-nie**) *f* (*pot: ustrój komunistyczny*) communist system; (*wspólnota*) commune
**komunalny** *adj* (*służby, gospodarka*) municipal; (*mieszkanie, budownictwo*) council *attr* (*Brit*), low-cost *attr* (*US*)
**komuni|a** (**-i, -e**) (*gen pl* **-i**) *f* communion; **Pierwsza K~ (Święta)** first (Holy) Communion; **iść (pójść** *perf*) **do komunii** to take communion
**komunikacj|a** (**-i**) *f* (*transport*) transport (*Brit*), transportation (*US*); (*porozumiewanie się*) communication; **~ miejska** public transport (*Brit*) *lub* transportation (*US*), transit (*US*); **środki komunikacji** means of transport (*Brit*) *lub* transportation (*US*)
**komunikacyjny** *adj* (*linia, sieć*) transport *attr* (*Brit*), transportation *attr* (*US*)
**komunika|t** (**-tu, -ty**) (*loc sg* **-cie**) *m* (*prasowy, oficjalny*) communiqué; (*informacyjny*) announcement
**komunikatywny** *adj* articulate
**komunik|ować się (-uję, -ujesz)** *vr* (*porozumiewać się*) to communicate; (*kontaktować się*) to be in touch (with one another)
**komuni|sta** (**-sty, -ści**) (*dat sg* **-ście**) *m decl like f in sg* communist
**komunist|ka** (**-ki, -ki**) (*dat sg* **-ce**, *gen pl* **-ek**) *f* communist
**komunistyczny** *adj* communist *attr*
**komuniz|m** (**-mu**) (*loc sg* **-mie**) *m* communism
**komuś** *pron dat sg od* **ktoś** somebody, someone; **dać** (*perf*) **coś ~** to give somebody sth, to give sth to somebody; **zabrać** (*perf*) **coś ~** to take sth away from somebody
**komuż** *pron dat od* **któż**
**komż|a** (**-y, -e**) (*gen pl* **-y**) *f* surplice
**kon|ać (-am, -asz)** *vi* to be dying; **~ ze śmiechu** (*przen*) to be dying of laughter
**kona|r** (**-ra** *lub* **-ru, -ry**) (*loc sg* **-rze**) *m* bough, branch
**koncentracj|a** (**-i**) *f* concentration
**koncentracyjny** *adj*: **obóz ~** concentration camp
**koncentra|t** (**-tu, -ty**) (*loc sg* **-cie**) *m* concentrate; **~ pomidorowy** tomato puree
**koncentr|ować (-uję, -ujesz)** (*perf* **s-**) *vt* to concentrate; **~ uwagę na czymś** to concentrate one's attention on sth; **koncentrować się** *vr*: **~ się (na** *+loc*) to concentrate (on)
**koncepcj|a** (**-i, -e**) (*gen pl* **-i**) *f* conception
**koncer|n** (**-nu, -ny**) (*loc sg* **-nie**) *m* concern
**koncer|t** (**-tu, -ty**) (*loc sg* **-cie**) *m* (*impreza*) concert; (*utwór muzyczny*) concerto; **~ życzeń** listeners' choice
**koncert|ować (-uję, -ujesz)** *vi* to give concerts
**koncertowy** *adj* (*sala, album*) concert *attr*; (*przen: popisowy*) masterly
**koncesj|a** (**-i, -e**) (*gen pl* **-i**) *f* licence (*Brit*), license (*US*)
**koncesjonowany** *adj* licenced
**kondensato|r** (**-ra, -ry**) (*loc sg* **-rze**) *m* capacitor, condenser

k

**kondens|ować (-uję, -ujesz)** (*perf* **s-**) *vt* to condense, to compress
**kondolencj|e** (-i) *pl* condolences; **składać (złożyć** *perf*) **komuś ~** to offer one's condolences to sb
**kondo|m** (-mu, -my) (*loc sg* **-mie**) *m* condom
**kondo|r** (-ra, -ry) (*loc sg* **-rze**) *m* condor
**konduk|t** (-tu, -ty) (*loc sg* **-cie**) *m*: **~ żałobny** *lub* **pogrzebowy** cortege, funeral procession
**kondukto|r** (-ra, -rzy) (*loc sg* **-rze**) *m* conductor, ticket inspector
**kondycj|a** (-i) *f* (*sprawność fizyczna*) fitness; **być w dobrej/słabej kondycji** to be in good/bad shape; **~ finansowa** financial standing
**kondygnacj|a** (-i) *f* (*budynku*) storey (*Brit*), story (*US*)
**koneksj|e** (-i) *pl* (*znajomości*) connections
**konese|r** (-ra, -rzy) (*loc sg* **-rze**) *m* connoisseur
**konew|ka** (-ki, -ki) (*dat sg* **-ce**, *gen pl* **-ek**) *f* watering can
**konfederacj|a** (-i, -e) (*gen pl* **-i**) *f* confederation; **K~ Polski Niepodległej** Confederation for Independent Poland
**konfekcj|a** (-i) *f* ready-to-wear clothes
**konferansje|r** (-ra, -rzy) (*loc sg* **-rze**) *m* host, compère (*Brit*), emcee (*US*)
**konferencj|a** (-i, -e) (*gen pl* **-i**) *f* conference; **~ prasowa** press conference
**konfesjona|ł** (-łu, -ły) (*loc sg* **-le**) *m* confessional (box)
**konfetti** *nt inv* confetti
**konfiden|t** (-ta, -ci) (*loc sg* **-cie**) *m* informer
**konfiguracj|a** (-i, -e) (*gen pl* **-i**) *f* configuration
**konfiska|ta** (-ty) (*loc sg* **-cie**) *f* confiscation
**konfisk|ować (-uję, -ujesz)** (*perf* **s-**) *vt* to confiscate
**konfitur|y** (-) *pl* conserve *sg*
**konflik|t** (-tu, -ty) (*loc sg* **-cie**) *m* conflict; **~ zbrojny** armed conflict; **wejść** (*perf*) **w ~ z prawem** to come into conflict with the law
**konfliktowy** *adj* (*człowiek*) abrasive, confrontational; **sytuacja konfliktowa** state of conflict, conflict situation (*US*)
**konformi|sta** (-sty, -ści) (*loc sg* **-ście**) *m decl like f in sg* conformist
**konformiz|m** (-mu) (*loc sg* **-mie**) *m* conformity
**konfrontacj|a** (-i, -e) (*gen pl* **-i**) *f* confrontation; (*porównanie*) comparison
**konfront|ować (-uję, -ujesz)** (*perf* **s-**) *vt* (*porównywać*) to compare; (*świadków*) to confront
**konglomera|t** (-tu, -ty) (*loc sg* **-cie**) *m* conglomerate
**kongre|s** (-su, -sy) (*loc sg* **-sie**) *m* (*zjazd*) congress; **K~ Stanów Zjednoczonych** the U.S. Congress
**konia|k** (-ku, -ki) (*instr sg* **-kiem**) *m* brandy; (*oryginalny*) cognac
**koniczy|na** (-ny, -ny) (*dat sg* **-nie**) *f* clover; **czterolistna ~** four-leaf clover
**ko|niec** (-ńca, -ńce) *m* end; (*ołówka*) tip; **do (samego) końca** until the (very) end; **od końca** in reverse order; **od końca do końca** from end to end; **pod ~ roku/miesiąca/życia** at the end of the year/month/life; **drugi od końca** last but one, next to last; **bez końca** (*dyskusja*) endless, interminable; (*dyskutować*) endlessly, interminably; **na** *lub* **w końcu** (*z tyłu*) at the end; **na ~** in the end; **w końcu** finally, at last; **~ końców** eventually; **mieć coś na końcu języka** (*przen*) to have sth on the tip of one's tongue; **wiązać ~ z końcem** (*przen*) to make ends meet
**koniecznie** *adv* absolutely, necessarily
**koniecznoś|ć** (-ci) *f* necessity; **w razie konieczności** if necessary; **robić (zrobić** *perf*) **coś z konieczności** to do sth out of necessity
**konieczny** *adj* essential, necessary
**koni|k** (-ka, -ki) (*instr sg* **-kiem**) *m dimin od* **koń**; (*figura szachowa*) knight; (*zainteresowanie*) hobby; (*pot: spekulant*) scalper; **~ morski** sea horse; **~ polny** grasshopper
**koni|na** (-ny) (*loc sg* **-nie**) *f* horse meat
**koniugacj|a** (-i, -e) (*gen pl* **-i**) *f* (*Jęz*) conjugation
**koniunktu|ra** (-ry) (*loc sg* **-rze**) *f* (*Ekon*) economic situation *lub* conditions; **zła/dobra ~ na rynku** slump/boom in the market
**koniusz|ek** (-ka, -ki) (*instr sg* **-kiem**) *m* tip
**konklawe** *nt inv* (*Rel*) conclave
**konkluzj|a** (-i, -e) (*gen pl* **-i**) *f* (*książk*) conclusion
**konkorda|t** (-tu, -ty) (*loc sg* **-cie**) *m* (*Pol*) concordat
**konkre|t** (-tu, -ty) (*loc sg* **-cie**) *m* fact; **przejść** (*perf*) **do ~ów** to get down to business, to get down to the nitty-gritty (*pot*)
**konkretny** *adj* (*przykład*) concrete; (*pytanie, sytuacja*) clear-cut, specific; (*człowiek*) businesslike
**konkretyz|ować (-uję, -ujesz)** (*perf* **s-**) *vt* to specify; **konkretyzować się** *vr* to take shape
**konkubi|na** (-ny, -ny) (*dat sg* **-nie**) *f* (*Prawo*) concubine
**konkurencj|a** (-i) *f* competition; (*Sport*) (*nom pl* **-e**, *gen pl* **-i**) event
**konkurencyjny** *adj* (*cena*) competitive; (*firma*) rival
**konkuren|t** (-ta, -ci) (*loc sg* **-cie**) *m* rival
**konkur|ować (-uję, -ujesz)** *vi*: **~ z** *+instr* to compete with

**konkur|s** (**-su, -sy**) (*loc sg* **-sie**) *m* competition, contest
**konno** *adv* on horseback
**konny** *adj* (*pojazd, zaprzęg*) horse-drawn; (*wyścig, przejażdżka*) horse *attr*; (*policja, oddział*) mounted; **jazda konna** horse riding
**kono|pie** (**-pi**) *pl* hemp *sg*
**konotacj|a** (**-i, -e**) (*gen pl* **-i**) *f* (*Jęz*) connotation
**konsekracj|a** (**-i, -e**) (*gen pl* **-i**) *f* consecration
**konsekr|ować (-uję, -ujesz)** *vt* to consecrate
**konsekwencj|a** (**-i**) *f* (*wynik, skutek*) (*nom pl* **-e**, *gen pl* **-i**) consequence; (*stanowczość, systematyczność*) consistency; **wyciągać (wyciągnąć** *perf*) **konsekwencje (w stosunku do kogoś)** to hold (sb) responsible; **ponosić (ponieść** *perf*) **konsekwencje czegoś** to take *lub* suffer the consequences of sth
**konsekwentny** *adj* consistent
**konsensu|s** (**-su, -sy**) (*loc sg* **-sie**) *m* consensus
**konser|wa** (**-wy, -wy**) (*dat sg* **-wie**) *f* tinned (*Brit*) *lub* canned (*US*) food
**konserwacj|a** (**-i**) *f* (*zabytków*) conservation; (*dróg, urządzeń*) maintenance
**konserwan|t** (**-tu, -ty**) (*loc sg* **-cie**) *m* preservative
**konserwato|r** (**-ra, -rzy**) (*loc sg* **-rze**) *m* restorer, conservator
**konserwatori|um** (**-um, -a**) (*gen pl* **-ów**) *nt inv in sg* conservatory
**konserwaty|sta** (**-sty, -ści**) (*loc sg* **-ście**) *m* conservative
**konserwatywny** *adj* conservative
**konserwatyz|m** (**-mu**) (*loc sg* **-mie**) *m* conservatism
**konserw|ować (-uję, -ujesz)** *vt* (*żywność*) (*perf* **za-**) to preserve; (*zabytki*) to restore, to conserve; (*maszyny*) to maintain
**konserwowy** *adj* (*szynka*) tinned (*Brit*), canned (*US*); (*ogórek*) pickled
**konsole|ta** (**-ty, -ty**) (*dat sg* **-cie**) *f* console
**konsolid|ować (-uję, -ujesz)** (*perf* **s-**) *vt* to consolidate; **konsolidować się** *vr* to consolidate
**konsorcj|um** (**-um, -a**) (*gen pl* **-ów**) *nt inv in sg* consortium
**konspek|t** (**-tu, -ty**) (*loc sg* **-cie**) *m* outline
**konspiracj|a** (**-i**) *f* (*tajność*) conspiracy; (*organizacja*) underground
**konspirato|r** (**-ra, -rzy**) (*loc sg* **-rze**) *m* (*działacz podziemia*) underground activist; (*spiskowiec*) conspirator
**konstelacj|a** (**-i, -e**) (*gen pl* **-i**) *f* constellation
**konsternacj|a** (**-i**) *f* consternation, dismay
**konstrukcj|a** (**-i**) *f* (*struktura*) (*nom pl* **-e**, *gen pl* **-i**) structure, construction; (*budowanie*) construction
**konstrukcyjny** *adj* structural
**konstrukto|r** (**-ra, -rzy**) (*loc sg* **-rze**) *m* (*wykonawca*) constructor; (*projektant*) designer
**konstruktywny** *adj* constructive
**konstru|ować (-uję, -ujesz)** (*perf* **s-**) *vt* (*wykonywać*) to construct; (*projektować*) to design
**konstytucj|a** (**-i, -e**) (*gen pl* **-i**) *f* constitution; **zgodny/niezgodny z konstytucją** constitutional/unconstitutional
**konstytucyjny** *adj* constitutional
**konsul** (**-a, -owie**) *m* consul; **~ generalny** consul general
**konsularny** *adj* consular
**konsula|t** (**-tu, -ty**) (*loc sg* **-cie**) *m* consulate
**konsultacj|a** (**-i, -e**) (*gen pl* **-i**) *f* (*porady*) consultation; (*wizyta u lekarza*) examination, consultation
**konsultan|t** (**-ta, -ci**) (*loc sg* **-cie**) *m* consultant
**konsultin|g** (**-gu**) (*instr sg* **-giem**) *m* (*Handel*) consultancy
**konsultingowy** *adj* consulting *attr*
**konsult|ować (-uję, -ujesz)** (*perf* **s-**) *vt*: **~ coś z kimś** to consult sth with sb; **konsultować się** *vr*: **~ się z kimś** to consult sb
**konsumen|t** (**-ta, -ci**) (*loc sg* **-cie**) *m* consumer
**konsum|ować (-uję, -ujesz)** (*perf* **s-**) *vt* to consume
**konsumpcj|a** (**-i**) *f* consumption
**konsumpcyjny** *adj* consumer *attr*
**konsystencj|a** (**-i**) *f* consistency
**konszacht|y** (**-ów**) *pl* secret dealings
**kontak|t** (**-tu, -ty**) (*loc sg* **-cie**) *m* (*styczność*) contact; (*Elektr: gniazdko*) socket, power point (*Brit*), (electrical) outlet (*US*); (*Elektr: pot: wyłącznik*) switch; **być z kimś w kontakcie** to be in contact *lub* touch with sb; **włączyć** (*perf*) **do ~u** to plug in; **kontakty** *pl* (*znajomości*) connections, contacts; **~y międzynarodowe** international contacts
**kontakt|ować (-uję, -ujesz)** (*perf* **s-**) *vt*: **~ kogoś z kimś** to put sb in touch with sb ▷ *vi* (*pot*): **żarówka nie kontaktuje** the bulb has a loose connection; **kontaktować się** *vr*: **~ się (z kimś)** to be in contact *lub* touch (with sb)
**kontaktowy** *adj* (*człowiek*) outgoing; **szkła** *lub* **soczewki kontaktowe** contact lenses; **lokal ~** safe house
**kontek|st** (**-stu, -sty**) (*loc sg* **-ście**) *m* context; **w kontekście** *+gen* in the context of
**kontemplacj|a** (**-i**) *f* contemplation
**kontempl|ować (-uję, -ujesz)** *vt/vi* to contemplate
**kontene|r** (**-ra, -ry**) (*loc sg* **-rze**) *m* container
**kontenero|wiec** (**-wca, -wce**) *m* container ship

**kon|to** (**-ta, -ta**) (*loc sg* **-cie**) *nt* account; **zakładać (założyć** *perf*) ~ to open an account; **mieć 10.000 złotych na koncie** to have 10,000 zloty in one's account; **mieć czyste ~** (*przen*) to have a clear record

**kont|ra** (**-ry, -ry**) (*dat sg* **-rze**) *f* (*Karty*) double; (*Sport: w boksie*) counter-punch, counterblow; (*Futbol*) counterattack ▷ *prep inv* (*przeciwko*): ~ +*nom* versus

**kontraban|da** (**-dy, -dy**) (*dat sg* **-dzie**) *f* contraband

**kontraba|s** (**-su, -sy**) (*loc sg* **-sie**) *m* double bass

**kontradmira|ł** (**-ła, -łowie**) (*loc sg* **-le**) *m* rear admiral

**kontrahen|t** (**-ta, -ci**) (*loc sg* **-cie**) *m* contracting party

**kontrak|t** (**-tu, -ty**) (*loc sg* **-cie**) *m* contract

**kontrapunk|t** (**-tu**) (*loc sg* **-cie**) *m* (*Muz*) counterpoint

**kontrargumen|t** (**-tu, -ty**) (*loc sg* **-cie**) *m* counter-argument

**kontra|st** (**-stu, -sty**) (*loc sg* **-ście**) *m* contrast

**kontrasygna|ta** (**-ty, -ty**) (*dat sg* **-cie**) *f* (*Ekon*) counter-signature

**kontrata|k** (**-ku, -ki**) (*instr sg* **-kiem**) *m* counterattack

**kontratak|ować (-uję, -ujesz)** *vi* to counterattack

**kontrkandyda|t** (**-ta, -ci**) (*loc sg* **-cie**) *m* opponent

**kontrofensy|wa** (**-wy, -wy**) (*loc sg* **-wie**) *f* (*Wojsk*) counter-offensive

**kontrol|a** (**-i**) *f* (*nadzór*) control; (*sprawdzenie*) (*nom pl* **-e**, *gen pl* **-i**) check; (*badanie kontrolne*) check-up; ~ **nad czymś** control of sth; ~ **biletów** ticket inspection; ~ **dokumentów** identity check; ~ **paszportowa/celna** passport/customs control

**kontrole|r** (**-ra, -rzy**) (*loc sg* **-rze**) *m* ticket inspector

**kontrol|ka** (**-ki, -ki**) (*dat sg* **-ce**, *gen pl* **-ek**) *f* indicator

**kontrolny** *adj* (*wieża*) control *attr*; (*przyrząd*) testing; **(lekarskie) badanie kontrolne** check-up; **obraz ~ TV** test card; **mecz ~** friendly (match); **spis ~** checklist

**kontrol|ować (-uję, -ujesz)** (*perf* **s-**) *vt* to control; **kontrolować się** *vr* (*czuwać nad sobą*) to control o.s.; (*sprawdzać jeden drugiego*) to check one another

**kontr|ować (-uję, -ujesz)** (*perf* **s-**) *vt* (*Karty*) to double; (*w piłce nożnej, boksie*) to counter

**kontrowersj|a** (**-i, -e**) (*gen pl* **-i**) *f* controversy

**kontrowersyjny** *adj* controversial

**kontrpropozycj|a** (**-i, -e**) (*gen pl* **-i**) *f* counter-proposal

**kontrwywia|d** (**-du, -dy**) (*loc sg* **-dzie**) *m* counter-intelligence *lub* -espionage

**kontrybucj|a** (**-i, -e**) (*gen pl* **-i**) *f* contribution

**kontua|r** (**-ru, -ry**) (*loc sg* **-rze**) *m* counter

**kontu|r** (**-ru, -ry**) (*loc sg* **-rze**) *m* contour, outline

**konturów|ka** (**-ki, -ki**) (*dat sg* **-ce**, *gen pl* **-ek**) *f* (*szminka*) lip liner

**kontuzj|a** (**-i, -e**) (*gen pl* **-i**) *f* (*Sport*) minor injury

**kontuzjowany** *adj* (*Sport*) injured

**kontynen|t** (**-tu, -ty**) (*loc sg* **-cie**) *m* continent

**kontynentalny** *adj* continental

**kontyngen|t** (**-tu, -ty**) (*loc sg* **-cie**) *m* (*Ekon*) quota; **~ bezcłowy** duty-free quota

**kontynuacj|a** (**-i, -e**) (*gen pl* **-i**) *f* continuation

**kontynuato|r** (**-ra, -rzy**) (*loc sg* **-rze**) *m* continuator

**kontynu|ować (-uję, -ujesz)** *vt* to continue

**konwali|a** (**-i, -e**) (*gen pl* **-i**) *f* lily of the valley

**konwekto|r** (**-ra, -ry**) (*loc sg* **-rze**) *m* convector

**konwenans|e** (**-ów**) *pl* (*książk*) etiquette

**konwencj|a** (**-i, -e**) (*gen pl* **-i**) *f* convention

**konwencjonalny** *adj* (*broń, metoda*) conventional; (*uśmiech*) polite

**konwen|t** (**-tu, -ty**) (*loc sg* **-cie**) *m* (*zgromadzenie*) caucus, assembly

**konwersacj|a** (**-i, -e**) (*gen pl* **-i**) *f* conversation

**konwersj|a** (**-i, -e**) (*gen pl* **-i**) *f* conversion

**konwojen|t** (**-ta, -ci**) (*loc sg* **-cie**) *m* escort

**konw|ój** (**-oju, -oje**) *m* convoy

**konwulsj|e** (**-i**) *pl* convulsions

**ko|ń** (**-nia, -nie**) (*gen pl* **-ni**, *instr pl* **-ńmi**) *m* horse; **żołnierz/policjant na koniu** mounted soldier/policeman; **koń mechaniczny** horsepower; **koń na biegunach** rocking horse; **na koń!** mount-up!; **zdrów jak koń** (*przen*) as sound as a bell; **zrobić** (*perf*) **kogoś w konia** (*pot*) to make a fool out of sb

**końca** *itd. n patrz* **koniec**

**końcowy** *adj* final; **końcowa stacja** *lub* **~ przystanek** terminus; **egzamin ~** (the) finals *pl*

**końców|ka** (**-ki, -ki**) (*dat sg* **-ce**, *gen pl* **-ek**) *f* (*filmu, zdania*) ending; (*sumy, liczby*) remainder; (*Jęz*) ending; (*Sport*) finish; (*narzędzia*) tip; (*kabla*) end

**kończ|yć (-ę, -ysz)** *vt* (*rozmowę*) (*perf* **s-**) to end; (*kawę, pracę*) (*perf* **s-**) to finish; (*szkołę, uniwersytet*) (*perf* **u-**) to graduate from; (*kurs*) (*perf* **u-** *lub* **s-**) to finish ▷ *vi* to finish; **~ coś robić** to finish doing sth; **muszę ~** I must end *lub* finish now; **s~** (*perf*) **ze sobą** to put an end to o.s.; **kończyć się** *vr* (*perf* **s-**) (*o wakacjach, dniu*) to end; **kończą nam się pieniądze/zapasy cukru** we are running out of money/sugar

**kończy|na** (**-ny, -ny**) (*dat sg* **-nie**) *f* limb
**koński** *adj*: **mucha końska** horsefly; **~ ogon** (*przen*: *fryzura*) ponytail
**kooperacj|a** (**-i, -e**) (*gen pl* **-i**) *f* co-operation
**kooper|ować (-uję, -ujesz)** *vi* to co-operate
**koordynacj|a** (**-i**) *f* co-ordination
**koordyn|ować (-uję, -ujesz)** (*perf* **s-**) *vt* to co-ordinate
**ko|pa** (**-py, -py**) (*dat sg* **-pie**) *f* (*60 sztuk*) threescore; (*siana*) stack; **kopę lat!** (*pot*) it's (been) ages!, long time no see! (*pot*)
**ko|pać (-pię, -piesz)** *vt* (*piłkę, przeciwnika*) (*perf* **-pnąć**) to kick; (*dół, norę*) (*perf* **wy-**) to dig; (*ziemniaki, buraki*) to dig up ▷ *vi* (*machać nogami*) to kick; (*w ziemi*) to dig
**kopal|nia** (**-ni, -nie**) (*gen pl* **-ni**) *f* mine; **~ węgla/soli** coal/salt mine; **~ odkrywkowa** strip mine; **~ wiedzy** (*przen*) mine of information
**kopar|ka** (**-ki, -ki**) (*dat sg* **-ce**, *gen pl* **-ek**) *f* excavator
**kop|cić (-cę, -cisz)** (*imp* **-ć**) *vi* (*dymić*) to smoke; (*pej*: *palić papierosy*) to smoke like a chimney; **kopcić się** *vr* (*pot*) to be smoking
**kopciusz|ek** (**-ka**) (*instr sg* **-kiem**) *m* Cinderella
**Kopenha|ga** (**-gi**) (*dat sg* **-dze**) *f* Copenhagen
**kop|er** (**-ru**) (*loc sg* **-rze**) *m* dill; **~ włoski** fennel
**koper|ek** (**-ku**) (*instr sg* **-kiem**) *m* dill
**koper|ta** (**-ty, -ty**) (*dat sg* **-cie**) *f* (*na listy*) envelope; (*zegarka*) watch-case; **~ ze znaczkiem** stamped envelope
**kopi|a** (**-i, -e**) (*gen pl* **-i**) *f* (*obrazu, oryginału*) reproduction; (*rzeźby, broni*) replica; (*dokumentu, listu*) copy; (*Komput*) backup (copy); (*broń*) (tilting) lance
**kopiar|ka** (**-ki, -ki**) (*dat sg* **-ce**, *gen pl* **-ek**) *f* copier
**ko|piec** (**-pca, -pce**) *m* (*wzgórek*) mound
**kopiej|ka** (**-ki, -ki**) (*dat sg* **-ce**, *gen pl* **-ek**) *f* kope(c)k
**kopi|ować (-uję, -ujesz)** *vt* (*powielać*) (*perf* **s-**) to copy; (*Komput*) (*perf* **prze-**) to copy
**kopiowy** *adj*: **ołówek ~** indelible pencil
**kop|nąć (-nę, -niesz)** (*imp* **-nij**) *vb perf od* **kopać**
**kopnia|k** (**-ka, -ki**) (*instr sg* **-kiem**) *m* kick
**kopnięty** *adj* (*pot*: *głupi*) insane
**kopulacj|a** (**-i, -e**) (*gen pl* **-i**) *f* copulation
**kopul|ować (-uję, -ujesz)** *vi* to copulate
**kopu|ła** (**-ły, -ły**) (*dat sg* **-le**) *f* dome, cupola
**kopyt|ka** (**-ek**) *pl* potato dumplings
**kopy|to** (**-ta, -ta**) (*loc sg* **-cie**) *nt* hoof; **wyciągnąć** (*perf*) **kopyta** (*pot*) to kick the bucket (*pot*); **robić wszystko na jedno ~** (*pot*) to do everything after one fashion
**ko|ra** (**-ry**) (*dat sg* **-rze**) *f* (*drzewa*) bark; (*tkanina*) seersucker; **~ mózgowa** cortex
**koral** (**-a, -e**) (*gen pl* **-i**) *m* (*Zool*) coral; (*paciorek*) bead; **korale** *pl* (*naszyjnik*) (necklace of) beads
**korali|k** (**-ka, -ki**) (*instr sg* **-kiem**) *m dimin od* **koral**
**koralowy** *adj* coral *attr*; **rafa koralowa** coral reef
**Kora|n** (**-nu**) (*loc sg* **-nie**) *m* (*Rel*) the Koran
**kor|ba** (**-by, -by**) (*dat sg* **-bie**) *f* crank
**korb|ka** (**-ki, -ki**) (*dat sg* **-ce**, *gen pl* **-ek**) *f dimin od* **korba**
**korbow|ód** (**-odu, -ody**) (*loc sg* **-odzie**) *m* (*Tech*) connecting rod
**korbowy** *adj*: **wał ~** crankshaft
**kor|cić (-ci)** *vt*: **korci mnie, żeby coś zrobić** I am itching to do sth
**kordo|n** (**-nu, -ny**) (*loc sg* **-nie**) *m* cordon; **otaczać (otoczyć** *perf*) **~em** to cordon off
**Kore|a** (**-i**) *f* Korea; **~ Północna/Południowa** North/South Korea
**Korean|ka** (**-ki, -ki**) (*dat sg* **-ce**, *gen pl* **-ek**) *f* Korean
**Koreańczy|k** (**-ka, -cy**) (*instr sg* **-kiem**) *m* Korean
**koreański** *adj* Korean
**kor|ek** (**-ka, -ki**) (*instr sg* **-kiem**) *m* cork; (*do wanny, umywalki*) (*nom pl* **-ki**) plug; (*zator na drodze*) traffic jam; (*pot*: *bezpiecznik*) fuse; **korki** *pl* (*pot*: *korepetycje*) private lessons
**korekcyjny** *adj* corrective
**korek|ta** (**-ty, -ty**) (*dat sg* **-cie**) *f* (*poprawka*) correction; (*Druk*) proofreading
**korekto|r** (**-ra, -rzy**) (*loc sg* **-rze**) *m* (*osoba*) proofreader; (*płyn*) Tipp-Ex® (*Brit*), whiteout (*US*)
**korelacj|a** (**-i, -e**) (*gen pl* **-i**) *f* correlation
**korel|ować (-uję, -ujesz)** *vi*: **~ z czymś** to correlate with sth
**korepetycj|e** (**-i**) *pl* private lessons; **udzielać korepetycji** to give private lessons, to coach
**korepetyto|r** (**-ra, -rzy**) (*loc sg* **-rze**) *m* coach
**korespondencj|a** (**-i**) *f* (*pisanie listów*) correspondence; (*listy*) mail, post (*Brit*); (*reportaż*) (*nom pl* **-e**, *gen pl* **-i**) report
**koresponden|t** (**-ta, -ci**) (*loc sg* **-cie**) *m* correspondent
**korespond|ować (-uję, -ujesz)** *vi*: **~ z** *+instr* to correspond with
**korkocią|g** (**-gu, -gi**) (*instr sg* **-giem**) *m* (*do butelek*) corkscrew; (*Lot*) spin
**kork|ować (-uję, -ujesz)** (*perf* **za-**) *vt* (*butelkę*) to cork up; (*przen*: *ruch*) to jam
**kormora|n** (**-na, -ny**) (*loc sg* **-nie**) *m* cormorant
**korne|r** (**-ra, -ry**) (*loc sg* **-rze**) *m* corner (kick)
**korni|k** (**-ka, -ki**) (*instr sg* **-kiem**) *m* woodworm
**korniszo|n** (**-na, -ny**) (*loc sg* **-nie**) *m* (*ogórek*) gherkin
**Kornwali|a** (**-i**) *f* Cornwall

**korod|ować (-uje)** (*perf* **s-**) *vi* to corrode
**koro|na** (**-ny, -ny**) (*loc sg* **-nie**) *f* (*królewska*) crown; (*drzewa*) crown, tree top; (*waluta*) krone; (*Med*) crown (*Brit*), cap (*US*); **~ cierniowa** crown of thorns
**koronacj|a** (**-i, -e**) (*gen pl* **-i**) *f* coronation
**koron|ka** (**-ki, -ki**) (*dat sg* **-ce**, *gen pl* **-ek**) *f* (*tkanina*) lace; (*dentystyczna*) crown (*Brit*), cap (*US*)
**koronkowy** *adj* (*szal, bielizna*) lacy; (*suknia*) lacy, crotchet; (*przen: robota, akcja*) meticulous
**koronny** *adj* (*dobra, klejnoty*) crown *attr*; **~ świadek** key witness
**koron|ować (-uję, -ujesz)** (*perf* **u-**) *vt* to crown; **koronować się** *vr* to be crowned
**korozj|a** (**-i**) *f* corrosion
**korporacj|a** (**-i, -e**) (*gen pl* **-i**) *f* corporation
**korpulentny** *adj* stout
**korpu|s** (**-su, -sy**) (*loc sg* **-sie**) *m* (*tułów*) trunk; (*Wojsk*) corps; **~ dyplomatyczny** diplomatic corps
**korri|da** (**-dy, -dy**) (*dat sg* **-dzie**) *f* bullfight
**korsarz** (**-a, -e**) (*gen pl* **-y**) *m* pirate
**Korsy|ka** (**-ki**) (*dat sg* **-ce**) *f* Corsica
**kor|t** (**-tu, -ty**) (*loc sg* **-cie**) *m*: **~ tenisowy** tennis court
**korump|ować (-uję, -ujesz)** (*perf* **s-**) *vt* to corrupt
**korupcj|a** (**-i**) *f* corruption
**koryg|ować (-uję, -ujesz)** (*perf* **s-**) *vt* to correct
**korytarz** (**-a, -e**) (*gen pl* **-y**) *m* (*w budynku*) corridor, passageway; (*skalny, podziemny*) tunnel
**kory|to** (**-ta, -ta**) (*loc sg* **-cie**) *nt* (*dla zwierząt*) trough; (*rzeki*) river bed
**korzenny** *adj* spicy
**korze|ń** (**-nia, -nie**) (*gen pl* **-ni**) *m* root; **korzenie** *pl* (*pochodzenie*) roots; (*przyprawy*) spice(s *pl*); **zapuścić** (*perf*) **korzenie** (*przen*) to put down roots; **wyrwać** (*perf*) **coś z korzeniami** to uproot sth
**korzon|ek** (**-ka, -ki**) (*instr sg* **-kiem**) *m dimin od* **korzeń**; **korzonki** *pl* (*Anat*) radicles
**korzyst|ać (-am, -asz)** (*perf* **s-**) *vi*: **~ z czegoś** (*z telefonu, łazienki*) to use sth; (*z praw*) to exercise sth; (*z sytuacji*) to take advantage of sth
**korzystny** *adj* (*interes*) profitable; (*wrażenie, warunki*) good, favourable (*Brit*), favorable (*US*)
**korzyś|ć** (**-ci, -ci**) (*gen pl* **-ci**) *f* (*pożytek*) advantage, benefit; (*zysk*) profit; **na czyjąś ~** to sb's advantage, in sb's favour (*Brit*) *lub* favor (*US*); **zmienić się** (*perf*) **na ~** to change for the better; **ciągnąć korzyści z** *+gen* to reap profit from
**ko|s** (**-sa, -sy**) (*loc sg* **-sie**) *m* blackbird
**ko|sa** (**-sy, -sy**) (*dat sg* **-sie**) *f* scythe
**kosiar|ka** (**-ki, -ki**) (*dat sg* **-ce**, *gen pl* **-ek**) *f* mower; (*do trawy*) lawn mower
**ko|sić (-szę, -sisz)** (*imp* **-ś**) *vt* (*perf* **s-**) to mow; (*pot: zabijać*) (*perf* **wy-**) to mow down
**kosmaty** *adj* hairy, shaggy
**kosmetycz|ka** (**-ki, -ki**) (*dat sg* **-ce**, *gen pl* **-ek**) *f* (*osoba*) beautician; (*torebka*) vanity bag *lub* case
**kosmetyczny** *adj* cosmetic; **gabinet ~** beauty salon *lub* parlor (*US*); **mleczko kosmetyczne** cleansing milk; **chusteczki kosmetyczne** (soft) tissues
**kosmety|k** (**-ku, -ki**) (*instr sg* **-kiem**) *m* cosmetic
**kosmiczny** *adj* (*statek, lot*) space *attr*; (*pył, promienie*) cosmic; **przestrzeń kosmiczna** (outer) space
**kosmi|ta** (**-ty, -ci**) (*dat sg* **-cie**) *m decl like f in sg* extraterrestrial
**kosmodro|m** (**-mu, -my**) (*loc sg* **-mie**) *m* launch(ing) pad
**kosmonau|ta** (**-ty, -ci**) (*loc sg* **-cie**) *m decl like f in sg* astronaut; (*w Rosji*) cosmonaut
**kosmopoli|ta** (**-ty, -ci**) (*dat sg* **-cie**) *m decl like f in sg* cosmopolitan
**kosmopolityczny** *adj* cosmopolitan
**kosmo|s** (**-su**) (*loc sg* **-sie**) *m* (*przestrzeń kosmiczna*) (outer) space; (*wszechświat*) cosmos
**kosmy|k** (**-ka, -ki**) (*instr sg* **-kiem**) *m* wisp, strand
**Kostary|ka** (**-ki**) *f* Costa Rica
**kostiu|m** (**-mu, -my**) (*loc sg* **-mie**) *m* (*ubiór kobiecy*) suit; (*teatralny*) costume; **~ karnawałowy** fancy dress; **~ gimnastyczny** sports outfit; **~ kąpielowy** bathing suit
**kost|ka** (**-ki, -ki**) (*dat sg* **-ce**, *gen pl* **-ek**) *f dimin od* **kość**; (*u nogi*) ankle; (*u ręki*) knuckle; (*do rzucania*) dice; (*do gry na gitarze*) pick; **~ cukru** sugar lump; **~ lodu** ice cube; **~ masła** slab of butter; **~ mydła** bar *lub* cake of soap; **~ brukowa** cobblestones *pl*; **woda do kostek** *lub* **po kostki** ankle-deep water; **suknia do kostek** an ankle-long dress; **krajać coś w kostkę** to dice sth
**kostnic|a** (**-y, -e**) *f* morgue, mortuary (*Brit*)
**kostnie|ć (-ję, -jesz)** (*perf* **s-**) *vi* (*z zimna*) to freeze, to grow stiff with cold
**kostny** *adj* bone *attr*
**kosz** (**-a, -e**) (*gen pl* **-y** *lub* **-ów**) *m* basket; (*pot: koszykówka*) basketball; **~ na śmieci** dustbin (*Brit*), garbage can (*US*); **~ plażowy** roofed wicker beach chair; **dostać** (*perf*) **~a** (*przen*) to be rejected; **grać w ~a** (*pot*) to play basketball
**koszar|y** (**-**) *pl* barracks *sg*
**koszerny** *adj* kosher
**koszma|r** (**-ru, -ry**) (*loc sg* **-rze**) *m* nightmare

**koszmarny** *adj* nightmarish, ghastly
**kosz|t** (**-tu, -ty**) (*loc sg* **-cie**) *m* (*Ekon*) cost, price; **koszty** *pl* (*nakład pieniężny*) expense, cost; (*wydatki*) expenses *pl*; **na ~ firmy** on the house; **~y utrzymania** cost of living; **~y podróży** travel(l)ing expenses; **~y eksploatacji** operating costs; **~em czegoś/kogoś** (*przen*) at the cost *lub* expense of sth/sb; **bawić się cudzym ~em** (*przen*) to have a laugh at somebody's expense *lub* cost
**kosztory|s** (**-su, -sy**) (*loc sg* **-sie**) *m* cost estimate *lub* calculation
**koszt|ować (-uję, -ujesz)** *vt* (*o towarze*) to cost; (*próbować*) (*perf* **s-**) to try, to taste; **pomidory kosztują 5 zł** tomatoes cost 5 zloty; **drogo** *lub* **dużo mnie to kosztowało** I paid through the nose for it
**kosztownoś|ci** (**-ci**) *pl* valuables *pl*
**kosztowny** *adj* dear, expensive
**koszul|a** (**-i, -e**) *f* shirt; **~ nocna** nightgown, nightdress
**koszul|ka** (**-ki, -ki**) (*dat sg* **-ce**, *gen pl* **-ek**) *f* T-shirt
**koszy|k** (**-ka, -ki**) (*instr sg* **-kiem**) *m dimin od* **kosz**
**koszykar|ka** (**-ki, -ki**) (*dat sg* **-ce**, *gen pl* **-ek**) *f* basketball player
**koszykarz** (**-a, -e**) (*gen pl* **-y**) *m* basketball player
**koszyków|ka** (**-ki**) (*dat sg* **-ce**) *f* basketball
**kościelny** *adj* church *attr* ▷ *m decl like adj* sexton, sacristan
**kościotru|p** (**-pa, -py**) (*loc sg* **-pie**) *m* (*pot*) skeleton
**koś|ciół** (**-cioła, -cioły**) (*loc sg* **-ciele**) *m* (*budynek*) church; (*organizacja*) Church; **chodzić do kościoła** to go to church
**kościsty** *adj* bony
**koś|ć** (**-ci, -ci**) (*gen pl* **-ci**) *f* (*Anat*) bone; (*Tech, Komput*) chip; **kości** *pl* (*do gry*) dice; **~ słoniowa** ivory; **~ niezgody** (*przen*) bone of contention; **skóra i kości** (*pot: chudzielec*) bag of bones (*pot*), (all) skin and bone (*pot*); **przy kości** plump; **dać** (*perf*) **komuś w ~** to give sb a hard time; **dostać** (*perf*) **w ~** to be put through it, to be given a hard time; **rozejść się** (*perf*) **po kościach** (*przen*) to flash in the pan, to come to nothing; **zmarznąć** (*perf*) **na ~** to be chilled to the bone *lub* marrow; **porachować** (*perf*) **komuś kości** (*przen*) to beat sb black and blue
**koślawy** *adj* crooked
**ko|t** (**-ta, -ty**) (*loc sg* **-cie**) *m* cat; **kupować (kupić** *perf*) **kota w worku** (*przen*) to buy a pig in a poke; **odwracać (odwrócić** *perf*) **kota ogonem** (*przen*) to move the goal posts
**kota|ra** (**-ry, -ry**) (*dat sg* **-rze**) *f* curtain
**kot|ek** (**-ka, -ki**) (*instr sg* **-kiem**) *m* (*pot: kot*) pussy-cat; (*młody kot*) kitten; **kotku!** honey!; **bawić się (z kimś) w kotka i myszkę** to play cat and mouse (with sb)
**kot|ka** (**-ki, -ki**) (*dat sg* **-ce**, *gen pl* **-ek**) *f* she-cat; **kotki** *pl* (*bazie*) catkins
**kotle** *n patrz* **kocioł**
**kotle|t** (**-ta, -ty**) (*loc sg* **-cie**) *m* (*Kulin*) chop; **~ schabowy** pork chop; **~ cielęcy** veal cutlet; **~ mielony** hamburger
**kotli|na** (**-ny, -ny**) (*dat sg* **-nie**) *f* valley
**kotła** *itd. n patrz* **kocioł**
**kotłow|nia** (**-ni, -nie**) (*gen pl* **-ni**) *f* boiler house
**kotur|n** (**-nu** *lub* **-na, -ny**) (*loc sg* **-nie**) *m* wedge heel
**kotwic|a** (**-y, -e**) *f* anchor; **rzucić** (*perf*) **kotwicę** to cast *lub* drop anchor; **podnieść** (*perf*) **kotwicę** to weigh anchor
**kotwicz|yć (-ę, -ysz)** (*perf* **za-**) *vt/vi* to anchor
**kowad|ło** (**-ła, -ła**) (*loc sg* **-le**, *gen pl* **-eł**) *nt* anvil; **między młotem a kowadłem** (*przen*) between the devil and the deep blue sea
**kowal** (**-a, -e**) (*gen pl* **-i**) *m* blacksmith
**kowboj** (**-a, -e**) *m* cowboy
**ko|za** (**-zy, -zy**) (*dat sg* **-zie**, *gen pl* **kóz**) *f* goat; **raz kozie śmierć!** (*przen*) sink or swim!
**kozacz|ki** (**-ków**) *pl dimin od* **kozaki**
**koza|k** (**-ka**) (*instr sg* **-kiem**) *m* (*grzyb*) (*nom pl* **-ki**) *kind of edible mushroom*; **Kozak** (*nom pl* **-cy**) Cossack; **kozaki** *pl* high boots
**kozet|ka** (**-ki, -ki**) (*dat sg* **-ce**, *gen pl* **-ek**) *f* couch
**kozi** *adj* goat's *attr*; **zapędzić** (*perf*) **kogoś w ~ róg** to knock sb into a cocked hat
**kozic|a** (**-y, -e**) *f* chamois
**ko|zioł** (**-zła, -zły**) (*loc sg* **-źle**) *m* billy-goat; (*przyrząd gimnastyczny*) horse; (*odbicie się piłki*) rebound; **~ ofiarny** (*przen*) scapegoat; **fikać (fiknąć** *perf*) **kozła** (*pot*) to do *lub* turn a somersault
**kozioł|ek** (**-ka, -ki**) (*instr sg* **-kiem**) *m dimin od* **kozioł**; (*przewrót*) somersault; **fikać** *lub* **wywracać koziołki** to turn somersaults
**koziołk|ować (-uję, -ujesz)** (*perf* **prze-**) *vi* to turn somersaults
**koziorożec** (**-ca, -ce**) *m* (*Zool*) ibex; **Koziorożec** (*Astrologia*) Capricorn; **Zwrotnik Koziorożca** the Tropic of Capricorn
**kozł|ować (-uję, -ujesz)** *vt* to dribble
**koźle** *n patrz* **kozioł**
**koźl|ę** (**-ęcia, -ęta**) (*gen pl* **-ąt**) *nt* kid
**kożuch** (**-a, -y**) *m* (*owcza skóra*) sheepskin; (*ubranie*) sheepskin coat; (*na mleku, farbie*) skin
**kój** *vb patrz* **koić**
**kół** *n patrz* **koło**
**kół|ko** (**-ka, -ka**) (*instr sg* **-kiem**) *nt dimin od* **koło**; (*przedmiot*) ring; (*narysowany znaczek*) circle; (*stowarzyszenie*) circle; **cztery kółka**

(*pot*) car; **stół na kółkach** a wheeled table; **w ~** (*biegać*) in circles, round and round; (*powtarzać*) over and over (again)

**kóz** *n patrz* **koza**

**kpić (kpię, kpisz)** (*perf* **za-**) *vi*: **~ (sobie) (z** *+gen*) to deride, to mock

**kpi|na** (**-ny, -ny**) (*dat sg* **-nie**) *f* mockery, scoffing

**KPN** *abbr* (*= Konfederacja Polski Niepodległej*) Confederation for Independent Poland

**kpr.** *abbr* (*= kapral*) Corp. (*= corporal*)

**kpt.** *abbr* (*= kapitan*) Capt. (*= captain*)

**kra** (**kry, kry**) (*dat sg* **krze**, *gen pl* **kier**) *f* ice float

**kra|b** (**-ba, -by**) (*loc sg* **-bie**) *m* crab

**krach** (**-u, -y**) *m* (*Ekon*) crash

**kraciasty** *adj* checquered (*Brit*) *lub* checkered (*US*)

**kradnę** *itd. vb patrz* **kraść**

**kradzież** (**-y, -e**) (*gen pl* **-y**) *f* theft, robbery; **~ tożsamości** identity theft; **~ z włamaniem** burglary

**krai|na** (**-ny, -ny**) (*loc sg* **-nie**) *f* (*książk: kraj*) land; (*geograficzna*) region

**kraj** (**-u, -e**) *m* (*państwo*) country; **w ~u** at home; **ciepłe ~e** warmer climes; **wiadomości z ~u** home news

**kraj|ać (-ę, -esz)** (*perf* **po-**) *vt* to cut; **~ na plasterki/w kostkę** to slice/dice; **~ mięso w plasterki** to carve meat; **krajać się** *vr*: **serce mi się kraje** my heart aches

**krajalnic|a** (**-y, -e**) *f* slicer

**krajobra|z** (**-zu, -zy**) (*loc sg* **-zie**) *m* scenery, landscape; (*Sztuka*) landscape

**krajo|wiec** (**-wca, -wcy**) *m* native

**krajowy** *adj* (*ogólnokrajowy*) national; (*wewnętrzny*) domestic; **towary produkcji krajowej** domestic *lub* home-made goods

**krajoznawczy** *adj*: **wycieczka krajoznawcza** sight-seeing tour

**krajoznawst|wo** (**-wa**) (*loc sg* **-wie**) *nt* touring, sightseeing

**kra|kać (-czę, -czesz)** *vi* (*o ptaku*) to caw, to croak; (*o człowieku*) to foretell evil, to croak (*pot*)

**kraker|s** (**-sa, -sy**) (*loc sg* **-sie**) *m* cracker

**krakowia|k** (**-ka, -ki**) (*instr sg* **-kiem**) *m kind of folk dance*

**Krak|ów** (**-owa**) (*loc sg* **-owie**) *m* Cracow

**krak|sa** (**-sy, -sy**) (*dat sg* **-sie**) *f* crash, accident

**kra|m** (**-mu, -my**) (*loc sg* **-mie**) *m* stall, booth

**kra|n** (**-nu, -ny**) (*loc sg* **-nie**) *m* (*kurek*) tap, faucet (*US*)

**kra|niec** (**-ńca, -ńce**) *m*: **~ świata** world's end; **~ miasta** city limits *lub* outskirts *pl*

**krańcowy** *adj* extreme

**krasnolud|ek** (**-ka, -ki**) (*instr sg* **-kiem**) *m* dwarf, gnome

**krasomówc|a** (**-y, -y**) *m decl like f in sg* orator

**krasomówst|wo** (**-wa**) (*loc sg* **-wie**) *nt* oratory, eloquence

**kra|ść (-dnę, -dniesz)** (*imp* **-dnij**, *perf* **u-**) *vt* to steal; **u~ coś komuś** to steal sth from sb

**kra|ta** (**-ty, -ty**) (*dat sg* **-cie**) *f* (*przegroda*) grating, grille; (*wzór*) check; (*w oknie*) bars *pl*; **spodnie w kratę** check trousers; **szkocka ~** tartan

**krate|r** (**-ru, -ry**) (*loc sg* **-rze**) *m* crater

**krat|ka** (**-ki, -ki**) (*dat sg* **-ce**, *gen pl* **-ek**) *f dimin od* **krata**; (*w formularzu*) blank; **w kratkę** (*tkanina*) checked, checkered; (*przen: nieregularnie*) irregularly; **za ~mi** behind bars

**kraul** (**-a**) *m* (*Sport*) crawl (stroke); **pływać ~em** to do *lub* swim the crawl

**krawa|t** (**-ta** *lub* **-tu, -ty**) (*loc sg* **-cie**) *m* (neck) tie

**krawco|wa** (**-wej, -we**) *f decl like adj* dressmaker

**krawę|dź** (**-dzi, -dzie**) (*gen pl* **-dzi**) *f* edge; **na krawędzi czegoś** (*przen*) on the verge of sth

**krawężni|k** (**-ka, -ki**) (*instr sg* **-kiem**) *m* kerb (*Brit*), curb (*US*)

**kra|wiec** (**-wca, -wcy**) *m* (*męski*) tailor; (*damski*) dressmaker

**krawiect|wo** (**-wa**) (*loc sg* **-wie**) *nt* (*damskie*) dressmaking; (*męskie*) tailoring

**kr|ąg** (**-ęgu, -ęgi**) (*instr sg* **-ęgiem**) *m* (*kształt, układ*) circle, ring; (*przen: ludzi, znajomych*) circle; (*przen: zainteresowań, badań*) range, sphere; **~ polarny** Polar circle; **kręgi pod oczyma** rings under eyes

**krąż|ek** (**-ka, -ki**) (*instr sg* **-kiem**) *m dimin od* **krąg**; (*przedmiot*) disc (*Brit*), disk (*US*); (*hokejowy*) puck

**krąże|nie** (**-nia**) *nt* circulation

**krążowni|k** (**-ka, -ki**) (*instr sg* **-kiem**) *m* cruiser

**krąż|yć (-ę, -ysz)** *vi* (*o ptakach, samolotach*) to make circles; (*o krwi*) to circulate; (*o przedmiocie*) to be passed around; (*o planetach*) to rotate

**kreacj|a** (**-i, -e**) (*gen pl* **-i**) *f* (*strój*) outfit

**kreatu|ra** (**-ry, -ry**) (*loc sg* **-rze**) *f* (*pej*) scoundrel

**kre|cha** (**-chy, -chy**) (*dat sg* **-sze**) *f*: **mieć krechę u kogoś** (*pot*) to be in sb's bad books

**kreci** *adj* (*przen*): **~a robota** scheming, machinations *pl*

**kre|da** (**-dy**) (*dat sg* **-dzie**) *f* (*do pisania*) (*nom pl* **-dy**) chalk; **biały jak ~** (as) white as a sheet

**kreden|s** (**-su, -sy**) (*loc sg* **-sie**) *m* cupboard

**kred|ka** (**-ki, -ki**) (*dat sg* **-ce**, *gen pl* **-ek**) *f* crayon; (*kolorowy ołówek*) coloured (*Brit*) *lub* colored (*US*) pencil; **~ do ust** lipstick; **~ do brwi** eyebrow pencil

**kredo** *nt inv* credo

**kredowy** *adj*: **papier ~** coated paper

**kredy|t (-tu, -ty)** (*loc sg* **-cie**) *m* credit; **~ inwestycyjny** investment credit; **~ hipoteczny** mortgage; **kupować na ~** to buy on credit; **~ zaufania** confidence, trust

**kredytobiorc|a (-y, -y)** *m decl like adj in sg* borrower

**kredytodawc|a (-y, -y)** *m decl like adj in sg* creditor, lender

**kredyt|ować (-uję, -ujesz)** (*perf* **s-**) *vt* to give credit for

**kre|m (-mu, -my)** (*loc sg* **-mie**) *m* cream; **ciastko z ~em** cream cake; **~ czekoladowy** chocolate cream; **~ do golenia/twarzy/rąk** shaving/face/hand cream; **~ nawilżający** moisturizing cream

**kremacj|a (-i, -e)** (*gen pl* **-i**) *f* cremation; **poddać** (*perf*) **kremacji** to cremate

**krematori|um (-um, -a)** (*gen pl* **-ów**) *nt inv in sg* crematory

**kremowy** *adj* cream *attr*; **śmietanka kremowa** whipping cream

**Kreol (-a, -e)** (*gen pl* **-i**) *m* Creole

**kre|ować (-uję, -ujesz)** (*perf* **wy-**) *vt* (*książk*) to create; (*Teatr, Film*) to perform the role of

**kre|pa (-py)** (*dat sg* **-pie**) *f* crepe

**kre|s (-su, -sy)** (*loc sg* **-sie**) *m* (*książk*: *koniec*) end; (*granica*) limit; **być u ~u sił** to be at the end of one's tether; **położyć** (*perf*) **czemuś ~** to put an end to sth; **kresy** *pl* (*pogranicze*) borderland

**kres|ka (-ki, -ki)** (*dat sg* **-ce**, *gen pl* **-ek**) *f* (*linia*) line; (*myślnik*) dash; (*łącznik*) hyphen; (*nad literą*) accent; (*na termometrze*) mark; (*w alfabecie Morse'a*) dash

**kresk|ować (-uję, -ujesz)** *vt* (*pokrywać kreskami*) to shade; **o** *lub* **ó kreskowane** the letter ó (*'o' with an acute accent*)

**kresków|ka (-ki, -ki)** (*dat sg* **-ce**, *gen pl* **-ek**) *f* (*Film*) (animated) cartoon

**kresowy** *adj* borderland *attr*

**kreślarski** *adj*: **deska kreślarska** drawing board

**kreślarz (-a, -e)** (*gen pl* **-y**) *m* draughtsman (*Brit*), draftsman (*US*)

**kreśl|ić (-ę, -isz)** *vt* (*projekt, rysunek*) to draw; (*wyrazy, zdania*) to cross out

**kre|t (-ta, -ty)** (*loc sg* **-cie**) *m* (*Zool*) mole

**Kre|ta (-ty)** (*dat sg* **-cie**) *f* Crete

**kretesem** *inv*: **z ~** (*przegrać*) completely

**kretowis|ko (-ka, -ka)** (*instr sg* **-kiem**) *nt* molehill

**krety|n (-na, -ni)** (*loc sg* **-nie**) *m* cretin

**kretyński** *adj* idiotic

**kr|ew (-wi)** *f* blood; **błękitna ~** (*przen*) blue blood; **nowa ~** new blood; **mieć coś we krwi** (*przen*) to be born with sth, to have sth in the *lub* one's blood; **zachować** (*perf*)**/stracić** (*perf*) **zimną ~** (*przen*) to keep/lose one's cool; **z zimną krwią** in cold blood; **koń czystej krwi** thoroughbred; **z krwi i kości** flesh and blood; **mrożący ~ w żyłach** bloodcurdling

**krewet|ka (-ki, -ki)** (*dat sg* **-ce**, *gen pl* **-ek**) *f* shrimp, prawn

**krewki** *adj* hot-blooded

**krewn|a (-ej) (-e)** *f decl like adj* relative

**krewnia|k (-ka, -cy)** (*instr sg* **-kiem**) *m* (*pot*) relative

**krew|ny (-nego, -ni)** *m decl like adj* relative

**kręc|ić (-cę, -cisz)** (*imp* **-ć**) *vt* (*włosy*) to curl; (*wąsa*) to twirl; (*masę, krem*) to mix ▷ *vi* (*pot*): **~ czymś** to turn sth; **~ (po~** *perf*) **głową** to shake one's head; **~ (na~** *perf*) **film** to shoot a film (*Brit*) *lub* movie (*US*); **~ nosem na coś** (*pot*) to sniff at sth (*pot*); **kręcić się** *vr* (*wirować*) to turn, to spin; (*wiercić się*) to squirm; **~ się koło kogoś** (*przen*) to hover round sb; **kręci mi się w głowie** my head is spinning

**kręcony** *adj* (*włosy*) curly; **kręcone schody** spiral staircase

**krę|g (-gu, -gi)** (*-instr sg* **-giem**) *m* (*Anat*) vertebra

**kręg|iel (-gla) (-gli)** (*gen pl* **-gli**) *m* skittle; **kręgle** *pl* (*gra*) skittles *pl*

**kręgiel|nia (-ni, -nie)** (*gen pl* **-ni**) *f* bowling alley

**kręgosłu|p (-pa, -py)** (*loc sg* **-pie**) *m* spine, backbone

**kręgo|wiec (-wca, -wce)** *m* (*Zool*) vertebrate

**kręgowy** *adj*: **rdzeń ~** spinal cord

**kręgu** *itd. n patrz* **krąg; kręg**

**kręp|ować (-uję, -ujesz)** *vt* (*przen*: *żenować*) to embarrass; (*przen*: *ograniczać*) to hamper; (*wiązać*) (*perf* **s-**) to tie up; **krępować się** *vr* to be bashful

**krępujący** *adj* embarrassing

**krępy** *adj* stocky

**krętact|wo (-wa, -wa)** (*loc sg* **-wie**) *nt* (*pot*) monkey business (*pot*)

**krętacz (-a, -e)** (*gen pl* **-y**) *m* (*pot*) cheater

**kręty** *adj* (*schody, uliczka*) winding

**krnąbrnoś|ć (-ci)** *f* defiance

**krnąbrny** *adj* defiant

**krochmal (-u)** *m* starch

**krochmal|ić (-ę, -isz)** (*perf* **wy-**) *vt* to starch

**kro|cie (-ci)** *pl*: **zarobić** (*perf*) **~ (na czymś)** to make a fortune (out of sth)

**krocz|e (-a, -a)** (*gen pl* **-y**) *nt* (*Anat*) crotch

**krocz|yć (-ę, -ysz)** *vi* to strut

**kr|oić (-oję, -oisz)** (*imp* **-ój**) *vt* (*kromkę chleba*) (*perf* **u-**) to cut; (*spodnie*) (*perf* **s-**) to tailor; **~ (po~** *perf*) **coś na kawałki** to cut sth to pieces; **~ (po~** *perf*) **coś w kostkę/na plasterki** to

dice/slice sth; **kroić się** *vr*: **coś komuś się kroi** sb has sth coming, sth is cooking for sb (*pot*)
**kro|k** (**-ku, -ki**) (*instr sg* **-kiem**) *m* (*ruch*) step; (*przen: czyn, działanie*) measure, step; (*krocze*) crotch; **co ~** every now and then; **~ po ~u** step by step; **o ~** *lub* **parę ~ów stąd** (just) a few steps from here; **spotykać coś na każdym ~u** to run into sth at every step; **podejmować (podjąć** *perf*) **~i w celu ...** to take steps *lub* measures to ...; **iść powolnym/żwawym/szybkim ~iem** to walk at a slow/brisk/quick pace; **przyśpieszyć** (*perf*) **~u** to speed up; **zwolnić** (*perf*) **~u** to slow down; **dotrzymywać (dotrzymać** *perf*) **komuś ~u** to keep pace with sb; **stawiać pierwsze ~i (w czymś)** to be taking one's first steps (at sth); **zrobić** (*perf*) **pierwszy ~** to make the first move
**krokie|t** (**-ta**) (*loc sg* **-cie**) *m* (*Sport*) croquet; (*Kulin*) (*nom pl* **-ty**) croquette
**krokodyl** (**-a, -e**) (*gen pl* **-i**) *m* crocodile
**kroku|s** (**-sa, -sy**) (*loc sg* **-sie**) *m* crocus
**krom|ka** (**-ki, -ki**) (*dat sg* **-ce**, *gen pl* **-ek**) *f* slice
**kroni|ka** (**-ki, -ki**) (*dat sg* **-ce**) *f* chronicle; **~ filmowa** newsreel; **~ towarzyska** gossip column
**kropel|ka** (**-ki, -ki**) (*dat sg* **-ce**, *gen pl* **-ek**) *f dimin od* **kropla**; (*przen: trochę*): **może jeszcze kropelkę kawy/wina?** a little more coffee/wine?; **kropelki** *pl* (*lekarstwo*) drops *pl*
**kro|pić (-pię, -pisz)** *vt* (*polewać*) (*perf* **s-**) to sprinkle ▷ *vi* (*o deszczu*) to spit
**kropid|ło** (**-ła, -ła**) (*loc sg* **-le**, *gen pl* **-eł**) *nt* aspergillum, aspersorium
**kropielnic|a** (**-y, -e**) *f* stoup
**krop|ka** (**-ki, -ki**) (*dat sg* **-ce**, *gen pl* **-ek**) *f* dot; (*znak przestankowy*) full stop (*Brit*), period (*US*); **sukienka w kropki** a dotted dress; **postawić** (*perf*) **kropkę nad i** (*przen*) to spell it out; **znaleźć się** (*perf*) **w kropce** to be put on the spot
**kropkowany** *adj*: **linia kropkowana** dotted line
**kropl|a** (**-i, -e**) (*gen pl* **-i**) *f* drop; **~ w morzu** (*przen*) a drop in the ocean; **podobni jak dwie krople wody** like as two peas *lub* as peas in a pod; **krople** *pl* (*lekarstwo*) drops *pl*; **krople do nosa/oczu** nose/eye drops *pl*
**kroplomierz** (**-a, -e**) (*gen pl* **-y**) *m* dropper
**kroplów|ka** (**-ki, -ki**) (*dat sg* **-ce**, *gen pl* **-ek**) *f* (*Med*) drip
**krop|nąć się (-nę, -niesz)** (*imp* **-nij**) *vr* (*pot: pomylić się*) to goof (*pot*)
**kro|sno** (**-sna, -sna**) (*loc sg* **-śnie**, *gen pl* **-sien**) *nt* loom
**kro|sta** (**-sty, -sty**) (*loc sg* **-ście**) *f* spot, pimple
**krost|ka** (**-ki, -ki**) (*loc sg* **-ce**, *gen pl* **-ek**) *f dimin od* **krosta**
**kr|owa** (**-owy, -owy**) (*dat sg* **-owie**, *gen pl* **-ów**) *f* cow
**krowi** *adj* cow's, cow *attr*
**krócej** *adv comp od* **krótko**
**kr|ój** (**-oju, -oje**) *m* (*ubrania, sukni*) cut; (*liter, pisma*) typeface; *patrz też* **kroić**
**król** (**-a**) *m* (*władca*) (*nom pl* **-owie**) king; (*Szachy, Karty*) (*nom pl* **-e**) king; **~ strzelców** (*Sport*) top scorer; **~ zwierząt** (*lew*) the king of the jungle; **(Święto) Trzech K~i** (*Rel*) Epiphany
**królest|wo** (**-wa, -wa**) (*loc sg* **-wie**) *nt* (*państwo*) kingdom; (*przen: teren działalności, władzy*) realm; **~ niebieskie** (*Rel*) kingdom of heaven
**królewicz** (**-a, -e**) *m* prince
**króle|wna** (**-wny, -wny**) (*dat sg* **-wnie**, *gen pl* **-wien**) *f* princess; **śpiąca ~** sleeping beauty
**królewski** *adj* royal; **Jego/Jej Królewska Mość** His/Her Majesty
**królicz|ek** (**-ka, -ki**) (*instr sg* **-kiem**) *m* bunny
**króli|k** (**-ka, -ki**) (*instr sg* **-kiem**) *m* rabbit; **~ doświadczalny** guinea pig
**królo|wa** (**-wej, -we**) *f decl like adj* queen
**król|ować (-uję, -ujesz)** *vi* to reign
**krót|ki** (*comp* **-szy**) *adj* (*włosy, sukienka*) short; (*odpowiedź, wizyta*) brief; **fale ~e** (*Radio*) shortwave; **mieć ~ wzrok** to be near-sighted *lub* short-sighted; **~e spięcie** (*Elektr*) short circuit; **~e spodnie** *lub* **spodenki** shorts *pl*; **na krótką metę** (*przen*) in the short term *lub* run; **w ~m czasie** in a short time, soon
**kró|tko** (*comp* **-cej**) *adv* (*ostrzyżony*) closely; (*mówić*) briefly; **~ mówiąc** briefly put; **trzymać kogoś ~** (*przen*) to keep a tight rein on sb
**krótkofalowy** *adj* (*Radio*) short-wave *attr*; (*przen: obliczony na krótki czas*) short-term
**krótkofalów|ka** (**-ki, -ki**) (*dat sg* **-ce**, *gen pl* **-ek**) *f* short-wave radio *lub* transmitter
**krótkometrażowy** *adj*: **film ~** short film, short subject (*US*)
**krótkoterminowy** *adj* short-term
**krótkotrwały** *adj* short-lived
**krótkowidz** (**-a, -e**) *m*: **być ~em** to be near-sighted *lub* short-sighted
**krótkowzroczność|ć** (**-ci**) *f* (*Med*) near-sightedness, short-sightedness; (*przen*) short-sightedness
**krótkowzroczny** *adj* (*Med*) near-sighted, short-sighted; (*przen*) short-sighted
**krów|ka** (**-ki, -ki**) (*dat sg* **-ce**, *gen pl* **-ek**) *f dimin od* **krowa**; (*cukierek*) fudge; **boża ~** (*Zool: biedronka*) ladybird (*Brit*), ladybug (*US*)
**krta|ń** (**-ni, -nie**) (*gen pl* **-ni**) *f* larynx
**krucho** *adv*: **~ z nim** he's in a spot; **~ u niego z pieniędzmi/czasem** he's (hard) pressed for money/time

**kruchoś|ć** (**-ci**) *f* fragility
**kruchy** *adj* (*lód, skała*) fragile; (*pieczywo*) crisp; (*mięso, drób*) tender; (*przen: wątły, nietrwały*) fragile
**krucja|ta** (**-ty, -ty**) (*dat sg* **-cie**) *f* crusade
**krucyfik|s** (**-su, -sy**) (*loc sg* **-sie**) *m* crucifix
**krucz|ek** (**-ka, -ki**) (*instr sg* **-kiem**) *m* (*pułapka*) catch; ~ **prawny** loophole
**kru|k** (**-ka, -ki**) (*instr sg* **-kiem**) *m* (*Zool*) raven; **biały** ~ (*przen*) collector's item
**krupie|r** (**-ra, -rzy**) (*loc sg* **-rze**) *m* croupier
**krupni|k** (**-ku, -ki**) (*instr sg* **-kiem**) *m* barley soup
**krusz|ec** (**-ca, -ce**) *m* ore
**krusze|ć (-je)** (*perf* **s-**) *vi* to become tender
**kruszon|ka** (**-ki, -ki**) (*dat sg* **-ce**, *gen sg* **-ek**) *f* short(crust) pastry
**krusz|yć (-ę, -ysz)** *vt* (*chleb*) (*perf* **po-**) to crumble; (*skałę*) (*perf* **s-**) to crush; **~ kopie o coś** (*przen*) to fight over sth; **kruszyć się** *vr* (*o chlebie*) (*perf* **po-**) to crumble; (*o skale*) to crumble
**kruszy|na** (**-ny, -ny**) (*loc sg* **-nie**) *f* crumb
**krużgan|ek** (**-ku** *lub* **-ka, -ki**) (*instr sg* **-kiem**) *m* (*Archit*) cloister
**krwa|wić (-wię, -wisz)** *vi* to bleed
**krwawie|nie** (**-nia, -nie**) (*gen pl* **-ń**) *nt* bleeding; **~ z nosa** nosebleed
**krwawy** *adj* bloody
**krwi** *itd. n patrz* **krew**
**krwia|k** (**-ka, -ki**) (*instr sg* **-kiem**) *m* (*Med*) h(a)ematoma
**krwin|ka** (**-ki, -ki**) (*dat sg* **-ce**, *gen pl* **-ek**) *f* blood cell
**krwiobie|g** (**-gu, -gi**) (*instr sg* **-giem**) *m* (*krążenie*) blood circulation; (*krążąca krew*) bloodstream
**krwiodawc|a** (**-y, -y**) *m decl like f in sg* blood donor; **honorowy** ~ volunteer blood donor
**krwiodawst|wo** (**-wa**) (*loc sg* **-wie**) *nt* blood donation
**krwionośny** *adj*: **układ** ~ circulatory *lub* cardiovascular system; **naczynie krwionośne** blood vessel
**krwiożerczy** *adj* bloodthirsty
**krwisty** *adj* (*befsztyk*) rare, underdone
**krwoto|k** (**-ku, -ki**) (*instr sg* **-kiem**) *m* bleeding, h(a)emorrhage
**kry|ć (-ję, -jesz)** *vt* (*chować*) (*perf* **u-**) to hide; (*uczucia, zamiary*) to hide, to conceal; (*dach, zwierzęta*) (*perf* **po-**) to cover; (*Sport: pilnować*) to cover, to mark (Brit); **~ kogoś** (*pot: chronić*) to cover up for sb (*pot*); **~ (w sobie)** (*zawierać*) to have in store; **kryć się** *vr* (*chować się*) (*perf* **u-** *lub* **s-**) to hide; (*zawierać się*) to lie hidden; **~ się z czymś** to keep sth secret; **coś się za tym kryje** there's more to it than meets the eye
**kryjomu** *inv*: **po** ~ in secret
**kryjów|ka** (**-ki, -ki**) (*dat sg* **-ce**, *gen pl* **-ek**) *f* hideout
**krykie|t** (**-ta**) (*loc sg* **-cie**) *m* (*Sport*) cricket
**Kry|m** (**-mu**) (*loc sg* **-mie**) *m* the Crimea
**kryminali|sta** (**-sty, -ści**) (*dat sg* **-ście**) *m decl like f in sg* criminal
**kryminalisty|ka** (**-ki**) (*dat sg* **-ce**) *f* crime detection
**kryminalny** *adj* (*przestępca, policja*) criminal; **film** ~ detective picture
**krymina|ł** (**-łu, -ły**) (*loc sg* **-le**) *m* (*książka*) detective story; (*film*) detective picture; (*pot: więzienie*) slammer (*pot*)
**kryp|ta** (**-ty, -ty**) (*dat sg* **-cie**) *f* crypt
**kryptoni|m** (**-mu, -my**) (*loc sg* **-mie**) *m* code name
**krystaliczny** *adj* crystalline; (*przen*) crystal clear
**krystalizacj|a** (**-i**) *f* crystallization
**krystaliz|ować się (-uje)** (*perf* **wy-**) *vr* to crystallize
**kryszta|ł** (**-łu, -ły**) (*loc sg* **-le**) *m* (*minerał*) crystal; (*szkło*) crystal (glass); (*wyrób*) crystal vase
**kryształowy** *adj* crystal; (*przen*) spotless
**kryteri|um** (**-um, -a**) (*gen pl* **-ów**) *nt inv in sg* criterion
**kryty** *adj* (*kort, wagon*) covered; **być ~m** (*pot*) to be clean (*pot*)
**krytycyz|m** (**-mu**) (*loc sg* **-mie**) *m* criticism
**krytyczny** *adj* critical; **pacjent jest w stanie ~m** the patient's condition is critical
**kryty|k** (**-ka, -cy**) (*instr sg* **-kiem**) *m* critic
**kryty|ka** (**-ki**) (*dat sg* **-ce**) *f* (*nom pl* **-ki**) (*ocena, analiza*) criticism; (*recenzja*) critique; **poddawać (poddać** *perf*) **coś krytyce** to express criticism of sth; **być poniżej wszelkiej krytyki** to be as bad as bad can be
**krytyk|ować (-uję, -ujesz)** (*perf* **s-**) *vt* to criticize
**kry|za** (**-zy, -zy**) (*dat sg* **-zie**) *f* (*Tech*) flange; (*kołnierz*) ruff
**kryzy|s** (**-su, -sy**) (*loc sg* **-sie**) *m* crisis; (*Ekon*) crisis, depression; **~ rządowy** cabinet crisis
**kryzysowy** *adj* crisis *attr*
**krzaczasty** *adj* (*brwi*) bushy
**krza|k** (**-ka** *lub* **-ku, -ki**) (*instr sg* **-kiem**) *m* bush, shrub; **krzaki** *pl* shrubbery
**krząt|ać się (-am, -asz)** *vr* to busy o.s., to bustle about
**krzątani|na** (**-ny**) (*dat sg* **-nie**) *f* bustle
**krze** *n patrz* **kra**
**krze|m** (**-mu**) (*loc sg* **-mie**) *m* silicon
**krzemie|ń** (**-nia, -nie**) (*gen pl* **-ni**) *m* flint
**krzemowy** *adj* silicon *attr*
**krze|pa** (**-py**) (*loc sg* **-pie**) *f* (*pot*) brawn

**krzepki** *adj* brawny
**krzep|nąć (-nie)** (*perf* **s-**) *vi* (*twardnieć*) to set; (*o krwi*) to clot; (*o wodzie*) to freeze
**krzesełkowy** *adj*: **wyciąg** ~ chairlift
**krze|sło** (**-sła, -sła**) (*loc sg* **-śle**, *gen pl* **-seł**) *nt* chair; ~ **składane** collapsible *lub* folding chair; ~ **elektryczne** electric chair
**krze|w** (**-wu, -wy**) (*loc sg* **-wie**) *m* bush, shrub
**krze|wić (-wię, -wisz)** *vi* (*książk*) to promote
**krz|ta** (**-ty**) (*dat sg* **-cie**) *f*: **ani krzty** not an ounce; **być bez krzty rozumu/honoru** not to have an ounce of reason/honour
**krztu|sić się (-szę, -sisz)** (*imp* **-ś**) *vr* to choke
**krztu|siec** (**-śca**) *m* (*Med*) whooping cough
**krzyczący** *adj* (*kolor*) garish; **krzycząca niesprawiedliwość** blatant injustice
**krzy|czeć (-czę, -czysz)** (*perf* **-knąć**) *vi* to shout, to scream; ~ **na kogoś** to shout at sb
**krzy|k** (**-ku, -ki**) (*instr sg* **-kiem**) *m* shout, scream; **podnieść** (*perf*) ~ to raise a hue and cry; **to jest ostatni ~ mody** (*przen*) it's all the rage
**krzykliwy** *adj* (*hałaśliwy*) noisy; (*zwracający uwagę*) gaudy
**krzyk|nąć (-nę, -niesz)** (*imp* **-nij**) *vb perf od* **krzyczeć**
**krzy|wa** (**-wej, -we**) *f decl like adj* (*Mat*) curve
**krzyw|da** (**-dy, -dy**) (*dat sg* **-dzie**) *f* harm, wrong; **wyrządzić** (*perf*) **komuś krzywdę** to harm sb; **naprawić** (*perf*) **krzywdę** to make up for the wrong
**krzyw|dzić (-dzę, -dzisz)** (*imp* **-dź**, *perf* **s-**) *vt* to harm, to wrong
**krzywic|a** (**-y**) *f* (*Med*) rickets
**krzy|wić (-wię, -wisz)** *vt* (*wyginać*) to bend; ~ **usta** *lub* **twarz** to make *lub* pull a face; **krzywić się** *vr* (*robić grymasy*) to make *lub* pull a face; ~ **się na kogoś/coś** to make *lub* pull a face at sb/sth
**krzywi|zna** (**-zny, -zny**) (*dat sg* **-źnie**) *f* curvature
**krzywo** *adv* (*stać*) askew; (*pisać*) clumsily; **patrzeć ~ na kogoś/coś** (*przen*) to frown at sb/sth
**krzywoprzysięst|wo** (**-wa, -wa**) (*loc sg* **-wie**) *nt* perjury
**krzywy** *adj* (*kij*) crooked; (*nogi*) knock-kneed; (*powierzchnia*) uneven; **patrzeć na kogoś/coś ~m okiem** (*przen*) to frown at sb/sth
**krzyż** (**-a, -e**) (*gen pl* **-y**) *m* (*przedmiot*) cross; (*część kręgosłupa*) lower back; **Czerwony K~** Red Cross; **wyglądać jak z ~a zdjęty** to look dead beat; **robić (zrobić** *perf*) **znak ~a** to make the sign of the cross; **parę osób na ~** (*pot*) just a handful of people, hardly a crowd
**krzyżacki** *adj* (*Hist*) Teutonic
**Krzyża|k¹** (**-ka, -cy**) (*instr sg* **-kiem**) *m* (*Hist*) Teutonic Knight, Knight of the Cross
**krzyża|k²** (**-ka, -ki**) (*instr sg* **-kiem**) *m* (*Tech*) cross; (*Zool*) cross spider
**krzyż|ować (-uję, -ujesz)** *vt* (*nogi, ramiona*) (*perf* **s-**) to cross; (*przybijać do krzyża*) (*perf* **u-**) to crucify; ~ **czyjeś plany** (*perf* **po-**) to thwart sb's plans; **krzyżować się** *vr* (*perf* **s-**) (*przecinać się*) to intersect
**krzyżo|wiec** (**-wca, -wcy**) *m* (*Hist*) crusader
**krzyżowy** *adj* (*mający kształt krzyża*) cross-shaped; (*kość, kręgi*) sacral; **droga krzyżowa** (*Rel*) the Way of the Cross; ~ **ogień** (*Wojsk*) crossfire; **wyprawa krzyżowa** (*Hist*) crusade; **brać (wziąć** *perf*) **kogoś w ~ ogień pytań** to cross-examine sb
**krzyżów|ka** (**-ki, -ki**) (*dat sg* **-ce**, *gen pl* **-ek**) *f* (*łamigłówka*) crossword (puzzle); (*Bio*) cross; (*pot: skrzyżowanie*) intersection; (*kaczka*) mallard
**krzyży|k** (**-ka, -ki**) (*instr sg* **-kiem**) *m dimin od* **krzyż**; (*Muz*) sharp; **położyć** *lub* **postawić na czymś ~** (*przen*) to give sth up; **ma szósty ~ na karku** (*pot*) he's pushing sixty (*pot*)
**KS** *abbr* (= *Klub Sportowy*) athletic club
**ks.** *abbr* (= *ksiądz*) Rev., Revd; (= *książę*) (*tytuł nadany*) Duke; (*syn króla*) Prince
**ksenofobi|a** (**-i**) *f* xenophobia
**ksero** *nt inv* (*pot: urządzenie*) Xerox® (machine); (*pot: odbitka*) Xerox (copy)
**kserograficzny** *adj* Xerox *attr*
**kserokopi|a** (**-i, -e**) (*gen pl* **-i**) *f* Xerox (copy)
**kserokopiar|ka** (**-ki, -ki**) (*dat sg* **-ce**, *gen pl* **-ek**) *f* Xerox machine
**kser|ować (-uję, -ujesz)** (*perf* **s-**) *vt* to Xerox
**ksiądz** (**księdza, księża**) (*voc sg* **księże**, *gen pl* **księży**, *instr pl* **księżmi**) *m* priest; **(Wielebny) ~ Jan Kowalski** the Reverend Jan Kowalski
**książecz|ka** (**-ki, -ki**) (*dat sg* **-ce**, *gen pl* **-ek**) *f dimin od* **książka**; ~ **czekowa** chequebook (*Brit*), checkbook (*US*); ~ **oszczędnościowa** savings book; ~ **wojskowa** military ID; ~ **do nabożeństwa** prayer book
**książę** (**księcia, książęta**) (*gen pl* **książąt**) *m* (*tytuł nadany*) duke; (*syn króla*) prince
**książęcy** *adj* duke's, prince's
**książ|ka** (**-ki, -ki**) (*dat sg* **-ce**, *gen pl* **-ek**) *f* book; ~ **kucharska** cookbook; ~ **telefoniczna** phone book, (telephone) directory; ~ **życzeń i zażaleń** book of complaints
**książkowy** *adj* (*wydanie*) in book form; (*wyrażenie*) bookish, formal; **mól ~** (*przen*) bookworm
**księga** (**księgi, księgi**) (*dat sg* **księdze**, *gen pl* **ksiąg**) *f* (*duża książka*) tome; ~ **gości** *lub* **pamiątkowa** visitors' book; ~ **wieczysta** (*Prawo*) land and mortgage book, ≈ land register (*Brit*); ~ **główna** (*Handel*) ledger;

**prowadzić księgi** (*Handel*) to keep accounts; **rewizja ksiąg** (*Handel*) audit; **zamykać (zamknąć** *perf*) **księgi** (*Handel*) to balance *lub* close the books

**księgar|nia** (**-ni, -nie**) (*gen pl* **-ń**) *f* bookshop (*Brit*), bookstore (*US*)

**księgarski** *adj* (*rynek*) book(selling) *attr*

**księgarz** (**-a, -e**) (*gen pl* **-y**) *m* bookseller

**księgo|wa** (**-wej, -we**) *f decl like adj* accountant

**księg|ować (-uję, -ujesz)** (*perf* **za-**) *vt* to enter in the books

**księgowani|e** (**-a**) *nt*: **~ pojedyncze/ podwójne** single/double entry book-keeping

**księgowoś|ć** (**-ci**) *f* (*prowadzenie ksiąg*) book-keeping, accounting; (*dział biura*) accounts

**księgo|wy** (**-wego, -wi**) *m decl like adj* accountant; **dyplomowany ~** chartered accountant ▷ *adj*: **kontroler** *lub* **rewident ~** auditor

**księgozbi|ór** (**-oru, -ory**) (*loc sg* **-orze**) *m* book collection; **~ podręczny** reference library

**księst|wo** (**-wa, -wa**) (*loc sg* **-wie**) *nt* duchy

**księż|na** (**-nej, -ne**) *f decl like adj* duchess

**księżnicz|ka** (**-ki, -ki**) (*dat sg* **-ce**, *gen pl* **-ek**) *f* princess

**księży** *adj* priest's *attr*

**księżyc** (**-a, -e**) *m* moon; **przy świetle ~a** by moonlight

**księżycowy** *adj* (*noc*) moonlit; (*pojazd*) lunar

**ksylofo|n** (**-nu, -ny**) (*loc sg* **-nie**) *m* (*Muz*) xylophone

**kształ|cić (-cę, -cisz)** (*imp* **-ć**, *perf* **wy-**) *vt* (*uczniów*) to educate; (*umysł, wolę*) to train; **kształcić się** *vr*: **~ się (na lekarza)** to study (to be a doctor) ▷ *vi*: **podróże kształcą** travel broadens the mind

**kształ|t** (**-tu, -ty**) (*loc sg* **-cie**) *m* shape; **kształty** *pl* (*pot*: *figura*) curves *pl* (*pot*); **w kształcie serca/cygara** heart/cigar-shaped; **coś na ~** *+gen* something like

**kształtny** *adj* shapely

**kształt|ować (-uję, -ujesz)** (*perf* **u-**) *vt* (*metal, glinę*) to shape; (*opinię, charakter*) to mould (*Brit*), to mold (*US*); **kształtować się** *vr*: **ceny kształtują się wysoko** prices are riding high; **bezrobocie kształtuje się na poziomie dwudziestu procent** unemployment is running at twenty per cent

 SŁOWO KLUCZOWE

**kto** *pron* **1** (*w zdaniach pytajnych lub ich równoważnikach*) who; **kto to (jest)?** who is it?; **kto tam?** who's there?, who is it?; **kto mówi?** who's speaking?

**2** (*w zdaniach podrzędnych*) who; **sprawdź, kto przyszedł** see who has arrived; **ten, kto ją znajdzie** whoever finds her; **kto chce, może iść** those who want to can go

**3**: **obojętnie kto** (*nieważne kto*) no matter who; (*ktokolwiek*) anybody, anyone; **mało kto** hardly anybody *lub* anyone

**ktokolwiek** (*jak*: **kto**) *pron* (*obojętnie kto*) anyone, anybody; **~ wie ...** whoever knows ...; **kimkolwiek jesteś** whoever you are

**ktoś** *pron* (*w zdaniach oznajmujących*) someone, somebody; (*w zdaniach pytających*) anyone, anybody; **czy zauważyłeś kogoś?** have you noticed anybody *lub* anyone?; **on myśli, że jest naprawdę kimś** he thinks he's really somebody; **~ inny** somebody *lub* someone else; **~, kogo nie znam** someone I don't know

**którędy** *pron* which way

 SŁOWO KLUCZOWE

**który** *pron decl like adj* **1** (*w zdaniach pytajnych*) which; **którą książkę chcesz?** which book do you want?; **którego dzisiaj mamy?** what's the date today?; **która godzina?** what time is it?, what's the time?; **o której (godzinie) masz pociąg?** what time is your train?; **który z was ...** which one of you ...

**2** (*w zdaniach podrzędnych*): **człowiek, którego widzisz ...** the man (that) you see ...; **nie wiem, którą wybrać** I don't know which to choose; **ludzie, z którymi pracuję** the people (that) I work with; **dziewczyna, z której siostrą rozmawiałem** the girl whose sister I was talking to

**3**: **mało** *lub* **rzadko który** hardly anyone *lub* anybody

**którykolwiek** (*jak*: **który**) *pron*: **~ (z** *+gen*) (*z wielu*) any (of); (*z dwu*) either (of)

**któryś** *pron*: **~ z nich/z moich ludzi** one of them/of my men; **któregoś dnia** one day, one of these days

**któż** *pron* who(ever)

**ku** *prep +dat* (*książk*): **ku morzu/niebu** toward(s) the sea/sky; **ku pamięci/czci** (*+gen*) in honour (*Brit*) *lub* honor (*US*) of; **ku mojemu zdziwieniu** to my surprise; **ku radości wszystkich** to everyone's joy; **ku końcowi** towards the end

**Ku|ba** (**-by**) (*dat sg* **-bie**) *f* Cuba

**Kuban|ka** (**-ki, -ki**) (*dat sg* **-ce**, *gen pl* **-ek**) *f* Cuban

**Kubańczy|k** (**-ka, -cy**) (*instr sg* **-kiem**) *m* Cuban

**kubański** *adj* Cuban

**kubatu|ra** (**-ry**) (*dat sg* **-rze**) *f* cubature, cubic content

**kub|ek** (**-ka, -ki**) (*instr sg* **-kiem**) *m* mug
**kub|eł** (**-ła, -ły**) (*loc sg* **-le**) *m* (*wiadro*) bucket, pail; (*kosz na śmieci*) (dust)bin (*Brit*), garbage can (*US*)
**kubiz|m** (**-mu**) (*loc sg* **-mie**) *m* cubism
**kuc|ać (-am, -asz)** (*perf* **-nąć**) *vi* to squat
**kuchar|ka** (**-ki, -ki**) (*dat sg* **-ce**, *gen pl* **-ek**) *f* cook
**kucharski** *adj*: **książka kucharska** cookbook; **sztuka kucharska** the art of cookery
**kucharz** (**-a, -e**) (*gen pl* **-y**) *m* cook, chef
**kuchen|ka** (**-ki, -ki**) (*dat sg* **-ce**, *gen pl* **-ek**) *f* cooker; (*też*: **kuchenka turystyczna**) camp stove; **~ mikrofalowa** microwave (oven)
**kuchenny** *adj* kitchen *attr*; **robot ~** food processor
**kuch|nia** (**-ni, -nie**) (*gen pl* **-ni**) *f* (*pomieszczenie*) kitchen; (*piec*) cooker, stove; (*tradycja kulinarna*) cuisine; (*gotowanie*) cooking
**kuc|nąć (-nę, -niesz)** (*imp* **-nij**) *vb perf od* **kucać**
**kucy|k** (**-ka, -ki**) (*instr sg* **-kiem**) *m* pony; (*kitka*) ponytail
**ku|ć (-ję, -jesz)** *vt* (*żelazo, miecz*) to forge; (*otwór*) (*perf* **wy-**) to chip, to chisel (out) ▷ *vi* (*rąbać*) to chisel; (*pot*: *uczyć się*) to cram, to swot (*pot*) (*Brit*)
**kudłaty** *adj* hairy, shaggy
**kuf|el** (**-la, -le**) (*gen pl* **-li**) *m* (*naczynie*) (beer) mug; (*porcja*) ≈ pint (of beer)
**kuf|er** (**-ra, -ry**) (*loc sg* **-rze**) *m* (*skrzynia*) trunk; (*pot*: *bagażnik samochodowy*) boot (*Brit*), trunk (*US*)
**kujawia|k** (**-ka, -ki**) (*instr sg* **-kiem**) *m Polish folk dance*
**kujo|n** (**-na, -ny**) (*loc sg* **-nie**) *m* (*pot*) swot (*Brit*) (*pot*), grind (*US*) (*pot*)
**kuk|ać (-am, -asz)** *vi* to cuckoo
**kukieł|ka** (**-ki, -ki**) (*dat sg* **-ce**, *gen pl* **-ek**) *f* puppet
**ku|kła** (**-kły, -kły**) (*dat sg* **-kle**, *gen pl* **-kieł**) *f* dummy
**kukuł|ka** (**-ki, -ki**) (*dat sg* **-ce**, *gen pl* **-ek**) *f* cuckoo; **zegar z kukułką** cuckoo clock
**kukurydz|a** (**-y**) *f* maize (*Brit*), corn (*US*); **prażona ~** popcorn
**kukurydziany** *adj* (*mąka, olej*) corn *attr*; **płatki kukurydziane** cornflakes
**kul|a** (**-i, -e**) *f* (*przedmiot*) ball; (*Geom*: *bryła*) sphere; (*pocisk*) bullet; **kule** *pl*: **chodzić o kuli/~ch** to walk on crutches; **pchnięcie kulą** (*Sport*) shot put; **~ ziemska** the globe; **~ u nogi** (*przen*) ball and chain
**kulawy** *adj* lame; (*stół*) rickety
**kule|ć (-ję, -jesz)** *vi* to limp
**kul|ić (-ę, -isz)** (*perf* **s-**) *vt* (*ramiona*) to hunch; (*głowę*) to duck; **kulić się** *vr* to shrink, to cringe
**kuli|g** (**-gu, -gi**) (*instr sg* **-giem**) *m* sleigh ride
**kulinarny** *adj* (*sztuka*) culinary; (*przepis*) cooking *attr*
**kulisty** *adj* spherical
**kulis|y** (**-**) *pl* (*Teatr*) wings *pl*; (*przen*: *nieznane okoliczności*) the behind-the-scenes *pl*; **za kulisami** (*przen*) behind the scenes, backstage
**kul|ka** (**-ki, -ki**) (*dat sg* **-ce**, *gen pl* **-ek**) *f dimin od* **kula**; (*papierowa, metalowa*) ball; (*lodów*) scoop; (*pot*: *pocisk*) slug (*pot*)
**kulkowy** *adj*: **łożysko kulkowe** ball bearing
**kulminacj|a** (**-i, -e**) (*gen pl* **-i**) *f* culmination
**kulminacyjny** *adj*: **moment/punkt ~** climax
**kuloodporny** *adj*: **kamizelka kuloodporna** bullet-proof vest
**kul|t** (**-tu, -ty**) (*loc sg* **-cie**) *m* cult; **~ jednostki** personality cult
**kultowy** *adj* cult *attr*; **obrzędy kultowe** rites
**kultu|ra** (**-ry, -ry**) (*dat sg* **-rze**) *f* culture; **dom kultury** ≈ community centre (*Brit*) *lub* center (*US*); **~ fizyczna** physical culture
**kulturalny** *adj* (*centrum, rozwój*) cultural; (*człowiek, sposób bycia*) well-mannered, cultured
**kulturowy** *adj* cultural
**kultury|sta** (**-sty, -ści**) (*dat sg* **-ście**) *m decl like f in sg* body-builder
**kulturysty|ka** (**-ki**) (*dat sg* **-ce**) *f* body-building
**kultyw|ować (-uję, -ujesz)** *vt* to cultivate
**kuluar|y** (**-ów**) *pl* lobby *sg*; **w kuluarach toczą się rozmowy** behind-the-scene talks are currently in progress
**kumoterst|wo** (**-wa**) (*loc sg* **-wie**) *nt* (*pot*) nepotism
**kump|el** (**-la, -le**) (*gen pl* **-li**) *m* (*pot*) mate (*pot*), pal (*pot*)
**kumulacj|a** (**-i, -e**) (*gen pl* **-i**) *f* accumulation
**kumul|ować (-uję, -ujesz)** (*perf* **s-**) *vt* to accumulate; **kumulować się** *vr* to pile up
**ku|na** (**-ny, -ny**) (*dat sg* **-nie**) *f* marten
**kund|el** (**-la, -le**) (*gen pl* **-li**) *m* mongrel
**kunsz|t** (**-tu, -ty**) (*loc sg* **-cie**) *m* artistry
**kunsztowny** *adj* elaborate
**ku|pa** (**-py, -py**) (*dat sg* **-pie**) *f* (*sterta*) pile, heap; (*pot!*) turd (*pot!*); **~ pieniędzy** (*pot*) loads of money (*pot*); **do kupy** (*pot*) together; **to się nie trzyma kupy** (*pot*) it doesn't stick (*pot*)
**kup|er** (**-ra, -ry**) (*loc sg* **-rze**) *m* rump
**ku|pić (-pię, -pisz)** *vb perf od* **kupować**
**ku|piec** (**-pca, -pcy**) *m* (*handlowiec*) merchant; (*nabywca*) buyer
**kup|ka** (**-ki, -ki**) (*dat sg* **-ce**, *gen pl* **-ek**) *f dimin od* **kupa**; (*stos*) heap; (*pot*) ca-ca (*pot*)
**kup|no** (**-na**) (*loc sg* **-nie**) *nt* purchase
**kupny** *adj* shop-bought (*Brit*), store-bought (*US*)

**kupo|n** (**-nu, -ny**) (*loc sg* **-nie**) *m* coupon, voucher
**ku|pować (-puję, -pujesz)** (*perf* **-pić**) *vt* to buy
**kupując|y** (**-ego, -y**) *m decl like adj* buyer, shopper
**ku|ra** (**-ry, -ry**) (*loc sg* **-rze**) *f* hen; **~ domowa** (*pej*) homebody
**kuracj|a** (**-i, -e**) (*gen pl* **-i**) *f* treatment
**kuracjusz** (**-a, -e**) (*gen pl* **-y**) *m* health resort visitor
**kuran|t** (**-ta, -ty**) (*loc sg* **-cie**) *m*: **zegar z ~em** chiming clock
**kuratel|a** (**-i**) *f* (*Prawo*) tutelage, wardship; **pod kuratelą** *+gen* under the tutelage of
**kurato|r** (**-ra, -rzy**) (*loc sg* **-rze**) *m* (*Prawo: opiekun*) warden; (*: nadzorca*) probation officer; (*Szkol*) superintendent of schools
**kuratori|um** (**-um, -a**) (*gen pl* **-ów**) *nt inv in sg* (local) department of education
**kurcz** (**-u, -e**) (*gen pl* **-y**) *m* cramp; **chwycił** *lub* **złapał go ~** he was seized with *lub* he got (a (US)) cramp
**kurcza|k** (**-ka, -ki**) (*instr sg* **-kiem**) *m* chicken
**kurcz|ę** (**-ęcia, -ęta**) (*gen pl* **-ąt**) *nt* chicken; **~ (pieczone)!** (*pot*) damn! (*pot*)
**kurczowo** *adv* tightly
**kurczowy** *adj* tight
**kurcz|yć się (-ę, -ysz)** (*perf* **s-**) *vr* (*o tkaninie, zapasach*) to shrink; (*o metalu, mięśniu*) to contract
**kur|ek** (**-ka, -ki**) (*instr sg* **-kiem**) *m* (*kran*) tap, faucet (US); (*pistoletu*) cock
**kuri|a** (**-i, -e**) (*gen pl* **-i**) *f* (*Rel*) curia
**kurie|r** (**-ra, -rzy**) (*loc sg* **-rze**) *m* courier, dispatch rider
**kurioz|um** (**-um, -a**) (*gen pl* **-ów**) *nt inv in sg* curiosity, oddity
**kur|ka** (**-ki, -ki**) (*dat sg* **-ce**, *gen pl* **-ek**) *f dimin od* **kura**; (*grzyb*) chanterelle; **~ wodna** water hen
**kurni|k** (**-ka, -ki**) (*instr sg* **-kiem**) *m* hen house, chicken coop
**kuropat|wa** (**-wy, -wy**) (*dat sg* **-wie**) *f* partridge
**kuror|t** (**-tu, -ty**) (*loc sg* **-cie**) *m* spa, health resort
**kur|ować (-uję, -ujesz)** (*perf* **wy-**) *vt* to treat; **kurować się** *vr* (*pot*) to undergo treatment
**kur|s** (**-su, -sy**) (*loc sg* **-sie**) *m* (*przejazd*) ride; (*kierunek*) course; (*waluty*) exchange rate; (*Giełda*) price; (*Uniw, Szkol*) course; **zboczyć** (*perf*) **z ~u** to go off course; **~ prawa jazdy** driving course
**kurso|r** (**-ra, -ry**) (*loc sg* **-rze**) *m* cursor
**kurs|ować (-uję, -ujesz)** *vi* to run
**kursy|wa** (**-wy, -wy**) (*dat sg* **-wie**) *f* (*Druk*) italics
**kurt|ka** (**-ki, -ki**) (*dat sg* **-ce**, *gen pl* **-ek**) *f* jacket
**kurtuazj|a** (**-i**) *f* courtesy
**kurtuazyjny** *adj* (*uprzejmy*) courteous; (*symboliczny*) token *attr*
**kurty|na** (**-ny, -ny**) (*dat sg* **-nie**) *f* curtain; **Żelazna K~** the Iron Curtain
**kur|wa** (**-wy, -wy**) (*dat sg* **-wie**, *gen pl* **-ew**) *f* (*pot!: prostytutka*) whore (*pot!*); **~ (mać)!** (*pot!*) fuck! (*pot!*), bugger! (*pot!*) (*Brit*)
**kurz** (**-u, -e**) *m* dust
**kurzaj|ka** (**-ki, -ki**) (*dat sg* **-ce**, *gen pl* **-ek**) *f* wart
**kurzy** *adj* (*ferma*) chicken *attr*; (*jajko*) hen's *attr*; **kurza pamięć** bad memory; **kurza ślepota** night blindness; **kurze łapki** crow's feet; **~ móżdżek** (*pot*) chicken head
**kurz|yć (-ę, -ysz)** *vi* (*podnosić tumany kurzu*) to raise dust; (*pot: palić papierosa*) to smoke, to puff; **kurzyć się** *vr*: **kurzyło się za samochodem** the car raised a cloud of dust; **kurzyło się z komina** smoke was spilling from the chimney
**ku|sić (-szę, -sisz)** (*imp* **-ś**, *perf* **s-**) *vt* to tempt; **kusi mnie, żeby to zrobić** I am tempted to do it; **~ los** to tempt fate *lub* providence
**kustosz** (**-a, -e**) (*gen pl* **-y**) *m* curator
**kusy** *adj* (*sukienka*) skimpy
**kusz|a** (**-y, -e**) *f* crossbow
**kuszący** *adj* tempting
**kuszet|ka** (**-ki, -ki**) (*dat sg* **-ce**, *gen pl* **-ek**) *f* berth, couchette
**kuśnierz** (**-a, -e**) (*gen pl* **-y**) *m* furrier
**kuśtyk|ać (-am, -asz)** *vi* (*utykać*) to limp; (*iść niezdarnie*) to hobble (along)
**kuta|s** (**-sa, -sy**) (*loc sg* **-sie**) *m* (*pot!*) prick (*pot!*)
**kut|er** (**-ra, -ry**) (*loc sg* **-rze**) *m* (*też:* **kuter rybacki**) fishing boat; (*też:* **kuter torpedowy**) torpedo boat
**kuty** *adj*: **kute żelazo** wrought iron; **on jest ~ na cztery nogi** (*pot*) he's a sly old fox (*pot*)
**kuwejcki** *adj* Kuwaiti
**Kuwej|t** (**-tu**) (*loc sg* **-cie**) *m* Kuwait
**kuzy|n** (**-na, -ni**) (*loc sg* **-nie**) *m* cousin
**kuzyn|ka** (**-ki, -ki**) (*dat sg* **-ce**, *gen pl* **-ek**) *f* cousin
**kuź|nia** (**-ni, -nie**) (*gen pl* **-ni**) *f* smithy, forge
**kw.** *abbr* (*= kwadratowy*): **120 m kw.** 120 sq. m.
**kwad|ra** (**-ry, -ry**) (*dat sg* **-rze**) *f* (*Astron*) quarter
**kwadran|s** (**-sa, -se**) (*loc sg* **-sie**) *m* quarter (*of an hour*); **~ po pierwszej** a quarter past (Brit) *lub* after (US) one; **za ~ pierwsza** a quarter to one
**kwadra|t** (**-tu, -ty**) (*loc sg* **-cie**) *m* (*figura*) square; (*potęga*): **pięć do ~u** five squared; **podnieść** (*perf*) **(liczbę) do ~u** to square (a number)
**kwadratowy** *adj* square
**kwa|kać (-cze)** *vi* to quack

k

**kwalifikacj|e** (**-i**) *pl* qualifications *pl*
**kwalifik|ować (-uję, -ujesz)** *vt* (*perf* **za-**) (*zaliczać*) to classify; (*określać*) to describe; (*oceniać*) to evaluate; **kwalifikować się** *vr*: **~ się (do czegoś)** to be qualified (for sth); **~ się na ministra** to qualify for the ministerial position; **to się kwalifikuje do sądu** this is a matter for the court
**kwan|t** (**-tu, -ty**) (*loc sg* **-cie**) *m* (*Fiz*) quantum
**kwa|pić się (-pię, -pisz)** (*perf* **po-**) *vr*: **nie kwapić się do czegoś/z czymś** not to be eager for sth/to do sth
**kwarantan|na** (**-ny, -ny**) (*dat sg* **-nie**) *f* quarantine
**kwarc** (**-u, -e**) *m* quartz
**kwarców|ka** (**-ki, -ki**) (*dat sg* **-ce**, *gen pl* **-ek**) *f* (*lampa kwarcowa*) sunlamp
**kwartalni|k** (**-ka, -ki**) (*instr sg* **-kiem**) *m* quarterly
**kwartalny** *adj* quarterly *attr*
**kwarta|ł** (**-łu, -ły**) (*loc sg* **-le**) *m* quarter (*of a year*)
**kwarte|t** (**-tu, -ty**) (*loc sg* **-cie**) *m* (*Muz*) quartet
**kwa|s** (**-su, -sy**) (*loc sg* **-sie**) *m* acid
**kwas|ek** (**-ku, -ki**) (*instr sg* **-kiem**) *m*: **~ cytrynowy** citric acid
**kwaszony** *adj*: **kapusta kwaszona** sauerkraut
**kwaśnie|ć (-je)** (*perf* **s-**) *vi* (*o mleku*) to turn (sour)
**kwaśny** *adj* (*owoc, smak*) sour, acid; (*mina*) sour; (*gleba*) acidic; **kwaśne mleko** sour milk; **~ deszcz** acid rain; **zbić** (*perf*) **kogoś na kwaśne jabłko** to beat sb black and blue
**kwate|ra** (**-ry, -ry**) (*dat sg* **-rze**) *f* (*prywatna*) lodgings *pl*; (*Wojsk*) billet, quarters *pl*; **~ główna** (*Wojsk*) headquarters
**kwatermistrz** (**-a, -owie** *lub* **-e**) *m* (*Wojsk*) quartermaster
**kwater|ować (-uję, -ujesz)** (*perf* **za-**) *vt* to quarter ▷ *vi* to be quartered
**kwaterunkowy** *adj*: **mieszkanie kwaterunkowe** ≈ council flat (*Brit*), ≈ public housing (*US*)
**kwe|sta** (**-sty, -sty**) (*dat sg* **-ście**) *f* collection (*of money for charity*)
**kwesti|a** (**-i, -e**) (*gen pl* **-i**) *f* (*sprawa*) issue; (*Teatr*) line(s *pl*); **~ czasu/pieniędzy** a matter *lub* question of time/money; **to (tylko) ~ czasu** it's (only) a matter of time; **to nie ulega kwestii** there is no doubt about it
**kwestionariusz** (**-a, -e**) (*gen pl* **-y**) *m* questionnaire
**kwestion|ować (-uję, -ujesz)** (*perf* **za-**) *vt* to (call into) question
**kwesto|r** (**-ra, -rzy**) (*loc sg* **-rze**) *m* (*Uniw*) bursar
**kwestu|ra** (**-ry, -ry**) (*dat sg* **-rze**) *f* (*Uniw*) bursar's office
**kwiaciar|ka** (**-ki, -ki**) (*dat sg* **-ce**, *gen pl* **-ek**) *f* flower girl
**kwiaciar|nia** (**-ni, -nie**) (*gen pl* **-ni**) *f* florist('s)
**kwia|t** (**-tu, -ty**) (*loc sg* **kwiecie**) *m* (*cięty, polny*) flower; (*roślina doniczkowa*) plant; (*na drzewie*) blossom; **~ młodzieży** the flower *lub* cream of youth; **w kwiecie wieku** (*przen*) in the flower *lub* prime of life
**kwiat|ek** (**-ka, -ki**) (*instr sg* **-kiem**) *m dimin od* **kwiat**
**kwi|czeć (-czę, -czysz)** (*perf* **-knąć**) *vi* to squeak
**kwie|cień** (**-tnia, -tnie**) (*gen pl* **-tni**) *m* April
**kwiecisty** *adj* (*łąka*) flowery; (*tkanina, sukienka*) flowered; (*przen*: *styl*) florid
**kwietni|k** (**-ka, -ki**) (*instr sg* **-kiem**) *m* flowerbed
**kwietniowy** *adj* April *attr*
**kwil|ić (-ę, -isz)** *vi* to whimper
**kwin|ta** (**-ty, -ty**) (*dat sg* **-cie**) *f*: **spuścić** (*perf*) **nos na kwintę** to make *lub* pull a long face
**kwintal** (**-a, -e**) (*gen pl* **-i**) *m* (*Rol*) quintal (*= 100 kg*)
**kwintesencj|a** (**-i**) *f* quintessence
**kwinte|t** (**-tu, -ty**) (*loc sg* **-cie**) *m* (*Muz*) quintet
**kwi|t** (**-tu, -ty**) (*loc sg* **-cie**) *m* receipt; **~ bagażowy** luggage receipt *lub* check (*US*)
**kwita** *inv*: **jesteśmy ~** (*pot*) we're quits *lub* square (*pot*)
**kwit|ek** (**-ka, -ki**) (*instr sg* **-kiem**) *m dimin od* **kwit**; **z kwitkiem** empty-handed
**kwitnący** *adj* (*kwiat*) blooming; (*drzewo*) blossoming; (*przen*) flourishing, thriving
**kwit|nąć (-nie)** *vi* (*o kwiatach*) to bloom; (*o drzewach*) to blossom; (*przen*) to flourish, to thrive
**kwit|ować (-uję, -ujesz)** *vt* (*perf* **po-**); **~ odbiór czegoś** to sign for sth, to acknowledge receipt of sth; **~ (s~** *perf*) **coś uśmiechem** to greet sth with a wry smile
**kwi|z** (**-zu, -zy**) (*loc sg* **-zie**) *m* = **quiz**
**kworum** *nt inv* quorum
**kwo|ta** (**-ty, -ty**) (*dat sg* **-cie**) *f* sum, amount; **~ 100 złotych** the amount of 100 zloty
**kynologiczny** *adj*: **związek ~** kennel club

# Ll

**L, l**[1] *nt inv (litera)* L, l; **L jak Leon** ≈ L for Lucy (*Brit*), ≈ L for Love (*US*)

**l**[2] *abbr* (= *litr*) l (= *litre*)

**labiryn|t** (**-tu, -ty**) (*loc sg* **-cie**) *m* labyrinth, maze

**laboran|t** (**-ta, -ci**) (*loc sg* **-cie**) *m* lab(oratory) assistant

**laborant|ka** (**-ki, -ki**) (*dat sg* **-ce**, *gen pl* **-ek**) *f* lab(oratory) assistant

**laboratori|um** (**-um, -a**) (*gen pl* **-ów**) *nt inv in sg* lab(oratory); ~ **językowe** language lab(oratory)

**laboratoryjny** *adj* lab(oratory) *attr*

**lać (leję, lejesz)** *vt (płyn)* to pour; *(pot: bić)* (*perf* **z-**) to beat, to belt (*pot*) ▷ *vi (o deszczu)* to pour; *(pot!: oddawać mocz)* to piss (*pot!*); **leje jak z cebra** *(przen: pot)* the rain's *lub* it's pouring down; **lać wodę** *(pot: mówić, pisać nieściśle)* to waffle (*pot*); **lać się** *(o wodzie, krwi)* *vr* to pour; *(pot: bić się)* to fight

**la|da** (**-dy, -dy**) (*dat sg* **-dzie**) *f* (*też:* **lada sklepowa**) counter ▷ *inv:* ~ **dzień/chwila** any day/moment; **spod lady** *(kupować, sprzedawać)* under the counter; **nie ~ sukces** a huge success; ~ **kto/co** anyone/anything

**lagu|na** (**-ny, -ny**) (*dat sg* **-nie**) *f* lagoon

**laicki** *adj* lay

**laicyzacj|a** (**-i**) *f* secularization

**lai|k** (**-ka, -cy**) (*instr sg* **-kiem**) *m* layman

**la|k** (**-ku, -ki**) (*instr sg* **-kiem**) *m* sealing wax

**lakie|r** (**-ru, -ry**) (*loc sg* **-rze**) *m* varnish, lacquer; ~ **do paznokci** nail polish; ~ **do włosów** hair spray

**lakier|ki** (**-ek**) *pl* patent leather shoes *pl*

**lakierni|k** (**-ka, -cy**) (*instr sg* **-kiem**) *m* painter

**lakier|ować (-uję, -ujesz)** (*perf* **po-**) *vt (paznokcie)* to polish; *(meble)* to varnish; *(samochód)* to paint

**lakmusowy** *adj*: **papierek ~** litmus *lub* test paper

**lakoniczny** *adj* laconic

**lak|ować (-uję, -ujesz)** (*perf* **za-**) *vt* to seal

**lal|ka** (**-ki, -ki**) (*dat sg* **-ce**, *gen pl* **-ek**) *f (zabawka)* doll; *(kukiełka)* puppet

**la|ma**[1] (**-my**) (*dat sg* **-mie**) *f (Zool)* (*nom pl* **-my**) llama; *(materiał)* lamé

**la|ma**[2] (**-my, -mowie**) (*dat sg* **-mie**) *m decl like f in sg (mnich)* lama

**lamen|t** (**-tu, -ty**) (*loc sg* **-cie**) *m* lament

**lament|ować (-uję, -ujesz)** *vi* to lament

**lamina|t** (**-tu, -ty**) (*loc sg* **-cie**) *m* laminate

**lamin|ować (-uję, -ujesz)** (*perf* **z-**) *vt* to laminate

**lam|ować (-uję, -ujesz)** (*perf* **ob-**) *vt* to trim

**lamów|ka** (**-ki, -ki**) (*dat sg* **-ce**, *gen pl* **-ek**) *f* trimming

**lam|pa** (**-py, -py**) (*dat sg* **-pie**) *f* lamp; *(Elektr)* valve (*Brit*), (vacuum) tube (*US*); ~ **błyskowa** flash(light); ~ **naftowa** paraffin lamp; ~ **kwarcowa** sunlamp

**lampar|t** (**-ta, -ty**) (*loc sg* **-cie**) *m* leopard

**lampa|s** (**-sa, -sy**) (*loc sg* **-sie**) *m* stripe (*on trousers*)

**lampio|n** (**-nu, -ny**) (*loc sg* **-nie**) *m* Chinese lantern

**lamp|ka** (**-ki, -ki**) (*dat sg* **-ce**, *gen pl* **-ek**) *f (mała lampa)* lamp; *(kieliszek)* glass; ~ **nocna** bedside lamp; ~ **kontrolna** control light

**lamu|s** (**-sa**) (*loc sg* **-sie**) *m*: **złożyć** (*perf*) **coś do ~a** to scrap *lub* discard sth

**lanc|a** (**-y, -e**) *f* lance

**lance|t** (**-tu, -ty**) (*loc sg* **-cie**) *m (Med)* lancet

**landryn|ka** (**-ki, -ki**) (*dat sg* **-ce**, *gen pl* **-ek**) *f* fruit drop

**langu|sta** (**-sty, -sty**) (*dat sg* **-ście**) *f (Zool)* spiny lobster

**lani|e** (**-a**) *nt* hiding, beating; **dostać** (*perf*) ~ to take a hiding; **spuścić** (*perf*) **komuś ~** to give sb a thrashing

**lans|ować (-uję, -ujesz)** (*perf* **wy-**) *vt* to promote, to launch

**lany** *adj*: **lane żelazo** cast iron; **lane kluski** egg noodles; ~ **poniedziałek** *Easter Monday, on which a custom in Poland is for people to sprinkle each other with water*

**lapidarny** *adj* terse, curt

**Laponi|a** (**-i**) *f* Lapland

**Lapończy|k** (**-ka, -cy**) (*instr sg* **-kiem**) *m* Lapp

**lapsu|s** (**-su, -sy**) (*loc sg* **-sie**) *m* gaffe, slip

**lapto|p** (**-pa, -py**) (*loc sg* **-pie**) *m* laptop (computer)

**lar|wa** (**-wy**, **-wy**) (*dat sg* **-wie**) *f* larva
**laryngolo|g** (**-ga**, **-gowie** *lub* **-dzy**) (*instr sg* **-giem**) *m* (ear, nose and) throat specialist
**laryngologi|a** (**-i**) *f* otolaryngology
**la|s** (**-su**, **-sy**) (*loc sg* **lesie**) *m* (*duży*) forest; (*mały*) wood; (*przen*: *rąk*, *sztandarów*) forest; **las iglasty/liściasty** coniferous/deciduous forest
**las|ek** (**-ku**, **-ki**) (*instr sg* **-kiem**) *m* grove, wood
**lase|r** (**-ra**, **-ry**) (*loc sg* **-rze**) *m* laser
**laserowy** *adj* laser *attr*
**las|ka** (**-ki**, **-ki**) (*dat sg* **-ce**, *gen pl* **-ek**) *f* cane, walking stick; (*pot*: *dziewczyna*) chick (*pot*); **chodzić o lasce** to use a stick *lub* cane (for walking); **~ marszałkowska** speaker's staff (*in parliament*)
**laskowy** *adj*: **orzech ~** hazelnut
**las|so** (**-sa**, **-sa**) (*loc sg* **-sie**) *nt* lasso
**lastry|ko** (**-ka**) (*instr sg* **-kiem**) *nt or inv* terrazzo, Venetian mosaic
**lat|a** (**-**) *pl* years *pl*; (*wiek*) age; **~ dwudzieste/trzydzieste** the twenties/thirties; **od wielu lat** for many years; **przed laty** many years ago; **ostatnimi laty** in recent years; **sto lat!** many happy returns (of the day)!; **ile masz lat?** how old are you?; **mam 10 lat** I'm ten (years old); *patrz też* **rok**
**lat|ać** (**-am**, **-asz**) *vi* to fly; (*pot*: *biegać*) to run
**latający** *adj*: **~ talerz** flying saucer; **L~ Holender** Flying Dutchman
**latar|ka** (**-ki**, **-ki**) (*dat sg* **-ce**, *gen pl* **-ek**) *f* torch (*Brit*), flashlight (*US*)
**latar|nia** (**-ni**, **-nie**) (*gen pl* **-ni**) *f* (*uliczna*) street lamp; (*przenośna*) lantern; **~ morska** lighthouse
**lata|wiec** (**-wca**, **-wce**) *m* kite
**la|to** (**-ta**, **-ta**) (*loc sg* **lecie**) *nt* summer; **latem** *lub* **w lecie** in (the) summer; **babie ~** (*pajęczyna*) gossamer; (*pora roku*) Indian Summer
**latorośl** (**-i**, **-e**) (*gen pl* **-i**) *f* (*roślina*) vine; (*przen*: *potomek*) offspring
**latry|na** (**-ny**, **-ny**) (*dat sg* **-nie**) *f* latrine
**latynoamerykański** *adj* Latin American
**Latyno|s** (**-sa**, **-si**) (*loc sg* **-sie**) *m* Latin American
**latynoski** *adj* Latin American
**laurea|t** (**-ta**, **-ci**) (*loc sg* **-cie**) *m* prizewinner, laureate
**laureat|ka** (**-ki**, **-ki**) (*dat sg* **-ce**, *gen pl* **-ek**) *f* prizewinner, laureate
**laur|ka** (**-ki**, **-ki**) (*dat sg* **-ce**, *gen pl* **-ek**) *f* card
**laurowy** *adj* (*wieniec*, *drzewo*) laurel *attr*; **liść ~** bay leaf
**laur|y** (**-ów**) *pl*: **zdobywać** *lub* **zbierać ~** to win *lub* reap laurels (*przen*); **~ olimpijskie** (*Sport*) Olympic laurels; **spoczywać (spocząć** *perf*) **na laurach** to rest on one's laurels
**la|wa** (**-wy**) (*dat sg* **-wie**) *f* lava
**lawen|da** (**-dy**, **-dy**) (*dat sg* **-dzie**) *f* lavender
**lawi|na** (**-ny**, **-ny**) (*dat sg* **-nie**) *f* avalanche; (*przen*) cornucopia
**lawir|ować (-uję, -ujesz)** *vi* (*kluczyć*) to swerve; (*przen*) to steer a middle course (*pot*)
**lazł** *itd. vb patrz* **leźć**
**lazu|r** (**-ru**) (*loc sg* **-rze**) *m* azure
**lazurowy** *adj* azure
**lą|d** (**-du**, **-dy**) (*loc sg* **-dzie**) *m* land; **stały ląd** mainland, dry land; **schodzić (zejść** *perf*) **na ląd** to disembark, to go ashore
**ląd|ować (-uję, -ujesz)** (*perf* **wy-**) *vi* to land
**lądowa|nie** (**-nia**, **-nia**) (*gen pl* **-ń**) *nt* landing, touchdown
**lądowis|ko** (**-ka**, **-ka**) (*instr sg* **-kiem**) *nt* landing field *lub* strip
**lądowy** *adj* (*wojska*) ground *attr*; (*zwierzęta*) terrestrial; (*granica*, *obszar*) land *attr*; (*klimat*) continental; (*transport*) overland; (*budownictwo*) land; **szczur ~** (*przen*) landlubber (*pot*)
**lągł** *itd. vb patrz* **lęgnąć się**
**leasin|g** (**-gu**) (*instr sg* **-giem**) *m* (*Ekon*) leasing
**le|c, le|gnąć (-gnę, -gniesz)** (*imp* **-gnij**, *pt* **-gł**) *vi* (*książk*: *położyć się*) to lie down; (: *zginąć*) to fall
**lecie** *n patrz* **lato**
**le|cieć (-cę, -cisz)** (*imp* **-ć**) *vi* (*o ptaku*, *samolocie*) (*perf* **po-**) to fly; (*o wodzie*, *krwi*) (*perf* **po-**) to flow; (*o liściach*, *kamieniach*) (*perf* **z-**) to fall (down); (*pot*: *pędzić*) (*perf* **po-**) to run; (*pot*: *w radiu*, *telewizji*) to air, to be on
**lecz** *conj* but, yet
**leczeni|e** (**-a**) *nt* treatment
**lecznic|a** (**-y**, **-e**) *f* clinic; **~ dla zwierząt** animal *lub* veterinary clinic
**lecznict|wo** (**-wa**) (*loc sg* **-wie**) *nt* health care
**leczniczy** *adj* (*ziele*, *środek*) medicinal; (*działanie*) therapeutic
**lecz|yć (-ę, -ysz)** (*perf* **wy-**) *vt* (*o człowieku*) to treat; (*o substancji*) to cure; **leczyć się** *vr* to get treatment
**ledwo, ledwie** *adv*: **~ widoczny/słyszalny** barely visible/audible; **~ umie czytać** he can hardly read; **~ (co) wyszedł, a już ...** he's only just left, and ..., no sooner had he left than ...; **~ ~** (*pot*) only just (*pot*)
**legalizacj|a** (**-i**) *f* legalization
**legaliz|ować (-uję, -ujesz)** (*perf* **za-**) *vt* to legalize
**legalnie** *adv* legally, lawfully
**legalnoś|ć** (**-ci**) *f* legality, lawfulness
**legalny** *adj* legal, lawful
**legen|da** (**-dy**, **-dy**) (*dat sg* **-dzie**) *f* legend
**legendarny** *adj* legendary
**leggins|y** (**-ów**) *pl* leggings *pl*

**legi|a** (**-i, -e**) (*gen pl* **-i**) *f* legion; **L~ Cudzoziemska** Foreign Legion; **L~ Honorowa** Legion of Honour (*Brit*) *lub* Honor (*US*)
**legio|n** (**-nu, -ny**) (*loc sg* **-nie**) *m* legion
**legislacj|a** (**-i, -e**) (*gen pl* **-i**) *f* legislation
**legislacyjny** *adj* legislative
**legitymacj|a** (**-i, -e**) (*gen pl* **-i**) *f* (*identyfikująca*) ID, identity card; (*członkowska*) membership card
**legitym|ować (-uję, -ujesz)** (*perf* **wy-**) *vt*: **~ kogoś** to check sb's ID; **legitymować się** *vr* (*okazywać legitymację*) (*perf* **wy-**) to show one's ID; **~ się tytułem** to hold a title
**leg|nąć (-nę, -niesz)** (*imp* **-nij**, *pt* **-ł**) *vb patrz* **lec**
**legowis|ko** (**-ka, -ka**) (*instr sg* **-kiem**) *nt* (*miejsce do leżenia*) bed; (*zwierzęce*) den, lair
**legumi|na** (**-ny, -ny**) (*dat sg* **-nie**) *f* pudding
**le|j** (**-ja, -je**) *m* (*gen pl* **-jów**) (*zagłębienie*) crater
**lejc|e** (**-ów**) *pl* reins *pl*
**lej|ek** (**-ka, -ki**) (*instr sg* **-kiem**) *m* funnel
**leję** *itd. vb patrz* **lać**
**lejkowaty** *adj* funnel-shaped
**le|k** (**-ku, -ki**) (*instr sg* **-kiem**) *m* medicine, drug
**lek.** *abbr* (= *lekarz*) ≈ MD
**lekar|ka** (**-ki, -ki**) (*dat sg* **-ce**, *gen pl* **-ek**) *f* (woman) physician *lub* doctor
**lekarski** *adj* (*gabinet, porada*) physician's *attr*, doctor's *attr*; (*badanie*) physical, medical; (*zaświadczenie, zwolnienie*) doctor's *attr*; **piłka lekarska** medicine ball
**lekarst|wo** (**-wa, -wa**) (*loc sg* **-wie**) *nt* medicine, drug; (*przen*: *środek*) cure; **(jak) na ~** almost nonexistent
**lekarz** (**-a, -e**) (*gen pl* **-y**) *m* doctor, physician; **~ ogólny** general practitioner; **~ rodzinny** family doctor
**lekceważąco** *adv* disrespectfully
**lekceważący** *adj* disrespectful
**lekceważeni|e** (**-a**) *nt* disrespect
**lekceważ|yć (-ę, -ysz)** (*perf* **z-**) *vt* (*traktować pogardliwie*) to scorn; (*bagatelizować*) to disregard
**lekcj|a** (**-i, -e**) (*gen pl* **-i**) *f* lesson; (*szkolna, prywatna*) lesson, class; **lekcje** *pl* (*zadanie domowe*): **odrabiać (odrobić** *perf*) **lekcje** to do (one's) homework; **~ angielskiego/ matematyki** English/math lesson *lub* class
**lekcyjny** *adj* (*dziennik, godzina*) teaching *attr*
**lekki** (*comp* **lżejszy**) *adj* light; (*mróz, zmęczenie*) slight; (*zapach*) faint; **lekką ręką** recklessly
**lekko** (*comp* **lżej**) *adv* lightly; (*nieznacznie*) slightly; **~ licząc** at least; **~ ubrany** dressed lightly; **~ ranny** slightly wounded; **z lekka** a little
**lekkoatle|ta** (**-ty, -ci**) (*dat sg* **-cie**) *m decl like f in sg* athlete
**lekkoatlet|ka** (**-ki, -ki**) (*dat sg* **-ce**, *gen pl* **-ek**) *f* athlete
**lekkoatletyczny** *adj* (*meeting, konkurencja*) athletic (*Brit*), track-and-field *attr* (*US*)
**lekkoatlety|ka** (**-ki**) *f* (*dat sg* **-ce**) athletics *pl* (*Brit*), track and field sports *pl* (*US*)
**lekkomyślnie** *adv* recklessly
**lekkomyślnoś|ć** (**-ci**) *f* recklessness
**lekkomyślny** *adj* reckless
**lekkostrawny** *adj* light (*food*)
**lekoma|n** (**-na, -ni**) (*loc sg* **-nie**) *m* pill taker *lub* addict
**lekoman|ka** (**-ki, -ki**) (*dat sg* **-ce**, *gen pl* **-ek**) *f* pill taker *lub* addict
**leksyko|n** (**-nu, -ny**) (*loc sg* **-nie**) *m* lexicon
**lekto|r** (**-ra, -rzy**) (*loc sg* **-rze**) *m* (*Szkol*) instructor; (*spiker*) announcer
**lektora|t** (**-tu, -ty**) (*loc sg* **-cie**) *m* (*Szkol*) (foreign language) course
**lektu|ra** (**-ry, -ry**) (*dat sg* **-rze**) *f* (*czytanie*) reading; (*materiały do czytania*) reading material *lub* matter; (: *Szkol*) suggested reading; **spis lektur** reading list
**lekty|ka** (**-ki, -ki**) (*dat sg* **-ce**) *f* litter (*vehicle*)
**lemonia|da** (**-dy, -dy**) (*dat sg* **-dzie**) *f* lemonade
**len** (**lnu, lny**) (*loc sg* **lnie**) *m* (*roślina*) flax; (*tkanina*) linen
**le|nić się (-nię, -nisz)** (*imp* **-ń**) *vr* to be (bone) idle
**lenist|wo** (**-wa**) (*loc sg* **-wie**) *nt* laziness
**leniuch** (**-a, -y**) *m* (*pot*) lazybones *sg* (*pot*)
**leniuch|ować (-uję, -ujesz)** *vi* to laze (away)
**leni|wiec** (**-wca, -wce**) *m* (*Zool*) sloth; (*pot*: *leniuch*) (*voc sg* **-wcze**) lazybones *sg* (*pot*)
**leniwy** *adj* lazy; **pierogi leniwe** cottage cheese dumplings
**len|no** (**-na, -na**) (*loc sg* **-nie**) *nt* (*Hist*) feud
**lentek|s**® (**-su, -sy**) (*loc sg* **-sie**) *m* ≈ linoleum
**le|ń** (**-nia, -nie**) (*gen pl* **-ni** *lub* **-niów**) *m* idler, sluggard
**le|p** (**-pu, -py**) (*loc sg* **-pie**) *m*: **lep na muchy** fly paper; **brać (wziąć** *perf*) **kogoś na lep (czegoś)** (*przen*) to lure sb (by sth)
**le|pić (-pię, -pisz)** *vt* (*formować*) (*perf* **u-**) to model; (*kleić*) (*perf* **z-**) to glue (together); **lepić się** *vr* (*przyklejać się*) (*perf* **przy-**) to stick; (*być lepkim*) to stick, to be sticky
**lepiej** *adv comp od* **dobrze** better; **coraz ~** better and better; **im prędzej tym ~** the sooner the better; **~ już pójdę** I'd better go now; **tym ~!** that's even better!
**lepki** *adj* sticky
**lepsz|e** (**-ego**) *nt decl like adj*; **zmiana na ~** a change for the better; **zmierzać ku ~mu** to improve

l

**lepszy** *adj comp od* **dobry** better; **pierwszy ~** (*pot*) any old one; **kto pierwszy ten ~** first come, first served
**lesbij|ka** (**-ki, -ki**) (*dat sg* **-ce**, *gen pl* **-ek**) *f* lesbian
**lese|r** (**-ra, -rzy**) (*loc sg* **-rze**) *m* (*pot*: *pej*) layabout (*pot*)
**lesie** *n patrz* **las**
**leszcz** (**-a, -e**) (*gen pl* **-y** *lub* **-ów**) *m* bream (*freshwater fish*)
**leszczy|na** (**-ny, -ny**) (*dat sg* **-nie**) *f* (*Bot*) hazel
**leśnict|wo** (**-wa**) (*loc sg* **-wie**) *nt* forestry
**leśniczów|ka** (**-ki, -ki**) (*dat sg* **-ce**, *gen pl* **-ek**) *f* forester's lodge
**leśnicz|y** (**-ego, -owie**) *m decl like adj* forest ranger
**leśni|k** (**-ka, -cy**) (*instr sg* **-kiem**) *m* forester
**leśny** *adj* forest *attr*
**letar|g** (**-gu**) (*instr sg* **-giem**) *m* lethargy
**letni** *adj* (*wakacje, sukienka*) summer *attr*; (*woda, herbata*) lukewarm, tepid; **czas ~** Daylight Saving Time
**letnis|ko** (**-ka, -ka**) (*instr sg* **-kiem**) *nt* summer resort
**letniskowy** *adj* summer-resort *attr*, holiday *attr*
**leukocy|t** (**-tu, -ty**) (*loc sg* **-cie**) *m* leucocyte
**lew** (**lwa, lwy**) (*loc sg* **lwie**) *m* (*Zool*) lion; **Lew** (*Astrologia*) Leo; **odważny jak lew** (as) brave as a lion
**le|wa** (**-wy, -wy**) (*dat sg* **-wie**) *f* (*Karty*) trick
**lewacki** *adj* (extreme) leftist
**lewar|ek** (**-ka, -ki**) (*instr sg* **-kiem**) *m* (*Mot*) jack
**lewaty|wa** (**-wy, -wy**) (*dat sg* **-wie**) *f* enema
**lewic|a** (**-y**) *f* (*Pol*) the left
**lewicowy** *adj* left-wing, leftist
**lewitacj|a** (**-i**) (*dat sg* **-i**) *f* levitation
**lewkoni|a** (**-i, -e**) (*gen pl* **-i**) *f* (*Bot*) stock, gillyflower
**lewo** *adv*: **w** *lub* **na ~** (to the) left; **na prawo i ~** right and left, all over the place; **na ~** (*pot*: *sprzedawać, załatwiać*) on the q.t. (*pot*), under the table (*pot*); **w ~** (*o ruchu obrotowym*) anticlockwise
**lewobrzeżny** *adj* left-bank *attr*
**leworęczny** *adj* left-handed
**lewoskrzydło|wy** (**-wego, -wi**) *m decl like adj* (*Sport*) left wing(er)
**lewostronny** *adj*: **ruch ~** left-hand driving *lub* traffic
**lewy** *adj* (*bok, but*) left; (*strona tkaniny*) inside *attr*; (*pot*: *sfałszowany*) phoney (*pot*); **~ pas** (*Mot*) outside *lub* fast lane
**le|źć** (**-zę, -ziesz**) (*imp* **-ź**, *pt* **lazł, leźli**) *vi* (*pot*) to straggle
**leża|k** (**-ka, -ki**) (*instr sg* **-kiem**) *m* deckchair (*Brit*), beach chair (*US*)
**leżak|ować** (**-uję, -ujesz**) *vi* (*o trunkach*) to mature
**leżąco** *adv*: **na ~** lying down
**leż|eć** (**-ę, -ysz**) (*pt* **-ał**) *vi* to lie; (*o ubraniu*) to fit; **~ w łóżku/szpitalu** to stay in bed/in (the (*US*)) hospital; **~ odłogiem** (*o ziemi*) to lie fallow; **~ na pieniądzach** (*pot*) to be rolling in it (*pot*); **leży mi to na sercu** I have it at heart; **leży mi to na sumieniu** it lies heavy on my conscience; **jeśli tak, to leżę** (*pot*) if so, I'm cooked (*pot*); **to nie leży w moim interesie** it's not in my interest
**lędź|wie** (**-wi**) *pl* loins *pl*
**lęg|nąć się** (**-nie**) (*imp* **-nij**, *pt* **lągł, lęgła**) *vi* (*o zwierzętach*: *z jaja*) to hatch; (*: żyworodnie*) to be born; (*przen*: *o myślach*) to keep coming
**lę|k** (**-ku, -ki**) (*instr sg* **-kiem**) *m* fear, anxiety; **lęk przestrzeni/wysokości** a fear of open spaces/heights
**lęk|ać się** (**-am, -asz**) *vr* to fear
**lękliwy** *adj* apprehensive
**lg|nąć** (**-nę, -niesz**) (*imp* **-nij**) *vi* (*przylepiać się*) (*perf* **przy-**); **~** (**do** *+gen*) to cling (to)
**lia|na** (**-ny, -ny**) (*dat sg* **-nie**) *f* liana
**libacj|a** (**-i, -e**) (*gen pl* **-i**) *f* drinking spree
**Liba|n** (**-nu**) (*loc sg* **-nie**) *m* Lebanon
**Libańczy|k** (**-ka, -cy**) (*instr sg* **-kiem**) *m* Lebanese
**libański** *adj* Lebanese
**liberaliz|m** (**-mu**) (*loc sg* **-mie**) *m* liberalism
**liberaliz|ować** (**-uję, -ujesz**) (*perf* **z-**) *vt* to liberalize
**liberalny** *adj* liberal
**libera|ł** (**-ła, -łowie**) (*loc sg* **-le**) *m* liberal
**Libi|a** (**-i**) *f* Libya
**Libijczy|k** (**-ka, -cy**) (*instr sg* **-kiem**) *m* Libyan
**libijski** *adj* Libyan
**liceali|sta** (**-sty, -ści**) (*dat sg* **-ście**) *m decl like f in sg* secondary school student (*Brit*), high school student (*US*)
**licealist|ka** (**-ki, -ki**) (*dat sg* **-ce**, *gen pl* **-ek**) *f* secondary school student (*Brit*), high school student (*US*)
**licealny** *adj* secondary school *attr* (*Brit*), high school *attr* (*US*)
**licencj|a** (**-i, -e**) (*gen pl* **-i**) *f* licence (*Brit*), license (*US*)
**licencja|t** (**-tu, -ty**) (*loc sg* **-cie**) *m* ≈ Bachelor's degree
**licencjonowany** *adj* licensed
**lice|um** (**-um, -a**) (*gen pl* **-ów**) *nt inv in sg* secondary school (*Brit*), high school (*US*); **~ zawodowe** vocational school; **~ ogólnokształcące** ≈ grammar school (*Brit*), ≈ high school (*US*)
**lich|o** (**-a**) *nt* devil; **do licha!** for God's sake!; **co u licha ...?** what on earth ...?; **niech cię ~**

**(porwie)!** to hell with you!; **~ nie śpi** accidents will happen
**lichtarz** (**-a, -e**) (*gen pl* **-y**) *m* candlestick
**lich|wa** (**-wy, -wy**) (*dat sg* **-wie**) *f* usury
**lichwiarz** (**-a, -e**) *m* usurer
**lichy** *adj* (*kiepski*) shoddy; (*niepozorny*) flimsy
**lic|ować (-uję, -ujesz)** *vi*: **nie ~ z czymś** (*książk*) to be incompatible with sth
**licytacj|a** (**-i, -e**) (*gen pl* **-i**) *f* (*przetarg*) auction; (*Karty*) bidding
**licyt|ować (-uję, -ujesz)** *vt* (*sprzedać na aukcji*) (*perf* **z-**) to auction; (*Karty*) (*perf* **za-**) to bid
**licz|ba** (**-by, -by**) (*dat sg* **-bie**) *f* number; (*Jęz*): **~ pojedyncza/mnoga** singular/plural (number); **w liczbie 40 osób** forty strong
**liczbowy** *adj* numerical; **gra liczbowa** (number) lottery
**liczebnie** *adv* in number; **przeważać ~ nad** *+instr* to outnumber
**liczebni|k** (**-ka, -ki**) (*instr sg* **-kiem**) *m* numeral; **~ główny/porządkowy** cardinal/ordinal number
**liczebnoś|ć** (**-ci**) *f* number
**liczebny** *adj* (*przewaga*) measured in numbers; **stan ~** number
**licznie** *adv* in large numbers
**liczni|k** (**-ka, -ki**) (*instr sg* **-kiem**) *m* (*gazowy, telefoniczny, prądu*) meter; (*Mat*) numerator
**liczny** *adj* numerous
**licz|yć (-ę, -ysz)** *vt* (*perf* **po-**) to count ▷ *vi* (*rachować*) (*perf* **po-**) to calculate; (*wynosić*): **klasa liczy 20 osób** the class numbers 20; **~ na** *+acc* to count on; **nie licząc** *+gen* not counting; **liczyć się** *vr* (*mieć znaczenie*) to matter; **~ się z** *+instr* to take into account; **(nie) ~ się ze słowami** (not) to watch one's tongue
**liczyd|ło** (**-ła, -ła**) (*loc sg* **-le**, *gen pl* **-eł**) *nt* abacus
**lide|r** (**-ra, -rzy**) (*loc sg* **-rze**) *m* leader
**Liechtenstei|n** (**-nu**) (*loc sg* **-nie**) *m* Liechtenstein
**liftin|g** (**-gu, -gi**) (*instr sg* **-giem**) *m* facelift
**li|ga** (**-gi, -gi**) (*dat sg* **-dze**) *f* league; **pierwsza ~** (*Futbol*) ≈ premier league (*Brit*); **druga ~** (*Futbol*) ≈ division one (*Brit*)
**ligowy** *adj* league *attr*
**likie|r** (**-ru, -ry**) (*loc sg* **-rze**) *m* liqueur
**likwidacj|a** (**-i, -e**) (*gen pl* **-i**) *f* liquidation; (*zniesienie*) abolition
**likwid|ować (-uję, -ujesz)** (*perf* **z-**) *vt* (*usuwać*) to eliminate; (*zabijać*) to liquidate
**lila** *inv*: **kolor ~** lilac; **sukienka ~** lilac dress
**lili|a** (**-i, -e**) (*gen pl* **-i**) *f* lily
**liliowy** *adj* lilac
**lim|fa** (**-fy**) (*dat sg* **-fie**) *f* lymph
**limfatyczny** *adj* lymphatic; **węzeł ~** lymph node
**limi|t** (**-tu, -ty**) (*loc sg* **-cie**) *m* limit
**limit|ować (-uję, -ujesz)** *vt* to limit
**limuzy|na** (**-ny, -ny**) (*dat sg* **-nie**) *f* limo(usine)
**li|n** (**-na, -ny**) (*loc sg* **-nie**) *m* (*Zool*) tench
**li|na** (**-ny, -ny**) (*dat sg* **-nie**) *f* rope; **~ holownicza** towline; **przeciąganie liny** tug-of-war
**lincz** (**-u, -e**) *m* lynch
**lincz|ować (-uję, -ujesz)** (*perf* **z-**) *vt* to lynch
**lingwi|sta** (**-sty, -ści**) (*dat sg* **-ście**) *m decl like f in sg* linguist
**lini|a** (**-i, -e**) (*gen pl* **-i**) *f* line; (*trasa*) line, route; (*ród*) line of descent; (*sylwetka, zarys*) contour; **w linie** (*zeszyt*) lined; **~ stacjonarna** (*Tel*) landline; **porażka na całej linii** across-the-board defeat; **iść (pójść** *perf*) **po linii najmniejszego oporu** to take the line of least resistance; **dbać o linię** to watch one's weight
**lini|eć (-eje)** (*perf* **wy-**) *vi* to moult (*Brit*), to molt (*US*)
**linij|ka** (**-ki, -ki**) (*dat sg* **-ce**, *gen pl* **-ek**) *f* (*przyrząd*) ruler; (*wiersz tekstu*) line
**linio|wiec** (**-wca, -wce**) *m* liner
**liniowy** *adj* linear; **sędzia ~** linesman
**lin|ka** (**-ki, -ki**) (*dat sg* **-ce**, *gen pl* **-ek**) *f* cord, line; **~ holownicza** towline
**linole|um** (**-um, -a**) (*gen pl* **-ów**) *nt inv in sg* linoleum
**linowy** *adj*: **kolejka linowa** (*system transportu*) cable railway; (*wagonik*) cable car
**li|pa** (**-py, -py**) (*dat sg* **-pie**) *f* (*Bot*) lime (tree), linden; (*pot: tandeta*) trash (*pot*); (*pot: oszustwo*) eyewash (*pot*)
**lipcowy** *adj* July *attr*
**li|piec** (**-pca, -pce**) *m* July
**lipny** *adj* (*pot: fałszywy*) phoney (*pot*); (*pot: tandetny*) trashy (*pot*)
**li|r** (**-ra, -ry**) (*loc sg* **-rze**) *m* (*waluta*) lira
**li|ra** (**-ry, -ry**) (*dat sg* **-rze**) *f* lyre
**liryczny** *adj* lyrical
**liry|k** (**-ku, -ki**) (*instr sg* **-kiem**) *m* (*wiersz*) lyric
**liry|ka** (**-ki**) (*dat sg* **-ce**) *f* lyric verse
**liryz|m** (**-mu**) (*loc sg* **-mie**) *m* lyricism
**li|s** (**-sa, -sy**) (*loc sg* **-sie**) *m* fox; **chytry jak lis** (as) sly as a fox
**lisic|a** (**-y, -e**) *f* vixen
**li|st** (**-stu, -sty**) (*loc sg* **-ście**) *m* letter; **~ zwykły** surface-mail letter; **~ polecony** registered letter, recorded delivery letter (*Brit*), certified letter (*US*); **~ lotniczy** airmail letter; **~ miłosny** love letter; **~ gończy** (arrest) warrant; **~ pasterski** (*Rel*) pastoral; **~ polecający** letter of recommendation
**li|sta** (**-sty, -sty**) (*dat sg* **-ście**) *f* list; **~ przebojów** (*spis utworów*) the charts *pl*; (*program*) hit parade; **~ obecności** roll; **~ płac**

payroll; ~ **wyborcza** register of voters; **znajdować się/znaleźć się** *perf* **na czarnej liście** to be/go on the black list
**list|ek** (**-ka, -ki**) (*instr sg* **-kiem**) *m dimin od* **liść**
**listew|ka** (**-ki, -ki**) (*dat sg* **-ce**, *gen pl* **-ek**) *f* strip (of wood)
**listonosz** (**-a, -e**) (*gen pl* **-y**) *m* postman (Brit), mailman (US)
**listopa|d** (**-da, -dy**) (*loc sg* **-dzie**) *m* November
**listopadowy** *adj* November *attr*
**listownie** *adv* by mail
**listowny** *adj* written
**listowy** *adj*: **papier** ~ writing paper
**list|wa** (**-wy, -wy**) (*dat sg* **-wie**) *f* (*podkładowa*) batten; (*zewnętrzna*) slat
**lisza|j** (**-ja, -je**) (*gen pl* **-jów** *lub* **-i**) *m* (*Med*) lichen
**liściasty** *adj* deciduous
**liście** *n patrz* **list, lista**
**liś|ć** (**-cia, -cie**) (*gen pl* **-ci**, *instr pl* **-ćmi**) *m* leaf; ~ **bobkowy** *lub* **laurowy** bay leaf
**litani|a** (**-i, -e**) (*gen pl* **-i**) *f* litany
**lite|ra** (**-ry, -ry**) (*loc sg* **-rze**) *f* letter; **wielka** *lub* **duża** ~ capital (letter); **mała** ~ small *lub* lowercase letter; **litery drukowane** printed characters; **cztery litery** (*pot: przen*) bum (*pot*)
**literacki** *adj* literary
**litera|t** (**-ta, -ci**) (*loc sg* **-cie**) *m* man of letters
**literatu|ra** (**-ry, -ry**) (*dat sg* **-rze**) *f* literature; ~ **piękna** belles-lettres
**literaturoznawst|wo** (**-wa**) (*loc sg* **-wie**) *nt* literary studies *pl*
**liter|ować (-uję, -ujesz)** (*perf* **prze-**) *vt* to spell
**literów|ka** (**-ki, -ki**) (*dat sg* **-ce**, *gen pl* **-ek**) *f* misprint
**litewski** *adj* Lithuanian
**litościwy** *adj* merciful
**litoś|ć** (**-ci**) *f* (*łaska*) mercy; (*współczucie*) compassion; **bez litości** without mercy; **robić (zrobić** *perf*) **coś z litości** to do sth out of pity; **na ~ boską!** for heaven's sake!
**lit|ować się (-uję, -ujesz)** (*perf* **z-**) *vr*: **litować się (nad** *+instr*) to have mercy (on)
**lit|r** (**-ra, -ry**) (*loc sg* **-rze**) *m* litre (Brit), liter (US)
**litrowy** *adj* (*butelka, słoik*) one-litre *attr* (Brit), one-liter *attr* (US)
**liturgi|a** (**-i, -e**) (*gen pl* **-i**) *f* liturgy
**liturgiczny** *adj* liturgical
**Lit|wa** (**-wy**) (*dat sg* **-wie**) *f* Lithuania
**Litwi|n** (**-na, -ni**) (*loc sg* **-nie**) *m* Lithuanian
**Litwin|ka** (**-ki, -ki**) (*dat sg* **-ce**, *gen pl* **-ek**) *f* Lithuanian
**li|zać (-żę, -żesz)** (*perf* **-znąć**) *vt* to lick; **palce ~!** scrumptious!, yum-yum! (*pot*), yummy! (*pot*)
**liza|k** (**-ka, -ki**) (*instr sg* **-kiem**) *m* lollipop
**Lizbo|na** (**-ny**) (*dat sg* **-nie**) *f* Lisbon
**li|znąć (-znę, -źniesz)** (*imp* **-źnij**) *vb perf od* **lizać** ▷ *vt perf*: ~ **czegoś** (*pot: poznać, nauczyć się*) to get a smattering of sth
**lizu|s** (**-sa, -sy**) (*loc sg* **-sie**) *m* toady
**lm.** *abbr* (= *liczba mnoga*) pl (= *plural*)
**lniany** *adj* (*płótno*) linen *attr*; (*olej*) linseed *attr*; **siemię lniane** flaxseed, linseed
**lnu** *itd. n patrz* **len**
**lo|b** (**-bu, -by**) (*loc sg* **-bie**) *m* (*Sport*) lob
**lobbin|g** (**-gu, -gi**) (*instr sg* **-giem**) *m* lobbying
**lobby** *nt inv* lobby
**loch** (**-u, -y**) *m* dungeon
**locie** *n patrz* **lot**
**lodołamacz** (**-a, -e**) (*gen pl* **-y**) *m* icebreaker
**lodowaty** *adj* ice-cold; (*przen*) icy
**lodowcowy** *adj* glacial
**lodo|wiec** (**-wca, -wce**) *m* glacier
**lodowis|ko** (**-ka, -ka**) (*instr sg* **-kiem**) *nt* skating *lub* ice rink
**lodowy** *adj* (*twór*) glacial; (*epoka, powłoka*) ice *attr*; (*tort*) ice-cream *attr*; **góra lodowa** iceberg
**lodów|ka** (**-ki, -ki**) (*dat sg* **-ce**, *gen pl* **-ek**) *f* fridge, refrigerator
**lodu** *itd. n patrz* **lód**
**lod|y** (**-ów**) *pl* ice cream; *patrz też* **lód**
**logaryt|m** (**-mu, -my**) (*loc sg* **-mie**) *m* logarithm
**logiczny** *adj* logical
**logi|ka** (**-ki**) (*dat sg* **-ce**) *f* logic
**logo** *nt inv* logo
**logope|da** (**-dy, -dzi**) (*loc sg* **-dzie**) *m* speech therapist
**lojalnie** *adv* loyally
**lojalnoś|ć** (**-ci**) *f* loyalty
**lojalny** *adj* loyal
**lo|k** (**-ku, -ki**) (*instr sg* **-kiem**) *m* curl, lock
**loka|j** (**-ja, -je**) (*gen pl* **-jów** *lub* **-i**) *m* butler
**lokal** (**-u, -e**) (*gen pl* **-i** *lub* **-ów**) *m* (*ogólnie*) premises *pl*; (*restauracja*) restaurant; ~ **mieszkalny** private accommodation; ~ **wyborczy** polling station; ~ **biurowy** office (space); **nocny** ~ night club
**lokalizacj|a** (**-i, -e**) (*gen pl* **-i**) *f* location
**lokaliz|ować (-uję, -ujesz)** (*perf* **z-**) *vt* (*umieszczać*) to situate; (*znajdować*) to locate
**lokalny** *adj* local; **wizja lokalna** (*Prawo*) *inspection at the scene of the crime*
**loka|ta** (**-ty, -ty**) (*dat sg* **-cie**) *f* (*pozycja*) place; (*też*: **lokata kapitału**) (capital) investment; (*też*: **lokata pieniężna**) deposit
**lokato|r** (**-ra, -rzy**) (*loc sg* **-rze**) *m* occupant
**lokator|ka** (**-ki, -ki**) (*dat sg* **-ce**, *gen pl* **-ek**) *f* occupant
**lokomocj|a** (**-i**) *f*: **środek lokomocji** means of transport (Brit) *lub* transportation (US)

**lokomoty|wa** (**-wy, -wy**) (*dat sg* **-wie**) *f* engine, locomotive
**lok|ować (-uję, -ujesz)** (*perf* **u-**) *vt* (*umieszczać*) to place; (*Ekon*) to invest
**loków|ka** (**-ki, -ki**) (*dat sg* **-ce**, *gen pl* **-ek**) *f* curler; ~ **elektryczna** curling tongs *lub* irons
**lokum** *nt inv* (*książk*) venue
**lombar|d** (**-du, -dy**) (*loc sg* **-dzie**) *m* pawnshop
**Londy|n** (**-nu**) (*loc sg* **-nie**) *m* London
**londyńczy|k** (**-ka, -cy**) (*instr sg* **-kiem**) *m* Londoner
**londyński** *adj* London *attr*
**longplay** (**-a, -e**) *m* LP
**lon|t** (**-tu, -ty**) (*loc sg* **-cie**) *m* fuse (*Brit*), fuze (*US*)
**lor|d** (**-da, -dowie**) (*loc sg* **-dzie**) *m* lord
**lornet|ka** (**-ki, -ki**) (*dat sg* **-ce**, *gen pl* **-ek**) *f* binoculars *pl*
**lo|s** (**-su, -sy**) (*loc sg* **-sie**) *m* (*koleje życia*) lot; (*przeznaczenie*) fate; (*na loterii*) (lottery) ticket; **zły los** bad fortune; **ironia losu** (*przen*) an ironic twist of fate; **ciągnąć losy** to draw lots; **masz ci los!** too bad!; **jego losy się ważą** his fate hangs in the balance
**los|ować (-uję, -ujesz)** *vt* (*perf* **wy-**) to draw ▷ *vi* to draw lots
**losowa|nie** (**-nia, -nia**) (*gen pl* **-ń**) *nt* drawing
**losowo** *adv* at random
**losowy** *adj* (*wybór, próba*) random; **zdarzenie losowe** act of God
**lo|t** (**-tu, -ty**) (*loc sg* **-cie**) *m* flight; **widok z lotu ptaka** bird's eye view; **lotem błyskawicy** in a flash; **w lot** instantly
**loteri|a** (**-i, -e**) (*gen pl* **-i**) *f* lottery
**lot|ka** (**-ki, -ki**) (*dat sg* **-ce**, *gen pl* **-ek**) *f* (*Zool*) flight feather; (*Lot*) aileron; (*Sport*) shuttlecock, (badminton) bird
**lot|nia** (**-ni, -nie**) (*gen pl* **-ni**) *f* hang-glider
**lotnict|wo** (**-wa**) (*loc sg* **-wie**) *nt* (*cywilne*) aviation; (*wojskowe*) air force
**lotniczy** *adj* air *attr*; **linia lotnicza** (air) carrier, airline
**lotni|k** (**-ka, -cy**) (*instr sg* **-kiem**) *m* aviator
**lotnis|ko** (**-ka, -ka**) (*instr sg* **-kiem**) *nt* (*pasażerskie*) airport; (*lądowisko*) airfield
**lotnisko|wiec** (**-wca, -wce**) *m* aircraft carrier
**lotny** *adj* (*Chem, Fiz*) volatile; (*bystry*) nimble
**loż|a** (**-y, -e**) (*gen pl* **lóż**) *f* box (*in a theatre*); ~ **masońska** masonic lodge
**lód** (**lodu, lody**) (*loc sg* **lodzie**) *m* ice; **zimny jak lód** (as) cold as ice; **mieć pieniędzy jak lodu** (*pot*) to be rolling in money (*pot*), to have money to burn (*pot*); (*przen*): **zostać** (*perf*) **na lodzie** to be left out in the cold (*przen*); (*przen*): **przełamać** (*perf*) **pierwsze lody** to break the ice (*przen*); *patrz też* **lody**
**lp.** *abbr* (= *liczba porządkowa*) (Item) No.; (*Jęz*: = *liczba pojedyncza*) sg (= *singular*)
**lśniący** *adj* glittering, glistening
**lś|nić (-nię, -nisz)** (*imp* **-nij**) *vi* to glitter, to glisten
**lub** *conj* or; **lub też** or else
**lubiany** *adj* popular
**lu|bić (-bię, -bisz)** *vt* to like; ~ **coś robić** to like doing sth *lub* to do sth; **lubić się** *vr* to like one another
**lubieżni|k** (**-ka, -cy**) (*instr sg* **-kiem**) *m* lecher
**lubieżny** *adj* lascivious; **czyn** ~ lewd conduct
**luboś|ć** (**-ci**) *f*: **robić coś z lubością** to delight in doing sth
**lub|ować się (-uję, -ujesz)** *vr*: **lubować się w czymś** (*książk*) to take delight in sth
**lucer|na** (**-ny, -ny**) (*dat sg* **-nie**, *gen pl* **-n**) *f* (*Bot*) lucerne (*Brit*), alfalfa (*US*)
**lu|d** (**-du**) (*loc sg* **-dzie**) *m* (*masy*) people; (*plemię, szczep*) (*nom pl* **-dy**) people
**ludnoś|ć** (**-ci**) *f* population
**ludobójczy** *adj* genocidal
**ludobójst|wo** (**-wa, -wa**) (*loc sg* **-wie**) *nt* genocide
**ludoja|d** (**-da, -dy**) (*loc sg* **-dzie**) *m*: **rekin** ~ man-eating shark
**ludowy** *adj* (*strój, taniec, muzyka*) folk *attr*; (*władza, republika*) people's *attr*; (*Pol*: *partia, stronnictwo*) peasant *attr*
**ludożerc|a** (**-y, -y**) *m* cannibal
**ludożerst|wo** (**-wa**) (*loc sg* **-wie**) *nt* cannibalism
**lu|dzie** (**-dzi**) (*instr pl* **-dźmi**) *pl* people; **przy ludziach** in public; *patrz też* **człowiek**
**ludzki** *adj* (*ciało, istota, natura*) human; (*traktowanie, stosunek*) humane; **po ludzku** (*życzliwie*) decently; (*należycie*) properly
**ludzkoś|ć** (**-ci**) *f* humankind, humanity
**lu|fa** (**-fy, -fy**) (*dat sg* **-fie**) *f* barrel
**lufci|k** (**-ka, -ki**) (*instr sg* **-kiem**) *m* window vent
**lu|k** (**-ku, -ki**) (*instr sg* **-kiem**) *m* hatch (*opening*)
**lu|ka** (**-ki, -ki**) (*dat sg* **-ce**) *f* gap; ~ **w prawie** loophole
**lu|kier** (**-kru, -kry**) (*loc sg* **-krze**) *m* icing
**lukr|ować (-uję, -ujesz)** (*perf* **po-**) *vt* to ice
**Luksembur|g** (**-ga**) (*instr sg* **-giem**) *m* Luxembourg
**luksu|s** (**-su, -sy**) (*loc sg* **-sie**) *m* luxury
**luksusowy** *adj* luxury *attr*
**lumbago** *nt inv* lumbago
**luminescencj|a** (**-i**) *f* (*Fiz*) luminescence
**lunapar|k** (**-ku, -ki**) (*instr sg* **-kiem**) *m* funfair (*Brit*), amusement park (*US*)
**lunaty|k** (**-ka, -cy**) (*instr sg* **-kiem**) *m* sleepwalker
**lu|nąć (-nie)** (*imp* **-ń**) *vi perf* (*o deszczu*) to lash down

**lune|ta** (**-ty, -ty**) (*dat sg* **-cie**) *f* telescope
**lu|pa** (**-py, -py**) (*loc sg* **-pie**) *f* magnifying glass
**lu|ra** (**-ry, -ry**) (*dat sg* **-rze**) *f* (*pot*) dishwater (*pot*)
**luster|ko** (**-ka, -ka**) (*instr sg* **-kiem**, *gen pl* **-ek**) *nt* mirror; ~ **wsteczne** rear-view mirror; ~ **boczne** wing (*Brit*) *lub* outside (*US*) mirror
**lustracj|a** (**-i, -e**) (*gen pl* **-i**) *f* (*oględziny*) inspection; (*Pol*) vetting
**lust|ro** (**-ra, -ra**) (*loc sg* **-rze**, *gen pl* **-er**) *nt* mirror; ~ **wody** water level
**lustr|ować (-uję, -ujesz)** (*perf* **z-**) *vt* (*kontrolować*) to inspect; (*Pol*) to vet
**lustrzan|ka** (**-ki, -ki**) (*dat sg* **-ce**, *gen pl* **-ek**) *f* reflex camera
**lustrzany** *adj* mirror *attr*
**lu|t** (**-tu, -ty**) (*loc sg* **-cie**) *m* solder
**luterański** *adj* Lutheran
**lut|nia** (**-ni, -nie**) (*gen pl* **-ni**) *f* lute
**lutni|k** (**-ka, -cy**) (*instr sg* **-kiem**) *m* violin maker
**lut|ować (-uję, -ujesz)** (*perf* **z-**) *vt* to solder
**lutownic|a** (**-y, -e**) *f* soldering iron
**lutowy** *adj* February *attr*
**lut|y** (**-ego**) *m decl like adj* February
**lu|z** (**-zu, -zy**) (*loc sg* **-zie**) *m* (*wolny czas*) (free) time; (*wolne miejsce*) room; (*Tech*) play, clearance; (*Mot*) neutral; (*pot: swoboda*) elbow room (*pot*); **luz psychiczny** (*pot*) relaxation; **na luzie** (*pot*) laid back (*pot*); **luzem** (*towar*) loose
**luz|ować (-uję, -ujesz)** *vt* (*wartę, zmiennika*) (*perf* **z-**) to relieve; (*linę*) (*perf* **po-**) to slacken
**luźno** *adv* loosely
**luźny** *adj* (*spodnie, obuwie*) loose(-fitting); (*lina, wodze*) slack; (*kartka*) loose; (*przen: uwaga*) casual, detached; (*kontakt*) occasional; (*pot: rozmowa, atmosfera*) casual; **luźna zabudowa** scattered buildings *pl*; (*Archit*) dispersed development
**lwa** *itd. n patrz* **lew**
**lwi** *adj*: **lwia część** (*przen*) lion's share
**lwic|a** (**-y, -e**) *f* lioness
**Lw|ów** (**-owa**) (*loc sg* **-owie**) *m* Lvov
**lyc|ra** (**-ry**) (*loc sg* **-rze**) *f* Lycra®
**lżej** *adv comp od* **lekko**
**lżejszy** *adj comp od* **lekki**
**lż|yć (-ę, -ysz)** (*imp* **-yj**) *vt* to revile

# Łł

**Ł, ł** *nt inv* (*litera*) Ł, ł; **Ł jak Łukasz** L with a bar, L-bar
**Ła|ba** (**-by**) (*loc sg* **-bie**) *f* the Elbe
**łabę|dź** (**-dzia, -dzie**) (*gen pl* **-dzi**) *m* swan
**łac.** *abbr* (= *łaciński*) Lat. (= *Latin*)
**łach** (**-a, -y**) *m* (*pot*) rag (*pot*)
**łachma|n** (**-na, -ny**) (*loc sg* **-nie**) *m* (*pot*) rag (*pot*)
**łaciaty** *adj* piebald
**łacie** *n patrz* **łata**
**łaci|na** (**-ny**) (*dat sg* **-nie**) *f* Latin
**łaciński** *adj* Latin; **Ameryka Łacińska** Latin America
**ła|d** (**-du**) (*loc sg* **-dzie**) *m* order; **bez ładu i składu** without rhyme or reason; **dojść** (*perf*) **z kimś do ładu** (*pot*) to come to terms with sb
**ładnie** *adv* (*ubierać się, prosić, czytać*) nicely; (*zarabiać*) quite a lot; **to ~ wygląda/pachnie** it looks/smells nice *lub* pretty; **~ ci w tym kapeluszu** that hat suits you very well
**ładny** *adj* pretty, nice; (*dziewczyna*) pretty; (*pogoda, dzień*) nice
**ład|ować (-uję, -ujesz)** *vt* (*paczki, ciężarówkę, broń*) (*perf* **za-**) to load; (*akumulator*) (*perf* **na-**) to charge; **~ w coś pieniądze** to pump money into sth; **ładować się** *vr* (*pot*: *wchodzić*) to barge in
**ładow|nia** (**-ni, -nie**) (*gen pl* **-ni**) *f* (cargo) hold
**ładownoś|ć** (**-ci**) *f* carrying capacity
**ładowny** *adj* capacious
**ładun|ek** (**-ku, -ki**) (*instr sg* **-kiem**) *m* load; (*towary*) cargo; (*bomba*) bomb; (*materiał wybuchowy*) charge; (*Elektr*) charge
**ła|gier** (**-gru, -gry**) (*loc sg* **-grze**) *m* (*Hist*) labour (*Brit*) *lub* labor (*US*) camp
**łagodnie** *adv* (*mówić, spoglądać*) softly; (*skręcać, hamować*) gently
**łagodni|eć (-eję, -ejesz)** (*perf* **z-**) *vi* (*o osobie, wyrazie twarzy*) to soften; (*o wietrze*) to ease off *lub* up
**łagodnoś|ć** (**-ci**) *f* gentleness; (*klimatu*) mildness
**łagodny** *adj* (*człowiek, uwaga, zakręt*) gentle; (*wyrok, zima, klimat*) mild; (*proszek, lek, działanie*) mild, gentle
**łagodzący** *adj*: **okoliczności łagodzące** extenuating *lub* mitigating circumstances
**łag|odzić (-odzę, -odzisz)** (*imp* **-odź** *lub* **-ódź**, *perf* **z-** *lub* **za-**) *vt* (*żal*) to soothe, to ease; (*cierpienie, ból*) to alleviate; (*spór*) to mitigate, to moderate
**łaj|ać (-ę, -esz)** (*perf* **z-**) *vt* to scold
**łajdacki** *adj* rascally
**łajda|k** (**-ka, -cy**) (*instr sg* **-kiem**) *m* rascal, scoundrel
**łaj|no** (**-na, -na**) (*loc sg* **-nie**, *gen pl* **-en**) *nt* (*pot*) dung
**łak|nąć (-nę, -niesz)** (*imp* **-nij**) *vt*: **~ czegoś** (*przen*) to hunger *lub* be hungry for sth, to crave sth
**łaknieni|e** (**-a**) *nt* hunger
**łako|cie** (**-ci**) *pl* sweets *pl*, candy (*US*)
**łakomczuch** (**-a, -y**) *m* glutton
**łakomst|wo** (**-wa**) (*loc sg* **-wie**) *nt* gluttony, greediness
**łakomy** *adj* (*żarłoczny*) gluttonous, greedy; **~ na coś** greedy for sth; **~ kąsek** (*przen*) titbit (*Brit*), tidbit (*US*)
**ła|m** (**-mu, -my**) (*loc sg* **-mie**) *m* column; **na łamach gazet** *lub* **prasy** in the papers
**ła|mać (-mię, -miesz)** (*perf* **z-**) *vt* (*gałąź, obietnicę, prawo*) to break; (*opór*) to break (down); **~ sobie głowę (nad czymś)** to puzzle one's head (over sth); **łamie mnie w kościach** my bones are aching; **łamać się** *vr* (*o gałęzi*) to break; (*o głosie*) to falter
**łamany** *adj* broken; **mówić łamaną angielszczyzną** to speak in broken English; **5 łamane przez 8** five stroke eight
**łamigłów|ka** (**-ki, -ki**) (*dat sg* **-ce**, *gen pl* **-ek**) *f* puzzle; (*układanka*) jigsaw (puzzle)
**łamistraj|k** (**-ka, -ki**) (*instr sg* **-kiem**) *m* strikebreaker, blackleg (*Brit*)
**łamliwy** *adj* breakable
**ła|n** (**-nu, -ny**) (*loc sg* **-nie**) *m* field
**ła|nia** (**-ni, -nie**) (*gen pl* **-ni** *lub* **-ń**) *f* doe
**łańcuch** (**-a, -y**) *m* chain; **~ górski** mountain range; **~ zdarzeń** sequence of events
**łańcuchowy** *adj*: **reakcja łańcuchowa** chain reaction

**łańcusz|ek** (**-ka, -ki**) (*instr sg* **-kiem**) *m dimin od* **łańcuch**
**ła|pa** (**-py, -py**) (*dat sg* **-pie**) *f* (*kota, psa*) paw; (*pot: ręka*) paw (*pot*); **dać** (*perf*) **komuś w łapę** (*pot*) to grease sb's palm (*pot*); **dostać** (*perf*) **po ~ch** to get a rap on one's knuckles; **precz z ~mi!** (*pot!*) hands off!; **żyć (z kimś) na kocią łapę** (*pot*) to shack up (with sb)
**ła|pać (-pię, -piesz)** (*perf* **z-**) *vt* to catch; **kurcz mnie złapał** I was seized with (a (US)) cramp; **~ kogoś za coś** to grasp sb by sth; **z~ oddech** to catch one's breath; **łapać się** *vr*: **~ się za głowę** to clutch one's head; **~ się za kolano/guzik** to grasp one's knee/button; **~ się na czymś** to catch o.s. doing sth
**łapczywie** *adv* greedily
**łapczywy** *adj* greedy
**łap|ka** (**-ki, -ki**) (*dat sg* **-ce**, *gen pl* **-ek**) *f dimin od* **łapa**; (*na myszy*) mousetrap; **kurze łapki** crow's feet
**łapów|ka** (**-ki, -ki**) (*dat sg* **-ce**, *gen pl* **-ek**) *f* bribe; **dawać (dać** *perf*) **komuś łapówkę** to bribe sb
**łapówkarst|wo** (**-wa**) (*loc sg* **-wie**) *nt* bribery
**łapu-capu** *adv*: **na ~** helter-skelter
**łasic|a** (**-y, -e**) *f* weasel
**ła|sić się (-szę, -sisz)** (*imp* **-ś**) *vr*: **łasić się do kogoś** to fawn on sb
**łas|ka** (**-ki, -ki**) (*dat sg* **-ce**, *gen pl* **-k**) *f* (*przychylność*) favour (Brit), favor (US); (*ułaskawienie*) pardon; **~ boża** God's grace; **bez łaski!** (*pot*) I can do without it!, big deal! (*pot*); **zrobić** (*perf*) **coś z łaski** to do sth reluctantly; **być na łasce kogoś/czegoś** to be at the mercy of sb/sth; **proszę z łaski swojej zamknąć drzwi** close the door, if you please; **prawo łaski** the right to reprieve
**łaskawie** *adv*: **czy mógłby Pan ~ ...?** would you be so kind as to ...?
**łaskawy** *adj* (*uśmiech, los*) favourable (Brit) *lub* favorable (US); **bądź łaskaw położyć to tam** be so kind and put it there
**łasko|tać (-czę, -czesz)** *vt* to tickle; **~ kogoś w szyję** to tickle sb's neck
**łaskot|ki** (**-ek**) *pl* (*pot*): **mieć ~** to be ticklish
**łasy** *adj*: **~ na coś** greedy for sth
**ła|ta** (**-ty, -ty**) (*dat sg* **-cie**) *f* patch
**łat|ać (-am, -asz)** (*perf* **za-**) *vt* to patch
**łat|ka** (**-ki, -ki**) (*dat sg* **-ce**, *gen pl* **-ek**) *f dimin od* **łata**
**łatwi|zna** (**-zny**) (*dat sg* **-źnie**) *f*: **iść (pójść** *perf*) **na łatwiznę** to follow the line of least resistance; **ten egzamin to ~** this exam is a piece of cake (*pot*)
**łatwo** *adv* easily; **~ zrozumiały** easy to understand
**łatwopalny** *adj* (in)flammable
**łatwoś|ć** (**-ci**) *f*: **z łatwością** easily, with ease
**łatwowiernoś|ć** (**-ci**) *f* gullibility
**łatwowierny** *adj* gullible, credulous
**łatwy** *adj* easy; **~ w obsłudze** (*maszyna*) easy to use; (*program komputerowy*) user-friendly
**ła|wa** (**-wy, -wy**) (*dat sg* **-wie**) *f* (*stolik*) coffee table; (*do siedzenia*) bench; **~ oskarżonych** dock (*in court*); **~ przysięgłych** jury (box)
**ławic|a** (**-y, -e**) *f* (*ryb*) shoal, school
**ław|ka** (**-ki, -ki**) (*dat sg* **-ce**, *gen pl* **-ek**) *f* (*w parku*) bench; (*w szkole*) desk; (*w kościele*) pew; **~ kar** (*Sport*) sin bin; **~ rezerwowych** (*Sport*) substitute bench
**ławni|k** (**-ka, -cy**) (*instr sg* **-kiem**) *m* juror
**ła|zić (-żę, -zisz)** (*imp* **-ź**, *perf* **po-**) *vi* (*pot*) to walk
**łazien|ka** (**-ki, -ki**) (*dat sg* **-ce**, *gen pl* **-ek**) *f* bathroom
**łazi|k** (**-ka, -ki**) (*instr sg* **-kiem**) *m* jeep
**łaź|nia** (**-ni, -nie**) (*gen pl* **-ni**) *f* baths *sg lub pl*
**łącz|e** (**-a, -a**) (*gen pl* **-y**) *nt* (*Tel*) link
**łącznie** *adv*: **~ z** *+instr* (*wliczając*) including; **pisać coś ~** to write sth as one word
**łączni|k** (**-ka**) (*instr sg* **-kiem**) *m* (*znak graficzny*) (*nom pl* **-ki**) hyphen; (*Wojsk*) (*nom pl* **-cy**) liaison officer; (*czynnik*) (*nom pl* **-ki**) link
**łącznoś|ć** (**-ci**) *f* (*kontakt*) contact; (*wspólnota*) unity; (*komunikacja*) communication(s *pl*)
**łączny** *adj* total
**łącz|yć (-ę, -ysz)** (*perf* **po-**) *vt* (*elementy*) to join; (*punkty, miasta*) to link, to connect; (*Tel*) to connect, to put through; (*mieszać*) to mix, to blend; (*jednoczyć*) to unite; (*przewody, rury*) (*perf* **po-** *lub* **z-**) to connect; **~ coś w sobie** to combine sth; **~ przyjemne z pożytecznym** to mix *lub* combine business with pleasure; **(już) łączę!** I'm putting you through!; **łączyć się** *vr* (*stykać się: o elementach*) to be joined; (*o dłoniach, gałęziach*) to meet, to join; (*o rzekach, drogach*) to merge; (*kojarzyć się*) to be associated; (*Radio, TV*) to link up; (*Chem*) to combine
**łą|ka** (**-ki, -ki**) (*dat sg* **-ce**) *f* meadow
**łeb** (**łba, łby**) (*loc sg* **łbie**) *m* (*zwierzęcy*) head; (*pot: głowa ludzka*) nut (*pot*); **łeb w łeb** neck and neck; **kocie łby** cobblestones *pl*
**łeb|ek, łep|ek** (**-ka, -ki**) (*instr sg* **-kiem**) *m dimin od* **łeb**; (*gwoździa, szpilki*) head; **od łebka** (*pot*) per head, each
**łechtacz|ka** (**-ki, -ki**) (*dat sg* **-ce**, *gen pl* **-ek**) *f* clitoris
**łech|tać (-czę, -czesz** *lub* **-tam, -tasz)** (*imp* **-cz** *lub* **-taj**, *perf* **po-**) *vt* to tickle
**łep|ek** (**-ka, -ki**) (*instr sg* **-kiem**) *m* = **łebek**
**łepety|na** (**-ny, -ny**) (*dat sg* **-nie**) *f* (*pot*) nut (*pot*), bean (*pot*)
**łez** *n patrz* **łza**

**łękot|ka, łąkot|ka** (**-ki, -ki**) (*dat sg* **-ce**, *gen pl* **-ek**) *f* meniscus
**łgać (łżę, łżesz)** (*imp* **łżyj**, *perf* **ze-**) *vi* to lie
**łgarz** (**-a, -e**) (*gen pl* **-y**) *m* liar
**łk|ać (-am, -asz)** *vi* to sob
**łkani|e** (**-a, -a**) *nt* sobbing
**łobu|z** (**-za, -zy**) (*loc sg* **-zie**) *m* (*urwis*) urchin; (*chuligan*) hooligan
**łody|ga** (**-gi, -gi**) (*dat sg* **-dze**) *f* stem, stalk
**łodzi** *itd. n patrz* **łódź**
**ło|ić (-ję, -isz)** (*imp* **łój**, *perf* **z-**) *vt* (*przen*): ~ **komuś skórę** to tan sb's hide
**łoju** *itd. n patrz* **łój**
**ło|kieć** (**-kci, -kcie**) (*gen pl* **-kci**) *m* elbow
**ło|m** (**-mu, -my**) (*loc sg* **-mie**) *m* crowbar
**łomo|t** (**-tu, -ty**) (*loc sg* **-cie**) *m* (*hałas*) din; (*dudnienie*) rumble; (*głuchy odgłos*) thud; (*huk*) bang
**łomo|tać (-czę, -czesz)** (*perf* **za-**) *vi* (*hałasować*) to knock; (*o sercu*) to thud; ~ **do drzwi/w ścianę** to bang *lub* hammer on the door/wall
**ło|no** (**-na, -na**) (*loc sg* **-nie**) *nt* (*Anat*) womb; (*pierś*) bosom; **na łonie natury** (*przen*) in the open
**łopa|ta** (**-ty, -ty**) (*dat sg* **-cie**) *f* shovel
**łopat|ka** (**-ki, -ki**) (*dat sg* **-ce**, *gen pl* **-ek**) *f dimin od* **łopata**; (*Kulin*) spatula; (*Anat*) shoulder blade
**łopo|tać (-czę, -czesz)** (*perf* **za-**) *vi* to flap, to flutter
**łosko|t** (**-tu, -ty**) (*loc sg* **-cie**) *m* (*hałas*) din; (*huk*) bang; (*stukot*) clatter
**łosko|tać (-czę, -czesz)** *vi* (*hałasować*) to rumble, to bang; (*stukać*) to clatter
**łoso|ś** (**-sia, -sie**) (*gen pl* **-si**) *m* salmon
**ło|ś** (**-sia, -sie**) (*gen pl* **-si**) *m* elk; **łoś amerykański** moose
**łotewski** *adj* Latvian
**łot|r** (**-ra, -ry**) (*loc sg* **-rze**) *m* scoundrel
**Łot|wa** (**-wy**) (*dat sg* **-wie**) *f* Latvia
**Łotysz** (**-a, -e**) (*gen pl* **-y** *lub* **-ów**) *m* Latvian
**Łotysz|ka** (**-ki, -ki**) (*dat sg* **-ce**, *gen pl* **-ek**) *f* Latvian
**łowc|a** (**-y, -y**) *m* hunter; ~ **autografów/głów** autograph/head hunter
**ło|wić (-wię, -wisz)** (*imp* **łów**, *perf* **z-**) *vt* (*zwierzynę*) to hunt; (*ryby, motyle*) to catch; ~ **ryby** to fish
**łowiecki** *adj* hunting *attr*
**łowiect|wo** (**-wa**) (*loc sg* **-wie**) *nt* hunting
**łowis|ko** (**-ka, -ka**) (*instr sg* **-kiem**) *nt* (*miejsce połowu ryb*) fishery
**łow|y** (**-ów**) *pl* hunt
**łoż|e** (**-a, -a**) (*gen pl* **łóż**) *nt* bed; **dziecko z nieprawego łoża** illegitimate child; **na łożu śmierci** on one's deathbed
**łoż|yć (-ę, -ysz)** (*imp* **łóż**) *vt*: ~ **na** *+acc* to provide for
**łożys|ko** (**-ka, -ka**) (*instr sg* **-kiem**) *nt* (*Tech*) bearing; (*Anat*) placenta; (*rzeki*) bed
**łód|ka** (**-ki, -ki**) (*dat sg* **-ce**, *gen pl* **-ek**) *f* boat
**łódź** (**łodzi, łodzie**) (*gen pl* **łodzi**) *f* boat; ~ **ratunkowa** lifeboat; ~ **podwodna** submarine; ~ **motorowa** motor boat; ~ **żaglowa** sailing boat (*Brit*), sailboat (*US*)
**łój** (**łoju**) *m* (*przemysłowy*) tallow; (*jadalny*) suet
**łóżecz|ko** (**-ka, -ka**) (*instr sg* **-kiem**, *gen pl* **-ek**) *nt* cot (*Brit*), crib (*US*)
**łóż|ko** (**-ka, -ka**) (*instr sg* **-kiem**, *gen pl* **-ek**) *nt* bed; ~ **piętrowe** bunk beds *pl*; ~ **polowe** camp bed (*Brit*), cot (*US*); **iść (pójść** *perf*) **z kimś do łóżka** to go to bed with sb
**łubi|n** (**-nu, -ny**) (*loc sg* **-nie**) *m* lupin (*Brit*), lupine (*US*)
**łucznict|wo** (**-wa**) (*loc sg* **-wie**) *nt* archery
**łuczni|k** (**-ka, -cy**) (*instr sg* **-kiem**) *m* archer
**łu|dzić (-dzę, -dzisz)** (*imp* **-dź**) *vt* to deceive; **łudzić się** *vr*: ~ **się, że ...** to be under the illusion that ...
**łu|k** (**-ku, -ki**) (*instr sg* **-kiem**) *m* (*krzywizna*) curve; (*broń*) bow; (*Archit*) arch; (*Geom, Elektr*) arc; **łuk brwiowy** eyebrow ridge
**łu|na** (**-ny, -ny**) (*dat sg* **-nie**) *f* glow
**łu|p** (**-pu, -py**) (*loc sg* **-pie**) *m* loot; **paść łupem** *+gen* to fall prey to; **łupy** *pl* spoils *pl*
**łu|pać (-pię, -piesz)** *vt* to crack; **łupie mnie w kościach** (*pot*) my bones are aching
**łup|ek** (**-ka, -ki**) (*instr sg* **-kiem**) *m* (*Geol*) slate
**łu|pić (-pię, -pisz)** (*perf* **z-**) *vt* to loot, to plunder
**łupież** (**-u**) *m* dandruff
**łupi|na** (**-ny, -ny**) (*dat sg* **-nie**) *f* (*orzecha*) (nut) shell; (*ziemniaka*) skin
**łup|nąć (-nę, -niesz)** (*imp* **-nij**) *vt perf* (*pot: uderzyć*) to bang; **łupnąć się** (*pot*): ~ **się w głowę** to bang one's head
**łus|ka** (**-ki, -ki**) (*dat sg* **-ce**, *gen pl* **-ek**) *f* (*ryby*) scale; (*nasiona, zboża*) husk; (*grochu, fasoli*) shell; (*Wojsk*) shell
**łusk|ać (-am, -asz)** *vt* to shell
**łuszcz|yć się (-y)** (*perf* **z-**) *vr* to peel off
**łu|t** (**-ta, -ty**) (*loc sg* **-cie**) *m*: **łut szczęścia** a stroke of luck
**łycz|ek** (**-ka, -ki**) (*instr sg* **-kiem**) *m* sip; **pić coś (małymi) łyczkami** to sip sth
**łyd|ka** (**-ki, -ki**) (*dat sg* **-ce**, *gen pl* **-ek**) *f* calf
**ły|k** (**-ku, -ki**) (*instr sg* **-kiem**) *m* swallow
**łyk|ać (-am, -asz)** (*perf* **-nąć**) *vt* to swallow
**łyk|nąć (-nę, -niesz)** (*imp* **-nij**) *vb perf od* **łykać**
**łykowaty** *adj* stringy, fibrous
**ły|pać (-pię, -piesz)** (*perf* **-pnąć**) *vi* to glance
**łyp|nąć (-nę, -niesz)** (*imp* **-nij**) *vb perf od* **łypać**

Ł

**łysi|eć (-eję, -ejesz)** (*perf* **wy-**) *vi* to go *lub* grow bald
**łysiejący** *adj* balding
**łysieni|e** (**-a**) *nt* baldness
**łysi|na** (**-ny, -ny**) (*loc sg* **-nie**) *f* (*miejsce*) bald patch; (*łysa głowa*) bald head
**łysy** *adj* bald
**łyżecz|ka** (**-ki, -ki**) (*dat sg* **-ce**, *gen pl* **-ek**) *f dimin od* **łyżka**; (*też*: **łyżeczka do herbaty**) teaspoon; (*zawartość*) teaspoonful
**łyż|ka** (**-ki, -ki**) (*dat sg* **-ce**, *gen pl* **-ek**) *f* spoon; (*zawartość*) spoonful; **~ do butów** shoehorn; **~ do zupy** soup spoon; **~ wazowa** ladle
**łyż|wa** (**-wy, -wy**) (*dat sg* **-wie**, *gen pl* **-ew**) *f* skate; **jeździć na ~ch** to skate
**łyżwiar|ka** (**-ki, -ki**) (*dat sg* **-ce**, *gen pl* **-ek**) *f* skater
**łyżwiarski** *adj* skating *attr*
**łyżwiarst|wo** (**-wa**) (*loc sg* **-wie**) *nt* skating; **~ figurowe/szybkie** figure/speed skating
**łyżwiarz** (**-a, -e**) (*gen pl* **-y**) *m* skater
**łyżworol|ka** (**-ki, -ki**) (*dat sg* **-ce**, *gen pl* **-ek**) *f* Rollerblade®
**łza** (**łzy, łzy**) (*dat sg* **łzie**, *gen pl* **łez**) *f* tear; **czysty jak łza** as pure as the driven snow; **ze łzami w oczach** with tears in one's eyes
**łzawiący** *adj*: **gaz ~** tear gas
**łza|wić (-wi)** *vi*: **oczy mi łzawią** my eyes are running
**łzawy** *adj* sentimental
**łżę** *itd. vb patrz* **łgać**

# Mm

**M, m**[1] *nt inv (litera)* M, m; **M jak Maria** ≈ M for Mary *(Brit)*, ≈ M for Mike *(US)*
**m²** *abbr (= metr)* m
**m.** *abbr (= miasto)* t. *(= town)*; *(= mieszkanie)* flat *(Brit)*, apt. *(US)*; *(= morze)* S. *(= Sea)*
**ma** *vb patrz* **mieć**
**mac|ać (-am, -asz)** *vt (badać)* to feel, to finger; *(pot: dotykać lubieżnie)* to paw *(pot)*, to grope *(pot)*
**Macedoni|a (-i)** *f* Macedonia
**macedoński** *adj* Macedonian
**macek** *n patrz* **macka**
**mach|ać (-am, -asz)** *vi (perf* **-nąć***) (chusteczką, ręką)* to wave; *(ogonem)* to wag; *(skrzydłami)* to flap; *(szablą)* to brandish
**machi|na (-ny, -ny)** *(dat sg* **-nie***) f* machine
**machinacj|e (-i)** *pl* machinations *pl*
**machinalny** *adj* automatic
**machloj|ka (-ki, -ki)** *(dat sg* **-ce**, *gen pl* **-ek***) f (pot)* fraud
**mach|nąć (-nę, -niesz)** *(imp* **-nij***) vb perf od* **machać** ▷ *vi perf*: **~ na coś ręką** *(przen)* not to bother with sth
**macic|a (-y, -e)** *f (Anat)* uterus; **~ perłowa** mother of pearl
**macie** *patrz* **mat, mata, mieć**
**maciej|ka (-ki, -ki)** *(dat sg* **-ce**, *gen pl* **-ek***) f* night-scented stock
**macierz (-y, -e)** *f (Mat, Tech)* matrix
**macierzyński** *adj (instynkt)* maternal; *(miłość)* motherly; **urlop ~** maternity leave
**macierzyńst|wo (-wa)** *(loc sg* **-wie***) nt* maternity; **świadome ~** planned parenthood
**macierzysty** *adj* mother *attr*
**macio|ra (-ry, -ry)** *(dat sg* **-rze***) f* sow
**mac|ka (-ki, -ki)** *(dat sg* **-ce**, *gen pl* **-ek***) f* tentacle, feeler
**maco|cha (-chy, -chy)** *(dat sg* **-sze***) f* stepmother
**macoszemu** *adj*: **traktować kogoś/coś po ~** to neglect sb/sth
**macz|ać (-am, -asz)** *(perf* **zamoczyć***) vt*: **~ (coś w czymś)** to dip (sth in sth); **na pewno maczał w tym palce** *(przen)* he must have had a hand in this
**macz|ek (-ku, -ki)** *(instr sg* **-kiem***) m*: **pisać maczkiem** to write a tiny hand
**macze|ta (-ty, -ty)** *(dat sg* **-cie***) f* machet(e)
**maczu|ga (-gi, -gi)** *(dat sg* **-dze***) f* club
**ma|ć (-ci)** *f*: **psia mać!** *(pot)* damn (it)! *(pot)*; **kurwa mać!** *(pot!)* fuck (it)! *(pot!)*
**Madon|na (-ny)** *(dat sg* **-nie***) f* Madonna
**madryga|ł (-łu, -ły)** *(loc sg* **-le***) m* madrigal
**Madry|t (-tu)** *(loc sg* **-cie***) m* Madrid
**maest|ro (-ra, -rowie)** *(loc sg* **-rze***) m* maestro
**mafi|a (-i, -e)** *(gen pl* **-i***) f* mob; *(sycylijska)* the Mafia; *(przen)* mafia
**mafio|zo (-za, -zi)** *(loc sg* **-zie***) m* mobster; *(sycylijski)* Mafioso; *(pot)* slicker *(pot)*
**magazy|n (-nu, -ny)** *(loc sg* **-nie***) m (budynek)* warehouse, storehouse; *(pomieszczenie)* store(room), stockroom; *(czasopismo, program)* magazine
**magazyn|ek (-ku, -ki)** *(instr sg* **-kiem***) m (Wojsk)* magazine
**magazynie|r (-ra, -rzy)** *(loc sg* **-rze***) m* warehouse manager *lub* attendant
**magazyn|ować (-uję, -ujesz)** *vt (przechowywać)* to store; *(gromadzić) (perf* **z-***)* to store up
**magi|a (-i, -e)** *(gen pl* **-i***) f* magic; **to dla mnie czarna ~** it's (all) Greek to me
**magiczny** *adj (sztuka, obrzęd)* magic; *(siła, wpływ)* magical
**ma|giel (-gla, -gle)** *(gen pl* **-gli***) m* linen press
**magi|k (-ka, -cy)** *(instr sg* **-kiem***) m* magician
**magist|er (-ra, -rzy** *lub* **-rowie)** *(loc sg* **-rze***) m (nauk ścisłych, przyrodniczych)* Master of Science; *(nauk humanistycznych)* Master of Arts
**magisteri|um (-um, -a)** *(gen pl* **-ów***) nt inv in sg* master's degree
**magisterski** *adj* master's *attr*
**magistral|a (-i, -e)** *f (szlak komunikacyjny)* route; *(Komput)* bus; **~ kolejowa** main line; **~ wodna/gazowa** gas/water main
**magistran|t (-ta, -ci)** *(loc sg* **-cie***) m* master's student
**magla** *itd. n patrz* **magiel**
**magl|ować (-uję, -ujesz)** *(perf* **wy-***) vt* to press; *(pot: męczyć pytaniami)* to grill *(pot)*
**magna|t (-ta, -ci)** *(loc sg* **-cie***) m* magnate
**magnateri|a (-i)** *f* the nobility

**magne|s** (**-su, -sy**) (*loc sg* **-sie**) *m* magnet
**magnes|ować (-uję, -ujesz)** (*perf* **na-**) *vt* to magnetize
**magnetofo|n** (**-nu, -ny**) (*loc sg* **-nie**) *m* (*ze wzmacniaczem*) tape recorder; (*bez wzmacniacza*) tape deck; ~ **kasetowy** cassette recorder *lub* deck
**magnetofonowy** *adj* (*taśma*) magnetic; **zapis** ~ tape recording
**magnetowi|d** (**-du, -dy**) (*loc sg* **-dzie**) *m* video (cassette recorder), VCR
**magnetyczny** *adj* magnetic
**magnetyz|m** (**-mu**) (*loc sg* **-mie**) *m* magnetism
**magne|z** (**-zu**) (*loc sg* **-zie**) *m* magnesium
**magnificencj|a** (**-i, -e**) (*gen pl* **-i**) *m decl like f*; **Jego M~** Rector Magnificus
**magnoli|a** (**-i, -e**) (*gen pl* **-i**) *f* magnolia
**mahometa|nin** (**-nina, -nie**) (*loc sg* **-ninie**, *gen pl* **-n**) *m* Muslim
**mahometański** *adj* Muslim
**mahoniowy** *adj* mahogany *attr*
**maho|ń** (**-niu, -nie**) (*gen pl* **-ni** *lub* **-niów**) *m* mahogany
**maj** (**-a, -e**) *m* May
**majacz|yć (-ę, -ysz)** *vi* (*bredzić*) to be delirious; (*ukazywać się*) (*perf* **za-**) to emerge
**maja|ki** (**-ków**) *pl* illusion
**mają** *vb patrz* **mieć**
**mająt|ek** (**-ku**) (*instr sg* **-kiem**) *m* (*mienie*) property, possessions *pl*; (*bogactwo*) fortune; (*ziemski*) (**-ki**) estate; **zbić** (*perf*) ~ to make a fortune; **to kosztuje** ~ it costs a fortune; ~ **narodowy** national heritage
**majątkowy** *adj*: **prawo majątkowe** property law; **sytuacja majątkowa** financial situation
**majeran|ek** (**-ku, -ki**) (*instr sg* **-kiem**) *m* marjoram
**majesta|t** (**-tu**) (*loc sg* **-cie**) *m* majesty; **obraza ~u** lèse-majesté
**majestatyczny** *adj* majestic
**majętny** *adj* moneyed, monied
**majone|z** (**-zu, -zy**) (*loc sg* **-zie**) *m* mayonnaise
**majo|r** (**-ra, -rowie** *lub* **-rzy**) (*loc sg* **-rze**) *m* major
**Major|ka** (**-ki**) (*dat sg* **-ce**) *f* Majorca
**majowy** *adj* May *attr*
**majów|ka** (**-ki, -ki**) (*dat sg* **-ce**, *gen pl* **-ek**) *f* picnic
**majst|er** (**-ra, -rowie** *lub* **-rzy**) (*loc sg* **-rze**) *m* (*w przemyśle*) foreman; (*w rzemiośle*) master; **~-klepka** DIY man; (*pej*) jack-of-all-trades
**majsterk|ować (-uję, -ujesz)** *vi* to do (some) DIY
**majsterkowicz** (**-a, -e**) *m* DIY man
**majstersztу|k** (**-ku, -ki**) (*instr sg* **-kiem**) *m* masterpiece
**majstr|ować (-uję, -ujesz)** *vi*: ~ **przy czymś** (*pot*) to tinker *lub* fiddle with sth (*pot*)
**majt|ek** (**-ka, -kowie**) (*instr sg* **-kiem**) *m* deck hand
**majt|ki** (**-ek**) *pl* (*damskie, dziecięce*) panties *pl*; (*męskie*) briefs *pl*
**ma|k** (**-ku**) *m* (*roślina*) (*pl* **-ki**) poppy; (*nasiona*) poppyseed; **było cicho jak makiem zasiał** the place was as silent as the grave; **rozbić się** (*perf*) **w drobny mak** to smash to smithereens
**makab|ra** (**-ry, -ry**) (*dat sg* **-rze**) *f* (*pot*) horror
**makabryczny** *adj* macabre
**makaro|n** (**-nu, -ny**) (*loc sg* **-nie**) *m* (*ogólnie*) pasta; (*nitki*) spaghetti; (*rurki*) macaroni; (*muszelki*) shells *pl*; (*paski*) noodles *pl*; (*kolanka*) elbows *pl*
**makaroniarz** (**-a, -e**) (*gen pl* **-y**) *m* (*pot!*: *Włoch*) wop, Eyetie (*Brit*) (*pot!*)
**makie|ta** (**-ty, -ty**) (*dat sg* **-cie**) *f* (*Archit*) model; (*Tech*) mock-up; (*Druk*) dummy
**makijaż** (**-u, -e**) (*gen pl* **-y** *lub* **-ów**) *m* make-up; **robić (zrobić** *perf*) **komuś** ~ to make sb up; **robić (zrobić** *perf*) **sobie** ~ to make (o.s.) up
**makle|r** (**-ra, -rzy**) (*loc sg* **-rze**) *m* (stock)broker
**maklerski** *adj* stockbroking; **dom** ~ brokerage house
**mako|wiec** (**-wca, -wce**) *m* poppyseed cake
**makowy** *adj* (*kolor, sukienka*) poppy (red); **olej** ~ poppyseed oil
**maków|ka** (**-ki, -ki**) (*dat sg* **-ce**, *gen pl* **-ek**) *f* poppy-head; (*pot: głowa*) bean (*pot*)
**makrel|a** (**-i, -e**) (*gen pl* **-** *lub* **-i**) *f* mackerel
**makro...** *pref* macro...
**makroekonomi|a** (**-i**) *f* macro-economics
**maksim|um** (**-um, -a**) (*gen pl* **-ów**) *nt inv in sg* maximum ▷ *adv* maximum
**maksy|ma** (**-my, -my**) (*dat sg* **-mie**) *f* maxim
**maksymaliz|ować (-uję, -ujesz)** (*perf* **z-**) *vt* to maximize
**maksymalny** *adj* maximum
**makulatu|ra** (**-ry**) (*dat sg* **-rze**) *f* recycling paper; (*po przetworzeniu*) recycled paper
**Malaj** (**-a, -e**) *m* Malay
**malajski** *adj* Malay
**malari|a** (**-i**) *f* malaria
**malar|ka** (**-ki, -ki**) (*dat sg* **-ce**, *gen pl* **-ek**) *f* painter
**malarski** *adj* (*pracownia*) painter's *attr*; (*technika*) painting *attr*
**malarst|wo** (**-wa**) (*loc sg* **-wie**) *nt* (*sztuka*) painting; (*obrazy*) paintings *pl*
**malarz** (**-a, -e**) (*gen pl* **-y**) *m* painter; (*też*: **malarz pokojowy**) decorator, painter
**mal|ec** (**-ca, -cy**) (*voc sg* **-cze**) *m* kid
**mal|eć (-eję, -ejesz)** (*perf* **z-**) *vi* to diminish, to decrease

**Malediw|y** (**-ów**) *pl* the Maldives *pl*
**malejący** *adj* diminishing, decreasing
**maleńki** *adj* tiny
**maleńst|wo** (**-wa, -wa**) (*loc sg* **-wie**) *nt* (*pot*) little one (*pot*)
**Malezj|a** (**-i**) *f* Malaysia
**mali|na** (**-ny, -ny**) (*dat sg* **-nie**) *f* raspberry; **wpuszczać (wpuścić** *perf*) **kogoś w maliny** (*pot*) to lead sb up the garden path
**malinowy** *adj* raspberry *attr*
**malkonten|t** (**-ta, -ci**) (*loc sg* **-cie**) *m* grumbler
**mal|ować (-uję, -ujesz)** *vt* (*płot, kaloryfer, ścianę*) (*perf* **po-**) to paint; (*mieszkanie*) (*perf* **wy-**) to decorate, to paint; (*obraz*) (*perf* **na-**) to paint; (*usta*) (*perf* **po-** *lub* **u-**) to paint; **malować się** *vr* (*nakładać makijaż*) to make up; (*o uczuciach*) to appear; (*o przyszłości*) to look; (*o szczytach gór*) to stand out; **~ (po~** *perf*) **coś na czerwono** to paint sth red; **~ coś w ciemnych/jasnych barwach** (*przen*) to paint a gloomy/bright picture of sth
**malowany** *adj*: **„świeżo malowane"** "wet paint"
**malowid|ło** (**-ła, -ła**) (*loc sg* **-le**, *gen pl* **-eł**) *nt* painting; **~ ścienne** mural
**malowniczy** *adj* (*krajobraz, widok*) picturesque; (*opis*) vivid
**Mal|ta** (**-ty**) (*dat sg* **-cie**) *f* Malta
**maltańczy|k** (**-ka**) (*instr sg* **-kiem**) (*pies*) (*nom pl* **-ki**) Maltese dog; **Maltańczyk** (*nom pl* **-cy**) *m* Maltese
**maltański** *adj*: **krzyż ~** Maltese Cross
**maltret|ować (-uję, -ujesz)** (*perf* **z-**) *vt* to maltreat, to abuse
**maluch** (**-a, -y**) *m* toddler; (*pot*) Fiat 126 (*a compact car popular in Poland*)
**malusieńki** *adj* minuscule
**malutki** *adj* tiny, diminutive
**mal|wa** (**-wy, -wy**) (*dat sg* **-wie**) *f* hollyhock
**malwersacj|a** (**-i, -e**) (*gen pl* **-i**) *f* embezzlement
**malwersan|t** (**-ta, -ci**) (*loc sg* **-cie**) *m* embezzler
**mał|a**[1] (**-ej, -e**) *f decl like adj* (*pot*) babe (*pot*); **~ czarna** small black coffee
**mała**[2] *inv*: **bez ~** virtually
**mał|e** (**-ego, -e**) *nt decl like adj* (*potomstwo*) young
**mało** (*comp* **mniej**) *adv* (*ludzi, drzew*) few; (*czasu, światła, wody*) little; (*mówić, wiedzieć*) little; (*zniszczony, prawdopodobny*) hardly; **~ kto wie, że ...** (very) few people know that ...; **~ tego** that's not all; **o ~ (co) nie upadłem** I nearly fell
**małodusznoś|ć** (**-ci**) *f* meanness
**małoduszny** *adj* mean
**małola|t** (**-ta, -ty**) (*loc sg* **-cie**) *m* (*pot*) teenager
**małola|ta** (**-ty, -ty**) (*dat sg* **-cie**) *f* (*pot*) teenager
**małoletni** *adj* teenage
**małolitrażowy** *adj*: **samochód ~** small-engine car
**małomiasteczkowy** *adj* provincial, parochial
**małomówny** *adj* taciturn, reticent
**małoobrazkowy** *adj*: **aparat ~** 35mm camera
**Małopols|ka** (**-ki**) (*dat sg* **-ce**) *f a province in southern Poland*
**małorolny** *adj*: **chłop ~** smallholder
**małosolny** *adj* low-salt *attr*
**małostkowoś|ć** (**-ci**) *f* pettiness
**małostkowy** *adj* petty
**mał|pa** (**-py, -py**) (*dat sg* **-pie**) *f* monkey; (*też*: **małpa człekokształtna**) ape; (*pot!*: *kobieta*) bitch (*pot!*)
**małpolu|d** (**-da, -dy**) (*loc sg* **-dzie**) *m* (*pot*: *człowiek pierwotny*) hominid; (*przen*) bozo (*pot*)
**małp|ować (-uję, -ujesz)** *vi* to ape
**ma|ły** (*comp* **mniejszy**) *adj* small; (*palec, spacer, chwilka*) little; (*dziecko, chłopiec*) small, little; (*litera*) lower-case, small ▷ *m decl like adj* kid; **mieć coś w ~m palcu** (*przen*) to have sth at one's fingertips; **małe piwo** (*przen*) a piece of cake, no big deal; **od małego** from childhood; **o ~ włos nie zrobić czegoś** to be within a hair's breadth of doing sth
**małż** (**-a, -e**) (*gen pl* **-y** *lub* **-ów**) *m* (*Zool*) shellfish; (*też*: **małż jadalny**) mussel
**małżeński** *adj* (*para*) married; (*pożycie, przysięga*) marital; **związek ~** marriage, matrimony
**małżeńst|wo** (**-wa, -wa**) (*loc sg* **-wie**) *nt* (*związek prawny*) marriage; (*para*) (married) couple; (*stan*) matrimony, wedlock; **zawierać (zawrzeć** *perf*) **~** to marry; **unieważniać (unieważnić** *perf*) **~** to annul a marriage
**małżon|ek** (**-ka, -kowie**) (*instr sg* **-kiem**) *m* spouse, husband; **małżonkowie** *pl* husband and wife, both spouses *pl*
**małżon|ka** (**-ki, -ki**) (*dat sg* **-ce**, *gen pl* **-ek**) *f* spouse, wife
**małżowi|na** (**-ny, -ny**) (*dat sg* **-nie**) *f* (*też*: **małżowina uszna**) auricle
**mam** *vb patrz* **mieć**
**ma|ma** (**-my, -my**) (*dat sg* **-mie**) *f* mum
**ma|mić (-mię, -misz)** (*perf* **o-**) *vt* to beguile
**maminsyn|ek** (**-ka, -kowie** *lub* **-ki**) (*instr sg* **-kiem**) *m* (*pej*) mother's boy (*pej*)
**mam|ka** (**-ki, -ki**) (*dat sg* **-ce**, *gen pl* **-ek**) *f* wet nurse
**mammografi|a** (**-i**) *f* mammography
**mamro|tać (-czę, -czesz)** (*perf* **wy-**) *vi* to mutter
**mamu|sia** (**-si, -sie**) (*gen pl* **-ś**) *f* mummy
**mamu|t** (**-ta, -ty**) (*loc sg* **-cie**) *m* mammoth
**mamy** *vb patrz* **mieć**

m

**manat|ki** (**-ków**) *pl* (*pot*) stuff, clobber (*Brit*) (*pot*)
**mandaryn|ka** (**-ki, -ki**) (*dat sg* **-ce**, *gen pl* **-ek**) *f* tangerine, mandarin
**manda|t** (**-tu, -ty**) (*loc sg* **-cie**) *m* (*kara*) ticket; (*poselski*) seat; (*pełnomocnictwo*) mandate; **ukarać** (*perf*) **kogoś ~em** to give sb a ticket
**mandoli|na** (**-ny, -ny**) (*dat sg* **-nie**) *f* mandolin(e)
**maneki|n** (**-na, -ny**) (*loc sg* **-nie**) *m* (*u krawca*) (tailor's) dummy; (*w sklepie*) mannequin, dummy
**manel|e** (**-i**) *pl* (*pot*) gear (*pot*)
**manew|r** (**-ru, -ry**) (*loc sg* **-rze**) *m* manoeuvre (*Brit*), maneuver (*US*); **manewry** *pl* (*Wojsk*) man(o)euvres *pl*
**manewr|ować (-uję, -ujesz)** *vi* to manoeuvre (*Brit*), to maneuver (*US*)
**mango** *nt inv* mango
**mani|a** (**-i, -e**) (*gen pl* **-i**) *f* mania; **~ prześladowcza** persecution complex; **~ wielkości** megalomania; (*przen*) delusions of grandeur
**maniacki** *adj* (*upór*) maniac(al)
**mania|k** (**-ka, -cy**) (*instr sg* **-kiem**) *m* maniac
**maniakalny** *adj* manic; **maniakalno-depresyjny** manic-depressive
**manicure** *m inv* manicure
**manie|ra** (**-ry, -ry**) (*dat sg* **-rze**) *f* (*zmanierowanie*) mannerism; (*styl*) manner; **maniery** *pl* manners *pl*
**manier|ka** (**-ki, -ki**) (*dat sg* **-ce**, *gen pl* **-ek**) *f* canteen, (water-)flask
**manieryczny** *adj* manneristic
**manife|st** (**-stu, -sty**) (*loc sg* **-ście**) *m* manifesto
**manifestacj|a** (**-i, -e**) (*gen pl* **-i**) *f* (*uczuć*) expression; (*zgromadzenie*) demonstration
**manifest|ować (-uję, -ujesz)** (*perf* **za-**) *vt* to manifest, to demonstrate ▷ *vi* to demonstrate
**manikiu|r** (**-ru**) (*loc sg* **-rze**) *m* = **manicure**
**manikiurzyst|ka** (**-ki, -ki**) (*dat sg* **-ce**, *gen pl* **-ek**) *f* manicurist
**manipulacj|a** (**-i, -e**) (*gen pl* **-i**) *f* manipulation; **manipulacje** *pl* (*finansowe, handlowe*) dishonest dealings *pl*
**manipulacyjny** *adj*: **opłaty manipulacyjne** handling charges
**manipul|ować (-uję, -ujesz)** *vi* to manipulate
**mankamen|t** (**-tu, -ty**) (*loc sg* **-cie**) *m* shortcoming
**mankie|t** (**-tu, -ty**) (*loc sg* **-cie**) *m* (*u koszuli*) cuff; (*u spodni*) turn-up
**man|ko** (**-ka, -ka**) (*instr sg* **-kiem**) *nt* cash shortage
**man|na** (**-ny**) (*dat sg* **-nie**) *f* (*też*: **kasza manna**) semolina; **~ z nieba** manna from heaven
**manomet|r** (**-ru, -ry**) (*loc sg* **-rze**) *m* manometer
**manowc|e** (**-ów**) *pl*: **sprowadzić** (*perf*) **kogoś na ~** to lead sb astray; **zejść** (*perf*) **na ~** to go astray
**mansar|da** (**-dy, -dy**) (*dat sg* **-dzie**) *f* attic, garret
**manualny** *adj* manual
**manufaktu|ra** (**-ry, -ry**) (*dat sg* **-rze**) *f* workshop
**manuskryp|t** (**-tu, -ty**) (*loc sg* **-cie**) *m* manuscript
**mańku|t** (**-ta, -ci**) (*loc sg* **-cie**) *m* left-hander; **jestem ~em** I'm left-handed
**Maory|s** (**-sa, -si**) (*loc sg* **-sie**) *m* Maori
**ma|pa** (**-py, -py**) (*loc sg* **-pie**) *f* map; **~ samochodowa** road map
**mar.** *abbr* (= *marynarz*) seaman
**marato|n** (**-nu, -ny**) (*loc sg* **-nie**) *m* marathon
**maratończy|k** (**-ka, -cy**) (*instr sg* **-kiem**) *m* marathon runner
**maraz|m** (**-mu**) (*loc sg* **-mie**) *m* torpor
**marca** *n patrz* **marzec**
**marce** *n patrz* **marka**
**marcepa|n** (**-na, -ny**) (*loc sg* **-nie**) *m* marzipan
**march|ew** (**-wi, -wie**) (*gen pl* **-wi**) *f* carrot
**marcowy** *adj* March *attr*
**mar|ek** (**-ka, -ki**) (*instr sg* **-kiem**) *m*: **nocny ~** (*pot*) night owl *lub* hawk (*US*) (*pot*); *patrz też* **marka**
**margary|na** (**-ny, -ny**) (*dat sg* **-nie**) *f* margarine
**marginalny** *adj* marginal
**margine|s** (**-su, -sy**) (*loc sg* **-sie**) *m* margin; **na ~ie** (*zauważyć, powiedzieć coś*) in passing; **~ społeczny** the dregs *pl* of society
**marginesowy** *adj* marginal
**marihua|na** (**-ny**) (*dat sg* **-nie**) *f* marihuana
**marionet|ka** (**-ki, -ki**) (*dat sg* **-ce**, *gen pl* **-ek**) *f* puppet
**marionetkowy** *adj* (*teatr, rząd*) puppet *attr*
**mar|ka** (**-ki, -ki**) (*dat sg* **-ce**, *gen pl* **-ek**) *f* (*znak fabryczny*) brand; (*waluta*) mark; (*samochodu*) make; **mieć dobrą/złą markę** to have a good/bad name; **wyrób dobrej/złej marki** a product of good/poor quality
**marke|r** (**-ra, -ry**) (*loc sg* **-rze**) *m* (*pisak*) highlighter
**marketin|g** (**-gu**) (*instr sg* **-giem**) *m* marketing
**marketingowy** *adj* marketing *attr*
**marki|z** (**-za, -zowie**) (*loc sg* **-zie**) *m* marquis, marquess (*Brit*)
**marki|za** (**-zy, -zy**) (*dat sg* **-zie**) *f* (*daszek*) awning; (*ciastko*) cream-filled biscuit (*Brit*) *lub* cookie (*US*); (*żona markiza*) marchioness
**markotny** *adj* moody, out of sorts
**mark|ować (-uję, -ujesz)** (*perf* **za-**) *vt/vi* to feign
**markowy** *adj* brand-name *attr*

**marksi|sta** (**-sty, -ści**) (*dat sg* **-ście**) *m decl like f in sg* Marxist
**marksistowski** *adj* Marxist
**marksiz|m** (**-mu**) (*loc sg* **-mie**) *m* Marxism
**marmola|da** (**-dy, -dy**) (*dat sg* **-dzie**) *f* jam; (*z owoców cytrusowych*) marmalade
**marmu|r** (**-ru, -ry**) (*loc sg* **-rze**) *m* marble
**marmurowy** *adj* marble *attr*
**marnie** *adv* poorly
**marni|eć (-eję, -ejesz)** (*perf* **z-**) *vi* (*o człowieku*) to waste *lub* pine away; (*o roślinie*) to wither (away)
**marnotra|wić (-wię, -wisz)** (*perf* **z-**) *vt* to squander
**marnotrawny** *adj*: **syn ~** prodigal son
**marnotrawst|wo** (**-wa**) (*loc sg* **-wie**) *nt* waste
**marn|ować (-uję, -ujesz)** (*perf* **z-**) *vt* to waste; **marnować się** *vr* to go to waste
**marny** *adj* (*pensja, grosz*) paltry; (*zdrowie, kucharz*) poor; **iść (pójść** *perf*) **na marne** to go to waste; **~ twój los** you're in real trouble; **nie powiedzieć komuś marnego słowa** never to say an angry word to sb
**Maro|ko** (**-ka**) (*instr sg* **-kiem**) *nt* Morocco
**Mar|s** (**-sa**) (*loc sg* **-sie**) *m* Mars
**Marsja|nin** (**-nina, -nie**) (*loc sg* **-ninie**, *gen pl* **-n**) *m* Martian
**marskoś|ć** (**-ci**) *f*: **~ wątroby** cirrhosis
**marsowy** *adj* (*mina, spojrzenie*) stern
**Marsyli|a** (**-i**) *f* Marseilles
**marsz** (**-u, -e**) *m* march; **naprzód ~!** quick march!; **biegiem ~!** double (time)!; **~ weselny/żałobny** wedding/funeral march; **kiszki mi ~a grają** (*pot*) I'm starving (*pot*)
**marszał|ek** (**-ka, -kowie**) (*instr sg* **-kiem**) *m* (*Wojsk*) marshal; (*sejmu, senatu*) speaker
**marszcz|yć (-ę, -ysz)** (*perf* **z-**) *vt* (*czoło, nos*) to wrinkle; (*sukienkę*) to gather; **~ brwi** to knit one's brows; **marszczyć się** *vr* (*o twarzy*) to wrinkle; (*o materiale*) to crease
**marszru|ta** (**-ty, -ty**) (*dat sg* **-cie**) *f* itinerary
**martwic|a** (**-y**) *f* (*Med*) necrosis
**mart|wić (-wię, -wisz)** (*perf* **z-**) *vt* to upset; **martwić się** *vr* to worry; **~ się czymś** to worry about *lub* over sth; **~ się o** *+acc* to be concerned about; **nie martw się!** don't worry!
**martwy** *adj* dead; **martwa natura** still life; **utknąć** (*perf*) *lub* **stanąć** (*perf*) **w ~m punkcie** to come to a standstill
**martyrologi|a** (**-i**) *f* martyrdom
**maru|da** (**-dy, -dy**) (*dat sg* **-dzie**) *f lub m decl like f* (*zrzęda*) grumbler; (*guzdrała*) dawdler
**marude|r** (**-ra, -rzy**) (*loc sg* **-rze**) *m* (*żołnierz*) marauder; (*spóźnialski*) straggler
**marudny** *adj* grumpy
**maru|dzić (-dzę, -dzisz)** (*imp* **-dź**) *vi* (*zrzędzić*) to whine, to grumble; (*guzdrać się*): **~ (z czymś)** to dawdle (over sth)
**maryjny** *adj relating to the cult of the Virgin Mary*
**marynar|ka** (**-ki**) (*dat sg* **-ce**) *f* (*ubiór*) (*nom pl* **-ki**, *gen pl* **-ek**) jacket; (*też*: **marynarka wojenna**) navy; (*też*: **marynarka handlowa**) merchant marine *lub* navy
**marynarski** *adj* (*stopień*) naval; (*czapka, ubranie*) sailor *attr*
**marynarz** (**-a, -e**) (*gen pl* **-y**) *m* seaman, sailor
**maryna|ta** (**-ty, -ty**) (*dat sg* **-cie**) *f* (*do mięs*) marinade; (*do ogórków itp.*) pickle
**maryn|ować (-uję, -ujesz)** (*perf* **za-**) *vt* (*konserwować*) to pickle; (*przed gotowaniem*) to marinate
**marynowany** *adj* pickled
**ma|rzec** (**-rca, -rce**) *m* March
**marze|nie** (**-nia, -nia**) (*gen pl* **-ń**) *nt* dream; **~ ściętej głowy** pipe dream
**marz|nąć (-nę, -niesz)** (*imp* **-nij**) *vi* (*o człowieku*) (*perf* **z-**) to freeze; (*o deszczu, mżawce*) (*perf* **za-**) to freeze
**marzyciel** (**-a, -e**) (*gen pl* **-i**) *m* (day)dreamer
**marzycielski** *adj* dreamy
**marzycielst|wo** (**-wa**) (*loc sg* **-wie**) *nt* daydreaming
**marz|yć (-ę, -ysz)** *vi* to (day)dream; **~ o** *+loc* to dream of; **marzyć się** *vr*: **marzy mu się sława** he has dreams of fame
**marż|a** (**-y, -e**) *f* (*Handel*) (profit) margin
**ma|sa** (**-sy, -sy**) (*dat sg* **-sie**) *f* mass; (*Elektr*) earth (*Brit*), ground (*US*); **~ plastyczna** plastic; **(cała) ~** *+gen* masses of; **ciemna ~** (*pot*) numbskull (*pot*); **masy** *pl* (*lud*) the masses *pl*
**masak|ra** (**-ry, -ry**) (*dat sg* **-rze**) *f* massacre
**masakr|ować (-uję, -ujesz)** (*perf* **z-**) *vt* to massacre
**masaż** (**-u, -e**) (*gen pl* **-y**) *m* massage
**masaży|sta** (**-sty, -ści**) (*dat sg* **-ście**) *m decl like f in sg* masseur
**masażyst|ka** (**-ki, -ki**) (*dat sg* **-ce**, *gen pl* **-ek**) *f* masseuse
**masce** *n patrz* **maska**
**masecz|ka** (**-ki, -ki**) (*dat sg* **-ce**, *gen pl* **-ek**) *f* mask
**masek** *n patrz* **maska**
**maselnicz|ka** (**-ki, -ki**) (*dat sg* **-ce**, *gen pl* **-ek**) *f* butter dish
**mas|ka** (**-ki, -ki**) (*dat sg* **-ce**, *gen pl* **-ek**) *f* mask; (*Mot*) bonnet (*Brit*), hood (*US*); **~ gazowa** gas mask; **pod maską** *+gen* under the guise of
**maskara|da** (**-dy, -dy**) (*loc sg* **-dzie**) *f* masquerade
**maskot|ka** (**-ki, -ki**) (*dat sg* **-ce**, *gen pl* **-ek**) *f* mascot
**mask|ować (-uję, -ujesz)** (*perf* **za-**) *vt* to camouflage; (*przen*) to mask; **maskować się** *vr* to assume a disguise

**maskowy** *adj*: **bal ~** masked ball
**ma|sło** (**-sła**) (*loc sg* **-śle**) *nt* butter; **~ orzechowe** peanut butter; **~ kakaowe** cocoa butter; **jak po maśle** swimmingly; **~ maślane** (*pot*) tautology
**masochi|sta** (**-sty, -ści**) (*dat sg* **-ście**) *m decl like f in sg* masochist
**masochistyczny** *adj* masochistic
**masochiz|m** (**-mu**) (*loc sg* **-mie**) *m* masochism
**maso|n** (**-na, -ni**) (*loc sg* **-nie**) *m* freemason
**masoneri|a** (**-i**) *f* freemasonry
**masoński** *adj*: **loża masońska** masonic lodge
**mas|ować (-uję, -ujesz)** (*perf* **po-**) *vt* to massage
**maso|wiec** (**-wca, -wce**) *m* bulk carrier
**masowy** *adj* mass *attr*; **środki (masowego) przekazu** the (mass) media; **broń masowej zagłady** weapons of mass destruction
**masów|ka** (**-ki, -ki**) (*dat sg* **-ce**, *gen pl* **-ek**) (*pot*) *f* (*wiec*) rally; (*produkcja*) mass production
**mass-medi|a** (**-ów**) *pl* the (mass) media *pl*
**masturbacj|a** (**-i**) *f* masturbation
**masy|w** (**-wu, -wy**) (*loc sg* **-wie**) *m* (*górski*) massif
**masywny** *adj* (*budowla*) massive; (*człowiek*) hefty
**masz** *vb patrz* **mieć**
**maszer|ować (-uję, -ujesz)** (*perf* **po-**) *vi* to march
**masz|t** (**-tu, -ty**) (*loc sg* **-cie**) *m* pole; (*Żegl*) mast
**maszy|na** (**-ny, -ny**) (*dat sg* **-nie**) *f* machine; **~ cyfrowa** (digital) computer; **~ do pisania** typewriter; **~ do szycia** sewing machine; **pisać na maszynie** to type; **hala maszyn** (*w fabryce*) engine house; (*w biurze*) typing pool; **pracować jak ~** to work like a robot
**maszyneri|a** (**-i, -e**) (*gen pl* **-i**) *f* machinery
**maszyni|sta** (**-sty, -ści**) (*dat sg* **-ście**) *m decl like f in sg* engine driver (Brit), engineer (US)
**maszynist|ka** (**-ki, -ki**) (*dat sg* **-ce**, *gen pl* **-ek**) *f* typist
**maszyn|ka** (**-ki, -ki**) (*dat sg* **-ce**, *gen pl* **-ek**) *f* machine; (*kuchenka*) cooker; **~ do golenia** razor; **~ do mięsa** mincer
**maszynopi|s** (**-su, -sy**) (*loc sg* **-sie**) *m* typescript
**maszynow|nia** (**-ni, -nie**) (*gen pl* **-ni**) *f* engine room
**maszynowy** *adj* (*dotyczący maszyny*) machine *attr*; (*wykonany maszyną*) machine-made; **karabin/pistolet ~** machine/submachine gun; **papier ~** typing paper
**maś|ć** (**-ci, -ci**) (*gen pl* **-ci**) *f* (*Med*) ointment; (*konia, krowy*) colour (Brit), color (US); **wszelkiej maści** of every description
**maślan|ka** (**-ki**) (*dat sg* **-ce**) *f* buttermilk
**maślany** *adj* butter *attr*
**maśle** *n patrz* **masło**
**ma|t** (*loc sg* **-cie**) *m* (*gen sg* **-tu**) (*wykończenie*) mat(t) (finish); (*Szachy*) (*gen sg* **-ta**) checkmate; **dać** (*perf*) **komuś mata** to checkmate sb
**ma|ta** (**-ty, -ty**) (*dat sg* **-cie**) *f* mat
**matact|wo** (**-wa, -wa**) (*loc sg* **-wie**) *nt* hocus-pocus
**matado|r** (**-ra, -rzy**) (*loc sg* **-rze**) *m* matador
**matczyny** *adj* motherly
**matematyczny** *adj* (*wzór*) mathematical; (*maszyna*) calculating, computing
**matematy|k** (**-ka, -cy**) *m* mathematician
**matematy|ka** (**-ki**) (*dat sg* **-ce**) *f* mathematics; (*przedmiot, lekcja*) maths (*Brit*), math (US)
**matera|c** (**-ca, -ce**) (*gen pl* **-cy** *lub* **-ców**) *m* mattress; **~ dmuchany** air mattress
**materi|a** (**-i**) *f* matter; **przemiana materii** metabolism
**materiali|sta** (**-sty, -ści**) (*dat sg* **-ście**) *m decl like f in sg* materialist
**materialistyczny** *adj* materialistic
**materializ|m** (**-mu**) (*loc sg* **-mie**) *m* materialism
**materializ|ować się (-uję, -ujesz)** (*perf* **z-**) *vr* to materialize
**materialny** *adj* (*świat, kultura*) material; (*środki, sytuacja*) financial
**materia|ł** (**-łu, -ły**) (*loc sg* **-le**) *m* material; (*tkanina*) fabric; **~ wybuchowy** explosive; **~ dowodowy** the evidence
**mat|ka** (**-ki, -ki**) (*dat sg* **-ce**, *gen pl* **-ek**) *f* mother; **~ chrzestna** godmother; **M~ Boska** the Virgin Mary
**mato|ł** (**-ła, -ły**) (*loc sg* **-le**) *m* (*pot*) dumbhead (*pot*)
**mato|wieć (-wieje)** (*perf* **z-**) *vi* to tarnish
**matowy** *adj* (*szkło*) frosted; (*głos*) dull; (*farba, odbitka*) mat(t) *attr*
**matriarcha|t** (**-tu**) (*loc sg* **-cie**) *m* matriarchy
**matro|na** (**-ny, -ny**) (*dat sg* **-nie**) *f* matron
**matryc|a** (**-y, -e**) *f* matrix
**matrymonialny** *adj* matrimonial; **biuro matrymonialne** marriage bureau; **ogłoszenie matrymonialne** singles ad
**matu|ra** (**-ry, -ry**) (*dat sg* **-rze**) *f* ≈ GCSE (*Brit*), ≈ high school finals (US); **zdać** (*perf*) **maturę** ≈ to pass the GCSE (*Brit*), ≈ to graduate (*US*)
**maturalny** *adj*: **świadectwo maturalne** ≈ GCSE (*Brit*), ≈ High School Diploma (*US*); **bal ~** graduation ball; **egzamin ~ = matura**
**maturzy|sta** (**-sty, -ści**) (*dat sg* **-ście**) *m decl like f in sg* ≈ secondary school leaver (Brit), ≈ high school graduate (US)
**maturzyst|ka** (**-ki, -ki**) (*dat sg* **-ce**, *gen pl* **-ek**) *f* ≈ secondary school leaver (Brit), ≈ high school graduate (US)

**mauzole|um** (**-um, -a**) (*gen pl* **-ów**) *nt inv in sg* mausoleum
**mawi|ać (-am, -asz)** *vi*: **jak mawiał mój dziadek** as my Grandpa used to say
**ma|zać (-żę, -żesz)** *vt* (*brudzić*) (*perf* **-znąć** *lub* **po-**) to smear; (*ścierać*) (*perf* **z-**) to erase
**maza|k** (**-ka, -ki**) (*instr* **-kiem**) *m* felt-tip (pen)
**mazga|j** (**-ja, -je**) (*gen pl* **-jów** *lub* **-i**) *m* (*pot*) cry-baby (*pot*)
**ma|znąć (-znę, -źniesz)** (*imp* **-źnij**) *vb perf od* **mazać**
**mazu|r** (**-ra, -ry**) (*loc sg* **-rze**) *m* mazurka (*dance*); **Mazur** (*nom pl* **-rzy**) *an inhabitant of Mazury*
**mazur|ek** (**-ka, -ki**) (*instr sg* **-kiem**) *m* (*Muz*) mazurka; (*Kulin*) *a frosted cake traditionally eaten at Easter*
**Mazur|y** (-) *pl a region in north-eastern Poland*
**mazu|t** (**-tu**) (*loc sg* **-cie**) *m* mazout
**ma|ź** (**-zi, -zie**) (*gen pl* **-zi**) *f* gunk; **maź stawowa** synovia
**mące** *n patrz* **mąka**
**mąciciel** (**-a, -e**) (*gen pl* **-i**) *m* troublemaker
**mą|cić (-cę, -cisz)** (*imp* **-ć**, *perf* **z-**) *vt* (*wodę*) to stir; (*przen: spokój, radość*) to disturb; **mącić się** *vr*: **~ komuś w głowie** to put ideas in sb's head
**mącz|ka** (**-ki, -ki**) (*dat sg* **-ce**, *gen pl* **-ek**) *f*: **~ ziemniaczana** potato starch; **~ kostna** bone meal; **~ rybna** fish meal *lub* flour
**mączny** *adj* flour *attr*
**mądral|a** (**-i, -e**) (*gen pl* **-i**) *m decl like f* (*pot*) know-all (*pot*)
**mądroś|ć** (**-ci, -ci**) (*gen pl* **-ci**) *f* wisdom; **ząb mądrości** wisdom tooth
**mąd|ry** (*comp* **-rzejszy**) *adj* wise; **nie bądź taki ~!** don't try to be so smart!
**mądrze** *adv* wisely
**mądrz|eć (-eję, -ejesz)** (*perf* **z-**) *vi* to grow wise
**mądrz|yć się (-ę, -ysz)** *vr* (*pot*) to play the wise guy (*pot*)
**mąk** *n patrz* **męka**
**mą|ka** (**-ki, -ki**) (*dat sg* **-ce**) *f* flour; (*grubo zmielona*) meal
**mąż** (**męża, mężowie**) *m* husband; **wyjść** (*perf*) **za mąż** to get married, to marry; **mąż stanu** statesman; **mąż zaufania** intermediary; **jak jeden mąż** with one accord
**m.b.** *abbr* (= *metr bieżący*) m (= *metre*)
**mchu** *itd. n patrz* **mech**
**mdl|eć (-eję, -ejesz)** (*perf* **ze-**) *vi* to faint
**mdl|ić (-i)** *vt* to nauseate, to make sick; **mdli mnie** I feel sick
**mdłości** (-) *pl* nausea; **mieć ~** to feel nauseous; **wywoływać (wywołać** *perf*) **~** to cause nausea
**mdły** *adj* (*nijaki*) bland; (*mdlący*) nauseating
**meb|el** (**-la, -le**) (*gen pl* **-li**) *m* a piece of furniture; **meble** *pl* furniture
**meblościan|ka** (**-ki, -ki**) (*dat sg* **-ce**, *gen pl* **-ek**) *f* wall unit (set)
**mebl|ować (-uję, -ujesz)** (*perf* **u-**) *vt* to furnish
**meblowy** *adj* furniture *attr*
**mecena|s** (**-sa, -si** *lub* **-sowie**) (*loc sg* **-sie**) *m* patron; (*Prawo*) *polite term used when addressing a lawyer*
**mecena|t** (**-tu, -ty**) (*loc sg* **-cie**) *m* patronage
**mech** (**mchu, mchy**) *m* moss
**mechaniczny** *adj* mechanical; **pojazd ~** motor vehicle; **koń ~** horsepower
**mechani|k** (**-ka, -cy**) *m* mechanic
**mechani|ka** (**-ki**) (*dat sg* **-ce**) *f* mechanics
**mechanizacj|a** (**-i**) *f* mechanization
**mechaniz|m** (**-mu, -my**) (*loc sg* **-mie**) *m* (*maszyny*) mechanism; (*zjawiska*) mechanics
**mechaniz|ować (-uję, -ujesz)** (*perf* **z-**) *vt* to mechanize
**mecz** (**-u, -e**) *m* match, game
**meczbol** (**-a, -e**) (*gen pl* **-i**) *m* match point
**mecze|t** (**-tu, -ty**) (*loc sg* **-cie**) *m* mosque
**med.** *abbr* = **medyczny**; **medycyna**
**medal** (**-u, -e**) (*gen pl* **-i**) *m* medal; **odwrotna strona ~u** (*przen*) the other side of the coin
**medali|k** (**-ka, -ki**) (*instr sg* **-kiem**) *m small medallion worn by Catholics as a religious symbol*
**medalio|n** (**-nu, -ny**) (*loc sg* **-nie**) *m* medallion
**medali|sta** (**-sty, -ści**) (*dat sg* **-ście**) *m decl like f in sg* medallist (Brit), medalist (US); **złoty ~** gold medal(l)ist
**medi|a** (**-ów**) *pl* the media *pl*
**mediacj|a** (**-i, -e**) (*gen pl* **-i**) *f* mediation
**mediato|r** (**-ra, -rzy**) (*loc sg* **-rze**) *m* mediator
**Mediola|n** (**-nu**) (*loc sg* **-nie**) *m* Milan
**medi|um** (**-um, -a**) (*gen pl* **-ów**) *nt inv in sg* medium
**medu|za** (**-zy, -zy**) (*dat sg* **-zie**) *f* jellyfish
**medycy|na** (**-ny**) (*dat sg* **-nie**) *f* medicine; **studiować medycynę** to study medicine
**medyczny** *adj* medical
**medytacj|a** (**-i, -e**) (*gen pl* **-i**) *f* meditation
**medyt|ować (-uję, -ujesz)** *vi* to meditate
**mega...** *pref* mega...
**megabaj|t** (**-ta, -ty**) (*loc sg* **-cie**) *m* megabyte
**megafo|n** (**-nu, -ny**) (*loc sg* **-nie**) *m* megaphone
**megaloma|n** (**-na, -ni**) (*loc sg* **-nie**) *m* megalomaniac
**megalomani|a** (**-i**) *f* megalomania
**megasa|m** (**-mu, -my**) (*loc sg* **-mie**) *m* superstore
**megawa|t** (**-ta, -ty**) (*loc sg* **-cie**) *m* megawatt
**Mek|ka** (**-ki**) (*dat sg* **-ce**) *f* Mecca; **mekka** (*przen*) Mecca

m

**Meksy|k** (**-ku**) (*instr sg* **-kiem**) *m* (*państwo*) Mexico; (*miasto*) Mexico City
**Meksyka|nin** (**-nina, -nie**) (*loc sg* **-ninie**, *gen pl* **-n**) *m* Mexican
**Meksykan|ka** (**-ki, -ki**) (*dat sg* **-ce**, *gen pl* **-ek**) *f* Mexican
**meksykański** *adj* Mexican
**melancholi|a** (**-i**) *f* melancholy
**melancholijny** *adj* melancholy, melancholic
**mela|sa** (**-sy**) *f* treacle (*Brit*), molasses (*US*)
**meld|ować (-uję, -ujesz)** (*perf* **za-**) *vi* to report ▷ *vt* to report; (*lokatora*) to register; **~ o** *+loc* to report of; **meldować się** *vr* to report; (*jako lokator*) to register
**meldun|ek** (**-ku, -ki**) (*instr sg* **-kiem**) *m* (*doniesienie*) report; (*zameldowanie*) registration
**meli|na** (**-ny, -ny**) (*dat sg* **-nie**) *f* (*pot: pijacka*) shebeen (*pot*); (*złodziejska*) den
**melioracj|a** (**-i, -e**) (*gen pl* **-i**) *f* land improvement
**meli|sa** (**-sy, -sy**) (*dat sg* **-sie**) *f* lemon balm
**melodi|a** (**-i, -e**) (*gen pl* **-i**) *f* melody
**melodrama|t** (**-tu, -ty**) (*loc sg* **-cie**) *m* melodrama
**melodramatyczny** *adj* melodramatic
**melodyjny** *adj* melodious
**meloma|n** (**-na, -ni**) (*loc sg* **-nie**) *m* music lover
**melo|n** (**-na, -ny**) (*loc sg* **-nie**) *m* melon
**meloni|k** (**-ka, -ki**) (*instr sg* **-kiem**) *m* bowler (hat)
**mełł** *itd. vb patrz* **mleć**
**membra|na** (**-ny, -ny**) (*dat sg* **-nie**) *f* membrane
**memorand|um** (**-um, -a**) (*gen pl* **-ów**) *nt inv in sg* memorandum
**memoria|ł** (**-łu, -ły**) (*loc sg* **-le**) *m* memorial; (*Sport*) memorial contest *lub* tournament
**MEN** *abbr* (= *Ministerstwo Edukacji Narodowej*) ≈ Department of Education and Science (*Brit*), ≈ Department of Education (*US*)
**menażeri|a** (**-i, -e**) (*gen pl* **-i**) *f* menagerie
**menaż|ka** (**-ki, -ki**) (*dat sg* **-ce**, *gen pl* **-ek**) *f* mess tin (*Brit*), mess kit (*US*)
**menedże|r** (**-ra, -rowie**) (*loc sg* **-rze**) *m* manager
**mennic|a** (**-y, -e**) *f* mint
**menopau|za** (**-zy, -zy**) (*dat sg* **-zie**) *f* the menopause
**menstruacj|a** (**-i, -e**) (*gen pl* **-i**) *f* menstruation
**mentalnoś|ć** (**-ci**) *f* mentality
**mentalny** *adj* mental
**menu** *nt inv* menu
**menue|t** (**-ta, -ty**) (*loc sg* **-cie**) *m* minuet
**menzur|ka** (**-ki, -ki**) (*dat sg* **-ce**, *gen pl* **-ek**) *f* measuring cylinder
**me|r** (**-ra, -rowie**) (*loc sg* **-rze**) *m* mayor
**merit|um** (**-um, -a**) *nt inv in sg*; **~ sprawy** heart of the matter
**merost|wo** (**-wa, -wa**) (*loc sg* **-wie**) *nt* (*urząd*) mayorship; (*kancelaria*) mayoralty; (*mer z żoną*) mayor and his wife
**meryno|s** (**-sa, -sy**) (*loc sg* **-sie**) *m* merino
**merytoryczny** *adj* content-related
**me|sa** (**-sy, -sy**) (*dat sg* **-sie**) *f* mess
**Mesjasz** (**-a**) *m* Messiah
**mesz|ek** (**-ku**) (*instr sg* **-kiem**) *m* (*na skórze, owocach*) down; (*na materiale*) fluff
**me|ta** (**-ty, -ty**) (*dat sg* **-cie**) *f* finish (line), finishing line; (*pot: melina*) dive (*pot*); **na dłuższą/krótszą metę** in the long/short run; **z mety** (*pot*) pronto (*pot*)
**metaboliz|m** (**-mu**) (*loc sg* **-mie**) *m* metabolism
**metafizyczny** *adj* metaphysical
**metafizy|ka** (**-ki**) (*dat sg* **-ce**) *f* metaphysics
**metafo|ra** (**-ry, -ry**) (*dat sg* **-rze**) *f* metaphor
**metaforyczny** *adj* metaphorical
**metal** (**-u, -e**) (*gen pl* **-i**) *m* metal
**metaliczny** *adj* metallic
**metali|k** (**-ka, -ki**) (*instr sg* **-kiem**) *m* metallic (finish)
**metalowy** *adj* metal *attr*; (*przemysł*) metallurgical
**metalurgi|a** (**-i**) *f* metallurgy
**metalurgiczny** *adj* metallurgical
**metamorfo|za** (**-zy, -zy**) (*dat sg* **-zie**) *f* metamorphosis
**meta|n** (**-nu**) (*loc sg* **-nie**) *m* methane
**meteo|r** (**-ru, -ry**) (*loc sg* **-rze**) *m* meteor
**meteorolo|g** (**-ga, -gowie** *lub* **-dzy**) *m* (*Radio, TV*) weatherman; (*naukowiec*) meteorologist
**meteorologi|a** (**-i**) *f* meteorology
**meteorologiczny** *adj* (*prognoza*) weather *attr*; (*stacja*) meteorological
**meteory|t** (**-tu, -ty**) (*loc sg* **-cie**) *m* meteorite
**met|ka** (**-ki, -ki**) (*dat sg* **-ce**, *gen pl* **-ek**) *f* (*etykietka: naklejana*) label; (*: przywieszana*) tag; (*kiełbasa*) meat spread
**metk|ować (-uję, -ujesz)** (*perf* **po-**) *vt* to label
**metkownic|a** (**-y, -e**) *f* labeller (*Brit*), labeler (*US*)
**meto|da** (**-dy, -dy**) (*dat sg* **-dzie**) *f* method
**metodologi|a** (**-i, -e**) (*gen pl* **-i**) *f* methodology
**metodyczny** *adj* (*systematyczny*) methodical; (*dotyczący metody*) methodological
**metody|ka** (**-ki**) (*dat sg* **-ce**) *f* methodology
**metody|sta** (**-sty, -ści**) (*loc sg* **-ście**) *m decl like f in sg* Methodist
**met|r** (**-ra, -ry**) (*loc sg* **-rze**) *m* metre (*Brit*), meter (*US*); **~ kwadratowy/sześcienny** square/cubic metre; **~ bieżący** running metre; **na ~y** by the metre
**metraż** (**-u, -e**) (*gen pl* **-y**) *m* (*pole powierzchni*) (metric) area; (*powierzchnia mieszkalna*) living area
**met|ro** (**-ra**) (*loc sg* **-rze**) *nt* tube (*Brit*), underground (*Brit*), subway (*US*)

**metrono|m** (**-mu, -my**) (*loc sg* **-mie**) *m* metronome
**metropoli|a** (**-i, -e**) (*gen pl* **-i**) *f* metropolis
**metropoli|ta** (**-ty, -ci**) (*dat sg* **-cie**) *m decl like f in sg* metropolitan
**metrum** *nt inv* (*Muz*) time; (*Lit*) metre (*Brit*), meter (*US*)
**metryczny** *adj* metric
**metry|ka** (**-ki, -ki**) (*dat sg* **-ce**) *f* (*chrztu, urodzenia*) certificate; (*rodowód zwierzęcia*) pedigree
**metylowy** *adj*: **alkohol ~** methyl alcohol, methanol
**Mety|s** (**-sa, -si**) (*loc sg* **-sie**) *m* mestizo
**me|wa** (**-wy, -wy**) (*dat sg* **-wie**) *f* seagull
**mezalian|s** (**-su, -se**) (*loc sg* **-sie**) *m* mésalliance, misalliance; **popełnić** (*perf*) **~** to marry below one's station
**męczar|nia** (**-ni, -nie**) (*gen pl* **-ni**) *f* (*duchowa*) torment; (*fizyczna*) torture
**męczący** *adj* tiring, tiresome
**męczennic|a** (**-y, -e**) *f* martyr
**męczenni|k** (**-ka, -cy**) (*instr sg* **-kiem**) *m* martyr
**męczeńst|wo** (**-wa**) (*loc sg* **-wie**) *nt* martyrdom
**męcz|yć (-ę, -ysz)** *vt* (*powodować zmęczenie*) (*perf* **z-**) to tire; (*znęcać się*) to torment; (*o kaszlu, hałasie*) to bother; **nie męcz mnie** stop pestering me; **męczyć się** *vr* (*odczuwać zmęczenie*) (*perf* **z-**) to get tired; (*cierpieć*) to suffer; **~ się nad czymś** to toil over sth
**mędrk|ować (-uję, -ujesz)** *vi* (*pot*) to play the wise guy (*pot*)
**męd|rzec** (**-rca, -rcy**) (*voc sg* **-rcze**) *m* sage
**mę|ka** (**-ki, -ki**) (*dat sg* **-ce**, *gen pl* **mąk**) *f* (*cierpienie fizyczne*) torture; (*cierpienie moralne*) torment
**męski** *adj* (*konfekcja, oddział, fryzjer*) men's *attr*; (*charakter, decyzja*) masculine, manly; (*osobnik, narządy*) male; **rodzaj ~** masculine (gender)
**męskoosobowy** *adj*: **rodzaj ~** (*Jęz*) virile gender
**męskoś|ć** (**-ci**) *f* masculinity, manhood
**męst|wo** (**-wa**) (*loc sg* **-wie**) *nt* bravery
**mętli|k** (**-ku**) (*instr sg* **-kiem**) *m* mess; **mieć ~ w głowie** to be all confused
**mętni|eć (-eje)** (*perf* **z-**) *vi* to cloud (up)
**mętny** *adj* (*woda, sok*) cloudy, murky; (*wzrok*) glassy; (*rozumowanie, wypowiedź*) cloudy
**męt|y** (**-ów**) *pl* dregs *pl*
**męża** *itd. n patrz* **mąż**
**mężat|ka** (**-ki, -ki**) (*dat sg* **-ce**, *gen pl* **-ek**) *f* married woman
**mężczy|zna** (**-zny, -źni**) (*dat sg* **-źnie**, *gen pl* **-zn**) *m decl like f in sg* man
**mężni|eć (-eję, -ejesz)** (*perf* **z-**) *vi* (*dorastać*) to grow into a man; (*nabierać siły*) to grow strong
**mężny** *adj* (*odważny*) brave; (*dzielny*) valiant
**MFW** *abbr* (= *Międzynarodowy Fundusz Walutowy*) IMF (= *International Monetary Fund*)
**mg** *abbr* (= *miligram*) mg
**mglisty** *adj* (*dzień*) foggy, misty; (*niewyraźny*) hazy; (*niejasny*) vague
**mg|ła** (**-ły, -ły**) (*dat sg* **-le**, *gen pl* **mgieł**) *f* (*gęsta*) fog; (*średnia*) mist; (*lekka*) haze; **pamiętać (coś) jak przez mgłę** to have a dim recollection (of sth)
**mgławic|a** (**-y, -e**) *f* (*Astron*) nebula; (*przen*) cloud
**mgnie|nie** (**-nia, -nia**) (*gen pl* **-ń**) *nt*: **w mgnieniu oka** in the twinkling of an eye
**mgr** *abbr* (= *magister*) (*nauk humanistycznych*) ≈ MA (= *Master of Arts*); (*nauk ścisłych, przyrodniczych*) ≈ MSc (= *Master of Science*)
**mia|ł**[1] (**-łu, -ły**) (*loc sg* **-le**) *m* dust
**miał**[2] *itd. vb patrz* **mieć**
**miałki** *adj* (*sypki*) fine; (*powierzchowny*) shallow
**mia|no** (**-na, -na**) (*loc sg* **-nie**) *nt* (*książk*) name
**mian|ować (-uję, -ujesz)** *vt* (*im*)*perf* to appoint, to nominate
**mianowicie** *adv*: **(a) ~** namely
**mianowni|k** (**-ka, -ki**) (*instr sg* **-kiem**) *m* (*Jęz*) nominative; (*Mat*) denominator; **wspólny ~** common denominator; **sprowadzać (sprowadzić** *perf*) **coś do wspólnego ~a** (*przen*) to find a common denominator for sth
**mia|ra** (**-ry, -ry**) (*dat sg* **mierze**) *f* measure; (*rozmiar*) size; (*umiarkowanie*) moderation, measure; **brać (wziąć** *perf*) **(czyjąś) miarę** to take sb's measurements; **w miarę jak** as; **w dużej mierze** to a large degree; **ze wszech miar** by all means; **żadną miarą** by no means
**miar|ka** (**-ki, -ki**) (*dat sg* **-ce**, *gen pl* **-ek**) *f* (*przyrząd*) (tape) measure
**miarodajny** *adj* authoritative, reliable
**miarowoś|ć** (**-ci**) *f* regularity
**miarowy** *adj* regular
**miastecz|ko** (**-ka, -ka**) (*gen pl* **-ek**, *instr sg* **-kiem**) *nt* (small) town; **wesołe ~** funfair (*Brit*), amusement park (*US*)
**miast|o** (**-a, -a**) (*loc sg* **mieście**) *nt* (*małe lub średnie*) town; (*duże*) city; **iść (pójść** *perf*) **do miasta** to go (in)to town (*Brit*), to go downtown (*US*); **jechać (pojechać** *perf*) **za ~** to take a drive out of town; **na mieście** (*pot*) in the high street (*Brit*), downtown (*US*)
**miau|czeć (-czy)** (*perf* **-knąć**) *vi* to mew, to miaow
**miaz|ga** (**-gi**) (*dat sg* **-dze**) *f* pulp; **zetrzeć** (*perf*) **coś na miazgę** to reduce sth to a pulp; **zetrzeć** (*perf*) **kogoś na miazgę** to make mincemeat of sb

m

**miażdżący** *adj* crushing
**miażdżyc|a** (**-y**) *f* atherosclerosis
**miażdż|yć (-ę, -ysz)** (*perf* **z-**) *vt* to crush
**miąć (mnę, mniesz)** (*imp* **mnij**, *perf* **z-**) *vt* to crumple (up); **miąć się** *vr* to crease, to crumple
**miąższ** (**-u**) *m* (*owocu*) pulp, flesh
**micie** *n patrz* **mit**
**miech** (**-a, -y**) *m* bellows *pl*
**miecz** (**-a, -e**) (*gen pl* **-ów** *lub* **-y**) *m* sword; (*Żegl*) centreboard (*Brit*), centerboard (*US*)
**mieczy|k** (**-ka, -ki**) (*instr sg* **-kiem**) *m* (*Bot*) gladiolus, sword lily; (*Zool*) sword-tail

 SŁOWO KLUCZOWE

**mieć (mam, masz)** (*imp* **miej**, *pt* **miał, mieli**) *vt* **1** (*posiadać*) to have; **mieć coś na sobie** to have sth on, to be wearing sth; **mam!** (*rozumiem*) (I) got it!
**2** (*składać się z czegoś*) to have; **kwadrat ma cztery boki** a square has four sides
**3** (*zmartwienie, trudności, grypę, operację*) to have; **mieć coś do kogoś** to have sth to ask sb; **mieć coś przeciw czemuś** to have sth against sth
**4** (*z różnymi dopełnieniami*) to have; **mieć miejsce** to take place; **masz (jeszcze) czas!** take your time!; **mieć ochotę na coś/zrobienie czegoś** to feel like sth/doing sth
**5** (*dla wyrażenia powinności*) to be supposed to, to be to; **masz spać** you're supposed to be sleeping
**6** (*dla wyrażenia zamiaru*) to be going to; **ona ma przyjść jutro** she's going to come tomorrow
**7** (*forma zaprzeczona czasownika być*): **nie ma** (*liczba pojedyncza*) there's no; (*liczba mnoga*) there are no; **nie ma czasu** there's no time; **nie ma ludzi** there are no people; **nie ma co czekać/żałować** there's no use waiting/regretting; **nie ma się czemu dziwić** (there's) no wonder; **nie ma za co!** you're welcome!; **cudów nie ma** (*pot*) miracles (simply) don't happen
**8** (*z imiesłowem biernym*): **miał to obiecane** it's been promised to him
**mieć się** *vr*: **jak się masz?** how are you?; **mieć się za** *+acc* to consider o.s. ...; **rzecz ma się tak ...** as things stand ...; **ma się na deszcz** it looks like rain

**miednic|a** (**-y, -e**) *f* basin, bowl; (*Anat*) pelvis
**miedziany** *adj* copper *attr*
**mie|dź** (**-dzi**) *f* copper
**miejsc|e** (**-a, -a**) *nt* (*wolna przestrzeń*) space, room; (*wycinek przestrzeni*) place, spot; (*położenie*) position; (*miejscowość*) place; (*w hotelu*) vacancy; (*siedzące*) seat; (*urywek tekstu*) passage; (*pozycja, ranga*) place, position; **~ publiczne** public place; **~ pracy** workplace; **~ przeznaczenia** destination; **~ zamieszkania** (place of) residence; **na miejscu** (*tam, gdzie coś lub ktoś jest*) on the spot; (*u celu*) there; **zginąć na miejscu** to die on the spot, to be killed on the spot; **mieć ~** to take place; **na/w ~ czegoś** in place of sth; **nie mogę sobie znaleźć miejsca** I can't find a place for myself; **ustąpić komuś miejsca** to yield a seat to sb; **na twoim miejscu** if I were you; **miejscami** in places; **z miejsca** right away
**miejscowni|k** (**-ka, -ki**) (*instr sg* **-kiem**) *m* locative
**miejscowoś|ć** (**-ci, -ci**) (*gen pl* **-ci**) *f* place
**miejscowy** *adj* local
**miejsców|ka** (**-ki, -ki**) (*dat sg* **-ce**, *gen pl* **-ek**) *f* seat reservation
**miejski** *adj* urban
**miel** *itd. vb patrz* **mleć**
**miel|ić (-ę, -isz)** (*perf* **z-**) *vb* = **mleć**
**mieli|zna** (**-zny, -zny**) (*dat sg* **-źnie**) *f* shallow; **osiąść** (*perf*) **na mieliźnie** to run aground
**mielone** (**-go**) *nt decl like adj* (*mięso*) mince (*Brit*), hamburger (*US*)
**mielony** *adj* (*kawa, pieprz*) ground; (*mięso*) minced ▷ *m decl like adj* (*też*: **kotlet mielony**) ≈ hamburger
**mie|nić się (-nię, -nisz)** (*imp* **-ń**) *vr* to sparkle
**mieni|e** (**-a**) *nt* property, possessions *pl*
**mierni|k** (**-ka, -ki**) (*instr sg* **-kiem**) *m* (*Tech*) meter, gauge; (*czasu, pracy*) measure; (*przen*) yardstick, touchstone
**miernoś|ć** (**-ci**) *f* mediocrity
**mierny** *adj* mediocre
**mierze** *n patrz* **miara**
**mierz|yć (-ę, -ysz)** (*perf* **z-**) *vt* (*dokonywać pomiaru*) to measure ▷ *vi* (*perf* **wy-**); **~ (do kogoś)** to aim (at sb); **~ (w coś)** to aim (at sth); **wysoko ~** (*przen*) to aim high; **mierzyć się** *vr*: **~ się z kimś/czymś** to set o.s. against sb/sth; **nie móc się ~ z kimś** to be no rival for sb; **~ się wzrokiem** to size each other up; **~ się z kimś** to pit o.s. against sb
**miesi|ąc** (**-ąca, -ące**) (*gen pl* **-ęcy**) *m* month; **miodowy ~** honeymoon
**miesiącz|ka** (**-ki, -ki**) (*dat sg* **-ce**, *gen pl* **-ek**) *f* period
**miesiączk|ować (-uję, -ujesz)** *vi* to menstruate
**miesięczni|k** (**-ka, -ki**) (*instr sg* **-kiem**) *m* monthly
**miesięczny** *adj* monthly
**miesz|ać (-am, -asz)** *vt* (*rozrabiać*) (*perf* **wy-** *lub* **za-**) to stir; (*łączyć*) (*perf* **z-**) to blend, to mix; (*potrząsać*) to shake; (*wplątywać*) (*perf* **w-**) to

involve; (*mylić*) (*perf* **po-**) to mix up, to confuse; **~ (z~** *perf***) kogoś z błotem** (*przen*) to sling mud at sb (*przen*); **~ (w~** *perf***) kogoś w coś** to involve sb in sth; **mieszać się** *vr* (*łączyć się*) to blend, to mix; (*wtrącać się*) to meddle; **wszystko mi się miesza** I got it all mixed up
**miesza|niec** (**-ńca, -ńce**) *m* cross-breed
**mieszani|na** (**-ny, -ny**) (*dat sg* **-nie**) *f* mixture, mix
**mieszan|ka** (**-ki, -ki**) (*dat sg* **-ce**, *gen pl* **-ek**) *f* mixture, mix; (*Mot*) mixture
**mieszany** *adj* mixed
**mieszcza|nin** (**-nina, -nie**) (*loc sg* **-ninie**, *gen pl* **-n**) *m* burgher, townsman; **mieszczanie** townspeople, townsfolk
**mieszczański** *adj* (*gust, moralność*) ≈ middle-class *attr*
**mieszczańst|wo** (**-wa**) (*loc sg* **-wie**) *nt* bourgeoisie
**mieszk|ać (-am, -asz)** *vi* (*stale*) to live; (*chwilowo*) to stay
**mieszkalny** *adj* (*dom, budynek*) residential; (*dzielnica*) residential, living *attr*
**mieszka|nie** (**-nia, -nia**) (*gen pl* **-ń**) *nt* flat (*Brit*), apartment (*US*)
**mieszka|niec** (**-ńca, -ńcy**) *m* (*domu*) occupant; (*miasta*) inhabitant; (*kraju*) resident
**mieszkaniowy** *adj* housing *attr*; **spółdzielnia mieszkaniowa** ≈ housing association
**mie|ścić (-szczę, -ścisz)** (*imp* **-ść**) *vt* (*zawierać: o naczyniu*) to hold; (*o budynku*) to house; (*o sali koncertowej*) to seat; **mieścić się** *vr* (*znajdować się*) to be situated; (*znajdować dość miejsca*) (*perf* **z-**) to fit; **to mi się nie mieści w głowie** it boggles my mind
**mieście** *n patrz* **miasto**
**miew|ać (-am, -asz)** *vt* to have (every now and then); **miewać się** *vr* to be feeling *lub* doing
**mięcza|k** (**-ka, -ki**) (*instr sg* **-kiem**) *m* (*Zool*) mollusc; (*pot: o człowieku*) wimp (*pot*)
**między** *prep +loc* (*dla oznaczenia miejsca: pomiędzy*) between; (*: wśród*) among; (*dla określenia przedziału czasu*) between ▷ *prep +acc* (*dla oznaczenia kierunku: pomiędzy*) between; (*: wśród*) among; (*przy podziale*) between; (*przy wyborze*) between; **~ (godziną) szóstą a siódmą** between six and seven (o'clock); **~ nami mówiąc** between you and me; **~ sobą** between ourselves/yourselves/themselves; **~ innymi** among other things
**międzycza|s** (**-su, -sy**) (*loc sg* **-sie**) *m* (*Sport*) lap time; **w ~ie** in the meantime
**międzykontynentalny** *adj* intercontinental
**międzylądowa|nie** (**-nia, -nia**) (*gen pl* **-ń**) *nt* intermediate landing
**międzyludzki** *adj* interpersonal
**międzymiastow|a** (**-ej, -e**) *f decl like adj* (*pot: też:* **rozmowa międzymiastowa**) long-distance call; (*pot: też:* **centrala międzymiastowa**) long-distance operator
**międzymiastowy** *adj* (*transport*) intercity *attr*; (*połączenie telefoniczne*) long-distance *attr*; **rozmowa międzymiastowa** long-distance call
**międzynarodowy** *adj* international
**międzypaństwowy** *adj* international
**międzywojenny** *adj* (*ogólnie*) interwar *attr*; (*dotyczący lat 1918-39*) between WW I and WW II
**miękki** (*comp* **miększy**) *adj* soft; **mieć ~e serce** to have a soft heart; **~e lądowanie** soft landing
**miękko** (*comp* **miękcej**) *adv* softly; **jajko na ~** soft-boiled egg
**miękkoś|ć** (**-ci**) *f* softness
**mięk|nąć (-nę, -niesz)** (*imp* **-nij**, *perf* **z-**) *vi* to soften
**mię|sień** (**-śnia, -śnie**) (*gen pl* **-śni**) *m* muscle
**mięsisty** *adj* fleshy
**mięsny** *adj* meat *attr*
**mię|so** (**-sa, -sa**) (*loc sg* **-sie**) *nt* meat; **~ armatnie** (*przen*) cannon fodder
**mięsożerny** *adj* carnivorous
**mięśnia|k** (**-ka, -ki**) (*instr sg* **-kiem**) *m* (*Med*) myoma
**mięśniowy** *adj* muscular
**mię|ta** (**-ty, -ty**) (*dat sg* **-cie**) *f* mint; **~ pieprzowa** peppermint; **~ kędzierzawa** spearmint
**miętowy** *adj* (pepper)mint; **likier ~** creme de menthe
**miętów|ka** (**-ki, -ki**) (*dat sg* **-ce**, *gen pl* **-ek**) *f* (*pot: cukierek*) (pepper)mint
**mi|g** (**-gu, -gi**) (*instr sg* **-giem**) *m*: **na migi** in sign language; **migiem** *lub* **w mig** in a jiffy
**migacz** (**-a, -e**) (*gen pl* **-y**) *m* (*Mot*) indicator (*Brit*), turn signal (*US*)
**mig|ać (-am, -asz)** (*perf* **-nąć**) *vi* to flash; **migać się** *vr* (*pot*) to swing the lead (*pot*)
**migaw|ka** (**-ki, -ki**) (*dat sg* **-ce**, *gen pl* **-ek**) *f* (*Fot*) shutter; **migawki** *pl* (*z podróży*) snapshots *pl*
**migda|ł** (**-ła, -ły**) (*loc sg* **-le**) *m* almond; **myśleć/marzyć o niebieskich ~ach** to daydream
**migdał|ek** (**-ka, -ki**) (*instr sg* **-kiem**) *m* tonsil
**migdałowy** *adj* almond *attr*
**mig|nąć (-nę, -niesz)** (*imp* **-nij**) *vb perf od* **migać**
**migo|tać (-cze)** (*imp* **-cz**) *vi* to flicker
**migowy** *adj*: **język ~** sign language
**migracj|a** (**-i, -e**) (*gen pl* **-i**) *f* migration
**migre|na** (**-ny**) (*dat sg* **-nie**) *f* migraine
**migr|ować (-uję, -ujesz)** *vi* to migrate
**mij|ać (-am, -asz)** (*perf* **minąć**) *vt* to pass, to go past; **to cię nie minie** you won't escape it

m

▷ *vi* (*o czasie*) to go by, to pass; (*o bólu*) to go away; **mijać się** *vr* (*wymijać się*) to pass (each other); (*rozmijać się*) to miss each other; **to się mija z celem** there's no point in it; **minąć się z powołaniem** to have missed one's vocation; **~ się z prawdą** (*o człowieku*) to depart from the truth; (*o informacji*) to be untrue

**mija|nie** (**-nia**) *nt*: **światła mijania** (*Mot*) dipped (*Brit*) *lub* dimmed (US) (head)lights; **włączyć** *perf* **światła mijania** to dip (*Brit*) *lub* dim (US) one's (head)lights

**mijan|ka** (**-ki, -ki**) (*dat sg* **-ce**, *gen pl* **-ek**) *f* passing place

**Mikołaj** (**-a, -e**) *m* (*też*: **Święty Mikołaj**) Father Christmas (*Brit*), Santa (Claus) (US)

**mikro|b** (**-ba, -by**) (*loc sg* **-bie**) *m* microbe

**mikrobiologi|a** (**-i**) *f* microbiology

**mikrobu|s** (**-su, -sy**) (*loc sg* **-sie**) *m* minibus

**mikrofalowy** *adj* microwave *attr*; **kuchenka mikrofalowa** microwave (oven)

**mikrofalów|ka** (**-ki, -ki**) (*dat sg* **-ce**, *gen pl* **-ek**) *f* (*pot*) microwave

**mikrofil|m** (**-mu, -my**) (*loc sg* **-mie**) *m* microfilm

**mikrofo|n** (**-nu, -ny**) (*loc sg* **-nie**) *m* microphone

**mikroklima|t** (**-tu, -ty**) (*loc sg* **-cie**) *m* microclimate

**mikrokompute|r** (**-ra, -ry**) (*loc sg* **-rze**) *m* microcomputer

**mikrokosmo|s** (**-su**) (*loc sg* **-sie**) *m* microcosm

**mikroproceso|r** (**-ra, -ry**) (*loc sg* **-rze**) *m* microprocessor, microchip

**mikrosko|p** (**-pu, -py**) (*loc sg* **-pie**) *m* microscope

**mikroskopijny** *adj* microscopic

**mikse|r** (**-ra, -ry**) (*loc sg* **-rze**) *m* (*kuchenny elektryczny*) food mixer, liquidizer (*Brit*), blender (US); (*Tech*) mixer

**miks|ować** (**-uję, -ujesz**) (*perf* **z-**) *vt* (*łączyć*) to blend; (*rozdrabniać*) to liquidize

**mik|st** (**-stu, -sty**) (*loc sg* **-ście**) *m* (*Sport*) mixed doubles

**mikstu|ra** (**-ry, -ry**) (*dat sg* **-rze**) *f* concoction

**mil|a** (**-i, -e**) *f* mile; **~ angielska** (statute) mile; **~ morska** nautical mile

**milczący** *adj* silent

**milcz|eć** (**-ę, -ysz**) *vi* to keep *lub* remain silent; **~ jak grób** *lub* **głaz** to be (as) silent *lub* quiet as the grave; **milcz!** be quiet!

**milczeni|e** (**-a**) *nt* silence; **pominąć** (*perf*) **coś ~m** to pass over sth (in silence)

**mile** *adv* (*uśmiechać się*) kindly; (*wspominać*) pleasantly; **~ widziany** (very) welcome

**mileni|um, millenni|um** (**-um, -a**) *nt inv in sg* millennium

**miliar|d** (**-da, -dy**) (*loc sg* **-dzie**) *m* billion

**miliarde|r** (**-ra, -rzy**) (*loc sg* **-rze**) *m* billionaire

**milicj|a** (**-i, -e**) (*gen pl* **-i**) *f* (*w Polsce*) police (*in Poland between 1944 and 1990*); (*rezerwa wojskowa*) militia

**milicjan|t** (**-ta, -ci**) (*loc sg* **-cie**) *m* policeman (*in Poland between 1944 and 1990*)

**miligra|m** (**-ma, -my**) (*loc sg* **-mie**) *m* milligram(me)

**mililit|r** (**-ra, -ry**) (*loc sg* **-rze**) *m* millilitre (*Brit*), milliliter (US)

**milimet|r** (**-ra, -ry**) (*loc sg* **-rze**) *m* millimetre (*Brit*), millimeter (US)

**milio|n** (**-na, -ny**) (*loc sg* **-nie**) *m* million

**milione|r** (**-ra, -rzy**) (*loc sg* **-rze**) *m* millionaire

**milionowy** *adj* (*obdarzony numerem milion*) one millionth; (*niezliczony*) countless; (*o milionowej wartości*) worth millions

**militarny** *adj* (*siła, działania*) military; (*państwo*) militaristic

**militaryz|m** (**-mu**) (*loc sg* **-mie**) *m* militarism

**milk|nąć** (**-nę, -niesz**) (*imp* **-nij**, *perf* **za-**) *vi* to fall silent

**milowy** *adj*: **kamień ~** (*przen*) milestone

**miło** (*comp* **milej**) *adv* (*przyjemnie*) pleasantly, nicely; (*serdecznie*) kindly; **~ mi (Pana/Panią) poznać** pleased to meet you; **to bardzo ~ z twojej strony** that's very kind of you; **było bardzo ~** it was very nice; **aż ~** it's worth seeing

**miłosierdzi|e** (**-a**) *nt* mercy

**miłosierny** *adj* merciful

**miłosny** *adj* amorous *attr*; **list ~** love letter

**miłoś|ć** (**-ci, -ci**) (*gen pl* **-ci**) *f* love; **~ bliźniego** brotherly love; **~ własna** self-love, pride; **na ~ boską!** (*pot*) for God's *lub* heaven's sake!

**miłośni|k** (**-ka, -cy**) (*instr sg* **-kiem**) *m* lover, fan

**mił|ować** (**-uję, -ujesz**) *vt* (*książk*) to love

**miły** (*comp* **milszy**) *adj* (*człowiek*) nice; (*widok, nastrój, niespodzianka*) nice, pleasant; **bądź tak ~ i ...** would you be so kind and ...; **~ch snów!** sweet dreams!; **~ w dotyku** nice to the touch; **~ sercu** dear; **stój, jeśli ci życie miłe!** stop, for God's sake!

**mi|m** (**-ma, -mowie**) (*loc sg* **-mie**) *m* mime (artist)

**mimi|ka** (**-ki**) (*dat sg* **-ce**) *f* facial expression; (*Teatr*) mime

**mimo** *prep +gen* despite, in spite of; **~ to** *lub* **wszystko** nevertheless, all the same; **~ woli** unintentionally, involuntarily; **~ że** *lub* **iż** although, (even) though

**mimochodem** *adv* incidentally, in passing

**mimowolnie** *adv* involuntarily, unintentionally

**mimowolny** *adj* (*ruch, gest*) involuntary; (*świadek*) unintentional

**Min.** *abbr* Min. (= *Ministry*)

**m.in.** *abbr* (= *między innymi*) among other things, inter alia

**min.** *abbr* (= *minuta*) min. (= *minute*); (= *minimum*) min. (= *minimum*); (= *minister*) Min. (= *Minister*)
**mi|na** (**-ny, -ny**) (*dat sg* **-nie**) *f* (*wyraz twarzy*) face, look (*on sb's face*); (*bomba*) mine; **stroić miny** to make *lub* pull faces
**mi|nąć** (**-nę, -niesz**) (*imp* **-ń**) *vb perf od* **mijać**
**mineralny** *adj* mineral
**mineralogi|a** (**-i**) *f* mineralogy
**minera|ł** (**-łu, -ły**) (*loc sg* **-le**) *m* mineral
**mini** *f inv* (*pot: spódniczka*) mini(skirt)
**miniatu|ra** (**-ry, -ry**) (*dat sg* **-rze**) *f* miniature
**miniaturowy** *adj* miniature
**minimaliz|ować** (**-uję, -ujesz**) (*perf* **z-**) *vt* to minimize
**minimalnie** *adv* (*wzrosnąć*) marginally; (*chybić, wygrać*) narrowly
**minimalny** *adj* minimum, minimal
**minim|um** (**-um, -a**) (*gen pl* **-ów**) *nt inv in sg* minimum ▷ *adv* (*przynajmniej*) at least; **przez ~ 5 minut** for a minimum of 5 minutes
**miniony** *adj* (*era, stulecia*) bygone, past; (*rok, miesiąc*) last, past; **w ~m tygodniu** last week
**minispódnicz|ka** (**-ki, -ki**) (*dat sg* **-ce**, *gen pl* **-ek**) *f* miniskirt
**minist|er** (**-ra, -rowie**) (*loc sg* **-rze**) *m* minister, Secretary of State (*Brit*), Secretary (*US*); **~ spraw zagranicznych** foreign minister, ≈ Foreign Secretary (*Brit*), ≈ Secretary of State (*US*); **~ spraw wewnętrznych** minister of the interior, ≈ Home Secretary (*Brit*), ≈ Secretary of the Interior (*US*); **~ finansów** finance minister, ≈ Chancellor of the Exchequer (*Brit*), ≈ Secretary of the Treasury (*US*); **~ obrony narodowej** minister of defence, ≈ Secretary of State for Defence (*Brit*), ≈ Secretary of Defense (*US*); **~ sprawiedliwości** minister of justice, ≈ Attorney General (*US, Brit*); **~ bez teki** minister without portfolio; **rada ministrów** the Cabinet
**ministerialny** *adj* ministerial *attr*
**ministerst|wo** (**-wa, -wa**) (*loc sg* **-wie**) *nt* ministry, department (*US*); **~ spraw wewnętrznych** ministry of the interior, ≈ Home Office (*Brit*), ≈ Department of the Interior (*US*); **~ spraw zagranicznych** ministry of foreign affairs, ≈ Foreign (and Commonwealth) Office (*Brit*), ≈ Department of State (*US*); **M~ Obrony Narodowej** ≈ Ministry of Defence (*Brit*), ≈ Department of Defense (*US*)
**ministran|t** (**-ta, -ci**) (*loc sg* **-cie**) *m* server, altar boy
**minorowy** *adj* (*Muz*) minor; (*nastrój*) melancholic
**min|ować** (**-uję, -ujesz**) (*perf* **za-**) *vt* to mine
**minu|s** (**-sa, -sy**) (*loc sg* **-sie**) *m* (*Mat*) minus; (*wada*) minus, drawback; **plus ~** more or less
**minusowy** *adj* (*temperatura*) subzero; (*wynik*) negative
**minu|ta** (**-ty, -ty**) (*dat sg* **-cie**) *f* minute; **za minutę** in a minute; **co do minuty** on the dot; **na minutę** a *lub* per minute
**minutni|k** (**-ka, -ki**) (*instr sg* **-kiem**) *m* timer
**minutowy** *adj* (*wskazówka*) minute *attr*; (*opóźnienie*) one-minute *attr*
**miodowy** *adj* (*cukierek*) honey-flavoured (*Brit*) *lub* flavored (*US*); (*kolor*) honey-coloured (*Brit*) *lub* colored (*US*); **~ miesiąc** honeymoon
**mio|t** (**-tu, -ty**) (*loc sg* **-cie**) *m* (*Zool*) litter
**miotacz** (**-a, -e**) (*gen pl* **-y**) *m* (*Sport*) shot putter; **~ ognia** flame thrower
**miot|ać** (**-am, -asz**) *vt* (*rzucać*) to hurl; (*uderzać*) to batter; **miotać się** *vr* to struggle
**miot|ła** (**-ły, -ły**) (*dat sg* **-le**, *gen pl* **-eł**) *f* broom
**miód** (**miodu**) (*loc sg* **miodzie**) *m* honey; (*napój*) mead
**miraż** (**-u, -e**) (*gen pl* **-y** *lub* **-ów**) *m* mirage
**mir|ra** (**-ry**) (*dat sg* **-rze**) *f* myrrh
**misecz|ka** (**-ki, -ki**) (*dat sg* **-ce**, *gen pl* **-ek**) *f* (*naczynie*) bowl; (*w staniku*) cup
**misj|a** (**-i, -e**) (*gen pl* **-i**) *f* mission
**misjonarz** (**-a, -e**) (*gen pl* **-y**) *m* missionary
**mis|ka** (**-ki, -ki**) (*dat sg* **-ce**, *gen pl* **-ek**) *f* bowl; **~ klozetowa** toilet bowl *lub* pan; **~ olejowa** (*Mot*) (oil) sump (*Brit*), oil pan (*US*)
**miss** *f inv* beauty queen; **M~ Polonia** Miss Poland
**misterny** *adj* (*robota*) meticulous; (*fryzura, plan*) elaborate; (*haft, rzeźba*) subtle, delicate
**mistrz** (**-a, -owie**) *m* master; (*Sport*) champion; **~ świata/Europy** World/European Champion; **~ ceremonii** Master of Ceremonies
**mistrzost|wo** (**-wa, -wa**) (*loc sg* **-wie**) *nt* (*kunszt*) mastery; (*Sport*) championship; **mistrzostwa** *pl* championships
**mistrzowski** *adj* (*gra, wyczyn*) masterly; (*drużyna*) champion *attr*; **tytuł ~** championship; **po mistrzowsku** excellently, superbly
**mistrzy|ni** (**-ni, -nie**) (*gen pl* **-ń**) *f* master; (*Sport*) champion
**mistyczny** *adj* mystic(al)
**mistyfikacj|a** (**-i, -e**) (*gen pl* **-i**) *f* mystification
**mi|ś** (**-sia, -sie**) *m* (*pot: niedźwiedź*) bear; (*zabawka*) teddy bear; (*tkanina*) fur
**mi|t** (**-tu, -ty**) (*loc sg* **-cie**) *m* myth
**mitologi|a** (**-i, -e**) (*gen pl* **-i**) *f* mythology
**mitologiczny** *adj* mythological
**mit|ra** (**-ry, -ry**) (*loc sg* **-rze**) *f* mitre (*Brit*), miter (*US*)
**mityczny** *adj* mythical

m

**mityn|g** (**-gu, -gi**) (*instr sg* **-giem**) *m* (*Sport*) meeting, meet (*US*)
**mizeri|a** (**-i, -e**) (*gen pl* **-i**) *f* (*Kulin*) cucumber salad
**mizerny** *adj* (*twarz, dziecko*) sickly; (*zarobek, żywot, wynik*) poor
**mjr** *abbr* (= *major*) Maj. (= *Major*)
**mk|nąć (-nę, -niesz)** (*imp* **-nij**) *vi* to speed
**MKOl** *abbr* (= *Międzynarodowy Komitet Olimpijski*) IOC (= *International Olympic Committee*)
**ml** *abbr* (= *mililitr*) ml
**mla|skać (-skam, -skasz** *lub* **-szczę, -szczesz)** (*perf* **mlasnąć**) *vi* to smack one's lips
**mla|snąć (-snę, -śniesz)** (*imp* **-śnij**) *vb perf od* **mlaskać**
**mld** *abbr* (= *miliard*) bn (= *billion*)
**mlecz** (**-a, -e**) (*gen pl* **-y** *lub* **-ów**) *m* (*Bot*) sow thistle; (*Zool*) (soft) roe, milt
**mleczar|nia** (**-ni, -nie**) (*gen pl* **-ni** *lub* **-ń**) *f* dairy, creamery
**mleczarski** *adj* dairy *attr*
**mleczarz** (**-a, -e**) (*gen pl* **-y**) *m* milkman
**mlecz|ko** (**-ka**) (*instr sg* **-kiem**) *nt* milk; **~ kosmetyczne** cleansing milk
**mleczny** *adj* (*czekolada, ząb*) milk *attr*; (*gruczoł*) mammary *attr*; (*szkło, żarówka*) frosted; **Droga Mleczna** the Milky Way; **krowa mleczna** dairy *lub* milk cow
**mleć (mielę, mielesz)** (*imp* **miel**, *pt* **mełł, mełła, mełli**) *vt* (*kawę, pieprz, ziarno*) to grind; (*mięso*) to mince; **~ ozorem** (*pot*) to prattle
**mle|ko** (**-ka**) *nt* milk; **kwaśne ~** sour milk; **~ w proszku** powdered milk
**mln** *abbr* (= *milion*) m, M (= *million*)
**mł.** *abbr* (= *młodszy*) jr.
**młocar|nia** (**-ni, -nie**) (*gen pl* **-ni**) *f* threshing machine
**młod|e** (**-ych**) *pl decl like adj* young *pl*, offspring *pl*
**młodni|eć (-eję, -ejesz)** (*perf* **wy-** *lub* **od-**) *vi* to get younger
**młodo** (*comp* **młodziej**) *adv* (*wyglądać, umrzeć*) young
**młodociany** *adj* juvenile ▷ *m decl like adj* juvenile
**młodoś|ć** (**-ci**) *f* youth; **być nie pierwszej młodości** not to be young any more
**młodszy** *adj comp od* **młody** younger; **moja młodsza siostra** my younger sister; **~ rangą/stopniem** junior; **Jan Kowalski ~** Jan Kowalski junior
**młody** (*comp* **młodszy**) *adj* young; (*ziemniaki*) new; **pan ~** (bride)groom; **panna młoda** bride; **młoda para** *lub* **państwo młodzi** (*przed ślubem*) bride and groom; (*po ślubie*) newlyweds; **za młodu** in one's youth
**młodzie|niec** (**-ńca, -ńcy**) *m* (*książk*) youth
**młodzieńczy** *adj* youthful
**młodzież** (**-y**) *f* youth; **~ szkolna** school children
**młodzieżowy** *adj* youth *attr*; **muzyka młodzieżowa** pop music
**młodzi|k** (**-ka, -cy**) (*instr sg* **-kiem**) *m* (*pot*) youngster; (*Sport*) *young athlete aged between 13-17*
**młoko|s** (**-sa, -sy**) (*loc sg* **-sie**) *m* (*pot*) kid (*pot*)
**mło|t** (**-ta, -ty**) (*loc sg* **-cie**) *m* (*narzędzie*) (big) hammer; (*Sport*) hammer; **~ pneumatyczny** pneumatic drill; **między ~em a kowadłem** (*przen*) between the devil and the deep blue sea; **rzut ~em** (*Sport*) hammer throw
**młotecz|ek** (**-ka, -ki**) (*instr sg* **-kiem**) *m* hammer
**młot|ek** (**-ka, -ki**) (*instr sg* **-kiem**) *m* hammer; (*drewniany*) mallet; **iść (pójść** *perf*) **pod ~** (*przen*) to come under the hammer
**młó|cić (-cę, -cisz)** (*imp* **-ć**, *perf* **wy-**) *vt* (*zboże*) to thresh; (*przen: uderzać*) to thrash
**mły|n** (**-na, -ny**) (*loc sg* **-nie**) *m* mill; (*Rugby*) scrum(mage); **~ wodny** water-mill
**młynarz** (**-a, -e**) (*gen pl* **-y**) *m* miller
**młyn|ek** (**-ka, -ki**) (*instr sg* **-kiem**) *m*: **~ do kawy** coffee-grinder *lub* -mill; **~ do pieprzu** pepper mill
**mm** *abbr* (= *milimetr*) mm
**mną** *pron instr od* **ja** me; **ze mną** with me
**mnę** *itd. vb patrz* **miąć**
**mni|ch** (**-cha, -si**) *m* monk
**mnie** *pron gen, dat, acc, loc od* **ja** me; **o ~** about me
**mniej** *adv comp od* **mało**; (*krzeseł, ludzi*) fewer; (*wody, pieniędzy*) less; **jest ich ~** there are fewer of them; **~ interesujący** less interesting; **~ więcej** more or less; **nie ~ niż** no fewer/less than; **ni ~, ni więcej, tylko X** X, no less, none other than X
**mniejszościowy** *adj* minority *attr*
**mniejszoś|ć** (**-ci, -ci**) (*gen pl* **-ci**) *f* minority
**mniejszy** *adj comp od* **mały**; **mniejsza o to** *lub* **mniejsza z tym** never mind; **Azja Mniejsza** Asia Minor
**mniem|ać (-am, -asz)** *vi* (*książk*) to suppose
**mniema|nie** (**-nie, -nia**) (*gen pl* **-ń**) *nt* opinion; **w czyimś mniemaniu** in sb's view *lub* judg(e)ment; **mieć wysokie ~ o** *+loc* to have a good *lub* high opinion of
**mnisz|ek** (**-ka, -ki**) (*instr sg* **-kiem**) *m* (*Bot*) dandelion
**mnisz|ka** (**-ki, -ki**) (*dat sg* **-ce**, *gen pl* **-ek**) *f* (*zakonnica*) nun
**mnogi** *adj*: **liczba mnoga** the plural
**mnogoś|ć** (**-ci**) *f* multitude
**mnoże|nie** (**-nia, -nia**) (*gen pl* **-ń**) *nt* multiplication; **tabliczka mnożenia** multiplication table

**mnoż|yć (-ę, -ysz)** (*imp* **mnóż**, *perf* **po-**) *vt* to multiply; **mnożyć się** *vr* to multiply
**mnóst|wo** (**-wa**) (*loc sg* **-wie**) *nt*: **~ ludzi/czasu** plenty *lub* lots of people/time; **on ~ zarabia** he earns a whole lot
**mobilizacj|a** (**-i, -e**) (*gen pl* **-i**) *f* (*wojsk, sił*) mobilization; (*gotowość*) eagerness
**mobiliz|ować (-uję, -ujesz)** (*perf* **z-**) *vt* (*wojsko, organizację*) to mobilize; (*siły*) to muster; **~ kogoś (do czegoś)** to stimulate sb (to sth); **mobilizować się** *vr* (*zbierać w sobie*) to pull o.s. together; (*organizować się*) to get o.s. organized
**mobilnoś|ć** (**-ci**) *f* mobility
**mobilny** *adj* mobile
**moc** (**-y, -e**) (*gen pl* **-y**) *f* power; (*argumentu, wybuchu*) force, power; (*mnóstwo*) plenty; **zrobić wszystko, co jest w czyjejś mocy** to do everything in one's power; **zmiana tego nie leży w mojej mocy** it's not within my power to change this; **moc prawna** legal force; **moc produkcyjna** capacity; **na mocy tego prawa/porozumienia** under this law/agreement; **z całej mocy** *lub* **z całą mocą** with all one's might
**mocarst|wo** (**-wa, -wa**) (*loc sg* **-wie**) *nt* superpower
**mocno** *adv* (*trzymać, przyklejać, wtykać*) firmly, fast; (*uderzać, kopnąć, naciskać*) hard; (*zakręcać, nakładać*) tightly; (*tęsknić, kochać*) very much; (*pachnieć, przesadzać, zawodzić*) strongly; (*zdziwiony, zaniedbany*) very; **wczoraj ~ padało** it rained hard *lub* heavily yesterday; **~ zbudowany** powerfully built; **~ poturbowany** badly injured; **~ spała** she was fast asleep; **~ przekonany** strongly convinced; **trzymaj się ~!** hold on tight!
**mocny** *adj* strong; (*ramię, cios, światło, argument*) strong, powerful; (*uścisk*) firm, tight; (*silnik*) powerful; **mieć mocną głowę** to have a strong head
**mocodawc|a** (**-y, -y**) *m* authority
**moc|ować (-uję, -ujesz)** *vt* (*zakładać*) (*perf* **za-**) to mount; (*przytwierdzać na stałe*) (*perf* **u-** *lub* **za-**) to fix; **mocować się** *vr*: **~ się (z** *+instr***)** to wrestle with
**mocz** (**-u**) *m* urine; **oddawać (oddać** *perf***) ~** to pass water
**moczar|y** (**-ów**) *pl* marsh
**moczopędny** *adj* diuretic
**moczow|ód** (**-odu, -ody**) (*loc sg* **-odzie**) *m* ureter
**moczowy** *adj* urinary; **układ ~** urinary tract; **pęcherz ~** urinary bladder
**mocz|yć (-ę, -ysz)** *vt* (*zwilżać*) (*perf* **z-**) to wet; (*zanurzać w płynie*) (*perf* **na-**) to soak; **moczyć się** *vr* (*być moczonym*) to soak; (*oddawać mocz*) (*perf* **z-**) to wet o.s.

**mo|da** (**-dy, -dy**) (*loc sg* **-dzie**, *gen pl* **mód**) *f* fashion; **być w modzie** to be in fashion *lub* vogue; **wyjść** (*perf*) **z mody** to go out of fashion
**modalny** *adj* (*Jęz*) modal
**model** (*nom pl* **-e**) *m* (*makieta, typ, wzór*) (*gen sg* **-u**, *gen pl* **-i**) model; (*osoba pozująca*) (*gen sg* **-a**, *gen pl* **-i**) model; **~ kolejki** model railway
**modelarst|wo** (**-wa**) (*loc sg* **-wie**) *nt* model making
**modelarz** (**-a, -e**) (*gen pl* **-y**) *m* modeller (*Brit*), modeler (*US*)
**model|ka** (**-ki, -ki**) (*dat sg* **-ce**, *gen pl* **-ek**) *f* model
**model|ować (-uję, -ujesz)** (*perf* **wy-**) *vt* (*w glinie*) to model; (*włosy*) to do, to set
**modelowy** *adj* model *attr*
**mode|m** (**-mu, -my**) (*loc sg* **-mie**) *m* modem
**modernistyczny** *adj* modernist
**modernizacj|a** (**-i**) *f* modernization
**moderniz|ować (-uję, -ujesz)** (*perf* **z-**) *vt* to modernize
**modl|ić się (-ę, -isz)** (*imp* **módl**) *vr* to pray
**modlisz|ka** (**-ki, -ki**) (*dat sg* **-ce**, *gen pl* **-ek**) *f* (*Zool*) (praying) mantis
**modlitewni|k** (**-ka, -ki**) (*instr sg* **-kiem**) *m* prayer book
**modlit|wa** (**-wy, -wy**) (*dat sg* **-wie**) *f* prayer
**mod|ła** (**-le, -ły**) (*dat sg* **-le**) *f*: **na taką modłę** after this fashion; **urobić** (*perf*) **kogoś na swoją modłę** to fashion sb after o.s.
**modł|y** (**-ów**) *pl* prayers
**modny** *adj* fashionable
**modry** *adj* (*książk*) bright-blue
**modrze|w** (**-wia, -wie**) (*gen pl* **-wi**) *m* larch
**modulacj|a** (**-i, -e**) (*gen pl* **-i**) *f* modulation
**modul|ować (-uję, -ujesz)** *vt* to modulate
**modu|ł** (**-łu, -ły**) (*loc sg* **-le**) *m* (*element*) unit, module; (*Mat*) absolute value
**modyfikacj|a** (**-i, -e**) (*gen pl* **-i**) *f* modification
**modyfik|ować (-uję, -ujesz)** (*perf* **z-**) *vt* to modify
**mogę** *itd.* *vb patrz* **móc**
**mogi|ła** (**-ły, -ły**) (*dat sg* **-le**) *f* (*książk*) grave
**mohe|r** (**-ru**) (*loc sg* **-rze**) *m* mohair
**moi** *itd.* *pron patrz* **mój**
**moja, moje** *itd.* *pron patrz* **mój**
**Mojżesz** (**-a**) *m* (*Rel*) Moses
**mokasy|n** (**-na, -ny**) (*loc sg* **-nie**) *m* moccasin
**mok|nąć (-nę, -niesz)** (*imp* **-nij**, *pt* **mókł**, *perf* **z-**) *vi* to get wet (*in rain*)
**mokrad|ła** (**-eł**) *pl* swamps
**mokro** *adv*: **jest ~** it is wet; **czesać włosy na ~** to comb one's hair while it is wet; **dziecko ma ~** (*pot*) the baby is wet
**mokry** *adj* wet; **mokra robota** (*pot*) (contract) killing

**mola** *itd. n patrz* **mól**
**molekularny** *adj* molecular
**moleku|ła** (**-ły, -ły**) (*dat sg* **-le**) *f* molecule
**molest|ować (-uję, -ujesz)** *vt* (*naprzykrzać się*) to pester; (*prześladować*) to harass; (*seksualnie, fizycznie*) to molest
**moll** *inv* (*Muz*) minor; **symfonia c-~** symphony in C-minor
**mol|o** (**-a, -a**) *nt* pier
**molowy** *adj* (*Muz*) minor
**Mołdawi|a** (**-i**) *f* Moldova
**mołdawski** *adj* Moldavian
**momenci|k** (**-ku, -ki**) (*instr sg* **-kiem**) *m dimin od* **moment**; **~!** just a minute!
**momen|t** (**-tu, -ty**) (*loc sg* **-cie**) *m* moment; **~ przełomowy** turning point; (*decydujący*) decisive moment; **na** *lub* **przez ~** for a while *lub* moment; **w tym momencie** (*teraz*) at the moment; (*wtedy*) at that moment; (*w tej sytuacji*) at this point *lub* juncture; **w momencie gdy** (*w czasie gdy*) while; (*skoro tylko*) the moment, the instant
**momentalnie** *adv* instantly
**momentalny** *adj* instant, instantaneous
**MON** *abbr* (= *Ministerstwo Obrony Narodowej*) ≈ MoD (Brit), ≈ DOD (US)
**Monachium** *nt inv* Munich
**Monako** *nt inv* Monaco
**monar|cha** (**-chy, -chowie**) (*dat sg* **-sze**) *m decl like f in sg* monarch, sovereign
**monarchi|a** (**-i, -e**) (*gen pl* **-i**) *f* monarchy
**monarchi|sta** (**-sty, -ści**) (*dat sg* **-ście**) *m decl like f in sg* monarchist
**monarchistyczny** *adj* monarchical
**mone|ta** (**-ty, -ty**) (*dat sg* **-cie**) *f* coin; **automat na monety** coin-operated public phone; **rzucać (rzucić** *perf***) monetę** *lub* **monetą** to toss a coin; **brać (wziąć** *perf***) coś za dobrą monetę** (*przen*) to take sth at face value
**monetarny** *adj* monetary
**Mongoli|a** (**-i**) *f* Mongolia
**mongoliz|m** (**-mu**) (*loc sg* **-mie**) *m* (*Med*) Down's syndrome
**mongolski** *adj* Mongolian
**Mongo|ł** (**-ła, -łowie**) (*loc sg* **-le**) *m* Mongolian
**moni|t** (**-tu, -ty**) (*loc sg* **-cie**) *m* reminder
**monito|r** (**-ra, -ry**) (*loc sg* **-rze**) *m* (*urządzenie*) monitor; (*ekran*) display
**monit|ować (-uję, -ujesz)** *vt*: **~ kogoś** to send sb a reminder
**mono** *adj inv* mono
**monochromatyczny** *adj* monochrome *attr*
**monofoniczny** *adj* mono(phonic)
**monogami|a** (**-i**) *f* monogamy
**monogamiczny** *adj* monogamous
**monografi|a** (**-i, -e**) (*gen pl* **-i**) *f* monograph
**monograficzny** *adj* monographic
**monogra|m** (**-mu, -my**) (*loc sg* **-mie**) *m* monogram
**monoli|t** (**-tu, -ty**) (*loc sg* **-cie**) *m* monolith
**monolo|g** (**-gu, -gi**) (*instr sg* **-giem**) *m* (*mówienie do siebie*) soliloquy; (*długa wypowiedź jednej osoby*) monologue (Brit), monolog (US)
**monopol** (**-u, -e**) (*gen pl* **-i**) *m* monopoly; **mieć ~ na coś** to have a monopoly on sth
**monopolistyczny** *adj* monopolistic
**monopoliz|ować (-uję, -ujesz)** (*perf* **z-**) *vt* to monopolize
**monopolowy** *adj* (*wyroby*) alcoholic; **sklep ~** off-licence (Brit), liquor store (US)
**monotoni|a** (**-i**) *f* monotony
**monotonny** *adj* monotonous
**monstrualny** *adj* monstrous
**monstr|um** (**-um, -a**) (*gen pl* **-ów**) *nt inv in sg* monster
**monsu|n** (**-nu, -ny**) (*loc sg* **-nie**) *m* monsoon
**montaż** (**-u, -e**) (*gen pl* **-y**) *m* (*składanie*) assembly; (*zakładanie*) instalment (Brit), installment (US); (*Film*: *obróbka filmu*) editing; (: *rodzaj filmu*) montage
**monte|r** (**-ra, -rzy**) (*loc sg* **-rze**) *m* fitter
**mont|ować (-uję, -ujesz)** *vt* (*składać*) (*perf* **z-**) to assemble; (*zakładać*) (*perf* **za-**) to install; (*pot*: *zespół*) (*perf* **z-**) to muster; (*Film*) (*perf* **z-**) to edit
**monumentalny** *adj* monumental
**morale** *nt inv* morale
**moralizatorski** *adj* moralistic
**moraliz|ować (-uję, -ujesz)** *vi* to moralize
**moralnoś|ć** (**-ci**) *f* morality
**moralny** *adj* moral
**mora|ł** (**-łu, -ły**) (*loc sg* **-le**) *m* moral; **prawić ~y (komuś)** to preach (at sb)
**moratori|um** (**-um, -a**) (*gen pl* **-ów**) *nt inv in sg* moratorium
**Moraw|y** (**-**) *pl* Moravia
**mor|d** (**-du, -dy**) (*loc sg* **-dzie**) *m* (*książk*) manslaughter
**mor|da** (**-dy, -dy**) (*dat sg* **-dzie**) *f* (*psia*) muzzle; (*pot!*: *twarz*) mug (*pot*); **dostać** (*perf*) **w mordę** (*pot*) to get beaten up; **dać** (*perf*) **komuś w mordę** (*pot*) to punch sb in the face
**morderc|a** (**-y, -y**) *m decl like f in sg* murderer; **zawodowy ~** contract killer
**morderczy** *adj* (*spojrzenie, skłonności*) murderous
**morderst|wo** (**-wa**) (*loc sg* **-wie**) *nt* murder
**mordę|ga** (**-gi**) (*dat sg* **-dze**) *f* (*pot*) drag
**mordobi|cie** (**-cia, -cia**) (*gen pl* **-ć**) *nt* (*pot*) fight
**mord|ować (-uję, -ujesz)** *vt* (*zabijać*) (*perf* **za-**) to murder; **mordować się** *vr*: **~ się z czymś** (*pot*) to struggle with sth
**morel|a** (**-i, -e**) (*gen pl* **-i**) *f* (*owoc*) apricot; (*drzewo*) apricot (tree)

**morfi|na** (**-ny**) (*dat sg* **-nie**) *f* morphine
**morfologi|a** (**-i**) *f* morphology; **~ krwi** blood count
**morfologiczny** *adj* morphologic(al); **skład ~ krwi** blood constituency
**mormo|n** (**-na, -ni**) (*loc sg* **-nie**) *m* Mormon
**mor|s** (**-sa, -sy**) (*loc sg* **-sie**) *m* (*Zool*) walrus; (*pot: alfabet Morse'a*) Morse code
**morski** *adj* sea *attr*; (*ubezpieczenie, oddział*) marine *attr*; (*klimat, prawo, muzeum*) maritime *attr*; (*szkoła, siły*) naval *attr*; **port ~** seaport; **choroba morska** seasickness; **mila morska** nautical mile; **świnka morska** guinea pig; **piechota morska** Royal Marines *pl* (*Brit*), Marine Corps (*US*), Marines *pl* (*US*); **wilk ~** (*przen*) sea dog; **drogą morską** by sea
**morszczu|k** (**-ka, -ki**) (*instr sg* **-kiem**) *m* hake
**mor|wa** (**-wy, -wy**) (*dat sg* **-wie**) *f* mulberry
**morz|e** (**-a, -a**) (*gen pl* **mórz**) *nt* sea; **~m** by sea; **M~ Północne/Bałtyckie** the North/Baltic Sea; **na morzu** (*pływać, znajdować się*) on the sea; (*służyć, przebywać*) at sea; **nad ~m** (*blisko morza*) by the sea; (*wakacje*) at *lub* by the seaside; **nad poziomem morza** above sea level; **jechać nad ~** to go to the seaside; **kropla w morzu** (*przen*) a drop in the ocean
**morz|yć (-ę, -ysz)** (*perf* **za-**) *vt*: **~ kogoś głodem** to starve sb
**mosiądz** (**-u, -e**) *m* brass
**mosiężny** *adj* brass *attr*
**Mosk|wa** (**-wy**) (*dat sg* **-wie**) *f* Moscow
**mo|st** (**-stu, -sty**) (*loc sg* **-ście**) *m* bridge; **~ zwodzony** drawbridge; **~ wiszący** suspension bridge; **~ powietrzny** airlift; **spalić** (*perf*) **za sobą ~y** (*przen*) to burn one's bridges *lub* boats; **powiedzieć** (*perf*) **coś komuś prosto z ~u** (*przen*) to tell sb sth straight out
**most|ek** (**-ku, -ki**) (*instr sg* **-kiem**) *m dimin od* **most**; (*Anat*) sternum, breastbone (*pot*); (*Sport, Żegl*) bridge; (*proteza stomatologiczna*) bridge
**mosz|na** (**-ny, -ny**) (*dat sg* **-nie**, *gen pl* **-en**) *f* scrotum
**mo|ścić (-szczę, -ścisz)** (*imp* **-ść**, *perf* **wy-**) *vt* to pad
**moś|ć** (**-ci, -ci**) (*gen pl* **-ci**) *f*: **Wasza Królewska M~** Your Majesty
**mot|ek** (**-ka, -ki**) (*instr sg* **-kiem**) *m* hank, skein
**motel** (**-u, -e**) (*gen pl* **-i**) *m* motel
**motłoch** (**-u**) *m* (*pej*) riffraff (*pej*)
**motocykl** (**-a, -e**) (*gen pl* **-i**) *m* motorcycle
**motocykli|sta** (**-sty, -ści**) (*dat sg* **-ście**) *m decl like f in sg* motorcyclist, motorcycle rider
**moto|r** (**-ru, -ry**) (*loc sg* **-rze**) *m* (*silnik*) motor; (*pot*) (motor)bike; **być ~em czegoś** (*przen*) to be the driving force behind sth
**motornicz|y** (**-ego, -owie**) *m decl like adj* tram driver (*Brit*), motorman (*US*)
**motorowe|r** (**-ru, -ry**) (*loc sg* **-rze**) *m* lightweight motorcycle, moped (*Brit*)
**motorowy** *adj* motor *attr*
**motorów|ka** (**-ki, -ki**) (*dat sg* **-ce**, *gen pl* **-ek**) *f* motorboat
**motoryzacj|a** (**-i**) *f* motorization
**motoryzacyjny** *adj* (*przemysł*) motor *attr*, auto(motive) *attr* (*US*); **sklep ~** motor (*Brit*) *lub* automobile (*US*) accessory shop
**mot|to** (**-ta, -ta**) (*loc sg* **-cie**) *nt* motto
**moty|ka** (**-ki, -ki**) (*dat sg* **-ce**) *f* hoe; **porywać się z motyką na słońce** (*pot*) to go on a wild-goose chase
**motyl** (**-a, -e**) (*gen pl* **-i**) *m* butterfly
**motyl|ek** (**-ka**) (*instr sg* **-kiem**) *m dimin od* **motyl**; (*Sport: pot*) butterfly (stroke)
**motylkowy** *adj*: **styl ~** (*Sport*) butterfly (stroke)
**moty|w** (**-wu, -wy**) (*loc sg* **-wie**) *m* (*postępowania, zbrodni*) motive; (*utworu, kompozycji*) motif; **~ przewodni** (*Lit*) leitmotiv, leitmotif
**motywacj|a** (**-i, -e**) (*gen pl* **-i**) *f* motivation
**motyw|ować (-uję, -ujesz)** (*perf* **u-**) *vt* (*popierać*) to support; (*uzasadniać*) to justify sth
**mo|wa** (**-wy**) (*dat sg* **-wie**) *f* (*język*) language, tongue; (*zdolność mówienia*) speech; (*przemówienie*) (*nom pl* **-wy**, *gen pl* **mów**) speech; **~ ojczysta** mother tongue; **~ potoczna** colloquial speech; **~ była o przyszłej współpracy** the subject (of the discussion) was future cooperation; **nie ma mowy!** that's out of the question!; **~ pogrzebowa** funeral oration; **człowiek, o którym ~** the man in question; **część mowy** (*Jęz*) part of speech; **~ zależna/niezależna** (*Jęz*) indirect/direct speech
**mozai|ka** (**-ki, -ki**) (*dat sg* **-ce**) *f* mosaic
**moz|olić się (-olę, -olisz)** (*imp* **-ól**) *vr*: **mozolić się (nad czymś)** to slog (away) (at sth)
**mozolny** *adj* arduous
**moz|ół** (**-ołu, -oły**) (*loc sg* **-ole**) *m*: **z mozołem** arduously
**moździerz** (**-a, -e**) (*gen pl* **-y**) *m* mortar
**może** *inv* perhaps, maybe; **być ~** maybe; **~ wyjdziemy?** how *lub* what about going out?; **~ byś coś zjadł?** why don't you eat something?
**możesz** *itd. vb patrz* **móc**
**możliwie** *adv*: **zrób to ~ szybko/dobrze** do it as soon/well as you possibly can; **wyglądali całkiem ~** they didn't look too bad
**możliwoś|ć** (**-ci, -ci**) (*gen pl* **-ci**) *f* possibility; (*sposobność*) chance, opportunity; **w miarę**

m

**możliwości** if at all possible; **miałem ~ rozmawiać z nim** I had a chance *lub* an opportunity to talk to him; **dwie możliwości do wyboru** two options *lub* possibilities to choose from; **możliwości** *pl* abilities *pl*; **w miarę naszych możliwości** to the best of our ability *lub* abilities

**możliwy** *adj* (*do wyobrażenia*) conceivable; (*ewentualny*) possible; (*pot: dość dobry*) passable; **możliwe, że zadzwonią jutro** they may give us a ring tomorrow; **o ile to możliwe** if that's possible; **~ do uniknięcia/rozpoznania** avoidable/recognizable

**można** *inv*: **~ stwierdzić, że ...** one *lub* you may say that ...; **~ już iść** you may *lub* can go now; **nie ~ tego kupić** you can't buy this; **nie ~ tak myśleć** you mustn't think that; **czy tu ~ palić?** may *lub* can I smoke here?; **~ wytrzymać** (*pot*) it's O.K. *lub* okay; **czy ~?** may I?; **tak nie ~!** that's wrong!

**możnoś|ć** (**-ci**) *f* opportunity; **mieć ~ coś zrobić** to have the opportunity to do sth; **w miarę możności** as far as possible

**możny** *adj* (*książk*) powerful and wealthy

 SŁOWO KLUCZOWE

**móc (mogę, możesz)** (*pt* **mógł, mogła, mogli**) *vi* **1** (*potrafić*) to be able; **czy możesz to zrobić na jutro?** can you do it for tomorrow?; **będzie mógł wam pomóc** he will be able to help you; **szkoda, że nie możesz przyjść** it is a pity that you can't come; **gdybym tylko mógł** if only I could

**2** (*mieć pozwolenie*): **móc coś zrobić** to be permitted *lub* allowed to do sth; **czy mogę wyjść wcześniej?** may *lub* can I leave early?; **czy mógłbym rozmawiać z Sue?** could I speak to Sue, please?

**3** (*dla wyrażenia przypuszczenia*): **on może się spóźnić** he may *lub* might be late; **kto to może być?** who can it be?; **mogła zapomnieć** she may have forgotten; **mógł cię zabić!** he could have killed you!; **nie może być!** this *lub* it can't be!

**4** (*w prośbach*): **czy mógłbyś zamknąć okno?** could you close the window?

**5** (*dla wyrażenia pretensji*): **mogłeś mi powiedzieć** you might have told me

**mód** *n patrz* **moda**

**módl** *itd. vb patrz* **modlić**

**mój** *possessive pron* (*z rzeczownikiem*) my; (*bez rzeczownika*) mine; **to są moje książki** these are my books; **te książki są moje** these books are mine

**mókł** *itd. vb patrz* **moknąć**

**mól** (**mola, mole**) (*gen pl* **moli**) *m* (*odzieżowy*) clothes moth; **mól książkowy** (*przen*) bookworm

**mórz** *n patrz* **morze**

**mów** *n patrz* **mowa**

**mówc|a** (**-y, -y**) *m decl like f in sg* speaker

**mó|wić (-wię, -wisz)** *vt* (*coś*) to say; (*prawdę, kłamstwa*) to tell ▷ *vi* (*przemawiać*) to speak; (*rozmawiać, opowiadać*) to talk; **on mówi, że ...** he says that ...; **mówił mi, że ...** he told me that ...; **~ po angielsku/polsku** to speak English/Polish; **nie mówiąc (już) o** *+loc* to say nothing of, let alone; **nie ma o czym ~** don't mention it; **prawdę mówiąc** to tell the truth; **mówiąc szczerze** frankly (speaking); **~ do siebie** to talk to o.s.; **między nami mówiąc** (just) between the two of us; **to nazwisko nic mi nie mówi** this name doesn't ring a bell; **to mówi samo za siebie** it speaks for itself

**mównic|a** (**-y, -e**) *f* rostrum

**mózg** (**-u, -i**) *m* brain; (*przen*) mastermind; **on jest ~iem organizacji** he is the brains of the organization

**mózgowy** *adj* cerebral

**móżdż|ek** (**-ka, -ki**) (*instr sg* **-kiem**) *m* (*Anat*) cerebellum; (*Kulin*) brains; **mieć ptasi ~** (*pot*) to be bird-brained (*pot*)

**MPK** *abbr* (= *Miejskie Przedsiębiorstwo Komunikacyjne*) *municipal transport company*, ≈ City Transport

**MPO** *abbr* (= *Miejskie Przedsiębiorstwo Oczyszczania*) ≈ sanitation department

**mroczny** *adj* dark

**mro|k** (**-ku, -ki**) (*instr sg* **-kiem**) *m* darkness

**mrowi|e** (**-a**) (*loc sg* **-u**) *nt* (*ludzi*) swarm; (*świateł*) myriad; (*ciarki*) chill

**mrowie|nie** (**-nia**) *nt* pins and needles *pl*

**mrowis|ko** (**-ka, -ka**) (*instr sg* **-kiem**) *nt* ant-hill

**mro|zić (-żę, -zisz)** (*imp* **-ź**) *vt* (*ziębić*) to chill; (*o lodówce*) to freeze; **~ (z~** *perf*) **krew w żyłach** (*przen*) to curdle one's blood

**mroźny** *adj* frosty

**mrożący** *adj*: **~ krew w żyłach** bloodcurdling

**mrożon|ki** (**-ek**) *pl* deep-frozen foods

**mrożony** *adj* (*owoce, warzywa*) deep-frozen; (*kawa, herbata*) iced

**mrów|ka** (**-ki, -ki**) (*dat sg* **-ce**, *gen pl* **-ek**) *f* ant; **pracowity jak ~** (as) busy as a bee; **mrówki** *pl* (*przen: ciarki*) pins and needles

**mrówkoja|d** (**-da, -dy**) (*loc sg* **-dzie**) *m* anteater

**mr|óz** (**-ozu, -ozy**) (*loc sg* **-ozie**) *m* frost; **5 stopni mrozu** 5 degrees below (zero); **Dziadek M~** ≈ Father Christmas

**mru|czeć (-czę, -czysz)** (*perf* **-knąć**) *vi* (*mamrotać*) to murmur; (*o kocie*) to purr

**mrug|ać (-am, -asz)** (*perf* **-nąć**) *vi* (*o gwiazdach, światłach*) to twinkle, to wink; **~ okiem (do kogoś)** to wink (at sb); **~ oczami** to blink (one's eyes); **~ światłami** (*Mot*) to flash one's headlights
**mrug|nąć (-nę, -niesz)** (*imp* **-nij**) *vb perf od* **mrugać** ▷ *vi perf*: **nawet nie mrugnął okiem** (*przen*) he didn't bat an eyelid
**mrugnię|cie** (**-cia**, **-cia**) (*gen pl* **-ć**) *nt* (*okiem*) wink; (*światłem*) flash; **bez mrugnięcia okiem** (*przen*) without batting *lub* blinking an eye
**mrukliwy** *adj* taciturn
**mruk|nąć (-nę, -niesz)** (*imp* **-nij**) *vb perf od* **mruczeć**
**mruż|yć (-ę, -ysz)** (*perf* **z-**) *vt*: **~ oczy** to squint
**mrzon|ka** (**-ki**, **-ki**) (*dat sg* **-ce**, *gen pl* **-ek**) *f* daydream
**MSW** *abbr* = **Ministerstwo Spraw Wewnętrznych**
**MSZ** *abbr* = **Ministerstwo Spraw Zagranicznych**
**msz|a** (**-y**, **-e**) (*gen pl* **-y**) *f* mass; (*Rel*): **iść (pójść** *perf*) **na mszę** to go to mass
**mszalny** *adj* (*wino*) Eucharistic; **kielich ~** chalice
**msza|ł** (**-łu**, **-ły**) (*loc sg* **-le**) *m* missal
**mszczę** *itd. vb patrz* **mścić**
**mszyc|a** (**-y**, **-e**) *f* aphid, greenfly
**mściciel** (**-a**, **-e**) (*gen pl* **-i**) *m* avenger
**mścić się (mszczę, mścisz)** (*imp* **mścij**, *perf* **ze-**) *vr*: **mścić się (na kimś)** to revenge o.s. (on sb); **mścić się (za coś)** to get one's revenge (for sth)
**mściwy** *adj* vindictive, revengeful
**MTP** *abbr* (= *Międzynarodowe Targi Poznańskie*) PIF (= *Poznań International Fair*)
**mu** *pron dat od* **on**; (*o osobie*) (to) him; (*o przedmiocie, zwierzęciu*) (to) it ▷ *pron dat od* **ono** (to) it; **dałem mu książkę** I gave him the book, I gave the book to him
**mu|cha** (**-chy**, **-chy**) (*dat sg* **-sze**) *f* (*Zool*) fly; (*krawat*) bow tie; **ruszać się jak ~ w smole** (*pot*) to move at a snail's pace; **padać** *lub* **ginąć jak muchy** to drop (off) like flies
**muchołap|ka** (**-ki**, **-ki**) (*dat sg* **-ce**, *gen pl* **-ek**) *f* flytrap
**muchomo|r** (**-ra**, **-ry**) (*loc sg* **-rze**) *m* (*Bot*) amanita; (*pot*) toadstool
**muf|ka** (**-ki**, **-ki**) (*dat sg* **-ce**, *gen pl* **-ek**) *f* muff
**Mula|t** (**-ta**, **-ci**) (*loc sg* **-cie**) *m* mulatto
**Mulat|ka** (**-ki**, **-ki**) (*dat sg* **-ce**, *gen pl* **-ek**) *f* mulatto
**mul|da** (**-dy**, **-dy**) (*dat sg* **-dzie**) *f* (*Sport*) mogul
**mulisty** *adj* muddy
**multimedi|a** (**-ów**) *pl* multimedia
**multimedialny** *adj* multimedia
**multimilione|r** (**-ra**, **-rzy**) (*loc sg* **-rze**) *m* multimillionaire
**multum** *nt inv* plenty
**mu|ł¹** (**-ła**, **-ły**) (*loc sg* **-le**) *m* (*Zool*) mule
**mu|ł²** (**-łu**, **-ły**) (*loc sg* **-le**) *m* (*szlam*) silt
**mumi|a** (**-i**, **-e**) (*gen pl* **-i**) *f* mummy
**mumifik|ować (-uję, -ujesz)** (*perf* **z-**) *vt* to mummify
**mundu|r** (**-ru**, **-ry**) (*loc sg* **-rze**) *m* uniform; **~ polowy** battledress
**mundur|ek** (**-ka**, **-ki**) (*instr sg* **-kiem**) *m* uniform
**municypalny** *adj* municipal; **policja municypalna** municipal police
**mu|r** (**-ru**, **-ry**) (*loc sg* **-rze**) *m* wall; **być przypartym** *lub* **przyciśniętym do muru** to have one's back to the wall; **stać (stanąć** *perf*) **murem za** *+instr* to give unanimous support to
**murarz** (**-a**, **-e**) (*gen pl* **-y**) *m* bricklayer
**mura|wa** (**-wy**, **-wy**) (*dat sg* **-wie**) *f* grass
**mur|ować (-uję, -ujesz)** (*perf* **wy-**) *vt* to build ▷ *vi* to lay bricks
**murowany** *adj* (*dom*: *z cegły*) brick *attr*; (*: z kamienia*) stone *attr*; (*pot*: *pewny*) absolutely sure
**mursz|eć (-eje)** (*perf* **z-**) *vt* (*o drewnie*) to rot
**Murzy|n** (**-na**, **-ni**) (*loc sg* **-nie**) *m* Black (man); **Murzyni** *pl* Blacks, Black people
**Murzyn|ka** (**-ki**, **-ki**) (*dat sg* **-ce**, *gen pl* **-ek**) *f* Black (woman)
**murzyński** *adj* Black
**mu|s** (**-su**) (*loc sg* **-sie**) *m* (*Kulin*) (*nom pl* **-sy**) mousse; (*konieczność*) necessity, must (*pot*); **z musu** out of necessity
**musical** (**-u**, **-e**) (*gen pl* **-i**) *m* musical comedy

 SŁOWO KLUCZOWE

**mu|sieć (-szę, -sisz)** *vi* **1** (*podlegać konieczności*): **musisz to zrobić** you have to do it, you've got to do it; **nie musisz przychodzić** you don't have *lub* need to come
**2** (*być zobowiązanym*): **muszę to zrobić** I must do it, I need to do it; **czy musisz już iść?** must you go just yet?; **nie musiałeś tutaj przychodzić** you needn't have come here
**3** (*dla wyrażenia prawdopodobieństwa*): **ona musi być w kuchni** she must be in the kitchen; **musiała mu powiedzieć** she must have told him

**muskularny** *adj* muscular
**musku|ł** (**-łu**, **-ły**) (*loc sg* **-le**) *m* muscle
**musli** *nt inv* muesli
**mus|ować (-uje)** *vi* to sparkle, to effervesce
**mustan|g** (**-ga**, **-gi**) (*instr sg* **-giem**) *m* mustang
**musujący** *adj* fizzy, sparkling

m

**musze** *n patrz* **mucha**
**muszel|ka** (**-ki, -ki**) (*dat sg* **-ce**, *gen pl* **-ek**) *f dimin od* **muszla**
**muszę** *itd. vb patrz* **musieć**
**musz|ka** (**-ki, -ki**) (*dat sg* **-ce**, *gen pl* **-ek**) *f dimin od* **mucha**; (*krawat*) bow tie; (*w broni palnej*) frontsight; **trzymać kogoś na muszce** to hold sb at gunpoint
**muszkatołowy** *adj*: **gałka muszkatołowa** nutmeg
**muszkiete|r** (**-ra, -rzy** *lub* **-rowie**) (*loc sg* **-rze**) *m* musketeer
**muszl|a** (**-i, -e**) (*gen pl* **-i**) *f* (*skorupka*) shell; **~ klozetowa** toilet bowl; **~ koncertowa** (concert) bowl
**musztar|da** (**-dy**) (*dat sg* **-dzie**) *f* mustard
**muszt|ra** (**-ry**) (*dat sg* **-rze**) *f* drill
**musztr|ować (-uję, -ujesz)** *vt* to drill
**muszy** *adj*: **waga musza** (*Sport*) flyweight
**muśli|n** (**-nu, -ny**) (*loc sg* **-nie**) *m* muslin
**mutacj|a** (**-i, -e**) (*gen pl* **-i**) *f* mutation; **przeszedł mutację głosu 2 lata temu** his voice broke 2 years ago
**mutan|t** (**-ta, -ty**) (*loc sg* **-cie**) *m* mutant
**mu|za** (**-zy, -zy**) (*dat sg* **-zie**) *f* muse; **dziesiąta ~** (*kino*) cinema
**muzealny** *adj* museum *attr*
**muze|um** (**-um, -a**) (*gen pl* **-ów**) *nt inv in sg* museum
**muzułma|nin** (**-nina, -nie**) (*loc sg* **-ninie**, *gen pl* **-nów**) *m* Muslim
**muzułmański** *adj* Muslim
**muzyczny** *adj* musical; **szkoła muzyczna** music school, school of music
**muzy|k** (**-ka, -cy**) (*instr sg* **-kiem**) *m* musician
**muzy|ka** (**-ki**) (*dat sg* **-ce**) *f* music
**muzykalny** *adj* musical
**my** *pron* we; **to my** it's us
**myci|e** (**-a**) *nt* washing; **~ naczyń** washing up
**my|ć (-ję, -jesz)** (*perf* **u-**) *vt* (*ręce, twarz, talerz*) to wash; (*okna, podłogę*) to clean; (*zęby*) to brush, to clean; **myć się** *vr* to wash (o.s.), to have a wash
**mydelnicz|ka** (**-ki, -ki**) (*dat sg* **-ce**, *gen pl* **-ek**) *f* soap dish
**mydlany** *adj* (*bańka*) soap *attr*; **płatki mydlane** soapflakes
**mydl|ić (-ę, -isz)** (*perf* **na-**) *vt* to soap; **~ komuś oczy** (*przen*) to pull the wool over sb's eyes; **mydlić się** *vr* (*o człowieku*) to soap o.s.; (*o mydle*) to lather
**mydlin|y** (**-**) *pl* (soap)suds, soapy water
**myd|ło** (**-ła, -ła**) (*loc sg* **-le**, *gen pl* **-eł**) *nt* soap
**myj|ka** (**-ki, -ki**) (*dat sg* **-ce**, *gen pl* **-ek**) *f* face cloth, (face) flannel (*Brit*), washcloth (*US*)
**myj|nia** (**-ni, -nie**) (*gen pl* **-ni**) *f*: **~ (samochodowa)** car wash
**myl|ić (-ę, -isz)** *vt* (*daty, twarze*) (*perf* **po-**) to confuse, to mix up; (*o wzroku, słuchu*) (*perf* **z-**) to mislead; **pozory mylą** appearances are misleading; **mylić się** *vr* (*popełniać błędy*) to make mistakes; (*być w błędzie*) to be wrong; **mylą mi się te daty** I mix up the dates; **jeśli się nie mylę** if I am not wrong *lub* mistaken
**mylnie** *adv* mistakenly, erroneously
**mylny** *adj* mistaken, erroneous
**mysz** (**-y, -y**) (*gen pl* **-y**) *f* mouse; **biedny jak ~ kościelna** (as) poor as a church-mouse; **siedzieć jak ~ pod miotłą** to be as still as a mouse; **myszy** *pl* mice
**mysz|ka** (**-ki, -ki**) (*dat sg* **-ce**, *gen pl* **-ek**) *f dimin od* **mysz**; **zabawa w kotka i myszkę** (*przen*) cat-and-mouse game; **trącić myszką** (*przen*) to be going grey (*Brit*) *lub* gray (*US*)
**myszk|ować (-uję, -ujesz)** *vi* to ferret
**myszoł|ów** (**-owa, -owy**) (*loc sg* **-owie**) *m* buzzard
**myśl** (**-i, -i**) (*gen pl* **-i**) *f* thought; **mieć kogoś/coś na ~i** to have sb/sth in mind; **co masz na ~i?** what do you mean?; **być dobrej ~i** to hope for the best; **robić coś z ~ą o kimś** to do sth for sb *lub* for sb's sake; **czytać w czyichś ~ach** to read sb's mind; **nosić się z ~ą o czymś** to contemplate sth; **na samą ~ o wyjeździe dostaję dreszczy** the mere thought of leaving gives me the shivers; **wszystko idzie po naszej ~i** everything is going according to the way we planned it; **w ~ tej zasady ...** according to this principle ...
**myślący** *adj* intelligent
**myśl|eć (-ę, -isz)** (*pt* **-ał, -eli**) *vi* to think; **~ o** *+loc* (*rozmyślać o*) to think about; (*rozważać, zamierzać*) to think of; (*troszczyć się*) to think of; **o czym myślisz?** what are you thinking about?; **myślę, że tak** I think so; **myślę, że nie** I don't think so; **niewiele myśląc** without much thought, not thinking much; **ani myślę to zrobić** I'm not going to do it
**myśleni|e** (**-a**) *nt* thinking; **to mi dało do myślenia** this made me think
**myśliciel** (**-a, -e**) (*gen pl* **-i**) *m* thinker
**myślist|wo** (**-wa**) (*loc sg* **-wie**) *nt* hunting
**myśli|wiec** (**-wca, -wce**) *m* (*samolot*) fighter (plane)
**myśliwski** *adj* hunting *attr*; **samolot ~** fighter (plane)
**myśli|wy** (**-wego, -wi**) *m* hunter
**myślni|k** (**-ka, -ki**) (*instr sg* **-kiem**) *m* (*w zdaniu*) dash; (*pot*: *w wyrazie*) hyphen
**mżaw|ka** (**-ki, -ki**) (*dat sg* **-ce**, *gen pl* **-ek**) *f* drizzle
**mż|yć (-y)** *vi*: **mży** it's drizzling

# Nn

**N, n** *nt inv (litera)* N, n; **N jak Natalia** ≈ N for Nellie *(Brit) lub* Nan *(US)*
**N.** *abbr (= Nowy)* N. *(= New)*
**n.** *abbr (= nad)* (up)on

**SŁOWO KLUCZOWE**

**na** *prep +loc* **1** *(miejsce)* on; **na stole/ścianie/Księżycu** on the table/wall/Moon; **na drzewie** in a tree; **na morzu** *(pływać, znajdować się)* on the sea; *(służyć, przebywać)* at sea; **na Węgrzech/Śląsku** in Hungary/Silesia; **na wsi/zachodzie** in the country/west; **na Kubie** in Cuba; **na obrazie/zdjęciu** in the picture/photograph; **na niebie** in the sky; **na ulicy** in *lub* on *(US)* the street; **na koncercie/wykładzie** at a concert/lecture; **mieć coś na sobie** to have sth on, to be wearing sth
**2** *(środek lokomocji)*: **na koniu** on horseback; **jeździć na rowerze/łyżwach** to cycle/skate
**3** *(narzędzie)*: **robić na drutach** to knit; **pisać na maszynie** to type
**4** *(instrument)*: **grać na gitarze/skrzypcach** to play the guitar/violin; **grać (zagrać** *perf***) coś na gitarze** to play sth on the guitar
▷ *prep +acc* **1** *(kierunek)* to; **na plażę/wieś** to the beach/country; **na Węgry/Kubę** to Hungary/Cuba; **wchodzić (wejść** *perf***) na drzewo** to climb a tree; **na zachód/północ** west/north, westward(s)/northward(s); **wpadać (wpaść** *perf***) na kogoś** to bump into sb
**2** *(okres)*: **na dwa dni** for two days; **na 5 minut przed** *+loc* five minutes before …
**3** *(termin)*: **na poniedziałek** for Monday; **na czwartą** *(zrobić coś)* by four (o'clock); *(przyjść)* at four (o'clock)
**4** *(okazja)*: **na śniadanie** for breakfast; **na wiosnę** in spring
**5** *(sposób)*: **na sztuki/tuziny** by the piece/the dozen; **na czyjś koszt** at sb's expense; **na raty** on hire purchase *(Brit) lub* installments *(US)*; **jajko na twardo** hard-boiled egg; **pranie na sucho** dry cleaning
**6** *(przyczyna)*: **na czyjąś prośbę/zaproszenie** at sb's request/invitation; **na czyjś sygnał/życzenie** on sb's signal/wish; **chory na grypę** ill *lub* sick *(US)* with flu
**7** *(miara)*: **100 km na godzinę** 100 km per hour; **dwa razy na tydzień** twice a *lub* per week; **stół na 20 osób** a table for twenty; **jeden na dziesięć** one in ten, one out of ten; **po trzy na raz** three at a time; **szeroki na dwa cale** two inches wide
**8** *(rezultat)*: **kroić (pokroić** *perf***) coś na kawałki** to cut sth into pieces; **malować (pomalować** *perf***) coś na biało** to paint sth white
**9** *(przeznaczenie)*: **album na znaczki** stamp album; **kosz na śmieci** dustbin *(Brit)*, garbage can *(US)*; **przerwa na kawę** coffee break
**10** *(zamiar)*: **iść na spacer** to go for a walk; **jechać na wakacje/wycieczkę** to go on holiday/a trip; **iść na wykład/koncert** to go to a lecture/concert
**11** *(z przysłówkami)*: **jeść obiad na stojąco** to eat lunch (while) standing

**naba|wić się (-wię, -wisz)** *vr perf*: **nabawić się** *+gen (choroby)* to catch, to develop
**nabia|ł (-łu)** *(loc sg* **-le***) m* dairy products *pl*
**nabiałowy** *adj* dairy *attr*
**na|bić (-biję, -bijesz)** *vb perf od* **nabijać**; **~ kogoś w butelkę** *(pot)* to make a fool of sb
**nabier|ać (-am, -asz)** *(perf* **nabrać***) vt*: **~** *+gen (wody, powietrza)* to take in; *(apetytu, zwyczaju)* to develop; *(szybkości)* to gather, to pick up; *(wysokości)* to gain; **~ sił** to get stronger; **~ kształtu** to take shape; **~ odwagi/otuchy** to take courage/heart; **~ przekonania** to become convinced; **~ wprawy** to become adept *lub* skilled; **~ kogoś** *(pot: żartować)* to pull sb's leg; *(pot: oszukiwać)* to deceive
**nabij|ać (-am, -asz)** *(perf* **nabić***) vt (broń)* to load; *(fajkę)* to fill; **nabijać się** *vr (pot)*: **~ się z kogoś** to make fun of sb
**nabity** *adj (broń)* loaded; *(fajka)* filled; *(pot: sala)* packed
**nabożeńst|wo (-wa)** *(loc sg* **-wie***) nt (Rel) (nom pl* **-wa***)* service; *(namaszczenie)* reverence

**nab|ój (-oju, -oje)** (*gen pl* **-oi** *lub* **-ojów**) *m* cartridge

**nab|ór (-oru, -ory)** (*loc sg* **-orze**) *m* recruitment

**na|brać (-biorę, -bierzesz)** *vb perf od* **nabierać** ▷ *vt perf*: ~ **wody w usta** (*przen*) to keep one's mouth shut

**nabrzeż|e (-a, -a)** (*gen pl* **-y**) *nt* (*rzeki, morza*) embankment; (*w porcie*) landing pier

**nabrzmiały** *adj* swollen; (*przen*: *problem*) pressing

**nabrzmi|eć (-eje)** *vb perf od* **nabrzmiewać**

**nabrzmiew|ać (-a)** (*perf* **nabrzmieć**) *vi* to swell

**na|być (-będę, -będziesz)** (*imp* **-bądź**) *vb perf od* **nabywać**

**nabyt|ek (-ku, -ki)** (*instr sg* **-kiem**) *m* (*zakup*) purchase; (*do kolekcji*) acquisition

**nabyty** *adj* acquired

**nabyw|ać (-am, -asz)** (*perf* **nabyć**) *vt* (*kupować*) to purchase, to buy; ~ **czegoś** (*zdobywać*) to acquire sth, to gain sth

**nabywc|a (-y, -y)** *m* buyer, purchaser

**nabywczy** *adj*: **siła nabywcza** purchasing *lub* buying power

**nacechowany** *adj*: ~ **czymś** characterized by sth, marked with sth

**nachalny** *adj* pushy

**nacho|dzić (-dzę, -dzisz)** (*imp* **-dź**, *perf* **najść**) *vt* (*o człowieku*: *przychodzić*) to keep coming to; (: *naprzykrzać się*) to intrude (up)on; (*o myślach, obawach*) to haunt, to pester ▷ *vi*: ~ **(na coś)** to overlap (sth)

**nachyl|ać się (-am, -asz)** *vr* (*o człowieku*) (*perf* **-ić**) to bend down; (*o terenie*) to slope

**nachyle|nie (-nia, -nia)** (*gen pl* **-ń**) *nt* slope, inclination

**na|ciąć (-tnę, -tniesz)** (*imp* **-tnij**) *vb perf od* **nacinać**; **nacinać się** *vr* (*pot*): **naciąłem się na tym** it let me down

**naciągacz (-a, -e)** (*gen pl* **-y**) *m* (*pot*) con man

**naciąg|ać (-am, -asz)** (*perf* **-nąć**) *vt* (*linę, strunę*) to tighten; (*łuk*) to draw; (*buty, sweter*) to pull on; (*mięsień*) to pull; (*pot*: *oszukiwać*) to fleece (*pot*) ▷ *vi* (*o herbacie*) to draw, to infuse; ~ **kołdrę/pokrowiec (na coś)** to pull the quilt/sleeve over (sth); **naciągnąć kogoś na 100 dolarów** (*pot*) to tap sb for 100 dollars; **naciągnąć kogoś na drinka** (*pot*) to cadge (*Brit*) *lub* mooch (*US*) a drink from sb

**naciągany** *adj* (*pot*: *argument, dowód*) far-fetched

**naciąg|nąć (-nę, -niesz)** (*imp* **-nij**) *vb perf od* **naciągać**

**nacier|ać (-am, -asz)** (*perf* **natrzeć**) *vt* to rub ▷ *vi*: ~ **(na** *+acc*) to charge (at); ~ **twarz kremem** to rub cream into one's face

**nacię|cie (-cia, -cia)** (*gen pl* **-ć**) *nt* cut, incision

**nacin|ać (-am, -asz)** (*perf* **naciąć**) *vt* to incise

**nacis|k (-ku, -ki)** (*instr sg* **-kiem**) *m* pressure; (*akcent*) stress; **pod czyimś ~iem** under pressure from sb; **wywierać (wywrzeć** *perf*) ~ **(na** *+acc*) to exert pressure (on); **kłaść (położyć** *perf*) ~ **na coś** to put *lub* place emphasis on sth; **grupa ~u** pressure group, lobby; **z ~iem** with emphasis

**nacis|kać (-kam, -kasz)** (*perf* **-nąć**) *vt* to press ▷ *vi*: ~ **na kogoś, żeby coś zrobił** (*przen*) to press sb to do sth

**naci|snąć (-snę, -śniesz)** (*imp* **-śnij**) *vb perf od* **naciskać**

**nacj|a (-i, -e)** (*gen pl* **-i**) *f* (*książk*) nation

**nacjonali|sta (-sty, -ści)** (*dat sg* **-ście**) *m decl like f in sg* nationalist

**nacjonalistyczny** *adj* nationalist

**nacjonalizacj|a (-i)** *f* nationalization

**nacjonaliz|m (-mu)** (*loc sg* **-mie**) *m* nationalism

**nacjonaliz|ować (-uję, -ujesz)** (*perf* **z-**) *vt* to nationalize

**naczelni|k (-ka, -cy)** (*instr sg* **-kiem**) *m* (*policji, straży pożarnej*) chief; (*więzienia*) governor; (*wydziału*) head; ~ **poczty** postmaster; ~ **stacji** station-master

**naczelny** *adj* (*główny*) chief *attr* ▷ *m decl like adj* (*pot*: *dyrektor naczelny*) manager; **dyrektor ~** general manager; ~ **wódz** commander-in-chief; ~ **redaktor** editor-in-chief; **lekarz ~** head doctor; **naczelne** *pl* (*Zool*) primates *pl*

**nacze|pa (-py, -py)** (*dat sg* **-pie**) *f* semitrailer

**naczy|nie (-nia, -nia)** (*gen pl* **-ń**) *nt* (*kuchenne*) dish; (*drewniane, gliniane*) vessel; ~ **krwionośne** blood vessel; **naczynia** *pl* dishes *pl*; **zmywać (pozmywać** *perf*) **naczynia** to wash *lub* do the dishes, to wash up

**naćpany** *adj* (*pot*) stoned

SŁOWO KLUCZOWE

**nad** *prep +instr* **1** (*powyżej*) over, above; **nad stołem/górami** over the table/mountains **2** (*o przewadze, władzy, kontroli*) over; **opieka nad starszymi ludźmi** the care of elderly people **3** (*w pobliżu*): **nad rzeką** by the river; **nad morzem** at the seaside; **nad ranem** at daybreak, in the small hours (of the morning) **4** (*na temat*): **myśleć nad czymś** to think about sth; **pracować nad czymś** to work on sth

▷ *prep +acc* (*kierunek*): **nad morze/rzekę** to the seaside/river

**nad|ać (-am, -asz)** (*3 pl* **-adzą**) *vb perf od* **nadawać**

**nadajni|k (-ka, -ki)** (*instr sg* **-kiem**) *m* transmitter

**nadal** *adv* still

**nada|nie** (**-nia, -nia**) (*gen pl* **-ń**) *nt* (*praw*) bestowal
**nadaremnie** *adv* in vain
**nadaremny** *adj* futile
**nadarz|ać się** (**-a**) (*perf* **-yć**) *vr* to occur, to come up
**nad|awać** (**-aję, -ajesz**) (*perf* **-ać**) *vt* (*audycję, program*) to broadcast; (*sygnał*) to transmit; (*list, paczkę*) to send, to mail (US); **~ (komuś) tytuł** to confer a title (on sb); **~ komuś odznaczenie/przywilej** to bestow a decoration/privilege on sb; **~ komuś imię** to give sb a name, to name sb; **~ czemuś kształt** to give shape to sth, to shape sth; **nadawać się** *vr*: **~ się (do czegoś)** to be fit (for sth); **ten materiał nadaje się na suknię** this material is suitable for a dress; **~ się do picia/użytku** to be drinkable/usable
**nadawc|a** (**-y, -y**) *m decl like f in sg* sender
**nad|ąć** (**-mę, -miesz**) (*imp* **-mij**) *vb perf od* **nadymać**
**nadąsany** *adj* sulky, petulant
**nadąż|ać** (**-am, -asz**) (*perf* **-yć**) *vi*: **nie ~ (z czymś)** to fall behind (with sth); **nie nadążałem (za nim)** I could not keep up (with him)
**nadbagaż** (**-u, -e**) (*gen pl* **-y**) *m* excess baggage *lub* luggage
**nadbrzeż|e** (**-a, -a**) (*gen pl* **-y**) *nt* waterside
**nadbud|owa** (**-owy, -owy**) (*dat sg* **-owie**, *gen pl* **-ów**) *f* superstructure
**nadbudów|ka** (**-ki, -ki**) (*dat sg* **-ce**, *gen pl* **-ek**) *f* (*budynku*) (upper) extension; (*statku*) superstructure
**nadchodzący** *adj* (forth)coming
**nadcho|dzić** (**-dzę, -dzisz**) (*imp* **-dź**, *perf* **nadejść**) *vi* (*o człowieku, burzy, śmierci*) to come; (*o liście*) to arrive, to come
**nadciąg|ać** (**-am, -asz**) (*perf* **-nąć**) *vi* to approach
**nadciąg|nąć** (**-nę, -niesz**) (*imp* **-nij**) *vb perf od* **nadciągać**
**nadciśnie|nie** (**-nia**) *nt* (*Med*) hypertension
**nadczłowiek** (**-a, nadludzie**) (*gen pl* **nadludzi**, *instr pl* **nadludźmi**) *m* superman
**naddat|ek** (**-ku, -ki**) (*instr sg* **-kiem**) *m* surplus; **płacić (zapłacić** *perf*) **z naddatkiem** to pay in excess; **pieniądze zwróciły mi się z naddatkiem** I got my money back with interest (*pot*)
**naddźwiękowy** *adj* supersonic
**nade** *prep* = **nad**; **~ wszystko** above all
**nadejś|cie** (**-cia**) *nt* arrival
**nadej|ść** (**-dę, -dziesz**) (*imp* **-dź**) *vb perf od* **nadchodzić**
**nadep|nąć** (**-nę, -niesz**) (*imp* **-nij**) *vb perf od* **nadeptywać**
**nadep|tywać** (**-tuję, -tujesz**) (*perf* **-nąć**) *vb* to tread on, to step on; **nadepnąć komuś na nogę** to step on sb's foot
**nader** *adv* (*książk*) most, highly
**nader|wać** (**-wę, -wiesz**) (*imp* **-wij**) *vb perf od* **nadrywać**
**nade|słać** (**-ślę, -ślesz**) (*imp* **-ślij**) *vb perf od* **nadsyłać**
**nadęty** *adj* (*pot: człowiek*) conceited; (*mina*) sulky
**nadg|aniać** (**-aniam, -aniasz**) (*perf* **-onić**) *vt* to make up for ▷ *vi* to catch up
**nadgarst|ek** (**-ka, -ki**) (*instr sg* **-kiem**) *m* wrist
**nadgodzin|y** (-) *pl* overtime
**nadgo|nić** (**-nię, -nisz**) (*imp* **-ń**) *vb perf od* **nadganiać**
**nadgorliwoś|ć** (**-ci**) *f* officiousness
**nadgorliwy** *adj* officious
**nadgraniczny** *adj* frontier *attr*, border *attr*
**nadinspekto|r** (**-ra, -rzy**) (*loc sg* **-rze**) *m* (*Policja*) ≈ chief constable
**nadj|echać** (**-adę, -edziesz**) (*imp* **-edź**) *vb perf od* **nadjeżdżać**
**nadjeżdż|ać** (**-am, -asz**) (*perf* **nadjechać**) *vi* to arrive, to come
**nadkład|ać** (**-am, -asz**) (*perf* **nadłożyć**) *vt*: **~ drogi** to take a roundabout way
**nadkomisarz** (**-a, -e**) (*gen pl* **-y**) *m* (*Policja*) ≈ assistant commissioner
**nadkwaśnoś|ć** (**-ci**) (*dat sg* **-ci**) *f* hyperacidity
**nadlat|ywać** (**-uję, -ujesz**) (*perf* **nadlecieć**) *vi* (*o samolocie*) to arrive; (*o pociskach, ptaku*) to come flying
**nadleśnict|wo** (**-wa, -wa**) (*loc sg* **-wie**) *nt* ≈ forestry management
**nadleśnicz|y** (**-ego, -y**) *m decl like adj* forest manager
**nadliczbowy** *adj* overtime *attr*
**nadludzki** *adj* superhuman
**nadłoż|yć** (**-ę, -ysz**) (*imp* **nadłóż**) *vb perf od* **nadkładać**
**nadmia|r** (**-ru**) (*loc sg* **-rze**) *m* excess; **w ~ze** in excess; **~ siły roboczej** overmanning
**nadmie|niać** (**-niam, -niasz**) (*perf* **-nić**) *vt/vi* to mention
**nadmie|nić** (**-nię, -nisz**) (*imp* **-ń**) *vb perf od* **nadmieniać**
**nadmiernie** *adv* excessively
**nadmierny** *adj* excessive
**nadmorski** *adj* seaside *attr*
**nadmuch** (**-u, -y**) *m* (*Mot*) demister, defogger
**nadmu|chiwać** (**-chuję, -chujesz**) (*perf* **-chać**) *vt* to inflate
**nadmuchiwany** *adj* inflatable
**nadobne** *inv*: **odpłacać (odpłacić** *perf*) **komuś pięknym za ~** to pay sb back in his own coin

n

**nadobowiązkowy** *adj* optional
**nadpła|ta** (**-ty, -ty**) (*dat sg* **-cie**) *f* excess payment
**nadpobudliwy** *adj* hyperactive
**nadprodukcj|a** (**-i, -e**) (*gen pl* **-i**) *f* overproduction
**nadprogramowy** *adj* additional, extra
**nadprzyrodzony** *adj* supernatural
**nadrabi|ać (-am, -asz)** (*perf* **nadrobić**) *vt* to make up for; **~ stracony czas** to make up for the lost time; **~ miną** (*przen*) to put on a brave face
**nadro|bić (-bię, -bisz)** (*imp* **nadrób**) *vb perf od* **nadrabiać**
**nadru|k** (**-ku, -ki**) (*instr sg* **-kiem**) *m* (*na książce, nalepce*) (printed) inscription; (*na koszulce*) printed design
**nadryw|ać (-am, -asz)** (*perf* **naderwać**) *vt* to rip, to tear (*partly*); (*linę, sznurowadło*) to fray
**nadrzędny** *adj* (*cel, racja*) overriding, imperative; (*wartość, władza*) superior; **zdanie nadrzędne** (*Jęz*) main clause
**nadska|kiwać (-kuję, -kujesz)** *vi*: **~ komuś** to fawn on sb
**nadsłu|chiwać (-chuję, -chujesz)** *vi* to listen; **~ czegoś** to listen (out) for sth
**nadspodziewany** *adj* unexpected
**nadsta|wiać (-wiam, -wiasz)** (*perf* **-wić**) *vt* (*policzek*) to present; **~ głowy** *lub* **karku** (*przen*) to risk one's neck; **~ uszu** (*przen*) to prick up one's ears
**nadsył|ać (-am, -asz)** (*perf* **nadesłać**) *vt* to send (in)
**nadszarp|nąć (-nę, -niesz)** (*imp* **-nij**) *vb perf od* **nadszarpywać**
**nadszarp|ywać (-uję, -ujesz)** (*perf* **-nąć**) *vt* (*majątek*) to make a dent in; (*nerwy, budżet*) to stretch; (*zdrowie*) to undermine; (*opinię, reputację*) to erode
**nadto** *adv*: **aż ~** more than enough
**nadużу|cie** (**-cia, -cia**) (*gen pl* **-ć**) *nt* abuse; **nadużycia finansowe** misuse of funds
**nadуż|yć (-yję, -yjesz)** *vb perf od* **nadużywać**
**nadużyw|ać (-am, -asz)** (*perf* **nadużyć**) *vt*: **~** *+gen* (*władzy, zaufania*) to abuse; (*alkoholu*) to overuse
**nadwa|ga** (**-gi**) (*dat sg* **-dze**) *f* overweight; **mieć nadwagę** to be overweight
**nadwątl|ać (-am, -asz)** (*perf* **-ić**) *vt* (*zdrowie*) to undermine
**nadweręż|ać (-am, -asz)** (*perf* **-yć**) *vt* (*zaufanie, cierpliwość*) to stretch; (*siły*) to overtax; **nadwerężać się** *vr* to overtax o.s.
**nadworny** *adj* court *attr*
**nadwo|zie** (**-zia, -zia**) (*gen pl* **-zi**) *nt* (*Mot*) body(work)
**nadwrażliwoś|ć** (**-ci**) *f* oversensitivity
**nadwrażliwy** *adj* oversensitive
**nadwyż|ka** (**-ki, -ki**) (*dat sg* **-ce**, *gen pl* **-ek**) *f* surplus; **wykonać** (*perf*) **plan z nadwyżką** to exceed the target figures
**nadym|ać (-am, -asz)** (*perf* **nadąć**) *vt* (*policzki*) to puff out; **nadymać się** *vr* (*przen*) to sulk
**na|dziać (-dzieję, -dziejesz)** *vb perf od* **nadziewać**
**nadziany** *adj* (*pot*) loaded (*pot*)
**nadzie|ja** (**-i, -je**) (*gen pl* **-i**) *f* hope; **mam nadzieję, że ...** I hope that ...; **mam nadzieję, że tu zostanę** I hope to stay here; **w nadziei, że ...** in the hope that ...; **pokładać nadzieję w** *+loc* to place one's faith in; **robić sobie nadzieje (na coś)** to build one's hopes (on sth); **pełen nadziei** hopeful
**nadziemny** *adj* overhead
**nadzie|nie** (**-nia, -nia**) (*gen pl* **-ń**) *nt* (*w cieście, czekoladzie*) filling; (*w mięsie, potrawie*) stuffing
**nadziew|ać (-am, -asz)** (*perf* **nadziać**) (*wbijać*) *vt*: **~ coś (na coś)** to impale sth (on sth); (*Kulin*) to skewer sth (on sth); **~ coś (czymś)** to stuff sth (with sth)
**nadzi|wić się (-wię, -wisz)** *vr perf*: **nie móc się nadziwić (czemuś)** to be amazed (at sth)
**nadzorc|a** (**-y, -y**) *m decl like f in sg* supervisor
**nadzorczy** *adj*: **rada nadzorcza** board of supervisors, supervisory board
**nadzor|ować (-uję, -ujesz)** *vt* to supervise
**nadz|ór** (**-oru**) (*loc sg* **-orze**) *m* supervision, inspection; **sprawować ~ nad kimś/czymś** to supervise sb/sth; **pod nadzorem** under surveillance
**nadzwyczaj** *adv* remarkably, extremely
**nadzwyczajnie** *adv* (*nadzwyczaj*) extremely; (*zmienić się*) remarkably
**nadzwyczajny** *adj* (*niezwykły*) extraordinary; (*specjalny*) special; **dodatek ~** special supplement; **profesor ~** ≈ professor (*Brit*), ≈ associate professor (*US*)
**naf|ta** (**-ty**) (*dat sg* **-cie**) *f* kerosene; (*pot*: *ropa naftowa*) oil
**naftowy** *adj* (*przemysł, szyb*) oil *attr*; (*lampa, piec*) paraffin *attr*; **ropa naftowa** petroleum, oil; **pole naftowe** oilfield
**nagab|nąć (-nę, -niesz)** (*imp* **-nij**) *vb perf od* **nagabywać**
**nagab|ywać (-uję, -ujesz)** (*perf* **-nąć**) *vt* (*zagadywać*) to approach; **~ kogoś o coś** to pester sb for sth
**nagad|ać (-am, -asz)** *vt perf*: **~ głupstw** to say a lot of silly things; **~ na kogoś** (*pot*) to backbite sb
**naga|na** (**-ny, -ny**) (*dat sg* **-nie**) *f* rebuke, reprimand; **udzielać (udzielić** *perf*) **komuś nagany** to reprimand sb
**naganny** *adj* reprehensible, blameworthy

**nagi** *adj* *(człowiek)* naked, nude; *(fakty, prawda)* plain
**na|giąć (-gnę, -gniesz)** *(imp* **-gnij***)* *vb perf od* **naginać**
**nagiet|ek (-ka, -ki)** *(instr sg* **-kiem***)* *m* marigold
**nagin|ać (-am, -asz)** *(perf* **nagiąć***)* *vt* *(gałąź)* to bend down; *(przen: prawo, reguły)* to bend
**naglący** *adj* urgent, pressing
**nagle** *adv* suddenly, all of a sudden; *(umrzeć)* unexpectedly; **co ~ to po diable** more haste less speed
**nagl|ić (-ę, -isz)** *(imp* **-ij***)* *vt*: **~ kogoś (do zrobienia czegoś)** to press *lub* urge sb (to do sth) ▷ *vi*: **nagliła, żeby wracać** she insisted on going back
**nagłaśni|ać (-am, -asz)** *(perf* **nagłośnić***)* *vt* *(salę)* to provide sound in; *(sprawę)* to publicize
**nagłoś|nić (-nię, -nisz)** *(imp* **-nij***)* *vb perf od* **nagłaśniać**
**nagłów|ek (-ka, -ki)** *(instr sg* **-kiem***)* *m* *(w tekście)* heading, title; *(w gazecie)* headline; *(na papierze listowym)* letterhead
**nagły** *adj* *(wyjazd, zgon)* sudden, unexpected; *(potrzeba)* urgent, pressing; **w ~m wypadku** *lub* **przypadku** in case of emergency
**nagminny** *adj* common
**nagniot|ek (-ka, -ki)** *(instr sg* **-kiem***)* *m* corn
**nago** *adv* in the nude
**nagon|ka (-ki, -ki)** *(dat sg* **-ce**, *gen pl* **-ek***)* *f* *(przen)* witch-hunt
**nagoś|ć (-ci)** *f* nudity
**nagr|ać (-am, -asz)** *vb perf od* **nagrywać**
**nagradz|ać (-am, -asz)** *(perf* **nagrodzić***)* *vt* to reward; **nagrodzić kogoś czymś/za coś** to reward sb with sth/for sth
**nagra|nie (-nia, -nia)** *(gen pl* **-ń***)* *nt* recording
**nagrob|ek (-ka, -ki)** *(instr sg* **-kiem***)* *m* *(pozioma płyta)* tombstone, gravestone; *(pionowa tablica)* headstone
**nagrobkowy, nagrobny** *adj*: **płyta nagrobna** tombstone, gravestone; **tablica nagrobna** headstone
**nagro|da (-dy, -dy)** *(loc sg* **-dzie**, *gen pl* **nagród***)* *f* *(w turnieju)* prize; *(za zasługi, pomoc)* reward; *(przyznawana przez organizacje)* award; **N~ Nobla** the Nobel prize; **w nagrodę za coś** in reward for sth
**nagr|odzić (-odzę, -odzisz)** *(imp* **-odź** *lub* **-ódź***)* *vb perf od* **nagradzać**
**nagrodzony** *adj* *(film, książka)* prizewinning *attr*
**nagromadzeni|e (-a)** *nt* accumulation
**nagroma|dzić (-dzę, -dzisz)** *(imp* **-dź***)* *vb perf od* **gromadzić**
**nagryw|ać (-am, -asz)** *(perf* **nagrać***)* *vt* *(płytę)* to record; *(na magnetofon)* to tape; *(na taśmę video)* to videotape
**nagrz|ać (-eję, -ejesz)** *vb perf od* **nagrzewać**
**nagrzew|ać (-am, -asz)** *(perf* **nagrzać***)* *vt* to warm, to heat; **nagrzewać się** *vr* to warm up
**naigraw|ać się (-am, -asz)** *vr*: **naigrawać się z** *+gen* to ridicule, to deride
**naiwnoś|ć (-ci)** *f* naivety, naïveté
**naiwny** *adj* naive
**naj...** *pref* *(tworzy stopień najwyższy)* the most, -est
**najazd (-u, -y)** *(loc sg* **najeździe***)* *m* invasion
**naj|ąć (-mę, -miesz)** *(imp* **-mij***)* *vb perf od* **najmować**
**najbardziej** *adv superl od* **bardzo** (the) most; **~ ze wszystkiego** most of all; **jak ~!** by all means!
**najbliższy** *adj superl od* **bliski**; *(o miejscu)* (the) nearest; *(o osobie)* (the) closest; *(o czasie)* (the) next; **w ~ch dniach** within the next few days; **w ~m czasie** very soon
**najdalej** *adv superl od* **daleko**; *(o miejscu)* (the) farthest, (the) furthest; *(w największym stopniu)* (the) furthest; *(najpóźniej)* at the latest
**naj|echać (-adę, -edziesz)** *(3 pl* **-adą**, *imp* **-edź***)* *vb perf od* **najeżdżać**
**najedzony** *adj* full, full up *(Brit)*
**naj|em (-mu)** *(loc sg* **-mie***)* *m* lease; **brać (wziąć** *perf***) coś w ~ (od kogoś)** to lease sth (from sb); **oddawać (oddać** *perf***) (komuś) coś w ~** to lease (sb) sth
**najemc|a (-y, -y)** *m decl like f in sg* lessee; **~ lokalu** occupier
**najemni|k (-ka, -cy)** *(instr sg* **-kiem***)* *m* *(żołnierz)* mercenary; *(robotnik)* hired hand
**najemny** *adj* *(pracownik)* hired *attr*; **żołnierz ~** mercenary
**naj|eść się (-em, -esz)** *(3 pl* **-edzą**, *imp* **-edz**, *pt* **-adł, -adła, -edli***)* *vr perf* to eat one's fill
**najeźdźc|a (-y, -y)** *m decl like f in sg* invader
**najeż|ać się (-am, -asz)** *(perf* **-yć***)* *vr* *(o człowieku)* to bristle; **kot najeżył się** the cat's hair bristled
**najeżdż|ać (-am, -asz)** *(perf* **najechać***)* *vt*: **~ na** *+acc* *(kraj)* to invade; *(krawężnik)* to run onto; *(słup)* to run into
**najeżony** *adj*: **~ niebezpieczeństwami** beset with dangers
**najgorszy** *adj superl od* **zły** (the) worst; **w ~m wypadku** *lub* **razie** at the worst; **najgorsze jest to, że ...** the worst (thing) is that ...
**najgorzej** *adv superl od* **źle** (the) worst; **nie ~** not too bad
**najlepiej** *adv superl od* **dobrze** (the) best
**najlepszy** *adj superl od* **dobry** (the) best; **w ~m wypadku** at best; **najlepsze, co możemy zrobić, to ...** the best (thing) we can do is ...; **najlepsze życzenia** best wishes
**najmniej** *adv superl od* **mało**; *(znać, kochać)* (the) least; **~ wody/kłopotu** the least water/

trouble; **~ ludzi/zabawek** the fewest people/ toys; **co ~** at least
**najmniejszy** *adj superl od* **mały** (the) smallest; (*prawie żaden*) the least; **nie mam najmniejszego pojęcia** (*pot*) I don't have the slightest *lub* foggiest idea
**najm|ować (-uję, -ujesz)** (*perf* **nająć**) *vt* (*lokal, sprzęt*) to lease; (*ludzi*) to hire; **najmować się** *vr* to get hired
**najnowszy** *adj superl od* **nowy**; (*najmłodszy*) (the) newest; (*ostatni*) (the) most recent, (the) latest
**najogólniej** *adv superl od* **ogólnie**; **~ mówiąc** speaking in the most general terms
**najpierw** *adv* first (of all), in the first place
**najpóźniej** *adv superl od* **późno** (the) latest; (*jako ostatni*) last; **~ we czwartek** on Thursday at the (very) latest
**najprawdopodobniej** *adv superl od* **prawdopodobnie** most probably, in all likelihood
**najstarszy** *adj superl od* **stary** (the) oldest; (*w rodzinie*) (the) eldest
**naj|ść (-dę, -dziesz)** (*imp* **-dź**, *pt* **naszedł, naszła, naszli**) *vb perf od* **nachodzić**
**najwidoczniej** *adv superl od* **widocznie**; (*wygląda na to, że*) clearly, evidently
**najwięcej** *adv superl od* **dużo, wiele** (the) most
**najwyraźniej** *adv superl od* **wyraźnie**; (*najwidoczniej*) clearly, evidently
**najwyżej** *adv superl od* **wysoko**; (*fruwać, latać*) (the) highest ▷ *adv*: **~ siedem** seven at the (very) most
**najwyższy** *adj superl od* **wysoki**; (*góra, liczba, dźwięk*) (the) highest; (*człowiek, drzewo, budynek*) (the) tallest; **~ czas, żebyśmy poszli** it's high time we left; **Sąd N~** ≈ the High Court (*Brit*), ≈ the Supreme Court (*US*); **najwyższe piętro** the top floor; **stopień ~** (*Jęz*) superlative degree; **sprawa najwyższej wagi** matter of paramount *lub* utmost importance
**nakar|mić (-mię, -misz)** *vb perf od* **karmić**
**naka|z (-zu, -zy)** (*loc sg* **-zie**) *m* order; (*Prawo*) warrant; **znak ~u** (*Mot*) regulatory sign; **~ aresztowania/rewizji** arrest/search warrant; **~ urzędowy** writ
**naka|zać (-żę, -żesz)** (*imp* **-ż**) *vb perf od* **nakazywać**
**nakaz|ywać (-uję, -ujesz)** (*perf* **-ać**) *vt* to order; **~ komuś coś zrobić** to order sb to do sth; **nakazać dietę** to prescribe a diet
**nakle|ić (-ję, -isz)** *vb perf od* **naklejać**
**nakle|jać (-jam, -jasz)** (*perf* **-ić**) *vt* to stick on; **nakleić znaczek na kopertę** to stamp an envelope
**naklej|ka (-ki, -ki)** (*dat sg* **-ce**, *gen pl* **-ek**) *f* (*etykieta*) label; (*nalepka*) sticker
**nakła|d (-du, -dy)** (*loc sg* **-dzie**) *m* (*książki*) edition; **książka ma wyczerpany ~** the book is out of print; **nakłady** *pl* expenditure, outlay
**nakład|ać (-am, -asz)** (*perf* **nałożyć**) *vt* (*farbę, krem*) to apply; (*ubranie, czapkę*) to put on; (*podatek, embargo*) to impose; (*obrazy na siebie*) to superimpose; **~ jedzenie na talerz** to put food on a plate; **nakładać się** *vr* to overlap
**nakłani|ać (-am, -asz)** (*perf* **nakłonić**) *vt* to induce sb to do sth
**nakło|nić (-nię, -nisz)** (*imp* **-ń**) *vb perf od* **nakłaniać**
**nakłu|ć (-ję, -jesz)** *vb perf od* **nakłuwać**
**nakłuw|ać (-am, -asz)** (*perf* **nakłuć**) *vt* to prick
**nakrapiany** *adj* speckled
**nakreśl|ać (-am, -asz)** (*perf* **-ić**) *vt* (*formułować*) to outline; (*rysować*) to draw
**nakrę|cać (-cam, -casz)** (*perf* **-cić**) *vt* (*zegar*) to wind up
**nakrę|cić (-cę, -cisz)** (*imp* **-ć**) *vb perf od* **nakręcać**
**nakręt|ka (-ki, -ki)** (*dat sg* **-ce**, *gen pl* **-ek**) *f* (*na śrubę*) nut; (*na butelkę*) (screw) top
**nakry|cie (-cia, -cia)** (*gen pl* **-ć**) *nt* covering; (*stołowe*) cover, place setting; **~ głowy** headgear
**nakry|ć (-ję, -jesz)** *vb perf od* **nakrywać** ▷ *vt perf* (*pot: przyłapać*) to nail (*pot*)
**nakryw|ać (-am, -asz)** (*perf* **nakryć**) *vt* to cover; **~ do stołu** to lay *lub* set the table
**nal|ać (-eję, -ejesz)** *vb perf od* **nalewać**
**naleciałoś|ć (-ci, -ci)** (*gen pl* **-ci**) *f* trace
**naleg|ać (-am, -asz)** *vi*: **~ na coś** to insist on (doing) sth; **~ na kogoś, żeby coś zrobił** to insist on sb's doing sth; **~, żeby ...** to insist that ...
**nale|piać (-piam, -piasz)** (*perf* **-pić**) *vt* to stick, to paste
**nalep|ka (-ki, -ki)** (*dat sg* **-ce**, *gen pl* **-ek**) *f* sticker
**naleśni|k (-ka, -ki)** (*instr sg* **-kiem**) *m* pancake (*Brit*), crepe (*US*)
**nalew|ać (-am, -asz)** (*perf* **nalać**) *vt* to pour
**nalew|ka (-ki, -ki)** (*dat sg* **-ce**, *gen pl* **-ek**) *f* (*alkohol*) liqueur; (*wyciąg*) tincture
**należ|eć (-ę, -ysz)** *vi*: **~ do** *+gen* to belong to; **należy ...** it's necessary to ..., one should ...; **to należy do jego obowiązków** it's his job; **należy sobie życzyć** one *lub* we can only hope; **należeć się** *vr*: **ile się należy?** how much do I owe you?; **to mi się należy** I deserve this; **należy mi się sześć dni urlopu** I am due 6 days' leave
**należnoś|ć (-ci, -ci)** (*gen pl* **-ci**) *f* amount due
**należny** *adj* due
**należycie** *adv* duly, appropriately
**należyty** *adj* appropriate
**nalo|t (-tu, -ty)** (*loc sg* **-cie**) *m* (*powietrzny*) air raid; (*policyjny*) raid; (*cienka warstwa*) coating; (*na języku*) fur

**naład|ować (-uję, -ujesz)** *vb perf od* **ładować**
**nałogo|wiec** (**-wca, -wcy**) *m* addict
**nałogowy** *adj* (*alkoholik*) chronic; (*palacz*) habitual, heavy
**nałoż|yć (-ę, -ysz)** (*imp* **nałóż**) *vb perf od* **nakładać**
**nał|óg** (**-ogu, -ogi**) (*instr pl* **-ogiem**) *m* (*zły nawyk*) bad habit; (*uzależnienie*) addiction
**nam** *pron dat od* **my** us
**namacalny** *adj* tangible
**namacz|ać (-am, -asz)** (*perf* **namoczyć**) *vt* to soak
**namal|ować (-uję, -ujesz)** *vb perf od* **malować**
**namaszcze|nie** (**-nia, -nia**) (*gen pl* **-ń**) *nt*: **ostatnie ~** the last rites *pl*; **z ~m** with deliberation
**namawi|ać (-am, -asz)** *vt* to urge, to encourage
**nami** *pron instr od* **my** us; **z ~** with us
**namia|r** (**-ru, -ry**) (*loc sg* **-rze**) *m* bearings *pl*
**namiast|ka** (**-ki, -ki**) (*dat sg* **-ce**, *gen pl* **-ek**) *f*: **~ czegoś** a poor substitute for sth
**namiętnie** *adv* passionately
**namiętnoś|ć** (**-ci, -ci**) (*gen pl* **-ci**) *f* passion
**namiętny** *adj* passionate
**namio|t** (**-tu, -ty**) (*loc sg* **-cie**) *m* tent; **~ tlenowy** oxygen tent; **~ cyrkowy** big top; **pod ~em** in a tent, under canvas (*Brit*)
**namiotowy** *adj*: **pole namiotowe** camping site (*Brit*), campsite (*Brit*), campground (*US*)
**namocz|yć (-ę, -ysz)** *vb perf od* **moczyć, namaczać**
**nam|owa** (**-owy, -owy**) (*dat sg* **-owie**, *gen pl* **-ów**) *f* suggestion; **za czyjąś namową** at sb's instigation, at sb's insistence
**namó|wić (-wię, -wisz)** *vt perf*: **~ kogoś do (zrobienia) czegoś** to coax *lub* talk sb into doing sth
**namydl|ać (-am, -asz)** (*perf* **-ić**) *vt* to apply soap to
**namy|sł** (**-słu, -sły**) (*loc sg* **-śle**) *m* thought, consideration; **bez ~u** without a second thought; **po namyśle** on second thoughts; **czas do ~u** time to think something over
**namyśl|ać się (-am, -asz)** (*perf* **-ić**) *vr* to think it over
**na|nieść (-niosę, -niesiesz)** (*imp* **-nieś**, *pt* **-niósł, -niosła, -nieśli**) *vb perf od* **nanosić**
**nano|sić (-szę, -sisz)** (*imp* **-ś**, *perf* **nanieść**) *vt* (*na wykres, mapę*) to plot
**naoczny** *adj*: **~ świadek** eye witness
**naokoło** *prep +gen* round, around ▷ *adv* round, around
**naostrz|yć (-ę, -ysz)** *vb perf od* **ostrzyć**
**napa|d** (**-du, -dy**) (*loc sg* **-dzie**) *m* (*agresja*) assault; (*choroby, szału, śmiechu*) fit; **~ z bronią w ręku** (*Prawo*) armed *lub* aggravated assault
**napad|ać (-am, -asz)** (*perf* **napaść**) *vt* to attack, to assault ▷ *vi*: **~ na kogoś** to attack sb, to assault sb; **co cię napadło?** whatever possessed you?
**napal|m** (**-mu**) (*loc sg* **-mie**) *m* napalm
**napalony** *adj* (*pot*) excited, horny (*pot*); **być ~m na coś** to be dying for sth
**napa|r** (**-ru, -ry**) (*loc sg* **-rze**) *m* infusion
**naparst|ek** (**-ka, -ki**) (*instr sg* **-kiem**) *m* thimble
**naparz|ać (-am, -asz)** (*perf* **-yć**) *vt* to infuse
**napastliwy** *adj* belligerent
**napastni|k** (**-ka, -cy**) (*instr sg* **-kiem**) *m* assailant, attacker; (*Sport*) forward
**napast|ować (-uję, -ujesz)** *vt* to harass, to pester; (*seksualnie*) to molest
**napaś|ć**[1] (**-ci, -ci**) (*gen pl* **-ci**) *f* assault
**napa|ść**[2] **(-dnę, -dniesz)** (*imp* **-dnij**) *vb perf od* **napadać**
**napaw|ać (-am, -asz)** *vt* to fill with; **napawać się** *vr*: **~ się czymś** (*widokiem*) to relish sth, to delight in sth; (*sukcesem, radością*) to savour (*Brit*) *lub* savor (*US*) sth
**napeł|niać (-niam, -niasz)** (*perf* **-nić**) *vt* to fill
**napeł|nić (-nię, -nisz)** (*imp* **-nij**) *vb perf od* **napełniać**
**napę|d** (**-du, -dy**) (*loc sg* **-dzie**) *m* (*elektryczny, spalinowy*) drive; (*rakietowy, odrzutowy*) propulsion; (*Komput*) disk drive; **~ na 4 koła** four wheel drive
**napędowy** *adj* (*siła*) driving; **olej ~** diesel oil; **wał ~** drive shaft
**napę|dzać (-dzam, -dzasz)** (*perf* **-dzić**) *vt* (*wprawiać w ruch*) to drive, to propel
**napę|dzić (-dzę, -dzisz)** (*imp* **-dź**) *vb perf od* **napędzać** ▷ *vt perf*: **~ komuś strachu** to give sb a scare
**na|piąć (-pnę, -pniesz)** (*imp* **-pnij**) *vb perf od* **napinać**
**napi|ć się (-ję, -jesz)** *vr perf* to have a drink; **czego się napijesz?** what would you like to drink?
**napię|cie** (**-cia, -cia**) (*gen pl* **-ć**) *nt* (*Elektr*) voltage; (*naprężenie*) tension; (*stan psychiczny*) tension; **wysokie ~** high voltage; **trzymać w napięciu** to keep in suspense
**napięty** *adj* (*plan*) tight; (*uwaga*) rapt; (*atmosfera, nerwy*) tense
**napin|ać (-am, -asz)** (*perf* **napiąć**) *vt* (*linę*) to tighten; (*mięśnie: na pokaz*) to flex; (*: z wysiłku*) to tense
**napi|s** (**-su, -sy**) (*loc sg* **-sie**) *m* caption, inscription; **napisy** *pl* (*Film: na początku lub końcu filmu*) the credits; (*: tłumaczenia dialogów*) subtitles
**napi|sać (-szę, -szesz)** (*imp* **-sz**) *vb perf od* **pisać**
**napiw|ek** (**-ku, -ki**) (*instr sg* **-kiem**) *m* tip
**naplet|ek** (**-ka, -ki**) (*instr sg* **-kiem**) *m* foreskin

n

**napły|nąć (-nę, -niesz)** *(imp* **-ń**) *vb perf od* **napływać**
**napły|w** (**-wu, -wy**) (*loc sg* **-wie**) *m* (*wody*) inflow; (*ludzi*) influx
**napływ|ać (-am, -asz)** (*perf* **napłynąć**) *vi* (*o wodzie*) to flow in; (*o ludziach, wiadomościach, listach*) to come flooding in
**napoleoński** *adj* Napoleonic
**napomk|nąć (-nę, -niesz)** (*imp* **-nij**) *vb perf od* **napomykać**
**napomp|ować (-uję, -ujesz)** *vb perf od* **pompować**
**napomyk|ać (-am, -asz)** (*perf* **napomknąć**) *vi*: **~ o** *+loc* to mention
**napotyk|ać (-am, -asz)** (*perf* **napotkać**) *vt* to encounter, to run into
**nap|ój (-oju, -oje)** (*gen pl* **-ojów**) *m* drink, beverage
**naprasz|ać się (-am, -asz)** *vr*: **napraszać się komuś z czymś** to importune sb with sth
**napra|wa** (**-wy, -wy**) (*dat sg* **-wie**) *f* repair; **w naprawie** under repair; **nie do naprawy** beyond repair
**naprawczy** *adj* repair *attr*
**naprawdę** *adv* really, truly; **~?** really?
**napra|wiać (-wiam, -wiasz)** (*perf* **-wić**) *vt* (*reperować*) to repair, to mend; (*przen: krzywdę*) to undo; (: *stratę*) to make good
**naprędce** *adv* hastily
**napręż|ać (-am, -asz)** *vt* to tighten; **naprężać się** *vr* (*o linie*) to tighten; (*o mięśniach*) to tense (up)
**napręże|nie** (**-nia, -nia**) (*gen pl* **-ń**) *nt* tension; (*Fiz*) stress
**naprowa|dzać (-dzam, -dzasz)** (*perf* **-dzić**) *vt* (*kierować*) to direct; (*dawać wskazówki*) to guide
**naprowa|dzić (-dzę, -dzisz)** (*imp* **-dź**) *vb perf od* **naprowadzać**
**naprzeciw** *prep +gen* opposite, across from; **wyjść komuś ~** to meet sb half way
**naprzeciwko** *adv* opposite
**naprzód** *adv* ahead, forward
**naprzykrz|ać się (-am, -asz)** *vr*: **naprzykrzać się komuś** to nag sb
**napuchnięty** *adj* swollen, bloated
**napuszcz|ać (-am, -asz)** (*perf* **napuścić**) *vt* (*wodę*) to pour; (*powietrze*) to let in; **~ kogoś na kogoś** (*pot*) to set sb against sb
**napuszony** *adj* (*przen: mina*) proud; (*człowiek*) puffed up; (*styl*) bombastic, pompous
**napu|ścić (-szczę, -ścisz)** (*imp* **-ść**) *vb perf od* **napuszczać**
**napyt|ać (-am, -asz)** *vt perf*: **~ sobie biedy** (*pot*) to get into trouble
**nara|da** (**-dy, -dy**) (*loc sg* **-dzie**) *f* (*zebranie*) conference, meeting; (*naradzanie się*) deliberation
**nara|dzać się (-dzam, -dzasz)** (*perf* **-dzić**) *vr* to confer, to deliberate
**nara|dzić się (-dzę, -dzisz)** (*imp* **-dź**) *vb perf od* **naradzać się**
**naramienni|k** (**-ka, -ki**) (*instr sg* **-kiem**) *m* (*Wojsk*) epaulette (*Brit*), epaulet (*US*)
**narast|ać (-a)** (*perf* **narosnąć**) *vt* to grow
**naraz** *adv* (*nagle*) suddenly, all at once; (*jednocześnie*) at the same time; **wszyscy ~** all together
**nara|zić (-żę, -zisz)** (*imp* **-ź**) *vb perf od* **narażać**
**naraż|ać (-am, -asz)** (*perf* **narazić**) *vt* to endanger, to jeopardize; **~ kogoś na coś** to expose sb to sth; **~ życie** to risk one's life; **narażać się** *vr*: **~ się na coś** to run the risk of sth; **narazić się komuś** to make o.s. unpopular with sb
**narażony** *adj*: **być ~m na coś** to be open *lub* subject to sth
**narciar|ka** (**-ki, -ki**) (*dat sg* **-ce**, *gen pl* **-ek**) *f* (*kobieta*) skier; (*czapka*) ski(ing) cap
**narciarski** *adj* ski *attr*
**narciarst|wo** (**-wa**) (*loc sg* **-wie**) *nt* skiing
**narciarz** (**-a, -e**) (*gen pl* **-y**) *m* skier
**narcie** *n patrz* **narta**
**narcy|z** (**-za, -zy**) (*loc sg* **-zie**) *m* (*Bot*) narcissus; (*człowiek*) narcissist
**narcyz|m** (**-mu**) (*loc sg* **-mie**) *m* narcissism
**nareszcie** *adv* at last
**narkoma|n** (**-na, -ni**) (*loc sg* **-nie**) *m* drug addict
**narkomani|a** (**-i**) *f* drug addiction
**narkoman|ka** (**-ki, -ki**) (*dat sg* **-ce**, *gen pl* **-ek**) *f* drug addict
**narkotyczny** *adj* narcotic; **głód ~** *drug-related withdrawal symptoms*
**narkoty|k** (**-ku, -ki**) (*instr sg* **-kiem**) *m* drug, narcotic
**narkotyz|ować się (-uję, -ujesz)** *vr* to take drugs
**narko|za** (**-zy, -zy**) (*dat sg* **-zie**) *f* (*Med*) anaesthesia; **pod narkozą** under an anaesthetic
**nar|obić (-obię, -obisz)** (*imp* **-ób**) *vt perf*: **~ hałasu** to make a noise; **~ szkody** to cause *lub* do damage
**narodowościowy** *adj* ethnic
**narodowoś|ć** (**-ci, -ci**) (*gen pl* **-ci**) *f* nationality; **być narodowości polskiej** to be of Polish nationality
**narodowy** *adj* national
**narodze|nie** (**-nia, -nia**) (*gen pl* **-ń**) *nt* birth; **Boże N~** Christmas
**nar|odzić się (-odzę, -odzisz)** (*imp* **-ódź**) *vr* to be born
**narodzin|y** (**-**) *pl* birth *sg*
**nar|osnąć (-ośnie)** (*pt* **-osł, -osła, -ośli**) *vb perf od* **narastać**

**narośl** (**-i, -e**) (*gen pl* **-i**) *f* growth
**narowisty** *adj* skittish
**narożni|k** (**-ka, -ki**) (*instr sg* **-kiem**) *m* (*domu, pokoju, obrusa*) corner; (*kanapa*) corner settee
**nar|ód** (**-odu, -ody**) (*loc sg* **-odzie**) *m* (*grupa etniczna*) nation; (*populacja kraju*) people; **Narody Zjednoczone** the United Nations
**narósł** *vb patrz* **narosnąć**
**narracj|a** (**-i, -e**) (*gen pl* **-i**) *f* narration
**narrato|r** (**-ra, -rzy**) (*loc sg* **-rze**) *m* narrator
**narrator|ka** (**-ki, -ki**) (*dat sg* **-ce**, *gen pl* **-ek**) *f* narrator
**nar|ta** (**-ty, -ty**) (*dat sg* **-cie**) *f* ski; **jeździć na ~ch** to ski; **narty biegowe/wodne/zjazdowe** cross-country/water/downhill skis
**narusz|ać (-am, -asz)** (*perf* **-yć**) *vt* (*granice, prawo, pokój*) to violate; (*równowagę*) to upset
**narusze|nie** (**-nia, -nia**) (*gen pl* **-ń**) *nt* violation, infringement
**narwany** *adj* (*pot*) hot-headed
**naryb|ek** (**-ku**) (*instr sg* **-kiem**) *m* (*Zool*) fry *pl*; (*przen*) new blood (*przen*)
**narys|ować (-uję, -ujesz)** *vb perf od* **rysować**
**narzą|d** (**-du, -dy**) (*loc sg* **-dzie**) *m* organ
**narzecz|e** (**-a, -a**) (*gen pl* **-y**) *nt* dialect
**narzeczon|a** (**-ej, -e**) *f decl like adj* fiancée
**narzecz|ony** (**-onego, -eni**) *m decl like adj* fiancé; **narzeczeni** the engaged couple
**narzek|ać (-am, -asz)** *vi*: **~ na** *+acc* to complain about
**narzędni|k** (**-ka, -ki**) (*instr sg* **-kiem**) *m* (*Jęz*) instrumental (case)
**narzę|dzie** (**-dzia, -dzia**) (*gen pl* **-dzi**) *nt* tool, instrument; **być ~m w czyichś rękach** to be a (mere) tool in the hands of sb
**narzu|cać (-cam, -casz)** (*perf* **-cić**) *vt* (*płaszcz*) to throw on; (*wolę, warunki*) to impose; **narzucać się** *vr*: **~ się komuś** to force o.s. upon sb
**narzu|cić (-cę, -cisz)** (*imp* **-ć**) *vb perf od* **narzucać**
**narzu|t** (**-tu, -ty**) (*loc sg* **-cie**) *m* mark-up; **z ~em** marked-up
**narzu|ta** (**-ty, -ty**) (*dat sg* **-cie**) *f* bedspread, coverlet
**nas** *pron gen, acc, loc od* **my**; **nie ma nas w domu** we're out (at the moment); **o nas** about us; **bez nas** without us
**nasad|ka** (**-ki, -ki**) (*dat sg* **-ce**) *f* (*pióra*) cap
**nasennie** *adv*: **działać ~** to induce sleep, to have a soporific effect
**nasenny** *adj*: **pigułka nasenna** sleeping pill
**nasi** *pron patrz* **nasz**
**nasiąk|ać (-am, -asz)** (*perf* **-nąć**) *vi*: **~ wodą** to soak up water
**nasiąk|nąć (-nę, -niesz)** (*imp* **-nij**) *vb perf od* **nasiąkać**
**na|sienie** (**-sienia**) *nt* (*Bot*) (*nom pl* **-siona**) seed; (*sperma*) semen
**nasil|ać się (-a)** (*perf* **-ić**) *vr* to intensify, to escalate
**naskór|ek** (**-ka**) (*instr sg* **-kiem**) *m* epidermis
**na|słać (-ślę, -ślesz)** (*imp* **-ślij**) *vb perf od* **nasyłać**
**nasłonecznieni|e** (**-a**) *nt* insolation
**nasłoneczniony** *adj* sunny, insolated
**nasłuch|ać się (-am, -asz)** *vr perf*: **nasłuchać się czegoś** to hear enough of sth; (*wymówek*) to get an earful of sth
**nasłuch|iwać (-uję, -ujesz)** *vt*: **~ kogoś/czegoś** to listen (out) for sb/sth
**nasmar|ować (-uję, -ujesz)** *vb perf od* **smarować**
**nasta|ć (-nę, -niesz)** (*imp* **-ń**) *vb perf od* **nastawać**
**nast|awać (-aję, -ajesz)** (*imp* **-awaj**, *perf* **-ać**) *vi* (*o porze, okresie*) to come; (*pot*: *o człowieku*) to take over; **nastała** (*perf*) **cisza** silence fell; **~ na czyjeś życie** to threaten sb's life
**nasta|wiać (-wiam, -wiasz)** (*perf* **-wić**) *vt* (*kawę, radio*) to put on; (*zegar, budzik*) to set; (*kość, ramię*) to set; **~ odbiornik na (stację)** to tune in (to a station); **~ ostrość** to focus; **~ uszu** to cock one's ears; **nastawiać się** *vr*: **~ się na coś** to expect sth
**nastawie|nie** (**-nia**) *nt*: **~ (do** *+gen***)** attitude (to *lub* towards)
**nastawiony** *adj*: **~ na karierę** career-minded; **liberalnie ~** liberally-minded
**nastą|pić (-pię, -pisz)** *vb perf od* **następować** ▷ *vi perf*: **~ na coś** to step *lub* tread on sth
**następc|a** (**-y, -y**) *m decl like f in sg* successor; **~ tronu** heir (to the throne), the Crown Prince
**następnie** *adv* then, next; **najpierw ..., ~ ...** first ..., next ...
**następny** *adj* next, following; **następnego dnia** the next *lub* following day; **za następne 5 lat** in another five years; **~ proszę!** next please!; **~m razem** next time
**następ|ować (-uję, -ujesz)** (*perf* **nastąpić**) *vi* (*pojawiać się kolejno*) to follow; (*o śmierci, zderzeniu, zmianie*) to ensue; **ciąg dalszy nastąpi** to be continued; **powiedział, co następuje ...** he said as follows ..., he said the following ...
**następst|wo** (**-wa, -wa**) (*loc sg* **-wie**) *nt* after-effect; **następstwa** after-effects *pl*, aftermath; **w następstwie czegoś** in the aftermath of sth
**następujący** *adj* following; **~ po sobie** successive
**nastolat|ek** (**-ka, -ki**) (*instr sg* **-kiem**) *m* teenager, adolescent
**nastolat|ka** (**-ki, -ki**) (*dat sg* **-ce**, *gen pl* **-ek**) *f* teenager, adolescent

n

**nastoletni** *adj* teenage, adolescent
**nastraj|ać (-a)** (*perf* **nastroić**) *vt* to incline
**nastr|oić (-oję, -oisz)** (*imp* **-ój**) *vb perf od* **nastrajać, stroić**
**nastrojowy** *adj* romantic
**nastrosz|yć (-ę, -ysz)** *vb perf od* **stroszyć**
**nastr|ój** (**-oju, -oje**) *m* (*stan psychiczny*) mood; (*panująca atmosfera*) atmosphere; **być w dobrym/złym nastroju** to be in a good/bad mood
**nasturcj|a** (**-i, -e**) (*gen pl* **-i**) *f* nasturtium
**nasu|nąć (-nę, -niesz)** (*imp* **-ń**) *vb perf od* **nasuwać**
**nasuw|ać (-am, -asz)** (*perf* **nasunąć**) *vt*: **~ kapelusz na oczy** to pull one's hat over one's eyes; **~ komuś coś na myśl** to suggest sth to sb; **nasuwać się** *vr* (*o myśli*) to come to mind
**nasy|cać (-cam, -casz)** (*perf* **-cić**) *vt* (*ciekawość, głód*) to satisfy
**nasyceni|e** (**-a**) *nt* saturation
**nasy|cić (-cę, -cisz)** (*imp* **-ć**) *vb perf od* **nasycać**; **nasycić się** *vr* (*najeść się*) to eat one's fill
**nasycony** *adj* (*syty*) replete, satiated; (*para, roztwór, barwa*) saturated
**nasy|p** (**-pu, -py**) (*loc sg* **-pie**) *m* embankment
**nasz** *possessive pron* (*przed rzeczownikiem*) our; (*bez rzeczownika*) ours; **to jest ~ samochód** this is our car; **ten samochód jest ~** this car is ours
**naszedł, naszła** *itd. vb patrz* **najść**
**naszkic|ować (-uję, -ujesz)** *vb perf od* **szkicować**
**naszyjni|k** (**-ka, -ki**) (*instr sg* **-kiem**) *m* necklace
**naszyw|ka** (**-ki, -ki**) (*dat sg* **-ce**, *gen pl* **-ek**) *f* badge
**naślad|ować (-uję, -ujesz)** *vt* (*wzorować się*) to copy, to emulate; (*imitować*) to imitate
**naśladowc|a** (**-y, -y**) *m decl like f in sg* imitator
**naśladownict|wo** (**-wa**) (*loc sg* **-wie**) *nt* imitation
**naśmiew|ać się (-am, -asz)** *vr*: **naśmiewać się z** *+gen* to mock, to laugh at
**naświetl|ać (-am, -asz)** (*perf* **-ić**) *vt* (*promieniami*) to irradiate; (*Med*) to give radiation treatment; (Fot) to expose; (*przen*) to throw *lub* cast light on
**naświetla|nie** (**-nia, -nia**) (*gen pl* **-ń**) *nt* (*promieniami*) irradiation; (Fot) exposure; **czas naświetlania** exposure time
**natar|cie** (**-cia, -cia**) (*gen pl* **-ć**) *nt* offensive, attack
**natarczywoś|ć** (**-ci**) *f* importunity
**natarczywy** *adj* importunate
**natch|nąć (-nę, -niesz)** (*imp* **-nij**) *vt perf* to inspire, to infuse
**natchnie|nie** (**-nia, -nia**) (*gen pl* **-ń**) *nt* inspiration
**natchniony** *adj* inspired
**natęż|ać (-am, -asz)** (*perf* **-yć**) *vt* (*wzrok, słuch*) to strain; **natężać się** *vr* to intensify
**natęże|nie** (**-nia, -nia**) (*gen pl* **-ń**) *nt* (*dźwięku*) volume; (*Elektr*) intensity
**nat|ka** (**-ki**) (*dat sg* **-ce**) *f* tops *pl*; **~ pietruszki** parsley
**natk|nąć się (-nę, -niesz)** (*imp* **-nij**) *vb perf od* **natykać się**
**natło|k** (**-ku**) (*instr sg* **-kiem**) *m*: **w ~u spraw/myśli** in the rush of events/ideas
**natomiast** *adv* however
**natra|fiać (-fiam, -fiasz)** (*perf* **-fić**) *vi*: **~ na** *+acc* to come across
**natrę|t** (**-ta, -ci**) (*loc sg* **-cie**) *m* pushy person
**natrętny** *adj* obtrusive
**natrys|k** (**-ku, -ki**) (*instr sg* **-kiem**) *m* shower; **brać (wziąć** *perf*) **~** to have (*Brit*) *lub* take (*US*) a shower
**nat|rzeć (-rę, -rzesz)** (*imp* **-rzyj**) *vb perf od* **nacierać**
**natu|ra** (**-ry**) (*loc sg* **-rze**) *f* nature; **rysować z natury** to draw from nature; **martwa ~** still life; **być bojaźliwym z natury** to be a coward by nature
**naturaliz|m** (**-mu**) (*loc sg* **-mie**) *m* naturalism
**naturalnie** *adv* naturally
**naturalnoś|ć** (**-ci**) *f* naturalness
**naturalny** *adj* natural; **przyrost ~** population growth (rate); **naturalnej wielkości** life-size(d); **umrzeć śmiercią naturalną** to die of natural causes
**natury|sta** (**-sty, -ści**) (*dat sg* **-ście**) *m decl like f in sg* naturist
**naturyst|ka** (**-ki, -ki**) (*dat sg* **-ce**, *gen pl* **-ek**) *f* naturist
**natychmiast** *adv* immediately, instantly
**natychmiastowy** *adj* immediate, instant
**natyk|ać się (-am, -asz)** (*perf* **natknąć**) *vr*: **natykać się na** *+acc* to encounter, to come up against
**nauce** *n patrz* **nauka**
**naucz|ać (-am, -asz)** *vt*: **~ kogoś (czegoś)** to teach sb (sth); **~ (kogoś) czegoś** to teach sth (to sb)
**naucza|nie** (**-nia**) *nt* teaching
**naucz|ka** (**-ki, -ki**) (*dat sg* **-ce**, *gen pl* **-ek**) *f* lesson; **dać** (*perf*) **komuś nauczkę** to teach sb a lesson; **dostać** (*perf*) **nauczkę** to learn a lesson
**nauczyciel** (**-a, -e**) (*gen pl* **-i**) *m* teacher; **~ angielskiego/fizyki** English/physics teacher
**nauczyciel|ka** (**-ki, -ki**) (*dat sg* **-ce**, *gen pl* **-ek**) *f* teacher
**nauczycielski** *adj*: **pokój ~** staff *lub* teachers' room; **kolegium ~e** teacher training college
**naucz|yć (-ę, -ysz)** *vb perf od* **uczyć**

**nau|ka** (**-ki, -ki**) (*dat sg* **-ce**) *f* (*wiedza, teoria*) science; (*uczenie się*) study; (*przestroga*) lesson; **~ jazdy** (*kurs*) driving school; (*kierowca*) learner *lub* student driver; **nauki przyrodnicze** natural science; **nauki humanistyczne** the humanities
**nauko|wiec** (**-wca, -wcy**) *m* scholar; (*w dyscyplinach przyrodniczych i ścisłych*) scientist, scholar
**naukowo** *adv*: **pracować ~** to do research; **~ udowodniony** scientifically proven
**naukowy** *adj* (*ekspedycja*) scientific; (*dyskusja, referat*) scholarly; **badania naukowe** research; **pracownik ~** research worker; **stopień ~** (university) degree; **pomoce naukowe** teaching aids
**naumyślnie** *adv* deliberately
**naumyślny** *adj* deliberate
**na|wa** (**-wy, -wy**) (*loc sg* **-wie**) *f*: **~ główna** nave; **~ boczna** aisle; **~ poprzeczna** transept
**nawad|niać (-niam, -niasz)** (*perf* **nawodnić**) *vt* to irrigate
**nawadniani|e** (**-a**) *nt* irrigation
**nawal|ać (-am, -asz)** (*perf* **-ić**) (*pot*) *vi* (*o urządzeniu*) to pack up (*pot*); (*o osobie*) to blow it (*pot*)
**nawa|ł** (**-łu**) (*loc sg* **-le**) *m*: **~ pracy** mountains *lub* a mountain of work (*pot*)
**nawałnic|a** (**-y, -e**) *f* (*wichura*) storm; (*śnieżyca*) snowstorm
**nawarst|wiać się (-wiam, -wiasz)** (*perf* **-wić**) *vr* to accumulate
**nawarz|yć (-ę, -ysz)** *vt*: **~** (*perf*) **sobie piwa** to get into trouble
**nawet** *adv* even
**na|wiać (-wieję, -wiejesz)** *vb perf od* **nawiewać**
**nawia|s** (**-su, -sy**) (*loc sg* **-sie**) *m* parenthesis, bracket (*Brit*); **~ okrągły** parenthesis, round bracket (*Brit*); **~ kwadratowy** square bracket; **~ klamrowy** brace, curly bracket; **w ~ie** in parentheses; **~em mówiąc** incidentally, by the way; **poza ~em** on the margin(s) of society
**nawią|zać (-żę, -żesz)** *vb perf od* **nawiązywać**
**nawiązani|e** (**-a**) *nt*: **w nawiązaniu do** *+gen* with reference to
**nawiąz|ka** (**-ki, -ki**) (*dat sg* **-ce**, *gen pl* **-ek**) *f*: **z nawiązką** with interest
**nawiąz|ywać (-uję, -ujesz)** *vt* (*stosunki, kontakty*) to establish; (*rozmowy, korespondencję*) to enter into ▷ *vi*: **~ do czegoś** to refer to sth
**nawie|dzać (-dzam, -dzasz)** (*perf* **-dzić**) *vt* (*o kataklizmie*) to hit, to descend (up)on; (*o chorobie, ataku*) to strike; (*o nieszczęściu, wspomnieniach*) to haunt
**nawiedzony** *adj* (*pot*) cranky (*pot*)
**nawieję** *itd. vb patrz* **nawiać**
**nawierzch|nia** (**-ni, -nie**) (*gen pl* **-ni**) *f* (*Mot*) surface
**nawie|w** (**-wu, -wy**) (*loc sg* **-wie**) *m* (*Tech, Mot*) ventilation
**nawiew|ać (-am, -asz)** (*perf* **nawiać**) *vi* (*pot: uciekać*) to scram (*pot*), to scoot (*pot*) ▷ *vt* (*o wietrze: liście, śnieg*) to blow (in)
**nawi|eźć (-ozę, -eziesz)** (*imp* **-eź**, *pt* **-ozł, -ozła, -eźli**) *vb perf od* **nawozić**
**nawigacj|a** (**-i**) *f* navigation
**nawigato|r** (**-ra, -rzy**) (*loc sg* **-rze**) *m* navigator
**nawij|ać (-am, -asz)** *vt* (*perf* **nawinąć**) to wind
**nawilżacz** (**-a, -e**) (*gen pl* **-y**) *m* (*też:* **nawilżacz powietrza**) humidifier; (*w żelazku*) steamer
**nawilż|ać (-am, -asz)** (*perf* **-yć**) *vt* (*skórę*) to moisturize; (*powietrze*) to humidify
**nawi|nąć (-nę, -niesz)** (*imp* **-ń**) *vb perf od* **nawijać**; **nawinąć się** *vr* (*pot*) to crop up
**nawi|s** (**-su, -sy**) (*loc sg* **-sie**) *m* overhang
**nawl|ec (-okę, -eczesz)** (*pt* **-ókł, -ekła, -ekli**) *vb perf od* **nawlekać**
**nawlek|ać (-am, -asz)** (*perf* **nawlec**) *vt* (*igłę*) to thread; (*korale itp.*) to string
**nawod|nić (-nię, -nisz)** (*imp* **-nij**) *vb perf od* **nawadniać**
**nawoł|ywać (-uję, -ujesz)** *vt* (*krzyczeć*) to call; **~ kogoś do (zrobienia) czegoś** to exhort sb to do sth
**naw|ozić (-ożę, -ozisz)** (*imp* **-oź** *lub* **-óź**, *perf* **-ieźć**) *vt* (*Rol*) to fertilize
**naw|óz** (**-ozu, -ozy**) (*loc sg* **-ozie**) *m* fertilizer
**nawrac|ać (-am, -asz)** (*perf* **nawrócić**) *vt* (*samochód*) to turn back; (*Rel*) to convert; **nawracać się** *vr*: **~ się na** *+acc* to be converted to
**nawróce|nie** (**-nia, -nia**) (*gen pl* **-ń**) *nt* (*z innego wyznania*) conversion; (*grzesznika*) reformation
**nawró|cić (-cę, -cisz)** (*imp* **-ć**) *vb perf od* **nawracać**
**nawrócony** *adj* (*z innego wyznania*) converted; (*grzesznik*) reformed
**nawr|ót** (**-otu, -oty**) (*loc sg* **-ocie**) *m* recurrence; (*choroby*) relapse
**nawy|k** (**-ku, -ki**) (*instr sg* **-kiem**) *m* habit
**nawykły** *adj*: **~ do czegoś** accustomed to sth
**nawzajem** *adv* (*obopólnie*) each other, one another; **dziękuję, ~!** thank you! same to you!
**nazajutrz** *adv* (*książk*) (on) the next *lub* following day
**Nazare|t** (**-tu**) (*loc sg* **-cie**) *m* Nazareth
**nazbyt** *adv* too, excessively
**nazewnict|wo** (**-wa**) (*loc sg* **-wie**) *nt* terminology, nomenclature
**naziemny** *adj*: **kontrola/stacja naziemna** ground control/station
**nazi|sta** (**-sty, -ści**) (*loc sg* **-ście**) *m decl like f in sg* Nazi

**nazistowski** *adj* Nazi
**naziz|m** (**-mu**) (*loc sg* **-mie**) *m* Nazism
**naznacz|ać (-am, -asz)** (*perf* **-yć**) *vt* (*opatrywać znakiem*) to mark; (*wyznaczać*) to set
**naz|wa** (**-wy, -wy**) (*dat sg* **-wie**) *f* name; **nosić nazwę X** to be named X; **nadawać (nadać** *perf***) czemuś nazwę** to give sth a name
**naz|wać (-wę, -wiesz)** (*imp* **-wij**) *vb perf od* **nazywać**
**nazwis|ko** (**-ka, -ka**) (*instr sg* **-kiem**) *nt* surname (*Brit*), last name (*US*); **~ panieńskie** maiden name; **czek na czyjeś ~** a cheque in sb's name; **człowiek o nazwisku ...** a man by the name of ...; **znać kogoś (tylko) z nazwiska** to know sb by name
**nazyw|ać (-am, -asz)** (*perf* **nazwać**) *vt* to call; **~ rzecz(y) po imieniu** to call a spade a spade; **nazywać się** *vr* to be called; **jak się Pan/Pani nazywa?** what's your name, please?; **jak to się nazywa?** what is it called?, what do you call it?
**NBP** *abbr* (= *Narodowy Bank Polski*) the National Bank of Poland
**n.e.** *abbr* (= *naszej ery*) AD, CE
**Neapol** (**-u**) *m* Naples
**Neapolitan|ka** (**-ki, -ki**) (*dat sg* **-ce**, *gen pl* **-ek**) *f* Neapolitan
**Neapolitańczy|k** (**-ka, -cy**) (*instr sg* **-kiem**) *m* Neapolitan
**neapolitański** *adj* Neapolitan
**necie** *n patrz* **net**
**negacj|a** (**-i, -i**) (*gen pl* **-i**) *f* negation
**negaty|w** (**-wu, -wy**) (*loc sg* **-wie**) *m* negative
**negatywny** *adj* negative
**negliż** (**-u, -e**) (*gen pl* **-y**) *m*: **w ~u** in a state of undress
**negocjacj|e** (**-i**) *pl* negotiations *pl*
**negocjato|r** (**-ra, -rzy**) (*loc sg* **-rze**) *m* negotiator
**negocj|ować (-uję, -ujesz)** *vi* to negotiate ▷ *vt* (*perf* **wy-**) to negotiate
**neg|ować (-uję, -ujesz)** (*perf* **za-**) *vt* (*zaprzeczać*) to deny; (*nie uznawać*) to negate
**nekrolo|g** (**-gu, -gi**) (*instr sg* **-giem**) *m* obituary
**nekta|r** (**-ru, -ry**) (*loc sg* **-rze**) *m* nectar
**nektaryn|ka** (**-ki, -ki**) (*dat sg* **-ce**) *f* nectarine
**nenufa|r** (**-ru, -ry**) (*loc sg* **-rze**) *m* water lily
**neo...** *pref* neo...
**neofaszy|sta** (**-sty, -ści**) (*dat sg* **-ście**) *m decl like f in sg* Neo-Nazi
**neofi|ta** (**-ty, -ci**) (*dat sg* **-cie**) *m* neophyte
**neogotycki** *adj* Neo-Gothic
**neoklasyczny** *adj* neoclassical
**neologiz|m** (**-mu**) (*loc sg* **-mie**) *m* (*Jęz*) neologism
**neo|n** (**-nu, -ny**) (*loc sg* **-nie**) *m* (*Chem*) neon; (*reklama*) neon sign *lub* light
**neonów|ka** (**-ki, -ki**) (*dat sg* **-ce**, *gen pl* **-ek**) *f* neon light
**nepotyz|m** (**-mu**) (*loc sg* **-mie**) *m* nepotism
**ner|ka** (**-ki, -ki**) (*dat sg* **-ce**, *gen pl* **-ek**) *f* kidney
**nerkowy** *adj* renal; **kamica nerkowa** nephrolithiasis
**ner|w** (**-wu, -wy**) (*loc sg* **-wie**) *m* nerve; **działać komuś na ~y** to get on sb's nerves; **mieć mocne/słabe ~y** to have strong/weak nerves; **kłębek ~ów** a bundle of nerves; **wojna ~ów** a war of nerves
**nerwic|a** (**-y, -e**) *f* neurosis
**nerwoból** (**-u, -e**) (*gen pl* **-ów** *lub* **-i**) *m* neuralgia
**nerwowoś|ć** (**-ci**) *f* nervousness
**nerwowy** *adj* nervous; **komórka nerwowa** nerve cell
**nerwu|s** (**-sa, -sy**) (*loc sg* **-sie**) *m* (*pot*) edgy fellow (*pot*)
**ne|t** (**-tu, -ty**) (*loc sg* **-necie**) *m* net; (*Comput*) the Net
**netto** *inv* net; **waga/cena ~** net weight/price; **to waży 300g ~** it weighs 300g net
**neurochirur|g** (**-ga, -dzy** *lub* **-gowie**) *m* neurosurgeon, brain surgeon
**neurolo|g** (**-ga, -dzy** *lub* **-gowie**) *m* neurologist
**neurologi|a** (**-i**) *f* neurology
**neuro|n** (**-nu, -ny**) (*loc sg* **-nie**) *m* neuron
**neurotyczny** *adj* neurotic
**neuroty|k** (**-ka, -cy**) (*instr sg* **-kiem**) *m* neurotic
**neutraliz|ować (-uję, -ujesz)** (*perf* **z-**) *vt* to neutralize
**neutralnoś|ć** (**-ci**) *f* neutrality
**neutralny** *adj* neutral; (*Pol*) non-aligned
**neutro|n** (**-nu, -ny**) (*loc sg* **-nie**) *m* neutron
**newralgiczny** *adj*: **punkt/rejon ~** trouble spot/area
**nęcący** *adj* tempting, seductive
**nę|cić (-cę, -cisz)** (*imp* **-ć**, *perf* **z-**) *vt* to tempt, to seduce
**nędz|a** (**-y, -e**) *f* misery; **obraz nędzy i rozpaczy** (*pot*) a pitiful *lub* sorry sight
**nędzarz** (**-a, -e**) (*gen pl* **-y**) *m* pauper
**nędzny** *adj* miserable, wretched
**nęk|ać (-am, -asz)** *vt* to plague, to haunt
**NFI** *abbr* (= *Narodowy Fundusz Inwestycyjny*) National Investment Fund
**ni** *conj*: **ni ... ni ...** neither ... nor ...; **ni stąd, ni zowąd** out of the blue; **ni mniej, ni więcej, tylko prezydent** the President, no less
**Niagara** *f inv*; **Wodospad ~** the Niagara Falls *pl*
**nia|nia** (**-ni, -nie**) (*gen pl* **-ń**) *f* nanny
**niańcz|yć (-ę, -ysz)** *vt* to nurse
**nią** *pron instr od* **ona** her; (*w odniesieniu do przedmiotu, zwierzęcia*) it
**niby** *part* (*rzekomo*) supposedly, allegedly; (*jak*) like; **~ przypadkiem** as if *lub* though by

accident; **robić coś na ~** to make believe one is doing sth
**nic** (*jak*: **co**) *pron* nothing; (*: z innym wyrazem przeczącym*) anything; **nic dziwnego** no wonder; **nic z tego** it's no use!; **to nic** (*nie szkodzi*) never mind; **to nic nie pomoże** it isn't going to help at all; **wszystko na nic** it's all for nothing; **za nic w świecie** not for anything; **nic mi nie jest** I'm OK; **nic jej nie będzie** she's going to be fine; **tyle co nic** next to nothing; **nic a nic** not a thing
**nici** *itd. n patrz* **nić**
**nicie** *n patrz* **nit**
**nicoś|ć** (**-ci**) *f* nothingness
**nicpo|ń** (**-nia, -nie**) (*gen pl* **-ni** *lub* **-niów**) *m* good-for-nothing
**niczego** *itd. pron patrz* **nic**; **niczego sobie** not bad
**niczyj** *adj* nobody's, no-one's; **ziemia ~a** no-man's-land
**ni|ć** (**-ci, -ci**) (*instr pl* **-ćmi**) *f* thread; **grubymi nićmi szyty** (*przen*) thinly disguised
**nie** *part* no; (*z czasownikiem*) not; **nie ma go tutaj** he's not here; **co to, to nie!** that is out of the question!; **nie ma co narzekać** it's no good complaining; **nie martw się!** don't worry!; **(to) anioł nie kobieta** (she's) an angel of a woman
**nie...** *pref* (*z przymiotnikami*) un..., in...; (*z rzeczownikami*) non-
**nieadekwatny** *adj* inappropriate
**nieagresj|a** (**-i**) *f*: **pakt o nieagresji** non-aggression pact
**nieaktualny** *adj* (*bilet*) invalid; (*oferta*) unavailable; (*informacja*) out-of-date
**nieapetyczny** *adj* unappetizing
**nieartykułowany** *adj* inarticulate
**nieautentyczny** *adj* inauthentic
**niebagatelny** *adj* considerable, substantial
**niebanalny** *adj* original
**niebawem** *adv* (*książk*) soon, by and by (*książk*)
**niebezpieczeńst|wo** (**-wa, -wa**) (*loc sg* **-wie**) *nt* (*zagrożenie*) danger, peril; (*narażenie*) risk, hazard; (*sytuacja awaryjna*) emergency
**niebezpieczny** *adj* (*sytuacja, bandyta*) dangerous; (*posunięcie*) risky; (*ładunek, substancja*) hazardous; **~ dla otoczenia** posing a threat to society
**niebiański** *adj* (*książk*) heavenly
**niebieski** *adj* (*kolor*) blue; (*ciało*) heavenly, celestial; (*królestwo*) heavenly; **benzyna niebieska** (*pot*) two-star petrol (*Brit*)
**niebi|osa** (**-os**) (*loc* **-osach**) *pl* heaven; **wychwalać kogoś pod ~** to praise sb to the skies
**nie|bo** (**-ba, -ba**) (*loc sg* **-bie**, *gen pl* **-bios**, *dat pl* **-biosom**, *instr pl* **-biosami**, *loc pl* **-biosach**) *nt* sky; (*Rel*) heaven; **na niebie** in the sky; **w niebie** in heaven; **spać pod gołym niebem** to sleep rough; **~ w gębie!** (*pot*) delicious!; **wielkie nieba!** good heavens!; **poruszyć ~ i ziemię** to move heaven and earth; **wołać o pomstę do nieba** to cry to heaven; **być w siódmym niebie** (*przen*) to be in seventh heaven; **o (całe) ~ lepszy** far better
**nieboracz|ka** (**-ki, -ki**) (*dat sg* **-ce**, *gen pl* **-ek**) *f* poor thing
**niebora|k** (**-ka, -cy** *lub* **-ki**) (*instr sg* **-kiem**) *m* poor thing
**nieboszcz|ka** (**-ki, -ki**) (*dat sg* **-ce**, *gen pl* **-ek**) *f* the deceased
**nieboszczy|k** (**-ka, -cy** *lub* **-ki**) (*instr sg* **-kiem**) *m* the deceased
**niebrzydki** *adj* rather pretty
**nieby|t** (**-tu**) (*loc sg* **-cie**) *m* non-existence
**niebywale** *adv* unusually
**niebywały** *adj* (most) unusual
**niecały** *adj*: **~ rok/tydzień** less than a year/week
**niecelny** *adj*: **~ strzał** miss
**niecelowy** *adj* inadvisable
**niecenzuralny** *adj* obscene
**niech** *part*: **~ wejdą** let them come in; **~ pomyślę** let me think *lub* see; **~ i tak będzie** so be it; **~ tylko spróbuje!** just let him try it!; **~ cię Bóg broni, jeśli ...** God help you if ...; **~ żyje ...!** three cheers for ...!; **~ żyje królowa** long live the Queen; **~ spojrzę** let me see (that); **a ~ to!** what a nuisance!
**niechcący** *adv* unintentionally, by accident
**niechcenia** *inv*: **od ~** casually, negligently
**niechciany** *adj* unwanted
**niechę|ć** (**-ci, -ci**) *f* dislike; **żywić ~ do kogoś** to dislike sb; **czuć ~ do pracy** to have an aversion to work; **z niechęcią** reluctantly
**niechętnie** *adv* reluctantly
**niechętny** *adj* reluctant
**niechlubny** *adj* (*książk*) shameful
**niechluj** (**-a, -e**) *m* (*pot*) slob
**niechlujny** *adj* sloppy
**niechlujst|wo** (**-wa**) (*loc sg* **-wie**) *nt* sloppiness
**niechodliwy** *adj* (*pot*: *towar*) unsaleable (*Brit*), unsalable (*US*)
**niechybny** *adj* certain
**niechże** *part* = **niech**
**nieciekawy** *adj* uninteresting
**niecierpli|wić (-wię, -wisz)** (*perf* **z-**) *vt* to make impatient; **niecierpliwić się** *vr* to grow impatient
**niecierpliwoś|ć** (**-ci**) *f* impatience; **z niecierpliwością** impatiently
**niecierpliwy** *adj* impatient
**niecny** *adj* (*książk*) ignoble
**nieco** *adv* somewhat; **~ większy** somewhat larger; **co ~** a little

n

**niecodzienny** *adj* unusual
**nieczęsty** *adj* infrequent
**nieczułoś|ć** (**-ci**) *f* insensitivity, insensibility
**nieczuły** *adj* (*obojętny*) insensitive, callous; (*odporny*) impervious; **~ na coś** insensitive to sth
**nieczynny** *adj* inactive, inoperative; (*sklep*) closed; (*urządzenie*) out of order *pred*; (*wulkan*) dormant; (*: wygasły*) extinct; (*Chem*) inert
**nieczysto** *adv* (*grać, śpiewać*) out of tune
**nieczystości** (**-**) *pl* (*śmieci*) rubbish (*Brit*), garbage (*US*); (*odpady*) waste
**nieczysty** *adj* (*skóra*) dirty, soiled; (*głos*) out of tune *pred*; (*myśli*) impure, unclean; (*zamiary*) dishonest; (*sumienie*) guilty
**nieczytelnoś|ć** (**-ci**) *f* illegibility
**nieczytelny** *adj* (*pismo*) illegible, unreadable; (*informacja*) unclear
**niedaleki** *adj* (*w przestrzeni*) nearby; (*w czasie*) near, prospective; **w ~ej przyszłości** in the near *lub* foreseeable future
**niedaleko** *adv* (*w małej odległości*) near (by); (*blisko w czasie*) soon; **już ~ do świąt** Christmas is quite near now
**niedawno** *adv* recently, not long ago
**niedawny** *adj* recent; **do niedawna** until recently; **od niedawna** since recently
**niedbalst|wo** (**-wa**) (*loc sg* **-wie**) *nt* negligence, neglect
**niedbały** *adj* (*pracownik*) negligent, inattentive; (*strój*) untidy; (*gest*) offhand
**niedelikatnoś|ć** (**-ci, -ci**) (*gen pl* **-ci**) *f* tactlessness
**niedelikatny** *adj* (*człowiek*) tactless; (*pytanie, uwaga*) indelicate, tactless
**niedługi** *adj* short; **w ~m czasie** in a short time, shortly
**niedługo** *adv* (*wkrótce*) soon, before long; (*krótko*) a little while
**niedobit|ki** (**-ków**) *pl* survivors *pl*
**niedob|ór** (**-oru, -ory**) (*loc sg* **-orze**) *m* (*witamin*) deficiency; (*pieniędzy, siły roboczej*) shortage; (*żywności*) scarcity, shortage; (*w budżecie*) deficit
**niedobrany** *adj* (*małżeństwo*) mismatched, ill-suited; (*meble*) mismatched, ill-matched
**niedobry** *adj* not good, bad; (*człowiek*) evil, wicked; (*wiadomość*) bad; (*jedzenie*) disgusting, yucky (*pot*); (*buty, okulary*) bad, ill-fitting; (*materiał, surowiec*) improper, substandard; (*przykład*) wrong
**niedobrze** *adv* (*niezdrowo*) sickly, unwell; (*niepomyślnie*) badly; (*niewłaściwie*) wrongly; (*nieprzyjaźnie*) unkindly; **~ mi** I feel sick; **robi mi się ~** I'm beginning to feel sick; **czuć się ~** to feel unwell; **~ z nim** he's (really) in trouble; **~ to wygląda** it looks pretty bad; **mieć ~ w głowie** to have a screw loose; **~ mu patrzy z oczu** he doesn't look like a good person
**niedoceniany** *adj* underestimated
**niedochodowy** *adj* (*interes*) unprofitable; (*organizacja*) non-profit
**niedociągnię|cie** (**-cia, -cia**) (*gen pl* **-ć**) *nt* shortcoming
**niedoczekanie** *nt inv*: **~ twoje!** that'll be the day!
**niedogodnoś|ć** (**-ci, -ci**) *f* inconvenience
**niedogodny** *adj* inconvenient
**niedogotowany** *adj* underdone, half-cooked
**niedojrzałoś|ć** (**-ci**) *f* immaturity
**niedojrzały** *adj* (*człowiek*) immature; (*zboże, owoc*) unripe, green; (*wino*) immature, green; (*ser*) immature, unripe
**niedokładnoś|ć** (**-ci, -ci**) (*gen pl* **-ci**) *f* inaccuracy
**niedokładny** *adj* (*człowiek*) careless, negligent; (*praca*) sloppy; (*nie sprecyzowany*) inaccurate
**niedokonany** *adj* (*Jęz*) imperfective
**niedokończony** *adj* unfinished, incomplete
**niedokrwistoś|ć** (**-ci**) *f* (*Med*) anaemia (*Brit*), anemia (*US*)
**niedol|a** (**-i, -e**) (*gen pl* **-i**) *f* misery
**niedołę|ga** (**-gi, -gi**) (*dat sg* **-dze**) *m/f decl like f in sg* (*pot*) twerp (*Brit*) (*pot*), goof (*US*) (*pot*)
**niedołęst|wo** (**-wa**) (*loc sg* **-wie**) *nt* (*brak sprawności*) infirmity; (*nieudolność*) incompetence
**niedołężny** *adj* (*niesprawny*) infirm; (*nieudolny*) incompetent; (*niezdarny*) awkward
**niedomag|ać (-am, -asz)** *vi* (*o człowieku*) to be ailing; (*o narządzie, urządzeniu*) to malfunction
**niedomagający** *adj* ailing
**niedomówie|nie** (**-nia, -nia**) (*gen pl* **-ń**) *nt* (*nieporozumienie*) misunderstanding; (*aluzja*) hint, undertone; **bez niedomówień** in plain terms
**niedomyślny** *adj* slow on the uptake
**niedopał|ek** (**-ka, -ki**) (*instr sg* **-kiem**) *m* (cigarette) butt, (cigarette) stub
**niedopatrze|nie** (**-nia, -nia**) (*gen pl* **-ń**) *nt* oversight
**niedopieczony** *adj* (*mięso, kotlet*) underdone, rare
**niedopowiedze|nie** (**-nia, -nia**) (*gen pl* **-ń**) *nt* allusion, understatement
**niedopracowany** *adj* half-baked (*przen*)
**niedopuszczalny** *adj* unacceptable, inadmissible
**niedoraj|da** (**-dy, -dy**) (*dat sg* **-dzie**) *m/f decl like f in sg* (*pot*) goof (*pot*), wimp (*pot*)
**niedorozwinięty** *adj* (*człowiek*) retarded, mentally handicapped *lub* deficient

**niedorozw|ój** (**-oju**) *m* (*umysłowy*) mental deficiency; (*Med: narządu*) underdevelopment
**niedorzecznoś|ć** (**-ci, -ci**) (*gen pl* **-ci**) *f* nonsense
**niedorzeczny** *adj* preposterous, absurd
**niedoskonałoś|ć** (**-ci, -ci**) (*gen pl* **-ci**) *f* imperfection, flaw
**niedoskonały** *adj* imperfect
**niedosłyszalny** *adj* inaudible
**niedosłysz|eć** (**-ę, -ysz**) *vi* to be hard of hearing
**niedostateczny** *adj* insufficient, inadequate ▷ *m decl like adj* (*Szkol: ocena*) unsatisfactory *lub* failing mark (*Brit*) *lub* grade (*US*)
**niedostat|ek** (**-ku, -ki**) (*instr sg* **-kiem**) *m* scarcity, shortage
**niedostępny** *adj* (*miejsce*) inaccessible; (*człowiek*) aloof, unapproachable
**niedostrzegalny** *adj* imperceptible, unnoticeable
**niedosy|t** (**-tu**) (*loc sg* **-cie**) *m* want, insufficiency; **mieć/odczuwać ~ czegoś** to be wanting in sth, to be in need of sth
**niedoszły** *adj* (*artysta, samobójca*) would-be
**niedościgły, niedościgniony** *adj* (*wzór, ideał*) unequalled, unattainable; (*mistrz*) unequalled
**niedoświadczony** *adj* inexperienced
**niedoświetlony** *adj* (*Fot*) underexposed
**niedotlenie|nie** (**-nia**) *adj* (*Med*) oxygen deficiency, anoxia
**niedowa|ga** (**-gi**) (*dat sg* **-dze**) *f* underweight
**niedowiar|ek** (**-ka, -ki**) (*instr sg* **-kiem**) *m* (*pot*) doubting Thomas (*pot*)
**niedowi|dzieć** (**-dzę, -dzisz**) (*imp* **-dź**) *vi*: **on niedowidzi** his sight is failing
**niedowierza|nie** (**-nia**) *nt*: **z ~m** in disbelief
**niedowła|d** (**-du**) (*loc sg* **-dzie**) *m* (*Med*) paresis; **~ organizacyjny** (*przen*) bureaucratic inertia
**niedozwolony** *adj* (*lektura, powieść*) banned; (*parkowanie*) prohibited
**niedożywie|nie** (**-nia**) *nt* malnutrition
**niedożywiony** *adj* undernourished
**niedrogi** *adj* inexpensive
**niedrożnoś|ć** (**-ci**) *f* (*Med*) obstruction
**niedrożny** *adj* obstructed
**niedużo** *adv* (*mleka, pieniędzy*) not much, little; (*książek, drzew*) not many, few
**nieduży** *adj* small
**niedwuznaczny** *adj* unambiguous
**niedyskrecj|a** (**-i, -e**) (*gen pl* **-i**) *f* indiscretion
**niedyskretny** *adj* indiscreet
**niedysponowany** *adj* indisposed
**niedyspozycj|a** (**-i, -e**) (*gen pl* **-i**) *f* indisposition
**niedziel|a** (**-i, -e**) *f* Sunday; **N~ Palmowa/Wielkanocna** Palm/Easter Sunday
**niedzielny** *adj* Sunday *attr*; **~ kierowca** Sunday driver; **szkółka niedzielna** Sunday school
**niedzisiejszy** *adj* (*przestarzały*) old-fashioned
**niedźwiad|ek** (**-ka, -ki**) (*instr sg* **-kiem**) *m* bear cub
**niedźwiedzi** *adj*: **~a przysługa** disservice
**niedźwiedzic|a** (**-y, -e**) *f* she-bear; **Wielka/Mała N~** (*Astron*) the Great/Little Bear
**niedźwie|dź** (**-dzia, -dzie**) (*gen pl* **-dzi**) *m* bear; **~ brunatny/polarny** brown/polar bear
**nieefektowny** *adj* unattractive
**nieefektywny** *adj* ineffective
**nieekonomiczny** *adj* uneconomical
**nieelegancki** *adj* (*niegustowny*) inelegant; (*nieuprzejmy*) impolite
**nieestetyczny** *adj* unsightly
**nieetatowy** *adj* (*praca, pracownik*) supernumerary
**nieetyczny** *adj* unethical
**niefachowy** *adj* incompetent, amateurish
**nieforemny** *adj* irregular
**nieformalny** *adj* (*nieoficjalny*) informal; (*niezgodny z przepisami*) illegal
**niefortunny** *adj* unfortunate
**niefrasobliwoś|ć** (**-ci**) *f* light-heartedness
**niefrasobliwy** *adj* light-hearted
**niefunkcjonalny** *adj* impractical
**niegazowany** *adj* (*napój*) still, noncarbonated
**niegdyś** *adv* (*książk*) formerly
**niegłupi** *adj* (quite) clever
**niegodny** *adj* (*czyn, postępowanie*) mean; **~ czegoś/kogoś** undeserving of sth/sb; **zachowanie niegodne dżentelmena** ungentlemanly conduct
**niegodzi|wiec** (**-wca, -wcy**) *m* villain
**niegodziwoś|ć** (**-ci, -ci**) (*gen pl* **-ci**) *f* wickedness
**niegodziwy** *adj* wicked, mean
**niegospodarny** *adj* uneconomical, wasteful
**niegościnnoś|ć** (**-ci**) *f* inhospitality
**niegościnny** *adj* inhospitable
**niegotowy** *adj* (*nie ukończony*) unfinished; (*nie przygotowany*) not ready
**niegramatyczny** *adj* ungrammatical
**niegroźny** *adj* (*dolegliwość*) mild
**niegrzeczny** *adj* (*nieuprzejmy*) impolite; (*dziecko*) bad, naughty
**niegustowny** *adj* tasteless
**niehigieniczny** *adj* unhygienic, insanitary
**niehonorowy** *adj* unsportsmanlike
**niehumanitarny** *adj* inhumane
**nieistotny** *adj* (*nieważny*) unimportant; (*nie powiązany*) irrelevant
**niej** *pron gen, dat, loc od* **ona**; (*w odniesieniu do osoby*) her; (*w odniesieniu do rzeczy, zwierzęcia*) it
**niejadalny** *adj* (*niesmaczny*) uneatable; (*niezdatny do jedzenia*) inedible

**niejaki** *adj* (*pewien*) some, a; **~ pan Smith** a Mr Smith
**niejasnoś|ć** (**-ci, -ci**) (*gen pl* **-ci**) *f* ambiguity, vagueness
**niejasny** *adj* (*sformułowanie*) unclear, vague; (*przeczucie*) indefinite
**niejeden** (*jak:* **jeden**) *pron* more than one; **~ raz** many a time; **niejedno mógłbym opowiedzieć** I could tell you a thing or two
**niejednokrotnie** *adv* more than once, many a time
**niejednolity** *adj* diversified
**niejednorodny** *adj* heterogenous
**niejednoznaczny** *adj* ambiguous
**niekiedy** *adv* sometimes
**niekłamany** *adj* genuine
**niekoleżeński** *adj* unsociable, unfriendly
**niekompatybilny** *adj* (*Komput*) incompatible
**niekompetencj|a** (**-i, -e**) (*gen pl* **-i**) *f* incompetence
**niekompetentny** *adj* (*nieumiejętny*) incompetent; (*nie uprawniony*) unauthorized
**niekompletny** *adj* incomplete
**niekomunikatywny** *adj* uncommunicative
**niekoniecznie** *adv* not necessarily
**niekonsekwencj|a** (**-i, -e**) (*gen pl* **-i**) *f* inconsistency
**niekonsekwentny** *adj* inconsistent
**niekonwencjonalny** *adj* unorthodox, unconventional; **medycyna niekonwencjonalna** alternative medicine
**niekorzystnie** *adv* (*wpływać*) unfavourably (*Brit*), unfavorably (*US*), adversely
**niekorzystny** *adj* unfavourable (*Brit*), unfavorable (*US*), disadvantageous
**niekorzyś|ć** (**-ci**) *f*: **na czyjąś ~** to sb's disadvantage
**niekrępujący** *adj* (*pokój*) private
**niektórzy** (*f, nt* **niektóre**) *pron* some; **~ mówią, że ...** some (people) say that ...
**niekulturalny** *adj* uncivil, rude
**niekurczliwy** *adj* (*materiał, tkanina*) non-shrink
**nielegalnie** *adv* illegally
**nielegalnoś|ć** (**-ci**) *f* illegality
**nielegalny** *adj* illegal
**nieletni** *adj* juvenile ▷ *m decl like adj* minor, juvenile; **sąd dla ~ch** juvenile court; **przestępczość ~ch** juvenile delinquency *lub* crime
**nieliczny** *adj* sparse, few
**nielogicznoś|ć** (**-ci, -ci**) (*gen pl* **-ci**) *f* illogicality
**nielogiczny** *adj* illogical
**nielojalnoś|ć** (**-ci**) *f* disloyalty
**nielojalny** *adj* disloyal
**nieludzki** *adj* (*okrutny*) inhuman(e); (*nadludzki*) superhuman
**nieludzko** *adv* (*traktować*) cruelly, inhumanly; **~ zmęczony** dead tired
**nieła|d** (**-du**) (*loc sg* **-dzie**) *m* disarray
**nieładnie** *adv* (*postępować*) unfairly; **~ się porusza** her/his movements are clumsy; **~ pisze** her/his handwriting is ugly
**nieładny** *adj* (*brzydki*) ugly; (*nieuczciwy*) unfair
**niełas|ka** (**-ki**) (*dat sg* **-ce**) *f* disgrace, disfavour (*Brit*), disfavor (*US*); **popaść** (*perf*) **w niełaskę** to fall into disgrace; **zdać się** (*perf*) **na czyjąś łaskę i niełaskę** to throw o.s. upon sb's mercy
**niełatwy** *adj* not easy, difficult; **~ w pożyciu** not easy to get along with
**niemal** *adv* almost, (very) nearly; **jestem ~ pewien** I am almost certain; **~ się nie spóźnił** he was very nearly late
**niemało** *adv*: **~ czegoś** quite a lot of sth
**niemały** *adj* substantial
**niemądry** *adj* unwise, silly
**Nie|mcy** (**-miec**) (*loc* **-mczech**) *pl* Germany; **Republika Federalna Niemiec** the Federal Republic of Germany
**niemiarodajny** *adj* unreliable
**Nie|miec** (**-mca, -mcy**) (*voc sg* **-mcze**) *m* German; *patrz też* **Niemcy**
**niemiecki** *adj* German; **Niemiecka Republika Demokratyczna** the German Democratic Republic; **owczarek ~** Alsatian (*Brit*), German shepherd (*US*)
**niemile, niemiło** *adv* (*zaskoczony*) unpleasantly; **~ widziany** unwelcome
**niemiłosierny** *adj* (*bezlitosny*) merciless; (*przen: okropny*) terrible, awful
**niemiły** *adj* (*wygląd, zapach*) unpleasant; (*człowiek*) unkind
**Niem|ka** (**-ki, -ki**) (*dat sg* **-ce**, *gen pl* **-ek**) *f* German
**niemłody** *adj* oldish
**niemnący** *adj* (*materiał*) crease-resistant
**niemniej** *adv* still, however; **tym ~** even so; **~ jednak** nevertheless
**niemoc** (**-y**) *f* incapacity; **~ płciowa** impotence
**niemodnie** *adv* (*ubierać się*) unfashionably
**niemodny** *adj* unfashionable, out-of-date
**niemoralny** *adj* immoral
**niemo|ta** (**-ty**) (*dat sg* **-cie**) *f* muteness
**niem|owa** (**-owy, -owy**) (*dat sg* **-owie**, *gen pl* **-ów**) *m/f decl like f in sg* mute
**niemowl|ę** (**-ęcia, -ęta**) (*gen pl* **-ąt**) *nt* baby
**niemowlęct|wo** (**-wa**) (*loc sg* **-wie**) *nt* babyhood
**niemowlęcy** *adj* baby *attr*
**niemożliwoś|ć** (**-ci**) *f* impossibility
**niemożliwy** *adj* impossible; **~ do zrobienia** unfeasible
**niemożnoś|ć** (**-ci**) *f* impossibility
**niemrawy** *adj* (*dyskusja, ruchy*) sluggish

**niemuzykalny** *adj* unmusical
**niemy** *adj* (*człowiek*) mute, dumb; (*film, aprobata*) silent
**nienadzwyczajny** *adj* ordinary, average
**nienagannie** *adv* (*zachowywać się*) faultlessly; **~ ubrany** impeccably dressed
**nienaganny** *adj* (*strój, zachowanie*) impeccable
**nienarodzony** *adj* unborn
**nienaruszalnoś|ć** (**-ci**) *f* sanctity
**nienaruszalny** *adj* (*Pol*) unalterable, inalienable
**nienaruszony** *adj* (*opakowanie, pieczęć*) intact
**nienasycony** *adj* insatiable; (*Chem*) unsaturated
**nienaturalnoś|ć** (**-ci**) *f* unnaturalness, artificiality
**nienaturalny** *adj* unnatural, artificial
**nienaumyślnie** *adv* (*zrobić coś*) unintentionally
**nienawi|dzić (-dzę, -dzisz)** (*imp* **-dź**) *vt* to hate, to detest
**nienawistny** *adj* (*pełen nienawiści*) hateful; (*znienawidzony*) odious
**nienawiś|ć** (**-ci**) *f* hatred, hate; **żywić ~** to feel hatred
**nienormalnoś|ć** (**-ci**) *f* abnormality
**nienormalny** *adj* (*niezgodny z normą*) abnormal; (*niezgodny z oczekiwanym rezultatem*) anomalous; (*chory psychicznie*) mad, insane
**nienowy** *adj* old
**nieobcy** *adj* (*znajomy*) familiar; **nieobce mu były ...** he was no stranger to ...
**nieobecnoś|ć** (**-ci**) *f* absence; **pod czyjąś ~** in sb's absence
**nieobecny** *adj* absent; **~ duchem** (*przen*) absent in soul
**nieobliczalny** *adj* unpredictable
**nieobyczajny** *adj* indecent
**nieobyty** *adj* unsophisticated, uncultured
**nieoceniony** *adj* invaluable
**nieoczekiwanie** *adv* unexpectedly, surprisingly
**nieoczekiwany** *adj* unexpected, surprising
**nieodgadniony** *adj* mysterious
**nieodłączny** *adj* inseparable, inherent
**nieodmienny** *adj* (*stały*) invariable; (*Jęz*) uninflected
**nieodparty** *adj* (*argument, dowód*) compelling, irrefutable; (*ochota, urok*) irresistible
**nieodpłatnie** *adv* free of charge, at no cost *lub* charge
**nieodpłatny** *adj* free
**nieodpowiedni** *adj* inappropriate, unsuitable
**nieodpowiedzialnoś|ć** (**-ci**) *f* irresponsibility
**nieodpowiedzialny** *adj* irresponsible
**nieodwołalnie** *adv* irrevocably, beyond recall
**nieodwołalny** *adj* irrevocable, unalterable
**nieodwracalny** *adj* (*decyzja*) irreversible; (*szkoda*) irreparable
**nieodzowny** *adj* indispensable, essential
**nieodżałowany** *adj* (*strata*) much regretted; (*o zmarłym*) late lamented
**nieoficjalnie** *adv* unofficially
**nieoficjalny** *adj* unofficial
**nieograniczony** *adj* (*możliwości, zaufanie*) unlimited, endless; (*swoboda, władza*) unrestricted
**nieokreślony** *adj* (*lęk, przeczucie*) vague; (*kolor, wiek*) indeterminate; **przedimek ~** (*Jęz*) indefinite article; **na czas ~** indefinitely
**nieokrzesany** *adj* coarse, crude
**nieomal** *adv* = **niemal**
**nieomylnoś|ć** (**-ci**) *f* infallibility
**nieomylny** *adj* infallible
**nieopanowany** *adj* (*człowiek*) quick-tempered, hot-blooded; (*gniew, śmiech*) unrestrained, uncontrollable
**nieopatrznie** *adv* recklessly, carelessly
**nieopatrzny** *adj* reckless, careless
**nieopisany** *adj* (*lęk*) untold, indescribable; (*bałagan*) indescribable
**nieopłacalny** *adj* unprofitable
**nieorganiczny** *adj* (*Chem*) inorganic
**nieosiągalny** *adj* unattainable
**nieostrożnoś|ć** (**-ci**) *f* carelessness
**nieostrożny** *adj* careless
**nieostry** *adj* (*nóż*) blunt; (*zdjęcie*) out of focus; (*obraz*) blurred
**niepalący** *adj* non-smoking ▷ *m decl like adj* non-smoker; **przedział dla ~ch** a non-smoking compartment
**niepalny** *adj* (*Tech*) non-flammable
**niepamię|ć** (**-ci**) *f*: **popaść** (*perf*) **w ~** to sink into oblivion; **puścić** (*perf*) **coś w ~** to forgive and forget sth
**niepamiętny** *adj*: **od ~ch czasów** from time immemorial
**nieparzysty** *adj* odd
**niepełnoletni** *adj* under age, under-age *attr*
**niepełnoletnoś|ć** (**-ci**) *f* (*Prawo*) minority
**niepełnosprawny** *adj* handicapped
**niepełnowartościowy** *adj* (*towar, materiał*) defective; (*pracownik*) incompetent
**niepełny** *adj* (*nie napełniony*) not (quite) full; (*niekompletny*) incomplete
**niepewnie** *adv* uncertainly
**niepewnoś|ć** (**-ci**) *f* uncertainty; **trzymać kogoś w niepewności** to keep sb in suspense; **żyć w niepewności** to live a life of uncertainty
**niepewny** *adj* (*człowiek*) hesitant; (*krok*) unsteady; (*pochodzenie, sytuacja*) uncertain; (*partner, sojusznik*) doubtful; **być ~m czegoś** to be unsure *lub* uncertain of sth

n

**niepijący** *m decl like adj* teetotaller (*Brit*), teetotaler (*US*) ▷ *adj* teetotal
**niepisany** *adj* (*prawo, umowa*) unwritten
**niepiśmienny** *adj* illiterate
**nieplanowy** *adj* unplanned
**niepłodnoś|ć** (**-ci**) *f* infertility, sterility
**niepłodny** *adj* infertile, sterile
**niepochlebny** *adj* unfavourable (*Brit*), unfavorable (*US*), critical
**niepocieszony** *adj* disconsolate
**niepoczytalnoś|ć** (**-ci**) *f* insanity
**niepoczytalny** *adj* insane
**niepodatny** *adj*: **~ na coś** impervious to sth
**niepodległoś|ć** (**-ci**) *f* independence
**niepodległy** *adj* independent
**niepodobieńst|wo** (**-wa, -wa**) (*loc sg* **-wie**) *nt* impossibility; **ucieczka była niepodobieństwem** escape was impossible
**niepodobna** *inv*: **~ wytrzymać w taki upał** such heat is impossible to stand
**niepodobny** *adj* unlike, dissimilar; **być ~m do kogoś** to be unlike sb; **to do niego niepodobne** it's very unlike him; **są do siebie zupełnie niepodobni** they have nothing in common
**niepodważalny** *adj* irrefutable, unquestionable
**niepodzielnie** *adv* (*panować, rządzić*) absolutely
**niepodzielny** *adj* (*liczba, całość*) indivisible; (*przen: władza*) absolute; **~ przez dwa/dziesięć** (*Mat*) indivisible by two/ten
**niepogo|da** (**-dy**) (*dat sg* **-dzie**) *f* bad weather
**niepohamowany** *adj* uncontrollable
**niepojęty** *adj* inconceivable
**niepokalany** *adj*: **niepokalane poczęcie** Immaculate Conception
**niepokaźny** *adj* insignificant
**niepok|oić (-oję, -oisz)** (*imp* **-ój**, *perf* **za-**) *vt* (*wzbudzać niepokój*) to worry; (*nie dawać spokoju*) to bother; **niepokoić się** *vr* to worry; **~ się o** *+acc* to worry about
**niepokojący** *adj* disturbing
**niepokonany** *adj* invincible
**niepok|ój** (**-oju**) *m* anxiety; **nie ma powodów do niepokoju** there's no reason for concern; **niepokoje** *pl* (*gen pl* **-ojów**) (*zamieszki*) unrest *sg*
**niepoliczalny** *adj* (*rzeczownik*) uncountable
**niepomyślny** *adj* (*wiadomość*) bad; (*wiatr*) adverse; (*próba*) unsuccessful
**niepoprawny** *adj* (*odpowiedź*) incorrect, wrong; (*człowiek*) incorrigible
**niepopularnoś|ć** (**-ci**) *f* unpopularity
**niepopularny** *adj* unpopular
**nieporadny** *adj* incapable, incompetent
**nieporęczny** *adj* unwieldy
**nieporozumie|nie** (**-nia, -nia**) (*gen pl* **-ń**) *nt* (*pomyłka*) misunderstanding; (*konflikt*) disagreement
**nieporząd|ek** (**-ku, -ki**) (*instr sg* **-kiem**) *m* mess
**nieporządny** *adj* (*człowiek*) untidy
**nieposkromiony** *adj* (*apetyt, temperament*) uncontrollable; (*ciekawość, ambicja*) unrestrained
**nieposłuszeńst|wo** (**-wa**) (*loc sg* **-wie**) *nt* disobedience
**nieposłuszny** *adj* disobedient
**niepostrzeżenie** *adv* imperceptibly; **wymknął się ~** he left unnoticed
**nieposzlakowany** *adj* (*charakter, opinia*) spotless
**niepotrzebnie** *adv* unnecessarily
**niepotrzebny** *adj* (*niekonieczny*) unnecessary; (*nie chciany*) unwanted
**niepoważny** *adj* (*człowiek*) silly; (*podejście*) unserious, frivolous
**niepowetowany** *adj* irreparable
**niepowodze|nie** (**-nia, -nia**) (*gen pl* **-ń**) *nt* failure; **skazany na ~** destined to fail; **doznać** (*perf*) **niepowodzenia** to fail; **niepowodzenia** *pl* misfortunes *pl*
**niepowołany** *adj*: **dostać się w niepowołane ręce** to fall into the wrong hands
**niepowszedni** *adj* unusual
**niepowtarzalny** *adj* unique
**niepoznaki** *inv* (*pot*): **dla ~** to distract (sb's) attention; **zmieniony do ~** changed beyond *lub* past (all) recognition
**niepozorny** *adj* inconspicuous
**niepożądany** *adj* undesirable, unwelcome
**niepraktyczny** *adj* impractical, unpractical
**niepraw|da** (**-dy**) (*dat sg* **-dzie**) *f* untruth; **to ~!** that's a lie!, that's not true!; **ten jest ładny, ~(ż)?** this one is pretty, isn't it?
**nieprawdopodobny** *adj* incredible, improbable
**nieprawdziwy** *adj* (*niezgodny z prawdą*) untrue; (*nierzeczywisty*) unreal; (*sztuczny*) artificial, false
**nieprawidłowoś|ć** (**-ci, -ci**) (*gen pl* **-ci**) *f* irregularity
**nieprawidłowy** *adj* (*niezgodny z normami*) against the rules *pred*; (*niepoprawny: odpowiedź*) incorrect
**nieprawny** *adj* unlawful, illegal
**nieprawomocny** *adj* (*Prawo*) pending appeal
**nieprawy** *adj*: **z nieprawego łoża** illegitimate
**nieprecyzyjny** *adj* imprecise
**nieprędko** *adv* not soon
**nieprofesjonalny** *adj* unprofessional
**nieproporcjonalny** *adj* disproportionate
**nieproszony** *adj*: **~ gość** unwelcome *lub* uninvited guest *lub* visitor, gatecrasher (*pot*)

**nieprzebrany** *adj* countless
**nieprzebyty** *adj* (*bagna, góry*) impassable
**nieprzechodni** *adj* (*Jęz*) intransitive
**nieprzeciętny** *adj* superior, outstanding
**nieprzejednany** *adj* intransigent, uncompromising
**nieprzejezdny** *adj* (*droga*: *z powodu robót*) closed; (: *z powodu złych warunków*) impassable
**nieprzejrzysty** *adj* (*nieprzezroczysty*) opaque; (*niezrozumiały*) obscure
**nieprzekonujący, nieprzekonywający** *adj* unconvincing
**nieprzekraczalny** *adj* (*granica*) impassable; **~ termin** deadline
**nieprzekupny** *adj* incorruptible
**nieprzemakalny** *adj* (*odzież*) rainproof; (*opakowanie*) waterproof; **płaszcz ~** raincoat
**nieprzenikniony** *adj* (*ciemność, mgła*) impenetrable; (*tajemnica*) unfathomable, inscrutable
**nieprzepisowy** *adj* (*Sport*) foul; (*Wojsk*) non-conforming, contrary to the regulations *pred*
**nieprzepuszczalny** *adj* (*dla wody*) waterproof; (*dla światła*) opaque; (*dla powietrza*) airtight
**nieprzerwanie** *adv* incessantly
**nieprzerwany** *adj* uninterrupted, continuous
**nieprzetłumaczalny** *adj* untranslatable
**nieprzewidywalny** *adj* unpredictable
**nieprzewidziany** *adj* unforeseen
**nieprzezroczysty** *adj* opaque
**nieprzezwyciężony** *adj* insurmountable
**nieprzychylnoś|ć** (**-ci**) *f* disfavour (*Brit*), disfavor (*US*)
**nieprzychylny** *adj* (*nieprzyjazny*) unfriendly; (*niesprzyjający*: *wiatr*) foul
**nieprzydatny** *adj* useless
**nieprzyja|ciel** (**-ciela, -ciele**) (*gen pl* **-ciół**, *dat pl* **-ciołom**, *instr pl* **-ciółmi**, *loc pl* **-ciołach**) *m* enemy
**nieprzyjacielski** *adj* enemy *attr*
**nieprzyjazny** *adj* unfriendly, hostile
**nieprzyjemnie** *adv* unpleasantly; **było mi ~** I felt bad; **~ zaskoczony/zdziwiony** unpleasantly surprised
**nieprzyjemności** (**-**) *pl* trouble; **mieć ~** to be in trouble
**nieprzyjemny** *adj* unpleasant
**nieprzypadkowo** *adv* not accidentally
**nieprzystępny** *adj* inaccessible
**nieprzytomny** *adj* (*człowiek*) unconscious; (*oczy, wzrok*) vacant; (*ze strachu, ze złości*) mad
**nieprzywykły** *adj* unaccustomed
**nieprzyzwoitoś|ć** (**-ci**) *f* obscenity
**nieprzyzwoity** *adj* obscene, indecent
**niepunktualnoś|ć** (**-ci**) *f* unpunctuality
**niepunktualny** *adj* unpunctual
**niepyszny** *adj*: **wyszedł jak ~** he left with his tail between his legs
**nieracjonalny** *adj* irrational
**nierad** *adv*: **rad ~** willy-nilly
**nierasowy** *adj*: **pies ~** mongrel (dog)
**nieraz** *adv* (*niejednokrotnie*) many times, many a time; (*niekiedy*) sometimes
**nierdzewny** *adj* stainless, rust-proof
**nierealistyczny** *adj* unrealistic
**nierealny** *adj* (*nierzeczywisty*) unreal; (*niewykonalny*) unfeasible
**nieregularnoś|ć** (**-ci, -ci**) (*gen pl* **-ci**) *f* irregularity
**nieregularny** *adj* irregular
**nierentowny** *adj* unprofitable
**nierozerwalnie** *adv* inseparably
**nierozerwalny** *adj* inseparable
**nierozgarnięty** *adj* slow-witted
**nierozłącz|ka** (**-ki, -ki**) (*dat sg* **-ce**, *gen pl* **-ek**) *f* (*Zool*) budgerigar, budgie (*pot*); **papużki nierozłączki** (*przen*: *pot*) conjoined twins
**nierozłączny** *adj* inseparable
**nierozmowny** *adj* quiet, taciturn
**nierozmyślny** *adj* unintentional
**nierozpuszczalny** *adj* insoluble
**nierozsądny** *adj* unreasonable
**nieroztropnoś|ć** (**-ci**) *f* imprudence
**nieroztropny** *adj* imprudent
**nierozumny** *adj* irrational
**nierozważnie** *adv* recklessly
**nierozważny** *adj* reckless
**nier|ób** (**-oba, -oby**) (*loc sg* **-obie**) *m* (*pot*) loafer (*pot*)
**nieróbst|wo** (**-wa**) (*loc sg* **-wie**) *nt* idleness
**nierówno** *adv* (*dzielić*) unevenly; (*oddychać*) irregularly; (*wisieć*) crookedly
**nierównomierny** *adj* (*podział*) unequal; (*puls*) irregular
**nierównoś|ć** (**-ci, -ci**) (*gen pl* **-ci**) *f* (*drogi*) unevenness; (*społeczna*) inequality
**nierówny** *adj* (*powierzchnia*) uneven, rough; (*droga*) bumpy; (*Mat*) not equal; (*podział*) unequal; (*pismo, rytm*) uneven; (*charakter*) inconsistent; (*walka*) one-sided
**nieruchomoś|ć** (**-ci, -ci**) (*gen pl* **-ci**) *f* (*dobra nieruchome*) property (*Brit*), real estate (*US*)
**nieruchomy** *adj* immobile, motionless; (*majątek*) immovable
**nierzadko** *adv* not infrequently
**nierzą|d** (**-du**) (*loc sg* **-dzie**) *m* prostitution
**nierządny** *adj*: **czyn ~** (*Prawo*) indecent assault
**nierzeczywisty** *adj* unreal
**nierzetelny** *adj* (*nieuczciwy*) dishonest; (*niesumienny*) unreliable
**niesamodzielny** *adj* (*człowiek*) dependent

n

**niesamowicie** *adv* (*pot*) incredibly, awfully
**niesamowity** *adj* (*przerażający*) eerie; (*niezwykły*) amazing
**niesforny** *adj* unruly
**niesiesz** *itd. vb patrz* **nieść**
**nieskazitelny** (*książk*) *adj* flawless
**nieskładny** *adj* incoherent
**nieskomplikowany** *adj* unsophisticated, uncomplicated
**nieskończenie** *adv* infinitely, extremely
**nieskończonoś|ć** (**-ci**) *f* (*Mat*) infinity; **w ~** ad infinitum
**nieskończony** *adj* (*bezmiar, lasy*) infinite, endless; (*Mat*) infinite
**nieskory** *adj*: **~ do czegoś** unwilling to do sth
**nieskromnoś|ć** (**-ci**) *f* (*zarozumialstwo*) immodesty; (*nieprzyzwoitość*) indecency
**nieskromny** *adj* (*zarozumiały*) immodest; (*nieprzyzwoity*) indecent
**nieskutecznoś|ć** (**-ci**) *f* ineffectiveness
**nieskuteczny** *adj* ineffective
**niesła|wa** (**-wy**) (*loc sg* **-wie**) *f* (*książk*) infamy, disgrace; **okryć się** (*perf*) **niesławą** to bring disgrace (up)on o.s.
**niesławny** *adj* (*książk*) infamous
**niesłownoś|ć** (**-ci**) *f* unreliability
**niesłowny** *adj* unreliable
**niesłusznie** *adv* unfairly, wrongly
**niesłusznoś|ć** (**-ci**) *f* (*oceny*) injustice, unfairness; (*stwierdzenia*) erroneousness
**niesłuszny** *adj* (*decyzja, wniosek*) erroneous; (*podejrzenie*) unfair
**niesłychanie** *adv* extremely
**niesłychany** *adj* (*niezwykły*) unheard-of; **to niesłychane!** I can't believe it!
**niesmaczny** *adj* (*nieapetyczny*) tasteless; (*żart*) sick, tasteless
**niesma|k** (**-ku**) (*instr sg* **-kiem**) *m*: **budzić (wzbudzić** *perf*) **~** to be disgusting; **czuć ~** to be disgusted
**niesnas|ki** (**-ek**) *pl* disputes *pl*, disagreements *pl*
**niesolidny** *adj* unreliable
**niespecjalnie** (*pot*) *adv* not really
**niespecjalny** *adj* (*pot: niezbyt dobry*) so-so, fair-to-middling (*pot*)
**niespełna** *adv* (*w przybliżeniu*) less than; **za ~ miesiąc** in less than a month; **~ rozumu** out of one's mind
**niespodzian|ka** (**-ki, -ki**) (*dat sg* **-ce**, *gen pl* **-ek**) *f* surprise; **zrobić** (*perf*) **komuś niespodziankę** to give sb a surprise
**niespodziewanie** *adv* unexpectedly
**niespodziewany** *adj* unexpected
**niespokojny** *adj* (*człowiek, spojrzenie, wzrok*) anxious; (*czasy*) turbulent; (*morze*) rough; (*sen*) restless; (*zatroskany: człowiek*): **być ~m o** *+acc* to be anxious about
**niesportowy** *adj* unsportsmanlike
**niespotykany** *adj* (*okaz*) rare; (*uprzejmość*) unprecedented
**niespójny** *adj* incoherent
**niesprawiedliwoś|ć** (**-ci, -ci**) (*gen pl* **-ci**) *f* injustice
**niesprawiedliwy** *adj* unfair, unjust; **być ~m dla** *lub* **wobec kogoś** to be unfair to sb
**niesprawny** *adj* (*zepsuty*) out of order; (*nie wyćwiczony*) unfit, out of shape
**niesprzyjający** *adj* (*okoliczność*) unfavourable (*Brit*), unfavorable (*US*); (*wiatr*) foul
**niestabilnoś|ć** (**-ci**) *f* instability
**niestabilny** *adj* unstable
**niestałoś|ć** (**-ci**) *f* (*przekonań, uczuć*) inconstancy
**niestały** *adj* changeable; **być ~m w miłości/ uczuciach** to be inconstant in one's love/ feelings
**niestarannoś|ć** (**-ci, -ci**) (*gen pl* **-ci**) *f* carelessness
**niestaranny** *adj* careless
**niestawiennict|wo** (**-wa**) (*loc sg* **-wie**) *nt* absence
**niestety** *adv* unfortunately
**niestosownoś|ć** (**-ci**) *f* impropriety
**niestosowny** *adj* improper
**niestrawnoś|ć** (**-ci**) *f* indigestion, dyspepsia
**niestrawny** *adj* (*pokarm*) indigestible; (*przen: nudny*) dry; (*: zbyt trudny*) indigestible
**niestrudzony** *adj* tireless, untiring
**niesubordynacj|a** (**-i, -e**) (*gen pl* **-i**) *f* insubordination
**niesumienny** *adj* unconscientious
**nieswojo** *adv*: **czuć się ~** to feel uneasy *lub* uncomfortable
**nieswój** *adj* ill at ease
**niesymetryczny** *adj* asymmetrical
**niesympatyczny** *adj* unpleasant
**niesystematyczny** *adj* (*uczeń*) unmethodical, disorganized; (*tryb życia*) irregular, disorganized
**nieszablonowy** *adj* unorthodox, original
**nieszczególnie** *adv* (*pot*): **wygląda ~** (s)he doesn't look very well
**nieszczególny** *adj* (*nijaki*) insignificant; (*niezbyt dobry*) mediocre
**nieszczelnoś|ć** (**-ci**) *f* (*brak szczelności*) leakiness; (*otwór*) (*nom pl* **-ci**, *gen pl* **-ci**) leak
**nieszczelny** *adj* leaky
**nieszczeroś|ć** (**-ci**) *f* insincerity
**nieszczery** *adj* insincere
**nieszczęsny** *adj* unfortunate
**nieszczęś|cie** (**-cia, -cia**) (*gen pl* **-ć**) *nt* (*zmartwienie*) unhappiness; (*zły los*) bad luck, misfortune; (*tragedia*) disaster; (*bieda*) misery; (*wypadek*) accident; **na ~** unfortunately

**nieszczęśliwy** *adj* unhappy; (*kaleka, mina*) miserable; (*zbieg okoliczności*) unfortunate
**nieszczęśni|k** (**-ka, -cy**) (*instr sg* **-kiem**) *m* poor thing *lub* soul
**nieszkodliwy** *adj* harmless; **~ dla środowiska** environment(ally) friendly
**nieszpor|y** (**-ów**) *pl* vespers
**nieściągalny** *adj* (*dług*) bad
**nieścisłoś|ć** (**-ci, -ci**) (*gen pl* **-ci**) *f* inaccuracy, imprecision
**nieścisły** *adj* inaccurate, imprecise
**nieść (niosę, niesiesz)** (*imp* **nieś**, *pt* **niósł, niosła, nieśli**) *vt* to carry; (*przynosić*) (*perf* **przy-**) to bring; (*zanosić*) (*perf* **za-**) to carry, to take; (*znosić: jaja*) (*perf* **z-**) to lay; **~ pociechę/pomoc** to bring comfort/help ▷ *vi*: **wieść niesie, że …** it is rumoured (*Brit*) *lub* rumored (*US*) that …; **nieść się** *vr* (*o dźwiękach, muzyce*) to carry; *patrz też* **nosić**
**nieślubny** *adj* illegitimate
**nieśmiałoś|ć** (**-ci**) *f* shyness, timidity
**nieśmiały** *adj* shy, timid
**nieśmiertelnoś|ć** (**-ci**) *f* immortality
**nieśmiertelny** *adj* immortal
**nieświadomoś|ć** (**-ci**) *f* (*brak świadomości*) unconsciousness; (*niewiedza*) ignorance, unawareness; **żyć w nieświadomości** to lead a life of ignorance; **utrzymywać kogoś w nieświadomości** to keep sb in ignorance *lub* the dark
**nieświadomy** *adj* (*bezwiedny*) unconscious; **być ~m czegoś** to be unaware of sth
**nieświeży** *adj* (*chleb*) stale; (*mięso, oddech*) bad; (*pościel*) dirty
**nietak|t** (**-tu, -ty**) (*loc sg* **-cie**) *m* faux pas, gaffe; **popełnić** (*perf*) **~** to commit *lub* make a faux pas, to make a blunder
**nietaktowny** *adj* tactless
**nietknięty** *adj* (*pieczęć, stan*) intact; (*człowiek*) unharmed, sound; (*praca*) untouched
**nietłukący** *adj* non-breakable, unbreakable
**nietoksyczny** *adj* nontoxic
**nietolerancj|a** (**-i**) *f* intolerance
**nietolerancyjny** *adj* intolerant
**nietoperz** (**-a, -e**) (*gen pl* **-y**) *m* bat
**nietowarzyski** *adj* unsociable
**nietrafny** *adj* (*uwaga*) irrelevant; **~ strzał/uderzenie** miss; **nietrafna ocena** misjudgement
**nietrudno** *adv*: **~ zgadnąć** it's an easy guess
**nietrudny** *adj* not difficult; **~ w pożyciu** easy to live with
**nietrwałoś|ć** (**-ci**) *f* (*żywności*) perishability; **~ uczuć** fickleness
**nietrwały** *adj* (*barwnik, kolor*) fast-fading; (*uczucie*) fleeting; (*żywność*) perishable
**nietrzeźwoś|ć** (**-ci**) *f* intoxication; **w stanie nietrzeźwości** in a state of drunkenness
**nietrzeźwy** *adj* drunk, intoxicated; **w stanie ~m** in a state of drunkenness
**nietutejszy** *adj* (*produkt*) non-domestic *lub* local; **jestem ~** I'm a stranger here
**nietuzinkowy** *adj* (*szef*) extraordinary, remarkable; (*talent*) uncommon
**nietykalnoś|ć** (**-ci**) *f* inviolability; **~ osobista** personal immunity; **~ poselska** parliamentary (*Brit*) *lub* congressional (*US*) immunity
**nietykalny** *adj* (*granica, własność*) inviolable; (*osoba*) untouchable
**nietypowy** *adj* atypical; (*rozmiar*) non-standard
**nieubłaganie** *adv* (*bezwzględnie*) unrelentingly; (*nieuchronnie*) inevitably
**nieubłagany** *adj* (*bezwzględny*) implacable; (*nieunikniony*) inevitable
**nieuchronnoś|ć** (**-ci**) *f* inevitability
**nieuchronny** *adj* inevitable
**nieuchwytny** *adj* (*złodziej*) elusive; (*czar, wpływ*) indefinable
**nieuct|wo** (**-wa**) (*loc sg* **-wie**) *nt* ignorance
**nieuczciwoś|ć** (**-ci, -ci**) (*gen pl* **-ci**) *f* dishonesty
**nieuczciwy** *adj* dishonest
**nieudaczni|k** (**-ka, -cy**) (*instr sg* **-kiem**) *m* loser
**nieudany** *adj* (*próba*) unsuccessful
**nieudolnoś|ć** (**-ci, -ci**) (*gen pl* **-ci**) *f* inefficiency, incompetence
**nieudolny** *adj* clumsy
**nieufnoś|ć** (**-ci**) *f* distrust, mistrust
**nieufny** *adj* distrustful
**nieugięty** *adj* unbending, relentless
**nieu|k** (**-ka, -ki**) (*instr sg* **-kiem**) *m* ignoramus
**nieuleczalnie** *adv*: **~ chory** incurably ill
**nieuleczalny** *adj* incurable
**nieumiarkowany** *adj* immoderate; (*apetyt, optymizm*) intemperate
**nieumiejętnoś|ć** (**-ci**) *f* inability, incapacity
**nieumiejętny** *adj* incompetent
**nieumyślnie** *adv* unintentionally, inadvertently
**nieumyślny** *adj* (*nie planowany*) unintentional, inadvertent; (*mimowolny*) involuntary
**nieunikniony** *adj* unavoidable, inevitable
**nieuprzejmoś|ć** (**-ci, -ci**) (*gen pl* **-ci**) *f* impoliteness, unkindness
**nieuprzejmy** *adj* impolite
**nieurodzaj** (**-u, -e**) *m* crop failure; **był ~ na jabłka/ziemniaki** the apple/potato crop failed
**nieurodzajny** *adj* (*rok*) lean; (*ziemia*) infertile
**nieustannie** *adv* unceasingly, continuously
**nieustanny** *adj* incessant, continuous
**nieustępliwoś|ć** (**-ci**) *f* tenacity

**nieustępliwy** *adj* persistent, tenacious
**nieustraszony** *adj* (*książk*) fearless
**nieuwa|ga** (**-gi**) (*dat sg* **-dze**) *f* inattention; **przez nieuwagę** through inattention
**nieuważny** *adj* (*roztargniony*) inattentive, absent-minded; (*nierozważny*) careless
**nieuzasadniony** *adj* groundless, unfounded
**nieużyt|ki** (**-ków**) *pl* (*Rol*) wastelands
**niewart** *adv*: **~ czegoś** not worth sth, unworthy of sth; **nic ~** worth nothing
**nieważkoś|ć** (**-ci**) *f*: **stan nieważkości** weightlessness
**nieważny** *adj* (*nieistotny*) unimportant, insignificant; (*przedawniony*) invalid; (*nieprawomocny*) invalid, null and void
**niewątpliwie** *adv* undoubtedly
**niewątpliwy** *adj* undoubted, unquestionable
**niewdzięcznoś|ć** (**-ci**) *f* ingratitude
**niewdzięczny** *adj* (*człowiek*) ungrateful; (*praca, temat*) unrewarding
**niewesoły** *adj* bleak
**niewiadom|a** (**-ej, -e**) *f decl like adj* (*Mat*) unknown; **równanie z dwoma niewiadomymi** equation with two unknowns; **ktoś/coś jest wielką niewiadomą** sb/sth is a great unknown
**niewiadomy** *adj* unknown
**niewi|ara** (**-ary**) (*dat sg* **-erze**) *f*: **~ (w coś)** disbelief (in sth)
**niewiarygodny** *adj* (*nie zasługujący na zaufanie*) unreliable; (*nieprawdopodobny*) incredible, unbelievable
**niewid|ka** (**-ki, -ki**) (*loc sg* **-ce**, *gen pl* **-ek**) *f*: **czapka ~** cap of invisibility
**niewidoczny** *adj* invisible, unseen
**niewidomy** *adj* blind ▷ *m decl like adj*; **niewidomi** the blind
**niewidzialny** *adj* invisible
**niewiedz|a** (**-y**) *f* ignorance
**niewiele** (*jak*: **ile**) *pron* (*światła, pieniędzy*) not much, little; (*osób, rzeczy*) not many, few ▷ *adv* (*trochę*) little; **~ brakowało, abym się utopił** I nearly drowned; **~ myśląc** without much thought, not thinking much; **~ mówiący tytuł** a title that doesn't say *lub* mean much; **~ sobie robić z czegoś** not to care much about sth
**niewielki** *adj* not big, not large
**niewielu** *pron patrz* **niewiele**
**niewiernoś|ć** (**-ci, -ci**) (*gen pl* **-ci**) *f* (*zdrada*) infidelity, unfaithfulness; (*nielojalność*) disloyalty, infidelity
**niewierny** *adj* (*mąż, żona*) unfaithful; (*pot*: *nieufny*) distrustful; **N~ Tomasz** doubting Thomas
**niewierzący** *adj* unbelieving ▷ *m decl like adj* non-believer
**niewiniąt|ko** (**-ka, -ka**) (*instr sg* **-kiem**, *gen pl* **-ek**) *nt* innocent; **rzeź niewiniątek** (*przen*) slaughter of innocents
**niewinnoś|ć** (**-ci**) *f* (*brak winy*) innocence; (*bezgrzeszność*) innocence, purity
**niewinny** *adj* innocent; **uznany za niewinnego** presumed innocent
**niewłaściwie** *adv* (*błędnie*) wrongly; (*niestosownie*) improperly
**niewłaściwy** *adj* (*błędny, nieprawidłowy*) wrong; (*niestosowny*) inappropriate, improper
**niewol|a** (**-i**) *f* captivity; **być w niewoli** to be in captivity; **dostać się** (*perf*) **do niewoli** to be taken captive *lub* prisoner; **brać (wziąć** *perf*) **kogoś do niewoli** to take sb captive *lub* prisoner
**niewolnic|a** (**-y, -e**) *f* slave
**niewolnict|wo** (**-wa**) (*loc sg* **-wie**) *nt* slavery
**niewolni|k** (**-ka, -cy**) (*instr sg* **-kiem**) *m* slave
**niewprawny** *adj* unskillful, inept
**niewrażliwoś|ć** (**-ci**) *f* (*brak reakcji*) insensitivity; (*odporność psychiczna*) insensibility
**niewrażliwy** *adj* (*nie reagujący*) insensitive; (*odporny*) insensible; **~ na coś** insensitive *lub* insensible to sth
**niewspółmierny** *adj*: **~ do czegoś** incommensurate with sth
**niewybaczalny** *adj* unforgivable, inexcusable
**niewybredny** *adj* (*czytelnik*) undemanding; (*gust*) unrefined
**niewyczerpany** *adj* inexhaustible
**niewyczuwalny** *adj* intangible, impalpable
**niewydarzony** *adj* mediocre
**niewydolnoś|ć** (**-ci**) *f* failure
**niewydolny** *adj* malfunctioning
**niewygodny** *adj* (*but, łóżko*) uncomfortable; (*obecność, świadek*) inconvenient
**niewyg|ody** (**-ód**) *pl* discomforts
**niewykluczony** *adj* (*prawdopodobny*) conceivable; **niewykluczone, że tak się stanie** it's not out of the question that this might happen
**niewykonalny** *adj* unworkable, unfeasible
**niewykształcony** *adj* uneducated
**niewykwalifikowany** *adj* unskilled, unqualified
**niewymierny** *adj* immeasurable
**niewymowny** *adj* unspeakable
**niewymuszony** *adj* casual
**niewypa|ł** (**-łu, -ły**) (*loc sg* **-le**) *m* dud
**niewyparzony** *adj*: **mieć niewyparzoną gębę** *lub* **język** to be foul-mouthed
**niewypłacalnoś|ć** (**-ci**) *f* insolvency
**niewypłacalny** *adj* insolvent
**niewypowiedziany** *adj* inexpressible, unspeakable

**niewyraźny** *adj* (*słabo słyszalny*) faint; (*słabo widzialny*) faint, dim; (*niepewny*) vague; (*niezrozumiały*) vague, obscure; (*podejrzany*) obscure
**niewyrobiony** *adj* unrefined, unsophisticated
**niewysłowiony** *adj* inexpressible
**niewysoki** *adj* not (very) tall *lub* high; (*człowiek*) not (very) tall, rather short
**niewystarczający** *adj* insufficient
**niewyszukany** *adj* simple, unrefined
**niewytłumaczalny** *adj* inexplicable
**niewyżyty** *adj* unfulfilled
**niewzruszony** *adj* (*postawa*) inflexible; (*człowiek*) inflexible, adamant
**niezaangażowany** *adj* (*państwo*) non-aligned
**niezadowole|nie** (**-nia**) *nt* discontent, dissatisfaction; **~ z** *+gen* discontent *lub* dissatisfaction with
**niezadowolony** *adj* dissatisfied, unhappy; **~ z** *+gen* discontented *lub* dissatisfied with
**niezależnie** *adv* independently; **~ od** *+gen* irrespective *lub* regardless of
**niezależnoś|ć** (**-ci**) *f* independence
**niezależny** *adj* independent; **mowa niezależna** (*Jęz*) direct speech; **być ~m materialnie** to be financially independent
**niezamężna** *adj*: **~ kobieta** unmarried *lub* single woman
**niezamierzony** *adj* unintentional
**niezamieszkały** *adj* uninhabited
**niezapominaj|ka** (**-ki, -ki**) (*dat sg* **-ce**, *gen pl* **-ek**) *f* forget-me-not
**niezapomniany** *adj* unforgettable
**niezaprzeczalny** *adj* undeniable, undisputed
**niezaradny** *adj* (*niezapobiegliwy*) resourceless; (*bezradny*) helpless
**niezasłużony** *adj* undeserved
**niezastąpiony** *adj* irreplaceable
**niezatapialny** *adj* unsinkable
**niezatarty** *adj* indelible
**niezauważalnie** *adv* imperceptibly
**niezauważalny** *adj* (*niedostrzegalny*) imperceptible; (*nie zwracający uwagi*) inconspicuous
**niezawisły** *adj* independent
**niezawodnie** *adv* unfailingly
**niezawodnoś|ć** (**-ci**) *f* reliability
**niezawodny** *adj* (*urządzenie, kuracja*) reliable, trustworthy; (*przyjaciel*) dependable, reliable; (*środek*) unfailing
**niezbadany** *adj* (*tajemnica, wyroki losu*) unfathomable, fathomless; (*terytorium*) unexplored
**niezbędni|k** (**-ka, -ki**) (*instr sg* **-kiem**) *m* *combination spoon and fork used when camping*
**niezbędny** *adj* essential, indispensable
**niezbity** *adj* (*argument, dowód*) irrefutable, incontrovertible
**niezbyt** *adv* not very *lub* too; **~ duży** not too big; **~ pomocny** unhelpful; **~ zachęcający** uninviting
**niezbywalny** *adj* (*prawo*) inalienable
**niezdarny** *adj* (*niezgrabny*) clumsy, awkward; (*nieudolny*) inept, ineffectual
**niezdatny** *adj* unfit; **~ do czegoś** unfit for sth; **~ do spożycia** unfit for human consumption
**niezdecydowa|nie** (**-nia**) *nt* (*stan*) indecision; (*cecha*) indecisiveness ▷ *adv* irresolutely
**niezdecydowany** *adj* undecided, irresolute
**niezdolnoś|ć** (**-ci**) *f* (*nieumiejętność*) inability; (*niezdatność*) unfitness
**niezdolny** *adj*: **~ do czegoś** incapable of sth; **~ do pracy/służby wojskowej** unfit for work/military service
**niezdrowy** *adj* (*chory*) unhealthy, unwell; (*chorobliwy*) unhealthy, sickly; (*szkodliwy*) unhealthy; **niezdrowa wyobraźnia** morbid imagination
**niezdyscyplinowany** *adj* undisciplined, recalcitrant
**niezgłębiony** *adj* unfathomable
**niezgo|da** (**-dy**) (*dat sg* **-dzie**) *f* disagreement, discord; **być w niezgodzie z czymś** to be in conflict *lub* at variance with sth; **siać niezgodę** to sow division, to spread discord; **kość** *lub* **jabłko niezgody** bone of contention, apple of discord
**niezgodnoś|ć** (**-ci, -ci**) (*gen pl* **-ci**) *f* (*charakterów*) incompatibility; **~ czegoś z czymś** discrepancy *lub* disagreement between sth and sth
**niezgodny** *adj* (*kłótliwy*) quarrelsome; (*sprzeczny ze sobą*) inconsistent; **~ z czymś** inconsistent with sth, not in agreement *lub* keeping with sth; **~ z prawdą/przepisami** contrary to the truth/regulations
**niezgrabny** *adj* (*niekształtny*) unshapely; (*niezręczny*) clumsy, awkward
**niezidentyfikowany** *adj*: **~ obiekt latający** unidentified flying object
**nieziemski** *adj* (*muzyka*) unearthly; (*piękność, rozkosz*) ethereal
**nieziszczalny** *adj* (*marzenia*) unrealizable; (*plany*) unworkable, unrealizable
**niezliczony** *adj* innumerable, countless
**niezłomny** *adj* (*bojownik*) steadfast; (*postanowienie, wiara*) unshaken, unwavering
**niezłośliwy** *adj* (*Med*) benign
**niezły** *adj* pretty good, not bad
**niezmącony** *adj* (*cisza, szczęście*) unbroken
**niezmienny** *adj* invariable
**niezmiernie** *adv* extremely, immensely
**niezmierny** *adj* extreme, immense

**niezmierzony** *adj* immeasurable
**niezmordowany** *adj* indefatigable
**niezmywalny** *adj* indelible
**nieznaczny** *adj* insignificant; **nieznaczna rola** bit part
**nieznajomoś|ć** (**-ci**) *f*: **~ czegoś** ignorance of sth
**nieznajomy** *adj* unknown, unfamiliar ▷ *m decl like adj* stranger
**nieznany** *adj* unknown; **Grób Nieznanego Żołnierza** tomb of the Unknown Soldier; **pójść/pojechać** (*perf*) **w nieznane** to go into the unknown
**niezniszczalny** *adj* indestructible
**nieznośny** *adj* (*ból*) unbearable, unendurable; (*dziecko*) unbearable
**niezręcznoś|ć** (**-ci, -ci**) (*gen pl* **-ci**) *f* (*niezaradność*) clumsiness, awkwardness; (*niezręczna wypowiedź*) blunder; **popełnić** (*perf*) **~** to blunder
**niezręczny** *adj* (*niezdarny*) clumsy, awkward; (*sytuacja*) awkward
**niezrozumiały** *adj* incomprehensible
**niezrozumie|nie** (**-nia**) *nt* lack of understanding, incomprehension; **spotkać się** (*perf*) **z ~m** to meet with incomprehension
**niezrównany** *adj* unmatched, unequalled
**niezrównoważony** *adj* unstable, unbalanced
**niezupełnie** *adv* not quite
**niezwłocznie** *adv* promptly, immediately
**niezwłoczny** *adj* prompt, immediate
**niezwyciężony** *adj* (*armia*) invincible; (*trudności*) insurmountable
**niezwykle** *adv* (*inaczej niż zwykle*) unusually; (*bardzo*) extremely
**niezwykły** *adj* unusual
**nieźle** *adv* pretty *lub* fairly well
**nieżonaty** *adj* unmarried, single
**nieżyciowy** *adj* (*człowiek*) unrealistic; (*plany*) unrealistic, unworkable
**nieżyczliwoś|ć** (**-ci**) *f* unkindness
**nieżyczliwy** *adj* unfriendly
**nieżyjący** *adj* deceased
**nieży|t** (**-tu**) (*loc sg* **-cie**) *m* (*Med*) inflammation; **~ krtani** laryngitis; **~ oskrzeli** bronchitis; **~ nosa** rhinitis; **~ żołądka** gastritis; **~ spojówek** conjunctivitis
**nieżywotny** *adj* (*Jęz*) inanimate
**nieżywy** *adj* dead
**nigdy** *adv* never; (*w pytaniach i przeczeniach*) ever; **~ więcej** never again; **już ~ (więcej)** never ever; **~ nie wiadomo** you never know *lub* can tell; **~ w życiu** never in my life; **teraz albo ~** (it's) now or never; **jak gdyby ~ nic** as if nothing had happened; **jak ~** as *lub* like never before
**nigdzie** *adv* nowhere; (*w pytaniach i przeczeniach*) anywhere; **~ indziej** nowhere else
**Nigeri|a** (**-i**) *f* Nigeria
**Nigeryjczy|k** (**-ka, -cy**) (*instr sg* **-kiem**) *m* Nigerian
**Nigeryj|ka** (**-ki, -ki**) (*dat sg* **-ce**, *gen pl* **-ek**) *f* Nigerian
**nigeryjski** *adj* Nigerian
**nihiliz|m** (**-mu**) (*loc sg* **-mie**) *m* nihilism
**nijak** *adv* (*pot*): **~ nie mogę tego zrobić** there is no way I can do it
**nijaki** *adj* nondescript; **rodzaj ~** (*Jęz*) neuter
**NIK** *abbr* (= *Najwyższa Izba Kontroli*) Supreme Control Chamber
**Nikaragu|a** (**-i**) *f* Nicaragua
**nikaraguański** *adj* Nicaraguan
**nikczemni|k** (**-ka, -cy**) (*instr sg* **-kiem**) *m* scoundrel, villain
**nikczemnoś|ć** (**-ci**) *f* meanness
**nikczemny** *adj* mean
**ni|kiel** (**-klu**) *m* nickel
**nikim** *pron instr, loc od* **nikt**; **być ~** to be a nobody
**nikl|ować (-uję, -ujesz)** (*perf* **po-**) *vt* to nickel, to nickel-plate
**niklowany** *adj* nickel-plated
**nikły** *adj* (*światło, zarys*) faint; (*nadzieja, szanse*) slender
**nik|nąć (-nę, -niesz)** (*imp* **-nij**) *vi* (*znikać*) (*perf* **z-**) to vanish; (*zanikać*) (*perf* **za-**) to fade away
**nikogo** *pron gen od* **nikt**; **~ tu nie ma** there is nobody here
**nikomu** *pron dat od* **nikt**; **nie dawaj tego ~** don't give it to anyone
**nikoty|na** (**-ny**) (*dat sg* **-nie**) *f* nicotine
**Nikozj|a** (**-i**) *f* Nicosia
**nikt** (*jak*: **kto**) *pron* nobody, no-one; (*w pytaniach i przeczeniach*) anyone, anybody; **~ z nas** none of us; **~ inny** nobody else; **~ inny tylko ...** nobody but ...; **~ a ~** not a soul
**Nil** (**-u**) *m* Nile
**nim**[1] *pron loc, instr od* **on, ono**; (*o mężczyźnie*) him; (*o dziecku, zwierzęciu, przedmiocie*) it
**nim**[2] *conj* before
**nim|fa** (**-fy, -fy**) (*dat sg* **-fie**) *f* nymph
**nimfomani|a** (**-i**) *f* (*Med*) nymphomania
**nimfoman|ka** (**-ki, -ki**) (*dat sg* **-ce**, *gen pl* **-ek**) *f* nymphomaniac
**nimi** *pron instr od* **oni, one** them
**niniejszy** *adj* (*książk*) present; **~m oświadczam ...** I hereby declare ...
**niosę** *itd. vb patrz* **nieść**
**niósł** *itd. vb patrz* **nieść**
**nirwa|na** (**-ny**) (*dat sg* **-nie**) *f* nirvana
**niski** (*comp* **niższy**) *adj* (*płot, drzewo, sufit, poziom*) low; (*człowiek*) short
**nisko** (*comp* **niżej**) *adv* low
**niskokaloryczny** *adj* low-calorie

**niskoprocentowy** *adj* (*roztwór*) weak; (*pożyczka*) low-interest
**nisz|a** (**-y, -e**) (*gen pl* **-y**) *f* niche
**niszcze|ć (-ję, -jesz)** (*perf* **z-**) *vi* to become spoiled *lub* ruined
**niszczyciel** (**-a, -e**) (*gen pl* **-i**) *m* destroyer
**niszczycielski** *adj* devastating, destructive
**niszcz|yć (-ę, -ysz)** (*perf* **z-**) *vt* to destroy; **niszczyć się** *vr patrz* **niszczeć**
**ni|t** (**-tu, -ty**) (*loc sg* **-cie**) *m* rivet
**nit|ka** (**-ki, -ki**) (*dat sg* **-ce**, *gen pl* **-ek**) *f* thread; **~ dentystyczna** dental floss; **nitki** *pl* (*makaron*) vermicelli; **przemoknięty do suchej nitki** dripping *lub* soaking wet; **nie zostawić** (*perf*) **na kimś suchej nitki** to pick sb to pieces
**nit|ować (-uję, -ujesz)** (*perf* **za-**) *vt* to rivet
**nitroglicery|na** (**-ny**) (*dat sg* **-nie**) *f* nitroglycerin
**niuan|s** (**-su, -se**) (*loc sg* **-sie**) *m* nuance
**niuch|ać (-am, -asz)** (*pot*) *vi* (*wąchać*) to sniff; (*szperać*) to nose about
**niwecz|yć (-ę, -ysz)** (*perf* **z-**) *vt* to thwart
**niwel|ować (-uję, -ujesz)** (*perf* **z-**) *vt* to level
**niz.** *abbr* (= *nizina*) lowland
**ni|zać (-żę, -żesz)** (*perf* **na-**) *vt* to thread, to string
**nizi|na** (**-ny, -ny**) (*dat sg* **-nie**) *f* lowland
**nizinny** *adj* lowland *attr*; (*rejon*) low-lying
**niż**[1] (**-u, -e**) *m* (*Meteo*) low, depression; (*Geog*) lowland
**niż**[2] *conj* than; **X jest starszy niż Y** X is older than Y
**niżej** *adv comp od* **nisko** lower; (*w tekście*) below; **~ wymieniony** mentioned below; **~ podpisany** the undersigned
**niższoś|ć** (**-ci**) *f* inferiority; **kompleks niższości** inferiority complex
**niższy** *adj comp od* **niski**; (*mur, poziom, drzewo*) lower; (*człowiek*) shorter; (*jakość*) inferior; (*ranga*) subordinate
**no** *part*: **no, no!** (*zdziwienie*) well, well!; (*uspokajająco*) there, now!; **no to idź!** so go!; **no to co?** so what?; **no nie?** right?
**Nob|el** (**-la**) *m*: **Nagroda Nobla** the Nobel prize
**nobilitacj|a** (**-i**) *f* ennoblement
**nobilit|ować (-uję, -ujesz)** *vt* to ennoble
**nobli|sta** (**-sty, -ści**) (*dat sg* **-ście**) *m decl like f in sg* Nobel prize winner
**nobliwy** *adj* dignified
**noc** (**-y, -e**) (*gen pl* **-y**) *f* night; **w nocy** at night; **co noc** every night; **Warszawa nocą** Warsaw by night; **nocami** at nights; **całą noc** the whole night; **dzień i noc** night and day; **dzisiejszej nocy** tonight; **przez całą noc** all night (long); **do późna w nocy** till late at night; **w środku nocy** in the middle of the night; **zostawać (zostać** *perf*) **na noc** to stay for the night
**nocie** *n patrz* **nota**
**nocle|g** (**-gu, -gi**) (*instr sg* **-giem**) *m* somewhere to spend the night; **dać** (*perf*) **komuś ~** to put sb up (for the night)
**nocni|k** (**-ka, -ki**) (*instr sg* **-kiem**) *m* chamber pot, potty (*pot*)
**nocny** *adj* night *attr*; (*zwierzę*) nocturnal; **~ marek** (*pot*) night owl *lub* hawk (*US*) (*pot*)
**noc|ować (-uję, -ujesz)** (*perf* **prze-**) *vi* to stay for the night
**no|ga** (**-gi, -gi**) (*dat sg* **-dze**, *gen pl* **nóg**) *f* (*kończyna*) leg; (*stopa*) foot; (*stołu, łóżka*) leg; **być na ~ch** to be on one's feet; **do góry ~mi** upside down; **do nogi!** here!; **brać nogi za pas** to take to one's heels; **być jedną nogą w grobie** to have one foot in the grave; **stać na własnych ~ch** to stand on one's own two feet; **wstać** (*perf*) **lewą nogą** to have got out on the wrong side of the bed; **postawić** (*perf*) **kogoś/coś na nogi** to get sb/sth back on their/its feet
**nogaw|ka** (**-ki, -ki**) (*dat sg* **-ce**, *gen pl* **-ek**) *f* (trouser) leg
**nokau|t** (**-tu, -ty**) (*loc sg* **-cie**) *m* knockout
**nokaut|ować (-uję, -ujesz)** (*perf* **z-**) *vt* to knock out
**noktur|n** (**-nu, -ny**) (*loc sg* **-nie**) *m* nocturne
**nomenklatu|ra** (**-ry, -ry**) (*dat sg* **-rze**) *f* (*nazewnictwo*) terminology; (*ludzie*) nomenclature
**nominacj|a** (**-i, -e**) (*gen pl* **-i**) *f* (*powołanie na stanowisko*) appointment; (*w wyborach, do nagrody*) nomination
**nominalnie** *adv* nominally
**nominalny** *adj* nominal; **wartość nominalna** face value; **płaca nominalna** nominal wages
**nomina|ł** (**-łu, -ły**) (*loc sg* **-le**) *m* denomination
**nomin|ować (-uję, -ujesz)** *vt* (*im*)*perf* (*na stanowisko*) to appoint; (*w wyborach, do nagrody*) to nominate
**non-iron** *adj* non-iron, drip dry
**nonkonformi|sta** (**-sty, -ści**) (*dat sg* **-ście**) *m decl like f in sg* nonconformist
**nonkonformiz|m** (**-mu**) (*loc sg* **-mie**) *m* nonconformism
**nonsen|s** (**-su, -sy**) (*loc sg* **-sie**) *m* nonsense
**nonsensowny** *adj* nonsensical
**non stop** *adv* non stop
**nonszalancj|a** (**-i**) *f* nonchalance
**nonszalancki** *adj* nonchalant
**no|ra** (**-ry, -ry**) (*dat sg* **-rze**) *f* (*królika, lisa*) burrow; (*myszy*) hole; (*pej*: *mieszkanie*) hole, hovel
**nordycki** *adj* Nordic

n

**nor|ka** (**-ki, -ki**) (*dat sg* **-ce**, *gen pl* **-ek**) *f dimin od* **nora**; (*Zool*) mink; **norki** *pl* (*futro*) mink coat
**nor|ma** (**-my, -my**) (*dat sg* **-mie**) *f* norm, standard; **poniżej/powyżej normy** below/above the norm; **normy moralne** moral standards
**normalizacj|a** (**-i**) *f* standardization
**normaliz|ować się (-uję, -ujesz)** (*perf* **z-**) *vr* to normalize
**normalnie** *adv* normally
**normalnoś|ć** (**-ci**) *f* normality
**normalny** *adj* normal; (*objaw, reakcja*) normal, usual; (*godziny odjazdu*) normal, regular; (*bilet*) full fare *attr*
**Normandi|a** (**-i**) *f* Normandy
**norm|ować się (-uję, -ujesz)** (*perf* **u-**) *vr* to normalize
**Norwe|g** (**-ga, -dzy**) (*instr sg* **-giem**) *m* Norwegian
**Norwegi|a** (**-i**) *f* Norway
**norweski** *adj* Norwegian ▷ *m decl like adj*; (**język**) ~ Norwegian; **kombinacja norweska** (*Sport*) Nordic combined
**Norweż|ka** (**-ki, -ki**) (*dat sg* **-ce**, *gen pl* **-ek**) *f* Norwegian
**norze** *n patrz* **nora**
**no|s** (**-sa, -sy**) (*loc sg* **-sie**) *m* nose; **mruczeć pod nosem** to mumble under one's breath; **zabrać** (*perf*) **coś komuś sprzed nosa** to snatch something from under sb's nose; **kręcić na coś nosem** (*przen*) to turn up one's nose at sth; **wtykać nos w nie swoje sprawy** (*przen*) to poke one's nose into other people's affairs; **mam to w nosie** (*przen*) I don't give a hoot; **mam tego po dziurki w nosie** (*przen*) I've had it up to here; **mieć nosa** (*przen*) to have a hunch
**nosiciel** (**-a, -e**) (*gen pl* **-i**) *m* carrier
**no|sić (-szę, -sisz)** (*imp* **noś**) *vt* (*ciężary, pieniądze*) to carry; (*spodnie, okulary*) to wear; (*brodę, długie włosy*) to have, to wear; (*nazwę*) to bear; (*nazwisko*) to use; **nosić się** *vr*: **~ się elegancko** to dress elegantly; **~ się z myślą zrobienia czegoś** to intend to do sth
**nosoroż|ec** (**-ca, -ce**) *m* rhinoceros, rhino (*pot*)
**nosowy** *adj* nasal
**nostalgi|a** (**-i**) *f* nostalgia
**nostalgiczny** *adj* nostalgic
**nostryfikacj|a** (**-i, -e**) (*gen pl* **-i**) *f an official recognition of a foreign diploma or scholarly degree*
**nostryfik|ować (-uję, -ujesz)** *vt (im)perf to grant an official recognition of a foreign diploma or a scholarly degree*
**nosz|e** (**-y**) *pl* stretcher *sg*
**noszę** *itd. vb patrz* **nosić**
**nośni|k** (**-ka, -ki**) (*instr sg* **-kiem**) *m* carrier
**nośnoś|ć** (**-ci**) *f* (*mostu*) load capacity; (*statku*) deadweight
**no|ta** (**-ty, -ty**) (*dat sg* **-cie**) *f* (*Pol*) note; (*ocena*) grade
**notabene** *inv* by the way, incidentally
**notabl|e** (**-i**) *pl* (*książk*) notables *pl*
**notacj|a** (**-i, -e**) (*gen pl* **-i**) *f* notation
**notarialny** *adj* (*akt*) notarized; (*biuro*) notary's
**notariusz** (**-a, -e**) (*gen pl* **-y**) *m* notary (public)
**notat|ka** (**-ki, -ki**) (*dat sg* **-ce**, *gen pl* **-ek**) *f* note; **robić notatki** to make notes
**notatni|k** (**-ka, -ki**) (*instr sg* **-kiem**) *m* notebook
**noteboo|k** (**-ka, -ki**) (*instr sg* **-kiem**) *m* (*Komput*) notebook computer
**note|s** (**-su, -sy**) (*loc sg* **-sie**) *m* notebook
**notoryczny** *adj* notorious
**not|ować (-uję, -ujesz)** (*perf* **za-**) *vt* (*zapisywać*) to write down; (*rejestrować*) to keep a record of ▷ *vi* to make notes
**notowa|nie** (**-nia, -nia**) (*gen pl* **-ń**) *nt* (*Giełda*) quotation
**novum** *nt inv* novelty
**Nowa Anglia** (**Nowej Anglii**) *f* New England
**Nowa Funlandia** (**Nowej Funlandii**) *f* Newfoundland
**Nowa Gwinea** (**Nowej Gwinei**) *f* New Guinea
**nowalij|ka** (**-ki, -ki**) (*dat sg* **-ce**, *gen pl* **-ek**) *f* early vegetable
**Nowa Szkocja** (**Nowej Szkocji**) *f* Nova Scotia
**nowato|r** (**-ra, -rzy**) (*loc sg* **-rze**) *m* innovator
**nowatorski** *adj* innovative
**Nowa Zelandia** (**Nowej Zelandii**) *f* New Zealand
**nowel|a** (**-i, -e**) *f* short story; (*Prawo*) amendment
**nowelizacj|a** (**-i, -e**) (*gen pl* **-i**) *f* amendment
**noweliz|ować (-uję, -ujesz)** (*perf* **z-**) *vt* to amend
**nowicja|t** (**-tu**) (*loc sg* **-cie**) *m* novitiate
**nowicjusz** (**-a, -e**) (*gen pl* **-y**) *m* novice
**nowicjusz|ka** (**-ki, -ki**) (*dat sg* **-ce**, *gen pl* **-ek**) *f* novice
**nowi|na** (**-ny, -ny**) (*dat sg* **-nie**) *f* news
**nowiu** *itd. n patrz* **nów**
**nowiutki** *adj* brand new
**nowo** *adv* newly; ~ **narodzony** newborn
**nowobogac|ki** (**-kiego, -cy**) *m decl like adj* nouveau riche
**nowoczesnoś|ć** (**-ci**) *f* modernity
**nowoczesny** *adj* modern
**nowojorczy|k** (**-ka, -cy**) (*instr sg* **-kiem**) *m* New Yorker
**nowojorski** *adj* New York *attr*
**nowomodny** *adj* new-fangled
**noworoczny** *adj* New Year's *attr*
**noworod|ek** (**-ka, -ki**) (*instr sg* **-kiem**) *m* baby, infant

**nowoś|ć** (**-ci, -ci**) (*gen pl* **-ci**) *f* (*coś nowego*) novelty; (*cecha*) newness
**nowotworowy** *adj* cancerous
**nowotw|ór** (**-oru, -ory**) (*loc sg* **-orze**) *m* (*Med*) tumour (*Brit*), tumor (*US*); **~ łagodny/złośliwy** benign/malicious tumo(u)r
**nowożeń|cy** (**-ców**) *pl* newlyweds *pl*
**nowożytny** *adj* modern
**nowy** *adj* new; **fabrycznie ~** brand new; **jak ~** as good as new; **na nowo** *lub* **od nowa** anew; **coś/nic nowego** something/nothing new; **co nowego?** what's new?; **N~ Testament** New Testament; **N~ Rok** New Year ▷ *m decl like adj* newcomer
**Nowy Jork** (**Nowego Jorku**) (*instr sg* **Nowym Jorkiem**) *m* (*miasto*) New York (City); (*stan*) New York (State)
**Nowy Meksyk** (**Nowego Meksyku**) (*instr sg* **Nowym Meksykiem**) *m* New Mexico
**Nowy Orlean** (**Nowego Orleanu**) (*loc sg* **Nowym Orleanie**) *m* New Orleans
**nozdrz|e** (**-a, -a**) (*gen pl* **-y**) *nt* nostril
**noża** *itd. n patrz* **nóż**
**nożny** *adj*: **hamulec ~** footbrake; **piłka nożna** (association) football, soccer
**nożyc|e** (-) *pl* shears *pl*
**nożycz|ki** (**-ek**) *pl* scissors *pl*; **~ do paznokci** nail scissors
**nóg** *n patrz* **noga**
**nów** (**nowiu**) *m* new moon
**nóż** (**noża, noże**) (*gen pl* **noży**) *m* knife; **nóż kuchenny** kitchen knife; **nóż sprężynowy** flick knife (*Brit*), switchblade (*US*); **mieć nóż na gardle** (*przen*) to be in a tight corner
**nóż|ka** (**-ki, -ki**) (*dat sg* **-ce**, *gen pl* **-ek**) *f dimin od* **noga**; (*grzyba, kieliszka*) stem; (*kurczaka*) drumstick
**np.** *abbr* (= *na przykład*) e.g.
**nr** *abbr* (= *numer*) no.
**NRD** *abbr* (= *Niemiecka Republika Demokratyczna*) GDR (= *the German Democratic Republic*)
**NSA** *abbr* (= *Naczelny Sąd Administracyjny*) Supreme Administrative Court
**n-ty** *adj*: **po raz ~** for the umpteenth time
**nu|cić** (**-cę, -cisz**) (*imp* **-ć**, *perf* **za-**) *vt* to hum
**nucie** *n patrz* **nuta**
**nu|da** (**-dy, -dy**) (*dat sg* **-dzie**, *gen pl* **-dów**) *f* boredom; **umierać z nudów** to be bored stiff *lub* to death; **robić coś z nudów** to do sth out of boredom
**nudnośc|i** (**-i**) *pl* nausea
**nudny** *adj* boring, dull; **~ jak flaki z olejem** (*pot*) (as) dull as ditch-water (*pot*)
**nudy|sta** (**-sty, -ści**) (*dat sg* **-ście**) *m decl like f in sg* nudist
**nudyst|ka** (**-ki, -ki**) (*dat sg* **-ce**, *gen pl* **-ek**) *f* nudist
**nudyz|m** (**-mu**) (*loc sg* **-mie**) *m* nudism
**nudziarz** (**-a, -e**) (*gen pl* **-y**) *m* bore
**nu|dzić** (**-dzę, -dzisz**) (*imp* **-dź**, *perf* **z-**) *vt* to bore; **nudzić się** *vr* to be bored
**nuklearny** *adj* nuclear
**nume|r** (**-ru, -ry**) (*loc sg* **-rze**) *m* (*liczba*) number; (*rozmiar*) size; (*czasopisma*) issue, number; (*w przedstawieniu*) act, turn (*Brit*); **~ rejestracyjny** registration number; **ten ~ nie przejdzie!** nothing doing!
**numeracj|a** (**-i, -e**) (*gen pl* **-i**) *f* numbering
**numer|ek** (**-ka, -ki**) (*instr sg* **-kiem**) *m* (*w szatni*) ticket
**numer|ować** (**-uję, -ujesz**) (*perf* **po-**) *vt* to number
**numizmaty|ka** (**-ki**) (*dat sg* **-ce**) *f* numismatics *sg*
**nuncjusz** (**-a, -e**) (*gen pl* **-y** *lub* **-ów**) *m* nuncio
**nur|ek** (**-ka**) (*instr sg* **-kiem**) *m* (*człowiek*) (*nom pl* **-kowie**) diver; (*skok do wody*) (*nom pl* **-ki**) dive; **dać** (*perf*) **nurka** to dive
**nur|ki** (**-ków**) *pl* (*futro*) mink coat
**nurk|ować** (**-uję, -ujesz**) (*perf* **za-**) *vi* to dive; (*o samolocie*) to nosedive
**nurkowa|nie** (**-nia**) *nt* diving; **aparat do nurkowania** scuba, aqualung
**nur|t** (**-tu, -ty**) (*loc sg* **-cie**) *m* (*rzeki, strumienia*) current; (*tendencja*) trend
**nurt|ować** (**-uję, -ujesz**) *vt* (*o pytaniu*) to bother; **nurtowało mnie uczucie niepewności** I felt a niggling doubt
**nurz|ać się** (**-am, -asz**) *vr* to wallow
**nu|ta** (**-ty, -ty**) (*dat sg* **-cie**) *f* note; **nuty** *pl* score; **grać/śpiewać z nut** to play/sing from the score; **kłamać jak z nut** to lie through one's teeth; **~ triumfu** note of triumph
**nut|ka** (**-ki, -ki**) (*dat sg* **-ce**, *gen pl* **-ek**) *f* (*odcień*) note
**nutowy** *adj*: **papier ~** music paper
**nutri|a** (**-i, -e**) (*gen pl* **-i**) *f* coypu; **futro z nutrii** coypu *lub* nutria coat
**nuworysz** (**-a, -e**) (*gen pl* **-y**) *m* nouveau riche
**nuż** *part*: **a nuż ...** what if ...; **a nuż nie przyjdzie?** what if he doesn't come?
**nużący** *adj* wearisome, tiresome
**nuż|yć** (**-ę, -ysz**) (*perf* **z-**) *vt* to tire
**nygu|s** (**-sa, -sy**) (*loc sg* **-sie**) *m* (*pot*) lazybones (*pot*)
**nylo|n** (**-nu**) (*loc sg* **-nie**) *m* nylon
**nylonowy** *adj* nylon *attr*

n

# Oo

**O, o**[1] *nt inv* (*litera*) O, o; **O jak Olga** ≈ O for Oliver (*Brit*), ≈ O for Olive (*US*)

SŁOWO KLUCZOWE

**o**[2] *prep +loc* **1** (*na temat*) about, on; **książka o wojnie** a book about *lub* on war; **mówić/myśleć/wiedzieć o czymś** to talk/think/know about sth
**2** (*za pomocą*): **o własnych siłach** on one's own; **o kulach** on crutches
**3** (*z określeniami czasu*) at; **o (godzinie) pierwszej** at one (o'clock); **o zmroku/północy/świcie** at dusk/midnight/dawn
**4** (*przy opisach*) with; **dziewczyna o długich włosach** a girl with long hair; **człowiek o dużych wymaganiach** a person of *lub* with high expectations
▷ *prep +acc* **1** (*przy porównaniach*) by; **o połowę krótszy** shorter by half; **starszy o rok** a year older
**2** (*z czasownikami*): **kłócić się o coś** to quarrel about sth; **niepokoić się o kogoś/coś** to worry about sb/sth; **prosić/pytać o coś** to ask for *lub* about sth
**3**: **opierać się o coś** to lean against sth; **rzucać czymś o coś** to throw sth against sth
▷ *excl* oh; **o, już idzie!** there he comes!

**oa|za (-zy, -zy)** (*loc sg* **-zie**) *f* oasis
**ob.** *abbr* (= *obywatel*) citizen
**oba** *num* both; **oba zdania/koty** both sentences/cats
**obaj** *num* both; **~ mężczyźni** both men
**obal|ać (-am, -asz)** (*perf* **-ić**) *vt* (*przeciwnika*) to knock down; (*drzewo*) to fell; (*ustrój, rząd*) to overthrow, to bring down; (*teorię, twierdzenie*) to refute, to disprove; (*testament*) to revise; (*wyrok*) to reverse; (*niewolnictwo*) to abolish; (*pot: piwo*) to knock back (*pot*)
**obandaż|ować (-uję, -ujesz)** *vb perf od* **bandażować**
**obarcz|ać (-am, -asz)** (*perf* **-yć**) *vt*: **~ kogoś czymś** to burden sb with sth; **~ kogoś obowiązkiem** to burden sb with a duty; **~ kogoś odpowiedzialnością (za coś)** to hold sb responsible (for sth)
**oba|wa (-wy, -wy)** (*dat sg* **-wie**) *f*: **~ (o kogoś/coś)** concern (for sb/sth); **~ (przed kimś/czymś)** fear (of sb/sth); **w obawie przed** *+instr* for fear of
**obawi|ać się (-am, -asz)** *vr*: **obawiać się kogoś/czegoś** to fear *lub* dread sb/sth; **obawiam się, że ...** I am afraid (that) ...; **obawiać się o kogoś/coś** to be concerned about sb/sth
**obca|s (-sa, -sy)** (*loc sg* **-sie**) *m* heel (*of a shoe*); **na (wysokim) ~ie** high-heeled
**obcąż|ki (-ków)** *pl* pliers *pl*
**obcesowy** *adj* off-hand, unceremonious
**obcę|gi (-gów)** *pl* pliers *pl*, pincers *pl*
**obcho|dzić (-dzę, -dzisz)** (*imp* **-dź**, *perf* **obejść**) *vt* (*dom, plac*) to walk round; (*przeszkodę*) to go *lub* walk round; (*zakaz, trudność*) to get round, to evade; (*rocznicę, imieniny*) to celebrate; (*interesować*) to interest, to concern; **co mnie to obchodzi?** what do I care?; **nic mnie to nie obchodzi** I don't care, I couldn't care less; **obchodzić się** *vr*: **~ się z czymś** to handle *lub* use sth; **~ się z kimś** to treat sb (*in some way*); **~ się bez czegoś** to do without sth; **~ się czymś** to make do with sth; **nie obejdzie się bez płaczu** tears will flow; **nie obejdzie się bez walki** fighting is inevitable; **obejdzie się!** thanks a lot! (*with irony*)
**obch|ód (-odu, -ody)** (*loc sg* **-odzie**) *m* (*inspekcja*) round; **obchody** *pl* (*uroczystości*) celebrations *pl*, festivities *pl*; **obchody Nowego Roku** New Year celebrations
**ob|ciąć (-etnę, -etniesz)** (*imp* **-etnij**) *vb perf od* **obcinać**
**obciąż|ać (-am, -asz)** (*perf* **-yć**) *vt* (*obładowywać*) to weigh down; (*zaopatrywać w balast*) to weight, to ballast; (*obowiązkami*) to burden, to saddle; (*pamięć*) to burden; (*o dowodach, faktach*) to incriminate; **~ czyjeś konto** to be charged to sb's account; **~ coś hipoteką** to mortgage sth
**obciąże|nie (-nia, -nia)** (*gen pl* **-ń**) *nt* load

**obcier|ać (-am, -asz)** (*perf* **obetrzeć**) *vt* (*łzy*) to wipe; (*kaleczyć*) to graze, to scrape; (*o butach*) to pinch

**obcin|ać (-am, -asz)** (*perf* **obciąć**) *vt* (*włosy, paznokcie*) to clip, to cut; (*gałąź*) to cut off; (*wydatki*) to cut (back), to cut down (on)

**obcisły** *adj* (skin)tight, close-fitting

**obco** *adv*: **czuję się tu ~** I feel like a stranger here, I don't belong here

**obcojęzyczny** *adj* foreign language *attr*

**obcokrajo|wiec** (**-wca, -wcy**) (*voc sg* **-wcze** *lub* **-wcu**) *m* foreigner

**obc|ować (-uję, -ujesz)** *vi*: **~ z** *+instr* to associate *lub* mix with; **~ z przyrodą** to commune with nature

**obcy** *adj* (*cudzy*) somebody else's *attr*, other people's *attr*; (*nietutejszy*) strange, alien; (*zagraniczny*) foreign ▷ *m decl like adj* (*obca osoba*) stranger, alien; **ciało obce** foreign body; **„~m wstęp wzbroniony"** (*w terenie*) "no trespassing"; (*w biurze, sklepie*) "private"; (*w budynku wojskowym itp.*) "authorized personnel only"

**obczy|zna** (**-zny**) (*dat* **-źnie**) *f* (*książk*: *zagranica*) foreign land(s *pl*); (*wygnanie*) exile

**obdar|ować (-uję, -ujesz)** *vb perf od* **obdarowywać**

**obdarow|ywać (-uję, -ujesz)** *vt*: **~ kogoś czymś** to present sb with sth

**obdartu|s** (**-sa, -sy**) (*loc sg* **-sie**) *m* (*pot*) scruff (*pot*)

**obdarty** *adj* ragged, tattered; **~ z czegoś** deprived *lub* stripped of sth

**obdarzony** *adj*: **być ~m czymś** to be endowed *lub* blessed with sth

**obdarz|yć (-ę, -ysz)** *vt perf*: **~ kogoś spojrzeniem/uśmiechem** to give sb a look/smile

**obdukcj|a** (**-i, -e**) (*gen pl* **-i**) *f* (*Med*: *badanie poszkodowanego*) forensic examination; (*: sekcja zwłok*) autopsy, postmortem (examination)

**obdziel|ać (-am, -asz)** (*perf* **-ić**) *vt*: **~ kogoś czymś** to hand out sth to sb

**obdzier|ać (-am, -asz)** (*perf* **obedrzeć**) *vt* to strip, to peel off; **~ kogoś z czegoś** (*pozbawiać*) to deprive sb of sth; **~ kogoś ze skóry** (*przen*) to rip sb off (*pot*)

**obecnie** *adv* at present, currently

**obecnoś|ć** (**-ci**) *f* (*bytność*) presence, attendance; (*istnienie*) existence; **sprawdzać ~** to check attendance, to call *lub* take the roll; **w czyjejś obecności** in sb's presence

**obecny** *adj* (*będący na miejscu*) present; (*teraźniejszy*) present, current; **być ~m na czymś** to attend sth, to be present at sth; **w chwili obecnej** at present; **~/obecna!** (*Szkol*) here!, present! ▷ *m*: **obecni** *pl* those present *pl*

**obed|rzeć (-rę, -rzesz)** (*imp* **-rzyj**, *pt* **obdarł**) *vb perf od* **obdzierać**

**obejmę** *itd. vb patrz* **objąć**

**obejm|ować (-uję, -ujesz)** (*perf* **objąć**) *vt* (*tulić*) to embrace, to hug; (*zawierać*) to include, to encompass; (*pojmować*) to comprehend; **~ urząd/władzę** to take office; **~ kierownictwo** to take charge; **~ kogoś/coś wzrokiem** *lub* **spojrzeniem** to take sb/sth in; **obejmować się** *vr* to embrace, to hug

**obejrz|eć (-ę, -ysz)** (*imp* **-yj**) *vb perf od* **oglądać**

**obejś|cie** (**-cia, -cia**) (*gen pl* **-ć**) *nt* (*podwórze*) farmyard; **miły w obejściu** well-mannered; **łatwy w obejściu** easy to deal with

**obej|ść (-dę, -dziesz)** (*imp* **-dź**, *pt* **obszedł, obeszła, obeszli**) *vb perf od* **obchodzić**

**obel|ga** (**-gi, -gi**) (*dat sg* **-dze**) *f* insult; **obelgi** *pl* abuse

**obelis|k** (**-ku, -ki**) (*instr* **-kiem**) *m* obelisk

**obelżywy** *adj* insulting, abusive

**ober|ek** (**-ka, -ki**) (*instr sg* **-kiem**) *m a lively Polish folk dance*

**ober|wać (-wę, -wiesz)** (*imp* **-wij**) *vb perf od* **obrywać**

**oberwa|nie (-nia)** (*gen pl* **-ń**) *nt*: **~ chmury** cloudburst

**oberż|nąć (-nę, -niesz)** (*imp* **-nij**) *vb perf od* **obrzynać**

**oberży|na** (**-ny, -ny**) (*dat sg* **-nie**) *f* aubergine (*Brit*), eggplant (*US*)

**obeszła** *itd. vb patrz* **obejść**

**obetnę** *itd. vb patrz* **obciąć**

**obet|rzeć (-rę, -rzesz)** (*imp* **-rzyj**, *pt* **obtarł**) *vb perf od* **obcierać**

**obeznany** *adj*: **~ z czymś** acquainted with sth

**obezwład|niać (-niam, -niasz)** (*perf* **-nić**) *vt* to overwhelm; (*przeciwnika*) to overpower

**obezwładniający** *adj* paralyzing, incapacitating

**obezwład|nić (-nię, -nisz)** (*imp* **-nij**) *vb perf od* **obezwładniać**

**obeżr|eć (-ę, -esz)** (*imp* **-yj**) *vb perf od* **obżerać**

**obędę** *itd. vb patrz* **obyć się**

**obficie** *adv* (*jeść*) heavily; (*padać*) hard, heavily; (*krwawić, pocić się*) profusely; (*kwitnąć*) richly

**obfitoś|ć** (**-ci**) *f* abundance

**obfit|ować (-uję, -ujesz)** *vi*: **~ w** *+acc* to abound in *lub* with

**obfitujący** *adj*: **~ w** *+acc* abounding in, replete with

**obfity** *adj* abundant, heavy; **~ (w** *+acc***)** rich (in)

**obgad|ywać (-uję, -ujesz)** (*perf* **-ać**) (*pot*) *vt* (*omawiać*) to talk over; (*obmawiać*) to backbite

O

**obgryz|ać (-am, -asz)** (*perf* **obgryźć**) *vt* (*kość: o psie*) to gnaw at; (*: o człowieku*) to pick; (*liście*) to eat (up); **~ paznokcie** to bite one's nails; **~ drzewo z liści** to strip a tree of leaves

**obgry|źć (-zę, -ziesz)** (*imp* **-ź**) *vb perf od* **obgryzać**

**obi|ad (-adu, -ady)** (*loc sg* **-edzie**) *m* (*wczesny*) lunch; (*późny*) dinner; (*też:* **obiad proszony**) dinner (party); **jeść ~** to have lunch/dinner, to lunch/dine; **co jest na ~?** what's for lunch/dinner?; **jestem po obiedzie** I've (already) eaten

**obiadowy** *adj* lunch *attr*, dinner *attr*; **pora obiadowa** lunchtime, dinnertime

**obi|cie (-cia, -cia)** (*gen pl* **-ć**) *nt* upholstery, padding

**obi|ć (-ję, -jesz)** *vb perf od* **obijać**

**obie** *num* both; **~ kobiety** both women

**obie|c (-gnę, -gniesz)** (*imp* **-gnij**, *pt* **-gł**) *vb perf od* **obiegać**

**obiec|ać (-am, -asz)** *vb perf od* **obiecywać**

**obiecan|ka (-ki, -ki)** (*dat sg* **-ce**, *gen pl* **-ek**) *f* (vain *lub* empty) promise; **„obiecanki cacanki!"** (*pot*) "promises, promises!" (*pot*)

**obiecujący** *adj* promising

**obiec|ywać (-uję, -ujesz)** (*perf* **-ać**) *vi* to promise ▷ *vt*: **~ coś (komuś)** to promise sth (to sb), to promise (sb) sth

**obie|g (-gu)** (*instr* **-giem**) *m* (*krwi, wody, pieniądza*) circulation; (*Astron: po orbicie*) orbiting; (*: wokół własnej osi*) rotation

**obieg|ać (-am, -asz)** (*perf* **-nąć** *lub* **obiec**) *vt* (*biec dookoła*) to run around; (*o planecie*) to orbit, to circle; (*o plotce, sławie*) to go round

**obieg|nąć (-nę, -niesz)** (*imp* **-nij**, *pt* **-ł**) *vb perf od* **obiegać**

**obiegowy** *adj* (*pieniądz*) current; (*opinia*) current, general; **karta obiegowa** clearance slip

**obiegów|ka (-ki, -ki)** (*gen pl* **-ek**) *f* (*pot*) clearance slip

**obiekcj|a (-i, -e)** (*gen pl* **-i**) *f* objection; **obiekcje** *pl* objection(s *pl*), reservation(s *pl*)

**obiek|t (-tu, -ty)** (*loc sg* **-cie**) *m* (*przedmiot*) object; (*budynek*) structure; **~ krytyki/plotek** target of criticism/gossip

**obiekty|w (-wu, -wy)** (*loc sg* **-wie**) *m* lens, objective

**obiektywiz|m (-mu)** (*loc sg* **-mie**) *m* objectivity

**obiektywnie** *adv* objectively

**obiektywnoś|ć (-ci)** *f* objectivity

**obiektywny** *adj* objective

**obiema** *num instr od* **obie**

**obier|ać (-am, -asz)** (*perf* **obrać**) *vt* (*jabłko, kartofel*) to peel; (*jajko*) to shell; (*rybę*) to bone; (*wybierać*) to adopt, to choose; **~ kogoś prezesem** *lub* **na prezesa** to elect sb chairperson

**obieralny** *adj* (*urzędnik*) elected; (*przedmiot*) elective

**obier|ki (-ek)** *pl* peelings *pl*

**obierze** *vb patrz* **obrać**

**obietnic|a (-y, -e)** *f* promise

**obieżyświa|t (-ta, -ty)** (*loc sg* **-cie**) *m* (*pot*) globetrotter

**obij|ać (-am, -asz)** (*perf* **obić**) *vt* (*obtłukiwać: garnek*) to chip, to crack; (*: jabłka*) to bruise; (*pokrywać materiałem: kanapę, stół*) to pad, to upholster; (*wykładać: ścianę*) to cover; **obijać się** *vr* (*obtłukiwać się: o garnku*) to chip, to crack; (*: o jabłkach*) to bruise; (*pot: wałkonić się*) to loaf (about *lub* around) (*pot*); **obiło mi się o uszy, że ...** I heard (that) ...

**obiorę** *itd. vb patrz* **obrać**

**obj.** *abbr* (= *objętość*) vol. (= *(cubic) volume*)

**objad|ać (-am, -asz)** (*perf* **objeść**) *vt*: **~ kogoś** (*przen*) to sponge on *lub* from sb; **objadać się** *vr* to gorge *lub* stuff o.s.

**objaś|niać (-niam, -niasz)** (*perf* **-nić**) *vt* (*wyjaśniać*) to explain; (*interpretować*) to explicate

**objaś|nić (-nię, -nisz)** (*imp* **-nij**) *vb perf od* **objaśniać**

**objaśnie|nie (-nia, -nia)** (*gen pl* **-ń**) *nt* explanation

**obja|w (-wu, -wy)** (*loc sg* **-wie**) *m* symptom, sign

**obja|wiać (-wiam, -wiasz)** (*perf* **-wić**) *vt* to display, to manifest; **objawiać się** *vr* to appear; **~ się czymś** to manifest o.s. in sth

**objawie|nie (-nia, -nia)** (*gen pl* **-ń**) *nt* (*Rel*) revelation

**objawowy** *adj*: **leczenie objawowe** (*Med*) symptomatic treatment

**obj|azd (-azdu, -azdy)** (*loc sg* **-eździe**) *m* (*objeżdżanie*) tour; (*droga okrężna: na stałe*) by-pass; (*: tymczasowo*) (traffic) diversion (*Brit*), detour (*US*); **„~"** "diverted traffic" (*Brit*), "diversion" (*Brit*), "detour" (*US*)

**objazdowy** *adj* (*teatr, wystawa, kino*) travelling *attr* (*Brit*), traveling *attr* (*US*); (*droga*) roundabout *attr*, bypass *attr*

**ob|jąć (-ejmę, -ejmiesz)** (*imp* **-ejmij**) *vb perf od* **obejmować**

**obj|echać (-adę, -edziesz)** (*imp* **-edź**) *vb perf od* **objeżdżać**

**obj|eść (-em, -esz)** (*pt* **-adł, -edli**) *vb perf od* **objadać**

**objeżdż|ać (-am, -asz)** (*perf* **objechać**) *vt* (*omijać*) to go round, to circle; (*odwiedzać*) to visit, to tour

**obję|cie (-cia)** *nt* (*uścisk*) (*nom pl* **-cia**, *gen pl* **-ć**) embrace, hug; (*przejęcie: władzy*) assumption;

(: *tronu*) accession; **brać kogoś w objęcia** to take sb in one's arms

**objętoś|ć** (**-ci**) *f* (*naczynia, torby*) capacity; (*odmierzona część*) part, measure; (*liczba stron*) length; (*Geom, Fiz*) (cubic) volume; **dwie objętości wody i jedna ~ kleju** two parts water and one part glue

**obkład|ać** (**-am, -asz**) (*perf* **obłożyć**) *vt* (*pokrywać*) to cover; (*owijać*) to wrap; **~ chleb serem** to spread bread with cheese; **obkładać się** *vr*: **~ się czymś** to cover o.s. with sth; **~ się książkami** to surround o.s. with books

**obku|ć** (**-ję, -jesz**) *vb perf od* **obkuwać**

**obl|ać** (**-eję, -ejesz**) *vb perf od* **oblewać**; **oblać się** *vr perf*: **~ się czymś** (*zupą, herbatą*) to spill sth on o.s.; **~ się (zimnym) potem** to break out into a (cold) sweat; **~ się rumieńcem** to blush, to redden

**oblamow|ywać** (**-uję, -ujesz**) (*perf* **-ać**) *vt* to trim

**oblat|ać** (**-am, -asz**) *vb perf od* **oblatywać**

**oblatany** *adj* (*pot*): **być ~m w czymś** to be at home in *lub* with sth

**oblatywacz** (**-a, -e**) (*gen pl* **-y**) *m* test pilot

**oblat|ywać** (**-uję, -ujesz**) (*perf* **oblatać**) *vt* (*samolot*) to test

**oble|c** (**-gnę, -gniesz**) (*imp* **-gnij**, *pt* **-gł**) *vb perf od* **oblegać**

**oble|cieć** (**-cę, -cisz**) (*imp* **-ć**) *vt perf*: **strach mnie obleciał** I got cold feet

**obleg|ać** (**-am, -asz**) (*perf* **-nąć** *lub* **oblec**) *vt* (*miasto*) to besiege, to lay siege to; (*przen: stoisko*) to crowd at, to mob

**oble|gnąć, oble|c** (**-gnę, -gniesz**) (*imp* **-gnij**, *pt* **-gł**) *vb perf od* **oblegać**

**oble|piać** (**-piam, -piasz**) (*perf* **-pić**) *vt*: **~ coś czymś** (*oklejać*) to paste *lub* stick sth all over sth; (*osmarowywać*) to smear sth with sth

**obleśny** *adj* (*lubieżny*) lecherous, lustful; (*obrzydliwy*) disgusting

**oblew|ać** (**-am, -asz**) (*perf* **oblać**) *vt* (*polewać: wodą*) to sprinkle; (*powlekać: czekoladą*) to coat; (*o morzu, jeziorze: otaczać*) to surround, to wash; (*pot: egzamin*) to fail, to flunk (*pot*); (: *mieszkanie, awans*) to celebrate; **oblać kogoś zimną wodą** (*przen*) to throw cold water on sb (*przen*)

**oblęże|nie** (**-nia, -nia**) (*gen pl* **-ń**) *nt* siege

**oblężony** *adj*: **~ (przez** *+acc***)** besieged (by), beleaguered (by)

**oblicz|ać** (**-am, -asz**) (*perf* **-yć**) *vt* (*pieniądze*) to count; (*sumę, prędkość*) to calculate, to work out; (*szacować*) to estimate; **obliczam straty na 1 mln zł** I estimate the losses at one million zloty

**oblicz|e** (**-a, -a**) (*gen pl* **-y**) *nt* (*twarz*) face; (*charakter*) side, facet; **w obliczu trudności/śmierci** in the face of difficulty/death; **w obliczu prawa** in the eye of the law; **ukazywać (ukazać** *perf***) prawdziwe ~** to show one's true nature

**oblicze|nie** (**-nia, -nia**) (*gen pl* **-ń**) *nt* (*rachunek*) calculation, computation; (*zliczenie*) count; (*ocena*) estimate

**obliczeniowy** *adj* computational

**oblicz|yć** (**-ę, -ysz**) *vb perf od* **obliczać**

**obligacj|a** (**-i, -e**) (*gen pl* **-i**) *f* (*Fin*) bond

**obligatoryjny** *adj* obligatory, mandatory

**obli|zać** (**-żę, -żesz**) (*imp* **-ż**) *vb perf od* **oblizywać**

**obliz|ywać** (**-uję, -ujesz**) (*perf* **-ać**) *vt* to lick; **oblizywać się** *vr* to lick one's lips

**oblodzeni|e** (**-a**) *nt* icing, ice-formation

**oblodzony** *adj* icy, covered with ice

**obluz|ować** (**-uję, -ujesz**) *vb perf od* **obluzowywać**

**obluzowany** *adj* slack, loose

**obluzow|ywać** (**-uję, -ujesz**) (*perf* **-ać**) *vt* to loosen (up), to slack(en); **obluzowywać się** *vr* to slack(en), to come loose

**obładow|ywać** (**-uję, -ujesz**) (*perf* **-ać**) *vt* to load, to burden

**obłaska|wiać** (**-wiam, -wiasz**) (*perf* **-wić**) *vt* to tame

**obła|wa** (**-wy, -wy**) (*dat sg* **-wie**) *f* (*polowanie*) hunt, chase; (*łapanka*) roundup, manhunt; (*policyjna*) raid

**obłąkany** *adj* insane, mad

**obłę|d** (**-du, -dy**) (*loc sg* **-dzie**) *m* (*szaleństwo*) insanity, madness; (*zamieszanie*) bedlam; **wpadać (wpaść** *perf***) w ~** to go insane *lub* mad

**obłędny** *adj* (*pot: wspaniały*) fantastic

**obło|k** (**-ku, -ki**) (*instr* **-kiem**) *m* cloud; **bujać w ~ach** (*przen*) to have one's head in the clouds (*przen*)

**obło|wić się** (**-wię, -wisz**) (*imp* **obłów**) *vr perf* (*pot: wzbogacić się*) to line one's pockets

**obłożnie** *adv*: **~ chory** bed-ridden

**obłoż|yć** (**-ę, -ysz**) (*imp* **obłóż**) *vb perf od* **okładać**

**obłu|da** (**-dy**) (*dat sg* **-dzie**) *f* hypocrisy

**obłudnic|a** (**-y, -e**) *f* hypocrite

**obłudni|k** (**-ka, -cy**) (*instr sg* **-kiem**) *m* hypocrite

**obłudny** *adj* false

**obłu|pać** (**-pię, -piesz**) *vb perf od* **obłupywać**

**obłu|pić** (**-pię, -pisz**) *vt perf* (*obrabować*) to rob; (*splądrować*) to plunder

**obłup|ywać** (**-uję, -ujesz**) (*perf* **-ać**) *vt* (*jajko*) to shell; (*korę, tynk*) to peel

**obły** *adj* (*walcowaty*) cylindrical; (*jajowaty*) oval

**obmac|ać** (**-am, -asz**) *vb perf od* **obmacywać**

**obmac|ywać** (**-uję, -ujesz**) (*perf* **-ać**) *vt* to feel, to finger; (*pej*) to paw, to grope

**obmawi|ać (-am, -asz)** (*perf* **obmówić**) *vt* to backbite
**obmy|ć (-ję, -jesz)** *vb perf od* **obmywać**
**obmyśl|ać (-am, -asz)** (*perf* **-ić**) *vt* to think over *lub* up
**obmyw|ać (-am, -asz)** (*perf* **obmyć**) *vt* (*myć*) to wash; (*przemywać*) to rinse; (*o morzu, jeziorze: otaczać*) to wash, to surround
**obnaż|ać (-am, -asz)** (*perf* **-yć**) *vt* to expose, to bare; **obnażać się** *vr* to expose o.s.
**obniż|ać (-am, -asz)** (*perf* **-yć**) *vt* (*poziom, głos*) to lower, to reduce; (*półkę, obraz*) to lower; **obniżać się** *vr* (*o wodzie, temperaturze*) to fall; (*o kosztach, cenach*) to fall, to drop
**obniż|ka** (**-ki, -ki**) (*dat sg* **-ce**) *f* reduction, cut
**obniż|yć (-ę, -ysz)** *vb perf od* **obniżać**
**obnośny** *adj*: **handel** ~ peddling
**obojczy|k** (**-ka, -ki**) (*instr* **-kiem**) *m* (*Anat*) collarbone, clavicle
**oboje** (*jak*: **dwoje**) *num* both; ~ **małżonkowie** both spouses
**obojętnie** *adv* (*z obojętnością*) indifferently; ~ **kto** (*nieważne kto*) no matter who; (*ktokolwiek*) anybody, anyone; ~ **kiedy** no matter when, any time
**obojętnie|ć (-ję, -jesz)** (*perf* **z-**) *vi*: ~ **na coś** to become *lub* grow indifferent to sth
**obojętnoś|ć** (**-ci**) *f* indifference
**obojętny** *adj* indifferent; (*Chem: roztwór*) neutral; (*: gaz*) inert; **coś/ktoś jest komuś ~m** sb is indifferent to sth/sb
**obojga** *itd. num patrz* **oboje**
**obojna|k** (**-ka, -ki**) (*instr* **-kiem**) *m* hermaphrodite
**obok** *prep +gen* (*blisko*) by, near, close to; (*oprócz*) beside ▷ *adv*: **(tuż)** ~ nearby, (very) close; **przeszła ~ (nas)** she walked past (us); ~ **siebie** side by side
**obolały** *adj* (*plecy, noga*) aching; (*gardło*) sore; (*pacjent*) suffering (from pain)
**oboma** *num instr od* **oba, obaj, obie**
**obopólny** *adj* mutual
**ob|ora** (**-ory, -ory**) (*dat sg* **-orze**, *gen pl* **-ór**) *f* cowshed
**oborni|k** (**-ka**) (*instr* **-kiem**) *m* manure
**obosieczny** *adj* two-edged, double-edged
**obostrz|ać (-am, -asz)** (*perf* **-yć**) *vt* (*przepisy, areszt*) to tighten; (*karę*) to augment
**obostrze|nie** (**-nia, -nia**) (*gen pl* **-ń**) *nt* restriction
**obostrz|yć (-ę, -ysz)** *vb perf od* **obostrzać**
**obowiąz|ek** (**-ku, -ki**) (*instr* **-kiem**) *m* duty, obligation; **obowiązki** *pl* duties *pl*; **pełniący obowiązki prezesa** acting chairperson
**obowiązkowo** *adv* (*przymusowo*) obligatorily; (*pot: koniecznie*) whatever happens
**obowiązkowy** *adj* (*służba wojskowa, zajęcia*) obligatory, mandatory; (*pracownik*) diligent, conscientious
**obowiązujący** *adj* (*rozkład jazdy*) (currently) valid, current; (*ustawa, umowa*) (currently) in force, (legally) binding
**obowiąz|ywać (-uje)** *vi* to be in force; **obowiązuje strój wieczorowy** ≈ black tie suggested
**oboz|ować (-uję, -ujesz)** *vi* to camp
**obozowis|ko** (**-ka, -ka**) (*instr* **-kiem**) *nt* camp(site)
**obozowy** *adj* camp *attr*
**ob|ój (-oju, -oje)** *m* oboe
**ob|óz** (**-ozu, -ozy**) (*loc sg* **-ozie**) *m* camp; ~ **koncentracyjny** concentration camp; ~ **dla uchodźców** refugee camp; ~ **jeniecki** prisoner-of-war camp, PoW camp; ~ **pracy** labour camp (*Brit*), labor camp (*US*)
**obrabi|ać (-am, -asz)** (*perf* **obrobić**) *vt* (*poddawać obróbce*) to machine; (*wykańczać: brzeg materiału*) to hem
**obrabiar|ka** (**-ki, -ki**) (*dat sg* **-ce**, *gen pl* **-ek**) *f* machine tool
**obrab|ować (-uję, -ujesz)** *vt perf* to rob
**obrac|ać (-am, -asz)** (*perf* **obrócić**) *vt* (*śrubę*) to turn, to rotate; (*wzrok*) to turn; (*szafę*) to move (around) ▷ *vi* (*iść tam i z powrotem*) to go there and back; **obrócić coś w gruzy** to bring sth to ruin, to lay waste to sth; ~ **pieniędzmi/kapitałem** to put money/capital to profit; **obracać się** *vr* (*o kole*) to turn, to revolve; (*w towarzystwie, środowisku*) to move; **obrócić się do kogoś przodem** to face sb; **obrócić się do kogoś tyłem** to turn one's back on sb; **obrócić się przeciwko komuś** to turn against sb
**obrachun|ek** (**-ku, -ki**) (*instr* **-kiem**) *m* account
**obrać (obiorę, obierzesz)** *vb perf od* **obierać**
**obrad|ować (-uję, -ujesz)** *vi*: ~ **(nad czymś)** to debate (sth)
**obrad|y** (**-**) *pl* proceedings *pl*
**obramow|ywać (-uję, -ujesz)** (*perf* **-ać**) *vt* (*otaczać*) to encircle; (*dorabiać ramę*) to frame; (*obszywać*) to hem
**obrast|ać (-am, -asz)** (*perf* **obrosnąć**) *vt* (*o roślinach*) to cover, to overgrow; (*: rosnąć dookoła*) to grow around; (*o zaroście*) to cover ▷ *vi*: ~ **czymś** to be covered with *lub* in sth; ~ **w piórka** (*bogacić się*) to feather one's nest; ~ **w sadło** to put on weight
**obra|z** (**-zu, -zy**) (*loc sg* **-zie**) *m* (*malowidło*) painting, picture; (*widok, scena*) sight; (*opis: epoki, wypadków*) picture; (*widok na ekranie*) image, picture; (*film*) film; (*Fiz, Fot*) image; **żywy ~ kogoś** a living *lub* spitting image of sb; ~ **nędzy i rozpaczy** (*pot*) a pitiful *lub* sorry sight; ~ **kontrolny** test pattern

**obra|za** (**-zy**) (*dat sg* **-zie**) *f* offence (Brit), offense (US); (*zniewaga*) insult; **~ moralności** scandal; **~ majestatu** lèse-majesté; **~ sądu** contempt of court
**obraz|ek** (**-ka, -ki**) (*instr sg* **-kiem**) *m* (*mały obraz*) (little) picture; (*ilustracja*) picture; (*scenka*) scene, picture
**obra|zić (-żę, -zisz)** (*imp* **-ź**) *vb perf od* **obrażać**
**obrazkowy** *adj* (*ilustrowany*) picture *attr*, pictorial; **pismo obrazkowe** picture writing
**obrazoburczy** *adj* iconoclastic
**obraz|ować (-uję, -ujesz)** *vt* (*opisywać*) to illustrate; (*wyrażać*) to represent
**obrazowo** *adv* graphically, vividly
**obrazowy** *adj* vivid
**obraźliwy** *adj* (*obrażający*) insulting, offensive; (*skłonny do obrażania się*) touchy, easily offended
**obraż|ać (-am, -asz)** (*perf* **obrazić**) *vt* to offend; **obrażać się** *vr*: **~ się na kogoś** to be offended with sb; **~ się o coś** to be offended at sth, to take offence (Brit) *lub* offense (US) at sth
**obrażals|ki** (**-kiego, -cy**) *m decl like adj* (*pot*) sulker
**obraże|nie** (**-nia, -nia**) (*gen pl* **-ń**) *nt* injury
**obrażony** *adj* offended; **być ~m na** *+acc* to be offended with
**obrącz|ka** (**-ki, -ki**) (*dat sg* **-ce**) *f* (*też*: **obrączka ślubna**) wedding ring; (*do znakowania zwierząt*) ring
**obręb** (**-bu**) (*loc sg* **-bie**) *m* (*obszar*: *miasta, fabryki*) grounds *pl*, limits *pl*; (*zakres*: *zainteresowań*) range, sphere; (*granica*: *społeczeństwa*) limits; (*brzeg tkaniny*) hem; **w ~ie czegoś** within (the limits of) sth
**obręb|iać (-biam, -biasz)** (*perf* **-bić**) *vt* to hem
**obręb|ić (-bię, -bisz)** (*imp* **obrąb**) *vb perf od* **obrębiać**
**obręcz** (**-y, -e**) (*gen pl* **-y**) *f* hoop; (*koła*) rim
**obro|bić (-bię, -bisz)** (*imp* **obrób**) *vb perf od* **obrabiać** ▷ *vt perf* (*pot*: *okraść*) to rob
**obro|dzić (-dzi)** *vi perf* (*o drzewie*) to bear a rich crop; (*o zbożu*) to give *lub* yield a good harvest; (*o owocach, warzywach*) to be plentiful
**obro|na** (**-ny**) (*dat sg* **-nie**) *f* defence (Brit), defense (US); (*ochrona*) protection; **w obronie własnej** in self-defence; **stawać (stanąć** *perf*) **w obronie kogoś/czegoś** to rise to sb's defence/in defence of sth, to stand up for sb/sth; **nie mam nic na swoją obronę** I have nothing in my defence; **~ pracy magisterskiej/doktorskiej** a defence of master's/doctoral thesis
**obro|nić (-nię, -nisz)** (*imp* **-ń**) *vb perf od* **bronić**
**obronnoś|ć** (**-ci**) *f*: **~ kraju** country's defences *pl*
**obronny** *adj* (*akcja, postawa*) defensive; (*mur, zamek*) fortified; **mury obronne** battlements, ramparts; **wyjść** (*perf*) **z czegoś obronną ręką** to get off sth lightly, to come off sth lightly *lub* well; **pies ~** guard dog
**obrońc|a** (**-y, -y**) *m decl like f in sg* defender; (*zwolennik*) advocate; (*Prawo*) barrister, counsel for the defence; **~ z urzędu** public defender (US), court-appointed lawyer (Brit)
**obrończy|ni** (**-ni, -nie**) (*gen pl* **-ń**) *f* defender; (*zwolenniczka*) advocate
**obr|osnąć (-osnę, -ośniesz)** (*imp* **-ośnij**, *pt* **-ósł, -osła, -ośli**) *vb perf od* **obrastać**
**obrotnoś|ć** (**-ci**) *f* (*przedsiębiorczość*) enterprise, industry; (*zaradność*) resourcefulness
**obrotny** *adj* (*przedsiębiorczy*) enterprising, industrious; (*zaradny*) resourceful
**obrotomierz** (**-a, -e**) (*gen pl* **-y**) *m* (*Tech*) tachometer, rev counter
**obrotowy** *adj* (*ruch*) rotary; (*drzwi, scena*) revolving; (*kapitał*) circulating; **podatek ~** turnover tax
**obroż|a** (**-y, -e**) (*gen pl* **-y**) *f* collar
**obrób|ka** (**-ki, -ki**) (*dat sg* **-ce**, *gen sg* **-ek**) *f* (*materiału*) processing; (*chemiczna*) treatment
**obró|cić (-cę, -cisz)** (*imp* **-ć**) *vb perf od* **obracać**
**obr|ót** (**-otu, -oty**) (*loc sg* **-ocie**) *m* (*śruby, planety*) revolution; (*tok sprawy*) turn; (*Ekon, Handel*) turnover; **obroty silnika** revolutions; **pracować na wysokich obrotach** to work at full capacity; **sytuacja przybrała nieoczekiwany ~** the situation took an unexpected turn
**obru|s** (**-sa** *lub* **-su, -sy**) (*loc sg* **-sie**) *m* tablecloth
**obrusz|ać się (-am, -asz)** (*perf* **-yć**) *vr*: **obruszać się na** *+acc* to bridle at
**obry|ć (-ję, -jesz)** *vt perf* (*pot*) to cram, to swot up on; **obryć się** *vr* to cram, to swot up on
**obry|s** (**-su, -sy**) (*loc sg* **-sie**) *m* contour, outline
**obrys|ować (-uję, -ujesz)** *vb perf od* **obrysowywać**
**obrysow|ywać (-uję, -ujesz)** (*perf* **-ać**) *vt* to outline
**obryw|ać (-am, -asz)** (*perf* **oberwać**) *vt* (*guziki*) to tear off; (*tynk*) to peel (off); (*owoce*) to pick ▷ *vi* (*pot*: *dostawać lanie*) to get a beating; **obrywać się** *vr* (*o guziku*) to tear off, to come off; **oberwało mu się** (*pot*) he caught it
**obryz|giwać (-guję, -gujesz)** (*perf* **-gać**) *vt* to splash
**obrząd|ek** (**-ku, -ki**) (*instr* **-kiem**) *m* (*ceremonia*) ceremony, ritual; (*obyczaj*) custom; (*Rel*) rite
**obrzeza|nie** (**-nia**) *nt* (*Rel*) circumcision
**obrzez|ywać (-uję, -ujesz)** (*perf* **-ać**) *vt* (*Rel*) to circumcise

O

**obrzeż|e** (**-a, -a**) (*gen pl* **-y**) *nt* edge
**obrzę|d** (**-du, -dy**) (*loc sg* **-dzie**) *m* (*ceremonia*) ceremony; (*rytuał*) ritual
**obrzędowy** *adj* (*muzyka*) ceremonial, ritual; (*taniec*) ritual; (*strój*) ceremonial
**obrzę|k** (**-ku, -ki**) (*instr* **-kiem**) *m* swelling
**obrzękły** *adj* swollen
**obrzmiały** *adj* swollen
**obrzmie|nie** (**-nia, -nia**) (*gen pl* **-ń**) *nt* swelling
**obrzu|cać (-cam, -casz)** (*perf* **-cić**) *vt*: **~ kogoś/coś czymś** to throw sth at sb/sth, to pelt sb/sth with sth; **~ kogoś błotem** (*przen*) to shower slander *lub* abuse at sb; **obrzucić kogoś/coś spojrzeniem** to cast a glance at sb/sth
**obrzu|cić (-cę, -cisz)** (*imp* **-ć**) *vb perf od* **obrzucać**
**obrzydliwoś|ć** (**-ci, -ci**) (*gen pl* **-ci**) *f* (*coś brzydkiego*) abomination; (*uczucie wstrętu*) disgust
**obrzydliwy** *adj* abominable, disgusting
**obrzydły** *adj* loathsome
**obrzyd|nąć (-nę, -niesz)** (*pt* **-ł**) *vi perf*: **obrzydło mi to** I'm sick (and tired) of it
**obrzy|dzać (-dzam, -dzasz)** (*perf* **-dzić**) *vt*: **~ komuś coś** to put sb off sth
**obrzydzeni|e** (**-a**) *nt* disgust, abomination
**obrzy|dzić (-dzę, -dzisz)** (*imp* **-dź**) *vb perf od* **obrzydzać**
**obrzyn|ać (-am, -asz)** (*perf* **oberżnąć**) *vt* (*okrawać*) to trim, to edge; (*odcinać*) to clip, to cut off
**obsa|da** (**-dy, -dy**) (*dat sg* **-dzie**) *f* (*obsadzenie stanowiska*) appointment, assignment; (*personel*) staff; (*załoga*) crew; (*Teatr, Film*) cast
**obsad|ka** (**-ki, -ki**) (*dat sg* **-ce**) *f* penholder
**obsa|dzać (-dzam, -dzasz)** (*perf* **-dzić**) *vt* (*teren: drzewami, trawą*) to plant; (*stanowisko*) to fill; **~ kimś stanowisko** to appoint sb to a post
**obsa|dzić (-dzę, -dzisz)** (*imp* **-dź**) *vb perf od* **obsadzać**
**obsceniczny** *adj* obscene
**obserwacj|a** (**-i, -e**) (*gen pl* **-i**) *f* (*obserwowanie*) observation; (*: przez policję*) observation, surveillance; (*spostrzeżenie, uwaga*) observation; **być pod obserwacją** to be under observation *lub* surveillance
**obserwacyjny** *adj* observational; **punkt ~** vantage point
**obserwato|r** (**-ra, -rzy**) (*loc sg* **-rze**) *m* observer
**obserwatori|um** (**-um, -a**) (*gen pl* **-ów**) *nt inv in sg* observatory
**obserwator|ka** (**-ki, -ki**) (*dat sg* **-ce**) *f* observer
**obserw|ować (-uję, -ujesz)** *vt* to observe, to watch
**obsesj|a** (**-i, -e**) (*gen pl* **-i**) *f* obsession
**obsesyjny** *adj* obsessive, obsessional
**obsi|ać (-eję, -ejesz)** *vb perf od* **obsiewać**
**obsiew|ać (-am, -asz)** (*perf* **obsiać**) *vt* to sow
**obska|kiwać (-kuję, -kujesz)** (*perf* **obskoczyć**) *vt*: **~ kogoś** (*otaczać, okrążać*) to surround sb; (*obsługiwać*) to wait on sb hand and foot
**obskurny** *adj* dilapidated, run down
**obsłu|ga** (**-gi**) (*dat sg* **-dze**) *f* (*maszyny*) service, maintenance; (*klientów*) service; (*personel, załoga*) staff, personnel; **~ naziemna** ground personnel; **~ hotelowa** hotel service
**obsłu|giwać (-guję, -gujesz)** (*perf* **-żyć**) *vt* (*klienta, gościa*) to serve, to attend to; (*maszynę*) to operate, to work ▷ *vi* (*obsługiwać do stołu*) to wait at the table; **obsługiwać się** *vr*: **obsłuż się sam** help yourself
**obsmaż|ać (-am, -asz)** (*perf* **-yć**) *vt* (*mięso*) to seal, to sear; (*cebulę*) to fry quickly
**obsta|wa** (**-wy, -wy**) (*dat sg* **-wie**) *f* (*więźnia*) guard; (*ważnej osoby*) bodyguard
**obsta|wać (-ję, -jesz)** (*imp* **-waj**) *vi*: **~ przy czymś** to persist in sth, to stick to sth; **~ przy swojej decyzji** to stick to one's decision; **~ przy swoich poglądach** to stick to one's point of view
**obsta|wiać (-wiam, -wiasz)** (*perf* **-wić**) *vt* (*otaczać*) to surround; (*na wyścigach, loterii*) to bet on, to back; (*Sport*) to surround, to guard
**obstęp|ować (-uję, -ujesz)** (*perf* **obstąpić**) *vt* to gather round, to surround
**obstrukcj|a** (**-i, -e**) (*gen pl* **-i**) *f* (*Pol*) obstruction; (*Med*) constipation
**obstrza|ł** (**-łu**) (*loc sg* **-le**) *m* (gun)fire; **być pod ~em** to be under fire
**obsu|nąć (-nę, -niesz)** (*imp* **-ń**) *vb perf od* **obsuwać**
**obsuw|ać się (-am, -asz)** (*perf* **obsunąć**) *vr* (*opadać*) to sink, to drop; (*o ziemi*) to slide, to cave in; **obsuwać się na kolana/ziemię** to drop *lub* sink to one's knees/the ground
**obsy|pać (-pię, -piesz)** *vb perf od* **obsypywać**
**obsyp|ywać (-uję, -ujesz)** (*perf* **-ać**) *vt*: **~ kogoś/coś czymś** (*śniegiem*) to throw *lub* tip sth onto sb/sth; (*cukrem, mąką*) to sprinkle sb/sth with sth; (*kamieniami, wyzwiskami*) to shower *lub* pelt sb/sth with sth; **~ kogoś prezentami** to shower sb with gifts *lub* presents
**obsza|r** (**-ru, -ry**) (*loc sg* **-rze**) *m* (*powierzchnia*) area; (*terytorium*) territory
**obszarni|k** (**-ka, -cy**) (*instr sg* **-kiem**) *m* landowner
**obszar|pać (-pię, -piesz)** *vb perf od* **obszarpywać**
**obszarpany** *adj* (*człowiek*) tattered; (*ubiór*) ragged, tattered

**obszarp|ywać (-uję, -ujesz)** (*perf* **-ać**) *vt* to fray
**obszedł** *vb patrz* **obejść**
**obszerny** *adj* (*mieszkanie*) large, spacious; (*płaszcz, koszula*) loose; (*artykuł, sprawozdanie*) extensive
**obszu|kiwać (-kuję, -kujesz)** (*perf* **-kać**) *vt* (*podejrzanego*) to search; (*kieszenie, dom*) to search, to go through
**obszy|cie (-cia, -cia)** (*gen pl* **-ć**) *nt* hem
**obtacz|ać (-am, -asz)** (*perf* **obtoczyć**) *vt* (*na tokarce*) to turn; (*w mące*) to coat; (*w bułce tartej*) to bread
**obtar|cie (-cia, -cia)** (*gen pl* **-ć**) *nt* sore
**obtarł** *itd. vb patrz* **obetrzeć**
**obtłu|c (-kę, -czesz)** (*imp* **-cz**, *pt* **-kł**) *vb perf od* **obtłukiwać**
**obtłu|kiwać (-kuję, -kujesz)** (*perf* **obtłuc**) *vt* to chip
**obu** *num gen, dat, loc, instr od* **oba, obaj, obie**
**obuch (-a, -y)** *m* head (*of an axe*)
**obud|owa (-owy, -owy)** (*gen pl* **-ów**) *f* casing, housing
**obud|ować (-uję, -ujesz)** *vb perf od* **obudowywać**
**obudow|ywać (-uję, -ujesz)** (*perf* **-ać**) *vt* (*otaczać budynkami*) to build round, to surround (with buildings); (*zaopatrywać w osłonę*) to encase; (*wyposażać w meble wbudowane na stałe*) to have fitted
**obu|dzić (-dzę, -dzisz)** (*imp* **-dź**) *vb perf od* **budzić**
**obumarły** *adj* dead
**obumier|ać (-am, -asz)** (*perf* **obumrzeć**) *vi* (*o tkankach*) to atrophy; (*o uczuciach*) to die; (*o tradycjach*) to die out
**obum|rzeć (-rę, -rzesz)** (*imp* **-rzyj**) *vb perf od* **obumierać**
**obunóż** *adv* with both feet
**oburącz** *adv* with both hands
**oburz|ać (-am, -asz)** (*perf* **-yć**) *vt* (*złościć*) to revolt, to appal (*Brit*), to appall (*US*); **oburzać się** *vr*: **~ się (na kogoś/coś)** to be *lub* feel indignant (with sb/at sth)
**oburzający** *adj* outrageous
**oburzeni|e (-a)** *nt* indignation
**oburzony** *adj*: **~ (na kogoś/coś)** indignant (with sb/at sth)
**obustronny** *adj* (*korzyść, porozumienie*) bilateral, mutual; (*pomoc, niechęć*) mutual, reciprocal
**obuwi|e (-a)** *nt* footwear
**obuwnict|wo (-wa)** (*loc sg* **-wie**) *nt* shoe industry
**obuwniczy** *adj* shoe *attr*
**obwarzan|ek (-ka, -ki)** (*instr sg* **-kiem**) *m* pretzel
**obwą|chiwać (-chuję, -chujesz)** (*perf* **-chać**) *vt* to sniff at
**obwią|zać (-żę, -żesz)** *vb perf od* **obwiązywać**
**obwiąz|ywać (-uję, -ujesz)** (*perf* **-ać**) *vt* (*sznurkiem, bandażem*) to tie; (*szalikiem*) to wrap round
**obwie|sić (-szę, -sisz)** (*imp* **-ś**) *vb perf od* **obwieszać**
**obwiesz|ać (-am, -asz)** (*perf* **obwiesić**) *vt*: **~ coś czymś** to decorate *lub* festoon sth with sth
**obwieszcz|ać (-am, -asz)** (*perf* **obwieścić**) *vt* to announce
**obwieszcze|nie (-nia, -nia)** (*gen pl* **-ń**) *nt* announcement
**obwie|ścić (-szczę, -ścisz)** (*imp* **-ść**) *vb perf od* **obwieszczać**
**obwi|eźć (-ozę, -eziesz)** (*imp* **-eź**, *pt* **-ózł, -ozła, -eźli**) *vb perf od* **obwozić**
**obwi|niać (-niam, -niasz)** (*perf* **-nić**) *vt*: **~ kogoś (o coś)** to accuse sb (of sth)
**obwi|nić (-nię, -nisz)** (*imp* **-ń**) *vb perf od* **obwiniać**
**obwisły** *adj* (*wąsy, uszy*) droopy; (*gałąź*) drooping
**obwodnic|a (-y, -e)** *f* bypass, ring road (*Brit*), beltway (*US*)
**obwodowy** *adj* district *attr*; **~ układ nerwowy** peripheral nervous system
**obwolu|ta (-ty, -ty)** (*dat sg* **-cie**) *f* dust cover
**obwoł|ywać (-uję, -ujesz)** (*perf* **-ać**) *vt*: **~ kogoś królem/przewodniczącym** to proclaim sb king/chair
**obwo|zić (-żę, -zisz)** (*perf* **obwieźć**) *vt*: **~ kogoś po mieście** to drive sb around town
**obwoźny** *adj*: **handel ~** house-to-house selling, door-to-door sales
**obw|ód (-odu, -ody)** (*loc sg* **-odzie**) *m* (*Geom: okręgu*) circumference; (*wielokąta*) periphery; (*Elektr*) circuit; (*okręg*) district; **~ drukowany** printed circuit
**obwód|ka (-ki, -ki)** (*dat sg* **-ce**) *f* border(ing)
**oby** *part*: **oby tak było** I wish it were so; **obyś był szczęśliwy** may you be happy ▹ *excl*: **oby!** if only it were so!
**obyci|e (-a)** *nt* manners *pl*; **~ z czymś** familiarity with sth
**obyczaj (-u, -e)** *m* (*zwyczaj*) custom; (*nawyk, przyzwyczajenie*) habit; **obyczaje** *pl* (*maniery*) manners *pl*; (*sposób życia*) morals *pl*; **kobieta lekkich ~ów** a woman of easy virtue
**obyczajowoś|ć (-ci)** *f* (*obyczaje*) customs *pl*; (*moralność*) morals *pl*; (*maniery*) manners *pl*
**obyczajowy** *adj* (*swoboda*) moral; **film ~** ≈ (film) drama; **powieść/komedia obyczajowa** a novel/comedy of manners; **policja obyczajowa** vice squad
**obyczajów|ka (-ki, -ki)** (*dat sg* **-ce**, *gen pl* **-ek**) *f* (*pot*) vice squad

O

**ob|yć się (-ędę, -ędziesz)** *(imp* **-ądź***) vb perf od* **obywać się**
**obydwa** *(jak:* **dwa***) num* both; *patrz też* **oba**
**obydwaj** *(jak:* **dwaj***) num* both; *patrz też* **obaj**
**obydwie** *(jak:* **dwie***) num* both; *patrz też* **obie**
**obydwoje** *(jak:* **dwoje***) num* both; *patrz też* **oboje**
**obyty** *adj (towarzysko)* well-mannered; **być ~m z czymś** to be familiar with sth
**obyw|ać się (-am, -asz)** *(perf* **obyć***) vr:* **obywać się bez czegoś** to do *lub* go without sth, to dispense with sth; **obywać się czymś** to make do with sth; **obyło się bez wypadku** an accident was avoided; **nie obyło się bez płaczu** tears flowed
**obywatel** (**-a, -e**) *(gen pl* **-i***) m* citizen; **~ Kowalski** citizen Kowalski; **~ honorowy** honorary citizen; **szary ~** the man in the street
**obywatel|ka** (**-ki, -ki**) *(dat sg* **-ce**, *gen pl* **-ek***) f* citizen
**obywatelski** *adj (prawo)* civil; *(obowiązek, komitet)* civic
**obywatelst|wo** (**-wa**) *(loc sg* **-wie***) nt* citizenship; **~ honorowe** honorary citizenship; **podwójne ~** dual citizenship
**obżarst|wo** (**-wa**) *(loc sg* **-wie***) nt* gluttony
**obżartuch** (**-a, -y**) *m* glutton, gourmand
**obżer|ać się (-am, -asz)** *(perf* **obeżreć***) vr:* **obżerać się czymś** *(pot)* to gorge o.s. on *lub* with sth
**ocal|ać (-am, -asz)** *(perf* **-ić***) vt* to save; **ocalić coś od zniszczenia/zapomnienia** to save sth from ruin/oblivion; **ocalić kogoś od śmierci** to deliver sb from death
**ocale|ć (-ję, -jesz)** *vi perf* to survive
**ocale|nie** (**-nia, -nia**) *nt* rescue, salvation
**ocal|ić (-ę, -isz)** *vb perf od* **ocalać**
**occie** *n patrz* **ocet**
**ocea|n** (**-nu, -ny**) *(loc sg* **-nie***) m* ocean; *(przen: mnóstwo)* oceans *pl*, sea; **za ~em** over the ocean; **O~ Atlantycki** the Atlantic (Ocean); **O~ Spokojny** the Pacific (Ocean); **O~ Indyjski** the Indian Ocean; **O~ Lodowaty** the Arctic Ocean
**Oceani|a** (**-i**) *f* Oceania, South Sea Islands *pl*
**oceaniczny** *adj (dno)* ocean *attr*; *(klimat, prąd)* oceanic; *(statek)* ocean-going
**oce|na** (**-ny, -ny**) *(dat sg* **-nie***) f (osąd)* assessment, opinion; *(Szkol: stopień)* mark *(Brit)*, grade *(US)*; *(oszacowanie)* estimate, evaluation
**oce|niać (-niam, -niasz)** *(perf* **-nić***) vt (osądzać)* to judge, to assess; *(szacować)* to estimate, to evaluate; **~ straty na 1 mln zł** to estimate the losses at 1 million zloty
**oce|nić (-nię, -nisz)** *(imp* **-ń***) vb perf od* **oceniać**
**oc|et** (**-tu, -ty**) *(loc sg* **-cie***) m (Kulin)* vinegar
**ochla|pać (-pię, -piesz)** *vb perf od* **ochlapywać**
**ochlapu|s** (**-sa, -sy**) *(loc sg* **-sie***) m (pot)* boozer *(pot)*
**ochlap|ywać (-uję, -ujesz)** *(perf* **-ać***) vt (opryskiwać)* to splash; *(plamić)* to splash, to spatter
**ochładz|ać (-am, -asz)** *(perf* **ochłodzić***) vt (mleko, wodę)* to cool; *(wino)* to chill; *(orzeźwiać)* to cool, to refresh; **ochładzać się** *vr (stawać się chłodnym)* to cool; *(oziębiać się)* to cool (down); *(orzeźwiać się)* to cool off; *(o stosunkach)* to cool, to chill; **ochładza się** it's getting colder
**ochła|p** (**-pu, -py**) *(loc sg* **-pie***) m (kawał mięsa)* scrap of meat; **ochłapy** *pl (resztki jedzenia)* scraps *pl*
**ochło|da** (**-dy**) *(dat sg* **-dzie***) f* refreshment; **dla ochłody** for refreshment
**ochłodze|nie** (**-nia**) *nt (Meteo)* cold(er) weather; *(stosunków)* cooling
**ochł|odzić (-odzę, -odzisz)** *(imp* **-odź** *lub* **-ódź***) vb perf od* **ochładzać**
**ochło|nąć (-nę, -niesz)** *(imp* **-ń***) vi perf (ochłodzić się)* to cool off; *(oprzytomnieć, uspokoić się)* to cool down; **~ z gniewu** to cool down; **~ ze strachu** to recover from fright
**ochmistrz** (**-a, -e** *lub* **-owie**) *m* chief steward
**ochoczy** *adj* cheerful
**ocho|ta** (**-ty**) *(dat sg* **-cie***) f (chęć)* willingness, readiness; *(radość)* cheerfulness; **z ochotą** eagerly, willingly; **mieć ochotę na coś** to feel like sth; **mieć ochotę coś zrobić** to feel like doing sth; **odbierać (odebrać** *perf***) komuś ochotę do czegoś** to put sb (right) off sth; **nabierać (nabrać** *perf***) ochoty do czegoś** to begin to like *lub* want sth; **czy masz ochotę na ...?** would you like ...?
**ochotnicz|ka** (**-ki, -ki**) *(dat sg* **-ce**, *gen pl* **-ek***) f* volunteer
**ochotniczy** *adj* voluntary, volunteer *attr*; **Ochotnicza Straż Pożarna** Voluntary Fire Brigade
**ochotni|k** (**-ka, -cy**) *(instr sg* **-kiem***) m* volunteer; **kto na ~a?** any volunteers?; **zgłosić się** *lub* **pójść** *(perf)* **na ~a** to volunteer
**och|ra** (**-ry**) *(dat sg* **-rze***) f* ochre
**ochraniacz** (**-a, -e**) *(gen pl* **-y***) m* guard; *(na kolano, ramię)* pad
**ochrani|ać (-am, -asz)** *(perf* **ochronić***) vt:* **~ kogoś/coś (od czegoś)** to protect sb/sth (from sth); **~ kogoś/coś przed kimś/czymś** to protect sb/sth against *lub* from sb/sth; **ochraniać się** *vr:* **~ się przed czymś** to protect o.s. from sth, to guard o.s. against sth
**ochro|na** (**-ny**) *(dat sg* **-nie***) f (zabezpieczenie)* protection; *(straż)* guard; **~ od czegoś** *lub*

**przed czymś** protection from *lub* against sth; ~ **przyrody** nature conservation *lub* preservation; ~ **środowiska** environment(al) protection; ~ **prawna** legal protection; **zwierzę/roślina pod ochroną** a protected species; ~ **osobista** bodyguard
**ochroniarz** (**-a, -e**) (*gen pl* **-y**) *m* (*pot*) bodyguard
**ochro|nić (-nię, -nisz)** (*imp* **-ń**) *vb perf od* **ochraniać**
**ochronny** *adj* protective; **znak** ~ (*Handel*) trademark; **okres** *lub* **czas** ~ (*łowiectwo*) close season (*Brit*), closed season (*US*); **barwa ochronna** (*Zool*) protective colo(u)ring
**ochrypły** *adj* hoarse
**ochryp|nąć (-nę, -niesz)** (*imp* **-nij**, *pt* **-nął** *lub* **-ł, -ła, -nęli** *lub* **-li**) *vi perf* to get hoarse
**ochrypnięty** *adj* hoarse
**ochrza|n** (**-nu**) (*loc sg* **-nie**) *m* (*pot*): **dostać** (*perf*) ~ to be given a dressing-down (*pot*)
**ochrza|nić (-nię, -nisz)** (*imp* **-ń**) *vt perf* (*pot*) to dress down (*pot*)
**ochrz|cić (-czę, -cisz)** (*imp* **-cij**) *vb perf od* **chrzcić**
**ociąg|ać się (-am, -asz)** *vr*: **ociągać się (z czymś)** to delay (doing sth)
**ociek|ać (-am, -asz)** (*perf* **-nąć**) *vi*: ~ **wodą/krwią** to drip with water/blood
**ociek|nąć (-nę, -niesz)** (*imp* **-nij**, *pt* **-ł** *lub* **-nął, -ła, -li**) *vb perf od* **ociekać**
**ociemniały** *adj* blind ▷ *m decl like adj* blind person; **ociemniali** the blind
**ocie|niać (-niam, -niasz)** (*perf* **-nić**) *vt* to shade
**ocie|nić (-nię, -nisz)** (*imp* **-ń**) *vb perf od* **ocieniać**
**ocieplacz** (**-a, -e**) (*gen pl* **-y**) *m* (*pot: podpinka*) (detachable) lining
**ocieplać (-am, -asz)** (*perf* **-ić**) *vt* (*ogrzewać*) to warm; (*izolować od zimna*) to insulate; **ocieplać się** *vr*: **ociepla się** it's getting warmer
**ocieplen|ie** (**-a**) *nt* (*klimatu*) warming up; (*w pogodzie*) warmer weather
**ocier|ać (-am, -asz)** (*perf* **otrzeć**) *vt* (*wycierać*) to wipe (away); (*ścierać skórę*) to graze; **ocierać się** *vr* (*wycierać się*) to wipe one's face; ~ **się o kogoś** to brush *lub* rub against sb; (*mieć kontakty*) to rub shoulders with sb; **otrzeć** (*perf*) **się o coś** (*dotknąć*) to brush *lub* rub against sth; (*poznać*) to come across sth
**ociężały** *adj* languid
**ock|nąć (-nę, -niesz)** (*imp* **-nij**) *vt perf* (*przebudzić*) to wake (up), to awake; (*wyrwać z zadumy*) to rouse; **ocknąć się** *vr* to rouse o.s.; ~ **się ze snu** to be roused from sleep, to awake
**ocl|ić (-ę, -isz)** *vb perf od* **clić**
**octu** *itd. n patrz* **ocet**
**ocuc|ać (-am, -asz)** (*perf* **ocucić**) *vt* to revive, to bring round
**ocu|cić (-cę, -cisz)** (*imp* **-ć**) *vb perf od* **cucić, ocucać**
**ocukrz|yć (-ę, -ysz)** *vb perf od* **cukrzyć**
**oczar|ować (-uję, -ujesz)** *vb perf od* **oczarowywać**
**oczarow|ywać (-uję, -ujesz)** (*perf* **-ać**) *vt* (*zachwycać*) to charm, to enchant; (*ujmować*) to put *lub* cast a spell on
**ocze|kiwać (-kuję, -kujesz)** *vt*: ~ **kogoś/czegoś** (*czekać*) to await sb/sth, to wait for sb/sth; (*spodziewać się*) to expect sb/sth; **oczekuje się, że ...** it is expected that ...
**oczekiwa|nie** (**-nia, -nia**) (*gen pl* **-ń**) *nt* awaiting; **oczekiwania** *pl* (*nadzieje*) expectations *pl*, hopes *pl*; (*przypuszczenia*) expectations *pl*; **moje oczekiwania sprawdziły się** my expectations were confirmed; **spełnić/zawieść** (*perf*) **czyjeś oczekiwania** to meet/fall short of sb's expectations; **przechodzić (przejść** *perf*) **wszelkie oczekiwania** to exceed *lub* surpass all expectation(s); **wbrew (wszelkim) oczekiwaniom** contrary to (all) expectation(s)
**oczer|niać (-niam, -niasz)** (*perf* **-nić**) *vt* to defame
**oczer|nić (-nię, -nisz)** (*imp* **-ń** *lub* **-nij**) *vb perf od* **oczerniać**
**ocz|ko** (**-ka, -ka**) (*instr sg* **-kiem**, *gen pl* **-ek**) *nt dimin od* **oko**; (*kamień w pierścionku*) stone; (*w sitku, tarce*) mesh; (*Dziewiarstwo*) stitch; (*w pończosze*) ladder (*Brit*), run (*US*); (*Karty*) blackjack; **pawie** ~ (*Zool*) guppy; **być czyimś oczkiem w głowie** to be the apple of sb's eye; **puszczać (puścić** *perf*) **do kogoś (perskie)** ~ to wink at sb, to make eyes at sb
**oczny** *adj* (*nerw*) optic; (*chirurgia*) ophthalmic; **gałka oczna** eyeball
**oczod|ół** (**-ołu, -oły**) (*loc sg* **-ole**) *m* eye socket *lub* hole, orbit (*Med*)
**oczy** *itd. n patrz* **oko**
**oczyszcz|ać (-am, -asz)** (*perf* **oczyścić**) *vt* (*ranę*) to clean; (*powietrze, wodę*) to purify; **oczyszczać się** *vr* to get cleaned; ~ **kogoś z winy/zarzutów** to clear sb of guilt/charges; ~ **się z winy/zarzutów** to be cleared of guilt/charges
**oczyszczal|nia** (**-ni, -nie**) (*gen pl* **-ni**) *f* (*też*: **oczyszczalnia ścieków**) sewage treatment plant
**oczy|ścić (-szczę, -ścisz)** (*imp* **-ść**) *vb perf od* **oczyszczać**
**oczytany** *adj* well-read
**oczywistoś|ć** (**-ci**) *f* obviousness

O

**oczywisty** *adj* (*twierdzenie, dowód*) obvious; (*kłamstwo, nonsens*) outright, obvious; **to oczywiste** it's obvious
**oczywiście** *adv* obviously, certainly; **~!** of course!

 SŁOWO KLUCZOWE

**od** *prep +gen* **1** (*kierunek*) from; **od okna** from the window; **od zachodu** from the west; **na zachód od Polski** west of Poland
**2** (*czas trwania*) for; **od trzech dni** for three days; **od dawna** for a long time
**3** (*początek*) since; **od poniedziałku** since Monday; **od wczoraj** since yesterday; **od jutra** starting tomorrow, as of *lub* from tomorrow; **od poniedziałku do piątku** Monday to Friday (*Brit*), Monday through Friday (*US*); **od rana do nocy** from morning till night
**4** (*odległość*) (away) from; **100 metrów od brzegu** a hundred meters off *lub* away from the shore
**5** (*dolna granica zakresu*) from; **od trzech do czterech godzin dziennie** (from) three to four hours a day
**6** (*początkowa granica skali*) (starting) from; **od wierszy (aż) po powieści** from poems to novels
**7** (*przyczyna*) with, from; **twarz mokra od łez/potu** face damp with tears/sweat; **ochrypł od krzyku** his voice grew hoarse from shouting
**8** (*pochodzenie*) from; **list od mojego brata** a letter from my brother
**9** (*przeznaczenie*): **kluczyki od samochodu** car keys; **pudełko od zapałek** matchbox; **syrop od kaszlu** cough mixture; **ubezpieczenie od ognia/kradzieży** insurance against theft/fire
**10** (*specjalizacja*): **nauczyciel od angielskiego** English teacher; **fachowiec od lodówek** fridge technician
**11** (*przy porównaniach*) than; **ona jest starsza od brata** she is older than her brother; **on jest wyższy ode mnie** he is taller than me *lub* I
**12**: **cena od sztuki** item price; **praca płatna od godziny** work paid by the hour
**13**: **zwolnienie od podatku** tax remission; **odstępstwo od reguły** exception to the rule

**oda** (**od, ody**) (*dat sg* **odzie**) *f* ode
**odbar|wiać (-wiam, -wiasz)** (*perf* **-wić**) *vt* to discolour (*Brit*), to discolor (*US*); **odbarwiać się** *vr* to discolour (*Brit*), to discolor (*US*)
**odbezpiecz|ać (-am, -asz)** (*perf* **-yć**) *vt* to unlock
**odbęb|niać (-niam, -niasz)** (*perf* **-nić**) *vt* (*pot: wykonywać niedbale*) to dash off (*pot*), to rattle off (*pot*); (*odgrywać na bębnie*) to drum; (*niedbale odgrywać na fortepianie*) to thump out
**odbęb|nić (-nię, -nisz)** (*imp* **-nij**) *vb perf od* **odbębniać**
**odbędzie** *itd. vb patrz* **odbyć się**
**odbi|cie** (**-cia, -cia**) (*gen pl* **-ć**) *nt* (*obraz odbity*) reflection; (*podobizna*) image; (*Fiz*) reflection; (*odcisk*) print; (*ciosu*) parry; (*piłki: odebranie*) return; (*: zakozłowanie*) bounce; (*więźniów*) rescue
**odbi|ć (-ję, -jesz)** *vb perf od* **odbijać**
**odbie|c (-gnę, -gniesz)** (*imp* **-gnij**, *pt* **-gł**) *vb perf od* **odbiegać**
**odbieg|ać (-am, -asz)** (*perf* **odbiec** *lub* **-nąć**) *vi* to run off *lub* away; **~ od czegoś** (*przen*) to depart *lub* differ from sth; **~ od tematu** to stray (away) from the subject
**odbie|gnąć (-gnę, -gniesz)** (*imp* **-gnij**, *pt* **-gł**) *vb perf od* **odbiegać**
**odbier|ać (-am, -asz)** (*perf* **odebrać**) *vt* (*odzyskiwać*) to get back, to reclaim; (*otrzymywać*) to receive; (*zgłaszać się po: paczkę, bagaż, list*) to collect; (*: dziecko, chorego, znajomego*) to pick up; (*telefon*) to pick up, to answer; (*pozbawiać: głos, rozum, apetyt, chęć*) to deprive of, to take away; (*: prawo, przywilej*) to withdraw, to take away; (*zabierać przemocą*) to seize, to confiscate; (*stację, fale*) to receive; (*odczuwać*) to experience; **~ coś od kogoś** to pick sth up from sb; **~ coś komuś** to take sth away from sb; **odebrać** (*perf*) **komuś/sobie życie** to take away sb's/one's life; **odebrać** (*perf*) **staranne wychowanie** to receive a thorough education; **jak odebrałeś ten film?** how did you like that film?
**odbij|ać (-am, -asz)** (*perf* **odbić**) *vt* (*światło, fale, obraz*) to reflect; (*piłkę: z powrotem*) to return; (*: o ziemię*) to bounce; (*pieczęć, stempel*) to put; (*ślady*) to leave; (*więźnia, jeńca*) to rescue; (*tynk*) to hammer down; (*drukować*) to print; (*odzyskiwać*) to retake, to recapture ▷ *vi* (*odłączać się od grupy*) to break away; **~ od czegoś** (*kontrastować*) to stand out against sth; **~ (od brzegu)** (*o łodzi*) to set sail, to cast off; **odbić komuś dziewczynę/chłopaka** to steal sb's girlfriend/boyfriend; **odbić kogoś w tańcu** to cut in on sb (*when dancing*); **odbijać się** *vr* to be reflected; (*o śladach, wzorze*) to leave traces; (*o piłce*) to bounce (off); **~ się na czymś** to have an impact on sth; **odbiło mu się** he belched *lub* burped; **odbić się głośnym echem** to reverberate; **~ sobie straty na kimś/czymś** to use sb/sth to make up for the losses; **~ na kimś swój gniew/złość** to vent one's anger on sb

**odbijan|y** (**-ego**) *m decl like adj* switch-partners (dance)
**odbiorc|a** (**-y, -y**) *m decl like f in sg* (*informacji*) recipient, receiver; (*przesyłki*) addressee; (*energii*) consumer; (*sztuki, literatury*) audience
**odbiorę** *itd. vb patrz* **odebrać**
**odbiornik** (**-a, -i**) *m* (*Elektr*) receiver; (*też*: **odbiornik radiowy**) radio set *lub* receiver; (*też*: **odbiornik telewizyjny**) TV set
**odbi|ór** (**-oru**) (*loc sg* **-orze**) *m* (*listu, bagażu, towaru*) receipt, collection; (*filmu, sztuki*) reception; (*Radio, TV, Tel*) reception; **~!** (*Tel*) over!
**odbit|ka** (**-ki, -ki**) (*dat sg* **-ce**) *f* print
**odblas|k** (**-ku, -ki**) *m* reflex, reflection
**odblaskowy** *adj*: **światło odblaskowe** reflector
**odblok|ować (-uję, -ujesz)** *vb perf od* **odblokowywać**
**odblokow|ywać (-uję, -ujesz)** (*perf* **-ać**) *vt* (*drogę*) to clear; (*koła, kierownicę*) to free; (*konto*) to unblock
**odbudo|wa** (**-wy**) (*dat sg* **-wie**) *f* reconstruction
**odbud|ować (-uję, -ujesz)** *vb perf od* **odbudowywać**
**odbudow|ywać (-uję, -ujesz)** (*perf* **-ać**) *vt* (*dom, miasto*) to reconstruct, to rebuild; (*przen*: *zaufanie, wiarę*) to restore
**odbur|kiwać (-kuję, -kujesz)** (*perf* **-knąć**) *vt* to answer back, to talk back
**odburk|nąć (-nę, -niesz)** *vb perf od* **odburkiwać**
**odb|yć (-ędę, -ędziesz)** (*imp* **-ądź**) *vb perf od* **odbywać**
**odby|t** (**-tu, -ty**) (*loc sg* **-cie**) *m* anus
**odbytnic|a** (**-y, -e**) *f* rectum
**odbyw|ać (-am, -asz)** (*perf* **odbyć**) *vt* (*kurs*) to do; (*służbę wojskową*) to serve; **~ praktykę** (*w fabryce*) to serve one's apprenticeship; (*w szkole*) to do teaching practice; **~ wartę** to stand watch; **odbywać się** *vr* to take place
**odce|dzać (-dzam, -dzasz)** (*perf* **-dzić**) *vt* to strain, to drain
**odce|dzić (-dzę, -dzisz)** (*imp* **-dź**) *vb perf od* **odcedzać**
**odchodnym** *inv*: **na ~** on leaving
**odchod|y** (**-ów**) *pl* (*ekskrementy*) excrement, faeces (Brit), feces (US)
**odcho|dzić (-dzę, -dzisz)** (*imp* **-dź**, *perf* **odejść**) *vi* (*oddalać się*) to go away, to walk away; (*o pociągu, transporcie*) to leave, to depart; (*umierać*) to pass away; (*zwalniać się z pracy*) to leave; (*o gałęziach*) to spread out; (*o ulicach*) to diverge, to branch off; (*o lakierze, farbie*) to come *lub* flake off, to peel (off); **odejść od kogoś** to leave sb; **odejść na emeryturę** to retire; **odejść ze stanowiska** to leave office; **~ od rozumu** *lub* **zmysłów ze zmartwienia** to be out of one's mind *lub* senses with worry
**odchrza|nić się (-nię, -nisz)** (*imp* **-ń**) (*pot*) *vr perf*: **odchrzanić się od kogoś/czegoś** to give sb/sth a break *lub* rest; **odchrzań się!** get off my back!, bugger off! (*pot*)
**odchrzą|kiwać (-kuję, -kujesz)** (*perf* **-knąć**) *vi* to clear one's throat ▷ *vt* (*flegmę*) to spit; (*krew*) to cough up
**odchrząk|nąć (-nę, -niesz)** (*imp* **-nij**) *vb perf od* **odchrząkiwać**
**odchu|dzać się (-dzam, -dzasz)** (*perf* **-dzić**) *vr* to slim, to diet
**odchudzani|e** (**-a**) *nt* slimming, dieting
**odchu|dzić (-dzę, -dzisz)** *vb perf od* **odchudzać się**
**odchyl|ać (-am, -asz)** (*perf* **-ić**) *vt* (*gałąź, firankę*) to pull *lub* draw back; (*głowę*) to tilt; **odchylać się** *vr* to bend *lub* swing (aside)
**odchyle|nie** (**-nia, -nia**) (*gen pl* **-ń**) *nt* deviation
**odciąć (odetnę, odetniesz)** (*imp* **odetnij**) *vb perf od* **odcinać**
**odciąg|ać (-am, -asz)** (*perf* **-nąć**) *vt* (*przesuwać*) to pull away; (*odwlekać*) to put off, to delay; **~ kogoś od czegoś** to pull sb away from sth; **~ czyjąś uwagę** to divert sb's attention
**odciąg|nąć (-nę, -niesz)** (*imp* **-nij**) *vb perf od* **odciągać**
**odciąż|ać (-am, -asz)** (*perf* **-yć**) *vt* (*osobę, konia*) to relieve; (*centralę*) to lighten the load of; **~ kogoś od obowiązków** to relieve sb of their duties
**odcie|c (-knie)** (*pt* **-kł**) *vb perf od* **odciekać**
**odciek|ać (-a)** (*perf* **odciec**) *vi* (*o cieczy*) to flow away; (*o ziemniakach, sałacie*) to drain
**odcie|ń** (**-nia, -nie**) (*gen pl* **-ni**) *m* (*barwa*) tint, shade; (*niuans*) shade
**odcięt|a** (**-ej, -e**) *f decl like adj* (*Mat*) abscissa
**odcięty** *adj*: **być ~m od świata** to be cut off from the rest of the world
**odcin|ać (-am, -asz)** (*perf* **odciąć**) *vt* to cut off; (*gałąź, przewód*) to cut off, to sever; (*rękę, palec*) to sever, to amputate; (*dostęp, odwrót*) to cut *lub* seal off; **odcinać się** *vr* (*ostro odpowiadać*) to retort, to answer back; **~ się od** *+gen* (*dystansować się*) to distance o.s. from; (*kontrastować*) to be in contrast with; **dałbym sobie rękę uciąć, że ...** I would give my right arm that ...
**odcin|ek** (**-ka, -ki**) (*instr sg* **-kiem**) *m* (*drogi, przewodu*) section; (*czasu*) period; (*kwit*) stub, receipt; (*powieści, serialu*) episode; (*Mat*) segment; (*dziedzina, zakres*) field, area
**odcinkowy** *adj* serialized
**odcis|k** (**-ku, -ki**) (*instr sg* **-kiem**) *m* (*ślad*) imprint; (*stopy*) footprint; (*palca*) fingerprint;

O

(*nagniotek*) corn; **nastąpić** (*perf*) *lub* **nadepnąć** (*perf*) **komuś na** ~ (*przen*) to tread on sb's corns
**odcis|kać (-kam, -kasz)** (*perf* **-nąć**) *vt* to impress
**odci|snąć (-snę, -śniesz)** (*imp* **-śnij**) *vb perf od* **odciskać**
**odcyfr|ować (-uję, -ujesz)** *vb perf od* **odcyfrowywać**
**odcyfrow|ywać (-uję, -ujesz)** (*perf* **-ać**) *vt* (*pismo, podpis*) to decipher, to make out; (*szyfr*) to decipher, to decode
**odczarow|ywać (-uję, -ujesz)** *vt* (*zdejmować czary*) to remove *lub* break a spell
**odcze|kiwać (-kuję, -kujesz)** (*perf* **-kać**) *vi* to wait
**odcze|piać (-piam, -piasz)** (*perf* **-pić**) *vt* (*odpinać*) to unfasten, to unbutton; (*łódkę, wagon*) to detach; **odczepiać się** *vr* (*odpinać się*) to come off, to become unfastened; (*o łódce, wagonie*) to become detached
**odcze|pić (-pię, -pisz)** *vb perf od* **odczepiać**; **odczepić się** *vr perf*: **~ się od kogoś** (*pot*) to get off sb's back; **odczep się (ode mnie)!** (*pot*) get lost! (*pot*)
**odczepnego** *inv*: **zrobić coś na** ~ to skimp sth
**odczu|cie** (**-cia, -cia**) (*gen pl* **-ć**) *nt* feeling; (*wrażenie*) feeling, sense; **w moim odczuciu** in my judgement; **jakie jest twoje ~?** how do you feel about it?
**odczu|ć (-ję, -jesz)** *vb perf od* **odczuwać**
**odczuw|ać (-am, -asz)** (*perf* **odczuć**) *vt* to feel; (*wrogość, zmiany*) to sense; **dawać (dać** *perf*) **komuś coś odczuć** to show sb how one feels about sth; **w pokoju dało się odczuć napięcie** a tension was felt in the room
**odczuwalny** *adj* noticeable
**odczynni|k** (**-ka, -ki**) (*instr sg* **-kiem**) *m* (*Chem*) reagent
**odczy|t** (**-tu, -ty**) (*loc sg* **-cie**) *m* (*wykład, prelekcja*) lecture; (*wyników, danych w komputerze*) reading
**odczyt|ywać (-uję, -ujesz)** (*perf* **-ać**) *vt* to read; (*czytać na głos*) to read out
**odd|ać (-am, -asz)** (*3 pl* **-adzą**) *vb perf od* **oddawać**
**oddal|ać (-am, -asz)** (*perf* **-ić**) *vt* (*wniosek, powództwo*) to dismiss; **oddalać się** *vr* (*odchodzić*) to walk *lub* go away; (*odjeżdżać*: *o samochodzie*) to drive away; (*o koniu, rowerze*) to ride away; (*odlatywać*) to fly away; (*odpływać*: *o statku*) to sail away; (*o brzegu*) to vanish away
**oddali** *inv*: **w** ~ in the distance; **z** ~ from a distance
**oddalony** *adj* remote, distant; **wioska jest oddalona 20 km od miasta** the village is 20 km away from the town
**oddani|e** (**-a**) *nt* (*poświęcenie*) devotion; (*gorliwość*) dedication
**oddany** *adj*: **być ~m komuś/czemuś** (*być przywiązanym*) to be devoted to sb/sth; (*być zaabsorbowanym*) to be dedicated to sb/sth
**odd|awać (-aję, -ajesz)** (*imp* **-awaj**, *perf* **-ać**) *vt* (*książkę*) to return; (*resztę*) to give; (*dług, pożyczkę*) to give *lub* pay back; (*zostawiać w celu wykonania usługi*: *buty, bagaż, film*) to leave; (*zostawiać na przechowanie*: *pieniądze, biżuterię*) to deposit; (*powierzać opiece*: *chorego, ucznia*) to send (*to school, hospital*); (*głos, pierwszeństwo*) to give; (*majątek, bogactwo*) to renounce; (*uścisk, pocałunek*) to return; (*cios*) to return, to hit back; (*uczucia, znaczenie*) to express; (*podobieństwo, nastrój*) to render; **~ komuś przysługę** to do sb a favour (*Brit*) *lub* favor (*US*); **~ życie (za kogoś/coś)** to lay down *lub* give one's life (for sb/sth); **~ krew** to give *lub* donate blood; **~ komuś sprawiedliwość** to do sb justice; **~ kogoś/coś w czyjeś ręce** to hand sb/sth over to sb; **oddawać się** *vr* (*poddawać się*) to give o.s. in; (*o kobiecie*) to give o.s.; **~ się czemuś** (*smutkowi, nałogowi*) to take to sth; (*pracy, rozmyślaniu*) to devote o.s. to sth; (*lenistwu*) to indulge in sth
**oddech** (**-u, -y**) *m* breath; **wstrzymywać (wstrzymać** *perf*) ~ to hold one's breath; **zaczerpnąć** (*perf*) **~u** to take a (deep) breath
**oddechowy** *adj* respiratory
**oddeleg|ować (-uję, -ujesz)** *vb perf od* **oddelegowywać**
**oddelegow|ywać (-uję, -ujesz)** (*perf* **-ać**) *vt*: **~ kogoś do** *+gen* to second *lub* assign sb to
**oddolny** *adj* rank-and-file
**oddych|ać (-am, -asz)** *vi* to breathe; **nie ma czym** ~ there is nothing to breathe with; **~ pełną piersią** (*głęboko*) to breathe deeply; (*swobodnie*) to breathe freely
**oddychani|e** (**-a**) *nt* breathing; **sztuczne ~** artificial respiration
**oddzia|ł** (**-łu, -ły**) (*loc sg* **-le**) *m* (*Wojsk*) unit; (*Policja*) squad; (*fabryki, urzędu*) department; (*banku, linii lotniczej*) branch; (*część szpitala*) ward, unit
**oddziałowy** *adj*: **siostra oddziałowa** ward sister
**oddział|ywać (-uję, -ujesz)** *vi*: **~ na** *+acc* to influence, to affect; (*Chem*) to react on
**oddziaływani|e** (**-a**) *nt* (*wpływ*) influence; (*działanie*) effect; (*wzajemne*) interaction
**oddziel|ać (-am, -asz)** (*perf* **-ić**) *vt* (*odgradzać*) to separate; (*odłączać od całości*) to separate, to detach; **oddzielać się** *vr* to separate, to part
**oddzielnie** *adv* separately, apart
**oddzielny** *adj* separate
**oddzier|ać (-am, -asz)** (*perf* **odedrzeć**) *vt* to tear off *lub* away

**oddzwani|ać (-am, -asz)** (*perf* **oddzwonić**) *vi*: ~ **(do kogoś)** to ring *lub* call (sb) back
**oddzwo|nić (-nię, -nisz)** (*imp* **-ń**) *vb perf od* **oddzwaniać**
**oddźwię|k** (**-ku, -ki**) *m* response
**ode** *prep* = **od; jest starszy ode mnie** he is older that I am *lub* me
**odebrać (odbiorę, odbierzesz)** (*imp* **odbierz**) *vb perf od* **odbierać**
**odech|cieć (-ce)** *vb perf od* **odechciewać się**
**odechciew|ać się (-a)** (*perf* **odechcieć**) *vr*: **komuś odechciewa się czegoś** sb feels no longer like doing sth; **odechciało mi się pić** I feel no longer thirsty
**oded|rzeć (-rę, -rzesz)** (*imp* **-rzyj**, *pt* **oddarł**) *vb perf od* **oddzierać**
**odegn|ać (-am, -asz)** *vb perf od* **odganiać**
**odegr|ać (-am, -asz)** *vb perf od* **odgrywać**
**odejm|ować (-uję, -ujesz)** (*perf* **odjąć**) *vt* (*Mat*) to subtract; (*podatek, nadwyżkę*) to deduct; (*szklankę od ust*) to take away; **pomogło jakby ręką odjął** it worked like a charm; **odjęło mu rozum** he lost his mind; **odjęło mi mowę** words failed me; **odbierać komuś apetyt** to spoil sb's appetite
**odejmowani|e** (**-a**) *nt* (*Mat*) subtraction
**odejści|e** (**-a**) *nt* departure, leaving; ~ **od zasad/norm** departure from principles/(the) norms *lub* (the) standards
**odej|ść (-dę, -dziesz)** (*imp* **-dź**, *pt* **odszedł, odeszła, odeszli**) *vb perf od* **odchodzić**
**odepch|nąć (-nę, -niesz)** (*imp* **-nij**) *vb perf od* **odpychać**
**odep|rzeć (-rę, -rzesz)** (*imp* **-rzyj**, *pt* **odparł**) *vb perf od* **odpierać** ▷ *vi perf* (*odpowiedzieć*) to reply; **odparł, że nic nie wie** he replied that he did not know anything; **nie wiem — odparła zdecydowanie** I do not know, she asserted *lub* said firmly
**oder|wać (-wę, -wiesz)** (*imp* **-wij**) *vb perf od* **odrywać**
**oderwanie** *nt*: **w oderwaniu od czegoś** in isolation from sth
**oderwany** *adj* (*fakty, słowa*) out of context; (*pojęcie*) abstract; ~ **od rzeczywistości** (*osoba*) starry-eyed; (*rzecz*) unrealistic
**oderż|nąć (-nę, -niesz)** (*imp* **-nij**) *vb perf od* **odrzynać**
**ode|słać (-ślę, -ślesz)** (*imp* **-ślij**) *vb perf od* **odsyłać**
**ode|spać (-śpię, -śpisz)** (*imp* **-śpij**) *vb perf od* **odsypiać**
**odetch|nąć (-nę, -niesz)** (*imp* **-nij**) *vi perf* (*uspokoić się*) to calm down; (*odpocząć*) to relax; ~ **z ulgą** to breathe a sigh of relief
**odetk|ać (-am, -asz)** *vt perf* (*butelkę*) to open; (*wannę, zlew*) to unblock
**odez|wa** (**-wy, -wy**) (*dat sg* **-wie**) *f* (*manifest*) manifesto
**odez|wać się (-wę, -wiesz)** (*imp* **-wij**) *vb perf od* **odzywać się**
**odfajk|ować (-uję, -ujesz)** *vb perf od* **odfajkowywać**
**odfajkow|ywać (-uję, -ujesz)** *vt* (*zaznaczać*) to tick (off); (*wykonywać byle jak*) to skimp
**odfru|nąć (-nę, -niesz)** *vi perf* to fly away
**odgad|nąć (-nę, -niesz)** (*imp* **-nij**, *pt* **-ł**) *vt perf* (*zagadkę*) to solve; (*prawdę, zamiary*) to guess
**odgałę|ziać się (-zia)** (*perf* **-zić**) *vr* (*o drodze*) to branch off, to fork; (*o kablach*) to branch off
**odgałęzie|nie** (**-nia, -nia**) (*gen pl* **-ń**) *nt* (*kabla*) offshoot; (*torów*) branch line; (*drogi*) fork
**odgani|ać (-am, -asz)** (*perf* **odgonić** *lub* **odegnać**) *vt* to drive away
**odgar|nąć (-nę, -niesz)** (*imp* **-nij**) *vb perf od* **odgarniać**
**odgarni|ać (-am, -asz)** (*perf* **odgarnąć**) *vt* (*śnieg*) to shove aside; (*włosy*) to brush aside
**od|giąć (-egnę, -egniesz)** (*imp* **-egnij**) *vb perf od* **odginać**
**odgin|ać (-am, -asz)** (*perf* **odgiąć**) *vt* (*gwóźdź, pręt*) to straighten, to unbend; (*mankiet*) to pull *lub* fold down
**odgło|s** (**-su, -sy**) (*loc sg* **-sie**) *m* sound
**odgo|nić (-nię, -nisz)** (*imp* **-ń**) *vb perf od* **odganiać**
**odgot|ować (-uję, -ujesz)** *vb perf od* **odgotowywać**
**odgotow|ywać (-uję, -ujesz)** (*perf* **-ać**) *vt* to boil off
**odgórny** *adj*: **odgórne zarządzenie** a directive from above
**odgradz|ać (-am, -asz)** (*perf* **odgrodzić**) *vt* (*płotem*) to fence off; (*murem*) to wall off
**odgraż|ać się (-am, -asz)** *vr* to make threats; **odgrażać się komuś** to threaten sb; **odgrażał się, że powie ojcu** he threatened to tell Father
**odgr|odzić (-odzę, -odzisz)** (*imp* **-odź** *lub* **-ódź**) *vb perf od* **odgradzać**
**odgruzow|ywać (-uję, -ujesz)** (*perf* **-ać**) *vt* to clear of rubble *lub* debris
**odgryw|ać (-am, -asz)** (*perf* **odegrać**) *vt* (*Muz, Teatr*) to play; (*wydarzenie, scenę*) to act out; **odgrywać się** *vr* (*po przegranej*) to get one's revenge; ~ **się na kimś (za coś)** to revenge o.s. *lub* take revenge on sb (for sth); ~ **rolę w czymś** to play a role *lub* part in sth
**odgryz|ać (-am, -asz)** (*perf* **odgryźć**) *vt* to bite off; **odgryzać się** *vr* (*przen: pot*) to strike back
**odgry|źć (-zę, -ziesz)** (*imp* **-ź**, *pt* **-zł, -zła, -źli**) *vb perf od* **odgryzać**
**odgrz|ać (-eję, -ejesz)** *vb perf od* **odgrzewać**

O

**odgrzeb|ywać (-uję, -ujesz)** (*perf* **-ać**) *vt* to dig up; (*przen: niepotrzebnie*) to rake up, to dredge up
**odgrzew|ać (-am, -asz)** (*perf* **odgrzać**) *vt* to warm up; (*przen: wspomnienia, dowcip*) to rehash
**odhacz|ać (-am, -asz)** (*perf* **-yć**) *vt* to check off, to tick off
**odj|azd (-azdu, -azdy)** (*loc sg* **-eździe**) *m* departure; **~!** all aboard!
**od|jąć (-ejmę, -ejmiesz)** (*imp* **-ejmij**) *vb perf od* **odejmować**
**od|jechać (-jadę, -jedziesz)** (*imp* **-jedź**) *vb perf od* **odjeżdżać**
**odjeżdż|ać (-am, -asz)** (*perf* **odjechać**) *vi* (*o osobie*) to leave; (*o autobusie, pociągu*) to depart, to leave; (*samochodem*) to drive away *lub* off; (*na rowerze, konno*) to ride away *lub* off; **pociąg odjechał (ze stacji)** the train drew *lub* pulled out (of the station)
**odkar|miać (-miam, -miasz)** (*perf* **-mić**) *vt* to feed up
**odkaszl|iwać (-uję, -ujesz)** (*perf* **-nąć**) *vi* to cough
**odka|zić (-żę, -zisz)** (*imp* **-ź**) *vb perf od* **odkażać**
**odkaż|ać (-am, -asz)** (*perf* **odkazić**) *vt* to disinfect; (*Wojsk*) to decontaminate
**odkąd** *pron* since; **~?** since when?; **~ mam zacząć?** where shall I start from?; **~ wyjechała** (ever) since she left; **~ pamiętam** for as long as I can remember
**odkle|ić (-ję, -isz)** (*imp* **-j**) *vb perf od* **odklejać**
**odklej|ać (-am, -asz)** (*perf* **odkleić**) *vt* to unstick; **odklejać się** *vr* to come unstuck
**odkład|ać (-am, -asz)** (*perf* **odłożyć**) *vt* (*książkę, pióro*) to put away *lub* aside; (*egzamin, podjęcie decyzji*) to postpone, to put off; (*pieniądze*) to put aside; **~ słuchawkę** to hang up (the phone); **odkładać się** *vr* to accumulate
**odkłani|ać się (-am, -asz)** (*perf* **odkłonić**) *vr*: **odkłaniać się komuś** to return sb's greeting
**odkło|nić się (-nię, -nisz)** (*imp* **-ń**) *vb perf od* **odkłaniać się**
**odko|chiwać się (-chuję, -chujesz)** (*perf* **-chać**) *vr*: **odkochiwać się (w kimś)** to fall out of love (with sb)
**odkop|ywać (-uję, -ujesz)** (*perf* **-ać**) *vt* to dig up, to unearth
**odkorkow|ywać (-uję, -ujesz)** (*perf* **-ać**) *vt* to uncork
**odkraj|ać (-ę, -esz)** *vb perf od* **odkrawać**
**odkraw|ać (-am, -asz)** (*perf* **odkroić** *lub* **odkrajać**) *vt* to cut off
**odkręc|ać (-am, -asz)** (*perf* **odkręcić**) *vt* (*śrubę itp.*) to unscrew; (*wieczko, zakrętkę*) to twist off; (*kurek, wodę, gaz*) to turn on; (*przen*) to undo
**odkrę|cić (-cę, -cisz)** (*imp* **-ć**) *vb perf od* **odkręcać**
**odkr|oić (-oję, -oisz)** (*imp* **-ój**) *vb perf od* **odkrawać**
**odkry|cie (-cia, -cia)** (*gen pl* **-ć**) *nt* discovery; **dokonać** (*perf*) **odkrycia** to make a discovery
**odkry|ć (-ję, -jesz)** *vb perf od* **odkrywać** *patrz też* **odkrycie**
**odkryty** *adj* (*wagon, samochód, teren*) open; (*basen*) outdoor
**odkryw|ać (-am, -asz)** (*perf* **odkryć**) *vt* (*twarz*) to uncover; (*garnek, skrzynię*) to open; (*nowy ląd, metodę, talent*) to discover; (*sekret, tajemnicę*) to uncover, to disclose; (*plany, zamiary*) to unveil, to reveal; **~ Amerykę** (*przen*) to reinvent the wheel; **odkryć karty** (*przen*) to lay *lub* put one's cards on the table
**odkrywc|a (-y, -y)** *m decl like f in sg* (*naukowiec*) discoverer; (*podróżnik*) explorer
**odkrywczy** *adj* (*wyprawa*) exploratory; (*spostrzeżenie*) revealing, insightful
**odkrywkowy** *adj*: **kopalnia odkrywkowa** strip mine
**odkrztu|sić (-szę, -sisz)** (*imp* **-ś**) *vb perf od* **odkrztuszać**
**odkrztusz|ać (-am, -asz)** (*perf* **odksztusić**) *vt* to cough up
**odkształc|ać (-am, -asz)** (*perf* **odkształcić**) *vt* to deform
**odkształ|cić (-cę, -cisz)** (*imp* **-ć**) *vb perf od* **odkształcać**
**odku|ć się (-ję, -jesz)** *vb perf od* **odkuwać się**
**odku|p (-pu)** (*loc sg* **-pie**) *m*: **prawo ~u** option *lub* right of repurchase
**Odkupiciel (-a)** *m* the Redeemer
**odku|pić (-pię, -pisz)** *vb perf od* **odkupywać**
**odkup|ywać (-uję, -ujesz)** (*perf* **odkupić**) *vt* (*odzyskiwać przez kupno*) to buy back, to repurchase; (*winę, zbrodnię*) to expiate, to atone for; **odkupić coś od kogoś** to buy sth from sb; **odkupię ci tę książkę** I'll replace that book
**odkurzacz (-a, -e)** (*gen pl* **-y**) *m* vacuum cleaner, hoover® (Brit)
**odkurz|ać (-am, -asz)** (*perf* **-yć**) *vt* (*wycierać z kurzu*) to dust; (*czyścić odkurzaczem*) to vacuum, to hoover (Brit)
**odkurz|yć (-ę, -ysz)** *vb perf od* **odkurzać**
**odkuw|ać się (-am, -asz)** *vr*: **odkuwać się na kimś** (*pot*) to take revenge on sb
**odl|ać (-eję, -ejesz)** *vb perf od* **odlewać**
**odlat|ywać (-uję, -ujesz)** (*perf* **odlecieć**) *vi* (*o samolocie*) to take off; (*o ptaku*) to fly away *lub* off; (*odpadać*) to fall off; **odleciał samolotem o 11:45** he took the 11:45 flight
**odle|cieć (-cę, -cisz)** (*imp* **-ć**) *vb perf od* **odlatywać**

**odległościomierz** (**-a, -e**) (*gen pl* **-y**) *m* (*Fot*) rangefinder

**odległoś|ć** (**-ci, -ci**) *f* distance; **na ~ ramienia** at arm's length; **w niewielkiej odległości od** *+gen* not far away from

**odległy** *adj* distant, remote; **~ o 300 metrów** 300 metres away

**odle|piać (-piam, -piasz)** (*perf* **-pić**) *vt* to unstick

**odle|w** (**-wu, -wy**) (*loc sg* **-wie**) *m* cast, casting

**odlew|ać (-am, -asz)** (*perf* **odlać**) *vt* (*wykonywać odlew*) to cast; (*: z metalu*) to cast, to found; (*wodę*) to drain off; (*ziemniaki*) to drain; **odlewać się** *vr* (*pot!*) to take *lub* have a leak (*pot!*)

**odlew|nia** (**-ni, -nie**) (*gen pl* **-ni**) *f* foundry

**odlewnict|wo** (**-wa**) (*loc sg* **-wie**) *nt* founding

**odleż|eć (-ę, -ysz)** *vt perf* (*chorobę*) to nurse; **odleżeć się** *vr perf* (*o produktach żywnościowych*) to mature; (*o piśmie, sprawie*) to lie gathering dust; **~ sobie plecy** to develop bedsores on one's back

**odleży|na** (**-ny, -ny**) (*dat sg* **-nie**) *f* bedsore

**odlicz|ać (-am, -asz)** (*perf* **-yć**) *vt* (*pieniądze, krople*) to count; (*koszty*) to deduct; **kolejno odlicz!** (*Wojsk*) count!

**odlo|t** (**-tu, -ty**) (*loc sg* **-cie**) *m* (*samolotu*) departure; (*ptaków*) migration; **godziny ~ów** departure times

**odlotowy** *adj* (*pot*) terrific

**odlud|ek** (**-ka, -ki**) (*instr sg* **-kiem**) *m* recluse

**odludny** *adj* (*dom*) desolate; (*okolica, droga, szlak*) lonely

**odlu|dzie** (**-dzia, -dzia**) (*gen pl* **-dzi**) *nt* secluded spot; **na odludziu** off the beaten track

**odła|m** (**-mu, -my**) (*loc sg* **-mie**) *m* (*skalny, lodu*) block; (*przen*) splinter group; (*Pol*) faction

**odła|mać (-mię, -miesz)** *vb perf od* **odłamywać**

**odłam|ek** (**-ka, -ki**) (*instr sg* **-kiem**) *m* (*szkła itp.*) sliver; (*granatu, pocisku*) shrapnel

**odłam|ywać (-uję, -ujesz)** (*perf* **-ać**) *vt* to break off

**odłącz|ać (-am, -asz)** (*perf* **-yć**) *vt* (*oddzielać*) to separate; (*wagon, prąd, telewizor*) to disconnect; **odłączyć dziecko od piersi** to wean a child; **odłączać się** *vr* (*od grupy, wycieczki*) to straggle

**odłoż|yć (-ę, -ysz)** (*imp* **odłóż**) *vb perf od* **odkładać**

**odł|óg** (**-ogu, -ogi**) *m* uncultivated land; **leżeć odłogiem** (*o ziemi*) to lie fallow

**odłup|ywać (-uję, -ujesz)** (*perf* **-ać**) *vt* to split off

**odmalow|ywać (-uję, -ujesz)** (*perf* **-ać**) *vt* (*ścianę*) to repaint; (*mieszkanie*) to redecorate; (*nastrój, sytuację*) to depict; **odmalowywać się** *vr* (*na czyjejś twarzy, w oczach*) to show

**odmarz|ać (-a)** (*perf* **-nąć**) *vi* (*o mięsie*) to defrost, to thaw; (*o rzece*) to thaw

**odmarz|nąć (-nie)** (*pt* **-ł**) *vb perf od* **odmarzać**

**odmawi|ać (-am, -asz)** (*perf* **odmówić**) *vi* to refuse, to decline ▷ *vt* (*wizytę, spotkanie*) to cancel; **~ modlitwę** to say one's prayers; **~ komuś czegoś** to refuse sb sth; **~ zrobienia czegoś** to refuse to do sth; **~ zgody** to refuse (to give one's) permission; **~ komuś prawa do czegoś** to dispute sb's right to sth; **~ komuś talentu/rozumu** to refuse to acknowledge sb's abilities/intelligence; **~ posłuszeństwa** (*o osobie*) to refuse to obey; **nerwy/nogi odmawiają mi posłuszeństwa** my nerves/legs are failing me; **~ sobie czegoś** to deny o.s. sth

**odmia|na** (**-ny, -ny**) (*dat sg* **-nie**) *f* (*zmiana*) change; (*wariant*) variety; (*Bot, Zool*) strain, variety; (*Jęz*) inflection; **dla odmiany** for a change

**odmie|niać (-niam, -niasz)** (*perf* **-nić**) *vt* (*człowieka, życie*) to transform; (*wyraz*) to inflect; (*czasownik*) to conjugate; (*rzeczownik, zaimek*) to decline; **odmieniać się** *vr* (*o wyrazach*) to inflect

**odmie|nić (-nię, -nisz)** (*imp* **-ń**) *vb perf od* **odmieniać**

**odmiennoś|ć** (**-ci**) *f* distinctness

**odmienny** *adj* (*inny*) different, dissimilar; (*odrębny*) distinct; (*Jęz*) inflected; **być odmiennego zdania** to be of a different opinion; **odmienna forma czasownika** finite verb

**odmierz|ać (-am, -asz)** (*perf* **-yć**) *vt* (*mierzyć*) to measure; (*wydzielać*) to measure out; **~ takt** to beat time; **~ słowa** to weigh one's words

**odmładz|ać (-am, -asz)** (*perf* **odmłodzić**) *vt* (*o fryzurze, uśmiechu*) to make look younger; (*czynić młodszym*) to rejuvenate; (*zespół, kadrę*) to bring new blood into

**odmładzający** *adj*: **kuracja odmładzająca** rejuvenating treatment

**odmłodnie|ć (-ję, -jesz)** *vi perf* (*poczuć się*) to feel younger; (*wyglądać*) to look younger

**odmło|dzić (-dzę, -dzisz)** (*imp* **odmłódź**) *vb perf od* **odmładzać**

**odmo|wa** (**-wy, -wy**) (*dat sg* **-wie**, *gen pl* **odmów**) *f* refusal; **spotkać się** (*perf*) **z odmową** to meet with a refusal

**odmownie** *adv*: **odpowiedzieć** (*perf*) **~ na czyjeś podanie/czyjąś prośbę** to reject *lub* turn down sb's application/request

**odmowny** *adj* (*odpowiedź*) negative

**odmó|wić (-wię, -wisz)** *vb perf od* **odmawiać**

**odmrażacz** (**-a, -e**) (*gen pl* **-y**) *m* defroster

**odmraż|ać (-am, -asz)** *(perf* **odmrozić***) vt* *(szybę, przewód)* to defrost; *(kadłub samolotu)* to de-ice; **odmroziłam sobie ręce/uszy** my hands/ears are frostbitten

**odmr|ozić (-ożę, -ozisz)** *(imp* **-oź** *lub* **-óź***) vb perf od* **odmrażać**

**odmroże|nie** (**-nia**) *nt (Med) (nom pl* **-nia**, *gen pl* **-ń**) frostbite; (*: na palcach rąk lub nóg*) chilblain; *(kapitału, rezerw)* release

**odnaj|ąć (-mę, -miesz)** *(imp* **-mij***) vb perf od* **odnajmować**

**odnajd|ować (-uję, -ujesz)** *(perf* **odnaleźć***) vt* to find; **odnajdować się** *vr (zjawiać się z powrotem)* to show up, to turn up; *(w nowych warunkach)* to find one's feet

**odnajm|ować (-uję, -ujesz)** *(perf* **odnająć***) vt* *(brać w użytkowanie)* to rent; *(odstępować)* to let (out), to rent out

**odna|leźć (-jdę, -jdziesz)** *(imp* **-jdź**, *pt* **-lazł, -lazła, -leźli***) vb perf od* **odnajdować**

**odnawi|ać (-am, -asz)** *(perf* **odnowić***) vt* *(budynek, mieszkanie)* to renovate, to refurbish; *(obraz)* to restore; *(sojusz, znajomość)* to renew

**odnawialny** *adj (zasoby naturalne, źródło energii)* renewable

**odniesie|nie** (**-nia, -nie**) *(gen pl* **-ń***) nt*: **w odniesieniu do** *+gen (książk)* with reference to; **punkt/układ odniesienia** point/frame of reference

**odni|eść (-osę, -esiesz)** *(imp* **-eś**, *pt* **-ósł, -osła, -eśli***) vb perf od* **odnosić**

**odno|ga** (**-gi, -gi**) *(dat sg* **-dze***) f (pnia, drogi)* branch; *(rzeki)* arm; *(łańcucha górskiego)* spur

**odno|sić (-szę, -sisz)** *(imp* **-ś**, *perf* **odnieść***) vt* *(zabierać z powrotem)* to take (back), to carry (back); *(zwycięstwo, sukces)* to achieve; *(porażkę)* to suffer; *(rany, obrażenia)* to sustain; **odnosić się** *vr*: **~ się do kogoś/czegoś** to treat sb/sth; *(ustosunkowywać się)* to feel about sb/sth; *(dotyczyć)* to relate to sb/sth, to apply to sb/sth; **~ skutek** to bring results, to work; **odnoszę wrażenie, że ...** I have a feeling *lub* an impression (that) ...; **~ coś do czegoś** to link sth to *lub* with sth

**odnośnie** *adv*: **~ do czegoś** *(książk)* regarding sth, with regard to sth

**odnośni|k** (**-ka, -ki**) *(instr sg* **-kiem***) m (znak)* reference (mark); *(przypis)* footnote

**odnośny** *adj (przepis)* pertinent; *(dane, literatura)* relevant

**odnotow|ywać (-uję, -ujesz)** *(perf* **-ać***) vt* to write down, to take down

**odno|wa** (**-wy**) *(dat sg* **-wie***) f (zabytków)* renovation, restoration; *(regeneracja)* renovation; **centrum odnowy (biologicznej)** fitness club

**odno|wić (-wię, -wisz)** *(imp* **odnów***) vb perf od* **odnawiać**

**odosabni|ać (-am, -asz)** *(perf* **odosobnić***) vt* to isolate

**odosob|nić (-nię, -nisz)** *(imp* **-nij***) vb perf od* **odosabniać**

**odosobnieni|e** (**-a**) *nt*: **żyć w odosobnieniu** to live in seclusion *lub* solitude

**odosobniony** *adj (miejsce)* secluded, isolated; *(życie)* secluded; *(fakt, przypadek, zjawisko)* isolated

**od|ór** (**-oru, -ory**) *(loc sg* **-orze***) m* stench, reek

**odpad|ać (-am, -asz)** *(perf* **odpaść***) vi* to come off; *(z zawodów, na egzaminie)* to drop out; *(w wyborach)* to lose (out), to be defeated; **ręce mi odpadają** *(przen)* I'm done in, I'm dead tired; **ktoś/coś odpada** *(pot: nie wchodzi w rachubę)* sb/sth is out (of the question)

**odpad|ki** (**-ków**) *pl (przemysłowe)* waste; *(kuchenne)* waste, garbage

**odpad|y** (**-ów**) *pl* waste (material), scrap material

**odpakow|ywać (-uję, -ujesz)** *(perf* **-ać***) vt* to unwrap

**odpal|ać (-am, -asz)** *(perf* **-ić***) vt (pocisk, torpedę)* to fire; *(rakietę)* to launch; *(pot: odstępować)* to cough up *(pot)* ▷ *vi (strzelać)* to fire; *(wybuchać)* to explode, to detonate; *(o silniku rakietowym)* to ignite, to blast off; *(pot: odpowiadać, odcinać się)* to riposte; **~ papierosa** to light a cigarette from another

**odparow|ywać (-uję, -ujesz)** *(perf* **-ać***) vt* *(roztwór, wodę)* to evaporate; *(cios, atak)* to parry, to ward off; *(zarzuty)* to refute ▷ *vi (o wilgoci, wodzie)* to evaporate; **odparować komuś** to chat back to sb

**odparz|ać (-am, -asz)** *(perf* **-yć***) vt (skórę, nogi)* to chafe

**odparze|nie** (**-nia, -nia**) *(gen pl* **-ń***) nt (Med)* chafe

**odparz|yć (-ę, -ysz)** *vb perf od* **odparzać**

**odpa|ść (-dnę, -dniesz)** *(imp* **-dnij**, *pt* **-dł***) vb perf od* **odpadać**

**odpędz|ać (-am, -asz)** *(perf* **odpędzić***) vt* *(odganiać)* to chase away, to repel; *(zmuszać do cofnięcia się)* to drive *lub* force back, to ward off; **~ głód** to suppress hunger; **~ sen** to keep the sleep away, to try to stay awake; **~ złe myśli** to chase away bad *lub* evil thoughts

**odpę|dzić (-dzę, -dzisz)** *(imp* **-dź***) vb perf od* **odpędzać**

**od|piąć (-epnę, -epniesz)** *(imp* **-epnij***) vb perf od* **odpinać**

**odpieczętow|ywać (-uję, -ujesz)** *(perf* **-ać***) vt* to unseal

**odpieprz|yć (-ę, -ysz)** *(pot!) vt perf (robotę)* to screw up *(pot!)*; **odpieprzyć się** *vr perf*: **~ się**

**od kogoś/czegoś** to leave sb/sth alone; **odpieprz się!** sod off! (*pot!*)

**odpier|ać (-am, -asz)** (*perf* **odeprzeć**) *vt* (*atak, natarcie*) to fight off, to ward off; (*nieprzyjaciela*) to fight back, to repulse; (*ciosy*) to fight off; (*argumenty*) to refute, to rebut

**odpiłow|ywać (-uję, -ujesz)** (*perf* **-ać**) *vt* (*piłą*) to saw off; (*pilnikiem*) to file off

**odpin|ać (-am, -asz)** (*perf* **odpiąć**) *vt* (*zamek, guzik*) to undo, to unfasten; (*koszulę, spodnie*) to unbutton, to undo; (*szelki, pas*) to unbuckle, to take off; (*broszkę*) to unclasp; **odpinać się** *vr* to get undone

**odpi|s (-su, -sy)** (*loc sg* **-sie**) *m* (*kopia*) copy, transcript; (*Księgowość*) deduction

**odpi|sać (-szę, -szesz)** *vb perf od* **odpisywać**

**odpis|ywać (-uję, -ujesz)** (*perf* **-ać**) *vt* (*tekst, zadanie*) to copy; (*Szkol: ściągać*) to copy, to crib; (*Księgowość*) to deduct ▷ *vi*: **~ (na list)** to answer (a letter)

**odplamiacz (-a, -e)** (*gen pl* **-y**) *m* (*do prania*) stain remover; (*przed praniem*) (laundry) prespotter

**odplą|tać (-czę, -czesz)** (*imp* **-cz**) *vb perf od* **odplątywać**

**odpląt|ywać (-uję, -ujesz)** (*perf* **-ać**) *vt* to disentangle

**odpła|cać (się) (-cam, -casz)** (*perf* **-cić**) *vt* (*vr*): **~ komuś za coś (czymś)** to repay sb for sth (with sth); **odpłacać pięknym za nadobne** to get even with sb; **odpłacać tą samą monetą** to give tit for tat

**odpła|cić (-cę, -cisz)** (*imp* **-ć**) *vb perf od* **odpłacać**

**odpłatnie** *adv* for a payment *lub* fee

**odpłatnoś|ć (-ci)** *f* payment

**odpłatny** *adj* payed

**odpły|nąć (-nę, -niesz)** (*imp* **-ń**) *vb perf od* **odpływać**

**odpły|w (-wu, -wy)** (*loc sg* **-wie**) *m* (*pary, gazu*) outflow; (*ludności*) emigration; (*morza*) low tide; (*ujście: rzeki*) mouth; (*: jeziora*) outlet

**odpływ|ać (-am, -asz)** (*perf* **odpłynąć**) *vi* (*o statku*) to sail away *lub* out; (*o pływaku, rybie*) to swim away; (*o przedmiocie*) to float away; (*o wodzie*) to flow away, to drain; (*o ludności*) to emigrate

**odpocz|ąć (-nę, -niesz)** (*imp* **-nij**) *vb perf od* **odpoczywać**

**odpoczyn|ek (-ku)** *m* rest; **nie dawać (dać** *perf*) **komuś odpoczynku** to keep pestering sb; **wieczny ~** eternal rest

**odpoczyw|ać (-am, -asz)** (*perf* **odpocząć**) *vi* to rest, to have *lub* take a rest

**odpokut|ować (-uję, -ujesz)** *vt perf* (*grzech*) to atone for; (*zbrodnię*) to pay a penalty for

**odpolitycz|niać (-niam, -niasz)** (*perf* **-nić**) *vt* to depoliticize

**odpolitycz|nić (-nię, -nisz)** (*imp* **-nij**) *vb perf od* **odpolityczniać**

**odpornościowy** *adj*: **układ ~** the immune system

**odpornoś|ć (-ci)** *f* resistance; (*Med*) resistance, immunity

**odporny** *adj*: **~ (na coś)** (*nie poddający się*) unaffected (by sth), resistant (to sth); (*wytrzymały*) resistant (to sth); (*Med*) immune (to sth); (*roślina*) tolerant (of sth)

**odpowiad|ać (-am, -asz)** (*perf* **odpowiedzieć**) *vi* to answer, to reply; (*Szkol: no perf*) to give a report, to say one's lesson; (*reagować*) to respond; **~ na coś** to answer sth, to reply to sth; **~ komuś** to answer sb, to reply to sb; **~ komuś na list/pytanie** to reply to *lub* answer sb's letter/question; **~ na apel/wezwanie** to respond to an appeal/a call; **~ na zarzuty/zaczepki** to respond to accusations/provocations; **~ na pukanie** to answer the door; **~ z matematyki** to give mathematics, to give a report in mathematics; **~ na czyjeś pozdrowienie** to acknowledge sb's greeting; **~ za coś** (*być odpowiedzialnym*) to be responsible for sth; (*ponosić karę*) to answer for sth; **~ warunkom/nadziejom** (*spełniać*) to fulfil(l) the conditions/hopes; **coś komuś odpowiada** sth suits sb; **~ rzeczywistości/prawdzie** to correspond with the facts/truth; **~ opisowi** to answer a description

**odpowiedni** *adj* (*kandydat, moment*) suitable, right; (*miejsce, rubryka*) appropriate, right; (*słowo*) right, adequate; (*kwalifikacje*) adequate; (*zachowanie, strój*) proper; **w ~m czasie** in due time

**odpowiedni|k (-ka, -ki)** (*instr sg* **-kiem**) *m* equivalent; (*przen: człowiek na takim samym stanowisku*) counterpart

**odpowiednio** *adv* suitably, adequately; **~ do czasu/okoliczności** in accordance with time/circumstances

**odpowiedzialnoś|ć (-ci)** *f* responsibility; **za coś grozi ~ sądowa** sth is punishable by law; **~ karna** criminal responsibility; **~ cywilna** civil liability; **spółka z ograniczoną odpowiedzialnością** (*Ekon*) limited (liability) company; **obarczać (obarczyć** *perf*) **kogoś odpowiedzialnością za coś** to hold sb responsible for sth; **pociągnąć** (*perf*) **kogoś do odpowiedzialności (za coś)** to bring *lub* call sb to account (for sth); **ponosić ~ (za coś)** to bear responsibility (for sth); **brać (wziąć** *perf*) **na siebie ~ (za coś)** to take (on) the responsibility (for sth); **na swoją ~** at one's own responsibility

O

**odpowiedzialny** *adj (pracownik, człowiek)* reliable, trustworthy; *(decyzja, praca)* responsible
**odpowi|edzieć (-em, -esz)** *(3 pl* **-edzą**, *imp* **-edz**) *vb perf od* **odpowiadać**
**odpowie|dź** (**-dzi, -dzi**) *(gen pl* **-dzi**) *f (na pytanie)* answer, reply; *(na list)* answer; *(na krytykę, cios)* response; *(na podanie, prośbę)* reply; *(Szkol)* report; **mieć na wszystko gotową ~** to have a reply to everything; **w odpowiedzi na Pański list** in reply to your letter; **wywoływać (wywołać** *perf***) kogoś do odpowiedzi** *(Szkol)* to hear sb's lesson
**odpracow|ywać (-uję, -ujesz)** *(perf* **-ać**) *vt (zaległą pracę)* to catch up on; *(wolny dzień)* to make up for
**odpra|wa** (**-wy, -wy**) *(dat sg* **-wie**) *f (zebranie instruktażowe)* briefing; *(wynagrodzenie)* severance pay; *(autobusu, samolotu)* clearance, dispatch; *(pasażerów)* check-in, clearance; **~ celna** customs (clearance)
**odpra|wiać (-wiam, -wiasz)** *(perf* **-wić**) *vt (odsyłać)* to send away *lub* off; *(zwalniać z pracy)* to dismiss, to discharge; *(ekspediować: samolot, pociąg)* to dispatch; *(clić: towar)* to declare, to pay duty on; *(modły, mszę)* to say
**odpręż|ać (-am, -asz)** *(perf* **-yć**) *vt (mięśnie, myśli)* to relax; *(sznur, sprężynę)* to release, to slacken; **odprężać się** *vr (o człowieku, nerwach, umyśle)* to relax, to unwind
**odprężający** *adj (kąpiel)* relaxing
**odpręże|nie** (**-nia**) *nt* relaxation; *(Pol)* détente
**odpręż|yć (-ę, -ysz)** *vb perf od* **odprężać**
**odprowadz|ać (-am, -asz)** *(perf* **odprowadzić**) *vt (towarzyszyć)* to escort, to accompany; *(gaz, ścieki, wodę)* to pipe away *lub* off; *(pieniądze, środki, fundusze)* to transfer; **~ kogoś do domu/na dworzec** to see sb home/ to the station; **~ kogoś wzrokiem** to follow sb with one's eyes
**odprowa|dzić (-dzę, -dzisz)** *(imp* **-dź**) *vb perf od* **odprowadzać**
**odpruw|ać (-am, -asz)** *(perf* **odpruć**) *vt* to rip away *lub* off; **odpruwać się** *vr* to come off
**odprys|k** (**-ku, -ki**) *(instr sg* **-kiem**) *m (szkła, kamienia)* splinter, chip; *(farby)* flake
**odprys|kiwać (-kuje)** *(perf* **-nąć**) *vi (o kamieniu, szkle)* to chip off; *(o farbie)* to flake
**odpry|snąć (-śnie)** *(pt* **-snął, -snęła, -snęli**) *vb perf od* **odpryskiwać**
**odpu|kiwać (-kuję, -kujesz)** *(perf* **-kać**) *vi (odpowiadać pukaniem)* to knock back *lub* in reply; **odpukać (w niemalowane drewno)!** touch wood!, knock on wood!
**odpu|st** (**-stu, -sty**) *(loc sg* **-ście**) *m (uroczystość kościelna, zabawa)* church fete; *(Rel: darowanie grzechów)* indulgence, pardon; **~ zupełny** plenary indulgence
**odpuszcz|ać (-am, -asz)** *(perf* **odpuścić**) *vt*: **~ komuś coś** to absolve sb of *lub* from sth
**odpu|ścić (-szczę, -ścisz)** *(imp* **-ść**) *vb perf od* **odpuszczać**
**odpych|ać (-am, -asz)** *vt (odsuwać pchnięciem) (perf* **odepchnąć**) to push back *lub* away; *(wywoływać niechęć)* to repel, to disgust; **odpychać się** *vr (odsuwać się pchnięciem)* to push back; *(przepychać się)* to push each other; *(Fiz: o ciałach)* to repel each other
**odpychający** *adj* disgusting, repulsive
**Od|ra** (**-ry**) *(dat sg* **-rze**) *f (Geog)* the Oder (river)
**od|ra** (**-ry**) *(dat sg* **-rze**) *f (Med)* measles
**odrabi|ać (-am, -asz)** *(perf* **odrobić**) *vt (pracę)* to catch up on; *(zaległości, dzień wolny)* to make up for; **~ lekcje** to do homework
**odracz|ać (-am, -asz)** *(perf* **odroczyć**) *vt (posiedzenie, sprawę)* to postpone, to adjourn; *(wykonanie wyroku)* to respite, to requite; *(służbę wojskową)* to defer
**odradz|ać[1] (-am, -asz)** *(perf* **odradzić**) *vt*: **~ komuś coś** to advise sb against sth, to dissuade sb from sth
**odradz|ać[2] (-am, -asz)** *(perf* **odrodzić**) *vt (dawać nowe życie)* to bring back to life, to revitalize; *(zainteresowanie, tradycje)* to revive; **odradzać się** *vr (odżywać)* to come back to life, to regenerate; *(Bio: o narządach)* to regenerate
**odra|dzić (-dzę, -dzisz)** *(imp* **-dź**) *vb perf od* **odradzać[1]**
**odrast|ać (-am, -asz)** *(perf* **odrosnąć**) *vi* to grow back *lub* again; **jeszcze nie odrósł od ziemi** he's still wet behind the ears; **ledwie odrósł od ziemi** he's just out of the cradle
**odratow|ywać (-uję, -ujesz)** *(perf* **-ać**) *vt* to save, to rescue
**odra|za** (**-zy**) *(dat sg* **-zie**) *f* disgust, repugnance; **budzić** *lub* **wzbudzać w kimś odrazę** to fill sb with disgust, to make sb sick; **czuć do kogoś/czegoś odrazę** to feel disgust for sb
**odrażający** *adj* disgusting, revolting
**odrą|bać (-bię, -biesz)** *vb perf od* **odrąbywać**
**odrąb|ywać (-uję, -ujesz)** *(perf* **-ać**) *vt* to chop off, to cut off
**odrdzewiacz** (**-a, -e**) *(gen pl* **-y**) *m* rust remover
**odreagow|ywać (-uję, -ujesz)** *(perf* **-ać**) *vt* to get over; **odreagowywać się** *vr* to recover from stress
**odredakcyjny** *adj*: **komentarz ~** *(długi)* editorial; *(krótki)* editor's note
**odremont|ować (-uję, -ujesz)** *vb perf od* **remontować**

**odrestaur|ować (-uję, -ujesz)** *vb perf od* **restaurować**
**odrębnoś|ć** (**-ci, -ci**) *f* (*właściwość*) autonomy; (*cecha różniąca*) distinction
**odrębny** *adj* separate, distinct
**odręcznie** *adv* by hand, manually
**odręczny** *adj* (*rysunek*) free-hand; (*podpis*) hand-written; (*sprzedaż, pożyczka*) instant; (*naprawa*) while-you-wait
**odrętwiały** *adj* numb
**odrętwieni|e** (**-a**) *nt* (*brak czucia*) numbness; (*otępienie*) stupor, trance; (*Med*) numbness
**odro|bić (-bię, -bisz)** (*imp* **odrób**) *vb perf od* **odrabiać**
**odrobi|na** (**-ny, -ny**) (*dat sg* **-nie**) *f* (*cząsteczka*) particle; (*mała ilość*) bit; **ani odrobinę** not a bit; **przy odrobinie szczęścia** with a bit of luck; **~ prawdy** a grain of truth; **odrobinę** a little (bit)
**odrocze|nie** (**-nia, -nia**) (*gen pl* **-ń**) *nt* (*posiedzenia, sprawy*) adjournment; (*wykonania wyroku*) respite, reprieve; (*służby wojskowej*) deferment
**odrocz|yć (-ę, -ysz)** *vb perf od* **odraczać**
**odrodzeni|e** (**-a**) *nt* rebirth, revival; **Odrodzenie** (*Hist*) Renaissance
**odr|odzić (-odzę, -odzisz)** (*imp* **-odź** *lub* **-ódź**) *vb perf od* **odradzać²**
**odro|snąć (-snę, -śniesz)** (*imp* **-śnij**) *vb perf od* **odrastać**
**odróż|niać (-niam, -niasz)** (*perf* **-nić**) *vt* (*rozpoznawać*) to distinguish; (*wyróżniać*) to differentiate, to discriminate; **odróżniać się** *vr* (*wyróżniać się*) to be distinct
**odróż|nić (-nię, -nisz)** (*imp* **-nij**) *vb perf od* **odróżniać**
**odróżnieni|e** (**-a**) *nt*: **w odróżnieniu od** *+gen* as opposed *lub* distinct from
**odruch** (**-u, -y**) *m* (*Med, Psych*) reflex; (*żywiołowa reakcja*) impulse; **~ warunkowy/bezwarunkowy** conditioned/unconditioned reflex
**odruchowo** *adv* involuntarily, instinctively
**odruchowy** *adj* (*czynność, skurcz*) reflex *attr*, reflexive; (*mimowolny, niezamierzony*) involuntary, instinctive
**odrysow|ywać (-uję, -ujesz)** (*perf* **-ać**) *vt* to copy
**odryw|ać (-am, -asz)** (*perf* **oderwać**) *vt* (*guzik, deskę*) to tear off, to rip off; **nie ~ od kogoś/czegoś oczu** *lub* **wzroku** to have one's eyes riveted to sb/sth; **~ kogoś od pracy/książki** to take *lub* draw sb away from sb's work/book; **odrywać się** *vr* (*odpadać*) to come off; **nie mogłem się oderwać od pracy/książki** I couldn't get away from my work/book; **oderwać się od ziemi** (*o samolocie*) to take off

**Odrze, odrze** *n patrz* **Odra; odra**
**odrze|c (-knę, -kniesz)** (*imp* **-knij**, *pt* **-kł**) *vi perf* to reply
**odrzuc|ać (-am, -asz)** (*perf* **odrzucić**) *vt* (*śnieg, kamienie*) to throw aside; (*piłkę*) to throw back; (*braki, śmieci*) to discard, to reject; (*dar, ofertę, zaproszenie*) to reject, to turn down; (*warunki, wniosek, artykuł, książkę*) to reject
**odrzu|cić (-cę, -cisz)** (*imp* **-ć**) *vb perf od* **odrzucać**
**odrzu|t** (**-tu, -ty**) (*loc sg* **-cie**) *m* (*broni palnej*) kick, recoil; (*brak*) reject; **~ z eksportu** export reject
**odrzuto|wiec** (**-wca, -wce**) *m* jet aeroplane (*Brit*) *lub* airplane (*US*)
**odrzutowy** *adj* jet *attr*
**odrzyn|ać (-am, -asz)** (*perf* **oderżnąć**) *vt* (*odcinać*) to cut off; (*piłą*) to saw off
**odsap|nąć (-nę, -niesz)** (*imp* **-nij**) *vi perf* (*westchnąć*) to sigh; (*odpocząć*) to take some rest
**odsącz|ać (-am, -asz)** (*perf* **-yć**) *vt* to drain off
**odsą|dzać (-dzam, -dzasz)** (*perf* **-dzić**) *vt*: **~ kogoś od talentu/rozumu** to deny sb (any) talent/reason; **~ kogoś od czci i wiary** to drag sb's name through muck and mire
**odsą|dzić (-dzę, -dzisz)** (*imp* **-dź**) *vb perf od* **odsądzać**
**odsepar|ować (-uję, -ujesz)** *vb perf od* **odseparowywać**
**odseparow|ywać (-uję, -ujesz)** (*perf* **-ać**) *vt* to separate; **odseparowywać się** *vr* to separate
**odset|ek** (**-ka, -ki**) (*instr sg* **-kiem**) *m* percentage; **znaczny ~ ludności** a significant percentage *lub* proportion of the people
**odset|ki** (**-ek**) *pl*: **~ (od** *+gen***)** interest (on)
**odsi|ać (-eję, -ejesz)** *vb perf od* **odsiewać**
**odsiad|ka** (**-ki, -ki**) (*dat sg* **-ce**, *gen pl* **-ek**) *f* (*pot*) term in prison, time (*pot*)
**odsiad|ywać (-uję, -ujesz)** (*perf* **odsiedzieć**) *vt* (*spędzać siedząc*) to sit out; (*wyrok*) to do (*pot*)
**odsiecz** (**-y, -e**) (*gen pl* **-y**) *f* relief
**odsie|dzieć (-dzę, -dzisz)** (*imp* **-dź**) *vb perf od* **odsiadywać**
**odsie|w** (**-wu, -wy**) (*log sg* **-wie**) *m* (*zboża, mąki*) sifting; (*kandydatów*) screening, selection
**odsiew|ać (-am, -asz)** (*perf* **odsiać**) *vt* to sift
**odska|kiwać (-kuję, -kujesz)** (*perf* **odskoczyć**) *vi* (*odsuwać się: w bok*) to dodge, to jump aside; (*: w tył*) to jump back; (*o zamku*) to snap *lub* spring back; (*o piłce: od nogi, rąk*) to run away; (*o broni palnej, sprężynie*) to recoil
**odskocz|nia** (**-ni, -nie**) (*gen pl* **-ni**) *f* springboard; (*okazja do wypoczynku*) retreat
**odskocz|yć (-ę, -ysz)** *vb perf od* **odskakiwać**

**odsłani|ać (-am, -asz)** (*perf* **odsłonić**) *vt* (*zęby, piersi, ramiona*) to expose, to bare; (*pomnik, tablicę pamiątkową*) to unveil; (*prawdę, tajemnicę*) to reveal, to disclose; (*firanki, zasłonę*) to draw back; **odsłaniać się** *vr* to come into view, to appear

**odsło|na** (**-ny, -ny**) (*dat sg* **-nie**) *f* (*Teatr*) scene; (*Szachy*) opening

**odsło|nić (-nię, -nisz)** (*imp* **-ń**) *vb perf od* **odsłaniać**

**odsłuż|yć (-ę, -ysz)** *vt perf*: **~ dwa lata w wojsku** to serve two years in the army

**odsprzed|awać (-aję, -ajesz)** (*imp* **-awaj**, *perf* **-ać**) *vt* to resell

**odsprzedaż** (**-y, -e**) (*gen pl* **-y**) *f* resale

**odst|ać się (-anie)** *vb perf od* **odstawać się**

**odstający** *adj*: **odstające uszy** protruding ears

**odsta|wać (-ję, -jesz)** (*imp* **-waj**) *vi* (*o uszach*) to protrude; (*odróżniać się*) to stand out; **odstawać się** (*perf* **odstać**) *vr* (*o cieczy*) to settle; (*o winie*) to mature; (*wracać do pierwotnego stanu*) to be undone; **co się stało, to się nie odstanie** what's done cannot be undone

**odsta|wiać (-wiam, -wiasz)** (*perf* **-wić**) *vt* (*odkładać na bok*) to put away; (*towar*) to deliver; (*lek, zastrzyki*) to discontinue; (*odwozić gdzieś*) to take; **~ dziecko (od piersi)** to wean a baby; **~ kogoś** (*pot*: *udawać*) to play *lub* act sb

**odstą|pić (-pię, -pisz)** *vb perf od* **odstępować**

**odstę|p (-pu, -py)** (*loc sg* **-pie**) *m* (*w przestrzeni*) distance, space; (*w czasie*) interval; (*w maszynie do pisania*) space; **w regularnych ~ach czasu** at regular intervals

**odstępc|a** (**-y, -y**) *m decl like f in sg* (*książk*) traitor, renegade

**odstępn|e** (**-ego**) *nt decl like adj* compensation

**odstęp|ować (-uję, -ujesz)** (*perf* **odstąpić**) *vt*: **~ coś komuś** (*udostępniać*) to give sb sth *lub* sth to sb; (*odsprzedawać*) to sell sb sth *lub* sth to sb ▷ *vi*: **~ (od** *+gen***)** (*o osobie*) to withdraw (from); **~ od czegoś** (*umowy*) to withdraw *lub* retract from sth; (*zamiaru*) to abandon sth; (*żądań*) to waive sth; (*zasad*) to depart from sth; **nie ~ kogoś na krok** to dog sb

**odstępst|wo** (**-wa, -wa**) (*loc sg* **-wie**) *nt* (*od zwyczaju, zasady, reguły*) departure; (*od wiary*) apostasy

**odstrasz|ać (-am, -asz)** (*perf* **-yć**) *vt* (*odpędzać*) to scare away; (*nie dopuszczać*) to keep away; **~ kogoś (od czegoś)** (*zniechęcać*) to deter sb (from sth)

**odstraszający** *adj*: **środek** *lub* **czynnik ~** deterrent; **środek ~ owady** insect repellent

**odstręcz|ać (-am, -asz)** (*perf* **-yć**) *vt* (*działać odstraszająco*) to deter; (*nie dopuszczać*) to keep off *lub* away; **~ kogoś od robienia czegoś** to deter *lub* dissuade sb from doing sth

**odstuk|ać (-am, -asz)** *vb perf od* **odstukiwać**

**odstu|kiwać (-kuję, -kujesz)** (*perf* **-kać**) *vi* to knock back *lub* in reply

**odsu|nąć (-nę, -niesz)** (*imp* **-ń**) *vb perf od* **odsuwać**

**odsuw|ać (-am, -asz)** *vt* (*krzesło, szafę*) to move away *lub* back; (*zasłonę*) to draw (back); (*zasuwkę*) to pull back; (*myśli*) to brush aside *lub* away; (*niebezpieczeństwo*) to ward off, to avert; **odsuwać się** *vr* (*cofać się*) to move *lub* stand back; (*robić miejsce*) to move *lub* step aside; **odsunąć kogoś od władzy** to remove sb from power; **proszę się odsunąć!** stand back, please!

**odsyłacz** (**-a, -e**) (*gen pl* **-y**) *m* (*znak graficzny*) reference mark; (*przypis*) reference; (*w słowniku, encyklopedii*) cross-reference

**odsył|ać (-am, -asz)** (*perf* **odesłać**) *vt* (*przesyłać*) to send, to forward; (*zwracać*) to send back, to return; (*kierować*) to refer, to send; (*o odsyłaczu*) to refer; **odesłać kogoś z kwitkiem** to send sb away empty-handed; **~ kogoś od Annasza do Kajfasza** (*pot*) to drive sb from pillar to post

**odsy|pać (-pię, -piesz)** *vb perf od* **odsypywać**

**odsypi|ać (-am, -asz)** (*perf* **odespać**) *vt* (*nie przespaną noc*) to make up for

**odsyp|ywać (-uję, -ujesz)** (*perf* **-ać**) *vt* to pour off

**odszczepie|niec** (**-ńca, -ńcy**) *m* dissident

**odszedł** *itd. vb patrz* **odejść**

**odszkodowa|nie** (**-nia, -nia**) (*gen pl* **-ń**) *nt* (*ubezpieczenie*) indemnity, compensation; (*kara*) damages *pl*, compensation; (*zadośćuczynienie*) settlement

**odszrani|ać (-am, -asz)** (*perf* **odszronić**) *vt* to defrost

**odszro|nić (-nię, -nisz)** (*imp* **-ń**) *vb perf od* **odszraniać**

**odszuk|ać (-am, -asz)** *vt perf* to find

**odszyfr|ować (-uję, -ujesz)** *vb perf od* **odszyfrowywać**

**odszyfrow|ywać (-uję, -ujesz)** (*perf* **-ać**) *vt* (*wiadomość*) to decode; (*pismo*) to decipher

**odśnież|ać (-am, -asz)** (*perf* **-yć**) *vt* to clear (of snow)

**odśpiew|ać (-am, -asz)** *vt perf* to sing

**odśrodkowy** *adj* (*tendencja*) decentralizing; (*siła*) centrifugal

**odświeżacz** (**-a, -e**) (*gen pl* **-y**) *m*: **~ powietrza** air freshener

**odśwież|ać (-am, -asz)** (*perf* **-yć**) *vt* (*twarz, ciało*) to refresh; (*mieszkanie*) to spruce up; (*ubranie*) to restore; (*wspomnienia, pamięć*) to refresh; (*wiadomości, znajomość czegoś*) to brush up (on); (*znajomość z kimś*) to renew; (*kadry, personel*) to infuse with new blood; **odświeżyć komuś pamięć** to refresh sb's memory; **odświeżać się** *vr* to refresh o.s., to freshen up

**odświętny** *adj* (*posiłek*) special; (*nastrój*) festive; **odświętne ubranie** one's (Sunday) best

**odtaj|ać (-ę, -esz)** *vi perf* (*o ziemi, lodzie*) to thaw; (*przen: o człowieku*) to get warm(er)

**odtąd** *adv* (*od tamtego czasu: do chwili obecnej*) since then; (*od tego momentu*) from now on; (*poczynając od tamtej chwili*) from that time on, from then on; (*od tego miejsca*) (starting) from here

**odtelefon|ować (-uję, -ujesz)** *vi perf* to phone *lub* ring back

**odtransport|ować (-uję, -ujesz)** *vb perf od* **odtransportowywać**

**odtransportow|ywać (-uję, -ujesz)** (*perf* **-ać**) *vt* (*towar*) to deliver; (*człowieka*) to take

**odtrą|cać (-cam, -casz)** (*perf* **-cić**) *vt* (*odpychać*) to shove away; (*pomoc, przyjaźń, kochankę*) to reject; (*myśli*) to brush off; (*odliczać*) to deduct

**odtrą|cić (-cę, -cisz)** (*imp* **-ć**) *vb perf od* **odtrącać**

**odtrut|ka (-ki, -ki)** (*dat sg* **-ce**, *gen pl* **-ek**) *f* antidote; **~ na coś** antidote to sth

**odtwarzacz (-a, -e)** (*gen pl* **-y**) *m* (*kasetowy*) (audio) cassette player; (*video*) video (cassette) player; (*kompaktowy*) CD player

**odtwarz|ać (-am, -asz)** (*perf* **odtworzyć**) *vt* (*odbudowywać: całkowicie*) to recreate; (*: częściowo*) to regenerate; (*skórę, nabłonek*) to regenerate; (*malowidło, bieg wypadków*) to reconstruct; (*rolę*) to perform; (*zapisany obraz, dźwięk*) to reproduce; (*o utworze, obrazie*) to reproduce, to capture; **odtwarzać się** *vr* (*o tkankach*) to regenerate

**odtwarzani|e (-a)** *nt* (*odradzanie: całkowite*) recreation; (*: częściowe*) regeneration; (*rekonstrukcja*) reconstruction; (*dźwięku, obrazu*) reproduction; **wysoka wierność odtwarzania** (*Tech*) high fidelity

**odtworz|yć (-ę, -ysz)** (*imp* **odtwórz**) *vb perf od* **odtwarzać**

**odtwórc|a (-y, -y)** *m decl like f in sg* (*wykonawca*) performer; (*imitator*) reproducer; **~ głównej roli** the leading man

**odtwórczy|ni (-ni, -nie)** (*gen pl* **-ń**) *f* (*wykonawczyni*) performer; **~ głównej roli** the leading lady

**oducz|ać (-am, -asz)** (*perf* **-yć**) *vt*: **~ kogoś robienia czegoś** to teach sb not to do sth; **oduczać się** *vr*: **~ się czegoś** to unlearn sth; **~ się robienia czegoś** to teach o.s. not to do sth

**odurz|ać (-am, -asz)** (*perf* **-yć**) *vt* (*o trunkach, narkotykach, powodzeniu*) to intoxicate; (*o powietrzu*) to make dizzy

**odurzający** *adj*: **środki odurzające** intoxicants *pl*, drugs *pl*

**odwadni|ać (-am, -asz)** (*perf* **odwodnić**) *vt* (*ziemię, grunty*) to drain; (*Chem, Med*) to dehydrate

**odwa|ga (-gi)** (*dat sg* **-dze**) *f* courage; **~ cywilna** moral courage; **brak mi odwagi** I don't have the heart *lub* courage; **mieć odwagę coś zrobić** to have the courage to do sth; **dodawać (dodać** *perf***) komuś odwagi** to bolster up sb's courage; **dodawać (dodać** *perf***) sobie odwagi** to screw up one's courage; **zdobyć się** (*perf*) **na odwagę** to muster up one's courage; **odwagi!** be brave!, take heart!

**odwal|ać (-am, -asz)** (*perf* **-ić**) *vt* (*śnieg, gruz*) to pull away; (*pot: wykonywać*) to do; (*pot: źle wykonywać: robotę*) to botch (up) (*pot*); **odwaliliśmy kawał roboty** (*pot*) we've done a whole lot of work

**odważ|ać (-am, -asz)** (*perf* **-yć**) *vt* (*ważyć*) to weigh out; **odważać się** *vr* to dare; **odważyć się coś zrobić** to dare (to) do sth, to have the courage to do sth; **odważyć się na coś** to risk sth

**odważni|k (-ka, -ki)** (*instr sg* **-kiem**) *m* weight

**odważny** *adj* (*człowiek*) brave, courageous; (*czyn, słowa*) brave, daring

**odwdzięcz|ać się (-am, -asz)** (*perf* **-yć**) *vr*: **odwdzięczać się komuś za coś** to pay sb back for sth, to repay sb for sth

**odwe|t (-tu)** (*loc sg* **-cie**) *m* retaliation; **brać (wziąć** *perf***) na kimś ~** to take revenge on sb; **w ~ za** *+acc* in retaliation for

**odwetowy** *adj* retaliatory

**odwią|zać (-żę, -żesz)** *vb perf od* **odwiązywać**

**odwiąz|ywać (-uję, -ujesz)** (*perf* **-ać**) *vt* to undo, to untie

**odwieczny** *adj* (*zamek, puszcza*) ancient; (*spór, zwyczaj*) everlasting

**odwie|dzać (-dzam, -dzasz)** (*perf* **-dzić**) *vt* (*przychodzić z wizytą*) to visit; (*: niespodziewanie*) to call on; (*bywać*) to frequent, to visit; **odwiedź mnie jutro** come and see me tomorrow

**odwie|dzić (-dzę, -dzisz)** (*imp* **-dź**) *vb perf od* **odwiedzać**

**odwiedzin|y (-)** *pl* visit; **przychodzić (przyjść** *perf***) do kogoś w ~** to come to visit sb; **jestem w odwiedzinach u rodziców** I'm visiting my parents

**odwie|sić (-szę, -sisz)** *vb perf od* **odwieszać**

**odwiesz|ać (-am, -asz)** (*perf* **odwiesić**) *vt* (*słuchawkę*) to hang up

**odwi|eść (-odę, -edziesz)** (*imp* **-edź**, *pt* **-ódł, -odła, -edli**) *vb perf od* **odwodzić**

O

**odwi|eźć (-ozę, -eziesz)** (*imp* **-eź**, *pt* **-ózł, -ozła, -eźli**) *vb perf od* **odwozić**
**odwij|ać (-am, -asz)** (*perf* **odwinąć**) *vt* (*paczkę*) to unwrap; (*sznurek, nici, film*) to unreel, to unwind; (*rękaw, mankiet*) to unroll
**odwilż** (**-y, -e**) (*gen pl* **-y**) *f* thaw
**odwi|nąć (-nę, -niesz)** (*imp* **-ń**) *vb perf od* **odwijać**
**odwir|ować (-uję, -ujesz)** *vb perf od* **odwirowywać**
**odwirow|ywać (-uję, -ujesz)** (*perf* **-ać**) *vt* (*pranie*) to spin(-dry)
**odwl|ec (-okę, -eczesz)** (*pt* **-ókł, -okła, -ekli**) *vb perf od* **odwlekać**
**odwlek|ać (-am, -asz)** (*perf* **odwlec**) *vt* (*opóźniać*) to delay, to stall; (*odciągać w inne miejsce*) to drag away; **odwlekać się** *vr* to be put off
**odwło|k** (**-ka** *lub* **-ku, -ki**) (*instr sg* **-kiem**) *m* (*Zool*) abdomen
**odwod|nić (-nię, -nisz)** (*imp* **-nij**) *vb perf od* **odwadniać**
**odwodnieni|e** (**-a**) *nt* dehydration
**odwo|dzić (-dzę, -dzisz)** (*imp* **odwódź**, *perf* **odwieść**) *vt* (*odprowadzać*) to take; (*kurek pistoletu*) to cock; **~ kogoś na bok** *lub* **na stronę** to take sb aside; **~ kogoś od zrobienia czegoś** to dissuade sb from doing sth
**odwoł|ać (-am, -asz)** *vb perf od* **odwoływać**
**odwoła|nie** (**-nia, -nia**) (*gen pl* **-ń**) *nt* (*urzędnika*) dismissal; (*ambasadora*) recall; (*zarządzenia, alarmu*) cancellation; (*od decyzji sądu*) appeal; **aż do odwołania** until further notice
**odwoławczy** *adj* appeal *attr*; **sąd ~** court of appeal
**odwoł|ywać (-uję, -ujesz)** (*perf* **-ać**) *vt* (*usuwać ze stanowiska*) to dismiss; (*: ambasadora*) to recall; (*alarm, rozkaz, zajęcia*) to cancel; (*obietnicę, słowa*) to retract, to withdraw; **odwoływać się** *vr* (*Prawo*) to appeal; **~ się od decyzji** to appeal against a decision
**odwo|zić (-żę, -zisz)** (*imp* **-ź**, *perf* **odwieźć**) *vt* (*zawozić*) to take; (*zawozić z powrotem*) to take back
**odw|ód** (**-odu, -ody**) (*loc sg* **-odzie**) *m* (*Wojsk*) reserve(s *pl*)
**odwrac|ać (-am, -asz)** (*perf* **odwrócić**) *vt* (*głowę*) to turn away; (*wzrok*) to avert; (*bieg rzeki*) to reverse; (*ubranie, pościel*) to turn over *lub* down; **~ czyjąś uwagę od czegoś** to divert sb's attention from sth; **~ kota ogonem** (*pot*) to put the cart before the horse; **odwracać się** *vr* to turn away; **odwrócić się na pięcie** to turn on one's heel; **odwrócić się od kogoś** (*porzucić*) to turn one's back on sb; (*o szczęściu*) to desert sb; **karta się odwróciła** (*przen*) my luck has run out *lub* turned
**odwracalny** *adj* reversible
**odwrotnie** *adv* (*na odwrót*) inversely; (*przeciwnie*) conversely; (*do góry nogami*) upside down; **~ proporcjonalny** inversely proportional; **i ~** and vice versa; **~ niż** contrary to
**odwrotnoś|ć** (**-ci**) *f* (*przeciwieństwo*) the opposite, the reverse; (*Mat*) reciprocal, inverse
**odwrotny** *adj* (*zjawisko, kierunek*) opposite, reverse; (*strona: ulicy*) opposite; (*: płaszczyzny*) reverse; **odwrotna strona medalu** (*przen*) the other side of the coin
**odwró|cić (-cę, -cisz)** (*imp* **-ć**) *vb perf od* **odwracać**
**odwr|ót** (**-otu, -oty**) (*loc sg* **-ocie**) *m* (*Wojsk*) retreat, withdrawal; **~ od czegoś** (*zmiana stanowiska*) a turn *lub* move away from sth
**odwy|k** (**-ku**) *m* (*instr sg* **-kiem**) (*pot: leczenie odwykowe*) drying-out (*pot*); **być na ~u** to be drying out (*pot*)
**odwyk|ać (-am, -asz)** (*perf* **-nąć**) *vi*: **~ od** *+gen* to lose the habit of, to get out of the habit of
**odwyk|nąć (-nę, -niesz)** (*imp* **-nij**, *pt* **-nął** *lub* **-ł, -ła, -li**) *vb perf od* **odwykać**
**odwyków|ka** (**-ki, -ki**) (*dat sg* **-ce**) *f* (*pot*) drying-out ward *lub* clinic (*pot*)
**odwzajem|niać (-niam, -niasz)** (*perf* **-nić**) *vt* (*uczucie, niechęć*) to reciprocate, to return; (*przysługę*) to return, to repay; (*uśmiech*) to return; **odwzajemniać się** *vr* to return, to reciprocate; **~ się komuś za coś** to repay sb for sth
**odwzajem|nić (-nię, -nisz)** (*imp* **-nij**) *vb perf od* **odwzajemniać**
**odze|w** (**-wu, -wy**) (*loc sg* **-wie**) *m* response; (*Wojsk*) countersign
**odzie** *n patrz* **oda**
**odziedzicz|yć (-ę, -ysz)** *vb perf od* **dziedziczyć** ▷ *vt perf* to inherit
**odzież** (**-y**) *f* clothing; **~ letnia/zimowa** summer/winter wear; **~ ochronna** protective clothing
**odzieżowy** *adj* (*sklep*) clothes *attr*; **przemysł ~** clothing industry
**odznacz|ać (-am, -asz)** (*perf* **-yć**) *vt* (*dekorować odznaczeniem*) to decorate, to honour (*Brit*), to honor (*US*); **odznaczać się** *vr*: **~ się czymś** to be characterized by sth
**odznacze|nie** (**-nia, -nia**) (*gen pl* **-ń**) *nt* decoration, distinction
**odznacz|yć (-ę, -ysz)** *vb perf od* **odznaczać**; **odznaczyć się** *vr perf* to distinguish o.s.
**odzna|ka** (**-ki, -ki**) (*dat sg* **-ce**) *f* (*wyróżnienie*) distinction, decoration; (*znak przynależności*) badge
**odzwierciedl|ać (-am, -asz)** (*perf* **-ić**) *vt* to reflect, to mirror; **odzwierciedlać się** *vr* to be reflected

**odzwierciedleni|e** (**-a**) *nt* reflection
**odzwierciedl|ić (-ę, -isz)** (*imp* **-ij**) *vb perf od* **odzwierciedlać**
**odzwyczа|ić (-ję, -isz)** *vb perf od* **odzwyczajać**
**odzwycza|jać (-jam, -jasz)** (*perf* **-ić**); **~ kogoś od czegoś** to break sb of their habit of doing sth; **odzwyczajać się** *vr*: **~ się (od czegoś)** to get out of the habit (of doing sth)
**odzys|k** (**-ku, -ki**) (*instr sg* **-kiem**) *m* recycling
**odzys|kiwać (-kuję, -kujesz)** (*perf* **-kać**) *vt* (*własność*) to get *lub* win back; (*niepodległość*) to regain; (*przytomność, spokój*) to recover, to regain; **odzyskać zdrowie** to recover
**odzyw|ać się (-am, -asz)** (*perf* **odezwać**) *vr* (*przemówić*) to speak; (*o uczuciach, doznaniach*) to awake; (*o dzwonku, głosie*) to sound; **on się jeszcze nie odezwał** we haven't heard from him yet; **nie odzywam się do ciebie!** I'm not speaking with *lub* to you!; **odezwać się (na coś)** to reply *lub* respond (to sth); **odezwij się!** speak to me!
**odzyw|ka** (**-ki, -ki**) (*dat sg* **-ce**, *gen pl* **-ek**) *f* (*Karty*) bid
**odżał|ować (-uję, -ujesz)** *vt perf* (*stratę*) to get over
**odżegn|ywać się (-uję, -ujesz)** (*perf* **-ać**) *vr*: **odżegnywać się od czegoś** to distance o.s. from sth
**odży|ć (-ję, -jesz)** *vb perf od* **odżywać**
**odżyw|ać (-am, -asz)** (*perf* **odżyć**) *vi* (*wracać do życia*) to come back to life; (*przen: o nadziei, wspomnieniach*) to be revived
**odżywczy** *adj* (*potrawa, produkty*) nutritious, nourishing; (*składnik, substancja*) nutritious; (*wartość*) nutritive; (*krem*) nourishing
**odży|wiać (-wiam, -wiasz)** (*perf* **-wić**) *vt* (*karmić, żywić*) to feed, to nourish; **odżywiać się** *vr* (*o człowieku*) to feed o.s., to eat; (*o zwierzęciu*) to feed
**odżywiani|e** (**-a**) *nt* nutrition, nourishment
**odżywiony** *adj*: **dobrze ~** well-fed, well-nourished; **źle ~** undernourished
**odżyw|ka** (**-ki, -ki**) (*dat sg* **-ce**, *gen pl* **-ek**) *f* (*pokarm*) nutrient; (*do włosów*) conditioner; (*dla dzieci*) baby-food, (baby) formula (*US*)
**oenzetowski** *adj* UN *attr*
**ofensy|wa** (**-wy, -wy**) (*dat sg* **-wie**) *f* offensive
**ofensywny** *adj* (*działalność*) aggressive; (*postawa*) pushy, aggressive
**ofer|ma** (**-my, -my**) (*dat sg* **-mie**) *m/f decl like f in sg* (*pot*) duffer (*pot*)
**ofer|ować (-uję, -ujesz)** (*perf* **za-**) *vt* to offer
**ofer|ta** (**-ty, -ty**) (*dat sg* **-cie**) *f* offer, proposal
**ofi|ara** (**-ary, -ary**) (*dat sg* **-erze**) *f* (*dar*) gift, present; (*: pieniężny*) contribution, donation; (*Rel*) offering; (*poświęcenie*) sacrifice; (*osoba poszkodowana*) victim; (*pot: niezdara*) duffer (*pot*); **~ losu** born loser (*pot*), hopeless case (*pot*); **paść** (*perf*) **ofiarą czegoś** to fall victim to sth; **składać (złożyć** *perf*) **coś w ofierze** to make an offering of sth
**ofiarnoś|ć** (**-ci**) *f* (*szczodrość*) generosity; (*gotowość do poświęceń*) dedication, devotion
**ofiarny** *adj* (*człowiek*) giving, selfless; (*praca*) hard, dedicated; (*ogień, stos, zwierzę*) sacrificial; **kozioł ~** (*przen*) scapegoat
**ofiarodawc|a** (**-y, -y**) *m decl like f in sg* benefactor, donor
**ofiarodawczy|ni** (**-ni, -nie**) (*gen pl* **-ń**) *f* benefactress, donor
**ofiar|ować (-uję, -ujesz)** *vb perf od* **ofiarowywać**
**ofiarow|ywać (-uję, -ujesz)** (*perf* **-ać**) *vt* (*dawać*) to give (as a present *lub* gift); (*proponować*) to offer; (*datki*) to donate; (*składać w ofierze*) to offer
**ofice|r** (**-ra, -rowie**) (*loc sg* **-rze**) *m* officer
**oficer|ki** (**-ek**) *pl* jackboots *pl*
**oficerski** *adj* officer's *attr*, officers' *attr*; **szkoła oficerska** military academy
**oficjalnie** *adv* officially, formally
**oficjalny** *adj* (*urzędowy*) official, formal; (*sztywny, bezduszny*) formal, proper
**oficjel** (**-a, -e**) (*gen pl* **-i**) *m* (*pot*) big wig (*pot*)
**oficy|na** (**-ny, -ny**) (*dat sg* **-nie**) *f* (*dobudówka*) lean-to, annexe (*Brit*), annex (*US*); (*wydawnictwo*) publishing house
**ofierze** *n patrz* **ofiara**
**ofsajdowy** *adj*: **pułapka ofsajdowa** offside
**ogani|ać (-am, -asz)** *vt* (*odganiać*) to brush away; **oganiać się** *vr*: **~ się przed kimś/czymś** to brush sb/sth away *lub* off
**ogar|nąć (-nę, -niesz)** (*imp* **-nij**) *vb perf od* **ogarniać** ▷ *vt perf* (*pot*) to straighten (up) (*pot*); **ogarnąć się** *vr* (*pot*) to spruce o.s. up (*pot*)
**ogarni|ać (-am, -asz)** (*perf* **ogarnąć**) *vt* (*o ciemnościach, mgle*) to surround, to encompass; (*o radości, niepokoju*) to overtake, to overcome; (*o wojnie, pożarze*) to spread across; **~ kogoś/coś wzrokiem** *lub* **spojrzeniem** to take sb/sth in
**ogień** (**ognia, ognie**) (*gen pl* **ogni**) *m* (*zjawisko*) fire; (*do papierosa*) light; (*przen: zapał*) fervour (*Brit*), fervor (*US*); (*: namiętność*) passion; **słomiany ~** a flash in the pan; **gotować na wolnym ogniu** cook on a low heat; **igrać z ogniem** to play with fire; **wpaść** (*perf*) **jak po ~** to come flying through; **stanąć** (*perf*) **w ogniu** to catch fire, to burst into flames; **sztuczne ognie** fireworks; **zimne ognie** sparklers *pl*; **ognia!** (*Wojsk*) fire!; **przerwij ~!** (*Wojsk*) cease fire!; **krzyżowy ~ pytań** cross-examination; **(gra w) dwa ognie** British bulldog (*Brit*), prison dodge ball (*US*); **dostać**

O

**się między dwa ognie** to get caught in the crossfire; **iść (pójść** *perf*) **na pierwszy ~** to go over the top first; **on skoczyłby dla niej w ~** he would go through fire and water for her
**ogie|r** (**-ra, -ry**) (*loc sg* **-rze**) *m* stallion
**ogląd|ać (-am, -asz)** (*perf* **obejrzeć**) *vt* (*obraz, książkę*) to look at, to examine; (*film*) to watch; (*wystawę, zabytki*) to see; **oglądać się** *vr* (*patrzeć na samego siebie*) to look at o.s.; (*spoglądać do tyłu*) to look back; (*spoglądać na boki*) to look around; **~ się na kogoś** (*przen*) to count on sb; **~ się na coś** (*przen*) to take sth into consideration
**oglądalnoś|ć** (**-ci**) *f* (*TV*) ratings *pl*, viewing figures *pl*
**oględny** *adj* (*ostrożny*) wary, guarded; (*umiarkowany*) moderate
**oględzin|y** (**-**) *pl* (*badanie*) examination; (*inspekcja*) survey, inspection; **~ zwłok** autopsy, post-mortem
**ogła|da** (**-dy**) (*dat sg* **-dzie**) *f* good manners *pl*
**ogłasz|ać (-am, -asz)** (*perf* **ogłosić**) *vt* to announce; (*manifest, odezwę*) to publish, to issue; (*amnestię, niepodległość*) to declare; (*konkurs*) to announce; (*wyrok, pracę naukową*) to publish; (*stan wyjątkowy*) to declare, to proclaim; **ogłaszać się** *vr* (*dawać ogłoszenie*) to advertise
**ogło|sić (-szę, -sisz)** (*imp* **-ś**) *vb perf od* **ogłaszać**
**ogłosze|nie** (**-nia, -nia**) (*gen pl* **-ń**) *nt* announcement; (*pisemne*) notice; (*wiadomość w gazecie*) ad, announcement; (*reklama*) ad, advertisement
**ogłuch|nąć (-nę, -niesz)** (*imp* **-nij**, *pt* **-ł** *lub* **-nął**) *vb perf od* **głuchnąć**
**ogłu|piać (-piam, -piasz)** (*perf* **-pić**) *vt* to stupefy
**ogłupiający** *adj* stupefying
**ogłupiały** *adj* confused, dazed
**ogłu|pić (-pię, -pisz)** *vb perf od* **ogłupiać**
**ogłusz|ać (-am, -asz)** (*perf* **-yć**) *vt* (*o hałasie*) to deafen; (*pozbawiać przytomności*) to knock unconscious *lub* out
**ogłuszający** *adj* deafening
**ogłusz|yć (-ę, -ysz)** *vb perf od* **ogłuszać**
**ognia** *itd. n patrz* **ogień**
**ogni|k** (**-ka, -ki**) (*instr sg* **-kiem**) *m* (*płomień*) flame; (*przen: blask oczu*) sparkle, glow; **błędny ~** will-o'-the-wisp
**ognioodporny** *adj* fire-resistant
**ogniotrwały** *adj* fireproof
**ogniowy** *adj* fire *attr*
**ognis|ko** (**-ka, -ka**) (*instr sg* **-kiem**) *nt* (*ogień*) bonfire; (*impreza harcerska*) (camp-)fire; (*ośrodek, centrum*) centre (*Brit*), center (*US*); (*kółko zainteresowań*) group, circle; (*Fiz, Fot, Med*) focus; **~ domowe** hearth and home; **~ niepokoju** hot spot
**ogniskow|a** (**-ej, -e**) *f decl like adj* (*Fiz, Fot*) focal length *lub* distance
**ognisk|ować (-uję, -ujesz)** (*perf* **z-**) *vt* to focus
**ognisty** *adj* (*rozżarzony*) fiery, flaming; (*rudy*) flaming red; (*pełen temperamentu*) fiery, passionate
**ogni|wo** (**-wa, -wa**) (*loc sg* **-wie**) *nt* link; (*komórka organizacji*) cell; (*Fiz, Chem*) cell
**ogol|ić (-ę, -isz)** (*imp* **ogol** *lub* **ogól**) *vb perf od* **golić**
**ogolony** *adj* shaved, shaven; **starannie ~** clean-shaven; **nie ~** unshaved, unshaven
**ogołac|ać (-am, -asz)** (*perf* **ogołocić**) *vt*: **~ coś z** *+gen* to strip sth of
**ogoło|cić (-cę, -cisz)** *vb perf od* **ogołacać**
**ogo|n** (**-na, -ny**) (*loc sg* **-nie**) *m* tail
**ogon|ek** (**-ka, -ki**) (*instr sg* **-kiem**) *m* (*mały ogon*) tail; (*pot: kolejka*) queue (*Brit*), line (*US*); (*liścia*) stalk; (*owocu*) stem; (*litery*) hook
**ogonowy** *adj*: **kość ogonowa** coccyx; **zupa ogonowa** oxtail soup
**ogorzały** *adj* tanned, tawny
**ogólnia|k** (**-ka, -ki**) (*instr sg* **-kiem**) *m* (*pot: liceum ogólnokształcące*) high school, comprehensive school (*Brit*)
**ogólnie** *adv* (*powszechnie*) generally, universally; (*ogólnikowo*) generally; **~ biorąc** in general, on the whole; **~ mówiąc** generally speaking
**ogólni|k** (**-ka, -ki**) (*instr sg* **-kiem**) *m* (*truizm*) generality; (*frazes*) cliché
**ogólnikowy** *adj* general, vague
**ogólnokrajowy** *adj* nationwide, country-wide
**ogólnokształcący** *adj* (*szkoła, przedmiot*) general education *attr*
**ogólnonarodowy** *adj* nationwide
**ogólnopolski** *adj* all-Poland
**ogólnoś|ć** (**-ci**) *f* generality
**ogólnoświatowy** *adj* worldwide, global
**ogólny** *adj* (*powszechny*) general, universal; (*publiczny*) public, common; (*nie szczegółowy*) general; (*suma, wynik*) total, global
**ogó|ł** (**-łu**) (*loc sg* **-le**) *m* (*całość*) totality; (*społeczeństwo*) the (general) public; **~ ludności** the community *lub* people at large; **dobro ~u** the common good; **~em** all in all, overall; **na ~** in general; **w ogóle** (*ogólnie biorąc*) generally; (*wcale*) (not) at all
**ogór|ek** (**-ka, -ki**) (*instr sg* **-kiem**) *m* cucumber
**ogórkowy** *adj* cucumber *attr*; **sezon ~** (*przen: pot*) the silly season
**ogra|biać (-biam, -biasz)** (*perf* **-bić**) *vt* to rob; **~ kogoś z czegoś** to rob sb of sth
**ogr|ać (-am, -asz)** *vb perf od* **ogrywać**

**ogradz|ać (-am, -asz)** (*perf* **ogrodzić**) *vt* (*płotem*) to fence in; (*murem*) to wall in

**ogranicz|ać (-am, -asz)** (*perf* **-yć**) *vt* (*pole, obszar*) to delimit, to mark off; (*zakres*) to limit; (*krępować*) to restrict, to constrain; (*wydatki*) to reduce, to cut down; (*prędkość, władzę*) to limit, to restrict; **ograniczać się** *vr* (*oszczędzać*) to cut down on spending; **~ się do** *+gen* (*zadowalać się*) to limit o.s. to; (*obejmować jedynie*) to be limited *lub* restricted to; (*sprowadzać się do*) to boil down to

**ogranicze|nie** (**-nia, -nia**) (*gen pl* **-ń**) *nt* (*przepis, norma*) restriction, limitation; (*tępota*) limitations *pl*; **~ prędkości** speed limit; **~ umysłowe** mental deficiency *lub* retardation

**ograniczony** *adj* (*widoczność, pole działania*) limited, restricted; (*środki, możliwości*) limited; (*tępy*) slow-witted

**ograny** *adj* (*temat*) worn out; (*dowcip*) corny

**ogrodnict|wo** (**-wa**) (*loc sg* **-wie**) *nt* horticulture, gardening

**ogrodnicz|ki** (**-ek**) *pl* (*spodnie*) dungarees *pl*

**ogrodniczy** *adj* (*narzędzie, sklep*) gardening *attr*, garden *attr*; (*szkoła*) gardening *attr*

**ogrodni|k** (**-ka, -cy**) (*instr sg* **-kiem**) *m* gardener

**ogrodowy** *adj* garden *attr*

**ogrodze|nie** (**-nia, -nia**) (*gen pl* **-ń**) *nt* fence

**ogro|dzić (-dzę, -dzisz)** (*imp* **-dź** *lub* **ogródź**) *vb perf od* **ogradzać**

**ogro|m** (**-mu**) (*loc sg* **-mie**) *m* (*wielki rozmiar*) enormity, vastness; (*wielka ilość*) multitude; **~ klęski/nieszczęść** the enormity of the calamity/disaster

**ogromnie** *adv* enormously, immensely

**ogromny** *adj* (*dom, drzewo, ilość*) huge; (*pustynia, ocean*) vast; (*znaczenie, radość, trudności*) immense, enormous

**ogr|ód** (**-odu, -ody**) (*loc sg* **-odzie**) *m* garden; **~ botaniczny** botanical garden(s *pl*); **~ zoologiczny** zoo, zoological garden(s *pl*)

**ogród|ek** (**-ka, -ki**) (*instr sg* **-kiem**) *m* (*mały ogród*) garden; (*przy kawiarni*) open-air café; **~ działkowy** allotment; **~ jordanowski** playground

**ogródek** *inv*: **mówić (powiedzieć** *perf*) **coś bez ~** to say sth bluntly

**ogryw|ać (-am, -asz)** (*perf* **ograć**) *vt* to beat, to outplay

**ogryzać** *vb* = **obgryzać**

**ogryz|ek** (**-ka, -ki**) (*instr sg* **-kiem**) *m* core

**ogrz|ać (-eję, -ejesz)** *vb perf od* **ogrzewać**

**ogrzewacz** (**-a, -e**) (*gen pl* **-y**) *m* heater

**ogrzew|ać (-am, -asz)** (*perf* **ogrzać**) *vt* (*wodę, pomieszczenie*) to heat; (*ręce*) to warm up; **ogrzewać się** *vr* to get warm

**ogrzewani|e** (**-a**) *nt* heating; **centralne ~** central heating

**ogumieni|e** (**-a**) *nt* (*Mot*) tyres *pl* (*Brit*), tires *pl* (*US*)

**ohy|da** (**-dy**) (*loc sg* **-dzie**) *f* monstrosity

**ohydny** *adj* hideous, monstrous

**oj|ciec** (**-ca, -cowie**) (*dat sg* **-cu**, *voc sg* **-cze**) *m* father; (*założyciel*) (founding) father, originator; **ojcowie** *pl* (*przodkowie*) forefathers, ancestors; **~ chrzestny** godfather; **Bóg O~** God the Father; **O~ Święty** Holy Father

**ojcost|wo** (**-wa**) (*loc sg* **-wie**) *nt* paternity, fatherhood

**ojcowski** *adj* (*dom, majątek*) father's *attr*; (*miłość, władza*) fatherly, paternal; **po ojcowsku** paternally

**ojczy|m** (**-ma, -mowie** *lub* **-mi**) (*loc sg* **-mie**) *m* stepfather

**ojczysty** *adj* native

**ojczy|zna** (**-zny, -zny**) (*dat sg* **-źnie**) *f* (*kraj*) homeland; (*przen: kolebka*) home

**ok.** *abbr* (= *około*) about, ca. (= *circa*)

**okabl|ować (-uję, -ujesz)** *vb perf od* **okablowywać**

**okablow|ywać (-uję, -ujesz)** (*perf* **-ać**) *vt* to wire (up)

**okalecz|ać (-am, -asz)** (*perf* **-yć**) *vt* (*czynić kaleką*) to cripple, to mutilate; (*ranić*) to injure

**okalecze|nie** (**-nia, -nia**) (*gen pl* **-ń**) *nt* wound, injury

**okalecz|yć (-ę, -ysz)** *vb perf od* **okaleczać**

**okamgnieni|e** (**-a**) *nt* twinkling of an eye; **w okamgnieniu** in a flash, in the twinkling of an eye

**oka|p** (**-pu, -py**) (*loc sg* **-pie**) *m* (*część dachu*) eaves *pl*; (*nad piecem*) hood

**oka|z** (**-zu, -zy**) (*loc sg* **-zie**) *m* (*egzemplarz*) specimen; (*wzór*) exemplar, paragon; **~ zdrowia** picture of health; **~ głupoty** a perfect fool

**oka|zać (-żę, -żesz)** *vb perf od* **okazywać**

**okazały** *adj* (*duży*) impressive; (*człowiek*) big; (*pałac*) magnificent; (*przyjęcie*) grand

**okaziciel** (**-a, -e**) (*gen pl* **-i**) *m* bearer; **czek na ~a** cheque (*Brit*) *lub* check (*US*) to bearer

**okazj|a** (**-i, -e**) (*gen pl* **-i**) *f* (*sposobność*) chance, opportunity; (*korzystnego kupna*) bargain; (*okoliczność*) occasion; **a przy okazji ...** by the way, ...; **z okazji** *+gen* on the occasion of; **gratulacje z okazji awansu** congratulations on your promotion; **skorzystać** (*perf*) **z okazji** to take *lub* grab an opportunity; **przepuścić** (*perf*) **okazję** to miss an opportunity

**okazyjnie** *adv* (*sprzedać*) at a good profit; (*kupić*) at a bargain price

**okazyjny** *adj* bargain *attr*

**okaz|ywać (-uję, -ujesz)** (*perf* **-ać**) *vt* (*kwit, bilet, paszport*) to present, to show; (*gniew,*

O

*niepokój, współczucie, zdumienie)* to demonstrate, to show; *(odwagę, zainteresowanie)* to demonstrate, to manifest; **okazywać się** *vr* to turn out (to be); **okazać pomoc** to provide help *lub* assistance; **okazało się, że ...** it turned out that ...; **jak się okazało** as it turned out; **jak się okazuje** apparently; **to się dopiero okaże** that is yet to be seen

**okiełzn|ać (-am, -asz)** *vt perf (konia)* to break in, to tame; *(temperament, fantazję)* to curb

**okien** *n patrz* **okno**

**okien|ko (-ka, -ka)** *(instr sg* **-kiem**, *gen pl* **-ek**) *nt dimin od* **okno**; *(w kasie, urzędzie, na poczcie)* counter; *(w kopercie)* window; *(Szkol: wolna godzina)* gap

**okiennic|a (-y, -e)** *f* shutter

**okienny** *adj* window *attr*

**oklap|nąć (-nę, -niesz)** *(imp* **-nij**, *pt* **-nął** *lub* **-ł**) *vi (o uszach)* to droop; *(o kwiatach)* to wilt; *(przen: o człowieku)* to sink

**oklas|ki (-ków)** *pl* applause, clapping

**oklas|kiwać (-kuję, -kujesz)** *vt* to applaud

**oklei|na (-ny, -ny)** *(dat sg* **-nie**) *f* veneer

**oklep** *inv*: **na ~** bareback

**oklepany** *adj (powszechnie znany)* commonplace; *(banalny)* trite

**okła|d (-du, -dy)** *(loc sg* **-dzie**) *m (Med)* compress; **z ~em** or more

**okład|ać (-am, -asz)** *(perf* **obłożyć**) *vt (pokrywać)* to cover; *(książkę, zeszyt)* to wrap; **~ chleb serem** to make a cheese sandwich; *(bić)* to beat; **~ podatkiem/grzywną** to impose tax/fine on

**okład|ka (-ki, -ki)** *(dat sg* **-ce**, *gen pl* **-ek**) *f* cover

**okładzi|na (-ny, -ny)** *(dat sg* **-nie**) *f* facing, lining

**okła|mać (-mię, -miesz)** *vb perf od* **okłamywać**

**okłam|ywać (-uję, -ujesz)** *(perf* **-ać**) *vt* to deceive, to lie to; **~ samego siebie** to deceive *lub* delude o.s.

**okno (okna, okna)** *(loc sg* **oknie**, *gen pl* **okien**) *nt* window; **~ wystawowe** shop window; **oglądać okna wystawowe** to window-shop; **~ na świat** *(przen)* a window on the world *(przen)*; **wyrzucać pieniądze przez ~** *(przen)* to throw money down the drain *(przen)*

**oko[1] (oka, oczy)** *(gen pl* **oczu**, *dat pl* **oczom**, *instr pl* **oczami** *lub* **oczyma**) *nt (narząd wzroku)* eye; *(wzrok)* (eye)sight; **oko w oko** face to face; **jak okiem sięgnąć** as far as the eye can see; **bez zmrużenia oka** without batting an eye(lid); **na czyichś oczach** before sb's very eyes; **na oko** roughly; **na pierwszy rzut oka** at first glance *lub* sight, on the face of it; **na piękne oczy** on trust; **pod czyimś okiem** under sb's supervision; **w cztery oczy** in private; **w oczach** *(z każdą chwilą)* rapidly; **w oczach prawa** in the eyes of the law; **kłamać w żywe oczy** to lie through one's teeth; **z zamkniętymi** *lub* **zawiązanymi oczami** *(bezbłędnie)* with one's eyes closed; *(bez namysłu)* without thinking; **cieszyć oko** to please the eye; **iść (pójść** *perf***) gdzie oczy poniosą** to go and never look back; **mieć dobre oko** to have a good eye; *(mieć dobry wzrok)* to have good eyes; **mieć kogoś/coś przed oczami** to have sb/sth before one's (very) eyes; **mieć kogoś/coś na oku** to keep an eye on sb/sth; **mieć oczy otwarte na** *+acc* to keep an eye out for; **mieć oko na** *+acc* to have an *lub* one's eye on; **nie spuszczać kogoś/czegoś z oka** to keep an eye on sb/sth; **nie wierzyć własnym oczom** not to believe one's own eyes; **nie zmrużyć** *(perf)* **oka** not to sleep a wink; **otworzyć komuś oczy na** *+acc* to open sb's eyes to; **patrzeć krzywym okiem na** *+acc* to frown upon, to look askance at; **pilnować kogoś/czegoś jak oka w głowie** to keep a close eye on sb/sth; **pożerać kogoś/coś oczami** to devour sb/sth with one's eyes; **przejrzałem na oczy** the scales fell back from my eyes; **przewracać oczami** to roll one's eyes; **przymykać (przymknąć** *perf***) na coś oczy** to turn a blind eye to sth; **puszczać (puścić** *perf***) do kogoś (perskie) oko** to wink at sb; **robić do kogoś słodkie oczy** to make eyes at sb; **rzucić** *(perf)* **okiem** to cast a glance; **rzucać się (rzucić się** *perf***) w oczy** to stand out, to be conspicuous; **wpaść** *(perf)* **komuś w oko** to catch sb's fancy; **zamknąć** *(perf)* **oczy** *(umrzeć)* to breathe one's last; **zginąć** *(perf)* **komuś z oczu** to disappear from sight; **dobrze/ źle mu patrzy z oczu** he has a kind/ forbidding look in his eyes; **dwoi mi się w oczach** I see double; **Pi razy oko** *(pot)* roughly, more or less; **zejdź mi z oczu!** get out of my sight!; **zrobiło mi się ciemno przed oczami** I'm seeing spots before my eyes

**oko[2] (oka, oka)** *nt (w sieci)* mesh; *(cyklonu)* eye; **pawie oko** peacock's eye, ocellus

**oko|cić się (-cę, -cisz)** *vr perf* to have kittens

**okolic|a (-y, -e)** *f (otoczenie)* surroundings *pl*, neighbourhood (Brit), neighborhood (US); *(obszar)* region, district; **w okolicy** *+gen* in the vicinity of

**okoliczni|k (-ka, -ki)** *(instr sg* **-kiem**) *m* adverbial

**okolicznościowy** *adj* occasional

**okolicznoś|ć (-ci, -ci)** *f (sytuacja)* circumstance; *(sposobność)* occasion; **okoliczności** *pl* circumstances; **w tych**

**okolicznościach** in *lub* under those circumstances; **okoliczności łagodzące** extenuating *lub* mitigating circumstances; **okoliczności obciążające** aggravating circumstances

**okoliczny** *adj* (*lasy, miasta*) surrounding, neighbouring (*Brit*), neighboring (*US*); (*ludność*) local

**około** *prep +gen* about

**oko|ń** (**-nia, -nie**) (*gen pl* **-ni**) *m* perch

**oko|p** (**-pu, -py**) (*loc sg* **-pie**) *m* trench

**oko|pać (-pię, -piesz)** *vb perf od* **okopywać**

**okop|ywać (-uję, -ujesz)** (*perf* **-ać**) *vt* (*ziemniaki, pomidory, drzewko*) to earth up; (*armatę, stanowisko ogniowe*) to dig in

**okostn|a** (**-ej**) *f decl like adj* periosteum

**okólni|k** (**-ka, -ki**) (*instr sg* **-kiem**) *m* circular

**okrad|ać (-am, -asz)** (*perf* **okraść**) *vt*: **~ kogoś (z czegoś)** to rob sb (of sth)

**okrakiem** *adv* astride

**okra|ść (-dnę, -dniesz)** (*imp* **-dnij**, *pt* **-dł**) *vb perf od* **okradać**

**okratowa|nie** (**-nia, -nia**) (*gen pl* **-ń**) *nt* grating, grille

**okraw|ać (-am, -asz)** (*perf* **okroić**) *vt* (*jabłko, chleb*) to trim; (*przen: referat, artykuł*) to abridge

**okr|ąg** (**-ęgu, -ęgi**) (*instr sg* **-ęgiem**) *m* circle; *patrz też* **okręg**

**okrągły** *adj* round, circular; (*liczba, suma*) round; (*człowiek*) plump

**okrąż|ać (-am, -asz)** (*perf* **-yć**) *vt* to surround; (*zataczać krąg*) to circle; (*przeszkodę*) to go (a) round

**okrąże|nie** (**-nia, -nia**) (*gen pl* **-ń**) *nt* (*Sport*) lap; (*Wojsk*) envelopment

**okrąż|yć (-ę, -ysz)** *vb perf od* **okrążać**

**okre|s** (**-su, -sy**) (*loc sg* **-sie**) *m* (*czas trwania*) period; (*pora*) time; (*stadium*) stage; (*epoka*) era; (*Szkol*) term, semester; (*miesiączka*) period; (*Astron, Fiz*) period; **~ gwarancji** warranty (coverage); **~ ochronny** close season (*Brit*), closed season (*US*); **~ urzędowania** term of office

**okresowo** *adv* periodically

**okresowy** *adj* (*badania, deszcze*) periodic(al); (*pobyt, zameldowanie*) temporary; **bilet ~** season ticket (*Brit*), commutation ticket (*US*); **~ układ pierwiastków** periodic system *lub* table

**określ|ać (-am, -asz)** (*perf* **-ić**) *vt* (*opisywać*) to describe, to characterize; (*wiek, pochodzenie*) to determine; (*datę, termin*) to determine, to specify; (*znaczenie*) to define

**określe|nie** (**-nie, -nia**) (*gen pl* **-ń**) *nt* (*epitet*) qualification; (*Jęz*) modifier

**określony** *adj* specific, given; **przedimek ~** definite article

**okręc|ać (-am, -asz)** (*perf* **okręcić**) *vt* (*owijać*) to wrap, to twist; (*obracać*) to turn (round *lub* around), to spin; **okręcać się** *vr* (*oplatać się*) to twist *lub* coil around; (*obracać się wkoło*) to turn (round *lub* around), to spin

**okrę|cić (-cę, -cisz)** (*imp* **-ć**) *vb perf od* **okręcać**

**okrę|g** (**-gu, -gi**) (*instr sg* **-giem**) *m* (*jednostka administracyjna*) district; (*obszar, region*) region; **~ wyborczy** constituency; *patrz też* **okrąg**

**okręgowy** *adj* district *attr*, regional

**okrę|t** (**-tu, -ty**) (*loc sg* **-cie**) *m* (*statek wojenny*) warship; (*pot: duży statek*) ship; **~ podwodny** submarine

**okrężny** *adj* (*droga, ulica*) roundabout; (*ruch*) circular; (*handel*) door-to-door *attr*

**okro|ić (-ję, -isz)** (*imp* **okrój**) *vb perf od* **okrawać**

**okropnie** *adv* (*zepsuć, zaśpiewać*) terribly, awfully; (*pot: bardzo*) awfully, terribly; **(on) wygląda/czuje się ~** he looks/feels awful *lub* terrible

**okropnoś|ć** (**-ci**) *f* horror; **okropności** *pl* atrocities *pl*

**okropny** *adj* (*widok*) terrible, horrible; (*ból, mróz, trema*) terrible; (*charakter, człowiek*) horrible; (*pogoda*) awful

**okruch|y** (**-ów**) *pl* (*chleba*) crumbs; (*szkła*) pieces; (*złota*) nuggets; (*przen: resztki*) scraps

**okrucieńst|wo** (**-wa**) (*loc sg* **-wie**) *nt* cruelty; **okrucieństwa** *pl* atrocities *pl*

**okrutny** *adj* cruel

**okry|cie** (**-cia, -cia**) (*gen pl* **-ć**) *nt* (*przykrycie*) cover(ing); (*ubranie*) coat

**okry|ć (-ję, -jesz)** *vb perf od* **okrywać**

**okryw|ać (-am, -asz)** (*perf* **okryć**) *vt* to cover; **~ kogoś hańbą/sławą** to bring disgrace/glory to sb; **okrywać się** *vr* to cover o.s.; **~ się żałobą** to go into mourning

**okrzyczany** *adj* (*osławiony*) famed; (*niesławny*) notorious

**okrzy|k** (**-ku, -ki**) (*instr sg* **-kiem**) *m* shout, cry; **wznosić (wznieść** *perf*) **~i na czyjąś cześć** to cheer sb

**okrzyk|nąć (-nę, -niesz)** (*imp* **-nij**) *vt perf*: **~ kogoś sknerą/zdrajcą** to declare sb a miser/traitor; **~ kogoś królem/wodzem** to proclaim sb king/chief

**Oksfor|d** (**-du**) (*loc sg* **-dzie**) *m* Oxford

**oksydowany** *adj* oxidized

**oktanowy** *adj*: **liczba** *lub* **zawartość oktanowa** octane number *lub* rating

**okta|wa** (**-wy, -wy**) (*dat sg* **-wie**) *f* octave

**oku|cie** (**-cia, -cia**) (*gen pl* **-ć**) *nt* fitting

**oku|ć (-ję, -jesz)** *vb perf od* **okuwać**

**okula|r** (**-ru, -ry**) (*loc sg* **-rze**) *m* (*w mikroskopie, teleskopie*) eyepiece

**okularni|k** (**-ka, -cy**) (*instr sg* **-kiem**) *m* (*pej*) four-eyes (*pej*)

O

**okular|y** (**-ów**) *pl* glasses *pl*, spectacles *pl*; **~ (przeciw)słoneczne** sunglasses *pl*; **~ ochronne** (safety) goggles *pl*; **patrzeć (na coś) przez różowe ~** to look (at sth) through rose-colo(u)red spectacles; *patrz też* **okular**
**okule|ć (-ję, -jesz)** *vi perf* to become lame
**okuli|sta** (**-sty, -ści**) (*dat sg* **-ście**) *m decl like f in sg* eye doctor, ophthalmologist, optometrist (US)
**okulisty|ka** (**-ki**) (*dat sg* **-ce**) *f* ophthalmology
**okultyz|m** (**-mu**) (*loc sg* **-mie**) *m* occultism
**oku|p** (**-pu**) (*loc sg* **-pie**) *m* ransom
**okupacj|a** (**-i, -e**) (*gen pl* **-i**) *f* (*Wojsk*) occupation; (*Prawo*) occupancy
**okupacyjny** *adj* (*siły, władze*) occupant *attr*, occupying *attr*; **strajk ~** sit-down (strike)
**okupan|t** (**-ta, -ci**) (*loc sg* **-cie**) *m* occupier
**okup|ować (-uję, -ujesz)** *vt* (*kraj, fabrykę, magazyn*) to occupy; (*pot: telefon, łazienkę*) to hog (*pot*)
**okuw|ać (-am, -asz)** (*perf* **okuć**) *vt* (*drzwi, okno, skrzynię*) to fit; (*konia*) to shoe
**ol|ać (-eję, -ejesz)** *vb perf od* **olewać**
**olbrzy|m** (**-ma, -my** *lub* **-mi**) (*loc sg* **-mie**) *m* giant
**olbrzymi** *adj* (*drzewo, budynek, kolekcja*) enormous, gigantic; (*dochód*) colossal, huge; (*powodzenie, siła*) enormous, huge; (*znaczący*) enormous
**ol|cha** (**-chy, -chy**) (*dat sg* **-sze**) *f* alder
**oldboj** (**-a, -e**) *m* (*Sport*) veteran (player)
**oleisty** *adj* (*ciecz*) oily
**ole|j** (**-ju, -je**) (*gen pl* **-i** *lub* **-jów**) *m* oil; (*obraz olejny*) oil painting; **~ jadalny** cooking oil; **~ napędowy** diesel oil; **nie mieć ~u w głowie** (*pot*) to be dead between the ears (*pot*)
**olejar|ka** (**-ki, -ki**) (*dat sg* **-ce**) *f* oiler
**olej|ek** (**-ku, -ki**) (*instr sg* **-kiem**) *m* oil; **~ do opalania** sun-tan oil; **~ smakowy** flavouring (*Brit*), flavoring (US)
**olejny** *adj* oil *attr*
**olejowy** *adj* oil *attr*; **miska olejowa** (*Mot*) (oil) sump (*Brit*), oil pan (US)
**olew|ać (-am, -asz)** (*perf* **olać**) *vt* (*pot!*) not to give a shit for (*pot!*)
**oligarchi|a** (**-i, -e**) (*gen pl* **-i**) *f* oligarchy
**olimpia|da** (**-dy, -dy**) (*dat sg* **-dzie**) *f* (*igrzyska olimpijskie*) the Olympics *pl*, the Olympic Games *pl*; (*konkurs*) contest
**olimpijczy|k** (**-ka, -cy**) (*instr sg* **-kiem**) *m* (*zawodnik*) Olympian (*male contender in the Olympics*)
**olimpij|ka** (**-ki, -ki**) (*dat sg* **-ce**) *f* (*zawodniczka*) Olympian (*female contender in the Olympics*); (*kurtka*) sports jacket
**olimpijski** *adj* (*medal, stadion*) Olympic; (*postawa, spokój*) Olympian; **igrzyska ~e** the Olympics, the Olympic Games
**oli|wa** (**-wy**) (*dat sg* **-wie**) *f* (*olej z oliwek*) olive oil; (*olej jadalny*) (salad *lub* cooking) oil; (*olej mineralny*) oil (lubricant); **dolewać (dolać** *perf*) **oliwy do ognia** to fan *lub* add fuel to the flames
**oliwiar|ka** (**-ki, -ki**) (*dat sg* **-ce**) *f* oilcan
**oli|wić (-wię, -wisz)** (*perf* **na-**) *vt* to oil, to lubricate
**oliw|ka** (**-ki, -ki**) (*dat sg* **-ce**, *gen pl* **-ek**) *f* (*drzewo*) olive (tree); (*owoc*) olive
**oliwkowy** *adj* olive *attr*; (*kolor*) olive (green)
**olsze** *n patrz* **olcha**
**olś|nić (-nię, -nisz)** (*imp* **-nij**) *vb perf od* **olśniewać**
**olśnie|nie** (**-nia, -nia**) (*gen pl* **-ń**) *nt* flash of insight
**olśniew|ać (-am, -asz)** (*perf* **olśnić**) *vt* (*oślepiać*) to blind, to dazzle; (*zachwycać*) to dazzle
**ołowiany** *adj* (*blacha, żołnierzyk*) lead *attr*; (*niebo, chmury*) leaden
**ołowic|a** (**-y**) *f* lead poisoning
**ołowiowy** *adj*: **benzyna ołowiowa** leaded petrol (*Brit*) *lub* gas(oline) (US)
**oł|ów** (**-owiu**) *m* lead
**ołów|ek** (**-ka, -ki**) (*instr sg* **-kiem**) *m* (lead) pencil; **~ automatyczny** propelling pencil; **~ do brwi** eyebrow pencil
**ołtarz** (**-a, -e**) (*gen pl* **-y**) *m* altar; **iść (pójść** *perf*) **z kimś do ~a** (*przen*) to tie the knot with sb; **wynosić (wynieść** *perf*) **kogoś na ~e** to glorify sb
**ołtarzy|k** (**-ka, -ki**) (*instr sg* **-kiem**) *m dimin od* **ołtarz**
**om** (**oma, omy**) (*loc sg* **omie**) *m* ohm
**omacku** *inv*: **po ~** blindfold; **szukać czegoś po ~** to grope for sth
**omal** *adv*: **~ nie** almost, (very) nearly; **~ nie upadł** he almost fell; **to jest ~ że niemożliwe** it's almost impossible
**oma|mić (-mię, -misz)** *vt perf* to beguile
**omam|y** (**-ów**) *pl* hallucinations *pl*
**Oma|n** (**-nu**) (*loc sg* **-nie**) *m* Oman
**omawi|ać (-am, -asz)** (*perf* **omówić**) *vt* to discuss, to talk over
**omdlały** *adj* faint
**omdle|ć (-ję, -jesz)** *vb perf od* **omdlewać**
**omdle|nie** (**-nia, -nia**) (*gen pl* **-ń**) *nt* fainting
**omdlew|ać (-am, -asz)** (*perf* **omdleć**) *vi* to faint
**ome|n** (**-nu**) (*loc sg* **-nie**) *m* omen, portent; **nomen ~** aptly named
**omiat|ać (-am, -asz)** (*perf* **omieść**) *vt* to sweep; **omieść coś spojrzeniem** to scan sth
**omieszk|ać (-am, -asz)** *vi perf*: **nie ~ coś zrobić** to remember to do sth
**omi|eść (-otę, -eciesz)** (*imp* **-eć**, *pt* **-ótł, -otła, -etli**) *vb perf od* **omiatać**

**omij|ać (-am, -asz)** (*perf* **ominąć**) *vt* (*okrążać*) to go (a)round, to skirt; (*unikać: sąsiadów*) to avoid; (*przeszkody, niebezpieczeństwa*) to avoid, to steer clear of; (*zakaz, prawo*) to dodge, to evade; (*nie uwzględniać*) to overlook, to pass over; **ominął go awans** he was passed over for promotion; **nie ominie go kara** he won't escape punishment

**omi|nąć (-nę, -niesz)** (*imp* **-ń**) *vb perf od* **omijać**

**omle|t** (**-tu** *lub* **-ta, -ty**) (*loc sg* **-cie**) *m* omelette (*Brit*), omelet (*US*)

**omomierz** (**-a, -e**) (*gen pl* **-y**) *m* ohmmeter

**omó|wić (-wię, -wisz)** *vb perf od* **omawiać**

**omówie|nie** (**-nia, -nia**) (*gen pl* **-ń**) *nt* (*recenzja*) report; (*dyskusja*) discussion; (*peryfraza*) circumlocution

**omszały, omszony** *adj* mossy

**omyl|ić się (-ę, -isz)** *vb perf od* **mylić się**

**omylny** *adj* fallible

**omył|ka** (**-ki, -ki**) (*dat sg* **-ce**, *gen pl* **-ek**) *f* (*błąd*) mistake; (*niedopatrzenie*) oversight; **przez omyłkę** by mistake

**omyłkowo** *adv* by mistake, wrongly

**on** *pron* (*o człowieku: w pozycji podmiotu*) he; (*w innych pozycjach*) him; (*o zwierzęciu, przedmiocie, pojęciu*) it; **to on!** that's him!

**ona** *pron* (*o człowieku: w pozycji podmiotu*) she; (*w innych pozycjach*) her; (*o zwierzęciu, przedmiocie, pojęciu*) it; **to ona!** that's her!

**onaniz|m** (**-mu**) (*loc sg* **-mie**) *m* masturbation

**onaniz|ować się (-uję, -ujesz)** *vr* to masturbate

**ondulacj|a** (**-i, -e**) (*gen pl* **-i**) *f* perm

**one** *pron* (*w pozycji podmiotu*) they; (*w innych pozycjach*) them

**oni** *pron* (*w pozycji podmiotu*) they; (*w innych pozycjach*) them

**oniemiały** *adj* speechless

**oniemie|ć (-ję, -jesz)** *vi perf* to be left speechless; **~ z zachwytu/przerażenia** to become speechless with delight/terror

**onieśmiel|ać (-am, -asz)** (*perf* **-ić**) *vt* to embarrass

**onieśmieleni|e** (**-a**) *nt* embarrassment

**onieśmielony** *adj* embarrassed, shy

**onkologi|a** (**-i**) *f* oncology

**onkologiczny** *adj* oncological

**ono** *pron* it

**onomatope|ja** (**-i, -je**) (*gen pl* **-i**) *f* onomatopoeia

**onyk|s** (**-su, -sy**) (*loc sg* **-sie**) *m* onyx

**ONZ** (**ONZ-etu**) (*loc sg* **ONZ-ecie**) *m abbr* (= *Organizacja Narodów Zjednoczonych*) UN

**op.** *abbr* (= *opus*) Op.

**opact|wo** (**-wa, -wa**) (*loc sg* **-wie**) *nt* abbey

**opaczny** *adj* wrong

**opa|d** (**-du, -dy**) (*loc* **-dzie**) *m* (*opadanie*) fall, drop; (*też:* **opad radioaktywny**) (radioactive) fallout; (*Sport*) bend; **opady** *pl* (*ogólnie*) precipitation; (*deszcz*) rain(fall), showers *pl*; (*śnieg*) snow(fall); **~ krwi** E.S.R. (= *erythrocyte sedimentation rate*)

**opad|ać (-am, -asz)** (*perf* **opaść**) *vi* (*o liściach*) to fall; (*o mgle*) to descend; (*o zawiesinie*) to settle; (*o kwiatach*) to die; (*o cieście*) to collapse; (*o terenie*) to sink, to descend; (*o temperaturze, poziomie*) to fall; (*o samolocie*) to descend; (*o gorączce, wietrze, entuzjazmie*) to subside; (*o sukni, włosach*) to hang loose; **ręce (mi) opadają** it's hopeless; **~ z sił** to lose one's strength; **zdenerwowanie/zmęczenie ze mnie opadło** the anger/fatigue is gone

**opak** *adv*: **na ~** wrong, the wrong *lub* other way round; **zrozumieć coś na ~** to get hold of the wrong end of the stick

**opak|ować (-uję, -ujesz)** *vb perf od* **opakowywać**

**opakowa|nie** (**-nia, -nia**) (*gen pl* **-ń**) *nt* (*paczka, pudełko*) box, packaging; (*wraz z zawartością*) packet

**opakow|ywać (-uję, -ujesz)** (*perf* **-ać**) *vt*: **~ coś (czymś)** to wrap sth up (in sth)

**opal** (**-u, -e**) (*gen pl* **-i**) *m* opal

**opal|ać (-am, -asz)** (*perf* **-ić**) *vt* (*mieszkanie*) to heat; (*osmalać*) to char; (*drób*) to singe; (*nogi, plecy*) to (sun)tan; **opalać się** *vr* to sunbathe

**opaleni|zna** (**-zny**) (*dat sg* **-źnie**) *f* (sun)tan

**opal|ić (-ę, -isz)** *vb perf od* **opalać**; **opalić się** *vr perf* to get a (sun)tan

**opalony** *adj* (sun)tanned

**opa|ł** (**-łu**) (*loc sg* **-le**) *m* fuel; **opały** *pl* trouble

**opałowy** *adj* fuel *attr*

**opamięt|ać się (-am, -asz)** *vr perf* to come to one's senses

**opamiętani|e** (**-a**) *nt* reflection, reason; **bez opamiętania** with abandon

**opancerzony** *adj* armoured (*Brit*), armored (*US*)

**opan|ować (-uję, -ujesz)** *vb perf od* **opanowywać**

**opanowani|e** (**-a**) *nt* self-control, composure

**opanowany** *adj* calm, composed

**opanow|ywać (-uję, -ujesz)** (*perf* **-ać**) *vt* (*miasto, twierdzę*) to capture; (*żywioł, sytuację*) to bring under control; (*gniew, radość*) to contain; (*język, technikę*) to master; (*o uczuciu, nastroju*) to overcome; **opanowywać się** *vr* (*zapanowywać nad sobą*) to control o.s.; (*uspokajać się*) to contain o.s.

**opa|r** (**-ru, -ry**) (*loc sg* **-rze**) *m* (*obłok pary*) vapour (*Brit*), vapor (*US*); (*mgła*) mist; **opary** *pl* (*woń*) fumes *pl*; (*wyziewy*) vapours *pl* (*Brit*), vapors *pl* (*US*)

**opar|cie** (**-cia, -cia**) (*gen pl* **-ć**) *nt* (*część mebla: na plecy*) back(rest); (*: na ramię*) arm(rest); (*: na głowę*) headrest; (*podpora*) support; (*przen*) support; **w oparciu o** *+acc* on the strength *lub* basis of
**oparł** *itd. vb patrz* **oprzeć**
**oparze|nie** (**-nia, -nia**) (*gen pl* **-ń**) *nt* burn; **~ pierwszego/drugiego stopnia** first-/second-degree burn
**oparz|yć (-ę, -ysz)** *vt perf* (*ogniem, gorącym przedmiotem*) to burn; (*gorącym płynem*) to scald; (*żrącą substancją*) to burn, to scorch; **oparzyć się** *vr perf* to get burned; **~ się w palec** to burn one's finger
**opa|sać (-szę, -szesz)** (*imp* **-sz**) *vb perf od* **opasywać**
**opas|ka** (**-ki, -ki**) (*dat sg* **-ce**, *gen pl* **-ek**) *f* band; (*na głowę*) (head)band; (*na oczy*) patch, blindfold; (*na czoło*) sweatband; (*na rękę*) armband; (*opatrunek*) bandage, dressing; **~ biodrowa** loincloth; **~ uciskowa** tourniquet; **~ żałobna** (black) armband
**opasły** *adj* obese; (*przen*) fat
**opas|ywać (-uję, -ujesz)** (*perf* **-ać**) *vt* (*pasem*) to belt, to gird(le); (*tasiemką*) to tie; (*przen*) to gird
**opa|ść (-dnę, -dniesz)** (*imp* **-dnij**, *pt* **-dł**) *vb perf od* **opadać** ▷ *vt perf* (*osaczyć, napaść*) to jump (on); **opadło mnie przeczucie** I got a feeling
**opa|t** (**-ta, -ci**) (*loc sg* **-cie**) *m* abbot
**opatent|ować (-uję, -ujesz)** *vt perf* to patent
**opatrun|ek** (**-ku, -ki**) (*instr sg* **-kiem**) *m* dressing, bandage
**opatr|ywać (-uję, -ujesz)** (*perf* **opatrzyć**) *vt* (*ranę*) to dress; (*rannego*) to bandage; **~ coś czymś** to provide *lub* equip sth with sth
**opatrznościowy** *adj* providential
**opatrznoś|ć** (**-ci**) *f* Providence
**opatrzony** *adj*: **~ czymś** equipped *lub* provided with sth
**opatrz|yć (-ę, -ysz)** *vb perf od* **opatrywać**; **opatrzyć się** *vr perf*: **coś się komuś opatrzyło** sb has seen too much of sth
**opch|ać się (-am, -asz)** *vb perf od* **opychać się**
**opch|nąć (-nę, -niesz)** (*imp* **-nij**) *vt perf* (*pot: sprzedać*) to sell, to flog (*Brit*) (*pot*)
**opcj|a** (**-i, -e**) (*gen pl* **-i**) *f* option; **~ zerowa** clean start (negotiations)
**ope|ra** (**-ry, -ry**) (*dat sg* **-rze**) *f* opera; (*gmach*) opera house
**operacj|a** (**-i, -e**) (*gen pl* **-i**) *f* (*zabieg*) operation, surgery; (*transakcja*) transaction; (*Wojsk*) operation; **~ plastyczna** (*Med*) plastic *lub* cosmetic surgery
**operacyjny** *adj* (*Med: sala, stół*) operating *attr*; (*maska, leczenie*) surgical; (*Wojsk*) combat *attr*
**operato|r** (**-ra, -rzy**) (*loc sg* **-rze**) *m* (*filmowy*) cameraman; (*dźwigu, maszyny*) operator; (*Mat, Logika*) operator
**operator|ka** (**-ki, -ki**) (*dat sg* **-ce**) *f* operator
**operatywny** *adj* efficient
**operet|ka** (**-ki, -ki**) (*dat sg* **-ce**, *gen pl* **-ek**) *f* operetta
**oper|ować (-uję, -ujesz)** *vi* to operate ▷ *vt* (*perf* **z-**) (*Med*) to operate on; **~ czymś** (*głosem, metaforą, narzędziem*) to use sth, to manipulate sth; (*kapitałem, papierami, kredytem*) to circulate sth
**operowy** *adj* (*tenor, przedstawienie, dzieło*) operatic; (*śpiewak, libretto*) opera *attr*
**opędz|ać (-am, -asz)** (*perf* **opędzić**) *vt* (*muchy, komary*) to bat away; **opędzać się** *vr*: **~ się od** *+gen* to drive *lub* chase away; **nie mogę się opędzić od** *+gen* I can't get rid of
**opę|dzić (-dzę, -dzisz)** (*imp* **-dź**) *vb perf od* **opędzać**
**opęt|ać (-am, -asz)** *vt perf* (*o gniewie, żądzy, idei*) to get a hold on, to come over; (*o człowieku*) to captivate; **diabeł go opętał** he is possessed (by the devil)
**opętany** *adj*: **jak ~** like crazy
**opi|ć (-ję, -jesz)** *vb perf od* **opijać**
**opie|c (-kę, -czesz)** (*imp* **-cz**, *pt* **-kł**) *vb perf od* **opiekać**
**opieczęt|ować (-uję, -ujesz)** *vb perf od* **pieczętować**
**opie|ka** (**-ki**) (*dat sg* **-ce**) *f* (*troszczenie się*) care, protection; (*dozór*) care, charge; (*pomoc: lekarska*) care, assistance; (*: prawna*) protection; (*Prawo*) custody, guardianship; **~ społeczna** social welfare; **być pod czyjąś opieką** to be in sb's care
**opiekacz** (**-a, -e**) (*gen pl* **-y**) *m* toaster
**opiek|ać (-am, -asz)** (*perf* **opiec**) *vt* (*w tłuszczu*) to braise; (*nad ogniem*) to barbecue, to roast
**opiekany** *adj* (*nad ogniem*) roasted; (*w tłuszczu*) braised
**opiek|ować się (-uję, -ujesz)** (*perf* **za-**) *vr*: **opiekować się kimś/czymś** (*troszczyć się*) to take care of sb/sth; (*zajmować się*) to look after sb/sth; (*sprawować dozór*) to guard sb/sth
**opieku|n** (**-na, -nowie**) (*loc sg* **-nie**) *m* (*osoba opiekująca się*) carer; (*kurator*) guardian; **~ społeczny** social worker
**opiekun|ka** (**-ki, -ki**) (*dat sg* **-ce**, *gen pl* **-ek**) *f* carer; **~ (do) dziecka** child-minder, baby-sitter
**opiekuńczy** *adj* (*troskliwy*) caring, protective; (*władza, instytucja*) welfare *attr*
**opieprz|ać (-am, -asz)** (*perf* **-yć**) (*pot!*) *vt*: **~ kogoś** to give sb (one bloody) hell (*pot*), to jump all over sb (*pot*); **opieprzać się** *vr* to fart about *lub* around (*pot!*)

**opier|ać (-am, -asz)** (*perf* **oprzeć**) *vt*: **~ coś o** *+acc* to prop *lub* lean sth against; **~ coś na** *+loc* to rest sth against, to put sth on; (*przen*) to base sth on; **opierać się** *vr*: **~ się komuś/ czemuś** to resist sb/sth; **~ się o** *+acc* to lean against; **~ się na** *+loc* (*lasce*) to lean on; (*dowodach, źródłach, zeznaniach*) to be based on; (*przyjaciołach, rodzicach*) to rely on; **sprawa oparła się o sąd** the matter went to court; **nie mogłem oprzeć się wrażeniu, że ...** I couldn't resist the impression that ...

**opieszały** *adj* sluggish

**opiew|ać (-am, -asz)** *vt* (*książk*) to exalt; **~ na** *+acc* (*o rachunku, czeku, wyroku*) to amount to

**opięty** *adj* skintight, clinging

**opij|ać (-am, -asz)** (*perf* **opić**) *vt* to celebrate (with drink), to drink to; **opijać się** *vr* to drink too much

**opił|ek (-ka, -ki)** (*instr* **-kiem**) *m* shaving; **opiłki** *pl* filings *pl*

**opini|a (-i, -e)** (*gen pl* **-i**) *f* (*pogląd*) opinion, view; (*reputacja*) opinion, reputation; (*ocena*) judgement; **~ publiczna** public opinion; **cieszyć się dobrą opinią** to enjoy a fine reputation; **psuć (zepsuć** *perf*) **komuś opinię** to give *lub* earn sb a bad name; **psuć (zepsuć** *perf*) **sobie opinię** to earn a bad name (for o.s.)

**opini|ować (-uję, -ujesz)** (*perf* **za-**) *vt* (*podanie*) to endorse; (*projekt*) to give an opinion on

**opi|s (-su, -sy)** (*loc sg* **-sie**) *m* description; (*relacja*) account; **~ techniczny** specification

**opi|sać (-szę, -szesz)** (*imp* **-sz**) *vb perf od* **opisywać**

**opisowy** *adj* descriptive; (*Jęz*) periphrastic

**opis|ywać (-uję, -ujesz)** (*perf* **-ać**) *vt* to describe; (*charakteryzować*) to characterize; (*Mat*) to circumscribe; **tego się nie da opisać** it defies description

**opity** *adj* (*alkoholem*) drunk, drunken; (*zbyt dużą ilością płynu*) bloated

**opium** (-) *nt inv* opium

**oplat|ać (-am, -asz)** (*perf* **opleść**) *vt* (*okręcać*) to entangle; (*o roślinie*) to twist around; (*o wężu*) to coil around; **~ kogoś ramionami** to wrap one's arms around sb

**opl|eść (-otę, -eciesz)** (*imp* **-eć**, *pt* **-ótł, -otła, -etli**) *vb perf od* **oplatać**

**oplu|ć (-ję, -jesz)** *vb perf od* **opluwać**

**opluw|ać (-am, -asz)** (*perf* **opluć**) *vt* to spit on; (*przen*) to throw *lub* sling mud at

**opłac|ać (-am, -asz)** (*perf* **opłacić**) *vt* (*czynsz, pracownika*) to pay; (*przekupywać*) to pay off; **opłacać się** *vr* to pay; **nie opłaca się tego robić** it's not worth doing; **to się nie opłaca** it's not worth the trouble; **opłaciło się!** it was worth my while!

**opłacalnoś|ć (-ci)** *f* profitability

**opłacalny** *adj* profitable

**opła|cić (-cę, -cisz)** (*imp* **-ć**) *vb perf od* **opłacać**

**opłakany** *adj*: **w ~m stanie** in a pitiful state

**opła|kiwać (-kuję, -kujesz)** *vt* (*stratę*) to lament, to bemoan; (*zmarłego*) to mourn (for)

**opła|ta (-ty, -ty)** (*dat sg* **-cie**) *f* (*kwota do zapłacenia*) payment, charge; (*za naukę*) fee; (*za przejazd*) fare; (*urzędowa*) payment; **~ celna** (customs) duty; **~ drogowa** toll; **~ pocztowa** postage; **~ skarbowa** stamp duty; **za niewielką** *lub* **drobną opłatą** for a small *lub* nominal fee

**opłat|ek (-ka, -ki)** (*instr sg* **-kiem**) *m* wafer

**opłucn|a (-ej)** *f decl like adj* pleura

**opłu|kać (-czę, -czesz)** (*imp* **-cz**) *vb perf od* **płukać**

**opły|nąć (-nę, -niesz)** (*imp* **-ń**) *vb perf od* **opływać**

**opływ|ać (-am, -asz)** (*perf* **opłynąć**) *vi*: **~ w dostatki** to live off the fat of the land ▷ *vt* (*o człowieku, rybie*) to (swim) round; (*o statku*) to (sail) round; (*o wodzie*) to flow round; **opłynąć kulę ziemską** to circumnavigate the world

**opływowy** *adj* streamlined

**opodal** *adv* nearby ▷ *prep +gen* near (to); **nie ~ (czegoś)** nearby (sth)

**opodatk|ować (-uję, -ujesz)** *vb perf od* **opodatkowywać**

**opodatkowani|e (-a)** *nt* taxation

**opodatkowany** *adj* taxed

**opodatkow|ywać (-uję, -ujesz)** (*perf* **-ać**) *vt* to tax; **opodatkowywać się** *vr*: **~ się (na rzecz** *+gen*) to subscribe (to) (*charities etc*)

**opo|ka (-ki, -ki)** (*dat sg* **-ce**) *f* (*książk*) rock; (*przen*) bedrock

**opo|na (-ny, -ny)** (*dat sg* **-nie**) *f* tyre (*Brit*), tire (*US*); **opony** *pl*: **zapalenie opon mózgowych** meningitis

**oponen|t (-ta, -ci)** (*loc sg* **-cie**) *m* opponent

**oporni|k (-ka, -ki)** (*instr sg* **-kiem**) *m* (*Elektr*) resistor

**opornoś|ć (-ci)** *f* resistance

**oporny** *adj* (*nieposłuszny*) disobedient; (*nieustępliwy*) unyielding, relentless; (*stawiający opór*) resistant

**oportuni|sta (-sty, -ści)** (*loc sg* **-ście**) *m decl like f in sg* opportunist

**oportuniz|m (-mu)** (*loc sg* **-mie**) *m* opportunism

**opowiad|ać (-am, -asz)** (*perf* **opowiedzieć**) *vi*: **~ (o** *+loc*) to talk (about) ▷ *vt* to tell; **opowiadać się** *vr*: **~ się za** *+instr* to opt for, to subscribe to

**opowiada|nie (-nia, -nia)** (*gen pl* **-ń**) *nt* (*opowieść*) story; (*utwór literacki*) short story

O

**opowi|edzieć (-em, -esz)** (*imp* **-edz**) *vb perf od* **opowiadać**
**opowieś|ć** (**-ci, -ci**) (*gen pl* **-ci**) *f* tale, story
**opozycj|a** (**-i, -e**) (*gen pl* **-i**) *f* opposition; **~ parlamentarna** parliamentary opposition, the Opposition
**opozycyjny** *adj* (*partia, ugrupowanie*) opposition *attr*; (*działanie*) oppositional
**op|ór** (**-oru**) (*loc sg* **-orze**) *m* resistance; **opory** *pl*: **mieć opory przed zrobieniem czegoś** to be reluctant to do sth; **ruch oporu** the Resistance; **iść (pójść** *perf*) **po linii najmniejszego oporu** to take the line of least resistance; **nie stawiać oporu** to put up *lub* offer no resistance
**opóź|niać (-niam, -niasz)** (*perf* **-nić**) *vt* (*wyjazd*) to postpone, to delay; (*dojrzewanie*) to retard; **opóźniać się** *vr* (*mieć zaległości*) to be behind time, to lag *lub* fall behind; (*o pociągu*) to be late; (*o zegarze*) to be slow
**opóź|nić (-nię, -nisz)** (*imp* **-nij**) *vb perf od* **opóźniać**
**opóźnie|nie** (**-nia, -nia**) (*gen pl* **-ń**) *nt* delay; **~ może ulec zmianie** the delay is subject to change
**opóźniony** *adj* (*pociąg*) delayed; (*w rozwoju*) retarded
**oprac|ować (-uję, -ujesz)** *vb perf od* **opracowywać**
**opracowa|nie** (**-nia, -nia**) (*gen pl* **-ń**) *nt* study
**opracow|ywać (-uję, -ujesz)** (*perf* **-ać**) *vt* to work out, to draw up
**opra|wa** (**-wy, -wy**) (*dat sg* **-wie**) *f* (*książki*) binding; (*obrazu, zdjęcia*) frame; (*klejnotu*) setting; (*okularów*) frame, rim; **~ muzyczna/plastyczna** musical/visual setting
**opra|wiać (-wiam, -wiasz)** (*perf* **-wić**) *vt* (*książkę*) to bind; (*obraz*) to frame; (*klejnot*) to set; (*rybę, kurę*) to flay
**opraw|ka** (**-ki, -ki**) (*dat sg* **-ce**, *gen pl* **-ek**) *f* (*okularów*) frame, rim; (*żarówki*) socket
**opresj|a** (**-i, -e**) (*gen pl* **-i**) *f*: **wybawić** (*perf*) **kogoś z opresji** to let sb off the hook
**oprocentowa|nie** (**-nia, -nia**) (*gen pl* **-ń**) *nt* interest (rate)
**oprogramowa|nie** (**-nia, -nia**) (*gen pl* **-ń**) *nt* software
**oprowadz|ać (-am, -asz)** (*perf* **oprowadzić**) *vt* to show round
**oprowa|dzić (-dzę, -dzisz)** (*imp* **-dź**) *vb perf od* **oprowadzać**
**oprócz** *prep +gen* (*w uzupełnieniu*) apart *lub* aside from, beside(s); (*z wyjątkiem*) except; **~ tego** besides
**opróż|niać (-niam, -niasz)** (*perf* **-nić**) *vt* (*butelkę, szufladę*) to empty; (*wagon*) to unload; (*mieszkanie*) to vacate; **opróżniać się** *vr* (*pustoszeć*) to empty, to become empty
**opróż|nić (-nię, -nisz)** (*imp* **-nij**) *vb perf od* **opróżniać**
**oprysk|ać (-am, -asz)** *vb perf od* **opryskiwać**
**opryskiwacz** (**-a, -e**) (*gen pl* **-y**) *m* (*do trawników*) sprinkler; (*do nawozów, środków ochrony*) sprayer
**oprys|kiwać (-kuję, -kujesz)** (*perf* **-kać**) *vt* (*wodą, błotem*) to splash; (*Rol*) to spray
**opryskliwy** *adj* surly
**opryszcz|ka** (**-ki, -ki**) (*dat sg* **-ce**, *gen pl* **-ek**) *f* cold sore
**oprysz|ek** (**-ka, -ki** *lub* **-kowie**) (*instr sg* **-kiem**) *m* (*pot*) thug, ruffian
**op|rzeć (-rę, -rzesz)** (*imp* **-rzyj**, *pt* **-arł**) *vb perf od* **opierać**
**oprzytomnie|ć (-ję, -jesz)** *vb perf od* **przytomnieć**
**optimum** *nt inv* optimum
**opt|ować (-uję, -ujesz)** *vi*: **~ za** *+instr* to opt for
**optyczny** *adj* optical
**opty|k** (**-ka, -cy**) (*instr sg* **-kiem**) *m* optician
**opty|ka** (**-ki**) (*dat sg* **-ce**) *f* optics
**optymalizacj|a** (**-i**) *f* optimization
**optymaliz|ować (-uję, -ujesz)** (*perf* **z-**) *vt* to optimize
**optymalny** *adj* optimal, optimum *attr*
**optymi|sta** (**-sty, -ści**) (*loc sg* **-ście**) *m decl like f in sg* optimist
**optymist|ka** (**-ki, -ki**) (*dat sg* **-ce**) *f* optimist
**optymistyczny** *adj* optimistic
**optymiz|m** (**-mu**) (*loc sg* **-mie**) *m* optimism
**opublik|ować (-uję, -ujesz)** *vb perf od* **publikować**
**opuchli|zna** (**-zny**) (*dat sg* **-źnie**) *f* swelling
**opuch|nąć (-nę, -niesz)** (*imp* **-nij**) *vb perf od* **puchnąć**
**opuchnięty** *adj* swollen
**opu|kiwać (-kuję, -kujesz)** (*perf* **-kać**) *vt* to tap; (*Med*) to percuss
**opu|s** (**-su, -sy**) (*loc sg* **-sie**) *nt decl like m*; **~ dziesiąte** opus 10
**opustoszały** *adj* deserted
**opustosze|ć (-je)** *vi perf* to empty, to become deserted
**opuszcz|ać (-am, -asz)** (*perf* **opuścić**) *vt* (*flagę, oczy, cenę*) to lower; (*szybę w samochodzie*) to wind down; (*rodzinę*) to abandon, to desert, to leave; (*pokój, szkołę, miejsce zamieszkania*) to leave; (*lekcje*) to cut *lub* miss; (*pomijać*) to skip, to leave out; **nie ~ kogoś** to stand *lub* stick by sb; **opuszczać się** *vr* (*obniżać się*) to lower; (*na linie*) to let o.s. down; (*zaniedbywać się*) to neglect one's duties; **odwaga mnie opuściła** my courage failed me; **opuścił się w nauce/pracy** he has lowered his standards

**opuszczony** *adj* (*dom, wieś*) deserted; (*człowiek*) desolate, forlorn
**opusz|ka** (**-ki, -ki**) (*dat sg* **-ce**) *f*: **opuszki palców** fingertips
**opu|ścić** (**-szczę, -ścisz**) (*imp* **-ść**) *vb perf od* **opuszczać**
**opych|ać się** (**-am, -asz**) (*perf* **opchać**) *vr* (*pot*): **opychać się (czymś)** to gorge (o.s.) (on sth)
**opyl|ać** (**-am, -asz**) (*perf* **-ić**) *vt* (*pokrywać proszkiem*) to sprinkle; (*pot: sprzedawać*) to flog (*pot*)
**orać** (**orzę, orzesz**) (*imp* **orz**) *vt* to plough (*Brit*), to plow (*US*) ▷ *vi* (*pot: ciężko pracować*) to sweat (*pot*)
**oranguta|n** (**-na, -ny**) (*loc sg* **-nie**) *m* orang-(o)utan(g)
**oranża|da** (**-dy, -dy**) (*dat sg* **-dzie**) *f* orangeade
**oranżeri|a** (**-i, -e**) (*gen pl* **-i**) *f* orangery
**orato|r** (**-ra, -rzy**) (*loc sg* **-rze**) *m* (*książk*) orator
**oratori|um** (**-um, -a**) (*gen pl* **-ów**) *nt inv in sg* oratorio
**oratorski** *adj* oratorical
**oraz** *conj* as well as
**orbi|ta** (**-ty, -ty**) (*dat sg* **-cie**) *f* orbit; (*Anat*) socket
**orce** *n patrz* **orka**
**orchide|a** (**-i, -e**) (*gen pl* **-i**) *f* orchid
**orczykowy** *adj*: **wyciąg ~** T-bar lift
**orde|r** (**-ru, -ry**) (*loc sg* **-rze**) *m* decoration, medal
**ordynacj|a** (**-i, -e**) (*gen pl* **-i**) *f*: **~ wyborcza** electoral law
**ordynarny** *adj* (*wulgarny*) vulgar; (*nieokrzesany*) rude; (*kłamstwo*) outright; (*fałszerstwo*) crude; (*w złym guście*) cheap
**ordynato|r** (**-ra, -rzy**) (*loc sg* **-rze**) *m head of a hospital ward*
**orę|dzie** (**-dzia, -dzia**) (*gen pl* **-dzi**) *nt*: **~ prezydenckie** presidential address
**oręż** (**-a**) *m* (*książk: broń*) arms *pl*; (*siły zbrojne*) army
**orga|n** (**-nu, -ny**) (*loc sg* **-nie**) *m* organ; **organy** *pl* (*Muz*) organ
**organiczny** *adj* organic
**organi|sta** (**-sty, -ści**) (*loc sg* **-ście**) *m decl like f in sg* organist
**organizacj|a** (**-i, -e**) (*gen pl* **-i**) *f* organization
**organizacyjny** *adj* (*działalność, zdolności*) organizational; (*komitet*) organizing
**organizato|r** (**-ra, -rzy**) (*loc sg* **-rze**) *m* organizer
**organiz|m** (**-mu, -my**) (*loc sg* **-mie**) *m* organism; **~ człowieka** the human body; **mieć silny ~** to have a strong constitution; **to był wstrząs dla jej ~u** it was a shock to her system
**organiz|ować** (**-uję, -ujesz**) (*perf* **z-**) *vt* (*wycieczkę, bal, pracę*) to organize; (*spotkanie*) to arrange; (*komitet, spółkę*) to set up; (*pot: załatwiać*) to fix (up); **organizować się** *vr* to organize
**organ|ki** (**-ków**) *pl* mouth organ, harmonica
**orgaz|m** (**-mu, -my**) (*loc sg* **-mie**) *m* orgasm, climax
**orgi|a** (**-i, -e**) (*gen pl* **-i**) *f* orgy
**orientacj|a** (**-i, -e**) (*gen pl* **-i**) *f* orientation; **zmysł orientacji** sense of direction; **bieg na orientację** orienteering; **tracić** (**stracić** *perf*) **orientację** to lose one's bearings
**orientacyjny** *adj* (*znak, punkt*) reference *attr*; (*przybliżony*) rough
**orientalny** *adj* oriental
**orient|ować** (**-uję, -ujesz**) (*perf* **z-**) *vt* (*osobę*) to inform, to brief; (*mapę*) to orientate; **orientować się** *vr* (*rozpoznawać strony świata*) to orientate o.s.; **~ się w** *+instr* to be at home in; **o ile się orientuję, ...** as far as I am aware, ...
**or|ka** (**-ki**) (*dat sg* **-ce**) *f* (*Rol*) ploughing (*Brit*), plowing (*US*); (*pot*) drudgery; (*Zool*) (*nom pl* **-ki**, *gen pl* **-ek**) orca, killer whale
**orkiest|ra** (**-ry, -ry**) (*dat sg* **-rze**) *f* orchestra; (*na dancingu*) band; **~ kameralna/symfoniczna** chamber/symphony orchestra; **~ dęta/jazzowa** brass/jazz band
**orle** *n patrz* **orzeł**
**orli** *adj* (*pióro, dziób*) eagle's *attr*; (*nos*) aquiline; **~ wzrok** eagle eye
**orła** *n patrz* **orzeł**
**Ormia|nin** (**-nina, -nie**) (*gen pl* **-n**) *m* Armenian
**Ormian|ka** (**-ki, -ki**) (*dat sg* **-ce**, *gen pl* **-ek**) *f* Armenian
**ormiański** *adj* Armenian
**ornamen|t** (**-tu, -ty**) (*loc sg* **-cie**) *m* ornament
**orna|t** (**-tu, -ty**) (*loc sg* **-cie**) *m* (*Rel*) vestments
**ornitologi|a** (**-i**) *f* ornithology
**orny** *adj* arable
**ORP** *abbr inv* (*= Okręt Rzeczypospolitej Polskiej*) ≈ HMS (*Brit*), ≈ USS (*US*)
**orsza|k** (**-ku, -ki**) (*instr sg* **-kiem**) *m* (*świta*) retinue; (*pochód*) procession
**ortodoksyjny** *adj* orthodox
**ortografi|a** (**-i, -e**) (*gen pl* **-i**) *f* (*nauka*) orthography; (*pisownia*) spelling
**ortograficzny** *adj*: **błąd/słownik ~** spelling mistake/dictionary
**ortope|da** (**-dy, -dzi**) (*loc sg* **-dzie**) *m decl like f in sg* orthop(a)edist
**oryginalnoś|ć** (**-ci, -ci**) *f* (*niezwykłość, osobliwość*) originality; (*swoistość*) uniqueness
**oryginalny** *adj* (*pierwotny, niezwykły, osobliwy*) original; (*autentyczny*) genuine; (*swoisty*) unique

O

**orygina|ł (-łu, -ły)** *(loc sg* **-le***)* *m* *(obrazu, dokumentu)* original; *(dziwak)* eccentric
**orze|c (-knę, -kniesz)** *(imp* **-knij**, *pt* **-kł***)* *vb perf od* **orzekać**
**orzech** **(-a, -y)** *m* *(owoc)* nut; *(drzewo: włoski)* walnut tree; *(: laskowy)* hazel; *(drewno)* walnut; **~ włoski** walnut; **~ laskowy** hazelnut; **~ ziemny** peanut; **twardy ~ do zgryzienia** a hard *lub* tough nut to crack
**orzechowy** *adj* *(kolor)* nut-brown; **masło orzechowe** peanut butter; **czekolada orzechowa** nut chocolate
**orzecze|nie** **(-nia, -nia)** *(gen pl* **-ń***)* *nt* *(opinia)* judg(e)ment; *(decyzja)* decree; *(Prawo)* verdict, ruling; *(Jęz)* predicate
**orzek|ać (-am, -asz)** *(perf* **orzec***)* *vi* *(oświadczać)* to state; *(Prawo)* to rule, to adjudicate ▷ *vt* *(stwierdzać)* to state
**orzekający** *adj*: **tryb ~** indicative mood
**orzeł** **(orła, orły)** *(loc sg* **orle***)* *m* eagle; *(przen)* high-flier; **~ czy reszka?** heads or tails?
**orzesz|ek** **(-ka, -ki)** *(instr sg* **-kiem***)* *m* (small) nut; **orzeszki ziemne** *lub* **arachidowe** peanuts
**orzeź|wiać (-wiam, -wiasz)** *(perf* **-wić***)* *vt* to refresh; **orzeźwiać się** *vr* to refresh o.s.
**orzeźwiający** *adj* refreshing; **napoje orzeźwiające** refreshments *(drinks)*
**orzeź|wić (-wię, -wisz)** *(imp* **-wij***)* *vb perf od* **orzeźwiać**
**orzę** *itd. vb patrz* **orać**
**osa** **(osy, osy)** *(dat sg* **osie***)* *f* wasp; **cienka jak osa** wasp-waisted; **cięty jak osa** waspish
**osacz|ać (-am, -asz)** *(perf* **-yć***)* *vt* *(otaczać)* to corner; *(o myślach, niepokoju)* to haunt
**osa|d** **(-du, -dy)** *(loc sg* **-dzie***)* *m* sediment; *(Chem)* precipitate
**osa|da** **(-dy, -dy)** *(dat sg* **-dzie***)* *f* *(wioska)* settlement; *(Sport)* team
**osadnicz|ka** **(-ki, -ki)** *(dat sg* **-ce**, *gen pl* **-ek***)* *f* settler
**osadni|k** **(-ka, -cy)** *(instr sg* **-kiem***)* *m* settler
**osadz|ać (-am, -asz)** *(perf* **osadzić***)* *vt* *(osiedlać)* to settle; *(w areszcie, na tronie)* to put; *(umiejscawiać)* to place; *(nanosić osad)* to deposit; *(przytwierdzać)* to fix, to secure; *(oprawiać)* to set; **osadzać się** *vr* *(Chem)* to precipitate
**osa|dzić (-dzę, -dzisz)** *(imp* **-dź***)* *vb perf od* **osadzać**
**osamotnieni|e** **(-a)** *nt* *(samotność)* solitude, loneliness; *(odosobnienie)* seclusion
**osamotniony** *adj* *(samotny)* lonely; *(opuszczony)* forlorn
**osą|d** **(-du, -dy)** *(loc sg* **-dzie***)* *m* *(książk)* judg(e) ment
**osądz|ać (-am, -asz)** *(perf* **osądzić***)* *vt* *(podejrzanego)* to adjudge; *(sytuację)* to appraise
**osą|dzić (-dzę, -dzisz)** *(imp* **-dź***)* *vb perf od* **osądzać**
**oschły** *adj* dry
**oscyl|ować (-uję, -ujesz)** *vi* to oscillate; **~ między A a B** *(o temperaturze)* to vary from A to B; *(o człowieku)* to oscillate between A and B
**oseł|ka** **(-ki, -ki)** *(dat sg* **-ce***)* *f* whetstone
**oses|ek** **(-ka, -ki)** *(instr sg* **-kiem***)* *m* suckling
**oset** **(ostu, osty)** *(loc sg* **oście***)* *m* thistle
**osępiały** *adj* crestfallen
**osi** *itd. n patrz* **oś**
**osiad|ać (-am, -asz)** *(perf* **osiąść***)* *vi* to settle; **osiąść na mieliźnie** to run aground
**osiadły** *adj* *(człowiek)* settled; *(ptak)* resident
**osiąg|ać (-am, -asz)** *(perf* **-nąć***)* *vt* *(sukces, cel, wynik)* to achieve, to accomplish; *(szczyt, nakład)* to reach; **nic (przez to) nie osiągniesz** you will gain nothing (by this)
**osiągalny** *adj* attainable
**osią|gi** **(-gów)** *pl* *(Mot)* performance
**osiąg|nąć (-nę, -niesz)** *(imp* **-nij***)* *vb perf od* **osiągać**
**osiągnię|cie** **(-cia, -cia)** *(gen pl* **-ć***)* *nt* achievement
**osią|ść (-dę, -dziesz)** *(imp* **-dź**, *pt* **osiadł, osiadła, osiedli***)* *vb perf od* **osiadać**
**osiedl|ać (-am, -asz)** *(perf* **-ić***)* *vt* to settle; **osiedlać się** *vr* to settle
**osiedl|e** **(-a, -a)** *(gen pl* **-i***)* *nt* *(też:* **osiedle mieszkaniowe***)* (housing) estate *(Brit)*, housing development *(US)*; *(Hist)* settlement
**osiedle|niec** **(-ńca, -ńcy)** *(voc sg* **-ńcze***)* *m* settler
**osiem** *(jak:* **pięć***)* *num* eight
**osiemdziesiąt** *(jak:* **dziesięć***)* *num* eighty
**osiemdziesiąt|ka** **(-ki, -ki)** *(dat sg* **-ce**, *gen pl* **-ek***)* *f* eighty
**osiemdziesiąty** *adj* eightieth
**osiemnast|ka** **(-ki, -ki)** *(dat sg* **-ce***)* *f* eighteen; *(pot: urodziny)* eighteenth birthday; *(pot: przyjęcie)* eighteenth birthday party
**osiemnastoletni** *adj* eighteen-year-old *attr*
**osiemnastowieczny** *adj* 18th century *attr*
**osiemnasty** *adj* eighteenth; **(godzina) osiemnasta** 6 p.m.
**osiemnaście** *(jak:* **jedenaście***)* *num* eighteen
**osiemset** *(jak:* **pięćset***)* *num* eight hundred
**osiemsetny** *adj* eight hundredth
**osier|dzie** **(-dzia, -dzia)** *(gen pl* **-dzi***)* *nt* *(Anat)* pericardium
**osiero|cić (-cę, -cisz)** *(imp* **-ć***)* *vt perf* to orphan
**osi|ka** **(-ki, -ki)** *(dat sg* **-ce***)* *f* *(Bot)* aspen; **trząść się** *lub* **drżeć jak ~** to shake like a jelly *lub* leaf
**osił|ek** **(-ka, -ki)** *(instr sg* **-kiem***)* *m* *(pot)* bruiser *(pot)*
**osiodł|ać (-am, -asz)** *vb perf od* **siodłać**

**osioł** (**osła, osły**) (*loc sg* **ośle**) *m* donkey, ass; (*pot: głupi człowiek*) ass (*pot*); **uparty jak ~** (as) stubborn as a mule
**osiwi|eć (-eję, -ejesz)** (*imp* **-ej**) *vb perf od* **siwieć**
**oskalp|ować (-uję, -ujesz)** *vb perf od* **skalpować**
**oskar|d** (**-da, -dy**) (*loc sg* **-dzie**) *m* pick(axe) (*Brit*), pick(ax) (*US*)
**oskarż|ać (-am, -asz)** (*perf* **-yć**) *vt*: **~ kogoś (o coś)** to accuse sb (of sth); (*Prawo*) to charge sb (with sth)
**oskarże|nie** (**-nia, -nia**) (*gen pl* **-ń**) *nt* (*zarzut*) accusation; (*Prawo: strona oskarżająca*) prosecution; **akt oskarżenia** indictment; **świadek oskarżenia** witness for the prosecution; **postawić** (*perf*) **kogoś w stan oskarżenia** to indict sb, to bring sb to trial
**oskarżon|a** (**-ej, -e**) *f decl like adj* (*Prawo*) (the) accused, (the) defendant
**oskarż|ony** (**-onego, -eni**) *m decl like adj* (*Prawo*) (the) accused, (the) defendant
**oskarżyciel** (**-a, -e**) *m* (*Prawo*) prosecutor; **~ publiczny** Public Prosecutor
**oskarżycielski** *adj* (*ton, spojrzenie*) accusatory
**oskro|bać (-bię, -biesz)** *vb perf od* **oskrobywać, skrobać**
**oskrob|ywać (-uję, -ujesz)** (*perf* **-ać**) *vt* (*warzywa*) to scrape; (*rybę*) to scale; **oskrobać rurę z rdzy** to scrape the rust off the pipe
**oskrzel|a** (**-i**) *pl* (*Anat*) bronchial tubes *pl*, bronchi *pl*; **zapalenie oskrzeli** bronchitis
**osku|bać (-bię, -biesz)** *vb perf od* **oskubywać, skubać**; (*pot: oszukać*) to fleece (*pot*)
**oskub|ywać (-uję, -ujesz)** (*perf* **-ać**) *vt* to pluck
**osła|biać (-biam, -biasz)** (*perf* **-bić**) *vt* (*człowieka, serce, fundament*) to weaken; (*wrażenie*) to reduce, to lessen; (*cios, upadek*) to soften, to cushion
**osłabieni|e** (**-a**) *nt* weakness
**osłabiony** *adj* weak
**osłab|nąć (-nę, -niesz)** *vb perf od* **słabnąć**
**osładz|ać (-am, -asz)** (*perf* **osłodzić**) *vt* to sweeten
**osłani|ać (-am, -asz)** (*perf* **osłonić**) *vt* to cover; **~ kogoś (przed czymś)** to shield *lub* shelter sb (from sth)
**osławiony** *adj* renowned, famed
**osło|da** (**-dy**) (*dat sg* **-dzie**) *f* (*pociecha*) comfort; **na osłodę** as a comfort
**osł|odzić (-odzę, -odzisz)** (*imp* **-odź** *lub* **-ódź**) *vb perf od* **osładzać, słodzić**
**osło|na** (**-ny, -ny**) (*dat sg* **-nie**) *f* (*okrycie*) cover, shield; (*ochrona*) protection; (*Wojsk*) cover; **pod osłoną nocy** under cover of darkness
**osłonek** *inv*: **bez ~** openly
**osło|nić (-nię, -nisz)** (*imp* **-ń**) *vb perf od* **osłaniać**
**osłuch|ać (-am, -asz)** *vb perf od* **osłuchiwać**; **osłuchać się** *vr perf*: **~ się z czymś** (*poznać*) to get a feel for sth; **już mi się osłuchała ta piosenka** I've grown tired of this song
**osłu|chiwać (-chuję, -chujesz)** (*perf* **-chać**) *vt* (*Med*) to auscultate
**osłupi|eć (-eję, -ejesz)** *vi perf* to be stunned
**osłupieni|e** (**-a**) *nt* bewilderment; **wprawiać (wprawić** *perf*) **kogoś w ~** to bewilder sb
**osn|owa** (**-owy, -owy**) (*gen pl* **-ów**) *f* (*w tkaninie*) warp; (*Lit*) fabric
**osnuty** *adj*: **~ na** *+instr* based (up)on
**os|oba** (**-oby, -oby**) (*dat sg* **-obie**, *gen pl* **-ób**) *f* (*człowiek*) person, individual; (*kobieta*) woman; (*Jęz*) person; (*postać dramatu*) character; **stół/obiad na cztery osoby** table/dinner for four; **prezydent we własnej osobie** the president himself; **w jednej osobie** rolled into one; **~ fizyczna** private person; **~ prawna** legal entity *lub* person, body corporate; **~ trzecia** third party
**osobistoś|ć** (**-ci, -ci**) (*gen pl* **-ci**) *f* (*znana osoba*) celebrity, personality; (*ważna osoba*) personage
**osobisty** *adj* personal; **komputer ~** personal computer; **dowód ~** ≈ identity card; **rewizja osobista** body search
**osobiście** *adv* personally, in person; **~ uważam, że ...** personally, I think that ...
**osobliwoś|ć** (**-ci, -ci**) (*gen pl* **-ci**) *f* (*rzecz dziwna*) curiosity; (*dziwność*) oddity; (*specyficzność*) peculiarity
**osobliwy** *adj* (*dziwny*) odd, curious; (*specyficzny*) peculiar
**osobni|k** (**-ka**) (*instr sg* **-kiem**) *m* (*Bio*) (*nom pl* **-ki**) specimen; (*mężczyzna*) (*nom pl* **-cy**) individual
**osobno** *adv* separately
**osobności** *inv*: **na ~** in private
**osobny** *adj* separate; **z osobna** separately, individually
**osobowoś|ć** (**-ci, -ci**) (*gen pl* **-ci**) *f* personality; **~ prawna** legal personality
**osobowy** *adj* (*winda, pojazd*) passenger *attr*; (*Jęz*) personal; **pociąg ~** slow train; **dział ~** personnel department
**osocz|e** (**-a**) *nt* (*Bio*) plasma
**osol|ić (-ę, -isz)** (*imp* **osól**) *vb perf od* **solić**
**osowiały** *adj* dejected
**os|pa** (**-py**) (*dat sg* **-pie**) *f* (*Med*) smallpox; **~ wietrzna** chickenpox
**ospały** *adj* (*senny*) drowsy; (*powolny*) sluggish
**ospowaty** *adj* (*twarz*) pockmarked
**osprzę|t** (**-tu**) (*loc sg* **-cie**) *m* equipment
**osta|ć się (-nę, -niesz)** (*imp* **-ń**) *vr perf* (*książk*) to survive

**ostatecznie** *adv* (*w końcu*) finally, ultimately; (*ewentualnie*) after all
**ostatecznoś|ć** (**-ci**) *f* (*konieczność*) necessity; (*wyjątkowa sytuacja*) extremity; **w ostateczności** as a last resort; **doprowadzić** (*perf*) **kogoś do ostateczności** to drive sb to extremes
**ostateczny** *adj* final; **sąd ~** (*Rel*) the Final *lub* Last Judgement
**ostat|ek** (**-ka, -ki**) (*instr sg* **-kiem**) *m* (*resztka*) remainder; **do ostatka** to the bitter end; **na ~** at the end; **ostatki** *pl* (*ostatnie dni karnawału*) Shrovetide
**ostatni** *adj* (*końcowy*) last; (*najnowszy*) latest; (*ostateczny*) final; (*spośród wymienionych*) (the) latter; (*najgorszy*) out-and-out *attr*; **w ~ch latach** in recent years; **~e słowo** the last word; **~a wola** last will; **~e namaszczenie** the last rites *pl*; **on jest ~ą osobą, która ...** he'd be the last (person) to ...; **w pierwszym/~m przypadku ...** in the former/latter case ...
**ostatnio** *adv* recently, lately
**ostentacyjny** *adj* ostentatious
**osteoporo|za** (**-zy**) (*dat sg* **-zie**) *f* osteoporosis
**osto|ja** (**-i**) *f* mainstay
**ostro** (*comp* **ostrzej**) *adv* sharply
**ostro|ga** (**-gi, -gi**) (*dat sg* **-dze**) *f* spur
**ostrokątny** *adj*: **trójkąt ~** acute triangle
**ostrokrze|w** (**-wu, -wy**) (*loc sg* **-wie**) *m* (*Bot*) holly
**ostrosłu|p** (**-pa, -py**) (*loc sg* **-pie**) *m* (*Geom*) pyramid
**ostroś|ć** (**-ci**) *f* sharpness; (*Fot*) focus; **~ wzroku** sharpness of vision
**ostrożnie** *adv* carefully, cautiously; **~!** watch out!; **„~"** (*na paczce*) "(handle) with care"
**ostrożnoś|ć** (**-ci**) *f* caution; **przedsięwziąć** (*perf*) **środki ostrożności** to take precautions
**ostrożny** *adj* (*człowiek, postępowanie*) careful, cautious; (*oszacowanie, prognoza*) conservative
**ostr|ów** (**-owu, -owy**) (*loc sg* **-owie**) *m* (*książk*) islet
**ostrug|ać** (**-am, -asz**) *vb perf od* **strugać**
**ostry** (*comp* **ostrzejszy**) *adj* sharp; (*zima*) severe, hard; (*papryka*) hot; (*kąt*) acute; (*Med*) acute; (*gra*) rough
**ostry|ga** (**-gi, -gi**) (*dat sg* **-dze**) *f* oyster
**ostrza|ł** (**-łu**) (*loc sg* **-le**) *m* fire, shelling; **znajdować się** *lub* **być pod ~em** to be under fire
**ostrz|e** (**-a, -a**) (*gen pl* **-y**) *nt* (*podłużne*) blade, edge; (*spiczaste*) point; **postawić** (*perf*) **coś na ostrzu noża** to bring sth to a head
**ostrze|c** (**-gę, -żesz**) (*imp* **-ż**, *pt* **-gł**) *vb perf od* **ostrzegać**
**ostrzeg|ać** (**-am, -asz**) (*perf* **ostrzec**) *vt*: **~ kogoś (o czymś)** to warn sb (of sth); **~ kogoś przed kimś/czymś** to warn *lub* caution sb against sb/sth
**ostrzegawczy** *adj* warning *attr*
**ostrzeliw|ać** (**-uję, -ujesz**) (*perf* **ostrzelać**) *vt* to shell
**ostrzeże|nie** (**-nia, -nia**) (*gen pl* **-ń**) *nt* warning
**ostrzy|c** (**-gę, -żesz**) (*imp* **-ż**, *pt* **-gł**) *vb perf od* **strzyc**
**ostrz|yć** (**-ę, -ysz**) (*perf* **na-**) *vt* to sharpen; **~ sobie zęby na coś** to set one's sights on sth
**ostu** *itd. n patrz* **oset**
**ostudz|ać** (**-am, -asz**) (*perf* **ostudzić**) *vt* to cool down
**ostu|dzić** (**-dzę, -dzisz**) (*imp* **-dź**) *vb perf od* **studzić, ostudzać**
**ostyg|nąć** (**-nę, -niesz**) (*imp* **-nij**, *pt* **-ł**) *vb perf od* **stygnąć**
**osu|nąć się** (**-nę, -niesz**) (*imp* **-ń**) *vb perf od* **osuwać się**
**osusz|ać** (**-am, -asz**) (*perf* **-yć**) *vt* (*oczy, łzy*) to wipe, to dry; (*bagno*) to drain
**osuw|ać się** (**-am, -asz**) (*perf* **osunąć**) *vr* (*o ziemi, brzegu*) to slide; (*o nodze*) to slip; (*upadać*) to slump
**oswabadz|ać** (**-am, -asz**) (*perf* **oswobodzić**) *vb* = **oswobadzać**
**oswaj|ać** (**-am, -asz**) (*perf* **oswoić**) *vt* (*zwierzę*) to tame, to domesticate; **~ kogoś z czymś** to accustom sb to sth; **oswajać się** *vr* (*o zwierzęciu*) to become tame; **~ się z czymś** to get used to sth, to grow accustomed to sth
**oswobadz|ać, oswabadz|ać** (**-am, -asz**) (*perf* **oswobodzić**) *vt* (*przywracać wolność*) to liberate, to (set) free; (*uwalniać: od obowiązku*) to release, to free; **oswobadzać się** *vr* to free *lub* liberate o.s.
**oswobodziciel** (**-a, -e**) (*gen pl* **-i**) *m* (*książk*) liberator
**oswobo|dzić** (**-dzę, -dzisz**) (*imp* **-dź**) *vb perf od* **oswobadzać**
**oswo|ić** (**-ję, -isz**) (*imp* **oswój**) *vb perf od* **oswajać**
**oswojony** *adj* tame, domesticated
**oszac|ować** (**-uję, -ujesz**) *vb perf od* **szacować**
**oszalały** *adj* mad
**oszale|ć** (**-ję, -jesz**) *vi perf* to go mad
**oszałami|ać** (**-am, -asz**) (*perf* **oszołomić**) *vt* (*odurzać*) to stupefy; (*urzekać*) to stun
**oszałamiający** *adj* stunning
**oszcze|nić się** (**-ni**) *vr perf* to have pups, to pup
**oszcze|p** (**-pu, -py**) (*loc sg* **-pie**) *m* (*Sport*) javelin; (*dzida*) spear; **rzut ~em** javelin throw
**oszczerc|a** (**-y, -y**) *m decl like f in sg* slanderer
**oszczerczy** *adj* slanderous

**oszczerst|wo** (**-wa, -wa**) (*loc sg* **-wie**) *nt* slander
**oszczędnościowy** *adj* (*model, wersja*) economy *attr*; (*rachunek*) savings *attr*
**oszczędnoś|ć** (**-ci**) *f* (*cecha charakteru*) thrift(iness); (*oszczędne używanie*) economy; **oszczędności** *pl* savings *pl*
**oszczędny** *adj* (*człowiek*) thrifty; (*gospodarka, metoda*) economical; (*samochód*) fuel-efficient
**oszczędz|ać (-am, -asz)** *vt* (*czas*) to save; (*pieniądze*) to put away, to save; (*energię, wodę*) to conserve, to save; (*siły, ręce, człowieka, konia*) to spare ▷ *vi* (*oszczędzać pieniądze*) to save (up); (*żyć oszczędnie*) to economize; **~ na czymś** to economize on sth; **oszczędzać się** *vr* to take it easy; **nie ~ się** to pull one's weight
**oszczę|dzić (-dzę, -dzisz)** (*imp* **-dź**) *vt perf*: **~ kogoś** to spare sb; **katastrofa nie oszczędziła nikogo** the catastrophe spared nobody; **~ komuś kłopotów** to save sb trouble
**oszlif|ować (-uję, -ujesz)** *vb perf od* **szlifować**
**oszoło|m** (**-ma, -my**) (*loc sg* **-mie**) *m* (*pot*) fanatic
**oszoło|mić (-mię, -misz)** *vb perf od* **oszałamiać**
**oszołomieni|e** (**-a**) *nt* (*stan zamroczenia*) stupor; (*szok*) stupefaction
**oszpec|ać (-am, -asz)** (*perf* **oszpecić**) *vt* to mar
**oszpe|cić (-cę, -cisz)** (*imp* **-ć**) *vb perf od* **oszpecać**
**oszroniony** *adj* frosted
**oszuk|ać (-am, -asz)** *vb perf od* **oszukiwać**; **oszukać się** *vr perf* to be disappointed
**oszu|kiwać (-kuję, -kujesz)** (*perf* **-kać**) *vi* to cheat ▷ *vt* to deceive
**oszu|st** (**-sta, -ści**) (*loc sg* **-ście**) *m* fraud, cheat
**oszust|ka** (**-ki, -ki**) (*dat sg* **-ce**, *gen pl* **-ek**) *f* fraud, cheat
**oszust|wo** (**-wa, -wa**) (*loc sg* **-wie**) *nt* deception, fraud
**oś** (**osi, osie**) (*gen pl* **osi**) *f* axis; (*Tech*) axle; (*przen*) pivot
**oście** *n patrz* **oset**
**ościenny** *adj* neighbouring (*Brit*), neighboring (*US*)
**oścież** *inv*: **otwarty na ~** wide open
**ościsty** *adj* bony
**oś|ć** (**-ci, -ci**) (*gen pl* **-ci**) *f* fishbone; **stanąć** (*perf*) **komuś ością w gardle** to stick in sb's throat
**ośka** (**ośki, ośki**) (*dat sg* **ośce**, *gen pl* **osiek**) *f* axle
**ośle** *n patrz* **osioł**
**oślep** *adv* blindly; **robić coś na ~** to do sth blindfold
**ośle|piać (-piam, -piasz)** (*perf* **-pić**) *vt* to blind; (*razić*) to dazzle
**oślepiający** *adj* dazzling, glaring
**oślep|nąć (-nę, -niesz)** (*imp* **-nij**) *vb perf od* **ślepnąć**
**ośli** *adj* donkey *attr*; **posadzić kogoś w oślej ławce** (*Szkol*) ≈ to put sb in the corner; **ośla łączka** (*Narty: pot*) bunny hill, nursery slope; **~ upór** mulishness; **ośla głowa** (*pot*) dimwit; **ośle uszy** (*pot*) dog ears
**ośliz(g)ły** *adj* slimy
**ośmiel|ać (-am, -asz)** (*perf* **-ić**) *vt* to encourage; **ośmielać się** *vr* (*nabierać odwagi*) to gain confidence; (*zdobywać się na odwagę*) to dare; (*mieć czelność*) to dare; **ośmielę się zauważyć, że ...** please, allow me to say that ...; **ona nie ośmieliłaby się tego zrobić** she wouldn't dare to do it
**ośmiesz|ać (-am, -asz)** (*perf* **-yć**) *vt* to ridicule; **ośmieszać się** *vr* to make a fool of o.s.
**ośmio...** *itd. patrz* **osiem...**
**ośmiokrotny** *adj* eight-time
**ośmioletni** *adj* eight-year-old
**ośmiopiętrowy** *adj* eight-storeyed (*Brit*), eight-storied (*US*)
**ośmiornic|a** (**-y, -e**) *f* octopus
**ośmioro** (*jak:* **czworo**) *num* eight
**ośmiu** *itd. num patrz* **osiem**
**ośnieżony** *adj* snow-covered, snowy
**ośrod|ek** (**-ka, -ki**) (*instr sg* **-kiem**) *m* centre (*Brit*), center (*US*); **~ zdrowia** health centre (*Brit*) *lub* center (*US*); **~ wypoczynkowy** resort, holiday camp
**ośrodkowy** *adj*: **~ układ nerwowy** central nervous system
**oświadcz|ać (-am, -asz)** (*perf* **-yć**) *vt* to state, to declare; **oświadczać się** *vr*: **~ się komuś** to propose to sb
**oświadcze|nie** (**-nia, -nia**) (*gen pl* **-ń**) *nt* statement, announcement
**oświadczyn|y** (**-**) *pl* proposal (*of marriage*)
**oświa|ta** (**-ty**) (*dat sg* **-cie**) *f* education
**oświatowy** *adj* educational
**oświe|cać (-cam, -casz)** (*perf* **-cić**) (*książk*) *vt* to enlighten
**oświeceni|e** (**-a**) *nt*: **O~** the Enlightenment
**oświe|cić (-cę, -cisz)** (*imp* **-ć**) *vb perf od* **oświecać**
**oświecony** *adj* enlightened
**oświetl|ać (-am, -asz)** (*perf* **-ić**) *vt* to light (up)
**oświetleni|e** (**-a**) *nt* (*światło*) lighting, illumination; (*instalacja oświetleniowa*) lighting system
**Oświęci|m** (**-mia**) (*loc sg* **-miu**) *m* Auschwitz
**otacz|ać (-am, -asz)** (*perf* **otoczyć**) *vt* to surround; (*o płocie, lesie*) to enclose; **otaczać**

O

**się** *vr*: **~ się kimś/czymś** to surround o.s. with sb/sth; **~ coś tajemnicą** to wrap sth in mystery

**otar|cie** (**-cia, -cia**) (*gen pl* **-ć**) *nt* (*Med*) abrasion; **na ~ łez** as a consolation

**otchła|ń** (**-ni, -nie**) (*gen pl* **-ni**) *f* (*przepaść*) abyss; (*głębia*) the depths *pl*; (*przen: piekielna*) abyss; (*: rozpaczy*) the depths *pl*

**otępiały** *adj* (*człowiek*) stupefied; (*wzrok*) dull

**otępieni|e** (**-a**) *nt* (*zobojętnienie*) stupefaction; (*Med*) dementia

**oto** *part*: **oto nasz dom** that's our house; **oto jestem** here I am; **oto wszystko, co wiem** that's all I know; **ten oto samochód** this (very) car; **oto prawdziwy dżentelmen** that's what I call a real gentleman

**otoczeni|e** (**-a**) *nt* (*okolica*) surroundings *pl*; (*środowisko*) environment

**otóż** *part*: **~, ...** well, ...; **~ i ona** there she is; **~ to** exactly!, that's just it!

**otręb|y** (**-ów**) *pl* bran; **~ pszenne** wheat bran

**otru|ć (-ję, -jesz)** *vt perf* to poison; **otruć się** *vr perf* to poison o.s.

**otrzask|ać się (-am, -asz)** *vr perf*: **otrzaskać się z czymś** (*pot: przyzwyczaić się*) to get the hang of sth; **jest otrzaskany z** *+instr* (*pot*) he is familiar with

**otrząs|ać (-am, -asz)** (*perf* **-nąć**) *vt* (*strząsać*) to shake off; **otrząsać się** *vr*: **~ się z czegoś** to shake sth off

**otrzą|snąć (-snę, -śniesz)** (*imp* **-śnij**) *vb perf od* **otrząsać**; **otrząsnąć się** *vr*: **~ się z czegoś** (*przen*) to recover from sth; **~ się** (*perf*) **z przygnębienia** to get over a depression

**otrzeć (otrę, otrzesz)** (*imp* **otrzyj**, *pt* **otarł**) *vb perf od* **ocierać**

**otrze|pać (-pię, -piesz)** *vb perf od* **otrzepywać**

**otrzep|ywać (-uję, -ujesz)** (*perf* **-ać**) *vt*: **~ coś (z czegoś)** to brush sth (off sth); **otrzepywać się** *vr*: **~ się z czegoś** to brush sth off

**otrzewn|a** (**-ej**) *f decl like adj* peritoneum

**otrzeź|wiać (-wiam, -wiasz)** (*perf* **-wić**) *vt* to sober up

**otrzeźwie|ć (-ję, -jesz)** *vb perf od* **trzeźwieć**

**otrzym|ywać (-uję, -ujesz)** (*perf* **-ać**) *vt* to receive; **~ coś z czegoś** to obtain sth out of sth

**otu|cha** (**-chy**) (*dat sg* **-sze**) *f* comfort, reassurance; **dodawać (dodać** *perf***) komuś otuchy** to cheer sb up; **nabrać** (*perf*) **otuchy** to take heart; **tracić (stracić** *perf***) otuchę** to lose heart

**otul|ać (-am, -asz)** (*perf* **-ić**) *vt* (*osobę*) to wrap; (*krzew, drzewo*) to sheathe

**otuma|nić (-nię, -nisz)** (*imp* **-ń**) *vt perf* (*obałamucić*) to stupefy, to con; (*odurzyć*) to daze

**otwarcie**[1] *adv* openly

**otwar|cie**[2] (**-cia, -cia**) (*gen pl* **-ć**) *nt* opening; **godziny otwarcia** opening hours, opening time

**otwartoś|ć** (**-ci**) *f* openness, frankness

**otwarty** *adj* open; **dni otwarte** (*Szkol*) ≈ open day; **dom ~** open house; **pod ~m niebem** in the open air; **z otwartą głową** open-minded; **z ~mi ramionami** with open arms; **list ~** open letter; **grać w otwarte karty** (*przen*) to play with one's cards on the table; **posiedzenie przy drzwiach ~ch** open meeting; **prowadzą ze sobą otwartą wojnę** they are in open conflict; **u otwarte** (*Jęz*) the letter u

**otwieracz** (**-a, -e**) (*gen pl* **-y**) *m* opener; **~ do puszek** *lub* **konserw** tin-opener (*Brit*), can-opener (*US*); **~ do butelek** bottle-opener

**otwier|ać (-am, -asz)** (*perf* **otworzyć**) *vt* to open; (*zamek, kłódkę*) to unlock; (*wodę, gaz*) to turn on; **otwierać się** *vr* to open; (*o widoku, perspektywach*) to open up

**otworz|yć (-ę, -ysz)** (*imp* **otwórz**) *vb perf od* **otwierać**

**otw|ór (-oru, -ory)** (*loc sg* **-orze**) *m* opening; (*dziura*) hole; (*szpara*) slot; (*luka*) gap; **stać otworem** to be open

**otyłoś|ć** (**-ci**) *f* obesity

**otyły** *adj* obese

**otynk|ować (-uję, -ujesz)** *vb perf od* **tynkować**

**owa** *pron* (*książk*) that

**owacj|a** (**-i, -e**) (*gen pl* **-i**) *f* ovation

**owacyjny** *adj* enthusiastic

**owa|d** (**-da, -dy**) (*loc sg* **-dzie**) *m* insect

**owadobójczy** *adj*: **środek ~** insecticide

**owak** *adv*: **tak czy ~** (*pot*) anyhow, in any case

**owaki** (*pot*) *adj*: **taki czy ~** this or that

**owal** (**-u, -e**) (*gen pl* **-i**) *m* oval

**owalny** *adj* oval

**owca** (**owcy, owce**) (*gen pl* **owiec**) *f* sheep; **czarna ~** (*przen*) black sheep

**owczar|ek** (**-ka, -ki**) (*instr sg* **-kiem**) *m* sheepdog, shepherd dog; **~ alzacki** *lub* **niemiecki** Alsatian (*Brit*), German shepherd (*US*); **~ szkocki** collie

**owczy** *adj* sheep's; **robić coś ~m pędem** to follow the herd *lub* crowd

**owdowiały** *adj* widowed

**owdowie|ć (-ję, -jesz)** *vi perf* (*o żonie*) to become a widow; (*o mężu*) to become a widower

**owego** *itd. pron patrz* **ów, owo**

**owiec** *n patrz* **owca**

**owiecz|ka** (**-ki, -ki**) (*dat sg* **-ce**) *f* lamb

**owies** (**owsa, owsy**) (*loc sg* **owsie**) *m* oats *pl*

**owij|ać (-am, -asz)** (*perf* **owinąć**) *vt* (*sznurkiem, bandażem*) to wrap around;

(*papierem*) to wrap up; (*okrywać, otulać*) to wrap (up); **nie owijaj w bawełnę** don't beat about the bush; **owinąć kogoś dookoła małego palca** to twist *lub* wrap sb round one's little finger
**owi|nąć (-nę, -niesz)** (*imp* **-ń**) *vb perf od* **owijać**
**owład|nąć (-nę, -niesz)** (*imp* **-nij**) *vt perf*: **~ kimś** (*o uczuciu*) to overwhelm sb
**owłosieni|e** (**-a**) *nt* hair; (*na zwierzęciu*) coat
**owłosiony** *adj* hairy
**owo** *pron* (*książk*) that
**owoc** (**-u, -e**) *m* fruit; **owoce** *pl* fruit, fruits *pl*
**owocny** *adj* fruitful
**owoc|ować (-uje)** (*perf* **za-**) *vi* (*rodzić owoce*) to fruit; (*przen*) to bear fruit
**owocowy** *adj* fruit *attr*
**owrzodze|nie** (**-nia, -nia**) (*gen pl* **-ń**) *nt* ulceration
**owsa** *itd. n patrz* **owies**
**owsian|ka** (**-ki, -ki**) (*dat sg* **-ce**) *f* porridge
**owsiany** *adj* oat *attr*; **płatki owsiane** oatmeal
**owsi|ki** (**-ków**) *pl* pinworms *pl*
**owszem** *adv* (*książk*) naturally, of course
**owulacj|a** (**-i**) *f* ovulation
**ozdabi|ać (-am, -asz)** (*perf* **ozdobić**) *vt* to decorate
**ozd|oba** (**-oby, -oby**) (*dat sg* **-obie**, *gen pl* **-ób**) *f* (*dekoracja*) decoration; (*chluba*) jewel; **dla ozdoby** as a decoration
**ozdo|bić (-bię, -bisz)** (*imp* **ozdób**) *vb perf od* **ozdabiać**
**ozdobni|k** (**-ka, -ki**) (*instr sg* **-kiem**) *m* ornament
**ozdobny** *adj* decorative
**ozię|biać (-biam, -biasz)** (*perf* **-bić**) *vt* to cool (down); **oziębiać się** *vr* to cool down; **oziębia się** (*o pogodzie*) it's getting colder
**oziębieni|e** (**-a**) *nt* (*Meteo*) cold weather; (*przen: w stosunkach itp.*) cooling
**oziębłoś|ć** (**-ci**) *f* (*obojętność*) coldness; **~ płciowa** frigidity
**oziębły** *adj* (*obojętny*) cold; (*płciowo*) frigid
**ozimi|na** (**-ny, -ny**) (*dat sg* **-nie**) *f* winter crops *pl*
**ozłac|ać (-am, -asz)** (*perf* **ozłocić**) *vt* to shed golden light on; **ozłocić kogoś za coś** (*przen*) to cover sb in gold for (doing) sth
**ozło|cić (-cę, -cisz)** (*imp* **-ć**) *vb perf od* **ozłacać**
**oznacz|ać (-am, -asz)** *vt* (*znaczyć*) to mean; (*wyrażać*) to represent, to signify; (*o literze, skrócie*) to stand for; (*robić znak*) (*perf* **-yć**) to mark; **co to oznacza?** what does this mean?; **oznacza to, że ...** this means that ...
**oznacze|nie** (**-nia, -nia**) (*gen pl* **-ń**) *nt* sign, symbol
**oznaczony** *adj* (*godzina*) appointed
**oznacz|yć (-ę, -ysz)** *vb perf od* **oznaczać**
**oznaj|miać (-miam, -miasz)** (*perf* **-mić**) *vt* to announce ▷ *vi* to declare; **~ komuś coś** to inform sb about sth
**oznaj|mić (-mię, -misz)** (*imp* **-mij**) *vb perf od* **oznajmiać**
**oznajmujący** *adj* (*Jęz*) indicative
**ozna|ka** (**-ki, -ki**) (*dat sg* **-ce**) *f* (*choroby*) symptom; (*gniewu, postępu*) sign
**oznak|ować (-uję, -ujesz)** *vb perf od* **znakować**
**ozo|n** (**-nu**) (*loc sg* **-nie**) *m* ozone
**ozonowy** *adj*: **warstwa** *lub* **powłoka ozonowa** the ozone layer
**ozor|ek** (**-ka, -ki**) (*instr sg* **-kiem**) *m* (*Kulin*) tongue
**oz|ór** (**-ora, -ory**) (*loc sg* **-orze**) *m* tongue
**ożaglowa|nie** (**-nia, -nia**) (*gen pl* **-ń**) *nt* (*Żegl*) rig
**ożebrowa|nie** (**-nia, -nia**) (*gen pl* **-ń**) *nt* (*Archit, Tech*) ribbing
**oże|nić (-nię, -nisz)** (*imp* **-ń**) *vb perf od* **żenić**
**ożyw|ać (-am, -asz)** (*perf* **ożyć**) *vi* (*o człowieku, przyrodzie*) to come to life; (*o wspomnieniach, urazach*) to come back
**ożywczy** *adj* invigorating, refreshing
**oży|wiać (-wiam, -wiasz)** (*perf* **-wić**) *vt* (*przywracać do życia*) to revive; (*urozmaicać*) to enliven; (*gospodarkę*) to revive, to liven up; **ożywiać się** *vr* (*nabierać życia*) to liven up; (*o oczach*) to light up; (*o twarzy*) to brighten up
**ożywieni|e** (**-a**) *nt* (*podniecenie*) liveliness; **~ gospodarcze** economic revival
**ożywiony** *adj* (*intensywny*) animated, lively; (*żyjący*) living

O

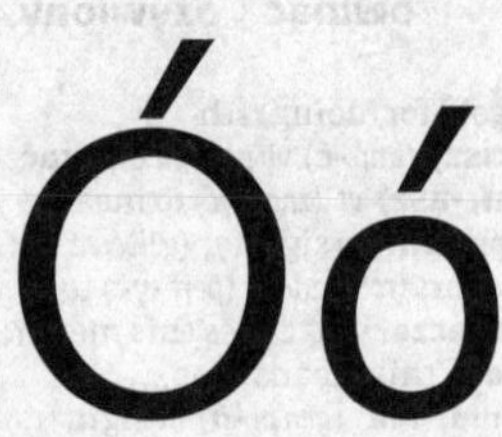

**Ó, ó** *nt inv* (*litera*) Ó, ó

**ósem|ka** (**-ki, -ki**) (*dat sg* **-ce**) *f* eight; (*kształt, ewolucja*) figure of eight (*Brit*), figure eight (*US*); (*Muz*) quaver (*Brit*), eighth note (*US*); **cała ~** all eight of them

**ósmy** *adj* eighth; **jedna ósma** one-eighth; **jest (godzina) ósma** it's eight o'clock

**ów** *pron* (*książk*) that; **w owych czasach** in those days, at that time; **ni z tego, ni z owego** out of the blue

**ówczesny** *adj*: **~ premier** the then Prime Minister; **~m zwyczajem** according to the customs of the time

**ówdzie** *adv*: **tu i ~** here and there

# Pp

**P, p** *nt inv* (*litera*) P, p; **P jak Paweł** ≈ P for Peter
**p.** *abbr* (= *pan*) Mr; (= *pani*) Mrs; (= *patrz*) cf.
**pa|cha** (**-chy, -chy**) (*dat sg* **-sze**) *f* armpit; **pod pachą** under one's arm
**pach|nieć (-nę, -niesz)** (*imp* **-nij**) *vi* to smell; **~ czymś** to smell of sth
**pachoł|ek** (**-ka, -ki**) (*instr sg* **-kiem**) *m* (*słupek*) bollard
**pachwi|na** (**-ny, -ny**) (*dat sg* **-nie**) *f* groin
**pacierz** (**-a, -e**) (*gen pl* **-y**) *m* prayer
**pacior|ek** (**-ka, -ki**) (*instr sg* **-kiem**) *m dimin od* **pacierz**; (*koralik*) bead
**paciorko|wiec** (**-wca, -wce**) *m* (*Bio*) streptococcus
**pacjen|t** (**-ta, -ci**) (*loc sg* **-cie**) *m* patient
**pacjent|ka** (**-ki, -ki**) (*dat sg* **-ce**, *gen pl* **-ek**) *f* patient
**pac|ka** (**-ki, -ki**) (*dat sg* **-ce**, *gen pl* **-ek**) *f* (fly) swatter
**Pacyfi|k** (**-ku**) (*instr sg* **-kiem**) *m* the Pacific
**pacyfikacj|a** (**-i, -e**) (*gen pl* **-i**) *f* pacification
**pacyfik|ować (-uję, -ujesz)** (*perf* **s-**) *vt* to pacify
**pacyfi|sta** (**-sty, -ści**) (*dat sg* **-ście**) *m decl like f in sg* pacifist
**pacyfistyczny** *adj* (*ruch*) pacifist *attr*
**pacyn|ka** (**-ki, -ki**) (*dat sg* **-ce**, *gen pl* **-ek**) *f* glove puppet
**pacz|ka** (**-ki, -ki**) (*dat sg* **-ce**, *gen pl* **-ek**) *f* (*pakunek*) package; (*Poczta*) parcel; (*papierosów, płatków*) packet (Brit), pack(age) (US); (*pot: grupa ludzi*) gang, pack
**paczk|ować (-uję, -ujesz)** (*perf* **po-**) *vt* to package
**padacz|ka** (**-ki**) (*dat sg* **-ce**) *f* epilepsy
**pad|ać (-am, -asz)** (*perf* **paść**) *vi* (*przewracać się*) to drop, to fall; (*ginąć*) to fall, to perish; (*o świetle, podejrzeniu*) to fall; **~ ze zmęczenia** to be dead on one's feet; **paść na twarz** to prostrate o.s.; **paść na kolana** to fall to one's knees; **pada (deszcz)** it's raining; **pada śnieg/grad** it's snowing/hailing; **paść ofiarą czegoś** to fall victim to sth; **padł rozkaz** an order was given; **padł strzał** a shot was fired; **los padł na niego** the lot fell to him, it fell to his lot; **nie padło ani jedno słowo** not a word was spoken *lub* said
**padal|ec** (**-ca, -ce**) *m* (*Zool*) blindworm, slow-worm
**padli|na** (**-ny**) (*dat sg* **-nie**) *f* carrion
**padlinożerny** *adj*: **zwierzę padlinożerne** scavenger
**padnę** *itd. vb patrz* **paść**
**pado|k** (**-ku, -ki**) (*instr sg* **-kiem**) *m* (*Sport*) paddock
**page|r** (**-ra, -ry**) (*loc sg* **-rze**) *m* (*Tel*) pager
**pagi|na** (**-ny, -ny**) (*dat sg* **-nie**) *f* (*Druk*) folio; **żywa ~** (*Druk*) running head
**pagon|y** (**-ów**) *pl* shoulder boards
**pagór|ek** (**-ka, -ki**) (*instr sg* **-kiem**) *m* hillock, knoll
**pagórkowaty** *adj* (*teren*) hilly; (*krajobraz*) rolling
**pajac** (**-a, -e**) *m* (*błazen, arlekin*) clown; (*zabawka*) puppet; (*pot: przen*) buffoon; (*ćwiczenie gimnastyczne*) star jumps
**pają|k** (**-ka, -ki**) (*instr sg* **-kiem**) *m* spider
**pajęczy|na** (**-ny, -ny**) (*dat sg* **-nie**) *f* cobweb
**pa|ka** (**-ki, -ki**) (*dat sg* **-ce**) *f* (*pot: więzienie*) clink (Brit), can (US)
**pakie|t** (**-tu, -ty**) (*loc sg* **-cie**) *m* packet; (*spraw*) package; **kontrolny ~ akcji** (*Giełda*) controlling interest *lub* share
**Pakista|n** (**-nu**) (*loc sg* **-nie**) *m* Pakistan
**Pakistańczy|k** (**-ka, -cy**) (*instr sg* **-kiem**) *m* Pakistani
**pakistański** *adj* Pakistani
**pak|ować (-uję, -ujesz)** *vt* (*walizkę, plecak*) (*perf* **s-** *lub* **za-**) to pack; (*owijać*) (*perf* **o-**) to wrap (up); (*pot: wpychać*) (*perf* **w-**) to stuff; **~ pieniądze w coś** (*pot*) to pour money into sth; **w~ kogoś do więzienia** (*pot*) to clap sb in prison; **pakować się** *vr* (*perf* **s-** *lub* **za-**) (*pakować swoje rzeczy*) to pack (up); (*pot: wchodzić*) (*perf* **w-**) to barge (into); **w~ się w kłopoty** *lub* **tarapaty** (*pot*) to get o.s. into trouble
**pakowny** *adj* capacious
**pakowy** *adj*: **papier ~** brown paper
**pak|t** (**-tu, -ty**) (*loc sg* **-cie**) *m* pact

**pakuł|y** (**-ów** *lub* **-**) *pl* (*Tech*) oakum
**pakun|ek** (**-ku, -ki**) (*instr sg* **-kiem**) *m* package
**pal** (**-a, -e**) (*gen pl* **-i** *lub* **-ów**) *m* (*słup ogrodzeniowy*) pale, stake; (*słup konstrukcyjny*) pile
**palacz** (**-a, -e**) (*gen pl* **-y**) *m* (*robotnik*) stoker; (*tytoniu*) smoker; **~ nałogowy** chain smoker
**palan|t** (**-ta**) (*loc sg* **-cie**) *m* (*Sport*) ≈ baseball
**palar|nia** (**-ni, -nie**) (*gen pl* **-ni**) *f* smoke *lub* smoking room; **~ kawy** coffee roasting plant
**palący** *adj* (*słońce*) blazing; (*smak*) pungent; (*przen: wstyd*) burning; (*przen: problem*) urgent ▷ *m decl like adj* (*palacz*) smoker; **przedział/wagon dla ~ch** smoking compartment/carriage
**pal|ec** (**-ca, -ce**) *m* (*u ręki*) finger; (*u nogi*) toe; **mały ~** little finger; **~ serdeczny** ring finger; **~ środkowy** middle finger; **~ wskazujący** index finger, forefinger; **wielki ~** big toe; **pokazywać coś palcem** to point a finger at sth; **maczać w czymś palce** (*przen*) to have a hand in sth; **mieć coś w małym palcu** (*przen*) to know sth inside out; **nie kiwnąć** *lub* **ruszyć** (*perf*) **palcem** not to lift *lub* raise a finger; **patrzeć na coś przez palce** (*przen*) to turn a blind eye on *lub* to sth; **chodzić na palcach** to tiptoe, to walk on tiptoe; **wyssać** (*perf*) **coś z palca** to fabricate sth; **palce lizać!** scrumptious!, yum-yum! (*pot*), yummy! (*pot*); **owinąć** (*perf*) **sobie kogoś dookoła palca** to twist sb round one's little finger
**paleni|e** (**-a**) *nt* (*tytoniu*) smoking; (*zwłok, śmieci*) incineration; **„~ wzbronione"** "no smoking"
**palenis|ko** (**-ka, -ka**) (*instr sg* **-kiem**) *nt* hearth
**paleontologi|a** (**-i**) *f* palaeontology
**Palesty|na** (**-ny**) (*dat sg* **-nie**) *f* Palestine; **Organizacja Wyzwolenia Palestyny** Palestine Liberation Organization
**Palestyńczy|k** (**-ka, -cy**) (*instr sg* **-kiem**) *m* Palestinian
**palestyński** *adj* Palestinian
**pale|ta** (**-ty, -ty**) (*dat sg* **-cie**) *f* palette
**paliatywny** *adj* (*Med*) palliative
**pal|ić** (**-ę, -isz**) *vt* (*papierosy, fajkę*) to smoke; (*świecę*) to burn; (*światło*) to keep on; (*niszczyć ogniem*) (*perf* **s-**) to burn (down) ▷ *vi* (*palić papierosy*) to smoke; (*o słońcu, gorączce*) to burn; **pali mnie (w gardle)** my throat is on fire; **~ w piecu** to heat with a stove; **palić się** *vr* (*płonąć*) to burn; (*o domu, mieście*) to be on fire; (*o świetle*) to be on; **pali się!** fire!; **pali mu się grunt** *lub* **ziemia pod nogami** (*przen*) the heat is on for him; **~ się do czegoś** to be keen on (doing) sth; **nie pali się!** (*pot*) no (great) hurry!
**palisa|da** (**-dy, -dy**) (*dat sg* **-dzie**) *f* stockade
**pali|wo** (**-wa, -wa**) (*loc sg* **-wie**) *nt* fuel; (*Mot*) petrol (*Brit*), gas(oline) (*US*)
**pal|ma** (**-my, -my**) (*dat sg* **-mie**) *f* palm (tree); **~ pierwszeństwa** the victor's palm
**palmiar|nia** (**-ni, -ni**) (*gen pl* **-ni**) *f* greenhouse
**palmowy** *adj* palm *attr*; **Niedziela Palmowa** Palm Sunday
**palni|k** (**-ka, -ki**) (*instr sg* **-kiem**) *m* burner; (*Tech*) torch
**palny** *adj* (*materiał*) flammable; **łatwo ~** (highly) flammable; **broń palna** firearms *pl*
**pal|to** (**-ta, -ta**) (*loc sg* **-cie**) *nt* overcoat
**paluch** (**-a, -y**) *m* (*pej*) finger; (*wielki palec u nogi*) big toe
**palusz|ek** (**-ka, -ki**) (*instr sg* **-kiem**) *m dimin od* **palec**; **paluszki** *pl*: **słone paluszki** savoury sticks; **paluszki rybne** (*Kulin*) fish fingers, fish sticks (*US*)
**pałac** (**-u, -e**) *m* palace
**pał|ać** (**-am, -asz**) (*perf* **za-**) *vi*: **~ nienawiścią/gniewem** to be burning *lub* inflamed with hatred/anger
**pałasz|ować** (**-uję, -ujesz**) (*perf* **s-**) *vt* (*pot*) to eat
**pałecz|ka** (**-ki, -ki**) (*dat sg* **-ce**, *gen pl* **-ek**) *f dimin od* **pałka**; (*do gry na bębnie*) (drum)stick; (*dyrygenta, sztafetowa*) baton; **pałeczki** *pl* (*do jedzenia*) chopsticks
**pał|ka** (**-ki, -ki**) (*dat sg* **-ce**, *gen pl* **-ek**) *f* club; (*Policja*) baton, truncheon (*Brit*), nightstick (*US*)
**pamfle|t** (**-tu, -ty**) (*loc sg* **-cie**) *m* lampoon
**pamiąt|ka** (**-ki, -ki**) (*dat sg* **-ce**, *gen pl* **-ek**) *f* (*przedmiot*) souvenir, memento; (*znak, symbol*) token; **sklep z ~mi** souvenir shop; **na pamiątkę (czegoś)** in memory (of sth); **dać** (*perf*) **coś komuś na pamiątkę** to give sb sth as a keepsake *lub* memento
**pamiątkowy** *adj* commemorative
**pamięciowy** *adj*: **portret ~** identikit (picture) (*Brit*), composite sketch (*US*)
**pamię|ć** (**-ci**) *f* memory; (*wspomnienie*) memory, remembrance; **z pamięci** from memory; **mieć dobrą/słabą ~ (do czegoś)** to have a good/bad memory (for sth); **~ stała** (*Komput*) read-only memory; **~ operacyjna** (*Komput*) random-access memory; **uczyć się (nauczyć się** *perf***) czegoś na ~** to learn sth by heart; **o ile mnie ~ nie myli** if my memory serves me right; **świętej pamięci ...** (the) late ...
**pamięt|ać** (**-am, -asz**) *vt* (*perf* **za-**) to remember ▷ *vi*: **~ o kimś/czymś** to keep sb/sth in mind; **~(, żeby) coś zrobić** to remember to do sth; **pamiętam, że go widziałem** I remember seeing him
**pamiętliwy** *adj* (*pej*) unforgiving

**pamiętni|k** (**-ka, -ki**) (*instr sg* **-kiem**) *m* diary; **pamiętniki** *pl* (*Lit*) memoirs *pl*
**pamiętny** *adj* memorable
**PAN** *abbr* (= *Polska Akademia Nauk*) Polish Academy of Sciences
**pa|n** (**-na, -nowie**) (*dat sg* **-nu**, *voc sg* **-nie**) *m* (*mężczyzna*) gentleman, man; (*przy zwracaniu się*) you; (*arystokrata*) lord; (*Bóg*) Lord; (*pot: nauczyciel*) master, teacher; (*właściciel psa*) master; **Pan Kowalski** Mr Kowalski; **czy wiedział Pan o tym?** did you know about it, sir?; **czy to Pana parasol?** is this your umbrella?; **być panem czegoś/kogoś** to be master of sth/sb; **proszę Pana!** excuse me, sir!; **Panie Przewodniczący/Prezydencie** Mr Chairman/President; **Pan Bóg** Lord; **pan domu** host; **pan młody** (bride)groom; **Szanowny Panie!** (*w korespondencji*) Dear Sir; **być z kimś za pan brat** to be on familiar terms with sb
**panace|um** (**-um, -a**) (*gen pl* **-ów**) *nt inv in sg* cure-all, panacea
**Pana|ma** (**-my**) (*dat sg* **-mie**) *f* Panama
**panamski** *adj* Panamanian; **Kanał P~** the Panama Canal
**pancerni|k** (**-ka, -ki**) (*instr sg* **-kiem**) *m* (*okręt*) battleship; (*Zool*) armadillo
**pancerny** *adj* (*wojska, samochód*) armoured (*Brit*), armored (*US*); **szafa** *lub* **kasa pancerna** safe
**pancerz** (**-a, -e**) (*gen pl* **-y**) *m* armour (*Brit*), armor (*US*); (*żółwia*) shell; (*przen: osłona*) shield
**panczeni|sta** (**-sty, -ści**) (*loc sg* **-ście**) *m* (*Sport*) speed skater
**pan|da** (**-dy, -dy**) (*dat sg* **-dzie**) *f* panda
**panegiry|k** (**-ku, -ki**) (*instr sg* **-kiem**) *m* eulogy
**panel** (**-u, -e**) (*gen pl* **-i**) *m* (*publiczna dyskusja*) panel
**pa|ni** (**-ni, -nie**) (*acc sg* **-nią**, *gen pl* **-ń**) *f* (*kobieta*) lady, woman; (*przy zwracaniu się*) you; (*pot: nauczycielka*) mistress, teacher; **P~ Kowalska** Mrs Kowalski; **czy wiedziała P~ o tym?** did you know about it (, madam)?; **czy to P~ płaszcz?** is this your coat, madam?; **~ domu** hostess; **~ doktor/profesor** Doctor/Professor; **proszę P~!** madam!; **Szanowna P~!** Dear Madam
**panicznie** *adv*: **bać się ~ (kogoś/czegoś)** to be terrified (of sb/sth)
**paniczny** *adj* (*strach*) mortal
**panien|ka** (**-ki, -ki**) (*dat sg* **-ce**, *gen pl* **-ek**) *f* (*pej*): **~ do towarzystwa** *lub* **na telefon** call girl
**panieński** *adj*: **nazwisko ~e** maiden name; **wieczór ~** hen night
**panier|ować (-uję, -ujesz)** *vt* to bread, to coat in breadcrumbs
**panierowany** *adj* breaded, in breadcrumbs
**pani|ka** (**-ki**) (*dat sg* **-ce**) *f* panic; **wpadać (wpaść** *perf*) **w panikę** to panic
**panikarski** *adj* (*pot*) panicky
**panik|ować (-uję, -ujesz)** (*perf* **s-**) *vi* (*pot*) to panic
**pa|nna** (**-nny, -nny**) (*dat sg* **-nnie**, *gen pl* **-nien**) *f* girl; (*stan cywilny*) unmarried woman; **P~ Kowalska** Miss Kowalski; **~ młoda** bride; **stara ~** (*pej*) old maid, spinster; **Panna** (*Astrologia*) Virgo; **Najświętsza Maria P~** Virgin Mary
**panora|ma** (**-my, -my**) (*dat sg* **-mie**) *f* (*widok*) panorama; (*Sztuka*) cyclorama
**panoramiczny** *adj* (*ekran*) wide; (*widok*) panoramic; (*film*) wide-screen
**panosz|yć się (-ę, -ysz)** *vr* (*rządzić się*) to throw one's weight about; (*przen: grasować*) to be rampant
**pan|ować (-uję, -ujesz)** *vi* (*o królu, dynastii*) to rule, to reign; (*o ciszy, terrorze*) (*perf* **za-**) to reign; (*o zwyczajach, poglądach*) to prevail; **~ nad kimś/czymś** to be master of sb/sth; **~ nad sytuacją** to be master of the situation; **~ nad sobą** to be in control of o.s.; **panowało przekonanie, że ...** it was generally believed that ...
**panowani|e** (**-a**) *nt* (*rządy*) rule, reign; (*kontrola*) control; **za panowania** *+gen* during the reign of; **(stracić** *perf*) **~ nad sobą** to lose one's temper
**pantałyku** *inv*: **zbić** (*perf*) **kogoś z ~** (*pot*) to throw sb off balance
**pante|ra** (**-ry, -ry**) (*dat sg* **-rze**) *f* leopard, panther
**panter|ka** (**-ki, -ki**) (*dat sg* **-ce**, *gen pl* **-ek**) *f* (*ubiór wojskowy*) camouflage jacket
**pantof|el** (**-la, -le**) (*gen pl* **-li**) *m* slipper; **być pod pantoflem (żony)** (*pot*) to be henpecked
**pantofel|ek** (**-ka, -ki**) (*instr sg* **-kiem**) *m dimin od* **pantofel**; (*Zool*) paramecium
**pantoflarz** (**-a, -e**) (*gen pl* **-y**) *m* (*pot*) henpecked husband
**pantoflowy** *adj* (*pot*): **poczta pantoflowa** the grapevine; **doszło to do mnie pocztą pantoflową** I heard it on the grapevine
**pantogra|f** (**-fu, -fy**) (*loc sg* **-fie**) *m* pantograph
**pantomi|ma** (**-my, -my**) (*dat sg* **-mie**) *f* mime show
**panujący** *adj* (*monarcha, dynastia*) reigning, ruling; (*klasa*) ruling; (*upały, susza*) current; (*pogląd, religia*) prevailing ▷ *m decl like adj* (*władca*) ruler
**pański** *adj* your; (*gest, maniery*) lordly; **Roku P~ego 1791** Anno Domini 1791
**państ|wo** (**-wa**) (*loc sg* **-wie**) *nt* (*kraj*) (*pl* **-wa**) state; (*forma grzecznościowa*) you; **P~ Kowalscy**

P

the Kowalskis; **czy mają P~ rezerwację?** have you got a reservation?; **proszę Państwa!** Ladies and Gentlemen!; **~ młodzi** the bride and the bridegroom; (*po ślubie*) the newly-weds

**państwowy** *adj* (*hymn, święto*) national; (*szkoła, przedsiębiorstwo*) state *attr*, state-owned

**pańszczy|zna** (**-zny**) (*dat sg* **-źnie**) *f* (*Hist*) serfdom, serfhood; (*pot: przymusowe zajęcie*) drudgery

**PAP** *abbr* (= *Polska Agencja Prasowa*) Polish Press Agency

**pa|pa** (**-py, -py**) (*dat sg* **-pie**) *f* (*Bud*) asphalt roofing

**papeteri|a** (**-i, -e**) (*gen pl* **-i**) *f* stationery

**papie|r** (**-ru, -ry**) (*loc sg* **-rze**) *m* paper; **arkusz ~u** a sheet of paper; **~ firmowy** letterhead; **~ listowy** writing paper; **~ pakowy** brown paper; **~ ścierny** sandpaper; **~ toaletowy** toilet *lub* lavatory paper; **na ~ze** (*pisemnie*) in writing, on paper; (*teoretycznie*) on paper only; **papiery** *pl* (*dokumenty, notatki*) papers *pl*; **~y wartościowe** (*Fin*) securities *pl*

**papier|ek** (**-ka, -ki**) (*instr sg* **-kiem**) *m* piece of paper; **~ lakmusowy** litmus *lub* test paper; **papierki od cukierków** sweet wrappers

**papierkowy** *adj*: **papierkowa robota** paperwork

**papierniczy** *adj* (*przemysł, zakład*) paper *attr*; **sklep ~** stationer('s)

**papiero|s** (**-sa, -sy**) (*loc sg* **-sie**) *m* cigarette; **palić ~y** to smoke cigarettes

**papierośnic|a** (**-y, -e**) *f* cigarette case

**papierowy** *adj* paper *attr*; (*Sport*): **waga papierowa** light flyweight

**papieski** *adj* papal

**papież** (**-a, -e**) (*gen pl* **-y**) *m* pope

**papilarny** *adj*: **linie papilarne** fingerprints *pl*

**papilot|y** (**-ów**) *pl* curlpapers *pl*

**papiru|s** (**-su**) (*loc sg* **-sie**) *m* papyrus

**pap|ka** (**-ki, -ki**) (*dat sg* **-ce**, *gen pl* **-ek**) *f* (*masa*) pulp; (*do jedzenia*) pap

**papl|ać** (**-ę, -esz**) *vi* (*pot: dużo mówić*) to prattle

**paplani|na** (**-ny**) (*dat sg* **-nie**) *f* prattle

**pap|rać** (**-rzę, -rzesz**) *vt* (*pot: brudzić*) (*perf* **u-**) to smear; (*: robić niechlujnie*) (*perf* **s-**) to botch, to bungle; **paprać się** *vr* (*pot: brudzić się*) (*perf* **u-**) to dirty o.s.; (*o ranie*) to fester

**papro|ć** (**-ci, -cie**) (*gen pl* **-ci**) *f* fern

**papry|ka** (**-ki, -ki**) (*dat sg* **-ce**) *f* (*suszona*) paprika; **~ czerwona/zielona** red/green pepper

**paprykarz** (**-u, -e**) *m a kind of goulash*

**papu|ga** (**-gi, -gi**) (*dat sg* **-dze**) *f* parrot; (*przen*) copycat; **powtarzać jak ~** to parrot

**papug|ować** (**-uję, -ujesz**) (*perf* **s-**) *vt* (*pot*) to parrot

**papuż|ka** (**-ki, -ki**) (*dat sg* **-ce**, *gen pl* **-ek**) *f*: **~ falista** budgerigar, budgie (*pot*); *patrz też* **papuga**

**pa|r** (**-ra, -rowie**) (*loc sg* **-rze**) *m* peer

**par.** *abbr* (= *paragraf*) art. (= *article*)

**pa|ra** (**-ry**) (*dat sg* **-rze**) *f* (*butów, rąk, zwierząt*) (*nom pl* **-ry**) pair; (*dwoje ludzi*) (*nom pl* **-ry**) pair, couple; (*Fiz*) vapour (*Brit*), vapor (*US*); (*też:* **para wodna**) steam; **pełną parą** (at) full blast; **gotować na parze** to steam; **nie puszczać (puścić** *perf*) **pary z ust** (*przen*) not to breathe a word; **młoda ~** (*w czasie ślubu*) the bride and the bridegroom; (*po ślubie*) the newly-weds; **~mi** (*iść, siedzieć*) in twos *lub* pairs; **czegoś jest nie do pary** there's an odd number of sth; **iść w parze z czymś** (*przen*) to go hand in hand with sth

**parabol|a** (**-i, -e**) (*gen pl* **-i** *lub* **-**) *f* (*Mat*) parabola; (*Lit*) parable

**par|ać się** (**-am, -asz**) *vr*: **parać się czymś** to dabble in sth

**para|da** (**-dy, -dy**) (*dat sg* **-dzie**) *f* parade

**paradok|s** (**-su, -sy**) (*loc sg* **-sie**) *m* paradox

**paradoksalnie** *adv* paradoxically

**paradoksalny** *adj* paradoxical

**parad|ować** (**-uję, -ujesz**) *vi* to parade

**parafi|a** (**-i, -e**) (*gen pl* **-i**) *f* parish

**parafialny** *adj* parish *attr*

**parafia|nin** (**-nina, -nie**) (*loc sg* **-ninie**, *gen pl* **-n**) *m* parishioner

**parafi|na** (**-ny**) (*dat sg* **-nie**) *f* paraffin

**paraf|ka** (**-ki, -ki**) (*loc sg* **-ce**, *gen pl* **-ek**) *f* (*podpis*) initials *pl*; **stawiać (postawić** *perf*) **parafkę na czymś** to initial sth

**paraf|ować** (**-uję, -ujesz**) *vt* to initial

**parafra|za** (**-zy, -zy**) (*dat sg* **-zie**) *f* paraphrase

**parafraz|ować** (**-uję, -ujesz**) (*perf* **s-**) *vt* to paraphrase

**parago|n** (**-nu, -ny**) (*loc sg* **-nie**) *m* receipt

**paragra|f** (**-fu, -fy**) (*loc sg* **-fie**) *m* (*Prawo*) article; (*akapit*) paragraph

**Paragwaj** (**-u**) *m* Paraguay

**Paragwajczy|k** (**-ka, -cy**) (*instr sg* **-kiem**) *m* Paraguayan

**paragwajski** *adj* Paraguayan

**paralel|a** (**-i, -e**) (*gen pl* **-i** *lub* **-**) *f* parallel(ism)

**paralelny** *adj* parallel

**parality|k** (**-ka, -cy**) (*instr sg* **-kiem**) *m* paralytic

**paraliż** (**-u**) *m* paralysis; **~ dziecięcy** polio(myelitis)

**paraliż|ować** (**-uję, -ujesz**) (*perf* **s-**) *vt* to paralyse (*Brit*), to paralyze (*US*)

**paramet|r** (**-ru, -ry**) (*loc sg* **-rze**) *m* parameter

**paramilitarny** *adj* paramilitary

**paranoiczny** *adj* paranoid

**paranoi|k** (**-ka, -cy**) (*instr sg* **-kiem**) *m* paranoiac

**parano|ja** (**-i**) *f* paranoia
**paranormalny** *adj* paranormal
**parape|t** (**-tu, -ty**) (*loc sg* **-cie**) *m* (window)sill
**parapetów|ka** (**-ki, -ki**) (*dat sg* **-ce**, *gen pl* **-ek**) *f* housewarming
**parapsychologi|a** (**-i**) *f* parapsychology
**parasol** (**-a, -e**) (*gen pl* **-i**) *m* (*od deszczu*) umbrella; (*od słońca*) parasol, sunshade
**parasol|ka** (**-ki, -ki**) (*dat sg* **-ce**, *gen pl* **-ek**) *f* umbrella
**parawa|n** (**-nu, -ny**) (*loc sg* **-nie**) *m* screen; **coś służy komuś za ~** (*przen*) sb hides behind sth
**parcel|a** (**-i, -e**) (*gen pl* **-i** *lub* **-**) *f* plot
**parcel|ować (-uję, -ujesz)** (*perf* **roz-**) *vt* to parcel out
**parci|e** (**-a**) *nt* (*wody*) pressure; (*Med*) pushing; (*Fiz*) thrust
**pardo|n** (**-nu**) (*loc sg* **-nie**) *m*: **bez ~u** unceremoniously
**pard|wa** (**-wy, -wy**) (*dat sg* **-wie**) *f* (*Zool*) grouse
**parę** (*jak*: **ile**) *num* a few, several; **~ dni temu** the other day; **~ godzin/dni/miesięcy** a few hours/days/months; **od paru godzin/dni/miesięcy** for a few hours/days/months; **za ~ minut** in a few minutes; **sześćdziesiąt ~ lat** over sixty years; **~ groszy** a few pennies; **napisać** (*perf*) **do kogoś ~ słów** to drop sb a line
**par|k** (**-ku, -ki**) (*instr sg* **-kiem**) *m* park; **~ narodowy** national park
**parka|n** (**-nu, -ny**) (*loc sg* **-nie**) *m* fence
**parkie|t** (**-tu, -ty**) (*loc sg* **-cie**) *m* (*posadzka*) parquet floor(ing); (*do tańca*) dance-floor
**parkin|g** (**-gu, -gi**) (*instr sg* **-giem**) *m* car park (*Brit*), parking lot (*US*); **~ strzeżony/nie strzeżony** attended/unattended car park; **~ płatny/bezpłatny** paid/free parking
**parkomet|r** (**-ru, -ry**) (*loc sg* **-rze**) *m* parking meter
**park|ować (-uję, -ujesz)** (*perf* **za-**) *vt/vi* to park
**parkowani|e** (**-a**) *nt* parking; **„~ zabronione"** "no parking"
**parkowy** *adj* park *attr*
**parlamen|t** (**-tu, -ty**) (*loc sg* **-cie**) *m* parliament
**parlamentariusz** (**-a, -e**) (*gen pl* **-y**) *m* peace-maker
**parlamentarny** *adj* parliamentary
**parlamentarzy|sta** (**-sty, -ści**) (*dat sg* **-ście**) *m decl like f in sg* parliamentarian
**parmeza|n** (**-nu, -ny**) (*loc sg* **-nie**) *m* Parmesan (cheese)
**parno** *adv*: **jest ~** it's close *lub* sultry
**parny** *adj* sultry
**parob|ek** (**-ka, -ki** *lub* **-cy**) (*instr sg* **-kiem**) *m* farm-hand
**parodi|a** (**-i, -e**) (*gen pl* **-i**) *f* parody; **~ sprawiedliwości** a travesty of justice
**parodi|ować (-uję, -ujesz)** (*perf* **s-**) *vt* to parody
**parodniowy** *adj* a few days' *attr*
**parody|sta** (**-sty, -ści**) (*dat sg* **-ście**) *m decl like f in sg* impressionist
**parokrotny** *num* repeated
**paroletni** *adj* (*trwający parę lat*) a few years' *attr*; (*mający parę lat*) a few-year-old *attr*
**par|ować (-uję, -ujesz)** *vt* (*cios, uderzenie, atak*) (*perf* **od-**) to parry ▷ *vi* (*zamieniać się w parę*) (*perf* **wy-**) to evaporate
**parowani|e** (**-a**) *nt* evaporation
**paro|wiec** (**-wca, -wce**) *m* steamer
**parow|óz** (**-ozu, -ozy**) (*loc sg* **-ozie**) *m* steam engine
**parowy** *adj* steam *attr*
**par|ów** (**-owu, -owy**) (*loc sg* **-owie**) *m* ravine
**parów|ka** (**-ki, -ki**) (*dat sg* **-ce**, *gen pl* **-ek**) *f* (breakfast) sausage (*Brit*), hot dog (*US*)
**parsk|ać (-am, -asz)** (*perf* **-nąć**) *vi* to snort
**parsk|nąć (-nę, -niesz)** (*imp* **-nij**) *vb perf od* **parskać**; **~ śmiechem** to burst out laughing
**parszywy** *adj* (*pot*) lousy (*pot*), rotten (*pot*); **parszywa owca** (*przen*) black sheep (*przen*)
**partacki** *adj* (*rzemieślnik*) bungling; (*robota*) bungled
**partacz** (**-a, -e**) (*gen pl* **-y**) *m* (*pej*) bungler
**partacz|yć (-ę, -ysz)** (*perf* **s-**) *vt* to bungle, to botch (up)
**parte|r** (**-ru, -ry**) (*loc sg* **-rze**) *m* (*najniższe piętro*) ground floor *lub* level (*Brit*), first floor (*US*); (*w kinie, teatrze*) stalls *pl* (*Brit*), orchestra (*US*)
**parterowy** *adj*: **dom ~** bungalow
**parti|a** (**-i, -e**) (*gen pl* **-i**) *f* (*Pol*) party; (*towaru*) batch; (*szachów, warcabów*) game; (*rola*) part; **~ rządząca/opozycyjna** ruling/opposition party; **wstąpić** *lub* **zapisać się do partii** to join a party; **dostarczać coś ~mi** to deliver sth in several shipments; **zagrać** (*perf*) **partię szachów** to play a game of chess
**partne|r** (**-ra, -rzy**) (*loc sg* **-rze**) *m* partner
**partner|ka** (**-ki, -ki**) (*dat sg* **-ce**, *gen pl* **-ek**) *f* partner
**partnerski** *adj* based on partnership
**partnerst|wo** (**-wa**) (*loc sg* **-wie**) *nt* partnership
**party** *nt inv* (*przyjęcie*) party
**partycyp|ować (-uję, -ujesz)** *vi* to participate
**partyjny** *adj* party *attr*
**partyku|ła** (**-ły, -ły**) (*dat sg* **-le**) *f* (*Jęz*) particle
**partytu|ra** (**-ry, -ry**) (*dat sg* **-rze**) *f* score
**partyzancki** *adj* guerrilla *attr*
**partyzan|t** (**-ta, -ci**) (*loc sg* **-cie**) *m* guerrilla
**partyzant|ka** (**-ki, -ki**) (*dat sg* **-ce**, *gen pl* **-ek**) *f* (*wojna partyzancka*) guerrilla warfare; (*kobieta partyzant*) guerrilla

P

**paru** *itd. num patrz* **parę**
**paryski** *adj* Parisian; **bułka paryska** French stick, French loaf (*Brit*)
**paryte|t** (**-tu, -ty**) (*loc sg* **-cie**) *m* (*Ekon*) parity; ~ **złota** gold standard *lub* parity
**Paryż** (**-a**) *m* Paris
**parz|yć (-ę, -ysz)** *vt* (*o słońcu, piasku*) (*perf* **po-**) to burn; (*o pokrzywie*) (*perf* **po-**) to sting; (*kapustę, pomidory*) (*perf* **s-**) to blanch; (*herbatę, kawę*) (*perf* **za-**) to brew; **parzyć się** *vr* (*o zwierzętach*) to mate
**parzysty** *adj* even
**pa|s** (**-sa, -sy**) (*loc sg* **-sie**) *m* (*do spodni*) belt; (*lasu, materiału*) strip; (*talia*) waist; (*też*: **pas ruchu**) lane; **pas bezpieczeństwa** seat belt; **pas bezwładnościowy** inertia-reel seat belt; **pas do pończoch** garter belt; **pas ratunkowy** lifebelt; **pas napędowy** *lub* **transmisyjny** transmission belt; **zaciskać pasa** (*przen*) to tighten one's belt; **wiosna/egzaminy za pasem** spring is/exams are (near) at hand; **pas zieleni** green belt; **pas startowy** runway; **w pasy** (*materiał, sukienka*) striped; **rozebrać się** (*perf*) **do pasa** to undress from the waist up; **brać (wziąć** *perf*) **nogi za pas** to show a clean pair of heels; **pasy** *pl* (*dla pieszych*) zebra crossing ▷ *excl* (*w brydżu*) no bid; (*w pokerze*) pass
**pasa|t** (**-tu, -ty**) (*loc sg* **-cie**) *m* trade wind
**pasaż** (**-u, -e**) (*gen pl* **-y**) *m* (*przejście*) passage(way); (*Muz*) passage; ~ **handlowy** shopping arcade
**pasaże|r** (**-ra, -rowie**) (*loc sg* **-rze**) *m* passenger; ~ **na gapę** (*w autobusie, pociągu*) fare dodger; (*na statku*) stowaway
**pasażer|ka** (**-ki, -ki**) (*loc sg* **-ce**, *gen pl* **-ek**) *f* passenger
**pasażerski** *adj* passenger *attr*
**Pas|cha** (**-chy, -chy**) (*dat sg* **-sze**) *f* (*Rel*) Passover
**pas|ek** (**-ka, -ki**) (*instr sg* **-kiem**) *m dimin od* **pas**; (*do spodni*) belt; ~ **do zegarka** watch strap; ~ **klinowy** (*Mot*) fan belt; **w paski** (*materiał, sukienka*) striped
**pasem|ko** (**-ka, -ka**) (*instr sg* **-kiem**, *gen pl* **-ek**) *nt dimin od* **pasmo**; **pasemka** *pl* highlights *pl*, streaks *pl*
**pase|r** (**-ra, -rzy**) (*loc sg* **-rze**) *m* fence (*pot*)
**paserst|wo** (**-wa**) (*loc sg* **-wie**) *nt* fencing
**pasę** *itd. vb patrz* **paść**
**pasiasty** *adj* striped
**pasi|eka** (**-eki, -eki**) (*dat sg* **-ece**, *gen pl* **-ek**) *f* apiary
**pasier|b** (**-ba, -bowie**) (*loc sg* **-bie**) *m* stepson
**pasierbic|a** (**-y, -e**) *f* stepdaughter
**pasikoni|k** (**-ka, -ki**) (*instr sg* **-kiem**) *m* grasshopper

**pasj|a** (**-i, -e**) (*gen pl* **-i**) *f* passion; (*gniew*) rage; **czytanie to jego** ~ reading is his passion; **lubić coś ~mi** to have a passion for sth; **wpadać (wpaść** *perf*) **w pasję** to fly into a fury *lub* rage; **szewska** ~ blind rage, white heat
**pasjan|s** (**-sa, -se**) (*loc sg* **-sie**) *m* (*Karty*) patience (*Brit*), solitaire (*US*)
**pasjon|ować (-uję, -ujesz)** *vt* to fascinate; **pasjonować się** *vr*: ~ **się czymś** to be very keen on sth
**pasjonujący** *adj* fascinating, thrilling
**paskarst|wo** (**-wa**) (*loc sg* **-wie**) *nt* profiteering
**paskowy** *adj*: **kod** ~ bar code
**paskudny** *adj* nasty
**paskudzt|wo** (**-wa, -wa**) (*loc sg* **-wie**) *nt* (*pot*) filth (*pot*)
**pasmanteri|a** (**-i**) *f* haberdashery (*Brit*), dry goods (*US*)
**pa|smo** (**-sma, -sma**) (*loc sg* **-smie** *lub* **-śmie**, *gen pl* **-sm** *lub* **-sem**) *nt* (*włosów*) strand; (*nici*) thread; (*lądu, lasu*) strip; (*przen*: *wydarzeń, nieszczęść*) series; ~ **gór** *lub* **górskie** mountain range; ~ **(wysokiej) częstotliwości** (*Radio*) (high) frequency band
**pas|ować (-uję, -ujesz)** *vt*: ~ **kogoś na rycerza** to knight sb ▷ *vi* to fit; (*Karty*) (*perf* **s-**) to pass; **pasuje jak ulał** it fits like a glove
**pasoży|t** (**-ta, -ty**) (*loc sg* **-cie**) *m* parasite
**pasożytniczy** *adj* parasitic
**pas|sa** (**-sy, -sy**) (*dat sg* **-sie**) *f*: **dobra/zła** ~ a run of good/bad luck, winning/losing streak
**pa|sta** (**-sty, -sty**) (*dat sg* **-ście**) *f*: ~ **mięsna/pomidorowa** meat/tomato spread; ~ **do zębów** toothpaste; ~ **do butów** shoe polish; ~ **do podłóg** floor polish
**pastel** (**-u, -e**) (*gen pl* **-i** *lub* **-ów**) *m* pastel
**pastelowy** *adj* pastel
**paster|ka** (**-ki, -ki**) (*dat sg* **-ce**, *gen pl* **-ek**) *f* (*osoba*) shepherdess; (*Rel*) Christmas midnight mass
**pasterski** *adj* shepherd's *attr*, shepherds' *attr*; **pies** ~ shepherd dog; **list** ~ (*Rel*) pastoral
**pasteryzacj|a** (**-i**) *f* pasteurization
**pasteryz|ować (-uję, -ujesz)** *vt* to pasteurize
**pasteryzowany** *adj* pasteurized
**pasterz** (**-a, -e**) (*gen pl* **-y**) *m* shepherd
**pastewny** *adj* (*roślina*) fodder *attr*
**pastisz** (**-u, -e**) (*gen pl* **-y** *lub* **-ów**) *m* pastiche
**pasto|r** (**-ra, -rzy** *lub* **-rowie**) (*loc sg* **-rze**) *m* pastor
**past|ować (-uję, -ujesz)** (*perf* **wy-**) *vt* (*buty*) to polish; (*podłogę*) to wax
**past|wa** (**-wy**) (*dat sg* **-wie**) *f*: **zostawić** (*perf*) **kogoś/coś na pastwę losu** to leave sb/sth to their/its own fate

**past|wić się (-wię, -wisz)** *vr*: **pastwić się nad kimś** to torment sb
**pastwis|ko** (**-ka, -ka**) (*instr sg* **-kiem**) *nt* pasture
**pastyl|ka** (**-ki, -ki**) (*dat sg* **-ce**, *gen pl* **-ek**) *f* (*lek*) pill, tablet; (*cukierek*) pastille, drop; **~ na kaszel/gardło** lozenge, pastille
**pasyw|a** (**-ów**) *pl* (*Ekon*) liabilities *pl*
**pasywny** *adj* passive
**pasz|a** (**-y, -e**) *f* fodder
**paszcz|a** (**-y, -e**) *f* jaws *pl*
**pasze** *n patrz* **pacha**
**paszkwil** (**-u, -e**) (*gen pl* **-i** *lub* **-ów**) *m* lampoon
**paszpor|t** (**-tu, -ty**) (*loc sg* **-cie**) *m* passport
**paszportowy** *adj* passport *attr*; **kontrola paszportowa** passport control
**pasztecí|k** (**-ka, -ki**) (*instr sg* **-kiem**) *m dimin od* **pasztet**; (*do barszczu, rosołu*) patty, pasty (*Brit*)
**paszte|t** (**-tu, -ty**) (*loc sg* **-cie**) *m* pâté
**pasztetow|a** (**-ej, -e**) *f decl like adj* liver sausage (*Brit*), liverwurst (*US*)
**paście** *n patrz* **pasta**
**pa|ść**[1] **(-dnę, -dniesz)** (*imp* **-dnij**, *pt* **-dł**) *vb perf od* **padać**
**pa|ść**[2] **(-sę, -siesz)** (*imp* **-ś**, *pt* **-sł, -śli**) *vt* (*pilnować na pastwisku*) to graze; (*tuczyć*) to fatten; **paść się** *vr* to graze
**pa|t** (**-ta, -ty**) (*loc sg* **-cie**) *m* (*Szachy*) stalemate; (*przen*) stalemate, deadlock
**patel|nia** (**-ni, -nie**) (*gen pl* **-ni**) *f* frying pan
**paten|t** (**-tu, -ty**) (*loc sg* **-cie**) *m* patent; **~ oficerski** (officer's) commission
**patentowy** *adj*: **urząd ~** patent office; **zamek ~** yale lock
**patetyczny** *adj* pompous
**pati|o** (**-a, -a**) (*gen pl* **-ów**) *nt* patio
**pat|ka** (**-ki, -ki**) (*dat sg* **-ce**, *gen pl* **-ek**) *f* flap
**patologi|a** (**-i**) *f* pathology
**patologiczny** *adj* pathological
**pato|s** (**-su**) (*loc sg* **-sie**) *m* pathos
**patowy** *adj*: **sytuacja patowa** stalemate, deadlock
**patriar|cha** (**-chy, -chowie**) (*dat sg* **-sze**) *m decl like f in sg* patriarch
**patrio|ta** (**-ty, -ci**) (*dat sg* **-cie**) *m decl like f in sg* patriot
**patriot|ka** (**-ki, -ki**) (*dat sg* **-ce**, *gen pl* **-ek**) *f* patriot
**patriotyczny** *adj* patriotic
**patriotyz|m** (**-mu**) (*loc sg* **-mie**) *m* patriotism
**patrol** (**-u, -e**) (*gen pl* **-i**) *m* patrol
**patrol|ować (-uję, -ujesz)** *vt* to patrol
**patro|n** (**-na, -nowie** *lub* **-ni**) (*loc sg* **-nie**) *m* (*opiekun*) patron; (*Rel*) patron saint
**patrona|t** (**-tu**) (*loc sg* **-cie**) *m* patronage
**patron|ka** (**-ki, -ki**) (*loc sg* **-ce**, *gen pl* **-ek**) *f* (*Rel*) patron saint
**patron|ować (-uję, -ujesz)** *vt +dat* to patronize
**patrosz|yć (-ę, -ysz)** (*perf* **wy-**) *vt* to gut
**patrz|eć, patrz|yć (-ę, -ysz)** *vi* to look; **~ na coś trzeźwo/optymistycznie** to view sth with objectivity/optimism; **~ na kogoś jak na wroga/intruza** to look on sb as an enemy/intruder; **dobrze/źle mu z oczu patrzy** he has kind/mean eyes; **~ wstecz/w przyszłość** to look back/ahead; **~ krzywym okiem na kogoś/coś** to look askance at sb/sth; **~ na coś przez palce** (*przen*) to turn a blind eye to sth; **~ na kogoś z góry** (*przen*) to look down on sb
**patrz|yć (-ę, -ysz)** *vi* = **patrzeć**
**patyczk|ować się (-uję, -ujesz)** *vr*: **patyczkować się z kimś** to handle sb with kid gloves
**paty|k** (**-ka, -ki**) (*instr sg* **-kiem**) *m* stick
**patykowaty** *adj* spindly
**paty|na** (**-ny**) (*dat sg* **-nie**) *f* patina
**pau|za** (**-zy, -zy**) (*dat sg* **-zie**) *f* (*przerwa*) pause; (*Szkol*) break; (*Muz*) rest; (*myślnik*) dash
**pa|w** (**-wia, -wie**) (*gen pl* **-wi**) *m* peacock; **dumny jak paw** (as) proud as a peacock; **puścić** (*perf*) **pawia** (*pot: zwymiotować*) to puke (*pot*)
**pawia|n** (**-na, -ny**) (*loc sg* **-nie**) *m* baboon
**pawilo|n** (**-nu, -ny**) (*loc sg* **-nie**) *m* pavilion
**pawlacz** (**-a, -e**) (*gen pl* **-y**) *m* storage place
**pazerny** *adj* (*pot*): **~ (na coś)** greedy (for sth)
**pazno|kieć** (**-kcia, -kcie**) (*gen pl* **-kci**) *m* (*u ręki*) (finger)nail; (*u nogi*) (toe)nail
**pazu|cha** (**-chy**) (*dat sg* **-sze**) *f*: **za pazuchą** in one's breast pocket
**pazu|r** (**-ra, -ry**) (*loc sg* **-rze**) *m* claw; **pokazać** (*perf*) **~y** (*przen*) to show one's claws; **walczyć o coś zębami i ~ami** (*przen*) to fight tooth and nail for sth
**pa|ź** (**-zia, -ziowie**) *m* (*Hist*) page
**październi|k** (**-ka, -ki**) (*instr sg* **-kiem**) *m* October
**październikowy** *adj* October *attr*
**październzowy** *adj*: **płyta paździerzowa** fibreboard (*Brit*), fiberboard (*US*)
**pącz|ek** (**-ka, -ki**) (*instr sg* **-kiem**) *m* (*Bot: pąk*) bud; (*ciastko*) doughnut, donut (*US*)
**pączk|ować (-uje)** *vi* to bud
**pączkowani|e** (**-a**) *nt* budding
**pą|k** (**-ka, -ki**) (*instr sg* **-kiem**) *m* bud; **wypuszczać (wypuścić** *perf*) **pąki** to bud
**pą|s** (**-su, -sy**) (*loc sg* **-sie**) *m*: **oblać się** (*perf*) **pąsem** to blush
**pąsowy** *adj* crimson
**pch|ać (-am, -asz)** *vt* (*perf* **-nąć**) to push; (*przen: skłaniać*) (*perf* **-nąć**) to prod; (*wpychać*) to thrust, to stuff; **„~"** "push"; **zazdrość**

P

**pchnęła go do morderstwa** he was driven to murder by jealousy; **~ nos w nie swoje sprawy** to poke *lub* stick one's nose into somebody else's business; **pchać się** *vr* (*tłoczyć się*) to force *lub* push one's way

**pcheł|ka** (**-ki, -ki**) (*dat sg* **-ce**, *gen pl* **-ek**) *f dimin od* **pchła**; **pchełki** *pl* (*gra*) tiddlywinks *pl*

**pchli** *adj*: **~ targ** flea market

**pch|ła** (**-ły, -ły**) (*dat sg* **-le**, *gen pl* **-eł**) *f* flea

**pch|nąć (-nę, -niesz)** (*imp* **-nij**) *vb perf od* **pchać** ▷ *vt perf* (*nożem, sztyletem*) to stab

**pchnię|cie** (**-cia, -cia**) (*gen pl* **-ć**) *nt* (*nożem, sztyletem*) stab; **~ kulą** (*Sport*) shot put

**PCK** *abbr* (= *Polski Czerwony Krzyż*) Polish Red Cross

**pece|t** (**-ta, -ty**) (*loc sg* **-cie**) *m* (*pot: komputer*) PC

**pech** (**-a**) *m* bad luck; **mieć ~a** to be unlucky; **a to ~!** bad *lub* tough luck!

**pecho|wiec** (**-wca, -wcy**) *m* unlucky person

**pechowy** *adj* unlucky

**pedago|g** (**-ga, -gowie** *lub* **-dzy**) (*instr sg* **-giem**) *m* educator

**pedagogiczny** *adj* pedagogic(al)

**pedagogi|ka** (**-ki**) (*dat sg* **-ce**) *f* pedagogy

**peda|ł** (*loc sg* **-le**, *nom pl* **-ły**) *m* (*przy rowerze, pianinie*) (*gen sg* **-łu**) pedal; (*pej: homoseksualista*) (*gen sg* **-ła**) queer (*pej*); **~ gazu/hamulca** accelerator/brake pedal

**pedał|ować (-uję, -ujesz)** *vi* to pedal

**pedan|t** (**-ta, -ci**) (*loc sg* **-cie**) *m* pedant

**pedantyczny** *adj* pedantic

**pedera|sta** (**-sty, -ści**) (*dat sg* **-ście**) *m decl like f in sg* pederast

**pediat|ra** (**-ry, -rzy**) (*dat sg* **-rze**) *m decl like f in sg* paediatrician (*Brit*), pediatrician (*US*)

**pediatri|a** (**-i**) *f* paediatrics (*Brit*), pediatrics (*US*)

**pediatryczny** *adj* paediatric (*Brit*), pediatric (*US*)

**pedicu|re** (**-re'u**) (*instr sg* **-re'em**, *loc sg* **-rze**) *m* = **pedikiur**

**pedikiu|r** (**-ru**) (*loc sg* **-rze**) *m* pedicure

**pedikiurzyst|ka** (**-ki, -ki**) (*dat sg* **-ce**) *f* pedicurist

**pedofi|l** (**-la, -le**) *m* paedophile (*Brit*), pedophile (*US*)

**pedofil|ka** (**-ki, -ki**) (*dat sg* **-ce**) *f* paedophile (*Brit*), pedophile (*US*)

**Pega|z** (**-za**) (*loc sg* **-zie**) *m* Pegasus

**pejcz** (**-a, -e**) (*gen pl* **-y**) *m* whip

**pejoratywny** *adj* pejorative

**pej|s** (**-sa, -sy**) (*loc sg* **-sie**) *m* sidelock

**pejzaż** (**-u, -e**) (*gen pl* **-y**) *m* landscape

**Peki|n** (**-nu**) (*loc sg* **-nie**) *m* Beijing, Peking

**pekińczy|k** (**-ka, -ki**) (*instr sg* **-kiem**) *m* (*pies*) pekin(g)ese, peke (*pot*)

**pekl|ować (-uję, -ujesz)** (*perf* **za-**) *vt* to corn

**pelargoni|a** (**-i, -e**) (*gen pl* **-i**) *f* geranium

**pelery|na** (**-ny, -ny**) (*dat sg* **-nie**) *f* cloak, cape

**peleto|n** (**-nu, -ny**) (*loc sg* **-nie**) *m* (*Sport*) main group (*of cyclists*)

**pelika|n** (**-na, -ny**) (*loc sg* **-nie**) *m* pelican

**pełen** *adj* = **pełny**

**pełł** *itd. vb patrz* **pleć**

**peł|nia** (**-ni, -nie**) (*gen pl* **-ni**) *f* (*księżyca*) full moon; (*obfitość*) fullness; **~ sezonu** high *lub* peak season; **~ lata** the height of summer; **księżyc jest w pełni** the moon is full; **być w pełni sił** to be sound in body; **być w pełni władz umysłowych** to be of sound mind; **~ szczęścia/zadowolenia** complete happiness/satisfaction; **w pełni się z tobą zgadzam** I fully agree with you

**peł|nić (-nię, -nisz)** (*imp* **-nij** *lub* **-ń**) *vt* (*rolę, obowiązki*) to fulfil (*Brit*), to fulfill (*US*); **~ służbę** to serve; **~ wartę** to keep guard; **pełniący obowiązki premiera** acting prime minister

**pełno** *adv* (*wiele*) a lot *lub* plenty of; **w butelce jest ~ wody** the bottle is full of water; **w autobusie było ~** the bus was full

**pełnoetatowy** *adj* full-time *attr*

**pełnokrwisty** *adj* thoroughbred

**pełnoletni** *adj* of age; **być ~m** to be of age

**pełnoletnoś|ć** (**-ci**) *f* majority; **osiągnąć** (*perf*) **~** to come of age

**pełnometrażowy** *adj*: **film ~** feature film

**pełnomocnict|wo** (**-wa, -wa**) (*loc sg* **-wie**) *nt* power of attorney, proxy; **udzielić** (*perf*) **komuś pełnomocnictwa do zrobienia czegoś** to authorize sb to do sth, to give sb power of attorney to do sth

**pełnomocni|k** (**-ka, -cy**) (*instr sg* **-kiem**) *m* proxy, plenipotentiary; **przez ~a** by proxy

**pełnomocny** *adj* plenipotentiary

**pełnomorski** *adj* (*jacht*) ocean-going; **rejs ~** off-shore sailing

**pełnopłatny** *adj* full price *lub* payment *attr*

**pełnoprawny** *adj* rightful

**pełnotłusty** *adj* (*mleko*) full-cream *attr*

**pełnowartościowy** *adj* (*pożywienie, dieta*) balanced

**pełnoziarnisty** *adj* (*chleb*) wholemeal

**pełny, pełen** *adj* (*kubek, worek*) full; (*szczęście, zaufanie*) complete; **ten kubek jest pełen (wody)** this cup is full (of water); **pełen entuzjazmu** enthusiastic; **pełen nadziei** hopeful; **pełne mleko** full-cream milk; **pełne morze** open *lub* high sea; **pełna cegła** solid brick; **koń pełnej krwi** thoroughbred; **w ~m toku** in full swing; **jechać na ~m gazie** to floor it (*pot*); **do pełna proszę!** fill her *lub* it up, please!

**pełz|ać (-am, -asz)** *vi* (*o ludziach, zwierzętach*) to crawl; (*o ogniu, mgle*) to creep
**peł|znąć (-znę, -zniesz** *lub* **-źniesz)** (*imp* **-znij** *lub* **-źnij**, *pt* **-znął** *lub* **-zł, -zła, -zli** *lub* **-źli**) *vi* = **pełzać**
**penetr|ować (-uję, -ujesz)** (*perf* **s-**) *vt* to penetrate
**penicyli|na** (**-ny**) (*dat sg* **-nie**) *f* penicillin
**peni|s** (**-sa, -sy**) (*loc sg* **-sie**) *m* penis
**penitencjarny** *adj* (*zakład*) penal; (*system*) penal, penitentiary
**pen|s** (**-sa, -sy**) (*loc sg* **-sie**) *m* penny; **20 ~ów** 20 pence
**pensj|a** (**-i, -e**) (*gen pl* **-i**) *f* (*płaca*) salary, pay
**pensjona|t** (**-tu, -ty**) (*loc sg* **-cie**) *m* guest-house, boarding-house
**percepcj|a** (**-i, -e**) (*gen pl* **-i**) *f* (Psych) perception
**perfekcj|a** (**-i**) *f* perfection; **dojść** (*perf*) **w czymś do perfekcji** to attain *lub* achieve perfection at *lub* in sth
**perfekcjoni|sta** (**-sty, -ści**) (*dat sg* **-ście**) *m decl like f in sg* perfectionist
**perfekcyjny** *adj* perfect
**perfidi|a** (**-i**) *f* perfidy
**perfidny** *adj* perfidious
**perforacj|a** (**-i, -e**) (*gen pl* **-i**) *f* perforation
**perfumeri|a** (**-i, -e**) (*gen pl* **-i**) *f* perfume shop
**perfum|ować (-uję, -ujesz)** (*perf* **wy-**) *vt* to perfume; **perfumować się** *vr* to put on (a) perfume
**perfum|y** (-) *pl* perfume
**pergami|n** (**-nu, -ny**) (*loc sg* **-nie**) *m* parchment
**periodyczny** *adj* periodic
**periody|k** (**-ku, -ki**) (*instr sg* **-kiem**) *m* periodical
**perkal** (**-u, -e**) (*gen pl* **-i** *lub* **-ów**) *m* percale
**perko|z** (**-za, -zy**) (*loc sg* **-zie**) *m* grebe
**perkusi|sta** (**-sty, -ści**) (*dat sg* **-ście**) *m decl like f in sg* drummer
**perkusj|a** (**-i, -e**) (*gen pl* **-i**) *f* drums *pl*
**perkusyjny** *adj*: **instrumenty perkusyjne** percussion instruments
**perlicz|ka** (**-ki, -ki**) (*dat sg* **-ce**, *gen pl* **-ek**) *f* (*Zool*) guinea fowl
**perlisty** *adj* pearly
**per|ła** (**-ły, -ły**) (*dat sg* **-le**, *gen pl* **-eł**) *f* pearl
**perłowy** *adj* (*z pereł: naszyjnik*) pearl *attr*; (*srebrzystobiały*) pearly; **masa perłowa** mother-of-pearl
**permanentny** *adj* (*książk*) permanent
**permutacj|a** (**-i, -e**) (*gen pl* **-i**) *f* (*Mat*) permutation
**pero|n** (**-nu, -ny**) (*loc sg* **-nie**) *m* platform; **pociąg odjeżdża z ~u siódmego** the train departs from platform seven
**Per|s** (**-sa, -sowie**) (*loc sg* **-sie**) *m* Persian
**Persj|a** (**-i**) *f* Persia
**perski** *adj* Persian; **Zatoka Perska** the (Persian) Gulf
**personali|a** (**-ów**) *pl* personal data
**personalny** *adj* (*dane*) personal; (*dział, polityka*) personnel *attr*; **zmiany personalne w rządzie** Cabinet reshuffle
**personel** (**-u**) *m* personnel, staff
**personifik|ować (-uję, -ujesz)** *vt* to personify
**perspekty|wa** (**-wy, -wy**) (*dat sg* **-wie**) *f* (*w obrazie*) perspective; (*widok, panorama*) view, vista; (*odległość w czasie*) prospect; (*przen: możliwość*) prospect; **mieć coś w perspektywie** to have sth in prospect
**perspektywiczny** *adj* (*myślenie, planowanie*) far-reaching; (*zadanie*) future *attr*
**perswad|ować (-uję, -ujesz)** (*perf* **wy-**) *vt*: **~ komuś coś** to try to persuade sb of sth
**perswazj|a** (**-i**) *f* persuasion
**pertraktacj|e** (**-i**) *pl* negotiations *pl*
**pertrakt|ować (-uję, -ujesz)** *vi* to negotiate
**Peru** *nt inv* Peru
**peru|ka** (**-ki, -ki**) (*dat sg* **-ce**) *f* wig
**Peruwiańczy|k** (**-ka, -cy**) (*instr sg* **-kiem**) *m* Peruvian
**peruwiański** *adj* Peruvian
**perwersj|a** (**-i, -e**) (*gen pl* **-i**) *f* perversion
**perwersyjny** *adj* perverse
**peryferi|e** (**-i**) *pl* (*zewnętrzne części*) periphery; (*krańce miasta*) outskirts *pl*
**peryferyjny** *adj* (*leżący na uboczu*) peripheral; **urządzenie peryferyjne** (*Komput*) peripheral (device)
**perypeti|e** (**-i**) *pl* ups and downs *pl*, vicissitudes *pl*
**perysko|p** (**-pu, -py**) (*loc sg* **-pie**) *m* periscope
**perz** (**-u**) *m* couch grass
**perzy|na** (**-ny**) (*dat sg* **-nie**) *f*: **obrócić** (*perf*) **coś w perzynę** to lay waste to sth
**pest|ka** (**-ki, -ki**) (*dat sg* **-ce**, *gen pl* **-ek**) *f* (*śliwki, wiśni*) stone; (*jabłka, pomarańczy*) pip; (*dyni, słonecznika*) seed; **zalać się** (*perf*) **w pestkę** (*pot*) to get blind drunk (*pot*); **to (dla mnie) ~** (*pot*) it's a piece of cake (*pot*)
**pestycy|d** (**-du, -dy**) (*loc sg* **-dzie**) *m* pesticide
**pesymi|sta** (**-sty, -ści**) (*dat sg* **-ście**) *m decl like f in sg* pessimist
**pesymistyczny** *adj* pessimistic
**pesymiz|m** (**-mu**) (*loc sg* **-mie**) *m* pessimism
**pesz|yć (-ę, -ysz)** (*perf* **s-**) *vt* to disconcert, to put off balance; **peszyć się** *vr* to get disconcerted, to lose countenance
**pe|t** (**-ta, -ty**) (*loc sg* **-cie**) *m* (*pot*) fag end (*pot*)
**petar|da** (**-dy, -dy**) (*dat sg* **-dzie**) *f* firecracker, squib
**peten|t** (**-ta, -ci**) (*loc sg* **-cie**) *m* inquirer

P

**petrochemiczny** *adj* petrochemical
**pettin|g** (**-gu**) (*instr sg* **-giem**) *m* petting
**petycj|a** (**-i, -e**) (*gen pl* **-i**) *f* petition; **wnosić (wnieść** *perf*) **petycję** to petition
**pewien** (*f* **pewna**, *nt* **pewne**) *adj* (*jakiś*) a (certain); (*pewny*) sure, certain; **~ pan** a (certain) gentleman; **~ nasz znajomy** an acquaintance of ours; **pewnego dnia** one day; **pewnego razu** once (upon a time); **przez ~ czas** for some time; **w pewnym stopniu** to some extent; **w pewnym sensie** in a sense
**pewnia|k** (**-ka**) (*instr sg* **-kiem**) *m* (*pot: kandydat*) (*nom pl* **-cy**) safe bet, dead cert (*pot*); (*: koń itp.*) (*nom pl* **-ki**) safe bet, dead cert (*pot*)
**pewnie** *adv* (*zdecydowanie*) firmly; (*sprawnie*) confidently; (*niezawodnie*) dependably, reliably; (*prawdopodobnie*) probably; **czuć się ~** to feel confident; **~ znów się spóźni** he'll probably be late again; **~, że…** surely, …; **(no) ~!** (*pot*) you bet! (*pot*), sure! (*pot*)
**pewni|k** (**-ka, -ki**) (*instr sg* **-kiem**) *m* (a) certainty; **przyjmować (przyjąć** *perf*) **coś za ~** to take sth as read
**pewno** *adv* (*prawdopodobnie*) probably; **na ~** certainly, surely
**pewnoś|ć** (**-ci**) *f* (*przekonanie*) certainty; (*zdecydowanie*) firmness; (*sprawność*) confidence; (*niezawodność*) dependability, reliability; **dla pewności** to be on the safe side, to make sure; **~ siebie** self-assurance, self-confidence; **z pewnością** surely
**pewny** *adj* (*zguba, śmierć*) certain, sure; (*dowód, wniosek*) unquestionable; (*krok, ruch*) firm; (*ręka, oko*) steady; (*urządzenie, człowiek*) dependable, reliable; (*bezpieczny*) secure; **być ~m czegoś** to be sure of sth, to be positive about sth; **to pewne** that's for sure, that's certain; **~ siebie** self-assured, self-confident; **być ~m kogoś** to have confidence in sb; **on jest ~** *lub* **pewien, że …** he's sure (that) …
**pęcherz** (**-a, -e**) (*gen pl* **-y**) *m* (*na skórze*) blister; (*Anat*) bladder
**pęcherzy|k** (**-ka, -ki**) (*instr sg* **-kiem**) *m* (*na skórze*) blister; (*powietrza*) bubble; **~ żółciowy** gall bladder; **~ płucny** alveolus
**pęcz|ek** (**-ka, -ki**) (*instr sg* **-kiem**) *m* bunch; **mieć czegoś na pęczki** (*pot*) to have heaps of sth (*pot*)
**pęczni|eć (-eję, -ejesz)** (*perf* **na-**) *vi* to swell
**pę|d** (**-du**) (*loc sg* **-dzie**) *m* (*szybki ruch*) speed; (*Bot*) (*nom pl* **-dy**) shoot; **pęd do czegoś** drive for sth
**pędz|el** (**-la, -le**) (*gen pl* **-li**) *m* (*do malowania*) (paint)brush; (*do golenia*) (shaving) brush
**pędzel|ek** (**-ka, -ki**) (*instr sg* **-kiem**) *m dimin od* **pędzel**
**pę|dzić (-dzę, -dzisz)** (*imp* **-dź**) *vt* (*bydło, więźniów*) to drive; (*alkohol*) to distil (Brit), to distill (US) ▷ *vi* (*perf* **po-**) to speed along, to race
**pę|k** (**-ku, -ki**) (*instr sg* **-kiem**) *m* bunch
**pęk|ać (-am, -asz)** (*perf* **-nąć**) *vi* (*o lodzie, szybie*) to crack; (*o sznurku, strunie*) to burst; (*o koszuli, worku*) to rip; **głowa mi pęka** (*przen*) my head is splitting; **~ w szwach** to be bursting at the seams; **~ ze śmiechu** (*przen*) to burst with laughter, to be in stitches
**pękaty** *adj* (*beczka*) squat; (*portfel*) bulging
**pęk|nąć (-nę, -niesz)** (*imp* **-nij**, *pt* **-ł**) *vb perf od* **pękać**
**pęknię|cie** (**-cia, -cia**) (*gen pl* **-ć**) *nt* (*kości*) fracture; (*rysa*) crack
**pęp|ek** (**-ka, -ki**) (*instr sg* **-kiem**) *m* navel; **~ świata** (*pot*) the hub of the universe
**pępowi|na** (**-ny, -ny**) (*dat sg* **-nie**) *f* umbilical cord
**pęse|ta** (**-ty, -ty**) (*dat sg* **-cie**) *f* tweezers *pl*
**pęt|a** (**-**) *pl* (*więzy*) fetters *pl*
**pęt|ać (-am, -asz)** (*perf* **s-**) *vt* (*konie, bydło*) to hog-tie; **pętać się** *vr* (*pot*) to hang around (*pot*)
**pętel|ka** (**-ki, -ki**) (*dat sg* **-ce**) *f* loop
**pętl|a** (**-i, -e**) (*gen pl* **-i**) *f* (*na sznurze*) loop, noose; (*autobusowa, tramwajowa*) terminus; (*Lot, Komput*) loop
**PGR** *abbr* (*= Państwowe Gospodarstwo Rolne*) *a state-owned farm in former Poland*
**piać (pieję, piejesz)** (*pt* **piali** *lub* **pieli**, *perf* **za-**) *vi* (*o kogucie*) to crow
**pia|na** (**-ny**) (*dat sg* **-nie**) *f* foam, froth; (*z mydła*) lather; (*na powierzchni piwa*) head, froth
**piani|no** (**-na, -na**) (*loc sg* **-nie**) *nt* piano
**piani|sta** (**-sty, -ści**) (*dat sg* **-ście**) *m decl like f in sg* pianist
**pianist|ka** (**-ki, -ki**) (*dat sg* **-ce**, *gen pl* **-ek**) *f* pianist
**pian|ka** (**-ki**) (*dat sg* **-ce**) *f dimin od* **piana**; **~ do włosów** styling mousse; **~ do golenia** shaving foam; **~ poliuretanowa** polyurethane foam
**pianowy** *adj*: **gaśnica pianowa** foam extinguisher
**pias|ek** (**-ku, -ki**) (*instr sg* **-kiem**) *m* sand; **chować (schować** *perf*) **głowę w ~** (*przen*) to bury one's head in the sand
**piaskar|ka** (**-ki, -ki**) (*dat sg* **-ce**, *gen pl* **-ek**) *f* (*pojazd*) sand (and salt) spreader
**piasko|wiec** (**-wca, -wce**) *m* sandstone
**piaskownic|a** (**-y, -e**) *f* sandpit, sandbox
**piaskowy** *adj* (*gleba, kolor*) sandy; **burza piaskowa** sandstorm
**pia|sta** (**-sty, -sty**) (*dat sg* **-ście**) *f* (*Tech*) hub
**piast|ować (-uję, -ujesz)** (*książk*) *vt*: **~ urząd/godność** to hold an office/a position

**piaszczysty** *adj* sandy
**piąć się (pnę, pniesz)** (*imp* **pnij**) *vr* to climb (up)
**piąt|ek** (**-ku, -ki**) (*instr sg* **-kiem**) *m* Friday; **Wielki P~** Good Friday
**piąt|ka** (**-ki, -ki**) (*dat sg* **-ce**, *gen pl* **-ek**) *f* five; (*Szkol*) ≈ A
**piątkowy** *adj* Friday *attr*
**piąty** *num decl like adj* fifth; **piąte koło u wozu** (*przen*) odd-man-out
**pice** *n patrz* **pika**
**pich|cić (-cę, -cisz)** (*imp* **-ć**, *perf* **u-**) *vt* (*pot*) to cook up; **coś tam upichcę** I'll throw sth together (*pot*)
**pi|cie** (**-cia**) *nt* (*czynność*) drinking; (*pot: napój*) drink; **ta woda jest do picia** this water is drinkable; **daj mi coś do picia** give me sth to drink
**pi|ć (-ję, -jesz)** *vt* (*perf* **wy-**) to drink ▷ *vi* to drink; **chce mi się pić** I'm thirsty; **pić (wypić** *perf*) **(za) czyjeś zdrowie** to drink (to) sb's health
**piec**[1] (**-a, -e**) *m* (*grzewczy, kuchenny*) stove; (*piekarniczy*) oven; (*hutniczy, odlewniczy*) furnace
**pie|c**[2] **(-kę, -czesz)** (*imp* **-cz**) *vt* (*ciasto*) (*perf* **u-**) to bake; (*mięso*) (*perf* **u-**) to roast ▷ *vi* (*o słońcu*) to beat down; **oczy mnie pieką** my eyes are stinging; **piec się** *vr* (*perf* **u-**) (*o cieście*) to bake; (*o mięsie*) to roast
**piecho|ta** (**-ty**) (*dat sg* **-cie**) *f* (*Wojsk*) infantry; **~ morska** Royal Marines *pl* (*Brit*), Marine Corps (*US*), Marines *pl* (*US*); **iść piechotą** *lub* **na piechotę** to walk, to go on foot
**piechu|r** (**-ra, -rzy** *lub* **-ry**) (*loc sg* **-rze**) *m* walker, hiker
**piecy|k** (**-ka, -ki**) (*instr sg* **-kiem**) *m* heater
**piecz|a** (**-y**) *f* (*książk*): **mieć kogoś/coś w swojej pieczy** *lub* **pod swoją pieczą** to be responsible for sb/sth
**piecza|ra** (**-ry, -ry**) (*dat sg* **-rze**) *f* cave, cavern
**pieczar|ka** (**-ki, -ki**) (*dat sg* **-ce**, *gen pl* **-ek**) *f* (meadow) mushroom
**piecząt|ka** (**-ki, -ki**) (*dat sg* **-ce**, *gen pl* **-ek**) *f* (*przyrząd*) (rubber) stamp; (*znak*) stamp
**piecze|ń** (**-ni, -nie**) (*gen pl* **-ni**) *f* roast; **~ wołowa** roast beef
**pieczę|ć** (**-ci, -cie**) (*gen pl* **-ci**) *f* stamp; (*lakowa*) seal
**pieczęt|ować (-uję, -ujesz)** *vt* (*meble, mieszkanie*) (*perf* **za-**) to seal; (*przen: przyjaźń*) (*perf* **przy-**) to seal
**pieczołowity** *adj* careful
**pieczy|wo** (**-wa**) (*loc sg* **-wie**) *nt* bread
**piedesta|ł** (**-łu, -ły**) (*loc sg* **-le**) *m* pedestal; **postawić** (*perf*) **kogoś na piedestale** (*przen*) to place *lub* put sb on a pedestal
**pie|gi** (**-gów**) *pl* freckles *pl*
**piegowaty** *adj* freckled
**pieję** *itd. vb patrz* **piać**
**piekar|nia** (**-ni, -nie**) (*gen pl* **-ni**) *f* (*zakład*) bakery; (*sklep*) the baker's (shop), bakery
**piekarni|k** (**-ka, -ki**) (*instr sg* **-kiem**) *m* oven
**piekarz** (**-a, -e**) (*gen pl* **-y**) *m* baker; **u ~a** at the baker's
**piekący** *adj* (*słońce*) scorching; (*ból*) stinging
**piekielnie** *adv* (*pot: zdolny*) terribly, incredibly; (*trudny*) hellishly, fiendishly
**piekielny** *adj* (*ogień, moce*) infernal; (*ból, hałas*) dreadful, hellish
**piekl|ić się (-ę, -isz)** *vr* (*pot*) to rage
**piek|ło** (**-ła**) (*loc sg* **-le**) *nt* hell; **on jest z piekła rodem** (*przen*) he's got a hellish temper; **robić (zrobić** *perf*) **~** to raise hell (*pot*); **urządzać (urządzić** *perf*) **komuś ~** to give sb hell (*pot*)
**pielęgnacj|a** (**-i**) *f* (*roślin*) nurturing; (*chorych*) nursing; (*zwierząt*) tending; **krem do pielęgnacji twarzy/rąk** face/hand cream
**pielęgniar|ka** (**-ki, -ki**) (*dat sg* **-ce**, *gen pl* **-ek**) *f* nurse
**pielęgniarst|wo** (**-wa**) (*loc sg* **-wie**) *nt* nursing
**pielęgniarz** (**-a, -e**) (*gen pl* **-y**) *m* male nurse
**pielęgn|ować (-uję, -ujesz)** *vt* (*ludzi*) to nurse; (*rośliny*) to take care of, to look after; (*ogródek*) to tend; (*ręce, twarz*) to take care of; (*tradycje, obyczaje*) to foster
**pielgrzy|m** (**-ma, -mi**) (*loc sg* **-mie**) *m* pilgrim
**pielgrzym|ka** (**-ki, -ki**) (*dat sg* **-ce**, *gen pl* **-ek**) *f* pilgrimage
**pielić, pleć (pielę, pielisz)** *vt* (*perf* **wy-**) to weed ▷ *vi* to weed
**pielu|cha** (**-chy, -chy**) (*dat sg* **-sze**) *f* nappy (*Brit*), diaper (*US*)
**pielusz|ka** (**-ki, -ki**) (*dat sg* **-ce**, *gen pl* **-ek**) *f* nappy (*Brit*), diaper (*US*); **~ jednorazowa** disposable nappy *lub* diaper
**pieni|ądz** (**-ądza, -ądze**) (*gen pl* **-ędzy**) *m* (*moneta, banknot*) money; **pieniądze** *pl* money; **mam mało pieniędzy** I have little money; **być bez pieniędzy** to have no money; **mieć pieniędzy jak lodu** (*pot*) to be rolling in money (*pot*), to have money to burn (*pot*); **robić ~e (na czymś)** (*pot*) to make money (out of sth); **wyrzucać ~e w błoto** (*przen*) to throw money down the drain
**pieniąż|ek** (**-ka, -ki**) (*instr sg* **-kiem**) *m* coin; **pieniążki** *pl* (*pot*) money
**pie|nić się (-nię, -nisz)** (*imp* **-ń**) *vr* (*perf* **s-**) (*o mydle*) to lather; (*o piwie*) to froth; (*o zwierzęciu*) to foam *lub* froth at the mouth; (*pot: złościć się*) to be frothing at the mouth (*pot*)
**pie|niek** (**-ńka, -ńki**) (*instr sg* **-ńkiem**) *m dimin od* **pień**; **mieć z kimś na pieńku** (*przen*) to be at daggers drawn with sb, to have a bone to pick with sb

P

**pieniężny** *adj* money *attr*; (*finansowy*) financial; (*kara*) pecuniary; (*zasoby*) monetary, pecuniary; **świadczenia pieniężne** (cash) benefits; **wygrana pieniężna** prize money

**pień** (**pnia, pnie**) (*gen pl* **pni**) *m* (*część drzewa*) trunk; (*drzewo po ścięciu*) stump; **głuchy jak ~** (as) deaf as a post, stone-deaf; **wyciąć** (*perf*) *lub* **wyrżnąć** (*perf*) **w ~** to wipe out

**pieprz** (**-u**) *m* pepper; **~ naturalny/biały** black/white pepper; **~ ziołowy** *a mixture of pepper and herbs used as seasoning*; **suchy jak ~** (as) dry as a bone; **uciekać, gdzie ~ rośnie** to run away like hell (*pot*)

**pieprznicz|ka** (**-ki, -ki**) (*dat sg* **-ce**, *gen pl* **-ek**) *f* pepperpot *lub* pepper pot (*Brit*), pepper shaker (*US*)

**pieprzny** *adj* (*potrawa*) hot, spicy; (*dowcip*) dirty, bawdy

**pieprzów|ka** (**-ki, -ki**) (*dat sg* **-ce**, *gen pl* **-ek**) *f* (*wódka*) *pepper-flavo(u)red vodka*

**pieprz|yć (-ę, -ysz)** *vt* (*posypywać pieprzem*) (*perf* **po-**) to pepper; (*pot!: psuć*) (*perf* **s-**) to screw up (*pot!*); (*pot!: o mężczyźnie: odbywać stosunek płciowy*) (*perf* **prze-** *lub* **wy-**) to screw (*pot!*) ▷ *vi* (*pot: mówić od rzeczy*) to talk nonsense; **pieprzyć się** *vr* (*pot!*) to fuck (*pot!*)

**pieprzy|k** (**-ka** *lub* **-ku, -ki**) (*instr sg* **-kiem**) *m* (*na skórze*) mole

**pierd|nąć (-nę, -niesz)** (*imp* **-nij**) *vb perf od* **pierdzieć**

**pierdol|ić (-ę, -isz)** *vt* (*pot!*) to fuck (*pot!*) ▷ *vi* (*pot!: pleść bzdury*) to bullshit (*pot!*); **nie pierdol!** (*pot!*) don't bullshit me! (*pot!*); **pierdolić się** *vr* (*pot!: odbywać stosunek płciowy*) to fuck (*pot!*)

**pier|dzieć (-dzę, -dzisz)** (*imp* **-dź**, *perf* **-dnąć**) *vi* (*pot!*) to fart (*pot!*)

**pierni|k** (**-ka, -ki**) (*instr sg* **-kiem**) *m* gingerbread; **co ma ~ do wiatraka?** (*pot*) what's that got to do with anything?

**piero|gi** (**-gów**) *pl boiled dough pockets filled with meat, cheese or fruit*

**piersiowy** *adj*: **klatka piersiowa** chest; (*Anat*) ribcage

**piersiów|ka** (**-ki, -ki**) (*dat sg* **-ce**, *gen pl* **-ek**) *f* (*pot*) ≈ hip flask

**pier|ś** (**-si, -si**) (*gen pl* **-si**) *f* (*klatka piersiowa*) chest, breast; (*u kobiety*) breast; **bić się** *lub* **uderzać się w piersi** (*przen*) to beat one's breast; **karmić dziecko piersią** to breast-feed a child; **~ kurza/indycza** chicken/turkey breast

**pierście|ń** (**-nia, -nie**) (*gen pl* **-ni**) *m* ring

**pierścion|ek** (**-ka, -ki**) (*instr sg* **-kiem**) *m* ring; **~ zaręczynowy** engagement ring

**pierwiast|ek** (**-ka, -ki**) (*instr sg* **-kiem**) *m* (*Chem*) element; (*Mat*) root; **~ śladowy** trace element; **~ kwadratowy** square root; **~ sześcienny** cube root

**pierwiosn|ek** (**-ka, -ki**) (*instr sg* **-kiem**) *m* primrose

**pierwoku|p** (**-pu**) (*loc sg* **-pie**) *m*: **prawo ~u** pre-emption

**pierworodny** *adj* (*syn*) first-born; **grzech ~** the original sin

**pierwotnia|k** (**-ka, -ki**) (*instr sg* **-kiem**) *m* protozoan

**pierwotnie** *adv* originally

**pierwotny** *adj* (*człowiek, kultura*) primitive; (*las, puszcza*) primeval, primaeval (*Brit*); (*plan, kolor*) original

**pierwowz|ór** (**-oru, -ory**) (*loc sg* **-orze**) *m* (*urządzenie*) prototype; (*archetyp*) archetype; (*oryginał*) original

**pierwszeńst|wo** (**-wa**) (*loc sg* **-wie**) *nt* (*prawo, przywilej*) precedence; (*Mot*): **~ przejazdu** right of way; **mieć ~ nad** *+instr* to take precedence over; **ustąpić** (*perf*) **pierwszeństwa** to yield, to give way

**pierwszoplanowy** *adj* (*sprawa, zadanie*) crucial; (*postać*) leading

**pierwszorzędny** *adj* first-class, first-rate

**pierwszy** *num decl like adj* first; **~ stycznia** the first of January; **pierwsze piętro** first floor (*Brit*), second floor (*US*); **pierwsza pomoc** first aid; **pierwsze danie** first course; **pierwsza litera** initial; **pierwsza wojna światowa** the First World War, World War One; **pierwsza w prawo/lewo** the next on the right/left; **~ lepszy** (*pot*) any old one; **Pan ~!** after you!; **po pierwsze** first, firstly; **~ raz** *lub* **po raz ~** for the first time; **na ~ rzut oka** at first glance *lub* sight, on the face of it; **miłość od pierwszego wejrzenia** love at first sight; **z pierwszej ręki** (*wiadomość, informacja*) first-hand; (*słyszeć, dowiedzieć się*) at first hand; **relacja z pierwszej ręki** inside story; **artykuły pierwszej potrzeby** necessities

**pierwszy|zna** (**-zny**) (*dat sg* **-źnie**) *f*: **to dla mnie nie ~** that's nothing new for me; **to dla mnie ~** that's something new for me

**pierzch|ać (-am, -asz)** (*perf* **-nąć**) *vi* (*o ludziach*) to take (to) flight; (*o drobnej zwierzynie*) to scamper away

**pierzch|nąć (-nę, -niesz)** (*imp* **-nij**) *vb perf od* **pierzchać** ▷ *vi* (*perf* **s-**) (*o skórze*) to chap

**pierz|e** (**-a**) *nt* feathers *pl*

**pierzy|na** (**-ny, -ny**) (*dat sg* **-nie**) *f* feather bed

**pies** (**psa, psy**) (*loc sg* **psie**) *m* dog; (*pot!*): **ty psie!** you dirty dog! (*pot!*); **~ z rodowodem** pedigree dog; **schodzić (zejść** *perf***) na psy** (*pot*) to go to the dogs (*pot*); **żyją jak ~ z kotem** they lead a cat-and-dog life; **wieszać**

**psy na kimś** to slander sb; **pogoda pod psem** wretched weather; **on jest ~ na czekoladę** he's crazy about chocolate

**pieszczo|ta** (**-ty, -ty**) (*dat sg* **-cie**) *f* caress

**pieszczotliwy** *adj* (*głos*) gentle; (*spojrzenie*) tender

**pieszo** *adv* on foot; **iść (pójść** *perf*) **~** to go on foot, to walk

**pieszy** *adj* (*żołnierz*) foot *attr*; (*oddział*) infantry *attr*; **piesza wycieczka** hike; **~ turysta** hiker, backpacker ▷ *m decl like adj* pedestrian; **przejście dla ~ch** (pedestrian) crossing

**pie|ścić (-szczę, -ścisz)** (*imp* **-ść**) *vt* to pet, to caress; **pieścić się** *vr* to pet, to caress; **nie ~ się z kimś** (*przen*) to be hard on sb

**pieśniarz** (**-a, -e**) *m* singer

**pieś|ń** (**-ni, -ni**) (*gen pl* **-ni**) *f* song

**piet|er** (**-ra**) *m*: **mieć pietra** (*pot*) to be scared; **dostać pietra** to get the wind up

**pietrusz|ka** (**-ki, -ki**) (*dat sg* **-ce**, *gen pl* **-ek**) *f* (*roślina*) parsley; (*korzeń*) parsley-root

**pietyz|m** (**-mu**) (*loc sg* **-mie**) *m*: **robić coś z (wielkim) ~em** to do sth with (great) reverence

**piewc|a** (**-y, -y**) *m decl like f in sg* (*książk*) eulogist

**pięciobo|k** (**-ku, -ki**) (*instr sg* **-kiem**) *m* pentagon

**pięciob|ój** (**-oju, -oje**) (*gen pl* **-oi** *lub* **-ojów**) *m*: **~ nowoczesny** pentathlon

**pięciodniowy** *adj* five-day *attr*, five-days' *attr*

**pięciogwiazdkowy** *adj* five-star *attr*

**pięcioką|t** (**-ta, -ty**) (*loc sg* **-cie**) *m* pentagon

**pięciokrotny** *adj* five-times *attr*

**pięcioletni** *adj* (*chłopiec, samochód*) five-year-old *attr*; (*plan, studia*) five-year *attr*, five years' *attr*

**pięciolini|a** (**-i, -e**) (*gen pl* **-i**) *f* (*Muz*) staff, stave (*Brit*)

**pięcioracz|ki** (**-ków**) *pl* quintuplets *pl*

**pięcioro** *num* (*dzieci*) five

**pięć** *num* five; **za ~ dwunasta** (*przen*) at the eleventh hour

**pięćdziesiąt** (*jak*: **dziesięć**) *num* fifty

**pięćdziesiąty** *num decl like adj* fiftieth

**pięćdziesięciolеci|e** (**-a, -a**) *nt* fiftieth anniversary *lub* jubilee

**pięćset** *num* five hundred

**pięćsetny** *num decl like adj* five-hundredth

**pięknie** *adv* beautifully; **~ wyglądać** to look beautiful

**piękni|eć (-eję, -ejesz)** (*perf* **wy-**) *vi* to become more and more beautiful

**pięk|no** (**-na**) (*loc sg* **-nie**) *nt* beauty

**pięknoś|ć** (**-ci**) *f* (*cecha*) beauty; (*piękna kobieta*) (*nom pl* **-ci**, *gen pl* **-ci**) beauty; **salon piękności** beauty salon; **konkurs piękności** beauty contest

**piękny** *adj* beautiful; (*wynik, czas*) excellent; **literatura piękna** belles-lettres; **sztuki piękne** fine arts; **płeć piękna** the fair sex

**pięściarst|wo** (**-wa**) (*loc sg* **-wie**) *nt* boxing

**pięściarz** (**-a, -e**) (*gen pl* **-y**) *m* boxer

**pięś|ć** (**-ci, -ci**) (*gen pl* **-ci**) *f* fist; **walka na pięści** fistfight; **prawo pięści** might is right, law of the jungle

**pię|ta** (**-ty, -ty**) (*dat sg* **-cie**) *f* heel; **~ Achillesa** *lub* **achillesowa** Achilles heel; **deptać komuś po ~ch** (*przen*) to be hot on sb's heels, to tread hard on sb's heels

**piętnastoletni** *adj* (*chłopiec, urządzenie*) fifteen-year-old *attr*; (*okres czasu*) fifteen years' *attr*

**piętnasty** *num decl like adj* fifteenth

**piętnaście** *num* fifteen; **za ~ czwarta** a quarter to four

**pięt|no** (**-na, -na**) (*loc sg* **-nie**) *nt* (*znak na zwierzęciu*) brand; (*przen*) stamp, imprint; **odciskać (odcisnąć** *perf*) **na kimś/czymś swoje ~** to leave one's stamp on sb/sth

**piętn|ować (-uję, -ujesz)** (*perf* **na-**) *vt* to stigmatize

**pięt|ro** (**-ra, -ra**) (*loc sg* **-rze**, *gen pl* **-er**) *nt* (*budynku*) floor, storey (*Brit*), story (*US*); **mieszkać na drugim piętrze** to live on the second (*Brit*) *lub* third (*US*) floor; **na piętrze** upstairs; **iść na ~** to go upstairs

**piętrowy** *adj*: **dom ~** storeyed (*Brit*) *lub* storied (*US*) house; **łóżko piętrowe** bunk beds *pl*; **autobus ~** double-decker

**piętrz|yć (-ę, -ysz)** (*perf* **s-**) *vt* (*wodę*) to dam up; (*przen*: *trudności*) to pile up; **piętrzyć się** *vr* to accumulate

**Pigmej** (**-a, -e**) *m* (*mieszkaniec Afryki*) Pygmy, Pigmy; (*niski człowiek*) pygmy, pigmy

**pigmen|t** (**-tu, -ty**) (*loc sg* **-cie**) *m* pigment

**piguł|ka** (**-ki, -ki**) (*dat sg* **-ce**, *gen pl* **-ek**) *f* pill; **~ nasenna** sleeping pill; **~ antykoncepcyjna** contraceptive pill, the pill; **przełknąć** (*perf*) **gorzką pigułkę** (*przen*) to swallow a bitter pill

**pig|wa** (**-wy, -wy**) (*dat sg* **-wie**) *f* (*Bot*) quince

**pijacki** *adj* drunken

**pija|k** (**-ka, -cy** *lub* **-ki**) (*instr sg* **-kiem**) *m* drunk, drunkard

**pijal|nia** (**-ni, -nie**) (*gen pl* **-ni**) *f* (*w uzdrowisku*) pump room

**pijany** *adj* drunk(en) ▷ *m decl like adj* drunk; **po pijanemu** under the influence (of alcohol); **jazda po pijanemu** drink driving (*Brit*), drunk driving (*US*); **~ sukcesem/szczęściem** (*przen*) drunk with success/happiness

**pijańst|wo** (**-wa**) (*loc sg* **-wie**) *nt* (*nałóg*) drunkenness; (*libacja*) drunken party

**pijaw|ka** (**-ki, -ki**) (*dat sg* **-ce**, *gen pl* **-ek**) *f* (*Zool*) leech

P

**piję** *itd. vb patrz* **pić**
**pi|k** (**-ka, -ki**) (*instr sg* **-kiem**) *m* (*Karty*) spade; **dama pik** the queen of spades
**pi|ka** (**-ki, -ki**) (*dat sg* **-ce**) *f* pike (*weapon*); *patrz też* **pik**
**pikado|r** (**-ra, -rzy**) *m* picador
**pikanteri|a** (**-i**) *f*: **dodawać (dodać** *perf*) **czemuś pikanterii** to spice sth up
**pikantny** *adj* (*sos*) piquant; (*przyprawa*) hot; (*przen: szczegół, historia*) juicy; (*dowcip*) bawdy
**pikie|ta** (**-ty, -ty**) (*dat sg* **-cie**) *f* picket
**pikiet|ować (-uję, -ujesz)** *vt* to picket
**pikni|k** (**-ku, -ki**) (*instr sg* **-kiem**) *m* picnic
**pik|ować (-uję, -ujesz)** *vt* (*Krawiectwo*) (*perf* **prze-**) to quilt ▷ *vi* (*Lot*) to nose-dive
**pikowany** *adj* quilted
**piksel** (**-a, -e**) *m* (*Komput*) pixel
**pile** *n patrz* **piła**
**pilni|k** (**-ka, -ki**) (*instr sg* **-kiem**) *m* file; **~ do paznokci** nail file
**pilnoś|ć** (**-ci**) *f* diligence
**piln|ować (-uję, -ujesz)** *vt* (*dzieci, domu*) to look after, to mind; (*interesów*) to look after; (*uczniów, robotników*) (*perf* **przy-**) to supervise; (*porządku, prawa*) to maintain; **pilnuj swego nosa!** (*pot*) mind your own business!; **pilnować się** *vr* to look after o.s., to take care of o.s.
**pilny** *adj* (*uczeń*) diligent; (*sprawa*) urgent; **pilna sprawa** a matter of urgency
**pilo|t** (**-ta**) (*loc sg* **-cie**) *m* (*samolotu*) (*nom pl* **-ci**) pilot; (*wycieczek*) (*nom pl* **-ci**) guide; (*do telewizora*) (*nom pl* **-ty**) remote control
**pilotaż** (**-u**) *m* pilotage
**pilotażowy** *adj* pilot *attr*
**pilot|ka** (**-ki, -ki**) (*dat sg* **-ce**, *gen pl* **-ek**) *f* (*kobieta pilot*) pilot
**pilot|ować (-uję, -ujesz)** *vt* (*samolot, statek*) to pilot; (*wycieczkę*) to guide
**pilśniowy** *adj* (*kapelusz*) felt *attr*; **płyta pilśniowa** fibreboard (Brit), fiberboard (US)
**pi|ła** (**-ły, -ły**) (*dat sg* **-le**) *f* saw
**pił|ka** (**-ki, -ki**) (*dat sg* **-ce**, *gen pl* **-ek**) *f* (*do gier i zabaw*) ball; (*do piłowania*) saw; **grać w piłkę** to play ball; **~ nożna** (association) football, soccer; **~ ręczna** (*Sport*) handball; **~ wodna** water-polo
**piłkarski** *adj* football *attr*, soccer *attr*
**piłkarz** (**-a, -e**) (*gen pl* **-y**) *m* football *lub* soccer player, footballer
**pił|ować (-uję, -ujesz)** *vt* (*piłą*) to saw; (*pilnikiem*) (*perf* **s-**) to file
**PIN** *abbr*: **numer PIN** PIN (= *personal identification number*)
**pince|ta** (**-ty, -ty**) *f* (*dat sg* **-cie**) tweezers *pl*
**pinez|ka** (**-ki, -ki**) (*dat sg* **-ce**, *gen pl* **-ek**) *f* drawing pin (Brit), thumbtack (US)
**ping-pon|g** (**-ga**) (*instr sg* **-giem**) *m* ping-pong
**pingwi|n** (**-na, -ny**) (*loc sg* **-nie**) *m* penguin
**piołu|n** (**-nu, -ny**) (*loc sg* **-nie**) *m* wormwood
**pio|n** (**-nu, -ny**) (*loc sg* **-nie**) *m* (*kierunek*) the perpendicular; (*przyrząd*) plumb-line; (*Szachy*) pawn; (*wodociągowy*) riser; (*dział, resort*) department
**pion|ek** (**-ka, -ki**) (*instr sg* **-kiem**) *m* pawn; (*w warcabach*) draughtsman (Brit), checker (US)
**pionie|r** (**-ra, -rzy**) (*loc sg* **-rze**) *m* pioneer
**pionierski** *adj* pioneer(ing) *attr*
**pionowo** *adv* vertically; (*w krzyżówce*) down
**pionowy** *adj* vertical, perpendicular; (*stojący w pozycji pionowej*) upright
**pioru|n** (**-na, -ny**) (*loc sg* **-nie**) *m* (thunder)bolt, lightning; **uderzenie ~a** a clap of thunder; **burza z ~ami** thunderstorm; **niech to ~ trzaśnie!** (*pot*) blast it!; **~em** (*pot: szybko*) in a jiffy
**piorunochro|n** (**-nu, -ny**) (*loc sg* **-nie**) *m* lightning conductor *lub* rod
**piorunujący** *adj* (*wiadomość, spojrzenie*) electrifying
**piosen|ka** (**-ki, -ki**) (*dat sg* **-ce**, *gen pl* **-ek**) *f* song
**piosenkar|ka** (**-ki, -ki**) (*dat sg* **-ce**, *gen pl* **-ek**) *f* singer
**piosenkarz** (**-a, -e**) (*gen pl* **-y**) *m* singer
**piór|ko** (**-ka, -ka**) (*instr sg* **-kiem**) *nt* feather; **lekki jak ~** (as) light as a feather; **obrastać w piórka** (*przen*) to feather one's nest
**piórni|k** (**-ka, -ki**) (*instr sg* **-kiem**) *m* pencil case
**pió|ro** (**-ra, -ra**) (*loc sg* **-rze**) *nt* (*ptaka*) feather; (*też*: **wieczne pióro**) fountain pen; (*wiosła, wycieraczki*) blade; **gęsie ~** quill(pen)
**pióropusz** (**-a, -e**) (*gen pl* **-y**) *m* plume
**pipet|ka** (**-ki, -ki**) (*dat sg* **-ce**) *f* pipette
**piracki** *adj* (*statek, radiostacja*) pirate *attr*; (*nagranie*) pirated
**piract|wo** (**-wa**) (*loc sg* **-wie**) *nt* piracy
**pirami|da** (**-dy, -dy**) (*dat sg* **-dzie**) *f* pyramid
**pirani|a** (**-i, -e**) (*gen pl* **-i**) *f* piranha
**pira|t** (**-ta, -ci**) (*loc sg* **-cie**) *m* pirate; **~ drogowy** speeder
**Pirenej|e** (**-ów**) *pl* the Pyrenees
**pirenejski** *adj* Pyrenean
**piroma|n** (**-na, -ni**) (*loc sg* **-nie**) *m* pyromaniac
**pirotechni|ka** (**-ki**) (*dat sg* **-ce**) *f* pyrotechnics
**pirue|t** (**-tu, -ty**) (*loc sg* **-cie**) *m* pirouette
**pi|sać (-szę, -szesz)** *vt* (*perf* **na-**) to write ▷ *vi* to write; **~ drukowanymi literami** to print; **~ na maszynie** to type; **to mu było pisane** it was his destiny; **pisać się** *vr*: **jak to się pisze?** how do you spell it?; **~ się (na coś)** to be on (for sth)
**pisa|k** (**-ka, -ki**) (*instr sg* **-kiem**) *m* felt-tip (pen)
**pisan|ka** (**-ki, -ki**) (*dat sg* **-ce**, *gen pl* **-ek**) *f* Easter egg

**pisar|ka** (**-ki, -ki**) (*dat sg* **-ce**, *gen pl* **-ek**) *f* writer
**pisarski** *adj* literary
**pisarst|wo** (**-wa**) (*loc sg* **-wie**) *nt* writing
**pisarz** (**-a, -e**) (*gen pl* **-y**) *m* writer
**pisemnie** *adv* in writing, on paper
**pisemny** *adj* written
**pis|k** (**-ku, -ki**) (*instr sg* **-kiem**) *m* (*opon*) screech; (*dzieci, myszy*) squeak, squeal
**piskl|ę** (**-ęcia, -ęta**) (*gen pl* **-ąt**) *nt* nestling
**piskliwy** *adj* shrill, squeaky
**pi|smo** (**-sma**) (*loc sg* **-śmie**) *nt* writing; (*alfabet*) alphabet; (*charakter pisma*) hand(writing); (*dokument*) (*nom pl* **-sma**) letter; (*czasopismo*) (*nom pl* **-sma**) magazine; (*dzieło*) (*nom pl* **-sma**) work; **na piśmie** in writing, on paper; **mieć ładny/czytelny charakter pisma** to write a good/legible hand(writing); **P~ Święte** the (Holy) Scriptures; **~ pochyłe** italics; **~ techniczne** lettering
**pi|snąć (-snę, -śniesz)** (*imp* **-śnij**) *vb perf od* **piszczeć**; **nie ~ (ani) słowa** (*przen*) not to breathe a word
**pisow|nia** (**-ni, -nie**) (*gen pl* **-ni**) *f* spelling
**pistacjowy** *adj* pistachio *attr*
**pistole|t** (**-tu, -ty**) (*loc sg* **-cie**) *m* gun; **~ maszynowy** submachine gun
**pisua|r** (**-ru, -ry**) (*loc sg* **-rze**) *m* urinal
**pis|ywać (-uję, -ujesz)** *vt* to write
**piszczał|ka** (**-ki, -ki**) (*dat sg* **-ce**, *gen pl* **-ek**) *f* pipe (*musical instrument*)
**piszcz|eć (-ę, -ysz)** (*perf* **pisnąć**) *vi* (*o dziecku, myszy*) to squeal; (*o kole, zawiasach*) to screech; **u nich bieda aż piszczy** they can't make both ends meet; **wiedzieć, co w trawie piszczy** to know which way the wind is blowing (*przen*)
**piszczel** (**-a** *lub* **-i, -e**) (*gen pl* **-i** *lub* **-ów**) *m lub f* (*Anat*) tibia
**piśmie** *n patrz* **pismo**
**piśmienny** *adj* (*umiejący pisać*) literate; **artykuły** *lub* **materiały piśmienne** stationery
**PIT** *n* tax return
**pitny** *adj* (*woda*) drinking *attr*; **miód ~** mead
**pius|ka** (**-ki, -ki**) (*dat sg* **-ce**, *gen pl* **-ek**) *f* (*czapka*) skullcap
**piwiar|nia** (**-ni, -nie**) (*gen pl* **-ni**) *f* pub
**piwnic|a** (**-y, -e**) *f* cellar
**piwny** *adj* beer *attr*; (*oczy*) hazel
**pi|wo** (**-wa, -wa**) (*loc sg* **-wie**) *nt* (*napój*) beer; (*porcja*) pint, beer; **~ jasne/ciemne** lager/brown ale; **wypić** (*perf*) **małe/duże ~** to have a half/a pint; **nawarzyć** (*perf*) **sobie piwa** (*przen*) to get (o.s.) into trouble; **(to dla mnie) małe ~** it's a piece of cake
**piwoni|a** (**-i, -e**) (*gen pl* **-i**) *f* peony; **czerwony jak ~** (as) red as a beetroot
**piwosz** (**-a, -e**) (*gen pl* **-y**) *m* beer drinker
**pi|zda** (**-zdy, -zdy**) (*dat sg* **-ździe**) *f* (*pot!*) cunt (*pot!*)
**pizz|a** (**-y, -e**) *f* pizza
**pizzeri|a** (**-i, -e**) (*dat sg* **-i**) *f* pizzeria, pizza place
**piża|ma** (**-my, -my**) (*dat sg* **-mie**) *f* pyjamas *pl* (*Brit*), pajamas *pl* (*US*)
**piż|mo** (**-ma**) (*loc sg* **-mie**) *nt* musk
**piżmowy** *adj* (*zapach*) musky; (*olejek*) musk *attr*
**PKB** *abbr* (= *produkt krajowy brutto*) GNP, gross national product
**PKOl** *abbr* (= *Polski Komitet Olimpijski*) Polish Olympic Committee
**PKP** *abbr* (= *Polskie Koleje Państwowe*) Polish State Railways
**PKS** *abbr* (= *Państwowa Komunikacja Samochodowa*) National Transport Company
**pkt** *abbr* (= *punkt*) pt. (= *point*)
**pl.** *abbr* (= *plac*) sq. (= *square*)
**plac** (**-u, -e**) *m* square; **~ budowy** building site; **~ zabaw** playground
**plac|ek** (**-ka, -ki**) (*instr sg* **-kiem**) *m* (*ciasto*) cake; **~ drożdżowy** yeast cake; **placki kartoflane** potato pancakes; **padać/leżeć plackiem** (*przen*) to fall/lie flat
**placów|ka** (**-ki, -ki**) (*dat sg* **-ce**, *gen pl* **-ek**) *f* (*przedstawicielstwo*) post; **~ naukowa/kulturalna** research/cultural institution; **~ handlowa** business establishment; **~ służby zdrowia** health-care institution
**pla|ga** (**-gi, -gi**) (*dat sg* **-dze**) *f* plague
**plagia|t** (**-tu, -ty**) (*loc sg* **-cie**) *m* plagiarism
**plaj|ta** (**-ty, -ty**) (*dat sg* **-cie**) *f* (*pot*) bankruptcy; **zrobić** (*perf*) **plajtę** to go broke (*pot*)
**plajt|ować (-uję, -ujesz)** (*perf* **s-**) *vi* (*pot*) to go broke (*pot*)
**plaka|t** (**-tu, -ty**) (*loc sg* **-cie**) *m* poster
**plakatów|ka** (**-ki, -ki**) (*dat sg* **-ce**, *gen pl* **-ek**) *f* (*pot*) poster paint, poster colour (*Brit*) *lub* color (*US*)
**plakiet|ka** (**-ki, -ki**) (*dat sg* **-ce**, *gen pl* **-ek**) *f* badge
**pla|ma** (**-my, -my**) (*dat sg* **-mie**) *f* stain; **tłusta ~** greasy spot; **~ na honorze** a blot on sb's escutcheon; **dać** (*perf*) **plamę** (*pot*) to drop a brick (*pot*); **biała ~** (*przen*) blank spot
**pla|mić (-mię, -misz)** *vt* (*brudzić*) (*perf* **po-**) to stain; (*okrywać hańbą*) (*perf* **s-**) to stain, to tarnish; **plamić się** *vr* (*brudzić się*) (*perf* **po-**) to soil; (*okrywać się hańbą*) (*perf* **s-**) to tarnish one's reputation
**plamisty** *adj* blotchy, spotty
**plam|ka** (**-ki, -ki**) (*dat sg* **-ce**) *f dimin od* **plama**

P

**pla|n (-nu, -ny)** (*loc sg* **-nie**) *m* (*zamiar*) plan; (*urlopów*) schedule; (*działania*) scheme; (*wypracowania, wykładu*) outline; (*mapa*) street map; (*Film*) set; (*: plener*) location; **mieć coś w ~ie** to plan to do sth; **pokrzyżować** (*perf*) **czyjeś ~y** to thwart sb's plans; **~ zajęć** (*godzinowy*) timetable; (*tematyczny*) syllabus; **według ~u** *lub* **zgodnie z ~em** according to plan; **~ miasta** street map; **pierwszy ~** foreground; **drugi** *lub* **dalszy ~** background; **wysuwać się na pierwszy ~** (*przen*) to come to the fore; **zejść** (*perf*) **na drugi** *lub* **dalszy ~** to recede into the background

**plande|ka (-ki, -ki)** (*dat sg* **-ce**) *f* tarpaulin

**plane|ta (-ty, -ty)** (*dat sg* **-cie**) *f* planet

**planetari|um (-um, -a)** (*gen pl* **-ów**) *nt inv in sg* planetarium

**planetarny** *adj* planetary

**plankto|n (-nu)** (*loc sg* **-nie**) *m* plankton

**plan|ować (-uję, -ujesz)** (*perf* **za-**) *vt* (*zamierzać*) to plan; (*ustalać czas*) to schedule

**planowani|e (-a)** *nt* planning

**planowy** *adj* (*przyjazd*) on time *lub* schedule; (*gospodarka*) planned

**plansz|a (-y, -e)** *f* (*z rysunkiem, fotografią*) chart; (*do gier*) board

**planszowy** *adj*: **gra planszowa** board game

**plantacj|a (-i, -e)** (*gen pl* **-i**) *f* plantation

**plantato|r (-ra, -rzy)** (*loc sg* **-rze**) *m* grower

**plant|y (-)** *pl* park

**plas|ować się (-uję, -ujesz)** (*perf* **u-**) *vr*: **plasować się na drugiej pozycji** to come in second

**plasteli|na (-ny)** (*dat sg* **-nie**) *f* Plasticine®

**plast|er (-ra, -ry)** (*loc sg* **-rze**) *m* (*przylepiec*) (sticking) plaster (*Brit*), bandaid® (*US*); (*szynki, sera*) slice; (*miodu*) honeycomb; **pokroić** (*perf*) **coś w plastry** to slice sth

**plaster|ek (-ka, -ki)** (*instr sg* **-kiem**) *m dimin od* **plaster**

**plasti|k (-ku, -ki)** (*instr sg* **-kiem**) *m* plastic

**plastikowy** *adj* plastic

**plastycz|ka (-ki, -ki)** (*dat sg* **-ce**) *f* artist

**plastycznoś|ć (-ci)** *f* plasticity

**plastyczny** *adj* (*substancja*) plastic; (*praca*) artistic; (*gestykulacja, opis*) vivid; **oprawa plastyczna** decoration; **sztuki plastyczne** fine *lub* plastic arts; **operacja plastyczna** (*Med*) plastic *lub* cosmetic surgery; **mapa plastyczna** relief map

**plasty|k (-ka, -cy)** (*instr sg* **-kiem**) *m* artist

**plasty|ka (-ki)** (*dat sg* **-ce**) *f* fine *lub* plastic arts *pl*

**plata|n (-na, -ny)** (*loc sg* **-nie**) *m* (*Bot*) plane(-tree)

**platfor|ma (-my, -my)** (*dat sg* **-mie**) *f* platform; **~ wiertnicza** drilling rig

**platfu|s (-sa, -sy)** (*loc sg* **-sie**) *m* flatfoot

**platoniczny** *adj* platonic

**platy|na (-ny)** (*dat sg* **-nie**) *f* platinum

**platynowy** *adj* (*naszyjnik*) platinum *attr*; (*włosy*) platinum blond

**playba|ck (-cku, -cki)** (*instr sg* **-ckiem**) *m*: **śpiewać z ~u** to lip-sync, to mime

**plaz|ma (-my)** (*dat sg* **-mie**) *f* plasma

**plaż|a (-y, -e)** *f* beach; **~ strzeżona** guarded beach; **dzika ~** unguarded beach

**plaż|ować (-uję, -ujesz)** *vi* to lie on the beach

**plażowy** *adj* beach *attr*

**plądr|ować (-uję, -ujesz)** (*perf* **s-**) *vt* to plunder

**plą|tać (-czę, -czesz)** *vt* (*włosy, nici*) (*perf* **po-** *lub* **za-**) to tangle (up); (*pot: daty, nazwiska*) (*perf* **po-**) to mix up (*pot*); **plątać się** *vr* (*o niciach, włosach*) (*perf* **po-** *lub* **za-**) to tangle; (*o mówcy*) to falter; (*pot: krążyć*) to hang around (*pot*); **wszystko mi się plącze** (*przen*) I'm all confused; **język mu się plącze** he can't find his tongue

**plątani|na (-ny)** (*dat sg* **-nie**) *f* (*nici, myśli*) tangle; (*ulic*) maze

**plebani|a (-i, -e)** (*gen pl* **-i**) *f* presbytery

**plebiscy|t (-tu, -ty)** (*loc sg* **-cie**) *m* plebiscite

**pleb|s (-su)** (*loc sg* **-sie**) *m* mob, the pleb(eian)s

**pleca|k (-ka, -ki)** (*instr sg* **-kiem**) *m* rucksack, backpack (*US*)

**plec|y (-ów)** *pl* back; **mieć ~** to have friends in high places; **odwrócić się do kogoś plecami** (*przen*) to turn one's back on sb; **robić coś za czyimiś plecami** (*przen*) to do sth behind sb's back

**pleć (pielę, pielesz)** (*pt* **pełł, pełli**) *vt* = **pielić**

**ple|d (-du, -dy)** (*loc sg* **-dzie**) *m* blanket

**pleksigla|s (-su)** (*loc sg* **-sie**) *m* Plexiglas®

**plemienny** *adj* tribal

**plemi|ę (-enia, -ona)** (*gen pl* **-on**) *nt* tribe

**plemni|k (-ka, -ki)** (*instr sg* **-kiem**) *m* sperm (cell)

**plenarny** *adj* plenary

**plene|r (-ru, -ry)** (*loc sg* **-rze**) *m* (*Sztuka*) open air; (*Film*) location; **w ~ze** on location

**ple|nić się (-ni)** (*perf* **roz-**) *vr* (*o zwierzętach*) to multiply; (*o roślinach*) to spread

**plenipoten|t (-ta, -ci)** (*loc sg* **-cie**) *m* plenipotentiary

**plen|um (-um, -a)** (*gen pl* **-ów**) *nt inv in sg* joint assembly

**pl|eść (-otę, -eciesz)** (*imp* **-eć**, *pt* **plótł, plotła, pletli**) *vt* (*łączyć*) (*perf* **s-** *lub* **za-**) to plait; (*pot: mówić bez sensu*) (*perf* **na-**) to blabber (*pot*); **~ głupstwa** *lub* **bzdury** to talk through one's hat

**pleśnie|ć (-je)** (*perf* **s-**) *vi* to get *lub* grow mouldy (*Brit*), to get *lub* grow moldy (*US*)

**pleś|ń (-ni)** *f* mould (*Brit*), mold (*US*)

**ple|wa** (**-wy, -wy**) (*dat sg* **-wie**) *f* chaff; **odróżniać ziarno od plewy** (*przen*) to separate the wheat from the chaff
**pli|k** (**-ku, -ki**) (*instr sg* **-kiem**) *m* bundle; (*Komput*) file
**pli|sa** (**-sy, -sy**) (*dat sg* **-sie**) *f* pleat
**plisz|ka** (**-ki, -ki**) (*dat sg* **-ce**, *gen pl* **-ek**) *f* wagtail
**plom|ba** (**-by, -by**) (*dat sg* **-bie**) *f* (*zabezpieczenie*) seal; (*w zębie*) filling
**plomb|ować (-uję, -ujesz)** (*perf* **za-**) *vt* (*towary*) to seal; (*ząb*) to fill
**plo|n** (**-nu, -ny**) (*loc sg* **-nie**) *m* crop; (*wydajność*) yield; (*przen*) fruit
**plotę** *itd. vb patrz* **pleść**
**plot|ka** (**-ki, -ki**) (*dat sg* **-ce**, *gen pl* **-ek**) *f* rumour (*Brit*), rumor (*US*); **plotki** *pl* gossip *sg*
**plotkarz** (**-a, -e**) (*gen pl* **-y**) *m* gossip(monger)
**plotk|ować (-uję, -ujesz)** *vi* to gossip
**plu|cha** (**-chy, -chy**) (*dat sg* **-sze**) *f* wet weather
**pl|uć (-uję, -ujesz)** (*perf* **-unąć**) *vi* to spit; **~ sobie w brodę** (*przen*) to be kicking o.s.; **pluję na to!** (*pot*) I don't give a damn! (*pot*)
**plugawy** *adj* filthy, foul
**plu|nąć (-nę, -niesz)** (*imp* **-ń**) *vb perf od* **pluć**
**pluralistyczny** *adj* pluralist(ic)
**pluraliz|m** (**-mu**) (*loc sg* **-mie**) *m* pluralism
**plu|s** (**-sa, -sy**) (*loc sg* **-sie**) *m* (*Mat*) plus; (*zaleta*) plus, advantage; **dwa ~ dwa równa się cztery** two plus two equals four; **~ cztery stopnie** four degrees above zero; **~ minus** more or less; **~y i minusy** pros and cons
**plus|k** (**-ku, -ki**) (*instr sg* **-kiem**) *m* splash
**plus|kać (-kam, -kasz)** (*imp* **-kaj**, *perf* **-nąć**) *vi* to splash; **pluskać się** *vr* to splash about
**pluskiew|ka** (**-ki, -ki**) (*dat sg* **-ce**, *gen pl* **-ek**) *f* drawing pin (*Brit*), thumbtack (*US*)
**plus|kwa** (**-kwy, -kwy**) (*dat sg* **-kwie**, *gen pl* **-kiew**) *f* bedbug
**plu|snąć (-snę, -śniesz)** (*imp* **-śnij**) *vb perf od* **pluskać**
**plusz** (**-u, -e**) *m* plush
**pluszowy** *adj* plush *attr*; **~ niedźwiadek** teddy bear
**pluto|n** (**-nu**) (*loc sg* **-nie**) *m* (*Wojsk*) (*nom pl* **-ny**) platoon; (*Chem*) plutonium; **~ egzekucyjny** firing squad
**plutono|wy** (**-wego, -wi**) *m decl like adj military rank above corporal and below sergeant*
**plwoci|na** (**-ny**) (*dat sg* **-nie**) *f* spit, spittle
**płac|a** (**-y, -e**) *f* (*ogólnie*) pay, earnings *pl*; (*pracownika fizycznego*) wage, wages *pl*; (*pracownika umysłowego*) salary
**płach|ta** (**-ty, -ty**) (*dat sg* **-cie**) *f* (*płótna, materiału*) cloth; (*papieru*) sheet
**pła|cić (-cę, -cisz)** (*imp* **-ć**, *perf* **za-**) *vt/vi* to pay; **~ za coś** to pay for sth; **~ gotówką/czekiem** to pay in cash/by cheque (*Brit*) *lub* check (*US*); **~ za coś życiem/zdrowiem** to pay for sth with one's life/health
**płacowy** *adj* wage *attr*
**płacz** (**-u, -e**) *m* crying, weeping; **wybuchnąć** (*perf*) **~em** to burst into tears
**płaczliwy** *adj* (*dziecko*) weepy, tearful; (*głos*) tearful; (*melodia*) moving, touching
**pła|kać (-czę, -czesz)** *vi* to cry, to weep; **~ nad kimś** to mourn (for) sb; **~ nad czymś** to mourn for sth; **~ z radości** to cry for joy; **~ się chce** (*pot*) this is pathetic (*pot*)
**płaski** *adj* flat; **~ talerz** dinner plate
**płaskorzeź|ba** (**-by, -by**) (*dat sg* **-bie**) *f* bas-relief
**płaskosto|pie** (**-pia, -pia**) (*gen pl* **-pi**) *nt*: **mieć ~** to be flat-footed
**płaskowyż** (**-u, -e**) *m* plateau
**płastu|ga** (**-gi, -gi**) (*gen sg* **-dze**) *f* plaice
**płaszcz** (**-a, -e**) (*gen pl* **-y**) *m* (*okrycie*) (over)coat; (*przen*) cloak; **~ kąpielowy** bath robe; **~ przeciwdeszczowy** raincoat
**płaszcz|ka** (**-ki, -ki**) (*dat sg* **-ce**, *gen pl* **-ek**) *f* (*Zool*) ray
**płaszcz|yć się (-ę, -ysz)** *vr*: **płaszczyć się przed kimś** to crawl to sb, to fawn on sb
**płaszczy|k** (**-ka, -ki**) (*instr sg* **-kiem**) *m dimin od* **płaszcz**; **pod ~iem czegoś** (*przen*) under the pretence of sth
**płaszczy|zna** (**-zny, -zny**) (*loc sg* **-źnie**) *f* (*Geom*) plane; **~ porozumienia** common ground
**pła|t** (**-ta, -ty**) (*loc sg* **-cie**) *m* (*materiału*) piece; (*szynki, sera*) slice; (*farby*) flake; (*Anat*) lobe
**płat|ać (-am, -asz)** (*perf* **s-**) *vt*: **~ (komuś) figle** to play tricks (on sb)
**płat|ek** (**-ka, -ki**) (*instr sg* **-kiem**) *m* (*kwiatu*) petal; **~ śniegu** snowflake; **płatki kukurydziane** cornflakes; **płatki owsiane** oatmeal; **płatki mydlane** soapflakes; **idzie jak z płatka** (*pot*) everything is going on smoothly
**płatniczy** *adj*: **środek ~** legal tender; **bilans ~** balance of payments; **nakaz ~** demand for payment
**płatni|k** (**-ka, -cy**) (*instr sg* **-kiem**) *m* payer
**płatnoś|ć** (**-ci, -ci**) (*gen pl* **-ci**) *f* payment
**płatny** *adj* paid; **dobrze/nisko ~** well-/low-paid; **~ morderca** contract killer (*pot*); **płatne gotówką** paid in cash; **płatne z góry** paid in advance; **płatne przy odbiorze** cash on delivery
**pła|wić się (-wię, -wisz)** *vr*: **pławić się we krwi/w luksusie** to wallow in blood/luxury
**pławny** *adj*: **pęcherz ~** air bladder
**pła|z** (**-za, -zy**) (*loc sg* **-zie**) *m* amphibian; **puścić** (*perf*) **coś komuś ~em** (*przen*) to let sb

P

get away with sth; **to ci nie ujdzie ~em!** you won't get away with it!
**płciowy** *adj* sexual
**płd.** *abbr* (= *południowy*) s., S. (= *southern, South*)
**pł|eć (-ci, -ci)** (*gen pl* **-ci**) *f* sex, gender; **~ męska/żeńska** the male/female sex; **~ piękna** the fair sex; **niemowlę płci męskiej** a male infant
**płet|wa (-wy, -wy)** (*dat sg* **-wie**) *f* (*ryby*) fin; (*płetwonurka*) flipper
**płetwonur|ek (-ka, -kowie** *lub* **-ki)** (*instr sg* **-kiem**) *m* scuba diver
**płk** *abbr* (= *pułkownik*) Col. (= *Colonel*)
**płn.** *abbr* (= *północny*) n., N. (= *northern, North*)
**płochliwy** *adj* (*człowiek*) timid, nervous; (*zwierzę*) skittish
**pło|ć (-ci, -cie)** (*gen pl* **-ci**) *f* (*Zool*) roach
**płodnoś|ć (-ci)** *f* fertility; (*przen*) productivity
**płodny** *adj* fertile; (*pisarz*) prolific
**płodozmia|n (-nu, -ny)** (*loc sg* **-nie**) *m* crop rotation
**płodu** *itd.* *n patrz* **płód**
**pł|odzić (-odzę, -odzisz)** (*imp* **-ódź**, *perf* **s-**) *vt* (*książk: syna*) to beget; (*przen*) to produce
**płomie|ń (-nia, -nie)** (*gen pl* **-ni**) *m* (*ogień*) flame; (*blask*) blaze; (*namiętność*) flame, passion; (*żarliwość*) fire, ardour (*Brit*), ardor (*US*); **stanąć** (*perf*) **w płomieniach** to burst into flames
**płomy|k (-ka, -ki)** (*instr sg* **-kiem**) *m dimin od* **płomień**; **~ nadziei** a flicker of hope
**pło|nąć (-nę, -niesz)** (*imp* **-ń**) *vi* to burn; (*przen: o gwiazdach*) to shine; **~ ze wstydu** to burn with shame
**płonny** *adj* vain *attr*
**płosz|yć (-ę, -ysz)** (*perf* **s-**) *vt* to frighten away *lub* off; **płoszyć się** *vr* (*wpadać w popłoch*) to take fright, to panic; (*uciekać*) to flee, to take flight; (*o koniu*) to shy
**pło|t (-tu, -ty)** (*loc sg* **-cie**) *m* fence
**płot|ek (-ka, -ki)** (*instr sg* **-kiem**) *m dimin od* **płot**; (*Sport*) hurdle; **bieg przez płotki** (*Sport*) hurdles *pl*
**płot|ka (-ki, -ki)** (*dat sg* **-ce**, *gen pl* **-ek**) *f* (*płoć*) roach; (*przen*) small fry
**płowi|eć (-eję, -ejesz)** (*perf* **wy-**) *vi* (*o tkaninie, papierze*) to fade, to lose colour (*Brit*) *lub* color (*US*); (*o trawie, włosach*) to bleach
**płowy** *adj* fawn; **zwierzyna płowa** deer
**pł|oza (-ozy, -ozy)** (*dat sg* **-ozie**, *gen pl* **-óz**) *f* (*sań*) runner; (*samolotu*) ski
**pł|ód (-odu, -ody)** (*loc sg* **-odzie**) *m* foetus (*Brit*), fetus (*US*); **płody** *pl* (*rolne*) produce *sg*
**płó|tno (-tna, -tna)** (*loc sg* **-tnie**, *gen pl* **-cien**) *nt* (*na pościel, obrusy*) linen; (*żaglowe, namiotowe*) canvas; (*obraz*) canvas; **blady jak ~** (as) white as a sheet
**płuc|o (-a, -a)** *nt* lung; **zapalenie płuc** pneumonia
**płu|g (-ga, -gi)** (*instr sg* **-giem**) *m* plough (*Brit*), plow (*US*); **~ śnieżny** snowplough (*Brit*), snowplow (*US*)
**płu|kać (-czę, -czesz)** *vt* (*bieliznę*) (*perf* **wy-**) to rinse; (*warzywa, naczynia*) (*perf* **o-** *lub* **wy-**) to rinse; (*usta*) (*perf* **wy-** *lub* **prze-**) to rinse, to wash; **~ gardło** to gargle
**płukani|e (-a)** *nt* (*bielizny, owoców*) rinsing; **~ gardła** gargle
**Płw.** *abbr* (= *półwysep*) Pen. (= *Peninsula*)
**płycej** *adv comp od* **płytko**
**pły|n (-nu, -ny)** (*loc sg* **-nie**) *m* liquid; **~ do mycia naczyń** washing-up liquid; **~ po goleniu** aftershave lotion; **~ hamulcowy** brake fluid; **~ do kąpieli** bubble bath, bath foam; **lekarstwo w ~ie** liquid medicine; **~ do płukania gardła** gargle; **~ do płukania jamy ustnej** mouthwash
**pły|nąć (-nę, -niesz)** (*imp* **-ń**) *vi* to flow; (*o człowieku, rybie, ptaku*) to swim; (*o statku, jachcie*) to sail; (*o czasie, życiu*) (*perf* **u-**) to go by; **~ (statkiem)** to sail, to go by boat; **~ (łodzią)** to row (a boat); **~ z czegoś** (*wynikać*) to follow from sth
**płynnie** *adv* (*mówić, czytać*) fluently; (*poruszać się*) smoothly; **ona mówi ~ po angielsku** she speaks English fluently
**płynnoś|ć (-ci)** *f* (*ruchów, kroku*) smoothness; (*stylu, mowy*) fluency; (*Fin*) liquidity
**płynny** *adj* (*ciekły*) liquid; (*ruch, krok*) smooth; (*styl, wymowa*) fluent
**pły|ta (-ty, -ty)** (*dat sg* **-cie**) *f* (*z kamienia, metalu: cienka*) plate; (*: gruba*) slab; (*gramofonowa*) record; **~ kompaktowa** compact disc; **~ chodnikowa** flag(stone); **~ nagrobkowa** tombstone, gravestone; **~ pamiątkowa** commemorative *lub* memorial plaque
**płyt|ka (-ki, -ki)** (*dat sg* **-ce**, *gen pl* **-ek**) *f* plate; (*ceramiczna*) tile; **~ nazębna** plaque
**płytki** *adj* shallow; (*przen*) superficial; **~ talerz** dinner plate
**pły|tko** (*comp* **-cej**) *adv* (*oddychać*) shallowly; (*zakopywać, leżeć*) near the surface; (*przen: powierzchownie*) superficially
**płytote|ka (-ki, -ki)** (*dat sg* **-ce**) *f* record collection
**pływacz|ka (-ki, -ki)** (*dat sg* **-ce**, *gen pl* **-ek**) *f* swimmer
**pływ|ać (-am, -asz)** *vi* (*o człowieku, zwierzęciu*) to swim; (*o statku, jachcie*) to sail; (*o korku, oliwie*) to float
**pływa|k (-ka)** (*instr sg* **-kiem**) *m* (*człowiek*) (*nom pl* **-cy**) swimmer; (*przyrząd*) (*nom pl* **-ki**) float
**pływal|nia (-ni, -nie)** (*gen pl* **-ni**) *f* swimming-pool

**pływani|e** (**-a**) *nt* swimming
**pływ|y** (**-ów**) *pl* (*Geog*) tides
**pnącz|e** (**-a, -a**) (*gen pl* **-y**) *nt* climber, creeper
**p.n.e.** *abbr* (= *przed naszą erą*) B.C.
**pneumatyczny** *adj* pneumatic; **młot ~** pneumatic drill
**pnę** *itd. vb patrz* **piąć się**
**pnia** *itd. n patrz* **pień**
**PO** *abbr* (*Szkol*: = *Przysposobienie Obronne*) *civil defence course*
**p.o.** *abbr* (= *pełniący obowiązki*) acting *attr*

SŁOWO KLUCZOWE

**po** *prep +loc* **1** (*czas*) after; **po obiedzie** after dinner; **po chwili** after a while, a moment later; **pięć po ósmej** five past *lub* after (*US*) eight
**2** (*kolejność*) after; **jeden po drugim** one after another; **butelka po piwie/winie** beer/wine bottle
**3** (*na podstawie*) by; **rozpoznać kogoś po głosie** to recognize sb by his voice
**4** (*dziedziczenie*) from; **ma urodę po matce** she gets her beauty from her mother; **spadek po dziadku** inheritance from one's grandfather; **objąć** (*perf*) **stanowisko po kimś** to take over sb's position
**5** (*hierarchia*) after; **po Szekspirze** after Shakespeare; **pierwszy po Bogu** next to God
**6**: **chodzić po lesie/górach** to walk in the woods/mountains; **po niebie** in the sky; **chodzić po trawie/piasku** to walk on grass/sand; **po szynach** on rails; **jeździć po mieście/kraju** to travel around the town/country; **spacerować po korytarzu** to walk in *lub* along the corridor; **po całym pokoju** all over the room; **po drugiej stronie** on the other side; **głaskać kogoś po włosach** to stroke sb's hair; **schodzić po drabinie/schodach** to go down the ladder/stairs
**7**: **po kawałku** piece by piece
▷ *prep +acc* **1** (*kres, zasięg*) to; **wody było po kolana** the water was knee-deep; **po brzegi** to the rim
**2** (*cel*) for; **przyjść po książkę** to come to get a book; **posłać po lekarza** to send for a doctor; **po co?** what for?; **po dwadzieścia sztuk w paczce** twenty items per pack; **po dwa złote za sztukę** (at) two zloty a piece
▷ *prep +dat*; **po cichu** (*bezgłośnie*) quietly, silently; (*potajemnie*) on the quiet, secretly; **po trochu** bit by bit, little by little; **po polsku/angielsku** in Polish/English; **mówić po polsku/angielsku** to speak Polish/English

**po|bić** (**-biję, -bijesz**) *vb perf od* **pobijać** ▷ *vt perf* (*pokonać*) to defeat, to beat; (*zbić*) to beat up; **pobić się** *vr perf* to have a fight
**pobie|c** (**-gnę, -gniesz**) (*imp* **-gnij**, *pt* **-gł**) *vi perf* (*o człowieku, zwierzęciu*) to run; (*o wzroku, spojrzeniu*) to go
**pobier|ać** (**-am, -asz**) (*perf* **pobrać**) *vt* (*pensję, narzędzia*) to collect; (*krew, próbkę*) to take; (*tlen, pokarm*) to take (in); **~ opłatę** to charge a fee; **~ nauki** to study; **pobierać się** *vr* to get married, to marry
**pobieżnie** *adv* cursorily; (*zapoznawać się*) briefly; **przeczytać** (*perf*) **coś ~** to read sth through *lub* over; **~ rzucić okiem na coś** to have a cursory look at sth
**pobieżny** *adj* cursory
**pobij|ać** (**-am, -asz**) (*perf* **pobić**) *vt* (*rekordy*) to beat, to break
**pobliski** *adj* nearby *attr*
**pobliż|e** (**-a**) *nt*: **w pobliżu** nearby; **w pobliżu wioski** in the vicinity of the village
**pobłaż|ać** (**-am, -asz**) *vi*: **~ komuś** to be lenient with sb
**pobłażliwie** *adv* (*ze zrozumieniem*) tolerantly; (*z wyższością*) condescendingly
**pobłażliwoś|ć** (**-ci**) *f* forbearance
**pobłażliwy** *adj* indulgent, forgiving
**pobocz|e** (**-a, -a**) (*gen pl* **-y**) *nt* (*miękkie*) verge (*Brit*), shoulder (*US*); (*twarde*) hard shoulder (*Brit*), shoulder (*US*)
**pobojowis|ko** (**-ka, -ka**) (*instr sg* **-kiem**) *nt* (*przen*) shambles *sg*
**poborowy** *adj* (*wiek*) military *attr*; **komisja poborowa** recruitment board ▷ *m decl like adj* conscript
**pobor|y** (**-ów**) *pl* (*pensja*) salary
**pobożnoś|ć** (**-ci**) *f* piety
**pobożny** *adj* pious, devout; **pobożne życzenie** wishful thinking
**pob|ór** (**-oru, -ory**) (*loc sg* **-orze**) *m* (*Wojsk*) conscription, draft (*US*); (*energii, gazu, mocy*) consumption; (*opłat, podatków*) collection; **prawa poboru** (*Giełda*) subscription rights
**po|brać** (**-biorę, -bierzesz**) *vb perf od* **pobierać**
**pobru|dzić** (**-dzę, -dzisz**) (*imp* **-dź**) *vb perf od* **brudzić**
**pobud|ka** (**-ki, -ki**) (*dat sg* **-ce**, *gen pl* **-ek**) *f* (*sygnał*) reveille; **pobudki** *pl* (*powody*) motives; **~!** wake up!
**pobudliwy** *adj* excitable
**pobu|dzać** (**-dzam, -dzasz**) (*perf* **-dzić**) *vt* (*apetyt, organizm*) to stimulate; **~ kogoś do działania** to prompt sb to act
**pobudzający** *adj*: **środek ~** stimulant
**pobu|dzić** (**-dzę, -dzisz**) (*imp* **-dź**) *vb perf od* **pobudzać**
**pob|yć** (**-ędę, -ędziesz**) (*imp* **-ądź**) *vi perf* to stay

P

**poby|t** (**-tu, -ty**) (*loc sg* **-cie**) *m* stay; **~ stały/tymczasowy** permanent/temporary residence
**pobytowy** *adj*: **wiza pobytowa** temporary visa
**pocał|ować (-uję, -ujesz)** *vb perf od* **całować**; **pocałuj mnie gdzieś** (*pot!*) kiss my arse (*Brit*) (*pot!*) *lub* ass (*US*) (*pot!*)
**pocałun|ek** (**-ku, -ki**) (*instr sg* **-kiem**) *m* kiss
**pochlebc|a** (**-y, -y**) *m decl like f in sg* flatterer
**pochle|biać (-biam, -biasz)** (*perf* **-bić**) *vt +dat* (*podlizywać się*) to flatter; (*chwalić*) to speak highly of; **pochlebiało mi, że ...** it flattered me that ...
**pochlebny** *adj* flattering
**pochlebst|wo** (**-wa, -wa**) (*loc sg* **-wie**) *nt* compliment; **pochlebstwa** *pl* flattery *sg*
**pochłani|ać (-am, -asz)** (*perf* **pochłonąć**) *vt* to absorb; (*pot: jedzenie, książki*) to devour; **wojna pochłonęła wiele ofiar** the war took a heavy toll of (human) lives; **~ wielkie koszty** to involve a lot of expense
**pochmurno** *adv*: **jest ~** it's cloudy
**pochmurny** *adj* (*dzień*) cloudy; (*twarz, wzrok*) gloomy
**pochodn|a** (**-ej, -e**) *f* (*Mat*) derivative
**pochod|nia** (**-ni, -nie**) (*gen pl* **-ni**) *f* torch
**pochodny** *adj* derivative; **instrumenty pochodne** (*Fin*) derivatives
**pochodzeni|e** (**-a**) *nt* origin; **on jest Polakiem z pochodzenia** he is of Polish descent
**pocho|dzić (-dzę, -dzisz)** *vi*: **pochodzę z Polski/bogatej rodziny** I come from Poland/a rich family; **~ od** *+gen* (*o gatunku*) to be descended from; (*o słowie*) to derive from
**pochopnie** *adv* rashly, recklessly
**pochopny** *adj* rash
**pochow|ać (-am, -asz)** *vb perf od* **chować**
**poch|ód** (**-odu, -ody**) (*loc sg* **-odzie**) *m* parade
**poch|wa** (**-wy, -wy**) (*dat sg* **-wie**, *gen pl* **-ew**) *f* (*Anat*) vagina; (*książk: futerał*) sheath
**pochwal|ać (-am, -asz)** *vt* (*aprobować*) to approve of; **nie ~ czegoś** to disapprove of sth
**pochwal|ić (-ę, -isz)** *vb perf od* **chwalić**
**pochwalny** *adj* laudatory; **hymn ~** eulogy; **list ~** letter of commendation
**pochwa|ła** (**-ły, -ły**) (*dat sg* **-le**) *f* (*wyraz uznania*) praise; (*na piśmie*) citation; **godny pochwały** praiseworthy
**pochyl|ać (-am, -asz)** (*perf* **-ić**) *vt* (*głowę*) to bend, to incline; (*słup*) to tip; **pochylać się** *vr* (*o człowieku, drzewie*) to bend down; (*o budynku*) to lean; **~ się nad kimś/czymś** to lean over sb/sth
**pochyl|nia** (**-ni, -nie**) (*gen pl* **-ni**) *f* (*Tech*) ramp; (*Żegl*) slipway
**pochyły** *adj* (*drzewo*) leaning; (*pismo*) slanting; (*grunt*) sloping; **~m drukiem** in italics
**po|ciąć (-tnę, -tniesz)** (*imp* **-tnij**) *vt perf* to cut up
**pocią|g** (**-gu, -gi**) (*instr sg* **-giem**) *m* (*pojazd*) train; (*skłonność*) attraction; **jechać ~iem** to go by train; **~ towarowy** goods (*Brit*) *lub* freight (*US*) train; **mieć ~ do** *+gen* to be attracted to
**pociąg|ać (-am, -asz)** *vt* to attract ▷ *vi* (*perf* **-nąć**); **~ za coś** to pull (at) sth; **~ za sobą** to entail; **~ nosem** to sniff; **~ kogoś do odpowiedzialności za coś** to bring *lub* call sb to account for sth
**pociągły** *adj* (*twarz*) oval; (*nos*) long
**pociąg|nąć (-nę, -niesz)** (*imp* **-nij**) *vb perf od* **pociągać, ciągnąć** ▷ *vt perf* (*pomalować*: *też*: **pociągnąć farbą**) to coat with paint; **on długo nie pociągnie** (*pot*) he won't last long
**pociągnię|cie** (**-cia, -cia**) (*gen pl* **-ć**) *nt* (*pędzla, pióra*) stroke; (*posunięcie*) move
**pociągowy** *adj*: **zwierzę pociągowe** beast of burden
**po|cić się (-cę, -cisz)** (*imp* **-ć**) *vr* (*o człowieku, rękach*) (*perf* **s-**) to sweat; (*o szkle, okularach*) (*perf* **za-**) to steam up; **pocić się nad czymś** (*pot*) to sweat over sth
**pocie|c (-knie)** (*pt* **-kł**) *vb perf od* **ciec**
**pocie|cha** (**-chy**) (*dat sg* **-sze**) *f* (*pocieszenie*) comfort, consolation; (*pot: dziecko*) (*nom pl* **-chy**) kid; **mała** *lub* **niewielka z tego ~** (it's) cold comfort; **szukać pociechy w czymś** to seek comfort in sth
**pocier|ać (-am, -asz)** (*perf* **potrzeć**) *vt* to rub; **~ czoło dłonią** to rub one's hand against one's forehead; **potrzeć zapałkę** to strike a match
**pociesz|ać (-am, -asz)** (*perf* **-yć**) *vt* to comfort, to console; **pocieszać się** *vr* to console o.s.
**pocieszeni|e** (**-a**) *nt* consolation, comfort; **nagroda pocieszenia** consolation prize
**pocieszny** *adj* funny
**pocis|k** (**-ku, -ki**) (*instr sg* **-kiem**) *m* (*karabinowy*) bullet; (*artyleryjski*) shell; (*rakietowy*) missile
**pocz|ąć (-nę, -niesz)** (*imp* **-nij**) (*książk*) *vi perf* to conceive; **co ja mam (teraz) ~?** what shall I do?
**począt|ek** (**-ku, -ki**) (*instr sg* **-kiem**) *m* beginning, start; **na ~** for a start, to begin with; **na początku** at the beginning; **od początku** from the beginning; **z początku** at first; **z początkiem maja** as of *lub* from the beginning of May; **brać ~ od** *+gen* to originate from; **dać** (*perf*) **~ czemuś** to give rise to sth
**początkowo** *adv* initially, originally

**początkowy** *adj* initial
**początkujący** *adj (literat, dziennikarz)* novice *attr* ▷ *m decl like adj* beginner
**począwszy** *inv*: **~ od środy** *(w przeszłości)* as early as Wednesday; *(w przyszłości)* as of *lub* from Wednesday, from Wednesday on
**poczciwy** *adj* kind-hearted
**poczek|ać (-am, -asz)** *vb perf od* **czekać**
**poczekal|nia (-ni, -nie)** *(gen pl* **-ni)** *f* waiting-room
**poczekaniu** *inv*: **na ~** while you wait
**poczerwieni|eć (-eję, -ejesz)** *vb perf od* **czerwienieć**
**poczesny** *adj (książk)* prominent
**pocz|et (-tu, -ty)** *(loc sg* **-cie)** *m*: **~ sztandarowy** colour *(Brit) lub* color *(US)* guard; **~ królów** *a pictorial guide to the kings and queens of Poland*; **wpłacać na ~ czegoś** to pay towards sth
**poczę|cie (-cia, -cia)** *(gen pl* **-ć)** *nt* conception; **regulacja poczęć** birth control
**poczęst|ować (-uję, -ujesz)** *vb perf od* **częstować**
**poczęstun|ek (-ku, -ki)** *(instr sg* **-kiem)** *m* food and drinks
**pocz|ta (-ty, -ty)** *(dat sg* **-cie)** *f (urząd pocztowy)* post office; *(korespondencja)* post *(Brit)*, mail *(US)*; **~ elektroniczna** e-mail; **pocztą lotniczą** (by) airmail; **wysyłać (wysłać** *perf***) coś pocztą** to send sth by post, to post *(Brit) lub* mail *(US)* sth
**pocztowy** *adj* postal; **urząd ~** post office; **znaczek ~** postage stamp; **skrzynka pocztowa** *lub* **na listy** *(na drzwiach domu, przed domem)* letter-box *(Brit)*, mailbox *(US)*; **skrzynka pocztowa** *(na poczcie, ulicy)* post-box *(Brit)*, mailbox *(US)*; **opłata pocztowa** postage; **karta/kartka pocztowa** postcard; **gołąb ~** carrier pigeon; **wagon ~** mail coach
**pocztów|ka (-ki, -ki)** *(dat sg* **-ce**, *gen pl* **-ek)** *f* postcard
**poczuci|e (-a)** *nt (bezpieczeństwa, winy, niższości)* feeling; *(obowiązku, czasu, sprawiedliwości)* sense; **~ humoru** sense of humo(u)r; **~ wspólnoty** community spirit
**pocz|uć (-uję, -ujesz)** *vb perf od* **czuć**
**poczuw|ać się (-am, -asz)** *vr*: **poczuwać się do winy** to feel guilty; **poczuwać się do odpowiedzialności** to feel responsible
**poczwar|ka (-ki, -ki)** *(dat sg* **-ce**, *gen pl* **-ek)** *f (Zool)* chrysalis
**poczyna|nia (-ń)** *pl* actions
**poczy|nić (-nię, -nisz)** *(imp* **-ń)** *vb perf od* **czynić**
**poczytalnoś|ć (-ci)** *f* soundness of mind; **ograniczona ~** diminished responsibility
**poczytalny** *adj* of sound mind
**poczytny** *adj* widely read
**poczyt|ywać (-uję, -ujesz)** *(perf* **-ać)** *vt (książk)*: **~ kogoś/coś za** *+acc* to consider sb/sth to be ..., to regard sb/sth as ...

 SŁOWO KLUCZOWE

**pod** *prep +instr* **1** *(poniżej)* under; **pod stołem** under the table; **pod wodą/ziemią** underwater/underground; **pod spodem** below, underneath
**2** *(obok)* by; **pod ścianą** by the wall; **pod drzwiami** at the door
**3** *(w pobliżu)* near; **wieś pod Warszawą** a village near Warsaw; **bitwa pod Grunwaldem** the Battle of Grunwald
**4** *(dla wyrażenia przyczyny)* under; **pod wpływem/przymusem** under the influence/pressure
▷ *prep +acc* **1** *(kierunek)* under; **kot wszedł pod stół** the cat went under the table; **pod wiatr/prąd** against the wind/stream; **iść pod górę** to walk uphill; **wpaść** *(perf)* **pod samochód** to be hit by a car, to get run over by a car
**2** *(dla wyrażenia czasu)*: **pod wieczór/koniec** towards the evening/end; **pod czyjąś nieobecność** in sb's absence; **mężczyzna pod czterdziestkę** a man approaching forty
**3**: **pod kierunkiem nauczyciela** under the teacher's supervision; **pod czyjąś opieką** in sb's care; **pod nazwiskiem Kowalski** under the name of Kowalski; **pod warunkiem, że ...** on condition (that) ..., provided *lub* providing (that) ...; **książka pod tytułem ...** a book entitled ...; **pod przysięgą** under *lub* on *(Brit)* oath; **pod karą/groźbą czegoś** on pain of/under threat of sth

**pod|ać (-am, -asz)** *vb perf od* **podawać**
**podajni|k (-ka, -ki)** *(instr sg* **-kiem)** *m (Tech)* feeder
**poda|nie (-nia, -nia)** *(gen pl* **-ń)** *nt (wniosek)* application; *(Sport: w piłce nożnej, hokeju)* pass; *(: w tenisie, siatkówce)* service; **składać (złożyć** *perf***) ~ o** *+acc* to apply for
**podar|ować (-uję, -ujesz)** *vt perf*: **~ coś komuś** *(dać w prezencie)* to give sth to sb as a present; *(przebaczyć)* to forgive sb sth
**podarty** *adj* torn, tattered
**podarun|ek (-ku, -ki)** *(instr sg* **-kiem)** *m* gift
**podat|ek (-ku, -ki)** *(instr sg* **-kiem)** *m* tax; **~ dochodowy** income tax; **~ od wartości dodanej** value added tax, VAT
**podatkowy** *adj (system, przepisy, rok)* tax *attr*; **zeznanie podatkowe** *lub* **deklaracja podatkowa** tax return
**podatni|k (-ka, -cy)** *(instr sg* **-kiem)** *m* taxpayer

P

**podatnoś|ć** (**-ci**) *f*: **~ (na coś)** susceptibility (to sth)
**podatny** *adj*: **~ (na coś)** susceptible (to sth)
**pod|awać (-aję, -ajesz)** (*perf* **-ać**) *vt* (*książkę, cukier*) to pass; (*nazwisko, cenę, przykład*) to give; (*wiadomość, rezultaty*) to announce; (*lekarstwo*) to administer; (*piłkę*: *w tenisie, siatkówce*) to serve; (: *w piłce nożnej*) to pass; **~ coś komuś** to pass sb sth *lub* sth to sb; **podali sobie ręce** they shook hands; **~ do stołu** to wait at table; **~ (do wiadomości), że ...** to announce that ...; **~ kogoś do sądu** to take sb to court; **podawać się** *vr*: **~ się za kogoś** to pose as sb; **podać się do dymisji** to hand in one's resignation
**podaż** (**-y**) *f* supply
**podąż|ać (-am, -asz)** (*perf* **-yć**) *vi* to proceed; **~ za kimś** to follow sb
**podbi|cie** (**-cia, -cia**) (*gen pl* **-ć**) *nt* (*stopy*) instep
**pod|bić (-biję, -bijesz)** *vb perf od* **podbijać** ▷ *vt perf*: **~ komuś oko** to give sb a black eye
**podbie|c (-gnę, -gniesz)** (*imp* **-gnij**) *vb perf od* **podbiegać**
**podbieg|ać (-am, -asz)** (*perf* **podbiec**) *vi*: **~ do** *+gen* to run up to
**podbiegunowy** *adj* polar; **koło podbiegunowe północne/południowe** Arctic/Antarctic Circle
**podbiera|k** (**-ka, -ki**) (*instr sg* **-kiem**) *m* landing net
**podbij|ać (-am, -asz)** (*perf* **podbić**) *vt* (*kraj*) to conquer; (*piłkę*: *posyłać w górę*) to flick up; (: *żonglować*) to juggle (with); (*cenę*) to push up; (*pot*: *legitymację*) to stamp; **podbić czyjeś serce** to win sb's heart; **podbić obcas w bucie** to reheel a shoe
**podb|ój** (**-oju, -oje**) *m* conquest
**podbród|ek** (**-ka, -ki**) (*instr sg* **-kiem**) *m* chin
**podbrzusz|e** (**-a, -a**) (*gen pl* **-y**) *nt* (*u człowieka*) abdomen; (*u zwierzęcia*) underbelly
**podbud|owa** (**-owy, -owy**) (*dat sg* **-owie**, *gen pl* **-ów**) *f* foundation
**podburz|ać (-am, -asz)** (*perf* **-yć**) *vt* to instigate
**podca|st (-stu, -sty)** (*loc sg* **-ście**) *m* (*Komput*) podcast
**podchmielony** *adj* (*pot*) tipsy
**podcho|dzić (-dzę, -dzisz)** (*imp* **-dź**, *perf* **podejść**) *vt* (*tropić*: *zwierzynę, przestępcę*) to stalk ▷ *vi*: **~ do** *+gen* to approach, to come up to
**podchorąż|y** (**-ego, -owie**) *m decl like adj* (*Wojsk*) officer trainee (*Brit*) *lub* cadet (*US*)
**podchwytliwy** *adj*: **podchwytliwe pytanie** trick question
**pod|ciąć (-etnę, -etniesz)** (*imp* **-etnij**) *vb perf od* **podcinać**
**podciąg|ać (-am, -asz)** (*perf* **-nąć**) *vt* (*spodnie, rękaw, kolana*) to pull up; (*poziom*) to raise; **podciągać się** *vr* (*na rękach*) to pull o.s. up; (*przen*: *w nauce*) to lift one's grades
**podciąg|nąć (-nę, -niesz)** (*imp* **-nij**) *vb perf od* **podciągać**
**podcie|ń** (**-nia, -nie**) (*gen pl* **-ni**) *m* (*Archit*) arcade
**podcin|ać (-am, -asz)** (*perf* **podciąć**) *vt* (*włosy, drzewo*) to cut; (*piłkę*) to slash; (*osobę, zawodnika*) to cut *lub* hack (*pot*) down; **~ komuś skrzydła** (*przen*) to clip sb's wings; **podciąć sobie żyły** to slash *lub* slit one's wrists
**podczas** *prep +gen* during; **~ gdy** ((*wtedy*) *kiedy*) while; (*natomiast*) whereas
**podczerwie|ń** (**-ni**) (*gen pl* **-ni**) *f* infrared light
**podczerwony** *adj* infra-red
**podda|ny** (**-nego, -ni**) *m decl like adj* subject
**poddasz|e** (**-a, -a**) (*gen pl* **-y**) *nt* loft; **pokój na poddaszu** attic, garret
**podd|awać (-aję, -ajesz)** (*perf* **-ać**) *vt* (*miasto*) to surrender; (*myśl, temat*) to suggest; (*projekt, wniosek*) to put forward, to propose; **~ kogoś/coś próbie** to put sb/sth to the test; **~ kogoś/coś krytyce/ocenie** to subject sb/sth to criticism/assessment; **~ coś pod dyskusję** to submit sth to discussion; **~ coś pod głosowanie** to put sth to the vote; **~ coś w wątpliwość** to question sth, to bring *lub* call sth into question; **~ kogoś/coś działaniu czegoś** to expose sb/sth to sth; **poddawać się** *vr* (*rezygnować*) to give up; **~ się** (*+dat*) (*nieprzyjacielowi*) to surrender (to); (*wpływowi, urokowi*) to surrender *lub* give in (to); **poddać się operacji** to undergo an operation
**podejm|ować (-uję, -ujesz)** (*perf* **podjąć**) *vt* (*kroki, wezwanie, ryzyko*) to take; (*pracę*) to take up; (*walkę*) to put up; (*dyskusję, wątek*) to take up; (*gości*) to receive; (*pieniądze*) to withdraw; **~ decyzję** to take *lub* make a decision; **~ próbę zrobienia czegoś** to make an attempt *lub* effort to do sth; **~ starania** *lub* **wysiłki** to make an effort; **podejmować się** *vr*: **~ się czegoś/coś zrobić** to undertake sth/to do sth
**podejrzany** *adj* suspicious ▷ *m decl like adj* suspect; **być ~m o coś** to be suspected of sth
**podejrz|eć (-ę, -ysz)** *vb perf od* **podglądać**
**podejrze|nie** (**-nia, -nia**) (*gen pl* **-ń**) *nt* suspicion; **wzbudzać podejrzenia** to arouse suspicion; **nabierać (nabrać** *perf***) podejrzeń** to become suspicious
**podejrzew|ać (-am, -asz)** *vt* to suspect; **~ kogoś o coś** to suspect sb of sth; **nie podejrzewam cię o taką złośliwość** I wouldn't expect you to be so malicious

**podejrzliwoś|ć** (**-ci**) *f* suspiciousness, distrust

**podejrzliwy** *adj* suspicious; **~ wobec** *lub* **w stosunku do kogoś** suspicious about sb, mistrustful of sb

**podejś|cie** (**-cia, -cia**) (*gen pl* **-ć**) *nt* (*droga pod górę*) climb; **~ (do** *+gen*) (*stosunek*) attitude (to *lub* towards); (*interpretacja*) approach (to)

**pod|ejść (-ejdę, -ejdziesz)** (*imp* **-ejdź**, *pt* **-szedł, -eszła, -eszli**) *vb perf od* **podchodzić** ▷ *vt perf* (*pot: oszukać*) to trick

**podekscytowany** *adj* excited

**podenerwowany** *adj* nervous

**podep|rzeć (-rę, -rzesz)** (*imp* **-rzyj**) *vb perf od* **podpierać**

**podep|tać (-czę, -czesz)** *vb perf od* **deptać**

**poder|wać (-wę, -wiesz)** (*imp* **-wij**) *vb perf od* **podrywać**

**poderż|nąć (-nę, -niesz)** (*imp* **-nij**) *vt perf*: **~ komuś gardło** to cut *lub* slit sb's throat

**pode|st** (**-stu, -sty**) (*loc sg* **-ście**) *m* (*na schodach*) landing; (*dla mówcy*) podium

**podeszły** *adj*: **w ~m wieku** advanced in years, of advanced years *lub* age; **osoby w ~m wieku** the aged

**podesz|wa** (**-wy, -wy**) (*dat sg* **-wie**) *f* sole

**podgląd|ać (-am, -asz)** (*perf* **podejrzeć**) *vt* to spy on

**podgłów|ek** (**-ka, -ki**) (*instr sg* **-kiem**) *m* bolster

**podgrz|ać (-eję, -ejesz)** *vb perf od* **podgrzewać**

**podgrzewacz** (**-a, -e**) (*gen pl* **-y**) *m* heater

**podgrzew|ać (-am, -asz)** (*perf* **podgrzać**) *vt* (*wodę*) to heat; (*zupę, obiad*) to heat up

**podi|um** (**-um, -a**) (*gen pl* **-ów**) *nt inv in sg* podium

**podj|azd** (**-azdu, -azdy**) (*loc sg* **-eździe**) *m* (*do budynku*) drive(way)

**pod|jąć (-ejmę, -ejmiesz)** (*imp* **-ejmij**) *vb perf od* **podejmować**

**podj|echać (-adę, -edziesz)** (*imp* **-edź**) *vb perf od* **podjeżdżać**

**podjeżdż|ać (-am, -asz)** (*perf* **podjechać**) *vt* (*do miejsca*) to draw up, to drive up; (*pod górę*) to go uphill; **podjadę autobusem** I'll take a bus

**podju|dzać (-dzam, -dzasz)** (*perf* **-dzić**) *vt* to incite

**podju|dzić (-dzę, -dzisz)** (*imp* **-dź**) *vb perf od* **podjudzać**

**podkła|d** (**-du, -dy**) (*loc sg* **-dzie**) *m* (*pod farbę*) undercoat; (*pod makijaż*) foundation (cream); (*Kolej*) sleeper (*Brit*), tie (*US*); **~ muzyczny** incidental music

**podkład|ać (-am, -asz)** (*perf* **podłożyć**) *vt* (*kłaść*): **~ coś pod** *+acc* to put sth under; **~ bombę** to plant a bomb; **~ ogień pod coś** to set fire to sth; **podłożyć komuś nogę** to trip sb (up)

**podkład|ka** (**-ki, -ki**) (*dat sg* **-ce**, *gen pl* **-ek**) *f* (*pod talerz*) mat; (*pod kieliszek*) coaster; (*Tech*) washer

**podkolanów|ki** (**-ek**) *pl* knee-length socks

**podko|p** (**-pu, -py**) (*loc sg* **-pie**) *m* tunnel

**podko|pać (-pię, -piesz)** *vb perf od* **podkopywać**

**podkop|ywać (-uję, -ujesz)** (*perf* **-ać**) *vt* (*pot*) to undermine; **podkopywać się** *vr* to tunnel one's way

**podkoszul|ek** (**-ka, -ki**) (*instr sg* **-kiem**) *m* vest (*Brit*), undershirt (*US*)

**podk|owa** (**-owy, -owy**) (*dat sg* **-owie**, *gen pl* **-ów**) *f* horseshoe

**podkrad|ać (-am, -asz)** (*perf* **podkraść**) *vt* to steal; **podkradać się** *vr*: **~ się (do kogoś)** to creep up (on sb)

**podkra|ść (-dnę, -dniesz)** (*pt* **-dł**) *vb perf od* **podkradać**

**podkrążony** *adj*: **mieć podkrążone oczy** to have dark rings round one's eyes

**podkreśl|ać (-am, -asz)** (*perf* **-ić**) *vt* (*tekst, błąd*) to underline, to underscore; (*uwydatniać*) to emphasize, to stress

**podkrę|cać (-cam, -casz)** (*perf* **-cić**) *vt* (*wąsa*) to curl up

**podkrę|cić (-cę, -cisz)** (*imp* **-ć**) *vb perf od* **podkręcać**

**podk|uć (-uję, -ujesz)** *vb perf od* **podkuwać**

**podkuw|ać (-am, -asz)** (*perf* **podkuć**) *vt* (*konia*) to shoe; (*buty*) to hobnail

**podl|ać (-eję, -ejesz)** *vb perf od* **podlewać**

**podle** *adv* (*postępować*) despicably, vilely; (*pot: czuć się*) lousy, rotten

**podleg|ać (-am, -asz)** *vi*: **~ komuś/czemuś** (*instytucji, kierownictwu*) to be subordinate to sb/sth; **~ czemuś** (*karze, obowiązkowi, wpływowi*) to be subject to sth

**podległy** *adj*: **~ komuś/czemuś** subordinate to sb/sth

**podlew|ać (-am, -asz)** (*perf* **podlać**) *vt* to water

**podlicz|ać (-am, -asz)** (*perf* **-yć**) *vt* to count (up)

**podli|zać się (-żę, -żesz)** *vb perf od* **podlizywać się**

**podliz|ywać się (-uję, -ujesz)** (*perf* **-ać**) *vr*: **podlizywać się komuś** (*pot*) to suck up to sb (*pot*), to toady to sb

**podlot|ek** (**-ka, -ki**) (*instr sg* **-kiem**) *m* teenage girl, schoolgirl

**podłącz|ać (-am, -asz)** (*perf* **-yć**) *vt* to connect, to hook up

**podł|oga** (**-ogi, -ogi**) (*dat sg* **-odze**, *gen pl* **-óg**) *f* floor

**podłoś|ć** (**-ci**) *f* (*cecha*) meanness; (*uczynek*) mean trick
**podłoż|e** (**-a, -a**) (*gen pl* **-y**) *nt* (*ziemia*) ground; (*podstawa*) basis; **~ kwiatowe** compost
**podł|ożyć (-ożę, -ożysz)** (*imp* **-óż**) *vb perf od* **podkładać**
**podłużny** *adj* (*kształt*) elongated; (*przekrój*) longitudinal
**podły** *adj* (*człowiek*) mean; (*czyn*) mean, base
**podmiejski** *adj* suburban
**podmin|ować (-uję, -ujesz)** *vb perf od* **podminowywać**
**podminow|ywać (-uję, -ujesz)** (*perf* **-ać**) *vt* to mine
**podmio|t** (**-tu, -ty**) (*loc sg* **-cie**) *m* (*Jęz*) subject; (*Prawo*) entity
**podmokły** *adj* boggy, marshy
**podmu|ch** (**-chu, -chy**) *m* (*wiatru*) gust
**podnaj|ąć (-mę, -miesz)** (*imp* **-mij**) *vb perf od* **podnajmować**
**podnaj|mować (-muję, -mujesz)** (*perf* **-ąć**) *vt* to sublet
**podniebie|nie** (**-nia, -nia**) (*gen pl* **-ń**) *nt* palate; **~ miękkie/twarde** soft/hard palate
**podnie|cać (-cam, -casz)** (*perf* **-cić**) *vt* (*ożywiać*) to excite, to thrill; (*pobudzać seksualnie*) to excite, to arouse; (*wyobraźnię, nadzieję, apetyt*) to stimulate; **podniecać się** *vr* (*ożywiać się*) to get excited; (*pobudzać się seksualnie*) to become excited *lub* aroused; **~ się czymś** (*pot*) to get excited about sth
**podniecający** *adj* exciting
**podniece|nie** (**-nia**) *nt* excitement; (*seksualne*) arousal
**podnie|cić (-cę, -cisz)** (*imp* **-ć**) *vb perf od* **podniecać**
**podniecony** *adj* (*ożywiony*) excited; (*pobudzony seksualnie*) excited, aroused
**podniesieni|e** (**-a**) *nt* (*Rel*) Elevation; **głosować przez ~ rąk** to vote by a show of hands
**pod|nieść (-niosę, -niesiesz)** (*imp* **-nieś**, *pt* **-niósł, -niosła, -nieśli**) *vb perf od* **podnosić**
**podnie|ta** (**-ty, -ty**) (*dat sg* **-cie**) *f* stimulus
**podniosły** *adj* (*styl*) lofty, elevated; (*nastrój, chwila*) solemn
**podno|sić (-szę, -sisz)** (*imp* **-ś**, *perf* **podnieść**) *vt* (*unosić*) to raise; (*z wysiłkiem*) to lift; (*zbierać*) to pick up; (*pomagać wstać*) to lift; (*poziom, płace, alarm*) to raise; (*problem, kwestię*) to raise, to bring up; **~ głos** to raise one's voice; **~ rękę na kogoś** to raise one's hand against sb; **~ krzyk** *lub* **wrzawę** to raise a rumpus; **~ liczbę do kwadratu/sześcianu** to square/cube a number; **~ kotwicę** to weigh anchor; **~ kogoś na duchu** to lift *lub* raise sb's spirits *lub* heart; **podnosić się** *vr* (*wstawać*) to lift o.s.; (*o dochodach, cenach*) to rise; (*o krzyku, hałasie*) to erupt
**podnoszeni|e** (**-a**) *nt*: **~ ciężarów** weight lifting
**podnośni|k** (**-ka, -ki**) (*instr sg* **-kiem**) *m* (*Tech*) lift; (*lewarek*) jack; **~ widłowy** fork-lift truck
**podnóż|e** (**-a, -a**) (*gen pl* **-y**) *nt*: **u podnóża góry** at the foot of the mountain
**podnóż|ek** (**-ka, -ki**) (*instr sg* **-kiem**) *m* footstool
**podob|ać się (-am, -asz)** *vr*: **ona mi się podoba** I like her; **to mi się nie podoba** I don't like it; **podobać się komuś** to appeal to sb; **rób, co ci się podoba** do as you like
**podobieńst|wo** (**-wa, -wa**) (*loc sg* **-wie**) *nt* similarity; (*wyglądu*) likeness, resemblance
**podobnie** *adv* (*w podobny sposób*) similarly, alike; (*równie*) as; **~ jak** like
**podobno** *adv* supposedly, reportedly
**podobny** *adj* similar; (*o dwóch lub więcej osobach/rzeczach*) alike, similar; **być ~m do kogoś/czegoś** to resemble sb/sth; **i tym podobne** and the like; **coś podobnego!** really!; **nic podobnego!** nothing of the sort!
**podofice|r** (**-ra, -rowie**) (*loc sg* **-rze**) *m* non-commissioned officer; (*w marynarce*) petty officer
**podoł|ać (-am, -asz)** *vi perf*: **nie podołam temu** I'm not up to it
**podom|ka** (**-ce, -ki**) (*gen pl* **-ek**) *f* housecoat
**podopiecz|ny** (**-nego, -ni**) *m decl like adj*; **mój ~** my charge
**podpad|ać (-am, -asz)** (*perf* **podpaść**) *vi* (*pot*): **~ komuś** to get into sb's bad *lub* black books (*pot*)
**podpalacz** (**-a, -e**) (*gen pl* **-y**) *m* arsonist
**podpal|ać (-am, -asz)** (*perf* **-ić**) *vt*: **~ coś** to set fire to sth, to set sth on fire
**podpas|ka** (**-ki, -ki**) (*dat sg* **-ce**, *gen pl* **-ek**) *f* (*też*: **podpaska higieniczna**) sanitary towel (Brit) *lub* napkin (US)
**podpa|ść (-dnę, -dniesz)** (*imp* **-dnij**, *pt* **-dł**) *vb perf od* **podpadać**
**podpatr|ywać (-uję, -ujesz)** (*perf* **podpatrzyć**) *vt* to watch
**podpatrz|yć (-ę, -ysz)** *vb perf od* **podpatrywać** ▷ *vt perf* (*podejrzeć*) to (e)spy
**podpier|ać (-am, -asz)** *vt* (*głowę, chorego*) (*perf* **podeprzeć**) to support; (*stół, biurko*) (*perf* **podeprzeć**) to prop up; (*stanowić podporę*) to support
**podpin|ka** (**-ki, -ki**) (*dat sg* **-ce**, *gen pl* **-ek**) *f* (detachable) lining
**podpi|s** (**-su, -sy**) (*loc sg* **-sie**) *m* (*czyjś*) signature; (*pod ilustracją*) caption; **składać** (**złożyć** *perf*) **~ pod czymś** to put one's signature to sth

**podpis|ywać (-uję, -ujesz)** (*perf* **-ać**) *vt* to sign; **podpisywać się** *vr* to sign one's name
**podpity** *adj* tipsy
**podpiw|ek** (**-ka** *lub* **-ku, -ki**) (*instr sg* **-kiem**) *m* home-brew
**podpły|nąć (-nę, -niesz)** (*imp* **-ń**) *vb perf od* **podpływać**
**podpływ|ać (-am, -asz)** (*perf* **podpłynąć**) *vi*: ~ **do czegoś** to approach sth (*about swimmer, boat etc*)
**podp|ora** (**-ory, -ory**) (*loc sg* **-orze**, *gen pl* **-ór**) *f* support
**podporuczni|k** (**-ka, -cy**) (*instr sg* **-kiem**) *m* Second Lieutenant; (*w marynarce wojennej*) Acting Sub-Lieutenant (*Brit*), Ensign (*US*)
**podporządkowany** *adj*: **droga podporządkowana** minor road
**podporządkow|ywać (-uję, -ujesz)** (*perf* **-ać**) *vt* to subordinate; **podporządkowywać się** *vr*: ~ **się czemuś** to conform to sth, to comply with sth; ~ **się komuś** to defer to sb
**podpowiad|ać (-am, -asz)** (*perf* **podpowiedzieć**) *vt* to suggest ▷ *vi*: ~ **komuś** to prompt sb; **podpowiedzieć komuś, jak coś zrobić** to tell sb how to do sth
**podpowi|edzieć (-em, -esz)** (*3 pl* **-edzą**) *vb perf od* **podpowiadać**
**podpór|ka** (**-ki, -ki**) (*dat sg* **-ce**, *gen pl* **-ek**) *f* support
**podpułkowni|k** (**-ka, -cy**) (*instr sg* **-kiem**) *m* Lieutenant Colonel
**podpuszcz|ać (-am, -asz)** (*perf* **podpuścić**) *vt* (*pot*): ~ **kogoś** to put sb on (*pot*)
**podpyt|ywać (-uję, -ujesz)** (*perf* **-ać**) *vt* (*pot*) to pump (*pot*)
**podrabi|ać (-am, -asz)** (*perf* **podrobić**) *vt* to forge
**podrabiany** *adj* fake
**podra|pać (-pię, -piesz)** *vb perf od* **drapać**
**podraż|ać (-am, -asz)** (*perf* **podrożyć**) *vt* to raise the cost of
**podraż|niać (-niam, -niasz)** (*perf* **-nić**) *vt* to irritate
**podraż|nić (-nię, -nisz)** (*imp* **-nij**) *vb perf od* **podrażniać**
**podrażnie|nie** (**-nia, -nia**) (*gen pl* **-ń**) *nt* irritation
**podręczni|k** (**-ka, -ki**) (*instr sg* **-kiem**) *m* textbook
**podręczny** *adj* (*słownik*) concise; **bagaż** ~ hand *lub* carry-on luggage; **księgozbiór** ~ reference library
**podr|obić (-obię, -obisz)** (*imp* **-ób**) *vb perf od* **podrabiać**
**podrobiony** *adj* forged, counterfeit
**podrob|y** (**-ów**) *pl* offal; (*drobiowe*) giblets *pl*
**podroż|eć (-eje)** *vb perf od* **drożeć**
**podroż|yć (-ę, -ysz)** *vb perf od* **podrażać**
**podrób|ka** (**-ki, -ki**) (*dat sg* **-ce**, *gen pl* **-ek**) *f* fake
**podróż** (**-y, -e**) (*gen pl* **-y**) *f* (*długa*) journey; (*krótka*) trip; ~ **poślubna** honeymoon; ~ **służbowa** business trip; **biuro ~y** travel agency; **szczęśliwej ~y!** have a safe journey *lub* trip!; **podróże** *pl* travels *pl*, voyages *pl*
**podróżniczy** *adj* travel *attr*
**podróżni|k** (**-ka, -cy**) (*instr sg* **-kiem**) *m* traveller (*Brit*), traveler (*US*)
**podróżny** *adj*: **torba podróżna** travelling (*Brit*) *lub* traveling (*US*) bag; **czek** ~ traveller's cheque (*Brit*), traveler's check (*US*) ▷ *m decl like adj* passenger
**podróż|ować (-uję, -ujesz)** *vi* to travel
**podrywacz** (**-a, -e**) (*gen pl* **-y**) *m* (*pot*) lady-killer (*pot*)
**podryw|ać (-am, -asz)** (*perf* **poderwać**) *vt* (*pot*) to pick up (*pot*); **podrywać się** *vr* (*podnosić się*) to jump to one's feet; (*wzlatywać*) to take off
**pod|rzeć (-rę, -rzesz)** (*imp* **-rzyj**) *vb perf od* **drzeć**
**podrzędny** *adj* second-rate; **zdanie podrzędne** subordinate clause
**podrzu|cać (-cam, -casz)** (*perf* **-cić**) *vt* (*w górę*) to toss *lub* throw (into the air); (*podsuwać ukradkiem*) to plant; (*dostarczać*) to drop round; **podrzucić kogoś (do domu/szkoły)** to give sb a lift (home/to school)
**podrzu|cić (-cę, -cisz)** (*imp* **-ć**) *vb perf od* **podrzucać**
**podrzut|ek** (**-ka, -ki**) (*instr sg* **-kiem**) *m* foundling
**podsa|dzać (-dzam, -dzasz)** (*perf* **-dzić**) *vt* to help up
**podsa|dzić (-dzę, -dzisz)** (*imp* **-dź**) *vb perf od* **podsadzać**
**podsekretarz** (**-a, -e**) (*gen pl* **-y**) *m* undersecretary; ~ **stanu** ≈ junior minister (*Brit*), ≈ undersecretary (*US*)
**podska|kiwać (-kuję, -kujesz)** (*perf* **podskoczyć**) *vi* to jump (up); **nie podskakuj** (*pot*) don't be cheeky (*pot*)
**podskocz|yć (-ę, -ysz)** *vb perf od* **podskakiwać** ▷ *vi perf* (*o cenach, inflacji*) to shoot up; (*o temperaturze*) to soar
**podskórny** *adj* (*zastrzyk*) hypodermic; (*tkanka, wylew*) subcutaneous
**podsłuch** (**-u, -y**) *m* (*na linii*) tap; (*w pomieszczeniu*) bug; **zakładać (założyć** *perf*) **u kogoś** ~ (*na linii*) to tap sb's phone; (*w pomieszczeniu*) to bug sb's house
**podsłuch|ać (-am, -asz)** *vb perf od* **podsłuchiwać** ▷ *vt perf* (*przypadkiem*) to overhear
**podsłuch|iwać (-uję, -ujesz)** (*perf* **-ać**) *vt* to eavesdrop on ▷ *vi* to eavesdrop

**podsta|wa** (**-wy, -wy**) (*loc sg* **-wie**) *f* basis; (*Geom*) base; **podstawy** *pl* the basics *pl*; **na podstawie czegoś** on the basis of sth; **mieć podstawy do czegoś** to have (sufficient) grounds for (doing) sth; **na jakiej podstawie?** on what grounds?; **nie bez podstaw** not without reason

**podsta|wiać (-wiam, -wiasz)** (*perf* **-wić**) *vt* (*naczynie*) to place; (*liczby*) to provide; (*agenta*) to plant; ~ **A za B** to substitute A for B; **podstawić komuś nogę** to trip sb (up)

**podsta|wić (-wię, -wisz)** *vb perf od* **podstawiać** ▷ *vt perf*: **pociąg jest podstawiony na peronie drugim** the train is (already) waiting at platform two

**podstawowy** *adj* basic; **szkoła podstawowa** primary (*Brit*) *lub* elementary (*US*) school

**podstę|p** (**-pu, -py**) (*loc sg* **-pie**) *m* ruse, trick

**podstępny** *adj* (*człowiek*) sneaky, insidious; (*pytanie*) tricky

**podsum|ować (-uję, -ujesz)** *vb perf od* **podsumowywać**

**podsumowa|nie** (**-nia, -nia**) (*gen pl* **-ń**) *nt* summary, résumé

**podsumow|ywać (-uję, -ujesz)** (*perf* **podsumować**) *vt* (*dodawać*) to add up; (*streszczać*) to sum up

**podsu|nąć (-nę, -niesz)** (*imp* **-ń**) *vb perf od* **podsuwać**

**podsuw|ać (-am, -asz)** (*perf* **podsunąć**) *vt* to offer

**podsy|cać (-cam, -casz)** (*perf* **-cić**) *vt* to fuel

**podsy|cić (-cę, -cisz)** (*imp* **-ć**) *vb perf od* **podsycać**

**podszedł** *itd. vb patrz* **podejść**

**podszew|ka** (**-ki, -ki**) (*dat sg* **-ce**, *gen pl* **-ek**) *f* lining; **znać coś od podszewki** to know sth inside out

**podszkol|ić (-ę, -isz)** *vt perf* to coach; **podszkolić się** *vr perf*: ~ **się w czymś** to brush up on sth

**podszy|cie** (**-cia, -cia**) (*gen pl* **-ć**) *nt* (*leśne*) undergrowth

**podszyw|ać (-am, -asz)** (*perf* **podszyć**) *vt* (*płaszcz*) to line; **podszywać się** *vr*: ~ **się pod kogoś** to pretend to be sb, to impersonate sb

**podśmiew|ać się (-am, -asz)** *vr*: **podśmiewać się z kogoś** to make fun of sb

**podświadomoś|ć** (**-ci**) *f* the subconscious

**podświadomy** *adj* subconscious

**podtrzym|ywać (-uję, -ujesz)** (*perf* **-ać**) *vt* (*chorego*) to support; (*rozmowę*) to keep going; (*przyjaźń*) to maintain; (*żądania, opinię*) to stand by; ~ **kogoś na duchu** to buoy sb up

**podtytu|ł** (**-łu, -ły**) (*loc sg* **-le**) *m* (*utworu*) subtitle; (*w gazecie*) subheading

**podupad|ać (-am, -asz)** (*perf* **podupaść**) *vi* (*o przedsiębiorstwie*) to go downhill, to fall into decline; (*o autorytecie*) to erode

**podupa|ść (-dnę, -dniesz)** (*pt* **-dł**) *vb perf od* **podupadać**

**poduszecz|ka** (**-ki, -ki**) (*dat sg* **-ce**, *gen pl* **-ek**) *f dimin od* **poduszka**; ~ **do igieł/szpilek** pincushion

**podusz|ka** (**-ki, -ki**) (*dat sg* **-ce**, *gen pl* **-ek**) *f* (*część pościeli*) pillow; (*na kanapie, fotelu*) cushion; (*do stempli*) ink-pad; ~ **powietrzna** airbag

**poduszko|wiec** (**-wca, -wce**) *m* hovercraft

**podwaj|ać (-am, -asz)** (*perf* **podwoić**) *vt* to double

**podwalin|y** (-) *pl*: **kłaść (położyć** *perf*) ~ **pod coś** to lay the foundations of sth

**podważ|ać (-am, -asz)** (*perf* **-yć**) *vt* (*wieko, pokrywę*) to lever up; (*wiarę, zaufanie*) to undermine; (*hipotezę, teorię*) to challenge; (*czyjąś wiarygodność*) to question

**podwiąz|ka** (**-ki, -ki**) (*dat sg* **-ce**, *gen pl* **-ek**) *f* garter

**podwieczor|ek** (**-ku, -ki**) (*instr sg* **-kiem**) *m* tea (*meal*)

**pod|wieźć (-wiozę, -wieziesz)** (*imp* **-wieź**, *pt* **-wiózł, -wiozła, -wiozły**) *vb perf od* **podwozić**

**podwij|ać (-am, -asz)** (*perf* **podwinąć**) *vt* (*rękaw, nogawkę*) to roll up

**podwi|nąć (-nę, -niesz)** (*imp* **-ń**) *vb perf od* **podwijać**

**podwład|ny** (**-nego, -ni**) *m decl like adj* subordinate

**podwodny** *adj* (*świat, skała*) underwater *attr*; **okręt** ~ submarine

**podw|oić (-oję, -oisz)** (*imp* **-ój**) *vb perf od* **podwajać**

**podw|ozić (-ożę, -ozisz)** (*imp* **-oź** *lub* **-óź**) *vt*: ~ **kogoś (do domu/szkoły)** to give sb a lift (home/to school)

**podwo|zie** (**-zia, -zia**) (*gen pl* **-zi**) *nt* (*Mot*) chassis; (*Lot*) undercarriage

**podwójnie** *adv* doubly; **płacić/kosztować** ~ to pay/cost double

**podwójny** *adj* double; **podwójne obywatelstwo** dual citizenship; **gra podwójna** (*Tenis*) doubles *pl*

**podwór|ko** (**-ka, -ka**) (*instr sg* **-kiem**, *gen pl* **-ek**) *nt* yard; (*za domem*) backyard

**podwórz|e** (**-a, -a**) (*gen pl* **-y**) *nt* yard

**podwyż|ka** (**-ki, -ki**) (*dat sg* **-ce**, *gen pl* **-ek**) *f* (*pensji*) rise (*Brit*), raise (*US*); (*cen*) rise

**podwyższ|ać (-am, -asz)** (*perf* **-yć**) *vt* to raise; (*walory, zalety*) to increase

**podwyższe|nie** (**-nia, -nia**) (*gen pl* **-ń**) *nt* platform

**podwyższ|yć (-ę, -ysz)** *vb perf od* **podwyższać**

**podykt|ować (-uję, -ujesz)** *vb perf od* **dyktować**
**podyplomowy** *adj* postgraduate *attr*
**podzesp|ół (-ołu, -oły)** (*loc sg* **-ole**) *m* component
**podzia|ł (-łu, -ły)** (*loc sg* **-le**) *m* division; (*Bio*) fission
**podziałka** (**-ki, -ki**) (*dat sg* **-ce**, *gen pl* **-ek**) *f* scale
**podziel|ać (-am, -asz)** *vt*: **~ czyjś smutek/czyjeś zdanie** to share sb's grief/sb's opinion
**podziel|ić (-ę, -isz)** *vb perf od* **dzielić**
**podzielny** *adj* divisible; **podzielna uwaga** divided attention
**podzie|mie** (**-mia, -mia**) (*gen pl* **-mi**) *nt* (*Pol*) the underground; **podziemia** *pl* (*zamku, budynku*) basement
**podziemny** *adj* underground *attr*; **przejście podziemne** subway (*Brit*), underpass (*US*)
**podziew|ać się (-am, -asz)** (*perf* **podziać**) *vr*: **gdzieś ty się podziewał?** where (on earth) have you been?
**podzięk|ować (-uję, -ujesz)** *vb perf od* **dziękować**
**podziękowa|nie** (**-nia, -nia**) (*gen pl* **-ń**) *nt* thanks *pl*
**podziura|wić (-wię, -wisz)** *vb perf od* **dziurawić**
**podzi|w** (**-wu**) (*loc sg* **-wie**) *m* admiration; **nad ~** admirably; **godny ~u** admirable; **nie móc wyjść z ~u** to be lost in admiration
**podziwi|ać (-am, -asz)** *vt* to admire
**podzwrotnikowy** *adj* subtropical
**podżeg|ać (-am, -asz)** *vt*: **~ kogoś do czegoś** to incite sb to (do) sth
**poema|t** (**-tu, -ty**) (*loc sg* **-cie**) *m* poem
**poe|ta** (**-ty, -ci**) (*dat sg* **-cie**) *m decl like f in sg* poet
**poet|ka** (**-ki, -ki**) (*dat sg* **-ce**, *gen pl* **-ek**) *f* poet
**poetycki** *adj* poetic(al)
**poetyczny** *adj* poetic(al)
**poezj|a** (**-i, -e**) (*gen pl* **-i**) *f* poetry
**pofałdowany** *adj* (*teren*) undulating; (*skóra*) wrinkled
**pofarb|ować (-uję, -ujesz)** *vb perf od* **farbować**
**pofatyg|ować się (-uję, -ujesz)** *vr perf*: **pofatygować się dokądś** to kindly go somewhere
**pogadan|ka** (**-ki, -ki**) (*dat sg* **-ce**, *gen pl* **-ek**) *f* talk
**pogadusz|ki** (**-ek**) *pl* chit-chat
**pogani|ać (-am, -asz)** (*perf* **pogonić**) *vt* to urge; **nie poganiaj mnie!** don't rush me!
**poga|nin** (**-nina, -nie**) (*loc sg* **-ninie**, *gen pl* **-n**) *m* pagan, heathen
**pogan|ka** (**-ki, -ki**) (*dat sg* **-ce**, *gen pl* **-ek**) *f* pagan, heathen
**pogański** *adj* pagan, heathen
**pogar|da** (**-dy**) (*dat sg* **-dzie**) *f* contempt; **godny pogardy** contemptible
**pogardliwy** *adj* contemptuous
**pogar|dzać (-dzam, -dzasz)** (*perf* **-dzić**) *vi*: **~ kimś/czymś** (*odnosić się z pogardą*) to hold sb/sth in contempt; (*lekceważyć*) to disdain sb/sth; **~ czymś** (*wyrzekać się*) to renounce sth
**pogardzenia** *inv*: **nie do ~** not to be sneezed at
**pogar|dzić (-dzę, -dzisz)** (*imp* **-dź**) *vb perf od* **pogardzać**
**pogarsz|ać (-am, -asz)** (*perf* **pogorszyć**) *vt* to worsen; **pogarszać się** *vr* to deteriorate, to worsen; **pogorszyło mu się** his condition deteriorated
**pogawęd|ka** (**-ki, -ki**) (*dat sg* **-ce**, *gen pl* **-ek**) *f* chat
**pogięty** *adj* twisted
**poglą|d** (**-du, -dy**) (*loc sg* **-dzie**) *m* view; **~ na świat** outlook, world view; **wymiana ~ów** exchange of views *lub* ideas
**pogła|skać (-szczę, -szczesz)** *vb perf od* **głaskać**
**pogłę|biać (-biam, -biasz)** (*perf* **-bić**) *vt* to deepen; **pogłębiać się** *vr* to deepen
**pogłębiar|ka** (**-ki, -ki**) (*dat sg* **-ce**, *gen pl* **-ek**) *f* dredger
**pogło|s** (**-su, -sy**) (*loc sg* **-sie**) *m* echo, reverberation
**pogłos|ka** (**-ki, -ki**) (*dat sg* **-ce**, *gen pl* **-ek**) *f* rumour (*Brit*), rumor (*US*)
**pogni|eść (-otę, -eciesz)** (*imp* **-ećć**) *vb perf od* **gnieść**
**pogo|da** (**-dy**) (*dat sg* **-dzie**) *f* weather; (*słoneczna pora*) sunny weather; **~ ducha** cheerfulness; **jaka jest ~?** what's the weather like?
**pogodny** *adj* bright; (*niebo*) clear
**pog|odzić (-odzę, -odzisz)** (*imp* **-ódź**) *vb perf od* **godzić**; **pogodzić się** *vr perf*: **~ się z kimś** to be reconciled with sb; **~ się z czymś** to reconcile o.s. to sth
**pogo|nić (-nię, -nisz)** (*imp* **-ń**) *vb perf od* **poganiać**
**pogo|ń** (**-ni, -nie**) (*gen pl* **-ni**) *f* (*pościg*) chase, pursuit; **~ za czymś** pursuit of sth; **ruszyć** (*perf*) **w ~ za kimś/czymś** to set off in pursuit of sb/sth
**pogorszeni|e** (**-a**) *nt* deterioration
**pogorsz|yć (-ę, -ysz)** *vb perf od* **pogarszać**
**pogotowi|e** (**-a**) *nt* (*stan gotowości*) alert; (*instytucja*) emergency service; (*karetka*) ambulance; **być w pogotowiu** to be on stand-by; **~ ratunkowe** ambulance service; **~ techniczne** public utilities emergency service; **górskie ~ ratunkowe** mountain rescue team; **mieć coś w pogotowiu** to have sth at the ready; **stan pogotowia** alert

P

**pogórz|e** (**-a, -a**) (*gen pl* **-y**) *nt* foothills *pl*
**pogranicz|e** (**-a, -a**) (*gen pl* **-y**) *nt* borderland
**pogratul|ować (-uję, -ujesz)** *vb perf od* **gratulować**
**pogrąż|ać (-am, -asz)** (*perf* **-yć**) *vt* (*w wodzie*) to sink; (*przen*: *w rozpaczy, ciemności*) to plunge; **to mnie pogrążyło** this finished me; **pogrążać się** *vr* (*w wodzie*) to sink; (*w myślach, pracy*) to be immersed; (*w rozpaczy, bólu*) to plunge
**pogro|m** (**-mu, -my**) (*loc sg* **-mie**) *m* (*książk*: *klęska*) rout; (*Żydów*) pogrom
**pogromc|a** (**-y, -y**) *m decl like f in sg* (*zwycięzca*) conqueror; (*treser*) tamer
**pogróż|ka** (**-ki, -ki**) (*dat sg* **-ce**, *gen pl* **-ek**) *f* threat
**pogry|źć (-zę, -ziesz)** (*imp* **-ź**) *vt perf* (*pokąsać*) to bite; (*rozdrobnić zębami*) to chew
**pogrze|b** (**-bu, -by**) (*loc sg* **-bie**) *m* funeral
**pogrzebacz** (**-a, -e**) (*gen pl* **-y**) *m* poker
**pogrzebowy** *adj* funeral *attr*; **dom** *lub* **zakład** ~ funeral parlour (*Brit*) *lub* home (*US*)
**pogwał|cać (-cam, -casz)** (*perf* **-cić**) *vt* to violate
**pogwałceni|e** (**-a**) *nt* breach, violation
**pogwał|cić (-cę, -cisz)** (*imp* **-ć**) *vb perf od* **pogwałcać**
**poham|ować (-uję, -ujesz)** *vt perf* to check, to repress; **pohamować się** *vr perf* to check o.s.
**po|ić (-ję, -isz)** (*imp* **pój**) *vt* (*dawać pić*) (*perf* **na-**) to water; (*pot*: *upijać*) (*perf* **s-**); ~ **kogoś** to ply sb with drink
**poinform|ować (-uję, -ujesz)** *vb perf od* **informować**
**poinformowany** *adj*: **dobrze/źle** ~ well-/ill-informed
**poinstru|ować (-uję, -ujesz)** *vb perf od* **instruować**
**poin|ta** (**-ty, -ty**) (*dat sg* **-cie**) *f patrz* **puenta**
**pointe|r** (**-ra, -ry**) (*loc sg* **-rze**) *m* pointer
**poiryt|ować (-uję, -ujesz)** *vb perf od* **irytować**
**poja|wiać się (-wiam, -wiasz)** (*perf* **-wić**) *vr* to appear
**poj|azd** (**-azdu, -azdy**) (*loc sg* **-eździe**) *m* vehicle; ~ **kosmiczny** spacecraft; ~ **mechaniczny** motor vehicle
**poj|ąć (-mę, -miesz)** (*imp* **-mij**) *vb perf od* **pojmować**
**poj|echać (-adę, -edziesz)** (*imp* **-edź**) *vi perf* to go
**pojedn|ać (-am, -asz)** *vb perf od* **pojednywać**
**pojedna|nie** (**-nia, -nia**) (*gen pl* **-ń**) *nt* reconciliation
**pojednawczy** *adj* conciliatory
**pojedn|ywać (-uję, -ujesz)** (*perf* **-ać**) *vt* to reconcile
**pojedynczo** *adv* singly, individually
**pojedynczy** *adj* single; (*jeden z wielu*) individual; **liczba pojedyncza** the singular; **gra pojedyncza** singles *pl*
**pojedyn|ek** (**-ku, -ki**) (*instr sg* **-kiem**) *m* duel
**pojedynkę** *inv*: **w** ~ by oneself, solo
**pojedynk|ować się (-uję, -ujesz)** *vr* to duel
**pojemni|k** (**-ka, -ki**) (*instr sg* **-kiem**) *m* container, receptacle; ~ **na śmieci** rubbish bin (*Brit*), trash *lub* garbage can (*US*)
**pojemnoś|ć** (**-ci**) *f* capacity; ~ **pamięci** (*Komput*) storage capacity; ~ **akumulatora** battery capacity; ~ **skokowa silnika** engine cubic capacity
**pojemny** *adj* capacious, voluminous
**poję|cie** (**-cia, -cia**) (*gen pl* **-ć**) *nt* concept; (*pot*) idea; **nie mieć (zielonego** *lub* **najmniejszego) pojęcia o czymś** not to have the foggiest *lub* faintest idea of sth; **to przechodzi ludzkie** ~ it's beyond belief
**pojętny** *adj* clever
**poj|mać (-mę, -miesz)** (*imp* **-mij**) *vt perf* (*książk*) to capture
**pojm|ować (-uję, -ujesz)** (*perf* **pojąć**) *vt* to comprehend, to grasp
**pojutrze** *adv* the day after tomorrow
**pokar|m** (**-mu, -my**) (*loc sg* **-mie**) *m* (*pożywienie*) food; (*mleko matki*) milk
**pokarmowy** *adj*: **treść pokarmowa** chyme; **zatrucie pokarmowe** food poisoning; **przewód** ~ alimentary canal
**poka|z** (**-zu, -zy**) (*loc sg* **-zie**) *m* demonstration; **robić coś na** ~ to do sth for show; ~ **mody/lotniczy** fashion/air show
**poka|zać (-żę, -żesz)** *vb perf od* **pokazywać**
**pokazowy** *adj* display *attr*; **lekcja pokazowa** object lesson
**pokaz|ywać (-uję, -ujesz)** (*perf* **-ać**) *vt* to show; **pokazać komuś język** to poke *lub* stick one's tongue out at sb; **pokazać komuś drzwi** to show sb the door; **nie ~ czegoś po sobie** not to show sth; **ja ci pokażę!** I'll teach you!; **pokazywać się** *vr* (*pojawiać się*) to turn up; **nie pokazał się** he didn't show up (*pot*); **pokazać się z najlepszej strony** to show one's best side
**pokaźny** *adj* sizeable
**pokątny** *adj* (*sprzedawca*) illegal; (*handel*) illicit; (*doradca, lekarz*) back-street *attr*
**poke|r** (**-ra**) (*loc sg* **-rze**) *m* poker
**pokier|ować (-uję, -ujesz)** *vb perf od* **kierować**
**pokiw|ać (-am, -asz)** *vb perf od* **kiwać**
**pokle|pać (-pię, -piesz)** *vb perf od* **poklepywać**
**poklep|ywać (-uję, -ujesz)** (*perf* **-ać**) *vt* to pat; **poklepać kogoś po plecach/ramieniu** to pat sb's back/shoulder

**pokła|d (-du, -dy)** *(loc sg* **-dzie***)* *m* *(na statku)* deck; *(warstwa)* layer; *(Geol)* bed, stratum; **na ~zie (statku/samolotu)** on board (a ship/a plane)

**pokład|ać (-am, -asz)** *vt:* **~ w kimś nadzieję** to put one's hopes in sb; **~ w kimś ufność** to place trust in sb; **pokładać się** *vr:* **~ się ze śmiechu** to double up with laughter

**pokło|n (-nu, -ny)** *(loc sg* **-nie***)* *m* *(książk)* bow

**pokłó|cić (-cę, -cisz)** *(imp* **-ć***)* *vt perf:* **~ kogoś z kimś** to turn sb against sb; **pokłócić się** *vr perf:* **~ się z kimś** to have a row *lub* quarrel with sb

**pokoch|ać (-am, -asz)** *vt perf* to come to love

**pokojowy** *adj* *(polityka)* peaceful; *(traktat)* peace *attr*; *(temperatura)* room *attr*; **malarz ~** painter

**pokojów|ka (-ki, -ki)** *(dat sg* **-ce**, *gen pl* **-ek***)* *f* (chamber)maid

**pokole|nie (-nia, -nia)** *(gen pl* **-ń***)* *nt* generation

**pokolor|ować (-uję, -ujesz)** *vb perf od* **kolorować**

**pokon|ać (-am, -asz)** *vb perf od* **pokonywać**

**pokonani|e (-a)** *nt:* **nie do pokonania** *(przeciwnik)* unbeatable; *(przeszkoda)* insurmountable, insuperable

**pokon|ywać (-uję, -ujesz)** *(perf* **-ać***)* *vt* *(wroga)* to defeat; *(rywali)* to beat; *(przen: strach, nieśmiałość)* to overcome; **~ odległość** to cover a distance

**poko|ra (-ry)** *(dat sg* **-rze***)* *f* humility

**pokornie** *adv* humbly

**pokorny** *adj* humble

**poko|st (-stu)** *(loc sg* **-ście***)* *m* varnish

**pok|ój (-oju)** *m* *(część mieszkania)* *(nom pl* **-oje**, *gen pl* **-oi** *lub* **-ojów***)* room; *(Pol, Wojsk)* peace; **~ gościnny** living room; **~ jadalny** dining room; **~ jednoosobowy/dwuosobowy** single/double room; **~ dziecinny** nursery; **~ nauczycielski** staff *lub* teachers' room; **~ z łazienką** room with en suite bathroom; **niech odpoczywa w pokoju** let him/her rest in peace

**pokraczny** *adj* clumsy

**pokrewieńst|wo (-wa)** *(loc sg* **-wie***)* *nt* *(między ludźmi)* kinship; *(przen: podobieństwo)* affinity; *(Bio, Zool)* affinity

**pokrewny** *adj* *(nauki, języki)* related; *(charaktery)* similar

**pokrę|cić (-cę, -cisz)** *(imp* **-ć***)* *vb perf od* **kręcić** ▷ *vt perf* *(pot: pogmatwać)* to muddle up; **~ głową** to shake one's head; **żeby cię pokręciło!** *(pot)* damn you! *(pot)*; **pokręcić się** *vr* *(pomieszać się)* to get mixed up; **coś mi się pokręciło** I've got it (all) wrong

**pokręt|ło (-ła, -ła)** *(loc sg* **-le**, *gen pl* **-eł***)* *nt* *(regulator)* dial; **~ siły głosu** volume control

**pokrętny** *adj* twisted

**pokr|oić (-oję, -oisz)** *(imp* **-ój***)* *vb perf od* **kroić**

**pokro|wiec (-wca, -wce)** *m* cover

**pokr|ój (-oju)** *m:* **ludzie tego pokroju** people of this sort; **ona jest tego samego pokroju** she is of the same character

**pokrótce** *adv* briefly

**pokrusz|yć (-ę, -ysz)** *vb perf od* **kruszyć**

**pokry|cie (-cia, -cia)** *(gen pl* **-ć***)* *nt:* **~ dachu** roofing; **~ ściany** facing; **czek bez pokrycia** dud cheque; **słowa/obietnice bez pokrycia** *(przen)* empty words/promises

**pokry|ć (-ję, -jesz)** *vb perf od* **pokrywać**

**pokry|wa (-wy, -wy)** *(loc sg* **-wie***)* *f* *(wieko)* lid; *(lodowa)* sheet; *(śnieżna)* layer

**pokryw|ać (-am, -asz)** *(perf* **pokryć***)* *vt* to cover; *(farbą)* to coat; *(fotel)* to upholster; **pokrywać się** *vr* *(powlekać się)* to become covered; *(być zbieżnym)* to agree; **teoria pokrywa się z faktami** the theory agrees with the facts

**pokryw|ka (-ki, -ki)** *(dat sg* **-ce**, *gen pl* **-ek***)* *f* lid

**pokrze|piać (-piam, -piasz)** *vt* *(wzmacniać)* to sustain; *(orzeźwiać)* to refresh; **~ kogoś na duchu** to lift *lub* raise sb's spirits

**pokrzy|wa (-wy, -wy)** *(loc sg* **-wie***)* *f* nettle

**pokrzywdz|ony (-onego, -eni)** *m decl like adj* sufferer

**pokrzyż|ować (-uję, -ujesz)** *vb perf od* **krzyżować**

**poku|sa (-sy, -sy)** *(dat sg* **-sie***)* *f* temptation

**poku|sić się (-szę, -sisz)** *(imp* **-ś***)* *vr perf:* **pokusić się o coś** to venture to do sth

**poku|ta (-ty, -ty)** *(dat sg* **-cie***)* *f* penance; **odprawiać (odprawić** *perf***) pokutę** to do penance

**pokut|ować (-uję, -ujesz)** *(perf* **od-***)* *vi:* **~ za coś** to pay for sth *(przen)*

**pokwitani|e (-a)** *nt* puberty

**pokwit|ować (-uję, -ujesz)** *vb perf od* **kwitować**

**pokwitowa|nie (-nia, -nia)** *(gen pl* **-ń***)* *nt* receipt

**pol|ać (-eję, -ejesz)** *vb perf od* **polewać**; **polać się** *vr perf* to flow; **polała się krew** *(książk)* there was bloodshed; **polały się łzy** tears flowed

**Pola|k (-ka, -cy)** *(instr sg* **-kiem***)* *m* Pole

**polakier|ować (-uję, -ujesz)** *vb perf od* **lakierować**

**pola|na (-ny, -ny)** *(dat sg* **-nie***)* *f* clearing

**pola|r (-ru, -ry)** *(loc sg* **-rze***)* *m* *(materiał, kurtka)* fleece

**polarny** *adj* polar; **zorza polarna** aurora; *(na biegunie północnym)* northern lights; *(na biegunie południowym)* southern lights; **Gwiazda Polarna** Pole Star

**polaryzacj|a** (**-i, -e**) (*gen pl* **-i**) *f* polarization
**pol|e** (**-a, -a**) (*gen pl* **pól**) *nt* field; (*Mat*) area; **~ naftowe** oilfield; **~ bramkowe/karne** goal/penalty field; **~ namiotowe** camping site (*Brit*), campsite (*Brit*), campground (*US*); **~ bitwy** battlefield; **~ widzenia** field of vision; **wywieść** (*perf*) **kogoś w ~** to hoodwink sb; **~ do popisu** room to display one's talents
**pole|c (-gnę, -gniesz)** (*imp* **-gnij**, *pt* **-gł**) *vi perf* (*książk*) to fall, to be killed
**pole|cać (-cam, -casz)** (*perf* **-cić**) *vt* (*rekomendować*) to recommend; (*kazać*) to command; (*powierzać*) to entrust; **~ coś komuś** to recommend sth to sb; **polecić komuś, żeby coś zrobił** to command sb to do sth
**polecający** *adj*: **list ~** letter of recommendation
**polece|nie** (**-nia, -nia**) (*gen pl* **-ń**) *nt* (*rozkaz*) command, order; (*rekomendacja*) recommendation; **z czyjegoś polecenia** on sb's recommendation
**pole|cić (-cę, -cisz)** (*imp* **-ć**) *vb perf od* **polecać**
**pole|cieć (-cę, -cisz)** (*imp* **-ć**) *vb perf od* **lecieć**
**polecony** *adj*: **list ~** registered letter, recorded delivery letter (*Brit*), certified letter (*US*); **przesyłka polecona** registered mail, recorded delivery (*Brit*), certified mail (*US*)
**poleg|ać (-am, -asz)** *vi*: **~ na** *+loc* (*ufać*) to depend on, to rely on; (*zasadzać się*) to consist in; **nie można na nim ~** he is unreliable; **różnica polega na tym, że ...** the difference lies in the fact that ...; **na czym to polega?** what does it consist in?
**poleg|ły** (**-łego, -li**) *m decl like adj* casualty
**polemi|ka** (**-ki, -ki**) (*dat sg* **-ce**) *f* polemic
**polemiz|ować (-uję, -ujesz)** *vi*: **~ z kimś** to argue with sb
**polepsz|ać (-am, -asz)** (*perf* **-yć**) *vt* to improve; **polepszać się** *vr* to improve; **polepszyło mu się** he is much better
**polepszeni|e** (**-a**) *nt* improvement
**poler|ować (-uję, -ujesz)** (*perf* **wy-**) *vt* to polish
**pole|wa** (**-wy, -wy**) (*dat sg* **-wie**) *f* (*glazura, szkliwo*) glaze; (*na cieście*) icing
**polewacz|ka** (**-ki, -ki**) (*dat sg* **-ce**, *gen pl* **-ek**) *f* (*samochód*) street-cleaning lorry (*Brit*) *lub* truck (*US*); (*konewka*) watering can, watering pot (*US*)
**polew|ać (-am, -asz)** (*perf* **polać**) *vt* to pour water on; (*emaliować*) to glaze
**polędwic|a** (**-y**) *f* loin; (*befsztyk*) sirloin (steak)
**policj|a** (**-i**) *f* police; **~ drogowa** traffic police; **tajna ~** secret police; **~ kryminalna** CID (*Brit*), FBI (*US*)
**policjan|t** (**-ta, -ci**) (*loc sg* **-cie**) *m* policeman, (police) officer
**policjant|ka** (**-ki, -ki**) (*dat sg* **-ce**, *gen pl* **-ek**) *f* policewoman, (police) officer
**policyjny** *adj* police *attr*; **godzina policyjna** curfew
**policzalny** *adj* countable
**policz|ek** (**-ka, -ki**) (*instr sg* **-kiem**) *m* (*część twarzy*) cheek; (*uderzenie*) slap on the cheek *lub* face; (*zniewaga*) slap in the face; **wymierzyć** (*perf*) **komuś ~** to give sb a slap on the cheek *lub* face
**policzk|ować (-uję, -ujesz)** (*perf* **s-**) *vt*: **s~** (*perf*) **kogoś** to slap sb across the face
**policzkowy** *adj*: **kość policzkowa** cheekbone
**policz|yć (-ę, -ysz)** *vb perf od* **liczyć** ▷ *vt perf*: **~ komuś 100 złotych (za coś)** to charge sb 100 zloty (for sth); **jego dni są policzone** his days are numbered; **policzyć się** *vr perf*: **~ się z kimś** to get even with sb
**poliest|er** (**-ru, -ry**) (*loc sg* **-rze**) *m* polyester
**polietyle|n** (**-nu**) *m* polythene
**poligami|a** (**-i**) *f* polygamy
**poliglo|ta** (**-ty, -ci**) (*dat sg* **-cie**) *m* polyglot
**poligo|n** (**-nu, -ny**) (*loc sg* **-nie**) *m* military training ground
**poligrafi|a** (**-i**) *f* printing
**Polinezj|a** (**-i**) *f* Polynesia
**polio** *nt inv* polio
**poli|p** (**-pa, -py**) (*loc sg* **-pie**) *m* polyp
**poli|sa** (**-sy, -sy**) (*dat sg* **-sie**) *f*: **~ ubezpieczeniowa** insurance policy
**polistyre|n** (**-nu**) (*loc sg* **-nie**) *m* polystyrene
**poliszynel** (**-a, -e**) (*gen pl* **-i** *lub* **-ów**) *m*: **tajemnica ~a** open secret
**politechni|ka** (**-ki, -ki**) (*dat sg* **-ce**) *f* polytechnic
**politologi|a** (**-i**) *f* political science
**politowani|e** (**-a**) *nt* disdain; **godny politowania** pitiable; **spojrzeć** (*perf*) **na kogoś z ~m** to give sb a pitying look
**politu|ra** (**-ry**) (*dat sg* **-rze**) *f* furniture polish
**polityczny** *adj* political
**polity|k** (**-ka, -cy**) (*instr sg* **-kiem**) *m* politician
**polity|ka** (**-ka**) (*dat sg* **-ce**) *f* politics; (*plan działania*) policy; **~ gospodarcza/zagraniczna** foreign/economic policy
**poliureta|n** (**-nu**) (*loc sg* **-nie**) *m* polyurethane
**poli|zać (-żę, -żesz)** *vt perf* to have a lick of
**pol|ka** (**-ki, -ki**) (*dat sg* **-ce**, *gen pl* **-ek**) *f* polka; **Polka** Pole, Polish woman
**polny** *adj*: **polne kwiaty** wild flowers; **konik ~** grasshopper; **polna droga** dirt road (*in the countryside*)
**polo** *nt inv* (*Sport*) polo; (*bluzka*) polo shirt
**polodowcowy** *adj* glacial
**polone|z** (**-za, -zy**) (*loc sg* **-zie**) *m* polonaise (*dance*)
**Poloni|a** (**-i**) *f* Polonia; **~ Amerykańska** Polish Americans *pl*

**polonijny** *adj*: **działacz/ośrodek ~** Polish community activist/centre (*Brit*) *lub* center (*US*)
**polonisty|ka (-ka, -ki)** (*dat sg* **-ce**) *f* (*dyscyplina*) Polish language and literature; (*wydział*) Polish Department *lub* Faculty
**polo|t (-tu)** (*loc sg* **-cie**) *m* imaginativeness; **bez ~u** unimaginative
**pol|ować (-uję, -ujesz)** *vi* to hunt; **~ na** *+acc* to hunt; (*pot: szukać*) to hunt for
**polowa|nie (-nia, -nia)** (*gen pl* **-ń**) *nt* hunt
**polowy** *adj*: **łóżko polowe** camp bed (*Brit*), cot (*US*); **mundur ~** battledress; **kuchnia polowa** soup kitchen
**Pols|ka (-ki)** (*dat sg* **-ce**) *f* Poland
**polski** *adj* Polish; **Rzeczpospolita Polska** the Republic of Poland
**polu|bić (-bię, -bisz)** *vt perf* to come to like, to take (a liking) to; **polubić się** *vr perf* to grow to like each other
**polubownie** *adv* out of court
**polubowny** *adj* arbitrational; **sąd ~** arbitration (court)
**poła|mać (-mię, -miesz)** *vb perf od* **łamać**
**poła|pać się (-pię, -piesz)** *vr perf* (*pot*) to catch on (*pot*); **nie móc się w czymś połapać** not to be able to make head or tail of sth
**połącze|nie (-nia, -nia)** (*gen pl* **-ń**) *nt* (*kolejowe, telefoniczne*) connection; (*zespół elementów*) combination; (*element łączący*) joint
**połącz|yć (-ę, -ysz)** *vb perf od* **łączyć** ▷ *vt perf*: **~ kogoś z kimś** (*Tel*) to put sb through to sb; **połączyć się** *vr perf*: **~ się z kimś** (*Tel*) to get through to sb
**połk|nąć (-nę, -niesz)** (*imp* **-nij**) *vb perf od* **połykać**
**poło|wa (-wy, -wy)** (*dat sg* **-wie**) *f* (*część*) half; (*środek*) middle; **do połowy pusty** half empty; **na połowę** in half; **o połowę więcej** half as much again; **o połowę mniej** half as much; **po połowie** fifty-fifty; **w połowie drogi** halfway, midway; **w połowie czerwca** in mid-June, in the middle of June; **za połowę ceny** half-price
**połowiczny** *adj*: **~ środek** half-measure; **~ sukces** qualified success; **okres połowicznego rozpadu** half-life
**położe|nie (-nia)** *nt* (*miejsce*) location; (*warunki*) position, situation
**położn|a (-ej, -e)** *f decl like adj* midwife
**położnict|wo (-wa)** (*loc sg* **-wie**) *nt* obstetrics
**położniczy** *adj*: **oddział/szpital ~** maternity *lub* obstetric ward/hospital
**położni|k (-ka, -cy)** (*instr sg* **-kiem**) *m* obstetrician
**położony** *adj*: **wieś położona jest nad rzeką** the village is situated on the river
**poł|ożyć (-ożę, -ożysz)** (*imp* **-óż**) *vb perf od* **kłaść**
**poł|óg (-ogu, -ogi)** (*instr sg* **-ogiem**) *m* puerperium
**poł|ów (-owu, -owy)** (*loc sg* **-owie**) *m* (*łowienie*) fishing; (*ryby*) catch
**połów|ka (-ki, -ki)** (*dat sg* **-ce**, *gen pl* **-ek**) *f* half; (*pot*) *a half litre bottle of vodka*
**południ|e (-a)** *nt* (*godzina dwunasta*) noon, midday; (*strona świata*) south; (*kraje południowe*) the South; **przed ~m** in the morning; **po południu** in the afternoon; **w ~** at noon *lub* midday; **na ~ od** *+gen* south of
**południ|k (-ka, -ki)** (*instr sg* **-kiem**) *m* meridian; **~ zerowy** Greenwich *lub* prime meridian
**południo|wiec (-wca, -wcy)** *m* southerner
**południowoamerykański** *adj* South American
**południowo-wschodni** *adj* south-east(ern)
**południowo-zachodni** *adj* south-west(ern)
**południowy** *adj* (*kraj, półkula, akcent*) southern; (*wiatr*) south, southerly; **przerwa południowa** midday break; **~ zachód** south-west; **~ wschód** south-east; **biegun ~** the South Pole; **Korea/Ameryka Południowa** South Korea/America; **południowa Polska** southern Poland
**połyk|ać (-am, -asz)** (*perf* **połknąć**) *vt* to swallow; (*pot: książkę, wiedzę*) to devour; **~ łzy** to gulp back one's tears
**połys|k (-ku)** (*instr sg* **-kiem**) *m* gloss; (*metalu*) lustre; **z ~iem** glossy
**połys|kiwać (-kuję, -kujesz)** *vi* to glisten; (*o słońcu*) to shine
**pomad|ka (-ki, -ki)** (*dat sg* **-ce**, *gen pl* **-ek**) *f*: **~ (do ust)** lipstick
**pomag|ać (-am, -asz)** (*perf* **pomóc**) *vi* to help; **~ komuś w czymś** to help sb with sth; **w czym mogę pomóc?** how can I help you?; **~ sobie rękami/nogami** to use one's hands/feet; **~ na kaszel/ból głowy** to relieve coughs/headaches; **płacz/krzyk nic nie pomoże** crying/shouting won't help (you)
**pomal|ować (-uję, -ujesz)** *vb perf od* **malować**
**pomału** *adv* slowly; **~!** slow down!
**pomarańcz|a (-y, -e)** (*gen pl* **-y**) *f* orange
**pomarańczowy** *adj* orange *attr*
**pomarszczony** *adj* wrinkled
**pomarszcz|yć (-ę, -ysz)** *vb perf od* **marszczyć**
**pomaturalny** *adj*: **szkoła pomaturalna** ≈ college
**pomawi|ać (-am, -asz)** (*perf* **pomówić**) *vt*: **~ kogoś o coś** to unjustly accuse sb of sth
**pomia|r (-ru, -ry)** (*loc sg* **-rze**) *m* measurement
**pomiat|ać (-am, -asz)** *vt*: **~ kimś** to push sb around

**pomido|r** (**-ra, -ry**) (*loc sg* **-rze**) *m* tomato
**pomidorowy** *adj* tomato *attr*
**pomiesz|ać (-am, -asz)** *vb perf od* **mieszać**; **pomieszać się** *vr perf*: **coś mi się pomieszało** I got mixed up
**pomieszcze|nie** (**-nia, -nia**) (*gen pl* **-ń**) *nt* room
**pomie|ścić (-szczę, -ścisz)** (*imp* **-ść**) *vb perf od* **mieścić**
**pomiędzy** *prep +instr* = **między**
**pomij|ać (-am, -asz)** (*perf* **pominąć**) *vt* (*opuszczać*) to omit; (*nie uwzględniać*) to pass over; **pominąć coś milczeniem** to pass over sth in silence; **pomijając** *lub* **pominąwszy X** excepting X, X excepted
**pomimo** *prep +gen* in spite of, despite; ~ **że** even though; ~ **to** *lub* **wszystko** all the same, nevertheless; *patrz też* **mimo**
**pomi|nąć (-nę, -niesz)** (*imp* **-ń**) *vb perf od* **pomijać**
**pomnaż|ać (-am, -asz)** (*perf* **pomnożyć**) *vt* (*majątek*) to amass; (*zbiory*) to build up
**pomniejsz|ać (-am, -asz)** (*perf* **-yć**) *vt* to diminish, to lessen; (*przen*) to diminish, to belittle
**pomni|k** (**-ka, -ki**) (*instr sg* **-kiem**) *m* monument
**pomn|ożyć (-ożę, -ożysz)** (*imp* **-óż**) *vb perf od* **pomnażać**; **mnożyć**
**pomoc** (**-y**) *f* (*pomaganie*) help, assistance; (*ratunek*) help, rescue; (*wsparcie*) aid; (*osoba*) (*nom pl* **-e**) help; (*Sport*) full(-)backs *pl*; **na ~!** help!; **przy ~y** *+gen* with the help *lub* aid of; **za ~ą** *+gen* by means of; ~ **drogowa** emergency road service; ~ **domowa** domestic (help); **pierwsza** ~ first aid; ~ **humanitarna** humanitarian aid; **~e dydaktyczne** *lub* **naukowe** teaching aids; **mieć kogoś do ~y** to have sb to help one; **przychodzić (przyjść** *perf*) **komuś z ~ą** to come to sb's aid
**pomocnic|a** (**-y, -e**) *f* helper
**pomocniczy** *adj* auxiliary
**pomocni|k** (**-ka, -cy**) (*instr sg* **-kiem**) *m* helper; (*Sport*) full(-)back
**pomocny** *adj* helpful; **podawać (podać** *perf*) **komuś pomocną dłoń** to give *lub* lend sb a helping hand
**pomocz|yć (-ę, -ysz)** *vt perf* to wet; **pomoczyć się** *vr perf* to get wet
**Pomorz|e** (**-a**) *nt* Pomerania (*region in north-western Poland*)
**pomo|st** (**-stu, -sty**) (*loc sg* **-ście**) *m* (*na jeziorze*) pier, jetty; (*w tramwaju*) platform
**pom|óc (-ogę, -ożesz)** (*imp* **-óż**) *vb perf od* **pomagać**
**pomó|wić (-wię, -wisz)** *vb perf od* **pomawiać** ▷ *vi perf* (*porozmawiać*) to talk
**pomówie|nie** (**-nia, -nia**) (*gen pl* **-ń**) *nt* slander; **mam z tobą do pomówienia** I've got to have a word with you
**pom|pa** (**-py**) (*dat sg* **-pie**) *f* (*urządzenie*) (*nom pl* **-py**) pump; (*wystawność*) pomp; ~ **paliwowa** fuel pump; **z pompą** in grand style
**pompatyczny** *adj* pompous
**pomp|ka** (**-ki, -ki**) (*dat sg* **-ce**, *gen pl* **-ek**) *f* pump; (*ćwiczenie*) press-up (*Brit*), push-up (*US*); ~ **rowerowa** bicycle pump
**pompo|n** (**-nu, -ny**) (*loc sg* **-nie**) *m* pompom
**pomp|ować (-uję, -ujesz)** (*perf* **na-**) *vt* to pump (up)
**pomst|ować (-uję, -ujesz)** *vi*: ~ **na** *+acc* to execrate
**pom|ścić (-szczę, -ścisz)** (*imp* **-ścij**) *vt perf* to avenge
**pomyj|e** (-) *pl* swill
**pomyl|ić (-ę, -isz)** *vb perf od* **mylić**; **coś mu się pomyliło** he must have got it wrong
**pomylony** *adj* (*pot*) crazy (*pot*), loony (*pot*)
**pomył|ka** (**-ki, -ki**) (*dat sg* **-ce**, *gen pl* **-ek**) *f* mistake; (*Tel*) wrong number; **przez pomyłkę** by mistake
**pomyłkowo** *adv* by mistake
**pomy|sł** (**-słu, -sły**) (*loc sg* **-śle**) *m* idea; **dobry ~!** (what a) good idea!; **wpaść** (*perf*) **na** ~ to hit (up)on an idea
**pomysłodawc|a** (**-y, -y**) (*loc sg* **-y**) *m decl like f* originator
**pomysłowoś|ć** (**-ci**) *f* ingenuity, inventiveness
**pomysłowy** *adj* (*rozwiązanie*) ingenious; (*człowiek*) inventive, ingenious
**pomyślany** *adj*: **dobrze/źle** ~ well/badly designed
**pomyśl|eć (-ę, -isz)** *vi perf*: ~ **o** *+instr* (*zastanowić się*) to think of *lub* about; (*zatroszczyć się*) to think of; **kto by pomyślał, że ...** who would have thought (that) ...
**pomyśleni|e** (**-a**) *nt*: **nie do pomyślenia** unthinkable
**pomyślnoś|ć** (**-ci**) *f* well-being; **życzyć komuś pomyślności** to wish sb luck
**pomyślny** *adj* (*początek, wróżba, znak*) auspicious, favourable (*Brit*), favorable (*US*); (*wiadomość*) good
**pomywacz** (**-a, -e**) (*gen pl* **-y**) *m* dishwasher (*person*)
**ponad** *prep +instr* (*dla oznaczenia miejsca*) above, over ▷ *prep +acc* (*dla oznaczenia kierunku*) over; (*więcej niż*) above, over; (*dłużej niż*) over; ~ **miarę** excessively; **być ~ czyjeś siły** to be beyond sb; ~ **wszystko** above all
**ponadczasowy** *adj* timeless
**ponaddźwiękowy** *adj* supersonic
**ponadpodstawowy** *adj* (*szkoła*) secondary (*Brit*), high (*US*); (*wykształcenie*) higher

**ponadprogramowy** *adj* (*Szkol*) extracurricular; (*ponadplanowy*) extra
**ponadto** *adv* (*książk*) further(more), moreover
**ponagl|ać (-am, -asz)** (*perf* **-ić**) *vt*: **~ kogoś** to hurry *lub* rush sb; **~ kogoś, żeby coś zrobił** to press sb to do sth
**ponagl|ić (-ę, -isz)** (*imp* **-ij**) *vb perf od* **ponaglać**
**ponawi|ać (-am, -asz)** (*perf* **ponowić**) *vt* to renew, to repeat
**poncz** (**-u, -e**) (*gen pl* **-ów**) *m* punch
**ponętny** *adj* alluring
**poniech|ać (-am, -asz)** *vt perf*: **~ czegoś** (*książk*) to abandon sth
**poniedział|ek** (**-ku, -ki**) (*instr sg* **-kiem**) *m* Monday; **lany ~** *Easter Monday, on which a custom in Poland is for people to sprinkle each other with water*
**poniedziałkowy** *adj* Monday *attr*
**poniekąd** *adv* in a way
**poni|eść (-osę, -esiesz)** (*imp* **-eś**, *pt* **-ósł, -osła, -eśli**) *vb perf od* **ponosić** ▷ *vt perf*: **~ śmierć** to meet one's death; **koń poniósł** the horse bolted
**ponieważ** *conj* because, since
**poniewier|ać (-am, -asz)** *vt*: **~ kimś** to treat sb badly; **poniewierać się** *vr* (*tułać się*) to knock about *lub* around; (*o rzeczach*) to lie about *lub* around
**poniż|ać (-am, -asz)** (*perf* **-yć**) *vt* to demean, to put down (*pot*); **poniżać się** *vr* to demean o.s.
**poniżej** *prep +gen* (*niżej niż*) below, beneath; (*mniej niż*) below, under ▷ *adv* (*w tekście*) below; **pięć stopni ~ zera** five degrees below zero *lub* freezing; **cios ~ pasa** a low blow; **~ krytyki** beneath criticism
**poniżeni|e** (**-a**) *nt* humiliation
**poniższy** *adj*: **poniższe uwagi** the following remarks
**poniż|yć (-ę, -ysz)** *vb perf od* **poniżać**
**pono|sić (-szę, -sisz)** (*imp* **-ś**, *perf* **ponieść**) *vt* (*odpowiedzialność, koszty*) to bear; (*ryzyko, stratę*) to incur; (*porażkę*) to suffer; **poniosło go** he got carried away; **iść, gdzie oczy poniosą** to wander aimlessly
**pon|owić (-owię, -owisz)** (*imp* **-ów**) *vb perf od* **ponawiać**
**ponownie** *adv* again
**ponowny** *adj* renewed, repeated
**ponto|n** (**-nu, -ny**) (*loc sg* **-nie**) *m* pontoon
**pontyfika|t** (**-tu, -ty**) (*loc sg* **-cie**) *m* pontificate
**ponumer|ować (-uję, -ujesz)** *vb perf od* **numerować**
**ponury** *adj* (*osoba, wiadomość*) gloomy; (*wygląd*) bleak; (*miejsce*) bleak, dreary; (*myśli*) dismal
**pończo|cha** (**-chy, -chy**) (*dat sg* **-sze**) *f* stocking
**poobiedni** *adj* after-dinner *attr*
**pooperacyjny** *adj*: **opieka pooperacyjna** postoperative care
**po|p** (**-pa, -pi**) (*loc sg* **-pie**) *m* pope (*parish priest in the Orthodox Church*)
**popad|ać (-am, -asz)** (*perf* **popaść**) *vi*: **~ w długi** to fall into debt; **~ w nędzę/ruinę/niełaskę** to fall into poverty/disrepair/disgrace
**popamięt|ać (-am, -asz)** *vt perf*: **jeszcze mnie popamiętasz!** I'll show you!
**poparci|e** (**-a**) *nt* support, backing; **udzielać (udzielić** *perf*) **komuś poparcia** to give sb (one's) support
**poparze|nie** (**-nia, -nia**) (*gen pl* **-ń**) *nt* burn
**poparz|yć (-ę, -ysz)** *vt perf* to burn; **poparzyć się** *vr perf* to burn o.s.
**popa|ść (-dnę, -dniesz)** (*imp* **-dnij**) *vb perf od* **popadać**; **gdzie/jak popadnie** just anywhere/anyhow
**popatrz|eć, popatrz|yć (-ę, -ysz)** *vb perf* to look; **popatrz!** look!
**popch|nąć (-nę, -niesz)** (*imp* **-nij**) *vb perf od* **popychać**
**popeli|na** (**-ny, -ny**) (*dat sg* **-nie**) *f* poplin
**popeł|niać (-niam, -niasz)** (*perf* **-nić**) *vt* (*grzech, przestępstwo*) to commit; (*błąd, nietakt*) to make; **popełnić samobójstwo** to commit suicide
**popeł|nić (-nię, -nisz)** (*imp* **-nij**) *vb perf od* **popełniać**
**popę|d** (**-du, -dy**) (*loc sg* **-dzie**) *m*: **~ płciowy** sex(ual) drive
**popędliwoś|ć** (**-ci**) *f* impetuosity
**popędliwy** *adj* impetuous, short-tempered
**popę|dzać (-dzam, -dzasz)** (*perf* **-dzić**) *vt* to rush, to hurry
**popę|dzić (-dzę, -dzisz)** (*imp* **-dź**) *vb perf od* **popędzać** ▷ *vi perf* to rush *lub* dash (off), to run
**popi|ć (-ję, -jesz)** *vb perf od* **popijać** ▷ *vt perf*: **~ wody/mleka** to take a sip of water/milk ▷ *vi perf*: **on lubi ~** he likes a drink
**popielaty** *adj* grey, gray (US)
**popielcowy** *adj*: **środa popielcowa** Ash Wednesday
**Popiel|ec** (**-ca**) *m* Ash Wednesday
**popielnicz|ka** (**-ki, -ki**) (*dat sg* **-ce**, *gen pl* **-ek**) *f* ashtray
**popier|ać (-am, -asz)** (*perf* **poprzeć**) *vt* to support, to back up; (*wniosek*) to second; (*prośbę: ustnie*) to back; (*: na piśmie*) to support
**popier|sie** (**-sia, -sia**) (*gen pl* **-si**) *nt* bust
**popij|ać (-am, -asz)** *vt* (*pić wolno*) to sip; (*jedzenie, tabletkę*) (*perf* **popić**) to wash down ▷ *vi* (*upijać się*) to booze
**popiln|ować (-uję, -ujesz)** *vb perf od* **pilnować**

**popi|ół** (**-ołu, -oły**) (*loc sg* **-ele**) *m* ash; **popioły** *pl* ashes *pl*

**popi|s** (**-su, -sy**) (*loc sg* **-sie**) *m* show; **mieć pole do ~u** to have an ideal setting in which to demonstrate one's skills

**popi|sać się (-szę, -szesz)** *vb perf od* **popisywać się**

**popisowy** *adj* spectacular

**popis|ywać się (-uję, -ujesz)** (*perf* **-ać**) *vr* to show off; **popisywać się odwagą/talentem** to show off one's courage/talent

**popiw|ek** (**-ku**) (*instr sg* **-kiem**) *m* (*Ekon*) *remuneration increase tax*

**popla|mić (-mię, -misz)** *vb perf od* **plamić**

**poplą|tać (-czę, -czesz)** *vb perf od* **plątać**

**popleczni|k** (**-ka, -cy**) (*instr sg* **-kiem**) *m* partisan, henchman

**popłac|ać (-a)** *vi* to pay

**popłatny** *adj* (*zawód, zajęcie*) well-paid; (*interes*) profitable

**popłoch** (**-u**) *m* panic; **wpaść** (*perf*) **w ~** to panic

**popły|nąć (-nę, -niesz)** (*imp* **-ń**) *vi perf* (*o wodzie, łzach*) (to begin) to flow; (*o statku*) to sail away; (*o pływaku*) to swim away

**popływ|ać (-am, -asz)** *vi perf* to have a swim; **chodźmy ~** let's go for a swim

**popojutrze** *adv* in three days' time

**popołudni|e** (**-a, -a**) *nt* afternoon

**popołudniowy** *adj* afternoon *attr*

**popołudniów|ka** (**-ki, -ki**) (*dat sg* **-ce**, *gen pl* **-ek**) *f* (*gazeta*) evening paper; (*Teatr*) matinée

**popra|wa** (**-wy, -wy**) (*dat sg* **-wie**) *f* improvement

**poprawcza|k** (**-ka, -ki**) (*instr sg* **-kiem**) *m* (*pot*) borstal (Brit), reformatory (US)

**poprawczy** *adj*: **dom ~** borstal (Brit), reformatory (US)

**popra|wiać (-wiam, -wiasz)** (*perf* **-wić**) *vt* (*strój, krawat*) to adjust, to straighten; (*wynik, rekord*) to better, to improve (up)on; (*błąd, rozmówcę*) to correct; **poprawiać się** *vr* (*polepszać się*) to improve; (*wyrażać się inaczej*) to correct o.s.; (*siadać wygodniej*) to settle o.s.; (*o człowieku: zmieniać się na lepsze*) to reform, to mend one's ways

**popraw|ka** (**-ki, -ki**) (*dat sg* **-ce**, *gen pl* **-ek**) *f* correction; (*do konstytucji*) amendment; (*pot: egzamin*) repeat exam; **brać (wziąć** *perf***) poprawkę na** *+acc* to make allowances for

**poprawkowy** *adj*: **egzamin ~** repeat *lub* resit examination

**poprawnie** *adv* correctly

**poprawnoś|ć** (**-ci**) *f* correctness

**poprawny** *adj* (*odpowiedź*) correct; (*maniery*) proper

**popręg|g** (**-gu, -gi**) (*instr sg* **-giem**) *m* girth

**popromienny** *adj*: **choroba popromienna** radiation sickness

**popro|sić (-szę, -sisz)** (*imp* **-ś**) *vb perf od* **prosić**

**poprzecz|ka** (**-ki, -ki**) (*dat sg* **-ce**, *gen pl* **-ek**) *f* (*belka*) crossbeam; (*Sport*) crossbar

**poprzeczny** *adj* (running) crosswise, cross *attr*; (*Tech*) transverse

**pop|rzeć (-rę, -rzesz)** (*imp* **-rzyj**) *vb perf od* **popierać**

**poprzedni** *adj* (*dyrektor, małżeństwo*) previous; (*rozdział, miesiąc*) preceding, previous

**poprzednicz|ka** (**-ki, -ki**) (*dat sg* **-ce**, *gen pl* **-ek**) *f* predecessor

**poprzedni|k** (**-ka, -cy**) (*instr sg* **-kiem**) *m* predecessor

**poprzednio** *adv* previously, before

**poprze|dzać (-dzam, -dzasz)** (*perf* **-dzić**) *vt* to precede

**poprzedzający** *adj*: **~ (coś)** preceding (sth)

**poprze|dzić (-dzę, -dzisz)** (*imp* **-dź**) *vb perf od* **poprzedzać**

**poprzek**; **w ~** *adv* crosswise

**poprzesta|ć (-nę, -niesz)** (*imp* **-ń**) *vb perf od* **poprzestawać**

**poprzest|awać (-aję, -ajesz)** (*perf* **-ać**) *vi*: **~ na czymś** to confine *lub* limit o.s. to sth

**poprzez** *prep +acc* through; *patrz też* **przez**

**popsu|ć (-ję, -jesz)** *vb perf od* **psuć**; **popsuć się** *vr* (*o samochodzie itp.*) to break down; (*o pogodzie, atmosferze*) to deteriorate

**populacj|a** (**-i, -e**) (*gen pl* **-i**) *f* population

**popularnonaukowy** *adj* popular science *attr*

**popularnoś|ć** (**-ci**) *f* popularity; **cieszyć się popularnością wśród** *+gen* to be popular with

**popularny** *adj* popular

**popularyzacj|a** (**-i**) *f* popularization

**popularyz|ować (-uję, -ujesz)** (*perf* **s-**) *vt* to popularize

**populiz|m** (**-mu**) (*loc sg* **-mie**) *m* populism

**popuszcz|ać (-am, -asz)** (*perf* **popuścić**) *vt* to loosen; **nie popuszczę mu** (*pot*) I won't let him get away with it

**popu|ścić (-szczę, -ścisz)** (*imp* **-ść**) *vb perf od* **popuszczać**

**popych|ać (-am, -asz)** (*perf* **popchnąć**) *vt* to push, to shove; **~ kogoś do czegoś** (*przen*) to push sb into sth; *patrz też* **pchać**

**popychad|ło** (**-ła, -ła**) (*loc sg* **-le**, *gen pl* **-eł**) *nt* (*pot*) doormat (*przen*)

**popy|t** (**-tu**) (*loc sg* **-cie**) *m* (*Handel*) demand; **~ na coś** demand for sth; **cieszyć się ~em** to be in (great) demand

**po|r** (**-ra, -ry**) (*loc sg* **-rze**) *m* (*Anat, Bio*) (*gen sg also* **-ru**) pore; (*Bot, Kulin*) leek

**por.** *abbr* (= *porucznik*) Lt, Lieut (= *lieutenant*); (= *porównaj*) cf. (= *confer (compare)*)

**po|ra** (**-ry, -ry**) (*dat sg* **-rze**, *gen pl* **pór**) *f* (*okres, właściwy moment*) time; **~ roku** season; **~ deszczowa** rainy season; **do tej pory** until now, so far; **nie ~ (teraz) na** *+acc* this is no time for; **o każdej porze (dnia i nocy)** any time (night or day); **od tej pory** from now on; **w porze obiadu/kolacji** at lunchtime/ dinnertime; **w (samą) porę** (just) in time, in the nick of time; **wizyta/uwaga nie w porę** an untimely *lub* ill-timed visit/remark

**porabi|ać (-am, -asz)** *vi*: **co porabiasz?** what are you up to (these days)?

**porachun|ki** (**-ków**) *pl*: **mieć z kimś ~** to have a bone to pick with sb; **załatwiać (załatwić** *perf***) (z kimś) ~** to settle a(n old) score (with sb)

**pora|da** (**-dy, -dy**) (*dat sg* **-dzie**) *f* (piece of) advice; **~ lekarska/prawna** medical/legal advice; **za czyjąś poradą** on sb's advice; **udzielać (udzielić** *perf***) komuś porady** to give sb counsel *lub* advice; **zasięgać (zasięgnąć** *perf***) czyjejś porady** to seek sb's advice

**porad|nia** (**-ni, -nie**) (*gen pl* **-ni**) *f*: **~ lekarska** out-patient clinic; **~ małżeńska** marriage guidance service; **~ zawodowa** vocational guidance service

**poradnict|wo** (**-wa**) (*loc sg* **-wie**) *nt* guidance, counselling (*Brit*), counseling (*US*)

**poradni|k** (**-ka, -ki**) (*instr sg* **-kiem**) *m* guide, handbook

**pora|dzić (-dzę, -dzisz)** (*imp* **-dź**) *vb perf od* **radzić** ▷ *vi perf*: **~ sobie z czymś** to manage sth; **nic na to nie poradzę** I cannot help it

**poran|ek** (**-ka, -ki**) (*instr sg* **-kiem**) *m* morning

**poranny** *adj* morning *attr*

**porast|ać (-a)** (*perf* **porosnąć**) *vt* (*o roślinności*) to overgrow

**pora|zić (-żę, -zisz)** (*imp* **-ź**) *vb perf od* **porażać**

**poraż|ać (-am, -asz)** (*perf* **porazić**) *vt* (*o truciźnie*) to paralyse (*Brit*), to paralyze (*US*); (*o prądzie*) to give a shock; (*o blasku*) to dazzle

**poraże|nie** (**-nia, -nia**) (*gen pl* **-ń**) *nt* (*prądem*) electric shock; (*Med*) paralysis; **~ słoneczne** sunstroke; **~ mózgowe** cerebral palsy

**poraż|ka** (**-ki, -ki**) (*dat sg* **-ce**, *gen pl* **-ek**) *f* (*przegrana bitwa*) defeat; (*niepowodzenie*) failure; **ponieść** (*perf*) **porażkę** *lub* **doznać** (*perf*) **porażki** to be defeated, to suffer defeat

**porą|bać (-bię, -biesz)** *vb perf od* **rąbać**

**porcela|na** (**-ny**) (*dat sg* **-nie**) *f* china, porcelain

**porcelanowy** *adj* china *attr*, porcelain *attr*

**porcj|a** (**-i, -e**) (*gen pl* **-i**) *f* portion, helping; (*dawka*) dose

**poręcz** (**-y, -e**) (*gen pl* **-y**) *f* (*schodów*) banister, handrail; (*fotela*) arm; (*na balkonie*) railing, balustrade; **poręcze** *pl* (*Sport*) parallel bars *pl*

**poręcz|ać (-am, -asz)** (*perf* **-yć**) *vt* (*weksel, kwit*) to guarantee, to underwrite ▷ *vi*: **~ za kogoś** to vouch for sb

**poręcze|nie** (**-nia, -nia**) (*gen pl* **-ń**) *nt* guarantee

**poręczny** *adj* handy

**poręczyciel** (**-a, -e**) (*gen pl* **-i**) *m* guarantor

**poręcz|yć (-ę, -ysz)** *vb perf od* **poręczać**

**porno** *adj inv* (*pot*): **film/czasopismo ~** porn(ographic) movie/magazine

**pornografi|a** (**-i**) *f* pornography

**pornograficzny** *adj* pornographic

**porodowy** *adj*: **bóle porodowe** labour (*Brit*) *lub* labor (*US*) pains; **sala porodowa** delivery room

**poro|nić (-nię, -nisz)** (*imp* **-ń**) *vi perf* to miscarry

**poronie|nie** (**-nia, -nia**) (*gen pl* **-ń**) *nt* miscarriage; (*sztuczne*) abortion

**poroniony** *adj* (*pot*: *pomysł*) silly, foolish

**poro|snąć (-snę, -śniesz)** (*imp* **-śnij**) *vb perf od* **porastać**

**poro|st** (**-stu, -sty**) (*loc sg* **-ście**) *m* (*wzrost*) growth; (*Bot*) lichen

**porowaty** *adj* porous

**porozmawi|ać (-am, -asz)** (*imp* **-aj**) *vi perf*: **~ (z kimś o czymś)** to talk *lub* speak (to sb about *lub* of sth)

**porozu|mieć się (-miem, -miesz)** (*imp* **-miej** *lub* **-m**) *vb perf od* **porozumiewać się**

**porozumie|nie** (**-nia, -nia**) (*gen pl* **-ń**) *nt* agreement; **w porozumieniu z kimś** in consultation with sb; **dojść** (*perf*) **(z kimś) do porozumienia** to reach an agreement *lub* understanding (with sb)

**porozumiew|ać się (-am, -asz)** (*perf* **porozumieć**) *vr* (*komunikować się*) to communicate; (*dogadywać się*) to come to *lub* reach an agreement

**porozumiewawczy** *adj* (*spojrzenie*) knowing

**por|ód** (**-odu, -ody**) (*loc sg* **-odzie**) *m* (child) birth, delivery

**porówn|ać (-am, -asz)** *vb perf od* **porównywać**

**porówna|nie** (**-nia, -nia**) (*gen pl* **-ń**) *nt* comparison; (*Lit*) simile; **w porównaniu z** *+instr* in comparison with *lub* to, compared with *lub* to; **bez porównania lepszy/ ładniejszy** better/prettier by far

**porównawczy** *adj* comparative

**porówn|ywać (-uję, -ujesz)** (*perf* **-ać**) *vt* to compare; **~ kogoś/coś z** *+instr* to compare sb/ sth with *lub* to

**porównywalny** *adj* comparable

**poróż|nić (-nię, -nisz)** (*imp* **-nij**) *vt perf*: **~ kogoś z kimś** to set *lub* turn sb against sb else; **poróżnić się** *vr*: **~ się z kimś** to fall out with sb

P

**por|t (-tu, -ty)** (*loc sg* **-cie**) *m* port, harbour (*Brit*), harbor (*US*); **~ lotniczy** airport
**portal (-u, -e)** (*gen pl* **-i**) *m* (*Archit*) portal
**porte|r (-ra, -ry)** (*loc sg* **-rze**) *m* (*piwo*) porter
**portfel (-a, -e)** (*gen pl* **-i**) *m* wallet, billfold (*US*); (*Ekon*) portfolio
**portie|r (-ra, -rzy)** (*loc sg* **-rze**) *m* (*odźwierny*) porter, doorman; (*recepcjonista*) receptionist
**portier|nia (-ni, -nie)** (*gen pl* **-ni**) *f* porter's lodge, reception desk
**port|ki (-ek)** *pl* (*pot*) trousers (*Brit*), pants (*US*); **trząść portkami** (*pot*) to be scared stiff
**portmonet|ka (-ki, -ki)** (*dat sg* **-ce**, *gen pl* **-ek**) *f* purse
**por|to (-ta)** (*loc sg* **-cie**) *nt* (*wino*) port
**portow|iec (-ca, -cy)** *m* docker
**portowy** *adj* (*urządzenia, robotnik*) dock *attr*; (*miasto*) port *attr*
**portre|t (-tu, -ty)** (*loc sg* **-cie**) *m* portrait; **~ pamięciowy** identikit (picture) (*Brit*), composite sketch (*US*)
**portret|ować (-uję, -ujesz)** (*perf* **s-**) *vt* to paint a portrait of; (*przen*) to portray
**Portugalczy|k (-ka, -cy)** (*instr sg* **-kiem**) *m* Portuguese
**Portugali|a (-i)** *f* Portugal
**Portugal|ka (-ki, -ki)** (*dat sg* **-ce**, *gen pl* **-ek**) *f* Portuguese
**portugalski** *adj* Portuguese
**porty|k (-ku, -ki)** (*instr sg* **-kiem**) *m* portico
**poruczni|k (-ka, -cy)** (*instr sg* **-kiem**) *m* lieutenant (*Brit*), (1st) lieutenant (*US*)
**porusz|ać (-am, -asz)** (*perf* **-yć**) *vt*: **~ czymś** to move sth; **~ coś** (*omawiać*) to bring sth up, to touch (up)on sth; (*napędzać*) to drive *lub* propel sth; **~ kogoś** to move sb; **poruszyć niebo i ziemię** to move heaven and earth; **poruszyć kogoś do żywego** to cut *lub* sting sb to the quick; **poruszać się** *vr* to move; **nie ~ się** to keep still, to be motionless; **~ się w czymś łatwo** *lub* **swobodnie** (*przen*) to be *lub* feel at home in sth
**poruszeni|e (-a)** *nt* (*wzburzenie*) agitation; (*zamieszanie*) commotion, stir
**poruszony** *adj* (*wzburzony*) agitated; (*wzruszony*) touched, moved
**porusz|yć (-ę, -ysz)** *vb perf od* **poruszać**
**por|wać (-wę, -wiesz)** (*imp* **-wij**) *vb perf od* **porywać** ▷ *vt perf* (*podrzeć*) to tear up
**porwa|nie (-nia, -nia)** (*gen pl* **-ń**) *nt* (*człowieka*) abduction, kidnapping; (*samolotu itp.*) hijacking
**pory|w (-wu, -wy)** (*loc sg* **-wie**) *m* (*wiatru*) gust; (*nagłe uczucie*) outburst, flush
**porywacz (-a, -e)** (*gen pl* **-y**) *m* (*ludzi*) kidnapper; (*samolotu*) hijacker
**poryw|ać (-am, -asz)** (*perf* **porwać**) *vt* (*człowieka*) to abduct, to kidnap; (*samolot itp.*) to hijack; (*o wietrze*) to sweep away; (*przen*) to carry away; **porywać się** *vr*: **~ się na kogoś** to make an attempt on sb's life; **~ się na coś** to attempt sth; **~ się z motyką na słońce** (*pot*) to go on a wild-goose chase
**porywający** *adj* rousing, inspiring
**porywczoś|ć (-ci)** *f* quick temper, impetuosity
**porywczy** *adj* impetuous, quick- *lub* hot-tempered
**porywisty** *adj* (*wiatr*) gusty
**porząd|ek (-ku, -ki)** (*instr sg* **-kiem**) *m* order; **w porządku!** all right!; **doprowadzać (doprowadzić** *perf***) coś do porządku** to put sth in order, to clean *lub* tidy sth up; **~ dzienny/obrad** the agenda; (*Pol*) the order of the day; **być na porządku dziennym** to be the order of the day; **~ prawny/publiczny** legal/public order; **przechodzić (przejść** *perf***) nad czymś do porządku (dziennego)** to wave sth aside; **porządki** *pl* (*sprzątanie*) cleaning
**porządk|ować (-uję, -ujesz)** (*perf* **u-**) *vt* (*układać*) to order; (*sprzątać*) to clean, to tidy
**porządkowy** *adj* (*liczebnik*) ordinal; (*numer*) serial
**porządnie** *adv* (*starannie*) neatly; (*przyzwoicie*) decently; (*pot: mocno*) properly
**porządny** *adj* (*lubiący porządek*) tidy; (*obywatel*) respectable; (*mróz*) severe; (*pot: ulewa*) heavy; (*: posiłek*) square, decent
**porzecz|ka (-ki, -ki)** (*dat sg* **-ce**, *gen pl* **-ek**) *f* currant; **czarna ~** blackcurrant; **czerwona ~** redcurrant
**porzu|cać (-cam, -casz)** (*perf* **-cić**) *vt* (*kraj, dzieci*) to abandon, to leave; (*pracę, naukę*) to quit; **porzucić szkołę** to drop out of school
**porzu|cić (-cę, -cisz)** (*imp* **-ć**) *vb perf od* **porzucać**
**pos.** *abbr* (= *poseł*) MP (Brit) (= *Member of Parliament*), Rep. (US) (= *Representative*)
**posa|da (-dy, -dy)** (*dat sg* **-dzie**) *f* job, situation; **wolna ~** vacancy
**posa|dzić (-dzę, -dzisz)** (*imp* **-dź**) *vb perf od* **sadzać; sadzić**
**posadz|ka (-ki, -ki)** (*dat sg* **-ce**, *gen pl* **-ek**) *f* floor
**posa|g (-gu, -gi)** (*instr sg* **-giem**) *m* dowry
**posą|dzać (-dzam, -dzasz)** (*perf* **-dzić**) *vt*: **~ kogoś (o coś)** to suspect sb (of sth)
**posą|dzić (-dzę, -dzisz)** (*imp* **-dź**) *vb perf od* **posądzać**
**posą|g (-gu, -gi)** (*instr sg* **-giem**) *m* statue
**posegreg|ować (-uję, -ujesz)** *vb perf od* **segregować**
**poselski** *adj* parliamentary
**poselst|wo (-wa, -wa)** (*loc sg* **-wie**) *nt* (*przedstawicielstwo*) legation; (*wysłannicy*) mission

**po|seł** (**-sła, -słowie**) (*loc sg* **-śle**) *m* (*członek parlamentu*) ≈ Member of Parliament (*Brit*), ≈ Representative (*US*); (*wysłannik*) envoy
**posesj|a** (**-i, -e**) (*gen pl* **-i**) *f* property
**posępny** *adj* (*człowiek, nastrój*) gloomy, sombre (*Brit*), somber (*US*); (*krajobraz*) bleak, forbidding
**posiadacz** (**-a, -e**) (*gen pl* **-y**) *m* owner
**posiad|ać** (**-am, -asz**) *vt* (*majątek*) to own; (*właściwości, umiejętności*) to possess; **posiadać się** *vr*: **nie ~ się z radości/ze złości** to be beside o.s. with joy/rage
**posiadani|e** (**-a**) *nt* possession, ownership; **brać (wziąć** *perf*) **coś w ~** to take possession of sth; **być w posiadaniu czegoś** to be in possession of sth
**posiadłoś|ć** (**-ci, -ci**) (*gen pl* **-ci**) *f* estate, property
**posią|ść** (**-dę, -dziesz**) (*imp* **-dź**) *vt perf* (*znajomość języka, wiedzę*) to acquire
**posiedze|nie** (**-nia, -nia**) (*gen pl* **-ń**) *nt* sitting, session; **za jednym ~m** at one sitting
**posił|ek** (**-ku, -ki**) (*instr sg* **-kiem**) *m* meal; **posiłki** *pl* reinforcements *pl*
**posiłkowy** *adj*: **czasownik ~** auxiliary verb
**poską|pić** (**-pię, -pisz**) *vb perf od* **skąpić**
**poskrami|ać** (**-am, -asz**) (*perf* **poskromić**) *vt* (*gniew*) to curb; (*namiętność, ciekawość*) to restrain; (*zwierzęta*) to tame
**po|słać**[1] (**-ślę, -ślesz**) (*imp* **-ślij**) *vb perf od* **posyłać**
**po|słać**[2] (**-ścielę, -ścielisz**) *vb perf od* **słać**
**posła|nie** (**-nia, -nia**) (*gen pl* **-ń**) *nt* (*legowisko*) bedding; (*pismo*) message
**posła|niec** (**-ńca, -ńcy**) *m* messenger
**posłan|ka** (**-ki, -ki**) (*dat sg* **-ce**, *gen pl* **-ek**) *f* ≈ Member of Parliament (*Brit*), ≈ Representative (*US*)
**posłannict|wo** (**-wa, -wa**) (*loc sg* **-wie**) *nt* mission
**posł|odzić** (**-odzę, -odzisz**) (*imp* **-odź** *lub* **-ódź**) *vb perf od* **słodzić**
**posło|wie** (**-wia, -wia**) (*gen pl* **-wi**) *nt* afterword
**posłuch|ać** (**-am, -asz**) *vb perf od* **słuchać**
**posłu|giwać się** (**-guję, -gujesz**) (*perf* **posłużyć**) *vr*: **posługiwać się czymś/kimś** to use sth/sb
**posłuszeńst|wo** (**-wa**) (*loc sg* **-wie**) *nt* obedience; **nogi odmawiają mi posłuszeństwa** my feet are killing me; **silnik odmówił posłuszeństwa** the engine wouldn't work
**posłusznie** *adv* obediently
**posłuszny** *adj* obedient; **być ~m komuś/ rozkazowi** to obey sb/an order
**posłuż|yć** (**-ę, -ysz**) *vb perf od* **posługiwać** ▷ *vi perf*: **~ komuś** (*o wypoczynku itp.*) to do sb good; **~ (komuś) za/jako coś** to serve (sb) for/as sth
**posma|k** (**-ku**) (*instr sg* **-kiem**) *m* aftertaste
**posmar|ować** (**-uję, -ujesz**) *vb perf od* **smarować**
**posmutni|eć** (**-eję, -ejesz**) *vi perf* to become sad
**pos|olić** (**-olę, -olisz**) (*imp* **-ól**) *vb perf od* **solić**
**posort|ować** (**-uję, -ujesz**) *vb perf od* **sortować**
**pospieszny** *itd. patrz* **pośpieszny** *itd.*
**pospolity** *adj* common; **rzeczownik ~** common noun
**posprząt|ać** (**-am, -asz**) *vb perf od* **sprzątać**
**posprzecz|ać się** (**-am, -asz**) *vr perf*: **posprzeczać się (z kimś) (o coś)** to have a tiff (with sb) (over sth)
**posrebrzany** *adj* silver-plated
**po|st** (**-stu, -sty**) (*loc sg* **-ście**) *m* fast; **wielki ~** Lent
**posta|ć** (**-ci, -cie** *lub* **-ci**) (*gen pl* **-ci**) *m* (*forma*) form; (*sylwetka, osoba*) figure; (*w utworze literackim*) character; **w postaci czegoś** in the form of sth; **to zmienia ~ rzeczy** that puts a different complexion on things
**postanawi|ać** (**-am, -asz**) (*perf* **postanowić**) *vt* to decide on ▷ *vi* to decide; **postanowić coś zrobić** to decide to do *lub* on doing sth; **postanowić czegoś nie robić** to decide against doing sth; **postanowić, że ...** to decide that ...; (*Prawo*) to rule that ...
**postan|owić** (**-owię, -owisz**) (*imp* **-ów**) *vb perf od* **postanawiać**
**postanowie|nie** (**-nia, -nia**) (*gen pl* **-ń**) *nt* (*decyzja*) decision; (*zamiar*) resolution, resolve; (*Prawo*) ruling
**postar|ać się** (**-am, -asz**) *vb perf od* **starać się** ▷ *vr perf*: **postarać się o coś** (*uzyskać, zdobyć*) to obtain sth; **postaram się to zrobić** I'll try to do this
**postarz|ać** (**-am, -asz**) (*perf* **-yć**) *vt*: **~ kogoś** to age sb
**postarz|eć się** (**-eję, -ejesz**) *vb perf od* **starzeć się**
**posta|wa** (**-wy, -wy**) (*loc sg* **-wie**) *f* (*wygląd człowieka*) bearing, stance; (*postura*) posture; (*stosunek*) attitude, stance; **~ wobec kogoś/ czegoś** attitude towards sb/sth
**posta|wić** (**-wię, -wisz**) *vb perf od* **stawiać**; **postawić się** *vr perf* (*przeciwstawić się*) to put one's foot down; **postaw się w mojej sytuacji** put yourself in my position
**postawny** *adj* strapping
**postą|pić** (**-pię, -pisz**) *vb perf od* **postępować**
**poste restante** *inv* poste restante (*Brit*), general delivery (*US*)
**posterun|ek** (**-ku, -ki**) (*instr sg* **-kiem**) *m* post; **~ policji/straży pożarnej** police/fire station

P

**postę|p** (**-pu**) (*loc sg* **-pie**) *m* progress; **postępy** *pl* progress; **robić ~y (w czymś)** to make progress *lub* headway (in sth); **iść z ~em** to keep abreast of the times; **~ arytmetyczny/ geometryczny** arithmetic/geometric progression
**postęp|ek** (**-ku, -ki**) (*instr sg* **-kiem**) *m* deed; (*też*: **zły postępek**) misdeed
**postęp|ować (-uję, -ujesz)** *vi* (*perf* **postąpić**) (*o pracy*) to proceed; (*o chorobie*) to progress; (*zachowywać się*) to act, to behave; (*kroczyć*) to walk; **~ naprzód** to advance; **jak postępuje praca?** how is the work progressing?; **źle/ dobrze ~ z kimś** to treat sb badly/well
**postępowa|nie** (**-nia**) *nt* conduct, behaviour (*Brit*), behavior (*US*); **~ prawne/sądowe** legal action *lub* proceedings; **wszczynać (wszcząć** *perf*) **~** to institute *lub* initiate proceedings
**postępowy** *adj* (*działacz, umysł*) progressive
**postępujący** *adj* (*choroba*) progressive
**postkomuni|sta** (**-sty, -ści**) (*dat sg* **-ście**) *m decl like f in sg* post-communist
**postkomunistyczny** *adj* postcommunist
**postny** *adj*: **dzień ~** a fast day; **potrawy postne** Lenten fare
**postojowy** *adj*: **światła postojowe** parking lights
**post|ój** (**-oju, -oje**) (*gen pl* **-ojów** *lub* **-oi**) *m* (*przerwa w podróży*) stopover; (*miejsce*) (road) stop; **~ taksówek** taxi rank; **„zakaz postoju"** "no waiting"
**postrach** (**-u**) *m* terror; **budzić (wzbudzić** *perf*) **~** to inspire terror; **być ~em (dla)** *+gen* to be the terror of; **na ~** as a deterrent
**postrad|ać (-am, -asz)** *vt perf* (*życie, majątek*) to lose; **~ zmysły** to take leave of one's senses
**postronny** *adj*: **osoba postronna** outsider
**postrza|ł** (**-łu, -ły**) (*loc sg* **-le**) *m* (*rana*) gunshot wound; (*Med*) lumbago
**postrzałowy** *adj*: **rana postrzałowa** gunshot wound
**postrzeg|ać (-am, -asz)** (*perf* **postrzec**) *vt* to perceive
**postrzegani|e** (**-a**) *nt* perception
**postrzel|ić (-ę, -isz)** *vt perf* to shoot
**postrzelony** *adj* (*pot*: *szalony*) wacky (*pot*)
**postscriptum** *nt inv* postscript
**postula|t** (**-tu, -ty**) (*loc sg* **-cie**) *m* postulate
**postul|ować (-uję, -ujesz)** *vt* to postulate
**postumen|t** (**-tu, -ty**) (*loc sg* **-cie**) *m* plinth
**postu|ra** (**-ry, -ry**) (*dat sg* **-rze**) *f* (*książk*) posture
**posu|nąć (-nę, -niesz)** (*imp* **-ń**) *vb perf od* **posuwać**
**posunię|cie** (**-cia, -cia**) (*gen pl* **-ć**) *nt* move
**posunięty** *adj*: **daleko ~** advanced
**posuw|ać (-am, -asz)** (*perf* **posunąć**) *vt* to move forward ▷ *vi*: **~ nogami** to shuffle one's feet; **posunąć pracę/sprawę naprzód** to move the job/matter along *lub* forward; **posunąć żart za daleko** to carry a joke too far; **posuwać się** *vr* to move along *lub* forward; **~ się do czegoś** not to stop short of (doing) sth; **~ się za daleko** (*przen*) to go too far
**posył|ać (-am, -asz)** (*perf* **posłać**) *vt* to send; **posłać (kogoś) po coś/kogoś** to send (sb) for sth/sb; **posłać kogoś dokądś** to send sb somewhere
**posył|ka** (**-ki, -ki**) (*dat sg* **-ce**, *gen pl* **-ek**) *f*: **chłopiec na posyłki** (*przen*) errand boy; **chodzić na posyłki** to run errands
**posy|pać (-pię, -piesz)** *vb perf od* **posypywać**; **posypać się** *vr perf* (*o pytaniach*) to pour in; (*o oklaskach*) to ring out
**posyp|ywać (-uję, -ujesz)** (*perf* **-ać**) *vt*: **~ coś czymś** to sprinkle sth with sth
**poszanowani|e** (**-a**) *nt* (*książk*) respect; **~ prawa** observance of the law
**poszczególny** *adj* individual
**poszczę** *itd. vb patrz* **pościć**
**poszczę|ścić się (-ści)** *vr perf*: **(nie) poszczęściło mu się** he was (un)lucky
**poszedł** *itd. vb patrz* **pójść**
**poszerz|ać (-am, -asz)** (*perf* **-yć**) *vt* to widen, to broaden; (*spodnie, sukienkę*) to let out; **poszerzać się** *vr* to widen
**poszerz|yć (-ę, -ysz)** *vb perf od* **poszerzać**
**poszew|ka** (**-ki, -ki**) (*dat sg* **-ce**, *gen pl* **-ek**) *f* pillowcase
**poszkodowa|ny** (**-nego, -ni**) *m decl like adj* (*Prawo*) injured party; **być ~m w wypadku/ przez los** to be injured in an accident/ wronged by fate
**poszla|ka** (**-ki, -ki**) (*dat sg* **-ce**) *f* circumstantial evidence
**poszlakowy** *adj*: **dowody poszlakowe** circumstantial evidence; **proces ~** a process based on circumstantial evidence
**poszła** *itd. vb patrz* **pójść**
**poszuk|ać (-am, -asz)** *vt perf*: **~ kogoś/czegoś** to find sb/sth
**poszukiwacz** (**-a, -e**) (*gen pl* **-y**) *m* searcher; **~ złota** gold-digger; **~ przygód** adventure-seeker, adventurer
**poszu|kiwać (-kuję, -kujesz)** *vt*: **~ kogoś/ czegoś** to search for sb/sth
**poszukiwa|nie** (**-nia, -nia**) (*gen pl* **-ń**) *nt* (*pracy*) search, hunt; (*złota*) digging; (*prawdy, szczęścia*) quest; **poszukiwania** *pl* (*zaginionej osoby*) search; (*zbiega*) hunt; **poszukiwania geologiczne** prospecting
**poszukiwany** *adj* (*mający popyt, ceniony*) sought-after; (*ścigany*) wanted
**posz|wa** (**-wy, -wy**) (*loc sg* **-wie**, *gen pl* **-ew**) *f* quilt cover

**poszy|cie** (**-cia, -cia**) (*gen pl* **-ć**) *nt* (*dachu*) roofing; (*samolotu, statku*) sheathing, plating; (*leśne*) undergrowth
**po|ścić** (**-szczę, -ścisz**) (*imp* **-ść**) *vi* to fast
**poście** *n patrz* **post**
**pościel** (**-i, -e**) (*gen pl* **-i**) *f* bedclothes, bedding
**pościel|ić** (**-ę, -isz**) *vt perf* = **posłać**
**pościelowy** *adj*: **bielizna pościelowa** bed linen
**pości|g** (**-gu, -gi**) (*instr sg* **-giem**) *m* chase, pursuit; (*przen*) pursuit
**poślad|ek** (**-ka, -ki**) (*instr sg* **-kiem**) *m* buttock
**pośle** *n patrz* **poseł**
**pośledni** *adj* mediocre
**poślę** *itd. vb patrz* **posłać**[2]
**pośli|nić** (**-nię, -nisz**) (*imp* **-ń**) *vt perf* (*chustkę, palce*) to moisten (*with saliva*); (*znaczek*) to lick
**pośliz|g** (**-gu, -gi**) (*instr sg* **-giem**) *m* skid; (*pot*) delay; **wpaść** (*perf*) **w ~** to go into a skid
**poślizg|nąć się** (**-nę, -niesz**) (*imp* **-nij**) *vr perf* to slip
**poślu|bić** (**-bię, -bisz**) *vt perf* to wed
**poślubny** *adj*: **noc poślubna** wedding night; **podróż poślubna** honeymoon
**pośmiertny** *adj* posthumous; **stężenie pośmiertne** rigor mortis
**pośmiewis|ko** (**-ka**) (*instr sg* **-kiem**) *nt*: **być pośmiewiskiem** *+gen* to be the laughing stock of; **robić (zrobić** (*perf*)**) z kogoś/siebie ~** to make a laughing stock of sb/o.s.
**pośpiech** (**-u**) *m* hurry, haste; **bez ~u** without haste; **w ~u** hurriedly, in haste; **nie ma ~u** there's no hurry; **po co ten ~?** what's the hurry?
**pośpieszny** *adj* hurried, hasty; **pociąg ~** fast train
**pośpiesz|yć** (**-ę, -ysz**) *vb perf od* **śpieszyć**; **pośpieszyć się** *vr perf*: **pośpiesz się!** hurry up!
**pośredni** *adj* (*wpływ, związek, skutek*) indirect; (*stadium, etap*) intermediate; **coś ~ego między A a B** something halfway between A and B
**pośrednict|wo** (**-wa**) (*loc sg* **-wie**) *nt* mediation; (*Handel*) agency; **za pośrednictwem kogoś/czegoś** through *lub* by the agency of sb/sth; **biuro pośrednictwa pracy** employment agency
**pośrednicz|yć** (**-ę, -ysz**) *vi* to mediate
**pośredni|k** (**-ka, -cy**) (*instr sg* **-kiem**) *m* mediator; (*Handel*) agent; (*też*: **pośrednik handlu nieruchomościami**) (real) estate agent
**pośrednio** *adv* indirectly
**pośrodku** *prep +gen* in the middle of
**pośród** *prep +gen* in the midst of
**poświadcz|ać** (**-am, -asz**) (*perf* **-yć**) *vt* to authenticate, to certify
**poświadcze|nie** (**-nia, -nia**) (*gen pl* **-ń**) *nt* authentication, certification
**poświadcz|yć** (**-ę, -ysz**) *vb perf od* **poświadczać**
**poświa|ta** (**-ty, -ty**) (*dat sg* **-cie**) *f* glow
**poświe|cić** (**-cę, -cisz**) (*imp* **-ć**) *vi perf*: **poświeć (mi)!** shine the light for me!
**poświę|cać** (**-cam, -casz**) (*perf* **-cić**) *vt* (*Rel*) to consecrate; **~ coś komuś** (*składać w ofierze*) to sacrifice sth to sb; (*dedykować*) to dedicate sth to sb; **poświęcić czas/wysiłki na coś** to spend time/effort on sth; **konferencja była poświęcona energii atomowej** the conference was devoted to nuclear energy; **poświęcać się** *vr*: **~ się dla kogoś** to make sacrifices for sb; **~ się czemuś** to devote *lub* dedicate o.s. to sth
**poświęce|nie** (**-nia**) *nt* (*oddanie*) dedication, devotion; (*ofiara*) sacrifice; (*Rel*) consecration; **robić coś z ~m** to do sth with dedication
**poświę|cić** (**-cę, -cisz**) (*imp* **-ć**) *vb perf od* **poświęcać**
**po|t** (**-tu, -ty**) (*loc sg* **-cie**) *m* sweat, perspiration; **w pocie czoła** by the sweat of one's brow; **zlany potem** drenched with sweat
**pot.** *abbr* (*= potocznie*) inf. (*= informally*)
**potajemnie** *adv* secretly
**potajemny** *adj* secret
**pota|kiwać** (**-kuję, -kujesz**) (*perf* **-knąć**) *vi* to nod in agreement
**potak|nąć** (**-nę, -niesz**) (*imp* **-nij**) *vb perf od* **potakiwać**
**potani|eć** (**-eje**) *vb perf od* **tanieć**
**potarg|ać** (**-am, -asz**) *vt perf* to tousle; **potargać się** *vr* to get tousled
**pota|s** (**-su**) (*loc sg* **-sie**) *m* potassium
**potas|ować** (**-uję, -ujesz**) *vb perf od* **tasować**
**potąd** *adv*: **mam tego ~!** I've had it up to here!; **mam jej ~!** I can't take her any more!
**potem** *adv* (*następnie*) then, next, afterwards; (*później*) later, afterwards; **na ~** for later
**potencj|a** (**-i**) *f* potency
**potencjalny** *adj* potential
**potencja|ł** (**-łu, -ły**) (*loc sg* **-le**) *m* potential
**potencjomet|r** (**-ru, -ry**) (*loc sg* **-rze**) *m* (*Elektr*) potentiometer; (*pokrętło*) dial
**potenta|t** (**-ta, -ci**) (*loc sg* **-cie**) *m* potentate
**potę|ga** (**-gi**) (*dat sg* **-dze**) *f* power; (*mocarstwo*) (*nom pl* **-gi**) power; **dwa do potęgi trzeciej** two to the power of three; **do n-tej potęgi** (*Mat*) to the power of n; (*przen*) to the nth degree
**potęg|ować** (**-uję, -ujesz**) (*perf* **s-**) *vt* (*Mat*) to exponentiate, to raise to a power; (*wzmacniać*) to heighten; **potęgować się** *vr* to heighten

P

**potę|piać (-piam, -piasz)** (*perf* **-pić**) *vt*: **~ coś** to condemn sth; **~ kogoś (za coś)** to condemn sb (for sth)
**potę|pić (-pię, -pisz)** *vb perf od* **potępiać**
**potępie|nie** (**-nia**) *nt* condemnation; (*Rel*) damnation
**potężny** *adj* (*władca, cios*) powerful, mighty; (*drzewo*) mighty, huge; (*huk, wrażenie, uczucie*) powerful
**potk|nąć się (-nę, -niesz)** (*imp* **-nij**) *vb perf od* **potykać się**
**potknię|cie** (**-cia, -cia**) (*gen pl* **-ć**) *nt* stumble; (*przen*) slip-up
**potłu|c się (-kę, -czesz)** (*pt* **-kł, -kła, -kli**) *vr perf* to get bruised
**potnę** *itd. vb patrz* **pociąć**
**potocznie** *adv* popularly
**potoczny** *adj* (*nazwa, rozumienie*) popular; (*język*) colloquial, informal
**potocz|yć (-ę, -ysz)** *vb perf od* **toczyć (się)**
**potoczysty** *adj* flowing
**poto|k** (**-ku, -ki**) (*instr sg* **-kiem**) *m* stream; (*przen*: *łez, deszczu*) flood; (: *słów*) stream; (: *wyzwisk*) volley
**potom|ek** (**-ka, -kowie**) (*instr sg* **-kiem**) *m* descendant
**potomnoś|ć** (**-ci**) *f*: **przejść** (*perf*) **do potomności** to be passed on to posterity
**potomst|wo** (**-wo**) (*loc sg* **-wie**) *nt* offspring
**poto|p** (**-pu**) (*loc sg* **-pie**) *m* deluge; (*Rel*) the Flood
**potra|fić (-fię, -fisz)** *vi*: **on potrafi to zrobić** (*umie*) he can do it; (*jest zdolny*) he can do it, he is capable of doing it
**potraj|ać (-am, -asz)** (*perf* **potroić**) *vt* to treble, to triple; **potrajać się** *vr* to treble, to triple
**potrakt|ować (-uję, -ujesz)** *vb perf od* **traktować**
**potra|wa** (**-wy, -wy**) (*dat sg* **-wie**) *f* dish; **spis potraw** menu
**potraw|ka** (**-ki, -ki**) (*dat sg* **-ce**, *gen pl* **-ek**) *f* fricassee
**potrą|cać (-cam, -casz)** (*perf* **-cić**) *vt* (*szturchać*) to jostle, to jog; (*odliczać*) to deduct
**potrą|cić (-cę, -cisz)** (*imp* **-ć**) *vb perf od* **potrącać** ▷ *vt perf*: **~ kogoś** (*o pojeździe*) to run sb down
**potr|oić (-oję, -oisz)** (*imp* **-ój**) *vb perf od* **potrajać**
**potrójny** *adj* treble, triple
**potrw|ać (-a)** *vi perf* (*zająć czas*) to take; (*przetrwać*) to last; **jak długo to potrwa?** how long is it going to take?; **to nie potrwa długo** it won't take long
**potrzas|k** (**-ki, -ki**) (*instr sg* **-kiem**) *m*: **być w ~u** to be trapped; **znaleźć się** (*perf*) **w ~u** to get into a trap
**potrząs|ać (-am, -asz)** (*perf* **-nąć**) *vt* to shake
**potrzą|snąć (-snę, -śniesz)** (*imp* **-śnij**) *vb perf od* **potrząsać**
**potrze|ba**[1] (**-by, -by**) (*dat sg* **-bie**) *f* need; **potrzeby** *pl* needs *pl*; **bez potrzeby** unnecessarily; **w razie potrzeby** if necessary *lub* required, should the need arise; **nie ma potrzeby się spieszyć** there's no need to hurry; **w potrzebie** in need; **potrzeby fizjologiczne/cielesne** physiological/bodily needs; **artykuły pierwszej potrzeby** necessities
**potrzeba**[2] *inv*: **~ nam pieniędzy/czasu** we need money/time; **czego ci ~?** what do you need?
**potrzebny** *adj* necessary, needed; **to mi jest potrzebne** I need that; **jestem ci ~?** do you need me?; **to nie jest potrzebne** this isn't necessary
**potrzeb|ować (-uję, -ujesz)** *vt perf*: **~ czegoś** *lub* **coś** to need sth; **nie potrzebujesz tego robić** you don't need to do this
**pot|rzeć (-rę, -rzesz)** (*imp* **-rzyj**) *vb perf od* **pocierać**
**potrzym|ać (-am, -asz)** *vt perf* to hold
**potulny** *adj* meek
**poturb|ować (-uję, -ujesz)** *vt perf* to maul
**potwarz** (**-y, -e**) *f* slander, calumny
**potwier|dzać (-dzam, -dzasz)** (*imp* **-dź**, *perf* **-dzić**) *vt* to confirm; (*odbiór przesyłki*) to acknowledge; **potwierdzać się** *vr* to be confirmed
**potwierdze|nie** (**-nia, -nia**) (*gen pl* **-ń**) *nt* confirmation
**potwier|dzić (-dzę, -dzisz)** (*imp* **-dź**) *vb perf od* **potwierdzać**
**potwornie** *adv*: **wyglądać/czuć się ~** to look/feel awful; **~ brzydki/głodny** terribly ugly/hungry
**potwornoś|ć** (**-ci**) *f* monstrosity
**potworny** *adj* monstrous
**potw|ór** (**-ora, -ory**) (*loc sg* **-orze**) *m* monster
**potycz|ka** (**-ki, -ki**) (*dat sg* **-ce**, *gen pl* **-ek**) *f* skirmish
**potyk|ać się (-am, -asz)** (*perf* **potknąć**) *vr* to stumble, to trip (up); (*przen*) to slip
**potylic|a** (**-y, -e**) *f* (*Anat*) occiput
**poucz|ać (-am, -asz)** (*perf* **-yć**) *vt* (*informować*) to instruct; (*upominać*) to admonish; (*dawać niepotrzebne rady*) to patronize
**pouczający** *adj* (*bogaty w informacje*) instructive; (*budujący, umoralniający*) edifying; (*upominający*) admonishing
**poucze|nie** (**-nia, -nia**) (*gen pl* **-ń**) *nt* (*informacja*) instruction; (*ostrzeżenie*) admonition
**poucz|yć (-ę, -ysz)** *vb perf od* **pouczać**

**poufałoś|ć** (**-ci**) *f* familiarity
**poufały** *adj* familiar
**poufny** *adj* confidential
**pow.** *abbr* (= *powierzchnia*) area
**powa|b** (**-bu, -by**) (*loc sg* **-bie**) *m* (*książk*) allure
**powabny** *adj* (*książk*) alluring
**powa|ga** (**-gi**) (*dat sg* **-dze**) *f* seriousness; (*urzędu, stanowiska*) authority; **z powagą** seriously; **zachować** (*perf*) **powagę** to keep serious
**powal|ić (-ę, -isz)** *vt perf* to strike down
**poważ|ać (-am, -asz)** *vt* (*cenić*) to esteem, to hold in high regard; (*szanować*) to respect
**poważa|nie** (**-nia**) *nt* esteem; **cieszyć się ~m** to be held in high esteem; **„z ~m"** "yours sincerely *lub* faithfully"
**poważany** *adj* esteemed
**poważnie** *adv* seriously; **wyglądać ~** to look serious; **~?** seriously?; **mówisz ~?** are you serious?; **na ~** seriously
**poważny** *adj* (*mina, błąd, strata, choroba*) serious; (*rola*) substantial; (*instytucja*) reputable; **muzyka poważna** classical music
**powąch|ać (-am, -asz)** *vb perf od* **wąchać**
**powątpiew|ać (-am, -asz)** *vi*: **~ w coś** to be dubious about sth
**powątpiewa|nie** (**-nia**) *nt* doubt
**powesel|eć (-eję, -ejesz)** *vi perf* to cheer up
**powet|ować (-uję, -ujesz)** *vt perf*: **~ (sobie) coś** to make up for sth
**powi|ać (-eje)** *vb perf od* **powiewać**
**powiadami|ać (-am, -asz)** (*perf* **powiadomić**) *vt*: **~ kogoś (o czymś)** to notify sb (of sth)
**powi|at** (**-atu, -aty**) (*loc sg* **-ecie**) *m Polish administrative unit*
**powią|zać (-żę, -żesz)** *vb perf od* **wiązać**
**powiąza|nie** (**-nia, -nia**) (*gen pl* **-ń**) *nt* connection; **mieć ~ z** *+instr* to be connected with; **powiązania** *pl*: **(mieć) powiązania z** *+instr* (to have) connections with
**powiązany** *adj*: **~ z** *+instr* connected with *lub* to, related to
**po|wić (-wiję, -wijesz)** *vt perf* (*książk*: *urodzić*) to bear
**powid|ła** (**-eł**) *pl* (*Kulin*) plum jam
**powiedze|nie** (**-nia, -nia**) (*gen pl* **-ń**) *nt* (*aforyzm*) saying; **mieć coś do powiedzenia** (*chcieć coś wyjaśnić*) to have sth to say; (*liczyć się*) to have some say
**powiedziany** *adj*: **nie jest powiedziane, że przyjdzie** you can't bank on his coming; **to mało powiedziane!** that's an understatement!
**powi|edzieć (-em, -esz)** (*3 pl* **-edzą**, *imp* **-edz**) *vt perf*: **~ coś/, że ...** to say sth/(that) ... ▷ *vi perf* to say; **~ komuś coś/o czymś/, że ...** to tell sb sth/about sth/(that) ...; **co chcesz przez to ~?** what do you mean by that?; **co powiesz na** *+acc*? how *lub* what about ...?; **powiedz sam** *lub* **sam powiedz** wouldn't you agree?; **powiedzmy** (let's) say; **że tak powiem** so to speak
**powie|ka** (**-ki, -ki**) (*dat sg* **-ce**) *f* eyelid
**powielacz** (**-a, -e**) (*gen pl* **-y**) *m* (*Tech*) duplicator
**powiel|ać (-am, -asz)** (*perf* **-ić**) *vt* to duplicate
**powierniczy** *adj*: **fundusz ~** trust fund
**powierni|k** (**-ka, -cy**) (*instr sg* **-kiem**) *m* trustee
**powierz|ać (-am, -asz)** (*perf* **-yć**) *vt*: **~ coś komuś** to entrust sth to sb, to entrust sb with sth
**powierzch|nia** (**-ni, -nie**) (*gen pl* **-ni**) *f* (*strona zewnętrzna*) surface; (*obszar, teren*) area; (*Mat, Geom*) area
**powierzchownie** *adv* superficially
**powierzchownoś|ć** (**-ci**) *f* (*wygląd*) exterior; (*pobieżność*) superficiality
**powierzchowny** *adj* superficial
**powierz|yć (-ę, -ysz)** *vb perf od* **powierzać**
**powie|sić (-szę, -sisz)** (*imp* **-ś**) *vt perf* to hang; **powiesić się** *vr perf* to hang o.s.
**powieściopisarz** (**-a, -e**) (*gen pl* **-y**) *m* novelist
**powieś|ć**[1] (**-ci, -ci**) (*gen pl* **-ci**) *f* novel; **~ telewizyjna** TV series, soap opera
**powi|eść**[2] **(-odę, -edziesz)** (*imp* **-edź**, *pt* **-ódł, -odła, -edli**) *vb perf od* **wieść** ▷ *vt perf* (*przesunąć*): **powiódł wzrokiem po pokoju** his eyes *lub* gaze swept round the room; **powiódł palcem po mapie** he traced the route on the map with his finger; **powieść się** *vb perf od* **wieść się** ▷ *vr perf* (*udać się*) to succeed, to be successful; **nie powiodło mi się** I didn't succeed; **powiodło mi się** I made it
**powietrz|e** (**-a**) *nt* air; **na (wolnym) powietrzu** in the open air, outdoors; **w powietrzu** in the air
**powietrzny** *adj* air *attr*; **obszar ~** airspace; **trąba powietrzna** whirlwind; **poduszka powietrzna** (*Mot*) airbag; **siły powietrzne** Air Force; **most ~** airlift
**powie|w** (**-wu, -wy**) (*loc sg* **-wie**) *m* breath, puff
**powiew|ać (-a)** *vi* (*o wietrze*) (*perf* **powiać**) to blow; (*o fladze*) to fly, to wave; **~ chusteczką** to wave a handkerchief
**powiększ|ać (-am, -asz)** (*perf* **-yć**) *vt* (*teren, obszar*) to expand; (*ilość, dostawy, deficyt*) to increase; (*organizację, zespół*) to enlarge; (*obraz*) to magnify; (*Fot*) to enlarge, to blow up; **powiększać się** *vr* (*o zasobach*) to increase; (*o obszarze*) to expand; (*o grupie*) to grow
**powiększający** *adj*: **szkło powiększające** magnifying glass

P

**powiększalni|k** (**-ka, -ki**) (*instr sg* **-kiem**) *m* (*Fot*) enlarger
**powiększe|nie** (**-nia, -nia**) (*gen pl* **-ń**) *nt* (*obszaru*) expansion; (*deficytu*) increase; (*Fot*) enlargement, blow-up; **w (dwukrotnym) powiększeniu** enlarged *lub* blown up (to twice the size)
**powiększ|yć (-ę, -ysz)** *vb perf od* **powiększać**
**powija|ki** (**-ków**) *pl*: **nasz projekt nadal znajduje się w powijakach** our project is still in its infancy
**powikła|nie** (**-nia, -nia**) (*gen pl* **-ń**) *nt* complication
**powi|nąć się (-nie)** *vr perf*: **noga mu się powinęła** he slipped up
**powinien** (*f* **powinna**, *nt* **powinno**); **on ~/ona powinna tam pójść** he/she should go there, he/she ought to go there; **~eś (powinnaś** *f*) **mu powiedzieć** you should tell him; **~em był (powinnam była** *f*) **zaczekać** I should have waited; **on ~ zaraz wrócić** he should be back any moment; **słońce powinno zajść o dziewiątej** the sun should set at nine; **powinno się pomagać innym** one *lub* you should help others
**powinnoś|ć** (**-ci, -ci**) (*gen pl* **-ci**) *f* (*książk*) duty
**powinowact|wo** (**-wa, -wa**) (*loc sg* **-wie**) *nt* kinship
**powinowa|ty** (**-tego, -ci**) *m decl like adj* kinsman; **powinowata** *f decl like adj* kinswoman; **powinowaci** *pl* kin
**powit|ać (-am, -asz)** *vb perf od* **witać**
**powitalny** *adj* (*gest, uśmiech*) welcoming *attr*; (*oklaski*) greeting *attr*; (*mowa*) opening *attr*
**powita|nie** (**-nia, -nia**) (*gen pl* **-ń**) *nt* welcome, greeting
**powle|c (-kę, -czesz)** (*pt* **-kł**) *vb perf od* **powlekać**
**powlek|ać (-am, -asz)** (*perf* **powlec**) *vt*: **~ (czymś)** to coat (with sth); **~ poduszki** to change pillowcases
**powłocz|ka** (**-ki, -ki**) (*dat sg* **-ce**, *gen pl* **-ek**) *f* (*poszewka*) pillowcase
**powło|ka** (**-ki, -ki**) (*dat sg* **-ce**) *f* (*farby*) coat(ing); (*ozonu*) layer; (*balonu*) envelope
**powłócz|yć (-ę, -ysz)** *vt*: **~ nogami** to drag one's feet
**powod|ować (-uję, -ujesz)** (*perf* **s-**) *vt* to cause, to bring about; **s~, że coś się stanie** to cause sth to happen; **powodować się** *vr* (*książk*): **~ się czymś** to be motivated by sth
**powodze|nie** (**-nia**) *nt* (*sukces*) success; (*popularność*) popularity; **powodzenia!** good luck!; **mieć ~ u młodzieży** to be popular with the young; **z ~m** successfully; **bez powodzenia** unsuccessfully, without success
**powo|dzić się (-dzi)** *vr*: **dobrze/źle jej się powodzi** she is doing well/badly; (*finansowo*) she is well/badly off
**powodziowy** *adj* flood *attr*
**powojenny** *adj* postwar *attr*
**powoli** *adv* slowly
**powolny** *adj* slow
**powoł|ać (-am, -asz)** *vb perf od* **powoływać**
**powoła|nie** (**-nia, -nia**) (*gen pl* **-ń**) *nt* (*rządu*) formation; (*ministra*) appointment; (*zamiłowanie*) calling; **~ do wojska** call-up (*Brit*) *lub* draft (*US*) (papers); **~ do czegoś** calling *lub* vocation for sth; **lekarz z powołania** a born doctor
**powołany** *adj* (*kompetentny*) competent, qualified
**powoł|ywać (-uję, -ujesz)** (*perf* **-ać**) *vt* (*wyznaczać*) to appoint; **~ kogoś do wojska** to conscript sb (*Brit*), to call sb up (*Brit*), to draft sb (*US*); **powołać kogoś (na stanowisko)** to appoint sb (to a post); **~ kogoś na świadka** (*Prawo*) to call sb as a witness; **~ coś do życia** to bring sth into being *lub* existence; **powoływać się** *vr*: **~ się na** *+acc* (*źródło*) to cite, to quote; (*przywilej, prawo*) to invoke; **powołaj się na mnie** tell them I sent you
**powonieni|e** (**-a**) *nt* (sense of) smell
**pow|ozić (-ożę, -ozisz)** (*imp* **-oź** *lub* **-óź**) *vi* *+instr* to drive (*a horse-drawn vehicle*)
**pow|ód**[1] (**-odu, -ody**) (*loc sg* **-odzie**) *m* (*przyczyna*) cause; (*uzasadnienie*) reason; **z powodu** *+gen* because of, due to; **z tego powodu** for this reason; **bez powodu** for no reason; **nie bez powodu** with good reason; **mieć ~ do radości** to have (every) reason to be happy
**pow|ód**[2] (**-oda, -odowie**) (*loc sg* **-odzie**) *m* (*Prawo*) plaintiff
**powództ|wo** (**-wa, -wa**) (*loc sg* **-wie**) *nt* (*Prawo*) complaint
**pow|ódź** (**-odzi, -odzie**) (*gen pl* **-odzi**) *f* (*woda*) flood(ing); (*przen*: *mnóstwo*) flood
**pow|ój** (**-oju, -oje**) (*gen pl* **-oi** *lub* **-ojów**) *m* (*Bot*) bindweed
**pow|óz** (**-ozu, -ozy**) (*loc sg* **-ozie**) *m* carriage
**powrac|ać (-am, -asz)** (*perf* **powrócić**) *vi* to return, to come back; **~ do rozmowy** to resume a conversation; **~ do tematu** to return *lub* go back to a topic
**powrotny** *adj*: **bilet ~** return (*Brit*) *lub* round-trip (*US*) ticket; **w drodze powrotnej** on the way back
**powró|cić (-cę, -cisz)** (*imp* **-ć**) *vb perf od* **powracać**
**powr|ót** (**-otu, -oty**) (*loc sg* **-ocie**) *m* return; **~ do domu** homecoming; **~ do zdrowia** recovery; **z powrotem** (*w kierunku powrotnym*)

back; (*na nowo*) again; **tam i z powrotem** back and forth

**powr|óz** (**-ozu, -ozy**) (*loc sg* **-ozie**) *m* rope

**powst|ać (-anę, -aniesz)** (*imp* **-ań**) *vb perf od* **powstawać**

**powsta|nie** (**-nia**) *nt* (*utworzenie*) rise, origin; (*rewolta*) (*nom pl* **-nia**, *gen pl* **-ń**) uprising

**powsta|niec** (**-ńca, -ńcy**) *m* insurgent

**powst|awać (-aję, -ajesz)** (*imp* **-awaj**, *perf* **-ać**) *vi* (*zaczynać istnieć*) to arise, to come into being; (*wstawać*) to stand (up); (*buntować się*) to rise (up)

**powstrzym|ywać (-uję, -ujesz)** (*perf* **-ać**) *vt* (*zatrzymywać*) to restrain, to hold back; (*śmiech, łzy*) to hold back, to check; (*nieprzyjaciela*) to hold off; **~ kogoś od (robienia) czegoś** to stop *lub* keep sb from (doing) sth; **powstrzymywać się** *vr*: **~ się od** *+gen* (*picia*) to abstain from; (*komentarza*) to refrain from; **~ się od (robienia) czegoś** to refrain from (doing) sth

**powszechnie** *adv* (*znany, lubiany*) generally; (*używany*) commonly; **~ wiadomo, że …** it's common knowledge that …

**powszechny** *adj* (*opinia*) common; (*wybory*) general; (*szkoła, edukacja*) primary *attr* (*Brit*), elementary *attr* (*US*)

**powszedni** *adj* commonplace; **dzień ~** weekday; (*przen*) average day; **chleb ~** daily bread; **to dla mnie chleb ~** (*przen*) I'm used to this kind of thing

**powściągliwoś|ć** (**-ci**) *f* (*umiar*) restraint, moderation; (*opanowanie*) reserve, self-restraint

**powściągliwy** *adj* (*wymijający*) evasive; (*opanowany*) restrained

**powtarz|ać (-am, -asz)** (*perf* **powtórzyć**) *vt* to repeat; (*TV, Radio*) to repeat, to rebroadcast; (*materiał, lekcje*) to revise (*Brit*), to review (*US*); **czy mógłbyś powtórzyć?** could you say that again?; **~ za kimś** *lub* **po kimś** to echo sb's words; **powtarzaj(cie) za mną!** repeat after me!; **powtarzać się** *vr* (*odbywać się ponownie*) to recur; (*o historii*) to repeat itself; (*o człowieku*) to repeat o.s.

**powtarzający się** *adj* recurrent

**powtór|ka** (**-ki, -ki**) (*dat sg* **-ce**, *gen pl* **-ek**) *f* (*Szkol*) revision (*Brit*), review (*US*); (*programu*) repeat, re-run; **~ akcji** action replay

**powtórnie** *adv* again, a second time; **~ przekraczać granicę** to re-enter; **~ napełniać** to refill

**powtórny** *adj* second

**powtórze|nie** (**-nia, -nia**) (*gen pl* **-ń**) *nt* repetition; (*materiału*) revision (*Brit*), review (*US*); (*programu*) repeat, re-run

**powtórz|yć (-ę, -ysz)** *vb perf od* **powtarzać**

**powyżej** *prep +gen* (*wyżej niż*) above, over; (*ponad*) over ▷ *adv* above

**powyższe** (**-go**) *nt decl like adj* (*książk*): **zgodnie z powyższym/wobec ~go** for this reason

**powyższy** *adj* (*książk*) above-mentioned, foregoing

**pow|ziąć (-ezmę, -eźmiesz)** (*imp* **-eźmij**) *vt perf*: **~ decyzję** to take *lub* make a decision; **~ postanowienie** *lub* **zamiar** to make up one's mind

**poz.** *abbr* (= *pozycja*) item

**po|za**[1] (**-zy, -zy**) (*dat sg* **-zie**, *gen pl* **póz**) *f* pose

**poza**[2] *prep +acc* (*dalej niż*) beyond ▷ *prep +instr* (*na zewnątrz*) outside; (*oprócz*) apart from, beside; **przebywać ~ domem** to be out; **~ tym** (*zresztą*) besides; (*również*) also; **~ zasięgiem** out of reach; **mieć coś ~ sobą** to be over sth

**pozagrobowy** *adj*: **życie pozagrobowe** the afterlife

**pozazdroszcze|nie** (**-nia**) *nt*: **godny pozazdroszczenia** enviable; **nie do pozazdroszczenia** unenviable

**pozaziemski** *adj* extraterrestrial; **istota pozaziemska** alien

**pozba|wiać (-wię, -wisz)** (*perf* **-wić**) *vt*: **~ kogoś czegoś** to deprive sb of sth; **pozbawić kogoś złudzeń** to disillusion sb; **pozbawiać się** *vr +gen* (*przyjemności*) to deny o.s.; (*szansy*) to lose; **pozbawić się/kogoś życia** to take one's own/sb's life

**pozbawie|nie** (**-nia**) *nt*: **kara pozbawienia wolności** (*Prawo*) imprisonment

**pozbawiony** *adj*: **~ czegoś** devoid of sth

**pozbier|ać (-am, -asz)** *vb perf od* **zbierać**; **pozbierać się** *vr perf* (*pot*) to pull o.s. together

**pozb|yć się (-ędę, -ędziesz)** (*imp* **-ądź**) *vb perf od* **pozbywać się**

**pozbyw|ać się (-am, -asz)** (*perf* **pozbyć**) *vr +gen* to get rid of

**pozdrawi|ać (-am, -asz)** (*perf* **pozdrowić**) *vt* to greet; **pozdrów (ode mnie) Janka** give my regards to John, remember me to John

**pozdr|owić (-owię, -owisz)** (*imp* **-ów**) *vb perf od* **pozdrawiać**

**pozdrowie|nie** (**-nia, -nia**) (*gen pl* **-ń**) *nt* (*powitanie*) greeting; **pozdrowienia** *pl* regards *pl*; **„Pozdrowienia z wakacji przesyła Tomek"** (*na kartce*) "Having a great holiday. Wish you were here. Tom"; **przekaż (moje) pozdrowienia żonie** give my regards to your wife

**poze|r** (**-ra, -rzy**) (*loc sg* **-rze**) *m* (*pej*) pose(u)r

**poz|ew** (**-wu, -wy**) (*loc sg* **-wie**) *m* (*Prawo*) suit, petition; **wnosić (wnieść** *perf*) **~ (do sądu)** to file a suit *lub* petition

**pozio|m** (**-mu, -my**) (*loc sg* **-mie**) *m* (*wysokość*) level; (*stopień*) standard; (*zawartość*) content;

P

**~ życia** living standards; **~ morza** sea level; **coś (nie) jest na ~ie** (*pot*) sth is (not) up to scratch
**poziomic|a (-y, -e)** *f* (*Geog*) contour (line); (*Tech*) spirit level
**poziom|ka (-ki, -ki)** (*dat sg* **-ce**, *gen pl* **-ek**) *f* wild strawberry
**poziomo** *adv* horizontally; (*w krzyżówce*) across
**poziomy** *adj* horizontal
**pozłacany** *adj* (*rama*) gilt, gilded; (*pierścionek, styki*) gold-plated
**pozmyw|ać (-am, -asz)** *vb perf od* **zmywać**
**pozn|ać (-am, -asz)** *vb perf od* **poznawać** ▷ *vt perf* (*zawrzeć znajomość*) to meet; **~ kogoś z kimś drugim** to introduce sb to sb else; **miło mi Pana/Panią ~** nice *lub* pleased to meet you; **miło (mi) było Pana/Panią ~** it was nice meeting you; **poznać się** *vr perf* (*zawrzeć znajomość*) to meet; **~ się dobrze/bliżej** to get to know each other well/better; **poznajcie się ...** have you met ...?, let me introduce ...
**pozna|nie (-nia)** *nt* (*zapoznanie się*) meeting; (*Filozofia*) cognition; **nie do poznania** (*być*) unrecognizable; (*zmienić się*) beyond recognition
**pozn|awać (-aję, -ajesz)** (*perf* **-ać**) *vt* (*miasto, ludzi*) to get to know; (*świat*) to see; (*języki*) to learn; (*rozpoznawać*) to recognize; (*doświadczać*) to experience; (*plany, tajemnice*) to find out; **poznawać się** *vr* (*rozpoznawać siebie*) to recognize o.s.; (*rozpoznawać jeden drugiego*) to recognize one another; (*dowiadywać się o sobie*) to get to know one another; **poznałem się na nim** I knew him for what he was
**pozornie** *adv* seemingly
**pozorny** *adj* seeming, apparent
**pozor|ować (-uję, -ujesz)** (*perf* **u-**) *vt* (*chorobę, śmierć*) to feign; (*wypadek, walkę*) to simulate
**pozost|ać (-anę, -aniesz)** (*imp* **-ań**) *vb perf od* **pozostawać**
**pozostałoś|ć (-ci, -ci)** (*gen pl* **-ci**) *f* remnant; (*relikt*) relic; **pozostałości** *pl* (*resztki*) remains *pl*
**pozostały** *adj* remaining; (*drugi*) the other *attr*; **osoby pozostałe przy życiu** the survivors
**pozost|awać (-aję, -ajesz)** (*imp* **-awaj**, *perf* **-ać**) *vi* (*przebywać*) to stay; (*być nadal*) to remain, to continue; **~ niedostępnym/wiernym/na wolności** to remain inaccessible/faithful/at large; **~ w tyle** to lag behind; **do rozpoczęcia igrzysk pozostały trzy dni** the opening of the Olympics is three days away; **pozostaje mi (tylko) ...** all that's left for me to do is ...
**pozosta|wiać (-wiam, -wiasz)** *vt* (*perf* **-wić**) to leave; **nie ~ (żadnych) wątpliwości** to leave no doubts (whatsoever); **to pozostawia wiele do życzenia** this leaves a lot to be desired
**poz|ować (-uję, -ujesz)** *vi* (*do zdjęcia*) to pose; (*o modelce*) to model; (*zachowywać się sztucznie*) to pose; **~ do zdjęcia** to pose for a photograph
**poz|ór (-oru, -ory)** (*loc sg* **-orze**) *m* pretence (*Brit*), pretense (*US*), false appearance; **na ~** *lub* **z pozoru** on the surface, outwardly; **zachowywać (zachować** *perf*) **pozory** to keep up appearances; **pod pozorem czegoś** under a pretence of sth; **pod żadnym pozorem** on no account
**poz|wać (-wę, -wiesz)** (*imp* **-wij**) *vb perf od* **pozywać**
**pozwal|ać (-am, -asz)** (*perf* **pozwolić**) *vi*: **~ komuś coś robić** to allow sb to do sth, to let sb do sth; **~ na coś** to permit sth; **~ komuś na coś** to allow *lub* permit sb sth; **nie mogę sobie na to pozwolić** I can't afford it; **~ sobie na zrobienie czegoś** to take the liberty of doing sth; **pozwalam sobie zauważyć, że ...** allow me to say that ...; **za dużo sobie pozwalasz!** you've gone too far!
**pozwa|ny (-nego, -ni)** *m decl like adj* defendant (*in civil suit*)
**pozwole|nie (-nia, -nia)** (*gen pl* **-ń**) *nt* (*zgoda*) permission; (*zezwolenie*) permit
**pozw|olić (-olę, -olisz)** (*imp* **-ól**) *vb perf od* **pozwalać**; **Pan/Pani pozwoli do środka** please, come inside; **Pan/Pani pozwoli za mną** follow me, please; **Pan/Pani pozwoli, że się przedstawię** let me introduce myself
**pozycj|a (-i, -e)** (*gen pl* **-i**) *f* position; (*w spisie, kolekcji*) item
**pozycyjny** *adj*: **światła pozycyjne** (*Mot*) sidelights *pl* (*Brit*), parking lights *pl* (*US*); **wojna pozycyjna** (*Wojsk*) positional warfare
**pozys|kiwać (-kuję, -kujesz)** (*perf* **-kać**) *vt* (*przychylność, zaufanie*) to win; (*przyjaciół*) to win over
**pozyty|w (-wu, -wy)** (*loc sg* **-wie**) *m* positive
**pozytywiz|m (-mu)** (*loc sg* **-mie**) *m* positivism
**pozytyw|ka (-ki, -ki)** (*dat sg* **-ce**, *gen pl* **-ek**) *f* musical box (*Brit*), music box (*US*)
**pozytywnie** *adv* favourably (*Brit*), favorably (*US*)
**pozytywny** *adj* (*reakcja, nastawienie*) positive; (*rezultat*) favourable (*Brit*), favorable (*US*)
**pozyw|ać (-am, -asz)** (*perf* **pozwać**) *vt* (*Prawo*) to sue
**pożal|ić się (-ę, -isz)** *vb perf od* **żalić się**
**pożał|ować (-uję, -ujesz)** *vb perf od* **żałować**
**pożałowa|nie (-nia)** *nt*: **godny pożałowania** pitiful

**poża|r** (**-ru, -ry**) (*loc sg* **-rze**) *m* fire (*of building etc*)
**pożarny** *adj*: **straż pożarna** (*instytucja*) fire brigade (*Brit*), fire department (*US*); (*budynek*) fire station; (*wóz*) fire engine (*Brit*), fire truck (*US*)
**pożąd|ać (-am, -asz)** *vt* to covet, to lust after
**pożąda|nie** (**-nia**) *nt* desire
**pożądany** *adj* (*skutek*) desirable; (*gość*) welcome
**pożądliwy** *adj* lustful
**pożegn|ać (-am, -asz)** *vb perf od* **żegnać**
**pożegnalny** *adj* farewell *attr*
**pożegna|nie** (**-nia, -nia**) (*gen pl* **-ń**) *nt* farewell, leave-taking
**pożer|ać (-am, -asz)** (*perf* **pożreć**) *vt* to devour; **~ kogoś wzrokiem** (*przen*) to devour sb with one's eyes
**pożr|eć (-ę, -esz)** (*imp* **-yj**) *vb perf od* **pożerać**
**poży|cie** (**-cia**) *nt*: **~ małżeńskie/seksualne** married/sex life
**pożycz|ać (-am, -asz)** (*perf* **-yć**) *vt*: **~ coś komuś** to lend sb sth, to lend sth to sb; **~ coś (od kogoś)** to borrow sth (from sb)
**pożycz|ka** (**-ki, -ki**) (*dat sg* **-ce**, *gen pl* **-ek**) *f* loan; **udzielać (udzielić** *perf*) **komuś pożyczki** to give sb a loan; **zaciągać (zaciągnąć** *perf*) **pożyczkę** to take out *lub* get a loan
**pożyczkodaw|ca** (**-cy, -cy**) *m decl like f in sg* lender
**pożycz|yć (-ę, -ysz)** *vb perf od* **pożyczać**
**poż|yć (-yję, -yjesz)** *vi perf*: **on pożyje jeszcze kilka lat** he'll live another couple of years
**pożyteczny** *adj* useful
**pożyt|ek** (**-ku, -ki**) (*instr sg* **-kiem**) *m* benefit, advantage; **mieć ~ z** *+gen* to benefit from, to profit by *lub* from; **z pożytkiem dla kogoś** to sb's benefit; **z pożytkiem dla** *+gen* to the benefit of
**pożywie|nie** (**-nia**) *nt* food, nourishment
**pożywny** *adj* nourishing, nutritious
**pój** *vb patrz* **poić**
**pój|ść (-dę, -dziesz)** (*imp* **-dź**, *pt* **poszedł, poszła, poszli**) *vb perf od* **iść**
**póki** *conj* as long as; **~ nie** until; **~ nie wrócę** until I come back; **~ czas** before it's too late; **~ nie wróci** before he comes back; **~ co** for the moment
**pól** *n patrz* **pole**
**pół** *inv* half; **pół jabłka/szklanki** half an apple/a glass; **pół godziny** half an hour; **dwa i pół** two and a half; **na pół** in half; **w pół drogi** half(-)way; **za pół ceny** (*sprzedawać*) at half price *lub* half-price; (*kupować*) for half price *lub* half-price; **przerywać (przerwać** *perf*) **komuś w pół zdania** *lub* **słowa** to interrupt sb; **(to) pół biedy** (*pot*) it could be worse; **pracować na pół etatu** to work part-time; **dzielić się pół na pół** to go fifty-fifty
**półbu|t** (**-ta, -ty**) (*loc sg* **-cie**) *m* (low) shoe
**półciężarów|ka** (**-ki, -ki**) (*dat sg* **-ce**, *gen pl* **-ek**) *f* van
**półciężki** *adj*: **waga półciężka** (*Sport*) light-heavy weight
**półeta|t** (**-tu, -ty**) (*loc sg* **-cie**) *m* part-time job
**półfabryka|t** (**-tu, -ty**) (*loc sg* **-cie**) *m* semi-finished product
**półfinali|sta** (**-sty, -ści**) (*loc sg* **-ście**) *m decl like f in sg* semi-finalist
**półfina|ł** (**-łu, -ły**) (*loc sg* **-le**) *m* the semi-finals *pl*
**półfinałowy** *adj*: **mecz ~** semi-final
**półgłosem** *adv* (*mówić*) in an undertone
**półgłów|ek** (**-ka, -ki**) (*instr sg* **-kiem**) *m* (*pej*) dimwit (*pej*), blockhead (*pot*)
**półgodzinny** *adj* thirty-minute *attr*, thirty minutes' *attr*; **przyszedł z ~m opóźnieniem** he was half an hour late
**pół|ka** (**-ki, -ki**) (*dat sg* **-ce**, *gen pl* **-ek**) *f* shelf; (*na książki*) bookshelf; (*na bagaż*) rack; (*skalna*) ledge
**półkol|e** (**-a, -a**) (*gen pl* **-i**) *nt* semicircle
**półkolisty** *adj* semicircular
**półksiężyc** (**-a, -e**) *m* crescent
**półkul|a** (**-i, -e**) *f* hemisphere
**półmet|ek** (**-ka**) (*instr sg* **-kiem**) *m* half-way point
**półmis|ek** (**-ka, -ki**) (*instr sg* **-kiem**) *m* platter, dish
**półmro|k** (**-ku**) (*instr sg* **-kiem**) *m* semidarkness
**północ** (**-y**) *f* (*godzina*) midnight; (*strona świata*) north; **na ~ od** *+gen* (to the) north of
**północno-wschodni** *adj* north-east(ern)
**północno-zachodni** *adj* north-west(ern)
**północny** *adj* (*klimat, półkula*) northern; (*wiatr, kierunek*) northerly; **~ wschód** north-east; **~ zachód** north-west; **Ameryka Północna** North America; **Irlandia Północna** Northern Ireland; **biegun ~** the North Pole; **północna Polska** northern Poland
**półnu|ta** (**-ty, -ty**) (*loc sg* **-cie**) *f* minim (*Brit*), half-note (*US*)
**półokr|ąg** (**-ęgu, -ęgi**) (*instr sg* **-ęgiem**) *m* semicircle
**półpa|siec** (**-śca**) *m* (*Med*) shingles
**półpięt|ro** (**-ra, -ra**) (*loc sg* **-rze**, *gen pl* **-er**) *nt* landing
**półproduk|t** (**-tu, -ty**) (*loc sg* **-cie**) *m* semi-finished article
**półprzewodni|k** (**-ka, -ki**) (*instr sg* **-kiem**) *m* semiconductor

P

**półprzytomny** *adj* semiconscious
**półrocz|e** (**-a, -a**) (*gen pl* **-y**) *nt* half (*of the year*); (*Szkol*) term, semester (US)
**półroczny** *adj* (*zdarzający się co pół roku*) half-yearly, semi-annual; (*trwający pół roku*) six-month *attr*; (*liczący pół roku*) six-month-old *attr*
**półsłodki** *adj* semi-sweet
**półśrod|ek** (**-ka, -ki**) (*instr sg* **-kiem**) *m* half-measure
**półświat|ek** (**-ka**) (*instr sg* **-kiem**) *m* underworld
**półtłusty** *adj* semi-skimmed
**półto|n** (**-nu, -ny**) (*loc sg* **-nie**) *m* (*odcień*) halftone; (*Muz*) semitone, halftone (US)
**półtora** *num* one and a half; **~ kilograma** one and a half kilogram; **półtorej godziny** an hour and a half
**półwys|ep** (**-pu, -py**) (*loc sg* **-pie**) *m* peninsula
**półwytrawny** *adj* semi-dry
**pór** *n patrz* **pora**
**póty** *conj*: **~ ... póki nie ...** until, till; **~ tu zostaniesz, póki nam nie powiesz wszystkiego** you will stay here until you have told us everything
**póz** *n patrz* **poza'**
**później** *adv comp od* **późno**; (*następnie*) later; **prędzej czy ~** sooner or later; **dwa dni ~** two days later; **nie ~ niż** no later than; **odkładać (odłożyć** *perf*) **coś na ~** to put sth off until *lub* till later
**późniejszy** *adj comp od* **późny**; (*następny*) subsequent; **~ prezydent** the future president
**późno** (*comp* **później**) *adv* late; **za ~** too late; **robi się ~** it's getting late; **do późna** till late
**późny** *adj* late; **późna starość** advanced old age
**pp.** *abbr* = **panie; panowie; państwo**
**ppłk** *abbr* (= *podpułkownik*) Lt-Col
**p.p.m.** *abbr* (= *poniżej poziomu morza*) below see level
**ppor.** *abbr* (= *podporucznik*) 2nd Lt.
**PPP** *abbr* (= *Program Powszechnej Prywatyzacji*) National Privatization Programme (*Brit*) *lub* Program (US)
**PR** *abbr* = **Polskie Radio**
**prabab|ka** (**-ki, -ki**) (*dat sg* **-ce**, *gen pl* **-ek**) *f* great-grandmother
**prac|a** (**-y, -e**) *f* work; **~ klasowa** (classroom) test, test paper; **~ domowa** homework; **~ magisterska** M.A. thesis; **~ doktorska** doctoral *lub* Ph.D. dissertation; **iść do pracy** to go to work; **być w pracy** to be at work; **być bez pracy** to be out of work; **prace badawcze** research
**pracobiorc|a** (**-y, -y**) *m decl like f in sg* employee
**pracochłonny** *adj* laborious
**pracodawc|a** (**-y, -y**) *m decl like f in sg* employer
**prac|ować (-uję, -ujesz)** *vi* (*wykonywać pracę*) to work; (*mieć posadę*) to have a job; (*funkcjonować*) to work, to operate; **~ nad kimś/czymś** to work on sb/sth; **~ fizycznie/umysłowo** to do manual/mental work
**pracowitoś|ć** (**-ci**) *f* diligence
**pracowity** *adj* (*uczeń*) hard-working, diligent; (*dzień*) arduous
**pracow|nia** (**-ni, -nie**) (*gen pl* **-ni**) *f* (*malarza, rzeźbiarza*) studio, atelier; (*chemiczna, techniczna*) laboratory; (*warsztat*) workshop
**pracownic|a** (**-y, -e**) *f* (woman) worker
**pracowni|k** (**-ka, -cy**) (*instr sg* **-kiem**) *m* worker, employee; **~ biurowy** office worker, clerk; **~ naukowy** research worker; **~ fizyczny** labourer (*Brit*), laborer (US), blue-collar worker; **~ umysłowy** office worker, white-collar worker
**pracz|ka** (**-ki, -ki**) (*dat sg* **-ce**, *gen pl* **-ek**) *f* washerwoman, laundress
**prać (piorę, pierzesz)** *vt* (*usuwać brud*) (*perf* **wy-**) to wash; (*chemicznie*) to dry-clean; (*pot: bić*) (*perf* **s-**) to thrash ▷ *vi* to wash (clothes), to do the laundry; **prać się** *vr* (*być pranym*) (*perf* **wy-**) to wash
**pradawny** *adj* primeval
**pradziad|ek** (**-ka, -kowie**) (*instr sg* **-kiem**) *m* great-grandfather
**Pra|ga** (**-gi**) (*dat sg* **-dze**) *f* Prague
**pragmatyczny** *adj* pragmatic
**pragmatyz|m** (**-mu**) (*loc sg* **-mie**) *m* pragmatism
**prag|nąć (-nę, -niesz)** (*imp* **-nij**) *vt* (*życzyć sobie*) to desire; (*pożądać*) to lust for; **~ coś zrobić** to wish to do sth
**pragnie|nie** (**-nia**) *nt* (*suchość w ustach*) thirst; (*gorąca chęć*) (*nom pl* **-nia**, *gen pl* **-ń**) desire; **mieć ~** to be thirsty
**praktycznie** *adv* practically; (*doświadczalnie*) practically, in practice
**praktyczny** *adj* (*człowiek, metoda*) practical; (*strój*) practical, sensible
**prakty|k** (**-ka, -cy**) (*instr sg* **-kiem**) *m* (*osoba z doświadczeniem*) experienced person; (*osoba zaradna*) pragmatist, practical person; **lekarz/inżynier ~** practising (*Brit*) *lub* practicing (US) doctor/engineer
**prakty|ka** (**-ki**) (*dat sg* **-ce**) *f* practice; (*staż: w firmie*) training period; (*: w szkole*) teacher practice; (*: u rzemieślnika*) apprenticeship; **w praktyce** in practice; **zastosować** (*perf*) **coś w praktyce** to put sth into practice; **praktyki** *pl* (*zabiegi*) practices *pl*; **praktyki religijne** religious practices

**praktykan|t** (**-ta, -ci**) (*loc sg* **-cie**) *m* (*w firmie*) trainee; (*w szkole*) practice teacher; (*u rzemieślnika*) apprentice

**praktykant|ka** (**-ki, -ki**) (*dat sg* **-ce**, *gen pl* **-ek**) *f* (*w firmie*) trainee; (*w szkole*) practice teacher; (*u rzemieślnika*) apprentice

**praktyk|ować** (**-uję, -ujesz**) *vi* (*o lekarzu*) to practise (*Brit*) *lub* practice (*US*) medicine; (*o adwokacie*) to practise (*Brit*) *lub* practice (*US*) law; (*być na praktyce*) to be in training; (*jako Chrześcijanin*) to be a practising (*Brit*) *lub* practicing (*US*) Christian

**pral|ka** (**-ki, -ki**) (*dat sg* **-ce**, *gen pl* **-ek**) *f* washing machine

**pral|nia** (**-ni, -nie**) (*gen pl* **-ni**) *f* laundry; (*chemiczna*) dry-cleaner's; (*samoobsługowa*) launderette, laundromat (*US*)

**prała|t** (**-ta, -ci**) (*loc sg* **-cie**) *m* prelate

**pra|nie** (**-nia**) *nt* (*czynność*) washing; (*porcja bielizny*) (*nom pl* **-nia**, *gen pl* **-ń**) washing, laundry; **oddawać (oddać** *perf*) **coś do prania** to take sth to the laundry; **~ brudów** (*przen*) muckraking

**prapremie|ra** (**-ry, -ry**) (*dat sg* **-rze**) *f* world premiere

**pra|sa** (**-sy**) (*dat sg* **-sie**) *f* press; (*dziennikarze*) the Press; **~ drukarska** printing press

**pras|ować** (**-uję, -ujesz**) *vt* (*bieliznę*) (*perf* **wy-**) to iron, to press; (*blachę*) (*perf* **s-**) to press

**prasownic|a** (**-y, -e**) *f*: **~ do spodni** trouser press

**prasowy** *adj* press *attr*; **agencja prasowa** press *lub* news agency

**prastary** *adj* (*las*) primeval; (*ród, pomnik*) ancient

**praw|da** (**-dy, -dy**) (*dat sg* **-dzie**) *f* truth; **prawdę mówiąc** to tell the truth; **co ~** as a matter of fact; **to ~** it's true; **czy to ~?** is that true?; **jest zimno, ~?** it's cold, isn't it?; **lubisz go, ~?** you like him, don't you?; **zgodny z prawdą** truthful; **mijać (minąć** *perf*) **się z prawdą** to depart from the truth; **spojrzeć** (*perf*) **prawdzie w oczy** to face the truth

**prawdomównoś|ć** (**-ci**) *f* truthfulness

**prawdomówny** *adj* truthful

**prawdopodobieńst|wo** (**-wa**) (*loc sg* **-wie**) *nt* probability, likelihood; **rachunek prawdopodobieństwa** probability calculus; **według wszelkiego prawdopodobieństwa** in all probability; **istnieje małe ~, że ...** it is unlikely that ...

**prawdopodobnie** *adv* (*chyba*) probably; (*autentycznie*) plausibly

**prawdopodobny** *adj* (*bliski prawdy*) probable; (*możliwy*) probable, likely; **mało ~** unlikely

**prawdziw|ek** (**-ka, -ki**) (*instr sg* **-kiem**) *m* boletus

**prawdziwy** *adj* (*kłopot, przyjemność*) real; (*skóra, perła*) genuine; (*opowieść*) true, truthful; (*zdarzenie*) authentic; **to prawdziwa niespodzianka** it's a real surprise; **szef z prawdziwego zdarzenia** real boss

**prawic|a** (**-y**) *f* (*Pol*) the Right; (*książk: prawa ręka*) (*nom pl* **-e**) right hand; **po prawicy** (*z prawej strony*) on the right

**prawicowy** *adj* rightist, right-wing

**pra|wić** (**-wię, -wisz**) *vt* (*książk*): **~ komplementy** to pay compliments; **~ komuś kazania** *lub* **morały** to sermonize sb

**prawid|ło** (**-ła, -ła**) (*loc sg* **-le**, *gen pl* **-eł**) *nt* (*zasada*) rule; (*do butów*) shoetree

**prawidłowoś|ć** (**-ci, -ci**) (*gen pl* **-ci**) *f* regularity

**prawidłowy** *adj* (*poprawny*) correct; (*należyty*) proper; (*normalny*) normal

**prawie** *adv* almost, nearly; **~ go nie znam** I hardly know him; **~ nic** next to nothing; **~ nigdzie/nigdy** hardly anywhere/ever; **~ nikt** scarcely anybody; **~ skończyłem** I've just about finished

**prawniczy** *adj* (*zawód, wykształcenie*) legal; (*studia, wydział*) law *attr*

**prawnie** *adv* legally, lawfully

**prawni|k** (**-ka, -cy**) (*instr sg* **-kiem**) *m* lawyer

**prawnucz|ka** (**-ki, -ki**) (*dat sg* **-ce**, *gen pl* **-ek**) *f* great-granddaughter

**prawnu|k** (**-ka, -ki**) (*instr sg* **-kiem**) *m* great-grandson; **prawnuki** *pl* great-grandchildren

**prawny** *adj* (*radca, porada, moc*) legal; (*akt*) legislative; (*właściciel*) lawful, rightful; **osoba prawna** legal entity *lub* person, body corporate

**pra|wo**[1] (**-wa**) (*loc sg* **-wie**) *nt* (*prawodawstwo*) law; (*ustawa*) (*nom pl* **-wa**) law; (*: zapisana w dzienniku ustaw*) statute; (*uprawnienie*) (*nom pl* **-wa**) right; (*zasada*) principle, law; **~ cywilne/karne** civil/criminal law; **~ jazdy** (*Mot*) driving licence (*Brit*), driver's license (*US*); **prawa człowieka** human rights; **~ autorskie** copyright; **mieć ~ do czegoś/coś zrobić** to be entitled to sth/to do sth, to have a right to sth/to do sth; **nie masz prawa tak mówić!** you have no right to talk like this!; **zgodnie z prawem** in compliance with the law; **prawa obywatelskie** civil rights; **~ poboru** (*Giełda*) subscription right; **~ wyborcze** voting rights; **~ łaski** the right to reprieve; **jakim prawem?** by what right?

**prawo**[2] *adv*: **w ~** (*w prawą stronę*) to the right; **na ~** (*w prawą stronę*) to the right; (*po prawej stronie*) on *lub* to the right; **na ~ i lewo** right and left, all over the place

**prawodawc|a** (**-y, -y**) *m decl like f in sg* legislator

**prawodawczy** *adj* legislative

P

**prawodawst|wo** (**-wie**) *nt* legislation
**prawomocny** *adj* legally valid; **wyrok jest ~** the sentence is final and binding
**prawomyślny** *adj* law-abiding
**praworęczny** *adj* right-handed
**praworządnoś|ć** (**-ci**) *f* law and order
**praworządny** *adj* (*postępujący zgodnie z prawem*) law-abiding; (*zgodny z prawem*) legal
**prawoskrzydło|wy** (**-wego, -wi**) *m decl like adj* (*Sport*) right winger (*Brit*), outside right (*US*)
**prawosławi|e** (**-a**) *nt* Orthodox Church
**prawosławny** *adj* Orthodox
**prawostronny** *adj* right-hand
**prawoś|ć** (**-ci**) *f* (*książk*) integrity
**prawowity** *adj* (*książk*) legitimate, rightful
**prawy** *adj* right; (*uczciwy*) honest; **prawa strona** the right-hand side; (*tkaniny*) right side; **prawe oczko** plain; **z prawej strony** *lub* **po prawej stronie** on the right side; **czyjaś prawa ręka** (*przen*) sb's right hand
**prażony** *adj*: **prażona kukurydza** popcorn
**praż|yć (-ę, -ysz)** *vt* (*perf* **u-**) to roast ▷ *vi* (*o słońcu*) to beat down
**prażyn|ki** (**-ek**) *pl* crisps *pl* (*Brit*), chips *pl* (*US*)
**prą|cie** (**-cia, -cia**) (*gen pl* **-ci**) *nt* penis
**prą|d** (**-du, -dy**) (*loc sg* **-dzie**) *m* current, stream; (*elektryczny*) current; (*elektryczność*) electricity; (*przen*: *kierunek*) current, trend; **iść pod ~** to go against the stream *lub* tide; **iść z ~em** to go with the stream *lub* tide; **~ stały/zmienny** (*Elektr*) direct/alternating current
**prądnic|a** (**-y, -e**) *f* generator; **~ prądu stałego** dynamo; **~ prądu zmiennego** alternator
**prąż|ek** (**-ka, -ki**) (*instr sg* **-kiem**) *m* line, stripe; **spodnie w prążki** striped trousers
**prążkowany** *adj* striped
**preceden|s** (**-su, -sy**) (*loc sg* **-sie**) *m* precedent; **bez ~u** unprecedented
**precel|ek** (**-ka, -ki**) (*instr sg* **-kiem**) *m* pretzel
**precyzj|a** (**-i**) *f* precision, accuracy
**precyz|ować (-uję, -ujesz)** (*perf* **s-**) *vt* to specify
**precyzyjny** *adj* (*ruch, definicja*) precise; (*narzędzia, instrumenty*) precision *attr*; **mechanika precyzyjna** precision engineering
**precz** *excl*: **~!** go away!; **~ z X!** down with X!
**predestyn|ować (-uje)** *vt*: **~ kogoś do czegoś** (*książk*) to predestine sb to sth
**predyspozycj|a** (**-i, -e**) (*gen pl* **-i**) *f* predisposition
**prefabryka|t** (**-tu, -ty**) (*loc sg* **-cie**) *m* prefabricated element
**preferencj|a** (**-i, -e**) (*gen pl* **-i**) *f* (*książk*) preference
**prefer|ować (-uję, -ujesz)** *vt* (*książk*) to prefer, to favour (*Brit*), to favor (*US*)
**prefik|s** (**-su, -sy**) (*loc sg* **-sie**) *m* (*Jęz*) prefix
**prehistori|a** (**-i**) *f* prehistory
**prehistoryczny** *adj* prehistoric(al)
**prekurso|r** (**-ra, -rzy**) (*loc sg* **-rze**) *m* (*poprzednik*) predecessor, precursor; (*zwiastun*) harbinger, forerunner
**prelegen|t** (**-ta, -ci**) (*loc sg* **-cie**) *m* speaker
**prelekcj|a** (**-i, -e**) (*gen pl* **-i**) *f* (*książk*) (public) lecture
**preludi|um** (**-um, -a**) (*gen pl* **-ów**) *nt inv in sg* prelude
**premedytacj|a** (**-i**) *f* premeditation; **morderstwo z premedytacją** premeditated murder
**premi|a** (**-i, -e**) (*gen pl* **-i**) *f* (*dodatek do płacy*) bonus; (*nagroda*) prize
**premie|r** (**-ra, -rzy**) (*loc sg* **-rze**) *m* prime minister, premier
**premie|ra** (**-ry, -ry**) (*dat sg* **-rze**) *f* premiere
**prenumera|ta** (**-ty, -ty**) (*loc sg* **-cie**) *f* subscription
**prenumerato|r** (**-ra, -rzy**) (*loc sg* **-rze**) *m* subscriber
**prenumer|ować (-uję, -ujesz)** (*perf* **za-**) *vt*: **~ czasopismo** to subscribe to a magazine
**prepara|t** (**-tu, -ty**) (*loc sg* **-cie**) *m* (*substancja*) preparation; (*Bio, Med*) specimen
**preri|a** (**-i, -e**) (*gen pl* **-i**) *f* prairie
**prerogatyw|y** (-) *pl* (*książk*) prerogatives *pl*
**presj|a** (**-i**) *f* pressure; **wywierać presję na kogoś** to put pressure on sb
**prestiż** (**-u**) *m* prestige
**prestiżowy** *adj* prestigious
**pretek|st** (**-stu, -sty**) (*loc sg* **-ście**) *m* pretext; **pod ~em czegoś** under the pretext of sth
**pretenden|t** (**-ta, -ci**) (*loc sg* **-cie**) *m* (*do tronu*) pretender; (*do urzędu*) candidate
**pretend|ować (-uję, -ujesz)** *vi*: **~ do czegoś** to aspire to sth; **~ do urzędu** (*w wyborach*) to run for an office
**pretensj|a** (**-i, -e**) (*gen pl* **-i**) *f* (*roszczenie*) claim; (*żal*) resentment; **rościć sobie pretensje do czegoś** to lay claim to sth; **mieć pretensję do kogoś** to hold a grudge against sb
**pretensjonalnoś|ć** (**-ci**) *f* (*nacechowanie pretensją*) pretentiousness; (*sztuczność*) affectation
**pretensjonalny** *adj* (*pełen pretensji*) pretentious; (*sztuczny*) affected
**prewencj|a** (**-i**) *f*: **oddziały prewencji** riot police
**prewencyjny** *adj* preventive
**prez.** *abbr* = **prezes; prezydent**
**prezbiteri|um** (**-um, -a**) (*gen pl* **-ów**) *nt inv in sg* (*Rel*) chancel
**prezencj|a** (**-i**) *f* (*książk*) appearance
**prezen|t** (**-tu, -ty**) (*loc sg* **-cie**) *m* present, gift; **dać** (*perf*)**/dostać** (*perf*) **coś w prezencie** to give/receive sth as a present

**prezentacj|a** (**-i, -e**) (*gen pl* **-i**) *f* (*osób*) introduction; (*pokaz*) presentation; **dokonać** (*perf*) **prezentacji kogoś** to (formally) introduce sb

**prezente|r** (**-ra, -rzy**) (*loc sg* **-rze**) *m* (*TV, Radio*) presenter (*Brit*), announcer (*US*)

**prezent|ować (-uję, -ujesz)** (*perf* **za-**) *vt* (*ludzi*) to introduce; **~ coś (komuś)** to show sth (to sb); **~ broń** to present arms; **prezentować się** *vr*: **dobrze się ~** to look presentable

**prezerwaty|wa** (**-wy, -wy**) (*dat sg* **-wie**) *f* condom, sheath (*Brit*)

**preze|s** (**-sa, -si**) (*loc sg* **-sie**) *m* chairman (*Brit*), president (*US*); **~ Rady Ministrów** Prime Minister

**prezydencki** *adj* presidential

**prezyden|t** (**-ta, -ci**) (*loc sg* **-cie**) *m* (*państwa*) president; (*miasta*) mayor

**prezydentu|ra** (**-ry, -ry**) (*dat sg* **-rze**) *f* presidency

**prezydi|um** (**-um, -a**) (*gen pl* **-ów**) *nt inv in sg* presidium

**pręci|k** (**-ka, -ki**) (*instr sg* **-kiem**) *m dimin od* **pręt**; (*Bot*) stamen

**prędki** *adj* (*nurt, chód*) fast; (*koniec, reakcja*) quick

**pręd|ko** (*comp* **-dzej**) *adv* (*szybko*) quickly; (*niebawem*) soon; **~!** quick(ly)!

**prędkościomierz** (**-a, -e**) (*gen pl* **-y**) *m* speedometer

**prędkoś|ć** (**-ci**) *f* (*samochodu, zmian*) speed; (*Fiz*) velocity; **~ dźwięku/światła** the speed of sound/light; **jechać z prędkością 100 km/h** to drive at 100 km an hour

**prędzej** *adv comp od* **prędko**; **~ czy później** sooner or later; **im ~ tym lepiej** the sooner the better

**pręg|a** (**-gi, -gi**) (*dat sg* **-dze**) *f* streak; **krwawa ~** a bloody welt *lub* weal

**pręgierz** (**-a, -e**) (*gen pl* **-y**) *m* pillory, whipping post; **znalazł się pod ~em (opinii publicznej)** he was (publicly) pilloried

**pręt** (**-ta, -ty**) (*loc sg* **-cie**) *m* rod

**prężnoś|ć** (**-ci**) *f* (*umysłu, działania*) vigour (*Brit*), vigor (*US*); (*firmy, gospodarki*) resilience

**prężny** *adj* (*mięśnie, krok*) springy; (*przen: gospodarka itp.*) resilient, buoyant

**pręż|yć (-ę, -ysz)** *vt* (*ramiona, grzbiet*) (*perf* **na-**) to flex; **prężyć się** *vr* (*napinać mięśnie*) (*perf* **na-**) to flex one's muscles; (*prostować się*) (*perf* **wy-**) to stand upright *lub* erect

**prima aprilis** *m inv* April Fool's Day

**primabaleri|na** (**-ny, -ny**) (*dat sg* **-nie**) *f* prima ballerina

**primadon|na** (**-ny, -ny**) (*dat sg* **-nie**) *f* prima donna

**prioryte|t** (**-tu, -ty**) (*loc sg* **-cie**) *m* priority; **priorytety** *pl* priorities *pl*

**priorytetowy** *adj* priority *attr*

**PRL** *abbr* (= *Polska Rzeczpospolita Ludowa*) (*Hist*) the Polish People's Republic

**pro...** *pref* (*z przymiotnikami*) pro-; **~unistyczny** pro-communist

**probierczy** *adj*: **znak ~** hallmark, plate mark; **urząd ~** assay office; **kamień ~** touchstone

**proble|m** (**-mu, -my**) (*loc sg* **-mie**) *m* problem; **bez ~u** without any problem; **nie ma ~u** (*pot*) no problem; **~ polega na tym, że...** the problem *lub* thing is (that) ...; **robić z czegoś ~** to make an issue out of sth

**problematyczny** *adj* (*budzący wątpliwości*) questionable

**problematy|ka** (**-ki**) (*dat sg* **-ce**) *f*: **~ społeczna/polityczna** social/political issues

**probost|wo** (**-wa, -wa**) (*loc sg* **-wie**) *nt* (*urząd, budynek: w Kościele katolickim*) presbytery; (*: w Kościele anglikańskim*) rectory

**proboszcz** (**-a, -owie**) *m* rector

**probów|ka** (**-ki, -ki**) (*dat sg* **-ce**, *gen pl* **-ek**) *f* test tube; **dziecko z probówki** test-tube baby

**proc.** *abbr* (= *procent*) percent

**proc|a** (**-y, -e**) *f* sling, catapult (*Brit*), slingshot (*US*)

**procede|r** (**-ru, -ry**) (*loc sg* **-rze**) *m* (*pej*): **niecny ~** shady business *lub* dealings

**procedu|ra** (**-ry, -ry**) (*dat sg* **-rze**) *f* procedure

**proceduralny** *adj* procedural

**procen|t** (**-tu, -ty**) (*loc sg* **-cie**) *m* (*setna część*) percent, per cent (*Brit*); (*odsetki*) interest; **pewien/duży ~** a certain/high percentage; **być pewnym (czegoś) na sto ~** to be one hundred percent sure (of sth)

**procent|ować (-uje)** *vi* (*perf* **za-**) to pay dividends, to bear *lub* yield interest; (*przen*) to pay (dividends)

**procentowy** *adj*: **stopa procentowa** interest rate; **punkt ~** percentage point

**proce|s** (**-su, -sy**) (*loc sg* **-sie**) *m* process; (*Prawo*) (law)suit; **wytoczyć** (*perf*) **komuś ~** to bring a suit against sb

**procesj|a** (**-i, -e**) (*gen pl* **-i**) *f* (*Rel*) procession

**proceso|r** (**-ra, -ry**) (*loc sg* **-rze**) *m* (*Komput*) processor

**proces|ować się (-uję, -ujesz)** *vr*: **procesować się (z kimś) (o coś)** to fight (sb) in court (over sth)

**proch** (**-u**) *m* (*strzelniczy*) gunpowder; (*pył*) dust; **prochy** *pl* (*książk: szczątki ludzkie*) remains *pl*; (*popioły*) ashes *pl*; (*pot: narkotyki*) dope

**procho|wiec** (**-wca, -wce**) *m* trench coat

**prodiż** (**-a** *lub* **-u, -e**) (*gen pl* **-ów** *lub* **-y**) *m electric baking tin*

P

**producen|t** (**-ta, -ci**) (*loc sg* **-cie**) *m* producer, manufacturer; ~ **(filmowy)** (film) producer
**produkcj|a** (**-i**) *f* (*wytwarzanie*) production, manufacture; (*wyroby*) production, output, manufacture; (*Film*) production
**produkcyjny** *adj*: **linia/jednostka produkcyjna** production line/unit
**produk|ować (-uję, -ujesz)** (*perf* **wy-**) (*wytwarzać*) *vt* to produce, to manufacture, to make; (*tworzyć*) to produce; **produkować się** *vr* (*pot*: *występować*) to perform
**produk|t** (**-tu, -ty**) (*loc sg* **-cie**) *m* product; **~y rolne** farm produce; **~y spożywcze** foodstuffs; ~ **uboczny** by-product; ~ **końcowy** end-product
**produktywnoś|ć** (**-ci**) *f* productivity
**produktywny** *adj* productive
**prof.** *abbr* (= *profesor*) prof.
**profanacj|a** (**-i**) *f* profanation, desecration
**profan|ować (-uję, -ujesz)** (*perf* **s-**) *vt* to profane, to desecrate
**profesj|a** (**-i, -e**) (*gen pl* **-i**) *f* profession
**profesjonali|sta** (**-sty, -ści**) (*loc sg* **-ście**) *m decl like f in sg* professional
**profesjonaliz|m** (**-mu**) (*loc sg* **-mie**) *m* professionalism
**profesjonalnie** *adv* professionally
**profesjonalny** *adj* professional
**profeso|r** (**-ra, -rowie**) (*loc sg* **-rze**) *m* professor; ~ **uniwersytetu** university professor; ~ **prawa** professor of law
**profesorski** *adj* professorial
**profil** (**-u, -e**) *m* profile; (*kontur, zarys*) outline
**profilaktyczny** *adj* (*leczniczy*) prophylactic; (*działalność*) preventive
**profilakty|ka** (**-ki**) (*dat sg* **-ce**) *f* (*Med*) prevention, prophylaxis
**profi|t** (**-tu, -ty**) (*loc sg* **-cie**) *m* (*książk*) profit
**progi** *n patrz* **próg**
**progno|za** (**-zy, -zy**) (*dat sg* **-zie**) *f* (*przewidywanie*) forecast; (*zapowiedź*) prognosis; ~ **pogody** weather forecast
**progra|m** (**-mu, -my**) (*loc sg* **-mie**) *m* programme (*Brit*), program (*US*); (*wyborczy*) manifesto, platform; (*spotkania*) agenda; (*nauczania*) curriculum, syllabus; (*Komput*) program; ~ **rozrywkowy** show; **mieć coś w ~ie** to have sth on the agenda
**programi|sta** (**-sty, -ści**) (*loc sg* **-ście**) *m decl like f in sg* (*Komput*) programmer
**program|ować (-uję, -ujesz)** (*perf* **za-**) *vt* to programme (*Brit*), to program (*US*) ▷ *vi* (*Komput*) to program
**programowy** *adj* (*artykuł, założenia*) manifesto *attr*; (*działalność, audycja*) policy *attr*; (*utwór*) exemplary *attr*; (*rada*) programming policy *attr*
**progresywny** *adj* progressive
**prohibicj|a** (**-i**) *f* prohibition
**projekcj|a** (**-i, -e**) (*gen pl* **-i**) *f* projection
**projek|t** (**-tu, -ty**) (*loc sg* **-cie**) *m* (*plan działania*) project; (*rysunek*) design; ~ **ustawy** bill
**projektan|t** (**-ta, -ci**) (*loc sg* **-cie**) *m* designer; ~ **mody/wnętrz** fashion/interior designer
**projekto|r** (**-ra, -ry**) (*loc sg* **-rze**) *m* (cine-) projector
**projekt|ować (-uję, -ujesz)** (*perf* **za-**) *vt* to design
**proklamacj|a** (**-i, -e**) (*gen pl* **-i**) *f* proclamation
**proklam|ować (-uję, -ujesz)** *vt* to proclaim
**prokreacj|a** (**-i**) *f* (*książk*) procreation
**prokurato|r** (**-ra, -rzy**) (*loc sg* **-rze**) *m* prosecutor, prosecuting attorney
**prokuratu|ra** (**-ry, -ry**) (*dat sg* **-rze**) *f* public prosecutor's office
**proletaria|t** (**-tu**) (*loc sg* **-cie**) *m* the proletariat
**prolo|g** (**-gu, -gi**) (*instr sg* **-giem**) *m* prologue; (*wyścigu kolarskiego*) opening stage
**prolong|ować (-uję, -ujesz)** (*perf* **s-**) *vt* (*umowę itp.*) to prolong
**pro|m** (**-mu, -my**) (*loc sg* **-mie**) *m* ferry; ~ **kosmiczny** space shuttle
**promena|da** (**-dy, -dy**) (*dat sg* **-dzie**) *f* (*książk*) promenade, boardwalk (*US*)
**promienie|ć (-ję, -jesz)** *vi*: ~ **radością** *itp.* to radiate joy *itp.*
**promieniotwórczoś|ć** (**-ci**) *f* radioactivity
**promieniotwórczy** *adj* radioactive
**promieni|ować (-uję, -ujesz)** *vt* to radiate ▷ *vi* (*o bólu*) to radiate; **promieniowała z niego energia** he radiated energy
**promieniowani|e** (**-a**) *nt* radiation; ~ **słoneczne** solar radiation
**promienisty** *adj* (*układ*) radial; (*światło*) radiant
**promienny** *adj* (*uśmiech*) beaming, radiant
**promie|ń** (**-nia, -nie**) (*gen pl* **-ni**) *m* (*światła, Roentgena*) ray; (*okręgu*) radius; ~ **słońca** sunbeam; **w promieniu stu metrów od** *+gen* within a radius of 100 m from
**promil** (**-a, -e**) (*gen pl* **-i**) *m* per mill
**prominen|t** (**-ta, -ci**) (*loc sg* **-cie**) *m* (*książk*) high-ranking official
**prominentny** *adj* prominent
**promocj|a** (**-i, -e**) (*gen pl* **-i**) *f* promotion
**prom|ować (-uję, -ujesz)** *vt* (*perf* **wy-**) to promote; (*przen*: *nagradzać*) to reward
**promy|k** (**-ka, -ki**) (*instr sg* **-kiem**) *m dimin od* **promień** ray; (*przen*): ~ **nadziei** a ray *lub* gleam of hope
**propagan|da** (**-dy**) (*dat sg* **-dzie**) *f* propaganda
**propagandowy** *adj* propaganda *attr*
**propagato|r** (**-ra, -rzy**) (*loc sg* **-rze**) *m* propagator

**propag|ować (-uję, -ujesz)** (*perf* **roz-**) *vt* to propagate, to disseminate
**propa|n (-nu)** (*loc sg* **-nie**) *m* (*Chem*) propane; **~-butan** bottled gas, LPG (= *liquefied petroleum gas*), Calor gas® (Brit)
**propon|ować (-uję, -ujesz)** (*perf* **za-**) *vt* to suggest, to propose; **~ coś komuś** to offer sth to sb
**proporcj|a (-i, -e)** (*gen pl* **-i**) *f* proportion
**proporcjonalnie** *adv*: **~ do czegoś** in proportion to *lub* with sth; **wzrastać/maleć ~** to increase/decrease in proportion
**proporcjonalny** *adj* (*harmonijny*) well-proportioned; **(wprost/odwrotnie) ~ (do** *+gen*) (directly/inversely) proportional (to)
**proporczy|k (-ka, -ki)** (*instr sg* **-kiem**) *m* pennant
**propo|rzec (-rca, -rce)** *m* banner
**propos** *inv*: **a ~** by the way
**propozycj|a (-i, -e)** (*gen pl* **-i**) *f* (*pomysł*) suggestion, proposal; (*oferta*) offer, proposal
**prorekto|r (-ra, -rzy)** (*loc sg* **-rze**) *m* (*Uniw*) vice-rector (Brit), vice-president (US)
**proroct|wo (-wa, -wa)** (*loc sg* **-wie**) *nt* prophecy
**proroczy** *adj* prophetic
**prorodzinny** *adj* pro-family
**proro|k (-ka, -cy)** (*instr sg* **-kiem**) *m* prophet
**prorok|ować (-uję, -ujesz)** *vt*: **~ (komuś) coś/, że ...** to prophesy (sb) sth/that ...
**prosektori|um (-um, -a)** (*gen pl* **-ów**) *nt inv in sg* dissection room
**prosia|k (-ka, -ki)** (*instr sg* **-kiem**) *m* piglet
**pro|sić (-szę, -sisz)** (*imp* **-ś**) *vt, perf* **po**; **~ kogoś (o coś/, żeby coś zrobił)** to ask sb ((for) sth/ to do sth); **~ kogoś do pokoju/na herbatę** to ask sb in/to tea; **proszę Pana/Pani** sir/ madam; **proszę Pani, ...** (*Szkol*) please miss, ...; **proszę Państwa** ladies and gentlemen; **proszę (bardzo)** (*odpowiedź na dziękuję*) not at all, you're welcome; (*podając coś*) here you are; (*wyrażając zgodę*) please do, go ahead; **~ kogoś o rękę** to propose to sb; **proszę?** (*prośba o powtórzenie*) pardon?, excuse me?; (*czym mogę służyć?*) can I help you?; **proszę usiąść** please be seated; **proszę za mną** follow me, please
**prosi|ę (-ęcia, -ęta)** (*gen pl* **-ąt**) *nt* piglet
**pro|so (-sa)** (*loc sg* **-sie**) *nt* millet
**prospek|t (-tu, -ty)** (*loc sg* **-cie**) *m* (*broszura*) prospectus, brochure
**prosper|ować (-uję, -ujesz)** *vi* to prosper, to thrive; **~ dobrze/źle** to do well/badly
**prost|a (-ej, -e)** *f decl like adj* (*też*: **linia prosta**) straight line; (*Sport*) straight (Brit), straightaway (US)
**prostacki** *adj* (*pej*) boorish, coarse
**prosta|k (-ka, -cy)** (*instr sg* **-kiem**) *m* (*pej*) boor, simpleton
**prosta|ta (-ty, -ty)** (*dat* **-cie**) *f* prostate
**prosto** *adv* (*iść, jechać*) straight (ahead); (*chodzić, trzymać się*) upright; (*tłumaczyć*) clearly; (*bezpośrednio*) straight; **(powiedzieć komuś coś) ~ z mostu** (to tell sb sth) straight out *lub* from the shoulder
**prostoduszny** *adj* simple(-hearted), guileless
**prostoką|t (-ta, -ty)** (*loc sg* **-cie**) *m* rectangle
**prostokątny** *adj* rectangular
**prostolinijny** *adj* (*człowiek*) straightforward
**prostopadły** *adj*: **~ (do** *+gen*) perpendicular (to)
**prosto|ta (-ty)** (*loc sg* **-cie**) *f* simplicity
**prost|ować (-uję, -ujesz)** *vt* (*wyrównywać*) (*perf* **wy-**) to straighten; (*błąd, wiadomość*) (*perf* **s-**) to straighten out, to rectify; **prostować się** *vr* (*perf* **wy-**) (*o człowieku*) to straighten up
**prostowni|k (-ka, -ki)** (*instr sg* **-kiem**) *m* (*Tech*) rectifier; (*do akumulatorów*) battery charger
**prostu** *inv*: **po ~** (*zwyczajnie*) simply; (*wprost*) straight
**prosty** *adj* (*włosy, droga*) straight; (*człowiek, maszyna, zdanie*) simple; (*wyprostowany*) erect ▷ *m decl like adj* (*Sport*): **prawy/lewy ~** right/left straight; **kąt ~** right angle
**prostytucj|a (-i)** *f* prostitution
**prostytut|ka (-ki, -ki)** (*dat sg* **-ce**, *gen pl* **-ek**) *f* prostitute
**prosz|ek (-ku, -ki)** (*instr sg* **-kiem**) *m* (*substancja*) powder; (*lekarstwo*) pill; **~ do prania** washing powder; **mleko w proszku** powdered milk; **~ do pieczenia** baking powder
**pr|ośba (-ośby, -ośby)** (*dat sg* **-ośbie**, *gen pl* **-óśb**) *f* request; **mam do ciebie prośbę** I have a favour (Brit) *lub* favor (US) to ask of you; **(zrobić coś) na czyjąś prośbę** (to do sth) at sb's request
**proteg|ować (-uję, -ujesz)** *vt*: **~ kogoś** to pull strings *lub* open doors for sb
**protegowa|ny (-nego, -ni)** *m decl like adj* protégé
**protekcj|a (-i, -e)** (*gen pl* **-i**) *f* favouritism (Brit), favoritism (US)
**protekcjonalny** *adj* patronizing, condescending
**protekcjoniz|m (-mu)** (*loc sg* **-mie**) *m* (*Ekon*) protectionism
**protekcyjny** *adj* (*polityka, cło*) protective
**protektora|t (-tu, -ty)** (*loc sg* **-cie**) *m* (*Pol*) protectorate
**prote|st (-stu, -sty)** (*loc sg* **-ście**) *m* protest; **wystosować** (*perf*) *lub* **złożyć** (*perf*) **~** to lodge a protest; **na znak ~u (przeciwko czemuś)** in protest (against sth)
**protestacyjny** *adj*: **marsz ~** protest march; **list ~** a letter of protest

P

**protestancki** *adj* Protestant
**protestan|t** (**-ta, -ci**) (*loc sg* **-cie**) *m* Protestant
**protestantyz|m** (**-mu**) (*loc sg* **-mie**) *m* Protestantism
**protest|ować (-uję, -ujesz)** (*perf* **za-**) *vi*: **~ (przeciwko czemuś)** to protest (against *lub* about sth)
**prote|za** (**-zy, -zy**) (*dat sg* **-zie**) *f* (*ortopedyczna*) artificial limb; (*zębowa*) dentures *pl*
**protokoł|ować, protokół|ować (-uję, -ujesz)** *vt* (*perf* **za-**) to minute ▷ *vi* to take the minutes
**protok|ół** (**-ołu, -oły**) (*loc sg* **-ole**) *m* (*pisemne sprawozdanie*) minutes *pl*; (*akt urzędowy*) (official) report; **~ dyplomatyczny** diplomatic protocol; **poza protokołem** off the record
**prototy|p** (**-pu, -py**) (*loc sg* **-pie**) *m* prototype
**prototypowy** *adj* prototype *attr*
**prowadnic|a** (**-y, -e**) *f* (*Tech*) runner
**prowadzący** *adj* leading ▷ *m decl like adj* (*TV, Radio*) compere, host
**prowadzeni|e** (**-a**) *nt* (*domu, sklepu*) running; (*samochodu*) driving; (*też*: **prowadzenie się**) conduct; **obejmować (objąć** *perf*) **~** to take the lead; **(być) na prowadzeniu** (*Sport*) (to be) in the lead
**prowa|dzić (-dzę, -dzisz)** (*imp* **-dź**) *vt* (*dziecko, życie*) to lead; (*samochód*) to drive; (*samolot*) to fly; (*rozmowę*) to carry on; (*spotkanie*) to chair; (*badania*) to conduct; (*śledztwo*) to hold; (*dom*) to keep, to run; (*zakład*) to run; (*interesy*) to do; (*korespondencję, dokumentację*) to keep; (*wojnę*) to wage ▷ *vi* (*o drodze, korytarzu*) to lead; (*Sport*) to lead, to be in the lead; **~ (partnera)** (*w tańcu*) to lead (one's partner); **~ kogoś za rękę** to lead sb by the hand; **~ (do~** *perf*) **do czegoś** to lead (up) to sth; **prowadzić się** *vr*: **dobrze/ źle się ~** to conduct o.s well/badly
**prowian|t** (**-tu, -ty**) (*loc sg* **-cie**) *m* provisions *pl*; **suchy ~** packed lunch
**prowincj|a** (**-i, -e**) (*gen pl* **-i**) *f* (*jednostka administracyjna*) province; (*część kraju poza stolicą*) provinces *pl*
**prowincjonalny** *adj* (*pej*) provincial
**prowizj|a** (**-i, -e**) (*gen pl* **-i**) *f* (*Handel*) commission
**prowizor|ka** (**-ki, -ki**) (*dat sg* **-ce**, *gen pl* **-ek**) *f* (*pot*) makeshift, improvisation
**prowizoryczny** *adj* makeshift *attr*, rough-and-ready
**prowody|r** (**-ra, -rowie** *lub* **-rzy**) (*loc sg* **-rze**) *m* (*pej*) ringleader
**prowokacj|a** (**-i, -e**) (*gen pl* **-i**) *f* provocation
**prowokato|r** (**-ra, -rzy**) (*loc sg* **-rze**) *m* (agent) provocateur
**prowok|ować (-uję, -ujesz)** (*perf* **s-**) *vt* to provoke; **~ kogoś do dyskusji/działania** to provoke sb into discussion/action
**pro|za** (**-zy**) (*dat sg* **-zie**) *f* (*Lit*) prose
**prozaiczny** *adj* (*Lit*) prose *attr*; (*powszedni*) prosaic
**prozai|k** (**-ka, -cy**) (*instr sg* **-kiem**) *m* prose writer
**pró|ba** (**-by, -by**) (*loc sg* **-bie**) *f* (*wytrzymałości itp.*) test; (*Teatr*) rehearsal; **~ głosu** voice check; **~ (zrobienia czegoś)** attempt (at doing sth); **poddawać (poddać** *perf*) **coś próbie** to put sth to the test; **wystawiać (wystawić** *perf*) **kogoś na próbę** to tax *lub* try sb; **~ generalna** dress rehearsal; **ciężka ~** (*przen*) ordeal; **metodą prób i błędów** by (a process of) trial and error; **(robić coś) na próbę** (to do sth) on a trial basis
**prób|ka** (**-ki, -ki**) (*dat sg* **-ce**, *gen pl* **-ek**) *f* (*towaru*) sample; (*gleby itp.*) specimen; (*krwi*) sample, specimen
**próbny** *adj*: **lot ~** test flight; **zdjęcia próbne** screen test; **okres ~** trial period
**prób|ować (-uję, -ujesz)** (*perf* **s-**) *vt* (*zupę*) to taste; (*samochód, instrument*) to test; **~ coś zrobić** to try to do sth; **~ szczęścia/sił (w czymś)** to try one's luck/hand (at sth)
**próchnic|a** (**-y**) *f* (*Med*) caries; (*Rol*) humus
**próchni|eć (-eje)** (*perf* **s-**) *vt* (*o drzewach*) to rot; (*o zębie*) to decay
**próch|no** (**-na**) (*loc sg* **-nie**) *nt* (*produkt rozkładu*) rotten wood
**prócz** *prep +gen* (*książk*) = **oprócz**
**pr|óg** (**-ogu, -ogi**) (*instr sg* **-ogiem**) *m* (*domu, drzwi*) doorstep, threshold; (*przen*: *życia, dojrzałości*) threshold; (*Sport*) take-off board; **~ słyszalności** auditory threshold; **~ świadomości** threshold of consciousness; **u progu śmierci** on the verge of death; **to dla mnie za wysokie progi** (*przen*) it's quite out of my league
**prósz|yć (-y)** *vi*: **prószy śnieg** it's snowing lightly
**próśb** *n patrz* **prośba**
**próż|nia** (**-ni, -nie**) (*gen pl* **-ni**) *f* (*Fiz*) vacuum; (*pot*: *pustka*) void; **trafiać w próżnię** (*przen*) to fall on deaf ears
**próżnia|k** (**-ka, -cy** *lub* **-ki**) (*instr sg* **-kiem**) *m* idler
**próżniowy** *adj* vacuum *attr*
**próżno** *adv* (*książk*): **na ~** in vain, to no avail
**próżn|ować (-uję, -ujesz)** *vi* to loaf
**próżny** *adj* (*człowiek, trud*) vain; (*gadanie, słowa*) futile; (*pusty*) empty; **odejść** (*perf*) **z ~mi rękami** to leave empty-handed; **przelewać z pustego w próżne** to talk for the sake of talking
**pru|ć (-ję, -jesz)** *vt* (*sweter*) (*perf* **s-**) to undo, to unravel; (*sukienkę*) (*perf* **s-**) to unpick; (*fale*) to

plough (Brit), to plow (US) ▷ *vi* (*pot*: *pędzić*) to belt (*pot*); **pruć się** *vr* (*perf* **po-**) (*o swetrze*) to run; (*o sukience*) to come apart
**pruderi|a** (**-i**) *f* prudery
**pruderyjny** *adj* prudish
**prusa|k** (**-ka**) (*instr sg* **-kiem**) *m* (*karaluch*) (*nom pl* **-ki**) cockroach; **Prusak** (*nom pl* **-cy**) (*Hist*) Prussian
**pruski** *adj* Prussian; **kwas ~** prussic acid
**Prus|y** (**-**) *pl* Prussia
**prych|ać (-am, -asz)** (*perf* **-nąć**) *vi* to snort
**prych|nąć (-nę, -niesz)** (*imp* **-nij**) *vb perf od* **prychać**
**prycz|a** (**-y, -e**) (*gen pl* **-** *lub* **-y**) *f* bunk
**pry|m** (**-mu**) (*loc sg* **-mie**) *m*: **wieść ~** to make the running (*przen*)
**pryma|s** (**-sa, -si** *lub* **-sowie**) (*loc sg* **-sie**) *m* primate
**pryma|t** (**-tu**) (*loc sg* **-cie**) *m* primacy
**prymitywny** *adj* primitive
**prymul|a** (**-i, -e**) (*gen pl* **-** *lub* **-i**) *f* primrose
**prymu|s** (**-sa, -si**) (*loc sg* **-sie**) *m* top student
**pryncypialny** *adj*: **~ człowiek** a man of principle
**prys|kać (-kam, -kasz)** (*perf* **-nąć**) *vt*: **~ czymś** (*wodą*) to splash, to spray; (*środkiem owadobójczym*) to spray ▷ *vi* to splutter; (*przen*: *znikać*) to vanish; (*pot*: *uciekać*) to scram
**pry|snąć (-snę, -śniesz)** (*imp* **-śnij**) *vb perf od* **pryskać**
**pryszcz** (**-a, -e**) (*gen pl* **-y**) *m* spot, pimple
**pryszczaty** *adj* pimply, spotty
**pryszczyc|a** (**-y**) *f* (*Med*) foot-and-mouth disease
**prysznic** (**-u, -e**) *m* shower; **brać (wziąć** *perf*) **~** to shower, to take *lub* have a shower
**prywaciarz** (**-a, -e**) (*gen pl* **-y**) *m* (*pot*) private entrepreneur
**prywat|ka** (**-ki, -ki**) (*dat sg* **-ce**, *gen pl* **-ek**) *f* party
**prywatnie** *adv* privately
**prywatnoś|ć** (**-ci**) *f* privacy
**prywatny** *adj* private; (*szkoła*) private, public (*Brit*); (*użytek*) personal
**prywatyzacj|a** (**-i**) *f* privatization
**prywatyz|ować (-uję, -ujesz)** (*perf* **s-**) *vt* to privatize
**pryz|ma** (**-my, -my**) (*dat sg* **-mie**) *f* pile, heap
**pryzma|t** (**-tu, -ty**) (*loc sg* **-cie**) *m* prism
**przaśny** *adj* unleavened
**prząd|ka** (**-ki, -ki**) (*dat sg* **-ce**, *gen pl* **-ek**) *f* spinner
**prz|ąść (-ędę, -ędziesz)** (*imp* **-ędź** *lub* **-ądź**) *vt* (*perf* **u-**) to spin ▷ *vi*: **cienko ~** (*pot*) to live from hand to mouth
**przeanaliz|ować (-uję, -ujesz)** *vt perf* to analyse (*Brit*) *lub* analyze (*US*) (thoroughly)
**przebacz|ać (-am, -asz)** (*perf* **-yć**) *vt*: **przebaczyć (coś) komuś** to forgive sb (sth)
**przebaczeni|e** (**-a**) *nt* forgiveness
**przebad|ać (-am, -asz)** *vt perf* to give a thorough examination to
**przebar|wiać (-wiam, -wiasz)** (*perf* **-wić**) *vt* to discolour (*Brit*), to discolor (*US*)
**przebi|ć (-ję, -jesz)** *vb perf od* **przebijać**
**przebie|c (-gnę, -gniesz)** (*imp* **-gnij**) *vb perf od* **przebiegać**
**przebie|g** (**-gu**) (*instr sg* **-giem**) *m* (*rozmowy, procesu*) course; (*szlaku*) route; (*Mot*) mil(e)age
**przebieg|ać (-am, -asz)** (*perf* **przebiec**) *vt* (*trasę, odcinek*) to run ▷ *vi* (*o zjawisku, chorobie, rozmowie*) to proceed; (*o człowieku, zwierzęciu*: *przemykać*) to rush *lub* dash (across); (*o linii, drodze*) to go; **przebiec komuś drogę** to cross sb's path; **przebiec coś wzrokiem** *lub* **oczami** to run one's eyes over sth
**przebiegłoś|ć** (**-ci**) *f* cunning, guile
**przebiegły** *adj* cunning, crafty
**przebier|ać (-am, -asz)** *vt* (*sortować*) (*perf* **przebrać**) to sift; **~ (przebrać** *perf*) **kogoś** (*zmieniać ubranie*) to change sb's clothes; **~ kogoś za** *+acc* to disguise sb as ▷ *vi*: **~ (w czymś)** to be fussy (about sth); **~ palcami** to tap one's fingers; **~ nogami** to hop from one leg to the other; **nie ~ w słowach** not to mince one's words; **nie przebierając w środkach** by hook or by crook; **przebierać się** (*perf* **przebrać**) *vr* to change (one's clothes); **~ się (za kogoś)** to dress up *lub* disguise o.s. (as sb)
**przebieralni|a** (**-, -e**) (*gen pl* **-**) *f* dressing room
**przebij|ać (-am, -asz)** (*perf* **przebić**) *vt* (*deskę, skórę*) to pierce; (*oponę, zbiornik*) to puncture; (*przekopywać*: *ulicę*) to dig up; (*przewiercać*) to drill; (*Karty*) to beat ▷ *vi* (*o świetle, farbie*) to show through; **przebijać się** *vr* (*przez gąszcz*) to fight *lub* push one's way through; (*przez tłum*) to elbow one's way through; (*przez wrogie oddziały*) to fight one's way through
**przebiśnie|g** (**-gu, -gi**) (*instr sg* **-giem**) *m* snowdrop
**przebłag|ać (-am, -asz)** *vt perf* to conciliate, to appease
**przebłys|k** (**-ku, -ki**) (*instr sg* **-kiem**) *m* (*światła*) glimmer; (*geniuszu*) stroke; (*intuicji, świadomości*) flash
**przebojowy** *adj* (*osoba*) go-ahead *attr*; (*piosenka, nagranie*) hit *attr*
**przebol|eć (-eję, -ejesz)** *vt perf* to get over
**przeb|ój** (**-oju, -oje**) *m* (*piosenka*) hit; (*sukces*) success; **iść przebojem** to be a go-getter; **lista przebojów** (*spis utworów*) the charts *pl*; (*program*) hit parade
**prze|brać (-biorę, -bierzesz)** *vb perf od* **przebierać** ▷ *vt perf*: **~ miar(k)ę** to go too far,

P

to overstep the mark; **miarka się przebrała** this is the last straw
**przebra|nie** (**-nia, -nia**) (*gen pl* **-ń**) *nt* (*kostium*) disguise; **w przebraniu** in disguise
**przebr|nąć** (**-nę, -niesz**) (*imp* **-nij**) *vb perf od* **brnąć** ▷ *vi perf*: **~ przez szkołę/książkę** to wade through school/a book
**przebudo|wa** (**-wy**) (*dat sg* **-wie**) *f* (*domu*) conversion; (*ulicy*) rebuilding
**przebud|ować** (**-uję, -ujesz**) *vb perf od* **przebudowywać**
**przebudow|ywać** (**-uję, -ujesz**) (*perf* **-ać**) *vt* (*dom*) to convert; (*ulicę*) to rebuild
**przebudze|nie** (**-nia, -nia**) (*gen pl* **-ń**) *nt* awakening
**przebu|dzić** (**-dzę, -dzisz**) (*imp* **-dź**) *vb perf* to rouse, to awaken; **przebudzić się** *vr* to awaken
**przeb|yć** (**-ędę, -ędziesz**) (*imp* **-ądź**) *vb perf od* **przebywać**
**przebyty** *adj* (*odległość, dystans*) covered; (*choroba*) past
**przebyw|ać** (**-am, -asz**) *vt* (*perf* **przebyć**) (*granicę, rzekę*) to cross; (*trudny okres, chorobę*) to suffer, to go through ▷ *vi* to stay; **~ z kimś** to spend time with sb; **~ w szpitalu** to be in hospital (*Brit*) *lub* the hospital (*US*); **~ za granicą** to stay abroad; **~ w areszcie** to be in custody; **~ na wolności** to be at large, to be on the loose
**przece|dzać** (**-dzam, -dzasz**) (*perf* **-dzić**) *vt* to strain
**przece|dzić** (**-dzę, -dzisz**) (*imp* **-dź**) *vb perf od* **przecedzać**
**przece|na** (**-ny**) (*dat sg* **-nie**) *f* reduction in prices; **towar z przeceny** cut-price *lub* discounted goods *pl*
**przece|niać** (**-niam, -niasz**) (*perf* **-nić**) *vt* (*oceniać zbyt wysoko*) to overestimate; (*towar*) to reduce; **przeceniać się** *vr* to overrate o.s., to think too highly of o.s.
**przece|nić** (**-nię, -nisz**) (*imp* **-ń**) *vb perf od* **przeceniać**
**przeceniony** *adj* discounted, cut-price, cut-rate (*US*)
**przechadz|ać się** (**-am, -asz**) *vr* to stroll
**przechadz|ka** (**-ki, -ki**) (*dat sg* **-ce**, *gen pl* **-ek**) *f* stroll
**przechodni** *adj* (*pokój*) connecting; (*nagroda*) challenge *attr*; (*Jęz*) transitive
**przecho|dzić** (**-dzę, -dzisz**) (*imp* **-dź**, *perf* **przejść**) *vt* (*rzekę, ulicę*) to cross; (*chorobę, wstrząs*) to suffer, to go through; (*trasę*) to cover; (*koleje losu*) to experience; (*operację*) to undergo, to go through ▷ *vi* (*iść dalej*) to pass on, to move on; (*iść obok*) to pass by; (*przedostawać się*) to go *lub* pass through; (*mijać: o bólu*) to pass, to ease; (*: o czasie*) to pass, to go by; (*zostawać zaakceptowanym: o propozycji, wniosku*) to go through; (*o ustawie*) to be passed; (*o pomyśle*) to be accepted; **przejść do następnej klasy** to go on to the next form (*Brit*) *lub* grade (*US*); **przejść na katolicyzm** to convert to catholicism; **przejść na inne stanowisko** to take up a different post; **~ przez ulicę** to cross the street; **~ obok czegoś** to pass sth, to go past sth; **~ do historii** to go down in history; **przejść do sprawy/konkretów** to get down to business/brass tacks; **~ samego siebie** to excel o.s.; **~ na czyjąś własność** to become sb's property; **przejść nad czymś do porządku dziennego** to wave sth aside; **przejść z kimś na „ty"** *to agree to address one another by first names*; **to przechodzi wszelkie granice!** (*pot*) there are limits! (*pot*); **przejdzie mu** (*pot*) he'll get over it; **przeszło mi przez myśl, że ...** it's just occurred to me that ...
**przecho|dzień** (**-dnia, -dnie**) *m* passer-by
**przechow|ać** (**-am, -asz**) *vb perf od* **przechowywać**
**przechowal|nia** (**-ni, -nie**) (*gen pl* **-ni**) *f*: **~ bagażu** left-luggage office (*Brit*), checkroom (*US*)
**przechowani|e** (**-a**) *nt*: **oddać** (*perf*) **coś (komuś) na ~** to give sth (to sb) for safekeeping
**przechow|ywać** (**-uję, -ujesz**) (*perf* **-ać**) *vt* (*żywność*) to keep, to store; (*pamiątki, dokumenty*) to keep; (*przen: wspomnienia*) to retain, to hold; (*zbiega*) to hide
**przechowywani|e** (**-a**) *nt* storage; **okres przechowywania** shelf life
**przechwal|ać się** (**-am, -asz**) *vr*: **przechwalać się (czymś)** to boast (of *lub* about sth)
**przechwy|cić** (**-cę, -cisz**) (*imp* **-ć**) *vb perf od* **przechwytywać**
**przechwyt|ywać** (**-uję, -ujesz**) (*perf* **przechwycić**) *vt* to intercept; (*władzę*) to seize; (*piłkę*) to win
**przechyl|ać** (**-am, -asz**) (*perf* **-ić**) *vt* (*przedmiot, głowę*) to tilt; **~ szalę (na czyjąś stronę)** to tip the balance *lub* scales (in sb's favour (*Brit*) *lub* favor (*US*)); **przechylać się** *vr* (*przekrzywiać się*) to tilt; (*wychylać się*) to lean (over)
**przechytrz|yć** (**-ę, -ysz**) *vt perf* (*oszukać*) to outwit, to outsmart
**prze|ciąć** (**-tnę, -tniesz**) (*imp* **-tnij**) *vb perf od* **ciąć, przecinać**
**przecią|g** (**-gu, -gi**) (*instr sg* **-giem**) *m* (*prąd powietrza*) draught (*Brit*), draft (*US*); **w ~u tygodnia/roku** in the course of a week/year
**przeciąg|ać** (**-am, -asz**) (*perf* **-nąć**) *vt*

(*przewlekać: nić*) to thread; (*: sznur*) to pull through; (*przesuwać*) to drag; (*rozmowę, zebranie*) to prolong, to protract; (*słowa, sylaby*) to draw out ▹ *vi* (*o chmurach*) to drift by *lub* past; (*o ptakach*) to fly overhead; (*o armii*) to march past; (*o pojazdach*) to file past; **przeciągnąć ręką po czymś** to run one's hand across sth; **~ strunę** (*przen*) to overstep the mark; **~ kogoś (na swoją stronę)** to win sb over (to one's side); **przeciągać się** *vr* (*o zebraniu: przedłużać się*) to overrun, to be drawn out; (*o człowieku: prostować kości*) to stretch (o.s.)

**przeciągani|e** (**-a**) *nt*: **~ liny** tug-of-war

**przeciągły** *adj* (*dźwięk*) drawn-out; (*spojrzenie*) lingering

**przeciąg|nąć (-nę, -niesz)** (*imp* **-nij**) *vb perf od* **przeciągać**

**przeciąż|ać (-am, -asz)** (*perf* **-yć**) *vt* (*pojazd*) to overload; (*pracą, obowiązkami*) to overburden; (*sieć, obwód*) to overload, to overcharge

**przeciąże|nie** (**-nia**) *nt* (*Lot*) G-force; (*Elektr*) overload

**przeciążony** *adj*: **~ pracą/obowiązkami** overburdened with work/responsibilities

**przecie|c (-knie)** *vb perf od* **przeciekać**

**przecie|k** (**-ku, -ki**) (*instr sg* **-kiem**) *m* (*awaria*) leak(age); (*miejsce*) leak; (*przen: informacji*) leak

**przeciek|ać (-a)** (*perf* **przeciec**) *vi* (*o dachu, naczyniu*) to leak; (*pot: o informacjach*) to leak out; **~ przez coś/do wnętrza czegoś** to leak through/into sth

**przecie|r** (**-ru, -ry**) (*loc sg* **-rze**) *m* purée

**przecier|ać (-am, -asz)** (*perf* **przetrzeć**) *vt* (*jarzyny, owoce*) to purée, to rice (*US*); **~ coś (czymś)** to wipe sth (with sth); **~ drogę** *lub* **szlak** (*przen*) to blaze a trail; **przecierać się** *vr* (*o tkaninie*) to wear through; **przeciera się** it's clearing up

**przecież** *adv* but, yet; **nie wierzycie mi, a ~ to prawda** you don't believe me, but *lub* yet it's true; **~ wiesz** you do know, don't you?; **~ go nie znam** but I don't know him; **to ~ jasne** it's obvious, isn't it?, why, it's obvious

**przecię|cie** (**-cia, -cia**) (*gen pl* **-ć**) *nt* (*przecięte miejsce*) slit; (*skrzyżowanie*) intersection

**przeciętnie** *adv* (*wynosić, zarabiać*) on (the) average; (*wyglądać*) plain; (*nie najlepiej*) indifferently

**przeciętny** *adj* (*pensja, obywatel*) average; (*zdolności*) mediocre

**przecin|ać (-am, -asz)** (*perf* **przeciąć**) *vt* (*nitkę, skórę*) to cut; (*ciszę*) to break; (*dyskusję*) to cut short; (*ulicę, polanę*) to cross; (*las: o drodze, rzece*) to cut through; (*równinę, niebo: o linii, błyskawicy*) to cut across; (*o wielu liniach, drogach*) to criss-cross; **~ komuś drogę** to block sb's way; **przeciąć zakład** (*pot*) to seal a bet; **przecinać się** *vr* (*o dwóch ulicach, liniach*) to cross; (*o wielu ulicach, liniach*) to criss-cross

**przecin|ek** (**-ka, -ki**) (*instr sg* **-kiem**) *m* (*Jęz*) comma; (*Mat*) ≈ (decimal) point; **do trzech miejsc po przecinku** to three decimal places

**przecisk|ać (-am, -asz)** (*perf* **przecisnąć**) *vt*: **~ coś (przez** *+acc*) to squeeze *lub* force sth (through); **przeciskać się** *vr*: **przecisnąć się pod czymś/przez coś** to squeeze o.s. under/ through sth

**przeci|snąć (-snę, -śniesz)** (*imp* **-śnij**) *vb perf od* **przeciskać**

**przeciw, przeciwko** *prep +dat* against; **sprawa Kramer ~ Kramerowi** (*Prawo*) the case Kramer versus Kramer; **(argumenty) za i ~** pros and cons; **nie mam nic ~ko temu** I don't mind it; **czy ma Pan(i) coś ~ko temu, żebym zapalił?** would you mind if I smoked?; **jeśli nie masz nic ~ko temu** if you have no objection

**przeciw...** *pref* anti-, counter-; **pocisk ~niczy** anti-aircraft missile

**przeciwatomowy** *adj*: **schron ~** (nuclear) fall-out shelter

**przeciwbólowy** *adj* (*Med*) analgesic; **środek ~** painkiller, analgesic

**przeciwciał|a** (**-**) *pl* (*Bio*) antibodies *pl*

**przeciwdeszczowy** *adj*: **płaszcz ~** raincoat

**przeciwdział|ać (-am, -asz)** *vi*: **~ czemuś** to counteract sth

**przeciwieńst|wo** (**-wa, -wa**) (*loc sg* **-wie**) *nt* (*sprzeczność*) contrast; (*coś odwrotnego*) opposite, contradiction; **w przeciwieństwie do** *+gen* in contrast to, unlike; **~ kogoś/ czegoś** the opposite of sb/sth

**przeciwko** *prep* = **przeciw**

**przeciwległy** *adj* opposite

**przeciwlotniczy** *adj* (*działo, obrona*) anti-aircraft; (*schron*) air-raid *attr*

**przeciwmgielny** *adj* (*światła*) fog *attr*

**przeciwnie** *adv* (*na odwrót*) in reverse; (*w przeciwnych kierunkach*) in opposite directions; **wprost** *lub* **wręcz ~** on the contrary; **~ do ruchu wskazówek zegara** anticlockwise (*Brit*), counterclockwise (*US*)

**przeciwni|k** (**-ka, -cy**) (*instr sg* **-kiem**) *m* (*wróg*) enemy; (*oponent*) adversary, opponent; (*współzawodnik*) opponent; **być ~iem czegoś** to oppose sth

**przeciwnoś|ci** (**-ci**) *pl*: **~ losu** adversities *pl*

**przeciwny** *adj* (*ściana, płeć*) opposite; (*poglądy, zdania*) contrary; **w ~m razie** otherwise, or else; **być ~m czemuś** to oppose sth, to be against sth; **~ wiatr** headwind, opposing wind

P

**przeciwpancerny** *adj* antitank
**przeciwpożarowy** *adj* fire *attr*
**przeciwsłoneczny** *adj*: **okulary przeciwsłoneczne** sunglasses, dark glasses
**przeciwsta|wiać (-wiam, -wiasz)** (*perf* **-wić**) *vt*: **~ coś czemuś** to contrast sth with sth; **przeciwstawiać się** *vr*: **~ się komuś** to stand up to sb, to oppose sb; **~ się czemuś** to oppose sth
**przeciwstawieni|e (-a)** *nt* (*porównanie*) contrast; **być ~m kogoś** to be the opposite of sb
**przeciwstawny** *adj* opposing
**przeciwwa|ga (-gi)** (*dat sg* **-dze**) *f* counterweight, counterbalance
**przeciwwskaza|nie (-nia, -nia)** (*gen pl* **-ń**) *nt* (*Med*) contraindication
**przeczący** *adj* (*zdanie, odpowiedź*) negative; **~ ruch głową** a shake of the head
**przeczek|ać (-am, -asz)** *vt perf* to wait for the end of; **~ deszcz/burzę** to wait until the rain/storm stops
**przecze|nie (-nia, -nia)** (*gen pl* **-ń**) *nt* (*Jęz*) negative
**przecze|sać (-szę, -szesz)** *vb perf od* **przeczesywać**
**przeczes|ywać (-uję, -ujesz)** (*perf* **-ać**) *vt* (*przen: przeszukiwać*) to comb through, to scour
**przecznic|a (-y, -e)** *f*: **druga ~** the second street across; **trzy przecznice stąd** three blocks from here
**przeczu|cie (-cia, -cia)** (*gen pl* **-ć**) *nt* intuition, hunch; **złe ~** premonition; **mam ~, że ...** I have a hunch that ...
**przeczu|ć (-ję, -jesz)** *vb perf od* **przeczuwać**
**przeczulony** *adj*: **~ (na punkcie** *+gen*) oversensitive (about), touchy (about)
**przeczuw|ać (-am, -asz)** (*perf* **przeczuć**) *vt* to sense, to have an inkling of
**przecz|yć (-ę, -ysz)** (*perf* **za-**) *vi*: **~ czemuś** to deny sth; **fakty temu przeczą** the facts contradict it
**przeczyszczający** *adj*: **środek ~** laxative
**przeczyt|ać (-am, -asz)** *vb perf od* **czytać**
**przeć (prę, przesz)** (*imp* **przyj**, *pt* **parł**) *vi* (*Med*) to push; **~ na coś** to exert pressure on sth; (*: w dół*) to push sth down; **~ na kogoś, żeby coś zrobił** to pressure *lub* urge sb to do sth; **~ do czegoś** to push for sth; **parli naprzód** they pressed on

**SŁOWO KLUCZOWE**

**przed** *prep +instr* **1** (*miejsce*) in front of; **przed domem** in front of the house
**2** (*czas*) before; **przed obiadem/wojną** before dinner/the war; **przed czasem** ahead of time; **przed dwoma miesiącami** two months ago
**3** (*w obronie przed*): **przed chorobą/zimnem** against disease/cold; **uciekać/chronić się przed czymś** to flee/shelter from sth
**4** (*wobec*): **stawić się przed sędzią** to appear before the judge; **ukrywać coś przed kimś** to hide sth from sb
▷ *prep +acc* (*kierunek*): **zajechać** (*perf*) **przed dom** to pull up in front of the house; **iść przed siebie** to walk ahead

**przed...** *pref* pre...
**przedawk|ować (-uję, -ujesz)** *vt perf* to overdose
**przedawkowani|e (-a)** *nt* overdose
**przedawnie|nie (-nia, -nia)** (*gen pl* **-ń**) *nt* (*Prawo*) limitation, prescription
**przedawniony** *adj* (*Prawo*): **dług ~** prescribed debt
**przedbie|gi (-gów)** *pl* (*Sport*) heat
**przed|dzień** (*loc sg* **-edniu**) *m*: **w ~** *lub* **przededniu** *+gen* the day before, on the eve of; (*przen: tuż przed*) shortly before
**przede** *prep* = **przed**; **~ mną** (*w czasie*) before me; (*w przestrzeni*) in front of me; **~ wszystkim** (*w pierwszej kolejności*) first of all, first and foremost
**przedim|ek (-ka, -ki)** (*instr sg* **-kiem**) *m* (*Jęz*) article; **~ określony/nieokreślony** definite/indefinite article
**przedkład|ać (-am, -asz)** *vt* (*wniosek, plan*) (*perf* **przedłożyć**) to submit, to put forward; (*argumenty, racje*) (*perf* **przedłożyć**) to present; **~ coś (nad** *+acc*) (*woleć*) to prefer sth (to sth)
**przedłużacz (-a, -e)** (*gen pl* **-y**) *m* (*Elektr*) extension lead (*Brit*), extension cord (*US*)
**przedłuż|ać (-am, -asz)** (*perf* **-yć**) *vt* (*ulicę, paszport*) to extend; (*urlop, pobyt*) to extend, to prolong; **przedłużać się** *vr* to overrun, to get drawn out
**przedłuże|nie (-nia, -nia)** (*gen pl* **-ń**) *nt* extension
**przedmieś|cie (-cia, -cia)** (*gen pl* **-ć**) *nt* suburb(s) (*pl*); **na przedmieściu** in the suburbs
**przedmio|t (-tu, -ty)** (*loc sg* **-cie**) *m* object; (*dyskusji*) topic; (*badań*) subject
**przedm|owa (-owy, -owy)** (*dat sg* **-owie**, *gen pl* **-ów**) *f* preface, foreword
**przedmówc|a (-y, -y)** *m decl like adj in sg* the preceding speaker
**przedni** *adj* (*znajdujący się z przodu*) front *attr*; (*książk: wyśmienity*) exquisite, outstanding; **~a szyba** (*Mot*) windscreen (*Brit*), windshield (*US*); **~a noga** foreleg; **~ napęd** *lub* **napęd na ~e koła** front wheel drive; **straż ~a** advance guard

**przedosta|ć się (-nę, -niesz)** (*imp* **-ń**) *vb perf od* **przedostawać się**
**przedostatni** *adj* last but one (*Brit*), next to last (*US*); (*sylaba*) penultimate
**przedost|awać się (-aję, -ajesz)** (*imp* **-awaj**, *perf* **-ać**) *vr*: **przedostawać się gdzieś** to find one's way somewhere; (*przenikać*) to penetrate, to get through
**przedpła|ta** (**-ty, -ty**) (*dat sg* **-cie**) *f* advance *lub* down payment
**przedpok|ój** (**-oju, -oje**) (*gen pl* **-oi** *lub* **-ojów**) *m* hall
**przedpołud|nie** (**-nia, -nia**) (*gen pl* **-ni**) *nt* morning
**przedpołudniowy** *adj* morning *attr*
**przedpotopowy** *adj* (*pot*) obsolete
**przedrami|ę** (**-enia, -ona**) (*gen pl* **-on**) *nt* forearm
**przedrost|ek** (**-ka, -ki**) (*instr sg* **-kiem**) *m* (*Jęz*) prefix
**przedru|k** (**-ku, -ki**) (*instr sg* **-kiem**) *m* reprint
**przedruk|ować (-uję, -ujesz)** *vb perf od* **przedrukowywać**
**przedrukow|ywać (-uję, -ujesz)** (*perf* **-ać**) *vt* to reprint
**przed|rzeć (-rę, -rzesz)** (*imp* **-rzyj**) *vb perf od* **przedzierać**
**przedrzeźni|ać (-am, -asz)** *vt* to mimic, to mock
**przedsiębiorc|a** (**-y, -y**) *m decl like adj in sg* entrepreneur; **~ budowlany** (building) contractor; **~ pogrzebowy** undertaker (*Brit*), funeral director (*US*)
**przedsiębiorczoś|ć** (**-ci**) *f* (*cecha*) enterprise; (*działalność gospodarcza*) entrepreneurship; **drobna/wolna ~** small/free enterprise
**przedsiębiorczy** *adj* enterprising
**przedsiębiorst|wo** (**-wa, -wa**) (*loc sg* **-wie**) *nt* enterprise, company
**przedsię|brać (-biorę, -bierzesz)** (*perf* **-wziąć**) *vt* to undertake; **przedsięwziąć kroki** to take steps
**przedsięw|ziąć (-ezmę, -eźmiesz)** (*imp* **-eźmij**) *vb perf od* **przedsiębrać**
**przedsięwzię|cie** (**-cia, -cia**) (*gen pl* **-ć**) *nt* undertaking, venture
**przedsion|ek** (**-ka, -ki**) (*instr sg* **-kiem**) *m* (*pomieszczenie*) vestibule; (*serca*) atrium
**przedsma|k** (**-ku**) (*instr sg* **-kiem**) *m*: **mieć ~ czegoś** to have a foretaste of sth
**przedsprzedaż** (**-y, -e**) (*gen pl* **-y**) *f* advance sale, pre-booking
**przedsta|wiać (-wiam, -wiasz)** (*perf* **-wić**) *vt* (*gościa*) to introduce; (*plany, wniosek*) to put forward, to present; (*film, sytuację*) to present; (*ukazywać*) to depict, to show; **przedstawić kogoś (komuś)** to introduce sb (to sb); **~ kogoś do awansu/odznaczenia** to put sb forward for a promotion/decoration; **Pan pozwoli, że Panu przedstawię ...** let me introduce to you ...; **przedstawiać się** *vr* (*wymieniać swoje nazwisko*) to introduce o.s.; (*o widoku*) to show itself
**przedstawiciel** (**-a, -e**) (*gen pl* **-i**) *m* representative; (*Prawo*) proxy; (*Handel*) representative, agent; **~ handlowy/regionalny** sales/regional representative
**przedstawicielski** *adj* (*organ, system*) representative
**przedstawicielst|wo** (**-wa, -wa**) (*gen pl* **-wie**) *nt* (*Handel*) sales *lub* branch office, agency; (*Pol*) diplomatic post
**przedstawie|nie** (**-nia, -nia**) (*gen pl* **-ń**) *nt* (*widowisko*) show; **robić ~** (*przen*) to make a spectacle of o.s.
**przedszkola|k** (**-ka, -ki**) (*instr sg* **-kiem**) *m* nursery school pupil (*Brit*), kindergartener (*US*)
**przedszkolan|ka** (**-ki, -ki**) (*dat sg* **-ce**, *gen pl* **-ek**) *f* nursery school (*Brit*) *lub* kindergarten (*US*) teacher
**przedszkol|e** (**-a, -a**) (*gen pl* **-i**) *nt* nursery school (*Brit*), kindergarten (*US*)
**przedtem** *adv* (*wcześniej*) earlier, before; (*dawniej*) formerly, before
**przedterminowy** *adj* early
**przedwczesny** *adj* premature, untimely
**przedwcześnie** *adv* prematurely
**przedwczoraj** *adv* the day before yesterday
**przedwioś|nie** (**-nia, -nia**) (*gen pl* **-ni**) *nt* early spring
**przedwojenny** *adj* pre-war *attr*
**przedwyborczy** *adj* (*walka, spotkanie*) election *attr*; (*sondaż*) pre-election *attr*
**przedyskut|ować (-uję, -ujesz)** *vt perf* to discuss, to talk over
**przedzia|ł** (**-łu, -ły**) (*loc sg* **-le**) *m* (*Kolej*) compartment; (*liczbowy, cenowy*) range, bracket; **~ dla palących/niepalących** smoking/non-smoking compartment
**przedziałł|ek** (**-ka, -ki**) (*instr sg* **-kiem**) *m* parting
**przedzie** *n patrz* **przód**
**przedziel|ać (-am, -asz)** (*perf* **-ić**) *vt* (*pokój*) to divide; (*wyraz*) to hyphenate
**przedzier|ać (-am, -asz)** (*perf* **przedrzeć**) *vt* to tear; **przedzierać się** *vr* (*o papierze itp.*) to tear; (*o słońcu*) to break through; (*o człowieku*): **~ się przez coś** to struggle through sth
**przedziura|wić (-wię, -wisz)** *vb perf od* **dziurawić**
**przedziwny** *adj* bizarre
**przedzwo|nić (-nię, -nisz)** (*imp* **-ń**) *vi perf* (*pot*): **~ do kogoś** to give sb a ring (*pot*)

P

**przeegzamin|ować (-uję, -ujesz)** *vb perf od* **egzaminować**
**przefors|ować (-uję, -ujesz)** *vb perf od* **forsować**
**przegad|ać (-am, -asz)** *vt perf (godzinę)* to talk away; *(kogoś)* to outtalk
**przegadany** *adj (pot: książka itp.)* wordy
**przegani|ać (-am, -asz)** *vt (wypędzać) (perf* **przegnać** *lub* **przegonić**) to chase away; *(prześcigać) (perf* **przegonić**) to outrun
**przega|pić (-pię, -pisz)** *vt perf (pot)* to overlook
**prze|giąć (-gnę, -gniesz)** *(imp* **-gnij**) *vb perf od* **przeginać**
**przegię|cie** (**-cia, -cia**) *nt (pot)*: **to jest ~** this is a bit over the top *(pot)*
**przegin|ać (-am, -asz)** *vt (perf* **przegiąć**) *(wyginać)* to bend; **~ (pałę)** *(pot)* to go over the top *(pot)*; **przeginać się** *vr* to bend over
**przeglą|d** (**-du, -dy**) *(loc sg* **-dzie**) *m (kontrola)* inspection; *(filmów, prasy)* review; *(wiadomości)* roundup; *(literatury na dany temat)* survey; **~ techniczny** service; **dokonać** *(perf)* **~u samochodu** to service a car
**przegląd|ać (-am, -asz)** *(perf* **przejrzeć**) *vt* to look through; **przeglądać się** *vr*: **~ się (w lustrze)** to examine o.s. in the mirror
**przeglądar|ka** (**-ki, -ki**) *(dat sg* **-ce**, *gen pl* **-ek**) *f* (web) browser
**przegłosow|ywać (-uję, -ujesz)** *(perf* **-ać**) *vt (projekt, ustawę)* to put to the vote; *(osobę)* to outvote; *(oponentów)* to vote down
**przegn|ać (-am, -asz)** *vb perf od* **przeganiać**
**przego|nić (-nię, -nisz)** *(imp* **-ń**) *vb perf od* **przeganiać**
**przegot|ować (-uję, -ujesz)** *vt perf (mleko, wodę)* to boil
**przegr|ać (-am, -asz)** *vb perf od* **przegrywać**
**przegran|a (-ej, -e)** *f decl like adj (kwota, rzecz)* loss; *(porażka)* defeat
**przegrany** *adj (mecz, zakład, sprawa)* lost; *(człowiek)* defeated
**przegr|oda (-ody, -ody)** *(dat sg* **-odzie**, *gen pl* **-ód**) *f (ściana)* partition; *(bariera)* division; **~ nosowa** nasal septum
**przegród|ka** (**-ki, -ki**) *(dat sg* **-ce**, *gen pl* **-ek**) *f* compartment
**przegrup|ować (-uję, -ujesz)** *vt perf (siły)* to redeploy
**przegryw|ać (-am, -asz)** *(perf* **przegrać**) *vt (mecz, zakład, wybory)* to lose; *(kasetę, utwór)* to copy ▷ *vi* to lose
**przegryz|ać (-am, -asz)** *(perf* **przegryźć**) *vt* to bite through; **przegryzać się** *vr (przen)*: **~ się przez** *+acc* to struggle through
**przegry|źć (-zę, -ziesz)** *(imp* **-ź**) *vb perf od* **przegryzać**; **~ coś** *(pot)* to have a bite to eat *(pot)*; **przegryźć się** *vr perf (Kulin)* to mature

**przegrzew|ać (-am, -asz)** *(perf* **przegrzać**) *vt* to overheat; **przegrzewać się** *vr* to overheat
**przegu|b** (**-bu, -by**) *(loc sg* **-bie**) *m (dłoni)* wrist; *(Tech)* joint
**przegubowy** *adj* articulated
**przehol|ować (-uję, -ujesz)** *vi perf (pot)* to go over the top *(pot)*
**przeinacz|ać (-am, -asz)** *(perf* **-yć**) *vt* to misrepresent
**przeistacz|ać (-am, -asz)** *(perf* **przeistoczyć**) *vt* to transform; **przeistaczać się** *vr*: **~ się (w kogoś/coś)** to transform o.s. (into sb/sth)
**przejad|ać (-am, -asz)** *(perf* **przejeść**) *vt (pieniądze, oszczędności)* to spend on food; **przejadać się** *vr* to overeat
**przejaskra|wiać (-wiam, -wiasz)** *(perf* **-wić**) *vt* to exaggerate
**przejaś|niać się (-nia)** *(perf* **-nić**) *vr*: **przejaśnia/przejaśniło się** it's clearing/it's cleared up
**przejaśnie|nia** (**-ń**) *pl* sunny intervals *pl*
**przeja|w** (**-wu, -wy**) *(loc sg* **-wie**) *m* manifestation; *(choroby)* symptom
**przeja|wiać (-wiam, -wiasz)** *(perf* **-wić**) *vt* to display; **przejawiać się** *vr*: **~ się w czymś** to manifest itself in sth
**przej|azd** (**-azdu, -azdy**) *(loc sg* **-eździe**) *m (samochodem)* drive; *(pociągiem)* ride; *(miejsce)* crossing; **opłata za ~** fare; **~ kolejowy (strzeżony/niestrzeżony)** (protected/unprotected) level *(Brit) lub* grade *(US)* crossing; **są w mieście ~em** they're passing through town
**przejażdż|ka** (**-ki, -ki**) *(dat sg* **-ce**, *gen pl* **-ek**) *f* ride
**przej|ąć (-mę, -miesz)** *(imp* **-mij**) *vb perf od* **przejmować**
**przej|echać (-adę, -edziesz)** *(imp* **-edź**) *vb perf od* **przejeżdżać**; *(przebyć)* to travel; *(najechać, rozjechać)* to run over; **przejechać się** *vr* to go for a ride
**przejedzeni|e** (**-a**) *nt*: **z przejedzenia** from overeating
**przej|eść (-em, -esz)** *(3 pl* **-edzą**, *imp* **-edz**, *pt* **-adł, -edli**) *vb perf od* **przejadać**; **przejeść się** *vr perf* to overeat; **ziemniaki mi się przejadły** *(przen)* I'm tired of potatoes
**przejezdny** *adj* passable
**przejeżdż|ać (-am, -asz)** *(perf* **przejechać**) *vt (przekraczać)* to cross; *(mijać)* to pass; **przejechać przystanek/stację** to miss one's stop/station
**przeję|cie** (**-cia**) *nt (władzy)* taking over; *(piłki, krążka, pałeczki) (nom pl* **-cia**, *gen pl* **-ć**) taking over; *(wzruszenie)* excitement; **z ~m** with excitement
**przejęty** *adj* excited

**przejęzycz|ać się (-am, -asz)** (*perf* **-yć**) *vr* to make a slip
**przejęzycze|nie** (**-nia, -nia**) (*gen pl* **-ń**) *nt* a slip of the tongue
**przejm|ować (-uję, -ujesz)** (*perf* **przejąć**) *vt* (*majątek, obowiązki, piłkę*) to take over; (*list, przesyłkę, transport*) to intercept, to seize; (*obyczaje, tradycje*) to adopt; (*o dreszczach, smutku itp.*) to take hold of; (*wzruszać*) to move; **przejmować się** *vr*: **~ się (czymś)** to be concerned (about sth); **nie przejmuj się** don't worry
**przejmujący** *adj* piercing
**przejrz|eć (-ę, -ysz)** (*imp* **-yj**) *vb perf od* **przeglądać** ▷ *vt perf* (*osobę, zamiary*) to see through ▷ *vi perf* to see the light
**przejrzysty** *adj* transparent
**przejś|cie** (**-cia, -cia**) (*gen pl* **-ć**) *nt* (*miejsce*) passage; (*stadium pośrednie*) transition; (*przeżycie*) ordeal; (*Sport*) transfer; **~ dla pieszych** (pedestrian) crossing; **~ podziemne** subway (*Brit*), underpass (*US*); **~ graniczne** border checkpoint; **„~ wzbronione"** *lub* **„przejścia nie ma"** "no entry"; **robić (zrobić** *perf*) **komuś ~** to make way for sb; **stać (stanąć** *perf*) **w przejściu** to stand in the way
**przejściowy** *adj* (*krótkotrwały*) passing, transitory; (*pośredni*) transitional
**przej|ść (-dę, -dziesz)** (*imp* **-dź**) *vb perf od* **przechodzić**; **przejść się** *vr* to take a walk
**przeka|z** (**-zu, -zy**) (*loc sg* **-zie**) *m* (*też*: **przekaz pieniężny** *lub* **pocztowy**) money *lub* postal order; (*obrazu, dźwięku, tradycji*) transmission; **środki (masowego) ~u** the (mass) media
**przekaz|ywać (-uję, -ujesz)** (*perf* **-ać**) *vt* (*list, wiadomość, polecenie*) to pass on; (*urząd, uprawnienia*) to hand over; (*pieniądze*: *nadawać*) to transfer; **przekazać w spadku** to will, to bequeath; **przekazać coś komuś** (*ofiarować*) to donate sth to sb; **~ komuś pozdrowienia** to give one's regards to sb
**przekaźni|k** (**-ka, -ki**) (*instr sg* **-kiem**) *m* (*Tech*) relay
**przeką|s** (**-su**) (*loc sg* **-sie**) *m*: **z ~em** mockingly
**przeką|sić (-szę, -sisz)** (*imp* **-ś**) *vt perf*: **~ coś** to have a bite to eat (*pot*)
**przekąs|ka** (**-ki, -ki**) (*dat sg* **-ce**, *gen pl* **-ek**) *f* snack
**przekątn|a** (**-ej, -e**) *f decl like adj* diagonal; **po przekątnej** diagonally
**przekl|ąć (-nę, -niesz)** (*imp* **-nij**) *vb perf od* **przeklinać**
**przekleńst|wo** (**-wa, -wa**) (*loc sg* **-wie**) *nt* (*wyraz*) swearword; (*książk*: *klątwa*) curse
**przeklęty** *adj* (*okropny*) damn
**przeklin|ać (-am, -asz)** (*perf* **przekląć**) *vt* to curse ▷ *vi* to swear
**przekła|d** (**-du, -dy**) (*loc sg* **-dzie**) *m* translation
**przekład|ać (-am, -asz)** (*perf* **przełożyć**) *vt* (*układać inaczej*) to rearrange; (*wkładać w środek*) to sandwich; (*zmieniać termin*) to reschedule; (*tłumaczyć*) to translate; **~ nogę/rękę (nad** *+instr*) to step/reach (over); **przełóżmy spotkanie na jutro/piątek** let's reschedule the meeting for tomorrow/Friday
**przekład|nia** (**-ni, -nie**) (*gen pl* **-ni**) *f* transmission (gear)
**przekłama|nie** (**-nia, -nia**) (*gen pl* **-ń**) *nt* distortion
**przekłamany** *adj* distorted
**przekłuw|ać (-am, -asz)** (*perf* **przekłuć**) *vt* (*balonik*) to prick; (*uszy*) to pierce
**przekomarz|ać się (-am, -asz)** *vr* to banter
**przekon|ać (-am, -asz)** *vb perf od* **przekonywać**; **przekonać się** *vr perf*: **~ się do kogoś/czegoś** to get to like sb/sth
**przekona|nie** (**-nia, -nia**) (*gen pl* **-ń**) *nt* belief, conviction; **przekonania polityczne/religijne** political/religious beliefs; **dochodzić (dojść** *perf*) **do przekonania, że …** to become convinced that …; **nie mieć przekonania do** *+gen* to be wary of; **trafiać komuś do przekonania** to appeal to sb; **z ~m/bez przekonania** whole-/half-heartedly
**przekonany** *adj* convinced; **być ~m o czymś** to be convinced of sth
**przekonujący** *adj* convincing
**przekon|ywać (-uję, -ujesz)** (*perf* **-ać**) *vt* to convince; **~ kogoś o czymś** to convince sb of sth; **~ kogoś do czegoś** to sell sb on sth *lub* sth to sb (*pot*); **przekonywać się** *vr* to become convinced
**przekonywający** *adj* = **przekonujący**
**przekop|ywać (-uję, -ujesz)** (*perf* **-ać**) *vt* to dig
**przeko|ra** (**-ry**) (*dat sg* **-rze**) *f* perversity
**przekorny** *adj* perverse, contrary
**przekór** *inv*: **na ~** *+dat* in defiance of
**przekracz|ać (-am, -asz)** (*perf* **przekroczyć**) *vt* (*próg, granicę*) to cross; (*normę, limit, wiek*) to exceed; (*prawo*) to transgress; **~ wszelkie granice** to go way too far; **przekroczyć saldo/stan konta** to overdraw one's account
**przekraw|ać (-am, -asz)** (*perf* **przekroić**) *vt* to cut (in half)
**przekreśl|ać (-am, -asz)** (*perf* **-ić**) *vt* to cross out; (*przen*) to write off
**przekrę|cać (-cam, -casz)** (*perf* **-cić**) *vt* to turn; (*przen*) to twist; **przekręcać się** *vr* (*ustawiać się krzywo*) to twist; (*obracać się*) to turn

P

**przekrocze|nie** (**-nia, -nia**) (*gen pl* **-ń**) *nt* (*prawa, przepisów*) infringement; (*granicy państwa*) crossing; **~ salda** overdraft; **~ szybkości** speeding
**przekrocz|yć (-ę, -ysz)** *vb perf od* **przekraczać**
**przekr|oić (-oję, -oisz)** (*imp* **-ój**) *vb perf od* **przekrawać**
**przekrojowy** *adj* (*rysunek*) sectional; (*przen: analiza, ujęcie*) cross-sectional
**przekr|ój** (**-oju, -oje**) *m* section; **~ pionowy/poziomy/poprzeczny** vertical/horizontal/cross section
**przekrwiony** *adj* bloodshot
**przekrzy|wiać (-wiam, -wiasz)** (*perf* **-wić**) *vt* to tilt; **przekrzywiać się** *vr* to tilt
**przekształ|cać (-cam, -casz)** (*perf* **-cić**) *vt* (*zakład, pomieszczenie*) to convert; (*produkcję*) to reprofile; (*rzeczywistość*) to reshape, to transform; (*Mat*) to transform; **przekształcać się** *vr*: **~ się (w coś)** to evolve (into sth)
**przekształce|nie** (**-nia, -nia**) (*gen pl* **-ń**) *nt* (*pomieszczenia, zakładu*) conversion; (*matematyczne, ustrojowe*) transformation
**przekształ|cić (-cę, -cisz)** (*imp* **-ć**) *vb perf od* **przekształcać**
**przeku|pić (-pię, -pisz)** *vb perf od* **przekupywać**
**przekup|ka** (**-ki, -ki**) (*dat sg* **-ce**, *gen pl* **-ek**) *f* tradeswoman
**przekupny** *adj* corruptible
**przekupst|wo** (**-wa, -wa**) (*loc sg* **-wie**) *nt* bribery
**przeku|pywać (-puję, -pujesz)** (*perf* **-pić**) *vt* to bribe
**przekwalifik|ować (-uję, -ujesz)** *vt perf* to retrain; **przekwalifikować się** *vr perf* to retrain
**przekwit|ać (-a)** (*perf* **-nąć**) *vi* to lose *lub* shed blossom; (*przen: o urodzie*) to wither
**przekwitani|e** (**-a**) *nt* (*Med*) menopause
**przekwit|nąć (-nie)** (*imp* **-nij**) *vb perf od* **przekwitać**
**przel|ać (-eję, -ejesz)** *vb perf od* **przelewać**
**przelat|ywać (-uję, -ujesz)** (*perf* **przelecieć**) *vi* (*o samolocie, ptaku*) to fly (past); (*o wodzie, piasku: przedostawać się*) to seep through; (*pot: przebiegać*) to run; **różne myśli przelatywały mi przez głowę** various thoughts were crossing my mind
**przele|cieć (-cę, -cisz)** (*imp* **-ć**) *vb perf od* **przelatywać** ▷ *vi perf* (*pot: o czasie*) to fly (by)
**przele|w** (**-wu, -wy**) (*loc sg* **-wie**) *m* (*Ekon*) transfer; **dokonać** (*perf*) **~u** to make a transfer
**przelew|ać (-am, -asz)** (*perf* **przelać**) *vt* (*płyn*) to pour; (*prawa, uprawnienia*) to transfer, to convey; (*pieniądze*) to transfer; **~ krew** (*książk*) to spill blood; **~ łzy** (*książk*) to shed tears; **~ coś na papier** to commit sth to paper; **przelewać się** *vr* to overflow; **nie przelewa nam się** (*pot*) we can barely make ends meet
**przelew|ki** (**-ek**) *pl*: **to nie ~** this is no joke
**przelęk|nąć się (-nę, -niesz)** (*imp* **-nij**, *pt* **przeląkł, przelękła, przelękli**) *vr perf* (*książk*): **przelęknąć się** *+gen* to take fright at
**przelicz|ać (-am, -asz)** (*perf* **-yć**) *vt* (*zamieniać*) to convert; (*zliczać*) to count
**przeliczeniowy** *adj*: **tabele przeliczeniowe** conversion tables
**przeliczni|k** (**-ka, -ki**) (*instr sg* **-kiem**) *m* conversion rate
**przelicz|yć (-ę, -ysz)** *vb perf od* **przeliczać**; **przeliczyć się** *vr* to miscalculate
**przelo|t** (**-tu, -ty**) (*loc sg* **-cie**) *m* (*samolotu*) flight; **przeloty** *pl* (*ptaków*) passage; **~em** *lub* **w przelocie** in passing
**przelotnie** *adv* fleetingly
**przelotny** *adj* (*chwila, znajomość*) fleeting; (*deszcz, opady*) occasional
**przelotowy** *adj*: **trasa przelotowa** arterial highway
**przeludnieni|e** (**-a**) *nt* overpopulation
**przeludniony** *adj* overpopulated
**przeładowany** *adj* overloaded
**przeładun|ek** (**-ku, -ki**) (*instr sg* **-kiem**) *m* reloading
**przełaj** (**-u, -e**) *m* (*Sport*) cross-country; **iść/biec na ~** to take a short cut; **bieg na ~** cross-country (race)
**przełajowy** *adj*: **bieg/wyścig ~** cross-country (race)
**przełam|ywać (-uję, -ujesz)** (*perf* **-ać**) *vt* to break; (*przen*) to overcome; **~ (pierwsze) lody** (*przen*) to break the ice; **przełamywać się** *vr* to break; (*o człowieku*) to conquer one's fears
**przełącz|ać (-am, -asz)** (*perf* **-yć**) *vt* to switch (over)
**przełączni|k** (**-ka, -ki**) (*instr sg* **-kiem**) *m* switch
**przełącz|yć (-ę, -ysz)** *vb perf od* **przełączać**
**przełęcz** (**-y, -e**) (*gen pl* **-y**) *f* pass
**przełk|nąć (-nę, -niesz)** (*imp* **-nij**) *vb perf od* **przełykać**
**przeło|m** (**-mu, -my**) (*loc sg* **-mie**) *m* (*moment zwrotny*) breakthrough; (*Geol*) gorge; (*Med*) crisis; **na ~ie wieków** at the turn of the century
**przełomowy** *adj* (*moment, znaczenie*) crucial, critical; (*dzieło*) breakthrough *attr*
**przełoże|nie** (**-nia, -nia**) (*gen pl* **-ń**) *nt* (*Tech*) transmission ratio
**przełożony** *adj*: **siostra przełożona** (*zakonnica*) Mother Superior; (*pielęgniarka*) matron ▷ *m decl like adj* superior

**przeł|ożyć (-ożę, -ożysz)** (*imp* **-óż**) *vb perf od* **przekładać**
**przeły|k** (**-ku, -ki**) (*instr sg* **-kiem**) *m* gullet, oesophagus
**przełyk|ać (-am, -asz)** (*perf* **przełknąć**) *vt* to swallow
**przemag|ać (-am, -asz)** (*perf* **przemóc**) *vt* to overcome; **przemagać się** *vr* to conquer one's fears
**przemak|ać (-am, -asz)** (*perf* **przemoknąć**) *vi* (*moknąć*) to get soaked *lub* drenched; (*przepuszczać wilgoć*) to let water through; **mój płaszcz kompletnie przemókł** my coat is completely soaked
**przemarsz** (**-u, -e**) *m* march past
**przemarz|ać (-am, -asz)** (*perf* **-nąć**) *vi* to freeze
**przemarz|nąć (-nę, -niesz)** (*imp* **-nij**) *vb perf od* **przemarzać**
**przemarznięty** *adj* (*ziemia*) frozen; (*człowiek*) chilled
**przemawi|ać (-am, -asz)** (*perf* **przemówić**) *vi* (*wygłaszać mowę*) to give *lub* make a speech; (*odzywać się*) to speak; ~ **komuś do rozumu** to reason with sb; ~ **za czymś** to support sth; **to do mnie nie przemawia** it doesn't appeal to me
**przemądrzały** *adj* bigheaded
**przemebl|ować (-uję, -ujesz)** *vt perf* to rearrange
**przemęcz|ać (-am, -asz)** (*perf* **-yć**) *vt* to (over) strain; **przemęczać się** *vr* to overexert o.s.; **nie przemęczaj się!** take it easy!
**przemęczeni|e** (**-a**) *nt* exhaustion, fatigue
**przemęczony** *adj* exhausted, fatigued
**przemęcz|yć (-ę, -ysz)** *vb perf od* **przemęczać**
**przemian** *inv*: **na** ~ alternately
**przemia|na** (**-ny, -ny**) (*dat sg* **-nie**) *f* transformation; ~ **materii** metabolism
**przemianow|ywać (-uję, -ujesz)** (*perf* **-ać**) *vt* to rename
**przemie|niać (-niam, -niasz)** (*perf* **-nić**) *vt* to transform, to change; **przemieniać się** *vr*: **przemienić się w** *+acc* to change into
**przemierz|ać (-am, -asz)** (*perf* **-yć**) *vt* to traverse
**przemieszcz|ać (-am, -asz)** (*perf* **przemieścić**) *vt* to move; **przemieszczać się** *vr* to get about *lub* around
**przemieszcze|nie** (**-nia, -nia**) (*gen pl* **-ń**) *nt* (*kości*) dislocation
**przemie|ścić (-szczę, -ścisz)** (*imp* **-ść**) *vb perf od* **przemieszczać**
**przemij|ać (-a)** (*perf* **przeminąć**) *vi* (*o życiu, czasie*) to go by; (*o urodzie*) to fade
**przemilcz|ać (-am, -asz)** (*perf* **-eć**) *vt* (*zbywać milczeniem*) to pass over (in silence); (*nie wspominać*) to leave unsaid
**przemiły** *adj* amiable
**przemi|nąć (-nie)** (*imp* **-ń**) *vb perf od* **przemijać**
**przemk|nąć (-nę, -niesz)** (*imp* **-nij**) *vb perf od* **przemykać; przemknęło mi przez myśl, że ...** it crossed my mind that ...
**przemoc** (**-y**) *f* violence; **~ą** forcibly, through violence
**przemocz|yć (-ę, -ysz)** *vt perf*: ~ **płaszcz** to get one's coat soaked through
**przemok|nąć (-nę, -niesz)** (*imp* **-nij**) *vb perf od* **przemakać**
**przemoknięty** *adj* soaked, drenched
**przem|owa** (**-owy, -owy**) (*dat sg* **-owie**, *gen pl* **-ów**) *f* speech
**przem|óc (-ogę, -ożesz)** (*imp* **-óż**, *pt* **-ógł, -ogła, -ogli**) *vb perf od* **przemagać**
**przemó|wić (-wię, -wisz)** *vb perf od* **przemawiać**
**przemówie|nie** (**-nia, -nia**) (*gen pl* **-ń**) *nt* speech; **wygłosić** (*perf*) ~ to give *lub* make a speech
**przemy|cać (-cam, -casz)** (*perf* **-cić**) *vt* to smuggle
**przemy|cić (-cę, -cisz)** (*imp* **-ć**) *vb perf od* **przemycać**
**przemy|ć (-ję, -jesz)** *vb perf od* **przemywać**
**przemyk|ać (-am, -asz)** (*perf* **przemknąć**) *vi* (*o człowieku, zwierzęciu, cieniu*) to steal by; (*o myśli, wspomnieniu*) to flit
**przemy|sł** (**-słu, -sły**) (*loc sg* **-śle**) *m* industry; ~ **ciężki/lekki** heavy/light industry
**przemysło|wiec** (**-wca, -wcy**) *m* industrialist
**przemysłowy** *adj* industrial
**przemyślany** *adj* well-thought-out
**przemyśl|eć (-ę, -isz)** *vb perf od* **przemyśliwać** ▷ *vt perf*: ~ **sprawę** to think the matter over
**przemyśliw|ać (-am, -asz)** (*perf* **przemyśleć**) *vt* to think over *lub* through ▷ *vi*: ~ **nad czymś** to ponder upon sth
**przemyślny** *adj* clever
**przemy|t** (**-tu**) (*loc sg* **-cie**) *m* smuggling
**przemytni|k** (**-ka, -cy**) (*instr sg* **-kiem**) *m* smuggler
**przemyw|ać (-am, -asz)** (*perf* **przemyć**) *vt* to bathe
**przen.** *abbr* (= *przenośnie*) fig.
**przeniesie|nie** (**-nia, -nia**) (*gen pl* **-ń**) *nt* (*pracownika*) transfer; **kwota z/do przeniesienia** balance brought/carried forward
**prze|nieść (-niosę, -niesiesz)** (*imp* **-nieś**, *pt* **-niósł, -niosła**) *vb perf od* **przenosić**
**przenigdy** *adv* never ever
**przenik|ać (-a)** (*perf* **-nąć**) *vt* (*przedostawać się*) to penetrate; (*nasycać*) to pervade; **przeniknął go strach** he was overcome by fear

P

**przenikliwoś|ć** (**-ci**) *f* (*myślenia*) perspicacity
**przenikliwy** *adj* penetrating
**przenik|nąć** (**-nę, -niesz**) (*imp* **-nij**) *vb perf od* **przenikać** ▷ *vt perf* (*tajemnicę itp.*) to fathom
**przenoc|ować** (**-uję, -ujesz**) *vb perf od* **nocować** ▷ *vt perf* to put up
**przeno|sić** (**-szę, -sisz**) (*imp* **-ś**, *perf* **przenieść**) *vt* (*dziecko, bagaż*) to carry; (*siedzibę, stolicę*) to move; (*zarazki*) to transmit; (*wyraz*) to hyphenate; (*przerysowywać*) to copy; **przeniosła wzrok na** *+acc* her eyes shifted to; **~ kogoś na inne stanowisko** to transfer sb (to another position); **przenosić się** *vr* (*przeprowadzać się*) to move; (*o ogniu, wojnie*) to spread
**przenoś|nia** (**-ni, -nie**) (*gen pl* **-ni**) *f* metaphor; **w przenośni** metaphorically speaking
**przenośny** *adj* (*radio, komputer*) portable; (*wyrażenie, zwrot*) figurative, metaphorical; **w znaczeniu ~m** in a figurative sense
**przeobra|zić** (**-żę, -zisz**) (*imp* **-ź**) *vb perf od* **przeobrażać**
**przeobraż|ać** (**-am, -asz**) (*perf* **przeobrazić**) *vt* to transform; **przeobrażać się** *vr* to be transformed
**przeocze|nie** (**-nia, -nia**) (*gen pl* **-ń**) *nt* oversight
**przeocz|yć** (**-ę, -ysz**) *vt perf* to overlook
**przeo|r** (**-ra, -rzy** *lub* **-rowie**) (*loc sg* **-rze**) *m* prior
**przepad|ać** (**-am, -asz**) (*perf* **przepaść**) *vi* (*o osobie, przedmiocie*) to disappear; (*o majątku, szansie*) to be lost; **~ za** *+instr* to be very fond of; **wszystko przepadło** it's all gone
**przepad|ek** (**-ku**) (*instr sg* **-kiem**) *m*: **~ (mienia)** forfeiture (of property)
**przepal|ać** (**-a**) (*perf* **-ić**) *vt* to burn (through); **przepalać się** *vr* (*o żarówce, bezpieczniku*) to blow
**przepa|sać** (**-szę, -szesz**) *vb perf od* **przepasywać**
**przepas|ka** (**-ki, -ki**) (*dat sg* **-ce**, *gen pl* **-ek**) *f* (*na czoło*) sweatband; (*na oczy*) blindfold; (*na jedno oko*) patch; (*na biodra*) loincloth
**przepas|ywać** (**-uję, -ujesz**) (*perf* **-ać**) *vt*: **~ coś czymś** to tie sth (a)round sth; **przepasywać się** *vr*: **~ się czymś** to tie sth (a) round one's waist
**przepaścisty** *adj* precipitous
**przepaś|ć**[1] (**-ci, -ci**) (*gen pl* **-ci**) *f* precipice; (*przen*) gap, gulf; **stać (stanąć** *perf*) **nad przepaścią** (*przen*) to stand on the edge of a precipice
**przepa|ść**[2] (**-dnę, -dniesz**) (*imp* **-dnij**) *vb perf od* **przepadać**
**przepch|ać** (**-am, -asz**) *vb perf od* **przepychać**
**przepch|nąć** (**-nę, -niesz**) (*imp* **-nij**) *vb perf od* **przepychać**
**przepełniony** *adj* (*ludźmi*) overcrowded; (*wodą itp.*) overflowing
**przepę|dzać** (**-dzam, -dzasz**) (*perf* **-dzić**) *vt* (*bydło*) to drive; (*wyganiać*) to drive off
**przepę|dzić** (**-dzę, -dzisz**) (*imp* **-dź**) *vb perf od* **przepędzać**
**przepici|e** (**-a**) *nt*: **z przepicia** from drinking too much
**prze|pić** (**-piję, -pijesz**) (*imp* **-pij**) *vb perf od* **przepijać**
**przepier|ka** (**-ki, -ki**) (*dat* **-ce**, *gen pl* **-ek**) *f* (*pot*) hand wash
**przepierze|nie** (**-nia, -nia**) (*gen pl* **-ń**) *nt* partition
**przepiękny** *adj* exquisite
**przepij|ać** (**-am, -asz**) (*perf* **przepić**) *vt* (*pieniądze*) to spend on drink
**przepiłow|ywać** (**-uję, -ujesz**) (*perf* **-ać**) *vt* to saw (in half)
**przepiór|ka** (**-ki, -ki**) (*dat sg* **-ce**, *gen pl* **-ek**) *f* quail
**przepi|s** (**-su, -sy**) (*loc sg* **-sie**) *m* (*Kulin*) recipe; (*zarządzenie*) regulation; **~y ruchu drogowego** traffic regulations; **„wydaje się z ~u lekarza"** "only available on prescription"
**przepi|sać** (**-szę, -szesz**) *vb perf od* **przepisywać**
**przepisowy** *adj*: **~ mundur/strój** regulation uniform/outfit
**przepis|ywać** (**-uję, -ujesz**) (*perf* **-ać**) *vt* (*pisać jeszcze raz*) to copy out; (*na maszynie, komputerze*) to type out; (*Med*) to prescribe; **~ coś na kogoś** to sign *lub* make sth over to sb
**przepity** *adj* (*głos*) hoarse from drinking; (*człowiek*) hung over
**przeplat|ać** (**-am, -asz**) (*perf* **przepleść**) *vt* (*przen*): **~ coś czymś** to alternate sth and sth; **przeplatać się** *vr*: **~ się z czymś** (*przen*) to alternate with sth
**przepl|eść** (**-otę, -eciesz**) (*imp* **-eć**, *pt* **-ótł, -otła, -etli**) *vb perf od* **przeplatać**
**przepła|cać** (**-cam, -casz**) (*perf* **-cić**) *vi* to pay too much
**przepła|cić** (**-cę, -cisz**) (*imp* **-ć**) *vb perf od* **przepłacać**
**przepłu|kiwać** (**-kuję, -kujesz**) (*perf* **-kać**) *vt* to rinse; **przepłukać gardło** (*pot*: *napić się*) to wet one's whistle (*pot*)
**przepły|nąć** (**-nę, -niesz**) (*imp* **-ń**) *vb perf od* **przepływać**
**przepły|w** (**-wu**) (*loc sg* **-wie**) *m* flow
**przepływ|ać** (**-am, -asz**) (*perf* **przepłynąć**) *vt* (*o człowieku*) to swim; (*o statku*) to sail ▷ *vi* (*o człowieku*) to swim; (*o statku*) to sail; (*o prądzie, wodzie*) to flow
**przepocony** *adj* sweaty
**przepojony** *adj* (*książk*): **~ czymś** imbued with sth

**przepoła|wiać (-wiam, -wiasz)** (*perf* **przepołowić**) *vt* to halve

**przepoł|owić (-owię, -owisz)** (*imp* **-ów**) *vb perf od* **przepoławiać**

**przepo|na** (**-ny, -ny**) (*dat sg* **-nie**) *f* diaphragm

**przepowiad|ać (-am, -asz)** (*perf* **przepowiedzieć**) *vt* to prophesy, to foretell; (*pogodę*) to predict

**przepowied|nia** (**-ni, -nie**) (*gen pl* **-ni**) *f* (*proroctwo*) prophecy; (*prognoza*) prediction

**przepowi|edzieć (-em, -esz)** (*3 pl* **-edzą**, *imp* **-edz**) *vb perf od* **przepowiadać**

**przepracowany** *adj* overworked

**przepracow|ywać (-uję, -ujesz)** (*perf* **-ać**) *vt* (*godzinę, rok*) to work for; **przepracowywać się** *vr* to overwork

**przeprasz|ać (-am, -asz)** (*perf* **przeprosić**) *vt*: **~ (kogoś/za coś)** to apologize (to sb/for sth); **przepraszam!** (I'm) sorry!; **przepraszam, która (jest) godzina?** excuse me, what's the time?; **przepraszam, że przeszkadzam** sorry to disturb you; **przepraszać się** *vr* (*godzić się*) to make up

**przepraszająco** *adv* apologetically

**przepra|wa** (**-wy, -wy**) (*dat sg* **-wie**) *f* (*podróż*) crossing; **mieć ciężką przeprawę (z kimś)** to have a hard time (with sb)

**przepra|wiać (-wiam, -wiasz)** (*perf* **-wić**) *vt* to ferry; **przeprawiać się** *vr* to get to the other side; **~ się przez rzekę** to ford a river

**przepro|sić (-szę, -sisz)** (*imp* **-ś**) *vb perf od* **przepraszać**

**przeprosi|ny** (**-n**) *pl* apology

**przeproszeni|e** (**-a**) *nt*: **za ~m** (if you'll) pardon the expression

**przeprowa|dzać (-dzam, -dzasz)** (*perf* **-dzić**) *vt* (*z miejsca na miejsce*) to take; (*realizować*) to carry out; **przeprowadzać się** *vr* to move

**przeprowa|dzić (-dzę, -dzisz)** (*imp* **-dź**) *vb perf od* **przeprowadzać**

**przeprowadz|ka** (**-ki, -ki**) (*dat sg* **-ce**, *gen pl* **-ek**) *f* move

**przepukli|na** (**-ny, -ny**) (*dat sg* **-nie**) *f* hernia, rupture

**przepust|ka** (**-ki, -ki**) (*dat sg* **-ce**, *gen pl* **-ek**) *f* pass; **być na przepustce** (*pot*) to be on a pass

**przepustnic|a** (**-y, -e**) *f* throttle; (*Mot*)

**przepustowoś|ć** (**-ci**) *f* capacity

**przepuszcz|ać (-am, -asz)** (*perf* **przepuścić**) *vt* (*pozwalać przejść/przejechać*) to let through; (*przez maszynkę, filtr*) to put; (*światło, wilgoć*) to let in; (*pieniądze, majątek*) to throw away; **nie ~ wody/światła** to keep (the) water/light out

**przepu|ścić (-szczę, -ścisz)** (*imp* **-ść**) *vb perf od* **przepuszczać** ▷ *vt perf* (*błąd*) to miss; (*okazję*) to pass up; **on ci tego nie przepuści** he won't let you get away with it

**przepych** (**-u**) *m* splendour (*Brit*), splendor (*US*)

**przepych|ać (-am, -asz)** (*perf* **przepchać** *lub* **przepchnąć**) *vt* (*przesuwać*) to shove (through); (*rurę*) to unclog; (*fajkę*) to clean out; **przepychać się** *vr* to elbow one's way

**przepyszny** *adj* (*smaczny*) delicious; (*okazały*) splendid

**przepyt|ywać (-uję, -ujesz)** (*perf* **-ać**) *vt*: **przepytać kogoś (z czegoś)** to quiz sb (on sth)

**przerabi|ać (-am, -asz)** (*perf* **przerobić**) *vt* (*płaszcz*) to alter; (*powieść*) to rewrite; (*surowiec*) to process; (*Szkol: materiał, lekturę*) to do

**przeradz|ać się (-a)** (*perf* **przerodzić**) *vr*: **przeradzać się w** *+acc* to turn into

**przerast|ać (-am, -asz)** (*perf* **przerosnąć**) *vt* (*wzrostem*) to outgrow; (*przen: umiejętnościami*) to surpass; **to przerasta ich możliwości** it is beyond their capabilities

**przera|zić (-żę, -zisz)** (*imp* **-ź**) *vb perf od* **przerażać**

**przeraźliwie** *adv* frightfully

**przeraźliwy** *adj* frightful

**przeraż|ać (-am, -asz)** (*perf* **przerazić**) *vt* to horrify, to terrify; **przerażać się** *vr* to be terrified

**przerażający** *adj* horrifying, terrifying

**przerażeni|e** (**-a**) *nt* terror

**przerażony** *adj* terrified

**przereklamowany** *adj* overrated

**przer|obić (-obię, -obisz)** (*imp* **-ób**) *vb perf od* **przerabiać**

**przero|dzić się (-dzi)** *vb perf od* **przeradzać się**

**przero|snąć (-snę, -śniesz)** (*imp* **-śnij**) *vb perf od* **przerastać**

**przero|st** (**-stu, -sty**) (*loc sg* **-ście**) *m* (*przen*) excess; **~ formy nad treścią** excess of form

**przer|ób** (**-obu, -oby**) (*loc sg* **-obie**) *m* processing

**przeróbk|a** (**-ki, -ki**) (*dat sg* **-ce**, *gen pl* **-ek**) *f* (*odzieży*) alteration; (*książki na film itp.*) adaptation

**przeróżny** *adj* various

**przer|wa** (**-wy, -wy**) (*dat sg* **-wie**) *f* (*pauza*) break; (*Szkol*) break, playtime (*Brit*), recess (*US*); (*Teatr*) interval; (*Film*) intermission; (*Sport*) half-time; (*luka, szpara*) gap; **bez przerwy** (*bez odpoczynku*) without a break; (*ciągle*) continuously; **~ obiadowa** lunch break; **roczna ~ (przed podjęciem studiów)** (*Scol*) gap year; **~ na kawę** coffee break; **robić (zrobić** *perf*) **przerwę** to take a break; **z ~mi** on and off

**przer|wać (-wę, -wiesz)** (*imp* **-wij**) *vb perf od* **przerywać**

**przeryw|ać (-am, -asz)** (*perf* **przerwać**) *vt* (*nitkę, front*) to break; (*połączenie, rozmowę*) to interrupt; (*produkcję*) to discontinue;

P

(*marchew, buraki*) to thin ▷ *vi* (*milknąć*) to pause; **~ komuś (w pół słowa)** to interrupt sb (in the middle of a sentence); **~ ciążę** to have an abortion *lub* a termination; **silnik przerywa** the engine splutters; **przerywać się** *vr* to break

**przerywany** *adj* (*oddech, głos*) broken; (*linia*) dashed

**przerywni|k** (**-ka, -ki**) (*instr sg* **-kiem**) *m* interlude

**przerze|dzać (-dzam, -dzasz)** (*imp* **-dź**, *perf* **-dzić**) *vt* to thin; (*przen*: *zapasy itp.*) to deplete; **przerzedzać się** *vr* (*o roślinach, włosach*) to thin; (*przen*: *o tłumie*) to thin out

**przerze|dzić (-dzę, -dzisz)** (*imp* **-dź**) *vb perf od* **przerzedzać**

**przerzu|cać (-cam, -casz)** (*perf* **-cić**) *vt* (*piłkę itp.*) to throw (over); (*broń, żołnierzy*) to redeploy; (*strony*) to leaf *lub* thumb through; (*ubrania, rzeczy*) to dig through; (*pot*: *pracowników*) to transfer; **~ bieg** to change (*Brit*) *lub* shift (*US*) gear; **~ most przez rzekę** to bridge a river; **~ na kogoś obowiązki** to pass one's duties on to sb; **~ na kogoś odpowiedzialność** to shift the responsibility onto sb; **~ książkę/ czasopismo** to flip through a book/ magazine; **przerzucać się** *vr*: **~ się na** *+acc* to switch over to; (*o ogniu itp.*) to spread to

**przerzu|cić (-cę, -cisz)** (*imp* **-ć**) *vb perf od* **przerzucać**

**przerzu|t** (**-tu, -ty**) (*loc sg* **-cie**) *m* (*żołnierzy*) redeployment; (*Med*) metastasis; (*Sport*) swing pass

**przerzut|ka** (**-ki, -ki**) (*dat sg* **-ce**, *gen pl* **-ek**) *f* (derailleur) gears *pl*

**przesa|da** (**-dy**) (*dat sg* **-dzie**) *f* exaggeration; **do przesady** to a fault; **to już ~!** this is going too far!

**przesadnie** *adv* excessively

**przesadny** *adj* exaggerated

**przesa|dzać (-dzam, -dzasz)** (*perf* **-dzić**) *vt* (*rośliny*) to transplant; (*ucznia, widza*) to move (to another seat) ▷ *vi* to exaggerate

**przesa|dzić (-dzę, -dzisz)** (*imp* **-dź**) *vb perf od* **przesadzać**

**przesą|d** (**-du, -dy**) (*loc sg* **-dzie**) *m* (*zabobon*) superstition; (*uprzedzenie*) prejudice

**przesądny** *adj* superstitious

**przesą|dzać (-dzam, -dzasz)** (*perf* **-dzić**) *vt* (*sprawę*) to settle; **~ o czymś** to determine sth

**przesą|dzić (-dzę, -dzisz)** (*imp* **-dź**) *vb perf od* **przesądzać**

**prze|siać (-sieję, -siejesz)** *vb perf od* **przesiewać**

**przesiad|ać się (-am, -asz)** (*perf* **przesiąść**) *vr* (*zmieniać miejsce*) to move to another seat; (*zmieniać środek lokomocji*) to change; **przesiąść się na autobus** to change to a bus; **przesiąść się do innego autobusu** to change buses

**przesiad|ka** (**-ki, -ki**) (*dat sg* **-ce**, *gen pl* **-ek**) *f* change

**przesiad|ywać (-uję, -ujesz)** *vi* to hang about *lub* around

**przesiąk|ać (-am, -asz)** (*perf* **-nąć**) *vi* to soak (through)

**przesiąk|nąć (-nę, -niesz)** (*imp* **-nij**) *vb perf od* **przesiąkać** ▷ *vt perf +instr* to become saturated with

**przesią|ść się (-dę, -dziesz)** (*imp* **-dź**) *vb perf od* **przesiadać się**

**przesiedl|ać (-am, -asz)** (*perf* **-ić**) *vt* to displace; **przesiedlać się** *vr* to migrate

**przesiew|ać (-am, -asz)** (*perf* **przesiać**) *vt* to sift

**przesile|nie** (**-nia, -nia**) (*gen pl* **-ń**) *nt* turning point; (*Astron*) solstice; (*Med*) crisis

**przeska|kiwać (-kuję, -kujesz)** (*perf* **przeskoczyć**) *vt* to jump (over); (*przen*) to skip; **~ z tematu na temat** to jump from one thing to another

**przesko|k** (**-ku, -ki**) (*instr sg* **-kiem**) *m* jump

**prze|słać (-ślę, -ślesz)** (*imp* **-ślij**) *vb perf od* **przesyłać**

**przesłani|ać (-am, -asz)** (*perf* **przesłonić**) *vt* (*zakrywać*) to conceal; **~ coś komuś** (*przen*) to make sb blind to sth

**przesła|nie** (**-nia, -nia**) (*gen pl* **-ń**) *nt* (*książk*) message

**przesłan|ka** (**-ki, -ki**) (*dat sg* **-ce**, *gen pl* **-ek**) *f* (*okoliczność*) circumstance; (*Filozofia*) premise

**przesło|na** (**-ny, -ny**) (*dat sg* **-nie**) *f* (*zasłona*) screen; (*Fot*) aperture

**przesło|nić (-nię, -nisz)** (*imp* **-ń**) *vb perf od* **przesłaniać**

**przesłuch|ać (-am, -asz)** *vb perf od* **przesłuchiwać**

**przesłucha|nie** (**-nia, -nia**) (*gen pl* **-ń**) *nt* (*świadków*) examination; (*zatrzymanego*) interrogation, questioning; (*artysty*) audition

**przesłu|chiwać (-chuję, -chujesz)** (*perf* **-chać**) *vt* (*świadka*) to examine; (*zatrzymanego*) to interrogate, to question; (*artystę*) to audition; (*płytę*) to listen to

**przesłysz|eć się (-ę, -ysz)** *vr perf* to mishear

**przesmy|k** (**-ku, -ki**) (*instr sg* **-kiem**) *m* pass; (*Geog*) isthmus

**prze|solić (-olę, -olisz)** (*imp* **-ól**) *vt perf* to put too much salt in

**prze|spać (-śpię, -śpisz)** (*imp* **-śpij**) *vb perf od* **przesypiać**; **przespać się** *vr perf* to get some sleep; **~ się z kimś** to sleep with sb

**przesta|ć (-nę, -niesz)** (*imp* **-ń**) *vb perf od* **przestawać**

**przestankowy** *adj*: **znak ~** punctuation mark
**przestarzały** *adj* obsolete
**przest|awać (-aję, -ajesz)** (*imp* **-awaj**) *vi* (*perf* **-ać**); **~ coś robić** to stop doing sth; **przestań!** stop it!; **nie przestawał pytać** he kept asking questions ▷ *vt imperf*: **~ z kimś** to associate with sb
**przesta|wiać (-wiam, -wiasz)** (*perf* **-wić**) *vt* (*mebel, wazon*) to move; (*meble*) to rearrange; (*zmieniać kolejność*) to reorder; **przestawiać się** *vr*: **~ się (z czegoś) na coś** to switch (over) (from sth) to sth
**przestawny** *adj*: **szyk ~** inversion
**przestą|pić (-pię, -pisz)** *vb perf od* **przestępować**
**przestępc|a** (**-y, -y**) *m decl like f in sg* criminal
**przestępczoś|ć** (**-ci**) *f* crime
**przestępczy** *adj* criminal
**przestępny** *adj*: **rok ~** leap year
**przestęp|ować (-uję, -ujesz)** (*perf* **przestąpić**) *vt* (*próg, granicę*) to cross; **~ z nogi na nogę** to shuffle one's feet
**przestępst|wo** (**-wa, -wa**) (*loc sg* **-wie**) *nt* crime; **popełniać** (**popełnić** *perf*) **~** to commit a crime
**przest|ój** (**-oju, -oje**) *m* stoppage
**przestrach** (**-u**) *m* fright
**przestraj|ać (-am, -asz)** (*perf* **przestroić**) *vt* to retune
**przestraszony** *adj* frightened
**przestrasz|yć (-ę, -ysz)** *vt perf* to frighten, to scare; **przestraszyć się** *vr perf* to get scared
**przestr|oga** (**-ogi, -ogi**) (*dat sg* **-odze**, *gen pl* **-óg**) *f* (fore)warning
**przestr|oić (-oję, -oisz)** (*imp* **-ój**) *vb perf od* **przestrajać**
**przestronny** *adj* spacious
**przestrze|c (-gę, -żesz)** (*pt* **-gł**) *vb perf od* **przestrzegać**
**przestrzeg|ać (-am, -asz)** *vt* (*przepisów*) to obey; (*prawa*) to abide by; (*zwyczaju*) to observe; (*udzielać przestrogi*) (*perf* **przestrzec**); **~ kogoś (przed czymś)** to (fore)warn sb (of sth)
**przestrzenny** *adj* (*figura*) three-dimensional; (*planowanie*) spatial
**przestrze|ń** (**-ni, -nie**) (*gen pl* **-ni**) *f* (*obszar*) space; (*powierzchnia*) expanse; **~ kosmiczna** (outer) space; **na przestrzeni pięciu lat** within the space of five years; **~ życiowa** living space; **lęk przestrzeni** a fear of heights; **~ powietrzna** air space
**przestudi|ować (-uję, -ujesz)** *vb perf od* **studiować**
**przestworz|a** (**-y**) *pl* (*książk*) skies *pl*
**przesu|nąć (-nę, -niesz)** (*imp* **-ń**) *vb perf od* **przesuwać**
**przesunię|cie** (**-cia, -cia**) (*gen pl* **-ć**) *nt* (*ruch*) shift; (*Fiz*) displacement
**przesu|w** (**-wu, -wy**) (*loc sg* **-wie**) *m* (*taśmy, rolki*) travel
**przesuw|ać (-am, -asz)** (*perf* **przesunąć**) *vt* (*przestawiać*) to move, to shift; (*przen*: *zmieniać termin*) to reschedule; (*przenosić*: *pracownika*) to transfer; **~ zegarek do przodu/tyłu** to put the clock forward/back; **przesuwać się** *vr* (*o przedmiotach*) to shift; (*o człowieku*) to move over
**przesycony** *adj*: **~ czymś** permeated with sth
**przesył|ać (-am, -asz)** (*perf* **przesłać**) *vt* to send; **~ komuś pozdrowienia** *lub* **ukłony** to give one's regards to sb; **~ coś faksem/teleksem** to send sth by fax/telex
**przesył|ka** (**-ki, -ki**) (*dat sg* **-ce**, *gen pl* **-ek**) *f* (*pocztowa*) (piece of) mail; **~ lotnicza/polecona** air/registered mail; **~ pieniężna** money *lub* postal order
**przesy|pać (-pię, -piesz)** *vb perf od* **przesypywać**
**przesypi|ać (-am, -asz)** (*perf* **przespać**) *vt* (*noc*) to sleep through; (*przen*: *okazję*) to let slip ▷ *vi*: **~ do rana** to sleep until morning
**przesyp|ywać (-uję, -ujesz)** (*perf* **-ać**) *vt* to pour
**przesy|t** (**-tu**) (*loc sg* **-cie**) *m* surfeit
**przeszcze|p** (**-pu, -py**) (*loc sg* **-pie**) *m* transplant; **~ skóry** skin graft
**przeszcze|piać (-piam, -piasz)** (*perf* **-pić**) *vt* to transplant
**przeszkadz|ać (-am, -asz)** (*perf* **przeszkodzić**) *vi*: **~ komuś** to disturb sb; **~ w czymś** to interfere with sth; **proszę sobie nie ~** don't let me disturb you; **mnie to nie przeszkadza** I don't mind (that)
**przeszk|oda** (**-ody, -ody**) (*dat sg* **-odzie**, *gen pl* **-ód**) *f* (*przedmiot*) obstruction; (*trudność*) obstacle; **bieg z ~mi** steeplechase; **stać (komuś) na przeszkodzie** to stand in (sb's)/the way; **bez (większych) przeszkód** with no (major) obstacles
**przeszko|dzić (-dzę, -dzisz)** (*imp* **-dź**) *vb perf od* **przeszkadzać**
**przeszkole|nie** (**-nia, -nia**) (*gen pl* **-ń**) *nt* training
**przeszkol|ić (-ę, -isz)** *vt perf* to train
**przeszło** *prep +acc* more than, over
**przeszłoś|ć** (**-ci**) *f* the past; **w przeszłości** in the past
**przeszły** *adj* past
**przeszpie|gi** (**-gów**) *pl*: **przyjść** (*perf*) **na ~** to come spying
**przeszu|kiwać (-kuję, -kujesz)** (*perf* **-kać**) *vt* to search
**przeszyw|ać (-am, -asz)** (*perf* **przeszyć**) *vt* (*o szpadzie, zimnie, bólu*) to pierce; (*zszywać*)

P

to stitch; ~ **kogoś wzrokiem** (*przen*) to look at sb piercingly

**prześcierad|ło (-ła, -ła)** (*loc sg* **-le**, *gen pl* **-eł**) *nt* sheet

**prześcig|ać (-am, -asz)** *vt* (*perf* **-nąć**) to outrun; ~ **kogoś w czymś** (*przen*) to beat sb at sth; **prześcigać się** *vr*: ~ **się w czymś** to try to outdo one another at sth

**prześcig|nąć (-nę, -niesz)** (*imp* **-nij**) *vb perf od* **prześcigać**

**prześlad|ować (-uję, -ujesz)** *vt* (*szykanować*) to persecute; (*przen: dręczyć*) to pester; (*o myśli, wspomnieniach itp.*) to haunt

**prześladowc|a (-y, -y)** *m decl like f in sg* persecutor

**prześladowczy** *adj*: **mania prześladowcza** persecution complex

**prześle|dzić (-dzę, -dzisz)** (*imp* **-dź**) *vt perf* to trace

**prześliczny** *adj* very lovely

**przeświadczeni|e (-a)** *nt* conviction

**przeświadczony** *adj*: ~ **(o czymś)** convinced (of sth)

**przeświec|ać (-a)** *vi*: ~ **(przez coś)** to show through (sth); (*o świetle*) to shine through (sth)

**prześwietl|ać (-am, -asz)** (*perf* **-ić**) *vt* (*Med*) to X-ray; (*Fot*) to overexpose; **prześwietlać się** *vr* (*Med*) to have an X-ray; (*Fot*) to be overexposed

**prześwietle|nie (-nia, -nia)** (*gen pl* **-ń**) *nt* X-ray

**prześwi|t (-tu, -ty)** (*loc sg* **-cie**) *m* gap

**przetacz|ać (-am, -asz)** (*perf* **przetoczyć**) *vt* (*beczki*) to roll; (*wagony*) to shunt; (*ropę, wino*) to decant; ~ **komuś krew** to give sb a (blood) transfusion; **przetaczać się** *vr* (*przejeżdżać*) to roll by; ~ **się przez** *+acc* (*o wozach, wojskach*) to trundle through; (*o wojnie*) to sweep across

**przetapi|ać (-am, -asz)** (*perf* **przetopić**) *vt* to melt down

**przetar|g (-gu, -gi)** (*instr sg* **-giem**) *m* (*wybór ofert*) tender; (*licytacja*) auction

**przetłumacz|yć (-ę, -ysz)** *vb perf od* **tłumaczyć**

**przetra|wić (-wię, -wisz)** *vt perf* (*strawić*) to digest; (*przen: przemyśleć*) to mull over

**przetrw|ać (-am, -asz)** *vt/vi perf* to survive; ~ **próbę czasu** to stand the test of time

**przetrząs|ać (-am, -asz)** (*perf* **-nąć**) *vt* to scour, to rummage through

**przetrzą|snąć (-snę, -śniesz)** (*imp* **-śnij**) *vb perf od* **przetrząsać**

**przet|rzeć (-rę, -rzesz)** (*imp* **-rzyj**) *vb perf od* **przecierać**

**przetrzym|ywać (-uję, -ujesz)** (*perf* **-ać**) *vt* (*książkę*) to keep; (*lekarstwa*) to hoard; (*osobę, zakładnika*) to hold, to detain; (*atak, ból*) to endure

**przetwarz|ać (-am, -asz)** (*perf* **przetworzyć**) *vt* to process

**przetwor|y (-ów)** *pl* (*Kulin*) preserves

**przetw|orzyć (-orzę, -orzysz)** (*imp* **-órz**) *vb perf od* **przetwarzać**

**przetwór|nia (-ni, -nie)** (*gen pl* **-ni**) *f* food processing plant *lub* factory

**przetwórst|wo (-wa)** (*loc sg* **-wie**) *nt* food processing industry

**przewa|ga (-gi)** (*dat sg* **-dze**) *f* advantage; (*wyższość*) superiority; ~ **(jednej minuty)** (one-minute) lead; **mieć przewagę liczebną nad kimś** to outnumber sb; **mieć przewagę nad kimś** (*dominować*) to dominate sb; (*być w lepszej sytuacji*) to have the advantage over sb

**przewal|ać (-am, -asz)** (*perf* **-ić**) *vt* (*pot: przewracać*) to topple; **przewalać się** *vr* (*pot: przewracać się*) to topple over

**przeważ|ać (-am, -asz)** (*perf* **-yć**) *vi* to overweigh, to prevail, to predominate

**przeważający** *adj* (*siła, liczba*) overwhelming; (*dominujący*) predominant, prevailing; **w przeważającej mierze** for the most part, predominantly

**przeważnie** *adv* mostly

**przewią|zać (-żę, -żesz)** *vb perf od* **przewiązywać**

**przewiąz|ywać (-uję, -ujesz)** (*perf* **-ać**) *vt* (*paczkę, suknię*) to tie; (*ranę*) to tie up; **przewiązywać się** *vr*: ~ **się czymś (w pasie)** to tie sth round one's waist

**przewidujący** *adj* foreseeing, far-sighted

**przewid|ywać (-uję, -ujesz)** (*perf* **przewidzieć**) *vt* (*przyszłość*) to foresee, to predict; (*pogodę*) to forecast; (*planować*) to anticipate, to expect; (*uwzględniać*) to provide for

**przewidywalny** *adj* predictable, foreseeable

**przewidywa|nie (-nia, -nia)** (*gen pl* **-ń**) *nt* expectation; **zgodnie z przewidywaniami** as anticipated; **umiejętność przewidywania** foresight

**przewidze|nie (-nia)** *nt*: **to było do przewidzenia** it was predictable *lub* foreseeable

**przewidziany** *adj*: ~ **umową/ustawą** provided for in the contract/bill

**przewi|dzieć (-dzę, -dzisz)** (*imp* **-dź**) *vb perf od* **przewidywać**

**przewietrz|yć (-ę, -ysz)** *vb perf od* **wietrzyć**; **przewietrzyć się** *vr perf* to take a breath of fresh air

**przewie|w (-wu, -wy)** (*loc sg* **-wie**) *m* draught (*Brit*), draft (*US*)

**przewiewny** *adj* (*mieszkanie*) airy; (*suknia*) cool

**prze|wieźć (-wiozę, -wieziesz)** (*imp* **-wieź**)

vb perf od **przewozić**

**przewij|ać (-am, -asz)** (*perf* **przewinąć**) *vt* (*bandaż, kabel*) to rewind; (*ranę*) to put a new dressing on; ~ **dziecko** to change a baby; ~ **taśmę do przodu/do tyłu** to fast-forward/rewind a tape; **przewijać się** *vr* (*przepływać*) to pass; (*pojawiać się i znikać*) to come and go

**przewi|nąć (-nę, -niesz)** (*imp* **-ń**) *vb perf od* **przewijać**

**przewinie|nie (-nia, -nia)** (*gen pl* **-ń**) *nt* (*wykroczenie*) offence (Brit), offense (US); (*Sport*) foul

**przewlekły** *adj* chronic

**przewodni** *adj* leading *attr*; **motyw** ~ (*Lit*) leitmotiv, leitmotif

**przewodnict|wo (-wa)** (*loc sg* **-wie**) *nt* (*kierownictwo*) leadership; (*w organizacji, obradach*) chairmanship

**przewodnicząc|a (-ej, -e)** *f decl like adj* (*kierująca obradami*) chair(woman); (*spółdzielni, związku*) chairwoman, president

**przewodnicząc|y (-ego, -y)** *m decl like adj* (*kierujący obradami*) chair(man); (*spółdzielni, samorządu*) chairman, president; (*Szkol*) class leader

**przewodnicz|yć (-ę, -ysz)** *vi* to be in the chair; ~ **zebraniu** to chair a meeting, to preside over a meeting

**przewodni|k (-ka)** (*instr sg* **-kiem**) *m* (*człowiek*) (*nom pl* **-cy**) guide; (*książka*) (*nom pl* **-ki**) guidebook; (*przywódca*) (*nom pl* **-cy**) leader; (*Fiz*) (*nom pl* **-ki**) conductor; ~ **wycieczek** tour guide

**przew|odzić (-odzę, -odzisz)** (*imp* **-ódź**) *vt* +*dat* (*dowodzić, kierować*) to lead ▷ *vt* +*acc* (*Fiz*) to conduct ▷ *vi* to be the leader

**przew|ozić (-ożę, -ozisz)** (*imp* **-oź** *lub* **-óź**, *perf* **przewieźć**) *vt* (*transportować*) to transport; (*zabierać*) to take

**przewozowy** *adj*: **przedsiębiorstwo przewozowe** haulage contractor (Brit), trucking company (US); **list** ~ way bill

**przewoźni|k (-ka, -cy)** (*instr sg* **-kiem**) *m* (*lotniczy*) carrier; (*spedycyjny*) haulier (Brit), hauler (US)

**przew|ód (-odu, -ody)** (*loc sg* **-odzie**) *m* (*Elektr*) wire; (*kanalizacyjny, gazowy*) pipe; (*paliwowy*) line; (*pokarmowy, oddechowy*) canal; ~ **doktorski** (*Uniw*) ≈ PhD course (Brit) *lub* program (US)

**przew|óz (-ozu, -ozy)** (*loc sg* **-ozie**) *m* transport; (*samochodowy*) haulage, trucking (US)

**przewrac|ać (-am, -asz)** (*perf* **przewrócić**) *vt* (*przestawiać do góry nogami*) to overturn; (*wywracać*) to knock over; (*kartkę*) to turn; (*łódź*) to capsize; ~ **coś do góry nogami** to turn sth upside down; ~ **komuś w głowie** to turn sb's head; **przewracać się** *vr* (*wywracać się*) to fall over; (*na plecy, bok*) to turn *lub* roll over; (*o łodzi*) to capsize

**przewrażliwiony** *adj* touchy

**przewrotnoś|ć (-ci)** *f* perversity

**przewrotny** *adj* perverse

**przewró|cić (-cę, -cisz)** (*imp* **-ć**) *vb perf od* **przewracać**

**przewr|ót (-otu, -oty)** (*loc sg* **-ocie**) *m* (*nagły zwrot*) revolution; (*Pol*) coup (d'etat); (*Sport*) somersault

**przewyższ|ać (-am, -asz)** *vt* (*być wyższym*) to be taller than; (*pod względem wartości, znaczenia*) (*perf* **-yć**) to outstrip, to surpass; (*być lepszym*) (*perf* **-yć**) to be better than; ~ **kogoś liczebnie** to outnumber sb; ~ **kogoś czymś/pod względem czegoś** to surpass sb in terms of sth

 SŁOWO KLUCZOWE

**przez** *prep* +*acc* **1** (*na drugą stronę*) across; **przechodzić (przejść** *perf*) **przez ulicę** to walk across the street, to cross the street; **przez granicę/rzekę** across *lub* over the border/river

**2** (*poprzez*) through; **przez park/pustynię** through *lub* across the park/desert; **przez Poznań do Warszawy** through *lub* via Poznań to Warsaw; **mówić przez sen** to talk in one's sleep

**3** (*ponad*) over; **przeskakiwać przez mur** to jump over the wall

**4** (*za pomocą*): **przez radio/telefon** over *lub* on the radio/phone; **to się pisze przez dwa „l"** it's spelt with double "l"; **co przez to rozumiesz?** what do you mean by that?

**5** (*czas trwania*) for; **chorowałem przez tydzień** I was ill for a week; **przez ten rok wiele się zmieniło** a lot has changed for *lub* in this past year; **przez cały (ten) czas** all this time; **robić (zrobić** *perf*) **coś przez niedzielę/wakacje** to do sth over Sunday/the holidays

**6** (*z powodu*): **przez niego** because of him; **przez pomyłkę/przypadek** by mistake/accident; **przez to** because of that; **przez to, że ...** because ...

**7** (*w konstrukcjach biernych*) by; **skomponowany przez Chopina** composed by Chopin

**8** (*w działaniach arytmetycznych*): **mnożyć/dzielić przez 2** to multiply/divide by 2

**przeze** *prep* = **przez**

**przezię|biać się (-biam, -biasz)** (*perf* **-bić**) *vr* to catch (a) cold

P

**przeziębie|nie** (**-nia, -nia**) (*gen pl* **-ń**) *nt* cold
**przeziębiony** *adj*: **być ~m** to have a cold
**przeznacz|ać (-am, -asz)** (*perf* **-yć**) *vt* to intend, to destine; (*pieniądze*) to allocate; **~ kogoś do robienia czegoś** to assign sb to do sth
**przeznacze|nie** (**-nia**) *nt* (*los*) destiny, fate; (*zastosowanie*) use; **miejsce przeznaczenia** destination
**przeznaczony** *adj*: **to jest przeznaczone do** *+gen* it is designed for; **to było przeznaczone dla** *+gen* it was meant for; **było im przeznaczone, że umrą** they were destined to die; **byli sobie przeznaczeni** they were meant for each other *lub* one another
**przezornoś|ć** (**-ci**) *f* foresight
**przezorny** *adj* (*człowiek*: *zapobiegliwy*) foreseeing, far-sighted; (: *ostrożny*) circumspect; (*rada*) cautious
**przezrocz|e, przeźrocz|e** (**-a, -a**) (*gen pl* **-y**) *nt* slide
**przezroczysty** *adj* (*woda, szyba*) transparent; (*suknia, materiał*) see-through, transparent
**przez|wać (-wę, -wiesz)** (*imp* **-wij**) *vb perf od* **przezywać**
**przezwis|ko** (**-ka, -ka**) (*instr sg* **-kiem**) *nt* nickname
**przezwycięż|ać (-am, -asz)** (*perf* **-yć**) *vt* to overcome
**przezyw|ać (-am, -asz)** *vt* (*nadawać przydomek*) (*perf* **przezwać**) to nickname; **~ kogoś** (*ubliżać*) to call sb names
**przeżegn|ać się (-am, -asz)** *vb perf od* **żegnać się**
**przeżer|ać (-a)** (*perf* **przeżreć**) *vt* (*o kwasie*) to eat away
**przeż|reć (-re)** (*pt* **-arł**) *vb perf od* **przeżerać**
**przeż|uć (-uję, -ujesz)** *vb perf od* **przeżuwać**
**przeżuw|ać (-am, -asz)** *vt* (*przed połknięciem*) (*perf* **przeżuć**) to chew ▷ *vi* (*o krowie*) to ruminate
**przeży|cie** (**-cia, -cia**) (*gen pl* **-ć**) *nt* experience
**przeż|yć (-yję, -yjesz)** *vb perf od* **przeżywać** ▷ *vt perf* (*wojnę, więzienie*) to survive; (*człowieka*) to outlive, to survive ▷ *vi perf* (*utrzymać się przy życiu*) to survive
**przeżyt|ek** (**-ku, -ki**) (*instr sg* **-kiem**) *m* anachronism
**przeżyw|ać (-am, -asz)** (*perf* **przeżyć**) *vt* (*doświadczać*) to experience, to live through; **ona bardzo to przeżywa** this is giving her a very difficult time; **przeżywać się** *vr* to become outdated
**przędz|a** (**-y, -e**) *f* yarn
**przę|sło** (**-sła, -sła**) (*loc sg* **-śle**, *gen pl* **-seł**) *nt* span (*in a bridge*)
**przod|ek** (**-ka, -kowie**) (*instr sg* **-kiem**) *m* ancestor, forefather
**przod|ować (-uję, -ujesz)** *vi*: **~ w czymś** to excel in *lub* at sth
**prz|ód** (**-odu, -ody**) (*loc sg* **-odzie**) *m* front; **do przodu** forward; **z przodu** in front; **na przedzie** in front; **wkładać (włożyć** *perf***) coś tył na ~** to put sth on back to front
**przytycz|ek** (**-ka, -ki**) (*instr sg* **-kiem**) *m* flick; **dać** (*perf*) **komuś prztyczka w nos** (*przen*) to take sb down a peg
**prztyk|ać (-am, -asz)** (*perf* **-nąć**) *vi*: **~ palcami** to snap one's fingers
**prztyk|nąć (-nę, -niesz)** (*imp* **-nij**) *vb perf od* **prztykać**

SŁOWO KLUCZOWE

**przy** *prep +loc* **1** (*w pobliżu*): **przy oknie** by the window; **przy biurku/stole** at the desk/table; **głowa przy głowie** head to head; **nie mam przy sobie pieniędzy** I don't have any money on me; **ręce przy sobie!** (keep your) hands off!
**2** (*w czasie, podczas*): **przy śniadaniu/pracy** at breakfast/work; **przy kawie** over coffee; **przy świecach** by candlelight; **przy cofaniu/skręcaniu należy ...** when reversing/turning, you should ...
**3** (*w obecności*) in front of; **przy świadkach** in the presence of witnesses
**4** (*w porównaniu do*): **przy bracie wydawał się niski** compared to *lub* with his brother he appeared short

**przy|bić (-biję, -bijesz)** *vb perf od* **przybijać** ▷ *vt perf* (*zmartwić*) to upset, to depress
**przybie|c, przybie|gnąć (-gnę, -gniesz)** (*imp* **-gnij**, *pt* **-gł**) *vb perf od* **przybiegać**
**przybieg|ać (-am, -asz)** (*perf* **-nąć** *lub* **przybiec**) *vi* to come running
**przybier|ać (-am, -asz)** (*perf* **przybrać**) *vt* (*tytuł, nazwisko, pozę*) to assume; (*stół, choinkę*) to decorate; (*potrawę*) to garnish ▷ *vi* (*o wodzie*) to rise; **~ na wadze** to put on weight, to gain weight; **~ na sile** to grow in strength; **sprawa przybrała zły obrót** the matter took a turn for the worse
**przybij|ać (-am, -asz)** (*perf* **przybić**) *vt* (*gwóźdź*) to hammer, to drive; (*deskę*) to nail ▷ *vi*: **~ do portu/brzegu** to reach port/the shore
**przybity** *adj* (*pot*: *zmartwiony*) dejected, downcast
**przybliż|ać (-am, -asz)** (*perf* **-yć**) *vt* to bring closer; (*termin, zwycięstwo*) to bring nearer; (*o lornetce*) to magnify; **przybliż nam jego sylwetkę** tell us a few words about him; **przybliżać się** *vr* to come closer

**przybliże|nie** (**-nia, -nia**) (*gen pl* **-ń**) *nt* (*wyniku*) approximation; **w przybliżeniu** approximately, roughly
**przybliżony** *adj* approximate
**przybłę|da** (**-dy, -dy**) (*loc sg* **-dzie**) *m/f decl like f in sg* (*człowiek*) vagrant, vagabond; (*zwierzę*) stray
**przybor|y** (**-ów**) *pl* (*osobno*) accessories; (*zestaw*) kit, gear; **~ piśmienne** *lub* **do pisania** stationery
**przy|brać (-biorę, -bierzesz)** *vb perf od* **przybierać**
**przybrany** *adj* (*dziecko, rodzice*) foster *attr*, adoptive; (*nazwisko*) assumed
**przybrzeżny** *adj* coastal
**przybudów|ka** (**-ki, -ki**) (*dat sg* **-ce**, *gen pl* **-ek**) *f* annexe (*Brit*), annex (*US*)
**przybyci|e** (**-a**) *nt* arrival
**przyb|yć (-ędę, -ędziesz)** (*imp* **-ądź**) *vb perf od* **przybywać**
**przybysz** (**-a, -e**) (*gen pl* **-ów**) *m* newcomer
**przybyt|ek** (**-ku, -ki**) (*instr sg* **-kiem**) *m* (*książk*) shrine
**przybyw|ać (-am, -asz)** (*perf* **przybyć**) *vi* (*przyjeżdżać*) to arrive; **przybywa ludzi** there are more and more people coming; **przybywa dnia** the days are getting longer; **przybyło jej lat** she's got older; **przybył nam pracownik** we have a new worker
**przychod|nia** (**-ni, -nie**) (*gen pl* **-ni**) *f* (*Med*) out-patient clinic; **~ rejonowa** ≈ community health centre (*Brit*) *lub* center (*US*)
**przycho|dzić (-dzę, -dzisz)** (*imp* **-dź**, *perf* **przyjść**) *vi* to come; (*o listach, przesyłkach*) to arrive; **~ na świat** to be born; **przyjść do siebie** to recover; **coś mi przyszło do głowy** I have an idea; **nauka raczej łatwo mu przychodzi** studying comes easy to him; **co ci z tego przyjdzie?** what will you get out of that?; **~ komuś z pomocą** to come to sb's help *lub* aid
**przych|ód** (**-odu, -ody**) (*loc sg* **-odzie**) *m* income
**przychyl|ać się (-am, -asz)** (*perf* **-ić**) *vr*: **przychylać się (do prośby)** to consent (to a request)
**przychylnoś|ć** (**-ci**) *f* favour (*Brit*), favor (*US*)
**przychylny** *adj* favourable (*Brit*), favorable (*US*)
**przy|ciąć (-tnę, -tniesz)** (*imp* **-tnij**) *vb perf od* **przycinać**
**przyciąg|ać (-am, -asz)** (*perf* **-nąć**) *vt* to attract; (*przysuwać*) to pull closer; **~ czyjąś uwagę/spojrzenie** to attract sb's attention/ eye; **przyciągać się** *vr* to attract one another
**przyciągający** *adj*: **~ wzrok** eye-catching
**przyciągani|e** (**-a**) *nt* attraction; **~ ziemskie** gravity
**przyciąg|nąć (-nę, -niesz)** (*imp* **-nij**) *vb perf od* **przyciągać**
**przycin|ać (-am, -asz)** (*perf* **przyciąć**) *vt* (*włosy, gałęzie*) to clip, to trim; (*blachę*) to cut (to size) ▷ *vi*: **~ komuś** to gibe at sb; **przyciąć sobie palec** to catch one's finger; **przyciąć sobie język** to bite one's tongue
**przycin|ek** (**-ka, -ki**) (*instr sg* **-kiem**) *m* gibe
**przycis|k** (**-ku, -ki**) (*instr sg* **-kiem**) *m* (*guzik*) button; **~ do papieru** paper-weight
**przycisk|ać (-am, -asz)** (*perf* **przycisnąć**) *vt* (*naciskać*) to press; (*pot: o nędzy, biedzie*) to grip; **przycisnąć coś do czegoś** to press sth against sth; **~ kogoś/coś do siebie** to hold sb/sth close to one's chest; **przycisnąć** (*perf*) **kogoś do muru** (*przen*) to nail *lub* pin sb down; **przyciskać się** *vr*: **~ się do czegoś** to press o.s. against sth
**przyci|snąć (-snę, -śniesz)** (*imp* **-śnij**) *vb perf od* **przyciskać**
**przycisz|ać (-am, -asz)** (*perf* **-yć**) *vt* to turn down
**przycza|ić się (-ję, -isz)** *vb perf od* **czaić się**
**przycze|pa** (**-py, -py**) (*dat sg* **-pie**) *f* trailer; (*motocyklowa*) sidecar; **~ kempingowa** *lub* **campingowa** caravan (*Brit*), trailer (*US*)
**przycze|piać (-piam, -piasz)** (*perf* **-pić**) *vt* to attach; **przyczepiać się** *vr* (*pot*): **~ się do kogoś** (*mieć pretensje*) to pick on sb; (*narzucać się*) to tag along with sb
**przyczół|ek** (**-ka** *lub* **-ku, -ki**) (*instr sg* **-kiem**) *m* bridgehead
**przyczy|na** (**-ny, -ny**) (*dat sg* **-nie**) *f* reason, cause; **~, dla której ...** the reason why *lub* for which ...; **być przyczyną czegoś** to cause sth, to be the cause of sth; **nie bez przyczyny** not without reason; **z tej przyczyny** for that reason
**przyczyn|ek** (**-ku, -ki**) (*instr sg* **-kiem**) *m* contribution
**przyczy|niać się (-niam, -niasz)** (*perf* **-nić**) *vr*: **przyczyniać się do czegoś** to contribute to sth
**przyczy|nić się (-nię, -nisz)** (*imp* **-ń**) *vb perf od* **przyczyniać się**
**przyczynowy** *adj* causal
**przyć|mić (-mię, -misz)** (*imp* **-mij**) *vb perf od* **przyćmiewać**
**przyćmiew|ać (-am, -asz)** (*perf* **przyćmić**) *vt* to eclipse
**przyd|ać (-am, -asz)** *vb perf od* **przydawać**
**przydarz|ać się (-a)** (*perf* **-yć**) *vr*: **coś mu się przydarzyło** something (has) happened to him
**przydatnoś|ć** (**-ci**) *f* usefulness
**przydatny** *adj* useful, helpful
**przyda|wać (-ję, -jesz)** (*imp* **-waj**, *perf* **przydać**) *vt +gen* (*powagi, autorytetu*) to add;

P

**przydawać się** *vr* (*być przydatnym*) to come in useful; **~ się do czegoś** to be of use for sth; **to mi się bardzo przydało** I found it very useful
**przydaw|ka** (**-ki, -ki**) (*dat sg* **-ce**, *gen pl* **-ek**) *f* (*Jęz*) attribute
**przydech** (**-u, -y**) *m* (*Jęz*) aspiration
**przydom|ek** (**-ka** *lub* **-ku, -ki**) (*instr sg* **-kiem**) *m* nickname
**przydrożny** *adj* wayside *attr*
**przydzia|ł** (**-łu, -ły**) (*loc sg* **-le**) *m* (*czynność*) allotment; (*przydzielona część*) ration; **~ pieniędzy** allocation
**przydziel|ać (-am, -asz)** (*perf* **-ić**) *vt* (*mieszkanie, pieniądze*) to allocate; (*stanowisko, zajęcie*) to assign; **~ kogoś do robienia czegoś** to assign sb to do sth
**przygad|ywać (-uję, -ujesz)** (*perf* **-ać**) *vi*: **~ komuś** (*pot*) to gibe at sb
**przygar|nąć (-nę, -niesz)** (*imp* **-nij**) *vb perf od* **przygarniać**
**przygarni|ać (-am, -asz)** (*perf* **przygarnąć**) *vt* (*tulić*) to take in one's arms; (*dawać schronienie*) to take in, to take under one's roof
**przygląd|ać się (-am, -asz)** (*perf* **przyjrzeć**) *vr*: **przyglądać się komuś/czemuś** to watch *lub* observe sb/sth
**przygnę|biać (-biam, -biasz)** (*perf* **-bić**) *vt* to depress
**przygnębiający** *adj* depressing
**przygnębieni|e** (**-a**) *nt* depression
**przygnębiony** *adj* depressed
**przygniat|ać (-am, -asz)** (*perf* **przygnieść**) *vt* (*o drzewie, ciężarze*) to crush, to squash; (*o odpowiedzialności*) to overwhelm
**przygniatający** *adj* overwhelming
**przyg|nieść (-niotę, -nieciesz)** (*imp* **-nieć**) *vb perf od* **przygniatać**
**przyg|oda** (**-ody, -ody**) (*dat sg* **-odzie**, *gen pl* **-ód**) *f* adventure; **~ miłosna** love affair
**przygodny** *adj*: **przygodna znajomość** a passing acquaintance
**przygodowy** *adj* adventure *attr*
**przygot|ować (-uję, -ujesz)** *vb perf od* **przygotowywać**
**przygotowa|nie** (**-nia, -nia**) (*gen pl* **-ń**) *nt* preparation; **bez przygotowania** impromptu
**przygotowany** *adj*: **~ (do** *+gen*/**na** *+acc*) prepared (for)
**przygotowawczy** *adj* preparatory
**przygotow|ywać (-uję, -ujesz)** (*perf* **-ać**) *vt* to prepare; **~ kogoś na coś** to prepare sb for sth; **przygotowywać się** *vr* to get (o.s.) ready, to prepare o.s.; **~ się do egzaminu** to study for an exam
**przygraniczny** *adj* border *attr*
**przygryw|ać (-am, -asz)** *vi*: **~ komuś** to accompany sb
**przygryw|ka** (**-ki, -ki**) (*dat sg* **-ce**, *gen pl* **-ek**) *f* prelude
**przyim|ek** (**-ka, -ki**) (*instr sg* **-kiem**) *m* preposition
**przyj** *itd. vb patrz* **przeć**
**przyjaci|el** (**-ela, -ele**) (*gen pl* **-ół**, *dat pl* **-ołom**, *instr pl* **-ółmi**, *loc pl* **-ołach**) *m* friend
**przyjacielski** *adj* friendly
**przyjaciół|ka** (**-ki, -ki**) (*dat sg* **-ce**, *gen pl* **-ek**) *f* (girl)friend
**przyj|azd** (**-azdu, -azdy**) (*loc sg* **-eździe**) *m* arrival
**przyjazny** *adj* friendly; (*Komput*) user-friendly
**przyjaź|nić się (-nię, -nisz)** (*imp* **-nij**) *vr* to be friends
**przyjaźnie** *adv* (*powitać, uśmiechać się*) amicably; (*nastawiony, usposobiony*) favourably (*Brit*), favorably (*US*)
**przyjaź|ń** (**-ni, -nie**) (*gen pl* **-ni**) *f* friendship; **żyć w przyjaźni (z kimś)** to live at peace (with sb)
**przyj|ąć (-mę, -miesz)** (*imp* **-mij**) *vb perf od* **przyjmować**
**przyj|echać (-adę, -edziesz)** (*imp* **-edź**) *vb perf od* **przyjeżdżać**
**przyjemnie** *adv* pleasantly; **jest ~** it is nice; **byłoby mi bardzo ~** I'd be delighted, I would be delighted
**przyjemnoś|ć** (**-ci, -ci**) (*gen pl* **-ci**) *f* pleasure; **z przyjemnością** with pleasure; **mam ~ powitać Państwa ...** I have the pleasure of welcoming you ...; **z kim mam ~?** with whom do I have the pleasure (of speaking)?; **cała ~ po mojej stronie** the pleasure is all mine, my pleasure; **sprawiać (sprawić** *perf*) **komuś ~** to please sb; **znajdować ~ w czymś** to take pleasure in sth
**przyjemny** *adj* pleasant; **~ dla oka/ucha** pleasing to the eye/ear; **łączyć przyjemne z pożytecznym** to combine business with pleasure
**przyjezdny** *adj* visiting ▷ *m decl like adj* visitor
**przyjeżdż|ać (-am, -asz)** (*perf* **przyjechać**) *vi* to arrive
**przyję|cie** (**-cia, -cia**) (*gen pl* **-ć**) *nt* reception; (*zamówienia*) taking; (*prezentu*) acceptance; (*kandydata, studenta*) admission; (*pomysłu, wniosku*) adoption; **to jest (nie) do przyjęcia** this is (un)acceptable; **~ towaru** delivery; **godziny przyjęć** (*Med*) surgery (*Brit*), office hours (*US*); **spotykać (spotkać** *perf*) **się z chłodnym ~m** to meet with a cold reception
**przyjęty** *adj* (*zwyczaj, praktyka*) established; (*kandydat*) admitted

**przyjm|ować (-uję, -ujesz)** (*perf* **przyjąć**) *vt* to accept; (*dostawę*) to receive; (*uchodźców, uciekinierów*) to admit; (*obywatelstwo*) to assume; (*propozycję, plan, wniosek, rezolucję*) to adopt; (*pracownika, ucznia, kandydata, chorego*) to admit; (*gości, delegację*) to receive; (*pacjentów*) to see; (*sytuację, rozwój wypadków*) to assume ▹ *vi* (*zakładać*) to assume; (*o lekarzu*) to see (one's) patients; **~ coś chłodno/z zainteresowaniem** to receive sth coldly/with interest; **~ (przyjąć** *perf*) **coś do wiadomości** to take note of sth; **~ (przyjąć** *perf*) **kogoś z otwartymi rękoma** to give sb a warm welcome; **przyjmować się** *vr* (*o modzie, zwyczajach*) to catch on; (*o sadzonkach, kwiatach*) to take root; (*o przeszczepie*) to be accepted

**przyjrz|eć się (-ę, -ysz)** (*imp* **-yj**) *vb perf od* **przyglądać się**

**przyj|ść (-dę, -dziesz)** (*imp* **-dź**) *vb perf od* **przychodzić**

**przykaza|nie** (**-nia, -nia**) (*gen pl* **-ń**) *nt* commandment; **dziesięcioro przykazań** the Ten Commandments

**przykle|ić (-ję, -isz)** *vb perf od* **przyklejać**

**przyklej|ać (-am, -asz)** (*perf* **przykleić**) *vt* to stick; **przyklejać się** *vr* to stick

**przykła|d** (**-du, -dy**) (*loc sg* **-dzie**) *m* example; **na ~** for example, for instance; **dla ~u** as an example; **brać (wziąć** *perf*) **z kogoś ~** to follow sb's example; **dawać (dać** *perf*) **dobry/zły ~** to set a good/bad example

**przykład|ać (-am, -asz)** (*perf* **przyłożyć**) *vt*: **~ coś (do** *+gen*) to put sth (against); **~ wagę** *lub* **znaczenie do czegoś** (*przen*) to attach importance *lub* weight to sth; **przykładać się** *vr*: **~ się do czegoś** to apply o.s. to sth

**przykładny** *adj* exemplary

**przykładowo** *adv* for example, for instance

**przykładowy** *adj* hypothetical

**przykrę|cać (-cam, -casz)** (*perf* **-cić**) *vt* (*śrubę, hak*) to screw in; (*półkę, osłonę*) to screw

**przykrę|cić (-cę, -cisz)** (*imp* **-ć**) *vb perf od* **przykręcać**

**przykro** *adv*: **~ mi** I'm sorry; **jest mi ~, gdy ...** I get upset when ...; **zrobiło jej się ~** she felt sorry; **~ mi to słyszeć** I'm sorry to hear that

**przykroś|ć** (**-ci**) *f* (*uczucie niezadowolenia*) distress; (*nieprzyjemne zdarzenie*) (*nom pl* **-ci**) unpleasantness, trouble; **z przykrością zawiadamiam, że ...** I regret to inform you that ...; **narażać kogoś na przykrości** to get sb into trouble

**przykry** *adj* unpleasant

**przykry|ć (-ję, -jesz)** *vb perf od* **przykrywać**

**przykryw|ać (-am, -asz)** (*perf* **przykryć**) *vt* to cover (up); (*zamykać od góry*) to cover; **przykrywać się** *vr*: **~ się (kocem)** to cover o.s. up (with a blanket)

**przykryw|ka** (**-ki, -ki**) (*dat sg* **-ce**, *gen pl* **-ek**) *f* lid, cover; **pod przykrywką czegoś** (*przen*) under the guise of sth

**przykrz|yć się (-y)** (*perf* **s-**) *vr*: **przykrzy mi się ta praca** I'm tired of this job

**przyku|ć (-ję, -jesz)** *vb perf od* **przykuwać**

**przykuty** *adj*: **~ do łóżka** bedridden

**przykuw|ać (-am, -asz)** (*perf* **przykuć**) *vt*: **~ kogoś do czegoś** to chain sb to sth; **~ (czyjąś) uwagę** to rivet (sb's) attention; **~ wzrok** *lub* **spojrzenie** to catch the eye

**przylat|ywać (-uję, -ujesz)** (*perf* **przylecieć**) *vi* (*o samolocie*) to arrive; (*o ptakach*) to fly in; (*o ludziach*) to arrive by plane; (*pot*) to come running

**przylądek** (**-ka, -ki**) (*instr sg* **-kiem**) *m* cape; **P~ Dobrej Nadziei** the Cape of Good Hope

**przyle|cieć (-cę, -cisz)** (*imp* **-ć**) *vb perf od* **przylatywać**

**przyleg|ać (-am, -asz)** *vi*: **~ do czegoś** (*przywierać*) to stick to sth; (*stykać się*) to border on sth

**przylegający** *adj*: **~ (do** *+gen*) adjacent (to)

**przyległy** *adj* (*sąsiedni*) adjoining; (*Mat, Geom*) adjacent

**przyle|piać (-piam, -piasz)** (*perf* **-pić**) *vt* to stick; **przylepiać się** *vr* to stick

**przylep|iec** (**-ca, -ce**) *m* (*rzep przy ubraniu*) Velcro®; (*plaster*) (sticking) plaster (*Brit*), Band-Aid® (*US*)

**przylg|nąć (-nę, -niesz)** (*imp* **-nij**) *vi perf*: **~ do** *+gen* to cling to

**przylo|t** (**-tu, -ty**) (*loc sg* **-cie**) *m* arrival

**przylut|ować (-uję, -ujesz)** *vt perf* to solder on

**przyła|pać (-pię, -piesz)** *vt perf*: **~ kogoś na czymś** to catch sb doing sth; **~ kogoś na gorącym uczynku** (*przen*) to catch sb red-handed *lub* in the act

**przyłącz|ać (-am, -asz)** (*perf* **-yć**) *vt* (*dołączać, dodawać*) to attach; (*budynek*) to wire; (*komputer*) to link; **przyłączać się** *vr* to join in; **przyłączyłem się do nich** I joined them

**przyłbic|a** (**-y, -e**) *f* visor

**przył|ożyć (-ożę, -ożysz)** (*imp* **-óż**) *vb perf od* **przykładać** ▹ *vi perf*: **~ komuś** (*pot*) to bash sb (*pot*)

**przymiar|ka** (**-ki, -ki**) (*dat sg* **-ce**, *gen pl* **-ek**) *f* (*próba*) trial run; (*u krawca*) fitting

**przymier|ać (-am, -asz)** *vi*: **~ głodem** to starve

**przymierz|ać (-am, -asz)** (*perf* **-yć**) *vt* to try on; **nie przymierzając** if I may say so, if you'll excuse the comparison; **przymierzać się** *vr*: **~ się do czegoś** to get ready for sth

P

**przymierzal|nia** (**-ni, -nie**) (*gen pl* **-ni**) *f* fitting room
**przymierz|e** (**-a, -a**) (*gen pl* **-y**) *nt* alliance
**przymiotni|k** (**-ka, -ki**) (*instr sg* **-kiem**) *m* adjective
**przymiotnikowy** *adj* adjectival
**przymiot|y** (**-ów**) *pl* attributes *pl*
**przymk|nąć (-nę, -niesz)** (*imp* **-nij**) *vb perf od* **przymykać** ▷ *vt perf*: **przymknij się!** (*pot!*) shut your trap (*pot!*)
**przymoc|ować (-uję, -ujesz)** *vb perf od* **przymocowywać**
**przymocow|ywać (-uję, -ujesz)** (*perf* **-ać**) *vt* to fasten, to fix; **przymocować coś do** *+gen* to attach *lub* fasten sth to
**przymroz|ek** (**-ku** *lub* **-ka, -ki**) (*instr sg* **-kiem**) *m* ground frost
**przymrużeni|e** (**-a**) *nt*: **z ~m oka** (*opowiadać*) with tongue in cheek; (*traktować*) with a pinch of salt
**przymu|s** (**-su**) (*loc sg* **-sie**) *m* compulsion; **pod ~em** under compulsion
**przymu|sić (-szę, -sisz)** (*imp* **-ś**) *vb perf od* **przymuszać**
**przymusowy** *adj* (*pobyt*) enforced; (*lądowanie, praca*) forced; (*bezrobocie*) compulsory
**przymusz|ać (-am, -asz)** (*perf* **przymusić**) *vt*: **~ kogoś do (robienia) czegoś** to force sb to do sth; **przymuszać się** *vr* to force o.s.
**przymyk|ać (-am, -asz)** (*perf* **przymknąć**) *vt* (*zamykać niecałkowicie*) to push to; (*pot: zamykać w areszcie*) to arrest, to pinch (*pot*); **~ na coś oczy** *lub* **oko** to turn a blind eye to sth
**przynagl|ać (-am, -asz)** (*perf* **-ić**) *vt* to rush
**przynagl|ić (-ę, -isz)** (*imp* **-ij**) *vb perf od* **przynaglać**
**przynajmniej** *adv* at least
**przynależnoś|ć** (**-ci, -ci**) (*gen pl* **-ci**) *f* membership
**przynęt|a** (**-ty, -ty**) (*dat sg* **-cie**) *f* bait
**przyni|eść (-osę, -esiesz)** (*imp* **-eś**, *pt* **-ósł, -osła, -eśli**) *vb perf od* **przynosić**
**przyno|sić (-szę, -sisz)** (*imp* **-ś**, *perf* **przynieść**) *vt* to bring
**przypad|ać (-am, -asz)** (*perf* **przypaść**) *vi*: **~ w niedzielę** to fall on (a) Sunday; **~ komuś** (*o zaszczycie, obowiązku*) to fall to sb; **przypadło jej to do gustu** she took a liking to it; **~ do zapłaty** to be due for payment
**przypad|ek** (*instr sg* **-kiem**, *nom pl* **-ki**) *m* (*traf*) (*gen sg* **-ku**) coincidence; (*Med*) (*gen sg* **-ku**) case; (*Jęz*) (*gen sg* **-ka**) case; **przypadkiem** *lub* **przez ~** by accident, by chance; **w przypadku** *+gen* in case of, in the event of
**przypadkowo** *adv* accidentally
**przypadkowy** *adj* accidental
**przypadłoś|ć** (**-ci, -ci**) (*gen pl* **-ci**) *f* ailment
**przypal|ać (-am, -asz)** (*perf* **-ić**) *vt* (*mleko, mięso*) to burn; (*materiał*) to singe; **przypalać się** *vr* to burn
**przypa|ść (-dnę, -dniesz)** (*imp* **-dnij**) *vb perf od* **przypadać**
**przypatr|ywać się (-uję, -ujesz)** (*perf* **przypatrzyć**) *vr*: **przypatrywać się (komuś/czemuś)** to scrutinize (sb/sth)
**przy|piąć (-pnę, -pniesz)** (*imp* **-pnij**) *vb perf od* **przypinać**
**przypi|ec (-ekę, -eczesz)** (*imp* **-ecz**) *vb perf od* **przypiekać**
**przypiek|ać (-am, -asz)** (*perf* **przypiec**) *vi* (*o słońcu*) to beat down; (*rumienić*) to brown
**przypieprz|ać się (-am, -asz)** (*perf* **-yć**) *vr* (*pot!*): **przypieprzać się do kogoś** (*czepiać się*) to climb all over sb (*pot*)
**przypieprz|yć (-ę, -ysz)** *vt perf* (*pot!*): **~ komuś** (*zbić*) to knock *lub* beat the shit out of sb (*pot!*)
**przypier|ać (-am, -asz)** (*perf* **przyprzeć**) *vt*: **~ kogoś do muru** to drive *lub* push sb to the wall
**przypin|ać (-am, -asz)** (*perf* **przypiąć**) *vt* (*broszkę*) to pin; (*narty*) to put on; (*pasami*) to strap
**przypi|s** (**-su, -sy**) (*loc sg* **-sie**) *m* note; (*na dole strony*) footnote; (*na końcu tekstu*) endnote
**przypi|sać (-szę, -szesz)** *vb perf od* **przypisywać**
**przypis|ywać (-uję, -ujesz)** (*perf* **-ać**) *vt*: **~ coś komuś** to ascribe *lub* attribute sth to sb
**przyplą|tać się (-czę, -czesz)** *vr perf* (*pej: o człowieku*) to drag one's arse (*Brit*) *lub* ass (*US*) in (*pot!*); **przyplątało mi się jakieś choróbsko** I caught a bug of some sort
**przypła|cać (-cam, -casz)** (*perf* **-cić**) *vt*: **~ coś czymś** to pay for sth with sth
**przypła|cić (-cę, -cisz)** (*imp* **-ć**) *vb perf od* **przypłacać**
**przypły|nąć (-nę, -niesz)** (*imp* **-ń**) *vb perf od* **przypływać**
**przypły|w** (**-wu, -wy**) (*loc sg* **-wie**) *m* (*morski*) high tide; (*energii, uczuć*) surge; **w ~ie natchnienia/gniewu** in a flash of inspiration/anger
**przypły|wać (-wam, -wasz)** (*perf* **-nąć**) *vi* (*o statku, pasażerach*) to arrive, to come in; (*o pływaku*) to swim up; **~ do brzegu** to come ashore; (*o pływaku*) to swim ashore
**przypomin|ać (-am, -asz)** (*perf* **przypomnieć**) *vt*: **~ kogoś/coś** to resemble sb/sth, to be like sb/sth; **~ komuś coś** to make sb think of sth; **~ sobie** to recall, to recollect; **przypomnieć komuś o czymś** to remind sb of sth; **przypomnieć komuś,**

**żeby coś zrobił** to remind sb to do sth; **przypomina mi swoją matkę** she reminds me of her mother; **przypominać się** *vr*: **przypomniało mi się, że ...** I remembered that ...

**przypom|nieć (-nę, -nisz)** (*imp* **-nij**) *vb perf od* **przypominać**

**przyporządk|ować (-uję, -ujesz)** *vb perf od* **przyporządkowywać**

**przyporządkow|ywać (-uję, -ujesz)** (*perf* **-ać**) *vt*: **~ coś czemuś** to assign sth to sth

**przypowieś|ć** (**-ci, -ci**) (*gen pl* **-ci**) *f* parable

**przypra|wa** (**-wy, -wy**) (*dat sg* **-wie**) *f* spice, seasoning

**przypra|wiać (-wiam, -wiasz)** (*perf* **-wić**) *vt* to spice (up); **~ kogoś o mdłości** to make sb sick

**przyprowa|dzać (-dzam, -dzasz)** (*perf* **-dzić**) *vt* to bring (along)

**przyprowa|dzić (-dzę, -dzisz)** (*imp* **-dź**) *vb perf od* **przyprowadzać**

**przyp|rzeć (-rę, -rzesz)** (*imp* **-rzyj**, *pt* **-arł**) *vb perf od* **przypierać**

**przypuszcz|ać (-am, -asz)** (*perf* **przypuścić**) *vt* (*atak, szturm*) to launch ▷ *vi* (*snuć domysły*) to suppose; (*zakładać*) to presume; **przypuśćmy, że ...** let's assume (that) ...; **jest gorzej niż przypuszczałam** it's worse than I thought

**przypuszczający** *adj* (*Jęz*) conditional

**przypuszczalnie** *adv* presumably

**przypuszczalny** *adj* presumable

**przypuszcze|nie** (**-nia, -nia**) (*gen pl* **-ń**) *nt* presumption; **snuć przypuszczenia** to make conjectures

**przypu|ścić (-szczę, -ścisz)** (*imp* **-ść**) *vb perf od* **przypuszczać**

**przyro|da** (**-dy**) (*dat sg* **-dzie**) *f* nature; **ochrona przyrody** nature conservation *lub* preservation

**przyrodni** *adj*: **~ brat** half-brother; **~a siostra** half-sister

**przyrodniczy** *adj* (*film*) nature *attr*; (*nauki*) natural

**przyrodni|k** (**-ka, -cy**) (*instr sg* **-kiem**) *m* naturalist

**przyro|st** (**-stu, -sty**) (*loc sg* **-ście**) *m* increase; **~ naturalny** population growth (rate)

**przyrost|ek** (**-ka, -ki**) (*instr sg* **-kiem**) *m* suffix

**przyrówn|ywać (-uję, -ujesz)** (*perf* **-ać**) *vt*: **~ kogoś/coś do** *+gen* to equate sb/sth to

**przyrzą|d** (**-du, -dy**) (*loc sg* **-dzie**) *m* instrument, device; **przyrządy** *pl* apparatus

**przyrzą|dzać (-dzam, -dzasz)** (*perf* **-dzić**) *vt* to prepare

**przyrzą|dzić (-dzę, -dzisz)** (*imp* **-dź**) *vb perf od* **przyrządzać**

**przyrze|c (-knę, -kniesz)** (*imp* **-knij**) *vb perf od* **przyrzekać**

**przyrzecze|nie** (**-nia, -nia**) (*gen pl* **-ń**) *nt* promise

**przyrzek|ać (-am, -asz)** (*perf* **przyrzec**) *vt*: **~ coś komuś** to promise sth to sb, to promise sb sth; **przyrzekł, że to zrobi** he promised to do it *lub* that he would do it

**przysad|ka** (**-ki, -ki**) (*dat sg* **-ce**, *gen pl* **-ek**) *f* (*też*: **przysadka mózgowa**) pituitary (gland)

**przysia|d** (**-du, -dy**) (*loc sg* **-dzie**) *m* knee bend

**przysiad|ać się (-am, -asz)** (*perf* **przysiąść**) *vr*: **przysiadać się (do kogoś)** to join (sb); **czy mogę się przysiąść?** can I join you?

**przysi|ąc (-ęgnę, -ęgniesz)** (*imp* **-ęgnij**, *pt* **-ągł, -ęgła, -ęgli**) *vb perf od* **przysięgać**

**przysi|ąść (-ądę, -ądziesz)** (*imp* **-ądź**, *pt* **-adł, -edli**) *vb perf od* **przysiadać się**

**przysi|ęga** (**-ęgi, -ęgi**) (*dat sg* **-ędze**, *gen pl* **-ąg**) *f* oath; **pod przysięgą** under oath; **składać (złożyć** *perf*) **przysięgę** to take *lub* swear an oath

**przysięg|ać (-am, -asz)** (*perf* **przysiąc**) *vt/vi* to swear

**przysięgły** *adj*: **tłumacz ~** certified translator; (*w sądzie*) court interpreter ▷ *m decl like adj* juror; **ława ~ch** jury(box)

**przy|słać (-ślę, -ślesz)** (*imp* **-ślij**) *vb perf od* **przysyłać**

**przysłani|ać (-am, -asz)** (*perf* **przysłonić**) *vt* (*oczy, lampę, słońce*) to shade; (*widok*) to obscure

**przysło|na** (**-ny, -ny**) (*dat sg* **-nie**) *f* aperture

**przysło|nić (-nię, -nisz)** (*imp* **-ń**) *vb perf od* **przysłaniać**

**przysł|owie** (**-owia, -owia**) (*gen pl* **-ów**) *nt* proverb

**przysłów|ek** (**-ka, -ki**) (*instr sg* **-kiem**) *m* adverb

**przysłuch|iwać się (-uję, -ujesz)** *vr*: **przysłuchiwać się (komuś/czemuś)** to listen in (to sb/sth)

**przysłu|ga** (**-gi, -gi**) (*dat sg* **-dze**) *f* favour (*Brit*), favor (*US*); **wyświadczać (wyświadczyć** *perf*) **komuś przysługę** to do sb a favo(u)r; **prosić (poprosić** *perf*) **kogoś o przysługę** to ask a favo(u)r of sb

**przysłu|giwać (-guje)** *vi*: **coś przysługuje komuś** sb is entitled to sth

**przysłuż|yć się (-ę, -ysz)** *vr perf*: **przysłużyć się komuś** to do sb a service

**przysma|k** (**-ku, -ki**) (*instr sg* **-kiem**) *m* delicacy

**przysparz|ać (-am, -asz)** (*perf* **przysporzyć**) *vt*: **~ komuś sławy** to make sb famous; **~ komuś kłopotów** to cause sb trouble; **~ sobie przyjaciół/wrogów** to make friends/ enemies

P

**przyspiesz|ać, przyśpiesz|ać (-am, -asz)** (*perf* **-yć**) *vt* (*tempo, działanie*) to speed up, to accelerate; (*wyjazd, egzaminy*) to advance ▷ *vi* (*zwiększać szybkość*) to speed up, to accelerate; **~ kroku** to quicken the pace
**przyspiesze|nie, przyśpiesze|nie (-nia)** *nt* (*zwiększenie tempa*) acceleration; (*przybliżenie terminu*) advancing; (Fiz) (*nom pl* **-nia**, *gen pl* **-ń**) acceleration
**przyspieszony, przyśpieszony** *adj* (*oddech, ruch*) accelerated; (*tryb*) summary; (*autobus*) ≈ express *attr*
**przyspiesz|yć, przyśpiesz|yć (-ę, -ysz)** *vb perf od* **przyspieszać**
**przysporz|yć (-ę, -ysz)** *vb perf od* **przysparzać**
**przysposa|biać (-biam, -biasz)** (*perf* **przysposobić**) *vt* (*przygotowywać*) to prepare; (*szkolić*) to train; **przysposabiać się** *vr* to prepare; **~ się do czegoś** to prepare for sth
**przyspos|obić (-obię, -obisz)** (*imp* **-ób**) *vb perf od* **przysposabiać**
**przyssaw|ka** (**-ki, -ki**) (*dat sg* **-ce**, *gen pl* **-ek**) *f* sucker
**przyst|ać (-anę, -aniesz)** (*imp* **-ań**) *vb perf od* **przystawać** ▷ *vi*: **takie zachowanie ci nie przystoi** that kind of behaviour is unworthy of you; **jak przystało na czterogwiazdkowy hotel** as befits a four-star hotel
**przysta|nąć (-nę, -niesz)** (*imp* **-ń**) *vb perf od* **przystawać**
**przystan|ek** (**-ku, -ki**) (*instr sg* **-kiem**) *m*: **~ autobusowy/tramwajowy** bus/tram stop
**przysta|ń** (**-ni, -nie**) (*gen pl* **-ni**) *f* marina; (*przen*) haven
**przyst|awać (-aję, -ajesz)** (*imp* **-awaj**) *vi* (*zatrzymywać się*) (*perf* **-anąć**) to stop; **~ do czegoś** to square with sth; **~ (przystać** *perf*) **na coś** to accede to sth
**przysta|wiać (-wiam, -wiasz)** (*perf* **-wić**) *vt*: **~ coś do** *+gen* to put sth against
**przystaw|ka** (**-ki, -ki**) (*dat sg* **-ce**, *gen pl* **-ek**) *f* (*potrawa*) starter, hors d'oeuvre (Brit), appetizer (US); (*urządzenie*) accessory
**przystą|pić (-pię, -pisz)** *vb perf od* **przystępować**
**przystępny** *adj* (*język, styl, sposób*) accessible; (*człowiek*) approachable; (*cena*) affordable
**przystęp|ować (-uję, -ujesz)** (*perf* **przystąpić**) *vi*: **~ do** *+gen* to begin, to start; **~ do egzaminu** to take an exam
**przystojny** *adj* handsome
**przystos|ować (-uję, -ujesz)** *vb perf od* **przystosowywać**
**przystosowani|e** (**-a**) *nt* (*Bio*) adaptation; (*Psych*) adjustment
**przystosow|ywać (-uję, -ujesz)** (*perf* **-ać**) *vt*: **~ coś do** *+gen* to adapt sth to;
**przystosowywać się** *vr*: **~ się (do czegoś)** to adapt (to sth)
**przysu|nąć (-nę, -niesz)** (*imp* **-ń**) *vb perf od* **przysuwać**
**przysuw|ać (-am, -asz)** (*perf* **przysunąć**) *vt*: **~ coś do czegoś** to push sth nearer to sth; **przysuwać się** *vr* to move closer
**przyswaj|ać (-am, -asz)** (*perf* **przyswoić**) *vt*: **~ coś sobie** (*wiedzę, wiadomości*) to absorb sth; (*język*) to learn sth
**przysw|oić (-oję, -oisz)** (*imp* **-ój**) *vb perf od* **przyswajać**
**przysył|ać (-am, -asz)** (*perf* **przysłać**) *vt* (*wiadomość*) to send; (*katalog*) to mail; (*mechanika*) to send in
**przyszłoroczny** *adj* next year,s
**przyszłoś|ć** (**-ci**) *f* future; **w (niedalekiej) przyszłości** in the (near) future
**przyszły** *adj* (*student*) prospective; (*czas*) future; (*poniedziałek, miesiąc*) next; **w ~m tygodniu/roku** next week/year; **przyszła żona** wife-to-be; **przyszłe dni** days to come
**przysz|yć (-yję, -yjesz)** *vb perf od* **przyszywać**
**przyszyw|ać (-am, -asz)** (*perf* **przyszyć**) *vt* to sew (on)
**przyś|nić się (-nię, -nisz)** (*imp* **-nij**) *vb perf od* **śnić się**
**przyśpiesz|ać (-am, -asz)** (*perf* **-yć**) *vt* = **przyspieszać**
**przyświec|ać (-a)** *vi* (*książk*): **przyświeca mu piękny cel** he has a noble purpose
**przytacz|ać (-am, -asz)** (*perf* **przytoczyć**) *vt* to quote
**przyta|kiwać (-kuję, -kujesz)** (*perf* **-knąć**) *vi* to nod; **~ komuś** to nod (in) agreement with sb
**przytak|nąć (-nę, -niesz)** (*imp* **-nij**) *vb perf od* **przytakiwać**
**przytk|nąć (-nę, -niesz)** (*imp* **-nij**) *vb perf od* **przytykać**
**przytłacz|ać (-am, -asz)** (*perf* **przytłoczyć**) *vt* to crush; (*przen*) to overwhelm
**przytłaczający** *adj* overwhelming
**przytłumiony** *adj* muffled
**przytocz|yć (-ę, -ysz)** *vb perf od* **przytaczać**
**przytomnoś|ć** (**-ci**) *f* consciousness; **~ umysłu** presence of mind; **tracić (stracić** *perf*) **~** to lose consciousness
**przytomny** *adj* (*świadomy*) conscious; (*bystry, rozsądny*) astute
**przytra|fiać się (-fia)** (*perf* **-fić**) *vr*: **przytrafiać się komuś** to happen to sb
**przytrzas|kiwać (-kuję, -kujesz)** (*perf* **przytrzasnąć**) *vt* to trap; **przytrzasnąć sobie palec (drzwiami)** to trap one's finger (in the door)
**przytrza|snąć (-snę, -śniesz)** (*imp* **-śnij**) *vb perf od* **przytrzaskiwać**

**przytrzym|ywać (-uję, -ujesz)** (*perf* **-ać**) *vt* (*wstrzymywać*) to hold back; (*obezwładniać*) to hold down; (*podtrzymywać*) to support; **przytrzymywać się** *vr +gen* to hold on to
**przytul|ać (-am, -asz)** (*perf* **-ić**) *vt* to hug, to give a hug *lub* cuddle; **przytulać się** *vr* to cuddle; **przytulić się do kogoś** to cuddle *lub* snuggle up to sb
**przytulnie** *adv*: **w pokoju było ~** the room was cosy *lub* cozy (*US*)
**przytulnoś|ć (-ci)** *f* cosiness, coziness (*US*)
**przytulny** *adj* cosy, cozy (*US*)
**przytwier|dzać (-dzam, -dzasz)** (*perf* **-dzić**) *vt* to attach
**przytwier|dzić (-dzę, -dzisz)** (*imp* **-dź**) *vb perf od* **przytwierdzać**
**przyty|ć (-ję, -jesz)** *vi perf* to put on weight
**przyty|k (-ku, -ki)** (*instr sg* **-kiem**) *m* dig (*remark*)
**przytyk|ać (-am, -asz)** (*perf* **przytknąć**) *vt*: **~ coś (do** *+gen*) to put sth (against)
**przywa|ra** (**-ry, -ry**) (*dat sg* **-rze**) *f* (*książk*) vice
**przywdziew|ać (-am, -asz)** (*perf* **przywdziać**) *vt* (*książk*) to don; **~ żałobę** to go into mourning
**przywią|zać (-żę, -żesz)** *vb perf od* **przywiązywać**
**przywiązani|e** (**-a**) *nt*: **~ (do kogoś/czegoś)** attachment (to sb/sth)
**przywiązany** *adj*: **~ (do kogoś/czegoś)** attached (to sb/sth)
**przywiąz|ywać (-uję, -ujesz)** (*perf* **-ać**) *vt*: **~ kogoś/coś do** *+gen* to tie sb/sth to; **~ wagę/znaczenie do czegoś** to attach weight/importance to sth; **przywiązywać się** *vr*: **~ się do czegoś** to tie o.s. to sth; **~ się do kogoś/czegoś** (*przen*) to become attached to sb/sth
**przywidze|nie** (**-nia, -nia**) (*gen pl* **-ń**) *nt* illusion
**przywi|dzieć się (-dzi)** *vr perf*: **coś mi się przywidziało** I must have been seeing things
**przywier|ać (-am, -asz)** (*perf* **przywrzeć**) *vi*: **~ do** *+gen* to cling to; (*garnka, patelni*) to stick to
**przywiesz|ka** (**-ki, -ki**) (*dat sg* **-ce**, *gen pl* **-ek**) *f* tag
**przywi|eść (-odę, -edziesz)** (*imp* **-edź**, *pt* **-ódł, -odła, -edli**) *vb perf od* **przywodzić**
**przywi|eźć (-ozę, -eziesz)** (*imp* **-eź**, *pt* **-ózł, -ozła, -eźli**) *vb perf od* **przywozić**
**przywilej** (**-u, -e**) *m* privilege
**przywit|ać (-am, -asz)** *vb perf od* **witać**
**przywłaszcz|ać (-am, -asz)** (*perf* **-yć**) *vt*: **~ coś sobie** to appropriate sth
**przyw|odzić (-odzę, -odzisz)** (*imp* **-ódź**, *perf* **przywieść**) *vt* (*książk*) to bring; **~ na myśl** to bring to mind
**przywoł|ywać (-uję, -ujesz)** (*perf* **-ać**) *vt* to call; **~ kogoś do porządku** to bring sb to heel
**przyw|ozić (-ożę, -ozisz)** (*imp* **-oź** *lub* **-óź**, *perf* **przywieźć**) *vt* to bring
**przywódc|a** (**-y, -y**) *m decl like f in sg* leader
**przywództw|o** (**-wa**) (*loc sg* **-wie**) *nt* leadership
**przyw|óz** (**-ozu, -ozy**) (*loc sg* **-ozie**) *m* (*dostawa*) delivery; (*import*) importation
**przywrac|ać (-am, -asz)** (*perf* **przywrócić**) *vt* to restore; **~ komuś życie** to bring sb back to life; **~ kogoś na stanowisko** to reinstate sb
**przywró|cić (-cę, -cisz)** (*imp* **-ć**) *vb perf od* **przywracać**
**przyw|rzeć (-rę, -rzesz)** (*imp* **-rzyj**, *pt* **-arł**) *vb perf od* **przywierać**
**przywyk|ać (-am, -asz)** (*perf* **-nąć**) *vi*: **~ do kogoś/czegoś** to get accustomed *lub* used to sb/sth
**przywykły** *adj*: **~ do** *+gen* accustomed to
**przywyk|nąć (-nę, -niesz)** (*imp* **-nij**, *pt* **-ł** *lub* **-nął, -ła, -li**) *vb perf od* **przywykać**
**przyziemny** *adj* down-to-earth, mundane
**przyzn|awać (-aję, -ajesz)** (*perf* **-ać**) *vt*: **~ coś komuś** (*kredyt, obywatelstwo, status*) to grant sb sth; (*nagrodę, wyróżnienie*) to award sb sth ▷ *vi*: **~, że ...** to admit *lub* grant that ...; **muszę przyznać, że ...** I must admit that ...; **przyznawać się** *vr*: **~ się do** *+gen* to own up *lub* confess to; **(nie) przyznać się do winy** (*Prawo*) to plead (not) guilty
**przyz|wać (-wę, -wiesz)** (*imp* **-wij**) *vb perf od* **przyzywać**
**przyzwal|ać (-am, -asz)** (*perf* **przyzwolić**) *vi* (*książk*): **~ na coś** to consent to sth
**przyzwalająco** *adv* in consent
**przyzwoicie** *adv* decently
**przyzwoit|ka** (**-ki, -ki**) (*dat sg* **-ce**, *gen pl* **-ek**) *f* chaperone
**przyzwoitoś|ć** (**-ci**) *f* decency
**przyzwoity** *adj* decent
**przyzwoleni|e** (**-a**) *nt* consent
**przyzw|olić (-olę, -olisz)** (*imp* **-ól**) *vb perf od* **przyzwalać**
**przyzwycza|ić (-ję, -isz)** (*imp* **-j**) *vb perf od* **przyzwyczajać**
**przyzwyczaj|ać (-am, -asz)** (*perf* **przyzwyczaić**) *vt*: **~ kogoś do czegoś** to accustom sb to sth; **przyzwyczajać się** *vr*: **~ się do czegoś** to get accustomed *lub* used to sth
**przyzwyczaje|nie** (**-nia, -nia**) (*gen pl* **-ń**) *nt* habit; **z przyzwyczajenia** out of habit
**przyzwyczajony** *adj*: **(nie) być ~m do** *+gen* (not) to be accustomed *lub* used to
**przyzyw|ać (-am, -asz)** (*perf* **przyzwać**) *vt* (*książk*) to summon

**PS** *abbr* (= *postscriptum*) P.S.
**psa** *itd. n patrz* **pies**
**psal|m** (**-mu, -my**) (*loc sg* **-mie**) *m* psalm
**psałterz** (**-a, -e**) (*gen pl* **-y**) *m* psalter
**pseudo...** *pref* pseudo...
**pseudoni|m** (**-mu, -my**) (*loc sg* **-mie**) *m* pseudonym; ~ **literacki** pen name
**psi** *adj* (*instynkt*) canine; **psia buda** (dog's) kennel
**psiakrew** *inv* (*pot*): ~! damn it! (*pot*)
**psiku|s** (**-sa, -sy**) (*loc sg* **-sie**) *m* prank
**psiocz|yć (-ę, -ysz)** *vi* (*pot*): ~ **na (kogoś/coś)** to gripe (about *lub* at sb/sth) (*pot*)
**PSL** *abbr* (= *Polskie Stronnictwo Ludowe*) Polish Peasant Party
**pso|cić (-cę, -cisz)** (*imp* **-ć**) *vi* to play tricks
**pso|ta** (**-ty, -ty**) (*dat sg* **-cie**) *f* prank
**psotni|k** (**-ka, -cy**) (*instr sg* **-kiem**) *m* prankster
**pstrą|g** (**-ga, -gi**) (*instr sg* **-giem**) *m* trout
**pstrokaty** *adj* (*pstry*) gaudy; (*koń*) dappled
**pstry** *adj* gaudy
**pstryk|ać (-am, -asz)** (*perf* **-nąć**) *vi* (*pot*) to click; ~ **palcami** to snap one's fingers
**pstryk|nąć (-nę, -niesz)** (*imp* **-nij**) *vb perf od* **pstrykać**
**psu|ć (-ję, -jesz)** (*perf* **ze-** *lub* **po-**) *vt* (*maszynę, zabawkę*) to break; (*nastrój, zabawę*) to spoil; (*reputację*) to ruin; ~ **sobie zdrowie/wzrok** to ruin one's health/eyes; **psuć się** *vr* (*o maszynach*) to break down; (*o żywności*) to go bad; (*o pogodzie*) to get worse; (*o stosunkach, układach, wzroku*) to deteriorate, to get worse
**psychiat|ra** (**-ry, -rzy**) (*loc sg* **-rze**) *m decl like f in sg* psychiatrist
**psychiatri|a** (**-i**) *f* psychiatry
**psychiatryczny** *adj* psychiatric
**psychicznie** *adv* mentally
**psychiczny** *adj* (*choroba, rozwój*) mental; (*uraz*) psychological
**psychi|ka** (**-ki**) (*dat sg* **-ce**) *f* psyche
**psychoanality|k** (**-ka, -cy**) (*instr sg* **-kiem**) *m* (psycho)analyst
**psychoanali|za** (**-zy**) (*dat sg* **-zie**) *f* (psycho) analysis
**psycholo|g** (**-ga, -dzy** *lub* **-gowie**) (*instr sg* **-giem**) *m* psychologist
**psychologi|a** (**-i**) *f* psychology
**psychologiczny** *adj* psychological
**psychopa|ta** (**-ty, -ci**) (*loc sg* **-cie**) *m decl like f in sg* psychopath
**psychosomatyczny** *adj* psychosomatic
**psychoterapi|a** (**-i**) *f* psychotherapy
**psychotropowy** *adj* psychotropic
**psycho|za** (**-zy**) (*dat sg* **-zie**) *f* psychosis
**pszczelarz** (**-a, -e**) (*gen pl* **-y**) *m* beekeeper
**pszczeli** *adj* bee's *attr*
**pszcz|oła** (**-oły, -oły**) (*dat sg* **-ole**, *gen pl* **-ół**) *f* bee
**pszenic|a** (**-y, -e**) *f* wheat
**pszenny** *adj*: **mąka pszenna** wheat-flour
**pt.** *abbr* (= *pod tytułem*) entitled
**ptact|wo** (**-wa**) (*loc sg* **-wie**) *nt* birds *pl*
**pta|k** (**-ka, -ki**) (*instr sg* **-kiem**) *m* bird; **widok z lotu ~a** bird's eye view; **niebieski** ~ (*pot*) layabout (*pot*)
**ptasi** *adj* (*gniazdo, dziób*) bird's *attr*; ~ **móżdżek** (*przen*) birdbrain
**ptaszar|nia** (**-ni, -nie**) (*gen pl* **-ni**) *f* aviary
**ptasz|ek** (**-ka, -ki**) (*instr sg* **-kiem**) *m dimin od* **ptak**; (*pot: znaczek*) tick (*Brit*), check (*US*); **ranny** ~ early bird
**PTTK** *abbr* (= *Polskie Towarzystwo Turystyczno-Krajoznawcze*) Polish Tourist and Sightseeing Society
**pty|ś** (**-sia, -sie**) (*gen pl* **-siów** *lub* **-si**) *m* (*ciastko*) cream puff
**pu|b** (**-bu, -by**) (*loc sg* **-bie**) *m* pub
**publicy|sta** (**-sty, -ści**) (*loc sg* **-ście**) *m decl like f in sg* (political) commentator
**publicysty|ka** (**-ki**) (*dat sg* **-ce**) *f* (political) commentary
**publicznie** *adv* publicly, in public
**publicznoś|ć** (**-ci**) *f* audience
**publiczny** *adj* public; **dom** ~ brothel
**publikacj|a** (**-i, -e**) (*gen pl* **-i**) *f* publication
**publik|ować (-uję, -ujesz)** (*perf* **o-**) *vt* to publish
**puch** (**-u**) *m* down; (*miękka warstwa*) fluff
**puchacz** (**-a, -e**) (*gen pl* **-y** *lub* **-ów**) *m* eagle owl
**pucha|r** (**-ru, -ry**) (*loc sg* **-rze**) *m* cup; **P~ Świata/Polski** World/Polish Cup; ~ **przechodni** challenge cup
**pucharowy** *adj*: **mecz/system** ~ cup match/ system
**puch|nąć (-nę, -niesz)** (*imp* **-nij**, *pt* **-ł** *lub* **-nął, -ła, -li**, *perf* **s-**) *vi* to swell
**puchowy** *adj*: **kurtka puchowa** down jacket; **kołdra puchowa** down-filled quilt
**pucołowaty** *adj* chubby
**puc|ować (-uję, -ujesz)** (*perf* **wy-**) *vt* (*pot: buty*) to shine
**pucybu|t** (**-ta, -ty** *lub* **-ci**) (*loc sg* **-cie**) *m* shoeblack (*US*), bootblack (*US*)
**pucz** (**-u, -e**) *m* coup
**puddin|g** (**-gu, -gi**) (*instr sg* **-giem**) *m* pudding
**pud|el** (**-la, -le**) (*gen pl* **-li**) *m* poodle
**pudeł|ko** (**-ka, -ka**) (*instr sg* **-kiem**, *gen pl* **-ek**) *nt* box; ~ **od zapałek** matchbox
**pud|er** (**-ru, -ry**) (*loc sg* **-rze**) *m* powder; **cukier** ~ icing sugar
**pudernicz|ka** (**-ki, -ki**) (*dat sg* **-ce**, *gen pl* **-ek**) *f* (powder) compact
**pud|ło** (**-ła, -ła**) (*loc sg* **-le**, *gen pl* **-eł**) *nt* box; (*pot: chybiony strzał*) miss; (*: więzienie*) klink (*Brit*) (*pot*), cooler (*US*) (*pot*)

**pudł|ować (-uję, -ujesz)** (*perf* **s-**) *vi* (*pot*) to miss

**pudr|ować (-uję, -ujesz)** (*perf* **wy-**) *vt* to powder; **pudrować się** *vr* to powder one's face

**puen|ta** (**-ty, -ty**) (*dat sg* **-cie**) *f* punchline

**pu|f** (**-fa** *lub* **-fu, -fy**) (*loc sg* **-fie**) *m* (*mebel*) pouf(fe)

**puk|ać (-am, -asz)** (*perf* **-nąć**) *vi* to knock; **~ do drzwi** to knock at *lub* on the door; **pukać się** *vr*: **puknij się w czoło** *lub* **głowę!** (*pot*) you must be out of your head! (*pot*)

**pu|kiel** (**-kla, -kle**) (*gen pl* **-kli**) *m* curl (of hair)

**puk|nąć (-nę, -niesz)** (*imp* **-nij**) *vb perf od* **pukać**

**pul|a** (**-i, -e**) *f* pool

**pulchny** *adj* (*twarz, ciało*) plump; (*ciasto*) spongy

**pulowe|r** (**-ru** *lub* **-ra, -ry**) (*loc sg* **-rze**) *m* pullover, jumper (*Brit*)

**pulpet|y** (**-ów**) *pl* meat balls *pl*

**pulpi|t** (**-tu, -ty**) (*loc sg* **-cie**) *m* (*do nut*) music stand; (*część ławki*) desk top; (*sterowniczy*) console

**pul|s** (**-su, -sy**) (*loc sg* **-sie**) *m* pulse; **badać (zbadać** *perf*) **komuś ~** to take sb's pulse; **trzymać rękę na ~ie** (*przen*) to have *lub* keep one's finger on the pulse (*przen*)

**pulsa|r** (**-ra, -ry**) (*loc sg* **-rze**) *m* pulsar

**puls|ować (-uje)** *vi* to pulsate

**pulsujący** *adj* pulsating

**puła|p** (**-pu, -py**) (*loc sg* **-pie**) *m* ceiling

**pułap|ka** (**-ki, -ki**) (*dat sg* **-ce**, *gen pl* **-ek**) *f* trap; **~ na myszy** mousetrap; **samochód-~** booby-trapped car; **zastawiać (zastawić** *perf*) **pułapkę na kogoś** to set a trap for sb

**puł|k** (**-ku, -ki**) (*instr sg* **-kiem**) *m* regiment

**pułkowni|k** (**-ka, -cy**) (*instr sg* **-kiem**) *m* colonel

**pu|ma** (**-my, -my**) (*dat sg* **-mie**) *f* puma

**pumek|s** (**-su, -sy**) (*loc sg* **-sie**) *m* pumice

**pumperni|kiel** (**-kla** *lub* **-klu, -kle**) (*gen pl* **-kli**) *m* pumpernickel

**pump|y** (**-** *lub* **-ów**) *pl* knee-breeches *pl*

**pun|k** (**-ka, -ki**) (*instr sg* **-kiem**) *m* punk

**punkcj|a** (**-i, -e**) (*gen pl* **-i**) *f* (*Med*) puncture

**punk|t[1]** (**-tu, -ty**) (*loc sg* **-cie**) *m* point; (*usługowy, sprzedaży*) outlet; (*programu, dokumentu*) item; **~ widzenia** viewpoint, point of view; **czyjś mocny/słaby ~** sb's strong/weak point; **(główny) ~ programu** (*imprezy rozrywkowej*) (main) event; (*zebrania*) (main) point on the agenda; **zdobyć** (*perf*) **~** to score (a point); **z ~u widzenia kogoś** from sb's point of view; **~ wyjścia** starting point; **być wrażliwym na punkcie** *+gen* to be sensitive about; **~ kontrolny** checkpoint; **~ zwrotny** turning point; **w martwym punkcie** at a standstill

**punkt[2]** *adv* (*pot*): **~ czwarta** four o'clock sharp

**punktacj|a** (**-i, -e**) (*gen pl* **-i**) *f* (*zasady*) grading scale; (*suma punktów*) score

**punktualnie** *adv* on time; **~ o drugiej** at two o'clock sharp

**punktualnoś|ć** (**-ci**) *f* punctuality

**punktualny** *adj* punctual

**pu|pa** (**-py, -py**) (*dat sg* **-pie**) *f* (*pot*) bottom (*pot*)

**pupil** (**-a, -e**) (*gen pl* **-ów**) *m* teacher's pet

**purchaw|ka** (**-ki, -ki**) (*dat sg* **-ce**, *gen pl* **-ek**) *f* puffball

**purée** *nt inv* (*też*: **purée ziemniaczane**) mashed potatoes

**purpu|ra** (**-ry, -ry**) (*dat sg* **-rze**) *f* purplish red; **~ kardynalska** cardinal red

**purpurowy** *adj* purplish red; **~ ze złości** purple with rage

**pury|sta** (**-sty, -ści**) (*dat sg* **-ście**) *m decl like f in sg* purist

**puryta|nin** (**-nina, -nie**) *m* puritan

**purytański** *adj* puritan *attr*; (*przen*) puritanical

**puryz|m** (**-mu**) (*loc sg* **-mie**) *m* (*też*: **puryzm językowy**) purism

**pusta|k** (**-ka, -ki**) (*instr sg* **-kiem**) *m* (*cegła*) hollow block

**pustel|nia** (**-ni, -nie**) (*gen pl* **-ni**) *f* hermitage

**pustelniczy** *adj* (*samotny*) secluded

**pustelni|k** (**-ka, -cy**) (*instr sg* **-kiem**) *m* hermit

**pust|ka** (**-ki, -ki**) (*dat sg* **-ce**, *gen pl* **-ek**) *f* emptiness; **mam pustkę w głowie** (*przen*) my mind is blank; **świecić ~mi** (*przen*) to be empty

**pustko|wie** (**-wia, -wia**) (*gen pl* **-wi**) *nt* wastes *pl*

**pusto** *adv*: **na ulicach jest ~** the streets are empty; **~ brzmiący** hollow

**pustosz|eć (-eje)** (*perf* **o-**) *vi* to empty

**pustosz|yć (-ę, -ysz)** (*perf* **s-**) *vt* to ravage

**pusty** *adj* empty; (*przen*: *człowiek, śmiech*) hollow; **~ w środku** hollow; **puste miejsce** (*w tekście*) blank; **z ~mi rękami** empty-handed; **na ~ żołądek** on an empty stomach

**pusty|nia** (**-ni, -nie**) (*gen pl* **-ń**) *f* desert; **P~ Gobi** the Gobi Desert

**pustynny** *adj* desert *attr*

**puszcz|a** (**-y, -e**) *f* (primeval) forest, jungle

**puszcz|ać (-am, -asz)** (*perf* **puścić**) *vt* (*linę, czyjąś rękę*) to let go of; (*więźnia, zakładnika*) to let go; (*sok itp.*) to ooze; (*wodę, strumień*) to let out; (*Bot*: *listki, pączki*) to send out; (*płytę, kasetę, piosenkę*) to play; (*pot*: *maszynę*) to run ▷ *vi* (*o zamku itp.*) to give way; (*o plamie*) to come off; (*pot*: *o bluzce itp.*) to bleed; **puścić coś w ruch** to set sth in motion; **~ latawca** to fly a kite; **nie ~ pary z ust** to keep one's

P

mouth shut; ~ **coś z dymem** to burn sth down; ~ **kogoś przodem** to let sb go first; **puszczać się** *vr* (*przestawać się trzymać*) to let go; (*pot: prowadzić rozwiązłe życie*) to sleep around

**puszczy|k** (**-ka, -ki**) (*instr sg* **-kiem**) *m* tawny owl

**pusz|ek** (**-ku, -ki**) (*instr sg* **-kiem**) *m* (*na policzkach itp.*) down; (*do pudru*) powder puff; *patrz też* **puszka**

**pusz|ka** (**-ki, -ki**) (*dat sg* **-ce**, *gen pl* **-ek**) *f* (*pojemnik*) tin (*Brit*), can (*US*); (*skarbonka*) collection box; ~ **piwa/coca-coli** a can of beer/coke; ~ **po piwie** beer can; **ryba z puszki** canned *lub* tinned fish

**pusz|yć się (-ę, -ysz)** (*perf* **na-**) *vr* (*o ptaku*) to puff out its feathers; (*przen: o człowieku*) to puff o.s. with pride

**puszysty** *adj* fluffy

**pu|ścić (-szczę, -ścisz)** (*imp* **-ść**) *vb perf od* **puszczać**

**puzo|n** (**-nu, -ny**) (*loc sg* **-nie**) *m* trombone

**PWN** *abbr* (= *Państwowe Wydawnictwo Naukowe*) Polish Scientific Publishers

**py|cha** (**-chy**) *f* (*duma*) (*dat sg* **-sze**) pride; **~!** (*pot*) yum(-yum)! (*pot*)

**pyk|ać (-am, -asz)** (*perf* **-nąć**) *vt/vi*: ~ **fajkę** *lub* **z fajki** to puff on a pipe

**pyk|nąć (-nę, -niesz)** (*imp* **-nij**) *vb perf od* **pykać**

**pyle** *n patrz* **pył**

**py|ł** (**-łu, -ły**) (*loc sg* **-le**) *m* dust; **pył wulkaniczny/węglowy** volcanic/coal dust; **rozbijać (rozbić** *perf*) **coś w pył** to smash sth to smithereens

**pył|ek** (**-ku, -ki**) (*instr sg* **-kiem**) *m* (*drobina*) a speck of dust; (*kwiatowy*) pollen

**pys|k** (**-ka, -ki**) (*instr sg* **-kiem**) *m* muzzle; **stul ~!** (*pot!*) shut your trap! (*pot!*); **dawać (dać** *perf*) **komuś w ~** *lub* **po ~u** (*pot*) to sock sb (*pot*); **jest mocny w ~u** (*pot*) he's got the gift of the gab (*pot*); **wyrzucić** (*perf*) **kogoś na zbity ~** (*pot*) to kick sb out (*pot*)

**pyskaty** *adj* (*pej*) cheeky

**pysk|ować (-uję, -ujesz)** *vi* (*pot*) to talk back

**pysków|ka** (**-ki, -ki**) (*dat sg* **-ce**, *gen pl* **-ek**) *f* (*pot*) row

**pysze** *n patrz* **pycha**

**pysz|nić się (-nię, -nisz)** (*imp* **-nij**) *vr*: **pysznić się czymś** to boast about sth

**pyszny** *adj* (*wyniosły*) proud; (*smaczny*) delicious, scrumptious (*pot*); (*zabawa*) excellent

**pyt|ać (-am, -asz)** (*perf* **za-** *lub* **s-**) *vt/vi* to ask; ~ **kogoś (o coś/czy ...)** to ask sb (about sth/if ...); ~ **kogoś z fizyki/z historii Anglii** to give sb an oral in physics/on English history; ~ **(kogoś) o drogę/godzinę** to ask (sb) the way/time; ~ **kogoś o radę** to ask sb's advice; **pytać się** *vr* to ask

**pytająco** *adv* questioningly

**pytający** *adj* (*wzrok*) questioning; (*Jęz*) interrogative

**pytajni|k** (**-ka, -ki**) (*instr sg* **-kiem**) *m* question mark

**pyta|nie** (**-nia, -nia**) (*gen pl* **-ń**) *nt* question; **zadawać (zadać** *perf*) ~ to ask a question

**pyto|n** (**-na, -ny**) (*loc sg* **-nie**) *m* python

**py|za** (**-zy, -zy**) (*dat sg* **-zie**) *f* dumpling

**pyzaty** *adj* chubby

**PZPR** *abbr* (= *Polska Zjednoczona Partia Robotnicza*) (*Hist*) Polish United Workers' Party

**PZU** *abbr* (= *Państwowy Zakład Ubezpieczeń*) *Polish insurance company*

**PŻM** *abbr* (= *Polska Żegluga Morska*) Polish Steamship Company

# Qq

**Q, q** *nt inv (litera)* Q, q; **Q jak Quebec** ≈ Q for Queen
**quasi...** *pref* quasi-
**Quebe|c** (**-cu**) (*instr sg* **-kiem**) *m* Quebec
**qui|z** (**-zu, -zy**) (*loc sg* **-zie**) *m* quiz (show)
**quor|um** (**-um, -a**) (*gen pl* **-ów**) *nt inv in sg* = **kworum**

q

# Rr

**R, r** *nt inv* (*litera*) R, r; **R jak Roman** ≈ R for Robert (*Brit*), ≈ R for Roger (*US*)
**r.** *abbr* y. (= *year*)
**rabarba|r** (**-ru, -ry**) (*loc sg* **-rze**) *m* rhubarb
**raba|t** (**-tu, -ty**) (*loc sg* **-cie**) *m* discount
**raba|ta** (**-ty, -ty**) (*dat sg* **-cie**) *f* flower bed
**rabi|n** (**-na, -ni**) (*loc sg* **-nie**) *m* rabbi
**rab|ować (-uję, -ujesz)** *vt* (*złoto, pieniądze*) (*perf* **z-**) to steal; (*osobę, bank*) (*perf* **ob-**) to rob
**rabun|ek** (**-ku, -ki**) (*instr sg* **-kiem**) *m* robbery
**rabunkowy** *adj*: **napad ~** hold-up
**rabu|ś** (**-sia, -sie**) *m* robber
**rac|a** (**-y, -e**) *f* flare, signal rocket
**rachu|ba** (**-by, -by**) (*dat sg* **-bie**) *f*: **stracić rachubę czasu** to lose count of time; **to nie wchodzi w rachubę** that's out of the question
**rachun|ek** (**-ku, -ki**) (*instr sg* **-kiem**) *m* (*obliczenie*) calculation; (*konto*) account; (*spis należności*) bill; (*w restauracji*) bill (*Brit*), check (*US*); **~ prawdopodobieństwa** probability calculus; **~ różniczkowy** differential calculus; **~ bieżący** current account; **~ oszczędnościowo-rozliczeniowy** cheque account; **kupować coś na ~** to buy sth on account; **na własny ~** on one's own account
**rachunkowoś|ć** (**-ci**) *f* (*dziedzina*) accountancy; (*dział*) accounting
**rachunkowy** *adj* (*działanie*) arithmetic; (*księgi*) account *attr*
**racic|a** (**-y, -e**) *f* (cloven) hoof
**racj|a** (**-i, -e**) (*gen pl* **-i**) *f* (*słuszność*) right; (*powód*) reason; (*porcja*) ration; **racje** *pl* (*argumenty*) arguments; **masz rację** you are right; **nie masz racji** you are wrong; **przyznać** (*perf*) **komuś rację** to accept sb's argument; **(święta) ~!** you can say that again!; **~ stanu** raison d'état; **~ bytu** raison d'etre; **z jakiej racji?** by what right?; **z racji czegoś** by virtue of sth
**racjonalizacj|a** (**-i**) *f* (*usprawnianie*) rationalization, streamlining
**racjonalnie** *adv* rationally
**racjonalnoś|ć** (**-ci**) *f* rationality
**racjonalny** *adj* rational
**racjon|ować (-uję, -ujesz)** *vt* to ration
**raczej** *adv* rather; **był wysoki, ~ chudy** he was tall, rather thin; **mówmy ~ o wakacjach** let's rather talk about holidays
**raczk|ować (-uję, -ujesz)** *vi* (*o dziecku*) to crawl; (*przen*) to be still in nappies
**racz|yć (-ę, -ysz)** *vt*: **~ kogoś czymś** (*książk*) (*perf* **u-**) to treat sb to sth; **nawet nie raczył odpowiedzieć** he wouldn't even bother to answer; **Bóg raczy wiedzieć** God only knows
**rad**[1] (*pl* **radzi**) *adj*: **rad jestem, że cię widzę** I am glad to see you; **rad bym ci pomóc** I would be glad to help you; **rad nierad** willy-nilly
**ra|d**[2] (**-du**) (*loc sg* **-dzie**) *m* radium
**ra|da** (**-dy, -dy**) (*dat sg* **-dzie**) *f* (*porada*) a piece of advice, tip; (*instytucja*) council; **nie ma rady** there's nothing we can do about it; **nie da rady** this can't be done; **nie ma innej rady, tylko ...** there is no other solution, but ...; **~ nadzorcza** board of supervisors, supervisory board; **R~ Ministrów** the Cabinet; **R~ Bezpieczeństwa** Security Council
**rada|r** (**-ru, -ry**) (*loc sg* **-rze**) *m* radar
**radc|a** (**-y, -y** *lub* **-owie**) *m decl like f in sg*; **~ prawny** legal adviser *lub* advisor, legal counsellor (*Brit*) *lub* counselor (*US*); **~ handlowy** commercial counsel(lor)
**radiacj|a** (**-i**) *f* radiation
**radialny** *adj*: **opona radialna** radial tyre (*Brit*) *lub* tire (*US*)
**radieste|ta** (**-ty, -ci**) (*dat sg* **-cie**) *m decl like f in sg* water diviner
**radiestezj|a** (**-i**) *f* (*różdżkarstwo*) water divining
**radi|o** (**-a, -a**) *nt* radio; **słuchać radia** to listen to the radio; **w ~** *lub* **radiu** on the radio; **przez ~** over the radio
**radioaktywnoś|ć** (**-ci**) *f* radioactivity
**radioaktywny** *adj* radioactive
**radioamato|r** (**-ra, -rzy**) (*loc sg* **-rze**) *m* ham (*Radio*)
**radiofoni|a** (**-i**) *f* (the) radio
**radiologi|a** (**-i**) *f* radiology

**radiologiczny** *adj* radiological *attr*
**radiomagnetofo|n** (**-nu, -ny**) (*loc sg* **-nie**) *m* cassette radio, radio cassette recorder
**radioodbiorni|k** (**-ka, -ki**) (*instr sg* **-kiem**) *m* radio
**radiosłuchacz** (**-a, -e**) (*gen pl* **-y**) *m* listener
**radiostacj|a** (**-i, -e**) (*gen pl* **-i**) *f* radio station
**radiotechni|ka** (**-ki**) (*dat sg* **-ce**) *f* radio engineering
**radiotelefo|n** (**-nu, -ny**) (*loc sg* **-nie**) *m* radiotelephone
**radioterapi|a** (**-i**) *f* radiotherapy
**radiow|óz** (**-ozu, -ozy**) (*loc sg* **-ozie**) *m* police car
**radiowy** *adj* radio *attr*
**radn|a** (**-ej, -e**) *f* councillor (*Brit*), councilor (*US*)
**rad|ny** (**-nego, -ni**) *m decl like adj* councillor (*Brit*), councilor (*US*)
**radosny** *adj* cheerful, joyful
**radoś|ć** (**-ci**) *f* happiness, joy; **sprawić** (*perf*) **komuś ~** to make sb happy; **z radością** with pleasure
**radośnie** *adv* merrily, joyfully
**rad|ować (-uję, -ujesz)** (*perf* **u-**) *vt* (*książk*) to gladden; **radować się** *vr* to rejoice
**radykalny** *adj* dramatic, radical *attr*
**radyka|ł** (**-ła, -łowie**) (*loc sg* **-le**) *m* radical
**radzi** *adj pl od* **rad**[1]
**ra|dzić (-dzę, -dzisz)** (*imp* **-dź**) *vt*: **~ komuś** (*perf* **po-**) to advise sb ▷ *vi* (*obradować*) to debate; **radzę ci to wziąć** I advise you to take it; **nie radzę ci tego robić** I wouldn't do that (if I were you); **~ sobie z czymś** to cope with sth; **radzić się** *vr*: **~ się (kogoś)** (*perf* **po-**) to seek (sb's) advice
**radziecki** *adj* Soviet *attr*; **Związek R~** the Soviet Union
**ra|fa** (**-fy, -fy**) (*loc sg* **-fie**) *f* reef; **~ koralowa** coral reef
**rafineri|a** (**-i, -e**) (*gen pl* **-i**) *f* refinery
**rafin|ować (-uję, -ujesz)** *vt* to refine
**raj** (**-u**) *m* paradise; **czuć się jak w raju** to feel like heaven, to be in heaven; **raj na ziemi** heaven on earth
**raj|d** (**-du, -dy**) (*loc sg* **-dzie**) *m* rally
**rajdow|iec** (**-ca, -cy**) *m* rally driver
**rajski** *adj* blissful; **~ ogród** Garden of Eden; **~ ptak** bird of paradise
**rajstop|y** (**-**) *pl* tights (*Brit*), pantihose (*US*)
**rajtuz|y** (**-ów**) *pl* tights (*Brit*), pantihose (*US*)
**ra|k** (**-ka, -ki**) (*instr sg* **-kiem**) *m* (*Zool*) crayfish, crawfish (*US*); (*nowotwór*) cancer; **Rak** (*Astrologia*) Cancer; **raki** *pl* (*przyczepy do butów*) crampons
**rakarz** (**-a, -e**) (*gen pl* **-y**) *m* dogwarden (*Brit*), dogcatcher (*US*)
**rakie|ta** (**-ty, -ty**) (*dat sg* **-cie**) *f* (*statek kosmiczny*) rocket; (*pocisk*) rocket; (*Sport*) racket, racquet
**rakiet|ka** (**-ki, -ki**) (*dat sg* **-ce**, *gen pl* **-ek**) *f* bat
**rakietnic|a** (**-y, -e**) *f* flare *lub* Very pistol
**rakietowy** *adj*: **pocisk/napęd ~** rocket missile/propulsion; **wyrzutnia rakietowa** rocket launcher; **baza rakietowa** missile base
**rakotwórczy** *adj* carcinogenic
**ra|ma** (**-my, -my**) (*dat sg* **-mie**) *f* frame; **ramy** *pl* (*granice*) confines *pl*, framework; **w ~ch** *+gen* within the confines of
**ramiącz|ko** (**-ka, -ka**) (*instr sg* **-kiem**) *nt* (*halki, stanika*) (shoulder) strap; (*wieszak*) (coat) hanger
**ra|mię** (**-mienia, -miona**) (*gen pl* **-mion**) *nt* arm; (*bark*) shoulder; (*świecznika*) branch; **~ w ~** shoulder to shoulder; **na ~ broń!** slope arms!; **mieć duszę na ramieniu** to have one's heart in one's mouth; **wzruszać (wzruszyć** *perf*) **ramionami** to shrug (one's shoulders); **brać (wziąć** *perf*) **kogoś w ramiona** to take sb in one's arms; **brać (wziąć** *perf*) **kogoś pod ~** to take sb by the arm; **z czyjegoś ramienia** on behalf of sb
**ram|ka** (**-ki, -ki**) (*dat sg* **-ce**, *gen pl* **-ek**) *f* frame; (*w tekście*) box
**ramol** (**-a, -e**) (*gen pl* **-i**) *m* (*pot*) (old) crock (*pot*)
**ram|pa** (**-py, -py**) (*dat sg* **-pie**) *f* (*pomost*) (loading) platform; (*Teatr*) footlights *pl*
**ra|na** (**-ny, -ny**) (*dat sg* **-nie**) *f* wound, injury; **rany boskie!** (*pot*) good(ness) gracious!
**rancz|o** (**-a, -a**) *nt* ranch
**rand|ka** (**-ki, -ki**) (*dat sg* **-ce**, *gen pl* **-ek**) *f* date; **mieć randkę z kimś** to have a date with sb; **~ w ciemno** blind date
**ran|ek** (**-ka, -ki**) (*instr sg* **-kiem**) *m* morning
**ran|ga** (**-gi, -gi**) (*dat sg* **-dze**) *f* rank; (*przen*) importance; **sprawa najwyższej rangi** a matter of (the) utmost importance
**ra|nić (-nię, -nisz)** (*imp* **-ń**, *perf* **z-**) *vt imperf* to wound, to injure; (*przen*) to hurt; **~ czyjeś uczucia** to hurt sb's feelings ▷ *vt perf* = **zranić**
**raniutko** *adv* in the small hours
**rankin|g** (**-gu, -gi**) (*instr sg* **-giem**) *m* ranking, rating
**ranny**[1] *adj* (*człowiek, zwierzę*) wounded ▷ *m decl like adj* casualty; **czterech zabitych i sześciu ~ch** four killed and six injured
**ranny**[2] *adj* (*spacer, słońce, rosa*) morning *attr*; **dziś we wczesnych godzinach ~ch** in the early hours of this morning
**ra|no**[1] (**-na**) (*loc sg* **-nie**) *nt* morning; **co ~** every morning; **nad ranem** at daybreak, in the small hours (of the morning); **od rana do wieczora** from morning until night

r

**rano²** *adv* in the morning; **dziś/jutro ~** this/ tomorrow morning
**rapor|t** (**-tu, -ty**) (*loc sg* **-cie**) *m* report
**rapsodi|a** (**-i, -e**) (*gen pl* **-i**) *f* rhapsody
**raptem** *adv* all of a sudden; **miał ~ siedemnaście lat** he was barely seventeen
**raptownie** *adv* abruptly, suddenly
**raptowny** *adj* (*hamowanie, zmiana*) abrupt, sudden; (*wiatr, deszcz*) sudden
**raryta|s** (**-su, -sy**) (*loc sg* **-sie**) *m* (*rzadkość*) rarity; (*smakołyk*) delicacy
**ra|sa** (**-sy, -sy**) (*dat sg* **-sie**) *f* (*ludzi*) race; (*zwierząt*) breed; **pies czystej rasy** pure-bred dog
**rasi|sta** (**-sty, -ści**) (*dat sg* **-ście**) *m decl like f in sg* racist
**rasistowski** *adj* racist
**rasiz|m** (**-mu**) (*loc sg* **-mie**) *m* racism
**rasowy** *adj* (*przesądy, dyskryminacja*) racial; **stosunki rasowe** race relations; **~ pies** pedigree dog
**ra|ta** (**-ty, -ty**) (*dat sg* **-cie**) *f* instalment (Brit), installment (US); **kupować (kupić** *perf*) **coś na raty** to buy sth on hire purchase (Brit) *lub* on the installment plan (US)
**ratalny** *adj*: **sprzedaż ratalna** hire purchase (Brit), installment plan (US)
**ratler|ek** (**-ka, -ki**) (*instr sg* **-kiem**) *m* ratter
**rat|ować (-uję, -ujesz)** (*perf* **u-**) *vt* to save; (*tonącego*) to rescue; (*chorego*) to resuscitate; (*mienie*) to salvage, to rescue; **u~** *perf* **komuś życie** to save sb's life; **~ sytuację** to save the day
**ratownict|wo** (**-wa**) (*loc sg* **-wie**) *nt*: **~ górskie** mountain rescue; **~ morskie** lifeboat service; **~ okrętowe** ship salvaging, wrecking
**ratowniczy** *adj*: **ekipa ratownicza** rescue party
**ratowni|k** (**-ka, -cy**) (*instr sg* **-kiem**) *m* (*na plaży*) lifeguard, life-saver; (*górski itp.*) rescuer
**ratun|ek** (**-ku, -ki**) (*instr sg* **-kiem**) *m* (*pomoc w niebezpieczeństwie*) help; (*wybawienie*) salvation, rescue; **ratunku!** help!; **ostatnia deska ratunku** the last resort; **przyjść** *perf* **komuś na ~** to come to sb's rescue
**ratunkowy** *adj*: **kamizelka ratunkowa** life jacket; **łódź ratunkowa** lifeboat; **pogotowie ratunkowe** ambulance service; **ekipa/akcja ratunkowa** rescue party/operation
**ratusz** (**-a, -e**) (*gen pl* **-y** *lub* **-ów**) *m* town hall
**ratyfikacj|a** (**-i, -e**) (*gen pl* **-i**) *f* ratification
**ratyfik|ować (-uję, -ujesz)** *vt* (*im*)*perf* to ratify
**rausz** (**-u**) *m*: **być na ~u** (*pot*) to be tipsy
**ra|z** (**-zu, -zy**) (*loc sg* **-zie**) *m* (*przy oznaczaniu wielokrotności, porównywaniu itp.*) time; (*cios*) blow; **(jeden) raz** once; **dwa razy** twice; **dwa razy więcej** (*osób, książek*) twice as many; (*wody, pieniędzy, rozumu*) twice as much; **dwa razy dwa** two times two; **ani razu** not (even) once; **raz na tydzień/rok** once a week/year; **ile razy?** how many times?; **jeszcze raz** one more time, once again; **na razie** (*do tej pory*) as yet; (*tymczasem*) for the moment, for the time being; **na razie!** (*pot*) so long! (*pot*); **od razu** straight away *lub* off, at once; **na raz** at a time; **chociaż raz** for once; **raz na zawsze** once and for all; **pewnego razu** once (upon a time); **po raz pierwszy/trzeci** for the first/ third time; **tym/innym razem** this/another time; **za każdym razem** each *lub* every time; **za jednym razem** at a time; **w razie** *+gen* in the event of; **w razie potrzeby** if necessary *lub* required, should the need arise; **w każdym (bądź) razie** at any rate, in any case; **w takim razie** in that case; **w najlepszym/ najgorszym razie** at best/worst; **w przeciwnym razie** otherwise, or else; **w sam raz** just right; **na drugi raz** next time ▷ *num* one; **raz, dwa, trzy ...** one, two, three ... ▷ *adv* (*pewnego razu*) once (upon a time)
**razem** *adv* together; **~ z** *+instr* along *lub* together with; **(to będzie) ~ sto złotych** (it's) one hundred zloty altogether
**ra|zić (-żę, -zisz)** (*imp* **-ź**) *vt* (*oślepiać*) to dazzle; (*obrażać*) to offend; (*książk*: *uderzać*) to smite; **raziło ją ostre słońce** the blazing sun dazzled her; **raził otoczenie swoim zachowaniem** his behaviour (Brit) *lub* behavior (US) antagonized people
**razow|iec** (**-ca, -ce**) *m* (*też*: **chleb razowy**) wholemeal (Brit) *lub* wholewheat (US) bread
**razowy** *adj*: **mąka razowa** wholemeal (Brit) *lub* wholewheat (US) flour
**raźnie, raźno** *adv* (*szybko, żwawo*) briskly, jauntily; (*ochoczo*) enthusiastically; **czułam się** *lub* **było mi raźniej** I felt safer
**raźny** *adj* (*szybki, ochoczy*) brisk, jaunty; (*rześki*) lively
**rażący** *adj* (*światło*) dazzling, glaring; (*kontrast*) glaring, striking; (*niesprawiedliwość*) glaring, flagrant; (*błąd*) glaring, gross; (*zachowanie*) gross, crass
**rażeni|e** (**-a**) *nt*: **pole rażenia** field of fire; **siła rażenia** explosive power; **środki masowego rażenia** weapons of mass destruction
**rą|bać (-bię, -biesz)** *vt* (*łupać*) (*perf* **po-**) to chop; (*uderzać*) (*perf* **rąbnąć**) to whack
**rąb|ek** (**-ka, -ki**) (*instr sg* **-kiem**) *m* (*chustki, spódnicy*) hem
**rąb|nąć (-nę, -niesz)** (*imp* **-nij**) *vb perf od* **rąbać** ▷ *vt perf* (*pot*: *ukraść*) to pinch (*pot*); **rąbnąć się** *vr perf* (*pot*: *uderzyć się*) to hit o.s.

**rącz|ka** (**-ki, -ki**) (*dat sg* **-ce**, *gen pl* **-ek**) *f dimin od* **ręka**; (*uchwyt*) handle; **złota ~** handyman
**rączy** *adj* (*książk*) swift
**rdz|a** (**-y**) *f* rust
**rdzawy** *adj* rust
**rdzenny** *adj* indigenous
**rdze|ń** (**-nia, -nie**) (*gen pl* **-ni**) *m* core; (*Jęz*) root; **~ kręgowy** spinal cord
**rdzewie|ć** (**-je**) (*perf* **za-**) *vi* to rust
**reag|ować** (**-uję, -ujesz**) (*perf* **za-**) *vi*: **~** (**na** *+acc*) to react *lub* respond (to); **~** (**z** *+instr*) (*Chem*) to react (with)
**reakcj|a** (**-i, -e**) (*gen pl* **-i**) *f* reaction, response; (*Bio, Chem*) reaction; **~ jądrowa/łańcuchowa** nuclear/chain reaction
**reakcjoni|sta** (**-sty, -ści**) (*dat sg* **-ście**) *m decl like f in sg* reactionary
**reakcyjny** *adj* reactionary
**reakto|r** (**-ra, -ry**) (*loc sg* **-rze**) *m* reactor
**reaktyw|ować** (**-uję, -ujesz**) *vt* (*im*)*perf* to reactivate
**reali|a** (**-ów**) *pl* realities *pl*
**reali|sta** (**-sty, -ści**) (*dat sg* **-ście**) *m decl like f in sg* realist
**realistyczny** *adj* realistic
**realizacj|a** (**-i, -e**) (*gen pl* **-i**) *f* (*marzeń, celów*) realization; (*planu*) execution; (*czeku*) cashing; (*Radio, TV*) production
**realizato|r** (**-ra, -rzy**) (*loc sg* **-rze**) *m* (*wykonawca*) executor; (*Radio, TV*) producer
**realiz|m** (**-mu**) (*loc sg* **-mie**) *m* realism
**realiz|ować** (**-uję, -ujesz**) (*perf* **z-**) *vt* (*cel, marzenie*) to realize; (*plan*) to execute; (*film, przedstawienie*) to produce; (*czek*) to cash
**realny** *adj* (*rzeczywisty*) real; (*wykonalny, osiągalny*) viable, feasible
**reanimacj|a** (**-i**) *f* resuscitation
**reanimacyjny** *adj* (*zabieg*) resuscitative; (*sala, sprzęt*) resuscitation *attr*; **karetka reanimacyjna** ambulance
**reanim|ować** (**-uję, -ujesz**) *vt* to resuscitate
**reasekuracj|a** (**-i**) *f* (*Ekon*) reinsurance
**reasum|ować** (**-uję, -ujesz**) (*perf* **z-**) *vt* to recapitulate; **reasumując, …** to recap(itulate), …
**rebeli|a** (**-i, -e**) (*gen pl* **-i**) *f* (*książk*) rebellion
**rebelian|t** (**-ta, -ci**) (*loc sg* **-cie**) *m* rebel
**rebu|s** (**-su, -sy**) (*loc sg* **-sie**) *m* rebus
**recenzen|t** (**-ta, -ci**) (*loc sg* **-cie**) *m* reviewer
**recenzent|ka** (**-ki, -ki**) (*dat sg* **-ce**, *gen pl* **-ek**) *f* reviewer
**recenzj|a** (**-i, -e**) (*gen pl* **-i**) *f* review
**recenz|ować** (**-uję, -ujesz**) (*perf* **z-**) *vt* to review
**recepcj|a** (**-i, -e**) (*gen pl* **-i**) *f* (*w hotelu*) reception (desk), front desk (US)
**recepcjoni|sta** (**-sty, -ści**) (*dat sg* **-ście**) *m decl like f in sg* receptionist
**recepcjonist|ka** (**-ki, -ki**) (*dat sg* **-ce**, *gen pl* **-ek**) *f* receptionist
**recep|ta** (**-ty, -ty**) (*dat sg* **-cie**) *f* prescription; (*przen*) recipe
**receptu|ra** (**-ry, -ry**) (*dat sg* **-rze**) *f* recipe
**recesj|a** (**-i**) *f* recession
**recho|t** (**-tu, -ty**) (*loc sg* **-cie**) *m* (*odgłos żaby*) croak; (*przen: śmiech*) cackle
**recho|tać** (**-czę, -czesz**) *vi* (*o żabach*) to croak; (*o człowieku: śmiać się*) to cackle
**recital** (**-u, -e**) (*gen pl* **-i**) *m* recital
**recydy|wa** (**-wy, -wy**) (*dat sg* **-wie**) *f* (*Prawo*) recidivism
**recydywi|sta** (**-sty, -ści**) (*dat sg* **-ście**) *m decl like f in sg* recidivist
**recyklin|g** (**-gu**) (*instr sg* **-giem**) *m* recycling
**recytacj|a** (**-i, -e**) (*gen pl* **-i**) *f* recitation
**recyt|ować** (**-uję, -ujesz**) (*perf* **wy-**) *vt* to recite
**red.** *abbr* = **redaktor, redakcja**
**re|da** (**-dy, -dy**) (*dat sg* **-dzie**) *f* (*Żegl*) roads *pl*
**redag|ować** (**-uję, -ujesz**) (*perf* **z-**) *vt* (*czasopismo, książkę*) to edit; (*list, odpowiedź*) to draw up
**redakcj|a** (**-i, -e**) (*gen pl* **-i**) *f* (*redagowanie*) editing; (*zespół redaktorski*) editorial staff; (*lokal redakcyjny*) editor's office; **pod czyjąś redakcją** edited by sb
**redakcyjny** *adj* editorial; **artykuł ~** editorial
**redakto|r** (**-ra, -rzy**) (*loc sg* **-rze**) *m* editor; (*Radio, TV: programu informacyjnego*) newscaster; (*: programu sportowego*) sportscaster; **~ naczelny** editor-in-chief
**redukcj|a** (**-i, -e**) (*gen pl* **-i**) *f* reduction; (*zwalnianie z pracy*) layoff, redundancy
**reduk|ować** (**-uję, -ujesz**) (*perf* **z-**) *vt* (*wydatki, dochody*) to reduce, to cut; (*pot: zwalniać z pracy*) to lay off, to make redundant; **~ biegi** (*Mot*) to reduce gears
**redu|ta** (**-ty, -ty**) (*dat sg* **-cie**) *f* redoubt
**redystrybucj|a** (**-i, -e**) (*gen pl* **-i**) *f* redistribution
**reelekcj|a** (**-i**) *f* re-election
**reemigracj|a** (**-i**) *f* repatriation
**reemigran|t** (**-ta, -ci**) (*loc sg* **-cie**) *m* repatriant
**refektarz** (**-a, -e**) (*gen pl* **-y**) *m* refectory
**refera|t** (**-tu, -ty**) (*loc sg* **-cie**) *m* (*naukowy*) paper; (*sprawozdanie*) report; (*dział instytucji*) department
**referencj|e** (**-i**) *pl* references, credentials
**referend|um** (**-um, -a**) (*gen pl* **-ów**) *nt inv in sg* referendum
**referen|t** (**-ta, -ci**) (*loc sg* **-cie**) *m* (*osoba referująca*) speaker; (*urzędnik*) head of department, department manager

r

**refer|ować (-uję, -ujesz)** (*perf* **z-**) *vt*: ~ **coś** to report on sth

**refinans|ować (-uję, -ujesz)** (*perf* **z-**) *vt* to refinance

**reflek|s (-su, -sy)** (*loc sg* **-sie**) *m* (*reakcja*) reflex; (*odblask*) reflection; **mieć dobry/słaby ~** to have good/slow reflexes

**refleksj|a (-i, -e)** (*gen pl* **-i**) *f* reflection; **nasunęła mi się ~** I had an afterthought

**refleksyjny** *adj* reflective

**reflekto|r (-ra, -ry)** (*loc sg* **-rze**) *m* (*lampa*) searchlight; (*Mot*) headlight; (*Tech, Radio*) reflector

**reflekt|ować (-uję, -ujesz)** *vi*: ~ **na coś** *lub* **kupno czegoś** to be interested in buying sth

**refor|ma (-my, -my)** (*dat sg* **-mie**) *f* reform

**reformacj|a (-i)** *f* (*Hist*) the Reformation

**reformato|r (-ra, -rzy)** (*loc sg* **-rze**) *m* reformer

**reformatorski** *adj* reformist

**reform|ować (-uję, -ujesz)** (*perf* **z-**) *vt* to reform

**refre|n (-nu, -ny)** (*loc sg* **-nie**) *m* refrain, chorus

**refundacj|a (-i, -e)** *f* reimbursement

**refund|ować (-uję, -ujesz)** (*perf* **z-**) *vt* to reimburse

**rega|ł (-łu, -ły)** (*loc sg* **-le**) *m* bookshelf

**regat|y (-)** *pl* regatta *sg*

**regeneracj|a (-i, -e)** (*gen pl* **-i**) *f* regeneration

**regener|ować (-uję, -ujesz)** (*perf* **z-**) *vt* to regenerate; **regenerować się** *vr* to regenerate

**regen|t (-ta, -ci)** (*loc sg* **-cie**) *m* regent

**regent|ka (-ki, -ki)** (*dat sg* **-ce**, *gen pl* **-ek**) *f* regent

**regio|n (-nu, -ny)** (*loc sg* **-nie**) *m* region

**regionaliz|m (-mu, -my)** *m* regionalism; (*Jęz*) localism, regionalism

**regionalny** *adj* regional

**reglamentacj|a (-i)** *f* rationing

**regre|s (-su)** (*loc sg* **-sie**) *m* (*książk*) regress, regression

**regulacj|a (-i, -e)** (*gen pl* **-i**) *f* (*normowanie*) control; (*należności, rachunków*) settlement; (*zegarka, przyrządu*) (re)adjustment; **~ siły głosu** volume control; **~ cen/płac** price/wage control; **~ urodzin** birth control

**regulami|n (-nu, -ny)** (*loc sg* **-nie**) *m* regulations *pl*

**regulaminowy** *adj* (*nagroda, obowiązki*) statutory; (*fryzura, ubiór*) regulation *attr*

**regularnie** *adv* regularly

**regularnoś|ć (-ci)** *f* regularity

**regularny** *adj* regular; **w ~ch odstępach czasu** at regular intervals

**regulato|r (-ra, -ry)** (*loc sg* **-rze**) *m* regulator; **na cały ~** (*pot*) at full blast

**regul|ować (-uję, -ujesz)** *vt* (*perf* **wy-**) (*nastawiać: grzejnik*) to regulate; (*: zegarek*) to set, to adjust; (*: radio, zapłon*) to tune; (*płacić*) (*perf* **u-**) to pay, to settle; **~ ruch** to control traffic

**regu|ła (-ły, -ły)** (*dat sg* **-le**) *f* rule; **z reguły** as a (general) rule; **reguły gry** rules of the game; **być/stać się** (*perf*) **regułą** to be/become the rule

**rehabilitacj|a (-i)** *f* rehabilitation

**rehabilit|ować (-uję, -ujesz)** (*perf* **z-**) *vt* to rehabilitate; **rehabilitować się** *vr* to rehabilitate o.s.

**reinkarnacj|a (-i)** *f* reincarnation

**rej** *m inv*; **wodzić rej** to call the tune

**rej.** *abbr* = **rejon, rejonowy**

**re|ja (-i, -je)** (*gen pl* **-j**) *f* (*Żegl*) yard

**rejen|t (-ta, -ci)** (*loc sg* **-cie**) *m* notary

**rejest|r (-ru, -ry)** (*loc sg* **-rze**) *m* register

**rejestracj|a (-i, -e)** (*gen pl* **-i**) *f* (*spisanie*) registration; (*w przychodni: czynność*) registration; (*: miejsce*) reception; (*Tech, Radio, TV*) recording; (*pot: Mot*) plates *pl*

**rejestracyjny** *adj*: **numer ~** registration number; **tablica rejestracyjna** number (*Brit*) *lub* license (*US*) plate; **dowód ~** registration

**rejestr|ować (-uję, -ujesz)** (*perf* **za-**) *vt* (*spisywać*) to register; (*Tech, Radio, TV*) to record; **rejestrować się** *vr* to register

**rejo|n (-nu, -ny)** (*loc sg* **-nie**) *m* (*jednostka administracyjna*) district, region; (*okolica*) area

**rejonowy** *adj* district *attr*

**rej|s (-su, -sy)** (*loc sg* **-sie**) *m* (*statku*) voyage; (*: turystyczny*) cruise; (*samolotu*) flight

**rejsowy** *adj* (*lot*) scheduled

**rekapitul|ować (-uję, -ujesz)** (*perf* **z-**) *vt* to recap, to recapitulate

**reki|n (-na, -ny)** (*loc sg* **-nie**) *m* shark

**rekla|ma (-my, -my)** (*loc sg* **-mie**) *f* (*reklamowanie*) advertising; (*kampania*) promotion; (*ogłoszenie w TV, radiu*) commercial; (*ogłoszenie w prasie*) advertisement; (*tablica reklamowa*) billboard; (*rozgłos*) publicity

**reklamacj|a (-i, -e)** (*gen pl* **-i**) *f* complaint; **składać (złożyć** *perf***) reklamację** to complain

**reklam|ować (-uję, -ujesz)** (*perf* **za-**) *vt* (*propagować*) to advertise; (*składać reklamację*) to complain about

**reklamowy** *adj* advertising *attr*; **tablica reklamowa** billboard

**reklamów|ka (-ki, -ki)** (*dat sg* **-ce**, *gen pl* **-ek**) *f* (*pot: film reklamowy*) commercial, infomercial (*pot*); (*: torba plastikowa*) plastic bag

**rekolekcj|e (-i)** *pl* (*Rel*) retreat

**rekomendacj|a** (**-i, -e**) (*gen pl* **-i**) *f* recommendation
**rekomend|ować** (**-uję, -ujesz**) (*perf* **za-**) *vt* to recommend
**rekompensa|ta** (**-ty**) (*dat sg* **-cie**) *f* compensation; **tytułem rekompensaty (za coś)** in compensation (for sth)
**rekompens|ować** (**-uję, -ujesz**) (*perf* **z-**) *vt*: **~ coś komuś** to compensate sb for sth
**rekonesan|s** (**-su, -se**) (*loc sg* **-sie**) *m* reconnaissance
**rekonstrukcj|a** (**-i, -e**) (*gen pl* **-i**) *f* reconstruction
**rekonstru|ować** (**-uję, -ujesz**) (*perf* **z-**) *vt* to reconstruct
**rekonwalescencj|a** (**-i**) *f* convalescence
**rekonwalescen|t** (**-ta, -ci**) (*loc sg* **-cie**) *m* convalescent
**rekonwalescent|ka** (**-ki, -ki**) (*dat sg* **-ce**, *gen pl* **-ek**) *f* convalescent
**rekor|d** (**-du, -dy**) (*loc sg* **-dzie**) *m* record; **~ świata/kraju** world/national record; **pobić** (*perf*) **~** to break a record; **poprawić** (*perf*) **~** to better a record; **ustanowić** (*perf*) **~** to set a record
**rekordowy** *adj* record(-breaking) *attr*
**rekordzi|sta** (**-sty, -ści**) (*dat sg* **-ście**) *m decl like f in sg* record holder; **~ świata** world-record holder
**rekreacj|a** (**-i**) *f* recreation
**rekreacyjny** *adj* recreational
**rekru|t** (**-ta, -ci**) (*loc sg* **-cie**) *m* recruit
**rekrutacj|a** (**-i, -e**) (*gen pl* **-i**) *f* (*Szkol*) enrolment; (*Wojsk*) recruitment, conscription (*Brit*), draft (*US*)
**rekrut|ować się** (**-uję, -ujesz**) *vr*: **rekrutować się spośród** *+gen* (*pochodzić*) to come from
**rekto|r** (**-ra, -rzy**) (*loc sg* **-rze**) *m* (*Uniw*) ≈ vice chancellor (*Brit*), ≈ president (*US*)
**rektora|t** (**-tu, -ty**) (*loc sg* **-cie**) *m* (*Uniw*) ≈ vice chancellor's office (*Brit*), ≈ president's office (*US*)
**rekultywacj|a** (**-i**) *f* reclamation
**rekultyw|ować** (**-uję, -ujesz**) (*perf* **z-**) *vt* to reclaim
**rekwir|ować** (**-uję, -ujesz**) (*perf* **za-**) *vt* to requisition, to commandeer
**rekwizy|t** (**-tu, -ty**) (*loc sg* **-cie**) *m* (*Film, Teatr*) prop
**relacj|a** (**-i, -e**) (*gen pl* **-i**) *f* (*sprawozdanie*) report; (*związek*) relationship; **zdawać (zdać** *perf*) **relację (z czegoś)** to report (on sth); **pociąg relacji Warszawa-Zakopane** a Warsaw-to-Zakopane train
**relacjon|ować** (**-uję, -ujesz**) (*perf* **z-**) *vt* to report on, to relate
**relak|s** (**-su**) (*loc sg* **-sie**) *m* relaxation
**relaksacyjny** *adj* relaxation *attr*
**relaks|ować się** (**-uję, -ujesz**) (*perf* **z-**) *vr* to relax
**relatywnie** *adv* (*książk*) relatively
**relatywny** *adj* (*książk*) relative
**releg|ować** (**-uję, -ujesz**) *vt* (*im*)*perf* (*książk*) to relegate
**relie|f** (**-fu, -fy**) (*loc sg* **-fie**) *m* (*Sztuka*) relief
**religi|a** (**-i, -e**) (*gen pl* **-i**) *f* religion; (*nauka religii*) religious instruction
**religijny** *adj* religious
**relik|t** (**-tu, -ty**) (*loc sg* **-cie**) *m* relic; **~ przeszłości** a relic of the past
**relikwi|a** (**-i, -e**) (*gen pl* **-i**) *f* relic
**relikwiarz** (**-a, -e**) (*gen pl* **-y**) *m* reliquary
**relin|g** (**-gu, -gi**) (*instr sg* **-giem**) *m* (*Żegl*) rail
**remanen|t** (**-tu, -ty**) (*loc sg* **-cie**) *m* (*Handel*) stocktaking
**remedi|um** (**-um, -a**) (*gen pl* **-ów**) *nt inv in sg* (*książk*) remedy
**reminiscencj|a** (**-i, -e**) (*gen pl* **-i**) *f* (*książk*) reminiscence
**remi|s** (**-su, -sy**) (*loc sg* **-sie**) *m* draw; **uzyskać ~** to draw
**remisj|a** (**-i, -e**) (*gen pl* **-i**) *f* (*Med*) remission
**remis|ować** (**-uję, -ujesz**) (*perf* **z-**) *vi* to draw
**remisowy** *adj* drawn
**remi|za** (**-zy, -zy**) (*dat sg* **-zie**) *f*: **~ strażacka** fire station
**remon|t** (**-tu, -ty**) (*loc sg* **-cie**) *m* (*mieszkania*) redecoration; (*maszyny, statku*) repair; **~ kapitalny** major overhaul
**remont|ować** (**-uję, -ujesz**) (*perf* **wy-** *lub* **od-**) *vt* (*mieszkanie*) to redecorate; (*maszynę, statek*) to repair
**Re|n** (**-nu**) (*loc sg* **-nie**) *m* (*Geog*) the Rhine
**renci|sta** (**-sty, -ści**) (*dat sg* **-ście**) *m decl like f in sg* pensioner
**rencist|ka** (**-ki, -ki**) (*dat sg* **-ce**, *gen pl* **-ek**) *f* pensioner
**renega|t** (**-ta, -ci**) (*loc sg* **-cie**) *m* renegade
**renesan|s** (**-su**) (*loc sg* **-sie**) *m* Renaissance; (*rozkwit*) renaissance
**renesansowy** *adj* Renaissance
**renife|r** (**-ra, -ry**) (*loc sg* **-rze**) *m* reindeer
**renklo|da** (**-dy, -dy**) (*dat sg* **-dzie**) *f* greengage
**reno|ma** (**-my**) (*dat sg* **-mie**) *f* reputation; **cieszyć się dobrą renomą** to hold a good reputation; **zdobyć** (*perf*) **sobie renomę** to make a reputation for o.s.
**renomowany** *adj* famous
**renowacj|a** (**-i, -e**) (*gen pl* **-i**) *f* renovation; **przeprowadzać (przeprowadzić** *perf*) **renowację budynku** to renovate a building

**ren|ta** (**-ty, -ty**) (*dat sg* **-cie**) *f* pension; **~ emerytalna/inwalidzka** old age/disability pension; **być na rencie** to receive a pension
**rentge|n** (**-na, -ny**) (*loc sg* **-nie**) *m* (*pot: aparat*) X-ray machine; (*prześwietlenie*) X-ray
**rentgenowski** *adj* X-ray *attr*
**rentownoś|ć** (**-ci**) *f* (*Ekon*) profitability
**rentowny** *adj* profitable
**reorganizacj|a** (**-i, -e**) (*gen pl* **-i**) *f* reorganization
**reorganiz|ować** (**-uję, -ujesz**) (*perf* **z-**) *vt* to reorganize
**reparacj|e** (**-i**) *pl*: **~ wojenne** war reparations *pl*
**repatriacj|a** (**-i**) *f* repatriation
**repatrian|t** (**-ta, -ci**) (*loc sg* **-cie**) *m* repatriate
**reperkusj|e** (**-i**) *pl* (*książk*) repercussions *pl*
**reper|ować** (**-uję, -ujesz**) (*perf* **z-**) *vt* to repair, to mend
**repertua|r** (**-ru, -ry**) (*loc sg* **-rze**) *m* repertoire
**repet|ować** (**-uję, -ujesz**) *vt* (*klasę*) to repeat; (*broń*) (*perf* **za-**) to cock
**repetytori|um** (**-um, -a**) (*gen pl* **-ów**) *nt inv in sg* (*powtórka materiału*) review; (*podręcznik*) review textbook
**repli|ka** (**-ki, -ki**) (*dat sg* **-ce**) *f* (*odpowiedź*) rejoinder; (*kopia*) replica
**reportaż** (**-u, -e**) (*gen pl* **-y**) *m* report, reportage
**reporte|r** (**-ra, -rzy**) (*loc sg* **-rze**) *m* reporter
**reporter|ka** (**-ki, -ki**) (*dat sg* **-ce**, *gen pl* **-ek**) *f* reporter
**represj|e** (**-i**) *pl* repressive measures
**represjon|ować** (**-uję, -ujesz**) *vt* to persecute, to victimize
**represyjny** *adj* repressive
**reprezentacj|a** (**-i, -e**) (*gen pl* **-i**) *f* representation; (*Sport*): **~ kraju** national team
**reprezentacyjny** *adj* (*fundusz*) entertainment *attr*; (*strój, dzielnica*) elegant
**reprezentan|t** (**-ta, -ci**) (*loc sg* **-cie**) *m* (*przedstawiciel*) representative; **Izba R~ów** the House of Representatives
**reprezentant|ka** (**-ki, -ki**) (*dat sg* **-ce**, *gen pl* **-ek**) *f* (*przedstawicielka*) representative
**reprezentatywny** *adj*: **~ (dla** *+gen***)** representative (of)
**reprezent|ować** (**-uję, -ujesz**) *vt* to represent; **~ pogląd** to hold an opinion
**reprodukcj|a** (**-i, -e**) (*gen pl* **-i**) *f* reproduction
**reproduk|ować** (**-uję, -ujesz**) (*perf* **z-**) *vt* to reproduce
**reprymen|da** (**-dy, -dy**) (*dat sg* **-dzie**) *f* reprimand; **udzielać (udzielić** *perf***) komuś reprymendy** to reprimand sb
**reprywatyzacj|a** (**-i**) *f* reprivatization
**reprywatyz|ować** (**-uję, -ujesz**) (*perf* **z-**) *vt* to reprivatize
**republi|ka** (**-ki, -ki**) (*dat sg* **-ce**) *f* republic; **R~ Czeska** the Czech Republic; **R~ Federalna Niemiec** the Federal Republic of Germany
**republika|nin** (**-nina, -nie**) (*loc sg* **-ninie**) *m* republican
**republikański** *adj* republican
**reputacj|a** (**-i**) *f* reputation; **dbać o (swoją) reputację** to guard one's reputation; **psuć (popsuć** *perf***) komuś reputację** to damage sb's reputation; **psuć (popsuć** *perf***) sobie reputację** to blot one's copybook; **mieć złą reputację** to have a bad reputation
**requiem** (**-**) *nt inv* requiem
**reset|ować** (**-uję, -ujesz**) (*perf* **z-**) *vt* (*Komput*) to reboot, to reset
**resocjalizacj|a** (**-i**) *f* rehabilitation
**resocjaliz|ować** (**-uję, -ujesz**) (*perf* **z-**) *vt* to rehabilitate; **resocjalizować się** *vr* to rehabilitate
**reso|r** (**-ru, -ry**) (*loc sg* **-rze**) *m* (*Mot*) (suspension) spring
**resor|t** (**-tu, -ty**) (*loc sg* **-cie**) *m* department
**respek|t** (**-tu**) (*loc sg* **-cie**) *m* (*poważanie*) respect; (*obawa*) awe; **mieć dla kogoś ~** to have respect for sb; **budzić ~** to command respect
**respekt|ować** (**-uję, -ujesz**) *vt* to respect
**responden|t** (**-ta, -ci**) (*loc sg* **-cie**) *m* respondent
**restauracj|a** (**-i, -e**) (*gen pl* **-i**) *f* (*lokal gastronomiczny*) restaurant; (*renowacja*) restoration; (*Hist*) the Restoration
**restauracyjny** *adj*: **wagon ~** dining *lub* restaurant car
**restaur|ować** (**-uję, -ujesz**) (*perf* **od-**) *vt* to restore
**restrukturyzacj|a** (**-i**) *f* restructuring
**restrukturyz|ować** (**-uję, -ujesz**) (*perf* **z-**) *vt* to restructure
**restrykcj|e** (**-i**) *pl* restrictions *pl*
**restrykcyjny** *adj* restrictive
**resz|ka** (**-ki, -ki**) (*dat sg* **-ce**, *gen pl* **-ek**) *f* heads; **orzeł czy ~?** heads or tails?
**resz|ta** (**-ty, -ty**) (*dat sg* **-cie**) *f* (*pozostałość*) rest, remainder; (*pieniądze*) change; **reszty nie trzeba!** keep the change!; **bez reszty** completely
**reszt|ka** (**-ki, -ki**) (*dat sg* **-ce**, *gen pl* **-ek**) *f* remainder; **resztki** *pl* leftovers *pl*; **gonić ~mi sił** to be on one's last legs
**retoryczny** *adj*: **pytanie retoryczne** rhetorical question; **figura retoryczna** figure of speech
**retory|ka** (**-ki**) (*dat sg* **-ce**) *f* rhetoric
**retransmisj|a** (**-i, -e**) (*gen pl* **-i**) *f* rebroadcast

**retransmit|ować (-uję, -ujesz)** *vt im(perf)* to rebroadcast
**retro** *adj inv* retro *attr*; **w stylu ~** (in a) retro (style)
**retrospekcj|a (-i, -e)** *(gen pl* **-i**) *f (Film, Lit)* flashback
**retrospektywny** *adj (scena, wątek)* retrospective, flashback *attr*
**retusz (-u, -e)** *m* touch-up, retouch
**retusz|ować (-uję, -ujesz)** *(perf* **wy-**) *vt* to touch up, to retouch
**reumatolo|g (-ga, -dzy** *lub* **-gowie**) *(instr sg* **-giem**) *m* rheumatologist
**reumatyczny** *adj* rheumatic
**reumatyz|m (-mu)** *(loc sg* **-mie**) *m* rheumatism
**rewaloryzacj|a (-i)** *f (Ekon)* revaluation
**rewaloryz|ować (-uję, -ujesz)** *(perf* **z-**) *vt (Ekon)* to revalue
**rewaluacj|a (-i)** *f* revaluation
**rewanż (-u, -e)** *m (Sport)* return match
**rewanż|ować się (-uję, -ujesz)** *(perf* **z-**) *vr*: **rewanżować się komuś za coś** to repay sb for sth; **rewanżować się komuś czymś** to repay sb with sth
**rewanżowy** *adj (mecz, pojedynek)* return *attr*
**rewelacj|a (-i, -e)** *(gen pl* **-i**) *f* hit, revelation
**rewelacyjny** *adj* amazing, sensational
**rewer|s (-su, -sy)** *(loc sg* **-sie**) *m (monety)* reverse; *(pokwitowanie)* receipt; *(w bibliotece)* (check-out) slip
**rewi|a (-i, -e)** *(gen pl* **-i**) *f (widowisko)* revue; *(przegląd, pokaz)* parade
**rewiden|t (-ta, -ci)** *(loc sg* **-cie**) *m (też:* **rewident księgowy**) auditor
**rewid|ować (-uję, -ujesz)** *(perf* **z-**) *vt (przeszukiwać)* to search, to frisk; *(zmieniać)* to revise; *(Fin)* to audit
**rewizj|a (-i, -e)** *(gen pl* **-i**) *f (przeszukiwanie)* search; *(modyfikacja)* review; *(Prawo)* appeal; **nakaz rewizji** search warrant; **wnosić (wnieść** *perf***) rewizję** to appeal
**rewizjoniz|m (-mu)** *(loc sg* **-mie**) *m* revisionism
**rewizy|ta (-ty, -ty)** *(dat sg* **-cie**) *f* return visit
**rewol|ta (-ty, -ty)** *(dat sg* **-cie**) *f* revolt
**rewolucj|a (-i, -e)** *(gen pl* **-i**) *f* revolution
**rewolucjoni|sta (-sty, -ści)** *(dat sg* **-ście**) *m decl like f in sg* revolutionary
**rewolucjoniz|ować (-uję, -ujesz)** *(perf* **z-**) *vt* to revolutionize
**rewolucyjny** *adj* revolutionary
**rewolwe|r (-ru, -ry)** *(loc sg* **-rze**) *m* revolver
**rezer|wa (-wy)** *(dat sg* **-wie**) *f (zapas) (nom pl* **-wy**) reserve; *(powściągliwość)* reserve; *(Wojsk)* (the) reserve; **trzymać coś w rezerwie** to keep sth in reserve
**rezerwacj|a (-i, -e)** *(gen pl* **-i**) *f* reservation, booking *(Brit)*; **zrobić** *(perf)* **rezerwację** *lub* **dokonać** *(perf)* **rezerwacji** to make a reservation
**rezerwa|t (-tu, -ty)** *(loc sg* **-cie**) *m (przyrody)* reserve; *(Indian)* reservation
**rezerwi|sta (-sty, -ści)** *(dat sg* **-ście**) *m decl like f in sg* reservist
**rezerw|ować (-uję, -ujesz)** *(perf* **za-**) *vt (pokój, stolik, czas)* to reserve; *(pieniądze)* to earmark
**rezerwowy** *adj* reserve ▷ *m (Sport) decl like adj* sub(stitute), reserve player
**rezerwua|r (-ru, -ry)** *(loc sg* **-rze**) *m* reservoir
**rezolucj|a (-i, -e)** *(gen pl* **-i**) *f* resolution; **uchwalić** *(perf)* **rezolucję** to adopt *lub* pass a resolution
**rezolutnoś|ć (-ci)** *f* self-assurance; *(bystrość)* cleverness
**rezolutny** *adj* self-assured; *(bystry)* clever
**rezonan|s (-su, -se)** *(loc sg* **-sie**) *m* resonance
**rezonansowy** *adj*: **płyta rezonansowa** sounding board; **pudło rezonansowe** resonance box
**rezon|ować (-uję, -ujesz)** *vi (Fiz)* to resonate
**rezulta|t (-tu, -ty)** *(loc sg* **-cie**) *m* result; **w rezultacie** as a result, consequently; **bez ~u** without result
**rezurekcj|a (-i, -e)** *(gen pl* **-i**) *f (Rel)* resurrection
**rezydencj|a (-i, -e)** *(gen pl* **-i**) *f* residence
**rezyd|ować (-uję, -ujesz)** *vi (książk)* to reside
**rezygnacj|a (-i, -e)** *(gen pl* **-i**) *f* resignation; **złożyć** *(perf)* **rezygnację** to hand in one's resignation
**rezygn|ować (-uję, -ujesz)** *(perf* **z-**) *vi (dać za wygraną)* to give up; **~ z czegoś** to give sth up; **~ ze stanowiska** to resign from one's post
**reżi|m, reży|m (-mu, -my)** *(loc sg* **-mie**) *m* regime
**reżimowy, reżymowy** *adj* regime *attr*
**reżyse|r (-ra, -rzy)** *(loc sg* **-rze**) *m* director
**reżyseri|a (-i)** *f*: **„~: Steven Spielberg"** "directed by Steven Spielberg"
**reżyser|ować (-uję, -ujesz)** *(perf* **wy-**) *vt* to direct
**ręce** *n patrz* **ręka**
**ręcznie** *adv* manually, by hand; **~ malowany** hand-painted
**ręczni|k (-ka, -ki)** *(instr sg* **-kiem**) *m* towel; **~ kąpielowy** bath towel
**ręczny** *adj* hand *attr*; **piłka ręczna** *(Sport)* handball; **~ hamulec** handbrake *(Brit)*, emergency brake *(US)*; **ręcznej roboty** handmade
**ręcz|yć (-ę, -ysz)** *(perf* **za-**) *vi*: **~ za kogoś/coś** to vouch for sb/sth

r

**ręk|a** (**-ki, -ce**) (*dat sg* **-ce**, *loc sg* **-ce**, *gen pl* **rąk**, *instr pl* **-kami** *lub* **-koma**, *loc pl* **-kach**) *f* hand; (*ramię*) arm; (*dłoń*) palm; **na ręce** *lub* **do rąk ...** care of ...; **od ręki** while you wait; **pod ręką** (close *lub* near) at hand; **to mi jest nie na rękę** it isn't convenient for me; **własnymi rękoma** with one's own hands; **z pierwszej ręki** (*wiadomość, informacja*) first-hand; (*słyszeć, dowiedzieć się*) at first hand; **iść (pójść** *perf***) komuś na rękę** to be accommodating with sb; **z pustymi rękoma** empty-handed; **siedzieć z założonymi rękoma** to sit on one's hands; **ręce do góry!** hands up!; **iść z kimś pod rękę** to walk arm in arm with sb; **dawać (dać** *perf***) komuś wolną rękę** to give sb a free hand; **mieć związane ręce** (*przen*) to have one's hands tied; **prosić kogoś o rękę** to propose to sb; **wziąć coś w swoje ręce** to take sth into one's hands; **precz z ~mi!** hands off!; **ręce przy sobie!** (keep your) hands off!

**rękа|w** (**-wa, -wy**) (*loc sg* **-wie**) *m* sleeve; **bez ~ów** sleeveless

**rękawic|a** (**-y, -e**) *f* glove; **rękawice bokserskie** boxing gloves

**rękawicz|ka** (**-ki, -ki**) (*dat sg* **-ce**, *gen pl* **-ek**) *f* glove; (*z jednym palcem*) mitten

**rękoczy|n** (**-nu, -ny**) (*loc sg* **-nie**) *m* fist fight

**rękodzie|ło** (**-ła, -ła**) (*loc sg* **-le**) *nt* handicraft

**rękojeś|ć** (**-ci, -ci**) (*gen pl* **-ci**) *f* (*noża, łopaty*) handle; (*pistoletu*) grip; (*miecza*) hilt

**rękoj|mia** (**-mi, -mie**) (*gen pl* **-mi**) *f* (*gwarancja*) guarantee; (*Prawo*) warranty

**rękopi|s** (**-su, -sy**) (*loc sg* **-sie**) *m* manuscript

**RFN** (**RFN-u**) *abbr* (= *Republika Federalna Niemiec*) FRG (= *the Federal Republic of Germany*)

**Rh** *abbr*: **mieć dodatnie/ujemne Rh** to be rhesus positive/negative

**riksz|a** (**-y, -e**) (*gen pl* **-y**) *f* rickshaw

**rin|g** (**-gu, -gi**) (*instr sg* **-giem**) *m* ring

**ripo|sta** (**-sty, -sty**) (*dat sg* **-ście**) *f* riposte

**ripost|ować (-uję, -ujesz)** (*perf* **z-**) *vi* to retort, to riposte

**risot|to** (**-ta**) (*loc sg* **-cie**) *nt* risotto

**r-k** *abbr* (= *rachunek*) a/c

**r.m.** *abbr* (= *rodzaj męski*) m (= *masculine*)

**r.nij.** *abbr* (= *rodzaj nijaki*) nt (= *neuter*)

**robact|wo** (**-wa**) (*loc sg* **-wie**) *nt* bugs *pl*

**robacz|ek** (**-ka, -ki**) (*instr sg* **-kiem**) *m*: **~ świętojański** glow-worm

**robaczkowy** *adj*: **wyrostek ~** (vermiform) appendix; **zapalenie wyrostka robaczkowego** appendicitis

**robaczywy** *adj* wormy

**roba|k** (**-ka, -ki**) (*instr sg* **-kiem**) *m* worm; **robaki** *pl* (*pasożyty*) worms *pl*

**ro|bić (-bię, -bisz)** (*imp* **rób**, *perf* **z-**) *vt* (*herbatę, meble, majątek*) to make; (*pranie, zakupy, lekcje*) to do; (*wywoływać: zamieszanie, hałas*) to cause ▷ *vi* (*działać*) to act, to act; (*pot: pracować*) to work; **co robisz?** what are you doing?; **~ komuś miejsce** to make room for sb; **~ na drutach** to knit; **~ komuś nadzieje** to raise sb's hopes; **~ komuś przyjemność** to please sb; **to ci dobrze zrobi** it will do you good; **robić się** *vr* (*stawać się*) to become; **robi się ciemno/zimno** it's getting dark/cold; **robi mi się niedobrze** I'm beginning to feel sick; **już się robi!** (*pot*) (I/we) will get right down to it! (*pot*); **tak się nie robi** it's not fair

**robоci|zna** (**-zny**) (*dat sg* **-źnie**) *f* (*Ekon*) labour (*Brit*) *lub* labor (*US*) (cost)

**roboczogodzi|na** (**-ny, -ny**) (*dat sg* **-nie**) *f* man-hour

**roboczy** *adj* (*ubranie, tytuł*) working; (*spotkanie, wizyta*) working, business *attr*; **dzień ~** weekday; **siła robocza** workforce, labour (*Brit*) *lub* labor (*US*) force

**robo|t** (**-ta, -ty**) (*loc sg* **-cie**) *m* robot; **~ kuchenny** food processor

**rob|ota** (**-oty, -oty**) (*dat sg* **-ocie**, *gen pl* **-ót**) *f* (*robienie czegoś*) job; (*praca*) work; (*pot: zatrudnienie*) job; **roboty** *pl*: **roboty drogowe** road works *pl* (*Brit*), roadwork (*US*); **mokra ~** (*pot*) (contract) killing; **mieć dużo do roboty** to have a lot of things to do; **rozglądać się za robotą** to be looking for a job; **roboty publiczne** public works; **5 lat ciężkich robót** 5 years hard labour (*Brit*) *lub* labor (*US*)

**robotnic|a** (**-y, -e**) *f* (*pracownica*) worker; (*mrówka*) worker ant; (*pszczoła*) worker bee

**robotniczy** *adj* working-class *attr*; **klasa robotnicza** working class; **hotel ~** workers hostel

**robotni|k** (**-ka, -cy**) (*instr sg* **-kiem**) *m* worker; **~ rolny** farmhand

**robót|ki** (**-ek**) *pl*: **~ ręczne** knitting

**rockowy** *adj* rock *attr*

**rocznic|a** (**-y, -e**) *f* anniversary; **~ ślubu** wedding anniversary

**roczni|k** (**-ka, -ki**) (*instr sg* **-kiem**) *m* (*pokolenie*) generation; (*Szkol*) class; (*wina*) vintage; (*czasopism*) a year's issue; **~ statystyczny** statistical yearbook

**roczny** *adj* (*trwający rok*) year-long; (*liczący rok*) year-old

**rodacz|ka** (**-ki, -ki**) (*dat sg* **-ce**, *gen pl* **-ek**) *f* compatriot, fellow countrywoman

**roda|k** (**-ka, -cy**) (*instr sg* **-kiem**) *m* compatriot, fellow countryman

**rode|o** (**-o, -a**) (*gen pl* **-ów**) *nt* rodeo

**rodowity** *adj* native

**rodow|ód** (**-odu, -ody**) (*loc sg* **-odzie**) *m* (*dzieła, wyrazu*) origin; (*genealogia*) lineage; (*psa, konia*) pedigree; **pies z rodowodem** pedigree dog

**rodowy** *adj* ancestral
**rodu** *itd. n patrz* **ród**
**rodza|j (-ju, -je)** *(gen pl* **-jów***) m (gatunek)* kind, type; *(Bio)* genus; *(Jęz: też:* **rodzaj gramatyczny***)* gender; *(Sztuka, Lit)* genre; **coś w tym ~u** something of that sort; **tego ~u** of this kind; **~ ludzki** humankind
**rodzajni|k (-ka, -ki)** *(instr sg* **-kiem***) m* article; **~ określony/nieokreślony** definite/ indefinite article
**rodzeńst|wo (-wa, -wa)** *(loc sg* **-wie***) nt* siblings *pl*; **czy masz jakieś ~?** do you have any brothers or sisters?
**rodzic|e (-ów)** *pl* parents *pl*
**rodzicielski** *adj* parental; **komitet ~** ≈ parent-teacher association, ≈ PTA
**ro|dzić (-dzę, -dzisz)** *(imp* **rodź** *lub* **ródź***) vt (wydawać na świat) (perf* **u-***) (o kobiecie, samicy)* to give birth to; *(o ziemi)* to bear; *(przen: wywoływać) (perf* **z-***)* to give rise to; **rodzić się** *vr (przychodzić na świat) (perf* **u-***)* to be born; *(przen: powstawać) (perf* **z-***)* to be born *(przen)*, to arise
**rodzimy** *adj* native; **~ użytkownik języka** native speaker
**rodzi|na (-ny, -ny)** *(dat sg* **-nie***) f* family
**rodzinny** *adj (miasto)* home *attr*; *(uroczystość, wartości)* family *attr*; **zasiłek ~** child benefit
**rodzony** *adj*: **mój ~ brat** my own brother
**rodzyn|ek (-ka, -ki)** *(instr sg* **-kiem***) m* raisin
**rodzyn|ka (-ki, -ki)** *(dat sg* **-ce**, *gen pl* **-ek***) f* = **rodzynek**
**rogacz (-a, -e)** *(gen pl* **-y** *lub* **-ów***) m* stag; *(przen)* cuckold
**rogal (-a, -e)** *(gen pl* **-i** *lub* **-ów***) m (Kulin)* croissant
**rogali|k (-ka, -ki)** *(instr sg* **-kiem***) m* croissant
**rogat|ka (-ki, -ki)** *(dat sg* **-ce**, *gen pl* **-ek***) f* barrier
**rogaty** *adj* horned
**rogi** *itd. n patrz* **róg**
**rogowacie|ć (-je)** *(perf* **z-***) vi* to become horny
**rogowy** *adj* horn *attr*; **okulary w rogowej oprawie** horn-rimmed glasses *lub* spectacles
**rogów|ka (-ki, -ki)** *(dat sg* **-ce**, *gen pl* **-ek***) f (Anat)* cornea
**ro|ić (-ję, -isz)** *(imp* **rój***) vi*: **~ o czymś** *(marzyć) (perf* **u-***)* to dream of sth; **roić się** *vr (o owadach)* to swarm; *(przen: występować licznie)* to swarm, to crawl; **list roi się od błędów** the letter is full of mistakes
**rojalistyczny** *adj* royalist
**ro|k (-ku, lata)** *(instr sg* **-kiem***) m decl like nt in pl* year; **co roku** every *lub* each year; **w zeszłym/ przyszłym roku** last/next year; **w tym roku** this year; **rok szkolny/akademicki** school/ academic year; **Nowy Rok** New Year; **z roku na rok** year in, year out; *patrz też* **lata**
**rokokowy** *adj* rococo *attr*
**rok|ować (-uję, -ujesz)** *vi (pertraktować)* to negotiate ▷ *vt (zapowiadać)* to augur; **~ nadzieje** to hold promise
**rokowa|nie (-nia, -nia)** *(gen pl* **-ń***) nt* prognosis; **rokowania** *pl* negotiations *pl*
**rokrocznie** *adv* every year
**rol|a (-i, -e)** *(gen pl* **ról***) f* part, role; *(ziemia, gleba)* soil; **~ główna/tytułowa** leading/title role *lub* part; **„w ~ch głównych"** "starring"; **to nie gra roli** it doesn't matter; **pracować na roli** to work on the land
**rola|da (-dy, -dy)** *(dat sg* **-dzie***) f (Kulin: danie mięsne)* roulade; *(ciasto)* Swiss roll *(Brit)*, (jelly) roll *(US)*
**role|ta (-ty, -ty)** *(dat sg* **-cie***) f* roller blind
**rol|ka (-ki, -ki)** *(dat sg* **-ce**, *gen pl* **-ek***) f* roll
**rolmop|s (-sa, -sy)** *(loc sg* **-sie***) m* rollmop
**rolnict|wo (-wa)** *(loc sg* **-wie***) nt* agriculture
**rolniczy** *adj (kraj, wystawa, produkt)* agricultural; *(spółdzielnia)* farming
**rolni|k (-ka, -cy)** *(instr sg* **-kiem***) m* farmer
**rolny** *adj (produkt, reforma)* agricultural; **gospodarstwo rolne** farm
**rol|ować (-uję, -ujesz)** *(perf* **z-***) vt* to roll
**romanisty|ka (-ki)** *(dat sg* **-ce***) f* Romance studies *pl*
**roman|s (-su, -se)** *(loc sg* **-sie***) m (Lit)* love story; *(Muz)* romance; *(przygoda miłosna)* (love) affair
**romans|ować (-uję, -ujesz)** *vi*: **~ z kimś** to have an affair with sb
**romantycz|ka (-ki, -ki)** *(dat sg* **-ce**, *gen pl* **-ek***) f* romantic
**romantycznoś|ć (-ci)** *f* romanticism
**romantyczny** *adj* romantic
**romanty|k (-ka, -cy)** *(instr sg* **-kiem***) m* romantic(ist)
**romantyz|m (-mu)** *(loc sg* **-mie***) m* romanticism
**romański** *adj* Romanesque
**rom|b (-bu, -by)** *(loc sg* **-bie***) m* rhombus
**rond|el (-la, -le)** *(gen pl* **-li***) m* saucepan
**ron|do (-da, -da)** *(loc sg* **-dzie***) nt (kapelusza)* brim; *(skrzyżowanie)* roundabout *(Brit)*, traffic circle *(US)*; *(Muz)* rondo
**ro|nić (-nię, -nisz)** *(imp* **-ń***) vt (perf* **u-***) (łzy)* to shed
**ro|pa (-py)** *(dat sg* **-pie***) f (Med)* pus; *(Chem: też:* **ropa naftowa***)* (crude) oil, petroleum
**ropie|ć (-je)** *(perf* **za-***) vi* to suppurate, to fester
**rop|ień (-nia, -nie)** *(gen pl* **-ni***) m (Med)* abscess
**ropnia|k (-ka, -ki)** *(instr sg* **-kiem***) m (pot: samochód na ropę)* Diesel
**ropu|cha (-chy, -chy)** *(dat sg* **-sze***) f* toad
**ro|sa (-sy)** *(dat sg* **-sie***) f* dew
**Rosj|a (-i)** *f* Russia

r

**Rosja|nin** (**-nina, -nie**) (*loc sg* **-ninie**, *gen pl* **-n**) *m* Russian
**Rosjan|ka** (**-ki, -ki**) (*dat sg* **-ce**, *gen pl* **-ek**) *f* Russian
**rosły** *adj* robust
**ro|snąć (-snę, -śniesz)** (*imp* **-śnij**) *vi* (*o żywych organizmach, roślinach*) (*perf* **u-**) to grow; (*dorastać*) (*perf* **wy-**) to grow up; (*o cenach, o stratach*) (*perf* **wz-**) to rise; (*potęgować się*) to grow
**rosołowy** *adj*: **kostka rosołowa** stock (Brit) *lub* bouillon (US) cube
**ros|ół** (**-ołu, -oły**) (*loc sg* **-ole**) *m* broth, consommé
**rostbe|f** (**-fu, -fy**) (*loc sg* **-fie**) *m* (*potrawa*) roast beef; (*część tuszy wołowej*) rump cut
**rosyjski** *adj* Russian; **mówić po rosyjsku** to speak Russian
**rosza|da** (**-dy, -dy**) (*dat sg* **-dzie**) *f* (*Szachy*) castling; (*przen*) reshuffle
**roszcze|nie** (**-nia, -nia**) (*gen pl* **-ń**) *nt* claim; **roszczenia płacowe** wage claims
**ro|ścić (-szczę, -ścisz)** (*imp* **-ść**) *vt*: ~ **sobie prawo do czegoś** to claim a right to sth
**rośli|na** (**-ny, -ny**) (*dat sg* **-nie**) *f* plant
**roślinnoś|ć** (**-ci**) *f* vegetation
**roślinny** *adj* vegetable *attr*
**roślinożerc|a** (**-y, -y**) *m decl like f in sg* herbivore
**roślinożerny** *adj* herbivorous
**rotacj|a** (**-i, -e**) (*gen pl* **-i**) *f* rotation
**rotacyjny** *adj* (*ruch, silnik*) rotary
**row|ek** (**-ka, -ki**) (*instr sg* **-kiem**) *m* groove
**rowe|r** (**-ru, -ry**) (*loc sg* **-rze**) *m* bicycle, bike; **jechać na ~ze** to cycle; ~ **górski/treningowy** mountain/exercise bike; ~ **wodny** pedal boat
**rowerowy** *adj* bicycle *attr*
**rowerzy|sta** (**-sty, -ści**) (*loc sg* **-ście**) *m* cyclist
**rowu** *itd. n patrz* **rów**
**rozba|wiać (-wiam, -wiasz)** (*perf* **-wić**) *vt* to amuse
**rozbawiony** *adj* amused
**rozbecz|eć się (-ę, -ysz)** *vr perf* to burst into tears
**rozbest|wiać się (-wiam, -wiasz)** (*perf* **-wić**) *vr* to get out of hand
**rozbestwiony** *adj* unruly
**rozbi|ć (-ję, -jesz)** (*imp* **-j**) *vb perf od* **rozbijać**
**rozbie|c się (-gną)** *vb perf od* **rozbiegać się**
**rozbie|g** (**-gu, -gi**) (*instr sg* **-giem**) *m* run-up; **brać (wziąć** *perf*) ~ to take a run-up
**rozbieg|ać się (-ają)** (*perf* **rozbiec**) *vr* (*o ludziach*) to disperse; (*o drogach*) to diverge
**rozbier|ać (-am, -asz)** (*perf* **rozebrać**) *vt* (*zdejmować ubranie*) to undress; (*rozkładać*) to take apart, to disassemble; (*budynek*) to pull down; **rozbierać się** *vr* to undress, to take off one's clothes
**rozbieżnoś|ć** (**-ci, -ci**) (*gen pl* **-ci**) *f* discrepancy
**rozbieżny** *adj* divergent
**rozbij|ać (-am, -asz)** (*perf* **rozbić**) *vt* (*tłuc na kawałki*) to break; (*ranić*) to bruise; (*rozgramiać*) to crush; (*przen*: *rodzinę*) to break up; **rozbić samochód** to smash a car; **rozbić bank** to break the bank; ~ **namiot** to pitch a tent; ~ **obóz** to pitch camp; **rozbijać się** *vr* (*o talerzu, jajku*) to break; (*o samochodzie*) to smash; (*o samolocie*) to crash; ~ **się samochodem po mieście** to cruise around town
**rozbi|ór** (**-oru, -ory**) (*loc sg* **-orze**) *m* (*badanie*) analysis; (*Hist*) partition; ~ **zdania** parsing
**rozbiór|ka** (**-ki, -ki**) (*dat sg* **-ce**, *gen pl* **-ek**) *f* demolition; **budynek przeznaczony do rozbiórki** building due for demolition
**rozbit|ek** (**-ka, -kowie**) (*instr sg* **-kiem**) *m* castaway
**rozbity** *adj* (*talerz, rodzina, dom*) broken; (*samochód*) smashed; (*nos*) bruised
**rozbol|eć (-i)** *vi perf*: **rozbolała go głowa** he got a headache
**rozb|ój** (**-oju, -oje**) (*gen pl* **-ojów**) *m*: ~ **w biały dzień** daylight robbery
**rozbójni|k** (**-ka, -cy**) (*instr sg* **-kiem**) *m* highwayman
**rozbraj|ać (-am, -asz)** (*perf* **rozbroić**) *vt* to disarm; (*pocisk, minę*) to defuse; **rozbrajać się** *vr* to disarm
**rozbrajający** *adj* disarming
**rozbr|oić (-oję, -oisz)** (*imp* **-ój**) *vb perf od* **rozbrajać**
**rozbroje|nie** (**-nia**) *nt* disarmament
**rozbrojeniowy** *adj* disarmament *attr*
**rozbrykany** *adj* frisky
**rozbryz|giwać (-guję, -gujesz)** (*perf* **rozbryznąć**) *vt* to splash; **rozbryzgiwać się** *vr* to splash
**rozbry|znąć (-znę, -źniesz)** (*imp* **-źnij**) *vb perf od* **rozbryzgiwać**
**rozbrzmiew|ać (-a)** (*perf* **rozbrzmieć**) *vi*: ~ **(czymś)** to resound (with sth)
**rozbudo|wa** (**-wy**) (*dat sg* **-wie**) *f* (*dzielnicy, miasta*) extension; (*gospodarki, potencjału*) development
**rozbud|ować (-uję, -ujesz)** *vb perf od* **rozbudowywać**
**rozbudowany** *adj* (*złożony*) complex
**rozbudow|ywać (-uję, -ujesz)** (*perf* **-ać**) *vt* (*dzielnicę, miasto*) to extend; (*potencjał, przemysł*) to develop
**rozbu|dzać (-dzam, -dzasz)** (*perf* **-dzić**) *vt* to arouse
**rozbu|dzić (-dzę, -dzisz)** (*imp* **-dź**) *vb perf od* **rozbudzać**

**rozbudzony** *adj perf (obudzony)* wide awake
**rozchmurz|ać się (-am, -asz)** *(perf* **-yć***) vr (o pogodzie)* to clear up; *(przen: o człowieku)* to cheer up
**rozcho|dzić (-dzę, -dzisz)** *(imp* **-dź***) vt perf (buty)* to break in
**rozcho|dzić się (-dzę, -dzisz)** *(imp* **-dź***, perf* **rozejść***) vr (o tłumie)* to disperse, to scatter; *(o małżeństwie)* to split; *(o wiadomościach, plotkach)* to spread; *(o głosie, zapachu)* to travel; *(o drogach)* to diverge; *(o towarze)* to sell; *(o pieniądzach)* to disappear
**rozchor|ować się (-uję, -ujesz)** *vr perf* to fall ill, to be taken ill
**rozch|ód** (**-odu, -ody**) *(loc sg* **-odzie***) m* expenditure
**rozchwyt|ywać (-uje)** *(perf* **-ać***) vt* to snatch away
**rozchwytywany** *adj* (much) sought-after; **być ~m** to be much in demand
**rozchyl|ać (-am, -asz)** *(perf* **-ić***) vt* to part; **rozchylać się** *vr* to part
**roz|ciąć (-etnę, -etniesz)** *(imp* **-etnij***) vb perf od* **rozcinać** ▷ *vt perf (skaleczyć)* to cut; **rozciąłem sobie nogę** I cut my leg
**rozciąg|ać (-am, -asz)** *(perf* **-nąć***) vt (sprężynę, sweter)* to stretch; *(koc)* to spread; *(władzę)* to extend; **rozciągać się** *vr (o swetrze)* to stretch; *(o polach, o widoku)* to spread, to extend; *(kłaść się, przewracać się)* to sprawl (out)
**rozciągliwy** *adj* stretchy
**rozciągłoś|ć** (**-ci**) *f*: **w całej rozciągłości** to the/its full extent
**rozciąg|nąć (-nę, -niesz)** *(imp* **-nij***) vb perf od* **rozciągać**
**rozcieńcz|ać (-am, -asz)** *(perf* **-yć***) vt* to dilute, to thin (down); **rozcieńczyć farbę wodą** to water the paint down, to thin the paint down with water
**rozcieńczalni|k** (**-ka, -ki**) *(imp* **-kiem***) m (Chem)* thinner
**rozcieńcz|yć (-ę, -ysz)** *vb perf od* **rozcieńczyć**
**rozcier|ać (-am, -asz)** *(perf* **rozetrzeć***) vt* to rub; **rozetrzeć żółtka z cukrem** to mix the egg yolks with sugar
**rozcię|cie** (**-cia, -cia**) *(gen pl* **-ć***) nt (skaleczenie)* cut; *(szpara)* slit; **spódnica z ~m** slit skirt
**rozcin|ać (-am, -asz)** *(perf* **rozciąć***) vt* to cut; *patrz też* **rozciąć**
**rozczar|ować (-uję, -ujesz)** *vb perf od* **rozczarowywać**
**rozczarowa|nie** (**-nia, -nia**) *(gen pl* **-ń***) nt* disappointment
**rozczarowany** *adj*: **być ~m (kimś/czymś)** to be disappointed (with sb/sth)
**rozczarow|ywać (-uję, -ujesz)** *(perf* **-ać***) vt* to disappoint; **rozczarowywać się** *vr*: **rozczarować się (co do kogoś/czegoś)** to become disappointed *lub* disillusioned (with sb/sth)
**rozczes|ywać (-uję, -ujesz)** *(perf* **-ać***) vt* to comb through
**rozczochrany** *adj (włosy)* unkempt, tousled; *(człowiek)* unkempt, dishevelled *(Brit)*, disheveled *(US)*
**rozd|ać (-am, -asz)** *(3 pl* **-adzą***) vb perf od* **rozdawać**
**rozdar|cie** (**-cia, -cia**) *(gen pl* **-ć***) nt (w materiale)* rip, tear; *(rozterka)* dilemma; **przeżywać wewnętrzne ~** to be on the horns of a dilemma
**rozdarty** *adj* torn
**rozd|awać (-aję, -ajesz)** *(perf* **-ać***) vt (prospekty, ulotki)* to distribute, to give *lub* hand out; *(pieniądze)* to give away; *(karty)* to deal
**roz|dąć (-edmę, -edmiesz)** *(imp* **-edmij***) vb perf od* **rozdymać**
**rozdep|tać (-czę, -czesz)** *vb perf od* **rozdeptywać**
**rozdept|ywać (-uję, -ujesz)** *(perf* **-ać***) vt (ścieżkę, uprawy)* to trample down; *(niedopałek)* to trample on
**rozdmu|chiwać (-chuję, -chujesz)** *(perf* **-chać***) vt (liście, śmieci)* to blow about; *(ogień, ognisko)* to fan; *(przen: aferę, sprawę)* to blow up
**rozdrabni|ać (-am, -asz)** *(perf* **rozdrobnić***) vt (chleb)* to crumble; *(majątek)* to break up; **rozdrabniać się** *vr (pot: rozpraszać się)* to get sidetracked *lub* distracted; **nie rozdrabniaj się w szczegółach** don't get bogged down in details
**rozdrap|ywać (-uję, -ujesz)** *(perf* **-ać***) vt (krostę, ranę)* to scratch (raw); *(przen: majątek, spadek)* to snatch away
**rozdrażni|ać (-am, -asz)** *(perf* **-ć***) vt* to irritate, to annoy
**rozdraż|nić (-nię, -nisz)** *(imp* **-nij***) vb perf od* **rozdrażniać**
**rozdrażniony** *adj* irritated, annoyed
**rozdrob|nić (-nię, -nisz)** *(imp* **-nij***) vb perf od* **rozdrabniać**
**rozdroż|e** (**-a, -a**) *(gen pl* **-y***) nt*: **na rozdrożu** *(przen)* at a crossroads
**rozdwaj|ać (-am, -asz)** *(perf* **rozdwoić***) vt* to split; **rozdwajać się** *vr (o drodze)* to fork; *(o włosach)* to split
**rozdw|oić (-oję, -oisz)** *(imp* **-ój***) vb perf od* **rozdwajać**
**rozdwoje|nie** (**-nia, -nia**) *(gen pl* **-ń***) nt*: **~ jaźni** split personality
**rozdygotany** *adj (ręce)* shaking; *(człowiek)* wobbly
**rozdym|ać (-am, -asz)** *(perf* **rozdąć***) vt (żagle)* to puff out; *(brzuch)* to distend; *(przen: incydent, sprawę)* to blow up

r

**rozdyspon|ować (-uję, -ujesz)** *vt perf (książk)* to dispense, to allocate
**rozdzia|ł (-łu, -ły)** *(loc sg* **-le***)* *m (część książki)* chapter; *(rozdzielanie)* distribution; *(rozgraniczenie)* separation; **~ kościoła od państwa** separation of Church and State
**rozdzielacz (-a, -e)** *(gen pl* **-y***)* *m (Mot)* distributor
**rozdziel|ać (-am, -asz)** *(perf* **-ić***)* *vt (rozdawać)* to distribute; *(dzielić)* to separate; **~ coś (po) między kogoś** to distribute sth among sb; **rozdzielać się** *vr (o grupie)* to split up; *(o rzece)* to fork, to branch
**rozdzielczy** *adj*: **deska rozdzielcza** dashboard; **tablica rozdzielcza** control panel
**rozdziel|ić (-ę, -isz)** *vb perf od* **rozdzielać**
**rozdzier|ać (-am, -asz)** *(perf* **rozedrzeć***)* *vt* to tear (apart); **rozdzierać się** *vr* to tear, to rip
**rozdzierający** *adj (ból)* excruciating; *(krzyk)* piercing
**rozdźwię|k (-ku, -ki)** *(instr sg* **-kiem***)* *m* dissonance, discrepancy
**roz|ebrać (-biorę, -bierzesz)** *vb perf od* **rozbierać**
**rozebrany** *adj* undressed
**roze|dma (-my)** *(dat sg* **-mie***)* *f (też:* **rozedma płuc***)* emphysema
**roze|drzeć (-rę, -rzesz)** *(imp* **-rzyj***)* *vb perf od* **rozdzierać**; **rozedrzeć się** *vr perf (pot)* to start yelling
**rozegn|ać (-am, -asz)** *vb perf od* **rozganiać**
**rozegr|ać (-am, -asz)** *vb perf od* **rozgrywać**
**rozej|m (-mu, -my)** *(loc sg* **-mie***)* *m* truce, armistice
**rozejrz|eć się (-ę, -ysz)** *(imp* **-yj***)* *vb perf od* **rozglądać się**; **rozejrzeć się w sytuacji** to see how the land lies
**rozej|ść się (-dę, -dziesz)** *(imp* **-dź**, *pt* **rozszedł, rozeszła, rozeszli***)* *vb perf od* **rozchodzić się**
**rozentuzjazmowany** *adj* enthusiastic
**rozepch|ać (-am, -asz)** *vb perf od* **rozpychać**
**rozepch|nąć (-nę, -niesz)** *(imp* **-nij***)* *vb perf od* **rozpychać**
**rozep|rzeć (-rę, -rzesz)** *(imp* **-rzyj**, *pt* **rozparł***)* *vb perf od* **rozpierać**
**rozer|wać (-wę, -wiesz)** *(imp* **-wij***)* *vb perf od* **rozrywać**
**roz|esłać[1] (-eślę, -eślesz)** *(imp* **-eślij***)* *vb perf od* **rozsyłać**
**roz|esłać[2] (-ścielę, -ścielisz)** *vb perf od* **rozścielać**
**roześmi|ać się (-eję, -ejesz)** *vr perf* to laugh out loud
**roześmiany** *adj (twarz)* smiling; *(głos)* laughing
**roze|ta (-ty, -ty)** *(dat sg* **-cie***)* *f (ornament)* rosette; *(okno)* rose window
**rozetkowy** *adj*: **drukarka rozetkowa** daisy-wheel printer
**rozetnę** *itd. vb patrz* **rozciąć**
**rozet|rzeć (-rę, -rzesz)** *(imp* **-rzyj***)* *vb perf od* **rozcierać**
**rozew|rzeć (-rę, -rzesz)** *(imp* **-rzyj***)* *vb perf od* **rozwierać**
**rozezn|ać się (-am, -asz)** *vi perf*: **rozeznać się w czymś** to find one's way around in sth
**rozezna|nie (-nia)** *nt*: **nie mam rozeznania w czymś** I am not at home in sth
**rozezn|awać się (-aję, -ajesz)** *(perf* **-ać***)* *vr*: **rozeznawać się w czymś** to know one's way around in sth
**rozeźl|ić (-ę, -isz)** *(imp* **-ij***)* *vt perf* to madden, to infuriate; **rozeźlić się** *vr perf* to go mad
**rozgad|ać się (-am, -asz)** *vr perf* to start chattering away
**rozgałęziacz (-a, -e)** *(pl* **-y***)* *m (z kablem)* trailing socket *(Brit)*, extension cord *(US)*; *(bez kabla)* 2-way/3-way *itp.* adapter
**rozgałę|ziać (-ziam, -ziasz)** *(perf* **-zić***)* *vt (przewody)* to split, to branch; **rozgałęziać się** *vr* to branch, to fork
**rozgałę|zić (-żę, -zisz)** *(imp* **-ź***)* *vb perf od* **rozgałęziać**
**rozgani|ać (-am, -asz)** *(perf* **rozgonić** *lub* **rozegnać***)* *vt* to disperse
**rozgardiasz (-u)** *m* commotion, bustle
**rozgarni|ać (-am, -asz)** *(perf* **rozgarnąć***)* *vt (trawę, włosy)* to part; *(kupkę liści)* to brush *lub* rake aside
**rozgarnięty** *adj (pojętny)* sharp-witted; **mało ~** slow-witted
**roz|giąć (-egnę, -egniesz)** *(imp* **-egnij***)* *vb perf od* **rozginać**
**rozgin|ać (-am, -asz)** *(perf* **rozgiąć***)* *vt (drut)* to unbend; *(palce)* to unclasp; **rozginać się** *vr* to straighten
**rozgląd|ać się (-am, -asz)** *(perf* **rozejrzeć***)* *vr* to (have a) look around; **rozglądać się za pracą** to be on the lookout *lub* be looking for a job
**rozgłasz|ać (-am, -asz)** *(perf* **rozgłosić***)* *vt*: **~ coś** to make sth known *lub* public
**rozgło|s (-su)** *(loc sg* **-sie***)* *m* publicity; **bez ~u** without publicity; **nadawać (nadać** *perf***) czemuś ~** to give sth wide publicity; **zdobywać (zdobyć** *perf***) ~** to gain publicity
**rozgło|sić (-szę, -sisz)** *(imp* **-ś***)* *vb perf od* **rozgłaszać**
**rozgłoś|nia (-ni, -nie)** *(gen pl* **-ni***)* *f* broadcasting station
**rozgniat|ać (-am, -asz)** *(perf* **rozgnieść***)* *vt* to crush; *(orzech)* to crack; *(robaka)* to squash; *(niedopałek)* to stub out

**rozgni|eść (-otę, -eciesz)** (*imp* **-eć**) *vb perf od* **rozgniatać**
**rozgniew|ać (-am, -asz)** *vt perf*: **~ kogoś** to make sb angry, to anger sb; **rozgniewać się** *vr* to get angry
**rozgniewany** *adj* angry, angered
**rozgo|nić (-nię, -nisz)** (*imp* **-ń**) *vb perf od* **rozganiać**
**rozgorączkowany** *adj* frantic, feverish
**rozgorycz|ać (-am, -asz)** (*perf* **-yć**) *vt* to embitter
**rozgorycze|nie** (**-nia**) *nt* bitterness
**rozgoryczony** *adj* embittered
**rozgo|ścić się (-szczę, -ścisz)** (*imp* **-ść**) *vr perf* to make o.s. comfortable; **proszę się rozgościć!** make yourself at home!
**rozgot|ować się (-uję, -ujesz)** *vr perf* to be overcooked
**rozgotowany** *adj* overboiled
**rozgotow|ywać (-uję, -ujesz)** (*perf* **-ać**) *vt* to overcook; **rozgotowywać się** *vr*: **to się łatwo rozgotowuje** it cooks quickly
**rozgra|biać (-biam, -biasz)** (*perf* **-bić**) *vt* (*rozkradać*) to steal (away); (*grabiami*) to rake (over)
**rozgrami|ać (-am, -asz)** (*perf* **rozgromić**) *vt* to rout
**rozgranicz|ać (-am, -asz)** (*perf* **-yć**) *vt* to differentiate, to discriminate
**rozgranicze|nie** (**-nia, -nia**) (*gen pl* **-ń**) *nt* distinction
**rozgryw|ać (-am, -asz)** (*perf* **rozegrać**) *vt* to play; **rozgrywać się** *vr*: **akcja filmu rozgrywa się w Londynie** the film is set in London
**rozgryw|ka** (**-ki, -ki**) (*dat sg* **-ce**, *gen pl* **-ek**) *f* (*Sport*) game; **rozgrywki** *pl* (*Pol*) games *pl*
**rozgry|zać (-zam, -zasz)** (*perf* **-źć**) *vt* to crack (*with one's teeth*)
**rozgry|źć (-zę, -ziesz)** (*imp* **-ź**, *pt* **-zł, -zła, -źli**) *vb perf od* **rozgryzać** ▷ *vt perf* (*pot*: *zagadkę, tajemnicę*) to solve
**rozgrz|ać (-eję, -ejesz)** *vb perf od* **rozgrzewać**
**rozgrzany** *adj* hot; **~ do czerwoności** red-hot
**rozgrze|bać (-bię, -biesz)** *vb perf od* **rozgrzebywać**
**rozgrzeb|ywać (-uję, -ujesz)** *vt* (*rozkopywać*) to dig up; (*rozwalać*) to turn upside down
**rozgrzesz|ać (-am, -asz)** (*perf* **-yć**) *vt* (*Rel*) to absolve
**rozgrzesze|nie** (**-nia, -nia**) (*gen pl* **-ń**) *nt* (*Rel*) absolution; **udzielać (udzielić** *perf***) komuś rozgrzeszenia** to grant absolution to sb
**rozgrzew|ać (-am, -asz)** (*perf* **rozgrzać**) *vt* (*dłonie*) to warm (up); (*blachę*) to heat (up); **rozgrzewać się** *vr* (*o człowieku*) to warm o.s. up; (*o dachu*) to heat up; (*o silniku*) to warm up
**rozgrzew|ka** (**-ki, -ki**) (*dat sg* **-ce**, *gen pl* **-ek**) *f* warm-up
**rozgwi|azda** (**-azdy, -azdy**) (*dat sg* **-eździe**) *f* starfish
**rozhisteryzowany** *adj* hysterical
**rozjaśni|ać (-am, -asz)** (*perf* **-ć**) *vt* (*oświetlać*) to light up; (*czynić jaśniejszym*) to brighten; **~ włosy** to bleach one's hair; **uśmiech rozjaśnił mu twarz** a smile lit up his face; **rozjaśniać się** *vr*: **rozjaśnia się** (*dnieje*) it's getting light; (*przejaśnia się*) it's clearing up
**rozjaś|nić (-nię, -nisz)** (*imp* **-nij**) *vb perf od* **rozjaśniać**
**rozj|azd** (**-azdu, -azdy**) (*loc sg* **-eździe**) *m* junction; **być w ~ach** to be out of town
**rozjątrz|ać (-am, -asz)** (*perf* **-yć**) *vt* (*ranę, spór*) to inflame; **rozjątrzać się** *vr* (*o ranie*) to fester
**rozj|echać (-adę, -edziesz)** (*imp* **-edź**) *vt perf* to run over
**rozjemc|a** (**-y, -y**) *m* (*Pol*) peacemaker; (*Prawo*) arbiter, arbitrator
**rozkapryszony** *adj* capricious
**rozka|z** (**-zu, -zy**) (*loc sg* **-zie**) *m* order; **wydać** (*perf*) **~** to give an order; **wykonać** (*perf*) **~** to obey an order; **~!** (*Wojsk*) yes sir!
**rozka|zać (-żę, -żesz)** *vb perf od* **rozkazywać**
**rozkazujący** *adj* (*głos, ton*) commanding; **tryb ~** (*Jęz*) the imperative
**rozkaz|ywać (-uję, -ujesz)** (*perf* **-ać**) *vt* to order; **rozkazać komuś, żeby coś zrobił** to order sb to do sth
**rozkle|ić się (-ję, -isz)** (*imp* **-j**) *vb perf od* **rozklejać się**
**rozklej|ać (-am, -asz)** (*perf* **rozkleić**) *vt* (*plakaty*) to put up; (*coś sklejonego*) to unstick; **rozklejać się** *vr* (*rozlatywać się*) to fall apart; (*przen*) to go to pieces, to fall apart
**rozkła|d** (**-du, -dy**) (*loc sg* **-dzie**) *m* (*harmonogram*) schedule, timetable; (*mieszkania, biura*) layout; (*Bio*) decomposition, decay; (*upadek*) disintegration; (*Mat*) distribution; **~ zajęć** routine; **~ jazdy** timetable (*Brit*), schedule (*US*)
**rozkład|ać (-am, -asz)** (*perf* **rozłożyć**) *vt* (*obrus*) to spread, to unfold; (*towar*) to lay out; (*parasol*) to open; (*tapczan*) to unfold; (*pracę, koszty*) to divide; (*maszynę*) to take to pieces; (*powodować rozkład*) to break up; **~ ramiona** to spread one's arms; **rozkładać się** *vr* (*o krześle, stole*) to unfold; (*Bio, Chem*) to decompose; (*pot*: *kłaść się*) to stretch out
**rozkojarzony** *adj* absent-minded
**rozko|pać (-pię, -piesz)** *vb perf od* **rozkopywać**
**rozkop|ywać (-uję, -ujesz)** (*perf* **-ać**) *vt* (*ziemię, grób*) to dig (up); (*pościel*) to tumble

r

**rozkosz** (**-y, -e**) (*gen pl* **-y**) *f* (*radość*) joy, delight; (*przyjemność*) pleasure; **~e wiejskiego życia** the delights *lub* joys of country life
**rozkoszny** *adj* delightful
**rozkosz|ować się (-uję, -ujesz)** *vr*: **rozkoszować się czymś** to delight in sth, to relish sth
**rozkrę|cać (-cam, -casz)** (*perf* **-cić**) *vt* (*maszynę, mebel*) to take apart *lub* to pieces; (*sznurek*) to untwist; **~ interes** to start up a business; **rozkręcać się** *vr* (*o interesie, firmie*) to be thriving
**rozkro|k** (**-ku, -ki**) (*instr sg* **-kiem**) *m*: **w ~u** astride, with one's legs apart
**rozkrusz|ać (-am, -asz)** (*perf* **-yć**) *vt* to crush
**rozkurczowy** *adj* (*ciśnienie*) diastolic; **lek** *lub* **środek ~** relaxant
**rozkwi|t** (**-tu**) *m* heyday, prime; **w rozkwicie** in full bloom
**rozkwit|ać (-a)** (*perf* **-nąć**) *vt* (*o kwiatach*) to bloom; (*o drzewach*) to blossom; (*o handlu, przemyśle*) to flourish
**rozkwit|nąć (-nie)** *vb perf od* **rozkwitać**
**rozl|ać (-eję, -ejesz)** *vb perf od* **rozlewać**
**rozle|c się (-gnie)** *vb perf od* **rozlegać się**
**rozleg|ać się (-a)** (*perf* **rozlec**) *vr* to ring out, to reverberate; **rozległ się huk wystrzału** a shot was heard
**rozległy** *adj* (*równina, widok*) wide, broad; (*plany, projekty*) extensive
**rozle|w** (**-wu**) (*loc sg* **-wie**) *m*: **~ krwi** bloodshed
**rozlew|ać (-am, -asz)** (*perf* **rozlać**) *vt* (*na stół*) to spill; (*do naczyń*) to pour (out); **rozlał wszystkim po kieliszku** he poured a drink for everybody; **rozlewać się** *vr* to spill
**rozlew|nia** (**-ni, -nie**) (*gen pl* **-ni**) *f* bottling plant
**rozlicz|ać (-am, -asz)** (*perf* **-yć**) *vt* (*koszty*) to account for; **~ delegację** to present an account of expenses (*incurred during a business trip*); **~ kogoś z pieniędzy** to clear accounts with sb; **rozliczać się** *vr*: **~ się z kimś** to settle *lub* square up with sb; **~ się z czegoś** to account for sth
**rozliczeniowy** *adj* accounting *attr*; **rachunek oszczędnościowo-~** checking account
**rozliczny** *adj* (*książk*) various, manifold
**rozlicz|yć (-ę, -ysz)** *vb perf od* **rozliczać**
**rozlok|ować (-uję, -ujesz)** *vb perf od* **rozlokowywać**
**rozlokow|ywać (-uję, -ujesz)** (*perf* **-ać**) *vt* (*żołnierzy*) to quarter
**rozlos|ować (-uję, -ujesz)** *vb perf od* **rozlosowywać**
**rozlosow|ywać (-uję, -ujesz)** (*perf* **-ać**) *vt*: **~ nagrody** to distribute prizes by lot
**rozluź|niać (-niam, -niasz)** (*perf* **-nić**) *vt* (*kołnierzyk, pasek*) to loosen; (*mięśnie, dyscyplinę*) to relax; **rozluźniać się** *vr* (*o człowieku*) to loosen up; (*o śrubach, związkach*) to loosen
**rozluź|nić (-nię, -nisz)** (*imp* **-nij**) *vb perf od* **rozluźniać**
**rozład|ować (-uję, -ujesz)** *vb perf od* **rozładowywać**
**rozładow|ywać (-uję, -ujesz)** (*perf* **-ać**) *vt* (*towar, wagon, broń*) to unload; (*kondensator*) to discharge; **rozładować napiętą atmosferę** to relieve the tension; **rozładowywać się** *vr* (*o akumulatorze, baterii*) to go flat (*Brit*) *lub* dead (*US*); (*o atmosferze*) to be defused
**rozładun|ek** (**-ku, -ki**) (*instr sg* **-kiem**) *m* unloading
**rozła|m** (**-mu, -my**) (*loc sg* **-mie**) *m* split
**rozłącz|ać (-am, -asz)** (*perf* **-yć**) *vt* (*przewody*) to disconnect; (*rodzinę, walczących*) to separate; **rozłączać się** *vr* (*o przewodach*) to disconnect; (*Tel*) to ring off (*Brit*), to hang up (*US*)
**rozłą|ka** (**-ki**) (*dat sg* **-ce**) *f* separation
**rozł|ożyć (-ożę, -ożysz)** (*imp* **-óż**) *vb perf od* **rozkładać**
**rozłu|pać (-pię, -piesz)** *vb perf od* **rozłupywać**
**rozłup|ywać (-uję, -ujesz)** (*perf* **-ać**) *vt* to crack, to split; **rozłupywać się** *vr* to crack
**rozmach** (**-u**) *m* (*energiczny ruch*) swing; (*dynamika*) momentum; **brać (wziąć** *perf***) ~** to take a swing; **nabierać (nabrać** *perf***) ~u** to gather momentum; **z ~em** with a flourish
**rozmaitoś|ć** (**-ci**) *f* variety
**rozmaity** *adj* various, diverse
**rozmary|n** (**-nu, -ny**) (*loc sg* **-nie**) *m* (*Bot, Kulin*) rosemary
**rozmarz|yć się (-ę, -ysz)** *vt perf* to fall into a reverie
**rozmas|ować (-uję, -ujesz)** *vt perf* to massage
**rozmawi|ać (-am, -asz)** *vi* to speak, to talk; **~ z kimś (o czymś)** to talk to *lub* with sb (about sth); **~ przez telefon** to be on the phone; **oni ze sobą nie rozmawiają** they are not on speaking terms
**rozma|z** (**-zu, -zy**) (*loc sg* **-zie**) *m* (*Med*) smear
**rozma|zać (-żę, -żesz)** (*imp* **-ż**) *vb perf od* **rozmazywać**
**rozmaz|ywać (-uję, -ujesz)** (*perf* **-ać**) *vt* to smear, to smudge; **rozmazywać się** *vr* (*o plamie*) to smudge; (*o konturach*) to blur
**rozmia|r** (**-ru, -ry**) (*loc sg* **-rze**) *m* (*wielkość*) size; (*zakres*) extent
**rozmie|niać (-niam, -niasz)** (*perf* **-nić**) *vt* to change
**rozmie|nić (-nię, -nisz)** (*imp* **-ń**) *vb perf od* **rozmieniać**

**rozmieszcz|ać (-am, -asz)** (*perf* **rozmieścić**) *vt* to place, to site; (*oddziały*) to deploy
**rozmie|ścić (-szczę, -ścisz)** (*imp* **-ść**) *vb perf od* **rozmieszczać**
**rozmięk|ać (-a)** (*perf* **-nąć**) *vi* to soften
**rozmiękcz|ać (-am, -asz)** (*perf* **-yć**) *vt* to soften
**rozmięk|nąć (-nie)** *vb perf od* **rozmiękać**
**rozmij|ać się (-am, -asz)** (*perf* **rozminąć**) *vr*: **rozmijać się z prawdą** to deviate from the truth
**rozmiłowany** *adj*: **być ~m w czymś** to be an ardent lover of sth
**rozmi|nąć (-nę, -niesz)** (*imp* **-ń**) *vb perf od* **rozmijać się**; **rozminąć się** *vr perf*: **~ się z kimś** (*nie spotkać się*) to miss sb; (*przejść obok*) to pass sb
**rozmnaż|ać (-am, -asz)** (*perf* **rozmnożyć**) *vt* to reproduce; **rozmnażać się** *vr* (*Bio*) to reproduce; (*zwiększać się liczebnie*) to multiply
**rozmnaża|nie** (**-nia**) *nt* reproduction
**rozmn|ożyć (-ożę, -ożysz)** (*imp* **-óż**) *vb perf od* **rozmnażać**
**rozmont|ować (-uję, -ujesz)** *vb perf od* **rozmontowywać**
**rozmontow|ywać (-uję, -ujesz)** (*perf* **-ać**) *vt* to disassemble, to take apart
**rozm|owa** (**-owy, -owy**) (*dat sg* **-owie**, *gen pl* **-ów**) *f* conversation, talk; **rozmowy** *pl* negotiations *pl*; **~ telefoniczna** phone call; **~ międzymiastowa** long-distance call; **~ kwalifikacyjna** interview; **prowadzić rozmowy** to conduct negotiations, to negotiate
**rozmowny** *adj* talkative
**rozmówc|a** (**-y, -y**) *m decl like f in sg* interlocutor
**rozmówczy|ni** (**-ni, -nie**) (*gen pl* **-ń**) *f* interlocutor
**rozmó|wić się (-wię, -wisz)** *vr perf*: **rozmówić się z kimś** to have a word with sb
**rozmów|ki** (**-ek**) *pl* phrase book; **~ polsko-angielskie** Polish-English phrase book
**rozmraż|ać (-am, -asz)** (*perf* **rozmrozić**) *vt* to defrost
**rozmr|ozić (-ożę, -ozisz)** (*imp* **-óź**) *vb perf od* **rozmrażać**
**rozmysł** (**-u**) *m*: **z ~em** with intent
**rozmyśl|ać (-am, -asz)** *vi imperf*: **~ o** *+loc lub* **nad** *+loc* to meditate on, to ponder on
**rozmyśla|nia** (**-ń**) *pl* meditations *pl*
**rozmyśl|ić się (-ę, -isz)** *vr perf* to change one's mind
**rozmyślnie** *adv* on purpose, deliberately
**rozmyślny** *adj* calculated, deliberate
**roznegliżowany** *adj* in a state of undress
**roznie|cać (-cam, -casz)** (*perf* **-cić**) *vt* (*ogień*) to start, to kindle; (*uczucie*) to stir up
**roznie|cić (-cę, -cisz)** (*imp* **-ć**) *vb perf od* **rozniecać**
**rozni|eść (-osę, -esiesz)** (*imp* **-eś**, *pt* **-ósł, -osła, -eśli**) *vb perf od* **roznosić**
**roznosiciel** (**-a, -e**) (*gen pl* **-i**) *m* distributor
**rozno|sić (-szę, -sisz)** (*imp* **-ś**) *vt* (*dostarczać*) to deliver; (*rozgłaszać*) to spread; **roznosiła ją duma** she was bursting with pride
**rozpacz** (**-y**) *f* despair; **wpadać (wpaść** *perf***) w ~** to fall *lub* sink into despair
**rozpacz|ać (-am, -asz)** *vi* to despair
**rozpaczliwy** *adj* (*walka, sytuacja*) desperate; (*krzyk*) anguished
**rozpa|d** (**-du**) (*loc sg* **-dzie**) *m* (*imperium*) break-up; (Fiz) disintegration, decay; **okres połowicznego ~u** half-life
**rozpad|ać się (-am, -asz)** (*perf* **rozpaść**) *vr* (*o budynku, meblu*) to fall apart; (*o małżeństwie*) to disintegrate ▷ *vr perf*: **rozpadało się na dobre** the rain has set in for the day
**rozpadli|na** (**-ny, -ny**) (*dat sg* **-nie**) *f* fissure
**rozpakow|ywać (-uję, -ujesz)** (*perf* **-ać**) *vt* to unpack; **rozpakowywać się** *vr* to unpack
**rozpal|ać (-am, -asz)** (*perf* **-ić**) *vt* (*ogień*) to light; (*uczucia, zapał*) to kindle ▷ *vi*: **~ w piecu** to light the stove; **rozpalać się** *vr* to start burning
**rozpał|ka** (**-ki**) (*dat sg* **-ce**) *f*: **drewno na rozpałkę** kindling
**rozpamięt|ywać (-uję, -ujesz)** *vt imperf* to brood on
**rozparcelow|ywać (-uję, -ujesz)** (*perf* **-ać**) *vt* to parcel out
**rozpasani|e** (**-a**) *nt* debauchery
**rozpa|ść się (-dnę, -dniesz)** (*imp* **-dnij**) *vb perf od* **rozpadać się**
**rozpatr|ywać (-uję, -ujesz)** (*perf* **rozpatrzyć**) *vt* to consider
**rozpatrz|yć (-ę, -ysz)** *vb perf od* **rozpatrywać**
**rozpę|d** (**-du**) (*loc sg* **-dzie**) *m* momentum; **nabierać (nabrać** *perf***) ~u** to gather momentum
**rozpę|dzać (-dzam, -dzasz)** (*perf* **-dzić**) *vt* (*pojazd*) to speed up, to accelerate; (*tłum*) to disperse; **rozpędzać się** *vr* (*nabierać szybkości*) to speed up, to pick up speed; **samochód rozpędza się od 0 do 100 km/h w 10 sekund** the car goes from 0 to 100 kph in ten seconds
**rozpę|dzić (-dzę, -dzisz)** (*imp* **-dź**) *vb perf od* **rozpędzać**
**rozpęt|ać (-am, -asz)** *vt perf* (*kłótnię, dyskusję*) to spark off; **rozpętać się** *vr perf* (*o wojnie, kłótni*) to break out
**roz|piąć (-epnę, -epniesz)** (*imp* **-epnij**) *vb perf od* **rozpinać**

r

**rozpi|ć (-ję, -jesz)** *vb perf od* **rozpijać**
**rozpieprz|ać (-am, -asz)** (*perf* **-yć**) *vt* (*pot!*: *psuć*) to fuck up (*pot!*)
**rozpier|ać (-am, -asz)** (*perf* **rozeprzeć**) *vr*: **duma/radość kogoś rozpiera** sb is bursting with pride/joy; **rozpierać się** *vr* to lounge
**rozpierzch|ać się (-a)** (*perf* **-nąć**) *vr* to scamper (away), to disperse
**rozpierzch|nąć się (-nie)** (*pt* **-nął** *lub* **-ł, -ła, -nęli** *lub* **-li**) *vb perf od* **rozpierzchać się**
**rozpieszcz|ać (-am, -asz)** (*perf* **rozpieścić**) *vt* to pamper, to spoil
**rozpieszczony** *adj* pampered, spoilt (Brit), spoiled (US)
**rozpie|ścić (-szczę, -ścisz)** (*imp* **-ść**) *vb perf od* **rozpieszczać**
**rozpiętoś|ć** (**-ci**) *f* (*odległość*) span; (*skala*) range; **~ skrzydeł** wingspan; **~ cen** price range; **~ płac** wage differential
**rozpij|ać (-am, -asz)** (*perf* **rozpić**) *vt*: **~ kogoś** to push sb into drinking; **rozpijać się** *vr* to take to drink
**rozpin|ać (-am, -asz)** (*perf* **rozpiąć**) *vt* (*guzik, zamek*) to undo; (*bluzkę*) to unbutton; (*spodnie*) to unzip; (*pasek*) to unbuckle; (*skrzydła*) to spread; **rozpinać się** *vr* to come undone
**rozpis|ywać (-uję, -ujesz)** (*perf* **-ać**) *vt*: **rozpisać konkurs (na coś)** to invite tenders (for sth); **rozpisać wybory** to call an election; **rozpisywać się** *vr* to write at length
**rozplanow|ywać (-uję, -ujesz)** (*perf* **-ać**) *vt* (*dzień, pracę*) to plan (out); (*wnętrze*) to design; (*ulice*) to lay out
**rozplat|ać (-am, -asz)** (*perf* **rozpleść**) *vt* to unbraid
**rozpląt|ywać (-uję, -ujesz)** (*perf* **-ać**) *vt* (*nici, węzeł*) to untangle; (*zagadkę*) to unravel
**rozple|niać się (-nia)** (*perf* **-nić**) *vr* to proliferate
**rozpl|eść (-otę, -eciesz)** (*imp* **-eć**, *pt* **-ótł, -otła, -etli**) *vb perf od* **rozplatać**
**rozpła|kać się (-czę, -czesz)** *vr perf* to burst into tears
**rozpłaszcz|yć (-ę, -ysz)** *vt perf* to flatten; **rozpłaszczyć się** *vr* to flatten o.s.
**rozpłat|ać (-am, -asz)** *vt perf* (*brzuch*) to slash; (*głowę*) to cleave
**rozpły|nąć się (-nę, -niesz)** (*imp* **-ń**) *vb perf od* **rozpływać się**
**rozpływ|ać się (-am, -asz)** (*perf* **rozpłynąć**) *vt* (*rozlewać się*) to spread out; (*topić się*) to melt; **rozpływać się nad czymś** to go into ecstasies about *lub* over sth
**rozpocz|ąć (-nę, -niesz)** (*imp* **-nij**) *vb perf od* **rozpoczynać**
**rozpoczęci|e (-a)** *nt* beginning, start
**rozpoczyn|ać (-am, -asz)** (*perf* **rozpocząć**) *vt* to begin, to start; **rozpoczynać się** *vr* to begin, to start
**rozpogadz|ać się (-a)** (*perf* **rozpogodzić**) *vr*: **wieczorem rozpogodziło się** it cleared up in the evening
**rozpogodze|nie** (**-nia, -nia**) (*gen pl* **-ń**) *nt* bright *lub* sunny spell
**rozpor|ek** (**-ka, -ki**) (*instr sg* **-kiem**) *m* flies *pl* (Brit), fly (US)
**rozporzą|dzać (-dzam, -dzasz)** (*perf* **-dzić**) *vt*: **~ czymś** (*zarządzać*) to manage sth; (*mieć do dyspozycji*) to have sth at one's disposal
**rozporządze|nie** (**-nia, -nia**) (*gen pl* **-ń**) *nt* (*akt prawny*) decree; (*polecenie*) order
**rozporzą|dzić (-dzę, -dzisz)** (*imp* **-dź**) *vb perf od* **rozporządzać**
**rozpost|rzeć (-rę, -rzesz)** (*imp* **-rzyj**, *pt* **-arł**) *vb perf od* **rozpościerać**
**rozpościer|ać (-am, -asz)** (*perf* **rozpostrzeć**) *vt* to spread; **rozpościerać się** *vr* to stretch
**rozpowiad|ać (-am, -asz)** (*perf* **rozpowiedzieć**) *vt*: **~ coś** to put sth about *lub* around
**rozpowi|edzieć (-em, -esz)** (*3 pl* **-edzą**, *imp* **-edz**) *vb perf od* **rozpowiadać**
**rozpowszech|niać (-niam, -niasz)** (*perf* **-nić**) *vt* (*wiadomości*) to diffuse, to spread; (*film*) to screen; **rozpowszechniać się** *vr* (*o plotce*) to get around, to spread
**rozpowszech|nić (-nię, -nisz)** (*imp* **-nij**) *vb perf od* **rozpowszechniać**
**rozpowszechniony** *adj*: **(szeroko) ~** widespread
**rozpozna|nie** (**-nia, -nia**) (*gen pl* **-ń**) *nt* (*Med*) diagnosis; (*Wojsk*) reconnaissance; **przeprowadzać (przeprowadzić** *perf*) **~** to reconnoitre (Brit), to reconnoiter (US)
**rozpozn|awać (-aję, -ajesz)** (*perf* **-ać**) *vt* (*ludzi, twarze*) to recognize, to identify; (*chorobę*) to diagnose; (*sprawę*) to probe (into)
**rozpoznawczy** *adj* (*samolot*) reconnaissance *attr*; (*znak*) identification *attr*; **hasło rozpoznawcze** password
**rozprac|ować (-uję, -ujesz)** *vb perf od* **rozpracowywać**
**rozpracow|ywać (-uję, -ujesz)** (*perf* **-ać**) (*pot*) *vt* to work out, to suss out (*pot*)
**rozprasz|ać (-am, -asz)** (*perf* **rozproszyć**) *vt* (*człowieka, uwagę*) to distract; (*tłum*) to disperse; (*wątpliwości*) to dispel; **nie rozpraszaj mnie** don't distract me; **rozpraszać się** *vr* to get distracted
**rozpra|wa** (**-wy, -wy**) (*dat sg* **-wie**) *f* (*Prawo*) trial, hearing; (*praca naukowa*) dissertation, thesis; **~ doktorska** doctoral dissertation *lub* thesis

**rozpra|wiać (-wiam, -wiasz)** *vi* (*opowiadać*): ~ (**o** *+instr*) to speak at length (about); ~ **nad czymś** to debate sth; **rozprawiać się** (*perf* **-wić**) *vr*: ~ **się z kimś** to get even with sb; ~ **się z czymś** to crack down on sth

**rozpromieniony** *adj* radiant, beaming

**rozpropag|ować (-uję, -ujesz)** *vb perf od* **propagować**

**rozprost|ować (-uję, -ujesz)** *vb perf od* **rozprostowywać**

**rozprostow|ywać (-uję, -ujesz)** (*perf* **-ać**) *vt* to stretch; **rozprostować nogi** *lub* **kości** to stretch one's legs

**rozprosz|yć (-ę, -ysz)** *vb perf od* **rozpraszać**

**rozprowa|dzać (-dzam, -dzasz)** (*perf* **-dzić**) *vt* to distribute; (*masło, farbę*) to spread; (*rozcieńczać*) to dilute

**rozprowa|dzić (-dzę, -dzisz)** (*imp* **-dź**) *vb perf od* **rozprowadzać**

**rozpru|ć (-ję, -jesz)** *vb perf od* **rozpruwać**

**rozpruw|ać (-am, -asz)** (*perf* **rozpruć**) *vt* (*rękaw, brzuch*) to rip; (*szew*) to unpick; (*kasę*) to crack; **rozpruwać się** *vr* to come undone

**rozprys|kiwać (-kuję, -kujesz)** (*perf* **-kać**) *vt* to splatter, to spatter; **rozpryskiwać się** *vr* (*o cieczy*) to splatter, to spatter; (*o talerzu*) to shatter

**rozprzestrze|niać (-niam, -niasz)** (*perf* **-nić**) *vt* to spread; **rozprzestrzeniać się** *vr* to spread

**rozprzestrze|nić (-nię, -nisz)** (*imp* **-ń**) *vb perf od* **rozprzestrzeniać**

**rozprzęże|nie** (**-nia**) *nt* (*chaos*) disorder; (*brak dyscypliny*) indiscipline; (*obyczajów*) laxity

**rozpuku** *inv*: **śmiać się do** ~ to roar with laughter

**rozpu|sta** (**-sty**) (*dat sg* **-ście**) *f* debauchery

**rozpustny** *adj* immoral

**rozpuszcz|ać (-am, -asz)** (*perf* **rozpuścić**) *vt* (*rozcieńczać*) to dissolve; (*topić*) to melt; (*rozpowszechniać*) to spread; ~ **włosy** to let loose one's hair; **rozpuszczać się** *vr* (*o cukrze*) to dissolve; (*o lodzie*) to melt

**rozpuszczalni|k** (**-ka, -ki**) (*instr sg* **-kiem**) *m* (*Tech*) solvent

**rozpuszczalny** *adj* (*kawa*) instant; (*Chem*) soluble

**rozpu|ścić (-szczę, -ścisz)** (*imp* **-ść**) *vb perf od* **rozpuszczać**

**rozpych|ać (-am, -asz)** *vt* to jostle; **rozpychać się** *vr* to jostle

**rozpylacz** (**-a, -e**) (*gen pl* **-y**) *m* (*Tech*) atomizer, sprayer

**rozpyl|ać (-am, -asz)** (*perf* **-ić**) *vt* to spray

**rozrabi|ać (-am, -asz)** *vt* (*Kulin*) (*perf* **rozrobić**) to cream, to mix together; (*farbę*) (*perf* **rozrobić**) to dilute ▷ *vi* (*pot*) to stir things up (*pot*)

**rozrachun|ek** (**-ku, -ki**) (*instr sg* **-kiem**) *m* reckoning; **być na własnym rozrachunku** to be self-financing; **dokonać** (*perf*) **rozrachunku z kimś** to square up with sb; **w ostatecznym rozrachunku** in the final analysis

**rozrachunkowy** *adj* (*Fin*) clearing *attr*; **izba rozrachunkowa** clearing house

**rozradowany** *adj* jubilant

**rozrast|ać się (-am, -asz)** (*perf* **rozrosnąć**) *vr* to grow

**rozreklam|ować (-uję, -ujesz)** *vt perf* to publicize (extensively), to advertise (widely)

**rozr|obić (-obię, -obisz)** (*imp* **-ób**) *vb perf od* **rozrabiać**

**rozrodczy** *adj* reproductive

**rozro|snąć się (-snę, -śniesz)** (*imp* **-śnij**) *vb perf od* **rozrastać się**

**rozró|ba** (**-by, -by**) (*dat sg* **-bie**) *f* (*pot*) brawl

**rozr|ód** (**-odu**) (*loc sg* **-odzie**) *m* (*Bio*) reproduction

**rozróż|niać (-niam, -niasz)** (*perf* **-nić**) *vt* to distinguish

**rozróż|nić (-nię, -nisz)** (*imp* **-nij**) *vb perf od* **rozróżniać**

**rozróżnie|nie** (**-nia, -nia**) (*gen pl* **-ń**) *nt* distinction

**rozruch** (**-u**) *m* (*silnika*) starting; (*produkcji*) start; **rozruchy** *pl* (*zamieszki*) riots *pl*

**rozrusz|ać (-am, -asz)** *vt perf* (*towarzystwo*) to liven up; ~ **nogi/nadgarstek** to work off the stiffness in one's legs/wrist; **rozruszać się** *vr* (*poprzez ćwiczenia*) to loosen up; (*ożywić się*) to liven up

**rozruszni|k** (**-ka, -ki**) (*instr sg* **-kiem**) *m* (*Mot*) starter; (*Med*) pacemaker

**rozryw|ać (-am, -asz)** (*perf* **rozerwać**) *vt* (*materiał*) to tear (apart); (*tamę, linę*) to burst; (*o bombie*) to tear apart; **rozrywać się** *vr* (*o materiale*) to tear (apart); (*o tamie, linie*) to burst; (*zabawiać się*) to have fun

**rozrywany** *adj* sought-after

**rozryw|ka** (**-ki, -ki**) (*dat sg* **-ce**, *gen pl* **-ek**) *f* entertainment; ~ **umysłowa** mental exercise

**rozrywkowy** *adj*: **lokal** ~ nightclub; **muzyka rozrywkowa** light music; **program** ~ show; **przemysł** ~ entertainment industry, show business

**rozrzą|d** (**-du, -dy**) (*loc sg* **-dzie**) *m* (*Mot*: *też*: **wał rozrządu**) camshaft

**rozrze|dzać (-dzam, -dzasz)** (*perf* **-dzić**) *vt* to dilute, to thin down

**rozrze|dzić (-dzę, -dzisz)** (*imp* **-dź**) *vb perf od* **rozrzedzać**

r

**rozrzedzony** *adj* (*sok*) diluted; (*powietrze*) rare(fied)
**rozrzew|niać (-niam, -niasz)** (*perf* **-nić**) *vt* to move, to stir; **rozrzewniać się** *vr* to be moved *lub* stirred
**rozrzew|nić (-nię, -nisz)** (*imp* **-nij**) *vb perf od* **rozrzewniać**
**rozrzewnie|nie** (**-nia**) *nt*: **wspominać coś z ~m** to have fond memories of sth
**rozrzu|cać (-cam, -casz)** (*perf* **-cić**) *vt* (*zabawki*) to scatter; (*nawóz*) to spread; (*ulotki*) to drop
**rozrzu|cić (-cę, -cisz)** (*imp* **-ć**) *vb perf od* **rozrzucać**
**rozrzutnoś|ć** (**-ci**) *f* wastefulness, extravagance
**rozrzutny** *adj* wasteful, extravagant
**rozsa|dzać (-dzam, -dzasz)** (*perf* **-dzić**) *vt* (*rośliny*) to plant out; (*uczniów*) to separate; (*gości*) to seat; (*lód, skałę*) to blow up
**rozsa|dzić (-dzę, -dzisz)** (*imp* **-dź**) *vb perf od* **rozsadzać**
**rozsąd|ek** (**-ku**) (*instr sg* **-kiem**) *m* reason, sense; **zdrowy ~** common sense; **przemawiać (przemówić** *perf*) **komuś do rozsądku** to bring sb to their senses, to talk some sense into sb
**rozsądny** *adj* reasonable, sensible
**rozsą|dzać (-dzam, -dzasz)** (*perf* **-dzić**) *vt* to settle, to adjudicate (upon)
**rozsą|dzić (-dzę, -dzisz)** (*imp* **-dź**) *vb perf od* **rozsądzać**
**roz|siać (-sieję, -siejesz)** *vb perf od* **rozsiewać**
**rozsiad|ać się (-am, -asz)** (*perf* **rozsiąść**) *vr* (*siadać wygodnie*) to sit back; (*rozlokowywać się*) to sit (down)
**rozsią|ść się (-dę, -dziesz)** (*imp* **-dź**) *vb perf od* **rozsiadać się**
**rozsiew|ać (-am, -asz)** (*perf* **rozsiać**) *vt* (*nasiona*) to sow; (*zarazki, plotki*) to spread; (*zapach*) to give out *lub* off
**rozsła|wiać (-wiam, -wiasz)** (*perf* **-wić**) *vt* to praise
**rozsmar|ować (-uję, -ujesz)** *vb perf od* **rozsmarowywać**
**rozsmarow|ywać (-uję, -ujesz)** (*perf* **-ać**) *vt* to spread
**rozsta|ć się (-nę, -niesz)** (*imp* **-ń**) *vb perf od* **rozstawać się**
**rozsta|je** (**-jów** *lub* **-i**) *pl*: **na rozstaju** *lub* **rozstajach dróg** at a *lub* the crossroads
**rozsta|nie** (**-nia, -nia**) (*gen pl* **-ń**) *nt* parting
**rozsta|w** (**-wu, -wy**) (*loc sg* **-wie**) *m* span, distance; **~ osi** (*Mot*) wheelbase
**rozst|awać się (-aję, -ajesz)** (*perf* **-ać**) *vt*: **rozstawać się z kimś** to part from sb, to part company with sb; **(nie) rozstawać się z czymś** (not) to part with sth; **rozstać się** (*perf*) **z mężem/żoną** to split up with one's husband/wife
**rozsta|wiać (-wiam, -wiasz)** (*perf* **-wić**) *vt* (*talerze*) to lay out; (*krzesła*) to arrange; (*leżak, stół*) to set up; **~ nogi** to spread one's feet *lub* legs
**rozstęp|ować się (-uję, -ujesz)** (*perf* **rozstąpić**) *vr* (*o tłumie*) to part; (*o ziemi*) to open up
**rozstęp|y** (**-ów**) *pl* (*Med*) stretch marks
**rozstraj|ać (-am, -asz)** (*perf* **rozstroić**) *vt* (*instrument*) to put out of tune; (*nerwy*) to upset
**rozstr|oić (-oję, -oisz)** (*imp* **-ój**) *vb perf od* **rozstrajać**
**rozstrojony** *adj* out of tune, out-of-tune *attr*
**rozstr|ój** (**-oju, -oje**) *m*: **~ nerwowy** nervous breakdown; **~ żołądka** stomach upset
**rozstrzeliw|ać (-uję, -ujesz)** (*perf* **rozstrzelać**) *vt* to put before the firing squad, to execute by firing squad
**rozstrzelony** *adj* (*druk*) spaced-out
**rozstrzyg|ać (-am, -asz)** (*perf* **-nąć**) *vt* to decide, to settle
**rozstrzygający** *adj* (*bitwa*) decisive; **~ głos** casting vote
**rozstrzyg|nąć (-nę, -niesz)** (*imp* **-nij**) *vb perf od* **rozstrzygać**
**rozsu|nąć (-nę, -niesz)** (*imp* **-ń**) *vb perf od* **rozsuwać**
**rozsupł|ywać (-uję, -ujesz)** (*perf* **-ać**) *vt* to untangle, to disentangle
**rozsuw|ać (-am, -asz)** (*perf* **rozsunąć**) *vt* (*firanki, zasłony*) to draw (aside); (*stół*) to extend; **rozsuwać się** *vr* (*o kurtynie*) to draw aside
**rozsy|pać (-pię, -piesz)** *vb perf od* **rozsypywać**
**rozsyp|ywać (-uję, -ujesz)** (*perf* **-ać**) *vt* to spill; **rozsypywać się** *vr* to spill
**rozszalały** *adj* raging
**rozszale|ć się (-je)** *vr perf* (*o tłumie, zwierzętach*) to go wild; (*o epidemii, burzy*) to break out
**rozszar|pać (-pię, -piesz)** *vb perf od* **rozszarpywać**
**rozszarp|ywać (-uję, -ujesz)** (*perf* **-ać**) *vt* to tear (to pieces)
**rozszcze|p** (**-pu, -py**) (*loc sg* **-pie**) *m*: **~ podniebienia** cleft palate
**rozszcze|piać (-piam, -piasz)** (*perf* **-pić**) *vt* to split
**rozszczepie|nie** (**-nia**) *nt*: **~ jądra atomowego** (*Fiz*) atomic *lub* nuclear fission
**rozszerz|ać (-am, -asz)** (*perf* **-yć**) *vt* to widen, to broaden; **rozszerzać się** *vr* (*powiększać się*) to widen; (*rozprzestrzeniać się*) to expand, to spread (out)

**rozsznurow|ywać (-uję, -ujesz)** (*perf* **-ać**) *vt* to unlace

**rozszyfr|ować (-uję, -ujesz)** *vb perf od* **rozszyfrowywać**

**rozszyfrow|ywać (-uję, -ujesz)** (*perf* **-ać**) *vt* (*wiadomość*) to decipher, to decode; (*tajemnicę, zagadkę*) to unravel; **rozszyfrować kogoś** to see through sb

**rozściel|ać, rozściel|ać (-am, -asz)** (*perf* **rozesłać**) *vt* to spread

**rozśmiesz|ać (-am, -asz)** (*perf* **-yć**) *vt*: **~ kogoś** to make sb laugh

**rozświetl|ać (-am, -asz)** (*perf* **-ić**) *vt* to light (up)

**roztacz|ać (-am, -asz)** (*perf* **roztoczyć**) *vt* (*perspektywy, wizję*) to unfold; (*blask, zapach*) to spread; **~ nad kimś opiekę** to have sb under one's protection

**roztapi|ać (-am, -asz)** (*perf* **roztopić**) *vt* to melt

**roztargnie|nie (-nia)** *nt* absent-mindedness; **przez ~** absent-mindedly

**roztargniony** *adj* absent-minded

**rozter|ka (-ki, -ki)** (*dat sg* **-ce**, *gen pl* **-ek**) *f* quandary, dilemma; **być w rozterce** to be in a quandary *lub* dilemma

**roztkli|wiać się (-wiam, -wiasz)** (*perf* **-wić**) *vr*: **roztkliwiać się (nad** *+instr*) to get sentimental (over)

**roztocz|yć (-ę, -ysz)** *vb perf od* **roztaczać**

**rozto|pić (-pię, -pisz)** *vb perf od* **roztapiać**

**roztop|y (-ów)** *pl* thaw

**roztrą|cać (-cam, -casz)** (*perf* **-cić**) *vt* to jostle

**roztrą|cić (-cę, -cisz)** (*imp* **-ć**) *vb perf od* **roztrącać**

**roztropnoś|ć (-ci)** *f* prudence

**roztropny** *adj* prudent

**roztrwo|nić (-nię, -nisz)** (*imp* **-ń**) *vb perf od* **trwonić**

**roztrzas|kiwać (-kuję, -kujesz)** (*perf* **-kać**) *vt* to smash (up); **roztrzaskać na** *lub* **w kawałki** to smash to pieces; **roztrzaskiwać się** *vr* (*o samolocie*) to crash; (*o wazonie*) to smash

**roztrząs|ać (-am, -asz)** *vt* (*kwestie, zagadnienie*) to deliberate over; (*obornik, siano*) (*perf* **-nąć**) to spread

**roztrzą|snąć (-snę, -śniesz)** (*imp* **-śnij**) *vb perf od* **roztrząsać**

**roztrzepany** *adj* scatterbrained

**roztrzęsiony** *adj* jittery

**roztw|ór (-oru, -ory)** (*loc sg* **-orze**) *m* solution; **~ wodny** water solution

**rozty|ć się (-ję, -jesz)** *vr perf* to grow fat

**rozu|m (-mu, -my)** (*loc sg* **-mie**) *m* reason; **na chłopski** *lub* **zdrowy ~, ...** common sense suggests that ...; **być niespełna ~u** to be out of one's mind

**rozumi|eć (-em, -esz)** (*perf* **z-**) *vt* to understand; **rozumiem** I understand *lub* see; **co przez to rozumiesz?** what do you mean by that?; **to rozumiem!** now you're talking!; **~ po angielsku** to understand English; **rozumiem, że nie przyjdziesz** I understand you won't be coming; **rozumieć się** *vr*: **~ się (ze sobą)** to understand each other; **~ się bez słów** to be on the same wavelength; **to się rozumie samo przez się** it goes without saying; **ma się ~!** by all means!

**rozumny** *adj* rational; **istota rozumna** rational being

**rozum|ować (-uję, -ujesz)** *vi imperf* to reason

**rozumowa|nie (-nia)** *nt* reasoning

**rozwadni|ać (-am, -asz)** (*perf* **rozwodnić**) *vt* to water down

**rozwa|ga (-gi)** (*dat sg* **-dze**) *f* judiciousness; **brać (wziąć** *perf*) **coś pod rozwagę** to take sth into consideration; **z rozwagą** with deliberation

**rozwal|ać (-am, -asz)** (*perf* **-ić**) (*pot*) *vt* (*rozbijać*) to smash up, to shatter; (*rozrzucać*) to throw about; **rozwalać się** *vr* (*rozpadać się*) to fall apart; (*siedzieć, leżeć*) to loll (about)

**rozwałkow|ywać (-uję, -ujesz)** (*perf* **-ać**) *vt* to roll (out)

**rozwarst|wiać się (-wiam, -wiasz)** (*perf* **-wić**) *vr* (*o społeczeństwie*) to stratify; (*o materiale*) to separate

**rozwarstwie|nie (-nia, -nia)** (*gen pl* **-ń**) *nt* (*społeczeństwa*) stratification

**rozwarty** *adj*: **kąt ~** obtuse angle

**rozważ|ać (-am, -asz)** (*perf* **-yć**) *vt* to consider; **rozważam taką możliwość** I'm considering the possibility

**rozważny** *adj* judicious

**rozważ|yć (-ę, -ysz)** *vb perf od* **rozważać**

**rozwesel|ać (-am, -asz)** (*perf* **-ić**) *vt* to cheer up; **rozweselać się** *vr* to cheer *lub* brighten up

**rozwi|ać (-eję, -ejesz)** *vb perf od* **rozwiewać**

**rozwią|zać (-żę, -żesz)** *vb perf od* **rozwiązywać**

**rozwiąza|nie (-nia, -nia)** (*gen pl* **-ń**) *nt* (*zadania, zagadki, problemu*) solution; (*parlamentu, małżeństwa*) dissolution; (*Med*) delivery

**rozwiązłoś|ć (-ci)** *f* promiscuity

**rozwiązły** *adj* promiscuous

**rozwiąz|ywać (-uję, -ujesz)** (*perf* **-ać**) *vt* (*sznurowadło, węzeł*) to undo, to untie; (*kogoś/coś związanego*) to untie; (*zadanie, zagadkę, równanie*) to solve; (*umowę*) to terminate; (*parlament, małżeństwo*) to dissolve

**rozwidl|ać się (-a)** (*perf* **-ić**) *vr* to fork

r

**rozwidle|nie** (-nia, -nia) (*gen pl* -ń) *nt* fork
**rozwiedziony** *adj* divorced
**rozwie|sić (-szę, -sisz)** (*imp* -ś) *vb perf od* **rozwieszać**
**rozwiesz|ać (-am, -asz)** (*perf* **rozwiesić**) *vt* (*bieliznę*) to hang out; (*obrazy*) to hang
**rozwi|eść się (-odę, -edziesz)** (*imp* -**edź**, *pt* -**ódł, -odła, -edli**) *vb perf od* **rozwodzić się**
**rozwiew|ać (-am, -asz)** (*perf* **rozwiać**) *vt* (*dym, mgłę*) to disperse; (*przen: nadzieje, wątpliwości*) to dispel; (*włosy*) to blow through; **rozwiewać się** *vr* (*o dymie, mgle*) to disperse; (*o nadziejach, wątpliwościach*) to be dispelled
**rozwi|eźć (-ozę, -eziesz)** (*imp* -**eź**, *pt* -**ózł, -ozła, -eźli**) *vb perf od* **rozwozić**
**rozwi|jać (-jam, -jasz)** (*perf* -**nąć**) *vt* (*rolkę, film*) to unroll; (*skrzydła*) to spread; (*sztandar*) to unfurl; (*paczkę*) to unwrap; (*temat, zamiłowanie, zdolności*) to develop; (*działalność*) to expand; **rozwijać się** *vr* (*o drucie*) to uncoil; (*o wątku*) to unfold; (*rosnąć*) to grow; (*doskonalić się, przybierać na sile*) to develop
**rozwikł|ać (-am, -asz)** *vt perf* to unravel
**rozwi|nąć (-nę, -niesz)** (*imp* -**ń**) *vb perf od* **rozwijać**
**rozwinięty** *adj* (fully) developed
**rozwlekły** *adj* verbose, wordy
**rozwod|nić (-nię, -nisz)** (*imp* -**nij**) *vb perf od* **rozwadniać**
**rozwodni|k** (-ka, -cy) (*instr sg* -**kiem**) *m* divorcee
**roz|wodzić się (-wodzę, -wodzisz)** (*imp* -**wódź**, *perf* -**wieść**) *vr* to get divorced; **rozwodzić się z kimś** to divorce sb; **rozwodzić się nad czymś** to dwell on sth
**rozwojowy** *adj* developmental; **prace badawczo-rozwojowe** research and development
**rozwolnie|nie** (-nia) *nt* diarrhoea (Brit), diarrhea (US)
**rozwo|zić (-żę, -zisz)** (*perf* **rozwieźć**) *vt* to deliver
**rozw|ód** (-odu, -ody) (*loc sg* -**odzie**) *m* divorce; **wziąć** (*perf*) ~ to get a divorce
**rozwód|ka** (-ki, -ki) (*dat sg* -**ce**, *gen pl* -**ek**) *f* divorcee
**rozw|ój** (-oju) *m* (*techniki, organizmu*) development; (*akcji, wypadków*) progress
**rozwściecz|yć (-ę, -ysz)** *vt perf* to enrage, to infuriate
**rozwydrzony** *adj* (*dziecko*) spoilt; (*tłum*) rowdy
**rozzie|w** (-wu) (*loc sg* -**wie**) *m* (*rozbieżność*) disparity; (*Jęz*) hiatus
**rozzłoszczony** *adj* angered, angry
**rozzło|ścić (-szczę, -ścisz)** (*imp* -**ść**) *vt perf* to anger; **rozłościć się** *vr* to get angry
**rozzuchwal|ać się (-am, -asz)** (*perf* -**ić**) *vr* to grow impudent
**rozzuchwalony** *adj* impudent
**rozżale|nie** (-nia) *nt* bitterness
**rozżalony** *adj* embittered
**rozżarzony** *adj* glowing-hot; ~ **do białości/czerwoności** white-/red-hot
**roż|en** (-na, -ny) (*loc sg* -**nie**) *m* (rotating) spit; **kurczak/pieczeń z rożna** spitroasted chicken/meat
**rożny** *adj*: **rzut** ~ (*Sport*) corner kick
**rób** *itd. vb patrz* **robić**
**ród** (**rodu, rody**) (*loc sg* **rodzie**) *m* (*rodzina*) family; (*dynastia, linia*) house; **ród Jagiellonów** the house of Jagiellonians
**róg** (**rogu, rogi**) (*instr sg* **rogiem**) *m* (*u bydła*) horn; (*u jelenia, sarny*) antler, horn; (*kąt*) corner; (*zbieg ulic*) corner; (*Muz*) horn; (*Sport*) corner; **na rogu** on *lub* at the corner; **za rogiem** round the corner; **w rogu pokoju** in the corner of the room; **róg obfitości** cornucopia
**rój** (**roju, roje**) *m* swarm
**ról** *n patrz* **rola**
**rósł** *vb patrz* **rosnąć**
**rów** (**rowu, rowy**) (*loc sg* **rowie**) *m* ditch; (*Geol*) trough; **rów melioracyjny** drainage ditch; **rów oceaniczny** oceanic trench
**rówieśnic|a** (-y, -e) *f* = **rówieśniczka**
**rówieśnicz|ka** (-ki, -ki) (*dat sg* -**ce**, *gen pl* -**ek**) *f* peer
**rówieśni|k** (-ka, -cy) (*instr sg* -**kiem**) *m* peer
**równ|ać (-am, -asz)** *vt* (*powierzchnię*) (*perf* **wy-**) to level, to flatten; (*prawa, obowiązki*) (*perf* **z-**) to equalize; ~ (**z**~ *perf*) **coś z ziemią** to raze sth to the ground; **równać się** *vr*: **dwa plus dwa równa się cztery** two plus two equals four; ~ **się z kimś/czymś** (*dorównywać*) to equal sb/sth; ~ **się z czymś** (*być jednoznacznym*) to be tantamount to sth, to amount to sth
**równa|nie** (-nia, -nia) (*gen pl* -**ń**) *nt* (*Mat*) equation; **układ równań** a system of equations
**rów|nia** (-ni, -nie) (*gen pl* -**ni**) *f*: ~ **pochyła** inclined plane; **stawiać coś na równi z** +*instr* to put sth on a par with
**równie** *adv* (*tak samo*): ~ **... (jak...)** as ... (as ...); (*aż tak*) equally; **nigdy nie widziałem nic ~ strasznego** I've never seen anything as horrible; ~ **dobrze możesz wcale nie przychodzić** you might as well not come at all
**również** *adv* also, as well; **jak** ~ ... and also ...
**równi|k** (-ka, -ki) (*instr sg* -**kiem**) *m* equator
**równikowy** *adj* (*las: obszar, strefa*) equatorial; **las** ~ rain forest
**równi|na** (-ny, -ny) (*dat sg* -**nie**) *f* plain

**równo** *adv* (*gładko*) evenly; (*jednakowo*) evenly, equally; (*dokładnie*) exactly
**równoboczny** *adj*: **trójkąt ~** equilateral triangle
**równoczesny** *adj* simultaneous
**równocześnie** *adv* (*w tym samym czasie*) at the same time, simultaneously; (*zarazem*) at the same time
**równolegle** *adv* (*jednocześnie*) simultaneously; **studiować ~ dwa przedmioty** to study two subjects concurrently
**równoległy** *adj* parallel; **~ do** *+gen* parallel to
**równoleżni|k** (**-ka, -ki**) (*instr sg* **-kiem**) *m* parallel
**równomiernie** *adv* evenly
**równomierny** *adj* even
**równonoc** (**-y, -e**) (*dat sg* **-y**) *f* equinox
**równoprawny** *adj* equal
**równoramienny** *adj*: **trójkąt ~** isosceles triangle
**równorzędny** *adj* equivalent; **~ przeciwnik** a match
**równoś|ć** (**-ci**) *f* equality; **znak równości** equals sign
**równouprawnie|nie** (**-nia**) *nt* equality of rights; **~ kobiet** women's rights, equal rights for women
**równowa|ga** (**-gi**) (*dat sg* **-dze**) *f* balance; (*opanowanie*) balance, poise; (*Tenis*) deuce; **tracić (stracić** *perf*) **równowagę** to lose one's balance; **wyprowadzić** *lub* **wytrącić** (*perf*) **kogoś z równowagi** to throw sb off balance
**równowartoś|ć** (**-ci**) *f* equivalent
**równoważ|nia** (**-ni, -nie**) (*gen pl* **-ni**) *f* (*Sport*) beam
**równoważny** *adj*: **~ (z** *+instr*) equivalent (to)
**równoważ|yć (-ę, -ysz)** (*perf* **z-**) *vt* to balance; **równoważyć się** *vr* to be in balance
**równoznaczny** *adj*: **~ (z** *+instr*) equivalent (to)
**równy** *adj* (*gładki*) even, flat; (*jednakowy*) equal; (*rytmiczny*) even, steady; **stopień ~** (*Jęz*) positive degree; **wszyscy obywatele są równi wobec prawa** all citizens are equal before the law; **on nie ma sobie równego** he has no match/equal; **równe sto lat temu** a hundred years ago today; **jak ~ z ~m** on equal terms; **w równej mierze** equally; **~ gość** (*pot*) good sort
**róz|ga** (**-gi, -gi**) (*dat sg* **-dze**) *f* (*gałąź*) twig; (*narzędzie kary*) birch, rod
**róż** (**-u, -e**) *m* (*kolor*) pink; (*kosmetyk*) rouge, blusher
**róż|a** (**-y, -e**) *f* rose; **dzika ~** briar
**róża|niec** (**-ńca, -ńce**) *m* rosary
**różdż|ka** (**-ki, -ki**) (*dat sg* **-ce**, *gen pl* **-ek**) *f* (*rozwidlony pręt*) divining rod; **~ czarodziejska** magic wand
**różdżkarst|wo** (**-wa**) (*loc sg* **-wie**) *nt* dowsing, water divining
**różdżkarz** (**-a, -e**) (*gen pl* **-y**) *m* water diviner, water finder (*US*)
**różnic|a** (**-y, -e**) *f* difference; (*Mat*) remainder, difference; **~ czasu** time difference; **~ zdań** difference of opinion; **z tą różnicą, że ...** except that ...; **~ polega na tym, że ...** the difference lies in the fact that ...; **to mi nie robi** *lub* **sprawia różnicy** this makes no difference to me
**różnic|ować się (-uje)** (*perf* **z-**) *vr* to become different
**różnicz|ka** (**-ki, -ki**) (*dat sg* **-ce**, *gen pl* **-ek**) *f* (*Mat*) differential
**różniczkowy** *adj*: **rachunek ~** (*Mat*) differential calculus
**róż|nić (-nię, -nisz)** (*imp* **-nij**) *vt*: **~ kogoś/coś od** *+gen* to distinguish sb/sth from; **różnić się** *vr*: **~ się (od kogoś/czegoś)** to differ (from sb/sth)
**różnie** *adv* variously; **~ w życiu bywa** you have your ups and downs
**różnobarwny** *adj* multicoloured (*Brit*), multicolored (*US*)
**różnokolorowy** *adj* multicoloured (*Brit*), multicolored (*US*)
**różnoraki** *adj* varied, diverse
**różnorodnoś|ć** (**-ci**) *f* diversity, variety
**różnorodny** *adj* varied, diverse
**różnoś|ć** (**-ci**) *f* (*różnorodność*) diversity, variety; **różności** *pl* various things
**różny** *adj* (*rozmaity*) various, different; (*odmienny*) different, distinct
**różowy** *adj* (*kolor*) pink; (*przen*: *przyszłość*) rosy; **widzieć coś w ~ch barwach** to see sth through rose-coloured (*Brit*) *lub* -colored (*US*) spectacles
**różycz|ka** (**-ki**) (*dat sg* **-ce**) *f* (*Med*) German measles
**RP** *abbr* = **Rzeczpospolita Polska**
**rtę|ć** (**-ci**) *f* mercury
**RTV** *abbr* = **Radio i Telewizja**
**rubaszny** *adj* coarse
**rub|el** (**-la, -le**) (*gen pl* **-li**) *m* rouble, ruble
**rubi|n** (**-nu, -ny**) (*loc sg* **-nie**) *m* ruby
**rubry|ka** (**-ki, -ki**) (*dat sg* **-ce**) *f* (*w formularzu*) blank, blank space; (*w gazecie*) column
**ruch** (**-u, -y**) *m* (*zmiana położenia*) movement, motion; (*wysiłek fizyczny*) exercise; (*ożywienie*) boom; (*na drogach*) traffic; (*w grze*) move; (*Fiz*) motion; (*Sztuka, Pol*) movement; **~ oporu** the Resistance; **być w ~u** to be running; **wprawiać (wprawić** *perf*) **coś w ~** to set sth in motion; **zgodnie z ~em wskazówek zegara** clockwise; **odwrotnie do ~u wskazówek zegara** anticlockwise (*Brit*), counterclockwise (*US*)

r

**ruchliwy** *adj* *(oczy)* restless; *(ulica, port)* busy; *(dziecko)* lively, active
**ruchomoś|ci** **(-ci)** *pl* movables
**ruchomy** *adj* *(cel, punkt)* moving; *(przegroda, majątek, święto)* movable; **ruchome schody** escalator
**ru|da** **(-dy, -dy)** *(dat sg* **-dzie***)* *f* ore
**rude|ra** **(-ry, -ry)** *(dat sg* **-rze***)* *f* ruin
**rudowłosy** *adj* redheaded
**rudy** *adj* red
**rudziel|ec** **(-ca, -cy)** *m (pot)* redhead
**rudzi|k** **(-ka, -ki)** *(instr sg* **-kiem***)* *m (Zool)* robin
**ru|fa** **(-fy, -fy)** *(dat sg* **-fie***)* *f* stern; **na rufie** aft, astern
**rug|ać (-am, -asz)** *(perf* **z-***)* *vt* to tell off
**rugby** *nt inv (Sport)* rugby
**rui|na** **(-ny)** *(dat sg* **-nie***)* *f* ruin
**ru|ja** **(-i)** *f* rut
**rujn|ować (-uję, -ujesz)** *(perf* **z-***)* *vt* to ruin
**rulet|ka** **(-ki, -ki)** *(dat sg* **-ce**, *gen pl* **-ek***)* *f* roulette
**rulo|n** **(-nu, -ny)** *(loc sg* **-nie***)* *m* roll
**ru|m** **(-mu, -my)** *(loc sg* **-mie***)* *m* rum
**ruma|k** **(-ka, -ki)** *(instr sg* **-kiem***)* *m (książk)* steed
**rum|ba** **(-by, -by)** *(dat sg* **-bie***)* *f* rumba
**rumian|ek** **(-ku, -ki)** *(instr sg* **-kiem***)* *m (Bot)* c(h)amomile
**rumiany** *adj* *(twarz)* ruddy; *(jabłko)* red; *(pieczywo, mięso z kurczaka)* golden brown
**rumie|nić (-nię, -nisz)** *(imp* **-ń***)* *vt (przypiekać)* *(perf* **przy-***)* to brown; **rumienić się** *(perf* **za-***)* *vr* to blush, to flush
**rumie|niec** **(-ńca, -ńce)** *m* blush
**rumo|r** **(-ru, -ry)** *(loc sg* **-rze***)* *m* rumble
**rumowis|ko** **(-ka, -ka)** *(instr sg* **-kiem***)* *nt* rubble
**rumszty|k** **(-ku, -ki)** *(instr sg* **-kiem***)* *m* rump steak
**Rumu|n** **(-na, -ni)** *(loc sg* **-nie***)* *m* Romanian
**Rumuni|a** **(-i)** *f* Romania
**Rumun|ka** **(-ki, -ki)** *(dat sg* **-ce**, *gen pl* **-ek***)* *f* Romanian
**rumuński** *adj* Romanian
**ru|n** **(-nu)** *(loc sg* **-nie***)* *m (pot)*: **jest run na coś** there's a run on sth
**ru|nąć (-nę, -niesz)** *(imp* **-ń***)* *vi perf (o budynku, człowieku)* to collapse; *(o samolocie)* to plummet (down); *(przen: o planach)* to collapse, to fall to the ground
**run|da** **(-dy, -dy)** *(dat sg* **-dzie***)* *f* round; **~ honorowa** lap of honour *(Brit) lub* honor *(US)*
**ru|no** **(-na, -na)** *(loc sg* **-nie***)* *nt* fleece; **~ leśne** undergrowth
**rupi|a** **(-i, -e)** *(gen pl* **-i***)* *f* rupee
**rupieciar|nia** **(-ni, -nie)** *(gen pl* **-ni***)* *f* lumber room
**rupie|ć** **(-cia, -cie)** *(gen pl* **-ci***)* *m* (piece of) junk; **rupiecie** *pl* junk, lumber
**ru|ra** **(-ry, -ry)** *(dat sg* **-rze***)* *f* pipe; **~ wydechowa** exhaust (pipe) *(Brit)*, tailpipe *(US)*
**rur|ka** **(-ki, -ki)** *(dat sg* **-ce**, *gen pl* **-ek***)* *f* tube
**rurocią|g** **(-gu, -gi)** *(instr sg* **-giem***)* *m* pipeline
**rusał|ka** **(-ki, -ki)** *(dat sg* **-ce**, *gen pl* **-ek***)* *f* water-nymph
**Rus|ki** **(-kiego, -cy)** *m (pot!) decl like adj* Russki *(pot!)*
**ruski** *adj (pot!)* Russian; **pierogi ~e** cheese(-filled) pierogi
**rusycysty|ka** **(-ki)** *(dat sg* **-ce***)* *f* Russian studies
**rusz|ać (-am, -asz)** *(perf* **-yć***)* *vt*: **~ czymś** to move sth ▷ *vi (o samochodzie, pociągu)* to pull out; *(o człowieku)* to set off; *(o maszynie, silniku)* to start; *(o budowie, przedsięwzięciu)* to get off the ground; **co rusz** every second; **rusz głową!** use your head!; **rusz się!** get a move on!; **nie ~ się!** freeze!; **nie ruszył palcem** *(przen)* he didn't lift a finger; **nie ruszaj tego** keep your hands off (this thing); **sumienie go ruszyło** his conscience began to nag him; **ruszać się** *vr (być w ruchu)* to move; *(wyruszać)* to get moving; *(o haku, zębie: chwiać się)* to be loose
**rusznikarz** **(-a, -e)** *(gen pl* **-y***)* *m* gunsmith
**rusz|t** **(-tu, -ty)** *(loc sg* **-cie***)* *m (na jedzenie)* grill; *(na opał)* grate; **mięso/ryba z ~u** grilled meat/fish
**rusztowa|nie** **(-nia, -nia)** *(gen pl* **-ń***)* *nt* scaffolding
**rusz|yć (-ę, -ysz)** *vb perf od* **ruszać**
**ruty|na** **(-ny)** *(dat sg* **-nie***)* *f (doświadczenie, wprawa)* experience; **popadać (popaść** *perf***) w rutynę** to fall *lub* get into a rut
**rutynowany** *adj* experienced
**rutynowy** *adj*: **postępowanie rutynowe** routine procedure
**rwać (rwę, rwiesz)** *(imp* **rwij***)* *vt (kwiaty) (perf* **ze-***)* to pick; *(zęby) (perf* **wy-***)* to pull (out); *(ubranie, sieć) (perf* **po-***)* to tear ▷ *vi imperf (o zębie, stawach)* to shoot; *(pot: pędzić)* to tear; **~ sobie włosy z głowy** *(przen)* to tear one's hair (out); **rwać się** *vr (o tkaninie)* to tear; *(o głosie, wątku)* to break (off); **~ się do walki** to be spoiling for a fight
**ry|ba** **(-by, -by)** *(dat sg* **-bie***)* *f* fish; **zdrów jak ~** (as) right as rain; **gruba ~** *(przen)* bigwig *(pot)*, big shot *(pot)*; **iść na ryby** to go fishing; **Ryby** *pl (Astrologia)* Pisces
**rybacki** *adj*: **sieć/łódź rybacka** fishing net/boat
**ryba|k** **(-ka, -cy)** *(instr sg* **-kiem***)* *m* fisherman
**rybit|wa** **(-wy, -wy)** *(dat sg* **-wie***)* *f* tern

**ryb|ka** (**-ki, -ki**) (*dat sg* **-ce**, *gen pl* **-ek**) *f dimin od* **ryba**; **złota** ~ goldfish
**rybny** *adj* fish *attr*; **sklep** ~ fishmonger's (shop)
**rybołówst|wo** (**-wa**) (*loc sg* **-wie**) *nt* fishing, fishery
**ryc.** *abbr* (= *rycina, rysunek*) fig. (= *figure*)
**rycerski** *adj* (*turniej, zbroja*) knight's *attr*; (*zachowanie*) knightly, chivalrous; **zakon** ~ order of knights
**rycerskoś|ć** (**-ci**) *f* chivalry
**rycerst|wo** (**-wa**) (*loc sg* **-wie**) *nt* knighthood
**rycerz** (**-a, -e**) (*gen pl* **-y**) *m* knight
**rychły** *adj* (*książk: wczesny*) early
**ryci|na** (**-ny, -ny**) (*dat sg* **-nie**) *f* print
**rycynowy** *adj*: **olej** ~ castor oil
**ryczał|t** (**-tu, -ty**) (*loc sg* **-cie**) *m* lump sum
**ryczałtowy** *adj* flat-rate *attr*
**rycz|eć (-ę, -ysz)** (*perf* **ryknąć**) *vi* (*o lwie*) to roar; (*o ośle*) to bray; (*o byku*) to bellow; (*o krowie*) to moo; (*o syrenie, radiu*) to blare; (*wrzeszczeć*) to yell; (*pot: płakać*) to blubber; **~ ze śmiechu** to roar with laughter
**ry|ć (-ję, -jesz)** *vt* (*kopać*) (*perf* **z-**) to burrow; (*rzeźbić*) (*perf* **wy-**) to engrave
**rydwa|n** (**-nu, -ny**) (*loc sg* **-nie**) *m* chariot
**rydz** (**-a, -e**) *m*: **zdrów jak** ~ as fit as a fiddle
**ry|giel** (**-gla, -gle**) (*gen pl* **-gli** *lub* **-glów**) *m* bolt
**rygl|ować (-uję, -ujesz)** (*perf* **za-**) *vt* to bolt
**rygo|r** (**-ru, -ry**) (*loc sg* **-rze**) *m* strict discipline; **pod ~em aresztu** (*Prawo*) on penalty of arrest
**rygorystyczny** *adj* rigorous
**ryj** (**-a, -e**) *m* (*świni*) snout; (*pot!: twarz*) mug (*pot*)
**ry|k** (**-ku, -ki**) (*instr sg* **-kiem**) *m* (*lwa*) roar; (*krowy*) moo; (*osła*) bray; (*syreny, radia*) blare; (*pot: płacz*) howl (*pot*)
**rykosze|t** (**-tu, -ty**) (*loc sg* **-cie**) *m* ricochet; **odbić** (*perf*) **się ~em** to ricochet
**ryksz|a** (**-y, -y**) *f* rickshaw
**ry|m** (**-mu, -my**) (*loc sg* **-mie**) *m* rhyme
**rymarz** (**-a, -e**) (*gen pl* **-y**) *m* leatherworker
**rym|ować (-uję, -ujesz)** *vt* to rhyme; **rymować się** *vr* to rhyme
**ryn|ek** (**-ku, -ki**) (*instr sg* **-kiem**) *m* (*plac*) marketplace; (*Fin, Handel*) market; **czarny** ~ black market; **wolny** ~ free market; **Wspólny R~** the Common Market
**rynkowy** *adj*: **cena/wartość rynkowa** market price/value
**ry|nna** (**-nny, -nny**) (*dat sg* **-nnie**, *gen pl* **-nien**) *f* gutter
**rynszto|k** (**-ka** *lub* **-ku, -ki**) (*instr sg* **-kiem**) *m* gutter
**rynsztun|ek** (**-ku, -ki**) (*instr sg* **-kiem**) *m* gear; **w pełnym rynsztunku** in full gear
**ry|s** (**-su, -sy**) (*loc sg* **-sie**) *m* (*charakteru*) trait, feature; (*streszczenie*) outline; **rysy** *pl* (*też:* **rysy twarzy**) (facial) features *pl*
**rys.** *abbr* (= *rysunek*) fig. (= *figure*)
**ry|sa** (**-sy, -sy**) (*dat sg* **-sie**) *f* (*zadrapanie*) scratch; (*pęknięcie*) crack
**rysi|k** (**-ka, -ki**) (*instr sg* **-kiem**) *m* pencil lead
**rys|ować (-uję, -ujesz)** (*perf* **na-**) *vt* to draw; (*przen: przedstawiać*) to picture; (*robić rysy*) to scratch; **rysować się** (*perf* **za-**) *vr* (*uwidaczniać się*) to appear; (*pokrywać się rysami*) to scratch
**rysownic|a** (**-y, -e**) *f* drawing board
**rysowni|k** (**-ka, -cy**) (*instr sg* **-kiem**) *m* draughtsman
**rysun|ek** (**-ku, -ki**) (*instr sg* **-kiem**) *m* drawing; (*kształt, zarys*) shape; **~ techniczny** mechanical drawing
**rysunkowy** *adj* drawing *attr*; **film** ~ cartoon
**ry|ś** (**-sia, -sie**) *m* lynx
**ryt|m** (**-mu, -my**) (*loc sg* **-mie**) *m* rhythm
**rytmiczny** *adj* (*piosenka, wiersz, oddech*) rhythmic(al); (*dostawy*) regular
**rytmi|ka** (**-ki**) (*dat sg* **-ce**) *f* (*Muz*) rhythmics
**rytualny** *adj* ritual
**rytua|ł** (**-łu, -ły**) (*loc sg* **-le**) *m* ritual
**rywal** (**-a, -e**) (*gen pl* **-i**) *m* rival
**rywalizacj|a** (**-i**) *f* rivalry
**rywaliz|ować (-uję, -ujesz)** *vi*: **~ z kimś o coś** to compete with sb for sth; **~ (ze sobą)** to compete
**rywal|ka** (**-ki, -ki**) (*dat sg* **-ce**, *gen pl* **-ek**) *f* rival
**ry|za** (**-zy, -zy**) (*dat sg* **-zie**) *f* (*papieru*) ream; **trzymać kogoś w ~ch** to keep a tight rein on sb
**ryzykancki** *adj* reckless
**ryzykan|t** (**-ta, -ci**) (*loc sg* **-cie**) *m* risk-taker
**ryzy|ko** (**-ka**) (*instr sg* **-kiem**) *nt* risk; **na własne** ~ at one's own risk; **~ zawodowe** occupational hazard
**ryzyk|ować (-uję, -ujesz)** (*perf* **za-**) *vt* to risk ▷ *vi* to take a risk *lub* chance
**ryzykowny** *adj* risky
**ryż** (**-u**) *m* rice
**ryżowy** *adj*: **pole ryżowe** rice field *lub* paddy, paddy (field); **szczotka ryżowa** scrubbing brush
**rz.** *abbr* (= *rzeka*) R. (= *river*)
**rzad|ki** (*comp* **-szy**) *adj* (*nie gęsty*) thin; (*nieczęsty*) rare
**rza|dko** (*comp* **rzadziej**) *adv* (*nieczęsto*) rarely, seldom; (*w dużych odstępach*) sparsely; **~ kto** hardly anyone; **~ kiedy** hardly ever
**rzadkoś|ć** (**-ci**) *f* rarity
**rząd**[1] (**rzędu, rzędy**) (*loc sg* **rzędzie**) *m* (*szereg*) row, line; (*Bot, Zool*) order; **suma rzędu czterech milionów** a sum of *lub* in the order of four million; **cztery razy z rzędu** four

r

times running *lub* in a row; **w pierwszym rzędzie** primarily
**rzą|d²** (**-du, -dy**) (*loc sg* **-dzie**) *m* government; **rządy** *pl* rule
**rządowy** *adj* government *attr*
**rządzący** *adj* ruling
**rzą|dzić (-dzę, -dzisz)** (*imp* **-dź**) *vt*: **~** *+instr* to rule over, to govern ▷ *vi* (*sprawować rządy*) to rule, to govern; (*kierować*) to be in charge; **rządzić się** *vr* to throw one's weight about; **~ się sercem/rozumem** to listen to one's heart/reason
**rze|c (-knę, -kniesz)** (*imp* **-knij**, *pt* **-kł**) *vi perf* (*książk*) to say
**rzecz** (**-y, -y**) (*gen pl* **-y**) *f* thing; **rzeczy** *pl* (*dobytek, ubrania*) things *pl*; **~ jasna ...** needless to say ...; **on jest do ~y** he's all right; **co to ma do ~y?** what's that got to do with it?; **to nie ma nic do ~y** that's beside the point; **mówić od ~y** to talk nonsense; **na ~** *+gen* (*składka*) in aid of; (*zrzeczenie się*) in favour (*Brit*) *lub* favor (*US*) of; **znać się na ~y** to know the ropes; **nazywać ~y po imieniu** to call a spade a spade; **ogólnie ~ biorąc** in general; **siłą ~y** by the force of events; **w gruncie ~y** in fact, essentially
**rzecznicz|ka** (**-ki, -ki**) (*dat sg* **-ce**, *gen pl* **-ek**) *f* spokeswoman
**rzeczni|k** (**-ka, -cy**) (*instr sg* **-kiem**) *m* spokesman; **~ prasowy** spokesperson
**rzeczny** *adj* river *attr*
**rzeczowni|k** (**-ka, -ki**) (*instr sg* **-kiem**) *m* noun
**rzeczownikowy** *adj* nominal
**rzeczowo** *adv* to the point
**rzeczowoś|ć** (**-ci**) *f* matter-of-factness
**rzeczowy** *adj* matter-of-fact; **dowód ~** (*Prawo*) exhibit; **nagroda rzeczowa** prize gift
**rzeczoznawc|a** (**-y, -y**) *m* expert
**rzeczpospolit|a** (**-ej, -e**) *f* republic; **R~ Polska** the Republic of Poland; **Polska R~ Ludowa** (*Hist*) the Polish People's Republic
**rzeczywistoś|ć** (**-ci**) *f* reality; **odpowiadać rzeczywistości** to correspond with the facts; **w rzeczywistości** in reality *lub* fact; **~ wirtualna** virtual reality
**rzeczywisty** *adj* real
**rzeczywiście** *adv* really
**rzed|nąć (-nie)** (*pt* **-nął** *lub* **-ł, -ła, -li**, *perf* **z-**) *vi* to be thinning; **mina mu zrzedła** (*przen*) his face fell
**rze|ka** (**-ki, -ki**) (*dat sg* **-ce**) *f* river; **nad rzeką** on *lub* by the river; **w dół/górę rzeki** up/down the river
**rzekł** *itd. vb patrz* **rzec**
**rzekomo** *adv* allegedly
**rzekomy** *adj* alleged
**rzemie|ń** (**-nia, -nie**) (*gen pl* **-ni**) *m* (leather) strap
**rzemieślniczy** *adj*: **cech ~** craft guild
**rzemieślni|k** (**-ka, -cy**) (*instr sg* **-kiem**) *m* craftsman, artisan
**rzemio|sło** (**-sła, -sła**) (*loc sg* **-śle**) *nt* (*drobna wytwórczość*) craftsmanship, artisanship; (*zawód*) trade
**rzemy|k** (**-ka, -ki**) (*instr sg* **-kiem**) *m* thong
**rze|p** (**-pu, -py**) (*loc sg* **-pie**) *m* (*Bot*) burr; (*zapięcie*) Velcro®; **przyczepić się jak ~ do psiego ogona** (*pot*) to stick like a leech
**rze|pa** (**-py, -py**) (*dat sg* **-pie**) *f* turnip
**rzepa|k** (**-ku, -ki**) (*instr sg* **-kiem**) *m* (*Bot*) rape
**rzepakowy** *adj*: **olej ~** rape(seed) oil
**rzep|ka** (**-ki, -ki**) (*dat sg* **-ce**, *gen pl* **-ek**) *f* (*Anat*) kneecap
**rzesz|a** (**-y, -e**) (*gen pl* **-y**) *f*: **szeroka ~ odbiorców** a wide audience; **Trzecia R~** (*Hist*) the Third Reich
**rześki** *adj* brisk
**rzetelnoś|ć** (**-ci**) *f* reliability
**rzetelny** *adj* reliable
**rzewny** *adj* doleful
**rze|ź** (**-zi, -zie**) (*gen pl* **-zi**) *f* (*ubój zwierząt*) slaughter; (*przen*) slaughter, carnage; **iść (pójść** *perf*) **na ~** to go to slaughter
**rzeź|ba** (**-by, -by**) (*dat sg* **-bie**) *f* sculpture; **~ terenu** relief
**rzeźbiar|ka** (**-ki, -ki**) (*dat sg* **-ce**, *gen pl* **-ek**) *f* sculptor
**rzeźbiarski** *adj* (*praca, pracownia*) sculptor's *attr*; **mieć talent ~** to have an aptitude for sculpture
**rzeźbiarst|wo** (**-wa**) (*loc sg* **-wie**) *nt* sculpture
**rzeźbiarz** (**-a, -e**) (*gen pl* **-y**) *m* sculptor
**rzeź|bić (-bię, -bisz)** (*perf* **wy-**) *vt* to sculpt
**rzeź|nia** (**-ni, -nie**) (*gen pl* **-ni**) *f* slaughterhouse, abattoir
**rzeźni|k** (**-ka, -cy**) (*instr sg* **-kiem**) *m* butcher; (*pot: sklep*) butcher's (shop)
**rzeżącz|ka** (**-ki**) (*dat sg* **-ce**) *f* gonorrhoea (*Brit*), gonorrhea (*US*)
**rzeżu|cha** (**-chy, -chy**) (*dat sg* **-sze**) *f* cress
**rzędu** *n patrz* **rząd¹**
**rzępol|ić (-ę, -isz)** *vi imperf* (*pot*) to scrape away (*pot*)
**rzę|sa** (**-sy, -sy**) (*dat sg* **-sie**) *f* (eye)lash; (*też*: **rzęsa wodna**) duckweed
**rzęsisty** *adj* (*deszcz*) torrential; (*oklaski*) thunderous
**rzę|zić (-żę, -zisz)** (*imp* **-ź**) *vi* to wheeze
**rzodkiew|ka** (**-ki, -ki**) (*dat sg* **-ce**, *gen pl* **-ek**) *f* radish
**rzu|cać (-cam, -casz)** (*perf* **-cić**) *vt* (*piłkę, kamień*) to throw; (*cień, kostkę, spojrzenie*) to throw, to cast; (*rodzinę, dom*) to abandon, to desert; (*chłopaka, dziewczynę*) to drop, to jilt; (*palenie, wódkę, pracę*) to quit; (*uwagę, słówko*)

to throw in ▷ *vi* (*o autobusie, o samochodzie*) to toss; **rzuć broń!** drop it!; ~ **kotwicę** to drop anchor; ~ **monetą** to toss a coin; ~ **czar** *lub* **urok** to cast a spell; ~ **podejrzenie na kogoś** to cast suspicion on sb; ~ **oskarżenia** to make accusations; **rzucać się** *vr* (*miotać się*) to thrash about *lub* around; (*z mostu, pod pociąg, na łóżko*) to fling o.s.; ~ **się na kogoś** to pounce on sb; **(nie)** ~ **się w oczy** (not) to stand out; ~ **się do ucieczki** to turn tail; **nie rzucaj się!** (*pot*) cool it! (*pot*)

**rzu|cić (-cę, -cisz)** (*imp* **-ć**) *vb perf od* **rzucać**

**rzu|t** (**-tu, -ty**) (*loc sg* **-cie**) *m* (*rzucenie*) throw; (*porcja, etap*) batch; (*Geom*) projection; (*Tech, Archit*) projection, view; ~ **dyskiem/ oszczepem** the discus/javelin; ~ **młotem** (*Sport*) hammer throw; ~ **karny/rożny/wolny** penalty/corner/free kick; **na pierwszy ~ oka** at first glance *lub* sight, on the face of it; ~ **pionowy/poziomy** vertical/horizontal projection

**rzut|ka** (**-ki, -ki**) (*dat sg* **-ce**, *gen pl* **-ek**) *f* dart

**rzutki** *adj* enterprising, go-ahead

**rzutni|k** (**-ka, -ki**) (*instr sg* **-kiem**) *m* projector

**rzut|ować (-uje)** *vi*: ~ **na coś** to impinge on sth

**rzyg|ać (-am, -asz)** (*perf* **-nąć**) *vi* (*pot*) to puke (*pot*)

**rzyg|nąć (-nę, -niesz)** (*imp* **-nij**) *vb perf od* **rzygać**

**Rzy|m** (**-mu**) (*loc sg* **-mie**) *m* Rome

**Rzymia|nin** (**-nina, -nie**) (*loc sg* **-ninie**, *gen pl* **-n**) *m* Roman

**Rzymian|ka** (**-ki, -ki**) (*dat sg* **-ce**, *gen pl* **-ek**) *f* Roman

**rzymski** *adj* Roman; **pieczeń rzymska** meat loaf

**rzymskokatolicki** *adj* Roman Catholic

**r.ż.** *abbr* (= *rodzaj żeński*) f (= *feminine*)

**rż|eć (-ę, -ysz)** (*imp* **-yj**, *perf* **za-**) *vi* to neigh

**rż|nąć (-nę, -niesz)** (*imp* **-nij**, *perf* **u-**) *vt* (*piłować*) to saw; (*ciąć*) to cut; (*pot!*: *mieć stosunek z*) (*perf* **ze-**) to screw (*pot!*); (*pot*): ~ **w brydża/pokera** to play bridge/poker

**rżnięty** *adj* (*szkło*) cut

r

# Ss

**S, s** *nt inv* (*litera*) S, s; **S jak Stanisław** ≈ S for sugar
**s.** *abbr* (*= strona*) p. (*= page*)
**SA, S.A.** *abbr* (*= spółka akcyjna*) Co. (*= Company*)
**saba|t** (**-tu, -ty**) (*loc sg* **-cie**) *m* Sabbath
**sabotaż** (**-u, -e**) (*gen pl* **-y**) *m* sabotage
**sabotaży|sta** (**-sty, -ści**) (*dat sg* **-ście**) *m decl like f in sg* saboteur
**sabot|ować (-uję, -ujesz)** *vt* to sabotage
**sachary|na** (**-ny**) (*dat sg* **-nie**) *f* saccharine
**sa|d** (**-du, -dy**) (*loc sg* **-dzie**) *m* orchard; **sad jabłkowy** apple orchard
**sad|ło** (**-ła**) (*loc sg* **-le**) *nt* (*na ciele*) fat; (*produkt*) suet; **zalać** (*perf*) **komuś sadła za skórę** to make sb's life hell
**sad|owić się (-owię, -owisz)** (*imp* **-ów**, *perf* **u-**) *vr* to settle (o.s.)
**sadownict|wo** (**-wa**) (*loc sg* **-wie**) *nt* fruit-growing
**sadowni|k** (**-ka, -cy**) (*instr sg* **-kiem**) *m* fruit-grower
**sady|sta** (**-sty, -ści**) (*loc sg* **-ście**) *m decl like f in sg* sadist
**sadystyczny** *adj* sadistic
**sadyz|m** (**-mu**) (*loc sg* **-mie**) *m* sadism
**sadz|a** (**-y, -e**) (*gen pl* **-y**) *f* soot
**sadz|ać (-am, -asz)** *vt* (*gości*) to seat
**sadzaw|ka** (**-ki, -ki**) (*dat sg* **-ce**, *gen pl* **-ek**) *f* pond
**sa|dzić (-dzę, -dzisz)** (*imp* **-dź**) *vt* (*perf* **po-** *lub* **za-**) to plant
**sadzon|ka** (**-ki, -ki**) (*dat sg* **-ce**, *gen pl* **-ek**) *f* (*flanca*) seedling; (*pęd*) cutting
**sadzony** *adj*: **jajko sadzone** fried egg
**safari** *nt inv* safari
**sa|ga** (**-gi, -gi**) (*dat sg* **-dze**) *f* saga
**Saha|ra** (**-ry**) (*dat sg* **-rze**) *f* the Sahara
**sakiew|ka** (**-ki, -ki**) (*dat sg* **-ce**, *gen pl* **-ek**) *f* pouch
**sakralny** *adj*: **muzyka/sztuka sakralna** sacred music/art
**sakramen|t** (**-tu, -ty**) (*loc sg* **-cie**) *m* (*Rel*) sacrament
**sakramentalny** *adj* (*formuła itp.*) time-honoured (*Brit*), time-honored (*US*)
**saksofo|n** (**-nu, -ny**) (*loc sg* **-nie**) *m* sax(ophone)
**saksofoni|sta** (**-sty, -ści**) (*loc sg* **-ście**) *m decl like f in sg* saxophonist, sax(ophone) player
**Saksoni|a** (**-i**) *f* Saxony
**saks|y** (**-ów**) *pl*: **jeździć na ~** (*pot*) *to do seasonal work abroad*
**sal|a** (**-i, -e**) *f* (*duża*) hall; (*mała*) room; (*przen: publiczność*) (the) audience; **~ lekcyjna** classroom; **~ wykładowa** lecture hall; **~ gimnastyczna** gymnasium, gym (*pot*); **~ operacyjna** (operating) theatre (*Brit*), operating room (*US*); **~ balowa** ballroom; **~ koncertowa** concert hall; **~ obrad** conference hall *lub* room; **~ sądowa** *lub* **rozpraw** courtroom
**salamand|ra** (**-ry, -ry**) (*dat sg* **-rze**, *gen pl* **-er**) *f* salamander
**salami** *nt inv* (*wędlina*) salami; (*ser*) *type of mild hard cheese*
**salater|ka** (**-ki, -ki**) (*dat sg* **-ce**, *gen pl* **-ek**) *f* salad bowl
**salceso|n** (**-nu, -ny**) (*loc sg* **-nie**) *m* (*czarny*) black *lub* blood pudding (*Brit*), blood sausage (*US*); (*biały*) brawn (*Brit*), headcheese (*US*)
**sal|do** (**-da, -da**) (*loc sg* **-dzie**) *nt* (*Księgowość*) balance; **~ dodatnie/ujemne** positive/negative balance, credit/debit balance
**salet|ra** (**-ry, -ry**) (*dat sg* **-rze**) *f* (*też*: **saletra potasowa**) saltpetre (*Brit*), saltpeter (*US*); (*też*: **saletra amonowa**) ammonium nitrate, Norway saltpetre (*Brit*) *lub* saltpeter (*US*)
**salicylowy** *adj*: **kwas ~** salicylic acid; **spirytus ~** salicyl alcohol
**salmonell|a** (**-i, -e**) (*gen pl* **-i**) *f* salmonella
**salo|n** (**-nu, -ny**) (*loc sg* **-nie**) *m* (*pokój*) living *lub* sitting *lub* drawing room, lounge; (*też*: **salon wystawowy**) showroom; **~ fryzjerski** hair(dressing) salon; **~ samochodowy** car showroom; **~ piękności** *lub* **kosmetyczny** beauty salon *lub* parlour (*Brit*) *lub* shop (*US*); **~ mody** boutique; **~ gier** amusement arcade; **~ gry** casino
**salow|a** (**-ej, -e**) *f decl like adj* orderly
**sal|to** (**-ta, -ta**) (*loc sg* **-cie**) *nt* somersault

**salu|t** (**-tu, -ty**) (*loc sg* **-cie**) *m* (*Wojsk*) salute
**salut|ować** (**-uję, -ujesz**) (*perf* **za-**) *vi* (*Wojsk*): ~ **(komuś)** to salute (sb)
**sal|wa** (**-wy, -wy**) (*dat sg* **-wie**) *f* volley, salvo; **salwy śmiechu** peals of laughter
**sała|ta** (**-ty, -ty**) (*dat sg* **-cie**) *f* lettuce
**sałat|ka** (**-ki, -ki**) (*dat sg* **-ce**, *gen pl* **-ek**) *f* salad; ~ **owocowa/warzywna** *lub* **z warzyw** fruit/ vegetable salad

SŁOWO KLUCZOWE

**sam**[1] *pron decl like adj* **1** (*samodzielnie*): **sam to zrobiłem** I did it myself; **talerz sam się rozbił** the plate broke by itself
**2** (*samotny*): **przyszła sama** she came alone *lub* on her own; **byłam tam sama jedna** I was there all alone *lub* all by myself; **zostali sami na świecie** they were left (all) alone in the world; **być sam na sam (z** *+instr*) to be alone (with)
**3** (*uściśla czas, miejsce, termin*): **na samej górze** at the very top; **do samego końca** to the very end; **to jest w sam raz** this is just right; **w samą porę** just in time
**4** (*bez dodatków*): **same kłopoty** nothing but trouble; **same drobne (pieniądze)** only small change
**5** (*o wystarczającej przyczynie/racji*): **na samą myśl o czymś** at the very *lub* mere thought of sth
**6** (*podkreślenie ważności*): **sam prezydent tam był** the President himself was there; **w rzeczy samej** indeed
**7** (*w połączeniach z „sobie", „siebie", „się"*): **sam sobie wszystko zawdzięczam** I owe everything to myself; **sam z siebie** of my/his *itp.* own accord; **to jest ciekawe samo w sobie** this is interesting in its own right; **to się rozumie samo przez się** it goes without saying; **przechodzić (przejść** *perf*) **samego siebie** to excel o.s.; **zostawiać (zostawić** *perf*) **kogoś samemu sobie** to leave sb to himself/ herself
**8** (*w połączeniach z „ten", „taki"*): **taki sam** identical; **ten sam** the same; **w tym samym czasie** at the same time; **tym samym** thereby, thus

**sa|m**[2] (**-mu, -my**) (*loc sg* **-mie**) *m* self-service shop
**Samaryta|nin** (**-nina, -nie**) (*loc sg* **-ninie**) *m* Samaritan
**sam|ba** (**-by, -by**) (*dat sg* **-bie**) *f* (*Muz*) samba
**samic|a** (**-y, -e**) *f* female; ~ **wieloryba** female whale
**sa|miec** (**-mca, -mce**) *m* male
**samo** *pron decl like adj patrz* **sam** ▷ *pron inv*; **tak ~** (*podobnie*) similarly, likewise; (*w ten sam sposób*) in the same way; **tak ~ mądry jak ...** as clever as ...
**samo...** *pref*: **~tarczalny** self-sufficient
**samobieżny** *adj* self-propelled
**samobójc|a** (**-y, -y**) *m* suicide (*person*)
**samobójczy** *adj* (*akt, nastrój*) suicidal; **gol ~** *lub* **bramka samobójcza** own goal
**samobójst|wo** (**-wa, -wa**) (*loc sg* **-wie**) *nt* suicide; **popełniać (popełnić** *perf*) **~** to commit suicide; **próba samobójstwa** suicide attempt *lub* bid
**samochodowy** *adj*: **wypadek ~** car crash *lub* accident; **myjnia samochodowa** car wash; **pojazd/przemysł ~** motor vehicle/industry; **mapa samochodowa** road map; **wyścigi samochodowe** motor racing; **warsztat ~** service station, garage (*Brit*)
**samochodzi|k** (**-ku, -ki**) (*instr sg* **-kiem**) *m dimin od* **samochód**; (*zabawka*) toy car; **samochodziki** *pl* (*w wesołym miasteczku*) dodgems *pl* (*Brit*), bumper cars *pl* (*US*)
**samoch|ód** (**-odu, -ody**) (*loc sg* **-odzie**) *m* (motor)car, automobile; **~ ciężarowy** lorry (*Brit*), truck (*US*); **~ osobowy** car; **(jechać) samochodem** (to go) by car; **~ terenowy** off-road vehicle; **~ sportowy** sports car; **prowadzić ~** to drive (a car)
**samochwa|ła** (**-ły, -ły**) (*dat sg* **-le**) *m/f* (*pot*) braggart
**samoczynny** *adj* (*drzwi*) automatic; **zapłon ~** (*Mot*) spontaneous ignition
**samodzielnie** *adv* (*bez pomocy*) single-handed(ly), unaided; (*odrębnie*) independently
**samodzielnoś|ć** (**-ci**) *f* independence
**samodzielny** *adj* (*człowiek*) independent, self-reliant; (*praca, dzieło*) independent; (*mieszkanie*) self-contained
**samofinansowani|e** (**-a**) *nt* self-financing
**samogłos|ka** (**-ki, -ki**) (*dat sg* **-ce**, *gen pl* **-ek**) *f* vowel
**samogo|n** (**-nu**) (*loc sg* **-nie**) *m* moonshine (*esp US*)
**samogwał|t** (**-tu**) (*loc sg* **-cie**) *m* masturbation
**samoistny** *adj* (*zjawisko*) spontaneous; (*dzieło*) self-contained
**samokontrol|a** (**-i**) *f* self-control
**samokrytycyz|m** (**-mu**) (*loc sg* **-mie**) *m* self-criticism
**samokrytyczny** *adj* self-critical
**samokryty|ka** (**-ki**) (*dat sg* **-ce**) *f* self-criticism
**samolo|t** (**-tu, -ty**) (*loc sg* **-cie**) *m* (aero)plane (*Brit*), (air)plane (*US*); **(lecieć) ~em** (to go) by plane; **~ pasażerski/wojskowy** passenger/ military plane; **~ odrzutowy** jet (plane)

S

**samolu|b** (**-ba, -by**) (*loc sg* **-bie**) *m* egoist
**samolubny** *adj* selfish
**samoobro|na** (**-ny**) (*dat sg* **-nie**) *f* (*obrona samego siebie*) self-defence; (*obrona cywilna*) civil defence
**samoobsłu|ga** (**-gi**) (*dat sg* **-dze**) *f* self-service
**samoobsługowy** *adj* self-service *attr*
**samopas** *adv* (*bez opieki/dozoru*) uncared-for
**samopoczuci|e** (**-a**) *nt* mood; **mieć dobre/złe ~** to be in a good/bad mood
**samoprzylepny** *adj* self-adhesive
**samorzą|d** (**-du, -dy**) (*loc sg* **-dzie**) *m*: **~ miejski** town/city council; **~ terytorialny** local government; **~ klasowy/szkolny** (*Szkol*) student council; **~ studencki** (*Uniw*) student government
**samorządnoś|ć** (**-ci**) *f* self-government
**samorządny** *adj* self-governing
**samorządowy** *adj* council *attr*
**samorzutny** *adj* spontaneous
**samosą|d** (**-du**) (*loc sg* **-dzie**) *m* lynch law
**samostanowieni|e** (**-a**) *nt* (*Pol*) self-determination
**samotni|k** (**-ka, -cy**) (*instr sg* **-kiem**) *m* loner
**samotnoś|ć** (**-ci**) *f* loneliness, solitude
**samotny** *adj* (*człowiek, spacer, życie*) lonely; (*drzewo, dom*) solitary, lone; (*matka, ojciec*) single, lone
**samoucz|ek** (**-ka, -ki**) (*instr sg* **-kiem**) *m*: **~ języka angielskiego** a "Teach Yourself English" book
**samou|k** (**-ka, -cy** *lub* **-ki**) (*instr sg* **-kiem**) *m*: **być ~iem** to be self-educated *lub* self-taught
**samouwielbieni|e** (**-a**) *nt* self-admiration
**samowa|r** (**-ra, -ry**) (*loc sg* **-rze**) *m* samovar
**samowol|a** (**-i**) *f* licence (Brit), license (US), wilfulness (Brit), willfulness (US)
**samowolny** *adj* (*człowiek*) wilful (Brit), willful (US), self-willed; (*decyzja, postępowanie*) arbitrary
**samowystarczalny** *adj* self-sufficient
**samowyzwalacz** (**-a, -e**) (*gen pl* **-y**) *m* (*Fot*) self-timer
**samozachowawczy** *adj*: **instynkt ~** the instinct of *lub* for self-preservation
**samozadowoleni|e** (**-a**) *nt* self-satisfaction, complacency
**samozaparci|e** (**-a**) *nt* persistence
**samozapło|n** (**-nu**) (*loc sg* **-nie**) *m* spontaneous combustion *lub* ignition
**samozwa|niec** (**-ńca, -ńcy**) *m* usurper
**samozwańczy** *adj* self-appointed, self-styled
**samuraj** (**-a, -owie** *lub* **-e**) *m* samurai
**sanatori|um** (**-um, -a**) (*gen pl* **-ów**) *nt inv in sg* sanatorium
**sandacz** (**-a, -e**) (*gen pl* **-y**) *m* zander
**sandał** (**-a, -y**) *m* sandal; **sandały** *pl* sandals *pl*
**sandałowy** *adj*: **drzewo sandałowe** sandalwood; **olejek ~** sandalwood (oil)
**saneczkarst|wo** (**-wa**) (*loc sg* **-wie**) *nt* (*Sport*) tobogganing
**saneczkarz** (**-a, -e**) (*gen pl* **-y**) *m* tobogganer, tobogganist
**sa|nie** (**-ń** *lub* **-ni**) *nt* sleigh
**sanitariusz** (**-a, -e**) (*gen pl* **-y**) *m* orderly
**sanitariusz|ka** (**-ki, -ki**) (*dat sg* **-ce**, *gen pl* **-ek**) *f* nurse (*in a military hospital or on the front*)
**sanitar|ka** (**-ki, -ki**) (*dat sg* **-ce**, *gen pl* **-ek**) *f* ambulance
**sanitarny** *adj* (*warunki, urządzenia*) sanitary; **punkt ~** (*Wojsk*) dressing station
**sankcj|a** (**-i, -e**) (*gen pl* **-i**) *f* sanction
**sankcjon|ować (-uję, -ujesz)** (*perf* **u-**) *vt* to sanction, to legitimize
**san|ki** (**-ek**) *pl* sledge (Brit), sled (US); **jeździć na sankach** to sledge (Brit), to sled (US)
**sanktuari|um** (**-um, -a**) (*gen pl* **-ów**) *nt inv in sg* shrine, sanctuary
**San Marino** *nt inv* San Marino
**sanskry|t** (**-tu**) (*loc sg* **-cie**) *m* Sanskrit
**sa|pać (-pię, -piesz)** (*perf* **-pnąć**) *vi* to pant, to puff
**sape|r** (**-ra, -rzy**) (*loc sg* **-rze**) *m* sapper
**saper|ka** (**-ki, -ki**) (*dat sg* **-ce**, *gen pl* **-ek**) *f* camp shovel
**sap|nąć (-nę, -niesz)** (*imp* **-nij**) *vb perf od* **sapać**
**sardoniczny** *adj* sardonic
**Sardyni|a** (**-i**) *f* Sardinia
**sardyn|ka** (**-ki, -ki**) (*dat sg* **-ce**, *gen pl* **-ek**) *f* sardine
**sark|ać (-am, -asz)** (*perf* **-nąć**) *vi* to grumble
**sarkastyczny** *adj* sarcastic
**sarkaz|m** (**-mu**) (*loc sg* **-mie**) *m* sarcasm
**sarkofa|g** (**-gu, -gi**) (*instr sg* **-giem**) *m* sarcophagus
**sar|na** (**-ny, -ny**) (*loc sg* **-nie**, *gen pl* **-en**) *f* (roe) deer
**sasan|ka** (**-ki, -ki**) (*dat sg* **-ce**, *gen pl* **-ek**) *f* pasqueflower
**saski** *adj* Saxon
**saszet|ka** (**-ki, -ki**) (*dat sg* **-ce**, *gen pl* **-ek**) *f* travel document organizer
**sataniczny** *adj* satanic
**satani|sta** (**-sty, -ści**) (*loc sg* **-ście**) *m decl like f in sg* Satanist
**sataniz|m** (**-mu**) (*loc sg* **-mie**) *m* Satanism
**satelicki** *adj*: **państwa/kraje ~e** satellite states/countries
**sateli|ta** (**-ty, -ty**) (*loc sg* **-cie**) *m decl like f in sg* (*obiekt, państwo*) satellite; (*pot: antena satelitarna*) (satellite) dish; **sztuczny ~** artificial satellite; **~ (tele)komunikacyjny** communications satellite

**satelitarny** *adj*: **telewizja/antena satelitarna** satellite television/dish
**saty|na (-ny, -ny)** (*dat sg* **-nie**) *f* (*jedwabna, sztuczna*) satin; (*bawełniana*) sateen
**saty|ra (-ry, -ry)** (*dat sg* **-rze**) *f* satire
**satyryczny** *adj* (*program*) comedy *attr*; (*utwór*) satirical
**satyry|k (-ka, -cy)** (*instr sg* **-kiem**) *m* (*występujący*) comedian; (*piszący*) satirist
**satysfakcj|a (-i)** *f* satisfaction
**satysfakcjon|ować (-uję, -ujesz)** (*perf* **u-**) *vt* to satisfy
**sau|na (-ny, -ny)** (*dat sg* **-nie**) *f* sauna
**sawan|na (-ny, -ny)** (*dat sg* **-nie**) *f* savanna(h)
**są** *vb patrz* **być**
**sącz|ek (-ka, -ki)** (*instr sg* **-kiem**) *m* (*Med*) drain
**sącz|yć (-ę, -ysz)** *vt* (*pić powoli*) (*perf* **wy-**) to sip; **sączyć się** *vr* (*wypływać*) to ooze, to trickle; (*przeciekać*) to leak
**są|d (-du, -dy)** (*loc sg* **-dzie**) *m* (*instytucja, budynek*) court (of justice *lub* law), law court; (*rozprawa*) trial; (*książk: opinia*) judg(e)ment; **Sąd Najwyższy** ≈ the High Court (*Brit*), ≈ the Supreme Court (*US*); **sąd wojenny** court martial; **sąd ostateczny** (*Rel*) the Final *lub* Last Judgement; **oddawać (oddać** *perf*) **sprawę do sądu** to go to court; **stawać (stanąć** *perf*) **przed sądem** to appear before court; **postawić** (*perf*) **kogoś przed sądem** to bring sb before court; **podawać (podać** *perf*) **kogoś do sądu** to take sb to court; **proszę Wysokiego Sądu!, Wysoki Sądzie!** Your Honour! (*Brit*), Your Honor! (*US*)
**sądny** *adj*: **~ dzień** (*Rel*) Doomsday; (*przen*) doomsday
**sądownict|wo (-wa)** (*loc sg* **-wie**) *nt* the judiciary, judicature
**sądowniczy** *adj* judiciary
**sądownie** *adv* (*zająć lokal*) legally; (*dochodzić praw*) through legal action, in court; **ścigać kogoś ~** to prosecute *lub* sue sb
**sądowy** *adj* (*system*) judicial; (*procedura, koszty*) legal; (*medycyna*) forensic; **proces ~** lawsuit; **na drodze sądowej** in court
**są|dzić (-dzę, -dzisz)** (*imp* **-dź**) *vt* (*perf* **o-**) (*Prawo*) to try; (*oceniać*) to judge ▷ *vi* to suppose, to think; **tak sądzę** I suppose so; **nie sądzę** (*raczej nie*) I don't think so; **co o tym sądzisz?** what do you think (of that)?
**sąsi|ad (-ada, -edzi)** *m* neighbour (*Brit*), neighbor (*US*)
**sąsiad|ować (-uję, -ujesz)** *vi*: **~ z** *+instr* (*być sąsiadem*) to live next door to; (*graniczyć*) to neighbour (*Brit*) *lub* neighbor (*US*) on
**sąsiedni** *adj* (*pokój*) next, adjoining; (*kraj*) neighbouring (*Brit*), neighboring (*US*)
**sąsiedzki** *adj* neighbourly (*Brit*), neighborly (*US*)
**sąsiedzt|wo (-wa)** (*loc sg* **-wie**) *nt* (*sąsiadowanie*) neighbourhood (*Brit*), neighborhood (*US*); (*pobliże*): **w sąsiedztwie** *+gen* in the neighbo(u)rhood *lub* vicinity of
**sążnisty** *adj* (*list itp.*) lengthy
**SB** *abbr* (= *Służba Bezpieczeństwa*) Secret Police
**S.C.** *abbr* = **spółka cywilna**
**scal|ać (-am, -asz)** (*perf* **-ić**) *vt* to integrate, to consolidate; (*Komput: pliki*) to merge
**scalony** *adj*: **układ** *lub* **obwód ~** integrated circuit
**sced|ować (-uję, -ujesz)** *vb perf od* **cedować**
**scement|ować (-uję, -ujesz)** *vb perf od* **cementować**
**sce|na (-ny, -ny)** (*dat sg* **-nie**) *f* scene; (*podwyższenie w teatrze*) stage; (*przen: teatr*) the stage; **~ polityczna** political scene; **występować na scenie** to appear on (the) stage; **(po)za sceną** behind the scenes, backstage; **zrobić** (*perf*) **scenę** to make a scene
**scenariusz (-a, -e)** (*gen pl* **-y**) *m* (*filmowy*) screenplay, script; (*przen*) scenario
**scenarzy|sta (-sty, -ści)** (*loc sg* **-ście**) *m decl like f in sg* screenwriter, scriptwriter
**sceneri|a (-i, -e)** (*gen pl* **-i**) *f* scenery
**sceniczny** *adj* stage *attr*
**scen|ka (-ki, -ki)** (*dat sg* **-ce**, *gen pl* **-ek**) *f dimin od* **scena**
**scenogra|f (-fa, -fowie)** (*loc sg* **-fie**) *m* (*Teatr*) set *lub* stage designer; (*Film*) set designer *lub* decorator
**scenografi|a (-i, -e)** (*gen pl* **-i**) *f* (*Teatr*) set *lub* stage design; (*Film*) set design *lub* decoration
**scentraliz|ować (-uję, -ujesz)** *vb perf od* **centralizować**
**scentralizowany** *adj* centralized
**sceptycyz|m (-mu)** (*loc sg* **-mie**) *m* scepticism, skepticism (*US*)
**sceptycznie** *adv* sceptically, skeptically (*US*)
**sceptyczny** *adj* sceptical, skeptical (*US*)
**scepty|k (-ka, -cy)** (*instr sg* **-kiem**) *m* sceptic, skeptic (*US*)
**scha|b (-bu, -by)** (*loc sg* **-bie**) *m* pork loin
**schabowy** *adj*: **(kotlet) ~** pork chop
**schadz|ka (-ki, -ki)** (*dat sg* **-ce**, *gen pl* **-ek**) *f* (*książk*) tryst
**scharakteryz|ować (-uję, -ujesz)** *vb perf od* **charakteryzować**
**schema|t (-tu, -ty)** (*loc sg* **-cie**) *m* (*postępowania*) pattern; (*urządzenia*) diagram, chart
**schematycznie** *adv* (*przedstawić*) schematically; (*działać, grać*) conventionally
**schematyczny** *adj* (*rysunek, mapa*) schematic; (*szablonowy*) conventional
**scher|zo (-za, -za)** (*gen pl* **-z**) *nt* (*Muz*) scherzo

S

**schiz|ma** (**-my**) (*dat sg* **-mie**) *f* (*Rel*) schism
**schizofreni|a** (**-i**) *f* schizophrenia
**schizofreniczny** *adj* schizophrenic
**schizofreni|k** (**-ka, -cy**) (*instr sg* **-kiem**) *m* schizophrenic
**schl|ać się (-am, -asz)** *vr perf* (*pot: upić się*) to get canned (*pot*)
**schlany** *adj* (*pot*) canned (*pot*)
**schle|biać (-biam, -biasz)** (*perf* **-bić**) *vi*: **~ komuś** to flatter sb
**schludny** *adj* neat, tidy
**schładz|ać (-am, -asz)** (*perf* **schłodzić**) *vt* to chill
**schł|odzić (-odzę, -odzisz)** (*imp* **-odź** *lub* **-ódź**) *vb perf od* **schładzać**
**schłodzony** *adj* chilled
**sch|nąć (-nę, -niesz)** (*imp* **-nij**) *vi* (*o bieliźnie, farbie*) (*perf* **wy-**) to dry; (*o chlebie*) to become *lub* get stale; (*o kwiatach*) (*perf* **u-**) to wither
**schod|ek** (**-ka, -ki**) (*instr sg* **-kiem**) *m* (*stopień*) step
**schodowy** *adj*: **klatka schodowa** staircase
**schod|y** (**-ów**) *pl* stairs *pl*; **ruchome ~** escalator; **wchodzić/schodzić po schodach** to go up/down the stairs; **schodami w górę/dół** up/down the stairs
**scho|dzić (-dzę, -dzisz)** (*imp* **-dź**, *perf* **zejść**) *vi* (*iść w dół*) to go down; (*z konia, roweru*) to dismount, to get off; (*z fotela, kanapy*) to get off; (*o samolocie, drodze*) to descend; (*o łodzi podwodnej*) to submerge; (*pot: sprzedawać się*) to sell; (*o plamie, pierścionku*) to come off; **~ na dalszy plan** to recede into the background; **~ komuś z drogi** to get out of sb's way; **~ z kursu** to stray *lub* swerve from the course; **uśmiech nie schodził jej z ust** a smile never left her face; **rozmowa zeszła na inny temat** the conversation went on to a different topic; **schodzić się** *vr* (*gromadzić się*) to gather; (*o drogach, liniach*) to join; (*pot: odbywać się jednocześnie*) to coincide
**schorowany** *adj* ailing
**schorze|nie** (**-nia, -nia**) (*gen pl* **-ń**) *nt* illness
**schow|ać (-am, -asz)** *vb perf od* **chować**
**schow|ek** (**-ka, -ki**) (*instr sg* **-kiem**) *m* (*kryjówka*) hiding place; (*w samochodzie*) glove compartment
**schro|n** (**-nu, -ny**) (*loc sg* **-nie**) *m* (*Wojsk*) shelter; **~ przeciwlotniczy/atomowy** air-raid/fallout shelter
**schro|nić się (-nię, -nisz)** (*imp* **-ń**) *vb perf od* **chronić się**
**schronie|nie** (**-nia, -nia**) (*gen pl* **-ń**) *nt* shelter; **znaleźć** (*perf*) **~** to find shelter
**schronis|ko** (**-ka, -ka**) (*instr sg* **-kiem**) *nt* (*górskie*) chalet, hut; (*turystyczne, młodzieżowe*) hostel; (*dla zwierząt*) shelter
**schrza|nić (-nię, -nisz)** (*imp* **-ń**) *vt* (*pot*) to botch (*pot*)
**schud|nąć (-nę, -niesz)** (*imp* **-nij**) *vb perf od* **chudnąć**
**schwy|cić (-cę, -cisz)** (*imp* **-ć**) *vt perf* (*złapać*) to catch
**schwyt|ać (-am, -asz)** *vb perf od* **chwytać** ▷ *vt perf* (*zbiega, przestępcę*) to capture; **~ kogoś na gorącym uczynku** to catch sb red-handed *lub* in the act
**schyl|ać (-am, -asz)** (*perf* **-ić**) *vt*: **~ głowę** to bow one's head; **schylać się** *vr* to stoop
**schył|ek** (**-ku**) (*instr sg* **-kiem**) *m* (*książk*) twilight (*przen*); **u schyłku życia** in one's declining years
**schyłkowy** *adj* (*książk*) decadent
**scysj|a** (**-i, -e**) (*gen pl* **-i**) *f* squabble
**scyzory|k** (**-ka, -ki**) (*instr sg* **-kiem**) *m* penknife
**scze|piać (-piam, -piasz)** (*perf* **-pić**) *vt* to join; **sczepiać się** *vr* (*zahaczyć się*) to get stuck together
**sczerni|eć (-eje)** *vb perf od* **czernieć**
**scze|znąć (-znę, -źniesz)** *vi perf* (*książk: zginąć*) to perish
**SdRP** *abbr* (= *Socjaldemokracja Rzeczypospolitej Polskiej*) Social Democratic Party of Poland
**sean|s** (**-su, -se**) (*loc sg* **-sie**) *m* (*Film, TV*) show; **~ spirytystyczny** séance
**secesj|a** (**-i**) *f* (*książk*) secession; (*Sztuka*) art nouveau
**secesyjny** *adj* (*Sztuka*) art nouveau *attr*; **wojna secesyjna** (*Hist*) the Civil War (*1861-65*)
**secie** *n patrz* **set**
**seda|n** (**-nu, -ny**) (*loc sg* **-nie**) *m* (*Mot*) saloon (*Brit*), sedan (*US*)
**sede|s** (**-su, -sy**) (*loc sg* **-sie**) *m* (*muszla klozetowa*) toilet bowl; (*deska klozetowa*) toilet seat
**sed|no** (**-na**) (*loc sg* **-nie**) *nt* (*istota*) essence; **~ sprawy** heart of the matter; **trafić** (*perf*) **w (samo) ~** to hit the nail on the head
**segmen|t** (**-tu, -ty**) (*loc sg* **-cie**) *m* (*element*) segment; (*mebel*) wall unit set
**segmentacj|a** (**-i**) *f* (*Bio*) segmentation
**segregacj|a** (**-i**) *f* segregation
**segregato|r** (**-ra, -ry**) (*loc sg* **-rze**) *m* (*teczka*) file binder
**segreg|ować (-uję, -ujesz)** (*perf* **po-**) *vt* to file
**sej|f** (**-fu, -fy**) (*loc sg* **-fie**) *m* safe
**sej|m** (**-mu, -my**) (*loc sg* **-mie**) *m* the Seym (*lower house of the Polish Parliament*)
**sejmowy** *adj* parliamentary
**sejsmiczny** *adj* seismic
**sejsmogra|f** (**-fu, -fy**) (*loc sg* **-fie**) *m* seismograph
**sejsmologiczny** *adj* seismological
**sek.** *abbr* (= *sekunda*) sec.

**sekato|r** (**-ra, -ry**) (*loc sg* **-rze**) *m* garden shears *pl*
**sekciarst|wo** (**-wa**) (*loc sg* **-wie**) *nt* (*Rel*) sectarianism
**sekcj|a** (**-i, -e**) (*gen pl* **-i**) *f* (*dział, oddział*) section; (*też*: **sekcja zwłok**) autopsy, post-mortem
**sekre|t** (**-tu, -ty**) (*loc sg* **-cie**) *m* secret; **w sekrecie** in secret
**sekretaria|t** (**-tu, -ty**) (*loc sg* **-cie**) *m* (*zespół ludzi*) secretarial staff, secretariat; (*pomieszczenie*) secretary's office, secretariat
**sekretar|ka** (**-ki, -ki**) (*dat sg* **-ce**, *gen pl* **-ek**) *f* secretary; **automatyczna ~** answering machine
**sekretarz** (**-a, -e**) (*gen pl* **-y**) *m* secretary; **~ stanu** secretary of state
**sekretarzy|k** (**-ka, -ki**) (*instr sg* **-kiem**) *m* writing desk
**sekretny** *adj* (*tajny*) secret
**sek|s** (**-su**) (*loc sg* **-sie**) *m* sex
**seksbom|ba** (**-by, -by**) (*dat sg* **-bie**) *f* (*pot*) bombshell (*pot*)
**seksistowski** *adj* sexist
**seksowny** *adj* (*pot*) sexy
**sekstan|s** (**-su, -sy**) (*loc sg* **-sie**) *m* (*Żegl*) sextant
**sekste|t** (**-tu, -ty**) (*loc sg* **-cie**) *m* sextet
**seksualny** *adj* sexual
**seksuolo|g** (**-ga, -dzy** *lub* **-gowie**) (*instr sg* **-giem**) *m* sexologist
**seksuologi|a** (**-i**) *f* sexology
**sek|ta** (**-ty, -ty**) (*loc sg* **-cie**) *f* sect
**sekto|r** (**-ra, -ry**) (*loc sg* **-rze**) *m* sector; **~ prywatny/państwowy** private/public sector
**sekularyzacj|a** (**-i**) *f* secularization
**sekun|da** (**-dy, -dy**) (*dat sg* **-dzie**) *f* second; **sekundę!** (*pot*) just a sec(ond)! (*pot*)
**sekundan|t** (**-ta, -ci**) (*loc sg* **-cie**) *m* second (*in boxing, duelling*)
**sekundni|k** (**-ka, -ki**) (*instr sg* **-kiem**) *m* second hand
**sekund|ować** (**-uję, -ujesz**) *vi*: **~ komuś** to second sb
**Sekwa|na** (**-ny**) (*dat sg* **-nie**) *f* the Seine
**sekwencj|a** (**-i, -e**) (*gen pl* **-i**) *f* sequence
**sekwen|s** (**-su, -sy**) (*loc sg* **-sie**) *m* (*Karty*) straight
**sekwo|ja** (**-i, -je**) (*gen pl* **-i**) *f* (*Bot*) sequoia
**seledynowy** *adj* celadon (green), willow-green
**selekcj|a** (**-i**) *f* selection
**selekcjone|r** (**-ra, -rzy**) (*loc sg* **-rze**) *m* (*Sport*) selector
**selekcjon|ować** (**-uję, -ujesz**) (*perf* **wy-**) *vt* to sort, to size
**selektywny** *adj* selective
**sele|n** (**-nu**) (*loc sg* **-nie**) *m* (*Chem*) selenium
**sele|r** (**-ra, -ry**) (*loc sg* **-rze**) *m* (*korzeniowy*) celeriac; (*łodygowy*) celery
**semafo|r** (**-ra, -ry**) (*loc sg* **-rze**) *m* semaphore
**semantyczny** *adj* (*Jęz*) semantic
**semanty|ka** (**-ki**) (*dat sg* **-ce**) *f* (*Jęz*) semantics
**semest|r** (**-ru, -ry**) (*loc sg* **-rze**) *m* semester
**semicki** *adj* Semitic
**seminari|um** (**-um, -a**) (*gen pl* **-ów**) *nt inv in sg* seminar; (*też*: **seminarium duchowne**) seminary
**semioty|ka** (**-ki**) (*dat sg* **-ce**) *f* (*Jęz*) semiotics
**sen** (**snu, sny**) (*loc sg* **śnie**) *m* sleep; (*marzenie senne*) dream; **mieć zły sen** to have a bad dream; **we śnie** in one's sleep; **sen zimowy** (*Zool*) hibernation; **jak we śnie** as *lub* like in a dream; **pamiętać coś jak przez sen** to have a hazy recollection of sth; **spędzać komuś sen z powiek** to keep sb awake at night; **zapadać (zapaść** *perf*) **w sen** to fall asleep
**senacki** *adj* (*komisja*) senate *attr*
**sena|t** (**-tu, -ty**) (*loc sg* **-cie**) *m* senate
**senato|r** (**-ra, -rowie** *lub* **-rzy**) (*loc sg* **-rze**) *m* senator
**senatorski** *adj* (*godność, mandat*) senatorial
**senio|r** (**-ra, -rzy**) (*loc sg* **-rze**) *m* senior
**senni|k** (**-ka, -ki**) (*instr sg* **-kiem**) *m* dream book
**sennoś|ć** (**-ci**) *f* sleepiness, drowsiness
**senny** *adj* sleepy, drowsy
**sen|s** (**-su**) (*loc sg* **-sie**) *m* (*racjonalność*) point; (*znaczenie*) sense; **bez ~u** pointless; **w pewnym ~ie** in a sense; **to nie ma ~u** there's no point in it; **nie ma ~u płakać** there's no point in crying, it *lub* there is no use crying
**sensacj|a** (**-i, -e**) (*gen pl* **-i**) *f* sensation; **sensacje** *pl*: **sensacje żołądkowe** stomach trouble; **wywołać** (*perf*) **sensację** to cause a sensation
**sensacyjny** *adj* (*wiadomość, artykuł*) sensational; (*film, powieść*) detective *attr*
**senso|r** (**-ra, -ry**) (*loc sg* **-rze**) *m* (*Elektr*) sensor
**sensownoś|ć** (**-ci**) *f* reasonableness
**sensowny** *adj* sensible, reasonable
**sentencj|a** (**-i, -e**) (*gen pl* **-i**) *f* maxim, saying
**sentymen|t** (**-tu, -ty**) (*loc sg* **-cie**) *m* fondness; **mieć ~ do** *+gen* to have a fondness for, to be fond of
**sentymentalnoś|ć** (**-ci**) *f* sentimentality
**sentymentalny** *adj* sentimental
**separacj|a** (**-i**) *f* (*Prawo*) separation; **być/żyć w separacji** to be separated
**separat|ka** (**-ki, -ki**) (*dat sg* **-ce**, *gen pl* **-ek**) *f* (*Med*) isolation room
**separatystyczny** *adj* (*Pol*) separatist
**separatyz|m** (**-mu**) (*loc sg* **-mie**) *m* (*Pol*) separatism

S

**separ|ować (-uję, -ujesz)** (*perf* **od-**) *vt* (*chorych*) to isolate; (*małżonków*) to separate; **separować się** *vr*: **~ się (od kogoś/czegoś)** to isolate o.s. (from sb/sth)
**sepi|a** (**-i, -e**) (*gen pl* **-i**) *f* (*barwnik*) sepia
**seple|nić (-nię, -nisz)** (*imp* **-ń**) *vi* to lisp
**septe|t** (**-tu, -ty**) (*loc sg* **-cie**) *m* (*Muz*) septet
**septyczny** *adj* (*Med*) septic
**se|r** (**-ra, -ry**) (*loc sg* **-rze**) *m* cheese; **biały ser** cottage cheese; **żółty ser** hard cheese
**Ser|b** (**-ba, -bowie**) (*loc sg* **-bie**) *m* Serb
**Serbi|a** (**-i**) *f* Serbia
**Serb|ka** (**-ki, -ki**) (*dat sg* **-ce**, *gen pl* **-ek**) *f* Serb
**serbski** *adj* Serb(ian)
**serbsko-chorwacki** *adj* Serbo-Croat(ian) ▷ *m decl like adj* (*język*) Serbo-Croat(ian)
**serc|e** (**-a, -a**) *nt* (*nom pl* **-a**) heart; (*dzwonu*) clapper, tongue; **okazywać komuś ~** to have a heart for sb; **atak** *lub* **zawał serca** coronary (attack), heart attack; **bez serca** heartless; **całym ~m** *lub* **z całego serca** wholeheartedly, with all one's heart; **z ręką na sercu, nie wiem** cross my heart, I don't know; **z dobrego serca** out of the goodness of one's heart; **brać (wziąć** *perf*) **(sobie) coś do serca** to take sth to heart; **z ciężkim ~m** with a heavy heart; **z głębi serca** from the bottom of one's heart; **w głębi serca** deep in one's heart; **wkładać w coś dużo serca** to put one's heart and soul into sth; **złamać** (*perf*) **komuś ~** to break sb's heart; **ktoś nie ma do czegoś serca** sb's heart is not in sth; **kamień spadł mi z serca** (*przen*) it's a weight *lub* load off my mind; **~ mi się kraje** my heart breaks *lub* bleeds, it breaks my heart; **leży mi to sercu** I care deeply about it; **przyjaciel od serca** a bosom friend
**sercowy** *adj* (*Anat*: *mięsień, choroba*) cardiac; (*pot*: *zawód, sprawa*) romantic
**serdecznie** *adv* (*witać, dziękować*) cordially, warmly; (*uśmiać się, ubawić się*) heartily; **pozdrawiać kogoś ~** to greet sb sincerely *lub* wholeheartedly
**serdecznoś|ć** (**-ci, -ci**) (*gen pl* **-ci**) *f* warmth
**serdeczny** *adj* (*przyjaciel*) bosom *attr*; (*list*) warm; (*śmiech*) hearty; **~ palec** ring finger; **serdeczne pozdrowienia** best greetings
**serdel|ek** (**-ka, -ki**) (*instr sg* **-kiem**) *m a kind of short frankfurter*
**serdusz|ko** (**-ka, -ka**) (*instr sg* **-kiem**, *gen pl* **-ek**) *nt dimin od* **serce**
**ser|ek** (**-ka, -ki**) (*instr sg* **-kiem**) *m dimin od* **ser** cheese; **~ topiony** processed cheese; **~ grani** cottage cheese
**serena|da** (**-dy, -dy**) (*dat sg* **-dzie**) *f* serenade
**seri|a** (**-i, -e**) (*gen pl* **-i**) *f* (*nieszczęść, wypadków*) series; (*zastrzyków*) course; (*znaczków*) set; (*rozmów*) round; (*produktu*) batch; **~ wystrzałów** a burst of fire; **~ wydawnicza** book series; **film z serii ...** another episode of ...; **program z serii ...** a programme in the series ...
**serial** (**-u, -e**) (*gen pl* **-i**) *m* series, serial
**serio** *adv* seriously; **traktować kogoś/coś (na) ~** to treat sb/sth seriously; **mówisz (na) ~?** are you (being) serious?
**serni|k** (**-ka, -ki**) (*instr sg* **-kiem**) *m* cheesecake
**serologiczny** *adj* (*Bio, Med*) serologic(al)
**serpenty|na** (**-ny, -ny**) (*dat sg* **-nie**) *f* (*droga*) hairpin road, switchback; (*taśma*) streamer
**ser|w** (**-wu, -wy**) (*loc sg* **-wie**) *m* (*Sport*) serve
**serwat|ka** (**-ki, -ki**) (*dat sg* **-ce**, *gen pl* **-ek**) *f* whey
**serwe|r** (**-ra, -ry**) (*loc sg* **-rze**) *m* (*Komput*) server
**serwe|ta** (**-ty, -ty**) (*dat sg* **-cie**) *f* tablecloth
**serwet|ka** (**-ki, -ki**) (*dat sg* **-ce**, *gen pl* **-ek**) *f dimin od* **serweta**; (*do ust, rąk*) napkin; **~ papierowa** paper napkin
**serwi|s** (**-su, -sy**) (*loc sg* **-sie**) *m* (*komplet naczyń*) service, set; (*też*: **serwis informacyjny**) news bulletin; (*obsługa*) service; (*Tenis*) serve; **~ społecznościowy** (*Internet*) social networking site
**serwisowy** *adj* (*ekipa, punkt*) service *attr*; (*informacje*) headline *attr*; **(podwójny) błąd ~** (*Tenis*) (double) fault
**serw|ować (-uję, -ujesz)** (*perf* **za-**) *vt* to serve; (*dowcipy, wiadomości*) to tell ▷ *vi* (*Sport*) to serve
**serwus** *inv*: **~!** (*pot*: *cześć!*) hi! (*pot*), howdy! (*pot*) (*US*)
**seryjnie** *adv*: **produkować ~** to mass-produce
**seryjny** *adj* (*numer*) serial; (*produkcja*) mass *attr*; (*produkt*) mass-produced
**sesj|a** (**-i, -e**) (*gen pl* **-i**) *f* session; (*Uniw*: *też*: **sesja egzaminacyjna**) end-of-term examinations *pl*; (*Giełda*) trading session
**se|t** (**-ta, -ty**) (*loc sg* **-cie**) *m* set
**setbol** (**-a, -e**) (*gen pl* **-i**) *m* setball
**sete|r** (**-ra, -ry**) (*loc sg* **-rze**) *m* setter
**set|ka** (**-ki, -ki**) (*dat sg* **-ce**, *gen pl* **-ek**) *f* hundred; (*pot*: *kieliszek alkoholu*) shot; **setki** (*+gen*) hundreds (of); **jechać setką** (*pot*: *Mot*) to hit *lub* top 70 mph
**setn|a** (**-ej, -e**) *f decl like adj*; **pięć setnych** five hundredths
**setny** *num decl like adj* hundredth
**Seul** (**-u**) *m* Seoul
**seza|m** (**-mu, -my**) (*loc sg* **-mie**) *m* sesame; **~ie otwórz się!** open, sesame!
**sezam|ki** (**-ków**) *pl* sesame seed snaps
**sezo|n** (**-nu, -ny**) (*loc sg* **-nie**) *m* season; **w/po ~ie** in/off season; **~ ogórkowy** (*przen*: *pot*) the silly season; **martwy ~** dead season

**sezonowy** *adj* seasonal

**sę|dzia** (**-dziego** *lub* **-dzi, -dziowie**) *m decl like adj lub f in sg* (*w sądzie*) judge; (*w konkursie*) juror; (*w piłce nożnej, boksie, hokeju*) referee; (*w tenisie, krykiecie*) umpire; **~ polubowny** arbitrator; **~ liniowy** linesman

**sędzi|ować (-uję, -ujesz)** *vi* (*w meczu piłki nożnej, hokeja*) to referee; (*w meczu tenisowym, krykieta*) to umpire; (*Prawo*) to judge

**sędziowski** *adj* (*egzamin, ława*) judge's *attr*; **rzut ~** (*w koszykówce*) drop ball; (*w hokeju*) face-off

**sędziwy** *adj* aged

**sę|k** (**-ku, -ki**) (*instr sg* **-kiem**) *m* knot (*in wood*); **w tym sęk** (*pot*) that's the problem *lub* hitch

**sękaty** *adj* gnarled

**sę|p** (**-pa, -py**) (*loc sg* **-pie**) *m* vulture; (*przen*) predator

**sfabryk|ować (-uję, -ujesz)** *vb perf od* **fabrykować**

**sfałsz|ować (-uję, -ujesz)** *vb perf od* **fałszować**

**sfałszowany** *adj* forged

**sfaul|ować (-uję, -ujesz)** *vb perf od* **faulować**

**sfe|ra** (**-ry, -ry**) (*dat sg* **-rze**) *f* (*obszar, strefa*) zone; (*dziedzina, krąg, kula*) sphere; (*warstwa społeczna*) class; **wyższe/niższe sfery** upper/lower classes

**sferyczny** *adj* spherical

**sfilm|ować (-uję, -ujesz)** *vb perf od* **filmować**

**sfinaliz|ować (-uję, -ujesz)** *vb perf od* **finalizować**

**sfinans|ować (-uję, -ujesz)** *vb perf od* **finansować**

**sfing|ować (-uję, -ujesz)** *vb perf od* **fingować**

**sfink|s** (**-sa, -sy**) (*loc sg* **-sie**) *m* sphinx

**sflaczały** *adj* flabby

**sfo|ra** (**-ry, -ry**) (*dat sg* **-rze**) *f* pack

**sformat|ować (-uję, -ujesz)** *vb perf od* **formatować**

**sformatowany** *adj* (*Komput*) formatted

**sform|ować (-uję, -ujesz)** *vb perf od* **formować**

**sformuł|ować (-uję, -ujesz)** *vb perf od* **formułować**

**sformułowa|nie** (**-nia, -nia**) (*gen pl* **-ń**) *nt* expression

**sfotograf|ować (-uję, -ujesz)** *vb perf od* **fotografować**

**sfrustrowany** *adj* frustrated

**show-bizne|s** (**-su**) (*loc sg* **-sie**) *m* show business

**siać (sieję, siejesz)** *vt* (*rzucać ziarno*) (*perf* **za-** *lub* **po-**) to sow; (*przen: szerzyć*) (*perf* **za-**) (*panikę*) to spread; **~ strach** to arouse *lub* inspire fear

**sia|d** (**-du, -dy**) (*loc sg* **-dzie**) *m* squat

**siad|ać (-am, -asz)** (*perf* **siąść**) *vi* to sit (down); **proszę ~!** please sit down; **~ do stołu/obiadu/kart** to sit down to table/dinner/cards

**siak** *inv*: **tak czy ~** one way or the other; **ni tak, ni ~** neither one way nor the other

**siaki** *inv*: **ni taki, ni ~** neither this nor that

**sia|no** (**-na**) (*loc sg* **-nie**) *nt* hay; (*pot: pieniądze*) bread (*pot*), dough (*pot*)

**sianokos|y** (**-ów**) *pl* haymaking

**siarcza|n** (**-nu, -ny**) (*loc sg* **-nie**) *m* (*Chem*) sulphate (*Brit*) *lub* sulfate (*US*)

**siarczysty** *adj* (*mróz*) biting, sharp; (*policzek*) stinging; (*uderzenie*) powerful

**siar|ka** (**-ki**) (*dat sg* **-ce**) *f* (*Chem*) sulphur (*Brit*) *lub* sulfur (*US*)

**siarkowod|ór** (**-oru**) (*loc sg* **-orze**) *m* hydrogen sulphide (*Brit*) *lub* sulfide (*US*)

**siarkowy** *adj*: **kwas ~** sulphuric (*Brit*) *lub* sulfuric (*US*) acid

**siat|ka** (**-ki, -ki**) (*dat sg* **-ce**, *gen pl* **-ek**) *f* (*materiał z plecionki*) mesh, net; (*ogrodzenie*) (wire) fence; (*rozmieszczenie, rozkład*) network; (*Sport*) net; **~ na zakupy** string bag; **~ druciana** wire mesh; **~ geograficzna** geographical grid; **~ płac** payroll

**siatkarz** (**-a, -e**) (*gen pl* **-y**) *m* volleyball player

**siatkowy** *adj*: **piłka siatkowa** volleyball

**siatków|ka** (**-ki**) (*dat sg* **-ce**) *f* (*Anat*) (*nom pl* **-ki**, *gen pl* **-ek**) retina; (*Sport*) volleyball

**sią|pić (-pi)** *vi*: **siąpi (deszcz)** it's drizzling

**sią|ść (-dę, -dziesz)** (*imp* **-dź**) *vb perf od* **siadać**

**sicie** *n* = **sito**

**sid|ła** (**-eł**) *pl* snare; (*przen*) trap

**siebie** *pron* (*też*: **siebie samego**) oneself; (*też*: **siebie wzajemnie**) each other, one another; **przed ~** right *lub* straight ahead; **być u ~** (*w domu*) to be at home; (*w swoim pokoju*) to be in one's room; **czuj się jak u ~ (w domu)** make yourself at home; **powiedzieć** (*perf*) **coś od ~** to express one's own opinion; **brać (wziąć** *perf*) **coś do ~** to take sth personally; **być pewnym ~** to be sure of o.s.; **pewny ~** self-assured, self-confident; **daleko od ~** a long way apart; **dochodzić (dojść** *perf*) **do ~** to recover; **jak mają się do ~ ceny?** how do the prices compare?; **jesteście o ~ zazdrośni** you are jealous of each other; **mów za ~!** speak for yourself!; **obok ~** side by side

**sie|c (-kę, -czesz)** *vt* (*nożem, szablą*) to hack, to slash; (*batem, kijem*) to lash, to slash ▷ *vi*: **~ze deszcz** it's lashing down

**siecz|ka** (**-ki**) (*dat sg* **-ce**) *f* chaff; **mieć sieczkę w głowie** (*pot*) to be empty-headed

**sie|ć** (**-ci, -ci**) (*gen pl* **-ci**) *f* (*do połowu ryb*) net; (*pająka*) (cob)web; (*telefoniczna, komputerowa*) network; (*sklepów, restauracji*) chain; (*przen:*

S

*pułapka*) trap; ~ **rybacka** fishing net; **włączać (włączyć** *(perf)*) **coś do sieci** to plug sth in; **wyłączać (wyłączyć** *(perf)*) **coś z sieci** to unplug sth; **łączyć (połączyć** *perf*) **w** ~ *(Tel)* to network; ~ **wodno-kanalizacyjna** plumbing

**siedem** (*jak*: **pięć**) *num* seven

**siedemdziesiąt** (*jak*: **dziesięć**) *num* seventy

**siedemdziesiąty** *num decl like adj* seventieth; ~ **pierwszy** seventy-first

**siedemnasty** *num decl like adj* seventeenth; **jest (godzina) siedemnasta** it's 5 P.M.

**siedemnaście** (*jak*: **jedenaście**) *num* seventeen

**siedemset** (*jak*: **pięćset**) *num* seven hundred

**siedemsetny** *num decl like adj* seven-hundredth

**siedlis|ko** (**-ka, -ka**) (*instr sg* **-kiem**) *nt* (*miejsce zamieszkania*) home; (*przen*) hotbed

**siedmiokrotny** *adj* (*wzrost*) sevenfold; (*zwycięzca*) seven-times *attr*

**siedmioletni** *adj* (*dziecko, samochód*) seven-year-old; (*plan*) seven-year

**siedmioro** (*jak*: **czworo**) *num* seven

**siedząco** *adv*: **robić coś na** ~ to do sth sitting down

**siedzący** *adj* (*osoba*) sitting; (*praca*) sedentary; (*postawa*) sitting, sedentary; **miejsce siedzące** seat

**siedze|nie** (**-nia, -nia**) (*gen pl* **-ń**) *nt* (*miejsce siedzące*) seat; (*pot*: *pośladki*) bottom; **przednie/tylne** ~ front/back seat; ~ **rozkładane** reclining seat

**siedzi|ba** (**-by, -by**) (*dat sg* **-bie**) *f* seat, base; **główna** ~ headquarters *pl*, head office; **firma ma swoją siedzibę w Warszawie** the firm is based *lub* seated in Warsaw

**sie|dzieć (-dzę, -dzisz)** (*imp* **-dź**) *vi* (*znajdować się w pozycji siedzącej*) to sit; (*pot*: *przebywać*) to stay; (*pot*: *być w więzieniu*) to do time; (*Szkol*: *powtarzać rok*) to repeat; ~ **cicho** to sit still *lub* quiet; ~ **nad czymś** (*przen*) to work on sth; ~ **w czymś** (*przen*) to know sth inside out

**siego** *inv*: **do** ~ **roku!** Happy New Year!

**sieję** *itd. vb patrz* **siać**

**siekacz** (**-a, -e**) (*gen pl* **-y**) *m* (*Anat*) incisor

**siek|ać (-am, -asz)** (*perf* **po-**) *vt* to chop

**siekie|ra** (**-ry, -ry**) (*dat sg* **-rze**) *f* axe (*Brit*), ax (*US*)

**sielan|ka** (**-ki, -ki**) (*dat sg* **-ce**, *gen pl* **-ek**) *f* idyll

**sielankowy** *adj* idyllic

**sielski** (*książk*) *adj* (*sielankowy*) idyllic; (*wiejski*) rural

**sie|mię** (**-mienia**) *nt* birdseed; ~ **lniane** flaxseed, linseed

**sienni|k** (**-ka, -ki**) (*instr sg* **-kiem**) *m* straw mattress

**sienny** *adj*: **katar** ~ hay fever

**sie|ń** (**-ni, -nie**) (*gen pl* **-ni**) *f* hall, vestibule

**sieroci|niec** (**-ńca, -ńce**) *m* orphanage

**siero|ta** (**-ty, -ty**) (*dat sg* **-cie**) *m/f decl like f* orphan

**sier|p** (**-pa, -py**) (*loc sg* **-pie**) *m* (*narzędzie*) sickle; (*cios*) hook

**sier|pień** (**-pnia, -pnie**) *m* August

**sierpniowy** *adj* August *attr*

**sierpowy** *adj*: **prawy/lewy** ~ (*Sport*) right/left hook

**sierś|ć** (**-ci**) *f* fur, coat

**sierż.** *abbr* (= *sierżant*) serg(t) (= *sergeant*)

**sierżan|t** (**-ta, -ci**) (*loc sg* **-cie**) *m* sergeant

**sie|w** (**-wu, -wy**) (*loc sg* **-wie**) *m* sowing

**siewc|a** (**-y, -y**) *m* (*Rol*) sower; (*przen*) propagator

**siewni|k** (**-ka, -ki**) (*instr sg* **-kiem**) *m* (*Rol*) seeder

 SŁOWO KLUCZOWE

**się** *pron inv* **1** (*siebie samego*) oneself; **widział/widzieli się w lustrze** he saw himself/they saw themselves in the mirror

**2** (*siebie wzajemnie*) each other, one another; **X i Y znają się dobrze** X and Y know each other very well

**3** (*tworzy stronę zwrotną czasownika*): **położyć się** to lie down; **czesać się** to comb one's hair; **zgubiłem się** I got lost

**4** (*jako odpowiednik strony biernej*): **ta książka sprzedaje się świetnie** this book sells very well; **to się dobrze nosi/pierze** it wears/washes well; **tak się tego nie robi** that's not the way to do it

**5** (*bezosobowo*): **zrobiło się późno** it's got late

**sięg|ać (-am, -asz)** (*perf* **-nąć**) *vt/vi* to reach; ~ **po coś** to reach (out) for sth; **sięgnąć do kieszeni** to reach into one's pocket; **czy możesz mi sięgnąć słownik z półki?** can you reach me the dictionary from the bookshelf?; **włosy sięgały jej do pasa** her hair came *lub* reached down to her waist; **woda sięgała mi do szyi** the water came up *lub* reached to my neck; **straty sięgały milionów** losses ran into millions; ~ **do słownika/notatek** to refer to a dictionary/one's notes; **nasza współpraca sięga roku 1980** our cooperation goes *lub* dates back to 1980; ~ **po władzę** to strive for power; **jak okiem sięgnąć** as far as the eye can see; ~ **pamięcią (wstecz) (do czegoś)** to go back in one's mind (to sth)

**sięg|nąć (-nę, -niesz)** (*imp* **-nij**) *vb perf od* **sięgać**

**sik|ać (-am, -asz)** *(perf* **-nąć***)* *vi* *(pot: tryskać)* to squirt; *(pot: oddawać mocz)* to piss
**Sikh (-a, -owie)** *m* Sikh
**sikhijski** *adj* Sikh *attr*
**si|ki (-ków)** *pl (pot!)* piss *(pot!)*
**sik|nąć (-nę, -niesz)** *(imp* **-nij***)* *vb perf od* **sikać**
**sikor|ka (-ki, -ki)** *(dat sg* **-ce**, *gen pl* **-ek***)* *f (Zool)* tit
**sile** *n patrz* **siła**
**sil|ić się (-ę, -isz)** *(perf* **wy-***)* *vr* to exert o.s.; **silić się na dowcip** to try to be funny
**siliko|n (-nu, -ny)** *(loc sg* **-nie***)* *m* silicone
**sil|nia (-ni, -nie)** *(gen pl* **-ni***)* *f (Mat)*: **cztery ~** factorial four
**silnie** *adv (uderzać)* hard; *(oddziaływać)* strongly; **~ to przeżyła** she took it badly
**silni|k (-ka, -ki)** *(instr sg* **-kiem***)* *m* engine; **~ elektryczny** electric motor; **~ parowy** steam engine; **~ spalinowy** internal combustion engine; **~ odrzutowy** jet engine
**silnikowy** *adj* motor *attr*; **olej ~** engine *lub* motor oil
**silny** *adj* strong; *(ból)* intense; *(lekarstwo, okulary)* strong, powerful; *(akcent)* strong, thick
**silo|s (-su, -sy)** *(loc sg* **-sie***)* *m* silo
**si|ła (-ły, -ły)** *(dat sg* **-le***)* *f (moc)* strength, power; *(intensywność)* intensity, strength; *(Fiz)* force; **siłą** by force; **~ robocza** workforce, labour *(Brit) lub* labor *(US)* force; **~ woli** willpower; **~ wiatru** wind strength; **~ wybuchu** strength of explosion; **w sile wieku** in one's prime; **~ nabywcza** purchasing *lub* buying power; **na siłę** *(pot)* by force; **siłą rzeczy** by the force of events; **siły** *pl* forces; **siły zbrojne** armed forces; **siły przyrody** the forces of nature; **o własnych ~ch** on one's own, unaided; **próbować (spróbować** *perf***) swoich sił (w czymś)** to try one's hand at sth; **pracować co sił** to work as hard as one can; **to ponad moje siły** this is too much for me; **(nie) czuć się na ~ch (coś zrobić)** (not) to feel up to doing sth
**siłacz (-a, -e)** *(gen pl* **-y***)* *m* strongman
**sił|ować się (-uję, -ujesz)** *vr* to wrestle
**siłow|nia (-ni, -nie)** *(gen pl* **-ni***)* *f (Sport)* body building gym; *(zakład energetyczny)* power plant
**siłowy** *adj*: **ćwiczenia siłowe** weight training; **sport ~** weight lifting; **uciec się** *(perf)* **do siłowego rozwiązania sprawy** to resolve a matter by force; **pole siłowe** *(Tech)* field of force
**Singapu|r (-ru)** *(loc sg* **-rze***)* *m* Singapore
**sin|gel, sin|giel (-gla, -gle)** *(gen pl* **-gli***)* *m (płyta)* single; *(Sport)* singles *pl*; *(Karty)* singleton
**sinia|k (-ka, -ki)** *(instr sg* **-kiem***)* *m* bruise; *(pod okiem)* black eye
**sinic|a (-y)** *f (Med)* cyanosis
**si|niec (-ńca, -ńce)** *m* bruise
**sini|eć (-eję, -ejesz)** *(perf* **z-** *lub* **po-***)* *vi* to become *lub* turn blue
**sinu|s (-sa, -sy)** *(loc sg* **-sie***)* *m (Mat)* sine
**siny** *adj* blue; **pojechać** *(perf)* **w siną dal** to vanish into thin air
**siodeł|ko (-ka, -ka)** *(instr sg* **-kiem***)* *nt* saddle
**siodł|ać (-am, -asz)** *(perf* **o-***)* *vt* to saddle
**siod|ło (-ła, -ła)** *(loc sg* **-le**, *gen pl* **-eł***)* *nt* saddle; **wysadzić** *(perf)* **kogoś z siodła** *(przen)* to knock sb off his perch
**sior|bać (-bię, -biesz)** *(perf* **-bnąć***)* *vi* to slurp
**siorb|nąć (-nę, -niesz)** *(imp* **-nij***)* *vb perf od* **siorbać**
**si|ostra (-ostry, -ostry)** *(dat sg* **-ostrze**, *gen pl* **-óstr***)* *f* sister; *(też:* **siostra zakonna***)* nun, sister; *(pielęgniarka)* nurse; **~ oddziałowa** ward sister; **~ cioteczna/stryjeczna** cousin; **~ przyrodnia** stepsister, half-sister
**siostrzany** *adj (uczucia)* sisterly; *(instytucje, miasta)* sister *attr*
**siostrzenic|a (-y, -e)** *f* niece
**siostrze|niec (-ńca, -ńcy)** *m* nephew
**siódem|ka (-ki, -ki)** *(dat sg* **-ce**, *gen pl* **-ek***)* *f* seven
**siódmy** *num decl like adj* seventh; **jest (godzina) siódma** it is seven (o'clock); **na stronie siódmej** on page seven; **być w ~m niebie** *(przen)* to be in seventh heaven
**sit|ko (-ka, -ka)** *(instr sg* **-kiem***)* *nt dimin od* **sito**; **~ do herbaty** tea strainer
**si|to (-ta, -ta)** *(loc sg* **-cie***)* *nt* sieve; *(kuchenne)* sieve, strainer
**sitodru|k (-ku, -ki)** *(instr sg* **-kiem***)* *m* silk-screen printing
**sitowi|e (-a)** *nt* bulrush
**sit|wa (-wy, -wy)** *(dat sg* **-wie***)* *f (pot)* clique, coterie
**siusi|ać (-am, -asz)** *vi (pot)* to pee *(pot)*
**siusiu** *nt inv (pot)*: **robić (zrobić** *perf***) ~** to pee *(pot)*
**siwi|eć (-eję, -ejesz)** *(perf* **o-** *lub* **po-***)* *vi* to grey *(Brit) lub* gray *(US)*, to turn grey *(Brit) lub* gray *(US)*
**siwi|zna (-zny)** *(dat sg* **-źnie***)* *f* grey *(Brit) lub* gray *(US)* hair
**siwy** *adj* grey *(Brit)*, gray *(US)*
**sje|sta (-sty, -sty)** *(dat sg* **-ście***)* *f* siesta
**s-ka, ska** *abbr (= spółka)* Co. *(= company)*
**skacowany** *adj (pot)* hung over
**skafand|er (-ra, -ry)** *(loc sg* **-rze***)* *m (kurtka)* anorak *(Brit)*, wind breaker *(US)*; *(nurka)* diving suit; *(astronauty)* spacesuit
**skaj (-u)** *m* artificial leather, leatherette *(Brit)*

S

**ska|kać (-czę, -czesz)** (*perf* **skoczyć**) *vi* (*wykonywać skok*) to jump; (*podskakiwać*) to skip, to jump up and down; (*o cenach*) to shoot up, to jump; **~ koło kogoś** (*przen*) to fawn on *lub* upon sb; **~ komuś do oczu** to fly at sb's throat; **~ z tematu na temat** to jump from one subject to another

**skakan|ka (-ki, -ki)** (*dat sg* **-ce**, *gen pl* **-ek**) *f* (*zabawka*) skipping rope (Brit), jump rope (US); **skakać przez skakankę** to skip

**skal|a (-i, -e)** *f* scale; (*przen: zainteresowań, barw*) range; (*talentu*) breadth; **na małą/wielką skalę** on a small/large scale

**skalecze|nie (-nia, -nia)** (*gen pl* **-ń**) *nt* cut

**skalecz|yć (-ę, -ysz)** *vt perf* to cut; **skaleczyć się** *vr perf* to cut o.s.; **~ się w palec** to cut one's finger

**skalisty** *adj* rocky

**skalny** *adj* rocky; **ogród ~** rock-garden, rockery

**skal|ować (-uję, -ujesz)** *vt* to calibrate

**skal|p (-pu, -py)** (*loc sg* **-pie**) *m* scalp

**skalpel (-a, -e)** (*gen pl* **-i** *lub* **-ów**) *m* scalpel

**skalp|ować (-uję, -ujesz)** (*perf* **o-**) *vt* to scalp

**ska|ła (-ły, -ły)** (*dat sg* **-le**) *f* rock

**skamieli|na (-ny, -ny)** (*dat sg* **-nie**) *f* fossil

**skamieniałoś|ć (-ci)** *f* fossil

**skamieniały** *adj* (*rośliny, zwierzęta*) fossilized; (*przen: ze strachu*) petrified

**skamieni|eć (-eję, -ejesz)** *vi perf* (*zamienić się w kamień*) to petrify, to fossilize; (*przen: osłupieć*) to become petrified

**skaml|ać, skaml|eć (-am, -asz** *lub* **-ę, -esz)** *vi* (*o psie*) to whine; (*pot*) to whimper

**skandal (-u, -e)** (*gen pl* **-i** *lub* **-ów**) *m* scandal

**skandaliczny** *adj* scandalous

**skand|ować (-uję, -ujesz)** *vt* to chant

**Skandyna|w (-wa, -wowie)** (*loc sg* **-wie**) *m* Scandinavian

**Skandynawi|a (-i)** *f* Scandinavia

**skandynawisty|ka (-ki)** (*dat sg* **-ce**) *f* (*Uniw*) Scandinavian studies *pl*

**Skandynaw|ka (-ki, -ki)** (*dat sg* **-ce**, *gen pl* **-ek**) *f* Scandinavian

**skandynawski** *adj* Scandinavian; **Półwysep S~** Scandinavian Peninsula

**skane|r (-ra, -ry)** (*loc sg* **-rze**) *m* (*Komput*) scanner

**skan|ować (-uję, -ujesz)** (*perf* **ze-**) *vt* (*Komput*) to scan

**skanse|n (-nu, -ny)** (*loc sg* **-nie**) *m* heritage park

**skapitul|ować (-uję, -ujesz)** *vb perf od* **kapitulować**

**skapt|ować (-uję, -ujesz)** *vb perf od* **kaptować**

**skarabeusz (-a, -e)** (*gen pl* **-y** *lub* **-ów**) *m* scarab

**skar|b (-bu, -by)** (*loc sg* **-bie**) *m* treasure; **~ państwa** (*Ekon*) the treasury; **za żadne ~y (świata)** (*pot*) not for all the money in the world (*pot*)

**skar|biec (-bca, -bce)** *m* vault

**skarbnic|a (-y, -e)** *f* (*przen*) treasure house

**skarbni|k (-ka, -cy)** (*instr sg* **-kiem**) *m* treasurer

**skarbon|ka (-ki, -ki)** (*dat sg* **-ce**, *gen pl* **-ek**) *f* money-box, piggy bank

**skarbowy** *adj* (*przepisy*) treasury *attr*; **urząd ~** (*Ekon*) ≈ Inland Revenue (Brit), ≈ Internal Revenue Service (US)

**skar|cić (-cę, -cisz)** (*imp* **-ć**) *vb perf od* **karcić**

**skar|ga (-gi, -gi)** (*dat sg* **-dze**) *f* complaint; **wnosić (wnieść** *perf*) **skargę (na kogoś)** to file *lub* lodge a complaint (against sb); **złożyć** (*perf*) **skargę (z powodu czegoś)** to complain (about sth), to file *lub* lodge a complaint (about sth)

**skar|pa (-py, -py)** (*dat sg* **-pie**) *f* slope

**skarpe|ta (-ty, -ty)** (*dat sg* **-cie**) *f* sock

**skarpet|ka (-ki, -ki)** (*dat sg* **-ce**, *gen pl* **-ek**) *f* sock

**skarż|yć (-ę, -ysz)** *vt*: **~ kogoś (do sądu)** to sue sb ▷ *vi* (*perf* **na-**); **~ na kogoś** to tell on sb; **skarżyć się** *vr* (*perf* **po-**) to complain; (*Med*): **~ się na coś** to complain of sth; **~ się na kogoś/coś** to complain about sb/sth

**skarżypy|ta (-ty, -ty)** (*dat sg* **-cie**) *m decl like f in sg* (*pot*) telltale (*pot*)

**skas|ować (-uję, -ujesz)** *vb perf od* **kasować**

**skatalog|ować (-uję, -ujesz)** *vb perf od* **katalogować**

**skat|ować (-uję, -ujesz)** *vb perf od* **katować**

**skau|t (-ta, -ci)** (*loc sg* **-cie**) *m* (boy) scout

**ska|za (-zy, -zy)** (*dat sg* **-zie**) *f* flaw; (*Med*) diathesis; **bez skazy** (*bez wad*) flawless

**ska|zać (-żę, -żesz)** *vb perf od* **skazywać**

**skaza|niec (-ńca, -ńcy)** *m* (death row) convict

**skazany** *adj* (*Prawo*) convicted; (*przen*): **~ na porażkę** *lub* **niepowodzenie** doomed to failure ▷ *m decl like adj* (*Prawo*) convict; **być ~m na własne siły** to be thrown back on one's own resources

**ska|zić (-żę, -zisz)** (*imp* **-ź**) *vb perf od* **skażać**

**skazujący** *adj*: **wyrok ~** verdict of guilty

**skaz|ywać (-uję, -ujesz)** (*perf* **-ać**) *vt* (*Prawo*) to sentence; **skazać kogoś na 5 lat więzienia** to sentence sb to 5 years' imprisonment; **skazywać się** *vr*: **~ się (na wygnanie)** to condemn o.s. (to exile)

**skaż|ać (-am, -asz)** (*perf* **skazić**) *vt* to contaminate

**skażeni|e (-a)** *nt* contamination

**skażony** *adj* contaminated

**skąd** *pron* where ... from; **~ jesteś?** where are you from?; **~ wiesz?** how do you know?; **(ależ) ~!** not at all!

**skądinąd** *adv*: **wiem ~, że ...** I know from other sources that ...; **człowiek ~ znany** a man who isn't unknown
**skądś** *pron* from somewhere
**skądże** *pron*: **~ (znowu)!** but of course not!
**skąpany** *adj*: **~ w** *+loc* bathed in
**ską|pić (-pię, -pisz)** (*perf* **po-**) *vt*: **~ komuś czegoś** to grudge sb sth; **nie ~ wysiłków** to spare no pains *lub* trouble
**ską|piec (-pca, -pcy)** *m* miser
**skąpo** *adv* (*oszczędnie*) sparingly; (*biednie*) poorly; (*ubrany*) scantily
**skąpst|wo (-wa)** (*loc sg* **-wie**) *nt* miserliness, tight-fistedness
**skąpy** *adj* (*człowiek*) stingy, miserly; (*strój, informacje, światło*) scant
**skecz (-u, -e)** (*gen pl* **-y** *lub* **-ów**) *m* skit
**skib|ka (-ki, -ki)** (*dat sg* **-ce**, *gen pl* **-ek**) *f* (*chleba*) slice
**skier|ować (-uję, -ujesz)** *vb perf od* **kierować**
**skierowa|nie (-nia, -nia)** (*gen pl* **-ń**) *nt* (*do lekarza, szpitala*) referral; (*do pracy*) appointment
**ski|n (-na, -ni** *lub* **-ny)** (*loc sg* **-nie**) *m* skinhead
**ski|nąć (-nę, -niesz)** (*imp* **-ń**) *vi perf* (*ręką*) to beckon; (*głową*) to nod; **~ na kogoś** to beckon sb
**skinieni|e (-a)** *nt* (*gest ręką*) wave; (*gest głową*) nod; **jest gotowa na każde jego ~** she is at his beck and call
**sklasyfik|ować (-uję, -ujesz)** *vb perf od* **klasyfikować**
**sklasyfikowany** *adj* (*Sport*): **~ na siódmym miejscu** listed seventh
**skle|ić (-ję, -isz)** *vb perf od* **sklejać**
**sklej|ać (-am, -asz)** (*perf* **skleić**) *vt* to glue together; **sklejać się** *vr* to get stuck together
**sklej|ka (-ki, -ki)** (*dat sg* **-ce**, *gen pl* **-ek**) *f* plywood
**skle|p (-pu, -py)** (*loc sg* **-pie**) *m* shop (*Brit*), store (*US*); **~ spożywczy** grocer's shop, grocery; **~ mięsny** butcher's shop
**sklepie|nie (-nia, -nia)** (*gen pl* **-ń**) *nt* (*Archit*) vault; **~ czaszki** skull cap; **~ niebieskie** firmament
**sklepikarz (-a, -e)** (*gen pl* **-y**) *m* shopkeeper (*Brit*), storekeeper (*US*)
**sklero|za (-zy)** (*dat sg* **-zie**) *f* sclerosis
**skła|d (-du, -dy)** (*loc sg* **-dzie**) *m* (*węgla, złomu*) yard; (*magazyn*) warehouse; (*zbiór składników*) makeup, composition; (*Chem*) composition; (*Druk*) typesetting; (*drużyny*) lineup; (*komisji*) makeup; **mieć coś na ~zie** to have sth in store *lub* stock; (*Sport*): **w pełnym/niepełnym ~zie** at full strength/below strength; **orkiestra w pełnym ~zie** full orchestra; **wchodzić (wejść** *perf*) **w ~ czegoś** to be part of sth, to be included in sth; **(robić coś) bez ładu i ~u** (to do sth) without rhyme or reason
**skład|ać (-am, -asz)** (*perf* **złożyć**) *vt* (*papier, leżak*) to fold; (*parasol*) to furl; (*silnik, mebel*) to put together, to assemble; (*węgiel, towar*) to store; (*dokumenty*) to turn *lub* hand in; (*ofertę, obietnicę*) to make; (*zażalenie*) to file; (*podziękowanie, kondolencje*) to offer, to express; (*wizytę, hołd*) to pay; **~ jaja** to lay eggs; **~ komuś wizytę** to pay sb a visit; **~ wniosek** to apply; **~ broń** to lay down one's arms; **~ do druku** to send to press; **~ podpis** to put one's signature, to sign; **~ przysięgę** to take *lub* swear an oath; **~ zeznania** to testify, to give evidence; **składać się** *vr* (*o krześle, leżaku*) to fold up; (*pot*: *robić składkę*) to chip in (*pot*); **~ się z czegoś** to be made up of sth, to consist of sth; **dobrze/źle się składa, że ...** it's fortunate/unfortunate that ...; **tak się składa, że ...** as it turns out, ...; **składa się na to wiele przyczyn** many factors are involved here; **~ się do strzału** to take aim
**składa|k (-ka, -ki)** (*instr sg* **-kiem**) *m* (*rower*) folding *lub* fold-up *lub* collapsible bike; (*kajak*) inflatable canoe
**składan|ka (-ki, -ki)** (*dat sg* **-ce**, *gen pl* **-ek**) *f* medley
**składany** *adj* (*urządzenie, mebel*) folding, fold-up, collapsible; **łóżko składane** foldaway bed
**skład|ka (-ki, -ki)** (*dat sg* **-ce**, *gen pl* **-ek**) *f* (*członkowska*) fee; (*ubezpieczeniowa*) premium; (*publiczna*) collection
**skład|nia (-ni)** *f* (*Jęz*) syntax
**składnic|a (-y, -e)** *f* (*skład, magazyn*) storehouse; **~ złomu** scrapyard
**składni|k (-ka, -ki)** (*instr sg* **-kiem**) *m* (*element*) component, ingredient; (*Mat*) element
**składniowy** *adj* (*Jęz*) syntactic
**składny** *adj* neat
**skład|ować (-uję, -ujesz)** *vt* to store
**składowy** *adj* component *attr*
**skła|mać (-mię, -miesz)** *vb perf od* **kłamać**
**skłani|ać (-am, -asz)** (*perf* **skłonić**) *vt*: **~ kogoś do zrobienia czegoś** to induce *lub* persuade sb to do sth; **~ głowę (przed kimś)** to bow *lub* lower one's head (before sb); **skłaniać się** *vr*: **~ się ku czemuś** *lub* **do czegoś** to incline *lub* lean towards sth
**skło|n (-nu, -ny)** (*loc sg* **-nie**) *m* (*ćwiczenie*) (forward) bend
**skło|nić (-nię, -nisz)** (*imp* **-ń**) *vb perf od* **skłaniać**
**skłonnoś|ć (-ci, -ci)** (*gen pl* **-ci**) *f* (*podatność*) susceptibility; (*zamiłowanie, pociąg*) penchant; **mieć ~ do czegoś** to have a penchant for sth

S

**skłonny** *adj*: **~ do przeziębień** prone *lub* susceptible to colds; **~ do płaczu** given to crying; **~ do kompromisu** willing to compromise; **być ~m coś zrobić** to be willing to do sth
**skłó|cać (-cam, -casz)** (*perf* **-cić**) *vt* to divide
**skłó|cić (-cę, -cisz)** (*imp* **-ć**) *vb perf od* **skłócać**
**skne|ra** (**-ry, -ry**) (*dat sg* **-rze**) *m/f decl like f* (*pot*) skinflint (*pot*)
**sknerst|wo** (**-wa**) (*loc sg* **-wie**) *nt* miserliness, stinginess
**skno|cić (-cę, -cisz)** (*imp* **-ć**) *vb perf od* **knocić**
**skob|el** (**-la, -le**) (*gen pl* **-li**) *m* (*do kłódki*) staple
**skocz|ek** (**-ka**) (*instr sg* **-kiem**) *m* (*Sport*) (*nom pl* **-kowie**) jumper; (*Szachy*) (*nom pl* **-ki**) knight; **~ spadochronowy** parachutist
**skocz|nia** (**-ni, -nie**) (*gen pl* **-ni**) *f* (*też*: **skocznia narciarska**) ski jump
**skoczny** *adj* (*taniec, muzyka*) lively
**skocz|yć (-ę, -ysz)** *vb perf od* **skakać**; (*pot*: *podążyć śpiesznie*) to pop out (*pot*), to nip out (*pot*); **~ na równe nogi** to jump *lub* leap *lub* spring to one's feet
**skojarze|nie** (**-nia, -nia**) (*gen pl* **-ń**) *nt* association
**skojarz|yć (-ę, -ysz)** *vb perf od* **kojarzyć**
**sko|k** (**-ku, -ki**) (*instr sg* **-kiem**) *m* jump; (*napad rabunkowy*) robbery; **~ w bok** (*pot*) one-night stand (*pot*); **~ w dal/wzwyż** long/high jump; **~i narciarskie** ski-jumping; **~ o tyczce** pole vault; **~i do wody** diving
**skokowy** *adj*: **staw ~** ankle joint; **pojemność skokowa** cubic capacity
**skoligacony** *adj*: **~ z** *+instr* related to
**skomas|ować (-uję, -ujesz)** *vb perf od* **komasować**
**skombin|ować (-uję, -ujesz)** *vt perf* (*pot*: *załatwić*) to wangle (*pot*)
**skoment|ować (-uję, -ujesz)** *vb perf od* **komentować**
**skomercjaliz|ować (-uję, -ujesz)** *vb perf od* **komercjalizować**
**skoml|eć (-ę, -isz)** *vi* = **skamlać**
**skomplet|ować (-uję, -ujesz)** *vb perf od* **kompletować**
**skomplik|ować (-uję, -ujesz)** *vb perf od* **komplikować**
**skomplikowany** *adj* complicated
**skompon|ować (-uję, -ujesz)** *vb perf od* **komponować**
**skompromit|ować (-uję, -ujesz)** *vb perf od* **kompromitować**
**skomputeryz|ować (-uję, -ujesz)** *vb perf od* **komputeryzować**
**skon|ać (-am, -asz)** *vb perf od* **konać**; **niech skonam!** (*pot*) I'll be damned! (*pot*)
**skonany** *adj* (*pot*: *zmęczony*) bushed (*pot*)
**skoncentr|ować (-uję, -ujesz)** *vb perf od* **koncentrować**
**skoncentrowany** *adj* (*sok*) concentrated; (*uwaga*) concentrated, focused
**skondensowany** *adj* (*zagęszczony*) condensed; **mleko skondensowane** evaporated milk
**skonfisk|ować (-uję, -ujesz)** *vb perf od* **konfiskować**
**skonfront|ować (-uję, -ujesz)** *vb perf od* **konfrontować**
**skonsult|ować (-uję, -ujesz)** *vb perf od* **konsultować**
**skonsum|ować (-uję, -ujesz)** *vb perf od* **konsumować**
**skontakt|ować (-uję, -ujesz)** *vb perf od* **kontaktować**
**skontrol|ować (-uję, -ujesz)** *vb perf od* **kontrolować**
**skończony** *adj* (*zakończony*) finished; (*kompletny*) utter, absolute; (*Mat*) finite; **jesteś ~** (*pot*) you're finished
**skończ|yć (-ę, -ysz)** *vb perf od* **kończyć**
**skoordyn|ować (-uję, -ujesz)** *vb perf od* **koordynować**
**sko|pać (-pię, -piesz)** *vt perf* (*ogródek*) to dig; **~ kogoś** to kick sb black and blue
**skopi|ować (-uję, -ujesz)** *vb perf od* **kopiować**
**skor|ek** (**-ka, -ki**) (*instr sg* **-kiem**) *m* (*Zool*) earwig
**skoro** *conj* (*ponieważ*) since, as; **~ tylko** as soon as; **~ świt** at the break of day, at daybreak
**skorod|ować (-uje)** *vb perf od* **korodować**
**skoroszy|t** (**-tu, -ty**) (*loc sg* **-cie**) *m* file
**skorowidz** (**-a, -e**) *m* index
**skorpio|n** (**-na, -ny**) (*loc sg* **-nie**) *m* (*Zool*) scorpion; (*Astrologia*) Scorpio
**skorumpowany** *adj* corrupt
**skoru|pa** (**-py, -py**) (*dat sg* **-pie**) *f* (*orzecha, ślimaka*) shell; **~ ziemska** the earth's crust
**skorupia|k** (**-ka, -ki**) (*instr sg* **-kiem**) *m* (*Zool*) crustacean
**skorup|ka** (**-ki, -ki**) (*dat sg* **-ce**, *gen pl* **-ek**) *f* shell; **~ (od) jajka** eggshell; **obrać** (*perf*) **ze skorupki** to shell
**skory** *adj*: **~ do nauki/pomocy** willing to learn/help
**skoryg|ować (-uję, -ujesz)** *vb perf od* **korygować**
**skorzyst|ać (-am, -asz)** *vb perf od* **korzystać**
**sko|s** (**-su, -sy**) (*loc sg* **-sie**) *m* (*ukośna powierzchnia*) slant; **na** *lub* **w ~** at *lub* on a slant
**sko|sić (-szę, -sisz)** (*imp* **-ś**) *vb perf od* **kosić**
**skostniały** *adj* (*zdrętwiały*) stiff; (*tradycyjny, stały*) fossilized
**skoszt|ować (-uję, -ujesz)** *vb perf od* **kosztować**
**skośnie** *adv* aslant

**skośnooki** *adj* slant-eyed
**skośny** *adj* (*oczy*) slanting; (*pasek, promień*) diagonal
**skowron|ek** (**-ka, -ki**) (*instr sg* **-kiem**) *m* lark
**skowycz|eć (-y)** (*perf* **za-**) *vi* (*o psie*) to yelp
**skowy|t** (**-tu, -ty**) (*loc sg* **-cie**) *m* yelp
**skó|ra** (**-ry, -ry**) (*dat sg* **-rze**) *f* (*u człowieka, zwierząt*) skin; (*u zwierząt gruboskórnych*) hide; (*materiał*) leather; **torba ze skóry** leather bag; **~ i kości** (*pot: chudzielec*) bag of bones (*pot*), (all) skin and bone (*pot*); **dać** *perf* **komuś w skórę** to tan sb's hide; **przekonać się** *perf* **o czymś na własnej skórze** to learn sth the hard way; **być w czyjejś skórze** (*przen*) to be in sb's shoes; **wychodzić** *lub* **wyłazić ze skóry** (*przen*) to bend over backwards
**skór|ka** (**-ki, -ki**) (*dat sg* **-ce**, *gen pl* **-ek**) *f dimin od* **skóra**; (*przy paznokciu*) cuticle; (*zadzior przy paznokciu*) hangnail; (*chleba*) crust; (*cytryny, pomarańczy, banana*) peel; (*winogrona, ziemniaka*) skin; (*melona*) rind; (*futerko*) pelt; **gęsia ~** gooseflesh, goose(-)pimples
**skórkowy** *adj* leather *attr*
**skórzany** *adj* leather *attr*
**skrac|ać (-am, -asz)** (*perf* **skrócić**) *vt* to shorten; (*artykuł, książkę, film*) to shorten, to abridge; (*wyraz*) to abbreviate; **skrócić referat do pięciu minut/dwóch stron** to shorten *lub* cut the paper down to five minutes/two pages; **~ sobie drogę** to take a short cut; **~ (sobie) czymś czas** to keep o.s. occupied with sth
**skrad|ać się (-am, -asz)** *vr* to sneak, to steal
**skraj** (**-u, -e**) *m* edge; **na ~u nędzy/przepaści** on the brink of poverty/a precipice
**skrajnoś|ć** (**-ci, -ci**) (*gen pl* **-ci**) *f* extremity; **z jednej skrajności w drugą** from one extreme to the other
**skrajny** *adj* extreme
**skrapi|ać (-am, -asz)** (*perf* **skropić**) *vt* to sprinkle
**skrapl|ać (-am, -asz)** (*perf* **skroplić**) *vt* to condense; **skraplać się** *vr* to condense
**skra|ść (-dnę, -dniesz)** (*imp* **-dnij**, *pt* **-dł, -dli**) *vb perf od* **kraść**
**skrawani|e** (**-a**) *nt* (*Tech*) machine cutting
**skraw|ek** (**-ka, -ki**) (*instr sg* **-kiem**) *m* (*papieru, tkaniny*) scrap; (*nieba, ziemi*) patch
**skreśl|ać (-am, -asz)** (*perf* **-ić**) *vt* (*usuwać*) to delete, to remove; (*zaznaczać*) to cross out, to strike off
**skrę|cać (-cam, -casz)** (*perf* **-cić**) *vt* (*linę, sznurek*) to weave, to twine; (*papierosa*) to roll; (*meble*) to screw together ▷ *vi* (*o pojeździe, drodze*) to turn; **~ w lewo/ulicę Długą** to turn left/into Długa street; **skręć w drugą w prawo** take the second (turn to the) right; **skręca mnie z głodu** (*pot*) I'm starving (*pot*); **skręcać się** *vr* (*zwijać się*) to writhe; **~ się z bólu** to writhe in pain; **~ się ze śmiechu** to double up with laughter
**skrę|cić (-cę, -cisz)** (*imp* **-ć**) *vb perf od* **skręcać** ▷ *vt perf* (*nogę, ramię*) to sprain; **~ nogę w kostce** to sprain *lub* twist an ankle; **~ kark** to break one's neck
**skręp|ować (-uję, -ujesz)** *vb perf od* **krępować**
**skrępowani|e** (**-a**) *nt* embarrassment
**skrępowany** *adj* (*onieśmielony*) ill-at-ease, embarrassed; (*związany*) tied (up)
**skrę|t** (**-tu, -ty**) (*loc sg* **-cie**) *m* (*ruch*) turn; (*miejsce*) bend, turn; (*pot: skręcony papieros*) roll-up (*pot*), roll-your-own (*pot*); **zakaz ~u w lewo** no left turn; **wykonać** (*perf*) **~** to make a turn; **~ jelit** *lub* **kiszek** (*Med*) volvulus
**skro|bać (-bię, -biesz)** *vt* (*farbę, brud*) (*perf* **ze-**) to scrape off; (*ziemniaki, rybę*) (*perf* **o-**) to scrape; (*drapać*) (*perf* **po-**) to scratch; (*pot: bazgrać*) (*perf* **na-**) to scribble, to scrawl
**skroban|ka** (**-ki, -ki**) (*dat sg* **-ce**, *gen pl* **-ek**) *f* (*zabieg*) abortion
**skro|bia** (**-bi**) *f* starch
**skrob|nąć (-nę, -niesz)** (*imp* **-nij**) *vt perf* (*pot: napisać*) to dash down *lub* off (*pot*)
**skr|oić (-oję, -oisz)** (*imp* **-ój**) *vb perf od* **kroić, skrawać**; (*Krawiectwo*) to tailor
**skrojony** *adj* (*Krawiectwo*): **dobrze ~** well-tailored
**skromnie** *adv* modestly
**skromnoś|ć** (**-ci**) *f* modesty
**skromny** *adj* modest
**skro|ń** (**-ni, -nie**) (*gen pl* **-ni**) *f* temple
**skro|pić (-pię, -pisz)** *vb perf od* **skrapiać**
**skropl|ić (-ę, -isz)** *vb perf od* **skraplać**
**skró|cić (-cę, -cisz)** (*imp* **-ć**) *vb perf od* **skracać**
**skrócony** *adj* shortened; (*wersja książki*) abridged
**skró|t** (**-tu, -ty**) (*loc sg* **-cie**) *m* (*Jęz*) abbreviation; (*przemówienia, artykułu*) summary; (*w powieści, filmie*) cut; (*krótsza droga*) short cut; **w skrócie** in short; **iść (pójść** *perf*) **na ~y** to take a short cut
**skrótowy** *adj* shortened
**skru|cha** (**-chy**) (*dat sg* **-sze**) *f* repentance; **okazywać (okazać** *perf*) **skruchę** to repent
**skrupulatnie** *adv* meticulously
**skrupulatnoś|ć** (**-ci**) *f* meticulousness, precision
**skrupulatny** *adj* meticulous
**skrupuł|y** (**-ów**) *pl* scruples *pl*; **robić coś bez skrupułów** not to have scruples about doing sth; **pozbawiony skrupułów** unscrupulous
**skrusz|eć (-eje)** *vi perf* (*o murze, skale*) to crumble; (*o mięsie*) to become tender
**skruszony** *adj* apologetic

S

**skrusz|yć (-ę, -ysz)** *vb perf od* **kruszyć**
**skrycie** *adv* secretly
**skry|ć (-ję, -jesz)** *vb perf od* **skrywać**
**skryp|t** (**-tu, -ty**) (*loc sg* **-cie**) *m printed series of course lectures*
**skryt|ka** (**-ki, -ki**) (*dat sg* **-ce**, *gen pl* **-ek**) *f* (*w biurku, ścianie*) hiding place; (*w samochodzie*) glove compartment; ~ **pocztowa** post-office box
**skrytobójc|a** (**-y, -y**) *m* assassin
**skrytobójczy** *adj* treacherous
**skrytoś|ć** (**-ci**) *f* secretiveness; **w skrytości ducha** *lub* **serca** in one's heart of hearts, at heart
**skryty** *adj* (*człowiek*) secretive; (*uczucia, zamiary*) secret
**skrytyk|ować (-uję, -ujesz)** *vb perf od* **krytykować**
**skryw|ać (-am, -asz)** (*perf* **skryć**) *vt* to conceal; **skrywać się** *vr* to hide (away *lub* up)
**skrza|t** (**-ta, -ty**) (*loc sg* **-cie**) *m* goblin
**skrzecz|eć (-ę, -ysz)** *vi* to croak
**skrze|k** (**-ku**) (*instr sg* **-kiem**) *m* (*odgłos*) croak; (*Zool*) spawn
**skrzel|e** (**-a, -a**) (*gen pl* **-i**) *nt* (*Zool*) gill
**skrze|p** (**-pu, -py**) (*loc sg* **-pie**) *m* (*też*: **skrzep krwi**) blood clot
**skrzep|nąć (-nie)** *vb perf od* **krzepnąć**
**skrzętny** *adj* thrifty
**skrzycz|eć (-ę, -ysz)** *vt perf* to scold
**skrz|yć się (-y)** *vr* to sparkle
**skrzydeł|ko** (**-ka, -ka**) (*instr sg* **-kiem**, *gen pl* **-ek**) *nt dimin od* **skrzydło**
**skrzydlaty** *adj* winged
**skrzyd|ło** (**-ła, -ła**) (*loc sg* **-le**, *gen pl* **-eł**) *nt* wing; (*wentylatora, śruby*) blade; (*okna*) sash; (*Wojsk*) flank; **brać (wziąć** *perf***) kogoś pod swoje skrzydła** to take sb under one's wing; **dodawać (dodać** *perf***) komuś skrzydeł** to lend wings to sb; **pędzić jak na skrzydłach** to run like the wind
**skrzydłowy** *adj* (*Sport*) wing *attr*; (*Wojsk*) flank *attr* ▷ *m decl like adj* (*Sport*) wing(er)
**skrzy|nia** (**-ni, -nie**) (*gen pl* **-ń**) *f* chest, crate; (*nadwozie ciężarówki*) (loading) platform; (*urządzenie gimnastyczne*) box; ~ **biegów** (*Mot*) gearbox
**skrzyn|ka** (**-ki, -ki**) (*dat sg* **-ce**, *gen pl* **-ek**) *f dimin od* **skrzynia**; (*na rośliny*) window box; (*obudowa*) case; ~ **pocztowa** *lub* **na listy** (*na drzwiach domu*) letter-box (Brit), mailbox (US); ~ **pocztowa** (*na poczcie, ulicy*) post-box (Brit), mailbox (US); **czarna** ~ black box
**skrzy|p** (**-pu, -py**) (*loc sg* **-pie**) *m* (*Bot*) horsetail
**skrzypacz|ka** (**-ki, -ki**) (*dat sg* **-ce**, *gen pl* **-ek**) *f* violinist
**skrzy|pce** (**-piec**) *pl* violin *sg*; **pierwsze/drugie** ~ (*Muz*) first/second violin; **grać pierwsze/drugie** ~ (*przen*) to play first/second fiddle
**skrzypcowy** *adj* violin *attr*
**skrzyp|ek** (**-ka, -kowie**) (*instr sg* **-kiem**) *m* violinist
**skrzy|pieć (-pi)** (*perf* **-pnąć**) *vi* (*o drzwiach*) to creak; (*o butach*) to squeak; (*o śniegu*) to crunch
**skrzyp|nąć (-nie)** *vb perf od* **skrzypieć**
**skrzyw|dzić (-dzę, -dzisz)** (*imp* **-dź**) *vb perf od* **krzywdzić**
**skrzy|wić (-wię, -wisz)** *vb perf od* **krzywić** ▷ *vt perf* (*prawdę, słowa*) to twist; (*rzeczywistość, prawdę*) to distort
**skrzywieni|e** (**-a**) *nt* (*grymas*) (wry) face; ~ **kręgosłupa** curvature of the spine
**skrzyż|ować (-uję, -ujesz)** *vb perf od* **krzyżować**
**skrzyżowa|nie** (**-nia, -nia**) (*gen pl* **-ń**) *nt* intersection
**skser|ować (-uję, -ujesz)** *vb perf od* **kserować**
**sku|bać (-bię, -biesz)** *vt* (*szarpać*) (*perf* **-bnąć**) to pluck; (*wyrywać*) (*perf* **wy-**) to pluck; (*o zwierzętach: zrywać i jeść*) (*perf* **-bnąć**) to nibble; (*odzierać z piór*) (*perf* **wy-**) to pluck
**skub|nąć (-nę, -niesz)** (*imp* **-nij**) *vb perf od* **skubać**
**sku|ć (-ję, -jesz)** *vb perf od* **skuwać**
**skul|ić (-ę, -isz)** *vb perf od* **kulić**
**skunk|s** (**-sa, -sy**) (*loc sg* **-sie**) *m* skunk
**sku|p** (**-pu, -py**) (*loc sg* **-pie**) *m* purchase; ~ **butelek** bottle return; ~ **makulatury** *paper recycling*
**sku|piać (-piam, -piasz)** (*perf* **-pić**) *vt* (*gromadzić*) to assemble, to gather; (*koncentrować*) to concentrate; ~ **myśli** to collect one's thoughts; ~ **uwagę na czymś** to focus one's attention on sth; ~ **na sobie uwagę** to attract attention; **skupiać się** *vr* (*gromadzić się*) to assemble, to gather; (*o życiu, działalności*) to concentrate; (*o człowieku*) to concentrate
**skupie|nie** (**-nia**) *nt* concentration
**skupiony** *adj* (*człowiek*) focused, concentrated; (*wyraz twarzy*) intent
**skupis|ko** (**-ka, -ka**) (*instr sg* **-kiem**) *nt* cluster
**sku|pować (-puję, -pujesz)** (*perf* **-pić**) *vt* to buy; (*butelki*) to buy (back)
**skurcz** (**-u, -e**) *m* cramp; ~ **szyi** crick in the neck; ~ **mnie złapał** I've got (a) cramp
**skurczyby|k** (**-ka, -ki**) (*instr sg* **-kiem**) *m* (*pot*) son of a gun (*pot*)
**skurcz|yć (-ę, -ysz)** *vb perf od* **kurczyć**
**skurwysy|n** (**-na, -ny**) (*loc sg* **-nie**) *m* (*pot!*) motherfucker (*pot!*)
**sku|sić (-szę, -sisz)** (*imp* **-ś**) *vt perf* to tempt; **skusić się** *vr*: ~ **się (na coś)** to feel *lub* be tempted (to do sth)

**skutecznoś|ć** (**-ci**) *f* effectiveness, efficacy
**skuteczny** *adj* (*działanie, lekarstwo*) effective, efficacious; (*broń*) effective
**skut|ek** (**-ku, -ki**) (*instr sg* **-kiem**) *m* result, effect; **(aż) do skutku** to the bitter end; **bez skutku** to no effect; **dojść** (*perf*) **do skutku** to come into effect; **nie dojść** (*perf*) **do skutku** not to come into effect, to come to nothing; **na ~ czegoś** as a result of sth; **ponosić (ponieść** (*perf*)**) skutki czegoś** to bear consequences of sth
**skute|r** (**-ra, -ry**) (*loc sg* **-rze**) *m* scooter
**skutk|ować (-uje)** (*perf* **po-**) *vi* to be effective *lub* efficacious, to work
**skuw|ać (-am, -asz)** (*perf* **skuć**) *vt* (*w łańcuchy*) to chain; (*w kajdanki*) to handcuff
**skwapliwie** *adv* eagerly
**skwapliwoś|ć** (**-ci**) *f* eagerness
**skwapliwy** *adj* eager
**skwa|r** (**-ru**) (*loc sg* **-rze**) *m* heat
**skwar|ki** (**-ków** *lub* **-ek**) *pl* (*Kulin*) pork scratchings *pl* (*Brit*)
**skwarny** *adj* sweltering
**skwaszony** *adj* sour
**skwe|r** (**-ru, -ry**) (*loc sg* **-rze**) *m* square
**skwiercz|eć (-y)** *vi* to sizzle
**skwit|ować (-uję, -ujesz)** *vb perf od* **kwitować**
**slaj|d** (**-du, -dy**) (*loc sg* **-dzie**) *m* slide
**slalo|m** (**-mu, -my**) (*loc sg* **-mie**) *m* slalom
**slan|g** (**-gu, -gi**) (*instr sg* **-giem**) *m* (*Jęz*) slang
**slawisty|ka** (**-ki**) (*dat sg* **-ce**) *f* Slavic studies
**SLD** *abbr* (= *Sojusz Lewicy Demokratycznej*) Democratic Left Alliance
**slip|y** (**-ów**) *pl* briefs *pl*
**sloga|n** (**-nu, -ny**) (*loc sg* **-nie**) *m* slogan
**slums|y** (**-ów**) *pl* slums *pl*
**słabeusz** (**-a, -e**) (*gen pl* **-y** *lub* **-ów**) *m* weakling
**słab|nąć (-nę, -niesz)** (*imp* **-nij**, *perf* **o-**) *vi* (*tracić siły*) to weaken, to grow weaker; (*o zainteresowaniu*) to diminish, to decline; (*o wietrze, ruchu*) to die down; (*o bólu, trudnościach*) to ease off
**słabo** *adv* weakly; (*widoczny, zaludniony*) poorly; (*marnie*) poorly; **~ mi** I feel faint
**słaboś|ć** (**-ci**) *f* weakness; (*wada*) (*nom pl* **-ci**, *gen pl* **-ci**) weakness; **mieć ~ do** *+gen* to have a weakness for
**słabowity** *adj* frail
**słaby** *adj* weak; (*uczeń, zdrowie*) poor; **mieć słabą głowę** to have a weak head; **~ punkt** *lub* **słaba strona** (*przen*) a weak point; **być ~m z czegoś** *lub* **w czymś** to be poor *lub* weak in *lub* at sth
**słać**[1] **(ślę, ślesz)** (*imp* **ślij**, *perf* **po-** *lub* **wy-**) *vt* (*książk*) to send
**słać**[2] **(ścielę, ścielisz)** (*perf* **po-** *lub* **za-**) *vt*: **~ łóżko** to make the bed; **słać się** *vr* to float
**słani|ać się (-am, -asz)** *vr* (*też*: **słaniać się na nogach**) to stagger
**sła|wa** (**-wy**) (*dat sg* **-wie**) *f* (*rozgłos*) fame; (*reputacja*) reputation; **światowej sławy muzyk** a world-famous musician; (*pot: sławny człowiek*) celebrity, celeb (*pot*); **cieszyć się dobrą/złą sławą** to have a good/bad reputation; **zdobyć** (*perf*) **sławę** to make a name for o.s.
**sławetny** *adj* glorious
**sła|wić (-wię, -wisz)** *vt* to praise
**sławny** *adj* famous
**słodki** *adj* sweet; **słodka woda** fresh water
**słodko-kwaśny** *adj* (*Kulin*) sweet and sour
**słodkoś|ć** (**-ci**) *f* sweetness; **słodkości** *pl* (*pot: słodycze*) sweets *pl* (*Brit*), candy (*US*)
**słodkowodny** *adj* fresh-water *attr*
**słodu** *itd. n patrz* **słód**
**słodycz** (**-y**) *f* sweetness; (*przen*) bliss; **słodycze** *pl* sweets *pl* (*Brit*), candy (*US*)
**sł|odzić (-odzę, -odzisz)** (*imp* **-ódź** *lub* **-odź**, *perf* **o-** *lub* **po-**) *vt* to sweeten; **czy słodzisz herbatę?** do you take sugar in your tea?
**słodzi|k** (**-ku, -ki**) (*instr sg* **-kiem**) *m* sweetener
**słoi** *n patrz* **słój**
**słoi|k** (**-ka, -ki**) (*instr sg* **-kiem**) *m* jar
**słoja** *itd. n patrz* **słój**
**sło|ma** (**-my**) (*dat sg* **-mie**) *f* straw
**słomian|ka** (**-ki, -ki**) (*dat sg* **-ce**, *gen pl* **-ek**) *f* doormat
**słomiany** *adj* straw *attr*; **~ zapał** *lub* **ogień** (*przen*) a flash in the pan; **~ wdowiec** (*przen*) grass widower
**słom|ka** (**-ki, -ki**) (*dat sg* **-ce**, *gen pl* **-ek**) *f* straw
**słomkowy** *adj* (*kapelusz*) straw *attr*; **w kolorze ~m** straw-coloured (*Brit*), straw-colored (*US*)
**słonawy** *adj* (slightly) salty
**słonecznie** *adv*: **jest ~** it is sunny
**słoneczni|k** (**-ka, -ki**) (*instr sg* **-kiem**) *m* sunflower
**słoneczny** *adj* (*dzień, pokój*) sunny; (*energia*) solar; **światło słoneczne** sunlight; **porażenie słoneczne** sunstroke; **zegar ~** sundial; **okulary słoneczne** sunglasses *pl*; **Układ S~** solar system; **splot ~** (*Anat*) solar plexus
**słonic|a** (**-y, -e**) *f* cow elephant
**słoni|na** (**-ny**) (*dat sg* **-nie**) *f* pork fat
**słoniowy** *adj*: **kość słoniowa** ivory
**słono** *adv* (*przyprawić*) saltily; **płacić (zapłacić** *perf*) **~** to pay through the nose
**słony** *adj* (*potrawa*) salty; (*woda*) salt *attr*; (*przen: cena*) steep; **~ dowcip** a spicy joke
**sło|ń** (**-nia, -nie**) (*gen pl* **-ni**) *m* (*Zool*) elephant
**słońc|e** (**-a**) *nt* (*Astron*) (*nom pl* **-a**) sun; (*światło słoneczne*) sun(light), sunshine; **w** *lub* **na słońcu** in the sun *lub* sunshine; **jasne jak ~**

S

(as) clear as day; **najlepszy pod ~m** the best under the sun
**sło|ta** (**-ty, -ty**) (*dat sg* **-cie**) *f* drizzly weather
**Słowacj|a** (**-i**) *f* Slovakia
**słowacki** *adj* Slovak(ian) ▷ *m decl like adj* (*język*) Slovak
**Słowacz|ka** (**-ki, -ki**) (*dat sg* **-ce**, *gen pl* **-ek**) *f* Slovak
**Słowa|k** (**-ka, -cy**) (*instr sg* **-kiem**) *m* Slovak
**Słoweni|a** (**-i**) *f* Slovenia
**Słowe|niec** (**-ńca, -ńcy**) *m* Slovene, Slovenian
**Słowen|ka** (**-ki, -ki**) (*dat sg* **-ce**, *gen pl* **-ek**) *f* Slovene, Slovenian
**słoweński** *adj* Slovene, Slovenian ▷ *m decl like adj* (*język*) Slovene
**Słowia|nin** (**-nina, -nie**) (*loc sg* **-ninie**, *gen pl* **-n**) *m* Slav
**Słowian|ka** (**-ki, -ki**) (*dat sg* **-ce**, *gen pl* **-ek**) *f* Slav
**słowiański** *adj* (*rasa, kultura*) Slavic; (*język*) Slavonic
**słowi|k** (**-ka, -ki**) (*instr sg* **-kiem**) *m* nightingale
**słownict|wo** (**-wa**) (*loc sg* **-wie**) *nt* vocabulary
**słownicz|ek** (**-ka, -ki**) (*instr sg* **-kiem**) *m* glossary
**słownie** *adv*: **napisać** *perf* **sumę ~** to write the amount in words
**słowni|k** (**-ka, -ki**) (*instr sg* **-kiem**) *m* (*książka*) dictionary; (*słownictwo*) vocabulary; **~ polsko-angielski** a Polish-English dictionary
**słowny** *adj* (*wyjaśnienie*) verbal; (*człowiek*) dependable, reliable; **~ człowiek** a man of his word
**sł|owo** (**-owa, -owa**) (*loc sg* **-owie**, *gen pl* **-ów**) *nt* word; **słowem** in a word; **innymi słowy** in other words; **~ w ~** word for word; **~ honoru!** my word of honour (*Brit*) *lub* honor (*US*)!; **dawać (dać** *perf***) (komuś) ~** to give (sb) one's word; **~ wstępne** foreword, preface; **w dwóch słowach** in a word, in short *lub* brief; **gra słów** pun, play on words; **przerywać (przerwać** *perf***) komuś w pół słowa** to cut sb short; **brak mi słów** I'm lost for words; **trzymać kogoś za ~** to hold sb to their promise; **wierzyć komuś na ~** to take sb's word (for it); **dotrzymywać (dotrzymać** *perf***) słowa** to keep one's word; **on nie przebiera w słowach** he does not mince his words; **czy mógłbym zamienić z tobą dwa słowa?** could I have a word with you?; **wyrażać (wyrazić** *perf***) coś słowami** to put sth into words; **słowa** *pl* (*tekst piosenki*) lyrics *pl*
**słowotwórst|wo** (**-wa**) (*loc sg* **-wie**) *nt* (*Jęz*) word formation
**sł|ód** (**-odu**) (*loc sg* **-odzie**) *m* malt
**słódź** *itd. vb patrz* **słodzić**
**sł|ój** (**-oja, -oje**) (*gen pl* **-ojów** *lub* **-oi**) *m* (*naczynie*) jar; (*w drewnie*) ring
**słów** *n patrz* **słowo**
**słów|ko** (**-ka, -ka**) (*instr sg* **-kiem**) *nt dimin od* **słowo**; **czułe słówka** terms of endearment; **piękne słówka** (*pej*) glib words; **słówka** *pl* (*Szkol*) vocabulary
**słuch** (**-u**) *m* (*zmysł*) hearing; (*muzyczny*) (an) ear for music; **mieć dobry ~** to have a good ear for music; **mieć słaby ~** to be hard of hearing; **grać ze ~u** to play by ear; **zamieniać się (zamienić się** *perf***) w ~** (*pot*) to be all ears; **~ o nim zaginął** he was not heard of any more; **słuchy** *pl*: **chodzą ~y, że ...** rumour (*Brit*) *lub* rumor (*US*) has it that ...
**słuchacz** (**-a, -e**) (*gen pl* **-y**) *m* (*radiowy*) listener; (*uczestnik studium*) student; (*uczestnik kursu*) (course) participant
**słuch|ać** (**-am, -asz**) *vt +gen* to listen to; (*być posłusznym*) (*perf* **u-** *lub* **po-**) to obey ▷ *vi* to obey; **~ radia** to listen to the radio; **~ muzyki** to listen to music; **słucham?** (*halo?*) hallo?, hello?; (*nie dosłyszałem*) sorry?, pardon?; **słuchaj!** look (here)!; **nie ~ (po~** *perf***)** to disobey
**słuchaw|ka** (**-ki, -ki**) (*dat sg* **-ce**, *gen pl* **-ek**) *f* (*telefoniczna*) receiver; (*do radia*) earphone; (*Med*) stethoscope; **podnosić słuchawkę** to pick up *lub* answer the phone; **proszę nie odkładać słuchawki!** hold the line!, hold on!; **słuchawki** *pl* (*na uszy*) headphones *pl*, earphones *pl*
**słuchowis|ko** (**-ka, -ka**) (*instr sg* **-kiem**) *nt* radio drama
**słuchowy** *adj* auditory *attr*; **aparat ~** hearing aid
**słu|ga** (**-gi, -dzy**) (*dat sg* **-dze**) *m decl like f* (*książk*) servant; **~ boży** servant of God
**słu|p** (**-pa, -py**) (*loc sg* **-pie**) *m* (*telefoniczny*) pole; (*wysokiego napięcia*) pylon; (*latarni*) post; (*dymu, ognia*) column
**słup|ek** (**-ka, -ki**) (*instr sg* **-kiem**) *m* (*mały słup*) post; (*blokujący wjazd*) bollard; (*Sport: bramki*) (goal)post; (*liczb, cyfr*) column; (*Bot*) pistil; **~ rtęci** mercury column
**słupkowy** *adj*: **wykres ~** bar chart
**słusznie** *adv* (*sprawiedliwie*) rightly; **~!** (that's) right!
**słusznoś|ć** (**-ci**) *f* (*uzasadnienie*) legitimacy; **mieć ~** to be right; **nie mieć słuszności** to be wrong; **przyznawać (przyznać** *perf***) komuś ~** to admit that sb is right
**słuszny** *adj* (*rozumowanie, pogląd*) correct; (*pretensje*) legitimate; (*wyrok*) justified
**służalczy** *adj* (*pej*) servile
**służąc|a** (**-ej, -e**) *f decl like adj* servant, maid
**służąc|y** (**-ego, -y**) *m decl like adj* servant

**służ|ba** (**-by, -by**) (*dat sg* **-bie**) *f* service; (*obowiązki, dyżur*) duty; (*służący*) servants *pl*; **~ zdrowia/wojskowa** health/military service; **być na służbie/po służbie** to be on/ off duty
**służbi|sta** (**-sty, -ści**) (*dat sg* **-ście**) *m decl like f in sg* bureaucrat
**służbowo** *adv* on business
**służbowy** *adj* (*wyjazd*) business *attr*; (*stopień, tajemnica*) official; **samochód ~** company car; **drogą służbową** through official channels
**służ|yć (-ę, -ysz)** *vi* to serve; (*o psie*) to beg; (*o odzieży, sprzęcie*) to be useful; **~ (komuś) radą/ pomocą** to offer one's advice/help (to sb); **~ do czegoś** to be designed for sth; **~ u kogoś** to be in sb's service; **~ za coś** to serve as *lub* for sth; **~ w wojsku** to serve in the army; **~ ojczyźnie/sprawie** to serve the country/ cause; **~ komuś** (*o klimacie, powietrzu*) to do sb good; **zdrowie jej służy** she enjoys good health; **czym mogę (Panu/Pani) ~?** can I help you (, Sir/Madam)?; **do czego to służy?** what's this for?
**słychać** *vi inv*; **~ było muzykę** music could be heard; **~, że ...** there's news that ...; **nic nie ~** I can't hear a thing; **co ~?** how are things? (*Brit*), what's up? (*US*)
**sły|nąć (-nę, -niesz)** (*imp* **-ń**) *vi*: **~ (z czegoś)** to be famous (for sth)
**słynny** *adj* famous
**słyszalnoś|ć** (**-ci**) *f* audibility
**słyszalny** *adj* audible
**słysz|eć (-ę, -ysz)** *vt* (*perf* **u-**) (*głos, hałas*) to hear ▷ *vi* (*mieć słuch*) to hear; **słyszysz mnie?** can you hear me?; **nie chcę o tym ~** I don't want to hear about it; **czy słyszałeś o tym?** have you heard about it?; **nigdy nie słyszałam o tym filmie** I've never heard of that film; **pierwsze słyszę** this is news to me
**słyszeni|e** (**-a**) *nt*: **znać kogoś/coś ze słyszenia** to have heard of sb/sth
**smaczny** *adj* (*obiad, zupa*) tasty; **smacznego!** bon appétit!; (*kelner do gościa*) enjoy your meal!
**smag|ać (-am, -asz)** (*perf* **-nąć**) *vt* (*batem*) to whip; (*o deszczu, wietrze*) to lash
**smagły** *adj* swarthy
**smag|nąć (-nę, -niesz)** (*imp* **-nij**) *vb perf od* **smagać**
**sma|k** (**-ku**) (*instr sg* **-kiem**) *m* taste; (*potrawy*) (*nom pl* **-ki**) taste, flavour (*Brit*), flavor (*US*); **bez ~u** tasteless; **przyprawić** (*perf*) **coś do ~u** to season sth to taste; **ze ~iem** (*przyrządzać, ozdabiać*) tastefully; (*jeść*) with gusto
**smakoły|k** (**-ku, -ki**) (*instr sg* **-kiem**) *m* delicacy
**smakosz** (**-a, -e**) (*gen pl* **-y** *lub* **-ów**) *m* gourmet
**smak|ować (-uję, -ujesz)** *vt* (*próbować*) (*perf* **po-**) to taste ▷ *vi*: **~ świetnie** to taste excellent; **to mi nie smakuje** I don't like it
**smakowity** *adj* appetizing
**smal|ec** (**-cu**) *m* lard
**sma|r** (**-ru, -ry**) (*loc sg* **-rze**) *m* (*Tech*) grease, lubricant
**smar|k** (**-ku, -ki**) (*instr sg* **-kiem**) *m* (*pot*) snot (*pot*)
**smarkacz** (**-a, -e**) (*gen pl* **-y** *lub* **-ów**) *m* (*pot: pej*) snotnose (*pot*)
**smark|ać (-am, -asz)** (*perf* **-nąć**) *vi* (*pot*) to blow one's nose
**smarkaty** *adj* (*pot*) wet behind the ears (*pot*)
**smark|nąć (-nę, -niesz)** (*imp* **-nij**) *vb perf od* **smarkać**
**smarkul|a** (**-i, -e**) *f* (*pot*) teenybopper (*pot*)
**smar|ować (-uję, -ujesz)** *vt* (*chleb masłem*) (*perf* **po-**) to butter; (*zawiasy*) (*perf* **na-**) to grease, to lubricate; (*pot: mazać, brudzić*) (*perf* **wy-**) to smear; **~ chleb margaryną/dżemem** to spread margarine/jam on one's bread; **~ stół farbą** to smear paint all over the table; **~ palec maścią** to apply ointment to a finger; **smarować się** *vr* (*kremem, olejkiem*) (*perf* **na-**) to put on cream/oil
**smarownic|a** (**-y, -e**) *f* (*Tech*) grease gun
**smartpho|ne** (**-ne'a, -ne'y**) (*loc sg* **-ne'ie**) *m* smartphone
**smażal|nia** (**-ni, -nie**) (*gen pl* **-ni**) *f* fried food stand
**smażony** *adj* fried
**smaż|yć (-ę, -ysz)** (*perf* **u-**) *vt* to fry; **smażyć się** *vr* to fry
**smecz** (**-u, -e**) (*gen pl* **-ów**) *m* (*Sport*) smash
**smętny** *adj* (*książk*) cheerless
**smocz|ek** (**-ka, -ki**) (*instr sg* **-kiem**) *m* dummy (*Brit*), pacifier (*US*), comforter (*US*); (*na butelkę*) teat
**smo|g** (**-gu, -gi**) (*instr sg* **-giem**) *m* smog
**smo|k** (**-ka, -ki**) (*instr sg* **-kiem**) *m* dragon
**smokin|g** (**-gu, -gi**) (*instr sg* **-giem**) *m* dinner jacket (*Brit*), tuxedo (*US*)
**sm|oła** (**-oły, -oły**) (*dat sg* **-ole**, *gen pl* **-ół**) *f* tar; **czarny jak ~** pitch-black; **ruszać się jak mucha w smole** (*pot*) to move at a snail's pace
**smoł|ować (-uję, -ujesz)** (*perf* **wy-**) *vt* to tar
**smrodliwy** *adj* stinky
**smro|dzić (-dzę, -dzisz)** (*imp* **-dź**) *vi* to give off a stench
**smr|ód** (**-odu, -ody**) (*loc sg* **-odzie**) *m* stench, stink
**SMS** (**SMS-a, SMS-y**) (*loc sg* **SMS-ie**) *m* text message
**smu|cić (-cę, -cisz)** (*imp* **-ć**, *perf* **za-**) *vt* to sadden; **smucić się** *vr* to be sad

S

**smu|ga** (**-gi, -gi**) (*dat sg* **-dze**) *f* (*samolotu, dymu*) trail

**smukły** *adj* slender

**smut|ek** (**-ku, -ki**) (*instr sg* **-kiem**) *m* sadness, sorrow; **ze smutkiem** with sadness

**smutni|eć (-eję, -ejesz)** (*pt* **-ał, -eli**, *perf* **po-**) *vi* to grow sad

**smutno** *adv* (*patrzeć, kiwać głową*) sadly, sorrowfully; **~ mi** I feel sad

**smutny** *adj* sad

**smycz** (**-y, -e**) (*gen pl* **-y**) *f* lead, leash

**smycz|ek** (**-ka, -ki**) (*instr sg* **-kiem**) *m* (*Muz*) bow; **smyczki** *pl* (*w orkiestrze*) strings *pl*

**smyczkowy** *adj*: **kwartet ~** string quartet; **instrumenty smyczkowe** stringed instruments

**smy|k** (**-ka, -ki**) (*instr sg* **-kiem**) *m* (*pot*) kid (*pot*)

**smykał|ka** (**-ki**) (*dat sg* **-ce**) *f* (*pot*): **mieć smykałkę do czegoś** to have a flair for sth

**snajpe|r** (**-ra, -rzy**) (*loc sg* **-rze**) *m* sniper

**sno|b** (**-ba, -bi** *lub* **-by**) (*loc sg* **-bie**) *m* snob

**snobistyczny** *adj* snobbish

**snobiz|m** (**-mu**) (*loc sg* **-mie**) *m* snobbery

**sno|p** (**-pa, -py**) (*loc sg* **-pie**) *m* (*żyta*) sheaf; (*światła*) beam

**snopowiązał|ka** (**-ki, -ki**) (*dat sg* **-ce**, *gen pl* **-ek**) *f* sheaf-binder

**snowboar|d** (**-du, -dy**) (*loc sg* **-dzie**) *m* snowboard

**snu** *itp. n patrz* **sen**

**snu|ć (-ję, -jesz)** *vt* (*perf* **u-**) (*nitkę, pajęczynę, opowieść*) to spin; (*intrygę, spisek*) to devise; (*plany*) to make; **~ domysły** to speculate; **snuć się** *vr* (*ciągnąć się*) to trail; (*chodzić bez celu*) to moon *lub* mope around *lub* about

**sobą** *pron* (*sobą samym*) oneself; (*sobą wzajemnie*) each other, one another; **być ~** to be oneself; **chodzili ze ~ przez trzy lata** they went out for 3 years; **mamy ze ~ coś wspólnego** we have sth in common; **mieszkać ze ~** to live together

**sob|ek** (**-ka, -ki**) (*instr sg* **-kiem**) *m* egoist

**sobie** *pron* (*sobie samemu*) oneself; (*sobie nawzajem*) each other, one another; **idź ~!** go away!; **ręce przy ~!** hands off!; **czego Pan ~ życzy?** what would you like, sir?; **mieć coś na ~** to wear sth, to have sth on; **mówić o ~** to talk about oneself; **nie mam przy ~ pieniędzy** I don't have any money on me; **przypomnieć** (*perf*) **~** to remember; **tak ~** (*pot*) so-so (*pot*); **taki ~** (*pot*) so-so (*pot*); **wyobrażać ~** to imagine; **życzyć ~** to desire

**sob|ota** (**-oty, -oty**) (*dat sg* **-ocie**, *gen pl* **-ót**) *f* Saturday; **Wielka S~** Holy Saturday

**sobotni** *adj* Saturday *attr*

**sobowtó|r** (**-ra, -ry**) (*loc sg* **-rze**) *m* double, look-alike

**sob|ól** (**-ola, -ole**) (*gen pl* **-oli**) *m* sable

**sob|ór** (**-oru, -ory**) (*loc sg* **-orze**) *m* (*Rel*: *zgromadzenie*) council; (: *cerkiew*) cathedral (*in the Orthodox Church*); **~ powszechny** *lub* **ekumeniczny** ecumenical council

**socjaldemokracj|a** (**-i, -e**) (*gen pl* **-i**) *f* (*Pol*) social democratic party; **S~ Rzeczypospolitej Polskiej** Social Democracy for the Republic of Poland

**socjaldemokra|ta** (**-ty, -ci**) (*dat sg* **-cie**) *m decl like f in sg* social democrat

**socjaldemokratyczny** *adj* social democratic

**socjali|sta** (**-sty, -ści**) (*dat sg* **-ście**) *m decl like f in sg* socialist

**socjalistyczny** *adj* socialist

**socjaliz|m** (**-mu**) (*loc sg* **-mie**) *m* socialism

**socjalny** *adj* social

**socjolo|g** (**-ga, -gowie** *lub* **-dzy**) (*instr sg* **-giem**) *m* sociologist

**socjologi|a** (**-i**) *f* sociology

**socjologiczny** *adj* sociological

**soczewic|a** (**-y**) *f* (*roślina*) lentil; (*nasiona*) lentils *pl*

**soczew|ka** (**-ki, -ki**) (*dat sg* **-ce**, *gen pl* **-ek**) *f* lens; **soczewki kontaktowe** contact lenses

**soczystoś|ć** (**-ci**) *f* juiciness

**soczysty** *adj* (*owoc, dowcip*) juicy; (*barwa*) rich

**so|da** (**-dy**) (*dat sg* **-dzie**) *f* soda; **~ oczyszczona** bicarbonate of soda

**sodomi|a** (**-i**) *f* sodomy

**sodowy** *adj*: **woda sodowa** soda (water); **chlorek ~** sodium chloride; **woda sodowa uderzyła mu do głowy** success went to his head

**sodu** *itp. n patrz* **sód**

**so|fa** (**-fy, -fy**) (*dat sg* **-fie**) *f* sofa, couch

**Sofi|a** (**-i**) *f* Sofia

**softwa|re** (**-re'u**) (*loc sg* **-rze**) *m* (*Komput*) software

**so|ja** (**-i**) *f* soya bean (*Brit*), soybean (*US*)

**sojowy** *adj*: **sos ~** soya (*Brit*) *lub* soy (*US*) sauce; **olej ~** soya (*Brit*) *lub* soybean (*US*) oil

**sojusz** (**-u, -e**) *m* alliance

**sojuszniczy** *adj*: **państwa/siły sojusznicze** allied countries/forces

**sojuszni|k** (**-ka, -cy**) (*instr sg* **-kiem**) *m* ally

**so|k** (**-ku, -ki**) (*instr sg* **-kiem**) *m* (*owocowy, warzywny*) juice; (*roślinny*) sap; **soki żołądkowe/trawienne** gastric/digestive juices

**sokoli** *adj*: **~ wzrok** eagle eye

**sokowirów|ka** (**-ki, -ki**) (*dat sg* **-ce**, *gen pl* **-ek**) *f* juice extractor (*Brit*), juicer (*US*)

**sok|ół** (**-oła, -oły**) (*loc sg* **-ole**) *m* falcon

**solari|um** (**-um, -a**) (*gen pl* **-ów**) *nt inv in sg* solarium

**solenizan|t** (**-ta, -ci**) (*loc sg* **-cie**) *m person celebrating his birthday or nameday*

**solennie** *adv* (*przyrzekać, zapewniać*) solemnly
**solenny** *adj* (*książk: obietnica*) solemn
**soli** *itp. n patrz* **sól**
**solić (solę, solisz)** (*imp* **sól**, *perf* **o-** *lub* **po-**) *vt* (*podczas gotowania, konserwowania*) to salt, to add salt to; (*potrawę na talerzu, kanapkę*) to put salt on
**solidarnościowy** *adj*: **przeprowadzać (przeprowadzić** *perf*) **strajk ~** to come out in sympathy
**solidarnoś|ć (-ci)** *f* solidarity
**solidarny** *adj* solid; **związkowcy byli solidarni w tej kwestii** the unionists were solid on this issue
**solidaryz|ować się (-uję, -ujesz)** *vr imp*: **solidaryzować się z kimś** to be on sb's side, to sympathize with sb
**solidnoś|ć (-ci)** *f* (*człowieka*) solidity, reliability; (*budowli*) solidity, sturdiness
**solidny** *adj* (*firma, człowiek*) solid, reliable; (*budowla*) solid, sturdy; (*podstawy*) solid; (*wiedza*) deep, thorough; (*posiłek, porcja*) substantial
**soli|sta (-sty, -ści)** (*dat sg* **-ście**) *m decl like f in sg* soloist
**solist|ka (-ki, -ki)** (*dat sg* **-ce**, *gen pl* **-ek**) *f* soloist
**solnicz|ka (-ki, -ki)** (*dat sg* **-ce**, *gen pl* **-ek**) *f* salt cellar, saltshaker (US)
**solny** *adj* (*roztwór, złoża*) saline; **kwas ~** hydrochloric acid; **zalewa solna** brine
**sol|o (-a, -a)** *nt lub inv* (*utwór*) solo ▷ *adv* solo
**solony** *adj* (*orzeszki, masło*) salted
**solowy** *adj* solo *attr*
**solów|ka (-ki, -ki)** (*dat sg* **-ce**, *gen pl* **-ek**) *f* (*pot: występ*) solo
**sołty|s (-sa, -si)** (*loc sg* **-sie**) *m elected chair of a village council*
**Somali|a (-i)** *f* Somalia
**Somalijczy|k (-ka, -cy)** (*instr sg* **-kiem**) *m* Somali
**Somalij|ka (-ki, -ki)** (*dat sg* **-ce**, *gen pl* **-ek**) *f* Somali
**somalijski** *adj* Somali
**sombre|ro (-ra, -ra)** (*loc sg* **-rze**) *nt lub inv* sombrero
**sona|ta (-ty, -ty)** (*dat sg* **-cie**) *f* sonata
**son|da (-dy, -dy)** (*dat sg* **-dzie**) *f* (*Tech, Med*) probe; (*sondaż*) (opinion) poll; **~ kosmiczna** space probe
**sondaż (-u, -e)** (*gen pl* **-y**) *m* (opinion) poll
**sond|ować (-uję, -ujesz)** (*perf* **wy-**) *vt* to probe; (*przen*) to probe, to sound out; **~ kogoś wzrokiem** to give sb a probing look
**sone|t (-tu, -ty)** (*loc sg* **-cie**) *m* sonnet
**son|g (-gu, -gi)** (*instr* **-giem**) *m* song (*cabaret, political etc*)
**sop|el (-la, -le)** (*gen pl* **-li**) *m* icicle
**sopra|n (-nu, -ny)** (*loc sg* **-nie**) *m* soprano
**sort|ować (-uję, -ujesz)** (*perf* **po-**) *vt* to sort
**SOS** *nt inv* SOS (call), mayday, distress signal
**so|s (-su, -sy)** (*loc sg* **-sie**) *m* sauce; (*mięsny*) gravy; (*do sałatek*) dressing; **sos pomidorowy/miętowy** tomato/mint sauce; **nie w sosie** (*pot*) out of sorts (*pot*)
**sosjer|ka (-ki, -ki)** (*dat sg* **-ce**, *gen pl* **-ek**) *f* gravy boat
**so|sna (-sny, -sny)** (*dat sg* **-śnie**, *gen pl* **-sen**) *f* pine
**sosnowy** *adj*: **meble/lasy sosnowe** pine furniture/forests
**soul** *m inv* (*też*: **muzyka soul** *lub* **soulowa**) soul (music)
**so|wa (-wy, -wy)** (*loc sg* **-wie**, *gen pl* **sów**) *f* owl
**sowiecki** *adj* (*pej: radziecki*) Soviet
**sowity** *adj* (*książk: nagroda, zapłata*) generous, lavish
**sód (sodu)** (*loc sg* **sodzie**) *m* sodium
**sój|ka (-ki, -ki)** (*dat sg* **-ce**, *gen pl* **-ek**) *f* jay
**sól (soli)** *f* salt; **sól kamienna/kuchenna** rock/table salt; **sól ziemi** (*przen*) the salt of the earth; **być komuś solą w oku** to be a thorn in sb's side *lub* flesh; **sole** *pl* (*Chem*) salts *pl*; **sole mineralne** mineral salts; *patrz też* **solić**
**sów** *n patrz* **sowa**
**space|r (-ru, -ry)** (*loc sg* **-rze**) *m* walk, stroll; **iść (pójść** *perf*) **na ~** to go for a walk *lub* stroll, to take a walk *lub* stroll
**spacer|ować (-uję, -ujesz)** *vi* to stroll
**spacerowicz (-a, -e)** *m* stroller (*person*)
**spacerowy** *adj*: **krok ~** leisurely pace; **statek ~** excursion boat; **wózek ~** pushchair (*Brit*), stroller (*US*)
**spacerów|ka (-ki, -ki)** (*dat sg* **-ce**, *gen pl* **-ek**) *f* pushchair (*Brit*), stroller (US)
**spacj|a (-i, -e)** (*gen pl* **-i**) *f* (*Druk*) space
**spacz|yć (-ę, -ysz)** *vb perf od* **paczyć**
**spać (śpię, śpisz)** (*imp* **śpij**) *vi* to sleep; **ona śpi/nie śpi** she's asleep/awake; **iść (pójść** *perf*) **~** to go to bed; **chce mi się ~** I am *lub* feel sleepy; **~ z kimś** to sleep with sb
**spa|d (-du, -dy)** (*loc sg* **-dzie**) *m* (*powierzchnia*) slope; (*owoc*) windfall
**spad|ać (-am, -asz)** *vi* (*perf* **spaść**) (*o przedmiocie, człowieku*) to fall (down); (*o cenach, temperaturze*) to fall, to drop; (*o drodze*) to descend; **~ na kogoś** (*o ciosie, kiju*) to come down on sb; (*o odpowiedzialności, obowiązku*) to fall on sb; **spadło na niego wielkie nieszczęście** a great misfortune befell him; **~ gwałtownie** to plummet, to fall *lub* drop sharply; **z nieba mi spadasz!** (*pot*) you're a godsend!; **ciężar** *lub* **kamień spadł mi z serca** it is/was a load *lub* weight off my mind; **spadaj!** (*pot!*) get lost! (*pot!*)

S

**spad|ek** (**-ku, -ki**) (*instr sg* **-kiem**) *m* (*temperatury, cen*) fall, drop; (*terenu*) slope; (*gospodarczy*) decline; (*Prawo*) inheritance, legacy; **dostać** (*perf*) **coś w spadku (po kimś)** to inherit sth (from sb); **zostawić** (*perf*) **komuś coś w spadku** to bequeath *lub* leave sb sth

**spadkobierc|a** (**-y, -y**) *m decl like f in sg* heir

**spadkobierczy|ni** (**-ni, -nie**) (*gen pl* **-ń**) *f* heiress

**spadkowy** *adj* (*prawo, postępowanie*) inheritance *attr*; (*tendencja*) downward

**spadochro|n** (**-nu, -ny**) (*loc sg* **-nie**) *m* parachute; **skakać ze ~em** to parachute

**spadochroniarz** (**-a, -e**) (*gen pl* **-y**) *m* parachutist

**spadochronowy** *adj* (*sport, wieża*) parachuting

**spadzisty** *adj* (*dach, zbocze*) steep

**spaghetti** *nt inv* spaghetti

**spaj|ać (-am, -asz)** (*perf* **spoić**) *vt* to join

**spak|ować (-uję, -ujesz)** *vb perf od* **pakować**

**spal|ać (-am, -asz)** (*perf* **-ić**) *vt* to burn; **spalić za sobą mosty** to burn one's bridges *lub* boats (behind one); **spalać się** *vr* (*płonąć*) to burn; (*eksploatować się*) to burn o.s. out

**spalani|e** (**-a**) *nt* (*Tech*) combustion

**spaleni|zna** (**-zny, -zny**) (*dat sg* **-źnie**) *f*: **czuję spaleniznę** I can smell something burning

**spal|ić (-ę, -isz)** *vb perf od* **palić, spalać** ▷ *vt perf* (*skórę, pieczeń*) to burn; (*bezpiecznik*) to blow; (*silnik, żarówkę*) to burn (out); **spalić się** *vb perf od* **palić się**

**spalinowy** *adj*: **silnik ~** internal combustion engine; **gazy spalinowe** combustion gases; **lokomotywa spalinowa** diesel locomotive

**spali|ny** (**-n**) *pl* (exhaust) fumes *pl*

**spalony** *adj* burnt; (*pot: zdekonspirowany*) hot (*pot*); (*Sport*) offside ▷ *m decl like adj* (*też*: **pozycja spalona**) offside; **być na ~m** to be offside

**spa|m** (**-mu**) *m* (*Komput*) spam

**spa|nie** (**-nia, -nia**) (*gen pl* **-ń**) *nt* (*posłanie*) bed

**spaniel** (**-a, -e**) (*gen pl* **-i**) *m* spaniel

**spap|rać (-rzę, -rzesz)** *vt perf* (*pot: zepsuć*) to mess *lub* louse up (*pot*)

**sparafraz|ować (-uję, -ujesz)** *vb perf od* **parafrazować**

**sparaliż|ować (-uję, -ujesz)** *vb perf od* **paraliżować**

**sparin|g, sparrin|g** (**-gu, -gi**) (*instr sg* **-giem**) *m* sparring

**spartacz|yć (-ę, -ysz)** *vb perf od* **partaczyć**

**spartański** *adj* spartan

**sparz|yć (-ę, -ysz)** *vb perf od* **parzyć** to burn; (*pokrzywą*) to sting; (*wrzątkiem*) to blanch; **sparzyć się** *vr* to get burnt, to burn o.s.; (*przen*) to get one's fingers burnt

**spasiony** *adj* (*pot*) cornfed (*pot*)

**spas|ować (-uję, -ujesz)** *vb perf od* **pasować**

**spa|ść (-dnę, -dniesz)** (*imp* **-dnij**, *pt* **-dł**) *vb perf od* **spadać**

**spa|w** (**-wu, -wy**) (*loc sg* **-wie**) *m* weld

**spawacz** (**-a, -e**) (*gen pl* **-y**) *m* welder

**spaw|ać (-am, -asz)** (*perf* **ze-**) *vt* to weld

**spawani|e** (**-a**) *nt* welding

**spaz|m** (**-mu, -my**) (*loc sg* **-mie**) *m* spasm; **spazmy** *pl* (*płacz*) sobbing

**spazmatyczny** *adj* spasmodic

**spec** (**-a, -e**) *m* (*pot*) w(h)iz(z) (*pot*)

**specjali|sta** (**-sty, -ści**) (*dat sg* **-ście**) *m decl like f in sg* (*znawca*) expert, specialist; (*lekarz*) specialist

**specjalistyczny** *adj* (*sprzęt, badanie*) specialist; (*doradztwo*) expert, specialist

**specjalizacj|a** (**-i, -e**) (*gen pl* **-i**) *f* specialization

**specjaliz|ować się (-uję, -ujesz)** (*perf* **wy-**) *vr*: **specjalizować się w czymś** to specialize in sth

**specjalnie** *adv* specially

**specjalnoś|ć** (**-ci, -ci**) (*gen pl* **-ci**) *f* specialty, speciality (*Brit*); **~ zakładu** (*w restauracji*) special(i)ty of the house; (*w barze*) chef's special

**specjalny** *adj* special; **nic specjalnego** nothing special

**specja|ł** (**-łu, -ły**) (*loc sg* **-le**) *m* delicacy

**specyficzny** *adj* (*zapach, smak*) peculiar; **~ dla czegoś** specific *lub* peculiar to sth

**specyfi|k** (**-ku, -ki**) (*instr sg* **-kiem**) *m* patent medicine

**specyfi|ka** (**-ki**) (*dat sg* **-ce**) *f* specificity, peculiarity

**specyfikacj|a** (**-i, -e**) (*gen pl* **-i**) *f* (*Handel*) specification

**spedycj|a** (**-i**) *f* forwarding, shipping

**spedycyjny** *adj* forwarding, shipping

**spedyto|r** (**-ra, -rzy**) (*loc sg* **-rze**) *m* forwarder, shipper

**spektakl** (**-u, -e**) (*gen pl* **-i**) *m* (*Teatr*) performance

**spektakularny** *adj* spectacular

**spekulacj|a** (**-i, -e**) (*gen pl* **-i**) *f* (*myślenie*) speculation; (*nieuczciwe przedsięwzięcie*) speculation, profiteering

**spekulan|t** (**-ta, -ci**) (*loc sg* **-cie**) *m* speculator, profiteer

**spekul|ować (-uję, -ujesz)** *vi* (*uprawiać spekulację*) to speculate, to profiteer; **~ (na temat czegoś)** to speculate (about sth)

**speleolo|g** (**-ga, -gowie** *lub* **-dzy**) (*instr sg* **-giem**) *m* speleologist

**speleologi|a** (**-i**) *f* speleology

**spelun|ka** (**-ki, -ki**) (*dat sg* **-ce**, *gen pl* **-ek**) *f* (*pot*) dive (*pot*)

**speł|niać (-niam, -niasz)** (*perf* **-nić**) *vt* (*obowiązek*) to fulfil (Brit), to fulfill (US); (*prośbę, polecenie*) to carry out; (*wymagania*) to meet; (*oczekiwania*) to live *lub* come up to; **spełniać się** *vr* to come true

**speł|nić (-nię, -nisz)** (*imp* **-nij**) *vb perf od* **spełniać**

**spełnieni|e** (**-a**) *nt* fulfilment (Brit), fulfillment (US)

**speł|znąć (-znę, -zniesz** *lub* **-źniesz)** (*imp* **-znij** *lub* **-źnij**, *pt* **-znął** *lub* **-zł, -zła, -zły**) *vi perf*: **~ na niczym** to come to nothing

**sper|ma** (**-my**) (*loc sg* **-mie**) *f* sperm

**speszony** *adj* abashed

**spesz|yć (-ę, -ysz)** *vb perf od* **peszyć**

**spę|d** (**-du, -dy**) (*loc sg* **-dzie**) *m* roundup

**spędz|ać (-am, -asz)** (*perf* **-ić**) *vt* (*czas, wakacje*) to spend; (*owce, ludzi*) to round up; **spędziliśmy trzy godziny na rozmowie** we spent three hours talking

**spę|dzić (-dzę, -dzisz)** (*imp* **-dź**) *vb perf od* **spędzać**

**spęt|ać (-am, -asz)** *vb perf od* **pętać**

**spiąć (zepnę, zepniesz)** (*imp* **zepnij**) *vb perf od* **spinać**

**spichlerz, spichrz** (**-a, -e**) (*gen pl* **-y** *lub* **-ów**) *m* granary

**spiczasty** *adj* pointed

**spi|ć (-ję, -jesz)** *vb perf od* **spijać** ▷ *vt perf* (*alkoholem*) to make drunk; **spić się** *vr perf* to get drunk

**spie|c (-kę, -czesz)** (*pt* **-kł**) *vb perf od* **spiekać**

**spiek|ać (-am, -asz)** (*perf* **spiec**) *vt* to parch; **spiec się** *vr* (*opalić się*) to get sunburnt

**spieko|ta** (**-ty, -ty**) (*dat sg* **-cie**) *f* searing heat

**spie|niać (-niam, -niasz)** (*perf* **-nić**) *vt* to froth; **spieniać się** *vr* (*o wodzie itp.*) to froth

**spienięż|ać (-am, -asz)** (*perf* **-yć**) *vt* to cash in

**spieprz|ać (-am, -asz)** (*perf* **-yć**) *vi* (*pot!*: *uciekać*) to sod off (*pot!*)

**spieprz|yć (-ę, -ysz)** *vb perf od* **spieprzać**; (*pot!*: *zrobić źle*) to screw up (*pot!*)

**spier|ać (-am, -asz)** (*perf* **sprać**) *vt* to wash out

**spier|ać się (-am, -asz)** *vr*: **spierać się (o coś)** to argue (about sth)

**spierd|alać (-alam, -alasz)** (*perf* **-olić**) (*pot!*) *vi* (*uciekać*) to get the fuck out (*pot!*); (*odczepiać się*) to fuck off (*pot!*)

**spierdol|ić (-ę, -isz)** *vb perf od* **spierdalać**; (*pot!*) *vt* (*zrobić źle*) to fuck up (*pot!*)

**spierzch|nąć (-nie)** (*pt* **-nął** *lub* **-ł, -ła**) *vb perf od* **pierzchnąć**

**spierzchnięty** *adj* chapped

**spierzesz** *itd. vb patrz* **sprać**

**spiesz|yć (-ę, -ysz)** *vi* = **śpieszyć**

**spię|cie** (**-cia, -cia**) (*gen pl* **-ć**) *nt* (*też*: **krótkie spięcie**) short (circuit); (*sprzeczka*) clash

**spiętrz|ać (-am, -asz)** (*perf* **-yć**) *vt* (*włosy*) to pile up; (*wody rzeki*) to dam up; **spiętrzać się** *vr* (*o trudnościach*) to pile up

**spięty** *adj* (*pot*: *zdenerwowany*) uptight (*pot*)

**spij|ać (-am, -asz)** (*perf* **spić**) *vt* to drink (off)

**spike|r** (**-ra, -rzy**) (*loc sg* **-rze**) *m* announcer

**spił|ować (-uję, -ujesz)** *vb perf od* **piłować**

**spinacz** (**-a, -e**) (*gen pl* **-y**) *m* paper clip

**spin|ać (-am, -asz)** (*perf* **spiąć**) *vt* (*kartki*) to clip; (*włosy*) to pin

**spin|ka** (**-ki, -ki**) (*dat sg* **-ce**, *gen pl* **-ek**) *f* pin; **~ do krawata** tie pin; **~ do mankietu** cuff link; **~ do włosów** (*wsuwka*) hairpin; (*ozdoba*) hair clip

**spinnin|g** (**-gu, -gi**) (*instr sg* **-giem**) *m* (*wędka*) spinning rod; (*sposób łowienia*) spinning, spin fishing

**spiorę** *itd. vb patrz* **sprać**

**spiral|a** (**-i, -e**) *f* spiral; (*też*: **spirala grzejna**) heating coil

**spiralny** *adj* spiral

**spirytu|s** (**-su, -sy**) (*loc sg* **-sie**) *m* spirit; **~ skażony/rektyfikowany** methylated/rectified spirit

**spirytusowy** *adj*: **ocet ~** spirit vinegar

**spirytystyczny** *adj*: **seans ~** seance

**spi|s** (**-su, -sy**) (*loc sg* **-sie**) *m* list; **~ treści** (table of) contents; **~ ludności** census; **~ potraw** menu

**spi|sać (-szę, -szesz)** *vb perf od* **spisywać**

**spis|ek** (**-ku, -ki**) (*instr sg* **-kiem**) *m* conspiracy, plot

**spisk|ować (-uję, -ujesz)** *vi* to conspire, to plot

**spisko|wiec** (**-wca, -wcy**) *m* conspirator

**spiskowy** *adj* conspiratorial

**spis|ywać (-uję, -ujesz)** (*perf* **-ać**) *vt* (*sporządzać wykaz*) to make a list of; (*umowę, protokół*) to draw up; **~ na straty** to write off; **spisywać się** *vr*: **dobrze/źle się ~** (*o człowieku*) to do well/badly; (*o samochodzie*) to run well/badly

**spity** *adj* (*pot*) soaked (*pot*)

**spiżar|nia** (**-ni, -nie**) (*gen pl* **-ni**) *f* pantry

**splajt|ować (-uję, -ujesz)** *vb perf od* **plajtować**

**spla|mić (-mię, -misz)** *vb perf od* **plamić**

**splat|ać (-am, -asz)** (*perf* **spleść**) *vt* to plait (Brit), to braid (US); **~ dłonie** to clasp one's hands; **splatać się** *vr* to intertwine

**splądr|ować (-uję, -ujesz)** *vb perf od* **plądrować**

**splą|tać (-czę, -czesz)** *vb perf od* **plątać**

S

**splendo|r** (**-ru, -ry**) (*loc sg* **-rze**) *m* (*książk*) splendour (*Brit*), splendor (*US*)
**spl|eść (-otę, -eciesz)** (*imp* **-eć**, *pt* **-ótł, -otła, -etli**) *vb perf od* **splatać**
**spleśniały** *adj* mouldy (*Brit*), moldy (*US*)
**spleśni|eć (-eje)** *vb perf od* **pleśnieć**
**splo|t** (**-tu, -ty**) (*loc sg* **-cie**) *m* (*liny*) coil; (*gałęzi, korzeni*) tangle; (*przen: wydarzeń*) series; **~ słoneczny** solar plexus
**splu|nąć (-nę, -niesz)** (*imp* **-ń**) *vb perf od* **spluwać**
**splu|wać (-wam, -wasz)** (*perf* **-nąć**) *vi* to spit
**spła|cać (-cam, -casz)** (*perf* **-cić**) *vt* to pay off; **~ dług/pożyczkę** to pay off a debt/loan; **~ coś ratami** *lub* **w ratach** to pay sth off in instalments (*Brit*) *lub* installments (*US*)
**spła|cić (-cę, -cisz)** (*imp* **-ć**) *vb perf od* **spłacać**
**spłaszcz|ać (-am, -asz)** (*perf* **-yć**) *vt* to flatten
**spła|ta** (**-ty, -ty**) (*dat sg* **-cie**) *f* repayment
**spłat|ać (-am, -asz)** *vt*: **~ komuś figla** to play a trick on sb
**spławi|ać (-am, -asz)** (*perf* **-ć**) *vt* (*człowieka: pot*) to get rid of; (*drzewo*) to float
**spła|wić (-wię, -wisz)** *vb perf od* **spławiać**
**spławi|k** (**-ka, -ki**) (*instr sg* **-kiem**) *m* float
**spławny** *adj* navigable
**spł|odzić (-odzę, -odzisz)** (*imp* **-ódź**) *vb perf od* **płodzić**
**spło|nąć (-nę, -niesz)** (*imp* **-ń**) *vb perf od* **płonąć**
**spło|nić się (-nię, -nisz)** (*imp* **-ń**) *vb perf od* **płonić się**
**spłoszony** *adj* frightened
**spłosz|yć (-ę, -ysz)** *vb perf od* **płoszyć**
**spłowi|eć (-eje)** *vb perf od* **płowieć**
**spłucz|ka** (**-ki, -ki**) (*dat sg* **-ce**, *gen pl* **-ek**) *f* (toilet) cistern
**spłu|kać (-czę, -czesz)** *vb perf od* **spłukiwać**; **spłukać się** *vr perf* (*pot*) to blow all one's cash (*pot*)
**spłu|kiwać (-kuję, -kujesz)** (*perf* **-kać**) *vt* to rinse off
**spły|cać (-cam, -casz)** (*perf* **-cić**) *vt* (*upraszczać*) to (over)simplify
**spły|cić (-cę, -cisz)** (*imp* **-ć**) *vb perf od* **spłycać**
**spły|nąć (-nę, -niesz)** (*imp* **-ń**) *vb perf od* **spływać**
**spły|w** (**-wu, -wy**) (*loc sg* **-wie**) *m* (*tratwą*) (white-water) rafting; (*też:* **spływ kajakowy**) canoeing trip; (*zbieg rzek*) confluence
**spły|wać (-wam, -wasz)** (*perf* **-nąć**) *vi* (*o wodzie, kroplach*) to flow (down); (*o łodzi, barce*) to float; (*o włosach, grzywie*) to fall; **spływaj!** (*pot*) beat it! (*pot*)
**spochmurni|eć (-eję, -ejesz)** *vb perf od* **pochmurnieć**
**spo|cić się (-cę, -cisz)** (*imp* **-ć**) *vb perf od* **pocić się**
**spocony** *adj* sweaty
**spocz|ąć (-nę, -niesz)** (*imp* **-nij**) *vb perf od* **spoczywać**; **spocznij!** (*Wojsk*) at ease!; **proszę ~!** take *lub* have a seat, please!; **~ na laurach** to rest on one's laurels; **nie spocznę, dopóki ...** I won't rest until ...
**spoczyn|ek** (**-ku**) (*instr sg* **-kiem**) *m* (*odpoczynek, brak ruchu*) rest; (*sen*) sleep; **oficer w stanie spoczynku** a retired officer; **udawać się (udać się** *perf*) **na ~** to retire
**spoczyw|ać (-am, -asz)** (*perf* **spocząć**) *vi* (*książk: siedzieć*) to sit; (*leżeć*) to lie; (*o przedmiocie*) to sit; (*o wzroku*) to fall
**spod** *prep +gen* from under; **~ Warszawy** from somewhere around Warsaw; **~ czyjejś opieki** from under sb's care; **być ~ znaku Skorpiona** to be Scorpio; **~ lady** under the counter
**spodecz|ek** (**-ka, -ki**) (*instr sg* **-kiem**) *m dimin od* **spodek**
**spod|ek** (**-ka, -ki**) (*instr sg* **-kiem**) *m* saucer
**spoden|ki** (**-ek**) *pl dimin od* **spodnie**; (*też:* **krótkie spodenki**) shorts *pl*
**spodni** *adj*: **~a warstwa** bottom layer
**spod|nie** (**-ni**) *pl* trousers *pl* (*Brit*), pants *pl* (*US*)
**spodob|ać się (-am, -asz)** *vb perf od* **podobać się**
**spodu** *itd. n patrz* **spód**
**spodziew|ać się (-am, -asz)** *vr*: **spodziewać się kogoś/czegoś** to be expecting sb/sth; **spodziewać się czegoś po kimś** to expect sth of sb; **Maria spodziewa się dziecka** Maria is expecting
**spogląd|ać (-am, -asz)** (*perf* **spojrzeć**) *vi* to look; **~ na kogoś z góry** (*przen*) to look down on sb; **~ po sobie** to look at one another
**spoić**[1] **(spoję, spoisz)** (*imp* **spój**) *vb perf od* **spajać**
**spoić**[2] **(spoję, spoisz)** (*imp* **spój**) *vt perf* (*upić*) to make drunk
**spoi|na** (**-ny, -ny**) (*dat sg* **-nie**) *f* joint
**spoje|nie** (**-nia, -nia**) (*gen pl* **-ń**) *nt* joint
**spojów|ka** (**-ki, -ki**) (*dat sg* **-ce**, *gen pl* **-ek**) *f*: **zapalenie spojówek** conjunctivitis
**spojrz|eć (-ę, -ysz)** (*imp* **spójrz** *lub* **spojrzyj**) *vb perf od* **spoglądać**
**spojrze|nie** (**-nia, -nia**) (*gen pl* **-ń**) *nt* look, glance; **obrzucić** (*perf*) **kogoś/coś ~m** to throw a glance at sb/sth; **mieć trzeźwe ~ na coś** (*przen*) to hold a sober view of sth
**spoko** *interj* (*pot: w porządku*) no problem; (*nie denerwuj się*) chill out
**spokojnie** *adv* (*z opanowaniem*) calmly; (*powoli*) slowly; (*w spokoju*) quietly; (*bez pośpiechu*) at leisure; (*bez problemów*) smoothly; **(tylko) ~!** stay cool!

**spokojny** *adj* (*człowiek, morze*) calm; (*charakter*) placid; (*kolor*) sober; **być ~m o kogoś/coś** to be confident of sb/sth; **możesz być ~** rest assured; **spokojna głowa!** (*pot*) not to worry! (*pot*)

**spok|ój** (**-oju**) *m* (*stan psychiczny*) calmness; (*cisza*) calm, quiet; (*pokój*) peace; **daj ~!** come off it! (*pot*); **dać** (*perf*) **komuś ~, zostawić** (*perf*) **kogoś w spokoju** to leave sb alone; **dać sobie ~ z kimś/czymś** to forget sb/sth; **ta myśl nie dawała mi spokoju** the thought kept nagging me; **proszę o ~!** quiet, please!, order!

**spokrewniony** *adj* related

**spolaryz|ować (-uję, -ujesz)** *vb perf od* **polaryzować**

**spoliczk|ować (-uję, -ujesz)** *vb perf od* **policzkować**

**spolszcz|ać (-am, -asz)** (*perf* **-yć**) *vt* to polonize

**społeczeńst|wo** (**-wa, -wa**) (*loc sg* **-wie**) *nt* society; **~ polskie** (*ogół Polaków*) the Polish people; (*struktura*) Polish society; **ogół społeczeństwa** the general public; **nauka o społeczeństwie** social science

**społecznie** *adv* (*szkodliwy, nieprzystosowany*) socially; **pracować ~** to do community service

**społecznoś|ć** (**-ci, -ci**) (*gen pl* **-ci**) *f* community

**społeczny** *adj*: **klasa/drabina/opieka społeczna** social class/ladder/welfare; **dobro/poparcie społeczne** public good/ support; **margines ~** the dregs *pl* of society; **pochodzenie społeczne** social background; **ubezpieczenie społeczne** national insurance (*Brit*), social security (*US*); **niepokoje społeczne** civil unrest; **praca społeczna** community service

**spomiędzy** *prep +gen* from among

**sponad** *prep +gen* from above

**sponiewier|ać (-am, -asz)** *vb perf od* **poniewierać**

**sponso|r** (**-ra, -rzy**) (*loc sg* **-rze**) *m* sponsor

**sponsor|ować (-uję, -ujesz)** *vt* to sponsor

**sponsorowani|e** (**-a**) *nt* sponsorship

**spontanicznoś|ć** (**-ci**) *f* spontaneity

**spontaniczny** *adj* spontaneous

**spopularyz|ować (-uję, -ujesz)** *vb perf od* **popularyzować**

**sporadycznie** *adv* sporadically

**sporadyczny** *adj* sporadic

**sporny** *adj*: **punkt ~** moot point; **kwestie sporne** contentious issues

**sporo** *adv* a good *lub* great deal

**spor|t** (**-tu, -ty**) (*loc sg* **-cie**) *m* sport(s *pl*); **~ wyczynowy** professional athletics; **~y wodne/zimowe** aquatic/winter sports; **uprawiać ~** to practice (*Brit*) *lub* practise (*US*) sports; **dla ~u** (*przen*) for sport

**sporto|wiec** (**-wca, -wcy**) *m* athlete

**sportowy** *adj* (*klub, samochód, marynarka*) sports *attr*; (*zachowanie*) sporting *attr*

**sportret|ować (-uję, -ujesz)** *vb perf od* **portretować**

**sporu** *itd. n patrz* **spór**

**spory** *adj* substantial

**sporzą|dzać (-dzam, -dzasz)** (*perf* **-dzić**) *vt* (*testament, umowę*) to draw up

**sporzą|dzić (-dzę, -dzisz)** (*imp* **-dź**) *vb perf od* **sporządzać**

**sposobnoś|ć** (**-ci**) *f* opportunity; **przy każdej/pierwszej sposobności** at every/the earliest opportunity

**spos|ób** (**-obu, -oby**) (*loc sg* **-obie**) *m* (*metoda*) way, manner; (*środek*) means; **w ten ~** in this way; **~ bycia** manners; **w jaki ~, jakim sposobem** how, in what way; **w jakiś ~** somehow; **w taki czy inny ~** somehow or other, one way or another; **nie ~ nie zauważyć, że ...** one cannot help noticing that ...; **~ zapłaty** method of payment

**spostrze|c (-gę, -żesz)** (*imp* **-ż**, *pt* **-gł**) *vb perf od* **spostrzegać**

**spostrzeg|ać (-am, -asz)** (*perf* **spostrzec**) *vt* (*zauważać*) to notice; (*zdawać sobie sprawę*) to become aware of; **spostrzegła, że była sama** she realized (that) she was alone; **spostrzegać się** *vr*: **~ się, że ...** to realize that ...; **(za)nim się spostrzegłem, ...** the next thing I knew, ...

**spostrzegawczoś|ć** (**-ci**) *f* perceptiveness

**spostrzegawczy** *adj* perceptive, observant

**spostrzeże|nie** (**-nia, -nia**) (*gen pl* **-ń**) *nt* (*uwaga*) observation; (*akt psychiczny*) perception

**spośród** *prep +gen* from among

**spotęg|ować (-uję, -ujesz)** *vb perf od* **potęgować**

**spotk|ać (-am, -asz)** *vb perf od* **spotykać**

**spotka|nie** (**-nia, -nia**) (*gen pl* **-ń**) *nt* meeting; (*zawody sportowe*) meet(ing); **przyjść** (*perf*) **na ~** to come to a meeting, to meet an appointment; **umówić się** (*perf*) **na ~** to make an appointment

**spotyk|ać (-am, -asz)** (*perf* **spotkać**) *vt* (*natykać się*) to come across; (*poznawać*) to meet; (*zdarzać się*) to happen to; **spotykać się** *vr* to meet; **~ się z czyjąś aprobatą** to meet with sb's approval

**spoufal|ać się (-am, -asz)** (*perf* **-ić**) *vr*: **spoufalać się z kimś** to take liberties with sb

**spoważni|eć (-eję, -ejesz)** *vb perf od* **poważnieć**

S

**spowiad|ać (-am, -asz)** (*perf* **wy-**) *vt*: **~ kogoś** to hear sb's confession; **spowiadać się** *vr* to confess; **~ się komuś z czegoś** to confide sth to sb
**spowiedni|k** (**-ka, -cy**) (*instr sg* **-kiem**) *m* confessor
**spowie|dź** (**-dzi, -dzi**) (*gen pl* **-dzi**) *f* confession
**spowod|ować (-uję, -ujesz)** *vb perf od* **powodować**
**spowszedni|eć (-eję, -ejesz)** *vb perf od* **powszednieć**
**spoza** *prep +gen* (*zza*) from behind; (*z innego środowiska*) (from) outside
**spożyci|e** (**-a**) *nt* (*alkoholu, paliwa*) consumption; (*witamin, tłuszczów*) intake; **„termin przydatności do spożycia:"** "best before:"
**spożyw|ać (-am, -asz)** (*perf* **spożyć**) *vt* (*książk*) to consume
**spożywczy** *adj*: **przemysł ~** food industry; **sklep ~** grocer's (shop) (*Brit*), grocery (store) (*US*); **artykuły spożywcze** groceries
**sp|ód** (**-odu, -ody**) (*loc sg* **-odzie**) *m* (*dno*) bottom; (*spodnia strona*) underside; **na (samym) spodzie** at the (very) bottom; **od spodu** from below; **pod spodem** below, underneath
**spódnic|a** (**-y, -e**) *f* skirt
**spódnicz|ka** (**-ki, -ki**) (*dat sg* **-ce**, *gen pl* **-ek**) *f* *dimin od* **spódnica**
**spójni|k** (**-ka, -ki**) (*instr sg* **-kiem**) *m* (*Jęz*) conjunction
**spójnoś|ć** (**-ci**) *f* (*teorii*) cohesion
**spójny** *adj* (*teoria*) coherent
**spółdzielczy** *adj* cooperative; **mieszkanie spółdzielcze** ≈ housing association flat
**spółdziel|nia** (**-ni, -nie**) (*gen pl* **-ni**) *f* cooperative; **~ mieszkaniowa** ≈ housing association
**spółgłos|ka** (**-ki, -ki**) (*dat sg* **-ce**, *gen pl* **-ek**) *f* consonant
**spół|ka** (**-ki, -ki**) (*dat sg* **-ce**, *gen pl* **-ek**) *f* company; **~ akcyjna** joint-stock company; **~ z ograniczoną odpowiedzialnością** (*Ekon*) limited (liability) company; **~ cywilna** civil partnership; **~ joint venture** joint venture; **do spółki z kimś** together with sb; **wchodzić (wejść** *perf*) **z kimś w spółkę** to go into partnership with sb
**spółk|ować (-uję, -ujesz)** *vi* to copulate
**sp|ór** (**-oru, -ory**) (*loc sg* **-orze**) *m* dispute; (*Prawo*) litigation
**spóź|niać się (-niam, -niasz)** (*perf* **-nić**) *vr* (*o osobie, pociągu*) to be late; (*o zegarze*) to be late *lub* slow; (*odbywać się z opóźnieniem*) to be (running) late; **spóźnić się na pociąg** to miss one's train
**spóźnials|ki** (**-kiego, -cy**) *m decl like adj* latecomer
**spóź|nić się (-nię, -nisz)** (*imp* **-nij**) *vb perf od* **spóźniać się**
**spóźnie|nie** (**-nia, -nia**) (*gen pl* **-ń**) *nt* (*niepunktualność*) lateness; (*zaległość*) delay; **pociąg ma ~** the train is delayed *lub* late
**spóźniony** *adj* (*pociąg, wiosna*) late; (*przesyłka, samolot*) delayed; (*życzenia*) belated
**spracowany** *adj* (*osoba*) tired out; (*ręce*) work-worn
**sprać (spiorę, spierzesz)** (*imp* **spierz**) *vb perf od* **spierać**; (*pot*: *zbić*) to work over (*pot*)
**spragniony** *adj* thirsty; **~ czegoś** avid *lub* eager for sth
**sprasz|ać (-am, -asz)** (*perf* **sprosić**) *vt* to invite
**spra|wa** (**-wy, -wy**) (*dat sg* **-wie**) *f* (*wydarzenie*) matter, affair; (*interes*) business; (*Prawo*) case; (*wzniosły cel*) cause; **Ministerstwo Spraw Wewnętrznych** Ministry of the Interior, ≈ Home Office (*Brit*); **Ministerstwo Spraw Zagranicznych** Ministry of Foreign Affairs, ≈ Foreign Office (*Brit*), ≈ Department of State (*US*); **(to) nie twoja ~** it's none of your business; **zdawać (zdać** *perf*) **sobie sprawę z czegoś** to be (become) aware of sth; **to ~ tygodnia** it's a matter of one week; **to inna ~** that's another matter; **brać (wziąć** *perf*) **sprawę w swoje ręce** to take the matter into one's hands; **robić z czegoś (wielką) sprawę** to make an issue of sth; **zajmować się swoimi ~mi** to go about one's business; **~ cywilna/karna/sądowa** civil/criminal/court case; **wnosić (wnieść** *perf*) **sprawę do sądu** to bring *lub* file a suit
**sprawc|a** (**-y, -y**) *m decl like f in sg* perpetrator; **~ wypadku** the guilty party
**spraw|dzać (-dzam, -dzasz)** (*perf* **-dzić**) *vt* (*zabezpieczenia, paszport*) to check; (*wyraz w słowniku*) to look up; **sprawdzać się** *vr* (*spełniać się*) to come true; (*okazywać się przydatnym*) to turn out to be useful
**sprawdzalny** *adj* verifiable
**sprawdzia|n** (**-nu, -ny**) (*loc sg* **-nie**) *m* (*Szkol*) test (*Brit*), quiz (*US*); (*miernik*) test
**spraw|dzić (-dzę, -dzisz)** (*imp* **-dź**) *vb perf od* **sprawdzać**
**spra|wiać (-wiam, -wiasz)** (*perf* **-wić**) *vt* (*ból*) to inflict; (*niespodziankę*) to give; (*kłopot*) to cause; (*książk*: *kupować*) to purchase; **sprawić, że coś się stanie** to make sth happen; **~ dobre/złe wrażenie** to make a good/bad impression; **sprawiać się** *vr*: **dobrze/źle się sprawić** to do well/badly
**spra|wić (-wię, -wisz)** *vb perf od* **sprawiać**
**sprawiedliwie** *adv* fairly, justly

**sprawiedliwoś|ć** (**-ci**) *f* fairness, justice; (*sądownictwo*) (system of) justice; **wymiar sprawiedliwości** (system of) justice; **minister sprawiedliwości** minister of justice, ≈ Attorney General (*US, Brit*); **oddać komuś/czemuś ~** to do justice to sb/sth; **wymierzyć** (*perf*) **komuś ~** to bring sb to justice

**sprawiedliwy** *adj* fair, just

**spraw|ka** (**-ki, -ki**) (*dat sg* **-ce**, *gen pl* **-ek**) *f*: **to twoja ~** this is your doing

**sprawnoś|ć** (**-ci, -ci**) (*gen pl* **-ci**) *f* (*kondycja fizyczna*) fitness; (*zręczność*) dexterity; (*sprawne działanie*) efficiency

**sprawny** *adj* (*zdolny do działania*) fit; (*zręczny*) adroit; (*dobrze działający: człowiek*) efficient; (*: maszyna, urządzenie*) in working order

**spraw|ować (-uję, -ujesz)** *vt* (*urząd*) to hold; (*władzę*) to wield; **sprawować się** *vr* to behave

**sprawowani|e** (**-a**) *nt* (*urzędu*) holding; (*władzy*) wielding; (*Szkol*) conduct

**sprawozda|nie** (**-nia, -nia**) (*gen pl* **-ń**) *nt* report; **~ roczne** annual report; **~ telewizyjne/radiowe** television/radio coverage

**sprawozdawc|a** (**-y, -y**) *m decl like f in sg*; **~ radiowy/telewizyjny** radio/television commentator

**sprawun|ek** (**-ku, -ki**) (*instr sg* **-kiem**) *m* purchase; **iść (pójść** *perf*) **po sprawunki** to go shopping

**spray** (**-u, -e**) (*gen pl* **-ów**) *m* spray; **dezodorant w ~u** spray deodorant

**sprecyz|ować (-uję, -ujesz)** *vb perf od* **precyzować**

**sprepar|ować (-uję, -ujesz)** *vb perf od* **preparować**

**spręż|ać (-am, -asz)** (*perf* **-yć**) *vt* to compress; **sprężać się** *vr* (*zwierać się w sobie*) to brace o.s.; (*Tech*) to be compressed

**sprężar|ka** (**-ki, -ki**) (*dat sg* **-ce**, *gen pl* **-ek**) *f* compressor

**sprężony** *adj* (*powietrze*) compressed

**spręży|na** (**-ny, -ny**) (*dat sg* **-nie**) *f* spring

**sprężyn|ować (-uje)** *vi* to spring back

**sprężynowy** *adj*: **materac ~** spring mattress; **nóż ~** flick knife (*Brit*), switchblade (*US*)

**sprężynujący** *adj* (*mechanizm*) spring-loaded

**sprężystoś|ć** (**-ci**) *f* resilience

**sprężysty** *adj* springy, resilient; **chodzić ~m krokiem** to walk with a spring in one's step

**sprin|t** (**-tu, -ty**) (*loc sg* **-cie**) *m* sprint

**sprinte|r** (**-ra, -rzy**) (*loc sg* **-rze**) *m* sprinter

**sprofan|ować (-uję, -ujesz)** *vb perf od* **profanować**

**spro|sić (-szę, -sisz)** (*imp* **-ś**) *vb perf od* **spraszać**

**sprost|ać (-am, -asz)** *vi perf*: **~ czemuś** to be up to sth; **~ komuś** to match sb

**sprost|ować (-uję, -ujesz)** *vb perf od* **prostować**

**sprostowa|nie** (**-nia, -nia**) (*gen pl* **-ń**) *nt* correction

**sproszk|ować (-uję, -ujesz)** *vb perf od* **proszkować**

**sprośny** *adj* bawdy

**sprowa|dzać (-dzam, -dzasz)** (*perf* **-dzić**) *vt* (*lekarza, pomoc*) to get; (*towary*) to import; (*cierpienie, głód*) to bring; (*pomagać zejść w dół*) to take down; **~ coś do czegoś** to reduce sth to sth; **co was tu sprowadza?** what brings you here?; **sprowadzić kogoś na złą drogę** to lead sb astray; **sprowadzać się** *vr* (*o ludziach*) to move in; **~ się do czegoś** to boil down *lub* amount to sth

**sprowa|dzić (-dzę, -dzisz)** (*imp* **-dź**) *vb perf od* **sprowadzać**

**sprowok|ować (-uję, -ujesz)** *vb perf od* **prowokować**

**sprób|ować (-uję, -ujesz)** *vb perf od* **próbować**

**spróchniały** *adj* rotten

**spru|ć (-ję, -jesz)** *vb perf od* **pruć**

**spryciarz** (**-a, -e**) (*gen pl* **-y**) *m* (*pot*) smooth operator (*pot*)

**spryskiwacz** (**-a, -e**) (*gen pl* **-y**) *m* (*w ogrodzie*) sprinkler, spray(er); (*Mot*) windscreen (*Brit*) *lub* windshield (*US*) washer

**sprys|kiwać (-kuję, -kujesz)** (*perf* **-kać**) *vt* (*włosy, bieliznę*) to sprinkle; (*rośliny, pole*) to spray

**spry|t** (**-tu**) (*loc sg* **-cie**) *m* shrewdness

**sprytny** *adj* (*człowiek*) shrewd; (*mechanizm, rozwiązanie*) clever

**sprywatyz|ować (-uję, -ujesz)** *vb perf od* **prywatyzować**

**sprz|ąc (-ęgę, -ężesz)** (*imp* **-ęż** *lub* **-ąż**) *vb perf od* **sprzęgać**

**sprzącz|ka** (**-ki, -ki**) (*dat sg* **-ce**, *gen pl* **-ek**) *f* buckle

**sprzątacz** (**-a, -e**) (*loc sg* **-u**, *gen pl* **-y**) *m* cleaner

**sprzątacz|ka** (**-ki, -ki**) (*dat sg* **-ce**, *gen pl* **-ek**) *f* cleaning lady, charlady

**sprząt|ać (-am, -asz)** (*perf* **-nąć**) *vt* (*mieszkanie, ulice*) to clean; (*książki*) to clear ▷ *vi* to clean; **~ ze stołu** to clear the table

**sprzątani|e** (**-a**) *nt* cleaning

**sprząt|nąć (-nę, -niesz)** (*imp* **-nij**) *vb perf od* **sprzątać**; (*pot: zabrać*) to snatch; (*pot: zabić*) to knock off (*pot*)

**sprzeci|w** (**-wu, -wy**) (*loc sg* **-wie**) *m* (*opór*) opposition; (*Prawo*) objection; **bez ~u** without demur; **zgłaszać (zgłosić** *perf*) **~** to raise *lub* voice an objection

S

**sprzeci|wiać się (-wiam, -wiasz)** (*perf* **-wić**) *vr*: **sprzeciwiać się komuś/czemuś** (*przeciwstawiać się*) to oppose sb/sth; **sprzeciwiać się czemuś** (*wyrażać sprzeciw*) to object to sth
**sprzeci|wić się (-wię, -wisz)** *vb perf od* **sprzeciwiać się**
**sprzecz|ać się (-am, -asz)** (*perf* **po-**) *vr* to argue
**sprzecz|ka (-ki, -ki)** (*dat sg* **-ce**, *gen pl* **-ek**) *f* argument
**sprzecznoś|ć (-ci, -ci)** (*gen pl* **-ci**) *f* contradiction; **być** *lub* **stać w sprzeczności z czymś** to contradict sth
**sprzeczny** *adj* (*uczucia*) conflicting; (*opinie, interesy*) contradictory; **to jest sprzeczne z prawem** it's illegal *lub* against the law; **być ~m z czymś** to be at variance with sth
**sprzed** *prep +gen* (*domu, sklepu*) from in front of; **budynki ~ wojny** prewar buildings; **gazeta ~ tygodnia** a week-old newspaper
**sprzed|ać (-am, -asz)** *vb perf od* **sprzedawać**
**sprzedajny** *adj* corruptible
**sprzedany** *adj* sold
**sprzed|awać (-aję, -ajesz)** (*imp* **-awaj**, *perf* **-ać**) *vt* to sell ▷ *vi* to sell; **~ coś detalicznie/hurtem** to sell sth at retail/wholesale prices; **~ coś na sztuki** to sell sth by the item; **~ coś na raty** to sell sth on hire purchase (*Brit*) *lub* on installments (*US*); **~ coś z zyskiem/ze stratą** to sell sth at a profit/at a loss; **sprzedawać się** *vr* (*o towarze*) to sell; (*o człowieku*) to sell out
**sprzedawc|a (-y, -y)** *m decl like f in sg* salesman, shop *lub* sales assistant (*Brit*), salesclerk (*US*)
**sprzedawczy|ni (-ni, -nie)** (*gen pl* **-ń**) *f* saleswoman, shop *lub* sales assistant (*Brit*), salesclerk (*US*)
**sprzedaż (-y)** *f* sale; **na ~** for sale; **~ detaliczna** retail; **~ hurtowa** wholesale; **~ na raty** hire purchase (*Brit*), installment plan (*US*); **~ wysyłkowa** mail order
**sprzeniewierz|ać (-am, -asz)** (*perf* **-yć**) *vt* to misappropriate, to embezzle; **sprzeniewierzać się** *vr*: **~ się komuś/czemuś** to betray sb/sth
**sprzęg|ać (-am, -asz)** (*perf* **sprząc** *lub* **sprzęgnąć**) *vt* to couple; **sprzęgać się** *vr* to engage
**sprzę|gło (-gła, -gła)** (*loc sg* **-gle**, *gen pl* **-gieł**) *nt* clutch
**sprzęg|nąć (-nę, -niesz)** (*imp* **-nij**) *vb perf od* **sprzęgać**
**sprzę|t (-tu)** (*loc sg* **-cie**) *m* (*zestaw przedmiotów*) equipment; (*mebel*) (*nom pl* **-ty**) piece of furniture; **~ sportowy** sports equipment; **~ elektroniczny** home electronics; **~ komputerowy** (computer) hardware
**sprzęże|nie (-nia, -nia)** (*gen pl* **-ń**) *nt* coupling; **~ zwrotne** feedback
**sprzyj|ać (-am, -asz)** *vi*: **~ komuś** (*być przychylnym*) to favour (*Brit*) *lub* favor (*US*) sb; (*dopisywać*) to be favourable (*Brit*) *lub* favorable (*US*) to sb; **~ czemuś** to be conducive to sth
**sprzyjający** *adj* favourable (*Brit*), favorable (*US*)
**sprzykrz|yć się (-ę, -ysz)** *vr perf*: **sprzykrzyło mi się ...** I am tired of ...
**sprzymierz|ać się (-am, -asz)** (*perf* **-yć**) *vr*: **sprzymierzać się z kimś** to ally o.s. with sb
**sprzymierze|niec (-ńca, -ńcy)** *m* ally
**sprzymierzony** *adj* allied
**sprzymierz|yć się (-ę, -ysz)** *vb perf od* **sprzymierzać się**
**sprzysi|ąc się (-ęgnę, -ęgniesz)** (*imp* **-ęgnij**) *vb perf od* **sprzysięgać się**
**sprzysięg|ać się (-am, -asz)** (*perf* **sprzysiąc**) *vr* to conspire
**spuch|nąć (-nę, -niesz)** (*imp* **-nij**, *pt* **-ł**) *vb perf od* **puchnąć**
**spuchnięty** *adj* swollen
**spudł|ować (-uję, -ujesz)** *vb perf od* **pudłować**
**spulch|niać (-niam, -niasz)** (*perf* **-nić**) *vt* (*glebę*) to loosen; (*ciasto*) to leaven
**spulch|nić (-nię, -nisz)** (*imp* **-nij**) *vb perf od* **spulchniać**
**spu|st (-stu, -sty)** (*loc sg* **-ście**) *m* (*rewolweru*) trigger; **~ migawki** (*Fot*) shutter release; **mieć ~** (*pot*) to be a heavy eater
**spustosze|nie (-nia, -nia)** (*gen pl* **-ń**) *nt* devastation; **siać ~ (wśród kogoś/w czymś)** to wreak havoc (with sb/on sth)
**spustosz|yć (-ę, -ysz)** *vb perf od* **pustoszyć**
**spuszcz|ać (-am, -asz)** (*perf* **spuścić**) *vt* (*opuszczać*) to lower; (*odprowadzać*: *wodę, powietrze*) to let out; **~ cenę** to bring down the price; **~ psa ze smyczy** to unleash a dog; **~ wodę** (*w toalecie*) to flush the toilet; **~ oczy** *lub* **wzrok** to lower one's eyes; **nie ~ kogoś/czegoś z oczu** to keep an eye on sb/sth; **spuścić z tonu** to come down a peg or two; **spuszczać się** *vr* (*opuszczać się*) to come down
**spu|ścić (-szczę, -ścisz)** (*imp* **-ść**) *vb perf od* **spuszczać**
**spuści|zna (-zny)** (*loc sg* **-źnie**) *f* legacy
**spychacz (-a, -e)** (*gen pl* **-y**) *m* bulldozer
**spych|ać (-am, -asz)** (*perf* **zepchnąć**) *vt* to push aside; (*zmuszać do wycofania się*) to drive back; **~ coś na kogoś** (*odpowiedzialność, pracę*) to shift sth onto sb
**spyt|ać (-am, -asz)** *vb perf od* **pytać**
**sp. z o.o.** *abbr* (*= spółka z ograniczoną odpowiedzialnością*) Ltd

**sracz|ka** (**-ki, -ki**) (*dat sg* **-ce**, *gen pl* **-ek**) *f* (*pot!*): **mieć sraczkę** to have the shits (*pot!*)
**sr|ać (-am, -asz)** *vi* (*pot!*) to crap (*pot!*); **sram na to** I don't give a shit (about it)
**srebrny** *adj* silver; **srebrne wesele** silver wedding (anniversary)
**sreb|ro** (**-ra, -ra**) (*loc sg* **-rze**, *gen pl* **-er**) *nt* silver; **srebra** *pl*: **srebra stołowe** silver(ware)
**srebrz|yć się (-y)** *vr* to shimmer
**srebrzysty** *adj* silvery
**srogi** *adj* (*władca*) stern; (*mróz*) severe
**sro|ka** (**-ki, -ki**) (*dat sg* **-ce**) *f* magpie
**srokaty** *adj* piebald
**sro|m** (**-mu, -my**) (*loc sg* **-mie**) *m* vulva
**sromotny** *adj* ignominious
**sromowy** *adj*: **wargi sromowe** labia
**ssać (ssę, ssiesz)** (*imp* **ssij**) *vt* to suck (on)
**ssa|k** (**-ka, -ki**) (*instr sg* **-kiem**) *m* mammal
**ssani|e** (**-a**) *nt* (*Mot*) choke; (*zasysanie*) suction
**ssaw|ka** (**-ki, -ki**) (*dat sg* **-ce**, *gen pl* **-ek**) *f* (*do odkurzacza*) attachment
**ssący** *adj*: **pompa ssąca** suction pump
**st.** *abbr* (= *starszy*) Sr (= *Senior*); (= *stacja*) sta. (= *station*)
**stabilizacj|a** (**-i**) *f* stabilization
**stabilizato|r** (**-ra, -ry**) (*loc sg* **-rze**) *m* (*Elektr*) stabilizer
**stabiliz|ować (-uję, -ujesz)** (*perf* **u-**) *vt* to stabilize; **stabilizować się** *vr* to stabilize
**stabilnoś|ć** (**-ci**) *f* stability
**stabilny** *adj* stable
**stacj|a** (**-i, -e**) (*gen pl* **-i**) *f* station; **~ kolejowa/autobusowa** railway (*Brit*) *lub* railroad (*US*)/bus station; **~ telewizyjna/radiowa** TV/radio station; **~ benzynowa** filling station, petrol (*Brit*) *lub* gas (*US*) station; **~ obsługi** service station; **~ dysków** (*Komput*) disk drive
**stacjonarny** *adj* stationary
**stacjon|ować (-uję, -ujesz)** *vi* to be stationed
**stacyj|ka** (**-ki, -ki**) (*dat sg* **-ce**, *gen pl* **-ek**) *f dimin od* **stacja**; (*pot*: *Mot*) ignition
**stacz|ać (-am, -asz)** (*perf* **stoczyć**) *vt* (*kamień, bryłę*) to roll down; (*walkę, pojedynek*) to fight; **staczać się** *vr* to roll down, to tumble (down); (*przen*) to go downhill
**st|ać (-oję, -oisz)** (*imp* **-ój**, *perf* **-anąć**) *vi* to stand; (*o fabryce*) to be at a standstill; **stój!** halt!; **mój zegarek stoi** my watch has stopped; **~ w miejscu** to stand still; **~ na czele** *+gen* to (spear)head; **~ w kolejce** to queue (up) (*Brit*), to line up (*US*); **~ źle/dobrze** (*o sprawach, interesach*) to be going badly/well; **umowa stoi!** you got a deal!; **nie ~ mnie na to** I can't afford it
**sta|ć się (-nę, -niesz)** (*imp* **-ń**) *vb perf od* **stawać się**
**stadio|n** (**-nu, -ny**) (*loc sg* **-nie**) *m* stadium
**stadi|um** (**-um, -a**) (*gen pl* **-ów**) *nt inv in sg* stage
**stad|ko** (**-ka, -ka**) (*instr sg* **-kiem**, *gen pl* **-ek**) *nt dimin od* **stado**
**stadni|na** (**-ny, -ny**) (*dat sg* **-nie**) *f* stud (farm)
**stadny** *adj* (*zwierzę*) gregarious, social; **instynkt ~** herd instinct
**sta|do** (**-da, -da**) (*loc sg* **-dzie**) *nt* (*bydła*) herd; (*wilków*) pack; (*ptaków*) flock
**stagnacj|a** (**-i**) *f* stagnation
**staj|ać (-e)** *vb perf od* **tajać**
**stajenny** *adj* stable *attr* ▷ *m decl like adj* groom
**staj|nia** (**-ni, -nie**) (*gen pl* **-ni**) *f* stable
**stal** (**-i**) *f* steel; **~ nierdzewna** stainless steel
**stalagmi|t** (**-tu, -tu**) (*loc sg* **-cie**) *m* stalagmite
**stalakty|t** (**-tu, -ty**) (*loc sg* **-cie**) *m* stalactite
**stale** *adv* constantly
**stalow|nia** (**-ni, -nie**) (*gen pl* **-ni**) *f* steelworks
**stalowy** *adj* (*ze stali*) steel; (*w kolorze stali*) steely; **mieć stalowe nerwy** to have nerves of steel
**stalów|ka** (**-ki, -ki**) (*dat sg* **-ce**, *gen pl* **-ek**) *f* nib
**stał|a** (**-ej, -e**) *f decl like adj* constant
**stałoś|ć** (**-ci**) *f* (*uczuć, charakteru*) constancy; (*zatrudnienia, dochodów*) permanence
**stały** *adj* (*ciało, stan skupienia*) solid; (*mieszkaniec, praca, pobyt*) permanent; (*klient*) regular; (*komisja*) standing; (*wysokość, uczucie, charakter*) constant; (*cena*) fixed; (*postęp*) steady; **na stałe** permanently; **prąd ~** direct current
**stamtąd** *adv* from (over) there; **niedaleko ~** near there
**sta|n** (**-nu**) (*loc sg* **-nie**) *m* (*położenie*) state; (*kondycja*) (*nom pl* **-ny**) condition; (*część państwa*) (*nom pl* **-ny**) state; **w dobrym/złym ~ie** in good/poor condition; **~ konta** balance (of account); **~ zdrowia** (state of) health, condition; **~ podgorączkowy** slight temperature; **~ cywilny** marital status; **~ wojenny** martial law; **~ wyjątkowy** state of emergency; **być w ~ie coś zrobić** to be capable of doing sth; **mąż ~u** statesman; **zamach ~u** coup (d'état)
**sta|nąć (-nę, -niesz)** (*imp* **-ń**) *vb perf od* **stać, stawać** ▷ *vi perf* (*o pomniku, budynku*) to be erected; **stanęło na tym, że ...** it was decided that ...
**stancj|a** (**-i, -e**) (*dat sg* **-i**, *gen pl* **-i**) *f* digs *pl*; **mieszkać na stancji** to live in digs
**standar|d** (**-du, -dy**) (*loc sg* **-dzie**) *m* standard
**standardowy** *adj* standard
**standaryzacj|a** (**-i**) *f* standardization
**stanic|a** (**-y, -e**) (*dat sg* **-y**) *f simple campsite on a river or lake*
**stani|eć (-eje)** *vb perf od* **tanieć**
**stani|k** (**-ka, -ki**) (*instr sg* **-kiem**) *m* bra
**stanowczo** *adv* firmly

S

**stanowczoś|ć** (**-ci**) *f* firmness
**stanowczy** *adj* firm
**stan|owić** (**-owię, -owisz**) (*imp* **-ów**) *vt* (*całość*) to make up; (*problem*) to pose, to present; (*naruszenie praw, wyjątek*) to constitute; ~ **przykład czegoś** to exemplify sth; ~ **o czymś** to determine sth; ~ **prawo** to make law
**stanowis|ko** (**-ka, -ka**) (*instr sg* **-kiem**) *nt* (*posada*) position, post; (*miejsce*) position; (*na dworcu autobusowym*) bay; (*pogląd*) stance, standpoint; **stać na stanowisku, że ...** to take the position *lub* view that ...; **zajmować (zająć** *perf*) ~ **w jakiejś sprawie** to take a stand on sth; **zwolnić** (*perf*) *lub* **usunąć** (*perf*) **kogoś ze stanowiska** to remove sb from the post
**stanowy** *adj*: **administracja stanowa** state administration; **społeczeństwo stanowe** class society
**Stany Zjednoczone (Ameryki)** (**Stanów Zjednoczonych**) *pl* the United States (of America)
**stapi|ać** (**-am, -asz**) (*perf* **stopić**) *vt* (*rozpuszczać*) to melt; (*łączyć*) to fuse; **stapiać się** *vr* (*rozpuszczać się*) to melt; (*łączyć się*) to fuse
**star|a** (**-ej, -e**) *f* (*pot*) *decl like adj* (*koleżanka*) old girl (*pot*); (*szefowa*) boss; (*matka*) old lady (*pot*); *patrz też* **stary**
**star|ać się** (**-am, -asz**) (*perf* **po-**) *vr* to try; **staram się o pracę** I'm looking for a job
**stara|nia** (**-ń**) *pl* efforts *pl*; **dokładać (dołożyć** *perf*) **(wszelkich) starań (, aby ...)** to do one's (very) best (to ...)
**starannie** *adv* carefully
**staranność|ć** (**-ci**) *f* care
**staranny** *adj* careful
**staran|ować** (**-uję, -ujesz**) *vb perf od* **taranować**
**star|cie** (**-cia, -cia**) (*gen pl* **-ć**) *nt* (*bitwa*) clash, scuffle; (*kłótnia*) squabble
**starcz|ać** (**-a**) (*perf* **-yć**) *vi* to be enough; (*do końca miesiąca, na długo*) to last; **starczy!** that's enough!, that'll do!
**starczy** *adj* senile; **zniedołężnienie starcze** senility
**starcz|yć** (**-y**) *vb perf od* **starczać**
**staro|cie** (**-ci**) *pl* (*antyki*) antiques *pl*; (*graty*) (old) junk
**starodawny** *adj* antique
**staromodny** *adj* old-fashioned
**staropolski** *adj* Old Polish
**staroś|ć** (**-ci**) *f* (*człowieka*) old age; (*budynku*) age; **ze starości** (*pomarszczony*) with age; (*umrzeć*) of old age; **na** ~ (*zabezpieczenie*) for old age
**staroświecki** *adj* (*człowiek, poglądy*) old-fashioned, antiquated; (*dom, ubranie*) old-fashioned
**starożytnoś|ć** (**-ci**) *f* antiquity
**starożytny** *adj* ancient
**starszeńst|wo** (**-wa**) (*loc sg* **-wie**) *nt* seniority
**starszy** *adj comp od* **stary**; ~ **brat** elder *lub* older brother; ~ **rangą** senior, superior
**star|t** (**-tu, -ty**) (*loc sg* **-cie**) *m* (*początek działalności, biegu*) start; (*samolotu*) take-off; (*rakiety*) launch, lift-off; **~!** go!
**starte|r** (**-ra**) (*loc sg* **-rze**) *m* (*Sport*) (*nom pl* **-rzy**) starter; (*rozrusznik*) (*nom pl* **-ry**) starter
**start|ować** (**-uję, -ujesz**) (*perf* **wy-**) *vi* to start; (*rozpoczynać lot*) to take off; ~ **w zawodach** to take part in a competition
**startowy** *adj* (*stanowisko*) take-off *attr*; **pas** ~ runway
**starusz|ek** (**-ka, -kowie**) (*instr sg* **-kiem**) *m* old man
**starusz|ka** (**-ki, -ki**) (*dat sg* **-ce**, *gen pl* **-ek**) *f* old lady
**stary** *adj* old; (*chleb itp.*) stale; **co nowego? — wszystko po staremu** what's new? — nothing much ▷ *m* (*pot*) *decl like adj* (*kolega*) old boy (*pot*); (*szef*) boss; (*ojciec*) old man (*pot*)
**sta|rzec** (**-rca, -rcy**) *m* old man; **dom starców** old people's home; **dom spokojnej starości** nursing *lub* rest home
**starz|eć się** (**-eję, -ejesz**) *vr* (*perf* **ze-**) (*o człowieku*) to age; (*o tytoniu, żywności*) to go stale; (*przen: o dziele, teorii*) to become stale
**sta|rzy** (**-rych**) *pl decl like adj* (*pot: rodzice*) folks *pl* (*pot*); *patrz też* **stary**
**starzy|zna** (**-zny**) (*dat sg* **-źnie**) *f* junk; **handlarz starzyzną** junk dealer
**stateczni|k** (**-ka, -ki**) (*instr sg* **-kiem**) *m* (*Lot*) tail fin
**stateczny** *adj* (*człowiek, zachowanie*) staid, sedate; (*łódź, samolot*) stable
**stat|ek** (**-ku, -ki**) (*instr sg* **-kiem**) *m* (*Żegl*) ship; ~ **handlowy/pasażerski** merchant/ passenger ship; ~ **kosmiczny** spaceship; **wsiąść** (*perf*) **na** ~ to board a ship; **płynąć statkiem** to sail
**statu|a** (**-y** *lub* **-i, -y**) (*dat sg* **-i**, *gen pl* **-i**) *f* statue
**statuet|ka** (**-ki, -ki**) (*dat sg* **-ce**, *gen pl* **-ek**) *f* statuette
**statu|s** (**-su**) (*loc sg* **-sie**) *m* status
**statu|t** (**-tu, -ty**) (*loc sg* **-cie**) *m* (*organizacji*) charter; (*też:* **statut spółki**) statute(s *pl*) *lub* articles *pl* of association
**statutowy** *adj* statutory; **kapitał nominalny** *lub* ~ authorized capital
**statyczny** *adj* static
**staty|sta** (**-sty, -ści**) (*dat sg* **-ście**) *m decl like f in sg* (*Film*) extra

**statystyczny** *adj* (*badanie, tabela*) statistical; (*Polak, czytelnik*) average

**statysty|ka** (**-ki, -ki**) (*dat sg* **-ce**) *f* (*nauka*) statistics; (*dane*) statistics *pl*

**staty|w** (**-wu, -wy**) (*loc sg* **-wie**) *m* tripod

**sta|w** (**-wu, -wy**) (*loc sg* **-wie**) *m* (*zbiornik wodny*) pond; (*Anat*) joint

**sta|wać (-ję, -jesz)** (*imp* **-waj**, *perf* **-nąć**) *vi* (*wstawać*) to stand up; (*być ustawianym pionowo*) to stand; (*zatrzymywać się, przestawać funkcjonować*) to stop; **~ rzędem/szeregiem** *lub* **w rzędzie/szeregu** to stand in a line/row; **~ do wyborów (prezydenckich)** to run (for president); **~ na głowie** (*przen*) to bend over backwards; **stanąć na nogi** (*przen*) to get back on one's feet; **~ dęba** (*o koniu*) to rear; (*o włosach*) to stand on end; **stanąć po czyjejś stronie** to side with sb, to take sb's side; **stanąć w czyjejś obronie** to stand up for sb; **stanął jak wryty** he stopped dead; **stanąć na wysokości zadania** to rise to the occasion; **stanąć wobec trudności/problemu** to face difficulties/a problem; **~ przed sądem** to stand trial

**sta|wać się (-ję, -jesz)** (*imp* **-waj**, *perf* **stać**) *vr* (*przed przymiotnikiem*) to get, to grow, to become; (*przed rzeczownikiem, zaimkiem*): **stawać się kimś/czymś** to become sb/sth; (*zdarzać się*) to happen; **co się stało?** what happened?

**stawi|ać (-am, -asz)** (*perf* **postawić**) *vt* (*umieszczać*) to put, to place; (*budowlę*) to put up; (*kołnierz*) to raise; (*pytanie*) to ask; (*diagnozę, wniosek*) to make; (*dawać jako stawkę*) to bet, to wager; (*fundować*) to stand, to buy ▹ *vi*: **~ na kogoś/coś** to place a bet on sb/sth; (*przen*) to back sb/sth; **~ kogoś/coś za przykład** to make an example of sb/sth; **~ kogoś w trudnym położeniu** to put sb on the spot; **~ na swoim** to get one's own way; **~ stopnie** to give grades; **~ opór** to put up resistance; **~ coś pod znakiem zapytania** to put sth in question; **to cię postawi na nogi** this will put you back on your feet

**stawi|ać się (-am, -asz)** *vr* (*zgłaszać się*) (*perf* **stawić**) to report; (*pot: przeciwstawiać się*) (*perf* **postawić**) to put one's foot down; **stawiać się w czyimś położeniu** to put o.s. into sb's shoes

**sta|wić (-wię, -wisz)** *vt perf*: **~ czoło komuś/czemuś** to face (up to) sb/sth

**sta|wić się (-wię, -wisz)** *vb perf od* **stawiać się**

**staw|ka** (**-ki, -ki**) (*dat sg* **-ce**, *gen pl* **-ek**) *f* (*podstawa płatności*) rate; (*w grze, rozgrywce*) stake; (*biegaczy, koni*) the field

**staż** (**-u**) *m* (*praktyka*) training; **~ pracy** (job) seniority; **odbywać ~** to receive training

**staży|sta** (**-sty, -ści**) (*dat sg* **-ście**) *m decl like f in sg* trainee; **lekarz ~** houseman (*Brit*), intern (*US*)

**stąd** *adv* (*z tego miejsca*) from here; (*z tego powodu*) hence; **niedaleko ~** not far from here, near here; **to daleko ~** it's far from here, it's a long way off *lub* away; **wyszła ~ o piątej** she left here at five; **~ dotąd** from here to here; **nie jestem ~** I'm a stranger here; **ni ~, ni zowąd** out of the blue

**stąp|ać (-am, -asz)** (*perf* **-nąć**) *vi* to tread; **(mocno) ~ po ziemi** (*przen*) to have one's feet (firmly) on the ground

**stąp|nąć (-nę, -niesz)** (*imp* **-nij**) *vb perf od* **stąpać**

**stchórz|yć (-ę, -ysz)** *vb perf od* **tchórzyć**

**ste|k** (**-ku**) (*instr sg* **-kiem**) *m* (*Kulin*) (*nom pl* **-ki**) steak; **~ kłamstw** a pack of lies; **~ wyzwisk** a hail of abuse

**stelaż** (**-a** *lub* **-u, -e**) (*gen pl* **-y**) *m* (*rama*) frame; (*podstawka*) stand; **plecak ze ~em zewnętrznym/wewnętrznym** external/internal frame rucksack (*Brit*) *lub* backpack (*US*)

**stemp|el** (**-la, -le**) (*gen pl* **-li**) *m* stamp; **~ pocztowy** postmark

**stempl|ować (-uję, -ujesz)** (*perf* **o-** *lub* **pod-**) *vt* to stamp

**stenogra|f** (**-fa, -fowie**) (*loc sg* **-fie**) *m* shorthand typist (*Brit*), stenographer (*US*)

**stenografi|a** (**-i**) *f* shorthand (*Brit*), stenography (*US*)

**stenograficzny** *adj* shorthand *attr* (*Brit*), stenographic (*US*)

**stenograf|ować (-uję, -ujesz)** *vt* to take down in shorthand, to stenograph

**stenogra|m** (**-mu, -my**) (*loc sg* **-mie**) *m* stenographic record

**stenotypist|ka** (**-ki, -ki**) (*dat sg* **-ce**, *gen pl* **-ek**) *f* shorthand typist, stenotypist

**ste|p** (**-pu, -py**) (*loc sg* **-pie**) *m* steppe

**step|ować (-uję, -ujesz)** *vi* to tap-dance

**ste|r** (**-ru, -ry**) (*loc sg* **-rze**) *m* (*Żegl, Lot*) rudder; (*przen: kierowanie*) helm; **u ~u** at the helm

**stercz|eć (-ę, -ysz)** *vi* (*wystawać*) to jut *lub* stick out, to protrude; (*pot: tkwić w jednym miejscu*) to hang around (*pot*)

**stereo** *nt inv* (*efekt*) stereo ▹ *adj inv* stereo *attr*

**stereofoni|a** (**-i**) *f* stereo(phony)

**stereofoniczny** *adj* stereo(phonic)

**stereoskopi|a** (**-i**) *f* (*Fot*) stereoscopy

**stereoty|p** (**-pu, -py**) (*loc sg* **-pie**) *m* stereotype

**stereotypowy** *adj* stereotypical, stereotyped

**sterni|k** (**-ka, -cy**) (*instr sg* **-kiem**) *m* (*Żegl*) helmsman; (*Sport*) cox(swain)

**ster|ować (-uję, -ujesz)** *vt +instr* (*statkiem*) to steer; (*mechanizmem*) to control

S

**sterowani|e** (**-a**) *nt*: **zdalne ~** remote control
**sterowany** *adj*: **~ zdalnie/radiem** remote-/radio-controlled; **pocisk zdalnie ~** guided missile
**stero|wiec** (**-wca, -wce**) *m* airship, dirigible
**sterow|nia** (**-ni, -nie**) (*gen pl* **-ni**) *f* (*Żegl*) pilot house, wheelhouse; (*Tech*) control room
**sterowniczy** *adj*: **pulpit ~** control panel
**sterowni|k** (**-ka, -ki**) (*instr sg* **-kiem**) *m* (*Komput*) driver
**sterowy** *adj*: **koło sterowe** steering wheel; **drążek ~** joystick
**sterroryz|ować (-uję, -ujesz)** *vb perf od* **terroryzować**
**ster|ta** (**-ty, -ty**) (*dat sg* **-cie**) *f* (*książek, ubrań*) heap, pile; (*słomy*) stack
**stery|d** (**-du, -dy**) (*loc sg* **-dzie**) *m* (*Chem*) steroid
**sterylizacj|a** (**-i**) *f* sterilization
**steryliz|ować (-uję, -ujesz)** (*perf* **wy-**) *vt* to sterilize
**sterylnoś|ć** (**-ci**) *f* sterility
**sterylny** *adj* sterile
**stetosko|p** (**-pu, -py**) (*loc sg* **-pie**) *m* (*Med*) stethoscope
**stewar|d** (**-da, -dzi** *lub* **-dowie**) (*loc sg* **-dzie**) *m* (*Żegl*) steward; (*Lot*) flight attendant
**stewardes|sa** (**-sy, -sy**) (*dat sg* **-sie**) *f* (*Lot*) flight attendant; (*Żegl*) stewardess
**stęchli|zna** (**-zny**) (*dat sg* **-źnie**) *f* mustiness
**stęchły** *adj* musty
**stęk|ać (-am, -asz)** (*perf* **-nąć**) *vi* (*wzdychać, jęczeć*) to groan, to moan; (*pot*: *narzekać*) to moan (*pot*), to bellyache (*pot*)
**stę|p** (**-pa**) (*loc sg* **-pie**) *m* (*chód konia*) walk; **jechać ~a** to walk
**stę|piać (-piam, -piasz)** (*perf* **-pić**) *vt* to blunt; **stępiać się** *vr* to become blunt
**stępie|ć (-ję, -jesz)** *vb perf od* **tępieć**
**stęp|ka** (**-ki, -ki**) (*dat sg* **-ce**, *gen pl* **-ek**) *f* (*Żegl*) keel
**stęsk|nić się (-nię, -nisz)** (*imp* **-nij**) *vr perf*: **stęskniłam się za Markiem/domem** I miss Mark/home
**stęskniony** *adj*: **~ (za kimś/czymś)** longing (for sb/sth)
**stęż|eć (-eje)** (*pt* **-ał**) *vb perf od* **tężeć**
**stęże|nie** (**-nia, -nia**) (*gen pl* **-ń**) *nt* (*Chem*) concentration; **~ pośmiertne** rigor mortis; **~ pyłków (w powietrzu)** pollen count
**stężony** *adj* concentrated
**stiu|k** (**-ku, -ki**) (*instr sg* **-kiem**) *m* stucco
**stłacz|ać (-am, -asz)** (*perf* **stłoczyć**) *vt* to cram, to crowd; **stłaczać się** *vr* to crowd
**stłam|sić (-szę, -sisz)** (*imp* **-ś**) *vb perf od* **tłamsić**
**stłu|c (-kę, -czesz)** *vb perf od* **tłuc**
**stłucze|nie** (**-nia, -nia**) (*gen pl* **-ń**) *nt* bruise
**stłucz|ka** (**-ki, -ki**) (*dat sg* **-ce**, *gen pl* **-ek**) *f* (*wypadek*) bump, fender bender (US) (*pot*); (*złom*) cullet, broken glass
**stłu|mić (-mię, -misz)** *vb perf od* **tłumić**
**stłumiony** *adj* (*odgłos itp.*) muted, muffled
**sto** (*jak*: **dwadzieścia**) *num* hundred; **sto dwadzieścia** a hundred and twenty; **sto osób/stu mężczyzn** a hundred people/men; **„sto lat!”** (*życzenie*) “many happy returns (of the day)”; (*piosenka*: *urodzinowa*) ≈ “Happy Birthday”; (: *śpiewana przy różnych okazjach*) ≈ “For He’s a Jolly Good Fellow”; **sto razy** (*przen*) a hundred times
**stocz|nia** (**-ni, -nie**) (*gen pl* **-ni**) *f* shipyard
**stocznio|wiec** (**-wca, -wcy**) *m* shipyard worker
**stoczniowy** *adj*: **przemysł ~** shipbuilding (industry)
**stocz|yć (-ę, -ysz)** *vb perf od* **staczać**
**stod|oła** (**-oły, -oły**) (*dat sg* **-ole**, *gen pl* **-ół**) *f* barn
**stoicki** *adj* stoic(al)
**stoicyz|m** (**-mu**) (*loc sg* **-mie**) *m* stoicism
**stois|ko** (**-ka, -ka**) (*instr sg* **-kiem**) *nt* (*w sklepie*) department; (*stragan*) stall, stand; (*na targach handlowych*) stand; **~ z kwiatami** flower stand *lub* stall
**stoisz** *itp. vb patrz* **stać**
**stoja|k** (**-ka, -ki**) (*instr sg* **-kiem**) *m* (*na ubrania, parasole, do mikrofonu*) stand; (*na rowery, buty*) rack; **~ na nuty** music stand
**stojąco** *adv*: **na ~** standing up; **owacja na ~** standing ovation
**stojący** *adj*: **lampa stojąca** standard lamp (*Brit*), floor lamp (*US*); **miejsca stojące** standing room; **dom wolno ~** detached house
**stoję** *itp. vb patrz* **stać**
**sto|k** (**-ku, -ki**) (*instr sg* **-kiem**) *m* slope
**stokrot|ka** (**-ki, -ki**) (*dat sg* **-ce**, *gen pl* **-ek**) *f* daisy
**stokrotnie** *adv* (*sto razy*) a hundred times; **~ dziękuję** thank you (ever) so much
**stokrotny** *adj* hundredfold; **stokrotne dzięki!** (*pot*) thanks a million! (*pot*)
**stolar|ka** (**-ki**) (*dat sg* **-ce**) *f* (*elementy drewniane*) carpentry, woodwork; (*stolarstwo*) carpentry
**stolar|nia** (**-ni, -nie**) (*gen pl* **-ni**) *f* carpenter’s (work)shop
**stolarski** *adj* carpenter’s *attr*
**stolarst|wo** (**-wa**) (*loc sg* **-wie**) *nt* carpentry; (*artystyczne*) cabinet-making
**stolarz** (**-a, -e**) (*gen pl* **-y**) *m* carpenter; (*artystyczny*) cabinet-maker
**stole** *n patrz* **stół**

**stol|ec** (**-ca, -ce**) *m* (*Med*) stool
**stolic|a** (**-y, -e**) *f* capital
**stoli|k** (**-ka, -ki**) (*instr sg* **-kiem**) *m* (small) table; (*w restauracji*) table
**stolnic|a** (**-y, -e**) *f* moulding (*Brit*) *lub* molding (*US*) board
**stołeczny** *adj* (*miasto*) capital *attr*; (*urząd*) central
**stoł|ek** (**-ka, -ki**) (*instr sg* **-kiem**) *m* (*mebel*) stool; (*pot: stanowisko*) berth (*pot*)
**stoł|ować się (-uję, -ujesz)** *vr*: **tu się stołuję** this is where I go for my meals
**stołowy** *adj* (*woda, wino, tenis*) table *attr*; **zastawa/łyżka stołowa** tableware/ tablespoon; **pokój ~** dining room; **meble stołowe** dining-room furniture
**stołów|ka** (**-ki, -ki**) (*dat sg* **-ce**, *gen pl* **-ek**) *f* canteen
**stołu** *itp. n patrz* **stół**
**stomatolo|g** (**-ga, -dzy** *lub* **-gowie**) (*instr sg* **-giem**) *m* (*Med*) dental surgeon, dentist
**stomatologi|a** (**-i**) *f* (*Med*) dentistry
**stomatologiczny** *adj*: **gabinet ~** dentist's (surgery); **leczenie stomatologiczne** dental treatment
**ston|ka** (**-ki, -ki**) (*dat sg* **-ce**, *gen pl* **-ek**) *f* (*też:* **stonka ziemniaczana**) Colorado *lub* potato beetle
**ston|oga** (**-ogi, -ogi**) (*dat sg* **-odze**, *gen pl* **-óg**) *f* wood louse, centipede
**ston|ować (-uję, -ujesz)** *vb perf od* **tonować**
**stonowany** *adj* (*barwa, światło*) subdued
**sto|p**[1] (**-pu, -py**) (*loc sg* **-pie**) *m* (*metali*) alloy; (*pot: też:* **światło stopu**) brake light
**stop**[2] *excl*: **~!** (*stój!*) hold it!, stop!; (*w telegramie*) stop
**st|opa** (**-opy, -opy**) (*dat sg* **-opie**, *gen pl* **-óp**) *f* foot; **od stóp do głów** from head to foot; **~ życiowa** standard of living, living standard; **~ procentowa/inflacji** interest/inflation rate; **u stóp czegoś** at the foot of sth; **pod ~mi** underfoot; **odpowiadać z wolnej stopy** (*Prawo*) to be released pending trial
**stope|r** (**-ra, -ry**) (*loc sg* **-rze**) *m* (*zegarek*) stopwatch; (*Futbol*) centre-half (*Brit*), center halfback (*US*)
**sto|pić (-pię, -pisz)** *vb perf od* **stapiać**
**sto|pień** (**-pnia, -pnie**) (*gen pl* **-pni**) *m* (*schodów*) stair, step; (*w hierarchii*) rank; (*ocena*) mark (*Brit*), grade (*US*); (*jednostka miary*) degree; (*poziom, intensywność*) degree, extent; **~ równy/ wyższy/najwyższy** positive/comparative/ superlative degree; **~ naukowy** (university) degree; **~ wojskowy** military rank; **20 stopni Celsjusza** 20 degrees centigrade *lub* Celsius; **poparzenia drugiego stopnia** second-degree burns; **zakręt** *lub* **zwrot o 180 stopni** U-turn; **zwrot o 180 stopni** (*przen*) about-face, volte-face; **w pewnym stopniu** *lub* **do pewnego stopnia** to some degree *lub* extent; **w dużym stopniu** to a large extent; **„uwaga ~!"** "mind the step"
**stop|ka** (**-ki, -ki**) (*dat sg* **-ce**, *gen pl* **-ek**) *f* copyright note
**stopni|eć (-eje)** (*pt* **-ał**) *vb perf od* **topnieć**
**stopni|ować (-uję, -ujesz)** *vt* (*stopniowo zwiększać*) to increase *lub* raise gradually; (*różnicować*) to graduate; (*Jęz*) to compare
**stopniowani|e** (**-a**) *nt* (*Jęz*) comparison; (*zwiększanie*) gradual increase; (*gradacja*) gradation
**stopniowo** *adv* gradually
**stopniowy** *adj* gradual
**stop|ować (-uję, -ujesz)** *vt* (*perf* **za-** *lub* **przy-**) to halt, to stop
**sto|ra** (**-ry, -ry**) (*dat sg* **-rze**) *f* curtain (*Brit*), drape (*US*)
**storczy|k** (**-ka, -ki**) (*instr sg* **-kiem**) *m* orchid
**sto|s** (**-su, -sy**) (*loc sg* **-sie**) *m* (*śmieci, ubrań*) heap, pile; (*talerzy, książek*) stack; (*ofiarny*) pyre; **spalić** (*perf*) **kogoś na ~ie** to burn sb at the stake
**stos|ować (-uję, -ujesz)** (*perf* **za-**) *vt* (*metody, przepisy, siłę*) to apply; (*leki*) to administer; **stosować się** *vr*: **~ się do** *+gen* (*mieć zastosowanie*) to apply to; (*przestrzegać*) to comply with
**stosowany** *adj* applied
**stosownie** *adv* (*odpowiednio*) appropriately, suitably; (*przyzwoicie*) properly; **~ do czegoś** in accordance with sth; **~ do tego** accordingly
**stosowny** *adj* appropriate, suitable; **uważać** *lub* **uznać za stosowne coś zrobić** to see *lub* think fit to do sth
**stosun|ek** (**-ku, -ki**) (*instr sg* **-kiem**) *m* (*zależność*) relation, relationship; (*traktowanie*) attitude; (*liczbowy*) ratio; (*też:* **stosunek płciowy**) intercourse; **w stosunku do** *+gen* (*w porównaniu z*) in *lub* with relation to; (*w odniesieniu do*) with reference to; **w stosunku 3 do 2** in the ratio of 3 to 2; **stosunki** *pl* (*kontakty*) relations *pl*, relationships *pl*; (*znajomości*) connections *pl*; (*warunki*) conditions *pl*; **stosunki dyplomatyczne** diplomatic relations; **być z kimś w dobrych/złych stosunkach** to be on good/ bad terms with sb
**stosunkowo** *adv* relatively, comparatively
**stosunkowy** *adj* relative, comparative
**stowarzysz|ać się (-am, -asz)** (*perf* **-yć**) *vr* to form an association
**stowarzysze|nie** (**-nia, -nia**) (*gen pl* **-ń**) *nt* association

S

**stowarzysz|yć się (-ę, -ysz)** *vb perf od* **stowarzyszać się**

**stoż|ek** (**-ka, -ki**) (*instr sg* **-kiem**) *m* cone

**stożkowy** *adj* conical, cone-shaped

**st|óg** (**-ogu, -ogi**) (*instr sg* **-ogiem**) *m* haystack; **szukać igły w stogu siana** (*przen*) to look *lub* search for a needle in a haystack

**stój** *itp. vb patrz* **stać**

**stój|ka** (**-ki, -ki**) (*dat sg* **-ce**, *gen pl* **-ek**) *f* (*kołnierzyk*) stand-up *lub* turnup collar; **~ na rękach/na głowie** handstand/headstand

**st|ół** (**-ołu, -oły**) (*loc sg* **-ole**) *m* table; **przy stole** at the table; **proszę do stołu** dinner *itp.* is served; **sprzątać ze stołu** to clear the table

**stóp** *n patrz* **stopa**

**stó|wa** (**-wy, -wy**) (*dat sg* **-wie**) *f* (*pot*) a hundred

**str.** *abbr* (= *strona*) p. (= *page*); (= *strony*) pp. (= *pages*)

**stracenі|e** (**-a**) *nt*: **nie mieć nic/chwili do stracenia** to have nothing/no time to lose

**strace|niec** (**-ńca, -ńcy**) *m* desperado

**stra|ch** (**-chu**) *m* (*lęk*) fear; (*kukła*) (*nom pl* **-chy**); **~ na wróble** scarecrow; **blady ~** mortal fear; **mieć ~a** (*pot*) to have cold feet (*pot*); **~ pomyśleć** I shudder to think

**strachliwy** *adj* (*zwierzę*) skittish; (*człowiek*) cowardly

**stra|cić (-cę, -cisz)** (*imp* **-ć**) *vb perf od* **tracić**

**stracony** *adj* (*przegrany*) lost; (*skazany na porażkę*) doomed; **(jeszcze) nic straconego** all is not lost (yet); **stoją na straconej pozycji** they're fighting a losing battle

**straga|n** (**-nu, -ny**) (*loc sg* **-nie**) *m* stall

**straganiarz** (**-a, -e**) (*gen pl* **-y**) *m* stallholder

**straj|k** (**-ku, -ki**) (*instr sg* **-kiem**) *m* strike; **~ okupacyjny/głodowy** sit-down/hunger strike

**strajk|ować (-uję, -ujesz)** *vi*: **~** to be on strike, to strike

**strajkowy** *adj*: **akcja strajkowa** industrial action; **płaca strajkowa** strike pay

**strapie|nie** (**-nia, -nia**) (*gen pl* **-ń**) *nt* heartache, worry

**strapiony** *adj* crestfallen

**strasza|k** (**-ka, -ki**) (*instr sg* **-kiem**) *m* (*imitacja rewolweru*) toy gun

**straszliwy** *adj* (*przejmujący lękiem*) horrendous, horrifying; (*bardzo zły*) horrible; (*pot: niezmierny, intensywny*) horrendous

**strasznie** *adv* terribly, awfully

**straszny** *adj* (*przerażający*) scary, frightening; (*zły, okropny*) dreadful, terrible; (*bardzo duży*) tremendous

**strasz|yć (-ę, -ysz)** *vt* to scare, to frighten ▷ *vi*: **w tym domu straszy** this house is haunted

**straszyd|ło** (**-ła, -ła**) (*loc sg* **-le**, *gen pl* **-eł**) *nt*: **wyglądać jak ~** (*pot*) to look a fright (*pot*)

**stra|ta** (**-ty, -ty**) (*dat sg* **-cie**) *f* (*materialna, moralna*) loss; **~ czasu/pieniędzy** a waste of time/money; **ponieść** (*perf*) **stratę** to incur *lub* suffer a loss; **(sprzedać** (*perf*) **coś) ze stratą** (to sell sth) at a loss; **zyski i straty** profit and loss; **spisać** (*perf*) **kogoś/coś na straty** to write sb/sth off; **straty w ludziach** casualties

**strate|g** (**-ga, -dzy**) (*instr sg* **-giem**) *m* strategist

**strategi|a** (**-i, -e**) (*gen pl* **-i**) *f* strategy

**strategiczny** *adj* strategic

**stratny** *adj*: **być ~m** to be the loser

**stratosfe|ra** (**-ry**) (*dat sg* **-rze**) *f* stratosphere

**strat|ować (-uję, -ujesz)** *vb perf od* **tratować**

**stra|wa** (**-wy**) (*dat sg* **-wie**) *f* (*książk*) fare (*książk*)

**stra|wić (-wię, -wisz)** *vb perf od* **trawić**

**strawny** *adj* digestible; **lekko/ciężko ~** easy/hard to digest

**straż** (**-y, -e**) (*gen pl* **-y**) *f* guard; **trzymać** *lub* **pełnić ~** to stand guard, to be on guard; **~ pożarna** (*instytucja*) fire brigade (*Brit*), fire department (*US*); (*budynek*) fire station; (*wóz*) fire engine (*Brit*), fire truck (*US*); **~ miejska** municipal police; **~ graniczna** border guard; **~ przednia** advance guard; **~ tylna** rearguard; **pod ~ą** under guard; **na ~y** on guard; **stać na ~y czegoś** (*przen*) to guard sth

**strażacki** *adj*: **wóz ~** fire engine

**straża|k** (**-ka, -cy**) (*instr sg* **-kiem**) *m* fireman, fire fighter

**strażniczy** *adj*: **budka strażnicza** sentry box; **wieża strażnicza** watchtower

**strażni|k** (**-ka, -cy**) (*instr sg* **-kiem**) *m* (*w instytucji*) (security) guard; (*więzienny*) warder; **~ leśny** (forest) ranger

**strą|cać (-cam, -casz)** (*perf* **-cić**) *vt* (*wazon*) to knock off; (*liść: z rękawa*) to shake off; (*samolot*) to shoot *lub* bring down

**strą|cić (-cę, -cisz)** (*imp* **-ć**) *vb perf od* **strącać**

**strączkowy** *adj*: **roślina strączkowa** leguminous plant, legume; **fasola strączkowa** string *lub* runner (*Brit*) bean

**strą|k** (**-ka, -ki**) (*instr sg* **-kiem**) *m* pod

**stre|fa** (**-fy, -fy**) (*dat sg* **-fie**) *f* zone; **~ podzwrotnikowa** the subtropics, the subtropical region(s); **~ czasowa/klimatyczna** time/climatic zone; **szara ~** (*gospodarcza*) (the) black economy, (economic) twilight zone; **~ wolnocłowa/przygraniczna** free(-trade)/border zone

**strem|ować (-uję, -ujesz)** *vb perf od* **tremować**

**stre|s (-su, -sy)** (*loc sg* **-sie**) *m* stress; **żyć w ~ie** to live under stress
**stres|ować (-uję, -ujesz)** (*perf* **ze-**) *vt* to stress out, to put under stress
**stresowy** *adj* stressful
**stresujący** *adj* stressful
**streszcz|ać (-am, -asz)** (*perf* **streścić**) *vt* to summarize; **streszczać się** *vr* (*pot*) to keep it short, to be brief
**streszcze|nie** (**-nia, -nia**) (*gen pl* **-ń**) *nt* summary
**stre|ścić (-szczę, -ścisz)** (*imp* **-ść**) *vb perf od* **streszczać**
**stręczyciel** (**-a, -e**) (*gen pl* **-i**) *m* procurer
**stręczycielst|wo** (**-wa**) (*loc sg* **-wie**) *nt* procuration
**stripti|z** (**-zu**) (*loc sg* **-zie**) *m* striptease
**striptizer|ka** (**-ki, -ki**) (*dat sg* **-ce**, *gen pl* **-ek**) *f* stripper
**strobosko|p** (**-pu, -py**) (*loc sg* **-pie**) *m* stroboscope
**stro|fa** (**-fy, -fy**) (*dat sg* **-fie**) *f* (*Lit*) verse, stanza
**strof|ować (-uję, -ujesz)** *vt* to scold, to rebuke
**stroiciel** (**-a, -e**) (*gen pl* **-i**) *m* (*też*: **stroiciel fortepianów**) piano tuner
**str|oić (-oję, -oisz)** (*imp* **-ój**) *vt* (*dziecko*) (*perf* **wy-**) to dress up; (*radio, instrument*) (*perf* **na-**) to tune; (*choinkę*) (*perf* **u-**) to decorate; **~ miny** to make *lub* pull faces; **stroić się** *vr* (*ubierać się*) (*perf* **wy-**) to dress up
**stroi|k** (**-ka, -ki**) (*instr sg* **-kiem**) *m* (*Muz*) reed; (*świąteczny*) Christmas wreath; (*na głowę*) headdress
**strojny** *adj* ornate
**stromi|zna** (**-zny, -zny**) (*dat sg* **-źnie**) *f* steep slope
**stromo** *adv* (*wznosić się*) steeply; **tu jest bardzo ~** it's very steep here
**stromy** *adj* steep
**stro|na** (**-ny, -ny**) (*dat sg* **-nie**) *f* side; (*stronica*) page; (*kierunek*) direction; (*Prawo*) party; **~ czynna/bierna** (*Jęz*) active/passive voice; **po lewej/prawej stronie** on the left/right(-hand) side; **po obu ~ch** on either side; **po drugiej stronie ulicy** across the street; **przejść** (*perf*) **na drugą stronę (ulicy)** to cross the street; **~ zewnętrzna/wewnętrzna** the outside/inside; **na lewej stronie** (*ubranie*) inside out; **z drugiej strony** (*z drugiego końca*) from the opposite direction; **z jednej strony ..., z drugiej strony ...** on (the) one hand ..., on the other hand ...; **być po czyjejś stronie** to be on sb's side; **to jej słaba/mocna ~** it's her weak/strong point; **dziadek ze strony ojca** paternal grandfather; **(cztery) strony świata** the (four) cardinal points; **bilet w jedną stronę/w obie strony** single/return ticket (*Brit*), one-way/round-trip ticket (*US*); **w którą stronę?** which way?; **druga ~** (*odwrotna*) the reverse (side); **druga** *lub* **odwrotna ~ medalu** the other side of the coin; **na** *lub* **we wszystkie strony** in all directions; **ze wszystkich stron** from all directions; **to ładnie z twojej strony** it's nice of you; **stawać po czyjejś stronie** to side with sb; **strony** *pl* (*okolica*) parts *pl*
**stronic|a** (**-y, -e**) *f* page
**stro|nić (-nię, -nisz)** (*imp* **-ń**) *vi*: **~ od** *+gen* to shun
**stronnict|wo** (**-wa, -wa**) (*loc sg* **-wie**) *nt* (*Pol*) party; **Polskie S~ Ludowe** Polish Peasant Party
**stronniczoś|ć** (**-ci**) *f* partiality, bias
**stronniczy** *adj* partial, biased
**stronni|k** (**-ka, -cy**) (*instr sg* **-kiem**) *m* supporter, backer
**stro|p** (**-pu, -py**) (*loc sg* **-pie**) *m* ceiling
**stro|pić (-pię, -pisz)** *vt perf* to disconcert; **stropić się** *vr perf* to become disconcerted
**strosz|yć (-ę, -ysz)** (*perf* **na-**) *vt* to ruffle; **stroszyć się** *vr* to bristle
**str|ój** (**-oju, -oje**) *m* (*ubiór*) dress, attire; (*Muz*) key; **~ kąpielowy** bathing *lub* swimming costume (*Brit*), swimsuit (*US*); **~ ludowy/narodowy** national dress; **~ wieczorowy** evening dress *lub* wear
**stróż** (**-a, -e**) *m* porter (*Brit*), janitor (*US*); (*przen*) guardian; **~ nocny** night watchman; **Anioł S~** guardian angel
**struchl|eć (-eję, -ejesz)** (*pt* **-ał, -eli**) *vb perf od* **truchleć**
**stru|ć (-ję, -jesz)** *vt perf* to poison; **struć się** *vr perf* to upset one's stomach
**stru|g** (**-ga, -gi**) (*instr sg* **-giem**) *m* plane (*tool*)
**stru|ga** (**-gi, -gi**) (*dat sg* **-dze**) *f* stream
**strug|ać (-am, -asz)** *vt* (*deskę*) (*perf* **o-**) to plane; (*kij*) (*perf* **o-**) to whittle; (*figurkę*) (*perf* **wy-**) to carve; **~ wariata** (*pot*) to play dumb (*pot*); **~ ważniaka** (*pot*) to put on airs
**struktu|ra** (**-ry, -ry**) (*dat sg* **-rze**) *f* structure
**strukturalny** *adj* structural
**strumie|ń** (**-nia, -nie**) (*gen pl* **-ni**) *m* stream; **lać się strumieniami** to stream; (*o deszczu*) to come down in sheets
**strumy|k** (**-ka, -ki**) (*instr sg* **-kiem**) *m* brook
**stru|na** (**-ny, -ny**) (*dat sg* **-nie**) *f* string; **struny głosowe** vocal cords; **przeciągać (przeciągnąć** *perf*) **strunę** (*przen*) to go too far
**strunowy** *adj*: **instrument ~** stringed instrument
**stru|p** (**-pa, -py**) (*loc sg* **-pie**) *m* scab
**stru|ś** (**-sia, -sie**) *m* ostrich
**struż|ka** (**-ki, -ki**) (*dat sg* **-ce**, *gen pl* **-ek**) *f* trickle

S

**strych** (**-u, -y**) *m* attic, loft (*Brit*)
**strychni|na** (**-ny**) (*dat sg* **-nie**) *f* strychnine
**strycz|ek** (**-ka, -ki**) (*instr sg* **-kiem**) *m* (*sznur*) halter; (*pot: kara śmierci*) the rope
**stryj** (**-a, -owie**) *m* uncle (*father's brother*)
**strza|ł** (**-łu, -ły**) (*loc sg* **-le**) *m* shot; **broń gotowa do ~u** weapon ready to fire; **oddawać (oddać** *perf*) ~ (*Sport*) to take a shot
**strza|ła** (**-ły, -ły**) (*dat sg* **-le**) *f* arrow
**strzał|ka** (**-ki, -ki**) (*dat sg* **-ce**, *gen pl* **-ek**) *f* (*znak*) arrow; (*kompasu, barometru*) pointer
**strząs|ać (-am, -asz)** (*perf* **-nąć**) *vt* (*owoce*) to shake off; (*popiół*) to flick (off)
**strzą|snąć (-snę, -śniesz)** (*imp* **-śnij**) *vb perf od* **strząsać**
**strze|c (-gę, -żesz)** *vt +gen* to guard; **strzec się** *vr +gen* to beware of
**strze|cha** (**-chy, -chy**) (*dat sg* **-sze**) *f* thatched roof, thatch; **kryty strzechą** thatched
**strzel|ać (-am, -asz)** (*perf* **-ić**) *vt* (*bramkę*) to shoot ▷ *vi* (*z broni*) to shoot; (*palcami*) to snap; (*obcasami*) to click; (*Sport*) to shoot; (*o ogniu*) to crackle; (*o korku*) to pop; **~ do kogoś** to shoot at sb; **co ci strzeliło do głowy?** (*pot*) what came over you?
**strzelani|na** (**-ny**) (*dat sg* **-nie**) *f* shoot-out, shooting
**strzel|ba** (**-by, -by**) (*dat sg* **-bie**) *f* rifle
**strzel|ec** (**-ca, -cy**) *m* shooter; (*Wojsk*) rifleman; (*Sport*) scorer; **Strzelec** (*Astrologia*) Sagittarius; **być dobrym strzelcem** to be a good shot; **~ wyborowy** sharpshooter, marksman; **wolny ~** (*przen*) freelancer
**strzelecki** *adj* shooting *attr*
**strzelect|wo** (**-wa**) (*loc sg* **-wie**) *nt* shooting
**strzel|ić (-ę, -isz)** *vb perf od* **strzelać**
**strzelisty** *adj* (*budynek*) soaring
**strzelnic|a** (**-y, -e**) *f* rifle-range; (*w wesołym miasteczku*) shooting gallery
**strzelniczy** *adj*: **proch ~** gunpowder
**strzemienne** (**-go**) *nt decl like adj*; **pić (wypić** *perf*) **~go** to drink one for the road, to drink a stirrup cup
**strzemi|ę** (**-enia, -ona**) *nt* stirrup
**strzep|nąć (-nę, -niesz)** (*imp* **-nij**) *vb perf od* **strzepywać**
**strzep|ywać (-uję, -ujesz)** (*perf* **-nąć**) *vt* (*okruchy*) to shake off; (*kurz, śnieg*) to brush off; (*termometr*) to shake down
**strzeżony** *adj* guarded
**strzę|p** (**-pu, -py**) (*loc sg* **-pie**) *m* (*kawałek*) shred; **podrzeć** (*perf*) **na ~y** to rip *lub* tear to shreds; **w ~ach** in shreds; **~y rozmowy** snatches of conversation
**strzę|pić (-pię, -pisz)** (*perf* **wy-**) *vt* (*materiał*) to fray; **~ sobie język** (*pot*) to waste one's breath; **strzępić się** *vr* to fray
**strzy|c (-gę, -żesz)** *vt* (*perf* **o-**) (*człowieka*): **~ kogoś** to cut sb's hair; (*owcę*) to shear; (*trawę*) to mow; **strzyc się** *vr* (*perf* **o-**) to have one's hair cut
**strzykaw|ka** (**-ki, -ki**) (*dat sg* **-ce**, *gen pl* **-ek**) *f* syringe
**strzyk|nąć (-nę, -niesz)** (*imp* **-nij**) *vb perf od* **strzykać**
**strzyże|nie** (**-nia, -nia**) (*gen pl* **-ń**) *nt* (*włosów, głowy*) hair-cutting; (*owiec*) shearing; (*trawy*) mowing
**strzyży|k** (**-ka, -ki**) (*instr sg* **-kiem**) *m* (*Zool*) wren
**stu** *itd. num patrz* **sto** *itd.*
**studencki** *adj* (*teatr, stołówka*) students'; (*życie*) student *attr*; **dom ~** hall of residence (*Brit*), dormitory (*US*)
**studen|t** (**-ta, -ci**) (*loc sg* **-cie**) *m* student; **~ prawa/medycyny** a law/medical student; **~ pierwszego roku** a first-year student, fresher (*Brit*) (*pot*), freshman (*US*) (*pot*)
**student|ka** (**-ki, -ki**) (*dat sg* **-ce**, *gen pl* **-ek**) *f* student
**studi|a** (**-ów**) *pl* (*nauka na uczelni*) studies *pl*; (*praca badawcza*) research; **skończyć** (*perf*) **~** to graduate
**studi|o** (**-a, -a**) (*gen pl* **-ów**) *nt/inv* studio
**studi|ować (-uję, -ujesz)** *vt* (*prawo, chemię*) to study; (*mapę, rozkład jazdy*) (*perf* **prze-**) to study; **on studiuje medycynę** he's a medical student
**studi|um** (**-um, -a**) (*gen pl* **-ów**) *nt inv in sg* (*rozprawa, dzieło*) study; (*uczelnia*) college; (*Sztuka*) study
**stu|dnia** (**-dni, -dnie**) (*gen pl* **-dni** *lub* **-dzien**) *f* well; **~ bez dna** (*przen*) a bottomless pit
**studniów|ka** (**-ki, -ki**) (*dat sg* **-ce**, *gen pl* **-ek**) *f* *traditional party organized by secondary school students a hundred days before final exams*
**studyjny** *adj* studio *attr*
**stu|dzić (-dzę, -dzisz)** (*imp* **-dź**, *perf* **o-**) *vt* to cool (down)
**studzien|ka** (**-ki, -ki**) (*dat sg* **-ce**, *gen pl* **-ek**) *f* (*niewielka studnia*) well; (*właz kanalizacyjny*) manhole, inspection chamber; **~ ściekowa** catch pit (*Brit*), catch basin (*US*)
**stu|k** (**-ku, -ki**) (*instr sg* **-kiem**) *m* clatter
**stuk|ać (-am, -asz)** (*perf* **-nąć**) *vi* (*pukać*) to knock; (*uderzać*) to clatter; **~ do drzwi** to knock at *lub* on the door; **stuknęła mu czterdziestka** (*pot*) he's past the magic forty; **stukać się** *vr*: **stuknąć się w łokieć** to hit one's elbow; **stuknij się!** (*pot*) get wise! (*pot*); **~ się kieliszkami** to clink glasses
**stuk|nąć (-nę, -niesz)** (*imp* **-nij**) *vb perf od* **stukać** ▷ *vi perf* (*pot: o samochodzie*) to hit, to bump (into)

**stuknięty** *adj* (*pot*) cracked (*pot*)
**stuko|t** (**-tu, -ty**) (*loc sg* **-cie**) *m* clatter
**stuko|tać (-czę, -czesz)** *vi* to clatter
**stule|cie** (**-cia, -cia**) (*gen pl* **-ci**) *nt* (*wiek*) century; (*setna rocznica*) centenary
**stuletni** *adj* (*człowiek*) hundred-year-old; (*okres*) hundred-year *attr*
**stul|ić (-ę, -isz)** *vt perf* (*płatki, skrzydła*) to close up; **stul gębę** *lub* **pysk!** (*pot!*) shut your trap! (*pot!*)
**stuprocentowy** *adj* (*wełna, spirytus*) 100 per cent *attr*; (*pot: mężczyzna*) complete; (*zaufanie*) absolute, complete
**stuzłotów|ka** (**-ki, -ki**) (*dat sg* **-ce**, *gen pl* **-ek**) *f* a hundred zloty note
**stwardni|eć (-eje)** (*pt* **-ał, -ała, -eli**) *vb perf od* **twardnieć**
**stwardnieni|e** (**-a**) *nt* (*skóry*) callus; **~ rozsiane** (*Med*) multiple sclerosis
**stwarz|ać (-am, -asz)** (*perf* **stworzyć**) *vt* to create; (*warunki*) to offer
**stwier|dzać (-dzam, -dzasz)** (*perf* **-dzić**) *vt* to affirm ▷ *vi* to state
**stwierdze|nie** (**-nia, -nia**) (*gen pl* **-ń**) *nt* (*poświadczenie*) assertion; (*wypowiedź*) statement
**stwier|dzić (-dzę, -dzisz)** (*imp* **-dź**) *vb perf od* **stwierdzać**
**stworze|nie** (**-nia, -nia**) (*gen pl* **-ń**) *nt* (*czynność*) creation; (*istota*) creature
**stworzony** *adj*: **być ~m do czegoś/dla kogoś** to be meant for sth/sb
**stw|orzyć (-orzę, -orzysz)** (*imp* **-órz**) *vb perf od* **stwarzać**
**stw|ór** (**-ora, -ory**) (*loc sg* **-orze**) *m* creature
**stwórc|a** (**-y, -y**) *m decl like f in sg* creator; **S~** (*Rel*) the Creator
**stycz|eń** (**-nia, -nie**) *m* January
**styczniowy** *adj* January *attr*
**styczność|ć** (**-ci**) *f*: **mieć ~ z** *+instr* to be in contact with
**styg|nąć (-nie)** (*perf* **o-**) *vi* to cool (down)
**sty|k** (**-ku, -ki**) (*instr sg* **-kiem**) *m* point of contact; (*Elektr*) contact; **robić coś na ~** (*przen*) to cut it fine
**styk|ać (-am, -asz)** (*perf* **zetknąć**) *vt* (*przykładać, przytykać*) to connect; **~ kogoś z kimś** to put sb in touch *lub* contact with sb; **stykać się** *vr* (*przylegać*) to adjoin, to adhere; **~ się z kimś/czymś** to encounter sb/sth
**styl** (**-u, -e**) *m* style; (*w pływaniu*) stroke; **~ życia** life style; **~ wolny** (*Sport*) free style; **to (nie) w jego ~u** it's (not) like him
**stylistyczny** *adj* stylistic
**stylizowany** *adj* stylized, stylised (*Brit*)
**stylowy** *adj* period *attr*
**stymulacj|a** (**-i, -e**) (*gen pl* **-i**) *f* stimulation
**stymulato|r** (**-ra, -ry**) (*loc sg* **-rze**) *m* (*książk*) stimulus; **~ serca** pacemaker
**stymul|ować (-uję, -ujesz)** *vt* to stimulate
**stymulujący** *adj* stimulating
**sty|pa** (**-py, -py**) (*dat sg* **-pie**) *f funeral banquet*
**stypendi|um** (**-um, -a**) (*gen pl* **-ów**) *nt inv in sg* (*pieniądze*) scholarship, stipend; (*studia*) scholarship
**stypendy|sta** (**-sty, -ści**) (*loc sg* **-ście**) *m decl like f in sg* scholarship *lub* grant holder, stipendiary
**styropia|n** (**-nu**) (*loc sg* **-nie**) *m* polystyrene (foam) (*Brit*), Styrofoam® (*US*)
**subiektywnoś|ć** (**-ci**) *f* subjectivity
**subiektywny** *adj* subjective
**subkultu|ra** (**-ry, -ry**) (*dat sg* **-rze**) *f* subculture
**sublokato|r** (**-ra, -rzy**) (*loc sg* **-rze**) *m* lodger, subtenant
**subordynacj|a** (**-i**) *f* discipline
**subskryben|t** (**-ta, -ci**) (*loc sg* **-cie**) *m* subscriber
**subskryb|ować (-uję, -ujesz)** *vt* to subscribe to
**subskrypcj|a** (**-i, -e**) (*gen pl* **-i**) *f* subscription
**substancj|a** (**-i, -e**) (*gen pl* **-i**) *f* substance; **~ chemiczna** chemical; **~ trująca** toxin
**substytu|t** (**-tu, -ty**) (*loc sg* **-cie**) *m* substitute, stopgap
**subsydi|ować (-uję, -ujesz)** *vt* to subsidize
**subtelnoś|ć** (**-ci**) *f* subtlety
**subtelny** *adj* subtle
**subtropikalny** *adj* subtropical
**subwencj|a** (**-i, -e**) (*gen pl* **-i**) *f* subsidy, subvention
**suchar|ek** (**-ka, -ki**) (*instr sg* **-kiem**) *m* rusk
**sucho** *adv* drily; **zrobiło się ~** it dried up; **pranie na ~** dry cleaning; **na ~** on an empty stomach; **mam ~ w gardle/ustach** my throat/mouth is dry; **to ci nie ujdzie na ~!** (*pot*) you'll never get away with it!
**suchy** *adj* dry; **wycierać coś do sucha** to wipe sth dry; **zmoknąć** (*perf*) **do suchej nitki** to be dripping wet, to get drenched *lub* soaked to the skin; **nie zostawić** (*perf*) **na kimś suchej nitki** to pick sb to pieces
**Suda|n** (**-nu**) (*loc sg* **-nie**) *m* Sudan
**Sudet|y** (**-ów**) *pl* the Sudety Mountains *pl*
**Sueski** *adj*: **Kanał ~** the Suez Canal
**sufik|s** (**-su, -sy**) (*loc sg* **-sie**) *m* suffix
**sufi|t** (**-tu, -ty**) (*loc sg* **-cie**) *m* ceiling
**sufle|r** (**-ra, -rzy**) (*loc sg* **-rze**) *m* prompter
**sufle|t** (**-tu, -ty**) (*loc sg* **-cie**) *m* soufflé
**sufrażyst|ka** (**-ki, -ki**) (*dat sg* **-ce**, *gen pl* **-ek**) *f* suffragette
**suger|ować (-uję, -ujesz)** (*perf* **za-**) *vt*: **~ coś (komuś)** to suggest sth (to sb), to imply sth (to sb); **~, że ...** to hint that ...; **sugerować się** *vr +instr* to be influenced by

S

**sugesti|a** (**-i, -e**) (*gen pl* **-i**) *f* hint, suggestion
**sugestywny** *adj* eloquent, suggestive
**sui|ta** (**-ty, -ty**) (*dat sg* **-cie**) *f* suite
**su|ka** (**-ki, -ki**) (*dat sg* **-ce**) *f* bitch
**sukce|s** (**-su, -sy**) (*loc sg* **-sie**) *m* success; **odnieść** (*perf*) ~ to succeed, to be a success; **to połowa ~u** that's half the battle; **odnosić ~y jako** to be successful as
**sukcesj|a** (**-i, -e**) (*gen pl* **-i**) *f* succession
**sukceso|r** (**-ra, -rzy**) (*loc sg* **-rze**) *m* (*następca*) successor; (*następca tronu*) heir to the throne
**sukcesywny** *adj* successive
**sukien|ka** (**-ki, -ki**) (*dat sg* **-ce**, *gen pl* **-ek**) *f* dress
**sukinsy|n** (**-na, -ny**) (*loc sg* **-nie** *lub* **-nu**) *m* (*pot!*) son of a bitch (*pot!*)
**su|knia** (**-kni, -knie**) (*gen pl* **-kni** *lub* **-kien**) *f* dress, gown; ~ **wieczorowa** evening *lub* party dress; ~ **ślubna** wedding dress; ~ **ciążowa** maternity dress
**su|kno** (**-kna, -kna**) (*loc sg* **-knie**, *gen pl* **-kien**) *nt* cloth
**sukur|s** (**-su**) (*loc sg* **-sie**) *m*: **iść (pójść** *perf*) **komuś w** ~ (*książk*) to come to sb's aid
**sułta|n** (**-na, -ni** *lub* **-nowie**) (*loc sg* **-nie**) *m* sultan
**su|m** (**-ma, -my**) (*loc sg* **-mie**) *m* catfish
**su|ma** (**-my, -my**) (*dat sg* **-mie**) *f* sum, total; (*kwota*) amount, sum of money; (*Rel*) high mass; **w sumie** all things considered, all in all; ~ **częściowa** subtotal
**sumie|nie** (**-nia, -nia**) (*gen pl* **-ń**) *nt* conscience; **czyste/nieczyste** ~ a clear/guilty conscience; **wyrzuty sumienia** remorse, pangs of conscience; **mieć kogoś/coś na sumieniu** to have sb/sth on one's conscience; **z czystym ~m** with a clear conscience; **rachunek sumienia** (*Rel*) examination of conscience
**sumiennoś|ć** (**-ci**) *f* conscientiousness
**sumienny** *adj* conscientious
**sum|ować (-uję, -ujesz)** (*perf* **z-**) *vt* (*liczby*) to add (up); (*pieniądze*) to total (up), to sum (up); (*doświadczenia, wrażenia*) to accumulate; **sumować się** *vr* to sum up
**sump|t** (**-tu**) (*loc sg* **-cie**) *m*: **własnym ~em** at one's own expense
**su|nąć (-nę, -niesz)** (*imp* **-ń**) *vi* to glide, to slide
**sup|eł** (**-ła, -ły**) (*loc sg* **-le**) *m* knot, tangle; **zawiązać** (*perf*) **coś na** ~ to knot sth
**super** *adj inv* (*pot*) super; **etylina** ~ premium gasoline
**superlatyw|y** (**-**) *pl*: **wyrażać się o kimś w (samych) superlatywach** to speak highly of sb
**supermarke|t** (**-tu, -ty**) (*loc sg* **-cie**) *m* supermarket
**supermocarst|wo** (**-wa, -wa**) (*loc sg* **-wie**) *nt* superpower
**supernowoczesny** *adj* ultramodern, high-tech
**supersa|m** (**-mu, -my**) (*loc sg* **-mie**) *m* supermarket
**suplemen|t** (**-tu, -ty**) (*loc sg* **-cie**) *m* supplement
**supłać (-am, -asz)** (*perf* **za-**) *vt* (*plątać*) to knot, to tangle
**supremacj|a** (**-i, -e**) (*gen pl* **-i**) *f* supremacy
**surfin|g** (**-gu**) (*instr sg* **-giem**) *m* surfing
**surfingowy** *adj*: **deska surfingowa** surfboard
**suroga|t** (**-tu, -ty**) (*loc sg* **-cie**) *m* surrogate
**surowic|a** (**-y, -e**) *f* (*też*: **surowica krwi**) serum
**suro|wiec** (**-wca, -wce**) *m* (*do produkcji*) raw material; **surowce** *pl* (*do produkcji*) raw materials; (*zasoby*) resources; **surowce naturalne** natural resources; **surowce wtórne** recyclable materials
**surowo** *adv* (*kategorycznie*) harshly, severely; (*urządzony, ubrany*) austerely; **„Palenie ~ wzbronione"** "No smoking"; **jeść coś na ~** to eat sth raw
**surowoś|ć** (**-ci**) *f* (*przepisów, prawa*) rigidity, strictness; (*klimatu*) severity; **z całą surowością** with severity
**surowy** *adj* (*mleko, owoce, mięso*) raw, uncooked; (*drewno*) unseasoned; (*mina*) stern; (*nauczyciel*) strict, severe; (*krytyka, wyrok*) severe; (*wnętrze, strój*) austere; (*klimat, zima*) harsh, severe; (*warunki, życie*) severe, austere
**surów|ka** (**-ki, -ki**) (*dat sg* **-ce**, *gen pl* **-ek**) *f* (*Kulin*) salad; (*Tech*) pig-iron
**surrealistyczny** *adj* (*sztuka, malarz*) surrealist; (*nierealny*) surrealistic, surreal
**surrealiz|m** (**-mu**) (*loc sg* **-mie**) *m* surrealism
**su|s** (**-sa, -sy**) (*loc sg* **-sie**) *m* (*skok*) leap; **dać** (*perf*) **susa** to leap, to take a leap
**su|seł** (**-sła, -sły**) (*loc sg* **-śle**) *m* (*Zool*) gopher; **spać jak** ~ to sleep like a log
**susz|a** (**-y, -e**) *f* drought, dry weather
**suszar|ka** (**-ki, -ki**) (*dat sg* **-ce**, *gen pl* **-ek**) *f* dryer; ~ **do włosów** hair dryer; ~ **do naczyń** dish drainer
**suszar|nia** (**-ni, -nie**) (*gen pl* **-ni**) *f* drying room
**suszony** *adj* dried; (*owoc*) desiccated
**susz|yć (-ę, -ysz)** *vt* (*włosy, bieliznę*) (*perf* **wy-**) to dry; (*kwiaty, grzyby*) (*perf* **u-**) to dry; **suszyć się** *vr* to dry, to get dry
**sutan|na** (**-ny, -ny**) (*dat sg* **-nie**) *f* cassock, soutane
**sut|ek** (**-ka, -ki**) (*instr sg* **-kiem**) *m* (*pierś*) breast; (*brodawka*) nipple
**sutene|r** (**-ra, -rzy**) (*loc sg* **-rze**) *m* pimp
**sutere|na** (**-ny, -ny**) (*loc sg* **-nie**) *f* basement

**suty** *adj* (*książk*: *napiwek*) generous; (*posiłek, przyjęcie*) sumptuous
**su|w** (**-wu, -wy**) (*loc sg* **-wie**) *m* (*Mot*) stroke
**suwa|k** (**-ka, -ki**) (*instr sg* **-kiem**) *m* (*pot*: *zamek błyskawiczny*) zip (*Brit*), zipper (*US*); (*przesuwana część przyrządu*) slide control; **~ logarytmiczny** slide rule
**suwerennoś|ć** (**-ci**) *f* sovereignty, independence
**suwerenny** *adj* sovereign
**suwmiar|ka** (**-ki, -ki**) (*dat sg* **-ce**, *gen pl* **-ek**) *f* vernier calliper gauge (*Brit*) *lub* caliper gage (*US*)
**suwnic|a** (**-y, -e**) *f* gantry
**swa** *pron* = **swoja**
**swasty|ka** (**-ki, -ki**) (*dat sg* **-ce**) *f* swastika
**swat|ać (-am, -asz)** (*perf* **wy-**) *vt*: **~ kogoś z kimś** to arrange for sb to marry sb
**swat|ka** (**-ki, -ki**) (*dat sg* **-ce**, *gen pl* **-ek**) *f* matchmaker
**swawol|a** (**-i**) *f* frolic
**swawol|ić (-ę, -isz)** *vi* to frolic
**swawolny** *adj* rollicking
**sw|ąd** (**-ędu**) (*loc sg* **-ędzie**) *m* smell of burning
**swe** *pron* = **swoje**
**swet|er** (**-ra, -ry**) (*loc sg* **-rze**) *m* sweater, jumper (*Brit*); **~ rozpinany** cardigan
**swędzeni|e** (**-a**) *nt* itch
**swę|dzić, swę|dzieć (-dzi)** (*pt* **-dził** *lub* **-dział**) *vi* to itch; **swędzi mnie szyja** my neck is itching
**swin|g** (**-gu**) (*instr sg* **-giem**) *m* swing
**swobo|da** (**-dy**) (*dat sg* **-dzie**) *f* (*wolność*) liberty; (*niezależność*) freedom; (*śmiałość*) familiarity; (*łatwość*) ease; **swobody obywatelskie** civil liberties; **mieć swobodę działania** to have leeway, to have a free hand
**swobodnie** *adv* freely; (*zachowywać się*) freely, without restraint; (*czuć się*) at ease, comfortable; (*ubrany*) informally, casually
**swobodny** *adj* (*wybór*) free; (*rozwój*) unconstrained; (*rytm, akcent*) free; (*nastrój, rozmowa*) casual, informal; (*strój*) informal; (*frywolny*) uninhibited, risqué; **mieć wolną** *lub* **swobodną rękę** to have a free hand; **pamięć o dostępie ~m** (*Komput*) random access memory
**swoisty** *adj* peculiar
**swoja** *itd. pron patrz* **swój**
**swoje** *pron patrz* **swój** ▷ *nt decl like adj*; **ona dba o ~** she takes care of her interests; **mieszkać na swoim** to live in one's own home; **wyjść** (*perf*) **na ~** to come out on top; **dopiąć** (*perf*) **swego** to accomplish one's ends; **robić ~** to do one's job; **zrobię to po ~mu** I'll do it my way
**swojski** *adj* (*znajomy*) familiar; (*domowej roboty*) home-made
**swojsko** *adv*: **brzmieć ~** to sound familiar; **czuć się ~** to feel at home
**sworz|eń** (**-nia, -nie**) (*gen pl* **-ni**) *m* pivot
**swój** (*jak*: **mój**) *pron* one's; (*mój*) my; (*twój*) your; (*jego*) his; (*jej*) her; (*nasz*) our; (*wasz*) your; (*ich*) their; (*pot*: *swojski*) home-made ▷ *m decl like adj* friend; **pojechaliśmy swoim samochodem** we took our car; **na ~ sposób** in a way; **swoją drogą ...** still, ...; **w swoim czasie** in due time *lub* course; **to jest ~ chłop** (*pot*) he is one of us; **konfitury swojej roboty** (*pot*) home-made jam
**Syberi|a** (**-i**) *f* Siberia
**syberyjski** *adj* Siberian
**sy|cić (-cę, -cisz)** (*imp* **-ć**, *perf* **na-**) *vt* to satiate; **~ czymś wzrok** *lub* **oczy** (*książk*) to feast one's eyes (up) on sth
**Sycyli|a** (**-i**) *f* Sicily
**sycylijski** *adj* Sicilian
**sycz|eć (-ę, -ysz)** *vi* (*wydawać syk*) (*perf* **syknąć** *lub* **za~**) to hiss; (*mówić ze złością*) (*perf* **syknąć**) to hiss
**sy|f** (**-fu, -fy**) (*loc sg* **-fie**) *m* (*pot!*) syphilis; (*pot!*: *brud*) shit (*pot!*)
**syfili|s** (**-su**) (*loc sg* **-sie**) *m* syphilis
**syfo|n** (**-nu, -ny**) (*loc sg* **-nie**) *m* (*butelka*) siphon bottle; (*Tech*) U-bend
**sygnalizacj|a** (**-i**) *f* (*przekazywanie sygnałów*) signalling; (*urządzenia sygnalizacyjne*) signalling equipment; **~ świetlna** traffic lights *lub* signals
**sygnalizacyjny** *adj* signalling
**sygnaliz|ować (-uję, -ujesz)** (*perf* **za-**) *vt* (*dawać sygnały*) to signal; (*wskazywać*) to indicate
**sygna|ł** (**-łu, -ły**) (*loc sg* **-le**) *m* signal; (*Tel*) tone; (*programu*) signature tune; **jechać na sygnale** (*pot*) to drive with the siren going
**sygnatariusz** (**-a, -e**) (*gen pl* **-y**) *m* signatory
**sygnatu|ra** (**-ry, -ry**) (*loc sg* **-rze**) *f* (*podpis*) signature; (*na książce*) catalogue number
**sygne|t** (**-tu, -ty**) (*loc sg* **-cie**) *m* signet ring
**sygn|ować (-uję, -ujesz)** *vt* to sign
**Syja|m** (**-mu**) (*loc sg* **-mie**) *m* Siam
**syjamski** *adj* Siamese
**syjoni|sta** (**-sty, -ści**) (*dat sg* **-ście**) *m decl like f in sg* Zionist
**syjonistyczny** *adj* Zionist
**syjoniz|m** (**-mu**) (*loc sg* **-mie**) *m* Zionism
**sy|k** (**-ku, -ki**) (*instr sg* **-kiem**) *m* (*pojedynczy*) hiss; (*ciągły*) hissing
**syk|nąć (-nę, -niesz)** (*imp* **-nij**) *vb perf od* **syczeć**
**syla|ba** (**-by, -by**) (*dat sg* **-bie**) *f* syllable

S

**sylabiz|ować (-uję, -ujesz)** (*perf* **prze-**) *vt* to read letter by letter
**sylwest|er** (**-ra, -ry**) (*loc sg* **-rze**) *m* New Year's Eve
**sylwestrowy** *adj* New Year's *attr*
**sylwet|ka** (**-ki, -ki**) (*dat sg* **-ce**, *gen pl* **-ek**) *f* (*figura*) figure; (*zarys postaci*) silhouette, profile; (*opis osoby*) profile
**symbio|za** (**-zy**) (*dat sg* **-zie**) *f* symbiosis
**symbol** (**-u, -e**) *m* symbol; **być ~em czegoś** to represent sth
**symbolicznie** *adv* (*przedstawiać, rozumieć*) metaphorically, symbolically; (*wynagradzać, płacić*) nominally
**symboliczny** *adj* (*sens, znaczenie, powieść*) symbolic; (*upominek, wynagrodzenie*) nominal
**symboliz|m** (**-mu**) (*dat sg* **-mie**) *m* symbolism
**symboliz|ować (-uje)** *vt* to symbolize, to represent
**symetri|a** (**-i**) *f* symmetry
**symetryczny** *adj* symmetrical
**symfoni|a** (**-i, -e**) (*gen pl* **-i**) *f* symphony
**symfoniczny** *adj* (*utwór, poemat*) symphonic; **orkiestra symfoniczna** symphony orchestra
**sympati|a** (**-i, -e**) (*gen pl* **-i**) *f* (*uczucie*) liking; (*pot*: *dziewczyna*) girlfriend; (*: chłopak*) boyfriend; **cieszyć się czyjąś sympatią** to be liked by sb; **czuć sympatię do kogoś** to feel attracted to sb; **darzyć kogoś sympatią** to feel affinity with *lub* for sb; **nabierać do kogoś sympatii** to take a fancy to sb
**sympatyczny** *adj* pleasant, nice; **atrament ~** invisible ink
**sympaty|k** (**-ka, -cy**) (*instr sg* **-kiem**) *m* sympathizer
**sympatyz|ować (-uję, -ujesz)** *vi*: **~ z** *+instr* to sympathize with
**sympozj|um** (**-um, -a**) (*gen pl* **-ów**) *nt inv in sg* symposium
**sympto|m** (**-mu, -my**) (*loc sg* **-mie**) *m* symptom
**symptomatyczny** *adj* symptomatic
**symulacj|a** (**-i, -e**) (*gen pl* **-i**) *f* simulation
**symulan|t** (**-ta, -ci**) (*loc sg* **-cie**) *m* malingerer
**symulato|r** (**-ra, -ry**) (*loc sg* **-rze**) *m* simulator; **~ lotu** flight simulator
**symul|ować (-uję, -ujesz)** *vt* (*udawać*) to fake; (*naśladować*) to simulate ▷ *vi* to malinger
**sy|n** (**-na, -nowie**) (*loc sg* **-nu**) *m* son; **Syn Boży** Son of God
**synago|ga** (**-gi, -gi**) (*dat sg* **-dze**) *f* synagogue
**Synaj** (**-u**) *m* Sinai
**synchroniczny** *adj* synchronous; **pływanie synchroniczne** synchronized swimming
**synchronizacj|a** (**-i**) *f* synchronization
**synchroniz|ować (-uję, -ujesz)** (*perf* **z-**) *vt* to synchronize
**syndro|m** (**-mu, -my**) (*loc sg* **-mie**) *m* syndrome
**syndy|k** (**-ka, -cy**) (*instr sg* **-kiem**) *m*: **~ masy upadłościowej** official receiver
**syndyka|t** (**-tu, -ty**) (*loc sg* **-cie**) *m* syndicate
**synko|pa** (**-py, -py**) (*loc sg* **-pie**) *f* syncopation
**syno|d** (**-du, -dy**) (*loc sg* **-dzie**) *m* synod
**synoni|m** (**-mu, -my**) (*loc sg* **-mie**) *m* synonym
**synonimiczny** *adj* synonymous
**synopty|k** (**-ka, -cy**) (*instr sg* **-kiem**) *m* weatherman
**synow|a** (**-ej, -e**) *f decl like adj* daughter-in-law
**syntetyczny** *adj* synthetic
**syntetyz|ować (-uję, -ujesz)** (*perf* **z-**) *vt* to synthetize
**synte|za** (**-zy, -zy**) (*dat sg* **-zie**) *f* synthesis; **~ jądrowa** fusion
**syntezato|r** (**-ra, -ry**) (*loc sg* **-rze**) *m* synthesizer
**sy|pać (-pię, -piesz)** (*perf* **-pnąć**) *vt* (*piasek, mąkę*) to pour, to sprinkle; (*pot*: *zdradzać*) to inform on *lub* against ▷ *vi* (*pot*) to inform against one's accomplices; **śnieg sypie** it's snowing; **~ żartami/faktami** to reel off jokes/facts; **sypać się** *vr* (*o tynku*) to fall off; (*o iskrach*) to fly; (*o liściach*) to fall; (*o ciosach*) to rain down; (*pot*: *rozpadać się*) (*perf* **roz-**) to fall apart
**sypi|ać (-am, -asz)** *vi* to sleep
**sypial|nia** (**-ni, -nie**) (*gen pl* **-ni**) *f* bedroom
**sypialny** *adj*: **wagon ~** sleeping car; **pokój ~** bedroom
**sypki** *adj* loose
**syp|nąć (-nę, -niesz)** (*imp* **-nij**) *vb perf od* **sypać**
**syre|na** (**-ny, -ny**) (*dat sg* **-nie**) *f* (*przyrząd*) siren; (*nimfa*) mermaid, siren
**Syri|a** (**-i**) *f* Syria
**syro|p** (**-pu, -py**) (*loc sg* **-pie**) *m* syrup; **~ na kaszel** cough syrup
**Syryjczy|k** (**-ka, -cy**) (*instr sg* **-kiem**) *m* Syrian
**Syryj|ka** (**-ki, -ki**) (*dat sg* **-ce**, *gen pl* **-ek**) *f* Syrian
**syryjski** *adj* Syrian
**syste|m** (**-mu, -my**) (*loc sg* **-mie**) *m* system; **~ operacyjny** operating system; **~ ratalny** installment plan; **~ wczesnego ostrzegania** early warning system
**systematycznoś|ć** (**-ci**) *f* (*regularność*) regularity; (*cecha charakteru*) orderly manner
**systematyczny** *adj* (*praca, nauka*) systematic; (*uczeń*) methodical
**systematyz|ować (-uję, -ujesz)** (*perf* **u-**) *vt* to systematize
**systemowy** *adj* (*rozwiązanie*) comprehensive; **dysk ~** system disk

**sytoś|ć** (**-ci**) *f*: **uczucie sytości** feeling of satiety
**sytuacj|a** (**-i, -e**) (*gen pl* **-i**) *f* situation; **w tej sytuacji ...** in such a situation ..., under such circumstances ...; **być w lepszej/gorszej sytuacji (niż)** to be in a better/worse position (than), to be better/worse off (than)
**sytuacyjny** *adj* situational
**sytu|ować (-uję, -ujesz)** (*perf* **u-**) *vt* to locate, to place
**sytuowany** *adj*: **dobrze/źle ~** well/badly off
**syty** *adj* replete, satiated; **najeść/napić się do syta** to eat/drink one's fill
**syzyfowy** *adj*: **syzyfowa praca** a never-ending job
**szaba|s** (**-su, -sy**) (*loc sg* **-sie**) *m* the Sabbath (day)
**szabl|a** (**-i, -e**) (*gen pl* **-i**) *f* sword, sabre (*Brit*), saber (*US*)
**szablo|n** (**-nu, -ny**) (*loc sg* **-nie**) *m* (*literniczy*) stencil; (*techniczny*) template; (*wzór*) pattern; (*przen*) stereotype, routine
**szablonowy** *adj* run-of-the-mill, commonplace
**szach** *m* (*w szachach*) (*gen sg* **-u** *lub* **-a**) check; (*tytuł władcy*) (*gen sg* **-a**, *nom pl* **-owie**) Shah; **trzymać kogoś w ~u** (*przen*) to keep sb in check; **~-mat** checkmate
**szachi|sta** (**-sty, -ści**) (*dat sg* **-ście**) *m decl like f in sg* chess player
**szachownic|a** (**-y, -e**) *f* chessboard
**szach|y** (**-ów**) *pl* (*gra*) chess; (*zestaw do gry*) chess set
**szac|ować (-uję, -ujesz)** (*perf* **o-**) *vt* (*majątek, straty*) to estimate, to assess; **~ coś na** *+acc* to assess sth at, to value sth at
**szacowny** *adj* respectable, venerable
**szacun|ek** (**-ku**) (*instr sg* **-kiem**) *m* (*poważanie*) respect, reverence; (*ocena*) assessment, estimate; **mieć ~ dla** *+gen* to have respect for; **z wyrazami szacunku** (*w liście*) with kindest regards
**szacunkowy** *adj* estimated
**sza|fa** (**-fy, -fy**) (*dat sg* **-fie**) *f* (*na ubrania*) wardrobe; (*na akta, dokumenty*) cabinet; **~ grająca** jukebox, music box; **~ pancerna** safe
**szafi|r** (**-ru, -ry**) (*loc sg* **-rze**) *m* (*kamień*) sapphire; (*kolor*) sapphire blue
**szafirowy** *adj* sapphire *attr*
**szaf|ka** (**-ki, -ki**) (*dat sg* **-ce**, *gen pl* **-ek**) *f* (*na buty*) cabinet; **~ ścienna** wall cupboard; **~ kuchenna** kitchen unit, cupboard; **~ nocna** bedside table
**szafo|t** (**-tu, -ty**) (*loc sg* **-cie**) *m* scaffold
**szaf|ować (-uję, -ujesz)** *vt*: **~ czymś** to be careless with sth
**szafra|n** (**-nu, -ny**) (*loc sg* **-nie**) *m* saffron
**szaj|ba** (**-by**) (*dat sg* **-bie**) *f*: **~ mu odbiła** (*pot*) he's got a screw loose
**szaj|ka** (**-ki, -ki**) (*dat sg* **-ce**, *gen pl* **-ek**) *f* band (*of thieves*)
**szakal** (**-a, -e**) (*gen pl* **-i**) *m* jackal
**szal** (**-a, -e**) (*gen pl* **-i**) *m* scarf, shawl
**szal|a** (**-i, -e**) *f* (*wagi*) scale (pan); **przechylić** (*perf*) **szalę zwycięstwa na czyjąś stronę** to tip the scales in favo(u)r of sb
**szal|eć (-eję, -ejesz)** *vi* (*wariować*) (*perf* **o-**) to go mad; (*o burzy, powodzi, epidemii*) to rage; (*hulać*) to revel; **~ z rozpaczy** to be frantic with worry; **~ za kimś** to be crazy about sb
**szalenie** *adv* extremely
**szale|niec** (**-ńca, -ńcy**) *m* madman, maniac
**szaleńczy** *adj* (*myśl, zamiar*) mad, insane; (*radość, gniew*) mad
**szaleńst|wo** (**-wa, -wa**) (*loc sg* **-wie**) *nt* (*szalony czyn*) madness, insanity; (*szał*) frenzy; **zakochany do szaleństwa** madly in love
**szale|t** (**-tu, -ty**) (*loc sg* **-cie**) *m* public toilet
**szali|k** (**-ka, -ki**) (*instr sg* **-kiem**) *m* scarf
**szalony** *adj* (*człowiek*) mad, insane; (*zamiar, myśl*) mad, crazy; (*życie, taniec, gniew*) mad; (*pot: niesłychany*) terrible
**szalun|ek** (**-ku, -ki**) (*instr sg* **-kiem**) *m* formwork, shuttering (*Brit*)
**szalu|pa** (**-py, -py**) (*dat sg* **-pie**) *f* lifeboat
**sza|ł** (**-łu**) (*loc sg* **-le**) *m* (*furia*) madness; (*stan podniecenia*) frenzy, rage; (*mania: zakupów, porządków*) folly; **wpaść** (*perf*) **w ~** to fly into a rage, to go berserk; **doprowadzać (doprowadzić** *perf*) **kogoś do ~u** (*pot*) to drive sb mad, to drive sb into a frenzy
**szała|s** (**-su, -sy**) (*dat sg* **-sie**) *m* shelter
**szałowy** *adj* (*pot*) smashing
**szałwi|a** (**-i, -e**) (*gen pl* **-i**) *f* sage
**szama|n** (**-na, -ni**) (*loc sg* **-nie**) *m* witch doctor, medicine man
**szam|bo** (**-ba, -ba**) (*loc sg* **-bie**) *nt* cesspool, cesspit
**szamo|tać się (-czę, -czesz)** *vr* to struggle, to tussle
**szampa|n** (**-na, -ny**) (*loc sg* **-nie**) *m* champagne
**szampański** *adj* (*humor, nastrój*) sparkling; (*zabawa*) lively
**szampo|n** (**-nu, -ny**) (*loc sg* **-nie**) *m* shampoo; **myć włosy ~em** to shampoo one's hair
**Szanghaj** (**-u**) *m* Shanghai
**szan|ować (-uję, -ujesz)** *vt* (*cenić*) to respect, to look up to; (*chronić*) to take care of; **szanować się** *vr* (*mieć poczucie własnej godności*) to have self-respect; (*poważać jeden drugiego*) to respect one another

S

**szanowny** *adj* honourable, respectable; **S~ Panie!/Szanowna Pani!** *(w liście)* Dear Sir/ Madam,, Dear Mr/Mrs X,; **Szanowni Państwo!** Ladies and Gentlemen!
**szan|sa** (**-sy, -se**) *(dat sg* **-sie***)* *f* chance; **~ na wygranie meczu** a chance of winning *lub* to win the match; **~ na sukces** a chance to succeed; **życiowa ~** the chance of a lifetime; **mieć szansę coś zrobić** to have a chance to do *lub* of doing sth
**szantaż** (**-u**) *m* blackmail
**szantaż|ować (-uję, -ujesz)** *vt*: **~ kogoś (czymś)** to blackmail sb (with sth)
**szantaży|sta** (**-sty, -ści**) *(dat sg* **-ście***)* *m decl like f in sg* blackmailer
**szara|da** (**-dy, -dy**) *(dat sg* **-dzie***)* *f* charade
**szarańcz|a** (**-y**) *f* locust
**szar|fa** (**-fy, -fy**) *(dat sg* **-fie***)* *f* sash
**szarlata|n** (**-na, -ni**) *(loc sg* **-nie***)* *m* charlatan
**szarlot|ka** (**-ki, -ki**) *(dat sg* **-ce**, *gen pl* **-ek***)* *f* apple-pie
**szarmancki** *adj* gallant
**szaro** *adv (w szarym kolorze)*: **pomalować coś na ~** to paint sth grey (Brit) *lub* gray (US); **zrobiło się ~** it got gloomy
**szaroś|ć** (**-ci, -ci**) *(gen pl* **-ci***)* *f* grey(ness) (Brit), gray(ness) (US); *(przen)* dullness
**szarot|ka** (**-ki, -ki**) *(dat sg* **-ce**, *gen pl* **-ek***)* *f (Bot)* edelweiss
**szar|pać (-pię, -piesz)** *vt (ciągnąć) (perf* **-pnąć***)* to pull at; *(rozdzierać) (perf* **po-***)* to tear (apart) ▷ *vi (o pojazdach) (perf* **-pnąć***)* to jerk; **~ kogoś za włosy/rękaw** to pull sb's hair/sleeve; **~ (z~** *perf***) komuś nerwy** to fray sb's nerves; **szarpać się** *vr* to struggle; *(pot: martwić się)* to fret
**szarpani|na** (**-ny**) *(dat sg* **-nie***)* *f* struggle
**szarp|nąć (-nę, -niesz)** *(imp* **-nij***)* *vb perf od* **szarpać** ▷ *vr perf*: **~ się na coś** *(pot)* to splash out on sth
**szarpnię|cie** (**-cia, -cia**) *(gen pl* **-ć***)* *nt* jerk, jolt
**szary** *adj (kolor)* grey (Brit), gray (US); *(dzień)* gloomy; *(papier, koperta)* brown; *(życie)* ordinary; **szara eminencja** éminence grise; **szara strefa** twilight zone; **na ~m końcu** at the tail end
**szarz|eć (-eje)** *(perf* **z-** *lub* **po-***)* *vi* to grow grey (Brit) *lub* gray (US)
**szarż|a** (**-y, -e**) *f (atak)* charge; *(stopień wojskowy)* rank
**szarż|ować (-uję, -ujesz)** *vi (nacierać)* to charge; *(przen: przesadzać)* to go over the top
**szast|ać (-am, -asz)** *vt*: **~ pieniędzmi** to be extravagant with one's money; **~ obietnicami** to be lavish with promises
**szaszły|k** (**-ka, -ki**) *(instr sg* **-kiem***)* *m* shashlik, shish kebab
**sza|ta** (**-ty, -ty**) *(dat sg* **-cie***)* *f (książk)* garment, vestment; **~ graficzna** layout; **~ roślinna** flora; **królewskie szaty** regal gowns; **rozdzierać szaty (nad** *+instr***)** to rend one's garments over
**szata|n** (**-na, -ny** *lub* **-ni**) *(loc sg* **-nie***)* *m (Rel)* satan; *(pot: człowiek nieznośny)* devil; *(: człowiek energiczny)* ball of fire
**szatański** *adj* fiendish
**szatk|ować (-uję, -ujesz)** *(perf* **po-***)* *vt* to shred
**szat|nia** (**-ni, -nie**) *(gen pl* **-ni***)* *f (przebieralnia)* changing room; *(w teatrze, kinie)* cloakroom
**szatniarz** (**-a, -e**) *(gen pl* **-y***)* *m* cloakroom attendant
**szaty|n** (**-na, -ni**) *(loc sg* **-nie***)* *m* dark-haired man
**szatyn|ka** (**-ki, -ki**) *(dat sg* **-ce**, *gen pl* **-ek***)* *f* dark-haired woman
**szcz|ać (-am, -asz)** *vi (pot!)* to piss *(pot!)*
**szcza|pa** (**-py, -py**) *(dat sg* **-pie***)* *f (drewna)* chip, sliver; **chudy jak ~** *(pot)* as thin as a lath *lub* rake
**szcza|w** (**-wiu, -wie**) *m* sorrel
**szcząt|ki** (**-ków**) *pl (samolotu)* debris *sg*; *(ludzkie)* remains
**szczeb|el** (**-la, -le**) *(gen pl* **-li***)* *m (drabiny)* rung; *(hierarchii)* grade; **rozmowy na najwyższym szczeblu** summit talks; **urzędnik niskiego/ wysokiego szczebla** low/top level official; **na szczeblu centralnym** at the minister level
**szczebio|t** (**-tu, -ty**) *(loc sg* **-cie***)* *m* chirp
**szczebio|tać (-czę, -czesz)** *vi* to chirp
**szczeci|na** (**-ny**) *(dat sg* **-nie***)* *f* bristle; *(przen: zarost)* stubble
**szczeciniasty** *adj* bristly
**szczególnie** *adv (zwłaszcza)* especially, particularly; *(osobliwie)* peculiarly
**szczególnoś|ć** (**-ci**) *f*: **w szczególności** in particular
**szczególny** *adj (uprawnienia)* special; *(gust, zamiłowania)* peculiar; *(cecha)* characteristic; **nic szczególnego** nothing special
**szczegó|ł** (**-łu, -ły**) *(loc sg* **-le***)* *m* detail; **szczegóły** *pl* details *pl*, particulars *pl*
**szczegółowo** *adv* in detail
**szczegółowy** *adj* detailed
**szczek|ać (-a)** *(perf* **-nąć***)* *vi* to bark
**szczek|nąć (-nie)** *(imp* **-nij***)* *vb perf od* **szczekać**
**szczeli|na** (**-ny, -ny**) *(dat sg* **-nie***)* *f* crack
**szczelnie** *adv (zamykać)* tight(ly); *(wypełniać)* to capacity
**szczelnoś|ć** (**-ci**) *f* tightness
**szczelny** *adj* tight
**szczeniacki** *adj (pot)* infantile

**szczenia|k** (**-ka, -ki**) (*instr sg* **-kiem**) *m* pup(py); (*pej*) whippersnapper
**szcze|nić się (-ni)** (*perf* **o-**) *vr* to have puppies
**szczeni|ę** (**-ęcia, -ęta**) (*gen pl* **-ąt**) *nt* pup(py)
**szczenięcy** *adj*: **szczenięca miłość** puppy love; **szczenięce lata** salad days
**szcze|p** (**-pu, -py**) (*loc sg* **-pie**) *m* (*plemię*) tribe; (*Bio*) strain; (*drzewko*) graft
**szcze|pić (-pię, -pisz)** (*perf* **za-**) *vt* (*ludzi*) to vaccinate, to inoculate; (*drzewa*) to graft
**szczepie|nie** (**-nia, -nia**) (*gen pl* **-ń**) *nt* vaccination, inoculation; **szczepienia ochronne** immunization
**szczepion|ka** (**-ki, -ki**) (*dat sg* **-ce**, *gen pl* **-ek**) *f* vaccine; **~ przeciw(ko) ospie/wściekliźnie** smallpox/rabies vaccine
**szczer|ba** (**-by, -by**) (*dat sg* **-bie**) *f* (*w zębach*) gap; (*w ostrzu, murze*) chip
**szczerbaty** *adj* (*bez zębów*) gap-toothed; (*wyszczerbiony*) jagged
**szczeroś|ć** (**-ci**) *f* sincerity
**szczerozłoty** *adj* pure gold
**szczery** *adj* (*przyjaciel, uśmiech*) sincere; (*podziw, żal*) genuine; (*prawda*) plain; (*złoto*) pure; **jeśli mam być ~** to be honest (with you); **w ~m polu** in the middle of nowhere
**szczerze** *adv* sincerely; **~ mówiąc** frankly, in all honesty
**szczerz|yć (-ę, -ysz)** (*perf* **wy-**) *vt*: **~ zęby** to bare one's teeth; (*pot: uśmiechać się*) to grin
**szczę|dzić (-dzę, -dzisz)** (*imp* **-dź**) *vt*: **nie ~ czegoś** to be generous with sth
**szczę|k** (**-ku, -ki**) (*instr sg* **-kiem**) *m* (*zbroi*) clash; (*klucza w zamku*) clatter
**szczę|ka** (**-ki, -ki**) (*dat sg* **-ce**) *f* jaw; **sztuczna ~** false teeth, dentures; **~ hamulcowa** (brake) shoe
**szczęk|ać (-am, -asz)** (*perf* **-nąć**) *vi* to clash; **szczękałem zębami** my teeth were chattering
**szczęk|nąć (-nę, -niesz)** (*imp* **-nij**) *vb perf od* **szczękać**
**szczękościs|k** (**-ku**) (*instr sg* **-kiem**) *m* lockjaw
**szczękowy** *adj*: **kość szczękowa** jawbone
**szczęściarz** (**-a, -e**) (*gen pl* **-y**) *m* (*pot*) lucky chap (*pot*); **~ z ciebie!** lucky you!
**szczęś|cić (-ci)** *vi*: **szczęść Boże!** God bless (you); **szczęścić się** (*perf* **po-**) *vr*: **szczęści mu się** he's lucky
**szczęści|e** (**-a**) *nt* (*pomyślny traf*) (good) luck; (*stan ducha*) happiness; **mieć ~** to be lucky *lub* in luck; **nie mieć szczęścia** to be unlucky *lub* of luck; **na ~** fortunately, luckily; **przynosić (komuś) ~** to bring (sb) luck
**szczęśliwie** *adv* (*skończyć się*) happily; (*składać się*) fortunately; (*na szczęście*) luckily, fortunately; **żyli długo i ~** they lived happily ever after
**szczęśliwy** *adj* (*pomyślny*) fortunate, lucky; (*zadowolony*) happy; **Szczęśliwego Nowego Roku!** Happy New Year!; **szczęśliwej podróży!** have a safe journey *lub* trip!
**szczodroś|ć** (**-ci**) *f* (*książk*) generosity
**szczodry** *adj* (*książk*) generous
**szczodrze** *adv* (*książk*) generously
**szczotecz|ka** (**-ki, -ki**) (*dat sg* **-ce**, *gen pl* **-ek**) *f* brush; **~ do zębów** toothbrush
**szczot|ka** (**-ki, -ki**) (*dat sg* **-ce**, *gen pl* **-ek**) *f* (*do zamiatania*) broom; (*Elektr*) brush; **~ do włosów** hairbrush; **~ do butów** shoebrush; **~ do ubrania** clothes brush
**szczotk|ować (-uję, -ujesz)** (*perf* **wy-**) *vt* to brush
**szczu|ć (-ję, -jesz)** *vt* (*perf* **po-**); **~ kogoś psem** to set a dog on sb
**szczud|ła** (**-eł**) *pl* stilts *pl*; **chodzić na ~ch** to walk on stilts
**szczupa|k** (**-ka, -ki**) (*instr sg* **-kiem**) *m* pike
**szczupl|eć (-eję, -ejesz)** (*perf* **wy-**, *pt* **-ał, -eli**) *vi* to grow slim
**szczupły** *adj* (*człowiek, nogi*) slim; (*fundusze, zapasy*) slender
**szczu|r** (**-ra, -ry**) (*loc sg* **-rze**) *m* rat; **~ lądowy** (*przen*) landlubber (*pot*)
**szczwany** *adj* cunning; **~ lis** slyboots
**szczy|cić się (-cę, -cisz)** (*imp* **-ć**, *perf* **po-**) *vr*: **szczycić się** *+instr* to pride o.s. on, to boast of
**szczy|gieł** (**-gła, -gły**) (*loc sg* **-gle**) *m* goldfinch
**szczy|pać (-pię, -piesz)** *vt* to pinch; **dym szczypie mnie w oczy** the smoke is stinging my eyes; **oczy mnie szczypią** my eyes are stinging
**szczypaw|ka** (**-ki, -ki**) (*dat sg* **-ce**, *gen pl* **-ek**) *f* (*pot*) earwig
**szczy|pce** (**-piec** *lub* **-pców**) *pl* (*narzędzie*) pliers *pl*, pincers *pl*; (*Zool*) pincers *pl*
**szczypior|ek** (**-ku**) (*instr sg* **-kiem**) *m* chives *pl*
**szczyp|ta** (**-ty, -ty**) (*dat sg* **-cie**) *f* pinch; (*przen: rozumu, szczęścia*) speck
**szczy|t** (**-tu, -ty**) (*loc sg* **-cie**) *m* (*góry*) top, peak; (*drzewa, schodów*) top; (*sławy, kariery, formy*) peak; (*stołu*) head; (*Archit*) gable; **godziny ~u** peak *lub* rush hours; **spotkanie na szczycie** summit (meeting); **~ luksusu** the ultimate in luxury
**szczytny** *adj* (*książk*) noble
**szczytowy** *adj*: **okres ~** peak period; **punkt ~** climax
**szedł** *itd. vb patrz* **iść**
**sze|f** (**-fa, -fowie**) (*loc sg* **-fie**) *m* boss; **~ rządu** Prime Minister; **~ sztabu** Chief of Staff; **~ kuchni** chef
**szej|k** (**-ka, -kowie**) (*instr sg* **-kiem**) *m* sheik(h)
**szele|st** (**-stu, -sty**) (*loc sg* **-ście**) *m* rustle

S

**szele|ścić (-szczę, -ścisz)** *(imp* **-ść)** *vi (o liściach itp.)* to rustle; **~ papierami** to rustle the papers
**szel|f** (**-fu, -fy**) *(loc sg* **-fie**) *m (Geol)* shelf
**szel|ki** (**-ek**) *pl (do spodni)* braces *pl (Brit)*, suspenders *pl (US)*; *(przy fartuchu, sukience)* straps *pl*
**szem|rać (-rzę, -rzesz)** *vi* to murmur
**szemrani|e** (**-a**) *nt*: **bez szemrania** without a murmur
**szep|nąć (-nę, -niesz)** *(imp* **-nij**) *vb perf od* **szeptać**
**szep|t** (**-tu**) *(loc sg* **-cie**) *m* whisper; **~em** in a whisper; **mówić ~em** to whisper; **szepty** *pl* whispering
**szep|tać (-czę, -czesz)** *(perf* **-nąć)** *vt* to whisper ▷ *vi* to whisper
**szer.** *abbr (= szeregowiec)* Pvt. *(= private)*; *(= szerokość)* w. *(= width)*
**szere|g** (**-gu, -gi**) *(instr sg* **-giem**) *m (liczb, krzeseł, ludzi)* row; *(Mat)* series; *(osób, spraw, dni)* a number of; **ustawiać się w ~u** to line up; **szeregi** *pl* ranks *pl*
**szereg|ować (-uję, -ujesz)** *(perf* **u-**) *vt* to rank
**szerego|wiec** (**-wca, -wcy**) *m (Wojsk)* private; *(pot: dom szeregowy)* terrace house *(Brit)*, row house *(US)*; **starszy ~** Lance Corporal *(Brit)*, Private First Class *(US)*
**szeregowy** *adj (domek, zabudowa)* terrace *attr (Brit)*, row *attr (US)*; *(Elektr)* serial; *(przen: członkowie itp.)* rank-and-file ▷ *m decl like adj (szeregowiec)* private
**szermier|ka** (**-ki**) *(dat sg* **-ce**) *f* fencing; **~ słowna** war of words
**szermierz** (**-a, -e**) *(gen pl* **-y**) *m* fencer; *(przen: bojownik)* champion
**szer|oki** *(comp* **-szy**) *adj (rzeka, brama, ekran, rękaw)* wide; *(widok, uśmiech, gest ręki, czoło)* broad; *(przen: plany, zakres, horyzonty)* broad; *(: publiczność, grono)* wide; **~ na 2 metry** two metres *(Brit) lub* meters *(US)* wide; **jak kraj długi i ~** all across the country; **mieć ~ gest** *(przen)* to be open-handed; **wypłynąć** *(perf)* **na ~e wody** *(przen)* to rise to prominence
**sze|roko** *(comp* **-rzej**) *adv (rozlegle wszerz)* widely; *(na wszystkie strony)* broadly; *(obszernie)* at length; **otworzyć** *(perf)* **~ okno/usta** to open the window/mouth wide; **mieć oczy ~ otwarte** *(przen)* to keep one's eyes peeled
**szerokokątny** *adj*: **obiektyw ~** wide-angle lens
**szerokopasmowy** *adj (Komput)* broadband; **łącze** *nt* **szerokopasmowe** broadband connection, broadband access
**szerokoś|ć** (**-ci, -ci**) *(gen pl* **-ci**) *f* width, breadth; **mieć 5 m szerokości** to be 5 m wide; **~ geograficzna** latitude; **otworzyć** *(perf)* **coś na całą ~** to open sth wide
**szersze|ń** (**-nia, -nie**) *(gen pl* **-ni**) *m* hornet
**szery|f** (**-fa, -fowie**) *(loc sg* **-fie**) *m* sheriff
**szerz|yć (-ę, -ysz)** *vt (oświatę, hasła)* to disseminate, to propagate; *(plotki)* to spread; *(zniszczenie, postrach)* to cause; **szerzyć się** *vr* to spread
**szesnast|ka** (**-ki, -ki**) *(dat sg* **-ce**, *gen pl* **-ek**) *f* sixteen; *(Muz)* semiquaver *(Brit)*, sixteenth note *(US)*
**szesnasty** *num decl like adj* sixteenth; **strona szesnasta** page sixteen; **(godzina) szesnasta** 4 p.m.
**szesnaście** *(jak:* **jedenaście**) *num* sixteen
**sześc.** *abbr (= sześcienny)* cubic
**sześcia|n** (**-nu, -ny**) *(loc sg* **-nie**) *m* cube; **podnosić do ~u** to cube
**sześcienny** *adj*: **metr ~** cubic metre *(Brit) lub* meter *(US)*; **pierwiastek ~** cube root
**sześcioką|t** (**-ta, -ty**) *(loc sg* **-cie**) *m* hexagon
**sześciokrotny** *adj* six-time *attr*
**sześcioletni** *adj (dziecko, samochód)* six-year-old; *(plan, studia)* six-year *attr*
**sześcioro** *(jak:* **czworo**) *num* six
**sześć** *(jak:* **pięć**) *num* six; **pal ~!** *(pot)* to hell with it! *(pot)*
**sześćdziesiąt** *(jak:* **dziesięć**) *num* sixty
**sześćdziesiąty** *num* sixtieth; **lata sześćdziesiąte** the sixties
**sześćset** *(jak:* **pięćset**) *num* six hundred
**sześćsetny** *num* six hundredth
**Szetland|y** (**-ów**) *pl* the Shetland Islands *pl*, the Shetlands *pl*
**szetlandzki** *adj* Shetland
**szew** (**szwu, szwy**) *(loc sg* **szwie**) *m (Krawiectwo)* seam; *(Med)* suture, stitch; **sala pękała w szwach** the hall was bursting at the seams
**szewc** (**-a, -y**) *m* shoemaker, cobbler; **kląć jak ~** to swear like a trooper
**szewski** *adj (zakład, warsztat, młotek)* shoemaker's *attr*, cobbler's *attr*; **szewska pasja** blind rage, white heat
**szkal|ować (-uję, -ujesz)** *(perf* **o-**) *vt* to vilify
**szka|pa** (**-py, -py**) *(dat sg* **-pie**) *f* nag
**szkaradny** *adj* hideous
**szkarlaty|na** (**-ny**) *(dat sg* **-nie**) *f* scarlet fever
**szkarłatny** *adj* dark red
**szkatuł|ka** (**-ki, -ki**) *(dat sg* **-ce**, *gen pl* **-ek**) *f* casket
**szkic** (**-u, -e**) *m (plan, projekt)* draft; *(Sztuka)* sketch
**szkic|ować (-uję, -ujesz)** *(perf* **na-**) *vt* to sketch
**szkicowni|k** (**-ka, -ki**) *(instr sg* **-kiem**) *m* sketchbook

**szkicowy** *adj* (*omówienie*) sketchy; **~ plan/rysunek** sketch
**szkiele|t** (**-tu, -ty**) (*loc sg* **-cie**) *m* (*człowieka, zwierzęcia*) skeleton; (*budowli, konstrukcji*) frame(work)
**szkieł|ko** (**-ka, -ka**) (*instr sg* **-kiem**) *nt* glass
**szklan|ka** (**-ki, -ki**) (*dat sg* **-ce**, *gen pl* **-ek**) *f* glass; (*Kulin: miarka*) ≈ cup; **burza w szklance wody** a storm in a teacup
**szklany** *adj* glass *attr*; **~ ekran** (*przen*) the small screen
**szklar|nia** (**-ni, -nie**) (*gen pl* **-ni**) *f* glasshouse, greenhouse
**szklarz** (**-a, -e**) (*gen pl* **-y**) *m* glazier
**szkl|ić (-ę, -isz)** (*perf* **o-**) *vt* to glaze
**szklisty** *adj* (*powierzchnia*) glassy; (*oczy*) glassy, glazed
**szkli|wo** (**-wa, -wa**) (*loc sg* **-wie**) *nt* (*glazura*) glaze; (*na zębach*) enamel
**sz|kło** (**-kła**) (*loc sg* **-kle**) *nt* glass; (*szklane przedmioty*) (*nom pl* **-kła**, *gen pl* **-kieł**) glass(ware); **pod szkłem** under glass; **~ powiększające** magnifying glass; **szkła** *pl* glasses *pl*; **szkła kontaktowe** contact lenses
**Szkocj|a** (**-i**) *f* Scotland
**szkocki** *adj* Scottish, Scots; **szkocka krata** tartan; **szkocka** *f decl like adj* (*pot: też:* **szkocka whisky**) Scotch
**szk|oda** (**-ody, -ody**) (*dat sg* **-odzie**, *gen pl* **-ód**) *f* damage ▷ *adv*: **~, że ...** (it's a) pity (that) ...; **~ majątkowa** damage to property; **ze szkodą dla** *+gen* to the detriment of; **działać na szkodę** *+gen* to be detrimental to; **~ twoich słów/twego czasu** you're wasting your breath/time; **(jaka) ~!** what a pity!; **~ gadać!** (*pot*) what can I say?
**szkodliwie** *adv* harmfully
**szkodliwoś|ć** (**-ci**) *f* harm(fulness)
**szkodliwy** *adj* harmful, damaging; **~ dla** *+gen* harmful *lub* damaging to
**szkodni|k** (**-ka, -ki**) (*instr sg* **-kiem**) *m* pest
**szko|dzić (-dzę, -dzisz)** *vi*: **~ komuś/czemuś** to be bad for sb/sth; **palenie szkodzi** smoking is bad for you *lub* your health; **(nic) nie szkodzi!** never mind!, that's OK!; **czosnek mi szkodzi** garlic disagrees with me; **co ci szkodzi?** (*pot*) what's the harm?
**szkole|nie** (**-nia, -nia**) (*gen pl* **-ń**) *nt* training; **~ zawodowe** professional training
**szkoleniowy** *adj*: **kurs/ośrodek ~** training course/centre (*Brit*) *lub* center (*US*)
**szk|olić (-olę, -olisz)** (*imp* **-ol** *lub* **-ól**, *perf* **wy-**) *vt* to train; **szkolić się** *vr* to train
**szkolnict|wo** (**-wa**) (*loc sg* **-wie**) *nt* education
**szkolny** *adj* (*rok, budynek, świadectwo*) school *attr*; (*statek, samolot*) training *attr*; **dziecko w wieku ~m** schoolchild
**szk|oła** (**-oły, -oły**) (*dat sg* **-ole**, *gen pl* **-ół**) *f* school; **~ podstawowa** primary (*Brit*) *lub* elementary (*US*) school; **~ średnia** secondary (*Brit*) *lub* high (*US*) school; **~ wieczorowa** night school; **chodzić do szkoły** to go to school; **w szkole** at school; **dać** (*perf*) **komuś szkołę** (*pot*) to put sb through a mill (*pot*)
**szko|p** (**-pa, -py**) (*loc sg* **-pie**) *m* (*pej, pot: Niemiec*) jerry (*pej, pot*)
**szkopu|ł** (**-łu**) (*loc sg* **-le**) *m* hitch; **~ w tym, że ...** the hitch is that ...
**szkorbu|t** (**-tu**) (*loc sg* **-cie**) *m* scurvy
**Szko|t** (**-ta, -ci**) (*loc sg* **-cie**) *m* Scot(sman)
**Szkot|ka** (**-ki, -ki**) (*dat sg* **-ce**, *gen pl* **-ek**) *f* Scot(swoman)
**szkół|ka** (**-ki, -ki**) (*dat sg* **-ce**, *gen pl* **-ek**) *f* school; **~ leśna** nursery
**szkra|b** (**-ba, -by**) (*loc sg* **-bie**) *m* (*pot*) tot
**szkune|r** (**-ra, -ry**) (*loc sg* **-rze**) *m* schooner
**szkutnict|wo** (**-wa**) (*loc sg* **-wie**) *nt* boatbuilding
**szkutni|k** (**-ka, -cy**) (*instr sg* **-kiem**) *m* boatbuilder
**szkwa|ł** (**-łu, -ły**) (*loc sg* **-le**) *m* squall
**szlaba|n** (**-nu, -ny**) (*loc sg* **-nie**) *m* barrier, gate
**szlachcic** (**-a, -e**) *m* nobleman
**szlachecki** *adj* noble
**szlachect|wo** (**-wa**) (*loc sg* **-wie**) *nt* nobility
**szlachetnie** *adv* nobly; **~ urodzony** of noble birth
**szlachetnoś|ć** (**-ci**) *f* (*urodzenia*) nobility; (*człowieka, czynu, charakteru*) nobleness
**szlachetny** *adj* noble; (*kamień*) precious
**szlach|ta** (**-ty**) (*dat sg* **-cie**) *f* nobility
**szlafro|k** (**-ka, -ki**) (*instr sg* **-kiem**) *m* dressing gown, (bath)robe
**szla|g** (**-gu**) (*instr sg* **-giem**) *m* (*pot*): **~ mnie trafia** it gets my goat (*pot*); **niech to ~!** (*pot*) damnation! (*pot*)
**szlagie|r** (**-ra** *lub* **-ru, -ry**) (*loc sg* **-rze**) *m* (*piosenka*) hit; (*książka*) bestseller; (*film*) blockbuster
**szla|k** (**-ku, -ki**) (*instr sg* **-kiem**) *m* (*komunikacyjny*) route; (*turystyczny*) trail
**szla|m** (**-mu, -my**) (*loc sg* **-mie**) *m* slime
**szle|m** (**-ma, -my**) (*loc sg* **-mie**) *m* grand slam
**szlemi|k** (**-ka, -ki**) (*instr sg* **-kiem**) *m* little *lub* small slam
**szli** *vb patrz* **iść**
**szli|f** (**-fu, -fy**) (*loc sg* **-fie**) *m* (*kamienia*) cut
**szlifier|ka** (**-ki, -ki**) (*dat sg* **-ce**, *gen pl* **-ek**) *f* grinder
**szlifierski** *adj*: **kamień ~** grindstone
**szlifierz** (**-a, -e**) (*gen pl* **-y**) *m* grinder
**szlif|ować (-uję, -ujesz)** *vt* (*nadawać kształt*) (*perf* **o-**) (*kamień, szkło*) to grind; (*kryształ*) to cut; (*polerować*) (*perf* **wy-**) (*kamień, szkło*)

S

to polish; (*kryształ*) to sand; (*przen: wykańczać, doskonalić*) (*perf* **wy-**) to polish up

**szloch** (**-u**) *m* sob

**szloch|ać (-am, -asz)** *vi* to sob

**szluf|ka** (**-ki, -ki**) (*dat sg* **-ce**, *gen pl* **-ek**) *f* (*część odzieży*) belt loop (Brit), belt carrier (US); (*część paska*) keeper (Brit), carrier (US)

**szła** *itd. vb patrz* **iść**

**szmaciany** *adj*: **szmaciana lalka** rag doll

**szmal** (**-u**) *m* (*pot*) dough (*pot*)

**szmarag|d** (**-du, -dy**) (*loc sg* **-dzie**) *m* emerald

**szmaragdowy** *adj* emerald

**szma|t** (**-tu**) (*loc sg* **-cie**) *m*: **~ drogi/czasu** a long way/time

**szma|ta** (**-ty, -ty**) (*dat sg* **-cie**) *f* rag; (*pej: o człowieku*) toe-rag (*pej*); (*pej: o gazecie*) rag (*pej*); **szmaty** *pl* (*pot*) rags *pl* (*pot*)

**szmat|ka** (**-ki, -ki**) (*dat sg* **-ce**, *gen pl* **-ek**) *f* cloth, rag

**szmatławy** *adj* (*pej*) shabby (*pej*)

**szmelc** (**-u**) *m* (*pot*) junk (*pot*)

**szme|r** (**-ru, -ry**) (*loc sg* **-rze**) *m* murmur

**szmin|ka** (**-ki, -ki**) (*dat sg* **-ce**, *gen pl* **-ek**) *f* (*też:* **szminka do ust**) lipstick; (*do charakteryzacji*) greasepaint

**szmink|ować (-uję, -ujesz)** (*perf* **u-**) *vt*: **~ usta** to put on lipstick; **szminkować się** *vr* to wear lipstick

**szmi|ra** (**-ry, -ry**) (*dat sg* **-rze**) *f* (*pot*) trash (*pot*), rubbish (*pot*)

**szmirowaty** *adj* (*pot*) trashy (*pot*), rubbishy (*pot*)

**szmu|giel** (**-glu**) *m* smuggling

**szmugl|ować (-uję, -ujesz)** (*perf* **prze-**) *vt* to smuggle

**sznu|r** (**-ra, -ry**) (*loc sg* **-rze**) *m* (*cienki powróz*) string; (*samochodów*) line; (*ptaków, korali*) string; (*pot: elektryczny*) lead, cord; **~ do bielizny** washing line (Brit), clothes line (US)

**sznur|ek** (**-ka, -ki**) (*instr sg* **-kiem**) *m* string

**sznur|ować (-uję, -ujesz)** (*perf* **za-**) *vt* to lace (up)

**sznurowad|ło** (**-ła, -ła**) (*loc sg* **-le**, *gen pl* **-eł**) *nt* shoelace

**sznurowany** *adj*: **buty sznurowane** laced shoes *pl*, lace-ups *pl*

**sznurowy** *adj*: **drabinka sznurowa** rope ladder

**sznyc|el** (**-la, -le**) (*gen pl* **-li** *lub* **-lów**) *m* rissole

**szofe|r** (**-ra, -rzy**) (*loc sg* **-rze**) *m* chauffeur

**szo|k** (**-ku**) (*instr sg* **-kiem**) *m* shock

**szok|ować (-uję, -ujesz)** (*perf* **za-**) *vt* to shock

**szokujący** *adj* shocking

**szo|p** (**-pa, -py**) (*loc sg* **-pie**) *m* (*też:* **szop pracz**) raccoon

**szo|pa** (**-py, -py**) (*dat sg* **-pie**) *f* (*pomieszczenie*) shed; (*pot: czupryna*) mop (*of hair*)

**szop|ka** (**-ki, -ki**) (*dat sg* **-ce**, *gen pl* **-ek**) *f dimin od* **szopa**; (*Rel: żłóbek*) crib; (*: jasełka*) nativity play; (*pot*) carry-on (*pot*)

**szor|ować (-uję, -ujesz)** *vt* (*perf* **wy-**) to scrub ▷ *vi*: **~ o** *+acc* to rub against; **szoruj stąd!** (*pot*) beat it! (*pot*)

**szorstki** *adj* (*powierzchnia*) rough; (*materiał, człowiek, uwaga*) coarse; (*dźwięk, głos*) harsh

**szort|y** (**-ów**) *pl* shorts *pl*

**szo|sa** (**-sy, -sy**) (*dat sg* **-sie**) *f* road

**szosowy** *adj*: **kolarstwo szosowe** (bicycle) road racing

**szowini|sta** (**-sty, -ści**) (*dat sg* **-ście**) *m decl like f in sg* chauvinist

**szowinistyczny** *adj* chauvinistic

**szowiniz|m** (**-mu**) (*loc sg* **-mie**) *m* chauvinism

**szóst|ka** (**-ki, -ki**) (*dat sg* **-ce**, *gen pl* **-ek**) *f* six; (*Szkol*) outstanding (*mark*); **~ osób** six people, a half-dozen people

**szósty** *num decl like adj* sixth; **strona szósta** page six; **~ zmysł** (*przen*) sixth sense

**szpachl|a** (**-i, -e**) (*gen pl* **-i**) *f* spatula

**szpachl|ować (-uję, -ujesz)** (*perf* **za-**) *vt* (*otwory*) to fill (*perf* **wy-**) *vt*: **wy~ ścianę** to fill holes in a wall

**szpachlów|ka** (**-ki, -ki**) (*dat sg* **-ce**, *gen pl* **-ek**) *f* filler

**szpa|da** (**-dy, -dy**) (*dat sg* **-dzie**) *f* (*broń*) sword; (*Sport*) épée

**szpad|el** (**-la, -le**) (*gen pl* **-li**) *m* spade

**szpadzi|sta** (**-sty, -ści**) (*loc sg* **-ście**) *m decl like f in sg* épéeist

**szpaga|t** (**-tu, -ty**) (*loc sg* **-cie**) *m* (*sznurek*) twine; (*Sport*) the splits *pl*; **robić (zrobić** *perf***) ~** to do the splits

**szpa|k** (**-ka, -ki**) (*instr sg* **-kiem**) *m* starling

**szpakowaty** *adj* grizzled

**szpale|r** (**-ru, -ry**) (*loc sg* **-rze**) *m* line

**szpal|ta** (**-ty, -ty**) (*dat sg* **-cie**) *f* column

**szpa|n** (**-nu**) (*loc sg* **-nie**) *m* (*pot*) swank (*pot*)

**szpanerski** *adj* (*pot*) swanky (*pot*)

**szpan|ować (-uję, -ujesz)** *vi* (*pot*) to swank (*pot*)

**szpa|ra** (**-ry, -ry**) (*dat sg* **-rze**) *f* gap, space

**szpara|g** (**-ga, -gi**) (*instr sg* **-giem**) *m* asparagus; **szparagi** *pl* (*Kulin*) asparagus (spears *pl*)

**szparagowy** *adj*: **fasolka szparagowa** string *lub* runner (Brit) bean

**szpargał|y** (**-ów**) *pl* (*pot*) old stuff (*pot*)

**szpatuł|ka** (**-ki, -ki**) (*dat sg* **-ce**, *gen pl* **-ek**) *f* spatula

**szpe|cić (-cę, -cisz)** (*imp* **-ć**, *perf* **o-** *lub* **ze-**) *vt* to mar

**szperacz** (**-a, -e**) (*gen pl* **-y**) *m* (*poszukiwacz*) explorer; (*reflektor*) spotlight

**szper|ać (-am, -asz)** (*perf* **wy-**) *vi* to browse; **~ po kieszeniach** to rummage through one's pockets
**szpetny** *adj* unsightly
**szpic** (**-a, -e**) *m* (*czubek*) point; (*pies*) spitz; **sweter w ~** V-necked sweater; **wycięcie w ~** V-neck
**szpic|el** (**-la, -le**) (*gen pl* **-li** *lub* **-lów**) *m* (*pej*: *szpieg*) snooper
**szpicl|ować (-uję, -ujesz)** *vi* to snoop
**szpicru|ta** (**-ty, -ty**) (*dat sg* **-cie**) *f* horsewhip, crop
**szpie|g** (**-ga, -dzy**) (*instr sg* **-giem**) *m* spy
**szpiegost|wo** (**-wa**) (*loc sg* **-wie**) *nt* espionage
**szpieg|ować (-uję, -ujesz)** (*perf* **wy-**) *vt*: **~ kogoś** to spy on sb ▷ *vi* to spy
**szpiegowski** *adj*: **film/satelita ~** spy movie/ satellite
**szpi|k** (**-ku**) (*instr sg* **-kiem**) *m* (*też*: **szpik kostny**) (bone) marrow; **zepsuty do ~u kości** rotten to the core; **zmarznięty do ~u kości** chilled to the marrow
**szpik|ować (-uję, -ujesz)** (*perf* **na-**) *vt*: **na~ coś cytatami/wiadomościami** to lard sth with quotations/bits of information
**szpikul|ec** (**-ca, -ce**) *m* skewer
**szpil|a** (**-i, -e**) *f* (*duża szpilka*) pin
**szpil|ka** (**-ki, -ki**) (*dat sg* **-ce**, *gen pl* **-ek**) *f* (*Krawiectwo*) pin; (*też*: **szpilka do włosów**) hairpin; (*obcas*) stiletto heel (*Brit*), spike heel (*US*); **szpilki** *pl* (*buty*) stilettos *pl*
**szpina|k** (**-ku**) (*instr sg* **-kiem**) *m* spinach
**szpital** (**-a, -e**) (*gen pl* **-i**) *m* hospital; **być** *lub* **leżeć w ~u** to be in (the (*US*)) hospital; **zabrać** (*perf*) **kogoś do ~a** to take sb to (the (*US*)) hospital
**szpitalny** *adj* hospital *attr*
**szpo|n** (**-na** *lub* **-nu, -ny**) (*loc sg* **-nie**) *m* talon, claw; **w czyichś ~ach** (*przen*) in sb's clutches
**szprot|ka** (**-ki, -ki**) (*dat sg* **-ce**, *gen pl* **-ek**) *f* sprat
**szpry|cha** (**-chy, -chy**) (*dat sg* **-sze**) *f* spoke
**szpryc|ować się (-uję, -ujesz)** (*perf* **na-**) *vr* (*pot*: *narkotyzować się*) to shoot up (*pot*)
**szpul|a** (**-i, -e**) *f* spool, reel
**szpul|ka** (**-ki, -ki**) (*dat sg* **-ce**, *gen pl* **-ek**) *f* bobbin
**szpulowy** *adj*: **magnetofon ~** reel-to-reel tape recorder
**szra|ma** (**-my, -my**) (*dat sg* **-mie**) *f* scar
**szran|ki** (**-ków**) *pl*: **stawać (stanąć** *perf*) **w ~ z kimś** to enter the lists against sb
**szrapnel** (**-a, -e**) (*gen pl* **-i**) *m* shrapnel
**szro|n** (**-nu**) (*loc sg* **-nie**) *m* (white) frost, hoarfrost
**szta|b** (**-bu, -by**) (*loc sg* **-bie**) *m* staff; **~ główny** *lub* **generalny** general headquarters; **~ doradców** board of advisers; **~ ekspertów** panel of experts
**szta|ba** (**-by, -by**) (*dat sg* **-bie**) *f* bar; **złoto w ~ch** gold bullion
**sztab|ka** (**-ki, -ki**) (*dat sg* **-ce**, *gen pl* **-ek**) *f* bar
**sztabowy** *adj*: **oficer ~** staff officer; **mapa sztabowa** ≈ ordnance map (*Brit*)
**sztache|ta** (**-ty, -ty**) (*dat sg* **-cie**) *f* pale
**sztafe|ta** (**-ty, -ty**) (*dat sg* **-cie**) *f* relay
**sztafetowy** *adj*: **bieg ~** relay (race); **pałeczka sztafetowa** baton
**sztalu|gi** (**-g**) *pl* easel
**sztampowy** *adj* run-of-the-mill
**sztanda|r** (**-ru, -ry**) (*loc sg* **-rze**) *m* standard (*flag*)
**sztandarowy** *adj* (*główny*) leading; **poczet ~** colour (*Brit*) *lub* color (*US*) guard
**sztan|ga** (**-gi, -gi**) (*dat sg* **-dze**) *f* (*Sport*) weight
**sztangi|sta** (**-sty, -ści**) (*loc sg* **-ście**) *m decl like f in sg* weight-lifter
**szterlin|g** (**-ga, -gi**) (*instr sg* **-giem**) *m*: **funt ~** (pound) sterling
**sztok** *inv*: **pijany w ~** (*pot*) pie-eyed (*pot*)
**Sztokhol|m** (**-mu**) (*loc sg* **-mie**) *m* Stockholm
**sztol|nia** (**-ni, -nie**) (*gen pl* **-ni**) *f* tunnel (*in a mine*)
**sztorc** (**-a, -e**) *m*: **na ~** on end
**sztorc|ować (-uję, -ujesz)** (*perf* **ob-**) *vt* to scold
**sztor|m** (**-mu, -my**) (*loc sg* **-mie**) *m* storm
**sztormowy** *adj* (*pogoda*) stormy
**sztruk|s** (**-su, -sy**) (*loc sg* **-sie**) *m* corduroy, cord; **sztruksy** *pl* cords *pl*
**sztruksowy** *adj* corduroy
**sztuce|r** (**-ra, -ry**) (*loc sg* **-rze**) *m* rifle
**sztucz|ka** (**-ki, -ki**) (*dat sg* **-ce**, *gen pl* **-ek**) *f* (*fortel*) ploy, trick; (*karciana, magiczna*) trick; **tylko bez sztuczek!** (*pot*) don't try anything funny! (*pot*)
**sztucznie** *adv* artificially
**sztucznoś|ć** (**-ci**) *f* artificiality
**sztuczny** *adj* artificial; **tworzywo sztuczne** plastic; **sztuczne ognie** fireworks; **sztuczne oddychanie** artificial respiration; **sztuczne oddychanie z masażem serca** CPR
**sztućc|e** (**-ów**) *pl* cutlery
**sztu|ka** (**-ki, -ki**) (*dat sg* **-ce**) *f* (*twórczość, kunszt, umiejętność*) art; (*Teatr*) play; (*karciana, cyrkowa*) trick; (*egzemplarz*) piece; **~ ludowa** folk art; **sztuki piękne/plastyczne** the fine/plastic arts; **po 2 złote ~** *lub* **za sztukę** 2 zloty apiece; **~ użytkowa** craft; **sztuki walki** martial arts; **~ dla sztuki** art for art's sake; **(cała) ~ w tym** *lub* **~ polega na tym, żeby ...** the (whole) trick is to ...; **płacić od sztuki** to pay by the piece; **do trzech razy ~** (*pot*) third time lucky
**sztukateri|a** (**-i, -e**) (*gen pl* **-i**) *f* moulding

S

**sztukmistrz** (**-a, -e**) *m* conjurer
**sztuk|ować** (**-uję, -ujesz**) (*perf* **nad-**) *vt* to lengthen
**szturch|ać** (**-am, -asz**) (*perf* **-nąć**) *vt* to nudge
**szturcha|niec** (**-ńca, -ńce**) *m* nudge
**szturch|nąć** (**-nę, -niesz**) (*imp* **-nij**) *vb perf od* **szturchać**
**sztur|m** (**-mu, -my**) (*loc sg* **-mie**) *m*: **przypuścić** (*perf*) **~ na** *+acc* to launch an assault against; **wziąć** (*perf*) **coś ~em** to take sth by storm
**szturm|ować** (**-uję, -ujesz**) *vt* (*Wojsk*) to storm; (*przen*) to invade
**szturmowy** *adj* (*Wojsk*) assault *attr*
**sztyf|t** (**-tu, -ty**) (*loc sg* **-cie**) *m* (*bolec*) pin; **dezodorant w sztyfcie** deodorant stick
**sztyga|r** (**-ra, -rzy**) (*loc sg* **-rze**) *m* foreman (*in a mine*)
**sztyle|t** (**-tu, -ty**) (*loc sg* **-cie**) *m* dagger
**sztywnia|k** (**-ka, -cy**) (*instr sg* **-kiem**) *m* (*pot*) stuffed shirt (*pot*)
**sztywni|eć** (**-eję, -ejesz**) (*perf* **ze-**) *vi* to stiffen; **kark mi zesztywniał** I have a stiff neck
**sztywno** *adv* (*sterczeć, zamocować*) rigidly; (*chodzić, zachowywać się*) stiffly
**sztywnoś|ć** (**-ci**) *f* (*nóg, ruchów, zachowania*) stiffness; (*cen, przepisów, konstrukcji*) rigidity
**sztywny** *adj* (*kołnierzyk, część ciała, ruch*) stiff; (*konstrukcja, przepisy*) rigid; (*ceny*) fixed; (*wygląd*) prim; **książka w sztywnej oprawie** hardback
**szubienic|a** (**-y, -e**) *f* gallows
**szubra|wiec** (**-wca, -wcy**) *m* rascal, rogue
**szufel|ka** (**-ki, -ki**) (*dat sg* **-ce**, *gen pl* **-ek**) *f* (*do śmieci*) dustpan; (*do węgla*) shovel
**szufl|a** (**-i, -e**) (*gen pl* **-i**) *f* shovel
**szufla|da** (**-dy, -dy**) (*dat sg* **-dzie**) *f* drawer
**szufladk|ować** (**-uję, -ujesz**) (*perf* **za-**) *vt* to pigeonhole
**szu|ja** (**-i, -je**) *m decl like f* (*pej*) rat (*pej*)
**szuk|ać** (**-am, -asz**) (*perf* **po-**) *vt +gen* (*miejsca, złodzieja, okazji, pociechy*) to look for; (*przygód, sprawiedliwości, zemsty, szczęścia*) to seek; **szukałam wszędzie** I've looked everywhere
**szule|r** (**-ra, -rzy**) (*loc sg* **-rze**) *m* cardsharp
**szu|m** (**-mu, -my**) (*loc sg* **-mie**) *m* (*fal, głosów, miasta*) hum; (*drzew, deszczu*) rustle; (*nieuzasadniona popularność*) hype; (*w głośniku*) noise; **~ w uszach** buzzing in the ears; **narobić** (*perf*) **~u (wokół czegoś)** (*pot*) to raise a stink (about sth) (*pot*); **szumy** *pl* (*Radio*) static
**szumi|eć** (**-**) (*pt* **-ał**) *vi* (*o falach, wietrze, wentylatorze*) to hum; **szumi mi w głowie** my head is buzzing
**szumny** *adj* high-sounding
**szumowin|y** (**-**) *pl* scum
**szur|ać** (**-am, -asz**) (*perf* **-nąć**) *vi* to make a scraping noise; **~ butami** to shuffle one's feet
**szur|nąć** (**-nę, -niesz**) (*imp* **-nij**) *vb perf od* **szurać**
**szu|s** (**-su** *lub* **-sa, -sy**) (*loc sg* **-sie**) *m* run
**szuwar|y** (**-ów**) *pl* rushes *pl*
**szwacz|ka** (**-ki, -ki**) (*dat sg* **-ce**, *gen pl* **-ek**) *f* seamstress
**szwadro|n** (**-nu, -ny**) (*loc sg* **-nie**) *m* squadron
**szwa|gier** (**-gra, -growie**) (*loc sg* **-grze**) *m* brother-in-law
**szwagier|ka** (**-ki, -ki**) (*dat sg* **-ce**, *gen pl* **-ek**) *f* sister-in-law
**Szwajca|r** (**-ra, -rzy**) (*loc sg* **-rze**) *m* Swiss
**Szwajcari|a** (**-i**) *f* Switzerland
**Szwajcar|ka** (**-ki, -ki**) (*dat sg* **-ce**, *gen pl* **-ek**) *f* Swiss
**szwajcarski** *adj* Swiss
**szwan|k** (**-ku**) (*instr sg* **-kiem**) *m*: **narazić** (*perf*) **kogoś/coś na ~** to jeopardize sb/sth; **wyjść** (*perf*) **(z czegoś) bez ~u** to escape (sth) unharmed
**szwank|ować** (**-uje**) (*perf* **za-**) *vi* to be failing
**Szwecj|a** (**-i**) *f* Sweden
**Szwe|d** (**-da, -dzi**) (*loc sg* **-dzie**) *m* Swede
**Szwed|ka** (**-ki, -ki**) (*dat sg* **-ce**, *gen pl* **-ek**) *f* Swede
**szwedzki** *adj* Swedish ▷ *m decl like adj* Swedish
**szwend|ać się** (**-am, -asz**) *vr* to loiter
**szwie** *itd. n patrz* **szew**
**szwind|el** (**-lu, -le**) (*gen pl* **-li** *lub* **-lów**) *m* (*pot*) swindle (*pot*)
**szy|b** (**-bu, -by**) (*loc sg* **-bie**) *m* shaft; **~ naftowy** oil rig *lub* well; **~ wentylacyjny** ventilation shaft; *patrz też* **szyba**
**szy|ba** (**-by, -by**) (*dat sg* **-bie**) *f* (*szklana tafla*) (window) pane; (*okno*) window; **przednia ~** (*Mot*) windscreen (*Brit*), windshield (*US*)
**szyberdach** (**-u, -y**) *m* sliding *lub* sun roof
**szyb|ki** (*comp* **-szy**) *adj* fast; (*decyzja, koniec, zysk*) quick; **bar ~ej obsługi** fast food restaurant; **pas ~ego ruchu** the fast lane; **droga ~ego ruchu** clearway (*Brit*), freeway (*US*)
**szyb|ko** (*comp* **-ciej**) *adv* (*jechać, iść*) fast; (*reagować, odpowiadać*) quickly; **~!** (be) quick!
**szybkobieżny** *adj* fast-moving
**szybkościomierz** (**-a, -e**) (*gen pl* **-y**) *m* speedometer
**szybkoś|ć** (**-ci, -ci**) (*gen pl* **-ci**) *f* (*pojazdu, wiatru, zmian*) speed; (*decyzji*) promptness; (*wystrzałów*) rapidity; **z szybkością 100 mil na godzinę** at (the speed of) 100 miles per hour; **nabierać (nabrać** *perf*) **szybkości** to pick up speed; **zmniejszać (zmniejszyć** *perf*)**/zwiększać (zwiększyć** *perf*) **~** to reduce/increase speed

**szybkowa|r** (**-ru, -ry**) (*loc sg* **-rze**) *m* pressure cooker
**szyb|ować (-uję, -ujesz)** (*perf* **po-**) *vi* to glide
**szybo|wiec** (**-wca, -wce**) *m* glider
**szybownict|wo** (**-wa**) (*loc sg* **-wie**) *nt* gliding
**szy|cha** (**-chy, -chy**) (*dat sg* **-sze**) *f* (*pot*) big shot (*pot*)
**szyci|e** (**-a**) *nt* sewing; **maszyna do szycia** sewing machine
**szy|ć (-ję, -jesz)** *vt* (*wytwarzać*) (*perf* **u-**) to sew; (*zszywać*) (*perf* **z-**) to stitch; (*Med*) (*perf* **z-**) to suture, to stitch; ~ **na maszynie** to machine
**szydeł|ko** (**-ka, -ka**) (*instr sg* **-kiem**, *gen pl* **-ek**) *nt* crochet-hook
**szydełk|ować (-uję, -ujesz)** *vt* to crochet
**szyderczy** *adj* derisive, sneering
**szyderst|wo** (**-wa, -wa**) (*loc sg* **-wie**) *nt* derision, sneer
**szyd|ło** (**-ła, -ła**) (*loc sg* **-le**, *gen pl* **-eł**) *nt* awl; **wyszło ~ z worka** (*pot*) the cat is out of the bag (*pot*)
**szy|dzić (-dzę, -dzisz)** (*imp* **-dź**) *vi*: **~ z** *+gen* to deride, to sneer at
**szyfo|n** (**-nu, -ny**) (*loc sg* **-nie**) *m* chiffon
**szyf|r** (**-ru, -ry**) (*loc sg* **-rze**) *m* (secret) code, cipher
**szyfran|t** (**-ta, -ci**) (*loc sg* **-cie**) *m* coder
**szyfr|ować (-uję, -ujesz)** (*perf* **za-**) *vt* to code, to cipher
**szyfrowy** *adj*: **zamek ~** combination lock
**szyicki** *adj* Shiite
**szy|ja** (**-i, -je**) *f* neck; **rzucać się (rzucić się** *perf*) **komuś na szyję** to fling one's arms around sb; **na łeb, na szyję** headlong
**szyj|ka** (**-ki, -ki**) (*dat sg* **-ce**, *gen pl* **-ek**) *f* (*butelki, instrumentu*) neck; ~ **macicy** cervix
**szyjny** *adj* (*kręg, kręgosłup*) cervical; **tętnica szyjna** the carotid (artery)
**szy|k** (**-ku**) (*instr sg* **-kiem**) *m* (*elegancja*) style; (*Wojsk*) (*nom pl* **-ki**) formation; (*Jęz*) (*nom pl* **-ki**) word order; **ubierać się z ~iem** to dress in *lub* with style; **pokrzyżować** (*perf*) *lub* **popsuć** (*perf*) **komuś ~i** to thwart *lub* cross sb's plans
**szykan|ować (-uję, -ujesz)** *vt* to persecute
**szykan|y** (-) *pl* persecution
**szyk|ować (-uję, -ujesz)** *vt* (*śniadanie, obiad*) (*perf* **przy-** *lub* **na-** *lub* **u-**) to prepare; (*niespodziankę*) (*perf* **przy-**) to prepare; **szykować się** *vr* (*perf* **przy-**); **~ się (do czegoś)** to prepare (for sth); **coś się szykuje** (*pot*) something's cooking (*pot*)
**szykowny** *adj* chic, stylish
**szyl|d** (**-du, -dy**) (*loc sg* **-dzie**) *m* sign (board); **pod ~em** *+gen* behind the façade of
**szylin|g** (**-ga, -gi**) (*instr sg* **-giem**) *m* shilling
**szympan|s** (**-sa, -sy**) (*loc sg* **-sie**) *m* chimp(anzee)
**szy|na** (**-ny, -ny**) (*dat sg* **-nie**) *f* rail; (*Med*) splint; **szyny** *pl* rail(s *pl*)
**szyn|ka** (**-ki, -ki**) (*dat sg* **-ce**, *gen pl* **-ek**) *f* ham
**szynszyl|a** (**-i, -e**) (*gen pl* **-i**) *f* chinchilla
**szyp|er** (**-ra, -rowie**) (*loc sg* **-rze**) *m* skipper
**szypuł|ka** (**-ki, -ki**) (*dat sg* **-ce**, *gen pl* **-ek**) *f* stalk
**szysz|ka** (**-ki, -ki**) (*dat sg* **-ce**, *gen pl* **-ek**) *f* cone
**szyszyn|ka** (**-ki, -ki**) (*dat sg* **-ce**, *gen pl* **-ek**) *f* (*Anat*) pineal body *lub* gland
**szyty** *adj*: **~ na miarę** tailor-made, made-to-measure

S

# Śś

**Ś, ś** *nt inv (litera)* Ś, ś; **Ś jak Światowid** s acute
**ścia|na (-ny, -ny)** *(dat sg* **-nie***) f* wall; *(strome zbocze)* face; **za ścianą** next door
**ścian|ka (-ki, -ki)** *(dat sg* **-ce**, *gen pl* **-ek***) f dimin od* **ściana**; *(naczynia, pudełka)* side
**ściąć (zetnę, zetniesz)** *(imp* **zetnij***) vb perf od* **ścinać**
**ścią|ga (-gi, -gi)** *(dat sg* **-dze***) f* crib sheet
**ściągacz (-a, -e)** *(gen pl* **-y***) m* welt
**ściąg|ać (-am, -asz)** *(perf* **-nąć***) vt (buty, koszulę)* to pull off; *(flagę)* to take down; *(mocno związywać)* to pull tight; *(pot: odpisywać)* to crib ▷ *vi (przybywać)* to come flocking; *(pot: odpisywać)* to crib; **~ coś ze stołu** to pull sth off the table; **~ podatki/opłaty** to collect taxes/fees; **~ na siebie uwagę/podejrzenie** to draw attention/suspicion upon o.s.
**ściągaw|ka (-ki, -ki)** *(dat sg* **-ce**, *gen pl* **-ek***) f* crib sheet
**ściąg|nąć (-nę, -niesz)** *(imp* **-nij***) vb perf od* **ściągać**
**ściągnięty** *adj (twarz)* drawn, pinched; **forma ściągnięta** *(Jęz)* contracted form
**ście|c (-knie)** *vb perf od* **ściekać**
**ście|g (-gu, -gi)** *(instr sg* **-giem***) m* stitch; **~ prosty** plain
**ście|k (-ku, -ki)** *(instr sg* **-kiem***) m (kanał)* sewer; **ścieki** *pl* sewage *sg*
**ściek|ać (-a)** *(perf* **ściec** *lub* **ścieknąć***) vi* to trickle (down)
**ściek|nąć (-nie)** *(pt* **-ł***) vb perf od* **ściekać**
**ściekowy** *adj*: **rura ściekowa** waste pipe; **kanał ~** *(otwarty)* drainage ditch; *(podziemny)* sewer; **studzienka ściekowa** drain
**ściel|ić (-ę, -isz)** *vt (perf* **po-***);* **~ łóżko** to make the bed; **ścielić się** *vr (przen)* to spread
**ściem|niać się (-niam, -niasz)** *(perf* **-nić***) vr (o obrazie)* to go dark; **ściemnia się** it is getting dark
**ściem|nić (-nię, -nisz)** *(imp* **-nij***) vb perf od* **ściemniać się**
**ściemni|eć (-eje)** *vi perf (o kolorze)* to darken; *(o obrazie, niebie)* to go dark, to darken; *(o świetle)* to dim
**ścienny** *adj* wall *attr*
**ścier|ać (-am, -asz)** *(perf* **zetrzeć***) vt (napis, rysunek)* to rub off; *(resztki cieczy)* to wipe away *lub* off; **~ kurze** to dust; **ścierać się** *vr (o armiach, poglądach)* to clash; *(o materiale, dywanie)* to get worn, to wear thin; *(o butach)* to wear out
**ścierecz|ka (-ki, -ki)** *(dat sg* **-ce**, *gen pl* **-ek***) f dimin od* **ścierka**
**ścier|ka (-ki, -ki)** *(dat sg* **-ce**, *gen pl* **-ek***) f* cloth; *(do naczyń)* dishcloth; *(do kurzu)* duster
**ściernis|ko (-ka, -ka)** *(instr sg* **-kiem***) nt* stubble
**ścierny** *adj*: **papier ~** sandpaper
**ścier|pieć (-pię, -pisz)** *vt perf*: **nie mogę go ~** I can't stand him
**ścierp|nąć (-nę, -niesz)** *(imp* **-nij**, *pt* **-ł***) vb perf od* **cierpnąć**
**ścierpnięty** *adj* numb(ed)
**ścier|wo (-wa)** *(loc sg* **-wie***) nt* carcass
**ścieś|niać (-niam, -niasz)** *(perf* **-nić***) vt (litery)* to squeeze together; **~ szeregi** to move in closer, to get closer together
**ścież|ka (-ki, -ki)** *(dat sg* **-ce**, *gen pl* **-ek***) f* path; *(na taśmie magnetofonowej)* track; **~ rowerowa** bicycle path; **~ dźwiękowa** soundtrack; **~ zdrowia** fitness trail; **chodzić własnymi ~mi** *(przen)* to be independent
**ścię|cie (-cia, -cia)** *(gen pl* **-ć***) nt (egzekucja)* beheading; *(Sport)* smash
**ścię|gno (-gna, -gna)** *(loc sg* **-gnie**, *gen pl* **-gien***) nt (Anat)* tendon; **~ Achillesa** Achilles tendon
**ścig|ać (-am, -asz)** *vt (gonić)* to chase, to pursue; *(o policji)* to hunt for; **ścigany przez prawo** wanted by the law; **ścigać się** *vr* to race; **~ się z kimś** to race against sb
**ścigani|e (-a)** *nt*: **organy ścigania** ≈ the police
**ścin|ać (-am, -asz)** *(perf* **ściąć***) vt (drzewo)* to cut down, to fell; *(włosy)* to cut; *(skazańca)* to behead ▷ *vi (Sport)* to smash (the ball); **~ kogoś z nóg** *(przen)* to knock sb sideways; **~ zakręt** to cut a corner; **ścinać się** *vr (o białku)* to set; *(przen: o krwi w żyłach)* to curdle
**ścin|ek (-ka, -ki)** *(instr sg* **-kiem***) m (papieru)* clipping; *(materiału)* off-cut

**ściół|ka** (**-ki, -ki**) (*dat sg* **-ce**, *gen pl* **-ek**) *f* (*dla zwierząt*) bedding; **~ leśna** forest bed
**ścis|k** (**-ku**) (*instr sg* **-kiem**) *m* (*pot*) crush
**ścis|kać (-kam, -kasz)** *vt* (*dłońmi*) (*perf* **-nąć**) to squeeze; (*imadłem*) (*perf* **-nąć**) to grip; (*mocno trzymać*) (*perf* **-nąć**) to clasp tightly; (*obejmować*) (*perf* **u-**) to hug; **ściskała mi** *lub* **moją rękę** she was squeezing my hand; **żal ściska mi serce** it grieves my heart; **ściskać się** *vr* (*obejmować się*) (*perf* **u-**) to hug
**ścisłoś|ć** (**-ci**) *f* (*dokładność*) exactness; **jeśli chodzi o ~** to be precise *lub* exact
**ścisły** *adj* (*instrukcja, informacja, nauka*) exact; (*dyscyplina, dieta*) strict; (*związek, zależność*) close; (*druk*) condensed; (*umysł*) exact, scientific; **nauki ścisłe** the sciences; **ścisłe grono** small group
**ści|snąć (-snę, -śniesz)** (*imp* **-śnij**) *vb perf od* **ściskać**
**ścisz|ać (-am, -asz)** (*perf* **-yć**) *vt* (*radio*) to turn down; **ściszył głos** he lowered his voice
**ściśle** *adv* (*określać, wyrażać, przestrzegać*) exactly; (*wykonywać, badać*) rigorously; (*przylegać, pakować*) closely, tightly; **~ tajny** top-secret; **~ związany (z** *+instr*) closely connected (with) *lub* related (to); **~ mówiąc** to be precise *lub* exact, strictly speaking
**Śl.** *abbr* (= *Śląski*) Silesian
**śla|d** (**-du, -dy**) (*loc sg* **-dzie**) *m* (*stopy*) footprint, footmark; (*zwierzęcia*) track; (*kopyta*) hoof-print; (*pozostałość*) trace; **znikać (zniknąć** *perf*) **bez ~u** to vanish *lub* disappear without trace; **podążać (podążyć** *perf*) **w ~ za kimś/czymś** to follow sb/sth; **iść w czyjeś ~y** (*przen*) to follow in sb's footsteps; **ani ~u strachu** no trace of fear
**śladowy** *adj* (*ilość*) vestigial; **pierwiastek ~** trace element
**ślamazarny** *adj* sluggish
**Śląs|k** (**-ka**) (*instr sg* **-kiem**) *m* Silesia
**śląski** *adj* Silesian
**Ślązacz|ka** (**-ki, -ki**) (*dat sg* **-ce**, *gen pl* **-ek**) *f* Silesian
**Ślęza|k** (**-ka, -cy**) (*instr sg* **-kiem**) *m* Silesian
**śledczy** *adj*: **oficer ~** investigating officer; **areszt ~** custody
**śle|dzić (-dzę, -dzisz)** (*imp* **-dź**) *vt* to follow; (*ruchy wojsk*) to monitor; (*o radarze*) to track
**śledzio|na** (**-ny, -ny**) (*loc sg* **-nie**) *f* spleen
**śledzt|wo** (**-wa, -wa**) (*loc sg* **-wie**) *nt* investigation, inquiry
**śle|dź** (**-dzia, -dzie**) (*gen pl* **-dzi**) *m* (*Zool*) herring; (*do namiotu*) tent peg
**śle|pia** (**-piów** *lub* **-pi**) *pl* (*pot*) eyes
**śle|piec** (**-pca, -pcy**) *m* blind man
**ślep|nąć (-nę, -niesz)** (*imp* **-nij**, *pt* **-ł**, *perf* **o-**) *vi* to go blind
**ślepo** *adv* blindly; **na ~** randomly
**ślepo|ta** (**-ty**) (*dat sg* **-cie**) *f* blindness
**ślepy** *adj* blind; **ślepa ulica** cul-de-sac, dead end; **ślepa kiszka** (*Anat: pot*) (vermiform) appendix; **~ zaułek** (*przen*) blind alley, dead end; **~ na jedno oko** blind in one eye; **być ~m na coś** (*przen*) to be blind to sth; **~ nabój** blank (cartridge) ▷ *m decl like adj* (*pot*) blind man; **ślepi** *pl* the blind
**ślę, ślesz** *itd. vb patrz* **słać**
**ślęcz|eć (-ę, -ysz)** *vi*: **~ nad czymś** (*aktami, książką*) to pore over sth; (*szyciem*) to labour (*Brit*) *lub* labor (*US*) over sth
**ślicznot|ka** (**-ki, -ki**) (*dat sg* **-ce**, *gen pl* **-ek**) *f* (*pot*) beauty, pretty face (*pot*)
**śliczny** *adj* (*bardzo ładny*) lovely; (*przen: zły*) pretty, fine
**ślimacz|yć się (-ę, -ysz)** *vr* (*pot*) to move at a snail's pace
**ślima|k** (**-ka, -ki**) (*instr sg* **-kiem**) *m* (*Zool*) snail; (*bez skorupy*) slug; (*Mot*) *a loop-shaped access road*
**śli|na** (**-ny**) (*dat sg* **-nie**) *f* saliva, spit; **mówić co komuś ~ na język przyniesie** to talk off the top of one's head
**ślinia|k** (**-ka, -ki**) (*instr sg* **-kiem**) *m* bib
**śli|nić (-nię, -nisz)** (*imp* **śliń**, *perf* **po-**) *vt* (*palec*) to moisten (*with saliva*); **ślinić się** *vr* (*o człowieku, zwierzęciu*) to drool; (*o dziecku*) to dribble
**ślin|ka** (**-ki**) (*dat sg* **-ce**, *gen pl* **-ek**) *f*: **~ mi leci na samą myśl** it makes my mouth water
**śliski** *adj* (*droga, posadzka*) slippery; (*przen: sprawa*) dodgy
**ślisko** *adv*: **na drogach jest ~** the roads are slippery
**śli|wa** (**-wy, -wy**) (*dat sg* **-wie**) *f* plum (tree)
**śliw|ka** (**-ki, -ki**) (*dat sg* **-ce**, *gen pl* **-ek**) *f* (*owoc*) plum; (*drzewo*) plum tree; **suszona ~** prune
**śliwowic|a** (**-y**) *f* slivovitz (*plum brandy*)
**śliz|g** (**-gu, -gi**) (*instr sg* **-giem**) *m* (*Lot*) side-slip; (*Sport: zjazd*) run
**ślizgacz** (**-a, -e**) (*gen pl* **-y**) *m* hydroplane, speedboat
**ślizg|ać się (-am, -asz)** *vr* (*na łyżwach*) to skate; (*na butach*) to slide; (*nie móc utrzymać równowagi*) to slither; (*o samochodzie*) to skid
**ślizgawic|a** (**-y**) *f* (*pot*) icy roads conditions *pl*
**ślizgaw|ka** (**-ki, -ki**) (*dat sg* **-ce**, *gen pl* **-ek**) *f* slide
**ślu|b** (**-bu, -by**) (*loc sg* **-bie**) *m* marriage, wedding; **~ kościelny** church wedding; **~ cywilny** civil marriage; **brać (wziąć** *perf*) **~** to get married, to marry; **~y zakonne** (*Rel*) holy orders
**ślubny** *adj* wedding *attr*
**ślub|ować (-uję, -ujesz)** *vt* (*miłość*) to pledge; (*zemstę*) to swear

**ślusarz** (**-a, -e**) (*gen pl* **-y**) *m* locksmith
**ślu|z** (**-zu, -zy**) (*loc sg* **-zie**) *m* mucus
**ślu|za** (**-zy, -zy**) (*dat sg* **-zie**) *f* (*zapora*) sluice; (*na szlaku wodnym*) lock
**śluzowy** *adj*: **błona śluzowa** mucous membrane
**śmiać się (śmieję, śmiejesz)** (*perf* **za-**) *vr* to laugh; **śmiać się z kogoś/czegoś** to laugh at sb/sth
**śmiał|ek** (**-ka, -kowie** *lub* **-ki**) (*instr sg* **-kiem**) *m* daredevil
**śmi|ało** *adv* (*comp* **-elej**) (*odważnie*) boldly; (*bez trudu*) easily; **~!** come on!; **mogę ~ powiedzieć, że ...** I can safely say that ...; **możesz ~ pytać** don't hesitate to ask
**śmiałoś|ć** (**-ci**) *f* boldness; **mieć ~ coś zrobić** to have the cheek to do sth
**śmi|ały** (*comp* **-elszy**) *adj* bold, daring
**śmiech** (**-u, -y**) *m* laughter; **wywołać** (*perf*) **~** to raise a laugh; **wybuchać (wybuchnąć** *perf*) **~em** to burst out laughing; **robić (zrobić** *perf*) **coś dla ~u** to do sth for a laugh; **to (jest) ~u warte** it's ludicrous
**śmieciar|ka** (**-ki, -ki**) (*dat sg* **-ce**, *gen pl* **-ek**) *f* dustcart (*Brit*), garbage truck (*US*)
**śmieciarz** (**-a, -e**) (*gen pl* **-y**) *m* dustman (*Brit*), garbage collector (*US*)
**śmie|cić (-cę, -cisz)** (*imp* **-ć**) *vi* to throw litter about
**śmieć**[1] (**śmiecia, śmieci** *lub* **śmiecie**) *m* (*odpadek*) piece of litter; (*rzecz bez wartości*) rubbish, trash; **śmieci** *pl* (*odpadki*) rubbish, garbage (*US*); (*na ulicy, w parku*) litter *sg*
**śmieć**[2] **(śmiem, śmiesz)** (*3 pl* **śmią** *lub* **śmieją**, *imp* **śmiej**) *vi* to dare; **jak śmiesz!** how dare you!
**śmieć**[3] *vb patrz* **śmiecić**
**śmiercionośny** *adj* lethal, deadly
**śmier|ć** (**-ci**) *f* death; **ponieść** (*perf*) **~** to die; **skazywać (skazać** *perf*) **kogoś na ~** to sentence sb to death; **wyrok śmierci** death sentence; **kara śmierci** capital punishment, the death penalty; **umrzeć** (*perf*) **śmiercią naturalną** to die of natural causes; **walczyć na ~ i życie** to fight to the death; **zagłodzić się** (*perf*) **na ~** to starve o.s. to death; **nie wybaczy ci tego do śmierci** he won't forgive you to his dying day; **na ~ zapomniałem** (*pot*) I clean forgot (*pot*)
**śmierdzący** *adj* stinking; **śmierdząca sprawa** (*pot*) stinking business
**śmier|dzieć (-dzę, -dzisz)** (*imp* **-dź**) *vi*: **~ (czymś)** to stink (of sth); **śmierdzi tutaj** this place stinks
**śmiertelnie** *adv* (*blady, zimny*) deathly; (*chory*) terminally; (*ranny*) mortally, fatally; **~ nudny** deadly dull; **~ znudzony/przerażony** bored/frightened to death
**śmiertelni|k** (**-ka, -cy**) (*instr sg* **-kiem**) *m* mortal
**śmiertelnoś|ć** (**-ci**) *f* mortality; **~ noworodków** infant mortality
**śmiertelny** *adj* (*dawka*) lethal; (*trucizna*) deadly; (*bladość, cisza*) deathly; (*choroba*) terminal, fatal; (*istota, niebezpieczeństwo, wróg*) mortal; (*rana*) fatal, mortal; **wypadek ~** fatality; **grzech ~** mortal sin
**śmiesznie** *adv* (*zabawnie*) comically; **~ tani** ridiculously cheap
**śmieszny** *adj* (*zabawny*) funny, amusing; (*absurdalny*) ridiculous, laughable
**śmiesz|yć (-ę, -ysz)** (*perf* **roz~**) *vt* to amuse
**śmieta|na** (**-ny**) (*dat sg* **-nie**) *f* cream; **kwaśna ~** sour cream; **~ kremowa** double (*Brit*) *lub* rich (*US*) cream; **bita ~** whipped cream
**śmietan|ka** (**-ki**) (*dat sg* **-ce**, *gen pl* **-ek**) *f* cream; **kawa ze śmietanką** coffee with cream; **~ kosmetyczna** cleansing milk; **~ towarzyska** (*przen*) the cream of society
**śmietankowy** *adj*: **serek ~** cream cheese; **masło śmietankowe** cream butter
**śmietnicz|ka** (**-ki, -ki**) (*dat sg* **-ce**, *gen pl* **-ek**) *f* (*szufelka*) dustpan
**śmietni|k** (**-ka, -ki**) (*instr sg* **-kiem**) *m* (*miejsce*) the bins *pl*; (*pojemnik*) skip (*Brit*), dumpster (*US*); (*przen*: *bałagan*) mess; (*: miejsce*) pigsty; **wyrzucić** (*perf*) **coś na ~** to dump sth
**śmietnis|ko** (**-ka, -ka**) (*instr sg* **-kiem**) *nt* rubbish (*Brit*) *lub* garbage (*US*) dump
**śmig|ać (-am, -asz)** (*perf* **-nąć**) *vi* to whoosh, to whizz
**śmi|gło** (**-gła, -gła**) (*loc sg* **-gle**, *gen pl* **-gieł**) *nt* propeller
**śmigło|wiec** (**-wca, -wce**) *m* helicopter, chopper (*pot*)
**śmig|nąć (-nę, -niesz)** (*imp* **-nij**) *vb perf od* **śmigać**
**śmigu|s** (**-sa** *lub* **-su, -sy**) (*loc sg* **-sie**) *m*: **~-dyngus** *the custom of dousing women with water on Easter Monday*
**śniada|nie** (**-nia, -nia**) (*gen pl* **-ń**) *nt* breakfast; **jeść ~** to have breakfast; **drugie ~** (*posiłek*) elevenses (*Brit*), midmorning snack (*US*); (*kanapki*) packed lunch (*Brit*), box *lub* bag lunch (*US*)
**śniadaniowy** *adj*: **płatki śniadaniowe** breakfast cereal; **papier ~** sandwich paper
**śniady** *adj* tawny
**śnić (śnię, śnisz)** *vt* (*perf* **wy-**) to dream ▷ *vi*: **~ o kimś/czymś** to dream of *lub* about sb/sth; **śnić się** *vr* (*perf* **przy-**); **śniło mu się, że ...** he dreamt that ...; **śniłaś mi się** I had a dream about you; **ani mi się śni!** (*pot*) no way! (*pot*)
**śnie** *n patrz* **sen**
**śnie|dź** (**-dzi**) *f* patina, verdigris

**śnie|g** (**-gu, -gi**) (*instr sg* **-giem**) *m* snow; **pada ~** it's snowing; **~ z deszczem** sleet; **opady ~u** snowfall

**śniego|wiec** (**-wca, -wce**) *m* overshoe

**śnież|ka** (**-ki, -ki**) (*dat sg* **-ce**, *gen pl* **-ek**) *f* snowball; **Królewna Ś~** Snow White

**śnieżnobiały** *adj* snow-white

**śnieżny** *adj*: **zamieć śnieżna** snowstorm, blizzard; **pług ~** snowplough (*Brit*), snowplow (*US*)

**śnieżyc|a** (**-y, -e**) *f* snowstorm

**śnieżyn|ka** (**-ki, -ki**) (*dat sg* **-ce**, *gen pl* **-ek**) *f* snowflake

**śnięty** *adj*: **śnięta ryba** dead fish

**śp.** *abbr* (= *świętej pamięci*) *abbreviation put before the name of a late Christian*

**śpiący** *adj* (*pogrążony we śnie*) asleep, sleeping; (*senny*) sleepy, drowsy; **Śpiąca Królewna** Sleeping Beauty

**śpiącz|ka** (**-ki**) (*dat sg* **-ce**) *f* (*Med*) coma

**śpiesznie** *adv* hurriedly

**śpieszny** *adj* hurried; **~m krokiem** hurriedly

**śpiesz|yć, spiesz|yć** (**-ę, -ysz**) (*perf* **po-**) *vi*: **~ komuś z pomocą** to rush to the aid of sb; **~ na ratunek** to go to the rescue; **śpieszę dodać** I hasten to add; **śpieszyć się** *vr* (*o człowieku*) to (be in a) rush, to (be in a) hurry; (*o zegarze*) to be fast; **~ się dokądś** to be in a hurry to get somewhere; **śpieszy mi się** I'm in a hurry; **nie śpiesz się!** take your time!

**śpie|w** (**-wu, -wy**) (*loc sg* **-wie**) *m* singing; (*napis na płycie, kasecie*) vocals *pl*; **łabędzi ~** swansong

**śpiewacz|ka** (**-ki, -ki**) (*dat sg* **-ce**, *gen pl* **-ek**) *f* singer

**śpiew|ać** (**-am, -asz**) (*perf* **za-**) *vt/vi* to sing

**śpiewająco** *adv*: **zdał egzamin ~** he sailed through the exam

**śpiewa|k** (**-ka, -cy**) (*instr sg* **-kiem**) *m* singer

**śpiewni|k** (**-ka, -ki**) (*instr sg* **-kiem**) *m* songbook

**śpiewny** *adj* melodious

**śpioch** (**-a, -y**) *m* late riser; **wstawaj, ~u!** wake up, sleepyhead!

**śpiosz|ki** (**-ków**) *pl* rompers *pl*

**śpiw|ór** (**-ora, -ory**) (*loc sg* **-orze**) *m* sleeping bag

**śr.** *abbr* (= *średni, średnio*) av. (= *average*) (= *on average*); (= *średnica*) d. (= *diameter*); (= *środa*) Wed. (= *Wednesday*)

**średni** *adj* (*przeciętny*) average; (*rozmiar*) medium; **~ego wzrostu** of medium *lub* average height; **w ~m wieku** middle-aged; **klasa ~a** the middle class; **szkoła ~a** secondary (*Brit*) *lub* high (*US*) school; **~e wykształcenie** secondary education; **fale ~e** medium wave; **waga ~a** middleweight; **Wieki Ś~e** the Middle Ages

**średni|a** (**-ej, -e**) *f decl like adj* mean, average; **poniżej/powyżej średniej** below/above (the) average

**średnic|a** (**-y, -e**) *f* diameter; **mieć 10 cm średnicy** to be 10 cm in diameter

**średni|k** (**-ka, -ki**) (*instr sg* **-kiem**) *m* semicolon

**średnio** *adv* on average; **~ utalentowany** of average talents

**średniodystanso|wiec** (**-wca, -wcy**) *m* middle-distance runner

**średniowiecz|e** (**-a**) *nt* the Middle Ages

**średniowieczny** *adj* (*Hist*) medieval; (*przestarzały*) antiquated

**średnio zaawansowany** *adj* intermediate

**śr|oda** (**-ody, -ody**) (*dat sg* **-odzie**, *gen pl* **-ód**) *f* Wednesday; **~ popielcowa** Ash Wednesday

**środ|ek** (**-ka, -ki**) (*instr sg* **-kiem**) *m* (*punkt centralny*) middle, centre (*Brit*), center (*US*); (*wnętrze*) inside; (*sposób*) means; (*forma działania*) measure; (*preparat chemiczny*) agent; (*lek: Med*) medication; (*: przen*) remedy; **w środku** (*w centrum*) in the middle; (*wewnątrz*) inside; **do środka** (*do wewnątrz*) inward(s); **poprosić** (*perf*) **kogoś do środka** to ask sb in; **wejść** (*perf*) **do środka** to go inside; **ze środka** from within; **~ ciężkości** centre (*Brit*) *lub* center (*US*) of gravity; **~ tygodnia/lata** the middle of the week/summer, midweek/midsummer; **muzyka środka** middle-of-the-road music; **~ antykoncepcyjny** contraceptive; **~ nasenny** soporific (drug); **~ uspakajający** tranquillizer (*Brit*), tranquilizer (*US*); **~ przeciwbólowy** painkiller, analgesic; **~ transportu** means of transport (*Brit*) *lub* transportation (*US*); **~ płatniczy** legal tender; **środki** *pl* (*zasoby materialne*) means *pl*; **środki finansowe** *lub* **pieniężne** finance *sg*, (financial) resources; **środki ostrożności** precautions; **środki masowego przekazu** mass-media; **środki obrotowe/płynne** (*Ekon*) current/liquid assets

**środkowoeuropejski** *adj* Central European

**środkowy** *adj* central, middle *attr*; (*Sport: obrońca, napastnik*) centre *attr* (*Brit*), center *attr* (*US*)

**środowis|ko** (**-ka, -ka**) (*instr sg* **-kiem**) *nt* environment; **~ naturalne** the environment; **ochrona środowiska** environment(al) protection

**środowiskowy** *adj* environmental; **badania środowiskowe** research into the environment

**śródlądowy** *adj* inland *attr*

**śródmiejski** *adj* central (*Brit*), downtown *attr* (*US*)

Ś

**śródmieś|cie** (**-cia, -cia**) (*gen pl* **-ci**) *nt* city centre (*Brit*), downtown (*US*)
**śródziemnomorski** *adj* Mediterranean *attr*
**śródziemny** *adj*: **Morze Śródziemne** the Mediterranean (sea)
**śru|ba** (**-by, -by**) (*dat sg* **-bie**) *f* screw; (*do łączenia elementów*) bolt; (*okrętowa*) propeller
**śrub|ka** (**-ki, -ki**) (*dat sg* **-ce**) *f dimin od* **śruba**
**śrubokrę|t** (**-tu, -ty**) (*loc sg* **-cie**) *m* screwdriver
**śrub|ować (-uję, -ujesz)** (*perf* **wy-**) *vt* (*ceny*) to jack up
**śru|t** (**-tu**) (*loc sg* **-cie**) *m* shot
**św.** *abbr* (= *święty, święta*) St
**świadcze|nie** (**-nia, -nia**) (*gen pl* **-ń**) *nt*: **~ usług** provision of services; **świadczenia** *pl* (*obowiązkowe usługi*) services *pl*; (*pomoc materialna*) benefit *sg*; **świadczenia socjalne** welfare benefit *sg*
**świadcz|yć (-ę, -ysz)** *vt* (*usługi*) to provide ▷ *vi* (*zeznawać*) to testify; (*wskazywać*) to show; **jego uwagi świadczyły o tym, że nic nie zrozumiał** his remarks showed he didn't understand anything; **to tylko świadczy o tym, że...** it just goes to show that ...; **to dobrze o tobie świadczy** it is to your credit
**świadect|wo** (**-wa, -wa**) (*loc sg* **-wie**) *nt* (*dokument*) certificate; (*dowód, wypowiedź*) testimony; **~ szkolne** school report (*Brit*), report card (*US*); **~ dojrzałości** *certificate of secondary education*, ≈ GCSE (*Brit*), ≈ High School Diploma (*US*); **~ urodzenia** birth certificate; **być świadectwem czegoś** (*książk*) to be (a) testimony to sth, to testify to sth
**świad|ek** (**-ka, -kowie**) (*instr sg* **-kiem**) *m* witness; (*na ślubie: mężczyzna*) ≈ best man; (*: kobieta*) ≈ maid of honour (*Brit*) *lub* honor (*US*); **być świadkiem czegoś** to witness sth; **naoczny ~** eye witness; **~ oskarżenia/obrony** witness for the prosecution/defence (*Brit*) *lub* defense (*US*); **przy świadkach** in the presence of witnesses
**świadomie** *adv* knowingly
**świadomoś|ć** (**-ci**) *f* consciousness, awareness
**świadomy** *adj* (*celowy*) conscious; **~ czegoś** aware *lub* conscious of sth
**świa|t** (**-ta, -ty**) (*loc sg* **świecie**) *m* world; **na całym świecie** all over the world; **~ przestępczy** the criminal world, the underworld; **przyjść** (*perf*) **na ~** to be born; **mistrz ~a** world champion; **Trzeci Ś~** the Third World; **wielki ~** high society; **~a poza kimś nie widzieć** (*przen*) to think the world of sb; **za nic w świecie!** not for the whole world!
**świateł|ko** (**-ka, -ka**) (*instr sg* **-kiem**, *gen pl* **-ek**) *nt dimin od* **światło**
**świat|ło** (**-ła, -ła**) (*loc sg* **świetle**, *gen pl* **-eł**) *nt* light; **~ dzienne** daylight; **przy świetle księżyca/gwiazd** by moonlight/starlight; **w świetle czegoś** (*przen*) in the light of sth; **rzucić** (*perf*) **~ na coś** (*przen*) to cast *lub* throw light on sth; **~ przednie/tylne** (*Mot*) headlight/rear light; **~ odblaskowe** reflector; **wydobyć** (*perf*) **coś na ~ dzienne** to unearth sth; **przedstawiać kogoś/coś w korzystnym świetle** (*przen*) to present sb/sth in a favourable (*Brit*) *lub* favorable (*US*) light; **światła** *pl* (*pot: na skrzyżowaniu*) traffic lights; **światła drogowe** *lub* **długie** full (*Brit*) *lub* high (*US*) beam; **światła mijania** *lub* **krótkie** dipped (*Brit*) *lub* dimmed (*US*) (head)lights; **światła awaryjne** hazard (warning) lights; **światła cofania** reversing lights; **światła postojowe** parking lights; **światła stopu** stoplights
**światłoczuły** *adj* light-sensitive
**światłomierz** (**-a, -e**) (*gen pl* **-y**) *m* light *lub* exposure meter
**światłow|ód** (**-odu, -ody**) (*loc sg* **-odzie**) *m* (*materiał*) optical fibre (*Brit*) *lub* fiber (*US*)
**światły** *adj* (*książk*) enlightened
**światopoglą|d** (**-du, -dy**) (*loc sg* **-dzie**) *m* outlook
**świato|wiec** (**-wca, -wcy**) *m* man of the world
**światowy** *adj* (*wojna, potęga, premiera*) world *attr*; (*sława, rozgłos, kryzys*) world-wide; (*życie, towarzystwo*) high *attr*; **pierwsza/druga wojna światowa** World War One/Two, the First/Second World War; **artysta światowej sławy** a world-famous artist; **człowiek ~** a man of the world
**świąt** *n patrz* **święto**
**świąteczny** *adj* (*odświętny*) festive; (*bożonarodzeniowy*) Christmas *attr*; (*wielkanocny*) Easter *attr*; **dzień ~** holiday; **życzenia świąteczne** (*na Boże Narodzenie*) Season's *lub* Christmas greetings; (*na Wielkanoc*) Easter greetings; **świąteczne ubranie** Sunday best
**świątobliwoś|ć** (**-ci, -ci**) (*gen pl* **-ci**) *f*: **Jego Ś~** His Holiness
**świątobliwy** *adj* saintly
**świąty|nia** (**-ni, -nie**) (*gen pl* **-ń**) *f* temple
**świcie** *n patrz* **świt**
**świd|er** (**-ra, -ry**) (*loc sg* **-rze**) *m* drill
**świdr|ować (-uję, -ujesz)** *vt* (*deski, skałę*) to drill holes in ▷ *vi* to drill; **~ kogoś oczami** *lub* **wzrokiem** to bore one's eyes into sb
**świdrujący** *adj* (*dźwięk*) piercing, penetrating; (*ból*) piercing
**świec|a** (**-y, -e**) *f* candle; **~ (zapłonowa)** (*Mot*) spark plug, sparking plug (*Brit*); **przy ~ch** by candlelight

**świecący** *adj* (*palący się: słońce, lampa*) shining; (*błyszczący*) shiny; (*fosforyzujący*) luminous
**świe|cić (-cę, -cisz)** (*imp* **-ć**) *vi* (*wysyłać światło: o lampie, słońcu*) to shine; (*lśnić*) to gleam, to shine; **~ przykładem** to be a shining example; **świecić się** *vr* (*o lampie*) to be on; (*lśnić*) to shine, to gleam
**świecideł|ko** (**-ka, -ka**) (*instr sg* **-kiem**, *gen pl* **-ek**) *nt* trinket
**świecie** *n patrz* **świat**
**świecki** *adj* (*szkoła, władza*) secular; (*człowiek*) lay ▷ *m decl like adj* (*Rel*) layman
**świecowy** *adj*: **kredki świecowe** wax crayons
**świecz|ka** (**-ki, -ki**) (*dat sg* **-ce**, *gen pl* **-ek**) *f* candle; **to gra (nie)warta świeczki** (*przen*) the game is (not) worth the candle, it's (not) worth it
**świeczni|k** (**-ka, -ki**) (*instr sg* **-kiem**) *m* candlestick
**świergo|t** (**-tu, -ty**) (*loc sg* **-cie**) *m* twitter
**świergo|tać (-cze)** *vi* to twitter
**świer|k** (**-ku** *lub* **-ka, -ki**) (*instr sg* **-kiem**) *m* spruce
**świerszcz** (**-a, -e**) (*gen pl* **-y**) *m* cricket
**świerz|bić (-bi)** *vi* to itch; **ręka mnie świerzbi (na niego)** (*przen*) I'm itching to hit him
**świetlany** *adj* bright; **świetlana przyszłość** a rosy future
**świetle** *n patrz* **światło**
**świetlic|a** (**-y, -e**) *f* (*Szkol*) common room
**świetli|k** (**-ka, -ki**) (*instr sg* **-kiem**) *m* (*Zool*) glow-worm; (*okno w dachu*) skylight
**świetlisty** *adj* bright, shining
**świetlny** *adj* (*sygnał, rok, pióro*) light *attr*; (*efekt*) luminous; **napis ~** *lub* **reklama świetlna** neon sign; **sygnalizacja świetlna** traffic lights
**świetlów|ka** (**-ki, -ki**) (*dat sg* **-ce**, *gen pl* **-ek**) *f* fluorescent light
**świetnie** *adv*: **czuć się ~** to feel great; **~ nam idzie** we're doing very well; **ona ~ gotuje/gra** she's an excellent cook/player; **~!** great!
**świetnoś|ć** (**-ci**) *f* (*pałacu*) magnificence, splendour (*Brit*), splendor (*US*); (*tradycji, rodu*) glory, greatness
**świetny** *adj* (*pomysł, praca, pisarz*) excellent; (*ród, tradycja*) fine
**świeżo** *adv* (*przygotowany*) freshly; (*odkryty*) newly; **czuć się/pachnieć ~** to feel/smell fresh; **on jest ~ po studiach** he's fresh from university; **„~ malowane"** "wet paint"
**świeżoś|ć** (**-ci**) *f* freshness
**świeży** *adj* fresh; **na ~m powietrzu** in the open (air); **praca/ćwiczenia na ~m powietrzu** outdoor work/exercises
**święce|nia** (**-ń**) *pl*: **~ kapłańskie** ordination
**świę|cić (-cę, -cisz)** (*imp* **-ć**) *vt* (*jubileusz, rocznicę*) to celebrate; (*kaplicę, kościół*) (*perf* **po-**) to consecrate; (*mieszkanie, potrawy*) (*perf* **po-**) to bless; **~ sukcesy** *lub* **triumfy** to be very successful; **święcić się** *vr*: **coś się święci** there's something in the air
**święcie** *adv* (*przekonany*) absolutely
**święcon|ka** (**-ki, -ki**) (*dat sg* **-ce**, *gen pl* **-ek**) *f* *food traditionally blessed in church before Easter*
**święcony** *adj*: **woda święcona** holy water
**święt|a** (**-ej, -e**) *f decl like adj* saint
**świę|to** (**-ta, -ta**) (*loc sg* **-cie**, *gen pl* **świąt**) *nt* holiday; **~ państwowe/kościelne** national/religious holiday; **od święta** once in a blue moon; **święta** *pl*: **święta (Bożego Narodzenia)** Christmas; **Święta Wielkanocne** Easter; **Wesołych Świąt!** (*Bożego Narodzenia*) Merry *lub* Happy Christmas!; (*Wielkanocnych*) Happy Easter!
**świętojański** *adj* (*noc*) midsummer *attr*; **robaczek ~** glow-worm
**świętokradzt|wo** (**-wa, -wa**) (*loc sg* **-wie**) *nt* sacrilege
**świętosz|ek** (**-ka, -ki**) (*instr sg* **-kiem**) *m* goody-goody
**świętoszkowaty** *adj* sanctimonious
**świętoś|ć** (**-ci**) *f* (*cecha*) holiness, sacredness; **to dla mnie ~** it's sacred to me
**święt|ować (-uję, -ujesz)** *vt* to celebrate ▷ *vi* (*obchodzić święto*) to have a holiday; (*bawić się*) to celebrate
**święty** *adj* (*Rel: księga, obraz*) holy, sacred; (*: przed imieniem*) saint; (*człowiek: cnotliwy*) saintly; (*prawo*) sacred, sacrosanct; (*obowiązek*) clear; **Pismo Święte** the (Holy) Scriptures; **Duch Ś~** Holy Spirit *lub* Ghost; **Ojciec Ś~** Holy Father; **Ś~ Mikołaj** Father Christmas (*Brit*), Santa (Claus) (*US*); **świętej pamięci pan Kowalski** the late Mr Kowalski; **daj mi ~ spokój!** (*pot*) leave me alone!; **Ziemia Święta** the Holy Land; **święte przekonanie** absolute conviction; **święta racja/święte słowa!** (*pot*) you're absolutely right! ▷ *m decl like adj* saint; **Wszystkich Ś~ch** All Saints' Day
**świ|nia** (**-ni, -nie**) (*gen pl* **-ń**) *f* (*Zool*) pig; (*pot!: o człowieku*) pig (*pot!*), swine (*pot*)
**świ|nić (-nię, -nisz)** (*imp* **-ń**, *perf* **na-**) *vi* (*pot*) to make a mess; **świnić się** *vr* (*perf* **u-**) (*pot*) to get mucked up (*pot*)
**świniobi|cie** (**-cia, -cia**) (*gen pl* **-ć**) *nt* pig slaughter
**świn|ka** (**-ki, -ki**) (*dat sg* **-ce**, *gen pl* **-ek**) *f dimin od* **świnia**; (*Med*) mumps; **~ morska** guinea pig
**świntuch** (**-a, -y**) *m* (*pot*) dirty old man (*pot*)

Ś

**świński** *adj* (*pot: żart*) dirty (*pot*); (*pot: postępek*) dirty (*pot*), rotten (*pot*); **świńska skóra** pigskin; **postąpiłeś po świńsku** (*pot*) that was a rotten thing to do (*pot*), that was rotten of you (*pot*)

**świńst|wo (-wa, -wa)** (*loc sg* **-wie**) *nt* (*pot: podły czyn*) dirty *lub* rotten trick (*pot*); (*: obrzydliwe jedzenie*) muck (*pot*); **co za ~!** that's disgusting!; **zrobić** (*perf*) **komuś ~** to play a dirty *lub* rotten trick on sb; **świństwa** *pl* filth

**świ|r (-ra, -ry)** (*loc sg* **-rze**) *m* (*pot: wariat*) nut (*pot*); **mieć ~a (na punkcie czegoś)** (*pot*) to be nuts (about sth) (*pot*)

**świrnięty** *adj* (*pot*) nuts, nutty

**świ|snąć (-snę, -śniesz)** (*imp* **-śnij**) *vb perf od* **świstać** ▷ *vt perf* (*pot: ukraść*) to pinch (*pot*)

**świ|st (-stu, -sty)** (*loc sg* **-ście**) *m* (*bata, pocisku*) swish; (*wiatru*) whistle

**świ|stać (-szczę, -szczysz)** *vi* (*perf* **-snąć**) to whistle

**śwista|k (-ka, -ki)** (*instr sg* **-kiem**) *m* marmot

**świst|ek (-ka, -ki)** (*instr sg* **-kiem**) *m*: **~ papieru** a scrap of paper

**świszcz|eć (-y)** *vi* to whistle

**świ|t (-tu, -ty)** (*loc sg* **-cie**) *m* dawn, daybreak; **o świcie** at dawn; **od ~u do nocy** from dawn to dusk

**świ|ta (-ty, -ty)** (*dat sg* **-cie**) *f* retinue, entourage

**świt|ać (-a)** (*perf* **za-**) *vi* (*o dniu*) to dawn; **coś mi (w głowie) świta** it sounds familiar; **zaświtała mi myśl, że/żeby ...** it crossed my mind that/to ...; **świtało** the dawn was breaking

# Tt

**T, t** *nt inv* (*litera*) T, t; **T jak Tadeusz** ≈ T for Tommy
**ta** *pron* (*bliżej*) this; (*dalej*) that
**tab.** *abbr* (= *tabela*) tab. (= *table*)
**taba|ka** (**-ki, -ki**) (*dat sg* **-ce**) *f* snuff
**tabakier|ka** (**-ki, -ki**) (*dat sg* **-ce**, *gen pl* **-ek**) *f* snuffbox
**tabel|a** (**-i, -e**) *f* table
**tabel|ka** (**-ki, -ki**) (*dat sg* **-ce**, *gen pl* **-ek**) *f dimin od* **tabela**
**tabernakul|um** (**-um, -a**) (*gen pl* **-ów**) *nt inv in sg* tabernacle
**tabl.** *abbr* (= *tablica*) chart
**tablet|ka** (**-ki, -ki**) (*dat sg* **-ce**, *gen pl* **-ek**) *f* tablet; **~ nasenna** sleeping pill
**tablic|a** (**-y, -e**) *f* (*Szkol*) blackboard; (*tabela*) chart; **~ ogłoszeń** noticeboard (*Brit*), bulletin board (*US*); **~ pamiątkowa** plaque; **tablice rejestracyjne** (number) plates *pl* (*Brit*), (license) plates *pl* (*US*); **tablice matematyczne/logarytmiczne** mathematical/logarithmic tables
**tablicz|ka** (**-ki, -ki**) (*dat sg* **-ce**, *gen pl* **-ek**) *f dimin od* **tablica**; (*z nazwiskiem na drzwiach*) nameplate; **~ czekolady** a bar of chocolate; **~ mnożenia** multiplication table
**tabo|r** (**-ru, -ry**) (*loc sg* **-rze**) *m* (*Kolej*) rolling stock; (*cygański*) camp
**tabore|t** (**-tu, -ty**) (*loc sg* **-cie**) *m* stool
**tabu** *nt inv* taboo
**tabulato|r** (**-ra, -ry**) (*loc sg* **-rze**) *m* tabulator
**tabu|n** (**-nu, -ny**) (*loc sg* **-nie**) *m* (*koni*) herd; (*pot: ludzi*) horde
**tac|a** (**-y, -e**) *f* tray; **zbierać na tacę** (*w kościele*) to collect the offertory, to take the collection
**tac|ka** (**-ki, -ki**) (*dat sg* **-ce**, *gen pl* **-ek**) *f dimin od* **taca**
**tacy** *pron decl like adj patrz* **taki**
**tacz|ka** (**-ki, -ki**) (*dat sg* **-ce**, *gen pl* **-ek**) *f* wheelbarrow
**taf|la** (**-li, -le**) (*gen pl* **-li**) *f* (*jeziora*) surface; (*lodu*) sheet
**taf|ta** (**-ty, -ty**) (*dat sg* **-cie**) *f* taffeta
**tahitański** *adj* Tahitian
**Tahiti** *nt inv* Tahiti
**ta|ić** (**-ję, -isz**) (*perf* **za-**) *vt* to conceal, to hide; **nie taję, że go nie lubię** frankly *lub* to be frank, I don't like him
**taj|ać** (**-e**) (*perf* **od-**) *vi* to thaw
**tajemnic|a** (**-y, -e**) *f* secret; (*zagadka*) mystery; **w tajemnicy** in secrecy, on the q.t.; **robić coś w tajemnicy** to do sth in secret; **trzymać coś w tajemnicy** to keep sth secret; **~ poliszynela** (*przen*) open secret
**tajemniczy** *adj* mysterious; **w ~ sposób** mysteriously
**tajemny** *adj* secret; **wiedza tajemna** the occult
**tajfu|n** (**-nu, -ny**) (*loc sg* **-nie**) *m* typhoon
**taj|ga** (**-gi, -gi**) (*dat sg* **-dze**) *f* taiga (*coniferous forest of subarctic Eurasia and North America*)
**Tajlandczy|k** (**-ka, -cy**) (*instr sg* **-kiem**) *m* Thai
**Tajlandi|a** (**-i**) *f* Thailand
**Tajland|ka** (**-ki, -ki**) (*dat sg* **-ce**, *gen pl* **-ek**) *f* Thai
**tajlandzki** *adj* Thai
**tajnia|k** (**-ka, -cy**) (*instr sg* **-kiem**) *m* (*pot*) undercover agent
**tajni|ki** (**-ków**) *pl* secrets *pl*; **~ sztuki** tricks of the trade; **~ nauki** secrets of science
**tajnoś|ć** (**-ci**) *f* secrecy
**tajny** *adj* (*układ, przejście, głosowanie, policja*) secret; (*dokument, akta*) classified; (*nauczanie, organizacja*) underground; **tajne służby** secret service; **„ściśle tajne"** "top secret"
**tajski** *adj* Thai
**Tajwa|n** (**-nu**) (*loc sg* **-nie**) *m* Taiwan
**Tajwan|ka** (**-ki, -ki**) (*dat sg* **-ce**, *gen pl* **-ek**) *f* Taiwanese
**Tajwańczy|k** (**-ka, -cy**) (*instr sg* **-kiem**) *m* Taiwanese
**tajwański** *adj* Taiwanese

 SŁOWO KLUCZOWE

**tak** *pron* (*potwierdzenie*) yes; **tak jest!** (*Wojsk*) yes, sir!
▷ *adv* **1** (*w taki sposób*): **zrób to tak** do it like this; **zrobił to tak, jak ja** he did it just like I did; **zrobił to tak jak kazali** he did it as he was told; **zrób to tak, żeby nikt nie**

**zauważył** do it in such a way that nobody should notice; **i tak dalej** and so on; **tak zwany** so-called; **tak już jest** that's the way it is; **tak czy owak** (*pot*) anyhow, in any case
**2** (*nasilenie*): **tak mocno/mocny (, że …)** so strongly/strong (that …); **tak sobie** (*pot*) so-so (*pot*)

SŁOWO KLUCZOWE

**taki** *pron decl like adj* **1** (*tego rodzaju*) such; **taki sam** the same; **taki jak** such as; **jest taki jak chciałeś** it's just what you wanted; **on już taki jest** that's the way he is; **taki a taki** (*pot*) so-and-so (*pot*); **w takim razie …** in that case …
**2** (*w połączeniach zdaniowych*): **była taka mgła, że …** it was so foggy that …, the fog was so dense that …
**3** (*wzmacniająco*): **on jest taki młody** he is so young; **taki mądry człowiek** such a wise man; **taka ładna pogoda** such nice weather; **taki jakiś senny/słaby** (*pot*) somewhat sleepy/weak; **taki sobie** (*pot*) so-so (*pot*); **taki jeden (facet)** one guy; **nic takiego** nothing (important)

**takielun|ek (-ku, -ki)** (*instr sg* **-kiem**) *m* rigging
**tako** *pron*: **jako ~** (*nieźle*) quite well; (*tak sobie*) so-so
**taksomet|r (-ru, -ry)** (*loc sg* **-rze**) *m* taximeter, clock
**taks|ować (-uję, -ujesz)** (*perf* **o-**) *vt* to estimate; **~ kogoś wzrokiem** to scrutinize sb
**taksów|ka (-ki, -ki)** (*dat sg* **-ce**, *gen pl* **-ek**) *f* (*osobowa*) taxi, cab; **~ bagażowa** ≈ removal van
**taksówkarz (-a, -e)** (*gen pl* **-y**) *m* taxi driver, cab driver
**tak|t (-tu)** (*loc sg* **-cie**) *m* tact; (*Muz*) (*nom pl* **-ty**) bar
**taktowny** *adj* tactful
**taktyczny** *adj* tactical
**takty|k (-ka, -cy)** (*instr sg* **-kiem**) *m* tactician
**takty|ka (-ki)** (*dat sg* **-ce**) *f* tactics *pl*
**także** *adv* also, too, as well
**talen|t (-tu, -ty)** (*loc sg* **-cie**) *m* (*zdolności*) talent, gift; (*człowiek uzdolniony*) talent; **mieć ~ do czegoś** to have a gift for sth
**talerz (-a, -e)** (*gen pl* **-y**) *m* plate; **latający ~** flying saucer; **talerze** *pl* (*Muz*) cymbals *pl*
**talerzy|k (-ka, -ki)** (*instr sg* **-kiem**) *m dimin od* **talerz**; (*pod filiżankę*) saucer
**tali|a (-i, -e)** (*gen pl* **-i**) *f* (*Karty*) deck, pack; (*kibić*) waist; **wąska w talii** slim-waisted; **obwód talii** waistline
**talizma|n (-nu, -ny)** (*loc sg* **-nie**) *m* charm, talisman
**tal|k (-ku)** (*instr sg* **-kiem**) *m* talc
**talo|n (-nu, -ny)** (*loc sg* **-nie**) *m* coupon, voucher (*Brit*); **~ książkowy** book token
**tam** *adv* there; **tu i tam** here and there; **tam i z powrotem** back and forth; **tam, skąd przyjechałem** the place where I came from; **co (mi) tam!** I don't care!; **gdzie tam!** (*pot*) nothing of the kind!; **jakiś tam aktor** some actor or other
**ta|ma (-my, -my)** (*loc sg* **-mie**) *f* dam
**tambury|n (-nu, -ny)** (*loc sg* **-nie**) *m* tambourine
**tamci** (*jak*: **ci**) *pron* those
**Tami|za (-zy)** (*dat sg* **-zie**) *f* the Thames
**tam|ować (-uję, -ujesz)** (*perf* **za-**) *vt* (*krew, krwotok*) to stem, to staunch; (*ruch*) to hamper
**tampo|n (-nu, -ny)** (*loc sg* **-nie**) *m* tampon
**tamta** (*jak*: **ta**) *pron* that
**tam-ta|m (-mu, -my)** (*loc sg* **-mie**) *m* tom-tom
**tamte** (*jak*: **te**) *pron* those
**tamtejszy** *adj* local
**tamten** (*jak*: **ten**) *pron* that; **nie ten, lecz ~** not this one but that one
**tamtędy** *adv* (down) that way
**tamto** (*jak*: **to**) *pron* that
**tamże** *adv* (*książk*) at the same place; (*odnośnik w tekście*) ibidem
**tancer|ka (-ki, -ki)** (*dat sg* **-ce**, *gen pl* **-ek**) *f* dancer
**tancerz (-a, -e)** (*gen pl* **-y**) *m* dancer
**tande|m (-mu, -my)** (*loc sg* **-mie**) *m* tandem
**tande|ta (-ty)** (*dat sg* **-cie**) *f* trash
**tandetny** *adj* (*wyrób*) tacky, shoddy; (*książka, film*) trashy
**taneczny** *adj*: **muzyka taneczna** dance music; **zespół ~** (dancing) chorus
**tangen|s (-sa, -sy)** (*loc sg* **-sie**) *m* tangent
**tan|go (-ga, -ga)** (*instr sg* **-giem**) *nt* tango
**ta|ni** (*comp* **-ńszy**) *adj* cheap; **~m kosztem** cheaply; **~ jak barszcz** (*przen*: *pot*) dirt-cheap (*pot*)
**ta|niec (-ńca, -ńce)** *m* (*czynność*) dancing; (*kompozycja*) dance; **prosić (poprosić** *perf***) kogoś do tańca** to ask sb to dance; **wybrać się** (*perf*) **na tańce** to go dancing
**tani|eć (-eje)** (*perf* **po-** *lub* **s-**) *vi* to get cheaper
**tanio** *adv*: **kupować/sprzedawać coś ~** to buy/sell sth cheaply *lub* cheap
**tank|ować (-uję, -ujesz)** *vt* (*wodę, paliwo*) (*perf* **za-**) to get; (*samochód*) (*perf* **za-**) to refuel ▷ *vi* (*perf* **za-**) to get fuel (*Brit*) *lub* gas (*US*); (*pot*: *pić alkohol*) to hit the bottle (*pot*)
**tanko|wiec (-wca, -wce)** *m* tanker
**tantiem|y (-)** *pl* royalties *pl*
**Tanzani|a (-i)** *f* Tanzania

**Tanzan|ka** (**-ki, -ki**) (*dat sg* **-ce**, *gen pl* **-ek**) *f* Tanzanian
**Tanzańczy|k** (**-ka, -cy**) (*instr sg* **-kiem**) *m* Tanzanian
**tanzański** *adj* Tanzanian
**tańca** *itd. n patrz* **taniec**
**tańcz|yć (-ę, -ysz)** (*perf* **za-**) *vt*: **~ walca/tango** to waltz/tango ▷ *vi* to dance
**tańszy** *itd. adj comp od* **tani**
**taoiz|m** (**-mu**) (*loc sg* **-mie**) *m* Taoism
**tapcza|n** (**-nu, -ny**) (*loc sg* **-nie**) *m backless sofa bed*
**tape|ta** (**-ty, -ty**) (*dat sg* **-cie**) *f* wallpaper; **kłaść (położyć** *perf*) **tapetę w pokoju** to wallpaper a room; **co jest teraz na tapecie?** (*pot*) what's being dealt with at the moment?
**tapet|ować (-uję, -ujesz)** *vt* (*perf* **wy-**) to wallpaper
**tapice|r** (**-ra, -rzy**) (*loc sg* **-rze**) *m* upholsterer
**tapicer|ka** (**-ki**) (*dat sg* **-ce**) *f* upholstery
**tapi|r** (**-ra, -ry**) (*loc sg* **-rze**) *m* tapir
**tapir|ować (-uję, -ujesz)** (*perf* **u-**) *vt* to backcomb
**tapl|ać się (-am, -asz)** *vr* (*pot*) to slosh around *lub* about (*pot*)
**ta|ra** (**-ry, -ry**) (*dat sg* **-rze**) *f* (*ciężar*) tare
**tara|n** (**-na, -ny**) (*loc sg* **-nie**) *m* battering ram
**taran|ować (-uję, -ujesz)** (*perf* **s-**) *vt* (*barykadę, drzwi*) to ram; (*osobę*) to crush
**tarantul|a** (**-i, -e**) *f* tarantula
**tarapat|y** (**-ów**) *pl* trouble; **ciężkie/finansowe ~** dire/financial straits; **być/znaleźć się** (*perf*) **w tarapatach** to be in/get into trouble
**tara|s** (**-su, -sy**) (*loc sg* **-sie**) *m* terrace; **~ widokowy** viewing area; (*na dachu*) observation deck
**taras|ować (-uję, -ujesz)** (*perf* **za-**) *vt* to block
**tarcic|a** (**-y, -e**) *f* lumber
**tar|cie** (**-cia**) *nt* friction; **tarcia** *pl* (*nieporozumienia*) friction
**tarcz|a** (**-y, -e**) *f* (*uzbrojenie, osłona*) shield; (*telefonu*) dial; (*zegar(k)a*) face; (*szkolna*) badge; (*słoneczna, szlifierska*) disc; (*strzelecka*) target
**tarczowy** *adj*: **hamulec ~** disc brake; **piła tarczowa** circular saw
**tarczyc|a** (**-y, -e**) *f* thyroid (gland)
**tar|g** (**-gu, -gi**) (*instr sg* **-giem**) *m* market; **targi** *pl* (trade) fair; **dobić** (*perf*) **~u (z kimś)** to strike a bargain (with sb)
**targ|ać (-am, -asz)** *vt* (*pot: dźwigać*) to lug (*pot*); (*szarpać*) (*perf* **-nąć**) to pull; **targać się** (*perf* **wy-**) *vr*: **~ się za włosy** *itp.* to pull each other's hair *itp.*
**targ|nąć (-nę, -niesz)** (*imp* **-nij**) *vb perf od* **targać**; **targnąć się**; **~ się na życie** to make an attempt on one's life
**targ|ować się (-uję, -ujesz)** (*perf* **po-**) *vr*: **targować się (z kimś/o coś)** to haggle (with sb/over sth)
**targowis|ko** (**-ka, -ka**) (*instr sg* **-kiem**) *nt* market(place)
**targowy** *adj*: **dzień ~** market day; **plac ~** marketplace
**tar|ka** (**-ki, -ki**) (*dat sg* **-ce**, *gen pl* **-ek**) *f* (*do owoców, warzyw*) grater; (*do bielizny*) washboard
**tarł** *itd. vb patrz* **trzeć**
**tar|ło** (**-ła**) (*loc sg* **-le**) *nt* spawning
**tarmo|sić (-szę, -sisz)** (*imp* **-ś**, *perf* **po-**) *vt* (*pot*) to pull about
**tarni|na** (**-ny, -ny**) (*dat sg* **-nie**) *f* blackthorn, sloe
**taro|t** (**-ta**) (*loc sg* **-cie**) *m* tarot
**tarpa|n** (**-na, -ny**) (*loc sg* **-nie**) *m* tarpan
**tarta|k** (**-ku, -ki**) (*instr sg* **-kiem**) *m* sawmill
**tarta|n** (**-nu**) (*loc sg* **-nie**) *m* tartan
**tarty** *adj* (*ser itp.*) grated; **bułka tarta** breadcrumbs
**tary|fa** (**-fy, -fy**) (*dat sg* **-fie**) *f* (*pocztowa, telekomunikacyjna*) rates *pl*; (*pot: taksówka*) cab; **~ kolejowa** table of fares; **~ opłat** scale of charges; **~ celna** tariff of duties; **~ ulgowa** (*przen*) leniency
**tarz|ać się (-am, -asz)** (*perf* **wy-**) *vr* to wallow; **tarzać się ze śmiechu** to be in stitches (*pot*)
**tasa|k** (**-ka, -ki**) (*instr sg* **-kiem**) *m* cleaver
**tasiemcowy** *adj* mile-long
**tasie|miec** (**-mca, -mce**) *m* tapeworm
**tasiem|ka** (**-ki, -ki**) (*dat sg* **-ce**, *gen pl* **-ek**) *f* tape
**Tasmani|a** (**-i**) *f* Tasmania
**tasmański** *adj* Tasmanian
**tas|ować (-uję, -ujesz)** (*perf* **po-**) *vt* to shuffle
**taszcz|yć (-ę, -ysz)** (*perf* **za-**) *vt* (*pot*) to lug (*pot*)
**taś|ma** (**-my, -my**) (*dat sg* **-mie**) *f* tape; (*w fabryce*) assembly line *lub* belt; (*do maszyny do pisania*) (fabric *lub* carbon) ribbon; **~ filmowa** film; **~ klejąca** Sellotape® (*Brit*), Scotch tape® (*US*); **nagranie z taśmy** taped recording
**taśmocią|g** (**-gu, -gi**) (*instr sg* **-giem**) *m* conveyor belt
**taśmote|ka** (**-ki, -ki**) (*dat sg* **-ce**) *f* tape collection
**taśmowy** *adj*: **produkcja taśmowa** assembly line production
**ta|ta, ta|to** (**-ty**) (*dat sg* **-cie**) *m decl like f* dad
**Tata|r** (**-ra**) (*loc sg* **-rze**, *nom pl* **-rzy**) *m* Tartar
**tata|r** (**-ra**) (*loc sg* **-rze**, *nom pl* **-ry**) *m* (*Kulin*) tartar(e) steak
**tatara|k** (**-ku, -ki**) (*instr sg* **-kiem**) *m* sweet flag
**tatarski** *adj* (*najazd, naród*) Tartar *attr*; (*Kulin*): **sos/befsztyk ~** tartar(e) sauce/steak

t

**taternict|wo** (**-wa**) (*loc sg* **-wie**) *nt* mountaineering
**taterni|k** (**-ka, -cy**) (*instr sg* **-kiem**) *m* mountaineer
**ta|to** (**-ty, -towie**) (*loc sg* **-cie**) *m* = **tata**
**Tatr|y** (-) *pl* the Tatra Mountains *pl*
**tatrzański** *adj*: **T~ Park Narodowy** Tatra National Park
**tatuaż** (**-u, -e**) (*gen pl* **-y**) *m* tattoo
**tatu|ować (-uję, -ujesz)** *vt* (*perf* **wy-**) to tattoo
**tatu|ś** (**-sia, -siowie**) *m* dad(dy)
**tautologi|a** (**-i**) *f* tautology
**tą** *pron acc, instr od* **ta**
**tchawic|a** (**-y, -e**) *f* windpipe, trachea
**tch|nąć (-nę, -niesz)** (*imp* **-nij**) *vt perf*: **~ nowe życie w** *+acc* to breathe new life into
**tchnie|nie** (**-nia, -nia**) (*gen pl* **-ń**) *nt* (*książk*) breath; **wydać** (*perf*) **ostatnie ~** to breathe one's last
**tchórz** (**-a, -e**) (*gen pl* **-y**) *m* (*osoba*) coward; (*Zool*) polecat; **~ go obleciał** (*pot*) he got cold feet (*pot*)
**tchórzliwoś|ć** (**-ci**) *f* cowardice
**tchórzliwy** *adj* cowardly
**tchórzost|wo** (**-wa**) (*loc sg* **-wie**) *nt* cowardice
**tchórz|yć (-ę, -ysz)** (*perf* **s-**) *vi* to chicken out
**tchu** *itd. n patrz* **dech**
**te** *pron* these; **te dzieci/książki** these children/books; **widziałem te, nie tamte** I saw these, not those
**tea|m** (**-mu, -my**) (*loc sg* **-mie**) *m* team
**teat|r** (**-ru, -ry**) (*loc sg* **-rze**) *m* theatre (*Brit*), theater (*US*)
**teatralny** *adj* (*aktor, przedstawienie*) theatre *attr* (*Brit*), theater *attr* (*US*); (*krytyk*) drama *attr*; (*mina, gest*) theatrical; **lornetka teatralna** opera glasses *pl*
**teatroma|n** (**-na, -ni**) (*loc sg* **-nie**) *m* theatregoer (*Brit*), theatergoer (*US*)
**teatrzy|k** (**-ku, -ki**) (*instr sg* **-kiem**) *m dimin od* **teatr**
**techniczny** *adj* (*literatura, opis, środki*) technical; (*postęp*) technological; **kalka techniczna** tracing paper; **pismo techniczne** lettering
**techni|k** (**-ka, -cy**) (*instr sg* **-kiem**) *m* technician; **~ laboratoryjny/dentystyczny** lab/dental technician
**techni|ka** (**-ki, -ki**) (*dat sg* **-ce**) *f* (*dział cywilizacji*) technology; (*metoda*) technique; **~ pisarska** writing technique; **~ komputerowa** computer technology; **mieć dobrą technikę** to have good technique
**technik|um** (**-um, -a**) (*gen pl* **-ów**) *nt inv in sg* (*Szkol*) technical college; **~ handlowe** commercial college
**technokra|ta** (**-ty, -ci**) (*dat sg* **-cie**) *m decl like f in sg* technocrat
**technolo|g** (**-ga, -dzy** *lub* **-gowie**) (*instr sg* **-giem**) *m* technologist
**technologi|a** (**-i**) *f* technology
**technologiczny** *adj* technological
**tecz|ka** (**-ki, -ki**) (*dat sg* **-ce**, *gen pl* **-ek**) *f* (*ze skóry*) briefcase, portfolio; (*z papieru*) folder
**teflo|n®** (**-nu**) (*loc sg* **-nie**) *m* Teflon®
**teflonowy** *adj* non-stick, Teflon-coated
**tego** *pron gen, acc od* **ten, to**
**tegoroczny** *adj* this year's
**tej** *pron gen, dat od* **ta**
**te|ka** (**-ki, -ki**) (*dat sg* **-ce**) *f* (*też*: **teka ministerialna**) portfolio; **minister bez teki** minister without portfolio
**Teksa|s** (**-su**) (*loc sg* **-sie**) *m* Texas
**tek|st** (**-stu, -sty**) (*loc sg* **-ście**) *m* text; (*piosenki*) lyrics *pl*
**tekstowy** *adj*: **plik ~** (*Komput*) text file
**tekstyli|a** (**-ów**) *pl* textiles *pl*
**tekstylny** *adj* textile
**tektu|ra** (**-ry, -ry**) (*dat sg* **-rze**) *f* cardboard
**tekturowy** *adj* cardboard *attr*
**tel.** *abbr* (= *telefon*) tel., ph.
**Tel-Awi|w** (**-wu**) (*loc sg* **-wie**) *m* Tel Aviv
**teledys|k** (**-ku, -ki**) (*instr sg* **-kiem**) *m* video clip
**telefo|n** (**-nu, -ny**) (*loc sg* **-nie**) *m* (*urządzenie*) telephone, phone; (*rozmowa*) phone call; (*numer telefonu*) phone number; **rozmawiać przez ~** to be on the phone; **rozmawiać z kimś przez ~** to talk to sb on the phone; **~ komórkowy** cell(ular) phone; **~ zaufania** helpline; **odbierać (odebrać** *perf*) **~** to pick up *lub* answer the phone; **~ do ciebie!** there's a (phone) call for you!, you're wanted on the phone; **podaj mi swój ~** give me your phone number
**telefonicznie** *adv* by (tele)phone
**telefoniczny** *adj* (*centrala, rozmowa*) (tele) phone *attr*; **budka/kabina telefoniczna** phone booth/box; **karta telefoniczna** phonecard; **książka telefoniczna** phone book, (telephone) directory; **telefoniczne centrum obsługi klienta** call centre (*Brit*) *lub* center (*US*)
**telefoni|sta** (**-sty, -ści**) (*dat sg* **-ście**) *m decl like f in sg* (switchboard) operator
**telefonist|ka** (**-ki, -ki**) (*dat sg* **-ce**, *gen pl* **-ek**) *f* (switchboard) operator
**telefon|ować (-uję, -ujesz)** (*perf* **za-**) *vi* (*korzystać z telefonu*) to make a (phone) call; **~ do kogoś** to phone *lub* call sb
**telegaze|ta** (**-ty, -ty**) (*dat sg* **-cie**) *f* teletext
**telegra|f** (**-fu, -fy**) (*loc sg* **-fie**) *m* telegraph
**telegraficznie** *adv* by telegraph *lub* cable

**telegraficzny** *adj* telegraph *attr*; **w ~m skrócie** with telegraphic brevity
**telegraf|ować (-uję, -ujesz)** (*perf* **za-**) *vi* to telegraph, to cable
**telegra|m** (**-mu, -my**) (*loc sg* **-mie**) *m* telegram, cable; **wysyłać (wysłać** *perf***) ~** to send a telegram, to wire
**telekomunikacj|a** (**-i**) *f* telecommunications
**telekonferencj|a** (**-i, -e**) (*gen pl* **-i**) *f* teleconference
**telek|s** (**-su, -sy**) (*loc sg* **-sie**) *m* telex
**teleks|ować (-uję, -ujesz)** (*perf* **za-**) *vi* to telex
**telenowel|a** (**-i, -e**) *f* soap opera
**teleobiekty|w** (**-wu, -wy**) (*loc sg* **-wie**) *m* (*Fot*) telephoto lens
**tele|pać się (-pię, -piesz)** *vr* (*pot*: *chwiać się*) to shake; (*: jechać*) to joggle along
**telepati|a** (**-i**) *f* telepathy
**telepatyczny** *adj* telepathic
**telesko|p** (**-pu, -py**) (*loc sg* **-pie**) *m* (*Astron*) telescope
**teletek|st** (**-stu**) (*loc sg* **-ście**) *m* teletext
**teleturniej** (**-u, -e**) *m* quiz show
**telewidz** (**-a, -owie**) (*gen pl* **-ów**) *m* viewer
**telewizj|a** (**-i, -e**) (*gen pl* **-i**) *f* television, TV; **oglądać telewizję** to watch TV; **~ satelitarna** satellite television; **~ kablowa** cable television; **~ przemysłowa** closed-circuit television; **~ reality** reality TV; **co dziś jest w telewizji?** what's on TV today?
**telewizo|r** (**-ra, -ry**) (*loc sg* **-rze**) *m* TV (set), television (set)
**telewizyjny** *adj* TV *attr*, television *attr*
**tema|t** (**-tu, -ty**) (*loc sg* **-cie**) *m* subject, topic; (*Muz*) theme; (*Jęz*) stem; **wykład/ wypracowanie na ~ czegoś** a lecture/ composition on sth; **(nie) na ~** (not) to the point; **odbiegać od ~u** to go off at a tangent; **zmieniać ~** to change the subject
**tematyczny** *adj* thematic
**tematy|ka** (**-ki**) (*dat sg* **-ce**) *f* subject matter
**temblа|k** (**-ka** *lub* **-ku, -ki**) (*instr sg* **-kiem**) *m* (*Med*) sling; **miał rękę na ~u** his arm was in a sling
**temp.** *abbr* (= *temperatura*) temp.
**temperamen|t** (**-tu, -ty**) (*loc sg* **-cie**) *m* temperament
**temperatu|ra** (**-ry, -ry**) (*dat sg* **-rze**) *f* temperature; (*pot*: *gorączka*) fever; **~ pokojowa** room temperature; **mieć temperaturę** (*Med*) to have *lub* run a temperature
**temper|ować (-uję, -ujesz)** (*perf* **za-**) *vt* to sharpen
**temperów|ka** (**-ki, -ki**) (*dat sg* **-ce**, *gen pl* **-ek**) *f* (pencil) sharpener
**tem|po** (**-pa, -pa**) (*loc sg* **-pie**) *nt* pace; (*Muz*) tempo; **w zwolnionym tempie** in slow motion; **nadawać ~** to set the pace
**temu** *pron dat od* **ten, to**
**temu** *adv*: **dwa lata ~** two years ago; **dawno ~** long ago; **jak dawno ~?** how long ago?; **parę dni ~** the other day
**ten** *pron* (*z rzeczownikiem*) this; (*bez rzeczownika*) this one; (*tamten*) that; **ten sam** the same; **ten jest zbyt drogi** this one is too expensive; **w ten czwartek** this Thursday
**tendencj|a** (**-i, -e**) (*gen pl* **-i**) *f* tendency, trend
**tendencyjny** *adj* biased
**teni|s** (**-sa**) (*loc sg* **-sie**) *m* (*Sport*) tennis; **~ stołowy** table tennis; **~ ziemny** lawn tennis
**tenisi|sta** (**-sty, -ści**) (*dat sg* **-ście**) *m decl like f in sg* tennis player; **łokieć tenisisty** tennis elbow
**tenisist|ka** (**-ki, -ki**) (*dat sg* **-ce**, *gen pl* **-ek**) *f* tennis player
**tenisowy** *adj* tennis *attr*
**tenisów|ki** (**-ek**) *pl* tennis shoes, plimsolls (*Brit*), sneakers (*US*)
**teno|r** (*loc sg* **-rze**) *m* (*głos*) (*gen sg* **-ru**, *nom pl* **-ry**) tenor; (*śpiewak*) (*gen sg* **-ra**, *nom pl* **-rzy**) tenor
**teolo|g** (**-ga, -gowie** *lub* **-dzy**) (*instr sg* **-giem**) *m* theologian
**teologi|a** (**-i**) *f* theology
**teologiczny** *adj* theological
**teoretycznie** *adv* theoretically, in theory
**teoretyczny** *adj* theoretical
**teorety|k** (**-ka, -cy**) (*instr sg* **-kiem**) *m* theoretician
**teoretyz|ować (-uję, -ujesz)** *vi* to theorize
**teori|a** (**-i, -e**) (*gen pl* **-i**) *f* theory
**terako|ta** (**-ty, -ty**) (*dat sg* **-cie**) *f* terracotta
**terapeu|ta** (**-ty, -ci**) (*dat sg* **-cie**) *m decl like f in sg* therapist
**terapeutyczny** *adj* therapeutic
**terapi|a** (**-i, -e**) (*gen pl* **-i**) *f* therapy
**teraz** *adv* (*w tej chwili*) now; (*obecnie*) nowadays; **nie ~** not now; **~, gdy ...** now that ...
**teraźniejszoś|ć** (**-ci**) *f* the present
**teraźniejszy** *adj* present, today's *attr*; **czas ~** (*Jęz*) present tense
**terce|t** (**-tu, -ty**) (*loc sg* **-cie**) *m* (*Muz*) trio
**tere|n** (**-nu, -ny**) (*loc sg* **-nie**) *m* ground, terrain; **~ budowy** building site; **~ szkoły** school grounds
**terenowy** *adj* (*pracownik, badanie*) field *attr*; (*władze*) local *attr*; **samochód ~** off-road vehicle
**terie|r** (**-ra, -ry**) (*loc sg* **-rze**) *m* terrier
**terko|t** (**-tu**) (*loc sg* **-cie**) *m* clatter
**terko|tać (-czę, -czesz)** (*perf* **za-**) *vi* to clatter; (*pot*: *mówić*) to rattle on *lub* away (*pot*)
**termiczny** *adj* thermal
**termi|n** (**-nu, -ny**) (*loc sg* **-nie**) *m* (*czas*) deadline, time limit; (*umówione spotkanie*) appointment; (*wyraz*) term; **ostateczny ~** the

t

final deadline, the closing date; **wyznaczyć** *(perf)* ~ to set a date; **skończyć** *(perf)* **coś w ~ie** to finish sth in time
**terminal** (**-u** *lub* **-a, -e**) *(gen pl* **-i** *lub* **-ów**) *m* *(Komput, Lot)* terminal
**terminarz** (**-a, -e**) *(gen pl* **-y**) *m* *(plan)* schedule; *(kalendarz)* diary
**terminato|r** (**-ra, -rzy**) *(loc sg* **-rze**) *m* apprentice
**terminologi|a** (**-i, -e**) *(gen pl* **-i**) *f* terminology
**terminologiczny** *adj* terminological
**termin|ować (-uję, -ujesz)** *vi* to serve one's apprenticeship
**terminowo** *adv* on time
**terminowy** *adj* *(praca, zadanie)* with a deadline; **rachunek** ~ deposit account
**termi|t** (**-ta, -ty**) *(loc sg* **-cie**) *m* termite
**termodynami|ka** (**-ki**) *(dat sg* **-ce**) *f* thermodynamics
**termofo|r** (**-ra, -ry**) *(loc sg* **-rze**) *m* hot-water bottle
**termojądrowy** *adj* thermonuclear
**termomet|r** (**-ru, -ry**) *(loc sg* **-rze**) *m* thermometer
**termo|s** (**-su, -sy**) *(loc sg* **-sie**) *m* Thermos® (flask), (vacuum *(Brit)*) flask
**termosta|t** (**-tu, -ty**) *(loc sg* **-cie**) *m* thermostat
**termowentylato|r** (**-ra, -ry**) *(loc sg* **-rze**) *m* fan heater
**terpenty|na** (**-ny, -ny**) *(dat sg* **-nie**) *f* turpentine
**terro|r** (**-ru**) *(loc sg* **-rze**) *m* terror
**terrory|sta** (**-sty, -ści**) *(loc sg* **-ście**) *m decl like f in sg* terrorist
**terrorystyczny** *adj* terrorist *attr*
**terroryz|m** (**-mu**) *(loc sg* **-mie**) *m* terrorism
**terroryz|ować (-uję, -ujesz)** *(perf* **s-**) *vt* to terrorize
**terytorialny** *adj* territorial
**terytori|um** (**-um, -a**) *(gen pl* **-ów**) *nt inv in sg* territory
**te|st** (**-stu, -sty**) *(loc sg* **-ście**) *m* test; ~ **ciążowy** pregnancy test
**testamen|t** (**-tu, -ty**) *(loc sg* **-cie**) *m* will, testament; **Stary/Nowy T~** the Old/New Testament; **zapisać** *(perf)* **coś komuś w testamencie** to will sth to sb
**test|ować (-uję, -ujesz)** *(perf* **prze-**) *vt* to test
**teściow|a** (**-ej, -e**) *f decl like adj* mother-in-law
**teś|ć** (**-cia, -ciowie**) *m* father-in-law; **teściowie** *pl* in-laws *pl*
**te|za** (**-zy, -zy**) *(dat sg* **-zie**) *f* thesis; *(Mat)* proposition
**tezauru|s** (**-sa, -sy**) *(loc sg* **-sie**) *m* thesaurus
**też** *adv* too, also; **ja też** me too; **ja też nie** me neither; **dlatego też** that is why; **też pomysł!** what a stupid idea!

**tę** *pron acc od* **ta**
**tęcz|a** (**-y, -e**) *f* rainbow
**tęczów|ka** (**-ki, -ki**) *(dat sg* **-ce**, *gen pl* **-ek**) *f* *(Anat)* iris
**tędy** *adv* this way
**tę|gi** *(comp* **-ższy**) *adj* stout
**tępa|k** (**-ka, -ki**) *(instr sg* **-kiem**) *m* *(pej)* moron *(pej)*
**tę|pić (-pię, -pisz)** *vt* *(szkodniki)* *(perf* **wy-**) to kill (off); *(poglądy)* *(perf* **wy-**) to eradicate; *(noże)* *(perf* **s-**) to blunt; **tępić się** *vr* *(o ludziach)* to fight one another; *(o nożu)* *(perf* **s-**) to become blunt
**tępo|ta** (**-ty**) *(dat sg* **-cie**) *f* obtuseness
**tępy** *adj* *(nóż, czubek)* blunt; *(człowiek)* dense, obtuse, dull; *(spojrzenie)* vacant; *(ból)* dull
**tęsk|nić (-nię, -nisz)** *(imp* **-nij**, *perf* **za-**) *vi*: ~ **za kimś/czymś** *lub* **do kogoś/czegoś** to miss sb/sth; ~ **za czymś** *lub* **do czegoś** *(pragnąć)* to long *lub* yearn for sth
**tęsknie** *adv* longingly
**tęskno|ta** (**-ty, -ty**) *(dat sg* **-cie**) *f*: ~ **(za czymś)** longing (for sth)
**tęskny** *adj* longing
**tęten|t** (**-tu**) *(loc sg* **-cie**) *m* rattle
**tętnic|a** (**-y, -e**) *f* artery
**tętniczy** *adj* arterial
**tęt|nić (-ni)** *vi* *(o krokach, kopytach)* to rattle; *(o krwi)* to pulsate; ~ **życiem** to be teeming with life
**tęt|no** (**-na, -na**) *(loc sg* **-nie**) *nt* pulse; **mierzyć (zmierzyć** *perf)* **komuś** ~ to take sb's pulse
**tęż|ec** (**-ca**) *m* *(Med)* tetanus
**tęż|eć (-eje)** *(perf* **s-**) *vi* *(o budyniu, galaretce)* to set; *(o twarzy)* to freeze
**tęższy** *adj comp od* **tęgi**
**tęży|zna** (**-zny**) *(dat sg* **-źnie**) *f*: ~ **(fizyczna)** (physical) fitness
**tia|ra** (**-ry, -ry**) *(dat sg* **-rze**) *f* tiara
**tie-brea|k** (**-ka, -ki**) *(instr sg* **-kiem**) *m* tie-break(er)
**ti|k** (**-ku, -ki**) *(instr sg* **-kiem**) *m* *(odruch)* tic
**ti|r** (**-ra, -ry**) *(loc sg* **-rze**) *m* heavy lorry *(Brit)* *lub* truck *(US)*, HGV *(Brit)*
**tiul** (**-u, -e**) *(gen pl* **-ów**) *m* tulle
**tiulowy** *adj* tulle *attr*
**tj.** *abbr* (= *to jest*) i.e.
**tkacki** *adj*: **warsztat** ~ *lub* **krosno ~e** loom
**tkact|wo** (**-wa**) *(loc sg* **-wie**) *nt* weaving
**tkacz|ka** (**-ki, -ki**) *(dat sg* **-ce**, *gen pl* **-ek**) *f* weaver
**tk|ać (-am, -asz)** *(perf* **u-**) *vt* to weave
**tkani|na** (**-ny, -ny**) *(dat sg* **-nie**) *f* fabric; ~ **bawełniana/wełniana** cotton/woollen fabric; ~ **drukowana** print
**tkan|ka** (**-ki, -ki**) *(dat sg* **-ce**, *gen pl* **-ek**) *f* tissue

**tkliwoś|ć** (**-ci**) *f* affection
**tkliwy** *adj* affectionate
**tk|nąć** (**-nę, -niesz**) (*imp* **-nij**) *vb perf od* **tykać**
▷ *vt perf*: **coś mnie tknęło** I got a strange feeling
**tk|wić** (**-wię, -wisz**) (*imp* **-wij**) *vi* (*o kluczu*) to be sitting; (*o strzale*) to be sticking; (*pot: o osobie*) to stick around (*pot*); (*o problemie itp.*): **~ w** *+loc* to lie *lub* reside in
**tle|n** (**-nu**) (*loc sg* **-nie**) *m* oxygen
**tlen|ek** (**-ku, -ki**) (*instr sg* **-kiem**) *m* oxide; **~ węgla** carbon monoxide
**tle|nić** (**-nię, -nisz**) (*imp* **-ń**, *perf* **u-**) *vt* to bleach
**tleniony** *adj* (*włosy*) bleached; **tleniona blondynka** peroxide blonde
**tlenowy** *adj* oxygen *attr*
**tl|ić się** (**-i**) *vr* to smoulder (*Brit*), to smolder (*US*); (*przen: o nadziei*) to flicker
**tłam|sić** (**-szę, -sisz**) (*imp* **-ś**, *perf* **s-**) *vt* (*przen*) to strangle, to suppress
**tło** (**tła, tła**) (*loc sg* **tle**, *gen pl* **teł**) *nt* background; **na niebieskim tle** against a blue background; **konflikt na tle religijnym** a religious conflict
**tłoczno** *adv*: **w pokoju było ~** the room was crowded
**tłocz|yć** (**-ę, -ysz**) *vt* (*olej*) (*perf* **wy-**) to press; (*wodę, gaz*) (*perf* **w-**) to force; (*wzór, napis*) (*perf* **wy-**) to (im)print; **tłoczyć się** (*perf* **s-**) *vr* to crowd
**tło|k** (*instr sg* **-kiem**) *m* (*ścisk*) (*gen sg* **-ku**) crowd; (*Tech*) (*gen sg* **-ka**, *nom pl* **-ki**) piston
**tłu|c** (**-kę, -czesz**) (*imp* **-cz**, *pt* **-kł**) *vt* (*szklanki, szkło*) (*perf* **s-**) to break; (*uderzać*): **~ w** *lub* **o coś** to pound at sth; (*pot*) (*perf* **s-**); **~ kogoś** to bash sb about (*pot*); **tłuc się** *vr* (*o szklance, szybie*) (*perf* **s-**) to break; (*pot: bić się*) (*perf* **s-**) to scrap (*pot*)
**tłucz|ek** (**-ka, -ki**) (*instr sg* **-kiem**) *m* (*do kartofli*) potato masher; (*do mięsa*) meat tenderizer
**tłucz|eń** (**-nia**) *m* rubble
**tłu|k** (**-ka, -ki**) (*instr sg* **-kiem**) *m* (*pot*) moron (*pot*)
**tłu|m** (**-mu, -my**) (*loc sg* **-mie**) *m* crowd
**tłum.** *abbr* (= *tłumaczył(a)*) transl. (by)
**tłumacz** (**-a, -e**) (*gen pl* **-y**) *m* (*pisemny*) translator; (*ustny*) interpreter; **~ przysięgły** certified translator; (*w sądzie*) court interpreter
**tłumacze|nie** (**-nia**) *nt* (*pisemne*) translation; (*ustne*) interpreting; (*tekst*) (*nom pl* **-nia**, *gen pl* **-ń**) translation
**tłumacz|yć** (**-ę, -ysz**) *vt* (*perf* **wy-**) (*wyjaśniać*) to explain; (*usprawiedliwiać*) to justify; (*przekładać*) (*perf* **prze-**) (*pisemnie*) to translate; (*ustnie*) to interpret; **tłumaczyć się** (*perf* **wy-**) *vr* to excuse o.s.
**tłu|mić** (**-mię, -misz**) (*perf* **s-**) *vt* (*ogień, uczucie, śmiech*) to smother; (*hałas*) to muffle; (*opozycję*) to suppress
**tłumi|k** (**-ka, -ki**) (*instr sg* **-kiem**) *m* (*Mot*) silencer (*Brit*), muffler (*US*); (*trąbki*) mute; (*pianina*) damper; (*pistoletu*) silencer
**tłumnie** *adv* in crowds
**tłusty** *adj* (*mięso, obiad*) fatty; (*talerz, plama, włosy*) greasy; (*osoba*) fat; (*druk, czcionka*) bold; **tłuste mleko** full-cream milk; **~ czwartek** *the last Thursday before Lent*
**tłuszcz** (**-u, -e**) *m* fat; **~ roślinny/zwierzęcy** vegetable/animal fat
**tłuszczowy** *adj*: **tkanka tłuszczowa** fatty tissue
**tłuścioch** (**-a, -y**) *m* (*pej*) fatty (*pej*)

 SŁOWO KLUCZOWE

**to** *pron* **1** (*zaimek wskazujący*) this; **to dziecko** this child
**2** (*w funkcji podmiotu*): **to fakt** it's a fact; **to jest lampa** this *lub* it is a lamp; **co/kto to jest?** what's/who's this?; **czy to ty?** is that you?; **to mi się podoba, a tamto nie** I like this one, but I don't like that one
**3** (*w funkcji ekspresywnej*): **a to łobuz!** what a rascal!
**4**: **jak to?** how so?, how come?; **no to co?** so what?; **otóż to!** exactly!
▷ *conj*: **jeśli chcesz, to idź** go if you like; **gdybyś czegoś potrzebował, to zadzwoń** call if you (should) need anything
▷ *inv* (*w funkcji łącznika*): **czas to pieniądz** time is money

**toale|ta** (**-ty, -ty**) (*dat sg* **-cie**) *f* toilet, lavatory (*Brit*), rest room (*US*); **~ damska** the ladies' (room); **~ męska** the gents
**toalet|ka** (**-ki, -ki**) (*dat sg* **-ce**, *gen pl* **-ek**) *f* dressing table
**toaletowy** *adj* toilet *attr*; **przybory toaletowe** toilet accessories, toiletries
**toa|st** (**-stu, -sty**) (*loc sg* **-ście**) *m* toast; **wznosić (wznieść** *perf*) **~ za kogoś/coś** to raise a glass to sb/sth
**tobie** *pron patrz* **ty**
**toboga|n** (**-nu, -ny**) (*loc sg* **-nie**) *m* toboggan
**tobołek** (**-ka, -ki**) (*instr sg* **-kiem**) *m* bundle
**tob|ół** (**-ołu, -oły**) (*loc sg* **-ole**) *m* (huge) bundle
**toczny** *adj*: **łożysko toczne** antifriction bearing
**tocz|yć** (**-ę, -ysz**) *vt* (*kulkę, beczkę*) (*perf* **po-**) to roll; (*rokowania*) to conduct; (*spór*) to carry on; (*wojnę*) to wage; (*bitwę*) to fight; (*Tech*) to turn; (*drążyć, trawić*) (*perf* **s-**) to gnaw at; **toczył pianę z ust** he was foaming at the

t

mouth; **toczyć się** *vr* (*perf* **po-**) (*turlać się*) to roll; (*dziać się*) to go on
**toffi** *nt lub m inv* toffee
**to|ga** (**-gi, -gi**) (*dat sg* **-dze**, *gen pl* **tóg**) *f* gown
**to|k** (**-ku**) (*instr sg* **-kiem**) *m* (*przebieg*) progress; (*wydarzeń*) course; (*myśli*) train; **być w toku** to be in progress; **nadać** (*perf*) **czemuś tok** to get sth under way
**tokaj** (**-u, -e**) *m* (*wino*) Tokay
**tokar|ka** (**-ki, -ki**) (*dat sg* **-ce**, *gen pl* **-ek**) *f* lathe
**tokarski** *adj*: **warsztat** ~ turnery; **nóż** ~ lathe tool, turning tool
**tokarst|wo** (**-wa**) (*loc sg* **-wie**) *nt* turnery (*trade*)
**tokarz** (**-a, -e**) (*gen pl* **-y**) *m* turner
**Tokio** *nt inv* Tokyo
**toksycznoś|ć** (**-ci**) *f* toxicity
**toksyczny** *adj* toxic
**toksykologi|a** (**-i**) *f* toxicology
**toksy|na** (**-ny, -ny**) (*dat sg* **-nie**) *f* toxin
**tolerancj|a** (**-i**) *f* tolerance, toleration; (*Tech*) (*nom pl* **-e**, *gen pl* **-i**) tolerance
**tolerancyjny** *adj* tolerant
**toler|ować (-uję, -ujesz)** *vt* to tolerate
**to|m** (**-mu, -my**) (*loc sg* **-mie**) *m* volume; **tom pierwszy/drugi** volume one/two; **(wydany) w czterech tomach** (published) in four volumes
**tomogra|f** (**-fu, -fy**) (*loc sg* **-fie**) *m* (*też*: **tomograf komputerowy**) CAT scanner
**tomografi|a** (**-i**) *f* (*też*: **tomografia komputerowa**) CAT scanning
**to|n** (**-nu, -ny**) (*loc sg* **-nie**) *m* (*Muz*) tone; (*brzmienie*) sound; (*styl mówienia*) tone (of voice); **tony niskie** bass; **tony wysokie** treble; **w dobrym/złym tonie** in good/poor taste; **spuścić** (*perf*) **z tonu** to come down a peg or two; **nie mów do mnie takim tonem!** don't talk to me like that!
**to|na** (**-ny, -ny**) (*dat sg* **-nie**) *f* tonne, (metric) ton; ~ **rejestrowa** (*Żegl*) register ton
**tonacj|a** (**-i, -e**) (*gen pl* **-i**) *f* (*Muz*) key; **(utrzymany) w czerwonej tonacji** predominantly red
**tonalny** *adj* (*Muz*) tonal
**tonaż** (**-u**) *m* tonnage
**to|nąć (-nę, -niesz)** (*imp* **-ń**) *vi* (*o statku*) (*perf* **za-**) to sink; (*o człowieku*) (*perf* **u-**) to drown; ~ **w śniegu** to be buried in snow; ~ **w kwiatach** to be smothered with flowers; ~ **w długach** to be up to one's ears in debt; ~ **we łzach** to be in floods of tears
**tone|r** (**-ra, -ry**) (*loc sg* **-rze**) *m* (*Tech*) toner
**toni** *itp. n patrz* **toń**
**toni|k** (**-ku, -ki**) (*instr sg* **-kiem**) *m* (*napój*) tonic (water); (*kosmetyk*) (skin) tonic
**ton|ować (-uję, -ujesz)** (*perf* **s-**) *vt* to tone down
**to|ń** (**-ni, -nie**) (*gen pl* **-ni**) *f* (*książk*) depths *pl*
**topa|z** (**-zu, -zy**) (*loc sg* **-zie**) *m* topaz
**to|pić (-pię, -pisz)** *vt* (*zanurzać*) (*perf* **u-**) to drown; (*rozpuszczać*) (*perf* **s-**) to melt; ~ **smutki (w alkoholu)** to drown one's sorrows; **topić się** *vr* (*tonąć*) (*perf* **u-**) to drown; (*rozpuszczać się*) (*perf* **s-**) to melt
**topiel|ec** (**-ca, -cy**) *m* drowned man
**topielic|a** (**-y, -e**) *f* drowned woman
**topikowy** *adj*: **bezpiecznik** ~ fuse; **drut** ~ fuse wire
**topni|eć (-eje)** (*perf* **s-**) *vi* (*o lodzie, śniegu*) to melt, to thaw; (*o metalu*) to melt; (*przen*: *o pieniądzach*) to dwindle (away); (: *o siłach*) to ebb (away)
**topografi|a** (**-i**) *f* topography
**topograficzny** *adj* topographical
**top|ola** (**-oli, -ole**) (*gen pl* **-oli** *lub* **-ól**) *f* poplar
**topor|ek** (**-ka, -ki**) (*instr sg* **-kiem**) *m* hatchet
**toporny** *adj* (*pej*) coarse, gross
**top|ór** (**-ora, -ory**) (*loc sg* **-orze**) *m* axe (*Brit*), ax (*US*); **pójść** (*perf*) **pod** ~ to get the ax(e), to be axed
**to|r** (**-ru, -ry**) (*loc sg* **-rze**) *m* (*trasa, droga*) path; (: *pocisku*) trajectory; (*kolejowy itp.*) track; (*wyścigowy*) racecourse (*Brit*), racetrack (*US*); (*na bieżni, basenie*) lane; (*saneczkowy, bobslejowy*) run, chute; **toczyć się** *lub* **biec zwykłym torem** (*przen*) to run *lub* take its course; **tory kolejowe** (railway (*Brit*) *lub* railroad (*US*)) track
**tor|ba** (**-by, -by**) (*dat sg* **-bie**, *gen pl* **-eb**) *f* bag; (*podróżna*) holdall; **puścić** (*perf*) **kogoś/pójść** (*perf*) **z ~mi** (*pot*) to reduce sb/to be reduced to beggary
**torbacz** (**-a, -e**) *m* (*Zool*) marsupial
**torbiel** (**-i, -e**) (*gen pl* **-i**) *f* (*Med*) cyst
**toreado|r** (**-ra, -rzy**) (*loc sg* **-rze**) *m* bullfighter
**toreb|ka** (**-ki, -ki**) (*dat sg* **-ce**, *gen pl* **-ek**) *f* (*papierowa*) (paper) bag; (*damska*) handbag, purse (*US*)
**tor|f** (**-fu, -fy**) (*loc sg* **-fie**) *m* peat
**torfowis|ko** (**-ka, -ka**) (*instr sg* **-kiem**) *nt* peat bog
**torfowy** *adj* peat *attr*
**torna|do** (**-da, -da**) (*loc sg* **-dzie**) *nt* tornado
**tornist|er** (**-ra, -ry**) (*loc sg* **-rze**) *m* satchel
**tor|ować (-uję, -ujesz)** (*perf* **u-**) *vt* (*drogę*) to clear; ~ **drogę do czegoś** (*przen*) to pave the way for sth; ~ **sobie drogę łokciami (w tłumie)** to fight *lub* elbow one's way (through a crowd)
**torowis|ko** (**-ka, -ka**) (*instr sg* **-kiem**) *nt* track
**torpe|da** (**-dy, -dy**) (*dat sg* **-dzie**) *f* torpedo
**torped|ować (-uję, -ujesz)** (*perf* **s-**) *vt* to torpedo
**torpedowy** *adj* torpedo *attr*

**torreado|r** (**-ra, -rzy**) (*loc sg* **-rze**) *m* = **toreador**
**tor|s** (**-su, -sy**) (*loc sg* **-sie**) *m* torso
**torsj|e** (**-i**) *pl* (*wymioty*) vomiting; (*odruchy wymiotne*) retching, heaving
**tor|t** (**-tu, -ty**) (*loc sg* **-cie**) *m* cream cake (*Brit*), layer cake (*US*)
**tortownic|a** (**-y, -e**) *f* springform (pan)
**tortowy** *adj*: **mąka tortowa** cake flour
**tortu|ra** (**-ry, -ry**) (*dat sg* **-rze**) *f* torture; **sala tortur** torture chamber
**tortur|ować** (**-uję, -ujesz**) *vt* to torture
**tory|s** (**-sa, -si**) (*loc sg* **-sie**) *m* Tory
**Toskani|a** (**-i**) *f* Tuscany
**to|st** (**-stu, -sty**) (*loc sg* **-ście**) *m* (a) piece *lub* slice of toast
**toste|r** (**-ra, -ry**) (*loc sg* **-rze**) *m* toaster
**totalitarny** *adj* totalitarian
**totalitaryz|m** (**-mu**) (*loc sg* **-mie**) *m* totalitarianism
**totalizato|r** (**-ra, -ry**) (*loc sg* **-rze**) *m* (*na wyścigach konnych*) sweepstake; (*piłkarski*) the pools *pl*; **~ sportowy** ≈ National Lottery (*Brit*), ≈ Lotto (*US*)
**totalnie** *adv* totally
**totalny** *adj* total
**tote|m** (**-mu, -my**) (*loc sg* **-mie**) *m* totem
**toteż** *conj* (and) so, which is why
**totolot|ek** (**-ka**) (*instr sg* **-kiem**) *m* ≈ National Lottery (*Brit*), ≈ Lotto (*US*)
**tournée** *nt inv* tour
**tow.** *abbr* (= *towarzystwo*) (*spółka*) Co. (= *Company*); (*stowarzyszenie*) Soc. (= *Society*); (= *towarzysz(ka)*) comrade
**towa|r** (**-ru, -ry**) (*loc sg* **-rze**) *m* commodity; **~y konsumpcyjne** consumer goods; **~ wybrakowany** second
**towarowy** *adj*: **pociąg ~** goods (*Brit*) *lub* freight (*US*) train; **wymiana towarowa** barter; **dom ~** department store; **znak ~** trademark; **rynek ~** commodity market
**towarzyski** *adj* (*człowiek*) sociable; (*kontakty, spotkanie, życie*) social; **rozmowa towarzyska** small talk; **gra towarzyska** parlour (*Brit*) *lub* parlor (*US*) game; **agencja towarzyska** escort agency; **kronika towarzyska** gossip column; **telefon ~** party line; **mecz ~** (*Sport*) friendly match
**towarzyst|wo** (**-wa**) (*loc sg* **-wie**) *nt* (*obecność*) company, companionship; (*otoczenie*) company; (*stowarzyszenie*) (*nom pl* **-wa**) society; (*Ekon: spółka*) (*nom pl* **-wa**) company; **być w czyimś towarzystwie** to be accompanied by sb; **wpaść** (*perf*) **w złe ~** to fall in with a bad company
**towarzysz** (**-a, -e**) (*gen pl* **-y**) *m* companion; (*w partii komunistycznej*) comrade; **~ zabaw** playmate; **~ podróży** fellow passenger
**towarzyszący** *adj*: **~ komuś/czemuś** accompanying sb/sth; **osoba towarzysząca** escort
**towarzysz|ka** (**-ki, -ki**) (*dat sg* **-ce**, *gen pl* **-ek**) *f* companion; (*w partii komunistycznej*) comrade
**towarzysz|yć** (**-ę, -ysz**) *vi*: **~ komuś/czemuś** to accompany sb/sth
**tożsamoś|ć** (**-ci**) *f* identity; **dowód tożsamości** (means of) identification, ID
**tóg** *n patrz* **toga**
**tra|cić** (**-cę, -cisz**) (*imp* **-ć**) *vt* (*przestawać mieć*) (*perf* **s-** *lub* **u-**) to lose; (*marnować*) (*perf* **s-**) (*okazję*) to miss; (*czas, pieniądze*) to waste ▷ *vi* (*ponosić stratę*) (*perf* **s-**) to suffer a loss, to lose out; **~ przytomność** to lose consciousness; **~ panowanie nad sobą** to lose one's temper; **~ kogoś/coś z oczu** to lose sight of sb/sth; **~ ważność** to expire, to run out; **~ głowę** (*przen*) to lose one's head; **~ na znaczeniu/wartości** to lose significance/(in) value
**tradycj|a** (**-i, -e**) (*gen pl* **-i**) *f* tradition
**tradycjonali|sta** (**-sty, -ści**) (*loc sg* **-ście**) *m decl like f in sg* traditionalist
**tradycyjny** *adj* traditional
**tra|f** (**-fu, -fy**) (*loc sg* **-fie**) *m* chance; **ślepy ~** pure chance; **szczęśliwym ~em** by a stroke of luck, by a lucky chance; **dziwnym ~em** funnily enough; **~ chciał, że ...** as luck would have it, ...
**tra|fiać** (**-fiam, -fiasz**) (*perf* **-fić**) *vt* to hit ▷ *vi* (*nie chybiać*) to hit the target; (*znajdować drogę*) to find one's way, to get there; **nie ~** to miss; **~ do szpitala/na posterunek policji** to land in (the (*US*)) hospital/at a police station; **trafić w dziesiątkę** to hit the bull's-eye; (*przen*) to be spot-on; **na chybił trafił** (*strzelać*) at random; (*strzał*) hit-or-miss; **trafić na kogoś** to run into sb; **trafiać się** *vr* to come up
**trafie|nie** (**-nia, -nia**) (*gen pl* **-ń**) *nt* (*trafny rzut itp.*) (direct) hit; (*w grze liczbowej*) lucky number
**trafiony** *adj* (*pot: decyzja*) right; **~ zakup** a good buy
**trafnoś|ć** (**-ci**) *f* (*ciosu, strzału*) accuracy; (*uwagi*) aptness; (*wyboru*) rightness
**trafny** *adj* (*cios, strzał*) accurate; (*uwaga*) apt; (*wybór*) right; (*słowo, wyrażenie*) felicitous, well-chosen
**tragarz** (**-a, -e**) (*gen pl* **-y**) *m* porter
**tragedi|a** (**-i, -e**) (*gen pl* **-i**) *f* tragedy; **nie rób (z tego) tragedii!** don't make a mountain out of a molehill!
**tragediopisarz** (**-a, -e**) (*gen pl* **-y**) *m* (*Lit*) tragic dramatist, tragedian
**tragicznie** *adv* tragically; (*pot: nieudolnie*) terribly (*pot*); **wyglądasz ~!** (*pot*) you look terrible! (*pot*)

t

**tragiczny** *adj* tragic; (*pot*: *wygląd*) terrible (*pot*)
**tragikomedi|a** (**-i, -e**) (*gen pl* **-i**) *f* (*Lit, Teatr*) tragicomedy
**tragiz|m** (**-mu**) (*loc sg* **-mie**) *m* tragic nature, tragedy
**trajektori|a** (**-i**) *f* trajectory
**trajko|tać (-czę, -czesz)** (*imp* **-cz**) *vi* (*pot*) to chatter
**trajl|ować (-uję, -ujesz)** *vi* (*pot*) to natter (*pot*)
**trakcj|a** (**-i, -e**) (*gen pl* **-i**) *f* (*napęd*) traction
**trakcyjny** *adj* (*silnik, koło*) traction *attr*; **sieć trakcyjna** trolley wires; **słup ~** pylon
**trak|t** (**-tu, -ty**) (*loc sg* **-cie**) *m* (*droga*) track; **być w trakcie (robienia) czegoś** to be in the middle of (doing) sth
**trakta|t** (**-tu, -ty**) (*loc sg* **-cie**) *m* (*Pol*) treaty; (*Lit*) treatise
**trakto|r** (**-ra, -ry**) (*loc sg* **-rze**) *m* tractor; **traktory** *pl* (*pot*) hiking boots *pl*
**traktorzy|sta** (**-sty, -ści**) (*dat sg* **-ście**) *m decl like f in sg* tractor driver
**trakt|ować (-uję, -ujesz)** *vt* (*perf* **po-**) to treat; **~ kogoś źle** to treat sb badly, to ill-treat sb; **~ kogoś z góry** to patronize sb ▷ *vi*: **~ o czymś** to deal with sth
**traktowa|nie** (**-nia**) *nt* treatment
**trało|wiec** (**-wca, -wce**) *m* (*Żegl*) minesweeper
**tram|p** (**-pa, -py** *lub* **-powie**) (*loc sg* **-pie**) *m* (*włóczęga*) tramp
**tramp|ek** (**-ka, -ki**) (*instr sg* **-kiem**, *gen pl* **-ek**) *m* gym shoe (*Brit*), sneaker (*US*); **trampki** *pl* gym shoes *pl* (*Brit*), sneakers *pl* (*US*)
**trampoli|na** (**-ny, -ny**) (*dat sg* **-nie**) *f* (*na basenie*) diving board, springboard; (*na sali gimnastycznej*) springboard, trampoline
**tramwa|j** (**-ju, -je**) (*gen pl* **-jów** *lub* **-i**) *m* tram (*Brit*), streetcar (*US*)
**tramwajarz** (**-a, -e**) (*gen pl* **-y**) *m* tram driver (*Brit*), streetcar driver (*US*)
**tramwajowy** *adj* (*bilet, przystanek*) tram *attr* (*Brit*), streetcar *attr* (*US*)
**tra|n** (**-nu, -ny**) (*loc sg* **-nie**) *m* cod-liver oil
**tran|s** (**-su, -sy**) (*loc sg* **-sie**) *m* trance; **wpadać (wpaść** *perf*) **w ~** to go into a trance
**transakcj|a** (**-i, -e**) (*gen pl* **-i**) *f* transaction; **dokonywać (dokonać** *perf*) **transakcji** to close a deal; **~ gotówkowa/wiązana** cash/tie-in transaction
**transatlantycki** *adj* transatlantic
**transatlanty|k** (**-ku, -ki**) (*instr sg* **-kiem**) *m* transatlantic (liner)
**transcendentalny** *adj* transcendental
**transfe|r** (**-ru, -ry**) (*loc sg* **-rze**) *m* transfer
**transformacj|a** (**-i, -e**) (*gen pl* **-i**) *f* transformation
**transformato|r** (**-ra, -ry**) (*loc sg* **-rze**) *m* (*Elektr*) transformer
**transfuzj|a** (**-i, -e**) (*gen pl* **-i**) *f* (*Med*) (blood) transfusion
**transkontynentalny** *adj* (*lot*) intercontinental
**transkrypcj|a** (**-i, -e**) (*gen pl* **-i**) *f* (*Muz, Jęz*) transcription
**transmisj|a** (**-i, -e**) (*gen pl* **-i**) *f* (*TV, Radio*) transmission; **~ danych** data transmission
**transmisyjny** *adj*: **wóz ~** mobile unit, outside broadcast van; **pas ~** transmission belt
**transmit|ować (-uję, -ujesz)** *vt* (*mecz, koncert*) to broadcast (live); (*sygnał*) to transmit; **mecz będzie transmitowany w telewizji** the game will be televised live
**transparen|t** (**-tu, -ty**) (*loc sg* **-cie**) *m* banner
**transplantacj|a** (**-i, -e**) (*gen pl* **-i**) *f* (*Med*) transplant; **operacja transplantacji serca** heart transplant operation
**transpor|t** (**-tu, -ty**) (*loc sg* **-cie**) *m* (*przewóz*) transport (*Brit*), transportation (*US*); (*ładunek*) shipment; **~ samochodowy** motor transport; **~ publiczny** public transport
**transporte|r** (**-ra, -ry**) (*loc sg* **-rze**) *m* (*Tech*) conveyor; (*też*: **transporter opancerzony**) armoured (*Brit*) *lub* armored (*US*) personnel carrier
**transport|ować (-uję, -ujesz)** (*perf* **prze-**) *vt* to transport
**transporto|wiec** (**-wca**) *m* (*Lot*) (*nom pl* **-wce**) cargo plane; (*Żegl*) (*nom pl* **-wce**) freighter; (*pracownik*) (*nom pl* **-wcy**) transport worker
**transportowy** *adj* (*firma, usługi*) shipping *attr*, forwarding *attr*
**transwesty|ta** (**-ty, -ci**) (*dat sg* **-cie**) *m decl like f in sg* transvestite
**tranzysto|r** (**-ra, -ry**) (*loc sg* **-rze**) *m* transistor
**tranzy|t** (**-tu**) (*loc sg* **-cie**) *m* transit; **jechać ~em przez Węgry** to go via Hungary
**tranzytowy** *adj* (*hala, wiza*) transit *attr*; (*przejazd, droga*) through *attr*
**tra|p** (**-pu, -py**) (*loc sg* **-pie**) *m* (*Żegl*) gangplank, gangway
**trape|r** (**-ra, -rzy**) (*loc sg* **-rze**) *m* trapper
**trape|z** (**-zu, -zy**) (*loc sg* **-zie**) *m* (*Geom*) trapezium (*Brit*), trapezoid (*US*); (*Sport*) trapeze
**tra|pić (-pię, -pisz)** *vt* to worry; **trapić się** *vr* to worry
**tra|sa** (**-sy, -sy**) (*loc sg* **-sie**) *f* route; (*wycieczki*) itinerary; **~ narciarska** ski run; **być w trasie** to be on the road
**trasa|t** (**-ta, -ci**) (*loc sg* **-cie**) *m* (*Fin*) drawee
**trasz|ka** (**-ki, -ki**) (*dat sg* **-ce**, *gen pl* **-ek**) *f* newt
**trat|ować (-uję, -ujesz)** (*perf* **s-**) *vt* to trample
**trat|wa** (**-wy, -wy**) (*loc sg* **-wie**) *f* raft; **~ ratunkowa** life raft

**traumatyczny** *adj* traumatic
**tra|wa** (**-wy, -wy**) (*loc sg* **-wie**) *f* (*roślina*) grass; (*trawnik*) lawn
**trawestacj|a** (**-i, -e**) (*gen pl* **-i**) *f* (*Lit*) travesty
**trawiasty** *adj* (*teren, kolor*) grassy; **kort ~** lawn *lub* grass court
**tra|wić (-wię, -wisz)** *vt* (*pokarm*) (*perf* **s-**) to digest; (*o chorobie, ogniu*) (*perf* **s-**) to consume; (*Chem, Tech*) (*perf* **wy-**) to etch; **~ czas na czymś** to waste (one's) time doing sth
**trawie|nie** (**-nia**) *nt* digestion; (*Chem, Tech*) etching
**trawienny** *adj* digestive
**traw|ka** (**-ki, -ki**) (*dat sg* **-ce**, *gen pl* **-ek**) *f dimin od* **trawa**; (*pot: marihuana*) grass (*pot*); **iść (pójść** *perf*) **na zieloną trawkę** (*pot*) to be fired (*pot*)
**trawle|r** (**-ra, -ry**) (*loc sg* **-rze**) *m* trawler
**trawni|k** (**-ka, -ki**) (*instr sg* **-kiem**) *m* lawn
**trą|ba** (**-by, -by**) (*dat sg* **-bie**) *f* (*Muz*) horn; (*słonia*) trunk; **~ powietrzna** whirlwind
**trą|bić (-bię, -bisz)** (*perf* **wy-**) *vt* (*pot: pić*) to guzzle (*pot*) ▷ *vi* (*perf* **za-**) (*grać na trąbce*) to blow the trumpet; (*używać klaksonu*) to blow *lub* sound the horn
**trąb|ka** (**-ki, -ki**) (*dat sg* **-ce**, *gen pl* **-ek**) *f* trumpet
**trąc|ać (-am, -asz)** (*imp* **-aj**, *perf* **trącić**) *vt* (*łokciem*) to nudge; (*strunę*) to strike
**trą|cić (-cę, -cisz)** (*imp* **-ć**) *vb perf od* **trącać** ▷ *vi*: **~ czymś** to smack of sth
**trą|d** (**-du**) (*loc sg* **-dzie**) *m* leprosy
**trądzi|k** (**-ku, -ki**) (*instr sg* **-kiem**) *m* acne
**trefl** (**-a, -e**) (*gen pl* **-i**) *m* clubs (*pl*); **dama ~** queen of clubs
**trefny** *adj* (*pot: towar*) hot (*pot*); (*niekoszerny*) tref
**trel** (**-u, -e**) (*gen pl* **-i** *lub* **-ów**) *m* (*słowika*) trill; **~e-morele** (*pot*) tittle-tattle (*pot*)
**tre|ma** (**-my**) (*dat sg* **-mie**) *f* stage fright
**tre|n** (**-nu, -ny**) (*loc sg* **-nie**) *m* (*sukni*) train; (*Lit*) threnody
**trencz** (**-a, -e**) (*gen pl* **-y** *lub* **-ów**) *m* trench coat
**tren|d** (**-du, -dy**) (*loc sg* **-dzie**) *m* trend
**trene|r** (**-ra, -rzy**) (*loc sg* **-rze**) *m* coach, trainer
**trenin|g** (**-gu, -gi**) (*instr sg* **-giem**) *m* training, practice (*Brit*), practise (*US*)
**treningowy** *adj* training *attr*; **rower ~** exercise bike
**tren|ować (-uję, -ujesz)** *vt* (*zawodników*) (*perf* **wy-**) to train, to coach; **on trenuje boks** he's a boxer; **w tej chwili trenuje w sali gimnastycznej** he's practising (*Brit*) *lub* practicing (*US*) in the gym now
**trepanacj|a** (**-i, -e**) (*dat sg* **-i**) *f* (*Med*) trepan(ation)
**trese|r** (**-ra, -rzy**) (*loc sg* **-rze**) *m* trainer
**treser|ka** (**-ki, -ki**) (*dat sg* **-ce**, *gen pl* **-ek**) *f* trainer
**tres|ować (-uję, -ujesz)** (*perf* **wy-**) *vt* to train
**tresowany** *adj* trained
**treściwy** *adj* (*artykuł*) pithy; (*zupa*) filling
**treś|ć** (**-ci, -ci**) (*gen pl* **-ci**) *f* (*wypowiedzi, artykułu*) content; (*książki*) contents *pl*; (*sens*) essence; **spis treści** (table of) contents
**trezo|r** (**-ra, -ry**) (*loc sg* **-rze**) *m* night safe
**trę** *itd. vb patrz* **trzeć**
**trębacz** (**-a, -e**) (*gen pl* **-y**) *m* trumpeter
**trędowa|ty** (**-tego, -ci**) *m decl like adj* leper
**tri|k** (**-ku, -ki**) (*instr sg* **-kiem**) *m* trick
**tri|o** (**-a, -a**) *nt* (*Muz*) trio
**trium|f** (**-fu, -fy**) (*instr sg* **-fie**) *m* triumph; **święcić ~y** to be successful
**triumfalny** *adj* (*okrzyk, uśmiech*) triumphant; (*marsz, łuk*) triumphal
**triumf|ować (-uję, -ujesz)** (*perf* **za-**) *vi* to triumph; **~ nad kimś** to triumph over sb
**trochę** *adv* a little, a bit; (*niedługo*) (for) a while; **zarobić** (*perf*) **~ pieniędzy** to earn a little money; **jestem ~ zmęczony** I'm a bit *lub* a little tired; **ani ~** not a bit; **musisz ~ poczekać** you'll have to wait a while; **po trochu** bit by bit, little by little
**trocin|y** (**-**) *pl* sawdust
**tro|ć** (**-ci, -cie**) (*gen pl* **-ci**) *f* (*Zool*) salmon trout
**trofe|um** (**-um, -a**) (*gen pl* **-ów**) *nt inv in sg* trophy
**tr|oić się (-oję, -oisz)** (*imp* **-ój**, *perf* **po-**) *vr* to triple; **troi mi się w oczach** I see double; **dwoić się i troić** to go out of one's way
**trojacz|ki** (**-ków**) *pl* triplets *pl*
**trojaki** *adj* threefold
**troje** (*jak*: **dwoje**) *num* three
**trolejbu|s** (**-su, -sy**) (*loc sg* **-sie**) *m* trolley bus
**trolejbusowy** *adj* (*bilet, przystanek*) trolley-bus *attr*
**tro|n** (**-nu, -ny**) (*loc sg* **-nie**) *m* (*fotel*) throne; (*władza królewska*) (the) throne; **następca ~u** heir (to the throne), the Crown Prince
**tro|p** (**-pu, -py**) (*loc sg* **-pie**) *m* tracks *pl*, trail; **być na czyimś ~ie** to be on sb's trail; **być na ~ie kogoś/czegoś** to be on the track of sb/sth; **być na właściwym/fałszywym ~ie** to be on the right/wrong track; **iść (pójść** *perf*) **fałszywym ~em** to go down a blind alley; **zbijać (zbić** *perf*) **kogoś z ~u** to throw sb off (their) balance
**tro|pić (-pię, -pisz)** *vt* to track, to trail
**tropi|k** (**-ku, -ki**) (*instr sg* **-kiem**) *m* (*Geog*) the tropics *pl*; (*nad namiotem*) flysheet
**tropikalny** *adj* (*klimat, choroba*) tropical; **hełm ~** pith helmet
**tros|ka** (**-ki, -ki**) (*dat sg* **-ce**) *f* (*kłopot*) worry, care; (*dbałość*) care, concern; **~ o kogoś** concern for sb; **~ o coś** concern with sth

t

**troskliwie** *adv* with care
**troskliwoś|ć** (**-ci**) *f* care
**troskliwy** *adj* caring, loving
**troszcz|yć się (-ę, -ysz)** *vr*: **troszczyć się o kogoś/coś** (*opiekować się*) to take care of sb/sth; (*martwić się*) to care about sb/sth
**troszkę** *adv dimin od* **trochę**
**trotyl** (**-u**) *m* TNT, trotyl
**trójc|a** (**-y**) *f*: **T~ Święta** the Holy Trinity
**trójdźwię|k** (**-ku, -ki**) (*instr sg* **-kiem**) *m* (*Muz*) triad
**trójfazowy** *adj*: **prąd ~** three-phase current
**trój|ka** (**-ki, -ki**) (*dat sg* **-ce**, *gen pl* **-ek**) *f* three; (*Szkol*) ≈ C; (*pot*: *tramwaj*) the number three; **zrobiliśmy to w trójkę** the three of us did it; **iść ~mi** to go in threes
**trójką|t** (**-ta, -ty**) (*loc sg* **-cie**) *m* triangle; **~ odblaskowy** *lub* **ostrzegawczy** warning triangle; **~ małżeński** the eternal triangle
**trójkątny** *adj* triangular
**trójkołowy** *adj*: **pojazd ~** three-wheeler; **rower ~** tricycle
**Trójmi|asto** (**-asta**) (*loc sg* **-eście**) *nt collective noun for the cities of Gdańsk, Sopot and Gdynia*
**trójni|k** (**-ka, -ki**) (*instr sg* **-kiem**) *m* (*Elektr*) (three-way) adapter
**trójn|óg** (**-ogu, -ogi**) (*instr sg* **-ogiem**) *m* tripod
**trójsko|k** (**-ku, -ki**) (*instr sg* **-kiem**) *m* triple jump
**trójstronny** *adj* tripartite
**trójwymiarowy** *adj* three-dimensional
**trójz|ąb** (**-ębu, -ęby**) (*loc sg* **-ębie**) *m* trident
**truchle|ć (-ję, -jesz)** (*perf* **s-**) *vi* to be terrified
**truch|t** (**-tu**) (*loc sg* **-cie**) *m* trot; **biec ~em** to trot
**truciciel** (**-a, -e**) (*gen pl* **-i**) *m* poisoner
**truci|zna** (**-zny, -zny**) (*dat sg* **-źnie**) *f* poison
**tru|ć (-ję, -jesz)** *vt* to give poison to ▷ *vi* (*pot*) to prattle (*pot*); **truć się** *vr* to take poison
**tru|d** (**-du, -dy**) (*loc sg* **-dzie**) *m* (*życiowy*) hardship; (*trudność*) difficulty; **z ~em** with difficulty; **zadawać (zadać** *perf*) **sobie ~ czegoś** to take pains to do sth
**trud|nić się (-nię, -nisz)** (*imp* **-nij**) *vr*: **trudnić się czymś** to do sth for a living; **on trudni się przemytem** he is into smuggling; **trudni się handlem** he is in trade
**trudno** *adv*: **~ powiedzieć** it's hard to tell; **(mówi się) ~** tough luck; **~ o dobrego hydraulika** a good plumber is hard to find; **~ mi uwierzyć, że...** I find it hard to believe that...
**trudnoś|ć** (**-ci, -ci**) (*gen pl* **-ci**) *f* difficulty; **mieć trudności z czymś** to have difficulty with sth; **mieć trudności ze zrobieniem czegoś** to have difficulty (in) doing sth; **robić komuś trudności** to cause difficulties for sb; **oddychać z trudnością/bez trudności** to breathe with/without difficulty
**trudny** *adj* difficult; **~ do zrozumienia** difficult to understand
**tru|dzić (-dzę, -dzisz)** (*imp* **-dź**) *vt* to bother, to trouble; **trudzić się** *vr* (*ciężko pracować*) to toil; **nie trudź się!** don't bother!
**trufl|a** (**-i, -e**) (*gen pl* **-i**) *f* truffle
**truiz|m** (**-mu, -my**) (*loc sg* **-mie**) *m* truism
**trujący** *adj* poisonous, toxic
**tru|mna** (**-mny, -mny**) (*dat sg* **-mnie**, *gen pl* **-mien**) *f* coffin, casket (US)
**trun|ek** (**-ku, -ki**) (*instr sg* **-kiem**) *m* alcoholic beverage
**tru|p** (**-pa, -py**) (*loc sg* **-pie**) *m* dead body, corpse; **paść** (*perf*) **~em** to drop (down) dead; **kłaść (położyć** *perf*) **kogoś ~em** to kill sb stone-dead; **po moim ~ie!** over my dead body!
**tru|pa** (**-py, -py**) (*dat sg* **-pie**) *f* troupe
**trupi** *adj* (*zapach*) putrid; (*cera*) deadly pale; **~a główka** skull
**truskaw|ka** (**-ki, -ki**) (*dat sg* **-ce**, *gen pl* **-ek**) *f* strawberry
**truskawkowy** *adj* strawberry *attr*; **o smaku ~m** strawberry-flavoured (Brit), strawberry-flavored (US)
**tru|st** (**-stu, -sty**) (*loc sg* **-ście**) *m* trust
**trut|eń** (**-nia, -nie**) (*gen pl* **-ni**) *m* drone
**trut|ka** (**-ki, -ki**) (*dat sg* **-ce**, *gen pl* **-ek**) *f* poison; **~ na szczury** rat poison
**trw|ać (-am, -asz)** *vt*: **~ godzinę/tydzień** to last (for) an hour/a week ▷ *vi* to last; (*o rozmowie, wymianie*) to go on; (*nie ulegać*) (*perf* **wy-**) to persist; **~ w bezruchu** to stay still; **~ w milczeniu** to keep *lub* stay silent; **~ przy swoim zdaniu** to stick to one's opinion
**trwał|a** (**-ej, -e**) *f decl like adj* (*pot*: *też*: **trwała ondulacja**) perm
**trwałoś|ć** (**-ci**) *f* durability
**trwały** *adj* (*produkt*) durable; (*pokój, uczucie*) lasting; **trwała ondulacja** perm
**trwani|e** (**-a**) *nt* duration
**trw|oga** (**-ogi, -ogi**) (*dat sg* **-odze**, *gen pl* **-óg**) *f* fear; **drżeć z trwogi** to shake with fear
**trwo|nić (-nię, -nisz)** (*imp* **-ń**) *vt* (*czas, zdolności*) to waste; (*zdrowie*) to ruin; (*pieniądze*) (*perf* **roz-**) to squander, to waste
**trw|ożyć (-ożę, -ożysz)** (*imp* **-óż**, *perf* **za-**) *vt* to frighten, to scare; **trwożyć się** *vr* to get frightened, to get scared
**try|b** (**-bu, -by**) (*loc sg* **-bie**) *m* mode; (*Jęz*) mood; **tryby** *pl* (*Tech*) gears *pl*, cog-wheels *pl*; **prowadzić spokojny ~ życia** to lead a quiet life; **siedzący ~ życia** a sedentary life; **~ postępowania** a course of action

**trybu|na** (**-ny, -ny**) (*dat sg* **-nie**) *f* (*mównica*) rostrum; (*na defiladzie*) parade stand; **trybuny** *pl* (*Sport*) (grand) stand
**trybuna|ł** (**-łu, -ły**) (*loc sg* **-le**) *m* tribunal; **T~ Konstytucyjny** Constitutional Tribunal
**trygonometri|a** (**-i**) *f* trigonometry
**tryko|t** (**-tu, -ty**) (*loc sg* **-cie**) *m* (*materiał*) tricot; (*strój gimnastyczny*) leotard
**trykotowy** *adj* tricot *attr*
**tryl** (**-u, -e**) (*gen pl* **-i** *lub* **-ów**) *m* (*Muz*) trill
**trylogi|a** (**-i, -e**) (*dat sg* **-i**) *f* trilogy
**trymest|r** (**-ru, -ry**) (*loc sg* **-rze**) *m* trimester
**Trypoli|s** (**-su**) (*loc sg* **-sie**) *m* Tripoli
**trypty|k** (**-ku, -ki**) (*instr sg* **-kiem**) *m* triptych
**trysk|ać** (**-am, -asz**) (*perf* **trysnąć**) *vi* (*o krwi*) to gush; (*o fontannie*) to spout water; **~ energią/zdrowiem** to be bursting with energy/health
**try|snąć** (**-snę, -śniesz**) (*imp* **-śnij**) *vb perf od* **tryskać**
**tryum|f** (**-fu, -fy**) (*loc sg* **-fie**) *m* = **triumf**
**tryumfalny** *adj* = **triumfalny**
**tryumf|ować** (**-uję, -ujesz**) (*perf* **za-**) *vi* = **triumfować**
**trywialny** *adj* (*banalny*) trivial; (*ordynarny*) vulgar
**trzas|k** (**-ku, -ki**) (*instr sg* **-kiem**) *m* (*drzwi*) bang, slam; (*gałęzi*) snap; (*ognia*) crackle; **trzaski** *pl* (*Radio*) static
**trzask|ać** (**-am, -asz**) (*perf* **trzasnąć**) *vt* (*pot: uderzać*) to hit, to smack ▷ *vi* (*o drzwiach*) to bang, to slam; (*o ogniu*) to crackle; **~ drzwiami** to slam the door; **~ pięścią w stół** to bang one's fist on the table; **~ obcasami** to click one's heels
**trza|snąć** (**-snę, -śniesz**) (*imp* **-śnij**) *vb perf od* **trzaskać**
**trz|ąść** (**-ęsę, -ęsiesz**) (*imp* **-ęś** *lub* **-ąś**, *pt* **-ąsł, -ęsła, -ęśli**) *vt/vi* to shake; (*rządzić*) to keep a firm grip on; **trząść się** (*perf* **za-**) *vr* (*o człowieku, ziemi*) to shake, to tremble; (*o głosie, ustach*) to quiver; **~ się ze śmiechu/strachu** to shake with laughter/fear; **~ się z zimna** to shake *lub* shiver with cold
**trzci|na** (**-ny, -ny**) (*dat sg* **-nie**) *f* (*Bot*) reed; (*surowiec*) cane; **~ cukrowa** sugar cane
**trzeba** *part inv* it is necessary to ...; **~ mu pomóc** we should help him, he's got to be helped; **~ było mu pomóc** we should have helped him; **~ przyznać, że ...** admittedly ..., it should be admitted that ...; **jeśli ~** if necessary; **~ ci czegoś?** do you need anything?; **dziękuję, nie ~** no, thanks
**trze|bić** (**-bię, -bisz**) (*perf* **wy-**) *vt* (*las*) to thin out; (*zwierzęta*) to exterminate; (*buhaja, ogiera*) to geld
**trzech** *num gen, loc od* **trzy, trzej, troje**
**trzechsetny** *adj* three-hundredth
**trzeci** *num* third; **jedna ~a** a *lub* one third; **~a potęga** (*Mat*) third power, cube; **kraje ~ego świata** the Third World countries; **po ~e** third(ly); **co ~ dzień** every three days
**trzeciorzę|d** (**-du**) (*loc sg* **-dzie**) *m* (*Geol*) Tertiary
**trzeciorzędny** *adj* third-rate *attr*
**trzeć** (**trę, trzesz**) (*imp* **trzyj**, *pt* **tarł**) *vt* (*czoło, powieki*) (*perf* **po-**) to rub; (*marchew, ziemniaki*) (*perf* **ze-**) to grate
**trzej** *pron* three
**trzepacz|ka** (**-ki, -ki**) (*dat sg* **-ce**, *gen pl* **-ek**) *f* (*do dywanów*) carpet beater; (*do ubijania jajek*) egg beater, whisk
**trze|pać** (**-pię, -piesz**) *vt* (*chodnik, dywan*) (*perf* **wy-**) to beat ▷ *vi*: **~ ogonem/skrzydłami** to beat one's tail/wings
**trzep|nąć** (**-nę, -niesz**) (*imp* **-nij**) *vb perf od* **trzepać**; **trzepnąć się** *vr perf* (*pot*) to hit o.s.
**trzepo|tać** (**-czę, -czesz**) *vi* to flutter; **trzepotać się** *vr* to flutter
**trzeszcz|eć** (**-ę, -ysz**) *vi* to creak; **~ w szwach** (*o marynarce, spódnicy*) to burst at the seams; (*o sali*) to be bursting with people
**trzewi|a** (**-**) *pl* intestines *pl*, guts *pl*
**trzeź|wić** (**-wię, -wisz**) *vt* to bring round, to sober up
**trzeźwie|ć** (**-ję, -jesz**) (*perf* **wy-**) *vi* to come round, to sober (up)
**trzeźwo** *adv* soberly
**trzeźwoś|ć** (**-ci**) *f* sobriety; **badanie trzeźwości** breathalyzing
**trzeźwy** *adj* sober
**trzęsawis|ko** (**-ka, -ka**) (*instr sg* **-kiem**) *nt* swamp
**trzęsie|nie** (**-nia, -nia**) (*gen pl* **-ń**) *nt*: **~ ziemi** earthquake
**trzmiel** (**-a, -e**) (*gen pl* **-i**) *m* bumblebee
**trz|oda** (**-ody**) (*dat sg* **-odzie**) *f*: **~ chlewna** swine *pl*, pigs *pl*
**trzo|n** (**-nu, -ny**) (*loc sg* **-nie**) *m* core, nucleus; (*organizacji*) hard core; (*grzyba*) stem
**trzon|ek** (**-ka, -ki**) (*instr sg* **-kiem**) *m* handle
**trzonowy** *adj*: **ząb ~** molar (tooth)
**trzust|ka** (**-ki, -ki**) (*dat sg* **-ce**, *gen pl* **-ek**) *f* (*Anat*) pancreas
**trzy** *num* three; **do trzech razy sztuka** third time lucky; **pleść ~ po ~** to talk nonsense
**trzyczęściowy** *adj* three-piece
**trzydziest|ka** (**-ki, -ki**) (*dat sg* **-ce**, *gen pl* **-ek**) *f* thirty; **ona jest po trzydziestce** she's in her thirties
**trzydziestoletni** *adj* (*okres*) thirty-year *attr*; (*osoba*) thirty-year-old
**trzydziesty** *num* thirtieth; **~ pierwszy** thirty-first

t

**trzydzieści** (*jak*: **dwadzieścia**) *num* thirty
**trzykrot|ka** (**-ki, -ki**) (*dat sg* **-ce**, *gen pl* **-ek**) *f* spiderwort
**trzykrotnie** *adv* (*wzrosnąć*) threefold; (*próbować*) three times
**trzyletni** *adj* (*okres*) three-year *attr*; (*dziecko*) three-year-old
**trzym|ać (-am, -asz)** *vt* (*w rękach*) to hold; (*jedzenie, zwierzęta, więźnia*) to keep ▷ *vi* (*o kleju, szwach*) to hold; **~ ręce w kieszeniach** to have one's hands in one's pockets; **~ kogoś w niepewności/napięciu** to keep sb in suspense; **~ coś (przed kimś) w sekrecie** to keep sth secret (from sb); **trzymam cię za słowo** I will hold you to your promise; **~ kogoś krótko** to keep a tight rein on sb; **~ język za zębami** (*przen*) to keep one's tongue (between one's teeth); **~ rękę na pulsie** (*przen*) to have *lub* keep one's finger on the pulse (*przen*); **~ z kimś** to join up with sb; **trzymać się** *vr*: **~ się** *+gen* (*poręczy, gałęzi*) to hold on to; (*drogi, szlaku*) to follow; (*przepisów, reguł*) to keep to, to stick to; **~ się za głowę** to hold one's head; **~ się razem** to stick together; **~ się kogoś** (*przen*) to keep with sb, to stick with sb; **trzymaj się!** take care!; **~ się prosto** to hold o.s. erect; **~ się z boku** to keep to o.s.; **~ się z dala od kogoś/czegoś** to stay away from sb/sth, to keep *lub* stay clear of sb/sth; **dobrze się ~** to be in good shape; **to się nie trzyma kupy** (*pot*) this doesn't hang together
**trzynasty** *num* thirteenth
**trzynaście** (*jak*: **jedenaście**) *num* thirteen
**trzysta** (*jak*: **dwadzieścia**) *num* three hundred
**tu** *adv* here; **tu (mówi) Nowak** this is Nowak (speaking); **tu i tam** here and there
**tu|ba** (**-by, -by**) (*dat sg* **-bie**) *f* (*kremu, pasty*) tube; (*do wzmacniania głosu*) loudhailer (Brit), bullhorn (US); (*Muz*) tuba
**tub|ka** (**-ki, -ki**) (*dat sg* **-ce**, *gen pl* **-ek**) *f* tube
**tubylczy** *adj* native
**tubyl|ec** (**-ca, -cy**) (*gen pl* **-ców**) *m* native
**tucz|yć (-ę, -ysz)** (*perf* **u-**) *vt* to fatten ▷ *vi* (*o pokarmach*) to be fattening
**tu|ja** (**-i, -je**) (*gen pl* **-i**) *f* (*Bot*) thuja
**tule|ja** (**-i, -je**) (*gen pl* **-i**) *f* (*Tech*) sleeve
**tulej|ka** (**-ki, -ki**) (*dat sg* **-ce**, *gen pl* **-ek**) *f dimin od* **tuleja**
**tul|ić (-ę, -isz)** *vt* (*obejmować*) to hug, to cuddle; **tulić się** *vr*: **~ się do kogoś/czegoś** (*perf* **przy-**) to nestle *lub* snuggle up to sb/sth
**tulipa|n** (**-na, -ny**) (*loc sg* **-nie**) *m* tulip
**tułacz** (**-a, -e**) (*gen pl* **-y**) *m* wanderer, drifter
**tułacz|ka** (**-ki, -ki**) (*dat sg* **-ce**, *gen pl* **-ek**) *f* wandering
**tuł|ać się (-am, -asz)** *vr* to wander, to drift
**tuł|ów** (**-owia, -owie**) (*gen pl* **-owi**) *m* trunk
**tuma|n** (**-nu, -ny**) (*loc sg* **-nie**) *m* (*kurzu*) cloud; (*pot*) (*gen sg* **-na**) twerp (*pot*), wally (*pot*) (Brit)
**tumul|t** (**-tu, -ty**) (*loc sg* **-cie**) *m* tumult
**tund|ra** (**-ry, -ry**) (*dat sg* **-rze**) *f* tundra
**tunel** (**-u, -e**) (*gen pl* **-i** *lub* **-ów**) *m* tunnel; **~ aerodynamiczny** wind tunnel; **~ foliowy** plastic tunnel
**tune|r** (**-ra, -ry**) (*loc sg* **-rze**) *m* tuner
**Tunezj|a** (**-i**) *f* Tunisia
**tunezyjski** *adj* Tunisian
**tuni|ka** (**-ki, -ki**) (*dat sg* **-ce**) *f* tunic
**tuńczy|k** (**-ka, -ki**) (*instr sg* **-kiem**) *m* tuna (fish)
**tu|pać (-pię, -piesz)** (*perf* **tupnąć**) *vi*: **~ (nogami)** to stamp one's feet
**tupeci|k** (**-ku, -ki**) (*instr sg* **-kiem**) *m* toupée
**tupe|t** (**-tu**) (*loc sg* **-cie**) *m* impudence, cheek; **mieć ~** to have a nerve
**tup|nąć (-nę, -niesz)** (*imp* **-nij**) *vb perf od* **tupać**
**tupo|t** (**-tu**) (*loc sg* **-cie**) *m* patter (*of feet*)
**tu|r** (**-ra, -ry**) (*loc sg* **-rze**) *m* (*Zool*) aurochs
**tu|ra** (**-ry, -ry**) (*dat sg* **-rze**) *f* round; **druga ~** run-off
**turba|n** (**-nu, -ny**) (*loc sg* **-nie**) *m* turban
**turbi|na** (**-ny, -ny**) (*dat sg* **-nie**) *f* turbine
**turboodrzutowy** *adj*: **samolot/silnik ~** turbojet
**turbośmigłowy** *adj* (*Lot*): **samolot/silnik ~** turboprop
**turbulencj|a** (**-i, -e**) (*dat sg* **-i**) *f* turbulence
**Turcj|a** (**-i**) *f* Turkey
**Turczyn|ka** (**-ki, -ki**) (*dat sg* **-ce**, *gen pl* **-ek**) *f* Turk
**turecki** *adj* Turkish ▷ *m* (*język*) Turkish; **kawa po turecku** Turkish coffee; **siedzieć po turecku** to sit cross-legged
**Tur|ek** (**-ka, -cy**) (*instr sg* **-kiem**) *m* Turk
**turko|t** (**-tu**) (*loc sg* **-cie**) *m* rattle
**turko|tać (-cze)** *vi* to rattle
**turku|s** (**-su** *lub* **-sa, -sy**) (*loc sg* **-sie**) *m* turquoise
**turkusowy** *adj* turquoise (blue)
**tur|nia** (**-ni, -nie**) (*gen pl* **-ni**) *f* crag
**turniej** (**-u, -e**) *m* tournament
**turnu|s** (**-su, -sy**) (*loc sg* **-sie**) *m* period
**Tury|n** (**-nu**) (*loc sg* **-nie**) *m* Turin
**tury|sta** (**-sty, -ści**) (*dat sg* **-ście**) *m decl like f in sg* tourist; **~ pieszy** backpacker, hiker; **~ zmotoryzowany** motoring tourist
**turystyczny** *adj* tourist *attr*; **biuro turystyczne** tourist (information) office; **klasa turystyczna** tourist *lub* economy class
**turysty|ka** (**-ki**) (*dat sg* **-ce**) *f* tourism; **~ górska** climbing; **~ piesza** hiking; **~ rowerowa** cycling

**tusz**[1] (**-u, -e**) *m* Indian ink; **~ do rzęs** mascara
**tusz**[2] (**-u, -e**) *m* (*Muz*) flourish
**tusz|a** (**-y**) *f* (*otyłość*) fatness; (*ubite zwierzę*) (*nom pl* **-e**) carcass, carcase (*Brit*)
**tusz|ować (-uję, -ujesz)** (*perf* **za-**) *vt* to gloss over
**tutaj** *adv* here
**tutejszy** *adj* local
**tuzi|n** (**-na, -ny**) (*loc sg* **-nie**) *m* dozen
**tuzinkowy** *adj* common, ordinary
**tuż** *adv* (*w przestrzeni*) close by, nearby; (*w czasie*) close on, just; **tuż obok kogoś/czegoś** right next to sb/sth; **tuż przed/po czymś** right before/after sth; **tuż za rogiem** just round the corner; **tuż, tuż** (*w przestrzeni*) close by; (*w czasie*) close on
**TVP** *abbr* (= *Telewizja Polska*) Polish Television
**twardnie|ć (-ję, -jesz)** (*perf* **s-**) *vi* to harden
**twardo** *adv* (*domagać się*) firmly; (*powiedzieć coś, spojrzeć*) sternly; (*walczyć*) hard; (*wychowywać*) strictly; **spać ~** to be fast *lub* sound asleep; **jajko na ~** hard-boiled egg
**twardoś|ć** (**-ci**) (*dat sg* **-ci**) *f* (*materiału*) hardness; (*przen: postępowania, człowieka*) toughness
**twardy** *adj* (*krzesło*) hard; (*mięso*) tough; (*zasady*) rigid, firm; (*zahartowany*) hardened, toughened; (*przen: spojrzenie*) stern; **~ facet** tough fellow *lub* guy; **~ sen** sound sleep; **mieć ~ orzech do zgryzienia** to have a hard *lub* tough nut to crack
**twardziel** (**-a, -e**) (*gen pl* **-i**) *m* (*pot*) tough guy (*pot*)
**twaroż|ek** (**-ku, -ki**) (*instr sg* **-kiem**) *m dimin od* **twaróg**
**twar|óg** (**-ogu, -ogi**) (*instr sg* **-ogiem**) *m* cottage cheese
**twarz** (**-y, -e**) (*gen pl* **-y**) *f* face; **być zwróconym ~ą do kogoś/czegoś** to face sb/sth; **jest ci w tym do ~y** it suits you; **nie jest ci w tym do ~y** it doesn't flatter you, it doesn't suit you; **stanąć** (*perf*) **z kimś/czymś ~ą w ~** to stand face to face with sb/sth; **stracić** (*perf*)**/zachować** (*perf*) **~** (*przen*) to lose/save face; **z kamienną ~ą** straight- *lub* poker-faced; **wyraz ~y** (facial) expression
**twarzowy** *adj* (*fryzura, kapelusz*) becoming, flattering; (*nerw*) facial
**twee|d** (**-du, -dy**) (*loc sg* **-dzie**) *m* tweed
**twee|t** (**-tu, -ty**) (*loc sg* **-cie**) *m* tweet
**tweet|ować (-uję, -ujesz)** *vt* to tweet
**twierdz|a** (**-y, -e**) *f* fortress
**twierdzący** *adj* affirmative
**twierdze|nie** (**-nia, -nia**) (*gen pl* **-ń**) *nt* (*zdanie*) statement; (*Mat*) theorem
**twier|dzić (-dzę, -dzisz)** (*imp* **-dź**, *perf* **s-**) *vi* to claim, to say
**twoja** *itd. pron patrz* **twój**
**tworzeni|e** (**-a**) *nt*: **~ (się)** formation
**tworz|yć (-ę, -ysz)** (*imp* **twórz**) *vt* (*świat, podstawy*) (*perf* **s-**) to create; (*oddział, rząd*) (*perf* **u-** *lub* **s-**) to form; (*komponować*) (*perf* **s-**) to produce; (*stanowić*) (*perf* **u-**) to form, to make up; **tworzyli dobraną parę** they made a well suited couple; **tworzyć się** *vr* (*powstawać*) to be formed; (*formować się*) to form
**tworzy|wo** (**-wa, -wa**) (*loc sg* **-wie**) *nt* (*materiał*) material; **~ sztuczne** plastic
**twój** (*jak:* **mój**) *possessive pron* (*przed rzeczownikiem*) your; (*bez rzeczownika*) yours; **czy to są twoje książki?** are these your books?; **czy te książki są twoje?** are these books yours?
**tw|ór** (**-oru, -ory**) (*loc sg* **-orze**) *m* (*wyobraźni, artysty*) creation; (*przyrody*) formation
**twórc|a** (**-y, -y**) *m decl like f in sg* creator; (*artysta*) artist; (*pisarz, autor*) author; (*inicjator, sprawca*) originator; (*organizacji*) founder
**twórczoś|ć** (**-ci**) *f* (*działanie*) creation, production; (*dzieła*) (artistic) works; **~ artystyczna** artistic *lub* creative activity
**twórczy** *adj* (*talent*) creative; (*środowisko, praca*) artistic
**ty** *pron* you; **być z kimś na** *lub* **per „ty"** to be on first-name terms with sb
**Tybe|t** (**-tu**) (*loc sg* **-cie**) *m* Tibet
**tybetański** *adj* Tibetan
**tych** *pron gen, loc od* **ci, te**
**tycz|ka** (**-ki, -ki**) (*dat sg* **-ce**, *gen pl* **-ek**) *f* pole; **skok o tyczce** pole vault
**tycz|yć się (-y)** *vr*: **tyczyć się kogoś/czegoś** to concern sb/sth; **co się tyczy ...** as regards ...
**tyć (tyję, tyjesz)** (*perf* **u-**) *vi* to get *lub* grow fat, to put on weight
**ty|dzień** (**-godnia, -godnie**) (*gen pl* **-godni**) *m* week; **co ~** every week, weekly; **za ~** in a week('s time); **od jutra za ~** a week from tomorrow, tomorrow week; **w ciągu tygodnia** within a week('s time); **raz/dwa razy w tygodniu** once/twice a week; **~ temu** a week ago; **w przyszłym/zeszłym tygodniu** next/last week; **od trzech tygodni** for the last three weeks; **Wielki T~** Holy Week
**tyfu|s** (**-su**) (*loc sg* **-sie**) *m* typhus
**ty|giel** (**-gla, -gle**) (*gen pl* **-gli**) *m* melting-pot
**tygodni|k** (**-ka, -ki**) (*instr sg* **-kiem**) *m* weekly
**tygodniowo** *adv* weekly
**tygodniowy** *adj* (*pobyt, urlop*) week's *attr*, week-long; (*zarobek*) weekly, week's *attr*
**tygry|s** (**-sa, -sy**) (*loc sg* **-sie**) *m* tiger
**tygrysic|a** (**-y, -e**) (*dat sg* **-y**) *f* tigress
**tyk|ać**[1] **(-am, -asz)** (*perf* **tknąć**) *vt* (*dotykać*) to touch
**tyk|ać**[2] **(-a)** (*perf* **-nąć**) *vi* (*o zegarze*) to tick

**tyk|nąć (-nie)** *vb perf od* **tykać²**

**tyle** (*jak*: **ile**) *pron* (*z rzeczownikiem: ludzi, samochodów, faktów*) so many; (*: mleka, miłości, pieniędzy*) so much; (*bez rzeczownika*) this many, this much; **straciłem ~ czasu** I wasted so much time; **tylu mężczyzn/chłopców** so many men/boys; **mam ~ pieniędzy/ problemów co i ty** I've got as much money/ as many problems as you; **ona ~ przeżyła!** she has been through so much!; **dwa razy ~ piwa/jabłek** twice as much beer/as many apples; **~ mogę dla ciebie zrobić** (*bardzo dużo*) I can do so much for you; (*tylko tyle*) I can do that much for you; **zarobił ~, że starczyło mu do końca życia** he had earned enough to last him till the end of his life; **robię ~, ile to możliwe** I am doing as much as possible; **~ co trzeba** as much/many as necessary; **~ co nic** next to nothing; **jesteś nie ~ kłamcą co durniem** you're not so much a liar as a fool; **~ (tylko) że lepszy** only better

**tylko** *part* only, just; **~ zacznij, ja będę kontynuował** just do begin, and I will take over; **zrobię wszystko, ~ nie to** I will do anything but this; **posłuchaj ~** just listen; **~ nie on!** anybody *lub* anyone but him! ▷ *conj*: **gdyby/jeśli ~** if only; **jak ~** as soon as; **kiedy ~ miałem okazję** whenever I had a chance; **kiedy ~ wstałem, on usiadł** as soon as I stood up, he sat down; **nie ~ ..., ale (również) ...** not only ..., but (also) ...; **~ że ...** only ...

**tylny** *adj* (*wyjście*) back, rear; (*koła, siedzenie*) rear; (*kieszeń*) hip, back; (*łapy*) hind, back; **tylne światło** tail light; **tylna straż** rearguard

**tylu** *pron patrz* **tyle**

**ty|ł (-łu, -ły)** (*loc sg* **-le**) *m* back; (*domu, samochodu*) back, rear; **tyłem do kogoś/ czegoś** with one's back towards sb/sth; **iść tyłem** to walk backwards, to retreat; **jechać tyłem** to drive backwards, to reverse; **założyć** (*perf*) **coś tyłem na przód** to put sth on back to front; **z tyłu** in the back *lub* rear; **zrobić** (*perf*) **krok w tył** *lub* **do tyłu** to step back; **pozostawać w tyle za kimś/czymś** to lag behind sb/sth; **w tył zwrot!** about turn (*Brit*) *lub* face! (*US*); **tyły** *pl* (*Wojsk*) rear

**tył|ek (-ka, -ki)** (*instr sg* **-kiem**) *m* (*pot*) bottom (*pot*)

**tym¹** *pron instr, loc od* **ten, to** ▷ *pron dat od* **ci, te**

**tym²** *part*: **im więcej, tym lepiej** the more, the better; **tym bardziej** all the more; **tym lepiej/ gorzej dla ciebie** all *lub* so much the better/ worse for you; **tym samym** thereby, thus

**tymczasem** *adv* (*w tym samym czasie*) meanwhile, while; (*na razie*) for the meantime ▷ *conj* (*jednak*) yet

**tymczasowo** *adv* temporarily

**tymczasowy** *adj* (*praca, rozwiązanie*) temporary; (*rząd*) interim, provisional; (*rozwiązanie, kontrakt*) provisional

**tymian|ek (-ku, -ki)** (*instr sg* **-kiem**) *m* thyme

**tyn|k (-ku, -ki)** (*instr sg* **-kiem**) *m* plaster

**tynk|ować (-uję, -ujesz)** (*perf* **o-**) *vt* to plaster

**ty|p** (*loc sg* **-pie**, *nom pl* **-py**) *m* (*gen sg* **-pu**) type; (*pej: człowiek*) (*gen sg* **-pa**) character; (*przewidywany zwycięzca*) (*gen sg* **-pu**) bet; **być w czyimś typie** to be sb's type

**typografi|a (-i)** (*dat sg* **-i**) *f* typography

**typ|ować (-uję, -ujesz)** (*perf* **wy-**) *vt* (*na wyścigach*) to put one's money on

**typowy** *adj* (*charakterystyczny*) typical; (*standardowy*) standard; **~ dla kogoś/czegoś** typical of sb/sth

**tyr|ać (-am, -asz)** *vi* (*pot*) to toil (away)

**tyra|n (-na, -ni)** (*loc sg* **-nie**) *m* tyrant

**tyrani|a (-i, -e)** (*dat sg* **-i**, *gen pl* **-i**) *f* tyranny

**tyraniz|ować (-uję, -ujesz)** *vt* to tyrannize

**tys.** *abbr* (*= tysiące*) thou. (*= thousand*)

**tysi|ąc (-ąca, -ące)** (*gen pl* **-ęcy**) *m* thousand; **tysiące** *pl* thousands

**tysiącle|cie (-cia, -cia)** (*gen pl* **-ci**) *nt* millennium

**tysięczny** *num* thousandth

**tyta|n** (*loc sg* **-nie**) *m* (*superman*) (*gen sg* **-na**, *nom pl* **-ni**) titan; (*Chem*) (*gen sg* **-nu**) titanium; **~ pracy** (*przen*) demon for work

**tytoniowy** *adj* (*przemysł, zakłady*) tobacco *attr*; **sklep z wyrobami ~mi** tobacconist's (shop)

**tyto|ń (-niu, -nie)** (*gen pl* **-ni** *lub* **-niów**) *m* tobacco

**tytularny** *adj* titular, nominal

**tytu|ł (-łu, -ły)** (*loc sg* **-le**) *m* title; **otrzymać** (*perf*) **pieniądze ~em czegoś** to receive money by way of sth; **książka pod ~em ...** a book entitled ...; **~ szlachecki** knighthood; **~y sportowe** sporting honours (*Brit*) *lub* honors (*US*); **~ magistra** Master's degree; **~ naukowy/hrabiego/mistrza** academic/ earl's/champion's title; **obrońca ~u** (*Sport*) defending champion; **~ własności** (*Prawo*) title deed

**tytuł|ować (-uję, -ujesz)** *vt* (*nadawać tytuł*) to entitle; (*zwracać się*) to address

**tytułowy** *adj* title *attr*

**tzn.** *abbr* (*= to znaczy*) i.e.

**tzw.** *abbr* (*= tak zwany*) so-called

# Uu

**U, u**[1] *nt inv (litera)* U, u; **U jak Urszula** ≈ U for Uncle

 **SŁOWO KLUCZOWE**

**u**[2] *prep +gen* **1** *(w pobliżu)* at; **stać u drzwi** to stand by the door; **być u władzy** to be in power; **szukać pomocy u kogoś** to seek help from sb
**2** *(część całości)*: **klamka u drzwi** doorhandle; **szyja długa jak u żyrafy** a neck as long as a giraffe's
**3** *(przynależność)*: **zostawić** *(perf)* **wiadomość u kogoś** to leave a message with sb; **u Dickensa** in Dickens; **co u ciebie słychać?** how are things with you?
**4** *(dla określenia miejsca)*: **u Marka** at Mark's (place); **u moich rodziców** at my parents' (place); **u siebie (w domu)** *(pot)* at one's place; **czuć się jak u siebie** to feel at home; **mieszkać u przyjaciół** to stay with friends; **wizyta u dentysty** a visit at the dentist

**uaktual|niać (-niam, -niasz)** *(perf* **-nić***) vt* to update, to bring up to date
**uaktual|nić (-nię, -nisz)** *(imp* **-nij***) vb perf od* **uaktualniać**
**uaktyw|niać (-niam, -niasz)** *(perf* **-nić***) vt* to rouse, to stimulate to action; **uaktywniać się** *vr* to become active
**uaktyw|nić (-nię, -nisz)** *(imp* **-nij***) vb perf od* **uaktywniać**
**uatrakcyj|niać (-niam, -niasz)** *(perf* **-nić***) vt* to make attractive
**uatrakcyj|nić (-nię, -nisz)** *(imp* **-nij***) vb perf od* **uatrakcyjniać**
**UB** *abbr (= Urząd Bezpieczeństwa) (Hist)* secret police
**ubar|wiać (-wiam, -wiasz)** *(perf* **-wić***) vt (historię, relację)* to embroider, to embellish
**ubarwieni|e (-a, -a)** *nt* coloration, colouring *(Brit)*, coloring *(US)*
**uba|w (-wu, -wy)** *(loc sg* **-wie***) m (pot)* great fun, ball *(pot)*
**uba|wić (-wię, -wisz)** *vt perf* to amuse; **ubawić się** *vr* to have fun
**ube|k (-ka, -cy)** *(instr sg* **-kiem***) m (Hist: pej) secret service agent*
**ubezpiecz|ać (-am, -asz)** *(perf* **-yć***) vt (mieszkanie, pracownika)* to insure; *(w czasie walki)* to cover; *(w czasie wspinaczki)* to cover for; **~ coś od kradzieży/pożaru** to insure sth against theft/fire; **być ubezpieczonym na 10 tys. zł** to be insured for 10,000 zloty; **ubezpieczaj mnie!** cover me!; **ubezpieczać się** *vr (ubezpieczać siebie)* to insure o.s.; *(w czasie walki)* to cover one another
**ubezpiecze|nie (-nia, -nia)** *(gen pl* **-ń***) nt* insurance; **~ od kradzieży/na życie** theft/life insurance; **~ międzynarodowe** *(Mot)* green card; **~ społeczne** national insurance *(Brit)*, social security *(US)*; **~ od nieszczęśliwych wypadków** accident insurance; **~ od odpowiedzialności cywilnej** third-party insurance
**ubezpieczyciel (-a, -e)** *(gen pl* **-i***) m* insurer
**ubezwłasnowol|niać (-niam, -niasz)** *(perf* **-nić***) vt (Prawo)* to incapacitate
**ubić (ubiję, ubijesz)** *vb perf od* **ubijać**
**ubie|c (-gnę, -gniesz)** *(imp* **-gnij***) vb perf od* **ubiegać**
**ubieg|ać (-am, -asz)** *(perf* **ubiec** *lub* **ubiegnąć***) vt* to forestall; **on mnie znowu ubiegł** he beat me to it again ▷ *vi (mijać: o czasie, latach)* to go by, to elapse; **ubiegać się** *vr*: **ubiegam się o pracę/wizę** I have applied for a job/visa; **~ się o azyl/wybór** to seek asylum/election; **~ się o prezydenturę** *lub* **urząd Prezydenta** to run for President; **~ się o czyjeś względy** to court sb
**ubiegłoroczny** *adj* last year's
**ubiegły** *adj* past, last; **w ~m roku/miesiącu** last year/month
**ubieg|nąć (-nę, -niesz)** *(imp* **-nij***) vb perf od* **ubiegać**
**ubier|ać (-am, -asz)** *vt (perf* **ubrać***) (dziecko, osobę)* to dress; *(płaszcz, spodnie)* to put on; *(choinkę, tort)* to decorate; **ubierać się** *vr (perf* **ubrać***) (wkładać ubranie)* to get dressed; **ładnie się ~** to dress well

**ubij|ać (-am, -asz)** (*perf* **ubić**) *vt* (*śmietanę*) to whip; (*jajko, białko*) to whisk, to beat; (*masło*) to churn; (*pot: zabijać*) to slay; **~ (ubić** *perf*) **interes** (*pot*) to strike a deal
**ubikacj|a (-i, -e)** (*dat sg* **-i**) *f* toilet
**ubiorę** *itd. vb patrz* **ubrać**
**ubi|ór (-oru, -ory)** (*loc sg* **-orze**) *m* clothing, dress
**ubliż|ać (-am, -asz)** (*perf* **-yć**) *vi*: **~ komuś** to insult sb; **~ czemuś** to offend sth
**ubłag|ać (-am, -asz)** *vt perf*: **~ kogoś, aby coś zrobił** to beg sb into doing sth
**ubocz|e (-a)** *nt*: **na uboczu** out of the way; **trzymać się na uboczu** to keep o.s. in the background
**uboczny** *adj*: **efekt ~** side effect; **produkt ~** by-product
**ubogi** *adj* poor
**ubolew|ać (-am, -asz)** *vi* to grieve, to lament; **~ nad czymś** (*żałować*) to lament sth; (*potępiać*) to deplore sth; **~ nad kimś** to feel sorry for sb, to deplore sb
**ubolewa|nie (-nia)** *nt* regret, sorrow; **wyrażać (wyrazić** *perf*) **~ z powodu ...** to express sorrow at ...; **godny ubolewania** deplorable; **wyrazy ubolewania** condolences
**uboż|eć (-eję, -ejesz)** (*perf* **z-**) *vi* to become impoverished
**ub|ój (-oju, -oje)** *m* slaughter
**ubóstwi|ać (-am, -asz)** *vt* (*uwielbiać*) to adore; (*uważać za bóstwo*) to idolize
**ubóst|wo (-wa)** (*loc sg* **-wie**) *nt* poverty
**ub|óść (-odę, -odziesz)** (*imp* **-ódź**, *pt* **-ódł, -odła, -odli**) *vb perf od* **bóść** ▷ *vt perf* (*przen: dotknąć, obrazić*) to hurt deeply
**ubrać (ubiorę, ubierzesz)** (*imp* **ubierz**) *vb perf od* **ubierać**
**ubra|nie (-nia, -nia)** (*gen pl* **-ń**) *nt* (*ubiór*) clothing; (*garnitur*) suit; **~ ochronne** protective clothing
**ubrany** *adj* dressed; **być ~m w** *+acc* to wear ..., to be dressed in ...
**ubru|dzić (-dzę, -dzisz)** (*imp* **-dź**) *vb perf od* **brudzić**
**ub|yć (-ędzie)** *vb perf od* **ubywać**
**ubyt|ek (-ku, -ki)** (*instr sg* **-kiem**) *m* (*krwi, paliwa*) loss; (*w zębie*) cavity
**ubyw|ać (-a)** (*perf* **ubyć**) *vi* (*odchodzić*) to go away; (*znikać*) to disappear; **ubywa wody** there is less and less water; **ubywa pracowników** there are fewer and fewer workers; **ubyło trzech** three are gone; **ubywa mi sił** my strength is declining; **ubyło mi na wadze** I (have) lost weight
**ubzdur|ać (-am, -asz)** *vt perf* (*pot*): **~ coś sobie** to get sth into one's head (*pot*)
**ucał|ować (-uję, -ujesz)** *vt perf* to kiss
**ucho**[1] **(ucha, uszy)** (*gen pl* **uszu**, *dat pl* **uszom**, *instr pl* **uszami**, *loc pl* **uszach**) *nt* ear; **nadstawiać (nadstawić** *perf*) **uszu** to prick up one's ears; **mieć czegoś/kogoś powyżej uszu** (*pot*) to be fed up with sth/sb (*pot*); **być po uszy w długach** to be up to one's ears in debt; **śmiać się/ziewać od ucha do ucha** to grin/yawn from ear to ear; **natrzeć** (*perf*) **komuś uszu** (*przen*) to give sb a dressing-down; **uszy do góry!** (*pot*) cheer up!; **zakochany po uszy** head over heels in love
**uch|o**[2] **(-a, -a)** *nt* (*garnka, kubka*) handle; (*igły*) eye
**ucho|dzić (-dzę, -dzisz)** (*imp* **-dź**, *perf* **ujść**) *vi* (*o dymie, gazie*) to escape; **~ za kogoś** to pass as sb; **~ czyjejś uwadze** to escape sb's attention; **coś komuś uchodzi bezkarnie** sb gets away with sth
**uchodźc|a (-y, -y)** *m decl like f in sg* refugee
**uchodźst|wo (-wa)** (*loc sg* **-wie**) *nt*: **na uchodźstwie** (*książk*) in exile
**uchow|ać (-am, -asz)** *vt perf* (*zachować*) to preserve; **uchowaj Boże!** God forbid!; **uchować się** *vr perf* (*przetrwać*) to survive, to stay alive; (*nie ulec zniszczeniu*) to stay untouched
**uchro|nić (-nię, -nisz)** (*imp* **-ń**) *vt perf* to save, to preserve; **~ kogoś przed czymś** to preserve sb from sth; **~ kogoś przed śmiercią** to preserve sb's life; **uchronić się** *vr* to protect o.s.
**uchwal|ać (-am, -asz)** (*perf* **-ić**) *vt* to pass
**uchwa|ła (-ły, -ły)** (*loc sg* **-le**) *f* resolution
**uchwy|cić (-cę, -cisz)** (*imp* **-ć**) *vt perf* (*ramię, władzę, sposobność*) to seize; (*myśl, intencję*) to grasp; (*podobieństwo, nastrój*) to capture; **uchwycić się** *vr*: **~ się czegoś** *lub* **za coś** to get hold of sth; **~ się nadziei/myśli** to cling to a hope/thought
**uchwy|t (-tu, -ty)** (*loc sg* **-cie**) *m* handle
**uchwytny** *adj* (*różnica, zmiana*) noticeable, perceptible; (*pot: człowiek*) reachable
**uchybie|nie (-nia, -nia)** (*gen pl* **-ń**) *nt* (*błąd*) inadvertence; (*niewłaściwy czyn*) transgression
**uchyl|ać (-am, -asz)** (*perf* **-ić**) *vt* (*Prawo: ustawę*) to repeal; (*: sprzeciw, decyzję*) to overrule; (*: wyrok*) to quash; **~ drzwi** to open the door a crack; **~ firankę** to pull the curtain a little to one side; **~ kapelusza** to raise one's hat; **uchylić rąbka tajemnicy** to lift the veil of secrecy; **uchylać się** *vr* (*o drzwiach, oknie*) to open a little; (*o człowieku*) to dodge; **~ się od odpowiedzialności** to evade responsibility
**uchylani|e się (-a)** *nt* evasion; **~ od podatków** tax evasion
**uciąć (utnę, utniesz)** (*imp* **utnij**, *pt* **uciął, ucięła, ucięli**) *vb perf od* **ucinać**

**uciążliwy** *adj* (*obowiązki, zadanie*) burdensome, onerous; (*człowiek, hałas*) bothersome, troublesome
**ucich|nąć (-nę, -niesz)** (*imp* **-nij**) *vb perf od* **cichnąć**
**ucie|c (-knę, -kniesz)** (*imp* **-knij**, *pt* **-kł**) *vb perf od* **uciekać**
**ucie|cha** (**-chy**) (*dat sg* **-sze**) *f* (*radość*) delight, joy; (*przyjemność*) (*nom pl* **-chy**) joy, pleasure; **ku czyjejś uciesze** to sb's delight
**uciecz|ka** (**-ki, -ki**) (*dat sg* **-ce**, *gen pl* **-ek**) *f* escape
**uciek|ać (-am, -asz)** (*perf* **uciec**) *vi* to run away, to escape; (*o czasie*) to fly; **~ od kogoś/czegoś** *lub* **przed kimś/czymś** to run away *lub* escape from sb/sth; **uciekł mi autobus** I missed my bus; **uciekać się** *vr*: **~ się do czegoś** to resort to sth
**uciekinie|r** (**-ra, -rzy**) (*loc sg* **-rze**) *m* runaway, fugitive
**ucieleś|niać (-niam, -niasz)** (*perf* **-nić**) *vt* (*książk*) to incarnate, to embody; **ucieleśniać się** *vr* to materialize
**ucieleśnie|nie** (**-nia**) *nt* incarnation, embodiment
**ucier|ać (-am, -asz)** (*perf* **utrzeć**) *vt* (*ciasto, żółtka*) to mix; (*buraki, marchew*) to grate
**ucier|pieć (-pię, -pisz)** *vi perf* to suffer; **nie ucierpieliśmy na tym** we're none the worse for it
**ucieszny** *adj* droll
**uciesz|yć (-ę, -ysz)** *vb perf od* **cieszyć**
**ucin|ać (-am, -asz)** (*perf* **uciąć**) *vt* (*gałąź, sznurek*) to cut (off); (*dyskusję, rozmowę*) to cut short; (*o owadach*) to sting; **dałbym sobie głowę uciąć, że ...** I would bet my bottom dollar that ...; **uciąć sobie pogawędkę/drzemkę** to have a chat/nap
**ucis|k** (**-ku**) (*instr sg* **-kiem**) *m* (*przyciskanie*) pressure; (*w gardle, piersiach*) constriction; (*polityczny*) oppression
**ucisk|ać (-am, -asz)** (*perf* **ucisnąć**) *vt* (*przyciskać*) to press; (*ograniczać wolność*) to oppress; (*o bucie*) to pinch; (*o pasku*) to squeeze
**uciskowy** *adj*: **opaska uciskowa** tourniquet
**uci|snąć (-snę, -śniesz)** (*imp* **-śnij**) *vb perf od* **uciskać**
**ucisz|ać (-am, -asz)** (*perf* **-yć**) *vt* to silence; **uciszać się** *vr* (*o morzu, wietrze*) to calm down; (*o ludziach*) to fall silent
**uciuł|ać (-am, -asz)** *vb perf od* **ciułać**
**ucz|cić (-czę, -cisz)** (*imp* **-cij**) *vt perf* to celebrate; *patrz też* **czcić**
**uczciwie** *adv* honestly
**uczciwoś|ć** (**-ci**) *f* honesty
**uczciwy** *adj* honest
**uczel|nia** (**-ni, -nie**) (*dat sg* **-ni**, *gen pl* **-ni**) *f* university, college
**uczelniany** *adj* university *attr*, college *attr*
**uczeni|e** (**-a**) *nt* teaching
**uczenie** *adv* learnedly
**uczennic|a** (**-e**) (**-y**) (*dat sg* **-y**) *f* (*w szkole*) schoolgirl, pupil, student (*US*); (*praktykantka*) apprentice
**ucz|eń** (**-nia, -niowie**) (*loc sg* **-niu**) *m* schoolboy, pupil, student (*US*); (*praktykant*) apprentice
**ucze|pić (-pię, -pisz)** *vt perf* to attach; **uczepić się** *vr*: **~ się** *+gen* (*uchwycić się*) to grab (hold of); (*krytykować*) to pick on; (*narzucić swoje towarzystwo*) to hang on; **~ się nadziei/myśli** to cling to hope/an idea
**ucze|sać (-szę, -szesz)** *vb perf od* **czesać**
**uczesa|nie** (**-nia, -nia**) (*gen pl* **-ń**) *nt* hairstyle, hairdo
**uczestnict|wo** (**-wa**) (*loc sg* **-wie**) *nt* participation
**uczestnicz|ka** (**-ki, -ki**) (*dat sg* **-ce**) *f* participant
**uczestnicz|yć (-ę, -ysz)** *vi* to participate
**uczestni|k** (**-ka, -cy**) (*instr sg* **-kiem**) *m* participant
**uczęszcz|ać (-am, -asz)** *vi* (*książk*): **~ do szkoły** to attend school; **~ na kursy/zebrania** to attend courses/meetings
**uczniowski** *adj*: **samorząd ~** student council
**uczony** *adj* learned
**ucz|ony** (**-onego, -eni**) *m decl like adj* scholar; (*w naukach przyrodniczych i ścisłych*) scientist, scholar
**ucz|ta** (**-ty, -ty**) (*dat sg* **-cie**) *f* feast
**uczt|ować (-uję, -ujesz)** *vi* (*książk*) to feast
**uczu|cie** (**-cia, -cia**) (*gen pl* **-ć**) *nt* (*miłość, nienawiść, smutek itp.*) emotion; (*samotności, strachu*) feeling; (*głodu, zimna*) sensation; (*miłość*) affection; **darzyć kogoś ~m** to feel affection for sb
**uczuciowo** *adv* emotionally
**uczuciowy** *adj* emotional
**uczul|ać (-am, -asz)** (*perf* **-ić**) *vt*: **~ kogoś na coś** to raise sb's awareness of sth
**uczule|nie** (**-nia**) *nt*: **~ (na coś)** allergy (to sth); **mieć ~ na coś** to be allergic to sth
**uczuleniowy** *adj* (*reakcja*) allergic
**uczul|ić (-ę, -isz)** *vb perf od* **uczulać**
**uczulony** *adj*: **~ na coś** allergic to sth
**ucz|yć (-ę, -ysz)** (*perf* **na-**) *vt* to teach ▷ *vi* to teach; **~ (kogoś) matematyki/polskiego** to teach (sb) mathematics/Polish; **uczyć się** *vr* to learn, to study; **~ się dobrze/źle** to be a good/bad student; **~ się do egzaminu** to study for an exam
**uczyn|ek** (**-ku, -ki**) (*instr sg* **-kiem**) *m*: **dobry/zły ~** a good/bad deed; **spełnić** (*perf*) **dobry ~** to do *lub* perform a good deed; **złapać** (*perf*)

U

**kogoś na gorącym uczynku** to catch sb red-handed
**uczy|nić (-nię, -nisz)** (*imp* **-ń**) *vb perf od* **czynić**
**uczynnoś|ć** (**-ci**) (*dat sg* **-ci**) *f* obligingness
**uczynny** *adj* obliging
**ud|ać (-am, -asz)** *vb perf od* **udawać**
**udany** *adj* (*taki, który się udał*) successful; (*udawany*) feigned; **spotkanie było udane** the meeting was a success
**uda|r** (**-ru, -ry**) (*loc sg* **-rze**) *m*: **~ cieplny** heat-stroke; **~ słoneczny** sunstroke; **~ mózgu** *lub* **mózgowy** stroke, apoplexy
**udarem|niać (-niam, -niasz)** (*perf* **-nić**) *vt* to foil
**udarem|nić (-nię, -nisz)** (*imp* **-nij**) *vb perf od* **udaremniać**
**udarł** *itd. vb patrz* **udrzeć**
**udarowy** *adj*: **wiertarka udarowa** hammer drill
**udawać (udaję, udajesz)** (*imp* **udawaj**, *perf* **udać**) *vt* (*symulować*) to fake, to pretend; (*naśladować*) to imitate; **~ Greka** to play dumb ▷ *vi*: **udawał, że śpi** he pretended to be asleep, he pretended he was sleeping; **udawała, że mnie nie zna** she pretended not to know me, she pretended (that) she didn't know me; **udawać się** *vr* (*o przyjęciu, wycieczce*) to be a success; (*o owocach, warzywach*) to bear a good crop; (*książk*: *iść, jechać*) to go; **udało mi się go odnaleźć** I managed to find him; **udało nam się** we've been lucky
**udawany** *adj* feigned
**udekor|ować (-uję, -ujesz)** *vb perf od* **dekorować**
**uderz|ać (-am, -asz)** (*perf* **-yć**) *vt*: **~ kogoś (w coś)** to hit sb (in *lub* on sth) ▷ *vi* (*pięścią*) to bang; (*narzędziem*) to hit; **~ (na kogoś/coś)** to strike (at sb/sth); **uderzyło mnie, że ...** it struck me (as strange) that ...; **~ komuś do głowy** (*o krwi*) to rush to sb's head; (*o alkoholu, sukcesie, sławie*) to go to sb's head; **uderzać się** *vr* (*samemu*) to hit o.s.; (*wzajemnie*) to hit one another; **uderzyłem się w łokieć/o biurko** I hit my elbow/the desk
**uderzająco** *adv* strikingly
**uderzający** *adj* striking
**uderze|nie** (**-nia, -nia**) (*gen pl* **-ń**) *nt* (*cios*) blow; (*dźwięk*) bang; (*atak*) strike; **~ serca/tętna** heart/pulse beat
**uderzeniowy** *adj*: **fala uderzeniowa** (*Fiz*) shock wave; **dawka uderzeniowa** (*Med*) loading dose
**uderz|yć (-ę, -ysz)** *vb perf od* **uderzać**
**ud|ko** (**-ka, -ka**) (*instr* **-kiem**) *nt* (*Kulin*) leg
**udła|wić się (-wię, -wisz)** *vr perf* to choke to death

**udo** (**uda, uda**) (*loc sg* **udzie**) *nt* thigh
**udobruch|ać (-am, -asz)** *vt perf* to placate, to mollify; **udobruchać się** *vr* to be placated *lub* mollified
**udogodnie|nie** (**-nia, -nia**) (*gen pl* **-ń**) *nt* convenience, help
**udokument|ować (-uję, -ujesz)** *vt perf* to substantiate
**udoma|wiać (-wiam, -wiasz)** (*perf* **udomowić**) *vt* to domesticate
**udomowiony** *adj* domesticated
**udoskonal|ać (-am, -asz)** (*perf* **-ić**) *vt* to refine, to improve
**udoskonale|nie** (**-nia, -nia**) (*gen pl* **-ń**) *nt* refinement, improvement
**udoskonal|ić (-ę, -isz)** *vb perf od* **udoskonalać**
**udostęp|niać (-niam, -niasz)** (*perf* **-nić**) *vt*: **~ coś komuś** to make sth available to sb
**udostęp|nić (-nię, -nisz)** (*imp* **-nij**) *vb perf od* **udostępniać**
**udowad|niać (-niam, -niasz)** (*perf* **udowodnić**) *vt* to prove
**udowod|nić (-nię, -nisz)** (*imp* **-nij**) *vb perf od* **udowadniać**
**udowy** *adj* (*Anat*): **kość udowa** thighbone, femur; **tętnica udowa** femoral artery
**udręcz|yć (-ę, -ysz)** *vt perf* to torment
**udrę|ka** (**-ki, -ki**) (*dat sg* **-ce**) *f* torment, distress
**udrzeć (udrę, udrzesz)** (*imp* **udrzyj**, *pt* **udarł**) *vb perf od* **udzierać**
**udu|sić (-szę, -sisz)** (*imp* **-ś**) *vb perf od* **dusić** ▷ *vt perf* to strangle
**udusze|nie** (**-nia**) *nt* (*zabójstwo*) strangulation; (*też*: **uduszenie się**) suffocation
**udzia|ł** (**-łu**) (*loc sg* **-le**) *m* participation; (*Fin*) (*nom pl* **-ły**) share; **brać ~ w czymś** to take part in sth; **~ członkowski** member share; **pierwotna wartość ~u** primary value of share; **mieć ~** *lub* **~y w X** to hold shares in X; **przypadło mu w udziale zrobienie tego** (*przen*) it fell to his lot to do it
**udziało|wiec** (**-wca, -wcy**) *m* shareholder
**udzie** *n patrz* **udo**
**udziec** (**udźca, udźce**) *m* (*Kulin*) leg
**udziel|ać (-am, -asz)** (*perf* **-ić**) *vt*: **~ czegoś (komuś)** to give sth (to sb), to give (sb) sth; **~ komuś głosu** to give the floor to sb; **udzielać się** *vr* (*o nastroju, chorobie*) to be infectious; **~ się komuś** to infect sb; **~ się towarzysko** to socialize
**udzier|ać (-am, -asz)** (*perf* **udrzeć**) *vt* to tear off
**udziwniony** *adj* bizarre, outlandish
**udźwi|g** (**-gu**) (*instr sg* **-giem**) *m* (*Tech*) capacity

**udźwig|nąć (-nę, -niesz)** (*imp* **-nij**) *vt perf*: **ledwo mógł to ~** he could barely carry it; **wzięła tyle, ile mogła ~** she took as much as she could carry
**uf|ać (-am, -asz)** (*perf* **za-**) *vi*: **~ komuś/czemuś** to trust sb/sth; **~, że ...** to trust (that) ...; **~ we własne siły** to be self-confident *lub* self-assured
**ufarb|ować (-uję, -ujesz)** *vb perf od* **farbować**
**uff** *excl* phew
**ufnie** *adv* trustingly
**ufnoś|ć** (**-ci**) *f* trust; **z ufnością** trustingly; **pokładać ~ w kimś/czymś** to put one's trust in sb/sth
**ufny** *adj* trusting
**UFO** *nt inv* UFO
**uform|ować (-uję, -ujesz)** *vb perf od* **formować**
**ufund|ować (-uję, -ujesz)** *vb perf od* **fundować**
**Ugan|da** (**-dy**) (*loc sg* **-dzie**) *f* Uganda
**Ugandyjczy|k** (**-ka, -cy**) (*instr sg* **-kiem**) *m* Ugandan
**Ugandyj|ka** (**-ki, -ki**) (*dat sg* **-ce**, *gen pl* **-ek**) *f* Ugandan
**ugandyjski** *adj* Ugandan
**uga|niać się (-niam, -niasz)** *vr* to run around; **uganiać się za kimś/czymś** to chase sb/sth; **uganiać się za sławą** to seek fame; **ugania się za spódniczkami** he's a womanizer
**uga|sić (-szę, -sisz)** (*imp* **-ś**) *vb perf od* **gasić** ▷ *vt perf*: **~ pragnienie** to quench one's thirst
**ugiąć się (ugnę, ugniesz)** (*imp* **ugnij się**) *vb perf od* **uginać się**
**ugin|ać się (-am, -asz)** (*perf* **ugiąć**) *vr* to bend; **uginać się od czegoś** to be laden with sth; **uginać się (ugiąć się** *perf*) **przed kimś/czymś** (*przen*) to bow to sb/sth
**ugłask|ać (-am, -asz)** *vb perf od* **ugłaskiwać**
**ugłas|kiwać (-kuję, -kujesz)** (*perf* **-kać**) *vt*: **~ kogoś** to placate sb
**ugniat|ać (-am, -asz)** *vt*: **te buty mnie ugniatają** these shoes pinch; **karabin ugniatał go w ramię** the gun dug into his shoulder
**ug|oda** (**-ody, -ody**) (*dat sg* **-odzie**, *gen pl* **-ód**) *f* compromise; **zawrzeć** (*perf*) **ugodę** to arrive at *lub* reach a compromise
**ugodowo** *adv*: **był ~ nastawiony** his attitude was conciliatory; **załatwić** (*perf*) **sprawę ~** to settle the matter in a conciliatory manner
**ugodowy** *adj* conciliatory
**ugodzić (ugodzę, ugodzisz)** (*imp* **ugódź**) *vt perf*: **~ kogoś (czymś)** to hit sb (with sth)
**ugo|ścić (-szczę, -ścisz)** (*imp* **-ść**) *vt perf*: **ugościli nas serdecznie** they were very hospitable; **ugościł nas kolacją** he gave us dinner
**ugot|ować (-uję, -ujesz)** *vb perf od* **gotować**
**ug|ór** (**-oru, -ory**) (*loc sg* **-orze**) *m* fallow land
**ugrunt|ować (-uję, -ujesz)** *vb perf od* **ugruntowywać**
**ugruntow|ywać (-uję, -ujesz)** (*perf* **-ać**) *vt* (*pozycję, wpływy*) to establish, to strengthen
**ugrupowa|nie** (**-nia, -nia**) (*gen pl* **-ń**) *nt* (*Pol*) group
**ugry|źć (-zę, -ziesz)** (*imp* **-ź**) *vb perf od* **gryźć**; **co cię ugryzło?** (*przen*) what came over you?; **ugryźć się** *vr*: **~ się w język** (*przen*) to bite it back
**ugrz|ąźć (-eznę, -ęźniesz)** (*imp* **-ęźnij**, *pt* **-ązł, -ęzła, -ęźli**) *vb perf* = **ugrzęznąć**
**ugrzeczniony** *adj* (*sprzedawca, uśmiech*) obsequious; (*list*) overly polite
**ugrz|ęznąć, ugrz|ąźć (-ęznę, -ęźniesz)** (*imp* **-ęźnij**, *pt* **-ązł, -ęzła, -ęźli**) *vb perf od* **grzęznąć**
**uhonor|ować (-uję, -ujesz)** *vt perf* to honour (*Brit*), to honor (*US*)
**uiszcz|ać (-am, -asz)** (*perf* **uiścić**) *vt* (*książk: należność, opłatę*) to pay
**uiścić (uiszczę, uiścisz)** (*imp* **uiść**) *vb perf od* **uiszczać**
**ujad|ać (-a)** *vi* to yap
**ujarz|miać (-miam, -miasz)** (*perf* **-mić**) *vt* (*kraj*) to conquer; (*naród*) to subjugate; (*przen*) to tame
**ujarz|mić (-mię, -misz)** (*imp* **-mij**) *vb perf od* **ujarzmiać**
**ujaw|niać (-niam, -niasz)** (*perf* **-nić**) *vt* (*dane, tajemnicę*) to disclose; **ujawniać się** *vr* (*o osobie*) to come out
**ujaw|nić (-nię, -nisz)** (*imp* **-nij**) *vb perf od* **ujawniać**
**ujawnieni|e** (**-a**) *nt* disclosure
**uj|ąć (-mę, -miesz)** (*imp* **-mij**) *vb perf od* **ujmować**; (*aresztować*) to capture
**ujdę** *itd. vb patrz* **ujść**
**ujechać (ujadę, ujedziesz)** (*imp* **ujedź**) *vt perf* to drive (*a distance*)
**ujednoli|cać (-cam, -casz)** (*perf* **-cić**) *vt* to standardize
**ujedno|licić (-licę, -licisz)** (*imp* **-lić**) *vb perf od* **ujednolicać**
**ujemny** *adj* (*wpływ, wynik, biegun, liczba*) negative; (*temperatura*) sub-zero; **bilans ~** (*Księgowość*) negative *lub* adverse balance
**ujeździć (ujeżdżę, ujeździsz)** (*imp* **ujeźdź**) *vb perf od* **ujeżdżać**
**ujeżdż|ać (-am, -asz)** (*perf* **ujeździć**) *vt* to break in
**ujeżdżal|nia** (**-ni, -nie**) (*gen pl* **-ni**) *f* riding stables *pl*

U

**uję|cie** (**-cia**, **-cia**) (*gen pl* **-ć**) *nt* (*postaci, tematu*) depiction; (*Film*) take
**uj|ma** (**-my**, **-my**) (*loc sg* **-mie**) *f*: **przynosić komuś ujmę** to be a blot on sb's reputation
**ujm|ować** (**-uję**, **-ujesz**) (*perf* **ująć**) *vt* (*brać*) to take; (*formułować*) to express; **ujmowała wszystkich swą uprzejmością** her kindness endeared her to everyone;
**ujmować się** *vr*: ~ **się za głowę** to hold one's head in one's hands; **ujęli się za ręce** they clasped hands; ~ **się za kimś** to plead sb's case
**ujmujący** *adj* winsome, charming
**ujrz|eć** (**-ę**, **-ysz**) (*imp* **-yj**) *vt perf* (*książk*) to see
**ujś|cie** (**-cia**, **-cia**) (*gen pl* **-ć**) *nt* (*rynny*) outlet; (*rzeki*) estuary, mouth; **dać** (*perf*) ~ **czemuś** to give vent to sth
**ujść** (**ujdę**, **ujdziesz**) (*imp* **ujdź**, *pt* **uszedł**, **uszła**, **uszli**) *vb perf od* **uchodzić**
**ukamien|ować** (**-uję**, **-ujesz**) *vt perf* to stone to death
**uka|rać** (**-rzę**, **-rzesz**) *vb perf od* **karać**
**ukart|ować** (**-uję**, **-ujesz**) *vt perf* to plot, to contrive
**uka|zać** (**-żę**, **-żesz**) (*imp* **-ż**) *vb perf od* **ukazywać**
**ukaz|ywać** (**-uję**, **-ujesz**) (*perf* **-ać**) *vt* (*prezentować*) to portray; **ukazywać się** *vr* (*o duchu, słońcu*) to appear; (*o publikacji*) to come out, to appear
**uką|sić** (**-szę**, **-sisz**) (*imp* **-ś**) *vb perf od* **kąsać**
**ukąsze|nie** (**-nia**, **-nia**) (*gen pl* **-ń**) *nt* bite
**UKF** *abbr* (= *ultrakrótkie fale*) ≈ FM (*frequency modulation*)
**ukierunk|ować** (**-uję**, **-ujesz**) *vb perf od* **ukierunkowywać**
**ukierunkow|ywać** (**-uję**, **-ujesz**) (*perf* **-ać**) *vt* (*książk*) to steer, to guide
**ukle|ja** (**-i**, **-je**) *f* (*Zool*) bleak
**uklęk|nąć** (**-nę**, **-niesz**) (*imp* **-nij**) *vb perf od* **klękać**
**ukła|d** (**-du**, **-dy**) (*loc sg* **-dzie**) *m* (*porządek*) arrangement; (*Anat, Tech, Chem*) system; (*umowa*) agreement; (: *Pol*) treaty; ~ **kierowniczy** (*Tech*) steering (mechanism); ~ **graficzny** layout; **U~ Słoneczny** solar system; ~ **scalony** integrated circuit; **prowadzić ~y** to conduct negotiations; **zerwać** (*perf*) **~y** to break off negotiations
**układ|ać** (**-am**, **-asz**) (*perf* **ułożyć**) *vt* (*książki, papiery, bukiet*) to arrange; (*wiersz, melodię*) to compose; (*rannego*) to lay down; ~ **plany** to make plans; ~ **sobie włosy** to have one's hair set *lub* styled; ~ **kogoś do snu** to put sb to bed; **układać się** *vr* (*kłaść się*) to lie down; (*o stosunkach, sprawach*) to shape up well; ~ **się** (**z kimś**) to negotiate *lub* bargain (with sb)
**układan|ka** (**-ki**, **-ki**) (*dat sg* **-ce**, *gen pl* **-ek**) *f* jigsaw (puzzle)
**układny** *adj* polite, courteous
**ukło|n** (**-nu**, **-ny**) (*loc sg* **-nie**) *m* (*głową*) nod; (*głęboki*) bow; **złożyć** (*perf*) ~ to make a bow; **~y dla** ... my compliments to ...
**ukło|nić się** (**-nię**, **-nisz**) (*imp* **-ń**) *vb perf od* **kłaniać się**
**ukłu|cie** (**-cia**, **-cia**) (*gen pl* **-ć**) *nt* (*igły, kolców*) prick; (*owada*) sting
**ukł|uć** (**-uję**, **-ujesz**) *vb perf od* **kłuć**
**ukn|uć** (**-uję**, **-ujesz**) *vb perf od* **knuć**
**ukochan|a** (**-ej**, **-e**) *f decl like adj* beloved, sweetheart
**ukochany** *adj* beloved ▷ *m decl like adj* beloved, sweetheart
**uk|oić** (**-oję**, **-oisz**) (*imp* **-ój**) *vb perf od* **koić**
**ukoje|nie** (**-nia**) *nt* solace; **znaleźć** *perf* ~ **w czymś** to find solace in sth
**ukoły|sać** (**-szę**, **-szesz**) (*imp* **-sz**) *vt perf*: ~ **dziecko do snu** to rock a baby to sleep
**ukończe|nie** (**-nia**) *nt* completion; **być na ukończeniu** to be near *lub* nearing completion
**ukończ|yć** (**-ę**, **-ysz**) *vt perf* to complete, to finish; ~ *perf* **szkołę** to finish school
**ukoron|ować** (**-uję**, **-ujesz**) *vb perf od* **koronować**
**ukoronowa|nie** (**-nia**) *nt* (*koronacja*) crowning; (*szczytowe osiągnięcie*) crowning achievement; **być ~m czegoś** to be the crown of sth
**ukorz|yć się** (**-ę**, **-ysz**) (*imp* **ukorz**) *vb perf od* **korzyć się**
**uko|s** (**-su**, **-sy**) (*loc sg* **-sie**) *m*: **na** ~ at a slant; **patrzeć na kogoś z ~a** (*przen*) to look askance at sb
**ukośnie** *adv* obliquely
**ukośni|k** (**-ka**, **-ki**) (*instr sg* **-kiem**) *m* slash; ~ **wsteczny** backslash
**ukośny** *adj* slanting, oblique
**ukrac|ać** (**-am**, **-asz**) (*perf* **ukrócić**) *vt* to curb
**ukradkiem** *adv* (*spoglądać*) furtively; (*przemykać się*) stealthily
**ukradkowy** *adj* (*spojrzenie*) furtive; (*spotkanie*) clandestine
**Ukrai|na** (**-ny**) (*loc sg* **-nie**) *f* the Ukraine
**Ukrai|niec** (**-ńca**, **-ńcy**) *m* Ukrainian
**Ukrain|ka** (**-ki**, **-ki**) (*dat sg* **-ce**, *gen pl* **-ek**) *f* Ukrainian
**ukraiński** *adj* Ukrainian ▷ *m* (*język*) Ukrainian
**ukra|ść** (**-dnę**, **-dniesz**) (*imp* **-dnij**, *pt* **-dł**) *vb perf od* **kraść**
**ukrę|cić** (**-cę**, **-cisz**) (*imp* **-ć**) *vt perf* (*guzik, gałkę*) to wrench off; (*krem*) to mix; (*powróz*) to plait
**ukr|oić** (**-oję**, **-oisz**) (*imp* **-ój**) *vb perf od* **kroić**

**ukro|p** (**-pu**) (*loc sg* **-pie**) *m* boiling water; **uwijać się jak w ~ie** (*biegając*) to dart around; (*pracując*) to work like crazy
**ukró|cić (-cę, -cisz)** (*imp* **-ć**) *vb perf od* **ukracać**
**ukrusz|yć (-ę, -ysz)** *vt perf* to break off; **ukruszyć się** *vr perf* to break off
**ukryci|e** (**-a, -a**) *nt*: **w ukryciu** in hiding; **z ukrycia** from hiding
**ukry|ć (-ję, -jesz)** *vb perf od* **ukrywać**
**ukryty** *adj* (*cel, myśl, wada*) hidden; (*motyw*) ulterior
**ukryw|ać (-am, -asz)** (*perf* **ukryć**) *vt* (*osobę, przedmiot*) to hide; (*niechęć, rozpacz*) to conceal, to hide; **~ coś przed kimś** to hide sth from sb; **nie ukrywam, że ...** I admit that ...; **ukrył twarz w dłoniach** he buried his face in his hands; **ukrywać się** *vr* (*chować się*) to hide (o.s.); (*przebywać w ukryciu*) to be in hiding; **~ się przed kimś** to hide from sb
**ukrzyż|ować (-uję, -ujesz)** *vt perf* to crucify
**ukrzyżowa|nie** (**-nia**) *nt* crucifixion
**ukształt|ować (-uję, -ujesz)** *vb perf od* **kształtować**
**uku|ć (-ję, -jesz)** *vt perf* (*wyraz, termin*) to coin
**ukwia|ł** (**-ła** *lub* **-łu, -ły**) (*loc sg* **-le**) *m* sea anemone
**ul** (**-a, -e**) (*gen pl* **-i** *lub* **-ów**) *m* (bee)hive
**ul.** *abbr* (= *ulica*) St (= *Street*)
**ul|ać (-eję, -ejesz)** (*imp* **-ej**) *vt perf*: **leży** *lub* **pasuje jak ulał** it fits like a glove
**ulatni|ać się (-am, -asz)** (*perf* **ulotnić**) *vr* (*o gazie*) to leak; (*przen: o złym nastroju*) to vanish, to evaporate; (*pot: o człowieku*) to make o.s. scarce
**ulat|ywać (-uję, -ujesz)** (*perf* **ulecieć**) *vt* (*o balonie*) to fly away; (*: z załogą*) to take off; (*o powietrzu, gazie*) to escape, to leak (out)
**uląc się (ulęknę, ulękniesz)** (*imp* **ulęknij**, *pt* **uląkł, ulękła**) *vi perf* = **ulęknąć się**
**uldze** *n patrz* **ulga**
**ule|c (-gnę, -gniesz)** (*imp* **-gnij**, *pt* **-gł**) *vb perf od* **ulegać**
**ule|cieć (-cę, -cisz)** (*imp* **-ć**) *vb perf od* **ulatywać**; **uleciało mi to z pamięci** it's slipped my mind *lub* memory
**uleczalny** *adj* curable
**ulecz|yć (-ę, -ysz)** *vt perf* (*książk*) to cure
**uleg|ać (-am, -asz)** (*perf* **ulec**) *vi*: **~ czemuś** (*naciskom, przemocy*) to give in *lub* yield to sth; (*pokusie, pragnieniu*) to yield *lub* succumb to sth; **ulec komuś** to be defeated by sb; **~ nastrojom** to be moody; **~ halucynacjom** to have hallucinations; **~ przemianom** to undergo changes; **~ wypadkowi** to meet with an accident; **~ zepsuciu** to go bad; **rana uległa zakażeniu** the wound became infected; **nie ulega wątpliwości, że ...** there's no doubt that ...
**uległoś|ć** (**-ci**) *f* docility, submission; **zmuszać (zmusić** *perf*) **do uległości** to bring into submission
**uległy** *adj* docile, submissive
**ule|pić (-pię, -pisz)** *vb perf od* **lepić**
**ulepsz|ać (-am, -asz)** (*perf* **-yć**) *vt* to improve, to better
**ulepsze|nie** (**-nia, -nia**) (*gen pl* **-ń**) *nt* improvement
**ulepsz|yć (-ę, -ysz)** *vb perf od* **ulepszać**
**ule|wa** (**-wy, -wy**) (*loc sg* **-wie**) *f* downpour, rainstorm
**ulewny** *adj* (*deszcz*) torrential, pouring
**ulęk|nąć się (-nę, -niesz)** (*imp* **-nij**, *pt* **uląkł, -ła, -li**) *vi perf* to take fright
**ul|ga** (**-gi**) (*dat sg* **-dze**) *f* (*uczucie*) relief; (*zniżka*) (*nom pl* **-gi**) concession, allowance; **odetchnąć** (*perf*) **z ulgą** to heave a sigh of relief; **~ podatkowa** tax relief *lub* allowance
**ulgowy** *adj* (*bilet*) reduced, cheap; (*traktowanie*) preferential; **opłata ulgowa** half *lub* reduced fare
**ulic|a** (**-y, -e**) *f* street; **na ulicy** in the street (*Brit*), on the street (*US*); **iść/jechać ulicą** to walk/drive down the street; **przechodzić przez ulicę** to cross the street; **po drugiej stronie ulicy** across the street; **pokój od ulicy** front room; **ślepa ~** cul-de-sac, dead end; **wyrzucić** (*perf*) **kogoś na ulicę** to turn sb out on the street
**ulicz|ka** (**-ki, -ki**) (*dat sg* **-ce**, *gen pl* **-ek**) *f dimin od* **ulica**; **ślepa ~** (*przen*) dead end, blind alley
**uliczny** *adj* street *attr*; **latarnia uliczna** streetlight, streetlamp; **ruch ~** traffic; **korek ~** traffic jam
**ulit|ować się (-uję, -ujesz)** *vr perf*: **ulitować się nad kimś/czymś** to have mercy on sb/sth
**ulok|ować (-uję, -ujesz)** *vb perf od* **lokować**
**ulot|ka** (**-ki, -ki**) (*dat sg* **-ce**, *gen pl* **-ek**) *f* leaflet
**ulot|nić się (-nię, -nisz)** *vb perf od* **ulatniać się**
**ulotny** *adj* (*woń*) faint; (*chwila*) transient, fleeting
**Ulste|r** (**-ru**) (*loc sg* **-rze**) *m* Ulster
**ultimatum** *nt inv* ultimatum; **postawić** (*perf*) **komuś ~** to give sb an ultimatum
**ultradźwię|k** (**-ku, -ki**) (*instr sg* **-kiem**) *m* ultrasound
**ultradźwiękowy** *adj* ultrasonic
**ultrafiole|t** (**-tu**) (*loc sg* **-cie**) *m* ultraviolet
**ultrafioletowy** *adj* ultraviolet
**ultrakrótki** *adj*: **fale ~e** ultra-high frequency waves
**ultrasonogra|f** (**-fu, -fy**) (*loc sg* **-fie**) *m* ultrasound scanner
**ulubienic|a** (**-y, -e**) *f* favourite (*Brit*), favorite (*US*)

U

**ulubie|niec** (**-ńca, -ńcy**) *m* favourite (*Brit*), favorite (*US*)
**ulubiony** *adj* favourite (*Brit*), favorite (*US*)
**ulż|yć (-ę, -ysz)** (*imp* **-yj**) *vi perf*: **~ komuś** to lighten sb's load; **~ czyimś cierpieniom** to ease sb's suffering; **ulżyło mi (na sercu)** what a relief!; **~ sobie** (*pot*) to get it off one's chest
**ułag|odzić (-odzę, -odzisz)** (*imp* **-odź** *lub* **-ódź**) *vt perf* to appease, to placate
**uła|mać (-mię, -miesz)** (*imp* **ułam**) *vb perf od* **łamać, ułamywać**
**ułam|ek** (**-ka, -ki**) (*instr sg* **-kiem**) *m* (*Mat*) fraction; (*część*) fragment (*small part*); **~ zwykły** vulgar fraction; **~ dziesiętny** decimal fraction; **przez ~ sekundy** for a fraction of a second, for a split second
**ułamkowy** *adj* (*liczba*) fractional; (*kreska*) horizontal
**ułam|ywać (-uję, -ujesz)** (*perf* **-ać**) *vt* to break off
**Ułan Bator** *m inv* Ulan Bator
**ułaska|wiać (-wiam, -wiasz)** (*perf* **-wić**) *vt* (*Prawo*) to pardon
**ułaskawie|nie** (**-nia, -nia**) (*gen pl* **-ń**) *nt* (*Prawo*) pardon
**ułat|wiać (-wiam, -wiasz)** (*perf* **-wić**) *vt* to make easier, to facilitate
**ułatwie|nie** (**-nia, -nia**) (*gen pl* **-ń**) *nt* help, convenience; **dla ułatwienia** to make it easier
**ułomnoś|ć** (**-ci**) *f* (*kalectwo*) handicap; (*wada*) (*nom pl* **-ci**, *gen pl* **-ci**) flaw
**ułomny** *adj* (*kaleki*) handicapped; (*niedoskonały*) flawed
**ułoże|nie** (**-nia**) *nt* arrangement
**ułożyć (ułożę, ułożysz)** (*imp* **ułóż**) *vb perf od* **układać**
**ułu|da** (**-dy, -dy**) (*dat sg* **-dzie**) *f* (*książk*) delusion
**umac|niać (-niam, -niasz)** (*perf* **umocnić**) *vt* (*mur, rusztowanie, przewagę*) to reinforce, to strengthen; (*przyjaźń*) to consolidate; (*Wojsk*) to fortify; **~ kogoś w czymś** to strengthen sb in sth; **umacniać się** *vr* to be strengthened; **umocniła się w przekonaniu, że ...** she was strengthened in her conviction that ...
**umal|ować (-uję, -ujesz)** *vt perf* (*twarz*) to make up; (*usta*) to paint; **umalować się** *vr* to make (o.s.) up
**umarł** *itd. vb patrz* **umrzeć**
**umar|ły** (**-łego, -li**) *m decl like adj* the deceased; **umarli** *pl* the dead ▷ *adj* dead
**umart|wiać (-wiam, -wiasz)** (*perf* **-wić**) *vt* (*ciało*) to mortify; **umartwiać się** *vr* to mortify
**umarz|ać (-am, -asz)** (*perf* **umorzyć**) *vt* (*dług, należność*) to write off; (*postępowanie, śledztwo*) to discontinue
**uma|wiać (-wiam, -wiasz)** (*perf* **umówić**) *vt*: **~ kogoś z kimś** to make an appointment for sb with sb; **umawiać się** *vr*: **~ się (z kimś)** to make an appointment (with sb)
**uma|zać (-żę, -żesz)** *vt perf* to smear; **umazać się** *vr perf* to smear o.s.
**umebl|ować (-uję, -ujesz)** *vb perf od* **meblować**
**umeblowani|e** (**-a**) *nt* furnishings *pl*
**umeblowany** *adj* furnished
**umia|r** (**-ru**) (*loc sg* **-rze**) *m* moderation; **z ~em** in moderation; **bez ~u** without moderation
**umiarkowa|nie** (**-nia**) *nt* moderation ▷ *adv* moderately
**umiarkowany** *adj* moderate; (*klimat, strefa*) temperate
**umieć (umiem, umiesz)** *vi*: **~ coś robić** to know how to do sth, to be able to do sth; **~ pisać i czytać** to be literate; **nie umiem pływać/prowadzić samochodu** I can't swim/drive; **~ po polsku** (*pot*) to know Polish
**umiejętnie** *adv* ably, skilfully (*Brit*), skillfully (*US*)
**umiejętnoś|ć** (**-ci, -ci**) (*gen pl* **-ci**) *f* (*zdolność*) ability; (*biegłość*) skill
**umiejętny** *adj* skilful (*Brit*), skillful (*US*)
**umiejsca|wiać (-wiam, -wiasz)** (*perf* **umiejscowić**) *vt* to locate
**umiejsc|owić (-owię, -owisz)** (*imp* **-ów**) *vb perf od* **umiejscawiać**
**umier|ać (-am, -asz)** (*perf* **umrzeć**) *vi* to die; **~ na raka** to die of cancer; **~ z głodu** to die of starvation; **~ z nudów** to be bored stiff *lub* to death; **~ ze strachu** to be frightened to death; **umieraliśmy ze śmiechu** (*pot*) we were laughing our heads off
**umieralnoś|ć** (**-ci**) *f* mortality; **~ niemowląt** infant mortality; **współczynnik umieralności** mortality rate
**umieszcz|ać (-am, -asz)** (*perf* **umieścić**) *vt* to place; **~ kogoś w szpitalu** to hospitalize sb
**umie|ścić (-szczę, -ścisz)** (*imp* **-ść**) *vb perf od* **umieszczać**
**umięśniony** *adj* muscular, brawny
**umil|ać (-am, -asz)** (*perf* **-ić**) *vt*: **~ komuś czas** to make the time pass more pleasantly for sb
**umilk|nąć (-nę, -niesz)** (*imp* **-nij**) *vb perf od* **milknąć**
**umiz|gi** (**-gów**) *pl* wooing, courtship
**umk|nąć (-nę, -niesz)** (*imp* **-nij**) *vb perf od* **umykać**
**umniejsz|ać (-am, -asz)** (*perf* **-yć**) *vt* (*wartość, zasługi*) to diminish
**umoc|nić (-nię, -nisz)** (*imp* **-nij**) *vb perf od* **umacniać**

**umocnie|nia** (**-ń**) *pl* fortifications
**umoc|ować (-uję, -ujesz)** *vb perf od* **mocować, umocowywać**
**umocow|ywać (-uję, -ujesz)** (*perf* **-ać**) *vt* to secure, to fasten
**umocz|yć (-ę, -ysz)** *vt perf* to dip, to soak
**umoral|niać (-niam, -niasz)** (*perf* **-nić**) *vt* to edify
**umorus|ać (-am, -asz)** *vt perf* to smudge (*with soot etc*); **umorusać się** *vr* to get all smudgy
**umorusany** *adj* smudgy
**umorzyć (umorzę, umorzysz)** (*imp* **umórz**) *vb perf od* **umarzać**
**umotyw|ować (-uję, -ujesz)** *vb perf od* **motywować**
**um|owa** (**-owy, -owy**) (*loc sg* **-owie**, *gen pl* **-ów**) *f* agreement; **zawierać (zawrzeć** *perf*) **umowę** to enter into an agreement; **~ handlowa** trade contract; **~ międzynarodowa** international agreement; **~ o pracę** contract of employment *lub* service; **naruszenie umowy** breach of contract
**umowny** *adj* (*zgodny z umową*) contracted, agreed; (*w teatrze, literaturze*) conventional
**umożli|wiać (-wiam, -wiasz)** (*perf* **-wić**) *vt* to make possible; **umożliwić komuś zrobienie czegoś** to enable sb to do sth
**umó|wić się (-wię, -wisz)** *vb perf od* **umawiać się**
**umówiony** *adj* prearranged
**um|rzeć (-rę, -rzesz)** (*imp* **-rzyj**, *pt* **-arł**) *vb perf od* **umierać**
**umundurowa|nie** (**-nia**) *nt* uniform
**umundurowany** *adj* (*policjant*) uniformed
**umy|ć (-ję, -jesz)** *vb perf od* **myć**
**umyk|ać (-am, -asz)** (*perf* **umknąć**) *vi* to escape, to make off; **umknąć czyjejś uwadze** to escape sb's attention
**umy|sł** (**-słu, -sły**) (*loc sg* **-śle**) *m* mind, intellect
**umysłowo** *adv* (*rozwijać się*) intellectually; **chory/upośledzony ~** mentally ill/handicapped
**umysłowy** *adj* (*rozwój*) intellectual; (*wysiłek, choroba*) mental; **pracownik ~** office worker, white-collar worker
**umyślnie** *adv* deliberately
**umyślny** *adj* deliberate
**umyw|ać (-am, -asz)** *vt*: **~ ręce od czegoś** to wash one's hands of sth; **umywać się** *vr*: **ich dom nie umywa się do naszego** their house does not compare with ours
**umywal|ka** (**-ki, -ki**) (*dat sg* **-ce**, *gen pl* **-ek**) *f* washbasin
**uncj|a** (**-i, -e**) (*gen pl* **-i**) *f* ounce
**uni|a** (**-i, -e**) (*loc sg* **-i**) *f* union; **U~ Europejska** European Union; **zawierać (zawrzeć** *perf*) **unię** to form a union; **U~ Pracy** Union of Labour; **U~ Wolności** Union for Freedom
**unicest|wiać (-wiam, -wiasz)** (*perf* **-wić**) *vt* to annihilate
**unicest|wić (-wię, -wisz)** (*imp* **-wij**) *vb perf od* **unicestwiać**
**uniemożli|wiać (-wiam, -wiasz)** (*perf* **-wić**) *vt* to make impossible, to prevent; **~ komuś zrobienie czegoś** to prevent sb from doing sth
**unierucha|miać (-miam, -miasz)** (*perf* **unieruchomić**) *vt* to immobilize
**uniesie|nie** (**-nie, -nia**) (*gen pl* **-ń**) *nt* (*euforia*) elation; (*poryw uczuć*) passion
**unieszczęśli|wiać (-wiam, -wiasz)** (*perf* **-wić**) *vt* to make unhappy
**unieszkodli|wiać (-wiam, -wiasz)** (*perf* **-wić**) *vt* (*napastnika*) to make powerless; (*truciznę*) to neutralize; (*bombę*) to defuse; (*broń nuklearną*) to disarm
**uni|eść (-osę, -esiesz)** (*imp* **-eś**, *pt* **-ósł, -osła, -eśli**) *vb perf od* **unosić** ▷ *vt perf* (*zdołać udźwignąć*) to be able to lift
**unieśmiertel|niać (-niam, -niasz)** (*perf* **-nić**) *vt* to immortalize
**unieważ|niać (-niam, -niasz)** (*perf* **-nić**) *vt* (*zapis, małżeństwo*) to annul; (*argument, kontrakt*) to invalidate; (*zamówienie*) to cancel
**unieważ|nić (-nię, -nisz)** (*imp* **-nij**) *vb perf od* **unieważniać**
**unieważnie|nie** (**-nia**) *nt* (*zapisu, małżeństwa*) annulment; (*argumentu, kontraktu*) invalidation; (*zamówienia*) cancellation
**uniewin|niać (-niam, -niasz)** (*perf* **-nić**) *vt* to acquit
**uniewin|nić (-nię, -nisz)** (*imp* **-nij**) *vb perf od* **uniewinniać**
**uniewinnieni|e** (**-a**) *nt* acquittal
**unijny** *adj* EU *attr*; **fundusze/przepisy unijne** EU funds/regulations
**uni|k** (**-ku, -ki**) (*instr sg* **-kiem**) *m* dodge, evasion; **robić (zrobić** *perf*) **~** to dodge, to evade
**unik|ać (-am, -asz)** (*perf* **-nąć**) *vt +gen* (*osoby, tematu, kłótni*) to avoid; (*ciosu*) to dodge; (*kary*) to escape
**unikalny** *adj* unique
**unika|t** (**-tu, -ty**) (*loc sg* **-cie**) *m* rarity
**unikatowy** *adj* unique
**unik|nąć (-nę, -niesz)** (*imp* **-nij**) *vb perf od* **unikać**
**unisono** *adv*: **śpiewać ~** to sing in unison ▷ *nt inv* (*Muz*) unison
**uniwersalny** *adj* universal; **klucz ~** master *lub* skeleton key
**uniwersytecki** *adj* university *attr*; **miasteczko ~e** campus

U

**uniwersyte|t** (-tu, -ty) (*loc sg* **-cie**) *m* university
**uniżony** *adj* (*postawa, zachowanie*) humble, servile
**unorm|ować (-uję, -ujesz)** *vb perf od* **normować**
**uno|sić (-szę, -sisz)** (*imp* **-ś**, *perf* **unieść**) *vt* (*głowę, rękę*) to raise; (*o rzece, wietrze*) to carry off *lub* away; **unosić się** *vr* (*nad ziemią*) to hover; (*na wodzie*) to float; (*o zapachu*) to waft; (*wstawać*) to rise; (*o kurtynie, mgle*) to go up; (*irytować się*) to get hot under the collar (*pot*), to get worked up (*pot*); **~ się z zachwytu nad kimś/czymś** to extol sb/sth
**unowocześ|niać (-niam, -niasz)** (*perf* **-nić**) *vt* to modernize
**uodpor|niać (-niam, -niasz)** (*perf* **-nić**) *vt*: **~ kogoś na coś** *lub* **przeciwko czemuś** to make sb immune to sth; **uodporniać się** *vr*: **~ się na coś** to become immune to sth
**uogól|niać (-niam, -niasz)** (*perf* **-nić**) *vt* to generalize
**uogól|nić (-nię, -nisz)** (*imp* **-nij**) *vb perf od* **uogólniać**
**uogólnie|nie** (-nia, -nia) (*gen pl* **-ń**) *nt* generalization
**UOP** *abbr* (= *Urząd Ochrony Państwa*) *Polish governmental agency responsible for state security*
**uosa|biać (-biam, -biasz)** (*perf* **uosobić**) *vt* (*reprezentować typ*) to epitomize; (*personifikować*) to personify, to embody
**uos|obić (-obię, -obisz)** (*imp* **-ób**) *vb perf od* **uosabiać**
**uosobie|nie** (-nia) *nt* (*ideał*) epitome; (*ucieleśnienie*) embodiment
**UP** *abbr* = **Unia Pracy**
**upad|ać (-am, -asz)** (*perf* **upaść**) *vi* (*przewracać się*) to fall (down); (*chylić się ku upadkowi*) to decline; **~ ze zmęczenia** to be dead tired; **~ na duchu** to lose heart; **projekt upadł** the proposal fell through
**upad|ek** (-ku, -ki) (*instr sg* **-kiem**) *m* (*przewrócenie się*) fall; (*sztuki, moralności*) decadence, decay; (*klęska*) downfall
**upadl|ać (-am, -asz)** (*perf* **upodlić**) *vt* to debase; **upadlać się** *vr* to debase o.s.
**upadłościowy** *adj*: **masa upadłościowa** bankrupt's assets *lub* estate
**upadłoś|ć** (-ci) *f* bankruptcy; **ogłaszać (ogłosić** *perf*) **~** to declare bankruptcy
**upaj|ać się (-am, -asz)** (*perf* **upoić**) *vr*: **upajać się czymś** (*sukcesem*) to revel in sth; (*pięknem*) to take delight in sth
**upalny** *adj* sweltering
**upa|ł** (-łu, -ły) (*loc sg* **-le**) *m* heat
**upamięt|niać (-niam, -niasz)** (*perf* **-nić**) *vt* to commemorate
**upamięt|nić (-nię, -nisz)** (*imp* **-nij**) *vb perf od* **upamiętniać**
**upaństw|awiać (-awiam, -awiasz)** (*perf* **-owić**) *vt* to nationalize
**upaństw|owić (-owię, -owisz)** (*imp* **-ów**) *vb perf od* **upaństwawiać**
**upaństwowieni|e** (-a) *nt* nationalization
**uparcie** *adv* stubbornly
**uparciuch** (-a, -y) *m* (*pot*) mule (*pot*)
**uparł** *itd. vb patrz* **uprzeć się**
**uparty** *adj* stubborn, obstinate; **~ jak osioł** (as) stubborn as a mule; **na upartego** (*pot*) when push comes to shove, at a push
**upa|ść (-dnę, -dniesz)** (*imp* **-dnij**, *pt* **-dł**) *vb perf od* **upadać** ▷ *vi perf* (*spaść*) to fall; **~ na głowę** (*pot*) to go off one's rocker (*pot*)
**upatrz|yć (-ę, -ysz)** *vt perf*: **~ sobie kogoś/coś** to set one's sights on sb/sth
**upch|ać (-am, -asz)** *vb perf od* **upychać**
**upch|nąć (-nę, -niesz)** (*imp* **-nij**) *vb perf od* **upychać**
**upew|niać (-niam, -niasz)** (*perf* **-nić**) *vt*: **~ kogoś o czymś** to assure sb of sth; **~ kogoś, że ...** to (re)assure sb that ...; **upewniać się** *vr* to make sure *lub* certain
**upew|nić (-nię, -nisz)** (*imp* **-nij**) *vb perf od* **upewniać**
**upiąć (upnę, upniesz)** (*imp* **upnij**) *vb perf od* **upinać**
**upi|ć (-ję, -jesz)** *vb perf od* **upijać**
**upie|c (-kę, -czesz)** (*pt* **-kł**) *vb perf od* **piec**
**upier|ać się (-am, -asz)** (*perf* **uprzeć**) *vr* to insist; **upierać się przy czymś** to insist on sth
**upierze|nie** (-nia) *nt* plumage
**upiększ|ać (-am, -asz)** (*perf* **-yć**) *vt* (*pokój*) to beautify; (*przen: fakty*) to embellish
**upij|ać (-am, -asz)** *vt* (*herbatę*) to take a sip of; (*osobę*) to make drunk; **upijać się** *vr* to get drunk
**upiln|ować (-uję, -ujesz)** *vt perf* (*dzieci*) to take good care of; (*samochód, dom*) to protect against
**upin|ać (-am, -asz)** (*perf* **upiąć**) *vt* to pin up
**upiorny** *adj* ghastly
**upi|ór** (-ora, -ory) (*loc sg* **-orze**) *m* ghost, spectre (*Brit*), specter (*US*)
**uplas|ować się (-uję, -ujesz)** *vb perf od* **plasować się**
**uplat|ać (-am, -asz)** (*perf* **upleść**) *vt* to plait
**upl|eść (-otę, -eciesz)** (*imp* **-eć**, *pt* **-ótł, -otła, -etli**) *vb perf od* **uplatać**
**upły|nąć (-nie)** *vb perf od* **upływać**
**upłyn|niać (-niam, -niasz)** (*perf* **-nić**) *vt* (*pot*) to sell
**upły|w** (-wu) (*loc sg* **-wie**) *m* (*czasu*) passage; **po ~ie godziny/miesiąca** after an hour/

a month; **przed ~em roku** *(przez rok)* within a *lub* one year; *(przed końcem roku)* before the end of the year; **zmarł z ~u krwi** he died of loss of blood; **z ~em lat** as the years go *lub* went by

**upływ|ać (-a)** *(perf* **upłynąć***)* *vi* *(o czasie)* to go by; *(o terminie)* to expire; **termin upływa pierwszego lipca** the deadline is July 1st

**upodabni|ać (-am, -asz)** *(perf* **upodobnić***)* *vt* to make alike; **upodabniać się** *vr*: **~ się do kogoś** to imitate sb

**upodleni|e** (**-a**) *nt* degradation

**upodl|ić (-ę, -isz)** *(imp* **-ij***)* *vb perf od* **upadlać**

**upodob|ać (-am, -asz)** *vt perf*: **~ sobie kogoś/coś** to take a liking to sb/sth

**upodoba|nie** (**-nia, -nia**) *(gen pl* **-ń***)* *nt* inclination; **robić coś z ~m** to delight in doing sth; **~ do czegoś** a liking for sth

**upodob|nić (-nię, -nisz)** *(imp* **-nij***)* *vb perf od* **upodabniać**

**up|oić (-oję, -oisz)** *(imp* **-ój***)* *vb perf od* **upajać**

**upoje|nie** (**-nia**) *nt* rapture, ecstasy; **~ alkoholowe** intoxication; **do upojenia** rapturously, ecstatically

**upojny** *adj* *(książk)* intoxicating

**upokarz|ać (-am, -asz)** *(perf* **upokorzyć***)* *vt* to humiliate; **upokarzać się** *vr* to humiliate o.s.

**upokarzający** *adj* humiliating

**upokorze|nie** (**-nia, -nia**) *(gen pl* **-ń***)* *nt* humiliation; **doznać** *(perf)* **upokorzenia** to suffer humiliation

**upok|orzyć (-orzę, -orzysz)** *(imp* **-órz***)* *vb perf od* **upokarzać**

**upol|ować (-uję, -ujesz)** *vt perf* *(zwierzynę)* to shoot, to kill

**upomin|ać (-am, -asz)** *(perf* **upomnieć***)* *vt* to rebuke, to admonish; **upominać się** *vr*: **~ się o coś** to demand *lub* claim sth

**upomin|ek** (**-ku, -ki**) *(instr sg* **-kiem***)* *m* gift; **otrzymała to w upominku od ojca** it was a gift from her father

**upom|nieć (-nę, -nisz)** *(imp* **-nij***)* *vb perf od* **upominać**

**upomnie|nie** (**-nia, -nia**) *(gen pl* **-ń***)* *nt* *(uwaga)* rebuke, reproof; *(pismo)* reminder; **udzielać (udzielić** *perf***) upomnienia** to administer a rebuke

**upor|ać się (-am, -asz)** *vr perf*: **uporać się z kimś/czymś** to deal with sb/sth (successfully)

**uporczywie** *adv* *(odmawiać)* persistently, repeatedly; *(wpatrywać się)* intensely

**uporczywoś|ć** (**-ci**) *f* persistence

**uporczywy** *adj* *(ból)* stubborn, persistent; *(hałas)* persistent

**uporządk|ować (-uję, -ujesz)** *vb perf od* **porządkować**

**uporządkowany** *adj* ordered, orderly

**uposaże|nie** (**-nia, -nia**) *(gen pl* **-ń***)* *nt* salary

**upośledze|nie** (**-nia, -nia**) *(gen pl* **-ń***)* *nt* *(słuchu)* defect, impairment; *(wzroku)* impairment; *(ograniczenie)* deprivation; **~ umysłowe** mental handicap

**upośledzony** *adj* handicapped ▷ *m decl like adj* handicapped person

**upoważ|niać (-niam, -niasz)** *(perf* **-nić***)* *vt*: **~ kogoś do zrobienia czegoś** to authorize sb to do sth

**upoważ|nić (-nię, -nisz)** *(imp* **-nij***)* *vb perf od* **upoważniać**

**upoważnie|nie** (**-nia, -nia**) *(gen pl* **-ń***)* *nt* authorization; **~ do zrobienia czegoś** authorization to do sth; **robić coś z czyjegoś upoważnienia** to be authorized by sb to do sth

**upowszech|niać (-niam, -niasz)** *(perf* **-nić***)* *vt* to disseminate; **upowszechniać się** *vr* to become widespread

**upowszech|nić (-nię, -nisz)** *(imp* **-nij***)* *vb perf od* **upowszechniać**

**upozor|ować (-uję, -ujesz)** *vb perf od* **pozorować**

**up|ór** (**-oru**) *(loc sg* **-orze***)* *m* obstinacy, stubbornness; **z uporem** obstinately, stubbornly

**upragniony** *adj* longed for

**upras|ować (-uję, -ujesz)** *vb perf od* **prasować**

**uprasz|ać (-am, -asz)** *vi*: **„uprasza się o ciszę"** "silence"

**upraszcz|ać (-am, -asz)** *(perf* **uprościć***)* *vt* *(czynić prostszym)* to simplify; *(spłycać)* to oversimplify

**upra|wa** (**-wy, -wy**) *(dat sg* **-wie***)* *f* *(zboża, warzyw, roli)* cultivation; *(uprawiana roślina)* crop

**uprawi|ać (-am, -asz)** *vt* *(warzywa, zboże, rolę)* to cultivate; *(sport, turystykę)* to go in for; **~ hazard** to gamble

**upraw|niać (-niam, -niasz)** *(perf* **-nić***)* *vt*: **~ kogoś do czegoś** to entitle sb to sth

**uprawnie|nie** (**-nia, -nia**) *(gen pl* **-ń***)* *nt* entitlement, right

**uprawniony** *adj* entitled; **być ~m do czegoś** to be entitled to sth

**uprawny** *adj* arable

**uproszcze|nie** (**-nia, -nia**) *(gen pl* **-ń***)* *nt* simplification

**uproszczony** *adj* simplified; **~ rachunek VAT** *simplified VAT invoice*

**upro|ścić (-szczę, -ścisz)** *(imp* **-ść***)* *vb perf od* **upraszczać**

**uprowadz|ać (-am, -asz)** *(perf* **uprowadzić***)* *vt* to abduct

U

**uprowadze|nie (-nia, -nia)** (*gen pl* **-ń**) *nt* abduction
**uprowa|dzić (-dzę, -dzisz)** (*imp* **-dź**) *vb perf od* **uprowadzać**
**uprząt|ać (-am, -asz)** (*perf* **-nąć**) *vt* (*mieszkanie*) to tidy (up); (*śmieci*) to remove
**uprząt|nąć (-nę, -niesz)** (*imp* **-nij**) *vb perf od* **uprzątać**
**uprz|ąż (-ęży, -ęże)** (*gen pl* **-ęży**) *f* harness
**up|rzeć się (-rę, -rzesz)** (*imp* **-rzyj**, *pt* **-arł**) *vb perf od* **upierać się**
**uprzedni** *adj* previous
**uprzednio** *adv* previously
**uprze|dzać (-dzam, -dzasz)** (*perf* **-dzić**) *vt* (*prośbę, zamiar*) to anticipate; (*ostrzegać*) to warn; **~ kogoś o czymś** to warn sb of *lub* about sth; **~ kogoś do kogoś/czegoś** to prejudice sb against sb/sth; **uprzedzić kogoś** (*ubiec*) to beat sb to it; **uprzedzać się** *vr*: **~ się do kogoś/czegoś** to get prejudiced against sb/sth
**uprzedzająco** *adv* suspiciously
**uprzedze|nie (-nia, -nia)** (*gen pl* **-ń**) *nt* prejudice, bias; **mieć ~ do kogoś/czegoś** to be prejudiced *lub* biased against sb/sth; **bez uprzedzenia** without warning; **bez uprzedzeń** impartially; **nie mieć uprzedzeń** to be free from prejudice
**uprze|dzić (-dzę, -dzisz)** (*imp* **-dź**) *vb perf od* **uprzedzać**
**uprzedzony** *adj*: **~ (do** *+gen*) prejudiced (against)
**uprzejmie** *adv* politely, courteously; **proszę ~** (*odpowiedź na „dziękuję"*) (it was) a pleasure, my pleasure; (*przy podawaniu czegoś*) here you are; **dziękuję ~** thank you very much
**uprzejmoś|ć (-ci)** *f* (*cecha*) politeness, courtesy; (*czyn*) (*nom pl* **-ci**, *gen pl* **-ci**) courtesy; **dzięki uprzejmości pana Kowalskiego** (by) courtesy of Mr Kowalski; **wyświadczyć** (*perf*) **komuś ~** to do sb a favour (*Brit*) *lub* favor (*US*); **wymieniać z kimś uprzejmości** to exchange courtesies with sb
**uprzejmy** *adj* (*człowiek, traktowanie*) polite, courteous; (*odmowa*) polite; **bądź tak ~ i zrób to teraz** would you be so kind as to do it now?
**uprzemysłowie|nie (-nia)** *nt* industrialization
**uprzemysłowiony** *adj* industrialized
**uprzyjem|niać (-niam, -niasz)** (*perf* **-nić**) *vt*: **~ coś** to make sth enjoyable
**uprzyjem|nić (-nię, -nisz)** (*imp* **-nij**) *vb perf od* **uprzyjemniać**
**uprzykrz|ać (-am, -asz)** (*perf* **-yć**) *vt* to spoil; **ktoś/coś uprzykrza komuś życie** sb/sth is a pain in the neck (*pot*)
**uprzykrzony** *adj* irritating
**uprzykrz|yć (-ę, -ysz)** *vb perf od* **uprzykrzać**
**uprzytom|nić (-nię, -nisz)** (*imp* **-nij**) *vt perf*: **uprzytamniać komuś coś** to make sb aware of sth; **uprzytomniłem sobie, że ...** I realized (that) ...
**uprzywilejowani|e (-a)** *nt* privilege; **klauzula najwyższego uprzywilejowania** most-favoured-nation clause
**uprzywilejowany** *adj* (*osoba, grupa*) privileged; **pojazd ~** (*Mot*) emergency vehicle; **akcje uprzywilejowane** (*Ekon*) preference shares
**upstrzony** *adj* (*pobrudzony*) flyblown (*Brit*), flyspecked (*US*); **~ czymś** speckled *lub* dotted with sth
**UPT** *abbr* (= *Urząd Pocztowo-Telekomunikacyjny*) ≈ post office
**upu|st (-stu, -sty)** (*loc sg* **-ście**) *m* (*pary, sprężonego powietrza*) bleeding; **~ krwi** bloodletting; **dać** (*perf*) **~ czemuś** to give vent to sth
**upuszcz|ać (-am, -asz)** (*perf* **upuścić**) *vt* to drop; **uważaj, nie upuść!** careful, don't drop it!
**upu|ścić (-szczę, -ścisz)** (*imp* **-ść**) *vb perf od* **upuszczać**
**upych|ać (-am, -asz)** (*perf* **upchnąć** *lub* **upchać**) *vt* to stuff
**ur.** *abbr* (= *urodzony*) b. (= *born*)
**urabi|ać (-am, -asz)** (*perf* **urobić**) *vt* (*ciasto*) to knead; (*glinę, osobę, opinię publiczną*) to mould (*Brit*), to mold (*US*)
**uracz|yć (-ę, -ysz)** *vb perf od* **raczyć**
**urad|ować (-uję, -ujesz)** *vb perf od* **radować**
**uradowany** *adj* joyful, overjoyed
**ura|dzić (-dzę, -dzisz)** (*imp* **-dź**) *vt perf* to decide
**Ural (-u)** *m* the Ural Mountains *pl*
**ura|n (-nu)** (*loc sg* **-nie**) *m* (*Chem*) uranium; **Uran** (*Astron*) Uranus
**urast|ać (-am, -asz)** (*perf* **urosnąć**) *vi*: **~ do rangi** *lub* **rozmiarów czegoś** to take on *lub* assume the proportions of sth
**urat|ować (-uję, -ujesz)** *vb perf od* **ratować**
**ura|z (-zu, -zy)** (*loc sg* **-zie**) *m* (*Med*) injury; (*Psych*) trauma; **mieć ~ na punkcie czegoś** to have a hang-up about sth
**ura|za (-zy, -zy)** (*dat sg* **-zie**) *f* resentment; **żywić do kogoś urazę** to bear sb a grudge; **bez urazy!** no hard feelings!
**ura|zić (-żę, -zisz)** (*imp* **-ź**) *vb perf od* **urażać**
**urazowy** *adj* traumatic; **oddział chirurgii urazowej** casualty ward
**ura|żać (-żam, -żasz)** (*perf* **-zić**) *vt* (*obrażać*) to offend; (*ranić*) to hurt

**urażony** *adj* (*człowiek*) offended; (*duma, ambicja*) hurt; **czuć się ~m** to feel offended
**urąg|ać (-am, -asz)** *vi*: **~ komuś** (*perf* **na-**) to hurl abuse at sb; **warunki urągające podstawowym zasadom higieny** appalling sanitary conditions; **~ zdrowemu rozsądkowi** to defy common sense
**urbani|sta (-sty, -ści)** (*dat sg* **-ście**) *m decl like f in sg* town planner
**urbanistyczny** *adj*: **projekt ~** town planning project
**urbanisty|ka (-ki)** (*dat sg* **-ce**) *f* town planning
**urbanizacj|a (-i)** *f* urban development
**uregul|ować (-uję, -ujesz)** *vb perf od* **regulować**
**urlo|p (-pu, -py)** (*loc sg* **-pie**) *m* (*przerwa w pracy*) leave (of absence); (*wakacje*) vacation, holiday; **iść (pójść** *perf*) **na ~** to go on leave; **być na ~ie** (*nie w pracy*) to be on leave; (*na wakacjach*) to be on vacation *lub* holiday; **~ dziekański** dean's leave; **~ macierzyński** maternity leave; **~ zdrowotny** sick leave
**urlopowicz (-a, -e)** *m* holiday-maker
**urlopowy** *adj*: **okres ~** holiday period
**URM** *abbr* (= *Urząd Rady Ministrów*) Office of the Council of Ministers
**ur|na (-ny, -ny)** (*dat sg* **-nie**) *f* urn; **~ wyborcza** ballot box
**uro|bić (-bię, -bisz)** (*imp* **urób**) *vb perf od* **urabiać**
**uroczy** *adj* charming
**uroczystoś|ć (-ci, -ci)** (*gen pl* **-ci**) *f* ceremony; **uroczystości weselne** wedding ceremony; **uroczystości żałobne** funeral service
**uroczysty** *adj* solemn
**uroczyście** *adv* solemnly
**uro|da (-dy)** (*dat sg* **-dzie**) *f* beauty
**urodzaj (-u, -e)** (*gen pl* **-ów**) *m* bumper crop; **~ na coś** (*przen*) a good year for sth
**urodzajny** *adj* (*ziemia*) fertile; (*rok*) good
**urodze|nie (-nia)** *nt* birth; **data/miejsce urodzenia** date/place of birth; **akt urodzenia** birth certificate; **od urodzenia** since birth
**uro|dzić (-dzę, -dzisz)** (*imp* **urodź** *lub* **uródź**) *vb perf od* **rodzić**
**urodzinowy** *adj* birthday *attr*
**urodzin|y (-)** *pl* birthday; **wszystkiego najlepszego w dniu urodzin!** happy birthday!
**urodziwy** *adj* comely
**urodzony** *adj* born; (*rodowity*) born and bred; **osoba szlachetnie urodzona** a person of noble birth
**urografi|a (-i)** *f* urography
**ur|oić (-oję, -oisz)** (*imp* **-ój**) *vt perf*: **~ sobie coś** to fantasize sth
**uroje|nie (-nia, -nia)** (*gen pl* **-ń**) *nt* (*wymysł*) fantasy; (*Psych*) delusion
**urojony** *adj* imaginary
**uro|k (-ku, -ki)** (*instr sg* **-kiem**) *m* (*piękno*) charm; (*czary*) spell; **być pod ~iem kogoś/czegoś** to be under the spell of sb/sth; **rzucać ~ na kogoś** to cast a spell on sb
**urokliwy** *adj* (*książk*) charming
**urolo|g (-ga, -dzy** *lub* **-gowie)** *m* urologist
**urologi|a (-i)** *f* urology
**urologiczny** *adj* urological
**uro|nić (-nię, -nisz)** (*imp* **-ń**) *vb perf od* **ronić**
**uro|snąć (-snę, -śniesz)** (*imp* **-śnij**) *vb perf od* **urastać, rosnąć**
**urozmai|cać (-cam, -casz)** (*perf* **-cić**) *vt* to vary
**urozmaiceni|e (-a, -a)** *nt* variety, diversity
**urozmai|cić (-cę, -cisz)** (*imp* **-ć**) *vb perf od* **urozmaicać**
**urozmaicony** *adj* varied, diversified
**urób** *vb patrz* **urobić**
**uródź** *vb patrz* **urodzić**
**uruch|amiać (-amiam, -amiasz)** (*perf* **-omić**) *vt* (*silnik, pojazd*) to start; (*mechanizm*) to activate; (*proces*) to set in motion
**Urugwaj (-u)** *m* Uruguay
**Urugwajczy|k (-ka, -cy)** (*instr sg* **-kiem**) *m* Uruguayan
**Urugwaj|ka (-ki, -ki)** (*dat sg* **-ce**, *gen pl* **-ek**) *f* Uruguayan
**urugwajski** *adj* Uruguayan
**ur|wać (-wę, -wiesz)** (*imp* **-wij**) *vb perf od* **urywać**
**urwani|e (-a)** *nt*: **~ głowy** (*pot*) hassle (*pot*)
**urwi|s (-sa, -sy)** (*loc sg* **-sie**) *m* urchin
**urwis|ko (-ka, -ka)** (*instr sg* **-kiem**) *nt* precipice
**urwisty** *adj* precipitous
**uryw|ać (-am, -asz)** (*perf* **urwać**) *vt* (*guzik, rękaw*) to tear off; (*rozmowę*) to cut short; **urywać się** *vr* (*o guziku*) to come off; (*o rozmowie*) to break off; (*o ścieżce itp.*) to end; (*pot: wychodzić przed czasem*) to push off (*pot*)
**urywany** *adj* (*dźwięk itp.*) interrupted
**uryw|ek (-ka, -ki)** (*instr sg* **-kiem**) *m* fragment
**urz|ąd (-ędu, -ędy)** (*loc sg* **-ędzie**) *m* (*organ władzy*) department; (*biuro*) office; (*stanowisko*) post; **~ pocztowy** post office; **~ zatrudnienia** employment agency; **U~ Skarbowy** ≈ Internal Revenue (*Brit*), ≈ the IRS (*US*); **U~ Rady Ministrów** Office of the Council of Ministers; **Główny U~ Ceł** Central Board of Customs; **Główny U~ Statystyczny** Central Statistical Office; **~ stanu cywilnego** register *lub* registry (*Brit*) office; **pełnić** *lub* **sprawować ~** *+gen* to hold the office of; **obrońca z urzędu** public defender (*US*), court-appointed lawyer (*Brit*)

**urzą|dzać (-dzam, -dzasz)** (*perf* **-dzić**) *vt* (*mieszkanie*) to furnish; (*wycieczkę, koncert*) to organize; **~ przyjęcie** to throw a party; **to mnie urządza** (*pot*) it suits me; **to mnie nie urządza** (*pot*) it doesn't suit me; **urządzać się** *vr* (*w nowym mieszkaniu itp.*) to settle down

**urządze|nie** (-nia, -nia) (*gen pl* **-ń**) *nt* device, appliance; **~ pomiarowe** measuring instrument; **~ peryferyjne** (*Komput*) peripheral (device); **urządzenia** *pl* equipment; **urządzenia klimatyzacyjne** air-conditioning equipment

**urzą|dzić (-dzę, -dzisz)** (*imp* **-dź**) *vb perf od* **urządzić**; **~ kogoś** (*pot*) to get sb into a pretty mess (*pot*); **urządzić się** *vr* (*pot*) to get (o.s.) into a pretty mess (*pot*)

**urze|c (-knę, -kniesz)** (*imp* **-knij**) *vb perf od* **urzekać**

**urzeczony** *adj* bewitched

**urzeczywist|niać (-niam, -niasz)** (*perf* **-nić**) *vt* (*plany*) to implement; (*marzenia*) to realize

**urzeczywist|nić (-nię, -nisz)** (*imp* **-nij**) *vb perf od* **urzeczywistniać**

**urzek|ać (-am, -asz)** (*perf* **urzec**) *vt* to bewitch, to captivate

**urzekający** *adj* bewitching, captivating

**urzędnicz|ka** (-ki, -ki) (*dat sg* **-ce**, *gen pl* **-ek**) *f* clerk, office worker

**urzędniczy** *adj* (*posada*) clerical; (*pensja*) clerk's *attr*

**urzędni|k** (-ka, -cy) (*instr sg* **-kiem**) *m* clerk, office worker; (*wysoki rangą*) official; **~ administracji państwowej** civil servant; **~ stanu cywilnego** registrar

**urzęd|ować (-uję, -ujesz)** *vi* to work (*in an office*)

**urzędowani|e** (-a) *nt*: **godziny urzędowania** office hours

**urzędowy** *adj* official; (*czas*) standard; **nakaz ~** writ

**urż|nąć (-nę, -niesz)** (*imp* **-nij**) *vt perf* to cut off; **urżnąć się** *vr perf* (*pot*) to get drunk

**urżnięty** *adj* (*pot: pijany*) stoned

**usadawi|ać (-am, -asz)** (*perf* **usadowić**) *vt*: **~ kogoś w fotelu/przy stole** to put *lub* place sb in an armchair/by the table; **usadawiać się** *vr* to settle (o.s.)

**usado|wić (-wię, -wisz)** (*imp* **usadów**) *vb perf od* **usadawiać**

**usamodziel|niać się (-niam, -niasz)** (*perf* **-nić**) *vr* to become self-dependent

**usamodziel|nić się (-nię, -nisz)** (*imp* **-nij**) *vb perf od* **usamodzielniać się**

**usatysfakcjonowany** *adj* satisfied

**USC** *abbr* (= *Urząd Stanu Cywilnego*) register *lub* registry (Brit) office

**usch|nąć (-nę, -niesz)** (*imp* **-nij**, *pt* **-nął** *lub* **usechł, -ła**) *vb perf od* **usychać**

**usiany** *adj* (*gwiazdami*) speckled with; (*plamami*) covered in

**usią|ść (-dę, -dziesz)** (*imp* **-dź**) *vb perf od* **siadać**

**usidl|ać (-am, -asz)** (*perf* **usidlić**) *vt* to ensnare

**usie|dzieć (-dzę, -dzisz)** (*imp* **-dź**) *vt perf*: **nie móc ~** (*przen*) to be restless

**usilnie** *adv* (*prosić*) insistently; (*starać się*) hard, strenuously

**usilny** *adj* (*praca*) hard; (*prośba, żądanie*) insistent

**usił|ować (-uję, -ujesz)** *vt*: **~ coś zrobić** to try *lub* attempt to do sth

**usiłowa|nie** (-nia, -nia) (*gen pl* **-ń**) *nt* attempt; **~ zabójstwa** attempted murder

**uska|kiwać (-kuję, -kujesz)** (*perf* **uskoczyć**) *vi* to dodge

**uskarż|ać się (-am, -asz)** *vr*: **uskarżać się na kogoś/coś** to complain about *lub* of sb/sth

**uskocz|yć (-ę, -ysz)** *vb perf od* **uskakiwać**

**usko|k** (-ku, -ki) (*instr sg* **-kiem**) *m* (*skok*) dodge; (*Geol*) fault

**uskrzydl|ać (-am, -asz)** (*perf* **-ić**) *vt* (*przen*): **~ kogoś** to boost sb's confidence

**usłany** *adj*: **(nie) być ~m różami** (not) to be all roses

**usłuch|ać (-am, -asz)** *vb perf od* **słuchać**

**usłu|ga** (-gi, -gi) (*dat sg* **-dze**) *f* (*przysługa*) favour (Brit), favor (US); **wyświadczyć** (*perf*) **komuś usługę** to do sb a favour (Brit) *lub* favor (US); **usługi** *pl* services; **korzystać z usług** *+gen* to be a customer of

**usłu|giwać (-guję, -gujesz)** *vi*: **~ komuś** (*o kelnerze, służącym*) to wait on sb; (*choremu, potrzebującemu*) to minister to sb

**usługowy** *adj*: **punkt** *lub* **zakład ~** shop; **działalność usługowa** service, services *pl*

**usłużny** *adj* attentive

**usłysz|eć (-ę, -ysz)** *vb perf od* **słyszeć** ▷ *vt perf*: **źle ~** to mishear; **~ przypadkiem** to overhear

**usmaż|yć (-ę, -ysz)** *vb perf od* **smażyć**

**usnąć (usnę, uśniesz)** (*imp* **uśnij**) *vb perf od* **usypiać**

**uspokaj|ać (-am, -asz)** (*perf* **uspokoić**) *vt* to calm down; (*dzieci*) to quieten (Brit), to quiet (US); (*nerwy*) to calm; **uspokajać się** *vr* to calm down; (*o dzieciach*) to quieten (Brit), to quiet (US); (*o wietrze*) to calm

**uspokajający** *adj*: **lek** *lub* **środek ~** tranquillizer (Brit), tranquilizer (US)

**uspok|oić (-oję, -oisz)** (*imp* **-ój**) *vb perf od* **uspokajać**

**uspołeczniony** *adj* (*gospodarka*) planned; (*przedsiębiorstwo*) state-owned

**usposabi|ać (-am, -asz)** (*perf* **usposobić**) *vt*: **~ kogoś przychylnie/nieprzychylnie do** *+acc* to leave sb well-/ill-disposed towards; **~ kogoś do marzeń/płaczu** to make sb feel like dreaming/crying

**uspos|obić (-obię, -obisz)** (*imp* **-ób**) *vb perf od* **usposabiać**

**usposobie|nie** (**-nia**) *nt* (*natura*) disposition; (*nastrój*) mood

**usposobiony** *adj* disposed; **być przyjaźnie/wrogo ~m do kogoś** to be well-/ill-disposed towards sb

**usprawiedli|wiać (-wiam, -wiasz)** (*perf* **-wić**) *vt* (*tłumaczyć*) to excuse; (*potwierdzać słuszność*) to justify; **usprawiedliwiać się** *vr* to excuse o.s.

**usprawiedliwie|nie** (**-nia, -nia**) (*gen pl* **-ń**) *nt* (*wymówka*) excuse; (*argument na uzasadnienie*) justification; (*Szkol*) excuse note; **mieć coś na swoje ~** to have sth to excuse o.s., to have an excuse to give; **powiedzieć coś na swoje ~** to say sth by way of excuse *lub* as an excuse

**usprawiedliwiony** *adj* (*żądanie, gniew*) justified; (*nieobecność*) excused; **niczym nie ~** (*niedopatrzenie*) inexcusable; (*wybuch gniewu*) unjustified

**uspraw|niać (-niam, -niasz)** (*perf* **-nić**) *vt* to rationalize; (*ulepszać*) to improve

**uspraw|nić (-nię, -nisz)** (*imp* **-nij**) *vb perf od* **usprawniać**

**usprawnie|nie** (**-nia**) (*gen pl* **-ń**) *nt* (*poprawienie*) rationalization; (*wynalazek*) improvement

**ust|a** (-) *pl* mouth *sg*; **oddychanie ~-~** mouth-to-mouth resuscitation, the kiss of life (*Brit*); **wyjąć** (*perf*) **coś komuś z ust** (*przen*) to take sth (right) out of sb's mouth; **być przekazywanym z ust do ust** (*przen*) to pass by word of mouth; **nabrać** (*perf*) **wody w ~** (*przen*) to keep one's mouth shut

**ustabiliz|ować (-uję, -ujesz)** *vb perf od* **stabilizować**

**ust|ać[1] (-anę, -aniesz)** (*imp* **-ań**) *vb perf od* **ustawać**

**ust|ać[2] (-oję, -oisz)** (*imp* **-ój**) *vi perf* (*nie przewrócić się*) to keep one's balance; **nie móc ~ na nogach** (*ze zmęczenia*) to be on one's last legs; **ustać się** *vr perf* (*o płynach*) to settle

**ustal|ać (-am, -asz)** (*perf* **-ić**) *vt* to establish; (*termin*) to fix; **ustalić swoją pozycję** to establish o.s.; **ustalać się** *vr* (*o zwyczaju*) to become established; **pogoda się ustaliła** the weather is settled

**ustale|nie** (**-nia, -nia**) (*gen pl* **-ń**) *nt* (*decyzja*) decision; **ustalenia** *pl* (*plan*) arrangement *sg*; (*werdykt*) findings

**ustalony** *adj* (*termin*) fixed; (*fakty*) established; (*zasady, normy*) set, established

**ustanawi|ać (-am, -asz)** (*perf* **ustanowić**) *vt* (*prawo, regułę*) to make; (*rekord*) to set

**ustan|owić (-owię, -owisz)** (*imp* **-ów**) *vb perf od* **ustanawiać**

**ustatk|ować się (-uję, -ujesz)** *vr perf* to settle down

**usta|wa** (**-wy, -wy**) (*dat sg* **-wie**) *f* act; **uchwalać (uchwalić** *perf*) **ustawę** to pass *lub* enact a bill; **projekt ustawy** bill; **~ zasadnicza** constitution

**usta|wać (-ję, -jesz)** (*imp* **-waj**, *perf* **ustać**) *vi* (*książk: kończyć się*) to cease; **nie ~ w wysiłkach** to persist in *lub* with one's efforts

**usta|wiać (-wiam, -wiasz)** (*perf* **-wić**) *vt* (*umieszczać*) to put, to place; (*rozmieszczać*) to arrange; (*wznosić*) to put up; (*regulować*) to adjust; **ustawiać się** *vr*: **~ się w szeregu** to line up; **~ się przodem do czegoś** to stand facing sth

**ustawicznie** *adv* persistently

**ustawiczny** *adj* persistent

**usta|wić (-wię, -wisz)** *vb perf od* **ustawiać**

**ustawieni|e** (**-a**) *nt* arrangement; (*drużyny*) line-up

**ustawodawc|a** (**-y, -y**) *m decl like f in sg* legislator

**ustawodawczy** *adj* legislative

**ustawodawst|wo** (**-wa, -wa**) (*loc sg* **-wie**) *nt* legislation

**ustawowo** *adv* by law

**ustawowy** *adj* statutory

**ustą|pić (-pię, -pisz)** *vb perf od* **ustępować**

**ustąpie|nie** (**-nia**) *nt* resignation

**uster|ka** (**-ki, -ki**) (*dat sg* **-ce**, *gen pl* **-ek**) *f* (*w urządzeniu*) fault; (*w wypracowaniu, raporcie*) error

**ustę|p** (**-pu, -py**) (*loc sg* **-pie**) *m* (*ubikacja*) toilet; (*urywek*) paragraph

**ustępliwoś|ć** (**-ci**) *f* compliance

**ustępliwy** *adj* compliant

**ustęp|ować (-uję, -ujesz)** *vi* (*perf* **ustąpić**) (*wycofywać się*) to retreat; (*ze stanowiska, urzędu*) to resign; (*mijać: o chorobie, gorączce*) to recede; (*: o bólu*) to subside; (*o zamku, bramie*) to yield; (*ulegać*) to give in; **~ komuś/czemuś** not to be as good as sb/sth; **~ (ustąpić** *perf*) **pierwszeństwa przejazdu** to give way (*Brit*), to yield (*US*); **~ komuś miejsce** (*w autobusie*) to give up one's seat to sb; **~ miejsca czemuś** to give way to sth

**ustępst|wo** (**-wa, -wa**) (*loc sg* **-wie**) *nt* concession; **iść na ustępstwa** to make concessions; **~ na czyjąś korzyść** *lub* **rzecz** concession to sb; **wzajemne ustępstwa** give-and-take *sg*

U

**ustępujący** *adj* (*dyrektor, rząd*) outgoing
**ustnie** *adv* (*przekazać, zawiadomić*) verbally; (*egzaminować*) orally
**ustni|k** (**-ka, -ki**) (*instr sg* **-kiem**) *m* (*papierosa*) filter tip; (*fajki, instrumentu*) mouthpiece
**ustny** *adj* (*egzamin*) oral; (*zgoda*) verbal; **jama ustna** the oral *lub* mouth cavity; **harmonijka ustna** harmonica, mouth organ
**ustosunkowany** *adj* well-connected
**ustosunkow|ywać się (-uję, -ujesz)** (*perf* **-ać**) *vr*: **ustosunkowywać się do czegoś** to take a position on sth
**ustrojowy** *adj* (*przemiana*) political; **płyn ~** body fluid
**ustro|nie** (**-nia, -nia**) (*gen pl* **-ni**) *nt* retreat, seclusion
**ustronny** *adj* secluded
**ustr|ój** (**-oju, -oje**) *m* (*Pol*) political system; (*organizm*) system
**ustrze|c (-gę, -żesz)** (*imp* **-ż**, *pt* **-gł**) *vt perf*: **~ kogoś od czegoś** to protect sb against *lub* from sth; **ustrzec się** *vr perf*: **~ się czegoś** to keep out of sth; **~ się przed czymś** to avoid sth
**usu|nąć (-nę, -niesz)** (*imp* **-ń**) *vb perf od* **usuwać**
**ususz|yć (-ę, -ysz)** *vb perf od* **suszyć**
**usu|wać (-wam, -wasz)** (*perf* **-nąć**) *vt* to remove; (*z partii, wojska*) to expel; (*pozbawiać urzędu*) to remove, to dismiss; (*ząb*) to extract; **~ ciążę** (*o kobiecie*) to have an abortion; (*o lekarzu*) to perform an abortion; **usuwać się** *vr* (*odchodzić*) to withdraw; (*o gruncie, ziemi*) to sink; **~ się na bok** to step aside; **~ się (usunąć się** *perf*) **na drugi plan** to take a back seat; **~ się (usunąć się** *perf*) **w cień** to efface o.s.
**usych|ać (-am, -asz)** (*perf* **uschnąć**) *vi* to wither; **~ z miłości** to be lovesick; **~ z tęsknoty za kimś/czymś** to pine for sb/sth
**usy|pać (-pię, -piesz)** *vb perf od* **usypywać**
**usypi|ać (-am, -asz)** *vt* (*perf* **uśpić**) to put to sleep ▷ *vi* (*perf* **usnąć**) to fall asleep, to go to sleep
**usypiająco** *adv*: **działać ~** to have a soporific effect, to induce sleep
**usyp|ywać (-uję, -ujesz)** (*perf* **-ać**) *vt* (*wał, kopiec*) to build, to raise; (*odsypywać*) to pour off
**usystematyz|ować (-uję, -ujesz)** *vb perf od* **systematyzować**
**usytu|ować (-uję, -ujesz)** *vb perf od* **sytuować**
**usytuowani|e** (**-a**) *nt* location
**uszan|ować (-uję, -ujesz)** *vb perf od* **szanować**
**uszanowani|e** (**-a**) *nt* respect; **moje ~!** good day!
**uszczel|ka** (**-ki, -ki**) (*dat sg* **-ce**, *gen pl* **-ek**) *f* gasket, seal; (*w kranie*) washer
**uszczel|niać (-niam, -niasz)** (*perf* **-nić**) *vt* to seal
**uszczel|nić (-nię, -nisz)** (*imp* **-nij**) *vb perf od* **uszczelniać**
**uszczerb|ek** (**-ku**) (*instr sg* **-kiem**) *m* damage; **doznać** (*perf*) **uszczerbku (na czymś)** to suffer damage (to sth); **z uszczerbkiem dla zdrowia** to the detriment of one's health
**uszczęśli|wiać (-wiam, -wiasz)** (*perf* **-wić**) *vt* to make happy
**uszczk|nąć (-nę, -niesz)** (*imp* **-nij**) *vt perf* (*oderwać*) to nip off; (*przen*) to snatch
**uszczupl|ać (-am, -asz)** (*perf* **-ić**) *vt* to reduce, to deplete
**uszczupl|ić (-ę, -isz)** (*imp* **-ij**) *vb perf od* **uszczuplać**
**uszczypliwie** *adv* bitingly
**uszczypliwoś|ć** (**-ci**) *nt* (*złośliwość*) acerbity; (*uwaga*) (*nom pl* **-ci**) biting remark
**uszczypliwy** *adj* biting, acerbic
**uszczyp|nąć (-nę, -niesz)** (*imp* **-nij**) *vb perf od* **szczypać**
**uszczypnię|cie** (**-cia, -cia**) (*gen pl* **-ć**) *nt* pinch
**uszedł** *itd. vb patrz* **ujść**
**uszkadz|ać (-am, -asz)** (*perf* **uszkodzić**) *vt* to damage; **uszkadzać się** *vr* to suffer damage
**usz|ko** (**-ka, -ka**) (*instr sg* **-kiem**, *gen pl* **-ek**) *nt dimin od* **ucho**; (*Kulin*) ravioli
**uszkodze|nie** (**-nia, -nia**) (*gen pl* **-ń**) *nt* (*maszyny, budynku*) damage; (*ciała*) injury, harm
**uszko|dzić (-dzę, -dzisz)** (*imp* **-dź**) *vb perf od* **uszkadzać**
**uszkodzony** *adj* damaged
**uszlachet|niać (-niam, -niasz)** (*perf* **-nić**) *vt* (*o cierpieniu, uczuciu*) to ennoble, to dignify; (*surowiec*) to purify, to refine
**uszlachet|nić (-nię, -nisz)** (*imp* **-nij**) *vb perf od* **uszlachetniać**
**uszła** *itd. vb patrz* **ujść**
**uszny** *adj* ear *attr*
**usztyw|niać (-niam, -niasz)** (*perf* **-nić**) *vt* to stiffen; (*przen: stanowisko*) to stiffen, to harden; **usztywniać się** *vr* to stiffen
**usztyw|nić (-nię, -nisz)** (*imp* **-nij**) *vb perf od* **usztywniać**
**uszy** *itd. n patrz* **ucho**
**uszy|ć (-ję, -jesz)** *vb perf od* **szyć**
**uszyk|ować (-uję, -ujesz)** *vb perf od* **szykować**
**uścis|k** (**-ku, -ki**) (*instr sg* **-kiem**) *m* grip; **~ dłoni** handshake; **przesyłać (przesłać** *perf*) **komuś ~i** to send love to sb

**uścisk|ać (-am, -asz)** *vt perf*: **~ kogoś** to hug sb; **uściskaj ode mnie swoją siostrę** give my love to your sister
**ści|snąć (-snę, -śniesz)** (*imp* **-śnij**) *vt perf* to hug; **~ czyjąś dłoń** to shake hands with sb
**uściśl|ać (-am, -asz)** (*perf* **-ić**) *vt* (*powody*) to specify; (*wypowiedź*) to qualify
**uściśl|ić (-ę, -isz)** (*imp* **-ij**) *vb perf od* **uściślać**
**uśmi|ać się (-eję, -ejesz)** *vr perf* to have a good laugh
**uśmiech** (**-u, -y**) *m* smile; **wywoływać** (**wywołać** *perf*) **~** to raise a smile; **~ losu** stroke of luck
**uśmiech|ać się (-am, -asz)** (*perf* **-nąć**) *vr* to smile; **uśmiechać się do kogoś** to smile to sb; **to mi się nie uśmiecha** I'm not happy about it
**uśmiech|nąć się (-nę, -niesz)** (*imp* **-nij**) *vb perf od* **uśmiechać się**
**uśmiechnięty** *adj* smiling
**uśmier|cać (-cam, -casz)** (*perf* **-cić**) *vt* to put to death
**uśmier|cić (-cę, -cisz)** (*imp* **-ć**) *vb perf od* **uśmiercać**
**uśmierz|ać (-am, -asz)** (*perf* **-yć**) *vt* (*ból*) to relieve, to soothe; (*rozruchy*) to quell
**uśnie** *itd. vb patrz* **usnąć**
**uś|pić (-pię, -pisz)** (*imp* **-pij**) *vb perf od* **usypiać**
**uświad|amiać (-amiam, -amiasz)** (*perf* **-omić**) *vt*: **~ coś komuś** to make sb aware of sth, to make sb realize sth; **~ sobie coś** to make o.s. aware of sth; **~ sobie, że ...** to realize that ...; **~ kogoś** to tell sb the facts of life
**uświado|mić (-mię, -misz)** *vb perf od* **uświadamiać**
**uświet|niać (-niam, -niasz)** (*perf* **-nić**) *vt* to add splendour (*Brit*) *lub* splendor (*US*) to
**uświet|nić (-nię, -nisz)** (*imp* **-nij**) *vb perf od* **uświetniać**
**uświę|cać (-cam, -casz)** (*perf* **-cić**) *vt* to sanctify; **cel uświęca środki** the end justifies the means
**uświę|cić (-cę, -cisz)** (*imp* **-ć**) *vb perf od* **uświęcać**
**utaj|niać (-niam, -niasz)** (*perf* **-nić**) *vt* to make classified *lub* top secret
**utaj|nić (-nię, -nisz)** (*imp* **-nij**) *vb perf od* **utajniać**
**utajony** *adj* latent
**utalentowany** *adj* talented, gifted
**utarcz|ka** (**-ki, -ki**) (*dat sg* **-ce**, *gen pl* **-ek**) *f* skirmish
**utar|g** (**-gu, -gi**) (*instr sg* **-giem**) *m* (*Handel*) takings *pl*
**utarg|ować (-uję, -ujesz)** *vt perf*: **~ 10 złotych** to knock the price down by 10 zloty
**utarty** *adj* (*opinia*) common; (*zwrot*) set *attr*
**utk|ać (-am, -asz)** *vb perf od* **tkać**
**utk|nąć (-nę, -niesz)** (*imp* **-nij**) *vb perf od* **utykać** ▷ *vi perf*: **~ w martwym punkcie** (*przen*) to come to a standstill
**utk|wić (-wię, -wisz)** (*imp* **-wij**) *vt perf* to stick; **coś utkwiło komuś w pamięci** sth stuck in sb's mind; **~ wzrok w kimś/czymś** to fix one's eyes on sb/sth
**utle|niać (-niam, -niasz)** (*perf* **-nić**) *vt* (*Chem*) to oxidize; (*włosy*) to bleach; **utleniać się** *vr* to oxidize
**utle|nić (-nię, -nisz)** (*imp* **-ń**) *vb perf od* **utleniać**
**utleniony** *adj*: **woda utleniona** hydrogen peroxide
**uto|nąć (-nę, -niesz)** (*imp* **-ń**) *vi perf* to drown
**utopi|a** (**-i, -e**) (*gen pl* **-i**) *f* utopia
**uto|pić (-pię, -pisz)** *vb perf od* **topić**
**utopijny** *adj* utopian
**utor|ować (-uję, -ujesz)** *vb perf od* **torować**
**utożsa|miać (-miam, -miasz)** (*perf* **-mić**) *vt* to identify; **utożsamiać się** *vr* to identify
**utra|cić (-cę, -cisz)** (*imp* **-ć**) *vb perf od* **tracić**
**utra|fić (-fię, -fisz)** *vi perf*: **~ (w** *+acc*) to hit
**utrapie|nie** (**-nia, -nia**) (*gen pl* **-ń**) *nt* nuisance; **mam z nim ~** he's causing me a lot of trouble
**utra|ta** (**-ty**) (*loc sg* **-cie**) *f* loss; **~ pamięci/ przytomności** loss of memory/ consciousness
**utrud|niać (-niam, -niasz)** (*perf* **-nić**) *vt*: **~ coś komuś** to make sth difficult for sb
**utrud|nić (-nię, -nisz)** (*imp* **-nij**) *vb perf od* **utrudniać**
**utrudnie|nie** (**-nia, -nia**) (*gen pl* **-ń**) *nt* difficulty
**utrwalacz** (**-a, -e**) (*gen pl* **-y**) *m* (*Fot*) fixative
**utrwa|lać (-lam, -lasz)** (*perf* **-lić**) *vt* (*pozycję*) to strengthen; (*przyjaźń*) to cement; (*Fot*) to fix; (*w kamieniu, powieści*) to preserve; (*na płycie, taśmie*) to record; **utrwalać się** *vr* to become established, to take root
**ut|rzeć (-rę, -rzesz)** (*imp* **-rzyj**) *vb perf od* **ucierać**; **utrzeć się** *vr* to become established
**utrzym|ać (-am, -asz)** *vb perf od* **utrzymywać**
**utrzyma|nie** (**-nia**) *nt* maintenance; (*środki do życia*) keep; **źródło utrzymania** livelihood; **być na czyimś utrzymaniu** to depend financially on sb
**utrzymany** *adj*: **dobrze ~** well-kept
**utrzym|ywać (-uję, -ujesz)** (*perf* **-ać**) *vt* (*ciężar*) to bear, to carry; (*dom, dzieci, rodzinę*) to provide for; (*równowagę, porządek*) to keep; (*bronić: miasto, twierdzę*) to hold; **~ kogoś przy życiu** to keep sb alive; **~ coś w dobrym stanie** to keep sth in good condition;

U

**utrzymać sekret** to keep a secret ▷ *vi* to claim; **utrzymywać się** *vr* (*w pewnej pozycji*) to remain; (*na stanowisku*) to stay; (*o pogodzie*) to hold; (*o zwyczaju*) to survive; **~ się z czegoś** to make a living by *lub* off doing sth; **~ się przy życiu** to stay alive
**utwar|dzać (-dzam, -dzasz)** (*perf* **-dzić**) *vt* to harden
**utwar|dzić (-dzę, -dzisz)** (*imp* **-dź**) *vb perf od* **utwardzać**
**utwier|dzać (-dzam, -dzasz)** (*perf* **-dzić**) *vt*: **~ kogoś w czymś** to strengthen sb in sth; **utwierdzać się** *vr*: **~ się w czymś** to strengthen o.s. in sth; **~ się w przekonaniu, że ...** to confirm o.s. in the conviction that ...
**utwier|dzić (-dzę, -dzisz)** (*imp* **-dź**) *vb perf od* **utwierdzać**
**utworz|yć (-ę, -ysz)** (*imp* **utwórz**) *vb perf od* **tworzyć**
**utw|ór (-oru, -ory)** (*loc sg* **-orze**) *m* piece, work
**uty|ć (-ję, -jesz)** *vb perf od* **tyć**
**utyk|ać (-am, -asz)** *vi* (*kuleć*) to limp; (*grzęznąć*) (*perf* **utknąć**) to get stuck; **utknąć na mieliźnie** to run aground
**utylitarny** *adj* utilitarian
**utylizacj|a (-i)** *f* recycling
**utyliz|ować (-uję, -ujesz)** *vt* to recycle
**utys|kiwać (-kuję, -kujesz)** *vi* to gripe; **~ na kogoś/coś** to gripe about sb/sth
**utytułowany** *adj* titled
**UW** *abbr* = **Unia Wolności**
**uwa|ga (-gi, -gi)** (*dat sg* **-dze**) *f* (*koncentracja świadomości*) attention; (*komentarz*) comment, remark; (*napomnienie*) reproof; **~!** (*ostrożnie!*) be careful!; (*w obliczu niebezpieczeństwa*) look out!; **„U~! Stopień!"** "Mind the step!"; **„U~! Wysokie napięcie!"** "Danger! High voltage!"; **„U~! Mokra podłoga!"** "Caution! Wet floor!"; **„U~! Zły pies!"** "Beware of the dog!"; **brać (wziąć** *perf***) coś pod uwagę** to take sth into consideration; **zwracać (zwrócić** *perf***) uwagę na kogoś/coś** to pay attention to sb/sth; **nie zwracać uwagi na kogoś/coś** to take no notice of sb/sth; **zwrócić** (*perf*) **komuś uwagę** to reprove sb; **uchodzić** *lub* **umykać uwadze** to escape notice; **robić (zrobić** (*perf*)**) uwagę na temat czegoś** to remark on sth; **z uwagi na coś** owing to sth
**uwal|niać (-niam, -niasz)** (*perf* **uwolnić**) *vt* to free; (*więźnia, zwierzę*) to free, to set free; **uwalniać się** *vr* (*wyzwalać się*) to free o.s.; **~ się od kogoś/czegoś** to free o.s. from sb/sth
**uwarunkow|ywać (-uję, -ujesz)** *vt*: **~ coś czymś** to condition sth on sth
**uważ|ać (-am, -asz)** *vt*: **~ kogoś za przyjaciela** to consider sb (to be) a friend; **~ uroczystość za rozpoczętą** to consider the ceremony open ▷ *vi* (*być ostrożnym*) to be careful; (*sądzić*) to think; **~ na kogoś/coś** to mind sb/sth; **uważaj, żebyś tego nie zgubił** mind you don't lose it; **uważaj, co robisz** mind what you are doing; **~ na drogę** mind the road; **rób jak uważasz** do as you wish; **uważaj na siebie** take care; **uważaj!** (*bądź ostrożny*) be careful!; (*w obliczu niebezpieczeństwa*) look out!; **uważać się** *vr*: **on się uważa za geniusza** he considers himself a genius
**uważnie** *adv* (*patrzeć*) attentively; (*czytać*) carefully
**uważny** *adj* (*spojrzenie*) attentive; (*obserwator*) careful
**uwertu|ra (-ry, -ry)** (*dat sg* **-rze**) *f* overture
**uwiarygod|nić (-nię, -nisz)** (*imp* **-nij**) *vt perf* (*podpis*) to authenticate; (*opowieść, usprawiedliwienie*) to give credence to
**uwią|zać (-żę, -żesz)** *vb perf od* **uwiązywać**
**uwiąz|ywać (-uję, -ujesz)** (*perf* **-ać**) *vt* to tie up
**uwi|ć (-ję, -jesz)** *vb perf od* **wić**
**uwidacz|niać, uwidocz|niać (-niam, -niasz)** (*perf* **uwidocznić**) *vt* to demonstrate; **uwidaczniać się** *vr* to appear
**uwidocz|nić (-nię, -nisz)** (*imp* **-nij**) *vb perf od* **uwidaczniać**
**uwiecz|niać (-niam, -niasz)** (*perf* **-nić**) *vt* to immortalize
**uwiecz|nić (-nię, -nisz)** (*imp* **-nij**) *vb perf od* **uwieczniać**
**uwiedzeni|e (-a)** *nt* seduction
**uwielbi|ać (-am, -asz)** *vt* to adore
**uwielbie|nie (-nia)** *nt* adoration
**uwieńcz|yć (-ę, -ysz)** *vt perf* (*ukoronować*) to crown; (*ozdobić*) to adorn
**uwier|ać (-a)** *vi* (*o kołnierzyku*) to pinch; (*o plecaku*) to dig into one's back; **buty mnie uwierają** my shoes pinch
**uwierzeni|e (-a)** *nt*: **nie do uwierzenia** unbelievable
**uwierz|yć (-ę, -ysz)** *vi perf* to start believing
**uwierzytel|niać (-niam, -niasz)** (*perf* **-nić**) *vt* (*dokument*) to authenticate
**uwierzytelniający** *adj*: **listy uwierzytelniające** credentials *pl*
**uwierzytel|nić (-nię, -nisz)** (*imp* **-nij**) *vb perf od* **uwierzytelniać**
**uwi|eść (-odę, -edziesz)** (*imp* **-edź**) *vb perf od* **uwodzić**
**uwię|zić (-żę, -zisz)** (*imp* **-ź**) *vt perf* (*w więzieniu*) to imprison; (*unieruchomić*) to trap
**uwięzieni|e (-a)** *nt* imprisonment
**uwię|znąć (-znę, -źniesz)** (*imp* **-źnij**, *pt* **uwiązł, uwięzła, uwięźli**) *vb perf od* **więznąć**

**uwię|ź** (**-zi**) *f*: **na uwięzi** (*pies: na smyczy*) on a leash; (*: na łańcuchu*) on a chain; (*krowa*) on a tether
**uwij|ać się (-am, -asz)** *vr* to bustle about
**uwikł|ać (-am, -asz)** *vb perf od* **wikłać**
**uwłacz|ać (-am, -asz)** *vt*: **~ komuś/czemuś** to bring discredit onto sb/sth
**uwłaczający** *adj* discreditable
**uwodziciel** (**-a, -e**) (*gen pl* **-i**) *m* seducer
**uwodziciel|ka** (**-ki, -ki**) (*dat sg* **-ce**, *gen pl* **-ek**) *f* seducer
**uwodzicielski** *adj* seductive
**uwodzicielsko** *adv* seductively
**uwo|dzić (-dzę, -dzisz)** (*imp* **uwódź**, *perf* **uwieść**) *vt* to seduce
**uwol|nić (-nię, -nisz)** (*imp* **-nij**) *vb perf od* **uwalniać**
**uwydat|niać (-niam, -niasz)** (*perf* **-nić**) *vt* to emphasize; **uwydatniać się** *vr* to be prominent
**uwydat|nić (-nię, -nisz)** (*imp* **-nij**) *vb perf od* **uwydatniać**
**uwypukl|ać (-am, -asz)** (*perf* **-ić**) *vt* (*podkreślać*) to emphasize; **uwypuklać się** *vr* to become prominent
**uwypukl|ić (-ę, -isz)** (*imp* **-ij**) *vb perf od* **uwypuklać**
**uwzględ|niać (-niam, -niasz)** (*perf* **-nić**) *vt* (*okoliczności, warunki*) to take into consideration; (*prośbę, życzenie*) to respect
**uwzględ|nić (-nię, -nisz)** (*imp* **-nij**) *vb perf od* **uwzględniać**
**uwzględnieni|e** (**-a**) *nt*: **z ~m czegoś** taking sth into consideration
**uw|ziąć się (-ezmę, -eźmiesz)** (*imp* **-eźmij**) *vi perf*: **uwziąć się na kogoś** to have it in for sb
**uzależ|niać (-niam, -niasz)** (*perf* **-nić**) *vt*: **~ coś od czegoś** to make sth dependent *lub* conditional on sth; **uzależniać się** *vr*: **~ się od kogoś/czegoś** to become dependent on sb/sth; **~ się od narkotyków** to become addicted to drugs
**uzależ|nić (-nię, -nisz)** (*imp* **-nij**) *vb perf od* **uzależniać**
**uzależnieni|e** (**-a**) *nt* addiction
**uzależniony** *adj*: **być ~m od kogoś/czegoś** to be dependent on sb/sth; **być ~m od narkotyków** to be addicted to drugs ▷ *m decl like adj* addict
**uzasad|niać (-niam, -niasz)** (*perf* **-nić**) *vt* to justify
**uzasad|nić (-nię, -nisz)** (*imp* **-nij**) *vb perf od* **uzasadniać**
**uzasadnie|nie** (**-nia, -nia**) (*gen pl* **-ń**) *nt* justification
**uzasadniony** *adj* justified
**Uzbekista|n** (**-nu**) (*loc sg* **-nie**) *m* Uzbekistan
**uzbraj|ać (-am, -asz)** (*perf* **uzbroić**) *vt* (*ludzi*) to arm; (*teren*) to develop; **uzbrajać się** *vr*: **~ się w coś** to arm o.s. with sth
**uzbr|oić (-oję, -oisz)** (*imp* **-ój**) *vb perf od* **uzbrajać**
**uzbrojeni|e** (**-a**) *nt* (*Wojsk*) weapons *pl*, armament; (*Tech*) fittings *pl*
**uzbrojony** *adj* (*posiadający broń*) armed; (*wyposażony w instalacje: teren*) developed; (*budynek*) mains connected; **być ~m w coś** to be armed with sth
**uz|da** (**-dy, -dy**) (*dat sg* **uździe**) *f* bridle
**uzdolnie|nie** (**-nia, -nia**) (*gen pl* **-ń**) *nt* aptitude, talent
**uzdolniony** *adj* talented, gifted
**uzdr|awiać (-awiam, -awiasz)** (*perf* **-owić**) *vt* to heal, to cure
**uzdrowiciel** (**-a, -e**) (*gen pl* **-i**) *m* healer
**uzdr|owić (-owię, -owisz)** (*imp* **-ów**) *vb perf od* **uzdrawiać**
**uzdrowi|sko** (**-ska, -ska**) (*instr sg* **-skiem**) *nt* health resort; (*z wodami mineralnymi*) spa
**uzewnętrz|niać (-niam, -niasz)** (*perf* **-nić**) *vt* to manifest; **uzewnętrzniać się** *vr* to manifest o.s.
**uzewnętrz|nić (-nię, -nisz)** (*imp* **-nij**) *vb perf od* **uzewnętrzniać**
**uzębieni|e** (**-a**) *nt* dentition
**uzgad|niać (-niam, -niasz)** (*perf* **uzgodnić**) *vt* (*treść, warunki*) to negotiate; **uzgodniliśmy, że ...** we have agreed that ...
**uzgod|nić (-nię, -nisz)** (*imp* **-nij**) *vb perf od* **uzgadniać**
**uzgodnie|nie** (**-nia, -nia**) (*gen pl* **-ń**) *nt* agreement; **do uzgodnienia** negotiable
**uzie|miać (-miam, -miasz)** (*perf* **-mić**) *vt* (*Tech*) to earth, to ground (*US*)
**uziemieni|e** (**-a**) *nt* (*Tech*) earth, ground (*US*)
**uzmysł|awiać (-awiam, -awiasz)** (*perf* **-owić**) *vt*: **~ coś komuś** to make sb aware of sth
**uzmysł|owić (-owię, -owisz)** (*imp* **-ów**) *vb perf od* **uzmysławiać**
**uzn|ać (-am, -asz)** *vb perf od* **uznawać**
**uzna|nie** (**-nia**) *nt* (*przyjęcie za słuszne*) recognition; (*poważanie*) respect; **w uznaniu czyichś osiągnięć** in recognition of sb's achievements; **zdobyć** (*perf*) **~** to gain *lub* win recognition; **cieszyć się ~m** to receive wide recognition; **pozostawić** (*perf*) **coś do czyjegoś uznania** to leave sth at sb's discretion; **według czyjegoś uznania** at sb's discretion
**uznany** *adj* recognized
**uzn|awać (-aję, -ajesz)** (*imp* **-awaj**, *perf* **-ać**) *vt* to recognize; **~ kogoś za oszusta** to regard sb as a crook; **~ coś za zaszczyt** to deem sth as

U

an honour (*Brit*) *lub* honor (*US*); **uznać coś za konieczne** to judge sth necessary; **uznawać się** *vr*: **uznać się za przywódcę** to consider o.s. the leader

**uzupeł|niać (-niam, -niasz)** (*perf* **-nić**) *vt* (*zapasy*) to replenish; (*dietę, wyposażenie*) to supplement; (*wypowiedź, strój*) to complete; **uzupełnić zapas wody/benzyny** to fill up with water/petrol (*Brit*) *lub* gas (*US*); **uzupełniać się** *vr*: **~ się wzajemnie** to complement one another

**uzupełniający** *adj*: **wybory uzupełniające** by-election

**uzupeł|nić (-nię, -nisz)** (*imp* **-nij**) *vb perf od* **uzupełniać**

**uzupełnie|nie** (**-nia, -nia**) (*gen pl* **-ń**) *nt* (*zapasów*) replenishment; (*diety, wyposażenia*) supplement; (*wypowiedzi, stroju*) completion

**uzurpato|r** (**-ra, -rzy**) (*loc sg* **-rze**) *m* usurper

**uzurp|ować (-uję, -ujesz)** *vt*: **~ coś sobie** to usurp sth

**uzysk|ać (-am, -asz)** *vb perf od* **uzyskiwać**

**uzys|kiwać (-kuję, -kujesz)** (*perf* **-kać**) *vt* (*pomoc*) to get; (*przewagę*) to gain; (*zgodę, stopień naukowy*) to get, to obtain; (*stypendium*) to get, to receive; **uzyskać połączenie** (*Tel*) to get through

**uździe** *n patrz* **uzda**

**użal|ać się (-am, -asz)** (*perf* **-ić**) *vr*: **użalać się na kogoś/coś** to complain about sb/sth; **użalać się nad kimś** to pity sb

**użądl|ić (-ę, -isz)** *vb perf od* **żądlić**

**użer|ać się (-am, -asz)** *vr*: **użerać się z kimś** (*pot*) to wrangle with sb

**uży|cie** (**-cia, -cia**) (*gen pl* **-ć**) *nt* use; **gotowy do użycia** ready for use; **łatwy w użyciu** easy to use; **wychodzić (wyjść** *perf***) z użycia** to go out of use; **sposób użycia** usage

**uży|ć (-ję, -jesz)** *vb perf od* **używać**

**użytecznoś|ć** (**-ci**) *f* (*przydatność*) usefulness; **zakład użyteczności publicznej** public utility

**użyteczny** *adj* useful; **ładunek handlowy** *lub* **~** payload

**użyt|ek** (**-ku**) *m* use; **do użytku wewnętrznego/zewnętrznego** for internal/external use; **zdatny do użytku** in working order; **robić (zrobić** *perf***) ~ z czegoś** to make use of sth; **użytki** *pl* arable lands

**użytk|ować (-uję, -ujesz)** *vt* to use

**użytkowa|nie** (**-nia**) *nt* use

**użytkowni|k** (**-ka, -cy**) (*instr sg* **-kiem**) *m* user; **~ drogi** road user; **rodzimy ~ języka** (*Jęz*) native speaker

**użytkowy** *adj* utilitarian; **rośliny użytkowe** *farm plants*; **powierzchnia użytkowa** *usable floor space*; **program ~** (*Komput*) application program

**używ|ać (-am, -asz)** *vt* (*perf* **użyć**) to use; (*lekarstwa*) to take ▷ *vi*: **~ sobie na kimś** to go hard on sb; **~ życia** to live it up

**używany** *adj* used, secondhand

**używ|ka** (**-ki, -ki**) (*dat sg* **-ce**, *gen pl* **-ek**) *f* ≈ stimulant

**użyź|niać (-niam, -niasz)** (*perf* **-nić**) *vt* to fertilize

**użyź|nić (-nię, -nisz)** (*imp* **-nij**) *vb perf od* **użyźniać**

# Vv

**V¹, v** *nt inv (litera)* V, v; **V jak Violetta** ≈ V for Victor
**V²** *abbr* = **Volt**
**vademecum** *nt inv* = **wademekum**
**VAT** (**VAT-u**) (*loc sg* **Vacie**) *m* VAT
**vel** *prep* also known as, a.k.a.
**verte** *inv* please turn over, PTO
**ve|to** (**-ta, -ta**) (*instr sg* **-cie**) *nt* = **weto**
**video** *nt inv* = **wideo**
**vis-à-vis** *prep* opposite
**vol|t** (**-ta, -ty**) (*instr sg* **-cie**) *m* = **wolt**

**W¹, w¹** *nt inv* (*litera*) W, w; **W jak Wacław** ≈ W for William

**W²** *abbr* (= *wat*) W. (= *watt*)

SŁOWO KLUCZOWE

**w²** *prep +loc* **1** (*położenie*) in; **w domu/szkole** at home/school; **w kinie/teatrze** at the cinema/theatre; **w telewizji/radiu** on television/the radio; **w górze/dole** above/below
**2** (*ubiór*): **człowiek w okularach** a man in glasses; **kobieta w czerni** a woman in black
**3** (*postać*): **cukier w kostkach** sugar cubes *lub* lumps; **mydło w płynie** liquid soap; **5 tys. zł w gotówce** 5,000 zloty in cash
**4** (*czas*): **w roku 2000** in the year 2000; **w poniedziałek** on Monday; **w maju** in May; **w dzień** during the day; **w nocy** at night; **w krótkim czasie** in a short time, soon
**5** (*ilość*): **powieść w trzech tomach** a novel in three volumes
**6** (*stan*): **w szoku/rozpaczy** in shock/despair; **w dobrej formie** in good form; **być w modzie** to be in fashion; **być w budowie** to be under construction
**7** (*sytuacja*): **żyć w biedzie** to live in poverty; **być w niebezpieczeństwie** to be in danger
**8** (*sposób*): **płacić w ratach** to pay in instalments; **dostać coś w prezencie** to get sth as a gift
▷ *prep +acc* **1** (*kierunek*) in(to); **patrzyć w niebo** to look into the sky; **wpadać (wpaść** *perf***) w kłopoty/kałużę** to get into trouble/a puddle; **złapać w pułapkę** to catch in a trap; **w lewo/prawo** to the left/right; **w dół/górę** up/down
**2** (*deseń, kształt*): **koszula w paski** striped shirt; **pokroić coś w kostkę/plasterki** to dice/slice sth
**3** (*cel*): **uderzyć kogoś w głowę** to hit sb on the head; **uderzyć w drzewo/mur** to hit a tree/wall; **zimno mi w nogi** my feet are cold
**4** (*czynność*): **grać w karty/tenisa** to play cards/tennis; **iść w odwiedziny** to go visiting
**5** (*wyposażenie*): **uzbrojony w rewolwer** armed with a gun
**6** (*sposób*): **śmiać się w głos** to laugh aloud; **biegać w kółko** *lub* **koło** to run in circles
**7** (*zakres czasu*): **w tydzień/pięć minut** within a week/five minutes

**w.** *abbr* (= *wiek*) c. (= *century*); (= *wewnętrzny*) ext. (= *extension*)

**wa|bić (-bię, -bisz)** (*perf* **z-**) *vt* to attract; (*zwierzę*) to lure; **wabić się** *vr imperf* to be called

**wachlarz** (**-a, -e**) (*gen pl* **-y**) *m* fan; (*przen*) range

**wachl|ować (-uję, -ujesz)** *vt* to fan; **wachlować się** *vr* to fan o.s.

**wach|ta** (**-ty, -ty**) (*dat sg* **-cie**) *f* watch

**waci|k** (**-ka, -ki**) (*instr sg* **-kiem**) *m* swab, cotton ball

**wa|da** (**-dy, -dy**) (*dat sg* **-dzie**) *f* (*ujemna cecha*) disadvantage; (*defekt*) defect; (*przywara*) fault, shortcoming

**wademekum** *nt inv* handbook, manual

**wadliwy** *adj* defective

**wadze** *n patrz* **waga**

**waf|el** (**-la, -le**) (*gen pl* **-li**) *m* (*do lodów*) cone, cornet (*Brit*); (*ciastko*) wafer

**wa|ga** (**-gi, -gi**) (*dat sg* **-dze**) *f* (*łazienkowa, kuchenna*) scales *pl*; (*laboratoryjna*) balance; (*ciężar*) weight; (*doniosłość*) importance, significance; (*Sport*) weight; **kupować/sprzedawać na wagę** to buy/sell by weight; **przybierać/tracić na wadze** to gain *lub* put on/lose weight; **być na wagę złota** (*przen*) to be worth one's weight in gold; **przywiązywać wagę do czegoś** to attach importance to sth; **sprawa najwyższej wagi** matter of paramount *lub* utmost importance; **Waga** (*Astrologia*) Libra

**wagar|ować (-uję, -ujesz)** *vi* (*pot*) to play truant (*Brit*) *lub* hooky (*US*)

**wagarowicz** (**-a, -e**) *m* (*pot*) truant

**wagar|y** (**-ów**) *pl* (*pot*) truancy; **iść (pójść** *perf***) na ~** to play truant (*Brit*) *lub* hooky (*US*)

**wago|n** (**-nu, -ny**) (*loc sg* **-nie**) *m* (*pasażerski*) carriage (*Brit*), coach (*Brit*), car (*US*);

(*towarowy*) wagon (*Brit*), truck; **~ sypialny** sleeping car; **~ restauracyjny** dining *lub* restaurant car

**wah|ać się (-am, -asz)** *vr (o człowieku) (perf* **za-**) to hesitate; (*o wskazówce*) (*perf* **-nąć**) to waver; (*o temperaturze*) to vary

**wahad|ło (-ła, -ła)** (*loc sg* **-le**, *gen pl* **-eł**) *nt* pendulum

**wahadłow|iec (-ca, -ce)** *m* space shuttle

**wahadłowy** *adj*: **drzwi wahadłowe** swing door

**waha|nie (-nia, -nia)** (*gen pl* **-ń**) *nt* hesitation; (*cen, temperatury*) fluctuations *pl*; **bez wahania** without hesitation

**wakacj|e (-i)** *pl* (*letnie, zimowe*) holiday(s) (*Brit*), vacation (*US*); **na wakacjach** on holidays *lub* vacation; **jechać (pojechać** *perf*) **na ~** to go on holidays *lub* vacation; **~ podatkowe** tax holidays

**waka|t (-tu, -ty)** (*loc sg* **-cie**) *m* vacancy

**walc (-a, -e)** *m* waltz

**walcow|nia (-ni, -nie)** (*gen pl* **-ni**) *f* steel mill

**walcz|yć (-ę, -ysz)** *vi* to fight; (*rywalizować*) to compete; (*zmagać się*) to struggle; **~ ze snem** to fight off sleep; **~ ze śmiercią** to be fighting with death; **~ o** *lub* **za coś** to fight for sth; **~ z czymś** to fight against sth

**wale** *n patrz* **wał**

**wal|ec (-ca, -ce)** *m* (*Geom*) cylinder; (*też:* **walec drogowy**) steamroller

**waleczność (-ci)** *f* bravery

**waleczny** *adj* brave

**walentyn|ka (-ki, -ki)** (*dat sg* **-ce**, *gen pl* **-ek**) *f* valentine (card)

**waleria|na (-ny)** (*dat sg* **-nie**) *f* valerian

**wale|t (-ta, -ty)** (*loc sg* **-cie**) *m* (*Karty*) jack, knave; **mieszkać na ~a** (*pot*) to reside illegally

**Wali|a (-i)** *f* Wales

**wal|ić (-ę, -isz)** (*perf* **-nąć**) *vt/vi* (*pot*) to bang; **serce mu waliło (jak młotem)** his heart was thumping *lub* pounding; **~ prosto z mostu** (*pot*) to talk straight from the shoulder; **walić się** *vr* (*rozpadać się*) to collapse; (*przewracać się*) to fall down, to collapse; **~ się (walnąć się** *perf*) **w piersi** to beat one's chest

**Walijczy|k (-ka, -cy)** (*instr sg* **-kiem**) *m* Welshman

**Walij|ka (-ki, -ki)** (*dat sg* **-ce**, *gen pl* **-ek**) *f* Welshwoman

**walijski** *adj* Welsh

**waliz|ka (-ki, -ki)** (*dat sg* **-ce**, *gen pl* **-ek**) *f* suitcase

**wal|ka (-ki, -ki)** (*dat sg* **-ce**, *gen pl* **-k**) *f* fight; (*ciągła*) warfare; **~ o władzę/niepodległość** struggle for power/independence

**walkma|n® (-na, -ny)** (*loc sg* **-nie**) *m* portable cassette player, walkman®

**walkowe|r (-ru)** (*loc sg* **-rze**) *m* walkover; **wygrać** (*perf*) **~em** to win by a walkover, to walk over

**wal|nąć (-nę, -niesz)** (*imp* **-nij**) *vb perf od* **walić**

**walnie** *adv* largely

**walny** *adj* (*zebranie, zgromadzenie*) general; (*zwycięstwo*) overwhelming

**walo|r (-ru, -ry)** (*loc sg* **-rze**) *m* virtue

**waloryzacj|a (-i)** *f* valorization

**waltor|nia (-ni, -nie)** (*gen pl* **-ni**) *f* French horn

**walu|ta (-ty, -ty)** (*dat sg* **-cie**) *f* currency; **waluty obce** foreign exchange

**walutowy** *adj* monetary; **kurs ~** foreign exchange rate; **Międzynarodowy Fundusz W~** International Monetary Fund

**wa|ł (-łu, -ły)** (*loc sg* **-le**) *m* (*wzdłuż rzeki, drogi*) embankment; **wał korbowy** crankshaft; **wał napędowy** drive shaft

**wał|ek (-ka, -ki)** (*instr sg* **-kiem**) *m* (*do ciasta*) rolling-pin; (*Tech*) roller; **wałki** *pl* (*do włosów*) rollers

**wałęs|ać się (-am, -asz)** *vr* to wander

**wałko|ń (-nia, -nie)** (*gen pl* **-ni** *lub* **-niów**) *m* (*pot*) loafer, idler

**wałk|ować (-uję, -ujesz)** *vt* (*ciasto*) (*perf* **roz-**) to roll out; (*pot: kwestię, temat*) to go over and over

**wam** *pron dat od* **wy** (to) you

**wam|p (-pa, -py)** (*loc sg* **-pie**) *m* vamp

**wampi|r (-ra, -ry)** (*loc sg* **-rze**) *m* vampire

**wandal (-a, -e)** (*gen pl* **-i** *lub* **-ów**) *m* vandal

**wandaliz|m (-mu)** (*loc sg* **-mie**) *m* vandalism

**wanili|a (-i)** *f* vanilla

**waniliowy** *adj* vanilla *attr*

**wan|na (-ny, -ny)** (*dat sg* **-nie**) *f* bath(tub)

**wapienny** *adj* limestone *attr*

**wapie|ń (-nia, -nie)** (*gen pl* **-ni**) *m* limestone

**wapni|eć (-eje)** (*perf* **z-**) *vi* (*o kościach*) to calcify; (*o żyłach*) to harden

**wap|no (-na)** (*loc sg* **-nie**) *nt* lime; **~ palone/ gaszone** burnt/slaked lime

**wap|ń (-nia)** *m* calcium

**warcab|y (-ów)** *pl* draughts (*Brit*), checkers (*US*)

**warchla|k (-ka, -ki)** (*instr sg* **-kiem**) *m* piglet

**warcho|ł (-ła, -ły)** (*loc sg* **-le**) *m* troublemaker

**war|czeć (-czę, -czysz)** (*perf* **-knąć** *lub* **za-**) *vi* to growl; (*o silniku*) to whir(r)

**war|ga (-gi, -gi)** (*dat sg* **-dze**) *f* lip; **dolna/ górna ~** lower/upper lip; **zajęcza ~** (*Med*) harelip

**wariacj|a (-i, -e)** (*gen pl* **-i**) *f* (*Muz*) variation

**wariacki** *adj* (*pot*) crazy; (*tempo*) breakneck *attr*; **kierować po wariacku** (*pot*) to drive like a madman

W

**wariact|wo** (**-wa, -wa**) (*loc sg* **-wie**) *nt* madness
**warian|t** (**-tu, -ty**) (*loc sg* **-cie**) *m* variant
**waria|t** (**-ta, -ci**) (*loc sg* **-cie**) *m* (*pot*) madman, lunatic (*pot*), nut (*pot*); **dom ~ów** (*pot*) madhouse; **robić (zrobić** *perf*) **z kogoś/siebie ~a** (*pot*) to make a fool of sb/o.s.
**wariat|ka** (**-ki, -ki**) (*dat sg* **-ce**, *gen pl* **-ek**) *f* (*pot*) madwoman (*pot*), lunatic (*pot*), nut (*pot*)
**wari|ować (-uję, -ujesz)** (*perf* **z-**) *vi* (*pot: tracić zmysły*) to go mad; **~ ze szczęścia** (*pot*) to be mad with joy (*pot*); **~ z rozpaczy** (*pot*) to go mad *lub* crazy with despair
**wark|nąć (-nę, -niesz)** (*imp* **-nij**) *vb perf od* **warczeć** ▷ *vi perf* (*powiedzieć opryskliwie*) to snarl
**warkocz** (**-a, -e**) (*gen pl* **-y**) *m* (*z włosów*) plait, braid (US); (*przen: dymu*) trail; (*komety*) tail
**warkoczy|k** (**-ka, -ki**) (*instr sg* **-kiem**) *m* pigtail
**warko|t** (**-tu, -ty**) (*loc sg* **-cie**) *m* throb, rattle
**warko|tać (-cze)** *vi* to throb, to rattle
**War|na** (**-ny**) (*dat sg* **-nie**) *f* Varna
**war|ować (-uję, -ujesz)** *vi* (*o psie*) to lie on guard
**warow|nia** (**-ni, -nie**) (*gen pl* **-ni**) *f* (*Hist*) stronghold
**warowny** *adj* fortified
**warst|wa** (**-wy, -wy**) (*dat sg* **-wie**) *f* (*pokład: atmosfery, izolacji*) layer; (*zewnętrzna: farby*) coat; **~ społeczna** social stratum
**Warsza|wa** (**-wy**) (*dat sg* **-wie**) *f* Warsaw
**warszawski** *adj* Warsaw *attr*
**warszta|t** (**-tu, -ty**) (*loc sg* **-cie**) *m* shop; (*Sztuka*) technique; **~ samochodowy** service station, garage (Brit); **mieć coś na warsztacie** (*przen*) to work on sth; **brać coś na ~** (*przen*) to get *lub* set to work on sth
**wart** *adj*: **~ 2000 złotych** worth 2,000 zloty; **~ zaufania** trustworthy; **ta książka jest ~a przeczytania** this book is worth reading; **ile to jest ~e?** how much is it worth?; **być ~ym czegoś** to be worthy of sth; **nic nie ~** worthless; **być ~ym zachodu** to be worthwhile; **to gra nie ~a świeczki** (*pot*) the game is not worth the candle
**war|ta** (**-ty, -ty**) (*dat sg* **-cie**) *f* (*oddział*) guard; (*służba*) guard (duty), sentry duty; **stać na warcie** to be on guard *lub* on sentry duty; **~ honorowa** guard of honour (Brit) *lub* honor (US); *patrz też* **wart**
**wartki** *adj* swift
**warto** *inv*: **~ spróbować/kupić** it's worth trying/buying; **~ było tu przyjechać** it was worth coming here
**wartości|ować (-uję, -ujesz)** *vt* to evaluate, to assess
**wartościowoś|ć** (**-ci**) *f* (*Chem*) valency (Brit), valence (US)
**wartościowy** *adj* valuable; **papiery wartościowe** (*Fin*) securities *pl*
**wartoś|ć** (**-ci**) *f* value, worth; **towar o wartości 100 funtów** goods worth 100 pounds, 100 pounds' worth of goods; **~ nabywcza** purchasing value; **~ rynkowa** market value; **~ użytkowa** utility value; **mieć poczucie własnej wartości** to have a high self-esteem; **wartości** *pl* values *pl*
**wartow|nia** (**-ni, -nie**) (*gen pl* **-ni**) *f* guardhouse
**wartowni|k** (**-ka, -cy**) (*instr sg* **-kiem**) *m* sentry
**warun|ek** (**-ku, -ki**) (*instr sg* **-kiem**) *m* condition; **pod warunkiem, że ...** on condition (that) ..., provided *lub* providing (that) ...; **pod żadnym warunkiem** on no account, under no circumstances; **~ wstępny** precondition, prerequisite; **warunki** *pl* conditions *pl*; **mieć warunki, żeby coś robić** to be predisposed to do sth
**warunk|ować (-uję, -ujesz)** (*perf* **u-**) *vt* to condition, to determine
**warunkowo** *adv* conditionally; **zostać zwolnionym ~** to be released on parole
**warunkowy** *adj* conditional; **zwolnienie warunkowe** parole
**warz|yć (-ę, -ysz)** *vt* (*perf* **u-**) (*piwo*) to brew; **warzyć się** (*perf* **z-**) *vr* (*o mleku*) to turn (sour)
**warzywnict|wo** (**-wa**) (*loc sg* **-wie**) *nt* ≈ market gardening (Brit), ≈ truck farming (US) (*vegetables only*)
**warzywniczy** *adj*: **sklep ~** greengrocer('s)
**warzywni|k** (**-ka, -ki**) (*instr sg* **-kiem**) *m* vegetable garden
**warzywny** *adj* vegetable *attr*; **sklep ~** greengrocer('s); **giełda owocowo-warzywna** fruit and vegetable market
**warzy|wo** (**-wa, -wa**) (*loc sg* **-wie**) *nt* vegetable
**was** *pron gen, acc, loc od* **wy** you
**wasal** (**-a, -e**) (*gen pl* **-i** *lub* **-ów**) *m* vassal
**wasz** (*jak:* **nasz**) *possessive pron* (*z rzeczownikiem*) your; (*bez rzeczownika*) yours; **~ samochód** your car; **~ jest większy** yours is bigger
**Waszyngto|n** (**-nu**) (*loc sg* **-nie**) *m* Washington
**waś|nić (-nię, -nisz)** (*imp* **-nij**, *perf* **z-** *lub* **po-**) *vt* (*książk*) to stir up discord between *lub* among
**waś|ń** (**-ni, -nie**) (*gen pl* **-ni**) *f* (*książk*) discord
**wa|t** (**-ta, -ty**) (*loc sg* **-cie**) *m* (*Fiz*) watt
**wa|ta** (**-ty, -ty**) (*dat sg* **-cie**) *f* cotton wool (Brit), (absorbent) cotton (US); **~ krawiecka** wad(ding); **~ szklana** glass wool; **~ cukrowa** candy-floss (Brit), cotton candy (US); **mieć nogi jak z waty** (*przen*) to be weak at the knees

**wat|ka (-ki, -ki)** (*dat sg* **-ce**, *gen pl* **-ek**) *f* cotton ball

**watoli|na (-ny)** (*dat sg* **-nie**) *f* wad(ding)

**watowany** *adj* wadded

**watowy** *adj*: **żarówka 60-watowa** a 60 watt bulb

**Watyka|n (-nu)** (*loc sg* **-nie**) *m* the Vatican

**wawrzy|n (-nu, -ny)** (*loc sg* **-nie**) *m* laurel

**wa|za (-zy, -zy)** (*dat sg* **-zie**) *f* (*do zupy*) tureen; (*ozdobna*) vase

**wazeli|na (-ny)** (*dat sg* **-nie**) *f* petroleum jelly, Vaseline®

**wazeliniarz (-a, -e)** (*gen pl* **-y**) *m* (*pot*) toady (*pot*), apple polisher (US) (*pot*)

**wazo|n (-nu, -ny)** (*loc sg* **-nie**) *m* vase

**wazoni|k (-ka, -ki)** (*instr sg* **-kiem**) *m dimin od* **wazon**

**waż|ka (-ki, -ki)** (*dat sg* **-ce**, *gen pl* **-ek**) *f* dragonfly

**ważki** *adj* (*książk*) important

**ważkoś|ć (-ci)** *f* (*książk*) importance

**ważnia|k (-ka, -cy)** (*instr sg* **-kiem**) *m* (*pot*) stuffed shirt

**ważnoś|ć (-ci)** *f* (*paszportu, wizy*) validity; (*doniosłość*) importance; **data ważności** sell-by date; **stracić** (*perf*) **~** (*o artykule spożywczym*) to be past the sell-by date; (*o wizie, paszporcie*) to expire

**ważny** *adj* important; (*paszport, wiza*) valid; (*pot: mina*) self-important; **ważna osobistość** VIP

**waż|yć (-ę, -ysz)** *vt* (*perf* **z-**) to weigh ▷ *vi*: **~ 70 kg** to weigh 70 kg; **ważyć się** *vr* to weigh o.s.; (*decydować się*) to hang in the balance; **~ się (od~ się** *perf*) **na coś** to venture (up)on sth; **ani mi się waż!** (*pot*) don't you dare! (*pot*)

**wąch|ać (-am, -asz)** (*perf* **po-**) *vt* to smell; (*o psie*) to sniff

**wą|gier (-gra, -gry)** (*loc sg* **-grze**) *m* blackhead

**wą|s (-sa, -sy)** (*loc sg* **-sie**) *m* moustache (*Brit*), mustache (US); **wąsy** *pl* (*u mężczyzny*) moustache (*Brit*), mustache (US); (*u kota, myszy*) whiskers *pl*

**wąsaty** *adj* moustached (*Brit*), mustached (US)

**wąsi|k (-ka, -ki)** (*instr sg* **-kiem**) *m* pencil moustache (*Brit*) *lub* mustache (US)

**wąski** (*comp* **węższy**) *adj* narrow; **~e gardło** (*przen*) bottleneck

**wąskotorowy** *adj* narrow-gauge *attr*

**wąt|ek (-ku, -ki)** (*instr sg* **-kiem**) *m* (*myśli*) train; (*wykładu, filmu, powieści*) thread; (*sztuki, książki*) plot, main story; **stracić** (*perf*) *lub* **zgubić** (*perf*) **~** to lose one's thread

**wątły** *adj* (*chłopiec, drzewko*) frail; (*płomień, ślad*) faint

**wąt|pić (-pię, -pisz)** *vi* to doubt; **~ w coś** to doubt sth; **~ o czymś** to be doubtful about sth; **wątpię** I doubt it

**wątpieni|e (-a)** *nt*: **bez wątpienia** undoubtedly

**wątpliwoś|ć (-ci, -ci)** (*gen pl* **-ci**) *f* doubt; **mieć wątpliwości (co do czegoś)** to have one's doubt(s) (about sth); **budzić wątpliwości** to be dubious *lub* questionable; **ponad wszelką ~** beyond all doubt; **nie ulega wątpliwości, że ...** there's no doubt that ...; **poddawać coś w ~** to question sth, to bring *lub* call sth into question

**wątpliwy** *adj* (*problematyczny*) questionable; (*podejrzany*) doubtful, dubious; (*mało prawdopodobny*) doubtful, debatable; (*honor, przyjemność*) dubious; **~ przypadek** borderline case

**wątr|oba (-oby, -oby)** (*dat sg* **-obie**, *gen pl* **-ób**) *f* liver; **zapalenie wątroby** hepatitis

**wątrobian|ka (-ki, -ki)** (*dat sg* **-ce**, *gen pl* **-ek**) *f* (*pot*) liver sausage, liverwurst (US)

**wątrób|ka (-ki, -ki)** (*dat sg* **-ce**, *gen pl* **-ek**) *f* (*Kulin*) liver

**wąw|óz (-ozu, -ozy)** (*loc sg* **-ozie**) *m* ravine

**wąż (węża, węże)** (*gen pl* **węży** *lub* **wężów**) *m* (*Zool*) snake; (*gumowy*) hose; **wąż ogrodowy** garden hose; **mieć węża w kieszeni** (*przen*) to be stingy

**w|bić (-biję, -bijesz)** *vb perf od* **wbijać**

**wbie|c (-gnę, -gniesz)** (*imp* **-gnij**, *pt* **-gł**) *vb perf od* **wbiegać**

**wbieg|ać (-am, -asz)** (*perf* **wbiec**) *vi* to run (into); **~ na boisko** to run onto the field; **~ na szczyt** to run up to the top

**wbij|ać (-am, -asz)** (*perf* **wbić**) *vt* (*gwóźdź, kołek*) to hammer in, to drive in; (*nóż, sztylet*) to plunge; (*zęby, paznokcie*) to sink, to dig; **~ gwóźdź w deskę** to drive *lub* hammer a nail into a plank; **wbić coś sobie do głowy** (*pot*) to get sth into one's head; **~ wzrok w coś** (*przen*) to fix one's eyes on sth; **wbijać się** *vr* to stick in

**wbrew** *prep +dat* contrary to, in defiance of; **~ czyjejś woli** against sb's will; **~ sobie** despite o.s.

**wbud|ować (-uję, -ujesz)** *vb perf od* **wbudowywać**

**wbudowany** *adj* built-in *attr*

**wbudow|ywać (-uję, -ujesz)** (*perf* **-ać**) *vt* to build in(to)

**WC, w.c.** *abbr* WC

**wcale** *adv* (*w ogóle*) (not) at all; (*całkiem*) quite; **~ tam nie poszedł** he didn't go there at all, he never went there; **~ niezły** quite good; **~ nie!** not at all!

**wchłani|ać (-am, -asz)** (*perf* **wchłonąć**) *vt* to absorb

W

**wchłaniani|e** (**-a**) *nt* absorption
**wchło|nąć (-nę, -niesz)** (*imp* **-ń**) *vb perf od* **wchłaniać**
**wcho|dzić (-dzę, -dzisz)** (*imp* **-dź**, *perf* **wejść**) *vi* (*do sali, budynku, wody*) to walk into, to enter; (*do samochodu*) to get in; **~ na drzewo/po schodach** to climb a tree/the stairs; **do sali wchodzi 100 osób** the room holds a hundred people; **(proszę) wejść!** come in!; **wejść do finału** (*Sport*) to get into the final; **w skład komisji wchodzą cztery osoby** the committee consists of four people; **w skład załogi wchodziło dwóch Brytyjczyków** the crew included two Britons; **~ w szczegóły** to go into details; **~ w życie** (*przen*) to come into effect, to take effect; **~ na ekrany** (*o filmie*) to be released; **~ na rynek** to come onto the market; **to nie wchodzi w grę** *lub* **rachubę** this is out of the question
**wciąć (wetnę, wetniesz)** (*imp* **wetnij**) *vb perf od* **wcinać**
**wciąg|ać (-am, -asz)** (*perf* **-nąć**) *vt* to pull (into); (*linę, żagiel, flagę*) to hoist; (*dym, powietrze*) to breathe in; (*o bagnie, wirze*) to suck in *lub* down; (*o książce, filmie*) to absorb; (*bluzę, spodnie*) to pull on; **~ coś do pokoju** to drag sth into the room; **~ brzuch** to pull in one's stomach; **~ kogoś (w coś)** to draw sb in(to sth); **~ kogoś/coś na listę** to put sb/sth on the list; **wciągać się** *vr*: **~ się w coś** to get into the swing of sth
**wciąg|nąć (-nę, -niesz)** (*imp* **-nij**) *vb perf od* **wciągać**
**wciąż** *adv* still
**wciel|ać (-am, -asz)** (*perf* **-ić**) *vt* (*włączać*) to incorporate; **~ kogoś do wojska** to enlist sb (into the army); **~ coś w życie** to put *lub* carry sth into effect; **wcielać się** *vr*: **~ się w kogoś** to impersonate sb
**wciele|nie** (**-nia, -nia**) (*gen pl* **-ń**) *nt* incarnation
**wcier|ać (-am, -asz)** (*perf* **wetrzeć**) *vt*: **~ coś (w coś)** to rub sth in(to sth)
**wcię|cie** (**-cia, -cia**) (*gen pl* **-ć**) *nt* (*wgłębienie*) notch; (*Druk*) indentation; **głębokie ~ w talii** slim waist
**wcin|ać (-am, -asz)** (*perf* **wciąć**) *vt* (*linię, wiersz*) to indent; (*pot: jeść*) to tuck in; **wcinać się** *vr*: **~ się w coś** to cut into sth
**wcisk|ać (-am, -asz)** (*perf* **wcisnąć**) *vt* (*wtłaczać*) to squeeze in; (*wsuwać*) to drive in; **~ książkę do torby** to squeeze *lub* cram a book into the bag; **wcisnąć coś komuś do ręki** to press sth into sb's hand; **~ coś komuś** (*pot: dawać*) to palm sth off on sb; **wciskać się** *vr*: **~ się (do sali)** to crowd in(to a room)
**wci|snąć (-snę, -śniesz)** (*imp* **-śnij**) *vb perf od* **wciskać**
**wczasowicz** (**-a, -e**) *m* holidaymaker (*Brit*), vacationer (*US*)
**wczas|y** (**-ów**) *pl* holiday *sg* (*Brit*), vacation *sg* (*US*); **jechać na ~** to go on holiday (*Brit*) *lub* vacation (*US*)
**wcze|sny** (*comp* **-śniejszy**) *adj* early; (*poród*) premature; **we ~ch godzinach rannych** in the small hours
**wcześnia|k** (**-ka, -ki**) (*instr sg* **-kiem**) *m* premature baby
**wcześnie** *adv* early
**wcześniej** *adv comp od* **wcześnie** earlier; (*uprzednio*) in advance
**wcześniejszy** *adj comp od* **wczesny** earlier; (*uprzedni*) prior
**wczoraj** *adv* yesterday ▷ *nt inv* (*przeszłość*) yesterday; **~ rano/wieczorem** yesterday morning/evening; **~ w nocy** last night
**wczorajszy** *adj* (*z wczoraj*) yesterday *attr*, yesterday's; (*książk: przeszły*) yesterday's, of yesterday; **~ dzień** yesterday; **~ wieczór** yesterday evening
**wcz|uć się (-uję, -ujesz)** *vb perf od* **wczuwać się**
**wczuw|ać się (-am, -asz)** (*perf* **wczuć**) *vr*: **wczuwać się w sytuację/rolę** to identify with a situation/role
**wczyt|ywać (-uję, -ujesz)** (*perf* **-ać**) *vt* (*Komput*) to load; **wczytywać się** *vr*: **~ się w coś** to pore over sth
**wd|ać się (-am, -asz)** *vb perf od* **wdawać się** ▷ *vi perf*: **on wdał się w ojca** he takes after his father
**wdarł** *itd. vb patrz* **wedrzeć się**
**wd|awać się (-aję, -ajesz)** (*perf* **-ać**) *vr*: **wdawać się w coś** (*bójkę, dyskusję*) to get into; (*szczegóły*) to go into
**wdech** (**-u, -y**) *m* inhalation; **robić (zrobić** *perf*) **~** to inhale, to breathe in
**wdep|nąć (-nę, -niesz)** (*imp* **-nij**) *vi perf*: **~ w coś** to step into sth; **~ w aferę/złe towarzystwo** (*pot*) to get mixed up in a scandal/with bad company
**wdep|tać (-czę, -czesz)** *vb perf od* **wdeptywać**
**wdept|ywać (-uję, -ujesz)** (*perf* **-ać**) *vt*: **~ coś w ziemię** to tread sth into the ground
**wd|owa** (**-owy, -owy**) (*dat sg* **-owie**, *gen pl* **-ów**) *f* widow; **~ po panu Kowalskim** Mr Kowalski's widow
**wdo|wiec** (**-wca, -wcy**) *m* widower
**wdra|pać się (-pię, -piesz)** *vb perf od* **wdrapywać się**
**wdrap|ywać się (-uję, -ujesz)** (*perf* **-ać**) *vr*: **wdrapywać się na coś** to climb (up) sth

**wdraż|ać (-am, -asz)** (*perf* **wdrożyć**) *vt* (*pracownika, śledztwo*) to initiate; (*technologię, wynalazek*) to put into practice; **~ kogoś do czegoś** to introduce sb to sth
**wdych|ać (-am, -asz)** *vt* to breathe in, to inhale
**wdzier|ać się (-am, -asz)** (*perf* **wedrzeć**) *vr* (*o żołnierzach*) to force one's way in; (*o wodzie*) to rush in; (*na mury*) to scale
**wdzięcznoś|ć** (**-ci**) *f* gratitude; **z wdzięcznością** gratefully, thankfully
**wdzięczny** *adj* grateful; (*ujmujący*) graceful; (*dający satysfakcję*) rewarding; **być ~m komuś za coś** to be grateful to sb for sth
**wdzięcz|yć się (-ę, -ysz)** *vr* (*pot*): **wdzięczyć się do kogoś** to flirt with sb
**wdzię|k** (**-ku, -ki**) (*instr sg* **-kiem**) *m* grace; **z ~iem** gracefully *lub* with grace; **wdzięki** *pl* charm *sg*
**we** *prep +acc* = **w**
**wedle** *prep* (*książk*) according to
**według** *prep +gen* according to; **~ mnie** in my opinion; **~ mojego zegarka** by my watch
**wed|rzeć się (-rę, -rzesz)** (*imp* **-rzyj**, *pt* **wdarł**) *vb perf od* **wdzierać się**
**weeken|d** (**-du, -dy**) (*loc sg* **-dzie**) *m* weekend
**wegetacj|a** (**-i**) *f* vegetation
**wegetaria|nin** (**-nina, -nie**) (*gen pl* **-n**) *m* vegetarian
**wegetarianiz|m** (**-mu**) (*loc sg* **-mie**) *m* vegetarianism
**wegetarian|ka** (**-ki, -ki**) (*dat sg* **-ce**, *gen pl* **-ek**) *f* vegetarian
**wegetariański** *adj* vegetarian
**weget|ować (-uję, -ujesz)** *vi* to vegetate
**wehiku|ł** (**-łu, -ły**) (*loc sg* **-le**) *m* (*książk*) vehicle; **~ czasu** time machine
**wejrze|nie** (**-nia, -nia**) (*-gen pl* **-ń**) *nt*: **miłość od pierwszego wejrzenia** love at first sight
**wejś|cie** (**-cia**) *nt* (*czynność*) entrance, entry; (*drzwi*) (*nom pl* **-cia**, *gen pl* **-ć**) entrance; (*wstęp*) entry; (*Tech*: *gniazdo*) (*nom pl* **-cia**, *gen pl* **-ć**) input; „~" "way in"
**wejściowy** *adj* (*drzwi*) front *attr*; (*bilet*) entrance *attr*; (*dane, gniazdo*) input *attr*
**wejściów|ka** (**-ki, -ki**) (*dat sg* **-ce**, *gen pl* **-ek**) *f* (*pot*) pass
**wej|ść (-dę, -dziesz)** (*imp* **-dź**, *pt* **wszedł, weszła, weszli**) *vb perf od* **wchodzić**
**we|k** (**-ku** *lub* **-ka, -ki**) (*instr sg* **-kiem**) *m* preserving jar
**weks|el** (**-la, -le**) (*gen pl* **-li**) *m* bill of exchange
**wekto|r** (**-ra, -ry**) (*loc sg* **-rze**) *m* vector
**welo|n** (**-nu, -ny**) (*loc sg* **-nie**) *m* (*część stroju*) veil; (*Zool*) goldfish
**welu|r** (**-ru, -ry**) (*loc sg* **-rze**) *m* velour
**welwe|t** (**-tu, -ty**) (*loc sg* **-cie**) *m* velvet
**weł|na** (**-ny, -ny**) (*dat sg* **-nie**, *gen pl* **-en**) *f* wool; **~ czesankowa** worsted
**wełniany** *adj* (*czapka, nić*) woollen; (*dywan*) wool *attr*
**wełnisty** *adj* fleecy
**wende|ta** (**-ty, -ty**) (*dat sg* **-cie**) *f* vendetta
**Wenecj|a** (**-i**) *f* Venice
**wenecki** *adj* Venetian
**wenerolo|g** (**-ga, -gowie** *lub* **-dzy**) (*instr sg* **-giem**) *m* venereologist
**weneryczny** *adj*: **choroba weneryczna** venereal disease
**Wenezuel|a** (**-i**) *f* Venezuela
**wenezuelski** *adj* Venezuelan
**wentyl** (**-a, -e**) (*gen pl* **-i** *lub* **-ów**) *m* valve
**wentylacj|a** (**-i**) *f* ventilation
**wentylacyjny** *adj* ventilation *attr*; **otwór ~** vent
**wentylato|r** (**-ra, -ry**) (*loc sg* **-rze**) *m* fan, ventilator
**wentyl|ować (-uję, -ujesz)** *vt* to air, to ventilate
**Wenus** *f inv* Venus
**wepch|nąć (-nę, -niesz)** (*imp* **-nij**) *vb perf od* **wpychać**
**weran|da** (**-dy, -dy**) (*dat sg* **-dzie**) *f* veranda, porch
**werbalny** *adj* verbal
**werb|el** (**-la, -le**) (*gen pl* **-li**) *m* (*instrument*) snare drum; (*odgłos*) drum roll
**werb|ować (-uję, -ujesz)** (*perf* **z-**) *vt* to recruit, to enlist
**werbun|ek** (**-ku, -ki**) (*instr sg* **-kiem**) *m* recruitment
**werdyk|t** (**-tu, -ty**) (*loc sg* **-cie**) *m* verdict
**wermiszel** (**-u**) *m* (*Kulin*) vermicelli
**wermu|t** (**-tu, -ty**) (*loc sg* **-cie**) *m* vermouth
**wernisaż** (**-u, -e**) (*gen pl* **-y**) *m* opening day (*of an exhibition*), vernissage
**wer|s** (**-su, -sy**) (*loc sg* **-sie**) *m* verse
**Wersal** (**-u**) *m* Versailles
**wersal|ka** (**-ki, -ki**) (*dat sg* **-ce**, *gen pl* **-ek**) *f* sofa bed
**wersalski** *adj*: **Traktat W~** (*Hist*) Treaty of Versailles
**werse|t** (**-tu, -ty**) (*loc sg* **-cie**) *m* verse
**wersj|a** (**-i, -e**) (*gen pl* **-i**) *f* version
**wertep|y** (**-ów**) *pl* (*pot*) rough terrain
**wert|ować (-uję, -ujesz)** (*perf* **prze-**) *vt* (*powierzchownie*) to browse through; (*pilnie*) to pore over
**wertykalny** *adj* (*książk*) vertical
**wer|wa** (**-wy**) (*dat sg* **-wie**) *f* verve; **pełen werwy** full of verve, spirited; **z werwą** with verve
**weryfikacj|a** (**-i**) *f* (*faktów, teorii*) verification; (*pracowników*) vetting

**weryfik|ować (-uję, -ujesz)** *(perf* **z-**) *vt (fakty, opinie)* to verify; *(pracowników)* to vet
**werż|nąć się (-nę, -niesz)** *(imp* **-nij**) *vb perf od* **wrzynać się**
**wesel|e** (**-a, -a**) *nt* wedding
**wesel|ić się (-ę, -isz)** *vr* to rejoice
**weselny** *adj* wedding *attr*
**wesoł|ek** (**-ka, -ki** *lub* **-kowie**) *(instr sg* **-kiem**) *m (pot)* joker, jester
**wes|oło** *(comp* **-elej**) *adv (śmiać się)* cheerfully; *(bawić się, spędzać czas)* happily; **było bardzo ~** there was a lot of fun
**wesołoś|ć** (**-ci**) *f* cheerfulness
**wesoły** *adj* cheerful; **wesołe miasteczko** funfair *(Brit)*, amusement park *(US)*; **„W~ch Świąt!"** *(na Boże Narodzenie)* "Merry Christmas!"; *(na Wielkanoc)* "Happy Easter!"
**wespół** *adv (książk)*: **~ z** *+instr* together with
**wesp|rzeć (-rę, -rzesz)** *(imp* **-rzyj**, *pt* **wsparł**) *vb perf od* **wspierać**
**wes|sać (-sę, -siesz)** *(imp* **-sij**) *vb perf od* **wsysać**
**westch|nąć (-nę, -niesz)** *(imp* **-nij**) *vb perf od* **wzdychać**
**westchnie|nie** (**-nia, -nia**) *(gen pl* **-ń**) *nt* sigh
**wester|n** (**-nu, -ny**) *(loc sg* **-nie**) *m* western
**westybul** (**-u, -e**) *(gen pl* **-i** *lub* **-ów**) *m* vestibule, lobby
**wesz** (**wszy, wszy**) *(dat sg, gen pl* **wszy**) *f* louse
**weszła** *itd. vb patrz* **wejść**
**wet** *inv*: **wet za wet** tit for tat
**wetera|n** (**-na, -ni**) *(loc sg* **-nie**) *m* veteran; *(pot: człowiek wiekowy)* old-timer
**weterynari|a** (**-i**) *f* veterinary medicine *lub* science; **lekarz weterynarii** vet *(Brit)*, veterinary surgeon *(Brit)*, veterinarian *(US)*
**weterynaryjny** *adj* veterinary
**weterynarz** (**-a, -e**) *(gen pl* **-y**) *m* vet *(Brit)*, veterinary surgeon *(Brit)*, veterinarian *(US)*
**wetk|nąć (-nę, -niesz)** *(imp* **-nij**) *vb perf od* **wtykać**
**wetnę** *itd. vb patrz* **wciąć**
**we|to** (**-ta, -ta**) *(loc sg* **-cie**) *nt* veto; **prawo weta** power of veto; **zgłaszać (zgłosić** *perf*) **~ (wobec** *+gen*) to place a veto (on)
**wet|ować (-uję, -ujesz)** *(perf* **za-**) *vt* to veto
**wet|rzeć (-rę, -rzesz)** *(imp* **-rzyj**, *pt* **wtarł**) *vb perf od* **wcierać**
**wew.** *abbr (= wewnętrzny)* ext. *(extension)*
**wewnątrz** *prep +gen* inside, within ▷ *adv* inside; **od** *lub* **z ~** from within, from the inside; **do ~** inward(s)
**wewnętrznie** *adv* internally; **zmienić się** *(perf)* **~** *(o człowieku)* to change inside
**wewnętrzny** *adj* internal; *(okno, drzwi)* interior; *(handel)* domestic; *(spokój, dyscyplina)* inner ▷ *m decl like adj (też:* **numer** *lub* **telefon wewnętrzny**) extension; **wewnętrzna strona** the inside; **wewnętrzna kieszeń** inside pocket; **Ministerstwo Spraw W~ch** Ministry of the Interior, ≈ Home Office *(Brit)*; **~ 220** *(Tel)* extension 220; **ucho wewnętrzne** inner ear; **„do użytku wewnętrznego"** *(Med)* "for internal use"; *(akta, dokumenty)* "confidential"
**wezbrać (wzbierze)** *vb perf od* **wzbierać**
**wezbrany** *adj* swollen; **wezbrana rzeka** a river in spate
**wezdmę** *itd. vb patrz* **wzdąć**
**wezmę** *itd. vb patrz* **wziąć**
**Wezuwiusz** (**-a**) *m* Vesuvius
**wez|wać (-wę, -wiesz)** *(imp* **-wij**) *vb perf od* **wzywać**
**wezwa|nie** (**-nia, -nia**) *(gen pl* **-ń**) *nt* summons; *(lekarza, policji)* call; **~ do sądu** citation, subpoena; **~ do wojska** call-up *(Brit)*, draft *(US)*; **kościół pod ~m Św. Marcina** St. Martin's Church
**wezy|r** (**-ra, -rowie**) *(loc sg* **-rze**) *m* vizier
**weź** *itd. vb patrz* **wziąć**
**weż|reć się (-re)** *(pt* **wżarł**) *vb perf od* **wżerać się**
**węch** (**-u**) *m (zmysł)* (sense of) smell; *(przen)* nose *(przen)*; **mieć dobry ~** to have a good sense of smell
**węchowy** *adj* olfactory
**węd|ka** (**-ki, -ki**) *(dat sg* **-ce**, *gen pl* **-ek**) *f* fishing rod
**wędkarst|wo** (**-wa**) *(loc sg* **-wie**) *nt* fishing, angling
**wędkarz** (**-a, -e**) *(gen pl* **-y**) *m* angler
**wędk|ować (-uję, -ujesz)** *vi* to fish
**wędli|na** (**-ny, -ny**) *(dat sg* **-nie**) *f* cured *lub* smoked meat(s *pl*)
**wędr|ować (-uję, -ujesz)** *vi (przemieszczać się)* to wander, to roam; *(podróżować)* to travel; *(: pieszo)* to hike; **~ po kraju** to wander *lub* roam (around) the country
**wędro|wiec** (**-wca, -wcy**) *m (podróżnik)* wanderer; *(turysta)* hiker
**wędrowny** *adj (ptak)* migratory; *(plemię, tryb życia)* nomadic; **wczasy wędrowne** walking holiday
**wędrów|ka** (**-ki, -ki**) *(dat sg* **-ce**, *gen pl* **-ek**) *f (podróż)* travel; *(piesza)* hike; **wędrówki ludów** *(Hist)* migration of peoples
**wędzar|nia** (**-ni, -nie**) *(gen pl* **-ni**) *f* smokehouse
**wę|dzić (-dzę, -dzisz)** *(imp* **-dź**, *perf* **u-**) *vt* to smoke; **wędzić się** *vr (o wędlinie)* to be smoked
**wędzid|ło** (**-ła, -ła**) *(dat sg* **-le**, *gen pl* **-eł**) *nt* bit
**wędzon|ka** (**-ki, -ki**) *(dat sg* **-ce**, *gen pl* **-ek**) *f* smoked bacon

**wędzony** *adj* smoked

**wę|giel** (**-gla**) *m* (*paliwo*) coal; (*Chem*) carbon; (*do rysowania, drzewny*) charcoal; **~ kamienny/ brunatny** hard/brown coal; **węgle** *pl* embers *pl*; **siedzieć jak na rozżarzonych węglach** (*przen*) to be on tenterhooks

**węgielny** *adj*: **kamień ~** cornerstone; (*przen*) cornerstone, keystone

**wę|gieł** (**-gła, -gły**) (*loc sg* **-gle**) *m*: **zza węgła** from round the corner

**Wę|gier** (**-gra, -grzy**) (*loc sg* **-grze**) *m* Hungarian; *patrz też* **Węgry**

**węgier|ka** (**-ki, -ki**) (*dat sg* **-ce**, *gen pl* **-ek**) *f a kind of plum*; **W~** Hungarian

**węgierski** *adj* Hungarian ▷ *m decl like adj* (*język*) Hungarian

**węglowoda|n** (**-nu, -ny**) (*loc sg* **-nie**) *m* carbohydrate

**węglowod|ór** (**-oru, -ory**) (*loc sg* **-orze**) *m* hydrocarbon

**węglowy** *adj*: **przemysł ~** coal industry; **stal węglowa** carbon steel; **zagłębie węglowe** coalfield

**węgorz** (**-a, -e**) (*gen pl* **-y**) *m* eel

**Wę|gry** (**-gier**) (*loc pl* **-grzech**) *pl* Hungary

**węsz|yć (-ę, -ysz)** *vt* (*perf* **z-**) (*zwierzynę, ślad, podstęp*) to scent ▷ *vi* (*o zwierzęciu*) to sniff; (*pot: o detektywie itp.*) to nose around *lub* about

**wę|zeł** (**-zła, -zły**) (*loc sg* **-źle**) *m* (*supeł, jednostka prędkości*) knot; (*kolejowy, komunikacyjny*) junction; **~ chłonny** lymph gland *lub* node; **~ gordyjski** (*przen*) the Gordian knot; **~ cieplny** heat distribution centre (*Brit*) *lub* center (*US*)

**węzeł|ek** (**-ka, -ki**) (*instr sg* **-kiem**) *m dimin od* **węzeł**; (*tobołek*) bundle

**węzłowaty** *adj*: **krótki i ~** brief

**węzłowy** *adj* (*punkt, stacja*) junction *attr*; (*problem, sprawa*) crucial

**węża** *itd. n patrz* **wąż**

**wężowy** *adj* (*ruch*) serpentine

**węższy** *adj comp od* **wąski**

**WF, wf.** *abbr* (= *wychowanie fizyczne*) PE (= *physical education*)

**wg** *abbr* (= *według*) according to

**wgiąć (wegnę, wegniesz)** (*imp* **wegnij**) *vb perf od* **wginać**

**wgię|cie** (**-cia, -cia**) (*gen pl* **-ć**) *nt* dent

**wgi|nać (-nam, -nasz)** (*perf* **-ąć**) *vt* to dent; **wginać się** *vr* to get dented

**wglą|d** (**-du**) (*loc sg* **-dzie**) *m* (*Psych*) insight; **mieć ~ do** *+gen*/**w** *+acc* to have the right to inspect; **być do ~u** to be (freely) available for inspection

**wgłę|biać się (-biam, -biasz)** (*perf* **-bić**) *vr*: **wgłębiać się w coś** (*w ziemię, skałę itp.*) to sink into sth; (*przen: wnikać*) to go into sth

**wgłębie|nie** (**-nia, -nia**) (*gen pl* **-ń**) *nt* hollow

**wgniat|ać (-am, -asz)** (*perf* **wgnieść**) *vt* (*wginać*) to dent; **~ coś w ziemię** to press sth into the ground

**wgniece|nie** (**-nia, -nia**) (*gen pl* **-ń**) *nt* dent

**wgni|eść (-otę, -eciesz)** (*imp* **-eć**, *pt* **-ótł, -otła, -etli**) *vb perf od* **wgniatać**

**wgramol|ić się (-ę, -isz)** *vb perf od* **gramolić się**

**wgryz|ać się (-am, -asz)** (*perf* **wgryźć**) *vr*: **wgryzać się w coś** to bite into sth; (*przen*) to get into sth

**wgry|źć się (-zę, -ziesz)** (*imp* **-ź**) *vb perf od* **wgryzać się**

**whisky** *f inv* (*szkocka*) whisky; (*irlandzka, amerykańska*) whiskey

**wi|ać (-eję, -ejesz)** *vi* (*o wietrze*) to blow; (*pot: uciekać*) (*perf* **z-**) to scram (*pot*); **wiał silny wiatr** there was a strong wind (blowing); **mocno wieje** it's very windy

**wiader|ko** (**-ka, -ka**) (*instr sg* **-kiem**, *gen pl* **-ek**) *nt* bucket

**wiadomo** *inv*: **~, że...** it's common knowledge that... ▷ *adv* (*oczywiście*) sure; **nie ~ gdzie/kiedy** nobody knows where/when; **~ było, że...** it was known that...; **o ile ~** as far as one can tell; **nic mi o tym nie ~** not to my knowledge, not that I know of; **nigdy (nic) nie ~** you never know

**wiadomoś|ć** (**-ci, -ci**) (*gen pl* **-ci**) *f* (*informacja*) a piece of news; (*dla/od kogoś*) message; (*Radio, TV*) news item; **wiadomości** *pl* (*wiedza*) knowledge; (*Radio, TV*) the news; **podawać coś (komuś) do wiadomości** to make sth known (to sb); **przyjąć** (*perf*) **coś do wiadomości** to accept sth as fact; **(to) dobra/zła ~** (it's) good/bad news; **masz od niej (jakieś) wiadomości?** have you heard from her?

**wiadomy** *adj*: **wiadoma osoba** you-know-who (*pot*)

**wiad|ro** (**-ra, -ra**) (*loc sg* **-rze**, *gen pl* **-er**) *nt* bucket; (*zawartość*) bucket(ful)

**wiaduk|t** (**-tu, -ty**) (*loc sg* **-cie**) *m* (*nad drogą*) flyover (*Brit*), overpass (*US*); (*nad doliną*) viaduct

**wian|ek** (**-ka, -ki**) (*instr sg* **-kiem**) *m* (*z kwiatów*) garland; (*czosnku itp.*) string

**wia|no** (**-na, -na**) (*loc sg* **-nie**) *nt* (*książk*) dowry

**wi|ara** (**-ary**) (*dat sg* **-erze**) *f* faith, belief; (*Rel: wyznanie*) (*nom pl* **-ary**) faith; **~ w kogoś/coś** faith in sb/sth; **~ w siebie** self-confidence; **to nie do wiary** it's unbelievable; **w dobrej/ złej wierze** in good/bad faith; **dawać czemuś wiarę** to give *lub* lend credence to sth; **przyjmować coś na wiarę** to take sth on trust

**wiarołomny** *adj* (*książk*) unfaithful

**wiarygodnoś|ć, wiarogodnoś|ć** (**-ci**) *f* credibility
**wiarygodny, wiarogodny** *adj* (*wiadomość, człowiek*) credible; (*źródło*) reliable
**wia|ta** (**-ty, -ty**) (*dat sg* **-cie**) *f*: **~ autobusowa** bus shelter
**wi|atr** (**-atru, -atry**) (*loc sg* **-etrze**) *m* wind; **pod ~** into *lub* against the wind; **z ~em** with the wind; **~ boczny** crosswind; **~ w plecy** tailwind; **rzucać słowa na ~** (*przen*) to make empty promises; **wystawić** (*perf*) **kogoś do ~u** (*pot*: *oszukać*) to double-cross sb; (*nie przyjść na randkę*) to stand sb up; **wiatry** *pl*: **puszczać ~y** to break wind
**wiatracz|ek** (**-ka, -ki**) (*instr sg* **-kiem**) *m* (*wentylator*) fan
**wiatra|k** (**-ka, -ki**) (*instr sg* **-kiem**) *m* windmill
**wiatrów|ka** (**-ki, -ki**) (*dat sg* **-ce**, *gen pl* **-ek**) *f* (*kurtka*) windcheater (Brit), windbreaker (US); (*broń*) airgun
**wiądł** *itd. vb patrz* **więdnąć**
**wią|z** (**-zu, -zy**) (*loc sg* **-zie**) *m* elm
**wią|zać** (**-żę, -żesz**) (*imp* **-ż**, *perf* **z-**) *vt* (*supeł, chustę, sznurowadło*) (*perf* **za-**) to tie; (*ręce, paczkę*) (*perf* **z-**) to tie; (*kojarzyć, łączyć*) (*perf* **z-**) to combine; (*o obietnicy, słowie*) to bind; (*o cemencie, kleju*) (*perf* **z-**) to bond; (*o atomach, cząsteczkach*) (*perf* **z-**) to bind; **~ koniec z końcem** (*przen*) to make ends meet; **~ z kimś nadzieje** to put *lub* place *lub* pin one's hopes on sb; **wiązać się** *vr* (*perf* **z-**); **~ się z kimś** to become involved with sb; **to się wiąże z wydatkami** it involves expenses; **~ się obietnicą** to bind o.s. to a promise
**wiązad|ło** (**-ła, -ła**) (*loc sg* **-le**, *gen pl* **-eł**) *nt* (*Anat*) ligament; **wiązadła głosowe** vocal cords
**wiąza|nie** (**-nia, -nia**) (*gen pl* **-ń**) *nt* (*narciarskie*) binding; (*Archit*) truss; (*Chem*) bond
**wiązan|ka** (**-ki, -ki**) (*dat sg* **-ce**, *gen pl* **-ek**) *f* (*kwiatów*) bunch; (*melodii*) medley; **~ wyzwisk/przekleństw** a volley of abuse/curses
**wiązany** *adj*: **buty wiązane** lace-up shoes, lace-ups; **sprzedaż wiązana** tie-in sale; **umowa wiązana** package deal
**wiąz|ka** (**-ki, -ki**) (*dat sg* **-ce**, *gen pl* **-ek**) *f* (*siana, słomy*) bundle; (*elektronów, światła*) beam
**wiążący** *adj* binding
**wibracj|a** (**-i, -e**) (*gen pl* **-i**) *f* vibration
**wibrato|r** (**-ra, -ry**) (*loc sg* **-rze**) *m* vibrator
**wibr|ować** (**-uję, -ujesz**) *vi* to vibrate
**wiceadmira|ł** (**-ła, -łowie**) (*loc sg* **-le**) *m* vice admiral
**wicedyrekto|r** (**-ra, -rzy**) (*loc sg* **-rze**) *m* deputy manager; (*szkoły*) deputy head
**wiceminist|er** (**-ra, -rowie**) (*loc sg* **-rze**) *m* ≈ under-secretary of state (Brit), ≈ undersecretary (US)
**wicemistrz** (**-a, -owie**) *m* (*Sport*) runner-up
**wicemistrzost|wo** (**-wa, -wa**) (*loc sg* **-wie**) *nt* second place (*in a championship*)
**wicepremie|r** (**-ra, -rzy**) (*loc sg* **-rze**) *m* ≈ deputy prime minister (Brit)
**wicepreze|s** (**-sa, -si**) (*loc sg* **-sie**) *m* vice-chairman (Brit), vice-president (US)
**wiceprezyden|t** (**-ta, -ci**) (*loc sg* **-cie**) *m* (*państwa*) vice-president; (*miasta*) deputy mayor
**wich|er** (**-ru, -ry**) (*loc sg* **-rze**) *m* gale
**wichrzyciel** (**-a, -e**) (*gen pl* **-i**) *m* troublemaker
**wichrzycielski** *adj* mutinous
**wichrz|yć** (**-ę, -ysz**) *vt* (*włosy, czuprynę*) (*perf* **z-**) to ruffle ▷ *vi* to stir up trouble; **wichrzyć się** *vr* (*perf* **z-**) (*o włosach*) to get ruffled
**wichu|ra** (**-ry, -ry**) (*dat sg* **-rze**) *f* gale
**wić**[1] (**wiję, wijesz**) *vt* (*perf* **u-**) (*gniazdo*) to build; (*wianek*) to weave; **wić się** *vr* (*o roślinach*) to twine; (*o rzece*) to meander; (*o człowieku*) to writhe
**wi|ć**[2] (**-ci, -ci**) (*gen pl* **-ci**) *f* (*Bio*) flagellum
**widać** *adv*: **~ nie mógł przyjść** apparently he couldn't come ▷ *inv*: **~ światło** I can see some light; **nie było go nigdzie ~** he was nowhere to be seen; **nic nie ~** I/we *itp.* can't see anything; **to ~** it shows; **jak ~** as you can see
**widel|ec** (**-ca, -ce**) *m* fork
**wideł|ki** (**-ek**) *pl* (*telefonu*) cradle; (*roweru*) fork; **~ płacowe** wage differential
**wideo** *nt inv* video ▷ *adj*: **kaseta ~** video cassette; **nagranie ~** video (recording); **kamera ~** camcorder; **nagrywać coś na ~** to videotape sth
**wideokli|p** (**-pu, -py**) (*loc sg* **-pie**) *m* video
**wideot|eka** (**-eki, -eki**) (*dat sg* **-ece**, *gen pl* **-ek**) *f* video collection
**widła|k** (**-ka, -ki**) (*instr sg* **-kiem**) *m* (*Bot*) club moss
**wid|ły** (**-eł**) *pl* fork; **robić z igły ~** to make a mountain out of a molehill
**wid|mo** (**-ma, -ma**) (*loc sg* **-mie**) *nt* (*zjawa*) phantom, spectre (Brit), specter (US); (*Fiz*) spectrum; **~ głodu/wojny** the spectre of hunger/war
**widni|eć** (**-eje**) (*pt* **-ał**) *vi* (*być widocznym*) to be visible; **(już) widnieje** day *lub* dawn is breaking
**widno** *adv*: **jest ~** it is light
**widnokr|ąg** (**-ęgu, -ęgi**) (*instr sg* **-ęgiem**) *m* horizon
**widny** *adj* (*mieszkanie, pokój*) light
**widocznie** *adv* (*zapewne*) apparently; (*wyraźnie*) clearly, visibly

**widocznoś|ć** (**-ci**) *f* visibility
**widoczny** *adj* visible; **być ~m** to show
**wido|k** (**-ku, -ki**) (*instr sg* **-kiem**) *m* (*panorama*) view; (*scena*) sight; **na ~ kogoś/czegoś** at the sight of sb/sth; **~ na jezioro** a view of *lub* over the lake; **być na ~u** to be exposed to view; **widoki** *pl* (*perspektywy*) prospects *pl*
**widokowy** *adj*: **taras ~** viewing area; (*na dachu*) observation deck; **punkt ~** viewpoint (*Brit*), overlook (*US*)
**widoków|ka** (**-ki, -ki**) (*dat sg* **-ce**, *gen pl* **-ek**) *f* (picture) postcard
**widomy** *adj* clear
**widowis|ko** (**-ka, -ka**) (*instr sg* **-kiem**) *nt* spectacle; **robić z siebie ~** (*pot*) to make a spectacle *lub* an exhibition of o.s.
**widowiskowy** *adj* spectacular
**widow|nia** (**-ni, -nie**) (*gen pl* **-ni**) *f* (*publiczność*) audience; (*miejsce*) auditorium
**wid|ywać** (**-uję, -ujesz**) *vt* to see (*occasionally*); **widywać się** *vr* to see one another
**widz** (**-a, -owie**) *m* viewer, spectator; (*świadek*) bystander, onlooker; **widzowie** *pl* (*publiczność*) audience
**widze|nie** (**-nia**) *nt* (*wizja*) vision; (*odwiedziny w więzieniu*) visit; **do widzenia!** good-bye!; **punkt widzenia** viewpoint, point of view; **znać kogoś z widzenia** to know sb by sight
**widzialnoś|ć** (**-ci**) *f* visibility
**widzialny** *adj* visible
**widziany** *adj*: **mile ~** (very) welcome; **mile ~ własny samochód** own car would be preferred; **źle ~** unwelcome
**wi|dzieć** (**-dzę, -dzisz**) *vt/vi* to see; **widzę dwoje ludzi** I (can) see two people; **widziałem już ten film** I have already seen this film; **źle/dobrze widzę** I see poorly/well; **widzę, że ...** I can see (that) ...; **co ty w niej widzisz?** what do you see in her?; **kto to widział!** (*pot*) well, I never!; **sam widzisz** there you are *lub* go; **widzieć się** *vr* (*samego siebie*) to see o.s.; (*spotykać się*) to see each other; **~ się z kimś** to see sb
**widzimisię** *nt inv* (*pot*) discretion; **według swego ~** at one's own discretion
**wiec** (**-u, -e**) *m* mass meeting, rally
**wieczerz|a** (**-y, -e**) (*gen pl* **-y**) *f* (*książk*) supper; **ostatnia ~** (*Rel*) Last Supper
**wiecz|ko** (**-ka, -ka**) (*instr sg* **-kiem**, *gen pl* **-ek**) *nt* (*pudełka*) top, cover; (*słoika*) lid
**wiecznie** *adv* (*trwać, żyć*) eternally, forever; (*narzekać, przeszkadzać*) always, perpetually
**wiecznoś|ć** (**-ci**) *f* eternity
**wieczny** *adj* eternal; **wieczne pióro** fountain pen; **na** *lub* **po wieczne czasy** (*książk*) for ever (and ever); **~ student** perpetual student
**wieczor|ek** (**-ku, -ki**) (*instr sg* **-kiem**) *m* (*muzyczny, literacki*) soirée
**wieczorny** *adj* (*wczesnym wieczorem*) evening *attr*; (*późnym wieczorem*) night *attr*
**wieczorowy** *adj* evening *attr*; (*szkoła*) night *attr*
**wieczorów|ka** (**-ki, -ki**) (*dat sg* **-ce**, *gen pl* **-ek**) *f* (*pot: szkoła wieczorowa*) night school
**wieczoryn|ka** (**-ki, -ki**) (*dat sg* **-ce**, *gen pl* **-ek**) *f a bedtime TV cartoon for children*
**wiecz|ór** (**-oru, -ory**) (*loc sg* **-orze**) *m* (*wczesny*) evening; (*późny*) night; (*impreza: muzyki, poezji*) soirée; **dobry ~!** good evening!; **(dzisiaj) wieczorem** tonight, this evening; **wczoraj wieczorem** last night; **co ~** every evening; **~ kawalerski** stag (*Brit*) *lub* bachelor (*US*) party
**wieczysty** *adj* (*książk: sława*) perpetual, eternal; **dzierżawa wieczysta** perpetual lease; **księga wieczysta** (*Prawo*) land and mortgage book, ≈ land register (*Brit*); **wyciąg z księgi wieczystej** abstract of title
**Wied|eń** (**-nia**) *m* (*Geog*) Vienna
**wiedeński** *adj* (*filharmonia, walc*) Viennese
**wiedli** *itd. vb patrz* **wieść**
**wiedz|a** (**-y**) *f* knowledge; (*specjalistyczna*) expertise; (*technologiczna*) know-how; **bez czyjejś wiedzy** without sb's knowledge; **bez niczyjej wiedzy** without anyone knowing; **za czyjąś wiedzą** with sb's knowledge
**wiedzie** *itd. vb patrz* **wieść**
**wiedzieć (wiem, wiesz)** (*imp* **wiedz**) *vt* to know ▷ *vi*: **~ (o kimś/czymś)** to know (about sb/sth); **wiem (to) od mamy** I know it from my mother; **wiesz co?** (*pot*) you know what? (*pot*), I'll tell you what! (*pot*); **bo** *lub* **czy ja wiem?** how can I tell?; **żebyś wiedział!** (*pot*) you bet! (*pot*); **o ile wiem** as far as I know; **jeśli chcesz wiedziesz, ...** for your information; **po raz nie wiem który** for the umpteenth time; **kto wie?** who knows?
**wiedź|ma** (**-my, -my**) (*loc sg* **-mie**) *f* witch
**wieję** *itd. vb patrz* **wiać**
**wiejski** *adj* (*droga, powietrze, okolica*) country *attr*; (*szkoła*) village *attr*; (*zwyczaje*) rural
**wie|k** (**-ku, -ki**) (*instr sg* **-kiem**) *m* age; (*stulecie*) century; **XX ~** the 20th century; **~ szkolny** school age; **całe ~i** for ages; **na ~i** for ages; **nie widzieliśmy się całe ~i** it's been ages since we last saw each other; **w ~u dwudziestu lat** at (the age of) twenty; **nie wyglądasz na swój ~** you don't look your age; **z ~iem** with age; **w moim ~u** at my age
**wie|ko** (**-ka, -ka**) (*instr sg* **-kiem**) *nt* lid
**wiekopomny** *adj* (*książk*) memorable
**wiekowy** *adj* (*dotyczący wieku*) age *attr*; (*stary*) aged
**wiekuisty** *adj* (*książk*) eternal, everlasting

**wielbiciel** (**-a, -e**) (*gen pl* **-i**) *m* (*miłośnik*) fan, enthusiast; (*adorator*) admirer
**wielbiciel|ka** (**-ki, -ki**) (*dat sg* **-ce**, *gen pl* **-ek**) *f* (*miłośniczka*) fan, enthusiast; (*adoratorka*) admirer
**wiel|bić (-bię, -bisz)** *vt* (*czcić*) to worship; (*uwielbiać*) to adore
**wielbłą|d** (**-da, -dy**) (*loc sg* **-dzie**) *m* camel; **~ jednogarbny** dromedary
**wielce** *adv* (*książk*) most, greatly
**wiele** (*jak*: **ile**) *pron* (*comp* **więcej**); **~** (*+gen*) (*z rzeczownikami policzalnymi*) a lot (of), many; (*z rzeczownikami niepoliczalnymi*) a lot (of), much; **~ kobiet** a lot of *lub* many women; **~ czasu/pieniędzy** a lot of *lub* much time/money; **~ rozumieć** to understand a lot; **wielu ludzi/studentów** a lot of *lub* many people/students ▷ *adv* much, a lot; **o ~ lepszy** much better, a lot better; **tego już za ~!** that's too much!
**wielebny** *adj*: **~ X** the Reverend X
**wielekroć** *pron* (*książk*) many a time
**Wielka Brytania** (**Wielkiej Brytanii**) *f* Great Britain, the United Kingdom
**Wielkanoc** (**-y, -e**) *f* Easter
**wielkanocny** *adj* Easter *attr*
**wielki** *adj* (*bardzo duży*) big, large; (*intensywny*) intense; (*przen*) great; **~ palec** (*u nogi*) big toe; **W~ Tydzień** (*Rel*) Holy Week; **W~ Piątek** (*Rel*) Good Friday; **W~ Czwartek** (*Rel*) Maundy Thursday; **Wielka Sobota** (*Rel*) Holy Saturday; **W~ Post** (*Rel*) Lent; **na wielką skalę** on a large scale; **w ~ej mierze** to a large extent; **nic ~ego** nothing much; **wielka szkoda!** too bad!; **Piotr W~** Peter the Great; **od ~ego święta** *lub* **dzwonu** once in a blue moon
**wielkodusznoś|ć** (**-ci**) *f* generosity
**wielkoduszny** *adj* (*książk*) big-hearted, generous
**wielkolu|d** (**-da, -dy**) (*loc sg* **-dzie**) *m* giant
**wielkomiejski** *adj* (big) city *attr*, urban
**wielkopański** *adj* lordly
**Wielkopols|ka** (**-ki**) (*dat sg* **-ce**) *f a province in western Poland*
**wielkoprzemysłowy** *adj* industrial
**wielkoś|ć** (**-ci**) *f* (*rozmiar*) (*nom pl* **-ci**, *gen pl* **-ci**) size; (*popytu, zamówienia*) scale; (*ogrom*) greatness; (*waga*) magnitude; (*Mat, Fiz*) quantity; **kraj wielkości Polski** a country the size of Poland; **portret naturalnej wielkości** life-size portrait; **gwiazda pierwszej wielkości** (*przen*) mega star
**wielobarwny** *adj* multicolour(ed) (*Brit*), multicolor(ed) (*US*)
**wielob|ój** (**-oju, -oje**) (*gen pl* **-ojów**) *m* (*Sport*) multi-discipline event (*a general term for biathlon, triathlon, pentathlon, heptathlon or decathlon*)
**wielodzietny** *adj with many children*
**wielofunkcyjny** *adj* versatile
**wielojęzyczny** *adj* multilingual
**wieloką|t** (**-ta, -ty**) (*loc sg* **-cie**) *m* (*Geom*) polygon
**wielokrop|ek** (**-ka, -ki**) (*instr sg* **-kiem**) *m* ellipsis, suspension points *pl*
**wielokrotnie** *pron* repeatedly
**wielokrotnoś|ć** (**-ci, -ci**) (*gen pl* **-ci**) *f* (*Fiz, Mat*) multiple
**wielokrotny** *adj* repeated *attr*, multiple *attr*; **test wielokrotnego wyboru** multiple-choice test
**wieloletni** *adj* long-term, of many years' standing; (*roślina*) perennial
**wielonarodowościowy** *adj* multinational
**wieloowocowy** *adj* multi-fruit *attr*
**wielopiętrowy** *adj* high-rise, multi-storey *attr* (*Brit*), multistory *attr* (*US*)
**wieloraki** *adj* multiple *attr*
**wielorasowy** *adj* multiracial
**wielory|b** (**-ba, -by**) (*loc sg* **-bie**) *m* whale
**wielorybnict|wo** (**-wa**) (*loc sg* **-wie**) *nt* whaling, whale fishing
**wielostronny** *adj* (*zainteresowania*) versatile; (*rokowania*) multilateral
**wielotomowy** *adj* multivolume(d) *attr*
**wielotorowy** *adj* (*przen*) multifarious, multifaceted
**wielotysięczny** *adj*: **~ tłum** a crowd of thousands
**wielowarzywny** *adj*: **sałatka wielowarzywna** mixed salad
**wielowiekowy** *adj* centuries old, of many centuries
**wielowymiarowy** *adj* multidimensional
**wielozmianowy** *adj*: **praca wielozmianowa** shiftwork
**wieloznacznoś|ć** (**-ci**) *f* ambiguity
**wieloznaczny** *adj* ambiguous
**wielożeńst|wo** (**-wa**) (*loc sg* **-wie**) *nt* polygamy
**wielu** *pron patrz* **wiele**
**wie|niec** (**-ńca, -ńce**) *m* wreath; **~ laurowy** (*przen*) laurels; **składać (złożyć** *perf*) **~** to lay a wreath
**wieńcowy** *adj* (*Anat*) coronary; **choroba wieńcowa** (*Med*) coronary heart disease
**wieńcz|yć (-ę, -ysz)** *vt* (*perf* **z-** *lub* **u-**) (*książk*) to crown
**wieprz** (**-a, -e**) (*gen pl* **-ów** *lub* **-y**) *m* hog
**wieprzowi|na** (**-ny**) (*dat sg* **-nie**) *f* pork
**wieprzowy** *adj* pork *attr*
**wierce|nie** (**-nia, -nia**) (*gen pl* **-ń**) *nt* drilling
**wier|cić (-cę, -cisz)** (*imp* **-ć**) *vt/vi* (*perf* **wy-**) to drill, to bore; **~ komuś dziurę w brzuchu**

(*pot*) to badger sb, to pester sb; **wiercić się** *vr* to fidget
**wiernie** *adv* faithfully
**wiernoś|ć** (**-ci**) *f* faithfulness; (*Tech*) fidelity
**wierny** *adj* faithful ▷ *m decl like adj*: **wierni** (*Rel*) the faithful
**wiersz** (**-a, -e**) (*gen pl* **-y**) *m* (*utwór*) poem; (*linijka pisma*) line; (*wers*) verse; **czytać między ~ami** to read between the lines
**wierszy|k** (**-ka, -ki**) (*instr sg* **-kiem**) *m*: **~ (dla dzieci)** (nursery) rhyme
**wiertar|ka** (**-ki, -ki**) (*dat sg* **-ce**, *gen pl* **-ek**) *f* drill
**wiert|ło** (**-ła, -ła**) (*loc sg* **-le**, *gen pl* **-eł**) *nt* drill, bit
**wiertniczy** *adj*: **platforma wiertnicza** drilling rig; **otwór ~** borehole
**wierutny** *adj* (*bzdura*) utter; (*kłamstwo*) downright
**wierzący** *adj*: **osoba wierząca** believer ▷ *m decl like adj* believer; **jestem ~** I'm a believer
**wierz|ba** (**-by, -by**) (*dat sg* **-bie**) *f* willow; **~ płacząca** weeping willow
**wierzch** (**-u, -y**) *m* (*stołu, pudełka*) top; (*dłoni*) back; (*ubrania*) outside; (*buta*) upper; **być/leżeć na ~u** to be/lie on top; **jechać ~em** to ride on horseback; **wkładać coś na ~** to put sth on top; **oczy mu wyszły na ~** (*pot*) his eyes popped out (*pot*)
**wierzchni** *adj* outer, top
**wierzchoł|ek** (**-ka, -ki**) (*instr sg* **-kiem**) *m* (*drzewa*) top; (*góry*) top, peak; (*figury geometrycznej*) point
**wierzcho|wiec** (**-wca, -wce**) *m* (*książk*) mount, saddle-horse
**wierze** *n patrz* **wiara**
**wierze|nie** (**-nia, -nia**) (*gen pl* **-ń**) *nt* belief
**wierzg|ać** (**-am, -asz**) (*perf* **-nąć**) *vi* to kick
**wierzg|nąć** (**-nę, -niesz**) (*imp* **-nij**) *vb perf od* **wierzgać**
**wierzyciel** (**-a, -e**) (*gen pl* **-i**) *m* creditor
**wierz|yć** (**-ę, -ysz**) *vi*: **~ w Boga/duchy** to believe in God/ghosts; **~ (u~** *perf*) **komuś** to believe sb; **~ w kogoś/coś** to have faith *lub* confidence in sb/sth; **nie wierzyłam własnym oczom** I couldn't believe my eyes
**wierzytelnoś|ć** (**-ci, -ci**) (*gen pl* **-ci**) *f* debt; **wierzytelności** *pl* receivables *pl*, (outstanding) liabilities *pl*
**wiesz** *vb patrz* **wiedzieć**
**wiesz|ać** (**-am, -asz**) (*perf* **powiesić**) *vt* to hang; **wieszać się** *vr* to hang o.s.
**wiesza|k** (**-ka, -ki**) (*instr sg* **-kiem**) *m* (*stojący*) stand; (*deska z kołkami*) (coat) rack; (*pojedynczy kołek*) peg; (*ramiączko*) (coat) hanger; (*przy płaszczu itp.*) loop
**wieszcz** (**-a, -owie** *lub* **-e**) *m* (*Lit*) bard
**wieś** (**wsi, wsie**) (*gen pl* **wsi**) *f* (*okolica*) country; (*miejscowość*) village; **na wsi** in the country
**wieś|ć**[1] (**-ci, -ci**) (*gen pl* **-ci**) *f* (*książk*) news
**wi|eść**[2] (**-odę, -edziesz**) (*imp* **-edź**, *pt* **-ódł, -odła, -edli**) *vt* (*życie*) to lead; (*spór*) to have; (*o przywódcy, przewodniku: kierować*) (*perf* **po-**) to lead; (*książk: o drodze itp.*) (*perf* **za-**) to lead ▷ *vi* (*książk: o drodze itp.*) to lead; **~ prym** to make the running (*przen*); **wieść się** *vr* (*perf* **po-**); **wiedzie mi się dobrze/źle** I'm doing well/badly
**wieśnia|k** (**-ka, -cy**) (*instr sg* **-kiem**) *m* peasant
**Wietna|m** (**-mu**) (*loc sg* **-mie**) *m* Vietnam
**Wietnamczy|k** (**-ka, -cy**) (*instr sg* **-kiem**) *m* Vietnamese
**Wietnam|ka** (**-ki, -ki**) (*dat sg* **-ce**, *gen pl* **-ek**) *f* Vietnamese
**wietnamski** *adj* Vietnamese ▷ *m decl like adj* (*język*) Vietnamese
**wietrze** *n patrz* **wiatr**
**wietrz|eć** (**-eje**) (*perf* **z-**) *vi* (*o skałach*) to weather; (*o piwie*) to go flat; (*o winie*) to go off; (*o perfumach*) to lose fragrance
**wietrzny** *adj* windy; **ospa wietrzna** chickenpox
**wietrz|yć** (**-ę, -ysz**) *vt* (*mieszkanie, pokój*) (*perf* **wy-** *lub* **prze-**) to air; (*wyczuwać*) (*perf* **z-**) to smell; **wietrzyć się** *vr* (*o mieszkaniu, ubraniu*) (*perf* **wy-** *lub* **prze-**) to be aired
**wietrzy|k** (**-ka** *lub* **-ku, -ki**) (*instr sg* **-kiem**) *m* breeze
**wiewiór|ka** (**-ki, -ki**) (*dat sg* **-ce**, *gen pl* **-ek**) *f* squirrel
**wi|eźć** (**-ozę, -eziesz**) (*imp* **-eź**, *pt* **-ózł, -ozła, -eźli**, *perf* **za-**) *vt* (*przewozić*) to carry, to transport; (*podwozić*) to drive
**wież|a** (**-y, -e**) *f* (*Archit*) tower; (*Szachy*) castle, rook; (*Pływanie*) diving tower; (*czołgu, okrętu*) turret; **~ kontrolna** control tower
**wieżo|wiec** (**-wca, -wce**) *m* high-rise (building), tower block (*Brit*)
**wieżycz|ka** (**-ki, -ki**) (*dat sg* **-ce**, *gen pl* **-ek**) *f* turret; (*ozdoba*) pinnacle
**więc** *conj* so; **tak ~** thus; **a ~, ...** well, ...; **wszyscy, a ~ dzieci, rodzice i nauczyciele, ...** everybody, that is children, parents and teachers, ...
**więcej** *adv comp od* **dużo, wiele** more; **nikt ~** nobody else; **nic ~** nothing more *lub* else; **nigdy ~!** never again!; **nigdy ~ wojny!** no more war!; **~ nie przyszła** she never came back; **co ~** what's more, furthermore; **im ~, tym lepiej** the more, the better; **mniej ~** more or less
**wi|ędnąć** (**-ędnie**) (*pt* **-ądł, -ędła, -ędły**, *perf* **z-**) *vi* (*o kwiatach*) to wilt, to wither; (*przen: o urodzie*) to fade

W

**większoś|ć** (**-ci**) *f* majority; **~ ludzi** most people; **w większości przypadków** in most cases; **wygrać** *(perf)* **większością głosów** to win by a majority of votes
**większy** *adj comp od* **duży, wielki**; *(budynek, część, objętość)* larger, bigger; *(doświadczenie, kłopot, wysiłek)* greater; *(znaczny: problem itp.)* major
**więzad|ło** (**-ła, -ła**) *(loc sg* **-le**, *gen pl* **-eł**) *nt* = **wiązadło**
**wię|zić** (**-żę, -zisz**) *(imp* **-ź**) *vt*: **~ kogoś** to keep sb in prison
**więzie|nie** (**-nia**) *nt (zakład karny) (nom pl* **-nia**, *gen pl* **-ń**) prison, jail, gaol *(Brit)*; *(kara)* imprisonment, prison; **siedzieć w więzieniu** to be in prison, to do time *(pot)*; **kara dwóch lat więzienia** two years imprisonment
**więziennict|wo** (**-wa**) *(loc sg* **-wie**) *nt (więzienia)* prison system; *(zarządzanie więzieniami)* prison management
**więzienny** *adj* prison *attr*
**wię|zień** (**-źnia, -źniowie**) *m* prisoner
**więz|y** (**-ów**) *pl (sznury)* bonds *pl*; *(przyjaźni, rodzinne)* ties *pl*
**wię|ź** (**-zi, -zi**) *(gen pl* **-zi**) *f* bond; *patrz też* **więzić**
**więźniar|ka** (**-ki, -ki**) *(dat sg* **-ce**, *gen pl* **-ek**) *f* prisoner
**WIG** *abbr (= Warszawski Indeks Giełdowy) Warsaw Stock Exchange index*
**wigili|a** (**-i, -e**) *(gen pl* **-i**) *f (święto)*: **W~** Christmas Eve; *(wieczerza)* Christmas Eve Supper; *(książk: przeddzień)* eve
**wigilijny** *adj*: **wieczór ~** Christmas Eve; **wieczerza wigilijna** Christmas Eve Supper
**wigo|r** (**-ru**) *(loc sg* **-rze**) *m* vigour *(Brit)*, vigor *(US)*
**wigwa|m** (**-mu, -my**) *(loc sg* **-mie**) *m* wigwam
**wiję, wijesz** *itd. vb patrz* **wić**
**wikariusz** (**-a, -e**) *(gen pl* **-y**) *m* = **wikary**
**wika|ry** (**-rego, -rzy**) *m decl like adj* curate
**wikin|g** (**-ga, -gowie**) *(instr sg* **-giem**) *m* viking
**wikli|na** (**-ny**) *(dat sg* **-nie**) *f* wicker
**wikliniarski** *adj*: **wyroby ~e** wickerwork
**wiklinowy** *adj*: **~ kosz/fotel** wicker basket/chair
**wikł|ać się** (**-am, -asz**) *vr (o akcji, wątku)* to become complicated; **wikłać się (uwikłać się** *perf*) **w coś** to become embroiled in sth
**wiktoriański** *adj* Victorian
**wilczu|r** (**-ra, -ry**) *(loc sg* **-rze**) *m* Alsatian *(Brit)*, German shepherd *(US)*
**wilczy** *adj (futro, trop)* wolf's *attr*; *(przen: apetyt)* wolfish
**wilczyc|a** (**-y, -e**) *f* she-wolf
**wil|ga** (**-gi, -gi**) *(dat sg* **-dze**) *f* golden oriole
**wilgo|ć** (**-ci**) *f (woda)* moisture; *(nasycenie wodą)* humidity; *(w piwnicy, na ścianie)* damp(ness)
**wilgotni|eć** (**-eje**) *(perf* **z-**) *vi (o soli, tytoniu)* to get damp; *(o oczach)* to moisten
**wilgotnoś|ć** (**-ci**) *f* humidity
**wilgotny** *adj (ubranie, ściana)* damp; *(powietrze, klimat)* humid, damp; *(oczy)* moist
**wil|k** (**-ka, -ki**) *(instr sg* **-kiem**) *m* wolf; **głodny jak ~** (as) hungry as a wolf *lub* horse; **~ morski** sea dog; **o ~u mowa!** speak *lub* talk of the devil!
**wilkoła|k** (**-ka, -ki**) *(instr sg* **-kiem**) *m* werewolf
**will|a** (**-i, -e**) *(gen pl* **-i** *lub* **-**) *f* (detached) house
**willowy** *adj*: **dzielnica willowa** ≈ residential area
**Wil|no** (**-na**) *(loc sg* **-nie**) *nt* Vilnius
**wi|na** (**-ny, -ny**) *(dat sg* **-nie**) *f (przewinienie)* fault; *(uczucie)* guilt; *(odpowiedzialność)* guilt, blame; **to (nie) twoja ~** it is (not) your fault; **to ~ systemu** the system is to blame; **z czyjejś winy** through sb's fault; **(nie) przyznać się** *(perf)* **do winy** *(o oskarżonym)* to plead (not) guilty; **zrzucać winę na kogoś** to pin the blame on sb
**win|da** (**-dy, -dy**) *(dat sg* **-dzie**) *f* lift *(Brit)*, elevator *(US)*
**wind|ować** (**-uję, -ujesz**) *(perf* **wy-**) *vt (podnosić)* to hoist; *(ceny)* to hike
**windsurfin|g** (**-gu**) *(instr sg* **-giem**) *m* windsurfing
**winia|k** (**-ku, -ki**) *(instr sg* **-kiem**) *m* brandy
**winiar|nia** (**-ni, -nie**) *(gen pl* **-ni**) *f* wine bar
**wi|nić** (**-nię, -nisz**) *(imp* **-ń**) *vt*: **~ kogoś za coś** to blame sb for sth
**winien**[1] *adj* = **winny**[1]
**winien**[2] *vi (książk)*: **~em/~ im podziękować** I/he ought to thank them
**winie|ta** (**-ty, -ty**) *(dat sg* **-cie**) *f (ozdobnik)* vignette
**winna** *adj patrz* **winny**[1] ▷ *vb patrz* **winien**[2]
**winnic|a** (**-y, -e**) *f* vineyard
**winny**[1] *adj*, **winien** *(f* **winna**, *nt* **winne**) *(odpowiedzialny)* guilty; *(dłużny)*: **jest mi winien 50 złotych** he owes me 50 zloty ▷ *m decl like adj* culprit; **być ~m czegoś** to be guilty of sth
**winny**[2] *adj (smak, zapach)* vinous; **przemysł/ocet ~** wine industry/vinegar
**wi|no** (**-na, -na**) *(loc sg* **-nie**) *nt* wine; **dzikie ~** Virginia creeper *(Brit)*, woodbine *(US)*
**winobra|nie** (**-nia, -nia**) *(gen pl* **-ń**) *nt* grape picking
**winogro|no** (**-na, -na**) *(loc sg* **-nie**) *nt* grape
**winorośl** (**-i, -e**) *(gen pl* **-i**) *f* (grape)vine

**winowajc|a** (**-y, -y**) *m decl like f in sg* culprit
**winsz|ować (-uję, -ujesz)** (*perf* **po-**) *vi*: **~ komuś czegoś** to congratulate sb on sth; **~ komuś z okazji imienin/rocznicy ślubu** to wish sb a happy nameday/anniversary; **winszuję!** congratulations!
**winyl** (**-u**) *m* vinyl; **polichlorek ~u** polyvinyl chloride
**wiodę, wiodła** *itp. vb patrz* **wieść**
**wiol|a** (**-i, -e**) (*gen pl* **-i** *lub* **-**) *f* viola
**wiolinowy** *adj*: **klucz ~** treble clef
**wiolonczel|a** (**-i, -e**) (*gen pl* **-i** *lub* **-**) *f* cello
**wiolonczeli|sta** (**-sty, -ści**) (*dat sg* **-ście**) *m decl like f in sg* cellist
**wiolonczelist|ka** (**-ki, -ki**) (*dat sg* **-ce**, *gen pl* **-ek**) *f* cellist
**wiolonczelowy** *adj* cello *attr*
**wiosenny** *adj* spring *attr*
**wios|ka** (**-ki, -ki**) (*dat sg* **-ce**, *gen pl* **-ek**) *f* village; **~ olimpijska** Olympic village
**wio|sło** (**-sła, -sła**) (*loc sg* **-śle**, *gen pl* **-seł**) *nt* (*do łodzi*) oar; (*do kajaka*) paddle
**wiosł|ować (-uję, -ujesz)** *vi* (*z łodzi*) to row; (*z kajaka*) to paddle
**wiosłowy** *adj*: **łódź wiosłowa** rowing boat (*Brit*), rowboat (*US*)
**wio|sna** (**-sny, -sny**) (*dat sg* **-śnie**, *gen pl* **-sen**) *f* spring; **wiosną** *lub* **na wiosnę** in the spring
**wioślar|ka** (**-ki, -ki**) (*dat sg* **-ce**, *gen pl* **-ek**) *f* rower, oarswoman
**wioślarski** *adj*: **zawody ~e** rowing competition
**wioślarst|wo** (**-wa**) (*loc sg* **-wie**) *nt* rowing
**wioślarz** (**-a, -e**) (*gen pl* **-y**) *m* rower, oarsman
**wiotcz|eć (-eje)** (*perf* **z-**) *vi* (*o mięśniach*) to grow flabby; (*o skórze*) to get slack
**wiotki** *adj* (*mięsień*) flabby; (*skóra*) slack; (*cienki, szczupły*) slender
**wiotkoś|ć** (**-ci**) *f* (*szczupłość*) slenderness
**wiozę** *itp. vb patrz* **wieźć**
**wiódł** *vb patrz* **wieść**
**wió|r** (**-ra, -ry**) (*loc sg* **-rze**) *m* shaving; **wióry** *pl* shavings *pl*; **suchy jak ~** dry as a bone, bone dry
**wiór|ki** (**-ków**) *pl* chips *pl*; **~ kokosowe** desiccated coconut
**wiórowy** *adj*: **płyta wiórowa** chipboard
**wiózł** *vb patrz* **wieźć**
**wi|r** (**-ru, -ry**) (*loc sg* **-rze**) *m* whirl; (*w wodzie*) whirlpool; **w wirze walki** in the thick of the battle; **wpaść** (*perf*) **w wir życia towarzyskiego** to fling o.s. into the social whirl
**wiraż** (**-u, -e**) (*gen pl* **-y** *lub* **-ów**) *m* (*zakręt*) tight bend; (*skręt*) turning
**Wirgini|a** (**-i**) *f* Virginia
**wirni|k** (**-ka, -ki**) (*instr sg* **-kiem**) *m* rotor
**wir|ować (-uję, -ujesz)** *vt* (*perf* **od-**) (*bieliznę*) to spin-dry; (*mleko*) to centrifuge ▹ *vi* (*perf* **za-**) to whirl
**wirowy** *adj* rotational
**wirów|ka** (**-ki, -ki**) (*dat sg* **-ce**, *gen pl* **-ek**) *f* (*do bielizny*) spin-dryer; (*do mleka*) centrifuge
**wirtualny** *adj* virtual
**wirtuo|z** (**-za, -zi** *lub* **-zowie**) (*loc sg* **-zie**) *m* virtuoso; **~ gitary/skrzypiec** guitar/violin virtuoso
**wirtuozeri|a** (**-i**) *f* (*książk*) virtuosity
**wiru|s** (**-sa, -sy**) (*loc sg* **-sie**) *m* virus
**wirusologi|a** (**-i**) *f* virology
**wirusowy** *adj* viral
**wi|sieć (-szę, -sisz)** (*imp* **-ś**) *vi* to hang; (*o helikopterze*) to hover; **za to można ~** you could hang for this; **~ na kimś** (*o ubraniu*) to hang loose on sb; **~ nad kimś** (*przen*) to hang over sb; **~ na włosku** (*przen*) to hang by a thread; **coś wisi w powietrzu** (*przen*) something is in the air; **wisi mi to** (*pot*) I don't give a damn (about it) (*pot*)
**wisielczy** *adj*: **~ humor** gallows humour (*Brit*) *lub* humor (*US*)
**wisiel|ec** (**-ca, -cy**) *m* hanged person; **grać w wisielca** to play hangman
**wisior|ek** (**-ka, -ki**) (*instr sg* **-kiem**) *m* pendant
**wisko|za** (**-zy**) (*dat sg* **-zie**) *f* viscose
**Wi|sła** (**-sły**) (*dat sg* **-śle**) *f* the Vistula
**wi|st** (**-sta, -sty**) (*loc sg* **-ście**) (*Karty*) *m* (*gra*) whist; (*wyjście, zagrywka*) lead
**wist|ować (-uję, -ujesz)** *vi* (*Karty*): **~ w piki** to lead (with) a spade
**wiszący** *adj*: **~ most** suspension bridge
**wi|śnia** (**-śni, -śnie**) (*gen pl* **-śni** *lub* **-sien**) *f* (*owoc*) cherry; (*drzewo*) cherry (tree)
**wiśnia|k** (**-ku, -ki**) (*instr sg* **-kiem**) *m* cherry vodka
**wiśniowy** *adj* (*sad, dżem, napój*) cherry *attr*; (*kolor*) cherry red
**wiśniów|ka** (**-ki, -ki**) (*dat sg* **-ce**, *gen pl* **-ek**) *f* cherry liqueur
**wit|ać (-am, -asz)** *vt* (*perf* **po-** *lub* **przy-**) (*pozdrawiać*) to greet; (*przybysza, zmiany*) to welcome; **witamy w Poznaniu!** welcome to Poznań!; **witaj/witajcie/witam!** nice to see you!; **witać się** *vr* (*perf* **przy-**); **~ się (z kimś)** to exchange greetings (with sb)
**witalnoś|ć** (**-ci**) *f* vitality
**witalny** *adj* vital
**witami|na** (**-ny, -ny**) (*dat sg* **-nie**) *f* vitamin; **~ C** vitamin C
**witaminizowany** *adj* with added vitamins
**wit|ka** (**-ki, -ki**) (*dat sg* **-ce**, *gen pl* **-ek**) *f* twig
**witraż** (**-a** *lub* **-u, -e**) (*gen pl* **-y**) *m* stained glass
**witrażowy** *adj*: **okno witrażowe** stained glass window; **szkło witrażowe** stained glass

W

**witry|na** (**-ny, -ny**) (*dat sg* **-nie**) *f* (shop) window; (*w muzeum, na wystawie*) glass case

**wiwa|t** (**-tu, -ty**) (*loc sg* **-cie**) *m* cheer; **~ młoda para!** long live the happy couple!; **strzelać na ~** to fire a salute

**wiwat|ować** (**-uję, -ujesz**) *vi* to cheer; **~ na czyjąś cześć** to cheer sb

**wiwisekcj|a** (**-i, -e**) (*gen pl* **-i**) *f* vivisection

**wi|za** (**-zy, -zy**) (*dat sg* **-zie**) *f* visa; **~ pobytowa/turystyczna** visitor's/tourist visa

**wizerun|ek** (**-ku, -ki**) (*instr sg* **-kiem**) *m* (*książk: osoby*) image; (*czasów*) picture

**wizj|a** (**-i, -e**) (*gen pl* **-i**) *f* (*wyobrażenie, majak*) vision; **~ lokalna** (*Prawo*) *inspection at the scene of the crime*; **być na wizji** (TV) to be on the air

**wizje|r** (**-ra, -ry**) (*loc sg* **-rze**) *m* (*Fot*) viewfinder; (*w drzwiach*) peephole; (*w broni*) sight

**wizjone|r** (**-ra, -rzy**) (*loc sg* **-rze**) *m* visionary

**wizjonerski** *adj* visionary

**wizowy** *adj*: **formularz ~** visa application form

**wizualnie** *adv* visually

**wizualny** *adj* (*książk*) visual

**wizy|ta** (**-ty, -ty**) (*dat sg* **-cie**) *f* visit; (*u lekarza itp.*) appointment; **składać (złożyć** *perf***) komuś wizytę** to pay sb a visit; **przyjść** (*perf*) **(do kogoś) z wizytą** to pay a call on sb, to pay sb a visit

**wizytacj|a** (**-i, -e**) (*gen pl* **-i**) *f* inspection

**wizytato|r** (**-ra, -rzy**) (*loc sg* **-rze**) *m* (*Szkol*) inspector

**wizyt|ować** (**-uję, -ujesz**) (*perf* **z-**) *vt* to inspect

**wizytowy** *adj* (*strój*) formal; **bilet ~** visiting card (Brit), calling card (US)

**wizytów|ka** (**-ki, -ki**) (*dat sg* **-ce**, *gen pl* **-ek**) *f* (business) card; (*przen*) showcase

**wj|azd** (**-azdu, -azdy**) (*loc sg* **-eździe**) *m* (*czynność*) entering; (*brama*) gateway; (*do garażu*) drive; (*na autostradę*) slip road (Brit), entrance ramp (US); **„zakaz ~u"** "no entry"

**wjazdowy** *adj*: **wiza/opłata wjazdowa** entry visa/fee; **brama wjazdowa** gateway

**wj|echać** (**-adę, -edziesz**) (*imp* **-edź**) *vb perf od* **wjeżdżać**

**wjeżdż|ać** (**-am, -asz**) (*perf* **wjechać**) *vi* (*do wewnątrz*) to drive in; (*windą*) to go up, to ascend; (*o pociągu: na stację*) to pull in; **~ na/w** *+acc* (*wpadać*) to drive into

**wkalkulow|ywać** (**-uję, -ujesz**) (*perf* **-ać**) *vt*: **~ coś w cenę/koszt** to include sth in the price/cost

**wkle|ić** (**-ję, -isz**) (*imp* **-j**) *vb perf od* **wklejać**

**wklej|ać** (**-am, -asz**) (*perf* **wkleić**) *vt* to stick in

**wklęsły** *adj* (*brzuch, klatka piersiowa*) hollow; (*zwierciadło, policzki*) concave; **druk ~** intaglio

**wklęśnię|cie** (**-cia, -cia**) (*gen pl* **-ć**) *nt* concavity

**wkła|d** (**-du, -dy**) (*loc sg* **-dzie**) *m* (*finansowy, pracy*) input, contribution; (*element wymienny*) refill (insert); (*w banku*) deposit; **~ (do długopisu)** (pen) refill; **~ do ołówka** refill lead

**wkład|ać** (**-am, -asz**) (*perf* **włożyć**) *vt* to insert, to put in; **~ coś do szuflady/na półkę** to put sth in the drawer/on the shelf; **~ buty/spodnie** to put on one's shoes/trousers; **włożyć w coś dużo wysiłku** to put great effort into sth

**wkład|ka** (**-ki, -ki**) (*dat sg* **-ce**, *gen pl* **-ek**) *f* insert; **~ antykoncepcyjna** intra-uterine device

**wkoło** *prep +gen* around

**wkomponow|ywać** (**-uję, -ujesz**) (*perf* **-ać**) *vt*: **~ się w coś** to blend (well) into sth

**wkop|ywać** (**-uję, -ujesz**) (*perf* **-ać**) *vt* (*słup, pal*) to sink into the ground; (*pot: zdradzać*) to rat on (*pot*); **wkopywać się** *vr* (*pot: zdradzać się*) to give o.s. away; **~ się w coś** (*wplątywać się*) to land o.s. in sth

**wkracz|ać** (**-am, -asz**) (*perf* **wkroczyć**) *vi* (*wchodzić uroczyście*) to enter, to make an entrance; (*o wojsku*) to move *lub* march in; (*przen: interweniować*) to step in; **~ do sali** to enter a room

**wkrad|ać się** (**-am, -asz**) (*perf* **wkraść**) *vr* (*o osobie*) to sneak in, to slip in; (*przen: o błędzie*) to creep in; **wkraść się w czyjeś łaski** to win sb's favour (Brit) *lub* favor (US)

**wkrapl|ać** (**-am, -asz**) (*perf* **wkroplić**) *vt* to instil (Brit), to instill (US)

**wkra|ść się** (**-dnę, -dniesz**) (*imp* **-dnij**, *pt* **-dł**) *vb perf od* **wkradać się**

**wkrę|cać** (**-cam, -casz**) (*perf* **-cić**) *vt* (*śrubkę, wkręt, żarówkę*) to screw in; (*papier maszynowy*) to load; **wkręcać się** *vr* (*o śrubie, wkręcie*) to screw; (*o materiale, włosach*) to catch, to get caught; **palce wkręciły mu się w tryby** he caught his fingers in the cogs

**wkrę|cić** (**-cę, -cisz**) (*imp* **-ć**) *vb perf od* **wkręcać**; **wkręcić się** *vr perf* (*pot: o człowieku*): **wkręcać się (do** *+gen***)** to wangle one's way (into)

**wkrę|t** (**-tu, -ty**) (*loc sg* **-cie**) *m* screw

**wkrocz|yć** (**-ę, -ysz**) *vb perf od* **wkraczać**

**wkro|ić** (**-ję, -isz**) *vt perf*: **~ warzywa** (*w przepisie*) add chopped vegetables

**wkropl|ić** (**-ę, -isz**) *vb perf od* **wkraplać**

**wkrótce** *adv* soon

**wk|uć** (**-uję, -ujesz**) *vb perf od* **wkuwać**

**wku|pić się** (**-pię, -pisz**) *vr perf*: **wkupić się (do** *+gen***)** to buy one's way (into); **wkupić się w czyjeś łaski** (*przen*) to buy sb's favours (Brit) *lub* favors (US)

**wkurz|ać (-am, -asz)** (*perf* **-yć**) *vt* (*pot*) to piss off (*pot*); **wkurzać się** *vr* (*pot*) to be pissed off (*pot*)
**wkurz|yć (-ę, -ysz)** *vb perf od* **wkurzać**
**wkuw|ać (-am, -asz)** (*perf* **wkuć**) *vt* (*pot: matematykę, chemię*) to swot up (on) ▷ *vi* (*pot*) to swot; **~ do egzaminów** to swot for exams
**wl|ać (-eję, -ejesz)** *vb perf od* **wlewać** ▷ *vi perf* (*pot*): **~ komuś** to give sb a thrashing
**wlat|ywać (-uję, -ujesz)** (*perf* **wlecieć**) *vi* (*o ptaku, owadzie*) to fly in; (*o dymie*) to get *lub* pour in; (*o piłce*) to shoot in; **~ na kogoś/coś** (*pot*) to bump into sb/sth
**wlazł** *itd. vb patrz* **wleźć**
**wl|ec (-okę, -eczesz)** (*pt* **-ókł, -okła, -ekli**) *vt* to drag, to haul; **wlec się** *vr* (*o człowieku*) to drag along; (*o czasie, sukni*) to drag; (*o pojeździe*) to crawl; (*o dymie*) to hang
**wle|cieć (-cę, -cisz)** (*imp* **-ć**) *vb perf od* **wlatywać**
**wle|piać (-piam, -piasz)** (*perf* **-pić**) *vt* (*wklejać*) to stick in; **wlepić komuś mandat** (*pot*) to give sb a ticket; **~ w kogoś wzrok** to fix one's eyes on *lub* upon sb
**wle|pić (-pię, -pisz)** *vb perf od* **wlepiać**
**wle|w (-wu, -wy)** (*loc sg* **-wie**) *m* inlet
**wlew|ać (-am, -asz)** (*perf* **wlać**) *vt*: **~ coś (do czegoś)** to pour sth (into sth); **~ w kogoś otuchę** (*przen*) to raise sb's spirits; **wlewać się** *vr* to flow in, to pour in
**wl|eźć (-ezę, -eziesz)** (*imp* **-eź**, *pt* **-azł, -eźli**) *vb perf od* **włazić**
**wlicz|ać (-am, -asz)** (*perf* **-yć**) *vt*: **~ coś w cenę/koszty** to include sth in the price/costs
**wlokę** *itd. vb patrz* **wlec**
**wlo|t (-tu, -ty)** (*loc sg* **-cie**) *m* inlet
**wlókł** *vb patrz* **wlec**
**wład|ać (-am, -asz)** *vt +instr* (*książk: krainą, państwem*) to rule; (*bronią, mieczem*) to wield; (*nogą, ręką*) to have the use of; (*obcym językiem*) to have a good command of
**władani|e (-a)** *nt*: **dostać** *lub* **objąć** (*perf*) **coś we ~** to come into *lub* take possession of sth; **mieć coś pod (swoim) ~m** to have sth under one's rule
**władc|a (-y, -y)** *m decl like f in sg* ruler
**władczy** *adj* lordly, imperious
**władczy|ni (-ni, -nie)** (*gen pl* **-ń**) *f* ruler
**władny** *adj*: **być ~m coś zrobić** (*książk*) to have the authority *lub* power to do sth
**wład|ować (-uję, -ujesz)** *vb perf od* **ładować**
**władz|a (-y)** *f* (*panowanie*) rule, reign; (*oddziaływanie*) power; **~ sądownicza** the judiciary; **~ ustawodawcza** the legislature; **~ wykonawcza** the executive; **sprawować władzę** to wield *lub* exercise power; **być u władzy** to be in power; **mieć nad kimś władzę** to have power over sb; **stracił władzę w nogach** he lost the use of his legs; **władze** *pl* (*państwowe, lokalne*) the authorities; **być w pełni władz umysłowych** to be of sound mind
**wła|mać się (-mię, -miesz)** *vb perf od* **włamywać się**
**włama|nie (-nia, -nia)** (*gen pl* **-ń**) *nt* burglary; **dokonywać (dokonać** *perf*) **włamania** to break in
**włamywacz (-a, -e)** (*gen pl* **-y**) *m* burglar
**włam|ywać się (-uję, -ujesz)** (*perf* **-ać**) *vr* to break in; **włamywać się do czegoś** to break into sth, to burgle (*pot*) *lub* burglarize sth
**własnoręczny** *adj*: **~ podpis** personal signature
**własnościowy** *adj*: **mieszkanie własnościowe** owner-occupied flat; **Ministerstwo Przekształceń W~ch** Ministry of Privatization
**własnoś|ć (-ci)** *f* (*mienie*) property; (*prawo do rozporządzania*) ownership
**własny** *adj*: **mój/jego/jej ~** my/his/her own; **nazwa własna** proper noun; **imię własne** proper name; **na własną rękę** unaided, under one's own steam; **z własnej woli** of one's own free will; **w obronie własnej** in self-defence; **na koszt ~** at one's own expense; **we własnej osobie** in person *lub* the flesh; **o ~ch siłach** on one's own, unaided; **„do rąk ~ch"** "private"
**właściciel (-a, -e)** (*gen pl* **-i**) *m* owner; (*domu*) landlord; (*firmy, hotelu, patentu*) proprietor; **zmieniać (zmienić** *perf*) **~a** to change hands
**właściciel|ka (-ki, -ki)** (*dat sg* **-ce**, *gen pl* **-ek**) *f* owner; (*domu*) landlady; (*firmy, hotelu, patentu*) proprietress
**właściwie** *adv* (*należycie*) properly; (*poprawnie*) correctly; (*prawdę mówiąc*) actually, as a matter of fact; **~ możesz już iść** you may as well go now
**właściwoś|ć (-ci, -ci)** (*gen pl* **-ci**) *f* property, characteristic
**właściwy** *adj* (*zachowanie, traktowanie*) proper; (*człowiek*) right; (*odpowiedź*) correct; (*faktyczny*) actual; **~ komuś** *lub* **dla kogoś** characteristic of sb; **ciężar ~** specific gravity; **we ~m czasie** at the right time, in due course
**właśnie** *adv*: **~ wtedy/tam/dlatego** this is when/where/why; **to ~** *lub* **~ to powiedział/zrobił** that's just what he said/did; **~ idzie/przyjechała** she is just coming/has just come; **~ miałem zatelefonować** I was (just) about to phone; **i o to ~ chodzi!** that's what it's all about!; **(no) ~!** quite (so)!; **nie było cię tam — ~ że byłam!** you weren't there — I was so!; **nie pójdziesz — ~ że pójdę!** you're

W

not going — I am too!; **tego nam ~ było potrzeba!** that's just what we needed!

**wła|z** (**-zu, -zy**) (*loc sg* **-zie**) *m* (*czołgu*) hatch(way); (*kanału*) manhole

**wła|zić (-żę, -zisz)** (*imp* **-ź**, *perf* **wleźć**) *vi* (*pot*): **~ do środka** to get inside; **~ na drzewo/po drabinie** to climb a tree/ladder; **wleźć w coś** to step into sth; **ile wlezie** to one's heart's content

**włącz|ać (-am, -asz)** (*perf* **-yć**) *vt* (*silnik, światło*) to switch *lub* turn on; **~ coś (do czegoś)** to include sth (in sth); **~ coś do sieci** *lub* **prądu** to plug sth in; **włączać się** *vr* (*o maszynie, świetle*) to come on; **~ się do dyskusji/pracy** to join in the discussion/work; **jak to się włącza?** how do you turn *lub* switch it on?

**włącznie** *adv*: **od poniedziałku do środy ~** (from) Monday to Wednesday inclusive; **~ ze mną** *lub* **ze mną ~** myself included

**włączony** *adj*: **być ~m** to be on; **przy ~m ogrzewaniu** with the heating on; **z ~mi światłami** with the lights on

**włącz|yć (-ę, -ysz)** *vb perf od* **włączać**

**Wło|ch** (**-cha, -si**) *m* Italian

**włochaty** *adj* (*dywan*) pile *attr*; (*niedźwiedź*) hairy

**Wło|chy** (**-ch**) (*loc* **-szech**) *pl* Italy

**wło|s** (**-sa, -sy**) (*loc sg* **-sie**) *m* hair; **o mały ~ nie oblałem** (*przen*) I only passed by the skin of my teeth; **jeśli choćby ~ mu z głowy spadnie, ...** if you harm a hair on his head, ...; **włosy** *pl* hair *no pl*

**włos|ek** (**-ka, -ki**) (*instr sg* **-kiem**) *m dimin od* **włos**; **wisieć na włosku** to hang by a thread

**Włosi** *n patrz* **Włoch**

**włosi|e** (**-a**) *nt* bristle, bristles *pl*

**włoski** *adj* Italian ▷ *m* (*język*) Italian; **orzech ~** walnut; **kapusta włoska** savoy (cabbage); **strajk ~** work-to-rule

**włosowaty** *adj*: **naczynie włosowate** capillary

**włoszczy|zna** (**-zny**) (*dat sg* **-źnie**) *f a bunch of mixed vegetables (usually carrot, leek, celeriac, parsley)*

**Włosz|ka** (**-ki, -ki**) (*dat sg* **-ce**, *gen pl* **-ek**) *f* Italian

**włoś|ci** (**-ci**) *pl* (*książk*) estate

**wł|ożyć (-ożę, -ożysz)** (*imp* **-óż**) *vb perf od* **wkładać**

**włóczę|ga¹** (**-gi, -gi**) (*dat sg* **-dze**) *f* (*wędrówka*) roaming, roving; (*długa wycieczka*) tramp, trek

**włóczę|ga²** (**-gi, -dzy** *lub* **-gi**) (*loc sg* **-dze**) *m decl like f in sg* (*osoba*) wanderer, vagabond

**włóczęgost|wo** (**-wa**) (*loc sg* **-wie**) *nt* vagrancy

**włócz|ka** (**-ki, -ki**) (*dat sg* **-ce**, *gen pl* **-ek**) *f* yarn (*knitting thread*)

**włócz|nia** (**-ni, -nie**) (*gen pl* **-ni**) *f* spear

**włócz|yć (-ę, -ysz)** *vt* to drag, to haul; **włóczyć się** *vr* to ramble, to rove

**włókienniczy** *adj* textile

**włó|kno** (**-kna, -kna**) (*loc sg* **-knie**, *gen pl* **-kien**) *nt* fibre (*Brit*), fiber (*US*)

**wmawi|ać (-am, -asz)** (*perf* **wmówić**) *vt*: **~ coś komuś** *lub* **w kogoś** to make sb believe sth; **~ sobie, że ...** to persuade o.s. that ...

**wmiesz|ać się (-am, -asz)** *vr perf*: **wmieszać się w coś** (*przen*) to get mixed up in sth

**wmó|wić (-wię, -wisz)** *vb perf od* **wmawiać**

**wmur|ować (-uję, -ujesz)** *vt perf* (*tablicę*) to fix; (*kamień węgielny*) to lay

**wmu|sić (-szę, -sisz)** (*imp* **-ś**) *vb perf od* **wmuszać**

**wmusz|ać (-am, -asz)** (*perf* **wmusić**) *vt*: **~ coś komuś/w kogoś** to force sth on *lub* upon sb

**wnet** *adv* (*książk*) soon

**wnę|ka** (**-ki, -ki**) (*dat sg* **-ce**) *f* recess

**wnętrz|e** (**-a, -a**) *nt* interior, inside; (*Archit*) interior

**wnętrznośc|i** (**-i**) *pl* entrails, bowels

**wniebogłosy** *adv* (*pot*) at the top of one's voice

**wniebowstąpieni|e** (**-a**) *nt* (*Rel*) Ascension

**wniebowzięci|e** (**-a**) *nt* (*Rel*) Assumption

**wniebowzięty** *adj* (*przen*) entranced

**wni|eść (-osę, -esiesz)** (*imp* **-eś**, *pt* **-ósł, -osła, -eśli**) *vb perf od* **wnosić**

**wnik|ać (-am, -asz)** (*perf* **-nąć**) *vi*: **~ w coś** (*o płynie, świetle*: *przenikać*) to penetrate sth; (*o człowieku*: *zgłębiać*) to get to the core of sth; **nie wnikając** *lub* **bez wnikania w szczegóły** without going into details

**wnikliwie** *adv* (*analizować*) carefully; (*patrzeć*) penetratingly

**wnikliwoś|ć** (**-ci**) *f* penetration

**wnikliwy** *adj* (*analiza, czytelnik*) careful; (*wzrok*) penetrating

**wnik|nąć (-nę, -niesz)** (*imp* **-nij**) *vb perf od* **wnikać**

**wnios|ek** (**-ku, -ki**) (*instr sg* **-kiem**) *m* (*propozycja*) motion, proposal; (*konkluzja*) conclusion; (*podanie*) application; **dochodzić (dojść** *perf***) do wniosku** to come to a conclusion; **wyciągać (wyciągnąć** *perf***) ~** to draw a conclusion; **zgłaszać (zgłosić** *perf***) ~** to make a motion, to move a proposal

**wnioskodawc|a** (**-y, -y**) *m decl like f in sg* mover

**wniosk|ować (-uję, -ujesz)** (*perf* **wy-**) *vt*: **~ (z czegoś), że ...** to conclude (from sth) that ...

**wno|sić (-szę, -sisz)** (*imp* **-ś**, *perf* **wnieść**) *vt* (*walizki, meble*) to carry in; (*zapach*) to bring in; (*przen*: *radość, życie*) to bring; (*opłatę, składkę*) to pay; (*podanie*) to put in; (*sprzeciw*) to raise; (*zażalenie*) to file ▷ *vi* (*książk*) to gather, to conclude; ~ **poprawki** to make amendments; ~ **sprawę do sądu** to bring a case to court

**WNP** *abbr (= Wspólnota Niepodległych Państw)* CIS (= *Commonwealth of Independent States*)

**wnucz|ek** (**-ka, -kowie**) (*instr sg* **-kiem**) *m* grandson

**wnucz|ka** (**-ki, -ki**) (*dat sg* **-ce**, *gen pl* **-ek**) *f* granddaughter

**wnu|k** (**-ka, -kowie** *lub* **-ki**) (*instr sg* **-kiem**) *m* grandson; **wnuki** *pl* grandchildren

**wny|ki** (**-ków**) *pl* snare

**woal** (**-u, -e**) (*gen pl* **-i** *lub* **-ów**) *m* voile

**woal|ka** (**-ki, -ki**) (*dat sg* **-ce**, *gen pl* **-ek**) *f* veil

**wobec** *prep +gen* (*w obecności*) in the presence of; (*w obliczu*) in the face of; (*w stosunku do*) to, toward(s); (*w porównaniu z*) in comparison with; (*z powodu*) because of; ~ **tego** in that case; **było to nic ~ tego, co zdarzyło się później** that was nothing in comparison to what happened later; ~ **braku wsparcia, musieli się wycofać** for the lack of support they had to withdraw

**wo|da** (**-dy, -dy**) (*dat sg* **-dzie**, *gen pl* **wód**) *f* water; ~ **sodowa/mineralna** soda/mineral water; ~ **słodka/morska** fresh/sea water; ~ **(zdatna) do picia** drinking water; **kolońska** (eau de) cologne; **pod wodą** underwater; **spuszczać (spuścić** *perf*) **wodę** to flush the toilet; **ryba z wody** (*Kulin*) boiled fish; **wody** *pl*: **wody płodowe** amniotic fluid *sg*; **wody terytorialne** territorial waters

**wodewil** (**-u, -e**) (*gen pl* **-ów**) *m* vaudeville

**wodni|k** (**-ka, -ki**) (*instr sg* **-kiem**) *m* (*w bajkach*) sprite; **Wodnik** (*Astrologia*) Aquarius

**wodnisty** *adj* watery

**wodny** *adj* (*zbiornik, turbina*) water *attr*; (*roztwór*) water *attr*, aqueous *attr*; (*sporty*) aquatic; **elektrownia wodna** hydroelectric power station; **narty wodne** water skis; **piłka wodna** water-polo; **znak** ~ watermark; **armatka wodna** water cannon

**wodocią|g** (**-gu, -gi**) (*instr sg* **-giem**) *m* water-supply (system); **wodociągi** *pl* (*pot*) waterworks *sg lub pl*

**wodociągowy** *adj* (*rura*) water *attr*; **sieć wodociągowa** water-supply system

**wodolejst|wo** (**-wa**) (*loc sg* **-wie**) *nt* (*pot*) wordiness

**wodolo|t** (**-tu, -ty**) (*loc sg* **-cie**) *m* hydrofoil

**wodomierz** (**-a, -e**) (*gen pl* **-y**) *m* water meter

**wodoodporny** *adj* waterproof, water-resistant; (*materiał, kurtka*) water-repellent

**wodop|ój** (**-oju, -oje**) *m* waterhole, watering place

**wodoro|st** (**-stu, -sty**) (*loc sg* **-ście**) *m* seaweed

**wodorotlen|ek** (**-ku, -ki**) (*instr sg* **-kiem**) *m* hydroxide

**wodorowy** *adj* (*Chem*) hydrogen *attr*; **bomba wodorowa** hydrogen bomb, H-bomb

**wodospa|d** (**-du, -dy**) (*loc sg* **-dzie**) *m* waterfall; **W~ Niagara** the Niagara Falls *pl*

**wodoszczelny** *adj* (*zegarek*) waterproof; (*łódź*) watertight

**wodotrys|k** (**-ku, -ki**) (*instr sg* **-kiem**) *m* fountain

**wod|ować (-uję, -ujesz)** *vt* (*perf* **z-**) (*Żegl*) to launch ▷ *vi* (*Kosmos*) to splash down

**wodowa|nie** (**-nia, -nia**) (*gen pl* **-ń**) *nt* (*Żegl*) launch, launching; (*Kosmos*) splashdown; (*Lot*) landing on water

**wodowstrę|t** (**-tu**) (*loc sg* **-cie**) *m* hydrophobia; (*wścieklizna*) rabies

**wod|ór** (**-oru**) (*loc sg* **-orze**) *m* hydrogen

**wodz|a** (**-y, -e**) (*gen pl* **-y**) *f*: **pod wodzą kogoś** under sb's command; **trzymać nerwy na wodzy** to keep one's temper; **wodze** *pl* reins *pl*; **puszczać (puścić** *perf*) **wodze fantazji** to give the reins to the imagination

**wo|dzić (-dzę, -dzisz)** (*imp* **wódź**) *vt* (*książk: prowadzić*) to lead; ~ **palcem/wzrokiem po czymś** to run one's finger/eye over sth; ~ **kogoś za nos** (*pot*) to lead sb by the nose

**wodzirej** (**-a, -e**) *m* (*na zabawie*) dance leader

**woj.** *abbr (= województwo)*: ~ **poznańskie** Poznań Province

**woja|k** (**-ka, -cy** *lub* **-ki**) (*instr sg* **-kiem**) *m* soldier

**wojaż** (**-u, -e**) (*gen pl* **-y**) *m* (*pot*) travel

**wojaż|ować (-uję, -ujesz)** *vi* (*pot*) to travel

**wojenny** *adj* (*korespondent, inwalida, weteran*) war *attr*; (*port*) military; **stan** ~ (*Pol*) martial law; **marynarka wojenna** navy; **okręt** ~ warship; **jeniec** ~ prisoner of war; **sąd** ~ court martial

**wojewo|da** (**-dy, -dowie**) (*dat sg* **-dzie**) *m decl like f in sg* governor (*of a province*); ~ **poznański** governor of the Poznań Province

**wojewódzki** *adj* provincial; **miasto ~e** provincial capital, capital of a province

**województ|wo** (**-wa, -wa**) (*loc sg* **-wie**) *nt* province; ~ **poznańskie** Poznań Province

**woj|na** (**-ny, -ny**) (*dat sg* **-nie**, *gen pl* **-en**) *f* war; **pierwsza/druga ~ światowa** World War One/Two, the First/Second World War; ~ **domowa** civil war; **zimna** ~ (*Hist*) the cold war; **wydawać (wydać** *perf*) **wojnę komuś/czemuś** to wage war on *lub* against sb/sth; **prowadzić** *lub* **toczyć wojnę (z kimś/czymś)** to be at war (with sb/sth); **(być) w stanie wojny z** *+instr* (to be) in the state of war with

**woj|ować (-uję, -ujesz)** *vi* (*pot*): ~ **z** *+instr* to wage war on *lub* against

W

**wojowniczoś|ć** (**-ci**) *f* (*narodu, plemienia*) warlike spirit; (*zachowania*) belligerence
**wojowniczy** *adj* (*naród, plemię*) warlike; (*zachowanie*) belligerent
**wojowni|k** (**-ka, -cy**) (*instr sg* **-kiem**) *m* warrior
**wojs|ko** (**-ka, -ka**) (*instr sg* **-kiem**) *nt* (*siły zbrojne*) (armed) forces *pl*; (*armia*) army; (*pot*) military service; **służyć w wojsku** to serve in the army; **wojska lądowe** army; **wojska lotnicze** air force
**wojskowoś|ć** (**-ci**) *f* military science
**wojskowy** *adj* military ▷ *m decl like adj* military man
**wojujący** *adj* militant
**wokali|sta** (**-sty, -ści**) (*dat sg* **-ście**) *m decl like f in sg* (*zespołu*) vocalist; (*indywidualny*) singer
**wokalist|ka** (**-ki, -ki**) (*dat sg* **-ce**, *gen pl* **-ek**) *f* (*zespołu*) vocalist; (*indywidualna*) singer
**wokalny** *adj* vocal
**wokan|da** (**-dy, -dy**) (*dat sg* **-dzie**) *f* (*Prawo*): **być na wokandzie (sądowej)** to come up for trial
**wokoło, wokół** *prep +gen* (*dokoła*) round ▷ *adv* (*dookoła*) all around; **rozglądać (rozejrzeć** *perf*) **się** ~ to look around
**wol|a** (**-i**) *f* will; **dobra** ~ goodwill; **zła** ~ ill will; **mieć silną/słabą wolę** to have strong/weak will; **ostatnia** ~ (*testament*) last will; **z własnej woli** voluntarily, of one's own free will; **mimo woli** unintentionally, involuntarily; **do woli** at will
**wol|e** (**-a, -a**) (*gen pl* **-i**) *nt* (*u ptaka*) crop; (*Med*) goitre
**wol|eć (-ę, -isz)** *vt/vi* to prefer; **wolę kawę niż herbatę** *lub* **od herbaty** I prefer coffee to tea; **wolę iść pieszo (niż jechać samochodem)** I prefer walking (to driving); **wolę o tym nie mówić** I'd rather not talk about it; **wolę, żebyś ty to zrobił** I'd rather you did it
**wolej** (**-a, -e**) *m* volley
**wolfra|m** (**-mu**) (*loc sg* **-mie**) *m* tungsten, wolfram
**woli** *adj* (*skóra*) bovine
**wolno**[1] *adv* (*pomału*) slowly; (*luzem*) freely; **dom ~ stojący** detached house
**wolno**[2] *inv*: **tu nie ~ palić** you are not allowed to smoke here; **nie ~ mu palić** he mustn't smoke; **jej wszystko** ~ she is allowed to do everything; **jeśli ~ spytać** if I may ask
**wolnocłowy** *adj* duty-free
**wolnomularst|wo** (**-wa**) (*loc sg* **-wie**) *nt* freemasonry
**wolnomularz** (**-a, -e**) (*gen pl* **-y**) *m* freemason
**wolnomyśliciel** (**-a, -e**) (*gen pl* **-i**) *m* freethinker
**wolnorynkowy** *adj*: **ceny wolnorynkowe** free-market prices
**wolnościowy** *adj*: **ruch** ~ liberation movement
**wolnoś|ć** (**-ci**) *f* freedom, liberty; **~ słowa/wyznania/zgromadzeń** freedom of speech/religion/assembly
**wolny** *adj* (*człowiek, rynek, wybór, przekład*) free; (*czas*) free, spare; (*etat, pokój*) free, vacant; (*krok, tempo*) slow; (*nieżonaty/niezamężna*) single; ~ **słuchacz** *auditing student*; ~ **dzień** a day off; **odpowiadać z wolnej stopy** (*Prawo*) to be released pending trial; **rzut** ~ free kick; **„wstęp ~"** "admission free"; **dawać (dać** *perf*) **komuś wolną rękę** to give sb a free hand; **gotować na ~m ogniu** cook on a low heat; **na ~m powietrzu** in the open air; **~ od cła** duty-free
**wolontariusz** (**-a, -e**) (*gen pl* **-y**) *m* volunteer
**wol|t** (**-ta, -ty**) (*loc sg* **-cie**) *m* volt
**wol|ta** (**-ty, -ty**) (*dat sg* **-cie**) *f* (*przen*) about-face
**woltyżer|ka** (**-ki, -ki**) (*dat sg* **-ce**, *gen pl* **-ek**) *f* bareback riding
**wolume|n** (**-nu, -ny**) (*loc sg* **-nie**) *m* (*Handel, Giełda*) volume
**wołacz** (**-a, -e**) (*gen pl* **-y**) *m* (*Jęz*) vocative
**woł|ać (-am, -asz)** (*perf* **za-**) *vt* to call ▷ *vi* to call; **~ o pomoc** to cry for help; **wołają na nią Aga** they call her Aga
**Woł|ga** (**-gi**) (*dat sg* **-dze**) *f* Volga
**wołowi|na** (**-ny**) (*dat sg* **-nie**) *f* beef
**wołowy** *adj*: **pieczeń wołowa** roast beef; **dupa wołowa** (*pot!*) ass (*pot!*)
**wołu** *itd. n patrz* **wół**
**won** *excl*: **won!** (*pot!*) (get) out! (*pot*)
**wonny** *adj* (*książk*) fragrant
**wo|ń** (**-ni, -nie**) (*gen pl* **-ni**) *f* scent, fragrance; **przykra woń** unpleasant odour (*Brit*) *lub* odor (*US*)
**WOPR** *abbr* (= *Wodne Ochotnicze Pogotowie Ratunkowe*) *Volunteer Lifeguards Association*
**worecz|ek** (**-ka, -ki**) (*instr sg* **-kiem**) *m* bag; **~ żółciowy** gall bladder
**wor|ek** (**-ka, -ki**) (*instr sg* **-kiem**) *m* sack; **worki** *pl*: **worki pod oczami** bags under the eyes
**workowaty** *adj* baggy
**wos|k** (**-ku, -ki**) (*instr sg* **-kiem**) *m* wax; **~ pszczeli** beeswax; **lać** ~ *to tell fortunes by pouring hot wax into water*
**wosk|ować (-uję, -ujesz)** (*perf* **wy-**) *vt* to wax
**woskowi|na** (**-ny**) (*dat sg* **-nie**) *f* (ear)wax
**woskowy** *adj* wax *attr*; (*przen*: *cera*) waxen
**wot|um** (**-um**) *nt inv in sg* (*Pol*): **~ zaufania/nieufności** a vote of confidence/no confidence; (*Rel*) (*nom pl* **-a**) vote offering
**wo|zić (-żę, -zisz)** (*imp* **woź** *lub* **wóź**) *vt* to transport; (*samochodem*) to drive
**wozu** *itd. n patrz* **wóz**

**woźn|a** (**-ej, -e**) *f decl like adj* caretaker (*Brit*), janitor (*US*)
**woźnic|a** (**-y, -e**) *m decl like f in sg* coachman
**woź|ny** (**-nego, -ni**) *m decl like adj* (*Szkol*) caretaker (*Brit*), janitor (*US*); (*sądowy*) usher
**wód** *n patrz* **woda**
**wód|ka** (**-ki, -ki**) (*dat sg* **-ce**, *gen pl* **-ek**) *f* vodka
**wódz** (**wodza, wodzowie**) *m* (*przywódca*) leader; (*plemienia, indiański*) chief; **~ naczelny** commander-in-chief
**wódź** *vb patrz* **wodzić**
**wój|t** (**-ta, -towie**) (*loc sg* **-cie**) *m administrator of a group of villages*
**wół** (**wołu, woły**) (*loc sg* **wole**) *m* ox; **wół roboczy** (*przen*) drudge
**wówczas** *adv* then
**wóz** (**wozu, wozy**) (*loc sg* **wozie**) *m* (*konny*) cart, wagon; (*ilość towaru*) cartload, wagonload; (*tramwajowy*) tram (*Brit*), streetcar (*US*); (*cygański*) caravan; (*pot: samochód*) car
**wóz|ek** (**-ka, -ki**) (*instr sg* **-kiem**) *m* (*głęboki*) pram (*Brit*), baby carriage (*US*); (*spacerówka*) pushchair (*Brit*), stroller (*US*); (*szpitalny*) trolley; (*inwalidzki*) wheelchair; **jechać na jednym** *lub* **tym samym wózku** (*przen*) to be in the same boat
**WP** *abbr* (= *Wojsko Polskie*) Polish Army; (= *Wielmożny Pan*) Mr; (= *Wielmożna Pani*) Mrs, Ms; (= *Wielmożni Państwo*) Mr and Mrs
**wpad|ać** (**-am, -asz**) (*perf* **wpaść**) *vt* (*do dołu, wody*) to fall; (*do bramki*) to go; (*do pokoju*) to rush; **~ do kogoś** to drop in on sb; **~ do morza** to flow into the sea; **~ we wściekłość** to fly into a rage; **~ w zachwyt** to rave, to enthuse
**wpad|ka** (**-ki, -ki**) (*dat sg* **-ce**, *gen pl* **-ek**) *f* (*pot: niepowodzenie*) slip-up (*pot*)
**wpadnę** *itd. vb patrz* **wpaść**
**wpaj|ać** (**-am, -asz**) (*perf* **wpoić**) *vt*: **~ coś komuś** to inculcate sth into sb
**wpak|ować** (**-uję, -ujesz**) *vt perf* (*pot: wepchnąć*) to stuff in; **~ kogoś do łóżka** to pack sb off to bed (*pot*); **~ kogoś do więzienia** to put sb away; **wpakować się** *vr perf* (*pot*) to barge in; **~ się na drzewo** to run into a tree; **~ się w błoto** to get into mud
**wpa|ść** (**-dnę, -dniesz**) (*imp* **-dnij**, *pt* **-dł, -dła, -dli**) *vb perf od* **wpadać**; **~ na drzewo** to run into a tree; **~ w poślizg** to go into a skid; **~ pod samochód** to be knocked down *lub* over by a car, to be run over by a car; **~ komuś w oko** to catch *lub* take sb's fancy; **coś mi wpadło do oka** sth has got into my eye; **wpadł mi do głowy pewien pomysł** I've hit (up)on an idea; **~ komuś w słowo** to interrupt sb; **~ w długi/nałóg** to fall *lub* get into debt/a habit; **~ w panikę** to panic
**wpatr|ywać się** (**-uję, -ujesz**) (*perf* **wpatrzyć**) *vr*: **wpatrywać się w** *+acc* to gaze *lub* stare at
**wpę|dzać** (**-dzam, -dzasz**) (*perf* **-dzić**) *vt*: **~ kogoś/coś gdzieś** to drive sb/sth in(to) sth; **~ kogoś do grobu** (*przen*) to drive sb to an early grave (*przen*)
**wpę|dzić** (**-dzę, -dzisz**) (*imp* **-dź**) *vb perf od* **wpędzać**; **~ kogoś w zakłopotanie** to embarrass sb
**wpiąć** (**wepnę, wepniesz**) (*imp* **wepnij**) *vb perf od* **wpinać**
**wpij|ać się** (**-am, -asz**) (*perf* **wpić**) *vr*: **wpijać się paznokciami/zębami w coś** to sink one's nails/teeth into sth
**wpin|ać** (**-am, -asz**) (*perf* **wpiąć**) *vt*: **~ kwiaty we włosy** to stick flowers in one's hair
**wpi|s** (**-su, -sy**) (*loc sg* **-sie**) *m* registration
**wpi|sać** (**-szę, -szesz**) *vb perf od* **wpisywać**
**wpisow|e** (**-ego**) *nt decl like adj* entrance fee (*to an organization*)
**wpis|ywać** (**-uję, -ujesz**) (*perf* **-ać**) *vt* to write down; (*wciągać do rejestru*) to list; (*Geom*) to inscribe
**wplat|ać** (**-am, -asz**) (*perf* **wpleść**) *vt*: **~ kwiaty/wstążki we włosy** to plait (*Brit*) *lub* braid (*US*) one's hair with flowers/ribbons
**wpląt|ywać** (**-uję, -ujesz**) (*perf* **-ać**) *vt*: **~ kogoś w coś** (*przen*) to entangle sb in sth; **wplątywać się** *vr*: **~ się w coś** to become entangled *lub* embroiled in sth
**wpl|eść** (**-otę, -eciesz**) (*imp* **-eć**, *pt* **-ótł, -otła, -etli**) *vb perf od* **wplatać**
**wpła|cać** (**-cam, -casz**) (*perf* **-cić**) *vt* to pay (in)
**wpła|cić** (**-cę, -cisz**) (*imp* **-ć**) *vb perf od* **wpłacać**
**wpła|ta** (**-ty, -ty**) (*dat sg* **-cie**) *f* payment; **dokonywać (dokonać** *perf*) **wpłaty** to make a payment
**wpław** *adv*: **przepłynąć rzekę ~** to swim across the river
**wpły|nąć** (**-nę, -niesz**) (*imp* **-ń**) *vb perf od* **wpływać**
**wpły|w** (**-wu, -wy**) (*loc sg* **-wie**) *m* influence, impact; **wpływy** *pl* (*przychody*) receipts *pl*, takings *pl*; (*znajomości*) influential friends *pl*; **mieć ~ na** *+acc* to have an influence on; **(łatwo) ulegać (ulec** *perf*) **~om** to be pliable; **być/pozostawać pod czyimś ~em** to be/remain under sb's influence; **być pod ~em alkoholu** to be under the influence of alcohol
**wpływ|ać** (**-am, -asz**) (*perf* **wpłynąć**) *vi* (*o korespondencji, pieniądzach*) to come in; **~ do portu** (*o statku*) to make port; **~ na** *+acc* to influence, to affect
**wpływowy** *adj* influential
**wpo|ić** (**-ję, -isz**) (*imp* **wpój**) *vb perf od* **wpajać**

W

**wpompow|ywać (-uję, -ujesz)** (*perf* **-ać**) *vt*: **~ coś (w coś)** to pump sth (into sth)

**wpół** *adv*: **trzymać kogoś ~** to hold sb round their waist; **zgiąć się ~** to bend double; **~ do szóstej** half past five; **na ~ żywy** half-alive

**wprasz|ać się (-am, -asz)** (*perf* **wprosić**) *vr*: **wpraszać się (do** *+gen***)** to invite o.s. (to)

**wpra|wa (-wy)** (*dat sg* **-wie**) *f* skill, proficiency; **mieć wprawę w czymś** to be adept at (doing) sth; **wychodzić (wyjść** *perf***) z wprawy** to be out of practice; **dla wprawy** for practice; **robić (zrobić** *perf***) coś z wprawą** to do sth skilfully

**wprawi|ać (-am, -asz)** (*perf* **-ć**) *vt* (*szybę, brylant*) to set; **~ kogoś w dobry nastrój** to put sb in a good mood; **~ kogoś w zakłopotanie** to disconcert sb; **wprawiać się** *vr*: **~ się (w czymś)** to get practice (in sth)

**wprawny** *adj* practised (*Brit*), practiced (*US*), expert

**wpro|sić się (-szę, -sisz)** (*imp* **-ś**) *vb perf od* **wpraszać się**

**wprost** *adv* directly; (*powiedzieć, spytać*) outright, point-blank; **iść ~ przed siebie** to go straight ahead; **na ~ kościoła** opposite the church; **~ proporcjonalny do** *+gen* directly proportional to; **jabłka ~ z drzewa** apples directly from the tree ▷ *part*: **~ przeciwnie** just the opposite; **(to jest) ~ nie do wiary** this is simply incredible

**wprowa|dzać (-dzam, -dzasz)** (*perf* **-dzić**) *vt* (*gości*) to bring *lub* show in; (*zwyczaj, reformy*) to introduce; (*umieszczać wewnątrz*) to insert; **wprowadzić kogoś w coś** (*zaznajomić*) to introduce sb to sth; **wprowadzić kogoś w dobry nastrój** to put sb in a good mood; **wprowadzić kogoś w błąd** to mislead sb; **~ samochód do garażu** to drive the car into the garage; **~ coś w życie** (*przen*) to put *lub* bring sth into effect; **~ kogoś w życie** (*przen*) to introduce sb to the world at large; **~ do obiegu** to bring into circulation; **wprowadzać się** *vr* to move in

**wprowadze|nie (-nia, -nia)** (*gen pl* **-ń**) *nt* (*wstęp*) introduction

**wprowa|dzić (-dzę, -dzisz)** (*imp* **-dź**) *vb perf od* **wprowadzać**

**wpuszcz|ać (-am, -asz)** (*perf* **wpuścić**) *vt* (*pozwalać wejść*) to let in; (*umieszczać*) to let in(to)

**wpu|ścić (-szczę, -ścisz)** (*imp* **-ść**) *vb perf od* **wpuszczać**

**wpych|ać (-am, -asz)** (*perf* **wepchnąć**) *vt* (*wtłaczać*) to shove in; **~ komuś coś** (*przen*) to push sth on sb (*przen*); **wpychać się** *vr* to push in; **~ się do kolejki** to jump the queue (*Brit*), to cut in line (*US*)

**wrabi|ać (-am, -asz)** (*perf* **wrobić**) *vt*: **~ kogoś w coś** (*pot*) to drop sb in sth; **wrabiać się** *vr*: **~ się w coś** (*pot*) to land o.s. into sth

**wrac|ać (-am, -asz)** (*perf* **wrócić**) *vi* (*przybywać ponownie*) to return, to come back; (*odchodzić z powrotem*) to go back; (*o książkach, rzeczach*) to be returned; **kiedy wrócisz?** when will you be back?; **~ do zdrowia** to recover, to recuperate; **~ do normy** to return to normal

**wra|k (-ku, -ki)** (*instr sg* **-kiem**) *m* wreck

**wrast|ać (-am, -asz)** (*perf* **wrosnąć** *lub* **wróść**) *vi*: **~ w** *+acc* (*o roślinach, paznokciu*) to grow into; (*przen: zespolić się*) to blend into

**wraz** *adv*: **~ z kimś/czymś** (*książk*) along with sb/sth

**wraże|nie (-nia, -nia)** (*gen pl* **-ń**) *nt* (*reakcja*) sensation; (*odczucie*) impression; **mam** *lub* **odnoszę ~, że ...** I have the impression that ...; **miałem ~, że ...** I was under the impression that ...; **robić (zrobić** *perf***) na kimś dobre/złe ~** to make a good/bad impression on sb; **z wrażenia** in amazement; **on robi** *lub* **sprawia ~ nieprzygotowanego** he seems unprepared

**wrażliwoś|ć (-ci)** *f* sensitivity, sensibility

**wrażliwy** *adj* sensitive; **~ na krzywdę** compassionate; **~ na ból** (*człowiek*) susceptible to pain; (*nos, oko*) sensitive to pain; **~ na wstrząsy/zmiany temperatury** sensitive to shocks/temperature changes

**wre** *itd. vb patrz* **wrzeć**

**wredny** *adj* (*pot*) vicious, mean (*US*)

**wreszcie** *adv* (*nareszcie*) at (long) last; **no ~ jesteście!** you're here at last!

**wrę** *vb patrz* **wrzeć**

**wręcz** *adj*: **walka ~** unarmed combat, hand-to-hand combat ▷ *adv*: **walczyć ~** to fight hand-to-hand ▷ *part* (*zupełnie*) completely; (*nawet*) not to say; **powiedzieć coś ~** to say sth plainly *lub* straight; **~ przeciwnie** on the contrary; **jego opowieść była ~ niewiarygodna** his story was just incredible

**wręcz|ać (-am, -asz)** (*perf* **-yć**) *vt*: **~ komuś coś** (*dyplom, medal*) to present sb with sth; (*kwiaty, prezent*) to give sb sth, to give sth to sb

**wr|obić (-obię, -obisz)** (*imp* **-ób**) *vb perf od* **wrabiać**

**wr|odzić się (-odzę, -odzisz)** (*imp* **-ódź**) *vr perf*: **wrodzić się w kogoś** to take after sb

**wrodzony** *adj* (*zdolności*) inborn, innate; (*wada, choroba*) congenital

**wroga** *itd. n patrz* **wróg**

**wrogi** *adj* (*państwo, wojsko*) enemy *attr*; (*stosunek, spojrzenie*) hostile

**wrogo** *adv* with hostility; **~ nastawiony** *lub* **usposobiony do kogoś** hostile to sb;

**~ usposabiać kogoś do** *+gen* to alienate sb against

**wrogoś|ć** (**-ci**) *f* hostility

**wro|na** (**-ny, -ny**) (*dat sg* **-nie**) *f* crow

**wr|osnąć (-osnę, -ośniesz)** (*imp* **-ośnij**, *pt* **-ósł, -osła, -ośli**) *vb perf od* **wrastać**

**wr|ota** (**wrót**) *pl* (*sali, stodoły*) door; (*zamku*) doors; **~ do sławy/sukcesu** gateway to fame/success

**wrot|ka** (**-ki, -ki**) (*dat sg* **-ce**, *gen pl* **-ek**) *f* roller skate; **jazda na ~ch** roller-skating; **jeździć na ~ch** to roller-skate

**wrób|el** (**-la, -le**) (*gen pl* **-li**) *m* sparrow

**wró|cić (-cę, -cisz)** (*imp* **-ć**) *vb perf od* **wracać**

**wr|óg** (**-oga, -ogowie**) (*instr sg* **-ogiem**) *m* (*nieprzyjaciel*) enemy; (*przeciwnik*) (fierce) opponent

**wr|óść (-osnę, -ośniesz)** (*imp* **-ośnij**, *pt* **-ósł, -osła, -ośli**) *vb perf od* **wrastać**

**wróż|ba** (**-by, -by**) (*dat sg* **-bie**) *f* (*przepowiednia*) prediction (*as told by a fortune-teller*); (*zapowiedź*) omen; **wróżby** *pl* fortune-telling

**wróżbiar|ka** (**-ki, -ki**) (*dat sg* **-ce**, *gen pl* **-ek**) *f* fortune-teller

**wróżbiarz** (**-a, -e**) (*gen pl* **-y**) *m* fortune-teller

**wróż|ka** (**-ki, -ki**) (*dat sg* **-ce**, *gen pl* **-ek**) *f* (*czarodziejka*) fairy; (*wróżbiarka*) fortune-teller

**wróż|yć** (**-ę, -ysz**) *vt* (*przepowiadać*) (*perf* **wy-**) (*przewidywać*) to predict, to foretell; (*być zapowiedzią*) to herald; **~ komuś wielką karierę** to foresee a brilliant career for sb; **to nie wróży nic dobrego** it doesn't augur *lub* bode well ▷ *vi*: **~ komuś** (*perf* **po-**) to tell sb's fortune; **to dobrze wróży dla kogoś/czegoś** it augurs *lub* bodes well for sb/sth; **~ z kart/fusów** to read the cards/tea leaves

**wry|ć się (-ję, -jesz)** *vr perf* (*o pojeździe*) to get bogged; (*o pocisku*) to sink; **wryć się (komuś) w pamięć** (*przen*) to be engraved *lub* etched in sb's memory

**wryty** *adj*: **stanąć** (*perf*) **jak ~** to stop dead

**wrzas|k** (**-ku, -ki**) (*instr sg* **-kiem**) *m* scream, yell; **podnieść ~** *lub* **narobić ~u** to start to scream; (*przen*) to raise *lub* cause a rumpus

**wrzaskliwy** *adj* noisy

**wrza|snąć (-snę, -śniesz)** (*imp* **-śnij**) *vb perf od* **wrzeszczeć**

**wrza|wa** (**-wy**) (*dat sg* **-wie**) *f* uproar; **wywoływać (wywołać** *perf*) **wrzawę** to create an uproar

**wrzący** *adj* boiling

**wrząt|ek** (**-ku**) (*instr sg* **-kiem**) *m* boiling water

**wrzecio|no** (**-na, -na**) (*loc sg* **-nie**) *nt* spindle

**wrzeć (wrę, wrzesz)** (*3 sg* **wre** *lub* **wrze**, *imp* **wrzyj**) *vi* to boil; (*przen: o bitwie, walce*) to rage; **~ z gniewu** to be boiling with anger *lub* rage

**wrzeni|e** (**-a**) *nt* boiling; **temperatura wrzenia** boiling point; **być w stanie wrzenia** (*przen*) to be in turmoil

**wrze|sień** (**-śnia, -śnie**) (*gen pl* **-śniów** *lub* **-śni**) *m* September

**wrzeszcz|eć (-ę, -ysz)** (*perf* **wrzasnąć**) *vi*: **~ (na kogoś)** to scream *lub* yell (at sb)

**wrześniowy** *adj* September *attr*

**wrzodowy** *adj*: **choroba wrzodowa** peptic ulcer disease

**wrzo|s** (**-su, -sy**) (*loc sg* **-sie**) *m* heather

**wrzosowis|ko** (**-ka, -ka**) (*instr sg* **-kiem**) *nt* heath, moors *pl* (*Brit*)

**wrz|ód** (**-odu, -ody**) (*loc sg* **-odzie**) *m* ulcer; (*pot: ropień*) abscess; **~ dwunastnicy/żołądka** duodenal/gastric ulcer

**wrzu|cać (-cam, -casz)** (*perf* **-cić**) *vt*: **~ coś do czegoś** to throw sth into sth

**wrzu|cić (-cę, -cisz)** (*imp* **-ć**) *vb perf od* **wrzucać**

**wrzyn|ać się (-am, -asz)** (*perf* **werżnąć**) *vr* to cut into; (*o kołnierzyku*) to pinch

**wsadowy** *adj*: **plik ~** (*Komput*) batch file

**wsa|dzać (-dzam, -dzasz)** (*perf* **-dzić**) *vt* (*umieszczać*) to put, to insert; (*pot: zamykać w więzieniu*) to lock up, to put away (*pot*); **~ kogoś do taksówki/na samolot** to put sb in a taxi/on a plane

**wsa|dzić (-dzę, -dzisz)** (*imp* **-dź**) *vb perf od* **wsadzać**

**wsch.** *abbr* (= *wschodni, wschód*) E. (= *Eastern, East*)

**wschodni** *adj* (*kierunek, wiatr*) easterly; (*półkula, obyczaj, potrawa*) eastern; **blok ~** Eastern bloc; **Europa W~a** Eastern Europe; **Berlin W~** East Berlin

**wschodnioeuropejski** *adj* Eastern European

**wscho|dzić (-dzi)** (*perf* **wzejść**) *vi* (*o księżycu, słońcu*) to rise; (*o roślinach*) to sprout

**wsch|ód** (**-odu**) (*loc sg* **-odzie**) *m* (*słońca*) (*nom pl* **-ody**) sunrise; (*strona świata*) (the) east; **Wschód** (*kraje wschodnie*) the East; **iść na ~** to go east *lub* eastward(s); **Bliski W~** the Middle East, the Near East; **Daleki W~** the Far East

**wsi** *itd. n patrz* **wieś**

**wsiad|ać (-am, -asz)** (*perf* **wsiąść**) *vi*: **~ (do czegoś)** (*autobusu, pociągu, samolotu*) to get on (sth); (*łodzi, samochodu*) to get in (sth); **~ na coś** (*statek*) to get on sth, to embark on sth; (*konia, motocykl, rower*) to get on sth

**wsiąk|ać (-am, -asz)** (*perf* **-nąć**) *vi*: **~ w coś** to soak into sth; (*pot: znikać*) to disappear *lub* vanish into thin air

**wsiąk|nąć (-nę, -niesz)** (*imp* **-nij**) *vb perf od* **wsiąkać**

**wsi|ąść (-ądę, -ądziesz)** (*imp* **-ądź**, *pt* **-adł, -adła, -edli**) *vb perf od* **wsiadać**

W

**wska|kiwać (-kuję, -kujesz)** (*perf* **wskoczyć**) *vi*: **~ na coś** (*ławkę*) to jump onto sth; (*konia, rower*) to leap on sth; **~ do czegoś** (*autobusu, pociągu*) to jump on sth; (*wody*) to plunge into sth; **wskoczyć do kogoś** (*pot*) to drop in on sb, to call on sb
**wska|zać (-żę, -żesz)** *vb perf od* **wskazywać**
**wskazany** *adj* advisable
**wskazów|ka (-ki, -ki)** (*dat sg* **-ce**, *gen pl* **-ek**) *f* (*zegara*) hand; (*rada*) hint; **~ minutowa/sekundowa** minute/second hand; **zgodnie z ruchem wskazówek zegara** clockwise; **przeciwnie do ruchu wskazówek zegara** anticlockwise (*Brit*), counterclockwise (*US*)
**wskazujący** *adj*: **palec ~** index finger, forefinger; **zaimek ~** demonstrative pronoun
**wskaz|ywać (-uję, -ujesz)** (*perf* **-ać**) *vt* to show ▷ *vi*: **~ na kogoś/coś** (*pokazywać*) to point at sb/sth; (*informować*) to point to sb/sth; (*oznaczać*) to indicate sth; **czy może mi Pan wskazać drogę do ...?** could you show me the way to ...?, could you tell me how to get to ...?; **wszystko wskazuje na to, że ...** the odds are that ...
**wskaźni|k (-ka, -ki)** (*instr sg* **-kiem**) *m* (*przyrząd*) pointer; (*kontrolka*) indicator; (*produkcji, rozwoju*) index; (*umieralności*) rate; **~ poziomu paliwa** fuel gauge *lub* gage (*US*); **~ kursów akcji** share index
**wskocz|yć (-ę, -ysz)** *vb perf od* **wskakiwać**
**wskór|ać (-am, -asz)** *vt perf* to accomplish; **nic nie wskórałem** I came back empty-handed
**wskroś** *adv*: **na ~** (*na wylot*) through; (*do głębi*) through and through
**wskrze|sić (-szę, -sisz)** (*imp* **-ś**) *vb perf od* **wskrzeszać**
**wskrzesz|ać (-am, -asz)** (*perf* **wskrzesić**) *vt* to raise from the dead; (*przen*) to revive
**wskutek** *prep*: **~ czegoś** as a result of sth
**wsła|wić się (-wię, -wisz)** *vr perf* to make a name for o.s., to become famous
**wsłuch|iwać się (-uję, -ujesz)** (*perf* **-ać**) *vr*: **wsłuchiwać się w kogoś/coś** to listen intently to sb/sth
**WSP** *abbr* (= *Wyższa Szkoła Pedagogiczna*) Teacher's Training College
**wspak** *adv* backwards
**wspaniale** *adv* magnificently, splendidly; **to ~!** that's fantastic!
**wspaniałomyślnie** *adv* generously
**wspaniałomyślnoś|ć (-ci)** *f* generosity
**wspaniałomyślny** *adj* generous, magnanimous
**wspaniałoś|ć (-ci, -ci)** (*gen pl* **-ci**) *f* (*natury, klejnotu*) magnificence; (*przyjęcia*) splendour (*Brit*), splendor (*US*); **wspaniałości** *pl* splendours *pl* (*Brit*), splendors *pl* (*US*)
**wspaniały** *adj* (*niepospolity*) wonderful; (*zwycięstwo*) splendid; (*przyjęcie*) grand; (*strój*) magnificent
**wsparci|e (-a)** *nt* support
**wsparł** *itd. vb patrz* **wesprzeć**
**wspiąć się (wespnę, wespniesz)** (*imp* **wespnij**) *vb perf od* **wspinać się**
**wspier|ać (-am, -asz)** (*perf* **wesprzeć**) *vt* (*podtrzymywać*) to support; (*pomagać*) to aid; **wspierać się** *vr* (*pomagać sobie nawzajem*) to support one another; **~ się na czymś** (*opierać się*) to lean on sth; (*spoczywać*) to rest (up)on sth
**wspinacz (-a, -e)** (*gen pl* **-y**) *m* mountaineer
**wspinacz|ka (-ki, -ki)** (*dat sg* **-ce**, *gen pl* **-ek**) *f* climbing; **~ górska** mountaineering
**wspin|ać się (-am, -asz)** (*perf* **wspiąć**) *vr* to climb; **wspinać się na palce** to stand on one's toes
**wspomag|ać (-am, -asz)** (*perf* **wspomóc**) *vt* to aid, to assist
**wspomagani|e (-a)** *nt* (*Mot*): **hamulce ze ~m** servo brakes; **kierownica ze ~m** power steering
**wspomin|ać (-am, -asz)** (*perf* **wspomnieć**) *vt* (*przypominać sobie*) to remember, to recall; (*napomykać*) to mention ▷ *vi*: **~ o czymś** to mention sth; **(wyżej) wspomniany** aforementioned, aforesaid; **nie wspominając o** *+loc* not to mention
**wspomin|ki (-ków)** *pl* (*pot*) reminiscences *pl*
**wspom|nieć (-nę, -nisz)** (*imp* **-nij**) *vb perf od* **wspominać**
**wspomnie|nie (-nia, -nia)** (*gen pl* **-ń**) *nt* memory, recollection; **na samo ~ (o tym)** at the mere mention of it; **wspomnienia** *pl* (*Lit*) memoirs *pl*
**wspom|óc (-ogę, -ożesz)** (*imp* **-óż**, *pt* **-ógł, -ogła, -ogli**) *vb perf od* **wspomagać**
**wsporni|k (-ka, -ki)** (*instr sg* **-kiem**) *m* (*Archit*) truss, corbel; (*Tech*) support, bracket
**wspólnicz|ka (-ki, -ki)** (*dat sg* **-ce**, *gen pl* **-ek**) *f* (*Ekon*) partner; (*Prawo*) accomplice
**wspólnie** *adv* jointly, together; **~ z kimś** together with sb
**wspólni|k (-ka, -cy)** (*instr sg* **-kiem**) *m* (*Ekon*) partner; (*Prawo*) accomplice
**wspólno|ta (-ty, -ty)** (*loc sg* **-cie**) *f* (*społeczność*) community; **~ interesów** community of interests; **(małżeńska) ~ majątkowa** joint property of spouses; **~ pierwotna** primitive community; **Europejska W~ Gospodarcza** the European Economic Community; **W~ Brytyjska** the Commonwealth (of Nations)
**wspólny** *adj* (*język, granica, cel*) common; (*kuchnia*) shared, communal; (*pokój*) shared;

(*zainteresowanie, znajomy*) mutual; (*przedsięwzięcie, fundusz, rachunek*) joint; **W~ Rynek** the Common Market; **~ mianownik/podzielnik** common denominator/factor; **to nie ma nic wspólnego z tobą** this has nothing to do with you; **mieć wiele wspólnego (z kimś)** to have a lot in common (with sb); **zrobiliśmy/zrobili to ~mi siłami** it was a joint effort; **nie możemy znaleźć wspólnego języka** we're not on the same wavelength

**współauto|r** (**-ra, -rzy**) (*loc sg* **-rze**) *m* co-author

**współautorst|wo** (**-wa**) (*loc sg* **-wie**) *nt* co-authorship, joint authorship

**współbrzm|ieć (-i)** *vi* to harmonize

**współbrzmie|nie** (**-nia, -nia**) (*gen pl* **-ń**) *nt* (*Muz*) sound combination

**współczesnoś|ć** (**-ci**) *f* the present day *lub* time

**współczesny** *adj* contemporary ▷ *m decl like adj*; **jemu/jej współcześni** his/her contemporaries

**współcześnie** *adv* (*obecnie*) today, these days

**współczuci|e** (**-a**) *nt* compassion, sympathy; **pełen współczucia** compassionate; **wyrazy współczucia** condolences

**współcz|uć (-uję, -ujesz)** *vi*: **~ komuś** to feel sorry for sb; **~ komuś (z powodu czegoś)** to commiserate with sb (over sth)

**współczująco** *adv* compassionately

**współczynni|k** (**-ka, -ki**) (*instr sg* **-kiem**) *m* coefficient

**współdział|ać (-am, -asz)** *vi* to co-operate

**współdziała|nie** (**-nia, -nia**) (*gen pl* **-ń**) *nt* co-operation

**współgospodarz** (**-a, -e**) (*gen pl* **-y**) *m* co-host, joint host

**współgr|ać (-am, -asz)** *vi*: **~ (z czymś)** to harmonize (with sth)

**współistnieni|e** (**-a**) *nt* coexistence

**współlokato|r** (**-ra, -rzy**) (*loc sg* **-rze**) *m* = **współmieszkaniec**

**współmałżon|ek** (**-ka, -kowie**) (*instr sg* **-kiem**) *m* spouse

**współmierny** *adj*: **~ do** *+gen* commensurate with

**współmieszka|niec** (**-ńca, -ńcy**) *m* (*w pokoju*) roommate; (*w mieszkaniu*) flatmate (*Brit*)

**współobywatel** (**-a, -e**) *m* fellow citizen

**współodpowiedzialnoś|ć** (**-ci**) *f* joint *lub* shared responsibility

**współodpowiedzialny** *adj*: **być ~m za coś** to share the responsibility for sth

**współorganizato|r** (**-ra, -rzy**) (*loc sg* **-rze**) *m* co-organizer

**współorganiz|ować (-uję, -ujesz)** *vt* to co-organize

**współpasaże|r** (**-ra, -rowie**) (*loc sg* **-rze**) *m* fellow passenger

**współprac|a** (**-y**) *f* cooperation; (*artystyczna, naukowa, z wrogiem*) collaboration

**współprac|ować (-uję, -ujesz)** *vi* to co-operate; (*o artystach, naukowcach, zdrajcach*) to collaborate; (*o częściach mechanizmu*) to interact

**współpracownic|a** (**-y, -e**) *f* = **współpracowniczka**

**współpracownicz|ka** (**-ki, -ki**) (*dat sg* **-ce**, *gen pl* **-ek**) *f* (*w pracy*) co-worker, associate; (*policji, wywiadu*) informer

**współpracowni|k** (**-ka, -cy**) (*instr sg* **-kiem**) *m* (*w pracy*) co-worker, associate; (*policji, wywiadu*) informer

**współrzędn|a** (**-ej, -e**) *f decl like adj* co-ordinate

**współrzędny** *adj*: **zdanie współrzędne** co-ordinate clause

**współtowarzysz** (**-a, -e**) (*gen pl* **-y**) *m* (*niedoli*) comrade; (*podróży*) companion

**współtworz|yć (-ę, -ysz)** (*imp* **współtwórz**) *vt* to co-author

**współuczestnicz|yć (-ę, -ysz)** *vi*: **~ w czymś** to participate in sth

**współuczestni|k** (**-ka, -cy**) (*instr sg* **-kiem**) *m* participant

**współudzia|ł** (**-łu**) (*loc sg* **-le**) *m*: **~ (w czymś)** participation (in sth); (*Prawo*) complicity (in sth)

**współwię|zień** (**-źnia, -źniowie**) *m* fellow prisoner, cellmate (*US*)

**współwłaściciel** (**-a, -e**) (*gen pl* **-i**) *m* co-owner, joint owner

**współzawodnict|wo** (**-wa**) (*loc sg* **-wie**) *nt* rivalry, competition; **stanąć** (*perf*) **do współzawodnictwa** to enter a competition

**współzawodnicz|yć (-ę, -ysz)** *vi*: **~ (z kimś) (o coś)** to compete (with sb) (for sth)

**współzawodni|k** (**-ka, -cy**) (*instr sg* **-kiem**) *m* competitor, contestant

**współżyci|e** (**-a**) *nt*: **~ społeczne/płciowe** social/sexual intercourse; **być trudnym we współżyciu** to be difficult to get along with

**współż|yć (-yję, -yjesz)** *vi*: **~ (z kimś)** (*obcować*) to interact (with sb); (*płciowo*) to have sex (with sb); (*Bio*) to live in symbiosis

**wst|ać (-anę, -aniesz)** (*imp* **-ań**) *vb perf od* **wstawać**

**wst|awać (-aję, -ajesz)** (*imp* **-awaj**, *perf* **-ać**) *vi* (*rano, z łóżka*) to get up, to rise; (*z krzesła, podłogi*) to stand up, to rise

**wsta|wiać (-wiam, -wiasz)** (*perf* **-wić**) *vt* (*szybę*) to set; (*ząb*) to replace; (*ryż, wodę, czajnik*) to put on; **~ coś do czegoś** to put sth in(to) sth; **wstawiać się** *vr*: **~ się za kimś** to put in a (good) word for sb, to plead sb's case

W

**wsta|wić (-wię, -wisz)** *vb perf od* **wstawiać**; **wstawić się** *vr perf (pot: upić się)* to have one over the eight *(pot)*

**wstawiennict|wo** (**-wa**) *(loc sg* **-wie**) *nt* intercession; **za czyimś wstawiennictwem** through sb's intercession

**wstawiony** *adj (pot)* tight *(pot)*

**wstaw|ka** (**-ki, -ki**) *(dat sg* **-ce**, *gen pl* **-ek**) *f (muzyczna, baletowa)* interlude; *(w odzieży: poszerzająca itp.)* gusset; *(: ozdobna)* insertion

**wstą|pić (-pię, -pisz)** *vb perf od* **wstępować**

**wstążecz|ka** (**-ki, -ki**) *(dat sg* **-ce**, *gen pl* **-ek**) *f* ribbon

**wstąż|ka** (**-ki, -ki**) *(dat sg* **-ce**, *gen pl* **-ek**) *f (do włosów)* ribbon; *(do kapelusza)* band

**wstecz** *adv (ruszyć, spojrzeć)* back(wards); **działać ~** *(Prawo)* to retroact

**wstecznict|wo** (**-wa**) *(loc sg* **-wie**) *nt* reaction, reactionism

**wsteczny** *adj (zacofany)* backward; *(poglądy, polityk)* reactionary; **~ bieg** reverse gear; **lusterko wsteczne** rear-view mirror

**wstę|ga** (**-gi, -gi**) *(dat sg* **-dze**) *f (z materiału)* band, ribbon; *(przen: drogi, rzeki, dymu)* ribbon; **przeciąć** *(perf)* **wstęgę** to cut the ribbon

**wstę|p** (**-pu, -py**) *(loc sg* **-pie**) *m (prawo wejścia)* entry, admission; *(przygotowanie, początek)* introduction; *(Lit)* preface; **„~ wzbroniony!"** "no entry"; **na ~ie** to begin with

**wstępnie** *adv (ocenić, opracować, ustalić)* tentatively, provisionally

**wstępny** *adj (przygotowawczy)* preliminary; *(początkowy)* initial; *(tymczasowy)* tentative, provisional; **egzamin ~** entrance exam(ination); **artykuł ~** editorial, leading article *(Brit)*; **słowo wstępne** foreword, preface; **warunek ~** precondition

**wstęp|ować (-uję, -ujesz)** *(perf* **wstąpić**) *vi*: **~ do biura/kawiarni** to stop by *lub* call (by) the office/café; **~ do organizacji** to join an organization; **~ po schodach** *(książk)* to ascend the stairs; **~ (do kogoś) na kawę** to drop in (on sb) for a cup of coffee; **wstąpić do wojska** to join the army, to join up *(Brit)*; **wstąpić na uniwersytet** to enrol *(Brit) lub* enroll *(US)* at the university; **~ na tron** to ascend the throne; **~ w związek małżeński** to enter into a marriage; **wstąpiły w niego nowe siły** he got a second wind

**wstrę|t** (**-tu**) *(loc sg* **-cie**) *m* revulsion, repulsion; **mieć** *lub* **czuć ~ do kogoś/czegoś** to find sb/sth repulsive

**wstrętny** *adj (człowiek, czyn)* repulsive; *(smak, zapach)* revolting

**wstrzą|s** (**-su, -sy**) *(loc sg* **-sie**) *m (tektoniczny)* tremor; *(psychiczny)* shock; **~ mózgu** concussion

**wstrząs|ać (-am, -asz)** *(perf* **-nąć**) *vt +instr (butelką)* to shake; *(człowiekiem)* to shake, to shock; **„przed użyciem wstrząsnąć"** "shake before use"

**wstrząsający** *adj* shocking

**wstrzą|snąć (-snę, -śniesz)** *(imp* **-śnij**) *vb perf od* **wstrząsać**

**wstrząsowy** *adj*: **kuracja wstrząsowa** shock treatment

**wstrząśnięty** *adj* shaken, shocked

**wstrzemięźliwoś|ć** (**-ci**) *f* temperance, abstinence

**wstrzemięźliwy** *adj (reakcja)* reserved; *(życie)* temperate, abstemious

**wstrzy|kiwać (-kuję, -kujesz)** *(perf* **-knąć**) *vt*: **~ coś komuś/sobie** to inject sb/o.s. with sth

**wstrzyk|nąć (-nę, -niesz)** *(imp* **-nij**) *vb perf od* **wstrzykiwać**

**wstrzym|ać (-am, -asz)** *vb perf od* **wstrzymywać**

**wstrzymujący się** *adj*: **cztery głosy wstrzymujące się** four abstentions

**wstrzym|ywać (-uję, -ujesz)** *(perf* **-ać**) *vt (bieg, napór, ruch)* to arrest; *(prace)* to discontinue; *(wypłatę, wydanie)* to withhold; **wstrzymywać się** *vr (podczas głosowania)* to abstain; **~ się z decyzją** to defer decision

**wsty|d** (**-du**) *(loc sg* **-dzie**) *m* shame; **~ mi, jest mi ~** I am *lub* feel ashamed; **jak ci nie ~?** you should be ashamed of yourself!; **przynosić (przynieść** *perf***) komuś ~** to bring shame on sb; **~ powiedzieć/się przyznać** I'm ashamed to say/admit

**wstydliwoś|ć** (**-ci**) *f* bashfulness, shyness

**wstydliwy** *adj* bashful, shy

**wsty|dzić się (-dzę, -dzisz)** *(imp* **-dź**) *vr*: **wstydzić się (za kogoś/coś)** to be ashamed (of sb/sth); **wstydzić się czegoś** to be ashamed of sth; **wstydzić się kogoś** to feel embarrassed in front of sb; **wstydzić się coś zrobić** to be ashamed to do sth

**wsu|nąć (-nę, -niesz)** *(imp* **-ń**) *vb perf od* **wsuwać**

**wsuw|ać (-am, -asz)** *(perf* **wsunąć**) *vt (kartkę: do książki)* to insert, to slip; *(: pod drzwiami)* to slip; *(monetę: do otworu)* to insert; *(: do kieszeni)* to slip; *(pot: jeść)* to tuck in *(pot)*; **~ obrączkę na palec** to slip a ring on one's finger; **~ ręce do kieszeni** to slide one's hands into one's pockets; **~ coś komuś** to slip sb sth; **wsuwać się** *vr (wchodzić cicho)* to slip in; *(wpełzać)* to creep in

**wsuw|ka** (**-ki, -ki**) *(dat sg* **-ce**, *gen pl* **-ek**) *f (też:* **wsuwka do włosów**) hairpin

**wsy|pać (-pię, -piesz)** *vb perf od* **wsypywać**; *(pot)*: **~ kogoś** to rat on sb *(pot)*

**wsyp|ywać (-uję, -ujesz)** (*perf* **-ać**) *vt* to pour (in)
**wszcz|ąć** *vb perf od* **wszczynać**
**wszcze|p (-pu, -py)** (*loc sg* **-pie**) *m* (*Med*) implant
**wszcze|piać (-piam, -piasz)** (*perf* **-pić**) *vt* to implant; (*roślinę*) to graft
**wszczyn|ać (-am, -asz)** (*perf* **wszcząć**) *vt* (*postępowanie prawne, śledztwo*) to institute, to initiate; (*poszukiwania*) to institute, to instigate; (*negocjacje*) to enter into; (*alarm, awanturę, wojnę*) to start
**wszechmocny** *adj* = **wszechmogący**
**wszechmogący** *adj*: **Bóg** ~ God Almighty
**wszechobecny** *adj* ubiquitous
**wszechogarniający** *adj* all-embracing
**wszechstronnie** *adv* (*wykształcony*) broadly; ~ **uzdolniony** multi-talented
**wszechstronnoś|ć (-ci)** *f* (*artysty, zawodnika*) versatility; (*wykształcenia*) comprehensiveness
**wszechstronny** *adj* (*artysta, zawodnik*) versatile; (*wykształcenie*) broad; (*zainteresowania*) wide-ranging
**wszechświ|at (-ata)** (*loc sg* **-ecie**) *m* universe
**wszechwładny** *adj* all-powerful, omnipotent
**wszedł** *itd. vb patrz* **wejść**
**wszelki** *adj* (*każdy*) every; (*jakikolwiek*) any; **na ~ wypadek** just in case, to be on the safe side; **za wszelką cenę** at all cost(s); **ponad wszelką wątpliwość** beyond (any) doubt; **~ego rodzaju** of every description; **„~e prawa zastrzeżone"** "all rights reserved"
**wszerz** *adv* (*przeciąć, przepłynąć*) widthways; **zjeździć** (*perf*) **Polskę wzdłuż i ~** to travel the length and breadth of Poland
**wszędobylski** *adj* ubiquitous
**wszędzie** *adv* everywhere
**wszy** *n patrz* **wesz**
**wszy|ć (-ję, -jesz)** *vb perf od* **wszywać**
**wszyscy** *pron decl like adj* all; (*wszyscy ludzie*) everybody, everyone; ~ **wiedzą** everybody *lub* everyone knows; ~ **wiemy/wiecie** we/you all know, all of us/you know; ~ **z wyjątkiem Pawła** everybody but Paul; ~ **studenci** all (the) students; ~ **inni** everybody else; ~ **razem** all together
**wszystek** *pron* (*cały*) all
**wszystkie** *pron decl like adj* all; ~ **książki** all (the) books; **czy masz ~?** do you have all of them?
**wszystko** *pron decl like adj* everything; **mimo ~** still; **nade ~** above all; **przede wszystkim** (*w pierwszej kolejności*) first of all, first and foremost; **~ mi jedno** it's all the same to me; **kawa czy herbata? — ~ jedno** tea or coffee? — I don't mind; **~ w porządku?** is everything all right *lub* O.K.?; **wszystkiego najlepszego!** all the best!; **już po wszystkim** it's all over; **on jest zdolny do wszystkiego** he will stop at nothing; **~ mnie boli** I'm all in pain; **~ wskazuje na to, że ...** the chances *lub* odds are that ...; **~, co mam** all *lub* everything (that) I have; **~ z wyjątkiem** *+gen* everything but; **zrobić ~, co możliwe/co jest w czyjejś mocy** to do everything possible/everything in one's power
**wszystkowiedzący** *adj* omniscient
**wszystkożerny** *adj* omnivorous
**wszyw|ać (-am, -asz)** (*perf* **wszyć**) *vt* to sew in
**wścibski** *adj* nosy
**wście|c się (-knę, -kniesz)** (*imp* **-knij**, *pt* **-kł, -kła, -kli**) *vr perf* (*pot*: *wpaść w złość*) to go mad (*pot*); (*o psie*: *dostać wścieklizny*) to come down with rabies
**wściek|ać się (-am, -asz)** *vr imperf* (*pot*) to rage; **wściekać się na kogoś** to be furious with sb
**wściekle** *adv* furiously, wildly; (*pot*: *bardzo*) madly
**wściekli|zna (-zny)** (*dat sg* **-źnie**) *f* rabies
**wściekłoś|ć (-ci)** *f* rage, fury; **doprowadzać (doprowadzić** *perf*) **kogoś do wściekłości** to drive sb mad; **wpadać (wpaść** *perf*) **we ~** to fly into a rage
**wściekły** *adj* (*rozgniewany*) furious, mad; (*chory na wściekliznę*) rabid; (*atak, kłótnia*) furious, fierce; (*ból, pośpiech*) mad; **być ~m na kogoś/coś** to be mad at *lub* furious with sb/sth
**wśliz|giwać się (-guję, -gujesz)** (*perf* **-gnąć**) *vr* (*o człowieku*) to slip in; (*o wężu*) to creep in
**wślizg|nąć się (-nę, -niesz)** (*imp* **-nij**) *vb perf od* **wślizgiwać się**
**wśród** *prep* among, amid; **popularny ~ młodzieży** popular with the young
**wtacz|ać (-am, -asz)** (*perf* **wtoczyć**) *vt* to roll in; **wtaczać się** *vr* to roll
**wtajemnicz|ać (-am, -asz)** (*perf* **-yć**) *vt*: **~ kogoś w coś** to initiate sb into sth
**wtajemnicze|nie (-nia, -nia)** (*gen pl* **-ń**) *nt* initiation
**wtajemniczony** *adj* initiated ▷ *m decl like adj*; **dla ~ch** for the initiated
**wtajemnicz|yć (-ę, -ysz)** *vb perf od* **wtajemniczać**
**wtapi|ać (-am, -asz)** (*perf* **wtopić**) *vt* (*Tech*) to set; **wtapiać się**; **~ się w krajobraz** to blend with *lub* into the scenery; **~ się w tłum** to melt into the crowd
**wtarg|nąć (-nę, -niesz)** (*imp* **-nij**) *vi perf*: **~ do** *+gen* (*o osobie, grupie*) to burst into; (*o wojsku*) to invade

W

**wtargnię|cie** (**-cia, -cia**) (*gen pl* **-ć**) *nt* (*osoby, grupy*) intrusion; (*obcych wojsk*) incursion
**wtarł** *itd. vb patrz* **wetrzeć**
**wtedy** *pron* then; **~, kiedy ...** when ...; **i co ~?** and then what?
**wtem** *adv* suddenly, all of a sudden
**wtłacz|ać (-am, -asz)** (*perf* **wtłoczyć**) *vt* (*powietrze, wodę*) to force in; (*ludzi, przedmioty*) to cram
**wtocz|yć (-ę, -ysz)** *vb perf od* **wtaczać**
**wto|pić (-pię, -pisz)** *vb perf od* **wtapiać**
**wtor|ek** (**-ku, -ki**) (*instr sg* **-kiem**) *m* Tuesday
**wtó|r** (**-ru**) (*loc sg* **-rze**) *m*: **do ~u** *lub* **przy ~ze** *+gen* to the accompaniment of
**wtórny** *adj* (*pochodny*) derivative; (*drugorzędny*) secondary; **surowce wtórne** recyclable materials; **~ analfabetyzm** functional illiteracy
**wtór|ować (-uję, -ujesz)** *vi*: **~ komuś** to accompany sb; **oklaskom wtórowały gwizdy** applause was mixed with *lub* accompanied by whistles
**wtóry** *adj*: **po wtóre** second(ly); **po raz ~** (*książk*) for the second time
**wtrą|cać (-cam, -casz)** (*perf* **-cić**) *vt* (*obce wyrazy*) to throw in; **~ kogoś do więzienia** to imprison sb; **wtrącić swoje trzy grosze** to put *lub* shove one's oar in; **wtrącać się** *vr*: **~ się (do czegoś)** to interfere *lub* meddle (in sth); **~ się w nie swoje sprawy** to pry (into other people's affairs); **nie wtrącaj się!** (*pot*) mind your own business! (*pot*)
**wtrące|nie** (**-nia, -nia**) (*gen pl* **-ń**) *nt* interpolation
**wtrą|cić (-cę, -cisz)** (*imp* **-ć**) *vb perf od* **wtrącać**
**wtrącony** *adj* (*uwaga*) interpolated; (*Jęz: wyraz, zdanie*) parenthetical
**wtrę|t** (**-tu, -ty**) (*loc sg* **-cie**) *m* insertion
**wtrys|k** (**-ku, -ki**) (*instr sg* **-kiem**) *m*: **~ paliwa** fuel injection
**wtrys|kiwać (-kuję, -kujesz)** (*perf* **wtrysnąć**) *vt* to inject
**wtryskowy** *adj*: **pompa wtryskowa** injection pump
**wtry|snąć (-snę, -śniesz)** (*imp* **-śnij**) *vb perf od* **wtryskiwać**
**wtul|ać (-am, -asz)** (*perf* **-ić**) *vt* (*głowę*) to nestle; **wtulać się** *vr*: **~ się w coś** to nestle in sth
**wtycz|ka** (**-ki, -ki**) (*dat sg* **-ce**, *gen pl* **-ek**) *f* plug; (*pot: szpieg*) mole (*pot*)
**wtyk|ać (-am, -asz)** (*perf* **wetknąć**) *vt* (*pot: wsadzać*) to stick (in); **~ coś komuś** (*po kryjomu*) to slip sb sth; (*na siłę*) to force *lub* press sth on sb; **~ nos w nie swoje sprawy** to poke one's nose into other people's affairs
**wuj** (**-a, -owie**) *m* uncle
**wujeczny** *adj*: **~ brat** cousin; **~ dziadek** great-uncle
**wuj|ek** (**-ka, -kowie**) (*instr sg* **-kiem**) *m* uncle
**wujost|wo** (**-wa**) (*loc sg* **-wie**) *nt* aunt and uncle
**wulgarnoś|ć** (**-ci**) *f* vulgarity
**wulgarny** *adj* vulgar
**wulka|n** (**-nu, -ny**) (*loc sg* **-nie**) *m* volcano
**wulkaniczny** *adj* volcanic
**wulkanizacj|a** (**-i**) *f* (*dętek, opon*) retreading; **oddać** (*perf*) **coś do wulkanizacji** to have sth retreaded
**wulkaniz|ować (-uję, -ujesz)** (*perf* **z-**) *vt* (*dętki, opony*) to retread
**ww.** *abbr* (*= wyżej wymieniony*) above-mentioned
**W-wa** *abbr* (*= Warszawa*) Warsaw
**wwi|eźć (-ozę, -eziesz)** (*imp* **-eź**, *pt* **-ózł, -ozła, -eźli**) *vb perf od* **wwozić**
**ww|ozić (-ożę, -ozisz)** (*imp* **-oź** *lub* **-óź**, *perf* **wwieźć**) *vt* (*na górę*) to bring up; (*do wnętrza*) to bring in; (*z zagranicy*) to bring in, to import
**ww|óz** (**-ozu**) (*loc sg* **-ozie**) *m* importation
**wy** *pron* you
**wyalienowany** *adj* alienated
**wyasygn|ować (-uję, -ujesz)** *vt perf*: **~ pieniądze na** *+acc* to allocate funds for
**wybacz|ać (-am, -asz)** (*perf* **-yć**) *vt*: **~ (komuś) coś** to forgive (sb) sth; **Pan/Pani wybaczy, ale ...** excuse me, but ...
**wybaczalny** *adj* excusable
**wybaczeni|e** (**-a**) *nt* forgiveness; **prosić/błagać kogoś o ~** to ask/beg sb's forgiveness; **nie do wybaczenia** unforgivable
**wybacz|yć (-ę, -ysz)** *vb perf od* **wybaczać**
**wybad|ać (-am, -asz)** *vt perf* (*osobę, zamiary*) to sound out
**wybałusz|ać (-am, -asz)** (*perf* **-yć**) *vt*: **~ oczy** (*pot*) to goggle (*pot*)
**wybawc|a** (**-y, -y**) *m decl like f in sg* saviour (Brit), savior (US)
**wyba|wiać (-wiam, -wiasz)** (*perf* **-wić**) *vt* to save; **~ kogoś z kłopotu** to get sb out of trouble
**wybawiciel** (**-a, -e**) (*gen pl* **-i**) *m* saviour (Brit), savior (US)
**wyba|wić (-wię, -wisz)** *vb perf od* **wybawiać**
**wy|bić (-biję, -bijesz)** *vb perf od* **bić, wybijać**
**wybie|c (-gnę, -gniesz)** (*imp* **-gnij**, *pt* **-gł**) *vb perf od* **wybiegać**
**wybie|g** (**-gu, -gi**) (*instr sg* **-giem**) *m* (*dla koni*) paddock; (*fortel*) subterfuge; (*na pokazie mody*) catwalk
**wybieg|ać (-am, -asz)** *vi* (*perf* **wybiec**); **~ (z domu/pokoju)** to run out (of the house/room); **~ komuś na spotkanie** to run out to meet sb; **~ myślą naprzód** to look ahead
**wybielacz** (**-a, -e**) (*gen pl* **-y**) *m* bleach

**wybiel|ać (-am, -asz)** (*perf* **-ić**) *vt* (*bieliznę, płótno*) to bleach; (*zęby*) to whiten
**wybier|ać (-am, -asz)** (*perf* **wybrać**) *vt* to choose; (*spośród innych osób/rzeczy tego samego rodzaju*) to select, to pick (out); (*posła, prezydenta*) to elect; (*piasek, monety*) to scoop; (*numer telefoniczny*) to dial; (*pieniądze z konta*) to draw; **wybierać się** *vr*: **wybieram się do biura/do Anglii** I'm going to the office/to England; **wybieramy się w podróż/na spacer** we're going away/for a walk; **~ się pod namiot/na narty** to go camping/skiing
**wybieralny** *adj* (*organ, rada*) elected; (*stanowisko*) elective
**wybij|ać (-am, -asz)** (*perf* **wybić**) *vt* (*czop, korek, gwóźdź*) to knock out; (*szybę*) to break; (*takt, rytm*) to beat; (*muchy, wilki*) to kill (off); (*piłkę: na aut, w pole*) to clear; (*o zegarze: siódmą itp.*) to strike; **wybić komuś ząb** to knock sb's tooth out; **wybić sobie palec** to dislocate one's finger; **wybić komuś coś z głowy** (*przen*) to get sth out of sb's head; **wybijać się** *vr* (*wyróżniać się*) to stand out; (*Sport: o skoczku*) to launch o.s.
**wybiórczo** *adv* selectively
**wybiórczy** *adj* selective
**wybitnie** *adv* outstandingly
**wybitny** *adj* outstanding
**wyblakły** *adj* faded
**wyblak|nąć (-nie)** (*pt* **-ł**) *vb perf od* **blaknąć** ▷ *vi perf* to fade (away)
**wybłag|ać (-am, -asz)** *vt perf* to get by begging
**wyboisty** *adj* bumpy
**wyborc|a** (**-y, -y**) *m decl like f in sg* voter
**wyborczy** *adj*: **kampania wyborcza** election campaign; **komisja wyborcza** electoral committee; **okręg ~** constituency; **bierne/czynne prawo wyborcze** right to be elected/to vote; **lokal ~** polling station; **urna wyborcza** ballot box
**wyborny** *adj* (*książk*) excellent
**wyborowy** *adj*: **strzelec ~** sharpshooter, marksman
**wyb|ój** (**-oju, -oje**) (*gen pl* **-oi** *lub* **-ojów**) *m* pothole
**wyb|ór** (**-oru, -ory**) (*loc sg* **-orze**) *m* (*zawodu*) choice; (*kandydata, prezydenta*) election; (*ćwiczeń, towarów*) selection; **nie mieć wyboru** to have no choice; **do wyboru mieliśmy ...** we could choose from ...; **(robić coś) z wyboru** (to do sth) by choice; **wybory** *pl* election(s *pl*); **wybory uzupełniające** by-election
**wy|brać (-biorę, -bierzesz)** *vb perf od* **wybierać**
**wybrakowany** *adj* defective; **towar ~** second
**wybra|niec** (**-ńca, -ńcy**) *m*: **wybrańcy** *pl* the elect; **garstka wybrańców** a select few
**wybrany** *adj* selected; **naród ~** (*Rel*) the chosen nation
**wybredny** *adj* choosy, fussy
**wybr|nąć (-nę, -niesz)** (*imp* **-nij**) *vi perf*: **~ z** *+gen* (*sytuacji, kłopotów*) to get out of
**wybro|nić (-nię, -nisz)** (*imp* **-ń**) *vt perf* to save
**wybruk|ować (-uję, -ujesz)** *vb perf od* **brukować**
**wybry|k** (**-ku, -ki**) (*instr sg* **-kiem**) *m* excess; **~ natury** a freak of nature
**wybrzeż|e** (**-a, -a**) (*gen pl* **-y**) *nt* coast; **u wybrzeża (Szkocji)** off the coast (of Scotland)
**Wybrzeż|e Kości Słoniowej** (**-a**) *nt* the Ivory Coast
**wybrzusze|nie** (**-nia, -nia**) (*gen pl* **-ń**) *nt* bulge
**wybrzydz|ać (-am, -asz)** *vi*: **~ na coś** to turn one's nose up at sth
**wybuch** (**-u, -y**) *m* (*gazu, bomby*) explosion; (*wulkanu*) eruption; (*pożaru, wojny, epidemii*) outbreak; (*płaczu, radości, śmiechu*) outburst; **Wielki W~** the Big Bang
**wybuch|ać (-am, -asz)** (*perf* **-nąć**) *vi* (*o bombie, granacie*) to explode, to go off; (*o wojnie, pożarze, epidemii*) to break out; (*o wulkanie*) to erupt; **~ płaczem** to burst into tears; **~ śmiechem** to burst out laughing
**wybuch|nąć (-nę, -niesz)** (*imp* **-nij**) *vb perf od* **wybuchać**
**wybuchowy** *adj* (*substancja*) explosive; (*człowiek, usposobienie*) short-tempered; **materiały wybuchowe** explosives
**wybud|ować (-uję, -ujesz)** *vb perf od* **budować**
**wybujały** *adj* (*roślinność*) rank, exuberant; (*ambicje*) exaggerated; (*wyobraźnia*) wild
**wybul|ić (-ę, -isz)** *vb perf od* **bulić**
**wyburz|ać (-am, -asz)** (*perf* **-yć**) *vt* to knock down
**wyburz|yć (-ę, -ysz)** *vb perf od* **burzyć, wyburzać**
**wyce|dzić (-dzę, -dzisz)** (*imp* **-dź**) *vb perf od* **cedzić**
**wycel|ować (-uję, -ujesz)** *vb perf od* **celować**
**wyce|na** (**-ny, -ny**) (*dat sg* **-nie**) *f* valuation
**wyce|niać (-niam, -niasz)** (*perf* **-nić**) *vt* to value
**wyce|nić (-nię, -nisz)** (*imp* **-ń**) *vb perf od* **wyceniać**
**wychl|ać (-am, -asz)** *vb perf od* **chlać**
**wychłep|tać (-czę, -czesz)** *vb perf od* **chłeptać**
**wychło|stać (-szczę, -szczesz)** *vb perf od* **chłostać**

W

**wychod|ek (-ka, -ki)** (*instr sg* **-kiem**) *m* (*pot*) privy (*pot*)
**wycho|dzić (-dzę, -dzisz)** (*imp* **-dź**, *perf* **wyjść**) *vi* (*z domu, pokoju, wojska*) to leave; (*spędzać czas poza domem*) to go out; (*o zdjęciach, słońcu, publikacji, włosach*) to come out; (*o planach*) to work (out); (*o żyłach, bieliźnie*) to show; **~ (z pokoju)** (*patrząc od wewnątrz*) to go out (of the room), to leave (the room); (*patrząc od zewnątrz*) to come out (of the room); **~ na spacer** to go out for a walk; **~ z opresji, długów** to get out of trouble/debt; **~ za mąż** to get married; **~ (za mąż) za kogoś** to marry sb; **~ na zachód/na morze** to look west/(out) onto the sea; **~ z użycia/mody** to go out of use/fashion; **~ w morze** to put out to sea; **~ od kogoś** (*o propozycji, inicjatywie*) to originate with sb; **~ na jaw** to come to light; **~ na idiotę** (*pot*) to be made to look like an idiot; **dobrze na czymś wyjść** to profit from sth; **wyjdzie mu to na dobre** it'll do him good; **~ na swoje** to break even; **~ z siebie** *lub* **ze skóry** (*pot: starać się*) to bend *lub* lean over backwards (*pot*); **wyjść z siebie** (*pot: stracić panowanie*) to be beside o.s.; **nic z tego nie wyszło** it came to nothing; **wszystko mu wychodzi** everything works out fine for him; **z tego materiału wyjdą dwie bluzki** this piece is big enough for two blouses; **wychodzi na to, że ...** it looks like ...
**wychow|ać (-am, -asz)** *vb perf od* **wychowywać**
**wychowan|ek (-ka, -kowie)** (*instr sg* **-kiem**) *m* (*absolwent*) old boy (Brit), alumnus (US); (*uczeń*) pupil; (*domu dziecka*) charge
**wychowani|e (-a)** *nt* (*nauka*) education; (*proces wychowawczy*) upbringing; (*ogłada*) manners *pl*; **~ fizyczne** physical education
**wychowan|ka (-ki, -ki)** (*dat sg* **-ce**, *gen pl* **-ek**) *f* (*absolwentka*) old girl (Brit), alumna (US); (*uczennica*) pupil; (*domu dziecka*) charge
**wychowany** *adj*: **dobrze/źle ~** well/ill-mannered
**wychowawc|a (-y, -y)** *m decl like f in sg* (*Szkol*) form tutor (Brit), home-room teacher (US); (*na obozie, koloniach*) (camp) counsellor (Brit) *lub* counselor (US); (*w domu dziecka*) house-father
**wychowawczy** *adj* (*metody, sukces*) educational; **urlop ~** parental leave, child care leave; **lekcja wychowawcza** *weekly class meeting*
**wychowawczy|ni (-ni, -nie)** (*gen pl* **-ń**) *f* (*Szkol*) form tutor (Brit), home-room teacher (US); (*w przedszkolu*) (nursery school) teacher; (*na obozie, koloniach*) (camp) counsellor (Brit) *lub* counselor (US); (*w domu dziecka*) house-mother
**wychow|ywać (-uję, -ujesz)** (*perf* **-ać**) *vt* (*o rodzicach*) to bring up; (*kształcić*) to educate; **wychowywać się** *vr* to be brought up
**wych|ów (-owu)** (*loc sg* **-owie**) *m* (*Rol*) raising
**wychuchany** *adj* (*jedynak*) pampered; (*mieszkanie*) spick-and-span
**wychudły** *adj* (*ręce*) skinny; (*twarz*) drawn
**wychudzony** *adj* emaciated
**wychwal|ać (-am, -asz)** *vt* to extol; **~ kogoś pod niebiosa** to praise sb to the skies
**wychwy|cić (-cę, -cisz)** (*imp* **-ć**) *vb perf od* **wychwytywać**
**wychwy|tywać (-tuję, -tujesz)** (*perf* **-cić**) *vt* (*błędy*) to pick out
**wychyl|ać (-am, -asz)** (*perf* **-ić**) *vt* (*wysunąć*) to stick out; (*wypić szybko*) to down; **wychylać się** *vr* (*wyglądać*): **~ się (z okna)** to lean out (of the window); (*o wskazówce, wahadle*) to swing; (*przen: o człowieku*) to stick one's neck out (*pot*)
**wy|ciąć (-tnę, -tniesz)** (*imp* **-tnij**) *vb perf od* **wycinać**
**wycią|g (-gu, -gi)** (*instr sg* **-giem**) *m* (*też*: **wyciąg narciarski**) ski lift; (*też*: **wyciąg z konta**) bank statement; (*dźwig*) hoist; (*wentylator*) extractor; (*z roślin itp.*) extract; (*wypis*) abstract; (*Med*) traction; **~ krzesełkowy** chairlift; **~ orczykowy** T-bar lift
**wyciąg|ać (-am, -asz)** (*perf* **-nąć**) *vt* (*wydobywać*) to pull out, to draw; (*prostować: nogi, ręce*) to stretch; (*pot: z łóżka, do kina*) to drag out (*pot*); **wyciągnąć rękę do kogoś** to reach out to sb; **~ kogoś z kłopotów/wody/** to get sb out of trouble/the water; **~ z czegoś wnioski** to draw conclusions from sth; **~ szyję** to crane one's neck; **~ od kogoś pieniądze** (*pot*) to scrounge money off sb (*pot*); **ten samochód wyciąga 180 km/godz.** (*pot*) this car does 180 kph (*pot*); **wyciągać się** *vr* (*pot: kłaść się*) to stretch out
**wyciąg|nąć (-nę, -niesz)** (*imp* **-nij**) *vb perf od* **wyciągać**; **wyciągnąć się** *vb perf od* **wyciągać się** ▷ *vr perf* (*o ubraniu*) to stretch
**wyciągnięty** *adj* (*ręka*) extended, outstretched; (*szyja*) craned; **leżał ~ na podłodze** he was lying flat on the floor
**wyci|e (-a)** *nt* howl(ing)
**wycie|c (-knie)** (*pt* **-kł**) *vb perf od* **wyciekać**
**wyciecz|ka (-ki, -ki)** (*dat sg* **-ce**, *gen pl* **-ek**) *f* trip, excursion; **~ piesza** hike; **~ po mieście** a tour of the city; **pojechać** (*perf*) **na wycieczkę** to go on a tour
**wycieczkowicz (-a, -e)** *m* tripper
**wycieczkowy** *adj*: **bilet ~** excursion ticket; **rejs ~** cruise; **statek ~** pleasure-boat
**wycie|k (-ku, -ki)** (*instr sg* **-kiem**) *m* leakage
**wyciek|ać (-a)** (*perf* **wyciec**) *vi* to leak

**wycieńcz|ać (-am, -asz)** (*perf* **-yć**) *vt* (*o chorobie*) to waste
**wycieńczeni|e** (**-a**) *nt* emaciation
**wycieńczony** *adj* emaciated
**wycieńcz|yć (-ę, -ysz)** *vb perf od* **wycieńczać**
**wycieracz|ka** (**-ki, -ki**) (*dat sg* **-ce**, *gen pl* **-ek**) *f* (*przed drzwiami*) doormat; (*Mot*) windscreen (*Brit*) *lub* windshield (*US*) wiper
**wycier|ać (-am, -asz)** (*perf* **wytrzeć**) *vt* (*ręce, tablicę*) to wipe; (*mleko, brud*) to wipe up; (*zużywać*) to wear out; **~ nos** to wipe one's nose; **~ kurze** to dust; **wycierać się** *vr* (*o człowieku*) to dry o.s.; (*o kołnierzyku*) to wear; (*o butach*) to wear out
**wycię|cie** (**-cia, -cia**) (*gen pl* **-ć**) *nt* (*otwór*) opening; (*dekolt*) neckline
**wycin|ać (-am, -asz)** (*perf* **wyciąć**) *vt* to cut out; (*migdały, wyrostek*) to take out; (*ryć*) to carve
**wycinan|ka** (**-ki, -ki**) (*dat sg* **-ce**, *gen pl* **-ek**) *f* cutout
**wycin|ek** (**-ka, -ki**) (*instr sg* **-kiem**) *m* (*z gazety*) cutting (*Brit*), clipping (*US*); (*Geom*) segment
**wycin|ka** (**-ki, -ki**) (*dat sg* **-ce**, *gen pl* **-ek**) *f* (*lasu*) logging
**wycinkowy** *adj* fragmentary
**wycis|k** (**-ku**) (*instr sg* **-kiem**) *m* (*pot*): **dać** (*perf*) **komuś ~** to give sb a hard time (*pot*)
**wyciskacz** (**-a, -e**) (*gen pl* **-y**) *m*: **~ do cytryn** lemon squeezer; **~ łez** (*pot*) tear-jerker (*pot*)
**wycisk|ać (-am, -asz)** (*perf* **wycisnąć**) *vt* (*cytrynę, pastę*) to squeeze (out); (*gąbkę, ubranie*) to wring out; (*pieczęć, znak*) to impress; **wycisnąć z kogoś pieniądze/prawdę** (*pot*) to squeeze money/the truth out of sb
**wyci|snąć (-snę, -śniesz)** (*imp* **-śnij**) *vb perf od* **wyciskać**
**wycisz|ać (-am, -asz)** (*perf* **-yć**) *vt* (*kroki, silnik*) to muffle; (*kabinę*) to soundproof
**wycofani|e** (**-a**) *nt* withdrawal; **~ się** withdrawal
**wycof|ywać (-uję, -ujesz)** (*perf* **-ać**) *vt* to withdraw; **wycofywać się** *vr* to withdraw; **~ się z życia publicznego** to retire *lub* withdraw from public life
**wyczar|ować (-uję, -ujesz)** *vt perf* to conjure up
**wycze|kiwać (-kuję, -kujesz)** *vt*: **~ kogoś/czegoś** to wait for sb/sth; **~ czegoś** (*z przyjemnością*) to look forward to sth ▷ *vi*: **~ na kogoś/coś** to wait for sb/sth
**wyczekująco** *adv* (*spoglądać*) expectantly, with anticipation
**wyczekujący** *adj* (*postawa*) expectant; (*polityka*) wait-and-see *attr*
**wyczer|pać (-pię, -piesz)** *vb perf od* **wyczerpywać**
**wyczerpani|e** (**-a**) *nt* (*zmęczenie*) exhaustion; **być na wyczerpaniu** (*o zapasach, cierpliwości*) to run low; (*o cierpliwości*) to wear thin
**wyczerpany** *adj* (*człowiek, zapasy*) exhausted; (*bateria*) flat, dead; **nakład książki jest ~** the book is out of print
**wyczerpująco** *adv* exhaustively
**wyczerpujący** *adj* (*praca*) exhausting; (*odpowiedź*) exhaustive
**wyczerp|ywać (-uję, -ujesz)** (*perf* **-ać**) *vt* to exhaust; **wyczerpywać się** *vr* (*o zapasach*) to run low; (*o baterii*) to run down; (*o cierpliwości*) to wear thin
**wyczuci|e** (**-a**) *nt*: **~ rytmu/sytuacji** a feeling for rhythm/the situation; **robić coś na ~** to follow one's nose in doing sth; **~ językowe** a feeling for language
**wycz|uć (-uję, -ujesz)** *vb perf od* **wyczuwać**
**wyczulony** *adj*: **być ~m na coś** to be sensitive to sth
**wyczuw|ać (-am, -asz)** (*perf* **wyczuć**) *vt* (*dotykiem*) to feel; (*węchem*) to smell, to scent; (*intuicyjnie*) to sense
**wyczuwalny** *adj* (*zapach, puls*) perceptible; (*nerwowość, smutek*) noticeable
**wyczy|n** (**-nu, -ny**) (*loc sg* **-nie**) *m* (*osiągnięcie*) achievement, feat; (*wybryk*) excess
**wyczyni|ać (-am, -asz)** *vt* (*cuda, sztuki*) to perform; **co ty wyczyniasz?** (*pot*) what on earth are you doing? (*pot*)
**wyczyno|wiec** (**-wca, -wcy**) *m* (*Sport*) professional
**wyczynowy** *adj* professional
**wyczy|ścić (-szczę, -ścisz)** (*imp* **-ść**) *vb perf od* **czyścić**
**wyczyt|ać (-am, -asz)** *vb perf od* **wyczytywać** ▷ *vt perf* (*przeczytać*) to read
**wyczyt|ywać (-uję, -ujesz)** (*perf* **-ać**) *vt* (*wymieniać*) to read out
**wyć (wyję, wyjesz)** *vi* (*o człowieku, psie*) to howl; (*o silniku, syrenie*) to scream; (*o syrenie*) to wail
**wyćwiczony** *adj* (*człowiek, wojsko*) trained; (*mięśnie*) exercised
**wyd|ać (-am, -asz)** *vb perf od* **wydawać**
**wydajnie** *adv* efficiently, effectively
**wydajnoś|ć** (**-ci**) *f* efficiency, productivity
**wydajny** *adj* (*praca*) efficient; (*Mot: silnik*) fuel-efficient; (*Rol: odmiana, zboże*) highly productive
**wydal|ać (-am, -asz)** (*perf* **-ić**) *vt* (*ze szkoły, kraju*) to expel; (*Bio*) to excrete
**wyda|nie** (**-nia, -nia**) (*gen pl* **-ń**) *nt* edition; (*opublikowanie*) publication; (*Prasa*) issue
**wydarz|ać się (-a)** (*perf* **-yć**) *vr* to happen, to occur
**wydarze|nie** (**-nia, -nia**) (*gen pl* **-ń**) *nt* event; **~ sezonu/roku** event of the season/year

**wydarz|yć się (-y)** *vb perf od* **wydarzać się**
**wydat|ek** (**-ku, -ki**) (*instr sg* **-kiem**) *m* expense; **wydatki** *pl* expenses *pl*, expenditure(s *pl*); **pieniądze na drobne wydatki** pocket money
**wydatk|ować (-uję, -ujesz)** (*perf* **-ować**) *vt* (*książk*) to expend
**wydatnie** *adv* considerably
**wydatny** *adj* (*biust, nos*) prominent; (*pomoc, wkład*) considerable
**wyd|awać (-aję, -ajesz)** (*perf* **-ać**) *vt* (*pieniądze, pensję*) to spend; (*gazetę, książkę*) to publish; (*posiłek*) to serve; (*kwit, zaświadczenie*) to give, to issue; (*dekret, proklamację*) to issue; (*opinię*) to give, to pass; (*werdykt*) to return, to deliver; (*wyrok*) to pass, to pronounce; (*polecenie, towar, przyjęcie*) to give; (*szpiega*) to give away; (*dźwięk*) to make, to utter; (*woń, zapach*) to give out; **~ okrzyk** to give a shout *lub* cry; **~ kogoś za mąż** to marry sb off; **~ na świat** to give birth to; **wydawać się** *vr* (*wyglądać*) to seem, to appear; (*o tajemnicy*) to come out; **wydaje mi się, że ...** it seems to me that ...; **wydaje się prawdopodobne, że ...** it seems probable that ...; **wydawałoby się, że ...** it would appear that ...
**wydawc|a** (**-y, -y**) *m* publisher
**wydawnict|wo** (**-wa, -wa**) (*loc sg* **-wie**) *nt* (*instytucja*) publishing house; (*publikacja*) publication
**wyd|ąć (-mę, -miesz)** (*imp* **-mij**) *vb perf od* **wydymać**
**wydech** (**-u, -y**) *m* exhalation; (*Tech, Mot*) exhaust
**wydechowy** *adj*: **rura wydechowa** exhaust (pipe) (*Brit*), tailpipe (*US*)
**wydekoltowany** *adj* (*suknia*) low-cut
**wydeleg|ować (-uję, -ujesz)** *vb perf od* **delegować**
**wydep|tać (-czę, -czesz)** (*imp* **-cz**) *vt perf* (*ścieżkę*) to tread
**wydęty** *adj* (*brzuch*) bulging; (*wargi*) pouted
**wydłu|bać (-bię, -biesz)** *vb perf od* **wydłubywać**
**wydłub|ywać (-uję, -ujesz)** (*perf* **-ać**) *vt* to pick
**wydłuż|ać (-am, -asz)** (*perf* **-yć**) *vt* (*cykl, krok*) to lengthen; (*czas, pobyt*) to prolong, to extend; (*podróż*) to prolong, to lengthen; **wydłużać się** *vr* to lengthen, to grow longer
**wydłużony** *adj* elongated
**wyd|ma** (**-my, -my**) (*dat sg* **-mie**) *f* (sand) dune
**wydmuch|ać (-am, -asz)** (*imp* **-nij**) *vb perf od* **wydmuchiwać**
**wydmu|chiwać (-chuję, -chujesz)** (*perf* **-chać** *lub* **-chnąć**) *vt* (*powietrze*) to exhale; **~ nos** to blow one's nose
**wydmuch|nąć (-nę, -niesz)** (*imp* **-nij**) *vb perf od* **wydmuchiwać**
**wydmusz|ka** (**-ki, -ki**) (*dat sg* **-ce**, *gen pl* **-ek**) *f* Easter egg shell
**wydobrz|eć (-eję, -ejesz)** *vi perf* to recover, to get better
**wydob|yć (-ędę, -ędziesz)** (*imp* **-ądź**) *vb perf od* **wydobywać**
**wydobyw|ać (-am, -asz)** (*perf* **wydobyć**) *vt* (*wyciągać*) to get *lub* bring out; (*rudę, węgiel*) to extract, to mine; **nie mogłem wydobyć głosu** I couldn't utter a sound; **wydobywać się** *vr* (*o gazie, płynie*) to get out, to escape; (*o jęku, płaczu*) to come out
**wydobywczy** *adj* mining *attr*
**wydolnoś|ć** (**-ci**) *f* efficiency
**wydorośl|eć (-eję, -ejesz)** *vi perf* to grow up
**wydost|ać (-anę, -aniesz)** (*imp* **-ań**) *vb perf od* **wydostawać**
**wydost|awać (-aję, -ajesz)** (*imp* **-awaj**, *perf* **-ać**) *vt*: **~ coś** (**z** *+gen*) get sth out (of); **~ coś od kogoś** to get sth out of sb; **wydostawać się** *vr* to get out
**wyd|ra** (**-ry, -ry**) (*dat sg* **-rze**) *f* otter
**wydra|pać (-pię, -piesz)** *vb perf od* **wydrapywać**
**wydrap|ywać (-uję, -ujesz)** (*perf* **-ać**) *vt* (*napis, rysunek*) to carve, to scratch; (*plamę*) to scrub off; (*błąd*) to scrape out; (*oczy*) to scratch out
**wydrąż|ać (-am, -asz)** (*perf* **-yć**) *vt* to hollow (out)
**wydrążony** *adj* hollow
**wydrąż|yć (-ę, -ysz)** *vb perf od* **drążyć, wydrążać**
**wydru|k** (**-ku, -ki**) (*instr sg* **-kiem**) *m* printout
**wydruk|ować (-uję, -ujesz)** *vb perf od* **drukować**
**wyd|rzeć (-rę, -rzesz)** (*imp* **-rzyj**) *vb perf od* **wydzierać**
**wydumany** *adj* (*problem*) invented
**wydu|sić (-szę, -sisz)** (*imp* **-ś**) *vb perf od* **wyduszać** ▷ *vt perf* (*pot*: *też*: **wydusić z siebie**) to stutter out
**wydusz|ać (-am, -asz)** (*perf* **wydusić**) *vt* (*wyciskać*) to squeeze out; **~ coś z kogoś** to extract sth from sb
**wydych|ać (-am, -asz)** *vt* to breathe out, to exhale
**wydym|ać (-am, -asz)** (*perf* **wydąć**) *vt* (*wargi, usta*) to pout
**wydze** *n patrz* **wyga**
**wydzia|ł** (**-łu, -ły**) (*loc sg* **-le**) *m* (*w urzędzie*) department; (*na uczelni*) faculty; **~ matematyczny** faculty of mathematics; **~ prawa** law school
**wydziedzicz|ać (-am, -asz)** (*perf* **-yć**) *vt* to disinherit

**wydziel|ać (-am, -asz)** (*perf* **-ić**) *vt* (*hormon, żółć*) to secrete; (*zapach*) to give off; (*ciepło, promieniowanie*) to emit; (*prowiant, pieniądze*) to ration out, to dispense; **wydzielać się** *vr* (*powstawać*) to be produced; (*o pocie, żywicy*) to exude

**wydzieli|na** (**-ny, -ny**) (*dat sg* **-nie**) *f* secretion

**wydzier|ać (-am, -asz)** (*perf* **wydrzeć**) *vt* (*kartkę*) to tear out; **~ coś (komuś)** to tear sth away (from sb); **~ coś sobie (z rąk)** to scramble for sth; **wydzierać się** *vr* (*pot*) to holler (*pot*); (*wyrywać się*) to (try to) wrench free

**wydzierża|wić (-wię, -wisz)** *vb perf od* **dzierżawić**

**wydziwi|ać (-am, -asz)** *vi* (*pot*): **~ (na coś)** to make a fuss (about sth)

**wydzwani|ać (-am, -asz)** *vi* (*o zegarze*) to strike; **~ do kogoś nieustannie** to bug *lub* pester sb with telephone calls

**wydźwię|k** (**-ku**) (*instr sg* **-kiem**) *m* overtone

**wydźwig|nąć (-nę, -niesz)** (*imp* **-nij**) *vt perf* to raise; **wydźwignąć się** *vr perf* to rise

**wyegzekw|ować (-uję, -ujesz)** *vb perf od* **egzekwować**

**wyeksmit|ować (-uję, -ujesz)** *vb perf od* **eksmitować**

**wyeksploat|ować (-uję, -ujesz)** *vt perf* to use up

**wyeksport|ować (-uję, -ujesz)** *vb perf od* **eksportować**

**wyelimin|ować (-uję, -ujesz)** *vb perf od* **eliminować**

**wyeliminowani|e** (**-a**) *nt* elimination

**wyemancyp|ować się (-uję, -ujesz)** *vr perf* to emancipate o.s.

**wyemancypowany** *adj* emancipated

**wyemigr|ować (-uję, -ujesz)** *vb perf od* **emigrować**

**wyfroter|ować (-uję, -ujesz)** *vb perf od* **froterować**

**wyfru|nąć (-nę, -niesz)** (*imp* **-ń**) *vi perf* to fly away

**wy|ga** (**-gi, -gi**) (*dat sg* **-dze**) *m*: **stary ~** (*pot*) an old stager

**wygad|ać (-am, -asz)** *vt perf* (*pot: sekret*) to let slip, to let out; **wygadać się** *vr* (*pot: nagadać się*) to chat *lub* talk to one's heart's content; (*: zdradzić się*) to spill the beans (*pot*), to blab (*pot*)

**wygadany** *adj* (*pot*): **być ~m** to have the gift of (the) gab

**wygad|ywać (-uję, -ujesz)** *vt* (*pot*): **~ bzdury** to talk nonsense; **co ty wygadujesz?** what are you talking about?

**wygani|ać (-am, -asz)** (*perf* **wygonić** *lub* **wygnać**) *vt* to drive (out), to chase (away)

**wygarb|ować (-uję, -ujesz)** *vb perf od* **garbować**

**wygar|nąć (-nę, -niesz)** (*imp* **-nij**) *vb perf od* **wygarniać** ▷ *vt perf* (*pot*): **~ komuś** to give it to sb straight (*pot*)

**wygarni|ać (-am, -asz)** (*perf* **wygarnąć**) *vt* to rake (out)

**wygas|ać (-a)** (*perf* **wygasnąć**) *vi* (*o ogniu*) to fizzle out; (*o uczuciach*) to fade; (*o epidemii*) to subside; (*o umowie*) to expire

**wyga|sić (-szę, -sisz)** (*imp* **-ś**) *vb perf od* **wygaszać**

**wyga|snąć (-śnie)** (*pt* **-sł**) *vb perf od* **wygasać**

**wygasz|ać (-am, -asz)** (*perf* **wygasić**) *vt* (*światła*) to put *lub* turn out; (*ogień*) to put out, to extinguish

**wygaśnięci|e** (**-a**) *nt* (*umowy, kontraktu*) expiry, termination

**wygener|ować (-uję, -ujesz)** *vb perf od* **generować**

**wy|giąć (-gnę, -gniesz)** (*imp* **-gnij**) *vb perf od* **wyginać**

**wygię|cie** (**-cia, -cia**) (*gen pl* **-ć**) *nt* curve

**wygięty** *adj* bent, curved

**wygimnastykowany** *adj* supple

**wygin|ać (-am, -asz)** (*perf* **wygiąć**) *vt* to bend; **wyginać się** *vr* to bend

**wygi|nąć (-nie)** *vi perf* to become extinct

**wyginięci|e** (**-a**) *nt* extinction

**wyglą|d** (**-du**) (*loc sg* **-dzie**) *m* (*zwierzęcia, przedmiotu*) appearance; (*człowieka*) appearance, looks *pl*; **~ zewnętrzny** outward appearance; **przypominać kogoś z ~u** to look like sb

**wygląd|ać (-am, -asz)** *vt*: **~ kogoś/czegoś** to be on the lookout for sb/sth ▷ *vi*: **~ (wyjrzeć** *perf*) **przez okno** to look through *lub* out (of) the window; **~ (wyjrzeć** *perf*) **zza/spod czegoś** to appear from behind/from beneath sth; **~ świetnie/źle** to look great/bad; **wygląda jak twój ojciec** he looks like your father; **wyglądasz na zmęczonego/zmartwionego** you look tired/worried; **jak ona wygląda?** what does she look like?; **wygląda na to, że ...** it looks as if ...; **na to wygląda** so it would seem

**wygła|dzać (-dzam, -dzasz)** (*perf* **-dzić**) *vt* to smooth out

**wygła|dzić (-dzę, -dzisz)** (*imp* **-dź**) *vb perf od* **wygładzać**

**wygłasz|ać (-am, -asz)** (*perf* **wygłosić**) *vt* to deliver (*a speech*)

**wygłodniały** *adj* ravenous, starving

**wygłodzony** *adj* starving

**wygło|sić (-szę, -sisz)** (*imp* **-ś**) *vb perf od* **wygłaszać**

W

**wygłupi|ać się (-am, -asz)** *vr* to fool about *lub* around; **nie wygłupiaj się!** stop acting *lub* playing the fool!
**wygłu|pić się (-pię, -pisz)** *vr perf* to make a fool of o.s.
**wygłup|y** (**-ów**) *pl* clowning *sg*, tomfoolery *sg*
**wygn|ać (-am, -asz)** *vb perf od* **wyganiać**
**wygnani|e** (**-a**) *nt* exile
**wygna|niec** (**-ńca, -ńcy**) *m* exile
**wygnieciony** *adj* wrinkled, crumpled
**wygni|eść (-otę, -eciesz)** (*imp* **-eć**, *pt* **-ótł, -otła, -etli**) *vt perf* to crumple; **wygnieść się** *vr perf* to crumple, to wrinkle
**wyg|oda** (**-ody, -ody**) (*dat sg* **-odzie**, *gen pl* **-ód**) *f* (*dogodność*) convenience; (*funkcjonalność*) comfort; **wygody** *pl* amenities *pl*
**wygodnict|wo** (**-wa**) (*loc sg* **-wie**) *nt* laziness
**wygodnie** *adv* comfortably
**wygodny** *adj* (*mebel, odzież*) comfortable; (*pretekst, tłumaczenie*) convenient; (*człowiek*) lazy
**wygolony** *adj*: **(gładko)** ~ (clean-)shaven
**wygo|nić (-nię, -nisz)** (*imp* **-ń**) *vb perf od* **wyganiać**
**wygospodar|ować (-uję, -ujesz)** *vt perf* to save up
**wygot|ować (-uję, -ujesz)** *vt perf* to boil; **wygotować się** *vr perf* to boil away
**wygórowany** *adj* (*suma*) exorbitant; (*ambicje, żądania*) excessive
**wygr|ać (-am, -asz)** *vb perf od* **wygrywać**
**wygran|a** (**-ej, -e**) *f decl like adj* (*rzecz*) prize; (*pieniądze*) winnings *pl*; (*zwycięstwo*) victory; **(nie) dawać (dać** *perf*) **za wygraną** (not) to give up
**wygraż|ać (-am, -asz)** *vi*: ~ **(komuś) pięścią/kijem** to shake one's fist/a stick (at sb)
**wygryw|ać (-am, -asz)** *vt* (*nagrodę, wojnę*) (*perf* **wygrać**) to win; (*melodię*) to play ▷ *vi* (*zwyciężać*) (*perf* **wygrać**) to win
**wygrywający** *adj* (*los, kupon*) winning ▷ *m decl like adj* (*zwycięzca*) winner
**wygry|źć (-zę, -ziesz)** (*imp* **-ź**, *pt* **-zł, -zła, -źli**) *vt perf*: ~ **kogoś** (*pot*) to boot sb out (*pot*)
**wygrze|bać (-bię, -biesz)** *vt perf* to dig out
**wygrzew|ać się (-am, -asz)** *vr* to warm o.s.; **wygrzewać się na słońcu** to bask in the sun
**wygwi|zdać (-żdżę, -żdżesz)** *vt perf* to boo
**wyhaft|ować (-uję, -ujesz)** *vb perf od* **haftować**
**wyham|ować (-uję, -ujesz)** *vb perf od* **hamować** ▷ *vt perf* (*pojazd, samochód*) to bring to a stop
**wyhod|ować (-uję, -ujesz)** *vb perf od* **hodować**
**wyidealizowany** *adj* idealized
**wyimagin|ować (-uję, -ujesz)** *vt perf* (*książk*): ~ **sobie coś** to dream sth up
**wyimaginowany** *adj* imaginary
**wyizol|ować (-uję, -ujesz)** *vb perf od* **izolować**
**wyjadacz** (**-a, -e**) (*gen pl* **-y**) *m* (*pot*): **stary** ~ an old stager
**wyjad|ać (-am, -asz)** (*perf* **wyjeść**) *vt* to eat up
**wyjadę** *itd. vb patrz* **wyjechać**
**wyjaławi|ać (-am, -asz)** (*perf* **wyjałowić**) *vt* (*ziemię*) to impoverish; (*sterylizować*) to sterilize
**wyjał|owić (-owię, -owisz)** (*imp* **-ów**) *vb perf od* **wyjaławiać**
**wyjałowiony** *adj* sterile; (*ziemia*) impoverished
**wyjaś|niać (-niam, -niasz)** (*perf* **-nić**) *vt* (*znaczenie, teorię*) to explain; (*sprawę, nieporozumienie*) to straighten out; **wyjaśniać się** *vr* (*o sytuacji*) to be cleared up
**wyjaś|nić (-nię, -nisz)** (*imp* **-nij**) *vb perf od* **wyjaśniać**
**wyjaśnie|nie** (**-nia, -nia**) (*gen pl* **-ń**) *nt* explanation, clarification
**wyja|wiać (-wiam, -wiasz)** (*perf* **-wić**) *vt* to reveal
**wyj|azd** (**-azdu, -azdy**) (*loc sg* **-eździe**) *m* (*odjazd*) departure; (*podróż*) trip; (*droga wyjazdowa*) exit
**wyjazdowy** *adj* exit *attr*; **mecz** ~ away game *lub* match
**wyj|ąć (-mę, -miesz)** (*imp* **-mij**) *vb perf od* **wyjmować**
**wyjąk|ać (-am, -asz)** *vt perf* to stammer (out)
**wyjąt|ek** (**-ku, -ki**) (*instr sg* **-kiem**) *m* (*odstępstwo*) exception; (*książk: urywek*) excerpt; **z(a) wyjątkiem** *+gen* except (for), with the exception of; **bez wyjątku** without exception; **z małymi wyjątkami** with some exceptions; ~ **od reguły** exception to the rule; **robić (zrobić** *perf*) **dla kogoś** ~ to make an exception for sb
**wyjątkowo** *adv* exceptionally; **wczoraj** ~ **nie padało** quite unusually, it did not rain yesterday
**wyjątkowoś|ć** (**-ci**) *f* exceptionality
**wyjątkowy** *adj* exceptional, unusual; **stan** ~ (*Pol*) state of emergency
**wyj|echać (-adę, -edziesz)** (*imp* **-edź**) *vb perf od* **wyjeżdżać**
**wyj|eść (-em, -esz)** (*imp* **-edz**, *pt* **-adł, -adła, -edli**) *vb perf od* **wyjadać**
**wyjeżdż|ać (-am, -asz)** (*perf* **wyjechać**) *vi* (*z bramy, garażu*) to go *lub* drive out; (*w podróż*) to leave; **jutro wyjeżdżamy** we're leaving tomorrow; **wyjechać do Stanów** to leave for

the States; **wyjechać na wakacje/w podróż** to go on holiday/on a trip; **moi sąsiedzi wyjechali do Kopenhagi** my neighbours are away in Copenhagen

**wyjm|ować (-uję, -ujesz)** (*perf* **wyjąć**) *vt* (*wyciągać*) to take out; (*wydostawać: kulę*) to get out; (*listy*) to collect; **~ coś z kieszeni** to take sth out of one's pocket

**wyjrz|eć (-ę, -ysz)** (*imp* **-yj**) *vb perf od* **wyglądać**

**wyjś|cie** (**-cia**) *nt* (*czynność*) departure; (*miejsce*) (*nom pl* **-cia**, *gen pl* **-ć**) exit, way out; (*rozwiązanie*) (*nom pl* **-cia**, *gen pl* **-ć**) solution; (*Tech: gniazdo*) (*nom pl* **-cia**, *gen pl* **-ć**) outlet; **po jej wyjściu ...** after she left, ...; **położenie** *lub* **sytuacja bez wyjścia** dead end; **nie miałem (innego) wyjścia, jak tylko to zrobić** I had no (other) choice, but to do it; **punkt wyjścia** starting point

**wyjściowy** *adj* (*drzwi*) exit *attr*; (*sytuacja, pozycja, materiał*) initial *attr*; (*moc, napięcie, dane*) output *attr*; (*pot: ubranie*) outdoor *attr*

**wyj|ść (-dę, -dziesz)** (*imp* **-dź**, *pt* **wyszedł, wyszła, wyszli**) *vb perf od* **wychodzić**

**wykałacz|ka** (**-ki, -ki**) (*dat sg* **-ce**, *gen pl* **-ek**) *f* toothpick

**wykańcz|ać (-am, -asz)** (*perf* **wykończyć**) *vt* (*doprowadzać do końca*) to put the finishing touches to; (*pot: zabijać*) to do in (*pot*); (*: męczyć*) to finish (off); **~ kogoś nerwowo** to shatter sb's nerves; **wykańczać się** *vr*: **~ się nerwowo** to become a nervous wreck

**wykapany** *adj* (*pot*): **~ ojciec** the very *lub* spitting image of his father

**wykar|mić (-mię, -misz)** *vt perf* (*nakarmić*) to feed; (*wychować*) to bring up

**wyka|z** (**-zu, -zy**) (*loc sg* **-zie**) *m* (*nazwisk, osób*) list, register; (*należności, kosztów*) statement

**wyka|zać (-żę, -żesz)** *vb perf od* **wykazywać**

**wykaz|ywać (-uję, -ujesz)** (*perf* **-ać**) *vt* (*przejawiać*) to show; (*udowadniać*) to prove; (*ujawniać*) to reveal; **wykazywać się** *vr* (*dowodzić swojej wartości*) to prove o.s.; **~ się czymś** to show sth

**wyką|pać (-pię, -piesz)** *vb perf od* **kąpać**

**wykit|ować (-uję, -ujesz)** *vi perf* (*pot*) to kick the bucket

**wykiw|ać (-am, -asz)** *vt perf* (*pot: oszukać*) to dupe, to fool

**wykl|ąć (-nę, -niesz)** (*imp* **-nij**) *vb perf od* **wyklinać**

**wyklin|ać (-am, -asz)** (*perf* **wykląć**) *vt* (*wyrzekać się*) to curse; (*Rel*) to excommunicate

**wyklucz|ać (-am, -asz)** (*perf* **-yć**) *vt* (*ewentualność: o człowieku*) to rule out, to exclude; (*: o okolicznościach*) to preclude; **~ kogoś (z organizacji/drużyny)** to disqualify sb (from an organization/a team); **~ zawodnika (z gry)** (*Sport*) to send a player off; **wykluczać się** *vr* (*też*: **wykluczać się wzajemnie**) to be mutually exclusive

**wykluczony** *adj*: **to jest wykluczone** it's out of the question

**wykl|uć się (-uje)** *vb perf od* **wykluwać się**

**wykluw|ać się (-a)** (*perf* **wykluć**) *vr* (*o kurczętach, ptakach*) to hatch (out); (*przen: o pomysłach*) to spring up

**wykła|d** (**-du, -dy**) (*loc sg* **-dzie**) *m* lecture; **prowadzić ~ (z +gen)** to lecture (on)

**wykład|ać (-am, -asz)** *vt* (*perf* **wyłożyć**) (*wyjmować*) to lay out; (*poglądy, plany*) to expound, to set forth; **~ podłogę kafelkami/dywanem** to tile/carpet the floor; **~ pudełko/szufladę czymś** to line a box/drawer with sth; **on wykłada literaturę** he lectures in literature

**wykład|nia** (**-ni, -nie**) (*gen pl* **-ni**) *f* (*Prawo*) interpretation

**wykładni|k** (**-ka, -ki**) (*instr sg* **-kiem**) *m* (*kultury, wartości*) indication, index; (*Mat: potęgi*) exponent, index; (*: pierwiastka*) degree, index

**wykładowc|a** (**-y, -y**) *m decl like f in sg* lecturer

**wykładowy** *adj*: **sala wykładowa** lecture hall; **język ~** language of instruction

**wykładzi|na** (**-ny, -ny**) (*dat sg* **-nie**) *f* (*dywanowa*) fitted carpet; (*podłogowa*) lino(leum)

**wykłó|cać się (-cam, -casz)** *vr*: **wykłócać się o coś** to argue about sth

**wykole|ić (-ję, -isz)** *vb perf od* **wykolejać**

**wykolej|ać (-am, -asz)** (*perf* **wykoleić**) *vt* (*pociąg*) to derail; **wykolejać się** *vr* (*o pociągu*) to be derailed

**wykombin|ować (-uję, -ujesz)** *vt perf* (*pot: sposób, pieniądze*) to come up with

**wykon|ać (-am, -asz)** *vb perf od* **wykonywać**

**wykonalnoś|ć** (**-ci**) *f* feasibility, practicability

**wykonalny** *adj* feasible, workable

**wykona|nie** (**-nia**) *nt* (*czynność*) execution; (*jakość*) workmanship; (*utworu, piosenki*) (*nom pl* **-nia**, *gen pl* **-ń**) performance, rendition; **niemożliwy do wykonania** unfeasible

**wykonany** *adj*: **~ z +gen** made of

**wykonawc|a** (**-y, -y**) *m decl like f in sg* (*robót*) contractor; (*testamentu, zlecenia, projektu*) executor; (*roli, utworu*) performer; **~ wyroku** executioner; **wykonawcą rzutu karnego będzie ...** the penalty (kick) will be taken by ...

**wykonawczy** *adj* executive *attr*; **władza wykonawcza** executive power

**wykonawczy|ni** (**-ni, -nie**) (*gen pl* **-ń**) *f* (*piosenki, roli*) performer; (*testamentu*) executrix

**wykon|ywać (-uję, -ujesz)** (*perf* **-ać**) *vt* (*plan, polecenie*) to carry out, to execute; (*operację, eksperyment, obowiązki*) to perform, to carry out; (*robotę, ćwiczenie*) to do; (*odlew, otwór, obrót*) to make; (*koncert, utwór, taniec*) to perform; (*rzut karny*) to take; **~ zawód prawnika** to work as a lawyer

**wykonywany** *adj*: **zawód ~** occupation, job

**wykończe|nie** (**-nia, -nia**) (*gen pl* **-ń**) *nt* (*domu*) decor; (*materiału, mebla*) finish; (*ozdobny brzeg*) trim

**wykończony** *adj* (*dom*) completed; (*przedmiot*) finished; (*pot: człowiek*) dog-tired (*pot*)

**wykończ|yć (-ę, -ysz)** *vb perf od* **wykańczać**

**wyko|p** (**-pu, -py**) (*loc sg* **-pie**) *m* (*pod fundamenty*) pit; (*pod instalację*) trench

**wyko|pać (-pię, -piesz)** *vt perf* to dig up

**wykopalis|ko** (**-ka, -ka**) (*instr sg* **-kiem**) *nt* (*przedmiot*) find; **wykopaliska** *pl* excavations *pl*

**wykork|ować (-uję, -ujesz)** *vi perf* (*pot*) to kick the bucket (*pot*)

**wykorze|niać (-niam, -niasz)** (*perf* **-nić**) *vt* to root out, to eradicate

**wykorze|nić (-nię, -nisz)** (*imp* **-ń**) *vb perf od* **wykorzeniać**

**wykorzyst|ywać (-uję, -ujesz)** (*perf* **-ać**) *vt* (*pożytkować*) to use, to make use of; (*korzystać z*) to take advantage of; (*wyzyskiwać*) to exploit; (*nadużywać*) to abuse; **maksymalnie coś wykorzystać** to make the most of sth; **~ urlop** to use one's holiday

**wykoszt|ować się (-uję, -ujesz)** *vr perf*: **wykosztować się (na coś)** to go to great expense (to buy sth)

**wyk|pić (-pię, -pisz)** (*imp* **-pij**) *vt perf* (*osobę, wady*) to ridicule, to mock; **wykpić się** *vr perf* (*pot*): **~ się od robienia czegoś** to get out of doing sth

**wykracz|ać (-am, -asz)** *vi* (*perf* **wykroczyć**); **~ przeciw(ko)** *+dat* to violate, to contravene; **~ poza** *+acc* to go beyond

**wykrad|ać (-am, -asz)** (*perf* **wykraść**) *vt* (*dokumenty*) to steal away; (*więźnia*) to abduct; **wykradać się** *vr* to steal out *lub* away

**wykra|ść (-dnę, -dniesz)** (*imp* **-dnij**, *pt* **-dł**) *vb perf od* **wykradać**

**wykraw|ać (-am, -asz)** (*perf* **wykroić**) *vt* to cut out

**wykre|s** (**-su, -sy**) (*loc sg* **-sie**) *m* (*rysunek*) chart, graph; (*Mat*) graph

**wykreśl|ać (-am, -asz)** (*perf* **-ić**) *vt* (*wymazywać*) to cross out *lub* off; (*rysować*) to draw

**wykrę|cać (-cam, -casz)** (*perf* **-cić**) *vt* (*śrubę, żarówkę*) to unscrew; (*głowę, szyję*) to turn; (*bieliznę*) to wring; (*numer*) to dial; **~ komuś rękę** to twist sb's arm; **wykręcać się** *vr* (*pot*): **~ się od obowiązków** to evade one's responsibilities; **wykręcił się z tego** he got out of it

**wykrę|cić (-cę, -cisz)** (*imp* **-ć**) *vb perf od* **wykręcać**

**wykrę|t** (**-tu, -ty**) (*loc sg* **-cie**) *m* (*wymówka*) excuse; (*unik*) hedge

**wykrętny** *adj* evasive

**wykrocze|nie** (**-nia, -nia**) (*gen pl* **-ń**) *nt* offence (Brit), offense (US)

**wykrocz|yć (-ę, -ysz)** *vb perf od* **wykraczać**

**wykr|oić (-oję, -oisz)** (*imp* **-ój**) *vb perf od* **wykrawać**

**wykr|ój** (**-oju, -oje**) *m* (*Krawiectwo*) pattern

**wykrusz|ać się (-am, -asz)** (*perf* **-yć**) *vr* (*o ludziach, zespole*) to drop off

**wykrwa|wić się (-wię, -wisz)** *vr perf* (*o człowieku*) to bleed to death

**wykr|yć (-yję, -yjesz)** *vb perf od* **wykrywać**

**wykrywacz** (**-a, -e**) (*gen pl* **-y**) *m* detector; **~ kłamstw** lie detector

**wykryw|ać (-am, -asz)** (*perf* **wykryć**) *vt* (*błąd, zarazki, oszustwa*) to detect; (*sprawcę*) to find

**wykrywalny** *adj* detectable

**wykrze|sać (-szę, -szesz)** *vb perf od* **krzesać** ▷ *vt perf*: **~ coś z siebie** to summon sth (up), to muster sth (up); **nie umiałam ~ z nich entuzjazmu** I was unable to fire them with enthusiasm

**wykrztu|sić (-szę, -sisz)** (*imp* **-ś**) *vt perf* to cough up

**wykrztuśny** *adj*: **środek ~** expectorant

**wykrzycz|eć (-ę, -ysz)** *vt perf* to shout (out); **wykrzyczeć się** *vr perf* (*pot*) to relieve one's feelings

**wykrzy|kiwać (-kuję, -kujesz)** (*perf* **-knąć**) *vt* to shout (out) ▷ *vi* to bellow, to shout

**wykrzyk|nąć (-nę, -niesz)** (*imp* **-nij**) *vb perf od* **wykrzykiwać**

**wykrzykni|k** (**-ka, -ki**) (*instr sg* **-kiem**) *m* (*znak interpunkcyjny*) exclamation mark; (*część mowy*) interjection

**wykrzy|wiać (-wiam, -wiasz)** (*perf* **-wić**) *vt* to contort, to twist; **ból wykrzywił jej twarz** her face (was) contorted *lub* twisted with pain; **wykrzywiać się** *vr* (*o twarzy, ustach*) to contort, to twist; (*o człowieku*) to grimace, to make *lub* pull a face

**wykrzy|wić (-wię, -wisz)** *vb perf od* **wykrzywiać**

**wykrzywiony** *adj* contorted, twisted

**wykształ|cać (-cam, -casz)** (*perf* **-cić**) *vt* (*rozwijać*) to develop; (*nadawać kształt*) to shape; **wykształcać się** *vr* (*rozwijać się*) to develop; (*nabierać kształtu*) to form, to take shape

**wykształceni|e** (**-a**) *nt* education; **~ podstawowe** primary *lub* elementary (*US*) education; **~ średnie** secondary education; **~ wyższe** higher education; **(ona) jest z wykształcenia prawnikiem** she is a lawyer by profession
**wykształ|cić (-cę, -cisz)** (*imp* **-ć**) *vb perf od* **kształcić, wykształcać** ▷ *vt perf* to educate
**wykształcony** *adj* (*człowiek*) educated; (*narząd*) (fully-)developed
**wyk|uć (-uję, -ujesz)** *vb perf od* **kuć, wykuwać** ▷ *vt perf*: **~ coś (na blachę)** (*pot*: *Szkol*) to cram (*pot*), to swot up (*Brit*) (*pot*)
**wyku|pywać (-puję, -pujesz)** (*perf* **-pić**) *vt* (*cały zapas, nakład*) to buy up; (*swoją własność*) to buy back; (*przedsiębiorstwo*) to buy out; (*abonament, prenumeratę*) to take out; (*z lombardu*) to redeem; (*więźnia, jeńca*) to ransom; **wykupywać się** *vr* to buy o.s. out
**wykur|ować (-uję, -ujesz)** *vb perf od* **kurować**
**wykusz** (**-a, -e**) (*gen pl* **-y**) *m* (*Archit*) bay window
**wykuw|ać (-am, -asz)** (*perf* **wykuć**) *vt* (*z metalu*) to forge; (*z kamienia*) to sculpture, to sculpt; (*otwór, tunel*) to cut
**wykwalifikowany** *adj* (*położna, pomoc domowa*) qualified; **robotnik ~** skilled worker
**wykwater|ować (-uję, -ujesz)** *vt perf* to evict
**wykwintnie** *adv* exquisitely
**wykwintny** *adj* (very) fine, exquisite
**wyl|ać (-eję, -ejesz)** *vb perf od* **wylewać**
**wylans|ować (-uję, -ujesz)** *vb perf od* **lansować**
**wylat|ywać (-uję, -ujesz)** (*perf* **wylecieć**) *vi* to fly out; (*o dymie, gazie*) to escape; (*pot*: *o szybie*) to fall out; (*o korku, pocisku*) to fly; **~ w powietrze** to blow up; **piłka wyleciała przez okno** (*pot*) the ball went flying through the window; **wyleciało mi to z głowy** (*pot*) it slipped my mind; **wylecieć (z pracy)** (*pot*) to get the sack (*pot*)
**wyl|ąc się (-ęgnie)** (*pt* **-ągł, -ęgła, -ęgły**) *vb perf od* **wylęgać się**
**wyląd|ować (-uję, -ujesz)** *vb perf od* **lądować**
**wyl|ąg** (**-ęgu, -ęgi**) (*instr sg* **-ęgiem**) *m* (*wylęganie się*) hatch(ing); (*pisklęta*) brood, hatch
**wyle|c (-gnie)** (*pt* **-gł, -gła, -gli**) *vb perf od* **wylegać**
**wyl|ecieć (-ecę, -ecisz)** (*imp* **-eć**) *vb perf od* **wylatywać**
**wylecz|yć (-ę, -ysz)** *vb perf od* **leczyć**
**wyleg|ać (-a)** (*perf* **wylec**) *vi* (*książk*): **~ na ulice** to take to the streets
**wylegitym|ować (-uję, -ujesz)** *vb perf od* **legitymować**
**wyle|giwać się (-guję, -gujesz)** *vr* to loll (about); **wylegiwać się w łóżku** to have a lie-in
**wyle|w** (**-wu, -wy**) (*loc sg* **-wie**) *m*: **~ krwi do mózgu** cerebral hemorrhage, stroke
**wylew|ać (-am, -asz)** (*perf* **wylać**) *vt* (*płyn*) to pour (out); (*: rozlewać*) to spill; (*łzy*) to shed; (*drogę*) to pave; (*pot*: *pracownika*) to fire; (*: członka, ucznia*) to expel ▷ *vi* (*o rzece*) to overflow; **wylewać się** *vr* (*rozlewać się*) to spill; **woda wylewała się z wiadra** water ran out of the bucket, the bucket ran over
**wylewnie** *adv* effusivelly, profusely
**wylewny** *adj* effusive
**wyl|eźć (-ezę, -eziesz)** (*imp* **-eź**, *pt* **-azł, -azła, -eźli**) *vb perf od* **wyłazić**
**wylę|g** (**-gu, -gi**) (*instr sg* **-giem**) *m* = **wyląg**
**wylęg|ać się (-a)** (*perf* **-nąć, wyląc**) *vr* (*o ptakach*) to hatch; (*przen*: *o pomysłach*) to be hatched
**wylęgar|nia** (**-ni, -nie**) (*gen pl* **-ni**) *f* hatchery; (*przen*) hotbed
**wyl|ęgnąć się (-ęgnie)** (*pt* **-ągł, -ęgła, -ęgły**) *vb perf od* **lęgnąć się, wylęgać się**
**wylękniony** *adj* frightened
**wylicz|ać (-am, -asz)** (*perf* **-yć**) *vt* (*wymieniać*) to enumerate; (*obliczać*) to calculate, to work out; (*Boks*) to count out; **wyliczać się** *vr*: **~ się z czegoś** to account for sth
**wyliczan|ka** (**-ki, -ki**) (*dat sg* **-ce**, *gen pl* **-ek**) *f* counting-out rhyme
**wylicze|nie** (**-nia, -nia**) (*gen pl* **-ń**) *nt* (*obliczenie*) estimate, calculation; (*zestawienie*) specification
**wylicz|yć (-ę, -ysz)** *vb perf od* **wyliczać**
**wyliniały** *adj* (*pies*) mangy; (*futro, kołnierz*) shabby
**wylini|eć (-eje)** *vb perf od* **linieć**
**wyli|zać (-żę, -żesz)** *vb perf od* **wylizywać**; **wylizać się** *vr perf*: **~ się (z choroby)** (*przen*) to pull through (an illness)
**wyliz|ywać (-uję, -ujesz)** (*perf* **-ać**) *vt* (*miskę*) to lick clean; (*mleko*) to lick out
**wylog|ować się (-uję, -ujesz)** *vi perf* to log out
**wylos|ować (-uję, -ujesz)** *vb perf od* **losować** ▷ *vt perf* (*los*) to draw; (*nagrodę*) to win
**wylo|t** (**-tu, -ty**) (*loc sg* **-cie**) *m* (*lufy*) muzzle; (*tunelu*) mouth; (*ulicy*) exit; **na ~** straight through; **znać kogoś na ~** (*pot*) to know sb through and through *lub* inside out
**wylotowy** *adj*: **droga** *lub* **trasa wylotowa z Warszawy** a road out of Warsaw
**wylud|niać (-niam, -niasz)** (*perf* **-nić**) *vt* to depopulate; **wyludniać się** *vr* to become depopulated
**wylud|nić (-nię, -nisz)** (*imp* **-nij**) *vb perf od* **wyludniać**

W

**wyludniony** *adj* depopulated
**wyluz|ować się (-uję, -ujesz)** *vr perf* to chill out
**wyluzowany** *adj* (*pot*) laid-back, easy-going
**wyładni|eć (-eję, -ejesz)** *vi perf* to grow prettier
**wyład|ować (-uję, -ujesz)** *vb perf od* **wyładowywać**
**wyładowa|nie** (**-nia, -nia**) (*gen pl* **-ń**) *nt* (*towaru*) unloading; **~ elektryczne** electric discharge; **~ atmosferyczne** lightning
**wyładowany** *adj* (*bateria, akumulator*) dead
**wyładow|ywać (-uję, -ujesz)** (*perf* **-ać**) *vt* (*towar, statek, wagon*) to unload; (*frustracje, złość*) to vent; **wyładowywać się** *vr* (*o człowieku*) to let off steam; (*o baterii*) to run down; **wyładować się na kimś** to vent one's anger on sb
**wyładun|ek** (**-ku, -ki**) (*instr sg* **-kiem**) *m* unloading, disembarkation
**wyła|mać (-mię, -miesz)** *vb perf od* **wyłamywać**
**wyłam|ywać (-uję, -ujesz)** (*perf* **-ać**) *vt* (*drzwi*) to break down; (*zamek*) to force; (*ząb*) to break; **~ palce** to crack one's knuckles; **wyłamywać się** *vr* (*o szczeblu, zębie*) to break; (*przen*) to break ranks
**wyłani|ać (-am, -asz)** (*perf* **wyłonić**) *vt* (*kandydata, komisję*) to appoint; **wyłaniać się** *vr* to emerge
**wyła|pać (-pię, -piesz)** *vb perf od* **wyłapywać**
**wyłap|ywać (-uję, -ujesz)** (*perf* **-ać**) *vt* to catch
**wyławi|ać (-am, -asz)** (*perf* **wyłowić**) *vt* to fish out; (*przen: błędy*) to pick up
**wyła|zić (-żę, -zisz)** (*imp* **-ź**, *perf* **wyleźć**) *vt* (*pot*) to get out
**wyłącz|ać (-am, -asz)** (*perf* **-yć**) *vt* (*silnik, telewizor, światło*) to switch *lub* turn off; (*prąd, gaz, telefon*) to cut off; **~ kogoś/coś (z** *+gen*) to exclude sb/sth (from); **~ z prądu** *lub* **sieci** to unplug, to disconnect; **~ sprzęgło** to declutch; **nie wyłączając** *+gen* not excluding; **wyłączać się** *vr* (*Tel*) to hang up; **jak to się wyłącza?** how do you turn *lub* switch it off?; **~ się wzajemnie** to be mutually exclusive *lub* incompatible
**wyłączeni|e** (**-a**) *nt*: **z ~m** *+gen* excluding, exclusive of
**wyłącznie** *adv* exclusively, solely; **~ do twojej wiadomości** for your information only
**wyłączni|k** (**-ka, -ki**) (*instr sg* **-kiem**) *m* switch
**wyłącznoś|ć** (**-ci**) *f*: **mieć ~ na coś** to have exclusive rights to sth
**wyłączny** *adj* exclusive
**wyłączony** *adj* (switched *lub* turned) off
**wyłącz|yć (-ę, -ysz)** *vb perf od* **wyłączać**
**wyło|gi** (**-gów**) *pl* lapels *pl*
**wyło|m** (**-mu, -my**) (*loc sg* **-mie**) *m* (*w murze*) breach; (*w szeregach*) break; **~ w tradycji** a break with tradition
**wyło|nić (-nię, -nisz)** (*imp* **-ń**) *vb perf od* **wyłaniać**
**wył|owić (-owię, -owisz)** (*imp* **-ów**) *vb perf od* **łowić, wyławiać**
**wyłożony** *adj*: **~ słomą/papierem** lined with straw/paper; **~ kafelkami** tiled
**wył|ożyć (-ożę, -ożysz)** (*imp* **-óż**) *vb perf od* **wykładać**
**wyłu|dzać (-dzam, -dzasz)** (*perf* **-dzić**) *vt*: **~ coś (od kogoś)** to wheedle sth (out of sb)
**wyłu|dzić (-dzę, -dzisz)** (*imp* **-dź**) *vb perf od* **wyłudzać**
**wyłupiasty** *adj* (*oczy*) bulging
**wyłu|pić (-pię, -pisz)** *vt perf*: **~ komuś oczy** to gouge out sb's eyes
**wyłu|skać (-skam, -skasz)** *vb perf od* **wyłuskiwać**
**wyłus|kiwać (-kuję, -kujesz)** (*perf* **-kać**) *vt* (*groch*) to shell; (*ziarno*) to husk; (*przen: fakty, prawdę*) to pick out
**wyłuszcz|ać (-am, -asz)** (*perf* **-yć**) *vt* (*argumenty, racje*) to set forth
**wyłuszcz|yć (-ę, -ysz)** *vb perf od* **wyłuszczać**
**wyłysi|eć (-eję, -ejesz)** *vb perf od* **łysieć**
**wymac|ać (-am, -asz)** *vt perf* (*odszukać*) to feel for, to grope for
**wymach** (**-u, -y**) *m* swing
**wyma|chiwać (-chuję, -chujesz)** *vt +instr* (*kijem, ręką*) to swing; (*szablą*) to brandish
**wymag|ać (-am, -asz)** *vt*: **~ czegoś** (*domagać się*) to require sth; (*potrzebować*) to need sth, to require sth; **~ od kogoś czegoś** to require sth of *lub* from sb; **~ od kogoś by coś zrobił** to require sb to do sth
**wymagający** *adj* demanding
**wymaga|nia** (**-ń**) *pl* demands, requirements; **mieć duże ~** (*o człowieku*) to be (very) demanding
**wymagany** *adj* required
**wymarły** *adj* (*zwierzę*) extinct; (*dom, miasto*) deserted
**wymarsz** (**-u, -e**) *m* departure
**wymarzony** *adj* ideal, dream *attr*
**wymarz|yć (-ę, -ysz)** *vt perf*: **~ coś sobie** to set one's heart on sth
**wymaszer|ować (-uję, -ujesz)** *vi perf* to march out
**wymawi|ać (-am, -asz)** (*perf* **wymówić**) *vt* (*dźwięk, głoskę*) to pronounce; (*nazwę, wyraz*) to utter; **~ zaklęcie** to make a spell; **~ komuś coś** to reproach sb for sth; **~ komuś pracę/pokój** to give sb notice; **wymawiać się** *vr*: **~ się (tym, że ...)** to excuse o.s. (by saying that ...)

**wyma|z** (**-zu, -zy**) (*loc sg* **-zie**) *m* (*Med*) smear test
**wyma|zać** (**-żę, -żesz**) *vb perf od* **wymazywać**
**wymaz|ywać** (**-uję, -ujesz**) (*perf* **-ać**) *vt* (*rysunek, napis*) to rub out, to erase; (*Tech: nagranie*) to erase; **~ coś z pamięci** to blot out the memory of sth
**wymądrz|ać się** (**-am, -asz**) *vr* to act a wise guy
**wymeld|ować** (**-uję, -ujesz**) *vb perf od* **wymeldowywać**
**wymeldow|ywać się** (**-uję, -ujesz**) (*perf* **-ać**) *vr* to check out
**wymęcz|yć** (**-ę, -ysz**) (*pot*) *vt perf* (*zwycięstwo*) to scrape; (*referat*) to scrape together; (*osobę*) to tire out
**wymia|na** (**-ny, -ny**) (*dat* **-nie**) *f* exchange; (*rury, części*) replacement, change; (*Tenis*) rally; **~ walut** (foreign) exchange; **~ oleju** oil change; **~ towarowa** (*Ekon*) barter
**wymia|r** (**-ru, -ry**) (*loc sg* **-rze**) *m* dimension, measurement; **~ sprawiedliwości** (system of) justice; **czwarty ~** fourth dimension; **pracować w pełnym/niepełnym ~ze godzin** to work full/part time; **pełny ~ kary** full sentence; **najwyższy ~ kary** capital punishment; **wymiary** *pl* (*człowieka*) measurements; (*boiska, maszyny*) dimensions, measurements
**wymiat|ać** (**-am, -asz**) (*perf* **wymieść**) *vt* to sweep out
**wymie|niać** (**-niam, -niasz**) (*perf* **-nić**) *vt* to exchange; (*olej, rurę*) to replace, to change; (*nazwisko, tytuł*) to mention; (*wyliczać*) to list, to enumerate; (*pieniądze, walutę*) to change; **~ coś na coś** to exchange sth for sth; **wymieniać się** *vr*: **~ się czymś** to exchange *lub* trade sth
**wymienialnoś|ć** (**-ci**) *f* convertibility
**wymienialny** *adj* convertible
**wymie|nić** (**-nię, -nisz**) (*imp* **-ń**) *vb perf od* **wymieniać**
**wymieniony** *adj*: **wyżej/niżej ~** mentioned above/below
**wymienny** *adj* (*element*) replaceable; **handel ~** barter
**wymier|ać** (**-a**) (*perf* **wymrzeć**) *vi* to die out
**wymierny** *adj* measurable; (*Mat*) rational
**wymierz|ać** (**-am, -asz**) (*perf* **-yć**) *vt* (*długość, deskę*) to measure; (*podatek, opłatę*) to assess; (*karę*) to mete out; (*cios*) to deliver; **~ sprawiedliwość** to administer justice
**wymierz|yć** (**-ę, -ysz**) *vb perf od* **mierzyć, wymierzać**; **~ komuś policzek** to give sb a slap on the face
**wymiesz|ać** (**-am, -asz**) *vb perf od* **mieszać**
**wymi|eść** (**-otę, -eciesz**) (*imp* **-eć**, *pt* **-ótł, -otła, -etli**) *vb perf od* **wymiatać**
**wymi|ę** (**-enia, -ona**) (*instr sg* **-eniem**) *nt* udder
**wymięty** *adj* (*koszula, gazeta*) crumpled
**wymi|giwać się** (**-guję, -gujesz**) (*perf* **-gać**) *vr*: **wymigiwać się od czegoś** (*pot*) to evade sth
**wymij|ać** (**-am, -asz**) (*perf* **wyminąć**) *vt* to pass; **wymijać się** *vr* to pass by one another
**wymijająco** *adv* evasively, noncommittally
**wymijający** *adj* evasive, noncommittal
**wymi|nąć** (**-nę, -niesz**) (*imp* **-ń**) *vb perf od* **wymijać**
**wymiociny** (**-**) *pl* vomit *sg*
**wymiotny** *adj*: **środek ~** emetic
**wymiot|ować** (**-uję, -ujesz**) (*perf* **z-**) *vi* to vomit
**wymiot|y** (**-ów**) *pl* vomiting *sg*
**wymk|nąć się** (**-nę, -niesz**) (*imp* **-nij**) *vb perf od* **wymykać się**
**wymont|ować** (**-uję, -ujesz**) *vb perf od* **wymontowywać**
**wymontow|ywać** (**-uję, -ujesz**) (*perf* **-ać**) *vt* to remove
**wymo|wa** (**-wy**) (*dat sg* **-wie**) *f* (*Jęz*) pronunciation; (*znaczenie*) significance
**wymownie** *adv* meaningfully
**wymowny** *adj* (*cisza, gest, spojrzenie*) meaningful; (*tytuł*) telling
**wym|óc** (**-ogę, -ożesz**) (*pt* **-ógł, -ogła, -ogli**) *vt perf*: **~ coś na kimś** to extract sth from sb
**wym|óg** (**-ogu, -ogi**) (*instr sg* **-ogiem**) *m* requirement
**wymó|wić** (**-wię, -wisz**) *vb perf od* **wymawiać**
**wymówie|nie** (**-nia, -nia**) (*gen pl* **-ń**) *nt* (*z pracy*) notice; **dostawać (dostać** *perf*) **~** to be given notice; **składać (złożyć** *perf*) **~** to hand in one's notice
**wymów|ka** (**-ki, -ki**) (*dat sg* **-ce**, *gen pl* **-ek**) *f* (*wykręt*) excuse; (*wyrzut*) reproach; **robić** *lub* **czynić komuś wymówki** to reproach sb
**wym|rzeć** (**-rze**) (*pt* **-arł**) *vb perf od* **wymierać**
**wymu|sić** (**-szę, -sisz**) (*imp* **-ś**) *vb perf od* **wymuszać**
**wymusz|ać** (**-am, -asz**) (*perf* **wymusić**) *vt* (*pieniądze, zeznania, okup*) to extract (by force); **~ coś na kimś** to extract sth from sb; **~ na kimś zrobienie czegoś** to force sb to do sth; **~ pierwszeństwo przejazdu** to violate the right of way
**wymuszony** *adj* forced
**wymyk|ać się** (**-am, -asz**) (*perf* **wymknąć**) *vr* to slip out; **wymykać się (komuś z rąk)** to slip through (sb's hands); **wymykać się spod kontroli** to get out of control
**wymy|sł** (**-słu, -sły**) (*loc sg* **-śle**) *m* invention

W

**wymyśl|ać (-am, -asz)** *vt (perf* **-ić**) (*wynajdywać*) to think up; (*zmyślać*) to invent, to make up ▷ *vi*: **~ komuś** to swear at sb
**wymyślny** *adj* sophisticated, fancy *attr*
**wymyw|ać (-a)** (*perf* **wymyć**) *vt* (*o rzece*) to wash away
**wynagradz|ać (-am, -asz)** (*perf* **wynagrodzić**) *vt*: **~ coś komuś** to recompense sb for sth; **~ komuś stratę** to make up for sb's loss; **~ kogoś (za coś)** to reward sb (for sth)
**wynagrodze|nie** (**-nia, -nia**) (*gen pl* **-ń**) *nt* pay
**wynagr|odzić (-odzę, -odzisz)** (*imp* **-odź** *lub* **-ódź**) *vb perf od* **wynagradzać**
**wynaj|ąć (-mę, -miesz)** (*imp* **-mij**) *vb perf od* **wynajmować**
**wynajd|ywać (-uję, -ujesz)** (*perf* **wynaleźć**) *vt* to find
**wynaj|em** (**-mu**) (*loc sg* **-mie**) *m* (*lokalu*) renting; (*maszyny, samochodu*) hiring
**wynajęci|e** (**-a**) *nt* = **wynajem; do wynajęcia** (*mieszkanie, pokój*) to let, for rent (US); (*samochód*) for hire
**wynajm|ować (-uję, -ujesz)** (*perf* **wynająć**) *vt* (*robotnika, mordercę*) to hire; (*dom, pokój*) to rent, to let; (*samochód*) to hire, to rent
**wynalazc|a** (**-y, -y**) *m decl like f in sg* inventor
**wynalaz|ek** (**-ku, -ki**) (*instr sg* **-kiem**) *m* invention
**wynalezieni|e** (**-a**) *nt* invention
**wyna|leźć (-jdę, -jdziesz)** (*imp* **-jdź**, *pt* **-lazł, -lazła, -leźli**) *vb perf od* **wynajdywać** ▷ *vt perf* (*wymyślić*) to invent
**wynaturze|nie** (**-nia, -nia**) (*gen pl* **-ń**) *nt* degeneration
**wynaturzony** *adj* degenerated
**wynegocj|ować (-uję, -ujesz)** *vt perf* to negotiate
**wynędzniały** *adj* (*człowiek*) emaciated, wasted; (*twarz*) drawn
**wyni|eść (-osę, -esiesz)** (*imp* **-eś**, *pt* **-ósł, -osła, -eśli**) *vb perf od* **wynosić**
**wyni|k** (**-ku, -ki**) (*instr sg* **-kiem**) *m* result; (*konferencji, śledztwa*) result, outcome; (*meczu*) score; **w ~u czegoś** as a result of sth; **w ~u tego** as a result (of that), consequently
**wynik|ać (-a)** (*perf* **-nąć**) *vi*: **~ z czegoś** (*o sytuacji*) to result from sth; (*o konflikcie, sprawie*) to ensue sth; (*o wniosku*) to follow *lub* stem from sth; **wynika z tego, że ...** it follows that ...
**wynik|nąć (-nie)** (*pt* **-ł** *lub* **-nął, -ła, -li**) *vb perf od* **wynikać**
**wyniosłoś|ć** (**-ci**) *f* (*terenu*) elevation; (*człowieka*) haughtiness
**wyniosły** *adj* (*człowiek, spojrzenie*) haughty; (*postać*) towering, lofty
**wyniośle** *adv* loftily, haughtily
**wyniszcz|ać (-am, -asz)** (*perf* **-yć**) *vt* (*organizm, człowieka, kraj*) to devastate, to destroy; (*naród*) to destroy, to annihilate
**wyniuch|ać (-am, -asz)** *vt perf* (*pot: intrygę, spisek*) to nose out
**wynocha** *inv*: **~!** (*pot!*) out! (*pot*)
**wynos** *inv*: **danie na ~** a take-away (*Brit*) *lub* take-out (US) meal
**wyno|sić (-szę, -sisz)** (*imp* **-ś**, *perf* **wynieść**) *vt* (*w inne miejsce*) to take *lub* carry away; (*na zewnątrz*) to take *lub* carry out; (*balon, rakietę*) to carry up; (*Mat*) to amount to; **~ śmieci** to take out the rubbish (*Brit*) *lub* garbage (US); **~ kogoś na urząd/tron** to elevate sb to an office/the throne; **koszty/straty wyniosły 1000 funtów** the cost/damage amounted *lub* came to 1,000 pounds; **wynosić się** *vr* (*pot: odchodzić*) to clear out; **~ się ponad innych** to look down on others; **wynoś się (stąd)!** get out (of here)!
**wynot|ować (-uję, -ujesz)** *vt perf* to copy down
**wynu|dzić się (-dzę, -dzisz)** (*imp* **-dź**) *vr perf* (*pot*) to get very bored
**wynurz|ać (-am, -asz)** (*perf* **-yć**) *vt* (*głowę, rękę*) to stick out of the water; **wynurzać się** *vr* (*z wody*) to surface, to emerge; (*z bramy, ciemności*) to emerge
**wynurze|nie** (**-nia**) *nt* (*z wody*) surfacing; **wynurzenia** *pl* (*książk*) revelations *pl*
**wyobc|ować się (-uję, -ujesz)** *vr perf*: **wyobcować się (z** *+gen*) to isolate o.s. (from)
**wyobcowani|e** (**-a**) *nt* alienation
**wyobcowany** *adj*: **~ (z czegoś)** alienated *lub* isolated (from sth)
**wyobra|zić (-żę, -zisz)** (*imp* **-ź**) *vb perf od* **wyobrażać**
**wyobraź|nia** (**-ni**) *f* imagination; **(człowiek) bez** *lub* **pozbawiony wyobraźni** unimaginative (person); **widzieć coś oczyma wyobraźni** to see sth in one's mind's eye; **to działa na moją wyobraźnię** it appeals to my imagination
**wyobraż|ać (-am, -asz)** (*perf* **wyobrazić**) *vt* (*przedstawiać*) to represent; **~ sobie** to imagine; **nie wyobrażam sobie, żeby ...** I can't imagine that ...; **wyobraź sobie, że znów się spóźnił** he was late again, would you believe it?; **nie tak wyobrażam sobie ...** that's not my idea of ...
**wyobrażalny** *adj* conceivable, imaginable
**wyobraże|nie** (**-nia, -nia**) (*gen pl* **-ń**) *nt* (*pogląd*) idea; (*obraz, wizerunek*) image
**wyodręb|niać (-niam, -niasz)** (*perf* **-nić**) *vt* (*części*) to separate; (*substancję*) to isolate; (*fragment*) to mark off; **wyodrębniać się** *vr* to emerge

**wyodręb|nić (-nię, -nisz)** (*imp* **-nij**) *vb perf od* **wyodrębniać**
**wyolbrzy|miać (-miam, -miasz)** (*perf* **-mić**) *vt* to exaggerate
**wypacz|ać (-am, -asz)** (*perf* **-yć**) *vt* (*intencje, obraz*) to distort; (*charakter, drzwi*) to warp; **wypaczać się** *vr* (*o drzwiach, oknie*) to warp; (*o charakterze*) to get warped
**wypa|d (-du, -dy)** (*loc sg* **-dzie**) *m* (*wycieczka*) outing; (*Wojsk*) sortie; **zrobić ~ do miasta** (*pot*) to go to town (*pot*), to hit the town (*pot*)
**wypad|ać (-am, -asz)** (*perf* **wypaść**) *vi* to fall out; (*wybiegać*): **~ (z pokoju)** to burst out (of the room); (*przypadać*): **~ w czwartek** to fall on (a) Thursday; (*w wyliczeniach*): **wypada po dwa na głowę** it works out at two each; **wypadł Pani długopis** your pen has slipped, you dropped your pen; **dobrze/źle wypaść** (*o egzaminie, próbie, operacji*) to go well/badly; (*o człowieku, kandydacie*) to do well/badly; **wypadło mi z ręki** it fell *lub* dropped out of my hand; **wypadło mi z głowy** it slipped my mind; **(spóźnił się, bo) coś mu wypadło** (*pot*) (he was late because) something came up *lub* cropped up; **~ (nie)korzystnie w porównaniu z** *+instr* to compare (un) favourably (*Brit*) *lub* (un)favorably (*US*) with; **wypada na nich poczekać** we should wait for them, the proper thing to do is wait for them; **wypadało na nich poczekać** we should have waited for them; **wypada mi tylko cię ostrzec, że ...** it seems only right to warn you that ...; **nie wypada ci tam iść** you shouldn't go there; **nie wypada zadawać takich pytań** it is awkward to ask such questions; **wypada, żebyś sam to zrobił** you should do it yourself
**wypad|ek (-ku, -ki)** (*instr sg* **-kiem**) *m* (*katastrofa*) accident; (*zdarzenie, fakt*) event; (*przykład*) instance; **~ drogowy** traffic accident; **na ~ wojny/pożaru** in case of war/ fire; **w żadnym wypadku** on no account; **w tym wypadku** in that case; **w najlepszym/ najgorszym wypadku** at best/worst, in the best/worst (possible) case; **w wielu wypadkach** on many occasions; **na wszelki ~** just in case; **~ przy pracy** accident at work
**wypadkow|a (-ej, -e)** *f decl like adj* (*wynik*) product; (*Geom, Fiz*) resultant
**wypadkowoś|ć (-ci)** *f* accident rate
**wypak|ować (-uję, -ujesz)** *vb perf od* **wypakowywać**
**wypakow|ywać (-uję, -ujesz)** (*perf* **-ać**) *vt* to unpack
**wypal|ać (-am, -asz)** (*perf* **-ić**) *vt* (*papierosa*) to smoke; (*dziurę*) to burn; (*cegły*) to bake; (*znak*) to brand
**wypal|ić (-ę, -isz)** *vb perf od* **wypalać** ▷ *vi perf* (*wystrzelić*) to fire; **nie ~** (*o broni, planie*) to misfire; **wypalić się** *vr perf* to burn out
**wypapl|ać (-am, -asz)** *vt perf* (*pot*) to blab (*pot*)
**wypar|ować (-uję, -ujesz)** *vb perf od* **parować, wyparowywać** ▷ *vi perf* (*przen: zniknąć*) to vanish into thin air
**wyparow|ywać (-uje)** (*perf* **-ać**) *vi* to evaporate
**wyparz|ać (-am, -asz)** (*perf* **-yć**) *vt* (*butelkę*) to scald
**wypa|s (-su, -sy)** (*loc sg* **-sie**) *m* (*Rol*) grazing, pasturage
**wypas|ać (-am, -asz)** *vt* to graze, to pasture
**wypa|ść (-dnę, -dniesz)** (*imp* **-dnij**, *pt* **-dł**) *vb perf od* **wypadać**
**wypatrosz|yć (-ę, -ysz)** *vb perf od* **patroszyć**
**wypat|rywać (-ruję, -rujesz)** *vt imperf*: **~ kogoś/czegoś** to look out for sb/sth
**wypatrz|yć (-ę, -ysz)** *vt perf* (*wykryć*) to spot
**wypch|ać (-am, -asz)** *vb perf od* **wypychać**; **wypchać się** *vr perf*: **wypchaj się!** (*pot!*) get stuffed! (*pot!*)
**wypch|nąć (-nę, -niesz)** (*imp* **-nij**) *vb perf od* **wypychać**
**wypełniacz (-a, -e)** *m* filler
**wypeł|niać (-niam, -niasz)** (*perf* **-nić**) *vt* (*naczynie, dziurę*) to fill; (*druk, formularz*) to fill in *lub* out; (*rozkaz, zobowiązanie*) to fulfil (*Brit*), to fulfill (*US*); **wypełniać się** *vr*: **sala wypełniła się (ludźmi)** the room filled (up) (with people)
**wypeł|nić (-nię, -nisz)** (*imp* **-nij** *lub* **-ń**) *vb perf od* **wypełniać**
**wypełniony** *adj* full
**wyperswad|ować (-uję, -ujesz)** *vt perf*: **~ komuś coś** to persuade sb out of doing sth
**wypę|dzać (-dzam, -dzasz)** (*perf* **-dzić**) *vt* (*z domu*) to throw out; (*z kraju*) to drive out
**wypę|dzić (-dzę, -dzisz)** (*imp* **-dź**) *vb perf od* **wypędzać**
**wy|piąć (-pnę, -pniesz)** (*imp* **-pnij**) *vb perf od* **wypinać**
**wy|pić (-piję, -pijesz)** *vb perf od* **pić, wypijać**
**wypieczony** *adj*: **dobrze/słabo ~** light/brown crusted
**wypie|k (-ku, -ki)** (*instr sg* **-kiem**) *m* (*pieczenie*) baking; (*porcja*) batch; **wypieki** *pl* (*rumieńce*) flush; **dostać** (*perf*) **~ów** to flush, to blush
**wypielęgnowany** *adj* well-groomed
**wypieprz|yć (-ę, -ysz)** *vt perf* (*pot!: wyrzucić*) to dump (*pot*); **wypieprzyć się** *vr perf* (*pot!*) to take a spill (*pot*)
**wypier|ać (-am, -asz)** (*perf* **wyprzeć**) *vt* (*nieprzyjaciela*) to dislodge; (*konkurencję, towary*) to squeeze out; (*ciecz, ciało*) to displace;

W

**wypierać się** *vr +gen (ojczyzny, rodziny)* to deny, to disown; *(obietnicy, danego słowa)* to go back on
**wypieszczony** *adj* ship-shape
**wypiękni|eć (-eję, -ejesz)** *vi perf* to grow pretty
**wypij|ać (-am, -asz)** (*perf* **wypić**) *vt* to drink up
**wypin|ać (-am, -asz)** (*perf* **wypiąć**) *vt* (*wysuwać*) to stick out; **wypinać się** *vr* (*pot: wypinać pośladki*) to stick out one's bum (*pot*), to do a moonie (*pot*)
**wypi|s (-su, -sy)** (*loc sg* **-sie**) *m* (*wyciąg*) extract; **wypisy** *pl* (*Szkol*) reader
**wypi|sać (-szę, -szesz)** *vb perf od* **wypisywać**
**wypis|ywać (-uję, -ujesz)** (*perf* **-ać**) *vt* (*czek*) to make out, to write out; (*dyplom*) to fill out; (*zapisywać*) to write down; (*pisać*) to write; **~ kogoś ze szpitala** to discharge sb from (a) hospital; **wypisz, wymaluj!** (*pot: ten sam*) dead spit! (*pot*), spitting image! (*pot*); (*to samo*) exactly the same!; **wypisywać się** *vr* (*o długopisie*) to run out; **wypisać się (z czegoś)** to withdraw (from sth)
**wyplat|ać (-am, -asz)** (*perf* **wypleść**) *vt* to weave
**wyplą|tać (-czę, -czesz)** *vt perf* to disentangle; **wyplątać się** *vr*: **~ się (z czegoś)** to disentangle o.s. (from sth), to extricate o.s. (from sth)
**wyple|nić (-nię, -nisz)** (*imp* **-ń**) *vt perf* (*chwasty*) to kill; (*nawyki*) to stamp out, to eradicate
**wypl|eść (-otę, -eciesz)** (*imp* **-eć**, *pt* **-ótł, -otła, -etli**) *vb perf od* **wyplatać**
**wypl|uć (-uję, -ujesz)** *vb perf od* **wypluwać**; **wypluj to słowo!** (*pot*) don't even think it! (*pot*)
**wypluw|ać (-am, -asz)** (*perf* **wypluć**) *vt* to spit out
**wypła|cać (-cam, -casz)** (*perf* **-cić**) *vt*: **~ coś (komuś)** to pay (sb) sth, to pay sth (to sb); **~ pieniądze z banku** to draw *lub* withdraw money from a bank
**wypłacalnoś|ć (-ci)** *f* solvency
**wypłacalny** *adj* solvent
**wypł|acić (-acę, -acisz)** (*imp* **-ać**) *vb perf od* **wypłacać**
**wypła|kać (-czę, -czesz)** *vb perf od* **wypłakiwać** ▷ *vt perf*: **~ coś u kogoś** (*pot*) to soft-soap sb into sth (with tears) (*pot*)
**wypła|kiwać (-kuję, -kujesz)** (*perf* **-kać**) *vt*: **~ oczy** to cry one's eyes out; **wypłakiwać się** *vr* to have a good cry
**wypła|ta (-ty, -ty)** (*dat sg* **-cie**) *f* (*wypłacanie, należność*) payment; (*podjęcie pieniędzy*) withdrawal; (*też:* **dzień wypłaty**) payday; **dostawać (dostać** *perf*) **wypłatę** to get paid; **dokonać** (*perf*) **wypłaty** to make a withdrawal; **suma** *lub* **kwota do wypłaty** the amount to be paid
**wypłosz|yć (-ę, -ysz)** *vb perf od* **płoszyć** ▷ *vt perf* to scare away *lub* off
**wypłowiały** *adj* faded
**wypłowi|eć (-eje)** *vb perf od* **płowieć**
**wypłu|kać (-czę, -czesz)** *vb perf od* **płukać, wypłukać**
**wypłu|kiwać (-kuję, -kujesz)** (*perf* **-kać**) *vt* to wash away
**wypły|nąć (-nę, -niesz)** (*imp* **-ń**) *vb perf od* **wypływać**; (*pot*) to make a name for o.s
**wypływ|ać (-am, -asz)** (*perf* **wypłynąć**) *vi* (*o łodzi, statku*) to set sail; (*o pływaku*) to set off; (*wynurzać się*) to surface; (*wydobywać się*) to flow (out); (*wychodzić na jaw*) to surface; (*wynikać*) to follow; **~ w morze** to put (out) to sea; **~ na powierzchnię** to surface
**wypo|cić się (-cę, -cisz)** (*imp* **-ć**) *vr perf* to sweat a lot
**wypoci|ny (-n)** *pl* (*pej*) (worthless) scribble
**wypocz|ąć (-nę, -niesz)** (*imp* **-nij**) *vi perf* to get some rest
**wypoczęty** *adj* rested, well-rested
**wypoczyn|ek (-ku)** (*instr sg* **-kiem**) *m* rest
**wypoczynkowy** *adj* holiday *attr*; **komplet** *lub* **zestaw ~** (living-room) suite
**wypoczyw|ać (-am, -asz)** (*perf* **wypocząć**) *vi* to rest
**wypogadz|ać się (-a)** (*perf* **wypogodzić**) *vr*: **wypogadza się** it's clearing up
**wypomin|ać (-am, -asz)** (*perf* **wypomnieć**) *vt*: **~ coś komuś** to rub sb's nose in sth (*przen*)
**wypom|nieć (-nę, -nisz)** (*imp* **-nij**) *vb perf od* **wypominać**
**wypomp|ować (-uję, -ujesz)** *vb perf od* **wypompowywać**
**wypompow|ywać (-uję, -ujesz)** (*perf* **-ać**) *vt* to pump out
**wypornoś|ć (-ci)** *f* (*Żegl*) draught, displacement
**wyposaż|ać (-am, -asz)** (*perf* **-yć**) *vt*: **~ coś w** *+acc* to fit sth with; **~ kogoś w coś** to equip sb with sth
**wyposażeni|e (-a)** *nt* (*biura*) furnishings *pl*; (*pracowni, szpitala, żołnierza*) equipment; (*roweru, miksera*) accessories *pl*; **mieć coś na wyposażeniu** to be equipped with sth; **kuchnia z ~m** fully-equipped kitchen
**wyposażony** *adj*: **dobrze ~** well-equipped; **być ~m w coś** to be equipped with sth
**wypowiad|ać (-am, -asz)** (*perf* **wypowiedzieć**) *vt* (*słowa, życzenie*) to utter; (*poglądy*) to voice; **~ komuś (mieszkanie/ pracę)** to give sb notice, to give notice to sb;

**wypowiedzieć wojnę Polsce** to declare war on Poland; **wypowiadać się** *vr* to express one's opinion

**wypowiedze|nie** (**-nia, -nia**) (*gen pl* **-ń**) *nt* notice; **dostać** (*perf*) ~ to be given notice; **dać** (*perf*) **komuś** ~ to give sb notice, to give notice to sb; ~ **wojny** declaration of war

**wypowi|edzieć** (**-em, -esz**) (*imp* **-edz**) *vb perf od* **wypowiadać**

**wypowie|dź** (**-dzi, -dzi**) (*gen pl* **-dzi**) *f* (*stwierdzenie*) statement; (*komentarz*) comment

**wypożycz|ać** (**-am, -asz**) (*perf* **-yć**) *vt*: ~ **coś (komuś)** to lend sth (to sb); ~ **coś (od kogoś)** to borrow sth (from sb)

**wypożyczal|nia** (**-ni, -nie**) (*gen pl* **-ni**) *f*: ~ **książek** lending library; ~ **samochodów** car hire (*Brit*), automobile rental (*US*)

**wypożycz|yć** (**-ę, -ysz**) *vb perf od* **wypożyczać**

**wyprac|ować** (**-uję, -ujesz**) *vb perf od* **wypracowywać**

**wypracowa|nie** (**-nia**) *nt* (*metody, stylu*) development; (*Szkol: praca pisemna*) (*nom pl* **-nia**, *gen pl* **-ń**) essay, composition

**wypracow|ywać** (**-uję, -ujesz**) (*perf* **-ać**) *vt* (*metody, zasady*) to work out, to develop; (*nadwyżkę, zysk*) to earn, to make

**wy|prać** (**-piorę, -pierzesz**) *vb perf od* **prać**

**wypras|ować** (**-uję, -ujesz**) *vb perf od* **prasować**

**wyprasz|ać** (**-am, -asz**) (*perf* **wyprosić**) *vt*: ~ **kogoś (z pokoju/domu)** to ask sb to leave (a room/house); **wypraszam sobie!** I beg your pardon! (*expressing anger*); ~ **kogoś za drzwi** to show sb the door

**wypra|wa** (**-wy, -wy**) (*dat sg* **-wie**) *f* (*ekspedycja*) expedition; (*ślubna*) trousseau

**wypra|wiać** (**-wiam, -wiasz**) (*perf* **-wić**) *vt* (*bal*) to organize; (*przyjęcie*) to give, to throw; (*skórę*) to tan; (*gońca*) to dispatch; ~ **kogoś w podróż** to send sb on a journey; **co ty wyprawiasz?** (*pot*) what do you think you're doing? (*pot*); **wyprawiać się** *vr*: ~ **się w podróż** to go on a trip

**wypraw|ka** (**-ki, -ki**) (*dat sg* **-ce**, *gen pl* **-ek**) *f* (*też*: **wyprawka niemowlęca**) layette

**wypręż|ać** (**-am, -asz**) (*perf* **-yć**) *vt* (*grzbiet*) to arch; (*ramiona*) to stiffen; **wyprężać się** *vr* to stiffen

**wyproduk|ować** (**-uję, -ujesz**) *vb perf od* **produkować**

**wyprom|ować** (**-uję, -ujesz**) *vb perf od* **promować**

**wypro|sić** (**-szę, -sisz**) (*imp* **-ś**) *vb perf od* **wypraszać** ▷ *vt perf*: ~ **coś u kogoś** to coax sb into sth

**wyprost|ować** (**-uję, -ujesz**) *vb perf od* **prostować**

**wyprostowany** *adj* erect

**wyprowa|dzać** (**-dzam, -dzasz**) (*perf* **-dzić**) *vt* (*na zewnątrz*) to take out; (*twierdzenie, wzór*) to derive; ~ **psa (na spacer)** to take a dog for a walk, to walk a dog; ~ **samochód (z garażu)** to take the/a car out (of the garage); ~ **kogoś z błędu** to put sb straight; ~ **kogoś z równowagi** to make sb's blood boil; **wyprowadzać się** *vr* to move out

**wyprowa|dzić** (**-dzę, -dzisz**) (*imp* **-dź**) *vb perf od* **wyprowadzać**

**wyprowadz|ka** (**-ki, -ki**) (*dat sg* **-ce**, *gen pl* **-ek**) *f* removal

**wypró|bować** (**-uję, -ujesz**) *vb perf od* **próbować** ▷ *vt perf* (*człowieka, odwagę*) to try out

**wypróbowany** *adj* tried, tested

**wypróż|niać** (**-niam, -niasz**) (*perf* **-nić**) *vt* to empty; **wypróżniać się** *vr* to defecate

**wypróż|nić** (**-nię, -nisz**) (*imp* **-nij**) *vb perf od* **wypróżniać**

**wypróżnie|nie** (**-nia, -nia**) (*gen pl* **-ń**) *nt* bowel movement, defecation, motion (*Brit*)

**wypr|uć** (**-uję, -ujesz**) *vb perf od* **wypruwać**

**wypruw|ać** (**-am, -asz**) (*perf* **wypruć**) *vt* (*nici, podszewkę*) to unstitch; (*wnętrzności*) to rip (out); ~ **sobie** *lub* **z siebie żyły** *lub* **flaki** (*pot*) to break one's back (*pot*)

**wyprys|k** (**-ku, -ki**) (*instr sg* **-kiem**) *m* eczema

**wyprz|ąc** (**-ęgę, -ężesz**) (*imp* **-ęż** *lub* **-ąż**, *pt* **-ągł, -ęgła, -ęgli**) *vb perf od* **wyprzęgać**

**wyp|rzeć** (**-rę, -rzesz**) (*imp* **-rzyj**, *pt* **-arł**) *vb perf od* **wypierać**

**wyprzed|ać** (**-am, -asz**) *vb perf od* **wyprzedawać**

**wyprzedany** *adj* sold out; **„bilety wyprzedane"** "(all tickets) sold out"

**wyprzed|awać** (**-aję, -ajesz**) (*imp* **-awaj**, *perf* **-ać**) *vt* (*towar*) to clear ▷ *vr*: ~ **się z majątku** to sell up

**wyprzedaż** (**-y, -e**) *f* (*Handel*) (clearance) sale

**wyprze|dzać** (**-dzam, -dzasz**) (*perf* **-dzić**) *vt* (*jechać szybciej*) to pass, to overtake; (*być bardziej postępowym*) to be ahead of; ~ **swoją epokę** to be ahead of one's times

**wyprzedzani|e** (**-a**) *nt* (*Mot*) passing, overtaking; **„zakaz wyprzedzania"** "passing prohibited", "no passing (zone)"

**wyprzedzeni|e** (**-a**) *nt*: **z ~m** in advance; **z tygodniowym ~m** a week in advance

**wyprze|dzić** (**-dzę, -dzisz**) (*imp* **-dź**) *vb perf od* **wyprzedzać**

**wyprzęg|ać** (**-am, -asz**) (*perf* **wyprząc, -nąć**) *vt* (*konie*) to unharness; (*wóz*) to unhitch

**wyprz|ęgnąć** (**-ęgnę, -ęgniesz**) (*imp* **-ęgnij**, *pt* **-ęgnął** *lub* **-ągł, -ęgła, -ęgli**) *vb perf od* **wyprzęgać**

W

**wyp|snąć się (-snie)** *vr perf (pot)*: **wypsnęło mi się** I let it slip
**wypukłoś|ć (-ci, -ci)** *(gen pl* **-ci**) *f (ściany)* protuberance; *(terenu, pagórka)* swelling
**wypukły** *adj (kształt)* convex; *(czoło)* protruding
**wypunkt|ować (-uję, -ujesz)** *vt perf* to enumerate
**wypust|ka (-ki, -ki)** *(dat sg* **-ce**, *gen pl* **-ek**) *f (w ubraniu)* inset
**wypuszcz|ać (-am, -asz)** *(perf* **wypuścić**) *vt (ptaka, więźnia)* to set free, to release; *(powietrze, wodę)* to let out; **~ coś (z ręki)** to let go of sth; *(liście, pędy)* to send out; *(znaczek, pieniądze)* to issue; **~ coś na rynek** to put sth on the market; **wypuszczać się** *vr* to wander off
**wypu|ścić (-szczę, -ścisz)** *(imp* **-ść**) *vb perf od* **wypuszczać**
**wypych|ać (-am, -asz)** *vt (wyciskać) (perf* **wypchnąć**) to push (out); *(zwierzę) (perf* **wypchać**) to stuff
**wypyt|ywać (-uję, -ujesz)** *(perf* **-ać**) *vt*: **~ kogoś (o** *+acc*) to question sb (about)
**wyrabi|ać (-am, -asz)** *(perf* **wyrobić**) *vt (produkować)* to produce; *(ciasto)* to knead; *(charakter, wolę)* to develop; *(paszport, przepustkę)* to obtain; **~ sobie pozycję** to establish one's reputation; **~ sobie pogląd** *lub* **opinię** to form an opinion; **co ty wyrabiasz?** *(pot)* what do you think you're doing? *(pot)*; **wyrabiać się** *vr (kształtować się)* to develop; *(Tech: wycierać się)* to wear (off); **nie wyrobię się (do jutra)** *(pot)* I won't make it (by tomorrow)
**wyrachowani|e (-a)** *nt* calculation
**wyrachowany** *adj (człowiek)* calculating; *(posunięcie)* calculated
**wyrafinowani|e (-a)** *nt* sophistication
**wyrafinowany** *adj* sophisticated
**wyrast|ać (-am, -asz)** *(perf* **wyrosnąć**) *vt* to grow; **~ z czegoś** to outgrow sth, to grow out of sth; **wyrósł na przystojnego mężczyznę** he grew up to become a handsome man
**wyrat|ować (-uję, -ujesz)** *vt perf* to rescue, to save; **wyratować się** *vr perf* to save o.s.
**wyra|z (-zu, -zy)** *(loc sg* **-zie**) *m (słowo)* word; *(objaw)* sign; *(ekspresja)* expression; **~ twarzy** (facial) expression; **„~y uznania"** "congratulations"; **„~y współczucia"** "my sympathies"; **bez ~u** expressionless, blank; **pełen ~u** full of expression; **nad ~ (interesujący/piękny)** extraordinarily (interesting/beautiful); **dawać czemuś ~** to give voice to sth
**wyraziciel (-a, -e)** *(gen pl* **-i**) *m* mouthpiece *(przen)*
**wyra|zić (-żę, -zisz)** *(imp* **-ź**) *vb perf od* **wyrażać**
**wyrazistoś|ć (-ci)** *f (siła wyrazu)* expressiveness; *(przejrzystość)* clarity
**wyrazisty** *adj (gest, rysy)* expressive; *(nos, podbródek)* distinct
**wyraźnie** *adv (słyszeć, czytać)* clearly; *(zdenerwowany)* visibly; **(mówić) głośno i ~** (to speak) loud and clear; **~ go nie lubiła** you could tell she didn't like him
**wyraźny** *adj (pismo, rozkaz, błąd)* clear; *(odgłos, ślad, zapach)* distinct
**wyraż|ać (-am, -asz)** *(perf* **wyrazić**) *vt* to express; **~ zgodę (na coś)** to give one's assent (to sth); **~ coś słowami** to put sth into words; **~ swoje zdanie** to speak one's mind; **wyrażać się** *vr (wysławiać się)* to express o.s.; *(pot: przeklinać)* to swear; **~ się dobrze/źle o kimś** to speak highly/ill of sb; **~ się w czymś** to find expression in sth; **że się tak wyrażę** so to say
**wyraże|nie (-nia, -nia)** *(gen pl* **-ń**) *nt* expression, phrase; *(Mat)* expression
**wyr|ąb (-ębu, -ęby)** *(loc sg* **-ębie**) *m* tree felling
**wyrą|bać (-bię, -biesz)** *vb perf od* **wyrąbywać**
**wyrąb|ywać (-uję, -ujesz)** *(perf* **-ać**) *vt (drzewa, las)* to cut (down); *(dziurę)* to hack
**wyregul|ować (-uję, -ujesz)** *vb perf od* **regulować**
**wyremont|ować (-uję, -ujesz)** *vb perf od* **remontować**
**wyretusz|ować (-uję, -ujesz)** *vb perf od* **retuszować**
**wyreżyser|ować (-uję, -ujesz)** *vb perf od* **reżyserować**
**wyręcz|ać (-am, -asz)** *(perf* **-yć**) *vt*: **~ kogoś (w czymś)** to help sb out (in doing sth); **wyręczać się** *vr*: **~ się kimś** to have one's work done by sb else
**wyr|obić (-obię, -obisz)** *(imp* **-ób**) *vb perf od* **wyrabiać**
**wyrobiony** *adj (publiczność)* discerning; *(mechanizm)* worn
**wyrobis|ko (-ka, -ka)** *(instr sg* **-kiem**) *nt (w kopalni)* heading *(in a mine)*
**wyrocz|nia (-ni, -nie)** *(gen pl* **-ni**) *f* oracle
**wyrod|ek (-ka, -ki)** *(instr sg* **-kiem**) *m (pej)* villain
**wyrodny** *adj (pej)* wayward
**wyr|odzić się (-odzę, -odzisz)** *(imp* **-odź** *lub* **-ódź**) *vr perf* to degenerate
**wyro|k (-ku, -ki)** *(instr sg* **-kiem**) *m* verdict, sentence; **wykonać** *(perf)* **~** to carry out *lub* execute a sentence; **~i losu** twists of fate; **~i opatrzności** acts of providence; **~ śmierci** death sentence

**wyrok|ować (-uję, -ujesz)** (*perf* **za-**) *vi*: **~ o czymś** to decide sth; **~ w kwestii czegoś** to settle the question of sth
**wyro|snąć (-snę, -śniesz)** (*imp* **-śnij**, *pt* **wyrósł, wyrosła, wyrośli**) *vb perf od* **rosnąć, wyrastać** ▷ *vi perf* (*o cieście*) to rise
**wyrost** *m*: **na ~** (*obawy*) premature; (*ubrania*) outsized
**wyrost|ek** (**-ka, -ki**) (*instr sg* **-kiem**) *m* (*też*: **wyrostek robaczkowy**) appendix; (*młokos*) youngster
**wyrośnięty** *adj* (*chłopak*) big; (*ciasto*) well-risen
**wyrozumiałoś|ć** (**-ci**) *f* understanding
**wyrozumiały** *adj* understanding
**wyr|ób** (**-obu**) (*loc sg* **-obie**) *m* (*produkt*) (*nom pl* **-oby**) product; (*wyrabianie*) production; **wyroby** *pl* products *pl*; **wyroby cukiernicze** confectionery; **wyroby garncarskie** earthenware; **wyroby tekstylne** textiles; *patrz też* **wyrobić**
**wyrówn|ać (-am, -asz)** *vb perf od* **równać, wyrównywać**
**wyrówna|nie** (**-nia, -nia**) (*gen pl* **-ń**) *nt* (*rekompensata*) compensation
**wyrównany** *adj* even
**wyrównawczy** *adj* compensatory
**wyrównujący** *adj*: **wyrównująca bramka, ~ gol** equalizer
**wyrówn|ywać (-uję, -ujesz)** (*perf* **-ać**) *vt* (*wygładzać*) to level; (*ujednolicać*) to even out; (*rekompensować*) to compensate ▷ *vi* (*Futbol*) to equalize; **~ z kimś rachunki** (*przen*) to get even with sb; **wyrównywać się** *vr* (*stabilizować się*) to even *lub* level out
**wyróż|niać (-niam, -niasz)** (*perf* **-nić**) *vt* (*zwracać uwagę na*) to single out; (*wyodrębniać*) to distinguish; (*nagradzać*) to honour (*Brit*), to honor (*US*); **jury wyróżniło ...** the jury has highly commended ...; **wyróżniać się** *vr*: **~ się czymś** to be distinguished by sth
**wyróżniający** *adj* (*Szkol*) very good; **~ się** (*wybitny*) outstanding; (*cecha*) distinctive, distinguishing
**wyróż|nić (-nię, -nisz)** (*imp* **-nij**) *vb perf od* **wyróżniać**
**wyróżnie|nie** (**-nia, -nia**) (*gen pl* **-ń**) *nt* (*w konkursie*) honourable (*Brit*) *lub* honorable (*US*) mention; **dyplom z ~m** (*Uniw*) ≈ first class hono(u)rs
**wyróżni|k** (**-ka, -ki**) (*instr sg* **-kiem**) *m* (*książk*) distinguishing feature
**wyrusz|ać (-am, -asz)** (*perf* **-yć**) *vi* to set out *lub* off; **~ w podróż** to set out on a journey
**wyr|wać (-wę, -wiesz)** (*imp* **-wij**) *vb perf od* **rwać, wyrywać**
**wyr|yć (-yję, -yjesz)** *vb perf od* **ryć**
**wyryw|ać (-am, -asz)** (*perf* **wyrwać**) *vt* to pull (out); **wyrwał mi (z ręki) książkę** he snatched the book from my hand; **wyrwać komuś ząb** to pull out sb's tooth; **~ drzewo z korzeniami** to uproot a tree; **~ kogoś ze snu/z odrętwienia** to rouse sb from sleep/from torpor; **wyrywać się** *vr* (*z okrążenia*) to break free; (*z czyichś rąk*) to wrench o.s. free; (*z domu, pracy*) to get away
**wyryw|ki** (**-ków**) *pl*: **znać coś na ~** to know *lub* have sth off pat (*Brit*), to have sth down pat (*US*)
**wyrywkowo** *adv* randomly, at random
**wyrywkowy** *adj* (*badania*) random; **wyrywkowa kontrola** spot check
**wyrzą|dzać (-dzam, -dzasz)** (*perf* **-dzić**) *vt*: **~ komuś krzywdę/szkodę** to inflict harm/damage on sb; **wyrządzić komuś przykrość** to upset sb
**wyrze|c (-knę, -kniesz)** (*imp* **-knij**, *pt* **-kł**) *vt perf* (*książk*) to utter; **wyrzec się** *vb perf od* **wyrzekać się**
**wyrzecze|nie** (**-nia, -nia**) (*gen pl* **-ń**) *nt* sacrifice; **~ się czegoś** renunciation of sth
**wyrzek|ać się (-am, -asz)** (*perf* **wyrzec**) *vr* +*gen* (*zrywać z*) to renounce; (*wypierać się*) to disown
**wyrzeź|bić (-bię, -bisz)** *vb perf od* **rzeźbić**
**wyrzu|cać (-cam, -casz)** *vt* (*perf* **-cić**) (*pozbywać się*) to throw away *lub* out; (*wypędzać*) to throw out; (*ciskać*) to throw; **~ coś komuś** to reproach sb for sth; **~ śmieci** to throw the rubbish (*Brit*) *lub* garbage (*US*) away *lub* out; **wyrzucić kogoś za drzwi** to throw sb out (of) the door; **fale wyrzuciły go/to na brzeg** he/it was washed ashore; **wyrzucić kogoś z pracy** to fire *lub* sack sb; **wyrzucić kogoś ze szkoły** to expel sb from school
**wyrzu|cić (-cę, -cisz)** (*imp* **-ć**) *vb perf od* **wyrzucać**
**wyrzu|t** (**-tu, -ty**) (*loc sg* **-cie**) *m* (*piłki*) throw; (*ramion*) fling; (*karcąca uwaga*) reproach; **(mieć) ~y sumienia** (to be full of) remorse; **robić komuś ~y** to reproach sb
**wyrzut|ek** (**-ka, -ki**) (*instr sg* **-kiem**) *m*: **~ (społeczeństwa)** outcast
**wyrzut|nia** (**-ni, -nie**) (*gen pl* **-ni**) *f* launcher
**wyrzyg|ać (-am, -asz)** *vt perf* (*pot!*) to puke (up) (*pot!*); **wyrzygać się** *vr perf* (*pot!*) to puke (up) (*pot!*)
**wyrzyn|ać (-am, -asz)** (*perf* **wyrżnąć**) *vt* (*rzeźbić*) to carve; (*pot: zabijać*) to slaughter; **wyrzynać się** *vr*: **wyrzynają jej się ząbki** she's teething; **wyrzyna mu się pierwszy ząb** he's cutting his first tooth
**wyrż|nąć (-nę, -niesz)** (*imp* **-nij**) *vb perf od* **wyrzynać**; (*pot: uderzyć*) to bash (*pot*);

W

**wyrżnąć się** *vr* (*pot*): ~ **się w głowę** to bang one's head
**wys.** *abbr* (= *wysokość*) alt. (= *altitude*)
**wysa|dzać (-dzam, -dzasz)** (*perf* **-dzić**) *vt* (*z samochodu*) to drop (off); (*ze statku*) to disembark; (*dziecko*) to put on the potty; (*też*: **wysadzać w powietrze**) to blow up
**wysadzany** *adj*: ~ **czymś** inset *lub* inlaid with sth
**wysa|dzić (-dzę, -dzisz)** (*imp* **-dź**) *vb perf od* **wysadzać**
**wysącz|yć (-ę, -ysz)** *vb perf od* **sączyć**
**wysch|nąć (-nę, -niesz)** (*imp* **-nij**, *pt* **-nął** *lub* **wysechł, -ła, -li**) *vb perf od* **schnąć, wysychać**
**wysep|ka** (**-ki, -ki**) (*dat sg* **-ce**, *gen pl* **-ek**) *f* island; (*tramwajowa itp.*) traffic (*Brit*) *lub* safety (*US*) island
**wysfor|ować się (-uję, -ujesz)** *vr perf*: **wysforować się (na czoło)** to take the lead
**wysi|ać (-eję, -ejesz)** *vb perf od* **wysiewać**
**wysiad|ać (-am, -asz)** (*perf* **wysiąść**) *vi* (*z autobusu/pociągu*) to get off; (*z samochodu*) to get out; (*pot*: *psuć się*) to pack up (*pot*)
**wysiad|ywać (-uję, -ujesz)** *vt* (*perf* **wysiedzieć**) (*jaja*) to incubate, to brood ▷ *vi*: ~ **gdzieś** to spend hours (sitting) somewhere
**wysią|ść (-dę, -dziesz)** (*imp* **-dź**, *pt* **wysiadł, wysiadła, wysiedli**) *vb perf od* **wysiadać**
**wysiedl|ać (-am, -asz)** (*perf* **-ić**) *vt* (*lokatorów*) to evict; (*ludność*) to displace
**wysiedle|niec** (**-ńca, -ńcy**) *m* displaced person
**wysiedl|ić (-ę, -isz)** *vb perf od* **wysiedlać**
**wysie|dzieć (-dzę, -dzisz)** (*imp* **-dź**) *vb perf od* **wysiadywać**; (*wytrzymać*): **nie mogłem ~ na filmie** (*pot*) I couldn't sit through the film
**wysiew|ać (-am, -asz)** (*perf* **wysiać**) *vt* to sow
**wysięgni|k** (**-ka, -ki**) (*instr sg* **-kiem**) *m* jib
**wysię|k** (**-ku, -ki**) (*instr sg* **-kiem**) *m* (*Med*) exudation
**wysil|ać (-am, -asz)** (*perf* **-ić**) *vt*: ~ **mózg/pamięć** to rack one's brains/memory; ~ **słuch** to strain one's ears; **wysilać się** *vr* to strain *lub* exert o.s.; ~ **się, by coś zrobić** to strain to do sth; **nie wysilaj się!** (*pot*) don't bother!
**wysił|ek** (**-ku, -ki**) (*instr sg* **-kiem**) *m* effort; **bez (żadnego) wysiłku** without (any) effort, effortlessly; **zmuszać (zmusić** *perf*) **kogoś do wysiłku** (*o człowieku*) to push sb; (*o zadaniu*) to stretch sb; **wkładać (włożyć** *perf*) **w coś dużo wysiłku** to put a lot of effort into (doing) sth; **wysiłki** *pl* efforts *pl*
**wyska|kiwać (-kuję, -kujesz)** (*perf* **wyskoczyć**) *vi*: ~ **(przez okno/z auta)** to jump out (of the window/of the car); ~ **z szyn** to come off the track; **wyskoczę po gazetę** (*pot*) I'll pop out for the paper (*pot*); **wyskoczył z głupią uwagą/niezwykłą propozycją** (*pot*) he came out with a silly remark/an unusual proposal (*pot*)
**wysko|k** (**-ku, -ki**) (*instr sg* **-kiem**) *m* (*w górę*) jump; (*pot*) excess
**wyskokowy** *adj*: **napoje wyskokowe** booze
**wyskro|bać (-bię, -biesz)** *vb perf* ▷ *vt perf* to scrape; (*pot*: *zdobyć*) to scrape up
**wysku|bać (-bię, -biesz)** *vb perf od* **skubać, wyskubywać**
**wyskub|ywać (-uję, -ujesz)** (*perf* **-ać**) *vt* to pluck
**wy|słać[1] (-ślę, -ślesz)** (*imp* **-ślij**) *vb perf od* **wysyłać**
**wy|słać[2] (-ścielę, -ścielisz)** (*imp* **-ściel**) *vb perf od* **wyściełać**
**wysłanni|k** (**-ka, -cy**) (*instr sg* **-kiem**) *m* (*Pol*) envoy; (*Prasa*) correspondent
**wysławi|ać (-am, -asz)** *vt* to glorify; **wysławiać się** (*perf* **wysłowić**) *vr* to express o.s.
**wysł|owić się (-owię, -owisz)** (*imp* **-ów**) *vb perf od* **wysławiać się**
**wysłuch|ać (-am, -asz)** *vt perf* (*koncertu, wykładu, próśb*) to hear; ~ **kogoś do końca** to hear sb out
**wysłu|chiwać (-chuję, -chujesz)**; **musieć ~** +*gen* *vt* to have to listen to
**wysłu|ga** (**-gi, -gi**) (*dat sg* **-dze**) *f*: ~ **lat** seniority
**wysłu|giwać się (-guję, -gujesz)** *vr*: **wysługiwać się komuś** to lackey sb; **wysługiwać się kimś** to use sb
**wysłużony** *adj* well-worn
**wysmakowany** *adj* (*dekoracja, kompozycja*) tasteful
**wysmark|ać się (-am, -asz)** *vr perf* (*pot*) to blow one's nose
**wysmar|ować (-uję, -ujesz)** *vb perf od* **smarować**
**wysmaż|yć (-ę, -ysz)** *vt perf* (*mięso*) to fry; (*pot*: *napisać z trudem*) to put together
**wysmukły** *adj* slender
**wysn|uć (-uję, -ujesz)** *vb perf od* **snuć, wysnuwać**
**wysnuw|ać (-am, -asz)** (*perf* **wysnuć**) *vt* (*wniosek*) to draw; ~ **domysł** to surmise
**wysoce** *adv* highly
**wy|soki** (*comp* **-ższy**) *adj* high; (*człowiek, drzewo, szklanka*) tall; (*urzędnik*) high(-ranking); (*głos, ton*) high(-pitched); ~ **na 2 metry** 2 metres (*Brit*) *lub* meters (*US*) high; **W~ Sądzie!** Your Honour!
**wy|soko** (*comp* **-żej**) *adv* high (up); ~ **kogoś cenić** to rate sb highly; ~ **na niebie** high in the sky
**wysokociśnieniowy** *adj* high-pressure *attr*

**wysokogatunkowy** *adj* high quality *attr*
**wysokogórski** *adj* (*klimat, roślinność*) alpine; **turystyka wysokogórska** mountaineering; **sprzęt** ~ mountaineering equipment; **wspinaczka wysokogórska** alpinism
**wysokokaloryczny** *adj* high-calorie *attr*
**wysokoobrotowy** *adj*: **wiertarka wysokoobrotowa** high-speed drill; **silnik** ~ high-revolution engine
**wysokooktanowy** *adj*: **paliwo wysokooktanowe** high octane fuel
**wysokopienny** *adj* standard
**wysokoprężny** *adj*: **silnik** ~ diesel engine
**wysokoprocentowy** *adj*: **ruda wysokoprocentowa** high-grade ore; **wysokoprocentowe napoje alkoholowe** high-proof spirits
**wysokościomierz** (**-a, -e**) (*gen pl* **-y**) *m* altimeter
**wysokościo|wiec** (**-wca, -wce**) *m* (*pot*) high-rise
**wysokościowy** *adj*: **prace wysokościowe** work at heights
**wysokoś|ć** (**-ci**) *f* (*domu, drzewa, figury geometrycznej*) height; (*lotu*) (*nom pl* **-ci**) altitude; (*dźwięku, głosu, tonu*) (*nom pl* **-ci**) pitch; **mieć 20 metrów wysokości** to be 20 metres (*Brit*) *lub* meters (*US*) high; **na wysokości oczu** at eye-level; **na wysokości trzeciego piętra** at third floor level; **na wysokości 3000 m** at 3000 m above sea level; **na wysokości** *+gen* (*naprzeciwko*) at the same level as; **jaka jest ~ grzywny/temperatury?** what is the fine/temperature?; **jaka jest ~ nakładu?** how big is the input?; **opłata w wysokości 50 złotych** a fee of 50 zloty; **Wasza/Jego W~** Your/His Highness; **stawać (stanąć** *perf*) **na wysokości zadania** to rise to the occasion
**wysond|ować (-uję, -ujesz)** *vb perf od* **sondować**
**wys|pa** (**-py, -py**) (*dat sg* **-pie**) *f* island; **Wyspy Brytyjskie** the British Isles; **Wyspy Kanaryjskie** the Canary Islands *pl*, the Canaries *pl*
**wy|spać się (-śpię, -śpisz)** (*imp* **-śpij**) *vb perf od* **wysypiać się**
**wyspany** *adj*: **jestem ~** I (have) had a good night's sleep; **jesteś ~?** did you get enough sleep?, did you sleep well?
**wyspecjaliz|ować się (-uję, -ujesz)** *vb perf od* **specjalizować się**
**wyspecjalizowany** *adj* specialized, dedicated
**wyspiarski** *adj* (*naród*) insular, island-living
**wyspiarz** (**-a, -e**) (*gen pl* **-y**) *m* islander
**wysportowany** *adj* athletic
**wyspowiad|ać (-am, -asz)** *vb perf od* **spowiadać**
**wysprząt|ać (-am, -asz)** *vt perf* to tidy (up)
**wysprzedany** *adj* = **wyprzedany**
**wysr|ać się (-am, -asz)** *vr perf* (*pot!*) to have a crap (*pot!*)
**wys|sać (-sę, -siesz)** (*imp* **-sij**) *vb perf od* **wysysać** ▷ *vt perf*: **~ coś z palca** (*przen*) to dream sth up
**wystający** *adj* protruding
**wystar|ać się (-am, -asz)** *vr perf*: **wystarać się o coś** to arrange sth, to fix sth up; **wystarać się komuś o coś** to fix sb up with sth
**wystarcz|ać (-a)** (*perf* **-yć**) *vt*: **wystarczy czasu/łóżek** we have enough time/beds; **dwa krzesła wystarczą** two chairs will be enough *lub* will do; **czy 5 wystarczy?** will 5 be enough?; **wystarczyło ci pieniędzy?** did you have enough money?; **to wystarczy** that will do, that's enough; **wystarczy, że ktoś się pomyli, a plan się nie uda** one person's mistake is enough to make the plan fail; **wystarczy zadzwonić (, a przyjadę)** just call me (and I will come)
**wystarczająco** *adv*: **~ długi** long enough; **~ dużo** enough; **~ szybko** quickly enough
**wystarczający** *adj* sufficient
**wystarcz|yć (-y)** *vb perf od* **wystarczać**
**wystart|ować (-uję, -ujesz)** *vb perf od* **startować**
**wysta|wa** (**-wy, -wy**) (*dat sg* **-wie**) *f* (*malarstwa, mebli*) exhibition; (*psów, kotów*) show; (*sklepowa*) shop window
**wysta|wać (-ję, -jesz)** (*imp* **-waj**) *vi* (*sterczeć*) to protrude, to stick out; **~ pod czyimś domem** to stick around outside sb's house
**wystawc|a** (**-y, -y**) *f decl like f in sg* (*na targach, wystawie*) exhibitor; (*rachunku, czeku*) drawer
**wysta|wiać (-wiam, -wiasz)** (*perf* **-wić**) *vt* (*głowę, nos*) to poke (out); (*meble, butelkę*) to put *lub* take out(side); (*obrazy*) to exhibit; (*komedię*) to stage; (*paszport, świadectwo*) to issue; (*rachunek, czek*) to make out, to write out; (*kandydata*) to put up; (*Myślistwo*) to point; **~ kogoś na działanie czegoś** to expose sb to sth; **~ coś na licytację/sprzedaż** to put sth up for auction/sale; **wystawić kogoś do wiatru** to lead sb up the garden path; **~ kogoś na próbę** to put sb to the test ▷ *vr*: **~ się na coś** to expose o.s. to sth
**wystawiony** *adj*: **wystawione towary/eksponaty** goods/items on display
**wystawnoś|ć** (**-ci**) *f* lavishness, pomp
**wystawny** *adj* sumptuous
**wystawowy** *adj* exhibition *attr*; **salon/teren ~** showroom/showground; **okno wystawowe** shop window

W

**wystą|pić (-pię, -pisz)** *vb perf od* **występować** ▷ *vi perf*: **~ z klubu/organizacji** to leave a club/an organization
**wystąpie|nie** (**-nia**, **-nia**) (*gen pl* **-ń**) *nt* (*przemowa*) speech; (*pojawienie się*) appearance
**wysteryliz|ować (-uję, -ujesz)** *vb perf od* **sterylizować**
**wystę|p** (**-pu**, **-py**) (*loc sg* **-pie**) *m* (*impreza*) performance; (*udział*) appearance; (*krawędź*) ledge, projection; **występy** *pl* show
**występ|ek** (**-ku**, **-ki**) (*instr sg* **-kiem**) *m* misdemeanour (*Brit*), misdemeanor (*US*)
**występny** *adj* (*książk*) wicked
**występ|ować (-uję, -ujesz)** (*perf* **wystąpić**) *vi* to occur; (*zabierać głos*) to speak, to take the floor; (*TV, Film, Teatr*) to appear, to star; (*Sport*) to take part; (*o objawach*) to appear; **wystąpić na środek** to step out to the center; **wystąpić z szeregu** to drop out of line; **~ z koncertem/recitalem** to give *lub* hold a concert/recital; **~ przeciwko komuś/czemuś** to come out against sb/sth; **~ w obronie kogoś/czegoś** to come out in support of sb/sth; **~ z wnioskiem/krytyką** to present a proposal/critique; **wystąpić o odszkodowanie** to sue for damages; **~ (do kogoś) o coś** to apply (to sb) for sth; **„występują/wystąpili:"** (*Film*) "starring:"; **~ w roli** *lub* **charakterze kogoś** to act as sb; **~ w czyimś imieniu** to represent sb
**występowani|e** (**-a**) *nt* (*roślinności*) occurrence; (*objawów*) appearance; (*przypadków choroby, przestępstw*) incidence
**wystos|ować (-uję, -ujesz)** *vt perf* (*książk*) to send in, to submit
**wystraszony** *adj* frightened, scared
**wystrasz|yć (-ę, -ysz)** *vt perf* to scare, to frighten; **wystraszyć się** *vr perf* to get scared, to get frightened
**wystrojony** *adj* (*sala*) adorned; (*człowiek*) spruced up, dressed up
**wystr|ój** (**-oju**, **-oje**) *m* decor
**wystrych|nąć (-nę, -niesz)** (*imp* **-nij**) *vt perf*: **~ kogoś na dudka** to make a fool of sb
**wystrza|ł** (**-łu**, **-ły**) (*loc sg* **-le**) *m* firing, (gun) shot
**wystrzałowy** *adj* (*pot*) sharp (*pot*), snazzy (*pot*)
**wystrzeg|ać się (-am, -asz)** *vr*: **wystrzegać się kogoś/czegoś** to beware of sb/sth
**wystrzel|ać (-am, -asz)** *vt perf* (*zużyć: amunicję*) to use up; (*pozabijać*) to shoot (dead)
**wystrzel|ić (-ę, -isz)** *vb perf od* **wystrzeliwać** ▷ *vi perf* (*z karabinu, pistoletu*) to fire
**wystrzeliw|ać (-uję, -ujesz)** (*perf* **wystrzelić**) *vt* (*strzałę, pocisk*) to shoot; (*rakietę*) to launch ▷ *vi* (*z broni palnej*) to fire, to shoot; (*o rakiecie, iskrach*) to shoot; (*o broni*) to fire
**wystu|dzić (-dzę, -dzisz)** (*imp* **-dź**) *vb perf od* **studzić**
**wystyg|nąć (-nie)** *vb perf od* **stygnąć**
**wysublimowany** *adj* sophisticated, sublime
**wysu|nąć (-nę, -niesz)** (*imp* **-ń**) *vb perf od* **wysuwać**
**wysunięty** *adj* advanced; **~ posterunek** *lub* **wysunięta placówka** outpost; **(najbardziej) ~ na północ/wschód** northernmost/easternmost
**wysupł|ać (-am, -asz)** *vt perf* (*pot: pieniądze*) to shell out (*pot*)
**wysusz|yć (-ę, -ysz)** *vb perf od* **suszyć**
**wysuw|ać (-am, -asz)** (*perf* **wysunąć**) *vt* (*szufladę*) to pull out; (*rękę, głowę*) to stick out; (*stół, szafkę*) to move; (*propozycje, zarzuty, żądania*) to put forward; **wysuwać się** *vr* (*ukazywać się*) to appear; (*dawać się przesuwać*) to pull out; **płyta wysunęła mu się z ręki** the record slipped out of his hand; **~ się na czoło** *lub* **prowadzenie** to take the lead
**wyswobadz|ać (-am, -asz)** (*perf* **wyswobodzić**) *vt* to liberate, to free; **wyswobadzać się** *vr* to free o.s.
**wyswob|odzić (-odzę, -odzisz)** (*imp* **-ódź** *lub* **-odź**) *vb perf od* **wyswobadzać**
**wysych|ać (-a)** (*perf* **wyschnąć**) *vi* to dry up
**wysył|ać (-am, -asz)** (*perf* **wysłać**) *vt* to send; (*promienie, światło*) to send (out); **~ coś komuś** to send sth to sb, to send sb sth; **~ coś pocztą** to send sth by post (*Brit*) *lub* mail (*US*), to mail sth
**wysył|ka** (**-ki**, **-ki**) (*dat sg* **-ce**, *gen pl* **-ek**) *f* dispatch
**wysyłkowy** *adj*: **sprzedaż wysyłkowa** mail order; **firma wysyłkowa** mail-order firm *lub* company
**wysy|pać (-pię, -piesz)** *vb perf od* **wysypywać**
**wysypi|ać się (-am, -asz)** (*perf* **wyspać**) *vr* to get enough sleep; **dobrze się wyspać** to get enough sleep
**wysypis|ko** (**-ka**, **-ka**) (*instr sg* **-kiem**) *nt* (*małe*) dump; (*: duże*) landfill (site)
**wysyp|ka** (**-ki**, **-ki**) (*dat sg* **-ce**, *gen pl* **-ek**) *f* rash
**wysyp|ywać (-uję, -ujesz)** (*perf* **-ać**) *vt* (*piasek, śmieci*) to dump; **wysypać ścieżkę piaskiem** to sprinkle a path with sand; **wysypywać się** *vr*: **~ się (z** *+gen*) to spill out (of)
**wysys|ać (-am, -asz)** (*perf* **wyssać**) *vt* to suck (out)
**wyszal|eć się (-eję, -ejesz)** *vr perf* (*pot*) to have one's fling (*pot*), to sow one's (wild) oats (*pot*)
**wyszarp|nąć (-nę, -niesz)** (*imp* **-nij**) *vt perf*: **~ coś z kieszeni** to jerk *lub* pull sth out of one's pocket; **~ coś komuś z ręki** to tear *lub* wrench sth away from sb's hand

**wyszczegól|niać (-niam, -niasz)** (*perf* **-nić**) *vt* to detail, to specify
**wyszczegól|nić (-nię, -nisz)** (*imp* **-nij**) *vb perf od* **wyszczególniać**
**wyszczególnie|nie** (**-nia, -nia**) (*gen pl* **-ń**) *nt* detailed list, inventory
**wyszczer|bić (-bię, -bisz)** *vt perf* to chip
**wyszczerz|ać (-am, -asz)** (*perf* **-yć**) *vt*: **~ zęby (w uśmiechu)** to grin; **~ zęby/kły** (*o zwierzęciu*) to bare its teeth/fangs
**wyszczotk|ować (-uję, -ujesz)** *vb perf od* **szczotkować**
**wyszczupl|ać (-a)** (*perf* **-ić**) *vt*: **~ kogoś** to make sb look slimmer
**wyszczupl|eć (-eję, -ejesz)** *vi perf* to slim down
**wyszedł** *itd. vb patrz* **wyjść**
**wyszep|tać (-czę, -czesz)** (*imp* **-cz**) *vb perf od* **szeptać**
**wyszkoleni|e** (**-a**) *nt* training
**wyszkol|ić (-ę, -isz)** *vb perf od* **szkolić**
**wyszkolony** *adj* trained
**wyszli** *itd. vb patrz* **wyjść**
**wyszlif|ować (-uję, -ujesz)** *vb perf od* **szlifować**
**wyszła** *itd. vb patrz* **wyjść**
**wyszor|ować (-uję, -ujesz)** *vb perf od* **szorować**
**wyszper|ać (-am, -asz)** *vt perf* to dig out, to ferret out
**wyszpieg|ować (-uję, -ujesz)** *vt perf* to spy out
**wyszuk|ać (-am, -asz)** *vb perf od* **wyszukiwać**
**wyszukany** *adj* sophisticated, fine
**wyszu|kiwać (-kuję, -kujesz)** *vt* (*perf* **-kać**) (*kandydata*) to search out; (*słówka*) to look up; (*odkrywać*) to discover
**wyszu|mieć się (-mię, -misz)** *vr perf* (*pot*) to have one's fling (*pot*), to sow one's (wild) oats (*pot*)
**wysz|yć (-yję, -yjesz)** *vb perf od* **wyszywać**
**wyszy|dzać (-dzam, -dzasz)** (*perf* **-dzić**) *vt* to scoff at
**wyszy|dzić (-dzę, -dzisz)** (*imp* **-dź**) *vb perf od* **wyszydzać**
**wyszyk|ować (-uję, -ujesz)** *vb perf od* **szykować**
**wyszyw|ać (-am, -asz)** (*perf* **wyszyć**) *vt/vi* to embroider
**wyszywany** *adj* embroidered
**wyściel|ać (-am, -asz)** (*perf* **wysłać**) *vt*: **~ coś (czymś)** to line sth (with sth); (*czymś miękkim*) to pad sth (with sth)
**wyściełany** *adj* padded
**wyści|g (-gu, -gi)** (*instr sg* **-giem**) *m* race; **~ zbrojeń** the arms race; **~ z czasem** (*przen*) a race against time; **robić coś na ~i** to vie with each another to do sth
**wyścigowy** *adj*: **koń ~** racehorse; **samochód/rower ~** racing car/bike; **tor ~** (*konny*) racecourse (*Brit*), racetrack (*US*); (*samochodowy*) racetrack
**wyściół|ka** (**-ki**) (*dat sg* **-ce**) *f* lining
**wyśle|dzić (-dzę, -dzisz)** (*imp* **-dź**) *vt perf* to track down
**wyślę** *itd. vb patrz* **wysłać**
**wyśliz|giwać się (-guję, -gujesz)** (*perf* **-nąć** *lub* **-gnąć**) *vr* to slip (out); **talerz wyśliz(g)nął jej się z ręki** the plate slipped from her hand
**wyślizg|nąć się (-nę, -niesz)** (*imp* **-nij**) *vb perf od* **wyślizgiwać się**
**wyśli|znąć się (-znę, -źniesz)** (*imp* **-źnij**) *vb perf od* **wyślizgiwać się**
**wyśmi|ać (-eję, -ejesz)** *vb perf od* **wyśmiewać**
**wyśmienicie** *adv* (*udać się, spisać się*) excellently; **smakować ~** to taste delicious; **~!** excellent!
**wyśmienity** *adj* (*humor, nastrój*) excellent; (*deser*) delicious
**wyśmiew|ać (-am, -asz)** (*perf* **wyśmiać**) *vt* to jeer (at); **wyśmiewać się** *vr*: **~ się z kogoś** to make fun of sb
**wyśniony** *adj* (*książk*) dream *attr*
**wyśpiew|ać (-am, -asz)** *vb perf od* **wyśpiewywać**; **wyśpiewał wszystko** (*pot*) he gave everything away
**wyśpiew|ywać (-uję, -ujesz)** (*perf* **-ać**) *vt* to sing
**wyśrub|ować (-uję, -ujesz)** *vt perf* (*pot*: *ceny*) to inflate; (*normy*) to raise
**wyśrubowany** *adj* (*cena*) inflated, steep (*pot*); (*normy, wymagania*) exacting
**wyświadcz|ać (-am, -asz)** (*perf* **-yć**) *vt*: **~ komuś grzeczność** *lub* **przysługę** to do sb a favour (*Brit*) *lub* favor (*US*)
**wyświechtany** *adj* shabby, threadbare; (*dowcip*) stale, threadbare; (*frazes*) hackneyed
**wyświetlacz** (**-a, -e**) *m* (*Tech*) display; **~ ciekłokrystaliczny** LCD (= *liquid-crystal display*)
**wyświetl|ać (-am, -asz)** (*perf* **-ić**) *vt* (*film, przezrocza*) to project, to show; (*komunikat, informację*) to display; (*okoliczności, tajemnice*) to clear up, to elucidate
**wyświę|cać (-cam, -casz)** (*perf* **-cić**) *vt* to ordain
**wyświę|cić (-cę, -cisz)** (*imp* **-ć**) *vb perf od* **wyświęcać**
**wytacz|ać (-am, -asz)** (*perf* **wytoczyć**) *vt* (*beczkę*) to roll out; (*armatę, wóz*) to wheel out; (*argumenty, racje*) to bring forward; (*Tech*) to lathe; **wytoczyć komuś sprawę** *lub* **proces** to bring an action *lub* a suit against sb
**wytapi|ać (-am, -asz)** (*perf* **wytopić**) *vt* (*Tech*) to smelt

W

**wytarg|ować (-uję, -ujesz)** *vt perf* to negotiate (*by haggling*)
**wytarty** *adj* (*obicie, spodnie*) threadbare; (*przen: zwrot, slogan*) hackneyed
**wytarz|ać się (-am, -asz)** *vb perf od* **tarzać się**
**wytaszcz|yć (-ę, -ysz)** *vt perf* (*pot*) to lug out
**wytatu|ować (-uję, -ujesz)** *vb perf od* **tatuować**
**wytch|nąć (-nę, -niesz)** (*imp* **-nij**) *vi perf* to pause (*for breath*)
**wytchnieni|e** (**-a**) *nt* pause, break; **bez wytchnienia** without pausing for breath
**wytę|pić (-pię, -pisz)** *vb perf od* **tępić**
**wytęż|ać (-am, -asz)** (*perf* **-yć**) *vt* (*siły, słuch, wzrok*) to strain
**wytężony** *adj* strenuous
**wytk|nąć (-nę, -niesz)** (*imp* **-nij**) *vb perf od* **wytykać**
**wytłacz|ać (-am, -asz)** (*perf* **wytłoczyć**) *vt* (*napis, znak*) to imprint, to impress; (*olej, sok*) to press; (*Tech*) to extrude
**wytłaczany** *adj* embossed
**wytłocz|yć (-ę, -ysz)** *vb perf od* **tłoczyć, wytłaczać**
**wytłu|c (-kę, -czesz)** *vt perf* (*pot: pozabijać*) to wipe out (*pot*)
**wytłumaczalny** *adj* explicable
**wytłumaczeni|e** (**-a**) *nt* explanation
**wytłumacz|yć (-ę, -ysz)** *vb perf od* **tłumaczyć**
**wytłu|miać (-miam, -miasz)** (*perf* **-mić**) *vt* (*pomieszczenie*) to sound-proof; (*urządzenie*) to muffle
**wytłu|ścić (-szczę, -ścisz)** (*imp* **-ść**) *vt perf* to grease; (*Druk*) to typeset *lub* print in boldface
**wytnę** *itd. vb patrz* **wyciąć**
**wytocz|yć (-ę, -ysz)** *vb perf od* **wytaczać**
**wyto|p** (**-pu, -py**) (*loc sg* **-pie**) *m* (*Tech*) smelting
**wyto|pić (-pię, -pisz)** *vb perf od* **wytapiać**
**wytra|wiać (-wiam, -wiasz)** (*perf* **-wić**) *vt* (*Chem, Tech*) to etch
**wytrawny** *adj* (*oszust, polityk*) expert *attr*, master *attr*; (*wino, wódka*) dry
**wytrą|cać (-cam, -casz)** (*perf* **-cić**) *vt*: **~ komuś coś (z ręki)** to knock sth out of sb's hand; **wytrącić coś (z roztworu)** (*Chem*) to precipitate sth (from a solution); **wytrącić kogoś ze snu/z zamyślenia** to break sb's sleep/thoughts; **wytrącić kogoś z równowagi** to throw sb off balance; **wytrącać się** *vr* (*Chem*) to precipitate
**wytrą|cić (-cę, -cisz)** (*imp* **-ć**) *vb perf od* **wytrącać**
**wytrenowany** *adj* trained
**wytres|ować (-uję, -ujesz)** *vb perf od* **tresować**
**wytro|pić (-pię, -pisz)** *vt perf* to track (down)
**wytr|uć (-uję, -ujesz)** *vt perf* to kill off (*with poison*)
**wytrw|ać (-am, -asz)** *vi perf* to hold out, to last out; **~ w czymś** to persevere in sth
**wytrwale** *adv* persistently
**wytrwałoś|ć** (**-ci**) *f* persistence, perseverance
**wytrwały** *adj* persistent; **być ~m w czymś/w robieniu czegoś** to be persistent in sth/doing sth
**wytrych** (**-a** *lub* **-u, -y**) *m* skeleton key
**wytrys|k** (**-ku, -ki**) (*instr sg* **-kiem**) *m* (*ropy, wody*) gush, spurt; (*Fizjologia*) ejaculation
**wytrys|kiwać (-kuje)** (*perf* **wytrysnąć**) *vi* (*o ropie, wodzie*) to gush, to spurt (out)
**wytry|snąć (-śnie)** *vb perf od* **wytryskiwać**
**wytrza|snąć (-snę, -śniesz)** (*imp* **-śnij**) *vt perf* (*pot: pieniądze*) to come up with
**wytrząs|ać (-am, -asz)** *vt* (*perf* **-nąć**) (*piasek*) to shake (out); (*kieszeń*) to empty
**wytrzą|snąć (-snę, -śniesz)** (*imp* **-śnij**) *vb perf od* **wytrząsać**
**wytrze|bić (-bię, -bisz)** *vb perf od* **trzebić**
**wyt|rzeć (-rę, -rzesz)** (*imp* **-rzyj**, *pt* **-arł**) *vb perf od* **wycierać**
**wytrze|pać (-pię, -piesz)** *vb perf od* **trzepać, wytrzepywać**
**wytrzep|ywać (-uję, -ujesz)** (*perf* **-ać**) *vt* (*piasek, popiół*) to shake off; (*dywan*) to beat
**wytrzeszcz|ać (-am, -asz)** (*perf* **-yć**) *vt*: **~ oczy** (*pot*) to goggle (*pot*)
**wytrzeźwi|eć (-eję, -ejesz)** *vb perf od* **trzeźwieć**
**wytrzym|ać (-am, -asz)** *vb perf od* **wytrzymywać** ▷ *vi perf*: **nie ~** (*o moście, budowli*) to give way; (*o człowieku*) to lose one's cool
**wytrzymałoś|ć** (**-ci**) *f* endurance; (*Tech*) durability; **być u kresu wytrzymałości** to be at the end of one's tether
**wytrzymały** *adj* (*człowiek*) tough, resilient; (*materiał*) durable; (*sprzęt, urządzenie*) heavy-duty; **~ na coś** tolerant of sth; **~ na wstrząsy** shockproof
**wytrzymani|e** (**-a**) *nt*: **nie do wytrzymania** unbearable
**wytrzym|ywać (-uję, -ujesz)** (*perf* **-ać**) *vt* to bear, to stand ▷ *vi* to hold on; **nie ~ krytyki** not to hold water; **nie ~ porównania** not to stand comparison; **nie ~ próby czasu** not to stand the test of time; **nie mogę już tego wytrzymać** I can't stand it any longer; **wytrzymać do końca** to stick it out
**wytwarz|ać (-am, -asz)** (*perf* **wytworzyć**) *vt* (*meble, energię, jad*) to produce; (*atmosferę, sytuację*) to create; **wytwarzać się** *vr* to be formed *lub* created
**wytwarzani|e** (**-a**) *nt* production

**wytwornoś|ć** (**-ci**) *f* refinement
**wytworny** *adj* (*osoba, maniery*) refined; (*apartament, kapelusz*) smart
**wytw|orzyć (-orzę, -orzysz)** (*imp* **-órz**) *vb perf od* **wytwarzać**
**wytw|ór** (**-oru, -ory**) (*loc sg* **-orze**) *m* product, creation; **~ czyjejś wyobraźni** a figment of sb's imagination
**wytwórc|a** (**-y, -y**) *m decl like f in sg* producer
**wytwórczoś|ć** (**-ci**) *f*: **drobna ~** (*Ekon*) small-scale production
**wytwór|nia** (**-ni, -nie**) (*gen pl* **-ni**) *f* factory; **~ filmowa/płytowa** film/record company
**wytycz|ać (-am, -asz)** (*perf* **wytyczyć**) *vt* (*drogę, szlak*) to mark out; (*przen: kierunek, linię postępowania*) to lay
**wytyczn|a** (**-ej, -e**) *f decl like adj* guideline
**wytyk|ać (-am, -asz)** (*perf* **wytknąć**) *vt* (*wysuwać*) to stick out; **~ coś komuś** to reproach sb for sth; **~ kogoś palcami** (*przen*) to point a *lub* the finger at sb; **nie wytykając palcem** without naming (any) names
**wytyp|ować (-uję, -ujesz)** *vb perf od* **typować**
**wyuczony** *adj*: **zawód ~** (skilled) trade
**wyucz|yć (-ę, -ysz)** *vt perf*: **~ kogoś zawodu** to teach sb a trade; **wyuczyć się** *vr perf +gen* to learn
**wyuzdani|e** (**-a**) *nt* promiscuity
**wyuzdany** *adj* promiscuous
**wywabiacz** (**-a, -e**) (*gen pl* **-y**) *m*: **~ plam** stain remover
**wywa|biać (-biam, -biasz)** (*perf* **-bić**) *vt* (*plamy*) to remove; (*człowieka, zwierzę*) to lure
**wywal|ać (-am, -asz)** (*perf* **-ić**) *vt* (*pot: wyrzucać*) to throw out; (*drzwi*) to smash down
**wywalcz|yć (-ę, -ysz)** *vt perf* to win
**wywal|ić (-ę, -isz)** *vb perf od* **wywalać**; **wywalić się** *vr* (*pot*) to fall
**wywa|r** (**-ru, -ry**) (*loc sg* **-rze**) *m* (*z jarzyn, mięsa*) stock; (*z ziół*) infusion
**wyważ|ać (-am, -asz)** (*perf* **-yć**) *vt* (*drzwi*) to force, to break down *lub* open; (*Mot: koła*) to balance; **~ otwarte drzwi** (*przen*) to state the obvious
**wywi|ać (-eje)** *vb perf od* **wywiewać**
**wywia|d** (**-du, -dy**) (*loc sg* **-dzie**) *m* (*rozmowa*) interview; (*Pol, Wojsk*) intelligence; **przeprowadzać (przeprowadzić** *perf*) **~ z kimś** to interview sb; **udzielać (udzielić** *perf*) **~u** to give an interview
**wywiadowc|a** (**-y, -y**) *m decl like f in sg* (secret) agent
**wywiadowczy** *adj*: **służba wywiadowcza** intelligence service
**wywiadów|ka** (**-ki, -ki**) (*dat sg* **-ce**, *gen pl* **-ek**) *f* (*pot: Szkol*) parents-teacher meeting
**wywiad|ywać się (-uję, -ujesz)** *vr*: **wywiadywać się (o kogoś/coś)** to make inquiries (about sb/sth)
**wywią|zać się (-żę, -żesz)** *vb perf od* **wywiązywać się**
**wywiąz|ywać się (-uję, -ujesz)** (*perf* **-ać**) *vr* (*powstawać*) to ensue; **wywiązywać się z obowiązków** to do one's duty; **wywiązywać się z obietnic** *lub* **obietnicy** to deliver (the goods) (*przen*)
**wywi|edzieć się (-em, -esz)** *vr perf*: **wywiedzieć się (o kogoś/coś)** to find out (about sb/sth)
**wywier|ać (-am, -asz)** (*perf* **wywrzeć**) *vt* to exert; **~ nacisk** *lub* **presję na kogoś** to put pressure on sb, to bring pressure to bear on sb; **~ wpływ na kogoś/coś** to exert an influence on sb/sth; **wywrzeć dobre wrażenie na kimś** to make a good impression on sb
**wywier|cić (-cę, -cisz)** (*imp* **-ć**) *vb perf od* **wiercić**
**wywie|sić (-szę, -sisz)** (*imp* **-ś**) *vb perf od* **wywieszać**
**wywiesz|ać (-am, -asz)** (*perf* **wywiesić**) *vt* (*flagę*) to display; (*ogłoszenie*) to post up
**wywiesz|ka** (**-ki, -ki**) (*dat sg* **-ce**, *gen pl* **-ek**) *f* sign, notice
**wywi|eść (-odę, -edziesz)** (*imp* **-edź**, *pt* **-ódł, -odła, -edli**) *vb perf od* **wywodzić** ▷ *vt perf*: **~ kogoś w pole** (*przen*) to outwit sb
**wywietrz|eć (-eje)** *vi perf* to evaporate
**wywietrzni|k** (**-ka, -ki**) (*instr sg* **-kiem**) *m* ventilator
**wywietrz|yć (-ę, -ysz)** *vb perf od* **wietrzyć**
**wywiew|ać (-a)** (*perf* **wywiać**) *vt* to blow away
**wywi|eźć (-ozę, -eziesz)** (*imp* **-eź**, *pt* **-ózł, -ozła, -eźli**) *vb perf od* **wywozić**
**wywij|ać (-am, -asz)** *vt* (*kołnierz*) (*perf* **wywinąć**) to turn down; **~ czymś** to brandish sth
**wywi|nąć (-nę, -niesz)** (*imp* **-ń**) *vb perf od* **wywijać**; **wywinąć się** *vr*: **~ się od czegoś** to wriggle out of sth
**wywl|ec (-okę, -eczesz)** (*imp* **-ecz**, *pt* **-ókł, -okła, -ekli**) *vb perf od* **wywlekać**
**wywlek|ać (-am, -asz)** (*perf* **wywlec**) *vt* (*pot*) to drag (out); **wywlec coś (na światło dzienne)** (*przen*) to drag sth up
**wywłaszcz|ać (-am, -asz)** (*perf* **-yć**) *vt* (*chłopów*) to expropriate; (*tereny*) to dispossess
**wywnętrz|ać się (-am, -asz)** *vr*: **wywnętrzać się (przed kimś)** to pour out one's heart (to sb)
**wywniosk|ować (-uję, -ujesz)** *vb perf od* **wnioskować**

**wyw|odzić (-odzę, -odzisz)** (*imp* **-ódź**, *perf* **wywieść**) *vt*: ~ **coś od czegoś** to derive sth from sth; **wywodzić się** *vr*: ~ **się z** *lub* **od** *+gen* to come from, to derive from

**wywoł|ać (-am, -asz)** *vb perf od* **wywoływać**

**wywoławczy** *adj*: **cena wywoławcza** starting price; **sygnał** ~ (*Radio*) call sign *lub* signal

**wywoływacz** (**-a, -e**) (*gen pl* **-y**) *m* (*Fot*) developer

**wywoł|ywać (-uję, -ujesz)** (*perf* **-ać**) *vt* (*wzywać*) to call; (*powodować: przerażenie, podziw*) to evoke; (*: powstanie, rozruchy, dyskusję*) to trigger off; (*Fot*) to develop; (*duchy*) to invoke

**wyw|ozić (-ożę, -ozisz)** (*imp* **-oź** *lub* **-óź**, *perf* **wywieźć**) *vt* (*gruz, śmieci*) to remove; (*ludzi*) to take away; (*towary*) to export

**wywozowy** *adj*: **cło wywozowe** export duty

**wyw|ód** (**-odu, -ody**) (*loc sg* **-odzie**) *m* argument

**wyw|óz** (**-ozu, -ozy**) (*loc sg* **-ozie**) *m* (*gruzu, śmieci*) removal, disposal; (*towarów*) export

**wywrac|ać (-am, -asz)** (*perf* **wywrócić**) *vt* (*domy, drzewa*) to overturn; (*łódź*) to capsize; (*kieszenie*) to turn out; ~ **coś na lewą stronę** to turn sth inside out; **wywracać się** *vr* (*o człowieku, drzewie*) to fall (down); (*o przedmiocie*) to overturn; (*o łodzi*) to capsize

**wywrot|ka** (**-ki, -ki**) (*dat sg* **-ce**, *gen pl* **-ek**) *f* (*ciężarówka*) dumper (truck) (*Brit*), dump truck (*US*); (*pot: upadek*) fall

**wywrotny** *adj* top-heavy

**wywroto|wiec** (**-wca, -wcy**) *m* subversive

**wywrotowy** *adj* subversive

**wywró|cić (-cę, -cisz)** (*imp* **-ć**) *vb perf od* **wywracać**

**wyw|rzeć (-rę, -rzesz)** (*imp* **-rzyj**, *pt* **-arł**) *vb perf od* **wywierać**

**wywyższ|ać (-am, -asz)** (*perf* **-yć**) *vt* to extol; **wywyższać się** *vr* to put on airs

**wyzb|yć się (-ędę, -ędziesz)** (*imp* **-ądź**) *vb perf od* **wyzbywać się**

**wyzbyw|ać się (-am, -asz)** (*perf* **wyzbyć**) *vr* *+gen* (*książk*) to divest o.s. of

**wyzdrowi|eć (-eję, -ejesz)** *vi perf* to recover

**wyziew|y** (**-ów**) *pl* (*zapachy*) smells *pl*; (*opary*) fumes *pl*

**wyzię|biać (-biam, -biasz)** (*perf* **-bić**) *vt* to chill

**wyzio|nąć (-nę, -niesz)** (*imp* **-ń**) *vt perf*: ~ **ducha** to give up the ghost

**wyznacz|ać (-am, -asz)** (*perf* **-yć**) *vt* (*miejsce, termin*) to fix, to determine; (*osobę*) to appoint, to designate; (*obliczać*) to calculate; **wyznaczyć nagrodę** to set a prize

**wyznaczni|k** (**-ka, -ki**) (*instr sg* **-kiem**) *m* determinant

**wyznaczony** *adj* appointed

**wyzn|ać (-am, -asz)** *vt perf*: ~ **coś (komuś)** to confess sth (to sb)

**wyzna|nie** (**-nia, -nia**) (*gen pl* **-ń**) *nt* (*miłości, sekretu*) confession; (*religia*) religion; ~ **wiary** (*Rel*) profession of faith

**wyzn|awać (-aję, -ajesz)** (*imp* **-awaj**) *vt* (*filozofię, pogląd*) to subscribe to

**wyznawc|a** (**-y, -y**) *m decl like f in sg* (*Rel*) believer; (*zwolennik*) advocate

**wyznawczy|ni** (**-ni, -nie**) (*gen pl* **-ń**) *f* (*Rel*) believer; (*zwolenniczka*) advocate

**wyzuty** *adj*: ~ **z czegoś** deprived of sth

**wyz|wać (-wę, -wiesz)** (*imp* **-wij**) *vb perf od* **wyzywać**

**wyzwal|ać (-am, -asz)** (*perf* **wyzwolić**) *vt* to release; (*kraj, więźniów*) to liberate; **wyzwalać się** *vr* (*o kraju*) to be liberated; ~ **się z czegoś** to free o.s. of sth

**wyzwa|nie** (**-nia, -nia**) (*gen pl* **-ń**) *nt* challenge; **rzucać (rzucić** *perf*) **komuś/czemuś** ~ to challenge sb/sth

**wyzwisk|a** (**-**) *pl* abuse, curses *pl*; **obrzucać (obrzucić** *perf*) **kogoś ~mi** to hurl abuse at sb

**wyzwoleni|e** (**-a**) *nt* liberation; **ruch wyzwolenia kobiet** women's liberation movement

**wyzwoliciel** (**-a, -e**) (*gen pl* **-i**) *m* liberator

**wyzw|olić (-olę, -olisz)** (*imp* **-ól**) *vb perf od* **wyzwalać**

**wyzwolony** *adj* liberated

**wyzys|k** (**-ku**) (*instr sg* **-kiem**) *m* exploitation

**wyzyskiwacz** (**-a, -e**) (*gen pl* **-y**) *m* exploiter

**wyzys|kiwać (-kuję, -kujesz)** (*perf* **-kać**) *vt* to exploit

**wyzyw|ać (-am, -asz)** (*perf* **wyzwać**) *vt* (*wymyślać*): ~ **kogoś** to call sb names; ~ **kogoś na pojedynek** to challenge sb to a duel

**wyzywająco** *adv* provocatively

**wyzywający** *adj* provocative

**wyż** (**-u, -e**) *m* high, anticyclone; **wyż demograficzny** population boom

**wyżal|ać się (-am, -asz)** (*perf* **-ić**) *vr*: **wyżalać się przed kimś** to confide in sb; **wyżalać się na coś** to complain about sth

**wyż|ąć (-mę, -miesz)** (*imp* **-mij**) *vb perf od* **wyżymać**

**wyżeb|rać (-rzę, -rzesz)** *vt perf* to cadge (*Brit*), to mooch (*US*)

**wyżej** *adv comp od* **wysoko** ▷ *adv* (*w tekście*) above; **jak** ~ ditto

**wyż|eł** (**-ła, -ły**) (*loc sg* **-le**) *m a breed of a gun dog*

**wyżer|ać (-am, -asz)** (*perf* **wyżreć**) (*pot*) *vt* (*o zwierzęciu, człowieku*) to eat up; (*o kwasie*) to eat away (at)

**wyżer|ka** (**-ki, -ki**) (*dat sg* **-ce**, *gen pl* **-ek**) *f* (*pot*) blow-out (*pot*)

**wyżł|obić (-obię, -obisz)** (*imp* **-ób**) *vb perf od* **żłobić**

**wyżłobie|nie** (**-nia, -nia**) (*gen pl* **-ń**) *nt* groove

**wyż|reć (-rę, -resz)** (*imp* **-ryj**, *pt* **-arł**) *vb perf od* **wyżerać**

**wyższoś|ć** (**-ci**) *f* superiority

**wyższy** *adj comp od* **wysoki** ▷ *adj* (*szkolnictwo, wykształcenie, stopień*) higher; (*urzędnik*) high-ranking; (*pobudki*) high; **uczucia/cele wyższe** lofty sentiments/goals *lub* aims; **szkoła wyższa** college; **siła wyższa** an act of God; **stopień ~** (*Jęz*) comparative degree

**wyż|yć (-yję, -yjesz)** *vi* to survive; **~ z czegoś** (*pot*) to get by on sth; **wyżyć się** *vb perf od* **wyżywać się**

**wyżymacz|ka** (**-ki, -ki**) (*dat sg* **-ce**, *gen pl* **-ek**) *f* mangle, wringer

**wyżym|ać (-am, -asz)** (*perf* **wyżąć**) *vt* to wring

**wyży|na** (**-ny, -ny**) (*dat sg* **-nie**) *f* (*Geog*) upland, uplands *pl*; (*przen*) summit

**wyżynny** *adj* upland *attr*

**wyżyw|ać się (-am, -asz)** (*perf* **wyżyć**) (*pot*) *vr* to let off steam (*pot*); **wyżywać się na kimś** to take it out on sb

**wyży|wić (-wię, -wisz)** *vr perf* to feed; **wyżywić się** *vr perf* to subsist

**wyżywieni|e** (**-a**) *nt* food; **pełne/niepełne ~** full/half board

**wzajemnie** *adv* mutually, reciprocally; **pomagamy sobie ~** we help each other; **dziękuję, ~!** thank you, the same to you!; **~ wykluczające się teorie** mutually exclusive theories

**wzajemnoś|ć** (**-ci**) *f* mutuality, reciprocation; **miłość ze wzajemnością/bez wzajemności** requited/unrequited love

**wzajemny** *adj* mutual, reciprocal; **wzajemne oddziaływanie** interaction

**wz|bić (-biję, -bijesz)** *vb perf od* **wzbijać**

**wzbier|ać (-a)** (*perf* **wezbrać**) *vi* to rise

**wzbierze** *itd. vb patrz* **wezbrać**

**wzbij|ać (-am, -asz)** (*perf* **wzbić**) *vt* (*kurz, tumany*) to raise, to stir *lub* kick up; **wzbijać się** *vr* to rise

**wzboga|cać (-cam, -casz)** (*perf* **-cić**) *vt* to enrich; **wzbogacać się** *vr* (*o człowieku*) to grow rich; **~ się (o coś)** (*o kolekcji*) to be enriched (by sth)

**wzbog|acić (-acę, -acisz)** (*imp* **-ać**) *vb perf od* **wzbogacać**

**wzbrani|ać (-am, -asz)** (*perf* **wzbronić**) *vt*: **~ komuś czegoś** to forbid sb to do sth; **wzbraniać się** *vr*: **~ się przed czymś/robieniem czegoś** to shrink from sth/doing sth

**wzbro|nić (-nię, -nisz)** (*imp* **-ń**) *vb perf od* **wzbraniać**

**wzbroniony** *adj* prohibited; **„palenie wzbronione"** "no smoking"; **„wstęp ~"** "no entry"; **„obcym wstęp ~"** (*w terenie*) "no trespassing"; (*w biurze, sklepie*) "private"; (*w budynku wojskowym itp.*) "authorized personnel only"

**wzbu|dzać (-dzam, -dzasz)** (*perf* **-dzić**) *vt* (*ciekawość, entuzjazm, gniew*) to arouse, to stir up; (*Elektr*) to induce

**wzbu|dzić (-dzę, -dzisz)** (*imp* **-dź**) *vb perf od* **wzbudzać**

**wzburz|ać (-am, -asz)** (*perf* **-yć**) *vt* to agitate, to whip up; **wzburzać się** *vr* (*o morzu*) to be agitated; (*o człowieku, umyśle, tłumie*) to become agitated

**wzburzeni|e** (**-a**) *nt* agitation

**wzburzony** *adj* (*morze, woda*) agitated, troubled; (*człowiek, umysł*) agitated

**wzdąć (wezdmę, wezdmiesz)** (*imp* **wezdmij**) *vb perf od* **wzdymać**

**wzdę|cie** (**-cia, -cia**) (*gen pl* **-ć**) *nt* (*Med*) flatulence

**wzdłuż** *prep +gen* along ▷ *adv* (*przeciąć*) lengthways; **~ korytarza/ulicy** down the corridor/street; **~ i wszerz** all over

**wzdrag|ać się (-am, -asz)** *vr*: **wzdragać się przed czymś/zrobieniem czegoś** to flinch from sth/doing sth

**wzdryg|ać się (-am, -asz)** (*perf* **-nąć**) *vr* to flinch, to shudder

**wzdryg|nąć się (-nę, -niesz)** (*imp* **-nij**) *vb perf od* **wzdrygać się**

**wzdych|ać (-am, -asz)** (*perf* **westchnąć**) *vi* to sigh; **westchnął z ulgą** he heaved a sigh of relief; **~ do czegoś** (*przen*) to hanker after *lub* for sth

**wzdym|ać (-am, -asz)** (*perf* **wzdąć**) *vt* (*żagle*) to fill, to swell; (*policzki*) to puff out; (*brzuch*) to distend, to bloat; **wzdymać się** *vr* (*o żaglu*) to fill, to swell; (*o brzuchu*) to distend

**wze|jść (-jdzie)** (*pt* **-szedł, -szła, -szli**) *vb perf od* **wschodzić**

**wzgar|da** (**-dy**) (*dat sg* **-dzie**) *f* (*książk*) disdain, scorn

**wzgardliwy** *adj* disdainful, scornful

**wzgar|dzić (-dzę, -dzisz)** (*imp* **-dź**) *vb perf od* **gardzić** ▷ *vt perf*: **~ czymś** to turn one's nose up at sth

**wzgl|ąd** (**-ędu, -ędy**) (*loc sg* **-ędzie**) *m*: **pod względem czegoś** as regards sth; **ze względu** *lub* **przez ~ na kogoś/coś** for the sake of sb/sth, for sb's/sth's sake; **z tego względu** for that reason; **bez względu na coś** regardless of sth; **bez względu na to, ile** no matter how much; **mieć ~ na coś** to take

W

sth into consideration; **pod tym względem** in this respect; **pod pewnym względem** in some respect; **pod każdym/żadnym względem** in every/no respect; **w tym względzie** on that score, in that regard; **względem czegoś** with respect to sth; **względy** *pl* (*okoliczności, powody*) considerations; (*przychylność*) favours (Brit), favors (US); **względy bezpieczeństwa** safety reasons

**względnie** *adv* (*stosunkowo*) relatively, comparatively; (*albo*) or; (*znośnie*) fairly

**względnoś|ć** (**-ci**) *f* relativity; **teoria względności** theory of relativity

**względny** *adj* (*wartość, wysokość*) relative; (*cisza, spokój*) comparative; **zaimek ~** (*Jęz*) relative pronoun

**wzgór|ek** (**-ka, -ki**) (*instr sg* **-kiem**) *m* hillock; **~ łonowy** pubes

**wzgórz|e** (**-a, -a**) *nt* hill

**wziąć (wezmę, weźmiesz)** (*imp* **weź**) *vb perf od* **brać**

**wzierni|k** (**-ka, -ki**) (*instr sg* **-kiem**) *m* (*Med*) speculum

**wzięci|e** (**-a**) *nt* (*powodzenie*) popularity; **cieszyć się ~m** to enjoy great popularity; **mieć ~ (u kogoś)** to be popular (with sb); **dziewczyna/panna do wzięcia** an eligible girl

**wzięty** *adj* (much) sought after; **wszyscy inni razem wzięci** all the rest (of them) put together

**wzlat|ywać (-uję, -ujesz)** (*perf* **wzlecieć**) *vi* (*o ptakach, owadach*) to fly up; (*o samolocie, balonie, fajerwerku*) to rise

**wzle|cieć (-cę, -cisz)** (*imp* **-ć**) *vb perf od* **wzlatywać**

**wzlo|t** (**-tu, -ty**) (*loc sg* **-cie**) *m*: **~y** (*myśli*) flights; **~y i upadki** (*przen*) ups and downs

**wzmacniacz** (**-a, -e**) (*gen pl* **-y**) *m* amplifier

**wzmacni|ać (-am, -asz)** (*perf* **wzmocnić**) *vt* (*siły, zdrowie, człowieka*) to strengthen; (*ścianę, tamę, straże*) to reinforce, to strengthen; (*głos, impuls, sygnał*) to amplify; **wzmacniać się** *vr* (*nabierać sił*) to get stronger

**wzmag|ać (-am, -asz)** (*perf* **wzmóc**) *vt* (*czujność, represje, wysiłki*) to increase; **wzmagać się** *vr* (*o wietrze, burzy*) to strengthen; (*o upale, gniewie*) to increase; (*o walce, ostrzale*) to escalate

**wzmian|ka** (**-ki, -ki**) (*dat sg* **-ce**, *gen pl* **-ek**) *f*: **~ (o kimś/czymś)** mention (of sb/sth)

**wzmiank|ować (-uję, -ujesz)** *vt* (*książk*): **~ coś/o czymś** to mention sth

**wzmoc|nić (-nię, -nisz)** (*imp* **-nij**) *vb perf od* **wzmacniać**

**wzmocnie|nie** (**-nia**) *nt* (*umocnienie*) reinforcement, strengthening; (*dodatkowy element*) (*nom pl* **-nia**, *gen pl* **-ń**) reinforcement; **lek na ~** restorative drug, tonic

**wzmożony** *adj* increased

**wzm|óc (-ogę, -ożesz)** (*imp* **-óż**, *pt* **-ógł, -ogła, -ogli**) *vb perf od* **wzmagać**

**wznak** *adv*: **leżeć na ~** to lie supine

**wznawi|ać (-am, -asz)** (*perf* **wznowić**) *vt* (*dyskusję, obrady*) to resume, to reopen; (*publikację*) to reissue

**wznie|cać (-cam, -casz)** (*perf* **-cić**) *vt* (*ogień, pożar*) to start; (*kurz, tuman*) to stir up, to kick up; (*przen: bunt, niepokój*) to incite

**wznie|cić (-cę, -cisz)** (*imp* **-ć**) *vb perf od* **wzniecać**

**wzniesie|nie** (**-nia, -nia**) (*gen pl* **-ń**) *nt* hill

**wzni|eść (-osę, -esiesz)** (*imp* **-eś**, *pt* **-ósł, -osła, -eśli**) *vb perf od* **wznosić**

**wzniosłoś|ć** (**-ci**) *f* loftiness

**wzniosły** *adj* lofty

**wzniośle** *adv* loftily

**wzno|sić (-szę, -sisz)** (*imp* **-ś**) *vt* (*perf* **wznieść**) (*podnosić*) to raise; (*budować*) to erect; **~ okrzyk** to raise a shout; (*na czyjąś cześć*) to give a cheer; **~ toast za kogoś/coś** to propose a toast to sb/sth, to toast sb/sth; **wznosić się** *vr* (*o ramionach, ptaku*) (*perf* **wznieść**) to rise; (*o drodze, schodach*) to rise, to ascend; (*o budowli, górach*) to tower

**wzn|owić (-owię, -owisz)** (*imp* **-ów**) *vb perf od* **wznawiać**

**wznowie|nie** (**-nia, -nia**) (*gen pl* **-ń**) *nt* (*książki*) reissue; (*sztuki teatralnej*) revival

**wzorcowy** *adj* model *attr*

**wzor|ek** (**-ku, -ki**) (*instr sg* **-kiem**) *m* pattern; **we wzorki** patterned

**wzornict|wo** (**-wa**) (*loc sg* **-wie**) *nt*: **~ przemysłowe** industrial design

**wzor|ować się (-uję, -ujesz)** *vr*: **wzorować się na kimś** to model o.s. on sb

**wzorowy** *adj* model *attr*, exemplary; **wzorowe sprawowanie** (*Szkol*) good conduct

**wzo|rzec** (**-rca, -rce**) *m* (*schemat*) pattern; (*pierwowzór*) prototype; (*godny naśladowania*) exemplar; (*masy itp.*) standard

**wz|ór** (**-oru, -ory**) (*loc sg* **-orze**) *m* (*rysunek, deseń*) pattern; (*konfekcji, obuwia*) model; (*cnót, skromności*) paragon; (*przejrzystości, jasności*) model; (*Mat, Chem, Fiz*) formula; **brać ~ z kogoś** to follow sb's example; **na ~ czegoś** on the model of sth; **~ podpisu** specimen signature; **~ cnót** a paragon of virtue

**wzrast|ać (-am, -asz)** (*perf* **wzrosnąć**) *vi* (*o dochodach, liczbie, spożyciu*) to rise; (*o człowieku*) to grow up; (*o gorączce, gniewie, hałasie*) to grow

**wzrastający** *adj* rising, growing

**wzro|k** (**-ku**) (*instr sg* **-kiem**) *m* (*zmysł*) (eye) sight, vision; (*spojrzenie*) gaze, eyes *pl*; **mieć**

**dobry/słaby ~** to have good/poor eyesight; **stracić/odzyskać** *(perf)* **~** to lose/regain one's sight; **jeśli mnie ~ nie myli** unless my eyes deceive me

**wzroko|wiec** (**-wca, -wcy**) *m* visualizer

**wzrokowo** *adv* visually

**wzrokowy** *adj* (*pamięć, wrażenie*) visual; (*nerw*) optic; (*zaburzenia*) optical

**wzro|snąć (-snę, -śniesz)** (*imp* **-śnij**) *vb perf od* **wzrastać**

**wzro|st** (**-stu**) (*loc sg* **-ście**) *m* (*człowieka*) height; (*organizmu, roślin*) growth; **być niskiego/średniego** to be short/medium height; **być wysokiego ~u** to be tall; **mieć 1,80 ~u** to be 180 centimetres tall; **ile masz ~u?** how tall are you?; **~ płac** salary increase; **~ gospodarczy** economic growth

**wzrusz|ać (-am, -asz)** (*perf* **-yć**) *vt* (*człowieka*) to move; (*ziemię*) to loosen; **~ ramionami** to shrug (one's shoulders)

**wzruszający** *adj* moving

**wzrusze|nie** (**-nia, -nia**) (*gen pl* **-ń**) *nt* emotion; **~ ramion** a shrug (of the shoulders); **ogarnęło go ~** he was overcome with emotion

**wzruszony** *adj* moved

**wzw|ód** (**-odu, -ody**) (*loc sg* **-odzie**) *m* erection

**wzwyż** *adv* up(wards); **skok ~** high jump; **od 5 ~** 5 and over

**wzyw|ać (-am, -asz)** (*perf* **wezwać**) *vt* (*lekarza, pogotowie, policję*) to call; **~ kogoś (do sądu)** to cite sb, to summon sb (before the magistrate); **~ kogoś do zrobienia czegoś** to call on sb to do sth; **~ pomocy** to call for help

**wżarł** *itd. vb patrz* **weżreć się**

**wże|nić się (-nię, -nisz)** (*imp* **-ń**) *vr perf*: **wżenić się w bogatą rodzinę** to marry into a rich family; **wżenić się w majątek** to marry money

**wżer|ać się (-am, -asz)** (*perf* **weżreć**) *vr*: **wżerać się w** *+acc* to eat into

W

**X, x** *nt inv* (*litera*) X, x; **X jak Xantypa** ≈ X for Xmas

**Y, y** *nt inv* (*litera*) Y, y; **Y jak Ypsylon** ≈ Y for Yellow, ≈ Y for Yoke (*US*)

**yachtin|g** **(-gu)** (*instr sg* **-giem**) *m* = **jachting**

**yeti** *m inv* yeti, abominable snowman

# Zz

**Z, z**[1] *nt inv* (*litera*) Z, z; **Z jak Zygmunt** ≈ Z for zebra

SŁOWO KLUCZOWE

**z**[2]**, ze** *prep +gen* **1** (*punkt wyjścia*) from; **z domu/góry/drzewa** from home/above/a tree
**2** (*źródło*) from; **z prasy/książki/doświadczenia** from the press/the book/experience
**3** (*czas*) from; **z grudnia/ubiegłego roku** from December/last year; **list z trzeciego sierpnia** a letter of August 3; **z rana** in the morning
**4** (*zbiorowość*) from; **kolega ze szkoły** friend from school; **niektórzy z was** some of you
**5** (*przyczyna*) (out) of; **z głodu/wdzięczności** (out) of hunger/gratitude; **ni z tego, ni z owego** all of a sudden
**6** (*materiał*): **stół z drewna** a wooden table; **zrobiony z drewna/wełny** made of wood/wool; **bukiet z róż** a bunch of roses; **sok z czarnych porzeczek** blackcurrant juice
**7** (*pod względem*): **ona jest dobra z matematyki** she is good at maths; **on jest z zawodu ślusarzem** he is a locksmith by profession; **egzamin z angielskiego** an examination in English
**8** (*nasilenie*): **z całych sił** with all one's might; **z całego serca** wholeheartedly
▷ *prep +instr* **1** (*w towarzystwie*) with; **chodź ze mną** come with me
**2** (*z dodatkiem*) with; **kawa z mlekiem** coffee with milk; **chleb z masłem** bread and butter
**3** (*z zawartością*) of; **dzbanek z wodą** a jar of water; **skrzynka z narzędziami** a toolbox
**4** (*określenie rzeczownika*) with; **chłopiec z długimi włosami** a boy with long hair; **sklep z zabawkami** toyshop; **problemy z koncentracją** problems with concentration
**5** (*skutek*) with; **z powodzeniem** successfully; **z dobrym wynikiem** with a good result
▷ *prep +acc* (*mniej więcej*) about; **z godzinę/kilometr** about an hour/a kilometre (*Brit*) *lub* kilometer (*US*)

SŁOWO KLUCZOWE

**za** *prep +instr* **1** (*miejsce*) behind; **za drzewem/oknem** behind the tree/window; **za burtą** overboard; **za miastem** out of town
**2** (*następstwo*) after; **jeden za drugim** one after another, one by one
**3** (*cel czynności*) for, after; **tęsknić za kimś** to miss sb; **gonić za zyskiem** to seek profit
▷ *prep +acc* **1** (*miejsce*) behind; **schować się za drzewo** to hide behind a tree; **wyjechać za miasto** to go out of town
**2**: **chwycić** (*perf*) **kogoś za rękę** to take hold of sb's hand, to grab sb's hand
**3** (*cel czynności*) for; **walczyć za wolność** to fight for freedom; **wznosić (wznieść** *perf***) toast za czyjeś zdrowie** to drink (a toast) to sb's health
**4** (*po upływie jakiegoś czasu*) in; **za trzy godziny** in three hours; **za dwa lata** in two years' time; **jest za dziesięć piąta** it's ten to five
**5** (*w zamian za*) for; **kupiłem to za 5 złotych** I bought this for 5 zloty; **za to, że ...** in return for ...
**6** (*w zastępstwie*) in place of; **pracować za dwóch** to do the work of two
**7** (*funkcja*) as; **uchodzić za specjalistę** to be regarded as an expert; **służyć za przykład** to serve as an example; **przebrać się za goryla** to dress up as a gorilla
▷ *prep +gen* (*w czasie*) in, during; **za młodu** in one's youth; **za (panowania) króla Ryszarda** during the reign of King Richard
▷ *adv* **1** (*zbyt*) too; **za późno/wcześnie** too late/early; **za dużo ludzi** too many people; **on jest za młody na to stanowisko** he's too young for the post
**2** (*w zdaniach wykrzyknikowych*): **co za dzień!** what a day!

**zaabsorb|ować (-uję, -ujesz)** *vb perf od* **absorbować**
**zaabsorbowany** *adj* preoccupied
**zaadapt|ować (-uję, -ujesz)** *vb perf od* **adaptować**

**zaadopt|ować (-uję, -ujesz)** *vb perf od* **adoptować**
**zaadres|ować (-uję, -ujesz)** *vb perf od* **adresować**
**zaadresowany** *adj* addressed
**zaaferowany** *adj* preoccupied
**zaakcent|ować (-uję, -ujesz)** *vb perf od* **akcentować**
**zaakcept|ować (-uję, -ujesz)** *vb perf od* **akceptować**
**zaalarm|ować (-uję, -ujesz)** *vb perf od* **alarmować**
**zaangaż|ować (-uję, -ujesz)** *vb perf od* **angażować**
**zaangażowany** *adj* (*literatura*) committed, engaged
**zaapel|ować (-uję, -ujesz)** *vb perf od* **apelować**
**zaareszt|ować (-uję, -ujesz)** *vb perf od* **aresztować**
**zaatak|ować (-uję, -ujesz)** *vb perf od* **atakować**
**zaawansowany** *adj* advanced ▷ *m decl like adj* advanced learner; **kurs angielskiego dla ~ch** English course for advanced learners
**zabar|wiać (-wiam, -wiasz)** (*perf* **-wić**) *vt* to dye; **~ coś na czerwono** to dye sth red; **zabarwiać się** *vr*: **~ się na niebiesko** to turn blue
**zabar|wić (-wię, -wisz)** *vb perf od* **barwić, zabarwiać**
**zabarwieni|e** (**-a**) *nt* (*barwa*) tint; (*brzmienie głosu*) tone; (*przen: charakter*) overtone
**zaba|wa** (**-wy, -wy**) (*dat sg* **-wie**) *f* (*zajęcie*) play; (*gra*) game; (*bal*) party; **coś do zabawy** something to play with; **dla zabawy** for fun; **plac zabaw** playground; **przyjemnej zabawy!** have a good time!
**zaba|wiać (-wiam, -wiasz)** (*perf* **-wić**) *vt* to entertain; **zabawiać się** *vr* to amuse o.s.; **~ się czyimś kosztem** to make jokes at sb's expense
**zaba|wić (-wię, -wisz)** *vb perf od* **zabawiać**
**zabaw|ka** (**-ki, -ki**) (*dat sg* **-ce**, *gen pl* **-ek**) *f* toy; **sklep z ~mi** toyshop
**zabawny** *adj* amusing
**zabezpiecz|ać (-am, -asz)** (*perf* **-yć**) *vt* (*chronić*) to protect, to guard; (*czynić bezpiecznym*) to secure; (*Prawo*) to secure; **~ coś przed czymś** to guard sth against sth; **zabezpieczać się** *vr*: **zabezpieczyć się (przed czymś)** to protect o.s. (against sth); **zabezpieczyć się na przyszłość** to secure one's future
**zabezpiecze|nie** (**-nia, -nia**) (*gen pl* **-ń**) *nt* protection
**zabi|ć (-ję, -jesz)** *vb perf od* **zabijać** ▷ *vi perf* (*o zegarze*) to strike; (*o sercu*) to start pounding; **zabić się** *vr perf* (*odebrać sobie życie*) to kill o.s.; (*stracić życie*) to get killed
**zabie|c (-gnę, -gniesz)** (*imp* **-gnij**, *pt* **-gł**) *vb perf od* **zabiegać**
**zabie|g** (**-gu, -gi**) (*instr sg* **-giem**) *m* procedure; (*operacja*) (minor) operation; **~ przerwania ciąży** abortion; **zabiegi** *pl* endeavours *pl* (*Brit*), endeavors *pl* (*US*)
**zabieg|ać (-am, -asz)** *vi*: **~** (**zabiec** *perf*) **komuś drogę** to bar sb's way; **~ o coś** to strive for sth
**zabiegany** *adj* busy
**zabiegowy** *adj* (*oddział*) surgical; (*gabinet*) surgery *attr*
**zabier|ać (-am, -asz)** (*perf* **zabrać**) *vt* (*brać ze sobą*) to take; (*przynosić ze sobą*) to bring; (*usuwać*) to take away; (*podnosić*) to pick up; (*miejsce, czas*) to take; (*o autobusie, statku: mieścić*) to take; **~ coś komuś** to take sth away from sb; **~ komuś czas** to take up sb's time; **~ głos** to take the floor; **zabierać się** *vr*: **~ się do czegoś** to get down to sth; **zabieraj się stąd!** (*pot*) get out of here! (*pot*)
**zabij|ać (-am, -asz)** (*perf* **zabić**) *vt* to kill; (*okno, otwór, skrzynię*) to nail up; **~ czas** to kill time; **zabić komuś klina** (*pot*) to put sb on the spot (*pot*); **zabijać się** *vr* to kill one another; **~ się o coś** (*pot*) to fight for sth tooth and nail
**zabity** *adj* killed; **spać jak ~** to sleep like a log
**zabłą|dzić (-dzę, -dzisz)** (*imp* **-dź**) *vi perf* to lose one's way, to get lost
**zabłąk|ać się (-am, -asz)** *vr perf* to stray
**zabły|snąć (-snę, -śniesz)** (*imp* **-śnij**) *vi perf* (*wydać błysk*) to flash; (*zapalić się*) to come on; (*przen*) to shine; *patrz też* **błysnąć**
**zabobo|n** (**-nu, -ny**) (*loc sg* **-nie**) *m* superstition
**zabobonny** *adj* superstitious
**zabol|eć (-i)** *vi perf* to hurt
**zaborc|a** (**-y, -y**) *m decl like f in sg* conqueror
**zaborczoś|ć** (**-ci**) *f* possessiveness
**zaborczy** *adj* (*polityka, władza*) aggressive; (*człowiek, charakter, miłość*) possessive
**zabójc|a** (**-y, -y**) *m decl like f in sg* killer, assassin
**zabójczy** *adj* (*kula, cios*) lethal, fatal; (*klimat, praca, tryb życia*) destructive; (*pot: uśmiech, spojrzenie*) seductive
**zabójst|wo** (**-wa, -wa**) (*loc sg* **-wie**) *nt* killing, assassination; **usiłowanie zabójstwa** attempted murder
**zab|ór** (**-oru, -ory**) (*loc sg* **-orze**) *m* (*przywłaszczenie*) seizure; (*Hist*) annexation
**za|brać (-biorę, -bierzesz)** *vb perf od* **zabierać**; **zabrać się** *vr perf*: **~ się z kimś** (*pot*) to get a lift from sb (*pot*)

**zabrak|nąć (-nie)** (*pt* **-ło**) *vi perf*: **zabrakło nam chleba/pieniędzy** we've run out of bread/money
**zabrani|ać (-am, -asz)** (*perf* **zabronić**) *vt*: **~ czegoś** to forbid *lub* prohibit sth; **~ komuś robić coś** to forbid sb to do sth, to prohibit sb from doing sth; **zabrania się palenia** smoking prohibited, no smoking
**zabro|nić (-nię, -nisz)** (*imp* **-ń**) *vb perf od* **zabraniać**
**zabroniony** *adj* prohibited; **przejście zabronione** no entry
**zabru|dzić (-dzę, -dzisz)** (*imp* **-dź**) *vb perf od* **brudzić**
**zabrz|mieć (-mi)** *vi perf* to resound
**zabudo|wa (-wy)** (*dat sg* **-wie**) *f* (*zabudowywanie*) development; (*budynki*) buildings *pl*
**zabud|ować (-uję, -ujesz)** *vb perf od* **zabudowywać**
**zabudowa|nia** (**-ń**) *pl* buildings *pl*
**zabudowany** *adj*: **teren ~** built-up area
**zabudow|ywać (-uję, -ujesz)** (*perf* **-ać**) *vt* (*teren*) to develop; (*ścianę, kuchnię*) to furnish
**zaburz|ać (-am, -asz)** (*perf* **-yć**) *vt* (*równowagę*) to upset; (*spokój*) to disturb
**zaburze|nia** (**-ń**) *pl* (*psychiczne*) disturbance; (*żołądkowe*) disorder, upset; (*atmosferyczne*) disturbance
**zabyt|ek** (**-ku, -ki**) (*instr sg* **-kiem**) *m* (historic) monument; **zabytki przyrody** monuments of nature
**zabytkowy** *adj* (*budynek*) historic; (*mebel*) antique
**zach.** *abbr* (= *zachodni*) W. (= *West, western*)
**zachcian|ka (-ki, -ki)** (*dat sg* **-ce**, *gen pl* **-ek**) *f* whim
**zach|cieć się (-ce)** *vb perf od* **zachciewać się**
**zachciew|ać się (-a)** (*perf* **zachcieć**) *vi*: **zachciało mi się spać/jeść** I got sleepy/ hungry
**zachę|cać (-cam, -casz)** (*perf* **-cić**) *vt*: **~ kogoś do czegoś** to encourage sb to do sth
**zachęcająco** *adv* encouragingly, invitingly
**zachęcający** *adj* encouraging, inviting
**zachę|cić (-cę, -cisz)** (*imp* **-ć**) *vb perf od* **zachęcać**
**zachę|ta** (**-ty, -ty**) (*dat sg* **-cie**) *f* encouragement, incentive; **~ do pracy/ nauki** incentive to work/study; **dawać (dać** *perf***) komuś zachętę do czegoś** to provide sb with an incentive to do sth
**zachłannoś|ć** (**-ci**) *f* avarice, avariciousness
**zachłanny** *adj* avaricious, acquisitive
**zachły|snąć się (-snę, -śniesz)** (*imp* **-śnij**) *vb perf od* **zachłystywać się**
**zachłyst|ywać się (-uję, -ujesz)** (*perf* **zachłysnąć**) *vr* to choke; **zachłystywać się czymś** (*przen*) to relish sth
**zachmurzeni|e** (**-a**) *nt* clouds *pl*
**zachmurzony** *adj* clouded
**zachmurz|yć się (-ę, -ysz)** *vr perf* (*o niebie, twarzy*) to cloud over; (*o człowieku*) to become gloomy
**zachodni** *adj* (*kierunek*) west, western; (*wiatr*) west, westerly; (*państwa, kultura, prasa, półkula*) western; **Europa Z~a** Western Europe; **Indie Z~e** the West Indies; **~a Polska** the west of Poland, western Poland
**zacho|dzić (-dzę, -dzisz)** (*imp* **-dź**, *perf* **zajść**) *vt*: **~ kogoś** to steal on sb ▷ *vi* (*o słońcu, księżycu*) to set; (*docierać*) to get; (*odwiedzać*) to look *lub* drop in; (*o zdarzeniu, pomyłce*) to occur; **~ na siebie** to overlap; **~ w głowę** to rack one's brains; **zajść daleko** *lub* **wysoko** to get ahead (in life); **zajść w ciążę** to become pregnant
**zachor|ować (-uję, -ujesz)** *vi perf* to be taken ill, to fall ill
**zachowani|e** (**-a**) *nt* (*sposób bycia*) behaviour (*Brit*), behavior (*US*); (*maniery*) manners *pl*; (*uchronienie*) preservation
**zachowawczoś|ć** (**-ci**) *f* conservatism
**zachowawczy** *adj* conservative; **instynkt ~** the instinct for self-preservation
**zachow|ywać (-uję, -ujesz)** (*perf* **-ać**) *vt* (*pamiątki, rzeczy*) to retain, to keep; (*siły, wdzięczność*) to retain; (*tradycje*) to preserve; **~ spokój** to keep one's cool; **zachować coś dla siebie** to keep sth to o.s.; **zachowywać się** *vr* (*postępować*) to act, to behave; (*o dokumentach, tradycjach, legendach*) to survive; **zachować się przy życiu** to stay alive
**zach|ód** (**-odu, -ody**) (*loc sg* **-odzie**) *m* (*też*: **zachód słońca**) sunset; (*strona świata*) west; (*Europa Zachodnia*) the West; **na ~ od** *+gen* west of; **Dziki Z~** Wild West; **coś jest niewarte zachodu** sth isn't worth the trouble
**zachrypnięty** *adj* hoarse
**zachwal|ać (-am, -asz)** *vt* to praise
**zachwi|ać (-eję, -ejesz)** *vt perf* (*równowagę*) to upset; (*wiarę, przekonanie*) to shake
**zachwy|cać (-cam, -casz)** (*perf* **-cić**) *vt* to delight, to enchant; **~ (kogoś) urodą/ wdziękiem** to delight (sb) with one's/its beauty/grace; **zachwycać się** *vr*: **~ się czymś** to marvel at sth
**zachwycający** *adj* delightful
**zachwy|cić (-cę, -cisz)** (*imp* **-ć**) *vb perf od* **zachwycać**
**zachwycony** *adj* delighted; **jestem ~ przedstawieniem** I am delighted with the performance

**zachwy|t (-tu, -ty)** (*dat sg* **-cie**) *m* delight; **budzić czyjś ~** to delight sb; **wpadać (wpaść** *perf*) **w ~** to go into raptures
**za|ciąć (-tnę, -tniesz)** (*imp* **-tnij**) *vb perf od* **zacinać**
**zaciąg|ać (-am, -asz)** (*perf* **-nąć**) *vt* (*wlec*) to drag; (*firankę*) to draw; (*pasek*) to tighten ▷ *vi* (*mówić rozciągając głoski*) to speak with a drawl; **zaciągnąć dług** to incur a debt; **zaciągać się** *vr* (*wstępować do służby*) to enlist; (*dymem papierosowym*) to inhale; (*o niebie*) to cloud over
**zaciąg|nąć (-nę, -niesz)** (*imp* **-nij**) *vb perf od* **zaciągać** ▷ *vt perf*: **~ kogoś do** *+gen* to drag sb to
**zacie|k (-ku, -ki)** (*instr sg* **-kiem**) *m* water stain (*on wall*)
**zacieka|wić (-wię, -wisz)** *vt perf*: **~ kogoś (czymś)** to arouse sb's interest (in sth); **zaciekawić się** *vr perf*: **~ się (czymś)** to become interested (in sth)
**zaciekawieni|e (-a)** *nt* (*zainteresowanie*) interest; (*ciekawość*) curiosity
**zaciekłoś|ć (-ci)** *f* ferocity
**zaciekły** *adj* (*walka, dyskusja*) fierce; (*atak*) ferocious; (*przeciwnik*) sworn
**zaciemnieni|e (-a)** *nt* blackout
**zacie|niać (-niam, -niasz)** (*perf* **-nić**) *vt* to shade
**zacieniony** *adj* (*miejsce*) shady
**zacier|ać (-am, -asz)** (*perf* **zatrzeć**) *vt* (*ślady, szczegóły*) to cover (up); (*złe wrażenie*) to efface; **~ ręce** to rub one's hands; (*przen*) to lick one's lips; **~ ślady** to cover one's tracks; **zacierać się** *vr* (*o napisie, wspomnieniach*) to fade (away); (*Tech*) to seize up
**zacieś|niać (-niam, -niasz)** (*perf* **-nić**) *vt* to tighten; **zacieśniać się** *vr* to tighten
**zacieś|nić (-nię, -nisz)** (*imp* **-nij**) *vb perf od* **zacieśniać**
**zacietrzewieni|e (-a)** *nt* fury
**zacietrzewiony** *adj* furious
**zacię|cie (-cia, -cia)** (*gen pl* **-ć**) *nt* (*predyspozycja*) bent; (*werwa, zapał*) verve; **robić coś z ~m** to do sth with verve
**zaciętoś|ć (-ci)** *f* stubbornness
**zacięty** *adj* (*opór*) stiff; (*bój*) hard-fought; (*mina, rysy, wróg*) implacable
**zacin|ać (-am, -asz)** (*perf* **zaciąć**) *vt* (*ranić*) to cut; (*wargi, usta*) to set; **zaciąć zęby** (*przen*) to set one's teeth ▷ *vi* (*o deszczu*) to whip; **zacinać się** *vr* (*kaleczyć się*) to cut o.s.; (*o mechanizmach, szufladzie*) to jam, to get stuck; (*jąkać się*) to stammer
**zacis|k (-ku, -ki)** (*instr sg* **-kiem**) *m* (*Elektr*) terminal; (*Tech*) clamp
**zacisk|ać (-am, -asz)** (*perf* **zacisnąć**) *vt* to tighten; **zacisnąć pasa** to tighten one's belt; **zacisnąć zęby** (*przen*) to clench *lub* set one's teeth; **zaciskać się** *vr* to tighten
**zaci|snąć (-snę, -śniesz)** (*imp* **-śnij**) *vb perf od* **zaciskać**
**zacisz|e (-a, -a)** (*gen pl* **-y**) *nt* (*miejsce osłonięte*) sheltered spot; (*miejsce ustronne*) secluded spot
**zaciszny** *adj* (*spokojny*) quiet; (*ustronny*) secluded
**zacofani|e (-a)** *nt* backwardness
**zacofany** *adj* backward
**zacza|dzić (-dzę, -dzisz)** (*imp* **-dź**) *vt perf* to poison with carbon monoxide; **zaczadzić się** *vr* to be poisoned with carbon monoxide
**zacza|ić się (-ję, -isz)** (*imp* **-j**) *vb perf od* **czaić, zaczajać się**
**zaczaj|ać się (-am, -asz)** (*perf* **zaczaić**) *vr*: **zaczajać się na** *+acc* to lie in ambush for
**zaczar|ować (-uję, -ujesz)** *vt perf* to cast *lub* put a spell on
**zaczarowany** *adj* magic
**zacz|ąć (-nę, -niesz)** (*imp* **-nij**) *vb perf od* **zaczynać**
**zaczą|tek (-ku, -ki)** (*instr sg* **-kiem**) *m* (*książk*) beginning, start
**zaczek|ać (-am, -asz)** *vb perf od* **czekać**
**zacze|p (-pu, -py)** (*loc sg* **-pie**) *m* fastener
**zacze|piać (-piam, -piasz)** (*perf* **-pić**) *vt* (*przyczepiać*) to fasten; (*zatrzymywać*) to accost; (*atakować*) to attack ▷ *vi*: **~ o coś** to catch on sth; **zaczepiłem ręką o klamkę** I caught my hand on the handle; **zaczepiać się** *vr*: **~ się o coś** (*chwytać się*) to catch hold of sth; (*zahaczać się*) to catch on sth
**zaczepieni|e (-a)** *nt*: **punkt zaczepienia** foothold
**zaczep|ka (-ki, -ki)** (*dat sg* **-ce**, *gen pl* **-ek**) *f* taunt; **szukać zaczepki** (*pot*) to look for a fight
**zaczepny** *adj* (*ton, uwaga*) aggressive; (*człowiek*) truculent, aggressive
**zaczer|niać (-niam, -niasz)** (*perf* **-nić**) *vt* to blacken
**zaczer|nić (-nię, -nisz)** (*imp* **-ń** *lub* **-nij**) *vb perf od* **zaczerniać**
**zaczerp|nąć (-nę, -niesz)** (*imp* **-nij**) *vb perf od* **czerpać** ▷ *vt perf* (*przykład*) to take; **~** *+gen* (*wody, zupy*) to ladle; (*piasku, mąki*) to scoop; (*informacji*) to gather; **~ powietrza** to take a breath
**zaczerwie|nić się (-nię, -nisz)** (*imp* **-ń**) *vr perf* to redden; (*zarumienić się*) to blush, to redden
**zaczerwienie|nie (-nia, -nia)** (*gen pl* **-ń**) *nt* (*na skórze*) red mark
**zaczyn|ać (-am, -asz)** (*perf* **zacząć**) *vt* to begin, to start; **~ coś robić** to begin *lub* start doing *lub* to do sth; **zaczyna nam brakować wody** we are running out of water; **~ od czegoś** to begin *lub* start with sth; **~ od nowa** to begin again, to start over (*US*); **~ od zera**

Z

(*przen*) to start from scratch; **zaczynać się** *vr* to start, to begin

**zać|ma** (**-my**) (*dat sg* **-mie**) *f* cataract

**zać|mić (-mię, -misz)** (*imp* **-mij**) *vb perf od* **zaćmiewać**

**zaćmie|nie** (**-nia, -nia**) (*gen pl* **-ń**) *nt* (*Słońca, Księżyca*) eclipse; (*pot: zamroczenie*) (mental) block

**zaćmiew|ać (-am, -asz)** (*perf* **zaćmić**) *vt* (*światło*) to darken; (*przen*) to outshine, to eclipse

**za|d** (**-du, -dy**) (*loc sg* **-dzie**) *m* rump

**zadamawi|ać się (-am, -asz)** (*perf* **zadomowić**) *vr* to get settled

**zada|nie** (**-nia, -nia**) (*gen pl* **-ń**) *nt* (*coś do wykonania*) task; (*Szkol*) task, exercise; (*z matematyki, fizyki*) problem; **~ domowe** homework; **stanąć** (*perf*) **na wysokości zadania** to rise to the occasion

**zadarty** *adj*: **~ nos** a snub nose

**zadat|ki** (**-ków**) *pl*: **mieć ~ na kogoś** to have the makings of sb

**zad|awać (-aję, -ajesz)** (*perf* **-ać**) *vt* (*pytanie*) to ask; (*lekcje, czytankę*) to assign; (*cios*) to deal; **zadać komuś pytanie** to ask sb a question; **~ komuś ból** to inflict pain on sb; **~ sobie trud, by coś zrobić** to take the trouble to do sth; **~ czemuś kłam** to give the lie to sth; **zadawać się** *vr* (*pot*): **~ się z kimś** to hang around with sb

**zadbany** *adj* (*człowiek*) well-groomed; (*ogród, dom*) neat (and tidy)

**zadecyd|ować (-uję, -ujesz)** *vb perf od* **decydować**

**zadedyk|ować (-uję, -ujesz)** *vb perf od* **dedykować**

**zad|ek** (**-ka** *lub* **-ku, -ki**) (*instr sg* **-kiem**) *m* (*pot*) backside (*pot*)

**zadeklar|ować (-uję, -ujesz)** *vb perf od* **deklarować**

**zademonstr|ować (-uję, -ujesz)** *vb perf od* **demonstrować**

**zadep|tać (-czę, -czesz)** *vb perf od* **zadeptywać**

**zadept|ywać (-uję, -ujesz)** (*perf* **-ać**) *vt* (*ścieżkę, kwiaty*) to trample; (*ogień*) to stamp out

**zadła|wić się (-wię, -wisz)** *vr perf* to choke; **zadławić się czymś** to choke on sth

**zadłuż|ać się (-am, -asz)** (*perf* **-yć**) *vr* to get into debt; **zadłużać się u kogoś** to get into a debt to sb

**zadłużeni|e** (**-a**) *nt* debt

**zadłużony** *adj* indebted; **być ~m** to be in debt

**zadom|owić się (-owię, -owisz)** (*imp* **-ów**) *vb perf od* **zadamawiać się**

**zadość** *inv*: **czynić (uczynić** *perf*) **~ prośbie/wymaganiom** to satisfy a request/demands; **sprawiedliwości stało się ~** it was poetic justice

**zadośćuczy|nić (-nię, -nisz)** (*imp* **-ń**) *vi perf* (*książk*): **~ prośbie/żądaniu** to satisfy a request/demand

**zadośćuczynieni|e** (**-a**) *nt* satisfaction

**zadowal|ać (-am, -asz)** (*perf* **zadowolić**) *vt* to satisfy; (*cieszyć*) to please; **zadowalać się** *vr*: **~ się czymś** to make do with sth, to settle for sth

**zadowalający** *adj* satisfactory

**zadowoleni|e** (**-a**) *nt* satisfaction; **z ~m** contentedly, with satisfaction

**zadow|olić (-olę, -olisz)** (*imp* **-ól**) *vb perf od* **zadowalać**

**zadowolony** *adj* (*szczęśliwy*) glad, pleased; (*usatysfakcjonowany*) satisfied, contented; **~ z czegoś** happy *lub* pleased with sth; **~ z siebie** complacent, self-satisfied

**zad|ra** (**-ry, -ry**) (*dat sg* **-rze**) *f* splinter

**zadra|pać (-pię, -piesz)** *vt perf* to scratch; **zadrapać się** *vr* to scratch o.s. (*by accident*)

**zadrapa|nie** (**-nia, -nia**) (*gen pl* **-ń**) *nt* scratch

**zadrap|nąć (-nę, -niesz)** (*imp* **-nij**) *vb perf od* **zadrapać**

**zadra|snąć (-snę, -śniesz)** (*imp* **-śnij**) *vt perf* to scratch; **zadrasnąć się** *vr perf*: **~ się w rękę** to graze one's hand

**zadraśnię|cie** (**-cia, -cia**) (*gen pl* **-ć**) *nt* graze

**zadraż|niać (-niam, -niasz)** (*perf* **-nić**) *vt* to strain

**zadrażnie|nia** (**-ń**) *pl* frictions *pl*

**zadręcz|ać (-am, -asz)** (*perf* **-yć**) *vt* to badger, to pester; **zadręczać się** *vr*: **~ się (czymś)** to torture *lub* torment o.s. (with sth)

**zadr|wić (-wię, -wisz)** (*imp* **-wij**) *vb perf od* **drwić**

**zad|rzeć (-rę, -rzesz)** (*imp* **-rzyj**) *vb perf od* **zadzierać** ▷ *vi perf*: **~ z kimś** (*pot*) to fall foul of sb

**zadrzewiony** *adj* wooded

**zadrż|eć (-ę, -ysz)** (*imp* **-yj**) *vb perf od* **drżeć**

**zaduch** (**-u**) *m* stuffy air

**zadufani|e** (**-a**) *nt* (*pot*) overconfidence

**zadufany** *adj* (*też*: **zadufany w sobie**) overconfident

**zadu|ma** (**-my**) (*dat sg* **-mie**) *f* reflection, meditation; **pogrążony w zadumie** lost in meditation *lub* thought

**zadum|ać się (-am, -asz)** *vr perf* (*książk*) to muse; **zadumać się nad czymś** to reflect *lub* muse on *lub* over sth

**zadumany** *adj* (*książk*) reflective, thoughtful

**zadurzony** *adj*: **~ w kimś** infatuated with sb

**zadurz|yć się (-ę, -ysz)** *vr perf* (*pot*): **zadurzyć się w kimś** to become infatuated with sb

**zadu|sić (-szę, -sisz)** (*imp* **-ś**) *vb perf od* **dusić**

**Zadusz|ki** (**-ek**) *pl* (*Rel*) All Souls' Day
**zaduszny** *adj*: **Dzień Z~** = **Zaduszki**
**zady|ma** (**-my, -my**) (*dat sg* **-mie**) *f* (*pot*) trouble (*disturbance*)
**zadymiony** *adj* smoky
**zadym|ka** (**-ki, -ki**) (*dat sg* **-ce**, *gen pl* **-ek**) *f* snowstorm, blizzard
**zadyszany** *adj* breathless
**zadysz|eć się (-ę, -ysz)** *vr perf* to run short *lub* out of breath
**zadysz|ka** (**-ki, -ki**) (*dat sg* **-ce**, *gen pl* **-ek**) *f* breathlessness; **dostać** (*perf*) **zadyszki** to lose one's breath
**zadział|ać (-am, -asz)** *vb perf od* **działać** ▷ *vi perf* (*podjąć działanie*) to take action
**zadzier|ać (-am, -asz)** *vt* (*perf* **zadrzeć**) (*paznokieć*) to tear; (*pot*: *spódnicę*) to pull up ▷ *vi*: **~ z kimś** (*pot*) to mess with sb (*pot*); **~ nosa** (*pot*) to put on airs; **~ głowę** to crane (one's neck)
**zadziorny** *adj* (*pot*: *kłótliwy*) quarrelsome; (: *nieustępliwy*) defiant
**zadzi|wiać (-wiam, -wiasz)** (*perf* **-wić**) *vt* to astonish, to amaze
**zadziwiający** *adj* astonishing, amazing
**zadzi|wić (-wię, -wisz)** *vb perf od* **zadziwiać**; **zadziwić się** *vr perf* to be astonished *lub* amazed
**zadzwo|nić (-nię, -nisz)** (*imp* **-ń**) *vb perf od* **dzwonić**
**zadźg|ać (-am, -asz)** *vt perf* (*pot*) to stab
**zafarb|ować (-uję, -ujesz)** *vb perf od* **farbować**
**zafascyn|ować (-uję, -ujesz)** *vb perf od* **fascynować**
**zafascynowani|e** (**-a**) *nt* fascination
**zafascynowany** *adj* fascinated
**zafrasowany** *adj* troubled, worried
**zafund|ować (-uję, -ujesz)** *vb perf od* **fundować**
**zagad|ać (-am, -asz)** *vb perf od* **zagadywać** ▷ *vi perf* to start talking; **zagadać się** *vr perf* (*pot*) to become lost in conversation
**zagad|ka** (**-ki, -ki**) (*dat sg* **-ce**, *gen pl* **-ek**) *f* (*zadanie*) riddle, puzzle; (*tajemnica*) mystery
**zagadkowy** *adj* puzzling, enigmatic
**zagad|nąć (-nę, -niesz)** (*imp* **-nij**) *vb perf od* **zagadywać**
**zagadnie|nie** (**-nia, -nia**) (*gen pl* **-ń**) *nt* problem, issue
**zagad|ywać (-uję, -ujesz)** *vt* (*zwracać się*) (*perf* **-nąć**) to speak to, to address; (*pot*: *zagłuszać*) (*perf* **zagadać**) to talk down ▷ *vi* (*odzywać się*) (*perf* **-nąć**) to start speaking; **~ kogoś o coś** to inquire sb about sth; **~ do kogoś** (*pot*) to chat up sb (*pot*)
**zaga|ić (-ję, -isz)** *vb perf od* **zagajać**
**zagaj|ać (-am, -asz)** (*perf* **zagaić**) *vt* (*zebranie*) to open; (*rozmowę*) to start
**zagajni|k** (**-ka, -ki**) (*instr sg* **-kiem**) *m* woods *pl*
**zagalopow|ywać się (-uję, -ujesz)** (*perf* **-ać**) *vr* (*przen*) to overstep the mark
**zagani|ać (-am, -asz)** (*perf* **zagnać** *lub* **zagonić**) *vt* to drive; **~ kogoś do robienia czegoś** to drive sb to do sth
**zaga|pić się (-pię, -pisz)** *vr perf* (*pot*): **zagapiłem się** I wasn't paying attention
**zagar|nąć (-nę, -niesz)** (*imp* **-nij**) *vb perf od* **zagarniać**
**zagar|niać (-niam, -niasz)** (*perf* **-nąć**) *vt* (*zbierać*) to gather; (*przywłaszczać*) to seize
**zagęszcz|ać (-am, -asz)** (*perf* **zagęścić**) *vt* to thicken; **~ zabudowę** to build up an area
**zagęszczeni|e** (**-a**) *nt* concentration
**zagęszczony** *adj*: **mleko zagęszczone** condensed milk
**zagę|ścić (-szczę, -ścisz)** (*imp* **-ść**) *vb perf od* **zagęszczać**
**za|giąć (-gnę, -gniesz)** (*imp* **-gnij**) *vb perf od* **zaginać**
**zagię|cie** (**-cia, -cia**) (*gen pl* **-ć**) *nt* (*materiału*) fold; (*drutu*) bend
**zagin|ać (-am, -asz)** (*perf* **zagiąć**) *vt* (*kartkę*) to fold; (*drut*) to bend; (*pot*: *osobę*) to confuse
**zagi|nąć (-nę, -niesz)** (*imp* **-ń**) *vi perf* to go missing, to disappear; **ślad po nim zaginął** there is no trace left of him
**zaginiony** *adj* missing ▷ *m decl like adj* missing person
**zaglą|dać (-am, -asz)** (*perf* **zajrzeć**) *vi* to look in; **~ do książki** to look into a book; **~ do kogoś** to look in on sb
**zagła|da** (**-dy, -dy**) (*dat sg* **-dzie**) *f* extermination, annihilation; **broń masowej zagłady** weapons of mass destruction
**zagła|dzać (-dzam, -dzasz)** (*perf* **zagłodzić**) *vt* to starve; **zagładzać się** *vr* to starve o.s.
**zagłę|biać (-biam, -biasz)** (*perf* **-bić**) *vt* (*w wodzie*) to immerse; (*w kieszeniach, masie czegoś*) to sink; **zagłębiać się** *vr* (*w wodzie*) to immerse o.s.; (*w fotelu*) to sink; **~ się w las** to go (deep) into a forest; **~ się w myślach/książce** to become absorbed *lub* engrossed in one's thoughts/a book
**zagłę|bie** (**-bia, -bia**) (*gen pl* **-bi**) *nt*: **~ węglowe** coalfield
**zagłębie|nie** (**-nia, -nia**) (*gen pl* **-ń**) *nt* hollow
**zagł|odzić (-odzę, -odzisz)** (*imp* **-odź** *lub* **-ódź**) *vb perf od* **głodzić, zagładzać**
**zagłos|ować (-uję, -ujesz)** *vb perf od* **głosować**
**zagłów|ek** (**-ka, -ki**) (*instr sg* **-kiem**) *m* headrest

**zagłusz|ać (-am, -asz)** (*perf* **-yć**) *vt* (*dźwięk, głos*) to drown out; (*wyrzuty sumienia*) to deaden; (*stację radiową*) to jam; **zagłuszać się** *vr* to drown one another out
**zagmatw|ać (-am, -asz)** *vb perf od* **gmatwać**
**zagmatwany** *adj* tangled, confused
**zagniat|ać (-am, -asz)** (*perf* **zagnieść**) *vt* (*ciasto*) to knead; (*tkaninę, kartkę*) to crease
**zagniece|nie** (**-nia, -nia**) (*gen pl* **-ń**) *nt* crease
**zagni|eść (-otę, -eciesz)** (*imp* **-eć**, *pt* **-ótł, -otła, -etli**) *vb perf od* **zagniatać**
**zagniewany** *adj* angry
**zagnieżdż|ać się (-a)** (*perf* **zagnieździć**) *vr* to nest
**zag|oić (-oję, -oisz)** (*imp* **-ój**) *vb perf od* **goić**
**zago|n** (**-nu, -ny**) (*loc sg* **-nie**) *m* patch (*of cabbages etc*)
**zago|nić (-nię, -nisz)** (*imp* **-ń**) *vb perf od* **zaganiać**
**zagoniony** *adj* (*pot*) busy, on the go
**zagorzały** *adj* (*zwolennik, fan*) ardent, fervent; (*przeciwnik*) fierce; (*dyskusja*) heated
**zagospodarowany** *adj* developed
**zagospodarow|ywać (-uję, -ujesz)** (*perf* **-ać**) *vt* (*teren*) to develop; **zagospodarowywać się** *vr* to settle in
**zago|ścić (-szczę, -ścisz)** (*imp* **-ść**) *vi perf* (*książk: o radości, spokoju*) to settle; **~ u kogoś** to honour (*Brit*) *lub* honor (*US*) sb with a visit
**zagot|ować (-uję, -ujesz)** *vb perf od* **gotować**
**zagra|biać (-biam, -biasz)** (*perf* **-bić**) *vt* (*liście, ścieżkę*) to rake; (*przen: ziemię, majątek*) to seize
**zagra|cać (-cam, -casz)** (*perf* **-cić**) *vt* (*pot*) to clutter
**zagra|cić (-cę, -cisz)** (*imp* **-ć**) *vb perf od* **zagracać**
**zagr|ać (-am, -asz)** *vb perf od* **grać, zagrywać**
**zagradz|ać (-am, -asz)** (*perf* **zagrodzić**) *vt* to obstruct, to bar
**zagranic|a** (**-y**) *f* foreign countries *pl*; **wracać z zagranicy** to return from abroad
**zagraniczny** *adj* foreign; **handel ~** foreign commerce *lub* trade; **Ministerstwo Spraw Z~ch** Ministry of Foreign Affairs, ≈ Foreign Office (*Brit*), ≈ State Department (*US*)
**zagra|nie** (**-nia, -nia**) (*gen pl* **-ń**) *nt* move
**zagraż|ać (-am, -asz)** (*perf* **zagrozić**) *vi*: **~ komuś/czemuś** to threaten sb/sth
**zagr|oda** (**-ody, -ody**) (*dat sg* **-odzie**, *gen pl* **-ód**) *f* (*gospodarstwo*) farm; (*dla krów itp.*) pen, corral (*US*)
**zagr|odzić (-odzę, -odzisz)** (*imp* **-odź** *lub* **-ódź**) *vb perf od* **zagradzać**
**zagr|ozić (-ożę, -ozisz)** (*imp* **-oź**) *vb perf od* **grozić, zagrażać**
**zagroże|nie** (**-nia, -nia**) (*gen pl* **-ń**) *nt* threat, danger; **~ społeczne** a public menace; **~ dla demokracji** a menace to democracy; **~ pożarowe/dla zdrowia** a fire/health hazard *lub* risk; **stanowić ~ dla kogoś/czegoś** to be a threat *lub* danger to sb/sth
**zagryw|ać (-am, -asz)** (*perf* **zagrać**) *vt* (*Sport*) to serve
**zagryw|ka** (**-ki, -ki**) (*dat sg* **-ce**, *gen pl* **-ek**) *f* (*Sport*) serve; (*przen*) (opening) gambit
**zagryz|ać (-am, -asz)** (*perf* **zagryźć**) *vt* (*o zwierzętach*) to bite to death; (*o człowieku: wargi*) to bite; **zagryzać się** *vr* (*o zwierzętach*) to bite each other to death; (*pot: martwić się*) to worry
**zagry|źć (-zę, -ziesz)** (*imp* **-ź**) *vb perf od* **zagryzać**
**zagrz|ać (-eję, -ejesz)** *vb perf od* **grzać, zagrzewać**
**Zagrze|b** (**-bia**) *m* Zagreb
**zagrze|bać (-bię, -biesz)** *vb perf od* **zagrzebywać**
**zagrzeb|ywać (-uję, -ujesz)** (*perf* **-ać**) *vt* to bury; **zagrzebywać się** *vr* to burrow, to bury o.s.
**zagrzew|ać (-am, -asz)** (*perf* **zagrzać**) *vt* (*podgrzewać*) to warm *lub* heat up; **~ kogoś do czegoś** to spur sb on to (do) sth; **nie zagrzała nigdzie miejsca** she never stayed anywhere long; **zagrzewać się** *vr* (*podgrzewać się*) to warm *lub* heat up
**zagu|bić (-bię, -bisz)** *vt perf* to lose; **zagubić się** *vr* to get lost
**zagubiony** *adj* (*człowiek*) lost; (*osada, wyspa*) remote
**zagwarant|ować (-uję, -ujesz)** *vb perf od* **gwarantować, zagwarantowywać**
**zagwarantow|ywać (-uję, -ujesz)** (*perf* **-ać**) *vt* to guarantee
**zahacz|ać (-am, -asz)** (*perf* **-yć**) *vt*: **~ coś o coś** to hook sth (on)to sth ▷ *vi*: **~ o coś** (*zaczepiać*) to catch on sth; (*pot: w rozmowie*) to touch (up) on sth; **zahaczyć o Pragę/znajomego** (*pot: wstąpić na krótko*) to stop off in Prague/at a friend's place; **zahaczać się** *vr* (*pot*): **zahaczyć się gdzieś** to land a job somewhere
**zaham|ować (-uję, -ujesz)** *vt perf* to bring to a stop ▷ *vi perf* to come to a stop
**zahamowa|nie** (**-nia, -nia**) (*gen pl* **-ń**) *nt* inhibition, hang-up (*pot*)
**zahart|ować (-uję, -ujesz)** *vb perf od* **hartować**
**zahartowany** *adj* hardened
**zahipnotyz|ować (-uję, -ujesz)** *vb perf od* **hipnotyzować**
**zahol|ować (-uję, -ujesz)** *vb perf od* **holować**
**zahukany** *adj* (*pot*) cowed
**ZAIKS** *abbr* (*= Związek Autorów i Kompozytorów Scenicznych*) *Association of Stage Writers and Composers*

**zaim|ek** (**-ka, -ki**) (*instr sg* **-kiem**) *m* pronoun; **~ dzierżawczy/pytający** possessive/ interrogative pronoun

**zaimpon|ować (-uję, -ujesz)** *vb perf od* **imponować**

**zaimprowiz|ować (-uję, -ujesz)** *vb perf od* **improwizować**

**zaimprowizowany** *adj* improvised, impromptu

**zainaugur|ować (-uję, -ujesz)** *vb perf od* **inaugurować**

**zainicj|ować (-uję, -ujesz)** *vb perf od* **inicjować**

**zainkas|ować (-uję, -ujesz)** *vb perf od* **inkasować**

**zainsceniz|ować (-uję, -ujesz)** *vb perf od* **inscenizować**

**zainspir|ować (-uję, -ujesz)** *vb perf od* **inspirować**

**zainstal|ować (-uję, -ujesz)** *vb perf od* **instalować**

**zainteres|ować (-uję, -ujesz)** *vb perf od* **interesować**; **zainteresować się** *vr perf*: **~ się czymś** to become interested in sth, to take an interest in sth

**zainteresowa|nie** (**-nia**) *nt* interest; **z ~m** with interest; **wzbudzać (wzbudzić** *perf***) ~** to arouse interest; **zainteresowania** *pl* interests *pl*

**zainteresowany** *adj*: **być czymś ~m** to be interested in sth

**zainton|ować (-uję, -ujesz)** *vb perf od* **intonować**

**zaintryg|ować (-uję, -ujesz)** *vb perf od* **intrygować**

**zainwest|ować (-uję, -ujesz)** *vb perf od* **inwestować**

**Zai|r** (**-ru**) (*loc sg* **-rze**) *m* Zaire

**zaistni|eć (-eję, -ejesz)** *vi perf* to come into being *lub* existence; (*o trudnościach*) to arise

**zajad|ać (-am, -asz)** *vt* (*pot*) to tuck into (*Brit*), to chow (down) (*US*); **zajadać się** *vr*: **~ się czymś** to gorge o.s. on *lub* with sth

**zajadłoś|ć** (**-ci**) *f* virulence

**zajadły** *adj* virulent

**zajaśni|eć (-eje)** *vi perf* (*o słońcu*) to come out; (*o oczach*) to brighten up; *patrz też* **jaśnieć**

**zaj|azd** (**-azdu, -azdy**) (*loc sg* **-eździe**) *m* wayside inn

**zaj|ąc** (**-ąca, -ące**) (*gen pl* **-ęcy**) *m* hare

**zajączk|ek** (**-ka, -ki**) (*instr sg* **-kiem**) *m dimin od* **zając**

**zaj|ąć (-mę, -miesz)** (*imp* **-mij**) *vb perf od* **zajmować**; **zająć się** *vr perf*: **zajmę się tym** I'll see to that; **~ się aktorstwem/medycyną** to take up acting/medicine

**zają|kiwać się (-kuję, -kujesz)** (*perf* **-knąć**) *vr* to stammer

**zająk|nąć się (-nę, -niesz)** (*imp* **-nij**) *vb perf od* **zająkiwać się**

**zaj|echać (-adę, -edziesz)** (*imp* **-edź**) *vb perf od* **zajeżdżać**

**zajezd|nia** (**-ni, -nie**) (*gen pl* **-ni**) *f* depot

**zaje|ździć (-żdżę, -ździsz)** (*imp* **-źdź**) *vb perf od* **zajeżdżać**

**zajeżdż|ać (-am, -asz)** *vt* (*konia*) (*perf* **zajeździć**) to override ▷ *vi* (*perf* **zajechać**); **~ do domu/na stację** to arrive home/at the station; **~ pod dom** to pull up outside the house; **~ do rodziny** to stop by one's relatives' house; **~ komuś drogę** (*Mot*) to cut in on sb

**zaję|cie** (**-cia, -cia**) (*gen pl* **-ć**) *nt* (*czynność*) occupation, pursuit; (*praca*) occupation; (*miasta, terytorium*) seizure; (*Prawo*) distraint; **zajęcia** *pl* (*Uniw*) classes *pl*; **(szkolny) plan** *lub* **rozkład zajęć** (school) timetable; **być na zajęciach** to be in class; **zajęcia praktyczno-techniczne** (*gotowanie itp.*) ≈ home economics

**zajęcz|eć (-ę, -ysz)** *vb perf od* **jęczeć**

**zajęczy** *adj*: **zajęcza warga** harelip

**zajęty** *adj* (*człowiek*) busy; (*miejsce*) taken, occupied; (*Tel*) busy, engaged (*Brit*); **teraz jestem zajęta** I'm busy now; **być ~m czymś** to be occupied with sth; **być ~m robieniem czegoś** to be busy doing sth

**zajm|ować (-uję, -ujesz)** (*perf* **zająć**) *vt* (*powierzchnię*) to occupy, to take up; (*pokój, dom*) to occupy; (*miasto, kraj*) to seize; (*wzbudzać ciekawość*) to engage; (*Prawo*) to distrain; **zajmie (mi) to dwie godziny** it'll take (me) two hours; **zająć miejsce** to take one's seat; **zająć komuś miejsce** to keep a seat for sb; **~ stanowisko w sprawie czegoś** to take a stand on sth; **zajmować się** *vr* (*zapalać się*) to catch fire; **~ się czymś/robieniem czegoś** to busy o.s. with sth/doing sth; **czym się zajmujesz?** what do you do (for a living)?; **~ się kimś/czymś** (*opiekować się*) to look after sb/sth; **~ się swoimi sprawami** to go about one's business

**zajmujący** *adj* (*opowieść*) engrossing, absorbing; (*praca*) absorbing; (*człowiek*) interesting

**zajrz|eć (-ę, -ysz)** (*imp* **-yj**) *vb perf od* **zaglądać**

**zajś|cie** (**-cia, -cia**) (*gen pl* **-ć**) *nt* incident

**zaj|ść (-dę, -dziesz)** (*imp* **-dź**) *vb perf od* **zachodzić**

**zakal|ec** (**-ca, -ce**) *m*: **ciasto z zakalcem** slack-baked cake

**zaka|ła** (**-ły, -ły**) (*dat sg* **-le**) *m/f* (*pot*): **być zakałą rodziny** to be a disgrace to one's family

**zakamar|ek** (**-ka, -ki**) (*instr sg* **-kiem**) *m* recess, corner

**zakamufl|ować (-uję, -ujesz)** *vb perf od* **kamuflować**

**zakańcz|ać (-am, -asz)** (*perf* **zakończyć**) *vt* to end

**zakas|ywać (-uję, -ujesz)** (*perf* **-ać**) *vt*: **zakasać rękawy** (*przen*) to roll one's sleeves up (*przen*)

**zakaszl|eć (-ę, -esz)** *vb perf od* **kaszleć**

**zakatalog|ować (-uję, -ujesz)** *vb perf od* **katalogować**

**zakatarzony** *adj*: **jest ~** he has a runny nose

**zaka|z** (**-zu, -zy**) (*loc sg* **-zie**) *m* ban, prohibition; **„~ postoju"** "no waiting"; **„~ skrętu w lewo/prawo"** "no left/right turn"; **„~ wjazdu"** "no entry"; **„~ wstępu"** "no entry"; **łamać (złamać** *perf*) **~** to break a ban

**zaka|zać (-żę, -żesz)** *vb perf od* **zakazywać**

**zakazany** *adj* (*działalność, praktyki*) illicit, forbidden; (*książka*) banned, forbidden; (*pot*: *typ, knajpa*) seedy; **~ owoc** (*przen*) forbidden fruit

**zaka|zić (-żę, -zisz)** (*imp* **-ź**) *vb perf od* **zakażać**

**zakaz|ywać (-uję, -ujesz)** (*perf* **-ać**) *vt* to forbid, to prohibit; **~ komuś czegoś** to forbid sb (to do) sth, to prohibit sb from doing sth

**zakaźny** *adj* (*choroba*) infectious; **oddział ~** isolation ward

**zakaż|ać (-am, -asz)** (*perf* **zakazić**) *vt* to infect

**zakaże|nie** (**-nia, -nia**) (*gen pl* **-ń**) *nt* infection; **ulegać (ulec** *perf*) **zakażeniu** to become infected

**zakażony** *adj* infected

**zakąs|ka** (**-ki, -ki**) (*dat sg* **-ce**, *gen pl* **-ek**) *f* (*zimna*) appetizer, hors d'oeuvre; (*ciepła*) appetizer

**zakąt|ek** (**-ka, -ki**) (*instr sg* **-kiem**) *m* nook

**zakichany** *adj* (*pot*) damned (*pot*)

**zakiełk|ować (-uje)** *vb perf od* **kiełkować**

**zaki|sić (-szę, -sisz)** (*imp* **-ś**) *vb perf od* **kisić**

**zakl|ąć (-nę, -niesz)** (*imp* **-nij**) *vb perf od* **kląć, zaklinać**

**zakl|eić (-eję, -eisz)** (*imp* **-ej**) *vb perf od* **zaklejać**

**zaklej|ać (-am, -asz)** (*perf* **zakleić**) *vt* to seal

**zaklę|cie** (**-cia, -cia**) (*gen pl* **-ć**) *nt* (*formuła*) spell, charm; (*prośba*) entreaty

**zaklin|ać (-am, -asz)** (*perf* **zakląć**) *vt* (*błagać*) to beg, to entreat; (*rzucać urok*) to put a spell on, to cast a spell over; **zaklinać się** *vr* to swear

**zaklin|ować (-uję, -ujesz)** *vb perf od* **klinować, zaklinowywać**

**zaklinow|ywać (-uję, -ujesz)** *vt* (*mocować klinem*) to wedge; (*blokować*) to block; **zaklinowywać się** *vr* to get stuck

**zakła|d** (**-du, -dy**) (*loc sg* **-dzie**) *m* (*umowa*) bet; **~ przemysłowy** industrial plant; **~ fryzjerski** hairdresser's; (*męski*) barber's; **~ badawczy** research institute; **~ poprawczy** borstal (*Brit*), reformatory (*US*); **~ karny** penal institute (*Brit*), penitentiary (*US*); **zawierać (zawrzeć** *perf*) **~** to make a bet; **wygrać** (*perf*)**/przegrać** (*perf*) **~** to win/lose a bet

**zakład|ać (-am, -asz)** (*perf* **założyć**) *vt* (*miasto*) to found; (*towarzystwo, spółkę*) to establish, to found; (*płaszcz, buty, okulary*) to put on; (*gaz, telefon*) to install; (*rewizję, protest*) to lodge; **założyć nogę na nogę** to cross one's legs; **założyć rodzinę** to set up home ▷ *vi* to assume, to suppose; **załóżmy, że wygrasz** suppose you win; **zakładać się** *vr* to bet; **założyć się z kimś o coś** to bet sb sth; **chcesz się założyć?** (do you) want to bet?

**zakład|ka** (**-ki, -ki**) (*dat sg* **-ce**, *gen pl* **-ek**) *f* (*do książki*) bookmark; (*Krawiectwo*) tuck

**zakładni|k** (**-ka, -cy**) (*instr sg* **-kiem**) *m* hostage

**zakładowy** *adj* (*teren, magazyn*) factory *attr*; **kapitał ~** initial capital

**zakłamani|e** (**-a**) *nt* hypocrisy

**zakłamany** *adj* hypocritical

**zakłopo|tać (-czę, -czesz)** *vt perf* to embarrass; **zakłopotać się** *vr* to get embarrassed

**zakłopotani|e** (**-a**) *nt* embarrassment; **wprawiać (wprawić** *perf*) **kogoś w ~** to embarrass sb

**zakłopotany** *adj* embarrassed

**zakłó|cać (-cam, -casz)** (*perf* **-cić**) *vt* (*ciszę, nastrój*) to disturb; (*działalność, proces*) to disrupt; (*sygnał, łączność*) to cause interference to

**zakłóce|nie** (**-nia, -nia**) (*gen pl* **-ń**) *nt* (*Radio*) interference; **zakłócenia w produkcji/transporcie** disruption in production/transport services; **~ porządku publicznego** breach *lub* disturbance of the peace; **zakłócenia atmosferyczne** atmospherics

**zakłó|cić (-cę, -cisz)** (*imp* **-ć**) *vb perf od* **zakłócać**

**zakłu|ć (-ję, -jesz)** *vt perf* (*zabić*) to stab to death; **zakłuło mnie w boku** I felt a stabbing pain in my side

**zakoch|ać się (-am, -asz)** *vb perf od* **zakochiwać się**

**zakochany** *adj*: **~ (w kimś/czymś)** in love (with sb/sth) ▷ *m decl like adj* lover; **~ po uszy** head over heels in love

**zakoch|iwać się (-uję, -ujesz)** (*perf* **zakochać**) *vr*: **zakochiwać się (w kimś/czymś)** to fall in love (with sb/sth)

**zakol|e** (**-a, -a**) (*gen pl* **-i**) *nt* (*drogi, rzeki*) bend; **zakola** *pl* (*we włosach*) receding hairline

**zakoły|sać (-szę, -szesz)** *vb perf od* **kołysać**
**zakomunik|ować (-uję, -ujesz)** *vt perf*: **~ komuś coś** to inform sb of *lub* about sth
**zako|n** (**-nu, -ny**) (*loc sg* **-nie**) *m* order; **~ rycerski** order of knights
**zakonnic|a** (**-y, -e**) *f* nun
**zakonni|k** (**-ka, -cy**) (*instr sg* **-kiem**) *m* friar
**zakonny** *adj* (*reguła, śluby*) monastic; **siostra zakonna** nun; **brat ~** friar
**zakończe|nie** (**-nia, -nia**) (*gen pl* **-ń**) *nt* (*pracy, współpracy*) end; (*opowiadania*) ending; (*wypracowania*) conclusion; **na ~** in closing *lub* conclusion
**zakończ|yć (-ę, -ysz)** *vb perf od* **kończyć, zakańczać**
**zako|pać (-pię, -piesz)** *vb perf od* **zakopywać**
**zakop|ywać (-uję, -ujesz)** (*perf* **-ać**) *vt* to bury; **zakopywać się** *vr* to bury o.s.
**zakork|ować (-uję, -ujesz)** *vb perf od* **korkować**
**zakorze|niać się (-nia)** (*perf* **-nić**) *vr* (*o roślinach*) to (take) root; (*przen: o zwyczajach, nawykach*) to take root
**zakorzeniony** *adj* (*szacunek, nienawiść*) ingrained; **głęboko ~** (*nienawiść*) deeply ingrained, deep-rooted; (*obawa*) deeply ingrained, deep-seated
**zakoszt|ować (-uję, -ujesz)** *vb perf od* **kosztować**
**zak|pić (-pię, -pisz)** (*imp* **-pij**) *vb perf od* **kpić**
**zakrad|ać się (-am, -asz)** (*perf* **zakraść**) *vr* to sneak in
**zakraplacz** (**-a, -e**) (*gen pl* **-y**) *m* dropper
**zakrapl|ać (-am, -asz)** (*perf* **zakroplić**) *vt*: **~ oczy/nos** to put eyedrops/nosedrops in
**zakra|ść się (-dnę, -dniesz)** (*imp* **-dnij**, *pt* **-dł, -dła, -dli**) *vb perf od* **zakradać się**
**zakraw|ać (-a)** *vi*: **to zakrawa na kpiny/dowcip** this sounds ridiculous/like a joke
**zakre|s** (**-su, -sy**) (*loc sg* **-sie**) *m* (*środków, obowiązków, działania*) range; (*uprawnień*) extent; (*tematyczny*) scope; (*Radio*) waveband; **wyżywienie we własnym ~ie** self-catering; **praca z ~u językoznawstwa** a paper in the field of linguistics
**zakreślacz** (**-a, -e**) (*gen pl* **-y**) *m* (*pisak*) highlighter, marker
**zakreśl|ać (-am, -asz)** (*perf* **-ić**) *vt* (*fragment tekstu*) to mark, to highlight; (*czek*) to cross
**zakrę|cać (-cam, -casz)** (*perf* **-cić**) *vt* (*słoik*) to twist on; (*kran*) to turn off; (*drut*) to twist; (*włosy*) to curl ▷ *vi* to turn
**zakrę|cić (-cę, -cisz)** (*imp* **-ć**) *vb perf od* **kręcić, zakręcać**
**zakrę|t** (**-tu, -ty**) (*loc sg* **-cie**) *m* bend, corner; **~ w lewo/prawo** left/right bend; **brać (wziąć** *perf*) **~** to take a bend *lub* corner
**zakręta|s** (**-sa, -sy**) (*loc sg* **-sie**) *m* flourish
**zakręt|ka** (**-ki, -ki**) (*dat sg* **-ce**, *gen pl* **-ek**) *f* (bottle) cap
**zakropl|ić (-ę, -isz)** *vb perf od* **zakraplać**
**zakrwawiony** *adj* bloody, bloodstained
**zakry|ć (-ję, -jesz)** *vb perf od* **zakrywać**
**zakrysti|a** (**-i, -e**) (*gen pl* **-i**) *f* sacristy, vestry
**zakryw|ać (-am, -asz)** (*perf* **zakryć**) *vt* to cover; **zakrywać się** *vr* to cover o.s.; **niebo zakryło się chmurami** the sky clouded over
**zakrze|p** (**-pu, -py**) (*loc sg* **-pie**) *m* (*Med*) clot
**zakrzep|nąć (-nie)** (*pt* **-ł** *lub* **-nął, -ła, -li**) *vb perf od* **krzepnąć**
**zakrztu|sić się (-szę, -sisz)** (*imp* **-ś**) *vb perf od* **krztusić się**
**zakrzy|kiwać (-kuję, -kujesz)** (*perf* **zakrzyczeć**) *vt* to shout down
**zakrzyk|nąć (-nę, -niesz)** (*imp* **-nij**) *vi perf* to shout
**zakrzy|wiać (-wiam, -wiasz)** (*perf* **-wić**) *vt* to bend; **zakrzywiać się** *vr* (*o gwoździu, gałęzi*) to bend; (*o drodze, ustach*) to curve
**zakrzy|wić (-wię, -wisz)** *vb perf od* **zakrzywiać**
**zakrzywiony** *adj* bent, curved
**zak|uć (-uję, -ujesz)** *vb perf od* **zakuwać**
**zakulisowy** *adj* backstage *attr*
**zaku|p** (**-pu, -py**) (*loc sg* **-pie**) *m* purchase; **iść na ~y** to go shopping; **robić ~y** to shop; **torba na ~y** shopping bag; **dobry/zły ~** good/bad buy; **cena/kurs ~u** purchase price; **~ hurtowy** bulk *lub* wholesale purchase
**zaku|pić (-pię, -pisz)** *vb perf od* **zakupywać**
**zaku|pywać (-puję, -pujesz)** (*perf* **-pić**) *vt* to purchase
**zakurzony** *adj* dusty
**zakurz|yć (-ę, -ysz)** *vb perf od* **kurzyć**
**zakus|y** (**-ów**) *pl*: **mieć ~ na coś** to have designs on sth
**zakuty** *adj*: **~ łeb** (*pot*) blockhead (*pot*)
**zakuw|ać (-am, -asz)** (*perf* **zakuć**) *vt* (*Szkol: pot*) to swot up (on) (*pot*) (*Brit*); (*więźnia*) to clap in irons *lub* chains; (*nit*) to close up, to clench ▷ *vi* (*pot*) to cram (*pot*), to swot (*pot*) (*Brit*)
**zakwalifik|ować (-uję, -ujesz)** *vb perf od* **kwalifikować**
**zakwa|sić (-szę, -sisz)** (*imp* **-ś**) *vb perf od* **kwasić, zakwaszać**
**zakwasz|ać (-am, -asz)** (*perf* **zakwasić**) *vt* (*kapustę*) to pickle
**zakwater|ować (-uję, -ujesz)** *vb perf od* **kwaterować, zakwaterowywać**
**zakwaterowani|e** (**-a**) *nt* accommodation, lodgings *pl*
**zakwaterow|ywać (-uję, -ujesz)** (*perf* **-ać**) *vt* (*turystów*) to accommodate; (*żołnierzy*) to quarter

Z

**zakwestion|ować (-uję, -ujesz)** *vb perf od* **kwestionować**
**zakwit|ać (-a)** (*perf* **-nąć**) *vi* to blossom, to bloom
**zakwit|nąć (-nie)** (*pt* **-ł** *lub* **-nął, -ła, -li**) *vb perf od* **kwitnąć, zakwitać**
**zal|ać (-eję, -ejesz)** *vb perf od* **zalewać**; **zalać się** *vr perf* (*pot*) to get stoned (*pot*); **~ się łzami** to dissolve in(to) tears
**zalak|ować (-uję, -ujesz)** *vb perf od* **lakować**
**zalany** *adj* flooded; (*pot*: *pijany*) drunk, sloshed (*pot*)
**zalatany** *adj* (*pot*) run off one's feet (*pot*)
**zalat|ywać (-uje)** (*perf* **zalecieć**) *vi* (*o zapachu*) to waft; **~ (czymś)** (*pot*) to smell (of sth)
**zal|ąc się (-ęgnie)** (*pt* **-ągł, -ęgła, -ęgli**) *vb perf od* **zalęgać się**
**zaląż|ek** (**-ka, -ki**) (*instr sg* **-kiem**) *m* germ
**zale|c (-gnę, -gniesz)** (*imp* **-gnij**) *vb perf od* **zalegać**; **zaległa cisza** a sudden silence fell
**zale|cać (-cam, -casz)** *vt* (*polecać*) (*perf* **-cić**); **~ coś (komuś)** to recommend sth (to sb); **zalecać się** *vr*: **~ się do kogoś** to court *lub* woo sb, to make advances to sb
**zalece|nie** (**-nia, -nia**) (*gen pl* **-ń**) *nt* recommendation; **godny zalecenia** advisable
**zale|cić (-cę, -cisz)** (*imp* **-ć**) *vb perf od* **zalecać**
**zale|cieć (-ci)** *vb perf od* **zalatywać**
**zalecz|yć (-ę, -ysz)** *vt perf* to cure (*temporarily or superficially*)
**zaledwie** *adv* merely ▷ *conj*: **~ przyjechał, ...** no sooner had he arrived than ...; **~ wczoraj** only yesterday
**zaleg|ać (-am, -asz)** *vi* (*o kurzu, śniegu, tłumie*) to linger; (*o węglu, torfie*) to occur; **~ z czymś** to be behind with sth
**zalegaliz|ować (-uję, -ujesz)** *vb perf od* **legalizować**
**zaległoś|ci** (**-ci**) *pl* (*w nauce, pracy*) backlog; (*w płaceniu*) arrears *pl*; **mieć ~ (w czymś)** to be behind (with sth)
**zaległy** *adj* overdue, outstanding
**zale|piać (-piam, -piasz)** (*perf* **-pić**) *vt* (*dziurę*) to block, to fill
**zale|pić (-pię, -pisz)** *vb perf od* **zalepiać**
**zale|siać (-siam, -siasz)** (*perf* **-sić**) *vt* to afforest
**zale|sić (-się, -sisz)** (*imp* **-ś**) *vb perf od* **zalesiać**
**zale|ta** (**-ty, -ty**) (*dat sg* **-cie**) *f* virtue, advantage
**zale|w** (**-wu, -wy**) (*loc sg* **-wie**) *m* (*sztuczne jezioro*) reservoir; (*zatoka morska*) bay; (*przen*) flood
**zale|wa** (**-wy, -wy**) (*dat sg* **-wie**) *f* (*octowa*) marinade; (*słona*) brine
**zalew|ać (-am, -asz)** (*perf* **zalać**) *vt* (*o rzece, świetle, tłumie*) to flood; (*o płynie*: *moczyć*) to drench; (: *plamić*) to stain; **~ coś wodą/mlekiem** to pour water/milk over sth; **~ otwór betonem** to fill a hole with concrete; **krew mnie zalewa** (*pot*) my blood is up
**zależ|eć (-y)** *vi*: **~ (od kogoś/czegoś)** to depend (on sb/sth); **bardzo jej na nim zależy** she cares deeply about him; **nie zależy mi (na tym)** I don't care; **to zależy** it depends; **to zależy od ciebie** it's up to you
**zależnie** *adv*: **~ od czegoś** depending on sth
**zależnoś|ć** (**-ci, -ci**) (*gen pl* **-ci**) *f* relationship, link; **~ (od** *+gen***)** dependence (on); **w zależności od czegoś** depending on sth
**zależny** *adj* dependent; (*Jęz*: *przypadek*) oblique; **mowa zależna** reported *lub* indirect speech
**zalęg|ać się (-a)** (*perf* **zaląc** *lub* **zalęgnąć**) *vr* (*o owadach, robakach*): **zalęgać się w piwnicy** *itp.* to infest the cellar *etc*
**zal|ęgnąć się (-ęgnie)** (*pt* **-ągł, -ęgła, -ęgli**) *vb perf od* **lęgnąć się, zalęgać się**
**zalękniony** *adj* (*książk*) frightened
**zalicz|ać (-am, -asz)** (*perf* **-yć**) *vt* (*Uniw*: *egzamin*) to pass; (: *semestr, rok*) to complete (successfully); (*pot*: *zwiedzać*: *miasto*) to do (*pot*); **~ kogoś/coś do** *+gen* to rate sb/sth among; **~ komuś coś** to give sb credit for sth; **zaliczać się** *vr*: **~ się do** *+gen* to be numbered among
**zalicze|nie** (**-nia, -nia**) (*gen pl* **-ń**) *nt* (*Szkol, Uniw*) credit; **za ~m pocztowym** ≈ COD
**zalicz|ka** (**-ki, -ki**) (*dat sg* **-ce**, *gen pl* **-ek**) *f* advance; **dawać komuś zaliczkę** to advance money to sb
**zaliczkowy** *adj*: **wpłata zaliczkowa** advance payment
**zalicz|yć (-ę, -ysz)** *vb perf od* **zaliczać**
**zalog|ować się (-uję, -ujesz)** *vi perf* to log in
**zalotni|k** (**-ka, -cy**) (*instr sg* **-kiem**) *m* suitor, wooer
**zalotny** *adj* coquettish
**zalot|y** (**-ów**) *pl* (*książk*) courtship, advances *pl*
**zalud|niać (-niam, -niasz)** (*perf* **-nić**) *vt* to populate, to people; **zaludniać się** *vr* to come alive (with people)
**zalud|nić (-nię, -nisz)** (*imp* **-nij**) *vb perf od* **zaludniać**
**zaludnieni|e** (**-a**) *nt* population; **gęstość zaludnienia** population density
**zał.** *abbr* (= *założony*) est., estab.
**załad|ować (-uję, -ujesz)** *vb perf od* **ładować, załadowywać**
**załadow|ywać (-uję, -ujesz)** (*perf* **-ać**) *vt* to load
**załadun|ek** (**-ku, -ki**) (*instr sg* **-kiem**) *m* loading
**załago|dzić (-dzę, -dzisz)** (*imp* **-dź**) *vb perf od* **łagodzić**

**zała|mać (-mię, -miesz)** *vb perf od* **załamywać**
**załama|nie** (**-nia, -nia**) (*gen pl* **-ń**) *nt* (*zagięcie*) bend; (*w gospodarce*) slump; **~ psychiczne** (nervous) breakdown; **~ światła/fal** refraction of light/waves; **~ się** (*dachu, mostu, lodu*) collapse
**załam|ywać (-uję, -ujesz)** (*perf* **-ać**) *vt* (*zaginać*) to bend; (*wpędzać w depresję*) to depress; (*dach, most*) to cause to collapse, to cave in; (*światło, promienie*) to refract; **~ ręce** to wring one's hands; **załamywać się** *vr* (*wyginać się*) to bend; (*o dachu, moście, lodzie*) to collapse, to cave in; (*o głosie*) to break; (*o człowieku*) to break down; (*o świetle, fali*) to be refracted
**załat|ać (-am, -asz)** *vb perf od* **łatać**
**załat|wiać (-wiam, -wiasz)** (*perf* **-wić**) *vt* (*sprawy, interesy*) to take care of; (*pot: klientów*) to serve; **załatwić komuś coś** (*pot*) to fix sb up with sth (*pot*); **ja to załatwię** let me handle that; **załatwiać się** *vr* (*pot*) to relieve o.s.
**załat|wić (-wię, -wisz)** *vb perf od* **załatwiać** ▹ *vt perf*: **~ kogoś** (*rozprawić się*) to fix sb (*pot*); (*zabić*) to dispose of sb, to take care of sb (*pot*)
**załatwieni|e** (**-a**) *nt*: **mam coś do załatwienia** I have some business to attend to; **to jest do załatwienia** it can be done
**załatwiony** *adj*: **załatwione!** done!; **jestem ~** (*pot*) I'm done for (*pot*)
**załącz|ać (-am, -asz)** (*perf* **-yć**) *vt* to enclose
**załącze|nie** (**-nia, -nia**) (*gen pl* **-ń**) *nt*: **w załączeniu ...** please find enclosed ...
**załączni|k** (**-ka, -ki**) (*instr sg* **-kiem**) *m* (*do listu*) enclosure
**załącz|yć (-ę, -ysz)** *vb perf od* **załączać**
**zał|oga** (**-ogi, -ogi**) (*dat sg* **-odze**, *gen pl* **-óg**) *f* (*statku, samolotu*) crew; (*fabryki*) staff
**załogowy** *adj* (*lot*) manned
**założe|nie** (**-nia, -nia**) (*gen pl* **-ń**) *nt* assumption, premise; **wychodzić (wyjść** *perf*) **z założenia, że ...** to assume that ...; **w założeniu** originally; **założenia** *pl* (*wytyczne*) guidelines *pl*
**założyciel** (**-a, -e**) (*gen pl* **-i**) *m* founder
**założycielski** *adj*: **komitet ~** founding committee
**zał|ożyć (-ożę, -ożysz)** (*imp* **-óż**) *vb perf od* **zakładać**
**załzawiony** *adj* watery
**zamach** (**-u, -y**) *m* (*próba zamordowania*) assassination attempt; (*zamordowanie*) assassination; (*bombowy*) attack; **~ stanu** coup (d'état); **dokonać** (*perf*) **~u na kogoś/na czyjeś życie** (*nieudanego*) to make an attempt on sb's life; (*udanego*) to assassinate sb; **za jednym ~em** at one go
**zamach|nąć się (-nę, -niesz)** (*imp* **-nij**) *vr perf* to swing one's arm
**zamacho|wiec** (**-wca, -wcy**) *m* (*zabójca*) assassin; (*napastnik*) attacker; (*podkładający bombę*) bomber
**zamachowy** *adj*: **koło zamachowe** flywheel
**zamacz|ać (-am, -asz)** (*perf* **zamoczyć**) *vt* (*przypadkowo*) to get wet; (*celowo*) to soak; **zamaczać się** *vr* to get wet
**zamak|ać (-am, -asz)** (*perf* **zamoknąć**) *vi* to get soaked
**zamart|wiać się (-wiam, -wiasz)** (*perf* **-wić**) *vr*: **zamartwiać się (czymś** *lub* **z powodu czegoś)** to worry (about sth)
**zamarz|ać (-am, -asz)** (*perf* **-nąć**) *vi* (*o wodzie*) to freeze; (*o rzece, jeziorze*) to freeze (over)
**zamarz|nąć (-nę, -niesz)** (*imp* **-nij**) *vb perf od* **marznąć, zamarzać** ▹ *vi perf* (*umrzeć*) to freeze to death
**zamarznięty** *adj* frozen
**zamask|ować (-uję, -ujesz)** *vb perf od* **maskować**
**zamaskowany** *adj* (*wejście*) concealed; (*twarz, bandyta*) masked
**zamaszysty** *adj* (*ruch, gest*) sweeping; (*krok*) vigorous
**zamawi|ać (-am, -asz)** (*perf* **zamówić**) *vt* (*danie, towar*) to order; (*bilety, stolik*) to book, to reserve; (*rozmowę telefoniczną*) to place; **~ wizytę** to make an appointment
**zama|zać (-żę, -żesz)** *vb perf od* **zamazywać**
**zamaz|ywać (-uję, -ujesz)** (*perf* **-ać**) *vt* (*napis*) to smear
**zamą|cić (-cę, -cisz)** (*perf* **-ć**) *vb perf od* **mącić**
**zamążpójści|e** (**-a**) *nt* marriage
**Zambi|a** (**-i**) *f* Zambia
**zambijski** *adj* Zambian
**zam|ek** (**-ku, -ki**) (*instr sg* **-kiem**) *m* (*budowla*) castle; (*w drzwiach, karabinie*) lock; (*też:* **zamek błyskawiczny**) zip (fastener), zipper (US)
**zameld|ować (-uję, -ujesz)** *vb perf od* **meldować**
**zamęcz|ać (-am, -asz)** (*perf* **-yć**) *vt*: **~ kogoś czymś** to badger *lub* plague sb with
**zamęcz|yć (-ę, -ysz)** *vb perf od* **zamęczać** ▹ *vt perf* (*pozbawić życia*) to martyr
**zamę|t** (**-tu**) (*loc sg* **-cie**) *m* confusion; **mieć ~ w głowie** to be confused *lub* in a muddle
**zamężna** *adj* married
**zamglony** *adj* misty, hazy
**zamian** *m inv*; **w ~ za** *+acc* in exchange *lub* return for
**zamia|na** (**-ny, -ny**) (*dat sg* **-nie**) *f* (*wymiana*) exchange; (*przekształcenie*) conversion
**zamia|r** (**-ru, -ry**) (*loc sg* **-rze**) *m* intention; **mieć ~ coś zrobić** to intend to do sth; **mieć dobre/złe ~y** to have good/evil *lub* bad intentions

Z

**zamiast** *prep +gen* instead of; **~ pójść z nami ...** instead of joining us ..., rather than go with us ...; **~ tego** instead
**zamiatacz** (**-a, -e**) (*gen pl* **-y**) *m* (*też:* **zamiatacz ulic**) streetsweeper (*Brit*), street cleaner (*US*)
**zamiat|ać (-am, -asz)** (*perf* **zamieść**) *vt* to sweep
**zamiatar|ka** (**-ki, -ki**) (*dat sg* **-ce**, *gen pl* **-ek**) *f* roadsweeper
**zamie|ć** (**-ci, -cie**) (*gen pl* **-ci**) *f* snowstorm, blizzard
**zamiejscowy** *adj* (*rozmowa*) long-distance; (*robotnik, pracownik: dojeżdżający*) commuting; (*: nie miejscowy*) out-of-town
**zamie|niać (-niam, -niasz)** (*perf* **-nić**) *vt*: **~ coś (na** *+acc*) to exchange sth (for); **~ kogoś/coś w** *+acc* to turn sb/sth into; **zamienić z kimś parę słów** to have a word with sb; **zamieniać się** *vr*: **~ się (czymś** *lub* **na coś)** to swap (sth); **~ się w** *+acc* to turn into; **zamieniłem się z nim miejscami** *lub* **na miejsca** I changed places with him; **zamieniam się w słuch** I'm all ears
**zamie|nić (-nię, -nisz)** (*imp* **-ń**) *vb perf od* **zamieniać**
**zamiennie** *adv* interchangeably
**zamienny** *adj*: **części zamienne** spare *lub* replacement parts
**zamier|ać (-am, -asz)** (*perf* **zamrzeć**) *vi* (*o dźwięku, głosie*) to die *lub* fade away; (*o człowieku: nieruchomieć*) to freeze; (*o życiu gospodarczym*) to come to a standstill; (*o żywych organizmach*) to decay, to die; **zamarł z przerażenia** he was petrified
**zamierz|ać (-am, -asz)** (*perf* **-yć**) *vt*: **~ coś zrobić** to intend to do sth; **zamierzać się** *vr*: **~ się na kogoś** to aim a blow at sb
**zamierze|nie** (**-nia, -nia**) (*gen pl* **-ń**) *nt* intention
**zamierzony** *adj* (*skutek, efekt*) intended; (*atak*) deliberate
**zamierz|yć (-ę, -ysz)** *vb perf od* **zamierzać**
**zamiesz|ać (-am, -asz)** *vb perf od* **mieszać** ▷ *vt perf*: **~ kogoś w coś** to implicate sb in sth; **~ komuś w głowie** to put ideas into sb's head
**zamieszani|e** (**-a**) *nt* confusion, chaos; **robić ~** to cause *lub* create confusion
**zamieszany** *adj*: **~ w** *+acc* implicated in
**zamieszcz|ać (-am, -asz)** (*perf* **zamieścić**) *vt* (*w prasie*) to run
**zamieszk|ać (-am, -asz)** *vi perf* to take up residence
**zamieszkały** *adj* (*dom, dzielnica*) inhabited; **~ w Londynie** resident in London
**zamieszkani|e** (**-a**) *nt*: **miejsce zamieszkania** (place of) residence
**zamiesz|ki** (**-ek**) *pl* riots *pl*
**zamiesz|kiwać (-kuję, -kujesz)** *vt* (*o zwierzętach*) to inhabit ▷ *vi* (*książk: mieszkać*) to dwell
**zamie|ścić (-szczę, -ścisz)** (*imp* **-ść**) *vb perf od* **zamieszczać**
**zami|eść (-otę, -eciesz)** (*imp* **-eć**, *pt* **-ótł, -otła, -etli**) *vb perf od* **zamiatać**
**zamilk|nąć (-nę, -niesz)** (*imp* **-nij**) *vb perf* to become silent
**zamiłowa|nie** (**-nia, -nia**) (*gen pl* **-ń**) *nt* passion; **mieć ~ do czegoś** to have a passion for sth; **ogrodnik z zamiłowania** a keen gardener
**zamiłowany** *adj* keen
**zamin|ować (-uję, -ujesz)** *vt perf* (*Wojsk*) to mine
**zamk|nąć (-nę, -niesz)** (*imp* **-nij**) *vb perf od* **zamykać**
**zamknię|cie** (**-cia**) *nt* (*na stałe*) closure; (*na noc*) closing; (*zamek*) (*nom pl* **-cia**, *gen pl* **-ć**) lock; **w zamknięciu** under lock and key
**zamknięty** *adj* closed; (*pokój, sala*) locked; (*system*) self-contained; **~ na klucz** locked; **~ w sobie** withdrawn; **(mógłbym to zrobić) z ~mi oczami** (*przen*) (I could do it) blindfold; **pokaz ~** preview; **przy drzwiach ~ch** (*Prawo*) in camera; **„zamknięte"** "closed"
**zamoc|ować (-uję, -ujesz)** *vb perf od* **mocować, zamocowywać**
**zamocow|ywać (-uję, -ujesz)** (*perf* **-ać**) *vt* to mount, to fix
**zamocz|yć (-ę, -ysz)** *vb perf od* **moczyć, zamaczać**
**zamok|nąć (-nę, -niesz)** (*imp* **-nij**) *vb perf od* **zamakać**
**zamont|ować (-uję, -ujesz)** *vb perf od* **montować, zamontowywać**
**zamontow|ywać (-uję, -ujesz)** (*perf* **-ać**) *vt* to fit, to mount
**zamord|ować (-uję, -ujesz)** *vb perf od* **mordować**
**zamorski** *adj* overseas *attr*
**zamortyz|ować (-uję, -ujesz)** *vb perf od* **amortyzować**
**zam|orzyć (-orzę, -orzysz)** (*imp* **-órz**) *vb perf od* **morzyć**
**zamożnoś|ć** (**-ci**) *f* affluence, wealth
**zamożny** *adj* affluent, wealthy
**zamó|wić (-wię, -wisz)** *vb perf od* **zamawiać**
**zamówie|nie** (**-nia, -nia**) (*gen pl* **-ń**) *nt* order; **zrobiony na ~** made to order, custom-made; **składać (złożyć** *perf*) **~ (u kogoś/na coś)** to place an order (with sb/for sth)
**zamraż|ać (-am, -asz)** (*perf* **zamrozić**) *vt* to freeze; **zamrażać się** *vr* (*o żywności*) to freeze
**zamrażalni|k** (**-ka, -ki**) (*instr sg* **-kiem**) *m* freezer compartment

**zamrażar|ka** (**-ki, -ki**) (*dat sg* **-ce**, *gen pl* **-ek**) *f* freezer, deep freeze

**zamroczeni|e** (**-a**) *nt* stupor, daze

**zamroczony** *adj* dazed

**zamrocz|yć (-ę, -ysz)** *vt perf* to daze

**zamro|zić (-żę, -zisz)** (*imp* **-ź**) *vb perf od* **zamrażać, mrozić**

**zam|rzeć (-rę, -rzesz)** (*imp* **-rzyj**, *pt* **-arł**) *vb perf od* **zamierać**

**zamsz** (**-u, -e**) *m* suede

**zamszowy** *adj* suede *attr*

**zamur|ować (-uję, -ujesz)** *vb perf od* **zamurowywać**

**zamurow|ywać (-uję, -ujesz)** (*perf* **-ać**) *vt* (*drzwi, okno*) to brick up; **zamurowało mnie** (*pot*) I was speechless

**zamydl|ać (-am, -asz)** (*perf* **-ić**) *vt*: **~ komuś oczy** (*przen*) to pull the wool over sb's eyes

**zamyk|ać (-am, -asz)** (*perf* **zamknąć**) *vt* (*drzwi, oczy, książkę*) to close, to shut; (*na klucz*) to lock; (*sklep, biuro, granicę*) to close; (*dyskusję, dochodzenie*) to close; (*wsadzać do więzienia*) to lock up; (*szkołę, fabrykę*) to close *lub* shut down; (*pot*: *gaz, prąd, wodę*) to turn off; **~ księgi** to balance the books; **„zamknąć cudzysłów"** "unquote"; **zamykać się** *vr* (*w pokoju, łazience*) to lock o.s.; (*o drzwiach*) to shut; (*o zamku*) to lock; (*o kwiatach*) to fold (up); (*o roku, działalności*) to close; **zamknąć się w sobie** (*przen*) to withdraw into o.s.; **usta mu się nie zamykają** he can't stop talking; **zamknij się!** (*pot*) shut up! (*pot*)

**zamy|sł** (**-słu, -sły**) (*loc sg* **-śle**) *m* (*książk*) intention, plan

**zamyśl|ać się (-am, -asz)** (*perf* **-ić**) *vr* to be lost in thought; **zamyślać się nad czymś** to muse over *lub* (up)on sth

**zamyśleni|e** (**-a**) *nt*: **w zamyśleniu** thoughtfully, pensively

**zamyśl|ić się (-ę, -isz)** *vb perf od* **zamyślać się**

**zamyślony** *adj* thoughtful, pensive

**zanadrzu** *inv*: (**trzymać/mieć coś) w ~** (to keep/have sth) up one's sleeve

**zanadto** *adv* excessively

**zanaliz|ować (-uję, -ujesz)** *vb perf od* **analizować**

**zaniech|ać (-am, -asz)** *vt perf +gen*; **~ czegoś** to give sth up, to desist from sth

**zanieczyszcz|ać (-am, -asz)** (*perf* **zanieczyścić**) *vt* to pollute, to contaminate

**zanieczyszcze|nie** (**-nia, -nia**) (*gen pl* **-ń**) *nt* (*stan*) pollution, contamination; (*domieszka*) impurity; **zanieczyszczenia** *pl* impurities *pl*, contaminants *pl*

**zanieczy|ścić (-szczę, -ścisz)** (*imp* **-ść**) *vb perf od* **zanieczyszczać**

**zaniedb|ać (-am, -asz)** *vb perf od* **zaniedbywać**

**zaniedba|nie** (**-nia, -nia**) (*gen pl* **-ń**) *nt* neglect, negligence

**zaniedbany** *adj* run-down, neglected

**zaniedb|ywać (-uję, -ujesz)** (*perf* **-ać**) *vt* to neglect; **zaniedbywać się** *vr* to let o.s. go; **~ się w obowiązkach** to be negligent in one's duty

**zaniem|óc (-ogę, -ożesz)** (*pt* **-ógł, -ogła, -ogli**) *vi perf* (*książk*) to fall ill

**zaniemó|wić (-wię, -wisz)** *vi perf*: **zaniemówił (z oburzenia)** he was speechless (with indignation)

**zaniepok|oić (-oję, -oisz)** (*imp* **-ój**) *vb perf od* **niepokoić** ▷ *vt perf* to alarm, to disturb; **zaniepokoić się** *vr perf* to become alarmed *lub* anxious

**zaniepokojeni|e** (**-a**) *nt* alarm

**zani|eść (-osę, -esiesz)** (*imp* **-eś**, *pt* **-ósł, -osła, -eśli**) *vb perf od* **nieść, zanosić**

**zani|k** (**-ku**) (*instr sg* **-kiem**) *m* disappearance; (*Med*) atrophy; **~ pamięci** memory loss; **~ mięśni** muscular atrophy

**zanik|ać (-a)** (*perf* **-nąć**) *vi* (*o tradycji, uczuciach, gatunku*) to disappear, to die out; (*o głosie, obrazie, tętnie*) to die away, to fade

**zanik|nąć (-nie)** (*pt* **-nął** *lub* **-ł, -ła, -li**) *vb perf od* **zanikać**

**zanim** *conj* before; **~ zadzwonię/zadzwoniłam ...** before I make/made the call ...; **~ nie sprawdzę** before I check *lub* have checked

**zaniż|ać (-am, -asz)** (*perf* **-yć**) *vt* (*stawki, poziom*) to lower; **~ cenę czegoś** to underprice sth

**zanoc|ować (-uję, -ujesz)** *vb perf od* **nocować**

**zano|sić (-szę, -sisz)** (*imp* **-ś**, *perf* **zanieść**) *vt* to take, to carry; **zanosić się** *vr*: **zanosi się na deszcz** it looks like (it's going to) rain; **~ się od płaczu/śmiechu** to cry/laugh hysterically

**zanot|ować (-uję, -ujesz)** *vb perf od* **notować**

**zanu|dzać (-dzam, -dzasz)** (*perf* **-dzić**) *vt* to bore; **~ kogoś pytaniami** to bore sb with questions

**zanu|dzić (-dzę, -dzisz)** (*imp* **-dź**) *vb perf od* **zanudzać**

**zanurz|ać (-am, -asz)** (*perf* **-yć**) *vt* to dip, to immerse; **zanurzać się** *vr* (*o pływaku*) to dive; (*o przedmiotach*) to sink; (*o łodzi podwodnej*) to submerge

**zanurzeni|e** (**-a**) *nt* (*Żegl*) draught (*Brit*), draft (*US*)

**zanurz|yć (-ę, -ysz)** *vb perf od* **zanurzać**

**zaobserw|ować (-uję, -ujesz)** *vb perf od* **obserwować**

**zaocznie** *adv* (*wybierać, sądzić*) in absentia; (*studiować*) part-time

Z

**zaoczny** *adj* (*wyrok*) in absentia; (*Uniw*) part-time, extramural
**zaofer|ować (-uję, -ujesz)** *vb perf od* **oferować**
**zaofiar|ować (-uję, -ujesz)** *vb perf od* **ofiarować**
**zaog|nić (-nię, -nisz)** (*imp* **-nij**) *vt perf* to inflame; **zaognić się** *vr* to become inflamed
**zaokrągl|ać (-am, -asz)** (*perf* **-ić**) *vt* (*nadawać okrągły kształt*) to round; (*ceny, liczby*: *w górę*) to round up; (: *w dół*) to round down; **zaokrąglać się** *vr* (*o twarzy, człowieku*) to fill out
**zaokrągle|nie** (**-nia, -nia**) (*gen pl* **-ń**) *nt* (*kształt*) curvature; **w zaokrągleniu** in round figures
**zaokrągl|ić (-ę, -isz)** (*imp* **-ij**) *vb perf od* **zaokrąglać**
**zaokręt|ować (-uję, -ujesz)** *vt perf* (*pasażera*) to embark; (*marynarza*) to enlist; **zaokrętować się** *vr* to enlist
**zaopatr|ywać (-uję, -ujesz)** (*perf* **zaopatrzyć**) *vt*: **~ kogoś w coś** (*dostarczać*) to provide *lub* supply sb with sth; (*wyposażać*) to supply *lub* equip sb with sth; **zaopatrywać się** *vr*: **~ się w wodę** to stock up on water
**zaopatrzeni|e** (**-a**) *nt* (*Handel*) delivery; **dział zaopatrzenia** delivery (department)
**zaopatrzony** *adj*: **dobrze/słabo ~** well/poorly stocked
**zaopatrz|yć (-ę, -ysz)** *vb perf od* **zaopatrywać**
**zaopiek|ować się (-uję, -ujesz)** *vb perf od* **opiekować się**
**zaopini|ować (-uję, -ujesz)** *vb perf od* **opiniować**
**zaor|ać (-am, -asz)** *vt perf* to plough (*Brit*), to plow (*US*)
**zaostrz|ać (-am, -asz)** (*perf* **-yć**) *vt* (*patyk, ołówek, kontury*) to sharpen; (*apetyt*) to whet, to sharpen; (*przepisy, sankcje*) to tighten; (*konflikt, polemikę*) to inflame; **zaostrzać się** *vr* to sharpen; (*o konflikcie, sporze*) to escalate
**zaostrz|yć (-ę, -ysz)** *vb perf od* **ostrzyć, zaostrzać**
**zaoszczę|dzić (-dzę, -dzisz)** (*imp* **-dź**) *vt perf* *+acc* (*pieniądze, czas*) to save ▷ *vt perf +gen*; **zaoszczędziło mu to pracy** it saved him some work; **~ na prądzie/opale** to save on electricity/fuel
**zaowoc|ować (-uje)** *vb perf od* **owocować**
**zapach** (**-u, -y**) *m* smell, odour (*Brit*), odor (*US*); (*kwiatów*) fragrance
**zapachowy** *adj* aromatic
**zapaćk|ać (-am, -asz)** (*pot*) *vt perf* (*pobrudzić*) to smudge; (*niedbale pomalować*) to slap paint on
**zapad|ać (-am, -asz)** (*perf* **zapaść**) *vi* (*o kurtynie, nocy, ciszy*) to fall; (*o decyzji*) to be made *lub* reached; (*o uchwale, rezolucji*) to be passed; **~ w głęboki sen** to fall into a deep sleep; **~ w sen zimowy** to hibernate; **zapaść na** *+acc* to fall *lub* be taken ill with; **(on) zapadł na zdrowiu** his health has declined; **klamka zapadła** (*przen*) it's too late now, it's past the point of no return; **zapadać się** *vr* (*w błocie, bagnie*) to sink; (*o dachu, podłodze*) to cave in, to fall in; **jakby się zapadł pod ziemię** he vanished into thin air
**zapad|ka** (**-ki, -ki**) (*dat sg* **-ce**, *gen pl* **-ek**) *f* (*Tech*) catch
**zapadły** *adj* (*pot*: *dziura, wioska*) godforsaken; (*boki, policzki*) sunken
**zapad|nia** (**-ni, -nie**) (*gen pl* **-ni**) *f* (*Teatr*) trapdoor
**zapadnięty** *adj* (*twarz, policzki*) sunken
**zapak|ować (-uję, -ujesz)** *vb perf od* **pakować**
**zapal|ać (-am, -asz)** (*perf* **-ić**) *vt* (*zapałkę, papierosa, fajkę*) to light; (*silnik*) to start; (*światło, lampę*) to turn on, to switch on; **zapalać się** *vr* (*zaczynać się palić*) to catch fire; (*włączać się*) to come on; **zapalić się do czegoś** (*przen*) to become enthusiastic over *lub* about sth
**zapalający** *adj* (*Wojsk*) incendiary
**zapalczywoś|ć** (**-ci**) *f* quick temper
**zapalczywy** *adj* (*człowiek*) quick-tempered; (*dyskusja*) heated
**zapaleni|e** (**-a**) *nt* (*Med*) inflammation; **~ płuc** pneumonia; **~ opon mózgowych** meningitis; **~ krtani** laryngitis; **~ wyrostka robaczkowego** appendicitis
**zapale|niec** (**-ńca, -ńcy**) *m* enthusiast
**zapal|ić (-ę, -isz)** *vb perf od* **zapalać**
**zapalnicz|ka** (**-ki, -ki**) (*dat sg* **-ce**, *gen pl* **-ek**) *f* lighter
**zapalni|k** (**-ka, -ki**) (*instr sg* **-kiem**) *m* (*Wojsk*) fuse, fuze (*US*)
**zapalny** *adj* (*materiał, substancja*) inflammable, flammable; (*charakter, stan*) inflammatory; **punkt ~** (*przen*) hot *lub* trouble spot
**zapalony** *adj* (*światło*) turned on, switched on; (*zapałka, świeca*) lighted, lit; (*zwolennik, myśliwy*) keen
**zapa|ł** (**-łu, -ły**) (*loc sg* **-le**) *m* zeal, eagerness; **z ~em** eagerly; **pełen ~u** zealous, eager; **słomiany ~** short-lived enthusiasm
**zapał|ać (-am, -asz)** *vb perf od* **pałać**
**zapał|ka** (**-ki, -ki**) (*dat sg* **-ce**, *gen pl* **-ek**) *f* match; **pudełko zapałek** a box of matches; **pudełko od zapałek** matchbox
**zapamięt|ać (-am, -asz)** *vb perf od* **zapamiętywać**
**zapamiętały** *adj* passionate

**zapamięt|ywać (-uję, -ujesz)** *(perf* **-ać***)* *vt* *(zachowywać w pamięci)* to remember; *(uczyć się na pamięć)* to memorize

**zapan|ować (-uję, -ujesz)** *vb perf od* **panować**

**zapar|cie** (**-cia, -cia**) *(gen pl* **-ć***)* *nt* *(Med)* constipation; **z ~m** with determination

**zapark|ować (-uję, -ujesz)** *vb perf od* **parkować**

**zapar|ować (-uje)** *vi perf* to mist over *(Brit)*, to steam *lub* fog over (US)

**zaparowany** *adj* misty *(Brit)*, steamy (US)

**zaparty** *adj*: **z ~m tchem** with bated breath

**zaparz|ać (-am, -asz)** *(perf* **-yć***)* *vt* *(herbatę, zioła)* to brew, to infuse

**zapa|s** (**-su, -sy**) *(loc sg* **-sie***)* *m* (spare) supply, reserve; **mieć coś w ~ie** to have sth in reserve; **na ~** *(martwić się, cieszyć się)* prematurely; **zapasy** *pl* provisions *pl*; *(Sport)* wrestling; **robić ~y (czegoś)** to stock up (on sth)

**zapasowy** *adj* *(koło, część)* spare; *(wyjście, schody)* emergency *attr*

**zapaś|ć**[1] (**-ci**) *f* *(Med)* collapse

**zapa|ść**[2] **(-dnę, -dniesz)** *(imp* **-dnij**, *pt* **-dł***)* *vb perf od* **zapadać**

**zapaśni|k** (**-ka, -cy**) *(instr sg* **-kiem***)* *m* wrestler

**zapatr|ywać się (-uję, -ujesz)** *vr*: **zapatrywać się na coś inaczej/sceptycznie** to take a different/sceptical view of sth

**zapatrywa|nia** (**-ń**) *pl* views *pl*

**zapatrzony** *adj*: **~ w siebie** self-centred *(Brit)*, self-centered (US); **być w kogoś ~m** *(przen)* to look up to sb

**zapatrz|yć się (-ę, -ysz)** *vr perf*: **zapatrzyć się (w** *+acc***)** to stare (at)

**zapch|ać (-am, -asz)** *vb perf od* **zapychać**

**zapchany** *adj* blocked (up)

**zapeł|niać (-niam, -niasz)** *(perf* **-nić***)* *vt* to fill; **zapełniać się** *vr* to fill (up)

**zapeł|nić (-nię, -nisz)** *(imp* **-nij** *lub* **-ń***)* *vb perf od* **zapełniać**

**zapesz|yć (-ę, -ysz)** *vi perf*: **nie chcę ~** *(pot)* I don't want to put a jinx on it *(pot)*

**zapewne** *adv* *(prawdopodobnie)* probably; *(niewątpliwie)* undoubtedly

**zapew|niać (-niam, -niasz)** *(perf* **-nić***)* *vt* *(osobę)* to assure; *(bezpieczeństwo)* to ensure; **~ kogoś o czymś** to assure sb of sth; **~ komuś coś** to secure sth for sb; **zapewniam cię, że ...** I assure you (that) ...

**zapewnie|nie** (**-nia, -nia**) *(gen pl* **-ń***)* *nt* assurance

**zapęd|y** (**-ów**) *pl* *(pot)* leanings *pl*, inclinations *pl*

**zapę|dzać (-dzam, -dzasz)** *(perf* **-dzić***)* *vt*: **zapędzić owce na pastwisko** to put out sheep to pasture; **~ kogoś do pracy** to drive sb to work; **zapędzić kogoś w kozi róg** *(przen)* to run rings round sb; **zapędzać się** *vr* to go too far

**zapę|dzić (-dzę, -dzisz)** *(imp* **-dź***)* *vb perf od* **pędzić, zapędzać**

**zapi|ać (-eje, -ejesz)** *vb perf od* **piać**

**za|piąć (-pnę, -pniesz)** *(imp* **-pnij***)* *vb perf od* **zapinać**

**zapie|c (-kę, -czesz)** *(pt* **-kł***)* *vb perf od* **zapiekać** ▷ *vi perf* *(o ranie)* to sting

**zapiek|ać (-am, -asz)** *(perf* **zapiec***)* *vt* to casserole

**zapiekan|ka** (**-ki, -ki**) *(dat sg* **-ce**, *gen pl* **-ek***)* *f* casserole

**zapieprz|ać (-am, -asz)** *vi* *(pot: iść)* to tear along *(pot)*; *(pracować)* to work one's butt off *(pot)*

**zapier|ać (-am, -asz)** *(perf* **zaprzeć***)* *vt* *(oddech)* to take away; **dech mi zaparło** it took my breath away; **zapierać się** *vr* to dig one's heels in

**zapierdal|ać (-am, -asz)** *(pot!)* *vi* *(iść)* to go full blast *(pot)*; *(pracować)* to bust one's arse *(Brit)* *(pot!)* *lub* ass (US) *(pot!)*

**zapię|cie** (**-cia, -cia**) *(gen pl* **-ć***)* *nt* *(czynność)* fastening; *(zamek, klamra)* fastener

**zapin|ać (-am, -asz)** *vt* *(perf* **zapiąć***)* *(ogólnie)* to fasten; *(na guziki)* to button up; *(na zamek)* to zip up; *(guziki, zamek)* to do up; **~ pasy (bezpieczeństwa)** to belt up; **czy wszystko jest zapięte na ostatni guzik?** *(przen)* (are you) all set?; **zapinać się** *vr* *(perf* **zapiąć***)* *(na guziki)* to button up; *(na zamek)* to zip up; *(mieć zapięcie)* to fasten

**zapin|ka** (**-ki, -ki**) *(dat sg* **-ce**, *gen pl* **-ek***)* *f* clasp

**zapi|s** (**-su, -sy**) *(loc sg* **-sie***)* *m* *(czynność)* recording; *(tekst)* record; *(nagranie)* record, recording; *(sposób zapisywania)* notation; *(w testamencie)* bequest; **zapisy** *pl* *(na uczelnię)* registration; *(kolejka)* waiting list

**zapi|sać (-szę, -szesz)** *vb perf od* **zapisywać** ▷ *vt perf* *(kartkę, zeszyt)* to use up

**zapis|ki** (**-ków**) *pl* *(notatki)* notes *pl*; *(pamiętnik)* diary

**zapis|ywać (-uję, -ujesz)** *(perf* **-ać***)* *vt* *(wiadomość, notatkę)* to write down, to take down; *(kandydatów)* to register; *(Tech)* to record; *(Komput)* to save, to write; **~ coś komuś** *(Prawo)* to bequeath sth to sb; *(o lekarzu)* to prescribe sth to sb; **zapisać dziecko do przedszkola** to enrol *(Brit)* *lub* enroll (US) a child at a nursery school; **zapisywać się** *vr*: **~ się do szkoły** to enrol *(Brit)* *lub* enroll (US) at a school; **~ się na kurs** to sign up for a course

**zapity** *adj* *(pot: człowiek)* sloshed *(pot)*; *(głos, wzrok)* boozy *(pot)*

**zapla|mić (-mię, -misz)** *vb perf od* **plamić**
**zaplan|ować (-uję, -ujesz)** *vb perf od* **planować**
**zaplanowany** *adj* (*wyjazd, wycieczka*) planned; (*konferencja, wykład*) scheduled
**zaplat|ać (-am, -asz)** (*perf* **zapleść**) *vt* (*warkocz*) to plait (Brit), to braid (US)
**zaplą|tać (-czę, -czesz)** *vb perf od* **plątać**; **zaplątać się** *vr perf* (*zostać unieruchomionym*) to become tangled (up) *lub* entangled; (*zgubić wątek*) to lose the thread; **~ się w coś** (*przen*) to become entangled in sth
**zaplecz|e** (**-a, -a**) (*gen pl* **-y**) *nt* (*sklepu, pracowni*) (the) back
**zapl|eść (-otę, -eciesz)** (*imp* **-eć**, *pt* **-ótł, -otła, -etli**) *vb perf od* **pleść, zaplatać**
**zaplomb|ować (-uję, -ujesz)** *vb perf od* **plombować**
**zapłaceni|e** (**-a**) *nt*: **„do zapłacenia"** "payment due"
**zapła|cić (-cę, -cisz)** (*imp* **-ć**) *vb perf od* **płacić**
**zapładni|ać (-am, -asz)** (*perf* **zapłodnić**) *vt* (*Bio*) to fertilize
**zapła|kać (-czę, -czesz)** *vi perf* to start crying
**zapłakany** *adj* tearful
**zapła|ta** (**-ty, -ty**) (*dat sg* **-cie**) *f* payment; (*przen*) reward
**zapłod|nić (-nię, -nisz)** (*imp* **-nij**) *vb perf od* **zapładniać**
**zapłodnie|nie** (**-nia, -nia**) (*loc sg* **-niu**, *gen pl* **-ń**) *nt* fertilization; **~ in vitro** in vitro fertilization
**zapło|n** (**-nu, -ny**) (*loc sg* **-nie**) *m* ignition
**zapło|nąć (-nę, -niesz)** (*imp* **-ń**) *vi perf* (*książk*) to flare up
**zapłonowy** *adj*: **świeca zapłonowa** spark(ing) plug
**zapobie|c (-gnę, -gniesz)** (*imp* **-gnij**, *pt* **-gł**) *vb perf od* **zapobiegać**
**zapobieg|ać (-am, -asz)** (*perf* **zapobiec**) *vi*: **~ czemuś** to prevent sth
**zapobiegani|e** (**-a**) *nt* prevention; **~ ciąży** contraception
**zapobiegawczy** *adj* preventive
**zapobiegliwoś|ć** (**-ci**) *f* forethought
**zapobiegliwy** *adj* far-sighted, provident
**zapoczątk|ować (-uję, -ujesz)** *vb perf od* **zapoczątkowywać**
**zapoczątkow|ywać (-uję, -ujesz)** (*perf* **-ać**) *vt* to initiate
**zapodzi|ać (-eję, -ejesz)** *vt perf* to misplace, to mislay; **zapodziać się** *vr* to be misplaced *lub* mislaid
**zapomin|ać (-am, -asz)** (*perf* **zapomnieć**) *vt* +*gen* (*przestawać pamiętać*) to forget; (*zostawiać*) to leave behind ▷ *vi*: **~ o** +*loc* to forget (about); **zapomnieć coś zrobić** to forget to do sth; **nie zapomnę ci tego** (*dziękując*) I'll never forget this; (*grożąc*) I won't let you get away with this; **~ o bożym świecie** to daydream; **na śmierć zapomniałam!** I forgot all about it!, I clean forgot!; **zapominać się** *vr* to forget o.s.
**zapominalski** *adj* (*pot*) scatterbrained (*pot*) ▷ *m decl like adj* (*pot*) scatterbrain (*pot*)
**zapom|nieć (-nę, -nisz)** (*imp* **-nij**) *vb perf od* **zapominać**
**zapomnieni|e** (**-a**) *nt* (*niepamięć*) oblivion; (*roztargnienie*) forgetfulness; **pójść** *lub* **odejść** (*perf*) **w ~** to sink *lub* fall into oblivion
**zapom|oga** (**-ogi, -ogi**) (*dat sg* **-odze**, *gen pl* **-óg**) *f* subsistence allowance
**zap|ora** (**-ory, -ory**) (*dat sg* **-orze**, *gen pl* **-ór**) *f* (*tama*) dam; (*przeszkoda*) barrier
**zaporowy** *adj* (*Wojsk*): **ogień ~** barrage; **balon ~** barrage balloon
**zapotrzebowa|nie** (**-nia, -nia**) (*gen pl* **-ń**) *nt*: **~ (na coś)** demand (for sth)
**zapowiad|ać (-am, -asz)** *vt* (*oznajmiać*) (*perf* **zapowiedzieć**) to announce; (*wróżyć*) to herald, to portend; **zapowiadać się** *vr* (*uprzedzać o przyjściu*) to announce one's visit; **zapowiada się mroźna zima** it looks we're going to have harsh winter; **ona się dobrze zapowiada** she shows promise
**zapowiadający się** *adj*: **dobrze ~ pisarze/muzycy** writers/musicians of promise
**zapowi|edzieć (-em, -esz)** (*imp* **-edz**) *vb perf od* **zapowiadać**
**zapowie|dź** (**-dzi, -dzi**) (*gen pl* **-dzi**) *f* (*ogłoszenie*) announcement; (*wiosny*) herald; (*wojny, nieszczęścia*) portent; **zapowiedzi** *pl* (*Rel*) banns *pl*
**zapozn|awać (-aję, -ajesz)** (*imp* **-awaj**, *perf* **-ać**) *vt*: **~ kogoś z czymś** to acquaint *lub* familiarize sb with sth; **~ kogoś z kimś** to introduce sb to sb; **zapoznawać się** *vr*: **~ się z czymś** to acquaint *lub* familiarize o.s. with sth; **~ się z kimś** to make sb's acquaintance
**zapożycz|ać (-am, -asz)** (*perf* **-yć**) *vt* to borrow; **zapożyczać się** *vr* to get into debt; **~ się u kogoś** to be in debt to sb
**zapożycze|nie** (**-nia, -nia**) (*gen pl* **-ń**) *nt* (*Jęz*) borrowing
**zaprac|ować (-uję, -ujesz)** *vb perf od* **zapracowywać**
**zapracowany** *adj* (*człowiek*) very busy, up to one's eyes in work (*pot*); (*sukces, pochwała*) well-earned
**zapracow|ywać (-uję, -ujesz)** (*perf* **-ać**) *vi*: **~ na coś** to earn sth; **zapracowywać się** *vr* to overwork
**zaprag|nąć (-nę, -niesz)** (*imp* **-nij**) *vt perf*: **~ kogoś/czegoś** to desire sb/sth; **~ coś zrobić** to desire to do sth; *patrz też* **pragnąć**

**zaprasz|ać (-am, -asz)** *vt* (*perf* **zaprosić**); **~ kogoś (na coś)** to invite sb (to sth); **~ kogoś do stołu** to invite sb to the table; **zaprosić kogoś na obiad do restauracji** to ask sb out to dinner; **zapraszać się** *vr* (*wpraszać się*) to invite o.s.; (*wzajemnie*) to exchange mutual invitations

**zapra|wa (-wy, -wy)** (*dat sg* **-wie**) *f* (*Bud*) mortar; (*Sport*) training, practice; **sucha ~ narciarska/wioślarska** dry skiing/rowing

**zapra|wiać (-wiam, -wiasz)** (*perf* **-wić**) *vt* (*przyprawiać*) to season; **~ kogoś do czegoś** to train sb for sth; **zaprawiać się** *vr*: **~ się do walki** to train o.s. to fight; (*pot*) to go on the booze (*pot*)

**zapra|wić (-wię, -wisz)** *vb perf od* **zaprawiać**; **~ kogoś** (*pot: uderzyć*) to whack sb (*pot*)

**zaprezent|ować (-uję, -ujesz)** *vb perf od* **prezentować**

**zaprogram|ować (-uję, -ujesz)** *vb perf od* **programować**

**zaprojekt|ować (-uję, -ujesz)** *vb perf od* **projektować**

**zapropon|ować (-uję, -ujesz)** *vb perf od* **proponować**

**zapro|sić (-szę, -sisz)** (*imp* **-ś**) *vb perf od* **zapraszać**

**zaprosze|nie (-nia, -nia)** (*gen pl* **-ń**) *nt* invitation; **na czyjeś ~** at sb's invitation; **wyłącznie za okazaniem zaproszenia** by invitation only

**zaprotest|ować (-uję, -ujesz)** *vb perf od* **protestować**

**zaprowa|dzać (-dzam, -dzasz)** (*perf* **-dzić**) *vt* (*osobę*) to lead, to take; (*porządek, ład*) to introduce; (*rejestr, dziennik*) to start

**zaprowa|dzić (-dzę, -dzisz)** (*imp* **-dź**) *vb perf od* **prowadzić, zaprowadzać**

**zaprósz|yć (-ę, -ysz)** *vt perf*: **piasek zaprószył mi oczy** sand got into my eyes; **~ ogień** to start a fire

**zaprz|ąc (-ęgę, -ężesz)** (*imp* **-ąż** *lub* **-ęż**, *pt* **-ągł, -ęgła, -ęgli**) *vb perf od* **zaprzęgać**

**zaprząt|ać (-am, -asz)** (*perf* **-nąć**) *vt* to occupy; **wciąż zaprząta sobie tym głowę** it is constantly on his mind

**zaprzecz|ać (-am, -asz)** (*perf* **-yć**) *vi* (*nie zgadzać się*) to disagree; **~ komuś** to contradict sb; **~ czemuś** to deny sth

**zaprzeczeni|e (-a)** *nt* denial

**zaprzecz|yć (-ę, -ysz)** *vb perf od* **przeczyć, zaprzeczać**

**zap|rzeć (-rę, -rzesz)** (*imp* **-rzyj**) *vb perf od* **zapierać**

**zaprzed|awać (-aję, -ajesz)** (*imp* **-awaj**, *perf* **-ać**) *vt* to betray; **zaprzedawać się** *vr* to sell o.s. (*przen*)

**zaprzepa|ścić (-szczę, -ścisz)** (*imp* **-ść**) *vt perf* to squander

**zaprzesta|ć (-nę, -niesz)** (*imp* **-ń**) *vb perf od* **zaprzestawać**

**zaprzestani|e (-a)** *nt* cessation

**zaprzest|awać (-aję, -ajesz)** (*imp* **-awaj**, *perf* **-ać**) *vt* to stop, to cease; **~ walki** to cease fighting; **~ robić coś** to cease to do *lub* doing sth

**zaprzeszły** *adj*: **czas ~** the past perfect

**zaprzę|g (-gu, -gi)** (*instr sg* **-giem**) *m* (horse-drawn) cart

**zaprzęg|ać (-am, -asz)** (*perf* **zaprząc** *lub* **zaprzęgnąć**) *vt* to harness

**zaprzęg|nąć (-nę, -niesz)** (*imp* **-nij**, *pt* **-nął** *lub* **zaprzągł, -ła, -li**) *vb perf od* **zaprzęgać**

**zaprzyjaź|nić się (-nię, -nisz)** (*imp* **-nij**) *vr perf*: **zaprzyjaźnić się (z kimś)** to make friends (with sb)

**zaprzyjaźniony** *adj*: **~ lekarz** a doctor friend; **kraje zaprzyjaźnione** friendly countries; **być ~m z kimś** to be friends *lub* friendly with sb

**zaprzysi|ąc (-ęgnę, -ęgniesz)** (*imp* **-ęgnij**, *pt* **-ągł, -ęgła, -ęgli**) *vb perf od* **zaprzysięgać**

**zaprzysięg|ać (-am, -asz)** (*perf* **zaprzysiąc** *lub* **zaprzysięgnąć**) *vt* (*posłuszeństwo, wierność*) to swear; (*świadków*) to swear in

**zaprzysięgły** *adj* avowed, confirmed; **zaprzysięgli wrogowie** sworn enemies

**zaprzysi|ęgnąć (-ęgnę, -ęgniesz)** (*imp* **-ęgnij**, *pt* **-ągł, -ęgła, -ęgli**) *vb perf od* **zaprzysięgać**

**zaprzysiężony** *adj* (*posłuszeństwo*) sworn; (*świadek*) sworn in

**zapuchnięty** *adj* swollen

**zapuk|ać (-am, -asz)** *vb perf od* **pukać**

**zapuszcz|ać (-am, -asz)** (*perf* **zapuścić**) *vt* (*włosy, brodę*) to grow; (*krople do oczu*) to instil; (*żaluzje*) to draw; (*pot: silnik*) to start; (*ogród, mieszkanie*) to neglect; **zapuszczać się** *vr*: **~ się gdzieś** to venture somewhere

**zapuszczony** *adj* run-down, neglected

**zapu|ścić (-szczę, -ścisz)** (*imp* **-ść**) *vb perf od* **zapuszczać**

**zapych|ać (-am, -asz)** (*perf* **zapchać**) *vt* (*odpływ, rurę*) to block up; (*samochód*) to push-start; **zapychać się** *vr* to block up

**zapyl|ać (-am, -asz)** (*perf* **-ić**) *vt* (*Bot*) to pollinate; (*pokrywać pyłem*) to cover with dust

**zapyleni|e (-a)** *nt* (*Bot*) pollination; (*zanieczyszczenie*) dust

**zapyt|ać (-am, -asz)** *vb perf od* **pytać, zapytywać**

**zapyta|nie (-nia, -nia)** (*gen pl* **-ń**) *nt* inquiry, enquiry; **znak zapytania** question mark; **być pod znakiem zapytania** to be in *lub* open to doubt; **jego przyszłość jest** *lub* **stoi pod znakiem zapytania** there is a question mark over his future; **stawiać (postawić** *perf***) pod znakiem zapytania** to call into question

**zapyt|ywać (-uję, -ujesz)** (*perf* **-ać**) *vt*: **~ kogoś o coś** to inquire *lub* enquire sth of sb ▷ *vi* to inquire, to enquire; **zapytywać się** *vr* to inquire, to enquire

**zarabi|ać (-am, -asz)** *vt* (*perf* **zarobić**) to earn; (*ciasto*) to knead ▷ *vi* (*osiągać zysk*) to make a profit; (*pracować za pieniądze*) to earn; **~ na czymś** to make money *lub* a profit on sth; **~ na siebie** to support o.s.; **~ na życie** to earn a living; **~ na czysto 1000 złotych** to have a net profit of 1000 zloty

**zarachow|ywać (-uję, -ujesz)** *vt* to calculate

**zaradczy** *adj*: **środki zaradcze** remedial measures *lub* steps

**zaradnoś|ć (-ci)** *f* resourcefulness

**zaradny** *adj* resourceful

**zara|dzić (-dzę, -dzisz)** (*imp* **-dź**) *vi perf*: **~ czemuś** to remedy sth

**zarani|e (-a)** *nt*: **od zarania czasu/dziejów** from the dawn of time/history

**zarast|ać (-a)** (*perf* **zarosnąć**) *vt* to overgrow ▷ *vi* (*o ranie*) to skin over; **~ chwastami/trzciną** to become overgrown with weeds/reeds

**zaraz** *adv* (*natychmiast*) at once, right away; (*za chwilę*) soon; **~ za rogiem** just round the corner; **~ po Świętach** right after Christmas; **od ~** starting right now; **~ wracam** I'll be right back; **~, ~!** wait a minute!

**zara|za (-zy, -zy)** (*dat sg* **-zie**) *f* plague

**zaraz|ek (-ka, -ki)** (*instr sg* **-kiem**) *m* germ

**zarazem** *adv* at the same time

**zara|zić (-żę, -zisz)** (*imp* **-ź**) *vb perf od* **zarażać**

**zaraźliwy** *adj* contagious, infectious

**zaraż|ać (-am, -asz)** (*perf* **zarazić**) *vt* to infect; **zarażać się** *vr* to get infected; **zarazić się czymś (od kogoś)** to catch sth (from sb)

**zardzewiały** *adj* rusty

**zardzewi|eć (-eje)** *vb perf od* **rdzewieć**

**zareag|ować (-uję, -ujesz)** *vb perf od* **reagować**

**zarejestr|ować (-uję, -ujesz)** *vb perf od* **rejestrować**

**zarejestrowany** *adj* (*samochód*) registered; **czy jest Pan ~?** have you made an appointment?

**zareklam|ować (-uję, -ujesz)** *vb perf od* **reklamować**

**zarezerw|ować (-uję, -ujesz)** *vb perf od* **rezerwować**

**zarezerwowany** *adj* reserved

**zarę|cz|ać (-am, -asz)** (*perf* **-yć**) *vt* to guarantee, to vouch for; **zaręczam (ci), że ...** I warrant (you) (that) ...; **zaręczać się** *vr*: **~ się (z kimś)** to get engaged (to sb)

**zaręczynowy** *adj*: **pierścionek ~** engagement ring

**zaręczyn|y (-)** *pl* engagement

**zarob|ek (-ku, -ki)** (*instr sg* **-kiem**) *m* (*wynagrodzenie*) earnings *pl*, wage; (*praca*) job; (*zysk*) profit; **zarobki** *pl* earnings *pl*

**zar|obić (-obię, -obisz)** (*imp* **-ób**) *vb perf od* **zarabiać**

**zarobkowy** *adj*: **praca zarobkowa** paid work

**zarod|ek (-ka, -ki)** (*instr sg* **-kiem**) *m* embryo; **niszczyć (zniszczyć** *perf***) coś w zarodku** to nip sth in the bud

**zarodni|k (-ka, -ki)** (*instr sg* **-kiem**) *m* (*Bot*) spore

**zar|osnąć (-ośnie)** (*imp* **-ośnij**, *pt* **-ósł, -osła, -ośli**) *vb perf od* **zarastać**

**zaro|st (-stu)** (*loc sg* **-ście**) *m* facial hair; **trzydniowy ~** three days' (growth of) stubble

**zarośl|a (-i)** *pl* thicket

**zarośnięty** *adj* unshaven

**zarozumial|ec (-ca, -cy)** *m* bighead

**zarozumialst|wo (-wa)** (*loc sg* **-wie**) *nt* conceit

**zarozumiałoś|ć (-ci)** *f* conceit, self-importance

**zarozumiały** *adj* conceited

**zarówno** *adv*: **~ X, jak (i) Y** both X and Y, X as well as Y

**zarumie|nić (-nię, -nisz)** (*imp* **-ń**) *vb perf od* **rumienić**

**zar|wać (-wę, -wiesz)** (*imp* **-wij**) *vb perf od* **zarywać**

**zary|biać (-biam, -biasz)** (*perf* **-bić**) *vt* to restock (with fish)

**zary|ć (-ję, -jesz)** *vi perf*: **zarył nartami w śnieg** his skis dug into the snow; **zaryć się** *vr* (*w błocie*) to be bogged (down)

**zarygl|ować (-uję, -ujesz)** *vb perf od* **ryglować, zaryglowywać**

**zaryglow|ywać (-uję, -ujesz)** (*perf* **-ać**) *vt* to bar (*a door*)

**zary|s (-su, -sy)** (*loc sg* **-sie**) *m* outline; **w ogólnych ~ach** in broad outline

**zarysow|ywać (-uję, -ujesz)** (*perf* **-ać**) *vt* (*arkusz, zeszyt*) to cover with drawings; (*posadzkę, karoserię*) to scratch; (*kształt, sytuację, tło*) to outline; **zarysowywać się** *vr* (*pękać*) to crack; (*stawać się widocznym*) to be outlined

**zaryw|ać (-am, -asz)** (*perf* **zarwać**) *vt* (*łóżko*) to break; **~ noce** (*pot*) to burn the midnight oil (*pot*); **zarywać się** *vr* to collapse

**zarzą|d (-du, -dy)** (*loc sg* **-dzie**) *m* (*zespół ludzi*) board (of directors); (*zarządzanie*) management; **być pod czyimś ~em** to be under sb's management; **sprawować ~ nad**

**czymś** to manage sth; **członek ~u** member of the board
**zarzą|dzać (-dzam, -dzasz)** *vt* (*kierować*): **~ czymś** to manage sth; (*wydawać polecenia*) (*perf* **-dzić**) to order
**zarządzani|e** (**-a**) *nt* management
**zarządze|nie** (**-nia, -nia**) (*gen pl* **-ń**) *nt* (*polecenie*) order, instruction; (*rozporządzenie*) regulation; (*sądu, sędziego*) order, ruling
**zarzą|dzić (-dzę, -dzisz)** (*imp* **-dź**) *vb perf od* **zarządzać**
**zarze|c się (-knę, -kniesz)** (*imp* **-knij**, *pt* **-kł, -kła, -kli**) *vb perf od* **zarzekać się**
**zarzek|ać się (-am, -asz)** (*perf* **zarzec**) *vr*: **zarzekać się, że ...** to vow that ...; **zarzekać się czegoś** to renounce sth
**zarzu|cać (-cam, -casz)** (*perf* **-cić**) *vt* (*rzucając zawieszać*) to throw over; (*nakładać na siebie*) to throw on; (*porzucać*) to give up, to abandon; **~ coś papierami/kwiatami** to scatter papers/ flowers all over sth; **~ komuś coś** to accuse sb of sth ▷ *vi* (*o pojeździe*) to skid; **~ wędkę** to cast (a fishing line); **zarzucić komuś ręce na szyję** to throw *lub* fling one's arms round sb's neck; **samochód zarzuciło** the car skidded
**zarzu|cić (-cę, -cisz)** (*imp* **-ć**) *vb perf od* **zarzucać**
**zarzu|t** (**-tu, -ty**) (*loc sg* **-cie**) *m* accusation; **robić komuś ~y** to reproach sb; **pod ~em czegoś** on a charge of sth; **bez ~u** beyond reproach
**zarzyn|ać (-am, -asz)** (*perf* **zarżnąć**) *vt* to butcher; **zarzynać się** *vr* (*kaleczyć się*) to cut o.s.
**zarż|nąć (-nę, -niesz)** (*imp* **-nij**) *vb perf od* **zarzynać**
**zasa|da** (**-dy, -dy**) (*dat sg* **-dzie**) *f* (*reguła*) principle; (*Chem*) alkali; **dla zasady** on principle; **w zasadzie** in principle
**zasadniczo** *adv* (*całkowicie*) fundamentally; (*w zasadzie*) in principle
**zasadniczy** *adj* (*podstawowy*) fundamental; (*pryncypialny*) principled; **zasadnicza służba wojskowa** national service; **ustawa zasadnicza** constitution; **postawa zasadnicza** (*Wojsk*) attention
**zasadnoś|ć** (**-ci**) *f* legitimacy
**zasadny** *adj* legitimate
**zasadowy** *adj* alkaline
**zasa|dzać się (-dzam, -dzasz)** (*perf* **-dzić**) *vr* (*książk*): **zasadzać się na kogoś/coś** to wait in ambush for sb/sth; **zasadzać się na czymś** to be based on sth
**zasa|dzić (-dzę, -dzisz)** (*imp* **-dź**) *vb perf od* **sadzić**
**zasadz|ka** (**-ki, -ki**) (*dat sg* **-ce**, *gen pl* **-ek**) *f* ambush; **wpadać (wpaść** *perf*) **w zasadzkę** to run into an ambush
**zasa|pać się (-pię, -piesz)** *vr perf* to lose one's breath
**zasapany** *adj* breathless
**zasą|dzać (-dzam, -dzasz)** (*perf* **-dzić**) *vt* to award, to adjudge
**zasą|dzić (-dzę, -dzisz)** (*imp* **-dź**) *vb perf od* **zasądzać**
**zasch|nąć (-nę, -niesz)** (*imp* **-nij**) *vb perf od* **zasychać**
**zasę|piać się (-piam, -piasz)** (*perf* **-pić**) *vr* to become gloomy
**zasępiony** *adj* gloomy
**zasi|ać (-eję, -ejesz)** *vb perf od* **siać**
**zasiad|ać (-am, -asz)** (*perf* **zasiąść**) *vi* (*siadać wygodnie*) to settle (o.s.); **~ do czegoś** to settle down to sth; **~ w komisji** to sit on a committee; **~ na ławie oskarżonych** to stand in the dock
**zasi|ąść (-ądę, -ądziesz)** (*imp* **-ądź**, *pt* **-adł, -adła, -edli**) *vb perf od* **zasiadać**
**zasiedl|ać (-am, -asz)** (*perf* **-ić**) *vt* to settle
**zasiedziały** *adj* settled
**zasie|dzieć się (-dzę, -dzisz)** (*imp* **-dź**) *vr perf* to linger
**zasie|ki** (**-ków**) *pl* wire entanglements *pl*
**zasię|g** (**-gu**) (*instr sg* **-giem**) *m* range; **w ~u wzroku/ręki** within sight/one's grasp; **być w czyimś ~u** to be within sb's reach; **kampania obejmująca swoim ~iem cały kraj** a nationwide campaign; **kryzys o światowym ~u** a worldwide crisis
**zasięg|ać (-am, -asz)** (*perf* **-nąć**) *vt*: **~ informacji/rady** to seek information/ advice; **zasięgnąć języka** to make inquiries; **zasięgnąć porady prawnej** to take legal advice
**zasięg|nąć (-nę, -niesz)** (*imp* **-nij**) *vb perf od* **zasięgać**
**zasilacz** (**-a, -e**) (*gen pl* **-y**) *m* (*też*: **zasilacz sieciowy**) power supply adaptor
**zasil|ać (-am, -asz)** (*perf* **-ić**) *vt* (*zaopatrywać*): **~ coś czymś** to supply sth with sth; (*wzmacniać, powiększać*) to reinforce
**zasilani|e** (**-a**) *nt* power (supply); **włączyć/ wyłączyć ~** to turn on/off the power
**zasil|ić (-ę, -isz)** *vb perf od* **zasilać**
**zasił|ek** (**-ku, -ki**) (*instr sg* **-kiem**) *m* benefit; **~ dla bezrobotnych** unemployment benefit, dole; **~ rodzinny/chorobowy** child/sickness benefit; **pobierać ~** to receive a benefit; **być na zasiłku** to be on the dole; **przechodzić (przejść** *perf*) **na ~** to go on the dole
**zaska|kiwać (-kuję, -kujesz)** (*perf* **zaskoczyć**) *vt* to surprise, to take by surprise ▷ *vi* (*o mechanizmie*) to click; (*o silniku*) to start

**zaskakujący** *adj* surprising
**zaskar|biać (-biam, -biasz)** (*perf* **-bić**) *vt*: **~ sobie czyjąś przyjaźń/czyjeś względy** to win sb's friendship/favours (*Brit*) *lub* favors (*US*)
**zaskarż|ać (-am, -asz)** (*perf* **-yć**) *vt* (*osobę*) to sue; (*wyrok*) to appeal against *lub* from
**zaskoczeni|e** (**-a**) *nt* surprise; **działać przez ~** to use the element of surprise, to use shock tactics
**zaskocz|yć (-ę, -ysz)** *vb perf od* **zaskakiwać**
**zaskórnia|k** (**-ka, -ki**) (*instr sg* **-kiem**) *m* (*pot*) *spouse's secret savings, usually not very big*
**zaskórni|k** (**-ka, -ki**) (*instr sg* **-kiem**) *m* blackhead
**zaskro|niec** (**-ńca, -ńce**) *m* grass snake
**zaskrzecz|eć (-ę, -ysz)** *vb perf od* **skrzeczeć**
**zaskrzy|pieć (-pię, -pisz)** *vb perf od* **skrzypieć**
**zasłab|nąć (-nę, -niesz)** (*imp* **-nij**, *pt* **-ł** *lub* **-nął, -ła, -li**) *vi perf* to collapse, to faint
**za|słać (-ścielę, -ścielisz)** *vb perf od* **słać**
**zasłani|ać (-am, -asz)** (*perf* **zasłonić**) *vt* (*twarz*) to cover; (*widok, światło*) to block (out); (*bronić*) to shield; **zasłaniać się** *vr* (*zakrywać się*) to cover o.s.; (*bronić się*) to shield o.s.; **~ się czymś** (*przen*) to hide behind sth
**zasło|na** (**-ny, -ny**) (*dat sg* **-nie**) *f* (*w oknie*) curtain (*Brit*), drape (*US*); **zasuwać/rozsuwać zasłony** to draw the curtains; **~ dymna** smokescreen
**zasło|nić (-nię, -nisz)** (*imp* **-ń**) *vb perf od* **zasłaniać**
**zasłuchany** *adj*: **~ (w coś)** engrossed (in sth)
**zasłu|ga** (**-gi, -gi**) (*dat sg* **-dze**) *f* merit; **to zwycięstwo jest ich zasługą** the credit for the victory goes to them; **zasługi dla kraju/organizacji** services to the country/organization
**zasłu|giwać (-guję, -gujesz)** (*perf* **zasłużyć**) *vi*: **~ na coś** to deserve sth; **zasłużyłeś sobie na to!** it serves you right!
**zasłużenie** *adv* deservedly
**zasłużony** *adj* (*obywatel*) of merit; (*order, zwycięstwo*) well-deserved, well-earned
**zasłuż|yć (-ę, -ysz)** *vb perf od* **zasługiwać**; **zasłużyć się** *vr*: **~ się komuś czymś** to bring credit to sb by doing sth
**zasły|nąć (-nę, -niesz)** (*imp* **-ń**) *vi perf*: **~ z czegoś** *lub* **czymś** to make o.s. *lub* become famous for sth; **~ jako mówca/kucharz** to make a name for o.s. as an orator/a chef
**zasmak|ować (-uję, -ujesz)** *vi perf*: **zasmakowało mu to** he found it tasty; (*przen*) he found it to his liking; **~ w czymś** to acquire *lub* develop a taste for sth
**zasmarkany** *adj* (*pot*) snotty (*pot*)
**zasmradz|ać (-am, -asz)** (*perf* **zasmrodzić**) *vt* (*pot*) to stink out (*Brit*) (*pot*), to stink up (*US*) (*pot*)
**zasmu|cać (-cam, -casz)** (*perf* **-cić**) *vt* to sadden, to make sad; **zasmucać się** *vr* to grow sad
**zasmu|cić (-cę, -cisz)** (*imp* **-ć**) *vb perf od* **zasmucać**
**za|snąć (-snę, -śniesz)** (*imp* **-śnij**) *vb perf od* **zasypiać**
**zasobny** *adj*: **~ (w coś)** rich (in sth)
**zasoleni|e** (**-a**) *nt* salinity
**zas|ób** (**-obu, -oby**) (*loc sg* **-obie**) *m* (*zapas*) reserve; **zasoby** *pl* resources *pl*; **bogaty ~ słów** a rich vocabulary; **zasoby naturalne** natural resources
**zas|pa** (**-py, -py**) (*dat sg* **-pie**) *f* snowdrift
**za|spać (-śpię, -śpisz)** (*imp* **-śpij**) *vb perf od* **zasypiać**
**zaspany** *adj* sleepy
**zaspokaj|ać (-am, -asz)** (*perf* **zaspokoić**) *vt* to satisfy
**zaspok|oić (-oję, -oisz)** (*imp* **-ój**) *vb perf od* **zaspokajać**
**zas|sać (-sie)** *vb perf od* **zasysać**
**zasta|ć (-nę, -niesz)** (*imp* **-ń**) *vb perf od* **zastawać**
**zastanawi|ać (-am, -asz)** (*perf* **zastanowić**) *vt* to puzzle; **zastanawia mnie jego odpowiedź** his answer puzzles me *lub* makes me wonder; **zastanawiać się** *vr* to think; **~ się nad czymś** to think sth over; **zastanawiam się, dlaczego to zrobił** I wonder why he did it; **zastanów się nad tym** think about it, think it over
**zastanawiający** *adj* puzzling
**zastan|owić (-owię, -owisz)** (*imp* **-ów**) *vb perf od* **zastanawiać**
**zastanowieni|e** (**-a**) *nt*: **bez zastanowienia** without thinking; **po zastanowieniu** upon reflection, on second thought(s)
**zasta|w** (**-wu, -wy**) (*loc sg* **-wie**) *m* deposit, security; **dawać (dać** *perf***) coś w ~** to give sth as collateral
**zasta|wa** (**-wy, -wy**) (*dat sg* **-wie**) *f*: **~ stołowa** tableware; **~ do herbaty** tea service
**zast|awać (-aję, -ajesz)** (*imp* **-awaj**, *perf* **-ać**) *vt* to find
**zasta|wiać (-wiam, -wiasz)** (*perf* **-wić**) *vt* (*drogę*) to block; (*pułapkę, sidła*) to lay, to set; (*oddawać w zastaw*) to pawn; (*otaczać*) to surround; **~ pokój meblami** to cram the room full of furniture
**zastaw|ka** (**-ki, -ki**) (*dat sg* **-ce**, *gen pl* **-ek**) *f* (*Anat*) valve
**zastą|pić (-pię, -pisz)** *vb perf od* **zastępować**
**zastę|p** (**-pu, -py**) (*loc sg* **-pie**) *m* (*Harcerstwo*) patrol; (*książk: ekspertów, dziennikarzy*) host

**zastępc|a** (**-y, -y**) *m decl like f in sg* replacement, substitute; **być czyimś zastępcą** to stand in *lub* deputize for sb; **~ dowódcy** second-in-command; **~ dyrektora** assistant *lub* deputy manager
**zastępczy** *adj* (*opakowanie, środek*) substitute *attr*; (*matka*) surrogate *attr*; **(globalny) znak ~** (*Komput*) wild card
**zastęp|ować (-uję, -ujesz)** (*perf* **zastąpić**) *vt*: **~ kogoś** to stand in *lub* fill in *lub* substitute for sb; **~ coś czymś innym** to replace sth with sth else, to substitute sth else for sth; **zastąpić komuś drogę** to bar sb's way *lub* path
**zastępow|y** (**-ego, -i**) *m decl like adj* (*w harcerstwie*) patrol leader
**zastępst|wo** (**-wa, -wa**) (*loc sg* **-wie**) *nt* replacement, substitution; **w zastępstwie kogoś** substituting for sb; **brać (wziąć** *perf*) **za kogoś ~** to substitute for sb
**zastos|ować (-uję, -ujesz)** *vb perf od* **stosować, zastosowywać**
**zastosowa|nie** (**-nia, -nia**) (*gen pl* **-ń**) *nt* application; **mieć/znajdować ~ w czymś** to have/find application in sth; **możliwy do zastosowania** practicable; **niemożliwy do zastosowania** impracticable
**zastosow|ywać (-uję, -ujesz)** (*perf* **-ać**) *vt* to apply; **zastosowywać się** *vr*: **~ się do czegoś** to comply with sth
**zast|ój** (**-oju**) *m*: **panuje ~ w interesach** business is slow *lub* slack *lub* at a standstill
**zastrajk|ować (-uję, -ujesz)** *vi perf* to go on strike, to come *lub* walk out
**zastrasz|ać (-am, -asz)** (*perf* **-yć**) *vt* to intimidate
**zastraszający** *adj* (*widok*) awesome, awe inspiring; (*brak rozwagi*) appalling
**zastrasz|yć (-ę, -ysz)** *vb perf od* **zastraszać**
**zastrze|c (-gę, -żesz)** (*imp* **-ż**, *pt* **-gł**) *vb perf od* **zastrzegać**
**zastrzeg|ać (-am, -asz)** (*perf* **zastrzec**) *vt*: **~ (sobie), że ...** to stipulate that ...; **~ sobie prawo do czegoś** to reserve the right to sth; **zastrzegać się** *vr*: **~ się, że ...** to make it clear that ...
**zastrzel|ić (-ę, -isz)** *vt perf*: **~ kogoś** to shoot sb (down *lub* dead); **~ kogoś trudnym pytaniem** to throw sb with a difficult question; **zastrzelić się** *vr* to shoot o.s.
**zastrzeże|nie** (**-nia, -nia**) (*gen pl* **-ń**) *nt* reservation; **bez zastrzeżeń** without reservation, unreservedly; **mieć zastrzeżenia co do czegoś/wobec kogoś** to have reservations about sth/sb
**zastrzeżony** *adj* (*numer, telefon*) ex-directory (*Brit*), unlisted (*US*); **wszelkie prawa zastrzeżone** all rights reserved; **znak handlowy prawnie ~** registered trademark
**zastrzy|k** (**-ku, -ki**) (*instr sg* **-kiem**) *m* injection, shot; (*przen*) boost, a shot in the arm; **zrobić** (*perf*) **komuś ~** to give sb an injection; **dostać** (*perf*) **~** to have an injection
**zastuk|ać (-am, -asz)** *vb perf od* **stukać**
**zastyg|ać (-am, -asz)** (*perf* **-nąć**) *vi* (*twardnieć*) to set; (*nieruchomieć*) to freeze
**zastyg|nąć (-nę, -niesz)** (*imp* **-nij**, *pt* **-ł** *lub* **-nął, -ła, -li**) *vb perf od* **zastygać**
**zasuger|ować (-uję, -ujesz)** *vb perf od* **sugerować**
**zasu|nąć (-nę, -niesz)** (*imp* **-ń**) *vb perf od* **zasuwać**
**zasusz|ać (-am, -asz)** (*perf* **-yć**) *vt* to dry out
**zasuszony** *adj* (*człowiek, twarz*) wizened
**zasusz|yć (-ę, -ysz)** *vb perf od* **zasuszać**
**zasu|wa** (**-wy, -wy**) (*dat sg* **-wie**) *f* bolt
**zasuw|ać (-am, -asz)** (*perf* **zasunąć**) *vt* (*firanki, zasuwę*) to draw; (*pot*: *iść lub biec szybko*) to go like the wind
**zasych|ać (-a)** (*perf* **zaschnąć**) *vi* (*o farbie, błocie*) to dry (out); (*o kwiatach*) to wither; **zaschło mi w gardle** my throat is dry
**zasycz|eć (-ę, -ysz)** *vb perf od* **syczeć** to hiss
**zasygnaliz|ować (-uję, -ujesz)** *vb perf od* **sygnalizować**
**zasył|ać (-am, -asz)** *vt*: **zasyłam pozdrowienia** best wishes (*in letter*)
**zasy|pać (-pię, -piesz)** *vb perf od* **zasypywać**
**zasypi|ać (-am, -asz)** *vi* (*zapadać w sen*) (*perf* **zasnąć**) to go (off) to sleep, to fall asleep; (*nie budzić się w porę*) (*perf* **zaspać**) to oversleep; **zaspać do pracy/na pierwszą lekcję** to oversleep for work/the first class
**zasyp|ka** (**-ki, -ki**) (*dat sg* **-ce**, *gen pl* **-ek**) *f* (*Med*) powder; **~ dla niemowląt** baby powder
**zasyp|ywać (-uję, -ujesz)** (*perf* **-ać**) *vt* (*wypełniać*: *dół, rów*) to fill; (*o śniegu, piasku*: *pokrywać*) to cover; (*o ziemi, węglu*: *przygniatać*) to bury; **~ kogoś prezentami/pochwałami** to shower sb with gifts/praise, to shower gifts/praise on sb; **~ kogoś pytaniami** to rain sb with questions
**zasys|ać (-a)** (*perf* **zassać**) *vt* to suck in
**zaszale|ć (-ję, -jesz)** *vi perf* (*pot*) to go on a spree
**zaszczek|ać (-a)** *vb perf od* **szczekać**
**zaszcze|piać (-piam, -piasz)** (*perf* **-pić**) *vt* (*drzewo*) to graft; (*Med*) to vaccinate, to inoculate; (*przen*) to inculcate, to instil (*Brit*) *lub* instill (*US*); **~ kogoś przeciwko czemuś** to vaccinate *lub* inoculate sb against sth; **zaszczepiać się** *vr*: **~ się (przeciwko czemuś)** to get vaccinated *lub* inoculated (against sth)

Z

**zaszczęk|ać (-am, -asz)** *vb perf od* **szczękać**
**zaszczy|cać (-cam, -casz)** (*perf* **-cić**) *vt*: **~ kogoś czymś** to honour (Brit) *lub* honor (US) sb with sth
**zaszczy|cić (-cę, -cisz)** (*imp* **-ć**) *vb perf od* **zaszczycać**
**zaszczy|t** (**-tu, -ty**) (*loc sg* **-cie**) *m* honour (Brit), honor (US); **dostąpić** (*perf*) **~u** to be hono(u)red; **mieć ~ coś zrobić** to have the hono(u)r *lub* privilege of doing sth; **zaszczyty** *pl* (*książk*) hono(u)rs *pl*; **obsypywać kogoś ~ami** to shower sb with hono(u)rs, to heap hono(u)rs on sb
**zaszczytny** *adj* honourable (Brit), honorable (US); **zaszczytne miejsce** a place of honour (Brit) *lub* honor (US)
**zaszele|ścić (-szczę, -ścisz)** (*imp* **-ść**) *vb perf od* **szeleścić**
**zaszeregow|ywać (-uję, -ujesz)** (*perf* **-ać**) *vt* to classify
**zaszko|dzić (-dzę, -dzisz)** (*imp* **-dź**) *vb perf od* **szkodzić**
**zasznur|ować (-uję, -ujesz)** *vb perf od* **sznurować**
**zaszok|ować (-uję, -ujesz)** *vb perf od* **szokować**
**zaszufladk|ować (-uję, -ujesz)** *vb perf od* **szufladkować**
**zaszumi|eć (-)** *vb perf od* **szumieć**
**zaszy|ć (-ję, -jesz)** *vb perf od* **zaszywać**
**zaszyfr|ować (-uję, -ujesz)** *vb perf od* **szyfrować**
**zaszyw|ać (-am, -asz)** (*perf* **zaszyć**) *vt* to sew up, to stitch up; **zaszywać się** *vr* (*ukrywać się*) to hole up; **zaszyć się na wsi** to bury o.s. in the country
**zaś** *conj* while; **niektórzy z nas ciągle mają wątpliwości, inni zaś już podjęli decyzję** some of us still have doubts, while others have already decided ▷ *part*: **szczególnie zaś** particularly, especially; **bardzo lubił polską poezję, zwłaszcza zaś Szymborską** he loved Polish poetry, particularly Szymborska
**zaścian|ek (-ka, -ki)** (*instr sg* **-kiem**) *m* backwater
**zaściankowy** *adj* parochial
**zaścielę** *itp. vb patrz* **zasłać**
**zaśle|piać (-piam, -piasz)** (*perf* **-pić**) *vt* (*o uczuciach*) to blind; (*rurę*) to blank off; (*otwór*) to stop, to plug
**zaślepieni|e (-a)** *nt* blindness (*przen*)
**zaślepiony** *adj* blind (*przen*)
**zaślu|biać (-biam, -biasz)** (*perf* **-bić**) *vt* (*książk*) to wed
**zaśmi|ać się (-eję, -ejesz)** (*pt* **-ali** *lub* **-eli**) *vb perf od* **śmiać się**
**zaśmie|cać (-cam, -casz)** *vt* (*perf* **-cić**) (*park*) to litter; (*pokój, pamięć*) to clutter (up)
**zaśmie|cić (-cę, -cisz)** (*imp* **-ć**) *vb perf od* **zaśmiecać**
**zaśmiew|ać się (-am, -asz)** *vr* to laugh one's head off
**zaśniedzi|eć (-eję, -ejesz)** *vb perf od* **śniedzieć**
**zaśnieżony** *adj* snowy, snow-covered *attr*
**zaśnięcie** *nt*: **przed ~m** before going (off) to sleep
**zaśpiew|ać (-am, -asz)** *vb perf od* **śpiewać**
**zaśpię** *itp. vb patrz* **zaspać**
**zaświadcz|ać (-am, -asz)** (*perf* **-yć**) *vt* (*pisemnie*) to certify; (*ustnie*) to testify
**zaświadcze|nie** (**-nia, -nia**) (*gen pl* **-ń**) *nt* certificate; **~ lekarskie** medical *lub* doctor's certificate
**zaświadcz|yć (-ę, -ysz)** *vb perf od* **zaświadczać**
**zaświat|y** (**-ów**) *pl* (*książk*) the (great) beyond
**zaświe|cić (-cę, -cisz)** (*imp* **-ć**) *vt perf* (*lampę*) to turn *lub* switch on; (*zapałkę*) to light ▷ *vi* (*o słońcu*) to come out; (*o oczach*) to light up; **zaświecić się** *vr* to light up
**zaświt|ać (-a)** *vb perf od* **świtać**
**zatacz|ać (-am, -asz)** (*perf* **zatoczyć**) *vt* (*koło, łuk*) to describe; (*beczkę, kamień*) to roll; **~ coraz szersze kręgi** (*przen*) to spread wider and wider; **zataczać się** *vr* to stagger
**zataj|ać (-am, -asz)** (*perf* **zataić**) *vt* to conceal, to withhold
**zatam|ować (-uję, -ujesz)** *vb perf od* **tamować**
**zatank|ować (-uję, -ujesz)** *vb perf od* **tankować**
**zatańcz|yć (-ę, -ysz)** *vb perf od* **tańczyć**
**zatapi|ać (-am, -asz)** (*perf* **zatopić**) *vt* (*statek, zęby*) to sink; (*piwnicę, ulice*) to flood; **zatapiać się** *vr*: **~ się w myślach/lekturze** to immerse o.s. in thought/a book
**zataras|ować (-uję, -ujesz)** *vb perf od* **tarasować**
**zatarci|e** (**-a, -a**) *nt* (*Tech*) seizing
**zatar|g** (**-gu, -gi**) (*instr sg* **-giem**) *m* dispute
**zataszcz|yć (-ę, -ysz)** *vb perf od* **taszczyć**
**zatelefon|ować (-uję, -ujesz)** *vb perf od* **telefonować**
**zatelegraf|ować (-uję, -ujesz)** *vb perf od* **telegrafować**
**zateleks|ować (-uję, -ujesz)** *vb perf od* **teleksować**
**zatem** *adv* (*książk*) therefore, thus; **a ~, zaczynajmy** let us begin then
**zatemper|ować (-uję, -ujesz)** *vb perf od* **temperować**
**zatęchły** *adj* musty, mouldy (Brit), moldy (US)

**zatęsk|nić (-nię, -nisz)** (*imp* **-nij**) *vi perf*: **~ za kimś/czymś** to begin longing *lub* yearning for sb/sth
**zatk|ać (-am, -asz)** *vb perf od* **zatykać**
**zatk|nąć (-nę, -niesz)** (*imp* **-nij**) *vb perf od* **zatykać**
**zatłoczony** *adj* crowded
**zatłu|c (-kę, -czesz)** (*imp* **-cz**) *vt* to beat to death
**zatłuszczony** *adj* greasy
**zatłu|ścić (-szczę, -ścisz)** (*imp* **-ść**) *vb perf od* **tłuścić**
**zatnę** *itp. vb patrz* **zaciąć**
**zatocz|ka** (**-ki, -ki**) (*dat sg* **-ce**, *gen pl* **-ek**) *f dimin od* **zatoka**
**zatocz|yć (-ę, -ysz)** *vb perf od* **zataczać**; **zatoczyć się** *vr* (*o beczce, kamieniu*) to roll
**zato|ka** (**-ki, -ki**) (*dat sg* **-ce**) *f* (*część morza*) bay, gulf; (*część jeziora*) bay; (*Anat*) sinus; (*Mot*) lay-by; **Z~ Gdańska** the Bay of Gdańsk; **Z~ Perska** the (Persian) Gulf
**zato|nąć (-nę, -niesz)** (*imp* **-ń**) *vb perf od* **tonąć**
**zato|pić (-pię, -pisz)** *vb perf od* **zatapiać**
**zatopiony** *adj* (*skarb, okręt*) sunken; **~ w myślach/lekturze** immersed in thought/a book
**zato|r** (**-ru, -ry**) (*loc sg* **-rze**) *m* (*Mot*) (traffic) jam, hold-up; (*Med*) embolism; **~ lodowy** ice-jam
**zatra|cać (-cam, -casz)** (*perf* **-cić**) *vt* to lose; **zatracać się** *vr* (*zanikać*) to vanish, to disappear
**zatra|cić (-cę, -cisz)** (*imp* **-ć**) *vb perf od* **zatracać**
**zatrą|bić (-bię, -bisz)** *vb perf od* **trąbić**
**zatrą|cać (-cam, -casz)** (*perf* **-cić**) *vi*: **~ z francuska** to speak with a French accent
**zatriumf|ować (-uję, -ujesz)** *vb perf od* **triumfować**
**zatroskany** *adj* worried
**zatroszcz|yć się (-ę, -ysz)** *vb perf od* **troszczyć się**; **zatroszczyć się o kogoś/coś** to take care of sb/sth
**zatru|cie** (**-cia, -cia**) (*gen pl* **-ć**) *nt* poisoning; **~ pokarmowe** food poisoning
**zatru|ć (-ję, -jesz)** *vb perf od* **zatruwać**
**zatrud|niać (-niam, -niasz)** (*perf* **-nić**) *vt* to employ; **„zatrudnię kucharza"** "cook wanted"; **zatrudniać się** *vr* to get a job
**zatrud|nić (-nię, -nisz)** (*imp* **-nij**) *vb perf od* **zatrudniać**
**zatrudnieni|e** (**-a**) *nt* employment; **miejsce zatrudnienia** place of employment; **pełne ~** full employment
**zatrudni|ony** (**-onego, -eni**) *m decl like adj* employee
**zatruw|ać (-am, -asz)** (*perf* **zatruć**) *vt* (*wodę, środowisko*) to poison; (*ząb*) to devitalize; **~ komuś życie** to be the bane of sb's life; **zatruwać się** *vr* to get poisoned; **~ się czymś** (*przen*) to brood on *lub* over sth
**zatrważ|ać (-am, -asz)** (*perf* **zatrwożyć**) *vt* (*książk*) to alarm; **zatrważać się** *vr* to be alarmed
**zatrważający** *adj* alarming
**zatrwożony** *adj* (*książk*) alarmed
**zatrwoż|yć (-ę, -ysz)** (*imp* **zatrwóż**) *vb perf od* **zatrważać**
**zatrzas|k** (**-ku, -ki**) (*instr sg* **-kiem**) *m* (*przy ubraniu*) press stud, snap fastener; (*w drzwiach*) latch
**zatrzas|kiwać (-kuję, -kujesz)** (*perf* **zatrzasnąć**) *vt* (*drzwi*) to slam; (*osobę*) to lock in; **zatrzaskiwać się** *vr* (*o drzwiach*) to slam; (*o osobie*) to lock o.s. in
**zatrza|snąć (-snę, -śniesz)** (*imp* **-śnij**) *vb perf od* **zatrzaskiwać**
**zatrz|ąść (-ęsę, -ęsiesz)** (*imp* **-ąś** *lub* **-ęś**) *vb perf od* **trząść**
**zat|rzeć (-rę, -rzesz)** (*imp* **-rzyj**) *vb perf od* **zacierać**
**zatrzepo|tać (-cze)** *vb perf od* **trzepotać**
**zatrzeszcz|eć (-y)** *vb perf od* **trzeszczeć**
**zatrzęsieni|e** (**-a**) *nt +gen* (*mnóstwo*) heaps of
**zatrzym|ać (-am, -asz)** *vb perf od* **zatrzymywać**
**zatrzymani|e** (**-a**) *nt* (*podejrzanego*) arrest
**zatrzym|ywać (-uję, -ujesz)** (*perf* **-ać**) *vt* (*osobę, maszynę*) to stop; (*o policji: podejrzanego*) to arrest; (*: samochód*) to pull over; (*zachowywać*) to keep; (*powodować spóźnienie*) to detain, to delay; **zatrzymaj tę wiadomość dla siebie** keep this to yourself; **zatrzymywać się** *vr* (*o osobie, samochodzie*) to stop; (*o urządzeniu, maszynie*) to (come to a) stop; (*zamieszkać chwilowo*) to put up
**zatusz|ować (-uję, -ujesz)** *vb perf od* **tuszować, zatuszowywać**
**zatuszow|ywać (-uję, -ujesz)** (*perf* **-ać**) *vt* to cover up
**zatwardzeni|e** (**-a**) *nt* constipation; **mieć ~** to be constipated
**zatwardziały** *adj* (*kawaler*) confirmed; (*przestępca*) hardened
**zatwier|dzać (-dzam, -dzasz)** (*perf* **-dzić**) *vt* to approve
**zatwier|dzić (-dzę, -dzisz)** (*imp* **-dź**) *vb perf od* **zatwierdzać**
**zatycz|ka** (**-ki, -ki**) (*dat sg* **-ce**, *gen pl* **-ek**) *f* stopper, plug; **zatyczki do uszu** earplugs
**zatyk|ać (-am, -asz)** *vt* (*perf* **zatkać**) (*zakorkowywać*) to stop (up); (*zapychać*) to clog (up); (*flagę*) (*perf* **zatknąć**) to put up; **aż mnie**

Z

zatkało I was speechless; **zatykać się** *vr* (*perf* **zatkać**) to get clogged

**zatytuł|ować (-uję, -ujesz)** *vb perf od* **tytułować**

**zauf|ać (-am, -asz)** *vb perf od* **ufać**

**zaufani|e** (**-a**) *nt* confidence, trust; **mieć do kogoś ~** to have confidence in sb; **cieszyć się czyimś ~m** to enjoy *lub* have sb's confidence; **w zaufaniu** in confidence; **godny zaufania** trustworthy; **telefon zaufania** helpline; **wotum zaufania** vote of confidence

**zaufany** *adj* trusted

**zauł|ek** (**-ka, -ki**) (*instr sg* **-kiem**) *m* lane; **ślepy ~** (*przen*) blind alley, dead end

**zauroczeni|e** (**-a**) *nt* enchantment

**zaurocz|yć (-ę, -ysz)** *vt perf* to enchant

**zautomatyz|ować (-uję, -ujesz)** *vb perf od* **automatyzować**

**zauważ|ać (-am, -asz)** (*perf* **-yć**) *vt* to notice, to spot ▷ *vi* to observe

**zauważalny** *adj* noticeable

**zauważ|yć (-ę, -ysz)** *vb perf od* **zauważać**

**zawa|da** (**-dy, -dy**) (*dat sg* **-dzie**) *f* obstacle

**zawadiacki** *adj* swashbuckling

**zawadia|ka** (**-ki, -ki** *lub* **-cy**) (*dat sg* **-ce**) *m decl like f* swashbuckler

**zawa|dzać (-dzam, -dzasz)** (*perf* **-dzić**) *vi*: **~ o coś** to knock against sth; **~ komuś** to be *lub* stand in sb's way; **~ komuś w czymś** to make it difficult for sb to do sth; **nie zawadzi spróbować** there's no harm in trying

**zawa|dzić (-dzę, -dzisz)** (*imp* **-dź**) *vb perf od* **zawadzać**

**zawah|ać się (-am, -asz)** *vb perf od* **wahać się**

**zawal|ać (-am, -asz)** *vt* (*zaśmiecać*) (*perf* **-ić**) to litter; (*tarasować*) to block; (*pot*: *plan, robotę*) (*perf* **-ić**) to botch (*pot*); **zawalać się** (*perf* **-ić**) *vr* to collapse

**zawal|ić (-ę, -isz)** *vb perf od* **walić, zawalać**

**zawa|ł** (**-łu, -ły**) (*loc sg* **-le**) *m* (*też*: **zawał serca**) coronary (attack), heart attack; **mieć ~** to have a heart attack

**zawartoś|ć** (**-ci**) *f* (*torebki, artykułu*) contents *pl*; (*alkoholu, tłuszczu*) content; **produkty o niskiej zawartości tłuszczu** low-fat products

**zaważ|yć (-ę, -ysz)** *vi perf*: **~ na czymś** to influence sth

**zawczasu** *adv* beforehand

**zawdzięcz|ać (-am, -asz)** *vt*: **~ coś komuś** to owe sth to sb

**zawę|zić (-żę, -zisz)** (*imp* **-ź**) *vb perf od* **zawężać**

**zawę|żać (-żam, -żasz)** (*perf* **-zić**) *vt* to narrow down; **~ coś do czegoś** to narrow sth down to sth

**zawi|ać (-eje)** *vb perf od* **zawiewać**

**zawiadami|ać (-am, -asz)** (*perf* **zawiadomić**) *vt* to notify, to inform; **~ kogoś o czymś** to notify *lub* inform sb of sth

**zawiado|mić (-mię, -misz)** *vb perf od* **zawiadamiać**

**zawiadomie|nie** (**-nia, -nia**) (*gen pl* **-ń**) *nt* notification

**zawiadowc|a** (**-y, -y**) *m decl like f in sg* stationmaster

**zawiany** *adj* (*pot*) tipsy (*pot*)

**zawia|s** (**-su, -sy**) (*loc sg* **-sie**) *m* hinge

**zawią|zać (-żę, -żesz)** *vb perf od* **wiązać, zawiązywać**

**zawiąz|ywać (-uję, -ujesz)** (*perf* **-ać**) *vt* to tie; **zawiązywać się** *vr* (*powstawać*) to form; **~ spółkę (z kimś)** to form a partnership (with sb); **~ komuś oczy** to blindfold sb

**zawiedziony** *adj* (*osoba*) disappointed; (*nadzieje*) dashed

**zawie|ja** (**-i, -je**) (*gen pl* **-i**) *f* snowstorm, blizzard

**zawier|ać (-am, -asz)** (*perf* **zawrzeć**) *vt* (*mieścić w sobie*) to include; (*umowę, kompromis*) to reach; (*pokój*) to make; **~ z kimś znajomość** to make sb's acquaintance

**zawieru|cha** (**-chy, -chy**) (*dat sg* **-sze**) *f* blustery weather

**zawierusz|ać (-am, -asz)** (*perf* **-yć**) *vt* to mislay; **zawieruszać się** *vr* (*o przesyłce*) to go astray; (*o długopisie, kluczach*) to disappear

**zawierz|ać (-am, -asz)** (*perf* **-yć**) *vt +dat* to trust

**zawie|sić (-szę, -sisz)** (*imp* **-ś**) *vb perf od* **zawieszać**

**zawiesi|na** (**-ny, -ny**) (*dat sg* **-nie**) *f* (*Chem*) suspension

**zawiesisty** *adj* thick

**zawiesz|ać (-am, -asz)** (*perf* **zawiesić**) *vt* (*obraz, firankę*) to hang; (*działalność, karę*) to suspend

**zawiesze|nie** (**-nia, -nia**) (*gen pl* **-ń**) *nt* (*Mot*) suspension; **wyrok z ~m** *lub* **w zawieszeniu** suspended sentence; **~ wykonania wyroku** stay of execution; **~ broni** ceasefire

**zawi|eść (-odę, -edziesz)** (*imp* **-edź**, *pt* **-ódł, -odła, -edli**) *vb perf od* **zawodzić**

**zawietrzn|a** (**-ej**) *f decl like adj* leeward; **na zawietrzną** to leeward

**zawietrzny** *adj* leeward

**zawiew|ać (-a)** (*perf* **zawiać**) *vt* (*o śniegu, piasku*: *zasypywać*) to cover ▷ *vi* (*o wietrze*) to blow; **zawiało mnie** (*pot*) I caught a bit of a chill (*pot*)

**zawi|eźć (-ozę, -eziesz)** (*imp* **-eź**) *vb perf od* **wieźć, zawozić**

**zawij|ać (-am, -asz)** (*perf* **zawinąć**) *vt* (*paczkę, kanapkę*) to wrap (up); (*rękawy, nogawki*) to roll

up ▷ *vi*: **~ do portu** to call at a port; **zawijać się** *vr* (*o kołnierzyku, rogu kartki*) to curl up
**zawija|s** (**-sa, -sy**) (*loc sg* **-sie**) *m* flourish
**zawikł|ać (-am, -asz)** *vb perf od* **wikłać**
**zawikłany** *adj* involved
**zawil|ec** (**-ca, -ce**) *m* anemone
**zawiłoś|ć** (**-ci, -ci**) (*gen pl* **-ci**) *f* complexity
**zawiły** *adj* complex, complicated
**zawi|nąć (-nę, -niesz)** (*imp* **-ń**) *vb perf od* **zawijać**
**zawiniąt|ko** (**-ka, -ka**) (*instr sg* **-kiem**, *gen pl* **-ek**) *nt* bundle
**zawi|nić (-nię, -nisz)** (*imp* **-ń**) *vi perf* to be at fault
**zawir|ować (-uję, -ujesz)** *vb perf od* **wirować**
**zawis|ać (-am, -asz)** (*perf* **-nąć**) *vi* (*zostawać zawieszonym*) to hang; **zawisnąć na włosku** (*przen*) to hang by a thread
**zawi|snąć (-snę, -śniesz)** (*imp* **-śnij**) *vb perf od* **zawisać**
**zawistny** *adj* envious
**zawiś|ć** (**-ci**) *f* envy; **budzić ~** to stir up *lub* arouse envy
**zawit|ać (-am, -asz)** *vi perf* (*książk*) to come
**zawl|ec (-okę, -eczesz)** (*pt* **-ókł, -okła, -ekli**) *vb perf od* **wlec, zawlekać**
**zawlecz|ka** (**-ki, -ki**) (*dat sg* **-ce**, *gen pl* **-ek**) *f* (*Tech*) pin; (*granatu*) safety pin
**zawlek|ać (-am, -asz)** (*perf* **zawlec**) *vt* (*prowadzić wlokąc*) to drag; (*chorobę, szkodnika*) to spread
**zawład|nąć (-nę, -niesz)** (*imp* **-nij**) *vi perf*: **~ czymś** (*o władcy, plemieniu*) to capture sth; **~ kimś** (*o myślach, uczuciach*) to take possession of sb
**zawłaszcz|yć (-ę, -ysz)** *vt perf* to appropriate
**zawoalowany** *adj* veiled
**zawodnicz|ka** (**-ki, -ki**) (*dat sg* **-ce**, *gen pl* **-ek**) *f* (*w sporcie*) competitor; (*w teleturnieju*) contestant
**zawodni|k** (**-ka, -cy**) (*instr sg* **-kiem**) *m* (*w lekkiej atletyce, tenisie*) competitor; (*w boksie, teleturnieju*) contestant
**zawodny** *adj* (*urządzenie*) unreliable; (*pamięć*) fallible
**zawodo|wiec** (**-wca, -wcy**) *m* professional
**zawodowo** *adv* professionally
**zawodowy** *adj* professional; **szkoła zawodowa** vocational school; **związek ~** trade union (*Brit*), labor union (*US*); **choroba zawodowa** occupational disease; **tajemnica zawodowa** trade secret
**zawod|y** (**-ów**) *pl* (*Sport*) competition, contest; *patrz też* **zawód**
**zaw|odzić (-odzę, -odzisz)** (*imp* **-ódź**) *vt* (*sprawiać zawód*) (*perf* **zawieść**) to let down, to disappoint; (*książk: prowadzić*) (*perf* **zawieść**) to lead ▷ *vi* (*o urządzeniu, pamięci*) (*perf* **zawieść**) to fail; (*o człowieku, wietrze: lamentować, wyć*) to wail; **zawodzić się** *vr* (*perf* **zawieść**); **~ się (na kimś/czymś)** to be disappointed (with sb/sth)
**zawoj|ować (-uję, -ujesz)** *vt perf* to conquer
**zawoł|ać (-am, -asz)** *vb perf od* **wołać**
**zawołani|e** (**-a**) *nt* call; **być na czyjeś (każde) ~** to be at sb's beck and call
**zawołany** *adj* (*mówca, myśliwy*) born
**zaw|ozić (-ożę, -ozisz)** (*imp* **-óź** *lub* **-oź**, *perf* **zawieźć**) *vt* (*samochodem*) to drive; (*pociągiem*) to take
**zaw|ód** (**-odu, -ody**) (*loc sg* **-odzie**) *m* (*fach*) profession; (*rozczarowanie*) letdown, disappointment; **kim Pan/Pani jest z zawodu?** what do you do for a living?; **doznawać (doznać** *perf*) **zawodu** to be disappointed; **sprawiać (sprawić** *perf*) **komuś ~** to disappoint sb
**zaw|ór** (**-oru, -ory**) (*loc sg* **-orze**) *m* valve; **~ bezpieczeństwa** safety valve; **~ odcinający** shut-off valve, stopcock
**zawrac|ać (-am, -asz)** (*perf* **zawrócić**) *vt* to turn round *lub* back ▷ *vi* to turn round *lub* back; **~ sobie głowę** to bother (one's head); **~ komuś głowę** to bother sb; **zawrócić komuś w głowie** to turn sb's head
**zawracani|e** (**-a**) *nt*: **~ głowy** bother
**zawrotny** *adj* staggering
**zawró|cić (-cę, -cisz)** (*imp* **-ć**) *vb perf od* **zawracać**
**zawr|ót** (**-otu, -oty**) (*loc sg* **-ocie**) *m*: **zawroty głowy** dizziness, vertigo; **mieć zawroty głowy** to suffer from vertigo *lub* dizzy spells
**zaw|rzeć[1] (-rę, -rzesz)** (*imp* **-rzyj**, *pt* **-arł, -arła, -arli**) *vb perf od* **zawierać**
**zaw|rzeć[2] (-rę, -rzesz)** (*imp* **-rzyj**) *vi perf* (*zagotować się*) to come to the (*Brit*) *lub* a (*US*) boil; (*wybuchnąć*) to break out; **~ gniewem/oburzeniem** to seethe with anger/indignation; *patrz też* **wrzeć**
**zawsty|dzać (-dzam, -dzasz)** (*perf* **-dzić**) *vt* to shame, to put to shame; **zawstydzać się** *vr* to be ashamed
**zawsty|dzić (-dzę, -dzisz)** (*imp* **-dź**) *vb perf od* **zawstydzać**
**zawstydzony** *adj* ashamed
**zawsze** *adv* always ▷ *part*: **ale ~** but still; **na ~** for ever; **tyle co ~** same as usual; **~ gdy** whenever; **raz na ~** once and for all
**zawy|ć (-ję, -jesz)** *vb perf od* **wyć**
**zawyrok|ować (-uję, -ujesz)** *vb perf od* **wyrokować**
**zawyż|ać (-am, -asz)** (*perf* **-yć**) *vt* (*ceny*) to inflate; (*dane*) to overstate
**zaw|ziąć się (-ezmę, -eźmiesz)** (*imp* **-eźmij**) *vr perf* to dig in one's heels; **zawziąć się na kogoś** to have it in for sb

Z

**zawzięcie** *adv* (*pracować*) relentlessly; (*kłócić się*) vehemently
**zawzięt|ość** (**-ci**) *f* doggedness
**zawzięty** *adj* (*opór*) dogged; (*mina*) determined; (*przeciwnik*) sworn
**zazdrosny** *adj* jealous; **~ o kogoś/coś** jealous of sb/sth
**zazdro|ścić (-szczę, -ścisz)** (*imp* **-ść**) *vi*: **~ komuś czegoś** to envy sb sth
**zazdroś|ć** (**-ci**) *f* jealousy
**zazę|biać się (-bia)** (*perf* **-bić**) *vr* (*o mechanizmach*) to mesh; (*przen: o sprawach, problemach*) to be interrelated *lub* interconnected
**zazię|biać się (-biam, -biasz)** (*perf* **-bić**) *vr* to catch a cold
**zazię|bić się (-bię, -bisz)** *vb perf od* **zaziębiać się**
**zaziębie|nie** (**-nia, -nia**) (*gen pl* **-ń**) *nt* cold
**zaziębiony** *adj*: **jestem ~** I have a cold
**zaznacz|ać (-am, -asz)** (*perf* **-yć**) *vt* (*wyróżniać znakiem*) to mark; (*uwydatniać*) to stress ▷ *vi*: **~, że ...** to stress that ...; **zaznaczać się** *vr* to be evident
**zazn|ać (-am, -asz)** *vb perf od* **zaznawać**
**zaznajami|ać (-am, -asz)** (*perf* **zaznajomić**) *vt*: **~ kogoś z czymś** to acquaint sb with sth; **zaznajamiać się** *vr*: **~ się z czymś** to familiarize o.s. with sth
**zaznajo|mić (-mię, -misz)** *vb perf od* **zaznajamiać**
**zazn|awać (-aję, -ajesz)** (*perf* **-ać**) *vt*: **~ czegoś** to experience sth
**zazwyczaj** *adv* usually
**zażale|nie** (**-nia, -nia**) (*gen pl* **-ń**) *nt* complaint; **składać (złożyć** *perf*) **~ (na kogoś/coś)** to file a complaint (against sb/about sth)
**zażarcie** *adv* fiercely
**zażart|ować (-uję, -ujesz)** *vb perf od* **żartować**
**zażarty** *adj* (*walka, dyskusja*) fierce; (*wróg*) sworn
**zażąd|ać (-am, -asz)** *vb perf od* **żądać**
**zażegn|ywać (-uję, -ujesz)** (*perf* **-ać**) *vt* to prevent, to head off
**zażenowani|e** (**-a**) *nt* embarrassment
**zażenowany** *adj* embarrassed
**zażycz|yć (-ę, -ysz)** *vi perf*: **~ sobie czegoś** to request sth
**zaży|ć (-ję, -jesz)** *vb perf od* **zażywać**
**zażyłoś|ć** (**-ci**) *f* intimacy
**zażyły** *adj* intimate; **być z kimś w ~ch stosunkach** to be intimate with sb
**zażyw|ać (-am, -asz)** (*perf* **zażyć**) *vt* (*tabletki itp.*) to take; **~ czegoś** (*przen: bogactw, przyjemności*) to enjoy sth
**zażywny** *adj* portly

**ząb** (**zęba, zęby**) (*loc sg* **zębie**) *m* tooth; **sztuczne zęby** false teeth; **boli mnie ząb** I have (a) toothache; **nie rozumiem ani w ząb** I don't understand a thing; **coś na ząb** (*pot*) a bite (*pot*); **zacisnąć** (*perf*) **zęby** to clench one's teeth; (*przen*) to grit one's teeth; **dać komuś w zęby** (*pot*) to punch sb in *lub* on the jaw
**ząb|ek** (**-ka, -ki**) (*instr sg* **-kiem**) *m dimin od* **ząb**; **~ czosnku** a clove of garlic; **ząbki** *pl* (*wycięcia*) notches *pl*; **w ząbki** notched
**ząbk|ować (-uję, -ujesz)** *vi* to teethe
**zbacz|ać (-am, -asz)** (*perf* **zboczyć**) *vi* to deviate, to diverge; **~ z tematu** to digress, to deviate from the subject
**zbad|ać (-am, -asz)** *vb perf od* **badać**
**zbankrut|ować (-uję, -ujesz)** *vb perf od* **bankrutować**
**zbawc|a** (**-y, -y**) *m decl like f in sg* saviour (Brit), savior (US)
**zba|wiać (-wiam, -wiasz)** (*perf* **-wić**) *vt* (*Rel*) to redeem; (*książk: wybawiać*) to save, to deliver
**Zbawiciel** (**-a**) *m* (*Rel*) Saviour (Brit), Savior (US)
**zbawieni|e** (**-a**) *nt* (*Rel*) redemption, salvation
**zbawienny** *adj* beneficial
**zbezcze|ścić (-szczę, -ścisz)** (*imp* **-ść**) *vb perf od* **bezcześcić**
**zbędny** *adj* (*wysiłek*) useless; (*słowa*) needless; (*rzecz*) superfluous, redundant
**zbi|ć (-ję, -jesz)** *vb perf od* **bić, zbijać** ▷ *vt perf* (*szybę*) to break; **~ kogoś** to give sb a thrashing; **zbić się** *vr perf* to break
**zbie|c (-gnę, -gniesz)** (*imp* **-gnij**, *pt* **-gł, -gła, -gli**) *vb perf od* **zbiegać** ▷ *vi perf* (*uciec*) to run away
**zbie|g¹** (**-ga, -gowie**) (*instr sg* **-giem**) *m* (*uciekinier*) fugitive, runaway
**zbie|g²** (**-gu, -gi**) (*instr sg* **-giem**) *m* (*ulic, alejek*) junction; **~ okoliczności** coincidence
**zbieg|ać (-am, -asz)** (*perf* **zbiec** *lub* **-nąć**) *vi* (*uciekać*) to run away; (*biec w dół*) to run downhill; **~ po schodach** to run downstairs; **zbiegać się** *vr* (*gromadzić się*) to gather; (*łączyć się w przestrzeni*) to converge; (*zdarzać się jednocześnie*) to coincide; (*kurczyć się*) to shrink
**zbieg|nąć (-nę, -niesz)** (*imp* **-nij**, *pt* **-ł**) *vb perf od* **zbiegać**
**zbiegowis|ko** (**-ka, -ka**) (*instr sg* **-kiem**) *nt* gathering, crowd
**zbieracz** (**-a, -e**) (*gen pl* **-y**) *m* (*kolekcjoner*) collector; (*grzybów*) picker
**zbier|ać (-am, -asz)** (*perf* **zebrać**) *vt* (*gromadzić*) to collect; (*zwoływać*) to gather, to assemble; (*sprzątać*) to gather; (*zrywać*) to

pick; (*wodę*) to mop up; **zebrać myśli** to gather *lub* collect one's thoughts; **~ siły** to gather one's strength; **zbierać się** *vr* (*gromadzić się*) to gather; **~ się (do czegoś)** to brace o.s. (for sth); **zebrać się na odwagę** to pluck up one's courage; **zebrać się w sobie** to brace o.s. (up); **zbiera się na deszcz** it's going to rain; **zbiera się na burzę** there is going to be a storm; **zbiera mi się na wymioty** I am going to be sick

**zbierani|na** (**-ny**) (*dat sg* **-nie**) *f* mixed lot

**zbieżnoś|ć** (**-ci**) (*gen pl* **-ci**) *f* convergence; **~ kół** (*Mot*) toe-in

**zbieżny** *adj* convergent

**zbij|ać (-am, -asz)** (*perf* **zbić**) *vt* (*gwoździami*) to nail together; (*piłkę*) to smash; **zbić majątek** to make a fortune; **zbić kogoś z tropu** to throw sb off the track; **~ czyjeś argumenty** to refute sb's arguments; **zbijać się** *vr* (*o ziemi, soli*) to lump

**zbiorczy** *adj* collective

**zbiorę** *itd. vb patrz* **zebrać**

**zbiorni|k** (**-ka, -ki**) (*instr sg* **-kiem**) *m* (*pojemnik*) container; (*Geog*) reservoir; **~ paliwa** (*Mot*) fuel tank

**zbiorniko|wiec** (**-wca, -wce**) *m* (oil) tanker

**zbiorowis|ko** (**-ka, -ka**) (*instr sg* **-kiem**) *nt* gathering

**zbiorowoś|ć** (**-ci, -ci**) (*gen pl* **-ci**) *f* community

**zbiorowy** *adj* (*wysiłek*) collective; **rezerwacja zbiorowa** block booking; **odpowiedzialność zbiorowa** collective responsibility; **umowa zbiorowa** (*Ekon*) collective agreement; **scena zbiorowa** crowd scene

**zbi|ór** (**-oru, -ory**) (*loc sg* **-orze**) *m* (*wierszy, znaczków*) collection; (*owoców, zboża*) harvest; (*Mat*) set; (*Komput*) file; **zbiory** *pl* (*plon*) crop

**zbiór|ka** (**-ki, -ki**) (*dat sg* **-ce**, *gen pl* **-ek**) *f* (*oddziału*) assembly; (*makulatury*) collection; (*pieniędzy*) fund-raising, collection; **~!** fall in!

**zbi|r** (**-ra, -ry**) (*loc sg* **-rze**) *m* thug, cutthroat

**zbit|ka** (**-ki, -ki**) (*dat sg* **-ce**, *gen pl* **-ek**) *f* cluster

**zbity** *adj* (*pobity*) beaten up; (*zwarty*) packed

**zblazowany** *adj* (*pot*) blasé

**zbled|nąć (-nę, -niesz)** (*imp* **-nij**, *pt* **zbladł, zbladła, -li**) *vb perf od* **blednąć**

**zbliż|ać (-am, -asz)** (*perf* **-yć**) *vt* (*przybliżać*) to bring nearer *lub* closer; (*przen*) to bring together; **zbliżać się** *vr* to approach; (*przen: zaprzyjaźniać się*) to become close; (*o terminie, godzinie, burzy*) to approach; **nie zbliżaj się!** stand away!

**zbliże|nie** (**-nia, -nia**) (*gen pl* **-ń**) *nt* (*bliskie stosunki*) close *lub* friendly relations; (*Fot*) close-up; **~ fizyczne** sexual intercourse

**zbliżony** *adj* similar

**zbliż|yć (-ę, -ysz)** *vb perf od* **zbliżać**

**zbłaź|nić się (-nię, -nisz)** (*imp* **-nij**) *vr perf* to make a fool of o.s.

**zbłą|dzić (-dzę, -dzisz)** (*imp* **-dź**) *vb perf od* **błądzić**

**zbłąkany** *adj* stray

**zbocz|e** (**-a, -a**) (*gen pl* **-y**) *nt* slope

**zbocze|nie** (**-nia, -nia**) (*gen pl* **-ń**) *nt* perversion

**zbocze|niec** (**-ńca, -ńcy**) *m* pervert

**zboczony** *adj* perverted

**zbocz|yć (-ę, -ysz)** *vb perf od* **zbaczać**

**zbojkot|ować (-uję, -ujesz)** *vb perf od* **bojkotować**

**zbombard|ować (-uję, -ujesz)** *vb perf od* **bombardować**

**zborny** *adj*: **punkt ~** rallying point

**zboru** *n patrz* **zbór**

**ZBoWiD** *abbr* (= *Związek Bojowników o Wolność i Demokrację*) *an association of Polish WW II veterans*

**zb|oże** (**-oża, -oża**) (*gen pl* **-óż**) *nt* cereal, corn (*Brit*); **~ jare/ozime** spring/winter crops

**zbożny** *adj* worthy

**zbożowy** *adj* cereal *attr*; **kawa zbożowa** chicory coffee

**zbój** (**-a, -e**) *m* robber

**zb|ór** (**-oru, -ory**) (*loc sg* **-orze**) *m* (*Rel*) (Protestant) church

**zbrod|nia** (**-ni, -nie**) (*gen pl* **-ni**) *f* crime

**zbrodniar|ka** (**-ki, -ki**) (*dat sg* **-ce**, *gen pl* **-ek**) *f* criminal

**zbrodniarz** (**-a, -e**) (*gen pl* **-y**) *m* criminal

**zbrodniczy** *adj* criminal

**zbr|oić¹ (-oję, -oisz)** (*imp* **-ój**, *perf* **u-**) *vt* (*wojsko*) to arm; (*beton*) to reinforce; (*teren*) to develop; **zbroić się** *vr* to arm

**zbr|oić² (-oję, -oisz)** (*imp* **-ój**) *vb perf od* **broić**

**zbro|ja** (**-i, -je**) (*gen pl* **-i**) *f* (a suit of) armour (*Brit*), armor (*US*)

**zbroje|nie** (**-nia, -nia**) (*gen pl* **-ń**) *nt* (*wojska*) armament; (*betonu*) reinforcement; **zbrojenia** *pl* armaments *pl*; **wyścig zbrojeń** the arms race

**zbrojeniowy** *adj* (*zakład*) arms *attr*; (*przemysł*) war *attr*

**zbrojny** *adj* armed, military

**zbrojow|nia** (**-ni, -nie**) (*gen pl* **-ni**) *f* armoury (*Brit*), armory (*US*)

**zbrzyd|nąć (-nę, -niesz)** (*imp* **-nij**, *pt* **-ł**) *vb perf od* **brzydnąć**

**zbud|ować (-uję, -ujesz)** *vb perf od* **budować**

**zbu|dzić (-dzę, -dzisz)** (*imp* **-dź**) *vb perf od* **budzić**

**zbu|k** (**-ka, -ki**) (*instr sg* **-kiem**) *m* addled egg

**zbulwers|ować (-uję, -ujesz)** *vb perf od* **bulwersować**

**zbulwersowany** *adj*: **być czymś ~m** to be appalled by sth

**zbunt|ować (-uję, -ujesz)** *vb perf od* **buntować**

Z

**zburz|yć (-ę, -ysz)** *vb perf od* **burzyć**
**zbutwi|eć (-eje)** *vb perf od* **butwieć**
**zb|yć (-ędę, -ędziesz)** (*imp* **-ądź**) *vb perf od* **zbywać**
**zby|t¹** (**-tu**) (*loc sg* **-cie**) *m* (*popyt*) market; (*sprzedaż*) sale(s *pl*); **cena ~u** selling price; **rynek ~u** market
**zbyt²** *adv* too; **~ szybki/szybko** too quick/ quickly
**zbyteczny** *adj* unnecessary
**zbyt|ek** (**-ku**) (*instr sg* **-kiem**) *m* (*przepych*) luxury; (*rzecz*) (*nom pl* **-ki**) luxury; **to ~ łaski!** that is too kind of you!
**zbytni** *adj* excessive
**zbytnio** *adv* excessively, unduly
**zbyw|ać (-am, -asz)** (*perf* **zbyć**) *vt* (*sprzedawać*) to sell off *lub* up; **~ kogoś** to get rid of sb; **na niczym mi nie zbywa** I have enough of everything
**zbywalny** *adj* transferable
**zbzikowany** *adj* (*pot*) crazy, loony
**ZChN** *abbr* (= *Zjednoczenie Chrześcijańsko-Narodowe*) Christian-Democratic Alliance
**zd|ać (-am, -asz)** *vb perf od* **zdawać** ▷ *vt perf*: **~ egzamin** to pass an exam; **~ na uniwersytet** to get into college; **~ do następnej klasy** to be promoted (*to a higher class*); **zdać się** *vr*: **to się na nic nie zda** it won't do any good
**zdalnie** *adv*: **~ kierowany** *lub* **sterowany** remote-controlled
**zdalny** *adj*: **zdalne sterowanie** remote control
**zda|nie** (**-nia, -nia**) (*gen pl* **-ń**) *nt* (*opinia*) opinion; (*Jęz*) sentence; **moim ~m** in my opinion; **być zdania, że ...** to be of the opinion that ...; **zmieniać (zmienić** *perf*) **~** to change one's mind; **różnica zdań** difference of opinion; **~ podrzędne/względne** subordinate/relative clause
**zdarł** *itd. vb patrz* **zedrzeć**
**zdarz|ać się (-a)** (*perf* **-yć**) *vr* to happen, to occur
**zdarze|nie** (**-nia, -nia**) (*gen pl* **-ń**) *nt* (*wydarzenie*) event, occurrence; **nauczyciel z prawdziwego zdarzenia** a true *lub* real teacher
**zdatny** *adj*: **~ do czegoś** fit *lub* suitable for sth; **„~ do spożycia"** "fit for human consumption"; **woda zdatna do picia** drinkable water; **~ do użytku** usable
**zda|wać (-ję, -jesz)** (*imp* **-waj**) *vt* (*przekazywać*) (*perf* **zdać**) to turn over; (*oddawać*) (*perf* **zdać**) to return ▷ *vi*: **~ (na uniwersytet/do liceum)** to take (one's) entrance exams (to college/secondary (*Brit*) *lub* high (*US*) school); **~ sobie sprawę z czegoś** to realize sth, to be aware of sth; **~ z czegoś sprawę** to relate *lub* recount sth; **~ egzamin (z fizyki)** to take an exam (in physics); **~ egzamin** (*przen*) to live up to its promise, to stand the test of time; **zdawać się** *vr* to seem, to appear; **dom zdawał się (być) ruiną** the house seemed (to be) a ruin; **gospodarz zdawał się drzemać** the host seemed *lub* appeared to be dreaming; **zdaje (mi) się, że ...** it seems (to me) that ...; **~ się na kogoś/coś** to depend on sb/sth; **zdawało ci się** you must have imagined it
**zdawkowy** *adj* (*odpowiedź, komentarz*) trite; (*uprzejmość*) superficial
**zdąż|ać (-am, -asz)** (*perf* **-yć**) *vi* (*przybywać na czas*) to be *lub* make it in time; (*dotrzymywać kroku*) to keep pace; **zdążyć coś zrobić** to manage to do sth (on time); **~ do ...** (*książk*) to head for ...; **nie zdążyć na samolot** to miss the plane; **nie zdążyć do szkoły** to be late for school
**zdąż|yć (-ę, -ysz)** *vb perf od* **zdążać**
**zdechły** *adj* dead
**zdech|nąć (-nę, -niesz)** (*imp* **-nij**, *pt* **-ł**) *vb perf od* **zdychać**
**zdecyd|ować (-uję, -ujesz)** *vb perf od* **decydować**
**zdecydowani|e¹** (**-a**) *nt* determination, resoluteness
**zdecydowanie²** *adv* (*stanowczo*) strongly, decidedly; (*wyraźnie*) definitely; **~ najlepszy** by far the best
**zdecydowany** *adj* (*człowiek*) firm, determined; (*posunięcie*) decisive; (*niewątpliwy*) unquestionable; **~ na coś** intent *lub* bent on doing sth, determined to do sth; **był ~ na wszystko** he would go to any lengths
**zdefini|ować (-uję, -ujesz)** *vb perf od* **definiować**
**zdeformowany** *adj* deformed
**zdegenerowany** *adj* degenerate
**zdegustowany** *adj* disgusted
**zdejmę** *itd. vb patrz* **zdjąć**
**zdejm|ować (-uję, -ujesz)** (*perf* **zdjąć**) *vt* (*ubranie*) to take off; (*książkę z półki*) to take down; **zdjąć nogę z pedału** to take one's foot off the pedal; **zdjąć kogoś ze stanowiska** to remove sb from a post
**zdeklarowany** *adj* avowed, professed
**zdelegaliz|ować (-uję, -ujesz)** *vb perf od* **delegalizować**
**zdemask|ować (-uję, -ujesz)** *vb perf od* **demaskować**
**zdement|ować (-uję, -ujesz)** *vb perf od* **dementować**
**zdemilitaryzowany** *adj*: **strefa zdemilitaryzowana** demilitarized zone

**zdemol|ować (-uję, -ujesz)** *vb perf od* **demolować**
**zdemont|ować (-uję, -ujesz)** *vb perf od* **demontować**
**zdenerw|ować (-uję, -ujesz)** *vb perf od* **denerwować**
**zdenerwowani|e** (**-a**) *nt* (*niepokój*) nervousness; (*złość*) anger, annoyance
**zdenerwowany** *adj* (*niespokojny*) nervous; **~ czymś/na kogoś** angry *lub* annoyed at sth/ with sb
**zderz|ać się (-am, -asz)** (*perf* **-yć**) *vr* to collide, to crash
**zderza|k** (**-ka, -ki**) (*instr sg* **-kiem**) *m* (*Mot*) bumper
**zderze|nie** (**-nia, -nia**) (*gen pl* **-ń**) *nt* (*wypadek*) collision, crash; (*przen: kultur, postaw*) clash; **~ czołowe** head-on collision
**zdesperowany** *adj* desperate
**zdeterminowany** *adj* determined; **być ~m coś zrobić** to be determined to do sth, to be intent on doing sth
**zdewast|ować (-uję, -ujesz)** *vb perf od* **dewastować**
**zdezorganiz|ować (-uję, -ujesz)** *vb perf od* **dezorganizować**
**zdezorganizowany** *adj* disorganized
**zdezorientowany** *adj* disorientated (*Brit*), disoriented (*US*)
**zdezynfek|ować (-uję, -ujesz)** *vb perf od* **dezynfekować**
**zdębi|eć (-eję, -ejesz)** *vi perf* (*pot*) to be dumbfounded
**zd|jąć (-ejmę, -ejmiesz)** (*imp* **-ejmij**) *vb perf od* **zdejmować**
**zdję|cie** (**-cia, -cia**) (*gen pl* **-ć**) *nt* (*fotografia*) photo(graph), picture; (*usunięcie*) removal; **robić (zrobić** *perf*) **komuś ~** to take a photo(graph) *lub* picture of sb; **~ rentgenowskie** X-ray (film *lub* photograph)
**zdła|wić (-wię, -wisz)** *vb perf od* **dławić**
**zdmuch|iwać (-uję, -ujesz)** (*perf* **-nąć**) *vt* (*kurz*) to blow off; (*zapałkę*) to blow out
**zdmuch|nąć (-nę, -niesz)** (*imp* **-nij**) *vb perf od* **zdmuchiwać** ▷ *vt perf*: **~ komuś coś sprzed nosa** (*pot*) to snatch sth from under sb's nose (*pot*)
**zd|obić (-obię, -obisz)** (*imp* **-ób**) *vt* (*ozdabiać*) to decorate; (*być ozdobą*) to grace
**zdobnict|wo** (**-wa**) (*loc sg* **-wie**) *nt* (*sztuka*) decorative art; (*ozdoby*) ornamentation
**zdobniczy** *adj* decorative
**zdobyci|e** (**-a**) *nt* (*miasta*) capture; (*majątku*) acquisition; (*szacunku*) earning, winning; (*bramki*) scoring; **nie do zdobycia** (*twierdza*) impregnable; (*bilety*) impossible to get
**zdobycz** (**-y, -e**) (*gen pl* **-y**) *f* (*łup*) loot, booty; (*drapieżnika*) prey; **zdobycze** *pl* achievements *pl*, accomplishments *pl*
**zdob|yć (-ędę, -ędziesz)** (*imp* **-ądź**) *vb perf od* **zdobywać**; **zdobyć się** *vr*: **~ się na zrobienie czegoś** to bring o.s. to do sth; **~ się na odwagę/wysiłek** to summon up the courage/strength
**zdobyw|ać (-am, -asz)** (*perf* **zdobyć**) *vt* (*łupy, miasto*) to capture; (*majątek*) to gain; (*bilety*) to get; (*szacunek, przyjaciół*) to win; (*bramkę*) to score; (*medal*) to earn; **zdobyć szczyt** to reach the summit
**zdobywc|a** (**-y, -y**) *m decl like f in sg* (*łupów, miasta*) conqueror; (*nagrody*) winner; (*bramki*) scorer
**zdolnoś|ć** (**-ci, -ci**) (*gen pl* **-ci**) *f* ability; **~ produkcyjna/prawna** economic/legal capacity; **zdolności** *pl* skills *pl*, gift; **mieć zdolności do czegoś** to have a gift for sth
**zdolny** *adj* (*uczeń*) capable, gifted; **~ do (zrobienia) czegoś** capable of (doing) sth
**zdoł|ać (-am, -asz)** *vi perf*: **~ coś zrobić** to be able to do sth, to manage to do sth
**zdrabni|ać (-am, -asz)** (*perf* **zdrobnić**) *vt* (*Jęz*) *to use the diminutive form of (a word, name etc)*
**zdra|da** (**-dy, -dy**) (*dat sg* **-dzie**) *f* (*nielojalność*) betrayal, treachery; (*przestępstwo*) treason; **~ małżeńska** adultery, marital infidelity *lub* unfaithfulness; **~ stanu** high treason
**zdradliwy** *adj* treacherous
**zdra|dzać (-dzam, -dzasz)** (*perf* **-dzić**) *vt* (*kraj, zasady*) to betray; (*dziewczynę, męża*) to be unfaithful to; (*tajemnicę*) to give away; (*zdolności, podobieństwo*) to show; **zdradzać się** *vr* (*wzajemnie*) to be unfaithful to each other; (*demaskować się*) to give o.s. away
**zdra|dzić (-dzę, -dzisz)** (*imp* **-dź**) *vb perf od* **zdradzać**
**zdradziecki** *adj* treacherous
**zdrajc|a** (**-y, -y**) *m decl like f in sg* traitor
**zdra|pać (-pię, -piesz)** *vb perf od* **zdrapywać**
**zdrap|ywać (-uję, -ujesz)** (*perf* **-ać**) *vt* to scrape off *lub* away
**zdrętwiały** *adj* numb
**zdrobniały** *adj* diminutive
**zdrob|nić (-nię, -nisz)** (*imp* **-nij**) *vb perf od* **zdrabniać**
**zdrobnie|nie** (**-nia, -nia**) (*gen pl* **-ń**) *nt* diminutive
**zdrowi|e** (**-a**) *nt* health; **ośrodek zdrowia** health centre (*Brit*) *lub* center (*US*); **służba zdrowia** health service, healthcare; **jak ~?** how are you (doing)?; **na ~!** (*toast*) cheers!; (*po kichnięciu*) (God) bless you!; **pić czyjeś ~** to drink (to) sb's health; **tryskać ~m** to be glowing with health; **szkodzić zdrowiu** to

Z

be bad for one's health; **wracać (wrócić** *perf*) **do zdrowia** to regain one's health, to recover; **(za) twoje ~!** here's to your health!

**zdrowi|eć (-eję, -ejesz)** (*perf* **wy-**) *vi* to get better

**zdrowo** *adv* (*odżywiać się*) healthily; (*wyglądać*) healthy, well; **~ sobie wypił** (*pot*) he got drunk something awful (*pot*)

**zdrowotny** *adj* (*warunki*) sanitary; (*klimat*) healthy; **opieka zdrowotna** healthcare; **urlop ~** sick leave

**zdrowy** *adj* healthy; **cały i ~** safe and sound; **~ rozsądek** common sense; **na ~ rozum ...** common sense tells us (that) ...; **być przy ~ch zmysłach** to be mentally sound, to be of sound mind

**zdroż|eć (-eje)** *vb perf od* **drożeć**

**zdrożny** *adj* (*książk*) sinful

**zdr|ój (-oju, -oje)** *m* spring

**zdrów** *adj patrz* **zdrowy**; **jest Pan ~** you are healthy *lub* in good health; **~ jak ryba** (as) right as rain; **bądź ~!** farewell!

**zdruzgo|tać (-czę, -czesz)** *vb perf od* **druzgotać**

**zdrzem|nąć się (-nę, -niesz)** (*imp* **-nij**) *vr perf* to have *lub* take a nap; (*mimowolnie*) to doze off

**zdubl|ować (-uję, -ujesz)** *vb perf od* **dublować**

**zdumi|eć (-eję, -ejesz)** *vb perf od* **zdumiewać**

**zdumieni|e (-a)** *nt* astonishment; **wprawiać (wprawić** *perf*) **kogoś w ~** to astonish *lub* amaze sb; **ku memu zdumieniu ...** to my astonishment, ...

**zdumiew|ać (-am, -asz)** (*perf* **zdumieć**) *vt* to astonish, to amaze; **zdumiewać się** *vr* to be amazed

**zdumiewający** *adj* astonishing, amazing

**zdumiony** *adj* astonished, amazed

**zdu|n (-na, -ni)** (*loc sg* **-nie**) *m* stove fitter

**zdu|sić (-szę, -sisz)** (*imp* **-ś**) *vb perf od* **dusić**

**zduszony** *adj* (*jęk, głos*) suppressed

**zdwaj|ać (-am, -asz)** (*perf* **zdwoić**) *vt* to double

**zdych|ać (-am, -asz)** (*perf* **zdechnąć**) *vi* to die; **~ z głodu** (*pot*) to be starved *lub* starving

**zdymisjon|ować (-uję, -ujesz)** *vb perf od* **dymisjonować**

**zdynamiz|ować (-uję, -ujesz)** *vb perf od* **dynamizować**

**zdyscyplinowani|e (-a)** *nt* discipline

**zdyscyplinowany** *adj* disciplined

**zdyskredyt|ować (-uję, -ujesz)** *vb perf od* **dyskredytować**

**zdyskwalifik|ować (-uję, -ujesz)** *vb perf od* **dyskwalifikować**

**zdystans|ować (-uję, -ujesz)** *vb perf od* **dystansować**

**zdyszany** *adj* breathless, winded

**zdział|ać (-am, -asz)** *vt perf* to accomplish, to achieve

**zdzicz|eć (-eję, -ejesz)** *vb perf od* **dziczeć**

**zdziecinni|eć (-eję, -ejesz)** *vb perf od* **dziecinnieć**

**zdziel|ić (-ę, -isz)** *vt perf* (*pot: uderzyć*) to clout (*pot*)

**zdzier|ać (-am, -asz)** (*perf* **zedrzeć**) *vt* (*zrywać*) to tear off; (*odzież, opony*) to wear out; (*zelówki*) to tear down ▷ *vi* (*pot*): **~ z kogoś** to rip sb off; **~ głos** to strain one's voice; **zedrzeć z kogoś skórę** (*przen*) to rip sb off, to fleece sb; **zdzierać się** *vr* (*o odzieży, oponach*) to wear out; (*o zelówkach*) to tear down

**zdzierst|wo (-wa)** (*loc sg* **-wie**) *nt* rip-off (*pot*)

**zdziesiątk|ować (-uję, -ujesz)** *vb perf od* **dziesiątkować**

**zdziwacz|eć (-eję, -ejesz)** *vb perf od* **dziwaczeć**

**zdzi|wić (-wię, -wisz)** *vb perf od* **dziwić**

**zdziwieni|e (-a)** *nt* surprise, astonishment; **ku swemu zdziwieniu znów ją zobaczył** to his surprise, he saw her again

**zdziwiony** *adj* surprised, astonished

**ze** *prep* = **z**

**zeb|ra (-ry, -ry)** (*dat sg* **-rze**) *f* (*Zool*) zebra; (*przejście*) zebra crossing (Brit), crosswalk (US)

**zebrać (zbiorę, zbierzesz)** *vb perf od* **zbierać**

**zebra|nie (-nia, -nia)** (*gen pl* **-ń**) *nt* meeting; **~ towarzyskie** (*w klubie itp.*) social; (*przyjaciół*) get-together

**zece|r (-ra, -rzy)** (*loc sg* **-rze**) *m* typesetter, compositor

**zech|cieć (-cę, -cesz)** (*imp* **-ciej**) *vi perf*: **~ coś zrobić** to be willing to do sth; **zechce Pan/Pani spocząć?** would you like to take a seat?; **kiedy tylko zechcesz** any time you like *lub* want

**zed|rzeć (-rę, -rzesz)** (*imp* **-rzyj**, *pt* **zdarł** *itp.*) *vb perf od* **zdzierać**

**zega|r (-ra, -ry)** (*loc sg* **-rze**) *m* clock; **~ słoneczny** sundial; **~ z kukułką** cuckoo clock; **~ parkingowy** parking meter

**zegar|ek (-ka, -ki)** (*instr sg* **-kiem**) *m* watch; **~ na rękę** wristwatch; **mój ~ się śpieszy/spóźnia** my watch is fast/slow; **na moim zegarku jest dwunasta** it's twelve by my watch; **jak w zegarku** like clockwork

**zegarmistrz (-a, -e** *lub* **-owie)** *m* watchmaker

**zegarowy** *adj*: **wieża zegarowa** clock tower; **bomba zegarowa** time bomb

**zegaryn|ka (-ki, -ki)** (*dat sg* **-ce**, *gen pl* **-ek**) *f* speaking clock

**zegn|ać (-am, -asz)** *vb perf od* **zganiać**

**zegnę** *itd. vb patrz* **zgiąć**

**zejś|cie (-cia, -cia)** (*gen pl* **-ć**) *nt* (*droga*) descent; (*Med*) decease; **~ do piwnicy/na**

**dolny pokład** stairs to the cellar/lower deck; **~ na ląd** disembarkation
**zej|ść (-dę, -dziesz)** (*imp* **-dź**, *pt* **zszedł** *lub* **zeszedł, zeszła, zeszli**) *vb perf od* **schodzić**
**zekraniz|ować (-uję, -ujesz)** *vb perf od* **ekranizować**
**zelektryfik|ować (-uję, -ujesz)** *vb perf od* **elektryfikować**
**zel|ować (-uję, -ujesz)** (*perf* **pod-**) *vt* to sole
**zelów|ka** (**-ki, -ki**) (*dat sg* **-ce**, *gen pl* **-ek**) *f* sole
**zelż|eć (-eje)** *vi perf* (*o bólu*) to ease, to subside; (*o gniewie*) to subside
**zelż|yć (-ę, -ysz)** (*imp* **-yj**) *vb perf od* **lżyć**
**zełg|ać (-am, -asz)** *vb perf od* **łgać**
**zemdl|eć (-eję, -ejesz)** *vb perf od* **mdleć**
**zemdleni|e** (**-a**) *nt* fainting
**zemdl|ić (-i)** *vb perf od* **mdlić**; **zemdliło mnie** I felt sick
**zemleć (zmielę, zmielesz)** (*pt* **zmełł** *lub* **zmielił, zmełła** *lub* **zmieliła, zmełli** *lub* **zmielili**) *vb perf od* **mleć**
**zem|sta** (**-sty**) (*dat sg* **-ście**) *f* revenge, vengeance
**zem|ścić się (-szczę, -ścisz)** (*imp* **-ścij**) *vb perf od* **mścić się**
**zeni|t** (**-tu**) (*loc sg* **-cie**) *m* zenith
**zepch|nąć (-nę, -niesz)** (*imp* **-nij**) *vb perf od* **spychać**
**zepnę** *itd. vb patrz* **spiąć**
**zepsuci|e** (**-a**) *nt* (*moralne*) depravity, corruption
**zepsu|ć (-ję, -jesz)** *vb perf od* **psuć**
**zepsuty** *adj* (*uszkodzony*) broken; (*zdemoralizowany*) depraved, corrupt; **~ do szpiku kości** (*przen*) rotten to the core
**zerk|ać (-am, -asz)** (*perf* **-nąć**) *vi* to peek, to peep; **~ na kogoś/coś** to peek at sb/sth, to have *lub* take a peek *lub* peep at sb/sth
**zerk|nąć (-nę, -niesz)** (*imp* **-nij**) *vb perf od* **zerkać**
**ze|ro** (**-ra, -ra**) (*loc sg* **-rze**) *nt* (*Mat*) zero; (*w numerach*) o(h), zero; (*nic*) nought; (*Sport: w piłce*) nil (*Brit*), nothing (*US*); (*w tenisie*) love; (*przen: o człowieku*) (a) nobody, nonentity (*Brit*), no-(ac)count (*US*); **5 stopni poniżej/powyżej zera** 5 (degrees) below/above freezing *lub* zero; **~ bezwzględne** *lub* **absolutne** (*Fiz*) absolute zero; **zaczynać** (**zacząć** *perf*) **od zera** to start from scratch; **wygrać** (*perf*) **dwa do zera** (*Sport*) to win two-nil (*Brit*) *lub* two-nothing (*US*); **„15 ~"** (*Tenis*) "15 love"
**zer|ować (-uję, -ujesz)** (*perf* **wy-**) *vt* to reset
**zerowy** *adj* (*godzina, punkt, przyrost*) zero *attr*; (*Elektr*) neutral; **południk ~** Greenwich *lub* prime meridian
**zerów|ka** (**-ki, -ki**) (*dat sg* **-ce**, *gen pl* **-ek**) *f* (*klasa zerowa*) *preparatory year of education for six-year-olds in Poland*
**zer|wać (-wę, -wiesz)** (*imp* **-wij**) *vb perf od* **zrywać**
**zes|chnąć (-chnie)** (*pt* **-chnął** *lub* **zsechł, -chła**) *vb perf od* **zsychać**
**zeschnięty** *adj* dried up
**zeska|kiwać (-kuję, -kujesz)** (*perf* **zeskoczyć**) *vi* to jump down
**zeskrob|ywać (-uję, -ujesz)** (*perf* **-ać**) *vt* to scrape (off)
**ze|słać (-ślę, -ślesz)** (*imp* **-ślij**) *vb perf od* **zsyłać**
**zesłani|e** (**-a**) *nt* exile; **Z~ Ducha Świętego** Pentecost
**zesła|niec** (**-ńca, -ńcy**) *m* exile (*person*)
**zespal|ać (-am, -asz)** (*perf* **zespolić**) *vt* to join
**zespaw|ać (-am, -asz)** *vb perf od* **spawać**
**zesp|olić (-olę, -olisz)** (*imp* **-ól**) *vb perf od* **zespalać**
**zespołowy** *adj*: **praca zespołowa** teamwork; **gry zespołowe** team games
**zesp|ół (-ołu, -oły)** (*loc pl* **-ole**) *m* (*ludzi*) group, team; (*budynków*) complex, set; (*Teatr*) company; (*część urządzenia*) unit; **~ ludowy/rockowy** folk/rock band *lub* group; **~ Downa** Down's syndrome; **~ miejski** conurbation
**zestarz|eć się (-eję, -ejesz)** *vb perf od* **starzeć się**
**zesta|w (-wu, -wy)** (*loc sg* **-wie**) *m* (*pytań*) set; (*kolorów*) combination; (*mebli*) suite; (*narzędzi*) kit
**zesta|wiać (-wiam, -wiasz)** (*perf* **-wić**) *vt* (*stawiać niżej*) to take down; (*stawiać blisko siebie*) to put *lub* set together; (*składać w całość*) to put together; **~ coś z czymś** to set sth against sth, to juxtapose sth with sth; **~ (złamaną) kość/nogę** (*Med*) to set a (broken) bone/leg
**zesta|wić (-wię, -wisz)** *vb perf od* **zestawiać**
**zestawie|nie** (**-nia, -nia**) (*gen pl* **-ń**) *nt* (*układ*) combination; (*wykaz*) breakdown; (*bilans*) balance sheet; **w zestawieniu z kimś/czymś** in comparison with sb/sth
**zestraj|ać (-am, -asz)** (*perf* **zestroić**) *vt* to put in tune, to tune (up); **zestrajać się** *vr* to tune up
**zestresowany** *adj* stressed (out)
**zestr|oić (-oję, -oisz)** (*imp* **-ój**) *vb perf od* **zestrajać**
**zestrzeliw|ać (-uję, -ujesz)** (*perf* **zestrzelić**) *vt* to shoot down
**zeszczupl|eć (-eję, -ejesz)** *vb perf od* **szczupleć**
**zeszłoroczny** *adj* last year's *attr*
**zeszły** *adj* last; **w ~m roku/tygodniu** last year/week; **w ~ czwartek** last Thursday; **zeszłej nocy** last night
**zeszpe|cić (-cę, -cisz)** (*imp* **-ć**) *vb perf od* **szpecić**

Z

**zesztywni|eć (-eję, -ejesz)** *vb perf od* **sztywnieć**
**zeszy|ć (-ję, -jesz)** *vb perf od* **szyć, zeszywać**
**zeszy|t** (**-tu, -ty**) (*loc sg* **-cie**) *m* (*do ćwiczeń*) exercise book (*Brit*), notebook (*Brit*); (*egzemplarz*) book
**zeszyw|ać (-am, -asz)** (*perf* **zeszyć**) *vt* to sew *lub* stitch together
**ześlę** *itp. vb patrz* **zesłać**
**ześliz|giwać się (-guję, -gujesz)** (*perf* **-gnąć** *lub* **ześliznąć**) *vr* to slide down
**ześlizg|nąć się (-nę, -niesz)** (*imp* **-nij**) *vb perf od* **ześlizgiwać się**
**ześli|znąć się (-znę, -źniesz)** (*imp* **-źnij**) *vb perf od* **ześlizgiwać się**
**zetk|nąć (-nę, -niesz)** (*imp* **-nij**) *vb perf od* **stykać**
**zet|rzeć (-rę, -rzesz)** (*imp* **-rzyj**, *pt* **starł**) *vb perf od* **ścierać**
**ze|w** (**-wu**) (*loc sg* **-wie**) *m* (*książk*) call; **zew morza/krwi** the call of the sea/wild
**zewnątrz** *adv*: **na ~** outside; **z** *lub* **od ~** from (the) outside
**zewnętrzny** *adj* (*ściana, powierzchnia*) outside, exterior; (*cecha, wygląd*) outward; (*Pol*) exterior; **strona zewnętrzna** the outside, the exterior; **„do użytku zewnętrznego"** "for external use only", "not to be taken internally"
**zew|rzeć (-rę, -rzesz)** (*imp* **-rzyj**, *pt* **zwarł, zwarła, zwarli**) *vb perf od* **zwierać**
**zewsząd** *adv* from everywhere, from far and wide
**ze|z** (**-za**) (*loc sg* **-zie**) *m* squint; **mieć zeza** to have a squint, to be cross-eyed
**zezło|ścić (-szczę, -ścisz)** (*imp* **-ść**) *vb perf od* **złościć**
**zezn|ać (-am, -asz)** *vb perf od* **zeznawać**
**zezna|nie** (**-nia, -nia**) (*gen pl* **-ń**) *nt* (*w sądzie*) testimony; **~ podatkowe** tax return; **składać** (**złożyć** *perf*) **~** to testify, to give evidence
**zezn|awać (-aję, -ajesz)** (*imp* **-awaj**, *perf* **-ać**) *vt* to testify ▷ *vi* to testify, to give evidence
**zez|ować (-uję, -ujesz)** *vi* to squint
**zezowaty** *adj* cross-eyed
**zezwal|ać (-am, -asz)** (*perf* **zezwolić**) *vi*: **~ na coś** to allow *lub* permit sth; **~ komuś na coś** to allow sb to do sth
**zezwole|nie** (**-nia, -nia**) (*gen pl* **-ń**) *nt* (*zgoda*) permission; (*dokument*) permit, licence (*Brit*), license (*US*)
**zezw|olić (-olę, -olisz)** (*imp* **-ól**) *vb perf od* **zezwalać**
**zeż|reć (-rę, -resz)** (*imp* **-ryj**, *pt* **zżarł** *lub* **zeżarł**) *vb perf od* **żreć**
**zęba** *itd. n patrz* **ząb**
**zębaty** *adj*: **koło zębate** cog(wheel)
**ZG** *abbr* (= *Zarząd Główny*) GHQ (= *General Headquarters*)
**zgad|nąć (-nę, -niesz)** (*imp* **-nij**, *pt* **-ł**) *vb perf od* **zgadywać**
**zgad|ywać (-uję, -ujesz)** (*perf* **-nąć**) *vt* to guess ▷ *vi* to guess, to take *lub* have a guess; **~ czyjeś myśli** (*przen*) to read sb's mind
**zgadz|ać się (-am, -asz)** (*perf* **zgodzić**) *vr*: **zgadzać się na coś** to agree *lub* consent to sth; **zgadzać się z kimś** to agree with sb; **zgadzać się, że ...** to agree that ...; **zgadzać się (z czymś)** (*wykazywać zgodność*) to tally (with sth); **te rachunki się nie zgadzają** the accounts don't square; **coś mi się tu nie zgadza** something's wrong here; **nie zgadzać się z kimś/czymś** to disagree with sb/sth; **zgadzać się ze sobą** (*żyć w zgodzie*) to get along fine (with each other), to get on (well) (with each other)
**zga|ga** (**-gi**) (*dat sg* **-dze**) *f* (*Med*) heartburn
**zgani|ać (-am, -asz)** (*perf* **zegnać, zgonić**) *vt* (*bydło*) to round up; (*muchę*) to drive away; **zganiać się** *vr perf* (*zmęczyć się*) to walk *lub* run o.s. into the ground
**zga|nić (-nię, -nisz)** (*imp* **-ń**) *vb perf od* **ganić**
**zga|pić się (-pię, -pisz)** *vr* to miss one's opportunity
**zgar|bić się (-bię, -bisz)** *vb perf od* **garbić się**
**zgar|nąć (-nę, -niesz)** (*imp* **-nij**) *vb perf od* **zgarniać**
**zgarni|ać (-am, -asz)** (*perf* **zgarnąć**) *vt* (*gromadzić*) to gather; (*odsuwać*) to push aside *lub* to the side; (*przen*: *wygraną itp.*) to rake in
**zga|sić (-szę, -sisz)** (*imp* **-ś**) *vb perf od* **gasić**
**zga|snąć (-snę, -śniesz)** (*imp* **-śnij**, *pt* **-sł, -sła, -śli**) *vb perf od* **gasnąć**
**zgaszony** *adj* (*człowiek*) downcast; (*kolor*) subdued
**zgęstni|eć (-eje)** *vb perf od* **gęstnieć**
**zgiąć (zegnę, zegniesz)** (*imp* **zegnij**, *pt* **zgiął, zgięła, zgięli**) *vb perf od* **zginać, giąć**
**zgieł|k** (**-ku**) (*instr sg* **-kiem**) *m* tumult
**zgiełkliwy** *adj* tumultuous
**zgię|cie** (**-cia, -cia**) (*gen pl* **-ć**) *nt* bend
**zgin|ać (-am, -asz)** (*perf* **zgiąć**) *vt* to bend; **zginać się** *vr* to bend
**zgi|nąć (-nę, -niesz)** (*imp* **-ń**) *vb perf od* **ginąć**
**zgliszcz|a** (**-y**) *pl* ashes *pl*
**zgła|dzić (-dzę, -dzisz)** (*imp* **-dź**) *vt perf* (*książk*) to slay
**zgłasz|ać (-am, -asz)** (*perf* **zgłosić**) *vt* (*projekt, wniosek*: *na piśmie*) to submit; (*ofertę*) to extend; (*kandydaturę*) to propose; **~ wniosek** (*na zebraniu*) to make a motion; **~ coś do oclenia** to declare sth; **zgłosić sprzeciw** to register a protest; **~ zastrzeżenia** to raise objections; **zgłaszać się** *vr* (*przychodzić*) to

report; (*zapisywać się*) to apply; (*Tel*) to answer; **~ się do kogoś** to report to sb; **~ się na ochotnika** to come forward, to volunteer; **~ się po coś** to call for sth
**zgłę|biać (-biam, -biasz)** (*perf* **-bić**) *vt* (*tajemnice*) to fathom; (*dziedzinę wiedzy*) to explore
**zgłę|bić (-bię, -bisz)** (*imp* **zgłęb**) *vb perf od* **zgłębiać**
**zgłodni|eć (-eję, -ejesz)** *vb perf od* **głodnieć**
**zgło|sić (-szę, -sisz)** (*imp* **-ś**) *vb perf od* **zgłaszać**
**zgłos|ka (-ki, -ki)** (*dat sg* **-ce**, *gen pl* **-ek**) *f* syllable
**zgłosze|nie (-nia, -nia)** (*gen pl* **-ń**) *nt* application; **Pan X proszony jest o ~ się do informacji** Mr X is requested to report to the information desk
**zgłupi|eć (-eję, -ejesz)** *vb perf od* **głupieć**
**zgnę|bić (-bię, -bisz)** *vb perf od* **gnębić**
**zgniat|ać (-am, -asz)** (*perf* **zgnieść**) *vt* (*miażdżyć*) to squash, to crush; (*miąć*) to crumple; (*przen: bunt, powstanie*) to quell
**zgni|ć (-ję, -jesz)** *vb perf od* **gnić**
**zgni|eść (-otę, -eciesz)** (*imp* **-eć**, *pt* **-ótł, -otła, -etli**) *vb perf od* **gnieść, zgniatać**
**zgnili|zna (-zny)** (*dat sg* **-źnie**) *f* (wet) rot; (*przen: moralna*) depravity, corruption
**zgniły** *adj* rotten
**zgn|oić (-oję, -oisz)** (*imp* **-ój**) *vb perf od* **gnoić**
**zgnuśni|eć (-eję, -ejesz)** *vb perf od* **gnuśnieć**
**zgo|da (-dy)** (*dat sg* **-dzie**) *f* (*brak konfliktów*) harmony, concord; (*pozwolenie*) assent, consent; (*wspólne zdanie*) agreement, consensus; (*pojednanie*) reconciliation; **być w zgodzie z kimś/czymś** to be in agreement with sb/sth; **wyrażać (wyrazić** *perf***) zgodę na coś** to assent *lub* consent to sth, to give one's assent *lub* consent to sth; **robić coś za czyjąś zgodą** to do sth with sb's consent
**zgodnie** *adv* (*bez konfliktów*) in harmony *lub* concord; **~ z planem** according to plan; **~ z przepisami/prawem** in accordance with the rules/law
**zgodnoś|ć (-ci)** *f* (*brak odstępstw, rozbieżności*) conformity; (*brak konfliktów*) harmony; (*jednomyślność*) unanimity; (*Komput*) compatibility
**zgodny** *adj* (*niekłótliwy*) agreeable; (*jednomyślny*) unanimous; (*pasujący*) compatible; (*niesprzeczny*): **~ z czymś** consistent with sth; **~ z prawem** legal
**zg|odzić się (-odzę, -odzisz)** (*imp* **-ódź**) *vb perf od* **zgadzać się**
**zg|olić (-olę, -olisz)** (*imp* **-ol** *lub* **-ól**) *vb perf od* **golić**
**zgo|n (-nu, -ny)** (*loc sg* **-nie**) *m* decease, demise; **świadectwo ~u** death certificate
**zgo|nić (-nię, -nisz)** (*imp* **-ń**) *vb perf od* **zganiać**
**zgorszeni|e (-a)** *nt* scandal; **siać ~ wśród kogoś** to scandalize sb
**zgorszony** *adj* scandalized
**zgorsz|yć (-ę, -ysz)** *vb perf od* **gorszyć**
**zgorzel (-i, -e)** (*gen pl* **-i**) *f* (*Med*) gangrene
**zgorzkniały** *adj* bitter
**zgorzkni|eć (-eję, -ejesz)** *vb perf od* **gorzknieć**
**zgot|ować (-uję, -ujesz)** *vt perf* (*książk: owację, powitanie*) to give
**zgra|biać (-biam, -biasz)** (*perf* **-bić**) *vt* to rake
**zgrabiały** *adj* (*ręce*) numb
**zgra|bić (-bię, -bisz)** *vb perf od* **grabić, zgrabiać**
**zgrabi|eć (-eję, -ejesz)** *vi perf* to go numb
**zgrabny** *adj* (*dziewczyna, nogi*) shapely; (*ruchy, kelner*) deft; (*sformułowanie*) neat
**zgr|ać (-am, -asz)** *vb perf od* **zgrywać**
**zgra|ja (-i, -je)** *f* (*pot*) crew (*pot*)
**zgrani|e (-a)** *nt* harmony
**zgrany** *adj* harmonious
**zgromadze|nie (-nia, -nia)** (*gen pl* **-ń**) *nt* gathering, assembly; (*Rel*) congregation; **Z~ Narodowe** National Assembly
**zgroma|dzić (-dzę, -dzisz)** (*imp* **-dź**) *vb perf od* **gromadzić**
**zgro|mić (-mię, -misz)** *vb perf od* **gromić**
**zgro|za (-zy)** (*dat sg* **-zie**) *f* horror
**zgrubiały** *adj* (*nabrzmiały*) swollen; (*stwardniały*) thickened; (*Jęz*) augmentative
**zgrubi|eć (-eję, -ejesz)** *vb perf od* **grubieć**
**zgrubie|nie (-nia, -nia)** (*gen pl* **-ń**) *nt* (*wypukłość*) swelling; (*Jęz*) augmentative form
**zgrup|ować (-uję, -ujesz)** *vb perf od* **grupować**
**zgrupowa|nie (-nia, -nia)** (*gen pl* **-ń**) *nt* group; (*Wojsk*) concentration
**zgry|wa (-wy, -wy)** (*dat sg* **-wie**) *f* (*pot: udawanie*) act
**zgryw|ać się (-am, -asz)** *vr* (*o aktorze*) to ham it up; (*pot: udawać*) to put on an act (*pot*); **zgrywać się na kogoś** (*pot*) to act *lub* play sb (*pot*)
**zgry|z (-zu)** (*loc sg* **-zie**) *m* bite
**zgryzo|ta (-ty)** (*dat sg* **-cie**) *f* grief
**zgry|źć (-zę, -ziesz)** (*imp* **-ź**, *pt* **-zł, -źli**) *vt perf* to crack; **twardy orzech do zgryzienia** a hard *lub* tough nut to crack
**zgryźliwy** *adj* (*człowiek*) snappish, snappy; (*uwaga*) cutting
**zgrz|ać (-eję, -ejesz)** *vb perf od* **zgrzewać**; **zgrzać się** *vr* to become hot
**zgrzany** *adj* hot
**zgrzesz|yć (-ę, -ysz)** *vb perf od* **grzeszyć**
**zgrz|ewać (-ewam, -ewasz)** (*perf* **-ać**) *vt* to seal (*by heating*)
**zgrzybiały** *adj* doddering

Z

**zgrzy|t (-tu, -ty)** (*loc sg* **-cie**) *m* grate, rasp; (*przen: nieprzyjemna sytuacja*) embarrassment
**zgrzyt|ać (-am, -asz)** (*perf* **-nąć**) *vi* to grate; ~ **zębami** to gnash *lub* grind one's teeth
**zgrzytliwy** *adj* grating, rasping
**zgrzyt|nąć (-nę, -niesz)** (*imp* **-nij**) *vb perf od* **zgrzytać**
**zgu|ba (-by, -by)** (*dat sg* **-bie**) *f* (*rzecz*) lost property; (*zagłada*) undoing
**zgu|bić (-bię, -bisz)** *vb perf od* **gubić**
**zgubny** *adj* (*wpływ, nałóg*) destructive; (*skutek*) pernicious
**zgwał|cić (-cę, -cisz)** (*imp* **-ć**) *vb perf od* **gwałcić**
**zhań|bić (-bię, -bisz)** *vb perf od* **hańbić**
**ZHP** *abbr* (= *Związek Harcerstwa Polskiego*) Polish Scouting Association
**ZHR** *abbr* (= *Związek Harcerstwa Rzeczpospolitej*) Scouting Association of the Polish Republic
**zi|ać (-eję, -ejesz)** *vi* (*dyszeć*) to pant; (*rozwierać się*) to gape; ~ **czymś** (*nienawiścią, chłodem itp.*) to emanate sth; ~ **ogniem** to belch fire
**ziaren|ko (-ka, -ka)** (*instr sg* **-kiem**, *gen pl* **-ek**) *nt dimin od* **ziarno**
**ziarnisty** *adj* (*zawierający nasiona*) grain *attr*; (*porowaty*) grainy; (*grubo mielony*) coarse-grained; **kawa ziarnista** coffee beans
**ziarn|ko (-ka, -ka)** (*instr sg* **-kiem**, *gen pl* **-ek**) *nt dimin od* **ziarno**
**ziar|no (-na, -na)** (*loc sg* **-nie**, *gen pl* **-en**) *nt* grain; (*nasienie*) seed; ~ **kawy** coffee bean; ~ **prawdy** a grain of truth
**zią|b (-bu)** (*loc sg* **-bie**) *m* chill
**zidentyfik|ować (-uję, -ujesz)** *vb perf od* **identyfikować**
**zidioci|eć (-eję, -ejesz)** *vb perf od* **idiocieć**
**zielarski** *adj*: **sklep** ~ herbalist's shop; **przemysł** ~ herbal industry
**zielarst|wo (-wa)** (*loc sg* **-wie**) *nt* herbalism
**zielarz (-a, -e)** (*gen pl* **-y**) *m* herbalist
**zi|ele (-ela, -oła)** (*gen pl* **-ół**) *nt* herb; ~ **angielskie** (*całe*) pimento; (*mielone*) allspice
**zielenia|k (-ka, -ki)** (*instr sg* **-kiem**) *m* (*sklep*) greengrocer; (*stragan*) greengrocer's stall
**ziele|nić się (-ni)** *vr* (*mieć zielony kolor*) to show green; (*stawać się zielonym*) to turn green
**zieleni|eć (-eje)** *vi* (*stawać się zielonym*) (*perf* **z-**) to turn green; (*mieć zielony kolor*) to show green
**zieleni|na** (*dat sg* **-nie**) *f* greens *pl*
**ziele|ń (-ni)** *f* (*kolor*) green; (*roślinność*) greenery
**zielonkawy** *adj* greenish
**zielono** *adv* green
**zielony** *adj* green; **Zielone Świątki** Pentecost, Whitsun(day); **nie mam zielonego pojęcia** (*pot*) I haven't the foggiest (idea) (*pot*)
**ziels|ko (-ka, -ka)** (*instr sg* **-kiem**) *nt* weed
**zie|mia (-mi)** *f* (*kula ziemska*): **Z~** earth, Earth; (*gleba*) (*pl* **-mie**) soil; (*grunt pod nogami*) ground; (*podłoga*) floor; (*własność, kraina*) (*pl* **-mie**) land; **trzęsienie ziemi** earthquake; **nie z tej ziemi** out of this world; **gryźć ziemię** (*przen: pot*) to bite the dust (*pot*); **poruszyć** (*perf*) **niebo i ziemię** to move heaven and earth; **wrócić** (*perf*) *lub* **zejść** (*perf*) **na ziemię** (*przen*) to come down *lub* back to earth; **do (samej) ziemi** (*zasłona, suknia*) full-length *attr*; **talerzyk spadł na ziemię** the plate fell to the floor; **pod ziemią** underground; ~ **pali im się pod nogami** (*przen*) things are getting hot for them; **zrównać** (*perf*) **coś z ziemią** to raze sth to the ground; **Z~ Święta** the Holy Land; ~ **ojczysta** homeland
**ziemia|nin (-nina, -nie)** (*gen pl* **-n**) *m* (*właściciel majątku*) landowner; (*mieszkaniec Ziemi*): **Z~** terrestrial; (*w science-fiction*) earthling
**ziemisty** *adj* (*cera, twarz*) sallow
**ziemniaczany** *adj*: **mąka/zupa ziemniaczana** potato flour/soup; **stonka ziemniaczana** Colorado (potato) beetle
**ziemnia|k (-ka, -ki)** (*instr sg* **-kiem**) *m* potato; **~i gotowane** boiled potatoes; **~i w mundurkach** jacket potatoes
**ziemny** *adj*: **roboty ziemne** earthwork; **gaz ~** natural gas; **orzeszki ziemne** peanuts
**ziemski** *adj* (*atmosfera, klimat, skorupa*) earth's *attr*; (*sprawy, troski*) earthly, worldly; **posiadłość ziemska** landed estate; **kula ziemska** the globe
**ziew|ać (-am, -asz)** (*perf* **-nąć**) *vi* to yawn
**ziew|nąć (-nę, -niesz)** (*imp* **-nij**) *vb perf od* **ziewać**
**ziewnięci|e (-a, -a)** *nt* yawn
**zię|ba (-by, -by)** (*dat sg* **-bie**) *f* chaffinch
**zię|bić (-bię, -bisz)** *vt* to chill; **to mnie ani ziębi, ani grzeje** it leaves me cold
**zięb|nąć (-nę, -niesz)** (*imp* **-nij**, *pt* **-nął** *lub* **ziąbł, -ła, -li**, *perf* **z-**) *vi* to freeze
**zię|ć (-cia, -ciowie)** *m* son-in-law
**zignor|ować (-uję, -ujesz)** *vb perf od* **ignorować**
**zilustr|ować (-uję, -ujesz)** *vb perf od* **ilustrować**
**zi|ma (-my, -my)** (*dat sg* **-mie**) *f* winter; **zimą** *lub* **w zimie** in winter
**Zimbabwe** *nt inv* Zimbabwe
**zim|no[1] (-na)** (*loc sg* **-nie**) *nt* (*niska temperatura*) cold; **drżeć z zimna** to shiver with cold; **w zimnie** in the cold
**zimno[2]** *adv* cold; (*przen: niechętnie*) coldly; ~ **mi** I am *lub* feel cold; ~ **mi w nogi** my feet are cold; ~ **mi się robi na samą myśl o tym** the mere thought of it sends shivers down my

spine; **na ~** (*bez emocji*) calmly; **jeść coś na ~** to eat sth cold
**zimnokrwisty** *adj* cold-blooded
**zimny** *adj* cold; **zimne ognie** sparklers *pl*; **zimna wojna** (*Hist*) the cold war; **z zimną krwią** in cold blood; **zachować** (*perf*) **zimną krew** to keep one's cool; **~ jak lód** *lub* **głaz** ice- *lub* stone-cold
**zimorod|ek** (**-ka, -ki**) (*instr sg* **-kiem**) *m* kingfisher
**zim|ować (-uję, -ujesz)** *vi* (*trwać przez zimę*) (*perf* **prze-**) to winter
**zimowis|ko** (**-ka, -ka**) (*instr sg* **-kiem**) *nt* winter camp
**zimowy** *adj* (*krajobraz, niebo, sport*) winter *attr*; **sen ~** (*Zool*) hibernation
**zintegr|ować (-uję, -ujesz)** *vb perf od* **integrować**
**zintensyfik|ować (-uję, -ujesz)** *vb perf od* **intensyfikować**
**zinterpret|ować (-uję, -ujesz)** *vb perf od* **interpretować**
**zi|oło** (**-oła, -oła**) (*loc sg* **-ole**, *gen pl* **-ół**) *nt* herb
**ziołolecznict|wo** (**-wa**) (*loc sg* **-wie**) *nt* herbalism
**ziołowy** *adj* herbal
**zio|nąć (-nę, -niesz)** (*imp* **-ń**) *vi* = **ziać**
**ziół|ko** (**-ka, -ka**) (*instr sg* **-kiem**, *gen pl* **-ek**) *nt dimin od* **zioło**; (*pot: człowiek*) scallywag (*pot*)
**ziryt|ować (-uję, -ujesz)** *vb perf od* **irytować**
**ziszcz|ać (-am, -asz)** (*perf* **ziścić**) *vt* (*książk*) to realize; **ziszczać się** *vr* to come true
**zi|ścić (-szczę, -ścisz)** (*imp* **-ść**) *vb perf od* **ziszczać**
**zjadacz** (**-a, -e**) (*gen pl* **-y**) *m*: **(przeciętny) ~ chleba** the (average) man in the street
**zjad|ać (-am, -asz)** (*perf* **zjeść**) *vt* (*spożywać*) to eat; (*przen: prąd, energię*) to use up, to consume; (*: o chorobie, zmartwieniach*) to consume
**zjadę** *itd. vb patrz* **zjechać**
**zjadliwoś|ć** (**-ci**) *f* virulence
**zjadliwy** *adj* (*krytyk, uwaga*) virulent, scathing; (*pot: dość smaczny*) eatable
**zjadł** *itd. vb patrz* **zjeść**
**zja|wa** (**-wy, -wy**) (*dat sg* **-wie**) *f* apparition, phantom
**zja|wiać się (-wiam, -wiasz)** (*perf* **-wić**) *vr* (*przybywać*) to show up, to turn up; (*pojawiać się*) to appear; **zjawić się na przyjęciu** to turn up at the party
**zja|wić się (-wię, -wisz)** *vb perf od* **zjawiać się**
**zjawis|ko** (**-ka, -ka**) (*instr sg* **-kiem**) *nt* phenomenon
**zj|azd** (**-azdu, -azdy**) (*loc sg* **-eździe**) *m* (*jazda z góry*) downhill drive; (*zgromadzenie*) convention; (*Sport*) run; **~ z autostrady** (*miejsce*) exit; (*droga*) slip road (*Brit*), (exit) ramp (*US*)
**zjazdowy** *adj* (*bieg, narciarstwo*) downhill *attr*
**zj|echać (-adę, -edziesz)** (*imp* **-edź**) *vb perf od* **zjeżdżać**; (*przemierzyć*) to travel all through; (*pot: skrytykować*) to slam (*pot*), to knock (*pot*)
**zjedn|ać (-am, -asz)** *vb perf od* **jednać, zjednywać**
**zjednocze|nie** (**-nia, -nia**) (*gen pl* **-ń**) *nt* (*partii, grup*) unification; (*organizacja*) union
**zjednoczony** *adj* united; **Zjednoczone Królestwo Wielkiej Brytanii i Irlandii Północnej** the United Kingdom of Great Britain and Northern Ireland
**zjednocz|yć (-ę, -ysz)** *vb perf od* **jednoczyć**
**zjedn|ywać (-uję, -ujesz)** (*perf* **-ać**) *vt* (*ludzi*) to win over; (*sympatię, poparcie*) to win
**zjełczały** *adj* rancid
**zjełcz|eć (-eje)** *vb perf od* **jełczeć**
**zj|eść (-em, -esz)** (*pt* **-adł, -adła, -edli**) *vb perf od* **jeść, zjadać**
**zje|ździć (-żdżę, -ździsz)** (*imp* **-źdź**) *vt perf* (*przemierzyć*) to travel all through
**zjeździe** *n patrz* **zjazd**
**zjeżdż|ać (-am, -asz)** (*perf* **zjechać**) *vi* (*windą*) to go down; (*na nartach, sankach*) to go downhill; (*samochodem*) to drive downhill; (*na rowerze*) to ride downhill; (*jadąc zboczyć*) to turn; (*przybywać*) to arrive; (*pot: zsuwać się: o okularach, torbie*) (*perf* **zjechać**) to slip off; **zjechać z drogi/na bok** to pull over; **zjeżdżaj (stąd)!** (*pot*) get out (of here)! (*pot*); **zjeżdżać się** *vr* (*przybywać*) to arrive
**zjeżdżal|nia** (**-ni, -nie**) (*gen pl* **-ni**) *f* slide
**zjeż|yć (-ę, -ysz)** *vb perf od* **jeżyć**; **zjeżyć się** *vr, vb perf od* **jeżyć się**; (*przen*) to be ruffled
**zl|ać (-eję, -ejesz)** *vb perf od* **lać, zlewać**; **zlać się** *vb perf od* **zlewać się**; (*pot*) to wet one's pants (*pot*)
**zlat|ywać (-uję, -ujesz)** (*perf* **zlecieć**) *vi* (*sfruwać*) to fly off *lub* down; (*spadać*) to fall off *lub* down; (*zbiegać*) to run down; **zlatywać się** *vr* to flock
**zlazł** *itp. vb patrz* **zleźć**
**zl|ąc się (-ęknę, -ękniesz)** (*imp* **-ęknij**, *pt* **-ąkł, -ękła, -ękli**) *vr perf* = **zlęknąć się**
**zle|cać (-cam, -casz)** (*perf* **-cić**) *vt* to commission; **~ komuś coś/zrobienie czegoś** to commission sb to do sth
**zlece|nie** (**-nia, -nia**) (*gen pl* **-ń**) *nt* order
**zleceniobiorc|a** (**-y, -y**) *m decl like f in sg firm accepting an order*; (*w robotach budowlanych*) contractor
**zleceniodawc|a** (**-y, -y**) *m decl like f in sg* client; (*firma*) customer
**zle|cić (-cę, -cisz)** (*imp* **-ć**) *vb perf od* **zlecać**

**zle|cieć (-cę, -cisz)** (*imp* **-ć**) *vb perf od* **zlatywać** ▷ *vi perf* (*o czasie*) to fly by
**zleję** *itd. vb patrz* **zlać**
**zlekceważ|yć (-ę, -ysz)** *vb perf od* **lekceważyć**
**zlep|ek (-ku, -ki)** (*instr sg* **-kiem**) *m* cluster; (*przen: pojęć itp.*) conglomeration
**zle|piać (-piam, -piasz)** (*perf* **-pić**) *vt* to glue *lub* stick together
**zle|pić (-pię, -pisz)** *vb perf od* **zlepiać**
**zle|w (-wu, -wy)** (*loc sg* **-wie**) *m* sink
**zlew|ać (-am, -asz)** (*perf* **zlać**) *vt* (*ulewać z wierzchu*) to decant; (*do jednego naczynia*) to pour together; **zlać kogoś wodą** to drench sb with water; **zlany potem** drenched with sweat; **zlewać się** *vr* to merge
**zlew|ki (-ków)** *pl* slops *pl*
**zlewozmywa|k (-ka, -ki)** (*instr sg* **-kiem**) *m* sink (unit)
**zl|eźć (-ezę, -eziesz)** (*imp* **-eź**, *pt* **-azł, -azła, -eźli**) *vb perf od* **złazić**
**zleżały** *adj* (*tytoń, żywność*) stale; (*jedwab, skóra*) fusty
**zlęk|nąć się (-nę, -niesz)** (*imp* **-nij**, *pt* **zląkł, zlękła, zlękli**) *vr perf*: **zlęknąć się (czegoś)** to take fright (at sth); **zlęknąć się, że ...** to begin to fear that ...
**zliberaliz|ować (-uję, -ujesz)** *vb perf od* **liberalizować**
**zlicyt|ować (-uję, -ujesz)** *vb perf od* **licytować**
**zlicz|ać (-am, -asz)** (*perf* **-yć**) *vt* to count
**zlicz|yć (-ę, -ysz)** *vb perf od* **liczyć, zliczać**
**zlikwid|ować (-uję, -ujesz)** *vb perf od* **likwidować**
**zlincz|ować (-uję, -ujesz)** *vb perf od* **linczować**
**zlit|ować się (-uję, -ujesz)** *vb perf od* **litować się**
**zli|zać (-żę, -żesz)** *vb perf od* **lizać, zlizywać**
**zliz|ywać (-uję, -ujesz)** (*perf* **-ać**) *vt* to lick up
**zlokaliz|ować (-uję, -ujesz)** *vb perf od* **lokalizować**
**zlo|t (-tu, -ty)** (*loc sg* **-cie**) *m* rally
**zlustr|ować (-uję, -ujesz)** *vb perf od* **lustrować**
**zlut|ować (-uję, -ujesz)** *vb perf od* **lutować**
**zluz|ować (-uję, -ujesz)** *vb perf od* **luzować**
**zł** *abbr* (= złoty) zl. (= zloty)
**złagodni|eć (-eję, -ejesz)** *vb perf od* **łagodnieć**
**złagodze|nie (-nia, -nia)** (*gen pl* **-ń**) *nt* (*napięcia*) relaxation; (*przepisów, obostrzeń*) liberalization; (*kary*) commutation
**złago|dzić (-dzę, -dzisz)** (*imp* **-dź**) *vb perf od* **łagodzić**
**złaknіony** *adj*: **~ czegoś** hungry for sth
**zła|mać (-mię, -miesz)** *vb perf od* **łamać**
**złama|nie (-nia, -nia)** (*gen pl* **-ń**) *nt* (*Med*) fracture; **~ otwarte/zamknięte** compound/simple fracture; **na ~ karku** at breakneck speed
**złamany** *adj* broken
**zła|pać (-pię, -piesz)** *vb perf od* **łapać**
**zła|zić (-żę, -zisz)** (*imp* **-ź**, *perf* **zleźć**) *vt perf* (*pot: przemierzyć*) to roam ▷ *vi* (*pot: z drzewa, po drabinie*) to climb down; (*: o farbie itp.*) to come off; **złazić się** *vr* (*pot: gromadzić się*) to crowd in
**złącz|e (-a, -a)** (*gen pl* **-y**) *nt* (*Tech*) joint, coupling
**złącz|yć (-ę, -ysz)** *vb perf od* **łączyć**
**zł|e (-ego)** *nt decl like adj*; **mieć coś komuś za złe** to hold sth against sb; **z dwojga złego** of (the) two evils; **na domiar złego** to make matters worse
**zł|o (-a)** *nt* evil; **zło konieczne** necessary evil; **wybierać (wybrać** *perf***) mniejsze zło** to choose the lesser evil; **naprawiać (naprawić** *perf***) zło** to right a wrong
**złoce|nie (-nia, -nia)** (*gen pl* **-ń**) *nt* (*powłoka*) gilt; (*ozdoba*) gilt ornament
**zło|cić (-cę, -cisz)** (*imp* **-ć**, *perf* **po-**) *vt* to gild
**złocisty** *adj* golden
**złocony** *adj* gilt *attr*, gilded; (*metal*) gold-plated
**złoczyńc|a (-y, -y)** *m decl like f in sg* (*książk*) villain
**złodzie|j (-ja, -je)** (*gen pl* **-i**) *m* thief; **~ kieszonkowy** pickpocket
**złodziejst|wo (-wa)** (*loc sg* **-wie**) *nt* thieving
**zł|oić (-oję, -oisz)** (*imp* **-ój**) *vb perf od* **łoić**
**zło|m (-mu)** (*loc sg* **-mie**) *m* scrap (metal); **oddawać (oddać** *perf***) coś na ~** to scrap sth
**złomowis|ko (-ka, -ka)** (*instr sg* **-kiem**) *nt* scrap yard
**złorzecz|yć (-ę, -ysz)** *vi* to curse; **~ komuś/czemuś** to curse sb/sth
**zło|ścić (-szczę, -ścisz)** (*imp* **-ść**, *perf* **roz-** *lub* **ze-**) *vt* to anger; **złościć się** *vr*: **~ się (na kogoś/o coś)** to be angry (with sb/about sth)
**złoś|ć (-ci)** *f* anger; **na ~ komuś** to spite sb; **jak na ~** as if out of spite; **wpadać (wpaść** *perf***) w ~** to lose one's temper
**złośliwie** *adv* maliciously
**złośliwoś|ć (-ci)** *f* malice
**złośliwy** *adj* malicious; (*Med*) malignant
**złośnic|a (-y, -e)** *f* shrew
**złot|ko (-ka, -ka)** (*instr sg* **-kiem**) *nt* (*pieszczotliwie*) honey
**złotnict|wo (-wa)** (*loc sg* **-wie**) *nt* goldsmithery
**złotni|k (-ka, -cy)** (*instr sg* **-kiem**) *m* goldsmith
**zło|to (-ta)** (*loc sg* **-cie**) *nt* gold; **być na wagę złota** to be worth one's weight in gold
**złotów|ka (-ki, -ki)** (*dat sg* **-ce**, *gen pl* **-ek**) *f* one zloty; (*moneta*) one zloty coin
**złot|y[1] (-ego, -e)** *m decl like adj* zloty

**złoty**[2] *adj* *(ze złota)* gold; *(w kolorze złota)* gold, golden; **~ medal** gold medal; **~ wiek** golden age; **mieć złote serce** to have a heart of gold; **znaleźć** *(perf)* **~ środek** to strike a happy medium; **złota rączka** handyman; **złota rybka** goldfish; **złote wesele** *lub* **gody** golden wedding; **obiecywać złote góry** to promise the earth
**zł|owić (-owię, -owisz)** *(imp* **-ów***)* *vb perf od* **łowić**
**złowieszczy** *adj* ominous, sinister
**złowrogi** *adj* ominous, sinister
**zł|oże** (**-oża, -oża**) *(gen pl* **-óż***)* *nt* deposit
**złoże|nie** (**-nia, -nia**) *(gen pl* **-ń***)* *nt* *(Jęz)* compound
**złożonoś|ć** (**-ci**) *f* complexity
**złożony** *adj* *(problem)* complex, complicated; *(układ)* complex; *(cząsteczka)* compound; **być ~m z** *+gen* to be composed of; **wyraz ~** compound (word); **zdanie złożone współrzędnie/podrzędnie** a sentence with co-ordinate clauses/with a subordinate clause
**zł|ożyć (-ożę, -ożysz)** *(imp* **-óż***)* *vb perf od* **składać**
**złóż** *n patrz* **złoże** ▷ *vb patrz* **złożyć**
**złu|da** (**-dy, -dy**) *(dat sg* **-dzie***)* *f* illusion
**złudny** *adj* illusory
**złudze|nie** (**-nia, -nia**) *(gen pl* **-ń***)* *nt* illusion; **~ optyczne** optical illusion; **pozbawiać (pozbawić** *perf***) kogoś złudzeń** to disillusion sb; **nie mieć złudzeń co do kogoś/czegoś** to have no illusions about sb/sth
**złu|pić (-pię, -pisz)** *vb perf od* **łupić**
**złuszcz|ać się (-a)** *(perf* **-yć***)* *vr* to flake, to peel (off)
**zły** *adj* *(niedobry, negatywny, niepomyślny)* bad; *(gniewny)* angry; *(niemoralny)* evil, wicked; *(niewłaściwy)* wrong; *(kiepski, nieudolny, słaby)* poor; **w złym humorze** in a (bad) mood; **w złym guście** in bad taste; **zła wola** ill will; **złe traktowanie** ill-treatment; **działać w złej wierze** to act in bad faith; **„uwaga, zły pies"** "beware of the dog"; **zrobić** *(perf)* **sobie coś złego** to hurt o.s.; **mieć zły sen** to have a bad dream; **sprowadzić** *(perf)* **kogoś na złą drogę** to lead sb astray
**zmag|ać się (-am, -asz)** *vr*: **zmagać się (z czymś)** to struggle (with sth)
**zmagazyn|ować (-uję, -ujesz)** *vb perf od* **magazynować**
**zmal|eć (-eję, -ejesz)** *vb perf od* **maleć**
**zmaltret|ować (-uję, -ujesz)** *vb perf od* **maltretować**
**zmałp|ować (-uję, -ujesz)** *vb perf od* **małpować**
**zmanierowany** *adj* mannered
**zmarł|a** (**-ej, -e**) *f decl like adj* the deceased
**zmarły** *adj* dead, deceased ▷ *m decl like adj* the deceased; **~ pan X** the late Mr X; **zmarli** *pl* the dead *pl*
**zmarni|eć (-eję, -ejesz)** *vb perf od* **marnieć**
**zmarnotra|wić (-wię, -wisz)** *vb perf od* **marnotrawić**
**zmarn|ować (-uję, -ujesz)** *vb perf od* **marnować**
**zmarszcze|nie** (**-nia**) *nt*: **~ brwi** frown
**zmarszcz|ka** (**-ki, -ki**) *(dat sg* **-ce**, *gen pl* **-ek***)* *f* *(na skórze)* wrinkle; *(na wodzie)* ripple; *(na materiale)* wrinkle, crease
**zmarszcz|yć (-ę, -ysz)** *vb perf od* **marszczyć**
**zmart|wić (-wię, -wisz)** *vb perf od* **martwić**
**zmartwie|nie** (**-nia, -nia**) *(gen pl* **-ń***)* *nt* worry; **mieć ~ z kimś/czymś** to have trouble with sb/sth
**zmartwiony** *adj* worried, troubled
**zmartwychwst|ać (-anę, -aniesz)** *(imp* **-ań***)* *vb perf od* **zmartwychwstawać**
**zmartwychwstani|e** (**-a**) *nt*: **Z~** the Resurrection
**zmartwychwst|awać (-aję, -ajesz)** *(imp* **-awaj**, *perf* **-ać***)* *vi* to rise from the dead
**zmarz|nąć (-nę, -niesz)** *(imp* **-nij**, *pt* **-ł***)* *vb perf od* **marznąć**
**zmarznięty** *adj* *(ziemia)* frozen; *(ręce, człowiek)* cold
**zmasakr|ować (-uję, -ujesz)** *vb perf od* **masakrować**
**zmaterializ|ować (-uję, -ujesz)** *vb perf od* **materializować**
**zmatowi|eć (-eje)** *vb perf od* **matowieć**
**zmawi|ać (-am, -asz)** *(perf* **zmówić***)* *vt*: **zmówić modlitwę/pacierz** to say a prayer/one's prayers; **zmawiać się** *vr* to conspire
**zma|zać (-żę, -żesz)** *vb perf od* **mazać, zmazywać**
**zmaz|ywać (-uję, -ujesz)** *(perf* **-ać***)* *vt* *(rysunek, napis: wykonany kredą)* to wipe off, to erase; *(: wykonany ołówkiem)* to rub out, to erase; *(przen: winę)* to wipe away, to expiate
**zmą|cić (-cę, -cisz)** *(imp* **-ć***)* *vb perf od* **mącić**
**zmądrz|eć (-eję, -ejesz)** *vb perf od* **mądrzeć**
**zmechaniz|ować (-uję, -ujesz)** *vb perf od* **mechanizować**
**zmęczeni|e** (**-a**) *nt* tiredness, fatigue; **~ metalu** metal fatigue
**zmęczony** *adj* tired
**zmęcz|yć (-ę, -ysz)** *vb perf od* **męczyć**
**zmętni|eć (-eje)** *vb perf od* **mętnieć**
**zmężni|eć (-eję, -ejesz)** *vb perf od* **mężnieć**
**zmia|na** (**-ny, -ny**) *(dat sg* **-nie***)* *f* change; **~ na lepsze/gorsze** a change for the better/worse; **~ czegoś na coś** substitution of sth for sth; **~ klimatu** climate change; **zmiany**

**personalne** job rotation; **robić coś na zmianę (z kimś)** to take turns in doing sth (with sb); **dzienna/nocna ~** day/night shift; **pracować na zmiany** to do shift work
**zmiat|ać (-am, -asz)** *vt* (*perf* **zmieść**) to sweep ▷ *vi* (*pot*): **zmiataj (stąd)!** clear off! (*pot*)
**zmiażdż|yć (-ę, -ysz)** *vb perf od* **miażdżyć**
**zmiąć (zemnę, zemniesz)** (*imp* **zemnij**, *pt* **zmiął, zmięła, zmięli**) *vb perf od* **miąć**
**zmie|niać (-niam, -niasz)** (*perf* **-nić**) *vt* to change; **~ zdanie** to change one's mind; **~ bieg/pas** (*Mot*) to change gear/lanes; **~ coś w coś innego** to change *lub* turn sth into sth else; **zmieniać się** *vr* (*przeobrażać się*) to change; (*wymieniać się*) to take turns; **~ się na lepsze/gorsze** to change for the better/ worse; **~ się przy czymś** to take turns at sth; **~ się wraz z czymś** to vary with sth
**zmie|nić (-nię, -nisz)** (*imp* **-ń**) *vb perf od* **zmieniać**
**zmienn|a** (**-ej, -e**) *f decl like adj* variable
**zmienni|k** (**-ka, -cy**) (*instr sg* **-kiem**) *m worker alternating with another at the same job*
**zmiennoś|ć** (**-ci**) *f* changeability
**zmienny** *adj* changeable; **prąd ~** alternating current
**zmierz|ać (-am, -asz)** *vi* (*książk*): **~ do** *+gen***/ w stronę** *+gen* to head for/towards; **do czego zmierzasz?** (*przen*) what are you driving at?
**zmierzch** (**-u, -y**) *m* dusk, twilight; (*przen*) twilight; **o ~u** at dusk
**zmierz|wiać (-wiam, -wiasz)** (*perf* **-wić**) *vt* to ruffle; **zmierzwiać się** *vr* to become ruffled
**zmierz|wić (-wię, -wisz)** *vb perf od* **mierzwić, zmierzwiać**
**zmierz|yć (-ę, -ysz)** *vb perf od* **mierzyć**
**zmiesz|ać (-am, -asz)** *vb perf od* **mieszać**
**zmieszani|e** (**-a**) *nt* confusion
**zmieszany** *adj* confused
**zmie|ścić (-szczę, -ścisz)** (*imp* **-ść**) *vb perf od* **mieścić**
**zmi|eść (-otę, -eciesz)** (*imp* **-eć**, *pt* **-ótł, -otła, -etli**) *vb perf od* **zmiatać**
**zmiękcz|ać (-am, -asz)** (*perf* **-yć**) *vt* to soften; (*Jęz*) to palatalize
**zmięk|nąć (-nę, -niesz)** (*imp* **-nij**, *pt* **-ł** *lub* **-nął, -ła, -li**) *vb perf od* **mięknąć**
**zmił|ować się (-uję, -ujesz)** *vr perf* (*książk*): **zmiłować się nad kimś** to have mercy on sb
**zminimaliz|ować (-uję, -ujesz)** *vb perf od* **minimalizować**
**zmizerni|eć (-eję, -ejesz)** *vb perf od* **mizernieć**
**zmniejsz|ać (-am, -asz)** (*perf* **-yć**) *vt* to decrease, to lessen; **zmniejszać się** *vr* to decrease, to lessen
**zmobiliz|ować (-uję, -ujesz)** *vb perf od* **mobilizować**
**zmocz|yć (-ę, -ysz)** *vb perf od* **moczyć**
**zmoderniz|ować (-uję, -ujesz)** *vb perf od* **modernizować**
**zmodyfik|ować (-uję, -ujesz)** *vb perf od* **modyfikować**
**zmogę** *itd. vb patrz* **zmóc**
**zmok|nąć (-nę, -niesz)** (*imp* **-nij**, *pt* **-nął** *lub* **zmókł, -ła, -li**) *vb perf od* **moknąć**
**zmoknięty** *adj* wet
**zmonopoliz|ować (-uję, -ujesz)** *vb perf od* **monopolizować**
**zmont|ować (-uję, -ujesz)** *vb perf od* **montować**
**zm|ora** (**-ory, -ory**) (*dat sg* **-orze**, *gen pl* **-or** *lub* **-ór**) *f* (*widmo, zjawa*) phantom, apparition; (*przen: bezrobocia, inflacji*) spectre (*Brit*), specter (*US*)
**zmotoryzowany** *adj* (*Wojsk*) motorized ▷ *m decl like adj* (*kierowca*) motorist
**zm|owa** (**-owy, -owy**) (*dat sg* **-owie**, *gen pl* **-ów**) *f* conspiracy; **być w zmowie z kimś** to be in league with sb; **~ milczenia** a conspiracy of silence
**zm|óc (-ogę, -ożesz)** (*imp* **-óż**, *pt* **-ógł, -ogła, -ogli**) *vt perf*: **zmogła go choroba/senność** his illness/sleepiness got the better of him
**zmór** *n patrz* **zmora**
**zmów** *vb patrz* **zmówić**
**zmó|wić (-wię, -wisz)** *vb perf od* **zmawiać**
**zmro|k** (**-ku**) (*instr sg* **-kiem**) *m* dusk, nightfall; **po ~u** after dark
**zmr|ozić (-ożę, -ozisz)** (*imp* **-óź** *lub* **-oź**) *vb perf od* **mrozić**
**zmruż|yć (-ę, -ysz)** *vb perf od* **mrużyć**
**zmursz|eć (-eje)** *vi perf* to rot
**zmu|sić (-szę, -sisz)** (*imp* **-ś**) *vb perf od* **zmuszać**
**zmusz|ać (-am, -asz)** (*perf* **zmusić**) *vt* to force; **~ kogoś do zrobienia czegoś** to force sb to do sth, to make sb do sth; **zmuszać się** *vr*: **~ się do zrobienia czegoś** to force o.s. to do sth
**zm|yć (-yję, -yjesz)** *vb perf od* **myć, zmywać**; **~ komuś głowę** (*przen*) to give sb a dressing-down
**zmyk|ać (-am, -asz)** *vi* to scamper away
**zmyl|ić (-ę, -isz)** *vb perf od* **mylić**
**zmy|sł** (**-słu, -sły**) (*loc sg* **-śle**) *m* sense; **~ artystyczny** artistic sense; **szósty ~** sixth sense; **zmysły** *pl*: **postradać** (*perf*) **~y** to take leave of one's senses; **być przy zdrowych ~ach** to be of sound mind
**zmysłowoś|ć** (**-ci**) *f* sensuality
**zmysłowy** *adj* (*wrażenie*) sensory; (*usta itp.*) sensual, sensuous
**zmyśl|ać (-am, -asz)** (*perf* **-ić**) *vt* to invent, to make up

**zmyślny** *adj* clever
**zmywacz** (**-a, -e**) (*gen pl* **-y**) *m*: **~ do paznokci** nail polish remover; **~ do farb** paint-stripper
**zmyw|ać (-am, -asz)** (*perf* **zmyć**) *vt* (*podłogę*) to wash; (*brud, krew*) to wash off; (*o rzece, powodzi: dom, most*) to wash away; (*przen: hańbę, winę*) to wipe away; **~ (po~** *perf*) **naczynia** to wash *lub* do the dishes, to wash up; **zmywać się** *vr* (*o brudzie, plamach*) to wash off; (*pot: uciekać*) to clear off (*pot*)
**zmywa|k** (**-ka, -ki**) (*instr sg* **-kiem**) *m* (*też:* **zmywak do naczyń**: *szmatka*) dishcloth; (*na rączce*) mop
**zmywalny** *adj* washable
**zmywar|ka** (**-ki, -ki**) (*dat sg* **-ce**, *gen pl* **-ek**) *f* dishwasher
**znacho|r** (**-ra, -rzy**) (*loc sg* **-rze**) *m* quack
**znacjonaliz|ować (-uję, -ujesz)** *vb perf od* **nacjonalizować**
**znaczący** *adj* (*mrugnięcie, uśmiech*) meaningful, significant; (*rola, pozycja*) significant; **niewiele ~** insignificant
**znacz|ek** (**-ka, -ki**) (*instr sg* **-kiem**) *m dimin od* **znak**; (*też:* **znaczek pocztowy**) (postage) stamp; (*odznaka*) badge; (*w tekście itp.*) mark; **naklejać (nakleić** *perf*) **~ na list** to stamp a letter
**znacze|nie** (**-nia, -nia**) (*gen pl* **-ń**) *nt* (*sens*) meaning; (*ważność*) importance, significance; **to nie ma znaczenia** it doesn't matter; **to jest bez znaczenia** it is of no importance *lub* significance; **mieć duże/małe ~** to be of great/little importance; **przywiązywać do czegoś ~** to consider sth important, to attach importance to sth
**znacznie** *adv* considerably, significantly; **~ lepiej** much better
**znaczny** *adj* considerable, significant
**znacz|yć (-ę, -ysz)** *vt* (*wyrażać*) to mean; (*mieć wagę*) to matter; (*znakować*) (*perf* **o-**) to mark; **co to znaczy?** what does this mean?; **to znaczy, ...** (*to jest*) that is (to say), ...; **co to ma ~?** what is that supposed to mean?; **to dla mnie wiele znaczy** it means a lot to me
**zn|ać (-am, -asz)** *vt* to know; **dawać (dać** *perf*) **komuś ~ (o czymś)** to let sb know (of sth); **~ kogoś z widzenia** to know sb by sight; **znać się** *vr* (*siebie samego*) to know o.s.; (*nawzajem*) to know each other; **~ się na czymś** to be knowledgeable about sth; **~ się na żartach** to know how to take a joke
**znad** *prep +gen* from above; **~ morza** from the seaside
**znajd|ować (-uję, -ujesz)** (*perf* **znaleźć**) *vt* to find; (*poparcie, zrozumienie*) to meet with; **~ przyjemność w czymś** to take pleasure in sth; **znajdować się** *vr* (*mieścić się*) to be located *lub* situated; (*zostawać odszukanym*) to be found; (*pojawiać się*) to turn up; **znajdujesz się wśród przyjaciół** you are among friends; **~ się w kłopotach/niebezpieczeństwie** to be in trouble/danger
**znajomoś|ć** (**-ci, -ci**) *f* (*z kimś*) acquaintance; (*wiedza*) knowledge; **mieć znajomości** to have connections; **zawierać (zawrzeć** *perf*) **z kimś ~** to make sb's acquaintance; **~ historii/polskiego** a knowledge of history/Polish
**znajomy** *adj* familiar ▷ *m decl like adj* acquaintance; **pewna moja znajoma** a woman I know; **~ lekarz powiedział mi ...** a doctor I know has told me ...
**zna|k** (**-ku, -ki**) (*instr sg* **-kiem**) *m* sign; **~ drogowy** traffic *lub* road sign; **~ zapytania** question mark; **~ interpunkcyjny** *lub* **przestankowy** punctuation mark; **~ dodawania/odejmowania** plus/minus sign; **~ towarowy** *lub* **fabryczny** trademark; **~ Zodiaku** sign of the Zodiac; **być spod ~u Barana** to be Aries; **~i szczególne** distinguishing marks; **na ~ protestu/przyjaźni** in token of protest/friendship; **dawać (dać** *perf*) **~** to signal; **dawać się (dać się** *perf*) **komuś we ~i** (*o osobie, sytuacji*) to make sb's life miserable; (*o pracy, wysiłku*) to take its toll on sb
**znakomicie** *adv* superbly
**znakomitoś|ć** (**-ci, -ci**) (*gen pl* **-ci**) *f* (*osoba*) celebrity
**znakomity** *adj* superb; (*książk: znaczny*) considerable
**znak|ować (-uję, -ujesz)** (*perf* **o-**) *vt* (*ołówkiem, długopisem*) to mark; (*naklejką*) to label; (*zwierzęta*) to brand
**znalazc|a** (**-y, -y**) *m decl like f in sg* finder
**znalezis|ko** (**-ka, -ka**) (*instr sg* **-kiem**) *nt* find
**zna|leźć (-jdę, -jdziesz)** (*imp* **-jdź**, *pt* **-lazł, -lazła, -leźli**) *vb perf od* **znajdować**
**znamienity** *adj* (*książk*) eminent
**znamienny** *adj*: **~ (dla** *+gen*) characteristic (of)
**zna|mię** (**-mienia, -miona**) (*gen pl* **-mion**) *nt* (*wrodzone*) birthmark; (*cecha*) trait
**znamion|ować (-uje)** *vt* to indicate
**znany** *adj* (*otoczenie, środowisko*) (well-)known, familiar; (*aktor, pisarz*) well-known, famous; (*oszust*) notorious; **mało ~** little-known; **być ~m z czegoś** to be famous for sth, to have a reputation for sth; (*w znaczeniu negatywnym*) to be notorious for sth, to have a reputation for sth
**znawc|a** (**-y, -y**) *m decl like f in sg*; **~ (czegoś)** expert (on sth)
**znawst|wo** (**-wa**) (*loc sg* **-wie**) *nt* competence

**znerwicowany** *adj* neurotic
**zneutraliz|ować (-uję, -ujesz)** *vb perf od* **neutralizować**
**znęc|ać się (-am, -asz)** *vr*: **znęcać się nad** *+instr* to abuse
**znęcani|e się** (**-a**) *nt* abuse
**znę|cić (-cę, -cisz)** (*imp* **-ć**) *vb perf od* **nęcić**
**znękany** *adj* harried
**znicz** (**-a, -e**) (*gen pl* **-y** *lub* **-ów**) *m* (*nagrobkowy*) candle; ~ **olimpijski** the Olympic torch
**zniechę|cać (-cam, -casz)** (*perf* **-cić**) *vt*: ~ **kogoś (do czegoś)** to discourage sb (from doing sth); **zniechęcać się** *vr* to become discouraged
**zniechęceni|e** (**-a**) *nt* discouragement
**zniechę|cić (-cę, -cisz)** (*imp* **-ć**) *vb perf od* **zniechęcać**
**zniecierpliwieni|e** (**-a**) *nt* impatience
**zniecierpliwiony** *adj* impatient
**znieczul|ać (-am, -asz)** (*perf* **-ić**) *vt* to anaesthetize (Brit), to anesthetize (US)
**znieczulający** *adj*: **środek** ~ anaesthetic (Brit), anesthetic (US)
**znieczule|nie** (**-nia, -nia**) (*gen pl* **-ń**) *nt* anaesthetic (Brit), anesthetic (US); ~ **miejscowe/ogólne** local/general an(a)esthetic; **w znieczuleniu** under an(a)esthetic
**znieczul|ić (-ę, -isz)** *vb perf od* **znieczulać**
**zniedołężni|eć (-eję, -ejesz)** *vb perf od* **niedołężnieć**
**zniedołężnieni|e** (**-a**) *nt* decrepitude; ~ **starcze** senility
**zniekształ|cać (-cam, -casz)** (*perf* **-cić**) *vt* to deform; (*słowa, prawdę*) to distort, to twist
**zniekształce|nie** (**-nia, -nia**) (*gen pl* **-ń**) *nt* (*obrazu, informacji*) distortion
**zniekształ|cić (-cę, -cisz)** (*imp* **-ć**) *vb perf od* **zniekształcać**
**znienacka** *adv* unawares
**znienawi|dzić (-dzę, -dzisz)** (*imp* **-dź**) *vb perf od* **nienawidzić**
**znieruchomi|eć (-eję, -ejesz)** *vb perf od* **nieruchomieć**
**zniesieni|e** (**-a**) *nt* (*prawa, przepisu*) abolition; **nie do zniesienia** unbearable, intolerable
**zniesła|wiać (-wiam, -wiasz)** (*perf* **-wić**) *vt* (*na piśmie*) to libel; (*w mowie*) to slander
**zniesła|wić (-wię, -wisz)** *vb perf od* **zniesławiać**
**zniesławieni|e** (**-a**) *nt* (*na piśmie*) libel; (*w mowie*) slander
**zni|eść (-osę, -esiesz)** (*imp* **-eś**, *pt* **-ósł, -osła, -eśli**) *vb perf od* **znosić**
**zniewa|ga** (**-gi, -gi**) (*dat sg* **-dze**) *f* insult
**zniewal|ać (-am, -asz)** (*perf* **zniewolić**) *vt* (*pozyskiwać sympatię*) to captivate; (*książk: zmuszać*) to constrain
**zniewalający** *adj* (*uśmiech*) captivating
**znieważ|ać (-am, -asz)** (*perf* **-yć**) *vt* to insult
**zniewieściały** *adj* effeminate
**zniew|olić (-olę, -olisz)** (*imp* **-ol**) *vb perf od* **zniewalać**
**znik|ać (-am, -asz)** (*perf* **-nąć**) *vi* to disappear, to vanish
**znik|nąć (-nę, -niesz)** (*imp* **-nij**, *pt* **-nął** *lub* **-ł, -nęła** *lub* **-ła, -nęli** *lub* **-li**) *vb perf od* **znikać**
**znikomy** *adj* slight
**zniszcz|eć (-eje)** *vb perf od* **niszczeć**
**zniszcze|nie** (**-nia, -nia**) (*gen pl* **-ń**) *nt* destruction; **siać** ~ to rampage
**zniszczony** *adj*: **zniszczone ręce** toil-worn hands
**zniszcz|yć (-ę, -ysz)** *vb perf od* **niszczyć**
**zniwecz|yć (-ę, -ysz)** *vb perf od* **niweczyć**
**zniwel|ować (-uję, -ujesz)** *vb perf od* **niwelować**
**zniż|ać (-am, -asz)** (*perf* **-yć**) *vt* to lower; ~ **głos** to lower one's voice; ~ **lot** to descend; **zniżać się** *vr* (*opuszczać się*) to descend; ~ **się do czegoś** to stoop to sth
**zniż|ka** (**-ki, -ki**) (*dat sg* **-ce**, *gen pl* **-ek**) *f* reduction, discount; **ze zniżką** at a discount; **10% zniżki** 10% off
**zniżk|ować (-uje)** *vi* (*o walucie*) to slip
**zniżkowy** *adj*: **cena zniżkowa** reduced *lub* discount price; **tendencja zniżkowa** downward trend; **bilet** ~ (*do kina, muzeum*) concession
**zniż|yć (-ę, -ysz)** *vb perf od* **zniżać**
**znokaut|ować (-uję, -ujesz)** *vb perf od* **nokautować**
**znormaliz|ować (-uję, -ujesz)** *vb perf od* **normalizować**
**zno|sić (-szę, -sisz)** (*imp* **-ś**, *perf* **znieść**) *vt* (*nieść w dół*) to carry down; (*gromadzić*) to gather; (*jajka*) to lay; (*o prądzie wody, powietrza*) to carry; (*ból, niewygody*) to endure, to tolerate; (*prawo, dekret*) to abolish; (*kontrolę, ograniczenia*) to lift; **nie znoszę go** I can't stand *lub* bear him; **pomarańcze źle znoszą transport** oranges travel badly; **znosić się** *vr* (*neutralizować się*) to cancel each other out; **oni się nie znoszą** they hate each other
**znoszony** *adj* (*odzież*) worn(-out)
**znośny** *adj* bearable, tolerable
**znoweliz|ować (-uję, -ujesz)** *vb perf od* **nowelizować**
**znowu** *adv* again ▷ *part* (*właściwie*) after all; ~ **to zrobił** he did it again; **to nie jest ~ taki zły pomysł** it's not such a bad idea after all; **(o) co ~ (chodzi)?** what (is it) now?
**znów** *adv* = **znowu**
**znudzeni|e** (**-a**) *nt* boredom; **do znudzenia** ad nauseam

**znu|dzić (-dzę, -dzisz)** (*imp* **-dź**) *vb perf od* **nudzić**
**znudzony** *adj* bored
**znużeni|e** (**-a**) *nt* weariness; **ze ~m** wearily
**znużony** *adj* weary; **być ~m kimś/czymś** to be tired of sb/sth
**znuż|yć (-ę, -ysz)** *vb perf od* **nużyć**
**zob.** *abbr* (= *zobacz*) see, cf.
**zobaczeni|e** (**-a**) *nt*: **do zobaczenia!** see you!; **do zobaczenia wkrótce/wieczorem!** (I'll) see you soon/tonight!
**zobacz|yć (-ę, -ysz)** *vt perf* to see; **zobaczę** (*namyślę się*) I'll see; **zobaczyć się** *vr*: **~ się z kimś** to see sb
**zoblig|ować (-uję, -ujesz)** *vb perf od* **obligować**
**zobligowany** *adj* obliged; **czuć się ~m, aby coś zrobić** feel obliged to do sth
**zobojęt|niać (-niam, -niasz)** (*perf* **-nić**) *vt* to render indifferent, to desensitize; (*Chem*) to neutralize
**zobojęt|nić (-nię, -nisz)** (*imp* **-nij**) *vb perf od* **zobojętniać**
**zobojętni|eć (-eję, -ejesz)** *vb perf od* **obojętnieć**
**zobowią|zać (-żę, -żesz)** *vb perf od* **zobowiązywać**
**zobowiąza|nie** (**-nia, -nia**) (*gen pl* **-ń**) *nt* commitment, obligation; **składać (złożyć** *perf*) **~** to make a commitment; **wywiązywać się (wywiązać się** *perf*) **z zobowiązań** to meet one's obligations; **zobowiązania bieżące** current liabilities
**zobowiązany** *adj*: **być ~m do czegoś** to be obliged to do sth; **jestem Panu/Pani bardzo ~** I'm much obliged (to you)
**zobowiąz|ywać (-uję, -ujesz)** (*perf* **-ać**) *vt*: **~ kogoś do czegoś** to oblige sb to do sth; **zobowiązywać się** *vr*: **~ się do czegoś** to commit o.s. to (doing) sth
**zobraz|ować (-uję, -ujesz)** *vb perf od* **obrazować**
**zodia|k** (**-ku**) (*instr sg* **-kiem**) *m* zodiac; **znak ~u** sign of the zodiac, zodiacal sign
**zognisk|ować (-uję, -ujesz)** *vb perf od* **ogniskować**
**zoo** *nt inv* zoo
**z o.o.** *abbr* (= *z ograniczoną odpowiedzialnością*) Ltd.
**zoolo|g** (**-ga, -gowie** *lub* **-dzy**) (*instr sg* **-giem**) *m* zoologist
**zoologi|a** (**-i**) *f* zoology
**zoologiczny** *adj* zoological; **ogród ~** zoo, zoological garden(s *pl*)
**zoper|ować (-uję, -ujesz)** *vb perf od* **operować**
**zorganiz|ować (-uję, -ujesz)** *vb perf od* **organizować**
**zorganizowany** *adj* (*grupa*) organized; (*wycieczka*) guided
**zorient|ować (-uję, -ujesz)** *vb perf od* **orientować**
**zorientowany** *adj*: **być (dobrze) ~m w czymś** to be well-versed in sth
**zorza** (**zorzy, zorze**) (*gen pl* **zórz**) *f*: **~ polarna** aurora; (*na biegunie północnym*) northern lights; (*na biegunie południowym*) southern lights
**zosta|ć (-nę, -niesz)** (*imp* **-ń**) *vi perf* (*lekarzem, ojcem*) to become; **~ zrozumianym** to be understood
**zost|awać (-aję, -ajesz)** (*imp* **-awaj**, *perf* **-ać**) *vi* (*pozostawać*) to stay, to remain; **~ w domu/łóżku** to stay at home/in bed; **zostać na noc** to stay overnight *lub* the night; **zostać na obiedzie** to stay for *lub* to dinner; **~ bez grosza/na bruku** to be left penniless/out in the street; **~ w tyle** to lag behind; **niech to zostanie między nami** let this remain between you and me
**zosta|wiać (-wiam, -wiasz)** (*perf* **-wić**) *vt* (*opuszczać, powodować*) to leave; (*nie zabierać*) to leave (behind); **zostaw ją w spokoju** leave her alone; **zostaw to mnie** leave it to me; **zostawić coś sobie** to keep sth; **zostawić komuś coś w spadku** to leave *lub* bequeath sth to sb; **zostawić wiadomość dla kogoś/u kogoś** to leave word *lub* a message for sb/with sb; **nie zostawić na czymś suchej nitki** (*przen*) to tear sth to pieces *lub* bits *lub* shreds
**zosta|wić (-wię, -wisz)** *vb perf od* **zostawiać**
**zowąd** *adv*: **ni stąd, ni ~** out of the blue
**ZOZ** *abbr* (= *Zespół Opieki Zdrowotnej*) *area health service administration*
**zórz** *n patrz* **zorza**
**zrab|ować (-uję, -ujesz)** *vb perf od* **rabować**
**zracjonaliz|ować (-uję, -ujesz)** *vb perf od* **racjonalizować**
**zramol|eć (-eję, -ejesz)** *vb perf od* **ramoleć**
**zra|nić (-nię, -nisz)** (*imp* **-ń**) *vb perf od* **ranić**
**zrast|ać się (-am, -asz)** (*perf* **zrosnąć**) *vr* (*o kościach*) to knit (together)
**zraszacz** (**-a, -e**) (*gen pl* **-y**) *m* sprinkler
**zrasz|ać (-am, -asz)** (*perf* **zrosić**) *vt* to sprinkle
**zra|z** (**-za, -zy**) (*loc sg* **-zie**) *m* (*Kulin*) beef roulade
**zra|zić (-żę, -zisz)** (*imp* **-ź**) *vb perf od* **zrażać**
**zraż|ać (-am, -asz)** (*perf* **zrazić**) *vt* to alienate, to antagonize; **zrażać się** *vr* (*rozczarowywać się*) to become disaffected; (*w obliczu trudności itp.*) to lose heart
**zrealiz|ować (-uję, -ujesz)** *vb perf od* **realizować**

Z

**zreasum|ować (-uję, -ujesz)** *vb perf od* **reasumować**
**zrecenz|ować (-uję, -ujesz)** *vb perf od* **recenzować**
**zredag|ować (-uję, -ujesz)** *vb perf od* **redagować**
**zreduk|ować (-uję, -ujesz)** *vb perf od* **redukować**
**zrefer|ować (-uję, -ujesz)** *vb perf od* **referować**
**zreform|ować (-uję, -ujesz)** *vb perf od* **reformować**
**zrefund|ować (-uję, -ujesz)** *vb perf od* **refundować**
**zregener|ować (-uję, -ujesz)** *vb perf od* **regenerować**
**zrehabilit|ować (-uję, -ujesz)** *vb perf od* **rehabilitować**
**zrekompens|ować (-uję, -ujesz)** *vb perf od* **rekompensować**
**zrekonstru|ować (-uję, -ujesz)** *vb perf od* **rekonstruować**
**zrelacjon|ować (-uję, -ujesz)** *vb perf od* **relacjonować**
**zrelaks|ować (-uję, -ujesz)** *vb perf od* **relaksować**
**zrelaksowany** *adj* relaxed
**zremis|ować (-uję, -ujesz)** *vb perf od* **remisować**
**zreorganiz|ować (-uję, -ujesz)** *vb perf od* **reorganizować**
**zreper|ować (-uję, -ujesz)** *vb perf od* **reperować**
**zresztą** *adv* in any case
**zrewaloryz|ować (-uję, -ujesz)** *vb perf od* **rewaloryzować**
**zrewanż|ować się (-uję, -ujesz)** *vb perf od* **rewanżować się**
**zrewid|ować (-uję, -ujesz)** *vb perf od* **rewidować**
**zrewolucjoniz|ować (-uję, -ujesz)** *vb perf od* **rewolucjonizować**
**zrezygn|ować (-uję, -ujesz)** *vb perf od* **rezygnować**
**zrezygnowany** *adj* resigned
**zręcznie** *adv* (*zwinnie*) adroitly; (*sprytnie*) cleverly, skilfully (*Brit*), skillfully (*US*)
**zręcznoś|ć** (**-ci, -ci**) (*gen pl* **-ci**) *f* (*zwinność*) agility; (*rąk*) dexterity; (*spryt*) cleverness
**zręczny** *adj* (*zwinny*) agile; (*sprytny*) clever, skilful (*Brit*), skillful (*US*)
**zr|obić (-obię, -obisz)** (*imp* **-ób**) *vb perf od* **robić**
**zr|odzić (-odzę, -odzisz)** (*imp* **-ódź**) *vb perf od* **rodzić**
**zrogowaciały** *adj* (*skóra*) callous
**zrol|ować (-uję, -ujesz)** *vb perf od* **rolować**
**zro|sić (-szę, -sisz)** (*imp* **-ś**) *vb perf od* **zraszać**
**zro|snąć się (-snę, -śniesz)** (*imp* **-śnij**, *pt* **zrósł, zrosła, zrośli**) *vb perf od* **zrastać się**
**zro|st** (**-stu, -sty**) (*loc sg* **-ście**) *m* (*Med*) adhesion
**zrozpaczony** *adj* (*człowiek, spojrzenie*) desperate; **być ~m** to be in despair
**zrozumiały** *adj* (*artykuł, wykład*) comprehensible, intelligible; (*niechęć, powód*) understandable
**zrozumi|eć (-em, -esz)** (*3 pl* **-eją**) *vb perf od* **rozumieć**
**zrozumieni|e** (**-a**) *nt* (*pojmowanie*) understanding, comprehension; (*uświadomienie sobie*) realization; (*współczucie*) understanding, empathy; **dawać (dać** *perf*) **komuś do zrozumienia, że ...** to give sb to understand that ...; **ze ~m** with understanding; **mieć ~ dla** *+gen* to have understanding for
**zrób** *vb patrz* **zrobić**
**zrówn|ać (-am, -asz)** *vb perf od* **zrównywać**
**zrównoważony** *adj* (*człowiek*) even-tempered; (*charakter*) equable; (*budżet*) balanced
**zrównoważ|yć (-ę, -ysz)** *vb perf od* **równoważyć**
**zrówn|ywać (-uję, -ujesz)** (*perf* **-ać**) *vt* to flatten, to level; **zrównać coś z ziemią** to raze sth (to the ground); **zrównywać się** *vr*: **~ się z kimś/czymś** to come *lub* draw level with sb/sth
**zróżnicowani|e** (**-a**) *nt* diversity
**zróżnicowany** *adj* diverse
**zrujn|ować (-uję, -ujesz)** *vb perf od* **rujnować**
**zryczałtowany** *adj* (*Ekon*) flat-rate *attr*
**zry|ć (-ję, -jesz)** *vb perf od* **ryć**
**zry|w** (**-wu, -wy**) (*loc sg* **-wie**) *m* spurt; **pracować ~ami** to work by *lub* in fits and starts
**zryw|ać (-am, -asz)** (*perf* **zerwać**) *vt* (*kwiaty, owoce*) to pick; (*plakat, plaster*) to tear off; (*o rzece*: *zaporę*) to burst; (: *most*) to wash away; (*o wietrze*: *dach*) to blow off; (*linię energetyczną, połączenie*) to cut off; (*więzy, linę*) to break; (*umowę, zaręczyny*) to break off; (*stosunki, związki*) to break off, to sever ▷ *vi*: **~ (z kimś)** to break *lub* split up (with sb); **~ z paleniem/piciem** to give up *lub* quit smoking/drinking; **zrywać się** *vr* (*o linie, nici*) to break; (*o człowieku*) to jump *lub* leap up; (*o wichurze, oklaskach*) to break out; **~ się na równe nogi** to jump to one's feet
**zrzą|dzać (-dza)** (*perf* **-dzić**) *vt*: **los zrządził, że ...** it was fated *lub* ordained that ...
**zrządze|nie** (**-nia, -nia**) (*gen pl* **-ń**) *nt*: **~ losu** (*książk*) a stroke of fate

**zrze|c się (-knę, -kniesz)** (*imp* **-knij**, *pt* **-kł, -kła, -kli**) *vb perf od* **zrzekać się**
**zrzed|nąć (-nie)** (*pt* **-nął** *lub* **-ł, -ła**) *vb perf od* **rzednąć**
**zrzedni|eć (-eje)** *vb perf od* **rzednieć**
**zrzek|ać się (-am, -asz)** (*perf* **zrzec**) *vr* (*tytułu, przywilejów*) to relinquish
**zrzesz|ać (-am, -asz)** (*perf* **-yć**) *vt* to associate; **zrzeszać się** *vr* to organize
**zrzesze|nie** (**-nia, -nia**) (*gen pl* **-ń**) *nt* association
**zrzesz|yć (-ę, -ysz)** *vb perf od* **zrzeszać**
**zrzę|da** (**-dy, -dy**) (*dat sg* **-dzie**) *m/f decl like f* (*pot*) grouch (*pot*)
**zrzę|dzić (-dzę, -dzisz)** (*imp* **-dź**) *vi* (*pot*) to grouch (*pot*)
**zrzu|cać (-cam, -casz)** (*perf* **-cić**) *vt* (*strącać, zdejmować*) to throw off; (*o koniu: jeźdźca*) to throw; (*liście, sierść*) to shed; **zrzucić parę kilogramów** to lose a few pounds *lub* kilos; **~ na kogoś winę** to pin the blame on sb; **zrzucać się** *vr* (*pot: robić składkę*) to chip in (*pot*)
**zrzu|cić (-cę, -cisz)** (*imp* **-ć**) *vb perf od* **zrzucać**
**zrzu|t** (**-tu, -ty**) (*loc sg* **-cie**) *m* (air-)drop
**zrzut|ka** (**-ki, -ki**) (*dat sg* **-ce**, *gen pl* **-ek**) *f* (*pot*) whip-round (*pot*); **robić zrzutkę** to have a whip-round
**zrzyn|ać (-am, -asz)** (*perf* **zerżnąć**) *vt* (*pot: odpisywać*) to crib (*pot*); (*ścinać*) to cut off
**zsa|dzać (-dzam, -dzasz)** (*perf* **-dzić**) *vt* to help down
**zsa|dzić (-dzę, -dzisz)** (*imp* **-dź**) *vb perf od* **zsadzać**
**zsechł** *vb patrz* **zeschnąć**
**zsiad|ać (-am, -asz)** (*perf* **zsiąść**) *vi*: **~ (z konia/roweru)** to get off (a horse/bicycle); **zsiadać się** *vr* (*o mleku*) to curdle
**zsiadły** *adj*: **zsiadłe mleko** curds *pl*
**zsią|ść (-dę, -dziesz)** (*imp* **-dź**, *pt* **zsiadł, zsiadła, zsiedli**) *vb perf od* **zsiadać**
**zsik|ać się (-am, -asz)** *vr perf* (*pot*) to pee in one's pants (*pot*)
**zsini|eć (-eję, -ejesz)** *vb perf od* **sinieć**
**zsiusi|ać się (-am, -asz)** *vr perf* (*pot*) to wet o.s. (*pot*)
**ZSP** *abbr* (= *Zrzeszenie Studentów Polskich*) Polish Students Association
**ZSRR** *abbr* (= *Związek Socjalistycznych Republik Radzieckich*) USSR
**zstą|pić (-pię, -pisz)** *vb perf od* **zstępować**
**zstęp|ować (-uję, -ujesz)** (*perf* **zstąpić**) *vi* to descend
**zsum|ować (-uję, -ujesz)** *vb perf od* **sumować, zsumowywać**
**zsumow|ywać (-uję, -ujesz)** (*perf* **-ać**) *vt* to total (up), to tot up
**zsu|nąć (-nę, -niesz)** (*imp* **-ń**) *vb perf od* **zsuwać**
**zsuw|ać (-am, -asz)** (*perf* **zsunąć**) *vt* (*w dół*) to slide (down); (*ławki, stoły*) to put together; **zsuwać się** *vr* (*z półki itp.*) to slide (off); (*o bucie*) to slip off
**zsył|ać (-am, -asz)** (*perf* **zesłać**) *vt* (*książk: ratunek, karę*) to send (down); (*deportować*) to send into exile
**zsył|ka** (**-ki, -ki**) (*dat sg* **-ce**, *gen pl* **-ek**) *f* exile
**zsynchroniz|ować (-uję, -ujesz)** *vb perf od* **synchronizować**
**zsyntetyz|ować (-uję, -ujesz)** *vb perf od* **syntetyzować**
**zsy|p** (**-pu, -py**) (*loc sg* **-pie**) *m* (rubbish (*Brit*) *lub* garbage (*US*)) chute
**zsy|pać (-pię, -piesz)** *vb perf od* **zsypywać**
**zszar|pać (-pię, -piesz)** *vt perf*: **~ komuś nerwy** to fray sb's nerves; **~ komuś zdrowie** to ruin sb's health
**zszedł** *itd. vb patrz* **zejść**
**zszokowany** *adj* shocked; **być ~m czymś** be shocked at sth
**zszywacz** (**-a, -e**) (*gen pl* **-y**) *m* stapler
**zszyw|ać (-am, -asz)** (*perf* **zszyć**) *vt* (*materiał*) to sew (together); (*ranę*) to suture, to stitch; (*kartki*) to staple
**zszyw|ka** (**-ki, -ki**) (*dat sg* **-ce**, *gen pl* **-ek**) *f* staple
**zubaż|ać (-am, -asz)** (*perf* **zubożyć**) *vt* to impoverish
**zuch** (**-a, -y**) *m* (*Harcerstwo*) Cub (Scout); **~ z ciebie!** well done!
**zuchwalst|wo** (**-wa, -wa**) (*loc sg* **-wie**) *nt* impudence, impertinence
**zuchwałoś|ć** (**-ci**) *f* impudence, impertinence
**zuchwały** *adj* (*bezczelny*) impertinent; (*brawurowy*) bold, daring
**zu|pa** (**-py, -py**) (*dat sg* **-pie**) *f* soup; **~ błyskawiczna** *lub* **w proszku** instant *lub* powdered soup; **~ w puszce** *lub* **z puszki** canned *lub* tinned soup
**zupełnie** *adv* completely, utterly; **podszedł do mnie, ~ jakby nic się nie stało** he walked up to me as if nothing had happened
**zupełnoś|ć** (**-ci**) *f*: **w zupełności** completely
**zupełny** *adj* complete, utter
**Zurych** (**-u**) *m* Zürich
**ZUS** *abbr* (= *Zakład Ubezpieczeń Społecznych*) ≈ Social Security
**zużyci|e** (**-a**) *nt* (*paliwa, energii*) consumption; (*stopień zniszczenia*) wear
**zuży|ć (-ję, -jesz)** *vb perf od* **zużywać**
**zużytk|ować (-uję, -ujesz)** *vt perf* (*zużyć*) to use (up); (*wykorzystać*) to utilize
**zużyty** *adj* worn out, used

**zużyw|ać (-am, -asz)** (*perf* **zużyć**) *vt* to use up; **zużywać się** *vr* to wear

**zw.** *abbr* (= *zwany*) a.k.a., aka

**zwa|biać (-biam, -biasz)** (*perf* **-bić**) *vt* to lure

**zwać (zwę, zwiesz)** (*imp* **zwij**) *vt* to call; **zwać się** *vr* (*książk*) to be called

**zwal|ać (-am, -asz)** (*perf* **-ić**) *vt* (*strącać: książki, doniczki*) to knock down; (*wyładowywać: węgiel*) to dump; (*pot: odpisywać*) to crib (*pot*); **~ coś na kogoś** (*pot: obowiązki, pracę*) to load sb down with sth; (*: winę*) to pin sth on sb; **zwalić kogoś z nóg** to knock sb off their feet; **zwalać się** *vr* (*pot: spadać*) to fall *lub* come down; (*: przewracać się*) to come a cropper (*pot*); (*: przybywać*) to show up (*pot*); **zwalić się z nóg** (*pot*) to take a spill (*pot*); **zwalić się komuś na głowę** *lub* **kark** to descend on sb

**zwalcz|ać (-am, -asz)** *vt imperf* to fight (against); **zwalczać się** *vr* to fight each other

**zwalcz|yć (-ę, -ysz)** *vt perf* to overcome; (*robactwo*) to exterminate

**zwal|ić (-ę, -isz)** *vb perf od* **zwalać**

**zwalni|ać (-am, -asz)** (*perf* **zwolnić**) *vt* (*tempo*) to slow (down); (*uścisk*) to relax; (*więźnia, zakładnika*) to release, to set free; (*pokój, miejsce*) to vacate; (*z pracy*) to dismiss, to fire ▷ *vi* (*zmniejszać szybkość*) to slow down; **~ kogoś z czegoś** to exempt sb from sth; **~ kogoś od odpowiedzialności** to absolve sb from responsibility; **zwalniać się** *vr* (*z pracy, zajęć*) to take a day *itp.* off; (*rezygnować z pracy*) to quit; (*o pokoju, miejscu*) to become vacant

**zwa|ł** (**-łu, -ły**) (*loc sg* **-le**) *m* (*śniegu, piasku*) heap

**zwany** *adj*: **tak ~** so-called

**zwarci|e** (**-a**) *nt* (*Elektr*) short circuit

**zwari|ować (-uję, -ujesz)** *vi perf* (*pot*) to go mad (*pot*); **nie daj się ~** keep your head!, keep a cool head!

**zwariowany** *adj* (*pot*) mad (*pot*); **~ na czyimś punkcie/punkcie czegoś** crazy about sb/sth

**zwarł** *itd. vb patrz* **zewrzeć**

**zwarty** *adj* (*zabudowa*) close; (*tłum*) tight; (*zarośla*) thick; (*kompozycja, struktura*) compact; (*Jęz*): **spółgłoska zwarta** stop (consonant)

**zwarz|yć się (-ę, -ysz)** *vr perf* (*o mleku*) to turn sour, to go sour

**zważ|ać (-am, -asz)** (*perf* **-yć**) *vi*: **(nie) ~ na kogoś/coś** (not) to pay attention to sb/sth; **zważywszy na jego przeszłość** considering his past; **zważywszy na to, że ...** considering the fact that ...

**zważ|yć (-ę, -ysz)** *vb perf od* **ważyć**

**zwąt|pić (-pię, -pisz)** *vb perf od* **wątpić**

**zwątpie|nie** (**-nia, -nia**) (*gen pl* **-ń**) *nt* pessimism

**zwerb|ować (-uję, -ujesz)** *vb perf od* **werbować**

**zwę** *itd. vb patrz* **zwać**

**zwę|dzić (-dzę, -dzisz)** (*imp* **-dź**) *vt* (*pot*) to pinch (*pot*)

**zwęgl|ić (-ę, -isz)** *vb perf od* **zwęglać**

**zwęglony** *adj* charred

**zwę|zić (-żę, -zisz)** (*imp* **-ź**) *vb perf od* **zwężać**

**zwęż|ać (-am, -asz)** (*perf* **zwęzić**) *vt* to narrow; (*sukienkę*) to take in; **zwężać się** *vr* to narrow

**zwęże|nie** (**-nia, -nia**) (*gen pl* **-ń**) *nt* narrowing

**zwi|ać (-eję, -ejesz)** *vb perf od* **zwiewać**

**zwiadowc|a** (**-y, -y**) *m decl like f in sg* scout

**zwiast|ować (-uję, -ujesz)** *vt* (*książk*) to herald, to portend

**zwiastu|n** (**-na, -ny**) (*loc sg* **-nie**) *m* (*książk*) omen; (TV) trailer

**zwią|zać (-żę, -żesz)** *vb perf od* **wiązać, związywać** ▷ *vt perf*: **nie mogliśmy ~ końca z końcem** we couldn't make ends meet; **związać się** *vr perf*: **~ się (z** *+instr***)** to associate (with)

**związany** *adj* (*sznurem*) tied (up); (*umową, obietnicą*) bound; **~ z** *+instr* connected with; **mieć związane ręce** (*przen*) to have one's hands tied

**związ|ek** (**-ku, -ki**) (*instr sg* **-kiem**) *m* (*powiązanie*) connection; (*organizacja*) association; (*stosunek*) relationship; (*Chem*) compound; **~ zawodowy** trade union (*Brit*), labor union (*US*); **~ małżeński** marriage, matrimony; **w związku z czymś** in connection with sth; **w związku z tym** in this connection; **mówić bez związku** to speak incoherently

**związko|wiec** (**-wca, -wcy**) *m* unionist

**związkowy** *adj* (trade) union *attr*

**związ|ywać (-uję, -ujesz)** (*perf* **-ać**) *vt* to tie (up)

**zwich|nąć (-nę, -niesz)** (*imp* **-nij**) *vt perf* (*nogę*) to dislocate

**zwichnię|cie** (**-cia, -cia**) (*gen pl* **-ć**) *nt* dislocation (*of bones*)

**zwie|dzać (-dzam, -dzasz)** (*perf* **-dzić**) *vt* to tour, to visit

**zwie|dzić (-dzę, -dzisz)** (*imp* **-dź**) *vb perf od* **zwiedzać**

**zwielokrot|niać (-niam, -niasz)** (*perf* **-nić**) *vt* to increase; **zwielokrotniać się** *vr* to increase, to mount

**zwielokrot|nić (-nię, -nisz)** (*imp* **-nij**) *vb perf od* **zwielokrotniać**

**zwieńcze|nie** (**-nia, -nia**) (*gen pl* **-ń**) *nt* (*Archit*) finial; (*przen*) crowning

**zwier|ać (-am, -asz)** (*perf* **zewrzeć**) *vt* (*mocno stykać*) to press together; (*zaciskać*) to clench; **zwierać się** *vr* (*zaciskać się*) to clench; (*o grupie ludzi*) to close ranks

**zwierciad|ło** (-ła, -ła) (*loc sg* **-le**, *gen pl* **-eł**) *nt* (*książk*) looking glass, mirror
**zwierz** (-a, -e) (*gen pl* **-ów**) *m* (*książk*) beast
**zwierz|ać (-am, -asz)** (*perf* **-yć**) *vt* to confide, to reveal; **zwierzać się** *vr*: **~ się komuś** to confide to *lub* in sb
**zwierza|k** (-ka, -ki) (*instr sg* **-kiem**) *m* (*pot*) animal
**zwierzchnict|wo** (-wa) (*loc sg* **-wie**) *nt* supervision; **pracować pod czyimś zwierzchnictwem** to work under sb's supervision
**zwierzchni|k** (-ka, -cy) (*instr sg* **-kiem**) *m* superior
**zwierze|nie** (-nia, -nia) (*gen pl* **-ń**) *nt* confession
**zwierz|ę** (-ęcia, -ęta) (*gen pl* **-ąt**) *nt* animal; (*przen*) beast, animal; **~ domowe** domestic animal
**zwierzęcy** *adj* animal *attr*
**zwierz|yć (-ę, -ysz)** *vb perf od* **zwierzać**
**zwierzy|na** (-ny) (*dat sg* **-nie**) *f* game; **gruba ~** big game
**zwie|sić (-szę, -sisz)** (*imp* **-ś**) *vb perf od* **zwieszać**
**zwiesz|ać (-am, -asz)** (*perf* **zwiesić**) *vt*: **zwiesić głowę** to hang one's head; **zwieszać się** *vr* to hang down
**zwi|eść (-odę, -edziesz)** (*imp* **-edź**, *pt* **-ódł, -odła, -edli**) *vb perf od* **zwodzić**
**zwietrzały** *adj* (*napój gazowany*) flat; (*kawa*) stale; (*skała*) weathered
**zwietrz|yć (-ę, -ysz)** *vt perf* to scent
**zwiew|ać (-am, -asz)** (*perf* **zwiać**) *vt* (*o wietrze*) to blow off *lub* away ▷ *vi* (*pot*: *uciekać*) to run away *lub* off
**zwiewny** *adj* (*tkanina*) airy; (*postać*) ethereal
**zwi|eźć (-ozę, -eziesz)** (*imp* **-eź**, *pt* **-ózł, -ozła, -eźli**) *vb perf od* **zwozić**
**zwięd|nąć (-nie)** (*pt* **zwiądł** *lub* **-nął, -ła**) *vb perf od* **więdnąć**
**zwiędnięty** *adj* withered
**zwiększ|ać (-am, -asz)** (*perf* **-yć**) *vt* to increase; **zwiększać się** *vr* to increase
**zwięzłoś|ć** (-ci) *f* conciseness, succinctness
**zwięzły** *adj* concise, succinct
**zwij|ać (-am, -asz)** (*perf* **zwinąć**) *vt* (*linę*) to coil; (*dywan*) to roll up; **~ obóz** to break camp; **zwijać się** *vr* (*skręcać się*) to coil; (*pot*: *krzątać się*) to rush about *lub* around; **~ się z bólu** to writhe in pain; **zwinąć się w kłębek** to curl into a ball
**zwilż|ać (-am, -asz)** (*perf* **-yć**) *vt* to moisten, to dampen
**zwi|nąć (-nę, -niesz)** (*imp* **-ń**) *vb perf od* **zwijać**
**zwinnoś|ć** (-ci) *f* agility
**zwinny** *adj* agile, nimble
**zwis|ać (-am, -asz)** (*perf* **-nąć**) *vi* to hang down; **zwisa mi to** (*pot!*) I don't give a shit (about it) (*pot!*)
**zwi|snąć (-snę, -śniesz)** (*imp* **-śnij**, *pt* **-snął** *lub* **-sł, -sła, -snęli**) *vb perf od* **zwisać**
**zwit|ek** (-ka, -ki) (*instr sg* **-kiem**) *m* roll
**zwl|ec (-okę, -eczesz)** (*pt* **-ókł, -okła, -ekli**) *vb perf od* **zwlekać**
**zwlek|ać (-am, -asz)** *vi*: **~ (z czymś)** to delay (doing sth); **zwlekać się** *vr*: **~ się z łóżka** to drag o.s. out of bed
**zwłaszcza** *adv* especially; **~, że ...** especially as ...
**zwło|ka** (-ki) (*dat sg* **-ce**) *f* delay; **bez zwłoki** without delay; **sprawa nie cierpiąca zwłoki** urgent matter; **grać na zwłokę** to play for time
**zwło|ki** (-k) *pl* (dead) body, corpse
**zwodniczy** *adj* deceptive, delusive
**zwodu** *itd. n patrz* **zwód**
**zw|odzić (-odzę, -odzisz)** (*imp* **-ódź**, *perf* **zwieść**) *vt* to delude; **zwodzić się** *vr* to delude o.s.
**zwodzony** *adj*: **most ~** drawbridge
**zwoju** *itp. n patrz* **zwój**
**zwolennicz|ka** (-ki, -ki) (*gen pl* **-ek**) *f* follower, supporter
**zwolenni|k** (-ka, -cy) (*instr sg* **-kiem**) *m* follower, supporter
**zwol|nić (-nię, -nisz)** (*imp* **-nij**) *vb perf od* **zwalniać**
**zwolnie|nie** (-nia, -nia) (*gen pl* **-ń**) *nt* (*wymówienie*) dismissal; **~ lekarskie** sick leave; **~ podatkowe** tax exemption; **~ warunkowe** parole
**zwolniony** *adj*: **~ od opłat** free of charge; **~ od podatku** exempt from tax(es) *lub* taxation, tax-exempt; **~ z zajęć/egzaminu** excused from classes/an exam; **~ z pracy** dismissed from work
**zwoł|ywać (-uję, -ujesz)** (*perf* **-ać**) *vt* (*ludzi*) to call together; (*zebranie*) to call; (*parlament*) to summon
**zw|ozić (-ożę, -ozisz)** (*imp* **-oź** *lub* **-óź**, *perf* **zwieźć**) *vt* (*na określone miejsce*) to bring; (*z góry na dół*) to take down
**zw|ód** (-odu, -ody) (*loc sg* **-odzie**) *m* (*Sport*) feint
**zw|ój** (-oju, -oje) *m* (*pętla*) coil, twist; (*papieru*) scroll
**zwrac|ać (-am, -asz)** (*perf* **zwrócić**) *vt* (*głowę, wzrok*) to turn; (*pieniądze, książkę*) to return; (*pokarm*) to bring up; **zwrócić komuś uwagę** to admonish sb; **zwrócić czyjąś uwagę na coś** to draw sb's attention to sth, to bring sth to sb's attention; **zwrócić uwagę (na kogoś/coś)** to take note (of sb/sth); **zwracać się** *vr*

Z

(*kierować się*) to turn (towards); (*o kosztach, inwestycji*) to pay off; ~ **się do kogoś** to turn to sb
**zwro|t** (**-tu, -ty**) (*loc sg* **-cie**) *m* (*obrót, odmiana*) turn; (*pieniędzy, książek*) return; (*wyrażenie*) expression; **w lewo/tył ~!** left/about turn!
**zwrot|ka** (**-ki, -ki**) (*dat sg* **-ce**, *gen pl* **-ek**) *f* stanza
**zwrotnic|a** (**-y, -e**) *f* (*Kolej*) points *pl* (*Brit*), switch (*US*)
**zwrotni|k** (**-ka, -ki**) (*instr sg* **-kiem**) *m* tropic; **Z~ Koziorożca/Raka** the tropic of Capricorn/ Cancer
**zwrotnikowy** *adj* tropical
**zwrotny** *adj* (*samochód*) responsive; (*Jęz*) reflexive; (*pożyczka*) returnable, repayable; **punkt** ~ (*przen*) turning point; **adres** ~ return address; **sprzężenie zwrotne** feedback
**zwró|cić (-cę, -cisz)** (*imp* **-ć**) *vb perf od* **zwracać**
**zwycięski** *adj* winning, victorious
**zwycięst|wo** (**-wa, -wa**) (*loc sg* **-wie**) *nt* victory; **odnieść** (*perf*) ~ **(nad kimś/czymś)** to win a victory (over sb/sth)
**zwycięzc|a** (**-y, -y**) *m decl like f in sg* winner
**zwycięż|ać (-am, -asz)** (*perf* **-yć**) *vt* to overcome ▷ *vi* to win
**zwyczaj** (**-u, -e**) *m* (*obyczaj*) custom; (*nawyk*) habit; **mieć ~ coś robić** to be in the habit of doing sth
**zwyczajnie** *adv* (*normalnie*) as usual; (*po prostu*) simply
**zwyczajny** *adj* (*normalny*) ordinary, regular; (*oczekiwany*) usual; (*często spotykany*) common, regular; (*niewyszukany*) common, simple; (*głupota, oszust*) downright, mere; **profesor** ~ professor
**zwyczajowy** *adj* customary; **prawo zwyczajowe** common law
**zwykle** *adv* usually; **jak** ~ as usual
**zwykły** *adj* (*normalny*) ordinary, regular; (*oczekiwany*) usual; (*częsty*) common; (*prosty*) common, simple; (*głupota, oszust*) downright, sheer
**zwymiot|ować (-uję, -ujesz)** *vb perf od* **wymiotować**
**zwymyśl|ać (-am, -asz)** *vt perf* to scold
**zwyrodniały** *adj* degenerate
**zwyrodnie|nie** (**-nia, -nia**) (*gen pl* **-ń**) *nt* degeneration
**zwyż|ka** (**-ki, -ki**) (*dat sg* **-ce**, *gen pl* **-ek**) *f* (*wzrost*) rise; (*gwałtowny wzrost*) surge
**zwyżk|ować (-uje)** *vi* (*rosnąć*) to rise; (*gwałtownie rosnąć*) to surge
**zygza|k** (**-ka, -ki**) (*instr sg* **-kiem**) *m* zigzag; **iść ~iem** to zigzag
**zys|k** (**-ku, -ki**) (*instr sg* **-kiem**) *m* (*Ekon*) profit; (*korzyść*) gain; ~ **brutto/netto** gross/net profit; **czysty** ~ clear profit; **stopa ~u** rate of profit, profit rate; **przynosić** ~ to bring in *lub* yield a profit; **sprzedawać coś z ~iem** to sell sth at a profit; **mieć ~ z czegoś** to make a profit on sth
**zys|kiwać (-kuję, -kujesz)** (*perf* **-kać**) *vt* (*popularność, zaufanie*) to gain, to earn; (*przyjaciół, zwolenników*) to win ▷ *vi*: **~ na czymś** to profit by *lub* from sth; **~ na wartości** to increase in value; **zyskać na czasie** to gain time
**zyskowny** *adj* profitable
**zza** *prep +gen*; **zza drzewa** from behind a tree; **zza rogu** from around the corner; **zza okna** through the window
**zziajany** *adj* breathless
**zzięb|nąć (-nę, -niesz)** (*imp* **-nij**) *vb perf od* **ziębnąć**
**zziębnięty** *adj* chilled, cold
**zżarł** *itd. vb patrz* **zeżreć**
**zżąć (zeżnę, zeżniesz)** (*imp* **zeżnij**, *pt* **zżął, zżęła, zżęli**) *vb perf od* **żąć**
**zżółk|nąć (-nę, -niesz)** (*imp* **-nij**, *pt* **-ł** *lub* **-nął, -ła, -li**) *vb perf od* **żółknąć**
**zży|ć się (-ję, -jesz)** *vb perf od* **zżywać się**
**zżyn|ać (-am, -asz)** *vt* (*pot: odpisywać*) (*perf* **zerżnąć**) to crib (*pot*)
**zżyty** *adj* intimate, close
**zżyw|ać się (-am, -asz)** (*perf* **zżyć**) *vr* (*o osobach*) to become close; **zżyć się z kimś** to become intimate with sb

# Źź

**Ź, ź** *nt inv* (*litera*) Ź, ź
**źdźb|ło** (**-ła, -ła**) (*loc sg* **-le**, *gen pl* **-eł**) *nt* (*trawy*) blade; (*zbóż*) straw
**źle** (*comp* **gorzej**) *adv* (*błędnie*) wrongly; (*byle jak*) poorly, badly; **źle wyglądasz** you look bad *lub* ill; **źle wychowany** bad-mannered, ill-mannered; **źle się czuć** to be *lub* feel unwell; **źle zrozumieć** to misunderstand; **źle, że tak się stało** (it's) too bad (that) this happened
**źreba|k** (**-ka, -ki**) (*instr sg* **-kiem**) *m* foal
**źreb|ić się (-i)** (*perf* **o-**) *vr* to foal
**źrebi|ę** (**-ęcia, -ęta**) (*gen pl* **-ąt**) *nt* foal
**źrenic|a** (**-y, -e**) *f* (*Anat*) pupil; **strzec czegoś jak źrenicy oka** to guard sth as if it were the crown jewels
**źródlany** *adj* spring *attr*
**źród|ło** (**-ła, -ła**) (*loc sg* **-le**, *gen pl* **-eł**) *nt* (*informacji, wiedzy, energii*) source; (*rzeki*) spring, source; (*zdrój*) spring; (*przyczyna*) source; **~ dochodów** source of income, income source; **wiedzieć coś z pewnego źródła** to know sth from a reliable source; **~ mineralne** *lub* **lecznicze** mineral spring
**źródłowy** *adj* source *attr*

# Żż

**Ż, ż** *nt inv (litera)* Ż, ż

**ża|ba** (**-by, -by**) (*dat sg* **-bie**) *f* frog

**żab|ka** (**-ki, -ki**) (*dat sg* **-ce**, *gen pl* **-ek**) *f dimin od* **żaba**; (*styl pływacki*) breaststroke; **pływać żabką** to do (the) breaststroke

**żaboja|d** (**-da, -dy**) (*loc sg* **-dzie**) *m* (*pej*) frog, Frog

**żach|nąć się (-nę, -niesz)** (*imp* **-nij**) *vr perf*: **żachnąć się (na coś)** to bridle (at sth)

**żaden** (*f* **żadna**, *nt* **żadne**) *pron* (*przed rzeczownikiem*) no; (*zamiast rzeczownika*) none; (*ani jeden ani drugi*) neither; **w ~ sposób** at all; **w żadnym razie** *lub* **wypadku** in no case, in *lub* under no circumstances; **w żadnym wypadku!** no way!; **jego zasługi są żadne** his merits are none; **~ z nich** none of them; (*spośród dwóch*) neither of them

**ża|giel** (**-gla, -gle**) (*gen pl* **-gli**) *m* sail; **zwijać (zwinąć** *perf*) **żagle** (*przen*) to call it quits

**żaglo|wiec** (**-wca, -wce**) *m* sailing ship

**żaglowy** *adj*: **płótno żaglowe** sailcloth; **statek ~** sailing ship

**żaglów|ka** (**-ki, -ki**) (*dat sg* **-ce**, *gen pl* **-ek**) *f* sailing boat (*Brit*), sailboat (*US*)

**żakie|t** (**-tu, -ty**) (*loc sg* **-cie**) *m* jacket

**żal** (**-u, -e**) *m* (*smutek*) sorrow; (*skrucha*) regret; (*rozgoryczenie*) bitterness; **było mi go żal** I felt sorry for him; **mieć do kogoś żal** to have *lub* bear a grudge against sb; **żal za grzechy** (*Rel*) repentance; **żale** *pl* complaints *pl*; **wylewać żale** to grumble

**żal|ić się (-ę, -isz)** (*perf* **po-**) *vr* to grumble; **żalić się na kogoś/coś** to grumble about sb/sth

**żaluzj|a** (**-i, -e**) (*gen pl* **-i**) *f* (*z listewek*) Venetian blind; (*roleta*) roller blind (*Brit*) *lub* shade (*US*)

**żało|ba** (**-by**) (*dat sg* **-bie**) *f* mourning; **nosić żałobę** to be in mourning

**żałobni|k** (**-ka, -cy**) (*instr sg* **-kiem**) *m* mourner

**żałobny** *adj* (*kondukt*) funeral *attr*; **ubiór ~** mourning; **msza żałobna** requiem (mass)

**żałosny** *adj* (*płacz*) piteous; (*spojrzenie, stan*) pitiful

**żałoś|ć** (**-ci**) *f* grief

**żałośnie** *adv* piteously; **wyglądasz ~!** you look a (real) sight!

**żał|ować (-uję, -ujesz)** (*perf* **po-**) *vt*: **~ czegoś** to regret sth; **~ kogoś** to feel sorry for sb; **~ komuś czegoś** to stint sb of sth ▷ *vi* to regret; **żałuję, że to zrobiłem** I wish I hadn't done that; **~ za grzechy** (*Rel*) to repent one's sins; **nie ~ wysiłków** to spare no pains

**żandar|m** (**-ma, -mi**) (*loc sg* **-mie**) *m* (*policjant wojskowy*) military policeman, MP; (*policjant francuski*) gendarme

**żandarmeri|a** (**-i**) *f* (*też*: **żandarmeria wojskowa**) military police; (*policja francuska*) gendarmerie

**ża|r** (**-ru**) (*loc sg* **-rze**) *m* (*upał*) heat; (*uczuć*) fervour (*Brit*), fervor (*US*); (*ogniska*) glow

**żarci|e** (**-a**) *nt* (*pot*: *jedzenie*) chow (*pot*), grub (*pot*)

**żarci|k** (**-ku, -ki**) (*instr sg* **-kiem**) *m dimin od* **żart**

**żargo|n** (**-nu, -ny**) (*loc sg* **-nie**) *m* (*język specjalistyczny*) jargon; (*język ulicy*) slang

**żarliwie** *adv* fervently

**żarliwoś|ć** (**-ci**) *f* fervour (*Brit*), fervor (*US*)

**żarliwy** *adj* (*zwolennik*) fervent; (*mowa*) impassioned

**żarłocznoś|ć** (**-ci**) *f* voracity, gluttony

**żarłoczny** *adj* voracious, gluttonous

**żarło|k** (**-ka, -cy**) (*instr sg* **-kiem**) *m* (*pot*) guzzler (*pot*)

**żaroodporny** *adj* (*naczynie*) ovenproof; (*szkło*) heat resistant

**żarów|ka** (**-ki, -ki**) (*dat sg* **-ce**, *gen pl* **-ek**) *f* (light) bulb

**żar|t** (**-tu, -ty**) (*loc sg* **-cie**) *m* joke; **dla ~u** for laughs; **powiedzieć** (*perf*) **coś ~em** to say sth in jest; **obrócić** (*perf*) **coś w ~** to make a joke out of sth; **robić sobie z kogoś ~y** to make fun of sb; **z nim nie ma ~ów** he is not someone to be trifled with

**żartobliwy** *adj* humorous

**żart|ować (-uję, -ujesz)** (*perf* **za-**) *vi* to joke; **~ z kogoś/czegoś** to make fun of sb/sth

**żartowni|ś** (**-sia, -sie**) *m* joker

**żarz|yć się (-y)** *vr* to glow

**żąć (żnę, żniesz)** (*imp* **żnij**, *perf* **z-**) *vt* (*zboże*) to reap; (*trawę*) to mow

**żąd|ać (-am, -asz)** (*perf* **za-**) *vt*: **~ czegoś** to demand sth, to insist upon sth

**żąda|nie** (**-nia, -nia**) (*gen pl* **-ń**) *nt* demand; **na ~** on demand; **przystanek na ~** request stop (*Brit*), flag stop (*US*); **wysuwać** *lub* **stawiać żądania** to put forward *lub* make demands

**żądl|ić (-i)** (*perf* **u-**) *vt* to sting

**żąd|ło** (**-ła, -ła**) (*loc sg* **-le**, *gen pl* **-eł**) *nt* sting

**żądny** *adj*: **~ czegoś** hungry for sth

**żądz|a** (**-y, -e**) *f* lust; **~ wiedzy/władzy** lust for knowledge/power

**żbi|k** (**-ka, -ki**) (*instr sg* **-kiem**) *m* (*Zool*) wildcat

**że** *conj* that; **dlatego że** because; **był tak słaby, że upadł** he was so weak that he collapsed ▷ *part*: **(po)mimo że** although; **jako że** as, since; **tyle że** but, only; **chyba że** unless

**żeber|ko** (**-ka, -ka**) (*instr sg* **-kiem**) *nt dimin od* **żebro**; **żeberka** *pl* (*Kulin*) (spare)ribs *pl*

**żebracz|ka** (**-ki, -ki**) (*dat sg* **-ce**, *gen pl* **-ek**) *f* beggar

**żeb|rać (-rzę, -rzesz)** *vi* to beg; **~ o coś** to beg (for) sth

**żebra|k** (**-ka, -cy**) (*instr sg* **-kiem**) *m* beggar

**żeb|ro** (**-ra, -ra**) (*loc sg* **-rze**, *gen pl* **-er**) *nt* rib

**żeby** *conj* (*cel*) (in order) to, so that; **jest zbyt nieśmiała, ~ próbować** she's too shy to try; **~ nie przestraszyć dziecka** so as not to frighten the child; **~ nie on, przegralibyśmy** but for him we would have lost, if it wasn't *lub* weren't for him we would have lost; **nie chcę, ~ś to robił** I don't want you to do it ▷ *part*: **~ tylko nam się udało** if only we could make it; **~ś mi był cicho!** keep quiet, understand?

**żeglarski** *adj* sailing *attr*

**żeglarst|wo** (**-wa**) (*loc sg* **-wie**) *nt* sailing, yachting

**żeglarz** (**-a, -e**) (*gen pl* **-y**) *m* (*Sport*) yachtsman; (*Hist*) sailor

**żegl|ować (-uję, -ujesz)** *vi* to sail

**żeglowny** *adj* navigable

**żeglu|ga** (**-gi**) (*dat sg* **-dze**) *f* navigation; **~ morska** maritime *lub* sea navigation; **~ powietrzna** air navigation

**żegn|ać (-am, -asz)** *vt* (*perf* **po-**); **~ kogoś** to say goodbye to sb; **żegnaj(cie)!** farewell!; **żegnać się** *vr* (*przy rozstaniu*) (*perf* **po-**) to say goodbye; (*Rel*: *kreślić znak krzyża*) (*perf* **prze-**) to cross o.s.

**żel** (**-u, -e**) (*gen pl* **-i**) *m* gel; **żel do włosów** hair gel, styling gel

**żelaty|na** (**-ny**) (*dat sg* **-nie**) *f* gelatine (*Brit*), gelatin (*US*)

**żelaz|ko** (**-ka, -ka**) (*instr sg* **-kiem**, *gen pl* **-ek**) *nt* iron (*for pressing clothes*)

**żelazny** *adj* iron; (*zdrowie*) robust; **żelazne nerwy** nerves of steel; **żelazna kurtyna** (*przen*) the Iron Curtain; **trzymać kogoś/coś żelazną ręką** to keep an iron grip on sb/sth

**żela|zo** (**-za**) (*loc sg* **-zie**) *nt* iron; **kute ~** wrought iron

**żelazobeto|n** (**-nu**) (*loc sg* **-nie**) *m* (*Bud*) reinforced concrete

**żelbe|t** (**-tu**) (*loc sg* **-cie**) *m* = **żelazobeton**

**żeliwny** *adj* cast iron *attr*

**żeli|wo** (**-wa**) (*loc sg* **-wie**) *nt* cast iron

**żenady** *inv*: **bez ~** blatantly, unceremoniously

**że|nić (-nię, -nisz)** (*imp* **-ń**, *perf* **o-**) *vt* to marry (off); **żenić się** *vr* to get married

**żen|ować (-uję, -ujesz)** (*perf* **za-**) *vt* to embarrass; **żenować się** *vr* to be embarrassed; **żenowała się wspomnieć o tym** it embarrassed her to mention it, she felt embarrassed to mention it

**żenujący** *adj* pathetic

**żeński** *adj* (*szkoła*) girls' *attr*; (*komórka, osobnik, chór*) female; **rodzaj ~** (*Jęz*) feminine (gender)

**żeń-sze|ń** (**-nia, -nie**) (*gen pl* **-ni**) *m* ginseng

**że|r** (**-ru**) (*loc sg* **-rze**) *m* (*pokarm*) food; (*czynność*) feeding

**żer|dź** (**-dzi, -dzie**) (*gen pl* **-dzi**) *f* (*tyczka*) pole; (*dla kury, papugi*) perch

**żeto|n** (**-nu, -ny**) (*loc sg* **-nie**) *m* (*do telefonu*) token; (*w kasynie*) chip

**żłob|ek** (**-ka, -ki**) (*instr sg* **-kiem**) *m* (*instytucja*) crèche (*Brit*), day nursery (*US*)

**żł|obić (-obię, -obisz)** (*imp* **-ób**, *perf* **wy-**) *vt* to groove

**żł|ób** (**-obu, -oby**) (*loc sg* **-obie**) *m* manger

**żłób|ek** (**-ka, -ki**) (*instr sg* **-kiem**) *m* (*Rel*) crib

**żmi|ja** (**-i, -je**) (*gen pl* **-i**) *f* viper, adder

**żmudny** *adj* arduous

**żniw|a** (**-**) *pl* harvest

**żniwiar|ka** (**-ki, -ki**) (*dat sg* **-ce**, *gen pl* **-ek**) *f* harvester, reaper

**żniwiarz** (**-a, -e**) (*gen pl* **-y**) *m* harvester, reaper

**żniwny** *adj* harvest *attr*

**żni|wo** (**-wa, -wa**) (*loc sg* **-wie**) *nt* (*przen*: *śmierci*) toll

**żołąd|ek** (**-ka, -ki**) (*instr sg* **-kiem**) *m* stomach; **żołądki** *pl* (*Kulin*) gizzards *pl*

**żołądkowy** *adj* stomach *attr*; (*soki*) gastric

**żoł|ądź** (**-ędzi, -ędzie**) (*gen pl* **-ędzi**) *f* (*Bot*) acorn; (*Anat*) glans

**żoł|d** (**-du**) (*loc sg* **-dzie**) *m* (soldier's) pay

**żołnierski** *adj* (*mundur, służba*) military *attr*; (*życie*) soldier's *attr*

**żołnierz** (**-a, -e**) (*gen pl* **-y**) *m* soldier

**żołnierzy|k** (**-ka, -ki**) (*instr sg* **-kiem**) *m* toy soldier

**żo|na** (**-ny, -ny**) (*dat sg* **-nie**) *f* wife

**żonaty** *adj* married ▷ *m decl like adj* married man
**żongle|r** (**-ra, -rzy**) (*loc sg* **-rze**) *m* juggler
**żongler|ka** (**-ki**) (*dat sg* **-ce**) *f* (*umiejętność*) jugglery
**żongl|ować (-uję, -ujesz)** *vt*: **~ czymś** to juggle with sth
**żonkil** (**-a, -e**) (*gen pl* **-i**) *m* jonquil
**żółciowy** *adj*: **kamień ~** gallstone; **pęcherzyk ~** gall bladder
**żół|ć** (**-ci**) *f* (*Anat*) bile; **wylewać na kogoś ~** (*przen*) to vent one's spleen on sb
**żółk|nąć (-nę, -niesz)** (*imp* **-nij**, *perf* **z-**) *vi* to yellow
**żółtacz|ka** (**-ki**) (*dat sg* **-ce**) *f* jaundice
**żółtawy** *adj* yellowish
**żółt|ko** (**-ka, -ka**) (*instr sg* **-kiem**, *gen pl* **-ek**) *nt* yolk
**żółtodzi|ób** (**-oba, -oby**) (*loc sg* **-obie**) *m* greenhorn
**żółty** *adj* yellow; **~ ser** hard cheese
**żół|w** (**-wia, -wie**) (*gen pl* **-wi**) *m* (*lądowy*) tortoise, turtle (US); **morski** turtle
**żółwi** *adj*: **w ~m tempie** at a snail's pace; **~e tempo** snail's pace
**żółwiowy** *adj*: **zupa żółwiowa** turtle soup
**żrący** *adj* caustic
**żr|eć (-ę, -esz)** (*imp* **-yj**, *perf vt* (*o zwierzęciu*) to eat; (*pot: o człowieku*) to gobble; (*o rdzy*) to eat into
**żub|r** (**-ra, -ry**) (*loc sg* **-rze**) *m* (European) bison, wisent
**żubrów|ka** (**-ki, -ki**) (*dat sg* **-ce**, *gen pl* **-ek**) *f* grass-flavo(u)red vodka
**żuch|wa** (**-wy, -wy**) (*dat sg* **-wie**) *f* (lower) jaw
**żuci|e** (**-a**) *nt* mastication, chew(ing); **guma do żucia** chewing gum
**żu|ć (-ję, -jesz)** *vt* to chew, to masticate
**żu|k** (**-ka, -ki**) (*instr sg* **-kiem**) *m* (*Zool*) beetle
**żura|w** (**-wia, -wie**) (*gen pl* **-wi**) *m* crane
**żurawi|na** (**-ny, -ny**) (*dat sg* **-nie**) *f* cranberry
**żur|ek** (**-ku, -ki**) (*instr sg* **-kiem**) *m* (*Kulin*) *traditional Polish soup made from fermented rye*
**żurnal** (**-a** *lub* **-u, -e**) (*gen pl* **-i**) *m* fashion magazine
**żurnali|sta** (**-sty, -ści**) (*dat sg* **-ście**) *m decl like f in sg* journalist
**żuż|el** (**-la** *lub* **-lu**) *m* (*substancja*) cinders *pl*, clinker; (*tor wyścigowy*) cinder track; **wyścigi na żużlu** speedway
**żużlo|wiec** (**-wca, -wcy**) *m* (*Sport*) speedway rider
**żużlowy** *adj* (*nawierzchnia*) cinder *attr*; (*wyścigi*) speedway *attr*
**żwawy** *adj* brisk
**żwi|r** (**-ru, -ry**) (*loc sg* **-rze**) *m* gravel
**żwirowy** *adj* gravelled
**życi|e** (**-a**) *nt* life; (*pot: utrzymanie, wyżywienie*) living, living costs; **tryb życia** life style; **~ osobiste** personal *lub* private life; **~ wieczne** (*Rel*) eternal life; **~ nocne** night life; **ubezpieczenie na ~** life insurance; **wprowadzać coś w ~** to put sth into effect; **zarabiać na ~** to earn one's living; **być bez środków do życia** to be down at heel; *patrz też* **żyto**
**życiodajny** *adj* life-giving
**życiory|s** (**-su, -sy**) (*loc sg* **-sie**) *m* (*dokument*) CV, curriculum vitae; (*opis życia*) biography
**życiowy** *adj* (*funkcje, energia*) vital; (*doświadczenie*) life *attr*; (*pot: praktyczny*) realistic; **stopa życiowa** standard of living, living standard; **rekord ~** PB, personal best
**życze|nie** (**-nia, -nia**) (*gen pl* **-ń**) *nt* (*pragnienie*) wish; **na ~** on request; **na czyjeś ~** at sb's request; **pozostawiać wiele do życzenia** to leave a lot to be desired; **życzenia** *pl* wishes; **składać komuś życzenia** to wish sb (all the best); **życzenia urodzinowe/imieninowe** birthday/nameday wishes *lub* greetings; **życzenia świąteczne** (*na Boże Narodzenie*) Season's *lub* Christmas greetings; (*na Wielkanoc*) Easter greetings
**życzliwoś|ć** (**-ci**) *f* kindness, friendliness
**życzliwy** *adj* kind, friendly
**życz|yć (-ę, -ysz)** *vt*: **~ komuś czegoś** to wish sb sth; **czego pan(i) sobie życzy?** can I help you?; **dobrze/źle komuś ~** to wish sb good/ill luck; **nie życzę sobie tego** I won't have it, I'm not having it
**ży|ć (-ję, -jesz)** *vi* to live; **niech żyje X!** long live X!; **żyć z czegoś** to make a living out of *lub* from sth, to live by sth; **żyć czymś** to be (totally) absorbed in sth; **żyć z kimś dobrze/źle** to get along well/badly with sb
**Ży|d** (**-da, -dzi**) (*loc sg* **-dzie**) *m* Jew
**żydowski** *adj* Jewish
**Żydów|ka** (**-ki, -ki**) (*dat sg* **-ce**, *gen pl* **-ek**) *f* Jew
**żyla|k** (**-ka, -ki**) (*instr sg* **-kiem**) *m* varicose vein
**żylasty** *adj* (*mięso*) stringy; (*człowiek, ręka*) veiny, sinewy
**żylet|ka** (**-ki, -ki**) (*dat sg* **-ce**, *gen pl* **-ek**) *f* razor blade
**żylny** *adj* venous
**ży|ła** (**-ły, -ły**) (*loc sg* **-le**) *f* vein; **~ złota** (*przen*) gold mine; **wypruwać z siebie żyły** (*przen*) to work one's fingers to the bone
**żył|ka** (**-ki, -ki**) (*dat sg* **-ce**, *gen pl* **-ek**) *f* small vein, veinlet; (*nić*) fishing line; (*przen: zamiłowanie*) bent; **mieć żyłkę do czegoś** to have a bent for sth
**żyra|fa** (**-fy, -fy**) (*loc sg* **-fie**) *f* giraffe
**żyrandol** (**-a, -e**) (*gen pl* **-i**) *m* chandelier
**żyran|t** (**-ta, -ci**) (*loc sg* **-cie**) *m* guarantor

**ży|ro** (**-ra, -ra**) (*loc sg* **-rze**) *nt* (*Handel*) guaranty, guarantee
**żyrokompa|s** (**-su, -sy**) (*loc sg* **-sie**) *m* gyro compass
**żyrosko|p** (**-pu, -py**) (*loc sg* **-pie**) *m* gyroscope
**żyr|ować (-uję, -ujesz)** (*perf* **pod-**) *vt* to guaranty, to guarantee
**żytni** *adj* rye *attr*
**żytniów|ka** (**-ki, -ki**) (*dat sg* **-ce**) *f vodka distilled from rye*
**ży|to** (**-ta, -ta**) (*loc sg* **-cie**) *nt* rye
**żywcem** *adv*: **brać (wziąć** *perf*) **kogoś ~** to take sb alive; **przepisać** (*perf*) **coś ~** (*pot*) to rip sth off
**żywic|a** (**-y, -e**) *f* resin
**żywiciel** (**-a, -e**) (*gen pl* **-i**) *m* (*rodziny*) breadwinner
**ży|wić (-wię, -wisz)** *vt* (*karmić*) to feed; (*przen*: *utrzymywać*) (*perf* **wy-**) to support; (: *nadzieję*) to cherish; (: *niechęć, nienawiść*) to feel; **żywić się** *vr*: **~ się czymś** to feed on sth
**ży|wiec** (**-wca**) *m* (*zwierzęta hodowlane*) livestock; (*przynęta*) (*nom pl* **-wce**, *gen pl* **-wców**) live-bait
**żywieni|e** (**-a**) *nt* feeding
**żywio|ł** (**-łu, -ły**) (*loc sg* **-le**) *m* element; **być w swoim żywiole** to be in one's element
**żywiołowo** *adv* (*reagować*) vigorously; (*rozwijać się*) spontaneously
**żywiołowy** *adj* (*rozwój*) spontaneous; (*temperament*) impetuous; **klęska żywiołowa** natural disaster
**żywnościowy** *adj* (*artykuł, produkt*) food *attr*; **kartka żywnościowa** food stamp
**żywnoś|ć** (**-ci**) *f* food
**żywo** *adv* (*energicznie*: *poruszać się*) briskly; (*intensywnie*: *interesować się*) keenly; (: *reagować*) strongly; **na ~** (*przekazywać, transmitować*) live
**żywopło|t** (**-tu, -ty**) (*loc sg* **-cie**) *m* hedge
**żywoś|ć** (**-ci**) *f* vitality
**żywo|t** (**-ta, -ty**) (*loc sg* **-cie**) *m* (*książk*) life
**żywotnie** *adv* vitally
**żywotny** *adj* vital
**żywy** *adj* (*żyjący*) living; (*dziecko, taniec, fabuła*) lively; (*kolor, wspomnienie*) vivid; **to on, jak ~** it's him to the life; **kłamać w żywe oczy** to lie through one's teeth; **żywa gotówka** (*pot*) hard *lub* ready cash; **dotknąć** (*perf*) **kogoś do żywego** to cut sb to the quick
**żyzny** *adj* fertile

# Polish Grammar

## Contents

# Polish Consonants chart

Polish is an inflected language. This means that – unlike in English – the relation between the words in the sentence is reflected in the word endings (suffixes). In Polish, the form of these endings depends on the last consonant in the word. For example, nouns in the declension system in the locative case, or adjectives in the comparative form, or plural form endings etc. all depend on the type of the last consonant in the word. It is therefore important to be familiar with the consonant types as this will make it easier to produce correct grammatical forms.

It is important to recognise the difference between letters with no special marks and letters with marks, which are called **diacritics**. Diacritics are marks that appear below the letter (**ę**, **ą**) or above it (e.g. **ó**, **ż**, **ń**, or **ł** – the last one in written language is highlighted on top of the letter **l**). Diacritics indicate a change in the pronunciation for the letter they are used with. The differences are reflected in the meaning, e.g. **że** = that, while **ze** = with; from. Diacritics do not have any influence over where the stress lies in a word – in Polish, this is usually on the penultimate syllable.

**Hard consonants** are those consonants that are either followed by another consonant or are not followed by any other letter/sound, and do not have any diacritics. However, consonants **–k**, and **–g** tend to often follow different rules from other hard consonants. The consonant **–ł** is a hard consonant (the dash through the **–'l'** is not treated as a diacritic), and the cluster **–ch** corresponds to one sound and is therefore treated as one consonant. Furthermore, letters **–j**, **–l**, and **–c** are semi-soft.

**Soft consonants** are those that are either followed by the vowel **–i** (**–pi**, **–bi**, **–mi**, **–si**, **–li** etc.) or have the apostrophe diacritic (**–ś**, **–ć**, **–ń** etc.).

The letters with diacritic ' replace the diacritic with an **–i** before taking on a suffix:

**młodość – młodości** [genitive] *youth – youth*

**gość – goście** *guest – guests*

**koń – konie** *horse – horses*

**Semi-soft consonants** are those that form clusters with the letter **–z** (**–cz**, **–sz**, **–dz**), letter **–ż** and the cluster **–dż**, and semi-consonants **–c**, **–j**, and **–l**. However, the letters **–j**, and **–l** tend to have different endings from the rest of the group.

The table below illustrates typical changes that occur in Polish, for instance **–k** changes into **–c** in

a) the plural masculine animate virile of nouns, e.g. **Polak – Polacy** *a Pole – Poles*
b) the plural masculine animate virile of adjectives, e.g. **wysoki – wysocy** *tall* [**sing – pl**]
c) singular feminine nouns in the locative, e.g. **Polska – w Polsce** *Poland – in Poland*

# Polish Consonants chart

| Spółgłoski twarde (hard consonants) | | | | | | | | | | | | | | |
|---|---|---|---|---|---|---|---|---|---|---|---|---|---|---|
| p | b | f | w | t | d | s | z | k | g | ch | m | n | r | ł |
| **Spółgłoski miękkie (soft consonants)** | | | | | | | | | | | | | | |
| pi | bi | fi | wi | ć<br>ci | dź<br>dzi | ś<br>si | ź<br>zi | ki | gi | chi<br>ś<br>si | mi | ń<br>ni | ri | li |
| **Spółgłoski funkcjonalnie miękkie (semi-soft consonants)** | | | | | | | | | | | | | | |
| (j) | | | | c<br>cz | dz<br>dż | sz | ż | c<br>cz | ż<br>dz | sz | | | rz | / |

# Nouns

## Gender of nouns

Polish nouns take two numbers: singular and plural. In the singular, there are three genders, and in the plural there are two genders. Without exception, all nouns in Polish are allocated a grammatical gender.

## Singular

There are three main types of grammatical gender that can be recognised by the ending of the noun.

## Masculine nouns

– usually end in a consonant, e.g.

| **paszport** | **komputer** | **samochód** | **Kraków** | **Lichtenstein** |
|---|---|---|---|---|
| *passport* | *computer* | *car* | *Cracow* | *Liechtenstein* |

– end in the vowel **–a** when denoting a male family relation or an occupation, e.g.

| **tata** | **kolega** | **dyplomata** | **artysta** | **ekonomista** |
|---|---|---|---|---|
| *Dad* | *friend* | *diplomat* | *artist* | *economist* |

There are further types of the masculine noun depending on what/who they denote. These nouns do not have a particular ending:

**Masculine inanimate nouns** denote objects and ideas, e.g.

| **tekst** | **dokument** | **kryminał** | **słownik** | **parasol** |
|---|---|---|---|---|
| *text* | *document* | *a crime story* | *dictionary* | *umbrella* |

**Masculine animate nouns** denote men and animals, e.g.

| **brat** | **sąsiad** | **uczeń** | **pies** | **kot** |
|---|---|---|---|---|
| *brother* | *neighbour* | *pupil* | *dog* | *cat* |

**Masculine animate virile nouns** denote men only, e.g.

| **ojciec** | **nauczyciel** | **premier** | **informatyk** |
|---|---|---|---|
| *father* | *teacher* | *prime minister* | *IT specialist* |

There are some proper names, e.g. **Jerzy**, **Kowalski** or words relating to family and occupations, e.g. **znajomy** acquaintance, **księgowy** accountant, that denote people but end in **–i** or **–y**. This ending indicates that such words are adjectives and will therefore follow a declension pattern of adjectives.

## Feminine nouns

– usually end in **–a**, e.g.

| **kobieta** | **dziewczyna** | **książka** | **Warszawa** | **Anglia** | **Europa** |
|---|---|---|---|---|---|
| *woman* | *young woman* | *book* | *Warsaw* | *England* | *Europe* |

– can end in a soft consonant especially when referring to abstract ideas, e.g.

| **solidarność** | **narodowość** | **powieść** | **noc** | **twarz** | **Białoruś** | **jesień** |
|---|---|---|---|---|---|---|
| *solidarity* | *nationality* | *novel* | *night* | *face* | *Bielarus* | *autumn* |

– rarely end in **–i**, e.g.

| **Pani** | **gospodyni** | **sprzedawczyni** | **bogini** |
|---|---|---|---|
| *formal form of address; Ms* | *hostess* | *female sales assistant* | *goddess* |

There are some proper names, e.g. **Kowalska**, or words relating to female family members and occupations, e.g. **znajoma** acquaintance, **teściowa** mother-in-law, **księgowa** accountant, that end in **–ska** or **–owa**. This ending indicates that these words are likely to be adjectives and therefore follow a declension pattern of adjectives.

## Neuter nouns

– usually end in **–o** or **–e**, e.g.

| **słowo** | **wino** | **kino** | **Gniezno** | **mieszkanie** | **zdjęcie** |
|---|---|---|---|---|---|
| *word* | *wine* | *cinema* | *(a Polish town)* | *flat* | *photo* |

– end in **–ę** (these nouns tend to have an irregular plural ending), e.g.

| **imię** | **zwierzę** | **niemowlę** |
|---|---|---|
| *first name* | *animal* | *infant* |

– are foreign words that end in **–i** (they are non-declinable), e.g.

| **pepsi** | **sushi** | **spaghetti** |
|---|---|---|
| *pepsi* | *sushi* | *spaghetti* |

– are foreign words that end in **–um** (they retain the same form for all singular forms in all cases in the singular), e.g.

| **centrum** | **stypendium** | **archiwum** | **akwarium** |
|---|---|---|---|
| *centre* | *scholarship* | *archives* | *fish tank, aquarium* |

## Plural

There are two genders in the plural: **masculine animate virile** (i.e. nouns denoting men or groups of people that include men) and the **non-masculine animate virile** group (i.e. masculine animate, masculine inanimate, feminine and neuter). There are two personal pronouns for **they** to denote the two groups:

**oni** (*they* for masculine animate virile), e.g.

| **Polacy** | **studenci** | **ludzie** |
|---|---|---|
| *Poles* | *students* | *people* |

**one** (*they* for all the other nouns), e.g.

| **filmy** | **psy** | **dziewczyny** | **dzieci** | **zdjęcia** |
|---|---|---|---|---|
| *films* | *dogs* | *young women* | *children* | *photos* |

The two plural forms require different endings of e.g. adjectives or verbs. The pronouns are rarely used explicitly in sentences, however, they are evident in the choice of the verb or adjective ending.

**Na premierę filmu przybyli aktorzy [=oni], którzy pozowali do zdjęć z fanami.**
*The first night was attended by actors who posed for pictures with their fans.*
**W naszym ogródku rosną truskawki [= one]. W tym roku zakwitły w maju.**
*There are strawberries in our garden. This year they bloomed in May.*

## Case system

The notion of case is crucial in Polish grammar. In a nutshell, it indicates the role nouns, adjectives and pronouns can play in a sentence. For example: **Adam mieszka z Anną**. (*Adam lives with Anna*) can be reordered to **Z Anną mieszka Adam**. (*With-Anna-lives-Adam*). The meaning of both sentences is the same.
What differs is the focus, which is usually on the last item of the clause. The same word takes a different ending depending on its role in a given context/sentence, for instance:

**Adam lubi grać w piłkę.**
*Adam* [nominative, subject] *likes playing football.*
**Piłka nożna interesuje Adama.**
*Football interests Adam* [accusative, direct object].
**Wczoraj grałem z Adamem w piłkę.**
*Yesterday I played football with Adam* [instrumental, prepositional phrase]

## Nouns

There are seven cases (*nominative*, *genitive*, *dative*, *accusative*, *instrumental*, *locative* and *vocative*) and two numbers (singular and plural) in the declension of Polish nouns. Since most endings are quite regular for each gender, they are not shown in this dictionary. However, each noun entry in the dictionary includes the genitive singular ending (or genitive plural for plural-only nouns). These endings are given in brackets right after the headword and separated with a comma, for example:

**pies (psa, psy)** *dog*
**kompute|r (–ra, –ry)** *computer*

If a given word has no plural form, only the genitive singular ending is shown after the headword, e.g.

**młodoś|ć (–ci)** *youth*

Irregular forms are given in smaller print before the part of speech information or, when limited to a specific sense of the word, inside the entry:

**ko|t (–ta, –ty)** (*loc sg* **–cie**) *m cat*

## Nominal phrase agreement

Adjectives, pronouns, numerals and other elements that describe a noun in a phrase have to agree with the noun in case, number and gender. This is called grammatical agreement and is an essential part of the Polish language.

## Nominative

The nominative is the form of the noun you find when you look up a Polish word in the dictionary. Nominative forms are also used:

– For the subject of the sentence:
**Słownik podaje wszystkie formy gramatyczne danego słowa.**
*The dictionary lists all grammatical forms of a given word.*

– After some prepositions, e.g. **niż** than,
**Dolar jest tańszy niż euro.**
*The dollar is cheaper than the euro.*

The plural form of the nominative is provided in the dictionary.

## Genitive

The genitive is the most frequent case in Polish and it has a variety of functions, including:

- the direct object of negative sentences if the direct object is in the accusative in statements, e.g.

  **Nie mam samochodu.** — *I do not have a car.*

  **Moja żona nie lubi kawy.** — *My wife does not like coffee.*

- the direct object after some verbs, (**uczyć się**, **potrzebować**, **chcieć**, **bać się** etc.)

  **Uczę się języka polskiego.** — *I am learning Polish.*

  **Potrzebuję urlopu.** — *I need a holiday.*

- to indicate possession, e.g.

  **wypowiedź prezydenta** — *the president's statement*

  **koniec filmu** — *the end of the film*

- after words denoting quantity or measure (including numerals of 5 and more),

  **dużo czasu** — *a lot of time*

  **wielu studentów** — *many students*

- after some prepositions (usually following verbs of motion). The dictionary will indicate when the genitive form is required by adding a note (+ *gen*):

– **do** to
**idę do pracy** *I'm going to work*
**pasta do zębów** *toothpaste*
**poprawka do ustawy** *bill amendment*

– **z** from [a place], in, (out of), of [often not translated by a preposition in English]
**przyjeżdżam z Polski** *I'm returning from Poland*
**ćwiczenie z gramatyki** *a grammar exercise*
**krzyknął z radości** *he cried out of joy*

– **od** from [a person],
**kartka od Ani** *a card from Ania*
**jak wrócę od dentysty** *when I come back from the dentist's*

– **koło / około / obok** next to, near, around
**siedzi koło okna** *she/he sits next to the window*

**mamy około godziny** *we have approximately an hour*
**usiądź obok mnie** *sit by me*

– **u** at sb's place
**spotkajmy się u mnie** *let's meet at my place*
**spotkanie u prezydenta** *the meeting at the president's [palace/office]*

– **dla** for
**jest wiadomość dla ciebie** *there is a message for you*

– **bez** without
**bez cukru / konsultacji** *without sugar/consultation*

– **oprócz** except for
**oprócz poniedziałków** *except for Mondays*

– **wśród / pośród** among
**nie było wśród nich ochotników** *there were no volunteers among them*

– **podczas** during
**podczas wojny / kadencji** *during the war / term*

The genitive singular form is given in the dictionary entry; the plural form for masculine nouns is usually **–ów** or, after semi soft consonants, **–i**, for feminine and neuter nouns the ending **–a**, **–e**, **–ę** or **–o** is dropped.

## Dative

The dative case is mainly used with personal pronouns:

- after some verbs
  **Czy ci się to podoba?** *Do you like it?*
  **Udało nam się dostać zniżkę.** *We managed to get a discount.*
  **Dziękuję państwu za uwagę.** *Thank you* [formal] *for your attention.*

- as indirect object
  **Kupiłam prezent ojcu.** *I bought my father a present.*
  **Czy możesz mi to wytłumaczyć?** *Can you explain this to me?*

- with adverbs to denote a certain state
  **Zimno mi.** *I'm cold.*
  **Przykro nam, że...** *We are sorry that...*

- after prepositions
  – **przeciw, przeciwko, wbrew** against
    **Jestem przeciwko Unii Europejskiej.** *I am against the EU.*
    **To jest wbrew naszym przekonaniom.** *This is against our convictions.*

  – **dzięki** thanks to
    **Zdałem egzamin dzięki ciężkiej pracy.** *I passed the exam thanks to hard work.*

The dative singular is formed as follows:

- monosyllabic masculine words and most neuter ones add the ending **–u**
- longer masculine words add the ending **–owi**
- feminine nouns ending in
  – soft consonants add **–i**
  – semi-soft consonants add **–y**
  – hard consonants add **–ie**; consonants **–k**, **–g**, **–r**, **–d**, **–t**, **–ł** require certain changes

The dative plural of all genders is formed by adding the ending **–om** to the nominative singular.

## Accusative

The accusative is used to fulfil the following functions:

- the direct object of the sentence after verbs that take the accusative case:
  **Lubię kawę.** *I like coffee.*
  **Czy często czytasz gazety?** *Do you read newspapers often?*

- after prepositions (usually following verbs of motion; please also consult the section on dual case prepositions for more information):
  – **na** for, to
    **Idę na koncert / film / kawę / zakupy.**
    *I'm going to a concert / to see a film / for a coffee/to do some shopping.*

  – **przez** through, via
    **patrzeć przez okno** *to look through the window*
    **rozmawiać przez telefon** *to talk on the phone*
    **przez godzinę** *for an hour*

  – **w** on, to:
    on days of the week
    **w poniedziałek / środę / niedzielę** *on Monday /Wednesday / Sunday*

to go to the mountains
**Jedziemy w góry / Tatry / Himalaje.**
*We are going to the mountains / the Tatras / the Himalayas.*

in, (in)to, up
**miły w dotyku** *nice to the touch*
**przyjść w odwiedziny** *to come with a visit; to pay a visit*
**wpaść w dobry humor** *get into a good mood*
**patrzeć w górę** *to look up[wards]*

– **po** to fetch something
**Idę [do sklepu] po chleb.** *I'm going [to the shops to buy] bread.*

– **między** between
**włóżyć gazetę między książki** *to put the newspaper in between books*

– **nad** to the sea / lake / ocean etc.
**Na wakacje jedziemy nad morze.** *We are going to the seaside for our holidays.*

– **pod** under, below
**Połóż torbę pod stół.** *Put the bag under the table.*

– **ponad** more than; above
**To jest ponad moje siły.** *This is more than I can do.*
**Samolot wzbił się ponad chmury.** *The plane went up above the clouds.*

– **poza** beyond
**To wychodzi poza moje obowiązki.** *This goes beyond my duties.*

– **za:**
outside; out of, away
**W weekend często jedziemy za miasto.**
*At the weekend we often go out of town [to the country].*

for, in favour of
**Przepraszam za spóźnienie.** *I'm sorry I'm late.*
**Dziękuję za prezent.** *Thank you for your present.*

in [amount of time]
**Za tydzień wyjeżdżamy na urlop.** *In a week we are going away on holiday.*
**Wyniki wyborów będą opublikowane za godzinę.**
*The election results will be released in an hour.*

In the singular, the accusative is formed as follows:

- Masculine nouns
  – Animate nouns that end in a consonant take the ending **–a**
  **brat – brata** *brother* **lekarz – lekarza** *doctor*
  **polityk – polityka** *politician* **nauczyciel – nauczyciela** *teacher*

  – Animate nouns that end in **–a** take the ending **–ę**
  **turysta – turystę** *tourist* **sprzedawca – sprzedawcę** *sales assistant*
  **tata – tatę** *dad* **ekonomista – ekonomistę** *economist*

- Feminine nouns
  – Nouns that end in **–a** replace the ending with an **–ę**
  **książka – książkę** book **komórka – komórkę** mobile phone
  **Czy możesz mi pożyczyć gazetę?** *Can you lend me a newspaper?*

  – Nouns that end in a consonant retain the same form as the nominative
  **Właśnie czytam tę powieść.** *I'm reading this novel at the moment.*
  **Najbardziej lubię jesień.** *I like the autumn the best.*

  – Neuter nouns retain the same form as the nominative
  **Do obiadu często piję wino.** *I often drink wine with my dinner.*

In the plural, the masculine animate virile group take the ending **–ów**, whereas the other group takes the same form of the plural as the plural nominative.

## Instrumental

The instrumental is used to fulfil the following functions:

- the direct object or verb complement, e.g.

| **być** | **stać się** | **interesować się** | **zajmować się** | **cieszyć się** |
|---|---|---|---|---|
| *to be* | *to became* | *to be interested in* | *to deal with* | *to be glad* |

**Jestem Polką / nauczycielką.** *I am Polish / a teacher.*
**Stolicą Polski jest Warszawa.** *The capital of Poland is Warsaw.*
**Interesuję się sportem.** *I'm interested in sport.*
**Czym się zajmujesz w wolnym czasie?** *What do you do in your free time?*

- the indirect object or an adverbial clause:
  - using a tool, instrument, material etc.
    **Piszę długopisem.** *I write in pen.*
    **Oni handlują narkotykami.** *They deal in narcotics.*
    **Do pracy jeżdżę metrem.** *I travel to work by tube.*

  - some time expressions
    **Wstałam rankiem.** *I got up early in the morning.*
    **Wrócił do domu wieczorem.** *He came back home in the evening.*

  - location of the event
    **Szliśmy ulicą Prostą.** *We walked along Prosta street.*
    **Spacerowaliśmy plażą.** *We walked along the beach.*

  - cause or result
    **Jesienią łatwo zarazić się grypą.** *It's easy to go down with a flu in the autumn.*
    **Uśmiechem zjednywała sobie ludzi.** *She won people over with her smile.*

  - manner
    **Ludzie napływali grupami.** *People came in groups.*
    **Zrobił to migiem.** *He did it in a flash.*

- after prepositions (usually following verbs of location):
  - **między** between, among
    **między książkami** *between/amongst books*
    **między nami mówiąc** *between you and me*

  - **nad / ponad** over; above
    **Mieszkanie jest nad sklepem.** *The flat is above the shop.*

  - **nad / ponad** on / about
    **Nad jakim projektem pracujesz?** *Which project are you working on?*

  - **pod** under / below
    **Sklep jest pod mieszkaniem.** *The shop is below the flat.*
    **pod przysięgą** *under oath*
    **pod moją opieką** *under my care*

  - **pod** at the foot of/at the outskirts of
    **Supermarket jest pod miastem.** *The supermarket is just outside the town.*
    **Mój dom stoi pod lasem.** *My house is located just outside the forest.*

– **poza** outside; beyond

**Sędzam dużo czasu <u>poza domem</u>.** *I spend a lot of time <u>away from home</u>.*

**To jest <u>poza moją kontrolą</u>.** *This is <u>beyond my control</u>.*

– **przed** in front of

**Sklep jest <u>przed bankiem</u>.** *The shop is <u>in front of the bank</u>.*

– **przed** before

**przed lekcją** *before the class*

**Reklamy wyświetlane są <u>przed filmem</u>.** *Adverts are shown <u>before the film</u>.*

– **z** together with

**z rodzicami** *with parents*

**Proszę o kanapkę <u>z serem</u>.** *A sandwich <u>with cheese</u> please.*

– **za** behind

**za stołem** *behind the table*

**za miastem** *out of town*

– **za** by

**za okazaniem paszportu** *by showing your passport*

**za pozwoleniem** *by permission*

Singular, masculine and neuter nouns take the ending **–(i)em**, while feminine nouns take the ending **–ą**. In the plural, all nouns take the ending **–ami**.

## Locative

The locative case is only used after certain prepositions to say where an activity takes place, and in some cases, when it takes place:

- location after prepositions

  – **w** in

  **Mieszkam <u>w Polsce</u>.** *I live <u>in Poland</u>.*

  **<u>W moim mieście</u> jest wiele interesujących zabytków.**
  *<u>In my town</u> there are many interesting tourist attractions.*

  – **na** on, at

  **Biuro szefa jest <u>na parterze</u>.** *The director's office is <u>on the ground floor</u>.*

  **Wczoraj byłam <u>na dobrym koncercie</u>.** *Last night I was <u>at a good concert</u>.*

– **przy** at, beside
**Przy rynku jest dobry bar.** *There is a good bar beside the market square.*

– **po** around
**W weekend często spaceruję po mieście.**
*At the weekend I often walk around/in the park.*
**Wielu młodych ludzi przed studiami podróżuje po świecie.**
*Many young people travel round the world during their gap year.*

- relation to time after prepositions
  – **po** after
  **Po pracy często chodzę na siłownię.** *After work I often go to the gym.*

  – **w** in (with months of the year)
  **W lipcu jeździmy na urlop.** *In July we go on annual leave.*
  **Najwięcej świąt przypada w grudniu.** *Most holidays fall in December.*

- introducing a topic after the preposition **o** about, on
  **artykuł o gramatyce** *an article on grammar*
  **książka o historii Polski** *a Polish history book / a book on Polish history*

The locative singular is formed by using many different consonant changes, all of which depend on the last consonant of the nominative form of the noun:

- semi soft and soft consonants
  – masculine and neuter nouns take the ending **–u**
  **hotel – w hotelu** *hotel – at the hotel*
  **korytarz – na korytarzu** *corridor – in the corridor*
  **mieszkanie – w mieszkaniu** *flat – in the flat*
  **zdjęcie – na zdjęciu** *picture – in the picture*

  – feminine nouns that end in soft and semisoft consonants take the same ending as in the genitive singular (these forms are provided in the dictionary)

- consonants **–k** and **–g**
  – masculine and neuter nouns take the ending **–u**
  **słownik – w słowniku** *dictionary – in the dictionary*
  **rok – w tym roku** *year – this year*
  **biurko – na biurku** *desk – on the desk*
  **radio – w radiu** *radio – on the radio*

–feminine nouns change:

**–ka** into **–ce**

**Polska – w Polsce** *Poland – in Poland*
**biblioteka – w bibliotece** *library – in the library*
**półka – na półce** *shelf – on the shelf*
**Ameryka – w Ameryce** *America – in America*

**–ga** into **–dze**

**Kopenhaga – w Kopenhadze** *Copenhagen – in Copenhagen*
**noga – na nodze** *leg – on the leg*

- Hard consonants

–The following consonants change:

**–t(a/o)** changes into **–cie**

**świat – na świecie** *world – in the world*
**Beata – o Beacie** *Beata – about Beata*
**miasto – w mieście** *town – in the town*

**–d(a/o)** changes into **–dzie**

**obiad – po obiedzie** *dinner – after dinner*
**wykład – na wykładzie** *lecture – at the lecture*
**moda – w modzie** *fashion – in fashion*

**–r(a/o)** changes to **–rze**

**teatr – w teatrze** *theatre – in the theatre*
**komputer – na komputerze** *computer – on computer*
**biuro – w biurze** *office – in the office*

**–ł(a/o)** changes into **–le**

**stół – na stole** *table – on the table*
**szkoła – w szkole** *at school*
**krzesło – na krześle** *chair – on the chair*

**–cha** changes to **–sze**

**mucha – w musze** *bow tie – in a bow tie*
**pycha – w pysze** *pride – in pride*

–Other hard consonants take the ending **–ie**

**Kraków – w Krakowie** *Kraków – in Cracow*
**Warszawa – w Warszawie** *Warsaw – in Warsaw*
**Londyn – w Londynie** *London – in London*

**dywan – na dywanie** *carpet – on the carpet*
**lampa – przy lampie** *lamp – at the lamp*
**kino – w kinie** *cinema – at the cinema*

The locative plural is formed by adding the ending **–ach** to the nominative singular form of all nouns.

## Vocative

The vocative is the least used case in Polish. Its main function is to be used in forms of address such as at the beginning of a letter, e.g. **Drogi Tomku** Dear Tomek, or when addressing someone, e.g.

**Tomku, podaj mi sól.** *Tomek, pass the salt please.*
**Pani Anno, co u pani słychać.** *Anna (formal way of address), how are you.*

In the singular, the vocative is formed as follows:

- Masculine nouns tend to have the same form as the locative singular
  **pan doktor – panie doktorze** *doctor*
  **człowiek – człowieku** *man*

  – There are some exceptions to this rule, e.g.
  **ojciec – ojcze** *father*
  **pan – panie** *Mr, Lord*

- Feminine nouns
  – that end in **–a** replace the ending with **–o**
  **mama – mamo** *mum*
  **Marta – Marto** *Marta*

  – that end in a consonant, just like in the genitive and locative, take the ending **–i**
  **młodość – młodości** *youth*
  **złość – złości** *anger*

- Neuter nouns have the same form as the nominative singular

In the plural, the vocative has the same form as the nominative plural.

## Overview of cases (nouns) – Singular

| | Masculine | | | Feminine | | | | | | Neuter | |
|---|---|---|---|---|---|---|---|---|---|---|---|
| | virile | animate | Inanimate | **–ka, –ga** | **–la, –ja** | **–ia** (Polish origin) | **–ia** (loan words) | Soft consonant | Hard consonant | **–o, –e, –ę** | **–um, –i** |
| **Nominative** | *Always shown in noun entry* | | | | | | | | | | |
| **Genitive** | *Always shown in noun entry* | | | | | | | | | | |
| **Dative** | **–u** *(monosyllabic) or* **–owi** *(longer words)* | | | *Change to* **–ce** *and* **–dze** | **–i** | **–i** | **–ii** | **–ii** | **–ie** *or consonant change* | **–u** | |
| **Accusative** | ***–a*** | ***–a*** | *As nominative* | **–ę** | **–ę** | **–ę** | **–ę** | *As nominative* | **–ę** | *As nominative* | |
| **Instrumental** | ***–(i)em*** | | | ***–ą*** | | | | | | ***–(i)em*** | |
| **Locative** | *Always shown in noun entry* | | | | | | | | | | |
| **Vocative** | ***–e*** *or* ***–u*** | | | ***–o*** | | | | **–i** | ***–o*** | *As nominative* | |

## Overview of cases (nouns) – Plural

| | Masculine | | | Feminine | | | | | | Neuter | |
|---|---|---|---|---|---|---|---|---|---|---|---|
| | virile | animate | Inanimate | **–ka, –ga** | **–la, –ja** | **–ia** (Polish origin) | **–ia** (loan words) | Soft consonant | Hard consonant | **–o, –e, –ę** | **–um, –i** |
| **Nominative** | *Always shown in noun entry* | | | | | | | | | | |
| **Genitive** | **–ów** *or* **–y** | | | *Dropped* **–a** | | | | **–i** | *Dropped* **–a** | *Dropped* **–o** *and* **–e** | **–ów** |
| **Dative** | **–om** | | | | | | | | | | |
| **Accusative** | **–ów** | *As nominative plural* | | | | | | | | | |
| **Instrumental** | **–ami** | | | | | | | | | | |
| **Locative** | **–ach** | | | | | | | | | | |
| **Vocative** | **–e** | | | **–ie** | | | | | **–y** | *As nominative* | |

## Pronouns

Pronouns are used instead of a noun, when you don't need or want to name someone or something directly. They help maintain the coherence of the text without unnecessary repetition. Just like nouns, pronouns are declined according to gender, case and number.

### Singular Nominative

**Ja** *I*
**Ty** *you* (informal singular)
**Pan** *you* (masculine formal singular)
**Pani** *you* (feminine formal singular)
**On** *he, it* (replaces all masculine nouns in the singular)
**Ona** *she, it* (replaces all feminine nouns in the singular)
**Ono** *it* (replaces all neuter nouns in the singular)

**„Kto chce pójść do kina?" „Ja!"**
*"Who wants to go to the cinema?" "I do!"*
**Czy pan mówi po polsku?**
*Do you* (formal masculine singular) *speak Polish?*

**To nasza nowa nauczycielka. Ona jest bardzo sympatyczna.**
*This is our new teacher* (feminine singular). *She is very nice.*
**To nasza nowa lodówka. Ona nie zajmuje dużo miejsca.**
*This is our new fridge* (feminine singular). *It does not take up too much space.*

**Spytaj się mojego brata, bo on powinien znać odpowiedź.**
*Ask my brother* (masculine animate virile singular) *as he* (masculine animate virile singular) *should know the answer.*
**Podoba mi się ten sweter. Ile on kosztuje?**
*I like this cardigan* (masculine inanimate singular). *How much is it?*

### Plural Nominative

**My** *we*
**Wy** *you* (informal plural)
**Panowie** *you* (masculine formal plural)
**Panie** *you* (feminine formal plural)
**Państwo** *you* (mixed gender formal plural)
**Oni** *they* (masculine virile animate)
**One** *they* (masculine animate non-virile, masculine inanimate, feminine and neuter)

**Czy panowie potrzebują pomocy?**
*Do you* (formal masculine animate virile plural) *need help?*
**To są nasi nowi sąsiedzi. Oni wydają się bardzo mili.**
*These are our new neighbours* (masculine animate virile plural). *They seem very nice.*
**Kupiłam te buty, bo były one na przecenie.**
*I bought these shoes* (mascule inanimate plulral) *as they were on sale.*

With the exception of the pronouns that are used for formal ways of address, other pronouns are not always used explicitly in sentences since the ending of the verb indicates the person and number, and sometimes the gender.

Where there is more than one form, the longest form is used after the preposition, the medium one is used at the beginning of the sentence (to emphasise the word), and the shortest form is used as a direct object in the middle or at the end of the sentence, e.g.

**Poczekaj na mnie.** *Wait for me.* (accusative after the preposition)
**Zrozum mnie.** *Try and understand me.* (accusative, direct object without the preposition)
**To duży supermarket, a obok niego jest parking dla klientów.**
*This is a large supermarket and next to it is a large car park for customers.* (genitive, with a preposition)
**To nasz nowy sąsiad. Lubię go bardzo.**
*This is our new neighbour. I like him a lot.*

## Personal pronouns

### Singular

| Nominative | Genitive | Dative | Accusative | Instrumental | Locative |
|---|---|---|---|---|---|
| ja | mnie | mi | mnie | mną | mnie |
| ty | ciebie, cię | tobie, ci | ciebie, cię | tobą | tobie |
| on | niego, jego, go | niemu, jemu, mu | niego, jego, go | nim | nim |
| pan | pana | panu | pana | panem | panu |
| ona | niej, jej | niej, jej | nią, ją | nią | niej |
| pani | pani | pani | pani | panią | pani |
| ono | niego, jego, go | niemu, jemu, mu | je | nim | nim |

## Plural

| Nominative | Genitive | Dative | Accusative | Instrumental | Locative |
|---|---|---|---|---|---|
| my | nas | nam | nas | nami | nas |
| wy | was | wam | was | wami | was |
| oni | nich, ich | nim, im | nich, ich | nimi | nich |
| panowie | panów | panom | panów | panami | panach |
| państwo | państwa | państwu | państwo | państwem | państwie |
| one | nich, ich | nim, im | nie, je | nimi | nich |
| panie | pań | paniom | panie | paniami | paniach |

# Demonstrative pronouns

**ten** *this one* (masculine singular)
**ta** *this one* (feminine singular)
**to** *this one* (neuter singular)
**ci** *these ones* (masculine viral plural)
**te** *these ones* (masculine non-viral animate and inanimate, feminine and neuter)

| Nominative | Genitive | Dative | Accusative | | Instrumental | Locative |
|---|---|---|---|---|---|---|
| | | | Animate | Inanimate | | |
| ten | tego | temu | tego | ten | tym | tym |
| ta | tej | tej | tę | | tą | tej |
| to | tego | temu | to | | tym | tym |
| ci | tych | tym | tych | | tymi | tych |
| te | tych | tym | te | | tymi | tych |

The same pattern is applied to:

**tamten** *that one* (masculine singular)
**tamta** *that one* (feminine singular)
**tamto** *that one* (neuter singular)
**tamci** *those ones* (masculine viral plural)
**tamte** *these ones* (masculine non-viral animate and inanimate, feminine and neuter)

## Possessive pronouns

Possessive pronouns must agree with the gender of the noun they modify:

**<u>mój</u> słownik** *<u>my</u> dictionary* (masculine singular)
**Ten słownik jest <u>mój</u>.** *This dictionary is <u>mine</u>.* (masculine singular)
**<u>moja</u> torebka** *<u>my</u> handbag* (feminine singular)
**<u>moje</u> pióro** *<u>my</u> pen* (neuter singular)
**<u>moi</u> rodzice** *<u>my</u> parents* (masculine animate virile plural)

| Nominative | Genitive | Dative | Accusative | | Instrumental | Locative |
|---|---|---|---|---|---|---|
| | | | Animate | Inanimate | | |
| **mój** | **mojego** | **mojemu** | **mojego** | **mój** | **moim** | **moim** |
| **moja** | **mojej** | **mojej** | **moją** | | **moją** | **mojej** |
| **moje** *(s)* | **mojego** | **mojemu** | **moje** | | **moim** | **moim** |
| **moi** | **moich** | **moim** | **moich** | | **moimi** | **moich** |
| **moje** *(pl)* | **moich** | **moim** | **moje** | | **moimi** | **moich** |

| Nominative | Genitive | Dative | Accusative | | Instrumental | Locative |
|---|---|---|---|---|---|---|
| | | | Animate | Inanimate | | |
| **twój** | **twojego** | **twojemu** | **twojego** | **twój** | **twoim** | **twoim** |
| **twoja** | **twojej** | **twojej** | **twoją** | | **twoją** | **twojej** |
| **twoje** *(s)* | **twojego** | **twojemu** | **twoje** | | **twoim** | **twoim** |
| **twoi** | **twoich** | **twoim** | **twoich** | | **twoimi** | **twoich** |
| **twoje** *(pl)* | **twoich** | **twoim** | **twoje** | | **twoimi** | **twoich** |

## Swój

The pronoun **swój** (one's own) refers to the subject of the sentence and can be used with all persons. Therefore it is essential to distinguish between **swój** and **jego** (his, someone else's), **jej** (her, someone else's) and **ich** (their, someone else's).

**Adam kocha <u>swoją</u> pracę.** *Adam loves <u>his (own)</u> job.*
**Tomek ma taką samą kurtkę. Adam musiał wziąć <u>jego</u> przez pomyłkę.**
*Tomek has the same jacket. Adam must have taken <u>his (Tomek's)</u> by mistake.*

**Państwo Kowalscy uczą <u>swoje</u> dzieci.** *The Kowalskis teach <u>their (own)</u> children.*
**Państwo Kowalscy znają państwa Nowaków, bo uczą <u>ich</u> dzieci.**
*The Kowalskis know the Nowaks because they teach <u>their (the Nowaks')</u> children.*

**Turystka pokazała celnikowi <u>swoje</u> dokumenty.**

*The tourist showed the immigration officer her (own) documents.*
**Celnik poprosił turystkę o jej dokumenty.**
*The immigration officer asked the tourist for her (the tourist's) documents.*

| Nominative | Genitive | Dative | Accusative | Instrumental | Locative |
|---|---|---|---|---|---|
| jego | | | | | |
| jej | | | | | |
| ich | | | | | |

| Nominative | Genitive | Dative | Accusative | | Instrumental | Locative |
|---|---|---|---|---|---|---|
| | | | Animate | Inanimate | | |
| **swój** | **swojego** | **swojemu** | **swojego** | **swój** | **swoim** | **swoim** |
| **swoja** | **swojej** | **swojej** | **swoją** | | **swoją** | **swojej** |
| **swoje** *(s)* | **swojego** | **swojemu** | **swój** | | **swoim** | **swoim** |
| **swoi** | **swoich** | **swoim** | **swoich** | | **swoimi** | **swoich** |
| **swoje** *(pl)* | **swoich** | **swoim** | **swoje** | | **swoimi** | **swoich** |

## Indefinite pronouns

Indefinite pronouns like *anyone*, *someone*, *something* or *nothing* refer to people or things in a general way without saying exactly who or what they are.

**Czy ktoś wie, gdzie jest toaleta?** *Does anyone know where the toilet is?*
**Potrzebuję czegoś do pisania.** *I need something to write with.*

| Nominative | Genitive | Dative | Accusative | Instrumental | Locative |
|---|---|---|---|---|---|
| ktoś | kogoś | komuś | kogoś | kimś | kimś |
| coś | czegoś | czemuś | coś | czymś | czymś |

## Relative and question pronouns

The relative pronouns *who*, *which*, *that* etc. relate groups of words to nouns or other pronouns and are usually used to introduce additional information about the person or thing being discussed. In Polish, they are declined in the same way as adjectives.

**To jest książka, o której ci opowiadałam.**
*This is the book that (which) I was telling you about.*
**Kandydatka, która odpowiedziała na wszystkie pytania, dostała tę pracę.**
*The candidate who answered all the questions got this job.*

**Która jest godzina?** *What time is it?*
**Którego słownika potrzebujesz?** *Which dictionary do you need?*

| Nominative | Genitive | Dative | Accusative | | Instrumental | Locative |
|---|---|---|---|---|---|---|
| | | | Animate | Inanimate | | |
| który | którego | którym | którego | który | którym | którym |
| która | której | której | którą | | którą | której |
| które (*s*) | którego | którego | które | | którym | którym |
| którzy | których | którym | których | | którymi | których |
| które (*pl*) | których | którym | które | | którymi | których |

**Kto to jest?** *Who is this?* (nominative)
**Kim jest ten pan?** *Who is this man?* (instrumental)
**Kogo szukasz?** *Who are you looking for?* (genitive)

**Co to jest?** *What is this?* (nominative)
**Z czym jest ta kanapka?** *What is this sandwich with? (What is in this sandwich?)* (instrumental)
**Czemu się przyglądasz?** *What are you looking at?* (dative)

| Nominative | Genitive | Dative | Accusative | Instrumental | Locative |
|---|---|---|---|---|---|
| kto | kogo | komu | kogo | kim | kim |
| co | czego | czemu | co | czym | czym |

**Czyj jest ten samochód?** *Whose car is this?* (masculine singular nominative)
**Czyja jest ta kawa?** *Whose is this coffee?* (feminine singular nominative)
**Czyjego adresu szukasz?** *Whose address are you looking for?* (masculine singular genitive)

| Nominative | Genitive | Dative | Accusative | | Instrumental | Locative |
|---|---|---|---|---|---|---|
| | | | Animate | Inanimate | | |
| jaki | jakiego | jakiemu | jakiego | jaki | jakim | jakim |
| jaka | jakiej | jakiej | jaką | | jaką | jakiej |
| jakie (*s*) | jakiego | jakim | jakie | | jakim | jakim |
| jacy | jakich | jakim | jakich | | jakimi | jakich |
| jakie (*pl*) | jakich | jakim | jakie | | jakimi | jakich |

**Jaka jest pogoda?** *What's the weather like?* (feminine singular nominative)
**Jakiej kawy się napijesz?** *What kind of coffee would you like?* (feminine singular genitive)
**Jakie macie cele?** *What aims do you have?* (masculine non-animate plural accusative)

## Agreement with nouns

When you look up a Polish adjective in the dictionary, you find the masculine singular nominative form. Adjectives need to agree with the noun or pronoun they are describing in gender, case and number. Therefore, just like nouns, adjectives take different endings, e.g.

| **nowy dom** | **nowa książka** | **nowe ćwiczenie** | **nowi sąsiedzi** | **nowe okna** |
|---|---|---|---|---|
| *a new house* | *a new book* | *a new exercise* | *new neighbours* | *new windows* |

**To czarna kawa. Lubię czarną kawę.**
*This is black coffee.* (nominative feminine singular) *I like black coffee.* (accusative feminine singular)

**Londyn jest starym miastem. Gniezno i Kraków są starymi miastami.**
*London is an old town.* (instrumental neuter singular) *Gniezno and Kraków are old towns.* (instrumental neuter plural)

Adjectives that end in **–k** or **–g** in the masculine form always retain **–i** before adding a suffix that starts in an **–e**.

**To jest długi film.**
*This is a long film.* (nominative masculine inaminate singular)

**Byłam na długiej przerwie.**
*I was on a long break.* (locative feminine singular)

**Ten reżyser nigdy nie nakręcił tak długiego filmu.**
*This director has never directed such a long film. (genitive masculine inanimate singular)*

There are some words that end in **–n** or **–p** that also take the ending **–i**; they require it before all suffixes in all cases, genders and numbers. However, it is important to remember that these adjectives, although frequently used, are exceptions, e.g.

| **ostatni dzień** | **ostatnia godzina** | **ostatnie spotkanie** | **ostatni dyrektor** |
|---|---|---|---|
| *the last day* | *the last hour* | *the last meeting* | *the last director* |
| **średni uczeń** | **średnia pensja** | **średni pracownicy** | **średnie frytki** |
| *an average pupil* | *average pay* | *average employees* | *medium fries* |
| **głupi pomysł** | **głupia uwaga** | **głupie zachowanie** | **głupi ludzie** |
| *silly idea* | *silly comment* | *foolish behaviour* | *stupid people* |

## Plural form

When you look up a Polish adjective in the dictionary, you find the masculine singular nominative form. The plural endings for all cases, genders and numbers are regular and are listed in the table below. However, masculine animate virile nouns cause the last consonant of the adjective to change:

- **–ry** changes into **–rzy**
  **dobry dentysta – dobrzy dentyści** *good dentist – good dentists*

- **–ki** changes into **–cy**
  **bliski kuzyn – bliscy kuzyni** *close cousin – close cousins*
  **elegancki kelner – eleganccy kelnerzy** *elegant waiter – elegant waiters*

- **–gi** changes into **–dzy**
  **drogi kolega – drodzy koledzy** *dear friend – dear friends*

- **–ty** changes into **–ci**
  **pracowity student – pracowici studenci** *dilligent student – diligent students*

- **–dy** changes into **–dzi**
  **młody specjalista – młodzi specjaliści** *young specialist – young specialists*

- **–ły** changes into **–li**
  **miły sąsiad – mili sąsiedzi** *nice neighbour – nice neighbours*
  **mały chłopiec – mali chłopcy** *small boy – small boys*

- **–ży** changes into **–zi**
  **duży chłopak– duzi chłopcy** *big boy – big boys*

- **–ch** changes into **–si**
  **cichy mężczyzna – cisi mężczyźni** *quiet man – quiet men*

- **–oły** changes into **–eli**
  **wesoły syn – weseli synowie** *cheerful son – cheerful sons*

- **–ony** changes into **–eni**
  **wykształcony kandydat – wykształceni kandydaci**
  *well educated candidate – well educated candidates*

- **-y** ending is usually replaced with **–i**
  **romantyczny chłopak – romantyczni chłopcy**
  *romantic man – romantic men*

- **–ący**, **–ni** or **–pi** retain the same form
  **wymagający nauczyciel – wymagający nauczyciele**
  *demanding teacher – demanding teachers*
  **tani fryzjer – tani fryzjerzy**
  *cheap hairdresser – cheap hairdressers*
  **głupi człowiek – głupi ludzie**
  *silly man – silly people*

- for the comparative and superlative forms, **–szy** changes into **–si**
  **starszy brat – starsi bracia**
  *elder brother – elder brothers*
  **najlepszy pracownik – najlepsi pracownicy**
  *the best employee – the best employees*

## Overview of cases (adjectives)

| | Singular | | | | Plural | |
|---|---|---|---|---|---|---|
| | Masculine | | Feminine | Neuter | Virile | Other |
| | Animate | Inanimate | | | | |
| **Nominative** | *Always shown in the entry* | | –a | –e | –i *or* –y | –e |
| **Genitive** | –(i)ego | | –(i)ej | –(i)ego | –ich *or* –ych | |
| **Dative** | –(i)emu | | –(i)ej | –(i)emu | –om | |
| **Accusative** | –(i)ego | *As nominative* | –ą | *As nominative* | | |
| **Instrumental** | –im *or* –ym | | –ą | –im *or* –ym | | |
| **Locative** | –im *or* –ym | | –(i)ej | –im *or* –ym | | |
| **Vocative** | *As nominative* | | | | | |

## Comparison of adjectives

To compare with other objects, ideas etc., adjectives can form their comparative and superlative forms by:

- adding the suffix **–szy** for the comparative and the prefix **naj–** for the superlative form. This is usually the form taken by short adjectives with one or two syllables
  **stary – starszy – najstarszy**
  *old – older – the oldest*
  **nowy – nowszy – najnowszy**
  *new – newer – the newest*

– Adjectives that end in two or more consonants usually add an additional syllable **–iej–** or **–zej–** to make pronunciation easier

**ładny – ładniejszy – najładniejszy**
*pretty – prettier – the prettiest*

**mądry – mądrzejszy – najmądrzejszy**
*clever – cleverer – the cleverest*

– Adjectives that end in **–gi** change the consonant to **–ż–**

**drogi – droższy – najdroższy**
*dear – dearer – the dearest*

**długi – dłuższy – najdłuższy**
*long – longer – the longest*

– Adjectives that end in **–ki** change the consonant to **–ż–** or drop it

**wysoki – wyższy – najwyższy**
*tall – taller – the tallest*

**słodki – słodszy – najsłodszy**
*sweet – sweeter – the sweetest*

– Adjectives that end in **–ły** change the consonant to **–l–**

**miły – milszy – najmilszy**
*nice – nicer – the nicest*

**ciepły – cieplejszy – najcieplejszy**
*warm – warmer – the warmest*

- using the descriptive form

  – add **bardziej** (more) to form the comparative and **najbardziej** (the most) to form the superlative. This form is used for longer words and also for words whose meaning is too abstract to compare

  **ciekawy – bardziej ciekawy – najbardziej ciekawy**
  *interesting – more interesting – the most interesting*
  **chory – bardziej chory – najbardziej chory**
  *ill – more ill – the most ill*

  – add **mniej** (less) to form the comparative and **najmniej** (the least) to form the superlative. This form is used with all adjectives

  **ładny – mniej ładny – najmniej ładny**
  *pretty – less pretty – the least pretty*

  **chory – mniej chory – najmniej chory**
  *ill – less ill – the least ill*

- irregular forms which are provided in the dictionary

  **dobry – lepszy – najlepszy**
  *good – better – the best*

  **zły – gorszy – najgorszy**
  *bad – worse – the worst*

## The infinitive and the finite verb form

When you look up a verb in the dictionary, you find the infinitive form. This usually ends in **–ć**, or in rare cases, **–c**, e.g.

| **pisać** | **mówić** | **grać** | **czytać** | **móc** | **biec** | **piec** |
|---|---|---|---|---|---|---|
| *to write* | *to speak* | *to play* | *to read* | *to be able to* | *to run* | *to bake* |

To conjugate the verb, the infinitive suffix is usually replaced with an ending that indicates the tense, person and number, and sometimes the gender of the performer of the action. This is the finite verb form.

| **pisać – piszę** | **móc – mogli** |
|---|---|
| *to write – I write* | *to be able to – they could* (+ the past tense ending) |

## Aspect of verbs – function

The Polish language has three tenses that indicate whether an action took place in the past, takes place in the present or will take place in the future. To convey more complex nuances of time, such as the length of the activity, its regularity, continuity or completion, the aspect of verbs are applied. Most Polish verbs come in pairs, one of them in each aspect, i.e. **niedokonany** (imperfective), which is the one provided as the entry in the dictionary, and **dokonany** (perfective):

The imperfective aspect is used to

- focus on the duration or length of an action (and not it's outcome), irrespective of how long (or short) the action is, e.g.
  **Czekaliśmy na autobus dwie godziny.** *We were waiting for the bus for two hours.*
  **Wczoraj wieczorem oglądałam wiadomości.** *Last night I was watching the news.*
  **Uczę się polskiego od miesiąca.** *I've been learning Polish for a month.*

- highlight a routine or a repeated action
  **Codziennie na śniadanie jem płatki z mlekiem.**
  *Everyday for breakfast I eat cereal with milk.*
  **Na wakacjach wstawaliśmy bardzo późno.** *On holiday we used to get up late.*

- provide background to another activity
  **Rozmawiałam przez telefon, gdy przyszedł listonosz.**
  *I was just talking on the phone when the postman arrived.*

**Będzie pracował za granicą, kiedy skończy 40 lat.**
*He'll be working abroad when he turns 40.*

The perfective aspect is used to

- focus on a single completed action, highlighting the outcome, result etc.
  **Wczoraj wieczorem obejrzałem wiadomości.** *Last night I watched the news.*
  **Kto napisał ten raport?** *Who wrote this report?*

- provide a list of activities that either were or will be completed
  **Przyszedł do pracy, włączył komputer i zaczął czytać emaile.**
  *He arrived at work, turned his computer on and started reading his emails.*
  **Jutro spotkam się z szefem, przedstawię nowy projekt i poproszę o podwyżkę.**
  *Tomorrow I'll meet with my boss, present my new project and ask for a pay rise.*

## Aspect of verbs – form

The imperfective form is the form that you find when you look up a Polish verb in the dictionary i.e. it's the same as the infinitive. The perfective is provided in the grammatical description of the entry. There is no set way of predicting how to form the perfective aspect and that is why it needs to be learned alongside the imperfective aspect. However, the perfective may be formed by:

- adding a prefix

| **pisać – napisać** | **czytać – przeczytać** | **jeść – zjeść** |
|---|---|---|
| *write* | *read* | *eat* |

  It should be noted that prefixes are also used to build families of verbs, i.e. produce words with (slightly) differing meanings.

  **pisać – napisać** *write* (imprefective – perfective)
  **dopisać** *add, write in* (perfective)
  **przepisać** *rewrite* (perfective)
  **podpisać** *sign, endorse* (perfective)

  Therefore you should not assume that a prefix always indicates a perfective form of the verb.

- changing the verb stem

| **zapraszać – zaprosić** | **kupować – kupić** | **wracać – wrócić** |
|---|---|---|
| *invite* | *buy* | *return* |

- using a different stem

| | | |
|---|---|---|
| **brać – wziąć** | **mówić – powiedzieć** | **kłaść – położyć** |
| *take* | *say* | *put* |

## Expressing the present

In Polish, there is only one present tense and it is used to indicate what has been done, is done regularly, and is being done at the moment. Only the imperfective aspect is used in the present tense as the actions described are either repeated, habitual or continuous.

**Raz w tygodniu <u>uczę się</u> polskiego.** *<u>I learn</u> Polish once a week.*
**<u>Uczę się</u> polskiego od roku.** *<u>I've been learning</u> Polish for a year.*
**Właśnie <u>uczę się</u> polskiego, dlatego korzystam ze słowika.**
*<u>I'm learning</u> Polish right now, that is why I'm using the dictionary.*

The present tense is formed by replacing the infinitive ending **–ć** or **–c** with the ending that indicates the person and number. Depending on the last syllable of the verb, the verbs follow one of several conjugation patterns:

| | **Verb endings** | | | |
|---|---|---|---|---|
| | **-ować** | **-ić** | **-yć** | **-ać** |
| **ja** | **-uję** | **-(i)ę** | **-ę** | **-am** |
| **ty** | **-ujesz** | **-isz** | **-ysz** | **-asz** |
| **on, pan, ona, pani, ono** | **-uje** | **-i** | **-y** | **-a** |
| **my** | **-ujemy** | **-imy** | **-ymy** | **-amy** |
| **wy** | **-ujecie** | **-icie** | **-ycie** | **-acie** |
| **oni, panowie, państwo, one, panie** | **-ują** | **-(i)ą** | **-ą** | **-ają** |

There are also a few irregular present tense conjugations

| | **być** (to be) | **jeść** (to eat) | **móc** (to be able) |
|---|---|---|---|
| **ja** | **jestem** | **jem** | **mogę** |
| **ty** | **jesteś** | **jesz** | **możesz** |
| **on, pan, ona, pani, ono** | **jest** | **je** | **może** |
| **my** | **jesteśmy** | **jemy** | **możemy** |
| **wy** | **jesteście** | **jecie** | **możecie** |
| **oni, panowie, państwo, one, panie** | **są** | **jedzą** | **mogą** |

Despite the irregularities or consonant and vowel changes, the personal endings are regular. Therefore the conjugation patterns tend to be easy to recreate once the first and the second person singular forms are established. The first person singular and the third person plural tend to have the same changes to the stem, and their form differs only by the last vowel (**-ę** and **–ą** respectively), e.g.

**Pisać – piszę – piszą** | **iść – idę – idą**
*to write – I write – they write* | *to go – I go – they go*

The second person singular ends in **–sz**, and this suffix is replaced with other regular endings to make the remaining three forms, for the third person singular the **–sz** is dropped and not replaced with any ending (so it is called the 'zero suffix'), for the first person plural it is replaced with **–my**, and for the second person plural with **–cie**, e.g.

**pisać – piszesz – pisze – piszemy – piszecie**
*to write – you (s) write – he writes – we write – you (pl) write*
**iść – idziesz – idzie – idziemy – idziecie**
*to go – you (s) go – he goes – we go – you (pl) go*

For this reason, the dictionary usually provides two conjugation forms in the grammar information after the verb infinitive as the other forms can be easily recreated, e.g.

**studi|ować (-uję, -ujesz)** | **rozumie|ć (-m, -sz)**
*to study* | *to understand*

## Expressing the past

In Polish, there is only one past tense but either of the aspects can be used to indicate difference in the time and completion of the activity. The imperfective aspect is used to focus on the regularity of the activity or on its length and duration, whereas the perfective aspect highlights the outcome of the activity. The verb aspect is chosen by the speaker to emphasise their intention.

**Wczoraj wieczorem czytałam tę książkę.**
*Last night I was reading this book.* (imperfective, focus on the activity, its duration)
**Wczoraj wieczorem przeczytałam tę książkę.**
*Last night I read this book.* (perfective, focus on the completion of the activity)

**Na wakacjach codziennie jedliśmy lody.**
*On holiday, we ate ice-cream every day.* (imperfective, regular activity)
**Kto zjadł wszystkie jabłka?**
*Who ate all the apples?* (perfective, focus on the outcome)

**Na uniwersytecie często chodziłem na koncerty.**
*When at the university, I often went to concerts.* (imperfective, regular activity)
**Spotkałem Adama, kiedy szedłem na koncert.**
*I met Adam, when I was (going) on my way to the concert.*
(imperfective, focus on the background activity)
**W weekend poszedłem na koncert.**
*At the weekend I went to a concert.* (pefective, a one-off activity in the past)

The past tense is formed by replacing the infinitive ending **–ć** or **–c** with the ending that indicates the person, number and also gender. Both perfective and imperfective verbs follow the same pattern, e.g.

**Przed chwilą zadzwonił twój szef.** *Your boss called a moment ago.*
(masculine animate virile singular)
**W weekend zadzwonili do mnie moi rodzice.**
*My parents called at the weekend.* (masculine animate virile plural)

**Moja siostra kupiła nowe buty.** *My sister bought new shoes.* (feminine singular)
**Moje koleżanki kupiły tanie bilety do kina.**
*My girlfriends bought cheap cinema tickets.* (feminine plural)

| | Masculine | | Feminine | Neuter |
|---|---|---|---|---|
| | Virile | Non-virile | | |
| **ja** | –łem | | –łam | |
| **ty** | –łeś | | –łaś | |
| **on, pan** | –ł | | | |
| **ona, pani** | | | –ła | |
| **ono** | | | | –ło |
| **my** | –liśmy | –łyśmy | | |
| **wy** | –liście | –łyście | | |
| **oni, panowie, państwo** | –li | | | |
| **one, panie** | | –ły | | |

There are just a few regular changes that occur in the past tense conjugation, e.g. the infinitives ending in **–eć** replace the vowel **–e–** with **–a–** before the suffix starting in **–ł–**. The infinitives ending in **–ść** replace the **–ś–** with **–d–**.

**mieć – miałem – miałam – miałeś**
*to have – I had* (m) *– I had* (f) *– you had* (m)
**jeść – jadłam – jadłeś – jadł – jadła**
*to eat – I ate* (f) *– you ate* (m) *– he ate – she ate*

There is only one irregular verb in the past tense, it is the verb **iść** (to go) and verbs related to it, e.g. **pójść** (to go to a place), **przyjść** (to arrive), **dojść** (to reach), **wyjść** (to leave).

**W weekend poszedłem do teatru.** *At the weekend I went to the theatre.*
**Wszyscy uczestnicy doszli do mety.** *All the participants reached the finishing line.*
**Dziś wyszłam dość późno z biura.** *Today I left the office quite late.*

| | Masculine | | Feminine | Neuter |
|---|---|---|---|---|
| | Virile | Non-virile | | |
| ja | –szedłem | | –szłam | |
| ty | –szedłeś | | –szłaś | |
| on, pan | –szedł | | | |
| ona, pani | | | –szła | |
| ono | | | | –szło |
| my | –szliśmy | –szłyśmy | | |
| wy | –szliście | –szłyście | | |
| oni, panowie, państwo | –szli | | | |
| one, panie | | –szły | | |

## Expressing the future

In Polish, the future can be expressed by using the present tense forms as well as future tense forms. There are two future tenses: imperfective and perfective. The imperfective future is used to focus on the regularity of the activity or on its length and duration, whereas the future perfective aspect highlights the outcome of an activity to be undertaken in the future. The verb aspect is chosen by the speaker to emphasise their intention.

## Future imperfective

The future imperfective is the only descriptive tense in Polish, i.e. it requires two words to be formed: the verb **być** (to be) plus a verb in its imperfective aspect, either in the infinitive form or in the past tense form. The difference relates to the form only, there is no difference in the meaning.

**Będę dzwonić / dzwonił(a) co tydzień.** *I'll be calling every week.*
**W tym roku będę regularnie uprawiać / uprawiał(a) sport.**
*This year I will do sport regularly.*

## Future imperfective (with the infinitive)

**grać** *(to play)*

| | Masculine | | Feminine | Neuter |
|---|---|---|---|---|
| | Virile | Non-virile | | |
| ja | będę grać | | | |
| ty | będziesz grać | | | |
| on, pan, ona, pani, ono | będzie grać | | | |
| my | będziemy grać | | | |
| wy | będziecie grać | | | |
| oni, panowie, państwo | będą grać | | | |
| one, panie | będą grać | | | |

## Future imperfective (with the past tense form)

**grać** *(to play)*

| | Masculine | | Feminine | Neuter |
|---|---|---|---|---|
| | Virile | Non-virile | | |
| ja | będę grał | | będę grała | |
| ty | będziesz grać | | będziesz grała | |
| on, pan | będzie grał | | | |
| ona, pani | | | będzie grała | |
| ono | | | | będzie grało |
| my | będziemy grali | będziemy grały | | |
| wy | będziecie grali | będziecie grały | | |
| oni, panowie, państwo | będą grali | | | |
| one, panie | | będą grały | | |

## Future perfective

The future perfective is formed by applying the present tense conjugation patterns to the perfective aspect of verbs. Thus, the future perfective tense is formed by replacing the infinitive ending **–ć** or **–c** with the ending that indicates the person and number. Depending on the last syllable of the verb, the verbs can follow one of several conjugation patterns.

**Kiedy <u>zrobisz</u> to zadanie?** *When <u>will you do</u> this exercise?*
**O której <u>zacznie się</u> film?** *What time <u>will</u> the film <u>start</u>?*
**Jutro <u>wstanę</u> wcześnie rano.** *Tomorrow <u>I will get up</u> early.*
**Czego <u>się napijesz</u>?** *What <u>will you drink</u>?*

| | Verb endings | | | |
|---|---|---|---|---|
| | -ować | -ić | -yć | -ać |
| ja | -uję | -(i)ę | -ę | -am |
| ty | -ujesz | -isz | -ysz | -asz |
| on, pan, ona, pani, ono | -uje | -i | -y | -a |
| my | -ujemy | -imy | -ymy | -amy |
| wy | -ujecie | -icie | -ycie | -acie |
| oni, panowie, państwo, one, panie | -ują | -(i)ą | -ą | -ają |

There are also a few irregular present tense conjugations

| | **być** (to be) | **zaczynać** (to start) | **wziąć** (to take) |
|---|---|---|---|
| ja | będę | zacznę | wezmę |
| ty | będziesz | zaczniesz | weźmiesz |
| on, pan, ona, pani, ono | będzie | zacznie | weźmie |
| my | będziemy | zaczniemy | weźmiemy |
| wy | będziecie | zaczniecie | weźmiecie |
| oni, panowie, państwo, one, panie | będą | zaczną | wezmą |

## Conditional Mood

The conditional mood sentences consist of two clauses, one of them starts with a conditional conjunction **jeżeli**, **jeśli** or **gdyby** (all meaning if) and provides a condition that should be fulfilled for another action to happen.

Sentences that start with **jeżeli** or **jeśli** indicate what action is likely to happen. They refer to the future or present situation and can describe:

- principles or advice; the clauses usually use the present tense or the imperative
  **Jeżeli temperatura jest poniżej zera, wówczas woda zamarza.**
  *If the temperature is below zero, the water freezes.*
  **Jeśli boli cię głowa, weź aspirynę.**
  *If you have a headache, take an aspirin.*

- a condition likely to be fulfilled; the sentences then use future tense forms or imperative forms
  **Jeśli będzie padać, zostanę w domu.**
  *If it rains (will be raining), I will stay (will stay) at home.*
  **Kupię nowy samochód, jeśli dostanę podwyżkę.**
  *I'll buy a new car, if I get (will get) a pay rise.*

Sentences that start with **gdyby** indicate what action is unlikely to happen. They often refer to the past or the present situation. An element of conditional mood is present in the structure of both clauses

**Gdybym się uczył, to zdałbym egzamin.**
*If I had studied, I would have passed the exam.*

The clause starting with **gdyby** provides the condition. It takes different endings to denote the person, and the main verb in the clause is in the third person singular or plural past tense form to denote number and gender.

| | |
|---|---|
| ja | gdybym |
| ty | gdybyś |
| on, ona, ono, pan, pani | gdyby |

| | |
|---|---|
| my | gdybyśmy |
| wy | gdybyście |
| oni, one, panowie, panie, państwo | gdyby |

**być** *(to be)*

| | Masculine | | Feminine | Neuter |
|---|---|---|---|---|
| | Virile | Non-virile | | |
| ja | gdybym był | | gdybym była | |
| ty | gdybyś był | | gdybyś była | |
| on, pan | gdyby był | | | |
| ona, pani | | | gdyby była | |
| ono | | | | gdyby było |
| my | gdybyśmy byli | gdybyśmy były | | |
| wy | gdybyście byli | gdybyście były | | |
| oni, panowie, państwo | gdyby byli | | | |
| one, panie | | gdyby były | | |

**Gdyby był punktualny...** *If he had been punctual...*
**Gdybyśmy były młode...** *If we were young...* (feminine plural)

The other clause provides information on what action could be carried out. The clause is formed by the third person singular or plural past tense to denote the gender and the number, followed by the suffix **–by–** to denote the condition, and by another suffix to denote the person

**być** *(to be)*

| | Masculine | | Feminine | Neuter |
|---|---|---|---|---|
| | Virile | Non-virile | | |
| ja | był-by-m | | była-by-m | |
| ty | był-by-ś | | była-by-ś | |
| on, pan | był-by | | | |
| ona, pani | | | była-by | |
| ono | | | | było-by |
| my | byli-by-śmy | były-by-śmy | | |
| wy | byli-by-ście | były-by-ście | | |
| oni, panowie, państwo | byli-by | | | |
| one, panie | | były-by | | |

**Gdybyśmy kupili bilety wcześnie, zapłacilibyśmy za nie mniej.**
*If we had bought the tickets earlier, we would have paid less for them.*
**Ta zupa smakowałaby lepiej, gdyby była lepiej doprawiona.**
*This soup would have tasted better if it had been seasoned.*

As there are two suffixes added to the verb, they can be detached from it and moved before it, usually attached to the pronoun **to** (then):

**Gdybyś znał wszystkie fakty, mógłbyś wziąć udział w dyskusji.**
**Gdybyś znał wszystkie fakty, tobyś mógł wziąć udział w dyskusji.**
*If you had known all the facts, you could have participated in the discussion.*

This form is also used in polite requests, e.g.

**Czy mógłbyś mi to wytłumaczyć?** *Could you explain this to me?*

## Imperative mood

The imperative is used to ask people to do something in a more direct way. It can be formed by using both the imperfective and perfective aspect, depending on whether a continuous/regular or one-off action is required.

## Formal imperative

The formal imperative can be formed by:

- using the infinitive form after the verb **proszę** *(I would like you to)*

| | | |
|---|---|---|
| **Proszę usiąść.** | **Proszę poczekać.** | **Proszę uważać.** |
| *Please sit down.* | *Please wait.* | *Be careful please.* |

- using the particle **niech** (let) followed by the third person singular or plural. The formal form of address **pan** (sir), **pani** (madam) etc. is then explicitly used in the structure.

**Niech pan usiądzie.**
*Please sit down (sir).*

**Niech pani poczeka.**
*Please wait (madam).*

**Niech państwo uważają.**
*Be careful please (ladies and gentleman).*

**Niech pan nie siada na tym krześle.**
*Do not sit on this chair (sir).*

**Niech pani nie czeka.**
*Do not wait (madam).*

## Informal imperative

Either the imperfective or perfective can be used to make the informal imperative form, e.g.

**Jedz codziennie owoce.**
*Eat fruit every day.*

**Zjedz to jabłko.**
*Eat this apple.*

**Czytaj regularnie gazety.**
*Read the newspapers regularly.*

**Przeczytaj ten artykuł. Jest bardzo ciekawy.**
*Read this article. It is very interesting.*

The negative imperative tends to use the imperfective aspect

**Nie jedz słodyczy.**
*Do not eat sweets.*

**Nie spóźniaj się do pracy.**
*Do not be late for work.*

The informal imperative is formed by adding a suffix to the third person singular present tense form of the verb. The second person singular is formed by adding the suffix **–j** or by dropping the last vowel. It then forms the basis for the first person plural, which adds a further suffix **–my**, and the second person plural, which adds a further suffix **–cie**. The third person singular and plural is formed by the particle **niech** (*let*) plus the third person singular or plural present tense form.

| Infinitive | 3rd person singular | Imperative | | | | |
|---|---|---|---|---|---|---|
| | | ty | on/ona/ono | my | wy | oni/one |
| | | +j | niech + 3rd *s* | +jmy | +jcie | niech + 3rd *pl* |
| **czytać** (to read) | **czyta** | **czytaj** | **niech czyta** | **czytajmy** | **czytajcie** | **niech czytają** |
| **dać** (to give) | **da** | **daj** | **niech da** | **dajmy** | **dajcie** | **niech dają** |
| **pisać** (to write) | **pisze** | **pisz** | **niech pisze** | **piszmy** | **piszcie** | **niech piszą** |
| **myśleć** (to think) | **myśli** | **myśl** | **niech myśli** | **myślmy** | **myślcie** | **niech myślą** |
| **myć** (to wash) | **myje** | **myj** | **niech myje** | **myjmy** | **myjcie** | **niech myją** |
| **zająć** (to save) | **zajmie** | **zajmij** | **niech zajmie** | **zajmijmy** | **zajmijcie** | **niech zajmą** |
| **wrócić** (to return) | **wróci** | **wróć** | **niech wróci** | **wróćmy** | **wróćcie** | **niech wrócą** |
| **chodzić** (to go) | **chodzi** | **chodź** | **niech chodzi** | **chodźmy** | **chodźcie** | **niech chodzą** |

## Irregular forms

Below are examples of some irregular forms.

| Infinitive | Imperative | | | | |
|---|---|---|---|---|---|
| | ty | on/ona/ono | my | wy | oni/one |
| **być** (to be) | **bądź** | **niech będzie** | **będziemy** | **będziecie** | **niech będą** |
| **brać** (to take) | **bierz** | **niech bierze** | **bierzmy** | **bierzcie** | **niech biorą** |
| **wziąć** (to take) | **weź** | **niech weź-mie** | **weźmy** | **weźcie** | **niech wezmą** |
| **jeść** (to eat) | **jedz** | **niech je** | **jedzmy** | **jedzcie** | **niech jedzą** |

## Impersonal structures

In Polish, the impersonal structure can be formed by either the passive voice, or more frequently by a subjectless form, i.e. a form that does not indicate who performs the action. In Polish the subjectless form is used much more frequently that the passive voice.

## Impersonal structures in the present tense

In the present tense, to form an impersonal structure, the verb is used in its third person singular form along with the reflexive pronoun **się**, e.g.

**W Polsce pije się herbatę z cytryną.**
*In Poland, one drinks tea with lemon.*
**W tej kawiarni zabrania się palić papierosy.**
*In this cafe, smoking is prohibited (one prohibits smoking).*

## Impersonal structures in the past tense

In the past tense, to form an impersonal structure:

- the infinitive suffix **–ć** is replaced with the suffix **–(o)no** or – **(o)mo**, e.g.
  **W Polsce mówiono wieloma językami.**
  *In Poland many languages were spoken (one spoke many languages).*
- the infinitive suffix **–ć** is replaced with suffix **–ło** and used with the pronoun **się**, e.g.
  **To się rozumiało samo przez się.** *This was clearly understood.*

## Impersonal structures in the future tense

In the future imperfective tense, to form an impersonal structure:

- the infinitive can be used, e.g.
  **Czy w Polsce będzie się organizować Olimpiadę?**
  *Will the Olympic Games be organised in Poland?*
- the infinitive suffix **–ć** can be replaced with suffix **–ło** and used with the pronoun **się**, e.g.
  **Dużo się będzie o tym mówiło.** *Much will be said about it.*

In the future perfective tense, to form an impersonal structure:

- the pefective verb is used in its third person singular form along with the reflexive pronoun **się**, e.g.
  **Gdzie wybuduje się nową szkołę?** *Where will the new school be built?*

## Structure of a sentence

In Polish, there is no fixed word order and the words forming a clause or a sentence can usually be placed at various points. What determines their position is the focus of the information; the initial and final positions are usually reserved for important or new information. For this reason, grammatical words such as pronouns tend to be placed in the middle of the sentence.

**Lubię muzykę klasyczną. Od dawna się nią interesuję.**
*I like classical music. I have been interested in it for a long time.*
(Since-long-[reflexive pronoun]-in-it-am interested.)

## Negations

Sentences in all tenses become negative by using the particle **nie** (not) which directly precedes the finite form of the verb. The verb form itself doesn't change.

**Nie lubię muzyki.** *I don't like music.*
**Nie zrozumieliśmy jego argumentu.** *We did not understand his argument.*

If the verb is negated, other parts of the sentence will automatically be used in their negative forms too. In Polish, there may be a double or triple negative form in a sentence.

**Nikt nie przyszedł na czas.** *No one came on time.* (No-one-did-not-come-on-time.)

## Negation of the verb **być** (to be)

The verb **być** (to be) is negated by the particle **nie** (not) preceding it when **być** (to be) refers to a quality or state. The structure of the sentence is not affected by this.

**Byłem zmęczony. Nie byłem zmęczony.** *I was tired. I was not tired.*

If the verb **być** (to be) refers to an existence or presence at a place, the structure changes as follows in the negative:

- For the present tense the structure **nie ma** (isn't, aren't, am not) with the genitive case is used for all persons
  **Jutro nie ma mnie w pracy.** *Tomorrow I am not at work.*
  **W tym artykule nie ma żadnych nowych argumentów.**
  *In this article, there are no new arguments.*
- For the past tense the structure **nie było** (wasn't, weren't) with the genitive case is used for all persons
  **Wczoraj nie było mnie w pracy.** *I was not at work yesterday.*
  **Na koncie nie było żadnych pieniędzy.** *There was no money in the account.*
- For the future tense the structure **nie będzie** (won't be) with the genitive case is used for all persons
  **Jutro nie będzie mnie w pracy.** *I will not be at work tomorrow.*
  **W weekend na pewno nie będzie takiej ładnej pogody.**
  *The weather will definitely not be so nice at the weekend.*

## Interrogative forms

Questions are usually formed by putting a question word at the beginning of the sentence. The pronoun **czy** (yes/no question pronoun) starts questions in all tenses.

**Czy mówi pan po polsku?** *Do you speak Polish?*
**Czy był pan kiedyś w Polsce?** *Have you ever been to Poland?*
**Kiedy będą ogłoszone wyniki?** *When will the results be announced?*

If the main verb requires a preposition, questions are often formed by moving the preposition to the start of the sentence.

**O czym myślisz?** *What are you thinking about?*

## Function and form

An adverb is a word that describes or modifies a verb, an adjective or another adverb. Adverbs indicate manner, quantity, time, place, and intensity. In Polish, adverbs change their form only in the comparative and superlative. A typical adverb ending is **–o** or **–(i)e**. The adverb rarely appears in the dictionary as a word or entry in its own right, however, it is usually provided as a grammatical form in the entry for the adjective.

- The suffix **–(i)e** is used most frequently, e.g.

| | | |
|---|---|---|
| **Ładnie wyglądasz.** | **Smacznie spał.** | **Dobrze się czuję.** |
| *You look nice.* | *He slept soundly.* | *I feel well.* |

- The suffix **–o** usually follows **–k**, **–g**, and some double consonants, e.g.

| | | |
|---|---|---|
| **Jest zimno.** | **Szybko odpowiedział.** | **Trudno to zrozumieć.** |
| *It's cold.* | *He responded quickly.* | *It's difficult to understand.* |

Sometimes both suffixes **–o** and **–(i)e** can be used with no difference to the meaning of the word.

| | |
|---|---|
| **Jest pochmurno / pochmurnie.** | **Na dworze było wietrznie / wietrzno.** |
| *It is overcast.* | *Outside it was windy.* |

- Suffix **–u** is usually used in fixed expressions following the preposition **po** (in a way/style)

| | | |
|---|---|---|
| **Czy mówisz po polsku?** | **Po mału doszli do domu.** | **Zrobimy to po naszemu.** |
| *Do you speak Polish?* | *Slowly they got home.* | *We'll do it in our own way.* |

Unlike in English, in Polish the form of the adverb is always different from the form of the adjective.

| | |
|---|---|
| **Pracujemy bardzo ciężko.** | **Ta praca jest ciężka.** |
| *We work very hard.* (adv) | *This work is hard.* (adj) |

In Polish, adverbs accompany verbs that do not take an object, such as **być** (to be), **wydawać się** (to seem), **stawać się** (to become) etc. to refer to a general state and not a specific object/person etc. The subject does not have to be explicitly stated in the clause. In English, the adjective is used in such structures.

**Jest (tu) ciepło / zimno.** *It is warm / cold (here).*

In English, some verbs of perception are used with an adjective, whereas in Polish verbs like **pachnieć** (to smell), **czuć** (to feel), **brzmieć** (to sound) and **wyglądać** (to look) take an adverb, just like all other Polish verbs.

**Ładnie dziś wyglądasz.** *You look nice today.*
**Ta zupa pachnie smacznie.** *This soup smells nice.*
**Czuję się świetnie.** *I feel great.*

## Comparison of adverbs

Adverbs can form their comparative and superlative forms by:

- adding the suffix **–(ie)j** to form the comparative and prefix **naj–** to form the superlative. This is usually the form taken by short adjectives (with one or two syllables)

**słabo – słabiej – najsłabiej**
*weakly – more weakly – most weakly*

**mocno – mocniej – najmocniej**
*strongly– more strongly – most strongly*

– Adverbs that end in **–ro** change this consonant to **–rz–** and take the ending **–ej**

**staro – starzej – najstarzej** *old – more old – most old*

– Adverbs that end in **–go** change the consonant to **–ż–**

**drogo – drożej – najdrożej**
*dearly – more dearly – most dearly*

**długo – dłużej – najdłużej**
*long – longer – the longest*

– Adverbs that end in **–ko** change the consonant to **–ż–** or **–ci**

**blisko – bliżej – najbliżej**
*closely – more closely – most closely*

**szybko – szybciej – najszybciej**
*quickly – more quickly – most quickly*

– Adverbs that end in **–dko** change the consonants to **–dz**

**prędko – prędzej – najprędzej**
*fast – more fast – most fast*

**rzadko – rzadziej – najrzadziej**
*rarely – more rarely – most rarely*

– Adverbs that end in **–tko** change the consonants to **–e**

**krótko – krócej – najkrócej**
*for a short period of time – for a shorter period of time – for the shortest period of time*

– Adverbs that end in **–ło** change the consonant to **–l-**

**miło – milej – najmilej**
*nicely – more nicely – most nicely*

**ciepło – cieplej – najcieplej**
*warmly – more warmly – most warmly*

– Adverbs that end in **–sto** change the consonant to **–ście–**

**prosto – prościej – najprościej** *simply – more simply – most simply*

– Adverbs that end in **–cho** change the consonant to **–sze–**
**cicho – ciszej – najciszej** *quietly – more quietly – most quietly*

- using the descriptive form, i.e .using a separate word **bardziej** (*more*) or **najbardziej** (*most*), **mniej** (*less*) or **najmniej** (*least*) to create the comparative and superlative forms
  – adding **bardziej** (*more*) and **najbardziej** (*most*). This form is used for longer words and also for words whose meaning is too abstract to compare

  **choro – bardziej choro – najbardziej choro** *ill – more ill – the most ill*

  – adding **mniej** (*less*) and **najmniej** (*least*). This form is used with all adjectives
  **ładnie – mniej ładnie – najmniej ładnie** *nicely – less nicely –least nicely*

- irregular forms are provided in the dictionary

**dobrze – lepiej – najlepiej**
*well – better – the best*
**dużo – więcej – najwięcej**
*many – more – the most*

**źle – gorzej – najgorzej**
*badly – worse – the worst*
**malo – mniej – najmniej**
*little – less – the least*

# Prepositions

Prepositions indicate the location of an object or activity, or a direction in which a movement is taking place. In Polish, prepositions take different cases depending on the verbs that they follow.

## Prepositions with verbs of movement

Verbs that indicate movement to or from a place are referred to as **czasowniki ruchu** (verbs of movement). Prepositions that follow them can take one of the following cases:

- the genitive case after the preposition **do** (*to*), **z** (*from a place*), **znad** (*from an area of water*), **od** (*from a person*) etc.
  **Jadę do Polski.** *I'm going to Poland.*
  **Pochodzę z Anglii.** *I come from England.*
  **Przesyłam pozdrowienia znad Bałtyku.**
  *I'm sending greetings from the Baltic Sea.*

- the accusative case after the preposition **na** (*to attend an activity, to a region or island*), **nad** (*to an area of water*), **w** (*to the mountain range*) etc.
  **Jutro idę na koncert.** *Tomorrow I'm going to a concert.*
  **Chciałabym pojechać na Kubę.** *I'd like to travel to Cuba.*
  **Wyprowadzili się na Śląsk.** *They have moved to Silesia (region).*
  **W sobotę jedziemy nad jezioro.** *On Saturday we are going to the lakeside.*

## Prepositions with verbs of location/state

Verbs that indicate location are referred to as **czasowniki statyczne** (non-movement verbs). Prepositions that follow them can take one of the following cases:

- the locative case after the preposition **w** (*in, at a place*), **na** (*at an event, on an island, in a region*) etc.
  **Wczoraj byliśmy w teatrze.** *We were at the theatre yesterday.*
  **Na wakacjach byliśmy w Polsce.** *We were in Poland on holiday.*

- the genitive case after the preposition **u** (*at a person's home*), **obok** (*next to*) etc.
  **W weekend byliśmy u rodziców.** *At the weekend we were at our parents'.*
  **Moje mieszkanie jest obok windy.** *My flat is next to the lift.*

- the instrumental case after the preposition **nad** (*at an area of water*), **za** (*out of, outside, behind*) etc.
  **Warszawa leży nad Wisłą.** *Warsaw is located on the Wisła river.*
  **Wakacje spędziliśmy nad morzem.** *We spent our holiday at the seaside.*
  **Mieszkamy za miastem.** *We live just out of town.*

## Dual case prepositions

The dictionary provides information on which cases prepositions take in each entry. Most prepositions take different cases depending on:

- their meaning, e.g.
  the preposition **w** (*on*, *in*) takes the accusative case for the days of the week, but the locative for the months of the year
  **Spotkajmy się w sobotę.** *Let's meet on Saturday.* (accusative)
  **Urodziłem się w lipcu.** *I was born in July.* (locative)

  the preposition **z** can mean either from and then takes the genitive case, or *with, by means of* and then takes the instrumental case
  **Jestem z Londynu.** *I come from London.* (genitive)
  **Mieszkam z rodzicami.** *I live with my parents.* (instrumental)

- the type of verb they are following e.g. the preposition **pod** (*under, below*) takes the accusative case after verbs of motion, and the instrumental after non-motion verbs
  **Postawiłam torbę pod stół.** *I put the bag under the table.* (motion, accusative)
  **Torba stoi pod stołem.** *The bag is under the table.* (location, instrumental)

## Clauses beginning with a preposition

If a verb takes a preposition, and the clause it is in is subordinate or in the form of a question, it often starts with the preposition. In Polish, the subordinate clause is always separated from the main clause by a comma, and it cannot exist on its own without the main clause.

**Na którym piętrze mieszkasz?** *What floor do you live on?*
**O czym jest ten film?** *What is this film about?*
**Nie wiem, do kogo zwrócić się po pomoc.** *I do not know to whom to turn for help.*

# Numbers

## Cardinal numbers

Cardinal numbers need to agree in gender, case and number with the nouns they modify.

**jeden słownik** *one dictionary* (masculine) **jedna kawa** *one coffee* (feminine) **jedno piwo** *one beer* (neuter)

**jeden** (one)

| Nominative | Genitive | Dative | Accusative | | Instrumental | Locative |
|---|---|---|---|---|---|---|
| | | | Animate | Inanimate | | |
| jeden | jednego | jednemu | jednego | jeden | jednym | jednym |
| jedna | jednej | jednej | jedną | | jedną | jednej |
| jedno | jednego | jednemu | jedno | | jednym | jednym |
| jedni | jednych | jednym | jednych | | jednymi | jednych |
| jedne | jednych | jednym | jedne | | jednymi | jednych |

**dwa słowniki** *two dictionaries* (masculine inanimate)
**dwóch braci = dwaj bracia** *two brothers* (masculine virile)
**dwie kawy** *two coffees* (feminine)
**dwa piwa** *two beers* (neuter)
**dwoje dzieci** *two children* (group)

| Nominative | **dwaj, dwóch** two (masculine virile) | **dwa** two (masculine animate non-virile and inanimate) | **dwie** two | **trzej, troje** three (masculine virile) | **trzy** three (masculine inanimate, masculine animate non-virile, feminine and neuter) |
|---|---|---|---|---|---|
| Genitive | dwóch | dwóch, dwu | dwóch, dwu | trzech | trzech |
| Dative | dwóm, dwu | dwóm, dwu | dwom, dwu | trzem | trzem |
| Accusative | dwóch | dwa | dwie | trzech | trzy |
| Instrumental | dwoma | dwoma | dwoma, dwiema | trzema | trzema |
| Locative | dwóch, dwu | dwóch, dwu | dwóch, dwu | trzech | trzech |

## Ordinal numbers

Ordinal numbers need to agree in gender, case and number with the nouns they modify.

**Pierwsza godzina pracy jest najgorsza.** *The first hour of work is the worst.*
**To moje pierwsze piwo.** *This is my first beer.*

**pierwszy** (first)

| Nominative | Genitive | Dative | Accusative | | Instrumental | Locative |
|---|---|---|---|---|---|---|
| | | | Animate | Inanimate | | |
| pierwszy | pierwszego | pierwszemu | pierwszego | pierwszy | pierwszym | pierwszym |
| pierwsza | pierwszej | pierwszej | pierwszą | | pierwszą | pierwszej |
| pierwsze *(s)* | pierwszego | pierwszemu | pierwsze | | pierwszym | pierwszym |
| pierwsi | pierwszych | pierwszym | pierwszych | | pierwszymi | pierwszych |
| pierwsze *(pl)* | pierwszych | pierwszym | pierwsze | | pierwszymi | pierwszych |

Ordinal numbers are used when, for instance, talking about the date or the time e.g.

**Dzisiaj jest <u>pierwszy</u> kwietnia.** *Today is the <u>first</u> of April.*
**Jest (godzina) <u>ósma</u>.** *It is <u>eight</u> (o'clock).*

# Gramatyka angielska

## Spis treści

## Rzeczowniki policzalne

Rzeczowniki odnoszące się do przedmiotów, które można policzyć, nazywamy **rzeczownikami policzalnymi**. Rzeczowniki policzalne mają dwie formy. Forma liczby pojedynczej odnosi się do jednej rzeczy lub osoby.

**a book** *książka* | **the teacher** *nauczyciel*

Forma liczby mnogiej odnosi się do więcej niż jednej rzeczy lub osoby.

**three books** *trzy książki* | **some teachers** *kilku nauczycieli*

Aby utworzyć formę liczby mnogiej, dodaje się końcówkę **–s** do większości rzeczowników.

**book → books** *książka → książki* | **school → schools** *szkoła → szkoły*

Do rzeczowników zakończonych na **–ss**, **–ch**, **–s**, **–sh**, lub **–x** dodaje się końcówkę **–es**.

**glass → glasses** *szklanka → szklanki* | **fox → foxes** *lis → lisy*

Niektóre rzeczowniki zakończone na **–o** przyjmują końcówkę **–s**, a inne **–es**.

**photo → photos** *zdjęcie → zdjęcia* | **hero → heroes** *bohater → bohaterowie*

Wszystkie rzeczowniki zakończone na **–y** po spółgłosce, zmieniają **–y** na **–i** przed dodaniem końcówki **–es**.

**lady → ladies** *pani → panie* | **country → countries** *kraj → kraje*

Niektóre rzeczowniki mają formę nieregularną.

**child → children** *dziecko → dzieci* | **tooth → teeth** *ząb → zęby*

**mouse → mice** *mysz → myszy* | **woman → women** *kobieta → kobiety*

W liczbie pojedynczej rzeczowniki policzalne zawsze są poprzedzone określnikiem, tj. wyrazem takim jak **a (an)**, **another** czy **the**.

**She was eating <u>an</u> apple.** *Jadła jabłko.*

**I've bought another dress.** *Kupiłam jeszcze jedną sukienkę.*
**I parked the car over there.** *Samochód zaparkowałam tam.*

Forma liczby mnogiej rzeczowników policzalnych nie jest poprzedzana określnikiem, jeśli rzeczowniki odnoszą się do ludzi czy rzeczy w ogóle.

**Does the hotel have large rooms?** *Czy ten hotel ma duże pokoje?*
**The film is not suitable for children.** *Ten film nie jest odpowiedni dla dzieci.*

Forma liczby mnogiej poprzedzona jest określnikiem, gdy rzeczownik odnosi się konkretnie do szczególnej rzeczy lub osoby.

**Their computers are very expensive.** *Ich komputery są bardzo drogie.*
**These cakes are delicious.** *Te ciastka są pyszne.*

## Liczba pojedyncza i mnoga rzeczowników

Niektóre rzeczowniki w formie liczby pojedynczej odnoszą się do rzeczy, które są niepowtarzalne, jedyne w swoim rodzaju. Ponieważ są użyte w konkretnym znaczeniu, zwykle poprzedza je przedimek **the**.

**The sun was shining.** *Świeciło słońce.*
**I'm afraid of the dark.** *Boję się ciemności.*

Inne rzeczowniki w formie liczby pojedynczej są zwykle poprzedzone przedimkiem **a (an)**, ponieważ odnoszą się do rzeczy, o których mówimy po raz pierwszy w danej chwili.

**I went upstairs and had a wash.** *Poszedłem na górę i umyłem się.*
**I felt I had to give him a chance.** *Czułem, że powinienem mu dać szansę.*

Niektóre rzeczowniki w formie liczby mnogiej są używane tylko w jednym konkretnym znaczeniu.

**His clothes looked terribly dirty.** *Jego ubrania wyglądały na bardzo brudne.*
**Troops will be sent to Afghanistan.** *Oddziały zostaną wysłane do Afganistanu.*

Niektóre z tych rzeczowników są używane z określnikami.

**I went to the pictures with Tina.** *Poszłam do kina z Tiną.*
**You hurt his feelings.** *Zraniłaś jego uczucia.*

Inne są używane bez określników.

**Refreshments are available inside.** *Napoje i przekąski są dostępne wewnątrz.*

Mała grupa rzeczowników w liczbie mnogiej odnosi się do pojedynczego przedmiotu składającego się z dwóch części.

**She was wearing brown trousers.** *Miała na sobie brązowe spodnie.*
**These binoculars are very light.** *Ta lornetka jest bardzo lekka.*

W przypadku rzeczowników, które odnoszą się do grupy osób lub rzeczy, ta sama forma rzeczownika może łączyć się z czasownikiem w formie liczby pojedynczej lub mnogiej. Te rzeczowniki często są określane mianem zbiorowych.

**Our little group is complete.** *Nasza mała grupa jest kompletna.*
**The largest group are the boys.** *Największą grupę stanowią chłopcy.*

## Rzeczowniki niepoliczalne

Niektóre rzeczowniki odnoszą się do rzeczy, których nie można policzyć. Są to rzeczowniki niepoliczalne. Nie mają one formy liczby mnogiej. Obejmują rzeczowniki, które odnoszą się do substancji, ilości, uczuć, czynności czy abstrakcyjnych koncepcji.

| **food** | **water** | **cruelty** | **honesty** | **anger** |
|---|---|---|---|---|
| *jedzenie* | *woda* | *okrucieństwo* | *uczciwość* | *złość* |
| **joy** | **sleep** | **travel** | **beauty** | **life** |
| *radość* | *sen* | *podróż* | *uroda* | *życie* |

**I was greeted with shouts of joy.** *Powitały mnie okrzyki radości.*
**All prices include travel to and from London.**
*Wszystkie ceny obejmują podróż do i z Londynu.*

Niektóre pospolite i często używane rzeczowniki, które tworzą formę liczby mnogiej w języku polskim, są niepoliczalne w języku angielskim i z tego powodu używane są tylko w formie liczby pojedynczej, ale bez przedimka.

| **advice** | **baggage** | **equipment** | **furniture** | **homework** |
|---|---|---|---|---|
| *rada* | *bagaż* | *sprzęt* | *mebel* | *zadanie domowe* |
| **information** | **traffic** | | | |
| *informacja* | *ruch uliczny* | | | |
| **knowledge** | **luggage** | **machinery** | **money** | **news** |
| *wiedza* | *bagaż* | *maszyna* | *pieniądze* | *wiadomość* |

**The airline lost my luggage.** *Linia lotnicza zgubiła mój bagaż.*
**For further information contact the number below.**
*W celu uzyskania dalszych informacji należy zadzwonić na poniższy numer.*

# Rzeczowniki

Niektóre rzeczowniki niepoliczalne mają końcówkę **–s** i dlatego wyglądają jak formy liczby mnogiej, którymi w rzeczywistości nie są. Odnoszą się one do dziedzin nauki, czynności, gier i chorób.

**Mathematics is too difficult for me.** *Matematyka jest dla mnie za trudna.*
**Measles is in most cases a harmless illness.**
*Odra jest w większości przypadków niegroźną chorobą.*

Kiedy rzeczownik niepoliczalny jest podmiotem zdania, czasownik przyjmuje formę liczby pojedynczej.

**Electricity is dangerous.** *Prąd jest niebezpieczny.*
**Food was very expensive.** *Jedzenie było bardzo drogie.*

Rzeczowniki niepoliczalne nie są używane z przedimkiem **a** (**an**).

**They resent having to give money to people like me.**
*Niechętnie daja pieniądze osobom takim jak ja.*
**My father started work when he was ten.**
*Mój ojciec rozpoczął pracę, gdy miał dziesięć lat.*

Rzeczowniki niepoliczalne są poprzedzone przedimkiem **the**, gdy odnoszą się do konkretnego lub znanego przypadku.

**I am interested in the education of young children.**
*Interesuję się nauczaniem małych dzieci.*

Rzeczowniki niepoliczalne nie są używane z liczebnikami. Można je poprzedzać słowami takimi jak **some** lub wyrażeniami typu **a piece of** czy **a bit of**.

**Let me give you a piece of advice.** *Pozwól, że udzielę ci rady.*
**They own a bit of land near Cambridge.**
*Posiadają kawałek ziemi niedaleko Cambridge.*

Niektóre rzeczowniki niepoliczalne odnoszą się do nazw jedzenia i picia, które mogą stać się policzalnymi, kiedy odnoszą się do konkretnych ilości lub porcji.

**Do you like coffee?** *Czy lubisz kawę?*
**We asked for two coffees.** *Poprosiliśmy o dwie kawy.*

Niektóre rzeczowniki są niepoliczalne, gdy odnoszą się do stanu ogólnego, czegoś w ogóle, ale stają się policzalne, gdy odnoszą się do konkretnego przykładu.

**Victory was now assured.** *Zwycięstwo było wówczas pewne.*
**In 1990, the party won a convincing victory.**
*W 1990 roku partia odniosła zdecydowane zwycięstwo.*

# Dzierżawczość

## Dopełniacz

Formy dopełniacza używa się, gdy chce się zaznaczyć, że jakaś osoba lub rzecz należy do innej osoby lub rzeczy lub jest z nią w jakiś sposób połączona. Formy dopełniacza i formy dzierżawcze to:

| **my** | **your** | **his** | **her** | **its** | **our** | **their** |
|---|---|---|---|---|---|---|
| *mój* | *twój / wasz* | *jego* | *jej* | *tego* | *nasz* | *ich* |

Forma **your** odnosi się zarówno do liczby pojedynczej i mnogiej.

**I'd been waiting a long time to park my car.**
*Długo czekałem, żeby zaparkować samochód.*
**They took off their shoes.** *Zdjęli swoje buty.*

UWAGA: Forma dzierżawcza **its** nie jest pisana z apostrofem. Forma **it's** to forma skrócona struktury **it is** lub **it has**.

## Zaimki dzierżawcze

Zaimków dzierżawczych używa się, gdy odnosi się do osoby lub rzeczy i chce się zaznaczyć, do kogo lub czego ta osoba lub rzecz należy, lub z kim czy czym jest połączona. Zaimki dzierżawcze to:

| **mine** | **yours** | **his** | **hers** | **ours** | **theirs** |
|---|---|---|---|---|---|
| *mój* | *twój / wasz* | *jego* | *jej* | *nasz* | *ich* |

Forma **yours** odnosi się zarówno do liczby pojedynczej i mnogiej. Nie istnieje forma dzierżawcza zaimka **its**.

**Is that coffee yours or mine?** *Czy ta kawa jest twoja czy moja?*
**It was his fault, not theirs.** *To była jego wina, nie ich.*

## Dopełniacz saksoński (apostrof 's)

Gdy chce się zaznaczyć, że jakaś osoba lub rzecz należy do innej osoby lub rzeczy, lub jest z nią w jakiś sposób połączona, można w tym celu użyć dopełniacza saksońskiego (**'s**). Na przykład, jeśli John posiada motocykl, można opisać ten motocykl jako **John's motorbike**.

**Sylvia put her hand on John's arm.** *Sylvia położyła rękę na ramieniu Johna.*
**I like the car's design.** *Podoba mi się model tego samochodu.*
**Have you met Jane's brother?** *Czy poznałeś brata Jane?*

## Dzierżawczość

Dopełniacz saksoński (**'s**) dodaje się do form liczby pojedynczej oraz do nieregularnych form liczby mnogiej, zwykle odnosząc się do ludzi raczej niż do przedmiotów.

**I wore a pair of my sister's boots.** *Miałam na sobie parę butów swojej siostry.*
**Children's birthday parties can be boring.** *Przyjęcia urodzinowe dzieci mogą być nudne.*

Do formy liczby mnogiej zakończonej na **–s** dodaje się jedynie apostrof (').

**It's not his parents' problem.** *To nie jest problem jego rodziców.*

## Przedimek określony

Wyraz **the** jest przedimkiem określonym. Używa się go, gdy osoba, z którą się rozmawia, zna osobę lub rzecz, o której mowa.

**The man began to run towards the boy.** *Mężczyzna zaczął biec w kierunku chłopca.*
**She dropped the can.** *Upuściła puszkę.*
**The girls were not at home.** *Dziewczyn nie było w domu.*

Przedimka **the** używa się, gdy odnosi się do rzeczy, która jest tylko jedna na świecie lub znajduje się w konkretnym miejscu.

**They all sat in the sun.** *Wszyscy siedzieli na słońcu.*
**The sky was a brilliant blue.** *Niebo było olśniewająco niebieskie.*
**He decided to put some words on the blackboard.**
*Zdecydował się napisać kilka słów na tablicy.*

Przedimka **the** używa się, gdy chce się wypowiedzieć ogólnie na jakiś temat.

**My father's favourite flower is the rose.** *Ulubionym kwiatem mojego ojca jest róża.*
**I don't like using the phone.** *Nie lubię korzystać z telefonu.*
**Shirin plays the piano very well.** *Shirin gra bardzo dobrze na fortepianie.*

Przedimka **the** używa się przed niektórymi tytułami oraz nazwami organizacji, budynków, gazet czy dzieł sztuki.

**...the Queen of England**
*...Królowa Anglii*
**...the Taj Mahal**
*...Tadź Mahal*
**...the Mona Lisa**
*...Mona Lisa*
**...the Times**
*...Times (dziennik)*
**...the United Nations**
*...Narody Zjednoczone*

Przedimka **the** używa się przed nazwami łańcuchów górskich i archipelagów.

**...the Alps**
*...Alpy*
**...the Canary Islands**
*...Wyspy Kanaryjskie*

Przedimka **the** używa się przed nazwami akwenów wodnych.

**...the Bay of Biscay**
*...Zatoka Biskajska*
**...the River Ganges**
*...Ganges*
**...the Atlantic Ocean**
*...Ocean Atlantycki*
**...the Panama Canal**
*...Kanał Panamski*

## Określinki

Przedimka **the** używa się przed nazwami krajów, które zawierają słowa takie jak **kingdom** czy **states**, oraz przed nazwami krajów, które mają formę liczby mnogiej.

| | |
|---|---|
| **...the Netherlands** | **...the United Kingdom** |
| *...Holandia* | *...Zjednoczone Królestwo* |

Przedimka **the** nie używa się przed nazwami większości krajów, kontynentów, miast, ulic, adresów i jezior.

| | |
|---|---|
| **...Turkey** | **...Asia** |
| *...Turcja* | *...Azja* |
| **...Tokyo** | **...Oxford Street** |
| *...Tokio* | *...ulica Oxford* |
| **...15 Park Street** | **...Lake Superior** |
| *...ulica Park(owa) 15* | *...Jezioro Górne* |

Przedimka **the** nie używa się przed nazwiskami i imionami ludzi lub przed tytułami, jeśli podane jest nazwisko.

| | |
|---|---|
| **...Queen Elizabeth** | **...President Obama** |
| *...Królowa Elżbieta* | *...Prezydent Obama* |
| **...Mr Brown** | **...Lord Olivier** |
| *...Pan Brown* | *...Lord Olivier* |

## Przedimek nieokreślony

Wyrazy **a** i **an** to przedimki nieokreślone. Przedimka **a** używa się przed wyrazem rozpoczynającym się od głoski wymawianej jak spółgłoska, nawet jeśli pierwsza litera wyrazu to samogłoska, na przykład **a university**, **a European language**. Przedimka **an** używa się przed wyrazem rozpoczynającym się w wymowie od samogłoski, nawet jeśli pierwszą literą wyrazu jest spółgłoska, na przykład **an honest man**. Przedimka **a** (**an**) używa się, gdy wspomina się o osobie lub rzeczy po raz pierwszy.

**She picked up a book.** *Wzięła książkę.*
**After weeks of looking, we eventually bought a house.**
*Po tygodniach poszukiwań w końcu kupiliśmy dom.*
**He was eating an apple.** *Jadł jabłko.*

Gdy odnosi się do tej samej osoby lub rzeczy po raz drugi, wówczas używa się przedimka **the**.

**She picked up a book. The book was lying on the table.**
*Wzięła książkę. Książka leżała na stole.*

Po czasowniku **to be** lub innym czasowniku łącznikowym, można użyć przedimka **a** (**an**) przed przymiotnikiem i rzeczownikiem, aby podać więcej informacji na temat kogoś lub czegoś.

**He seemed a worried man.** *Wydawał się być zmartwionym człowiekiem.*
**It was a really beautiful house.** *To był naprawdę piękny dom.*

Przedimka **a** (**an**) używa się po czasowniku **to be** lub innym czasowniku łącznikowym, kiedy podaje się nazwę zawodu.

**He became a school teacher.** *Został nauczycielem.*
**She is a model and an artist.** *Jest modelką i artystką.*

Przedimka **a** (**an**) używa się w znaczeniu wyrazu **one** z liczbami, ułamkami, pieniędzmi, określeniami miar i wag.

| | | | |
|---|---|---|---|
| **a hundred** | **a quarter** | **a pound** | **a kilo** |
| *sto* | *ćwierć* | *funt* | *kilo* |
| **a thousand** | **a half** | **a dollar** | **a litre** |
| *tysiąc* | *pół* | *dolar* | *litr* |

Przedimka **a** czy **an** nie używa się przed rzeczownikami niepoliczalnymi ani przed formą liczby mnogiej rzeczowników policzalnych.

**I love dogs.** *Uwielbiam psy.*
**Many adults don't listen to children.** *Wielu dorosłych nie słucha dzieci.*
**Money can't buy happiness.** *Pieniądze szczęścia nie dają.*

## Wyrażanie ilości (1): **much, little, many, few, more, less, fewer**

Wyrazu **much** używa się do określenia dużej ilości czegoś, a wyrazu **little** – małej. Wyrazów **much** oraz little używa się tylko z niepoliczalnymi rzeczownikami.

**I haven't got much time.** *Nie mam dużo czasu.*
**We've made little progress.** *Zrobiliśmy niewielki postęp.*

Wyrazu **many** używa się do określenia dużej ilości ludzi lub rzeczy, a wyrazu **few** – małej. Wyrazów **many** oraz **few** używa się z liczbą mnogą rzeczowników policzalnych.

**He wrote many novels.** *Napisał wiele powieści.*
**There were few visitors to our house.** *Mieliśmy niewielu gości w naszym domu.*

Zwykle wyrazu **much** używa się w zaprzeczeniach i pytaniach.

**He did not speak much English.** *Nie mówił dobrze po angielsku.*
**Why haven't I given much attention to this problem?**
*Dlaczego nie poświęciłem więcej uwagi temu problemowi?*

W zdaniach twierdzących zamiast wyrazu **much** używa się wyrażeń **a lot of**, **lots of**, czy **plenty of**. Można ich używać i przed rzeczownikami niepoliczalnymi i przed formą liczby mnogiej.

**I make a lot of mistakes.** *Popełniam mnóstwo błędów.*
**They spend lots of time on the project.** *Spędzają bardzo dużo czasu nad tym projektem.*
**I've got plenty of money.** *Mam mnóstwo pieniędzy.*

Wyrażeń **so much** oraz **too much** można używać w zdaniach twierdzących.

**She spends so much time here.** *Ona spędza tutaj tak dużo czasu.*
**There is too much chance of error.**
*Istnieje zbyt duże prawdopodobieństwo popełnienia błędu.*

Wyrazu **more** używa się z rzeczownikami niepoliczalnymi oraz formą liczby mnogiej rzeczowników policzalnych, gdy odnosi się do ilości czegoś lub liczby ludzi, która jest większa niż inna ilość lub liczba.

**His visit might do more harm than good.**
*Jego wizyta może wyrządzić więcej złego niż dobrego.*
**He does more hours than I do.** *On pracuje więcej godzin niż ja.*

Wyrazu **less** używa się, gdy odnosi się do ilości, która jest mniejsza niż ilość czegoś innego.

**The poor have less access to education.** *Ubodzy mają mniejszy dostęp do oświaty.*
**This machinery uses less energy.** *Ta maszyna zużywa mniej energii.*

Wyrazu **fewer** używa się z formą liczby mnogiej, gdy odnosi się do liczby ludzi lub rzeczy, która jest mniejsza niż liczebność innej grupy.

**There are fewer trees here.** *Tutaj jest mniej drzew.*

# Wyrażanie ilości (2): **some, any, another, other, each, every**

Wyrazu **some** używa się przed niepoliczalnymi rzeczownikami i formą liczby mnogiej, gdy określa się ogólnie ilość czegoś lub liczbę ludzi czy rzeczy.

**We have left some food for you in the fridge.**
*Zostawiliśmy ci w lodówce trochę jedzenia.*
**Some trains are running late.** *Niektóre pociągi mają opóźnienia.*

Wyrazu **some** używa się w pytaniach, jeśli oczekuje się odpowiedzi pozytywnej **yes**.

**Would you like some coffee?** *Czy chcesz trochę kawy?*
**Could you give me some examples?** *Czy mógłby mi pan podać kilka przykładów?*

Wyrazu **any** używa się przed rzeczownikami niepoliczalnymi lub formą liczby mnogiej, aby określić ilość czegoś, co istnieje lub nie. W pytaniach lub zaprzeczeniach zwykle wówczas używa się wyrazu **any**.

**Are there any jobs that men can do but women can't?**
*Czy są jakieś zawody, które mogą wykonywać mężczyźni, a kobiety nie?*
**It hasn't made any difference.** *To nie zrobiło żadnej różnicy.*

Wyrazu **another** używa się przed formą liczby pojedynczej, aby określić dodatkową osobę lub rzecz.

**Could I have another cup of coffee?** *Czy mogę poprosić o jeszcze jedną filiżankę kawy?*
**He opened another shop last month.** *Otworzył kolejny sklep w ubiegłym miesiącu.*

Wyrazu **another** można też użyć przed formą liczby mnogiej, by określić większą liczbę osób lub rzeczy.

**Another four years passed before we met again.**
*Minęły kolejne cztery lata, zanim znowu się spotkaliśmy.*
**I've got another three books to read.** *Mam jeszcze trzy książki do przeczytania.*

Wyrazu **other** używa się przed formą liczby mnogiej, a zwrotu **the other** albo przed formą liczby pojedynczej, albo mnogiej.

**I've got other things to think about.** *Mam inne rzeczy do przemyślenia.*
**The other man has gone.** *Ten drugi mężczyzna już wyszedł.*
**The other European countries have beaten us.** *Inne kraje europejskie nas pobiły.*

## Określinki

Wyrazów **each** lub **every** używa się przed formą liczby pojedynczej, aby zaznaczyć wszystkich członków danej grupy. Wyrazu **each** używa się, gdy chce się zaznaczyć członków grupy jako pojedyncze osoby czy części składowe, a wyrazu **every**, kiedy wypowiada się ogólne twierdzenie na temat całej grupy.

> **Each county is subdivided into several districts.**
> *Każde hrabstwo jest podzielone na kilka okręgów.*
> **Every child would have milk every day.**
> *Każde dziecko piło codziennie (każdego dnia) mleko.*

Wyraz **every** może być określony innymi przymiotnikami lub przysłówkami, natomiast wyraz **each** występuje tylko samodzielnie.

> **He spoke to them nearly every weekend.** *Rozmawiał z nimi niemal co weekend.*
> **We went out almost every evening.** *Wychodziliśmy gdzieś niemal każdego wieczoru.*

# Przymiotniki

## Pozycja przymiotnika w zdaniu

Większość przymiotników może pojawić się przed rzeczownikiem.

**He had a beautiful smile.** *Miał piękny uśmiech.*
**She bought a loaf of white bread.** *Kupiła bochenek pszennego chleba.*
**There was no clear evidence.** *Nie było żadnego niezbitego dowodu.*

Większość przymiotników może również być użyta po czasowniku łącznikowym takim jak **be**, **become** czy **feel**.

**I'm hungry.** *Jestem głodny.*
**I felt angry.** *Byłem zły.*
**Nobody seemed amused.** *Nikt nie zdawał się być rozbawiony.*

Niektóre przymiotniki są zwykle używane po czasowniku łącznikowym.

| **afraid** | **alive** | **alone** | **asleep** | **aware** |
|---|---|---|---|---|
| *bojaźliwy* | *żywy* | *sam* | *śpiący* | *świadomy* |
| **content** | **due** | **glad** | **ill** | **ready** |
| *zadowolony* | *należny* | *zadowolony* | *chory* | *gotowy* |
| **sorry** | **sure** | **unable** | **well** | |
| *zmartwiony* | *pewny* | *niezdolny* | *zdrowy* | |

Na przykład można powiedzieć **she was glad**, ale nie ~~**a glad woman**~~.

**I wanted to be alone.** *Chciałem być sam.*
**We are ready for bed.** *Jesteśmy gotowi do spania.*
**I'm not quite sure.** *Nie jestem do końca pewien.*

Niektóre przymiotniki zwykle są używane przed rzeczownikiem.

| **atomic** | **countless** | **indoor** | **introductory** | **occasional** |
|---|---|---|---|---|
| *atomowy* | *niezliczony* | *wewnętrzny* | *wstępny* | *okazjonalny* |
| **outdoor** | **eastern** | **northern** | **southern** | **western** |
| *zewnętrzny* | *wschodni* | *północny* | *południowy* | *zachodni* |

Na przykład można powiedzieć **an atomic bomb**, ale nie ~~**The bomb was atomic**~~.

**He sent countless letters to the newspapers.** *Wysyłał niezliczoną ilość listów do gazet.*
**This book includes a good introductory chapter on forests.**
*Ta książka zawiera dobry rozdział wprowadzający poświęcony lasom.*

## Przymiotniki

Niektóre przymiotniki mogą być użyte zaraz po rzeczowniku.

**She was now the president elect.** *I oto została prezydentem elektem.*
**There are empty houses galore.** *Jest mnóstwo pustych domów.*

## Stopniowanie przymiotników

W przypadku przymiotników jednosylabowych, formę wyższą przymiotnika tworzy się przez dodanie końcówki **–er**, a formę najwyższą przez dodanie końcówki **–est**. Jeśli w stopniu równym przymiotnik kończy się na **–e**, wówczas dodaje się odpowiednio **–r** i **–st**.

| | | | | |
|---|---|---|---|---|
| **cheap** | → | **cheaper** | → | **cheapest** |
| *tani* | → | *tańszy* | → | *najtańszy* |
| **safe** | → | **safer** | → | **safest** |
| *bezpieczny* | → | *bezpieczniejszy* | → | *najbezpieczniejszy* |

**Ben Nevis is the highest mountain in Britain.**
*Ben Nevis jest najwyższą górą w Wielkiej Brytanii.*
**I've found a nicer hotel.** *Znalazłem sympatyczniejszy hotel.*

Jeśli przymiotniki zakończone są na pojedynczą samogłoskę poprzedzającą pojedynczą spółgłoskę (za wyjątkiem spółgłoski **–w**), ostatnia spółgłoska zostaje podwojona.

| | | | | |
|---|---|---|---|---|
| **big** | → | **bigger** | → | **biggest** |
| *duży* | → | *większy* | → | *największy* |
| **hot** | → | **hotter** | → | **hottest** |
| *gorący* | → | *gorętszy* | → | *najgorętszy* |

**The day grew hotter.** *Dzień robił się coraz gorętszy.*
**Henry was the biggest of them.** *Henry był największym z nich.*

Przymiotniki dwusylabowe zakończone na **–y** po spółgłosce zamieniają **–y** na **–i**, zanim dodana zostanie końcówka **–er** lub **–est**.

| | | | | |
|---|---|---|---|---|
| **happy** | → | **happier** | → | **happiest** |
| *szczęśliwy* | → | *szczęśliwszy* | → | *najszczęśliwszy* |
| **dirty** | → | **dirtier** | → | **dirtiest** |
| *brudny* | → | *brudniejszy* | → | *najbrudniejszy* |

**It couldn't be easier.** *To nie mogło być prostsze.*
**That is the funniest bit of the film.** *To jest najzabawniejszy kawałek filmu.*

W przypadku większości przymiotników dwusylabowych oraz dłuższych przymiotników, formę wyższą tworzy się przez dodanie wyrazu **more**, a formę najwyższą przez dodanie wyrazu **most**. Zwykle dodaje się przedimek **the** przed formą najwyższą, gdy przymiotnik poprzedza rzeczownik. Jeśli przymiotnik użyty jest po czasowniku łącznikowym, wówczas można pominąć wyraz **the**.

| | | | | |
|---|---|---|---|---|
| **careful** | → | **more careful** | → | **most careful** |
| *uważny* | → | *bardziej uważny* | → | *najbardziej uważny* |
| **beautiful** | → | **more beautiful** | → | **most beautiful** |
| *piękny* | → | *piękniejszy* | → | *najpiękniejszy* |

**They are the most beautiful gardens in the world.**
*To są najpiękniejsze ogrody na świecie.*
**I was happiest when I was on my own.** *Byłem najszczęśliwszy, kiedy byłem sam.*

Dwusylabowe przymiotniki, które są często używane, mogą tworzyć stopień wyższy i najwyższy albo przez dodanie końcówek **–er** i **–est**, albo przez użycie wyrazów **more** i **most**. Wyrazy **clever** i **quiet** stopniowane są wyłącznie przez dodanie końcówek **–er** i **–est**.

**It was quieter outside.** *Na zewnątrz było ciszej.*
**He was the cleverest man I ever knew.** *Był najmądrzejszym człowiekiem, jakiego znałem.*

Niektóre często używane przymiotniki mają nieregularne formy.

| | | | | |
|---|---|---|---|---|
| **good** | → | **better** | → | **best** |
| *dobry* | → | *lepszy* | → | *najlepszy* |
| **bad** | → | **worse** | → | **worst** |
| *zły* | → | *gorszy* | → | *najgorszy* |

**There's nothing better than a cup of hot coffee.**
*Nie ma nic lepszego niż filiżanka gorącej kawy.*

# Przysłówki

## Przysłówki sposobu, miejsca i czasu

Przysłówków sposobu używa się, aby określić, w jaki sposób coś się dzieje lub jak jest wykonywane.

**Sit there quietly and listen to the music.** *Siedź cicho i słuchaj muzyki.*

Przysłówków miejsca używa się, aby określić, gdzie coś ma miejsce.

**A plane flew overhead.** *Nad naszymi głowami przeleciał samolot.*

Przysłówków czasu używa się, aby określić, kiedy coś się dzieje.

**She will be here soon.** *Będzie tu wkrótce.*

Przysłówki sposobu, miejsca i czasu zwykle występują po głównym czasowniku.

**She sang beautifully.** *Śpiewała ślicznie.*
**The car broke down yesterday.** *Samochód zepsuł się wczoraj.*

Jeśli po głównym czasowniku występuje dopełnienie, wówczas przysłówek pojawia się po nim.

**I did learn to play a few tunes very badly.** *Nauczyłem się grać kilka melodii bardzo źle.*
**Thomas made his decision immediately.** *Thomas podjął decyzję natychmiast.*

Przysłówek może również pojawić się na początku zdania, zwłaszcza w celu emfazy.

**Slowly, he opened his eyes.** *Powoli otworzył oczy.*

## Tworzenie przysłówków

Przysłówki sposobu zwykle tworzy się przez dodanie końcówki **–ly** do przymiotnika. Utworzone w ten sposób przysłówki zwykle mają znaczenie zbliżone do znaczenia przymiotnika.

**She is as clever as she is beautiful.** *Jest równie mądra, co piękna.*
**He talked so politely and danced so beautifully.**
*Wypowiadał się tak uprzejmie i tańczył tak pięknie.*

Czasami przy tworzeniu przysłówka z formy przymiotnika niezbędne jest wprowadzenie zmian w pisowni.

| | | | |
|---|---|---|---|
| **–le** *zmienia się na* **–ly**: | **gentle** | → | **gently** |
| | *delikatny* | → | *delikatnie* |
| **–y** *zmienia się na* **–ily**: | **easy** | → | **easily** |
| | *łatwy* | → | *łatwo* |
| **–ic** *zmienia się na* **–ically**: | **automatic** | → | **automatically** |
| | *automatyczny* | → | *automatycznie* |
| **–ue** *zmienia się na* **–uly**: | **true** | → | **truly** |
| | *prawdziwy* | → | *prawdziwie* |
| **–ull** *zmienia się na* **–uly**: | **full** | → | **fully** |
| | *pełen* | → | *w pełni* |

Forma niektórych przysłówków sposobu jest taka sama jak forma i znaczenie przymiotników, na przykład **fast**, **hard** i **late**.

> **I've always been interested in fast cars.** (*adjective*)
> *Zawsze interesowałem się szybkimi samochodami.* (przymiotnik)
> **The driver is driving too fast.** (*adverb*) *Kierowca jedzie za szybko.* (przysłówek)

Wyrazy **hardly** i **lately** nie są przysłówkami sposobu utworzonymi od przymiotników **hard** i **late**. Mają one inne znaczenie.

> **It was a hard decision to make.** *To była trudna decyzja do podjęcia.*
> **I hardly had any time to talk to her.** *Prawie nie miałem czasu z nią porozmawiać.*
> **The train was late as usual.** *Pociąg jak zwykle się spóźnił.*
> **Have you seen John lately?** *Czy widziałeś ostatnio Johna?*

## Stopniowanie przysłówków

Formę stopnia wyższego przysłówków jednosylabowych tworzy się przez dodanie końcówki **–er**, a formę stopnia najwyższego przez dodanie końcówki **–est**. Jeśli stopień równy zakończony jest na **–e**, wówczas dodaje się **–r** i **–st**.

> **They worked harder.** *Pracowali ciężej.*
> **Come closer.** *Podejdź bliżej.*

## Przysłówki

Przysłówki zakończone na **–ly** tworzą stopień wyższy przez dodanie wyrazu **more**, a stopień najwyższy przez dodanie wyrazu **most**.

**It affected Clive most seriously.** *To najpoważniej dotknęło Clive'a.*
**People should drive more carefully.** *Ludzie powinni jeździć uważniej.*

Niektóre często używane przysłówki mają nieregularne formy.

| | | | | |
|---|---|---|---|---|
| **well** | → | **better** | → | **best** |
| *dobrze* | → | *lepiej* | → | *najlepiej* |
| **badly** | → | **worse** | → | **worst** |
| *źle* | → | *gorzej* | → | *najgorzej* |

**Which one do you like best?** *Który najbardziej ci się podoba?*
**They played badly, but we played even worse.** *Grali źle, ale my graliśmy jeszcze gorzej.*

## Przechodniość: czasowniki przechodnie i nieprzechodnie

Niektóre czasowniki nie wymagają dopełnienia. Nazywają się one czasownikami nieprzechodnimi.

**An awful thing has happened.** *Straszna rzecz się zdarzyła.*
**The girl screamed.** *Dziewczyna krzyknęła.*
**I waited.** *Czekałem.*

Wiele czasowników zwykle wymaga wyrażenia rzeczownikowego w miejscu dopełnienia. Czasowniki takie nazywają się przechodnimi.

**He hit the ball really hard.** *Uderzył piłkę bardzo mocno.*
**Did you see the rainbow?** *Czy widziałeś tęczę?*
**Don't blame me.** *Nie obwiniaj mnie.*

Czasowniki przechodnie mogą tworzyć stronę bierną.

**They were blamed for everything.** *Byli obwiniani za wszystko.*

Wiele czasowników ma więcej niż jedno znaczenie. Niektóre mają jedno znaczenie w formie przechodniego czasownika, a inne jako czasowniki nieprzechodnie. Na przykład czasownik **run** jest nieprzechodni w znaczeniu **move quickly** (poruszać się szybko), a przechodni w znaczeniu **manage or operate** (zarządzać; prowadzić).

**The hare runs at enormous speed.** *Zając biegnie z olbrzymią prędkością.*
**She runs a hotel.** *Prowadzi hotel.*
**She moved gracefully.** *Poruszała się z gracją.*
**The whole incident had moved her profoundly.** *Cały incydent poruszył ją głęboko.*

## Czasowniki z dwoma dopełnieniami

Po niektórych czasownikach występują dwa dopełnienia, dopełnienie bliższe i dopełnienie dalsze. Na przykład w zdaniu **I gave John the book** [Dałem Johnowi książkę], **the book** [książka] to dopełnienie bliższe, a **John** – dalsze. Kiedy dopełnieniem dalszym jest zaimek lub krótkia grupa nominalna, pojawia się on przed dopełnieniem bliższym.

**Dad gave me a car.** *Tato dał mi samochód.*
**You promised the lad a job.** *Obiecałeś temu chłopakowi pracę.*
**He had lent my cousin the money.** *Pożyczył mojemu kuzynowi pieniądze.*

Aby wprowadzić dopełnienie dalsze, można również wykorzystać przyimki **to** i **for**, szczególnie gdy dopełnienie składa się z kilku słów. Wówczas dopełnienie dalsze występuje po dopełnieniu bliższym.

> **He handed his room key to the receptionist.** *Podał klucz do pokoju recepcjonistce.*
> **Bill saved a piece of cake for the children.** *Bill zostawił kawałek ciasta dla dzieci.*

# Czasy

## Czasowniki posiłkowe

Czasowniki posiłkowe to czasowniki **be**, **have** oraz **do**. Używane są wraz z czasownikiem głównym, przy tworzeniu czasów, zaprzeczeń i pytań.

**He <u>is</u> planning to get married soon.** *On planuje ożenić się wkrótce.*
**I <u>haven't</u> seen Peter since last night.** *Nie widziałem Peter'a od wczoraj wieczorem.*
**Which doctor <u>do</u> you want to see?** *Do której lekarki chce się pan umówić na wizytę?*

Czasownik **be** jako czasownik posiłkowy jest używany przy tworzeniu formy **–ing** głównego czasownika w czasach ciągłych.

**He <u>is</u> living in Germany.** *On mieszka w Niemczech.*
**They <u>were</u> going to phone you.** *Mieli do was zadzwonić.*

Czasownik **be** jako czasownik posiłkowy jest używany również wraz z imiesłowem przeszłym (*past participle*) przy tworzeniu strony biernej.

**These cars <u>are</u> made in Japan.** *Te samochody <u>są</u> produkowane w Japonii.*
**The walls of her flat <u>were</u> covered with posters.**
*Ściany jej mieszkania <u>były</u> pokryte plakatami.*

Czasownik **have** używany jest jako czasownik pomocniczy wraz z imiesłowem przeszłym przy tworzeniu czasów uprzednich (*perfect*).

**I <u>have</u> changed my mind.** *Zmieniłem zdanie.*
**I wish you <u>had</u> met Guy.** *Szkoda, że nie poznałeś Guya.*

Czas teraźniejszy uprzedni ciągły (*present perfect continuous*), przeszły uprzedni ciągły (*past perfect continuous*) oraz czasy uprzednie (*perfect*) w stronie biernej tworzone są przy użyciu zarówno czasownika **have** jak i czasownika **be**.

**He <u>has been</u> working very hard recently.** *Ostatnio pracuje bardzo ciężko.*
**She did not know how long she <u>had been</u> lying there.**
*Nie wiedziała, od jak dawna tam leżała.*
**The guest room window <u>has been</u> mended.**
*Okno w pokoju gościnnym zostało naprawione.*
**They <u>had been</u> taught by a young teacher.** *Uczył ich młody nauczyciel.*

Czasowniki **be** oraz **have** są również używane przy tworzeniu zaprzeczeń oraz pytań w czasach ciągłych (*continuous*) oraz uprzednich (*perfect*), jak również w stronie biernej.

**He isn't going.** *On nie idzie.*
**Hasn't she seen it yet?** *Czy jeszcze tego nie widziała?*
**Was it written in English?** *Czy to było napisane po angielsku?*

Czasownik **do** używany jest jako czasownik posiłkowy przy tworzeniu zaprzeczeń oraz pytań w czasie teraźniejszym prostym (*present simple*) i przeszłym prostym (*past simple*).

**He doesn't think he can come to the party.** *On nie sądzi, że może przyjść na przyjęcie.*
**Do you like her new haircut?** *Czy podoba ci się jej nowa fryzura?*
**She didn't buy the house.** *Nie kupiła tego domu.*
**Didn't he get the job?** *Czy nie dostał tej pracy?*

## Czasy teraźniejsze

W języku angielskim wyróżnia się cztery czasy teraźniejsze: czas teraźniejszy prosty (*the present simple*), czas teraźniejszy ciągły (*the present continuous*), czas teraźniejszy uprzedni (*the present perfect*) oraz czas teraźniejszy uprzedni ciągły (*the present perfect continuous*).

Czas teraźniejszy prosty oraz teraźniejszy ciągły odnoszą się do czasu teraźniejszego. Czas teraźniejszy prosty określa generalnie teraźniejszość oraz regularne, powtarzalne wydarzenia i czynności.

**George lives in Birmingham.** *George mieszka w Birmingham.*
**They often phone my mother.** *Często dzwonią do mojej matki.*

Aby określić coś wydarzającego się właśnie teraz, w danej chwili, używa się czasu teraźniejszego ciągłego.

**He's playing tennis at the university.** *Gra w tenisa na uniwersytecie.*
**I'm cooking the dinner.** *Gotuję obiad.*

Czas teraźniejszy ciągły używany jest często w opisach tymczasowej sytuacji.

**She's living in a small flat at present.** *Obecnie mieszka w małym mieszkaniu.*

Czasu teraźniejszego uprzedniego oraz teraźniejszego uprzedniego ciągłego używa się, gdy opisuje się obecne (teraźniejsze) rezultaty wydarzeń, które zdarzyły się w przeszłości lub gdy opisuje się wydarzenie, które rozpoczęło się w przeszłości, i trwa nadal.

**Have you seen the film at the Odeon?** *Czy widziałeś film w kinie Odeon?*
**We've been waiting here since two o'clock.** *Czekamy tutaj od drugiej.*

Czasu teraźniejszego prostego używa się również przy podawaniu informacji dotyczących wydarzenia zaplanowanego (przez instytucje itp.) na przyszłość i podanego na przykład w formie rozkładu jazdy.

**The next train leaves at two fifteen in the morning.**
*Następny pociąg odjeżdża o drugiej piętnaście w nocy.*
**It's Tuesday tomorrow.** *Jutro jest wtorek.*

Czasu teraźniejszego ciągłego, niemal zawsze z okolicznikiem czasu, używa się, by zaznaczyć plany prywatne.

**We're going on holiday with my parents this year.**
*W tym roku jedziemy na wakacje z moimi rodzicami.*
**The Browns are having a party next week.**
*Państwo Brown wydają przyjęcie w przyszłym tygodniu.*

Czas teraźniejszy prosty zwykle nie wymaga użycia czasownika posiłkowego w zdaniach twierdzących, ale przy zaprzeczeniach i pytaniach wykorzystuje czasownik posiłkowy **do**.

**Do you live round here?** *Czy mieszkasz gdzieś w okolicy?*
**Does your husband do most of the cooking?** *Czy twój mąż gotuje większość posiłków?*
**They don't often phone during the week.** *Nie dzwonią często w ciągu tygodnia.*
**She doesn't like being late if she can help it.**
*Ona nie lubi się spóźniać, jeśli może temu zaradzić.*

## Czasy przeszłe

W języku angielskim wyróżnia się cztery czasy przeszłe: czas przeszły prosty (*the past simple*), czas przeszły ciągły (*the past continuous*), czas przeszły uprzedni (*the past perfect*) oraz czas przeszły uprzedni ciągły (*the past perfect continuous*).

Czas przeszły prosty oraz przeszły ciągły odnoszą się do przeszłości. Czasu przeszłego prostego używa się przy opisywaniu wydarzeń, które odbyły się w przeszłości.

**I woke up early and got out of bed.** *Obudziłem się wcześnie i wstałem z łóżka.*

Czas przeszły prosty stosowany jest również do mówienia ogólnie o przeszłości, o przeszłych zwyczajach i regularnie powtarzających się zdarzeniach.

**She lived just outside London.** *Mieszkała tuż pod Londynem.*
**We often saw his dog sitting outside his house.**
*Często widzieliśmy, jak jego pies siedział przed domem.*

Czasu przeszłego ciągłego używa się, opisując wydarzenie, które odbywało się (działo się) przed i po pewnym punkcie w czasie.

**They were sitting in the kitchen, when they heard the explosion.**
*Siedzieli w kuchni, kiedy usłyszeli wybuch.*
**Jack arrived while the children were having their bath.**
*Jack przyjechał, kiedy dzieci brały kąpiel.*

Czas przeszły ciągły opisuje również tymczasową sytuację.

**He was working at home at the time.** *W tym czasie pracował w domu.*
**Bill was using my office until I came back from America.**
*Bill korzystał z mojego biura, dopóki nie wróciłem z Ameryki.*

Czasu przeszłego uprzedniego oraz przeszłego uprzedniego ciągłego używa się, gdy opisuje się wydarzenie, które miało miejsce przed innym wydarzeniem, lub rozpoczęło się wcześniej i trwało nadal.

**I had heard it was a good film so we decided to go and see it.**
*Słyszałam, że to dobry film, więc zdecydowaliśmy się go zobaczyć.*
**It was getting late. I had been waiting there since two o'clock.**
*Robiło się późno. Czekałam tam już od drugiej.*

Czasami wykorzystuje się czas przeszły zamiast czasu teraźniejszego, gdy chce się coś wyrazić w uprzejmy sposób.

**Did you want to see me now?** *Czy chciał pan ze mną porozmawiać teraz?*
**I was wondering if you could help me.** *Zastanawiałem się, czy mogłaby pani mi pomóc.*

## Czasy ciągłe

Czasów ciągłych używa się do zaznaczenia czynności, która trwa pomiędzy dwoma punktami w czasie, bez przerwy. Czasu teraźniejszego ciągłego używa się do opisania czynności, które rozpoczęły się przed czasem wypowiedzi i trwają po nim.

**I'm looking at the photographs my brother sent me.**
*Oglądam zdjęcia, które przysłał mi brat.*

Kiedy opisuje się dwa wydarzenia odbywające się w teraźniejszości, czasu ciągłego używa się do opisania tej czynności, która tworzy tło innej czynności, tj. czynności, która przerywa trwanie tej pierwszej. Druga czynność wyrażona jest czasem teraźniejszym prostym.

**The phone always rings when I'm having a bath.**
*Telefon dzwoni zawsze wtedy, kiedy biorę kąpiel.*

**Friends always talk to me when I'm trying to study.**
*Zawsze kiedy próbuję się uczyć, znajomi mnie zagadują.*

Opisując przeszłość, używa się czasu przeszłego ciągłego do opisania czynności, która rozpoczęła się przed inną czynnością, i trwała nieprzerwanie po zakończeniu tej drugiej czynności, która odbyła się w konkretnym punkcie czasu. Dla opisania drugiej czynności używa się czasu przeszłego prostego.

**He was watching television when the doorbell rang.**
*Oglądał telewizję, gdy zadzwonił dzwonek u drzwi.*
**It was 6 o'clock. The train was nearing London.**
*Była szósta. Pociąg zbliżał się do Londynu.*

UWAGA: Jeśli dwie czynności następują jedna po drugiej, wówczas obie opisane są w czasie przeszłym prostym.

**As soon as he saw me, he waved.** *Jak tylko mnie zobaczył, pomachał do mnie ręką.*

Czasów ciągłych używa się, gdy chce się podkreślić okres trwania czynności, gdy chce się podkreślić, jak długo coś trwało.

**We had been living in Athens for five years.** *Mieszkaliśmy w Atenach pięć lat.*
**They'll be staying with us for a couple of weeks.** *Zatrzymają się u nas na parę tygodni.*

Jednak dla zaznaczenia okresu trwania jakiejś czynności, nie trzeba używać czasu ciągłego.

**We had lived in Africa for five years.** *Mieszkaliśmy w Afryce pięć lat.*
**He worked for us for ten years.** *Pracował u nas dziesięć lat.*

Czasu ciągłego używa się do opisania tymczasowego stanu lub tymczasowej sytuacji.

**I'm living in London at the moment.** *W tej chwili mieszkam w Londynie.*
**He'll be working nights next week.** *W przyszłym tygodniu pracuje na nocki.*

Czasów ciągłych używa się dla zaznaczenia zmian i rozwoju jakiegoś stanu.

**Her English was improving.** *Jej angielski się poprawiał.*
**The children are growing up quickly.** *Dzieci rosną szybko.*

# Czasowniki

## Wyrażanie teraźniejszości

Kiedy wypowiada się ogólnie na temat teraźniejszości lub na temat właśnie trwającej chwili, zwykle używa się czasu teraźniejszego prostego.

**My dad works in Saudi Arabia.** *Mój tata pracuje w Arabii Saudyjskiej.*
**He lives in the French Alps near the Swiss border.**
*On mieszka w Alpach Francuskich niedaleko granicy szwajcarskiej.*

Czasu teraźniejszego prostego używa się również przy podawaniu ogólnie znanych zasad i praw.

**Water boils at 100 degrees centigrade.** *Woda wrze w temperaturze 100 stopni Celsjusza.*
**The bus takes longer than the train.** *Autobusem jedzie się dłużej niż pociągiem.*

Czasu teraźniejszego prostego używa się przy opisywaniu czynności wykonywanych regularnie lub zwyczajowo.

**Do you eat meat?** *Czy jesz mięso?*
**I get up early and eat my breakfast in bed.** *Wstaję wcześnie i jem śniadanie w łóżku.*

Czasu teraźniejszego używa się do opisania stanu, który uważany jest za tymczasowy.

**Do you know if she's still playing tennis these days?**
*Czy wiesz, czy ona ostatnio grywa w tenisa?*
**I'm working as a British Council officer.** *Pracuję jako urzędnik w British Council.*

Czasu teraźniejszego ciągłego używa się do opisania sytuacji mającej miejsce w danej chwili.

**We're having a meeting. Come and join us.** *Mamy zebranie. Przyłącz się do nas.*
**Wait a moment. I'm listening to the news.**
*Poczekaj chwilę. Właśnie słucham wiadomości.*

Niektóre czasowniki mogą być użyte tylko w czasie teraźniejszym prostym, nawet kiedy opisują sytuację odbywającą się w danej chwili. Te czasowniki zwykle nie mają formy ciągłej. Odnoszą się one do myślenia, upodobań, wyglądu, stanu posiadania, istnienia i odbierania zmysłami.

**I believe he was not to blame.** *Wierzę, że nie jest winny.*
**She hates going to parties.** *Ona nie znosi chodzić na przyjęcia.*
**Our neighbours have two cars.** *Nasi sąsiedzi mają dwa samochody.*

UWAGA: niektóre z tych czasowników mogą być użyte w czasach ciągłych, ale wówczas mają inne znaczenie.

**We're having a party tomorrow.** *Jutro organizujemy imprezę.*

**She's seeing an American guy.** *Spotyka się z Amerykaninem.*

## Wyrażanie przeszłości

Czasu przeszłego prostego używa się do opisania wydarzenia, które miało miejsce w konkretnym punkcie czasu w przeszłości.

**The Prime Minister flew into New York today.**
*Premier przyleciał dzisiaj do Nowego Jorku.*
**The new term started last week.** *Nowy semestr rozpoczął się w ubiegłym tygodniu.*

Czasu przeszłego używa się również do opisania sytuacji, która trwała przez pewien okres w przeszłości.

**We spent most of our time at home last winter.**
*Ubiegłej zimy większość czasu spędziliśmy w domu.*
**They earned their money quickly that year.** *Tego roku szybko zarobili pieniądze.*

Czasu przeszłego prostego używa się, gdy opisuje się zdarzenia odbywające się regularnie w przeszłości.

**They went for picnics most weekends.**
*Podczas większości weekendów chodzili na pikniki.*
**We usually spent the winter at Aunt Meg's house.**
*Zwykle spędzaliśmy zimę u cioci Meg.*

Do opisania regularnie odbywających się w przeszłości zdarzeń zamiast czasu przeszłego można użyć wyrażenia **used to**.

**People used to believe that the world was flat.** *Ludzie wierzyli, że świat jest płaski.*

Czasu przeszłego ciągłego używa się do opisania czynności, która trwała przed i po pewnym punkcie w czasie.

**I hurt myself when I was mending my bike.** *Zraniłem się, kiedy naprawiałem rower.*
**It was midnight. She was driving home.** *Była północ. Jechała samochodem do domu.*

Czasu przeszłego ciągłego używa się do opisania tymczasowej sytuacji mającej miejsce w przeszłości.

**Our team were losing 2-1 at the time.** *W tym czasie nasza drużyna przegrywała 2-1.*
**We were staying with friends in Italy.** *We Włoszech zatrzymaliśmy się u przyjaciół.*

Czasu teraźniejszego uprzedniego używa się do opisania widocznych w teraźniejszości skutków przeszłych czynności, albo do opisania czynności, która rozpoczęła się w przeszłości i trwa nadal.

**I'm afraid I've forgotten my book.** *Obawiam się, że zapomniałem książki.*
**Have you heard from Jill recently?** *Czy ostatnio byłeś w kontakcie z Jill?*
**He has been here since six o'clock.** *On jest tu od szóstej.*

Czasu przeszłego uprzedniego używa się do opisania skutków czynności, która wydarzyła się w przeszłości, ale przed inną czynnością, która też odbyła się w przeszłości.

**I apologized because I had left my wallet at home.**
*Przeprosiłem, bo zostawiłem portfel w domu.*
**They would have come if we had invited them.** *Przyszliby, gdybyśmy ich zaprosili.*

## Wyrażanie przyszłości z konstrukcjami z **will** i **going to**

Kiedy przedstawia się przypuszczenia dotyczące przyszłości, opierając się na ogólnie znanych prawach, opiniach i poglądach, wówczas stosuje się **will**.

**The weather tomorrow will be warm and sunny.** *Pogoda jutro będzie ciepła i słoneczna.*
**I'm sure you will enjoy your visit to the zoo.**
*Jestem pewna, że będziecie dobrze się bawić podczas wizyty w zoo.*

Kiedy w swoich przypuszczeniach wykorzystuje się fakty lub dowody, wtedy używa się **going to**.

**It's going to rain.** *Będzie padać.*
**I'm going to be late.** *Spóźnię się.*

Kiedy mówi się o swoich własnych zamiarach, używa się **will** lub **going to**.

**I'll ring you tonight.** *Zadzwonię do ciebie wieczorem.*
**I'm going to stay at home today.** *Dzisiaj zostanę w domu.*

Kiedy wypowiada się na temat tego, co ktoś inny zdecydował się zrobić, wówczas używa się **going to**.

**They're going to have a party.** *Urządzają przyjęcie.*

Kiedy ogłasza się decyzję, którą się właśnie podjęło lub ma się właśnie podjąć, używa się **will**.

**I think I'll go to bed.** *Chyba się położę.*

## Wyrażanie przyszłości: użycie czasów teraźniejszych

Kiedy mówi się o czymś, co będzie miało miejsce w przyszłości, ale jest oparte na oficjalnych rozkładach lub kalendarzu, wówczas używa się czasu teraźniejszego prostego wraz z odpowiednim okolicznikiem czasu.

**My last train leaves Euston at 11.30.** *Mój ostatni pociąg odjeżdża ze stacji Euston o 23.30.*
**Our next lesson is on Thursday.** *Nasza następna lekcja jest w czwartek.*

W twierdzeniach dotyczących ustalonych dat, zwykle używa się czasu teraźniejszego prostego.

**Tomorrow is Tuesday.** *Jutro jest wtorek.*
**It's my birthday next month.** *W przyszłym miesiącu są moje urodziny.*

Kiedy opisuje się czyjeś prywatne plany dotyczące przyszłości, wówczas używa się czasu teraźniejszego ciągłego.

**I'm meeting Bill next week.** *Spotykam się z Billem w przyszłym tygodniu.*
**They're getting married in June.** *Pobierają się w czerwcu.*

# Tryb warunkowy z **if**

Tryb warukowy używany jest do opisania sytuacji, która może się zdarzyć, oraz do opisania ewentulanych skutków tej sytuacji. Zdania określające warunek zaczynają się od **if**.

**If the light comes on, the battery is OK.** *Jeśli światełko się zapala, to bateria działa.*
**I'll call you if I need you.** *Zadzwonię do ciebie, jeśli będę cię potrzebować.*
**If I had known, I'd have told you.** *Gdybym wiedział, tobym ci powiedział.*
**If she asked me, I'd help her.** *Gdyby mnie poprosiła, tobym jej pomógł.*

Kiedy mówi się o ogólnych zasadach lub o czymś, co często się zdarza, wówczas w obu zdaniach używa się czasu teraźniejszego lub teraźniejszego uprzedniego.

**If you lose weight during an illness, you soon regain it afterwards.**
*Jeśli traci się wagę podczas choroby, szybko się ją odzyskuje po wyzdrowieniu.*
**If the baby is crying, it is probably hungry.** *Jeśli dziecko płacze, to pewnie jest głodne.*
**If they have lost any money, they report it to me.**
*Jeśli stracą pieniądze, zgłaszają to mnie.*

Kiedy w zdaniu określającym warunek używa się czasu teraźniejszego lub teraźniejszego uprzedniego, wtedy często w głównym zdaniu używa się trybu rozkazującego.

**Wake me up if you're worried.** *Obudź mnie, jeśli będziesz się martwić.*
**If he has finished, ask him to leave quietly.**
*Jeśli skończył, poproś go, by po cichu wyszedł.*

Kiedy swoje przypuszczenia odnosi się do przyszłości, wówczas w zdaniu wyrażającym warunek używa się czasu teraźniejszego lub teraźniejszego uprzedniego, a w zdaniu głównym – czasu przyszłego prostego.

**If I marry Celia, we will need the money.**
*Jeśli ożenię się z Celią, będziemy potrzebować tych pieniędzy.*
**If you are going to America, you will need a visa.**
*Jeśli jedziecie do Ameryki, będziecie potrzebować wizy.*

Kiedy mówi się o sytuacji, która prawdopodobnie nie będzie miała miejsca, w zdaniu podającym warunek używa się czasu teraźniejszego prostego lub przeszłego ciągłego, a w głównym zdaniu – **would**.

**If I had enough money, I would buy the car.**
*Gdybym miał dosyć pieniędzy, kupiłbym ten samochód.*
**If he was coming, he would ring.** *Gdyby miał przyjść, toby zadzwonił.*

Często używa się wyrażenia **if I were you**, kiedy udziela się rady.

**If I were you, I would take the money.**
*Na twoim miejscu wziąłbym te pieniądze, wziąłbym te pieniądze.*

Kiedy opisuje się wydarzenie, które mogło było się odbyć w przeszłości, ale się nie wydarzyło, wtedy używa się w zdaniu wyrażającym warunek czasu przeszłego uprzedniego, a w zdaniu głównym **would have** z imiesłowem przeszłym.

**If he had realized that, he would have run away.**
*Gdyby sobie wtedy zdał z tego sprawę, uciekłby.*
**I wouldn't have been so depressed if I had known that.**
*Nie byłbym tak przygnębiony, gdybym o tym wiedział wcześniej*

## Mowa zależna

Mowy zależnej używa się do przedstawiania myśli i opinii innych ludzi. Struktura mowy zależnej składa się z dwóch części. Jedną z nich jest wyrażenie wprowadzające, które zawiera odpowiedni dla mowy zależnej czasownik.

> **I told him nothing was going to happen to me.** *Powiedziałem mu, że nic mi się nie stanie.*
> **I agreed that he should do it.** *Zgodziłem się, ve powinien to zrobić.*

Druga część to zdanie zawierające relacjonowane informacje.

> **He felt that he had to do something.** *Poczuł, że musi coś zrobić.*
> **Henry said that he wanted to go home.** *Henry powiedział, że chce pójść do domu.*

Mowa zależna składa się z dwóch zdań. Pierwsze z nich to zdanie wprowadzające, które zawiera czasowniki takie jak **say**, **tell** czy **ask**.

> **She said that she'd been to Belgium.** *Powiedziała, że była w Belgii.*

Drugie zdanie to zdanie relacjonujące, które zawiera przekazywane informacje. Zdanie to tworzone jest przez zdanie podrzędne rozpoczynające się od **that** (że), **to** (żeby; lub wyrażenie bezokolicznikowe), **if** (czy) lub zaimka rozpoczynającego się od **wh–**, wprowadzającego pytanie szczegółowe.

> **She said that she didn't know.** *Powiedziała, że nie wie.*
> **He told me to do it.** *Kazał mi to zrobić.*
> **Mary asked if she could stay with us.**
> *Mary spytała, czy mogłaby się u nas zatrzymać.*
> **She asked where he'd gone.** *Spytała, dokąd poszedł.*

Kiedy relacjonuje się czyjąś wypowiedź, rzadko używa się dokładnych cytatów. Częściej przekazuje się informację własnymi słowami przy użyciu odpowiednich struktur.

> **Jim said he wanted to go home.** *Jim powiedział, że chce pójść do domu.*

Jim prawdopodobnie powiedział: **It's time I went** (Najwyższy czas, abym poszedł do domu) lub **I must go** (Muszę iść).

Forma czasownika w zdaniu podrzędnym powinna odpowiednio odzwierciedlać relacje czasowe. Ponieważ relacjonowana informacja zwykle dotyczy czegoś, co było powiedziane w przeszłości, czasowniki w obu zdaniach w mowie zależnej przybierają formę czasu przeszłego.

> **At the time we thought that he was mad.** *Wówczas myśleliśmy, że zwariował.*

## Pytania w mowie zależnej

Relacjonując pytanie zadane przez kogoś innego, używa się formy pytania w mowie zależnej.

**She asked me why I was so late.** *Spytała mnie, dlaczego się tak spóźniłem.*
**He wanted to know where I was going.** *Chciał wiedzieć, dokąd idę.*
**I demanded to know what was going on.** *Chciałem wiedzieć, co się działo.*

Kiedy relacjonuje się pytanie, czasownik w zdaniu podrzędnym podany jest często w czasie przeszłym. Jest tak dlatego, że pytanie to dotyczy przeszłości.

**She asked me why I was so late.** *Spytała mnie, dlaczego się tak spóźniłem.*
**Pat asked him if she had hurt him.** *Pat spytała go, czy go zraniła.*

Jeśli jednak pytanie odnosi się do teraźniejszości lub przyszłości, można użyć formy czasu teraźniejszego lub przyszłego.

**Mark was asking if you're enjoying your new job.**
*Mark pytał się, czy podoba ci się w nowej pracy.*
**They asked if you'll be there tomorrow night.** *Spytali, czy przyjdziecie jutro wieczorem.*

## Zdania twierdzące w mowie zależnej

Kiedy relacjonuje się zdanie twierdzące, używa się zdania podrzędnego rozpoczynającego się od **that** (**że**) po czasownikach takich jak **say**.

| | | | | |
|---|---|---|---|---|
| **admit** | **announce** | **complain** | **explain** | **mention** |
| *przyznać* | *ogłosić* | *narzekać* | *wyjaśnić* | *wspomnieć* |
| **say** | **suggest** | | | |
| *powiedzieć* | *zasugerować* | | | |

**He said that he would go.** *Powiedział, że pójdzie.*
**I replied that I had not read it yet.** *Odpowiedziałem, że jeszcze tego nie czytałem.*

Często wyraz **that** wprowadzający zdanie podrzędne może być pominięty, ale nie po czasownikach **answer**, **argue**, **explain** czy **reply**.

**They said I had to see a doctor.** *Powiedzieli, że muszę pójść do lekarza.*
**He answered that the price would be three pounds.**
*Odpowiedział, że cena wynosi trzy funty.*

Czasownik **tell** oraz inne czasowniki relacjonujące również używane są z zaimkiem **that** wprowadzającym zdanie podrzędne, ale w przypadku tych czasowników należy również wskazać adresata wypowiedzi poprzez podanie dopełnienia czasownika.

| | | | | |
|---|---|---|---|---|
| **convince** | **inform** | **notify** | **persuade** | **reassure** |
| *przekonywać* | *informować* | *powiadamiać* | *namawiać* | *zapewniać* |
| **remind** | **tell** | | | |
| *przypominać* | *mówić* | | | |

**He told me that he was a farmer.** *Powiedział mi, że jest rolnikiem.*
**I informed her that I couldn't come.** *Poinformowałam ją, że nie mogę przyjść.*

## Inne struktury w mowie zależnej

Zdanie relacjonujące rozkaz, żądanie czy radę zawiera czasowniki takie jak **tell**, **ask** czy **advise**, a zdanie podrzędne zawiera czasownik w formie bezokolicznika. W zdaniu głównym konieczne jest wskazanie adresata wypowiedzi.

**Johnson told her to wake him up.** *Johnson powiedział jej, żeby go obudziła.*
**He ordered me to fetch the books.** *Kazał mi przynieść książki.*
**He advised me to buy it.** *Poradził mi, żebym to kupił.*

Jeśli rozkaz, żądanie czy prośba są w formie zaprzeczenia, forma bezokolicznika w zdaniu podrzędnym zostaje poprzedzona wyrazem **not**.

**He had ordered his officers not to use weapons.**
*Rozkazał swoim oficerom, by nie używali broni.*
**She asked her staff not to discuss it publicly.**
*Poprosiła swoich pracowników, by nie dyskutowali o tym publicznie.*

Jeśli podmiotem zdania podrzędnego (rozpoczynającego się od bezokolicznika) jest podmiot zdania głównego, można użyć czasowników **ask** lub **beg**, aby zrelacjonować żądanie bez wskazywania adresata wypowiedzi.

**I asked to see the manager.** *Zażądałem spotkania z kierownikiem.*
**Both men begged not to be named.**
*Obydwaj mężczyźni błagali, by nie podawać ich nazwisk.*

## Strona bierna

Kiedy chce się mówić o osobie lub przedmiocie, który wykonuje jakąś czynność, wówczas używa się strony czynnej.

**Mr Smith locks the gate at 6 o'clock every night.**
*Pan Smith zamyka bramę co wieczór o 1800.*
**The storm destroyed dozens of trees.** *Burza zniszczyła kilkadziesiąt drzew.*

Kiedy chce się zwrócić większą uwagę na osobę lub rzecz, która jest celem (lub adresatem) czynności, a nie osobą czy rzeczą wykonującą tę czynność, wówczas używa się strony biernej.

> **The gate is locked at 6 o'clock every night.** *Brama jest zamykana co wieczór o 1800.*
> **Dozens of trees were destroyed.** *Kilkadziesiąt drzew zostało zniszczonych.*

Strona bierna tworzona jest przez użycie czasownika posiłkowego **be** oraz czasownika głównego w formie imiesłowu przeszłego.

> **Two new stores were opened this year.** *Dwa sklepy zostały otwarte w tym roku.*
> **The room had been cleaned.** *Pokój został posprzątany.*

Czasy ciągłe w stronie biernej tworzone są przez odpowiednią formę czasownika posiłkowego **be**, po którym podany jest wyraz **being** oraz czasownik główny w formie imiesłowu przeszłego.

> **Jobs are still being lost.** *Nadal wiele posad jest redukowanych.*

W zdaniach w stronie biernej często nie wskazuje się osoby lub rzeczy, która wykonuje daną czynność. Jeśli chce się zaznaczyć wykonawcę czynności, jego nazwę poprzedza się wyrazem **by**.

> **He had been poisoned by his girlfriend.** *Został otruty przez swoją dziewczynę.*
> **He was brought up by an aunt.** *Został wychowany przez ciocię.*

Jeśli zdanie w stronie czynnej ma dwa dopełnienia, może ono utworzyć dwa różne zdania w stronie biernej.

> **They were offered a new flat.** *Zaoferowano im nowe mieszkanie.*
> **A new flat was offered to them.** *Nowe mieszkanie zostało im zaoferowane.*

## Czasowniki modalne

Czasowniki modalne to następujące czasowniki: **can**, **could**, **may**, **might**, **must**, **ought**, **shall**, **should**, **will** oraz **would**.

Czasownik modalny jest czasownikiem pojawiającym się na pierwszej pozycji w grupie czasownikowej. Wszystkie czasowniki modalne za wyjątkiem **ought** wymagają formy czasownika w formie bezokolicznika bez wyznacznika **to**. **Ought** zawsze wymaga pełnej formy bezokolicznika (**to**-infinitive).

> **I must leave fairly soon.** *Muszę wyjść dość wcześnie.*
> **I think it will look very nice.** *Myślę, że to będzie wyglądać ładnie.*
> **She ought to go straight back to England.** *Powinna od razu wrócić do Anglii.*

Czasowniki modalne mają tylko jedną formę. Nie ma formy zakończonej na **–s** oznaczającej trzecią osobę liczby pojedynczej czasu teraźniejszego, nie ma też form zakończonych na **–ing** czy **–ed**.

**I'm sure he <u>can</u> do it.** *Jestem pewien, że <u>potrafi</u> to zrobić.*

## Zaprzeczenia i pytania

Zaprzeczenia tworzone są przez dodanie odpowiedniego słowa zaraz po czasowniku.

**You <u>must not</u> worry.** *<u>Nie powinieneś się</u> martwić.*
**I <u>can never</u> remember his name.** *<u>Nigdy nie mogę</u> sobie przypomnieć jego imienia.*

**Cannot** jest zawsze pisane jako jeden wyraz, **cannot**.

**I <u>cannot</u> go back.** *<u>Nie mogę</u> wrócić.*

W mówionym angielskim oraz w codziennym pisanym angielskim wyraz **not** często jest skracany do **n't**, który to skrót jest dołączany do czasownika modalnego.

| | |
|---|---|
| **could not** | **couldn't** |
| **should not** | **shouldn't** |
| **must not** | **mustn't** |
| **would not** | **wouldn't** |

**We <u>couldn't</u> leave the farm.** *<u>Nie mogliśmy</u> wyjechać z gospodarstwa.*
**You <u>mustn't</u> talk about Ron like that.** *<u>Nie wolno</u> ci mówić o Ronie w ten sposób.*

Poniżej podane są formy nieregularne zaprzeczeń.

| | |
|---|---|
| **shall not** | **shan't** |
| **will not** | **won't** |
| **cannot** | **can't** |

**I <u>shan't</u> let you go.** *Nie pozwolę ci odejść.*
**<u>Won't</u> you change your mind?** *Czy nie zmienisz zdania?*

## Możliwość

Kiedy chcemy powiedzieć, że coś jest możliwe, używa się czasownika modalnego **can**.

**Cooking <u>can</u> be a real pleasure.** *Gotowanie <u>może</u> być prawdziwą przyjemnością.*
**In some cases this <u>can</u> cause difficulty.**
*W niektórych przypadkach <u>może</u> to sprawiać trudność.*

Aby opisać coś jako niemożliwe, używa się **cannot** lub **can't**.

**This <u>cannot</u> be the answer.** *To <u>nie może</u> być właściwa odpowiedź.*
**You <u>can't</u> be serious.** *Nie <u>możesz</u> tego <u>chyba</u> mówić poważnie.*

Kiedy nie ma się pewności, czy dana rzecz jest możliwa, choć samemu tak się sądzi, używa się **could**, **might** czy **may**. **May** ma nieco bardziej formalne znaczenie.

**That could be the reason.** *To może być powodem.*
**He might come.** *Może przyjdzie.*
**They may help us.** *Może nam pomogą.*
**He might not be in England at all.** *Może wcale nie jest w Anglii.*

## Prawdopodobieństwo i pewność

Kiedy chce się powiedzieć, że coś prawdopodobnie jest prawdziwe lub prawdopodobnie się zdarzy, używa się **should** lub **ought**.

**We should arrive by dinner time.** *Powinniśmy przyjechać przed obiadem.*
**She ought to know.** *Powinna to wiedzieć.*

Kiedy chce się powiedzieć, że coś prawdopodobnie nie jest prawdziwe lub się nie wydarzy, używa się wówczas **should not** lub **ought not**.

**There shouldn't be any problem.** *Nie powinno być żadnego problemu.*
**That ought not to be too difficult.** *To nie powinno być zbyt trudne.*

## Umiejętność

Czasownik **can** używany jest w celu zaznaczenia, że ktoś posiada umiejętność wykonania czegoś.

**You can all read and write.** *Wszyscy potraficie czytać i pisać.*
**Anybody can become a qualified teacher.**
*Każdy może zostać wykwalifikowanym nauczycielem.*

Aby zaznaczyć, że ktoś nie posiada umiejętności wykonania jakiejś czynności, używa się **cannot** lub **can't**.

**He can't dance.** *On nie umie tańczyć.*

Kiedy opisuje się umiejętność, którą ktoś posiadał (lub nie posiadał) w przeszłości, używa się czasowników **could**, **couldn't** lub **could not**.

**He could run faster than anyone else.** *Biegał szybciej niż ktokolwiek inny.*
**A lot of them couldn't read or write.** *Wielu z nich nie potrafiło czytać ani pisać.*

## Zgoda

Czasownika **can** używa się, by prosić o udzielenie zgody lub gdy wyraża się zgodę.

**You can borrow that pen if you want to.** *Możesz pożyczyć ten długopis, jeśli chcesz.*
**She can go with you.** *Ona może pójść z tobą.*
**Can I ask a question?** *Czy mogę zadać pytanie?*

**Could** jest bardziej uprzejme niż **can**.

**Could I just interrupt a minute?** *Czy mógłbym na chwilę przerwać?*

**May** również jest stosowane przy udzielaniu zgody, ale jest znacznie bardziej formalne.

**You may leave as soon as you have finished.** *Możecie wyjść, jak tylko skończycie.*

Zdania wyrażające odmowę udzielenia zgody zawierają **cannot** lub **can't**.

**Can I have some sweets? No, you can't.** *Czy mogę się poczęstować cukierkami? Nie.*

## Polecenia i żądania

Kiedy chce się kogoś poprosić o zrobienie czegoś, używa się wyrażeń **could you**, **will you** lub **would you**. **Could you** oraz **would you** są bardziej uprzejme.

**Could you make out her bill, please?** *Czy mógłby pan wypisać jej rachunek?*
**Would you tell her that Adrian phoned?** *Czy mógłbyś jej przekazać, że dzwonił Adrian?*
**Will you please leave the room?** *Czy możecie wyjść z pokoju?*

Zwracając się do kogoś z prośbą o pomoc, używamy wyrażeń **can you**, **could you**, **will you** lub **would you**. **Could you** i **would you** są bardziej formalne i uprzejme.

**Could you show me how to do this?** *Czy mogłabyś mi pokazać, jak to się robi?*
**Would you do me a favour?** *Czy moglibyście mi oddać przysługę?*
**Will you post this for me on your way to work?**
*Czy mógłbyś to wysłać po drodze do pracy?*
**Can you make me a copy of that?** *Czy mogłabyś mi to skopiować?*

## Sugestie

Aby zaproponować zrobienie czegoś, używa się czasownika **could**.

**You could phone her.** *Mogłabyś do niej zadzwonić.*
**We could go on Friday.** *Moglibyśmy pojechać w piątek.*

Wyrażenia **Shall we** używamy, gdy proponujemy zrobienie czegoś wspólnie z kimś, natomiast **Shall I** używamy, gdy proponujemy, że zrobimy to sami.

**Shall we go and see a film?** *Może pójdziemy na film?*
**Shall I contact the chairman?** *Czy mam skontaktować się z przewodniczącym?*

## Propozycje i zaproszenia

Kiedy się coś komuś proponuje lub zaprasza na coś, używa się wyrażenia **Would you like**.

**Would you like a drink?** *Czy masz ochotę na drinka?*
**Would you like to come for a meal?** *Czy masz ochotę przyjść do nas coś zjeść?*

Można użyć wyrażenia **can I**, gdy oferuje się zrobienie czegoś za kogoś.

**Can I help you with the dishes?** *Czy mogę ci pomóc w zmywaniu naczyń?*

Można również użyć wyrażenia **shall I**, zwłaszcza gdy jest się dość pewnym, że oferta pomocy zostanie przyjęta.

**Shall I shut the door?** *Czy mam zamknąć drzwi?*

## Zobowiązanie i konieczność

Kiedy chce się przekazać, że ktoś ma obowiązek coś zrobić lub że zrobienie czegoś jest konieczne, używa się czasowników **must** lub **have to**. Kiedy podaje się swoje prywatne zdanie, zwykle używa się czasownika **must**.

**I must be very careful not to upset him.** *Muszę uważać, by go nie urazić.*
**We must eat before we go.** *Musimy coś zjeść, zanim wyjdziemy.*

Kiedy przekazujemy informację o czymś, co ktoś inny uważa za obowiązek lub konieczność, zwykle używamy **have to**.

**They have to pay the bill before next Thursday.**
*Muszą zapłacić rachunek do następnego czwartku.*
**She has to go now.** *Ona musi już iść.*

Kiedy odnosi się do konieczności wykonania czegoś, używa się **need to**.

**You might need to see a doctor.** *Możliwe, że będziesz musiał pójść do lekarza.*

Kiedy nie istnieje żadne zobowiązanie lub konieczność zrobienia czegoś, używamy **don't have to**.

**Some people don't have to work.** *Niektórzy ludzie nie muszą pracować.*

# Aa



**A¹, a¹** [eɪ] *n* (*letter*) A *nt*, a *nt*; (*Scol*) ≈ bardzo dobry *m*; **A for Andrew,** (*US*) **A for Able** ≈ A jak Adam; **A road** (*Brit*) ≈ droga główna; **A shares** (*Brit*: *Stock Exchange*) akcje klasy A
**A²** [eɪ] *n* (*Mus*) A *nt*, a *nt*

**KEYWORD**

**a²** [ə] (*przed samogłoską lub niemym h*: **an**) *indef art*
**1**: **a book/girl** książka/dziewczyna; **an apple** jabłko; **he's a doctor** on jest lekarzem
**2** (*some*): **a woman I know** pewna moja znajoma; **there's a Mr Cox on the phone** dzwoni jakiś pan Cox
**3** (*one*): **a year ago** rok temu; **a hundred/thousand pounds** sto/tysiąc funtów
**4** (*in expressing ratios*) na *+acc*; **three a day/week** trzy na dzień/tydzień; **10 km an hour** 10 km na godzinę
**5** (*in expressing prices*) za *+acc*; **30p a kilo** (po) 30 pensów za kilogram

**a.** *abbr* = **acre**
**AA** *n abbr* (*Brit*: = *Automobile Association*) ≈ PZM(ot) *m*; (*US*: = *Associate in/of Arts*) *stopień naukowy*; (= *Alcoholics Anonymous*) Anonimowi Alkoholicy *vir pl*, AA; (= *anti-aircraft*) plot
**AAA** *n abbr* (= *American Automobile Association*) ≈ PZM(ot) *m*; (*Brit*: = *Amateur Athletics Association*) ≈ PZLA *nt*
**A & R** (*Mus*) *n abbr* (= *artists and repertoire*): **~ person** *łowca talentów*
**AAUP** *n abbr* = **American Association of University Professors**
**AB** *abbr* (*Brit*) = **able-bodied seaman**; (*Canada*) = **Alberta**
**abaci** ['æbəsaɪ] *npl of* **abacus**
**aback** [ə'bæk] *adv*: **to be taken ~** być zaskoczonym
**abacus** ['æbəkəs] (*pl* **abaci**) *n* liczydło *nt*, abakus *m*
**abandon** [ə'bændən] *vt* (*person*) porzucać (porzucić *perf*), opuszczać (opuścić *perf*); (*car*) porzucać (porzucić *perf*); (*search, research*) zaprzestawać (zaprzestać *perf*) *+gen*; (*idea*) rezygnować (zrezygnować *perf*) z *+gen* ▷ *n*: **with ~** bez opamiętania; **with joyous ~** w radosnym uniesieniu; **to ~ ship** opuszczać (opuścić *perf*) statek
**abandoned** [ə'bændənd] *adj* (*child*) porzucony; (*house*) opuszczony; (*laugh*) niepohamowany
**abase** [ə'beɪs] *vt*: **to ~ o.s.** poniżać się (poniżyć się *perf*), upokarzać się (upokorzyć się *perf*)
**abashed** [ə'bæʃt] *adj* speszony
**abate** [ə'beɪt] *vi* słabnąć (osłabnąć *perf*)
**abatement** [ə'beɪtmənt] *n*: **noise ~ society** towarzystwo *nt* do walki z hałasem
**abattoir** ['æbətwɑːʳ] *n* rzeźnia *f*
**abbey** ['æbɪ] *n* opactwo *nt*
**abbot** ['æbət] *n* opat *m*
**abbreviate** [ə'briːvɪeɪt] *vt* (*word, essay*) skracać (skrócić *perf*)
**abbreviation** [əbriːvɪ'eɪʃən] *n* skrót *m*
**ABC** *n abbr* = **American Broadcasting Company**
**abdicate** ['æbdɪkeɪt] *vt* zrzekać się (zrzec się *perf*) *+gen* ▷ *vi* abdykować (abdykować *perf*)
**abdication** [æbdɪ'keɪʃən] *n* (*of right*) zrzeczenie się *nt*, wyrzeczenie się *nt*; (*of responsibility*) zrzeczenie się *nt*; (*monarch's*) abdykacja *f*
**abdomen** ['æbdəmɛn] *n* brzuch *m*
**abdominal** [æb'dɔmɪnl] *adj* brzuszny
**abduct** [æb'dʌkt] *vt* porywać (porwać *perf*), uprowadzać (uprowadzić *perf*)
**abduction** [æb'dʌkʃən] *n* porwanie *nt*, uprowadzenie *nt*
**Aberdonian** [æbə'dəunɪən] *adj dotyczący Aberdeen* ▷ *n* mieszkaniec(-nka) *m(f)* Aberdeen
**aberration** [æbə'reɪʃən] *n* odchylenie *nt*, aberracja *f*; **in a moment of mental ~** w chwili zachwiania równowagi umysłowej
**abet** [ə'bɛt] *vt see* **aid**
**abeyance** [ə'beɪəns] *n*: **in ~** w zawieszeniu
**abhor** [əb'hɔːʳ] *vt* brzydzić się *+instr*, odczuwać wstręt *or* odrazę do *+gen*
**abhorrent** [əb'hɔrənt] *adj* odrażający

**abide** [əˈbaɪd] *vt*: **I can't ~ it/him** nie mogę tego/go znieść
▸ **abide by** *vt fus* przestrzegać *+gen*
**ability** [əˈbɪlɪtɪ] *n* umiejętność *f*, zdolność *f*; **to the best of my ~** najlepiej jak potrafię
**abject** [ˈæbdʒɛkt] *adj* (*poverty*) skrajny; (*apology etc*) uniżony; (*coward*) nędzny
**ablaze** [əˈbleɪz] *adj* w płomieniach *post*; **~ with light** rozświetlony
**able** [ˈeɪbl] *adj* zdolny; **to be ~ to do sth** (*capable*) umieć coś (z)robić; (*succeed*) móc coś zrobić, zdołać (*perf*) coś zrobić
**able-bodied** [ˈeɪblˈbɔdɪd] *adj* zdrowy, krzepki; **~ seaman** (*Brit*) starszy marynarz
**ablutions** [əˈbluːʃənz] (*fml*) *npl* ablucje *pl*
**ably** [ˈeɪblɪ] *adv* umiejętnie, zręcznie
**ABM** *n abbr* = **anti-ballistic missile**
**abnormal** [æbˈnɔːml] *adj* nienormalny, anormalny
**abnormality** [æbnɔːˈmælɪtɪ] *n* (*condition*) nienormalność *f*; (*instance*) nieprawidłowość *f*, anomalia *f*
**aboard** [əˈbɔːd] *prep* (*Naut, Aviat*) na pokładzie *+gen*; (*train, bus*) w *+loc* ▷ *adv* na pokładzie
**abode** [əˈbəud] (*Jur*) *n*: **of no fixed ~** bez stałego miejsca zamieszkania
**abolish** [əˈbɔlɪʃ] *vt* (*system*) obalać (obalić *perf*); (*practice*) znosić (znieść *perf*)
**abolition** [æbəˈlɪʃən] *n* obalenie *nt*, zniesienie *nt*
**abominable** [əˈbɔmɪnəbl] *adj* wstrętny, odrażający
**abominably** [əˈbɔmɪnəblɪ] *adv* wstrętnie, odrażająco
**aborigine** [æbəˈrɪdʒɪnɪ] *n* aborygen(ka) *m(f)*, tubylec *m*
**abort** [əˈbɔːt] *vt* (*foetus*) usuwać (usunąć *perf*); (*activity*) przerywać (przerwać *perf*); (*plan*) zaniechać (*perf*) *+gen*; (*Comput*) przerywać (przerwać *perf*) (*zadanie, wykonywanie programu*)
**abortion** [əˈbɔːʃən] *n* aborcja *f*, przerywanie *nt* ciąży; **to have an ~** przerywać (przerwać *perf*) ciążę, poddawać się (poddać się *perf*) zabiegowi przerwania ciąży
**abortive** [əˈbɔːtɪv] *adj* nieudany, poroniony
**abound** [əˈbaund] *vi* (*be plentiful*) mnożyć się; (*possess in large numbers*): **to ~ in** *or* **with** obfitować w *+acc*

 KEYWORD

**about** [əˈbaut] *adv* **1** (*approximately*) około *+gen*; **about a hundred/thousand** około stu/tysiąca; **at about 2 o'clock** około (godziny) drugiej; **I've just about finished** prawie skończyłem
**2** (*referring to place*) dookoła; **to leave things lying about** zostawiać (zostawić *perf*) wszystko porozrzucane dookoła; **to run about** biegać dookoła
**3**: **to be about to do sth** mieć właśnie coś zrobić; **he was about to leave** właśnie miał wyjść
▷ *prep* **1** (*relating to*) o *+loc*; **we talked about it** rozmawialiśmy o tym; **what** *or* **how about going out tonight?** (a) może byśmy gdzieś wyszli (dziś) wieczorem?
**2** (*referring to place*) po *+loc*; **to walk about the town** spacerować po mieście

**about-face** [əˈbautˈfeɪs] *n* (*Mil*) w tył zwrot *m*; (*fig*) zwrot *m* o 180 stopni, wolta *f*
**about-turn** [əˈbautˈtəːn] *n* = **about-face**
**above** [əˈbʌv] *adv* (*higher up, overhead*) u góry, (po)wyżej; (*greater, more*) powyżej, więcej ▷ *prep* (*higher than*) nad *+instr*, ponad *+instr*; (*greater than, more than*) ponad *+acc*, powyżej *+gen*; **costing ~ 10 pounds** w cenie powyżej 10 funtów; **mentioned ~** wyżej wspomniany *or* wzmiankowany; **he's not ~ a bit of blackmail** byłby zdolny posunąć się do drobnego szantażu; **~ all** przede wszystkim, nade wszystko
**above board** *adj* jawny, uczciwy
**abrasion** [əˈbreɪʒən] *n* (*on skin*) otarcie *nt*
**abrasive** [əˈbreɪzɪv] *adj* (*substance*) ścierny; (*fig: person, manner*) irytujący
**abreast** [əˈbrɛst] *adv* ramię przy ramieniu, obok siebie; **three ~** trójkami; **to keep ~ of** (*fig: news etc*) nadążać za *+instr*, być na bieżąco z *+instr*
**abridge** [əˈbrɪdʒ] *vt* (*novel etc*) skracać (skrócić *perf*)
**abroad** [əˈbrɔːd] *adv* (*be*) za granicą; (*go*) za granicę; **there is a rumour ~ that ...** (*fig*) krążą plotki, że...
**abrupt** [əˈbrʌpt] *adj* (*action, ending*) nagły; (*person, behaviour*) obcesowy
**abruptly** [əˈbrʌptlɪ] *adv* (*leave, end*) nagle; (*speak*) szorstko, oschle
**abscess** [ˈæbsɪs] *n* ropień *m*, wrzód *m*
**abscond** [əbˈskɔnd] *vi*: **to ~ with** (*money*) zbiegać (zbiec *perf*) z *+instr*; **to ~ (from)** (*prison*) zbiegać (zbiec *perf*) (z *+gen*), uciekać (uciec *perf*) (z *+gen*); (*school*) uciekać (uciec *perf*) (z *+gen*)
**abseil** [ˈæbseɪl] *vi* spuszczać się (spuścić się *perf*) po linie
**absence** [ˈæbsəns] *n* (*of person*) nieobecność *f*, brak *m*; (*of thing*) brak *m*; **in the ~ of** (*person*) pod nieobecność *+gen*; (*thing*) wobec braku *+gen*
**absent** [*adj* ˈæbsənt, *vb* æbˈsɛnt] *adj* nieobecny ▷ *vt*: **to ~ o.s. from** (*school*) być nieobecnym w *+loc*; (*meeting*) być nieobecnym na *+loc*; **to be ~ without leave** (*Mil*) przebywać na samowolnym oddaleniu

**absentee** [æbsən'ti:] *n* nieobecny(-na) *m(f)*
**absenteeism** [æbsən'ti:ɪzəm] *n* absencja *f*
**absent-minded** ['æbsənt'maɪndɪd] *adj* roztargniony
**absent-mindedness** ['æbsənt'maɪndɪdnɪs] *n* roztargnienie *nt*
**absolute** ['æbsəlu:t] *adj* absolutny
**absolutely** [æbsə'lu:tlɪ] *adv (totally)* absolutnie, całkowicie; *(certainly)* oczywiście
**absolution** [æbsə'lu:ʃən] *n* rozgrzeszenie *nt*
**absolve** [əb'zɔlv] *vt*: **to ~ sb (from)** *(blame, sin)* odpuszczać (odpuścić *perf*) komuś *(+acc)*; *(responsibility)* zwalniać (zwolnić *perf*) kogoś (od *+gen*)
**absorb** [əb'zɔ:b] *vt (liquid)* wchłaniać (wchłonąć *perf*), absorbować (zaabsorbować *perf*); *(light)* pochłaniać (pochłonąć *perf*), absorbować (zaabsorbować *perf*); *(group, business)* wchłaniać (wchłonąć *perf*); *(changes, effects)* dostosowywać się (dostosować się *perf*) do *+gen*; *(information)* przyswajać (przyswoić *perf*) sobie; **to be ~ed in a book** być pochłoniętym lekturą
**absorbent** [əb'zɔ:bənt] *adj* chłonny, wchłaniający
**absorbent cotton** (US) *n* wata *f*
**absorbing** [əb'zɔ:bɪŋ] *adj (of task, work)* absorbujący; *(book, film)* zajmujący
**absorption** [əb'sɔ:pʃən] *n (of liquid)* absorpcja *f*, wchłanianie *nt*; *(of light)* absorpcja *f*, pochłanianie *nt*; *(assimilation)* asymilacja *f*; *(interest)* zainteresowanie *nt*, zaangażowanie *nt*
**abstain** [əb'steɪn] *vi (in vote)* wstrzymywać się (wstrzymać się *perf*); **to ~ from** powstrzymywać się (powstrzymać się *perf*) od *+gen*
**abstemious** [əb'sti:mɪəs] *adj* wstrzemięźliwy
**abstention** [əb'stɛnʃən] *n (action)* wstrzymanie *nt* się od głosu; *(result)* głos *m* wstrzymujący się
**abstinence** ['æbstɪnəns] *n* wstrzemięźliwość *f*, abstynencja *f*
**abstract** [*adj, n* 'æbstrækt, *vb* æb'strækt] *adj* abstrakcyjny ▷ *n* abstrakt *m*, wyciąg *m* ▷ *vt*: **to ~ sth (from)** wyławiać (wyłowić *perf*) *or* wychwytywać (wychwycić *perf*) coś (z *+gen*)
**abstruse** [æb'stru:s] *adj* zawiły
**absurd** [əb'sə:d] *adj* absurdalny
**absurdity** [əb'sə:dɪtɪ] *n* absurdalność *f*, absurd *m*
**ABTA** ['æbtə] *n abbr* = **Association of British Travel Agents**
**Abu Dhabi** ['æbu:'dɑ:bɪ] *n* Abu Zabi *nt inv*
**abundance** [ə'bʌndəns] *n* liczebność *f*, obfitość *f*; **an ~ of** mnóstwo *+gen*; **in ~** pod dostatkiem
**abundant** [ə'bʌndənt] *adj* obfity
**abundantly** [ə'bʌndəntlɪ] *adv (grow etc)* obficie; *(clear)* zupełnie
**abuse** [*n* ə'bju:s, *vb* ə'bju:z] *n (insults)* obelgi *pl*, przekleństwa *pl*; *(ill-treatment)* maltretowanie *nt*, znęcanie się *nt*; *(of power, drugs)* nadużywanie *nt* ▷ *vt (insult)* obrażać (obrazić *perf*), lżyć (zelżyć *perf*); *(ill-treat)* maltretować, znęcać się nad *+instr*; *(misuse)* nadużywać (nadużyć *perf*) *+gen*; **open to ~** podatny na nadużycia
**abusive** [ə'bju:sɪv] *adj* obelżywy, obraźliwy
**abysmal** [ə'bɪzməl] *adj (performance)* fatalny; *(failure)* sromotny; *(conditions, wages)* beznadziejny
**abysmally** [ə'bɪzməlɪ] *adv* sromotnie
**abyss** [ə'bɪs] *n* przepaść *f*, głębia *f*; *(fig)* przepaść *f*, otchłań *f*
**AC** *abbr* = **alternating current**; *(US: = athletic club)* KS *m (= Klub Sportowy)*
**a/c** *(Banking etc) abbr* = **account**; *(= account current)* rachunek *m* bieżący
**academic** [ækə'dɛmɪk] *adj (child)* dobrze się uczący; *(system, standard)* akademicki; *(book)* naukowy; *(pej: issue, discussion)* akademicki, jałowy ▷ *n* naukowiec *m*
**academic year** *n* rok *m* akademicki
**academy** [ə'kædəmɪ] *n* akademia *f*; **~ of music** akademia muzyczna; **military/naval ~** akademia wojskowa/marynarki wojennej
**ACAS** ['eɪkæs] *(Brit) n abbr (= Advisory, Conciliation and Arbitration Service) rządowa komisja pojednawcza i rozjemcza występująca w sporach dotyczących pracy*
**accede** [æk'si:d] *vi*: **to ~ to** przystawać (przystać *perf*) na *+acc*
**accelerate** [æk'sɛləreɪt] *vt* przyspieszać (przyspieszyć *perf*) ▷ *vi (Aut)* przyspieszać (przyspieszyć *perf*)
**acceleration** [æksɛlə'reɪʃən] *n* przyspieszenie *nt*
**accelerator** [æk'sɛləreɪtə^r] *n* pedał *m* przyspieszenia *or* gazu
**accent** ['æksɛnt] *n* akcent *m*; *(fig)* nacisk *m*, akcent *m*; **to speak with an Irish ~** mówić z irlandzkim akcentem; **he has a strong ~** mówi z silnym akcentem
**accentuate** [æk'sɛntjueɪt] *vt* akcentować (zaakcentować *perf*)
**accept** [ək'sɛpt] *vt (gift, invitation)* przyjmować (przyjąć *perf*); *(proposal)* przyjmować (przyjąć *perf*), akceptować (zaakceptować *perf*); *(fact, situation)* przyjmować (przyjąć *perf*) do wiadomości, godzić się (pogodzić się *perf*) z *+instr*; *(responsibility, blame)* brać (wziąć *perf*) na siebie
**acceptable** [ək'sɛptəbl] *adj* do przyjęcia *post*

**acceptance** [əkˈsɛptəns] *n* przyjęcie *nt*, akceptacja *f*; **to meet with general ~** spotykać się (spotkać się *perf*) z ogólną aprobatą

**access** [ˈæksɛs] *n* (*to building, room*) dojście *nt*; (*to information, papers*) dostęp *m* ▷ *vt* (*Comput*) uzyskiwać (uzyskać *perf*) dostęp do *+gen*; **this door gives ~ to...** te drzwi prowadzą do *+gen*; **to have ~ to** (*child etc*) mieć możliwość kontaktów z *+instr*; (*information, library*) mieć dostęp do *+gen*; **the burglars gained ~ through a window** włamywacze dostali się do środka przez okno

**accessible** [ækˈsɛsəbl] *adj* (*place, goods*) dostępny; (*person*) osiągalny; (*knowledge, art*) przystępny

**accession** [ækˈsɛʃən] *n* wstąpienie *nt* na tron, objęcie *nt* tronu

**accessory** [ækˈsɛsərɪ] *n* (*Aut, Comm*) wyposażenie *nt*, akcesoria *pl*; (*Dress*) dodatek *m*; (*Jur*): **~ to** współsprawca(-wczyni) *m(f)* *+gen*; **toilet accessories** (*Brit*) przybory toaletowe

**access road** *n* droga *f* dojazdowa

**access time** (*Comput*) *n* czas *m* dostępu

**accident** [ˈæksɪdənt] *n* (*chance event*) przypadek *m*; (*mishap, disaster*) wypadek *m*; **to meet with** *or* **to have an ~** ulegać (ulec *perf*) wypadkowi, mieć wypadek; **~s at work** wypadki przy pracy; **by ~** (*unintentionally*) niechcący, przez przypadek; (*by chance*) przez przypadek, przypadkiem

**accidental** [æksɪˈdɛntl] *adj* przypadkowy

**accidentally** [æksɪˈdɛntəlɪ] *adv* przypadkowo, przypadkiem

**accident insurance** *n* ubezpieczenie *nt* od następstw wypadku

**accident-prone** [ˈæksɪdəntˈprəun] *adj* podatny na wypadki

**acclaim** [əˈkleɪm] *n* uznanie *nt* ▷ *vt* darzyć uznaniem; **to be ~ed for one's achievements** wzbudzać uznanie swoimi osiągnięciami

**acclamation** [ækləˈmeɪʃən] *n* aklamacja *f*, aplauz *m*

**acclimate** [əˈklaɪmət] (*US*) *vt* = **acclimatize**

**acclimatize**, (*US*) **acclimate** [əˈklaɪmətaɪz] *vt*: **to become ~d (to)** przyzwyczaić się (*perf*) (do *+gen*)

**accolade** [ˈækəleɪd] *n* pochwała *f*, wyraz *m* uznania

**accommodate** [əˈkɔmədeɪt] *vt* (*provide with lodging*) kwaterować (zakwaterować *perf*); (*put up*) przenocowywać (przenocować *perf*); (*oblige*) iść (pójść *perf*) na rękę *+dat*; (*car, hotel etc*) mieścić (zmieścić *perf*), pomieścić (*perf*); **to ~ o.s. to sth** przystosowywać się (przystosować się *perf*) do czegoś

**accommodating** [əˈkɔmədeɪtɪŋ] *adj* uczynny, życzliwy

**accommodation** [əkɔməˈdeɪʃən] *n* zakwaterowanie *nt*, mieszkanie *nt*; **accommodations** (*US*) *npl* noclegi *pl*, zakwaterowanie *nt*; **he's found ~** znalazł zakwaterowanie *or* mieszkanie; **"~ to let"** „mieszkanie do wynajęcia"; **they have ~ for 500** dysponują 500 miejscami; **the hall has seating ~ for 600** (*Brit*) sala ma 600 miejsc siedzących

**accompaniment** [əˈkʌmpənɪmənt] *n* akompaniament *m*

**accompanist** [əˈkʌmpənɪst] *n* akompaniator(ka) *m(f)*

**accompany** [əˈkʌmpənɪ] *vt* (*escort, go along with*) towarzyszyć *+dat*; (*Mus*) akompaniować *or* towarzyszyć *+dat*

**accomplice** [əˈkʌmplɪs] *n* wspólnik(-iczka) *m(f)*, współwinny(-na) *m(f)*

**accomplish** [əˈkʌmplɪʃ] *vt* (*goal*) osiągać (osiągnąć *perf*); (*task*) realizować (zrealizować *perf*); **how did she ~ so much so quickly?** w jaki sposób udało jej się tyle dokonać w tak krótkim czasie?

**accomplished** [əˈkʌmplɪʃt] *adj* znakomity

**accomplishment** [əˈkʌmplɪʃmənt] *n* (*completion*) ukończenie *nt*; (*bringing about*) dokonanie *nt*; (*achievement*) osiągnięcie *nt*; (*skill*) umiejętności *pl*; **accomplishments** *npl* umiejętności *pl*

**accord** [əˈkɔːd] *n* porozumienie *nt*, uzgodnienie *nt* ▷ *vt*: **to ~ sb sth/sth to sb** obdarzać (obdarzyć *perf*) kogoś czymś, przyznawać (przyznać *perf*) komuś coś; **of his own ~** z własnej woli *or* inicjatywy; **with one ~** jak jeden mąż; **to be in ~** być w zgodzie

**accordance** [əˈkɔːdəns] *n*: **in ~ with** w zgodzie *or* zgodnie z *+instr*

**according** [əˈkɔːdɪŋ]: **~ to** *prep* według *+gen*; **~ to plan** zgodnie z planem

**accordingly** [əˈkɔːdɪŋlɪ] *adv* (*appropriately*) stosownie, odpowiednio; (*as a result*) w związku z tym

**accordion** [əˈkɔːdɪən] *n* akordeon *m*

**accost** [əˈkɔst] *vt* zaczepiać (zaczepić *perf*)

**account** [əˈkaunt] *n* (*Comm: bill*) rachunek *m*; (*also: monthly account*) rachunek *m* kredytowy; (*in bank*) konto *nt*, rachunek *m*; (*report*) relacja *f*, sprawozdanie *nt*; **accounts** *npl* (*Comm*) rozliczenie *nt*; (*Book-keeping*) księgi *pl* (rachunkowe); **"~ payee only"** (*Brit*) „na rachunek odbiorcy"; **to keep an ~ of** prowadzić zapis *+gen*; **to bring** *or* **call sb to ~ for sth** pociągać (pociągnąć *perf*) kogoś do odpowiedzialności za coś; **by all ~s** podobno; **of no ~** bez znaczenia; **to pay 10 pounds on ~**

wpłacać (wpłacić *perf*) 10 funtów zaliczki; **to buy sth on ~** kupować (kupić *perf*) coś na kredyt; **on no ~** pod żadnym pozorem; **on ~ of** z uwagi *or* ze względu na *+acc*; **to take into ~, take ~ of** brać (wziąć *perf*) pod uwagę *+acc*
▸ **account for** *vt fus* (*explain*) wyjaśniać (wyjaśnić *perf*); (*represent*) stanowić *+acc*; **all the children were ~ed for** żadnego z dzieci nie brakowało; **four people are still not ~ed for** los czterech osób ciągle nie jest znany
**accountability** [ə'kauntə'bɪlɪtɪ] *n* odpowiedzialność *f*
**accountable** [ə'kauntəbl] *adj*: **to be ~ (to)** odpowiadać (przed *+instr*)
**accountancy** [ə'kauntənsɪ] *n* księgowość *f*
**accountant** [ə'kauntənt] *n* księgowy(-wa) *m(f)*
**accounting** [ə'kauntɪŋ] *n* księgowość *f*, rachunkowość *f*
**accounting period** *n* okres *m* rozliczeniowy
**account number** *n* numer *m* konta *or* rachunku
**account payable** *n* rachunek *m* „wierzyciele"
**account receivable** *n* rachunek *m* „dłużnicy"
**accredited** [ə'krɛdɪtɪd] *adj* akredytowany
**accretion** [ə'kri:ʃən] *n* narastanie *nt*, nawarstwianie się *nt*
**accrue** [ə'kru:] *vi* gromadzić się (nagromadzić się *perf*), narastać (narosnąć *perf*); **to ~ to** przysługiwać *+dat*
**accrued interest** *n* narosłe odsetki *pl*
**accumulate** [ə'kju:mjuleɪt] *vt* gromadzić (nagromadzić *perf*) ▹ *vi* gromadzić się (nagromadzić się *perf*)
**accumulation** [əkju:mju'leɪʃən] *n* nagromadzenie *nt*
**accuracy** ['ækjurəsɪ] *n* precyzja *f*, dokładność *f*
**accurate** ['ækjurɪt] *adj* (*description, account*) dokładny, wierny; (*person, device*) dokładny; (*weapon, aim*) precyzyjny
**accurately** ['ækjurɪtlɪ] *adv* (*report, answer etc*) dokładnie, ściśle; (*shoot*) celnie
**accusation** [ækju'zeɪʃən] *n* (*act*) oskarżenie *nt*; (*instance*) zarzut *m*
**accusative** [ə'kju:zətɪv] (*Ling*) *n* biernik *m*
**accuse** [ə'kju:z] *vt*: **to ~ sb of** (*crime*) oskarżać (oskarżyć *perf*) kogoś o *+acc*; (*incompetence*) zarzucać (zarzucić *perf*) komuś *+acc*
**accused** [ə'kju:zd] *n*: **the ~** oskarżony(-na) *m(f)*
**accustom** [ə'kʌstəm] *vt* przyzwyczajać (przyzwyczaić *perf*); **to ~ o.s. to sth** przyzwyczajać się (przyzwyczaić się *perf*) do czegoś
**accustomed** [ə'kʌstəmd] *adj* zwykły, charakterystyczny; **~ to** przyzwyczajony *or* przywykły do *+gen*
**AC/DC** *abbr* (= *alternating current/direct current*) prąd *m* stały/prąd *m* zmienny
**ACE** [eɪs] *n abbr* = **American Council on Education**
**ace** [eɪs] *n* (*Cards*) as *m*; (*Tennis*) as *m* serwisowy
**acerbic** [ə'sə:bɪk] *adj* zgryźliwy, cierpki
**acetate** ['æsɪteɪt] *n* włókno *nt* celulozowe
**ache** [eɪk] *n* ból *m* ▹ *vi*: **my head ~s** boli mnie głowa; **I've got (a) stomach ~** boli mnie brzuch; **I'm aching all over** jestem cały obolały; **she was aching for a cigarette** marzyła o papierosie; **I was aching to tell you all my news** nie mogłam się doczekać, kiedy ci wszystko opowiem
**achieve** [ə'tʃi:v] *vt* (*aim, result*) osiągać (osiągnąć *perf*); (*victory, success*) odnosić (odnieść *perf*)
**achievement** [ə'tʃi:vmənt] *n* osiągnięcie *nt*
**acid** ['æsɪd] *adj* (*Chem*) kwaśny, kwasowy; (*taste*) kwaśny, kwaskowy ▹ *n* (*Chem*) kwas *m*; (*inf*) LSD *nt inv*
**acidity** [ə'sɪdɪtɪ] (*Chem*) *n* kwasowość *f*
**acid rain** *n* kwaśny deszcz *m*
**acid test** *n* (*Chem*) próba *f* kwasowa; (*fig*) próba *f* ogniowa
**acknowledge** [ək'nɔlɪdʒ] *vt* (*letter etc*) potwierdzać (potwierdzić *perf*) odbiór *+gen*; (*fact*) przyznawać (przyznać *perf*); (*situation*) uznawać (uznać *perf*); (*person*) zwracać (zwrócić *perf*) uwagę na *+acc*
**acknowledgement** [ək'nɔlɪdʒmənt] *n* (*of letter etc*) potwierdzenie *nt* odbioru; **acknowledgements** *npl* (*in book*) podziękowania *pl*
**ACLU** *n abbr* = **American Civil Liberties Union**
**acme** ['ækmɪ] *n* szczyt *m*
**acne** ['æknɪ] *n* trądzik *m*
**acorn** ['eɪkɔ:n] *n* żołądź *f*
**acoustic** [ə'ku:stɪk] *adj* akustyczny
**acoustic coupler** (*Comput*) *n* sprzęg *m* akustyczny
**acoustics** [ə'ku:stɪks] *n* (*science*) akustyka *f* ▹ *npl* (*of hall, room*) akustyka *f*
**acquaint** [ə'kweɪnt] *vt*: **to ~ sb with sth** zapoznawać (zapoznać *perf*) *or* zaznajamiać (zaznajomić *perf*) kogoś z czymś; **to be ~ed with** znać *+acc*
**acquaintance** [ə'kweɪntəns] *n* (*person*) znajomy(-ma) *m(f)*; (*with person, subject*) znajomość *f*; **to make sb's ~** zawierać (zawrzeć *perf*) z kimś znajomość
**acquiesce** [ækwɪ'ɛs] *vi*: **to ~ (to)** przystawać (przystać *perf*) (na *+acc*)
**acquire** [ə'kwaɪəʳ] *vt* (*obtain, buy*) nabywać (nabyć *perf*); (*develop: interest*) rozwijać (rozwinąć *perf*); (*learn: skill*) posiadać (posiąść *perf*), nabywać (nabyć *perf*)

**acquired** [ə'kwaɪəd] *adj* nabyty, zdobyty; **whisky is an ~ taste** do whisky trzeba się przyzwyczaić
**acquisition** [ækwɪ'zɪʃən] *n* (*of property, goods, skill*) nabywanie *nt*, nabycie *nt*; (*of language*) przyswajanie *nt* (sobie); (*purchase*) nabytek *m*
**acquisitive** [ə'kwɪzɪtɪv] *adj* zachłanny
**acquit** [ə'kwɪt] *vt* uniewinniać (uniewinnić *perf*); **to ~ o.s. well** dobrze się spisać (*perf*)
**acquittal** [ə'kwɪtl] *n* uniewinnienie *nt*
**acre** ['eɪkəʳ] *n* akr *m*
**acreage** ['eɪkərɪdʒ] *n* areał *m*
**acrid** ['ækrɪd] *adj* (*smell, smoke*) ostry, gryzący; (*fig: remark*) uszczypliwy
**acrimonious** [ækrɪ'məunɪəs] *adj* zjadliwy
**acrimony** ['ækrɪmənɪ] *n* zjadliwość *f*
**acrobat** ['ækrəbæt] *n* akrobata(-tka) *m(f)*
**acrobatic** [ækrə'bætɪk] *adj* akrobatyczny
**acrobatics** [ækrə'bætɪks] *npl* akrobacje *pl*
**acronym** ['ækrənɪm] *n* akronim *m*
**Acropolis** [ə'krɔpəlɪs] *n*: **the ~** Akropol *m*
**across** [ə'krɔs] *prep* w poprzek *+gen*; (*on the other side of*) po drugiej stronie *+gen* ▷ *adv*: **two kilometres ~** o szerokości dwóch kilometrów; **to walk ~ (the road)** przechodzić (przejść *perf*) przez ulicę; **to take sb ~ the road** przeprowadzać (przeprowadzić *perf*) kogoś przez ulicę; **a road ~ the wood** droga przez las; **the lake is 12 km ~** jezioro ma 12 km szerokości; **to run ~** przebiegać (przebiec *perf*); **they came ~ by plane** przylecieli samolotem; **~ from** naprzeciw(ko) *+gen*; **to get sth ~ (to sb)** uświadamiać (uświadomić *perf*) coś (komuś), wyjaśniać (wyjaśnić *perf*) coś (komuś)
**acrylic** [ə'krɪlɪk] *adj* akrylowy ▷ *n* akryl *m*; **acrylics** *npl*: **he paints in ~** maluje farbami akrylowymi
**ACT** *n abbr* (*= American College Test*) *standardowy test dla kandydatów na studia*
**act** [ækt] *n* (*action, document, part of play*) akt *m*; (*deed*) czyn *m*, postępek *m*; (*of performer*) numer *m*; (*Jur*) ustawa *f* ▷ *vi* (*do sth, take action, have effect*) działać; (*behave*) zachowywać się (zachować się *perf*); (*in play, film*) grać (zagrać *perf*); (*pretend*) grać ▷ *vt* (*Theat*) grać (zagrać *perf*); (*fig*) odgrywać (odegrać *perf*); **it's only an act** to tylko poza; **act of God** (*Jur*) klęska żywiołowa; (*fig*) siła wyższa; **in the act of** w trakcie *+gen*; **to catch sb in the act** łapać (złapać *perf*) kogoś na gorącym uczynku; **to act the fool** (*Brit*) udawać głupiego; **to act as** występować (wystąpić *perf*) w roli *+gen or* jako *+nom*; **it acts as a deterrent** to działa odstraszająco; **acting in my capacity as chairman, I wish to ...** (występując) jako przewodniczący, chciałbym *+infin*
▶ **act on** *vt fus* (*produce effect*) działać (podziałać *perf*) na *+instr*; (*behave according to*) postępować (postąpić *perf*) zgodnie z *+instr*
▶ **act out** *vt* (*event*) odgrywać (odegrać *perf*); (*fantasies*) urzeczywistniać (urzeczywistnić *perf*)
**acting** ['æktɪŋ] *adj* (*director etc*) pełniący obowiązki ▷ *n* (*profession*) aktorstwo *nt*; (*activity*) gra *f*
**action** ['ækʃən] *n* (*things happening*) akcja *f*; (*deed*) czyn *m*; (*of device, force, chemical*) działanie *nt*; (*movement*) ruch *m*; (*Mil*) działania *pl*; (*Jur*) powództwo *nt*; **to bring an ~ against sb** (*Jur*) wnosić (wnieść *perf*) powództwo przeciw(ko) komuś; **killed in ~** (*Mil*) poległy na polu chwały; **out of ~** (*person*) wyłączony z gry; (*machine*) niesprawny; **to take ~** podejmować (podjąć *perf*) działanie; **to put a plan into ~** wprowadzać (wprowadzić *perf*) plan w życie
**action replay** *n* powtórka *f* (w zwolnionym tempie)
**activate** ['æktɪveɪt] *vt* (*mechanism*) uruchamiać (uruchomić *perf*); (*Chem, Phys*) wzbudzać (wzbudzić *perf*)
**active** ['æktɪv] *adj* (*person, life*) aktywny; (*volcano*) czynny; **to play an ~ part in** odgrywać (odegrać *perf*) czynną rolę w *+loc*
**active duty** (*US: Mil*) *n* służba *f* czynna
**actively** ['æktɪvlɪ] *adv* (*be involved, participate*) czynnie, aktywnie; (*discourage*) usilnie
**active partner** *n* (*Comm*) wspólnik *m* rzeczywisty
**active service** (*Brit: Mil*) *n* służba *f* liniowa
**activist** ['æktɪvɪst] *n* aktywista(-tka) *m(f)*
**activity** [æk'tɪvɪtɪ] *n* (*being active*) działalność *f*; (*action*) działanie *nt*; (*pastime, pursuit*) zajęcie *nt*
**actor** ['æktəʳ] *n* aktor *m*
**actress** ['æktrɪs] *n* aktorka *f*
**actual** ['æktjuəl] *adj* (*real*) rzeczywisty, faktyczny; (*expressing emphasis*): **the ~ ceremony starts at 10** sama uroczystość zaczyna się o 10
**actually** ['æktjuəlɪ] *adv* (*really*) w rzeczywistości; (*in fact*) właściwie
**actuary** ['æktjuərɪ] *n* rachmistrz *m* ubezpieczeniowy
**actuate** ['æktjueɪt] (*Tech*) *vt* uruchamiać (uruchomić *perf*)
**acuity** [ə'kju:ɪtɪ] (*fml*) *n* ostrość *f*
**acumen** ['ækjumən] *n* przenikliwość *f*; **business ~** przedsiębiorczość
**acupuncture** ['ækjupʌŋktʃəʳ] *n* akupunktura *f*
**acute** [ə'kju:t] *adj* (*illness, angle*) ostry; (*pain*) ostry, przenikliwy; (*anxiety*) silny; (*mind, person, observer*) przenikliwy; (*Ling: accent*) akutowy

**AD** *adv abbr (= Anno Domini) (in contrast to BC)* n.e.; *(in religious texts etc)* A.D., R.P. (= *roku Pańskiego*) ▷ *n abbr (US: Mil)* = **active duty**
**ad** [æd] *(inf) n abbr (= advertisement)* ogł.
**adage** ['ædɪdʒ] *n* porzekadło *nt*
**adamant** ['ædəmənt] *adj* nieugięty, niewzruszony
**Adam's apple** ['ædəmz-] *n* jabłko *nt* Adama
**adapt** [ə'dæpt] *vt* adaptować (zaadaptować *perf*); **to ~ sth to** przystosowywać (przystosować *perf*) coś do *+gen* ▷ *vi*: **to ~ (to)** przystosowywać się (przystosować się *perf*) (do *+gen*)
**adaptability** [ədæptə'bɪlɪtɪ] *n* zdolności *pl* przystosowawcze
**adaptable** [ə'dæptəbl] *adj (person)* łatwo się przystosowujący; *(device)* dający się przystosować
**adaptation** [ædæp'teɪʃən] *n (of story, novel)* adaptacja *f*; *(of machine, equipment)* przystosowanie *nt*
**adapter** [ə'dæptə[r]] *n (Elec)* trójnik *m*
**adaptor** [ə'dæptə[r]] *n* = **adapter**
**ADC** *n abbr (Mil)* = **aide-de-camp**; *(US: = Aid to Dependent Children) pomoc finansowa dla rodzin o niskich dochodach*
**add** [æd] *vt* dodawać (dodać *perf*) ▷ *vi*: **to add to** powiększać (powiększyć *perf*) *+acc*
▶ **add on** *vt* dodawać (dodać *perf*)
▶ **add up** *vt* dodawać (dodać *perf*) ▷ *vi*: **it doesn't add up** *(fig)* to się nie zgadza; **it doesn't add up to much** *(fig)* to nie robi większego wrażenia
**addenda** [ə'dɛndə] *npl of* **addendum**
**addendum** [ə'dɛndəm] *(pl* **addenda***) n (in book)* addenda *pl*; *(document)* załącznik *m*
**adder** ['ædə[r]] *n* żmija *f*
**addict** ['ædɪkt] *n* osoba *f* uzależniona; *(also:* **drug addict***)* narkoman(ka) *m(f)*; *(devotee)* entuzjasta(-tka) *m(f)*
**addicted** [ə'dɪktɪd] *adj*: **to be ~ to** być uzależnionym od *+gen*; *(fig)* nie móc żyć bez *+gen*
**addiction** [ə'dɪkʃən] *n* uzależnienie *nt*; **drug ~** narkomania
**addictive** [ə'dɪktɪv] *adj (drug)* uzależniający; *(activity)* wciągający
**adding machine** ['ædɪŋ-] *n* maszyna *f* sumująca
**Addis Ababa** ['ædɪs'æbəbə] *n* Addis Abeba *f*
**addition** [ə'dɪʃən] *n (adding)* dodanie *nt*; *(thing added)* dodatek *m*; *(Math)* dodawanie *nt*; **in ~** w dodatku, na dodatek; **in ~ to** oprócz *+gen*
**additional** [ə'dɪʃənl] *adj* dodatkowy
**additive** ['ædɪtɪv] *n* dodatek *m (konserwujący, barwiący itp)*
**addled** ['ædld] *adj (Brit) adj (egg)* zepsuty; **his brain is ~** w głowie mu się pomieszało
**address** [ə'drɛs] *n (postal)* adres *m*; *(speech)* przemówienie *nt*, mowa *f* ▷ *vt (letter, parcel)* adresować (zaadresować *perf*); *(meeting, rally)* przemawiać (przemówić *perf*) do *+gen*; *(person)* zwracać się (zwrócić się *perf*) do *+gen*; **to ~ (o.s. to) a problem** zajmować się (zająć się *perf*) problemem; **form of ~** forma zwracania się; **what form of ~ do you use for ...?** jak należy zwracać się do *+gen?*; **absolute/relative ~** *(Comput)* adres bezwzględny/względny
**Aden** ['eɪdən] *n*: **Gulf of ~** Zatoka *f* Adeńska
**adenoids** ['ædɪnɔɪdz] *npl* trzeci migdałek *m*
**adept** ['ædɛpt] *adj*: **~ at** biegły w *+loc*
**adequacy** ['ædɪkwəsɪ] *n (quantitative)* dostateczność *f*; *(qualitative)* właściwość *f*, odpowiedniość *f*
**adequate** ['ædɪkwɪt] *adj (amount)* wystarczający, dostateczny; *(response)* właściwy, zadowalający
**adequately** ['ædɪkwɪtlɪ] *adv* właściwie
**adhere** [əd'hɪə[r]] *vi*: **to ~ to** przylegać (przylgnąć *perf*) do *+gen*; *(fig: rule, decision)* stosować się (zastosować się *perf*) do *+gen*; *(: opinion, belief)* obstawać przy *+loc*
**adhesion** [əd'hiːʒən] *n* przyleganie *nt*
**adhesive** [əd'hiːzɪv] *n* klej *m* ▷ *adj (sticky)* klejący się; *(gummed)* klejący
**adhesive tape** *n (Brit)* taśma *f* klejąca; *(US: Med)* plaster *m*, przylepiec *m*
**ad hoc** [æd'hɔk] *adj* ad hoc ▷ *adv* ad hoc
**ad infinitum** ['ædɪnfɪ'naɪtəm] *adv* w nieskończoność
**adjacent** [ə'dʒeɪsənt] *adj (room etc)* przyległy, sąsiedni; **~ to** przylegający do *+gen*, sąsiadujący z *+instr*
**adjective** ['ædʒɛktɪv] *n* przymiotnik *m*
**adjoining** [ə'dʒɔɪnɪŋ] *adj (room)* przyległy, sąsiedni; *(table)* sąsiedni ▷ *prep* obok *+gen*
**adjourn** [ə'dʒəːn] *vt* odraczać (odroczyć *perf*) ▷ *vi (meeting, trial)* zostawać (zostać *perf*) odroczonym; **they ~ed the meeting till the following week** odroczyli zebranie do następnego tygodnia; **they ~ed to the pub** *(Brit: fml)* udali się do pubu
**adjournment** [ə'dʒəːnmənt] *n (period)* przerwa *f* w obradach
**Adjt.** *(Mil) abbr* = **adjutant**
**adjudicate** [ə'dʒuːdɪkeɪt] *vt (contest)* rozstrzygać (rozstrzygnąć *perf*); *(claim, dispute)* rozsądzać (rozsądzić *perf*) ▷ *vi* orzekać (orzec *perf*)
**adjudication** [ədʒuːdɪ'keɪʃən] *n (Jur)* orzeczenie *nt*; **the matter is under ~** sprawa jest rozpatrywana
**adjudicator** [ə'djuːdɪkeɪtə[r]] *n* sędzia *m*

**adjust** [ə'dʒʌst] *vt* (*approach*) modyfikować (zmodyfikować *perf*); (*clothing*) poprawiać (poprawić *perf*); (*machine, device*) regulować (wyregulować *perf*) ▷ *vi*: **to ~ (to)** przystosowywać się (przystosować się *perf*) (do *+gen*)
**adjustable** [ə'dʒʌstəbl] *adj* regulowany
**adjuster** [ə'dʒʌstə^r] *n see* **loss**
**adjustment** [ə'dʒʌstmənt] *n* (*of machine, prices, wages*) regulacja *f*; (*of person*) przystosowanie się *nt*
**adjutant** ['ædʒətənt] *n* (*Mil*) adiutant *m*
**ad-lib** [æd'lɪb] *vi* improwizować (zaimprowizować *perf*) ▷ *vt* improwizować (zaimprowizować *perf*) ▷ *adv*: **ad lib** (*speak*) bez przygotowania
**adman** ['ædmæn] (*inf*) *n* autor *m* reklam
**admin** ['ædmɪn] (*inf*) *n abbr* = **administration**
**administer** [əd'mɪnɪstə^r] *vt* (*country, department*) administrować *+instr*; (*justice, punishment*) wymierzać (wymierzyć *perf*); (*test*) przeprowadzać (przeprowadzić *perf*); (*Med: drug*) podawać (podać *perf*)
**administration** [ədmɪnɪs'treɪʃən] *n* administracja *f*; **the A~** (*US*) rząd; **the Clinton A~** administracja Clintona
**administrative** [əd'mɪnɪstrətɪv] *adj* administracyjny
**administrator** [əd'mɪnɪstreɪtə^r] *n* administrator(ka) *m(f)*
**admirable** ['ædmərəbl] *adj* godny podziwu
**admiral** ['ædmərəl] *n* admirał *m*
**Admiralty** ['ædmərəltɪ] (*Brit*) *n*: **the ~** Admiralicja *f*
**admiration** [ædmə'reɪʃən] *n* podziw *m*; **to have great ~ for sth/sb** mieć wiele podziwu dla czegoś/kogoś
**admire** [əd'maɪə^r] *vt* podziwiać
**admirer** [əd'maɪərə^r] *n* (*suitor*) wielbiciel *m*; (*fan*) wielbiciel(ka) *m(f)*
**admission** [əd'mɪʃən] *n* (*admittance*) przyjęcie *nt*; (*to exhibition, night club*) wstęp *m*; (*entry fee*) opłata *f* za wstęp; (*confession*) przyznanie się *nt*; **"~ free", "free ~"** „wstęp wolny"; **by his own ~** jak sam przyznaje
**admit** [əd'mɪt] *vt* (*confess, accept*) przyznawać się (przyznać się *perf*) do *+gen*; (*permit to enter*) wpuszczać (wpuścić *perf*); (*to club, organization, hospital*) przyjmować (przyjąć *perf*); **"children not ~ted"** „(wstęp) tylko dla dorosłych"; **this ticket ~s two** to bilet wstępu dla dwóch osób; **I must ~ that ...** muszę przyznać, że ...
▸ **admit of** *vt fus* (*interpretation etc*) dopuszczać (dopuścić *perf*) *+acc*
▸ **admit to** *vt fus* (*murder etc*) przyznawać się (przyznać się *perf*) do *+gen*
**admittance** [əd'mɪtəns] *n* wstęp *m*; **"no ~"** „wstęp wzbroniony"
**admittedly** [əd'mɪtɪdlɪ] *adv* trzeba przyznać, co prawda
**admonish** [əd'mɔnɪʃ] *vt* upominać (upomnieć *perf*)
**ad nauseam** [æd'nɔ:sɪæm] *adv* do znudzenia
**ado** [ə'du:] *n*: **without (any) more ado** bez dalszych wstępów
**adolescence** [ædəu'lɛsns] *n* okres *m* dojrzewania
**adolescent** [ædəu'lɛsnt] *adj* młodociany ▷ *n* nastolatek(-tka) *m(f)*
**adopt** [ə'dɔpt] *vt* (*child*) adoptować (zaadoptować *perf*); (*position, attitude*) przyjmować (przyjąć *perf*); (*course of action, method*) obierać (obrać *perf*); (*tone etc*) przybierać (przybrać *perf*); **the party ~ed him as its candidate** partia wybrała go na swojego kandydata
**adopted** [ə'dɔptɪd] *adj* (*child*) adoptowany
**adoption** [ə'dɔpʃən] *n* (*of child*) adopcja *f*; (*of position, attitude*) przyjęcie *nt*; (*of course of action, method*) obranie *nt*; (*Pol: of candidate*) wybór *m*
**adoptive** [ə'dɔptɪv] *adj* przybrany
**adorable** [ə'dɔ:rəbl] *adj* (*child, kitten*) uroczy
**adoration** [ædə'reɪʃən] *n* uwielbienie *nt*
**adore** [ə'dɔ:^r] *vt* uwielbiać; **the audience will ~ the film** publiczność będzie filmem zachwycona
**adoringly** [ə'dɔ:rɪŋlɪ] *adv* z uwielbieniem
**adorn** [ə'dɔ:n] *vt* zdobić, przyozdabiać (przyozdobić *perf*)
**adornment** [ə'dɔ:nmənt] *n* (*act*) zdobienie *nt*; (*decoration*) ozdoba *f*
**ADP** *n abbr* = **automatic data processing**
**adrenalin** [ə'drɛnəlɪn] *n* adrenalina *f*; **to get the ~ going** podnosić (podnieść *perf*) ciśnienie
**Adriatic** [eɪdrɪ'ætɪk] *n*: **the ~ (Sea)** Adriatyk *m*, Morze *nt* Adriatyckie
**adrift** [ə'drɪft] *adj*: **to be ~** (*Naut*) dryfować; **to be** *or* **feel ~** (*fig*) być *or* czuć się zagubionym; **to come ~** (*rope, fastening*) poluzowywać się (poluzować się *perf*); **our plans have gone ~** nasze plany wzięły w łeb
**adroit** [ə'drɔɪt] *adj* zręczny, sprytny
**adroitly** [ə'drɔɪtlɪ] *adv* zręcznie, sprytnie
**ADT** (*US*) *abbr* = **Atlantic Daylight Time**
**adult** ['ædʌlt] *n* (*person*) dorosły *m*; (*animal, insect*) dorosły osobnik *m* ▷ *adj* (*grown-up*) dorosły; (*for adults*) dla dorosłych *post*
**adult education** *n* kształcenie *nt* dorosłych
**adulterate** [ə'dʌltəreɪt] *vt* fałszować (sfałszować *perf*), podrabiać (podrobić *perf*)
**adultery** [ə'dʌltərɪ] *n* cudzołóstwo *nt*
**adulthood** ['ædʌlthud] *n* dorosłość *f*

**advance** [əd'vɑːns] *n* (*movement*) posuwanie się *nt*; (*progress*) postęp *m*; (*money*) zaliczka *f* ▷ *adj* wcześniejszy, uprzedni ▷ *vt* (*money*) wypłacać (wypłacić *perf*) z góry *or* awansem; (*theory*) wysuwać (wysunąć *perf*) ▷ *vi* (*move forward*) posuwać się (posunąć się *perf*); (*make progress*) czynić (poczynić *perf*) postępy; **to make ~s (to sb)** podejmować (podjąć *perf*) próby zbliżenia (z kimś); (*amorously*) zalecać się (do kogoś); **in ~** (*arrive, notify*) z wyprzedzeniem; (*pay*) z góry; **to give sb ~ notice** dawać (dać *perf*) komuś wypowiedzenie z wyprzedzeniem

**advanced** [əd'vɑːnst] *adj* (*studies*) wyższy; (*course*) dla zaawansowanych *post*; (*country, child*) rozwinięty; **~ in years** w podeszłym wieku

**advancement** [əd'vɑːnsmənt] *n* (*furtherance*) wspieranie *nt*; (*in job*) awans *m*

**advantage** [əd'vɑːntɪdʒ] *n* (*benefit*) korzyść *f*; (*beneficial feature*) zaleta *f*, dobra strona *f*; (*supremacy, point in tennis*) przewaga *f*; **to take ~ of** (*person*) wykorzystywać (wykorzystać *perf*) *+acc*; (*opportunity*) korzystać (skorzystać *perf*) z *+gen*; **it's to our ~ to start learning Spanish** będzie dla nas korzystne, jeśli zaczniemy się uczyć hiszpańskiego

**advantageous** [ædvən'teɪdʒəs] *adj*: **~ (to)** korzystny (dla *+gen*)

**advent** ['ædvənt] *n* (*of era*) nastanie *nt*, nadejście *nt*; (*of innovation*) pojawienie się *nt*; (*Rel*): **A~** adwent *m*

**Advent calendar** *n* kalendarz *m* adwentowy

**adventure** [əd'vɛntʃə^r] *n* przygoda *f*

**adventurous** [əd'vɛntʃərəs] *adj* (*person*) odważny; (*action*) ryzykowny; (*life, journey*) pełen przygód

**adverb** ['ædvəːb] *n* przysłówek *m*

**adversary** ['ædvəsərɪ] *n* przeciwnik(-iczka) *m(f)*

**adverse** ['ædvəːs] *adj* niesprzyjający, niekorzystny; **~ to** wrogi *+dat*; **in ~ circumstances** w niesprzyjających okolicznościach

**adversity** [əd'vəːsɪtɪ] *n* przeciwności *pl* (losu)

**advert** ['ædvəːt] (*Brit*) *n abbr* = **advertisement**

**advertise** ['ædvətaɪz] *vi* reklamować się (zareklamować się *perf*) ▷ *vt* reklamować (zareklamować *perf*); **to ~ for** poszukiwać *+gen* (*przez ogłoszenie*)

**advertisement** [əd'vəːtɪsmənt] *n* (*for product*) reklama *f*; (*about job, accommodation etc*) ogłoszenie *nt*, anons *m*

**advertiser** ['ædvətaɪzə^r] *n* reklamujący(-ca) *m(f)*, ogłaszający(-ca) *m(f)*

**advertising** ['ædvətaɪzɪŋ] *n* reklama *f*

**advertising agency** *n* agencja *f* reklamowa

**advertising campaign** *n* kampania *f* reklamowa

**advice** [əd'vaɪs] *n* (*counsel*) rada *f*; (*: doctor's, lawyer's etc*) porada *f*; (*notification*) zawiadomienie *nt*; **a piece of ~** rada; **to ask sb for ~** prosić (poprosić *perf*) kogoś o radę; **to take legal ~** zasięgać (zasięgnąć *perf*) porady prawnej

**advice note** (*Brit*) *n* awizo *nt*

**advisable** [əd'vaɪzəbl] *adj* wskazany

**advise** [əd'vaɪz] *vt* (*person*) radzić (poradzić *perf*) *+dat*; (*company*) doradzać (doradzić *perf*) *+dat*; **to ~ sb of sth** powiadamiać (powiadomić *perf*) kogoś o czymś; **to ~ sb against sth/doing sth** odradzać (odradzić *perf*) komuś coś/zrobienie czegoś; **you would be well-/ill-~d to go** dobrze/źle byś zrobił, gdybyś pojechał

**advisedly** [əd'vaɪzɪdlɪ] *adv* celowo, rozmyślnie

**adviser** [əd'vaɪzə^r] *n* doradca(-dczyni) *m(f)*

**advisor** [əd'vaɪzə^r] *n* = **adviser**

**advisory** [əd'vaɪzərɪ] *adj* doradczy; **in an ~ capacity** w charakterze doradcy

**advocate** [*vb* 'ædvəkeɪt, *n* 'ædvəkɪt] *vt* (*support*) popierać (poprzeć *perf*); (*recommend*) zalecać (zalecić *perf*) ▷ *n* (*Jur*) adwokat(ka) *m(f)*; (*supporter*) zwolennik(-iczka) *m(f)*, orędownik(-iczka) *m(f)*

**advt.** *abbr* (= *advertisement*) ogł.

**AEA** (*Brit*) *n abbr* (= *Atomic Energy Authority*) *urząd sprawujący kontrolę nad wykorzystaniem energii atomowej*

**AEC** (*US*) *n abbr* (= *Atomic Energy Commission*) *komisja sprawująca kontrolę nad wykorzystaniem energii atomowej*

**AEEU** (*Brit*) *n abbr* = **Amalgamated Engineering and Electrical Union**

**Aegean** [iː'dʒiːən] *n*: **the ~ (Sea)** Morze *nt* Egejskie

**aegis** ['iːdʒɪs] *n*: **under the ~ of** pod egidą *+gen*

**aeon** ['iːən] *n* wiek *m*

**aerial** ['ɛərɪəl] *n* antena *f* ▷ *adj* lotniczy

**aero...** ['ɛərəu] *pref* aero...

**aerobatics** ['ɛərəu'bætɪks] *npl* akrobatyka *f* lotnicza

**aerobics** [ɛə'rəubɪks] *n* aerobik *m*

**aerodrome** ['ɛərədrəum] (*Brit*) *n* lądowisko *nt*, małe lotnisko *nt*

**aerodynamic** ['ɛərəudaɪ'næmɪk] *adj* aerodynamiczny

**aeronautics** [ɛərə'nɔːtɪks] *n* aeronautyka *f*

**aeroplane** ['ɛərəpleɪn] (*Brit*) *n* samolot *m*

**aerosol** ['ɛərəsɔl] *n* aerozol *m*

**aerospace industry** ['ɛərəuspeɪs-] *n* przemysł *m* aerokosmiczny

**aesthetic** [iːs'θɛtɪk] *adj* estetyczny
**aesthetically** [iːs'θɛtɪklɪ] *adv* estetycznie
**afar** [ə'fɑːʳ] *adv*: **from ~** z oddali
**AFB** (*US*) *n abbr* = **Air Force Base**
**AFDC** (*US*) *n abbr* (= *Aid to Families with Dependent Children*) *pomoc finansowa dla rodzin o niskich dochodach*
**affable** ['æfəbl] *adj* przyjemny, przyjazny
**affair** [ə'fɛəʳ] *n* sprawa *f*; (*also*: **love affair**) romans *m*; **affairs** *npl* sprawy *pl*
**affect** [ə'fɛkt] *vt* (*influence*) wpływać (wpłynąć *perf*) na *+acc*; (*afflict*) atakować (zaatakować *perf*); (*move deeply*) wzruszać (wzruszyć *perf*); (*concern*) dotyczyć *+gen*; (*feign*) udawać (udać *perf*)
**affectation** [æfɛk'teɪʃən] *n* poza *f*
**affected** [ə'fɛktɪd] *adj* sztuczny, afektowany
**affection** [ə'fɛkʃən] *n* uczucie *nt*
**affectionate** [ə'fɛkʃənɪt] *adj* czuły
**affectionately** [ə'fɛkʃənɪtlɪ] *adv* czule
**affidavit** [æfɪ'deɪvɪt] (*Jur*) *n* (pisemne) oświadczenie *nt* pod przysięgą
**affiliated** [ə'fɪlɪeɪtɪd] *adj* stowarzyszony
**affinity** [ə'fɪnɪtɪ] *n*: **to have an ~ with/for** (*attraction*) darzyć sympatią *+acc*, odczuwać więź z *+instr*; **to have an ~ with** (*resemblance*) zdradzać podobieństwo do *+gen*
**affirm** [ə'fəːm] *vt* stwierdzać (stwierdzić *perf*)
**affirmation** [æfə'meɪʃən] *n* (*of fact*) stwierdzenie *nt*; (*of belief*) afirmacja *f*
**affirmative** [ə'fəːmətɪv] *adj* (*statement*) twierdzący; (*nod, gesture*) potakujący ▷ *n*: **in the ~** twierdząco
**affix** [ə'fɪks] *vt* (*stamp*) naklejać (nakleić *perf*)
**afflict** [ə'flɪkt] *vt* dotykać (dotknąć *perf*)
**affliction** [ə'flɪkʃən] *n* nieszczęście *nt*; (*physical*) przypadłość *f*
**affluence** ['æfluəns] *n* dostatek *m*
**affluent** ['æfluənt] *adj* dostatni; **the ~ society** społeczeństwo dobrobytu
**afford** [ə'fɔːd] *vt* pozwalać (pozwolić *perf*) sobie na *+acc*; (*provide*) udzielać (udzielić *perf*) *+gen*; **can we ~ a car?** czy stać nas na samochód?; **I can't ~ the time** nie mam (na to) czasu
**affray** [ə'freɪ] (*Brit*: *Jur*) *n* zakłócenie *nt* spokoju publicznego
**affront** [ə'frʌnt] *n* zniewaga *f*, afront *m*
**affronted** [ə'frʌntɪd] *adj* urażony
**Afghan** ['æfgæn] *adj* afgański ▷ *n* Afgańczyk(-anka) *m(f)*
**Afghanistan** [æf'gænɪstæn] *n* Afganistan *m*
**afield** [ə'fiːld] *adv*: **far ~** daleko; **from far ~** z daleka
**AFL-CIO** *n abbr* (= *American Federation of Labor and Congress of Industrial Organizations*) *amerykańska federacja związków zawodowych*
**afloat** [ə'fləut] *adv* na wodzie, na powierzchni (wody) ▷ *adj* unoszący się na wodzie; **to stay ~** pozostawać (pozostać *perf*) wypłacalnym; **to get a business ~** uruchamiać (uruchomić *perf*) interes
**afoot** [ə'fut] *adv*: **there is something ~** coś się święci
**aforementioned** [ə'fɔːmɛnʃənd] *adj* wyżej wymieniony *or* wspomniany
**aforesaid** [ə'fɔːsɛd] *adj* = **aforementioned**
**afraid** [ə'freɪd] *adj* przestraszony; **to be ~ of** bać się *+gen*; **to be ~ to** bać się *+infin*; **she was ~ of offending anyone** bała się, że kogoś obrazi; **I am ~ that ...** obawiam się, że ...; **I am ~ so/not** obawiam się, że tak/nie
**afresh** [ə'frɛʃ] *adv* od nowa
**Africa** ['æfrɪkə] *n* Afryka *f*
**African** ['æfrɪkən] *adj* afrykański ▷ *n* Afrykańczyk(-anka) *m(f)*
**Afrikaans** [æfrɪ'kɑːns] *n* (język *m*) afrikaans *or* afrykańsko-burski
**Afrikaner** [æfrɪ'kɑːnəʳ] *n* Afrykaner(ka) *m(f)*
**Afro-American** ['æfrəuə'mɛrɪkən] *adj* afroamerykański
**AFT** (*US*) *n abbr* = **American Federation of Teachers**
**aft** [ɑːft] *adv* (*on ship*: *sit*) na rufie; (: *go*) ku rufie; (*on plane*: *sit*) z tyłu; (: *go*) ku tyłowi
**after** ['ɑːftəʳ] *prep* (*of time*) po *+loc*; (*of place, order*) po *+loc*, za *+instr*; (*artist, writer*) w stylu *+gen* ▷ *adv* potem, później ▷ *conj* gdy, po tym, jak; **~ dinner** po obiedzie; **the day ~ tomorrow** pojutrze; **what/who are you ~?** na co/kogo polujesz? (*inf*); **the police are ~ him** ściga go policja; **~ he left** po jego wyjeździe; **to name sb ~ sb** dawać (dać *perf*) komuś imię po kimś; **it's twenty ~ eight** (*US*) jest dwadzieścia po ósmej; **to ask ~ sb** pytać o kogoś; **~ all** (*it must be remembered that*) przecież, w końcu; (*in spite of everything*) mimo wszystko; **~ you!** proszę bardzo! (*przepuszczając kogoś w drzwiach*)
**aftercare** ['ɑːftəkɛəʳ] (*Brit*) *n* opieka *f* pooperacyjna *or* nad rekonwalescentem
**after-effects** ['ɑːftərɪfɛkts] *npl* następstwa *pl*
**afterlife** ['ɑːftəlaɪf] *n* życie *nt* pozagrobowe
**aftermath** ['ɑːftəmɑːθ] *n* następstwa *pl*, pokłosie *nt* (*literary*); **in the ~ of** w następstwie *+gen*
**afternoon** ['ɑːftə'nuːn] *n* popołudnie *nt*; **good ~!** (*hello*) dzień dobry!; (*goodbye*) do widzenia!
**afters** ['ɑːftəz] (*inf*) *n* deser *m*
**after-sales service** [ɑːftə'seɪlz-] (*Brit*: *Comm*) *n* serwis *m*
**after-shave (lotion)** ['ɑːftəʃeɪv-] *n* płyn *m* po goleniu
**aftershock** ['ɑːftəʃɔk] *n* trzęsienie *nt* następcze

**afterthought** ['ɑːftəθɔːt] *n*: **as an ~** machinalnie; **I had an ~** nasunęła mi się refleksja
**afterwards** ['ɑːftəwədz], *(US)* **afterward** *adv* później, potem
**again** [ə'gɛn] *adv (once more, on another occasion)* znowu, znów, ponownie *(fml)*; *(one more time)* jeszcze raz; **I won't be late ~** już (nigdy) się nie spóźnię; **never ~** nigdy więcej; **to begin ~** zaczynać (zacząć *perf*) od nowa; **he's opened it ~** znowu to otworzył; **~ and ~, time and ~** wielokrotnie, ciągle; **now and ~** od czasu do czasu
**against** [ə'gɛnst] *prep (lean, rub)* o *+acc*; *(fight)* z *+instr*; *(in opposition to)* przeciw(ko) *+dat*; *(in relation to)* w stosunku do *+gen*; **to press sth ~ sth** przyciskać (przycisnąć *perf*) coś do czegoś; **~ a blue background** na niebieskim tle; **(as) ~** w porównaniu z *+instr*
**age** [eɪdʒ] *n* wiek *m* ▷ *vi* starzeć się (zestarzeć się *perf or* postarzeć się *perf*) ▷ *vt* postarzać (postarzyć *perf*); **what age is he?** ile on ma lat?; **he is 20 years of age** ma dwadzieścia lat; **under age** nieletni, niepełnoletni; **to come of age** osiągać (osiągnąć *perf*) pełnoletniość; **it's been ages since we last saw each other** nie widzieliśmy się całe wieki
**aged**[1] ['eɪdʒd] *adj*: **~ 10** w wieku lat dziesięciu; **Bill Ash, ~ 62, ...** Bill Ash, lat 62, ...
**aged**[2] ['eɪdʒɪd] *npl*: **the ~** osoby *pl* w podeszłym wieku
**age group** *n* grupa *f* wiekowa; **the 40 to 50 ~** osoby w wieku od 40 do 50 lat
**ageless** ['eɪdʒlɪs] *adj (never growing old)* wiecznie młody; *(timeless)* wieczny
**age limit** *n* ograniczenie *nt or* limit *m* wieku
**agency** ['eɪdʒənsɪ] *n (Comm)* agencja *f*; *(government body)* urząd *m*, biuro *nt*; **through** *or* **by the ~ of** za pośrednictwem *+gen*
**agenda** [ə'dʒɛndə] *n* porządek *m* dzienny; **on the ~** w programie
**agent** ['eɪdʒənt] *n (person)* agent(ka) *m(f)*; *(Chem)* środek *m*; *(fig)* czynnik *m*
**aggravate** ['ægrəveɪt] *vt (worsen)* pogarszać (pogorszyć *perf*); *(annoy)* denerwować (zdenerwować *perf*)
**aggravating** ['ægrəveɪtɪŋ] *adj* denerwujący
**aggravation** [ægrə'veɪʃən] *n* zdenerwowanie *nt*
**aggregate** ['ægrɪgɪt] *n* suma *f* ▷ *vt* sumować (zsumować *perf*)
**aggression** [ə'grɛʃən] *n* agresja *f*
**aggressive** [ə'grɛsɪv] *adj* agresywny
**aggressiveness** [ə'grɛsɪvnɪs] *n* agresywność *f*
**aggrieved** [ə'griːvd] *adj* dotknięty
**aghast** [ə'gɑːst] *adj* przerażony; **to be ~ at sth** być przerażonym czymś
**agile** ['ædʒaɪl] *adj (physically)* zwinny; *(mentally)* sprawny
**agitate** ['ædʒɪteɪt] *vt (person)* poruszać (poruszyć *perf*); *(liquid)* wstrząsać (wstrząsnąć *perf*) *+instr* ▷ *vi*: **to ~ for/against** agitować za *+instr*/przeciw *+dat*
**agitated** ['ædʒɪteɪtɪd] *adj* poruszony
**agitator** ['ædʒɪteɪtə[r]] *n* agitator(ka) *m(f)*
**AGM** *n abbr (= annual general meeting)* WZA *nt inv*
**agnostic** [æg'nɔstɪk] *n* agnostyk(-yczka) *m(f)*
**ago** [ə'gəu] *adv*: **2 days ago** dwa dni temu; **not long ago** niedawno; **as long ago as 1960** już w roku 1960; **how long ago?** jak dawno (temu)?
**agog** [ə'gɔg] *adj* przejęty, podniecony; **she was all ~** była bardzo przejęta
**agonize** ['ægənaɪz] *vi*: **he ~d over the problem** zadręczał się tym problemem
**agonizing** ['ægənaɪzɪŋ] *adj (pain)* dręczący; *(cry)* rozdzierający; *(decision)* bolesny; *(wait)* męczący
**agony** ['ægənɪ] *n (pain)* (dotkliwy) ból *m*; *(torment)* udręka *f*, męczarnia *f*; **to be in ~** cierpieć katusze
**agony aunt** *n redaktorka rubryki porad osobistych dla czytelników*
**agony column** *n rubryka porad osobistych dla czytelników*
**agree** [ə'griː] *vt (price, date)* uzgadniać (uzgodnić *perf*) ▷ *vi* zgadzać się (zgodzić się *perf*); *(Ling)* zgadzać się; **to ~ with** *(person)* zgadzać się (zgodzić się *perf*) z *+instr*; *(food)* służyć *+dat*; *(statements etc)* pokrywać się (pokryć się *perf*) z *+instr*; **to ~ to sth/to do sth** zgadzać się (zgodzić się *perf*) na coś/zrobić coś; **to ~ on sth** uzgadniać (uzgodnić *perf*) coś; **to ~ that ...** przyznawać (przyznać *perf*), że ...; **garlic doesn't ~ with me** czosnek mi szkodzi *or* nie służy; **it was ~d that ...** uzgodniono, że ...; **they ~d on this** zgodzili się co do tego; **they ~d on going** uzgodnili, że pojadą
**agreeable** [ə'griːəbl] *adj (pleasant)* miły; *(willing)* skłonny; **are you ~ to this?** odpowiada ci to?
**agreed** [ə'griːd] *adj* uzgodniony; **to be ~** zgadzać się
**agreement** [ə'griːmənt] *n (consent)* zgoda *f*; *(contract)* porozumienie *nt*; **to be in ~ with sb** zgadzać się (zgodzić się *perf*) z kimś; **by mutual ~** za obopólną zgodą
**agricultural** [ægrɪ'kʌltʃərəl] *adj* rolniczy
**agriculture** ['ægrɪkʌltʃə[r]] *n* rolnictwo
**aground** [ə'graund] *(Naut) adv*: **to run ~** osiadać (osiąść *perf*) na mieliźnie

**ahead** [əˈhɛd] *adv* (*of place*) z przodu; (*of time*) z wyprzedzeniem, naprzód; (*into the future*) naprzód, do przodu; ~ **of** przed +*instr*; ~ **of schedule** przed terminem; **a year** ~ z rocznym wyprzedzeniem, na rok naprzód; **go right** *or* **straight** ~ proszę iść prosto przed siebie; **go ~!** (*fig*) proszę (bardzo)!; **they were (right) ~ of us** byli (tuż) przed nami; **we are a good ten years ~ of you** wyprzedzamy was o dobre dziesięć lat

**AI** *n abbr* = **Amnesty International**; (*Comput*) = **artificial intelligence**

**AIB** (*Brit*) *n abbr* = **Accident Investigation Bureau**

**AID** *n abbr* (= *artificial insemination by donor*) sztuczne zapłodnienie *nt* nasieniem dawcy; (*US*) = **Agency for International Development**

**aid** [eɪd] *n* pomoc *f* ▷ *vt* pomagać (pomóc *perf*) +*dat*, wspomagać (wspomóc *perf*); **with the aid of** (*thing*) za pomocą +*gen*; (*person*) przy pomocy +*gen*; **in aid of** na rzecz +*gen*; **to aid and abet** (*Jur*) udzielać (udzielić *perf*) pomocy w dokonaniu przestępstwa; *see also* **hearing**

**aide** [eɪd] (*Pol*, *Mil*) *n* doradca(-dczyni) *m(f)*

**aide-de-camp** [ˈeɪddəˈkɔŋ] (*Mil*) *n* adiutant(ka) *m(f)*

**AIDS** [eɪdz] *n abbr* (= *acquired immune deficiency syndrome*) AIDS *m inv*

**AIH** *n abbr* (= *artificial insemination by husband*) sztuczne zapłodnienie *nt* nasieniem męża

**ailing** [ˈeɪlɪŋ] *adj* (*person*) niedomagający; (*industry*) borykający się z trudnościami; (*economy*) kulejący

**ailment** [ˈeɪlmənt] *n* dolegliwość *f*

**aim** [eɪm] *vt*: **to aim sth (at)** (*gun*) celować (wycelować *perf*) z czegoś (do +*gen*); (*camera*) kierować (skierować *perf*) coś (na +*acc*); (*blow*) mierzyć (wymierzyć *perf*) coś (w +*acc*); (*remark*) kierować (skierować *perf*) coś (pod adresem +*gen*) ▷ *vi* celować (wycelować *perf*), mierzyć (wymierzyć *perf*) ▷ *n* cel *m*; (*skill*) celność *f*; **to aim at** (*with weapon*) celować (wycelować *perf*) w +*acc*; (*objective*) dążyć do +*gen*; **to aim to do sth** zamierzać coś zrobić

**aimless** [ˈeɪmlɪs] *adj* (*activity*) bezcelowy; (*person*) pozbawiony celu

**aimlessly** [ˈeɪmlɪslɪ] *adv* bez celu

**ain't** [eɪnt] (*inf*) = **am not**; (*inf*) = **aren't**; (*inf*) = **isn't**

**air** [ɛəʳ] *n* powietrze *nt*; (*aria*) aria *f*; (*tune*) melodia *f*; (*mood*) atmosfera *f*; (*appearance*) wygląd *m* ▷ *vt* (*room*) wietrzyć (przewietrzyć *perf or* wywietrzyć *perf*); (*views*) głosić, wygłaszać; (*grievances*) wylewać ▷ *cpd* (*currents*, *attack etc*) powietrzny; **to throw sth into the air** podrzucić (*perf*) coś do góry; **by air** drogą lotniczą, samolotem; **to be on the air** (*Radio*, *TV*: *programme*) być na antenie, być nadawanym; (: *station*) nadawać

**airbag** [ˈɛəbæg] *n* (*in car*) poduszka *f* powietrzna

**air base** *n* baza *f* lotnicza

**airbed** [ˈɛəbɛd] (*Brit*) *n* materac *m* nadmuchiwany

**airborne** [ˈɛəbɔːn] *adj* (*attack etc*) lotniczy; (*plane*) lecący; (*troops*) powietrznodesantowy; (*particles*) zawieszony w powietrzu; **as soon as the plane was ~** zaraz po starcie samolotu

**air cargo** *n* ładunek *m* lotniczy

**air-conditioned** [ˈɛəkənˈdɪʃənd] *adj* klimatyzowany

**air conditioning** *n* klimatyzacja *f*

**air-cooled** [ˈɛəkuːld] *adj* (*engine*) chłodzony powietrzem

**aircraft** [ˈɛəkrɑːft] *n inv* samolot *m*

**aircraft carrier** *n* lotniskowiec *m*

**air cushion** *n* poduszka *f* pneumatyczna

**airfield** [ˈɛəfiːld] *n* lotnisko *nt*

**Air Force** *n* siły *pl* powietrzne

**air freight** *n* fracht *m* lotniczy

**air freshener** *n* odświeżacz *m* powietrza

**airgun** [ˈɛəgʌn] *n* wiatrówka *f*

**air hostess** (*Brit*) *n* stewardessa *f*

**airily** [ˈɛərɪlɪ] *adv* beztrosko

**airing** [ˈɛərɪŋ] *n*: **to give an ~ to** wietrzyć (przewietrzyć *perf*) +*acc*; (*fig*: *ideas*, *views etc*) omawiać (omówić *perf*)

**air letter** (*Brit*) *n* list *m* lotniczy

**airlift** [ˈɛəlɪft] *n* most *m* powietrzny ▷ *vt* transportować (przetransportować *perf*) drogą lotniczą

**airline** [ˈɛəlaɪn] *n* linia *f* lotnicza

**airliner** [ˈɛəlaɪnəʳ] *n* samolot *m* pasażerski

**airlock** [ˈɛəlɔk] *n* (*in spacecraft*) śluza *f* powietrzna

**airmail** [ˈɛəmeɪl] *n*: **by ~** pocztą lotniczą

**air mattress** *n* materac *m* nadmuchiwany

**airplane** [ˈɛəpleɪn] (*US*) *n* samolot *m*

**airport** [ˈɛəpɔːt] *n* lotnisko *nt*, port *m* lotniczy

**air raid** *n* nalot *m*

**airsick** [ˈɛəsɪk] *adj*: **to be ~** mieć mdłości (*podczas lotu samolotem*)

**airspace** [ˈɛəspeɪs] *n* obszar *m* powietrzny

**airstrip** [ˈɛəstrɪp] *n* pas *m* startowy (*prowizoryczny*)

**air terminal** *n* terminal *m* (*lotniska*)

**airtight** [ˈɛətaɪt] *adj* szczelny (*nie przepuszczający powietrza*)

**air-traffic control** [ˈɛətræfɪk-] *n* kontrola *f* ruchu lotniczego

**air-traffic controller** [ˈɛətræfɪk-] *n* kontroler(ka) *m(f)* ruchu lotniczego

**airway** [ˈɛəweɪ] *n* trasa *f* lotnicza

a

**airy** [ˈɛərɪ] *adj* *(building)* przestronny, przewiewny; *(manner)* beztroski
**aisle** [aɪl] *n* *(of church)* nawa *f* boczna; *(of theatre, in plane)* przejście *nt*
**ajar** [əˈdʒɑːʳ] *adj* *(door)* uchylony
**AK** *(US: Post)* *abbr* = **Alaska**
**a.k.a.** *abbr* (= *also known as*) alias, v. (= *vel*)
**akin** [əˈkɪn] *adj*: **~ to** pokrewny *+dat*, przypominający *+acc*
**AL** *(US: Post)* *abbr* = **Alabama**
**ALA** *n abbr* = **American Library Association**
**alabaster** [ˈæləbɑːstəʳ] *n* alabaster *m*
**à la carte** [ɑːlɑːˈkɑːt] *adv* à la carte
**alacrity** [əˈlækrɪtɪ] *n* ochota *f*; **with ~** z ochotą
**alarm** [əˈlɑːm] *n* *(anxiety)* zaniepokojenie *nt*, niepokój *m*; *(in bank etc)* alarm *m*, system *m* alarmowy ▷ *vt* niepokoić (zaniepokoić *perf*)
**alarm call** *n* budzenie *nt* *(telefoniczne)*
**alarm clock** *n* budzik *m*
**alarming** [əˈlɑːmɪŋ] *adj* *(worrying)* niepokojący; *(frightening)* zastraszający, zatrważający
**alarmist** [əˈlɑːmɪst] *n* panikarz(-ara) *m(f)*
**alas** [əˈlæs] *excl* niestety
**Alaska** [əˈlæskə] *n* Alaska *f*
**Albania** [ælˈbeɪnɪə] *n* Albania *f*
**Albanian** [ælˈbeɪnɪən] *adj* albański ▷ *n* *(Ling)* (język *m*) albański; *(person)* Albańczyk(-anka) *m(f)*
**albeit** [ɔːlˈbiːɪt] *conj* aczkolwiek
**album** [ˈælbəm] *n* album *m*
**albumen** [ˈælbjumɪn] *n* białko *nt*
**alchemy** [ˈælkɪmɪ] *n* alchemia *f*
**alcohol** [ˈælkəhɔl] *n* alkohol *m*
**alcohol-free** [ˈælkəhɔlˈfriː] *adj* bezalkoholowy
**alcoholic** [ælkəˈhɔlɪk] *adj* alkoholowy ▷ *n* alkoholik(-iczka) *m(f)*
**alcoholism** [ˈælkəhɔlɪzəm] *n* alkoholizm *m*
**alcove** [ˈælkəuv] *n* wnęka *f*
**Ald.** *abbr* = **alderman**
**alderman** [ˈɔːldəmən] *(irreg: like* **man***)* *n* ≈ radny *m*
**ale** [eɪl] *n rodzaj piwa angielskiego*
**alert** [əˈləːt] *adj* czujny ▷ *n* stan *m* pogotowia *or* gotowości ▷ *vt* alarmować (zaalarmować *perf*); **to ~ sb (to sth)** uświadamiać (uświadomić *perf*) komuś (coś); **to ~ sb to the dangers of sth** ostrzegać (ostrzec *perf*) kogoś przed niebezpieczeństwami czegoś; **to be on the ~** być w pogotowiu; **~ to danger** świadomy niebezpieczeństwa
**Aleutian Islands** [əˈluːʃən-] *npl* Aleuty *pl*
**Alexandria** [ælɪgˈzɑːndrɪə] *n* Aleksandria *f*
**alfresco** [ælˈfrɛskəu] *adj* na świeżym powietrzu *(o posiłku)* ▷ *adv* na świeżym powietrzu *(spożywać posiłek)*
**algebra** [ˈældʒɪbrə] *n* algebra *f*
**Algeria** [ælˈdʒɪərɪə] *n* Algieria *f*
**Algerian** [ælˈdʒɪərɪən] *adj* algierski ▷ *n* Algierczyk(-rka) *m(f)*
**Algiers** [ælˈdʒɪəz] *n* Algier *m* *(miasto)*
**algorithm** [ˈælgərɪðəm] *n* algorytm *m*
**alias** [ˈeɪlɪəs] *prep* inaczej, alias ▷ *n* pseudonim *m*
**alibi** [ˈælɪbaɪ] *n* alibi *nt inv*
**alien** [ˈeɪlɪən] *n* *(foreigner)* cudzoziemiec(-mka) *m(f)*; *(extraterrestrial)* istota *f* pozaziemska, kosmita *m* ▷ *adj*: **~ (to)** obcy (*+dat*)
**alienate** [ˈeɪlɪəneɪt] *vt* zrażać (zrazić *perf*)
**alienation** [eɪlɪəˈneɪʃən] *n* wyobcowanie *nt*, alienacja *f*
**alight** [əˈlaɪt] *adj* płonący, zapalony; *(fig)* płomienny ▷ *adv* w płomieniach ▷ *vi* *(bird)* usiąść *(perf)*; *(passenger)* wysiadać (wysiąść *perf*)
**align** [əˈlaɪn] *vt* ustawiać (ustawić *perf*)
**alignment** [əˈlaɪnmənt] *n* ustawienie *nt*; **it's out of ~ (with)** to jest źle ustawione (względem *+gen*)
**alike** [əˈlaɪk] *adj* podobny ▷ *adv* *(similarly)* podobnie, jednakowo; **they all look ~** oni wszyscy są do siebie podobni; **men and women ~** zarówno mężczyźni, jak i kobiety; **winter and summer ~** tak zimą, jak i latem
**alimony** [ˈælɪmənɪ] *n* alimenty *pl*
**alive** [əˈlaɪv] *adj* *(living)* żywy; *(lively)* pełen życia; **the theatre is very much ~** teatr ma się bardzo dobrze; **to keep sb ~** utrzymywać (utrzymać *perf*) kogoś przy życiu; **to be ~ with** być wypełnionym *+instr*; **~ to** świadomy *+gen*
**alkali** [ˈælkəlaɪ] *n* *(Chem)* zasada *f*
**alkaline** [ˈælkəlaɪn] *adj* zasadowy, alkaliczny

KEYWORD

**all** [ɔːl] *adj* *(with sing)* cały; *(with pl)* wszystkie *(+nvir)*, wszyscy *(+vir)*; **all the food** całe jedzenie; **all day** cały dzień; **all night** całą noc; **all the books** wszystkie książki; **all men are equal** wszyscy ludzie są równi; **all five came** przyszła cała piątka
▷ *pron* **1** *(sg)* wszystko *nt*; *(pl)* wszystkie *nvir pl*, wszyscy *vir pl*; **I ate it all, I ate all of it** zjadłem (to) wszystko; **is that all?** czy to (już) wszystko?; **all of us went** wszyscy poszliśmy; **we all sat down** wszyscy usiedliśmy
**2**: **above all** przede wszystkim, nade wszystko; **after all** przecież, w końcu; **all in all** w sumie, ogółem
▷ *adv* zupełnie; **all alone** zupełnie sam; **it's not as hard as all that** to nie jest aż takie trudne; **all the more/the better** tym

więcej/lepiej; **all but** (*all except for*) wszyscy z wyjątkiem *or* oprócz *+gen*; (*almost*) już prawie; **all but the strongest** wszyscy z wyjątkiem najsilniejszych; **I had all but finished** już prawie skończyłam; **what's the score? — 2 all** jaki jest wynik? — dwa — dwa

**allay** [əˈleɪ] *vt* rozpraszać (rozproszyć *perf*)
**all clear** *n* koniec *m* niebezpieczeństwa (*odwołanie alarmu*); (*fig*) pozwolenie *nt*
**allegation** [ælɪˈgeɪʃən] *n* zarzut *m*
**allege** [əˈlɛdʒ] *vt* utrzymywać; **he is ~d to have said that ...** miał rzekomo powiedzieć, że ...
**alleged** [əˈlɛdʒd] *adj* rzekomy
**allegedly** [əˈlɛdʒɪdlɪ] *adv* rzekomo
**allegiance** [əˈliːdʒəns] *n* lojalność *f*
**allegory** [ˈælɪgərɪ] *n* alegoria *f*
**all-embracing** [ˈɔːlɪmˈbreɪsɪŋ] *adj* wszechogarniający
**allergic** [əˈləːdʒɪk] *adj* alergiczny; **~ to** uczulony na *+acc*
**allergy** [ˈælədʒɪ] *n* alergia *f*, uczulenie *nt*
**alleviate** [əˈliːvɪeɪt] *vt* łagodzić (złagodzić *perf*)
**alley** [ˈælɪ] *n* aleja *f*
**alliance** [əˈlaɪəns] *n* przymierze *nt*, sojusz *m*
**allied** [ˈælaɪd] *adj* (*Pol, Mil*) sprzymierzony, sojuszniczy; (*related*) pokrewny
**alligator** [ˈælɪgeɪtəʳ] *n* aligator *m*
**all-important** [ˈɔːlɪmˈpɔːtnt] *adj* bardzo ważny
**all-in** [ˈɔːlɪn] (*Brit*) *adj* (*cost etc*) łączny ▷ *adv* łącznie, ogółem
**all-in wrestling** *n* wolna amerykanka *f*
**alliteration** [əlɪtəˈreɪʃən] *n* aliteracja *f*
**all-night** [ˈɔːlˈnaɪt] *adj* (*café*) czynny całą noc; (*party*) całonocny
**allocate** [ˈæləkeɪt] *vt* przydzielać (przydzielić *perf*)
**allocation** [æləuˈkeɪʃən] *n* przydział *m*
**allot** [əˈlɔt] *vt*: **to ~ (to)** przyznawać (przyznać *perf*) *or* przydzielać (przydzielić *perf*) (na *+acc*); **in the ~ted time** w wyznaczonym czasie
**allotment** [əˈlɔtmənt] *n* (*garden*) działka *f*; (*share*) przydział *m*
**all-out** [ˈɔːlaut] *adj* (*effort*) zdecydowany; (*dedication*) całkowity; (*strike*) powszechny ▷ *adv*: **all out** wszelkimi środkami, na całego (*inf*); **to go all out for it** z całych sił do czegoś dążyć
**allow** [əˈlau] *vt* (*behaviour*) pozwalać (pozwolić *perf*) na *+acc*; (*sum*) przeznaczać (przeznaczyć *perf*); (*claim, goal*) uznawać (uznać *perf*); **to ~ that ...** przyznawać (przyznać *perf*), że ...; **to ~ sb to do sth** pozwalać (pozwolić *perf*) komuś coś zrobić; **he is ~ed to ...** wolno mu *+infin*; **smoking is not ~ed** nie wolno palić
▶ **allow for** *vt fus* uwzględniać (uwzględnić *perf*) *+acc*
**allowance** [əˈlauəns] *n* (*travelling etc*) dieta *f*; (*welfare payment*) zasiłek *m*; (*pocket money*) kieszonkowe *nt*; (*Tax*) ulga *f*; **fuel ~** dodatek paliwowy; **to make ~s for** brać (wziąć *perf*) poprawkę na *+acc*
**alloy** [ˈælɔɪ] *n* stop *m*
**all right** *adv* (*well*) w porządku, dobrze; (*correctly*) dobrze, prawidłowo; (*as answer*) dobrze
**all-rounder** [ɔːlˈraundəʳ] *n* osoba *f* wszechstronna; **to be a good ~** być bardzo wszechstronnym
**allspice** [ˈɔːlspaɪs] *n* ziele *nt* angielskie (*mielone*)
**all-time** [ˈɔːlˈtaɪm] *adj*: **an ~ record** rekord *m* wszech czasów; **an ~ high** najwyższy z dotychczas zanotowanych poziomów
**allude** [əˈluːd] *vi*: **to ~ to** robić (zrobić *perf*) aluzję do *+gen*
**alluring** [əˈljuərɪŋ] *adj* ponętny
**allusion** [əˈluːʒən] *n* aluzja *f*
**alluvium** [əˈluːvɪəm] *n* osady *pl* rzeczne
**ally** [*n* ˈælaɪ, *vb* əˈlaɪ] *n* (*friend*) sprzymierzeniec *m*; (*Pol, Mil*) sojusznik *m* ▷ *vt*: **to ~ o.s. with** sprzymierzać się (sprzymierzyć *perf* się) z *+instr*
**almighty** [ɔːlˈmaɪtɪ] *adj* (*omnipotent*) wszechmogący, wszechmocny; (*tremendous*) ogromny
**almond** [ˈɑːmənd] *n* (*fruit*) migdał *m*; (*tree*) migdałowiec *m*
**almost** [ˈɔːlməust] *adv* prawie; **he ~ fell** o mało nie upadł; **~ certainly** prawie na pewno
**alms** [ɑːmz] *npl* jałmużna *f*
**aloft** [əˈlɔft] *adv* (*carry*) w górę; (*hold*) w górze
**alone** [əˈləun] *adj* sam ▷ *adv* samotnie; **to leave sb ~** zostawiać (zostawić *perf*) kogoś w spokoju, dawać (dać *perf*) komuś spokój; **to leave sth ~** nie ruszać czegoś; **let ~ ...** nie mówiąc (już) o *+loc*
**along** [əˈlɔŋ] *prep* wzdłuż *+gen* ▷ *adv*: **is he coming ~ with us?** czy on idzie z nami?; **to drive ~ a street** jechać ulicą; **he was limping ~** posuwał się kulejąc; **~ with** razem *or* wraz z *+instr*; **all ~** od samego początku, przez cały czas
**alongside** [əˈlɔŋˈsaɪd] *prep* (*beside*) obok *+gen*; (*together with*) wraz z *+instr* ▷ *adv* obok; **we brought our boat ~ the pier** przybiliśmy do nabrzeża
**aloof** [əˈluːf] *adj* powściągliwy ▷ *adv*: **to stay** *or* **keep ~ from** trzymać się z dala od *+gen*
**aloofness** [əˈluːfnɪs] *n* powściągliwość *f*, rezerwa *f*

**aloud** [ə'laud] *adv* (*not quietly*) głośno; (*out loud*) na głos
**alphabet** ['ælfəbɛt] *n* alfabet *m*, abecadło *nt*
**alphabetical** [ælfə'bɛtɪkl] *adj* alfabetyczny; **in ~ order** w kolejności alfabetycznej
**alphanumeric** ['ælfənju:'mɛrɪk] *adj* alfanumeryczny
**alpine** ['ælpaɪn] *adj* alpejski
**Alps** [ælps] *npl*: **the ~** Alpy *pl*
**already** [ɔ:l'rɛdɪ] *adv* już
**alright** ['ɔ:l'raɪt] *adv* = **all right**
**Alsace** ['ælsæs] *n* Alzacja *f*
**Alsatian** [æl'seɪʃən] (*Brit*) *n* owczarek *m* alzacki *or* niemiecki, wilczur *m*
**also** ['ɔ:lsəu] *adv* też, także, również; **and ~** a także, jak również; **A~, ...** Poza tym ...
**altar** ['ɔltə[r]] *n* ołtarz *m*
**alter** ['ɔltə[r]] *vt* zmieniać (zmienić *perf*); (*clothes*) przerabiać (przerobić *perf*) ▷ *vi* zmieniać się (zmienić się *perf*)
**alteration** [ɔltə'reɪʃən] *n* (*to plans*) zmiana *f*; (*to clothes*) przeróbka *f*; (*to building*) przebudowa *f*; **alterations** *npl* przeróbki *pl*
**alternate** [*adj* ɔl'tə:nɪt, *vb* 'ɔltə:neɪt] *adj* (*processes, events*) naprzemienny; (*US*: *alternative*: *plans*) zastępczy, alternatywny ▷ *vi*: **to ~ (with)** występować na przemian (z *+instr*); **on ~ days** co drugi dzień
**alternately** [ɔl'tə:nɪtlɪ] *adv* na przemian, kolejno
**alternating current** ['ɔltə:neɪtɪŋ-] *n* prąd *m* zmienny
**alternative** [ɔl'tə:nətɪv] *adj* alternatywny ▷ *n* alternatywa *f*
**alternative energy** *n* energia *f* ze źródeł niekonwencjonalnych
**alternatively** [ɔl'tə:nətɪvlɪ] *adv*: **~ one could ...** ewentualnie można by...
**alternative medicine** *n* medycyna *f* alternatywna *or* niekonwencjonalna
**alternative society** *n*: **the ~** społeczeństwo *nt* alternatywne
**alternator** ['ɔltə:neɪtə[r]] (*Aut*) *n* alternator *m*
**although** [ɔ:l'ðəu] *conj* chociaż *or* choć, mimo że
**altitude** ['æltɪtju:d] *n* wysokość *f*
**alto** ['æltəu] *n* alt *m*
**altogether** [ɔ:ltə'gɛðə[r]] *adv* (*completely*) całkowicie, zupełnie; (*on the whole*) ogólnie biorąc, generalnie; **how much is that ~?** ile to będzie razem?; **not ~ true** niezupełnie prawdziwy
**altruistic** [æltru'ɪstɪk] *adj* altruistyczny
**aluminium** [ælju'mɪnɪəm], (*US*) **aluminum** [ə'lu:mɪnəm] *n* aluminium *nt*, glin *m*
**always** ['ɔ:lweɪz] *adv* zawsze
**Alzheimer's disease** ['æltshaɪməz-] *n* choroba *f* Alzheimera
**AM** *abbr* (= *amplitude modulation*) AM
**am** [æm] *vb see* **be**
**a.m.** *adv abbr* (= *ante meridiem*) przed południem
**AMA** *n abbr* = **American Medical Association**
**amalgam** [ə'mælgəm] *n* połączenie *nt*, amalgamat *m*
**amalgamate** [ə'mælgəmeɪt] *vi* (*companies etc*) łączyć się (połączyć się *perf*); **to ~ with** łączyć się (połączyć się *perf*) z *+instr*
**amalgamation** [əmælgə'meɪʃən] *n* połączenie *nt*
**amass** [ə'mæs] *vt* gromadzić (zgromadzić *perf*)
**amateur** ['æmətə[r]] *n* amator(ka) *m(f)* ▷ *adj* amatorski; **~ dramatics** teatr amatorski
**amateurish** ['æmətərɪʃ] (*pej*) *adj* amatorski
**amaze** [ə'meɪz] *vt* zdumiewać (zdumieć *perf*); **to be ~d (at)** być zdumionym (*+instr*)
**amazement** [ə'meɪzmənt] *n* zdumienie *nt*
**amazing** [ə'meɪzɪŋ] *adj* zdumiewający, niesamowity; (*bargain, offer*) fantastyczny
**amazingly** [ə'meɪzɪŋlɪ] *adv* niesamowicie
**Amazon** ['æməzən] *n* Amazonka *f*; **the ~ basin** dorzecze Amazonki; **the ~ jungle** dżungla amazońska
**Amazonian** [æmə'zəunɪən] *adj* amazoński
**ambassador** [æm'bæsədə[r]] *n* ambasador *m*
**amber** ['æmbə[r]] *n* (*substance*) bursztyn *m*; (*Brit*: *Aut*) żółte światło *nt*
**ambidextrous** [æmbɪ'dɛkstrəs] *adj* oburęczny
**ambience** ['æmbɪəns] *n* atmosfera *f*
**ambiguity** [æmbɪ'gjuɪtɪ] *n* dwuznaczność *f*, niejasność *f*
**ambiguous** [æm'bɪgjuəs] *adj* dwuznaczny, niejasny
**ambition** [æm'bɪʃən] *n* ambicja *f*; **to achieve one's ~** zrealizować (*perf*) swoje dążenia
**ambitious** [æm'bɪʃəs] *adj* ambitny
**ambivalent** [æm'bɪvələnt] *adj* ambiwalentny
**amble** ['æmbl] *vi* iść powoli
**ambulance** ['æmbjuləns] *n* karetka *f*
**ambulanceman** ['æmbjulənsmən] (*irreg*: *like* **man**) *n* sanitariusz *m*
**ambush** ['æmbuʃ] *n* zasadzka *f*, pułapka *f* ▷ *vt* (*Mil etc*) wciągać (wciągnąć *perf*) w zasadzkę
**ameba** [ə'mi:bə] (*US*) *n* = **amoeba**
**ameliorate** [ə'mi:lɪəreɪt] *vt* poprawiać (poprawić *perf*)
**amen** ['ɑ:'mɛn] *excl* amen
**amenable** [ə'mi:nəbl] *adj* (*person*) otwarty na sugestie; **~ to** (*flattery*) podatny na *+acc*; (*advice*) otwarty na *+acc*
**amend** [ə'mɛnd] *vt* wnosić (wnieść *perf*) poprawki do *+gen* ▷ *n*: **to make ~s for sth** naprawić (*perf*) coś
**amendment** [ə'mɛndmənt] *n* poprawka *f*

**amenities** [ə'mi:nɪtɪz] *npl* wygody *pl*, udogodnienia *pl*
**amenity** [ə'mi:nɪtɪ] *n* udogodnienie *nt*
**America** [ə'mɛrɪkə] *n* Ameryka *f*
**American** [ə'mɛrɪkən] *adj* amerykański ▷ *n* Amerykanin(-anka) *m(f)*
**americanize** [ə'mɛrɪkənaɪz] *vt* amerykanizować (zamerykanizować *perf*)
**amethyst** ['æmɪθɪst] *n* ametyst *m*
**Amex** ['æmɛks] *n abbr* = **American Stock Exchange**
**amiable** ['eɪmɪəbl] *adj* miły, uprzejmy
**amicable** ['æmɪkəbl] *adj* (*relationship*) przyjazny, przyjacielski; (*settlement*) polubowny
**amid(st)** [ə'mɪd(st)] *prep* wśród *+gen*
**amiss** [ə'mɪs] *adj*: **there's something ~** coś jest nie w porządku ▷ *adv*: **to take sth ~** poczuć się *(perf)* czymś urażonym
**ammeter** ['æmɪtə^r] *n* amperomierz *m*
**ammo** ['æməu] (*inf*) *n abbr* = **ammunition**
**ammonia** [ə'məunɪə] *n* amoniak *m*
**ammunition** [æmju'nɪʃən] *n* amunicja *f*; (*fig*) broń *f*
**ammunition dump** *n* (polowy) skład *m* amunicji
**amnesia** [æm'ni:zɪə] *n* amnezja *f*
**amnesty** ['æmnɪstɪ] *n* amnestia *f*; **to grant an ~ to** udzielać (udzielić *perf*) amnestii *+dat*
**amoeba**, (*US*) **ameba** [ə'mi:bə] *n* ameba *f*
**amok** [ə'mɔk] *adv*: **to run ~** dostawać (dostać *perf*) amoku
**among(st)** [ə'mʌŋ(st)] *prep* (po)między *+instr*, wśród *+gen*
**amoral** [æ'mɔrəl] *adj* amoralny
**amorous** ['æmərəs] *adj* (*feelings*) miłosny; (*person*) kochliwy
**amorphous** [ə'mɔ:fəs] *adj* (*cloud*) bezkształtny; (*organization, novel*) pozbawiony wyraźnej struktury
**amortization** [əmɔ:taɪ'zeɪʃən] (*Comm*) *n* amortyzacja *f*
**amount** [ə'maunt] *n* (*of food, work etc*) ilość *f*; (*of money*) suma *f*, kwota *f* ▷ *vi*: **to ~ to** (*total*) wynosić (wynieść *perf*) *+acc*; (*be same as*) sprowadzać się (sprowadzić się *perf*) do *+gen*; **this ~s to a refusal** to jest równoznaczne z odmową; **the total ~** (*of money*) całkowita kwota
**amp(ère)** ['æmp(ɛə^r)] *n* amper *m*; **a 13 amp plug** wtyczka na 13 amperów
**ampersand** ['æmpəsænd] *n* znak *&*
**amphetamine** [æm'fɛtəmi:n] *n* amfetamina *f*
**amphibian** [æm'fɪbɪən] *n* płaz *m*
**amphibious** [æm'fɪbɪəs] *adj* (*animal*) ziemnowodny; (*vehicle*) wodno-lądowy
**amphitheatre**, (*US*) **amphitheater** ['æmfɪθɪətə^r] *n* amfiteatr *m*
**ample** ['æmpl] *adj* (*large*) pokaźny; (*enough*) obfity; **this is ~** jest tego aż nadto; **to have ~ time/room** mieć pod dostatkiem czasu/miejsca
**amplifier** ['æmplɪfaɪə^r] *n* wzmacniacz *m*
**amplify** ['æmplɪfaɪ] *vt* wzmacniać (wzmocnić *perf*)
**amply** ['æmplɪ] *adv* wystarczająco
**ampoule**, (*US*) **ampule** ['æmpu:l] *n* ampułka *f*
**amputate** ['æmpjuteɪt] *vt* amputować (amputować *perf*)
**amputation** [æmpju'teɪʃən] *n* amputacja *f*
**Amsterdam** ['æmstədæm] *n* Amsterdam *m*
**amt** *abbr* = **amount**
**amuck** [ə'mʌk] *adv* = **amok**
**amuse** [ə'mju:z] *vt* (*entertain*) bawić (rozbawić *perf*), śmieszyć (rozśmieszyć *perf*); (*distract*) zabawiać (zabawić *perf*); **to ~ o.s. with sth/by doing sth** bawić się czymś/robieniem czegoś; **to be ~d at** bawić się (ubawić się *perf*) *+instr*; **he was not ~d** nie (roz)bawiło go to
**amusement** [ə'mju:zmənt] *n* (*mirth*) radość *f*; (*pleasure*) zabawa *f*, wesołość *f*; (*pastime*) rozrywka *f*; **much to my ~** ku memu rozbawieniu
**amusement arcade** *n* salon *m* gier automatycznych
**amusing** [ə'mju:zɪŋ] *adj* zabawny
**an** [æn, ən] *indef art see* **a**
**ANA** *n abbr* = **American Newspaper Association**; **American Nurses Association**
**anachronism** [ə'nækrənɪzəm] *n* anachronizm *m*, przeżytek *m*
**anaemia**, (*US*) **anemia** [ə'ni:mɪə] *n* anemia *f*, niedokrwistość *f*
**anaemic**, (*US*) **anemic** [ə'ni:mɪk] *adj* anemiczny
**anaesthetic**, (*US*) **anesthetic** [ænɪs'θɛtɪk] *n* środek *m* znieczulający; **under ~** pod narkozą, w znieczuleniu; **local/general ~** znieczulenie miejscowe/ogólne
**anaesthetist** [æ'ni:sθɪtɪst] *n* anestezjolog *m*
**anagram** ['ænəgræm] *n* anagram *m*
**analgesic** [ænæl'dʒi:sɪk] *adj* przeciwbólowy ▷ *n* środek *m* przeciwbólowy
**analog(ue)** ['ænəlɔg] *adj* analogowy
**analogy** [ə'nælədʒɪ] *n* analogia *f*; **to draw an ~ between** przeprowadzać (przeprowadzić *perf*) analogię pomiędzy *+instr*; **by ~** przez analogię
**analyse**, (*US*) **analyze** ['ænəlaɪz] *vt* (*situation, statistics*) analizować (przeanalizować *perf*); (*Chem, Med*) wykonywać (wykonać *perf*) analizę *+gen*; (*Psych*) poddawać (poddać *perf*) psychoanalizie

**analyses** [ə'næləsi:z] *npl of* **analysis**
**analysis** [ə'næləsɪs] (*pl* **analyses**) *n* analiza *f*; (*Psych*) psychoanaliza *f*; **in the last** *or* **final ~** w ostatecznym rozrachunku
**analyst** ['ænəlɪst] *n* (*political etc*) ekspert *m*, analityk *m*; (*Psych*) psychoanalityk *m*
**analytic(al)** [ænə'lɪtɪk(l)] *adj* analityczny
**analyze** ['ænəlaɪz] (US) *vt* = **analyse**
**anarchist** ['ænəkɪst] *n* anarchista(-tka) *m(f)* ▷ *adj* anarchistyczny
**anarchy** ['ænəkɪ] *n* anarchia *f*
**anathema** [ə'næθɪmə] *n*: **that is ~ to him** on tego nienawidzi
**anatomical** [ænə'tɔmɪkl] *adj* anatomiczny
**anatomy** [ə'nætəmɪ] *n* anatomia *f*
**ANC** *n abbr* (= *African National Congress*) Afrykański Kongres *m* Narodowy
**ancestor** ['ænsɪstə^r] *n* przodek *m*
**ancestral** [æn'sɛstrəl] *adj* rodowy
**ancestry** ['ænsɪstrɪ] *n* pochodzenie *nt*, rodowód *m*
**anchor** ['æŋkə^r] *n* kotwica *f* ▷ *vi* rzucać (rzucić *perf*) kotwicę, kotwiczyć (zakotwiczyć *perf*) ▷ *vt* (*fig*) przywiązywać (przywiązać *perf*); **to ~ sth to** przymocowywać (przymocować *perf*) coś do *+gen*; **to weigh ~** podnosić (podnieść *perf*) kotwicę
**anchorage** ['æŋkərɪdʒ] *n* miejsce *nt* (za) kotwiczenia
**anchovy** ['æntʃəvɪ] *n* anchois *nt inv*
**ancient** ['eɪnʃənt] *adj* (*civilization etc*) starożytny; (*person, car*) wiekowy
**ancient monument** *n* zabytek *m* historyczny
**ancillary** [æn'sɪlərɪ] *adj* pomocniczy
**and** [ænd] *conj* i; **and so on** i tak dalej; **try and come** spróbuj przyjść; **her marks are getting better and better** jej oceny są coraz lepsze
**Andes** ['ændi:z] *npl*: **the ~** Andy *pl*
**Andorra** [æn'dɔ:rə] *n* Andora *f*
**anecdote** ['ænɪkdəut] *n* anegdota *f*
**anemia** *etc* (US) = **anaemia** *etc*
**anemic** [ə'ni:mɪk] *adj* = **anaemic**
**anemone** [ə'nɛmənɪ] *n* anemon *m*, zawilec *m*
**anesthetic** *etc* [ænɪs'θɛtɪk] (*US*) = **anaesthetic** *etc*
**anew** [ə'nju:] *adv* na nowo, od nowa
**angel** ['eɪndʒəl] *n* anioł *m*
**angelic** [æn'dʒɛlɪk] *adj* anielski
**anger** ['æŋgə^r] *n* gniew *m*, złość *f* ▷ *vt* gniewać (rozgniewać *perf*), złościć (rozzłościć *perf*)
**angina** [æn'dʒaɪnə] *n* dusznica *f* bolesna
**angle** ['æŋgl] *n* (*Math*) kąt *m*; (*corner*) róg *m*, narożnik *m*; (*viewpoint*) strona *f* ▷ *vi*: **to ~ for** przymawiać się (przymówić się *perf*) o *+acc* ▷ *vt*: **to ~ sth towards/to** (*aim*) kierować (skierować *perf*) coś do *+gen*
**angler** ['æŋglə^r] *n* wędkarz(-arka) *m(f)*
**Anglican** ['æŋglɪkən] *adj* anglikański ▷ *n* anglikanin(-nka) *m(f)*
**anglicize** ['æŋglɪsaɪz] *vt* anglizować (zanglizować *perf*)
**angling** ['æŋglɪŋ] *n* wędkarstwo *nt*
**Anglo-** ['æŋgləu] *pref* anglo..., angielsko-
**Anglo-French** ['æŋgləu'frɛntʃ] *adj* (*Ling*) anglofrancuski; (*relations*) angielsko-francuski
**Anglo-Saxon** ['æŋgləu'sæksən] *adj* anglosaski ▷ *n* Anglosas(ka) *m(f)*
**Angola** [æŋ'gəulə] *n* Angola *f*
**Angolan** [æŋ'gəulən] *adj* angolski ▷ *n* Angolczyk(-lka) *m(f)*
**angrily** ['æŋgrɪlɪ] *adv* gniewnie, w złości
**angry** ['æŋgrɪ] *adj* (*person*) zły, rozgniewany; (*response, letter*) gniewny; (*fig*: *wound, rash*) zaogniony; **to be ~ with sb/at sth** złościć się na kogoś/o coś; **to get ~** rozgniewać się (*perf*), rozzłościć się (*perf*); **to make sb ~** rozzłościć (*perf*) kogoś, rozgniewać (*perf*) kogoś
**anguish** ['æŋgwɪʃ] *n* cierpienie *nt*
**angular** ['æŋgjulə^r] *adj* kanciasty
**animal** ['ænɪməl] *n* zwierzę *nt*; (*pej*: *person*) bydlę *nt* (*pej*) ▷ *adj* zwierzęcy
**animal rights** [-raɪts] *npl* prawa *pl* zwierząt
**animate** [*adj* 'ænɪmɪt, *vb* 'ænɪmeɪt] *adj* ożywiony ▷ *vt* ożywiać (ożywić *perf*)
**animated** ['ænɪmeɪtɪd] *adj* (*conversation*) ożywiony; (*Film*) animowany
**animosity** [ænɪ'mɔsɪtɪ] *n* animozja *f*, niechęć *f*
**aniseed** ['ænɪsi:d] *n* anyż *m*
**Ankara** ['æŋkərə] *n* Ankara *f*
**ankle** ['æŋkl] (*Anat*) *n* kostka *f*
**ankle sock** *n* skarpetka *f* do kostki
**annex** [*n* 'ænɛks, *vb* ə'nɛks], (*Brit*) **annexe** *n* przybudówka *f*, (nowe) skrzydło *nt* ▷ *vt* anektować (zaanektować *perf*), zajmować (zająć *perf*)
**annexation** [ænɛk'seɪʃən] *n* aneksja *f*, zajęcie *nt*
**annihilate** [ə'naɪəleɪt] *vt* unicestwiać (unicestwić *perf*)
**anniversary** [ænɪ'və:sərɪ] *n* rocznica *f*
**Anno Domini** ['ænəu'dɔmɪnaɪ] *adv* roku Pańskiego, ≈ naszej ery
**annotate** ['ænəuteɪt] *vt* robić (zrobić *perf*) przypisy do *+gen*
**announce** [ə'nauns] *vt* ogłaszać (ogłosić *perf*); **he ~d that he wasn't going** oświadczył, że nie pojedzie
**announcement** [ə'naunsmənt] *n* (*public declaration*) oświadczenie *nt*; (*in newspaper etc*) ogłoszenie *nt*; (*at airport, radio*) komunikat *m*, zapowiedź *f*; **I'd like to make an ~** chciałabym coś ogłosić

**announcer** [ə'naunsə^r] (*Radio, TV*) *n* spiker(ka) *m(f)*
**annoy** [ə'nɔɪ] *vt* irytować (zirytować *perf*), drażnić (rozdrażnić *perf*); **to be ~ed (at sth/ with sb)** być zdenerwowanym (czymś/na kogoś); **don't get ~ed!** nie irytuj się!
**annoyance** [ə'nɔɪəns] *n* irytacja *f*
**annoying** [ə'nɔɪɪŋ] *adj* irytujący
**annual** ['ænjuəl] *adj* (*meeting*) doroczny; (*income, rate*) roczny ▷ *n* (*Bot*) roślina *f* jednoroczna; (*book*) rocznik *m*
**annual general meeting** (*Brit*) *n* doroczne walne zgromadzenie *nt*
**annually** ['ænjuəlɪ] *adv* (*once a year*) co rok(u), corocznie, dorocznie; (*during a year*) rocznie
**annual report** *n* sprawozdanie *nt* roczne
**annuity** [ə'nju:ɪtɪ] *n* opłata *f or* rata *f* roczna; **life ~** renta dożywotnia
**annul** [ə'nʌl] *vt* (*contract*) unieważniać (unieważnić *perf*), anulować; (*law*) znosić (znieść *perf*)
**annulment** [ə'nʌlmənt] *n* (*of contract*) unieważnienie *nt*; (*of law*) zniesienie *nt*
**annum** ['ænəm] *n see* **per**
**Annunciation** [ənʌnsɪ'eɪʃən] *n* Zwiastowanie *nt*
**anode** ['ænəud] *n* anoda *f*
**anoint** [ə'nɔɪnt] *vt* namaszczać (namaścić *perf*)
**anomalous** [ə'nɔmələs] *adj* nieprawidłowy, nieregularny
**anomaly** [ə'nɔməlɪ] *n* anomalia *f*, nieprawidłowość *f*
**anon.** [ə'nɔn] *abbr* (= *anonymous*) anonim., anon.
**anonymity** [ænə'nɪmɪtɪ] *n* anonimowość *f*
**anonymous** [ə'nɔnɪməs] *adj* (*letter, gift*) anonimowy; (*place*) bezimienny; **to remain ~** zachowywać (zachować *perf*) anonimowość
**anorak** ['ænəræk] *n* skafander *m*
**anorexia** [ænə'rɛksɪə] *n* anoreksja *f*, jadłowstręt *m* psychiczny
**anorexic** [ænə'rɛksɪk] *adj* anorektyczny
**another** [ə'nʌðə^r] *adj* inny ▷ *pron* (*one more*) następny, drugi; (*a different one*) inny, drugi; **~ drink?** (czy) wypijesz jeszcze jednego?; **in ~ 5 years** za następne pięć lat; *see also* **one**
**ANSI** [eɪɛnɛs'aɪ] *n abbr* (= *American National Standards Institute*) *urząd normalizacyjny*
**answer** ['ɑ:nsə^r] *n* (*to question, letter*) odpowiedź *f*; (*to problem*) rozwiązanie *nt* ▷ *vi* odpowiadać (odpowiedzieć *perf*); (*Tel*) podnosić (podnieść *perf*) słuchawkę, odbierać (odebrać *perf*) (telefon) ▷ *vt* (*letter, question*) odpowiadać (odpowiedzieć *perf*) na *+acc*; (*problem*) rozwiązywać (rozwiązać *perf*); (*prayer*) wysłuchiwać (wysłuchać *perf*) *+gen*; **in ~ to your letter** w odpowiedzi na Pana/ Pani list; **to ~ the phone** odbierać (odebrać *perf*) telefon; **to ~ the bell** *or* **the door** otworzyć (*perf*) drzwi
▸ **answer back** *vi* odpyskowywać (odpyskować *perf*) (*inf*)
▸ **answer for** *vt fus* (*person etc*) ręczyć (poręczyć *perf*) za *+acc*; (*one's actions*) odpowiadać (odpowiedzieć *perf*) za *+acc*
▸ **answer to** *vt fus* (*description*) odpowiadać *+dat*
**answerable** ['ɑ:nsərəbl] *adj*: **~ to sb for sth** odpowiedzialny przed kimś za coś; **I am ~ to no-one** nie odpowiadam przed nikim
**answering machine** ['ɑ:nsərɪŋ-] *n* automatyczna sekretarka *f*
**ant** [ænt] *n* mrówka *f*
**ANTA** *n abbr* = **American National Theater and Academy**
**antagonism** [æn'tægənɪzəm] *n* wrogość *f*, antagonizm *m*
**antagonist** [æn'tægənɪst] *n* przeciwnik(-iczka) *m(f)*, antagonista(-tka) *m(f)*
**antagonistic** [æntægə'nɪstɪk] *adj* wrogi, antagonistyczny
**antagonize** [æn'tægənaɪz] *vt* zrażać (zrazić *perf*) sobie
**Antarctic** [ænt'ɑ:ktɪk] *n*: **the ~** Antarktyka *f*
**Antarctica** [ænt'ɑ:ktɪkə] *n* Antarktyda *f*
**Antarctic Circle** *n*: **the ~** koło *nt* podbiegunowe południowe
**Antarctic Ocean** *n*: **the ~** *wody antarktyczne*
**ante** ['æntɪ] *n*: **to up the ~** (*fig*) podnosić (podnieść *perf*) stawkę
**ante...** ['æntɪ] *pref* przed...
**anteater** ['ænti:tə^r] *n* mrówkojad *m*
**antecedent** [æntɪ'si:dənt] *n* poprzednik(-iczka) *m(f)*
**antechamber** ['æntɪtʃeɪmbə^r] *n* przedsionek *m*
**antelope** ['æntɪləup] *n* antylopa *f*
**antenatal** ['æntɪ'neɪtl] *adj* przedporodowy
**antenatal clinic** *n* klinika *f* przedporodowa
**antenna** [æn'tɛnə] (*pl* **~e**) *n* (*of insect*) czułek *m*; (*Radio, TV*) antena *f*
**anteroom** ['æntɪrum] *n* przedpokój *m*, poczekalnia *f*
**anthem** ['ænθəm] *n*: **national ~** hymn *m* państwowy
**ant-hill** ['ænthɪl] *n* mrowisko *nt*
**anthology** [æn'θɔlədʒɪ] *n* antologia *f*
**anthropologist** [ænθrə'pɔlədʒɪst] *n* antropolog *m*
**anthropology** [ænθrə'pɔlədʒɪ] *n* antropologia *f*
**anti...** ['æntɪ] *pref* przeciw..., anty...
**anti-aircraft** ['æntɪ'ɛəkrɑ:ft] *adj* przeciwlotniczy

**anti-aircraft defence** *n* obrona *f* przeciwlotnicza
**antiballistic** ['æntɪbə'lɪstɪk] *adj* przeciwbalistyczny
**antibiotic** ['æntɪbaɪ'ɔtɪk] *n* antybiotyk *m*
**antibody** ['æntɪbɔdɪ] *n* przeciwciało *nt*
**anticipate** [æn'tɪsɪpeɪt] *vt* (*foresee*) przewidywać (przewidzieć *perf*); (*look forward to*) czekać na *+acc*; (*do first*) antycypować; **this is worse than I ~d** jest gorzej, niż przewidywałem; **as ~d** zgodnie z przewidywaniami
**anticipation** [æntɪsɪ'peɪʃən] *n* (*expectation*) przewidywanie *nt*; (*eagerness*) niecierpliwość *f*; **thanking you in ~** z góry dziękuję
**anticlimax** ['æntɪ'klaɪmæks] *n* zawód *m*, rozczarowanie *nt*
**anticlockwise** ['æntɪ'klɔkwaɪz] (*Brit*) *adv* odwrotnie do ruchu wskazówek zegara
**antics** ['æntɪks] *npl* (*of animal, child*) błazeństwa *pl*, figle *pl*; (*of politicians etc*) wyskoki *pl*
**anticyclone** ['æntɪ'saɪkləun] *n* wyż *m*, układ *m* wysokiego ciśnienia
**antidote** ['æntɪdəut] *n* (*Med*) antidotum *nt*, odtrutka *f*; (*fig*) antidotum *nt*
**antifreeze** ['æntɪfri:z] (*Aut*) *n* płyn *m* nie zamarzający
**antihistamine** ['æntɪ'hɪstəmɪn] *n* środek *m* antyhistaminowy
**Antilles** [æn'tɪli:z] *npl*: **the ~** Antyle *pl*
**antipathy** [æn'tɪpəθɪ] *n* antypatia *f*
**Antipodean** [æntɪpə'di:ən] *adj dotyczący Australii i Nowej Zelandii*
**Antipodes** [æn'tɪpədi:z] *npl*: **the ~** antypody *pl*
**antiquarian** [æntɪ'kwɛərɪən] *adj*: **~ bookshop** antykwariat *m* ▷ *n* antykwariusz *m*
**antiquated** ['æntɪkweɪtɪd] *adj* przestarzały, staroświecki
**antique** [æn'ti:k] *n* antyk *m* ▷ *adj* zabytkowy
**antique dealer** *n* antykwariusz *m*
**antique shop** *n* sklep *m* z antykami, antykwariat *m*
**antiquity** [æn'tɪkwɪtɪ] *n* starożytność *f*
**anti-Semitic** ['æntɪsɪ'mɪtɪk] *adj* antysemicki
**anti-Semitism** ['æntɪ'sɛmɪtɪzəm] *n* antysemityzm *m*
**antiseptic** [æntɪ'sɛptɪk] *n* środek *m* odkażający *or* bakteriobójczy ▷ *adj* bakteriobójczy, antyseptyczny
**antisocial** ['æntɪ'səuʃəl] *adj* aspołeczny
**antitank** ['æntɪ'tæŋk] *adj* (*ditch*) przeciwczołgowy; (*rocket*) przeciwpancerny
**antitheses** [æn'tɪθɪsi:z] *npl of* **antithesis**
**antithesis** [æn'tɪθɪsɪs] (*pl* **antitheses**) *n* przeciwieństwo *nt*, antyteza *f*
**antitrust** ['æntɪ'trʌst] (*US*) *adj*: **~ legislation** ustawodawstwo *nt* przeciwtrustowe
**antlers** ['æntləz] *npl* rogi *pl* (*zwierzyny płowej*)
**Antwerp** ['æntwə:p] *n* Antwerpia *f*
**anus** ['eɪnəs] *n* odbyt *m*
**anvil** ['ænvɪl] *n* kowadło *nt*
**anxiety** [æŋ'zaɪətɪ] *n* (*concern*) niepokój *m*, obawa *f*; (*Med*) lęk *m*; **~ to do sth** pragnienie uczynienia czegoś; **the ~ not to offend** obawa, żeby nikogo nie urazić
**anxious** ['æŋkʃəs] *adj* (*worried*) zaniepokojony; (*worrying*) niepokojący; **she is ~ to go abroad** zależy jej na wyjeździe za granicę; **he is ~ that we should meet** zależy mu na tym, żebyśmy się spotkali; **I'm very ~ about you** bardzo się o ciebie martwię
**anxiously** ['æŋkʃəslɪ] *adv* z troską, z obawą

 KEYWORD

**any** ['ɛnɪ] *adj* **1** (*in questions etc*): **are there any tickets left?** czy zostały jakieś bilety?; **have you any sugar?** masz trochę cukru?
**2** (*with negative*): **I haven't any money/books** nie mam (żadnych) pieniędzy/książek; **they haven't any free time** nie mają (ani trochę) wolnego czasu
**3** (*no matter which*): **any excuse will do** każda wymówka będzie dobra; **ask any teacher** zapytaj jakiegokolwiek *or* któregokolwiek nauczyciela
**4**: **in any case** (*at any rate*) w każdym razie; (*besides*) zresztą, poza tym; (*no matter what*) tak czy owak; **any day now** lada dzień; **at any moment** lada chwila *or* moment, w każdej chwili; **at any rate** w każdym razie; **any time** (*at any moment*) lada chwila *or* moment; (*whenever*) zawsze gdy
▷ *pron* **1** (*in questions etc*): **I collect stamps, have you got any?** zbieram znaczki — masz jakieś?; **can any of you sing?** czy któreś z was umie śpiewać?; **there's some cake left, do you want any?** zostało trochę ciasta — chcesz trochę?
**2** (*with negative*): **I haven't any (of them)** nie mam ani jednego (z nich); **he's trying to lose weight, but so far hasn't lost any** stara się schudnąć, ale jak dotąd nie schudł ani trochę
**3** (*no matter which one(s)*) jakikolwiek, którykolwiek; **take any of them** weź którykolwiek z nich
▷ *adv* **1** (*in questions etc*) trochę; **are you feeling any better?** czy czujesz się (choć) trochę lepiej?
**2** (*with negative*) już; **I can't hear him any more** nie słyszę go już; **don't wait any longer** nie czekaj (już) dłużej

**anybody** ['ɛnɪbɔdɪ] *pron* = **anyone**

KEYWORD

**anyhow** ['ɛnɪhau] *adv* **1** (*at any rate*) i tak, tak czy owak; **I shall go anyhow** i tak pójdę
**2** (*haphazard*) byle jak, jak(kolwiek); **do it anyhow you like** zrób to, jak(kolwiek) chcesz; **she leaves things just anyhow** zostawia wszystko byle jak

KEYWORD

**anyone** ['ɛnɪwʌn] *pron* **1** (*in questions etc*) ktoś *m*, ktokolwiek *m*; **can you see anyone?** widzisz kogoś?; **if anyone should ask ...** gdyby ktoś *or* ktokolwiek pytał, ...
**2** (*with negative*) nikt *m*; **I can't see anyone** nikogo nie widzę
**3** (*no matter who*) każdy *m*, ktokolwiek *m*; **I could teach anyone to do it** każdego umiałabym tego nauczyć; **anyone could have done it** mógł to zrobić każdy *or* ktokolwiek

**anyplace** ['ɛnɪpleɪs] (US) *adv* = **anywhere**

KEYWORD

**anything** ['ɛnɪθɪŋ] *pron* **1** (*in questions etc*) coś *nt*, cokolwiek *nt*; **can you see anything?** widzisz coś?; **if anything happens to me ...** jeśli coś *or* cokolwiek mi się stanie, ...
**2** (*with negative*) nic *nt*; **I can't see anything** nic nie widzę
**3** (*no matter what*) co(kolwiek) *nt*, wszystko *nt*; **you can say anything you like** możesz mówić co(kolwiek) chcesz; **he'll eat anything** on wszystko zje

KEYWORD

**anyway** ['ɛnɪweɪ] *adv* **1** (*at any rate*) i tak, tak czy owak; **I shall go anyway** i tak pójdę
**2** (*besides*) w każdym razie, (a) poza tym, (a) tak w ogóle; **anyway, I'll let you know** w każdym razie dam ci znać; **anyway, I couldn't come even if I wanted to** (a) poza tym, nie mógłbym przyjść, nawet gdybym chciał; **why are you phoning, anyway?** a tak w ogóle, dlaczego dzwonisz?

KEYWORD

**anywhere** ['ɛnɪwɛəʳ] *adv* **1** (*in questions*) gdzieś; **can you see him anywhere?** widzisz go gdzieś?; **are you going anywhere?** wychodzisz gdzieś?
**2** (*with negative*) nigdzie; **I can't see him anywhere** nigdzie go nie widzę
**3** (*no matter where*) gdziekolwiek; **anywhere in the world** gdziekolwiek na świecie

**Anzac** ['ænzæk] *n abbr* = **Australia-New Zealand Army Corps**
**apace** [ə'peɪs] *adv*: **negotiations were continuing** ~ negocjacje toczyły się w szybkim tempie
**apart** [ə'pɑ:t] *adv* (*situate*) z dala, oddzielnie; (*move*) od siebie; (*aside*) osobno, na uboczu, z dala; **10 miles** ~ w odległości 10 mil od siebie; **a long way** ~ daleko od siebie; **they are living** ~ mieszkają oddzielnie; **with one's legs** ~ w rozkroku; **to take sth** ~ rozbierać (rozebrać *perf*) coś na części; ~ **from** (*excepting*) z wyjątkiem *or* oprócz *+gen*; (*in addition to*) oprócz *+gen*, poza *+instr*
**apartheid** [ə'pɑ:teɪt] *n* apartheid *m*
**apartment** [ə'pɑ:tmənt] *n* (US) mieszkanie *nt*; (*in palace etc*) apartament *m*
**apartment building** (US) *n* blok *m* mieszkalny
**apathetic** [æpə'θɛtɪk] *adj* apatyczny
**apathy** ['æpəθɪ] *n* apatia *f*
**APB** (US) *n abbr* (= *all points bulletin*) *rysopis przestępcy rozsyłany do wszystkich posterunków policji*
**ape** [eɪp] *n* małpa *f* człekokształtna ▷ *vt* małpować (zmałpować *perf*)
**Apennines** ['æpənaɪnz] *npl*: **the** ~ Apeniny *pl*
**aperitif** [ə'pɛrɪti:f] *n* aperitif *m*
**aperture** ['æpətʃjuəʳ] *n* otwór *m*, szczelina *f*; (*Phot*) przysłona *f*
**APEX** ['eɪpɛks] (*Aviat, Rail*) *n abbr* (= *advance passenger excursion*) APEX *m inv*
**apex** ['eɪpɛks] *n* (*of triangle etc*) wierzchołek *m*; (*fig*) szczyt *m*
**aphid** ['æfɪd] *n* mszyca *f*
**aphorism** ['æfərɪzəm] *n* aforyzm *m*
**aphrodisiac** [æfrəu'dɪzɪæk] *adj* pobudzający seksualnie ▷ *n* afrodyzjak *m*
**API** *n abbr* = **American Press Institute**
**apiece** [ə'pi:s] *adv* (*per thing*) za sztukę, sztuka; (*per person*) na osobę, na głowę
**aplomb** [ə'plɔm] *n* opanowanie *nt*
**APO** (US) *n abbr* = **Army Post Office**
**apocalypse** [ə'pɔkəlɪps] *n* apokalipsa *f*
**apolitical** [eɪpə'lɪtɪkl] *adj* apolityczny
**apologetic** [əpɔlə'dʒɛtɪk] *adj* (*person*) skruszony; (*tone, letter*) przepraszający; **to be** ~ **about ...** przepraszać za *+acc*
**apologize** [ə'pɔlədʒaɪz] *vi*: **to ~ (for sth to sb)** przepraszać (przeprosić *perf*) (kogoś za coś)

**apology** [ə'pɔlədʒɪ] *n* przeprosiny *pl*; **to send one's apologies** przepraszać (przeprosić *perf*) (*za niemożność przybycia*); **please accept my apologies** proszę o wybaczenie
**apoplectic** [æpə'plɛktɪk] *adj* (*Med*) apoplektyczny; (*fig*): **~ with rage** wściekły do granic wytrzymałości
**apoplexy** ['æpəplɛksɪ] *n* udar *m* mózgowy, apopleksja *f*
**apostle** [ə'pɔsl] *n* apostoł *m*
**apostrophe** [ə'pɔstrəfɪ] *n* apostrof *m*
**appal** [ə'pɔ:l] *vt* bulwersować (zbulwersować *perf*)
**Appalachian Mountains** [æpə'leɪʃən-] *npl*: **the ~** Appalachy *pl*
**appalling** [ə'pɔ:lɪŋ] *adj* przerażający; **she's an ~ cook** ona fatalnie gotuje
**apparatus** [æpə'reɪtəs] *n* (*equipment*) aparatura *f*, przyrządy *pl*; (*: in gymnasium*) przyrządy *pl*; (*of organization*) aparat *m*
**apparel** [ə'pærl] *n* strój *m*, szata *f* (*fml*)
**apparent** [ə'pærənt] *adj* (*seeming*) pozorny; (*obvious*) widoczny, oczywisty; **it is ~ that ...** jest oczywiste, że ...
**apparently** [ə'pærəntlɪ] *adv* najwidoczniej, najwyraźniej
**apparition** [æpə'rɪʃən] *n* zjawa *f*
**appeal** [ə'pi:l] *vi* (*Jur*) wnosić (wnieść *perf*) apelację, odwoływać się (odwołać się *perf*) ▷ *n* (*Jur*) apelacja *f*, odwołanie *nt*; (*request*) apel *m*; (*charm*) urok *m*, powab *m*; **to ~ (to sb) for** apelować (zaapelować *perf*) (do kogoś) o *+acc*; **to ~ to** podobać się (spodobać się *perf*) *+dat*; **to ~ to sb for mercy** prosić (poprosić *perf*) kogoś o łaskę; **it doesn't ~ to me** to do mnie nie przemawia; **right of ~** (*Jur*) prawo do odwołania; **on ~** (*Jur*) przy apelacji w sądzie wyższej instancji
**appealing** [ə'pi:lɪŋ] *adj* (*attractive*) pociągający; (*pleading*) błagalny
**appear** [ə'pɪəʳ] *vi* (*come into view*) pojawiać się (pojawić się *perf*), zjawiać się (zjawić się *perf*); (*Jur*) stawiać się (stawić się *perf*); (*be published*) ukazywać się (ukazać się *perf*) (*drukiem*); (*seem*) wydawać się (wydać się *perf*); **to ~ on TV/in "Hamlet"** występować (wystąpić *perf*) w telewizji/w „Hamlecie"; **it would ~ that ...** wydawałoby się, że ...
**appearance** [ə'pɪərəns] *n* (*arrival*) pojawienie się *nt*; (*look*) wygląd *m*; (*in public*) wystąpienie *nt*; **to put in** *or* **make an ~** pokazywać się (pokazać się *perf*); **in order of ~** (*Theat*) w kolejności pojawiania się na scenie; **to keep up ~s** zachowywać (zachować *perf*) pozory; **to all ~s** na pozór
**appease** [ə'pi:z] *vt* (*pacify*) uspokajać (uspokoić *perf*); (*satisfy*) zaspokajać (zaspokoić *perf*)
**appeasement** [ə'pi:zmənt] (*Pol*) *n* polityka *f* ustępstw
**append** [ə'pɛnd] (*Comput*) *vt* dołączać (dołączyć *perf*)
**appendage** [ə'pɛndɪdʒ] *n* dodatek *m*
**appendices** [ə'pɛndɪsi:z] *npl of* **appendix**
**appendicitis** [əpɛndɪ'saɪtɪs] *n* zapalenie *nt* wyrostka robaczkowego
**appendix** [ə'pɛndɪks] (*pl* **appendices**) *n* (*Anat*) wyrostek *m* robaczkowy; (*to publication*) dodatek *m*; **to have one's ~ out** mieć wycięty wyrostek
**appetite** ['æpɪtaɪt] *n* apetyt *m*; (*fig*) chętka *f*; **that walk has given me an ~** od tego spaceru nabrałem apetytu
**appetizer** ['æpɪtaɪzəʳ] *n* (*food*) przystawka *f*, zakąska *f*; (*drink*) aperitif *m*
**appetizing** ['æpɪtaɪzɪŋ] *adj* smakowity, apetyczny
**applaud** [ə'plɔ:d] *vi* bić brawo, klaskać ▷ *vt* (*actor etc*) oklaskiwać; (*action, attitude*) pochwalać (pochwalić *perf*); (*decision, initiative*) przyklaskiwać (przyklasnąć *perf*) *+dat*
**applause** [ə'plɔ:z] *n* (*clapping*) oklaski *pl*; (*praise*) aplauz *m*
**apple** ['æpl] *n* jabłko *nt*; **she is the ~ of his eye** ona jest jego oczkiem w głowie
**applet** ['æplɪt] (*Comput*) *n* aplet *m*
**apple tree** *n* jabłoń *f*
**apple turnover** *n* ciastko *nt* z jabłkami
**appliance** [ə'plaɪəns] *n* (*electrical, gas etc*) urządzenie *nt*
**applicable** [ə'plɪkəbl] *adj*: **~ (to)** odpowiedni (do *+gen*), mający zastosowanie (w *+loc*); **if ~** w stosownych przypadkach
**applicant** ['æplɪkənt] *n* kandydat(ka) *m(f)*
**application** [æplɪ'keɪʃən] *n* (*for job*) podanie *nt*; (*for grant*) podanie *nt*, wniosek *m*; (*of rules, theory*) zastosowanie *nt*; (*of cream*) nałożenie *nt*; (*of compress*) przyłożenie *nt*; (*of paint*) położenie *nt*; (*hard work*) pilność *f*; **on ~** na życzenie
**application form** *n* formularz *m* podania *or* wniosku
**application program** (*Comput*) *n* program *m* użytkowy
**applications package** (*Comput*) *n* pakiet *m* programów użytkowych
**applied** [ə'plaɪd] *adj* (*science, art*) stosowany
**apply** [ə'plaɪ] *vt* (*put on*) nakładać (nałożyć *perf*); (*put into practice*) stosować (zastosować *perf*) ▷ *vi* (*be applicable*) stosować się, mieć zastosowanie; (*ask*) składać (złożyć *perf*) podanie *or* wniosek, zgłaszać się (zgłosić się *perf*); **to ~ to** mieć zastosowanie do *+gen*; **to ~ for** ubiegać się o *+acc*; **to ~ the brakes** użyć hamulca; **to ~ o.s. to** przykładać się (przyłożyć się *perf*) do *+gen*

**appoint** [ə'pɔɪnt] *vt* (*to post*) mianować; (*date, place*) wyznaczać (wyznaczyć *perf*)
**appointed** [ə'pɔɪntɪd] *adj*: **at the ~ time** o wyznaczonym czasie
**appointee** [əpɔɪn'tiː] *n* osoba *f* wyznaczona *or* mianowana
**appointment** [ə'pɔɪntmənt] *n* (*of person*) mianowanie *nt*; (*post*) stanowisko *nt*; (*arranged meeting*: *with client*) spotkanie *nt*; (: *with doctor, hairdresser*) wizyta *f*; **to make an ~ (with sb)** ustalać (ustalić *perf*) termin spotkania (z kimś), umawiać się (umówić się *perf*) (z kimś); **by ~** po wcześniejszym uzgodnieniu terminu
**apportion** [ə'pɔːʃən] *vt* (*blame*) rozkładać (rozłożyć *perf*); (*praise*) rozdzielać (rozdzielić *perf*); **to ~ sth to sb** przydzielać (przydzielić *perf*) coś komuś
**appraisal** [ə'preɪzl] *n* (*of situation, market*) ocena *f*; (*of damage*) oszacowanie *nt*, wycena *f*
**appraise** [ə'preɪz] *vt* (*situation etc*) oceniać (ocenić *perf*); (*value*) szacować (oszacować *perf*), wyceniać (wycenić *perf*)
**appreciable** [ə'priːʃəbl] *adj* znaczny, znaczący
**appreciate** [ə'priːʃɪeɪt] *vt* (*like*) doceniać, cenić sobie; (*be grateful for*) być wdzięcznym za *+acc*, doceniać (docenić *perf*); (*be aware of*) rozumieć ▷ *vi* (*Comm*) zyskiwać (zyskać *perf*) na wartości; **I ~ your help** jestem ci wdzięczny za pomoc
**appreciation** [əpriːʃɪ'eɪʃən] *n* (*enjoyment*) uznanie *nt*; (*Comm*) wzrost *m* wartości; (*understanding*) zrozumienie *nt*, świadomość *f*; (*gratitude*) wdzięczność *f*
**appreciative** [ə'priːʃɪətɪv] *adj* (*person*) wdzięczny; (*audience, comment*) pełen uznania; **to be ~ of sth** doceniać coś
**apprehend** [æprɪ'hɛnd] *vt* (*arrest*) zatrzymywać (zatrzymać *perf*), ująć (*perf*); (*understand*) pojmować (pojąć *perf*)
**apprehension** [æprɪ'hɛnʃən] *n* (*fear*) obawa *f*; (*of criminal*) ujęcie *nt*, zatrzymanie *nt*
**apprehensive** [æprɪ'hɛnsɪv] *adj* pełen obawy; **to be ~ about sth** obawiać się czegoś
**apprentice** [ə'prɛntɪs] *n* (*carpenter etc*) uczeń/uczennica *m/f*, terminator *m* ▷ *vt*: **to be ~d to sb** terminować u kogoś
**apprenticeship** [ə'prɛntɪsʃɪp] *n* (*for trade*) nauka *f* rzemiosła, praktyka *f* (zawodowa); (*fig*) praktyka *f*; **to serve one's ~** odbywać (odbyć *perf*) praktykę, terminować
**appro.** ['æprəu] (*Brit*: *inf*: *Comm*) *abbr* (= *approval*): **on ~** na próbę
**approach** [ə'prəutʃ] *vi* nadchodzić (nadejść *perf*) ▷ *vt* (*place*) zbliżać się (zbliżyć się *perf*) do *+gen*; (*person, problem*) podchodzić (podejść *perf*) do *+gen*; (*ask, apply to*) zwracać się (zwrócić się *perf*) do *+gen* ▷ *n* (*of person*) nadejście *nt*; (*proposal*) propozycja *f*, oferta *f*; (*access, path*) droga *f*, dojście *nt*; (*to problem*) podejście *nt*; **to ~ sb about sth** zwracać się (zwrócić się *perf*) do kogoś o coś
**approachable** [ə'prəutʃəbl] *adj* (*person*) przystępny; (*place*) dostępny
**approach road** *n* droga *f* dojazdowa, podjazd *m*
**approbation** [æprə'beɪʃən] *n* aprobata *f*
**appropriate** [*adj* ə'prəuprɪɪt, *vb* ə'prəuprɪeɪt] *adj* (*remark etc*) stosowny, właściwy; (*tool*) odpowiedni ▷ *vt* przywłaszczać (przywłaszczyć *perf*) sobie; **it would not be ~ for me to comment** nie chciałbym się wypowiadać
**appropriately** [ə'prəuprɪɪtlɪ] *adv* odpowiednio, właściwie
**appropriation** [əprəuprɪ'eɪʃən] (*Comm*) *n* asygnowanie *nt*
**approval** [ə'pruːvəl] *n* (*approbation*) aprobata *f*; (*permission*) zgoda *f*; **to meet with sb's ~** spotykać się (spotkać się *perf*) z czyjąś aprobatą; **on ten days ~** (*Comm*) z możliwością zwrotu w ciągu dziesięciu dni
**approve** [ə'pruːv] *vt* zatwierdzać (zatwierdzić *perf*)
▸ **approve of** *vt fus* (*person, thing*) akceptować; (*behaviour*) pochwalać
**approved school** [ə'pruːvd-] (*Brit*) *n* ≈ zakład *m* poprawczy
**approvingly** [ə'pruːvɪŋlɪ] *adv* z aprobatą
**approx.** *abbr* (= *approximately*) ok.
**approximate** [*adj* ə'prɔksɪmɪt, *vb* ə'prɔksɪmeɪt] *adj* przybliżony ▷ *vi*: **to ~ to** (*in quality, nature*) być zbliżonym do *+gen*; (*in cost*) wynosić (wynieść *perf*) blisko *+acc*
**approximately** [ə'prɔksɪmɪtlɪ] *adv* około, w przybliżeniu
**approximation** [ə'prɔksɪ'meɪʃən] *n* przybliżenie *nt*
**APR** *n abbr* (= *annual percentage rate*) oprocentowanie *nt* w skali roku
**Apr.** *abbr* (= *April*) kwiec.
**apricot** ['eɪprɪkɔt] *n* morela *f*
**April** ['eɪprəl] *n* kwiecień *m*; **~ fool!** prima aprilis!; *see also* **July**
**April Fool's Day** *n* prima aprilis *m*
**apron** ['eɪprən] *n* (*clothing*) fartuch *m*, fartuszek *m*; (*Aviat*) płyta *f* lotniska
**apse** [æps] (*Archit*) *n* apsyda *f*
**APT** (*Brit*) *n abbr* (= *advanced passenger train*) *szybki pociąg pasażerski*
**apt** [æpt] *adj* (*comment etc*) trafny; (*person*) uzdolniony; **to be apt to do sth** mieć tendencję do robienia czegoś
**Apt.** *abbr* (= *apartment*) m.

**aptitude** ['æptɪtjuːd] *n* uzdolnienie *nt*
**aptitude test** *n* test *m* zdolności
**aptly** ['æptlɪ] *adv* trafnie
**aqualung** ['ækwəlʌŋ] *n* akwalung *m*
**aquarium** [ə'kwɛərɪəm] *n* (*fish tank*) akwarium *nt*; (*building*) oceanarium *nt*
**Aquarius** [ə'kwɛərɪəs] *n* Wodnik *m*; **to be ~** być spod znaku Wodnika
**aquatic** [ə'kwætɪk] *adj* wodny
**aqueduct** ['ækwɪdʌkt] *n* akwedukt *m*
**AR** (*US: Post*) *abbr* = **Arkansas**
**ARA** (*Brit*) *n abbr* = **Associate of the Royal Academy**
**Arab** ['ærəb] *adj* arabski ▷ *n* Arab(ka) *m(f)*
**Arabia** [ə'reɪbɪə] *n* Arabia *f*
**Arabian** [ə'reɪbɪən] *adj* (*Geog*) arabski
**Arabian Desert** *n*: **the ~** Pustynia *f* Arabska
**Arabian Sea** *n*: **the ~** Morze *nt* Arabskie
**Arabic** ['ærəbɪk] *adj* (*language, numerals*) arabski ▷ *n* (język *m*) arabski
**arable** ['ærəbl] *adj* uprawny, orny
**ARAM** (*Brit*) *n abbr* = **Associate of the Royal Academy of Music**
**arbiter** ['ɑːbɪtə^r] *n* arbiter *m*, rozjemca *m*
**arbitrary** ['ɑːbɪtrərɪ] *adj* (*attack*) przypadkowy; (*decision*) arbitralny
**arbitrate** ['ɑːbɪtreɪt] *vi* pełnić rolę arbitra *or* rozjemcy, rozstrzygać spory
**arbitration** [ɑːbɪ'treɪʃən] *n* arbitraż *m*; **the dispute went to ~** spór skierowano do arbitrażu
**arbitrator** ['ɑːbɪtreɪtə^r] *n* rozjemca(-mczyni) *m(f)*
**ARC** *n abbr* (= *American Red Cross*) ≈ PCK *nt inv*
**arc** [ɑːk] *n* łuk *m*
**arcade** [ɑː'keɪd] *n* (*covered passageway*) arkada *f*; (*shopping mall*) pasaż *m* handlowy
**arch** [ɑːtʃ] *n* (*Archit*) łuk *m*, sklepienie *nt* łukowe; (*: of bridge*) przęsło *nt*; (*of foot*) podbicie *nt* ▷ *vt* wyginać (wygiąć *perf*) w łuk ▷ *adj* figlarny, łobuzerski ▷ *pref* arcy...
**archaeological** [ɑːkɪə'lɔdʒɪkl] *adj* archeologiczny
**archaeologist** [ɑːkɪ'ɔlədʒɪst] *n* archeolog *m*
**archaeology** [ɑːkɪ'ɔlədʒɪ] *n* archeologia *f*
**archaic** [ɑː'keɪɪk] *adj* archaiczny
**archangel** ['ɑːkeɪndʒəl] *n* archanioł *m*
**archbishop** [ɑːtʃ'bɪʃəp] *n* arcybiskup *m*
**arch-enemy** ['ɑːtʃ'ɛnəmɪ] *n* zaciekły wróg *m*
**archeology** *etc* (*US*) = **archaeology** *etc*
**archery** ['ɑːtʃərɪ] *n* łucznictwo *nt*
**archetypal** ['ɑːkɪtaɪpəl] *adj* archetypowy
**archetype** ['ɑːkɪtaɪp] *n* archetyp *m*
**archipelago** [ɑːkɪ'pɛlɪgəu] *n* archipelag *m*
**architect** ['ɑːkɪtɛkt] *n* architekt *m*
**architectural** [ɑːkɪ'tɛktʃərəl] *adj* architektoniczny
**architecture** ['ɑːkɪtɛktʃə^r] *n* architektura *f*
**archive file** (*Comput*) *n* plik *m* zarchiwizowany
**archives** ['ɑːkaɪvz] *npl* archiwa *pl*, archiwum *nt*
**archivist** ['ɑːkɪvɪst] *n* archiwista(-tka) *m(f)*
**archway** ['ɑːtʃweɪ] (*Archit*) *n* sklepione przejście *nt*
**ARCM** (*Brit*) *n abbr* = **Associate of the Royal College of Music**
**Arctic** ['ɑːktɪk] *adj* arktyczny ▷ *n*: **the ~** Arktyka *f*
**Arctic Circle** *n*: **the ~** koło *nt* podbiegunowe północne
**Arctic Ocean** *n*: **the ~** Morze *nt* Arktyczne
**ARD** (*US: Med*) *n abbr* = **acute respiratory disease**
**ardent** ['ɑːdənt] *adj* (*admirer*) gorliwy, żarliwy; (*discussion*) ożywiony
**ardour**, (*US*) **ardor** ['ɑːdə^r] *n* zapał *m*
**arduous** ['ɑːdjuəs] *adj* żmudny
**are** [ɑː^r] *vb see* **be**
**area** ['ɛərɪə] *n* (*region, zone*) obszar *m*, rejon *m*; (*Math*) pole *nt* (powierzchni), powierzchnia *f*; (*part*) miejsce *nt*; (*of knowledge etc*) dziedzina *f*; **in the London ~** w rejonie Londynu
**area code** (*Tel*) *n* (numer *m*) kierunkowy
**arena** [ə'riːnə] *n* arena *f*; (*fig*) płaszczyzna *f*, niwa *f*
**aren't** [ɑːnt] = **are not**
**Argentina** [ɑːdʒən'tiːnə] *n* Argentyna *f*
**Argentinian** [ɑːdʒən'tɪnɪən] *adj* argentyński ▷ *n* Argentyńczyk(-tynka) *m(f)*
**arguable** ['ɑːgjuəbl] *adj* dyskusyjny; **it is ~ whether ... or not** jest kwestią do dyskusji, czy ..., czy nie; **it is ~ that ...** jest do wykazania, że ...
**arguably** ['ɑːgjuəblɪ] *adv* prawdopodobnie, być może; **it is ~ ...** jest to, być może, ...
**argue** ['ɑːgjuː] *vi* (*quarrel*) kłócić się, sprzeczać się; (*reason*) argumentować ▷ *vt* roztrząsać; **to ~ that ...** utrzymywać, że ...; **to ~ about sth** (*quarrel*) sprzeczać się na temat czegoś; (*debate*) dyskutować o czymś; **to ~ for/against sth** przedstawiać (przedstawić *perf*) argumenty za czymś/przeciw(ko) czemuś
**argument** ['ɑːgjumənt] *n* (*reason*) argument *m*; (*reasoning*) rozumowanie *nt*; (*quarrel*) kłótnia *f*, sprzeczka *f*; (*debate*) dyskusja *f*; **~ for/against** argument za *+instr*/przeciw *+dat*
**argumentative** [ɑːgju'mɛntətɪv] *adj* kłótliwy
**aria** ['ɑːrɪə] *n* aria *f*
**ARIBA** (*Brit*) *n abbr* = **Associate of the Royal Institue of British Architects**
**arid** ['ærɪd] *adj* suchy, jałowy
**aridity** [ə'rɪdɪtɪ] *n* suchość *f*, jałowość *f*
**Aries** ['ɛərɪz] *n* Baran *m*; **to be ~** być spod znaku Barana

**arise** [əˈraɪz] (*pt* **arose**, *pp* **~n**) *vi* powstawać (powstać *perf*), pojawiać się (pojawić się *perf*); **to ~ from** brać się (wziąć się *perf*) z *+gen*; **should the need ~** w razie potrzeby

**arisen** [əˈrɪzn] *pp of* **arise**

**aristocracy** [ærɪsˈtɔkrəsɪ] *n* arystokracja *f*

**aristocrat** [ˈærɪstəkræt] *n* arystokrata(-tka) *m(f)*

**aristocratic** [ærɪstəˈkrætɪk] *adj* arystokratyczny

**arithmetic** [əˈrɪθmətɪk] *n* (*Math*) arytmetyka *f*; (*calculation*) obliczenia *pl*, rachunki *pl*

**arithmetical** [ærɪθˈmɛtɪkl] *adj* rachunkowy, arytmetyczny

**ark** [ɑːk] *n*: **Noah's Ark** arka *f* Noego

**arm** [ɑːm] *n* (*Anat*) ręka *f*, ramię *nt*; (*of jacket*) rękaw *m*; (*of chair*) poręcz *f*; (*of organization etc*) ramię *nt* ▷ *vt* zbroić, uzbrajać (uzbroić *perf*); **arms** *npl* (*Mil*) broń *f*; **arm in arm** pod rękę

**armaments** [ˈɑːməmənts] *npl* zbrojenia *pl*

**armband** [ˈɑːmbænd] *n* opaska *f* (*na ramię*)

**armchair** [ˈɑːmtʃɛəʳ] *n* fotel *m*

**armed** [ɑːmd] *adj* (*soldier*) uzbrojony; (*conflict, action*) zbrojny; **the ~ forces** siły zbrojne

**armed robbery** *n* rabunek *m* z bronią w ręku

**Armenia** [ɑːˈmiːnɪə] *n* Armenia *f*

**Armenian** [ɑːˈmiːnɪən] *adj* ormiański, armeński ▷ *n* (*person*) Ormianin(-anka) *m(f)*, Armeńczyk(-enka) *m(f)*; (*Ling*) (język *m*) ormiański

**armful** [ˈɑːmful] *n* naręcze *nt*

**armistice** [ˈɑːmɪstɪs] *n* zawieszenie *nt* broni

**armour**, (*US*) **armor** [ˈɑːməʳ] *n* (*of knight*) zbroja *f*; (*also*: **armour-plating**) opancerzenie *nt*; (*tanks*) oddziały *pl* pancerne

**armoured car** [ˈɑːməd-] *n* samochód *m* opancerzony

**armoury** [ˈɑːmərɪ] *n* arsenał *m*

**armpit** [ˈɑːmpɪt] *n* pacha *f*

**armrest** [ˈɑːmrɛst] *n* podłokietnik *m*

**arms control** [ɑːmz-] *n* kontrola *f* zbrojeń

**arms race** [ɑːmz-] *n*: **the ~** wyścig *m* zbrojeń

**army** [ˈɑːmɪ] *n* (*Mil*) wojsko *nt*; (*: unit*) armia *f*; (*fig*) armia *f*

**aroma** [əˈrəumə] *n* aromat *m*

**aromatic** [ærəˈmætɪk] *adj* aromatyczny

**arose** [əˈrəuz] *pt of* **arise**

**around** [əˈraund] *adv* (*about*) dookoła; (*in the area*) w okolicy ▷ *prep* (*encircling*) wokół *or* dookoła *+gen*; (*near*) koło *+gen*; (*fig*: *about, roughly*) około *+gen*; **is he ~?** czy on tu (gdzieś) jest?; **~ 5 o'clock** (o)koło piątej

**arouse** [əˈrauz] *vt* (*from sleep*) budzić (obudzić *perf*); (*sexually*) pobudzać (pobudzić *perf*); (*interest, passion*) rozbudzać (rozbudzić *perf*), wzbudzać (wzbudzić *perf*)

**arpeggio** [ɑːˈpɛdʒɪəu] *n* arpeggio *nt*

**arrange** [əˈreɪndʒ] *vt* (*meeting, tour*) organizować (zorganizować *perf*); (*cards, papers*) układać (ułożyć *perf*); (*glasses, furniture*) ustawiać (ustawić *perf*); (*sth with/for sb*) załatwiać (załatwić *perf*); (*Mus*) aranżować (zaaranżować *perf*) ▷ *vi*: **we have ~d for a car to pick you up** załatwiliśmy, że podjedzie po ciebie samochód; **it was ~d that ...** ustalono, że ...; **they've ~d to meet her in the pub** umówili się (, że spotkają się) z nią w pubie

**arrangement** [əˈreɪndʒmənt] *n* (*agreement*) umowa *f*; (*order, layout*) układ *m*; (*Mus*) aranżacja *f*; **arrangements** *npl* (*plans*) ustalenia *pl*; (*preparations*) przygotowania *pl*; **to come to an ~ with sb** dochodzić (dojść *perf*) z kimś do porozumienia; **home deliveries by ~** możliwa dostawa do domu; **I'll make ~s for you to be met** załatwię, żeby ktoś po ciebie wyszedł

**array** [əˈreɪ] *n* (*Math*) macierz *f*, matryca *f*; (*Comput*) tablica *f*; (*Mil*) szyk *m*; **an ~ of** wachlarz *+gen*

**arrears** [əˈrɪəz] *npl* zaległości *pl* płatnicze; **to be in ~ with one's rent** zalegać z czynszem

**arrest** [əˈrɛst] *vt* (*criminal*) aresztować (zaaresztować *perf*); (*sb's attention*) przykuwać (przykuć *perf*) ▷ *n* aresztowanie *nt*; **you're under ~** jest Pan aresztowany

**arresting** [əˈrɛstɪŋ] *adj* (*fig*: *beauty etc*) uderzający

**arrival** [əˈraɪvl] *n* (*of person*) przybycie *nt*; (*of train, car*) przyjazd *m*; (*of plane*) przylot *m*; (*fig*: *of invention etc*) nadejście *nt*; **new ~** (*at college, work*) nowy(-wa) *m(f)*; (*baby*) nowo narodzone dziecko; **congratulations on the new ~** gratulacje z okazji powiększenia rodziny

**arrive** [əˈraɪv] *vi* (*person*) przybywać (przybyć *perf*); (*moment, news, letter*) nadchodzić (nadejść *perf*); (*baby*) przychodzić (przyjść *perf*) na świat

▸ **arrive at** *vt fus* (*fig*: *conclusion, agreement*) dochodzić (dojść *perf*) do *+gen*

**arrogance** [ˈærəgəns] *n* arogancja *f*

**arrogant** [ˈærəgənt] *adj* arogancki

**arrow** [ˈærəu] *n* (*weapon*) strzała *f*; (*sign*) strzałka *f*

**arse** [ɑːs] (*Brit*: *inf!*) *n* dupa *f* (*inf!*)

**arsenal** [ˈɑːsɪnl] *n* arsenał *m*

**arsenic** [ˈɑːsnɪk] *n* arszenik *m*

**arson** [ˈɑːsn] *n* podpalenie *nt*

**art** [ɑːt] *n* sztuka *f*; **arts** *npl* (*Scol*) nauki *pl* humanistyczne; **work of art** dzieło sztuki

**artefact** [ˈɑːtɪfækt] *n* wytwór *m* człowieka

**arterial** [ɑːˈtɪərɪəl] *adj* (*Anat*) tętniczy; (*road*) przelotowy

**artery** [ˈɑːtərɪ] *n* (*Med*) tętnica *f*; (*fig*: *road*) arteria *f*

**artful** [ˈɑːtful] *adj* chytry, przebiegły
**art gallery** *n* galeria *f* sztuki
**arthritic** [ɑːˈθrɪtɪk] *adj* (*pain*) artretyczny; (*person*): **to be ~** mieć artretyzm
**arthritis** [ɑːˈθraɪtɪs] *n* zapalenie *nt* stawów, artretyzm *m*
**artichoke** [ˈɑːtɪtʃəuk] *n* (*also*: **globe artichoke**) karczoch *m*; (*also*: **Jerusalem artichoke**) topinambur *m*
**article** [ˈɑːtɪkl] *n* artykuł *m*; (*Ling*) przedimek *m*, rodzajnik *m*; **articles** (*Brit*) *npl* (*Jur*) aplikacja *f*; **~ of clothing** część garderoby
**articles of association** (*Comm*) *npl* statut *m* spółki
**articulate** [*adj* ɑːˈtɪkjulɪt, *vb* ɑːˈtɪkjuleɪt] *adj* (*speech*) wyraźny; (*sth said or written*) zrozumiały, jasny; (*person*) elokwentny, wymowny ▷ *vt* wyrażać (wyrazić *perf*) ▷ *vi*: **to ~ well/badly** mówić wyraźnie/niewyraźnie
**articulated lorry** (*Brit*) *n* ciężarówka *f* przegubowa *or* naczepowa
**artifice** [ˈɑːtɪfɪs] *n* (*trick*) podstęp *m*; (*skill*) przebiegłość *f*
**artificial** [ɑːtɪˈfɪʃəl] *adj* sztuczny
**artificial insemination** [-ɪnsɛmɪˈneɪʃən] *n* sztuczne zapłodnienie *nt*, inseminacja *f*
**artificial intelligence** *n* sztuczna inteligencja *f*
**artificial respiration** *n* sztuczne oddychanie *nt*
**artillery** [ɑːˈtɪlərɪ] *n* artyleria *f*
**artisan** [ˈɑːtɪzæn] *n* rzemieślnik *m*
**artist** [ˈɑːtɪst] *n* artysta(-tka) *m(f)*
**artistic** [ɑːˈtɪstɪk] *adj* artystyczny; **she's very ~** (*creative*) jest bardzo uzdolniona artystycznie; (*appreciative*) jest wielką miłośniczką sztuki
**artistry** [ˈɑːtɪstrɪ] *n* artyzm *m*
**artless** [ˈɑːtlɪs] *adj* pozbawiony sztuczności
**art school** *n* ≈ akademia *f* sztuk pięknych
**ARV** *n abbr* (*Bible*: = *American Revised Version*) *amerykańskie tłumaczenie Biblii*
**AS** (US) *n abbr* (= *Associate in/of Science*) *stopień naukowy* ▷ *abbr* (Post) = **American Samoa**

KEYWORD

**as** [æz, əz] *conj* **1** (*referring to time*) kiedy, gdy; **he came in as I was leaving** wszedł, kiedy *or* gdy wychodziłem; **as the years went by** w miarę upływu lat; **as from tomorrow** (począwszy) od jutra
**2** (*in comparisons*): **as big as me** taki duży jak ja; **twice as big as you** dwa razy większy od ciebie; **she has as much money as I** ma tyle (samo) pieniędzy co ja; **as much as 200 pounds** aż 200 funtów; **as soon as you have finished** jak tylko skończysz
**3** (*since, because*) ponieważ; **he left early as he had to be home by ten** wyszedł wcześnie, ponieważ miał być w domu przed dziesiątą; **as you can't come I'll go without you** skoro nie możesz iść, pójdę bez ciebie
**4** (*referring to manner, way*) (tak) jak; **do as you wish** rób, jak chcesz; **as she said** (tak,) jak powiedziała; **he gave it to me as a present** dał mi to w prezencie
**5** (*in the capacity of*) jako; **he works as a driver** pracuje jako kierowca
**6** (*concerning*): **as for** *or* **to that** co do tego, jeśli o to chodzi
**7**: **as if** *or* **though** jak gdyby, jakby; **he looked as if he was ill** wyglądał, jakby był chory; *see also* **long**; **such**; **well**

**ASA** *n abbr* (= *American Standards Association*) *urząd normalizacyjny*
**a.s.a.p.** *adv abbr* (= *as soon as possible*) jak najszybciej
**asbestos** [æzˈbɛstəs] *n* azbest *m*
**ascend** [əˈsɛnd] *vt* (*hill*) wspinać się (wspiąć się *perf*) na *+acc*; (*stairs*) wspinać się (wspiąć się *perf*) po *+loc*; (*throne*) wstępować (wstąpić *perf*) na *+acc* ▷ *vi* (*path, stairs*) piąć się; (*person*: *on foot*) wspinać się (wspiąć się *perf*); (: *in lift*) wjeżdżać (wjechać *perf*)
**ascendancy** [əˈsɛndənsɪ] *n*: **~ (over sb)** dominacja *f or* panowanie *nt* (nad kimś)
**ascendant** [əˈsɛndənt] *n*: **to be in the ~** dominować
**ascension** [əˈsɛnʃən] (*Rel*) *n*: **the A~** Wniebowstąpienie *nt*
**Ascension Island** *n* Wyspa *f* Wniebowstąpienia
**ascent** [əˈsɛnt] *n* (*slope*) wzniesienie *nt*; (*climb*) wspinaczka *f*
**ascertain** [æsəˈteɪn] *vt* (*details, facts*) ustalać (ustalić *perf*)
**ascetic** [əˈsɛtɪk] *adj* ascetyczny
**asceticism** [əˈsɛtɪsɪzəm] *n* asceza *f*
**ASCII** [ˈæskiː] (*Comput*) *n abbr* (= *American Standard Code for Information Interchange*) (kod *m*) ASCII
**ascribe** [əˈskraɪb] *vt*: **to ~ sth to** przypisywać (przypisać *perf*) coś *+dat*
**ASCU** (US) *n abbr* = **Association of State Colleges and Universities**
**ASEAN** [ˈæsɪæn] *n abbr* (= *Association of South-East Asian Nations*) ASEAN *m*
**ASH** [æʃ] (*Brit*) *n abbr* (= *Action on Smoking and Health*) *stowarzyszenie antynikotynowe*
**ash** [æʃ] *n* (*of fire*) popiół *m*; (*tree, wood*) jesion *m*
**ashamed** [əˈʃeɪmd] *adj* zawstydzony; **to be ~ of/to do sth** wstydzić się *+gen*/coś zrobić;

**I'm ~ of myself for having done that** wstyd mi *or* wstydzę się, że to zrobiłam
**'A' shares** (*Brit*) *npl* akcje *pl* klasy A
**ashen** ['æʃən] *adj* śmiertelnie blady
**ashore** [ə'ʃɔːʳ] *adv* (*swim*) do brzegu; (*go*) na brzeg; (*be*) na brzegu
**ashtray** ['æʃtreɪ] *n* popielniczka *f*
**Ash Wednesday** *n* środa *f* popielcowa, Popielec *m*
**Asia** ['eɪʃə] *n* Azja *f*
**Asia Minor** *n* Azja *f* Mniejsza
**Asian** ['eɪʃən] *adj* azjatycki ▷ *n* Azjata(-tka) *m(f)*
**Asiatic** [eɪsɪ'ætɪk] *adj* azjatycki
**aside** [ə'saɪd] *adv* na bok ▷ *n* (*incidental remark*) uwaga *f* na marginesie; (*Theat*) uwaga *f* na stronie (*skierowana do publiczności*); **to brush objections ~** przechodzić (przejść *perf*) do porządku dziennego nad zastrzeżeniami
**aside from** *prep* oprócz *+gen*, poza *+instr*
**ask** [ɑːsk] *vt* (*question*) zadawać (zadać *perf*); (*invite*) zapraszać (zaprosić *perf*); **to ask sb sth/to do sth** prosić (poprosić *perf*) kogoś o coś/żeby coś zrobił; **to ask sb about sth** pytać (zapytać *perf or* spytać *perf*) kogoś o coś; **to ask sb the time** pytać (zapytać *perf*) kogoś o godzinę; **to ask about the price** pytać (zapytać *perf*) o cenę; **to ask sb out to dinner** zapraszać (zaprosić *perf*) kogoś do restauracji
▶ **ask after** *vt fus*: **she asked after you** pytała o ciebie, pytała, co u ciebie (słychać)
▶ **ask for** *vt fus* prosić (poprosić *perf*) o *+acc*; **it's just asking for trouble/it** to się może źle skończyć; **he asked for it!** sam się o to prosił!
**askance** [ə'skɑːns] *adv*: **to look ~ at sb/sth** spoglądać (spojrzeć *perf*) na kogoś/coś z ukosa
**askew** [ə'skjuː] *adv*: **his tie was ~** miał przekrzywiony krawat
**asking price** ['ɑːskɪŋ-] *n*: **the ~** cena *f* ofertowa
**asleep** [ə'sliːp] *adj* śpiący, pogrążony we śnie; **to be ~** spać; **to fall ~** zasypiać (zasnąć *perf*)
**ASLEF** ['æzlɛf] (*Brit*) *n abbr* (= *Associated Society of Locomotive Engineers and Firemen*) *związek zawodowy kolejarzy*
**asp** [æsp] *n* osika *f*
**asparagus** [əs'pærəgəs] *n* szparagi *pl*
**asparagus tips** *npl* główki *pl* szparagów
**ASPCA** *n abbr* = **American Society for the Prevention of Cruelty to Animals**
**aspect** ['æspɛkt] *n* aspekt *m*; **to take on a new/different ~** nabierać (nabrać *perf*) nowego/innego zabarwienia; **a room with a south-west ~** pokój z widokiem na południowy zachód
**aspersions** [əs'pəːʃənz] *npl*: **to cast ~ on** rzucać oszczerstwa na *+acc*
**asphalt** ['æsfælt] *n* asfalt *m*
**asphyxiate** [æs'fɪksɪeɪt] *vt*: **to be ~d** (*choke*) dusić się; (*die*) udusić się (*perf*)
**asphyxiation** [æsfɪksɪ'eɪʃən] *n* uduszenie *nt*
**aspirate** ['æspəreɪt] (*Ling*) *vt* aspirować, wymawiać (wymówić *perf*) z przydechem ▷ *n* aspirata *f*, głoska *f* przydechowa
**aspirations** [æspə'reɪʃənz] *npl* aspiracje *pl*
**aspire** [əs'paɪəʳ] *vi*: **to ~ to** aspirować do *+gen*
**aspirin** ['æsprɪn] *n* aspiryna *f*
**ass** [æs] *n* (*lit, fig*) osioł *m*; (*US: inf!*) dupa *f* (*inf!*)
**assail** [ə'seɪl] *vt* (gwałtownie) napadać (napaść *perf*) na *+dat*; **she was ~ed by doubts** nękały ją wątpliwości
**assailant** [ə'seɪlənt] *n* napastnik(-iczka) *m(f)*
**assassin** [ə'sæsɪn] *n* (*killer*) zabójca(-jczyni) *m(f)*; (*one who attempts to kill*) zamachowiec *m*
**assassinate** [ə'sæsɪneɪt] *vt* zabijać (zabić *perf*) (*w drodze zamachu*)
**assassination** [əsæsɪ'neɪʃən] *n* zabójstwo *nt* (*w drodze zamachu*)
**assault** [ə'sɔːlt] *n* (*Jur*) napad *m*, atak *m*; (*Mil*) atak *m*; (*fig*): **an ~ on** (*sb's beliefs, attitudes*) (gwałtowne) przeciwstawienie się *nt +dat* ▷ *vt* atakować (zaatakować *perf*), napadać (napaść *perf*); (*sexually*) gwałcić (zgwałcić *perf*); **~ and battery** (*Jur*) napaść z pobiciem, czynna napaść
**assemble** [ə'sɛmbl] *vt* gromadzić (zgromadzić *perf*); (*Tech*) montować (zmontować *perf*) ▷ *vi* zbierać się (zebrać się *perf*), gromadzić się (zgromadzić się *perf*)
**assembly** [ə'sɛmblɪ] *n* (*meeting, institution*) zgromadzenie *nt*; (*construction*) montaż *m*
**assembly language** (*Comput*) *n* asembler *m*
**assembly line** *n* linia *f* montażowa
**assent** [ə'sɛnt] *n* zgoda *f*, aprobata *f* ▷ *vi*: **to ~ (to)** godzić się (zgodzić się *perf*) (na *+acc*); **to give one's ~** wyrażać (wyrazić *perf*) (swoją) zgodę *or* aprobatę
**assert** [ə'səːt] *vt* (*opinion*) wyrażać (wyrazić *perf*) zdecydowanie; (*innocence*) zapewniać (zapewnić *perf*) o *+loc*; (*authority*) zaznaczać (zaznaczyć *perf*), podkreślać (podkreślić *perf*); **to ~ o.s.** zaznaczać (zaznaczyć *perf*) swój autorytet
**assertion** [ə'səːʃən] *n* twierdzenie *nt*
**assertive** [ə'səːtɪv] *adj* stanowczy; (*Psych*) asertywny
**assess** [ə'sɛs] *vt* (*situation, abilities, students*) oceniać (ocenić *perf*); (*tax*) naliczać (naliczyć *perf*), obliczać (obliczyć *perf*); (*damages, value*) szacować (oszacować *perf*)
**assessment** [ə'sɛsmənt] *n* (*of situation, abilities*) ocena *f*; (*of tax*) naliczenie *nt*, obliczenie *nt*; (*of damage, value*) oszacowanie *nt*; (*Scol*) ocena *f* (postępów)

**assessor** [ə'sɛsə^r] *(Jur)* *n* rzeczoznawca *m*, biegły *m*
**asset** ['æsɛt] *n* *(quality)* atut *m*; *(person)* cenny nabytek *m*; **assets** *npl* *(property, funds)* wkłady *pl* kapitałowe; *(Comm)* aktywa *pl*
**asset-stripping** ['æsɛt'strɪpɪŋ] *(Comm)* *n* wykup *m* majątku przedsiębiorstwa
**assiduous** [ə'sɪdjuəs] *adj* gorliwy
**assign** [ə'saɪn] *vt*: **to ~ (to)** *(task, resources)* przydzielać (przydzielić *perf*) *(+dat)*; *(person)* przydzielać (przydzielić *perf*) (do *+gen*), wyznaczać (wyznaczyć *perf*) (do *+gen*); *(cause, meaning)* przypisywać (przypisać *perf*) *(+dat)*
**assignment** [ə'saɪnmənt] *n* *(task)* zadanie *nt*; *(appointment)* wyznaczenie *nt*, przydzielenie *nt*; **heavy reading ~s** *(Scol)* duża liczba lektur obowiązkowych
**assimilate** [ə'sɪmɪleɪt] *vt* *(learn)* przyswajać (przyswoić *perf*) sobie; *(absorb)* wchłaniać (wchłonąć *perf*)
**assimilation** [əsɪmɪ'leɪʃən] *n* *(of ideas: by people)* przyswajanie *nt* (sobie); *(: in industry etc)* wdrażanie *nt*; *(of immigrants)* asymilacja *f*
**assist** [ə'sɪst] *vt* pomagać (pomóc *perf*) *+dat*
**assistance** [ə'sɪstəns] *n* pomoc *f*
**assistant** [ə'sɪstənt] *n* pomocnik(-ica) *m(f)*; *(Brit: also:* **shop assistant***)* sprzedawca(-wczyni) *m(f)*
**assistant manager** *n* ≈ zastępca *m* dyrektora
**assistant professor** *(US)* *n* ≈ docent *m*
**assizes** [ə'saɪzɪz] *(Brit)* *npl* *wyjazdowe sesje sądu*
**associate** [*n, adj* ə'səuʃɪɪt, *vb* ə'səuʃɪeɪt] *n* wspólnik(-iczka) *m(f)* ▷ *vt* kojarzyć (skojarzyć *perf*) ▷ *vi*: **to ~ with sb** zadawać się z kimś ▷ *adj*: **~ director** zastępca *m* dyrektora; **~ member** członek korespondent; **~ professor** *(US)* ≈ profesor nadzwyczajny
**associated company** [ə'səuʃɪeɪtɪd-] *n* przedsiębiorstwo *nt* zrzeszone
**association** [əsəusɪ'eɪʃən] *n* *(group)* stowarzyszenie *nt*, zrzeszenie *nt*; *(involvement, link)* związek *m*; *(Psych)* skojarzenie *nt*; **in ~ with** wspólnie z *+instr*
**association football** *n* piłka *f* nożna, futbol *m*
**assorted** [ə'sɔ:tɪd] *adj* mieszany; **in ~ sizes** w różnych rozmiarach
**assortment** [ə'sɔ:tmənt] *n* asortyment *m*
**Asst.** *abbr* (= *assistant*) asyst.
**assuage** [ə'sweɪdʒ] *vt* *(grief, pain)* łagodzić (złagodzić *perf*); *(thirst, appetite)* zaspokajać (zaspokoić *perf*)
**assume** [ə'sju:m] *vt* *(suppose)* zakładać (założyć *perf*); *(responsibilities etc)* brać (wziąć *perf*) (na siebie); *(appearance, name)* przybierać (przybrać *perf*)
**assumed name** [ə'sju:md-] *n* przybrane nazwisko *nt*
**assumption** [ə'sʌmpʃən] *n* *(supposition)* założenie *nt*; *(of power etc)* przejęcie *nt*; **on the ~ that** zakładając, że
**assurance** [ə'ʃuərəns] *n* *(promise)* zapewnienie *nt*; *(confidence)* przekonanie *nt*; *(insurance)* ubezpieczenie *nt* *(zwłaszcza na życie)*; **I can give you no ~s** nie mogę ci dać żadnej gwarancji
**assure** [ə'ʃuə^r] *vt* zapewniać (zapewnić *perf*)
**AST** *(US)* *abbr* = **Atlantic Standard Time**
**asterisk** ['æstərɪsk] *n* gwiazdka *f*, odsyłacz *m*
**astern** [ə'stə:n] *(Naut)* *adv* na rufie
**asteroid** ['æstərɔɪd] *n* asteroida *f*
**asthma** ['æsmə] *n* astma *f*
**asthmatic** [æs'mætɪk] *adj* astmatyczny ▷ *n* astmatyk(-yczka) *m(f)*
**astigmatism** [ə'stɪgmətɪzəm] *n* astygmatyzm *m*
**astir** [ə'stə:^r] *adv* na nogach
**astonish** [ə'stɔnɪʃ] *vt* zdumiewać (zdumieć *perf*), zadziwiać (zadziwić *perf*); **she was ~ed to hear that** zdumiała się, słysząc to
**astonishing** [ə'stɔnɪʃɪŋ] *adj* zdumiewający, zadziwiający; **I find it ~ that ...** uważam za zdumiewające, że ...
**astonishingly** [ə'stɔnɪʃɪŋlɪ] *adv* zdumiewająco
**astonishment** [ə'stɔnɪʃmənt] *n* zdumienie *nt*; **to my ~** ku memu zdumieniu
**astound** [ə'staund] *vt* zdumiewać (zdumieć *perf*)
**astounded** [ə'staundɪd] *adj* zdumiony
**astounding** [ə'staundɪŋ] *adj* zdumiewający
**astray** [ə'streɪ] *adv*: **to go ~** zawieruszyć się *(perf)*; **to lead ~** zwodzić (zwieść *perf*) (na manowce)
**astride** [ə'straɪd] *prep* okrakiem na *+loc*
**astringent** [əs'trɪndʒənt] *adj* ściągający; *(fig: remark etc)* uszczypliwy ▷ *n* tonik *m* *(kosmetyczny)*
**astrologer** [əs'trɔlədʒə^r] *n* astrolog *m*
**astrology** [əs'trɔlədʒɪ] *n* astrologia *f*
**astronaut** ['æstrənɔ:t] *n* astronauta(-tka) *m(f)*, kosmonauta(-tka) *m(f)*
**astronomer** [əs'trɔnəmə^r] *n* astronom *m*
**astronomical** [æstrə'nɔmɪkl] *adj* *(telescope, price)* astronomiczny; *(odds)* ogromny
**astronomy** [əs'trɔnəmɪ] *n* astronomia *f*
**astrophysics** ['æstrəu'fɪzɪks] *n* astrofizyka *f*
**astute** [əs'tju:t] *adj* przebiegły
**asunder** [ə'sʌndə^r] *adv*: **to tear ~** rozdzierać (rozedrzeć *perf*) na kawałki
**ASV** *n abbr* *(Bible: = American Standard Version)* *amerykańskie tłumaczenie Biblii*
**asylum** [ə'saɪləm] *n* *(refuge)* azyl *m*; *(hospital)* szpital *m* psychiatryczny; **to seek (political) ~** ubiegać się o azyl (polityczny)

a

**asymmetrical** [eɪsɪ'mɛtrɪkl] *adj* asymetryczny

 KEYWORD

**at** [æt] *prep* **1** (*referring to position, place*): **at the table** przy stole; **at home/school** w domu/ szkole; **at the top** na górze; **at my parents' (house)** u (moich) rodziców
**2** (*referring to direction*): **to look at sth** patrzeć (popatrzeć *perf*) na coś; **to throw sth at sb** rzucać (rzucić *perf*) czymś w kogoś
**3** (*referring to time*): **at 4 o'clock** o (godzinie) czwartej; **at night** w nocy; **at Christmas** na Boże Narodzenie; **at times** czasami, czasem
**4** (*referring to rates*) po *+acc*; **at 2 pounds a kilo** po 2 funty za kilogram; **two at a time** po dwa na raz
**5** (*referring to speed*): **at 50 km/h** z prędkością 50 km na godzinę
**6** (*referring to activity*): **to be at work** pracować; **to play at cowboys** bawić się w kowbojów; **to be good at sth** być dobrym w czymś
**7** (*referring to cause*): **shocked/surprised/ annoyed at sth** wstrząśnięty/zdziwiony/ rozdrażniony czymś; **at his command** na jego polecenie
**8**: **not at all** (*in answer to question*) wcale nie; (*in answer to thanks*) nie ma za co; **I'm not at all tired** nie jestem wcale zmęczony; **anything at all will do** może być obojętnie co

**ate** [eɪt] *pt of* **eat**
**atheism** ['eɪθɪɪzəm] *n* ateizm *m*
**atheist** ['eɪθɪɪst] *n* ateista(-tka) *m(f)*
**Athenian** [ə'θi:nɪən] *adj* ateński ▷ *n* Ateńczyk/Atenka *m/f*
**Athens** ['æθɪnz] *n* Ateny *pl*
**athlete** ['æθli:t] *n* (*man*) sportowiec *m*, sportsmen *m*; (*woman*) sportsmenka *f*
**athletic** [æθ'lɛtɪk] *adj* (*tradition, excellence*) sportowy; (*person*) wysportowany; (*build*) atletyczny
**athletics** [æθ'lɛtɪks] *n* lekkoatletyka *f*
**Atlantic** [ət'læntɪk] *adj* atlantycki ▷ *n*: **the ~ (Ocean)** Atlantyk *m*, Ocean *m* Atlantycki
**atlas** ['ætləs] *n* atlas *m*
**Atlas Mountains** *npl*: **the ~** góry *pl* Atlas
**ATM** *abbr* (*= Automated Telling Machine*) bankomat *m*
**atmosphere** ['ætməsfɪə[r]] *n* (*of planet, place*) atmosfera *f*; (*air*) powietrze *nt*
**atmospheric** [ætməs'fɛrɪk] *adj* atmosferyczny
**atmospherics** [ætməs'fɛrɪks] (*Radio*) *npl* zakłócenia *pl* atmosferyczne
**atoll** ['ætɔl] *n* atol *m*
**atom** ['ætəm] *n* atom *m*
**atomic** [ə'tɔmɪk] *adj* atomowy
**atom(ic) bomb** *n* bomba *f* atomowa
**atomizer** ['ætəmaɪzə[r]] *n* rozpylacz *m*
**atone** [ə'təun] *vi*: **to ~ for** odpokutowywać (odpokutować *perf*) za *+acc*
**atonement** [ə'təunmənt] *n* zadośćuczynienie *nt*
**ATP** *n abbr* = **Association of Tennis Professionals**
**atrocious** [ə'trəuʃəs] *adj* okropny
**atrocity** [ə'trɔsɪtɪ] *n* okrucieństwo *nt*
**atrophy** ['ætrəfɪ] *n* atrofia *f*, zanik *m* ▷ *vt* powodować (spowodować *perf*) atrofię *or* zanik *+gen* ▷ *vi* zanikać (zaniknąć *perf*), ulegać (ulec *perf*) atrofii
**attach** [ə'tætʃ] *vt* (*fasten, join*) przymocowywać (przymocować *perf*), przytwierdzać (przytwierdzić *perf*); (*document*) załączać (załączyć *perf*); (*employee, troops*) przyłączać (przyłączyć *perf*); (*importance etc*) przywiązywać (przywiązać *perf*); **to be ~ed to sb/sth** (*like*) być przywiązanym do kogoś/czegoś; **the ~ed letter** załączony list
**attaché** [ə'tæʃeɪ] *n* attaché *m*
**attaché case** *n* aktówka *f*
**attachment** [ə'tætʃmənt] *n* (*tool*) nasadka *f*, końcówka *f*; (*feeling*): **~ (to sb)** przywiązanie *nt* (do kogoś)
**attack** [ə'tæk] *vt* (*Mil*) atakować (zaatakować *perf*); (*assault*) atakować (zaatakować *perf*), napadać (napaść *perf*); (*criticize*) atakować (zaatakować *perf*), napadać (napaść *perf*) na *+acc*; (*tackle*) zabierać się (zabrać się *perf*) do *+gen* ▷ *n* (*Mil*) atak *m*; (*on sb's life*) napad *m*, napaść *f*; (*fig: criticism*) atak *m*, napaść *f*; (*of illness*) napad *m*, atak *m*; **heart ~** atak serca, zawał
**attacker** [ə'tækə[r]] *n* napastnik(-iczka) *m(f)*
**attain** [ə'teɪn] *vt* osiągać (osiągnąć *perf*); (*ambition*) zaspokajać (zaspokoić *perf*)
**attainments** [ə'teɪnmənts] *npl* osiągnięcia *pl*
**attempt** [ə'tɛmpt] *n* próba *f* ▷ *vt*: **to ~ sth/to** próbować (spróbować *perf*) czegoś/*+infin*; **to make an ~ on sb's life** dokonywać (dokonać *perf*) zamachu na czyjeś życie; **he made no ~ to help** nawet nie próbował pomóc
**attempted** [ə'tɛmptɪd] *adj* niedoszły; **~ murder** usiłowanie zabójstwa
**attend** [ə'tɛnd] *vt* (*school, church*) uczęszczać do *+gen*; (*lectures, course*) uczęszczać na *+acc*; (*patient*) zajmować się (zająć się *perf*) *+instr*; (*meeting*) brać (wziąć *perf*) udział w *+loc*
▶ **attend to** *vt fus* zajmować się (zająć się *perf*) *+instr*; (*customer*) obsługiwać (obsłużyć *perf*) *+acc*

**attendance** [ə'tɛndəns] *n* (*presence*) obecność *f*; (*people present*) frekwencja *f*
**attendant** [ə'tɛndənt] *n* pomocnik(-ica) *m(f)*; (*in garage, museum etc*) osoba *f* z obsługi ▷ *adj*: **...and its ~ dangers** ...i związane z tym niebezpieczeństwa
**attention** [ə'tɛnʃən] *n* (*concentration*) uwaga *f*; (*Med*) pomoc *f* (medyczna) ▷ *excl* (*Mil*) baczność; **for the ~ of** (*Admin*) do wiadomości *+gen*; **it has come to my ~ that ...** zwróciło moją uwagę, że ...; **to draw sb's ~ to sth** zwracać (zwrócić *perf*) czyjąś uwagę na coś; **to stand to/at ~** (*Mil*) stawać (stanąć *perf*)/ stać na baczność
**attentive** [ə'tɛntɪv] *adj* (*intent*) uważny; (*solicitous*) troskliwy; (*kind*) usłużny
**attentively** [ə'tɛntɪvlɪ] *adv* uważnie
**attenuate** [ə'tɛnjueɪt] *vt* osłabiać (osłabić *perf*) ▷ *vi* słabnąć (osłabnąć *perf*)
**attest** [ə'tɛst] *vi*: **to ~ to** (*demonstrate*) potwierdzać (potwierdzić *perf*) *+acc*; (*Jur*: *confirm*) świadczyć (poświadczyć *perf*) o *+loc*
**attic** ['ætɪk] *n* strych *m*
**attire** [ə'taɪəʳ] *n* strój *m*
**attitude** ['ætɪtjuːd] *n* (*posture, behaviour*) postawa *f*; (*view*): **~ (to)** pogląd *m* (na *+acc*), stosunek *m* (do *+gen*); **her arms flung out in an ~ of surrender** rozpostarła ramiona w geście rezygnacji
**attorney** [ə'təːnɪ] *n* (*US*) pełnomocnik *m*; **power of ~** pełnomocnictwo
**Attorney General** *n* (*Brit*) *minister sprawiedliwości i doradca prawny rządu i Korony*; (*US*) *minister sprawiedliwości i prokurator generalny*
**attract** [ə'trækt] *vt* (*people, attention*) przyciągać (przyciągnąć *perf*); (*support, publicity*) zyskiwać (zyskać *perf*); (*interest*) wzbudzać (wzbudzić *perf*); (*appeal to*) pociągać
**attraction** [ə'trækʃən] *n* (*appeal*) powab *m*, urok *m*; (*usu pl*: *amusements*) atrakcja *f*; (*Phys*) przyciąganie *nt*; (*fig*: *towards sb, sth*) pociąg *m*
**attractive** [ə'træktɪv] *adj* atrakcyjny
**attribute** [*n* 'ætrɪbjuːt, *vb* ə'trɪbjuːt] *n* atrybut *m* ▷ *vt*: **to ~ sth to** przypisywać (przypisać *perf*) coś *+dat*
**attrition** [ə'trɪʃən] *n*: **war of ~** wojna *f* na wyczerpanie
**Atty. Gen.** *abbr* = **Attorney General**
**ATV** *n abbr* (= *all terrain vehicle*) pojazd *m* terenowy
**aubergine** ['əubəʒiːn] *n* (*vegetable*) bakłażan *m*, oberżyna *f*; (*colour*) (kolor *m*) ciemnofioletowy, ciemny fiolet *m*
**auburn** ['ɔːbən] *adj* kasztanowaty, rudawobrązowy
**auction** ['ɔːkʃən] *n* licytacja *f*, aukcja *f* ▷ *vt* sprzedawać (sprzedać *perf*) na licytacji *or* aukcji
**auctioneer** [ɔːkʃə'nɪəʳ] *n* licytator(ka) *m(f)*
**auction room** *n* sala *f* aukcyjna
**audacious** [ɔː'deɪʃəs] *adj* śmiały, zuchwały (*pej*)
**audacity** [ɔː'dæsɪtɪ] *n* (*boldness, daring*) śmiałość *f*; (*impudence*) zuchwałość *f*, bezczelność *f*; **to have the ~ to do sth** mieć czelność coś (z)robić
**audible** ['ɔːdɪbl] *adj* słyszalny
**audience** ['ɔːdɪəns] *n* (*in theatre etc*) publiczność *f*, widownia *f*; (*Radio*) słuchacze *pl*; (*TV*) widzowie *pl*; (*with queen etc*) audiencja *f*; **to reach a wide ~** docierać (dotrzeć *perf*) do szerokiej rzeszy odbiorców
**audio-typist** ['ɔːdɪəu'taɪpɪst] *n maszynistka spisująca teksty z magnetofonu*
**audio-visual** ['ɔːdɪəu'vɪzjuəl] *adj* audiowizualny
**audio-visual aid** *n* pomoc *f* audiowizualna
**audit** ['ɔːdɪt] (*Comm*) *vt* rewidować (zrewidować *perf*), sprawdzać (sprawdzić *perf*) ▷ *n* rewizja *f* ksiąg (rachunkowych)
**audition** [ɔː'dɪʃən] *n* przesłuchanie *nt* (*do roli*) ▷ *vi*: **to ~ (for)** mieć przesłuchanie (do *+gen*)
**auditor** ['ɔːdɪtəʳ] *n* rewident *m* księgowy
**auditorium** [ɔːdɪ'tɔːrɪəm] *n* (*building*) audytorium *nt*; (*audience area*) widownia *f*
**Aug.** *abbr* (= *August*) sierp.
**augment** [ɔːg'mɛnt] *vt* powiększać (powiększyć *perf*), zwiększać (zwiększyć *perf*)
**augur** ['ɔːgəʳ] *vi*: **it ~s well (for)** to dobrze wróży (*+dat*)
**August** ['ɔːgəst] *n* sierpień *m*; *see also* **July**
**august** [ɔː'gʌst] *adj* (*figure, building*) majestatyczny; (*gathering*) dostojny
**aunt** [ɑːnt] *n* ciotka *f*; (*affectionately*) ciocia *f*
**auntie** ['ɑːntɪ], **aunty** *n dimin of* **aunt** ciocia *f*; (*jocularly, ironically*) cioteczka *f*, ciotunia *f*
**au pair** ['əu'pɛəʳ] *n* (*also*: **au pair girl**) *młoda cudzoziemka pomagająca w domu w zamian za utrzymanie i kieszonkowe*
**aura** ['ɔːrə] *n* (*fig*) atmosfera *f*
**auspices** ['ɔːspɪsɪz] *npl*: **under the ~ of** pod auspicjami *+gen*
**auspicious** [ɔːs'pɪʃəs] *adj* pomyślny
**austere** [ɔs'tɪəʳ] *adj* (*room, person, manner*) surowy; (*lifestyle*) prosty, skromny
**austerity** [ɔs'tɛrɪtɪ] *n* surowość *f*, prostota *f*; (*Econ*) trudności *pl* gospodarcze
**Australasia** [ɔːstrə'leɪzɪə] *n* Australazja *f*
**Australasian** [ɔːstrə'leɪzɪən] *adj* australazjatycki
**Australia** [ɔs'treɪlɪə] *n* Australia *f*
**Australian** [ɔs'treɪlɪən] *adj* australijski ▷ *n* Australijczyk(-jka) *m(f)*
**Austria** ['ɔstrɪə] *n* Austria *f*
**Austrian** ['ɔstrɪən] *adj* austriacki ▷ *n* Austriak(-aczka) *m(f)*

**AUT** *(Brit) n abbr* = **Association of University Teachers**
**authentic** [ɔːˈθɛntɪk] *adj* autentyczny
**authenticate** [ɔːˈθɛntɪkeɪt] *vt (painting)* ustalać (ustalić *perf*) autorstwo *+gen*; *(document, story)* poświadczać (poświadczyć *perf*)
**authenticity** [ɔːθɛnˈtɪsɪtɪ] *n* autentyczność *f*
**author** [ˈɔːθəʳ] *n* autor(ka) *m(f)*; *(profession)* pisarz(-arka) *m(f)*
**authoritarian** [ɔːθɔrɪˈtɛərɪən] *adj (attitudes, conduct)* władczy, apodyktyczny; *(government, rule)* autorytarny
**authoritative** [ɔːˈθɔrɪtətɪv] *adj (person, manner)* autorytatywny; *(source, account)* miarodajny, wiarygodny; *(study, treatise)* miarodajny
**authority** [ɔːˈθɔrɪtɪ] *n (power)* władza *f*; *(expert)* autorytet *m*; *(government body)* administracja *f*; *(official permission)* pozwolenie *nt*; **the authorities** *npl* władze *pl*; **to have the ~ to do sth** być władnym coś zrobić
**authorization** [ɔːθəraɪˈzeɪʃən] *n* pozwolenie *nt*
**authorize** [ˈɔːθəraɪz] *vt (publication)* autoryzować; *(loan)* zatwierdzać (zatwierdzić *perf*); *(course of action)* wyrażać (wyrazić *perf*) zgodę na *+acc*; **to ~ sb to do sth** upoważniać (upoważnić *perf*) kogoś *or* dawać (dać *perf*) komuś pełnomocnictwo do zrobienia czegoś
**authorized capital** [ˈɔːθəraɪzd-] *n* kapitał *m* statutowy
**authorship** [ˈɔːθəʃɪp] *n* autorstwo *nt*
**autistic** [ɔːˈtɪstɪk] *adj* autystyczny
**auto** [ˈɔːtəu] *(US) n* auto *nt*
**autobiographical** [ˈɔːtəbaɪəˈgræfɪkl] *adj* autobiograficzny
**autobiography** [ɔːtəbaɪˈɔgrəfɪ] *n* autobiografia *f*
**autocratic** [ɔːtəˈkrætɪk] *adj* autokratyczny
**autograph** [ˈɔːtəgrɑːf] *n* autograf *m* ▷ *vt* podpisywać (podpisać *perf*)
**automat** [ˈɔːtəmæt] *(US) n (vending machine)* automat *m*; *(restaurant) bar, w którym posiłki kupuje się w automatach*
**automata** [ɔːˈtɔmətə] *npl of* **automaton**
**automate** [ˈɔːtəmeɪt] *vt* automatyzować (zautomatyzować *perf*)
**automated** [ˈɔːtəmeɪtɪd] *adj* zautomatyzowany
**automatic** [ɔːtəˈmætɪk] *adj* automatyczny; *(reaction)* odruchowy ▷ *n (gun)* broń *f* automatyczna; *(washing machine)* pralka *f* automatyczna, automat *m (inf)*; *(car)* samochód *m* z automatyczną skrzynią biegów
**automatically** [ɔːtəˈmætɪklɪ] *adv (by itself)* automatycznie; *(without thinking)* machinalnie, odruchowo
**automatic data processing** *n* automatyczne przetwarzanie *nt* danych
**automation** [ɔːtəˈmeɪʃən] *n* automatyzacja *f*
**automaton** [ɔːˈtɔmətən] *(pl* **automata***) n* automat *m*, robot *m*
**automobile** [ˈɔːtəməbiːl] *(US) n* samochód *m*
**autonomous** [ɔːˈtɔnəməs] *adj (region, area)* autonomiczny; *(organization, person)* niezależny
**autonomy** [ɔːˈtɔnəmɪ] *n (of country)* autonomia *f*; *(of organization, person)* niezależność *f*
**autopsy** [ˈɔːtɔpsɪ] *n (post-mortem)* sekcja *f* zwłok, autopsja *f*
**autumn** [ˈɔːtəm] *n* jesień; **in ~** jesienią, na jesieni
**auxiliary** [ɔːgˈzɪlɪərɪ] *adj* pomocniczy ▷ *n* pomocnik(-ica) *m(f)*
**AV** *n abbr (Bible: = Authorized Version) angielskie tłumaczenie Biblii z roku 1611* ▷ *abbr* = **audiovisual**
**Av.** *abbr (= avenue)* al.
**avail** [əˈveɪl] *vt*: **to ~ o.s. of** korzystać (skorzystać *perf*) z *+gen* ▷ *n*: **to no ~** daremnie, na próżno
**availability** [əveɪləˈbɪlɪtɪ] *n (of goods, information)* dostępność *f*; *(of staff)* osiągalność *f*
**available** [əˈveɪləbl] *adj (article, service, information)* dostępny; *(person, time)* wolny; **every ~ means** wszelkie dostępne środki; **is the manager ~?** czy dyrektor jest wolny?; **to make sth ~ to sb** udostępniać (udostępnić *perf*) coś komuś
**avalanche** [ˈævəlɑːnʃ] *n (lit, fig)* lawina *f*
**avant-garde** [ˈævɑ̃ŋˈgɑːd] *adj* awangardowy
**avarice** [ˈævərɪs] *n* skąpstwo *nt*
**avaricious** [ævəˈrɪʃəs] *adj* skąpy
**avdp.** *abbr (= avoirdupois) angielski system wagowy*
**Ave.** *abbr (= avenue)* al.
**avenge** [əˈvɛndʒ] *vt* mścić (pomścić *perf*)
**avenue** [ˈævənjuː] *n* aleja *f*; *(fig)* możliwość *f*
**average** [ˈævərɪdʒ] *n* średnia *f* ▷ *adj (mean)* średni, przeciętny; *(ordinary)* przeciętny ▷ *vt* osiągać (osiągnąć *perf*) średnio; **on ~** średnio, przeciętnie; **above/below (the) ~** powyżej/poniżej średniej
▸ **average out** *vi*: **to ~ out at** wynosić (wynieść *perf*) średnio *+acc*
**averse** [əˈvəːs] *adj*: **to be ~ to sth/doing sth** być przeciwnym *or* niechętnym czemuś/robieniu czegoś; **I wouldn't be ~ to** nie miałbym nic przeciwko *+dat*
**aversion** [əˈvəːʃən] *n* niechęć *f*, awersja *f*; **to have an ~ to sb/sth** mieć awersję do kogoś/czegoś
**avert** [əˈvəːt] *vt (accident, war)* unikać (uniknąć *perf*) *+gen*; *(one's eyes)* odwracać (odwrócić *perf*)

**aviary** ['eɪvɪərɪ] *n* ptaszarnia *f*
**aviation** [eɪvɪ'eɪʃən] *n* lotnictwo *nt*
**avid** ['ævɪd] *adj* gorliwy; **~ for** spragniony *+gen*
**avidly** ['ævɪdlɪ] *adv* gorliwie
**avocado** [ævə'kɑːdəu] *n* (*Brit*: *also*: **avocado pear**) awokado *nt inv*
**avoid** [ə'vɔɪd] *vt* unikać (uniknąć *perf*) *+gen*; (*obstacle*) omijać (ominąć *perf*); **to ~ doing sth** unikać (uniknąć *perf*) (z)robienia czegoś
**avoidable** [ə'vɔɪdəbl] *adj* do uniknięcia *post*
**avoidance** [ə'vɔɪdəns] *n* unikanie *nt*; (*of tax*) uchylanie się *nt*
**avowed** [ə'vaud] *adj* (*feminist etc*) zaprzysięgły; (*aim*) obrany
**AVP** (*US*) *n abbr* = **assistant vice-president**
**avuncular** [ə'vʌŋkjulə^r] *adj* (*genial*) dobroduszny; (*fatherly*) ojcowski
**AWACS** ['eɪwæks] *n abbr* (= *airborne warning and control system*) (system *m*) AWACS
**await** [ə'weɪt] *vt* oczekiwać na *+acc*; **~ing attention/delivery** (*Comm*) do załatwienia/dostarczenia; **long ~ed** długo oczekiwany
**awake** [ə'weɪk] (*pt* **awoke**, *pp* **awoken** *or* **~ned**) *adj*: **to be ~** nie spać ▹ *vt* budzić (obudzić *perf*) ▹ *vi* budzić się (obudzić się *perf*); **he was still ~** jeszcze nie spał; **to be ~ to** być świadomym *+gen*, zdawać sobie sprawę z *+gen*
**awakening** [ə'weɪknɪŋ] *n* (*of emotion*) przebudzenie *nt*; (*of interest*) rozbudzenie *nt*
**award** [ə'wɔːd] *n* (*prize*) nagroda *f*; (*damages*) odszkodowanie *nt* ▹ *vt* (*prize*) przyznawać (przyznać *perf*); (*damages*) zasądzać (zasądzić *perf*)
**aware** [ə'wɛə^r] *adj*: **~ (of)** (*conscious*) świadomy (*+gen*); (*informed*) zorientowany (w *+loc*); **to become ~ of/that** uświadamiać (uświadomić *perf*) sobie *+acc*/, że; **politically/socially ~** świadomy politycznie/społecznie; **I am fully ~ that** zdaję sobie w pełni sprawę *or* jestem w pełni świadomy, że
**awareness** [ə'wɛənɪs] *n* świadomość *f*; **to develop people's ~ of** rozwijać (rozwinąć *perf*) wśród ludzi świadomość *+gen*
**awash** [ə'wɔʃ] *adj* zalany; (*fig*): **~ with** zalany *+instr*
**away** [ə'weɪ] *adv* (*be situated*) z dala, daleko; (*not present*): **to be ~** być nieobecnym; (*move*): **he walked ~ slowly** odszedł powoli; **two kilometres ~ from** w odległości dwóch kilometrów od *+gen*; **two hours ~ by car** dwie godziny jazdy samochodem; **the exam is two weeks ~** do egzaminu (po)zostały dwa tygodnie; **he's ~ for a week** nie będzie go przez tydzień, wyjechał na tydzień; **she's ~ in Milan** wyjechała do Mediolanu; **to take ~** (*remove*) zabierać (zabrać *perf*); (*subtract*) odejmować (odjąć *perf*); **to work/pedal** *etc* **~** zawzięcie pracować/pedałować *etc*; **to fade/wither ~** (*colour*) blaknąć (wyblaknąć *perf*); (*enthusiasm, light*) wygasać (wygasnąć *perf*); (*sound*) cichnąć (ucichnąć *perf*)
**away game** *n* mecz *m* wyjazdowy *or* na wyjeździe
**awe** [ɔː] *n* respekt *m*; **to be in awe of** czuć respekt przed *+instr*
**awe-inspiring** ['ɔːɪnspaɪərɪŋ] *adj* budzący respekt
**awesome** ['ɔːsəm] *adj* = **awe-inspiring**
**awestruck** ['ɔːstrʌk] *adj* pełen respektu
**awful** ['ɔːfəl] *adj* straszny, okropny; **an ~ lot (of)** strasznie dużo (*+gen*)
**awfully** ['ɔːfəlɪ] *adv* strasznie, okropnie
**awhile** [ə'waɪl] *adv* (przez) chwilę
**awkward** ['ɔːkwəd] *adj* (*person, movement, situation*) niezręczny; (*tool, machine*) niewygodny
**awkwardness** ['ɔːkwədnɪs] *n* niezręczność *f*
**awl** [ɔːl] *n* szydło *nt*
**awning** ['ɔːnɪŋ] *n* (*of tent, caravan*) daszek *m* płócienny; (*of shop, hotel*) markiza *f*
**awoke** [ə'wəuk] *pt of* **awake**
**awoken** [ə'wəukən] *pp of* **awake**
**AWOL** ['eɪwɔl] (*Mil*) *abbr* (= *absent without leave*) nieobecny nieusprawiedliwiony
**awry** [ə'raɪ] *adv*: **to be ~** (*clothes*) być w nieładzie; **to go ~** (*plan*) nie powieść się (*perf*)
**axe**, (*US*) **ax** [æks] *n* siekiera *f*, topór *m* ▹ *vt* robić (zrobić *perf*) cięcia w *+loc*; **to have an axe to grind** (*fig*) kierować się własnym interesem
**axes**[1] ['æksɪz] *npl of* **ax(e)**
**axes**[2] ['æksiːz] *npl of* **axis**
**axiom** ['æksɪəm] *n* aksjomat *m*
**axiomatic** [æksɪəu'mætɪk] *adj* aksjomatyczny
**axis** ['æksɪs] (*pl* **axes**) *n* oś *f*
**axle** ['æksl] (*Aut*) *n* (*also*: **axle-tree**) oś *f*
**aye** [aɪ] *excl* tak ▹ *n*: **the ayes** głosy *pl* „za"
**AYH** *n abbr* = **American Youth Hostels**
**AZ** (*US*: *Post*) *abbr* = **Arizona**
**azalea** [ə'zeɪlɪə] *n* azalia *f*, różanecznik *m*
**Azores** [ə'zɔːz] *npl*: **the ~** Azory *pl*
**AZT** *n abbr* (= *azidothymidine*) AZT *m inv*
**Aztec** ['æztɛk] *n* Aztek(-eczka) *m(f)* ▹ *adj*: **~ civilization/art** cywilizacja *f*/sztuka *f* Azteków
**azure** ['eɪʒə^r] *adj* lazurowy

# Bb

**B¹, b** [bi:] *n* (*letter*) B *nt*, b *nt*; (*Scol*) ≈ dobry *m*; **B for Benjamin,** (*US*) **B for Baker** ≈ B jak Barbara; **B road** (*Brit*) droga drugorzędna
**B²** [bi:] *n* (*Mus*) H *nt*, h *nt*
**b.** *abbr* (= *born*) ur.
**BA** *n abbr* (= *Bachelor of Arts*) *stopień naukowy*; = **British Academy**
**babble** ['bæbl] *vi* (*person*: *confusedly*) bełkotać; (: *thoughtlessly, continuously*) paplać; (*baby*) gaworzyć; (*brook*) szemrać ▷ *n*: **a ~ of voices** gwar *m*
**baboon** [bə'bu:n] *n* pawian *m*
**baby** ['beɪbɪ] *n* (*infant*) niemowlę *nt*; (: *affectionately*) dzidziuś *m*; (*US*: *inf*: *darling*) kochanie *nt*; **~ girl** dziewczynka; **~ boy** chłopczyk; **we're going to have a ~** będziemy mieli dziecko; **listen, ~** słuchaj, kochanie *or* dziecinko
**baby carriage** (*US*) *n* wózek *m* dziecięcy
**baby grand** *n* (*also*: **baby grand piano**) fortepian *m* salonowy
**babyhood** ['beɪbɪhud] *n* niemowlęctwo *nt*
**babyish** ['beɪbɪɪʃ] *adj* dziecinny
**baby-minder** ['beɪbɪ'maɪndə^r] (*Brit*) *n* opiekunka *f* do dziecka (*zajmująca się nim we własnym domu*)
**baby-sit** ['beɪbɪsɪt] *vi* pilnować (popilnować *perf*) dziecka *or* dzieci
**baby-sitter** ['beɪbɪsɪtə^r] *n* osoba *f* do pilnowania dziecka *or* dzieci, baby sitter *m*
**bachelor** ['bætʃələ^r] *n* kawaler *m*; **B~ of Arts/Science** *posiadacz stopnia naukowego odpowiadającego licencjatowi w dziedzinie nauk humanistycznych/ścisłych*; **B~ of Arts/Science degree** *stopień naukowy odpowiadający licencjatowi w dziedzinie nauk humanistycznych/ścisłych*
**bachelorhood** ['bætʃələhud] *n* stan *m* kawalerski
**bachelor party** (*US*) *n* wieczór *m* kawalerski
**back** [bæk] *n* (*of person*) plecy *pl*; (*of animal*) grzbiet *m*; (*of house, car, shirt*) tył *m*; (*of hand*) wierzch *m*; (*of chair*) oparcie *nt*; (*Football*) obrońca *m* ▷ *vt* (*candidate*) popierać (poprzeć *perf*); (*financially*) sponsorować; (*horse*) obstawiać (obstawić *perf*); (*car*) cofać (cofnąć *perf*) ▷ *vi* (*also*: **back up**) cofać się (cofnąć się *perf*) ▷ *cpd* (*payment, rent*) zaległy; (*seat, wheels*) tylny; (*garden*) za domem *post*; (*room*) od podwórza *post* ▷ *adv* do tyłu; **he's ~** wrócił; **throw the ball ~** odrzuć piłkę; **they ran ~** pobiegli z powrotem; **~ to front** (*wear*) tył(em) na przód; (*know*) na wylot; **an index at the ~ of the book** indeks na końcu *or* z tyłu książki; **pin the list on the ~ of the larder door** powieś listę na wewnętrznej stronie drzwi spiżarni; **to break the ~ of a job** (*Brit*) wychodzić (wyjść *perf*) na prostą; **to have one's ~ to the wall** (*fig*) być przypartym do muru; **to take a ~ seat** (*fig*) usuwać się (usunąć się *perf*) na drugi plan; **can I have them ~?** czy mogę je dostać z powrotem?
▸ **back down** *vi* wycofywać się (wycofać się *perf*)
▸ **back on to** *vt fus*: **the house ~s on to the golf course** tył budynku wychodzi na pole golfowe
▸ **back out** *vi* wycofywać się (wycofać się *perf*)
▸ **back up** *vt* (*support*) popierać (poprzeć *perf*); (*Comput*) robić (zrobić *perf*) (zapasową) kopię *+gen*
**backache** ['bækeɪk] *n* ból *m* pleców *or* krzyża
**backbencher** ['bæk'bɛntʃə^r] (*Brit*) *n członek brytyjskiego Parlamentu nie pełniący ważnej funkcji w rządzie ani w partii opozycyjnej i w związku z tym zasiadający w tylnych ławach Izby Gmin*
**backbiting** ['bækbaɪtɪŋ] *n* obgadywanie *nt* (za plecami)
**backbone** ['bækbəun] *n* kręgosłup *m*; (*fig*) odwaga *f*, siła *f* charakteru; **he's the ~ of the organization** jest filarem organizacji
**backchat** ['bæktʃæt] (*Brit*: *inf*) *n* pyskowanie *nt* (*inf*)
**backcloth** ['bækklɔθ] (*Brit*) *n* (*Theat*) kulisa *f* (*usu pl*); (*fig*) tło *nt*
**backcomb** ['bækkəum], (*Brit*) **back-comb** *vt* tapirować (utapirować *perf*)
**backdate** [bæk'deɪt] *vt* antydatować
**backdrop** ['bækdrɔp] *n* = **backcloth**
**backer** ['bækə^r] *n* stronnik(-iczka) *m*(*f*),

zwolennik(-iczka) *m(f)*; *(financial)* sponsor(ka) *m(f)*

**backfire** [bæk'faɪəʳ] *vi (Aut)* strzelać (strzelić *perf*); *(plans)* odnosić (odnieść *perf*) odwrotny skutek

**backgammon** ['bækgæmən] *n* trik-trak *m*

**background** ['bækgraund] *n (lit, fig)* tło *nt*; *(of person: origins)* pochodzenie *nt*; *(: educational)* wykształcenie *nt*; **he's from a working class ~** pochodzi z rodziny robotniczej; **my primary ~ is in marketing** mam doświadczenie głównie w marketingu; **we looked closely into her ~** zbadaliśmy dokładnie jej przeszłość; **against a ~ of** na tle *+gen*; **~ reading (on)** dodatkowa lektura (na temat *+gen*); **~ music** muzyka w tle

**backhand** ['bækhænd] *(Tennis etc) n* bekhend *m*

**backhanded** ['bæk'hændɪd] *adj (fig: compliment)* dwuznaczny

**backhander** ['bæk'hændəʳ] *(Brit: inf) n* łapówka *f*, wziątka *f (inf)*

**backing** ['bækɪŋ] *n (support)* poparcie *nt*; *(: Comm)* sponsorowanie *nt*; *(layer)* podklejka *f*; *(Mus)* akompaniament *m*

**backlash** ['bæklæʃ] *n (fig)* (gwałtowna) reakcja *f (atakująca określony trend, ideologię itp)*

**backlog** ['bæklɔg] *n*: **~ of work** zaległości *pl* w pracy

**back number** *n (of magazine etc)* stary numer *m*

**backpack** ['bækpæk] *n* plecak *m*

**backpacker** ['bækpækəʳ] *n* turysta(-tka) *m(f)* pieszy(-sza) *m(f)*

**back pay** *n* zaległa wypłata *f*

**backpedal** ['bækpɛdl] *vi (fig)* wycofywać się (wycofać się *perf*)

**backside** ['bæksaɪd] *(inf) n* tyłek *m (inf)*

**backslash** ['bækslæʃ] *n* ukośnik *m* wsteczny

**backslide** ['bækslaɪd] *vi* powracać (powrócić *perf*) na złą drogę

**backspace** ['bækspeɪs] *vi (in typing)* cofać się (cofnąć się *perf*) *(za pomocą cofacza)*

**backstage** [bæk'steɪdʒ] *adv (be)* za kulisami; *(go)* za kulisy

**back-street** ['bækstri:t] *n* uliczka *f (w uboższej części miasta)* ▷ *cpd*: **backstreet abortion** pokątna aborcja *f*

**backstroke** ['bækstrəuk] *n* styl *m* grzbietowy

**backtrack** ['bæktræk] *vi (fig)* wycofywać się (wycofać się *perf*)

**backup** ['bækʌp] *adj (staff, services)* pomocniczy; *(Comput)* zapasowy ▷ *n (people, machines)* zaplecze *nt*; *(also:* **backup file***)* zbiór *m* zapasowy *or* rezerwowy, kopia *f* zapasowa zbioru

**backward** ['bækwəd] *adj (movement)* do tyłu post; *(pej: country, person)* zacofany; *(fig)*: **a ~ step** krok *m* wstecz

**backwards** ['bækwədz] *adv (move, go)* do tyłu; *(fall)* na plecy; *(walk)* tyłem; *(fig)* wstecz; **~ and forwards** tam i z powrotem; **to know sth ~** *or (US)* **~ and forwards** znać coś na wylot

**backwater** ['bækwɔ:təʳ] *n (fig)* zaścianek *m*

**backyard** [bæk'jɑ:d] *n* podwórko *nt (za domem)*

**bacon** ['beɪkən] *n* bekon *m*

**bacteria** [bæk'tɪərɪə] *npl* bakterie *pl*

**bacteriology** [bæktɪərɪ'ɔlədʒɪ] *n* bakteriologia *f*

**bad** [bæd] *adj* zły; *(naughty)* niedobry, niegrzeczny; *(poor: work, health etc)* słaby; *(mistake, accident, injury)* poważny; **he has a bad back** ma chory kręgosłup; **to go bad** *(meat)* psuć się (zepsuć się *perf*); *(milk)* kwaśnieć (skwaśnieć *perf*); **I feel very bad about it** czuję się podle z tego powodu; **in bad faith** w złej wierze; **to be bad for** szkodzić *+dat*; **he's bad at maths** jest słaby z matematyki; **not bad** nieźle

**bad debt** *n* nieściągalny dług *m*

**bade** [bæd] *pt of* **bid**

**badge** [bædʒ] *n* odznaka *f*; *(with name, function)* identyfikator *m*; *(stick-on)* naklejka *f*; *(sew-on)* naszywka *f*; *(fig)* oznaka *f*

**badger** ['bædʒəʳ] *n* borsuk *m* ▷ *vt* wiercić dziurę w brzuchu *+dat*

**badly** ['bædlɪ] *adv* źle; **~ wounded** poważnie ranny; **he needs the money ~** bardzo potrzebuje tych pieniędzy; **things are going ~** sprawy idą źle; **they are ~ off (for money)** źle im się powodzi

**bad-mannered** ['bæd'mænəd] *adj* źle wychowany

**badminton** ['bædmɪntən] *n* badminton *m*, kometka *f*

**bad-tempered** ['bæd'tɛmpəd] *adj*: **to be ~** *(by nature)* mieć nieprzyjemne *or* przykre usposobienie; *(on one occasion)* być w złym humorze

**baffle** ['bæfl] *vt (puzzle)* zdumiewać (zdumieć *perf*), wprawiać (wprawić *perf*) w zdumienie; *(confuse)* wprawiać (wprawić *perf*) w zakłopotanie

**baffling** ['bæflɪŋ] *adj*: **I find his behaviour ~** jego zachowanie zdumiewa mnie; **a ~ problem** kłopotliwy problem

**bag** [bæg] *n (large)* torba *f*; *(small)* torebka *f*; *(also:* **handbag***)* (damska) torebka *f*; *(satchel)* tornister *m*; *(suitcase)* walizka *f*; *(pej: woman)* babsztyl *m (pej)*; **bags of** *(inf)* (cała) masa *+gen (inf)*; **to pack one's bags** pakować (spakować *perf*) manatki; **bags under the eyes** worki pod oczami ▷ *vt (animal, bird)* upolować *(perf)*

**bagful** ['bægful] *n* (pełna) torba *f*

**baggage** ['bægɪdʒ] *n* bagaż *m*

b

**baggage car** (US) *n* wagon *m* bagażowy
**baggage claim** *n (at airport)* odbiór *m* bagażu
**baggy** ['bægɪ] *adj* workowaty
**Baghdad** [bæg'dæd] *n* Bagdad *m*
**bagpipes** ['bægpaɪps] *npl* dudy *pl*
**bag-snatcher** ['bægsnætʃəʳ] (Brit) *n* złodziej(ka) *m(f)* torebek
**Bahamas** [bə'hɑ:məz] *npl*: **the ~** Wyspy *pl* Bahama
**Bahrain** [bɑ:'reɪn] *n* Bahrajn *m*
**bail** [beɪl] *n (Jur: payment)* kaucja *f*; *(: release)* zwolnienie *nt* za kaucją; **to grant ~ (to sb)** wyrażać (wyrazić *perf*) zgodę na zwolnienie (kogoś) za kaucją; **he was released on ~** został zwolniony za kaucją ▷ *vi (also:* **bail out**: *on boat)* wybierać (wybrać *perf*) wodę; *see also* **bale**
▸ **bail out** *vt (prisoner)* wpłacać (wpłacić *perf*) kaucję za *+acc*; *(friend, firm)* poratować *(perf)* (finansowo)
**bailiff** ['beɪlɪf] *n (Brit: of estate)* zarządca *m*; *(Jur: Brit)* ≈ komornik *m*; *(: esp US) niski rangą urzędnik sądowy pełniący funkcję gońca, który zajmuje się więźniami i pilnuje porządku*
**bait** [beɪt] *n* przynęta *f* ▷ *vt (tease)* drażnić; **to ~ a hook** zakładać (założyć *perf*) przynętę na haczyk
**bake** [beɪk] *vt (Culin)* piec (upiec *perf*); *(Tech)* wypalać (wypalić *perf*) ▷ *vi (bread etc)* piec się; *(person)* piec
**baked beans** [beɪkt-] *npl fasola z puszki w sosie pomidorowym*
**baker** ['beɪkəʳ] *n* piekarz *m*
**baker's dozen** *n* trzynaście *num*
**bakery** ['beɪkərɪ] *n* piekarnia *f*
**baking** ['beɪkɪŋ] *n (act)* pieczenie *nt*; *(food)* wypieki *pl* ▷ *adj (inf)* bardzo gorący; **a ~ hot day** upalny *or* skwarny dzień
**baking powder** *n* proszek *m* do pieczenia
**baking tin** *n (for cake)* forma *f* do pieczenia; *(for meat)* brytfanna *f*
**baking tray** *n* blacha *f* do pieczenia
**balaclava** [bælə'klɑ:və] *n (also:* **balaclava helmet**) kominiarka *f*
**balance** ['bæləns] *n (equilibrium)* równowaga *f*; *(of account: sum)* stan *m* konta; *(: remainder)* saldo *nt* rachunku; *(scales)* waga *f* ▷ *vt (budget)* bilansować (zbilansować *perf*); *(account)* zamykać (zamknąć *perf*); *(pros and cons)* rozważać (rozważyć *perf*); *(make equal, compensate)* równoważyć (zrównoważyć *perf*) ▷ *vi* balansować, utrzymywać równowagę; **on ~** po (głębszym) namyśle; **~ of trade/payments** bilans handlowy/płatniczy; **~ carried forward** *(Comm)* kwota do przeniesienia; **~ brought forward** *(Comm)* kwota z przeniesienia; **to ~ the books** *(Comm)* zamykać (zamknąć *perf*) księgi; **an ashtray was ~d on the arm of the chair** na poręczy fotela stała popielniczka
**balanced** ['bælənst] *adj (report, account)* wyważony; *(personality)* zrównoważony; *(diet)* pełnowartościowy
**balance sheet** *n* zestawienie *nt* bilansowe
**balcony** ['bælkənɪ] *n* balkon *m*
**bald** [bɔ:ld] *adj (person, head, tyre)* łysy; *(lie)* jawny; *(question)* bezceremonialny, bez ogródek *post*
**baldness** ['bɔ:ldnɪs] *n* łysina *f*
**bale** [beɪl] *n* bela *f*
▸ **bale out** *vi (of a plane)* wyskakiwać (wyskoczyć *perf*) ze spadochronem ▷ *vt (water)* wybierać (wybrać *perf*); *(boat)* wybierać (wybrać *perf*) wodę z *+gen*
**Balearic Islands** [bælɪ'ærɪk-] *npl*: **the ~** Baleary *pl*
**baleful** ['beɪlful] *adj (glance)* złowrogi; *(influence)* zły
**balk** [bɔ:k] *vi*: **to ~ (at)** *(person)* wzdragać się (przed *+instr*); *(horse)* zatrzymywać się (zatrzymać się *perf*) (przed *+instr*)
**Balkan** ['bɔ:lkən] *adj* bałkański ▷ *n*: **the ~s** Bałkany *pl*
**ball** [bɔ:l] *n (for football, tennis)* piłka *f*; *(of wool, string)* kłębek *m*; *(dance)* bal *m*; **to set the ~ rolling** *(fig)* puszczać (puścić *perf*) mechanizm w ruch; **to play ~ (with sb)** *(fig)* współpracować (z kimś); **to be on the ~** *(fig: competent)* znać się na rzeczy; *(alert)* mieć oczy otwarte; **the ~ is in your court** *(fig)* teraz twój ruch
**ballad** ['bæləd] *n* ballada *f*
**ballast** ['bæləst] *n* balast *m*
**ball bearings** *npl* łożysko *nt* kulkowe
**ballcock** ['bɔ:lkɔk] *n* zawór *m* kulowy
**ballerina** [bælə'ri:nə] *n* balerina *f*
**ballet** ['bæleɪ] *n* balet *m*
**ballet dancer** *n (male)* tancerz *m* baletowy; *(female)* tancerka *f* baletowa, baletnica *f*
**ballistic** [bə'lɪstɪk] *adj* balistyczny
**ballistic missile** *n* pocisk *m* balistyczny
**ballistics** [bə'lɪstɪks] *n* balistyka *f*
**balloon** [bə'lu:n] *n (child's)* balon *m*, balonik *m*; *(hot air balloon)* balon *m*; *(in comic strip)* dymek *m*
**balloonist** [bə'lu:nɪst] *n* pilot *m* balonowy, baloniarz *m*
**ballot** ['bælət] *n* tajne głosowanie *nt*
**ballot box** *n* urna *f* wyborcza; *(fig)* wybory *pl*
**ballot paper** *n* kartka *f* do głosowania
**ballpark** ['bɔ:lpɑ:k] (US) *n* boisko *nt* baseballowe
**ballpark figure** (US: *inf*) *n* orientacyjna liczba *f*

**ballpoint (pen)** ['bɔːlpɔɪnt(-)] *n* długopis *m*
**ballroom** ['bɔːlrum] *n* sala *f* balowa
**balls** [bɔːlz] (*inf!: testicles*) *npl* jaja *pl* (*inf!*)
**balm** [bɑːm] *n* balsam *m*
**balmy** ['bɑːmɪ] *adj* balsamiczny; (*Brit: inf*) = **barmy**
**BALPA** ['bælpə] *n abbr* (= *British Airline Pilots' Association*) *związek zawodowy pilotów*
**balsam** ['bɔːlsəm] *n* balsam *m*
**balsa (wood)** ['bɔːlsə-] *n* balsa *f*
**Baltic** [bɔːltɪk] *n*: **the ~ (Sea)** Bałtyk *m*, Morze *nt* Bałtyckie
**balustrade** [bæləs'treɪd] *n* balustrada *f*
**bamboo** [bæm'buː] *n* bambus *m*
**bamboozle** [bæm'buːzl] (*inf*) *vt*: **to ~ sb into sth** wrabiać (wrobić *perf*) kogoś w coś (*inf*)
**ban** [bæn] *n* zakaz *m* ▷ *vt* zakazywać (zakazać *perf*) +*gen*; **he was banned from driving** (*Brit*) odebrano mu prawo jazdy
**banal** [bə'nɑːl] *adj* banalny
**banana** [bə'nɑːnə] *n* banan *m*
**band** [bænd] *n* (*group*) banda *f* (*pej*), grupa *f*; (*rock*) grupa *f*, zespół *m*; (*jazz, military etc*) orkiestra *f*; (*strip, stripe*) pasek *m*, wstążka *f*; (*range*) przedział *m*; (*: of frequency*) pasmo *nt*, zakres *m*
▸ **band together** *vi* skrzykiwać się (skrzyknąć się *perf*)
**bandage** ['bændɪdʒ] *n* bandaż *m* ▷ *vt* (*wound, leg*) bandażować (zabandażować *perf*); (*person*) opatrywać (opatrzyć *perf*)
**Band-Aid**® ['bændeɪd] (*US*) *n* plaster *m*
**bandit** ['bændɪt] *n* bandyta *m*
**bandstand** ['bændstænd] *n* estrada *f*
**bandwagon** ['bændwægən] *n*: **to jump on the ~** (*fig*) przyłączać się (przyłączyć się *perf*) do większości
**bandy** ['bændɪ] *vt* (*jokes, ideas*) wymieniać (wymienić *perf*); (*insults*) obrzucać się +*instr*
▸ **bandy about** *vt* szafować +*instr*
**bandy-legged** ['bændɪ'lɛgɪd] *adj* krzywonogi
**bane** [beɪn] *n*: **it/he is the ~ of my life** to/on jest zmorą mojego życia
**bang** [bæŋ] *n* (*of door*) trzaśnięcie *nt*, trzask *m*; (*of gun, exhaust*) huk *m*, wystrzał *m*; (*blow*) uderzenie *nt*, walnięcie *nt* ▷ *vt* (*door*) trzaskać (trzasnąć *perf*) +*instr*; (*one's head etc*) uderzać (uderzyć *perf*) +*instr*, walić (walnąć *perf*) +*instr* ▷ *vi* (*door*) trzaskać (trzasnąć *perf*); (*fireworks*) strzelać (strzelić *perf*) ▷ *adv*: **to be ~ on time** (*Brit: inf*) być co do minuty; **to ~ at the door** walić w drzwi; **to ~ into sth** wpaść (*perf*) na coś; **~! ~! you're dead!** pif-paf! nie żyjesz!
**banger** ['bæŋəʳ] (*Brit: inf*) *n* (*car*) gruchot *m*; (*sausage*) kiełbaska *f*; (*firework*) petarda *f*
**Bangkok** [bæŋ'kɔk] *n* Bangkok *m*
**Bangladesh** [bæŋglə'dɛʃ] *n* Bangladesz *m*
**bangle** ['bæŋgl] *n* bransoletka *f*
**bangs** [bæŋz] (*US*) *npl* grzywka *f*
**banish** ['bænɪʃ] *vt* wygnać (*perf*), skazywać (skazać *perf*) na banicję *or* wygnanie
**banister(s)** ['bænɪstə(z)] *n*(*pl*) poręcz *f*, balustrada *f*
**banjo** ['bændʒəu] (*pl* **~es** *or* **~s**) *n* bandżo *nt inv*, banjo *nt inv*
**bank** [bæŋk] *n* bank *m*; (*of river, lake*) brzeg *m*; (*of earth*) skarpa *f*, nasyp *m*; (*of switches*) rząd *m* ▷ *vi* (*Aviat*) przechylać się (przechylić się *perf*); (*Comm*): **they ~ with Pitt's** mają konto w Pitt's
▸ **bank on** *vt fus* liczyć na +*acc*
**bank account** *n* konto *nt* bankowe
**bank card** *n* karta *f* bankowa
**bank charges** (*Brit*) *npl* koszty *pl* bankowe
**bank draft** *n* przekaz *m* bankowy
**banker** ['bæŋkəʳ] *n* bankier *m*
**banker's card** (*Brit*) *n* = **bank card**
**banker's order** (*Brit*) *n* polecenie *nt* wypłaty, przekaz *m* bankowy
**bank giro** *n* rozliczenie *nt* bezgotówkowe, żyro *nt*
**bank holiday** (*Brit*) *n jeden z ustawowo ustalonych dni, w które nieczynne są banki i wiele innych instytucji*
**banking** ['bæŋkɪŋ] *n* bankowość *f*
**banking hours** *npl* godziny *pl* otwarcia banku
**bank loan** *n* pożyczka *f* bankowa
**bank manager** *n* dyrektor *m* banku
**banknote** ['bæŋknəut] *n* banknot *m*
**bank rate** *n* stopa *f* procentowa od pożyczki bankowej
**bankrupt** ['bæŋkrʌpt] *adj* niewypłacalny ▷ *n* bankrut *m*; **to go ~** bankrutować (zbankrutować *perf*); **to be ~** być w stanie bankructwa, być bankrutem
**bankruptcy** ['bæŋkrʌptsɪ] *n* (*Comm*) bankructwo *nt*, upadłość *f*; (*fig*) upadek *m*, ruina *f*
**bank statement** *n* wyciąg *m* z konta
**banner** ['bænəʳ] *n* (*for decoration, advertising*) transparent *m*; (*in demonstration*) sztandar *m*, transparent *m*; (*Comput*) banner *n*, nagłówek *m*
**banner headline** *n* całostronicowy tytuł *m*
**bannister(s)** ['bænɪstə(z)] *n*(*pl*) = **banister(s)**
**banns** [bænz] *npl* zapowiedzi *pl*
**banquet** ['bæŋkwɪt] *n* bankiet *m*
**bantamweight** ['bæntəmweɪt] *n* waga *f* kogucia
**banter** ['bæntəʳ] *n* żarty *pl*, przekomarzanie się *nt*
**BAOR** *n abbr* = **British Army of the Rhine**
**baptism** ['bæptɪzəm] *n* chrzest *m*
**Baptist** ['bæptɪst] *n* baptysta(-tka) *m*(*f*)

**baptize** [bæp'taɪz] *vt* chrzcić (ochrzcić *perf*)
**bar** [bɑːʳ] *n* (*place for drinking*) bar *m*; (*counter*) kontuar *m*; (*of metal etc*) sztaba *f*; (*on window etc*) krata *f*; (*of soap*) kostka *f*; (*of chocolate*) tabliczka *f*; (*obstacle*) przeszkoda *f*; (*prohibition*) zakaz *m*; (*Mus*) takt *m* ▷ *vt* (*way, road*) zagradzać (zagrodzić *perf*); (*door, window*) barykadować (zabarykadować *perf*), ryglować (zaryglować *perf*); (*person*) odmawiać (odmówić *perf*) wstępu *+dat*; (*activity*) zabraniać (zabronić *perf*) *or* zakazywać (zakazać *perf*) *+gen*; **behind bars** za kratkami; **the Bar** (*Jur*) adwokatura; **bar none** bez wyjątku
**Barbados** [bɑː'beɪdɔs] *n* Barbados *m*
**barbaric** [bɑː'bærɪk] *adj* barbarzyński
**barbarous** ['bɑːbərəs] *adj* barbarzyński
**barbecue** ['bɑːbɪkjuː] *n* (*cooking device*) grill *m* (*ogrodowy*); (*meal, party*) przyjęcie *nt* z grillem
**barbed wire** ['bɑːbd-] *n* drut *m* kolczasty
**barber** ['bɑːbəʳ] *n* fryzjer *m* męski
**barbiturate** [bɑː'bɪtjurɪt] *n* barbituran *m*
**Barcelona** [bɑːsə'ləunə] *n* Barcelona *f*
**bar chart** *n* wykres *m* słupkowy, histogram *m*
**bar code** *n* (*on goods*) kod *m* kreskowy *or* paskowy
**bare** [bɛəʳ] *adj* (*body, trees, countryside*) nagi; (*feet*) bosy; (*minimum*) absolutny; (*necessities*) podstawowy ▷ *vt* obnażać (obnażyć *perf*); **the ~ essentials** najpotrzebniejsze rzeczy; **to ~ one's soul** odsłaniać (odsłonić *perf*) duszę
**bareback** ['bɛəbæk] *adv*: **to ride ~** jechać na oklep
**barefaced** ['bɛəfeɪst] *adj* bezczelny, bezwstydny
**barefoot** ['bɛəfut] *adj* bosy ▷ *adv* boso, na bosaka
**bareheaded** [bɛə'hɛdɪd] *adj* z gołą głową *post*, bez nakrycia głowy *post* ▷ *adv* z gołą głową, bez nakrycia głowy
**barely** ['bɛəlɪ] *adv* ledwo, ledwie
**Barents Sea** ['bærənts-] *n*: **the ~** Morze *nt* Barentsa
**bargain** ['bɑːgɪn] *n* (*deal, agreement*) umowa *f*, transakcja *f*; (*good buy*) okazja *f* ▷ *vi*: **to ~ (with sb)** (*negotiate*) negocjować (z kimś); (*haggle*) targować się (z kimś); **to drive a hard ~** twardo walczyć o swoje; **into the ~** w dodatku, na dodatek
▸ **bargain for** *vt fus*: **he got more than he ~ed for** tego się nie spodziewał
**bargaining** ['bɑːgənɪŋ] *n* negocjacje *pl*
**barge** [bɑːdʒ] *n* barka *f*
▸ **barge in** *vi* (*enter*) włazić (wleźć *perf*) (*inf*), pakować się (wpakować się *perf*) (*inf*); (*interrupt*) wtrącać się (wtrącić się *perf*)
▸ **barge into** *vt fus* (*room*) włazić (wleźć *perf*) do *+gen* (*inf*); (*person*) wpadać (wpaść *perf*) na *+acc*
**bargepole** ['bɑːdʒpəul] *n*: **I wouldn't touch it with a ~** (*fig*) nie chcę mieć z tym nic wspólnego, brzydzę się tym
**baritone** ['bærɪtəun] *n* baryton *m*
**barium meal** ['bɛərɪəm-] *n* papka *f* barytowa (*podawana przy prześwietleniach przewodu pokarmowego*)
**bark** [bɑːk] *n* (*of tree*) kora *f*; (*of dog*) szczekanie *nt* ▷ *vi* szczekać (szczeknąć *perf or* zaszczekać *perf*); **she's ~ing up the wrong tree** (*fig*) w ten sposób nic nie wskóra
**barley** ['bɑːlɪ] *n* jęczmień *m*
**barley sugar** *n twardy cukierek z parzonego cukru*
**barmaid** ['bɑːmeɪd] *n* barmanka *f*
**barman** ['bɑːmən] (*irreg: like* **man**) *n* barman *m*
**barmy** ['bɑːmɪ] (*Brit: inf*) *adj* kopnięty (*inf*), stuknięty (*inf*)
**barn** [bɑːn] *n* stodoła *f*
**barnacle** ['bɑːnəkl] *n* pąkla *f* (*gatunek skorupiaka wodnego*)
**barometer** [bə'rɔmɪtəʳ] *n* barometr *m*
**baron** ['bærən] *n* (*nobleman*) baron *m*; (*businessman*) magnat *m*
**baroness** ['bærənɪs] *n* baronowa *f*
**baronet** ['bærənɪt] *n* baronet *m*
**barracks** ['bærəks] *npl* koszary *pl*
**barrage** ['bærɑːʒ] *n* (*Mil*) ogień *m* zaporowy; (*dam*) zapora *f*; (*fig: of criticism, questions*) fala *f*
**barrel** ['bærəl] *n* (*of wine, beer*) beczka *f*, beczułka *f*; (*of oil*) baryłka *f*; (*of gun*) lufa *f*
**barrel organ** *n* katarynka *f*
**barren** ['bærən] *adj* jałowy
**barricade** [bærɪ'keɪd] *n* barykada *f* ▷ *vt* barykadować (zabarykadować *perf*); **to ~ o.s. (in)** zabarykadować się (*perf*)
**barrier** ['bærɪəʳ] *n* (*at frontier*) szlaban *m*, rogatka *f*; (*at entrance*) bramka *f*; (*Brit: also:* **crash barrier**) barierka *f*; (*fig: to progress, communication etc*) bariera *f*, przeszkoda *f*
**barrier cream** (*Brit*) *n* krem *m* ochronny
**barring** ['bɑːrɪŋ] *prep* wyjąwszy *+acc*, o ile nie będzie *+gen*
**barrister** ['bærɪstəʳ] (*Brit*) *n* adwokat(ka) *m(f)*, obrońca(-ńczyni) *m(f)*
**barrow** ['bærəu] *n* (*wheelbarrow*) taczka *f*; (*for selling vegetables etc*) wózek *m*
**bar stool** *n* stołek *m* barowy
**Bart.** (*Brit*) *abbr* (= *baronet*) *tytuł szlachecki*
**bartender** ['bɑːtɛndəʳ] (*US*) *n* barman *m*
**barter** ['bɑːtəʳ] *vt* wymieniać (wymienić *perf*), wymieniać się (wymienić się *perf*) *+instr* ▷ *n* wymiana *f* (towarowa)
**base** [beɪs] *n* (*of post, tree, system of ideas*) podstawa *f*; (*of cup, box*) spód *m*; (*of paint, make up*) podkład *m*; (*for military, individual,*

*organization)* baza *f* ▷ *vt*: **to ~ sth on** opierać (oprzeć *perf*) coś na *+loc* ▷ *adj* *(mind, thoughts)* podły, nikczemny; **to be ~d at** bazować w *+loc* *or* na *+loc*; **I'm ~d in London** mam siedzibę w Londynie; **a Paris-~d firm** firma z siedzibą w Paryżu; **coffee-~d** na bazie kawy

**baseball** ['beɪsbɔ:l] *n* baseball *m*

**baseboard** ['beɪsbɔ:d] (US) *n* listwa *f* przypodłogowa

**base camp** *n* baza *f*, główny obóz *m*

**Basel** [bɑ:l] *n* = **Basle**

**basement** ['beɪsmənt] *n* suterena *f*

**base rate** *(Fin)* *n* stopa *f* bazowa oprocentowania kredytu

**bases**[1] ['beɪsɪz] *npl of* **base**

**bases**[2] ['beɪsi:z] *npl of* **basis**

**bash** [bæʃ] *(inf)* *vt* walić (walnąć *perf*) *(inf)* ▷ *vi*: **to ~ into/against** walnąć *(perf)* w *+acc* *(inf)* ▷ *n*: **I'll have a ~ at it** *(Brit: inf)* przymierzę się do tego

▸ **bash up** *vt* *(car etc)* obijać (poobijać *perf*)

**bashful** ['bæʃful] *adj* wstydliwy, nieśmiały

**bashing** ['bæʃɪŋ] *n*: **Paki-/queer-~** *(inf)* nagonka *f* na Pakistańczyków/homoseksualistów

**BASIC** ['beɪsɪk] *(Comput)* *n* (język) BASIC *m*

**basic** ['beɪsɪk] *adj* *(problem)* zasadniczy, podstawowy; *(principles, wage, knowledge)* podstawowy; *(facilities)* prymitywny

**basically** ['beɪsɪklɪ] *adv* *(fundamentally)* zasadniczo; *(in fact, put simply)* w zasadzie

**basic rate** *n* *(of tax)* stopa *f* podstawowa; *(of pay)* stawka *f* zasadnicza

**basics** ['beɪsɪks] *npl*: **the ~** podstawy *pl*

**basil** ['bæzl] *n* bazylia *f*

**basin** ['beɪsn] *n* *(vessel)* miednica *f*; *(Brit: for food)* miska *f*; *(: bigger)* misa *f*; *(also:* **wash basin***)* umywalka *f*; *(of river)* dorzecze *nt*; *(of lake)* basen *m*

**basis** ['beɪsɪs] *(pl* **bases***)* *n* podstawa *f*; **on a part-time ~** na niecałym etacie; **on a voluntary ~** na zasadzie dobrowolności; **on the ~ of what you've said** na podstawie tego, co powiedziałeś

**bask** [bɑ:sk] *vi*: **to ~ in the sun** wygrzewać się na słońcu

**basket** ['bɑ:skɪt] *n* kosz *m*; *(smaller)* koszyk *m*

**basketball** ['bɑ:skɪtbɔ:l] *n* koszykówka *f*

**basketball player** *n* koszykarz(-arka) *m(f)*

**Basle** [bɑ:l] *n* Bazylea *f*

**Basque** [bæsk] *adj* baskijski ▷ *n* *(person)* Bask(ijka) *m(f)*; *(Ling)* (język *m*) baskijski

**bass** [beɪs] *n* *(singer)* bas *m*; *(part)* partia *f* basowa; *(also:* **bass guitar***)* gitara *f* basowa; *(on radio etc)* niskie tony *pl*, basy *pl*

**bass clef** *n* klucz *m* basowy

**bassoon** [bə'su:n] *n* fagot *m*

**bastard** ['bɑ:stəd] *n* *(offspring)* bękart *m*; *(inf!)* gnój *m* *(inf!)*

**baste** [beɪst] *vt* *(Culin)* polewać (polać *perf*) tłuszczem; *(Sewing)* fastrygować (sfastrygować *perf*)

**bastion** ['bæstɪən] *n* *(fig)* bastion *m*

**bat** [bæt] *n* *(Zool)* nietoperz *m*; *(for cricket, baseball)* kij *m*; *(Brit: for table tennis)* rakieta *f*, rakietka *f* ▷ *vt*: **he didn't bat an eyelid** nawet nie mrugnął; **off one's own bat** z własnej woli *or* inicjatywy

**batch** [bætʃ] *n* *(of bread)* wypiek *m*; *(of letters, papers)* plik *m*; *(of applicants)* grupa *f*; *(of work)* porcja *f*; *(of goods)* partia *f*

**batch processing** *(Comput)* *n* przetwarzanie *nt* partiowe

**bated** ['beɪtɪd] *adj*: **with ~ breath** z zapartym tchem

**bath** [bɑ:θ] *n* *(bathtub)* wanna *f*; *(act of bathing)* kąpiel *f* ▷ *vt* kąpać (wykąpać *perf*); **to have a ~** brać (wziąć *perf*) kąpiel, kąpać się (wykąpać się *perf*); *see also* **baths**

**bathe** [beɪð] *vi* *(swim)* kąpać się (wykąpać się *perf*), pływać (popływać *perf*); *(US: have a bath)* brać (wziąć *perf*) kąpiel, kąpać się (wykąpać się *perf*) ▷ *vt* *(wound)* przemywać (przemyć *perf*); *(fig: in light, love etc)* skąpać *(perf)*

**bather** ['beɪðə'] *n* kąpiący(-ca) się *m(f)*

**bathing** ['beɪðɪŋ] *n* kąpiel *f*

**bathing cap** *n* czepek *m* (kąpielowy)

**bathing costume**, (US) **bathing suit** *n* kostium *m* kąpielowy

**bath mat** *n* mata *f* łazienkowa

**bathrobe** ['bɑ:θrəub] *n* szlafrok *m* kąpielowy

**bathroom** ['bɑ:θrum] *n* łazienka *f*

**baths** [bɑ:ðz] *npl* kryta pływalnia *f*, kryty basen *m*

**bath towel** *n* ręcznik *m* kąpielowy

**bathtub** ['bɑ:θtʌb] *n* wanna *f*

**batman** ['bætmən] *(Brit: Mil)* *(irreg: like* **man***)* *n* ordynans *m*

**baton** ['bætən] *n* *(Mus)* batuta *f*; *(Athletics)* pałeczka *f* (sztafetowa); *(policeman's)* pałka *f*

**battalion** [bə'tælɪən] *n* batalion *m*

**batten** ['bætn] *n* *(Carpentry)* listwa *f*; *(Naut)* listwa *f* żagla

▸ **batten down** *vt*: **to ~ down the hatches** *(Naut)* zamykać (zamknąć *perf*) luki

**batter** ['bætə'] *vt* *(child, wife)* maltretować, bić; *(wind, rain)* targać *or* miotać *+instr* ▷ *n* *(Culin)* panier *m*

**battered** ['bætəd] *adj* *(hat, car)* sponiewierany; **~ wife** maltretowana żona

**battering ram** ['bætərɪŋ-] *n* taran *m*

**battery** ['bætərɪ] *n* *(for torch, radio etc)* bateria *f*; *(Aut)* akumulator *m*; *(of tests)* zestaw *m*, seria *f*; *(of cameras)* zespół *m*

**battery charger** *n* prostownik *m* do ładowania akumulatorów
**battery farming** *n* hodowla *f* fermowa
**battle** ['bætl] *n* (*Mil*) bitwa *f*; (*fig*) wojna *f* ▷ *vi* walczyć; **that's half the ~** to połowa sukcesu; **we're fighting a losing ~** toczymy beznadziejną walkę; **it's a losing ~** to jest beznadziejna walka
**battledress** ['bætldrɛs] *n* mundur *m* polowy
**battlefield** ['bætlfi:ld] *n* pole *nt* bitwy *or* walki
**battlements** ['bætlmənts] *npl* blanki *pl*
**battleship** ['bætlʃɪp] *n* pancernik *m*
**bauble** ['bɔ:bl] *n* błyskotka *f*, świecidełko *nt*
**baud** [bɔ:d] (*Comput*) *n* bod *m*
**baud rate** *n* szybkość *f* transmisji danych
**baulk** [bɔ:lk] *vi* = **balk**
**bauxite** ['bɔ:ksaɪt] *n* boksyt *m*
**Bavaria** [bə'vɛərɪə] *n* Bawaria *f*
**Bavarian** [bə'vɛərɪən] *adj* bawarski ▷ *n* Bawarczyk(-rka) *m(f)*
**bawdy** ['bɔ:dɪ] *adj* rubaszny, sprośny
**bawl** [bɔ:l] *vi* drzeć się (rozedrzeć się *perf*), ryczeć (ryknąć *perf*)
**bay** [beɪ] *n* zatoka *f*; (*Brit: for parking*) zatoczka *f*; (*: for loading*) podjazd *m*; (*horse*) gniadosz *m*; **to hold sb at bay** trzymać kogoś na dystans
**bay leaf** *n* liść *m or* listek *m* bobkowy *or* laurowy
**bayonet** ['beɪənɪt] *n* bagnet *m*
**bay tree** *n* wawrzyn *m*, laur *m*
**bay window** *n* okno *nt* wykuszowe
**bazaar** [bə'zɑ:ʳ] *n* (*market*) bazar *m*, jarmark *m*; (*fete*) kiermasz *m* dobroczynny
**bazooka** [bə'zu:kə] *n* pancerzownica *f*
**BB** (*Brit*) *n abbr* (= *Boys' Brigade*) *organizacja chłopięca*
**B & B** *n abbr* = **bed and breakfast**
**BBB** (*US*) *n abbr* (= *Better Business Bureau*) *biuro broniące praw konsumentów*
**BBC** *n abbr* (= *British Broadcasting Corporation*) BBC *nt inv*
**BC** *adv abbr* (= *before Christ*) p.n.e. ▷ *abbr* (*Canada*) = **British Columbia**
**BCG** *n abbr* (= *Bacillus Calmette-Guérin*) BCG *nt inv*
**BD** *n abbr* (= *Bachelor of Divinity*) *stopień naukowy*
**B/D** *abbr* = **bank draft**
**BDS** *n abbr* (= *Bachelor of Dental Surgery*) *stopień naukowy*

 KEYWORD

**be** [bi:] (*pt* **was, were**, *pp* **been**) *aux vb* **1** (*in continuous tenses*): **what are you doing?** co robisz?; **it is raining** pada (deszcz); **they're coming tomorrow** przyjeżdżają jutro; **I've been waiting for hours** czekam od dobrych paru godzin
**2** (*forming passives*) być, zostać (*perf*); **she was admired** była podziwiana; **he was killed** został zabity; **the thief was nowhere to be seen** złodzieja nigdzie nie było widać
**3** (*in tag questions*) prawda; **he's good-looking, isn't he?** jest przystojny, prawda?; **she's back again, is she?** a więc znów jest z powrotem?
**4** (*+to +infin*): **the house is to be sold** dom ma zostać sprzedany; **you are to report to the boss** masz się zgłosić do szefa; **he's not to open it** on ma tego nie otwierać
▷ *vb +complement* **1** być; **I'm English** jestem Anglikiem; **I am hot/cold** jest mi gorąco/zimno; **2 and 2 are 4** 2 i 2 jest 4; **be careful** bądź ostrożny
**2** (*of health*) czuć się; **how are you?** jak się czujesz?; **he's very ill** jest bardzo chory
**3** (*of age*): **how old are you?** ile masz lat?; **I'm sixteen (years old)** mam szesnaście lat
**4** (*cost*) kosztować; **how much was the dinner?** ile kosztował obiad?; **that'll be 5 pounds please** to będzie (razem) 5 funtów
▷ *vi* **1** (*exist, occur etc*) istnieć; **is there a God?** czy istnieje Bóg?; **so be it** niech tak będzie; **be that as it may** tak czy owak
**2** (*referring to place*) być; **I won't be here tomorrow** jutro mnie tu nie będzie; **where have you been?** gdzie byłeś?
▷ *impers vb* **1** (*referring to time, distance, weather*) być; **it's five o'clock** jest (godzina) piąta; **it's the 28th of April** jest 28 kwietnia; **it's 10 km to the village** do wsi jest 10 km; **it's too hot/cold** jest za gorąco/zimno
**2** (*emphatic*): **it's only me** to tylko ja; **it was Maria who paid the bill** to Maria uregulowała rachunek

**B/E** *abbr* = **bill of exchange**
**beach** [bi:tʃ] *n* plaża *f* ▷ *vt* (*boat*) wyciągać (wyciągnąć *perf*) na brzeg
**beach buggy** *n mały pojazd z silnikiem o dużej mocy i wielkimi oponami umożliwiającymi jazdę po wydmach*
**beachcomber** ['bi:tʃkəuməʳ] *n włóczęga zbierający wyrzucone przez fale przedmioty i utrzymujący się z ich sprzedaży*
**beachwear** ['bi:tʃwɛəʳ] *n* stroje *pl* plażowe
**beacon** ['bi:kən] *n* (*signal light*) znak *m* nawigacyjny; (*marker*) stawa *f*, pława *f*; (*radio beacon*) radiolatarnia *f*
**bead** [bi:d] *n* (*glass, plastic etc*) paciorek *m*, koralik *m*; (*of sweat*) kropla *f*; **beads** *npl* korale *pl*
**beady** ['bi:dɪ] *adj*: **~ eyes** oczy jak paciorki
**beagle** ['bi:gl] *n niewielki pies gończy*
**beak** [bi:k] *n* dziób *m*

**beaker** ['bi:kəʳ] *n* kubek *m* (*zwykle bez ucha i rozszerzający się ku górze*)
**beam** [bi:m] *n* (*Archit*) belka *f*, dźwigar *m*; (*of light*) snop *m*; (*Radio, Phys*) wiązka *f* ▷ *vi* rozpromieniać się (rozpromienić się *perf*) ▷ *vt* (*signal*) przesyłać (przesłać *perf*), nadawać (nadać *perf*); **to drive on full** *or* **main** *or* (*US*) **high ~** jechać z włączonymi światłami drogowymi
**beaming** ['bi:mɪŋ] *adj* (*sun*) jasny; (*smile*) promienny
**bean** [bi:n] *n* fasola *f*, fasolka *f*; **runner ~** fasol(k)a szparagowa; **broad ~** bób; **coffee ~** ziarn(k)o kawy
**beansprouts** ['bi:nsprauts] *npl* kiełki *pl* (*fasoli, soi itp*)
**bear**[1] [bɛəʳ] *n* niedźwiedź *m*; (*Stock Exchange*) gracz *m* na zniżkę; **a ~ market** okres intensywnej wyprzedaży akcji
**bear**[2] [bɛəʳ] (*pt* **bore**, *pp* **borne**) *vt* (*carry*) nieść, nosić; (*support*) podtrzymywać (podtrzymać *perf*); (*responsibility, cost*) ponosić (ponieść *perf*); (*tolerate, endure*) znosić (znieść *perf*); (*examination, scrutiny*) wytrzymywać (wytrzymać *perf*); (*traces, signs*) nosić; (*Comm: interest, dividend*) przynosić (przynieść *perf*); (*children, fruit*) rodzić (urodzić *perf*) ▷ *vi*: **to ~ right/left** (*Aut*) trzymać się prawej/lewej strony; **to ~ no relation to** nie mieć żadnego związku z *+instr*; **I can't ~ him** nie mogę go znieść, nie znoszę go; **to bring pressure to ~ on sb** wywierać (wywrzeć *perf*) na kogoś presję
▸ **bear out** *vt* (*claims, suspicions etc*) potwierdzać (potwierdzić *perf*); (*person*) popierać (poprzeć *perf*)
▸ **bear up** *vi* nie upadać na duchu, trzymać się; **he bore up well** trzymał się dzielnie
▸ **bear with** *vt fus* (*sb's decision, plan*) trwać (wytrwać *perf*) przy *+loc*; **~ with me a minute** posłuchaj mnie przez chwilę
**bearable** ['bɛərəbl] *adj* znośny
**beard** [bɪəd] *n* broda *f*, zarost *m*
**bearded** ['bɪədɪd] *adj* brodaty, z brodą *post*
**bearer** ['bɛərəʳ] *n* (*of letter, news*) doręczyciel(ka) *m(f)*; (*of cheque, passport, title*) posiadacz(ka) *m(f)*, właściciel(ka) *m(f)*
**bearing** ['bɛərɪŋ] *n* (*posture*) postawa *f*, postura *f*; (*connection*) związek *m*, powiązanie *nt*; (*Tech*) łożysko *nt*, ułożyskowanie *nt*; **bearings** *npl* łożysko *nt*; **to take a ~** wziąć (*perf*) namiar; **to get one's ~s** ustalić (*perf*) swoje położenie *or* swoją pozycję; (*fig*) zorientować się (*perf*), nabrać (*perf*) orientacji
**beast** [bi:st] *n* (*animal*) zwierzę *nt*, zwierz *m*; (*inf: person*) bestia *f*, potwór *m*
**beastly** ['bi:stlɪ] *adj* (*weather, trick etc*) paskudny; (*child*) nieznośny
**beat** [bi:t] (*pt* **~**, *pp* **~en**) *n* (*of heart*) bicie *nt*; (*Mus*) rytm *m*; (*of policeman*) obchód *m* ▷ *vt* (*wife, child*) bić (zbić *perf*); (*eggs, cream*) ubijać (ubić *perf*); (*opponent*) pokonywać (pokonać *perf*); (*record*) bić (pobić *perf*) ▷ *vi* (*heart, wind*) bić, uderzać (uderzyć *perf*); (*drum, rain*) bębnić (zabębnić *perf*); **to ~ time** wybijać rytm; **~ it!** (*inf*) spływaj! (*inf*), zmiataj! (*inf*); **that ~s everything** to przechodzi ludzkie pojęcie; **to ~ about the bush** owijać w bawełnę; **off the ~en track** z dala od cywilizacji
▸ **beat down** *vt* (*door*) wyważać (wyważyć *perf*); (*seller*) stargować (*perf*) ofertę *+gen* ▷ *vi* (*rain*) lać; (*sun*) prażyć
▸ **beat off** *vt* bronić się (obronić się *perf*) przed *+instr*
▸ **beat up** *vt* pobić (*perf*)
**beater** ['bi:təʳ] *n* trzepaczka *f*
**beating** ['bi:tɪŋ] *n* lanie *nt*; **to take a ~** (*fig*) doznawać (doznać *perf*) porażki *or* klęski, dostawać (dostać *perf*) lanie (*inf*); **she will take some ~** niełatwo będzie ją pokonać
**beat-up** ['bi:t'ʌp] (*inf*) *adj* (*car etc*) poobijany
**beautician** [bju:'tɪʃən] *n* kosmetyczka *f*
**beautiful** ['bju:tɪful] *adj* piękny
**beautifully** ['bju:tɪflɪ] *adv* (*play, sing, etc*) pięknie; (*quiet, empty etc*) doskonale
**beautify** ['bju:tɪfaɪ] *vt* upiększać (upiększyć *perf*)
**beauty** ['bju:tɪ] *n* (*quality*) piękno *nt*, uroda *f*; (*woman*) piękność *f*; (*object*) cudo *nt*; (*fig*) urok *m*; **the ~ of it is that ...** urok tego tkwi w tym, że ...
**beauty contest** *n* konkurs *m* piękności
**beauty queen** *n* miss *f inv* (*zwyciężczyni konkursu piękności*)
**beauty salon** *n* salon *m* kosmetyczny *or* piękności
**beauty spot** (*Brit*) *n* atrakcja *f* krajobrazowa
**beaver** ['bi:vəʳ] *n* bóbr *m*
**becalmed** [bɪ'kɑ:md] *adj* (*ship*) unieruchomiony (*z powodu braku wiatru*)
**became** [bɪ'keɪm] *pt of* **become**
**because** [bɪ'kɔz] *conj* ponieważ, dlatego, że; **~ of** z powodu *+gen*
**beck** [bɛk] *n*: **to be at sb's ~ and call** być na czyjeś zawołanie
**beckon** ['bɛkən] *vt* (*also*: **beckon to**) kiwać (kiwnąć *perf*) do *+gen*, skinąć (*perf*) na *+acc* ▷ *vi* (*fame, glory*) kusić
**become** [bɪ'kʌm] (*irreg: like* **come**) *vi* (*+noun*) zostawać (zostać *perf*) *or* stawać się (stać się *perf*) *+instr*; (*+adj*) stawać się (stać się *perf*) *+nom*; **to ~ fat** tyć (utyć *perf*); **to ~ thin** chudnąć (schudnąć *perf*); **to ~ angry** złościć się (rozzłościć się *perf*); **it became known that** stało się wiadome, że; **what has ~ of him?** co się z nim stało?

**becoming** [bɪ'kʌmɪŋ] *adj* (*behaviour*) stosowny, właściwy; (*clothes, colour*) twarzowy
**BECTU** ['bɛktu] (*Brit*) *n abbr* = **Broadcasting Entertainment Cinematographic and Theatre Union**
**BEd** *n abbr* (= *Bachelor of Education*) *stopień naukowy*
**bed** [bɛd] *n* (*furniture*) łóżko *nt*; (*of coal etc*) pokład *m*, złoże *nt*; (*of river, sea*) dno *nt*; (*of flowers*) klomb *m*, grządka *f*; **to go to bed** iść (pójść *perf*) do łóżka, iść (pójść *perf*) spać
▸ **bed down** *vi* przespać się (*perf*)
**bed and breakfast** *n* (*place*) ≈ pensjonat *m*; (*terms*) pokój *m* ze śniadaniem
**bedbug** ['bɛdbʌg] *n* pluskwa *f*
**bedclothes** ['bɛdkləuðz] *npl* pościel *f*
**bedding** ['bɛdɪŋ] *n* posłanie *nt*, pościel *f*
**bedevil** [bɪ'dɛvl] *vt* (*person*) prześladować; (*plans*) krzyżować (pokrzyżować *perf*)
**bedfellow** ['bɛdfɛləu] *n*: **they are strange ~s** (*fig*) dziwna z nich para
**bedlam** ['bɛdləm] *n* bałagan *m*, harmider *m*
**bedpan** ['bɛdpæn] *n* basen *m* (*dla chorego*)
**bedpost** ['bɛdpəust] *n* słupek *m* łóżka z baldachimem
**bedraggled** [bɪ'drægld] *adj* (*person*) przemoczony; (*clothes, hair*) w nieładzie *post* (*np. po deszczu*)
**bedridden** ['bɛdrɪdn] *adj* przykuty do łóżka, obłożnie chory
**bedrock** ['bɛdrɔk] *n* (*fig*) podstawa *f*, opoka *f*; (*Geol*) skała *f* macierzysta
**bedroom** ['bɛdrum] *n* sypialnia *f*
**Beds** [bɛdz] (*Brit: Post*) *abbr* = **Bedfordshire**
**bedside** ['bɛdsaɪd] *n*: **at sb's ~** u czyjegoś łoża; **a ~ lamp** lampka nocna
**bedsit(ter)** ['bɛdsɪt(əʳ)] (*Brit*) *n* ≈ kawalerka *f*
**bedspread** ['bɛdsprɛd] *n* narzuta *f*, kapa *f*
**bedtime** ['bɛdtaɪm] *n*: **it's ~** pora spać; **at ~** przed zaśnięciem; **it's long past her ~** już od dawna powinna spać
**bee** [bi:] *n* pszczoła *f*; **to have a bee in one's bonnet (about sth)** mieć bzika (na punkcie czegoś)
**beech** [bi:tʃ] *n* buk *m*
**beef** [bi:f] *n* wołowina *f*; **roast ~** pieczeń wołowa
▸ **beef up** *vt* (*inf: essay, programme*) uatrakcyjniać (uatrakcyjnić *perf*)
**beefburger** ['bi:fbə:gəʳ] *n* hamburger *m* z wołowiny
**Beefeater** ['bi:fi:təʳ] *n strażnik londyńskiej Tower w stroju historycznym*
**beehive** ['bi:haɪv] *n* ul *m*
**beeline** ['bi:laɪn] *n*: **to make a ~ for** ruszyć (*perf*) prosto do *+gen*
**been** [bi:n] *pp of* **be**
**beeper** ['bi:pəʳ] *n* brzęczyk *m*
**beer** [bɪəʳ] *n* piwo *nt*
**beer can** *n* puszka *f* po piwie
**beet** [bi:t] *n* burak *m* (pastewny); (*US: also:* **red beet**) burak *m* (ćwikłowy)
**beetle** ['bi:tl] *n* żuk *m*, chrząszcz *m*
**beetroot** ['bi:tru:t] (*Brit*) *n* burak *m* (ćwikłowy)
**befall** [bɪ'fɔ:l] (*irreg: like* **fall**) *vt* przytrafiać się (przytrafić się *perf*) *+dat*, spotykać (spotkać *perf*)
**befit** [bɪ'fɪt] *vt* wypadać *+dat*; **as ~s a four-star hotel** jak przystało na czterogwiazdkowy hotel
**before** [bɪ'fɔ:ʳ] *prep* (*of time*) przed *+instr*; (*of space*) przed *+instr*, naprzeciwko *+gen* ▹ *conj* zanim ▹ *adv* (*time*) (już) kiedyś, poprzednio; **~ going** przed wyjściem; **~ she goes** zanim wyjdzie; **the week ~** tydzień wcześniej, w poprzednim tygodniu; **I've never seen it ~** nigdy wcześniej tego nie widziałem
**beforehand** [bɪ'fɔ:hænd] *adv* wcześniej, z wyprzedzeniem
**befriend** [bɪ'frɛnd] *vt* okazywać (okazać *perf*) życzliwość *+dat*, przychodzić (przyjść *perf*) z pomocą *+dat*
**befuddled** [bɪ'fʌdld] *adj* zamroczony
**beg** [bɛg] *vi* żebrać ▹ *vt* (*also:* **beg for**: *food, money*) żebrać o *+acc*; (: *favour*) prosić o *+acc*; (: *mercy etc*) błagać o *+acc*; **to beg sb to do sth** błagać kogoś, żeby coś zrobił; **I beg your pardon** (*apologizing*) przepraszam; (*not hearing*) słucham?; **to beg the question** opierać się na nie dowiedzionych przesłankach
**began** [bɪ'gæn] *pt of* **begin**
**beggar** ['bɛgəʳ] *n* żebrak(-aczka) *m(f)*
**begin** [bɪ'gɪn] (*pt* **began**, *pp* **begun**) *vt* zaczynać (zacząć *perf*), rozpoczynać (rozpocząć *perf*) ▹ *vi* zaczynać się (zacząć się *perf*), rozpoczynać się (rozpocząć się *perf*); **to ~ doing** *or* **to do sth** zaczynać (zacząć *perf*) coś robić; **~ning (from) Monday** od poniedziałku; **I can't ~ to thank you** nie wiem, jak mam ci dziękować; **we'll have soup to ~ with** na początek będzie zupa; **to ~ with, I'd like to know ...** po pierwsze, chciałbym wiedzieć...
**beginner** [bɪ'gɪnəʳ] *n* początkujący(-ca) *m(f)*, nowicjusz(ka) *m(f)*
**beginning** [bɪ'gɪnɪŋ] *n* początek *m*; **right from the ~** od samego początku
**begrudge** [bɪ'grʌdʒ] *vt*: **to ~ sb sth** żałować (pożałować *perf*) komuś czegoś, zazdrościć (pozazdrościć *perf*) komuś czegoś
**beguile** [bɪ'gaɪl] *vt* mamić (omamić *perf*)

**beguiling** [bɪˈgaɪlɪŋ] *adj* (*voice, sight*) czarujący; (*prospect, promise*) złudny
**begun** [bɪˈgʌn] *pp of* **begin**
**behalf** [bɪˈhɑːf] *n*: **on ~ of,** (*US*) **in ~ of** (*as representative of*) w imieniu *+gen*; (*for benefit of*) na rzecz *+gen*; **on my/his ~** w swoim/jego imieniu
**behave** [bɪˈheɪv] *vi* (*person*) zachowywać się (zachować się *perf*), postępować (postąpić *perf*); (*object*) zachowywać się (zachować się *perf*); (*also*: **behave o.s.**) być grzecznym, zachowywać się (*poprawnie*); **~ yourself!** zachowuj się!
**behaviour**, (*US*) **behavior** [bɪˈheɪvjəʳ] *n* zachowanie *nt*, postępowanie *nt*
**behead** [bɪˈhɛd] *vt* ścinać (ściąć *perf*) głowę *+dat*
**beheld** [bɪˈhɛld] *pt, pp of* **behold**
**behind** [bɪˈhaɪnd] *prep* (*at the back of*) za *+instr*, z tyłu *+gen*; (*supporting*) za *+instr*, po stronie *+gen*; (*lower in rank etc*) za *+instr* ▷ *adv* z tyłu, w tyle ▷ *n* pupa *f* (*inf*), tyłek *m* (*inf*); **to be ~** być spóźnionym; **~ the scenes** (*fig*) za kulisami; **she asked me to stay ~** poprosiła, żebym został; **to leave sth ~** zapominać (zapomnieć *perf*) czegoś, zostawiać (zostawić *perf*) coś; **we're ~ them in technology** jesteśmy za nimi w tyle, jeśli idzie o technikę
**behold** [bɪˈhəuld] (*irreg*: *like* **hold**) (*old*) *vt* ujrzeć (*perf*)
**beige** [beɪʒ] *adj* beżowy
**Beijing** [ˈbeɪˈdʒɪŋ] *n* Pekin *m*
**being** [ˈbiːɪŋ] *n* (*creature*) istota *f*, stworzenie *nt*; (*existence*) istnienie *nt*, byt *m*; **to come into ~** powstawać (powstać *perf*), zaistnieć (*perf*)
**Beirut** [beɪˈruːt] *n* Bejrut *m*
**belated** [bɪˈleɪtɪd] *adj* (*thanks etc*) spóźniony
**belch** [bɛltʃ] *vi*: **he ~ed** odbiło mu się ▷ *vt* (*also*: **belch out**: *smoke etc*) buchać (buchnąć *perf*) *+instr*
**beleaguered** [bɪˈliːgɪd] *adj* (*city*) oblężony; (*army*) otoczony; (*fig*) zapracowany
**Belfast** [ˈbɛlfɑːst] *n* Belfast *m*
**belfry** [ˈbɛlfrɪ] *n* dzwonnica *f*
**Belgian** [ˈbɛldʒən] *adj* belgijski ▷ *n* Belg(ijka) *m(f)*
**Belgium** [ˈbɛldʒəm] *n* Belgia *f*
**Belgrade** [bɛlˈgreɪd] *n* Belgrad *m*
**belie** [bɪˈlaɪ] *vt* (*disprove*) przeczyć *+dat*, zadawać (zadać *perf*) kłam *+dat*; (*give false impression of*) maskować
**belief** [bɪˈliːf] *n* (*opinion*) przekonanie *nt*; (*trust, faith*) wiara *f*; (*religious*) wiara *f*, wierzenie *nt*; (*acceptance as true*) przekonanie *nt*, przeświadczenie *nt*; **beyond ~** nie do wiary; **in the ~ that ...** w nadziei, że ...
**believable** [bɪˈliːvəbl] *adj* wiarygodny
**believe** [bɪˈliːv] *vt* (*person*) wierzyć (uwierzyć *perf*) *+dat*; (*story*) wierzyć (uwierzyć *perf*) w *+acc* ▷ *vi* wierzyć (uwierzyć *perf*); **to ~ that...** uważać *or* wierzyć, że...; **to ~ in** wierzyć (uwierzyć *perf*) w *+acc*; **I don't ~ in corporal punishment** nie jestem zwolennikiem kar cielesnych; **he is ~d to be abroad** uważa się, że jest za granicą
**believer** [bɪˈliːvəʳ] *n* (*in idea*) zwolennik(-iczka) *m(f)*; (*Rel*) wyznawca(-wczyni) *m(f)*, wierzący(-ca) *m(f)*; **she's a great ~ in healthy eating** ona jest gorącą zwolenniczką zdrowego odżywiania się
**belittle** [bɪˈlɪtl] *vt* umniejszać (umniejszyć *perf*)
**Belize** [bɛˈliːz] *n* Belize *nt inv*
**bell** [bɛl] *n* (*of church*) dzwon *m*; (*small, electric*) dzwonek *m*; **that rings a ~** (*fig*) to mi coś przypomina
**bell-bottoms** [ˈbɛlbɔtəmz] *npl* dzwony *pl* (*spodnie*)
**bellboy** [ˈbɛlbɔɪ] (*Brit*) *n* goniec *m* hotelowy
**bellhop** [ˈbɛlhɔp] (*US*) *n* = **bellboy**
**belligerence** [bɪˈlɪdʒərəns] *n* wojowniczość *f*
**belligerent** [bɪˈlɪdʒərənt] *adj* wojowniczy
**bellow** [ˈbɛləu] *vi* (*bull*) ryczeć (ryknąć *perf or* zaryczeć *perf*); (*person*) grzmieć (zagrzmieć *perf*) ▷ *vt* (*orders*) wykrzykiwać (wykrzyczeć *perf*)
**bellows** [ˈbɛləuz] *npl* miech *m*, miechy *pl*
**bell push** (*Brit*) *n* przycisk *m* dzwonka
**belly** [ˈbɛlɪ] *n* brzuch *m*
**bellyache** [ˈbɛlɪeɪk] (*inf*) *n* ból *m* brzucha ▷ *vi* narzekać, stękać (*inf*)
**belly button** *n* pępek *m*
**belong** [bɪˈlɔŋ] *vi*: **to ~ to** należeć do *+gen*; **this book ~s here** miejsce tej książki jest tutaj
**belongings** [bɪˈlɔŋɪŋz] *npl* rzeczy *pl*, dobytek *m*
**beloved** [bɪˈlʌvɪd] *adj* ukochany ▷ *n* (*old*) ukochany(-na) *m(f)*
**below** [bɪˈləu] *prep* (*beneath*) pod *+instr*, poniżej *+gen*; (*less than*) poniżej *+gen* ▷ *adv* pod spodem, poniżej; **see ~** (*in letter etc*) patrz poniżej; **temperatures ~ normal** temperatury poniżej normy
**belt** [bɛlt] *n* (*clothing*) pasek *m*; (*of land, sea, air*) pas *m*, strefa *f*; (*Tech*) pas *m*, pasek *m* ▷ *vt* (*inf*) lać (zlać *perf*) (pasem) (*inf*) ▷ *vi* (*Brit*: *inf*) pędzić, pruć (*inf*); **industrial ~** okręg przemysłowy
▶ **belt out** *vt* (*inf*) wyśpiewywać (*na cały głos*)
▶ **belt up** (*Brit*: *inf*) *vi* zamknąć się (*perf*) (*inf*), przymknąć się (*perf*) (*inf*)
**beltway** [ˈbɛltweɪ] (*US*: *Aut*) *n* obwodnica *f*

**bemoan** [bɪ'məun] *vt* opłakiwać, żałować *+gen*
**bemused** [bɪ'mju:zd] *adj* zdezorientowany
**bench** [bɛntʃ] *n (seat)* ławka *f*, ława *f*; *(work bench)* warsztat *m*, stół *m* roboczy; *(Brit)* ława *f (w parlamencie)*; **the B~** sąd
**benchmark** ['bɛntʃmɑ:k] *n (fig)* miara *f*, kryterium *nt*; *(Comput)* test *m* sprawności; *(Fin)* cena *f* referencyjna
**bend** [bɛnd] *(pt, pp* **bent***) vt (leg)* zginać (zgiąć *perf*); *(pipe)* giąć, wyginać (wygiąć *perf*) ▷ *vi (person)* zginać się (zgiąć się *perf*), schylać się (schylić się *perf*); *(pipe)* zginać się (zgiąć się *perf*) ▷ *n (Brit: in road, river)* zakręt *m*; *(in pipe)* wygięcie *nt*; **bends** *npl*: **the bends** choroba *f* kesonowa
▶ **bend down** *vi* schylać się (schylić się *perf*)
▶ **bend over** *vi* nachylać się (nachylić się *perf*), pochylać się (pochylić się *perf*)
**beneath** [bɪ'ni:θ] *prep (in position)* pod *+instr*, poniżej *+gen*; *(in status)* poniżej *+gen* ▷ *adv* poniżej, pod spodem
**benefactor** ['bɛnɪfæktə^r] *n* dobroczyńca *m*, ofiarodawca *m*
**benefactress** ['bɛnɪfæktrɪs] *n* ofiarodawczyni *f*
**beneficial** [bɛnɪ'fɪʃəl] *adj* zbawienny, dobroczynny; **~ (to)** korzystny (dla *+gen*)
**beneficiary** [bɛnɪ'fɪʃərɪ] *(Jur) n* beneficjent *m*
**benefit** ['bɛnɪfɪt] *n (advantage)* korzyść *f*, pożytek *m*; *(money)* zasiłek *m*; *(also:* **benefit concert/match***)* impreza *f* na cele dobroczynne ▷ *vt* przynosić (przynieść *perf*) korzyść *or* pożytek *+dat* ▷ *vi*: **he'll ~ from it** skorzysta na tym
**Benelux** ['bɛnɪlʌks] *n* Beneluks *m*, kraje *pl* Beneluksu
**benevolent** [bɪ'nɛvələnt] *adj (person)* życzliwy; *(organization)* dobroczynny
**BEng** *n abbr (= Bachelor of Engineering) stopień naukowy*
**benign** [bɪ'naɪn] *adj (person, smile)* dobroduszny, dobrotliwy; *(Med)* łagodny, niezłośliwy
**bent** [bɛnt] *pt, pp of* **bend** ▷ *n* zacięcie *nt*, żyłka *f* ▷ *adj (wire, pipe)* zgięty, wygięty; *(inf: dishonest)* przekupny, skorumpowany; *(: pej: homosexual)* pedałowaty *(pej, inf)*; **to be ~ on** być zdecydowanym na *+acc*
**bequeath** [bɪ'kwi:ð] *vt* zapisywać (zapisać *perf*) *+dat*, zostawiać (zostawić *perf*) w spadku *+dat*
**bequest** [bɪ'kwɛst] *n*: **~ (to)** zapis *m* (na rzecz *+gen*)
**bereaved** [bɪ'ri:vd] *n*: **the ~** pogrążeni *pl* w smutku *or* żałobie ▷ *adj* osamotniony, osierocony
**bereavement** [bɪ'ri:vmənt] *n* strata *f* bliskiej osoby, żałoba *f*
**bereft** [bɪ'rɛft] *(fml) adj*: **~ of** pozbawiony *+gen*
**beret** ['bɛreɪ] *n* beret *m*
**Bering Sea** ['beɪrɪŋ-] *n*: **the ~** Morze *nt* Beringa
**Berks** [bɑ:ks] *(Brit: Post) abbr* = **Berkshire**
**Berlin** [bə:'lɪn] *n* Berlin *m*; **East/West ~** Berlin Wschodni/Zachodni
**berm** [bə:m] *(US) n* wał *m* ziemny *(na poboczu drogi)*
**Bermuda** [bə:'mju:də] *n* Bermudy *pl*
**Bermuda shorts** *npl* bermudy *pl*
**Bern** [bə:n] *n* Berno *nt*
**berry** ['bɛrɪ] *n* jagoda *f*
**berserk** [bə'sə:k] *adj*: **to go ~** wpadać (wpaść *perf*) w szał
**berth** [bə:θ] *n (on boat)* koja *f*; *(on train)* miejsce *nt* leżące; *(Naut)* miejsce *nt* postoju statku ▷ *vi* dobijać (dobić *perf*) do nabrzeża; **to give sb a wide ~** *(fig)* omijać kogoś szerokim łukiem
**beseech** [bɪ'si:tʃ] *(pt, pp* **besought***) vt* błagać
**beset** [bɪ'sɛt] *(pt, pp* **~***) vt* dręczyć, prześladować; **~ with dangers/difficulties** najeżony niebezpieczeństwami/trudnościami
**beside** [bɪ'saɪd] *prep (next to)* obok *+gen*; *(compared with)* oprócz *+gen*, poza *+instr*; **to be ~ o.s. (with rage)** nie posiadać się ze złości; **that's ~ the point** to nie ma nic do rzeczy
**besides** [bɪ'saɪdz] *adv* poza tym, oprócz tego ▷ *prep* poza *+instr*, oprócz *+gen*
**besiege** [bɪ'si:dʒ] *vt* oblegać (oblec *perf*); *(fig)* nagabywać; *(: with offers, requests)* zasypywać (zasypać *perf*)
**besmirch** [bɪ'smə:tʃ] *vt (person)* oczerniać (oczernić *perf*); *(reputation)* szargać (zszargać *perf*)
**besotted** [bɪ'sɔtɪd] *(Brit) adj*: **~ with** *(person)* ogłupiały na punkcie *+gen*; *(love, power)* zaślepiony *+instr*
**besought** [bɪ'sɔ:t] *pt, pp of* **beseech**
**bespectacled** [bɪ'spɛktɪkld] *adj* w okularach *post*
**bespoke** [bɪ'spəuk] *(Brit) adj (garment)* szyty na miarę; *(tailor)* szyjący na miarę
**best** [bɛst] *adj* najlepszy ▷ *adv* najlepiej; **the ~ thing to do is ...** najlepiej *+infin*; **the ~ part of** większa część *+gen*; **at ~** w najlepszym razie, co najwyżej; **to make the ~ of** robić (zrobić *perf*) jak najlepszy użytek z *+gen*; **to do one's ~** dawać (dać *perf*) z siebie wszystko; **to the ~ of my knowledge** o ile mi wiadomo; **to the ~ of my ability** najlepiej jak potrafię; **he's not exactly patient at the ~ of times** nigdy nie odznaczał się zbytnią cierpliwością

**bestial** ['bɛstɪəl] *adj* bestialski
**best man** *n* drużba *m*
**bestow** [bɪ'stəu] *vt*: **to ~ sth on sb** (*honour, title*) nadawać (nadać *perf*) coś komuś; (*affection, praise*) obdarzać (obdarzyć *perf*) czymś kogoś
**bestseller** ['bɛst'sɛlə$^r$] *n* bestseller *m*
**bet** [bɛt] (*pt, pp* **bet** *or* **betted**) *n* zakład *m* ▷ *vt* (*wager*): **to bet sb sth** zakładać się (założyć się *perf*) z kimś o coś; (*expect, guess*): **to bet that ...** zakładać się (założyć się *perf*), że ... ▷ *vi*: **to bet on** obstawiać (obstawić *perf*) *+acc*; **I wouldn't bet on it** nie liczyłbym na to; **it's a safe bet that ...** jest pewne jak w banku, że ...
**Bethlehem** ['bɛθlɪhɛm] *n* Betlejem *nt*
**betray** [bɪ'treɪ] *vt* (*person, country, emotion*) zdradzać (zdradzić *perf*); (*trust*) zawodzić (zawieść *perf*)
**betrayal** [bɪ'treɪəl] *n* zdrada *f*
**better** ['bɛtə$^r$] *adj* lepszy ▷ *adv* lepiej ▷ *vt* poprawiać (poprawić *perf*) ▷ *n*: **to get the ~ of** brać (wziąć *perf*) górę nad *+instr*; **a change for the ~** zmiana na lepsze; **I had ~ go** lepiej już (sobie) pójdę; **I'm much ~ now** czuję się teraz znacznie lepiej; **you had ~ do it** lepiej zrób to; **he thought ~ of it** rozmyślił się; **to get ~** (*Med*) zdrowieć (wyzdrowieć *perf*); **that's ~!** teraz lepiej!
**better off** *adj* zamożniejszy; **you can pay the money back when you are ~** możesz zwrócić pieniądze, gdy będziesz w lepszej sytuacji finansowej; **she'll be ~ in hospital/without him** lepiej jej będzie w szpitalu/bez niego
**betting** ['bɛtɪŋ] *n* (*gambling*) zakłady *pl*; (*odds*) prawdopodobieństwo *nt*
**betting shop** (*Brit*) *n* ajencja *f* bukmacherska
**between** [bɪ'twi:n] *prep* między *+instr*, pomiędzy *+instr* ▷ *adv*: **in ~** pośrodku; **the road ~ here and London** droga stąd do Londynu; **we only had 5 pounds ~ us** mieliśmy razem tylko 5 funtów; **~ you and me** między nami (mówiąc); **a man aged ~ 20 and 25** mężczyzna w wieku między 20 a 25 lat; **Penn Close, Court Road and all the little streets in ~** Penn Close, Court Road i wszystkie małe uliczki pomiędzy nimi
**bevel** ['bɛvəl] *n* (*also*: **bevel edge**) skos *m*, ukos *m*
**bevelled** ['bɛvəld] *adj*: **a ~ edge** fazowana krawędź *f*
**beverage** ['bɛvərɪdʒ] *n* napój *m*
**bevy** ['bɛvɪ] *n*: **a ~ of** stadko *nt +gen*
**bewail** [bɪ'weɪl] *vt* użalać się (użalić się *perf*) na *+acc*
**beware** [bɪ'wɛə$^r$] *vi*: **to ~ (of)** wystrzegać się (*+gen*); **"~ of the dog"** „uwaga zły pies"
**bewildered** [bɪ'wɪldəd] *adj* skonsternowany, zdezorientowany
**bewildering** [bɪ'wɪldrɪŋ] *adj* wprawiający w konsternację
**bewitching** [bɪ'wɪtʃɪŋ] *adj* czarujący, urzekający
**beyond** [bɪ'jɔnd] *prep* poza *+instr* ▷ *adv* dalej; **~ the age of 16** powyżej szesnastego roku życia; **~ doubt** ponad wszelką wątpliwość; **~ repair/recognition** nie do naprawienia/poznania; **to be ~ sb's wildest dreams** przechodzić czyjeś najśmielsze oczekiwania; **it's ~ me** nie mogę tego pojąć
**b/f** (*Comm*) *abbr* (*= brought forward*) do przeniesienia
**BFPO** *n abbr* = **British Forces Post Office**
**bhp** (*Aut*) *n abbr* (*= brake horsepower*) moc *f* użyteczna w koniach mechanicznych
**bi...** [baɪ] *pref* dwu...
**biannual** [baɪ'ænjuəl] *adj* odbywający się dwa razy do roku
**bias** ['baɪəs] *n* (*prejudice*) uprzedzenie *nt*; (*preference*) przychylność *f*
**bias(s)ed** ['baɪəst] *adj* stronniczy, tendencyjny; **to be ~ against** być uprzedzonym do *+gen*
**bib** [bɪb] *n* śliniaczek *m*
**Bible** ['baɪbl] *n* Biblia *f*
**biblical** ['bɪblɪkl] *adj* biblijny
**bibliography** [bɪblɪ'ɔgrəfɪ] *n* bibliografia *f*
**bicarbonate of soda** [baɪ'kɑ:bənɪt-] *n* soda *f* oczyszczona
**bicentenary** [baɪsɛn'ti:nərɪ] *n* dwóchsetlecie *nt*
**bicentennial** [baɪsɛn'tɛnɪəl] *n* = **bicentenary**
**biceps** ['baɪsɛps] *n* biceps *m*, bicepsy *pl*
**bicker** ['bɪkə$^r$] *vi* sprzeczać się
**bickering** ['bɪkərɪŋ] *n* sprzeczki *pl*
**bicycle** ['baɪsɪkl] *n* rower *m*
**bicycle path** *n* ścieżka *f* rowerowa
**bicycle pump** *n* pompka *f* rowerowa
**bicycle track** *n* tor *m* rowerowy
**bid** [bɪd] (*pt* **bade** *or* **bid**, *pp* **bid(den)**) *n* oferta *f* ▷ *vi* licytować ▷ *vt* oferować (zaoferować *perf*); **a bid for power** próba przejęcia władzy; **to bid sb good day** (*say hallo*) witać (przywitać *perf*) kogoś; (*say good-bye*) żegnać (pożegnać *perf*) kogoś
**bidder** ['bɪdə$^r$] *n*: **the highest ~** osoba *f* oferująca najwyższą cenę
**bidding** ['bɪdɪŋ] *n* licytacja *f*; **to do sb's ~** spełniać (spełnić *perf*) czyjeś rozkazy
**bide** [baɪd] *vt*: **to ~ one's time** czekać na właściwy moment
**bidet** ['bi:deɪ] *n* bidet *m*
**bidirectional** ['baɪdɪ'rɛkʃənl] *adj* dwukierunkowy

**biennial** [baɪ'ɛnɪəl] *adj* odbywający się co dwa lata ▷ *n* roślina *f* dwuletnia
**bier** [bɪəʳ] *n* mary *pl* (*nosze pogrzebowe*)
**bifocals** [baɪ'fəuklz] *npl* okulary *pl* dwuogniskowe
**big** [bɪg] *adj* duży; (*brother, sister*) starszy; (*ideas, plans*) ambitny; **a big woman in her early forties** rosła kobieta po czterdziestce; **to be big in** liczyć się w *+loc*; **in a big way** na wielką skalę
**bigamist** ['bɪgəmɪst] *n* bigamista(-tka) *m(f)*
**bigamous** ['bɪgəməs] *adj* bigamiczny
**bigamy** ['bɪgəmɪ] *n* bigamia *f*
**big dipper** [-'dɪpəʳ] *n* kolejka *f* górska (*w wesołym miasteczku*)
**big end** (*Aut*) *n* łeb *m* korbowy
**bigheaded** ['bɪg'hɛdɪd] *adj* przemądrzały
**big-hearted** ['bɪg'hɑ:tɪd] *adj* wielkiego serca *post*
**bigot** ['bɪgət] *n* bigot(ka) *m(f)*
**bigoted** ['bɪgətɪd] *adj* bigoteryjny
**bigotry** ['bɪgətrɪ] *n* bigoteria *f*
**big toe** *n* paluch *m*, duży *or* wielki palec *m* (u nogi)
**big top** *n* namiot *m* cyrkowy
**big wheel** *n* diabelski młyn *m*
**bigwig** ['bɪgwɪg] (*inf*) *n* gruba ryba *f* (*inf*)
**bike** [baɪk] *n* (*bicycle*) rower *m*; (*motorcycle*) motorower *m*
**bikini** [bɪ'ki:nɪ] *n* bikini *nt inv*
**bilateral** [baɪ'lætərl] *adj* dwustronny, bilateralny
**bile** [baɪl] *n* (*lit, fig*) żółć *f*
**bilingual** [baɪ'lɪŋgwəl] *adj* dwujęzyczny, bilingwalny
**bilious** ['bɪlɪəs] *adj* (*fig*) obrzydliwy; **I felt ~** było mi niedobrze
**bill** [bɪl] *n* rachunek *m*; (*Pol*) projekt *m* ustawy; (*US*) banknot *m*; (*of bird*) dziób *m*; (*Theat*): **on the ~** w programie ▷ *vt* (*item*) ewidencjonować (zaewidencjonować *perf*); (*customer*) wystawiać (wystawić *perf*) rachunek *+dat*; **"post no ~s"** „nie naklejać"; **to fit** *or* **fill the ~** (*fig*) nadawać się (nadać się *perf*); **~ me at my London address** proszę przysłać rachunek na mój londyński adres; **~ of exchange** weksel; **~ of fare** jadłospis; **~ of lading** konosament, list przewozowy; **~ of sale** akt sprzedaży
**billboard** ['bɪlbɔ:d] *n* billboard *m*
**billet** ['bɪlɪt] *n* (*Mil*) kwatera *f* ▷ *vt* kwaterować (zakwaterować *perf*)
**billfold** ['bɪlfəuld] (*US*) *n* portfel *m*
**billiards** ['bɪljədz] *n* bilard *m*
**billion** ['bɪljən] *n* (*Brit*) bilion *m*; (*US*) miliard *m*
**billow** ['bɪləu] *n* kłąb *m* ▷ *vi* (*smoke*) kłębić się; (*sail*) wydymać się
**billy goat** ['bɪlɪ-] *n* kozioł *m*
**bin** [bɪn] *n* (*Brit: for rubbish*) kosz *m*; (*for storing things*) pojemnik *m*
**binary** ['baɪnərɪ] (*Math*) *adj* dwójkowy, binarny
**bind** [baɪnd] (*pt, pp* **bound**) *vt* (*tie*) przywiązywać (przywiązać *perf*); (*tie together*) wiązać, związywać (związać *perf*); (*oblige*) zobowiązywać (zobowiązać *perf*); (*book*) oprawiać (oprawić *perf*) ▷ *n* (*inf*) zawracanie *nt* głowy (*inf*)
▸ **bind over** *vt* (*Jur*) zobowiązywać (zobowiązać *perf*) pod rygorem
▸ **bind up** *vt* (*wound*) bandażować (zabandażować *perf*); **to be bound up in** być zaangażowanym w *+acc*
**binder** ['baɪndəʳ] *n* segregator *m*
**binding** ['baɪndɪŋ] *adj* wiążący ▷ *n* (*of book*) oprawa *f*
**binge** [bɪndʒ] (*inf*) *n*: **to go on a ~** iść (pójść *perf*) w tango (*inf*)
**bingo** ['bɪŋgəu] *n* bingo *nt inv*
**binoculars** [bɪ'nɔkjuləz] *npl* lornetka *f*
**bio...** [baɪəu] *pref* bio...
**biochemistry** [baɪə'kɛmɪstrɪ] *n* biochemia *f*
**biodegradable** ['baɪəudɪ'greɪdəbl] *adj* ulegający biodegradacji
**biographer** [baɪ'ɔgrəfəʳ] *n* biograf *m*
**biographic(al)** [baɪə'græfɪk(l)] *adj* biograficzny
**biography** [baɪ'ɔgrəfɪ] *n* biografia *f*
**biological** [baɪə'lɔdʒɪkl] *adj* biologiczny; (*washing powder*) enzymatyczny
**biologist** [baɪ'ɔlədʒɪst] *n* biolog *m*
**biology** [baɪ'ɔlədʒɪ] *n* biologia *f*
**biophysics** ['baɪəu'fɪzɪks] *n* biofizyka *f*
**biopsy** ['baɪɔpsɪ] *n* biopsja *f*
**biotechnology** ['baɪəutɛk'nɔlədʒɪ] *n* biotechnologia *f*
**biped** ['baɪpɛd] *n* dwunożny *m*
**birch** [bə:tʃ] *n* brzoza *f*
**bird** [bə:d] *n* ptak *m*; (*Brit: inf: woman*) kociak *m*
**bird's-eye view** ['bə:dzaɪ-] *n* (*aerial view*) widok *m* z lotu ptaka; (*overview*) ogólne spojrzenie *nt*
**bird-watcher** ['bə:dwɔtʃəʳ] *n* obserwator(ka) *m(f)* ptaków
**Biro**® ['baɪərəu] *n* długopis *m*
**birth** [bə:θ] *n* (*lit, fig*) narodziny *pl*; **to give ~ to** rodzić (urodzić *perf*) *+acc*
**birth certificate** *n* metryka *f* (urodzenia)
**birth control** *n* (*policy*) planowanie *nt* rodziny; (*methods*) regulacja *f* urodzeń, zapobieganie *nt* ciąży
**birthday** ['bə:θdeɪ] *n* urodziny *pl* ▷ *cpd* urodzinowy; *see also* **happy**
**birthmark** ['bə:θmɑ:k] *n* znamię *nt* wrodzone

**birthplace** ['bə:θpleɪs] *n* miejsce *nt* urodzenia; (*fig*) miejsce *nt* narodzin, kolebka *f*
**birth rate** ['bə:θreɪt] *n* wskaźnik *m* urodzeń
**Biscay** ['bɪskeɪ] *n*: **the Bay of ~** Zatoka *f* Biskajska
**biscuit** ['bɪskɪt] *n* (*Brit*) herbatnik *m*, kruche ciasteczko *nt*; (*US*) biszkopt *m*, babeczka *f*
**bisect** [baɪ'sɛkt] *vt* przepoławiać (przepołowić *perf*), dzielić (podzielić *perf*) na połowę
**bisexual** [baɪ'sɛkʃuəl] *adj* biseksualny ▷ *n* biseksualista(-tka) *m(f)*
**bishop** ['bɪʃəp] *n* (*Rel*) biskup *m*; (*Chess*) goniec *m*
**bit** [bɪt] *pt of* **bite** ▷ *n* (*piece*) kawałek *m*; (*tool*) wiertło *nt*; (*Comput*) bit *m*; (*of horse*) wędzidło *nt*; (*US*) *12,5 centa*; **a bit of** trochę *or* odrobina *+gen*; **a bit mad** lekko stuknięty (*inf*); **bit by bit** kawałek po kawałku; **to come to bits** rozpaść się (*perf*) *or* rozlecieć się (*perf*) na kawałki; **bring all your bits and pieces** przynieś wszystkie swoje drobiazgi; **he did his bit** zrobił, co do niego należało
**bitch** [bɪtʃ] *n* suka *f*
**bite** [baɪt] (*pt* **bit**, *pp* **bitten**) *vt* gryźć (ugryźć *perf*) ▷ *vi* gryźć (ugryźć *perf*), kąsać (ukąsić *perf*) ▷ *n* (*from insect*) ukąszenie *nt*; (*mouthful*) kęs *m*; **to ~ one's nails** obgryzać paznokcie; **let's have a ~ (to eat)** (*inf*) przekąśmy coś (*inf*)
**biting** ['baɪtɪŋ] *adj* (*wind*) szczypiący; (*wit*) uszczypliwy
**bit part** (*Theat*) *n* rólka *f*
**bitten** ['bɪtn] *pp of* **bite**
**bitter** ['bɪtə[r]] *adj* (*person*) zgorzkniały; (*taste, experience, disappointment*) gorzki; (*cold, wind*) przejmujący, przenikliwy; (*struggle, criticism*) zawzięty ▷ *n* (*Brit*) *rodzaj piwa*; **to the ~ end** do samego końca; (*struggle etc*) do upadłego
**bitterly** ['bɪtəlɪ] *adv* gorzko; (*oppose, criticize*) zawzięcie; **it's ~ cold** jest przejmująco zimno
**bitterness** ['bɪtənɪs] *n* (*resentment*) gorycz *f*, rozgoryczenie *nt*; (*bitter taste*) gorycz *f*, gorzkość *f*
**bittersweet** ['bɪtəswi:t] *adj* gorzko-słodki; **~ memories** mieszanina złych i dobrych wspomnień
**bitty** ['bɪtɪ] (*Brit*: *inf*) *adj*: **the play was ~ in the second act** drugi akt nie trzymał się kupy (*inf*)
**bitumen** ['bɪtjumɪn] *n* bitum(in) *m*
**bivouac** ['bɪvuæk] *n* biwak *m*
**bizarre** [bɪ'zɑ:[r]] *adj* dziwaczny
**bk** *abbr* = **bank**; (= *book*) książ.
**BL** *n abbr* (= *Bachelor of Law, Bachelor of Letters, Bachelor of Literature*) *stopień naukowy*
**bl** *abbr* (= *bill of lading*) list *m* przewozowy
**blab** [blæb] (*inf*) *vi* wygadać się (*perf*) (*inf*)
**black** [blæk] *adj* czarny ▷ *n* (*colour*) (kolor *m*) czarny, czerń *f*; (*person*) czarnoskóry(-ra) *m(f)* ▷ *vt* (*Brit*: *Industry*) bojkotować (zbojkotować *perf*); **to give sb a ~ eye** podbić (*perf*) komuś oko; **~ and blue** posiniaczony; **in the ~** wypłacalny; **in ~ and white** (*fig*) czarno na białym
▶ **black out** *vi* (na krótko) tracić (stracić *perf*) przytomność
**black belt** *n* (*US*) dzielnica *f* murzyńska; (*Judo*) czarny pas *m*
**blackberry** ['blækbərɪ] *n* jeżyna *f*
**blackbird** ['blækbə:d] *n* kos *m*
**blackboard** ['blækbɔ:d] *n* tablica *f*
**black box** (*Aviat*) *n* czarna skrzynka *f*
**black coffee** *n* czarna kawa *f*
**Black Country** *n*: **the ~** *silnie uprzemysłowiony rejon środkowej Anglii*
**blackcurrant** ['blæk'kʌrənt] *n* czarna porzeczka *f*
**black economy** *n*: **the ~** szara strefa *f*
**blacken** ['blækn] *vt* (*fig*) oczerniać (oczernić *perf*)
**Black Forest** *n*: **the ~** Schwarzwald *m*
**blackhead** ['blækhɛd] *n* wągier *m*, zaskórnik *m*
**black ice** *n warstwa przezroczystego lodu na drodze*
**blackjack** ['blækdʒæk] *n* (*Cards*) oczko *nt*; (*US*) pałka *f*
**blackleg** ['blæklɛg] (*Brit*) *n* łamistrajk *m*
**blacklist** ['blæklɪst] *n* czarna lista *f* ▷ *vt* wciągać (wciągnąć *perf*) na czarną listę
**blackmail** ['blækmeɪl] *n* szantaż *m* ▷ *vt* szantażować (zaszantażować *perf*)
**blackmailer** ['blækmeɪlə[r]] *n* szantażysta(-tka) *m(f)*
**black market** *n* czarny rynek *m*
**blackout** ['blækaut] *n* (*in wartime*) zaciemnienie *nt*; (*power cut*) przerwa *f* w dostawie energii elektrycznej; (*TV, Radio*) zagłuszanie *nt*; (*faint*) (krótkotrwała) utrata *f* przytomności
**Black Sea** *n*: **the ~** Morze *nt* Czarne
**black sheep** *n* (*fig*) czarna owca *f*
**blacksmith** ['blæksmɪθ] *n* kowal *m*
**black spot** *n* (*Aut*) niebezpieczne miejsce *nt* na drodze; (*for unemployment etc*) rejon *m* zagrożony
**bladder** ['blædə[r]] (*Anat*) *n* pęcherz *m* (moczowy)
**blade** [bleɪd] *n* (*of knife*) ostrze *nt*; (*of sword*) klinga *f*, ostrze *nt*; (*of oar*) pióro *nt*; (*of propeller*) łopat(k)a *f*; (*of grass*) źdźbło *nt*
**blame** [bleɪm] *n* wina *f* ▷ *vt*: **to ~ sb for sth** obwiniać (obwinić *perf*) kogoś o coś; **to be to ~** być winnym, ponosić winę; **who's to ~?** kto jest winny?

**blameless** ['bleɪmlɪs] *adj* niewinny
**blanch** [blɑːntʃ] *vi* (*face*) blednąć (zblednąć *perf*) ▷ *vt* (*Culin*) parzyć (sparzyć *perf*), blanszować (zblanszować *perf*)
**blancmange** [blə'mɔnʒ] *n* ≈ budyń *m* (*na zimno*)
**bland** [blænd] *adj* (*taste*) mdły, nijaki
**blank** [blæŋk] *adj* (*paper*) czysty, nie zapisany; (*look*) bez wyrazu *post*, obojętny ▷ *n* (*of memory*) luka *f*; (*on form*) puste *or* wolne miejsce *nt*; (*cartridge*) ślepy nabój *m*; **we drew a** ~ (*fig*) nie doszliśmy do niczego
**blank cheque** *n* czek *m* in blanco; **to give sb a ~ to do sth** (*fig*) dawać (dać *perf*) komuś wolną rękę do zrobienia czegoś
**blanket** ['blæŋkɪt] *n* (*cloth*) koc *m*; (*of snow*) pokrywa *f*; (*of fog*) zasłona *f* ▷ *adj* całościowy
**blanket cover** *n* ubezpieczenie *nt* całościowe
**blare** [blɛəʳ] *vi* grzmieć (zagrzmieć *perf*)
▸ **blare out** *vi* ryczeć (*inf*)
**blarney** ['blɑːnɪ] *n* pochlebstwa *pl*
**blasé** ['blɑːzeɪ] *adj* zblazowany
**blaspheme** [blæs'fiːm] *vi* bluźnić
**blasphemous** ['blæsfɪməs] *adj* bluźnierczy
**blasphemy** ['blæsfɪmɪ] *n* bluźnierstwo *nt*
**blast** [blɑːst] *n* (*of wind, air*) podmuch *m*; (*of whistle*) gwizd *m*; (*explosion*) wybuch *m* ▷ *vt* wysadzać (wysadzić *perf*) w powietrze ▷ *excl* (*Brit: inf*) (o) kurczę! (*inf*); **at full** ~ na cały regulator
▸ **blast off** *vi* (*Space*) startować (wystartować *perf*), odpalać (odpalić *perf*)
**blast furnace** *n* piec *m* hutniczy
**blast-off** ['blɑːstɔf] (*Space*) *n* start *m*, odpalenie *nt*
**blatant** ['bleɪtənt] *adj* rażący, krzyczący
**blatantly** ['bleɪtəntlɪ] *adv*: **~ obvious** ewidentny; **to lie** ~ kłamać w żywe oczy
**blaze** [bleɪz] *n* pożar *m*; (*fig: of colour*) feeria *f*; (*: of glory*) blask *m* ▷ *vi* (*fire*) buchać (buchnąć *perf*); (*guns*) walić; (*fig: eyes*) płonąć (zapłonąć *perf*) ▷ *vt*: **to ~ a trail** (*fig*) przecierać (przetrzeć *perf*) szlak; **in a ~ of publicity** w blasku powszechnego zainteresowania
**blazer** ['bleɪzəʳ] *n* blezer *m*
**bleach** [bliːtʃ] *n* wybielacz *m* ▷ *vt* (*fabric*) wybielać (wybielić *perf*); (*hair*) tlenić (utlenić *perf*)
**bleached** [bliːtʃt] *adj* (*hair*) tleniony
**bleachers** ['bliːtʃəz] (*Sport: US*) *npl* trybuny *pl* (*nie osłonięte*)
**bleak** [bliːk] *adj* ponury, posępny
**bleary-eyed** ['blɪərɪ'aɪd] *adj*: **to be** ~ mieć zaczerwienione oczy
**bleat** [bliːt] *vi* beczeć (zabeczeć *perf*) ▷ *n* bek *m*, beczenie *nt*
**bled** [blɛd] *pt, pp of* **bleed**
**bleed** [bliːd] (*pt, pp* **bled**) *vi* (*Med*) krwawić; (*colour*) farbować, puszczać ▷ *vt* (*brakes, radiator*) odpowietrzać (odpowietrzyć *perf*); **my nose is ~ing** leci mi krew z nosa
**bleeper** ['bliːpəʳ] *n* brzęczyk *m* przywołujący
**blemish** ['blɛmɪʃ] *n* skaza *f*
**blend** [blɛnd] *n* mieszanka *f* ▷ *vt* (*Culin*) miksować (zmiksować *perf*); (*colours, styles*) mieszać (zmieszać *perf*) ▷ *vi* (*also*: **blend in**) wtapiać się (wtopić się *perf*)
**blender** ['blɛndəʳ] *n* mikser *m*
**bless** [blɛs] (*pt, pp* **~ed** *or* **blest**) *vt* błogosławić (pobłogosławić *perf*); **to be ~ed with** być obdarzonym +*instr*; **~ you!** na zdrowie!, sto lat!
**blessed** ['blɛsɪd] *adj* błogosławiony; **it rains every ~ day** (*inf*) nie ma dnia, żeby nie lało (*inf*)
**blessing** ['blɛsɪŋ] *n* błogosławieństwo *nt*; **you should count your ~s** powinieneś dziękować Bogu za to, co masz; **a ~ in disguise** błogosławione w skutkach nieszczęście
**blew** [bluː] *pt of* **blow**
**blight** [blaɪt] *vt* niweczyć (zniweczyć *perf*) ▷ *n* rdza *f* zbożowa
**blimey** ['blaɪmɪ] (*Brit: inf*) *excl* (o) kurczę! (*inf*)
**blind** [blaɪnd] *adj* niewidomy, ślepy; **~ (to)** (*fig*) ślepy (na +*acc*) ▷ *n* (*for window*) roleta *f*; (*also*: **Venetian blind**) żaluzja *f* ▷ *vt* oślepiać (oślepić *perf*); (*deaden*) zaślepiać (zaślepić *perf*); **the blind** *npl* niewidomi *vir pl*; **to turn a ~ eye (on** *or* **to)** przymykać (przymknąć *perf*) oko (na +*acc*)
**blind alley** *n* (*fig*) ślepa uliczka *f*
**blind corner** (*Brit*) *n* zakręt *m* z ograniczoną widocznością
**blind date** *n* randka *f* w ciemno
**blinders** ['blaɪndəz] (*US*) *npl* = **blinkers**
**blindfold** ['blaɪndfəuld] *n* przepaska *f* na oczy ▷ *adj* z zawiązanymi oczami *post* ▷ *adv* z zawiązanymi oczami ▷ *vt* zawiązywać (zawiązać *perf*) oczy +*dat*
**blindly** ['blaɪndlɪ] *adv* (*without seeing*) na oślep; (*without thinking*) ślepo
**blindness** ['blaɪndnɪs] *n* (*lit, fig*) ślepota *f*
**blind spot** *n* (*Aut*) martwy punkt *m*; (*fig: weak spot*) słabość *f*
**blink** [blɪŋk] *vi* (*person, animal*) mrugać (zamrugać *perf*); (*light*) migać (zamigać *perf*) ▷ *n*: **the TV's on the** ~ (*inf*) telewizor nawalił (*inf*)
**blinkers** ['blɪŋkəz] *npl* klapki *pl* na oczy
**blinking** ['blɪŋkɪŋ] (*Brit: inf*) *adj* cholerny (*inf*)
**bliss** [blɪs] *n* rozkosz *f*
**blissful** ['blɪsful] *adj* błogi; **in ~ ignorance** w błogiej niewiedzy

**blissfully** ['blɪsfəlɪ] *adv* błogo; **~ happy** bezgranicznie szczęśliwy; **~ unaware of** w błogiej nieświadomości *+gen*

**blister** ['blɪstə^r] *n* (*on skin*) pęcherz *m*; (*in paint, rubber*) pęcherzyk *m* ▷ *vi* (*paint*) pokrywać się (pokryć się *perf*) pęcherzykami

**blithely** ['blaɪðlɪ] *adv* beztrosko

**blithering** ['blɪðərɪŋ] (*inf*) *adj*: **~ idiot** skończony idiota (*inf*)

**BLit(t)** *n abbr* (= *Bachelor of Literature, Bachelor of Letters*) *stopień naukowy*

**blitz** [blɪts] *n* (*Mil*) bombardowanie *nt*; **to have a ~ on sth** (*fig*) ostro zabierać się (zabrać się *perf*) za coś

**blizzard** ['blɪzəd] *n* zamieć *f* (śnieżna)

**BLM** (*US*) *n abbr* (= *Bureau of Land Management*) *urząd federalny zajmujący się administracją gruntów i bogactw naturalnych*

**bloated** ['bləutɪd] *adj* (*face*) opuchnięty; (*stomach*) wydęty; (*person*) napchany (*inf*)

**blob** [blɔb] *n* (*of glue, paint*) kropelka *f*; (*sth indistinct*) plamka *f*

**bloc** [blɔk] (*Pol*) *n* blok *m*; **the Eastern ~** blok wschodni

**block** [blɔk] *n* (*large building, piece of stone*) blok *m*; (*toy*) klocek *m*; (*of ice*) bryła *f*; (*of wood*) kloc *m*; (*esp US: in town, city*) *obszar zabudowany, ograniczony ze wszystkich stron kolejnymi ulicami* ▷ *vt* (*road, agreement*) blokować (zablokować *perf*); (*Comput*) wyróżniać (wyróżnić *perf*); **~ of flats** (*Brit*) blok (mieszkalny); **three ~s from here** trzy przecznice stąd; **mental ~** zaćmienie (umysłu); **~ and tackle** wielokrążek

▸ **block up** *vt* zapychać (zapchać *perf*) ▷ *vi* zapychać się (zapchać się *perf*)

**blockade** [blɔ'keɪd] *n* blokada *f* ▷ *vt* blokować, zablokowywać (zablokować *perf*)

**blockage** ['blɔkɪdʒ] *n* (*in pipe, tube*) zator *m*

**block booking** *n* rezerwacja *f* zbiorowa

**blockbuster** ['blɔkbʌstə^r] *n* szlagier *m* (*film lub książka*)

**block capitals** *npl* drukowane litery *pl*

**blockhead** ['blɔkhɛd] (*inf*) *n* zakuty łeb *m* (*inf*)

**block letters** *npl* = **block capitals**

**block release** (*Brit*) *n* urlop *m* szkoleniowy

**block vote** (*Brit*) *n* głosowanie *nt* pośrednie

**blog** [blɔg] (*Comput*) *n* blog *m* ▷ *vi* blogować *imperf*

**bloke** [bləuk] (*Brit: inf*) *n* facet *m* (*inf*), gość *m* (*inf*)

**blond(e)** [blɔnd] *adj* blond ▷ *n*: **blonde** blondynka *f*

**blood** [blʌd] *n* krew *f*; **new ~** (*fig*) nowa krew

**bloodbath** ['blʌdbɑːθ] *n* rzeź *f*

**bloodcurdling** ['blʌdkəːdlɪŋ] *adj* mrożący krew w żyłach

**blood donor** *n* krwiodawca *m*

**blood group** *n* grupa *f* krwi

**bloodhound** ['blʌdhaund] *n* pies *m* św. Huberta

**bloodless** ['blʌdlɪs] *adj* (*victory*) bezkrwawy; (*cheeks*) blady

**bloodletting** ['blʌdlɛtɪŋ] *n* (*Med*) upust *m* krwi; (*fig*) rozlew *m* krwi

**blood poisoning** *n* posocznica *f*

**blood pressure** *n* ciśnienie *nt* (krwi); **to have high/low ~** mieć wysokie/niskie ciśnienie

**bloodshed** ['blʌdʃɛd] *n* rozlew *m* krwi

**bloodshot** ['blʌdʃɔt] *adj* nabiegły krwią

**blood sport** *n* łowiectwo *nt*

**bloodstained** ['blʌdsteɪnd] *adj* poplamiony krwią

**bloodstream** ['blʌdstriːm] *n* krwiobieg *m*

**blood test** *n* badanie *nt* krwi

**bloodthirsty** ['blʌdθəːstɪ] *adj* krwiożerczy

**blood transfusion** *n* transfuzja *f* (krwi)

**blood vessel** *n* naczynie *nt* krwionośne

**bloody** ['blʌdɪ] *adj* (*battle*) krwawy; (*hands*) zakrwawiony; (*Brit: inf!*) cholerny (*inf*); **~ strong/good** (*inf!*) cholernie silny/dobry (*inf*)

**bloody-minded** ['blʌdɪ'maɪndɪd] (*Brit: inf*) *adj* perfidny

**bloom** [bluːm] *n* kwiat *m* (*na drzewie itp*) ▷ *vi* (*be in flower*) kwitnąć; (*come into flower*) zakwitać (zakwitnąć *perf*); (*fig: talent, beauty*) rozkwitać (rozkwitnąć *perf*); **to be in ~** kwitnąć

**blooming** ['bluːmɪŋ] (*inf*) *adj* cholerny (*inf*)

**blossom** ['blɔsəm] *n* kwiat *m* ▷ *n inv* kwiecie *nt*, kwiaty *pl* ▷ *vi* zakwitać (zakwitnąć *perf*); **she has ~ed into a real beauty** zrobiła się z niej prawdziwa piękność

**blot** [blɔt] *n* kleks *m*; (*fig*) plama *f* ▷ *vt* osuszać (osuszyć *perf*) bibułą; **to be a ~ on the landscape** psuć widok; **to ~ one's copybook** (*fig*) psuć (zepsuć *perf*) sobie reputację

▸ **blot out** *vt* (*view*) przesłaniać (przesłonić *perf*); (*memory, thought*) wymazywać (wymazać *perf*) z pamięci

**blotchy** ['blɔtʃɪ] *adj* (*complexion*) plamisty

**blotter** ['blɔtə^r] *n* suszka *f*

**blotting paper** ['blɔtɪŋ-] *n* bibuła *f*

**blouse** [blauz] *n* bluzka *f*

**blow** [bləu] (*pt* **blew**, *pp* **~n**) *n* (*lit, fig*) cios *m* ▷ *vi* (*wind*) wiać; (*person*) dmuchać (dmuchnąć *perf*) ▷ *vt* (*instrument*) grać na *+loc*; (*whistle*) dmuchać (dmuchnąć *perf*) w *+acc*; (*fuse*) przepalać (przepalić *perf*); **to ~ one's nose** wydmuchiwać (wydmuchać *perf*) nos; **a gust of wind blew snow in her face** podmuch wiatru sypnął jej śniegiem w twarz; **they came to ~s** doszło (między nimi) do rękoczynów

▸ **blow away** *vt* wywiewać (wywiać *perf*) ▷ *vi* (*piece of paper etc*) odfruwać (odfrunąć *perf*)

▸ **blow down** *vt* (*tree*) powalać (powalić *perf*)
▸ **blow off** *vt* zwiewać (zwiać *perf*), zdmuchiwać (zdmuchnąć *perf*); **the washing blew off the line** wiatr zerwał pranie ze sznurka; **the ship was ~n off course** statek zniosło z kursu
▸ **blow out** *vt* (*fire, flame*) gasić (zgasić *perf*); (*candle*) zdmuchiwać (zdmuchnąć *perf*) ▹ *vi* gasnąć (zgasnąć *perf*)
▸ **blow over** *vi* (*storm, row*) ucichnąć (*perf*)
▸ **blow up** *vi* wybuchać (wybuchnąć *perf*) ▹ *vt* (*bridge, building*) wysadzać (wysadzić *perf*) (w powietrze); (*tyre*) pompować (napompować *perf*); (*balloon*) nadmuchiwać (nadmuchać *perf*); (*Phot*) powiększać (powiększyć *perf*)

**blow-dry** ['bləudraɪ] *n* modelowanie *nt* włosów (suszarką) ▹ *vt* modelować (wymodelować *perf*) (suszarką)
**blowlamp** ['bləulæmp] (*Brit*) *n* lampa *f* lutownicza
**blown** [bləun] *pp of* **blow**
**blow-out** ['bləuaut] *n* (*of tyre*) rozerwanie *nt*; (*of oil-well*) erupcja *f*; (*inf*: *big meal*) wyżerka *f* (*inf*)
**blowtorch** ['bləutɔ:tʃ] *n* = **blowlamp**
**blow-up** ['bləuʌp] *n* (*Phot*) powiększenie *nt*
**blowzy** ['blauzɪ] (*Brit*) *adj* flejtuchowaty
**BLS** (*US*) *n abbr* (= *Bureau of Labor Statistics*) *urząd federalny opracowujący statystyki rynku pracy*
**blubber** ['blʌbəʳ] *n* tłuszcz *m* wielorybi ▹ *vi* (*pej*) beczeć (*inf*), ryczeć (*inf*)
**bludgeon** ['blʌdʒən] *vt* tłuc (stłuc *perf*) pałką; **to ~ sb into doing sth** (*fig*) wymusić (*perf*) na kimś zrobienie czegoś
**blue** [blu:] *adj* niebieski; (*from cold*) siny; (*depressed*) smutny; (*joke*) pikantny; (*film*) porno *post* ▹ *n* (kolor *m*) niebieski, błękit *m*; **blues** *n*: **the blues** blues *m*; **(only) once in a ~ moon** (tylko) od wielkiego święta *or* dzwonu; **out of the ~** (*fig*) ni stąd, ni zowąd; **to have the ~s** mieć chandrę
**blue baby** *n* noworodek *m* z sinicą
**bluebell** ['blu:bɛl] *n* (*Bot*) dzwonek *m*
**bluebottle** ['blu:bɔtl] *n* mucha *f* mięsna
**blue cheese** *n* ser *m* pleśniowy
**blue-chip** ['blu:tʃɪp] *adj*: **~ investment** bezpieczna inwestycja *f*
**blue-collar worker** ['blu:kɔləʳ-] *n* pracownik *m* fizyczny
**blue jeans** *npl* dżinsy *pl*
**blueprint** ['blu:prɪnt] *n*: **a ~ (for)** (*fig*) projekt *m* (+*gen*)
**bluff** [blʌf] *vi* blefować (zablefować *perf*) ▹ *n* (*deception*) blef *m*; (*Geol*: *cliff*) urwisko *nt*; (: *promontory*) urwisty cypel *m*; **to call sb's ~** zmuszać (zmusić *perf*) kogoś do odkrycia kart
**blunder** ['blʌndəʳ] *n* gafa *f* ▹ *vi* popełniać (popełnić *perf*) gafę; **to ~ into sb/sth** wpadać (wpaść *perf*) na kogoś/coś
**blunt** [blʌnt] *adj* (*knife, pencil*) tępy; (*person, talk*) bezceremonialny ▹ *vt* tępić (stępić *perf*); **~ instrument** (*Jur*) tępe narzędzie; **to be ~, ...** mówiąc bez ogródek, ...
**bluntly** ['blʌntlɪ] *adv* bez ogródek, prosto z mostu
**bluntness** ['blʌntnɪs] *n* (*of person*) bezceremonialność *f*
**blur** [blə:ʳ] *n* (*shape*) niewyraźna plama *f*; (*memory*) mgliste wspomnienie *nt* ▹ *vt* (*vision*) zamglić (*perf*); (*distinction*) zacierać (zatrzeć *perf*), zamazywać (zamazać *perf*)
**blurb** [blə:b] *n* (*for book, concert*) notka *f* reklamowa
**blurred** [blə:d] *adj* zamazany
**blurt out** [blə:t-] *vt* wyrzucać (wyrzucić *perf*) z siebie
**blush** [blʌʃ] *vi* rumienić się (zarumienić się *perf*), czerwienić się (zaczerwienić się *perf*) ▹ *n* rumieniec *m*
**blusher** ['blʌʃəʳ] *n* róż *m* (*do makijażu*)
**bluster** ['blʌstəʳ] *n* (*threatening*) (głośne) pogróżki *pl*; (*boastful*) (głośne) przechwałki *pl* ▹ *vi* (*in anger*) grzmieć (zagrzmieć *perf*); (*boast*) przechwalać się (głośno)
**blustering** ['blʌstərɪŋ] *adj* (*tone*) grzmiący; (*person*): **to be ~** robić dużo hałasu
**blustery** ['blʌstərɪ] *adj*: **~ weather** zawierucha *f*
**Blvd** *abbr* = **boulevard**
**BM** *n abbr* (= *British Museum, Bachelor of Medicine*) *stopień naukowy*
**BMA** *n abbr* = **British Medical Association**
**BMJ** *n abbr* = **British Medical Journal**
**BMus** *n abbr* (= *Bachelor of Music*) *stopień naukowy*
**BMX** *n abbr* (= *bicycle motocross*) kros *m* rowerowy; **BMX bike** rower *m* krosowy, rower *m* BMX
**BO** *n abbr* (*inf*: = *body odour*) nieprzyjemny zapach *m* (ciała); (*US*) = **box office**
**boar** [bɔ:ʳ] *n* (*also*: **wild boar**) dzik *m*; (*male pig*) knur *m*
**board** [bɔ:d] *n* (*piece of wood*) deska *f*; (*piece of cardboard*) tektura *f*; (*also*: **notice board**) tablica *f*; (*for chess etc*) plansza *f*; (*committee*) rada *f*; (*in firm*) zarząd *m*; (*Naut, Aviat*): **on ~** na pokładzie ▹ *vt* (*ship*) wchodzić (wejść *perf*) na pokład +*gen*; (*train*) wsiadać (wsiąść *perf*) do +*gen*; **full/half ~** (*Brit*) pełne/niepełne wyżywienie; **~ and lodging** mieszkanie i wyżywienie; **the plan went by the ~** (*fig*) plan poszedł do kosza; **above ~** (*fig*) zgodny z prawem; **across the ~** (*fig*: *adv*) bez wyjątku; (: *adj*) dotyczący wszystkich

▸ **board up** *vt* (*door, window*) zabijać (zabić *perf*) deskami
**boarder** ['bɔːdə$^r$] (*Scol*) *n* mieszkaniec(-nka) *m(f)* internatu
**board game** *n* gra *f* planszowa
**boarding card** ['bɔːdɪŋ-] *n* = **boarding pass**
**boarding house** *n* pensjonat *m*
**boarding pass** *n* karta *f* pokładowa
**boarding school** *n* szkoła *f* z internatem
**board meeting** *n* zebranie *nt* zarządu
**board room** *n* sala *f* posiedzeń
**boardwalk** ['bɔːdwɔːk] (*US*) *n* promenada *f* (nadmorska)
**boast** [bəust] *vi*: **to ~ (about** *or* **of)** chwalić się *or* przechwalać się (*+instr*) ▹ *vt* (*fig*) szczycić się *+instr*
**boastful** ['bəustful] *adj* chełpliwy
**boastfulness** ['bəustfulnɪs] *n* chełpliwość *f*
**boat** [bəut] *n* łódź *f*; (*smaller*) łódka *f*; (*ship*) statek *m*; **to go somewhere by ~** płynąć (popłynąć *perf*) gdzieś statkiem; **to be in the same ~** (*fig*) jechać na tym samym wózku
**boater** ['bəutə$^r$] *n* kapelusz *m* słomkowy (*sztywny, z płaskim rondem*)
**boating** ['bəutɪŋ] *n* przejażdżka *f* łodzią
**boatswain** ['bəusn] *n* bosman *m*
**bob** [bɔb] *vi* (*also*: **bob up and down**: *boat*) huśtać się; (: *cork on water*) podskakiwać ▹ *n* (*Brit*: *inf*) = **shilling**
▸ **bob up** *vi* wyskakiwać (wyskoczyć *perf*)
**bobbin** ['bɔbɪn] *n* szpulka *f*
**bobby** ['bɔbɪ] (*Brit*: *inf*) *n policjant angielski*
**bobsleigh** ['bɔbsleɪ] *n* bobslej *m*
**bode** [bəud] *vi*: **to ~ well/ill (for)** wróżyć dobrze/źle (*+dat*)
**bodice** ['bɔdɪs] *n* góra *f* (sukienki)
**bodily** ['bɔdɪlɪ] *adj* (*functions*) fizjologiczny; (*needs, pain*) fizyczny ▹ *adv* (*move, lift etc*) w całości
**body** ['bɔdɪ] *n* (*Anat*) ciało *nt*; (*corpse*) zwłoki *pl*; (*main part*) główna część *f*; (*of car*) karoseria *f*, nadwozie *nt*; (*of plane*) kadłub *m*; (*fig*: *group*) grono *nt*; (: *organization*) ciało *nt*, gremium *nt*; (*of facts*) ilość *f*; (*of wine*) treść *f*, treściwość *f*; **ruling ~** ciało rządzące
**body-building** ['bɔdɪ'bɪldɪŋ] *n* kulturystyka *f*
**bodyguard** ['bɔdɪgɑːd] *n* członek *m* ochrony (osobistej), ochroniarz *m* (*inf*)
**body repairs** *npl* prace *pl* blacharskie
**bodywork** ['bɔdɪwəːk] *n* nadwozie *nt*
**boffin** ['bɔfɪn] *n* jajogłowy *m*
**bog** [bɔg] *n* bagno *nt* ▹ *vt*: **to get bogged down** (*fig*) grzęźć (ugrzęźć *perf*)
**bogey** ['bəugɪ] *n* (*worry*) zmora *f*; (*also*: **bogeyman**) strach *m*
**boggle** ['bɔgl] *vi*: **the mind ~s** w głowie się nie mieści
**bogie** ['bəugɪ] *n* straszydło *nt*
**Bogot** [bəugə'tɑː] *n* Bogota *f*
**bogus** ['bəugəs] *adj* fałszywy
**Bohemia** [bəu'hiːmɪə] *n* Czechy *pl*
**Bohemian** [bəu'hiːmɪən] *adj* czeski ▹ *n* Czech/Czeszka *m/f*; **bohemian cygan(ka)** *m(f)*
**boil** [bɔɪl] *vt* (*water*) gotować, zagotowywać (zagotować *perf*); (*eggs etc*) gotować (ugotować *perf*) ▹ *vi* (*liquid*) gotować się (zagotować się *perf*), wrzeć (zawrzeć *perf*); (*fig*: *with anger*) kipieć ▹ *n* czyrak *m*; **to come to the** (*Brit*) *or* **a** (*US*) **~** zagotować się (*perf*)
▸ **boil down to** *vt fus* (*fig*) sprowadzać się (sprowadzić się *perf*) do *+gen*
▸ **boil over** *vi* kipieć (wykipieć *perf*)
**boiled egg** [bɔɪld-] *n* gotowane jajko *nt*
**boiled potatoes** *npl* ziemniaki *pl* gotowane *or* z wody
**boiler** ['bɔɪlə$^r$] *n* kocioł *m*, bojler *m*
**boiler suit** *n* kombinezon *m*
**boiling** ['bɔɪlɪŋ] *adj*: **I'm ~ (hot)** (*inf*) umieram z gorąca, gotuję się (*inf*); **it's ~ in here** można się tu ugotować
**boiling point** *n* temperatura *f* wrzenia
**boisterous** ['bɔɪstərəs] *adj* hałaśliwy
**bold** [bəuld] *adj* (*person, action*) śmiały; (*pattern, colours*) krzykliwy; **if I may be so ~** jeśli wolno spytać
**boldly** ['bəuldlɪ] *adv* (*bravely*) śmiało; (*defiantly*) zuchwale
**boldness** ['bəuldnɪs] *n* śmiałość *f*
**bold type** *n* tłusta czcionka *f*
**Bolivia** [bə'lɪvɪə] *n* Boliwia *f*
**Bolivian** [bə'lɪvɪən] *adj* boliwijski ▹ *n* Boliwijczyk(-jka) *m(f)*
**bollard** ['bɔləd] *n* (*Brit*: *Aut*) słupek *m*; (*Naut*) pachołek *m*
**bolster** ['bəulstə$^r$] *n* wałek *m* (*pod głowę*)
▸ **bolster up** *vt* podbudowywać (podbudować *perf*)
**bolt** [bəult] *n* (*lock*) zasuwa *f*, rygiel *m*; (*with nut*) śruba *f*; (*of lightning*) piorun *m* ▹ *vt* (*door*) ryglować (zaryglować *perf*); (*food*) połykać (połknąć *perf*) (*nie żując*); **to ~ sth to sth** przykuwać (przykuć *perf*) coś do czegoś ▹ *vi* (*person*) pędzić (popędzić *perf*); (*horse*) ponosić (ponieść *perf*) ▹ *adv*: **~ upright** (prosto) jakby kij połknął; **a ~ from the blue** (*fig*) grom z jasnego nieba
**bomb** [bɔm] *n* bomba *f* ▹ *vt* bombardować (zbombardować *perf*)
**bombard** [bɔm'bɑːd] *vt* (*Mil*) bombardować (zbombardować *perf*); (*fig*: *with questions*) bombardować
**bombardment** [bɔm'bɑːdmənt] *n* bombardowanie *nt*
**bombastic** [bɔm'bæstɪk] *adj* (*person*) napuszony; (*language*) bombastyczny

**bomb disposal** *n*: **~ unit** oddział *m* saperski; **~ expert** saper

**bomber** ['bɔmə^r] *n* (*Aviat*) bombowiec *m*; (*terrorist*) zamachowiec *m*

**bombing** ['bɔmɪŋ] *n* atak *m* bombowy

**bombshell** ['bɔmʃɛl] *n* (*fig*) sensacja *f*

**bomb site** *n* lej *m* po bombie

**bona fide** ['bəunə'faɪdɪ] *adj* (*traveller etc*) prawdziwy; (*offer*) rzetelny

**bonanza** [bə'nænzə] *n* dobra *or* szczęśliwa passa *f*

**bond** [bɔnd] *n* (*of affection etc*) więź *f*; (*Fin*) obligacja *f*; (*Comm*): **in ~** na cle (*o wwożonym towarze*); **my word is my ~** daję słowo honoru

**bondage** ['bɔndɪdʒ] *n* niewola *f*; (*sexual*) krępowanie *nt* (*praktyka seksualna*)

**bonded warehouse** ['bɔndɪd-] *n* magazyn *m* *or* skład *m* celny

**bone** [bəun] *n* (*Anat*) kość *f*; (*of fish*) ość *f* ▷ *vt* (*meat*) oczyszczać (oczyścić *perf*) z kości; (*fish*) oczyszczać (oczyścić *perf*) z ości; **I've got a ~ to pick with you** mam z tobą do pomówienia

**bone china** *n* porcelana *f* kostna

**bone-dry** ['bəun'draɪ] *adj* suchy jak pieprz

**bone idle** *adj*: **he is ~** to śmierdzący leń

**boner** ['bəunə^r] (*US*) *n* byk *m*

**bonfire** ['bɔnfaɪə^r] *n* ognisko *nt*; **~ night** *wieczór 5 listopada, kiedy w Wielkiej Brytanii pali się kukłę Guya Fawkesa*

**Bonn** [bɔn] *n* Bonn *nt inv*

**bonnet** ['bɔnɪt] *n* (*hat*) czepek *m*; (*Brit*: *of car*) maska *f*

**bonny** ['bɔnɪ] *adj* (*Scottish, Northern English*) ładny

**bonus** ['bəunəs] *n* premia *f*; (*fig*) dodatkowa korzyść *f*

**bony** ['bəunɪ] *adj* (*arm, person*) kościsty; (*Med*: *tissue*) kostny; (*fish*) ościsty; **the meat is ~** to mięso ma dużo kości

**boo** [bu:] *excl* hu (*okrzyk mający na celu przestraszenie kogoś*) ▷ *vt* wygwizdywać (wygwizdać *perf*)

**boob** [bu:b] (*inf*) *n* (*breast*) cyc(ek) *m* (*inf*); (*Brit*: *mistake*) byk *m* (*inf*) ▷ *vi* strzelić (*perf*) byka (*inf*)

**booby prize** ['bu:bɪ-] *n* nagroda *f* pocieszenia

**booby trap** ['bu:bɪ-] *n* bomba *f* pułapka *f*; (*fig*: *practical joke*) głupi kawał *m*

**booby-trapped** ['bu:bɪtræpt] *adj* z podłączoną bombą-pułapką *post*; **a ~ car** samochód-pułapka

**book** [buk] *n* książka *f*; (*of stamps, tickets*) bloczek *m* ▷ *vt* (*ticket, seat, room*) rezerwować (zarezerwować *perf*); (*driver*) spisywać (spisać *perf*); (*Sport*: *player*) dawać (dać *perf*) kartkę *+dat*; **books** *npl* (*Comm*) księgi *pl* rachunkowe; **to keep the ~s** prowadzić księgowość; **by the ~** według przepisów; **to throw the ~ at sb** wymierzać (wymierzyć *perf*) komuś najwyższą karę

▸ **book in** (*Brit*) *vi* (*at hotel*) meldować się (zameldować się *perf*)

▸ **book up** *vt* wykupywać (wykupić *perf*); **all seats are ~ed up** wszystkie miejsca zostały wyprzedane; **the hotel is ~ed up** w hotelu nie ma wolnych miejsc

**bookable** ['bukəbl] *adj*: **all seats are ~** wszystkie miejsca są numerowane

**bookcase** ['bukkeɪs] *n* biblioteczka *f*, regał *m* na książki

**book ends** *npl* podpórki *pl* do książek

**booking** ['bukɪŋ] (*Brit*) *n* rezerwacja *f*

**booking office** (*Brit*) *n* kasa *f*

**book-keeping** ['buk'ki:pɪŋ] *n* księgowość *f*

**booklet** ['buklɪt] *n* broszur(k)a *f*

**bookmaker** ['bukmeɪkə^r] *n* bukmacher *m*

**bookmark** ['bukmɑ:k] *n* zakładka *f* (do książki); (*Comput*) zakładka *f* ▷ *vt* (*Comput*) dodawać (dodać *perf*) do ulubionych

**bookseller** ['buksɛlə^r] *n* księgarz *m*

**bookshop** ['bukʃɔp] *n* księgarnia *f*

**bookstall** ['bukstɔ:l] *n* stoisko *nt* księgarskie

**book store** *n* = **bookshop**

**book token** *n* talon *m* na książki

**book value** *n* wartość *f* księgowa

**boom** [bu:m] *n* (*noise*) huk *m*, grzmot *m*; (*in exports etc*) wzrost *m*, (dobra) koniunktura *f*; (*busy period*) ruch *m* ▷ *vi* grzmieć (zagrzmieć *perf*); (*business*) zwyżkować; **population ~** wyż demograficzny

**boomerang** ['bu:məræŋ] *n* bumerang *m* ▷ *vi* (*fig*): **to ~ on sb** obracać się (obrócić się *perf*) przeciwko komuś

**boom town** *n* świetnie prosperujące miasto *nt*

**boon** [bu:n] *n* dobrodziejstwo *nt*

**boorish** ['buərɪʃ] *adj* grubiański, gburowaty

**boost** [bu:st] *n*: **a ~ to sb's confidence** zastrzyk *m* pewności siebie ▷ *vt* (*sales, demand*) zwiększać (zwiększyć *perf*); (*confidence*) dodawać (dodać *perf*) *+gen*; (*morale*) podnosić (podnieść *perf*); **to give a ~ to sb's spirits** *or* **to sb** podnosić (podnieść *perf*) kogoś na duchu

**booster** ['bu:stə^r] *n* (*Med*) zastrzyk *m* przypominający; (*TV, Elec*) przetwornica *f*; (*also*: **booster rocket**) silnik *m* rakietowy pomocniczy

**booster seat** *n* fotelik *m* dziecięcy (*w samochodzie*)

**boot** [bu:t] *n* (*for winter*) kozaczek *m*; (*for football, walking*) but *m*; (*also*: **ankle boot**) trzewik *m*; (*Brit*: *of car*) bagażnik *m* ▷ *vt* (*Comput*) inicjować (zainicjować *perf*), zapuszczać (zapuścić *perf*) (*inf*); **... to ~** ...do tego (jeszcze), ...na dodatek; **to give sb the ~** *(inf)* wylewać (wylać *perf*) kogoś (z pracy) *(inf)*

**booth** [bu:ð] *n (at fair)* stoisko *nt*; *(for voting, telephoning)* kabina *f*

**bootleg** ['bu:tlɛg] *adj* nielegalny

**bootlegger** ['bu:tlɛgə^r] *n* przemytnik(-iczka) *m(f)* alkoholu

**booty** ['bu:tɪ] *n* łup *m*

**booze** [bu:z] *(inf) n* coś *nt* mocniejszego ▹ *vi* popijać (popić *perf*)

**boozer** ['bu:zə^r] *(inf) n (person)* ochlapus *m (inf)*; *(Brit)* knajpa *f (inf)*

**border** ['bɔ:də^r] *n (of country)* granica *f*; *(for flowers)* rabat(k)a *f*; *(on cloth)* lamówka *f*; *(on plate)* obwódka *f* ▹ *vt* leżeć wzdłuż *+gen*; *(also:* **border on**) graniczyć z *+instr*; **elm trees ~ the road** wzdłuż szosy rosną wiązy; **Borders** *n*: **the Borders** *pogranicze angielsko-szkockie*
▸ **border on** *vt fus (fig)* graniczyć z *+instr*

**borderline** ['bɔ:dəlaɪn] *n*: **on the ~** *(fig)* na granicy

**borderline case** *n* przypadek *m* wątpliwy

**bore** [bɔ:^r] *pt of* **bear** ▹ *vt (hole, tunnel)* wiercić (wywiercić *perf*); *(person)* zanudzać (zanudzić *perf*) ▹ *n (person)* nudziarz(-ara) *m(f)*; *(of gun)* kaliber *m*; **to be ~d** nudzić się; **he's ~d to tears** *or* **~d to death** *or* **~d stiff** umiera z nudów

**boredom** ['bɔ:dəm] *n (condition)* znudzenie *nt*; *(quality)* nuda *f*

**boring** ['bɔ:rɪŋ] *adj (tedious)* nudny; *(unimaginative)* nieciekawy

**born** [bɔ:n] *adj*: **to be ~** rodzić się (urodzić się *perf*); **I was ~ in 1960** urodziłem się w roku 1960; **~ blind** niewidomy od urodzenia; **a ~ comedian** urodzony komik

**borne** [bɔ:n] *pp of* **bear**

**Borneo** ['bɔ:nɪəu] *n* Borneo *nt inv*

**borough** ['bʌrə] *n* okręg *m* wyborczy

**borrow** ['bɔrəu] *vt (from sb)* pożyczać (pożyczyć *perf*); *(from library)* wypożyczać (wypożyczyć *perf*); **may I ~ your car?** czy mogę pożyczyć twój samochód?

**borrower** ['bɔrəuə^r] *n* kredytobiorca *m*

**borrowing** ['bɔrəuɪŋ] *n (Comm)* zaciąganie *nt* kredytów; *(Ling)* zapożyczenie *nt*

**borstal** ['bɔ:stl] *(Brit) n* dom *m or* zakład *m* poprawczy, poprawczak *m (inf)*

**bosom** ['buzəm] *n (Anat)* biust *m*; *(fig: of family)* łono *nt*

**bosom friend** *n* przyjaciel(-iółka) *m(f)* od serca

**boss** [bɔs] *n* szef(owa) *m(f)* ▹ *vt (also:* **boss around, boss about**) rozkazywać *+dat*; **stop ~ing everyone about!** przestań rozstawiać wszystkich po kątach!

**bossy** ['bɔsɪ] *adj* despotyczny

**bosun** ['bəusn] *(Naut) n* bosman *m*

**botanical** [bə'tænɪkl] *adj* botaniczny

**botanist** ['bɔtənɪst] *n* botanik(-iczka) *m(f)*

**botany** ['bɔtənɪ] *n* botanika *f*

**botch** [bɔtʃ] *vt (also:* **botch up**) knocić (sknocić *perf*) *(inf)*

**both** [bəuθ] *adj* obaj ▹ *pron (things: with plurals of neuter and masculine nouns)* oba; *(: with plurals of feminine nouns)* obie; *(people: male)* obaj; *(: female)* obie; *(: a male and a female)* oboje ▹ *adv*: **~ A and B** zarówno A, jak i B; **~ of us went, we ~ went** poszliśmy oboje; **they sell ~ meat and poultry** sprzedają mięso i drób; **they sell ~ the fabric and the finished curtains** sprzedają zarówno tkaniny, jak i gotowe zasłony

**bother** ['bɔðə^r] *vt (worry)* niepokoić; *(disturb)* przeszkadzać *+dat*, zawracać głowę *+dat (inf)* ▹ *vi (also:* **bother o.s.**) trudzić się, zawracać sobie głowę *(inf)* ▹ *n (trouble)* kłopot *m*; *(nuisance)*: **to be a ~** zawracać głowę *(inf)* ▹ *excl* kurczę *(inf)*; **it is a ~ to have to do** dużo z tym kłopotu; **to ~ doing sth** zadawać sobie trud robienia czegoś; **I'm sorry to ~ you** przepraszam, że przeszkadzam; **please don't ~** nie kłopocz się; **don't ~** nie zawracaj sobie głowy; **it's no ~** (to) żaden kłopot

**Botswana** [bɔt'swɑ:nə] *n* Botswana *f*

**bottle** ['bɔtl] *n* butelka *f*; *(small)* buteleczka *f*; *(Brit: inf)* odwaga *f* ▹ *vt (beer, wine)* rozlewać (rozlać *perf*) do butelek, butelkować; *(fruit)* zaprawiać (zaprawić *perf*); **a ~ of wine/milk** butelka wina/mleka; **wine/milk ~** butelka po winie/od mleka
▸ **bottle up** *vt* tłumić (stłumić *perf*) w sobie

**bottle bank** *n* pojemnik *m* na stłuczkę szklaną

**bottle-fed** ['bɔtlfɛd] *adj* karmiony butelką *or* sztucznie

**bottleneck** ['bɔtlnɛk] *n (Aut)* korek *m* (uliczny); *(fig)* wąskie gardło *nt*

**bottle-opener** ['bɔtləupnə^r] *n* otwieracz *m* do butelek

**bottom** ['bɔtəm] *n (of container, sea)* dno *nt*; *(buttocks)* pupa *f*, siedzenie *nt*; *(of page)* dół *m*; *(of chair)* siedzenie *nt*; *(of class etc)* szary koniec *m*; *(of mountain)* podnóże *nt* ▹ *adj* najniższy; **at the ~ of** *(mountain)* u stóp *or* podnóża *+gen*; *(situation, attitude)* u podłoża *+gen*; **to get to the ~ of sth** *(fig)* docierać (dotrzeć *perf*) do sedna czegoś

**bottomless** ['bɔtəmlɪs] *adj* bez dna *post*

**bough** [bau] *n* konar *m*

**bought** [bɔ:t] *pt, pp of* **buy**

**boulder** ['bəuldə^r] *n* głaz *m*

**boulevard** ['bu:ləvɑ:d] *n* bulwar *m*

**bounce** [bauns] *vi (ball)* odbijać się (odbić się *perf*); *(cheque)* nie mieć pokrycia ▹ *vt* odbijać

(odbić *perf*) ▷ *n* odbicie *nt*; **to ~ in/out** wpadać (wpaść *perf*)/wypadać (wypaść *perf*) w podskokach
**bouncer** ['baunsə[r]] (*inf*) *n* bramkarz *m* (*inf*) (*na dyskotece itp*)
**bound** [baund] *pt, pp of* **bind** ▷ *n* skok *m*; (*usu pl: of possibility etc*) granice *pl* ▷ *vi* podskakiwać (podskoczyć *perf*) ▷ *vt* otaczać (otoczyć *perf*), ograniczać (ograniczyć *perf*) ▷ *adj*: **~ by** (*law etc*) zobowiązany *+instr*; **to be/feel ~ to do sth** być/czuć się zobowiązanym zrobić coś; **he's ~ to fail** na pewno mu się nie uda; **~ for** (zdążający) do *+gen*; **out of ~s** (*fig*) w strefie zakazanej
**boundary** ['baundrı] *n* granica *f*
**boundless** ['baundlıs] *adj* nieograniczony, bezgraniczny
**bountiful** ['bauntıful] *adj* (*person*) szczodry; (*supply*) obfity
**bounty** ['bauntı] *n* (*generosity*) szczodrość *f*; (*reward*) premia *f*, nagroda *f*
**bounty hunter** *n* łowca *m* nagród
**bouquet** ['bukeı] *n* bukiet *m*
**bourbon** ['buəbən] (*US*) *n* burbon *m*
**bourgeois** ['buəʒwɑ:] *adj* burżuazyjny ▷ *n* członek *m* burżuazji, burżuj(ka) *m(f)* (*pej, inf*)
**bout** [baut] *n* (*of disease*) atak *m*; (*of activity*) napad *m*; (*Boxing*) walka *f*, mecz *m*
**boutique** [bu:'ti:k] *n* butik *m*
**bow**[1] [bəu] *n* (*knot*) kokarda *f*; (*weapon*) łuk *m*; (*Mus*) smyczek *m*
**bow**[2] [bau] *n* (*greeting*) ukłon *m*; (*Naut: also:* **bows**) dziób *m* ▷ *vi* kłaniać się (ukłonić się *perf*); **to bow to** *or* **before** (*pressure*) uginać się (ugiąć się *perf*) pod *+instr*; (*sb's wishes*) przystawać (przystać *perf*) na *+acc*; **to bow to the inevitable** godzić się (pogodzić się *perf*) z losem
**bowels** ['bauəlz] *npl* (*Anat*) jelita *pl*; (*of the earth etc*) wnętrze *nt*
**bowl** [bəul] *n* (*for/of food*) miska *f*; (*: small*) miseczka *f*; (*for washing*) miednica *f*; (*Sport*) kula *f*; (*of pipe*) główka *f*; (*US*) stadion *m* (*o budowie amfiteatralnej*) ▷ *vi* (*Cricket, Baseball*) rzucać (rzucić *perf*) (piłką)
▸ **bowl over** *vt* (*fig*) rzucać (rzucić *perf*) na kolana
**bow-legged** ['bəu'lɛgıd] *adj*: **to be ~** mieć pałąkowate nogi
**bowler** ['bəulə[r]] *n* (*Cricket, Baseball*) *gracz rzucający lub serwujący piłkę*; (*Brit: also:* **bowler hat**) melonik *m*
**bowling** ['bəulıŋ] *n* (*game*) kręgle *pl*
**bowling alley** *n* kręgielnia *f*
**bowling green** *n* trawnik *m* do gry w kule
**bowls** [bəulz] *n* gra *f* w kule
**bow tie** [bəu-] *n* muszka *f*
**box** [bɔks] *n* pudełko *nt*; (*cardboard box*) pudło *nt*, karton *m*; (*crate*) skrzynka *f*; (*Theat*) loża *f*; (*on form*) kratka *f*; (*Brit: Aut*) koperta *f* (*lub inne miejsce, w którym nie wolno się zatrzymywać*) ▷ *vt* pakować (zapakować *perf*) do pudełka/pudełek; (*Sport*) boksować się z *+instr* ▷ *vi* uprawiać boks; **to box sb's ears** dawać (dać *perf*) komuś po uszach
▸ **box in** *vt* blokować (zablokować *perf*)
▸ **box off** *vt* odgradzać (odgrodzić *perf*)
**boxer** ['bɔksə[r]] *n* bokser *m*
**box file** *n* segregator *m* (*w formie zamykanego pudła*)
**boxing** ['bɔksıŋ] (*Sport*) *n* boks *m*
**Boxing Day** (*Brit*) *n drugi dzień Świąt Bożego Narodzenia*
**boxing gloves** *npl* rękawice *pl* bokserskie
**boxing ring** *n* ring *m* bokserski
**box number** (*Press*) *n* numer *m* oferty
**box office** *n* kasa *f* (biletowa) (*w teatrze itp*)
**boxroom** ['bɔksrum] *n* rupieciarnia *f* (*służąca czasem jako dodatkowa sypialnia*)
**boy** [bɔı] *n* chłopiec *m*
**boycott** ['bɔıkɔt] *n* bojkot *m* ▷ *vt* bojkotować (zbojkotować *perf*)
**boyfriend** ['bɔıfrɛnd] *n* chłopak *m*; (*older woman's*) przyjaciel *m*
**boyish** ['bɔııʃ] *adj* chłopięcy
**boy scout** *n* ≈ harcerz *m*
**Bp** *abbr* (= *bishop*) bp
**BR** *abbr* (*formerly*) = **British Rail**
**bra** [brɑ:] *n* biustonosz *m*, stanik *m*
**brace** [breıs] *n* (*on teeth*) aparat *m* (korekcyjny); (*tool*) świder *m*; (*also:* **brace bracket**) nawias *m* klamrowy ▷ *vt* (*knees, shoulders*) napinać (napiąć *perf*); **braces** *npl* (*Brit*) szelki *pl*; **to ~ o.s.** podpierać się (podeprzeć się *perf*); (*fig*) zbierać (zebrać *perf*) siły
**bracelet** ['breıslıt] *n* bransoletka *f*
**bracing** ['breısıŋ] *adj* ożywczy, orzeźwiający
**bracken** ['brækən] *n* orlica *f* (*paproć*)
**bracket** ['brækıt] *n* (*Tech*) wspornik *m*, podpórka *f*; (*group, range*) przedział *m*; (*also:* **brace bracket**) nawias *m* klamrowy, klamra *f*; (*also:* **round bracket**) nawias *m* (okrągły); (*also:* **square bracket**) nawias *m* kwadratowy ▷ *vt* (*word, phrase*) brać (wziąć *perf*) w nawias; (*also:* **bracket together**) traktować (potraktować *perf*) razem; **income ~** przedział *or* grupa dochodu; **in ~s** w nawiasach
**brackish** ['brækıʃ] *adj* (*water*) słonawy
**brag** [bræg] *vi* chwalić się, przechwalać się
**braid** [breıd] *n* (*trimming*) galon *m*; (*plait*) warkocz *m*
**Braille** [breıl] *n* alfabet *m* Braille'a, brajl *m*

**brain** [breɪn] *n* mózg *m*; (*fig*) umysł *m*; **brains** *npl* (*Culin*) móżdżek *m*; (*intelligence*) głowa *f*; **he's got ~s** ma (dobrą) głowę
**brainchild** ['breɪntʃaɪld] *n*: **the project was the ~ of Max Nicholson** projekt narodził się w głowie Maxa Nicholsona
**brain drain** *n*: **the ~** drenaż *m* mózgów
**brainless** ['breɪnlɪs] *adj* głupi
**brainstorm** ['breɪnstɔːm] *n* (*aberration*) zaćmienie *nt* umysłu; (*US*: *brainwave*) olśnienie *nt*
**brainwash** ['breɪnwɔʃ] *vt* robić (zrobić *perf*) pranie mózgu +*dat*
**brainwave** ['breɪnweɪv] *n* olśnienie *nt*
**brainy** ['breɪnɪ] *adj* bystry, rozgarnięty
**braise** [breɪz] (*Culin*) *vt* dusić (udusić *perf*)
**brake** [breɪk] *n* hamulec *m*; (*fig*) ograniczenie *nt* ▷ *vi* hamować (zahamować *perf*)
**brake fluid** *n* płyn *m* hamulcowy
**brake light** *n* światła *pl* stopu *or* hamowania
**brake pedal** *n* pedał *m* hamulca
**bramble** ['bræmbl] *n* jeżyna *f* (*krzew*), ostrężyna *f*
**bran** [bræn] *n* otręby *pl*
**branch** [brɑːntʃ] *n* (*lit, fig*) gałąź *f*; (*Comm*) oddział *m* ▷ *vi* rozgałęziać się (rozgałęzić się *perf*)
▶ **branch out** *vi*: **to ~ out (into)** (*fig*) rozszerzać (rozszerzyć *perf*) działalność (o +*acc*)
**branch line** (*Rail*) *n* linia *f* boczna
**branch manager** *n* kierownik(-iczka) *m(f)* oddziału
**brand** [brænd] *n* (*make*) marka *f*; (*fig*) rodzaj *m*, odmiana *f* ▷ *vt* (*cattle*) znakować (oznakować *perf*); **to ~ sb a communist/traitor** przyczepiać (przyczepić *perf*) komuś etykietkę komunisty/zdrajcy
**brandish** ['brændɪʃ] *vt* wymachiwać *or* wywijać +*instr*
**brand name** *n* nazwa *f* firmowa
**brand-new** ['brænd'njuː] *adj* nowiutki, nowiuteńki; (*machine etc*) fabrycznie nowy
**brandy** ['brændɪ] *n* koniak *m*, winiak *m*
**brash** [bræʃ] *adj* zuchwały
**Brasilia** [brə'zɪlɪə] *n* Brasilia *f*
**brass** [brɑːs] *n* mosiądz *m*; **the ~** (*Mus*) instrumenty dęte blaszane
**brass band** *n* orkiestra *f* dęta
**brassière** ['bræsɪəʳ] *n* biustonosz *m*, stanik *m*
**brass tacks** *npl*: **to get down to ~** przechodzić (przejść *perf*) do rzeczy
**brat** [bræt] (*pej*) *n* bachor *m* (*pej, inf*)
**bravado** [brə'vɑːdəu] *n* brawura *f*
**brave** [breɪv] *adj* dzielny ▷ *n* wojownik *m* indiański ▷ *vt* stawiać (stawić *perf*) czoło +*dat*
**bravely** ['breɪvlɪ] *adv* dzielnie
**bravery** ['breɪvərɪ] *n* dzielność *f*, męstwo *nt*
**bravo** [brɑː'vəu] *excl* brawo
**brawl** [brɔːl] *n* bijatyka *f*, burda *f* ▷ *vi* bić się (pobić się *perf*)
**brawn** [brɔːn] *n* (*strength*) tężyzna *f* (fizyczna), krzepa *f* (*inf*); (*meat*) salceson *m*
**brawny** ['brɔːnɪ] *adj* krzepki
**bray** [breɪ] *vi* ryczeć (zaryczeć *perf*) ▷ *n* ryk *m* (*ośli lub podobny*)
**brazen** ['breɪzn] *adj* (*woman*) bezwstydny; (*lie, accusation*) bezczelny ▷ *vt*: **to ~ it out** nadrabiać tupetem
**brazier** ['breɪzɪəʳ] *n* koksownik *m*
**Brazil** [brə'zɪl] *n* Brazylia *f*
**Brazilian** [brə'zɪljən] *adj* brazylijski ▷ *n* Brazylijczyk(-jka) *m(f)*
**Brazil nut** *n* orzech *m* brazylijski
**breach** [briːtʃ] *vt* (*wall*) robić (zrobić *perf*) wyłom w +*loc*; (*defence*) przełamywać (przełamać *perf*) ▷ *n* (*gap*) wyłom *m*; (*estrangement*) różnica *f* zdań *or* poglądów; **~ of contract** naruszenie *or* pogwałcenie umowy; **~ of the peace** zakłócenie porządku publicznego; **~ of trust** nadużycie zaufania
**bread** [brɛd] *n* chleb *m*; (*inf*) forsa *f* (*inf*), siano *nt* (*inf*); **to earn one's daily ~** zarabiać (zarobić *perf*) na chleb; **he knows which side his ~ is buttered (on)** on wie, komu się przypodobać
**bread and butter** *n* chleb *m* z masłem; (*fig*) źródło *nt* utrzymania
**breadbin** ['brɛdbɪn] (*Brit*) *n* pojemnik *m* na chleb *or* pieczywo
**breadboard** ['brɛdbɔːd] *n* deska *f* do krojenia chleba; (*Comput*) płyta *f* montażowa
**breadbox** ['brɛdbɔks] (*US*) *n* = **breadbin**
**breadcrumbs** ['brɛdkrʌmz] *npl* okruszki *pl*; (*Culin*) bułka *f* tarta
**breadline** ['brɛdlaɪn] *n*: **on the ~** na skraju *or* granicy nędzy
**breadth** [brɛtθ] *n* szerokość *f*; (*fig*) rozmach *m*
**breadwinner** ['brɛdwɪnəʳ] *n* żywiciel(ka) *m(f)* (rodziny)
**break** [breɪk] (*pt* **broke**, *pp* **broken**) *vt* (*crockery, glass*) tłuc (stłuc *perf*); (*leg, promise, law*) łamać (złamać *perf*); (*record*) bić (pobić *perf*) ▷ *vi* (*crockery, glass*) tłuc się (stłuc się *perf*), rozbijać się (rozbić się *perf*); (*weather*) przełamywać się (przełamać się *perf*); (*storm*) zrywać się (zerwać się *perf*); (*story, news*) wychodzić (wyjść *perf*) na jaw ▷ *n* (*gap, pause, rest*) przerwa *f*; (*fracture*) złamanie *nt*; (*chance*) szansa *f*; **the day was about to ~ when ...** świtało, gdy ...; **to ~ the news to sb** przekazywać (przekazać *perf*) komuś (złą) wiadomość; **to ~ even** wychodzić (wyjść *perf*) na czysto *or* na zero; **to ~ with sb** zrywać (zerwać *perf*) z kimś; **to ~ free** *or* **loose**

wyrwać się *(perf)*, uwolnić się *(perf)*; **to ~ open** *(door)* wyważać (wyważyć *perf*); *(safe)* otwierać (otworzyć *perf*); **to take a ~** *(for a few minutes)* robić (zrobić *perf*) sobie przerwę; *(have a holiday)* brać (wziąć *perf*) wolne; **without a ~** bez przerwy; **her lucky ~ came in 1991** szczęście uśmiechnęło się do niej w 1991

▸ **break down** *vt* *(figures, data)* dzielić (podzielić *perf*), rozbijać (rozbić *perf*); *(door)* wyłamywać (wyłamać *perf*) ▹ *vi* *(machine, car)* psuć się (popsuć się *perf*); *(person, talks)* załamywać się (załamać się *perf*)

▸ **break in** *vt* *(horse)* ujeżdżać (ujeździć *perf*) ▹ *vi* *(burgle)* włamywać się (włamać się *perf*); *(interrupt)* wtrącać się (wtrącić się *perf*)

▸ **break into** *vt fus* włamywać się (włamać się *perf*) do *+gen*

▸ **break off** *vi* *(branch)* odłamywać się (odłamać się *perf*); *(speaker)* przerywać (przerwać *perf*) ▹ *vt* *(talks, engagement)* zrywać (zerwać *perf*)

▸ **break out** *vi* *(war, fight)* wybuchać (wybuchnąć *perf*); *(prisoner)* zbiegać (zbiec *perf*); **to ~ out in spots/a rash** pokrywać się (pokryć się *perf*) plamami/wysypką

▸ **break through** *vi*: **the sun broke through** wyszło *or* wyjrzało słońce

▸ **break through** *vt fus* przedzierać się (przedrzeć się *perf*) przez *+acc*

▸ **break up** *vi* *(object, substance, marriage)* rozpadać się (rozpaść się *perf*); *(couple)* zrywać (zerwać *perf*) ze sobą; *(crowd)* rozchodzić się (rozejść się *perf*); (*: in panic*) rozpierzchać się (rozpierzchnąć się *perf*); *(Scol)* kończyć (skończyć *perf*) naukę *or* zajęcia ▹ *vt* *(rocks, biscuit)* łamać (połamać *perf*), kruszyć (rozkruszyć *perf*); *(fight, meeting, monotony)* przerywać (przerwać *perf*); *(marriage)* doprowadzać (doprowadzić *perf*) do rozpadu *+gen*

**breakable** ['breɪkəbl] *adj* łamliwy, kruchy ▹ *n*: **~s** rzeczy *pl* łatwo tłukące się

**breakage** ['breɪkɪdʒ] *n* *(breaking)* uszkodzenie *nt*; (*: of glass etc object*) stłuczenie *nt*; *(damage)* szkoda *f*; **to pay for ~s** płacić (zapłacić *perf*) za szkody

**breakaway** ['breɪkəweɪ] *adj* frakcyjny

**break-dancing** ['breɪkdɑːnsɪŋ] *n* breakdance *m*

**breakdown** ['breɪkdaun] *n* *(Aut)* awaria *f*; *(of marriage, political system)* rozpad *m*; *(of talks)* załamanie się *nt*; *(of statistics)* rozbicie *nt*, analiza *f*; (*also*: **nervous breakdown**) załamanie *nt* (nerwowe)

**breakdown service** *(Brit)* *n* pomoc *f* drogowa

**breakdown van** *(Brit)* *n* samochód *m* pomocy drogowej

**breaker** ['breɪkəʳ] *n* fala *f* przybojowa

**breakeven** ['breɪk'iːvn] *cpd*: **~ chart** wykres *m* progu rentowności; **~ point** próg rentowności

**breakfast** ['brɛkfəst] *n* śniadanie *nt* ▹ *vi* jeść (zjeść *perf*) śniadanie

**breakfast cereal** *n* płatki *pl* śniadaniowe

**break-in** ['breɪkɪn] *n* włamanie *nt*

**breaking and entering** ['breɪkɪŋən'ɛntrɪŋ] *(Jur)* *n* wtargnięcie *nt* z włamaniem

**breaking point** ['breɪkɪŋ-] *n* granica *f* wytrzymałości

**breakthrough** ['breɪkθruː] *n* *(fig)* przełom *m*

**break-up** ['breɪkʌp] *n* rozpad *m*

**break-up value** *n suma wartości majątku spółki podzielona przez liczbę wyemitowanych akcji*

**breakwater** ['breɪkwɔːtəʳ] *n* falochron *m*

**breast** [brɛst] *n* pierś *f*; *(of lamb, veal)* mostek *m*

**breast-feed** ['brɛstfiːd] *(irreg: like* **feed***)* *vt* karmić (nakarmić *perf*) piersią ▹ *vi* karmić piersią

**breast pocket** *n* kieszeń *f* wewnętrzna

**breast-stroke** ['brɛststrəuk] *n* styl *m* klasyczny, żabka *f* *(inf)*

**breath** [brɛθ] *n* *(breathing)* oddech *m*; *(single intake of air)* wdech *m*; **to go out for a ~ of air** wychodzić (wyjść *perf*) zaczerpnąć powietrza *or* odetchnąć świeżym powietrzem; **to be out of ~** nie móc złapać tchu; **to get one's ~ back** odzyskać *(perf)* oddech; **to hold one's ~** wstrzymywać (wstrzymać *perf*) oddech

**breathalyze** ['brɛθəlaɪz], **breathalyse** *vt* mierzyć (zmierzyć *perf*) zawartość alkoholu (w organizmie) *+dat*, kazać (kazać *perf*) dmuchać w balonik *+dat* *(inf)*

**Breathalyzer**® ['brɛθəlaɪzəʳ], **Breathalyser** *n* ≈ alkomat *m*

**breathe** [briːð] *vt* oddychać (odetchnąć *perf*) *+instr* ▹ *vi* oddychać (odetchnąć *perf*); **I won't ~ a word about it** nie puszczę pary z ust na ten temat

▸ **breathe in** *vt* wdychać ▹ *vi* robić (zrobić *perf*) wdech

▸ **breathe out** *vt* wydychać ▹ *vi* wypuszczać (wypuścić *perf*) powietrze, robić (zrobić *perf*) wydech

**breather** ['briːðəʳ] *n*: **to take** *or* **have a ~** robić (zrobić *perf*) sobie przerwę (na złapanie oddechu)

**breathing** ['briːðɪŋ] *n* oddychanie *nt*, oddech *m*

**breathing space** *n* *(fig)* chwila *f* wytchnienia

**breathless** ['brɛθlɪs] *adj* *(from exertion)* z(a)dyszany; **he was ~ with excitement** z wrażenia zaparło mu dech

**breathtaking** ['brɛθteɪkɪŋ] *adj* zapierający dech (w piersiach)

**bred** [brɛd] *pt, pp of* **breed**

**-bred** [brɛd] *suff*: **well/ill~** dobrze/źle wychowany
**breed** [bri:d] (*pt, pp* **bred**) *vt* hodować (wyhodować *perf*); (*fig*) rodzić (zrodzić *perf*) ▷ *vi* rozmnażać się ▷ *n* (*Zool*) rasa *f*; (*of person*) typ *m*
**breeder** ['bri:dəʳ] *n* (*person*) hodowca *m*; (*also*: **breeder reactor**) reaktor *m* powielający
**breeding** ['bri:dɪŋ] *n* (*upbringing*) wychowanie *nt*
**breeding ground** *n* (*for birds*) lęgowisko *nt*; (*for fish*) tarlisko *nt*; (*fig*) wylęgarnia *f*
**breeze** [bri:z] *n* wietrzyk *m*
**breezeblock** ['bri:zblɔk] (*Brit*) *n* pustak *m*
**breezy** ['bri:zɪ] *adj* (*person*) żwawy; (*tone*) lekki; (*weather*) wietrzny
**Breton** ['brɛtən] *adj* bretoński ▷ *n* Bretończyk(-onka) *m(f)*
**brevity** ['brɛvɪtɪ] *n* (*of life*) krótkotrwałość *f*; (*of speech, writing*) zwięzłość *f*
**brew** [bru:] *vt* (*tea*) parzyć (zaparzyć *perf*); (*beer*) warzyć ▷ *vi* (*tea*) parzyć się (zaparzyć się *perf*); (*beer*) warzyć się; (*sth unpleasant*): **a storm/crisis is ~ing** zanosi się na burzę/kryzys
**brewer** ['bru:əʳ] *n* (*beer maker*) piwowar *m*; (*brewery owner*) właściciel *m* browaru
**brewery** ['bru:ərɪ] *n* browar *m*
**briar** ['braɪəʳ] *n* (*thorny bush*) wrzosiec *m*; (*wild rose*) dzika róża *f*
**bribe** [braɪb] *n* łapówka *f* ▷ *vt* przekupywać (przekupić *perf*); **to ~ sb to do sth** przekupić (*perf*) kogoś, żeby coś zrobił
**bribery** ['braɪbərɪ] *n* przekupstwo *nt*
**bric-a-brac** ['brɪkəbræk] *n* bibeloty *pl*
**brick** [brɪk] *n* cegła *f*
**bricklayer** ['brɪkleɪəʳ] *n* murarz *m*
**brickwork** ['brɪkwə:k] *n* mur *m* (ceglany)
**bridal** ['braɪdl] *adj* ślubny
**bride** [braɪd] *n* panna *f* młoda
**bridegroom** ['braɪdgru:m] *n* pan *m* młody
**bridesmaid** ['braɪdzmeɪd] *n* druhna *f*
**bridge** [brɪdʒ] *n* (*Tech, Archit*) most *m*; (*Naut*) mostek *m* kapitański; (*Cards*) brydż *m*; (*Dentistry*) most(ek) *m*; (*of nose*) grzbiet *m* ▷ *vt* (*river*) przerzucać (przerzucić *perf*) most nad *+instr*; (*fig: gap, gulf*) zmniejszać (zmniejszyć *perf*)
**bridging loan** ['brɪdʒɪŋ-] (*Brit*) *n* *krótkoterminowa pożyczka między transakcjami, np. na zakup nowego domu przed uzyskaniem wpływów ze sprzedaży starego*
**bridle** ['braɪdl] *n* uzda *f* ▷ *vt* (*horse*) zakładać (założyć *perf*) uzdę *+dat* ▷ *vi*: **to ~ (at)** obruszać się (obruszyć się *perf*) (na *+acc*)
**bridle path** *n* ścieżka *f* konna
**brief** [bri:f] *adj* krótki ▷ *n* (*Jur: documents*) akta *pl* (sprawy); (*task*) wytyczne *pl* ▷ *vt*: **to ~ sb (about sth)** (*give instructions*) instruować (poinstruować *perf*) kogoś (o czymś); (*give information*) informować (poinformować *perf*) kogoś (o czymś); **briefs** *npl* (*for men*) slipy *pl*; (*for women*) figi *pl*; **in ~** krótko mówiąc; **to give a ~ to sb** (*Jur*) powierzyć komuś prowadzenie sprawy
**briefcase** ['bri:fkeɪs] *n* aktówka *f*
**briefing** ['bri:fɪŋ] *n* instruktaż *m*; (*Mil*) odprawa *f*; (*Press*) briefing *m*
**briefly** ['bri:flɪ] *adv* (*smile, glance*) przelotnie; (*visit*) na krótko; (*explain*) pokrótce; **to glimpse sb/sth ~** ujrzeć (*perf*) kogoś/coś przelotnie
**Brig.** *abbr* (= *brigadier*) bryg.
**brigade** [brɪ'geɪd] *n* brygada *f*
**brigadier** [brɪgə'dɪəʳ] *n* brygadier *m* (*stopień pomiędzy pułkownikiem a generałem brygady*)
**bright** [braɪt] *adj* (*light, room, colour*) jasny; (*day*) pogodny; (*person*) bystry; (*idea*) błyskotliwy; (*outlook, future*) świetlany; (*lively*) ożywiony; **to look on the ~ side** podchodzić (podejść *perf*) do rzeczy optymistycznie
**brighten** ['braɪtn] (*also*: **brighten up**) *vt* (*place*) upiększać (upiększyć *perf*); (*person*) rozweselać (rozweselić *perf*); (*event*) ożywiać (ożywić *perf*) ▷ *vi* (*of weather*) rozpogadzać się (rozpogodzić się *perf*); (*person*) poweseleć (*perf*); (*face*) rozjaśniać się (rozjaśnić się *perf*); (*prospects*) polepszać się (polepszyć się *perf*)
**brightly** ['braɪtlɪ] *adv* (*shine*) jasno; (*smile*) promiennie; (*talk*) pogodnie
**brilliance** ['brɪljəns] *n* (*of light*) świetlistość *f*; (*of talent, skill*) błyskotliwość *f*
**brilliant** ['brɪljənt] *adj* (*person, idea, career*) błyskotliwy; (*smile*) promienny; (*light*) olśniewający; (*inf: holiday etc*) kapitalny (*inf*)
**brilliantly** ['brɪljəntlɪ] *adv* (*act, perform*) błyskotliwie; (*succeed, work*) znakomicie; (*illuminate*) rzęsiście
**brim** [brɪm] *n* (*of cup*) brzeg *m*; (*of hat*) rondo *nt*
**brimful** ['brɪm'ful] *adj*: **~ (of)** po brzegi napełniony (*+instr*); (*fig*) pełen (*+gen*)
**brine** [braɪn] *n* zalewa *f* solna
**bring** [brɪŋ] (*pt, pp* **brought**) *vt* (*thing, satisfaction*) przynosić (przynieść *perf*); (*person*) przyprowadzać (przyprowadzić *perf*); **to ~ sth to an end** zakończyć (*perf*) coś; **I can't ~ myself to fire him** nie mogę się przemóc, żeby go zwolnić
▸ **bring about** *vt* doprowadzać (doprowadzić *perf*) do *+gen*
▸ **bring back** *vt* (*restore*) przywracać (przywrócić *perf*); (*return*) odnosić (odnieść *perf*)
▸ **bring down** *vt* (*government*) obalać (obalić *perf*); (*price*) obniżać (obniżyć *perf*)

▸ **bring forward** *vt* (*meeting, proposal*) przesuwać (przesunąć *perf*) (*na wcześniejszy termin*); (*Book-keeping*) przenosić (przenieść *perf*)
▸ **bring in** *vt* (*money*) przynosić (przynieść *perf*); (*object, person*) sprowadzać (sprowadzić *perf*); (*Pol: legislation*) wprowadzać (wprowadzić *perf*); (*Jur: verdict*) ogłaszać (ogłosić *perf*)
▸ **bring off** *vt* (*task*) wykonywać (wykonać *perf*); (*deal, plan*) przeprowadzać (przeprowadzić *perf*)
▸ **bring out** *vt* (*person*) ośmielać (ośmielić *perf*); (*new product*) wypuszczać (wypuścić *perf*) (na rynek); **to ~ out the worst in sb** wyzwalać (wyzwolić *perf*) w kimś najgorsze instynkty
▸ **bring round** *vt* (*unconscious person*) cucić (ocucić *perf*)
▸ **bring up** *vt* (*carry up*) przynosić (przynieść *perf*) (*na górę*); (*children*) wychowywać (wychować *perf*); (*question, subject*) podnosić (podnieść *perf*); (*food*) zwracać (zwrócić *perf*)

**bring and buy sale** *n dobroczynna giełda rzeczy używanych*
**brink** [brɪŋk] *n* (*of disaster, war etc*) krawędź *f*; **to be on the ~ of doing sth** być bliskim zrobienia czegoś; **she was on the ~ of tears** była bliska łez
**brisk** [brɪsk] *adj* (*tone, person*) energiczny; (*pace*) dynamiczny; (*trade*) ożywiony; **~ walk** szybki spacer; **business is ~** interes kwitnie
**bristle** ['brɪsl] *n* (*on animal, chin*) szczecina *f*; (*of brush*) włosie *nt* ▹ *vi* (*in anger*) zjeżać się (zjeżyć się *perf*) (*inf*); (*at memory etc*) wzdrygać się (wzdrygnąć się *perf*); **bristling with** najeżony +*instr*
**bristly** ['brɪslɪ] *adj* (*beard, hair*) szczeciniasty; (*chin*) pokryty szczeciną
**Brit** [brɪt] (*inf*) *n abbr* (= *British person*) Brytyjczyk(-jka) *m(f)*
**Britain** ['brɪtən] *n* (*also*: **Great Britain**) Wielka Brytania *f*; **in ~** w Wielkiej Brytanii
**British** ['brɪtɪʃ] *adj* brytyjski ▹ *npl*: **the ~** Brytyjczycy *vir pl*
**British Isles** *npl*: **the ~** Wyspy *pl* Brytyjskie
**British Rail** *n* (*formerly*) Kolej *f* Brytyjska
**Briton** ['brɪtən] *n* Brytyjczyk(-jka) *m(f)*
**Brittany** ['brɪtənɪ] *n* Bretania *f*
**brittle** ['brɪtl] *adj* kruchy
**Br(o).** (*Rel*) *abbr* (= *brother*) br.
**broach** [brəutʃ] *vt* (*subject*) poruszać (poruszyć *perf*)
**broad** [brɔ:d] *adj* (*street, smile, range*) szeroki; (*outlines*) ogólny; (*accent*) silny ▹ *n* (*US: inf*) kobieta *f*; **in ~ daylight** w biały dzień; **~ hint** wyraźna aluzja
**broadband** ['brɔ:dbænd] (*Comput*) *n* łącze *nt* szerokopasmowe ▹ *adj* (*connection, access*) szerokopasmowy
**broad bean** *n* bób *m*
**broadcast** ['brɔ:dkɑ:st] (*pt, pp* **~**) *n* (*Radio*) audycja *f*, program *m*; (*TV*) program *m* ▹ *vt* (*Radio, TV*) nadawać (nadać *perf*), emitować (wyemitować *perf*) ▹ *vi* (*Radio, TV*) nadawać
**broadcasting** ['brɔ:dkɑ:stɪŋ] *n* nadawanie *nt* programów
**broadcasting station** *n* stacja *f* nadawcza
**broaden** ['brɔ:dn] *vt* rozszerzać (rozszerzyć *perf*), poszerzać (poszerzyć *perf*) ▹ *vi* rozszerzać się (rozszerzyć się *perf*); **to ~ sb's mind** poszerzać (poszerzyć *perf*) czyjeś horyzonty (myślowe); **travel ~s the mind** podróże kształcą
**broadly** ['brɔ:dlɪ] *adv* zasadniczo; **~ speaking** najogólniej biorąc
**broad-minded** ['brɔ:d'maɪndɪd] *adj* tolerancyjny
**broccoli** ['brɔkəlɪ] *n* brokuły *pl*
**brochure** ['brəuʃjuə^r] *n* broszura *f*, prospekt *m*
**brogue** [brəug] *n* (*accent*) *silny akcent, zwłaszcza irlandzki lub szkocki*; (*shoe*) *mocny, skórzany but*
**broil** [brɔɪl] *vt* opiekać (opiec *perf*)
**broiler** ['brɔɪlə^r] *n* brojler *m*
**broke** [brəuk] *pt of* **break** ▹ *adj* (*inf: person*) spłukany (*inf*); **to go ~** plajtować (splajtować *perf*) (*inf*)
**broken** ['brəukn] *pp of* **break** ▹ *adj* (*window, cup*) rozbity; (*machine*) zepsuty; (*leg, promise, vow*) złamany; (*marriage, home*) rozbity; **in ~ English/Polish** łamaną angielszczyzną/polszczyzną
**broken-down** ['brəukn'daun] *adj* (*car, machine*) zepsuty; (*house*) podupadły
**broken-hearted** ['brəukn'hɑ:tɪd] *adj*: **to be ~** mieć złamane serce
**broker** ['brəukə^r] *n* (*in shares*) makler *m*; (*insurance broker*) broker *m* ubezpieczeniowy
**brokerage** ['brəukrɪdʒ] *n* (*business*) usługi *pl* maklerskie; (*fee*) opłata *f* za usługi maklerskie
**brolly** ['brɔlɪ] (*Brit: inf*) *n* parasol *m*
**bronchitis** [brɔŋ'kaɪtɪs] *n* zapalenie *nt* oskrzeli, bronchit *m*
**bronze** [brɔnz] *n* (*metal*) brąz *m*; (*sculpture*) rzeźba *f* z brązu
**bronzed** [brɔnzd] *adj* opalony na brąz
**brooch** [brəutʃ] *n* broszka *f*
**brood** [bru:d] *n* (*baby birds*) wyląg *m*; (*sb's children*) trzódka *f*, gromadka *f* ▹ *vi* (*person*) rozmyślać; (*hen*) wysiadywać jajka
▸ **brood on** *or* **over** *vt fus* rozpamiętywać +*acc*
**broody** ['bru:dɪ] *adj* (*moody*) zasępiony; (*hen*) kwoczący; **to feel ~** (*woman*) pragnąć dziecka

**brook** [bruk] *n* strumyk *m*
**broom** [brum] *n* miotła *f*; (*Bot*) janowiec *m*
**broomstick** ['brumstɪk] *n* kij *m* od miotły
**Bros.** (*Comm*) *abbr* (= *brothers*) Bracia
**broth** [brɔθ] *n* rosół *m*
**brothel** ['brɔθl] *n* dom *m* publiczny, burdel *m* (*inf*)
**brother** ['brʌðə^r] *n* (*lit, fig*) brat *m*
**brotherhood** ['brʌðəhud] *n* braterstwo *nt*
**brother-in-law** ['brʌðərɪn'lɔː] *n* szwagier *m*
**brotherly** ['brʌðəlɪ] *adj* braterski
**brought** [brɔːt] *pt, pp of* **bring**
**brought forward** (*Book-keeping*) *adj* z przeniesienia *post*
**brow** [brau] *n* (*forehead*) czoło *nt*; (*old: eyebrow*) brew *f*; (*of hill*) grzbiet *m*
**browbeat** ['braubiːt] *vt*: **to ~ sb** zastraszać (zastraszyć *perf*) kogoś; **to ~ sb into doing sth** wymuszać (wymusić *perf*) na kimś zrobienie czegoś
**brown** [braun] *adj* brązowy ▷ *n* (kolor *m*) brązowy, brąz *m* ▷ *vi* (*Culin*) przyrumieniać się (przyrumienić się *perf*); **to go ~** (*person*) opalać się (opalić się *perf*); (*leaves*) brązowieć (zbrązowieć *perf*)
**brown bread** *n* ciemny chleb *m*
**Brownie** ['braunɪ] *n* (*also*: **Brownie Guide**) *dziewczynka należąca do drużyny zuchów*
**brownie** ['braunɪ] (*US*) *n czekoladowe ciasteczko z orzechami*
**brown paper** *n* szary papier *m*
**brown rice** *n* brązowy ryż *m*
**brown sugar** *n* cukier *m* nieoczyszczony
**browse** [brauz] *vi* (*in shop*) szperać; (*animal*) paść się ▷ *vt* (*Comput*) przeglądać (przejrzeć *perf*) ▷ *n*: **to have a ~ (around)** rozglądać się (rozejrzeć się *perf*); **to ~ through a book** przeglądać *or* przerzucać książkę
**browser** ['brauzə^r] (*Comput*) *n* przeglądarka *f*
**bruise** [bruːz] *n* (*on body*) siniec *m*, siniak *m*; (*on fruit*) obicie *nt* ▷ *vt* (*arm, leg*) stłuc (*perf*); (*person*) posiniaczyć (*perf*); (*fruit*) obijać (obić *perf*) ▷ *vi* (*fruit*) obijać się (obić się *perf*)
**Brum** [brʌm] (*Brit: inf*) *n abbr* = **Birmingham**
**Brummie** ['brʌmɪ] (*inf*) *n* mieszkaniec(-nka) *m(f)* Birmingham
**brunch** [brʌntʃ] *n połączenie późnego śniadania z lunchem*
**brunette** [bruː'nɛt] *n* brunetka *f*
**brunt** [brʌnt] *n*: **to bear the ~ of** (*attack, criticism*) najbardziej odczuwać (odczuć *perf*) *+acc*
**brush** [brʌʃ] *n* (*for cleaning*) szczotka *f*; (*for shaving, painting*) pędzel *m*; (*unpleasant encounter*) scysja *f* ▷ *vt* (*floor*) zamiatać (zamieść *perf*); (*hair*) szczotkować (wyszczotkować *perf*); (*also*: **brush against**) ocierać się (otrzeć się *perf*) o *+acc*; **to ~ one's teeth** myć (umyć *perf*) zęby; **to have a ~ with death** ocierać się (otrzeć się *perf*) o śmierć; **to have a ~ with the police** mieć do czynienia z policją
▶ **brush aside** *vt* odsuwać (odsunąć *perf*) na bok
▶ **brush past** *vt* przemykać (przemknąć *perf*) obok *+gen*
▶ **brush up (on)** *vt* (*language*) szlifować (podszlifować *perf*); (*knowledge*) odświeżać (odświeżyć *perf*)
**brushed** [brʌʃt] *adj* (*steel, chrome*) matowy; (*nylon, denim*) z meszkiem *post*
**brush-off** ['brʌʃɔf] *n*: **to give sb the ~** (*inf*) spławiać (spławić *perf*) kogoś (*inf*)
**brushwood** ['brʌʃwud] *n* chrust *m*
**brusque** [bruːsk] *adj* szorstki
**Brussels** ['brʌslz] *n* Bruksela *f*
**Brussels sprout** *n* brukselka *f*
**brutal** ['bruːtl] *adj* brutalny
**brutality** [bruː'tælɪtɪ] *n* brutalność *f*
**brute** [bruːt] *n* (*person*) brutal *m*; (*animal*) zwierz *m*, bydlę *nt* (*inf*) ▷ *adj*: **by ~ force** na siłę, na chama (*inf*)
**brutish** ['bruːtɪʃ] *adj* bydlęcy
**BS** (*US*) *n abbr* (= *Bachelor of Science*) *stopień naukowy*
**bs** *abbr* = **bill of sale**
**BSA** *n abbr* (= *Boy Scouts of America*) *chłopięca organizacja skautowska*
**BSc** *abbr* (= *Bachelor of Science*) *stopień naukowy*
**BSE** *n abbr* (= *bovine spongiform encephalopathy*) gąbczaste zwyrodnienie mózgu
**BSI** *n abbr* (= *British Standards Institution*) *urząd normalizacyjny*
**BST** *abbr* = **British Summer Time**
**Bt.** (*Brit*) *abbr* = **Bart.**
**btu** *n abbr* (= *British thermal unit*) brytyjska jednostka *f* cieplna
**bubble** ['bʌbl] *n* bańka *f* ▷ *vi* (*form bubbles: boiling liquid*) wrzeć; (*: champagne etc*) musować; (*gurgle*) bulgotać; (*: stream*) szemrać; (*fig: with energy*) kipieć; (*: with joy, confidence*) tryskać
**bubble bath** *n* (*liquid*) płyn *m* do kąpieli; (*bath*) kąpiel *f* w pianie
**bubble gum** *n* guma *f* balonowa
**bubble pack** *n opakowanie złożone z wymodelowanej przejrzystej pokrywy przymocowanej do kartonowej podstawy*
**Bucharest** [buːkə'rɛst] *n* Bukareszt *m*
**buck** [bʌk] *n* (*rabbit*) królik *m* (*samiec*); (*deer*) kozioł *m*; (*US: inf*) dolec *m* (*inf*) ▷ *vi* (*horse*) brykać (bryknąć *perf*); **to pass the ~** spychać (zepchnąć *perf*) odpowiedzialność na innych; **to pass the ~ to sb** spychać (zepchnąć *perf*) odpowiedzialność na kogoś

▸ **buck up** *vi* (*cheer up*) rozchmurzyć się (*perf*) ▹ *vt*: **to ~ one's ideas up** spinać się (spiąć się *perf*) (*inf*), sprężać się (sprężyć się *perf*) (*inf*)
**bucket** ['bʌkɪt] *n* wiadro *nt* ▹ *vi* (*Brit*: *inf*): **the rain is ~ing (down)** leje jak z cebra (*inf*)
**buckle** ['bʌkl] *n* sprzączka *f* ▹ *vt* (*shoe, belt*) zapinać (zapiąć *perf*) (na sprzączkę); (*wheel*) wyginać (wygiąć *perf*) ▹ *vi* (*wheel, bridge*) wyginać się (wygiąć się *perf*)
▸ **buckle down** *vi*: **to ~ down (to sth)** przykładać się (przyłożyć się *perf*) (do czegoś)
**Bucks** [bʌks] (*Brit*: *Post*) *abbr* = **Buckinghamshire**
**bud** [bʌd] *n* pąk *m*, pączek *m* ▹ *vi* wypuszczać (wypuścić *perf*) pąki *or* pączki
**Budapest** [bju:də'pɛst] *n* Budapeszt *m*
**Buddha** ['budə] *n* Budda *m*
**Buddhism** ['budɪzəm] *n* buddyzm *m*
**Buddhist** ['budɪst] *adj* buddyjski ▹ *n* buddysta(-tka) *m(f)*
**budding** ['bʌdɪŋ] *adj* (*fig*) dobrze się zapowiadający
**buddy** ['bʌdɪ] (*US*) *n* kumpel *m*; (*form of address*) kolego (*voc*)
**budge** [bʌdʒ] *vt* ruszać (ruszyć *perf*) (z miejsca) ▹ *vi* (*screw etc*) ruszać się (ruszyć się *perf*); (*fig*: *person*) ustępować (ustąpić *perf*); **he could not be ~d, he wouldn't ~** pozostawał niewzruszony
**budgerigar** ['bʌdʒərɪgɑ:ʳ] *n* papużka *f* falista
**budget** ['bʌdʒɪt] *n* budżet *m* ▹ *vi*: **to ~ for sth** preliminować (zapreliminować *perf*) coś; **I'm on a tight ~** mam napięty budżet; **she works out her ~ every month** co miesiąc planuje swoje wydatki
**budgie** ['bʌdʒɪ] *n* = **budgerigar**
**Buenos Aires** ['bweɪnɔs'aɪrɪz] *n* Buenos Aires *nt inv*
**buff** [bʌf] *adj* szary ▹ *n* (*inf*) znawca(-wczyni) *m(f)*
**buffalo** ['bʌfələu] (*pl* **~** *or* **~es**) *n* (*Brit*) bawół *m*; (*US*) bizon *m*
**buffer** ['bʌfəʳ] *n* (*Comput, Rail*) bufor *m*; (*fig*: *safeguard*) zabezpieczenie *nt*
**buffering** ['bʌfərɪŋ] (*Comput*) *n* buforowanie *nt*
**buffer state** *n* państwo *nt* buforowe
**buffet**[1] ['bufeɪ] (*Brit*) *n* bufet *m*
**buffet**[2] ['bʌfɪt] *vt* (*wind, waves*: *ship*) uderzać w *+acc or* o *+acc*
**buffet car** *n* wagon *m* restauracyjny
**buffet lunch** *n* stół *m* szwedzki
**buffoon** [bə'fu:n] *n* bufon *m*
**bug** [bʌg] *n* (*esp US*: *insect*) robak *m*; (*Comput*: *in program*) błąd *m*; (: *in equipment*) wada *f*; (*microphone*) ukryty mikrofon *m*; (*fig*: *germ*) wirus *m* ▹ *vt* (*inf*: *annoy*) wkurzać (*inf*); (: *bother*) gryźć; (*room, house*) zakładać (założyć *perf*) podsłuch w *+loc*; **to bug sb's telephone** zakładać (założyć *perf*) komuś *or* u kogoś podsłuch (telefoniczny); **to be bugged** (*room, telephone*) być na podsłuchu; **I've got the travel bug** (*fig*) złapałem bakcyla podróży
**bugbear** ['bʌgbɛəʳ] *n* problem *m*
**bugger** ['bʌgəʳ] (*inf!*) *n* gnój *m* (*inf!*) ▹ *vb*: **~ off!** odpierdol się! (*inf!*); **~ (it)!** (o) kurwa! (*inf!*)
**buggy** ['bʌgɪ] *n* (*also*: **baby buggy**) wózek *m* spacerowy, spacerówka *f* (*inf*)
**bugle** ['bju:gl] *n* trąbka *f* (*zwłaszcza używana w wojsku*)
**build** [bɪld] (*pt, pp* **built**) *n* (*of person*) budowa *f* (ciała) ▹ *vt* budować (zbudować *perf*)
▸ **build on** *vt fus* (*fig*) wykorzystywać (wykorzystać *perf*)
▸ **build up** *vt* (*production*) zwiększać (zwiększyć *perf*); (*forces*) wzmacniać (wzmocnić *perf*); (*morale*) podnosić (podnieść *perf*); (*stocks*) gromadzić (zgromadzić *perf*); (*business*) rozwijać (rozwinąć *perf*); **don't ~ your hopes up too soon** nie rób sobie przedwcześnie nadziei
**builder** ['bɪldəʳ] *n* budowniczy *m*
**building** ['bɪldɪŋ] *n* (*construction*) budowa *f*; (*structure*) budynek *m*
**building contractor** *n* przedsiębiorca *m* budowlany
**building industry** *n*: **the ~** przemysł *m* budowlany
**building site** *n* plac *m* budowy
**building society** (*Brit*) *n* kasa *f* mieszkaniowa *or* budowlana
**building trade** *n* = **building industry**
**build-up** ['bɪldʌp] *n* (*of gas etc*) nagromadzenie *nt*; **to give sb/sth a good ~** robić (zrobić *perf*) komuś/czemuś dobrą reklamę
**built** [bɪlt] *pt, pp of* **build** ▹ *adj*: **~-in** wbudowany; **well-~** dobrze zbudowany
**built-up area** ['bɪltʌp-] *n* obszar *m* zabudowany
**bulb** [bʌlb] *n* (*Bot*) bulwa *f*; (*Elec*) żarówka *f*
**bulbous** ['bʌlbəs] *adj* bulwiasty
**Bulgaria** [bʌl'gɛərɪə] *n* Bułgaria *f*
**Bulgarian** [bʌl'gɛərɪən] *adj* bułgarski ▹ *n* (*person*) Bułgar(ka) *m(f)*; (*Ling*) (język *m*) bułgarski
**bulge** [bʌldʒ] *n* (*bump*) wybrzuszenie *nt*; (*in birth rate, sales*) przejściowy wzrost *m* ▹ *vi*: **his pocket ~d** miał wypchaną kieszeń; **to be bulging with** (*box*) pękać od *+gen*; (*table, shelf*) uginać się od *+gen*; **population ~** wyż demograficzny
**bulimia** [bə'lɪmɪə] *n* bulimia *f*
**bulk** [bʌlk] *n* (*of object*) masa *f*; (*of person*) cielsko *nt*; **in ~** (*Comm*) hurtowo; **the ~ of** większość *+gen*
**bulk buying** [-'baɪɪŋ] *n* masowy skup *m*

**bulkhead** ['bʌlkhɛd] *n* przegroda *f*
**bulky** ['bʌlkɪ] *adj* nieporęczny
**bull** [bul] *n* (*Zool*) byk *m*; (*Stock Exchange*) gracz *m* na zwyżkę; (*Rel*) bulla *f*
**bulldog** ['buldɔg] *n* buldog *m*
**bulldoze** ['buldəuz] *vt* (*knock down*) burzyć (zburzyć *perf*) spychaczem; (*flatten*) wyrównywać (wyrównać *perf*) spychaczem; **I was ~d into it** (*inf*: *fig*) zmusili mnie do tego
**bulldozer** ['buldəuzəʳ] *n* spychacz *m*, buldożer *m*
**bullet** ['bulɪt] *n* kula *f*
**bulletin** ['bulɪtɪn] *n* (*TV etc*): **news ~** skrót *m* wiadomości; (*journal*) biuletyn *m*
**bulletin board** (*Comput*) *n* komputerowa tablica *f* ogłoszeń, BBS *m*; (*US*: *noticeboard*) tablica *f* ogłoszeń
**bulletproof** ['bulɪtpru:f] *adj* kuloodporny
**bullfight** ['bulfaɪt] *n* corrida *f*, walka *f* byków
**bullfighter** ['bulfaɪtəʳ] *n* torreador *m*
**bullfighting** ['bulfaɪtɪŋ] *n* walki *pl* byków
**bullion** ['buljən] *n* (*gold*) złoto *nt* w sztabach; (*silver*) srebro *nt* w sztabach
**bullock** ['bulək] *n* wół *m*
**bullring** ['bulrɪŋ] *n* arena *f* (*do walk byków*)
**bull's-eye** ['bulzaɪ] *n* środek *m* tarczy, dziesiątka *f* (*inf*)
**bullshit** ['bulʃɪt] (*inf*) *n* bzdury *pl* ▷ *vt* wciskać (wcisnąć) kit *+dat perf* ▷ *vi* chrzanić
**bully** ['bulɪ] *n*: **he was a ~ at school** w szkole znęcał się nad słabszymi ▷ *vt* tyranizować; **to ~ sb into doing sth** zmuszać (zmusić *perf*) kogoś do zrobienia czegoś
**bullying** ['bulɪɪŋ] *n* tyranizowanie *nt*
**bum** [bʌm] (*inf*) *n* (*Brit*: *backside*) zadek *m* (*inf*); (*esp US*: *tramp*) włóczęga *m*
▸ **bum around** (*inf*) *vi* (*drift*) włóczyć się; (*laze around*) obijać się
**bumblebee** ['bʌmblbi:] *n* trzmiel *m*
**bumf** [bʌmf], **bumph** (*inf*) *n* papierki *pl* (*inf*)
**bump** [bʌmp] *n* (*car accident*) stłuczka *f*; (*jolt*) wstrząs *m*; (*on head*) guz *m*; (*on road*) wybój *m* ▷ *vt*: **to ~ one's head on** *or* **against sth** uderzać (uderzyć *perf*) głową o coś ▷ *vi* (*car*) podskakiwać (podskoczyć *perf*)
▸ **bump into** *vt fus* wpadać (wpaść *perf*) na *+acc*
**bumper** ['bʌmpəʳ] *n* zderzak *m* ▷ *adj*: **~ crop/harvest** rekordowe zbiory *pl*
**bumper cars** *pl* samochodziki *pl* (*w wesołym miasteczku*)
**bumph** [bʌmf] *n* = **bumf**
**bumptious** ['bʌmpʃəs] *adj* przemądrzały
**bumpy** ['bʌmpɪ] *adj* wyboisty; **it was a ~ flight/ride** bardzo trzęsło (podczas lotu/jazdy)
**bun** [bʌn] *n* (*Culin*) (słodka) bułeczka *f*; (*hairstyle*) kok *m*
**bunch** [bʌntʃ] *n* (*of flowers*) bukiet *m*; (*of keys*) pęk *m*; (*of bananas, grapes*) kiść *f*; (*of people*) grupa *f*; **bunches** *npl* kitki *pl*, kucyki *pl*
**bundle** ['bʌndl] *n* (*of clothes, belongings*) zawiniątko *nt*, tobołek *m*; (*of sticks*) wiązka *f*; (*of papers*) paczka *f*, plik *m* ▷ *vt* (*also*: **bundle up**) pakować (spakować *perf*); (*put*): **to ~ sth/sb into** wpychać (wepchnąć *perf*) coś/kogoś do *+gen*
▸ **bundle off** *vt* (*person*) wyprawiać (wyprawić *perf*)
**bun fight** (*Brit*: *inf*) *n* bankiecik *m* (*inf*)
**bung** [bʌŋ] *n* (*of barrel*) szpunt *m*; (*of flask*) korek *m*, zatyczka *f* ▷ *vt* (*Brit*: *throw, put*) rzucać (rzucić *perf*); (*also*: **bung up**: *pipe, hole*) zatykać (zatkać *perf*); **my nose is ~ed up** mam zapchany nos
**bungalow** ['bʌŋgələu] *n* dom *m* parterowy, bungalow *m*
**bungle** ['bʌŋgl] *vt* spartaczyć (*perf*)
**bunion** ['bʌnjən] *n* (*Med*) paluch *m* sztywny
**bunk** [bʌŋk] *n* (*on ship*) koja *f*
**bunk beds** *npl* łóżko *nt* piętrowe
**bunker** ['bʌŋkəʳ] *n* (*coal store*) skład *m* na węgiel; (*Mil, Golf*) bunkier *m*
**bunny** ['bʌnɪ] *n* (*also*: **bunny rabbit**) króliczek *m*
**bunny girl** (*Brit*) *n hostessa w klubie nocnym w stroju króliczka*
**bunny hill** (*US*: *Ski*) *n* ośla łączka *f*
**bunting** ['bʌntɪŋ] *n* chorągiewki *pl*
**buoy** [bɔɪ] *n* boja *f*
▸ **buoy up** *vt* (*fig*) podtrzymywać (podtrzymać *perf*) na duchu
**buoyancy** ['bɔɪənsɪ] *n* (*of ship*) pływalność *f*
**buoyant** ['bɔɪənt] *adj* (*economy, market*) prężny; (*prices, currency*) zwyżkujący; **to be ~** utrzymywać się na powierzchni wody; (*fig*) cieszyć się życiem
**burden** ['bə:dn] *n* (*responsibility*) obciążenie *nt*; (*load, worry*) ciężar *m* ▷ *vt*: **to ~ sb with** (*trouble, worry*) martwić kogoś *+instr*; **to be a ~ to sb** być dla kogoś ciężarem
**bureau** ['bjuərəu] (*pl* **~x**) *n* (*Brit*) sekretarzyk *m*; (*US*) komoda *f*; (*for travel, information*) biuro *nt*
**bureaucracy** [bjuə'rɔkrəsɪ] *n* biurokracja *f*
**bureaucrat** ['bjuərəkræt] *n* biurokrata(-tka) *m(f)*
**bureaucratic** [bjuərə'krætɪk] *adj* biurokratyczny
**bureaux** ['bjuərəuz] *npl of* **bureau**
**burgeon** ['bə:dʒən] *vi* (*fig*) rozrastać się (rozrosnąć się *perf*)
**burger** ['bə:gəʳ] *n* hamburger *m*
**burglar** ['bə:gləʳ] *n* włamywacz(ka) *m(f)*
**burglar alarm** *n* alarm *m* antywłamaniowy *or* przeciwwłamaniowy

**burglarize** [ˈbə:gləraɪz] (*US*) *vt* włamywać się (włamać się *perf*) do +*gen*
**burglary** [ˈbə:glərɪ] *n* włamanie *nt*
**burgle** [ˈbə:gl] *vt* włamywać się (włamać się *perf*) do +*gen*
**Burgundy** [ˈbə:gəndɪ] *n* Burgundia *f*
**burial** [ˈbɛrɪəl] *n* pogrzeb *m*
**burial ground** *n* (*ancient*) cmentarzysko *nt*; (*of soldiers*) miejsce *nt* spoczynku
**burlesque** [bə:ˈlɛsk] *n* burleska *f*
**burly** [ˈbə:lɪ] *adj* krzepki
**Burma** [ˈbə:mə] *n* Birma *f*
**Burmese** [bə:ˈmi:z] *adj* birmański; (*person*) Birmańczyk(-anka) *m*(*f*); (*Ling*) (język *m*) birmański
**burn** [bə:n] (*pt, pp* **~ed** *or* **~t**) *vt* (*papers etc*) palić (spalić *perf*); (*fuel*) spalać (spalić *perf*); (*toast etc*) przypalać (przypalić *perf*); (*part of body*) parzyć (oparzyć *perf or* sparzyć *perf*) ▷ *vi* (*house, wood*) palić się (spalić się *perf*); (*fuel*) spalać się (spalić się *perf*); (*toast etc*) przypalać się (przypalić się *perf*); (*blister etc*) piec ▷ *n* oparzenie *nt*; **the cigarette ~t a hole in her dress** papieros wypalił jej dziurę w sukni; **I've ~t myself!** oparzyłem się!
▸ **burn down** *vt* spalić (*perf*) (doszczętnie)
▸ **burn out** *vi*: **to ~ (o.s.) out** wypalać się (wypalić się *perf*)
**burner** [ˈbə:nə[r]] *n* palnik *m*
**burning** [ˈbə:nɪŋ] *adj* (*house, forest*) płonący, palący się; (*sand, issue*) palący; (*interest, enthusiasm*) gorący
**burnish** [ˈbə:nɪʃ] *vt* polerować (wypolerować *perf*)
**burnt** [bə:nt] *pt, pp of* **burn**
**burnt sugar** (*Brit*) *n* karmel *m*
**burp** [bə:p] (*inf*) *n* odbicie *nt*, beknięcie *nt* (*inf*) ▷ *vi*: **he ~ed** odbiło mu się, beknął (*inf*)
**burrow** [ˈbʌrəu] *n* nora *f* (*np. królicza*) ▷ *vi* (*animal*) ryć *or* kopać norę; (*person*) szperać, grzebać
**bursar** [ˈbə:sə[r]] *n* kwestor *m*
**bursary** [ˈbə:sərɪ] (*Brit*) *n* stypendium *nt*
**burst** [bə:st] (*pt, pp* **~**) *vt* (*balloon, ball*) przebijać (przebić *perf*); (*pipe*) rozrywać (rozerwać *perf*) ▷ *vi* (*pipe, tyre*) pękać (pęknąć *perf*) ▷ *n* (*also*: **burst pipe**) pęknięta rura *f*; **to ~ into flames** stawać (stanąć *perf*) w płomieniach; **to ~ into tears** wybuchać (wybuchnąć *perf*) płaczem; **to ~ out laughing** wybuchać (wybuchnąć *perf*) śmiechem; **the river has ~ its banks** rzeka wystąpiła z brzegów; **~ blood vessel** pęknięte naczynie krwionośne; **to be ~ing with** (*container*) pękać od +*gen*; (*person*) tryskać +*instr*; **to ~ open** gwałtownie się otwierać (otworzyć *perf*); **a ~ of energy/enthusiasm** przypływ energii/entuzjazmu; **a ~ of laughter** wybuch śmiechu; **a ~ of applause** burza oklasków; **there was a ~ of gunfire** nagle otworzono ogień
▸ **burst into** *vt fus* wpadać (wpaść *perf*) do +*gen*
▸ **burst out of** *vt fus* wypadać (wypaść *perf*) z +*gen*
**bury** [ˈbɛrɪ] *vt* (*object*) zakopywać (zakopać *perf*); (*person*) chować (pochować *perf*); **to ~ one's face in one's hands** ukrywać (ukryć *perf*) twarz w dłoniach; **to ~ one's head in the sand** (*fig*) chować (schować *perf*) głowę w piasek; **to ~ the hatchet** (*fig*) zakopywać (zakopać *perf*) topór wojenny
**bus** [bʌs] *n* autobus *m*
**bush** [buʃ] *n* (*plant*) krzew *m*, krzak *m*; (*scrubland*) busz *m*; **to beat about the ~** owijać w bawełnę
**bushel** [ˈbuʃl] *n* buszel *m* (*36,4 litra*)
**bushy** [ˈbuʃɪ] *adj* (*eyebrows*) krzaczasty; (*tail*) puszysty; (*hair, plants*) bujny
**busily** [ˈbɪzɪlɪ] *adv* pracowicie
**business** [ˈbɪznɪs] *n* (*matter, question*) sprawa *f*; (*trading*) interesy *pl*, biznes *m*; (*firm*) firma *f*, biznes *m* (*inf*); (*trade*) branża *f*; **she's away on ~** wyjechała w interesach; **I'm here on ~** jestem tu w interesach *or* służbowo; **he's in the insurance ~** pracuje w branży ubezpieczeniowej; **to do ~ with sb** robić z kimś interesy; **it's my ~ to ...** moim obowiązkiem jest +*infin*; **it's none of my ~** to nie moja sprawa; **he means ~** on nie żartuje
**business address** *n* adres *m* firmy
**business card** *n* wizytówka *f*
**businesslike** [ˈbɪznɪslaɪk] *adj* rzeczowy
**businessman** [ˈbɪznɪsmən] (*irreg*: *like* **man**) *n* biznesman *m*
**business trip** *n* wyjazd *m* służbowy
**businesswoman** [ˈbɪznɪswumən] (*irreg*: *like* **woman**) *n* bizneswoman *f inv*
**busker** [ˈbʌskə[r]] (*Brit*) *n* grajek *m* uliczny
**bus lane** (*Brit*) *n* pas *m* (ruchu) wydzielony dla autobusów
**bus shelter** *n* wiata *f* (*na przystanku autobusowym*)
**bus station** *n* dworzec *m* autobusowy
**bus stop** *n* przystanek *m* autobusowy
**bust** [bʌst] *n* (*Anat*) biust *m*; (*measurement*) obwód *m* w biuście; (*sculpture*) popiersie *nt* ▷ *adj* (*inf*: *broken*) zepsuty ▷ *vt* (*inf*: *arrest*) przymykać (przymknąć *perf*) (*inf*); **to go ~** plajtować (splajtować *perf*) (*inf*)
**bustle** [ˈbʌsl] *n* krzątanina *f* ▷ *vi* krzątać się
**bustling** [ˈbʌslɪŋ] *adj* gwarny, ruchliwy
**bust-up** [ˈbʌstʌp] (*Brit*: *inf*) *n* kłótnia *f*; (*ending relationship*) zerwanie *nt*
**BUSWE** (*Brit*) *n abbr* = **British Union of Social Work Employees**

**busy** ['bɪzɪ] *adj (person, telephone line)* zajęty; *(street)* ruchliwy ▷ *vt*: **to ~ o.s. with** zajmować się (zająć się *perf*) *+instr*; **he's a ~ man** jest bardzo zapracowany; **she's ~** jest zajęta; **it's usually a very ~ shop** w tym sklepie panuje zwykle duży ruch
**busybody** ['bɪzɪbɔdɪ] *n* ciekawski(-ka) *m(f)*
**busy signal** *(US: Tel) n* sygnał *m* „zajęte"

KEYWORD

**but** [bʌt] *conj* **1** *(yet, however)* ale, lecz *(fml)*; **I'd love to come, but I'm busy** bardzo chciałabym przyjść, ale jestem zajęta; **I'm sorry, but I don't agree** przykro mi, lecz nie zgadzam się
**2** *(showing disagreement, surprise etc)* ależ; **but that's far too expensive!** ależ to o wiele za drogo!; **but that's fantastic!** ależ to wspaniale!
▷ *prep (apart from, except)*: **we've had nothing but trouble** mieliśmy same kłopoty; **no-one but him can do it** jedynie on może to zrobić; **but for your help** gdyby nie twoja pomoc; **I'll do anything but that** zrobię wszystko, tylko nie to
▷ *adv* tylko; **she's but a child** jest tylko dzieckiem; **had I but known** gdybym tylko wiedział; **I can but try** mogę tylko spróbować

**butane** ['bju:teɪn] *n (also:* **butane gas***)* butan *m*
**butcher** ['butʃəʳ] *n* rzeźnik(-iczka) *m(f)*; *(fig)* oprawca *m* ▷ *vt (cattle)* zarzynać (zarżnąć *perf*); *(people)* dokonywać (dokonać *perf*) rzezi na *+loc*
**butcher's (shop)** ['butʃəz-] *n* (sklep *m*) mięsny, rzeźnik *m*
**butler** ['bʌtləʳ] *n* kamerdyner *m*
**butt** [bʌt] *n (barrel)* beczka *f*; *(of spear)* rękojeść *f*; *(of gun)* kolba *f*; *(of cigarette)* niedopałek *m*; *(Brit: fig: of jokes, criticism)* obiekt *m*; *(US: inf!)* dupa *f (inf!)* ▷ *vt (person)* uderzać (uderzyć *perf*) głową; *(goat)* bóść (ubóść *perf*)
▸ **butt in** *vi* wtrącać się (wtrącić się *perf*)
**butter** ['bʌtəʳ] *n* masło *nt* ▷ *vt* smarować (posmarować *perf*) masłem
**buttercup** ['bʌtəkʌp] *n* jaskier *m*
**butter dish** *n* maselniczka *f*
**butterfingers** ['bʌtəfɪŋgəz] *(inf) n* niezdara *m/f*
**butterfly** ['bʌtəflaɪ] *n* motyl *m*; *(also:* **butterfly stroke***)* styl *m* motylkowy, motylek *m*
**buttocks** ['bʌtəks] *npl* pośladki *pl*
**button** ['bʌtn] *n (on clothes)* guzik *m*; *(on machine)* przycisk *m*, guzik *m*; *(US: badge)* znaczek *m (do przypinania)* ▷ *vt (also:* **button up***)* zapinać (zapiąć *perf*) ▷ *vi* zapinać się (zapiąć się *perf*)
**buttonhole** ['bʌtnhəul] *n* dziurka *f* ▷ *vt* przyczepiać się (przyczepić się *perf*) do *+gen*
**buttress** ['bʌtrɪs] *n* przypora *f*
**buxom** ['bʌksəm] *adj (woman)* dorodny
**buy** [baɪ] *(pt, pp* **bought***) vt* kupować (kupić *perf*) ▷ *n*: **good/bad buy** dobry *or* udany/zły *or* nieudany zakup *m*; **to buy sb sth** kupować (kupić *perf*) komuś coś; **to buy sth from sb/a shop** kupować (kupić *perf*) coś od kogoś/w sklepie; **to buy sth off sb** kupować (kupić *perf*) coś od kogoś; **to buy sb a drink** stawiać (postawić *perf*) komuś drinka
▸ **buy back** *vt* odkupić *(perf)* (z powrotem)
▸ **buy in** *(Brit) vt* zakupić *(perf)* (w dużych ilościach)
▸ **buy into** *(Brit: Comm) vt fus* zdobywać (zdobyć *perf*) udziały w *+loc*
▸ **buy off** *vt* przekupywać (przekupić *perf*)
▸ **buy out** *vt (business, partner)* wykupywać (wykupić *perf*)
▸ **buy up** *vt (land etc)* wykupywać (wykupić *perf*)
**buyer** ['baɪəʳ] *n (purchaser)* kupiec *m*, nabywca *m*; *(Comm)* zaopatrzeniowiec *m*
**buyer's market** ['baɪəz-] *n* rynek *m* nabywcy
**buy-out** ['baɪaut] *n*: **a management ~** wykup *m* przedsiębiorstwa przez kierownictwo
**buzz** [bʌz] *n* brzęczenie *nt* ▷ *vi (insect, saw)* brzęczeć ▷ *vt (person)* przywoływać (przywołać *perf*) *(za pomocą telefonu wewnętrznego, brzęczyka itp)*; *(Aviat)* przelatywać (przelecieć *perf*) lotem koszącym nad *+instr*; **to give sb a ~** *(inf)* przekręcić *(perf)* do kogoś *(inf)*; **my head is ~ing** mam mętlik w głowie; **my ears are ~ing** szumi mi w uszach
▸ **buzz off** *(inf) vi* spływać (spłynąć *perf*) *(inf)*
**buzzard** ['bʌzəd] *n* myszołów *m*
**buzzer** ['bʌzəʳ] *n* brzęczyk *m*
**buzz word** *(inf) n* modne określenie *nt (zwykle specjalistyczne i nadużywane w mediach)*

KEYWORD

**by** [baɪ] *prep* **1** *(referring to cause, agent)* przez *+acc*; **killed by lightning** zabity przez piorun; **surrounded by a fence** otoczony płotem; **a painting by Picasso** obraz Picassa
**2** *(referring to method, manner, means)*: **by bus** *etc* autobusem *itd.*; **to pay by cheque** płacić (zapłacić *perf*) czekiem; **by moonlight** przy świetle księżyca; **by candlelight** przy świecach; **by saving hard** oszczędzając każdy grosz
**3** *(via, through)* przez *+acc*; **he came in by the back door** wszedł tylnymi drzwiami

4 (*close to*): **she sat by his bed** usiadła przy jego łóżku; **the house by the river** dom nad rzeką
5 (*past*) obok *+gen*, koło *+gen*; **she rushed by me** przemknęła obok mnie; **I go by the post office every day** codziennie przechodzę koło poczty
6 (*not later than*) do *+gen*; **by 4 o'clock** do (godziny) czwartej; **by the time I got here it was too late** zanim tu dotarłem, było już za późno
7 (*amount*): **paid by the hour** opłacany za godzinę; **by the kilo/metre** na kilogramy/metry
8 (*Math*) przez *+acc*; **to divide by 3** dzielić (podzielić *perf*) przez 3
9 (*measure*): **a room 3 metres by 4** pokój o wymiarach 3 na 4 (metry); **it's broader by a metre** jest o metr szerszy
10 (*according to*) według *+gen*; **to play by the rules** grać według zasad; **it's all right by me** mnie to nie przeszkadza
11: **he did it (all) by himself** zrobił to (zupełnie) sam
12: **by the way** nawiasem mówiąc, à propos; **this wasn't my idea by the way** nawiasem mówiąc, to nie był mój pomysł; **by the way, did you know Claire was back?** à propos, czy wiesz, że Claire wróciła?
▷ *adv* **1** *see* **go**; **pass** *etc*
2: **by and by** wkrótce, niebawem; **by and by they came to a fork in the road** wkrótce dotarli do rozwidlenia dróg; **they'll come back by and by** niebawem wrócą
3: **by and large** ogólnie (rzecz) biorąc; **by and large I would agree with you** ogólnie (rzecz) biorąc, zgodziłbym się z tobą

**bye(-bye)** ['baɪ('baɪ)] *n excl* do widzenia; (*to child etc*) pa (pa)
**by(e)-law** ['baɪlɔː] *n* lokalne zarządzenie *nt*
**by-election** ['baɪɪlɛkʃən] (*Brit*) *n* wybory *pl* uzupełniające
**bygone** ['baɪgɔn] *adj* miniony ▷ *n*: **let ~s be ~s** puśćmy to w niepamięć, (co) było, minęło
**bypass** ['baɪpɑːs] *n* (*Aut*) obwodnica *f*; (*Med*) połączenie *nt* omijające, bypass *m* ▷ *vt* omijać (ominąć *perf*); (*fig*) obchodzić (obejść *perf*)
**by-product** ['baɪprɔdʌkt] *n* (*of industrial process*) produkt *m* uboczny; (*of situation*) skutek *m* uboczny
**byre** ['baɪə[r]] (*Brit*) *n* obora *f*
**bystander** ['baɪstændə[r]] *n* (*at accident etc*) świadek *m*, widz *m*
**byte** [baɪt] (*Comput*) *n* bajt *m*
**byway** ['baɪweɪ] *n* boczna droga *f*
**byword** ['baɪwəːd] *n*: **to be a ~ for** być symbolem *or* uosobieniem *+gen*
**by-your-leave** ['baɪjɔː'liːv] *n*: **without so much as a ~** nie pytając nikogo o zgodę

# Cc



**C[1], c[1]** [siː] *n* (*letter*) C *nt*, c *nt*; (*Scol*) ≈ dostateczny *m*; **C for Charlie** ≈ C jak Celina
**C[2]** [siː] *n* (*Mus*) C *nt*, c *nt*
**C[3]** *abbr* (= *Celsius, centigrade*) C, °C
**c[2]** *abbr* (= *century*) w.; (= *circa*) ok.; (*US etc*: = *cents*) c
**CA** *n abbr* (*Brit*) = **chartered accountant** ▷ *abbr* = **Central America**; (*US*: *Post*) = **California**
**ca.** *abbr* (= *circa*) ok.
**C/A** *abbr* (*Comm*) = **capital account**; **credit account**; **current account**
**CAA** *n abbr* (*Brit*: = *Civil Aviation Authority*, *US*: = *Civil Aeronautics Authority*) ≈ GILC *m* (= *Główny Inspektorat Lotnictwa Cywilnego*)
**CAB** (*Brit*) *n abbr* (= *Citizens' Advice Bureau*) *biuro porad dla obywateli*
**cab** [kæb] *n* (*taxi*) taksówka *f*; (*of truck etc*) kabina *f*, szoferka *f*; (*horse-drawn*) powóz *m*, dorożka *f*
**cabaret** ['kæbəreɪ] *n* kabaret *m*
**cabbage** ['kæbɪdʒ] *n* kapusta *f*
**cabin** ['kæbɪn] *n* (*on ship, plane*) kabina *f*; (*house*) chata *f*
**cabin cruiser** *n* turystyczny jacht *m* motorowy
**cabinet** ['kæbɪnɪt] *n* (*piece of furniture*) szafka *f*; (*also*: **display cabinet**) gablota *f*; (: *small*) gablotka *f*; (*Pol*) gabinet *m*; **cocktail ~** barek
**cabinet-maker** ['kæbɪnɪt'meɪkə[r]] *n* stolarz *m* meblowy *or* artystyczny
**cabinet minister** *n* minister *m* gabinetu, minister *m* w rządzie
**cable** ['keɪbl] *n* (*rope*) lina *f*; (*Elec*) przewód *m*; (*Tel, TV*) kabel *m* ▷ *vt* przesyłać (przesłać *perf*) telegraficznie
**cable-car** ['keɪblkɑː[r]] *n* wagon *m* kolei linowej
**cablegram** ['keɪblgræm] *n* depesza *f*
**cable railway** *n* kolej *f* linowa
**cable television** *n* telewizja *f* kablowa
**cache** [kæʃ] *n* tajny skład *m* (*broni itp*); **a ~ of food** ukryte zapasy żywności
**cackle** ['kækl] *vi* (*person*) rechotać (zarechotać *perf*) (*pej*); (*hen*) gdakać (zagdakać *perf*)
**cacti** ['kæktaɪ] *npl of* **cactus**
**cactus** ['kæktəs] (*pl* **cacti**) *n* kaktus *m*
**CAD** *n abbr* (= *computer-aided design*) CAD, projektowanie *nt* wspomagane komputerowo
**caddie** ['kædɪ] (*Golf*) *n osoba nosząca graczowi kije*
**caddy** ['kædɪ] *n* = **caddie**
**cadence** ['keɪdəns] *n* (*of voice*) kadencja *f*
**cadet** [kə'dɛt] *n* kadet *m*; **police ~** kadet szkoły policyjnej
**cadge** [kædʒ] (*inf*) *vt*: **to ~ (from** *or* **off)** wyłudzać (wyłudzić *perf*) (od +*gen*)
**cadger** ['kædʒə[r]] (*Brit*: *inf*) *n* żebrak(-aczka) *m*(*f*)
**cadre** ['kædrɪ] *n* kadra *f*
**Caesarean** [siː'zɛərɪən] *adj*: **~ (section)** cesarskie cięcie *nt*, cesarka *f* (*inf*)
**CAF** (*Brit*) *abbr* (= *cost and freight*) koszt *m* i fracht *m*
**café** ['kæfeɪ] *n* kawiarnia *f*
**cafeteria** [kæfɪ'tɪərɪə] *n* (*in school, factory*) stołówka *f*; (*in station*) bufet *m*
**caffein(e)** ['kæfiːn] *n* kofeina *f*
**cage** [keɪdʒ] *n* klatka *f* ▷ *vt* zamykać (zamknąć *perf*) w klatce
**cagey** ['keɪdʒɪ] (*inf*) *adj* wymijający
**cagoule** [kə'guːl] *n* (lekki) płaszcz *m* przeciwdeszczowy
**CAI** *n abbr* (= *computer-aided instruction*) nauczanie *nt* wspomagane komputerowo
**Cairo** ['kaɪərəu] *n* Kair *m*
**cajole** [kə'dʒəul] *vt* nakłaniać (nakłonić *perf*) (pochlebstwami)
**cake** [keɪk] *n* (*Culin*) ciasto *nt*; (: *small*) ciastko *nt*; (*of soap*) kostka *f*; **it's a piece of ~** (*inf*) to małe piwo (*inf*); **he wants to have his ~ and eat it (too)** (*fig*) on chce mieć wszystko naraz
**caked** [keɪkt] *adj*: **~ with** oblepiony +*instr*
**cake shop** *n* ciastkarnia *f*, cukiernia *f*
**calamine lotion** ['kæləmaɪn-] *n* płyn *m* kalaminowy (*mieszanina tlenku cynku i wody wapiennej*)
**calamitous** [kə'læmɪtəs] *adj* katastrofalny
**calamity** [kə'læmɪtɪ] *n* katastrofa *f*, klęska *f*
**calcium** ['kælsɪəm] *n* wapń *m*
**calculate** ['kælkjuleɪt] *vt* (*cost, distance, sum*) obliczać (obliczyć *perf*); (*chances*) oceniać (ocenić *perf*); (*consequences*) przewidywać (przewidzieć *perf*); **~d to attract shareholders** obliczony na przyciągnięcie akcjonariuszy

**calculated** ['kælkjuleɪtɪd] *adj* rozmyślny; **a ~ risk** wkalkulowane ryzyko
**calculating** ['kælkjuleɪtɪŋ] *adj* wyrachowany
**calculation** [kælkju'leɪʃən] *n* (*sum*) obliczenie *nt*; (*estimate*) rachuba *f*, kalkulacja *f*
**calculator** ['kælkjuleɪtə[r]] *n* kalkulator *m*
**calculus** ['kælkjuləs] *n*: **integral/differential ~** rachunek *m* całkowy/róż˙niczkowy
**calendar** ['kæləndə[r]] *n* kalendarz *m*
**calendar month/year** *n* miesiąc *m*/rok *m* kalendarzowy
**calf** [kɑːf] (*pl* **calves**) *n* (*of cow*) cielę *nt*; (*of elephant, seal*) młode *nt*; (*also*: **calfskin**) skóra *f* cielęca; (*Anat*) łydka *f*
**caliber** ['kælɪbə[r]] (*US*) *n* = **calibre**
**calibrate** ['kælɪbreɪt] *vt* (*gun etc*) kalibrować; (*measuring instrument*) skalować (wyskalować *perf*)
**calibre**, (*US*) **caliber** ['kælɪbə[r]] *n* kaliber *m*
**calico** ['kælɪkəu] *n* (*Brit*) surówka *f* (bawełniana); (*US*) perkal *m*
**California** [kælɪ'fɔːnɪə] *n* Kalifornia *f*
**calipers** ['kælɪpəz] (*US*) *npl* = **callipers**
**call** [kɔːl] *vt* (*name, label*) nazywać (nazwać *perf*); (*christen*) dawać (dać *perf*) na imię *+dat*; (*Tel*) dzwonić (zadzwonić *perf*) do *+gen*; (*summon*) przywoływać (przywołać *perf*), wzywać (wezwać *perf*); (*meeting*) zwoływać (zwołać *perf*); (*flight*) zapowiadać (zapowiedzieć *perf*); (*strike*) ogłaszać (ogłosić *perf*) ▷ *vi* (*shout*) wołać (zawołać *perf*); (*Tel*) dzwonić (zadzwonić *perf*); (*also*: **call in, call round**) wstępować (wstąpić *perf*), wpadać (wpaść *perf*) ▷ *n* (*shout*) wołanie *nt*; (*Tel*) rozmowa *f*; (*of bird*) głos *m*; (*visit*) wizyta *f*; (*demand*) wezwanie *nt*; (*for flight etc*) zapowiedź *f*; (*fig*) zew *m*; **to be on ~** dyżurować, mieć dyżur; **he's ~ed Hopkins** nazywa się Hopkins; **she's ~ed Suzanne** ma na imię Suzanne; **who is ~ing?** (*Tel*) kto mówi?; **London ~ing** (*Radio*) tu mówi Londyn; **please give me a ~ at 7** proszę zadzwonić do mnie o 7; **to make a ~** dzwonić (zadzwonić *perf*); **to pay a ~ on sb** składać (złożyć *perf*) komuś wizytę; **there's not much ~ for these items** nie ma dużego zapotrzebowania na te artykuły
▸ **call at** *vt fus* (*ship*: *town*) zawijać (zawinąć *perf*) do *+gen*; (*: island*) zawijać (zawinąć *perf*) na *+acc*; (*train*) zatrzymywać się (zatrzymać się *perf*) w *+loc*
▸ **call back** *vi* (*return*) wstępować (wstąpić *perf*) jeszcze raz; (*Tel*) oddzwaniać (oddzwonić *perf*) ▷ *vt* (*Tel*) oddzwaniać (oddzwonić *perf*) *+dat*
▸ **call for** *vt fus* (*demand*) wzywać (wezwać *perf*) do *+gen*; (*fetch*) zgłaszać się (zgłosić się *perf*) po *+acc*
▸ **call in** *vt* (*doctor, police*) wzywać (wezwać *perf*); (*library books*) wzywać (wezwać *perf*) do zwrotu *+gen*
▸ **call off** *vt* (*strike, meeting*) odwoływać (odwołać *perf*); (*engagement*) zrywać (zerwać *perf*)
▸ **call on** *vt fus* odwiedzać (odwiedzić *perf*) *+acc*; **to ~ on sb to do sth** wzywać (wezwać *perf*) kogoś do zrobienia czegoś
▸ **call out** *vi* krzyczeć (krzyknąć *perf*), wołać (zawołać *perf*) ▷ *vt* wzywać (wezwać *perf*)
▸ **call up** *vt* (*Mil*) powoływać (powołać *perf*) do wojska; (*Tel*) dzwonić (zadzwonić *perf*) do *+gen*
**callbox** ['kɔːlbɔks] (*Brit*) *n* budka *f* telefoniczna
**call centre**, (*US*) **call center** *n* centrum *nt* obsługi klienta
**caller** ['kɔːlə[r]] *n* (*visitor*) gość *m*, odwiedzający(-ca) *m(f)*; (*Tel*) telefonujący(-ca) *m(f)*; **hold the line, ~!** proszę nie odkładać słuchawki!
**call girl** *n* dziewczyna *f* do towarzystwa
**call-in** ['kɔːlɪn] (*US*: *Radio, TV*) *n program na żywo z telefonicznym udziałem słuchaczy/widzów*
**calling** ['kɔːlɪŋ] *n* (*trade, occupation*) fach *m*; (*vocation*) powołanie *nt*
**calling card** (*US*) *n* wizytówka *f*, bilet *m* wizytowy
**callipers**, (*US*) **calipers** ['kælɪpəz] *npl* (*Math*) cyrkiel *m* kalibrowy; (*Med*) cyrkiel *m* wyciągowy
**callous** ['kæləs] *adj* bezduszny
**callousness** ['kæləsnɪs] *n* bezduszność *f*
**callow** ['kæləu] *adj* niedoświadczony
**calm** [kɑːm] *adj* spokojny ▷ *n* spokój *m* ▷ *vt* (*person, fears*) uspokajać (uspokoić *perf*); (*grief, pain*) koić (ukoić *perf*)
▸ **calm down** *vt* uspokajać (uspokoić *perf*) ▷ *vi* uspokajać się (uspokoić się *perf*)
**calmly** ['kɑːmlɪ] *adv* spokojnie
**calmness** ['kɑːmnɪs] *n* spokój *m*
**Calor gas**® ['kælə[r]-] *n* ≈ propan-butan *m*
**calorie** ['kælərɪ] *n* kaloria *f*; **low ~ product** produkt niskokaloryczny
**calve** [kɑːv] *vi* cielić się (ocielić się *perf*)
**calves** [kɑːvz] *npl of* **calf**
**CAM** *n abbr* (= *computer-aided manufacturing*) CAM, produkcja *f* wspomagana komputerowo
**camber** ['kæmbə[r]] *n* (*of road*) wypukłość *f*
**Cambodia** [kæm'bəudɪə] *n* Kambodża *f*
**Cambodian** [kæm'bəudɪən] *adj* kambodżański ▷ *n* Kambodżanin(-anka) *m(f)*
**Cambs** (*Brit*: *Post*) *abbr* = **Cambridgeshire**
**camcorder** ['kæmkɔːdə[r]] *n* kamera *f* wideo
**came** [keɪm] *pt of* **come**
**camel** ['kæməl] *n* wielbłąd *m*

**cameo** ['kæmɪəu] *n* (*jewellery*) kamea *f*; (*performance*) *niewielka rola grana przez znanego aktora, często ograniczona do jednego wejścia*
**camera** ['kæmərə] *n* (*Phot*) aparat *m* (fotograficzny); (*Film, TV*) kamera *f*; (*also*: **cinecamera, movie camera**) kamera *f* filmowa; **35 mm ~** aparat małoobrazkowy; **in ~** (*Jur*) przy drzwiach zamkniętych
**cameraman** ['kæmərəmæn] (*irreg*: *like* **man**) *n* (*Film*) operator *m* (filmowy); (*TV*) kamerzysta *m*
**Cameroon** [kæmə'ru:n] *n* Kamerun *m*
**Cameroun** [kæmə'ru:n] *n* = **Cameroon**
**camomile** ['kæməumaɪl] *n* rumianek *m*
**camouflage** ['kæməflɑ:ʒ] *n* kamuflaż *m* ▷ *vt* (*Mil*) maskować (zamaskować *perf*)
**camp** [kæmp] *n* obóz *m* ▷ *vi* obozować, biwakować ▷ *adj* (*effeminate*) zniewieściały; (*exaggerated*) afektowany
**campaign** [kæm'peɪn] *n* kampania *f* ▷ *vi* prowadzić (przeprowadzić *perf*) kampanię; **to ~ for/against** prowadzić kampanię na rzecz *+gen*/przeciw(ko) *+dat*
**campaigner** [kæm'peɪnə<sup>r</sup>] *n*: **~ for/against sth** osoba *f* prowadząca kampanię na rzecz czegoś/przeciwko czemuś
**camp bed** (*Brit*) *n* łóżko *nt* polowe
**camper** ['kæmpə<sup>r</sup>] *n* (*person*) obozowicz(ka) *m(f)*, wczasowicz(ka) *m(f)*; (*vehicle*) samochód *m* kempingowy
**camping** ['kæmpɪŋ] *n* kemping *m*, obozowanie *nt*, biwakowanie *nt*; **to go ~** jechać (pojechać *perf*) na biwak *or* kemping
**camping site** *n* = **campsite**
**campsite** ['kæmpsaɪt] *n* kemping *m*, pole *nt* namiotowe
**campus** ['kæmpəs] *n* miasteczko *nt* uniwersyteckie
**camshaft** ['kæmʃɑ:ft] (*Aut*) *n* wał *m* rozrządowy
**can**[1] *n* (*for foodstuffs*) puszka *f*; (*for oil, water*) kanister *m* ▷ *vt* puszkować (zapuszkować *perf*); **a can of beer** puszka piwa; **he had to carry the can** (*Brit*: *inf*) musiał wziąć całą winę na siebie

KEYWORD

**can**[2] [kæn, kən] (*negative* **cannot, can't**, *conditional and pt* **could**) *aux vb* **1** (*be able to*) móc; **you can do it if you try** możesz to zrobić, jeśli się postarasz; **she couldn't sleep that night** nie mogła spać tej nocy; **I can't see you** nie widzę cię
**2** (*know how to*) umieć; **I can swim** umiem pływać; **can you speak French?** (czy) mówisz po francusku?
**3** (*expressing permission, disbelief, puzzlement, possibility*) móc; **could I have a word with you?** czy mógłbym zamienić z tobą dwa słowa?; **it can't be true!** to nie może być prawda!; **what CAN he want?** czego on może chcieć?; **she could have been delayed** mogło ją coś zatrzymać

**Canada** ['kænədə] *n* Kanada *f*
**Canadian** [kə'neɪdɪən] *adj* kanadyjski ▷ *n* Kanadyjczyk(-jka) *m(f)*
**canal** [kə'næl] *n* kanał *m*; (*Anat*) przewód *m*
**Canaries** [kə'nɛərɪz] *npl* = **Canary Islands**
**canary** [kə'nɛərɪ] *n* kanarek *m*
**Canary Islands** [kə'nɛərɪ 'aɪləndz] *npl*: **the ~** Wyspy *pl* Kanaryjskie
**Canberra** ['kænbərə] *n* Canberra *f*
**cancel** ['kænsəl] *vt* (*meeting, flight, reservation*) odwoływać (odwołać *perf*); (*contract, cheque*) anulować (anulować *perf*), unieważniać (unieważnić *perf*); (*order*) cofać (cofnąć *perf*); (*words, figures*) przekreślać (przekreślić *perf*)
▸ **cancel out** *vt* znosić (znieść *perf*); **they ~ each other out** wzajemnie się znoszą *or* niwelują
**cancellation** [kænsə'leɪʃən] *n* (*of appointment, reservation, flight*) odwołanie *nt*; (*Tourism*) zwrot *m*
**cancer** ['kænsə<sup>r</sup>] *n* rak *m*, nowotwór *m*; **C~** Rak; **to be C~** być spod znaku Raka
**cancerous** ['kænsrəs] *adj* nowotworowy
**cancer patient** *n* chory(-ra) *m(f)* na raka
**cancer research** *n* badania *pl* nad rakiem
**C and F** (*Brit*: *Comm*) *abbr* = **CAF**
**candid** ['kændɪd] *adj* szczery
**candidacy** ['kændɪdəsɪ] *n* kandydatura *f*
**candidate** ['kændɪdeɪt] *n* kandydat(ka) *m(f)*
**candidature** ['kændɪdətʃə<sup>r</sup>] (*Brit*) *n* = **candidacy**
**candied** ['kændɪd] *adj* kandyzowany
**candle** ['kændl] *n* (*in house*) świeczka *f*; (*in church*) świeca *f*; (*of tallow*) łojówka *f*
**candlelight** ['kændllaɪt] *n*: **by ~** przy świetle świec, przy świeczce *or* świecach
**candlestick** ['kændlstɪk] *n* świecznik *m*; (*big, ornate*) lichtarz *m*
**candour**, (*US*) **candor** ['kændə<sup>r</sup>] *n* szczerość *f*
**candy** ['kændɪ] *n* (*also*: **sugar-candy**) cukierek *m*; (*US*) słodycze *pl*
**candy-floss** ['kændɪflɔs] (*Brit*) *n* wata *f* cukrowa
**candy store** (*US*) *n* sklep *m* ze słodyczami
**cane** [keɪn] *n* trzcina *f*; (*for walking*) laska *f* ▷ *vt* (*Brit*: *Scol*) chłostać (wychłostać *perf*)
**canine** ['keɪnaɪn] *adj* psi
**canister** ['kænɪstə<sup>r</sup>] *n* (*for tea, sugar*) puszka *f*; (*of gas, chemicals*) kanister *m*
**cannabis** ['kænəbɪs] *n* marihuana *f*; **~ plant** konopie indyjskie

**canned** [kænd] *adj (fruit, vegetables)* z puszki *post*; *(inf: music)* z taśmy *post*; *(Brit: inf: drunk)* zalany *(inf)*
**cannibal** ['kænɪbəl] *n* kanibal *m*
**cannibalism** ['kænɪbəlɪzəm] *n* kanibalizm *m*
**cannon** ['kænən] *(pl ~ or ~s) n* armata *f*, działo *nt*
**cannonball** ['kænənbɔːl] *n* kula *f* armatnia
**cannon fodder** *n* mięso *nt* armatnie
**cannot** ['kænɔt] = **can not**
**canny** ['kænɪ] *adj* sprytny
**canoe** [kə'nuː] *n* kajak *m*, kanoe *or* kanu *nt inv*
**canoeing** [kə'nuːɪŋ] *n* kajakarstwo *nt*
**canon** ['kænən] *n (clergyman)* kanonik *m*; *(principle)* kanon *m*
**canonize** ['kænənaɪz] *vt* kanonizować (kanonizować *perf*)
**can opener** [-'əupnəʳ] *n* otwieracz *m* do puszek *or* konserw
**canopy** ['kænəpɪ] *n (above bed, throne)* baldachim *m*; *(of leaves, sky)* sklepienie *nt*
**cant** [kænt] *n* obłudne frazesy *pl*
**can't** [kænt] = **can not**
**Cantab.** *(Brit) abbr (in degree titles: = Cantabrigiensis) Uniwersytetu Cambridge*
**cantankerous** [kæn'tæŋkərəs] *adj* marudny
**canteen** [kæn'tiːn] *n (in workplace, school)* stołówka *f*; *(mobile)* kuchnia *f* polowa; **a ~ of cutlery** *(Brit)* komplet sztućców *(w pudełku)*
**canter** ['kæntəʳ] *vi (horse)* kłusować, biec kłusem ▷ *n* kłus *m*
**cantilever** ['kæntɪliːvəʳ] *n* wspornik *m*
**canvas** ['kænvəs] *n (fabric)* brezent *m*; *(painting)* płótno *nt*; *(Naut)* żagiel *m*; **under ~** pod namiotem
**canvass** ['kænvəs] *vi* agitować ▷ *vt (opinions, place)* badać (zbadać *perf*); *(person)* wybadać *(perf)*; **to ~ for** agitować za *+instr*
**canvasser** ['kænvəsəʳ] *n* agitator(ka) *m(f)*
**canvassing** ['kænvəsɪŋ] *n* agitacja *f*
**canyon** ['kænjən] *n* kanion *m*
**CAP** *n abbr (= Common Agricultural Policy)* Wspólna Polityka *f* Agrarna *(krajów Wspólnoty Europejskiej)*
**cap** [kæp] *n (hat)* czapka *f*; *(of pen)* nasadka *f*; *(of bottle)* nakrętka *f*, kapsel *m*; *(also:* **Dutch cap**) kapturek *m* dopochwowy; *(for toy gun)* kapiszon *m*; *(for swimming)* czepek *m* ▷ *vt (performance etc)* ukoronować *(perf)*, uwieńczyć *(perf)*; *(tax)* nakładać (nałożyć *perf*) ograniczenia na *+acc*; **he won his England cap** dostał się do reprezentacji (narodowej) Anglii; **she was capped twenty times** była w reprezentacji kraju dwadzieścia razy; **sweets capped with a cherry** słodycze przystrojone wiśnią; **and to cap it all, ...** a na domiar wszystkiego, ...
**capability** [keɪpə'bɪlɪtɪ] *n* zdolność *f*; *(Mil)* potencjał *m*; **it's beyond their capabilities** to przerasta ich możliwości
**capable** ['keɪpəbl] *adj* zdolny; **to be ~ of doing sth** *(able)* być w stanie coś zrobić; *(likely)* być zdolnym do zrobienia czegoś; **to be ~ of** być zdolnym do *+gen*; **moths are ~ of speeds of 50 kph** ćmy potrafią osiągać prędkość 50 km/h
**capacious** [kə'peɪʃəs] *adj* pojemny
**capacity** [kə'pæsɪtɪ] *n (of container)* pojemność *f*; *(of ship)* ładowność *f*; *(of pipeline)* przepustowość *f*; *(of lift)* udźwig *m*, obciążenie *nt*; *(capability)* zdolność *f*; *(position, role)* kompetencje *pl*, uprawnienia *pl*; *(of factory)* wydajność *f*; **seating ~** liczba miejsc siedzących; **filled to ~** wypełniony po brzegi; **in his ~ as a director** w ramach swoich dyrektorskich kompetencji *or* uprawnień; **this work is beyond my ~** ta praca przerasta moje możliwości; **in an advisory ~** w charakterze doradcy; **to work at full ~** pracować na pełnych obrotach
**cape** [keɪp] *n (Geog)* przylądek *m*; *(cloak)* peleryna *f*
**Cape of Good Hope** *n*: **the ~** Przylądek *m* Dobrej Nadziei
**caper** ['keɪpəʳ] *n (Culin: usu pl)* kapar *m*; *(prank)* psota *f*, figiel *m*
**Cape Town** *n* Kapsztad *m*
**capita** ['kæpɪtə] *n see* **per capita**
**capital** ['kæpɪtl] *n (city)* stolica *f*; *(money)* kapitał *m*; *(also:* **capital letter**) wielka litera *f*
**capital account** *n (Comm)* rachunek *m* kapitału, bilans *m*; *(of country)* bilans *m* płatniczy
**capital allowance** *n* odpisy *pl* amortyzacyjne
**capital assets** *npl* aktywa *pl* trwałe
**capital expenditure** *n* wydatki *pl* inwestycyjne
**capital gains tax** *n* podatek *m* od zysków kapitałowych
**capital goods** *(Comm) npl* dobra *pl* inwestycyjne
**capital-intensive** ['kæpɪtlɪn'tɛnsɪv] *(Comm) adj* kapitałochłonny
**capitalism** ['kæpɪtəlɪzəm] *n* kapitalizm *m*
**capitalist** ['kæpɪtəlɪst] *adj* kapitalistyczny ▷ *n* kapitalista(-tka) *m(f)*
**capitalize** ['kæpɪtəlaɪz] *vi*: **to ~ on** zbijać (zbić *perf*) kapitał na *+loc* ▷ *vt (Comm)* spieniężać (spieniężyć *perf*)
**capital punishment** *n* kara *f* śmierci
**capital transfer tax** *(Brit) n* podatek *m* od spadków *or* transferu kapitału
**capitulate** [kə'pɪtjuleɪt] *vi* kapitulować (skapitulować *perf*)
**capitulation** [kəpɪtju'leɪʃən] *n* kapitulacja *f*
**cappuccino** [kæpə'tʃiːnəu] *n* cappuccino *nt inv*

**capricious** [kəˈprɪʃəs] *adj* kapryśny
**Capricorn** [ˈkæprɪkɔːn] *n* Koziorożec *m*; **to be ~** być spod znaku Koziorożca
**caps** [kæps] *abbr* = **capital letters**
**capsize** [kæpˈsaɪz] *vt* wywracać (wywrócić *perf*) dnem do góry ▷ *vi* wywracać się (wywrócić się *perf*) dnem do góry
**capstan** [ˈkæpstən] *n* kabestan *m*
**capsule** [ˈkæpsjuːl] *n* (*Med*) kapsułka *f*; (*spacecraft*) kapsuła *f*; (*storage container*) pojemnik *m*
**Capt.** (*Mil*) *abbr* (= *captain*) kpt.
**captain** [ˈkæptɪn] *n* kapitan *m*; (*Naut*) komandor *m*; (*Brit*: *Scol*: *of debating team etc*) przewodniczący(-ca) *m*(*f*) ▷ *vt* być kapitanem +*gen*
**caption** [ˈkæpʃən] *n* (*to picture, photograph*) podpis *m*
**captivate** [ˈkæptɪveɪt] *vt* urzekać (urzec *perf*)
**captive** [ˈkæptɪv] *adj* schwytany, pojmany ▷ *n* jeniec *m*
**captivity** [kæpˈtɪvɪtɪ] *n* niewola *f*; **in ~** w niewoli
**captor** [ˈkæptəʳ] *n* (*unlawful*) porywacz *m*; (*lawful*) zdobywca *m*
**capture** [ˈkæptʃəʳ] *vt* (*animal*) schwytać (*perf*); (*person*) pojmać (*perf*), ująć (*perf*); (*town, country*) zdobywać (zdobyć *perf*); (*imagination*) zawładnąć (*perf*) +*instr*; (*market*) opanowywać (opanować *perf*); (*Comput*) wychwytywać (wychwycić *perf*) ▷ *n* (*of animal*) schwytanie *nt*; (*of person*) pojmanie *nt*, ujęcie *nt*; (*of town*) zdobycie *nt*; (*Comput*: *of data*) wychwytywanie *nt*
**car** [kɑːʳ] *n* (*Aut*) samochód *m*; (*Rail*) wagon *m*; **by car** samochodem
**Caracas** [kəˈrækəs] *n* Caracas *nt inv*
**carafe** [kəˈræf] *n* karafka *f*
**caramel** [ˈkærəməl] *n* (*sweet*) karmelek *m*; (*burnt sugar*) karmel *m*
**carat** [ˈkærət] *n* karat *m*; **18 ~ gold** 18-karatowe złoto
**caravan** [ˈkærəvæn] *n* (*Brit*: *vehicle*) przyczepa *f* kempingowa; (*in desert*) karawana *f*
**caravan site** (*Brit*) *n* pole *nt* kempingowe
**caraway** [ˈkærəweɪ] *n*: **~ seed** kminek *m*
**carbohydrate** [kɑːbəuˈhaɪdreɪt] *n* węglowodan *m*
**carbolic acid** [kɑːˈbɔlɪk-] *n* kwas *m* karbolowy
**carbon** [ˈkɑːbən] *n* (*Chem*) węgiel *m*
**carbonated** [ˈkɑːbəneɪtɪd] *adj* (*drink*) gazowany
**carbon copy** *n* kopia *f* (*przez kalkę*)
**carbon dioxide** *n* dwutlenek *m* węgla
**carbon monoxide** [mɔˈnɔksaɪd] *n* tlenek *m* węgla
**carbon paper** *n* kalka *f* (maszynowa *or* ołówkowa)
**carbon ribbon** *n* taśma *f* do maszyny do pisania
**carburettor**, (*US*) **carburetor** [kɑːbjuˈrɛtəʳ] *n* gaźnik *m*
**carcass** [ˈkɑːkəs] *n* padlina *f*, ścierwo *nt*; (*at butcher's*) tusza *f*
**carcinogen** [kɑːˈsɪnədʒən] *n* substancja *f* rakotwórcza
**carcinogenic** [kɑːsɪnəˈdʒɛnɪk] *adj* rakotwórczy
**card** [kɑːd] *n* (*index card, membership card, playing card*) karta *f*; (*material*) karton *m*, tektura *f*; (*greetings card*) kartka *f* (okolicznościowa); (*visiting card*) wizytówka *f*; **to play ~s** grać (zagrać *perf*) w karty
**cardamom** [ˈkɑːdəməm] *n* kardamon *m*
**cardboard** [ˈkɑːdbɔːd] *n* karton *m*, tektura *f*
**cardboard box** *n* pudełko *nt* tekturowe; (*large*) karton *m*
**cardboard city** (*inf*) *n miejsce (np. pod mostem), gdzie bezdomni sypiają w kartonach*
**card-carrying** [ˈkɑːdˈkærɪɪŋ] *adj* (*member*) pełnoprawny
**card game** *n* gra *f* karciana
**cardiac** [ˈkɑːdɪæk] *adj* sercowy; **~ arrest** zatrzymanie akcji serca
**cardigan** [ˈkɑːdɪgən] *n* sweter *m* rozpinany
**cardinal** [ˈkɑːdɪnl] *adj* główny ▷ *n* kardynał *m*
**card index** *n* katalog *m* alfabetyczny
**cardsharp** [ˈkɑːdʃɑːp] *n* szuler *m*
**card vote** (*Brit*) *n głosowanie za pośrednictwem przedstawiciela*
**CARE** [kɛəʳ] *n abbr* (= *Cooperative for American Relief Everywhere*) *organizacja charytatywna*
**care** [kɛəʳ] *n* (*attention*) opieka *f*; (*worry*) troska *f* ▷ *vi*: **to ~ about** (*person, animal*) troszczyć się o +*acc*; (*thing, idea*) przejmować się +*instr*; **would you ~ to/for ...?** czy masz ochotę +*infin*/na +*acc*?; **I don't ~ to remember** nie chcę pamiętać; **~ of Mr and Mrs. Brown** (*on letter*) u Państwa Brown; **"with ~"** „ostrożnie"; **in sb's ~** pod czyjąś opieką; **he took ~ not to offend the visitors** (bardzo) uważał, żeby nie urazić gości; **to take ~ of** (*person*) opiekować się (zaopiekować się *perf*) +*instr*; (*arrangements*) dopilnowywać (dopilnować *perf*) +*gen*; (*problem*) rozwiązywać (rozwiązać *perf*) +*acc*; **the boy has been taken into ~** chłopca zabrano do domu dziecka; **I don't ~** nic mnie to nie obchodzi; **I couldn't ~ less** wszystko mi jedno
▶ **care for** *vt fus* (*look after*) opiekować się +*instr*; (*like*): **does she still ~ for him?** czy nadal jej na nim zależy?
**career** [kəˈrɪəʳ] *n* kariera *f* ▷ *vi* (*also*: **career along**) pędzić (popędzić *perf*); **change/choice of ~** zmiana/wybór zawodu

**career girl** *n* = **career woman**
**careers officer** [kə'rɪəz-] *n osoba zajmująca się doradztwem zawodowym w szkole itp*
**career woman** (*irreg: like* **woman**) *n* kobieta *f* czynna zawodowo
**carefree** ['kɛəfri:] *adj* beztroski
**careful** ['kɛəful] *adj* (*cautious*) ostrożny; (*thorough*) uważny, staranny; **(be) ~!** uważaj!; **he's ~ with his money** nie szasta pieniędzmi
**carefully** ['kɛəfəlɪ] *adv* (*cautiously*) ostrożnie; (*methodically*) starannie
**careless** ['kɛəlɪs] *adj* (*not careful*) nieostrożny; (*negligent, heedless, casual*) niedbały; (*with money*) rozrzutny
**carelessly** ['kɛəlɪslɪ] *adv* niedbale
**carelessness** ['kɛəlɪsnɪs] *n* (*negligence*) niedbalstwo *nt*; (*casualness*) niedbałość *f*, nonszalancja *f*
**carer** ['kɛərəʳ] *n* opiekun(ka) *m(f)*
**caress** [kə'rɛs] *n* pieszczota *f* ▷ *vt* pieścić
**caretaker** ['kɛəteɪkəʳ] *n* dozorca(-rczyni) *m(f)*
**caretaker government** (*Brit*) *n* rząd *m* tymczasowy
**car-ferry** ['kɑ:fɛrɪ] *n* prom *m* samochodowy
**cargo** ['kɑ:gəu] (*pl* **~es**) *n* ładunek *m*
**cargo boat** *n* (*on river*) barka *f*; (*at sea*) frachtowiec *m*
**cargo plane** *n* samolot *m* towarowy *or* dostawczy
**car hire** (*Brit*) *n* wynajem *m* samochodów
**Caribbean** [kærɪ'bi:ən] *n*: **the ~ (Sea)** Morze *nt* Karaibskie ▷ *adj* karaibski
**caricature** ['kærɪkətjuəʳ] *n* karykatura *f*
**caring** ['kɛərɪŋ] *adj* opiekuńczy
**carnage** ['kɑ:nɪdʒ] *n* rzeź *f*
**carnal** ['kɑ:nl] *adj* cielesny
**carnation** [kɑ:'neɪʃən] (*Bot*) *n* goździk *m*
**carnival** ['kɑ:nɪvl] *n* karnawał *m*; (*US: funfair*) wesołe miasteczko *nt*
**carnivorous** [kɑ:'nɪvərəs] *adj* (*animal*) mięsożerny; (*plant*) owadożerny
**carol** ['kærəl] *n*: **(Christmas) ~** kolęda *f*
**carouse** [kə'rauz] *vi* hulać (pohulać *perf*)
**carousel** [kærə'sɛl] (*US*) *n* karuzela *f*
**carp** [kɑ:p] *n* karp *m*
▸ **carp at** *vt fus* utyskiwać na *+acc*, wydziwiać na *+acc* (*inf*)
**car park** (*Brit*) *n* parking *m*
**carpenter** ['kɑ:pɪntəʳ] *n* stolarz *m*
**carpentry** ['kɑ:pɪntrɪ] *n* stolarka *f*; (*at school*) obróbka *f* drewna
**carpet** ['kɑ:pɪt] *n* dywan *m*; (*fig*) kobierzec *m* ▷ *vt* wykładać (wyłożyć *perf*) dywanami; **fitted ~** (*Brit*) wykładzina (dywanowa)
**carpet slippers** *npl* bambosze *pl*
**carpet sweeper** [-'swi:pəʳ] *n* szczotka *f* do dywanów (*typu „kasia"*)
**car phone** *n* telefon *m* samochodowy
**car port** *n* wiata *f* samochodowa (*przy domu, zamiast garażu*)
**car rental** *n* wynajem *m* samochodów
**carriage** ['kærɪdʒ] *n* (*Brit: Rail*) wagon *m* (osobowy); (*horse-drawn*) (po)wóz *m*; (*of typewriter*) karetka *f*; (*transport costs*) przewóz *m*, koszt *m* przewozu; **~ forward/free** koszt przewozu ponosi odbiorca/dostawca; **~ paid** przewóz darmowy
**carriage return** *n* (*on typewriter etc*) powrót *m* karetki
**carriageway** ['kærɪdʒweɪ] (*Brit*) *n* nitka *f* (*autostrady*)
**carrier** ['kærɪəʳ] *n* (*Comm*) przewoźnik *m*, spedytor *m*; (*Med*) nosiciel *m*
**carrier bag** (*Brit*) *n* reklamówka *f*
**carrier pigeon** *n* gołąb *m* pocztowy
**carrion** ['kærɪən] *n* padlina *f*
**carrot** ['kærət] *n* marchew *f*, marchewka *f*; (*fig: incentive*) marchewka *f*
**carry** ['kærɪ] *vt* (*take*) nieść (zanieść *perf*); (*transport*) przewozić (przewieźć *perf*); (*involve*) nieść za sobą; (*disease, virus*) przenosić (przenieść *perf*); (*gun, donor card*) nosić (przy sobie); (*newspaper: report, picture*) zamieszczać (zamieścić *perf*) ▷ *vi* (*sound*) nieść się; **the motion was carried by 259 votes to 162** wniosek przeszedł stosunkiem 259 do 162 głosów; **he got carried away** (*fig*) poniosło go; **the placards carried the slogan: ...** na transparentach widniało hasło: ...; **this loan carries 10% interest** pożyczka jest oprocentowana na 10%
▸ **carry forward** *vt* (*book-keeping*) przenosić (przenieść *perf*)
▸ **carry on** *vi* kontynuować; (*inf*) zachowywać się ▷ *vt* prowadzić; **to ~ on with sth/doing sth** kontynuować coś/robienie czegoś; **am I boring you? — no, ~ on** nudzę cię? — nie, mów dalej
▸ **carry out** *vt* (*orders*) wykonywać (wykonać *perf*); (*investigation, experiments*) przeprowadzać (przeprowadzić *perf*); (*threat*) spełniać (spełnić *perf*)
**carrycot** ['kærɪkɔt] (*Brit*) *n* nosidełko *nt* (*torba do noszenia niemowlęcia*)
**carry-on** ['kærɪ'ɔn] (*inf*) *n*: **what a ~!** co za szopka! (*inf*)
**cart** [kɑ:t] *n* (*for grain, hay*) wóz *m*, furmanka *f*; (*for passengers*) powóz *m*; (*handcart*) wózek *m* ▷ *vt* (*inf*) wlec, włóczyć
**carte blanche** ['kɑ:t'blɔŋʃ] *n*: **to give sb ~** dawać (dać *perf*) komuś wolną rękę
**cartel** [kɑ:'tɛl] *n* kartel *m*
**cartilage** ['kɑ:tɪlɪdʒ] (*Anat*) *n* chrząstka *f*
**cartographer** [kɑ:'tɔgrəfəʳ] *n* kartograf *m*

**cartography** [kɑːˈtɔgrəfɪ] *n* kartografia *f*
**carton** [ˈkɑːtən] *n* karton *m*
**cartoon** [kɑːˈtuːn] *n* (*drawing*) rysunek *m* satyryczny, karykatura *f*; (*Film*) kreskówka *f*, film *m* rysunkowy; (*Brit*) komiks *m*
**cartoonist** [kɑːˈtuːnɪst] *n* karykaturzysta(-tka) *m(f)*
**cartridge** [ˈkɑːtrɪdʒ] *n* (*for gun, pen*) nabój *m*; (*for camera, tape recorder*) kaseta *f*; (*of record-player*) wkładka *f* (gramofonowa)
**cartwheel** [ˈkɑːtwiːl] *n* koło *nt* (wozu); **to turn a ~** (*Sport etc*) robić (zrobić *perf*) gwiazdę
**carve** [kɑːv] *vt* (*sculpt*) rzeźbić (wyrzeźbić *perf*); (*meat*) kroić (pokroić *perf*); (*initials, design*) wycinać (wyciąć *perf*)
▸ **carve up** *vt* (*land, property*) parcelować (rozparcelować *perf*); (*meat*) kroić (pokroić *perf*) (na kawałki)
**carving** [ˈkɑːvɪŋ] *n* (*object*) rzeźba *f*; (*design*) rzeźbienia *pl*; (*art of carving*) rzeźbiarstwo *nt*, snycerstwo *nt*
**carving knife** *n* nóż *m* do krojenia mięsa
**car wash** *n* myjnia *f* samochodowa
**Casablanca** [kæsəˈblæŋkə] *n* Casablanca *f*
**cascade** [kæsˈkeɪd] *n* kaskada *f* ▹ *vi* (*water*) spływać kaskadą; (*hair*) opadać kaskadą
**case** [keɪs] *n* (*also Med, Ling*) przypadek *m*; (*Jur*) sprawa *f*; (*for spectacles, nail scissors*) etui *nt inv*; (*for musical instrument*) futerał *m*; (*Brit: also:* **suitcase**) walizka *f*; (*of wine*) skrzynka *f*; **lower/upper ~** (*Typ*) małe/duże litery; **to have a good ~** (*Jur*) mieć duże szanse na wygranie sprawy; **to make (out) a ~ for/against** przedstawić argumenty za *+instr*/przeciw(ko) *+dat*; **there's a strong ~ for/against** wiele przemawia za *+instr*/przeciw(ko) *+dat*; **in ~ of** w przypadku *+gen*; **in ~ he comes** na wypadek, gdyby przyszedł; **in any ~** (*at any rate*) w każdym razie; (*besides*) zresztą, poza tym; (*no matter what*) tak czy owak; **just in ~** (tak) na wszelki wypadek
**case history** (*Med*) *n* historia *f* choroby
**case study** *n* studium *nt*, opracowanie *nt* (naukowe)
**cash** [kæʃ] *n* gotówka *f* ▹ *vt* (*cheque, money order*) realizować (zrealizować *perf*); **to pay (in) ~** płacić (zapłacić *perf*) gotówką; **~ on delivery** za pobraniem; **~ with order** zapłata rachunku przy zamówieniu
▸ **cash in** *vt* spieniężać (spieniężyć *perf*)
▸ **cash in on** *vt fus* zarabiać (zarobić *perf*) na *+loc*
**cash account** *n* konto *nt* gotówkowe
**cash-and-carry** [kæʃənˈkærɪ] *n* *skład (pół) hurtowy sprzedający za gotówkę i bez dostawy*
**cash-book** [ˈkæʃbuk] *n* księga *f* kasowa
**cash box** *n* sejf *m* sklepowy *or* przenośny, kasa *f* sklepowa
**cash card** (*Brit*) *n* karta *f* bankowa (*do wypłacania pieniędzy z bankomatu*)
**cash crop** *n* uprawa *f* rynkowa
**cash desk** (*Brit*) *n* kasa *f* (*w sklepie*)
**cash discount** (*Comm*) *n* rabat *m* przy zapłacie gotówką
**cash dispenser** (*Brit*) *n* bankomat *m*
**cashew** [kæˈʃuː] *n* (*also:* **cashew nut**) orzech *m* nerkowca
**cash flow** *n* przepływ *m* gotówki
**cashier** [kæˈʃɪəʳ] *n* kasjer(ka) *m(f)*
**cashmere** [ˈkæʃmɪəʳ] *n* kaszmir *m* ▹ *adj* kaszmirowy
**cashpoint** [ˈkæʃpɔɪnt] *n* bankomat *m*
**cash price** *n* cena *f* gotówkowa
**cash register** *n* kasa *f* rejestrująca *or* fiskalna
**cash sale** *n* sprzedaż *f* za gotówkę
**casing** [ˈkeɪsɪŋ] *n* obudowa *f*
**casino** [kəˈsiːnəu] *n* kasyno *nt*
**cask** [kɑːsk] *n* (*of wine, beer*) beczułka *f*
**casket** [ˈkɑːskɪt] *n* (*for jewellery*) szkatułka *f*, kasetka *f*; (*US: coffin*) trumna *f*
**Caspian Sea** [ˈkæspɪən-] *n*: **the ~** Morze *nt* Kaspijskie
**casserole** [ˈkæsərəul] *n* (*Culin*) zapiekanka *f*; (*container*) naczynie *nt* (żaroodporne) do zapiekanek
**cassette** [kæˈsɛt] *n* kaseta *f*
**cassette deck** *n* magnetofon *m* kasetowy (*bez wzmacniacza*)
**cassette player** *n* odtwarzacz *m* kasetowy
**cassette recorder** *n* magnetofon *m* kasetowy
**cast** [kɑːst] (*pt, pp* **~**) *vt* (*shadow, glance, spell, aspersions*) rzucać (rzucić *perf*); (*net, fishing-line*) zarzucać (zarzucić *perf*); (*skin*) zrzucać (zrzucić *perf*); (*metal*) odlewać (odlać *perf*); (*vote*) oddawać (oddać *perf*); (*Theat*): **to ~ sb as Hamlet** obsadzać (obsadzić *perf*) kogoś w roli Hamleta ▹ *vi* zarzucać (zarzucić *perf*) wędkę ▹ *n* (*Theat*) obsada *f*; (*mould*) odlew *m*; (*also:* **plaster cast**) gips *m*; **to ~ doubt on sth** podawać (podać *perf*) coś w wątpliwość
▸ **cast aside** *vt* odrzucać (odrzucić *perf*)
▸ **cast off** *vi* (*Naut*) odwiązywać (odwiązać *perf*) łódź; (*Knitting*) spuszczać (spuścić *perf*) oczka
▸ **cast on** (*Knitting*) *vi* nabierać (nabrać *perf*) oczka
**castanets** [kæstəˈnɛts] *npl* kastaniety *pl*
**castaway** [ˈkɑːstəweɪ] *n* rozbitek *m*
**caste** [kɑːst] *n* (*class*) kasta *f*; (*system*) kastowość *f*
**caster sugar** [ˈkɑːstə-] (*Brit*) *n* cukier *m* puder *m*
**casting vote** [ˈkɑːstɪŋ-] (*Brit*) *n* decydujący głos *m*
**cast iron** *n* żeliwo *nt* ▹ *adj*: **cast-iron** (*fig: alibi etc*) żelazny

C

**castle** ['kɑ:sl] *n* zamek *m*; (*Chess*) wieża *f*
**cast-off** ['kɑ:stɔf] *n*: **she wears her elder sister's ~s** nosi ubrania po starszej siostrze
**castor** ['kɑ:stə^r] *n* kółko *nt* (*u fotela, łóżka itp*)
**castor oil** *n* olej *m* rycynowy
**castrate** [kæs'treɪt] *vt* kastrować (wykastrować *perf*)
**casual** ['kæʒjul] *adj* (*accidental*) przypadkowy; (*irregular: work etc*) dorywczy; (*unconcerned*) swobodny, niezobowiązujący; **~ wear** odzież codzienna; **~ sex** przygodny seks
**casual labour** *n* praca *f* dorywcza
**casually** ['kæʒjulɪ] *adv* (*in a relaxed way*) swobodnie, od niechcenia; (*dress*) na sportowo; (*by chance*) przypadkowo
**casualty** ['kæʒjultɪ] *n* (*person*) ofiara *f*; (*in hospital*) izba *f* przyjęć (*dla przypadków urazowych*); **heavy casualties** duże straty (w ludziach)
**casualty ward** (*Brit*) *n* oddział *m* urazowy
**cat** [kæt] *n* kot *m*
**catacombs** ['kætəku:mz] *npl* katakumby *pl*
**catalogue**, (*US*) **catalog** ['kætəlɔg] *n* katalog *m*; (*of events*) seria *f*; (*of faults, sins*) litania *f* ▷ *vt* (*book, collection*) katalogować (skatalogować *perf*); (*events, qualities*) wyliczać (wyliczyć *perf*)
**catalyst** ['kætəlɪst] *n* katalizator *m*
**catalytic converter** [kætə'lɪtɪk kən'və:tə^r] (*Aut*) *n* katalizator *m*
**catapult** ['kætəpʌlt] *n* (*Brit: sling*) proca *f*; (*Mil*) katapulta *f* ▷ *vi* wyskakiwać (wyskoczyć *perf*) ▷ *vt* wyrzucać (wyrzucić *perf*)
**cataract** ['kætərækt] *n* zaćma *f*, katarakta *f*
**catarrh** [kə'tɑ:^r] *n* katar *m*
**catastrophe** [kə'tæstrəfɪ] *n* katastrofa *f*
**catastrophic** [kætə'strɔfɪk] *adj* katastrofalny
**catcall** ['kætkɔ:l] *n* gwizdy *pl*
**catch** [kætʃ] (*pt, pp* **caught**) *vt* (*capture, get hold of*) łapać (złapać *perf*); (*surprise*) przyłapywać (przyłapać *perf*); (*hit*) trafiać (trafić *perf*); (*hear*) dosłyszeć (*perf*); (*Med*) zarażać się (zarazić się *perf*) *+instr*, łapać (złapać *perf*) (*inf*); (*also*: **catch up**) zrównać się (*perf*) z *+instr*, doganiać (dogonić *perf*) ▷ *vi* (*fire*) zapłonąć (*perf*); (*in branches etc*) zaczepić się (*perf*) ▷ *n* (*of fish etc*) połów *m*; (*hidden problem*) kruczek *m*; (*of lock*) zapadka *f*; **to ~ sb's attention** *or* **eye** zwracać (zwrócić *perf*) (na siebie) czyjąś uwagę; **to ~ fire** zapalać się (zapalić się *perf*), zajmować się (zająć się *perf*); **to ~ sight of** dostrzegać (dostrzec *perf*) *+acc*; **she caught her breath** zaparło jej dech (w piersiach); **a difficult ~** trudna piłka
▶ **catch on** *vi* (*understand*) zaskakiwać (zaskoczyć *perf*) (*inf*); (*grow popular*) przyjmować się (przyjąć *perf* się), chwytać (chwycić *perf*) (*inf*); **to ~ on to sth** chwytać (chwycić *perf*) coś (*inf*)
▶ **catch out** (*Brit*) *vt* (*fig: with trick question*) zaginać (zagiąć *perf*) (*inf*)
▶ **catch up** *vi* (*with person*) doganiać (dogonić *perf*); **to ~ up on work/sleep** nadrabiać (nadrobić *perf*) zaległości w pracy/spaniu
▶ **catch up with** *vt fus* doganiać (dogonić *perf*) *+acc*
**catch-22** ['kætʃtwɛntɪ'tu:] *n*: **it's a ~ situation** to (jest) błędne koło
**catching** ['kætʃɪŋ] *adj* zaraźliwy
**catchment area** ['kætʃmənt-] (*Brit*) *n* (*of school, hospital*) rejon *m*
**catch phrase** *n* slogan *m*
**catchy** ['kætʃɪ] *adj* chwytliwy, wpadający w ucho
**catechism** ['kætɪkɪzəm] *n* katechizm *m*
**categoric(al)** [kætɪ'gɔrɪk(l)] *adj* kategoryczny
**categorize** ['kætɪgəraɪz] *vt* klasyfikować (sklasyfikować *perf*)
**category** ['kætɪgərɪ] *n* kategoria *f*
**cater** ['keɪtə^r] *vi*: **~ for** (*party etc*) zaopatrywać (zaopatrzyć *perf*); (*needs etc*) zaspokajać (zaspokoić *perf*); (*readers, consumers*) zaspokajać (zaspokoić *perf*) potrzeby *+gen*
**caterer** ['keɪtərə^r] *n* aprowizator(ka) *m(f)*
**catering** ['keɪtərɪŋ] *n* gastronomia *f*
**caterpillar** ['kætəpɪlə^r] *n* gąsienica *f*
**caterpillar tracks** *npl* gąsienice *pl* (*czołgu itp*)
**cathedral** [kə'θi:drəl] *n* katedra *f*
**cathode** ['kæθəud] *n* katoda *f*
**cathode ray tube** *n* lampa *f* kineskopowa *or* elektronopromieniowa
**catholic** ['kæθəlɪk] *adj* wszechstronny
**Catholic** ['kæθəlɪk] *adj* katolicki ▷ *n* katolik(-iczka) *m(f)*
**CAT scanner** (*Med*) *n abbr* (= *computerized axial tomography scanner*) tomograf *m* komputerowy
**cat's-eye** ['kæts'aɪ] (*Brit: Aut*) *n* kocie oko *nt*
**catsup** ['kætsəp] (*US*) *n* ketchup *m*, keczup *m*
**cattle** ['kætl] *npl* bydło *nt*
**catty** ['kætɪ] *adj* zjadliwy, złośliwy
**catwalk** ['kætwɔ:k] *n* wybieg *m*
**Caucasian** [kɔ:'keɪzɪən] *adj* kaukaski ▷ *n* mieszkaniec(nka) *m(f)* Kaukazu
**Caucasus** ['kɔ:kəsəs] *n*: **the ~** Kaukaz *m*
**caucus** ['kɔ:kəs] (*Pol*) *n* (*group*) komitet *m* wyborczy; (*meeting*) (zamknięte) zebranie *nt* komitetu wyborczego
**caught** [kɔ:t] *pt, pp of* **catch**
**cauliflower** ['kɔlɪflauə^r] *n* kalafior *m*
**cause** [kɔ:z] *n* (*of outcome, effect*) przyczyna *f*; (*reason*) powód *m*; (*aim, principle*) sprawa *f* ▷ *vt* powodować (spowodować *perf*), wywoływać (wywołać *perf*); **there is no ~ for concern** nie ma powodu do obaw; **to ~ sth to be done** sprawiać (sprawić *perf*), że coś zostanie

zrobione; **to ~ sb to do sth** sprawić *(perf)*, że ktoś coś zrobi

**causeway** ['kɔːzweɪ] *n* szosa *f* na grobli

**caustic** ['kɔːstɪk] *adj (Chem)* kaustyczny, żrący; *(fig: remark)* uszczypliwy

**cauterize** ['kɔːtəraɪz] *vt* przyżegać (przyżec *perf*)

**caution** ['kɔːʃən] *n (prudence)* ostrożność *f*; *(warning)* ostrzeżenie *nt* ▷ *vt* ostrzegać (ostrzec *perf*); *(policeman)* udzielać (udzielić *perf*) ostrzeżenia *+dat*

**cautious** ['kɔːʃəs] *adj* ostrożny

**cautiously** ['kɔːʃəslɪ] *adv* ostrożnie

**cautiousness** ['kɔːʃəsnɪs] *n* ostrożność *f*

**cavalier** [kævə'lɪə^r] *adj* nonszalancki

**cavalry** ['kævəlrɪ] *n* kawaleria *f*

**cave** [keɪv] *n* jaskinia *f*, grota *f* ▷ *vi*: **to go caving** chodzić po jaskiniach
▸ **cave in** *vi (roof etc)* zapadać się (zapaść *perf* się), załamywać się (załamać *perf* się); *(person)* uginać się (ugiąć się *perf*)

**caveman** ['keɪvmæn] *(irreg: like* **man**) *n* jaskiniowiec *m*

**cavern** ['kævən] *n* pieczara *f*

**caviar(e)** ['kævɪɑː^r] *n* kawior *m*

**cavity** ['kævɪtɪ] *n* otwór *m*; *(in tooth)* ubytek *m*, dziura *f (inf)*

**cavity wall insulation** *n* izolacja *f* murem szczelinowym *or* podwójnym

**cavort** [kə'vɔːt] *vi* baraszkować, hasać

**cayenne** [keɪ'ɛn] *n (also:* **cayenne pepper**) pieprz *m* cayenne

**CB** *n abbr (= Citizens' Band (Radio))* CB *nt inv*, CB radio *nt*; *(Brit: = Companion of (the Order of) the Bath) order brytyjski*

**CBC** *n abbr* = **Canadian Broadcasting Corporation**

**CBE** *(Brit) n abbr (= Commander of (the Order of) the British Empire) order brytyjski*

**CBI** *n abbr (= Confederation of British Industry) związek pracodawców*

**CBS** *(US) n abbr* = **Columbia Broadcasting System**

**CC** *(Brit) abbr* = **county council**

**cc** *abbr (= cubic centimetre)* cm³; = **carbon copy**

**CCA** *(US) n abbr (= Circuit Court of Appeals) okręgowy sąd apelacyjny*

**CCTV camera** *n (= closed-circuit television camera)* kamera *f* telewizji przemysłowej

**CCU** *(US) n abbr (= coronary care unit) oddział intensywnej opieki kardiologicznej*

**CD** *abbr (Brit: = Corps Diplomatique)* Korpus *m* Dyplomatyczny ▷ *n abbr (Mil: Brit: = Civil Defence (Corps))* ≈ OC *f inv*; *(: US: = Civil Defense)* ≈ OC *f inv*; *(= compact disc)* płyta *f* kompaktowa; **CD player** odtwarzacz *m* płyt kompaktowych

**CDC** *(US) n abbr* = **Center for Disease Control**

**Cdr** *(Mil) abbr (= commander)* dow., d-ca

**CD-ROM** *abbr (= compact disc read-only memory)* CD-ROM *m*

**CDT** *(US) abbr* = **Central Daylight Time**

**cease** [siːs] *vt* zaprzestawać (zaprzestać *perf*) *+gen*, przerywać (przerwać *perf*) ▷ *vi* ustawać (ustać *perf*)

**ceasefire** ['siːsfaɪə^r] *n* zawieszenie *nt* broni

**ceaseless** ['siːslɪs] *adj* nieustanny

**CED** *(US) n abbr* = **Committee for Economic Development**

**cedar** ['siːdə^r] *n* cedr *m*

**cede** [siːd] *vt* cedować (scedować *perf*)

**cedilla** [sɪ'dɪlə] *n* cedilla *f (haczyk nadający literze c brzmienie s)*

**CEEB** *(US) n abbr* = **College Entry Examination Board**

**ceiling** ['siːlɪŋ] *n (in room)* sufit *m*; *(on wages, prices etc)* (górny) pułap *m*

**celebrate** ['sɛlɪbreɪt] *vt (success, victory)* świętować; *(anniversary, birthday)* obchodzić; *(Rel: mass)* odprawiać (odprawić *perf*), celebrować ▷ *vi* świętować; **we ought to ~** powinniśmy to uczcić

**celebrated** ['sɛlɪbreɪtɪd] *adj* sławny

**celebration** [sɛlɪ'breɪʃən] *n* świętowanie *nt*

**celebrity** [sɪ'lɛbrɪtɪ] *n* (znana) osobistość *f*, sława *f*

**celeriac** [sə'lɛrɪæk] *n* seler *m*

**celery** ['sɛlərɪ] *n* seler *m* naciowy

**celestial** [sɪ'lɛstɪəl] *adj* niebiański, niebieski

**celibacy** ['sɛlɪbəsɪ] *n* celibat *m*

**cell** [sɛl] *n (in prison, monastery)* cela *f*; *(of revolutionaries)* komórka *f* (organizacyjna); *(Bio)* komórka *f*; *(Elec)* ogniwo *nt*

**cellar** ['sɛlə^r] *n* piwnica *f*

**cellist** ['tʃɛlɪst] *n* wiolonczelista(-tka) *m(f)*

**cello** ['tʃɛləu] *n* wiolonczela *f*

**cellophane** ['sɛləfeɪn] *n* celofan *m*

**cellphone** ['sɛlfəun] *n* telefon *m* komórkowy

**cellular** ['sɛljulə^r] *adj (structure, tissue)* komórkowy; *(fabrics)* luźno tkany

**cellulite** ['sɛljulaɪt] *n* cellulit *m*

**Celluloid**® ['sɛljulɔɪd] *n* celuloid *m*

**cellulose** ['sɛljuləus] *n* celuloza *f*

**Celsius** ['sɛlsɪəs] *adj*: **30 degrees ~** 30 stopni Celsjusza

**Celt** [kɛlt, sɛlt] *n* Celt *m*

**Celtic** ['kɛltɪk, 'sɛltɪk] *adj* celtycki ▷ *n* (język *m*) celtycki

**cement** [sə'mɛnt] *n (powder, concrete)* cement *m*; *(glue)* klej *m* cementowy ▷ *vt (path, floor)* cementować (wycementować *perf*); *(fig: relationship)* cementować (scementować *perf*); *(stick, glue)* przytwierdzać (przytwierdzić *perf*)

**cement mixer** *n* betoniarka *f*

**cemetery** ['sɛmɪtrɪ] *n* cmentarz *m*

**cenotaph** ['sɛnətɑ:f] *n symboliczny grobowiec upamiętniający poległych na wojnie*
**censor** ['sɛnsə^r] *n* cenzor(ka) *m(f)* ▷ *vt* cenzurować (ocenzurować *perf*)
**censorship** ['sɛnsəʃɪp] *n* cenzura *f*
**censure** ['sɛnʃə^r] *vt* (*reprove*) potępiać (potępić *perf*) ▷ *n* potępienie *nt*
**census** ['sɛnsəs] *n* spis *m* ludności
**cent** [sɛnt] (*US etc*) *n* cent *m*; *see also* **per**
**centenary** [sɛn'ti:nərɪ] *n* stulecie *nt*, setna rocznica *f*
**centennial** [sɛn'tɛnɪəl] *n* = **centenary**
**center** ['sɛntə^r] (US) = **centre**
**centigrade** ['sɛntɪgreɪd] *adj*: **23 degrees ~** 23 stopnie Celsjusza
**centilitre**, (US) **centiliter** ['sɛntɪli:tə^r] *n* centylitr *m*
**centimetre**, (US) **centimeter** ['sɛntɪmi:tə^r] *n* centymetr *m*
**centipede** ['sɛntɪpi:d] *n* wij *m*
**central** ['sɛntrəl] *adj* (*in the centre*) centralny, środkowy; (*close to city centre*) położony centralnie *or* w centrum; (*committee etc*) centralny; (*idea, figure*) główny
**Central African Republic** *n* Republika *f* Środkowoafrykańska
**Central America** *n* Ameryka *f* Środkowa
**central heating** *n* centralne ogrzewanie *nt*
**centralize** ['sɛntrəlaɪz] *vt* centralizować (scentralizować *perf*)
**central processing unit** (*Comput*) *n* mikroprocesor *m* centralny *or* główny
**central reservation** (*Brit*: *Aut*) *n* pas *m* zieleni *or* dzielący
**centre**, (US) **center** ['sɛntə^r] *n* (*of circle, room, line*) środek *m*; (*of town, attention, power*) centrum *m*; (*of action, belief*) podstawa *f*; (*of arts, industry*) ośrodek *m*, centrum *nt* ▷ *vt* (*weight*) umieszczać (umieścić *perf*) na środku; (*Phot, Typ*) centrować (wycentrować *perf*); (*ball*) dośrodkowywać (dośrodkować *perf*); **to ~ on** (*fig*) skupiać się (skupić się *perf*) na *+loc*
**centrefold** ['sɛntəfəuld], (US) **centerfold** *n* rozkładówka *f*
**centre-forward** ['sɛntə'fɔ:wəd] (*Football*) *n* środkowy napastnik *m*
**centre-half** ['sɛntə'hɑ:f] (*Football*) *n* środkowy pomocnik *m*
**centrepiece** ['sɛntəpi:s], (US) **centerpiece** *n dekoracja na środku stołu itp*; (*fig*) chluba *f*
**centre spread** (*Brit*) *n artykuł na dwóch środkowych stronach gazety lub czasopisma*
**centrifugal** [sɛn'trɪfjugl] *adj* odśrodkowy
**centrifuge** ['sɛntrɪfju:ʒ] *n* wirówka *f*
**century** ['sɛntjurɪ] *n* wiek *m*, stulecie *nt*; (*Cricket*) sto punktów; **in the twentieth ~** w dwudziestym wieku

**CEO** (*US*) *n abbr* = **chief executive officer**
**ceramic** [sɪ'ræmɪk] *adj* ceramiczny
**ceramics** [sɪ'ræmɪks] *npl* ceramika *f*
**cereal** ['si:rɪəl] *n* (*plant, crop*) zboże *nt*; (*food*) płatki *pl* zbożowe
**cerebral** ['sɛrɪbrəl] *adj* (*Med*) mózgowy; (*intellectual*) intelektualny; **~ hemorrhage** wylew krwi do mózgu
**ceremonial** [sɛrɪ'məunɪəl] *n* ceremoniał *m* ▷ *adj* ceremonialny, obrzędowy
**ceremony** ['sɛrɪmənɪ] *n* ceremonia *f*; **to stand on ~** robić ceremonie
**cert** [sə:t] (*Brit*: *inf*) *n*: **it's a dead ~** to pewniak (*inf*)
**certain** ['sə:tən] *adj* (*sure*) pewny, pewien; (*particular, some*) pewien; **a ~ Mr Smith** pewien *or* niejaki pan Smith; **~ days/places** pewne dni/miejsca; **a ~ coldness/pleasure** pewna oziębłość/przyjemność; **to make ~ that** upewniać się (upewnić się *perf*), że; **to be ~ of** być pewnym *+gen*; **for ~** na pewno
**certainly** ['sə:tənlɪ] *adv* (*undoubtedly*) na pewno, z pewnością; (*of course*) oczywiście, naturalnie
**certainty** ['sə:təntɪ] *n* (*assurance*) pewność *f*; (*inevitability*) pewnik *m*
**certificate** [sə'tɪfɪkɪt] *n* (*of birth, marriage etc*) akt *m*, świadectwo *nt*; (*diploma*) świadectwo *nt*, dyplom *m*
**certified letter** ['sə:tɪfaɪd-] (US) *n* list *m* polecony
**certified mail** (*US*) *n* poczta *f* polecona
**certified public accountant** ['sə:tɪfaɪd-] (US) *n* zaprzysiężony rewident *m* księgowy
**certify** ['sə:tɪfaɪ] *vt* (*fact*) poświadczać (poświadczyć *perf*); (*award diploma to*) przyznawać (przyznać *perf*) dyplom *or* patent *+dat*; **to ~ sb insane** orzekać (orzec *perf*) o czyjejś niepoczytalności ▷ *vi*: **to ~ that ...** zaświadczać (zaświadczyć *perf*), że ...
**cervical** ['sə:vɪkl] *adj* szyjny, karkowy; **~ cancer** rak szyjki macicy; **~ smear** wymaz z szyjki macicy
**cervix** ['sə:vɪks] *n* szyjka *f* macicy
**Cesarean** [si:'zɛərɪən] (US) *adj, n* = **Caesarean**
**cessation** [sə'seɪʃən] *n* (*of hostilities etc*) zaprzestanie *nt*
**cesspit** ['sɛspɪt] *n* szambo *nt*
**CET** *abbr* (= *Central European Time*) czas *m* środkowoeuropejski
**Ceylon** [sɪ'lɔn] *n* Cejlon *m*
**cf.** *abbr* (= *compare*) por.
**c/f** (*Comm*) *abbr* (= *carried forward*) do przeniesienia
**CFC** *n abbr* (= *chlorofluorocarbon*) chlorofluorokarbon *m*, CFC
**CG** (*US*) *n abbr* = **coastguard**
**cg** *abbr* (= *centigram*) cg

**CH** (Brit) *n abbr* (= *Companion of Honour*) *odznaczenie brytyjskie*
**ch.** *abbr* (= *chapter*) rozdz.
**c.h.** (Brit) *abbr* (= *central heating*) co
**Chad** [tʃæd] *n* Czad *m*
**chafe** [tʃeɪf] *vt* (*skin*) ocierać (otrzeć *perf*) ▷ *vi*: **to ~ at** (*fig*) irytować się (zirytować się *perf*) z powodu *+gen*
**chaffinch** ['tʃæfɪntʃ] *n* zięba *f*
**chagrin** ['ʃægrɪn] *n* rozgoryczenie *nt*
**chain** [tʃeɪn] *n* łańcuch *m*; (*piece of jewellery*) łańcuszek *m*; (*of shops, hotels*) sieć *f* ▷ *vt* (*also*: **chain up**: *prisoner*) przykuwać (przykuć *perf*) łańcuchem; (: *dog*) uwiązywać (uwiązać *perf*) na łańcuchu
**chain reaction** *n* (*fig*) reakcja *f* łańcuchowa
**chain-smoke** ['tʃeɪnsməuk] *vi* palić jednego (papierosa) za drugim
**chain store** *n* sklep *m* należący do sieci
**chair** [tʃɛəʳ] *n* (*seat*) krzesło *nt*; (*armchair*) fotel *m*; (*at university*) katedra *f*; (*of meeting etc*) przewodniczący(-ca) *m(f)* ▷ *vt* przewodniczyć *+dat*; **the ~** (US) krzesło elektryczne
**chairlift** ['tʃɛəlɪft] *n* wyciąg *m* krzesełkowy
**chairman** ['tʃɛəmən] (*irreg*: *like* **man**) *n* (*of committee*) przewodniczący *m*; (*Brit*: *of company*) prezes *m*
**chairperson** ['tʃɛəpə:sn] *n* przewodniczący(-ca) *m(f)*
**chairwoman** ['tʃɛəwumən] (*irreg*: *like* **woman**) *n* przewodnicząca *f*
**chalet** ['ʃæleɪ] *n* drewniana chata *f* (*najczęściej wczasowa, w górach*)
**chalice** ['tʃælɪs] *n* kielich *m*
**chalk** [tʃɔ:k] *n* kreda *f*
▸ **chalk up** *vt* zapisywać (zapisać *perf*); (*fig*) zapisywać (zapisać *perf*) na swoim koncie
**challenge** ['tʃælɪndʒ] *n* wyzwanie *nt*; (*to authority, received ideas*) kwestionowanie *nt* ▷ *vt* (*Sport*) rzucać (rzucić *perf*) wyzwanie *+dat*, wyzywać (wyzwać *perf*); (*rival*) stawiać (postawić *perf*) w obliczu wyzwania; (*authority, idea etc*) kwestionować (zakwestionować *perf*); **to ~ sb to do sth** wzywać (wezwać *perf*) kogoś do zrobienia czegoś; **to ~ sb to a fight/game** rzucać (rzucić *perf*) komuś wyzwanie do walki/gry
**challenger** ['tʃælɪndʒəʳ] *n* pretendent(ka) *m(f)*
**challenging** ['tʃælɪndʒɪŋ] *adj* (*career*) stawiający wysokie wymagania; (*task*) ambitny; (*tone, look etc*) wyzywający
**chamber** ['tʃeɪmbəʳ] *n* (*room*) komnata *f*; (*Pol*) izba *f*; (*Brit*: *usu pl*: *judge's office*) gabinet *m* sędziego; (: *barristers' offices*) kancelaria *f* adwokacka; **~ of commerce** izba handlowa; **torture ~** sala tortur
**chambermaid** ['tʃeɪmbəmeɪd] *n* pokojówka *f*
**chamber music** *n* muzyka *f* kameralna
**chamberpot** ['tʃeɪmbəpɔt] *n* nocnik *m*
**chameleon** [kə'mi:lɪən] *n* kameleon *m*
**chamois** ['ʃæmwɑ:] *n* (*Zool*) kozica *f*; (*also*: **chamois leather**) ircha *f*
**champagne** [ʃæm'peɪn] *n* szampan *m*
**champion** ['tʃæmpɪən] *n* (*of league, contest*) mistrz(yni) *m(f)*; (*of cause*) orędownik(-iczka) *m(f)*, szermierz *m*; (*of person*) obrońca(-ńczyni) *m(f)* ▷ *vt* bronić *+gen* (obronić *perf*)
**championship** ['tʃæmpɪənʃɪp] *n* (*contest*) mistrzostwa *pl*; (*title*) mistrzostwo *nt*
**chance** [tʃɑ:ns] *n* (*hope*) szansa *f*; (*likelihood*) prawdopodobieństwo *nt*; (*opportunity*) sposobność *f*, okazja *f*; (*risk*) ryzyko *nt*; (*accident*) przypadek *m* ▷ *vt* (*risk*): **to ~ it** zaryzykować (*perf*); (*happen*): **I ~d to overhear them talking** przez przypadek podsłuchałem ich rozmowę ▷ *adj* przypadkowy; **the ~s are that...** wszystko wskazuje na to, że...; **there is little ~ of his coming** prawdopodobieństwo, że przyjdzie, jest niewielkie; **to take a ~** ryzykować (zaryzykować *perf*); **by ~** przez przypadek, przypadkiem; **it's the ~ of a lifetime** to życiowa szansa
▸ **chance (up)on** *vt fus* natykać się (natknąć się *perf*) na *+acc*
**chancel** ['tʃɑ:nsəl] *n* prezbiterium *nt*
**chancellor** ['tʃɑ:nsələʳ] *n* (*head of government*) kanclerz *m*; (*Brit*: *of university*) (honorowy) rektor *m*
**Chancellor of the Exchequer** (Brit) *n* Minister *m* Skarbu
**chancy** ['tʃɑ:nsɪ] *adj* ryzykowny
**chandelier** [ʃændə'lɪəʳ] *n* żyrandol *m*
**change** [tʃeɪndʒ] *vt* zmieniać (zmienić *perf*); (*replace*) zamieniać (zamienić *perf*), wymieniać (wymienić *perf*); (*substitute, exchange*) wymieniać (wymienić *perf*); (*transform*): **to ~ sb/sth into** zamieniać (zamienić *perf*) *or* przemieniać (przemienić *perf*) kogoś/coś w *+acc* ▷ *vi* zmieniać się (zmienić się *perf*); (*on bus etc*) przesiadać się (przesiąść się *perf*); (*be transformed*): **to ~ into** zamieniać się (zamienić się *perf*) *or* przemieniać się (przemienić się *perf*) w *+acc* ▷ *n* (*alteration*) zmiana *f*; (*difference*) odmiana *f*; (*coins*) drobne *pl*; (*money returned*) reszta *f*; **to ~ trains/buses** przesiadać się (przesiąść się *perf*); **to ~ hands** (*person*) zmieniać (zmienić *perf*) rękę; (*money, house etc*) zmieniać (zmienić *perf*) właściciela; **to ~ a baby** przewijać (przewinąć *perf*) niemowlę; **to ~ one's mind** zmieniać (zmienić *perf*) zdanie, rozmyślić się (*perf*); **to ~ gear** (*Aut*) zmieniać (zmienić *perf*) bieg; **she ~d into an old skirt** przebrała się w starą spódnicę; **a ~ of clothes** ubranie na zmianę;

small ~ drobne; **to give sb ~ for** *or* **of ten pounds** rozmieniać (rozmienić *perf*) komuś dziesięć funtów; **keep the ~** proszę zatrzymać resztę; **for a ~** dla odmiany
**changeable** ['tʃeɪndʒəbl] *adj* zmienny
**change machine** *n* automat *m* do rozmieniania pieniędzy
**changeover** ['tʃeɪndʒəuvə^r] *n* (*to new system etc*) zmiana *f*
**changing** ['tʃeɪndʒɪŋ] *adj* zmieniający się
**changing room** (*Brit*) *n* (*in shop*) przymierzalnia *f*; (*Sport*) szatnia *f*
**channel** ['tʃænl] *n* kanał *m*; (*groove*) rowek *m*, wyżłobienie *nt* ▷ *vt* kierować (skierować *perf*); **to ~ sth into** (*fig*) kierować (skierować *perf*) coś w stronę *+gen*; **through the usual/normal ~s** zwykłymi/normalnymi kanałami; **green/red ~s** *stanowiska odprawy celnej dla podróżnych nie posiadających/posiadających rzeczy do oclenia*; **the (English) C~** kanał La Manche; **the C~ Islands** Wyspy Normandzkie
**chant** [tʃɑːnt] *n* (*of crowd, fans*) skandowanie *nt*; (*Rel*) pieśń *f*, śpiew *m* ▷ *vt* (*slogans etc*) skandować; (*song, prayer*) intonować (zaintonować *perf*) ▷ *vi* skandować; **the demonstrators ~ed their disapproval** demonstranci skandowaniem wyrażali swe niezadowolenie
**chaos** ['keɪɔs] *n* chaos *m*
**chaotic** [keɪ'ɔtɪk] *adj* (*jumble*) bezładny; (*situation*) chaotyczny
**chap** [tʃæp] (*Brit: inf*) *n* facet *m* (*inf*), gość *m* (*inf*); **old ~** (*term of address*) stary (*inf*)
**chapel** ['tʃæpl] *n* kaplica *f*; (*Brit: non-conformist chapel*) zbór *m*; (: *of union*) podstawowa organizacja *f* związkowa
**chaperone** ['ʃæpərəun] *n* (*for woman*) przyzwoitka *f*; (*for child*) opiekunka *f* ▷ *vt* (*woman*) towarzyszyć *+dat*; (*child*) opiekować się *+instr*
**chaplain** ['tʃæplɪn] *n* kapelan *m*
**chapped** [tʃæpt] *adj* spierzchnięty, spękany
**chapter** ['tʃæptə^r] *n* rozdział *m*; **a ~ of accidents** seria nieszczęść
**char** [tʃɑː^r] *vt* zwęglać (zwęglić *perf*) ▷ *vi* (*Brit*) sprzątać (*u kogoś*) ▷ *n* (*Brit*) = **charlady**
**character** ['kærɪktə^r] *n* charakter *m*; (*in novel, film*) postać *f*; (*eccentric*) oryginał *m*, dziwak(-aczka) *m(f)*; (*letter*) znak *m*; **a person of good ~** osoba o dobrej reputacji
**character code** (*Comput*) *n* kod *m* znaku
**characteristic** ['kærɪktə'rɪstɪk] *adj* charakterystyczny ▷ *n* cecha *f* (charakterystyczna), właściwość *f*; **~ of** charakterystyczny dla *+gen*
**characterize** ['kærɪktəraɪz] *vt* (*typify*) charakteryzować, cechować; (*describe character of*) charakteryzować (scharakteryzować *perf*); **to ~ sb/sth as** (*render*) nadawać (nadać *perf*) komuś/czemuś charakter *+gen*
**charade** [ʃə'rɑːd] *n* farsa *f*; **charades** *npl* szarady *pl*
**charcoal** ['tʃɑːkəul] *n* (*fuel*) węgiel *m* drzewny; (*for drawing*) węgiel *m* (rysunkowy)
**charge** [tʃɑːdʒ] *n* (*fee*) opłata *f*; (*Jur*) zarzut *m*, oskarżenie *nt*; (*attack*) natarcie *nt*, szarża *f*; (*responsibility*) odpowiedzialność *f*; (*Mil, Elec*) ładunek *m* ▷ *vt* (*person*) obciążać (obciążyć *perf*); (*sum*) pobierać (pobrać *perf*); (*gun*) ładować (załadować *perf*); (*Mil*) atakować (zaatakować *perf*), nacierać (natrzeć *perf*) na *+acc*; (*also*: **charge up**: *battery*) ładować (naładować *perf*); (*Jur*): **to ~ sb (with)** oskarżać (oskarżyć *perf*) kogoś (o *+acc*); **to ~ sb to do sth** zobowiązywać (zobowiązać *perf*) kogoś do zrobienia czegoś ▷ *vi* rzucać się (rzucić się *perf*) (do ataku), szarżować; **to ~ (up), to ~ (along), etc** ruszyć (ruszać *perf*), rzucać się (rzucić się *perf*); **charges** *npl* opłaty *pl*; **labour ~s** koszt robocizny; **to reverse the ~s** (*Brit*) *dzwonić na koszt osoby przyjmującej rozmowę*; **is there a ~?** czy jest jakaś opłata?; **there's no ~** nie ma żadnej opłaty; **at no extra ~** bez dodatkowej opłaty; **free of ~** nieodpłatnie; **they ~d us 20 pounds for the meal** policzyli nam 20 funtów za posiłek; **how much do you ~?** ile to u państwa kosztuje?; **to ~ an expense (up) to sb's account** dopisywać (dopisać *perf*) wydatek do czyjegoś rachunku; **under my ~** pod moją opieką; **to take ~ of** (*child*) zajmować się (zająć się *perf*) *+instr*; (*company*) obejmować (objąć *perf*) kierownictwo *+gen*; **to be in ~ of** (*person, machine*) odpowiadać za *+acc*; (*business*) kierować *+instr*
**charge account** *n* kredyt *m* (*w placówce lub sieci handlowej*)
**charge card** *n* karta *f* kredytowa *or* stałego klienta (*ważna w określonej placówce handlowej*)
**chargé d'affaires** ['ʃɑːʒeɪ dæ'fɛə] *n* chargé d'affaires *m inv*
**chargehand** ['tʃɑːdʒhænd] (*Brit*) *n* brygadzista(-tka) *m(f)*
**charger** ['tʃɑːdʒə^r] *n* (*also*: **battery charger**) urządzenie *nt* załadowcze; (*old*: *warhorse*) rumak *m*
**chariot** ['tʃærɪət] *n* rydwan *m*
**charisma** [kæ'rɪsmə] *n* charyzma *f*
**charitable** ['tʃærɪtəbl] *adj* (*organization*) charytatywny, dobroczynny; (*person, remark*) wyrozumiały, pobłażliwy
**charity** ['tʃærɪtɪ] *n* (*organization*) organizacja *f* charytatywna *or* dobroczynna; (*kindness,*

*generosity*) wyrozumiałość *f*; (*money, gifts*) jałmużna *f*
**charlady** ['tʃɑ:leɪdɪ] (*Brit*) *n* sprzątaczka *f*
**charlatan** ['ʃɑ:lətən] *n* szarlatan(ka) *m(f)*
**charm** [tʃɑ:m] *n* (*appeal, spell*) czar *m*, urok *m*; (*talisman*) talizman *m*, amulet *m*; (*on bracelet etc*) wisiorek *m*, breloczek *m* ▷ *vt* zauroczyć (*perf*)
**charm bracelet** *n* bransoletka *f* z wisiorkami
**charming** ['tʃɑ:mɪŋ] *adj* czarujący, uroczy
**chart** [tʃɑ:t] *n* (*graph, diagram*) wykres *m*; (*Naut*) mapa *f* (morska); (*weather chart*) mapa *f* (pogody) ▷ *vt* (*river etc*) nanosić (nanieść *perf*) na mapę; (*progress, movements*) rejestrować (*na wykresie*); **charts** *npl* listy *pl* przebojów
**charter** ['tʃɑ:tə^r] *vt* wynajmować (wynająć *perf*) ▷ *n* (*document, constitution*) karta *f*; (*of university, company*) statut *m*
**chartered accountant** ['tʃɑ:təd-] (*Brit*) *n* ≈ dyplomowany(-na) *m(f)* księgowy(-wa) *m(f)*
**charter flight** *n* lot *m* charterowy
**charwoman** ['tʃɑ:wumən] (*irreg: like* **woman**) *n* = **charlady**
**chary** ['tʃɛərɪ] *adj*: **to be ~ of** być ostrożnym przy *+loc*
**chase** [tʃeɪs] *vt* (*pursue*) gonić; (*also*: **chase away**) wyganiać (wygonić *perf*); (*job etc*) uganiać się za *+instr* ▷ *n* pościg *m*
▸ **chase down** (*US*) *vt* = **chase up**
▸ **chase up** (*Brit*) *vt* (*person*) przyciskać (przycisnąć *perf*) (*inf*); (*information*) odszukiwać (odszukać *perf*)
**chasm** ['kæzəm] *n* (*Geol*) rozpadlina *f*; (*between people*) przepaść *f*
**chassis** ['ʃæsɪ] *n* podwozie *nt*
**chaste** [tʃeɪst] *adj* czysty, cnotliwy
**chastened** ['tʃeɪsnd] *adj* skarcony, zawstydzony
**chastening** ['tʃeɪsnɪŋ] *adj* (*remark*) karcący; (*experience*) otrzeźwiający
**chastise** [tʃæs'taɪz] *vt* (*scold*) (surowo) upominać (upomnieć *perf*)
**chastity** ['tʃæstɪtɪ] *n* czystość *f*, cnota *f*
**chat** [tʃæt] *vi* (*also*: **have a chat**) gadać (pogadać *perf*), ucinać (uciąć *perf*) sobie pogawędkę ▷ *n* pogawędka *f*, pogaduszki *pl*; (*Comput*) czat *m* ▷ *vi* czatować przez internet
▸ **chat up** (*Brit: inf*) *vt* przygadać (*perf*) sobie (*inf*)
**chat show** (*Brit*) *n* talk show *m*
**chattel** ['tʃætl] *n see* **goods**
**chatter** ['tʃætə^r] *vi* (*person*) paplać (*inf*), trajkotać (*inf*); (*magpie etc*) skrzeczeć; (*teeth*) szczękać ▷ *n* (*of people*) paplanina *f*; (*of magpie etc*) skrzeczenie *nt*; **his teeth were ~ing** szczękał zębami
**chatterbox** ['tʃætəbɔks] (*inf*) *n* trajkotka *f* (*inf*)
**chatty** ['tʃætɪ] *adj* (*style, letter*) gawędziarski; (*person*) gadatliwy
**chauffeur** ['ʃəufə^r] *n* szofer *m*
**chauvinism** ['ʃəuvɪnɪzəm] *n* (*also*: **male chauvinism**) (męski) szowinizm *m*; (*Pol*) szowinizm *m*
**chauvinist** ['ʃəuvɪnɪst] *n* (*also*: **male chauvinist**) (męski) szowinista *m*; (*Pol*) szowinista(-tka) *m(f)*
**chauvinistic** [ʃəuvɪ'nɪstɪk] *adj* szowinistyczny
**ChE** *abbr* = **chemical engineer**
**cheap** [tʃi:p] *adj* (*lit, fig*) tani; (*ticket, fare*) ulgowy ▷ *adv*: **to buy/sell sth ~** kupować (kupić *perf*)/sprzedawać (sprzedać *perf*) coś tanio
**cheapen** ['tʃi:pn] *vt*: **I wouldn't ~ myself by doing such a thing** nie zniżyłbym się do czegoś takiego
**cheaper** ['tʃi:pə^r] *adj* tańszy
**cheaply** ['tʃi:plɪ] *adv* tanio
**cheat** [tʃi:t] *vi* oszukiwać (oszukać *perf*) ▷ *vt*: **to ~ sb out of sth** podstępem pozbawić (*perf*) kogoś czegoś ▷ *n* oszust(ka) *m(f)*
▸ **cheat on** (*inf*) *vt fus* (*husband, wife*) zdradzać *+acc*
**cheating** ['tʃi:tɪŋ] *n* oszustwo *nt*
**check** [tʃɛk] *vt* (*inspect, examine, verify*) sprawdzać (sprawdzić *perf*); (*halt, restrain*) powstrzymywać (powstrzymać *perf*) ▷ *vi*: **to ~ (with)** (*data, piece of information*) zgadzać się (z *+instr*) ▷ *n* (*inspection*) kontrola *f*; (*curb*) powstrzymanie *nt*; (*US: bill*) rachunek *m*; = **cheque**; (*Chess*) szach *m*; (*usu pl: pattern*) kratka *f* ▷ *adj* w kratkę *post*; **to ~ with sb** konsultować się (skonsultować się *perf*) z kimś; **to keep a ~ on sb/sth** kontrolować kogoś/coś; **a green jacket with sky-blue ~s** zielona marynarka w błękitną kratkę
▸ **check in** *vi* (*at hotel*) meldować się (zameldować się *perf*); (*at airport*) zgłaszać się (zgłosić się *perf*) do odprawy ▷ *vt* (*luggage*) nadawać (nadać *perf*)
▸ **check off** *vt* (*items on list*) odhaczać (odhaczyć *perf*)
▸ **check out** *vi* (*of hotel*) wymeldowywać się (wymeldować się *perf*) ▷ *vt* (*luggage*) odbierać (odebrać *perf*); (*person, story*) sprawdzać (sprawdzić *perf*), weryfikować (zweryfikować *perf*)
▸ **check up on** *vt fus*: **to ~ up on sb** zbierać (zebrać *perf*) informacje o kimś
**checkered** ['tʃɛkəd] (*US*) *adj* = **chequered**
**checkers** ['tʃɛkəz] (*US*) *npl* warcaby *pl*
**check guarantee card** (*US*) *n* = **cheque card**
**check-in (desk)** ['tʃɛkɪn-] *n* (*at airport*) punkt *m* odpraw

C

**checking account** ['tʃɛkɪŋ-] (US) *n* ≈ rachunek *m* oszczędnościowo-rozliczeniowy
**checklist** ['tʃɛklɪst] *n* lista *f* kontrolny
**checkmate** ['tʃɛkmeɪt] *n* szach-mat *m*
**checkout** ['tʃɛkaut] *n* kasa *f* (*w supermarkecie*)
**checkpoint** ['tʃɛkpɔɪnt] *n* punkt *m* kontroli granicznej
**checkroom** ['tʃɛkrum] (US) *n* przechowalnia *f* bagażu
**checkup** ['tʃɛkʌp], **check-up** (*Med*) *n* badanie *nt* lekarskie (*kontrolne*); (*at dentist's*) przegląd *m*
**cheek** [tʃi:k] *n* (*Anat*) policzek *m*; (*impudence*) bezczelność *f*, tupet *m*; **to have the ~ to do sth** mieć czelność coś zrobić
**cheekbone** ['tʃi:kbəun] *n* kość *f* policzkowa
**cheeky** ['tʃi:kɪ] *adj* bezczelny
**cheep** [tʃi:p] *vi* (*bird*) piszczeć (zapiszczeć *perf*) ▷ *n* pisk *m*
**cheer** [tʃɪəʳ] *vt* (*team, speaker*) zgotować (*perf*) owację *+dat*; (*gladden*) pocieszać (pocieszyć *perf*) ▷ *vi* wiwatować ▷ *n* wiwat *m*; **~s!** (*toast*) na zdrowie!; (*bye*) cześć!
▸ **cheer on** *vt* kibicować *+dat*
▸ **cheer up** *vi* rozchmurzać się (rozchmurzyć się *perf*) ▷ *vt* rozweselać (rozweselić *perf*)
**cheerful** ['tʃɪəful] *adj* wesoły, radosny
**cheerfulness** ['tʃɪəfulnɪs] *n* wesołość *f*
**cheerio** [tʃɪərɪ'əu] (Brit) *excl* cześć (*przy pożegnaniu*)
**cheerleader** ['tʃɪəli:dəʳ] *n* cheerleaderka *f*
**cheerless** ['tʃɪəlɪs] *adj* ponury
**cheese** [tʃi:z] *n* ser *m*
**cheeseboard** ['tʃi:zbɔ:d] *n* deska *f* do (krojenia) sera; (*with cheese on it*) półmisek *m* *or* wybór *m* serów
**cheesecake** ['tʃi:zkeɪk] *n* sernik *m*
**cheetah** ['tʃi:tə] *n* gepard *m*
**chef** [ʃɛf] *n* szef *m* kuchni
**chemical** ['kɛmɪkl] *adj* chemiczny ▷ *n* substancja *f* chemiczna; **~s** chemikalia
**chemical engineering** *n* inżynieria *f* chemiczna
**chemist** ['kɛmɪst] *n* (*Brit: pharmacist*) aptekarz(-arka) *m(f)*; (*scientist*) chemik(-iczka) *m(f)*
**chemistry** ['kɛmɪstrɪ] *n* chemia *f*
**chemist's (shop)** ['kɛmɪsts-] (Brit) *n* apteka *połączona z drogerią*
**cheque** [tʃɛk] (Brit) *n* czek *m*; **to pay by ~** płacić (zapłacić *perf*) czekiem
**chequebook** ['tʃɛkbuk] (Brit) *n* książeczka *f* czekowa
**cheque card** (Brit) *n* karta *f* czekowa (*gwarantująca czeki wystawiane przez jej posiadacza*)
**chequered**, (US) **checkered** ['tʃɛkəd] *adj* (*fig: career, history*) burzliwy

**cherish** ['tʃɛrɪʃ] *vt* (*person, freedom*) miłować (*literary*); (*right, privilege*) wysoko (sobie) cenić, przywiązywać wielką wagę do *+gen*; (*hope*) żywić; (*memory*) zachowywać (zachować *perf*) w pamięci
**cheroot** [ʃə'ru:t] *n* (krótkie) cygaro *nt*
**cherry** ['tʃɛrɪ] *n* czereśnia *f*; (*sour*) wiśnia *f*
**chervil** ['tʃə:vɪl] *n* (*Bot*) trybula *f*
**Ches** (*Brit: Post*) *abbr* = **Cheshire**
**chess** [tʃɛs] *n* szachy *pl*
**chessboard** ['tʃɛsbɔ:d] *n* szachownica *f*
**chessman** ['tʃɛsmən] (*irreg: like* **man**) *n* figura *f* szachowa
**chessplayer** ['tʃɛspleɪəʳ] *n* szachista(-tka) *m(f)*
**chest** [tʃɛst] *n* (*Anat*) klatka *f* piersiowa; (*box*) skrzynia *f*, kufer *m*; **I'm glad I got it off my ~** (*inf*) cieszę się, że zrzuciłam ten ciężar z serca
**chest measurement** *n* obwód *m* klatki piersiowej
**chestnut** ['tʃɛsnʌt] *n* kasztan *m*; (*also*: **chestnut tree**) kasztanowiec *m*, kasztan *m* ▷ *adj* kasztanowaty
**chest of drawers** *n* komoda *f*
**chew** [tʃu:] *vt* (*food*) żuć, przeżuwać; (*gum*) żuć; (*fingernails*) obgryzać; **to ~ a hole in sth** wygryźć (*perf*) dziurę w czymś
**chewing gum** ['tʃu:ɪŋ-] *n* guma *f* do żucia
**chic** [ʃi:k] *adj* (*dress, hat*) modny; (*person, place*) elegancki, szykowny
**chick** [tʃɪk] *n* pisklę *nt*; (*inf: girl*) laska *f* (*inf*)
**chicken** ['tʃɪkɪn] *n* kurczę *nt*, kurczak *m*; (*inf: person*) tchórz *m*
▸ **chicken out** (*inf*) *vi* tchórzyć (stchórzyć *perf*); **he ~ed out of going** stchórzył i nie poszedł
**chicken feed** *n* (*fig*) grosze *pl*
**chickenpox** ['tʃɪkɪnpɔks] *n* ospa *f* wietrzna
**chick pea** *n* ciecierzyca *f*
**chicory** ['tʃɪkərɪ] *n* cykoria *f*
**chide** [tʃaɪd] *vt*: **to ~ sb (for)** besztać (zbesztać *perf*) kogoś (za *+acc*)
**chief** [tʃi:f] *n* (*of tribe*) wódz *m*; (*of organization, department*) szef *m* ▷ *adj* główny
**chief constable** (Brit) *n* komisarz *m* *or* szef *m* policji (*w danym okręgu*)
**chief executive**, (US) **chief executive officer** *n* dyrektor *m* naczelny
**chiefly** ['tʃi:flɪ] *adv* głównie
**Chief of Staff** *n* szef *m* sztabu
**chiffon** ['ʃɪfɔn] *n* szyfon *m*
**chilblain** ['tʃɪlbleɪn] *n* odmrożenie *nt* (*palców rąk lub nóg*)
**child** [tʃaɪld] (*pl* **~ren**) *n* dziecko *nt*
**child benefit** (Brit) *n* ≈ zasiłek *m* rodzinny
**childbirth** ['tʃaɪldbə:θ] *n* poród *m*
**childhood** ['tʃaɪldhud] *n* dzieciństwo *nt*
**childish** ['tʃaɪldɪʃ] *adj* dziecinny
**childless** ['tʃaɪldlɪs] *adj* bezdzietny

**childlike** ['tʃaɪldlaɪk] *adj* (*behaviour*) dziecinny; (*eyes, figure*) dziecięcy
**child minder** (*Brit*) *n* opiekun(ka) *m(f)* do dziecka
**children** ['tʃɪldrən] *npl of* **child**
**child's play** ['tʃaɪldz-] *n* dziecinna igraszka *f or* zabawa *f*
**Chile** ['tʃɪlɪ] *n* Chile *nt inv*
**Chilean** ['tʃɪlɪən] *adj* chilijski ▷ *n* Chilijczyk(-jka) *m(f)*
**chill** [tʃɪl] *n* (*coldness*) chłód *m*; (*Med*) przeziębienie *nt*; (*shiver*) dreszcz *m* ▷ *adj* (*lit, fig*) chłodny ▷ *vt* (*food, drinks*) schładzać (schłodzić *perf*); (*person*): **to be ~ed** przemarzać (przemarznąć *perf*); **"serve ~ed"** „podawać schłodzone"
**chilli**, (*US*) **chili** ['tʃɪlɪ] *n* chili *nt inv*
**chilly** ['tʃɪlɪ] *adj* (*lit, fig*) chłodny; **I am/feel ~** jest mi bardzo zimno
**chime** [tʃaɪm] *n* (*of clock*) kurant *m*; (*of bells*) bicie *nt* ▷ *vi* dzwonić
**chimney** ['tʃɪmnɪ] *n* komin *m*
**chimney sweep** *n* kominiarz *m*
**chimpanzee** [tʃɪmpæn'zi:] *n* szympans *m*
**chin** [tʃɪn] *n* podbródek *m*
**China** ['tʃaɪnə] *n* Chiny *pl*
**china** ['tʃaɪnə] *n* (*clay*) glinka *f* porcelanowa; (*crockery*) porcelana *f*
**Chinese** [tʃaɪ'ni:z] *adj* chiński ▷ *n inv* (*person*) Chińczyk/Chinka *m/f*; (*Ling*) (język *m*) chiński
**chink** [tʃɪŋk] *n* (*in door, wall*) szczelina *f*; (*sound*) brzęk *m*
**chintz** [tʃɪnts] *n* perkal *m*
**chip** [tʃɪp] *n* (*of wood*) drzazga *f*, wiór *m*; (*of glass, stone*) odłamek *m*; (*in glass, cup*) szczerba *f*; (*in gambling*) żeton *m*; (*Comput*: *also*: **microchip**) kość *f*, układ *m* scalony; **chips** *npl* (*Brit*) frytki *pl*; (*US*: *also*: **potato chips**) chipsy *pl* ▷ *vt* wyszczerbiać (wyszczerbić *perf*); **when the ~s are down** (*fig*) kiedy przyjdzie co do czego
▸ **chip in** (*inf*) *vi* (*contribute*) zrzucać się (zrzucić się *perf*) (*inf*); (*interrupt*) wtrącać się (wtrącić się *perf*)
**chipboard** ['tʃɪpbɔ:d] *n* płyta *f* wiórowa
**chipmunk** ['tʃɪpmʌŋk] *n* (*Zool*) pręgowiec *m* amerykański
**chippings** ['tʃɪpɪŋz] *npl*: **"loose ~"** „uwaga żwir!"
**chiropodist** [kɪ'rɔpədɪst] (*Brit*) *n* specjalista *m* chorób stóp
**chiropody** [kɪ'rɔpədɪ] (*Brit*) *n* leczenie *nt* chorób stóp
**chirp** [tʃə:p] *vi* (*bird*) ćwierkać (zaćwierkać *perf*); (*crickets*) cykać
**chirpy** ['tʃə:pɪ] (*inf*) *adj* dziarski, żwawy
**chisel** ['tʃɪzl] *n* dłuto *nt*
**chit** [tʃɪt] *n* notka *f*, karteczka *f*
**chitchat** ['tʃɪttʃæt], **chit-chat** *n* pogawędka *f*
**chivalrous** ['ʃɪvəlrəs] *adj* rycerski
**chivalry** ['ʃɪvəlrɪ] *n* rycerskość *f*
**chives** [tʃaɪvz] *npl* szczypiorek *m*
**chloride** ['klɔ:raɪd] *n* chlorek *m*
**chlorinate** ['klɔrɪneɪt] *vt* chlorować
**chlorine** ['klɔ:ri:n] *n* chlor *m*
**chock** [tʃɔk] (*Aut, Aviat*) *n* klin *m* (*pod koła*)
**chock-a-block** ['tʃɔkə'blɔk] *adj*: **~ (with)** nabity *or* załadowany (*+instr*) (*inf*)
**chock-full** [tʃɔk'ful] *adj* = **chock-a-block**
**chocolate** ['tʃɔklɪt] *n* (*substance, drink*) czekolada *f*; (*sweet*) czekoladka *f* ▷ *cpd* czekoladowy
**choice** [tʃɔɪs] *n* (*selection*) wybór *m*; (*option*) możliwość *f* (do wyboru); (*person preferred*) typ *m*, kandydat *m* ▷ *adj* najlepszy; **by** *or* **from ~** z wyboru; **a wide ~** duży wybór; **I have no (other) ~** nie mam (innego) wyjścia; **this is a possible ~** to jeden z możliwych wariantów
**choir** ['kwaɪə[r]] *n* chór *m*
**choirboy** ['kwaɪə'bɔɪ] *n* chłopiec *m* śpiewający w chórze kościelnym
**choke** [tʃəuk] *vi* dławić się (zadławić się *perf*) ▷ *vt* (*strangle*) dusić ▷ *n* (*Aut*) ssanie *nt*; **the city centre was ~d with cars** centrum miasta było zapchane samochodami
**cholera** ['kɔlərə] (*Med*) *n* cholera *f*
**cholesterol** [kə'lɛstərɔl] *n* cholesterol *m*
**choose** [tʃu:z] (*pt* **chose**, *pp* **chosen**) *vt* wybierać (wybrać *perf*) ▷ *vi*: **to ~ between/ from** wybierać (wybrać *perf*) (po)między *+instr*/z *+gen*; **to ~ to do sth** postanawiać (postanowić *perf*) coś zrobić
**choosy** ['tʃu:zɪ] *adj* wybredny
**chop** [tʃɔp] *vt* rąbać (porąbać *perf*); (*also*: **chop up**) siekać (posiekać *perf*) ▷ *n* (*Culin*) kotlet *m*; **chops** (*inf*) *npl* wargi *pl* (*zwierzęcia*); **to lick one's ~s** (*fig*: *pej*) oblizywać się; **he got the ~** (*Brit*: *inf*) wylali go (z pracy) (*inf*)
▸ **chop down** *vt* zrąbać (*perf*)
**chopper** ['tʃɔpə[r]] (*inf*) *n* helikopter *m*
**choppy** ['tʃɔpɪ] *adj* (*sea*) lekko wzburzony
**chopsticks** ['tʃɔpstɪks] *npl* pałeczki *pl*
**choral** ['kɔ:rəl] *adj* chóralny
**chord** [kɔ:d] *n* (*Mus*) akord *m*; (*Math*) cięciwa *f*
**chore** [tʃɔ:[r]] *n* (*domestic task*) praca *f* domowa; (*routine task*) (przykry) obowiązek *m*; **household ~s** prace *or* obowiązki domowe
**choreographer** [kɔrɪ'ɔgrəfə[r]] *n* choreograf(ka) *m(f)*
**chorister** ['kɔrɪstə[r]] *n* chórzysta(-tka) *m(f)* (*w chórze kościelnym*)
**chortle** ['tʃɔ:tl] *vi* chichotać (zachichotać *perf*)
**chorus** ['kɔ:rəs] *n* chór *m*; (*part of song*) refren *m*; **she began her career in the ~ line of "Oklahoma"** zaczynała jako statystka w musicalu „Oklahoma"

**chose** [tʃəuz] *pt of* **choose**
**chosen** ['tʃəuzn] *pp of* **choose**
**chow** [tʃau] *n* chow-chow *m inv*
**chowder** ['tʃaudəʳ] *n* zupa *f* rybna (*lub ze skorupiaków*)
**Christ** [kraɪst] *n* Chrystus *m*
**christen** ['krɪsn] *vt* (*baby*) chrzcić (ochrzcić *perf*); (*with nickname*) ochrzcić (*perf*) (*fig*)
**christening** ['krɪsnɪŋ] *n* chrzest *m*
**Christian** ['krɪstɪən] *adj* chrześcijański ▹ *n* chrześcijanin(-anka) *m(f)*
**Christianity** [krɪstɪ'ænɪtɪ] *n* chrześcijaństwo *nt*
**Christian name** *n* imię *nt*
**Christmas** ['krɪsməs] *n* Święta *pl* (Bożego Narodzenia), Boże Narodzenie *nt*; **Happy** *or* **Merry ~!** Wesołych Świąt!
**Christmas card** *n* kartka *f* świąteczna
**Christmas Day** *n* dzień *m* Bożego Narodzenia
**Christmas Eve** *n* Wigilia *f* (Bożego Narodzenia)
**Christmas Island** *n* Wyspa *f* Bożego Narodzenia
**Christmas tree** *n* choinka *f*
**chrome** [krəum] *n* = **chromium**
**chromium** ['krəumɪəm] *n* chrom *m*; (*also*: **chromium plating**) chromowanie *pl*
**chromosome** ['krəuməsəum] *n* chromosom *m*
**chronic** ['krɔnɪk] *adj* chroniczny; (*fig*: *liar, drunkenness*) notoryczny
**chronicle** ['krɔnɪkl] *n* kronika *f*
**chronological** [krɔnə'lɔdʒɪkl] *adj* chronologiczny
**chrysanthemum** [krɪ'sænθəməm] *n* chryzantema *f*
**chubby** ['tʃʌbɪ] *adj* (*cheeks, child*) pucołowaty
**chuck** [tʃʌk] (*inf*) *vt* (*lit, fig*) rzucać (rzucić *perf*)
▸ **chuck out** *vt* wyrzucać (wyrzucić *perf*)
**chuckle** ['tʃʌkl] *vi* chichotać (zachichotać *perf*)
**chug** [tʃʌg] *vi* (*machine, car engine*) dyszeć, sapać; (*also*: **chug along**) telepać się (*inf*)
**chum** [tʃʌm] *n* kumpel *m*
**chump** [tʃʌmp] (*inf*) *n* matołek *m* (*inf*)
**chunk** [tʃʌŋk] *n* kawał *m*
**chunky** ['tʃʌŋkɪ] *adj* (*person*) krępy, przysadzisty; (*knitwear*) gruby; (*furniture*) masywny
**church** [tʃə:tʃ] *n* kościół *m*; **the C~ of England** Kościół *or* kościół anglikański
**churchyard** ['tʃə:tʃjɑ:d] *n* cmentarz *m* parafialny
**churlish** ['tʃə:lɪʃ] *adj* grubiański
**churn** [tʃə:n] *n* (*for butter*) maselnica *f*; (*also*: **milk churn**) bańka *f* (na mleko)
▸ **churn out** *vt* masowo produkować
**chute** [ʃu:t] *n* (*also*: **rubbish chute**) zsyp *m* (na śmieci); (*for coal*) zsuwnia *f*; (*Brit*: *in playground, into swimming pool*) zjeżdżalnia *f*
**chutney** ['tʃʌtnɪ] *n ostry, gęsty sos z owoców, cukru, octu i przypraw, spożywany jako dodatek do mięs i serów*
**CIA** (*US*) *n abbr* (= *Central Intelligence Agency*) CIA *f inv*
**cicada** [sɪ'kɑ:də] *n* cykada *f*
**CID** (*Brit*) *n abbr* (= *Criminal Investigation Department*) *brytyjska policja kryminalna*
**cider** ['saɪdəʳ] *n* cydr *m*, jabłecznik *m*
**c.i.f.** (*Comm*) *abbr* (= *cost, insurance and freight*) koszt *m*, ubezpieczenie *nt* i fracht *m*
**cigar** [sɪ'gɑ:ʳ] *n* cygaro *nt*
**cigarette** [sɪgə'rɛt] *n* papieros *m*
**cigarette case** *n* papierośnica *f*
**cigarette end** *n* niedopałek *m*
**cigarette holder** *n* cygarniczka *f*
**C-in-C** (*Mil*) *abbr* (= *commander-in-chief*) głównodowodzący *m*, naczelny wódz *m*
**cinch** [sɪntʃ] (*inf*) *n*: **it's a ~** to pestka (*inf*)
**Cinderella** [sɪndə'rɛlə] *n* Kopciuszek *m*
**cinders** ['sɪndəz] *npl* popiół *m*
**cine-camera** ['sɪnɪ'kæmərə] (*Brit*) *n* kamera *f* (filmowa)
**cine-film** ['sɪnɪfɪlm] (*Brit*) *n* taśma *f* filmowa
**cinema** ['sɪnəmə] *n* kino *nt*
**cine-projector** ['sɪnɪprə'dʒɛktəʳ] (*Brit*) *n* projektor *m* filmowy
**cinnamon** ['sɪnəmən] *n* cynamon *m*
**cipher** ['saɪfəʳ] *n* (*code*) szyfr *m*; (*fig*: *person*) pionek *m*; **in ~** szyfrem
**circa** ['sə:kə] *prep* około *+gen*
**circle** ['sə:kl] *n* (*curved line*) okrąg *m*; (*area enclosed by curved line*) koło *nt*; (*: smaller*) kółko *nt*; (*of friends*) krąg *m*; (*in cinema, theatre*) balkon *m* ▹ *vi* krążyć, zataczać koła (zatoczyć *perf* koło) ▹ *vt* (*move round*) okrążać (okrążyć *perf*); (*surround*) otaczać (otoczyć *perf*)
**circuit** ['sə:kɪt] *n* (*Elec*) obwód *m*; (*tour*) objazd *m*; (*track*) tor *m*; (*lap*) okrążenie *nt*
**circuit board** (*Comput, Elec*) *n* płytka *f* montażowa
**circuitous** [sə:'kjuɪtəs] *adj* okrężny
**circular** ['sə:kjuləʳ] *adj* (*plate, pond*) okrągły; (*route*) okrężny ▹ *n* (*letter*) okólnik *m*; (*advertisement*) ulotka *f* (reklamowa); **~ argument** błędne koło
**circulate** ['sə:kjuleɪt] *vi* krążyć ▹ *vt* (*report etc*) rozprowadzać (rozprowadzić *perf*); **the traffic ~s freely** ruch przebiega bez zakłóceń
**circulating capital** [sə:kju'leɪtɪŋ-] *n* kapitał *m* obrotowy
**circulation** [sə:kju'leɪʃən] *n* (*of report, book, newspaper*) nakład *m*; (*of air, money*) obieg *m*; (*of blood*) krążenie *nt*
**circumcise** ['sə:kəmsaɪz] *vt* obrzezywać (obrzezać *perf*)
**circumference** [sə'kʌmfərəns] *n* obwód *m*

**circumflex** ['sə:kəmflɛks] *n* (*also*: **circumflex accent**) cyrkumfleks *m*
**circumscribe** ['sə:kəmskraɪb] *vt* (*geometrical figure*) opisywać (opisać *perf*) okrąg na *+loc*; (*fig*: *authority, freedom*) ograniczać (ograniczyć *perf*)
**circumspect** ['sə:kəmspɛkt] *adj* ostrożny
**circumstances** ['sə:kəmstənsɪz] *npl* (*of accident, death etc*) okoliczności *pl*; (*conditions*) warunki *pl*; (*: financial, domestic*) sytuacja *f*; **in** *or* **under the ~** w tej sytuacji; **under no ~** w żadnym wypadku
**circumstantial** [sə:kəm'stænʃl] *adj* (*report, statement*) szczegółowy; **~ evidence** poszlaki
**circumvent** [sə:kəm'vɛnt] *vt* (*regulation, difficulty*) omijać (ominąć *perf*), obchodzić (obejść *perf*)
**circus** ['sə:kəs] *n* cyrk *m*; **C~** (*in place names*) plac *m*
**CIS** *n abbr* (= *Commonwealth of Independent States*) WNP *f inv*
**cistern** ['sɪstən] *n* (*water tank*) zbiornik *m*, cysterna *f*; (*of toilet*) spłuczka *f*, rezerwuar *m*
**citation** [saɪ'teɪʃən] *n* (*commendation*) (oficjalna) pochwała *f*; (*quotation*) cytat *m*; (*Jur*) wezwanie *nt* (do sądu)
**cite** [saɪt] *vt* (*sum*) wymieniać (wymienić *perf*); (*author, passage*) cytować (zacytować *perf*); (*example*) przytaczać (przytoczyć *perf*); (*Jur*) wzywać (wezwać *perf*) (do sądu)
**citizen** ['sɪtɪzn] *n* (*of country*) obywatel(ka) *m(f)*; (*of town*) mieszkaniec(-nka) *m(f)*
**citizenship** ['sɪtɪznʃɪp] *n* (*of country*) obywatelstwo *nt*
**citric** ['sɪtrɪk] *adj*: **~ acid** kwas *m* cytrynowy
**citrus fruit** ['sɪtrəs-] *n* owoc *m* cytrusowy, cytrus *m*
**city** ['sɪtɪ] *n* miasto *nt*; **the C~** (*Brit*) (londyńskie) City *nt inv*
**city centre** *n* centrum *nt* (miasta)
**civic** ['sɪvɪk] *adj* (*authorities*) miejski; (*duties, pride*) obywatelski
**civic centre** (*Brit*) *n* ≈ zarząd *m* miasta
**civil** ['sɪvɪl] *adj* (*disturbances, equality*) społeczny; (*authorities*) cywilny; (*rights, liberties*) obywatelski; (*behaviour, person*) uprzejmy
**Civil Aviation Authority** *n* ≈ Główny Inspektorat *m* Lotnictwa Cywilnego
**civil defence** *n* obrona *f* cywilna
**civil disobedience** *n* (*Jur*) nieposłuszeństwo *nt* obywatelskie
**civil engineer** *n* ≈ inżynier *m* budownictwa
**civil engineering** *n* ≈ inżynieria *f* wodno-lądowa
**civilian** [sɪ'vɪlɪən] *adj* (*casualties*) cywilny ▷ *n* cywil *m*
**civilization** [sɪvɪlaɪ'zeɪʃən] *n* cywilizacja *f*
**civilized** ['sɪvɪlaɪzd] *adj* (*society*) cywilizowany; (*person*) kulturalny; (*place, design*) w dobrym guście *post*
**civil law** *n* prawo *nt* cywilne
**civil rights** *npl* prawa *pl* obywatelskie
**civil servant** *n* urzędnik *m* służby cywilnej
**Civil Service** *n*: **the ~** Państwowa Służba *f* Cywilna
**civil war** *n* wojna *f* domowa
**cl** *abbr* (= *centilitre*) cl
**clad** [klæd] *adj*: **~ in** odziany w *+acc*
**claim** [kleɪm] *vt* (*rights, compensation*) żądać (zażądać *perf*) *+gen*, domagać się *+gen*; (*credit*) przypisywać (przypisać *perf*) sobie; (*expenses*) żądać (zażądać *perf*) zwrotu *+gen*; (*assert*): **he ~s (that)/to be ...** twierdzi, że/że jest *+instr* ▷ *n* (*assertion*) twierdzenie *nt*; (*for pension, wage rise*) roszczenie *nt*; (*to inheritance etc*) prawo *nt*, pretensje *pl*; **to ~ responsibility for** przyznawać się (przyznać się *perf*) do *+gen*; **she ~ed innocence** twierdziła, że jest niewinna; **to put in a ~ for** (*expenses*) przedstawiać (przedstawić *perf*) rachunek na *+acc*; **to lay a ~ to sth** rościć sobie prawo *or* pretensje do czegoś; **to ~ on the insurance** składać (złożyć *perf*) wniosek o odszkodowanie (*z tytułu polisy ubezpieczeniowej*); **the airline faced millions of dollars in ~s** linie lotnicze stanęły w obliczu wielomilionowych roszczeń o odszkodowania
**claimant** ['kleɪmənt] *n* osoba *f* wysuwająca roszczenie
**claim form** *n* formularz *m* podaniowy; (*completed*) podanie *nt*
**clairvoyant** [klɛə'vɔɪənt] *n* jasnowidz *m*
**clam** [klæm] *n* małż *m*
▸ **clam up** (*inf*) *vi* zamykać się (zamknąć się *perf*) w sobie
**clamber** ['klæmbə^r] *vi* (*aboard vehicle*) gramolić się (wgramolić się *perf*); (*up hill*) wdrapywać się (wdrapać się *perf*)
**clammy** ['klæmɪ] *adj* (*hands etc*) lepki, wilgotny
**clamour**, (*US*) **clamor** ['klæmə^r] *vi*: **to ~ for** głośno domagać się *+gen* ▷ *n* (*noise*) zgiełk *m*, wrzawa *f*; (*protest*) oburzenie *nt*
**clamp** [klæmp] *n* klamra *f*, zacisk *m* ▷ *vt* (*wheel, car*) zakładać (założyć *perf*) klamrę blokującą na *+acc*; **to ~ sth to sth** przymocowywać (przymocować *perf*) *or* przytwierdzać (przytwierdzić *perf*) coś do czegoś; **they ~ed handcuffs round my wrists** założyli mi kajdanki na ręce
▸ **clamp down on** *vt fus* przyhamowywać (przyhamować *perf*)
**clan** [klæn] *n* klan *m*
**clandestine** [klæn'dɛstɪn] *adj* (*radio station*) tajny; (*meeting, marriage*) potajemny

C

**clang** [klæŋ] *vi* (*bell*) dźwięczeć (zadźwięczeć *perf*); (*metal object*) szczękać (zaszczękać *perf*) ▷ *n* (*of bell*) brzęk *m*; (*of metal*) szczęk *m*
**clansman** ['klænzmən] *n* członek *m* klanu
**clap** [klæp] *vi* klaskać ▷ *vt*: **to ~ (one's hands)** klaskać (klasnąć *perf*) (w dłonie *or* ręce); **a ~ of thunder** uderzenie pioruna, grzmot
**clapping** ['klæpɪŋ] *n* oklaski *pl*
**claret** ['klærət] *n* bordo *nt inv* (*wino*)
**clarification** [klærɪfɪ'keɪʃən] *n* wyjaśnienie *nt*
**clarify** ['klærɪfaɪ] *vt* wyjaśniać (wyjaśnić *perf*)
**clarinet** [klærɪ'nɛt] *n* klarnet *m*
**clarity** ['klærɪtɪ] *n* jasność *f*
**clash** [klæʃ] *n* (*fight, disagreement*) starcie *nt*; (*of beliefs, cultures, styles*) zderzenie *nt*; (*of events, appointments*) nałożenie się *nt*; (*of weapons*) szczęk *m*; (*of cymbals*) brzęk *m* ▷ *vi* (*gangs, political opponents*) ścierać się (zetrzeć się *perf*); (*beliefs*) kolidować (ze sobą); (*colours, styles*) kłócić się (ze sobą); (*two events, appointments*) kolidować, nakładać się (nałożyć się *perf*) (na siebie); (*weapons*) szczękać (zaszczękać *perf*); (*cymbals*) brzękać (brzęknąć *perf*)
**clasp** [klɑ:sp] *n* (*hold, embrace*) uścisk *m*; (*of bag*) zatrzask *m*; (*of necklace*) zapięcie *nt* ▷ *vt* ściskać (ścisnąć *perf*)
**class** [klɑ:s] *n* klasa *f*; (*period of teaching*) lekcja *f*; (*: at university*) zajęcia *pl*, ćwiczenia *pl* ▷ *cpd* klasowy ▷ *vt* klasyfikować (zaklasyfikować *perf*)
**class-conscious** ['klɑ:s'kɔnʃəs] *adj* świadomy klasowo
**class-consciousness** ['klɑ:s'kɔnʃəsnɪs] *n* świadomość *f* klasowa
**classic** ['klæsɪk] *adj* klasyczny ▷ *n* (*film, novel*) klasyczne dzieło *nt*, klasyka *f*; (*author*) klasyk *m*; (*example*) klasyczny przykład *m*; **Classics** *npl* ≈ filologia *f* klasyczna
**classical** ['klæsɪkl] *adj* (*art, music, language*) klasyczny; (*times*) antyczny
**classification** [klæsɪfɪ'keɪʃən] *n* (*process*) klasyfikacja *f*; (*category*) zaklasyfikowanie *nt*
**classified** ['klæsɪfaɪd] *adj* (*information*) tajny, poufny
**classified advertisement** *n* ≈ ogłoszenie *nt* drobne
**classify** ['klæsɪfaɪ] *vt* klasyfikować (zaklasyfikować *perf*)
**classmate** ['klɑ:smeɪt] *n* kolega/koleżanka *m/f* z klasy
**classroom** ['klɑ:srum] *n* klasa *f*, sala *f* lekcyjna
**classy** ['klɑ:sɪ] (*inf*) *adj* z klasą *post*
**clatter** ['klætə^r] *n* (*of dishes, pots*) brzęk *m*; (*of hooves*) stukot *m* ▷ *vi* (*dishes, pots*) brzęczeć (zabrzęczeć *perf*); (*hooves*) stukotać (zastukotać *perf*)
**clause** [klɔ:z] *n* (*Jur*) klauzula *f*; (*Ling*) człon *m* zdania
**claustrophobia** [klɔ:strə'fəubɪə] *n* klaustrofobia *f*
**claw** [klɔ:] *n* (*of animal*) pazur *m*; (*of bird*) szpon *m*; (*of lobster*) szczypce *pl* (*no sg*)
▶ **claw at** *vt fus* (*curtains etc*) wczepiać się (wczepić się *perf*) w *+acc*; (*door etc*) drapać w *+acc*
**clay** [kleɪ] *n* glina *f*
**clean** [kli:n] *adj* (*lit, fig*) czysty; (*joke, story*) przyzwoity; (*edge*) gładki; (*Med: fracture*) prosty ▷ *vt* czyścić (wyczyścić *perf*) ▷ *adv*: **he ~ forgot** zupełnie *or* na śmierć zapomniał; **the thief got ~ away** złodziej zniknął bez śladu; **to come ~** (*inf*) przyznawać się (przyznać się *perf*); **to ~ one's teeth** (*Brit*) czyścić (wyczyścić *perf*) zęby; **to have a ~ driving licence** *or* (*US*) **record** ≈ nie mieć punktów karnych w ewidencji policji drogowej
▶ **clean out** *vt* (*cupboard, drawer*) opróżniać (opróżnić *perf*); (*inf: person*): **to be ~ed out** spłukać się (*perf*) (*inf*)
▶ **clean up** *vt* (*mess*) sprzątać (posprzątać *perf*); (*child*) doprowadzać (doprowadzić *perf*) do porządku; (*fig: police, authorities: city, area*) robić (zrobić *perf*) porządek w *+loc* ▷ *vi* sprzątać (posprzątać *perf*); (*fig*) zbijać (zbić *perf*) majątek
**clean-cut** ['kli:n'kʌt] *adj* (*person*) o miłej powierzchowności *post*; (*situation*) jasny
**cleaner** ['kli:nə^r] *n* (*person*) sprzątacz(ka) *m(f)*; (*substance*) środek *m* czyszczący
**cleaner's** ['kli:nəz] *n* (*also*: **dry cleaner's**) pralnia *f* chemiczna
**cleaning** ['kli:nɪŋ] *n* sprzątanie *nt*
**cleaning lady** *n* sprzątaczka *f*
**cleanliness** ['klɛnlɪnɪs] *n* czystość *f*, schludność *f*
**cleanly** ['kli:nlɪ] *adv* gładko
**cleanse** [klɛnz] *vt* (*face, cut*) oczyszczać (oczyścić *perf*), przemywać (przemyć *perf*); (*fig: image, memory*) wymazywać (wymazać *perf*)
**cleanser** ['klɛnzə^r] *n* płyn *m* do zmywania twarzy
**clean-shaven** ['kli:n'ʃeɪvn] *adj* gładko ogolony
**cleansing department** ['klɛnzɪŋ-] (*Brit*) *n* ≈ przedsiębiorstwo *nt* oczyszczania miasta
**clean-up** ['kli:nʌp] *n* gruntowne sprzątanie *nt or* porządki *pl*
**clear** [klɪə^r] *adj* (*report, argument*) jasny, klarowny; (*voice, photograph, commitment*) wyraźny; (*majority*) wyraźny, bezsporny; (*glass, plastic, water*) przezroczysty; (*road, way*) wolny; (*conscience, profit, sky*) czysty ▷ *vt* (*ground, suspect*) oczyszczać (oczyścić *perf*); (*building*) ewakuować (ewakuować *perf*);

(*weeds*) usuwać (usunąć *perf*); (*fence, wall*) przeskakiwać (przeskoczyć *perf*); (*cheque*) rozliczać (rozliczyć *perf*); (*goods*) wyprzedawać (wyprzedać *perf*) ▷ *vi* (*sky*) przejaśniać się (przejaśnić się *perf*); (*fog, smoke*) przerzedzać się (przerzedzić się *perf*) ▷ *adv*: **to be ~ of** nie dotykać *+gen*; **to be in the ~** (*free of suspicion*) być wolnym od podejrzeń; (*out of danger*) być bezpiecznym; **to ~ the table** sprzątać (sprzątnąć *perf*) ze stołu; **to ~ one's throat** odchrząkiwać (odchrząknąć *perf*); **to ~ a profit** osiągać (osiągnąć *perf*) zysk; **do I make myself ~?** czy wyrażam się jasno?; **to make it ~ to sb that ...** uzmysławiać (uzmysłowić *perf*) komuś, że ...; **to keep** *or* **stay** *or* **steer ~ of sb/sth** trzymać się z dala *or* daleka od kogoś/czegoś; **this weather should ~ any moment now** lada chwila powinno się rozpogodzić; **the cheque will take three days to ~** czek zostanie rozliczony w ciągu trzech dni

▶ **clear off** (*inf*) *vi* zmiatać (*inf*), zmywać się (zmyć się *perf*) (*inf*)

▶ **clear up** *vt* (*room, mess*) sprzątać (posprzątać *perf*); (*mystery, problem*) wyjaśniać (wyjaśnić *perf*) ▷ *vi* (*person*) sprzątać (posprzątać *perf*); (*illness*) przechodzić (przejść *perf*)

**clearance** ['klɪərəns] *n* (*removal*) usunięcie *nt*; (*permission*) pozwolenie *nt*, zgoda *f*; (*free space*) miejsce *nt*; (*Aviat*) zezwolenie *nt*

**clearance sale** *n* wyprzedaż *f* likwidacyjna

**clear-cut** ['klɪə'kʌt] *adj* (*decision, issue*) jednoznaczny

**clearing** ['klɪərɪŋ] *n* (*in wood*) polana *f*

**clearing bank** (*Brit*) *n* bank *m* clearingowy

**clearing house** (*Comm*) *n* izba *f* rozrachunkowa

**clearly** ['klɪəlɪ] *adv* (*distinctly*) wyraźnie; (*coherently*) jasno, klarownie; (*obviously*) najwyraźniej, najwidoczniej

**clearway** ['klɪəweɪ] (*Brit*) *n* droga *f* szybkiego ruchu

**cleavage** ['kli:vɪdʒ] *n* (*within group, society*) rozłam *m*; **she wore a dress which showed her ~** miała na sobie suknię z głębokim dekoltem

**cleaver** ['kli:vəʳ] *n* tasak *m*

**clef** [klɛf] (*Mus*) *n* klucz *m*

**cleft** [klɛft] *n* szczelina *f* (skalna)

**cleft palate** *n* rozszczep *m* podniebienia

**clemency** ['klɛmənsɪ] *n* (*Jur*) łaska *f*

**clement** ['klɛmənt] *adj* (*weather*) łagodny

**clench** [klɛntʃ] *vt* (*fist, teeth*) zaciskać (zacisnąć *perf*); (*object*) ściskać (ścisnąć *perf*)

**clergy** ['klə:dʒɪ] *n* duchowieństwo *nt*, kler *m*

**clergyman** ['klə:dʒɪmən] (*irreg: like* **man**) *n* duchowny *m*

**clerical** ['klɛrɪkl] *adj* (*worker, job*) biurowy; **~ opposition** sprzeciw duchownych *or* kleru; **~ collar** koloratka; **a ~ error** pomyłka urzędnika

**clerk** [klɑ:k] *n* (*office worker*) urzędnik(-iczka) *m(f)*; (*US: salesperson*) ekspedient(ka) *m(f)*

**Clerk of Court** *n* pisarz *m* sądowy, protokolant(ka) *m(f)*

**clever** ['klɛvəʳ] *adj* (*intelligent*) zdolny, bystry; (*deft, crafty*) sprytny; (*ingenious*) pomysłowy; (*device, gadget*) zmyślny

**clew** [klu:] *n* (*US*) = **clue**

**cliché** ['kli:ʃeɪ] *n* komunał *m*

**click** [klɪk] *vt* (*tongue*) mlaskać (mlasnąć *perf*) *+instr*; (*heels*) stukać (stuknąć *perf*) *or* trzaskać (trzasnąć *perf*) *+instr* ▷ *vi* (*camera, switch*) pstrykać (pstryknąć *perf*); (*fig: people*) przypaść (*perf*) sobie do gustu ▷ *n* **1** pstryknięcie *nt*

**2** (*Comput: of mouse*) kliknięcie *nt*

**client** ['klaɪənt] *n* klient(ka) *m(f)*

**clientele** [kli:ɑ̃:n'tɛl] *n* klientela *f*

**cliff** [klɪf] *n* wybrzeże *nt* klifowe, klif *m*

**cliffhanger** ['klɪfhæŋəʳ] *n* (*fig*) sytuacja *f* pełna napięcia

**climactic** [klaɪ'mæktɪk] *adj* szczytowy

**climate** ['klaɪmɪt] *n* (*lit, fig*) klimat *m*

**climate change** *n* zmiana *f* klimatu

**climax** ['klaɪmæks] *n* (*of battle*) punkt *m* kulminacyjny; (*of career*) szczyt *m*; (*of film, book*) scena *f* kulminacyjna; (*sexual*) szczytowanie *nt*, orgazm *m*

**climb** [klaɪm] *vi* (*person, sun*) wspinać się (wspiąć się *perf*); (*plant*) piąć się; (*plane*) wznosić się (wznieść się *perf*), wzbijać się (wzbić się *perf*); (*prices, shares*) wzrastać (wzrosnąć *perf*) ▷ *vt* (*stairs, ladder*) wdrapywać się (wdrapać się *perf*) po *+loc*; (*tree, hill*) wspinać się (wspiąć się *perf*) na *+acc* ▷ *n* wspinaczka *f*; **to ~ over a wall** przełazić (przeleźć *perf*) przez mur; **to ~ into a car** gramolić się (wgramolić się *perf*) do samochodu

▶ **climb down** (*Brit*) *vi* (*fig*) iść (pójść *perf*) na ustępstwa

**climb-down** ['klaɪmdaun] *n* ustępstwo *nt*

**climber** ['klaɪməʳ] *n* (*person*) alpinista(-tka) *m(f)*; (*plant*) pnącze *nt*

**climbing** ['klaɪmɪŋ] *n* wspinaczka *f* górska, alpinistyka *f*

**clinch** [klɪntʃ] *vt* (*deal*) finalizować (sfinalizować *perf*); (*argument*) rozstrzygać (rozstrzygnąć *perf*)

**cling** [klɪŋ] (*pt, pp* **clung**) *vi*: **to ~ to** (*mother, support*) trzymać się kurczowo *+gen*; (*idea, belief*) uporczywie trwać przy *+loc*; (*dress: body*) przylegać do *+gen*, opinać się na *+loc*

**clingfilm**® ['klɪŋfɪlm] *n (Brit)* folia *f* spożywcza
**clinic** ['klɪnɪk] *n (centre)* klinika *f*; *(session)* godziny *pl* przyjęć *or* konsultacji
**clinical** ['klɪnɪkl] *adj (tests etc)* kliniczny; *(building, white)* szpitalny; *(fig: dispassionate)* beznamiętny
**clink** [klɪŋk] *vi (glasses, cutlery)* brzęczeć, pobrzękiwać
**clip** [klɪp] *n (also:* **paper clip***)* spinacz *m*; *(Brit: also:* **bulldog clip***)* klips *m* do papieru; *(for hose etc)* klamra *f*, zacisk *m*; *(for hair)* spinka *f*; *(TV, Film)* clip *m* ▷ *vt (fasten)* przypinać (przypiąć *perf*); *(also:* **clip together***)* spinać (spiąć *perf*); *(hedge)* przycinać (przyciąć *perf*); *(nails)* obcinać (obciąć *perf*)
**clippers** ['klɪpəz] *npl (for gardening)* sekator *m*; *(also:* **nail clippers***)* cążki *pl* (do paznokci)
**clipping** ['klɪpɪŋ] *n (from newspaper)* wycinek *m*
**clique** [kli:k] *n* klika *f*
**clitoris** ['klɪtərɪs] *(Anat) n* łechtaczka *f*
**cloak** [kləuk] *n* peleryna *f* ▷ *vt (fig)*: **to be ~ed in** *(mist, secrecy)* być okrytym *+instr*
**cloakroom** ['kləukrum] *n (Brit: for coats)* szatnia *f*; *(bathroom)* toaleta *f (zwłaszcza w budynku publicznym)*
**clobber** ['klɔbə^r] *(inf) n* majdan *m (inf)*, manatki *pl (inf)* ▷ *vt (hit)* walnąć *(perf) (inf)*; *(defeat)* załatwić *(perf) (inf)*
**clock** [klɔk] *n* zegar *m*; *(of taxi)* taksometr *m*, licznik *m*; **round the ~** (przez) całą dobę, na okrągło *(inf)*; **a car with 30,000 miles on the ~** *(Brit)* samochód z przebiegiem 30.000 mil; **to work against the ~** walczyć z czasem
▸ **clock in** *(Brit) vi* odbijać (odbić *perf*) kartę (zegarową) *(po przyjściu do pracy)*
▸ **clock off** *(Brit) vi* odbijać (odbić *perf*) kartę (zegarową) *(przy wychodzeniu z pracy)*
▸ **clock on** *(Brit) vi* = **clock in**
▸ **clock out** *(Brit) vi* = **clock off**
▸ **clock up** *vt (hours, miles)* zaliczać (zaliczyć *perf*) *(inf)*
**clockwise** ['klɔkwaɪz] *adv* zgodnie z ruchem wskazówek zegara
**clockwork** ['klɔkwə:k] *n* mechanizm *m* zegarowy ▷ *adj* mechaniczny; **like ~** jak w zegarku
**clog** [klɔg] *n* chodak *m* ▷ *vt* zapychać (zapchać *perf*), zatykać (zatkać *perf*) ▷ *vi (also:* **clog up***)* zapychać się (zapchać się *perf*), zatykać się (zatkać się *perf*)
**cloister** ['klɔɪstə^r] *n* krużganek *m*
**clone** [kləun] *n* klon *m (potomstwo)* ▷ *vt* klonować
**close**¹ [kləus] *adj (near)*: **~ to** blisko *+gen*; *(friend, relative, ties)* bliski; *(writing, print)* drobny; *(texture)* gęsty, ścisły; *(examination, look)* dokładny; *(contest)* wyrównany; *(weather)* parny; *(room)* duszny ▷ *adv* blisko; **~ to** *or* **up** z bliska; **~ by** tuż obok; **~ at hand** = **close by**; **how ~ is Edinburgh to Glasgow?** jak daleko jest z Edynburga do Glasgow?; **it was a ~ shave** *(fig)* niewiele brakowało; **at ~ quarters** z bliska
**close**² [kləuz] *vt (door, window)* zamykać (zamknąć *perf*); *(sale, deal)* finalizować (sfinalizować *perf*); *(conversation, speech)* zakańczać (zakończyć *perf*) ▷ *vi (door, lid etc)* zamykać się (zamknąć się *perf*); *(film, speech etc)*: **to ~ (with)** kończyć się (zakończyć się *perf*) *(+instr)* ▷ *n* koniec *m*; **to bring sth to a ~** (stopniowo) zakańczać (zakończyć *perf*) coś; **the shops/libraries ~ on Saturdays at one p.m.** sklepy/biblioteki zamyka się w soboty o trzynastej
▸ **close down** *vi (factory, magazine)* zamykać (zamknąć *perf*)
▸ **close in** *vi (night, fog)* nadciągać (nadciągnąć *perf*); **to ~ in on sb/sth** otaczać (otoczyć *perf*) kogoś/coś; **the days are closing in** dni stają się coraz krótsze
▸ **close off** *vt* zamykać (zamknąć *perf*) (dla ruchu)
**closed** [kləuzd] *adj* zamknięty
**closed-circuit** ['kləuzd'sə:kɪt] *adj*: **~ television** telewizja *f* przemysłowa, sieć *f* telewizyjna zamknięta
**closed shop** *n zakład pracy wymagający od pracowników przynależności do określonego związku zawodowego*
**close-knit** ['kləus'nɪt] *adj (family, community)* zwarty, zżyty
**closely** ['kləuslɪ] *adv (examine, watch)* dokładnie; *(connected, related)* blisko; **a ~ guarded secret** pilnie strzeżona tajemnica
**closet** ['klɔzɪt] *n (cupboard)* szafa *f* ścienna
**close-up** ['kləusʌp] *(Phot) n* zbliżenie *nt*
**closing** ['kləuzɪŋ] *adj (stages, remarks)* końcowy
**closing price** *(Stock Exchange) n* kurs *m* zamknięcia
**closure** ['kləuʒə^r] *n* zamknięcie *nt*
**clot** [klɔt] *n (Med)* skrzep *m*; *(inf: person)* baran *m (inf)* ▷ *vi (blood)* krzepnąć (zakrzepnąć *perf*)
**cloth** [klɔθ] *n (material)* tkanina *f*; *(rag)* szmatka *f*; *(Brit: teacloth)* ścier(ecz)ka *f* (do naczyń); *(tablecloth)* obrus *m*
**clothe** [kləuð] *vt* ubierać (ubrać *perf*)
**clothes** [kləuðz] *npl* ubranie *nt*, ubrania *pl*; **to put one's ~ on** ubierać się (ubrać się *perf*); **to take one's ~ off** rozbierać się (rozebrać się *perf*); **to change one's ~** przebierać się (przebrać się *perf*)
**clothes brush** *n* szczotka *f* do ubrań
**clothes line** *n* sznur *m* do (suszenia) bielizny
**clothes peg**, *(US)* **clothes pin** *n* klamerka *f*

**clothing** ['kləuðɪŋ] *n* = **clothes**
**clotted cream** ['klɔtɪd-] (*Brit*) *n gęsta śmietana zbierana z podgrzewanego mleka*
**cloud** [klaud] *n* chmura *f*, obłok *m* ▷ *vt* (*liquid*) mącić (zmącić *perf*); **to ~ the issue** zaciemniać (zaciemnić *perf*) sprawę; **every ~ has a silver lining** (*proverb*) po burzy zawsze jest słońce
▸ **cloud over** *vi* (*sky*) chmurzyć się (zachmurzyć się *perf*); (*face, eyes*) pochmurnieć (spochmurnieć *perf*)
**cloudburst** ['klaudbə:st] *n* oberwanie *nt* chmury
**cloud-cuckoo-land** [klaud'kuku:lænd] (*Brit*) *n*: **he's living in ~** chodzi z głową w chmurach
**cloudy** ['klaudɪ] *adj* (*sky*) pochmurny; (*liquid*) mętny
**clout** [klaut] (*inf*) *vt* walnąć (*perf*) (*inf*) ▷ *n* (*fig*) siła *f* przebicia
**clove** [kləuv] (*Culin*) *n* goździki *pl*; **a ~ of garlic** ząbek czosnku
**clover** ['kləuvə^r^] *n* koniczyna *f*
**cloverleaf** ['kləuvəli:f] *n* liść *m* koniczyny; (*Aut*) koniczyn(k)a *f* (*dwupoziomowe skrzyżowanie bezkolizyjne*)
**clown** [klaun] *n* klown *m* ▷ *vi* (*also*: **clown about, clown around**) błaznować
**cloying** ['klɔɪɪŋ] *adj* mdły
**club** [klʌb] *n* (*society, place*) klub *m*; (*weapon*) pałka *f*; (*also*: **golf club**) kij *m* (golfowy) ▷ *vt* tłuc (stłuc *perf*) pałką, pałować (spałować *perf*) (*inf*) ▷ *vi*: **to ~ together (for sth)** składać się (złożyć się *perf*) *or* zrzucać się (zrzucić się *perf*) (*inf*) (na coś); **clubs** *npl* (*Cards*) trefle *pl*
**club car** (*US*: *Rail*) *n* salonka *f*
**clubhouse** ['klʌbhaus] (*Sport*) *n* siedziba *f* klubu
**cluck** [klʌk] *vi* (*hen*) gdakać
**clue** [klu:] *n* (*pointer, lead*) wskazówka *f*; (: *providing solution*) klucz *m*; (*in crossword*) hasło *nt*; **I haven't a ~** nie mam pojęcia
**clued up** (*US*), **clued in** *adj* (*inf*) dobrze poinformowany
**clueless** ['klu:lɪs] *adj* ciężko myślący
**clump** [klʌmp] *n* (*of trees, bushes*) kęp(k)a *f*; (*of people, buildings*) grupka *f*
**clumsy** ['klʌmzɪ] *adj* (*person, attempt*) niezdarny; (*object*) pokraczny
**clung** [klʌŋ] *pt, pp of* **cling**
**cluster** ['klʌstə^r^] *n* (*of people*) grupka *f*, gromadka *f*; (*of flowers*) pęk *m*; (*of stars*) skupisko *nt* ▷ *vi*: **to ~ (round)** skupiać się (skupić się *perf*) (wokół +*gen*)
**clutch** [klʌtʃ] *n* (*grip*) uścisk *m*; (*Aut*) sprzęgło *nt* ▷ *vt* ściskać (ścisnąć *perf*) kurczowo
▸ **clutch (at)** *vt fus* (*lit, fig*) chwytać się (chwycić się *perf*) (+*gen*)
**clutter** ['klʌtə^r^] *vt* (*also*: **clutter up**: *room, house*) zagracać (zagracić *perf*); (: *mind*) zaśmiecać (zaśmiecić *perf*) ▷ *n* graty *pl*
**CM** (*US*: *Post*) *abbr* = **North Mariana Islands**
**cm** *abbr* (= *centimetre*) cm
**CNAA** (*Brit*) *n abbr* (= *Council for National Academic Awards*) *rada przyznająca uprawnienia zawodowe*
**CND** *n abbr* = **Campaign for Nuclear Disarmament**
**CO** *n abbr* (= *commanding officer*) dow., d-ca; (*Brit*: = *Commonwealth Office*) *urząd do spraw brytyjskiej Wspólnoty Narodów* ▷ *abbr* (*US*: *Post*) = **Colorado**
**Co.** *abbr* = **county**; **company**
**c/o** *abbr* (= *care of*) na adres
**coach** [kəutʃ] *n* (*bus*) autokar *m*; (*horse-drawn*) powóz *m*, kareta *f*; (*Rail*) wagon *m*; (*Sport*) trener(ka) *m(f)*; (*Scol*) korepetytor(ka) *m(f)* ▷ *vt* (*sportsman/woman*) trenować; (*student*) udzielać korepetycji *or* dawać korepetycje +*dat*
**coach trip** *n* wycieczka *f* autokarowa
**coagulate** [kəu'ægjuleɪt] *vi* (*blood*) krzepnąć (zakrzepnąć *perf*); (*paint*) gęstnieć (zgęstnieć *perf*) ▷ *vt* powodować krzepnięcie +*gen*
**coal** [kəul] *n* (*substance*) węgiel *m*; (*piece of coal*) węgielek *m*
**coal face** *n* przodek *m* (węglowy)
**coalfield** ['kəulfi:ld] *n* zagłębie *nt* węglowe
**coalition** [kəuə'lɪʃən] *n* koalicja *f*
**coalman** ['kəulmən] (*irreg*: *like* **man**) *n* dostawca *m* węgla
**coalmine** ['kəulmaɪn] *n* kopalnia *f* (węgla)
**coal miner** *n* górnik *m*
**coal mining** *n* górnictwo *nt* (węgla)
**coarse** [kɔ:s] *adj* (*texture*) szorstki; (*person, laugh*) nieokrzesany; (*salt, sand*) gruboziarnisty; (*cloth*) surowy
**coast** [kəust] *n* wybrzeże *nt* ▷ *vi* (*car, bicycle etc*) jechać rozpędem
**coastal** ['kəustl] *adj* przybrzeżny
**coaster** ['kəustə^r^] *n* (*Naut*) statek *m* żeglugi przybrzeżnej, kabotażowiec *m*; (*for glass*) podkładka *f* pod kieliszek
**coastguard** ['kəustgɑ:d] *n* (*officer*) strażnik *m* straży przybrzeżnej; (*service*) straż *f* przybrzeżna
**coastline** ['kəustlaɪn] *n* linia *f* brzegowa
**coat** [kəut] *n* (*overcoat*) płaszcz *m*; (*of animal*) sierść *f*; (*of paint*) warstwa *f* ▷ *vt*: **to ~ sth with** pokrywać (pokryć *perf*) coś +*instr*
**coat hanger** *n* wieszak *m*
**coating** ['kəutɪŋ] *n* warstwa *f*
**coat of arms** *n* herb *m*
**co-author** ['kəu'ɔ:θə^r^] *n* współautor(ka) *m(f)*
**coax** [kəuks] *vt*: **to ~ sb (into doing sth)** namawiać (namówić *perf*) kogoś (do zrobienia czegoś) (*posługując się łagodną perswazją*)
**cob** [kɔb] *n see* **corn**

**cobbler** ['kɔbləʳ] *n* szewc *m*
**cobbles** ['kɔblz] *npl* bruk *m*
**cobblestones** ['kɔblstəunz] *npl* = **cobbles**
**COBOL** ['kəubɔl] (*Comput*) *n* COBOL *m*
**cobra** ['kəubrə] *n* kobra *f*
**cobweb** ['kɔbwɛb] *n* pajęczyna *f*
**cocaine** [kə'keɪn] *n* kokaina *f*
**cock** [kɔk] *n* kogut *m* ▷ *vt* repetować (zarepetować *perf*); **to ~ one's ears** (*fig*) nastawiać (nastawić *perf*) uszu
**cock-a-hoop** [kɔkə'hu:p] (*inf*) *adj* rozradowany
**cockerel** ['kɔkərl] *n* kogucik *m*
**cock-eyed** ['kɔkaɪd] *adj* (*fig: idea, method*) zwariowany
**cockle** ['kɔkl] *n* sercówka *f* jadalna (*małż*)
**cockney** ['kɔknɪ] *n* cockney *m* (*rdzenny mieszkaniec wschodniego Londynu lub dialekt, którym się posługuje*)
**cockpit** ['kɔkpɪt] *n* (*Aviat*) kabina *f* pilota; (*in racing car*) kabina *f*
**cockroach** ['kɔkrəutʃ] *n* karaluch *m*
**cocktail** ['kɔkteɪl] *n* koktajl *m*
**cocktail cabinet** *n* barek *m*
**cocktail party** *n* koktajl *m*
**cocktail shaker** [-'ʃeɪkəʳ] *n* shaker *m*
**cock-up** ['kɔkʌp] (*inf!*) *n* fuszerka *f* (*inf*)
**cocoa** ['kəukəu] *n* kakao *nt inv*
**coconut** ['kəukənʌt] *n* (*fruit*) orzech *m* kokosowy; (*flesh*) kokos *m*
**cocoon** [kə'ku:n] *n* kokon *m*; **in a ~ of love and warmth** otoczony miłością i ciepłem
**cod** [kɔd] *n* dorsz *m*
**COD** *abbr* (= *cash on delivery*) za pobraniem; (*US*: = *collect on delivery*) za pobraniem
**code** [kəud] *n* (*rules*) kodeks *m*; (*cipher*) szyfr *m*; (*also*: **dialling code**) (numer *m*) kierunkowy; (*also*: **post code**) kod *m* (pocztowy); **~ of behaviour/practice** kodeks zachowania/postępowania
**codeine** ['kəudi:n] *n* kodeina *f*
**codicil** ['kɔdɪsɪl] (*Jur*) *n* kodycyl *m*, testament *m* uzupełniający
**codify** ['kəudɪfaɪ] *vt* kodyfikować (skodyfikować *perf*)
**cod-liver oil** ['kɔdlɪvə-] *n* tran *m*
**co-driver** ['kəu'draɪvəʳ] *n* (*in race*) pilot *m*; (*of lorry*) zmiennik *m* (kierowcy)
**co-ed** ['kəu'ɛd] *adj abbr* (*Scol*) = **coeducational** ▷ *n abbr* (*US*: *female student*) studentka *f*; (*Brit*: *school*) szkoła *f* koedukacyjna
**coeducational** ['kəuɛdju'keɪʃənl] *adj* koedukacyjny
**coerce** [kəu'ə:s] *vt* przymuszać (przymusić *perf*)
**coercion** [kəu'ə:ʃən] *n* przymus *m*
**coexistence** ['kəuɪg'zɪstəns] *n* współistnienie *nt*
**C of C** *n abbr* (= *chamber of commerce*) Izba *f* Handlowa
**C of E** *abbr* = **Church of England**
**coffee** ['kɔfɪ] *n* kawa *f*; **black/white ~** czarna/biała kawa; **~ with cream** kawa ze śmietanką
**coffee bar** (*Brit*) *n* bar *m* kawowy
**coffee bean** *n* ziarenko *nt* kawy
**coffee break** *n* przerwa *f* na kawę
**coffee cake** (*US*) *n ciasto drożdżowe, często z bakaliami, lukrowane lub posypywane cukrem pudrem*
**coffee cup** *n* filiżanka *f* do kawy
**coffee pot** *n* dzbanek *m* do kawy
**coffee table** *n* ława *f*
**coffin** ['kɔfɪn] *n* trumna *f*
**C of I** *abbr* = **Church of Ireland**
**C of S** *abbr* = **Church of Scotland**
**cog** [kɔg] *n* (*wheel*) koło *nt* zębate; (*tooth*) ząb *m* (*koła zębatego*)
**cogent** ['kəudʒənt] *adj* przekonywający
**cognac** ['kɔnjæk] *n* koniak *m*
**cogwheel** ['kɔgwi:l] *n* koło *nt* zębate
**cohabit** [kəu'hæbɪt] (*fml*) *vi* mieszkać razem (*bez ślubu*)
**coherent** [kəu'hɪərənt] *adj* (*theory*) spójny; (*person*) komunikatywny
**cohesion** [kəu'hi:ʒən] *n* (*ideological, political*) jedność *f*; (*of text, performance*) spójność *f*
**cohesive** [kə'hi:sɪv] *adj* (*fig*) spójny
**COI** (*Brit*) *n abbr* (= *Central Office of Information*) *rządowe biuro informacji*
**coil** [kɔɪl] *n* (*of rope, wire*) zwój *m*; (*of smoke*) wstęga *f*; (*Elec*) cewka *f*; (*Aut*) cewka *f* zapłonowa; (*contraceptive*) spirala *f* ▷ *vt* zwijać (zwinąć *perf*); **to ~ sth round sth** owijać (owinąć *perf*) coś wokół czegoś
**coin** [kɔɪn] *n* moneta *f* ▷ *vt* (*word, slogan*) ukuć (*perf*)
**coinage** ['kɔɪnɪdʒ] *n* monety *pl* (*danego systemu monetarnego*); (*Ling*) neologizm *m*
**coin box** (*Brit*) *n* automat *m* telefoniczny (*na monety*)
**coincide** [kəuɪn'saɪd] *vi* (*events*) zbiegać się (zbiec się *perf*) (w czasie); (*ideas, views*) być zbieżnym
**coincidence** [kəu'ɪnsɪdəns] *n* zbieg *m* okoliczności
**coin-operated** ['kɔɪn'ɔpəreɪtɪd] *adj* na monety *post*
**Coke**® [kəuk] *n* coca cola *f*
**coke** [kəuk] *n* (*coal*) koks *m*
**Col.** *abbr* (= *Colonel*) płk
**COLA** (*US*) *n abbr* (= *cost-of-living adjustment*) ≈ indeksacja *f* (*świadczeń, zarobków*)
**colander** ['kɔləndəʳ] *n* cedzak *m*, durszlak *m*
**cold** [kəuld] *adj* zimny; (*person*: *in temperature*) zmarznięty; (*unemotional*) chłodny, oziębły

▷ *n* (*weather*) zimno *nt*; (*Med*) przeziębienie *nt*; **it's ~** jest zimno; **I am** *or* **feel ~** zimno mi; **to catch (a) ~** przeziębić się *(perf)*; **in ~ blood** z zimną krwią; **to get ~ feet (about)** *(fig)* przestraszyć się *(perf)* *(+gen)*; **to give sb the ~ shoulder** traktować (potraktować *perf*) kogoś ozięble

**cold-blooded** ['kəuld'blʌdɪd] *adj* (*Zool*) zmiennocieplny; (*murderer*) bezlitosny, bezwzględny; (*murder*) (popełniony) z zimną krwią

**cold cream** *n* krem *m* do oczyszczania twarzy

**coldly** ['kəuldlɪ] *adv* chłodno, ozięble

**cold-shoulder** [kəuld'ʃəuldə^r] *vt* zachowywać się (zachować się *perf*) ozięble wobec *+gen*

**cold sore** *n* opryszczka *f* (na wardze), febra *f* (*inf*)

**cold war** *n*: **the ~** zimna wojna *f*

**coleslaw** ['kəulslɔː] *n surówka z białej kapusty i innych warzyw z dodatkiem majonezu*

**colic** ['kɔlɪk] (*Med*) *n* kolka *f*

**collaborate** [kə'læbəreɪt] *vi* (*work together*): **to ~ (on)** pracować wspólnie (nad *+instr*); (*with enemy*) kolaborować

**collaboration** [kəlæbə'reɪʃən] *n* współpraca *f*

**collaborator** [kə'læbəreɪtə^r] *n* współpracownik(-iczka) *m(f)*; (*with enemy*) kolaborant(ka) *m(f)*

**collage** [kɔ'lɑːʒ] *n* collage *m*, kolaż *m*

**collagen** ['kɔlədʒən] *n* kolagen *m*

**collapse** [kə'læps] *vi* (*building*) zawalać się (zawalić się *perf*); (*table, resistance*) załamywać się (załamać się *perf*); (*marriage, system*) rozpadać się (rozpaść się *perf*); (*government, company*) upadać (upaść *perf*); (*hopes*) rozwiewać się (rozwiać się *perf*); (*plans*) runąć (*perf*); (*person*: *faint*) zemdleć (*perf*), zasłabnąć (*perf*); (*: from exhaustion*) padać (paść *perf*) ▷ *n* (*of building*) zawalenie się *nt*; (*of table, resistance*) załamanie się *nt*; (*of marriage, system*) rozpad *m*; (*of government, company*) upadek *m*; (*Med*) zapaść *f*

**collapsible** [kə'læpsəbl] *adj* składany

**collar** ['kɔlə^r] *n* (*of coat, shirt*) kołnierz *m*; (*of dog, cat*) obroża *f*; (*Tech*: *flange*) kołnierz *m*; (*: ring*) pierścień *m* ▷ *vt* (*inf*) dopadać (dopaść *perf*) (*inf*)

**collarbone** ['kɔləbəun] *n* obojczyk *m*

**collate** [kɔ'leɪt] *vt* zestawiać (zestawić *perf*)

**collateral** [kə'lætərl] (*Comm*) *n* (dodatkowe) zabezpieczenie *nt*

**collation** [kə'leɪʃən] *n* zestawienie *nt*; (*Culin*): **a cold ~** zimny bufet *m*

**colleague** ['kɔliːg] *n* kolega/koleżanka *m/f* (z pracy)

**collect** [kə'lɛkt] *vt* (*wood, litter*) zbierać (zebrać *perf*); (*stamps, coins*) zbierać, kolekcjonować; (*Brit*: *children from school etc*) odbierać (odebrać *perf*); (*debts, taxes*) ściągać (ściągnąć *perf*); (*mail*: *from box*) wybierać (wybrać *perf*), wyjmować (wyjąć *perf*) ▷ *vi* (*dust etc*) zbierać się (zebrać się *perf*); (*for charity etc*) prowadzić zbiórkę pieniędzy, kwestować; **to call ~** (*US*) dzwonić (zadzwonić *perf*) na koszt abonenta; **to ~ one's thoughts** zbierać (zebrać *perf*) myśli; **~ on delivery** (*US*: *Comm*) za pobraniem

**collected** [kə'lɛktɪd] *adj*: **~ works** dzieła *pl* zebrane

**collection** [kə'lɛkʃən] *n* (*of art, stamps*) kolekcja *f*, zbiór *m*; (*of poems, stories*) zbiór *m*; (*from place, person*) odbiór *m*; (*for charity*) zbiórka *f* pieniędzy, kwesta *f*; (*of mail*) wyjmowanie *nt* listów (*ze skrzynki pocztowej*)

**collective** [kə'lɛktɪv] *adj* zbiorowy ▷ *n* (zorganizowany) zespół *m*, kolektyw *m*; **~ farm** (*state-owned*) ≈ Państwowe Gospodarstwo Rolne; (*co-operative*) rolnicza spółdzielnia produkcyjna

**collective bargaining** *n* negocjacje *pl* w sprawie zbiorowego układu pracy

**collector** [kə'lɛktə^r] *n* (*of art, stamps*) kolekcjoner(ka) *m(f)*, zbieracz(ka) *m(f)*; (*of taxes, rent*) poborca *m*; **~'s item** *or* **piece** rzadki okaz

**college** ['kɔlɪdʒ] *n* (*in Oxford etc*) kolegium *nt*, college *m*; (*of agriculture, technology*) ≈ technikum *nt*; **to go to ~** ≈ iść (pójść *perf*) na studia; **~ of further education** *instytucja oświatowa, w której można uzupełnić wykształcenie średnie i/lub zdobyć kwalifikacje zawodowe*

**collide** [kə'laɪd] *vi* zderzać się (zderzyć się *perf*)

**collie** ['kɔlɪ] *n* owczarek *m* szkocki

**colliery** ['kɔlɪərɪ] (*Brit*) *n* kopalnia *f* węgla

**collision** [kə'lɪʒən] *n* zderzenie *nt*, kolizja *f*; **to be on a ~ course (with)** być na kursie kolizyjnym (z *+instr*); (*fig*) zmierzać do konfrontacji (z *+instr*)

**collision damage waiver** *n* zwolnienie *nt* z obowiązku wypłaty odszkodowania (*w następstwie wypadku drogowego*)

**colloquial** [kə'ləukwɪəl] *adj* potoczny

**collusion** [kə'luːʒən] *n* zmowa *f*; **in ~ with** w zmowie z *+instr*

**Cologne** [kə'ləun] *n* Kolonia *f*

**cologne** [kə'ləun] *n* (*also*: **eau de cologne**) woda *f* kolońska

**Colombia** [kə'lɔmbɪə] *n* Kolumbia *f*

**Colombian** [kə'lɔmbɪən] *adj* kolumbijski ▷ *n* Kolumbijczyk(-jka) *m(f)*

**colon** ['kəulən] *n* (*punctuation mark*) dwukropek *m*; (*Anat*) okrężnica *f*

**colonel** ['kəːnl] *n* pułkownik *m*

**colonial** [kə'ləunɪəl] *adj* kolonialny

**colonize** ['kɔlənaɪz] *vt* kolonizować (skolonizować *perf*)
**colony** ['kɔlənɪ] *n* kolonia *f*
**color** *etc* (US) = **colour** *etc*
**Colorado beetle** [kɔlə'rɑːdəu-] *n* stonka *f* ziemniaczana
**colossal** [kə'lɔsl] *adj* kolosalny
**colour**, (US) **color** ['kʌlə^r] *n* kolor *m*; (*skin colour*) kolor *m* skóry; (*of spectacle, place*) koloryt *m* ▷ *vt* (*paint*) malować (pomalować *perf*); (*dye*) farbować (ufarbować *perf*); (*fig*) mieć (pewien) wpływ na *+acc* ▷ *vi* czerwienić się (zaczerwienić się *perf*), poczerwienieć (*perf*) ▷ *cpd* kolorowy; **colours** *npl* (*of party, club*) barwy *pl*; **in ~** (*film, magazine*) kolorowy; (*illustrations*) barwny, kolorowy
▸ **colour in** *vt* kolorować (pokolorować *perf*)
**colour bar** *n* segregacja *f* rasowa
**colour-blind** ['kʌləblaɪnd] *adj*: **to be ~** być daltonistą(-tką) *m(f)*
**coloured** ['kʌləd] *adj* kolorowy
**colour film** *n* film *m* kolorowy
**colourful** ['kʌləful] *adj* kolorowy; (*fig: account, personality*) barwny
**colouring** ['kʌlərɪŋ] *n* (*complexion*) karnacja *f*; (*in food*) barwnik *m*; (*combination of colours*) kolorystyka *f*
**colour scheme** *n* kolorystyka *f*
**colour supplement** (*Brit: Press*) *n* kolorowy dodatek *m*
**colour television** *n* telewizja *f* kolorowa
**colt** [kəult] *n* źrebię *nt*, źrebak *m*
**column** ['kɔləm] *n* (*of building, people*) kolumna *f*; (*of smoke*) słup *m*; (*Press*) rubryka *f*; **the editorial ~** artykuł wstępny
**columnist** ['kɔləmnɪst] *n* felietonista(-tka) *m(f)* (*mający stałą rubrykę w gazecie lub czasopiśmie*)
**coma** ['kəumə] *n* śpiączka *f*
**comb** [kəum] *n* grzebień *m* ▷ *vt* (*hair*) rozczesywać (rozczesać *perf*); (*area*) przeczesywać (przeczesać *perf*); **to ~ one's hair** czesać się (uczesać się *perf*)
**combat** [*n* 'kɔmbæt, *vb* kɔm'bæt] *n* walka *f* ▷ *vt* walczyć z *+instr*, zwalczać
**combination** [kɔmbɪ'neɪʃən] *n* (*mixture*) połączenie *nt*, kombinacja *f*; (*for lock, safe*) szyfr *m*
**combination lock** *n* zamek *m* szyfrowy
**combine** [*vb* kəm'baɪn, *n* 'kɔmbaɪn] *vt* łączyć (połączyć *perf*) ▷ *vi* łączyć się (połączyć się *perf*) ▷ *n* (*Econ*) koncern *m*; **to ~ sth with sth** łączyć (połączyć *perf*) coś z czymś; **a ~d effort** wspólny wysiłek
**combine (harvester)** *n* kombajn *m*
**combo** ['kɔmbəu] *n* kapela *f* jazzowa
**combustible** [kəm'bʌstɪbl] *adj* łatwopalny
**combustion** [kəm'bʌstʃən] *n* spalanie *nt*

KEYWORD

**come** [kʌm] (*pt* **came**, *pp* **come**) *vi* **1** (*movement towards: on foot*) przychodzić (przyjść *perf*); (*: by car etc*) przyjeżdżać (przyjechać *perf*); **come here!** chodź tu(taj)!; **I've only come for an hour** przyszedłem tylko na godzinę; **are you coming to my party?** przyjdziesz na moje przyjęcie?; **to come running** przybiegać (przybiec *perf*)
**2** (*arrive*) przybywać (przybyć *perf*), przyjeżdżać (przyjechać *perf*); **he's just come from Aberdeen** właśnie przyjechał z Aberdeen; **he's come here to work** przybył tu do pracy
**3** (*reach*): **to come to** sięgać (sięgnąć *perf*) *or* dochodzić (dojść *perf*) do *+gen*; **her hair came to her waist** włosy sięgały jej do pasa; **to come to power** obejmować (objąć *perf*) władzę; **to come to a decision** podejmować (podjąć *perf*) decyzję
**4** (*occur*): **an idea came to me** przyszedł mi do głowy pewien pomysł
**5** (*be, become*): **to come loose** poluźniać się (poluźnić się *perf*); **I've come to like him** polubiłem go
▸ **come about** *vi*: **how did it come about?** jak do tego doszło?; **it came about that ...** stało się tak, że ...
▸ **come across** *vt fus* natknąć się (*perf*) na *+acc* ▷ *vi*: **to come across well/badly** (*idea, meaning*) zostać (*perf*)/nie zostać (*perf*) dobrze przekazanym
▸ **come along** *vi* (*arrive*) pojawiać się (pojawić się *perf*); (*make progress*) posuwać się (posunąć się *perf*) naprzód; **come along!** dalej!
▸ **come apart** *vi* rozpadać się (rozpaść się *perf*)
▸ **come away** *vi* (*leave*) odchodzić (odejść *perf*); (*become detached*) odpadać (odpaść *perf*), odrywać się (oderwać się *perf*)
▸ **come back** *vi* wracać (wrócić *perf*); **black is coming back into fashion** wraca moda na czerń
▸ **come by** *vt fus* (*find*) zdobyć (*perf*), znaleźć (*perf*)
▸ **come down** *vi* (*price*) obniżać się (obniżyć się *perf*); (*building, tree*) runąć (*perf*)
▸ **come forward** *vi* zgłaszać się (zgłosić się *perf*) (na ochotnika)
▸ **come from** *vt fus* pochodzić z *+gen*
▸ **come in** *vi* (*enter*) wchodzić (wejść *perf*); (*report, news*) nadchodzić (nadejść *perf*); (*on deal etc*) wchodzić (wejść *perf*); **come in!** proszę (wejść)!
▸ **come in for** *vt fus* (*criticism etc*) spotykać się (spotkać się *perf*) z *+instr*
▸ **come into** *vt fus* (*money*) dostawać (dostać

*perf*) w spadku; **to come into fashion** wchodzić (wejść *perf*) w modę; **money doesn't come into it** pieniądze nie mają z tym nic wspólnego

▸ **come off** *vi* (*become detached*) odpadać (odpaść *perf*); (*succeed*) powieść się (*perf*) ▹ *vt fus* (*inf*): **come off it!** daj spokój! (*inf*)

▸ **come on** *vi* (*pupil*) robić (zrobić *perf*) postęp(y); (*work, project*) postępować (postąpić *perf*) naprzód; (*electricity*) włączać się (włączyć się *perf*); **come on!** no już!, dalej!

▸ **come out** *vi* (*fact*) wychodzić (wyjść *perf*) na jaw; (*book*) wychodzić (wyjść *perf*); (*stain*) schodzić (zejść *perf*); (*sun*) wychodzić (wyjść *perf*), wyjrzeć (*perf*); (*workers*) strajkować (zastrajkować *perf*)

▸ **come over** *vt fus*: **I don't know what's come over him!** nie wiem, co go naszło!

▸ **come round** *vi* (*recover consciousness*) przychodzić (przyjść *perf*) do siebie; (*visit*) wpadać (wpaść *perf*); (*agree*) dawać (dać *perf*) się przekonać

▸ **come through** *vi* (*survive*) przetrwać (*perf*); **the call came through** połączenie zostało zrealizowane

▸ **come to** *vi* ocknąć się (*perf*) ▹ *vt fus*: **how much does it come to?** ile to (razem) wynosi?

▸ **come under** *vt fus* (*heading*) być zaliczanym do *+gen*; (*criticism, pressure*) zostawać (zostać *perf*) poddanym *+dat*

▸ **come up** *vi* (*approach*) podchodzić (podejść *perf*); (*sun*) wschodzić (wzejść *perf*); (*problem*) pojawiać się (pojawić się *perf*); (*event*) zbliżać się; (*in conversation*) padać (paść *perf*)

▸ **come up against** *vt fus* (*resistance, difficulties*) napotykać (napotkać *perf*)

▸ **come upon** *vt fus* natknąć się (*perf*) na *+acc*

▸ **come up to** *vt fus*: **the film didn't come up to our expectations** film nie spełnił naszych oczekiwań; **it's coming up to ten o'clock** zbliża się (godzina) dziesiąta

▸ **come up with** *vt fus* (*plan*) wymyślić (*perf*); (*money*) wykombinować (*perf*) *or* wytrzasnąć (*perf*) (skądś) (*inf*)

**comeback** ['kʌmbæk] *n* (*of film star, fashion*) powrót *m*, come-back *m*; **to have no ~** nie mieć prawa do rekompensaty

**Comecon** ['kɔmɪkɔn] *n abbr* (= *Council for Mutual Economic Aid*) RWPG *nt inv*

**comedian** [kə'mi:dɪən] *n* komik *m*

**comedienne** [kəmi:dɪ'ɛn] *n* kobieta *f*–komik *m*

**come-down** (*inf*) *n* degradacja *f*

**comedy** ['kɔmɪdɪ] *n* (*play, film*) komedia *f*; (*humour*) komizm *m*

**comet** ['kɔmɪt] *n* kometa *f*

**come-uppance** *n*: **to get one's ~** ponosić (ponieść *perf*) zasłużoną karę

**comfort** ['kʌmfət] *n* (*physical*) wygoda *f*; (*luxury, freedom from anxiety*) komfort *m*; (*consolation*) pociecha *f*, otucha *f* ▹ *vt* pocieszać (pocieszyć *perf*); **comforts** *npl* wygody *pl*

**comfortable** ['kʌmfətəbl] *adj* (*person*: *financially*) dobrze sytuowany; (: *physically*): **I'm ~** jest mi wygodnie; (: *when ill*): **she's ~** jej stan jest zadowalający; (*chair, bed*) wygodny; (*hotel, flat*) komfortowy; (*walk, climb*) łatwy; (*income*) wysoki; (*majority*) znaczny; **to be/feel ~** (*at ease*) czuć się swobodnie; **I don't feel very ~ about it** trochę mnie to niepokoi; **make yourself ~** rozgość się

**comfortably** ['kʌmfətəblɪ] *adv* wygodnie

**comforter** ['kʌmfətə^r] (*US*) *n* smoczek *m*

**comfort station** (*US*) *n* toaleta *f* publiczna

**comic** ['kɔmɪk] *adj* komiczny ▹ *n* (*person*) komik *m*; (*Brit*: *magazine*) komiks *m*

**comical** ['kɔmɪkl] *adj* komiczny

**comic strip** *n* historyjka *f* obrazkowa

**coming** ['kʌmɪŋ] *adj* nadchodzący, zbliżający się; **in the ~ weeks** w nadchodzących *or* najbliższych tygodniach

**comings and goings** *npl* (*arrivals and departures*) przyjazdy *pl* i wyjazdy *pl*; (*bustle*) ruch *m*, bieganina *f*

**Comintern** ['kɔmɪntə:n] *n* Międzynarodówka *f* Komunistyczna, Komintern *m*

**comma** ['kɔmə] *n* przecinek *m*

**command** [kə'ma:nd] *n* (*order*) polecenie *nt*, rozkaz *m*; (*control, charge*) kierownictwo *nt*; (*Mil*) dowództwo *nt*; (*of subject*) znajomość *f*, opanowanie *nt*; (*Comput*) polecenie *nt* ▹ *vt* (*troops*) dowodzić *+instr*; (*be able to get*) uzyskiwać (uzyskać *perf*); (*deserve*) zasługiwać na *+acc*; **to ~ sb to do sth** (*tell*) kazać (kazać *perf*) komuś coś zrobić; (*order*) rozkazywać (rozkazać *perf*) komuś coś zrobić; **to be in ~ of** dowodzić *+instr*; **to have/take ~ of** sprawować/obejmować (objąć *perf*) dowództwo nad *+instr*; **to have sth at one's ~** dysponować czymś

**commandant** ['kɔməndænt] *n* komendant(ka) *m(f)*

**commandeer** [kɔmən'dɪə^r] *vt* rekwirować (zarekwirować *perf*); (*fig*) przywłaszczać (przywłaszczyć *perf*) sobie; **to ~ sth from sb** odbierać (odebrać *perf*) coś komuś

**commander** [kə'ma:ndə^r] *n* dowódca *m*; (*Mil*) komandor *m* porucznik *m*

**commander-in-chief** [kə'ma:ndərɪn'tʃi:f] *n* głównodowodzący *m*, naczelny wódz *m*

**commanding** [kə'ma:ndɪŋ] *adj* (*voice*) rozkazujący, władczy; (*position*) dominujący; (*lead*) zdecydowany

**commanding officer** *n* dowódca *m*
**commandment** [kəˈmɑːndmənt] (*Rel*) *n* przykazanie *nt*
**command module** *n* człon *m* dowodzenia (*statku kosmicznego*)
**commando** [kəˈmɑːndəu] *n* (*group*) oddział *m* komandosów; (*soldier*) komandos *m*
**commemorate** [kəˈmɛməreɪt] *vt* (*with statue, monument*) upamiętniać (upamiętnić *perf*); (*with celebration*) obchodzić rocznicę *+gen*
**commemoration** [kəmɛməˈreɪʃən] *n* obchody *pl*; **in ~ of** dla upamiętnienia *+gen*
**commemorative** [kəˈmɛmərətɪv] *adj* pamiątkowy
**commence** [kəˈmɛns] *vt* rozpoczynać (rozpocząć *perf*) ▷ *vi* rozpoczynać się (rozpocząć się *perf*)
**commend** [kəˈmɛnd] *vt* pochwalać (pochwalić *perf*); **to ~ sth to sb** rekomendować (zarekomendować *perf*) coś komuś
**commendable** [kəˈmɛndəbl] *adj* godny pochwały
**commendation** [kɔmɛnˈdeɪʃən] *n* pochwała *f*
**commensurate** [kəˈmɛnʃərɪt] *adj*: **~ with/to** współmierny do *+gen*
**comment** [ˈkɔmɛnt] *n* (*remark*) uwaga *f*, komentarz *m*; (*event, situation*): **a ~ on** odbicie *nt or* odzwierciedlenie *nt +gen* ▷ *vi*: **to ~ (on)** komentować (skomentować *perf*) (*+acc*); **to ~ that ...** zauważyć (*perf*), że ...; **"no ~"** „bez komentarza"
**commentary** [ˈkɔməntərɪ] *n* komentarz *m*; (*genre*) publicystyka *f*
**commentator** [ˈkɔmənteɪtə^r] *n* (*Sport*) sprawozdawca *m*, komentator *m*; (*expert*) komentator(ka) *m(f)*
**commerce** [ˈkɔməːs] *n* handel *m*
**commercial** [kəˈməːʃəl] *adj* (*organization*) handlowy; (*success*) komercyjny ▷ *n* (*TV, Radio*) reklama *f*
**commercial bank** *n* bank *m* komercyjny
**commercial break** (*TV*) *n* przerwa *f* na reklamę
**commercial college** *n* ≈ technikum *nt* handlowe
**commercialism** [kəˈməːʃəlɪzəm] *n* komercjalizm *m*
**commercialized** [kəˈməːʃəlaɪzd] (*pej*) *adj* skomercjalizowany
**commercial radio** *n* prywatna *or* komercyjna stacja *f* radiowa
**commercial television** *n* telewizja *f* prywatna *or* komercyjna
**commercial traveller** *n* agent *m* handlowy, komiwojażer *m*
**commercial vehicle** *n* samochód *m* dostawczy
**commiserate** [kəˈmɪzəreɪt] *vi*: **to ~ with** współczuć *+dat*; (*verbally*) składać (złożyć *perf*) wyrazy współczucia *+dat*
**commission** [kəˈmɪʃən] *n* (*order for work*) zamówienie *nt*, zlecenie *nt*; (*Comm*) prowizja *f* (od sprzedaży); (*committee*) komisja *f*; (*Mil*) stanowisko *nt* oficerskie ▷ *vt* (*work of art*) zamawiać (zamówić *perf*); (*army officer*) mianować (mianować *perf*); **to be out of ~** nie funkcjonować; **I get 10% ~** dostaję 10% prowizji; **~ of inquiry** komisja dochodzeniowa; **to ~ sb to do sth** zlecać (zlecić *perf*) komuś zrobienie czegoś; **to ~ sth from sb** zamawiać (zamówić *perf*) coś u kogoś
**commissionaire** [kəmɪʃəˈnɛə^r] (*Brit*) *n* portier *m* (*w liberii*)
**commissioner** [kəˈmɪʃənə^r] *n* komisarz *m*
**commit** [kəˈmɪt] *vt* (*crime, murder*) popełniać (popełnić *perf*); (*money, resources*) przeznaczać (przeznaczyć *perf*); (*person*): **she was ~ted to a hospital/nursing home** umieszczono ją w szpitalu/prywatnym domu opieki; **to ~ o.s. (to do sth)** zobowiązywać się (zobowiązać się *perf*) (do zrobienia czegoś); **to ~ suicide** popełnić (*perf*) samobójstwo; **to ~ sth to writing** zapisywać (zapisać *perf*) *or* notować (zanotować *perf*) coś; **to ~ sb for trial** stawiać (postawić *perf*) kogoś w stan oskarżenia
**commitment** [kəˈmɪtmənt] *n* zobowiązanie *nt*; (*to ideology, system*) oddanie *nt*, zaangażowanie *nt*
**committed** [kəˈmɪtɪd] *adj* (*writer, politician*) zaangażowany; (*Christian*) wierny
**committee** [kəˈmɪtɪ] *n* komisja *f*, komitet *m*; **to be on a ~** zasiadać *or* być w komisji
**committee meeting** *n* posiedzenie *nt* komisji
**commodity** [kəˈmɔdɪtɪ] *n* towar *m*; **commodities** (*food*) artykuły *pl* spożywcze
**common** [ˈkɔmən] *adj* (*shared*) wspólny; (*ordinary*: *object, name, species*) pospolity; (: *experience, phenomenon*) powszechny; (*vulgar*) prostacki ▷ *n* błonia *pl* (wiejskie); **the Commons** (*Brit*) *npl* Izba *f* Gmin; **to have sth in ~ (with sb)** mieć coś wspólnego (z kimś); **we have sth in ~** mamy ze sobą coś wspólnego; **in ~ use** w powszechnym użyciu; **it's ~ knowledge that ...** powszechnie wiadomo, że ...; **for the ~ good** dla wspólnego dobra, dla dobra ogółu
**commoner** [ˈkɔmənə^r] *n* człowiek *m* z ludu
**common ground** *n* (*fig*) wspólna płaszczyzna *f*
**common law** *n* prawo *nt* zwyczajowe
**common-law** [ˈkɔmənlɔː] *adj*: **~ wife** konkubina *f*; **~ marriage** nieślubny związek
**commonly** [ˈkɔmənlɪ] *adv* powszechnie

**Common Market** *n*: **the ~** Wspólny Rynek *m*
**commonplace** ['kɔmənpleɪs] *adj* powszedni, zwykły
**common room** *n* (*Scol*) ≈ świetlica *f* (szkolna); (*Univ*) ≈ klub *m*
**common sense** *n* zdrowy rozsądek *m*
**Commonwealth** ['kɔmənwɛlθ] (*Brit*) *n*: **the ~** (Brytyjska) Wspólnota *f* Narodów
**commotion** [kə'məuʃən] *n* zamieszanie *nt*, rozgardiasz *m*
**communal** ['kɔmju:nl] *adj* (*property*) wspólny, społeczny; **~ life** życie we wspólnocie
**commune** [*n* 'kɔmju:n, *vb* kə'mju:n] *n* (*group*) wspólnota *f*; (*Pol*) komuna *f* ▷ *vi*: **to ~ with** (*nature, God*) obcować z *+instr*
**communicate** [kə'mju:nɪkeɪt] *vt* przekazywać (przekazać *perf*) ▷ *vi* (*by speech, gesture*) porozumiewać się (porozumieć się *perf*), komunikować się; (*by letter, telephone*) kontaktować się (skontaktować się *perf*), komunikować się
**communication** [kəmju:nɪ'keɪʃən] *n* (*process*) porozumiewanie się *nt*, komunikowanie się *nt*; (*message*) wiadomość *f*
**communication cord** (*Brit*) *n* (*on train*) ≈ hamulec *m* bezpieczeństwa
**communications network** [kəmju:nɪ'keɪʃənz-] *n* sieć *f* informacyjna
**communications satellite** *n* satelita *m* (tele) komunikacyjny
**communicative** [kə'mju:nɪkətɪv] *adj* (*person*) rozmowny
**communion** [kə'mju:nɪən] *n* (*also*: **Holy Communion**) komunia *f*, Komunia *f* (Święta)
**communiqué** [kə'mju:nɪkeɪ] *n* komunikat *m*
**communism** ['kɔmjunɪzəm] *n* komunizm *m*
**communist** ['kɔmjunɪst] *adj* komunistyczny ▷ *n* komunista(-tka) *m(f)*
**community** [kə'mju:nɪtɪ] *n* (*local*) społeczność *f*; (*national*) społeczeństwo *nt*; (*business etc*) środowisko *nt*
**community centre** *n* ≈ dom *m* *or* ośrodek *m* kultury
**community charge** (*Brit*) *n* *opłata na rzecz społeczności lokalnej uprawniająca do głosowania*
**community chest** (*US*) *n* lokalny fundusz *m* zapomogowy
**community health centre** *n* ≈ przychodnia *f* rejonowa
**community home** (*Brit*) *n* ≈ dom *m* poprawczy
**community service** *n* praca *f* społeczna (*wykonywana dobrowolnie lub jako kara za drobne wykroczenia*)
**community spirit** *n* poczucie *nt* *or* duch *m* wspólnoty
**commutation ticket** [kɔmju'teɪʃən-] (*US*) *n* bilet *m* okresowy (*dla dojeżdżających do pracy*)
**commute** [kə'mju:t] *vi* dojeżdżać (do pracy) ▷ *vt* (*Jur*: *sentence*) zamieniać (zamienić *perf*) (*na lżejszy*); (*pension*) zmieniać (zmienić *perf*) formę wypłaty *+gen*
**commuter** [kə'mju:tə<sup>r</sup>] *n* dojeżdżający(-ca) *m(f)* do pracy
**compact** [*adj* kəm'pækt, *n* 'kɔmpækt] *adj* niewielkich rozmiarów *post* ▷ *n* (*also*: **powder compact**) puderniczka *f*
**compact disc** *n* płyta *f* kompaktowa
**compact disc player** *n* odtwarzacz *m* kompaktowy
**companion** [kəm'pænjən] *n* towarzysz(ka) *m(f)*
**companionship** [kəm'pænjənʃɪp] *n* (*company*) towarzystwo *nt*; (*friendship*) przyjaźń *f*
**companionway** [kəm'pænjənweɪ] (*Naut*) *n* zejściówka *f*
**company** ['kʌmpənɪ] *n* (*Comm*) firma *f*, przedsiębiorstwo *nt*; (*Theat*) zespół *m* (teatralny), trupa *f* (*old*); (*Mil*) kompania *f*; (*companionship*) towarzystwo *nt*; **insurance ~** towarzystwo ubezpieczeniowe; **Smith and C~** Smith i spółka; **he's good ~** dobry z niego kompan; **we have ~** mamy towarzystwo; **to keep sb ~** towarzyszyć (potowarzyszyć *perf*) komuś; **to part ~ with** rozstawać się (rozstać się *perf*) z *+instr*
**company car** *n* samochód *m* służbowy
**company director** *n* dyrektor *m* spółki
**company secretary** (*Brit*) *n* sekretarz *m* spółki
**comparable** ['kɔmpərəbl] *adj* (*size, style etc*) porównywalny; (*car, property etc*) podobny, zbliżony; **~ to** porównywalny z *+instr*
**comparative** [kəm'pærətɪv] *adj* (*peace, safety*) względny; (*study, literature*) porównawczy; (*adjective, adverb*) w stopniu wyższym *post*; **a ~ stranger** ktoś stosunkowo mało znany
**comparatively** [kəm'pærətɪvlɪ] *adv* stosunkowo, względnie
**compare** [kəm'pɛə<sup>r</sup>] *vt*: **to ~ sb/sth with/to** (*contrast*) porównywać (porównać *perf*) kogoś/coś z *+instr*; **to ~ sb/sth to** (*liken*) porównywać (porównać *perf*) kogoś/coś z *+instr*, przyrównywać (przyrównać *perf*) kogoś/coś do *+gen* ▷ *vi*: **to ~ (un)favourably with** wypadać (wypaść *perf*) (nie)korzystnie w porównaniu z *+instr*; **how do the prices ~?** jak mają się do siebie ceny?; **~d with** *or* **to** w porównaniu z *+instr*
**comparison** [kəm'pærɪsn] *n* porównanie *nt*; **in ~ with** w porównaniu z *+instr*
**compartment** [kəm'pɑ:tmənt] *n* (*Rail*) przedział *m*; (*of wallet*) przegródka *f*; (*of fridge*) komora *f*

C

**compass** ['kʌmpəs] *n* (*Naut*) kompas *m*; (*Geom*) cyrkiel *m*; (*fig*: *of activity*) zasięg *m*; (: *of voice, musical instrument*) skala *f*; **compasses** *npl* (*also*: **pair of compasses**) cyrkiel *m*; **beyond/within the ~ of** poza zasięgiem/w zasięgu *+gen*
**compassion** [kəm'pæʃən] *n* współczucie *nt*
**compassionate** [kəm'pæʃənɪt] *adj* współczujący; **on ~ grounds** ze względów rodzinnych (*urlop itp*)
**compatibility** [kəmpætɪ'bɪlɪtɪ] *n* zgodność *f*; (*Comput*) kompatybilność *f*
**compatible** [kəm'pætɪbl] *adj* zgodny; (*Comput*) kompatybilny
**compel** [kəm'pɛl] *vt* zmuszać (zmusić *perf*), przymuszać (przymusić *perf*)
**compelling** [kəm'pɛlɪŋ] *adj* (*argument, reason*) nie do odparcia *post*; (*poem, painting*) przykuwający uwagę
**compendium** [kəm'pɛndɪəm] *n* kompendium *nt*
**compensate** ['kɔmpənseɪt] *vt* dawać (dać *perf*) odszkodowanie *+dat* ▷ *vi*: **to ~ for** rekompensować (zrekompensować *perf*) sobie *+acc*
**compensation** [kɔmpən'seɪʃən] *n* (*money*) odszkodowanie *nt*; (*for loss, disappointment*) rekompensata *f*; (*Psych etc*) kompensacja *f*
**compère** ['kɔmpɛəʳ] *n* (*TV, Radio*) gospodarz(-dyni) *m(f)* programu
**compete** [kəm'pi:t] *vi* (*in contest, game*) brać (wziąć *perf*) udział; **to ~ (with)** (*companies, theories*) rywalizować *or* konkurować (z *+instr*); (*sportsmen*) rywalizować *or* współzawodniczyć (z *+instr*); **to ~ (for)** walczyć (o *+acc*)
**competence** ['kɔmpɪtəns] *n* kompetencje *pl*, fachowość *f*
**competent** ['kɔmpɪtənt] *adj* (*person*) kompetentny, fachowy; (*piece of work*) fachowo wykonany
**competition** [kɔmpɪ'tɪʃən] *n* (*between firms, rivals*) rywalizacja *f*, współzawodnictwo *nt*; (*contest*) konkurs *m*, zawody *pl*; (*Econ*) konkurencja *f*; **to be in ~ with** konkurować *or* rywalizować z *+instr*
**competitive** [kəm'pɛtɪtɪv] *adj* (*industry, society*) oparty na współzawodnictwie; (*person*) nastawiony na współzawodnictwo; (*price, product*) konkurencyjny; (*sport*) wyczynowy
**competitive examination** *n* egzamin *m* konkursowy
**competitor** [kəm'pɛtɪtəʳ] *n* (*rival*) konkurent(ka) *m(f)*, rywal(ka) *m(f)*; (*participant*) zawodnik(-iczka) *m(f)*, uczestnik(-iczka) *m(f)*
**compile** [kəm'paɪl] *vt* (*report*) opracowywać (opracować *perf*); (*dictionary*) kompilować (skompilować *perf*)
**complacency** [kəm'pleɪsnsɪ] *n* samozadowolenie *nt*
**complacent** [kəm'pleɪsnt] *adj* (*person*) zadowolony z siebie; (*smile, attitude*) pełen samozadowolenia
**complain** [kəm'pleɪn] *vi*: **to ~ (about)** (*grumble*) narzekać (na *+acc*); (*protest*: *to authorities, bank*) składać (złożyć *perf*) zażalenie *or* skargę (z powodu *+gen*); (: *to shop*) zgłaszać (zgłosić *perf*) reklamację (*+gen*); **to ~ of** (*pain etc*) skarżyć się na *+acc*
**complaint** [kəm'pleɪnt] *n* (*activity*) narzekanie *nt*; (*instance*) skarga *f*; (*in shop etc*) reklamacja *f*; (*reason for complaining*) zarzut *m*; (*Med*) dolegliwość *f*; **a letter of ~** (pisemne) zażalenie
**complement** [*n* 'kɔmplɪmənt, *vb* 'kɔmplɪmɛnt] *n* (*supplement*) uzupełnienie *nt*; (*crew*) skład *m*, załoga *f* ▷ *vt*: **to ~ each other/one another** wzajemnie się uzupełniać; **to have a full ~ of** mieć komplet *+gen*
**complementary** [kɔmplɪ'mɛntərɪ] *adj* wzajemnie się uzupełniający; **to be ~** wzajemnie się uzupełniać; **~ medicine** lek wspomagający *or* pomocniczy
**complete** [kəm'pli:t] *adj* (*silence, change, success*) zupełny, całkowity; (*list, edition, set*) cały, kompletny; (*building, task*) ukończony ▷ *vt* (*building, task*) ukończyć (*perf*); (*set, group*) dopełniać (dopełnić *perf*); (*form*) wypełniać (wypełnić *perf*); **a silk tie ~d the outfit** stroju dopełniał jedwabny krawat
**completely** [kəm'pli:tlɪ] *adv* zupełnie, całkowicie, kompletnie
**completion** [kəm'pli:ʃən] *n* (*of building*) ukończenie *nt*; (*of sale*) sfinalizowanie *nt*; **to be nearing ~** być na ukończeniu; **on ~ of** po ukończeniu *+gen*
**complex** ['kɔmplɛks] *adj* złożony ▷ *n* kompleks *m*
**complexion** [kəm'plɛkʃən] *n* cera *f*, karnacja *f*; (*fig*: *of event, problem*) zabarwienie *nt*
**complexity** [kəm'plɛksɪtɪ] *n* złożoność *f*
**compliance** [kəm'plaɪəns] *n* uległość *f*; **~ with** podporządkowanie się *+dat*; **in ~ with** zgodnie z *+instr*
**compliant** [kəm'plaɪənt] *adj* uległy
**complicate** ['kɔmplɪkeɪt] *vt* komplikować (skomplikować *perf*)
**complicated** ['kɔmplɪkeɪtɪd] *adj* skomplikowany
**complication** [kɔmplɪ'keɪʃən] *n* (*problem*) szkopuł *m*; (*Med*) powikłanie *nt*, komplikacja *f*
**complicity** [kəm'plɪsɪtɪ] *n* współudział *m*
**compliment** [*n* 'kɔmplɪmənt, *vb* 'kɔmplɪmɛnt] *n* komplement *m* ▷ *vt* gratulować (pogratulować *perf*) *+dat*;

**compliments** *npl* uszanowanie *nt*, wyrazy *pl* uszanowania; **to pay sb a ~** powiedzieć *(perf)* komuś komplement; **to ~ sb (on sth/on doing sth)** gratulować (pogratulować *perf*) komuś (czegoś/zrobienia czegoś)

**complimentary** [kɔmplɪ'mɛntərɪ] *adj* *(remark)* pochlebny; *(ticket, copy of book)* bezpłatny, gratisowy

**compliments slip** *n* bilet *m* *or* bilecik *m* (grzecznościowy)

**comply** [kəm'plaɪ] *vi*: **to ~ (with)** stosować się (zastosować się *perf*) (do *+gen*)

**component** [kəm'pəunənt] *adj* składowy ▷ *n* składnik *m*

**compose** [kəm'pəuz] *vt*: **to be ~d of** składać się *or* być złożonym z *+gen* ▷ *vt* komponować (skomponować *perf*); **to ~ o.s.** opanowywać się (opanować się *perf*), uspokajać się (uspokoić się *perf*)

**composed** [kəm'pəuzd] *adj* opanowany, spokojny

**composer** [kəm'pəuzə[r]] *n* kompozytor(ka) *m(f)*

**composite** ['kɔmpəzɪt] *adj* *(fee)* łączny; *(resolution, character)* zbiorowy ▷ *n* połączenie *nt*

**composition** [kɔmpə'zɪʃən] *n* *(of substance, group)* skład *m*; *(essay)* wypracowanie *nt*; *(Mus)* kompozycja *f*

**compositor** [kəm'pɔzɪtə[r]] *n* zecer *m*, składacz *m*

**compos mentis** ['kɔmpɔs 'mentɪs] *adj* w pełni władz umysłowych *post*

**compost** ['kɔmpɔst] *n* *(decaying material)* kompost *m*; *(also:* **potting compost***)* podłoże *nt* kwiatowe

**composure** [kəm'pəuʒə[r]] *n* opanowanie *nt*, spokój *m*

**compound** [*n, adj* 'kɔmpaund, *vb* kəm'paund] *n* *(Chem)* związek *m*; *(enclosure)* ogrodzony *or* zamknięty teren *m*; *(Ling)* wyraz *m* złożony ▷ *adj* *(structure)* złożony; *(eye, leaf)* o złożonej budowie *post* ▷ *vt* *(fig: problem, difficulty)* pogłębiać; *(: error)* zwiększać

**compound fracture** *n* złamanie *nt* otwarte

**compound interest** *n* odsetki *pl* łączne

**comprehend** [kɔmprɪ'hɛnd] *vt* pojmować (pojąć *perf*)

**comprehension** [kɔmprɪ'hɛnʃən] *n* *(ability)* zdolność *f* pojmowania; *(understanding)* zrozumienie *nt*; **it's beyond my ~** nie jestem w stanie tego pojąć; **it's beyond all ~** to przechodzi ludzkie pojęcie; **listening ~** rozumienie ze słuchu

**comprehensive** [kɔmprɪ'hɛnsɪv] *adj* pełny

**comprehensive (school)** *(Brit)* *n* *państwowa szkoła średnia, do której przyjmuje się dzieci niezależnie od dotychczasowych wyników w nauce*

**compress** [*vb* kəm'prɛs, *n* 'kɔmprɛs] *vt* ściskać (ścisnąć *perf*); *(air, gas)* sprężać (sprężyć *perf*); *(text, information)* kondensować (skondensować *perf*) ▷ *n* kompres *m*

**compressed air** [kəm'prɛst-] *n* sprężone powietrze *nt*

**compression** [kəm'prɛʃən] *n* ściskanie *nt*; *(of gas, air)* sprężanie *nt*

**comprise** [kəm'praɪz] *vt* *(also:* **be comprised of***)* składać się *or* być złożonym z *+gen*; *(constitute)* stanowić, składać się na *+acc*

**compromise** ['kɔmprəmaɪz] *n* kompromis *m* ▷ *vt* *(beliefs, principles)* narażać (narazić *perf*) (na szwank) ▷ *vi* iść (pójść *perf*) na kompromis, zawierać (zawrzeć *perf*) kompromis ▷ *cpd* kompromisowy; **to ~ sb/o.s.** skompromitować *(perf)* kogoś/się

**compulsion** [kəm'pʌlʃən] *n* *(desire)* wewnętrzny przymus *m*; *(pressure)* przymus *m*; **under ~** pod przymusem

**compulsive** [kəm'pʌlsɪv] *adj* *(liar, gambler)* nałogowy; **it's ~ viewing/reading** *etc* nie można się od tego oderwać *(o filmie, książce itp)*

**compulsory** [kəm'pʌlsərɪ] *adj* *(attendance)* obowiązkowy; *(retirement)* przymusowy

**compulsory purchase** *n* wywłaszczenie *nt*

**compunction** [kəm'pʌŋkʃən] *n* skrupuły *pl*, wyrzuty *pl* (sumienia); **to have no ~ about doing sth** robić (zrobić *perf*) coś bez żadnych skrupułów

**computer** [kəm'pju:tə[r]] *n* komputer *m* ▷ *cpd* komputerowy

**computer game** *n* gra *f* komputerowa

**computerization** [kəmpju:təraɪ'zeɪʃən] *n* komputeryzacja *f*

**computerize** [kəm'pju:təraɪz] *vt* *(system, filing etc)* komputeryzować (skomputeryzować *perf*); *(information)* przetwarzać (przetworzyć *perf*) komputerowo

**computer programmer** *n* programista(-tka) *m(f)*

**computer programming** *n* programowanie *nt*

**computer science** *n* informatyka *f*

**computer scientist** *n* informatyk(-yczka) *m(f)*

**computing** [kəm'pju:tɪŋ] *n* *(activity)* praca *f* na komputerze; *(science)* informatyka *f*

**comrade** ['kɔmrɪd] *n* towarzysz(ka) *m(f)*

**comradeship** ['kɔmrɪdʃɪp] *n* koleżeństwo *nt*; **~ of war** braterstwo broni

**comsat** ['kɔmsæt] *n abbr* (= *communications satellite*) satelita *m* telekomunikacyjny

**con** [kɔn] *vt* nabierać (nabrać *perf*) *(inf)*, kantować (okantować *perf*) *(inf)* ▷ *n* kant *m* *(inf)*; **to con sb into doing sth** naciągać (naciągnąć *perf*) kogoś na zrobienie czegoś *(inf)*

**concave** ['kɔnkeɪv] *adj* wklęsły

**conceal** [kən'si:l] *vt* ukrywać (ukryć *perf*)
**concede** [kən'si:d] *vt* przyznawać (przyznać *perf*) ▷ *vi* ustępować (ustąpić *perf*), dawać (dać *perf*) za wygraną
**conceit** [kən'si:t] *n* zarozumiałość *f*
**conceited** [kən'si:tɪd] *adj* zarozumiały
**conceivable** [kən'si:vəbl] *adj* wyobrażalny; **there is no ~ reason why...** trudno wyobrazić sobie przyczynę, dla której ...; **it is ~ that ...** niewykluczone, że ...
**conceivably** [kən'si:vəblɪ] *adv*: **he may ~ be right** niewykluczone, że ma rację
**conceive** [kən'si:v] *vt* (*child*) począć (*perf*); (*plan*) obmyślić (*perf*), wymyślić (*perf*) ▷ *vi* (*Bio*) zajść (*perf*) w ciążę; **to ~ of sth/of doing sth** wyobrażać (wyobrazić *perf*) sobie coś/, że coś się zrobi
**concentrate** ['kɔnsəntreɪt] *vi* skupiać się (skupić się *perf*), koncentrować się (skoncentrować się *perf*) ▷ *vt* skupiać (skupić *perf*), koncentrować (skoncentrować *perf*)
**concentration** [kɔnsən'treɪʃən] *n* skupienie *nt*, koncentracja *f*; (*Chem*) stężenie *nt*
**concentration camp** *n* obóz *m* koncentracyjny
**concentric** [kɔn'sɛntrɪk] *adj* koncentryczny
**concept** ['kɔnsɛpt] *n* pojęcie *nt*
**conception** [kən'sɛpʃən] *n* (*idea*) koncepcja *f*; (*of child*) poczęcie *nt*
**concern** [kən'sə:n] *n* (*affair*) sprawa *f*; (*anxiety*) obawa *f*; (*worry*) zmartwienie *nt*, troska *f*; (*care*) troska *f*; (*Comm*) koncern *m* ▷ *vt* (*worry*) martwić (zmartwić *perf*); (*relate to*) dotyczyć *+gen*; **to be ~ed (about)** martwić się (o *+acc*); **to be ~ed with, ~ o.s. with** interesować się *+instr*; **"to whom it may ~"** „do wszystkich zainteresowanych"; **as far as I am ~ed** jeśli o mnie chodzi; **the people ~ed** zainteresowani
**concerning** [kən'sə:nɪŋ] *prep* dotyczący *+gen*
**concert** ['kɔnsət] *n* (*Mus*) koncert *m*; **to be in ~** (*Mus*) dawać koncert; **in ~** (*in cooperation*) wspólnie
**concerted** [kən'sə:tɪd] *adj* (*effort etc*) wspólny
**concert hall** *n* sala *f* koncertowa
**concertina** [kɔnsə'ti:nə] *n* (*instrument*) harmonia *f* ▷ *vi* (*fig*) składać się (złożyć się *perf*) w harmonijkę
**concerto** [kən'tʃə:təu] *n* koncert *m*; **piano/violin ~** koncert fortepianowy/skrzypcowy
**concession** [kən'sɛʃən] *n* (*compromise*) ustępstwo *nt*; (*Comm*) koncesja *f*; **tax ~** ulga podatkowa
**concessionaire** [kənsɛʃə'nɛəʳ] *n* koncesjonariusz(ka) *m(f)*
**concessionary** [kən'sɛʃənrɪ] *adj* (*fare etc*) ulgowy
**conciliation** [kənsɪlɪ'eɪʃən] *n* pojednanie *nt*
**conciliatory** [kən'sɪlɪətrɪ] *adj* pojednawczy
**concise** [kən'saɪs] *adj* zwięzły
**conclave** ['kɔnkleɪv] *n* tajne zebranie *nt*; (*Rel*) konklawe *nt inv*
**conclude** [kən'klu:d] *vt* (*speech, chapter*) kończyć (zakończyć *perf*); (*treaty, deal*) zawierać (zawrzeć *perf*); (*deduce*) wnioskować (wywnioskować *perf*) ▷ *vi*: **to ~ (with)** (*speaker*) kończyć (zakończyć *perf*) (*+instr*); (*event*) kończyć się (zakończyć się *perf*) (*+instr*); **"that," he ~d, "is why we did it"** „oto dlaczego to zrobiliśmy" — zakończył; **I ~ that ...** wnioskuję, że...
**conclusion** [kən'klu:ʒən] *n* (*of speech, chapter*) zakończenie *nt*; (*of treaty, deal*) zawarcie *nt*; (*deduction*) wniosek *m*, konkluzja *f*; **to come to the ~ that ...** dochodzić (dojść *perf*) do wniosku, że ...
**conclusive** [kən'klu:sɪv] *adj* (*evidence*) niezbity; (*defeat*) ostateczny
**concoct** [kən'kɔkt] *vt* (*excuse etc*) preparować (spreparować *perf*); (*meal*) zaimprowizować (*perf*)
**concoction** [kən'kɔkʃən] *n* (*mixture*) mikstura *f*; (*food, drink*) mieszanka *f*
**concord** ['kɔŋkɔ:d] *n* (*harmony, agreement*) zgoda *f*; (*treaty*) ugoda *f*
**concourse** ['kɔŋkɔ:s] *n* (*in building*) hol *m*; (*crowd*) zgromadzenie *nt*
**concrete** ['kɔŋkri:t] *n* beton *m* ▷ *adj* betonowy; (*fig*) konkretny
**concrete mixer** *n* betoniarka *f*
**concur** [kən'kə:ʳ] *vi* (*events*) zbiegać się (zbiec się *perf*); (*person*): **to ~ with** zgadzać się (zgodzić się *perf*) z *+instr*
**concurrently** [kən'kʌrntlɪ] *adv* w tym samym czasie, jednocześnie
**concussion** [kən'kʌʃən] *n* wstrząs *m* mózgu
**condemn** [kən'dɛm] *vt* (*action*) potępiać (potępić *perf*); (*prisoner*) skazywać (skazać *perf*); (*building*) przeznaczać (przeznaczyć *perf*) do rozbiórki
**condemnation** [kɔndɛm'neɪʃən] *n* potępienie *nt*
**condensation** [kɔndɛn'seɪʃən] *n* (*on wall, window*) skroplona para *f*
**condense** [kən'dɛns] *vi* skraplać się (skroplić się *perf*) ▷ *vt* (*report, information*) skondensować (*perf*)
**condensed milk** [kən'dɛnst-] *n* mleko *nt* zagęszczone
**condescend** [kɔndɪ'sɛnd] *vi* zniżać się (zniżyć się *perf*); **he ~ed to have dinner with us** raczył zjeść z nami obiad
**condescending** [kɔndɪ'sɛndɪŋ] *adj* protekcjonalny
**condition** [kən'dɪʃən] *n* (*state*) stan *m*; (*requirement*) warunek *m* ▷ *vt* (*person*)

formować (uformować *perf*); (*hair*) nakładać (nałożyć *perf*) odżywkę na *+acc*; **conditions** *npl* warunki *pl*; **in good/poor ~** w dobrym/złym stanie; **a heart ~** choroba serca; **weather ~s** warunki atmosferyczne; **on ~ that ...** pod warunkiem, że ...

**conditional** [kən'dɪʃənl] *adj* warunkowy; **to be ~ upon** być uzależnionym od *+gen*

**conditioner** [kən'dɪʃənə^r] *n* (*for hair*) odżywka *f*; (*for fabrics*) płyn *m* zmiękczający

**condo** ['kɔndəu] (*US: inf*) *n abbr* = **condominium**

**condolences** [kən'dəulənsɪz] *npl* kondolencje *pl*

**condom** ['kɔndəm] *n* prezerwatywa *f*, kondom *m* (*inf*)

**condominium** [kɔndə'mɪnɪəm] (*US*) *n* (*building*) *blok z mieszkaniami własnościowymi*; (*apartment*) ≈ mieszkanie *nt* własnościowe

**condone** [kən'dəun] *vt* akceptować, godzić się na *+acc*

**conducive** [kən'dju:sɪv] *adj*: **~ to** sprzyjający *+dat*

**conduct** [*n* 'kɔndʌkt, *vb* kən'dʌkt] *n* (*of person*) zachowanie *nt* ▷ *vt* (*survey, research*) przeprowadzać (przeprowadzić *perf*); (*life*) prowadzić; (*orchestra, choir*) dyrygować *+instr*; (*heat, electricity*) przewodzić; **to ~ o.s.** zachowywać się

**conducted tour** [kən'dʌktɪd-] *n* wycieczka *f* z przewodnikiem

**conductor** [kən'dʌktə^r] *n* (*of orchestra*) dyrygent *m*; (*on bus, train*) konduktor *m*; (*Elec*) przewodnik *m*

**conductress** [kən'dʌktrɪs] *n* (*on bus*) konduktorka *f*

**conduit** ['kɔndjuɪt] *n* przewód *m*, kanał *m*

**cone** [kəun] *n* (*shape*) stożek *m*; (*on road*) pachołek *m*; (*ice cream*) rożek *m*; (*Bot*) szyszka *f*

**confectioner** [kən'fɛkʃənə^r] *n* cukiernik *m*

**confectioner's (shop)** [kən'fɛkʃənəz-] *n* sklep *m* ze słodyczami

**confectionery** [kən'fɛkʃənrɪ] *n* (*sweets, candies*) słodycze *pl*; (*cakes*) ciasta *pl*

**confederate** [kən'fɛdrɪt] *n* (*accomplice*) wspólnik(-iczka) *m(f)*; (*US*) konfederat *m*

**confederation** [kənfɛdə'reɪʃən] *n* konfederacja *f*

**confer** [kən'fə:^r] *vt*: **to ~ sth on sb** nadawać (nadać *perf*) coś komuś ▷ *vi* (*jury, panel*) naradzać się; **to ~ with sb/about sth** naradzać się (naradzić się *perf*) z kimś/nad czymś

**conference** ['kɔnfərəns] *n* konferencja *f*; (*daily, routine*) narada *f*; **to be in ~** mieć naradę

**conference room** *n* pokój *m* konferencyjny

**confess** [kən'fɛs] *vt* (*sin, guilt*) wyznawać (wyznać *perf*); (*crime, ignorance, weakness*) przyznawać się (przyznać się *perf*) do *+gen* ▷ *vi* przyznawać się (przyznać się *perf*); **to ~ to** przyznawać się (przyznać się *perf*) do *+gen*; **I must ~ that I didn't enjoy it at all** muszę przyznać, że wcale mnie to nie bawiło

**confession** [kən'fɛʃən] *n* (*admission*) przyznanie się *nt*; (*Rel: of sins*) spowiedź *f*; (*: of faith*) wyznanie *nt*; **to make a ~** czynić (uczynić *perf*) wyznanie

**confessor** [kən'fɛsə^r] *n* spowiednik *m*

**confetti** [kən'fɛtɪ] *n* konfetti *nt inv*

**confide** [kən'faɪd] *vi*: **to ~ in** zwierzać się (zwierzyć się *perf*) *+dat*

**confidence** ['kɔnfɪdns] *n* (*faith*) zaufanie *nt*; (*self-assurance*) pewność *f* siebie; (*secret*) zwierzenie *nt*; **to have ~ in sb/sth** wierzyć w kogoś/coś; **to have (every) ~ that ...** być (święcie) przekonanym, że ...; **motion of no ~** wotum nieufności; **I'm telling you this in (strict) ~** mówię ci to w (największej) tajemnicy

**confidence trick** *n* oszustwo *nt*

**confident** ['kɔnfɪdənt] *adj* (*self-assured*) pewny siebie; (*positive*) pewny

**confidential** [kɔnfɪ'dɛnʃəl] *adj* (*information, tone*) poufny; (*secretary*) zaufany

**confidentiality** [kɔnfɪdɛnʃɪ'ælɪtɪ] *n* poufność *f*

**configuration** [kənfɪgju'reɪʃən] *n* konfiguracja *f*

**confine** [kən'faɪn] *vt*: **to ~ (to)** (*limit*) ograniczać (ograniczyć *perf*) (do *+gen*); (*shut up*) zamykać (zamknąć *perf*) (w *+loc*); **to ~ o.s. to doing sth/to sth** ograniczać się (ograniczyć się *perf*) do (z)robienia czegoś/do czegoś

**confined** [kən'faɪnd] *adj* ograniczony

**confinement** [kən'faɪnmənt] *n* (*imprisonment*) zamknięcie *nt*; (*Med*) poród *m*

**confines** ['kɔnfaɪnz] *npl*: **within the ~ of** (*area*) w granicach *+gen*; (*situation*) w ramach *+gen*

**confirm** [kən'fə:m] *vt* potwierdzać (potwierdzić *perf*); **to be ~ed** (*Rel*) być bierzmowanym

**confirmation** [kɔnfə'meɪʃən] *n* potwierdzenie *nt*; (*Rel*) bierzmowanie *nt*

**confirmed** [kən'fə:md] *adj* (*bachelor, teetotaller*) zaprzysięgły

**confiscate** ['kɔnfɪskeɪt] *vt* konfiskować (skonfiskować *perf*)

**confiscation** [kɔnfɪs'keɪʃən] *n* konfiskata *f*

**conflagration** [kɔnflə'greɪʃən] *n* pożoga *f*

**conflict** [*n* 'kɔnflɪkt, *vb* kən'flɪkt] *n* konflikt *m* ▷ *vi* ścierać się (zetrzeć się *perf*)

**conflicting** [kən'flɪktɪŋ] *adj* sprzeczny

**conform** [kən'fɔːm] *vi* dostosowywać się (dostosować się *perf*), podporządkowywać się (podporządkować się *perf*); **to ~ to** (*wish, ideal, standard*) odpowiadać *+dat*
**conformist** [kən'fɔːmɪst] *n* konformista(-tka) *m(f)*
**confound** [kən'faund] *vt* wprawiać (wprawić *perf*) w zakłopotanie
**confounded** [kən'faundɪd] *adj* przeklęty
**confront** [kən'frʌnt] *vt* (*problems, task*) stawać (stanąć *perf*) przed *+instr*; (*enemy, danger*) stawiać (stawić *perf*) czoło *+dat*
**confrontation** [kɔnfrən'teɪʃən] *n* konfrontacja *f*
**confuse** [kən'fjuːz] *vt* (*perplex*) wprawiać (wprawić *perf*) w zakłopotanie; (*mix up*) mylić (pomylić *perf*); (*complicate*) gmatwać (pogmatwać *perf*)
**confused** [kən'fjuːzd] *adj* (*bewildered*) zakłopotany, zmieszany; (*disordered*) pogmatwany; **to get ~** gubić się (pogubić się *perf*)
**confusing** [kən'fjuːzɪŋ] *adj* (*plot, instructions*) zagmatwany; (*signals*) mylący
**confusion** [kən'fjuːʒən] *n* (*mix-up*) pomyłka *f*; (*perplexity*) zakłopotanie *nt*, zmieszanie *nt*; (*disorder*) zamieszanie *nt*, zamęt *m*
**congeal** [kən'dʒiːl] *vi* (*blood*) krzepnąć (zakrzepnąć *perf*); (*sauce*) gęstnieć (zgęstnieć *perf*)
**congenial** [kən'dʒiːnɪəl] *adj* (*person*) sympatyczny; (*atmosphere*) przyjemny; (*work, company*) odpowiedni
**congenital** [kən'dʒɛnɪtl] *adj* (*Med*) wrodzony
**conger eel** ['kɔŋgər-] *n* węgorz *m* morski
**congested** [kən'dʒɛstɪd] *adj* (*nose*) zapchany; (*road, area*) zatłoczony
**congestion** [kən'dʒɛstʃən] *n* (*Med*) przekrwienie *nt*; (*of road*) zator *m*
**conglomerate** [kən'glɔmərɪt] *n* (*Comm*) konglomerat *m*
**conglomeration** [kənglɔmə'reɪʃən] *n* zlepek *m*, konglomerat *m*
**Congo** ['kɔŋgəu] *n* Kongo *nt*
**congratulate** [kən'grætjuleɪt] *vt*: **to ~ sb (on)** gratulować (pogratulować *perf*) komuś (*+gen*)
**congratulations** [kəngrætju'leɪʃənz] *npl* gratulacje *pl*; **~!** (moje) gratulacje!, gratuluję!; **~ on** gratulacje z okazji *+gen*
**congregate** ['kɔŋgrɪgeɪt] *vi* gromadzić się (zgromadzić się *perf*)
**congregation** [kɔŋgrɪ'geɪʃən] *n* kongregacja *f*
**congress** ['kɔŋgrɛs] *n* kongres *m*; (*US*): **C~** Kongres *m*
**congressman** ['kɔŋgrɛsmən] (*US*) (*irreg: like* **man**) *n* członek *m* Kongresu, kongresman *m*
**congresswoman** ['kɔŋgrɛswumən] (*US*) (*irreg: like* **woman**) *n* członkini *f* Kongresu
**conical** ['kɔnɪkl] *adj* stożkowy
**conifer** ['kɔnɪfə^r^] *n* drzewo *nt* iglaste
**coniferous** [kə'nɪfərəs] *adj* iglasty
**conjecture** [kən'dʒɛktʃə^r^] *n* domysł *m*, przypuszczenie *nt* ▷ *vi* snuć domysły *or* przypuszczenia, przypuszczać
**conjugal** ['kɔndʒugl] *adj* małżeński
**conjugate** ['kɔndʒugeɪt] *vt* (*Ling*) koniugować, odmieniać (odmienić *perf*)
**conjugation** [kɔndʒə'geɪʃən] *n* koniugacja *f*, odmiana *f* czasownika
**conjunction** [kən'dʒʌŋkʃən] *n* (*Ling*) spójnik *m*; **in ~ with** (*act, work*) wraz z *+instr*; (*treat, consider*) łącznie z *+instr*
**conjunctivitis** [kəndʒʌŋktɪ'vaɪtɪs] *n* zapalenie *nt* spojówek
**conjure** ['kʌndʒə^r^] *vi* pokazywać sztuczki (magiczne) ▷ *vt* (*lit, fig*) wyczarowywać (wyczarować *perf*)
▶ **conjure up** *vt* (*ghost, memories*) wywoływać (wywołać *perf*)
**conjurer** ['kʌndʒərə^r^] *n* sztukmistrz *m*, iluzjonista(-tka) *m(f)*
**conjuring trick** ['kʌndʒərɪŋ-] *n* sztuczka *f* magiczna
**conker** ['kɔŋkə^r^] (*Brit*) *n* kasztan *m*
**conk out** [kɔŋk-] (*inf*) *vi* (*machine, engine*) wysiadać (wysiąść *perf*) (*inf*)
**con man** (*irreg: like* **man**) *n* oszust *m*, kanciarz *m* (*inf*)
**connect** [kə'nɛkt] *vt* (*lit, fig*) łączyć (połączyć *perf*); (*Tel: telephone, subscriber*) podłączać (podłączyć *perf*); (*join*): **to ~ sth (to)** podłączać (podłączyć *perf*) coś (do *+gen*) ▷ *vi*: **to be ~ed with** być związanym z *+instr*; **this train ~s with a bus service to Worcester** z tego pociągu jest dogodna przesiadka na autobus do Worcester
**connection** [kə'nɛkʃən] *n* połączenie *nt*; (*of telephone, subscriber*) podłączenie *nt*; (*Elec*) styk *m*, połączenie *nt*; (*fig*) związek *m*; **in ~ with** w związku z *+instr*; **what is the ~ between them?** co oni mają ze sobą wspólnego?; **business ~s** stosunki handlowe; **I missed my ~** spóźniłem się *or* nie zdążyłem na przesiadkę
**connexion** [kə'nɛkʃən] (*Brit*) *n* = **connection**
**conning tower** ['kɔnɪŋ-] *n* (*Naut*) (pancerna) wieża *f* dowodzenia
**connive** [kə'naɪv] *vi*: **to ~ at** przymykać oczy na *+acc*
**connoisseur** [kɔnɪ'səː^r^] *n* koneser(ka) *m(f)*
**connotation** [kɔnə'teɪʃən] *n* konotacja *f*
**connubial** [kə'njuːbɪəl] *adj* małżeński
**conquer** ['kɔŋkə^r^] *vt* (*Mil*) zdobywać (zdobyć *perf*), podbijać (podbić *perf*); (*fig: fear, feelings*)

przemagać (przemóc *perf*), pokonywać (pokonać *perf*)
**conqueror** ['kɔŋkərə^r] *n* zdobywca *m*
**conquest** ['kɔŋkwɛst] *n* podbój *m*
**cons** [kɔnz] *npl see* **convenience**; **pro**
**conscience** ['kɔnʃəns] *n* sumienie *nt*; **to have a clear/guilty** *or* **bad ~** mieć czyste/nieczyste sumienie; **in all** *or* **good ~** z czystym sumieniem
**conscientious** [kɔnʃɪ'ɛnʃəs] *adj* sumienny
**conscientious objector** *n osoba odmawiająca służby wojskowej ze względu na przekonania*
**conscious** ['kɔnʃəs] *adj* (*awake*) przytomny; (*deliberate*) świadomy; (*aware*): **~ (of)** świadomy (*+gen*); **to become ~ of/that ...** zdać (*perf*) sobie sprawę z *+gen*/, że ...
**consciousness** ['kɔnʃəsnɪs] *n* świadomość *f*; (*Med*) przytomność *f*; **to lose/regain ~** tracić (stracić *perf*)/odzyskiwać (odzyskać *perf*) przytomność
**conscript** ['kɔnskrɪpt] *n* poborowy *m*
**conscription** [kən'skrɪpʃən] *n* pobór *m*
**consecrate** ['kɔnsɪkreɪt] *vt* święcić (poświęcić *perf*)
**consecutive** [kən'sɛkjutɪv] *adj* kolejny; **on three ~ occasions** trzy razy z rzędu
**consensus** [kən'sɛnsəs] *n* (powszechna) zgoda *f*, jednomyślność *f*; **~ (of opinion)** konsensus
**consent** [kən'sɛnt] *n* zgoda *f* ▷ *vi*: **to ~ to** zgadzać się (zgodzić się *perf*) na *+acc*; **by common ~** za obopólną zgodą; **age of ~** pełnoletność (*określona prawnie dolna granica wieku, przy której dopuszcza się współżycie płciowe i zawieranie związków małżeńskich*)
**consequence** ['kɔnsɪkwəns] *n* konsekwencja *f*; **of ~** znaczący, doniosły; **it's of little ~** to nie ma większego znaczenie; **in ~** w rezultacie
**consequently** ['kɔnsɪkwəntlɪ] *adv* w rezultacie
**conservation** [kɔnsə'veɪʃən] *n* (*of environment*) ochrona *f*; (*of paintings, books*) konserwacja *f*; (*of energy, mass, momentum*) zachowanie *nt*; **nature ~** ochrona przyrody; **energy ~** oszczędzanie energii
**conservationist** [kɔnsə'veɪʃnɪst] *n* działacz(ka) *m(f)* na rzecz ochrony przyrody
**conservative** [kən'sə:vətɪv] *adj* (*person, attitude*) konserwatywny, zachowawczy; (*estimate etc*) skromny; (Brit): **C~** konserwatywny ▷ *n* (Brit): **C~** konserwatysta(-tka) *m(f)*
**conservatory** [kən'sə:vətrɪ] *n* (*with plants*) oszklona weranda *f*; (*Mus*) konserwatorium *nt*
**conserve** [kən'sə:v] *vt* (*preserve*) utrzymywać (utrzymać *perf*), chronić; (*supplies, energy*) oszczędzać (zaoszczędzić *perf*) ▷ *n* konfitury *pl*
**consider** [kən'sɪdə^r] *vt* (*believe*): **to ~ sb/sth as** uważać kogoś/coś za *+acc*; (*study, take into account*) rozważać (rozważyć *perf*); (*regard, judge*) rozpatrywać (rozpatrzyć *perf*); **to ~ doing sth** rozważać (rozważyć *perf*) zrobienie czegoś; **they ~ themselves to be superior** uważają się za lepszych; **she ~ed it a disaster** uważała to za klęskę; **he is generally ~ed to have invented the first computer** powszechnie uważa się go za wynalazcę pierwszego komputera; **~ yourself lucky** masz *or* miałeś szczęście; **all things ~ed** wziąwszy wszystko pod uwagę
**considerable** [kən'sɪdərəbl] *adj* znaczny
**considerably** [kən'sɪdərəblɪ] *adv* znacznie
**considerate** [kən'sɪdərɪt] *adj* liczący się z innymi; **it was very ~ of you to remember her birthday** to bardzo ładnie, że pamiętałeś o jej urodzinach
**consideration** [kənsɪdə'reɪʃən] *n* (*deliberation*) namysł *m*; (*factor*) czynnik *m*, okoliczność *f*; (*fml*: *reward*) uznanie *nt*; **to show no ~ for sb** zupełnie nie liczyć się z czyimiś uczuciami; **out of ~ for** przez wzgląd na *+acc*; **under ~** rozważany; **my first ~ is my family** na pierwszym miejscu stoi u mnie (moja) rodzina
**considering** [kən'sɪdərɪŋ] *prep* zważywszy na *+acc*; **~ that ...** zważywszy (na to), że ...
**consign** [kən'saɪn] *vt* (*goods*) wysyłać (wysłać *perf*); (*person*): **to ~ sb to** (*sb's care*) powierzać (powierzyć *perf*) kogoś *+dat*; (*poverty*) skazywać (skazać *perf*) kogoś na *+acc*; **those old wheels had been ~ed to the loft** te stare koła wyniesiono na strych
**consignment** [kən'saɪnmənt] *n* partia *f* towaru
**consignment note** *n* (*Comm*) list *m* przewozowy
**consist** [kən'sɪst] *vi*: **to ~ of** składać się z *+gen*
**consistency** [kən'sɪstənsɪ] *n* (*of actions*) konsekwencja *f*; (*of yoghurt etc*) konsystencja *f*
**consistent** [kən'sɪstənt] *adj* (*person*) konsekwentny; (*argument*) spójny; **~ with** zgodny z *+instr*
**consolation** [kɔnsə'leɪʃən] *n* pocieszenie *nt*
**console** [*vb* kən'səul, *n* 'kɔnsəul] *vt* pocieszać (pocieszyć *perf*) ▷ *n* konsola *f*, konsoleta *f*
**consolidate** [kən'sɔlɪdeɪt] *vt* konsolidować (skonsolidować *perf*)
**consols** ['kɔnsɔlz] (Brit) *npl* konsole *pl*, obligacje *pl* państwowe
**consommé** [kən'sɔmeɪ] *n* bulion *m*
**consonant** ['kɔnsənənt] *n* spółgłoska *f*
**consort** [*n* 'kɔnsɔ:t, *vb* kən'sɔ:t] *n* (*also*: **prince consort**) książę *m* małżonek *m* ▷ *vi* (*often pej*): **to ~ with** zadawać się z *+instr*

**consortium** [kən'sɔ:tɪəm] *n* konsorcjum *nt*
**conspicuous** [kən'spɪkjuəs] *adj* rzucający się w oczy; **to make o.s. ~** zwracać (zwrócić *perf*) na siebie uwagę
**conspiracy** [kən'spɪrəsɪ] *n* spisek *m*
**conspiratorial** [kən'spɪrə'tɔ:rɪəl] *adj* (*group*) spiskowy; (*whisper, glance*) konspiracyjny
**conspire** [kən'spaɪə^r] *vi* (*criminals, revolutionaries*) spiskować; (*events*) sprzysięgać się (sprzysiąc się *perf*)
**constable** ['kʌnstəbl] (*Brit*) *n* posterunkowy *m*; **chief ~** naczelnik policji
**constabulary** [kən'stæbjulərɪ] (*Brit*) *n* siły *pl* policyjne (*danego miasta lub rejonu*)
**constant** ['kɔnstənt] *adj* stały
**constantly** ['kɔnstəntlɪ] *adv* stale
**constellation** [kɔnstə'leɪʃən] *n* gwiazdozbiór *m*, konstelacja *f*
**consternation** [kɔnstə'neɪʃən] *n* konsternacja *f*
**constipated** ['kɔnstɪpeɪtɪd] *adj*: **to be ~** cierpieć na zaparcie
**constipation** [kɔnstɪ'peɪʃən] *n* zaparcie *nt*
**constituency** [kən'stɪtjuənsɪ] *n* (*area*) okręg *m* wyborczy; (*electors*) wyborcy *vir pl*
**constituency party** *n* okręgowa organizacja *f* partyjna
**constituent** [kən'stɪtjuənt] *n* (*Pol*) wyborca *m*; (*component*) składnik *m*
**constitute** ['kɔnstɪtju:t] *vt* (*represent*) stanowić; (*make up*) stanowić, składać się na *+acc*
**constitution** [kɔnstɪ'tju:ʃən] *n* (*of country*) konstytucja *f*; (*of organization*) statut *m*; (*of committee etc*) skład *m*; **he has a strong ~** ma silny organizm
**constitutional** [kɔnstɪ'tju:ʃənl] *adj* konstytucyjny
**constrain** [kən'streɪn] *vt* ograniczać (ograniczyć *perf*)
**constrained** [kən'streɪnd] *adj* (*behaviour*) sztuczny; (*smile*) wymuszony; **he felt ~ to apologize** czuł się zmuszony przeprosić
**constraint** [kən'streɪnt] *n* (*restriction*) ograniczenie *nt*; (*compulsion*) przymus *m*
**constrict** [kən'strɪkt] *vt* (*person*) ograniczać (ograniczyć *perf*); (*breathing, movements*) utrudniać (utrudnić *perf*); (*blood vessels*) obkurczać (obkurczyć *perf*), zwężać (zwęzić *perf*)
**constriction** [kən'strɪkʃən] *n* (*restriction*) ograniczenie *nt*; (*in chest*) ucisk *m*
**construct** [kən'strʌkt] *vt* (*building*) budować (zbudować *perf*); (*machine, argument, theory*) budować (zbudować *perf*), konstruować (skonstruować *perf*)
**construction** [kən'strʌkʃən] *n* (*activity*) budowa *f*; (*structure*) konstrukcja *f*; (*fig*) interpretacja *f*; **to be under ~** być w budowie
**construction industry** *n* przemysł *m* budowlany
**constructive** [kən'strʌktɪv] *adj* konstruktywny
**construe** [kən'stru:] *vt* (*statement, event*) odbierać (odebrać *perf*), interpretować (zinterpretować *perf*)
**consul** ['kɔnsl] *n* konsul *m*
**consulate** ['kɔnsjulɪt] *n* konsulat *m*
**consult** [kən'sʌlt] *vt* (*friend*) radzić się (poradzić się *perf*) *+gen*; (*reference book*) sprawdzać (sprawdzić *perf*) w *+loc*; **to ~ sb (about sth)** (*doctor, lawyer etc*) konsultować się (skonsultować się *perf*) z kimś (w jakiejś sprawie)
**consultancy** [kən'sʌltənsɪ] *n* (*business*) firma *f* konsultacyjna; (*Med*) stanowisko *nt* lekarza specjalisty (*w szpitalu*)
**consultant** [kən'sʌltənt] *n* (*Med*) ≈ lekarz *m* specjalista *m*; (*other specialist*) doradca *m* ▷ *cpd*: **~ engineer** inżynier *m* specjalista *m*; **~ paediatrician** ≈ specjalista z zakresu pediatrii; **legal ~** radca prawny; **management ~** doradca do spraw zarządzania
**consultation** [kɔnsəl'teɪʃən] *n* konsultacja *f*; (*Jur*) porada *f* (prawna); **in ~ with** w porozumieniu z *+instr*; **the patient should feel at ease during a ~** podczas wizyty u lekarza pacjent powinien czuć się swobodnie
**consulting room** [kən'sʌltɪŋ-] (*Brit*) *n* gabinet *m* lekarski
**consume** [kən'sju:m] *vt* (*food, drink*) konsumować (skonsumować *perf*); (*fuel, energy*) zużywać (zużyć *perf*); (*time*) pochłaniać (pochłonąć *perf*); (*emotion: person*) trawić, żżerać; (*fire: city etc*) trawić (strawić *perf*)
**consumer** [kən'sju:mə^r] *n* konsument(ka) *m(f)*; **these machines are enormous ~s of electricity** te maszyny pożerają ogromne ilości prądu
**consumer credit** *n* kredyt *m* konsumpcyjny
**consumer durables** *npl* dobra *pl* konsumpcyjne trwałego użytku
**consumer goods** *npl* dobra *pl or* towary *pl* konsumpcyjne
**consumerism** [kən'sju:mərɪzəm] *n* obrona *f* interesów konsumenta
**consumer society** *n* społeczeństwo *nt* konsumpcyjne
**consummate** ['kɔnsʌmeɪt] *vt* (*marriage*) konsumować (skonsumować *perf*); (*achievements*) spożytkowywać (spożytkować *perf*)

**consumption** [kən'sʌmpʃən] *n* (*of food, drink*) konsumpcja *f*, spożycie *nt*; (*of fuel, energy, time*) zużycie *nt*; (*buying*) konsumpcja *f*; (*Med: old*) suchoty *pl*; **not fit for human ~** nie nadający się do spożycia
**cont.** *abbr* (= *continued*) c.d., cd
**contact** ['kɔntækt] *n* kontakt *m* ▷ *vt* kontaktować się (skontaktować się *perf*) z *+instr*; **to be in ~ with sb/sth** być w kontakcie z kimś/czymś; **business ~s** kontakty handlowe
**contact lenses** *npl* soczewki *pl or* szkła *pl* kontaktowe
**contagious** [kən'teɪdʒəs] *adj* (*disease*) zakaźny; (*fig: laughter, enthusiasm*) zaraźliwy
**contain** [kən'teɪn] *vt* (*objects, ingredients*) zawierać; (*growth, feeling*) powstrzymywać (powstrzymać *perf*); **to ~ o.s.** opanowywać się (opanować się *perf*)
**container** [kən'teɪnəʳ] *n* pojemnik *m*; (*Comm*) kontener *m*
**containerize** [kən'teɪnəraɪz] *vt* konteneryzować (skonteneryzować *perf*)
**container lorry** *n* ciężarówka *f* z kontenerem, ≈ TIR *m*
**container ship** *n* kontenerowiec *m*
**contaminate** [kən'tæmɪneɪt] *vt* zanieczyszczać (zanieczyścić *perf*)
**contamination** [kəntæmɪ'neɪʃən] *n* zanieczyszczenie *nt*; (*radioactive*) skażenie *nt*
**cont'd** *abbr* (= *continued*) c.d., cd
**contemplate** ['kɔntəmpleɪt] *vt* (*idea, course of action*) rozważać; (*subject*) rozmyślać o *+loc*; (*painting etc*) kontemplować
**contemplation** [kɔntəm'pleɪʃən] *n* rozmyślanie *nt*, kontemplacja *f*
**contemporary** [kən'tɛmpərərɪ] *adj* współczesny; **~ with** współczesny *+dat*; **Samuel Pepys and his contemporaries** Samuel Pepys i jemu współcześni
**contempt** [kən'tɛmpt] *n* pogarda *f*; **~ of court** (*disobedience*) niezastosowanie się do nakazu sądu; (*disrespect*) obraza sądu; **to have ~ for sb/sth, to hold sb/sth in ~** gardzić *or* pogardzać kimś/czymś
**contemptible** [kən'tɛmptəbl] *adj* godny pogardy
**contemptuous** [kən'tɛmptjuəs] *adj* pogardliwy
**contend** [kən'tɛnd] *vt*: **to ~ that ...** twierdzić *or* utrzymywać, że ... ▷ *vi*: **to ~ with** borykać się z *+instr* ▷ *vi*: **to ~ for** rywalizować o *+acc*; **to have to ~ with** musieć stawiać (stawić *perf*) czoło *+dat*; **he has a lot to ~ with** musi się uporać z wieloma problemami
**contender** [kən'tɛndəʳ] *n* (*in election*) kandydat(ka) *m(f)*; (*in competition*) uczestnik(-iczka) *m(f)*; (*for title*) pretendent(ka) *m(f)*
**content** [*vb* kən'tɛnt, *n* 'kɔntɛnt] *vt* zadowalać (zadowolić *perf*) ▷ *n* zawartość *f*; (*of book etc*) treść *f*; **contents** *npl* zawartość *f*; (*of book etc*) treść *f*; **(table of) ~s** spis treści; **to be ~ to do sth** chętnie coś (z)robić; **to be ~ with** być zadowolonym z *+gen*; **to ~ o.s. with sth/with doing sth** zadowalać się (zadowolić się *perf*) czymś/(z)robieniem czegoś
**contented** [kən'tɛntɪd] *adj* zadowolony
**contentedly** [kən'tɛntɪdlɪ] *adv* z zadowoleniem
**contention** [kən'tɛnʃən] *n* (*assertion*) twierdzenie *nt*; (*dispute*) spór *m*; **it is my ~ that...** twierdzę, że...; **bone of ~** kość niezgody
**contentious** [kən'tɛnʃəs] *adj* (*subject*) sporny; (*opinion*) kontrowersyjny; (*person*) kłótliwy
**contentment** [kən'tɛntmənt] *n* zadowolenie *nt*
**contest** [*n* 'kɔntɛst, *vb* kən'tɛst] *n* (*competition*) konkurs *m*; (*for control, power*) rywalizacja *f* ▷ *vt* (*election, competition*) uczestniczyć *or* startować w *+loc*; (*title*) ubiegać się *or* walczyć o *+acc*; (*decision, testament*) kwestionować (zakwestionować *perf*)
**contestant** [kən'tɛstənt] *n* (*in quiz, competition*) uczestnik(-iczka) *m(f)*; (*in election*) kandydat(ka) *m(f)*
**context** ['kɔntɛkst] *n* kontekst *m*; **in ~** całościowo; **in the ~ of** w kontekście *+gen*; **out of ~** w oderwaniu; **taken out of ~** wyrwany z kontekstu
**continent** ['kɔntɪnənt] *n* kontynent *m*; **the C~** (*Brit*) Europa *f* (*z wyłączeniem Wysp Brytyjskich*)
**continental** [kɔntɪ'nɛntl] (*Brit*) *adj* kontynentalny ▷ *n* Europejczyk(-jka) *m(f)*
**continental breakfast** *n* śniadanie *nt* kontynentalne (*pieczywo z dżemem i kawa*)
**continental quilt** (*Brit*) *n* kołdra *f*
**contingency** [kən'tɪndʒənsɪ] *n* ewentualność *f*
**contingency plan** *n*: **a ~ for** plan *m* na wypadek *+gen*
**contingent** [kən'tɪndʒənt] *n* reprezentacja *f*; (*Mil*) kontyngent *m* ▷ *adj*: **to be ~ on/upon** być uzależnionym od *+gen*
**continual** [kən'tɪnjuəl] *adj* ciągły, nieustający
**continually** [kən'tɪnjuəlɪ] *adv* ciągle, nieustannie
**continuation** [kəntɪnju'eɪʃən] *n* (*persistence*) ciągłość *f*; (*after interruption*) wznowienie *nt*; (*extension*) przedłużenie *nt*, kontynuacja *f*
**continue** [kən'tɪnju:] *vi* (*carry on*) trwać (nadal); (*after interruption*) zostawać (zostać

*perf)* wznowionym ▷ *vt* kontynuować; **to be ~d** ciąg dalszy nastąpi; **~d on page 10** ciąg dalszy na stronie 10

**continuity** [kɔntɪ'nju:ɪtɪ] *n* ciągłość *f* ▷ *cpd*: **~ announcer** ≈ prezenter(ka) *m(f)* telewizyjny(na) *m(f)*; **~ girl** *(Film)* inspicjentka

**continuous** [kən'tɪnjuəs] *adj (growth)* ciągły, stały; *(line, verb form)* ciągły; *(relationship)* stały; **~ performance** *(Film)* seans non-stop

**continuously** [kən'tɪnjuəslɪ] *adv* ciągle, stale

**continuous stationery** *n* składanka *f* komputerowa

**contort** [kən'tɔ:t] *vt (body)* wyginać (wygiąć *perf)*; *(face)* wykrzywiać (wykrzywić *perf)*

**contortion** [kən'tɔ:ʃən] *n (of body)* wygięcie *nt*; *(: unusual, complicated)* wygibas *m (usu pl)*; *(Med)* skręcenie *nt*

**contortionist** [kən'tɔ:ʃənɪst] *n (in circus etc)* kontorsjonista(-tka) *m(f)*

**contour** ['kɔntuə$^r$] *n (also:* **contour line**: *on map)* poziomica *f*, warstwica *f*; *(usu pl: outline)* kontur *m*

**contraband** ['kɔntrəbænd] *n* kontrabanda *f*, przemyt *m* ▷ *adj* z kontrabandy *or* przemytu *post*

**contraception** [kɔntrə'sɛpʃən] *n* antykoncepcja *f*, zapobieganie *nt* ciąży

**contraceptive** [kɔntrə'sɛptɪv] *adj* antykoncepcyjny ▷ *n* środek *m* antykoncepcyjny

**contract** [*n, cpd* 'kɔntrækt, *vb* kən'trækt] *n* kontrakt *m*, umowa *f* ▷ *vi (become smaller)* kurczyć się (skurczyć się *perf)*; *(Comm)*: **to ~ to do sth** zobowiązywać się (zobowiązać się *perf)* w drodze umowy do zrobienia czegoś ▷ *vt (illness)* nabawiać się (nabawić się *perf)* *+gen* ▷ *cpd (price)* umowny; *(work)* zlecony; **~ of employment/service** umowa o pracę

▸ **contract in** *(Brit) vi* zgłaszać się (zgłosić się *perf) (oficjalnie)*

▸ **contract out** *(Brit) vi* wycofywać się (wycofać się *perf) (oficjalnie)*

**contraction** [kən'trækʃən] *n (of muscle, uterus)* skurcz *m*; *(of metal, power)* kurczenie się *nt*; *(Ling)* forma *f* ściągnięta

**contractor** [kən'træktə$^r$] *n* zleceniobiorca *m*; *(for building)* wykonawca *m*; *(for supplies)* dostawca *m*

**contractual** [kən'træktʃuəl] *adj (obligation)* wynikający z umowy; *(agreement)* kontraktowy

**contradict** [kɔntrə'dɪkt] *vt (person, statement)* zaprzeczać (zaprzeczyć *perf) +dat*; *(be contrary to)* pozostawać w sprzeczności z *+instr*, przeczyć *+dat*; **these findings ~ each other** te odkrycia wzajemnie sobie przeczą

**contradiction** [kɔntrə'dɪkʃən] *n* sprzeczność *f*; **a ~ in terms** sprzeczność sama w sobie

**contradictory** [kɔntrə'dɪktərɪ] *adj* sprzeczny

**contralto** [kən'træltəu] *n* kontralt *m*

**contraption** [kən'træpʃən] *(pej) n* ustrojstwo *nt (inf)*

**contrary**[1] ['kɔntrərɪ] *adj* przeciwstawny ▷ *n* przeciwieństwo *nt*; **on the ~** przeciwnie; **unless you hear to the ~** jeśli nie otrzymasz innych instrukcji; **~ to what we thought** odwrotnie niż myśleliśmy

**contrary**[2] [kən'trɛərɪ] *adj* przekorny

**contrast** [*n* 'kɔntrɑ:st, *vb* kən'trɑ:st] *n* kontrast *m* ▷ *vt* zestawiać (zestawić *perf)*, porównywać (porównać *perf)*; **to ~ sth with sth** przeciwstawiać (przeciwstawić *perf)* coś czemuś; **in ~ to** *or* **with** w przeciwieństwie do *+gen*

**contrasting** [kən'trɑ:stɪŋ] *adj (colours)* kontrastowy; *(attitudes)* kontrastujący (ze sobą)

**contravene** [kɔntrə'vi:n] *vt (law, regulation)* naruszać (naruszyć *perf)*

**contravention** [kɔntrə'vɛnʃən] *n*: **in ~ of** z naruszeniem *+gen*

**contribute** [kən'trɪbju:t] *vi*: **to ~ to** *(charity etc)* zasilać (zasilić *perf)*; *(magazine)* pisywać do *+gen*, współpracować z *+instr*; *(situation, problem)* przyczyniać się (przyczynić się *perf)* do *+gen*; *(discussion, conversation)* brać (wziąć *perf)* udział w *+loc* ▷ *vt*: **to ~ 10 pounds to** *(charity)* wpłacać (wpłacić *perf) or* ofiarowywać (ofiarować *perf)* 10 funtów na *+acc*; **to ~ an article to** pisać (napisać *perf)* artykuł do *+gen*

**contribution** [kɔntrɪ'bju:ʃən] *n (donation)* datek *m*; *(to debate, campaign)* wkład *m*, przyczynek *m*; *(to magazine)* artykuł *m*; *(Brit: for social security)* składka *f*

**contributor** [kən'trɪbjutə$^r$] *n (to appeal)* ofiarodawca(-wczyni) *m(f)*; *(to magazine)* współpracownik(-iczka) *m(f)*

**contributory** [kən'trɪbjutərɪ] *adj*: **it was a ~ factor in ...** był to jeden z czynników, które złożyły się na *+acc*

**contributory pension scheme** *(Brit) n* składkowy fundusz *m* emerytalny

**contrite** ['kɔntraɪt] *adj* skruszony

**contrivance** [kən'traɪvəns] *n (scheme)* podstęp *m*; *(device)* urządzenie *nt*

**contrive** [kən'traɪv] *vt (device)* zmajstrować *(perf)*; *(meeting etc)* ukartować *(perf)* ▷ *vi*: **to ~ to do sth** znajdować (znaleźć *perf)* sposób na zrobienie czegoś

**control** [kən'trəul] *vt (country)* sprawować władzę w *+loc*; *(organization)* sprawować kontrolę nad *+instr*, kierować *+instr*; *(machinery, process)* sterować *+instr*; *(wages,* *prices*) kontrolować; (*one's emotions*) panować nad *+instr*; (*fire, disease*) opanowywać (opanować *perf*) ▷ *n* (*of country*) władza *f*; (*of organization, stocks*) kontrola *f*; (*also*: **control group**) grupa *f* kontrolna; **controls** *npl* (*of vehicle*) układ *m* sterowania; (*on radio, television*) przełączniki *pl*; (*governmental*) kontrola *f*; **to take ~ of** przejmować (przejąć *perf*) kontrolę nad *+instr*; **to be in ~ of** panować nad *+instr*; **~ yourself!** opanuj się!; **everything is under ~** panujemy nad sytuacją; **the car went out of ~** kierowca stracił kontrolę nad samochodem; **circumstances beyond our ~** okoliczności od nas niezależne; **to get out of ~** wymykać się (wymknąć się *perf*) spod kontroli

**control key** *n* (*Comput*) klawisz *m* sterujący

**controller** [kən'trəuləʳ] *n* (*of part of organization*) kierownik *m*; (*Comm*) rewident *m* księgowy

**controlling interest** [kən'trəulɪŋ-] *n* pakiet *m* kontrolny

**control panel** *n* pulpit *m* sterowniczy

**control room** *n* (*Naut, Mil*) sterownia *f*; (*Radio, TV*) pokój *m* aparatury

**control tower** *n* wieża *f* kontrolna

**control unit** *n* jednostka *f* sterująca

**controversial** [kɔntrə'vəːʃl] *adj* kontrowersyjny

**controversy** ['kɔntrəvəːsɪ] *n* kontrowersja *f*

**conurbation** [kɔnə'beɪʃən] *n* konurbacja *f*

**convalesce** [kɔnvə'lɛs] *vi* wracać (wrócić *perf*) do zdrowia

**convalescence** [kɔnvə'lɛsns] *n* rekonwalescencja *f*

**convalescent** [kɔnvə'lɛsnt] *adj* (*leave*) zdrowotny ▷ *n* rekonwalescent(ka) *m(f)*; **~ home** ≈ sanatorium

**convector** [kən'vɛktəʳ] *n* grzejnik *m* konwektorowy

**convene** [kən'viːn] *vt* (*meeting, conference*) zwoływać (zwołać *f*) ▷ *vi* (*parliament, jury*) zbierać się (zebrać się *perf*)

**convener** [kən'viːnəʳ] *n* (*Admin*) organizator *m* (*konferencji itp*)

**convenience** [kən'viːnɪəns] *n* wygoda *f*; **at your ~** w dogodnej (dla ciebie) chwili; **at your earliest ~** możliwie szybko *or* jak najszybciej; **all modern ~s**, (*Brit*) **all mod cons** z wygodami

**convenience foods** *npl łatwe do przygotowania produkty w puszkach, mrożonki itp*

**convenient** [kən'viːnɪənt] *adj* dogodny; **if it is ~ to you** jeśli ci to odpowiada

**conveniently** [kən'viːnɪəntlɪ] *adv* dogodnie

**convenor** [kən'viːnəʳ] *n* = **convener**

**convent** ['kɔnvənt] *n* klasztor *m*

**convention** [kən'vɛnʃən] *n* (*custom*) konwenans *m*; (*conference*) zjazd *m*; (*agreement*) konwencja *f*

**conventional** [kən'vɛnʃənl] *adj* konwencjonalny

**convent school** *n* szkoła *f* przyklasztorna

**converge** [kən'vəːdʒ] *vi* (*roads, interests*) zbiegać się (zbiec się *perf*); (*ideas*) upodabniać się (upodobnić się *perf*) do siebie; **to ~ on** przybywać (przybyć *perf*) do *+gen*

**conversant** [kən'vəːsnt] *adj*: **to be ~ with** posiadać gruntowną znajomość *+gen*

**conversation** [kɔnvə'seɪʃən] *n* rozmowa *f*

**conversational** [kɔnvə'seɪʃənl] *adj* (*language*) potoczny; (*Comput*) konwersacyjny, dialogowy; **~ skills** umiejętność prowadzenia rozmowy

**conversationalist** [kɔnvə'seɪʃnəlɪst] *n*: **(good) ~** (interesujący(-ca) *m(f)*) rozmówca(-wczyni) *m(f)*

**converse** [*n* 'kɔnvəːs, *vb* kən'vəːs] *n* odwrotność *f* ▷ *vi*: **to ~ (with sb) (about sth)** rozmawiać (z kimś) (o czymś)

**conversely** [kɔn'vəːslɪ] *adv* odwrotnie

**conversion** [kən'vəːʃən] *n* (*Chem*) zamiana *f*, konwersja *f*; (*Math*) przeliczenie *nt*; (*Rel*) nawrócenie *nt*; (*Brit*: *of house*) przebudowa *f*, adaptacja *f*

**conversion table** *n* tabela *f* przeliczeniowa

**convert** [*vb* kən'vəːt, *n* 'kɔnvəːt] *vt* (*change*): **to ~ sth into/to** zamieniać (zamienić *perf*) *or* przekształcać (przekształcić *perf*) coś w *+acc*; (*Rel, Pol*) nawracać (nawrócić *perf*); (*building, vehicle*) przebudowywać (przebudować *perf*), adaptować (zaadaptować *perf*); (*quantity*) zamieniać (zamienić *perf*), przeliczać (przeliczyć *perf*); (*Rugby*) podwyższać (podwyższyć *perf*) ▷ *n* nawrócony(-na) *m(f)*

**convertible** [kən'vəːtəbl] *adj* (*currency*) wymienialny ▷ *n* kabriolet *m*

**convex** ['kɔnvɛks] *adj* wypukły

**convey** [kən'veɪ] *vt* (*information, thanks*) przekazywać (przekazać *perf*); (*cargo, travellers*) przewozić (przewieźć *perf*)

**conveyance** [kən'veɪəns] *n* (*of goods*) przewóz *m*; (*vehicle*) pojazd *m*

**conveyancing** [kən'veɪənsɪŋ] (*Jur*) *n* przeniesienie *nt* własności

**conveyor belt** *n* przenośnik *m* taśmowy

**convict** [*vb* kən'vɪkt, *n* 'kɔnvɪkt] *vt* skazywać (skazać *perf*) ▷ *n* skazaniec *m*, skazany(-na) *m(f)*

**conviction** [kən'vɪkʃən] *n* (*belief, certainty*) przekonanie *nt*; (*Jur*) skazanie *nt*; **he had a long record of previous ~s** był przedtem wielokrotnie karany

**convince** [kən'vɪns] *vt* przekonywać (przekonać *perf*); **to ~ sb (of sth/that ...)** przekonać (*perf*) kogoś (o czymś/, że ...)

**convinced** [kən'vɪnst] *adj*: **~ of/that ...** przekonany o *+loc*/, że ...
**convincing** [kən'vɪnsɪŋ] *adj* przekonywający, przekonujący
**convincingly** [kən'vɪnsɪŋlɪ] *adv* przekonywająco, przekonująco
**convivial** [kən'vɪvɪəl] *adj* (*festive*) biesiadny; (*friendly*) serdeczny
**convoluted** ['kɔnvəlu:tɪd] *adj* (*statement, argument*) zawiły, zagmatwany; (*shape*) powykręcany
**convoy** ['kɔnvɔɪ] *n* konwój *m*
**convulse** [kən'vʌls] *vt*: **to be ~d with laughter/pain** skręcać się ze śmiechu/z bólu
**convulsion** [kən'vʌlʃən] *n* drgawki *pl*, konwulsje *pl*
**coo** [ku:] *vi* (*dove, pigeon*) gruchać (zagruchać *perf*); (*person*) gruchać
**cook** [kuk] *vt* gotować (ugotować *perf*) ▷ *vi* (*person*) gotować; (*meat etc*) gotować się (ugotować się *perf*) ▷ *n* kucharz(-arka) *m(f)*
▸ **cook up** (*inf*) *vt* spreparować (*perf*)
**cookbook** ['kukbuk] *n* książka *f* kucharska
**cook-chill** ['kuktʃɪl] *adj* (*food*) utrwalony przez szybkie schłodzenie
**cooker** ['kukəʳ] *n* kuchenka *f*
**cookery** ['kukərɪ] *n* sztuka *f* gotowania
**cookery book** (*Brit*) *n* = **cookbook**
**cookie** ['kukɪ] (*US*) *n* herbatnik *m*
**cooking** ['kukɪŋ] *n* gotowanie *nt*, kuchnia *f* ▷ *cpd* do gotowania *post*
**cookout** ['kukaut] (*US*) *n przyjęcie na wolnym powietrzu, podczas którego przyrządza się potrawy na ognisku lub rożnie*
**cool** [ku:l] *adj* (*temperature, drink*) chłodny; (*clothes*) lekki, przewiewny; (*person: calm*) spokojny, opanowany; (*: unfriendly*) chłodny ▷ *vt* ochładzać (ochłodzić *perf*) ▷ *vi* ochładzać się (ochłodzić się *perf*); **it's ~** jest chłodno; **to keep sth ~** *or* **in a ~ place** przechowywać coś w chłodnym miejscu; **to keep one's ~** zachowywać (zachować *perf*) spokój
▸ **cool down** *vi* ochładzać się (ochłodzić się *perf*); (*fig*) uspokajać się (uspokoić się *perf*)
**cool box**, (*US*) **cooler** *n* lodówka *f* turystyczna
**cooling tower** ['ku:lɪŋ-] *n* chłodnia *f* kominowa
**coolly** ['ku:lɪ] *adv* (*calmly*) spokojnie; (*in unfriendly way*) chłodno
**coolness** ['ku:lnɪs] *n* (*lit, fig*) chłód *m*; (*calmness*) spokój *m*
**coop** [ku:p] *n* klatka *f* (*dla drobiu, królików itp*) ▷ *vt*: **to ~ up** (*fig*) stłaczać (stłoczyć *perf*)
**co-op** ['kəuɔp] *n abbr* (= *cooperative (society)*) spółdz.
**cooperate** [kəu'ɔpəreɪt] *vi* (*collaborate*) współpracować; (*assist*) pomagać (pomóc *perf*); **to ~ with sb** współpracować z kimś
**cooperation** [kəuɔpə'reɪʃən] *n* (*collaboration*) współpraca *f*; (*assistance*) pomoc *f*
**cooperative** [kəu'ɔpərətɪv] *adj* (*enterprise*) wspólny; (*farm*) spółdzielczy; (*person*) pomocny ▷ *n* (*factory, business*) spółdzielnia *f*
**coopt** [kəu'ɔpt] *vt*: **to ~ sb onto a committee** dokooptowywać (dokooptować *perf*) kogoś do komisji
**coordinate** [*vb* kəu'ɔ:dɪneɪt, *n* kəu'ɔdɪnət] *vt* koordynować (skoordynować *perf*) ▷ *n* współrzędna *f*
**coordination** [kəuɔ:dɪ'neɪʃən] *n* koordynacja *f*
**co-ownership** ['kəu'əunəʃɪp] *n* współwłasność *f*
**cop** [kɔp] (*inf*) *n* glina *m* (*inf*), gliniarz *m* (*inf*)
**cope** [kəup] *vi*: **to ~ with** borykać się z *+instr*; (*successfully*) radzić sobie z *+instr*
**Copenhagen** ['kəupn'heɪgən] *n* Kopenhaga *f*
**copier** ['kɔpɪəʳ] *n* (*also*: **photocopier**) kopiarka *f*
**co-pilot** ['kəu'paɪlət] *n* drugi pilot *m*
**copious** ['kəupɪəs] *adj* obfity
**copper** ['kɔpəʳ] *n* miedź *f*; (*Brit: inf*) gliniarz *m* (*inf*); **coppers** *npl* miedziaki *pl*
**coppice** ['kɔpɪs] *n* zagajnik *m*
**copse** [kɔps] *n* = **coppice**
**copulate** ['kɔpjuleɪt] *vi* kopulować, spółkować
**copy** ['kɔpɪ] *n* (*duplicate*) kopia *f*, odpis *m*; (*of book, record*) egzemplarz *m*; (*material: for printing*) maszynopis *m* ▷ *vt* kopiować (skopiować *perf*); **to make good ~** (*Press*) nadawać się do gazety
▸ **copy out** *vt* przepisywać (przepisać *perf*)
**copycat** ['kɔpɪkæt] (*pej*) *n* papuga *f* (*pej*)
**copyright** ['kɔpɪraɪt] *n* prawo *nt* autorskie; **~ reserved** prawo autorskie zastrzeżone
**copy typist** *n* maszynistka *f*
**copywriter** ['kɔpɪraɪtəʳ] *n osoba zajmująca się układaniem haseł reklamowych*
**coral** ['kɔrəl] *n* koral *m*
**coral reef** *n* rafa *f* koralowa
**Coral Sea** *n*: **the ~** Morze *nt* Koralowe
**cord** [kɔ:d] *n* (*string*) sznur *m*; (*Elec*) przewód *m*; (*fabric*) sztruks *m*; **cords** *npl* sztruksy *pl*
**cordial** ['kɔ:dɪəl] *adj* serdeczny ▷ *n* (*Brit*) *słodki napój bezalkoholowy na bazie soku owocowego*
**cordless** ['kɔ:dlɪs] *adj* bezprzewodowy
**cordon** ['kɔ:dn] *n* kordon *m*
▸ **cordon off** *vt* odgradzać (odgrodzić *perf*) kordonem
**corduroy** ['kɔ:dərɔɪ] *n* sztruks *m*
**CORE** [kɔ:ʳ] (*US*) *n abbr* = **Congress of Racial Equality**
**core** [kɔ:ʳ] *n* (*of apple*) ogryzek *m*; (*of organization, earth*) jądro *nt*; (*of nuclear reactor*)

rdzeń *m*; (*of problem*) sedno *nt*; (*of building, place*) serce *nt* ▷ *vt* (*apple, pear*) wydrążać (wydrążyć *perf*); **rotten to the ~** (*fig*) zepsuty do szpiku kości

**Corfu** [kɔːˈfuː] *n* Korfu *nt inv*

**coriander** [kɔrɪˈændəʳ] *n* kolendra *f*

**cork** [kɔːk] *n* korek *m*

**corkage** [ˈkɔːkɪdʒ] *n opłata pobierana od klientów restauracji za podanie przyniesionego przez nich alkoholu*

**corked** [kɔːkt], (*US*) **corky** [ˈkɔːkɪ] *adj* smakujący *or* trącący korkiem

**corkscrew** [ˈkɔːkskruː] *n* korkociąg *m*

**cormorant** [ˈkɔːmərnt] *n* kormoran *m*

**Corn** (*Brit: Post*) *abbr* = **Cornwall**

**corn** [kɔːn] *n* (*Brit*) zboże *nt*; (*US*) kukurydza *f*; (*on foot*) odcisk *m*; **~ on the cob** gotowana kolba kukurydzy

**cornea** [ˈkɔːnɪə] *n* rogówka *f*

**corned beef** [ˈkɔːnd-] *n* peklowana wołowina *f*

**corner** [ˈkɔːnəʳ] *n* (*outside*) róg *m*; (*inside*) kąt *m*, róg *m*; (*in road*) zakręt *m*, róg *m*; (*Football*: *also*: **corner kick**) rzut *m* rożny, róg *m* (*inf*); (*Boxing*) narożnik *m* ▷ *vt* (*trap*) przypierać (przyprzeć *perf*) do muru; (*Comm*) monopolizować (zmonopolizować *perf*) ▷ *vi* (*car*) brać zakręty; **to cut ~s** (*fig*) iść (pójść *perf*) na łatwiznę

**corner flag** (*Football*) *n* chorągiewka *f* narożnikowa

**corner kick** (*Football*) *n* rzut *m* rożny

**cornerstone** [ˈkɔːnəstəun] *n* kamień *m* węgielny; (*fig*) podstawa *f*

**cornet** [ˈkɔːnɪt] *n* (*Mus*) kornet *m*; (*Brit*: *ice-cream*) rożek *m*

**cornflakes** [ˈkɔːnfleɪks] *npl* płatki *pl* kukurydziane

**cornflour** [ˈkɔːnflauəʳ] (*Brit*) *n* mąka *f* kukurydziana

**cornice** [ˈkɔːnɪs] *n* gzyms *m*

**Cornish** [ˈkɔːnɪʃ] *adj* kornwalijski

**corn oil** *n* olej *m* kukurydziany

**cornstarch** [ˈkɔːnstɑːtʃ] (*US*) *n* = **cornflour**

**cornucopia** [kɔːnjuˈkəupɪə] *n* (*abundance*) obfitość *f*; (*horn of plenty*) róg *m* obfitości

**Cornwall** [ˈkɔːnwəl] *n* Kornwalia *f*

**corny** [ˈkɔːnɪ] (*inf*) *adj* banalny; **~ joke** kawał z brodą

**corollary** [kəˈrɔlərɪ] *n* następstwo *nt*

**coronary** [ˈkɔrənərɪ] *n* (*also*: **coronary thrombosis**) zakrzepica *f* tętnicy wieńcowej

**coronation** [kɔrəˈneɪʃən] *n* koronacja *f*

**coroner** [ˈkɔrənəʳ] (*Jur*) *n* koroner *m* (*urzędnik zajmujący się ustalaniem przyczyn nagłych zgonów*)

**coronet** [ˈkɔrənɪt] *n* (*small crown*) korona *f*; (*jewellery*) diadem *m*

**Corp.** *abbr* (= *corporation*) Korp.; (*Mil*: = *corporal*) kpr.

**corporal** [ˈkɔːpərl] *n* kapral *m* ▷ *adj*: **~ punishment** kary *pl* cielesne

**corporate** [ˈkɔːpərɪt] *adj* (*Comm*) korporacyjny; (*action, effort, responsibility*) zbiorowy; **~ image** wizerunek firmy

**corporation** [kɔːpəˈreɪʃən] *n* (*Comm*) korporacja *f*; (*of town*) władze *pl* miejskie

**corporation tax** *n* ≈ podatek *m* dochodowy od osób prawnych

**corps** [kɔːʳ] (*pl* **~**) *n* korpus *m*; **the press ~** korpus prasowy

**corpse** [kɔːps] *n* zwłoki *pl*

**corpuscle** [ˈkɔːpʌsl] (*Bio*) *n* ciałko *nt*

**corral** [kəˈrɑːl] *n* zagroda *f*

**correct** [kəˈrɛkt] *adj* (*accurate*) poprawny, prawidłowy; (*proper*) prawidłowy ▷ *vt* poprawiać (poprawić *perf*); **you are ~** masz rację

**correction** [kəˈrɛkʃən] *n* (*act of correcting*) poprawa *f*; (*instance*) poprawka *f*

**correctly** [kəˈrɛktlɪ] *adv* poprawnie, prawidłowo

**correlate** [ˈkɔrɪleɪt] *vt* wiązać (powiązać *perf*) ze sobą ▷ *vi*: **to ~ with** być powiązanym z *+instr*, korelować z *+instr* (*fml*)

**correlation** [kɔrɪˈleɪʃən] *n* związek *m*, korelacja *f* (*fml*)

**correspond** [kɔrɪsˈpɔnd] *vi*: **to ~ (with)** (*write*) korespondować (z *+instr*); (*tally*) pokrywać się *or* zgadzać się (z *+instr*); **to ~ to** odpowiadać *+dat*

**correspondence** [kɔrɪsˈpɔndəns] *n* (*letters*) korespondencja *f*; (*relationship*) odpowiedniość *f*

**correspondence course** *n* kurs *m* korespondencyjny

**correspondent** [kɔrɪsˈpɔndənt] *n* korespondent(ka) *m(f)*

**corresponding** [kɔrɪsˈpɔndɪŋ] *adj* odpowiedni; **~ to** zgodny z *+instr*, odpowiadający *+dat*

**corridor** [ˈkɔrɪdɔːʳ] *n* korytarz *m*

**corroborate** [kəˈrɔbəreɪt] *vt* potwierdzać (potwierdzić *perf*)

**corrode** [kəˈrəud] *vt* powodować (spowodować *perf*) korozję *+gen*, korodować ▷ *vi* ulegać (ulec *perf*) korozji, korodować (skorodować *perf*)

**corrosion** [kəˈrəuʒən] *n* (*damage*) rdza *f*; (*process*) korozja *f*

**corrosive** [kəˈrəuzɪv] *adj* powodujący korozję

**corrugated** [ˈkɔrəgeɪtɪd] *adj* falisty

**corrugated iron** *n* blacha *f* stalowa falista

**corrupt** [kəˈrʌpt] *adj* (*dishonest*) skorumpowany; (*depraved*) zepsuty; (*Comput*: *data*) uszkodzony ▷ *vt* korumpować (skorumpować *perf*); (*Comput*: *data*)

C

uszkadzać (uszkodzić *perf*); **~ practices** nieuczciwe praktyki
**corruption** [kəˈrʌpʃən] *n* (*dishonesty*) korupcja *f*
**corset** [ˈkɔːsɪt] *n* gorset *m*
**Corsica** [ˈkɔːsɪkə] *n* Korsyka *f*
**Corsican** [ˈkɔːsɪkən] *adj* korsykański ▷ *n* Korsykanin(-anka) *m(f)*
**cortège** [kɔːˈteɪʒ] *n* (*also*: **funeral cortège**) kondukt *m or* orszak *m* pogrzebowy
**cortisone** [ˈkɔːtɪzəun] *n* kortyzon *m*
**coruscating** [ˈkɔrəskeɪtɪŋ] *adj* skrzący się, mieniący się
**c.o.s.** *abbr* (= *cash on shipment*) płatne gotówką przy załadowaniu
**cosh** [kɔʃ] (*Brit*) *n* pałka *f*
**cosignatory** [ˈkəuˈsɪgnətərɪ] *n* konsygnatariusz *m*
**cosiness** [ˈkəuzɪnɪs] *n* przytulność *f*
**cos lettuce** [ˈkɔs-] *n odmiana sałaty o długich i wąskich liściach*
**cosmetic** [kɔzˈmɛtɪk] *n* kosmetyk *m* ▷ *adj* (*lit, fig*) kosmetyczny; **~ surgery** operacja plastyczna
**cosmic** [ˈkɔzmɪk] *adj* kosmiczny
**cosmonaut** [ˈkɔzmənɔːt] *n* kosmonauta(-tka) *m(f)*
**cosmopolitan** [kɔzməˈpɔlɪtn] *adj* kosmopolityczny
**cosmos** [ˈkɔzmɔs] *n*: **the ~** kosmos *m*
**cosset** [ˈkɔsɪt] *vt* rozpieszczać (rozpieścić *perf*)
**cost** [kɔst] (*pt, pp* **~**) *n* koszt *m*; (*fig*) cena *f* ▷ *vt* (*be priced at*) kosztować; (*find out cost of*: *pt, pp costed*) ustalać (ustalić *perf*) koszt *+gen*; **costs** *npl* (*Comm*: *overheads*) koszty *pl* (stałe); (*Jur*) koszty *pl* (sądowe); **how much does it ~?** ile to kosztuje?; **it ~s 5 pounds/too much** to kosztuje 5 funtów/za dużo; **what will it ~ to have it repaired?** ile będzie kosztować naprawa?; **it ~ me time/effort** kosztowało mnie to wiele czasu/wysiłku; **it ~ him his life/job** kosztowało go to życie/pracę; **the ~ of living** koszty utrzymania; **at all ~s** za wszelką cenę
**cost accountant** *n* (*Comm*) kalkulator *m* (*osoba*)
**co-star** [ˈkəustɑːʳ] *n*: **his ~ was ...** obok niego główną rolę (w filmie) grała ...
**Costa Rica** [ˈkɔstəˈriːkə] *n* Kostaryka *f*
**cost centre** *n* dział *m* kalkulacji kosztów
**cost control** *n* kontrola *f* kosztów
**cost-effective** [ˈkɔstɪˈfɛktɪv] *adj* wydajny
**cost-effectiveness** [ˈkɔstɪˈfɛktɪvnɪs] *n* wydajność *f*
**costing** [ˈkɔstɪŋ] *n* sporządzanie *nt* kosztorysu
**costly** [ˈkɔstlɪ] *adj* kosztowny; (*in time*) czasochłonny; (*in effort*) pracochłonny
**cost-of-living** [ˈkɔstəvˈlɪvɪŋ] *adj*: **~ index** wskaźnik *m* kosztów utrzymania; **~ allowance** dodatek drożyźniany
**cost price** (*Brit*) *n* cena *f* własna; **to sell/buy at ~** sprzedawać (sprzedać *perf*)/kupować (kupić *perf*) po cenie własnej
**costume** [ˈkɔstjuːm] *n* (*outfit*) kostium *m*; (*style of dress*) strój *m*; (*Brit*: *also*: **swimming costume**) kostium *m* (kąpielowy)
**costume jewellery** *n* sztuczna biżuteria *f*
**cosy**, (*US*) **cozy** [ˈkəuzɪ] *adj* (*room, house*) przytulny; (*bed*) wygodny; (*atmosphere*) kameralny; (*evening, chat*) miły; **I am/feel very ~ here** jest mi tu bardzo wygodnie
**cot** [kɔt] *n* (*Brit*) łóżeczko *nt* (dziecięce); (*US*) łóżko *nt* polowe *or* rozkładane
**Cotswolds** [ˈkɔtswəuldz] *npl*: **the ~** *pasmo wzgórz w południowo-zachodniej Anglii*
**cottage** [ˈkɔtɪdʒ] *n* domek *m*
**cottage cheese** *n* ≈ serek *m* ziarnisty
**cottage industry** *n* chałupnictwo *nt*
**cottage pie** *n zapiekanka z mielonego mięsa i ziemniaków*
**cotton** [ˈkɔtn] *n* (*fabric, plant*) bawełna *f*; (*esp Brit*: *thread*) nici *pl*; **~ dress** bawełniana sukienka
▶ **cotton on** (*inf*) *vi*: **he ~ed on to the fact that ...** zorientował się, że ...
**cotton candy** (*US*) *n* wata *f* cukrowa
**cotton wool** (*Brit*) *n* wata *f*
**couch** [kautʃ] *n* kanapa *f*; (*doctor's*) leżanka *f* ▷ *vt* (*statement, question*) formułować (sformułować *perf*); **the booklet was ~ed in legal jargon** broszura napisana była żargonem prawniczym
**couchette** [kuːˈʃɛt] *n* kuszetka *f*
**cough** [kɔf] *vi* (*person*) kaszleć (zakaszleć *perf*); (*engine*) krztusić się ▷ *n* kaszel *m*
**cough drop** *n* pastylka *f* na kaszel
**cough mixture** *n* syrop *m* na kaszel
**cough syrup** *n* = **cough mixture**
**could** [kud] *pt of* **can**
**couldn't** [ˈkudnt] = **could not**
**council** [ˈkaunsl] *n* rada *f*; **city** *or* **town ~** rada miejska; **C~ of Europe** Rada Europy
**council estate** (*Brit*) *n osiedle mieszkaniowe należące do lokalnych władz samorządowych*
**council house** (*Brit*) *n budynek mieszkalny należący do lokalnych władz samorządowych*
**council housing** (*Brit*) *n* ≈ budownictwo *nt* komunalne
**councillor** [ˈkaunsləʳ] *n* radny(-na) *m(f)*
**counsel** [ˈkaunsl] *n* (*advice*) rada *f*; (*lawyer*) prawnik *m* (*mogący występować w sądach wyższej instancji*) ▷ *vt*: **to ~ sth/sb to do sth** doradzać (doradzić *perf*) coś/komuś, by coś zrobił; **~ for the defence/the prosecution** obrońca/oskarżyciel

**counsellor** ['kaunslə^r] *n (advisor)*: **marriage** *etc* ~ pracownik(-ica) *m(f)* poradni małżeńskiej *etc*; *(US: lawyer)* adwokat *m*

**count** [kaunt] *vt* liczyć (policzyć *perf*) ▷ *vi (matter, qualify)* liczyć się; *(enumerate)* wyliczać (wyliczyć *perf*) ▷ *n (of things, people)* liczba *f*; *(of cholesterol, pollen etc)* poziom *m*; *(nobleman)* hrabia *m*; **to ~ (up) to ten** liczyć (policzyć *perf*) do dziesięciu; **to keep ~ of sth** prowadzić rachunek czegoś; **not ~ing the children** nie licząc dzieci; **ten ~ing him** razem z nim dziesięciu; **to ~ the cost of** obliczać (obliczyć *perf*) koszt *+gen*; **it ~s for very little** to niewiele znaczy; **~ yourself lucky** uważaj się za szczęściarza

▸ **count on** *vt fus* liczyć na *+acc*; **to ~ on doing sth** liczyć na zrobienie czegoś

▸ **count up** *vt fus* liczyć (policzyć *perf*)

**countdown** ['kauntdaun] *n* odliczanie *nt*

**countenance** ['kauntınəns] *n* oblicze *nt* ▷ *vt* aprobować (zaaprobować *perf*)

**counter** ['kauntə^r] *n (in shop, café)* lada *f*, kontuar *m*; *(in bank, post office)* okienko *nt*; *(in game)* pionek *m*; *(Tech)* licznik *m* ▷ *vt (oppose)* przeciwstawiać się (przeciwstawić się *perf*) *+dat*; *(blow)* odparowywać (odparować *perf*) ▷ *adv*: **to run ~ to** być niezgodnym z *+instr*; **to buy under the ~** *(fig)* kupować (kupić *perf*) spod lady; **to ~ with sth/by doing sth** odparowywać (odparować *perf*) czymś/robiąc coś

**counteract** ['kauntər'ækt] *vt (effect, tendency)* przeciwdziałać *+dat*; *(poison, bitterness)* neutralizować (zneutralizować *perf*)

**counterattack** ['kauntərə'tæk] *n* kontratak *m* ▷ *vi* kontratakować

**counterbalance** ['kauntə'bæləns] *vt* równoważyć (zrównoważyć *perf*)

**counter-clockwise** ['kauntə'klɔkwaız] *adv* przeciwnie do ruchu wskazówek zegara

**counter-espionage** ['kauntər'ɛspıənɑ:ʒ] *n* kontrwywiad *m*

**counterfeit** ['kauntəfıt] *n* fałszerstwo *nt* ▷ *vt* fałszować (sfałszować *perf*) ▷ *adj* fałszywy

**counterfoil** ['kauntəfɔıl] *n (of cheque, money order)* odcinek *m*

**counter-intelligence** *n* kontrwywiad *m*

**countermand** ['kauntəmɑ:nd] *vt* odwoływać (odwołać *perf*)

**counter-measure** *n* środek *m* zaradczy

**counter-offensive** *n* kontrofensywa *f*

**counterpane** ['kauntəpeın] *n* kapa *f*

**counterpart** ['kauntəpɑ:t] *n (of person, company)* odpowiednik *m*; *(of document)* kopia *f*

**counter-productive** ['kauntəprə'dʌktıv] *adj*: **to be ~** przynosić (przynieść *perf*) skutki odwrotne do zamierzonych

**counter-proposal** *n* kontrpropozycja *f*

**countersign** ['kauntəsaın] *vt* kontrasygnować

**countersink** ['kauntəsıŋk] *vt* nawiercać (nawiercić *perf*)

**countess** ['kauntıs] *n* hrabina *f*

**countless** ['kauntlıs] *adj* niezliczony

**countrified** ['kʌntrıfaıd] *adj* prowincjonalny

**country** ['kʌntrı] *n (state, population, native land)* kraj *m*; *(rural area)* wieś *f*; *(region)* teren *m*; **in the ~** na wsi; **mountainous ~** górzysty teren

**country and western (music)** *n* country *nt inv*, muzyka *f* country

**country dancing** *(Brit) n* tańce *pl* ludowe

**country house** *n* posiadłość *f or* rezydencja *f* wiejska

**countryman** ['kʌntrımən] *(irreg: like* **man***) n (compatriot)* rodak *m*; *(country dweller)* wieśniak *m*

**countryside** ['kʌntrısaıd] *n* krajobraz *m* (wiejski); **in the ~** na wsi

**country-wide** ['kʌntrı'waıd] *adj* ogólnokrajowy ▷ *adv* w całym kraju

**county** ['kauntı] *n* hrabstwo *nt*

**county town** *(Brit) n* stolica *f* hrabstwa

**coup** [ku:] *(pl* **~s***) n (also:* **coup d'état***)* zamach *m* stanu; *(achievement)* osiągnięcie *nt*

**coupé** [ku:'peı] *(Aut) n* coupé *nt inv*

**couple** ['kʌpl] *n* para *f* ▷ *vt (ideas, names)* łączyć (połączyć *perf*); *(machinery)* sczepiać (sczepić *perf*); **a ~ of** *(two)* para *+gen*; *(a few)* parę *+gen*

**couplet** ['kʌplıt] *n* dwuwiersz *m*

**coupling** ['kʌplıŋ] *(Rail) n* łącznik *m*

**coupon** ['ku:pɔn] *n (voucher)* talon *m*; *(detachable form)* kupon *m*, odcinek *m*

**courage** ['kʌrıdʒ] *n* odwaga *f*

**courageous** [kə'reıdʒəs] *adj* odważny

**courgette** [kuə'ʒɛt] *(Brit) n* cukinia *f*

**courier** ['kurıə^r] *n (messenger)* goniec *m*, kurier *m*; *(for tourists)* pilot *m*

**course** [kɔ:s] *n (Scol, Naut)* kurs *m*; *(of life, events, river)* bieg *m*; *(of injections, drugs)* seria *f*; *(approach)* stanowisko *nt*; *(Golf)* pole *nt*; *(part of meal)*: **first/next/last ~** pierwsze/następne/ostatnie danie *nt*; **of ~** oczywiście; **(no) of ~ not!** oczywiście, że nie!; **in the ~ of the next few days** w ciągu kilku następnych dni; **in due ~** w swoim czasie, we właściwym czasie; **~ of action** sposób *or* tryb postępowania; **the best ~ would be to ...** najlepszym wyjściem byłoby *+infin*; **we have no other ~ but to ...** nie mamy innego wyjścia, jak tylko *+infin*; **~ of lectures** cykl wykładów; **~ of treatment** *(Med)* leczenie, kuracja

**court** [kɔ:t] *n (royal)* dwór *m*; *(Jur)* sąd *m*; *(for tennis etc)* kort *m* ▷ *vt (woman)* zalecać się do

*+gen*; (*fig*: *favour, popularity*) zabiegać o *+acc*; (: *death, disaster*) igrać z *+instr*; **out of ~** (*Jur*) polubownie; **to take sb to ~** (*Jur*) podawać (podać *perf*) kogoś do sądu
**courteous** ['kə:tɪəs] *adj* uprzejmy
**courtesan** [kɔ:tɪ'zæn] *n* kurtyzana *f*
**courtesy** ['kə:təsɪ] *n* grzeczność *f*, uprzejmość *f*; **(by) ~ of** dzięki uprzejmości *+gen*
**courtesy light** (*Aut*) *n lampka w samochodzie włączająca się przy otwieraniu drzwi*
**court-house** ['kɔ:thaus] (*US*) *n* budynek *m* sądu
**courtier** ['kɔ:tɪə^r] *n* dworzanin *m*
**court-martial** (*pl* **courts-martial**) *n* sąd *m* wojenny *or* wojskowy ▷ *vt* oddawać (oddać *perf*) pod sąd wojenny
**court of appeal** (*pl* **courts of appeal**) *n* sąd *m* apelacyjny
**court of inquiry** (*pl* **courts of inquiry**) *n* komisja *f* śledcza *or* dochodzeniowa
**courtroom** ['kɔ:trum] *n* sala *f* rozpraw
**court shoe** *n* but *m* na wysokim obcasie
**courtyard** ['kɔ:tjɑ:d] *n* dziedziniec *m*
**cousin** ['kʌzn] *n* kuzyn(ka) *m(f)*; **first ~** (*male*) brat cioteczny; (*female*) siostra cioteczna
**cove** [kəuv] *n* zatoczka *f*
**covenant** ['kʌvənənt] *n* umowa *f*, ugoda *f* ▷ *vt*: **to ~ 200 pounds per year to a charity** zobowiązywać się (zobowiązać się *perf*) w drodze umowy do płacenia 200 funtów rocznie na cele dobroczynne.
**Coventry** ['kɔvəntrɪ] *n*: **to send sb to ~** (*fig*) bojkotować (zbojkotować *perf*) kogoś
**cover** ['kʌvə^r] *vt* (*protect, hide*): **to ~ (with)** zakrywać (zakryć *perf*) (*+instr*); (*Insurance*): **to ~ (for)** ubezpieczać (ubezpieczyć *perf*) (od *+gen*); (*include*) obejmować (objąć *perf*); (*distance*) przemierzać (przemierzyć *perf*), pokonywać (pokonać *perf*); (*topic*) omawiać (omówić *perf*), poruszać (poruszyć *perf*); (*Press*) robić (zrobić *perf*) reportaż o *+loc* ▷ *n* (*for furniture, machinery*) pokrowiec *m*; (*of book, magazine*) okładka *f*; (*shelter*) schronienie *nt*; (*Insurance*) zwrot *m* kosztów; (*fig*: *for illegal activities*) przykrywka *f*; **to be ~ed in** *or* **with** być pokrytym *+instr*; **to take ~** kryć się (skryć się *perf*), chronić się (schronić się *perf*); **under ~** osłonięty; **under ~ of darkness** pod osłoną ciemności; **under separate ~** (*Comm*) osobną pocztą; **50 pounds will ~ my expenses** 50 funtów pokryje moje wydatki
▸ **cover up** *vt* przykrywać (przykryć *perf*); (*fig*: *facts, mistakes*) tuszować (zatuszować *perf*); (: *feelings*) maskować ▷ *vi*: **to ~ up for sb** (*fig*) kryć *or* osłaniać kogoś
**coverage** ['kʌvərɪdʒ] *n* (*TV, Press*) sprawozdanie *nt*; **television ~ of the conference** telewizyjne sprawozdanie z konferencji; **to give full ~ to sth** szczegółowo coś omawiać (omówić *perf*)
**coveralls** ['kʌvərɔ:lz] (*US*) *npl* kombinezon *m*
**cover charge** *n* cena *f* wstępu (*w restauracji, nocnym lokalu itp*)
**covering** ['kʌvərɪŋ] *n* (*layer*) powłoka *f*; (*of snow, dust*) warstwa *f*
**covering letter**, (*US*) **cover letter** *n* list *m* przewodni *or* towarzyszący
**cover note** (*Insurance*) *n* (maklerska) nota *f* kryjąca
**cover price** *n* cena *f* katalogowa (*książki*)
**covert** ['kʌvət] *adj* (*glance*) ukradkowy; (*threat*) ukryty; (*attack*) z ukrycia *post*
**cover-up** ['kʌvərʌp] *n* tuszowanie *nt*, maskowanie *nt*
**covet** ['kʌvɪt] *vt* pożądać *+gen*
**cow** [kau] *n* krowa *f*; (*inf!*: *woman*) krowa *f* (*inf!*), krówsko *nt* (*inf!*) ▷ *cpd*: **cow whale** *etc* samica *f* wieloryba *etc* ▷ *vt* zastraszać (zastraszyć *perf*)
**coward** ['kauəd] *n* tchórz *m*
**cowardice** ['kauədɪs] *n* tchórzostwo *nt*
**cowardly** ['kauədlɪ] *adj* tchórzliwy
**cowboy** ['kaubɔɪ] *n* kowboj *m*; (*pej*) partacz *m*
**cow elephant** *n* słonica *f*
**cower** ['kauə^r] *vi* kulić się (skulić się *perf*)
**cowshed** ['kauʃɛd] *n* obora *f*
**cowslip** ['kauslɪp] *n* pierwiosnek *m*
**cox** [kɔks] *n abbr* = **coxswain**
**coxswain** ['kɔksn] *n* sternik *m*
**coy** [kɔɪ] *adj* nieśmiały, wstydliwy
**coyote** [kɔɪ'əutɪ] *n* kojot *m*
**cozy** ['kəuzɪ] (*US*) *adj* = **cosy**
**CP** *n abbr* (= *Communist Party*) Partia *f* Komunistyczna
**cp.** *abbr* (= *compare*) zob.
**c/p** (*Brit*) *abbr* (= *carriage paid*) przewóz opłacony
**CPA** (*US*) *n abbr* = **certified public accountant**
**CPI** *n abbr* (= *Consumer Price Index*) wskaźnik *m* cen artykułów konsumpcyjnych
**Cpl.** (*Mil*) *abbr* (= *corporal*) kpr.
**CP/M** *n abbr* (= *Central Program for Microprocessors*) CP/M *m*
**c.p.s.** (*Comput, Typ*) *abbr* (= *characters per second*) znaków/s
**CPSA** (*Brit*) *n abbr* (= *Civil and Public Services Association*) *związek zawodowy pracowników administracji państwowej*
**CPU** (*Comput*) *n abbr* = **central processing unit**
**cr.** *abbr* = **credit**; **creditor**
**crab** [kræb] *n* krab *m*; (*meat*) kraby *pl*
**crab apple** *n* dzika jabłoń *f*
**crack** [kræk] *n* (*noise*) trzask *m*; (*gap*) szczelina *f*, szpara *f*; (*in bone*) pęknięcie *nt*; (*in wall, dish*) pęknięcie *nt*, rysa *f*; (*joke*) kawał *m*; (*drug*)

crack *m*; (*inf: attempt*): **to have a ~ (at sth)** próbować (spróbować *perf*) swoich sił (w czymś) ▹ *vt* (*whip, twig*) trzaskać (trzasnąć *perf*) +*instr*; (*knee etc*) stłuc (*perf*); (*nut*) rozłupywać (rozłupać *perf*); (*problem*) rozgryzać (rozgryźć *perf*); (*code*) łamać (złamać *perf*) ▹ *adj* (*athlete, expert*) pierwszorzędny; (*regiment*) elitarny; **to ~ jokes** (*inf*) opowiadać kawały; **I ~ed a glass** pękła mi szklanka; **to get ~ing** (*inf*) zabierać się (zabrać się *perf*) do roboty
▸ **crack down on** *vt fus* (*offenders etc*) rozprawiać się (rozprawić się *perf*) z +*instr*
▸ **crack up** *vi* (*Psych*) załamywać się (załamać się *perf*)

**crackdown** ['krækdaun] *n*: **~ (on)** rozprawa *f* (z +*instr*)

**cracked** [krækt] (*inf*) *adj* stuknięty (*inf*)

**cracker** ['krækə[r]] *n* (*biscuit*) krakers *m*; (*firework*) petarda *f*; (*Christmas cracker*) *kolorowy walec z papieru, zawierający niespodziankę i eksplodujący przy otwarciu*; **a ~ of a shot** (*Brit: inf*) pierwszorzędny strzał; **he's ~s** (*Brit: inf*) on jest stuknięty (*inf*)

**crackle** ['krækl] *vi* (*fire, twig*) trzaskać

**crackling** ['kræklıŋ] *n* (*of fire etc*) trzaskanie *nt*; (*on radio, telephone*) trzaski *pl*; (*pork*) (przypieczona) skórka *f*

**cradle** ['kreıdl] *n* kołyska *f* ▹ *vt* tulić

**craft** [krɑ:ft] *n* (*weaving etc*) rękodzieło *nt*; (*journalism etc*) sztuka *f*; (*skill*) biegłość *f*; (*pl inv: boat*) statek *m*; (*: plane*) samolot *m*

**craftsman** ['krɑ:ftsmən] (*irreg: like* **man**) *n* rzemieślnik *m*

**craftsmanship** ['krɑ:ftsmənʃıp] *n* kunszt *m*

**crafty** ['krɑ:ftı] *adj* przebiegły

**crag** [kræg] *n* grań *f*

**craggy** ['krægı] *adj* (*mountain, cliff*) urwisty; (*face*) wyrazisty

**cram** [kræm] *vt*: **to ~ sth with** wypełniać (wypełnić *perf*) coś (po brzegi) +*instr* ▹ *vi* kuć (*inf*), wkuwać (*inf*); **he ~med the bank notes into his pockets** poupychał banknoty po kieszeniach

**cramming** ['kræmıŋ] *n* kucie *nt* (*inf*), wkuwanie *nt* (*inf*)

**cramp** [kræmp] *n* (*Med*) skurcz *m* ▹ *vt* hamować (zahamować *perf*) rozwój +*gen*

**cramped** [kræmpt] *adj* (*accommodation*) ciasny

**crampon** ['kræmpən] (*for climbing*) *n* raki *pl*

**cranberry** ['krænbərı] *n* borówka *f*, żurawina *f*

**crane** [kreın] *n* (*machine*) dźwig *m*; (*bird*) żuraw *m* ▹ *vt*: **to ~ one's neck** wyciągać (wyciągnąć *perf*) szyję ▹ *vi*: **to ~ forward** wyciągać szyję

**cranium** ['kreınıəm] (*pl* **crania**) *n* czaszka *f*

**crank** [kræŋk] *n* (*person*) nawiedzony(-na) *m(f)* (*inf*); (*handle*) korba *f*

**crankshaft** ['kræŋkʃɑ:ft] (*Aut*) *n* wał *m* korbowy

**cranky** ['kræŋkı] *adj* nawiedzony (*inf*)

**cranny** ['krænı] *n see* **nook**

**crap** [kræp] (*inf!*) *n* gówno *nt* (*inf!*) ▹ *vi* srać (*inf!*); **to have a ~** wysrać się (*perf*) (*inf!*)

**crash** [kræʃ] *n* (*noise*) trzask *m*; (*Comm*) krach *m* ▹ *vt* rozbijać (rozbić *perf*) ▹ *vi* (*plane, car*) rozbijać się (rozbić się *perf*); (*two cars*) zderzać się (zderzyć się *perf*); (*glass, cup*) roztrzaskiwać się (roztrzaskać się *perf*); (*market, firm*) upadać (upaść *perf*); **car ~** wypadek samochodowy; **plane ~** katastrofa lotnicza; **to ~ into** wpadać (wpaść *perf*) na +*acc*; **he ~ed the car into a wall** rozbił samochód o mur; **the door ~ed open** drzwi otwarły się z trzaskiem

**crash barrier** (*Brit*) *n* bariera *f* ochronna *or* zabezpieczająca

**crash course** *n* błyskawiczny kurs *m*

**crash helmet** *n* kask *m* (*motocyklowy*)

**crash landing, crash-landing** *n* lądowanie *nt* awaryjne

**crass** [kræs] *adj* (*person, comment*) głupi, prymitywny; (*ignorance*) rażący

**crate** [kreıt] *n* (*of fruit, wine*) skrzynka *f*; (*inf: vehicle*) gruchot *m* (*inf*)

**crater** ['kreıtə[r]] *n* (*of volcano*) krater *m*; (*of bomb blast*) lej *m*

**cravat** [krə'væt] *n* apaszka *f*

**crave** [kreıv] *vt* (*also*: **crave for**: *drink, cigarette*) mieć nieprzepartą ochotę na +*acc*; (*: luxury, admiration*) być złaknionym +*gen*

**craving** ['kreıvıŋ] *n* (*for drink, cigarette*) ochota *f*; (*for luxury*) pragnienie *nt*

**crawl** [krɔ:l] *vi* (*adult*) czołgać się; (*baby*) raczkować; (*insect*) pełzać, pełznąć; (*vehicle*) wlec się; (*inf*): **to ~ (to sb)** czołgać się *or* płaszczyć się (przed kimś) ▹ *n* kraul *m*; **I ~ed in/out** wczołgałem się (do środka)/wyczołgałem się (na zewnątrz); **we were driving along at a ~** posuwaliśmy się bardzo powoli

**crayfish** ['kreıfıʃ] *n inv* (*freshwater*) rak *m*; (*saltwater*) langusta *f*

**crayon** ['kreıən] *n* kredka *f*

**craze** [kreız] *n* moda *f*, szaleństwo *nt* (*fig*)

**crazed** [kreızd] *adj* (*look, person*) szalony; (*pottery, glaze*) popękany

**crazy** ['kreızı] *adj* pomylony, zwariowany; **to be ~ about sb/sth** (*inf*) szaleć za kimś/czymś, mieć bzika na punkcie kogoś/czegoś (*inf*); **to go ~** wariować (zwariować *perf*)

**crazy paving** (*Brit*) *n* chodnik *m* z mozaiki

**creak** [kri:k] *vi* skrzypieć (zaskrzypieć *perf*)

**cream** [kri:m] *n* (*from milk*) śmietana *f*, śmietanka *f*; (*cake and chocolate filling, cosmetic*)

krem *m*; *(fig)* śmietanka *f* ▷ *adj* kremowy; **whipped** ~ bita śmietana
▸ **cream off** *vt (best talents)* wyławiać (wyłowić *perf*); *(part of profits)* zgarniać (zgarnąć *perf*)
**cream cake** *n* ciastko *nt* z kremem
**cream cheese** *n* serek *m* śmietankowy
**creamery** ['kri:mərɪ] *n* mleczarnia *f*
**creamy** ['kri:mɪ] *adj (colour)* kremowy; *(milk)* tłusty; *(coffee)* ze śmietanką *post*
**crease** [kri:s] *n (fold)* zgięcie *nt*; *(wrinkle)* zmarszczka *f*; *(in trousers)* kant *m* ▷ *vt* gnieść (pognieść *perf*), miąć (pomiąć *perf*) ▷ *vi* gnieść się (pognieść się *perf*), miąć się (pomiąć się *perf*)
**crease-resistant** ['kri:srɪzɪstənt] *adj* niemnący
**create** [kri:'eɪt] *vt* tworzyć (stworzyć *perf*); *(interest, fuss)* wywoływać (wywołać *perf*)
**creation** [kri:'eɪʃən] *n (bringing into existence)* tworzenie *nt*; *(production, design)* wyrób *m*; *(Rel)* stworzenie *nt* (świata)
**creative** [kri:'eɪtɪv] *adj (artistic)* twórczy; *(inventive)* twórczy, kreatywny
**creativity** [kri:eɪ'tɪvɪtɪ] *n* inwencja *f* (twórcza)
**creator** [kri:'eɪtə<sup>r</sup>] *n* twórca(-rczyni) *m(f)*; **the C**~ Stwórca *m*
**creature** ['kri:tʃə<sup>r</sup>] *n* stworzenie *nt*
**crèche** [krɛʃ] *n* ≈ żłobek *m*
**credence** ['kri:dns] *n*: **to lend** *or* **give ~ to** dawać (dać *perf*) wiarę *+dat*
**credentials** [krɪ'dɛnʃlz] *npl (references)* referencje *pl*; *(identity papers)* dokumenty *pl*
**credibility** [krɛdɪ'bɪlɪtɪ] *n* wiarygodność *f*
**credible** ['krɛdɪbl] *adj* wiarygodny
**credit** ['krɛdɪt] *n (Comm)* kredyt *m*; *(recognition)* uznanie *nt*; *(Scol)* ≈ zaliczenie *nt* ▷ *adj (Comm: balance etc)* dodatni ▷ *vt (believe)* dawać (dać *perf*) wiarę *+dat*; *(Comm)*: **to ~ sth to sb/sb's account** zapisywać (zapisać *perf*) coś na dobro czyjegoś rachunku; **credits** *npl (Film, TV)* napisy *pl* (końcowe); **to be in** ~ być wypłacalnym; **on the ~ side** po stronie „ma"; **to ~ sb with sth** *(fig)* przypisywać (przypisać *perf*) komuś coś; **to ~ 50 pounds to sb** zapisać *(perf)* 50 funtów na czyjeś konto; **on** ~ na kredyt; **it is to their ~ that ...** to ich zasługa, że..., to dzięki nim...; **to take the ~ for** przypisywać (przypisać *perf*) sobie *+acc*; **it does you** ~ to dobrze o tobie świadczy; **he's a ~ to his family** jest chlubą swojej rodziny
**creditable** ['krɛdɪtəbl] *adj* zaszczytny, godny uznania
**credit account** *n* konto *nt* kredytowe
**credit agency** *(Brit)* *n* biuro *nt* informacji kredytowej
**credit bureau** *(US)* *n* = **credit agency**
**credit card** *n* karta *f* kredytowa
**credit control** *(Econ)* *n* kontrola *f* kredytów
**credit facilities** *npl* udogodnienia *pl* kredytowe
**credit limit** *n* maksymalny kredyt *m*, limit *m* kredytu
**credit note** *(Brit)* *n pokwitowanie zwrotu zakupionego towaru, uprawniające do kupna towarów za tę samą sumę*
**creditor** ['krɛdɪtə<sup>r</sup>] *n* wierzyciel *m*
**credit transfer** *n* przelew *m* (bankowy)
**creditworthy** ['krɛdɪt'wə:ðɪ] *adj* rzetelny
**credulity** [krɪ'dju:lɪtɪ] *n* łatwowierność *f*
**creed** [kri:d] *n* wyznanie *nt*
**creek** [kri:k] *n (inlet)* wąska zatoka *f*; *(US: stream)* strumień *m*; **to be up the** ~ *(inf)* być w tarapatach
**creel** [kri:l] *n (also:* **lobster creel***)* kosz *m (na ryby, homary itp)*
**creep** [kri:p] *(pt, pp* **crept***)* *vi (person, animal)* skradać się; *(plant)* płozić się ▷ *n (inf)* lizus *m (inf)*; **it gives me the ~s** przyprawia mnie to o gęsią skórkę; **to ~ up on sb** podkradać się (podkraść się *perf*) do kogoś
**creeper** ['kri:pə<sup>r</sup>] *n* pnącze *nt*
**creepy** ['kri:pɪ] *adj* straszny
**creepy-crawly** ['kri:pɪ'krɔ:lɪ] *(inf)* *n* robal *m (inf)*
**cremate** [krɪ'meɪt] *vt* poddawać (poddać *perf*) kremacji
**cremation** [krɪ'meɪʃən] *n* kremacja *f*
**crematoria** [krɛmə'tɔ:rɪə] *npl of* **crematorium**
**crematorium** [krɛmə'tɔ:rɪəm] *(pl* **crematoria***)* *n* krematorium *nt*
**creosote** ['kri:əsəut] *n* kreozot *m*
**crepe** [kreɪp] *n* krepa *f (tkanina lub rodzaj kauczuku)*
**crepe bandage** *(Brit)* *n* bandaż *m* elastyczny
**crepe paper** *n* krepina *f*, bibułka *f* marszczona *or* krepowa
**crepe sole** *n* kauczukowa podeszwa *f*
**crept** [krɛpt] *pt, pp of* **creep**
**crescendo** [krɪ'ʃɛndəu] *n (Mus)* crescendo *nt inv*; *(noise)*: **in a** ~ coraz głośniej
**crescent** ['krɛsnt] *n (shape)* półksiężyc *m*; *(street)* ulica *f (w kształcie półkola)*
**cress** [krɛs] *n* rzeżucha *f*
**crest** [krɛst] *n (of hill)* szczyt *m*, wierzchołek *m*; *(of bird)* czub(ek) *m*, grzebień *m (z piór)*; *(coat of arms)* herb *m*
**crestfallen** ['krɛstfɔ:lən] *adj* strapiony
**Crete** [kri:t] *n* Kreta *f*
**crevasse** [krɪ'væs] *n* szczelina *f* lodowca
**crevice** ['krɛvɪs] *n* szczelina *f* (skalna)
**crew** [kru:] *n (Naut, Aviat)* załoga *f*; *(TV, Film)* ekipa *f*; *(gang)* zgraja *f*

**crew-cut** ['kru:kʌt] *n* fryzura *f* na jeża, jeżyk *m* (*inf*)
**crew-neck** ['kru:nɛk] *n* (*jersey*) pulower *m* (*z okrągłym wykończeniem przy szyi*)
**crib** [krɪb] *n* (*cot*) łóżeczko *nt* (dziecięce); (*Rel*) żłóbek *m* ▷ *vt* (*inf: copy*) ściągać (ściągnąć *perf*) (*inf*)
**cribbage** ['krɪbɪdʒ] *n gra karciana, w której jako tabeli wyników używa się drewnianej planszy z wtykanymi kołkami*
**crick** [krɪk] *n* (*in neck. back*) (bolesny) skurcz *m*, strzyknięcie *nt* (*inf*)
**cricket** ['krɪkɪt] *n* (*Sport*) krykiet *m*; (*insect*) świerszcz *m*
**cricketer** ['krɪkɪtəʳ] *n* gracz *m* w krykieta
**crime** [kraɪm] *n* (*illegal activities*) przestępczość *f*; (*illegal action*) przestępstwo *nt*; (*fig*) zbrodnia *f*
**crime wave** *n* fala *f* przestępczości
**criminal** ['krɪmɪnl] *n* przestępca(-pczyni) *m*(*f*) ▷ *adj* (*illegal*) kryminalny; (*morally wrong*) karygodny; **~ law** prawo karne; **C~ Investigation Department** (*Brit*) ≈ wydział kryminalny
**crimp** [krɪmp] *vt* (*fabric*) marszczyć (zmarszczyć *perf*) brzegi *+gen*; (*pastry*) zaginać (zagiąć *perf*) brzegi *+gen*; (*hair*) karbować
**crimson** ['krɪmzn] *adj* karmazynowy
**cringe** [krɪndʒ] *vi* kulić się (skulić się *perf*)
**crinkle** ['krɪŋkl] *vt* marszczyć (zmarszczyć *perf*) (lekko)
**cripple** ['krɪpl] *n* (*old*) kaleka *m* ▷ *vt* (*person*) okaleczać (okaleczyć *perf*), uczynić (*perf*) kaleką; (*ship, plane*) unieruchamiać (unieruchomić *perf*); (*production, exports*) paraliżować (sparaliżować *perf*); **~d with rheumatism** sparaliżowany przez reumatyzm
**crippling** ['krɪplɪŋ] *adj* (*disease*) wyniszczający; (*taxation, debts*) rujnujący
**crises** ['kraɪsi:z] *npl of* **crisis**
**crisis** ['kraɪsɪs] (*pl* **crises**) *n* kryzys *m*
**crisp** [krɪsp] *adj* (*vegetables*) kruchy; (*bacon, roll*) chrupiący; (*weather*) rześki; (*tone, reply*) rzeczowy
**crisps** [krɪsps] (*Brit*) *npl* chrupki *pl*, chipsy *pl*
**criss-cross** ['krɪskrɔs] *adj* (*pattern etc*) kratkowany ▷ *vt* przecinać (wzdłuż i wszerz)
**criteria** [kraɪ'tɪərɪə] *npl of* **criterion**
**criterion** [kraɪ'tɪərɪən] (*pl* **criteria**) *n* kryterium *nt*
**critic** ['krɪtɪk] *n* krytyk *m*
**critical** ['krɪtɪkl] *adj* krytyczny; **to be ~ of sb/sth** mieć krytyczny stosunek do kogoś/czegoś
**critically** ['krɪtɪklɪ] *adv* krytycznie; **he's ~ ill** jest w stanie krytycznym
**criticism** ['krɪtɪsɪzəm] *n* (*disapproval, complaint*) krytyka *f*; (*of book, play*) analiza *f* krytyczna; **literary ~** krytyka literacka
**criticize** ['krɪtɪsaɪz] *vt* krytykować (skrytykować *perf*)
**critique** [krɪ'ti:k] *n* krytyka *f*, analiza *f* krytyczna; **a ~ of Socialism** krytyka socjalizmu
**croak** [krəuk] *vi* (*frog*) rechotać (zarechotać *perf*); (*crow*) krakać (zakrakać *perf*); (*person*) chrypieć (zachrypieć *perf*)
**Croatia** [krəu'eɪʃə] *n* Chorwacja *f*
**crochet** ['krəuʃeɪ] *n* szydełkowanie *nt*
**crock** [krɔk] *n* garnek *m* gliniany; (*inf: vehicle*) grat *m* (*inf*); (*: person*) ramol *m* (*inf*)
**crockery** ['krɔkərɪ] (*also:* **crocks**) *n* naczynia *pl* stołowe
**crocodile** ['krɔkədaɪl] *n* krokodyl *m*
**crocus** ['krəukəs] *n* krokus *m*
**croft** [krɔft] (*Brit*) *n* małe gospodarstwo *nt*
**crofter** ['krɔftəʳ] (*Brit*) *n* właściciel *m* małego gospodarstwa, chłop *m* małorolny (*old*)
**crone** [krəun] *n* starucha *f*
**crony** ['krəunɪ] (*inf*) *n* kumpel *m* (*inf*)
**crook** [kruk] *n* (*criminal*) kanciarz *m*; (*of shepherd*) kij *m* pasterski; (*of arm*) zgięcie *nt*
**crooked** ['krukɪd] *adj* (*branch, table, smile*) krzywy; (*street, lane*) kręty; (*person*) nieuczciwy
**crop** [krɔp] *n* (*plant*) roślina *f* uprawna; (*harvest*) zbiór *m*, plon *m*; (*amount produced*) produkcja *f*; (*also:* **riding crop**) szpicruta *f* (*zakończona pętelką*); (*of bird*) wole *nt* ▷ *vt* (*hair*) przycinać (przyciąć *perf*) (krótko); (*animal: grass, leaves*) skubać
▸ **crop up** *vi* pojawiać się (pojawić się *perf*)
**crop circle** *n* (*Brit*) *tajemnicze koliste znaki ze złamanych kłosów pojawiające się na polu*
**cropper** ['krɔpəʳ] (*inf*) *n*: **to come a ~** dawać (dać *perf*) plamę (*inf*)
**crop spraying** [-'spreɪɪŋ] *n* opylanie *nt* zbiorów
**croquet** ['krəukeɪ] (*Brit*) *n* krokiet *m* (*gra*)
**croquette** [krə'kɛt] *n* krokiet *m* (*potrawa*)
**cross** [krɔs] *n* krzyż *m*; (*small*) krzyżyk *m*; (*Bio, Bot*) krzyżówka *f* ▷ *vt* (*street, room*) przechodzić (przejść *perf*) przez *+acc*; (*cheque*) zakreślać (zakreślić *perf*); (*arms, animals, plants*) krzyżować (skrzyżować *perf*); (*thwart: person*) psuć (popsuć *perf*) szyki *+dat*; (*: plan*) krzyżować (pokrzyżować *perf*) ▷ *vi*: **the boat ~es from ... to ...** łódź kursuje między *+instr* a *+instr* ▷ *adj* podenerwowany, poirytowany; **to ~ o.s.** żegnać się (przeżegnać się *perf*); **to ~ one's legs** zakładać (założyć *perf*) nogę na nogę; **we have a ~ed line** (*Brit: Tel*) mamy przebicia na linii; **they've got their lines** *or*

**wires ~ed** (*fig*) mówią o dwóch różnych rzeczach; **to be ~ with sb (about sth)** być poirytowanym na kogoś (o coś)
▶ **cross out** *vt* skreślać (skreślić *perf*)
▶ **cross over** *vi* przechodzić (przejść *perf*) na drugą stronę
**crossbar** ['krɔsbɑːʳ] (*Sport*) *n* poprzeczka *f*
**crossbreed** ['krɔsbriːd] *n* mieszaniec *m*
**cross-Channel ferry** ['krɔs'tʃænl-] *n* prom *m* kursujący po kanale La Manche
**crosscheck**, (*US*) **cross-check** ['krɔstʃɛk] *n* powtórne badanie *nt* ▷ *vt* powtórnie badać (zbadać *perf*)
**cross-country (race)** ['krɔs'kʌntrɪ-] *n* wyścig *m* przełajowy
**cross-examination** ['krɔsɪgzæmɪ'neɪʃən] (*Jur*) *n* przesłuchanie *nt* (*świadka strony przeciwnej*)
**cross-examine** ['krɔsɪg'zæmɪn] (*Jur*) *vt* przesłuchiwać (przesłuchać *perf*) (*świadka strony przeciwnej*)
**cross-eyed** ['krɔsaɪd] *adj* zezowaty
**crossfire** ['krɔsfaɪəʳ] *n* ogień *m* krzyżowy; **to get caught in the ~** dostać się (*perf*) w ogień krzyżowy; (*fig*) znaleźć się (*perf*) między młotem a kowadłem
**crossing** ['krɔsɪŋ] *n* (*sea passage*) przeprawa *f*; (*also*: **pedestrian crossing**) przejście *nt* dla pieszych
**crossing guard** (*US*) *n osoba przeprowadzająca dzieci przez jezdnię w drodze do/ze szkoły*
**cross-purposes** ['krɔs'pəːpəsɪz] *npl*: **we are at ~** nie rozumiemy się; **we're talking at ~** mówimy o różnych rzeczach
**cross-reference** ['krɔs'rɛfrəns] *n* odsyłacz *m*
**crossroads** ['krɔsrəudz] *n* skrzyżowanie *nt*
**cross section** *n* przekrój *m*
**crosswalk** ['krɔswɔːk] (*US*) *n* przejście *nt* dla pieszych
**crosswind** ['krɔswɪnd] *n* boczny wiatr *m*
**crosswise** ['krɔswaɪz] *adv* w poprzek
**crossword** ['krɔswəːd] *n* krzyżówka *f*
**crotch** [krɔtʃ], **crutch** *n* (*Anat*) krocze *nt*; (*of garment*) krok *m*
**crotchet** ['krɔtʃɪt] *n* ćwierćnuta *f*
**crotchety** ['krɔtʃɪtɪ] *adj* zrzędny
**crouch** [krautʃ] *vi* (*move*) kucać (kucnąć *perf*), przykucać (przykucnąć *perf*); (*sit*) siedzieć w kucki
**croup** [kruːp] (*Med*) *n* krup *m*, dławiec *m* rzekomy
**croupier** ['kruːpɪəʳ] *n* krupier *m*
**croutons** ['kruːtɔnz] *npl* grzanki *pl* (*małe, w zupie*)
**crow** [krəu] *n* wrona *f* ▷ *vi* piać (zapiać *perf*); (*fig*): **to ~ over sth** piać (z zachwytu) nad czymś
**crowbar** ['krəubɑːʳ] *n* łom *m*
**crowd** [kraud] *n* tłum *m* ▷ *vt*: **to ~ sb/sth in/into** wpychać (wepchnąć *perf*) kogoś/coś do środka/do *+gen* ▷ *vi*: **to ~ round sb/sth** tłoczyć się (stłoczyć się *perf*) dookoła kogoś/czegoś; **to ~ in/into** wpychać się (wepchnąć się *perf*) do środka/do *+gen*; **the/our ~** (nasza) paczka (*inf*); **~s of people** tłumy ludzi
**crowded** ['kraudɪd] *adj* (*full*) zatłoczony; (*densely populated*) przeludniony; **~ with** pełen *+gen*
**crowd scene** (*Film*) *n* scena *f* zbiorowa
**crown** [kraun] *n* (*of monarch, tooth*) korona *f*; (*of head*) ciemię *nt*; (*of hill*) wierzchołek *m*, szczyt *m*; (*of hat*) denko *nt* ▷ *vt* koronować (ukoronować *perf*); (*fig*) ukoronować (*perf*), uwieńczyć (*perf*); **the C~** (*monarchy*) Korona; **and to ~ it all ...** (*fig*) a na dodatek (jeszcze)...
**crown court** (*Brit*) *n Sąd Koronny do spraw karnych (w Anglii i Walii)*
**crowning** ['kraunɪŋ] *adj* (*achievement*) czołowy; (*ambition*) nadrzędny; **her hair is her ~ glory** włosy są jej głównym atutem
**crown jewels** *npl* klejnoty *pl* koronne
**crown prince** *n* następca *m* tronu
**crow's feet** *npl* kurze łapki *pl*
**crow's nest** *n* (*Naut*) bocianie gniazdo *nt*
**crucial** ['kruːʃl] *adj* (*vote*) rozstrzygający, decydujący; (*issue*) zasadniczy, kluczowy; **~ to** kluczowy dla *+gen*
**crucifix** ['kruːsɪfɪks] *n* krucyfiks *m*
**crucifixion** [kruːsɪ'fɪkʃən] *n* ukrzyżowanie *nt*
**crucify** ['kruːsɪfaɪ] *vt* krzyżować (ukrzyżować *perf*); **if he catches us he'll ~ us** jak nas złapie, to nas zamorduje
**crude** [kruːd] *adj* (*materials*) surowy; (*tool*) prosty, prymitywny; (*person*) niekrzesany
**crude (oil)** *n* ropa *f* naftowa
**cruel** ['kruəl] *adj* okrutny
**cruelty** ['kruəltɪ] *n* okrucieństwo *nt*
**cruet** ['kruːɪt] *n* komplet *m* do przypraw (*lub sam stojaczek, na którym umieszczone są pojemniki z solą, pieprzem itp*)
**cruise** [kruːz] *n* rejs *m* wycieczkowy ▷ *vi* (*ship*) płynąć (ze stałą prędkością); (*car*) jechać (ze stałą prędkością); (*aircraft*) lecieć (ze stałą prędkością); (*taxi*) krążyć
**cruise missile** *n* pocisk *m* samosterujący dalekiego zasięgu
**cruiser** ['kruːzəʳ] *n* (*motorboat*) łódź *f* motorowa; (*warship*) krążownik *m*
**cruising speed** *n* (stała) prędkość *f* jazdy
**crumb** [krʌm] *n* okruch *m*; (*small*) okruszek *m*; (*fig*: *of information, comfort*) odrobina *f*
**crumble** ['krʌmbl] *vt* kruszyć (pokruszyć *perf*) ▷ *vi* (*bread, plaster, brick*) kruszyć się (pokruszyć się *perf*); (*building, society, organization*) rozpadać się (rozpaść się *perf*)

**crumbly** ['krʌmblɪ] *adj* kruchy
**crummy** ['krʌmɪ] *(inf) adj* lichy
**crumpet** ['krʌmpɪt] *n okrągły placek spożywany na gorąco z masłem, konfiturami itp*
**crumple** ['krʌmpl] *vt (paper)* gnieść (zgnieść *perf*), miąć (zmiąć *perf*); *(clothes)* gnieść (pognieść *perf*), miąć (wymiąć *perf*)
**crunch** [krʌntʃ] *vt (food etc)* chrupać (schrupać *perf*); *(underfoot)* miażdżyć (zmiażdżyć *perf*) ▷ *n*: **the ~** *(fig)* krytyczny moment *m*; **if it comes to the ~** jak przyjdzie co do czego
**crunchy** ['krʌntʃɪ] *adj (food)* chrupiący, chrupki; *(snow, gravel)* skrzypiący, chrzęszczący
**crusade** [kru:'seɪd] *n* wyprawa *f* krzyżowa, krucjata *f*; *(fig)* kampania *f* ▷ *vi (fig)*: **to ~ for/against** prowadzić kampanię na rzecz *+gen*/przeciwko *+dat*
**crusader** [kru:'seɪdəʳ] *n* krzyżowiec *m*; *(fig)*: **moral ~** orędownik(-iczka) *m(f)* moralności
**crush** [krʌʃ] *n (crowd)* (gęsty) tłum *m*; *(drink)* sok *m (ze świeżych owoców i wody)* ▷ *vt (press, break)* miażdżyć (zmiażdżyć *perf*); *(grapes)* wyciskać (wycisnąć *perf*); *(paper)* gnieść (zgnieść *perf*), miąć (zmiąć *perf*); *(clothes)* gnieść (pognieść *perf*), miąć (wymiąć *perf*); *(garlic)* rozgniatać (rozgnieść *perf*); *(ice, rock)* kruszyć (skruszyć *perf*); *(enemy, opposition)* roznosić (roznieść *perf*); *(hopes, person)* zdruzgotać *(perf)*; **to have a ~ on sb** być zadurzonym w kimś
**crush barrier** *(Brit) n* = **crash barrier**
**crushing** ['krʌʃɪŋ] *adj (defeat, blow)* druzgocący
**crust** [krʌst] *n (of bread)* skórka *f*; *(of snow, ice)* skorupa *f*; **the earth's ~** skorupa ziemska
**crustacean** [krʌs'teɪʃən] *n* skorupiak *m*
**crusty** ['krʌstɪ] *adj* chrupiący
**crutch** [krʌtʃ] *n (Med)* kula *f*; *(fig)* podpora *f*; *see* **crotch**
**crux** [krʌks] *n* sedno *nt*
**cry** [kraɪ] *vi (weep)* płakać (zapłakać *perf*); *(also:* **cry out***)* krzyczeć (krzyknąć *perf*) ▷ *n (shriek)* (o)krzyk *m*; *(of bird)* krzyk *m*; *(of wolf)* wycie *nt*; **what are you crying about?** dlaczego płaczesz?; **to cry for help** wołać (zawołać *perf*) o pomoc; **she had a good cry** porządnie się wypłakała; **this is a far cry from ...** *(fig)* daleko temu do *+gen*
▸ **cry off** *(inf) vi* wycofywać się (wycofać się *perf*)
**crying** ['kraɪɪŋ] *adj (fig: need)* palący; **it's a ~ shame** to woła o pomstę do nieba
**crypt** [krɪpt] *n* krypta *f*
**cryptic** ['krɪptɪk] *adj* zagadkowy
**crystal** ['krɪstl] *n* kryształ *m*
**crystal clear** *adj (sky, air, sound)* kryształowo czysty; *(point, position)* absolutnie jasny
**crystallize** ['krɪstəlaɪz] *vt* krystalizować (skrystalizować *perf*) ▷ *vi (lit, fig)* krystalizować się (skrystalizować się *perf*); **~d fruits** *(Brit)* owoce kandyzowane
**CSA** *n abbr* = **Confederate States of America**
**CSC** *n abbr (= Civil Service Commission) komisja administracji państwowej*
**CSE** *(Brit) n abbr (formerly: = Certificate of Secondary Education) świadectwo ukończenia szkoły średniej*
**CS gas** *(Brit) n* gaz *m* łzawiący
**CST** *(US) abbr* = **Central Standard Time**
**CT** *(US: Post) abbr* = **Connecticut**
**ct** *abbr (= carat)* kt
**CTC** *(Brit) n abbr* = **city technology college**
**cu.** *abbr* = **cubic**
**cub** [kʌb] *n (of wild animal)* młode *nt*; *(also:* **cub scout***)* ≈ zuch *m*; **lion/wolf/bear cub** lwiątko/wilczek/niedźwiadek
**Cuba** ['kju:bə] *n* Kuba *f*
**Cuban** ['kju:bən] *adj* kubański ▷ *n* Kubańczyk(-anka) *m(f)*
**cubbyhole** ['kʌbɪhəul] *n* kącik *m*
**cube** [kju:b] *n (shape)* kostka *f*; *(Math)* sześcian *m*, trzecia potęga *f* ▷ *vt* podnosić (podnieść *perf*) do sześcianu
**cube root** *n* pierwiastek *m* sześcienny *or* trzeciego stopnia
**cubic** ['kju:bɪk] *adj (metre, foot)* sześcienny; **~ volume** *(of liquid, gas)* objętość; *(of container)* pojemność
**cubic capacity** *n* pojemność *f*
**cubicle** ['kju:bɪkl] *n (at pool)* kabina *f*; *(in hospital) część sali oddzielona zasłoną*
**cubism** ['kju:bɪzəm] *n* kubizm *m*
**cuckoo** ['kuku:] *n* kukułka *f*
**cuckoo clock** *n* zegar *m* z kukułką
**cucumber** ['kju:kʌmbəʳ] *n* ogórek *m*
**cud** [kʌd] *n*: **to chew the cud** *(fig)* rozmyślać, dumać
**cuddle** ['kʌdl] *vt (baby)* przytulać (przytulić *perf*); *(lover)* pieścić ▷ *n*: **to give sb a ~** przytulić *(perf)* kogoś
**cuddly** ['kʌdlɪ] *adj (person, animal)* milusi; **a ~ toy** przytulanka
**cudgel** ['kʌdʒl] *n* pałka *f* ▷ *vt*: **to ~ one's brains** zachodzić w głowę, łamać sobie głowę
**cue** [kju:] *n (snooker cue)* kij *m* bilardowy; *(hint)* sygnał *m*
**cuff** [kʌf] *n (of garment)* mankiet *m*; *(blow)* trzepnięcie *nt* ▷ *vt* trzepać (trzepnąć *perf*); **off the ~** (tak) z głowy
**cuff links** *npl* spinki *pl* do mankietów
**cu. in.** *abbr (= cubic inches)* cali sześciennych
**cuisine** [kwɪ'zi:n] *n* kuchnia *f (danego regionu, kraju itp)*
**cul-de-sac** ['kʌldəsæk] *n* ślepa uliczka *f*

**culinary** ['kʌlɪnərɪ] *adj* kulinarny
**cull** [kʌl] *vt* (*story, idea*) zaczerpnąć (*perf*); (*wild animals*) odstrzeliwać (odstrzelić *perf*); (*domestic animals*) dokonywać (dokonać *perf*) uboju *+gen* (*selektywnego*) ▷ *n* (*of wild animals*) odstrzał *m*; (*of domestic animals*) ubój *m* selektywny
**culminate** ['kʌlmɪneɪt] *vi*: **to ~ in** kończyć się (zakończyć się *perf*) *+instr*
**culmination** [kʌlmɪ'neɪʃən] *n* (*of career etc*) ukoronowanie *nt*; (*of process*) punkt *m* kulminacyjny
**culottes** [kju:'lɔts] *npl* spódnica *f* — spodnie *pl* (*o długości do kolan*)
**culpable** ['kʌlpəbl] *adj* winny
**culprit** ['kʌlprɪt] *n* (*of crime*) sprawca(-wczyni) *m(f)*
**cult** [kʌlt] *n* kult *m*
**cult figure** *n* bożyszcze *nt*
**cultivate** ['kʌltɪveɪt] *vt* (*land, crop*) uprawiać; (*attitude, feeling*) kultywować; (*: in o.s.*) rozwijać w sobie; (*person*) zabiegać o względy *+gen*
**cultivation** [kʌltɪ'veɪʃən] *n* uprawa *f*
**cultural** ['kʌltʃərəl] *adj* (*tradition, link*) kulturowy; (*concerning the arts*) kulturalny
**culture** ['kʌltʃə^r] *n* kultura *f*
**cultured** ['kʌltʃəd] *adj* (*person*) kulturalny; **~ pearl** *perła uzyskana w warunkach hodowlanych*
**cumbersome** ['kʌmbəsəm] *adj* (*object*) nieporęczny; (*system*) nieefektywny
**cumin** ['kʌmɪn] *n* kmin *m*, czarnuszka *f*
**cumulative** ['kju:mjulətɪv] *adj* (*effect*) kumulacyjny; (*result*) łączny
**cunning** ['kʌnɪŋ] *n* przebiegłość *f* ▷ *adj* przebiegły
**cunt** [kʌnt] (*inf!*) *n* pizda *f* (*inf!*)
**cup** [kʌp] *n* (*for drinking*) filiżanka *f*; (*trophy*) puchar *m*; (*of bra*) miseczka *f*; (*quantity*) ≈ szklanka *f*
**cupboard** ['kʌbəd] *n* kredens *m*
**cup final** (*Brit*) *n* finał *m* rozgrywek pucharowych
**cupful** ['kʌpful] *n* ≈ szklanka *f*
**Cupid** ['kju:pɪd] *n* Kupidyn *m* or Kupido *m*, Amor *m*; (*figurine*) kupidynek *m*, amorek *m*
**cupidity** [kju:'pɪdɪtɪ] *n* chciwość *f*
**cupola** ['kju:pələ] *n* kopuła *f*
**cup tie** (*Brit*) *n* rozgrywka *f* eliminacyjna (*w systemie pucharowym*)
**curable** ['kjuərəbl] *adj* uleczalny
**curate** ['kjuərɪt] *n* ≈ wikary *m* (*w kościele anglikańskim*)
**curator** [kjuə'reɪtə^r] *n* kustosz *m*
**curb** [kə:b] *vt* (*powers, expenditure*) ograniczać (ograniczyć *perf*); (*person*) okiełznywać (okiełznać *perf*) ▷ *n* (*restraint*) ograniczenie *nt*; (*US: kerb*) krawężnik *m*
**curd cheese** *n* twaróg *m*
**curdle** ['kə:dl] *vi* zsiadać się (zsiąść się *perf*)
**curds** [kə:dz] *npl* zsiadłe mleko *nt*
**cure** [kjuə^r] *vt* (*Med*) leczyć (wyleczyć *perf*); (*Culin*) konserwować (zakonserwować *perf*); (*problem*) zaradzać (zaradzić *perf*) *+dat* ▷ *n* lekarstwo *nt*; **to be ~d of sth** zostać (*perf*) z czegoś wyleczonym
**cure-all** ['kjuərɔ:l] *n* lekarstwo *nt* na wszystko; (*fig*) panaceum *nt*
**curfew** ['kə:fju:] *n* godzina *f* policyjna
**curio** ['kjuərɪəu] *n* osobliwość *f*
**curiosity** [kjuərɪ'ɔsɪtɪ] *n* (*interest*) ciekawość *f*, zaciekawienie *nt*; (*nosiness*) ciekawość *f*; (*unusual thing*) osobliwość *f*
**curious** ['kjuərɪəs] *adj* (*interested*) ciekawy, zaciekawiony; (*nosy*) ciekawski; (*strange, unusual*) dziwny; **I'm ~ about him** on mnie interesuje
**curiously** ['kjuərɪəslɪ] *adv* ciekawie, z ciekawością or zaciekawieniem; **~ enough, ...** co ciekawe, ...
**curl** [kə:l] *n* (*of hair*) lok *m*; (*of smoke*) kłąb *m* ▷ *vt* (*hair: loosely*) układać (ułożyć *perf*) w fale; (*: tightly*) zakręcać (zakręcić *perf*) ▷ *vi* (*hair*) kręcić się; (*smoke*) wić się
▸ **curl up** *vi* (*person*) kulić się (skulić się *perf*); (*animal*) zwijać się (zwinąć się *perf*) (w kłębek)
**curler** ['kə:lə^r] *n* wałek *m* (do włosów)
**curlew** ['kə:lu:] *n* kulik *m*
**curling** ['kə:lɪŋ] *n sport zimowy, polegający na toczeniu po lodzie płaskich kamieni, którymi gracze starają się trafić do celu*
**curling tongs**, (*US*) **curling irons** *npl* lokówka *f*
**curly** ['kə:lɪ] *adj* (*hair*) kręcony; (*leaf etc*) poskręcany
**currant** ['kʌrnt] *n* (*dried fruit*) rodzynek *m*; (*also:* **blackcurrant**) czarna porzeczka *f*; (*also:* **redcurrant**) czerwona porzeczka *f*
**currency** ['kʌrnsɪ] *n* waluta *f*; **to gain ~** (*fig*) zyskiwać (zyskać *perf*) popularność
**current** ['kʌrnt] *n* prąd *m* ▷ *adj* (*methods, rate*) obecny; (*month, year*) bieżący; (*beliefs etc*) powszechnie przyjęty; **direct/alternating ~** prąd stały/zmienny; **~ of opinion** trend; **the ~ issue of a magazine** bieżący numer czasopisma; **in ~ use** rozpowszechniony
**current account** (*Brit*) *n* rachunek *m* bieżący
**current affairs** *npl* aktualności *pl*
**current assets** *npl* środki *pl* obrotowe
**current liabilities** *npl* zobowiązania *pl* bieżące or krótkoterminowe
**currently** ['kʌrntlɪ] *adv* obecnie
**curricula** [kə'rɪkjulə] *npl of* **curriculum**
**curriculum** [kə'rɪkjuləm] (*pl* **~s** or **curricula**) *n* program *m* zajęć or nauczania

**curriculum vitae** [-'vi:taɪ] *n* życiorys *m*
**curry** ['kʌrɪ] *n* curry *nt inv* *(potrawa)* ▷ *vt*: **to ~ favour with** starać się przypodobać *+dat*, nadskakiwać *+dat*
**curry powder** *n* curry *nt inv* *(przyprawa)*
**curse** [kə:s] *vi* kląć (zakląć *perf*), przeklinać ▷ *vt* przeklinać (przekląć *perf*) ▷ *n* *(spell)* klątwa *f*, przekleństwo *nt*; *(swearword, scourge)* przekleństwo *nt*
**cursor** ['kə:səʳ] *(Comput)* *n* kursor *m*
**cursory** ['kə:sərɪ] *adj* pobieżny
**curt** [kə:t] *adj* *(reply, tone)* szorstki
**curtail** [kə:'teɪl] *vt* *(freedom, rights)* ograniczać (ograniczyć *perf*); *(visit)* skracać (skrócić *perf*); *(expenses)* redukować (zredukować *perf*)
**curtain** ['kə:tn] *n* zasłona *f*; *(Theat)* kurtyna *f*; **to draw the ~s** *(together)* zasuwać (zasunąć *perf*) zasłony; *(apart)* rozsuwać (rozsunąć *perf*) zasłony
**curtain call** *n*: **we took four ~s** wywoływano nas (oklaskami) cztery razy
**curts(e)y** ['kə:tsɪ] *vi* dygać (dygnąć *perf*) ▷ *n* dyg *m*
**curvature** ['kə:vətʃəʳ] *n* krzywizna *f*
**curve** [kə:v] *n* łuk *m*; *(Math)* krzywa *f* ▷ *vi* zataczać (zatoczyć *perf*) łuk
**curved** [kə:vd] *adj* zakrzywiony
**cushion** ['kuʃən] *n* poduszka *f* ▷ *vt* *(collision, fall)* amortyzować (zamortyzować *perf*); *(shock, effect)* osłabiać (osłabić *perf*)
**cushy** ['kuʃɪ] *(inf)* *adj* *(life, position)* wygodny; **a ~ job** ciepła posadka
**custard** ['kʌstəd] *n* *sos z mleka, cukru, mąki i jaj do polewania deserów*
**custard powder** *(Brit)* *n* *słodki sos w proszku do polewania deserów*
**custodian** [kʌs'təudɪən] *n* *(of building)* dozorca(-rczyni) *m(f)*; *(of museum)* kustosz *m*
**custody** ['kʌstədɪ] *n* *(Jur: of child)* opieka *f* nad dzieckiem; *(for offenders)* areszt *m*; **to take sb into ~** aresztować (zaaresztować *perf*) kogoś; **in the ~ of** pod opieką *+gen*; **the mother has ~ of the children** matce przyznano opiekę nad dziećmi
**custom** ['kʌstəm] *n* *(traditional activity)* obyczaj *m*, zwyczaj *m*; *(habit, convention)* zwyczaj *m*; **I shall take my ~ elsewhere** będę kupować gdzie indziej; **we get a lot of ~ from foreigners** kupuje u nas wielu obcokrajowców
**customary** ['kʌstəmərɪ] *adj* *(time, behaviour)* zwykły; *(method, celebration)* tradycyjny; **it is ~ to ...** przyjęło się *+infin*
**custom-built** ['kʌstəm'bɪlt] *adj* wykonany na zamówienie
**customer** ['kʌstəməʳ] *n* klient(ka) *m(f)*; **he's an odd ~** *(inf)* to dziwny gość *(inf)*
**customer profile** *n* charakterystyka *f* klienta
**customized** ['kʌstəmaɪzd] *adj* przerobiony *(na życzenie klienta)*
**custom-made** ['kʌstəm'meɪd] *adj* na zamówienie *post*
**customs** ['kʌstəmz] *npl* *(at border, airport)* punkt *m* odprawy celnej; **to go through (the) ~** odbywać (odbyć *perf*) odprawę celną
**Customs and Excise** *(Brit)* *n* ≈ Główny Urząd Ceł
**customs officer** *n* celnik(-iczka) *m(f)*
**cut** [kʌt] *(pt, pp* **cut***)* *vt* *(bread, meat)* kroić (pokroić *perf*); *(hand, knee)* rozcinać (rozciąć *perf*); *(grass)* przycinać (przyciąć *perf*); *(hair)* obcinać (obciąć *perf*); *(scene: from book)* usuwać (usunąć *perf*); *(: from film, broadcast)* wycinać (wyciąć *perf*); *(prices)* obniżać (obniżyć *perf*); *(spending, supply)* ograniczać (ograniczyć *perf*); *(garment)* kroić (skroić *perf*); *(line, path)* przecinać (przeciąć *perf*); *(inf: cancel)* odwoływać (odwołać *perf*) ▷ *vi* ciąć ▷ *n* *(in skin)* skaleczenie *nt*; *(in salary, spending)* cięcie *nt*; *(of meat)* płat *m*; *(of garment)* krój *m* ▷ *adj* *(jewel)* (o)szlifowany; **the baby is cutting a tooth** dziecku wyrzyna się ząb; **to cut one's finger** skaleczyć się *(perf)* w palec; **to get one's hair cut** obcinać (obciąć *perf*) sobie włosy; **to cut sth short** skracać (skrócić *perf*) coś; **to cut sb dead** udawać (udać *perf*), że się kogoś nie widzi; **cold cuts** *(US)* *różne rodzaje wędlin i zimnych mięs pokrojone w plasterki*; **power cut** przerwa w dopływie energii
▸ **cut back** *vt* *(plants)* przycinać (przyciąć *perf*); *(production, expenditure)* ograniczać (ograniczyć *perf*)
▸ **cut down** *vt* *(tree)* ścinać (ściąć *perf*); *(consumption)* ograniczać (ograniczyć *perf*); **to cut sb down to size** *(fig)* przytrzeć *(perf)* komuś nosa
▸ **cut down on** *vt fus* ograniczać (ograniczyć *perf*) *+acc*
▸ **cut in** *vi*: **to cut in (on)** *(interrupt)* wtrącać się (wtrącić się *perf*) (do *+gen*); **to cut in on sb** *(Aut)* zajeżdżać (zajechać *perf*) komuś drogę
▸ **cut off** *vt* *(piece, village, supply)* odcinać (odciąć *perf*); *(limb)* obcinać (obciąć *perf*); *(Tel)* rozłączać (rozłączyć *perf*); **we've been cut off** *(Tel)* rozłączono nas
▸ **cut out** *vt* *(shape, article from newspaper)* wycinać (wyciąć *perf*); *(scene, references: from book)* usuwać (usunąć *perf*); *(: from film, broadcast)* wycinać (wyciąć *perf*); **he ought to cut out the drinking** powinien przestać pić; **cut it out!** przestań!
▸ **cut up** *vt* *(paper)* ciąć (pociąć *perf*) na kawałki; *(meat)* kroić (pokroić *perf*) (na kawałki); **she still feels cut up about her**

**sister's death** (*inf*) jeszcze nie doszła do siebie po śmierci siostry

**cut-and-dried** ['kʌtən'draɪd] *adj* (*also*: **cut-and-dry**: *answer, solution*) gotowy

**cutaway** ['kʌtəweɪ] *n* (*coat*) frak *m*; (*drawing, model*) częściowy przekrój *m* perspektywiczny; (*Film, TV*) fragment *m* ujęcia

**cutback** ['kʌtbæk] *n* (*in services, business*) zwolnienia *pl*

**cute** [kju:t] *adj* (*sweet*) śliczny, milutki; (*clever*) sprytny; (*esp US: attractive*) fajny (*inf*)

**cut glass** *n* szkło *nt* rżnięte, kryształy *pl*

**cuticle** ['kju:tɪkl] *n* skórka *f* (*paznokcia*); ~ **remover** *płyn lub krem do usuwania skórek u paznokci*

**cutlery** ['kʌtlərɪ] *n* sztućce *pl*

**cutlet** ['kʌtlɪt] *n* kotlet *m*

**cutoff** ['kʌtɔf], **cut-off** *n* (*also*: **cutoff point**) (górna) granica *f*

**cutoff switch** *n* przełącznik *m* zamykający *or* odcinający

**cutout** ['kʌtaut] *n* (*switch*) wyłącznik *m*; (*paper figure*) wycinanka *f*

**cut-price** ['kʌt'praɪs], (*US*) **cut-rate** *adj* przeceniony

**cut-throat** *n* (*person*) rzezimieszek *m* ▷ *adj* (*competition*) bezwzględny; (*business*) niebezpieczny

**cutting** ['kʌtɪŋ] *adj* (*edge*) tnący; (*fig: remark*) kąśliwy ▷ *n* (*Brit: from newspaper*) wycinek *m*; (*: Rail*) wykop *m*; (*from plant*) sadzonka *f*; **to be at the ~ edge of** (*fig*) wyznaczać kierunek rozwoju *+gen*

**cuttlefish** ['kʌtlfɪʃ] *n* mątwa *f*

**CV** *n abbr* = **curriculum vitae**

**C & W** *n abbr* = **country and western music**

**c.w.o.** (*Comm*) *abbr* (= *cash with order*) płatne gotówką przy zamówieniu

**cwt.** *abbr* = **hundredweight**

**cyanide** ['saɪənaɪd] *n* cyjanek *m*

**cybernetics** [saɪbə'nɛtɪks] *n* cybernetyka *f*

**cyberspace** ['saɪbəspies] (*Comput*) *n* cyberprzestrzeń *f*

**cyclamen** ['sɪkləmən] *n* cyklamen *m*, fiołek *m* alpejski

**cycle** ['saɪkl] *n* (*bicycle*) rower *m*; (*series*) cykl *m*; (*movement*) obrót *m* ▷ *vi* jechać (pojechać *perf*) rowerem *or* na rowerze; (*: regularly*) jeździć na rowerze

**cycle race** *n* wyścig *m* kolarski *or* rowerowy

**cycle rack** *n* stojak *m* na rowery

**cycling** ['saɪklɪŋ] *n* jazda *f* na rowerze; (*Sport*) kolarstwo *nt*; **to go on a ~ holiday** (*Brit*) wybierać się (wybrać się *perf*) na wakacje rowerowe

**cyclist** ['saɪklɪst] *n* rowerzysta(-tka) *m(f)*; (*Sport*) kolarz *m*

**cyclone** ['saɪkləun] *n* cyklon *m*

**cygnet** ['sɪgnɪt] *n* łabędziątko *nt*

**cylinder** ['sɪlɪndə[r]] *n* (*shape*) walec *m*; (*of gas*) butla *f*; (*in engine, machine*) cylinder *m*

**cylinder block** *n* (*Aut*) blok *m* cylindrów

**cylinder head** *n* (*Aut*) głowica *f* cylindra

**cylinder-head gasket** ['sɪlɪndəhɛd-] *n* (*Aut*) uszczelka *f* pod głowicę cylindra

**cymbals** ['sɪmblz] *npl* (*Mus*) talerze *pl*

**cynic** ['sɪnɪk] *n* cynik(-iczka) *m(f)*

**cynical** ['sɪnɪkl] *adj* cyniczny

**cynicism** ['sɪnɪsɪzəm] *n* cynizm *m*

**CYO** (*US*) *n abbr* (= *Catholic Youth Organization*) *stowarzyszenie młodzieży katolickiej*

**cypress** ['saɪprɪs] *n* cyprys *m*

**Cypriot** ['sɪprɪət] *adj* cypryjski ▷ *n* Cypryjczyk(-jka) *m(f)*

**Cyprus** ['saɪprəs] *n* Cypr *m*

**cyst** [sɪst] *n* (*under skin*) pęcherz *m*; (*inside body*) torbiel *f*

**cystitis** [sɪs'taɪtɪs] *n* zapalenie *nt* pęcherza (moczowego)

**CZ** (*US*) *n abbr* = **Canal Zone**

**czar** [zɑ:[r]] *n* = **tsar**

**Czech** [tʃɛk] *adj* czeski ▷ *n* (*person*) Czech/Czeszka *m/f*; (*Ling*) (język *m*) czeski

**Czechoslovak** [tʃɛkə'sləuvæk] *adj, n* = **Czechoslovakian**

**Czechoslovakia** [tʃɛkəslə'vækɪə] (*old*) *n* Czechosłowacja *f*

**Czechoslovak(ian)** [tʃɛkəslə'vækɪən] (*old*) *adj* czechosłowacki ▷ *n* mieszkaniec(-nka) *m(f)* Czechosłowacji

**Czech Republic** *n*: **the ~** Republika *f* Czeska

# Dd

**D[1], d[1]** [di:] *n* *(letter)* D *nt*, d *nt*; **D for David,** *(US)* **D for Dog** ≈ D jak Dorota
**D[2]** [di:] *n* *(Mus)* D *nt*, d *nt*
**D[3]** *(US: Pol)* *abbr* = **democrat(ic)**
**d[2]** *(Brit: formerly)* *abbr* = **penny**
**d.** *abbr* (= *died*) zm.; **Henry Jones, d. 1754** Henry Jones, zm. 1754
**DA** *(US)* *n abbr* = **district attorney**
**dab** [dæb] *vt* *(wound)* (delikatnie) przemywać (przemyć *perf*); *(paint, cream)* nakładać (nałożyć *perf*) ▷ *n* odrobina *f*
▸ **dab at** *vt fus*: **she dabbed at her mouth with the lace handkerchief** kilkakrotnie dotknęła ust koronkową chusteczką; **to be a dab hand at sth/doing sth** być specem w czymś/robieniu czegoś
**dabble** ['dæbl] *vi*: **to ~ in** parać się *+instr*, zajmować się po amatorsku *+instr*
**dachshund** ['dækshund] *n* jamnik *m*
**dad** [dæd] *n* tata *m*, tatuś *m*
**daddy** ['dædɪ] *n* = **dad**
**daddy-long-legs** [dædɪ'lɔŋlɛgz] *(inf)* *n* *(Brit)* komarnica *f*; *(US)* kosarz *m*
**daffodil** ['dæfədɪl] *n* żonkil *m*
**daft** [dɑ:ft] *adj* *(person)* głupi; *(thing)* zwariowany; **to be ~ about sb/sth** mieć fioła na punkcie kogoś/czegoś *(inf)*
**dagger** ['dægəʳ] *n* sztylet *m*; **to be at ~s drawn with sb** być z kimś na noże; **to look ~s at sb** sztyletować kogoś wzrokiem
**dahlia** ['deɪljə] *n* dalia *f*
**daily** ['deɪlɪ] *adj* *(dose, wages)* dzienny; *(routine, life)* codzienny ▷ *n* *(paper)* dziennik *m*; *(Brit: also:* **daily help***)* (dochodząca) pomoc *f* domowa ▷ *adv* codziennie; **twice ~** dwa razy dziennie
**dainty** ['deɪntɪ] *adj* filigranowy
**dairy** ['dɛərɪ] *n* *(shop)* sklep *m* nabiałowy; *(company, building)* mleczarnia *f* ▷ *cpd* *(cattle, chocolate)* mleczny; *(industry)* mleczarski
**dairy farm** *n* gospodarstwo *nt* mleczarskie
**dairy products** *npl* nabiał *m*, produkty *pl* mleczne
**dairy store** *(US)* *n* sklep *m* nabiałowy
**dais** ['deɪɪs] *n* podium *nt*
**daisy** ['deɪzɪ] *n* stokrotka *f*
**daisy wheel** *n* *(on printer)* rozetka *f*
**daisy-wheel printer** ['deɪzɪwi:l-] *n* drukarka *f* rozetkowa
**Dakar** ['dækəʳ] *n* Dakar *m*
**dale** [deɪl] *(Brit)* *n* dolina *f*
**dally** ['dælɪ] *vi* ociągać się, marudzić; **to ~ with** rozważać *+acc* *(niezbyt poważnie)*
**dalmatian** [dæl'meɪʃən] *n* dalmatyńczyk *m*
**dam** [dæm] *n* *(on river)* tama *f*, zapora *f*; *(reservoir)* (sztuczny) zalew *m*, zbiornik *m* (zaporowy) ▷ *vt* stawiać (postawić *perf*) zaporę *or* tamę na *+loc*
**damage** ['dæmɪdʒ] *n* *(harm)* szkody *pl*; *(dents etc)* uszkodzenia *pl*; *(fig)* szkoda *f*, uszczerbek *m* ▷ *vt* *(physically)* uszkadzać (uszkodzić *perf*); *(affect)* narażać (narazić *perf*) na szwank, wyrządzać (wyrządzić *perf*) szkodę *+dat*;
**damages** *npl* *(Jur)* odszkodowanie *nt*; **~ to property** straty materialne; **to pay 5,000 pounds in ~s** wypłacać (wypłacić *perf*) 5 tys. funtów (tytułem) odszkodowania
**damaging** ['dæmɪdʒɪŋ] *adj*: **~ (to)** szkodliwy (dla *+gen*)
**Damascus** [də'mɑ:skəs] *n* Damaszek *m*
**dame** [deɪm] *n* *(Brit)* *tytuł nadawany kobietom nobilitowanym*; *(US: inf)* babka *f* *(inf)*, facetka *f* *(inf)*; *(Theat)* matrona *f*
**damn** [dæm] *vt* *(curse at)* przeklinać (przekląć *perf*); *(condemn)* potępiać (potępić *perf*) ▷ *n* *(inf)*: **I don't give a ~** mam to gdzieś *(inf)* ▷ *adj* *(inf: also:* **damned***)* cholerny *(inf)*; **~ (it)!** cholera! *(inf)*
**damnable** ['dæmnəbl] *adj* *(behaviour)* nikczemny, niecny; *(weather)* okropny
**damnation** [dæm'neɪʃən] *n* *(Rel)* potępienie *nt* ▷ *excl* *(inf)* niech to szlag *(inf)*
**damning** ['dæmɪŋ] *adj* *(evidence)* obciążający
**damp** [dæmp] *adj* wilgotny ▷ *n* wilgoć *f* ▷ *vt* *(also:* **dampen***: cloth, rag)* zwilżać (zwilżyć *perf*); *(: enthusiasm etc)* ostudzić *(perf)*
**damp course** *n* warstwa *f* izolacyjna (przeciwwilgociowa)
**damper** ['dæmpəʳ] *n* *(Mus)* tłumik *m*; *(of fire)* zasuwa *f*; **to put a ~ on** *(fig: enthusiasm etc)* ostudzić *(perf)* *+acc*

**dampness** ['dæmpnɪs] *n* wilgoć *f*
**damson** ['dæmzən] *n* śliwka *f* damaszka *or* damascenka
**dance** [dɑːns] *n* taniec *m*; *(social event)* potańcówka *f*, tańce *pl* ▷ *vi* tańczyć (zatańczyć *perf*); **to ~ about** podrygiwać
**dance hall** *n* sala *f* balowa
**dancer** ['dɑːnsəʳ] *n* tancerz(-rka) *m(f)*
**dancing** ['dɑːnsɪŋ] *n* taniec *m*, tańce *pl*
**D and C** *n abbr (Med: = dilation and curettage)* rozszerzenie *nt* i wyłyżeczkowanie *nt*
**dandelion** ['dændɪlaɪən] *n* dmuchawiec *m*, mlecz *m*
**dandruff** ['dændrəf] *n* łupież *m*
**dandy** ['dændɪ] *n* dandys *m* ▷ *adj (US: inf)* świetny
**Dane** [deɪn] *n* Duńczyk/Dunka *m/f*
**danger** ['deɪndʒəʳ] *n (unsafe situation)* niebezpieczeństwo *nt*; *(hazard)* zagrożenie *nt*; **there is a ~ of ...** istnieje niebezpieczeństwo *+gen*; **"~!"** „uwaga!"; **to be in ~** znajdować się (znaleźć się *perf*) w niebezpieczeństwie; **to put sb in ~** narażać (narazić *perf*) kogoś na niebezpieczeństwo; **he's in ~ of losing his job** grozi mu utrata pracy; **the patient is now out of ~** życiu pacjenta nie zagraża (już) niebezpieczeństwo
**danger list** *(Med) n*: **on the ~** w stanie zagrożenia życia
**dangerous** ['deɪndʒrəs] *adj* niebezpieczny
**dangerously** ['deɪndʒrəslɪ] *adv* niebezpiecznie; **~ ill** poważnie chory
**danger zone** *n* strefa *f* zagrożenia
**dangle** ['dæŋgl] *vt* wymachiwać *+instr* ▷ *vi* zwisać, dyndać *(inf)*
**Danish** ['deɪnɪʃ] *adj* duński ▷ *n* (język *m*) duński
**Danish pastry** *n* ciasto *nt* duńskie
**dank** [dæŋk] *adj (cellar)* zawilgocony; *(air)* wilgotny
**Danube** ['dænjuːb] *n*: **the ~** Dunaj *m*
**dapper** ['dæpəʳ] *adj* szykowny
**Dardanelles** [dɑːdə'nɛlz] *(Geog) npl*: **the ~** Dardanele *pl*, cieśnina *f* Dardanele
**dare** [dɛəʳ] *vt*: **to ~ sb to do sth** rzucać (rzucić *perf*) komuś wyzwanie do zrobienia czegoś, wzywać (wezwać *perf*) kogoś do zrobienia czegoś ▷ *vi*: **to ~ (to) do sth** ośmielać się (ośmielić się *perf*) coś zrobić, odważyć się *(perf)* coś zrobić; **I ~n't tell him** nie śmiem mu powiedzieć; **I ~ say...** zapewne..., przypuszczam, że...
**daredevil** ['dɛədɛvl] *n* śmiałek *m*
**Dar-es-Salaam** [dɑːrɛssə'lɑːm] *n* Dar es-Salaam *nt inv*
**daring** ['dɛərɪŋ] *adj* odważny, śmiały ▷ *n* odwaga *f*, śmiałość *f*

**dark** [dɑːk] *adj* ciemny; *(fig)* mroczny, ponury ▷ *n*: **in the ~** w ciemności, po ciemku; **to be in the ~ about sth** *(fig)* nic nie wiedzieć o czymś; **after ~** po zmroku; **~ blue** ciemnoniebieski; **~ green** ciemnozielony; **it is getting ~** ściemnia się; **~ chocolate** gorzka czekolada
**Dark Ages** *npl*: **the ~** wczesne średniowiecze *nt*; **in the ~** w mrokach średniowiecza
**darken** [dɑːkn] *vt* przyciemniać (przyciemnić *perf*) ▷ *vi* ciemnieć (ściemnieć *perf or* pociemnieć *perf*)
**dark glasses** *npl* ciemne okulary *pl*
**darkly** ['dɑːklɪ] *adv* złowrogo
**darkness** ['dɑːknɪs] *n* ciemność *f*, mrok *m*
**darkroom** ['dɑːkrum] *n* ciemnia *f*
**darling** ['dɑːlɪŋ] *adj* (u)kochany ▷ *n (as form of address)* kochanie *nt*; **to be the ~ of** być ulubieńcem/ulubienicą *m/f +gen*; **she is a ~** (ona) jest kochana
**darn** [dɑːn] *vt* cerować (zacerować *perf*)
**dart** [dɑːt] *n (in game)* rzutka *f*, strzałka *f*; *(in sewing)* zaszewka *f* ▷ *vi*: **to ~ towards** *(also:* **to make a dart towards**) rzucać się (rzucić się *perf*) w kierunku *or* w stronę *+gen*; **to ~ along** pędzić (popędzić *perf*)
**dartboard** ['dɑːtbɔːd] *n* tarcza *f* do gry w rzutki *or* strzałki
**darts** [dɑːts] *n* gra *f* w rzutki *or* strzałki
**dash** [dæʃ] *n (small quantity)* odrobina *f*; *(sign)* myślnik *m*, kreska *f*; *(journey)* wypad *m*; *(run)*: **to make a ~ for/towards** rzucać się (rzucić się *perf*) do *+gen*/w stronę *+gen* ▷ *vt (object)* ciskać (cisnąć *perf*); *(hopes)* grzebać (pogrzebać *perf*) ▷ *vi*: **to ~ towards** rzucać się (rzucić się *perf*) w kierunku *or* w stronę *+gen*; **a ~ of soda** odrobina wody sodowej; **we'll have to make a ~ for it** będziemy musieli się pospieszyć
▸ **dash away** *or* **off** *vi* popędzić *(perf)*, oddalać się (oddalić się *perf*) pędem ▷ *vt (essay etc)* pisać (napisać *perf*) na kolanie, odwalać (odwalić *perf*) *(inf)*
**dashboard** ['dæʃbɔːd] *n (Aut)* tablica *f* rozdzielcza
**dashing** ['dæʃɪŋ] *adj (person)* pełen fantazji; *(hat)* fantazyjny
**dastardly** ['dæstədlɪ] *adj* nikczemny, podły
**data** ['deɪtə] *npl* dane *pl*
**database** ['deɪtəbeɪs] *n* baza *f* danych
**data capture** *(Comput) n* zbieranie *nt* danych
**data processing** *n* przetwarzanie *nt* danych
**data transmission** *(Comput) n* przesyłanie *nt or* transmisja *f* danych
**date** [deɪt] *n (day)* data *f*; *(appointment)* (umówione) spotkanie *nt*; *(: with girlfriend, boyfriend)* randka *f*; *(fruit)* daktyl *m* ▷ *vt (event,*

*object)* określać (określić *perf)* wiek *+gen*; *(letter)* datować; *(person)* chodzić z *+instr*; **what's the ~ today?** którego dzisiaj mamy?; **~ of birth** data urodzenia; **closing ~** *(for application)* ostateczny termin; *(in accounting)* termin zamknięcia ksiąg (rachunkowych); **to ~** do chwili obecnej, do dzisiaj; **out-of-~** *(old-fashioned)* przestarzały; *(expired)* przeterminowany; **up-to-~** nowoczesny; **to bring up to ~** *(information)* uaktualniać (uaktualnić *perf)*; *(correspondence)* uzupełniać (uzupełnić *perf)*; *(person)* zapoznawać (zapoznać *perf)* z najnowszymi informacjami; **I have a ~ with Jill** umówiłem się z Jill; **letter ~d 5th July** *or (US)* **July 5th** list z piątego lipca

**dated** ['deɪtɪd] *adj*: **to be ~** trącić myszką

**dateline** ['deɪtlaɪn] *(Press)* *n nagłówek artykułu, podający datę i miejsce jego powstania*

**date stamp** *n* datownik *m*

**dative** ['deɪtɪv] *(Ling)* *n* celownik *m*

**daub** [dɔ:b] *vt*: **to ~ paint onto/over the wall, to ~ the wall with paint** mazać (pomazać *perf)* ścianę farbą

**daughter** ['dɔ:tə^r] *n* córka *f*

**daughter-in-law** ['dɔ:tərɪnlɔ:] *n* synowa *f*

**daunt** [dɔ:nt] *vt* *(intimidate)* onieśmielać (onieśmielić *perf)*; *(discourage)* zrażać (zrazić *perf)*, zniechęcać (zniechęcić *perf)*

**daunting** ['dɔ:ntɪŋ] *adj* *(task)* onieśmielający; *(prospect)* zniechęcający

**dauntless** ['dɔ:ntlɪs] *adj* nieustraszony

**dawdle** ['dɔ:dl] *vi* guzdrać się, grzebać się; **to ~ over one's work** grzebać się z robotą

**dawn** [dɔ:n] *n* *(of day)* świt *m*; *(of period, situation)* początek *m*, zaranie *nt (literary)* ▷ *vi* świtać (zaświtać *perf)*; **it ~ed on him that ...** zaświtało mu (w głowie), że ...; **from ~ to dusk** od świtu do zmierzchu *or* zmroku

**dawn chorus** *(Brit)* *n* poranne trele *pl*

**day** [deɪ] *n* *(as opposed to night)* dzień *m*; *(twenty-four hours)* doba *f*, dzień *m*; *(heyday)* czas *m*, dni *pl*; **the day before/after** poprzedniego/następnego dnia, dzień wcześniej/później; **the day after tomorrow** pojutrze; **the day before yesterday** przedwczoraj; **the following day** następnego dnia; **(on) the day that ...** w dniu, kiedy ...; **day by day** dzień po dniu; **by day** za dnia; **paid by the day** płatny od dniówki; **to work an 8 hour day** mieć ośmiogodzinny dzień pracy; **these days** w dzisiejszych czasach

**daybook** ['deɪbuk] *(Brit: Admin)* *n* dziennik *m* (kasowy)

**dayboy** ['deɪbɔɪ] *(Scol)* *n* ekstern(ista) *m*, uczeń *m* dochodzący

**daybreak** ['deɪbreɪk] *n* świt *m*, brzask *m*

**daydream** ['deɪdri:m] *vi* marzyć, fantazjować ▷ *n* marzenie *nt*, mrzonka *f*

**daygirl** ['deɪgə:l] *(Scol)* *n* eksternistka *f*, uczennica *f* dochodząca

**daylight** ['deɪlaɪt] *n* światło *nt* dzienne

**Daylight Saving Time** *(US)* *n* czas *m* letni

**day release** *n*: **to be on ~** kształcić się w godzinach pracy *(jeden dzień w tygodniu)*

**day return (ticket)** *(Brit)* *n* bilet *m* powrotny jednodniowy

**day shift** *n* dzienna zmiana *f*

**daytime** ['deɪtaɪm] *n*: **in the ~** za dnia

**day-to-day** ['deɪtə'deɪ] *adj* *(daily)* codzienny; *(planned a day at a time)* z dnia na dzień *post*

**day trip** *n* wycieczka *f* jednodniowa *or* całodzienna

**day tripper** *n* wycieczkowicz(ka) *m(f)*

**daze** [deɪz] *vt* *(stun)* oszałamiać (oszołomić *perf)*; *(blow)* ogłuszać (ogłuszyć *perf)* ▷ *n*: **in a ~** oszołomiony

**dazed** [deɪzd] *adj* oszołomiony

**dazzle** ['dæzl] *vt* *(bewitch)* olśniewać (olśnić *perf)*; *(blind)* oślepiać (oślepić *perf)*

**dazzling** ['dæzlɪŋ] *adj* *(light)* oślepiający; *(fig)* olśniewający

**DC** *abbr* = **direct current**; *(US: Post)* = **District of Columbia**

**DD** *n abbr (= Doctor of Divinity) stopień naukowy*, ≈ dr

**dd.** *(Comm)* *abbr (= delivered)* dostarczony

**D/D** *abbr* = **direct debit**

**D-day** ['di:deɪ] *n* godzina *f* zero

**DDS** *(US)* *n abbr (= Doctor of Dental Surgery) stopień naukowy*, ≈ dr

**DDT** *n abbr (= dichlorodiphenyl trichloroethane)* DDT *nt inv*, azotoks *m*

**DE** *(US: Post)* *abbr* = **Delaware**

**DEA** *(US)* *n abbr (= Drug Enforcement Administration)* ≈ urząd do walki z handlem narkotykami

**deacon** ['di:kən] *n* diakon *m*

**dead** [dɛd] *adj* *(person)* zmarły; *(animal)* zdechły, nieżywy; *(plant)* zwiędły; *(city)* wymarły; *(language)* martwy; *(body part)* zdrętwiały, ścierpnięty; *(engine)* zepsuty; *(telephone)* głuchy; *(battery)* wyładowany; *(silence)* zupełny ▷ *adv* *(completely)* całkowicie, zupełnie; *(directly, exactly)* akurat, dokładnie ▷ *npl*: **the ~** umarli *pl*, zmarli *pl*; **she's ~** (ona) nie żyje; **to shoot sb ~** zastrzelić *(perf)* kogoś; **to be ~ on time** być punktualnym co do minuty; **in the ~ centre, ~ in the centre** w samym środku; **~ tired** skonany; **he stopped ~** stanął jak wryty; **the line has gone ~** *(Tel)* połączenie zostało przerwane

**deaden** [dɛdn] *vt* tłumić (stłumić *perf)*, przytępiać (przytępić *perf)*

**dead end** *n* ślepa uliczka *f*
**dead-end** ['dɛdɛnd] *adj*: **a ~ job** praca *f* bez perspektyw
**dead heat** (*Sport*) *n* bieg *m* martwy *or* nierozstrzygnięty
**dead-letter office** [dɛd'lɛtə-] *n* dział *m* przesyłek nie doręczonych
**deadline** ['dɛdlaɪn] *n* nieprzekraczalny termin *m*; **I'm working to a ~** muszę wykonać tę pracę w terminie *or* na termin
**deadlock** ['dɛdlɔk] *n* impas *m*; **the meeting ended in ~** zebranie zakończyło się impasem
**dead loss** (*inf*) *n*: **to be a ~** być do niczego (*inf*)
**deadly** ['dɛdlɪ] *adj* (*weapon*) śmiercionośny; (*poison, insult*) śmiertelny; (*accuracy*) absolutny; (*logic*) nieubłagany ▷ *adv*: **~ dull** śmiertelnie nudny
**deadpan** ['dɛdpæn] *adj* udający powagę, śmiertelnie poważny
**Dead Sea** *n*: **the ~** Morze *nt* Martwe
**dead season** *n* martwy sezon *m*
**deaf** [dɛf] *adj* (*totally*) głuchy; (*partially*) niedosłyszący; **to turn a ~ ear to sth** być głuchym na coś
**deaf-aid** ['dɛfeɪd] (*Brit*) *n* aparat *m* słuchowy
**deaf-and-dumb** ['dɛfən'dʌm] *adj* głuchoniemy; **~ alphabet** alfabet głuchoniemych
**deafen** [dɛfn] *vt* ogłuszać (ogłuszyć *perf*)
**deafening** ['dɛfnɪŋ] *adj* ogłuszający
**deaf-mute** ['dɛfmju:t] *n* głuchoniemy(-ma) *m(f)*
**deafness** ['dɛfnɪs] *n* głuchota *f*
**deal** [di:l] (*pt, pp* **~t**) *n* (*Comm*) transakcja *f*, interes *m*; (*Pol*) porozumienie *nt*, układ *m* ▷ *vt* (*blow*) wymierzać (wymierzyć *perf*), zadawać (zadać *perf*); (*cards*) rozdawać (rozdać *perf*); **to strike a ~ with sb** ubijać (ubić *perf*) z kimś interes; **it's a ~!** (*inf*) zgoda!; **he got a fair/bad ~ from them** dobrze/źle go potraktowali; **a good/great ~** (bardzo) dużo *or* wiele; **a great ~ of concern** duże zaniepokojenie
▸ **deal in** *vt fus* handlować *+instr*
▸ **deal with** *vt fus* (*Comm*) utrzymywać stosunki handlowe z *+instr*, robić interesy z *+instr* (*inf*); (*handle*) radzić (poradzić *perf*) sobie z *+instr*, uporać się (*perf*) z *+instr*; (*be about*) dotyczyć *+gen*, traktować o *+instr*; **he was not easy to ~ with** nie był łatwy w obejściu
**dealer** ['di:lə^r] *n* (*Comm*) handlarz *m*; (*Cards*) rozdający(-ca) *m(f)*; **a drug ~** handlarz narkotyków
**dealership** ['di:ləʃɪp] *n* handel *m*
**dealings** ['di:lɪŋz] *npl* (*business*) interesy *pl*; (*relations*) kontakty *pl*, stosunki *pl*
**dealt** [dɛlt] *pt, pp of* **deal**
**dean** [di:n] *n* dziekan *m*
**dear** [dɪə^r] *adj* drogi ▷ *n* (*as form of address*) kochanie *nt*; **my ~** mój drogi *m*/moja droga *f* ▷ *excl*: **~ me!** ojej!; **D~ Sir/Madam** Szanowny Panie/Szanowna Pani; **D~ Mr/Mrs X** Drogi Panie X/Droga Pani X
**dearly** ['dɪəlɪ] *adv* (*love*) szczerze; (*pay*) drogo
**dear money** (*Comm*) *n* drogi pieniądz *m*
**dearth** [də:θ] *n*: **a ~ of** niedostatek *m +gen*
**death** [dɛθ] *n* (*Bio*) zgon *m*, śmierć *f*; (*fig*) śmierć *f*; (*fatality*) ofiara *f* (śmiertelna)
**deathbed** ['dɛθbɛd] *n*: **to be on one's ~** być na łożu śmierci
**death certificate** *n* świadectwo *nt or* akt *m* zgonu
**deathly** ['dɛθlɪ] *adj* (*paleness*) trupi; (*blow*) śmiertelny; (*silence*) grobowy ▷ *adv* trupio
**death penalty** *n* kara *f* śmierci
**death rate** *n* śmiertelność *f*
**death row** (*US*) *n* cela *f* śmierci; **to be on ~** oczekiwać na wykonanie wyroku śmierci
**death sentence** *n* wyrok *m* śmierci
**death toll** *n* liczba *f* ofiar, żniwo *nt* (*literary*)
**death trap** *n* śmiercionośna *or* śmiertelna pułapka *f*
**deb** [dɛb] (*inf*) *n abbr* = **debutante**
**debacle** [deɪ'bɑ:kl] *n* (*defeat*) klęska *f*; (*failure*) fiasko *nt*
**debar** [dɪ'bɑ:^r] *vt*: **to ~ sb from doing sth** zabraniać (zabronić *perf*) komuś robienia czegoś; **to ~ sb from a club** wykluczać (wykluczyć *perf*) kogoś z klubu
**debase** [dɪ'beɪs] *vt* (*value, quality*) deprecjonować (zdeprecjonować *perf*), dewaluować (zdewaluować *perf*); (*person*) poniżać (poniżyć *perf*), upokarzać (upokorzyć *perf*)
**debatable** [dɪ'beɪtəbl] *adj* dyskusyjny; **it is ~ whether** jest wątpliwe, czy
**debate** [dɪ'beɪt] *n* debata *f* ▷ *vt* (*topic*) debatować *or* dyskutować nad *+instr*; (*course of action*) zastanawiać się nad *+instr*; **to ~ whether** zastanawiać się (zastanowić się *perf*), czy
**debauchery** [dɪ'bɔ:tʃərɪ] *n* rozpusta *f*, rozpasanie *nt*
**debenture** [dɪ'bɛntʃə^r] (*Comm*) *n* obligacja *f*
**debilitate** [dɪ'bɪlɪteɪt] *vt* pozbawiać (pozbawić *perf*) sił, osłabiać (osłabić *perf*)
**debilitating** [dɪ'bɪlɪteɪtɪŋ] *adj* osłabiający
**debit** ['dɛbɪt] *n* debet *m* ▷ *vt*: **to ~ a sum to sb** *or* **to sb's account** obciążać (obciążyć *perf*) kogoś *or* czyjś rachunek kwotą; *see also* **direct**
**debit balance** *n* saldo *nt* debetowe
**debit note** *n* nota *f* debetowa, awizo *nt* debetowe
**debonair** [dɛbə'nɛə^r] *adj* elegancki i czarujący

**debrief** [diːˈbriːf] *vt* wysłuchiwać (wysłuchać *perf*) sprawozdania *+gen*
**debriefing** [diːˈbriːfɪŋ] *n* wysłuchanie *nt* sprawozdania
**debris** [ˈdɛbriː] *n* gruzy *pl*
**debt** [dɛt] *n* (*money owed*) dług *m*; (*state of owing money*) długi *pl*, zadłużenie *nt*; **to be in ~** mieć długi; **bad ~** nieściągalny dług
**debt collector** *n* poborca *m* należności
**debtor** [ˈdɛtəʳ] *n* dłużnik(-iczka) *m(f)*
**debug** [diːˈbʌg] (*Comput*) *vt* usuwać (usunąć *perf*) błędy z *+gen*
**debunk** [diːˈbʌŋk] *vt* (*myths, ideas, claim*) obalać (obalić *perf*); (*person, institution*) demaskować (zdemaskować *perf*)
**debut** [ˈdeɪbjuː] *n* debiut *m*
**debutante** [ˈdɛbjutænt] *n* debiutantka *f* (*młoda kobieta wprowadzana w towarzystwo*)
**Dec.** *abbr* (= *december*) grudz.
**decade** [ˈdɛkeɪd] *n* dziesięciolecie *nt*
**decadence** [ˈdɛkədəns] *n* (*period*) dekadencja *f*, schyłek *m*; (*of morals, standards*) dekadencja *f*, upadek *m*
**decadent** [ˈdɛkədənt] *adj* (*period*) dekadencki, schyłkowy; (*behaviour*) dekadencki
**decaffeinated** [dɪˈkæfɪneɪtɪd] *adj* bezkofeinowy
**decamp** [dɪˈkæmp] (*inf*) *vi* ulatniać się (ulotnić się *perf*) (*inf*)
**decant** [dɪˈkænt] *vt* (*wine*) przelewać (przelać *perf*) (*do karafki itp*)
**decanter** [dɪˈkæntəʳ] *n* karafka *f*
**decarbonize** [diːˈkɑːbənaɪz] *vt* usuwać (usunąć *perf*) osad węglowy z *+gen*, odwęglać (odwęglić *perf*)
**decay** [dɪˈkeɪ] *n* (*of organic matter, society, morals*) rozkład *m*, rozpad *m*; (*of building*) niszczenie *nt*; (*of tooth*) próchnica *f* ▷ *vi* (*body*) rozkładać się (rozłożyć się *perf*); (*leaves, wood*) gnić (zgnić *perf*); (*teeth*) psuć się; (*fig*) chylić się ku upadkowi
**decease** [dɪˈsiːs] (*Jur*) *n* zejście *nt* śmiertelne, zgon *m*
**deceased** [dɪˈsiːst] *n*: **the ~** zmarły(-ła) *m(f)*, nieboszczyk(-czka) *m(f)*
**deceit** [dɪˈsiːt] *n* (*quality*) fałsz *m*, nieuczciwość *f*; (*act*) oszustwo *nt*, kłamstwo *nt*
**deceitful** [dɪˈsiːtful] *adj* oszukańczy, kłamliwy
**deceive** [dɪˈsiːv] *vt* oszukiwać (oszukać *perf*), okłamywać (okłamać *perf*); **to ~ o.s.** oszukiwać się *or* samego siebie; **she ~d me into coming here** podstępem skłoniła mnie do przyjścia tutaj
**decelerate** [diːˈsɛləreɪt] (*Aut*) *vi* zmniejszać (zmniejszyć *perf*) szybkość
**December** [dɪˈsɛmbəʳ] *n* grudzień *m*; *see also* **July**
**decency** [ˈdiːsənsɪ] *n* przyzwoitość *f*, poczucie *nt* przyzwoitości
**decent** [ˈdiːsənt] *adj* przyzwoity; **we expect you to do the ~ thing** oczekujemy, że postąpisz właściwie; **they were very ~ about it** podeszli do sprawy bardzo uczciwie; **that was very ~ of him** to było bardzo poczciwe z jego strony; **are you ~?** jesteś ubrany?
**decently** [ˈdiːsəntlɪ] *adv* przyzwoicie
**decentralization** [ˈdiːsɛntrəlaɪˈzeɪʃən] *n* decentralizacja *f*
**decentralize** [diːˈsɛntrəlaɪz] *vt* decentralizować (zdecentralizować *perf*)
**deception** [dɪˈsɛpʃən] *n* oszustwo *nt*, podstęp *m*
**deceptive** [dɪˈsɛptɪv] *adj* złudny, zwodniczy
**decibel** [ˈdɛsɪbɛl] *n* decybel *m*
**decide** [dɪˈsaɪd] *vt* (*person*) przekonywać (przekonać *perf*); (*question, argument*) rozstrzygać (rozstrzygnąć *perf*) ▷ *vi* decydować (się) (zdecydować (się) *perf*); **to ~ to** decydować się (zdecydować się *perf*) *+infin*; **to ~ that ...** decydować (z(a)decydować *perf*), że ...; **to ~ on sth** decydować się (zdecydować się *perf*) na coś; **to ~ on/against doing sth** postanawiać (postanowić *perf*) coś zrobić/czegoś nie robić
**decided** [dɪˈsaɪdɪd] *adj* (*resolute*) zdecydowany, stanowczy; (*clear, definite*) zdecydowany, wyraźny
**decidedly** [dɪˈsaɪdɪdlɪ] *adv* (*emphatically*) zdecydowanie, stanowczo; (*distinctly*) zdecydowanie, wyraźnie
**deciding** [dɪˈsaɪdɪŋ] *adj* decydujący
**deciduous** [dɪˈsɪdjuəs] *adj* zrzucający liście
**decimal** [ˈdɛsɪməl] *adj* dziesiętny ▷ *n* ułamek *m* dziesiętny; **to three ~ places** do trzech miejsc po przecinku
**decimalize** [ˈdɛsɪməlaɪz] (*Brit*) *vt* decymalizować (zdecymalizować *perf*)
**decimal point** *n* ≈ przecinek *m* (*w ułamku dziesiętnym*)
**decimate** [ˈdɛsɪmeɪt] *vt* dziesiątkować (zdziesiątkować *perf*)
**decipher** [dɪˈsaɪfəʳ] *vt* (*coded message*) rozszyfrowywać (rozszyfrować *perf*); (*writing*) odcyfrowywać (odcyfrować *perf*)
**decision** [dɪˈsɪʒən] *n* (*choice*) decyzja *f*; (*decisiveness*) zdecydowanie *nt*, stanowczość *f*; **to make a ~** podejmować (podjąć *perf*) decyzję
**decisive** [dɪˈsaɪsɪv] *adj* (*action, intervention*) decydujący, rozstrzygający; (*person, reply*) zdecydowany, stanowczy; (*manner*) stanowczy
**deck** [dɛk] *n* (*Naut*) pokład *m*; (*of bus*) piętro *nt*; (*record deck*) gramofon *m* (*bez wzmacniacza*); (*of*

*cards*) talia *f*; **to go up on ~** wychodzić (wyjść *perf*) na pokład; **below ~** pod pokładem; **cassette ~** magnetofon kasetowy (*bez wzmacniacza*)
**deckchair** ['dɛktʃɛəʳ] *n* leżak *m*
**deck hand** *n* majtek *m*
**declaration** [dɛklə'reɪʃən] *n* (*statement, public announcement*) deklaracja *f*, oświadczenie *nt*; (*of love*) wyznanie *nt*; (*of war*) wypowiedzenie *nt*
**declare** [dɪ'klɛəʳ] *vt* (*intentions, result*) oznajmiać (oznajmić *perf*); (*income*) deklarować (zadeklarować *perf*); **have you anything to ~?** czy ma Pan/Pani coś do oclenia?
**declassify** [di:'klæsɪfaɪ] *vt* odtajniać (odtajnić *perf*)
**decline** [dɪ'klaɪn] *n*: **~ in/of** spadek *m* +*gen* ▷ *vt* (*invitation, offer*) nie przyjmować (nie przyjąć *perf*) +*gen* ▷ *vi* podupadać (podupaść *perf*); **to be on the ~** zanikać; **to fall into ~** podupadać (podupaść *perf*); **a ~ in living standards** spadek *or* obniżenie się poziomu życia *or* stopy życiowej; **when he asked me to dance, I politely ~d his invitation** gdy poprosił mnie do tańca, grzecznie odmówiłam
**declutch** ['di:'klʌtʃ] (*Aut*) *vi* wyłączać (wyłączyć *perf*) sprzęgło
**decode** ['di:'kəud] *vt* rozszyfrowywać (rozszyfrować *perf*)
**decoder** [di:'kəudəʳ] *n* dekoder *m*
**decompose** [di:kəm'pəuz] *vi* rozkładać się (rozłożyć się *perf*)
**decomposition** [di:kɔmpə'zɪʃən] *n* rozkład *m*
**decompression** [di:kəm'prɛʃən] *n* rozprężenie *nt*, dekompresja *f*
**decompression chamber** *n* komora *f* dekompresyjna
**decongestant** [di:kən'dʒɛstənt] *n* lek *m* zmniejszający przekrwienie
**decontaminate** [di:kən'tæmɪneɪt] *vt* odkażać (odkazić *perf*)
**decontrol** [di:kən'trəul] *vt* znosić (znieść *perf*) kontrolę +*gen* ▷ *n* zniesienie *nt* kontroli cen
**décor** ['deɪkɔ:ʳ] *n* wystrój *m* (wnętrza)
**decorate** ['dɛkəreɪt] *vt* (*room, flat: with paint*) malować (pomalować *perf or* wymalować *perf*); (*: with paper*) tapetować (wytapetować *perf*); **to ~ sth (with)** ozdabiać (ozdobić *perf*) *or* dekorować (udekorować *perf*) coś (+*instr*)
**decoration** [dɛkə'reɪʃən] *n* (*on dress, Christmas tree*) ozdoba *f*; (*of interior*) wystrój *m*; (*medal*) order *m*, odznaczenie *nt*
**decorative** ['dɛkərətɪv] *adj* ozdobny, dekoracyjny
**decorator** ['dɛkəreɪtəʳ] *n* malarz *m*
**decorum** [dɪ'kɔ:rəm] *n* przyzwoitość *f*
**decoy** ['di:kɔɪ] *n* przynęta *f*; **they used him as a ~ for the enemy** posłużyli się nim jako przynętą dla wroga
**decrease** [*n* 'di:kri:s, *vb* di:'kri:s] *n*: **~ (in)** zmniejszanie się *nt* (+*gen*) ▷ *vt* zmniejszać (zmniejszyć *perf*) ▷ *vi* zmniejszać się (zmniejszyć się *perf*), maleć (zmaleć *perf*); **to be on the ~** zmniejszać się, maleć
**decreasing** [di:'kri:sɪŋ] *adj* zmniejszający się, malejący
**decree** [dɪ'kri:] *n* (*Admin*) rozporządzenie *nt*, zarządzenie *nt*; (*Jur*) orzeczenie *nt*, wyrok *m*; (*Pol*) dekret *m*; (*Rel*) wyrok *m* ▷ *vt*: **to ~ (that)** zarządzać (zarządzić *perf*)(, że)
**decree absolute** *n* prawomocne orzeczenie *nt* sądu
**decree nisi** [-'naɪsaɪ] *n* warunkowy wyrok *m* rozwodowy
**decrepit** [dɪ'krɛpɪt] *adj* (*house*) walący się; (*person*) zniedołężniały
**decry** [dɪ'kraɪ] *vt* potępiać (potępić *perf*)
**dedicate** ['dɛdɪkeɪt] *vt*: **to ~ to** (*time*) poświęcać (poświęcić *perf*) +*dat*; (*book, record*) dedykować (zadedykować *perf*) +*dat*; **to ~ o.s. to** poświęcać się (poświęcić się *perf*) +*dat*, oddawać się (oddać się *perf*) +*dat*
**dedicated** ['dɛdɪkeɪtɪd] *adj* (*person*) oddany; (*Comput*) specjalistyczny
**dedication** [dɛdɪ'keɪʃən] *n* (*devotion*) oddanie *nt*, poświęcenie *nt*; (*in book, on radio*) dedykacja *f*
**deduce** [dɪ'dju:s] *vt*: **to ~ (that ...)** wnioskować (wywnioskować *perf*) *or* dedukować (wydedukować *perf*) (, że ...)
**deduct** [dɪ'dʌkt] *vt* potrącać (potrącić *perf*), odciągać (odciągnąć *perf*); **to ~ sth from** potrącać (potrącić *perf*) coś z +*gen*
**deduction** [dɪ'dʌkʃən] *n* (*reasoning*) wnioskowanie *nt*; (*: in logic*) dedukcja *f*; (*subtraction*) potrącenie *nt*
**deed** [di:d] *n* (*act*) czyn *m*, uczynek *m*; (*feat*) wyczyn *m*; (*Jur*) akt *m* prawny; **~ of covenant** zgoda notarialna
**deem** [di:m] (*fml*) *vt*: **to ~ sb/sth to be** uważać kogoś/coś za +*acc*, uznawać (uznać *perf*) kogoś/coś za +*acc*; **to ~ it wise to do sth** uważać zrobienie czegoś za rozsądne
**deep** [di:p] *adj* (*hole, thoughts, sleep*) głęboki; (*voice*) niski; (*trouble, concern*) poważny; (*colour*) ciemny, intensywny ▷ *adv*: **the spectators stood 20 ~** widzowie stali w 20 rzędach; **he took a ~ breath** wziął głęboki oddech; **in ~est sympathy** z wyrazami najgłębszego współczucia; **knee-~ in water** po kolana w wodzie; **~ down** w głębi duszy
**deepen** [di:pn] *vt* pogłębiać (pogłębić *perf*) ▷ *vi* pogłębiać się (pogłębić się *perf*)

**deep freeze** *n* zamrażarka *f*
**deep-fry** ['di:p'fraɪ] *vt* smażyć (usmażyć *perf*) w głębokim tłuszczu
**deeply** ['di:plɪ] *adv* głęboko
**deep-rooted** ['di:p'ru:tɪd] *adj* (głęboko) zakorzeniony
**deep-sea** ['di:p'si:] *adj* *(diving)* głębinowy; *(fishing)* dalekomorski
**deep-seated** ['di:p'si:tɪd] *adj* (głęboko) zakorzeniony
**deep-set** ['di:psɛt] *adj* *(eyes)* głęboko osadzony
**deer** [dɪəʳ] *n inv* zwierzyna *f* płowa; **(red) ~** jeleń *m*; **(roe) ~** sarna *f*; **(fallow) ~** daniel *m*
**deerskin** ['dɪəskɪn] *n* skóra *f* jelenia *or* sarnia
**deerstalker** ['dɪəstɔ:kəʳ] *n* kapelusz *m* myśliwski
**deface** [dɪ'feɪs] *vt* *(wall, notice)* niszczyć (zniszczyć *perf*); *(grave, monument)* bezcześcić (zbezcześcić *perf*)
**defamation** [dɛfə'meɪʃən] *n* zniesławienie *nt*
**defamatory** [dɪ'fæmətrɪ] *adj* zniesławiający
**default** [dɪ'fɔ:lt] *n* *(Comput: also:* **default value**) wartość *f* domyślna ▷ *vi*: **to ~ on a debt** nie spłacić *(perf)* długu; **to win by ~** wygrywać (wygrać *perf*) walkowerem
**defaulter** [dɪ'fɔ:ltəʳ] *n* strona *f* nie wywiązująca się ze zobowiązania
**default option** *(Comput)* *n* opcja *f* domyślna *or* standardowa
**defeat** [dɪ'fi:t] *n* *(in battle)* porażka *f*, klęska *f*; *(failure)* niepowodzenie *nt*, porażka *f* ▷ *vt* pokonywać (pokonać *perf*)
**defeatism** [dɪ'fi:tɪzəm] *n* defetyzm *m*
**defeatist** [dɪ'fi:tɪst] *adj* defetystyczny ▷ *n* defetysta(-tka) *m(f)*
**defecate** ['dɛfəkeɪt] *vi* oddawać (oddać *perf*) kał *or* stolec
**defect** [*n* 'di:fɛkt, *vb* dɪ'fɛkt] *n* wada *f*, defekt *m* ▷ *vi*: **to ~ to the enemy** przejść *(perf)* na stronę wroga; **to ~ to the West** uciec *(perf)* na Zachód; **physical ~** ułomność fizyczna; **mental ~** upośledzenie umysłowe
**defective** [dɪ'fɛktɪv] *adj* wadliwy, wybrakowany
**defector** [dɪ'fɛktəʳ] *n* zdrajca(-jczyni) *m(f)*
**defence**, (US) **defense** [dɪ'fɛns] *n* *(protection, justification)* obrona *f*; *(assistance)* pomoc *f*; **in ~ of** w obronie *+gen*; **witness for the ~** świadek obrony; **the Ministry of D~,** (US) **the Department of Defense** ≈ Ministerstwo Obrony Narodowej
**defenceless** [dɪ'fɛnslɪs] *adj* bezbronny
**defend** [dɪ'fɛnd] *vt* *(also Sport)* bronić *+gen* (obronić *perf +acc*); *(Jur)* bronić *+gen*
**defendant** [dɪ'fɛndənt] *(Jur)* *n* *(in criminal case)* oskarżony(-na) *m(f)*; *(in civil case)* pozwany(-na) *m(f)*
**defender** [dɪ'fɛndəʳ] *n* *(also Sport)* obrońca(-ńczyni) *m(f)*
**defending champion** [dɪ'fɛndɪŋ-] *(Sport)* *n* obrońca(-ńczyni) *m(f)* tytułu
**defending counsel** [dɪ'fɛndɪŋ-] *(Jur)* *n* obrona *f*
**defense** [dɪ'fɛns] (US) *n* = **defence**
**defensive** [dɪ'fɛnsɪv] *adj* obronny, defensywny ▷ *n*: **on the ~** w defensywie
**defer** [dɪ'fə:ʳ] *vt* odraczać (odroczyć *perf*), wstrzymywać (wstrzymać *perf*)
**deference** ['dɛfərəns] *n* szacunek *m*, poważanie *nt*; **out of** *or* **in ~ to** przez szacunek *or* z szacunku dla *+gen*
**deferential** [dɛfə'rɛnʃəl] *adj* pełen szacunku
**defiance** [dɪ'faɪəns] *n* bunt *m*; **in ~ of** *(rules, orders etc)* wbrew *or* na przekór *+dat*
**defiant** [dɪ'faɪənt] *adj* buntowniczy
**defiantly** [dɪ'faɪəntlɪ] *adv* buntowniczo
**deficiency** [dɪ'fɪʃənsɪ] *n* *(lack)* brak *m*, niedobór *m*; *(inadequacy)* niedostatki *pl*, słabość *f*; *(Comm)* deficyt *m*
**deficiency disease** *n* choroba *f* z niedoboru *(np. witamin)*
**deficient** [dɪ'fɪʃənt] *adj* *(service)* nie wystarczający; *(product)* wybrakowany; **to be ~ in** wykazywać niedobór *or* niedostatek *+gen*
**deficit** ['dɛfɪsɪt] *n* deficyt *m*
**defile** [*vb* dɪ'faɪl, *n* 'di:faɪl] *vt* bezcześcić (zbezcześcić *perf*) ▷ *n* wąwóz *m*
**define** [dɪ'faɪn] *vt* *(limits etc)* określać (określić *perf*), wyznaczać (wyznaczyć *perf*); *(word etc)* definiować (zdefiniować *perf*)
**definite** ['dɛfɪnɪt] *adj* *(fixed)* określony; *(clear)* wyraźny; *(certain)* pewny; **he was ~ about it** był stanowczy w tej sprawie
**definite article** *n* rodzajnik *m* *or* przedimek *m* określony
**definitely** ['dɛfɪnɪtlɪ] *adv* zdecydowanie
**definition** [dɛfɪ'nɪʃən] *n* *(of word)* definicja *f*; *(of photograph)* rozdzielczość *f*
**definitive** [dɪ'fɪnɪtɪv] *adj* ostateczny, rozstrzygający
**deflate** [di:'fleɪt] *vt* wypuszczać (wypuścić *perf*) *or* spuszczać (spuścić *perf*) powietrze z *+gen*; *(fig: person)* odbierać (odebrać *perf*) pewność siebie *+dat*; *(Econ)* przeprowadzać (przeprowadzić *perf*) deflację *+gen*
**deflation** [di:'fleɪʃən] *n* deflacja *f*
**deflationary** [di:'fleɪʃənrɪ] *adj* deflacyjny
**deflect** [dɪ'flɛkt] *vt* *(attention)* odwracać (odwrócić *perf*); *(criticism)* odpierać (odeprzeć *perf*); *(shot)* odbijać (odbić *perf*); *(light)* odchylać (odchylić *perf*)
**defog** ['di:'fɔg] (US: *Aut*) *vt* odparowywać (odparować *perf*) *(szybę)*
**defogger** ['di:'fɔgəʳ] (US: *Aut*) *n* nadmuch *m*

**deform** [dɪ'fɔ:m] *vt* zniekształcać (zniekształcić *perf*), deformować (zdeformować *perf*)
**deformed** [dɪ'fɔ:md] *adj* zniekształcony, zdeformowany
**deformity** [dɪ'fɔ:mɪtɪ] *n* (*condition*) kalectwo *nt*; (*distorted part*) deformacja *f*, zniekształcenie *nt*
**defraud** [dɪ'frɔ:d] *vt*: **to ~ sb (of sth)** okradać (okraść *perf*) kogoś (z czegoś) (*przez defraudację*)
**defray** [dɪ'freɪ] *vt*: **to ~ sb's expenses** zwracać (zwrócić *perf*) komuś koszty
**defrost** [di:'frɔst] *vt* rozmrażać (rozmrozić *perf*)
**defroster** [di:'frɔstə[r]] (*US*) *n* = **demister**
**deft** [dɛft] *adj* zręczny, zgrabny
**defunct** [dɪ'fʌŋkt] *adj* martwy
**defuse** [di:'fju:z] *vt* (*bomb*) rozbrajać (rozbroić *perf*); (*fig: tension*) rozładowywać (rozładować *perf*)
**defy** [dɪ'faɪ] *vt* (*disobey: person*) przeciwstawiać się (przeciwstawić się *perf*) *+dat*; (*: order*) ignorować (zignorować *perf*), postępować (postąpić *perf*) wbrew *+dat*; (*challenge*) wyzywać (wyzwać *perf*); (*fig*): **to ~ description/imitation** być nie do opisania/podrobienia, nie dawać się opisać/podrobić
**degenerate** [*vb* dɪ'dʒɛnəreɪt, *adj* dɪ'dʒɛnərɪt] *vi* pogarszać się (pogorszyć się *perf*) ▷ *adj* zwyrodniały, zdegenerowany
**degradation** [dɛgrə'deɪʃən] *n* upodlenie *nt*, poniżenie *nt*
**degrade** [dɪ'greɪd] *vt* (*person*) poniżać (poniżyć *perf*); (*environment etc*) powodować (spowodować *perf*) degradację *+gen*
**degrading** [dɪ'greɪdɪŋ] *adj* poniżający
**degree** [dɪ'gri:] *n* stopień *m*; (*Scol*) stopień *m* naukowy; **10 ~s below (zero)** 10 stopni poniżej zera, 10 stopni mrozu; **a considerable ~ of risk** znaczny stopień ryzyka *or* zagrożenia; **a ~ in maths** dyplom z matematyki; **by ~s** stopniowo; **to some ~, to a certain ~** w pewnym stopniu, do pewnego stopnia
**dehydrated** [di:haɪ'dreɪtɪd] *adj* (*Med*) odwodniony; (*milk etc*) w proszku *post*
**dehydration** [di:haɪ'dreɪʃən] (*Med*) *n* odwodnienie *nt*
**de-ice** ['di:'aɪs] *vt* (*windscreen*) usuwać (usunąć *perf*) lód z *+gen*
**de-icer** ['di:'aɪsə[r]] *n* skrobaczka *f* do lodu
**deign** [deɪn] *vi*: **to ~ to do sth** raczyć coś zrobić, zechcieć (*perf*) (łaskawie) coś zrobić
**deity** ['di:ɪtɪ] *n* boskość *f*, bóstwo *nt*
**déjà vu** [deɪʒɑ:'vu:] *n* déjà vu *nt inv*
**dejected** [dɪ'dʒɛktɪd] *adj* przygnębiony, przybity
**dejection** [dɪ'dʒɛkʃən] *n* przygnębienie *nt*
**del.** *abbr* = **delete**
**delay** [dɪ'leɪ] *vt* (*decision etc*) odwlekać (odwlec *perf*), odkładać (odłożyć *perf*) (na później); (*person*) zatrzymywać (zatrzymać *perf*); (*train etc*) powodować (spowodować *perf*) opóźnienie *+gen* ▷ *vi* zwlekać, ociągać się ▷ *n* (*waiting period*) opóźnienie *nt*, zwłoka *f*; (*postponement*) opóźnienie *nt*; **without ~** bezzwłocznie; **to be ~ed** (*person*) być spóźnionym; (*flight etc*) mieć opóźnienie, być opóźnionym
**delayed-action** [dɪ'leɪd'ækʃən] *adj* (*mechanism*) zwłoczny
**delectable** [dɪ'lɛktəbl] *adj* (*person*) powabny, rozkoszny; (*food*) wyśmienity
**delegate** [*n* 'dɛlɪgɪt, *vb* 'dɛlɪgeɪt] *n* delegat(ka) *m(f)*, wysłannik(-iczka) *m(f)* ▷ *vt* (*person*) delegować (wydelegować *perf*); (*task*) przekazywać (przekazać *perf*); **to ~ sth to sb/sb to do sth** udzielać (udzielić *perf*) komuś pełnomocnictwa do zrobienia czegoś
**delegation** [dɛlɪ'geɪʃən] *n* (*group*) delegacja *f*; (*by manager etc*) udzielanie *nt* pełnomocnictw, dzielenie się *nt* odpowiedzialnością (z podwładnymi)
**delete** [dɪ'li:t] *vt* (*cross out*) skreślać (skreślić *perf*), wykreślać (wykreślić *perf*); (*Comput*) kasować (skasować *perf*)
**Delhi** ['dɛlɪ] *n* Delhi *nt inv*
**deliberate** [*adj* dɪ'lɪbərɪt, *vb* dɪ'lɪbəreɪt] *adj* (*intentional*) umyślny, zamierzony; (*unhurried*) spokojny, nieśpieszny ▷ *vi* (*consider*) zastanawiać się; (*debate*) naradzać się
**deliberately** [dɪ'lɪbərɪtlɪ] *adv* (*on purpose*) umyślnie, celowo; (*carefully*) ostrożnie, rozważnie
**deliberation** [dɪlɪbə'reɪʃən] *n* namaszczenie *nt*, rozwaga *f*; (*usu pl*) obrady *pl*
**delicacy** ['dɛlɪkəsɪ] *n* delikatność *f*; (*choice food*) przysmak *m*
**delicate** ['dɛlɪkɪt] *adj* delikatny
**delicately** ['dɛlɪkɪtlɪ] *adv* delikatnie
**delicatessen** [dɛlɪkə'tɛsn] *n* delikatesy *pl*
**delicious** [dɪ'lɪʃəs] *adj* (*food, smell*) wyśmienity, (prze)pyszny; (*feeling, person*) rozkoszny, przemiły
**delight** [dɪ'laɪt] *n* (*feeling*) zachwyt *m*, radość *f*; (*experience etc*) (wielka) przyjemność *f*, rozkosz *f* ▷ *vt* cieszyć (ucieszyć *perf*), zachwycać (zachwycić *perf*); **to take (a) ~ in** lubować się w *+loc*, rozkoszować się *+instr*; **she was a ~ to interview** wywiad z nią to była sama przyjemność; **the ~s of country life** rozkosze życia na wsi
**delighted** [dɪ'laɪtɪd] *adj*: **~ at** *or* **with** zachwycony *+instr*; **he was ~ to meet them again** był zachwycony, że mógł ich znów

zobaczyć; **I'd be ~** byłoby mi bardzo przyjemnie
**delightful** [dɪ'laɪtful] *adj* zachwycający
**delimit** [di:'lɪmɪt] *vt* ograniczać (ograniczyć *perf*)
**delineate** [dɪ'lɪnɪeɪt] *vt* (*outline*) nakreślać (nakreślić *perf*); (*fig*) określać (określić *perf*)
**delinquency** [dɪ'lɪŋkwənsɪ] *n* (*criminality*) przestępczość *f*; (*criminal action*) przestępstwo *nt*, wykroczenie *nt*
**delinquent** [dɪ'lɪŋkwənt] *adj* winny przestępstwa *or* wykroczenia ▷ *n* (młodociany(-na) *m(f)*) przestępca(-pczyni) *m(f)*
**delirious** [dɪ'lɪrɪəs] *adj*: **to be ~** (*Med*) majaczyć, bredzić; (*fig*) szaleć (z radości)
**delirium** [dɪ'lɪrɪəm] (*Med*) *n* majaczenie *nt*, bredzenie *nt*
**deliver** [dɪ'lɪvə[r]] *vt* (*distribute*) dostarczać (dostarczyć *perf*), doręczać (doręczyć *perf*); (*hand over*) oddawać (oddać *perf*), przekazywać (przekazać *perf*); (*verdict etc*) wydawać (wydać *perf*); (*speech*) wygłaszać (wygłosić *perf*); (*blow*) zadawać (zadać *perf*); (*warning etc*) dawać (dać *perf*); **to ~ a baby** odbierać (odebrać *perf*) poród; **to ~ sb from** (*captivity*) oswobadzać (oswobodzić *perf*) kogoś spod *+gen*; (*evil, harm*) wybawiać (wybawić *perf*) kogoś od *+gen*; **to ~ the goods** (*fig*) wywiązać się (*perf*) z obietnic(y)
**deliverance** [dɪ'lɪvrəns] *n* uwolnienie *nt*, wyzwolenie *nt*
**delivery** [dɪ'lɪvərɪ] *n* (*distribution*) dostawa *f*; (*of speaker*) sposób *m* mówienia; (*Med*) poród *m*; **to take ~ of sth** obejmować (objąć *perf*) coś w posiadanie
**delivery note** (*Comm*) *n* dowód *m* wykonania dostawy
**delivery van**, (*US*) **delivery truck** *n* samochód *m* dostawczy
**delouse** ['di:'laus] *vt* odwszawiać (odwszawić *perf*)
**delta** ['dɛltə] *n* delta *f*
**delude** [dɪ'lu:d] *vt* zwodzić (zwieść *perf*), wprowadzać (wprowadzić *perf*) w błąd; **to ~ o.s.** łudzić się, oszukiwać samego siebie
**deluge** ['dɛlju:dʒ] *n* (*of rain*) ulewa *f*, potop *m*; (*fig: of petitions etc*) lawina *f*, zalew *m*
**delusion** [dɪ'lu:ʒən] *n* złudzenie *nt*, ułuda *f*; **to have ~s of grandeur** mieć złudzenie wielkości
**de luxe** [də'lʌks] *adj* luksusowy
**delve** [dɛlv] *vi*: **to ~ into** (*subject, past etc*) zagłębiać się (zagłębić się *perf*) w *+acc*; **to ~ into/among** grzebać w *+loc*/wśród *+gen*
**Dem.** (*US: Pol*) *abbr* = **democrat(ic)**
**demagogue** ['dɛməgɔg] *n* demagog *m*
**demand** [dɪ'mɑ:nd] *vt* (*ask for, insist on*) żądać (zażądać *perf*) *+gen*, domagać się *+gen*; (*need*) wymagać *+gen* ▷ *n* (*request*) żądanie *nt*; (*claim*) wymaganie *nt*; (*Econ*) popyt *m*; **to ~ sth (from *or* of sb)** żądać (zażądać *perf*) czegoś (od kogoś); **I ~ to see a doctor** żądam widzenia z lekarzem; **to be in ~** mieć powodzenie, być rozchwytywanym; **on ~** na żądanie
**demand draft** (*Comm*) *n* przekaz *m* na żądanie *or* na okaziciela *or* awista
**demanding** [dɪ'mɑ:ndɪŋ] *adj* wymagający
**demarcation** [di:mɑ:'keɪʃən] *n* rozgraniczenie *nt*
**demarcation dispute** (*Industry*) *n* spór *m* o rozdział między gałęziami
**demean** [dɪ'mi:n] *vt*: **to ~ o.s.** poniżać się (poniżyć się *perf*)
**demeanour**, (*US*) **demeanor** [dɪ'mi:nə[r]] *n* zachowanie (się) *nt*
**demented** [dɪ'mɛntɪd] *adj* obłąkany
**demilitarized zone** [di:'mɪlɪtəraɪzd-] *n* strefa *f* zdemilitaryzowana
**demise** [dɪ'maɪz] *n* (*death*) zgon *m*; (*end*) zanik *m*
**demist** [di:'mɪst] (*Brit*) *vt* (*windscreen*) usuwać (usunąć *perf*) parę z *+gen*
**demister** [di:'mɪstə[r]] (*Brit*) *n* nadmuch *m*
**demo** ['dɛməu] (*inf*) *n abbr* = **demonstration**
**demob** [di:'mɔb] (*inf*) *vt* zwalniać (zwolnić *perf*) do cywila (*inf*)
**demobilize** [di:'məubɪlaɪz] *vt* demobilizować (zdemobilizować *perf*)
**democracy** [dɪ'mɔkrəsɪ] *n* (*system*) demokracja *f*; (*country*) państwo *nt* demokratyczne
**democrat** ['dɛməkræt] *n* demokrata(-tka) *m(f)*
**democratic** [dɛmə'krætɪk] *adj* demokratyczny
**demography** [dɪ'mɔgrəfɪ] *n* demografia *f*
**demolish** [dɪ'mɔlɪʃ] *vt* (*building*) burzyć (zburzyć *perf*); (*fig: argument*) obalać (obalić *perf*)
**demolition** [dɛmə'lɪʃən] *n* (*of building*) zburzenie *nt*; (*of argument*) obalenie *nt*
**demon** ['di:mən] *n* demon *m* ▷ *cpd*: **~ player/driver** wytrawny gracz *m*/kierowca *m*
**demonstrate** ['dɛmənstreɪt] *vt* (*theory*) dowodzić (dowieść *perf*) *+gen*; (*principle*) pokazywać (pokazać *perf*); (*skill*) wykazywać (wykazać *perf*); (*appliance*) demonstrować (zademonstrować *perf*) ▷ *vi*: **to ~ (for/against)** demonstrować (zademonstrować *perf*) *or* manifestować (zamanifestować *perf*) (za *+instr*/przeciw(ko) *+dat*)
**demonstration** [dɛmən'streɪʃən] *n* (*Pol*) demonstracja *f*, manifestacja *f*; (*proof*)

dowód *m*; (*exhibition*) demonstracja *f*, pokaz *m*; **to hold a ~** (*Pol*) przeprowadzać (przeprowadzić *perf*) demonstrację *or* manifestację
**demonstration model** *n samochód używany do prób i pokazów, sprzedawany po niższej cenie*
**demonstrative** [dɪˈmɔnstrətɪv] *adj* (*person*) wylewny; (*pronoun*) wskazujący
**demonstrator** [ˈdɛmənstreɪtəʳ] *n* (*Pol*) demonstrant(ka) *m(f)*, manifestant(ka) *m(f)*; (*Comm: sales person*) demonstrator(ka) *m(f)*; (*: US*) = **demonstration model**
**demoralize** [dɪˈmɔrəlaɪz] *vt* zniechęcać (zniechęcić *perf*)
**demote** [dɪˈməut] *vt* degradować (zdegradować *perf*)
**demotion** [dɪˈməuʃən] *n* degradacja *f*
**demur** [dɪˈməːʳ] (*fml*) *vi* sprzeciwiać się (sprzeciwić się *perf*) ▷ *n*: **without ~** bez sprzeciwu; **they ~red at the suggestion** sprzeciwili się tej propozycji
**demure** [dɪˈmjuəʳ] *adj* skromny
**demurrage** [dɪˈmʌrɪdʒ] (*Comm*) *n* przestój *m*
**den** [dɛn] *n* (*of animal*) nora *f*, legowisko *nt*; (*of thieves*) melina *f*; (*room*) *mały, cichy pokój, w którym jego użytkownikowi nie przeszkadzają inni domownicy*
**denationalization** [ˈdiːnæʃnəlaɪˈzeɪʃən] *n* denacjonalizacja *f*
**denationalize** [diːˈnæʃnəlaɪz] *vt* denacjonalizować (zdenacjonalizować *perf*)
**denatured alcohol** [diːˈneɪtʃəd-] (*US*) *n* denaturat *m*
**denial** [dɪˈnaɪəl] *n* (*of allegation*) zaprzeczenie *nt*; (*of rights, liberties*) odmawianie *nt*; (*of country, religion etc*) wyparcie się *nt*
**denier** [ˈdɛnɪəʳ] *n* denier *m*, den *m* (*jednostka wagi przędzy*)
**denigrate** [ˈdɛnɪgreɪt] *vt* oczerniać (oczernić *perf*)
**denim** [ˈdɛnɪm] *n* dżins *m*, drelich *m*; **denims** *npl* dżinsy *pl*
**denim jacket** *n* kurtka *f* dżinsowa
**denizen** [ˈdɛnɪzn] *n* mieszkaniec *m*
**Denmark** [ˈdɛnmɑːk] *n* Dania *f*
**denomination** [dɪnɔmɪˈneɪʃən] *n* (*of money*) nominał *m*; (*Rel*) wyznanie *nt*
**denominator** [dɪˈnɔmɪneɪtəʳ] (*Math*) *n* mianownik *m*
**denote** [dɪˈnəut] *vt* oznaczać (oznaczyć *perf*)
**denounce** [dɪˈnauns] *vt* potępiać (potępić *perf*)
**dense** [dɛns] *adj* gęsty; (*inf: person*) tępy
**densely** [ˈdɛnslɪ] *adv* gęsto
**density** [ˈdɛnsɪtɪ] *n* gęstość *f*; **double-/high-~ disk** dyskietka o podwójnej/wysokiej gęstości
**dent** [dɛnt] *n* (*in metal*) wgniecenie *nt*; (*fig: to pride, ego*) uszczerbek *m* ▷ *vt* (*metal*) wgniatać (wgnieść *perf*); (*fig: pride, ego*) zadawać (zadać *perf*) cios *+dat*
**dental** [ˈdɛntl] *adj* (*treatment*) dentystyczny, stomatologiczny; (*sound*) zębowy; **~ hygiene** higiena jamy ustnej
**dental floss** [-flɔs] *n* nić *f* dentystyczna
**dental surgeon** *n* lekarz *m* dentysta *m or* stomatolog *m*
**dentifrice** [ˈdɛntɪfrɪs] *n* środek *m* do czyszczenia zębów
**dentist** [ˈdɛntɪst] *n* dentysta(-tka) *m(f)*, stomatolog *m*; **~'s** (*also*: **dentist's surgery**) gabinet dentystyczny *or* stomatologiczny
**dentistry** [ˈdɛntɪstrɪ] *n* stomatologia *f*
**dentures** [ˈdɛntʃəz] *npl* proteza *f* (zębowa), sztuczna szczęka *f* (*inf*)
**denuded** [diːˈnjuːdɪd] *adj*: **~ of** ogołocony z *+gen*
**denunciation** [dɪnʌnsɪˈeɪʃən] *n* potępienie *nt*
**deny** [dɪˈnaɪ] *vt* (*allegation*) zaprzeczać (zaprzeczyć *perf*) *+dat*; (*permission, rights*) odmawiać (odmówić *perf*) *+gen*; (*country, religion etc*) wypierać się (wyprzeć się *perf*) *+gen*; **he denies having said it** zaprzecza, że to powiedział
**deodorant** [diːˈəudərənt] *n* dezodorant *m*
**depart** [dɪˈpɑːt] *vi* (*visitor: on foot*) wychodzić (wyjść *perf*); (*: by train etc*) wyjeżdżać (wyjechać *perf*); (*train*) odjeżdżać (odjechać *perf*); (*plane*) odlatywać (odlecieć *perf*); **to ~ from** (*fig*) odchodzić (odejść *perf*) *or* odstępować (odstąpić *perf*) od *+gen*
**department** [dɪˈpɑːtmənt] *n* (*Comm*) dział *m*; (*Scol*) instytut *m*, wydział *m*; (*Pol*) departament *m*, ministerstwo *nt*; **that's not my ~** (*fig*) to nie moja działka (*inf*); **D~ of State** (*US*) Departament Stanu
**departmental** [diːpɑːtˈmɛntl] *adj* (*meeting etc*) wydziałowy; **~ manager** (*in company*) kierownik(-iczka) *m(f)* oddziału; (*in shop*) kierownik(-iczka) *m(f)* działu
**department store** *n* dom *m* towarowy
**departure** [dɪˈpɑːtʃəʳ] *n* (*of visitor: on foot*) wyjście *nt*; (*: by train etc*) wyjazd *m*; (*of train*) odjazd *m*; (*of plane*) odlot *m*; (*of employee, colleague*) odejście *nt*; (*fig*): **~ from** odejście *nt or* odstępstwo *nt* od *+gen*; **a new ~** (*in policy etc*) nowy kierunek
**departure lounge** *n* hala *f* odlotów
**depend** [dɪˈpɛnd] *vi*: **to ~ on** (*be supported by*) zależeć od *+gen*; (*rely on*) polegać na *+loc*; (*financially*) być zależnym od *+gen*; **it ~s** to zależy; **~ing on the result** w zależności od wyniku
**dependable** [dɪˈpɛndəbl] *adj* niezawodny

**dependant** [dɪ'pɛndənt], **dependent** *n*: **to be sb's ~** być na czyimś utrzymaniu
**dependence** [dɪ'pɛndəns] *n* uzależnienie *nt*
**dependent** [dɪ'pɛndənt] *adj*: **to be ~ on** być uzależnionym od *+gen* ▷ *n* = **dependant**
**depict** [dɪ'pɪkt] *vt* (*in picture*) przedstawiać (przedstawić *perf*); (*describe*) odmalowywać (odmalować *perf*)
**depilatory** [dɪ'pɪlətrɪ] *n* (*also*: **depilatory cream**) krem *m* do depilacji, depilator *m* (w kremie)
**depleted** [dɪ'pli:tɪd] *adj* (*stocks etc*) uszczuplony, naruszony
**deplorable** [dɪ'plɔ:rəbl] *adj* (*conditions*) żałosny; (*lack of concern*) godny ubolewania
**deplore** [dɪ'plɔ:ʳ] *vt* ubolewać *or* boleć nad *+instr*
**deploy** [dɪ'plɔɪ] *vt* rozmieszczać (rozmieścić *perf*) (strategicznie)
**depopulate** [di:'pɔpjuleɪt] *vt* wyludniać (wyludnić *perf*)
**depopulation** ['di:pɔpju'leɪʃən] *n* wyludnienie *nt*
**deport** [dɪ'pɔ:t] *vt* deportować (deportować *perf*)
**deportation** [di:pɔ:'teɪʃən] *n* deportacja *f*
**deportation order** *n* nakaz *m* deportacji *or* opuszczenia kraju
**deportment** [dɪ'pɔ:tmənt] *n* (*behaviour*) zachowanie się *nt*; (*way of walking etc*) sposób *m* poruszania się
**depose** [dɪ'pəuz] *vt* (*official*) dymisjonować (zdymisjonować *perf*); (*ruler*) detronizować (zdetronizować *perf*)
**deposit** [dɪ'pɔzɪt] *n* (*in account*) wkład *m*, lokata *f*; (*down payment*) pierwsza wpłata *f*, zadatek *m*; (*for hired goods etc*) kaucja *f*, zastaw *m*; (*Chem*) osad *m*; (*of ore, oil*) złoże *nt* ▷ *vt* (*money*) wpłacać (wpłacić *perf*), deponować (zdeponować *perf*); (*case etc*) oddawać (oddać *perf*) (na przechowanie); (*valuables*) deponować (zdeponować *perf*); (*river: sand etc*) osadzać (osadzić *perf*); **to put down a ~ of 50 pounds** wpłacać (wpłacić *perf*) kaucję w wysokości 50 funtów
**deposit account** *n* rachunek *m* terminowy
**depositor** [dɪ'pɔzɪtəʳ] *n* deponent *m*
**depository** [dɪ'pɔzɪtərɪ] *n* magazyn *m*, skład *m*
**depot** ['dɛpəu] *n* (*storehouse*) magazyn *m*, skład *m*; (*for vehicles*) zajezdnia *f*; (*US: station*) dworzec *m*
**depraved** [dɪ'preɪvd] *adj* (*conduct*) niemoralny; (*person*) zdeprawowany, zepsuty
**depravity** [dɪ'prævɪtɪ] *n* zdeprawowanie *nt*, zepsucie *nt*
**deprecate** ['dɛprɪkeɪt] *vt* potępiać
**deprecating** ['dɛprɪkeɪtɪŋ] *adj* wyrażający dezaprobatę
**depreciate** [dɪ'pri:ʃɪeɪt] *vi* tracić (stracić *perf*) na wartości
**depreciation** [dɪpri:ʃɪ'eɪʃən] *n* spadek *m* wartości, deprecjacja *f* (*fml*)
**depress** [dɪ'prɛs] *vt* (*person*) przygnębiać (przygnębić *perf*); (*price, wages*) obniżać (obniżyć *perf*); (*press down*) naciskać (nacisnąć *perf*)
**depressant** [dɪ'prɛsnt] *n* środek *m* uspokajający
**depressed** [dɪ'prɛst] *adj* (*person*) przygnębiony, przybity; (*industry etc*) dotknięty kryzysem; (*area*) dotknięty bezrobociem; **to get ~** popadać (popaść *perf*) w depresję *or* przygnębienie
**depressing** [dɪ'prɛsɪŋ] *adj* przygnębiający
**depression** [dɪ'prɛʃən] *n* (*Psych*) depresja *f*; (*Econ*) kryzys *m*, depresja *f*; (*weather system*) niż *m*; (*hollow*) zagłębienie *nt*
**deprivation** [dɛprɪ'veɪʃən] *n* (*poverty*) ubóstwo *nt*; (*of rights etc*) pozbawienie *nt*
**deprive** [dɪ'praɪv] *vt*: **to ~ sb of sth** pozbawiać (pozbawić *perf*) kogoś czegoś
**deprived** [dɪ'praɪvd] *adj* (*area*) upośledzony; (*children*) z ubogich rodzin *post*
**dept.** *abbr* (= *department*) wydz.
**depth** [dɛpθ] *n* (*of hole, water etc*) głębokość *f*; (*of emotion, knowledge*) głębia *f*; **the ~s** czeluść, otchłań; **in the ~s of despair** w skrajnej rozpaczy; **in the ~s of winter** w samym środku zimy; **at a ~ of 3 metres** na głębokości trzech metrów; **to be out of one's ~** (*fig*) nie czuć gruntu pod nogami; **to go out of one's ~** (*lit, fig*) tracić (stracić *perf*) grunt pod nogami; **to study sth in ~** studiować (przestudiować *perf*) coś dogłębnie
**depth charge** *n* bomba *f* głębinowa
**deputation** [dɛpju'teɪʃən] *n* (*assignment*) delegowanie *nt*; (*group*) delegacja *f*
**deputize** ['dɛpjutaɪz] *vi*: **to ~ for sb** zastępować (zastąpić *perf*) kogoś
**deputy** ['dɛpjutɪ] *cpd*: **~ chairman/leader** *etc* wiceprzewodniczący(-ca) *m(f)* ▷ *n* (*assistant, replacement*) zastępca(-pczyni) *m(f)*; (*Pol*) deputowany(-na) *m(f)*; (*US*: *also*: **deputy sheriff**) zastępca *m* szeryfa; **~ head** (*Brit*: *Scol*) wicedyrektor(ka) *m(f)*
**derail** [dɪ'reɪl] *vt*: **to be ~ed** wykolejać się (wykoleić się *perf*)
**derailment** [dɪ'reɪlmənt] *n* wykolejenie *nt*
**deranged** [dɪ'reɪndʒd] *adj* (*also*: **mentally deranged**) obłąkany
**derby** ['də:rbɪ] (*US*) *n* melonik *m*
**Derbys** (*Brit: Post*) *abbr* = **Derbyshire**
**deregulate** [dɪ'rɛgjuleɪt] *vt* wyjmować (wyjąć *perf*) spod kontroli państwowej

**deregulation** [dɪ'rɛgju'leɪʃən] *n* wyjęcie *nt* spod kontroli państwowej
**derelict** ['dɛrɪlɪkt] *adj* (*building*) opuszczony
**deride** [dɪ'raɪd] *vt* szydzić *or* drwić z *+gen*
**derision** [dɪ'rɪʒən] *n* szyderstwo *nt*, drwina *f*
**derisive** [dɪ'raɪsɪv] *adj* szyderczy, drwiący
**derisory** [dɪ'raɪsərɪ] *adj* (*sum*) śmiechu wart; (*laughter, person*) drwiący
**derivation** [dɛrɪ'veɪʃən] *n* (*Ling*) derywacja *f*
**derivative** [dɪ'rɪvətɪv] *n* (*Math, Chem*) pochodna *f*; (*Ling*) wyraz *m* pochodny, derywat *m* ▷ *adj* (*pej*) wtórny, nieoryginalny
**derive** [dɪ'raɪv] *vt*: **to ~ pleasure/benefit from** czerpać przyjemność/korzyści z *+gen* ▷ *vi*: **to ~ from** wywodzić się z *+gen*
**dermatitis** [də:mə'taɪtɪs] *n* zapalenie *nt* skóry
**dermatology** [də:mə'tɔlədʒɪ] *n* dermatologia *f*
**derogatory** [dɪ'rɔgətərɪ] *adj* uwłaczający
**derrick** ['dɛrɪk] *n* (*on ship*) żuraw *m*; (*on oil well*) wieża *f* wiertnicza
**derv** [də:v] (*Brit*) *n* olej *m* napędowy
**DES** (*Brit*) *n abbr* (= *Department of Education and Science*) Ministerstwo *nt* Oświaty i Nauki
**desalination** [di:sælɪ'neɪʃən] *n* odsalanie *nt*
**descend** [dɪ'sɛnd] *vt* (*stairs*) schodzić (zejść *perf*) po *+loc*; (*hill*) schodzić (zejść *perf*) z *+gen*; (*slope*) schodzić (zejść *perf*) w dół *+gen* ▷ *vi* schodzić (zejść *perf*); **to be ~ed from** wywodzić się z *+gen*, pochodzić od *+gen*; **to ~ to** (*lying etc*) zniżać się (zniżyć się *perf*) do *+gen*; **in ~ing order** (*Math*) w porządku malejącym; **in ~ing order of importance** od najważniejszych poczynając
▶ **descend on** *vt fus* (*enemy etc*) napadać (napaść *perf*) na *+acc*; (*silence etc*) zapanować (*perf*) nad *+instr*, zawładnąć (*perf*) *+instr*; **visitors ~ed (up)on us** zwalili nam się goście (*inf*)
**descendant** [dɪ'sɛndənt] *n* potomek *m*
**descent** [dɪ'sɛnt] *n* (*of stairs, hill etc*) schodzenie *nt*; (*Aviat*) opadanie *nt*, wytracanie *nt* wysokości; (*origin*) pochodzenie *nt*, rodowód *m*
**describe** [dɪs'kraɪb] *vt* opisywać (opisać *perf*)
**description** [dɪs'krɪpʃən] *n* (*account*) opis *m*; (*sort*) rodzaj *m*; **of every ~** wszelkiego rodzaju
**descriptive** [dɪs'krɪptɪv] *adj* opisowy
**desecrate** ['dɛsɪkreɪt] *vt* bezcześcić (zbezcześcić *perf*), profanować (sprofanować *perf*)
**desegregate** [di:'sɛgrɪgeɪt] *vt* (*school, area*) eliminować (wyeliminować *perf*) segregację rasową z *+gen*
**desert** [*n* 'dɛzət, *vb* dɪ'zə:t] *n* pustynia *f* ▷ *vt* opuszczać (opuścić *perf*), porzucać (porzucić *perf*) ▷ *vi* dezerterować (zdezerterować *perf*); *see also* **deserts**
**deserter** [dɪ'zə:tə[r]] *n* dezerter *m*
**desertion** [dɪ'zə:ʃən] *n* (*Mil*) dezercja *f*; (*Jur*) porzucenie *nt*
**desert island** *n* bezludna wyspa *f*
**deserts** [dɪ'zə:ts] *npl*: **to get one's just ~** dostawać (dostać *perf*) to, na co się zasłużyło
**deserve** [dɪ'zə:v] *vt* zasługiwać (zasłużyć *perf* na *+acc*
**deservedly** [dɪ'zə:vɪdlɪ] *adv* zasłużenie
**deserving** [dɪ'zə:vɪŋ] *adj* (*person*) zasłużony; (*action, cause*) chwalebny, godny poparcia; **~ o** zasługujący na *+acc*
**desiccated** ['dɛsɪkeɪtɪd] *adj* (*skin etc*) wysuszony; **~ coconut** wiórki kokosowe
**design** [dɪ'zaɪn] *n* (*art, process*) projektowanie *nt*; (*drawing*) projekt *m*; (*layout, shape*) zaprojektowanie *nt*; (*pattern*) deseń *m*; (*intention*) zamiar *m*, zamysł *m* ▷ *vt* (*house, product*) projektować (zaprojektować *perf*); (*test*) układać (ułożyć *perf*); **to have ~s on** mieć *or* robić zakusy na *+acc*; **well-~ed** dobrze zaprojektowany
**designate** [*vb* 'dɛzɪgneɪt, *adj* 'dɛzɪgnɪt] *vt* desygnować, wyznaczać (wyznaczyć *perf*) ▷ *adj*: **chairman/minister ~** desygnowany przewodniczący/minister
**designation** [dɛzɪg'neɪʃən] *n* określenie *nt*, oznaczenie *nt*
**designer** [dɪ'zaɪnə[r]] *n* projektant(ka) *m(f)*; (*Tech*) konstruktor(ka) *m(f)* ▷ *adj* (*clothes, label etc*) od znanego projektanta *post*
**desirability** [dɪzaɪərə'bɪlɪtɪ] *n*: **the ~ of** potrzeba *f +gen*
**desirable** [dɪ'zaɪərəbl] *adj* (*proper*) pożądany, wskazany; (*attractive*) godny pożądania; **it is ~ that** wskazane jest, by
**desire** [dɪ'zaɪə[r]] *n* (*urge*) chęć *f*, ochota *f*; (*sexual urge*) pożądanie *nt*, żądza *f* ▷ *vt* (*want*) pragnąć (zapragnąć *perf*) *+gen*, życzyć (zażyczyć *perf*) sobie *+gen*; (*lust after*) pożądać *+gen*; **to ~ to do sth** pragnąć coś (z)robić; **to ~ that** pragnąć, by
**desirous** [dɪ'zaɪərəs] (*fml*) *adj*: **to be ~ of** życzyć sobie *+infin*
**desist** [dɪ'zɪst] *vi*: **to ~ from** zaniechać (*perf*) *+gen*
**desk** [dɛsk] *n* (*in office*) biurko *nt*; (*for pupil*) ławka *f*; (*in hotel*) recepcja *f*; (*at airport*) informacja *f*; (*Brit*: *in shop, restaurant*) kasa *f*
**desk job** *n* praca *f* biurowa
**desk-top publishing** ['dɛsktɔp-] *n* komputerowe wspomaganie *nt* prac wydawniczych
**desolate** ['dɛsəlɪt] *adj* (*place*) wyludniony, opuszczony; (*person*) niepocieszony
**desolation** [dɛsə'leɪʃən] *n* (*of place*) pustka *f*; (*of person*) rozpacz *f*

**despair** [dɪs'pɛə^r] *n* rozpacz *f* ▷ *vi*: **to ~ of** tracić (stracić *perf*) nadzieję na *+acc*, wątpić (zwątpić *perf*) w *+acc*; **to be in ~** być zrozpaczonym *or* w rozpaczy
**despatch** *n, vt* = **dispatch**
**desperate** ['dɛspərɪt] *adj* (*person*) zdesperowany; (*action*) rozpaczliwy, desperacki; (*situation, cry*) rozpaczliwy; **to be ~ for sth/to do sth** rozpaczliwie potrzebować czegoś/pragnąć coś zrobić; **gang of ~ men** banda desperatów
**desperately** ['dɛspərɪtlɪ] *adv* (*struggle, shout*) z desperacją; (*ill, unhappy etc*) strasznie
**desperation** [dɛspə'reɪʃən] *n* desperacja *f*, rozpacz *f*; **in (sheer) ~** w desperacji
**despicable** [dɪs'pɪkəbl] *adj* nikczemny, podły
**despise** [dɪs'paɪz] *vt* gardzić (wzgardzić *perf*) *+instr*, pogardzać (pogardzić *perf*) *+instr*
**despite** [dɪs'paɪt] *prep* (po)mimo *+gen*; **~ o.s.** wbrew (samemu) sobie
**despondent** [dɪs'pɔndənt] *adj* przybity, przygnębiony
**despot** ['dɛspɔt] *n* despota(-tka) *m(f)*
**dessert** [dɪ'zə:t] *n* deser *m*
**dessert spoon** *n* (*object*) łyżka *f* deserowa; (*quantity*) *około 2 łyżeczek od herbaty*
**destabilize** [di:'steɪbɪlaɪz] *vt* destabilizować (zdestabilizować *perf*)
**destination** [dɛstɪ'neɪʃən] *n* (*of traveller*) cel *m* (podróży); (*of goods*) miejsce *nt* przeznaczenia; (*of letter*) adres *m*, adresat *m*
**destined** ['dɛstɪnd] *adj*: **~ for** przeznaczony do *+gen*; **~ for Warsaw** w drodze do Warszawy; **he was ~ to do it** było mu pisane *or* przeznaczone, że to zrobi
**destiny** ['dɛstɪnɪ] *n* przeznaczenie *nt*, los *m*
**destitute** ['dɛstɪtju:t] *adj* pozbawiony środków do życia
**destroy** [dɪs'trɔɪ] *vt* (*building, faith*) niszczyć (zniszczyć *perf*); (*animal*) uśmiercać (uśmiercić *perf*)
**destroyer** [dɪs'trɔɪə^r] (*Naut*) *n* niszczyciel *m*
**destruction** [dɪs'trʌkʃən] *n* zniszczenie *nt*, zagłada *f*
**destructive** [dɪs'trʌktɪv] *adj* (*force*) niszczący, niszczycielski; (*criticism, child*) destruktywny
**desultory** ['dɛsəltərɪ] *adj* (*reading*) pobieżny; (*conversation*) zdawkowy
**detach** [dɪ'tætʃ] *vt* odczepiać (odczepić *perf*), zdejmować (zdjąć *perf*)
**detachable** [dɪ'tætʃəbl] *adj* odczepiany, zdejmowany
**detached** [dɪ'tætʃt] *adj* (*attitude, person*) bezstronny; (*house*) wolno stojący
**detachment** [dɪ'tætʃmənt] *n* obojętność *f*, dystans *m*; (*Mil*) oddział *m* (specjalny)
**detail** ['di:teɪl] *n* szczegół *m*, detal *m* ▷ *vt* wyszczególniać (wyszczególnić *perf*); **in ~** szczegółowo; **to go into ~s** wdawać się (wdać się *perf*) w szczegóły
**detailed** ['di:teɪld] *adj* szczegółowy, drobiazgowy
**detain** [dɪ'teɪn] *vt* zatrzymywać (zatrzymać *perf*)
**detainee** [di:teɪ'ni:] *n* zatrzymany(-na) *m(f)*
**detect** [dɪ'tɛkt] *vt* wyczuwać (wyczuć *perf*); (*Med, Tech*) wykrywać (wykryć *perf*)
**detection** [dɪ'tɛkʃən] *n* wykrycie *nt*; **crime ~** wykrywanie *or* wykrywalność przestępstw; **to escape ~** (*criminal*) pozostawać (pozostać *perf*) na wolności; (*mistake*) pozostawać (pozostać *perf*) nie zauważonym, uchodzić (ujść *perf*) uwadze
**detective** [dɪ'tɛktɪv] *n* detektyw *m*, wywiadowca(-wczyni) *m(f)*; **private ~** prywatny detektyw
**detective story** *n* powieść *f* kryminalna *or* detektywistyczna, kryminał *m* (*inf*)
**detector** [dɪ'tɛktə^r] *n* detektor *m*, wykrywacz *m*
**détente** [deɪ'tɑ:nt] *n* odprężenie *nt*
**detention** [dɪ'tɛnʃən] *n* (*arrest*) zatrzymanie *nt*; (*Scol*): **to be in ~** zostawać (zostać *perf*) (za karę) po lekcjach
**deter** [dɪ'tə:^r] *vt* odstraszać (odstraszyć *perf*)
**detergent** [dɪ'tə:dʒənt] *n* detergent *m*
**deteriorate** [dɪ'tɪərɪəreɪt] *vi* pogarszać się (pogorszyć się *perf*), psuć się (popsuć się *perf*)
**deterioration** [dɪtɪərɪə'reɪʃən] *n* pogorszenie *nt*
**determination** [dɪtə:mɪ'neɪʃən] *n* (*resolve*) determinacja *f*, zdecydowanie *nt*; (*establishment*) określenie *nt*, ustalenie *nt*
**determine** [dɪ'tə:mɪn] *vt* (*facts, budget, quantity*) ustalać (ustalić *perf*); (*limits etc*) określać (określić *perf*), wyznaczać (wyznaczyć *perf*); **to ~ that** wykazywać (wykazać *perf*), że; **to ~ to do sth** postanawiać (postanowić *perf*) coś zrobić
**determined** [dɪ'tə:mɪnd] *adj* (*person*) zdecydowany, zdeterminowany; (*effort*) stanowczy; **~ to do sth** zdecydowany coś zrobić
**deterrence** [dɪ'tɛrəns] *n* odstraszanie *nt*, działanie *nt* odstraszające
**deterrent** [dɪ'tɛrənt] *n* czynnik *m* odstraszający; **to act as a ~** działać (podziałać *perf*) odstraszająco
**detest** [dɪ'tɛst] *vt* nienawidzić *+gen*, nie cierpieć *+gen*
**detestable** [dɪ'tɛstəbl] *adj* obrzydliwy, wstrętny
**detonate** ['dɛtəneɪt] *vi* wybuchać (wybuchnąć *perf*) ▷ *vt* detonować (zdetonować *perf*)
**detonator** ['dɛtəneɪtə^r] *n* detonator *m*

d

**detour** ['di:tuəʳ] *n* (*diversion*) objazd *m*; **to make a ~** zbaczać (zboczyć *perf*) z trasy
**detox** ['di:tɔks] (*Brit: inf*) *n* odwyk *m* (*inf*)
**detract** [dɪ'trækt] *vi*: **to ~ from** (*effect, achievement*) umniejszać (umniejszyć *perf*) *+acc*; (*pleasure*) zakłócać (zakłócić *perf*) *+acc*
**detractor** [dɪ'træktəʳ] *n* krytyk *m*
**detriment** ['dɛtrɪmənt] *n*: **to the ~ of** ze szkodą dla *+gen*; **without ~ to** bez szkody dla *+gen*
**detrimental** [dɛtrɪ'mɛntl] *adj*: **~ to** (wielce) szkodliwy dla *+gen*
**deuce** [dju:s] (*Tennis*) *n* równowaga *f*
**devaluation** [dɪvælju'eɪʃən] *n* dewaluacja *f*
**devalue** ['di:'vælju:] *vt* (*work, person*) lekceważyć (zlekceważyć *perf*); (*currency*) dewaluować (zdewaluować *perf*)
**devastate** ['dɛvəsteɪt] *vt* (doszczętnie) niszczyć (zniszczyć *perf*); (*fig*): **to be ~d by** być zdruzgotanym *+instr*
**devastating** ['dɛvəsteɪtɪŋ] *adj* (*weapon, storm*) niszczycielski, siejący spustoszenie; (*news, effect*) druzgocący
**devastation** [dɛvəs'teɪʃən] *n* zniszczenie *nt*, spustoszenie *nt*
**develop** [dɪ'vɛləp] *vt* (*business, idea*) rozwijać (rozwinąć *perf*); (*land*) zagospodarowywać (zagospodarować *perf*); (*resource*) wykorzystywać (wykorzystać *perf*); (*Phot*) wywoływać (wywołać *perf*); (*disease*) dostawać (dostać *perf*) *+gen*, nabawić się (*perf*) *+gen* ▷ *vi* (*advance, evolve*) rozwijać się (rozwinąć się *perf*); (*appear*) występować (wystąpić *perf*), pojawiać się (pojawić się *perf*); **the machine ~ed faults** w urządzeniu wystąpiły usterki; **to ~ a taste for sth** nabierać (nabrać *perf*) upodobania do czegoś, zasmakować (*perf*) w czymś; **to ~ into** rozwijać się (rozwinąć się *perf*) w *+acc*
**developer** [dɪ'vɛləpəʳ] *n* (*also*: **property developer**) inwestor *m* (budowlany)
**developing country** [dɪ'vɛləpɪŋ-] *n* kraj *m* rozwijający się
**development** [dɪ'vɛləpmənt] *n* (*advance*) rozwój *m*; (*in affair, case*) wydarzenie *nt*; (*of land*) zagospodarowanie *nt*
**development area** *n rejon wysokiego bezrobocia, w którym rząd zachęca do inwestowania*
**deviant** ['di:vɪənt] *adj* odbiegający od normy
**deviate** ['di:vɪeɪt] *vi*: **to ~ from** (*view*) odstępować (odstąpić *perf*) od *+gen*; (*norm*) odbiegać (odbiec *perf*) (od *+gen*); (*path*) zbaczać (zboczyć *perf*) (z *+gen*)
**deviation** [di:vɪ'eɪʃən] *n* odchylenie *nt*, dewiacja *f*
**device** [dɪ'vaɪs] *n* (*apparatus*) przyrząd *m*, urządzenie *nt*; (*stratagem*) sposób *m*, środek *m*; **explosive ~** bomba
**devil** ['dɛvl] *n* diabeł *m*; **go on, be a ~!** zaszalej sobie!; **talk of the ~!** o wilku mowa...; **poor ~** biedaczysko
**devilish** ['dɛvlɪʃ] *adj* diabelski
**devious** ['di:vɪəs] *adj* (*person*) przebiegły; (*path*) kręty
**devise** [dɪ'vaɪz] *vt* (*plan*) obmyślać (obmyślić *perf*); (*machine*) wynaleźć (*perf*)
**devoid** [dɪ'vɔɪd] *adj*: **~ of** pozbawiony *+gen*
**devolution** [di:və'lu:ʃən] *n* decentralizacja *f* (władzy)
**devolve** [dɪ'vɔlv] *vi*: **to ~ (up)on** przechodzić (przejść *perf*) na *+acc* ▷ *vt* (*power, duty etc*) przekazywać (przekazać *perf*)
**devote** [dɪ'vəut] *vt*: **to ~ sth to sb/sth** poświęcać (poświęcić *perf*) coś komuś/czemuś
**devoted** [dɪ'vəutɪd] *adj* (*service, friendship*) ofiarny; (*admirer, partner*) oddany; **to be ~ to sb** być komuś oddanym; **the book is ~ to politics** książka poświęcona jest polityce
**devotee** [dɛvəu'ti:] *n* entuzjasta(-tka) *m(f)*, wielbiciel(ka) *m(f)*; (*Rel*) wierny(-na) *m(f)*
**devotion** [dɪ'vəuʃən] *n* oddanie *nt*; (*Rel*) pobożność *f*
**devour** [dɪ'vauəʳ] *vt* pożerać (pożreć *perf*)
**devout** [dɪ'vaut] *adj* pobożny, nabożny
**dew** [dju:] *n* rosa *f*
**dexterity** [dɛks'tɛrɪtɪ] *n* (*manual*) sprawność *f*, zręczność *f*; (*mental*) sprawność *f*
**dext(e)rous** ['dɛkstrəs] *adj* sprawny, zręczny
**dg** *abbr* (*= decigram*) dkg
**DH** (*Brit*) *n abbr* (*= Department of Health*) Ministerstwo *nt* Zdrowia
**Dhaka** ['dækə] *n* Dakka *f*
**DHSS** (*Brit*) *n abbr* (*formerly*: *= Department of Health and Social Security*) Ministerstwo *nt* Zdrowia i Opieki Społecznej
**diabetes** [daɪə'bi:ti:z] *n* cukrzyca *f*
**diabetic** [daɪə'bɛtɪk] *adj* chory na cukrzycę; (*chocolate etc*) dla chorych na cukrzycę *post* ▷ *n* chory(-ra) *m(f)* na cukrzycę, cukrzyk *m*
**diabolical** [daɪə'bɔlɪkl] *adj* (*inf*: *behaviour, weather*) ohydny
**diaeresis** [daɪ'ɛrɪsɪs] *n* diereza *f*
**diagnose** [daɪəg'nəuz] *vt* rozpoznawać (rozpoznać *perf*), diagnozować (zdiagnozować *perf*)
**diagnoses** [daɪəg'nəusi:z] *npl of* **diagnosis**
**diagnosis** [daɪəg'nəusɪs] (*pl* **diagnoses**) *n* diagnoza *f*, rozpoznanie *nt*
**diagonal** [daɪ'ægənl] *adj* ukośny ▷ *n* przekątna *f*
**diagram** ['daɪəgræm] *n* wykres *m*, diagram *m*
**dial** ['daɪəl] *n* (*indicator*) skala *f* (tarczowa); (*tuner*) pokrętło *nt*, potencjometr *m*; (*of phone*) tarcza *f* ▷ *vt* (*number*) wykręcać (wykręcić

*perf*), wybierać (wybrać *perf*) (*fml*); **to ~ a wrong number** wykręcać (wykręcić *perf*) zły numer; **can I ~ London direct?** czy można zadzwonić do Londynu bezpośrednio?

**dial.** *abbr* = **dialect**

**dial code** (*US*) *n* = **dialling code**

**dialect** ['daɪəlɛkt] *n* dialekt *m*, gwara *f*

**dialling code** ['daɪəlɪŋ-], (*US*) **dial code** *n* (numer *m*) kierunkowy

**dialling tone**, (*US*) **dial tone** *n* sygnał *m* (zgłoszenia) (*w telefonie*)

**dialogue**, (*US*) **dialog** ['daɪəlɔg] *n* dialog *m*

**dial tone** (*US*) *n* = **dialling tone**

**dialysis** [daɪ'ælɪsɪs] *n* dializa *f*

**diameter** [daɪ'æmɪtə^r] *n* średnica *f*

**diametrically** [daɪə'mɛtrɪklɪ] *adv*: **~ opposed (to)** diametralnie różny (od *+gen*)

**diamond** ['daɪəmənd] *n* (*stone*) diament *m*; (*: polished*) brylant *m*; (*shape*) romb *m*; **diamonds** *npl* (*Cards*) karo *nt inv*

**diamond ring** *n* pierścionek *m* z brylantem

**diaper** ['daɪəpə^r] (*US*) *n* pieluszka *f*

**diaphragm** ['daɪəfræm] *n* (*Anat*) przepona *f*; (*contraceptive*) krążek *m* dopochwowy

**diarrhoea**, (*US*) **diarrhea** [daɪə'ri:ə] *n* biegunka *f*

**diary** ['daɪərɪ] *n* (*engagements book*) terminarz *m*, notatnik *m*; (*daily account*) pamiętnik *m*, dziennik *m*; **to keep a ~** pisać pamiętnik

**diatribe** ['daɪətraɪb] *n* diatryba *f*

**dice** [daɪs] *n inv* (*in game*) kostka *f* (do gry); (*game*) kości *pl* ▷ *vt* (*Culin*) kroić (pokroić *perf*) w kostkę

**dicey** ['daɪsɪ] (*inf*) *adj*: **it's a bit ~** to trochę ryzykowne

**dichotomy** [daɪ'kɔtəmɪ] *n* (*division*) dwudzielność *f*, dychotomia *f*; (*disagreement*) rozdźwięk *m*

**Dictaphone®** ['dɪktəfəun] *n* dyktafon *m*

**dictate** [*vb* dɪk'teɪt, *n* 'dɪkteɪt] *vt* dyktować (podyktować *perf*) ▷ *vi*: **to ~ to** narzucać (narzucić *perf*) swoją wolę *+dat* ▷ *n* nakaz *m*; **I won't be ~d to** nikt mi nie będzie rozkazywać

**dictation** [dɪk'teɪʃən] *n* (*of letter etc*) dyktowanie *nt*; (*order*) dyktat *m*; (*Scol*) dyktando *nt*; **to take ~ from** pisać pod dyktando *+gen*; **at ~ speed** w tempie dyktowania

**dictator** [dɪk'teɪtə^r] *n* dyktator(ka) *m(f)*

**dictatorship** [dɪk'teɪtəʃɪp] *n* dyktatura *f*

**diction** ['dɪkʃən] *n* dykcja *f*

**dictionary** ['dɪkʃənrɪ] *n* słownik *m*

**did** [dɪd] *pt of* **do**

**didactic** [daɪ'dæktɪk] *adj* dydaktyczny

**diddle** ['dɪdl] (*inf*) *vt* nabierać (nabrać *perf*) (*inf*)

**didn't** ['dɪdnt] = **did not**

**die** [daɪ] *vi* (*person*) umierać (umrzeć *perf*); (*animal*) zdychać (zdechnąć *perf*); (*plant*) usychać (uschnąć *perf*); (*fig*) umierać (umrzeć *perf*), ginąć (zginąć *perf*); **to die of** *or* **from** umierać (umrzeć *perf*) na *+acc*; (*fig*) umierać (umrzeć *perf*) z *+gen*; **he is dying** on umiera *or* jest umierający; **to be dying for sth/to do sth** bardzo chcieć czegoś/zrobić coś
▶ **die away** *vi* (*sound, light*) niknąć, zanikać (zaniknąć *perf*)
▶ **die down** *vi* cichnąć (ucichnąć *perf*), uspokajać się (uspokoić się *perf*)
▶ **die out** *vi* (*custom*) zanikać (zaniknąć *perf*); (*species*) wymierać (wymrzeć *perf*)

**diehard** ['daɪhɑ:d] *n* (zatwardziały(-ła) *m(f)*) konserwatysta(-tka) *m(f)*

**diesel** ['di:zl] *n* (*vehicle*) pojazd *m* napędzany ropą, diesel *m* (*inf*); (*also*: **diesel oil**) olej *m* napędowy

**diesel engine** *n* silnik *m* diesla, diesel *m* (*inf*)

**diet** ['daɪət] *n* (*food intake*) odżywianie *nt*, dieta *f*; (*restricted food*) dieta *f* ▷ *vi* (*also*: **to be on a diet**) być na diecie; **to live on a ~ of fish and rice** żywić się rybami i ryżem

**dietician** [daɪə'tɪʃən] *n* dietetyk(-yczka) *m(f)*

**differ** ['dɪfə^r] *vi*: **to ~ (from)** różnić się (od *+gen*); **to ~ (about)** nie zgadzać się (co do *+gen*); **they agreed to ~** uzgodnili, że pozostaną każdy przy swoim zdaniu

**difference** ['dɪfrəns] *n* (*dissimilarity*) różnica *f*; (*disagreement*) różnica *f* poglądów; **it makes no ~ to me** nie sprawia mi to różnicy; **to settle one's ~s** godzić się (pogodzić się *perf*)

**different** ['dɪfrənt] *adj* (*not the same, unlike*) inny, różny; (*various*) różny

**differential** [dɪfə'rɛnʃəl] *n* (*Math*) różniczka *f*; (*Brit: in wages*) zróżnicowanie *nt*

**differentiate** [dɪfə'rɛnʃɪeɪt] *vi*: **to ~ between** rozróżniać (rozróżnić *perf*) pomiędzy *+instr* ▷ *vt*: **to ~ sth from** odróżniać (odróżnić *perf*) coś od *+gen*

**differently** ['dɪfrəntlɪ] *adv* (*in a different way*) inaczej, odmiennie; (*in different ways*) różnie

**difficult** ['dɪfɪkəlt] *adj* trudny; **~ to understand** trudny do zrozumienia

**difficulty** ['dɪfɪkəltɪ] *n* trudność *f*; **to have difficulties with** mieć trudności z *+instr*; **to be in ~** być w tarapatach

**diffidence** ['dɪfɪdəns] *n* nieśmiałość *f*, rezerwa *f*

**diffident** ['dɪfɪdənt] *adj* nieśmiały

**diffuse** [*adj* dɪ'fju:s, *vb* dɪ'fju:z] *adj* (*idea, sense*) niejasny; (*light*) rozproszony ▷ *vt* (*information*) rozpowszechniać (rozpowszechnić *perf*), szerzyć

**dig** [dɪg] (*pt, pp* **dug**) *vt* (*hole etc*) kopać, wykopywać (wykopać *perf*); (*garden*) kopać w

*+loc*, przekopywać (przekopać *perf*) ▷ *n* (*prod*) kuksaniec *m*, szturchaniec *m*; (*also*: **archaeological dig**) wykopalisko *nt*; (*remark*) przytyk *m*; **to dig one's nails into sth** wbijać (wbić *perf*) w coś paznokcie
▶ **dig in** *vi* okopywać się (okopać się *perf*) ▷ *vt* (*compost*) zakopywać (zakopać *perf*); (*knife, claw*) wbijać (wbić *perf*); **to dig one's heels in** (*fig*) zapierać się (zaprzeć się *perf*)
▶ **dig into** *vt fus* (*savings*) sięgać (sięgnąć *perf*) do *+gen*
▶ **dig out** *vt* odkopywać (odkopać *perf*), odgrzebywać (odgrzebać *perf*)
▶ **dig up** *vt* (*plant*) wykopywać (wykopać *perf*); (*information*) wydobywać (wydobyć *perf*) na jaw
**digest** [*vb* daɪ'dʒɛst, *n* 'daɪdʒɛst] *vt* (*food*) trawić (strawić *perf*); (*fig*: *facts*) przetrawiać (przetrawić *perf*) ▷ *n* kompendium *nt*
**digestible** [dɪ'dʒɛstəbl] *adj* strawny
**digestion** [dɪ'dʒɛstʃən] *n* trawienie *nt*
**digestive** [dɪ'dʒɛstɪv] *adj* trawienny; (*Brit*) *n* *rodzaj herbatnika z mąki razowej*; **the ~ system** układ pokarmowy
**digit** ['dɪdʒɪt] *n* (*number*) cyfra *f*; (*finger*) palec *m*
**digital** ['dɪdʒɪtl] *adj* cyfrowy
**digital computer** *n* komputer *m* cyfrowy
**dignified** ['dɪgnɪfaɪd] *adj* dostojny, pełen godności
**dignitary** ['dɪgnɪtərɪ] *n* dygnitarz *m*, dostojnik *m*
**dignity** ['dɪgnɪtɪ] *n* godność *f*, dostojeństwo *nt*
**digress** [daɪ'grɛs] *vi*: **to ~ from** (*topic*) odbiegać (odbiec *perf*) od *+gen*
**digression** [daɪ'grɛʃən] *n* dygresja *f*
**digs** [dɪgz] (*Brit*: *inf*) *npl* kwatera *f*
**dike** [daɪk] *n* = **dyke**
**dilapidated** [dɪ'læpɪdeɪtɪd] *adj* walący się, w rozsypce *post*
**dilate** [daɪ'leɪt] *vi* rozszerzać się (rozszerzyć się *perf*) ▷ *vt* rozszerzać (rozszerzyć *perf*)
**dilatory** ['dɪlətərɪ] *adj* opieszały
**dilemma** [daɪ'lɛmə] *n* dylemat *m*; **to be in a ~** być w rozterce, mieć dylemat
**diligence** ['dɪlɪdʒəns] *n* pilność *f*
**diligent** ['dɪlɪdʒənt] *adj* pilny
**dill** [dɪl] *n* koper *m* ogrodowy, koperek *m*
**dilly-dally** ['dɪlɪ'dælɪ] *vi* ociągać się
**dilute** [daɪ'lu:t] *vt* (*liquid*) rozcieńczać (rozcieńczyć *perf*); (*fig*: *principle etc*) osłabiać (osłabić *perf*) ▷ *adj* rozcieńczony
**dim** [dɪm] *adj* (*room*) ciemny; (*outline, figure*) niewyraźny; (*light*) przyćmiony; (*memory*) niewyraźny, mglisty; (*eyesight*) osłabiony; (*prospects*) ponury; (*inf*: *person*) ciemny (*inf*) ▷ *vt* (*light*) przyciemniać (przyciemnić *perf*); (*US*): **to dim one's lights** włączać (włączyć *perf*) światła mijania; **to take a dim view of sth** niechętnie odnosić się do czegoś
**dime** [daɪm] (*US*) *n* dziesięciocentówka *f*
**dimension** [daɪ'mɛnʃən] *n* (*aspect, measurement*) wymiar *m*; (*also pl*: *scale, size*) rozmiary *pl*
**-dimensional** [dɪ'mɛnʃənl] *adj suff*: **two~** dwuwymiarowy
**diminish** [dɪ'mɪnɪʃ] *vi* zmniejszać się (zmniejszyć się *perf*), maleć (zmaleć *perf*) ▷ *vt* zmniejszać (zmniejszyć *perf*), pomniejszać (pomniejszyć *perf*)
**diminished** [dɪ'mɪnɪʃt] *adj*: **~ responsibility** ograniczona poczytalność *f*
**diminutive** [dɪ'mɪnjutɪv] *adj* malutki, maleńki ▷ *n* (*Ling*) zdrobnienie *nt*
**dimly** ['dɪmlɪ] *adv* (*shine*) blado; (*visible, lit*) słabo; (*remember*) mgliście; (*see*) niewyraźnie
**dimmer** ['dɪmə[r]] *n* (*also*: **dimmer switch**: *at home*) regulator *m* oświetlenia; (: *in car*) przełącznik *m* świateł mijania
**dimmers** ['dɪməz] (*US*: *Aut*) *npl* (*dipped headlights*) światła *pl* mijania; (*parking lights*) światła *pl* postojowe
**dimple** ['dɪmpl] *n* (*on cheek, chin*) dołeczek *m*
**dim-witted** ['dɪm'wɪtɪd] (*inf*) *adj* (*person*) ciemny (*inf*)
**din** [dɪn] *n* hałas *m*, gwar *m* ▷ *vt* (*inf*): **to din sth into sb** wbijać (wbić *perf*) coś komuś do głowy
**dine** [daɪn] *vi* jeść (zjeść *perf*) obiad
**diner** ['daɪnə[r]] *n* (*in restaurant*) gość *m*; (*US*) (tania) restauracja *f*
**dinghy** ['dɪŋgɪ] *n* (*also*: **rubber dinghy**) ponton *m*; (*also*: **sailing dinghy**) bączek *m*, bąk *m*
**dingy** ['dɪndʒɪ] *adj* (*streets, room*) obskurny; (*clothes, curtains*: *dirty*) przybrudzony; (: *faded*) wyblakły, wypłowiały
**dining car** ['daɪnɪŋ-] (*Brit*) *n* wagon *m* restauracyjny
**dining room** *n* (*in house*) pokój *m* jadalny *or* stołowy, jadalnia *f*; (*in hotel*) restauracja *f*
**dinner** ['dɪnə[r]] *n* (*evening meal*) ≈ kolacja *f*; (*lunch*) ≈ obiad *m*; (*banquet*) przyjęcie *nt*
**dinner jacket** *n* smoking *m*
**dinner party** *n* przyjęcie *nt*
**dinner service** *n* zastawa *f* stołowa
**dinner time** *n* (*midday*) pora *f* obiadowa; (*evening*) pora *f* kolacji
**dinosaur** ['daɪnəsɔ:[r]] *n* dinozaur *m*
**dint** [dɪnt] *n*: **by ~ of** dzięki *+dat*
**diocese** ['daɪəsɪs] *n* diecezja *f*
**dioxide** [daɪ'ɔksaɪd] *n* dwutlenek *m*
**Dip.** (*Brit*) *abbr* (= *diploma*) dypl.
**dip** [dɪp] *n* (*slope*) nachylenie *nt*, spadek *m*; (*Culin*) sos *m* (do maczania zakąsek), dip *m*; (*for sheep*) kąpiel *f* odkażająca ▷ *vt* zanurzać

(zanurzyć *perf*), zamaczać (zamoczyć *perf*) ▷ *vi* opadać (opaść *perf*); **to take a dip, go for a dip** iść (pójść *perf*) popływać; **to dip the headlights** (*Brit*) włączać (włączyć *perf*) światła mijania

**diphtheria** [dɪf'θɪərɪə] *n* błonica *f*, dyfteryt *m*

**diphthong** ['dɪfθɔŋ] (*Ling*) *n* dyftong *m*, dwugłoska *f*

**diploma** [dɪ'pləumə] *n* dyplom *m*

**diplomacy** [dɪ'pləuməsɪ] *n* dyplomacja *f*

**diplomat** ['dɪpləmæt] *n* dyplomata(-tka) *m(f)*

**diplomatic** [dɪplə'mætɪk] *adj* dyplomatyczny; **to break off ~ relations (with)** zrywać (zerwać *perf*) stosunki dyplomatyczne (z *+instr*)

**diplomatic corps** *n* korpus *m* dyplomatyczny

**dipstick** ['dɪpstɪk] (*Brit: Aut*) *n* (prętowy) wskaźnik *m* poziomu oleju

**dip switch** (*Brit: Aut*) *n* przełącznik *m* świateł (mijania)

**dire** [daɪəʳ] *adj* (*danger, misery*) skrajny; (*consequences*) zgubny; (*prediction*) złowieszczy

**direct** [daɪ'rɛkt] *adj* bezpośredni ▷ *vt* (*letter, remarks, attention*) kierować (skierować *perf*); (*company, project*) kierować (pokierować *perf*) *+instr*; (*play, film*) reżyserować (wyreżyserować *perf*); **to ~ sb to do sth** polecać (polecić *perf*) komuś zrobić coś ▷ *adv* bezpośrednio; **can you ~ me to ...?** czy może mi Pan/Pani wskazać drogę do *+gen*?

**direct access** (*Comput*) *n* dostęp *m* bezpośredni *or* swobodny

**direct cost** (*Comm*) *n* koszty *pl* bezpośrednie

**direct current** *n* prąd *m* stały

**direct debit** (*Brit*) *n* debet *m* bezpośredni

**direct dialling** *n* połączenie *nt* bezpośrednie

**direct hit** *n* trafienie *nt*

**direction** [dɪ'rɛkʃən] *n* (*way*) kierunek *m*, strona *f*; (*TV, Radio, Film*) reżyseria *f*; **directions** *npl* wskazówki *pl*; **sense of ~** orientacja (w terenie); **~s for use** przepis użytkowania; **to ask for ~s** pytać (spytać *perf*) o drogę; **in the ~ of** w kierunku *or* w stronę *+gen*

**directional** [dɪ'rɛkʃənl] *adj* kierunkowy

**directive** [dɪ'rɛktɪv] *n* dyrektywa *f*, wytyczna *f*

**direct labour** *n* zatrudnianie *nt* bezpośrednie

**directly** [dɪ'rɛktlɪ] *adv* bezpośrednio

**direct mail** *n* przesyłki *pl* reklamowe

**direct mailshot** (*Brit*) *n przesyłanie nie zamówionych materiałów reklamowych bezpośrednio na adres domowy lub służbowy potencjalnego klienta*

**directness** [daɪ'rɛktnɪs] *n* bezpośredniość *f*

**director** [dɪ'rɛktəʳ] *n* (*Comm*) członek *m* rady nadzorczej; (*of project*) kierownik(-iczka) *m(f)*; (*TV, Radio, Film*) reżyser *m*

**Director of Public Prosecutions** (*Brit*) *n* ≈ Prokurator *m* Generalny

**directory** [dɪ'rɛktərɪ] *n* (*Tel*) książka *f* telefoniczna; (*also*: **street directory**) księga *f* adresowa; (*Comput*) katalog *m*; (*Comm*) zarząd *m*

**directory enquiries**, (*US*) **directory assistance** *n* biuro *nt* numerów

**dirt** [də:t] *n* brud *m*; (*earth*) ziemia *f*; **to treat sb like ~** traktować (potraktować *perf*) kogoś jak szmatę

**dirt-cheap** ['də:t'tʃi:p] *adj* tani jak barszcz ▷ *adv* za psie pieniądze

**dirt road** *n* droga *f* gruntowa

**dirty** ['də:tɪ] *adj* brudny; (*joke, story*) nieprzyzwoity ▷ *vt* brudzić (zabrudzić *perf or* pobrudzić *perf*)

**dirty trick** *n* świństwo *nt*

**disability** [dɪsə'bɪlɪtɪ] *n* (*physical*) kalectwo *nt*, inwalidztwo *nt*; (*mental*) upośledzenie *nt* (umysłowe)

**disability allowance** *n* dodatek *m* inwalidzki

**disable** [dɪs'eɪbl] *vt* (*illness, accident*) powodować (spowodować *perf*) kalectwo *or* inwalidztwo *+gen*; (*tank, gun*) unieszkodliwiać (unieszkodliwić *perf*)

**disabled** [dɪs'eɪbld] *adj* (*physically*) kaleki; (*mentally*) upośledzony (umysłowo) ▷ *npl*: **the ~** niepełnosprawni *vir pl*

**disabuse** [dɪsə'bju:z] *vt*: **to ~ sb of** wyprowadzać (wyprowadzić *perf*) kogoś z błędu co do *+gen*

**disadvantage** [dɪsəd'vɑ:ntɪdʒ] *n* ujemna strona *f*, wada *f*; **to work to sb's ~** działać na czyjąś niekorzyść; **to be at a ~** być w niekorzystnym położeniu *or* sytuacji

**disadvantaged** [dɪsəd'vɑ:ntɪdʒd] *adj* społecznie upośledzony

**disadvantageous** [dɪsædvɑ:n'teɪdʒəs] *adj* niekorzystny

**disaffected** [dɪsə'fɛktɪd] *adj* (*estranged*) zrażony; (*disloyal*) nielojalny

**disaffection** [dɪsə'fɛkʃən] *n* nielojalność *f*, niezadowolenie *nt* (*polityczne*)

**disagree** [dɪsə'gri:] *vi* nie zgadzać się, być innego *or* odmiennego zdania; **to ~ with** (*action, proposal*) być przeciwnym *+dat*; **I ~ with you** nie zgadzam się z tobą; **garlic ~s with me** czosnek mi szkodzi *or* nie służy

**disagreeable** [dɪsə'gri:əbl] *adj* nieprzyjemny

**disagreement** [dɪsə'gri:mənt] *n* (*lack of consensus*) różnica *f* zdań; (*refusal to agree*) niezgoda *f*; (*between statements, reports*) niezgodność *f*; (*argument*) nieporozumienie *nt*; **to have a ~ with sb** nie zgadzać się z kimś

**disallow** ['dɪsə'lau] *vt* (*Jur: appeal*) odrzucać (odrzucić *perf*); (*Sport: goal*) nie uznawać (nie uznać *perf*) *+gen*

**disappear** [dɪsəˈpɪəʳ] *vi* znikać (zniknąć *perf*); (*custom etc*) zanikać (zaniknąć *perf*)
**disappearance** [dɪsəˈpɪərəns] *n* zniknięcie *nt*; (*of custom etc*) zanik *m*
**disappoint** [dɪsəˈpɔɪnt] *vt* rozczarowywać (rozczarować *perf*), zawodzić (zawieść *perf*)
**disappointed** [dɪsəˈpɔɪntɪd] *adj* rozczarowany, zawiedziony
**disappointing** [dɪsəˈpɔɪntɪŋ] *adj* (*result*) nie spełniający oczekiwań; (*book etc*) zaskakująco słaby
**disappointment** [dɪsəˈpɔɪntmənt] *n* rozczarowanie *nt*, zawód *m*
**disapproval** [dɪsəˈpruːvəl] *n* dezaprobata *f*
**disapprove** [dɪsəˈpruːv] *vi*: **to ~ of** nie pochwalać *+gen*
**disapproving** [dɪsəˈpruːvɪŋ] *adj*: **~ expression/gesture** wyraz *m*/gest *m* dezaprobaty
**disarm** [dɪsˈɑːm] *vt* (*lit, fig*) rozbrajać (rozbroić *perf*) ▷ *vi* rozbrajać się (rozbroić się *perf*)
**disarmament** [dɪsˈɑːməmənt] *n* rozbrojenie *nt*
**disarming** [dɪsˈɑːmɪŋ] *adj* rozbrajający
**disarray** *n* [dɪsəˈreɪ]: **in ~** w nieładzie; **to throw into ~** wprowadzać (wprowadzić *perf*) zamieszanie w *+loc*
**disaster** [dɪˈzɑːstəʳ] *n* (*natural*) klęska *f* żywiołowa; (*Aviat etc*) katastrofa *f*; (*fig*) nieszczęście *nt*, katastrofa *f*
**disaster area** *n* obszar *m* klęski żywiołowej; **he's a ~ as a politician** polityk z niego fatalny
**disastrous** [dɪˈzɑːstrəs] *adj* katastrofalny
**disband** [dɪsˈbænd] *vt* (*regiment, group*) rozwiązywać (rozwiązać *perf*) ▷ *vi* rozwiązywać się (rozwiązać się *perf*)
**disbelief** [ˈdɪsbəˈliːf] *n* niedowierzanie *nt*; **in ~** z niedowierzaniem
**disbelieve** [ˈdɪsbəˈliːv] *vt* (*person*) nie wierzyć *+dat*; (*story*) nie wierzyć w *+acc*; **I don't ~ you** wierzę ci
**disc** [dɪsk] *n* (*Anat*) dysk *m*; (*record*) płyta *f*, krążek *m*; (*Comput*) = **disk**
**disc.** (*Comm*) *abbr* = **discount**
**discard** [dɪsˈkɑːd] *vt* wyrzucać (wyrzucić *perf*), pozbywać się (pozbyć się *perf*) *+gen*; (*fig*) porzucać (porzucić *perf*), odrzucać (odrzucić *perf*)
**disc brake** *n* hamulec *m* tarczowy
**discern** [dɪˈsəːn] *vt* (*perceive*) (ledwie) dostrzegać (dostrzec *perf*); (*discriminate*) rozróżniać (rozróżnić *perf*); (*understand*) rozeznawać się (rozeznać się *perf*) w *+loc*
**discernible** [dɪˈsəːnəbl] *adj* dostrzegalny
**discerning** [dɪˈsəːnɪŋ] *adj* (*judgement, look*) wnikliwy; (*audience*) wyrobiony
**discharge** [*vb* dɪsˈtʃɑːdʒ, *n* ˈdɪstʃɑːdʒ] *vt* (*duties*) wypełniać (wypełnić *perf*); (*debt*) spłacać (spłacić *perf*); (*waste*) wydalać (wydalić *perf*); (*patient*) wypisywać (wypisać *perf*); (*employee, defendant, soldier*) zwalniać (zwolnić *perf*) ▷ *n* (*Chem*) emisja *f*; (*Elec*) wyładowanie *nt*, rozładowanie *nt*; (*Med*) wydzielina *f*, wysięk *m*; (*of patient*) wypisanie *nt* (ze szpitala); (*of defendant, soldier*) zwolnienie *nt*; **to ~ a gun** oddać (*perf*) strzał
**discharged bankrupt** [dɪsˈtʃɑːdʒd-] (*Jur*) *n* bankrut *m* z uregulowanymi długami
**disciple** [dɪˈsaɪpl] *n* (*Rel*) uczeń *m*; (*fig*) uczeń/uczennica *m/f*
**disciplinary** [ˈdɪsɪplɪnərɪ] *adj* dyscyplinarny; **to take ~ action against sb** stosować (zastosować *perf*) wobec kogoś środki dyscyplinarne
**discipline** [ˈdɪsɪplɪn] *n* dyscyplina *f* ▷ *vt* (*train*) narzucać (narzucić *perf*) dyscyplinę *+dat*; (*punish*) karać (ukarać *perf*) (dyscyplinarnie); **to ~ o.s. to do sth** mobilizować (zmobilizować *perf*) się do zrobienia czegoś
**disc jockey** *n* dyskdżokej *m*
**disclaim** [dɪsˈkleɪm] *vt* wypierać się (wyprzeć się *perf*) *+gen*
**disclaimer** [dɪsˈkleɪməʳ] *n* zaprzeczenie *nt*, dementi *nt inv* (*fml*); **to issue a ~** składać (złożyć *perf*) dementi
**disclose** [dɪsˈkləuz] *vt* ujawniać (ujawnić *perf*)
**disclosure** [dɪsˈkləuʒəʳ] *n* ujawnienie *nt*
**disco** [ˈdɪskəu] *n abbr* = **discothèque**
**discolour**, (*US*) **discolor** [dɪsˈkʌləʳ] *vt* przebarwiać (przebarwić *perf*) ▷ *vi* przebarwiać się (przebarwić się *perf*)
**discolo(u)ration** [dɪskʌləˈreɪʃən] *n* przebarwienie *nt*
**discolo(u)red** [dɪsˈkʌləd] *adj* przebarwiony
**discomfort** [dɪsˈkʌmfət] *n* (*unease*) zakłopotanie *nt*, zażenowanie *nt*; (*physical*) dyskomfort *m*; (*inconvenience*) niewygoda *f*
**disconcert** [dɪskənˈsəːt] *vt* (*perturb*) niepokoić (zaniepokoić *perf*); (*embarrass*) wprawiać (wprawić *perf*) w zakłopotanie
**disconcerting** [dɪskənˈsəːtɪŋ] *adj* (*perturbing*) niepokojący; (*embarrassing*) żenujący
**disconnect** [dɪskəˈnɛkt] *vt* odłączać (odłączyć *perf*); (*Tel*) rozłączać (rozłączyć *perf*)
**disconnected** [dɪskəˈnɛktɪd] *adj* (*speech, thoughts*) bezładny, chaotyczny
**disconsolate** [dɪsˈkɔnsəlɪt] *adj* niepocieszony
**discontent** [dɪskənˈtɛnt] *n* niezadowolenie *nt*
**discontented** [dɪskənˈtɛntɪd] *adj* niezadowolony
**discontinue** [dɪskənˈtɪnjuː] *vt* przerywać (przerwać *perf*); **"~d"** (*Comm*) „model *or* wzór już nie produkowany"

**discord** ['dɪskɔ:d] *n* niezgoda *f*; (*Mus*) dysonans *m*
**discordant** [dɪs'kɔ:dənt] *adj* (*fig: opinions*) niezgodny; (*note*) nieharmonijny
**discothèque** ['dɪskəutɛk] *n* dyskoteka *f*
**discount** [*n* 'dɪskaunt, *vb* dɪs'kaunt] *n* zniżka *f*, rabat *m* ▷ *vt* (*Comm*) udzielać (udzielić *perf*) rabatu w wysokości *+gen*; (*idea, fact*) pomijać (pominąć *perf*), nie brać (nie wziąć *perf*) pod uwagę *+gen*; **to give sb a ~ on sth** udzielać (udzielić *perf*) komuś zniżki na coś; **~ for cash** rabat przy zapłacie gotówką; **at a ~** ze zniżką
**discount house** *n* (*Fin*) bank *m* dyskontowy; (*also*: **discount store**) sklep *m* z towarami po obniżonych cenach
**discount rate** *n* stopa *f* dyskontowa
**discourage** [dɪs'kʌrɪdʒ] *vt* zniechęcać (zniechęcić *perf*); **to ~ sb from doing sth** zniechęcać (zniechęcić *perf*) kogoś do (z) robienia czegoś
**discouragement** [dɪs'kʌrɪdʒmənt] *n* (*act*) zniechęcanie *nt*, odradzanie *nt*; (*state*) zniechęcenie *nt*; **to act as a ~ to sb** działać (podziałać *perf*) na kogoś zniechęcająco
**discouraging** [dɪs'kʌrɪdʒɪŋ] *adj* zniechęcający
**discourteous** [dɪs'kə:tɪəs] *adj* nieuprzejmy, niegrzeczny
**discover** [dɪs'kʌvə^r] *vt* odkrywać (odkryć *perf*); (*missing person, object*) odnajdować (odnaleźć *perf*); **to ~ that ...** odkrywać (odkryć *perf*), że ...
**discovery** [dɪs'kʌvərɪ] *n* odkrycie *nt*; (*of missing person, object*) odnalezienie *nt*
**discredit** [dɪs'krɛdɪt] *vt* dyskredytować (zdyskredytować *perf*) ▷ *n*: **to be to sb's ~** przynosić (przynieść *perf*) komuś ujmę
**discreet** [dɪs'kri:t] *adj* dyskretny; (*distance*) bezpieczny
**discreetly** [dɪs'kri:tlɪ] *adv* dyskretnie
**discrepancy** [dɪs'krɛpənsɪ] *n* rozbieżność *f*
**discretion** [dɪs'krɛʃən] *n* dyskrecja *f*; **at the ~ of** według uznania *+gen*; **use your own ~** zdecyduj sam
**discretionary** [dɪs'krɛʃənrɪ] *adj* (*payment etc*) nieobowiązkowy, dobrowolny; **~ power(s)** prawo podejmowania decyzji
**discriminate** [dɪs'krɪmɪneɪt] *vi*: **to ~ between sth and sth** odróżniać (odróżnić *perf*) coś od czegoś; **to ~ against** dyskryminować *+acc*
**discriminating** [dɪs'krɪmɪneɪtɪŋ] *adj* (*public*) wyrobiony
**discrimination** [dɪskrɪmɪ'neɪʃən] *n* (*bias*) dyskryminacja *f*; (*discernment*) rozeznanie *nt*; **racial/sexual ~** dyskryminacja rasowa/pod względem płci
**discus** ['dɪskəs] (*Sport*) *n* (*object*) dysk *m*; (*event*) rzut *m* dyskiem
**discuss** [dɪs'kʌs] *vt* (*talk over*) omawiać (omówić *perf*); (*analyse*) dyskutować o *+loc or* nad *+instr* (przedyskutować *perf +acc*)
**discussion** [dɪs'kʌʃən] *n* dyskusja *f*; **under ~** omawiany, będący przedmiotem dyskusji
**disdain** [dɪs'deɪn] *n* pogarda *f* ▷ *vt* gardzić *+instr* ▷ *vi*: **to ~ to ...** nie raczyć *+infin*
**disease** [dɪ'zi:z] *n* (*lit, fig*) choroba *f*
**diseased** [dɪ'zi:zd] *adj* (*lit, fig*) chory
**disembark** [dɪsɪm'bɑ:k] *vt* (*freight*) wyładowywać (wyładować *perf*); (*passengers*) wysadzać (wysadzić *perf*) ▷ *vi* wysiadać (wysiąść *perf*)
**disembarkation** [dɪsɛmbɑ:'keɪʃən] *n* (*of freight*) wyładunek *m*; (*of passengers*) zejście *nt* na ląd
**disembodied** ['dɪsɪm'bɔdɪd] *adj* bezcielesny
**disembowel** ['dɪsɪm'bauəl] *vt* (*animal*) patroszyć (wypatroszyć *perf*); (*person*) wypruwać (wypruć *perf*) wnętrzności z *+gen*
**disenchanted** ['dɪsɪn'tʃɑ:ntɪd] *adj*: **~ (with)** rozczarowany (*+instr*), pozbawiony złudzeń (co do *+gen*)
**disenfranchise** ['dɪsɪn'fræntʃaɪz] *vt* (*Pol*) pozbawiać (pozbawić *perf*) praw obywatelskich; (*Comm*) pozbawiać (pozbawić *perf*) licencji *or* prawa wyłączności
**disengage** [dɪsɪn'geɪdʒ] *vt* (*Aut: clutch*) zwalniać (zwolnić *perf*)
**disentangle** [dɪsɪn'tæŋgl] *vt* (*person*) wyswobadzać (wyswobodzić *perf*); (*wool, string*) rozplątywać (rozplątać *perf*), rozsupływać (rozsupłać *perf*); (*truth from lies*) oddzielać (oddzielić *perf*)
**disfavour**, (*US*) **disfavor** [dɪs'feɪvə^r] *n* nieprzychylność *f*
**disfigure** [dɪs'fɪgə^r] *vt* oszpecać (oszpecić *perf*), zeszpecać (zeszpecić *perf*)
**disgorge** [dɪs'gɔ:dʒ] *vt* wypluwać (wypluć *perf*) (*fig*)
**disgrace** [dɪs'greɪs] *n* hańba *f* ▷ *vt* przynosić (przynieść *perf*) hańbę *+dat*, hańbić (zhańbić *perf*)
**disgraceful** [dɪs'greɪsful] *adj* haniebny, hańbiący
**disgruntled** [dɪs'grʌntld] *adj* rozczarowany
**disguise** [dɪs'gaɪz] *n* (*costume*) przebranie *nt*; (*art*) kamuflaż *m* ▷ *vt*: **to ~ sb (as)** przebierać (przebrać *perf*) kogoś (za *+acc*); **in ~** w przebraniu; **there's no disguising the fact that ...** nie da się ukryć faktu, że ...; **to ~ o.s. as** przebierać się (przebrać się *perf*) za *+acc*
**disgust** [dɪs'gʌst] *n* obrzydzenie *nt*, wstręt *m* ▷ *vt* wzbudzać (wzbudzić *perf*) obrzydzenie *or* wstręt w *+loc*, napawać obrzydzeniem *or* wstrętem; **she walked off in ~** oddaliła się ze wstrętem

d

**disgusting** [dɪsˈɡʌstɪŋ] *adj* obrzydliwy, wstrętny
**dish** [dɪʃ] *n* (*piece of crockery*) naczynie *nt*; (*shallow plate*) półmisek *m*; (*recipe, food*) potrawa *f*; (*also*: **satellite dish**) antena *f* satelitarna; **to do** *or* **wash the ~es** zmywać (pozmywać *perf*) (naczynia)
▸ **dish out** *vt* (*gifts*) rozdawać (rozdać *perf*); (*food*) nakładać (nałożyć *perf*) (na talerze); (*advice*) udzielać (udzielić *perf*) *+gen*; (*money*) rozdzielać (rozdzielić *perf*)
▸ **dish up** *vt* (*food*) podawać (podać *perf*)
**dishcloth** [ˈdɪʃklɔθ] *n* (*for drying*) ścier(ecz)ka *f* do naczyń; (*for washing*) zmywak *m* (do naczyń)
**dishearten** [dɪsˈhɑːtn] *vt* zniechęcać (zniechęcić *perf*)
**dishevelled**, (*US*) **disheveled** [dɪˈʃɛvəld] *adj* (*hair*) rozczochrany; (*clothes*) w nieładzie *post*
**dishonest** [dɪsˈɔnɪst] *adj* nieuczciwy
**dishonesty** [dɪsˈɔnɪstɪ] *n* nieuczciwość *f*
**dishonour**, (*US*) **dishonor** [dɪsˈɔnə^r] *n* hańba *f*
**dishono(u)rable** [dɪsˈɔnərəbl] *adj* haniebny, hańbiący
**dish soap** (*US*) *n* środek *m* do mycia naczyń
**dishtowel** [ˈdɪʃtauəl] (*US*) *n* ścier(ecz)ka *f* do naczyń
**dishwasher** [ˈdɪʃwɔʃə^r] *n* zmywarka *f* (do naczyń)
**disillusion** [dɪsɪˈluːʒən] *vt* pozbawiać (pozbawić *perf*) złudzeń ▹ *n* = **disillusionment**; **to become ~ed (with)** pozbywać się (pozbyć się *perf*) złudzeń (co do *+gen*)
**disillusionment** [dɪsɪˈluːʒənmənt] *n* rozczarowanie *nt*
**disincentive** [dɪsɪnˈsɛntɪv] *n*: **to be a ~ to work/investment** zniechęcać (zniechęcić *perf*) do pracy/inwestowania; **to be a ~ to sb** zniechęcać (zniechęcić *perf*) kogoś
**disinclined** [dɪsɪnˈklaɪnd] *adj*: **to be ~ to do sth** nie mieć ochoty czegoś (z)robić
**disinfect** [dɪsɪnˈfɛkt] *vt* odkażać (odkazić *perf*), dezynfekować (zdezynfekować *perf*)
**disinfectant** [dɪsɪnˈfɛktənt] *n* środek *m* odkażający *or* dezynfekujący
**disinflation** [dɪsɪnˈfleɪʃən] *n* zwalczanie *nt* inflacji
**disingenuous** [dɪsɪnˈdʒɛnjuəs] *adj* nieszczery
**disinherit** [dɪsɪnˈhɛrɪt] *vt* wydziedziczać (wydziedziczyć *perf*)
**disintegrate** [dɪsˈɪntɪɡreɪt] *vi* rozpadać się (rozpaść się *perf*)
**disinterested** [dɪsˈɪntrəstɪd] *adj* (*impartial*) bezinteresowny
**disjointed** [dɪsˈdʒɔɪntɪd] *adj* bezładny
**disk** [dɪsk] *n* dysk *m*; (*floppy*) dyskietka *f*; **double-/high-density ~** dyskietka o podwójnej/wysokiej gęstości
**disk drive** *n* stacja *f or* napęd *m* dysków
**diskette** [dɪsˈkɛt] (*US*) *n* dyskietka *f*
**disk operating system** *n* system *m* operacyjny
**dislike** [dɪsˈlaɪk] *n* (*feeling*) niechęć *f*; **one's ~s** rzeczy, których się nie lubi ▹ *vt* nie lubić *+gen*; **to take a ~ to sb/sth** zacząć (*perf*) odczuwać niechęć do kogoś/czegoś; **I ~ the idea** nie podoba mi się ten pomysł
**dislocate** [ˈdɪsləkeɪt] *vt* (*joint*) zwichnąć (*perf*); **he has ~d his shoulder** zwichnął (sobie) ramię
**dislodge** [dɪsˈlɔdʒ] *vt* wyrywać (wyrwać *perf*)
**disloyal** [dɪsˈlɔɪəl] *adj*: **~ (to)** nielojalny (wobec *or* w stosunku do *+gen*)
**dismal** [ˈdɪzml] *adj* (*weather, mood, prospects*) ponury; (*results*) fatalny
**dismantle** [dɪsˈmæntl] *vt* (*machine*) rozbierać (rozebrać *perf*), demontować (zdemontować *perf*)
**dismay** [dɪsˈmeɪ] *n* (wielki) niepokój *m*, konsternacja *f* ▹ *vt* napełniać (napełnić *perf*) niepokojem *or* konsternacją; **much to my ~** ku mojej konsternacji; **he gasped in ~** dech mu zaparło z przerażenia
**dismiss** [dɪsˈmɪs] *vt* (*worker*) zwalniać (zwolnić *perf*) (z pracy); (*pupils*) puszczać (puścić *perf*) (*do domu lub na przerwę*); (*soldiers*) rozpuszczać (rozpuścić *perf*); (*possibility, problem*) lekceważyć (zlekceważyć *perf*); (*Jur: case*) oddalać (oddalić *perf*)
**dismissal** [dɪsˈmɪsl] *n* zwolnienie *nt* (z pracy)
**dismount** [dɪsˈmaunt] *vi* zsiadać (zsiąść *perf*) (*z konia, roweru*)
**disobedience** [dɪsəˈbiːdɪəns] *n* nieposłuszeństwo *nt*
**disobedient** [dɪsəˈbiːdɪənt] *adj* nieposłuszny
**disobey** [dɪsəˈbeɪ] *vt* nie słuchać (nie posłuchać *perf*) *+gen*
**disorder** [dɪsˈɔːdə^r] *n* (*untidiness*) nieporządek *m*, bałagan *m*; (*rioting*) niepokoje *pl*, rozruchy *pl*; (*Med*) zaburzenia *pl*; **civil ~** niepokoje społeczne
**disorderly** [dɪsˈɔːdəlɪ] *adj* (*room*) nieporządny; (*meeting*) chaotyczny; (*behaviour*) rozpasany
**disorderly conduct** *n* zakłócenie *nt* porządku publicznego
**disorganize** [dɪsˈɔːɡənaɪz] *vt* dezorganizować (zdezorganizować *perf*)
**disorganized** [dɪsˈɔːɡənaɪzd] *adj* źle zorganizowany
**disorientated** [dɪsˈɔːrɪɛnteɪtɪd] *adj* zdezorientowany

**disown** [dɪs'əun] *vt* (*action*) wypierać się (wyprzeć się *perf*) *+gen*; (*child*) wyrzekać się (wyrzec się *perf*) *+gen*
**disparaging** [dɪs'pærɪdʒɪŋ] *adj* pogardliwy, lekceważący; **to be ~ about sb/sth** odnosić się do kogoś/czegoś z pogardą *or* lekceważeniem
**disparate** ['dɪspərɪt] *adj* (całkowicie) różny *or* odmienny, nieporównywalny
**disparity** [dɪs'pærɪtɪ] *n* nierówność *f*, różnica *f*
**dispassionate** [dɪs'pæʃənət] *adj* beznamiętny
**dispatch** [dɪs'pætʃ] *vt* (*send*) wysyłać (wysłać *perf*); (*deal with*) załatwiać (załatwić *perf*); (*kill*) uśmiercać (uśmiercić *perf*) ▷ *n* (*sending*) wysyłka *f*, wysłanie *nt*; (*Press*) doniesienie *nt*, depesza *f*; (*Mil*) meldunek *m*, komunikat *m*
**dispatch department** *n* dział *m* wysyłki
**dispatch rider** *n* kurier *m*, goniec *m*
**dispel** [dɪs'pɛl] *vt* rozwiewać (rozwiać *perf*)
**dispensary** [dɪs'pɛnsərɪ] *n* apteka *f* (*w szpitalu lub szkole*)
**dispensation** [dɪspən'seɪʃən] *n* (*of justice*) wymierzanie *nt*; (*of medicine*) wydawanie *nt*; (*permission*: *Rel*) dyspensa *f*; (: *royal etc*) specjalne pozwolenie *nt*
**dispense** [dɪs'pɛns] *vt* (*medicines*) wydawać (wydać *perf*); (*advice*) udzielać (udzielić *perf*) *+gen*; (*money*) rozdysponowywać (rozdysponować *perf*)
▸ **dispense with** *vt fus* (*do without*) obchodzić się (obejść się *perf*) *or* obywać się (obyć się *perf*) bez *+gen*; (*get rid of*) pozbywać się (pozbyć się *perf*) *+gen*
**dispenser** [dɪs'pɛnsə<sup>r</sup>] *n*: **drinks ~** automat *m* z napojami; **cash ~** bankomat; **soap ~** dozownik mydła
**dispensing chemist** [dɪs'pɛnsɪŋ-] (*Brit*) *n* (*shop*) apteka *f*; (*person*) farmaceuta(-tka) *m*(*f*) (*pracujący w aptece*)
**dispersal** [dɪs'pə:sl] *n* rozproszenie *nt*
**disperse** [dɪs'pə:s] *vt* rozpraszać (rozproszyć *perf*) ▷ *vi* rozpraszać się (rozproszyć się *perf*)
**dispirited** [dɪs'pɪrɪtɪd] *adj* zniechęcony
**displace** [dɪs'pleɪs] *vt* (*take place of*) wypierać (wyprzeć *perf*); (*force to move*) wysiedlać (wysiedlić *perf*)
**displaced person** [dɪs'pleɪst-] *n* wysiedleniec *m*
**displacement** [dɪs'pleɪsmənt] *n* (*of population*) wysiedlenie *nt*; (*of liquid*) wypieranie *nt*; (*of vessel*) wyporność *f*
**display** [dɪs'pleɪ] *n* (*in shop window*) wystawa *f*; (*of fireworks etc*) pokaz *m*; (*of feelings*) okazywanie *nt*; (*Comput*) monitor *m*; (*Tech*) wyświetlacz *m* ▷ *vt* (*collection, goods*) wystawiać (wystawić *perf*); (*feelings*) okazywać (okazać *perf*); (*departure times etc*: *on screen*) wyświetlać (wyświetlić *perf*); (*ostentatiously*) wystawiać (wystawić *perf*) na pokaz; **on ~** (*exhibits*) prezentowany; (*goods*) wystawiony
**display advertising** *n* reklama *f* na stojakach promocyjnych
**displease** [dɪs'pli:z] *vt* (*annoy*) drażnić, denerwować (zdenerwować *perf*); (*cause displeasure to*) wywoływać (wywołać *perf*) niezadowolenie *+gen*
**displeased** [dɪs'pli:zd] *adj*: **~ with** niezadowolony z *+gen*
**displeasure** [dɪs'plɛʒə<sup>r</sup>] *n* niezadowolenie *nt*
**disposable** [dɪs'pəuzəbl] *adj* (*lighter, bottle, syringe*) jednorazowy; **~ income** dochód netto
**disposable nappy** (*Brit*) *n* pieluszka *f* jednorazowa
**disposal** [dɪs'pəuzl] *n* (*of rubbish*) wywóz *m*; (*of radioactive waste*) usuwanie *nt*; (*of body, unwanted goods*) pozbycie się *nt*; **at one's ~** do (swojej) dyspozycji; **to put sth at sb's ~** oddawać (oddać *perf*) komuś coś do dyspozycji
**dispose** [dɪs'pəuz]: **~ of** *vt fus* (*body, unwanted goods*) pozbywać się (pozbyć się *perf*) *+gen*; (*problem, task*) radzić (poradzić *perf*) sobie z *+instr*; (*Comm*: *stock*) sprzedawać (sprzedać *perf*)
**disposed** [dɪs'pəuzd] *adj*: **to be ~ to do sth** (*inclined*) być skłonnym coś zrobić; (*willing*) mieć ochotę coś zrobić; **to be well ~ towards** być przyjaźnie usposobionym *or* nastawionym do *+gen*
**disposition** [dɪspə'zɪʃən] *n* (*nature*) usposobienie *nt*; (*inclination*) skłonność *f*
**dispossess** ['dɪspə'zɛs] *vt* wywłaszczać (wywłaszczyć *perf*); **to ~ sb of sth** pozbawiać (pozbawić *perf*) kogoś czegoś; **they were ~ed of the house** wysiedlono ich (z domu)
**disproportion** [dɪsprə'pɔ:ʃən] *n* dysproporcja *f*
**disproportionate** [dɪsprə'pɔ:ʃənət] *adj* nieproporcjonalny
**disprove** [dɪs'pru:v] *vt* (*belief, theory*) obalać (obalić *perf*)
**dispute** [dɪs'pju:t] *n* spór *m* ▷ *vt* (*fact, statement*) podawać (podać *perf*) w wątpliwość, kwestionować (zakwestionować *perf*); (*ownership etc*) spierać się o *+acc*; **to be in** *or* **under ~** (*matter*) być przedmiotem dyskusji; (*territory*) być przedmiotem sporu
**disqualification** [dɪskwɔlɪfɪ'keɪʃən] *n*: **~ (from)** dyskwalifikacja *f or* wykluczenie *nt* (z *+gen*); **~ (from driving)** (*Brit*) odebranie prawa jazdy

d

**disqualify** [dɪs'kwɔlɪfaɪ] *vt* (*Sport*) dyskwalifikować (zdyskwalifikować *perf*); **to ~ sb for sth** dyskwalifikować (zdyskwalifikować *perf*) *or* wykluczać (wykluczyć *perf*) kogoś za coś; **to ~ sb from doing sth** odbierać (odebrać *perf*) komuś prawo robienia czegoś; **he's been disqualified from driving** (*Brit*) odebrali mu prawo jazdy

**disquiet** [dɪs'kwaɪət] *n* zaniepokojenie *nt*

**disquieting** [dɪs'kwaɪətɪŋ] *adj* niepokojący

**disregard** [dɪsrɪ'gɑːd] *vt* lekceważyć, nie zważać na *+acc* ▷ *n*: **~ (for)** lekceważenie *nt* (*+gen*)

**disrepair** ['dɪsrɪ'pɛə^r] *n*: **to fall into ~** popadać (popaść *perf*) w ruinę

**disreputable** [dɪs'rɛpjutəbl] *adj* (*person*) podejrzany; (*behaviour*) naganny

**disrepute** ['dɪsrɪ'pjuːt] *n*: **to be in ~** cieszyć się złą sławą; **to bring sth into ~** przynosić (przynieść *perf*) czemuś złą sławę

**disrespectful** [dɪsrɪ'spɛktful] *adj* (*person*) lekceważący; (*conduct*) obraźliwy

**disrupt** [dɪs'rʌpt] *vt* (*plans*) krzyżować (pokrzyżować *perf*); (*conversation, proceedings*) przerywać (przerwać *perf*); (*event, process*) zakłócać (zakłócić *perf*)

**disruption** [dɪs'rʌpʃən] *n* zakłócenie *nt*

**disruptive** [dɪs'rʌptɪv] *adj* (*influence, action*) destrukcyjny

**dissatisfaction** [dɪssætɪs'fækʃən] *n* niezadowolenie *nt*

**dissatisfied** [dɪs'sætɪsfaɪd] *adj* niezadowolony; **~ with** niezadowolony z *+gen*

**dissect** [dɪ'sɛkt] *vt* przeprowadzać (przeprowadzić *perf*) sekcję *+gen*; (*fig: theory, article*) rozkładać (rozłożyć *perf*) na czynniki pierwsze

**disseminate** [dɪ'sɛmɪneɪt] *vt* rozpowszechniać (rozpowszechnić *perf*)

**dissent** [dɪ'sɛnt] *n* (*disagreement*) różnica *f* zdań *or* poglądów; (*protest*) protest *m*; **~ from the party line** odejście od linii partyjnej

**dissenter** [dɪ'sɛntə^r] *n* inaczej myślący(-ca) *m(f)*; (*Rel*) odszczepieniec *m*

**dissertation** [dɪsə'teɪʃən] *n* rozprawa *f*, dysertacja *f*

**disservice** [dɪs'səːvɪs] *n*: **to do sb a ~** źle się komuś przysłużyć (*perf*)

**dissident** ['dɪsɪdnt] *adj* dysydencki ▷ *n* dysydent(ka) *m(f)*

**dissimilar** [dɪ'sɪmɪlə^r] *adj* odmienny, różny; **~ to** niepodobny do *+gen*

**dissipate** ['dɪsɪpeɪt] *vt* (*heat*) odprowadzać (odprowadzić *perf*); (*clouds*) rozpraszać (rozproszyć *perf*); (*money, time*) trwonić (roztrwonić *perf*)

**dissipated** ['dɪsɪpeɪtɪd] *adj* (*person*) zniszczony rozpustą; (*behaviour*) rozpustny

**dissociate** [dɪ'səuʃɪeɪt] *vt* rozdzielać (rozdzielić *perf*), oddzielać (oddzielić *perf*); **to ~ o.s. from** odcinać się (odciąć się *perf*) od *+gen*

**dissolute** ['dɪsəluːt] *adj* rozwiązły

**dissolution** [dɪsə'luːʃən] *n* (*breaking up officially*) rozwiązanie *nt*; (*decay*) rozpad *m*

**dissolve** [dɪ'zɔlv] *vt* (*in liquid*) rozpuszczać (rozpuścić *perf*); (*organization, marriage*) rozwiązywać (rozwiązać *perf*) ▷ *vi* rozpuszczać się (rozpuścić się *perf*); **to ~ in(to) tears** zalewać się (zalać się *perf*) łzami

**dissuade** [dɪ'sweɪd] *vt*: **to ~ sb from** odwodzić (odwieść *perf*) kogoś od *+gen*

**distaff** ['dɪstɑːf] *n*: **on the ~ side** po kądzieli

**distance** ['dɪstns] *n* (*interval*) odległość *f*; (*remoteness*) oddalenie *nt*; (*reserve*) dystans *m* ▷ *vt*: **to ~ o.s. (from)** dystansować się (zdystansować się *perf*) (od *+gen*); **in the ~** w oddali; **what's the ~ to London?** jak daleko jest do Londynu?; **it's within walking ~** można tam dojść pieszo *or* piechotą; **at a ~ of two metres** w odległości dwóch metrów; **keep your ~!** nie zbliżać się!

**distant** ['dɪstnt] *adj* (*place, time*) odległy; (*relative*) daleki; (*manner*) chłodny

**distaste** [dɪs'teɪst] *n* wstręt *m*, obrzydzenie *nt*

**distasteful** [dɪs'teɪstful] *adj* wstrętny, obrzydliwy

**Dist. Atty.** (*US*) *abbr* = **district attorney**

**distemper** [dɪs'tɛmpə^r] *n* (*paint*) farba *f* klejowa; (*dog disease*) nosówka *f*

**distend** [dɪs'tɛnd] (*Med*) *vt* rozszerzać (rozszerzyć *perf*) ▷ *vi* (*stomach*) rozdymać się (rozdąć się *perf*); (*pupils*) rozszerzać się (rozszerzyć się *perf*)

**distended** [dɪs'tɛndɪd] *adj* (*stomach, intestine*) rozdęty

**distil**, (*US*) **distill** [dɪs'tɪl] *vt* destylować; (*fig: information etc*) czerpać, zaczerpywać (zaczerpnąć *perf*)

**distillery** [dɪs'tɪlərɪ] *n* gorzelnia *f*

**distinct** [dɪs'tɪŋkt] *adj* (*separate*) odrębny; (*different*) różny; (*clear*) wyraźny; (*unmistakable*) niewątpliwy, zdecydowany; **as ~ from** w odróżnieniu od *+gen*

**distinction** [dɪs'tɪŋkʃən] *n* (*difference*) różnica *f*; (*mark of respect, recognition of achievement*) wyróżnienie *nt*; **to draw a ~ between** przeprowadzać (przeprowadzić *perf*) rozróżnienie pomiędzy *+instr*; **a writer of ~** wybitny pisarz

**distinctive** [dɪs'tɪŋktɪv] *adj* wyróżniający

**distinctly** [dɪs'tɪŋktlɪ] *adv* wyraźnie

**distinguish** [dɪs'tɪŋgwɪʃ] *vt* (*differentiate*) odróżniać (odróżnić *perf*); (*identify*) rozpoznawać (rozpoznać *perf*); **to ~ between** rozróżniać (rozróżnić *perf*) pomiędzy *+instr*; **to ~ o.s.** (*in battle etc*) odznaczać się (odznaczyć się *perf*)

**distinguished** [dɪsˈtɪŋgwɪʃt] *adj* (*eminent*) wybitny; (*in appearance*) dystyngowany

**distinguishing** [dɪsˈtɪŋgwɪʃɪŋ] *adj* wyróżniający

**distort** [dɪsˈtɔːt] *vt* (*argument*) wypaczać (wypaczyć *perf*); (*sound, image, news*) zniekształcać (zniekształcić *perf*)

**distortion** [dɪsˈtɔːʃən] *n* (*of argument*) wypaczenie *nt*; (*of sound, image, news*) zniekształcenie *nt*

**distract** [dɪsˈtrækt] *vt* (*person, attention*) rozpraszać (rozproszyć *perf*); **to ~ sb's attention from sth** odrywać (oderwać *perf*) czyjąś uwagę od czegoś; **it ~ed them from their work** to im przeszkadzało w pracy

**distracted** [dɪsˈtræktɪd] *adj* (*dreaming*) nieuważny, roztargniony; (*anxious*) strapiony

**distraction** [dɪsˈtrækʃən] *n* (*diversion*) zakłócenie *nt*; (*amusement*) rozrywka *f*; **to drive sb to ~** doprowadzać (doprowadzić *perf*) kogoś do szału

**distraught** [dɪsˈtrɔːt] *adj*: **~ with** (*pain, worry*) oszalały z *+gen*

**distress** [dɪsˈtrɛs] *n* (*extreme worry*) rozpacz *f*; (*suffering*) cierpienie *nt* ▷ *vt* sprawiać (sprawić *perf*) ból *or* przykrość *+dat*; **in ~** (*ship*) w niebezpieczeństwie; (*person*) w niedoli *or* biedzie; **~ed area** (*Brit*) obszar dotknięty bezrobociem

**distressing** [dɪsˈtrɛsɪŋ] *adj* przykry

**distress signal** *n* (*Aviat, Naut*) sygnał *m* SOS

**distribute** [dɪsˈtrɪbjuːt] *vt* (*hand out*) rozdawać (rozdać *perf*); (*deliver*) rozprowadzać (rozprowadzić *perf*); (*share out*) rozdzielać (rozdzielić *perf*); (*spread out*) rozmieszczać (rozmieścić *perf*)

**distribution** [dɪstrɪˈbjuːʃən] *n* (*of goods*) rozprowadzanie *nt*; (*of profits etc*) rozdział *m*

**distribution cost** *n* koszt *m* dystrybucji

**distributor** [dɪsˈtrɪbjutəʳ] *n* (*Comm*) dystrybutor *m*; (*Aut, Tech*) rozdzielacz *m*

**district** [ˈdɪstrɪkt] *n* (*of country*) region *m*; (*of town*) dzielnica *f*; (*Admin*) okręg *m*

**district attorney** (*US*) *n* ≈ prokurator *m*

**district council** (*Brit*) *n* rada *f* okręgowa

**district nurse** (*Brit*) *n* ≈ pielęgniarka *f* środowiskowa

**distrust** [dɪsˈtrʌst] *n* nieufność *f*, podejrzliwość *f* ▷ *vt* nie ufać *or* nie dowierzać *+dat*

**distrustful** [dɪsˈtrʌstful] *adj*: **~ (of)** nieufny *or* podejrzliwy (wobec *or* w stosunku do *+gen*)

**disturb** [dɪsˈtəːb] *vt* (*interrupt*) przeszkadzać (przeszkodzić *perf*) *+dat*; (*upset*) martwić (zmartwić *perf*); (*rearrange*) naruszać (naruszyć *perf*); (*inconvenience*) niepokoić (zaniepokoić *perf*); **sorry to ~ you** przepraszam, że przeszkadzam

**disturbance** [dɪsˈtəːbəns] *n* (*emotional*) niepokój *m*; (*political etc*) niepokoje *pl*; (*violent event*) zajście *nt*; (*of mind*) zaburzenia *pl*; (*by drunks etc*) burda *f*; **to cause a ~** zakłócać (zakłócić *perf*) porządek (publiczny); **~ of the peace** zakłócenie spokoju *or* porządku (publicznego)

**disturbed** [dɪsˈtəːbd] *adj* (*worried, upset*) zaniepokojony, poruszony; (*childhood*) trudny; **mentally ~** umysłowo chory; **emotionally ~** niezrównoważony emocjonalnie

**disturbing** [dɪsˈtəːbɪŋ] *adj* niepokojący, poruszający

**disuse** [dɪsˈjuːs] *n*: **to fall into ~** wychodzić (wyjść *perf*) z użycia

**disused** [dɪsˈjuːzd] *adj* (*building*) opuszczony; (*airfield*) nie używany

**ditch** [dɪtʃ] *n* (*at roadside*) rów *m*; (*irrigation ditch*) kanał *m* ▷ *vt* (*inf: partner*) rzucać (rzucić *perf*); (*: plan*) zarzucać (zarzucić *perf*); (*: car*) porzucać (porzucić *perf*)

**dither** [ˈdɪðəʳ] (*pej*) *vi* wahać się

**ditto** [ˈdɪtəu] *adv* jak wyżej

**divan** [dɪˈvæn] *n* (*also:* **divan bed**) otomana *f*

**dive** [daɪv] *n* (*from board*) skok *m* (do wody); (*underwater*) nurkowanie *nt*; (*pej: place*) spelunka *f* (*pej*) ▷ *vi* (*into water*) skakać (skoczyć *perf*) do wody; (*under water*) nurkować (zanurkować *perf*); (*submarine*) zanurzać się (zanurzyć się *perf*); **to ~ into** (*bag, drawer*) sięgać (sięgnąć *perf*) do *+gen*; (*shop, car*) dawać (dać *perf*) nura do *+gen*

**diver** [ˈdaɪvəʳ] *n* (*from board*) skoczek *m* (do wody); (*deep-sea diver*) nurek *m*

**diverge** [daɪˈvəːdʒ] *vi* rozchodzić się (rozejść się *perf*)

**divergent** [daɪˈvəːdʒənt] *adj* (*interests, views*) rozbieżny; (*groups*) różnorodny

**diverse** [daɪˈvəːs] *adj* różnorodny, zróżnicowany

**diversification** [daɪvəːsɪfɪˈkeɪʃən] *n* różnorodność *f*, zróżnicowanie *nt*

**diversify** [daɪˈvəːsɪfaɪ] *vi* (*Comm*) poszerzać (poszerzyć *perf*) ofertę

**diversion** [daɪˈvəːʃən] *n* (*Brit: Aut*) objazd *m*; (*distraction*) urozmaicenie *nt*, rozrywka *f*; (*of investment etc*) zmiana *f* kierunku

**diversity** [daɪˈvəːsɪtɪ] *n* różnorodność *f*, urozmaicenie *nt*

**divert** [daɪˈvəːt] *vt* (*sb's attention*) odwracać (odwrócić *perf*); (*money*) zmieniać (zmienić

*perf)* przeznaczenie *+gen*; *(traffic)* zmieniać (zmienić *perf)* kierunek *+gen*, kierować (skierować *perf)* objazdem
**divest** [daɪ'vɛst] *vt*: **to ~ sb of** pozbawiać (pozbawić *perf)* kogoś *+gen*; **to ~ o.s. of** *(belief etc)* wyzbywać się (wyzbyć się *perf) +gen*
**divide** [dɪ'vaɪd] *vt* dzielić (podzielić *perf)* ▷ *vi* dzielić się (podzielić się *perf)* ▷ *n (gulf, rift)* przepaść *f (fig)*; **to ~ (between** *or* **among)** dzielić (podzielić *perf)* ((po)między *+acc)*; **40 ~d by 5** 40 podzielone przez 5
▶ **divide out** *vt*: **to ~ out (between** *or* **among)** rozdzielać (rozdzielić *perf)* ((po) między *+acc)*
**divided** [dɪ'vaɪdɪd] *adj (lit, fig)* podzielony
**divided highway** (US) *n* droga *f* dwupasmowa
**dividend** ['dɪvɪdɛnd] *n* dywidenda *f*; *(fig)*: **to pay ~s** procentować (zaprocentować *perf)*
**dividend cover** *n* gwarancja *f* dywidendy
**dividers** [dɪ'vaɪdəz] *npl (instrument)* cyrkiel *m* warsztatowy *or* pomiarowy; *(between pages)* separator *m*
**divine** [dɪ'vaɪn] *adj (Rel)* boski, boży; *(fig)* boski ▷ *vt (truth, future)* odgadywać (odgadnąć *perf)*; *(water, metal)* wykrywać (wykryć *perf)* (różdżką)
**diving** ['daɪvɪŋ] *n (underwater)* nurkowanie *nt*; *(from board)* skoki *pl* do wody
**diving board** *n* trampolina *f*
**diving suit** *n* skafander *m* (nurka)
**divinity** [dɪ'vɪnɪtɪ] *n (quality)* boskość *f*; *(god, goddess)* bóstwo *nt*; *(Scol)* teologia *f*
**divisible** [dɪ'vɪzəbl] *(Math) adj*: **~ (by)** podzielny (przez *+acc)*; **to be ~ into** dzielić się na *+acc*
**division** [dɪ'vɪʒən] *n (of cells, property, within party)* podział *m*; *(Math)* dzielenie *nt*; *(Mil)* dywizja *f*; *(esp Football)* liga *f*; *(department: in company)* dział *m*; *(: in bank)* oddział *m*; *(: in police)* wydział *m*; *(Brit: Pol) głosowanie polegające na przejściu członków Izby Gmin przez wyjścia oznaczające „za" i „przeciw"*; **~ of labour** podział pracy
**divisive** [dɪ'vaɪsɪv] *adj* stwarzający podziały
**divorce** [dɪ'vɔːs] *n* rozwód *m* ▷ *vt (spouse)* rozwodzić się (rozwieść się *perf)* z *+instr*; *(sth from sth else)* oddzielać (oddzielić *perf)*
**divorced** [dɪ'vɔːst] *adj* rozwiedziony
**divorcee** [dɪvɔː'siː] *n* rozwodnik(-wódka) *m(f)*
**divulge** [daɪ'vʌldʒ] *vt* wyjawiać (wyjawić *perf)*
**DIY** *(Brit) n abbr* = **do-it-yourself**
**dizziness** ['dɪzɪnɪs] *n* zawroty *pl* głowy
**dizzy** ['dɪzɪ] *adj (height)* zawrotny; **~ spell** *or* **turn** atak zawrotów głowy; **I feel ~** kręci mi się w głowie; **to make sb ~** przyprawiać (przyprawić *perf)* kogoś o zawroty głowy
**DJ** *n abbr (= disc jockey)* DJ *m*
**d.j.** *n abbr* = **dinner jacket**
**Djakarta** [dʒə'kɑːtə] *n* Dżakarta *f*
**DJIA** *(US) n abbr (= Dow-Jones Industrial Average)* indeks *m or* wskaźnik *m* Dow-Jones
**dl** *abbr (= decilitre)* dcl
**DLit(t)** *n abbr (= Doctor of Literature, Doctor of Letters) stopień naukowy*, ≈ dr hab.
**DLO** *n abbr (= dead-letter office) dział poczty zajmujący się niedoręczonymi przesyłkami*
**dm** *abbr (= decimetre)* dm
**DMus** *n abbr (= Doctor of Music) stopień naukowy*, ≈ dr
**DMZ** *n abbr (= demilitarized zone)* strefa *f* zdemilitaryzowana
**DNA** *n abbr (= deoxyribonucleic acid)* DNA *m inv*

KEYWORD

**do** [duː] *(pt* **did**, *pp* **done)** *aux vb* **1** *(in negative constructions)*: **I don't understand** nie rozumiem; **he didn't seem to care** wydawało się, że go to nie obchodzi
**2** *(to form questions)*: **didn't you know?** nie wiedziałaś?; **what do you think?** jak myślisz?
**3** *(for emphasis)* istotnie, rzeczywiście; **she does seem rather late** istotnie, wydaje się, że się spóźnia; **oh do shut up!** och, zamknij się wreszcie! *(inf)*
**4** *(in polite expressions)* (bardzo) proszę; **do sit down/help yourself** (bardzo) proszę usiąść/ poczęstować się
**5** *(used to avoid repeating vb)*: **she swims better than I do** ona pływa lepiej niż ja *or* ode mnie; **do you agree? — yes, I do/no, I don't** zgadzasz się? — tak/nie; **who made this mess? — I did** kto tak nabałaganił — ja
**6** *(in question tags)* prawda; **you like him, don't you?** lubisz go, prawda?; **I don't know him, do I?** przecież go nie znam
▷ *vt* **1** *(usu)* robić (zrobić *perf)*; **what are you doing tonight?** co robisz (dziś) wieczorem?; **what do you do (for a living)?** czym się Pan/ Pani zajmuje?; **have you done your homework?** (czy) odrobiłeś lekcje?; **I've got nothing to do** nie mam nic do roboty; **to do the cooking** gotować; **we're doing "Othello" at school** *(studying)* przerabiamy w szkole „Otella"; *(performing)* gramy w szkole „Otella"
**2** *(Aut etc: of distance)*: **we've done 200 km already** zrobiliśmy już 200 km; *(: of speed)*: **the car was doing 100** samochód jechał setką
▷ *vi* **1** *(act, behave)* robić (zrobić *perf)*; **do as I tell you** rób, jak ci każę; **you did well to**

**come so quickly** dobrze zrobiłeś, że tak szybko przyszedłeś
2 (*get on*) radzić sobie; **he's doing well/badly at school** dobrze/źle sobie radzi w szkole; **how do you do?** miło mi Pana/Panią poznać
3 (*suit*) nadawać się (nadać się *perf*); **will it do?** czy to się nada?
4 (*be sufficient*) starczać (starczyć *perf*), wystarczać (wystarczyć *perf*); **will 10 pounds do?** czy wystarczy dziesięć funtów?; **that'll do** (*is sufficient*) (to) wystarczy; **that'll do!** (*in annoyance*) starczy już!; **to make do with** zadowalać się (zadowolić się *perf*) +*instr* ▷ *n* (*inf*) impreza *f* (*inf*); **we're having a little do on Saturday** w sobotę robimy małą imprezę

**do.** *abbr* = **ditto**
**DOA** *abbr* = **dead on arrival**
**d.o.b.** *abbr* = **date of birth**
**docile** ['dəusaɪl] *adj* potulny
**dock** [dɔk] *n* (*Naut*) dok *m*; (*Jur*) ława *f* oskarżonych; (*Bot*) szczaw *m* ▷ *vi* (*ship*) wchodzić (wejść *perf*) do portu; (*two spacecraft*) łączyć się (połączyć się *perf*) ▷ *vt*: **they ~ed a third of his wages** potrącili mu jedną trzecią pensji; **docks** *npl* (*Naut*) port *m*
**dock dues** [-djuːz] *npl* opłaty *pl* dokowe *or* przystaniowe
**docker** ['dɔkə^r] *n* doker *m*
**docket** ['dɔkɪt] *n* (*Admin, Comm*) pokwitowanie *nt*, kwit *m*; (*on parcel etc*) wykaz *m or* opis *m* zawartości
**dockyard** ['dɔkjɑːd] *n* stocznia *f*
**doctor** ['dɔktə^r] *n* (*Med*) lekarz(-arka) *m(f)*; (*PhD etc*) doktor *m* ▷ *vt* (*figures, election results*) fałszować (sfałszować *perf*); **she ~ed his coffee with arsenic** dosypała mu arszeniku do kawy; **~'s office** (*US*) gabinet lekarski
**doctorate** ['dɔktərɪt] *n* doktorat *m*
**Doctor of Philosophy** *n* (*degree*) doktorat *m*; (*person*) doktor *m* (*nauk humanistycznych*)
**doctrine** ['dɔktrɪn] *n* doktryna *f*
**document** [*n* 'dɔkjumənt, *vb* 'dɔkjumɛnt] *n* dokument *m* ▷ *vt* opisywać (opisać *perf*)
**documentary** [dɔkju'mɛntərɪ] *n* film *m* dokumentalny ▷ *adj*: **~ evidence** dowody *pl* w postaci dokumentów
**documentation** [dɔkjumən'teɪʃən] *n* dokumentacja *f*
**DOD** (*US*) *n abbr* (= *Department of Defense*) Ministerstwo *nt* Obrony, ≈ MON *m*
**doddering** ['dɔdərɪŋ] *adj* trzęsący się (*ze starości*)
**Dodecanese (Islands)** [dəudɪkə'niːz ('aɪləndz)] *n(pl)*: **the ~** Dodekanez *m*
**dodge** [dɔdʒ] *n* unik *m* ▷ *vt* (*tax*) uchylać się (uchylić się *perf*) od +*gen*; (*blow, ball*) uchylać się (uchylić się *perf*) przed +*instr* ▷ *vi* robić (zrobić *perf*) unik; **he ~d the question** uchylił się od odpowiedzi; **to ~ out of the way** uskakiwać (uskoczyć *perf*); **to ~ through the traffic** przemykać się (przemknąć się *perf*) między samochodami
**dodgems** ['dɔdʒəmz] (*Brit*) *npl* samochodziki *pl* (*w wesołym miasteczku*)
**DOE** *n abbr* (*Brit*: = *Department of the Environment*) Ministerstwo *nt* Ochrony Środowiska; (*US*: = *Department of Energy*) Ministerstwo *nt* Energetyki
**doe** [dəu] *n* (*deer*) łania *f*; (*rabbit*) królica *f*
**does** [dʌz] *vb see* **do**
**doesn't** ['dʌznt] = **does not**
**dog** [dɔg] *n* pies *m* ▷ *vt* (*person*) chodzić za +*instr*; (*bad luck, memory*) prześladować; **to go to the dogs** schodzić (zejść *perf*) na psy
**dog biscuit** *n* sucharek *m* dla psów
**dog collar** *n* (*of dog*) obroża *f*; (*inf*: *of priest*) koloratka *f*
**dog-eared** ['dɔgɪəd] *adj* (*book etc*) zniszczony
**dog food** *n* pokarm *m* dla psów
**dogged** ['dɔgɪd] *adj* uparty, zawzięty
**dogma** ['dɔgmə] *n* dogmat *m*
**dogmatic** [dɔg'mætɪk] *adj* dogmatyczny
**do-gooder** [duː'gudə^r] (*pej*) *n* uszczęśliwiacz *m* (*pej*)
**dogsbody** ['dɔgzbɔdɪ] (*Brit*: *inf*) *n* posługacz(ka) *m(f)*
**doing** ['duɪŋ] *n*: **this is your ~** to twoja sprawka
**doings** ['duɪŋz] *npl* poczynania *pl*
**do-it-yourself** ['duːɪtjɔː'sɛlf] *n* majsterkowanie *nt*
**doldrums** ['dɔldrəmz] *npl*: **to be in the ~** (*person*) mieć chandrę; (*business*) podupadać
**dole** [dəul] (*Brit*: *inf*) *n* zasiłek *m*; **to be on the ~** być na zasiłku; **to go on the ~** iść (pójść *perf*) na zasiłek
▶ **dole out** *vt* wydzielać (wydzielić *perf*)
**doleful** ['dəulful] *adj* smętny, żałosny
**doll** [dɔl] *n* (*toy*) lalka *f*; (*US*: *inf*: *attractive woman*) laska *f* (*inf*)
**dollar** ['dɔlə^r] (*US etc*) *n* dolar *m*
**dolled up** (*inf*) *adj* odpicowany (*inf*)
**Dolomites** ['dɔləmaɪts] *npl*: **the ~** Dolomity *pl*
**dolphin** ['dɔlfɪn] *n* delfin *m*
**domain** [də'meɪn] *n* (*sphere*) dziedzina *f*; (*empire*) królestwo *nt* (*fig*)
**dome** [dəum] *n* kopuła *f*
**domestic** [də'mɛstɪk] *adj* (*trade, policy*) wewnętrzny; (*flight*) krajowy; (*news*) z kraju *post*; (*animals, tasks, happiness*) domowy
**domesticated** [də'mɛstɪkeɪtɪd] *adj* (*animal*) oswojony; **her husband is very ~** jej mąż dużo pomaga w domu

d

**domesticity** [dəumɛs'tɪsɪtɪ] *n* domatorstwo *nt*
**domestic servant** *n* służący(-ca) *m(f)*, pomoc *f* domowa
**domicile** ['dɔmɪsaɪl] *n* miejsce *nt* zamieszkania ▷ *vt*: **people ~d in Britain** ludzie zamieszkali (na stałe) w Wielkiej Brytanii
**dominant** ['dɔmɪnənt] *adj* (*share*) przeważający; (*role*) główny; (*partner*) dominujący
**dominate** ['dɔmɪneɪt] *vt* (*discussion*) dominować (zdominować *perf*); (*people, place*) mieć zwierzchnictwo nad *+instr*
**domination** [dɔmɪ'neɪʃən] *n* dominacja *f*, zwierzchnictwo *nt*
**domineering** [dɔmɪ'nɪərɪŋ] *adj* apodyktyczny
**Dominican Republic** [də'mɪnɪkən-] (*Geog*) *n*: **the ~** Dominikana *f*, Republika *f* Dominikańska
**dominion** [də'mɪnɪən] *n* (*territory*) dominium *nt*; (*authority*): **to have ~ over** mieć zwierzchnictwo nad *+instr*
**domino** ['dɔmɪnəu] (*pl* **~es**) *n* klocek *m* domina
**domino effect** *n* efekt *m* domina
**dominoes** ['dɔmɪnəuz] *n* domino *nt* (*gra*)
**don** [dɔn] *n* (*Brit*) nauczyciel *m* akademicki (*zwłaszcza w Oksfordzie lub Cambridge*) ▷ *vt* przywdziewać (przywdziać *perf*)
**donate** [də'neɪt] *vt*: **to ~ (to)** ofiarowywać (ofiarować *perf*) (na *+acc*)
**donation** [də'neɪʃən] *n* (*act of giving*) ofiarowanie *nt*; (*contribution*) darowizna *f*
**done** [dʌn] *pp of* **do**
**donkey** ['dɔŋkɪ] *n* osioł *m*
**donkey-work** ['dɔŋkɪwə:k] (*Brit*: *inf*) *n* czarna robota *f* (*inf*)
**donor** ['dəunə<sup>r</sup>] *n* (*Med*) dawca *m*; (*to charity*) ofiarodawca *m*
**don't** [dəunt] = **do not**
**donut** ['dəunʌt] (US) *n* = **doughnut**
**doodle** ['du:dl] *vi* gryzmolić, bazgrać ▷ *n* gryzmoły *pl*, bazgroły *pl*
**doom** [du:m] *n* fatum *nt* ▷ *vt*: **to be ~ed to failure** być skazanym na porażkę
**doomsday** ['du:mzdeɪ] *n* sądny dzień *m*; (*Rel*): **D~** dzień *m* Sądu Ostatecznego
**door** [dɔ:<sup>r</sup>] *n* (*of house, room, car*) drzwi *pl*; (*of cupboard*) drzwiczki *pl*; **to go from ~ to ~** chodzić od domu do domu *or* po domach
**doorbell** ['dɔ:bɛl] *n* dzwonek *m* u drzwi
**door handle** *n* klamka *f*
**doorman** ['dɔ:mən] (*irreg*: *like* **man**) *n* (*in hotel*) odźwierny *m*; (*in block of flats*) portier *m*
**doormat** ['dɔ:mæt] *n* wycieraczka *f*; (*fig*) popychadło *nt*
**doorpost** ['dɔ:pəust] *n* framuga *f* drzwiowa
**doorstep** ['dɔ:stɛp] *n* próg *m*; **on the ~** (*fig*) tuż za progiem
**door-to-door** ['dɔ:tə'dɔ:<sup>r</sup>] *adj*: **~ salesman** domokrążca *m*; **~ selling** handel obwoźny
**doorway** ['dɔ:weɪ] *n*: **in the ~** w drzwiach
**dope** [dəup] *n* (*inf*: *illegal drug*) narkotyk *m*; (*: medicine*) środek *m* odurzający; (*: person*) idiota(-tka) *m(f)*; (*: information*) cynk *m* (*inf*) ▷ *vt* odurzać (odurzyć *perf*) (*przez podanie narkotyku*)
**dopey** ['dəupɪ] (*inf*) *adj* (*groggy*) otumaniony, ogłupiały (*inf*); (*stupid*) głupkowaty (*inf*)
**dork** [dɔ:k] (US) *n* (*inf*) palant *m* (*inf*)
**dormant** ['dɔ:mənt] *adj* (*plant*) w okresie spoczynku *post*; (*volcano*) drzemiący; **to lie ~** (*idea, report etc*) pozostawać niewykorzystanym
**dormer** ['dɔ:mə<sup>r</sup>] *n* (*also*: **dormer window**) okno *nt* mansardowe
**dormice** ['dɔ:maɪs] *npl of* **dormouse**
**dormitory** ['dɔ:mɪtrɪ] *n* (*room*) sypialnia *f* (*wieloosobowa w internacie*); (US) dom *m* akademicki, akademik *m* (*inf*)
**dormouse** ['dɔ:maus] (*pl* **dormice**) *n* koszatka *f*
**Dors** (*Brit*: *Post*) *abbr* = **Dorset**
**DOS** [dɔs] (*Comput*) *n abbr* (= *disk operating system*) DOS *m*
**dosage** ['dəusɪdʒ] *n* (*Med*) dawka *f*; (*on label*) dawkowanie *nt*
**dose** [dəus] *n* (*of medicine*) dawka *f*; (*Brit*: *bout*) atak *m* ▷ *vt*: **to ~ o.s. with** aplikować (zaaplikować *perf*) sobie *+acc*; **a ~ of flu** atak grypy
**doss house** ['dɔs-] (*Brit*) *n* noclegownia *f*
**dossier** ['dɔsɪeɪ] *n* akta *pl*, dossier *nt inv*
**DOT** (US) *n abbr* (= *Department of Transportation*) Ministerstwo *nt* Transportu
**dot** [dɔt] *n* (*round mark*) kropka *f*; (*speck, spot*) punkcik *m* ▷ *vt*: **dotted with** (*pictures, decorations*) upstrzony *+instr*; (*stars, freckles*) usiany *+instr*; **on the dot** co do minuty
**dot command** (*Comput*) *n polecenie rozpoczynające się od znaku kropki*
**dote** [dəut]: **to ~ on** *vt fus* świata nie widzieć poza *+instr*, mieć bzika na punkcie *+gen* (*inf*)
**dot-matrix printer** [dɔt'meɪtrɪks-] *n* drukarka *f* igłowa
**dotted line** ['dɔtɪd-] *n* linia *f* kropkowana; **you must get them to sign on the ~** (*fig*) musisz ich nakłonić do podpisania się pod tym
**dotty** ['dɔtɪ] (*inf*) *adj* stuknięty (*inf*)
**double** ['dʌbl] *adj* podwójny ▷ *adv*: **to cost ~** kosztować podwójnie ▷ *n* sobowtór *m* ▷ *vt* (*offer, amount*) podwajać (podwoić *perf*); (*paper,*

*blanket*) składać (złożyć *perf*) na pół ▷ *vi* podwajać się (podwoić się *perf*); **to ~ as** spełniać (spełnić *perf*) równocześnie funkcję *+gen*; **on the ~**, (*Brit*) **at the ~** dwa razy szybciej; **~ five two six (5526)** (*Brit*: *Tel*) pięćdziesiąt pięć, dwadzieścia sześć; **it's spelt with a ~ "l"** to się pisze przez dwa „l"
▸ **double back** *vi* zawracać (zawrócić *perf*)
▸ **double up** *vi* (*with laughter, in pain*) skręcać się; (*share room*) ścieśniać się (ścieśnić się *perf*)

**double bass** *n* kontrabas *m*

**double bed** *n* łóżko *nt* dwuosobowe

**double-breasted** ['dʌbl'brɛstɪd] *adj* (*jacket etc*) dwurzędowy

**double-check** ['dʌbl'tʃɛk] *vt* ponownie sprawdzać (sprawdzić *perf*) ▷ *vi* podwójnie sprawdzać (sprawdzić *perf*)

**double-clutch** ['dʌbl'klʌtʃ] (*US*) *vi* zmieniać (zmienić *perf*) bieg z podwójnym wysprzęgleniem

**double cream** (*Brit*) *n* ≈ kremówka *f*

**double-cross** *vt* wystawiać (wystawić *perf*) do wiatru

**double-decker** *n* autobus *m* piętrowy

**double-declutch** ['dʌbldi:'klʌtʃ] (*Brit*) *vi* zmieniać (zmienić *perf*) bieg z podwójnym wysprzęgleniem

**double exposure** *n* podwójnie naświetlona klatka *f*

**double glazing** [-'gleɪzɪŋ] (*Brit*) *n* podwójne szyby *pl*

**double-page** ['dʌblpeɪdʒ] *adj*: **~ spread** rozkładówka *f*

**double parking** *n* parkowanie *nt* na drugiego (*inf*)

**double room** *n* pokój *m* dwuosobowy

**doubles** ['dʌblz] *n* debel *m*

**double time** *n* podwójna stawka *f* (*za pracę w dni świąteczne*)

**doubly** ['dʌblɪ] *adv* podwójnie

**doubt** [daut] *n* wątpliwość *f* ▷ *vt* (*disbelieve*) wątpić (zwątpić *perf*) w *+acc*; (*mistrust, suspect*) nie dowierzać *+dat*; **without (a) ~** bez wątpienia; **I ~ it (very much)** (bardzo) wątpię; **to ~ if** *or* **whether ...** wątpić, czy ...; **I don't ~ that ...** nie wątpię, że ...

**doubtful** ['dautful] *adj* (*fact*) niepewny; **to be ~ about sth** mieć wątpliwości co do czegoś; **I'm a bit ~** mam pewne wątpliwości

**doubtless** ['dautlɪs] *adv* niewątpliwie

**dough** [dəu] *n* (*Culin*) ciasto *nt*; (*inf*) forsa *f* (*inf*), szmal *m* (*inf*)

**doughnut** ['dəunʌt], (*US*) **donut** *n* ≈ pączek *m*

**dour** [duəʳ] *adj* oschły, surowy

**douse** [dauz] *vt* (*person*): **to ~ (with)** oblewać (oblać *perf*) (*+instr*); (*lamp*) gasić (zgasić *perf*)

**dove** [dʌv] *n* gołąb *m*; (*symbol of peace*) gołąb(ek) *m*

**Dover** ['dəuvəʳ] *n* Dover *nt inv*

**dovetail** ['dʌvteɪl] *vi* (*fig*) idealnie do siebie pasować ▷ *n*: **~ joint** połączenie *nt* na jaskółczy ogon

**dowager** ['dauədʒəʳ] *n* *wdowa dziedzicząca tytuł po mężu*

**dowdy** ['daudɪ] *adj* (*clothes*) niemodny; (*person*) zaniedbany

**Dow-Jones average** ['dau'dʒəunz-] (*US*) *n* wskaźnik *m* Dow-Jonesa

**down** [daun] *n* (*feathers*) puch *m*; (*hair*) meszek *m*; (*hill*) wzgórze *nt* ▷ *adv* w dół ▷ *prep* w dół *+gen* ▷ *vt* (*inf*: *drink*) wychylić (*perf*); **~ there/here** tam/tu na *or* w dole; **face ~** twarzą do ziemi; **~ the river** w dół rzeki; **~ the corridor** wzdłuż korytarza; **to walk ~ the road** iść drogą; **the price of meat is ~** cena mięsa spadła; **I've got it ~ in my diary** zapisałam to w pamiętniku; **to pay 5 pounds ~** zapłacić (*perf*) 5 funtów zadatku; **England are two goals ~** Anglia przegrywa dwoma bramkami; **to ~ tools** (*Brit*) przerywać (przerwać *perf*) pracę (*na znak protestu*); **~ with X!** precz z X!

**down-and-out** ['daunəndaut] *n* kloszard *m*

**down-at-heel** ['daunət'hi:l] *adj* (*shoes etc*) znoszony; (*appearance, person*) zabiedzony

**downbeat** ['daunbi:t] *n* (*Mus*) akcentowana miara *f* taktu ▷ *adj* (*inf*) powściągliwy

**downcast** ['daunkɑ:st] *adj* (*person*) przybity; (*eyes*) spuszczony

**downer** ['daunəʳ] (*inf*) *n* środek *m* uspokajający; **he is on a ~** jest przybity

**downfall** ['daunfɔ:l] *n* upadek *m*

**downgrade** ['daungreɪd] *vt* umniejszać (umniejszyć *perf*) znaczenie *+gen*

**downhearted** ['daun'hɑ:tɪd] *adj* przygnębiony

**downhill** ['daun'hɪl] *adv*: **to go ~** (*road*) biec w dół zbocza; (*person*) schodzić (zejść *perf*) ze zbocza; (*car*) zjeżdżać (zjechać *perf*) ze zbocza; (*fig*: *person*) staczać się (stoczyć się *perf*); (: *business, career*) podupadać (podupaść *perf*) ▷ *n* (*also*: **downhill race**) bieg *m* zjazdowy; **it was ~ after that** potem już było z górki (*inf*)

**Downing Street** ['daunɪŋ-] (*Brit*) *n*: **10 ~** *siedziba premiera Wielkiej Brytanii*

**download** ['daunləud] *vt* przesyłać (przesłać *perf*), ściągać (ściągnąć *perf*) (*dane, pliki itp.*) ▷ *n* dane *pl* ściągnięte z serwera

**down-market** ['daun'mɑ:kɪt] *adj* tandetny

**down payment** *n* zadatek *m*

**downplay** ['daunpleɪ] (*US*) *vt* bagatelizować (zbagatelizować) *perf*

**downpour** ['daunpɔ:ʳ] *n* ulewa *f*

**downright** ['daunraɪt] *adj* (*liar etc*) skończony; (*lie, insult*) jawny ▷ *adv* wręcz

**Downs** [daunz] (*Brit*) *npl*: **the ~** *porośnięte trawą wapienne wzgórza w południowej Anglii*
**downsize** ['daunsaɪz] *vt* zmniejszać (zmniejszyć *perf*) ▷ *vi* redukować (zredukować *perf*) zatrudnienie
**Down's syndrome** [daunz-] *n* zespół *m* Downa
**downstairs** ['daun'stɛəz] *adv* (*below, on ground floor*) na dole; (*downwards, to ground floor*) na dół (po schodach); (*on or to floor below*) piętro niżej
**downstream** ['daunstri:m] *adv* (*be*) w dole rzeki; (*go*) w dół rzeki
**downtime** ['dauntaɪm] *n* (*of machine etc*) okres *m* wyłączenia
**down-to-earth** ['dauntu'ə:θ] *adj* (*realistic*) praktyczny; (*direct*) bezpośredni; (*reason*) przyziemny
**downtown** ['daun'taun] *adv* (*in the centre*) w mieście *or* centrum; (*to the centre*) do miasta *or* centrum ▷ *adj* (*US*: *offices, buildings*) w śródmieściu *or* centrum *post*; **~ Chicago** śródmieście Chicago
**downtrodden** ['dauntrɔdn] *adj* poniewierany
**down under** *adv w Australii lub Nowej Zelandii*
**downward** ['daunwəd] *adj*: **~ movement** ruch *m* ku dołowi *or* w dół ▷ *adv* ku dołowi, w dół; **a ~ trend** tendencja zniżkowa
**downwards** ['daunwədz] *adv* = **downward**
**dowry** ['daurɪ] *n* posag *m*
**doz.** *abbr* = **dozen**
**doze** [dəuz] *vi* drzemać
▸ **doze off** *vi* zdrzemnąć się (*perf*)
**dozen** ['dʌzn] *n* tuzin *m*; **a ~ books** tuzin książek; **80p a ~** po 80 pensów za tuzin; **~s of** dziesiątki *+gen*
**DPh** *n abbr* (= *Doctor of Philosophy*) *stopień naukowy*, ≈ dr
**DPhil** *n abbr* (= *Doctor of Philosophy*) *stopień naukowy*, ≈ dr
**DPP** (*Brit*) *n abbr* (= *Director of Public Prosecutions*) ≈ Prokurator *m* Generalny
**DPT** *n abbr* (= *diphtheria, pertussis, tetanus*) DiPerTe *nt inv*
**DPW** (*US*) *n abbr* (= *Department of Public Works*) Ministerstwo *nt* Robót Publicznych
**Dr** *abbr* (= *doctor*) dr
**Dr.** *abbr* (*in street names*) = **Drive**
**dr** (*Comm*) *abbr* = **debtor**
**drab** [dræb] *adj* (*life, clothes*) szary, bezbarwny; (*weather*) ponury
**draft** [drɑ:ft] *n* (*first version*) szkic *m*; (*Pol*: *of bill*) projekt *m*; (*bank draft*) przekaz *m*; (*US*: *call-up*) pobór *m* ▷ *vt* (*plan*) sporządzać (sporządzić *perf*) projekt *or* szkic *+gen*; (*write roughly*) pisać (napisać *perf*) pierwszą wersję *+gen*; *see also* **draught**
**draftsman** ['drɑ:ftsmən] (*US*) (*irreg*: *like* **man**) *n* = **draughtsman**
**draftsmanship** ['drɑ:ftsmənʃɪp] (*US*) *n* = **draughtsmanship**
**drag** [dræg] *vt* (*bundle, person*) wlec (zawlec *perf*); (*river*) przeszukiwać (przeszukać *perf*) ▷ *vi* (*time, event*) wlec się ▷ *n* (*inf*: *bore*) męka *f*; (: *person*) nudziarz(-ara) *m*(*f*) (*inf*); (*Naut, Aviat*) opór *m*; **in ~** w damskim przebraniu
▸ **drag away** *vt*: **to ~ away (from)** odrywać (oderwać *perf*) (od *+gen*)
▸ **drag on** *vi* wlec się
**dragnet** ['drægnɛt] *n* włok *m*; (*fig*) obława *f*
**dragon** ['drægn] *n* smok *m*
**dragonfly** ['drægənflaɪ] *n* ważka *f*
**dragoon** [drə'gu:n] *n* dragon *m* ▷ *vt*: **to ~ sb into doing sth** (*Brit*) zmuszać (zmusić *perf*) kogoś do zrobienia czegoś
**drain** [dreɪn] *n* (*in street*) studzienka *f* ściekowa; (*fig*: *on resources*) odpływ *m* ▷ *vt* (*land*) drenować, osuszać (osuszyć *perf*); (*marshes, pond*) osuszać (osuszyć *perf*); (*vegetables*) osączać (osączyć *perf*); (*glass, cup*) wysączyć (*perf*) napój z *+gen* ▷ *vi* spływać (spłynąć *perf*); **to feel ~ed** czuć się (poczuć się *perf*) wyczerpanym; **I feel ~ed of energy** (cała) energia ze mnie odpłynęła
**drainage** ['dreɪnɪdʒ] *n* (*system*) system *m* odwadniający; (*process*) odwadnianie *nt*, drenaż *m*
**draining board** ['dreɪnɪŋ-], (*US*) **drainboard** *n* ociekacz *m*
**drainpipe** ['dreɪnpaɪp] *n* rura *f* odpływowa
**drake** [dreɪk] *n* kaczor *m*
**dram** [dræm] (*Scottish*) *n* ≈ kieliszeczek *m* (*czegoś mocniejszego*)
**drama** ['drɑ:mə] *n* (*lit, fig*) dramat *m*; (*of situation*) dramaturgia *f*
**dramatic** [drə'mætɪk] *adj* (*theatrical, exciting*) dramatyczny; (*marked*) radykalny; (*sudden*) gwałtowny
**dramatically** [drə'mætɪklɪ] *adv* (*theatrically*) dramatycznie; (*markedly*) radykalnie; (*suddenly*) gwałtownie
**dramatist** ['dræmətɪst] *n* dramaturg *m*, dramatopisarz(-arka) *m*(*f*)
**dramatize** ['dræmətaɪz] *vt* (*events*) dramatyzować (udramatyzować *perf*); (*book, story*) adaptować (zaadaptować *perf*)
**drank** [dræŋk] *pt of* **drink**
**drape** [dreɪp] *vt* drapować (udrapować *perf*)
**drapes** [dreɪps] (*US*) *npl* zasłony *pl*
**drastic** ['dræstɪk] *adj* drastyczny
**drastically** ['dræstɪklɪ] *adv* drastycznie
**draught**, (*US*) **draft** [drɑ:ft] *n* (*of wind*) podmuch *m*; (: *between open doors etc*) przeciąg *m*;

(*Naut*) zanurzenie *nt*; **beer on ~** piwo beczkowe

**draughtboard** ['drɑ:ftbɔ:d] (*Brit*) *n* plansza *f* do gry w warcaby, szachownica *f*

**draughts** [drɑ:fts] (*Brit*) *n* warcaby *pl*

**draughtsman** ['drɑ:ftsmən] (*irreg: like* **man**), (*US*) **draftsman** *n* (*Art*) rysownik(-iczka) *m(f)*; (*Tech*) kreślarz(-arka) *m(f)*

**draughtsmanship** ['drɑ:ftsmənʃɪp], (*US*) **draftsmanship** *n* rysunek *m*; **the ~ of the forgery was excellent** jakość falsyfikatu była wyśmienita

**draw** [drɔ:] (*pt* **drew**, *pp* **~n**) *vt* (*Art, Tech*) rysować (narysować *perf*); (*cart etc*) ciągnąć; (*curtain: close*) zaciągać (zaciągnąć *perf*), zasuwać (zasunąć *perf*); (*: open*) odsuwać (odsunąć *perf*); (*gun, conclusion*) wyciągać (wyciągnąć *perf*); (*tooth*) wyrywać (wyrwać *perf*); (*attention*) przyciągać (przyciągnąć *perf*); (*response*) spotykać się (spotkać się *perf*) z *+instr*; (*admiration*) wzbudzać (wzbudzić *perf*); (*money*) podejmować (podjąć *perf*); (*wages*) otrzymywać ▷ *vi* (*Art, Tech*) rysować; (*Sport*) remisować (zremisować *perf*) ▷ *n* (*Sport*) remis *m*; (*prize draw*) loteria *f*; **to ~ near** zbliżać się; **to ~ to a close** dobiegać końca; **to ~ a comparison (between sth and sth)** porównywać (porównać *perf*) (coś z czymś); **to ~ a distinction (between sth and sth)** rozróżniać (rozróżnić *perf*) (pomiędzy czymś a czymś)

▸ **draw back** *vi* cofać się (cofnąć się *perf*); **to ~ back from** odsuwać się (odsunąć się *perf*) od *+gen*

▸ **draw in** *vi* (*Brit: train*) wjeżdżać (wjechać *perf*) (na stację); **the nights are ~ing in** coraz wcześniej zapada zmierzch

▸ **draw on** *vt* (*resources, imagination*) sięgać (sięgnąć *perf*) do *+gen*; (*cigarette*) zaciągać się (zaciągnąć się *perf*) *+instr*

▸ **draw out** *vi* (*train*) ruszać (ruszyć *perf*) (*ze stacji*) ▷ *vt* (*money*) podejmować (podjąć *perf*)

▸ **draw up** *vi* (*car etc*) podjeżdżać (podjechać *perf*) ▷ *vt* (*chair*) przysuwać (przysunąć *perf*); (*plan*) kreślić (nakreślić *perf*)

**drawback** ['drɔ:bæk] *n* wada *f*, minus *m*

**drawbridge** ['drɔ:brɪdʒ] *n* most *m* zwodzony

**drawee** [drɔ:'i:] (*Fin*) *n* trasat *m*

**drawer** [drɔ:ʳ] *n* szuflada *f*

**drawing** ['drɔ:ɪŋ] *n* rysunek *m*

**drawing board** *n* deska *f* kreślarska, rysownica *f*; **back to the ~** (*fig*) trzeba zacząć od początku

**drawing pin** (*Brit*) *n* pinezka *f*

**drawing room** *n* salon *m*

**drawl** [drɔ:l] *n przeciągły sposób mówienia, charakterystyczny dla mieszkańców południowych Stanów* ▷ *vi mówić, przeciągając samogłoski*

**drawn** [drɔ:n] *pp of* **draw** ▷ *adj* wymizerowany

**drawstring** ['drɔ:strɪŋ] *n* sznurek *m* (*do zaciągania/luzowania*)

**dread** [drɛd] *n* strach *m* ▷ *vt* bać się *+gen*

**dreadful** ['drɛdful] *adj* straszny; **I feel ~!** czuję się okropnie!

**dreadlocks** ['drɛdlɔks] *npl* dredy *pl*

**dream** [dri:m] (*pt, pp* **~ed** *or* **~t**) *n* (*while asleep*) sen *m*; (*: Psych*) marzenie *nt* senne, sen *m*; (*ambition*) marzenie *nt* ▷ *vi* (*while asleep*): **I ~t about my father** śnił mi się ojciec; **she ~t that ...** śniło jej się, że ...; (*fantasize*): **he ~t about/that...** marzył o *+loc*/(o tym), że...; **to have a (strange) ~** mieć (dziwny) sen; **I had a ~ about you** śniłaś mi się; **to ~ of doing sth** marzyć o tym, żeby coś zrobić; **sweet ~s!** miłych snów!

▸ **dream up** *vt* wymyślić (*perf*), wydumać (*perf*) (*pej*)

**dreamer** ['dri:məʳ] *n* (*fig*) marzyciel(ka) *m(f)*

**dreamt** [drɛmt] *pt, pp of* **dream**

**dream world** *n*: **to live in a ~** żyć marzeniami

**dreamy** ['dri:mɪ] *adj* (*expression*) rozmarzony; (*person*) marzycielski; (*music*) kojący

**dreary** ['drɪərɪ] *adj* (*depressing*) ponury; (*boring*) drętwy

**dredge** [drɛdʒ] *vt* dragować, bagrować

▸ **dredge up** *vt* (*fig: unpleasant facts*) odgrzebywać (odgrzebać *perf*)

**dredger** ['drɛdʒəʳ] *n* draga *f*, pogłębiarka *f*

**dregs** [drɛgz] *npl* (*of wine, juice*) męty *pl*; (*of tea, coffee*) fusy *pl*; **the ~ of humanity** najgorsze męty *or* szumowiny

**drench** [drɛntʃ] *vt* przemoczyć (*perf*); **~ed to the skin** przemoczony do suchej nitki

**dress** [drɛs] *n* suknia *f*, sukienka *f*; (*no pl*) odzież *f* ▷ *vt* (*child*) ubierać (ubrać *perf*); (*wound*) opatrywać (opatrzyć *perf*) ▷ *vi* ubierać się (ubrać się *perf*); **she ~es very well** ona się bardzo dobrze ubiera; **to ~ a shop window** dekorować (udekorować *perf*) okno wystawowe; **to get ~ed** ubierać się (ubrać się *perf*)

▸ **dress up** *vi* stroić się (wystroić się *perf*); **to ~ up (as)** przebierać się (przebrać się *perf*) (za *+acc*)

**dress circle** (*Brit: Theat*) *n* pierwszy balkon *m*

**dress designer** *n* projektant(ka) *m(f)* odzieży

**dresser** ['drɛsəʳ] *n* (*Brit*) kredens *m*; (*US*) komoda *f* (z lustrem); (*Theat*) garderobiany(-na) *m(f)*

**dressing** ['drɛsɪŋ] *n* (*Med*) opatrunek *m*; (*Culin*) sos *m* (*sałatkowy*)

**dressing gown** (*Brit*) *n* szlafrok *m*

**dressing room** *n* (*Theat*) garderoba *f*; (*Sport*) szatnia *f*, przebieralnia *f*
**dressing table** *n* toaletka *f*
**dressmaker** ['drɛsmeɪkə^r] *n* krawiec/krawcowa *m/f*
**dressmaking** ['drɛsmeɪkɪŋ] *n* krawiectwo *nt*
**dress rehearsal** *n* próba *f* generalna
**dressy** ['drɛsɪ] (*inf*) *adj* elegancki
**drew** [dru:] *pt of* **draw**
**dribble** ['drɪbl] *vi* (*liquid*) spływać, ściekać; (*baby*) ślinić się; (*Football*) dryblować ▷ *vt* (*ball*) prowadzić (poprowadzić *perf*)
**dried** [draɪd] *adj* (*fruit*) suszony; (*eggs, milk*) w proszku *post*
**drier** ['draɪə^r] *n* = **dryer**
**drift** [drɪft] *n* (*of current*) prąd *m*; (*of snow*) zaspa *f*; (*of thought, argument*) sens *m* ▷ *vi* (*boat*) dryfować; (*sand, snow*) tworzyć zaspy; **to let things ~** pozostawiać (pozostawić *perf*) sprawy własnemu biegowi; **they have ~ed apart** stali się sobie obcy; **I get** *or* **catch your ~** rozumiem, o co ci chodzi
**drifter** ['drɪftə^r] *n* tułacz *m*
**driftwood** ['drɪftwud] *n* (*on water*) dryfujące drewno *nt*; (*on shore*) drewno *nt* wyrzucone na brzeg
**drill** [drɪl] *n* (*drill bit*) wiertło *nt*; (*machine: for DIY etc*) wiertarka *f*; (*: of dentist*) wiertarka *f* (dentystyczna); (*: for mining etc*) świder *m*; (*Mil*) musztra *f* ▷ *vt* (*hole*) wiercić (wywiercić *perf*); (*troops*) musztrować ▷ *vi* wiercić; **to ~ pupils in grammar/spelling** ćwiczyć z uczniami gramatykę/ortografię
**drilling** ['drɪlɪŋ] *n* wiercenia *pl*
**drilling rig** *n* (*on land*) wiertnica *f*; (*at sea*) platforma *f* wiertnicza
**drily** ['draɪlɪ] *adv* = **dryly**
**drink** [drɪŋk] (*pt* **drank**, *pp* **drunk**) *n* (*fruit etc*) napój *m*; (*alcoholic*) drink *m*; (*sip*) łyk *m* ▷ *vt* pić, wypijać (wypić *perf*) ▷ *vi* pić; **a (hot/cold) ~** coś (ciepłego/zimnego) do picia; **cold/hot ~s** (*on menu etc*) napoje zimne/gorące; **to have a ~** napić się (*perf*); **would you like a ~ of water?** czy chciałbyś się napić wody?; **would you like something to ~?** napijesz się czegoś?; **we had ~s before lunch** piliśmy przed obiadem
▸ **drink in** *vt* upajać się *+instr*, chłonąć *+acc*
**drinkable** ['drɪŋkəbl] *adj* (*not dangerous*) zdatny do picia, pitny; (*palatable*) nadający się do picia
**drinker** ['drɪŋkə^r] *n* pijący(-ca) *m(f)*; **to be a heavy ~** dużo pić
**drinking** ['drɪŋkɪŋ] *n* picie *nt*
**drinking fountain** *n automatyczny wodotrysk z wodą do picia*
**drinking water** *n* woda *f* pitna
**drip** [drɪp] *n* (*noise*) kapanie *nt*; (*Med*) kroplówka *f* ▷ *vi* (*water, rain*) kapać; (*tap*) cieknąć, ciec; (*washing*) ociekać
**drip-dry** ['drɪp'draɪ] *adj* nie wymagający prasowania
**drip-feed** ['drɪpfi:d] *vt* odżywiać dożylnie ▷ *n*: **she's on a ~** odżywiają ją dożylnie
**dripping** ['drɪpɪŋ] *n* tłuszcz *m* spod pieczeni ▷ *adj* ociekający wodą; **I'm ~** kapie ze mnie; **~ wet** przemoczony do suchej nitki
**drive** [draɪv] (*pt* **drove**, *pp* **~n**) *n* (*journey*) jazda *f or* podróż *f* (samochodem); (*also:* **driveway**) wjazd *m*, droga *f* dojazdowa; (*energy*) werwa *f*, zapał *m*; (*campaign*) działania *pl*; (*Sport*) uderzenie *nt*; (*also:* **disk drive**) stacja *f* dysków ▷ *vt* (*vehicle*) prowadzić, kierować *+instr*; (*Tech: motor, wheel*) napędzać; (*animal*) prowadzić (poprowadzić *perf*); (*ball*) posyłać (posłać *perf*); (*incite, encourage*) kierować *+instr*; (*nail, stake*): **to ~ sth into sth** wbijać (wbić *perf*) coś w coś ▷ *vi* (*as driver*) prowadzić (samochód), jeździć samochodem; (*travel*) jechać (pojechać *perf*) (samochodem); **to go for a ~** wybierać się (wybrać się *perf*) na przejażdżkę; **it's 3 hours' ~ from London** to trzy godziny jazdy z Londynu; **left-/right-hand ~** lewostronny/prawostronny układ kierowniczy; **front-/rear-/four-wheel ~** napęd na przednie/tylne/cztery koła; **he ~s a taxi** jest kierowcą taksówki; **to ~ at 50 km an hour** jechać z prędkością 50 km na godzinę; **to ~ sb home/to the airport** zawozić (zawieźć *perf*) *or* odwozić (odwieźć *perf*) kogoś do domu/na lotnisko; **to ~ sb mad** doprowadzać (doprowadzić *perf*) kogoś do szału; **to ~ sb to sth** doprowadzać (doprowadzić *perf*) kogoś do czegoś; **she drove him to move out** doprowadziła do tego, że się wyprowadził; **what are you driving at?** do czego zmierzasz?
▸ **drive off** *vt* (*enemy*) przepędzać (przepędzić *perf*); (*attack*) odpierać (odeprzeć *perf*)
▸ **drive out** *vt* (*evil spirits*) wypędzać (wypędzić *perf*)
**drive-in** ['draɪvɪn] (*esp US*) *adj obsługujący klientów siedzących w samochodach*
**drive-in cinema** (*US*) *n* kino *nt* dla zmotoryzowanych
**drivel** ['drɪvl] (*inf*) *n* brednie *pl*
**driven** ['drɪvn] *pp of* **drive**
**driver** ['draɪvə^r] *n* (*of car, bus*) kierowca *m*; (*Rail*) maszynista *m*
**driver's license** ['draɪvəz-] (*US*) *n* prawo *nt* jazdy
**driveway** ['draɪvweɪ] *n* wjazd *m*, droga *f* dojazdowa

**driving** ['draɪvɪŋ] *n* prowadzenie *nt* (samochodu), jazda *f* (samochodem) ▷ *adj* (*rain etc*) zacinający, siekący
**driving force** *n* siła *f* napędzająca
**driving instructor** *n* instruktor *m* nauki jazdy
**driving lesson** *n* lekcja *f* jazdy, jazda *f* (*inf*)
**driving licence** (*Brit*) *n* prawo *nt* jazdy
**driving school** *n* ≈ ośrodek *m* szkolenia kierowców
**driving test** *n* egzamin *m* na prawo jazdy
**drizzle** ['drɪzl] *n* mżawka *f* ▷ *vi* mżyć
**droll** [drəul] *adj* ucieszny
**dromedary** ['drɔmədərɪ] *n* dromader *m*
**drone** [drəun] *n* (*of insects*) bzyczenie *nt*, brzęczenie *nt*; (*of engine*) warkot *m*; (*of traffic*) szum *m*; (*male bee*) truteń *m* ▷ *vi* (*bee*) bzyczeć, brzęczeć; (*engine etc*) warczeć; (*also*: **drone on**) ględzić (*inf*), przynudzać (*inf*)
**drool** [dru:l] *vi* ślinić się; **to ~ over sth/sb** (*fig*) pożerać coś/kogoś wzrokiem
**droop** [dru:p] *vi* opadać (opaść *perf*), zwieszać się (zwiesić się *perf*)
**drop** [drɔp] *n* (*of liquid*) kropla *f*; (*reduction, distance*) spadek *m*; (*by parachute etc*) zrzut *m* ▷ *vt* (*object*) upuszczać (upuścić *perf*); (*voice*) zniżać (zniżyć *perf*); (*eyes*) spuszczać (spuścić *perf*); (*price*) zniżać (zniżyć *perf*), opuszczać (opuścić *perf*); (*set down from car: person*) wysadzać (wysadzić *perf*), wyrzucać (wyrzucić *perf*) (*inf*); (*: object*) podrzucać (podrzucić *perf*) (*inf*); (*omit*) opuszczać (opuścić *perf*) ▷ *vi* (*object, temperature*) spadać (spaść *perf*); (*wind*) ucichać (ucichnąć *perf*); **drops** *npl* krople *pl*; **cough ~s** krople na kaszel; **a 300 ft ~** stumetrowy spadek (terenu); **a ~ of 10%** spadek o 10%; **to ~ anchor** rzucać (rzucić *perf*) kotwicę; **to ~ sb a line** skrobnąć (*perf*) do kogoś parę słów (*inf*)
▸ **drop in** (*inf*) *vi*: **to ~ in (on sb)** wpadać (wpaść *perf*) (do kogoś)
▸ **drop off** *vi* zasypiać (zasnąć *perf*) (*mimowolnie*) ▷ *vt* podrzucać (podrzucić *perf*)
▸ **drop out** *vi* wycofywać się (wycofać się *perf*); **to ~ out of school** porzucać (porzucić *perf*) szkołę
**droplet** ['drɔplɪt] *n* kropelka *f*
**drop-out** ['drɔpaut] *n* (*from society*) odszczepieniec *m*; (*Scol*) *osoba, która nie ukończyła szkoły lub studiów*
**dropper** ['drɔpəʳ] *n* zakraplacz *m*
**droppings** ['drɔpɪŋz] *npl* odchody *pl* (*ptaków i małych zwierząt*)
**dross** [drɔs] *n* odpady *pl* żużlowe
**drought** [draut] *n* susza *f*
**drove** [drəuv] *pt of* **drive** ▷ *n*: **~s of people** tłumy *pl* ludzi
**drown** [draun] *vt* topić (utopić *perf*); (*fig*: *also*: **drown out**) zagłuszać (zagłuszyć *perf*) ▷ *vi* tonąć (utonąć *perf*), topić się (utopić się *perf*)
**drowse** [drauz] *vi* drzemać
**drowsy** ['drauzɪ] *adj* senny, śpiący
**drudge** [drʌdʒ] *n* (*person*) wół *m* roboczy
**drudgery** ['drʌdʒərɪ] *n* harówka *f*; **housework is sheer ~** prace domowe to ciągła harówka
**drug** [drʌg] *n* (*Med*) lek *m*; (*narcotic*) narkotyk *m* ▷ *vt* podawać (podać *perf*) środki nasenne +*dat*; **to be on ~s** (*Med*) brać leki; (*addicted*) brać narkotyki; **hard/soft ~s** twarde/miękkie narkotyki
**drug addict** *n* narkoman(ka) *m*(*f*)
**druggist** ['drʌgɪst] (*US*) *n* (*person*) aptekarz(-arka) *m*(*f*); (*shop*) apteka *f*
**drug peddler** *n* handlarz *m* narkotykami
**drugstore** ['drʌgstɔːʳ] (*US*) *n drogeria prowadząca też sprzedaż leków, napojów chłodzących i prostych posiłków*
**drum** [drʌm] *n* bęben *m*; (*for oil etc*) beczka *f* ▷ *vi* bębnić (zabębnić *perf*); **drums** *npl* perkusja *f*
▸ **drum up** *vt* (*support etc*) pozyskiwać (pozyskać *perf*)
**drummer** ['drʌməʳ] *n* perkusista(-tka) *m*(*f*)
**drum roll** *n* tusz *m* werbli, werbel *m*
**drumstick** ['drʌmstɪk] *n* (*Mus*) pałeczka *f*; (*of chicken*) pałka *f*
**drunk** [drʌŋk] *pp of* **drink** ▷ *adj* pijany ▷ *n* pijak(-aczka) *m*(*f*); **to get ~** upijać się (upić się *perf*)
**drunken** ['drʌŋkən] *adj* (*laughter etc*) pijacki; (*person*) pijany
**drunkenness** ['drʌŋkənnɪs] *n* pijaństwo *nt*
**dry** [draɪ] *adj* suchy; (*lake*) wyschnięty; (*humour*) ironiczny; (*wine*) wytrawny; (*subject*) nudny ▷ *vt* (*clothes, hair*) suszyć (wysuszyć *perf*); (*ground*) osuszać (osuszyć *perf*); (*hands, dishes*) wycierać (wytrzeć *perf*); (*tears*) ocierać (otrzeć *perf*) ▷ *vi* schnąć, wysychać (wyschnąć *perf*); **on dry land** na suchym lądzie
▸ **dry up** *vi* (*river, well*) wysychać (wyschnąć *perf*); (*in speech*) zaniemówić (*perf*)
**dry clean** *vt* czyścić (wyczyścić *perf*) *or* prać (wyprać *perf*) chemicznie
**dry cleaner** *n* (*person*) właściciel(ka) *m*(*f*) pralni chemicznej; (*shop*) pralnia *f* chemiczna
**dry-cleaner's** ['draɪ'kli:nəz] *n* pralnia *f* chemiczna
**dry-cleaning** ['draɪ'kli:nɪŋ] *n* czyszczenie *nt or* pranie *nt* chemiczne
**dry dock** *n* suchy dok *m*
**dryer** ['draɪəʳ] *n* suszarka *f*
**dry goods** (*US*) *npl* pasmanteria *f*

d

**dry ice** *n* suchy lód *m*
**dryness** ['draɪnɪs] *n* suchość *f*
**dry rot** *n* mursz *m*
**dry run** *n* (*fig*) próba *f*
**dry ski slope** *n* sztuczny stok *m*
**DSc** *n abbr* (= *Doctor of Science*) *stopień naukowy*, ≈ dr hab.
**DSS** (*Brit*) *n abbr* (= *Department of Social Security*) Ministerstwo *nt* Ubezpieczeń Społecznych
**DST** (*US*) *abbr* (= *Daylight Saving Time*) czas *m* letni
**DT** (*Comput*) *n abbr* (= *data transmission*) przesyłanie *nt* danych
**DTI** (*Brit*) *n abbr* (= *Department of Trade and Industry*) Ministerstwo *nt* Handlu i Przemysłu
**DTP** *n abbr* (= *desktop publishing*) DTP *nt inv*
**DT's** (*inf*) *npl abbr* (= *delirium tremens*) delirium *nt* tremens; **to have the ~** mieć delirium (tremens)
**dual** ['djuəl] *adj* podwójny
**dual carriageway** (*Brit*) *n* droga *f* dwupasmowa
**dual nationality** *n* podwójne obywatelstwo *nt*
**dual-purpose** ['djuəl'pə:pəs] *adj* dwufunkcyjny
**dubbed** [dʌbd] *adj* (*film*) dubbingowany; (*nicknamed*) ochrzczony
**dubious** ['dju:bɪəs] *adj* (*claim, reputation*) wątpliwy; (*past, company*) podejrzany; **to be ~ (about)** mieć wątpliwości (co do *+gen*)
**Dublin** ['dʌblɪn] *n* Dublin *m*
**Dubliner** ['dʌblɪnə[r]] *n* Dublińczyk/ Dublinianka *m/f*
**duchess** ['dʌtʃɪs] *n* księżna *f*
**duck** [dʌk] *n* kaczka *f* ▷ *vi* (*also*: **duck down**) uchylać się (uchylić się *perf*) ▷ *vt* uchylać się (uchylić się *perf*) przed *+instr*
**duckling** ['dʌklɪŋ] *n* (*Zool*) kaczątko *nt*, kaczuszka *f*; (*Culin*) kaczka *f*
**duct** [dʌkt] *n* przewód *m*, kanał *m*
**dud** [dʌd] *n* (*object*) bubel *m*; (*bomb*) niewypał *m*; (*note, coin*) podróbka *f* ▷ *adj*: **dud cheque** (*Brit*) czek *m* bez pokrycia
**due** [dju:] *adj* (*arrival*) planowy; (*publication, meeting*) planowany; (*money*) należny; (*attention*) należny, należyty ▷ *n*: **to give sb his (*or* her) due** oddawać (oddać *perf*) komuś sprawiedliwość ▷ *adv*: **due north** dokładnie na północ; **dues** *npl* (*for club, union*) składki *pl* (członkowskie); (*in harbour*) opłaty *pl* postojowe; **in due course** w swoim czasie, we właściwym czasie; **due to** z powodu *+gen*; **to be due to do sth** mieć coś zrobić; **the rent is due on the 30th** czynsz jest płatny (do) trzydziestego; **the train is due at 8** pociąg przyjeżdża o ósmej; **we were due in London at 2 a.m.** mieliśmy być w Londynie o drugiej w nocy.; **she is due back tomorrow** ma wrócić jutro; **I am due 6 days' leave** należy mi się sześć dni urlopu
**due date** *n* data *f* zwrotu (*książki z biblioteki itp*)
**duel** ['djuəl] *n* pojedynek *m*; (*fig*) konflikt *m*
**duet** [dju:'ɛt] *n* duet *m*
**duff** [dʌf] (*Brit*: *inf*) *adj* do niczego *post*
▶ **duff up** (*inf*) *vt* dołożyć (*perf*) *+dat* (*inf*)
**duffel bag** ['dʌfl-] *n* worek *m* marynarski
**duffel coat** *n* budrysówka *f*
**duffer** ['dʌfə[r]] (*inf*) *n* beztalencie *nt*
**dug** [dʌg] *pt, pp of* **dig**
**duke** [dju:k] *n* książę *m*
**dull** [dʌl] *adj* (*dark*) mroczny; (*boring*) nudny; (*pain, person*) tępy; (*sound*) głuchy; (*weather, day*) pochmurny ▷ *vt* przytępiać (przytępić *perf*)
**duly** ['dju:lɪ] *adv* (*properly*) należycie; (*on time*) zgodnie z planem
**dumb** [dʌm] *adj* niemy; (*pej*) głupi; **to be struck ~** oniemieć (*perf*)
**dumbbell** ['dʌmbɛl] *n* hantle *pl*
**dumbfounded** [dʌm'faundɪd] *adj* oniemiały
**dummy** ['dʌmɪ] *n* (*tailor's model*) manekin *m*; (*Comm, Tech*) atrapa *f*, makieta *f*; (*Cards*: *also*: **dummy hand**) dziadek *m*; (*Brit*: *for baby*) smoczek *m* ▷ *adj* (*bullet*) ślepy; (*firm*) fikcyjny
**dummy run** *n* bieg *m* pusty *or* jałowy
**dump** [dʌmp] *n* (*also*: **rubbish dump**) wysypisko *nt* (śmieci); (*inf*: *place*) nora *f* (*inf*); (*of ammunition*) skład *m* ▷ *vt* (*throw down*) rzucać (rzucić *perf*); (*get rid of*) wyrzucać (wyrzucić *perf*); (*Comput*: *data*) zrzucać (zrzucić *perf*) (*inf*); **to be down in the ~s** (*fig*: *inf*) być w dołku (*inf*); **"no ~ing"** „zakaz wysypywania śmieci"
**dumpling** ['dʌmplɪŋ] *n* knedel *m*, pyza *f*
**dumpy** ['dʌmpɪ] *adj* przysadzisty
**dunce** [dʌns] *n* (*Scol*) osioł *m* (*pej*)
**dune** [dju:n] *n* wydma *f*
**dung** [dʌŋ] *n* gnój *m*
**dungarees** [dʌŋgə'ri:z] *npl* (*for work*) kombinezon *m*; (*for child, woman*) ogrodniczki *pl*
**dungeon** ['dʌndʒən] *n* loch *m*
**dunk** [dʌŋk] *vt* maczać, zamaczać (zamoczyć *perf*)
**Dunkirk** [dʌn'kə:k] *n* Dunkierka *f*
**duo** ['dju:əu] *n* para *f*; (*Mus*) duet *m*
**duodenal** [dju:əu'di:nl] *adj*: **~ ulcer** wrzód *m* dwunastnicy
**duodenum** [dju:əu'di:nəm] *n* dwunastnica *f*
**dupe** [dju:p] *n* naiwniak *m* ▷ *vt* naciągać (naciągnąć *perf*) (*inf*)
**duplex** ['dju:plɛks] (*US*) *n* (*house*) bliźniak *m*; (*apartment*) mieszkanie *nt* dwupoziomowe

**duplicate** [*n* 'dju:plɪkət, *adj, vt* 'dju:plɪkeɪt] *n* kopia *f*, duplikat *m* ▷ *adj* zapasowy, dodatkowy ▷ *vt* powielać (powielić *perf*), kopiować (skopiować *perf*); **in ~** w dwóch egzemplarzach
**duplicating machine** ['dju:plɪkeɪtɪŋ-] *n* powielacz *m*
**duplicator** ['dju:plɪkeɪtə^r] *n* powielacz *m*
**duplicity** [dju:'plɪsɪtɪ] *n* obłuda *f*
**Dur** (*Brit: Post*) *abbr* = **Durham**
**durability** [djuərə'bɪlɪtɪ] *n* trwałość *f*, wytrzymałość *f*
**durable** ['djuərəbl] *adj* trwały, wytrzymały
**duration** [djuə'reɪʃən] *n* okres *m or* czas *m* (trwania)
**duress** [djuə'rɛs] *n*: **under ~** pod przymusem
**Durex**® ['djuərɛks] (*Brit*) *n* ≈ prezerwatywa *f*
**during** ['djuərɪŋ] *prep* podczas *+gen*, w czasie *+gen*
**dusk** [dʌsk] *n* zmierzch *m*, zmrok *m*
**dusky** ['dʌskɪ] *adj* mroczny
**dust** [dʌst] *n* kurz *m*, pył *m* ▷ *vt* (*furniture*) odkurzać (odkurzyć *perf*); (*cake etc*): **to ~ with** posypywać (posypać *perf*) *+instr*; **she ~ed her face with powder** upudrowała twarz
▸ **dust off** *vt* otrzepywać (otrzepać *perf*); (*fig*) odświeżać (odświeżyć *perf*)
**dustbin** ['dʌstbɪn] (*Brit*) *n* kosz *m* na śmieci
**dustbin liner** *n* worek *m* na śmieci (*wkładany do kosza*)
**duster** ['dʌstə^r] *n* ściereczka *f* (do kurzu)
**dust jacket** *n* obwoluta *f*
**dustman** ['dʌstmən] (*Brit*) (*irreg: like* **man**) *n* śmieciarz *m*
**dustpan** ['dʌstpæn] *n* szufelka *f*, śmietniczka *f*
**dusty** ['dʌstɪ] *adj* zakurzony
**Dutch** [dʌtʃ] *adj* holenderski ▷ *n* (język *m*) holenderski ▷ *adv*: **to go ~** (*inf*) płacić (zapłacić *perf*) każdy za siebie; **the Dutch** *npl* Holendrzy *vir pl*
**Dutch auction** *n* licytacja *f* zniżkowa (*polegająca na obniżaniu ceny wywoławczej*)
**Dutchman** ['dʌtʃmən] (*irreg: like* **man**) *n* Holender *m*
**Dutchwoman** ['dʌtʃwumən] (*irreg: like* **woman**) *n* Holenderka *f*
**dutiable** ['dju:tɪəbl] *adj* podlegający ocleniu
**dutiful** ['dju:tɪful] *adj* (*child*) posłuszny; (*husband, wife*) dobry; (*employee*) obowiązkowy
**duty** ['dju:tɪ] *n* (*responsibility*) obowiązek *m*; (*tax*) cło *nt*; **duties** *npl* obowiązki *pl*; **to make it one's ~ to do sth** zobowiązywać się (zobowiązać się *perf*) do zrobienia czegoś; **to pay ~ on sth** płacić (zapłacić *perf*) za coś cło; **on/off ~** na/po służbie
**duty-free** ['dju:tɪ'fri:] *adj* wolny od cła, wolnocłowy; **~ shop** sklep wolnocłowy
**duty officer** *n* oficer *m* służbowy
**duvet** ['du:veɪ] (*Brit*) *n* kołdra *f*
**DV** *abbr* (= *Deo volente*) jeśli Bóg pozwoli
**DVD** *n abbr* (= *digital video disc*) DVD *nt inv*
**DVLC** (*Brit*) *n abbr* = **Driver and Vehicle Licensing Centre**
**DVM** (*US*) *n abbr* (= *Doctor of Veterinary Medicine*) *stopień naukowy*, ≈ dr
**dwarf** [dwɔ:f] (*pl* **dwarves**) *n* karzeł *m* ▷ *vt*: **he was ~ed by a huge desk** wydawał się bardzo mały w porównaniu z wielkim biurkiem
**dwarves** [dwɔ:vz] *npl of* **dwarf**
**dwell** [dwɛl] (*pt, pp* **dwelt**) *vi* mieszkać
▸ **dwell on** *vt fus* rozpamiętywać *+acc*
**dweller** ['dwɛlə^r] *n* mieszkaniec(-nka) *m(f)*; **city ~** mieszkaniec miasta
**dwelling** ['dwɛlɪŋ] *n* mieszkanie *nt*
**dwelt** [dwɛlt] *pt, pp of* **dwell**
**dwindle** ['dwɪndl] *vi* (*interest, attendance*) maleć (zmaleć *perf*)
**dwindling** ['dwɪndlɪŋ] *adj* (*strength, interest*) malejący, słabnący; (*resources, supplies*) topniejący, kurczący się
**dye** [daɪ] *n* (*for hair*) farba *f*; (*for cloth*) barwnik *m* ▷ *vt* (*hair*) farbować (ufarbować *perf*); (*cloth*) barwić (zabarwić *perf*), farbować (zafarbować *perf*)
**dyestuffs** ['daɪstʌfs] *npl* barwniki *pl*
**dying** ['daɪɪŋ] *adj* umierający; (*moments, words*) ostatni (*przed śmiercią*)
**dyke** [daɪk] *n* (*Brit*) grobla *f*; (*channel*) rów *m*
**dynamic** [daɪ'næmɪk] *adj* dynamiczny
**dynamics** [daɪ'næmɪks] *n or npl* dynamika *f*
**dynamite** ['daɪnəmaɪt] *n* dynamit *m* ▷ *vt* wysadzać (wysadzić *perf*) (w powietrze)
**dynamo** ['daɪnəməu] *n* prądnica *f* (prądu stałego), dynamo *nt*
**dynasty** ['dɪnəstɪ] *n* dynastia *f*
**dysentery** ['dɪsntrɪ] *n* czerwonka *f*
**dyslexia** [dɪs'lɛksɪə] *n* dysleksja *f*
**dyslexic** [dɪs'lɛksɪk] *adj* cierpiący na dysleksję ▷ *n* dyslektyk(-yczka) *m(f)*
**dyspepsia** [dɪs'pɛpsɪə] *n* niestrawność *f*
**dystrophy** ['dɪstrəfɪ] *n* dystrofia *f*; **muscular ~** dystrofia mięśni

# Ee

**E¹, e** [iː] *n* *(letter)* E *nt*, e *nt*; **E for Edward,** *(US)* **E for Easy** ≈ E jak Ewa
**E²** [iː] *n* *(Mus)* E *nt*, e *nt*
**E³** *abbr* (= *east*) wsch.
**E111** *n abbr* (*also*: **form E111**) *formularz używany w krajach Wspólnoty Europejskiej przy ubieganiu się o zwrot wydatków związanych z leczeniem*
**E.A.** (US) *n abbr* (= *educational age*) wiek *m* szkolny
**ea.** *abbr* = **each**
**each** [iːtʃ] *adj* każdy ▷ *pron* każdy; **they blamed ~ other** oskarżali się nawzajem; **they hate/love ~ other** oni się nienawidzą/kochają; **you are jealous of ~ other** jesteście o siebie zazdrośni; **~ day** każdego dnia; **they have two books ~** mają po dwie książki każdy; **they cost 5 pounds ~** kosztują (po) 5 funtów za sztukę; **~ of us** każdy z nas
**eager** [ˈiːgəʳ] *adj* *(keen)* gorliwy; *(excited)* podniecony; **to be ~ to do sth** być chętnym do zrobienia czegoś; **to be ~ for** niecierpliwie oczekiwać *+gen*
**eagerly** [ˈiːgəlɪ] *adv* *(talk etc)* z zapałem; *(awaited)* niecierpliwie
**eagle** [ˈiːgl] *n* orzeł *m*
**ear** [ɪəʳ] *n* *(Anat)* ucho *nt*; *(of corn)* kłos *m*; **up to one's ears in debt** po uszy w długach; **to give sb a thick ear** trzepnąć *(perf)* kogoś w ucho; **we'll play it by ear** *(fig)* wymyślimy coś na poczekaniu
**earache** [ˈɪəreɪk] *n* ból *m* ucha
**eardrum** [ˈɪədrʌm] *n* błona *f* bębenkowa
**earl** [əːl] *(Brit)* *n* ≈ hrabia *m*
**earlier** [ˈəːlɪəʳ] *adj* wcześniejszy ▷ *adv* wcześniej; **in ~ times** dawniej, niegdyś; **I can't come any ~** nie mogę przyjść ani trochę wcześniej
**early** [ˈəːlɪ] *adv* *(not late)* wcześnie; *(ahead of time)* wcześniej ▷ *adj* *(hours, stage, lunch)* wczesny; *(death)* przedwczesny; *(Christians, settlers)* pierwszy; *(reply)* szybki; **~ last week/month** na początku zeszłego tygodnia/miesiąca; **~ in the morning** wcześnie rano, wczesnym rankiem; **in the ~** *or* **~ in the 19th century** w początkach 19. wieku; **in the ~** *or* **~ in the spring** wczesną wiosną; **to have an ~ night** kłaść się (położyć się *perf*) (spać) wcześniej; **take the ~ train** jechać (pojechać *perf*) wcześniejszym pociągiem; **you're ~** przyszedłeś za wcześnie; **she's in her ~ forties** jest trochę po czterdziestce, ma czterdzieści parę lat; **at your earliest convenience** możliwie szybko *or* jak najszybciej
**early retirement** *n*: **to take ~** iść (pójść *perf*) na wcześniejszą emeryturę
**early warning system** *n* system *m* wczesnego ostrzegania
**earmark** [ˈɪəmɑːk] *vt*: **to ~ (for)** rezerwować (zarezerwować *perf*) (na *+acc*)
**earn** [əːn] *vt* *(salary)* zarabiać (zarobić *perf*); *(Comm: profit)* przynosić (przynieść *perf*); *(praise)* zyskiwać (zyskać *perf*); *(hatred)* zasłużyć *(perf)* na *+acc*; **to ~ one's living** zarabiać (zarobić *perf*) na utrzymanie *or* życie; **this ~ed him much praise, he ~ed much praise for this** to przyniosło mu wiele uznania, zyskał tym sobie wiele uznania; **he's ~ed his rest/reward** zasłużył (sobie) na wypoczynek/nagrodę
**earned income** [əːnd-] *n* dochód *m* z pracy
**earnest** [ˈəːnɪst] *adj* *(wish, desire)* szczery; *(person, manner)* poważny ▷ *n* (*also*: **earnest money**) zadatek *m*; **in ~** *adv* na poważnie *or* serio ▷ *adj*: **she was in ~ about what she was to say** była (bardzo) przejęta tym, co miała powiedzieć; **do you think he was in ~?** (czy) myślisz, że mówił poważnie?
**earnings** [ˈəːnɪŋz] *npl* *(personal)* zarobki *pl*; *(of company)* dochody *pl*
**ear, nose and throat specialist** *n* specjalista *m* laryngolog *m*
**earphones** [ˈɪəfəunz] *npl* słuchawki *pl*
**earplugs** [ˈɪəplʌgz] *npl* zatyczki *pl* do uszu
**earring** [ˈɪərɪŋ] *n* kolczyk *m*
**earshot** [ˈɪəʃɔt] *n*: **to be within/out of ~** być dostatecznie blisko/za daleko, by słyszeć
**earth** [əːθ] *n* *(planet)* Ziemia *f*; *(land, surface, soil)* ziemia *f*; *(Brit: Elec)* uziemienie *nt*; *(of fox)* nora *f* ▷ *vt* *(Brit)* uziemiać (uziemić *perf*)

**earthenware** ['ə:θnwεə^r] *n* ceramika *f*, wyroby *pl* ceramiczne ▷ *adj* ceramiczny
**earthly** ['ə:θlɪ] *adj* doczesny, ziemski; **~ paradise** raj na ziemi; **there is no ~ reason to think that ...** nie ma najmniejszego powodu (, by) sądzić, że ...
**earthquake** ['ə:θkweɪk] *n* trzęsienie *nt* ziemi
**earth tremor** *n* wstrząs *m* podziemny
**earthworks** ['ə:θwə:ks] *npl* szańce *pl*
**earthworm** ['ə:θwə:m] *n* dżdżownica *f*
**earthy** ['ə:θɪ] *adj* (*fig: humour*) prymitywny
**earwig** ['ɪəwɪg] *n* skorek *m*
**ease** [i:z] *n* (*easiness*) łatwość *f*; (*comfort*) beztroska *f* ▷ *vt* (*pain*) łagodzić (złagodzić *perf*); (*tension, problem*) łagodzić (załagodzić *perf*) ▷ *vi* (*situation*) uspokajać się (uspokoić się *perf*); (*pain, grip*) zelżeć (*perf*); (*rain, snow*) słabnąć (osłabnąć *perf*); **to ~ sth in/out** włożyć/wyjąć coś; **at ~!** spocznij!; **with ~** z łatwością; **a life of ~** beztroskie życie
▸ **ease off** *vi* słabnąć (osłabnąć *perf*)
▸ **ease up** *vi* = **ease off**
**easel** ['i:zl] *n* sztaluga *f*
**easily** ['i:zɪlɪ] *adv* (*without difficulty, quickly*) łatwo; (*in a relaxed way*) swobodnie; (*by far*) bez wątpienia; (*possibly, well*) śmiało
**easiness** ['i:zɪnɪs] *n* łatwość *f*
**east** [i:st] *n* wschód *m* ▷ *adj* wschodni ▷ *adv* na wschód; **the E~** (*Orient, Eastern Europe*) Wschód *m*
**Easter** ['i:stə^r] *n* Wielkanoc *f* ▷ *cpd* wielkanocny
**Easter egg** *n* pisanka *f*
**Easter Island** *n* Wyspa *f* Wielkanocna
**easterly** ['i:stəlɪ] *adj* wschodni
**Easter Monday** *n* poniedziałek *m* wielkanocny, ≈ lany poniedziałek *m*
**eastern** ['i:stən] *adj* wschodni; **E~ Europe** Europa Wschodnia; **E~ philosophy** filozofia Wschodu; **the E~ bloc** blok wschodni
**Easter Sunday** *n* niedziela *f* wielkanocna
**East Germany** (*old*) *n* Niemcy *pl* Wschodnie, NRD *nt inv*
**eastward(s)** ['i:stwəd(z)] *adv* na wschód
**easy** ['i:zɪ] *adj* (*task, life, prey*) łatwy; (*conversation, manner*) swobodny ▷ *adv*: **to take it** *or* **things ~** (*go slowly*) nie przemęczać się; (*not worry*) nie przejmować się; (*for health*) oszczędzać się; **payment on ~ terms** spłata na dogodnych warunkach; **that's easier said than done** to się łatwo mówi; **I' m not ~** *or* **I do not feel ~ about** nie jestem przekonany do *+gen*; **I'm ~** (*inf*) ja się dostosuję
**easy chair** *n* fotel *m* klubowy
**easy-going** ['i:zɪ'gəuɪŋ] *adj* spokojny, opanowany

**eat** [i:t] (*pt* **ate**, *pp* **eaten**) *vt* jeść (zjeść *perf*) ▷ *vi* jeść
▸ **eat away** *vt* (*sea*) podmywać (podmyć *perf*); (*acid*) wyżerać (wyżreć *perf*)
▸ **eat away at** *vt fus* (*metal*) przeżerać (przeżreć *perf*); (*fig: savings*) pochłaniać (pochłonąć *perf*)
▸ **eat into** *vt fus* = **eat away at**
▸ **eat out** *vi* jeść (zjeść *perf*) poza domem
▸ **eat up** *vt* zjadać (zjeść *perf*) do końca; (*fig*) pożerać (pożreć *perf*)
**eatable** ['i:təbl] *adj* nadający się do jedzenia, zjadliwy (*inf*)
**eau de Cologne** ['əudəkə'ləun] *n* woda *f* kolońska
**eaves** [i:vz] *npl* okap *m*
**eavesdrop** ['i:vzdrɔp] *vi*: **to ~ (on)** podsłuchiwać (*+acc*)
**ebb** [εb] *n* odpływ *m* ▷ *vi* (*tidewater*) odpływać, opadać; (*fig: strength*) odpływać (odpłynąć *perf*); (*: feeling*) słabnąć (osłabnąć *perf*); **the ebb and flow** (*fig*) wzloty i upadki; **to be at a low ebb** (*fig*) przechodzić kryzys; **the tide is ebbing** jest odpływ
▸ **ebb away** *vi* (*fig*) = **ebb**
**ebb tide** *n* odpływ *m*
**ebony** ['εbənɪ] *n* heban *m*
**ebullient** [ɪ'bʌlɪənt] *adj* tryskający energią *or* entuzjazmem
**EC** *n abbr* (= *European Community*) Wspólnota *f* Europejska
**eccentric** [ɪk'sεntrɪk] *adj* ekscentryczny ▷ *n* ekscentryk(-yczka) *m(f)*
**ecclesiastic(al)** [ɪkli:zɪ'æstɪk(l)] *adj* kościelny
**ECG** *n abbr* (= *electrocardiogram*) EKG *nt inv*
**echo** ['εkəu] (*pl* **~es**) *n* echo *nt* ▷ *vt* powtarzać (powtórzyć *perf*) ▷ *vi* (*sound*) odbijać się (odbić się *perf*) echem; (*cave*) rozbrzmiewać (rozbrzmieć *perf*) echem
**éclair** ['eɪklεə^r] *n* ekler *m* (*ciastko*)
**eclipse** [ɪ'klɪps] *n* zaćmienie *nt* ▷ *vt* (*artist, performance*) przyćmiewać (przyćmić *perf*); (*competitor*) spychać (zepchnąć *perf*) na drugi *or* dalszy plan; (*problem*) przesłaniać (przesłonić *perf*)
**ECM** (US) *n abbr* (= *European Common Market*) Wspólny Rynek *m*
**ecofriendly** ['i:kəufrεndlɪ] *adj* przyjazny dla środowiska
**ecological** [i:kə'lɔdʒɪkəl] *adj* ekologiczny
**ecologist** [ɪ'kɔlədʒɪst] *n* ekolog *m*
**ecology** [ɪ'kɔlədʒɪ] *n* (*environment*) ekosystem *m*; (*discipline*) ekologia *f*
**economic** [i:kə'nɔmɪk] *adj* (*system, history*) gospodarczy, ekonomiczny; (*business*) rentowny

**economical** [i:kəˈnɔmɪkl] *adj (system, car)* oszczędny, ekonomiczny; *(person)* gospodarny, oszczędny
**economically** [i:kəˈnɔmɪklɪ] *adv (frugally)* oszczędnie; *(regarding economics)* gospodarczo, ekonomicznie
**economics** [i:kəˈnɔmɪks] *n* ekonomia *f* ▷ *npl* ekonomika *f*
**economist** [ɪˈkɔnəmɪst] *n* ekonomista(-tka) *m(f)*
**economize** [ɪˈkɔnəmaɪz] *vi* oszczędzać
**economy** [ɪˈkɔnəmɪ] *n (of country)* gospodarka *f*; *(financial prudence)* oszczędność *f*; **economies of scale** *(Comm)* obniżenie kosztów poprzez zwiększenie produkcji
**economy class** *n (Aviat)* klasa *f* turystyczna
**economy size** *n* duże opakowanie *nt*
**ecosystem** [ˈi:kəusɪstəm] *n* ekosystem *m*
**eco-warrior** [ˈi:kəuwɔrɪəʳ] *n* ekolog *m (protestujący w obronie środowiska)*
**ECSC** *n abbr (= European Coal & Steel Community)* EWWiS *f (= Europejska Wspólnota Węgla i Stali)*
**ecstasy** [ˈɛkstəsɪ] *n (rapture)* ekstaza *f*, uniesienie *nt*; *(drug)* ekstaza *f*; **in ~** w uniesieniu; **to go into ecstasies over** podniecać się *+instr*
**ecstatic** [ɛksˈtætɪk] *adj (welcome, reaction)* entuzjastyczny; *(person)* rozentuzjazmowany
**ECT** *n abbr* = **electro-convulsive therapy**
**ECU** [ˈeɪkju:] *n abbr (= European Currency Unit)* ECU *nt inv*
**Ecuador** [ˈɛkwədɔ:ʳ] *n* Ekwador *m*
**ecumenical** [i:kjuˈmɛnɪkl] *adj* ekumeniczny
**eczema** [ˈɛksɪmə] *n* egzema *f*
**eddy** [ˈɛdɪ] *n* zawirowanie *nt*
**edge** [ɛdʒ] *n (of forest, road)* skraj *m*; *(of table, chair)* krawędź *f*, brzeg *m*; *(of knife)* ostrze *nt* ▷ *vt* okrawać (okroić *perf*) ▷ *vi*: **to ~ forward** (powoli) przepychać się (przepchnąć się *perf*) (do przodu); **to ~ past** przeciskać się (przecisnąć się *perf*) przez *+acc*; **on ~** *(fig)* = **edgy**; **to ~ away from** (powoli) oddalać się (oddalić się *perf*) od *+gen*; **to have the ~ (over)** *(fig)* mieć przewagę (nad *+instr*)
**edgeways** [ˈɛdʒweɪz] *adv*: **he couldn't get a word in ~** nie mógł dojść do słowa
**edging** [ˈɛdʒɪŋ] *n* obramowanie *nt*
**edgy** [ˈɛdʒɪ] *adj* podenerwowany, poirytowany
**edible** [ˈɛdɪbl] *adj* jadalny
**edict** [ˈi:dɪkt] *n* edykt *m*
**edifice** [ˈɛdɪfɪs] *n* gmach *m*; *(fig)* struktura *f*, formacja *f*
**edifying** [ˈɛdɪfaɪɪŋ] *adj* budujący
**Edinburgh** [ˈɛdɪnbərə] *n* Edynburg *m*
**edit** [ˈɛdɪt] *vt (book)* redagować (zredagować *perf*); *(text)* adiustować (zadiustować *perf*); *(film, broadcast)* montować (zmontować *perf*); *(newspaper, magazine)* wydawać
**edition** [ɪˈdɪʃən] *n* wydanie *nt*
**editor** [ˈɛdɪtəʳ] *n (of newspaper, magazine)* redaktor *m* naczelny; *(of book, TV programme)* redaktor *m*; *(Film)* montażysta(-tka) *m(f)*; **foreign ~** redaktor działu zagranicznego
**editorial** [ɛdɪˈtɔ:rɪəl] *adj* redakcyjny ▷ *n* artykuł *m* redakcyjny *or* wstępny
**EDP** *(Comput) n abbr (= electronic data processing)* EPD *nt inv*
**EDT** *(US) abbr* = **Eastern Daylight Time**
**educate** [ˈɛdjukeɪt] *vt (teach)* kształcić (wykształcić *perf*), edukować *(literary)*; *(inform)* uświadamiać (uświadomić *perf*)
**education** [ɛdjuˈkeɪʃən] *n (process)* kształcenie *nt*, nauczanie *nt*; *(system, area of work)* oświata *f*; *(knowledge, culture)* wykształcenie *nt*; **primary** *or (US)* **elementary/secondary ~** szkolnictwo podstawowe/średnie
**educational** [ɛdjuˈkeɪʃənl] *adj (institution, policy)* oświatowy; *(toy)* edukacyjny; *(experience)* pouczający; **~ technology** technika kształcenia
**edutainment** [ɛdjuˈteɪnmənt] *(US) n (games)* gry *pl* edukacyjne; *(TV)* programy *pl* edukacyjno-rozrywkowe
**Edwardian** [ɛdˈwɔ:dɪən] *adj* edwardiański
**EE** *abbr* = **electrical engineer**
**EEC** *n abbr (= European Economic Community)* EWG *nt inv*
**EEG** *n abbr (= electroencephalogram)* EEG *nt inv*
**eel** [i:l] *n* węgorz *m*
**EENT** *(US: Med) n abbr (= eye, ear, nose and throat)* specjalista *m* z zakresu chorób oczu, uszu, nosa, gardła i krtani
**EEOC** *(US) n abbr (= Equal Employment Opportunities Commission) komisja do walki z dyskryminacją pracowników*
**eerie** [ˈɪərɪ] *adj* niesamowity
**EET** *abbr (= Eastern European Time)* czas *m* wschodnioeuropejski
**efface** [ɪˈfeɪs] *vt* zacierać (zatrzeć *perf*), wymazywać (wymazać *perf*); **to ~ o.s.** usuwać się (usunąć się *perf*) w cień
**effect** [ɪˈfɛkt] *n (result, consequence)* skutek *m*; *(impression)* efekt *m* ▷ *vt (repairs)* dokonywać (dokonać *perf*) *+gen*; *(savings)* czynić (poczynić *perf*); **effects** *npl (belongings)* rzeczy *pl* (osobiste); *(Theat, Film)* efekty *pl* (specjalne); **to take ~** *(law)* wchodzić (wejść *perf*) w życie; *(drug)* zaczynać (zacząć *perf*) działać; **to put into ~** wprowadzać (wprowadzić *perf*) w życie; **to have an ~ on sb/sth** mieć wpływ na kogoś/coś; **in ~** w praktyce; **his letter is to the ~ that ...** sens jego listu jest taki, że ...

**effective** [ɪ'fɛktɪv] *adj* (*successful*) skuteczny; (*actual*) faktyczny; **to become ~** (*Jur*) wchodzić (wejść *perf*) w życie; **~ date** data wejścia w życie
**effectively** [ɪ'fɛktɪvlɪ] *adv* (*successfully*) skutecznie; (*in reality*) faktycznie
**effectiveness** [ɪ'fɛktɪvnɪs] *n* skuteczność *f*
**effeminate** [ɪ'fɛmɪnɪt] *adj* zniewieściały
**effervescent** [ɛfə'vɛsnt] *adj* musujący
**efficacy** ['ɛfɪkəsɪ] *n* skuteczność *f*
**efficiency** [ɪ'fɪʃənsɪ] *n* (*of person, organization*) sprawność *f*; (*of machine*) wydajność *f*
**efficiency apartment** (US) *n* ≈ kawalerka *f*
**efficient** [ɪ'fɪʃənt] *adj* (*person*) sprawny; (*organization*) sprawnie działający; (*machine*) wydajny
**efficiently** [ɪ'fɪʃəntlɪ] *adv* (*competently*) sprawnie; (*without wasting time or energy*) wydajnie
**effigy** ['ɛfɪdʒɪ] *n* (*dummy*) kukła *f*; (*image*) wizerunek *m*, podobizna *f*
**effluent** ['ɛfluənt] *n* ściek *m*
**effort** ['ɛfət] *n* (*endeavour, exertion*) wysiłek *m*; (*determined attempt*) próba *f*, usiłowanie *nt*; **to make an ~ to do sth** dokładać (dołożyć *perf*) starań, żeby coś zrobić
**effortless** ['ɛfətlɪs] *adj* (*action*) nie wymagający wysiłku; (*style*) lekki, swobodny
**effrontery** [ɪ'frʌntərɪ] *n* bezczelność *f*, tupet *m*; **to have the ~ to do sth** mieć czelność coś zrobić
**effusive** [ɪ'fju:sɪv] *adj* wylewny
**EFL** (*Scol*) *n abbr* = **English as a Foreign Language**
**EFTA** ['ɛftə] *n abbr* (= *European Free Trade Association*) EFTA *f inv*, Europejskie Stowarzyszenie *nt* Wolnego Handlu
**e.g.** *adv abbr* (= *exempli gratia*) np.
**egalitarian** [ɪgælɪ'tɛərɪən] *adj* (*society*) egalitarny; (*principles*) egalitarystyczny ▷ *n* egalitarysta(-tka) *m(f)*
**egg** [ɛg] *n* jajo *nt*, jajko *nt*; **hard-boiled/soft-boiled egg** jajko na twardo/na miękko
▸ **egg on** *vt* podjudzać
**eggcup** ['ɛgkʌp] *n* kieliszek *m* do jajek
**eggplant** ['ɛgplɑ:nt] (*esp US*) *n* bakłażan *m*, oberżyna *f*
**eggshell** ['ɛgʃɛl] *n* skorupka *f* jajka ▷ *adj* (*paint, finish*) matowy
**egg white** *n* białko *nt*
**egg yolk** *n* żółtko *nt*
**ego** ['i:gəu] *n* ego *nt inv*
**egotism** ['ɛgəutɪzəm], **egoism** *n* egotyzm *m*, egoizm *m*
**egotist** ['ɛgəutɪst], **egoist** *n* egotysta(-tka) *m(f)*, egoista(-tka) *m(f)*
**Egypt** ['i:dʒɪpt] *n* Egipt *m*
**Egyptian** [ɪ'dʒɪpʃən] *adj* egipski ▷ *n* Egipcjanin(-anka) *m(f)*
**eiderdown** ['aɪdədaun] *n* pikowana narzuta *f*
**eight** [eɪt] *num* osiem; *see also* **five**
**eighteen** [eɪ'ti:n] *num* osiemnaście; *see also* **five**
**eighteenth** [eɪ'ti:nθ] *num* osiemnasty; *see also* **fifth**
**eighth** [eɪtθ] *num* ósmy; *see also* **fifth**
**eighty** ['eɪtɪ] *num* osiemdziesiąt; *see also* **fifty**
**Eire** ['ɛərə] *n* Irlandia *f*
**EIS** *n abbr* (= *Educational Institute of Scotland*) *szkocki związek zawodowy nauczycieli*
**either** ['aɪðə^r] *adj* (*one or other*) obojętnie który (*z dwóch*); (*both, each*) i jeden, i drugi ▷ *pron*: **~ (of them)** (oni) obaj; (*with negative*) żaden (z nich dwóch) ▷ *adv* też (nie) ▷ *conj*: **~ ... or** albo ... albo; (*with negative*) ani, ... ani; **she didn't say ~ yes or no** nie powiedziała ani tak, ani nie; **on ~ side** po obu stronach; **in ~ case** w obu przypadkach; **I don't like ~** nie lubię ani jednego, ani drugiego; **no, I don't ~** nie, ja też nie; **I haven't seen ~ one or the other** nie widziałem ani jednego, ani drugiego
**ejaculation** [ɪdʒækju'leɪʃən] *n* wytrysk *m*, ejakulacja *f*
**eject** [ɪ'dʒɛkt] *vt* (*object, gatecrasher*) wyrzucać (wyrzucić *perf*); (*tenant*) eksmitować (eksmitować *perf or* wyeksmitować *perf*) ▷ *vi* (*pilot*) katapultować się (katapultować się *perf*)
**ejector seat** [ɪ'dʒɛktə-] *n* fotel *m* wyrzucany
**eke** [i:k]: **to eke out** *vt* (*income*) podreperowywać (podreperować *perf*); **he eked out a living from writing** z trudem udawało mu się wyżyć z pisania
**EKG** (US) *n abbr* (= *electrocardiogram*) EKG *nt inv*
**el** [ɛl] (*US: inf*) *n abbr* (= *elevated railroad*) *kolejka miejska przebiegająca ponad poziomem ulic*
**elaborate** [*adj* ɪ'læbərɪt, *vb* ɪ'læbəreɪt] *adj* (*complex*) złożony; (*intricate*) zawiły; (*ornate*) misterny, kunsztowny ▷ *vt* (*expand*) rozwijać (rozwinąć *perf*); (*refine*) dopracowywać (dopracować *perf*) ▷ *vi*: **to ~ (on)** (*plan etc*) podawać (podać *perf*) szczegóły (*+gen*)
**elapse** [ɪ'læps] *vi* (*time*) mijać (minąć *perf*), upływać (upłynąć *perf*)
**elastic** [ɪ'læstɪk] *n* guma *f* ▷ *adj* rozciągliwy, elastyczny; (*fig*) elastyczny
**elastic band** (*Brit*) *n* gumka *f*
**elasticity** [ɪlæs'tɪsɪtɪ] *n* elastyczność *f*
**elated** [ɪ'leɪtɪd] *adj* rozradowany
**elation** [ɪ'leɪʃən] *n* rozradowanie *nt*
**elbow** ['ɛlbəu] *n* łokieć *m* ▷ *vt*: **to ~ one's way through the crowd** przepychać się (przepchnąć się *perf*) przez tłum

**elbow room** *n* pole *nt* manewru
**elder** ['ɛldəʳ] *adj* starszy ▷ *n* (*tree*) czarny bez *m*; (*usu pl*) starszyzna *f*
**elderly** ['ɛldəlɪ] *adj* starszy, w podeszłym wieku *post* ▷ *npl*: **the ~** ludzie *vir pl* starsi
**eldest** ['ɛldɪst] *adj* najstarszy ▷ *n* najstarsze dziecko *nt*
**elect** [ɪ'lɛkt] *vt* wybierać (wybrać *perf*) ▷ *adj*: **the president ~** prezydent *m* elekt *m*; **to ~ to do sth** zdecydować się (*perf*) coś (z)robić
**election** [ɪ'lɛkʃən] *n* (*voting*) wybory *pl*; (*installation*) wybór *m*; **to hold an ~** przeprowadzać (przeprowadzić *perf*) wybory
**election campaign** *n* kampania *f* wyborcza
**electioneering** [ɪlɛkʃə'nɪərɪŋ] *n* agitacja *f* (przed)wyborcza
**elector** [ɪ'lɛktəʳ] *n* wyborca *m*
**electoral** [ɪ'lɛktərəl] *adj* wyborczy
**electoral college** (*US*) *n* kolegium *nt* elektorskie
**electorate** [ɪ'lɛktərɪt] *n* wyborcy *vir pl*, elektorat *m*
**electric** [ɪ'lɛktrɪk] *adj* elektryczny
**electrical** [ɪ'lɛktrɪkl] *adj* elektryczny; **~ failure** awaria sieci elektrycznej
**electrical engineer** *n* inżynier *m* elektryk *m*
**electric blanket** *n* koc *m* elektryczny
**electric chair** *n* krzesło *nt* elektryczne
**electric cooker** *n* kuchenka *f* elektryczna
**electric current** *n* prąd *m* elektryczny
**electric fire** (*Brit*) *n* piecyk *m* elektryczny
**electrician** [ɪlɛk'trɪʃən] *n* elektryk *m*
**electricity** [ɪlɛk'trɪsɪtɪ] *n* elektryczność *f*, prąd *m*; **to switch on/off the ~** włączać (włączyć *perf*)/wyłączać (wyłączyć *perf*) dopływ prądu; **~ bill** rachunek za prąd; **~ meter** licznik prądu; **~ industry** przemysł energetyczny
**electricity board** (*Brit*) *n* zakład *m* energetyczny
**electric light** *n* światło *nt* elektryczne
**electric shock** *n* porażenie *nt* prądem
**electrify** [ɪ'lɛktrɪfaɪ] *vt* elektryfikować (zelektryfikować *perf*); (*fig*) elektryzować (zelektryzować *perf*)
**electro...** [ɪ'lɛktrəu] *pref* elektro...
**electrocardiogram** [ɪ'lɛktrə'kɑ:dɪəgræm] *n* elektrokardiogram *m*
**electroconvulsive therapy** [ɪ'lɛktrəkən'vʌlsɪv-] *n* leczenie *nt* elektrowstrząsami
**electrocute** [ɪ'lɛktrəkju:t] *vt* porażać (porazić *perf*) prądem
**electrode** [ɪ'lɛktrəud] *n* elektroda *f*
**electroencephalogram** [ɪ'lɛktrəuɛn'sɛfələgræm] *n* elektroencefalogram *m*
**electrolysis** [ɪlɛk'trɔlɪsɪs] *n* elektroliza *f*
**electromagnetic** [ɪ'lɛktrəmæg'nɛtɪk] *adj* elektromagnetyczny
**electron** [ɪ'lɛktrɔn] *n* elektron *m*
**electronic** [ɪlɛk'trɔnɪk] *adj* elektroniczny
**electronic data processing** *n* elektroniczne przetwarzanie *nt* danych
**electronic mail** *n* poczta *f* elektroniczna
**electronics** [ɪlɛk'trɔnɪks] *n* elektronika *f*
**electron microscope** *n* mikroskop *m* elektronowy
**electroplated** [ɪ'lɛktrə'pleɪtɪd] *adj* galwanizowany
**electrotherapy** [ɪ'lɛktrə'θɛrəpɪ] *n* elektroterapia *f*
**elegance** ['ɛlɪgəns] *n* elegancja *f*
**elegant** ['ɛlɪgənt] *adj* elegancki
**element** ['ɛlɪmənt] *n* (*part*) element *m*; (*Chem*) pierwiastek *m*; (*of heater, kettle etc*) element *m* grzejny; **to be in one's ~** być w swoim żywiole
**elementary** [ɛlɪ'mɛntərɪ] *adj* elementarny; (*school, education*) podstawowy
**elephant** ['ɛlɪfənt] *n* słoń *m*
**elevate** ['ɛlɪveɪt] *vt* (*to peerage etc*) wynosić (wynieść *perf*); (*physically*) podnosić (podnieść *perf*); (*Geol*) wypiętrzać (wypiętrzyć *perf*)
**elevated railroad** ['ɛlɪveɪtɪd-] (*US*) *n* nadziemna linia *f* kolejowa
**elevation** [ɛlɪ'veɪʃən] *n* (*to peerage etc*) wyniesienie *nt*; (*hill*) wzniesienie *nt*; (*of place*) wysokość *f* (nad poziomem morza); (*Archit*) elewacja *f*
**elevator** ['ɛlɪveɪtəʳ] *n* (*US*) winda *f*; (*in warehouse etc*) podnośnik *m*
**eleven** [ɪ'lɛvn] *num* jedenaście; *see also* **five**
**elevenses** [ɪ'lɛvnzɪz] (*Brit*) *npl* ≈ drugie śniadanie *nt*
**eleventh** [ɪ'lɛvnθ] *num* jedenasty; **at the ~ hour** (*fig*) za pięć dwunasta; *see also* **five**
**elf** [ɛlf] (*pl* **elves**) *n* elf *m*
**elicit** [ɪ'lɪsɪt] *vt*: **to ~ sth from sb** (*response, reaction*) wywoływać (wywołać *perf*) coś z czyjejś strony; (*information*) wydobywać (wydobyć *perf*) coś z kogoś
**eligible** ['ɛlɪdʒəbl] *adj* (*man, woman*) wolny, do wzięcia *post*; **an ~ bachelor** dobra partia; **to be ~ for sth** mieć prawo ubiegać się o coś; **to be ~ to do sth** mieć prawo coś robić
**eliminate** [ɪ'lɪmɪneɪt] *vt* (*poverty, smoking*) likwidować (zlikwidować *perf*); (*candidate, team, contestant*) eliminować (wyeliminować *perf*)
**elimination** [ɪlɪmɪ'neɪʃən] *n* (*of poverty, smoking*) likwidacja *f*; (*of candidate, team, contestant*) eliminacja *f*; **by a process of ~** przez eliminację
**élite** [eɪ'li:t] *n* elita *f*
**élitist** [eɪ'li:tɪst] (*pej*) *adj* elitarny
**elixir** [ɪ'lɪksəʳ] *n* eliksir *m*
**Elizabethan** [ɪlɪzə'bi:θən] *adj* elżbietański

**ellipse** [ɪ'lɪps] *n* elipsa *f*
**elliptical** [ɪ'lɪptɪkl] *adj* eliptyczny
**elm** [ɛlm] *n* wiąz *m*
**elocution** [ɛlə'kjuːʃən] *n* wymowa *f*
**elongated** ['iːlɔŋgeɪtɪd] *adj* wydłużony
**elope** [ɪ'ləup] *vi*: **to ~ (with sb)** uciekać (uciec *perf*) (z kimś)
**elopement** [ɪ'ləupmənt] *n* ucieczka *f* (*kochanków*)
**eloquence** ['ɛləkwəns] *n* (*of speech, description*) sugestywność *f*; (*of person*) krasomówstwo *nt*, elokwencja *f*
**eloquent** ['ɛləkwənt] *adj* (*speech, description*) sugestywny; (*person*) wymowny, elokwentny
**else** [ɛls] *adv*: **or ~** (*otherwise*) bo inaczej; (*threatening*) bo jak nie; **something ~** coś innego, coś jeszcze; **somewhere ~** gdzie(ś) indziej; **everywhere ~** wszędzie indziej; **where ~?** gdzie(ż) indziej?; **is there anything ~ I can do?** czy jest jeszcze coś, co mogę zrobić?; **there was little ~ to do** niewiele więcej można było zrobić; **everyone ~** wszyscy inni; **nobody ~ spoke** nikt więcej *or* inny się nie odezwał
**elsewhere** [ɛls'wɛəʳ] *adv* gdzie indziej
**ELT** (*Scol*) *n abbr* = **English Language Teaching**
**elucidate** [ɪ'luːsɪdeɪt] *vt* objaśniać (objaśnić *perf*)
**elude** [ɪ'luːd] *vt* (*captor*) umykać (umknąć *perf*) *+dat*; (*capture*) uciekać (uciec *perf*) przed *+instr*; **new ideas ~d them** nie byli w stanie pojąć nowych idei; **his name ~s me** nie mogę sobie przypomnieć jego nazwiska
**elusive** [ɪ'luːsɪv] *adj* (*person, animal*) nieuchwytny; (*quality*) ulotny
**elves** [ɛlvz] *npl of* **elf**
**emaciated** [ɪ'meɪsɪeɪtɪd] *adj* wychudzony
**email** *n abbr* (= *electronic mail*) poczta *f* elektroniczna, e-mail *m*
**email address** *n* adres *m* e-maila
**emanate** ['ɛməneɪt] *vi*: **to ~ from** (*idea*) wywodzić się od *+gen*; (*feeling*) emanować z *+gen*; (*sound, light, smell*) dochodzić z *+gen*; **he ~s concern** emanuje z niego troska
**emancipate** [ɪ'mænsɪpeɪt] *vt* (*slaves*) wyzwalać (wyzwolić *perf*); (*women*) emancypować (wyemancypować *perf*)
**emancipation** [ɪmænsɪ'peɪʃən] *n* (*of slaves*) wyzwolenie *nt*; (*of women*) emancypacja *f*
**emasculate** [ɪ'mæskjuleɪt] *vt* osłabiać (osłabić *perf*)
**embalm** [ɪm'bɑːm] *vt* balsamować (zabalsamować *perf*)
**embankment** [ɪm'bæŋkmənt] *n* (*of road, railway*) nasyp *m*; (*of river*) nabrzeże *nt*
**embargo** [ɪm'bɑːgəu] (*pl* **~es**) *n* embargo *nt* ▷ *vt* (*goods*) obejmować (objąć *perf*) embargiem; (*ship*) nakładać (nałożyć *perf*) sekwestr na *+acc*; **to put** *or* **impose** *or* **place an ~ on sth** nakładać (nałożyć *perf*) embargo na coś; **to lift an ~** znosić (znieść *perf*) embargo
**embark** [ɪm'bɑːk] *vi* (*Naut*): **to ~ (on)** zaokrętować się (*perf*) (na *+loc*)
▸ **embark on** *vt fus* (*journey*) wyruszać (wyruszyć *perf*) w *+acc*; (*task, course of action*) podejmować (podjąć *perf*)
**embarkation** [ɛmbɑː'keɪʃən] *n* (*of people*) zaokrętowanie *nt*; (*of cargo*) załadunek *m*
**embarrass** [ɪm'bærəs] *vt* (*emotionally*) wprawiać (wprawić *perf*) w zakłopotanie; (*politician, government*) stawiać (postawić *perf*) w trudnym położeniu
**embarrassed** [ɪm'bærəst] *adj* (*laugh, silence*) pełen zakłopotania *or* zażenowania; **to be ~** być zażenowanym *or* zakłopotanym; **to be ~ to do sth** krępować się coś zrobić
**embarrassing** [ɪm'bærəsɪŋ] *adj* (*situation*) kłopotliwy, krępujący; (*statement*) wprawiający w zakłopotanie
**embarrassment** [ɪm'bærəsmənt] *n* (*shame*) wstyd *m*; (*shyness*) zażenowanie *nt*, skrępowanie *nt*; (*problem*) kłopotliwa sytuacja *f*
**embassy** ['ɛmbəsɪ] *n* ambasada *f*; **the Polish E~** Ambasada Polski
**embedded** [ɪm'bɛdɪd] *adj* (*attitude, feeling*) zakorzeniony; (*object*): **~ in** wbity w *+acc*, osadzony w *+loc*
**embellish** [ɪm'bɛlɪʃ] *vt* (*place, dress*) ozdabiać (ozdobić *perf*); (*account*) upiększać (upiększyć *perf*); **lavishly ~ed** bogato zdobiony; **the house was ~ed with masterly paintings** dom zdobiły obrazy mistrzów
**embers** ['ɛmbəz] *npl* żar *m*
**embezzle** [ɪm'bɛzl] *vt* sprzeniewierzać (sprzeniewierzyć *perf*), defraudować (zdefraudować *perf*)
**embezzlement** [ɪm'bɛzlmənt] *n* malwersacja *f*, defraudacja *f*
**embezzler** [ɪm'bɛzləʳ] *n* malwersant *m*
**embitter** [ɪm'bɪtəʳ] *vt* (*fig*) wprawiać (wprawić *perf*) w rozgoryczenie
**embittered** [ɪm'bɪtəd] *adj* rozgoryczony
**emblem** ['ɛmbləm] *n* (*of country*) godło *nt*; (*of sports club etc*) emblemat *m*; (*mark, symbol*) symbol *m*
**embodiment** [ɪm'bɔdɪmənt] *n*: **to be the ~ of** być ucieleśnieniem *+gen*
**embody** [ɪm'bɔdɪ] *vt* (*express, manifest*) być ucieleśnieniem *+gen*, reprezentować; (*include*) zawierać w sobie
**embolden** [ɪm'bəuldn] *vt* podbudowywać (podbudować *perf*)

e

**embolism** ['ɛmbəlɪzəm] *n* (*Med*) zator *m*
**embossed** [ɪm'bɔst] *adj* (*design, word*) wytłoczony; **paper ~ with the royal insignia** papier z wytłoczonymi insygniami królewskimi
**embrace** [ɪm'breɪs] *vt* obejmować (objąć *perf*) ▷ *vi* obejmować się (objąć się *perf*) ▷ *n* uścisk *m*, objęcie *nt* (*usu pl*)
**embroider** [ɪm'brɔɪdə[r]] *vt* haftować (wyhaftować *perf*), wyszywać (wyszyć *perf*); (*fig: story*) ubarwiać (ubarwić *perf*); **she ~ed the tablecloth with flowers** wyhaftowała kwiaty na obrusie
**embroidery** [ɪm'brɔɪdərɪ] *n* haft *m*
**embroil** [ɪm'brɔɪl] *vt*: **to become ~ed (in sth)** wikłać się (uwikłać się *perf*) (w coś)
**embryo** ['ɛmbrɪəu] *n* zarodek *m*, embrion *m*; (*fig*) zalążek *m*
**emend** [ɪ'mɛnd] *vt* (*text*) wnosić (wnieść *perf*) poprawki do *+gen*
**emerald** ['ɛmərəld] *n* szmaragd *m*
**emerge** [ɪ'mə:dʒ] *vi* pojawiać się (pojawić się *perf*); **to ~ from** (*room, imprisonment*) wychodzić (wyjść *perf*) z *+gen*; (*sleep, reverie*) ocknąć się (*perf*) z *+gen*; (*discussion, investigation*) wyłaniać się (wyłonić się *perf*) z *+gen*; **it ~s that ...** (*Brit*) okazuje się, że ...
**emergence** [ɪ'mə:dʒəns] *n* pojawienie się *nt*
**emergency** [ɪ'mə:dʒənsɪ] *n* nagły wypadek *m* ▷ *cpd* (*repair*) awaryjny; (*talks, meeting*) nadzwyczajny; **in an ~** w razie niebezpieczeństwa; **a state of ~** stan wyjątkowy
**emergency cord** (*US*) *n* ≈ hamulec *m* bezpieczeństwa
**emergency exit** *n* wyjście *nt* awaryjne
**emergency landing** *n* lądowanie *nt* awaryjne
**emergency lane** (*US*) *n* pas *m* awaryjny (*na poboczu autostrady*)
**emergency road service** (*US*) *n* pomoc *f* drogowa
**emergency services** *npl*: **the ~** służby *pl* ratownicze
**emergency stop** (*Brit: Aut*) *n* nagłe zatrzymanie *nt*
**emergent** [ɪ'mə:dʒənt] *adj* (*country*) nowo powstały; (*group, movement, idea*) wyłaniający się
**emeritus** [ɪ'mɛrɪtəs] *adj* (*professor, chairman*) honorowy
**emery board** ['ɛmərɪ-] *n* pilnik *m* do paznokci (*szmerglowy*)
**emery paper** ['ɛmərɪ-] *n* papier *m* ścierny szmerglowy
**emetic** [ɪ'mɛtɪk] *n* środek *m* wymiotny
**emigrant** ['ɛmɪgrənt] *n* emigrant(ka) *m(f)*
**emigrate** ['ɛmɪgreɪt] *vi* emigrować (emigrować *perf or* wyemigrować *perf*)
**emigration** [ɛmɪ'greɪʃən] *n* emigracja *f*
**émigré** ['ɛmɪgreɪ] *n* uchodźca *m*
**eminence** ['ɛmɪnəns] *n* sława *f*
**eminent** ['ɛmɪnənt] *adj* znakomity, wybitny
**eminently** ['ɛmɪnəntlɪ] *adv* wybitnie
**emir** [ɛ'mɪə[r]] *n* emir *m*
**emirate** ['ɛmɪrɪt] *n* emirat *m*
**emission** [ɪ'mɪʃən] *n* emisja *f*
**emit** [ɪ'mɪt] *vt* emitować (emitować *perf or* wyemitować *perf*)
**emolument** [ɪ'mɔljumənt] (*fml*) *n* (*often pl: fee*) honorarium *nt*; (*salary*) wynagrodzenie *nt*
**emotion** [ɪ'məuʃən] *n* uczucie *nt*; (*as opposed to reason*) emocja *f* (*usu pl*); **he was overcome by** *or* **with ~** ogarnęło go wzruszenie
**emotional** [ɪ'məuʃənl] *adj* (*person*) uczuciowy; (*needs, attitude*) emocjonalny; (*issue*) budzący emocje; (*speech, plea*) wzruszający; **to be ~ about sth** podchodzić do czegoś emocjonalnie
**emotionally** [ɪ'məuʃnəlɪ] *adv* (*behave*) emocjonalnie; (*be involved*) uczuciowo; (*speak*) wzruszająco; **~ disturbed** niezrównoważony emocjonalnie
**emotive** [ɪ'məutɪv] *adj* (*subject*) budzący *or* wywołujący emocje; (*language*) odwołujący się do emocji
**empathy** ['ɛmpəθɪ] *n* zrozumienie *nt*; (*Psych*) empatia *f*; **to feel ~ with sb** wczuwać się (wczuć się *perf*) w czyjąś sytuację
**emperor** ['ɛmpərə[r]] *n* cesarz *m*, imperator *m*
**emphases** ['ɛmfəsi:z] *npl of* **emphasis**
**emphasis** ['ɛmfəsɪs] (*pl* **emphases**) *n* nacisk *m*; **to lay** *or* **place ~ on sth** (*fig*) kłaść (położyć *perf*) nacisk na coś; **the ~ is on reading** (największy) nacisk kładzie się na czytanie
**emphasize** ['ɛmfəsaɪz] *vt* (*word*) akcentować (zaakcentować *perf*); (*point, feature*) podkreślać (podkreślić *perf*); **I must ~ that ...** muszę podkreślić *or* zaznaczyć, że ...
**emphatic** [ɛm'fætɪk] *adj* dobitny, stanowczy
**emphatically** [ɛm'fætɪklɪ] *adv* (*forcefully*) stanowczo; (*certainly*) zdecydowanie; **"that'll be the day!", said Mike ~** „niedoczekanie!" — powiedział z naciskiem Mike
**emphysema** [ɛmfɪ'si:mə] *n* odma *f*
**empire** ['ɛmpaɪə[r]] *n* imperium *nt*, cesarstwo *nt*; (*fig*) imperium *nt*
**empirical** [ɛm'pɪrɪkl] *adj* (*study*) doświadczalny; (*knowledge*) empiryczny
**employ** [ɪm'plɔɪ] *vt* (*workforce, person*) zatrudniać (zatrudnić *perf*); (*tool, weapon*) stosować (zastosować *perf*); **he's ~ed in a bank** jest zatrudniony w banku
**employee** [ɪmplɔɪ'i:] *n* zatrudniony(-na) *m(f)*, pracownik(-ica) *m(f)*

**employer** [ɪm'plɔɪəʳ] *n* pracodawca *m*
**employment** [ɪm'plɔɪmənt] *n* zatrudnienie *nt*; **to find ~** znajdować (znaleźć *perf*) zatrudnienie; **without ~** bez zatrudnienia; **place of ~** miejsce zatrudnienia
**employment agency** *n* ≈ biuro *nt* pośrednictwa pracy
**employment exchange** (*Brit: old*) *n* giełda *f* pracy
**empower** [ɪm'pauəʳ] *vt*: **to ~ sb to do sth** uprawniać (uprawnić *perf*) kogoś do (z) robienia czegoś
**empress** ['ɛmprɪs] *n* cesarzowa *f*
**empties** ['ɛmptɪz] *npl* puste butelki *pl*
**emptiness** ['ɛmptɪnɪs] *n* (*of area, life*) pustka *f*; (*of sea, ocean*) bezkres *m*
**empty** ['ɛmptɪ] *adj* pusty; (*fig: threat, promise*) czczy, gołosłowny ▷ *vt* (*container*) opróżniać (opróżnić *perf*); (*liquid*) wylewać (wylać *perf*) ▷ *vi* (*house*) pustoszeć (opustoszeć *perf*); (*container*) opróżniać się (opróżnić się *perf*); **on an ~ stomach** na pusty żołądek; **to ~ into** (*river*) uchodzić *or* wpadać do *+gen*; **this kind of debate is guaranteed to ~ the House of Commons** podczas debat tego typu Izba Gmin zawsze pustoszeje
**empty-handed** ['ɛmptɪ'hændɪd] *adj*: **he returned ~** wrócił z pustymi rękami
**empty-headed** ['ɛmptɪ'hɛdɪd] *adj* głupiutki
**EMS** *n abbr* (= *European Monetary System*) Europejski System *m* Monetarny
**EMT** *n abbr* = **emergency medical technician**
**emu** ['i:mju:] *n* emu *m inv*
**emulate** ['ɛmjuleɪt] *vt* naśladować; (*Comput*) emulować
**emulsion** [ɪ'mʌlʃən] *n* (*Phot*) emulsja *f*; (*also*: **emulsion paint**) farba *f* emulsyjna
**enable** [ɪ'neɪbl] *vt*: **to ~ sb to do sth** umożliwiać (umożliwić *perf*) komuś (z) robienie czegoś; **the shell has to be porous to ~ oxygen to pass in** skorupa musi być porowata, żeby umożliwić przenikanie tlenu do wnętrza
**enact** [ɪ'nækt] *vt* (*law*) uchwalać (uchwalić *perf*); (*play, role*) grać (zagrać *perf*), odgrywać (odegrać *perf*)
**enamel** [ɪ'næməl] *n* emalia *f*; (*of tooth*) szkliwo *nt*
**enamoured** [ɪ'næməd] *adj*: **to be ~ of** być zakochanym *or* rozkochanym w *+loc*
**encampment** [ɪn'kæmpmənt] *n* obozowisko *nt*
**encased** [ɪn'keɪst] *adj*: **~ in** (*plaster*) pokryty *+instr*; (*shell*) zamknięty w *+loc*
**enchant** [ɪn'tʃɑ:nt] *vt* oczarowywać (oczarować *perf*)
**enchanted** [ɪn'tʃɑ:ntɪd] *adj* (*castle*) zaczarowany; (*person*) oczarowany
**enchanting** [ɪn'tʃɑ:ntɪŋ] *adj* czarujący
**encircle** [ɪn'sə:kl] *vt* otaczać (otoczyć *perf*)
**encl.** *abbr* (= *enclosed, enclosure*) zał.
**enclave** ['ɛnkleɪv] *n* enklawa *f*
**enclose** [ɪn'kləuz] *vt* (*land, space*) otaczać (otoczyć *perf*); (*letter, cheque*) załączać (załączyć *perf*); **please find ~d ...** w załączeniu przesyłamy *+acc*
**enclosure** [ɪn'kləuʒəʳ] *n* (*area*) ogrodzone miejsce *nt*; (*in letter*) załącznik *m*
**encoder** [ɪn'kəudəʳ] (*Comput*) *n* koder *m*
**encompass** [ɪn'kʌmpəs] *vt* (*subject, measure*) obejmować (objąć *perf*)
**encore** [ɔŋ'kɔ:ʳ] *n, excl* bis *m*; **as an ~** na bis
**encounter** [ɪn'kauntəʳ] *n* (*meeting*) spotkanie *nt*; (*experience*) zetknięcie się *nt* ▷ *vt* (*person*) spotykać (spotkać *perf*); (*problem*) napotykać (napotkać *perf*); (*new experience*) spotykać się (spotkać się *perf*) *or* stykać się (zetknąć się *perf*) z *+instr*
**encourage** [ɪn'kʌrɪdʒ] *vt* (*person*): **to ~ sb (to do sth)** zachęcać (zachęcić *perf*) kogoś (do zrobienia czegoś); (*activity*) zachęcać do *+gen*; (*attitude*) popierać (poprzeć *perf*); (*growth*) pobudzać (pobudzić *perf*)
**encouragement** [ɪn'kʌrɪdʒmənt] *n* (*inspiration*) zachęta *f*; (*support*) poparcie *nt*
**encouraging** [ɪn'kʌrɪdʒɪŋ] *adj* zachęcający
**encroach** [ɪn'krəutʃ] *vi*: **to ~ (up)on** (*rights*) naruszać (naruszyć *perf*) *+acc*; (*property*) wtargnąć (*perf*) *or* wdzierać się (wedrzeć się *perf*) na teren *+gen*; (*time*) zabierać (zabrać *perf*) *+acc*
**encrusted** [ɪn'krʌstɪd] *adj*: **~ with** (*gems*) inkrustowany *+instr*; (*snow, dirt*) pokryty skorupą *+gen*
**encumber** [ɪn'kʌmbəʳ] *vt*: **~ed with** (*baggage etc*) obarczony *+instr*; (*debts*) obciążony *+instr*
**encyclop(a)edia** [ɛnsaɪkləu'pi:dɪə] *n* encyklopedia *f*
**end** [ɛnd] *n* koniec *m*; (*purpose*) cel *m* ▷ *vt* kończyć (skończyć *perf*), zakańczać (zakończyć *perf*) ▷ *vi* kończyć się (skończyć się *perf*); **from end to end** od końca do końca; **to come to an end** kończyć się (zakończyć się *perf*); **to be at an end** kończyć się; **in the end** w końcu; **on end** na sztorc; **to stand on end** (*hair*) stawać (stanąć *perf*) dęba; **for hours on end** (całymi) godzinami; **to bring to an end, put an end to** kłaść (położyć *perf*) kres *+dat*; **for 5 hours on end** przez bite 5 godzin; **at the end of the street** na końcu ulicy; **at the end of the day** (*Brit: fig*) w ostatecznym rozrachunku; **to this end, with this end in view** w tym celu
▸ **end up** *vi*: **to end up in** (*prison etc*) kończyć (skończyć *perf*) w *+loc*, trafiać (trafić *perf*) do

*+gen*; **he ended up in tears** skończyło się na tym, że wybuchnął płaczem; **we ended up taking a taxi** koniec końców wzięliśmy taksówkę

**endanger** [ɪn'deɪndʒəʳ] *vt* zagrażać (zagrozić *perf*) *+dat*; **an ~ed species** gatunek zagrożony (wymarciem)

**endear** [ɪn'dɪəʳ] *vt*: **to ~ o.s. to sb** zdobywać (zdobyć *perf*) czyjeś względy

**endearing** [ɪn'dɪərɪŋ] *adj* ujmujący

**endearment** [ɪn'dɪəmənt] *n*: **term of ~** pieszczotliwe *or* czułe słowo *nt*; **to whisper ~s** szeptać czułe słowa

**endeavour**, (*US*) **endeavor** [ɪn'dɛvəʳ] *n* usiłowanie *nt*, próba *f* ▷ *vi*: **to ~ to do sth** usiłować coś zrobić, próbować (spróbować *perf*) coś zrobić; **an exciting new field of ~** nowa, pasjonująca dziedzina działań

**endemic** [ɛn'dɛmɪk] *adj* (*disease*) endemiczny; (*poverty*) powszechny

**ending** ['ɛndɪŋ] *n* (*of book, film*) zakończenie *nt*; (*Ling*) końcówka *f*

**endive** ['ɛndaɪv] *n* (*curly*) endywia *f*; (*smooth*) cykoria *f*

**endless** ['ɛndlɪs] *adj* (*argument, search*) nie kończący się; (*forest, beach*) bezkresny; (*patience, resources*) niewyczerpany; (*possibilities*) nieograniczony

**endorse** [ɪn'dɔːs] *vt* (*cheque*) podpisywać (podpisać *perf*) na odwrocie, indosować (indosować *perf*) (*fml*); (*proposal, candidate*) popierać (poprzeć *perf*), udzielać (udzielić *perf*) poparcia *+dat*

**endorsee** [ɪndɔː'siː] *n* indosatariusz *m*, indosat *m*

**endorsement** [ɪn'dɔːsmənt] *n* poparcie *nt*; (*Brit*: *on driving licence*) adnotacja *f* (*o wykroczeniu drogowym*)

**endow** [ɪn'dau] *vt* wspomagać (wspomóc *perf*) finansowo, dokonywać (dokonać *perf*) zapisu na rzecz *+gen*; **to be ~ed with** (*talent, ability*) być obdarzonym *+instr*

**endowment** [ɪn'daumənt] *n* (*money*) dar *m*, donacja *f*; (*of quality*) dar *m*

**endowment policy** *n* ubezpieczenie *nt* na życie z rentą kapitałową

**end product** *n* produkt *m* końcowy; (*fig*) rezultat *m* końcowy

**end result** *n* rezultat *m* (końcowy), wynik *m*

**endurable** [ɪn'djuərəbl] *adj* znośny

**endurance** [ɪn'djuərəns] *n* wytrzymałość *f*

**endurance test** *n* próba *f* wytrzymałości

**endure** [ɪn'djuəʳ] *vt* znosić (znieść *perf*) ▷ *vi* trwać (przetrwać *perf*)

**enduring** [ɪn'djuərɪŋ] *adj* trwały

**end user** (*Comput*) *n* użytkownik *m* (ostateczny)

**enema** ['ɛnɪmə] *n* lewatywa *f*

**enemy** ['ɛnəmɪ] *n* wróg *m*; (*Mil*) nieprzyjaciel *m* ▷ *cpd*: **~ forces/strategy** siły *pl*/strategia *f* nieprzyjaciela; **to make an ~ of sb** robić (zrobić *perf*) sobie z kogoś wroga

**energetic** [ɛnə'dʒɛtɪk] *adj* energiczny

**energy** ['ɛnədʒɪ] *n* energia *f*; **Department of E~** ≈ Departament Gospodarki Energetycznej i Paliwowej (*przy Ministerstwie Przemysłu*)

**energy crisis** *n* kryzys *m* energetyczny

**energy-saving** ['ɛnədʒɪ'seɪvɪŋ] *adj* energooszczędny

**enervating** ['ɛnəveɪtɪŋ] *adj* wyczerpujący

**enforce** [ɪn'fɔːs] *vt* (*Jur*: *impose*) wprowadzać (wprowadzić *perf*) w życie; (*compel observance of*) egzekwować

**enforced** [ɪn'fɔːst] *adj* przymusowy

**enfranchise** [ɪn'fræntʃaɪz] *vt* nadawać (nadać *perf*) prawo wyborcze *+dat*

**engage** [ɪn'geɪdʒ] *vt* (*attention*) zajmować (zająć *perf*); (*consultant, lawyer*) angażować (zaangażować *perf*); (*Aut*: *clutch*) włączać (włączyć *perf*); (*Mil*) nawiązywać (nawiązać *perf*) walkę z *+instr* ▷ *vi* (*Tech*) zaczepiać się (zaczepić się *perf*), sprzęgać się (sprząc się *perf*); **to ~ in** zajmować się (zająć się *perf*) *+instr*; **to ~ sb in conversation** zajmować (zająć *perf*) kogoś rozmową

**engaged** [ɪn'geɪdʒd] *adj* (*betrothed*) zaręczony; (*Brit*: *Tel*) zajęty; **to get ~ (to sb)** zaręczać się (zaręczyć się *perf*) (z kimś); **he is ~ in research** zajmuje się badaniami naukowymi

**engaged tone** (*Brit*: *Tel*) *n* sygnał *m* „zajęte"

**engagement** [ɪn'geɪdʒmənt] *n* (*appointment*) umówione spotkanie *nt*, zobowiązanie *nt* (towarzyskie); (*of actor*) angaż *m*; (*to marry*) zaręczyny *pl*; (*Mil*) potyczka *f*; **I have a previous ~** jestem już (z kimś) umówiony

**engagement ring** *n* pierścionek *m* zaręczynowy

**engaging** [ɪn'geɪdʒɪŋ] *adj* (*personality, trait*) ujmujący

**engender** [ɪn'dʒɛndəʳ] *vt* rodzić (zrodzić *perf*)

**engine** ['ɛndʒɪn] *n* (*Aut*) silnik *m*; (*Rail*) lokomotywa *f*

**engine driver** *n* maszynista(-tka) *m*(*f*)

**engineer** [ɛndʒɪ'nɪəʳ] *n* (*designer*) inżynier *m*; (*Brit*: *for repairs*) technik *m*; (*US*: *Rail*) maszynista *m*; (*on ship*) mechanik *m*; **civil ~** inżynier budownictwa; **mechanical ~** inżynier mechanik

**engineering** [ɛndʒɪ'nɪərɪŋ] *n* inżynieria *f*; (*of ships, machines*) budowa *f*; (*Scol*) nauki *pl* inżynieryjne ▷ *cpd*: **~ works** *or* **factory** zakład *m* produkcyjny; **mechanical ~** budowa maszyn

**engine failure** *n* awaria *f* silnika
**engine trouble** *n* = **engine failure**
**England** ['ɪŋglənd] *n* Anglia *f*
**English** ['ɪŋglɪʃ] *adj* angielski ▷ *n* (język *m*) angielski; **the English** *npl* Anglicy *vir pl*; **an ~ speaker** osoba mówiąca po angielsku
**English Channel** *n*: **the ~** kanał *m* La Manche
**Englishman** ['ɪŋglɪʃmən] (*irreg: like* **man**) *n* Anglik *m*
**English-speaking** ['ɪŋglɪʃspi:kɪŋ] *adj* anglojęzyczny
**Englishwoman** ['ɪŋglɪʃwumən] (*irreg: like* **woman**) *n* Angielka *f*
**engrave** [ɪn'greɪv] *vt* (*on jewellery*) grawerować (wygrawerować *perf*); (*for printing*) ryć (wyryć *perf*)
**engraving** [ɪn'greɪvɪŋ] *n* sztych *m*, rycina *f*
**engrossed** [ɪn'grəust] *adj*: **~ in** pochłonięty *+instr*
**engulf** [ɪn'gʌlf] *vt* (*fire, water*) pochłaniać (pochłonąć *perf*); (*panic, fear*) ogarniać (ogarnąć *perf*)
**enhance** [ɪn'hɑ:ns] *vt* (*value*) podnosić (podnieść *perf*); (*beauty*) uwydatniać (uwydatnić *perf*); (*reputation*) poprawiać (poprawić *perf*)
**enigma** [ɪ'nɪgmə] *n* zagadka *f*
**enigmatic** [ɛnɪg'mætɪk] *adj* enigmatyczny, zagadkowy
**enjoy** [ɪn'dʒɔɪ] *vt* (*like*): **I ~ dancing** lubię tańczyć; (*health, life*) cieszyć się *+instr*; **to ~ o.s.** dobrze się bawić; **I ~ed doing that** zrobiłam to z przyjemnością; **did you ~ the concert?** czy podobał ci się koncert?
**enjoyable** [ɪn'dʒɔɪəbl] *adj* przyjemny
**enjoyment** [ɪn'dʒɔɪmənt] *n* przyjemność *f*
**enlarge** [ɪn'lɑ:dʒ] *vt* powiększać (powiększyć *perf*) ▷ *vi*: **to ~ on** rozwodzić się nad *+instr*
**enlarged** [ɪn'lɑ:dʒd] *adj* (*edition*) rozszerzony; (*Med: organ, gland*) powiększony
**enlargement** [ɪn'lɑ:dʒmənt] *n* powiększenie *nt*
**enlighten** [ɪn'laɪtn] *vt* oświecać (oświecić *perf*)
**enlightened** [ɪn'laɪtnd] *adj* oświecony
**enlightening** [ɪn'laɪtnɪŋ] *adj* pouczający
**enlightenment** [ɪn'laɪtnmənt] *n*: **the E~** oświecenie *nt*, Oświecenie *nt*
**enlist** [ɪn'lɪst] *vt* (*soldier*) werbować (zwerbować *perf*); (*support, help*) pozyskiwać (pozyskać *perf*); (*person*) zjednywać (zjednać *perf*) sobie ▷ *vi*: **to ~ in** zaciągać się (zaciągnąć się *perf*) do *+gen*; **~ed man** (*US*) żołnierz
**enliven** [ɪn'laɪvn] *vt* ożywiać (ożywić *perf*)
**enmity** ['ɛnmɪtɪ] *n* wrogość *f*
**ennoble** [ɪ'nəubl] *vt* nadawać (nadać *perf*) tytuł szlachecki *+dat*; (*fig*) nobilitować (nobilitować *perf*)
**enormity** [ɪ'nɔ:mɪtɪ] *n* ogrom *m*
**enormous** [ɪ'nɔ:məs] *adj* ogromny
**enormously** [ɪ'nɔ:məslɪ] *adv* (*increase*) ogromnie; (*rich*) niezmiernie
**enough** [ɪ'nʌf] *adj* dosyć *or* dość (*+gen*) ▷ *pron* dosyć, dość ▷ *adv*: **big ~** dość *or* dostatecznie *or* wystarczająco duży; **he has not worked ~** nie pracował tyle, ile powinien; **have you had ~ to eat?** najadłeś się?; **will 5 be ~?** czy 5 wystarczy?; **I've had ~!** mam (tego) dosyć!; **he was kind ~ to lend me the money** był tak miły, że pożyczył mi pieniądze; **~!** dość (tego)!; **that's ~, thanks** dziękuję, wystarczy; **I've had ~ of him** mam go dosyć; **oddly/funnily ~, ...** dziwnym trafem, ...
**enquire** [ɪn'kwaɪə^r] *vt, vi* = **inquire**
**enrage** [ɪn'reɪdʒ] *vt* rozwścieczać (rozwścieczyć *perf*)
**enrich** [ɪn'rɪtʃ] *vt* wzbogacać (wzbogacić *perf*)
**enrol**, (*US*) **enroll** [ɪn'rəul] *vt*: **to ~ sb (at a school/on a course)** zapisywać (zapisać *perf*) kogoś (do szkoły/na kurs) ▷ *vi*: **to ~ (at a school/on a course)** zapisywać się (zapisać się *perf*) (do szkoły/na kurs)
**enrolment** [ɪn'rəulmənt], (*US*) **enrollment** *n* zapisanie (się) *nt*
**en route** [ɔn'ru:t] *adv* po drodze; **~ for** *or* **to/from** w drodze do *+gen*/z *+gen*
**ensconced** [ɪn'skɔnst] *adj*: **~ in** (*armchair etc*) usadowiony w *+loc*; (*town etc*) zadomowiony w *+loc*
**ensemble** [ɔn'sɔmbl] *n* (*Mus*) zespół *m*, grupa *f*; (*clothing*) strój *m*
**enshrine** [ɪn'ʃraɪn] *vt* chronić; **the universities' autonomy is ~d in their charters** autonomia uniwersytetów (za) gwarantowana jest w ich statutach
**ensue** [ɪn'sju:] *vi* następować (nastąpić *perf*), wywiązywać się (wywiązać się *perf*)
**ensuing** [ɪn'sju:ɪŋ] *adj* (*months*) następny; **in the ~ fight** w walce, która się (potem) wywiązała
**en suite** [ɔn'swi:t] *adj*: **room with ~ bathroom** pokój *m* z łazienką
**ensure** [ɪn'ʃuə^r] *vt* zapewniać (zapewnić *perf*)
**ENT** (*Med*) *n abbr* (= *Ear, Nose and Throat*) specjalista *m* z zakresu chorób uszu, nosa, gardła i krtani
**entail** [ɪn'teɪl] *vt* pociągać (pociągnąć *perf*) za sobą
**entangled** [ɪn'tæŋgld] *adj*: **to become ~ (in)** zaplątywać się (zaplątać się *perf*) (w *+acc*)
**enter** ['ɛntə^r] *vt* (*room, building*) wchodzić (wejść *perf*) do *+gen*; (*club, army*) wstępować (wstąpić *perf*) do *+gen*; (*university*) wstępować (wstąpić *perf*) na *+acc*; (*race, contest*) brać (wziąć *perf*) udział w *+loc*; (*person: for competition*) zgłaszać (zgłosić *perf*); (*write down*)

e

zapisywać (zapisać *perf*); (*Comput*) wprowadzać (wprowadzić *perf*) ▷ *vi* wchodzić (wejść *perf*)
▸ **enter for** *vt fus* zapisywać się (zapisać się *perf*) na *+acc*
▸ **enter into** *vt fus* (*discussion*) wdawać się (wdać się *perf*) w *+acc*; (*correspondence*) nawiązywać (nawiązać *perf*) *+acc*; (*agreement*) zawierać (zawrzeć *perf*) *+acc*
▸ **enter (up)on** *vt fus* zapoczątkowywać (zapoczątkować *perf*) *+acc*

**enteritis** [ɛntəˈraɪtɪs] *n* zapalenie *nt* jelit(a)

**enterprise** [ˈɛntəpraɪz] *n* (*company*) przedsiębiorstwo *nt*; (*venture*) przedsięwzięcie *nt*; (*initiative*) przedsiębiorczość *f*; **free ~** wolna konkurencja (rynkowa); **private ~** sektor prywatny

**enterprising** [ˈɛntəpraɪzɪŋ] *adj* (*person*) przedsiębiorczy, rzutki; (*scheme*) pomysłowy

**entertain** [ɛntəˈteɪn] *vt* (*amuse*) zabawiać (zabawić *perf*); (*play host to*) przyjmować (przyjąć *perf*); (*consider*) brać (wziąć *perf*) pod uwagę

**entertainer** [ɛntəˈteɪnəʳ] *n* artysta(-tka) *m(f)* estradowy(-wa) *m(f)*

**entertaining** [ɛntəˈteɪnɪŋ] *adj* zabawny ▷ *n*: **to do a lot of ~** często przyjmować gości

**entertainment** [ɛntəˈteɪnmənt] *n* (*amusement*) rozrywka *f*; (*show*) widowisko *nt*

**entertainment allowance** *n* fundusz *m* reprezentacyjny

**enthralled** [ɪnˈθrɔːld] *adj* zafascynowany

**enthralling** [ɪnˈθrɔːlɪŋ] *adj* fascynujący

**enthuse** [ɪnˈθuːz] *vi*: **to ~ about** *or* **over** zachwycać się *+instr*

**enthusiasm** [ɪnˈθuːzɪæzəm] *n* entuzjazm *m*

**enthusiast** [ɪnˈθuːzɪæst] *n* entuzjasta(-tka) *m(f)*; **a jazz ~** entuzjasta(-tka) *m(f)* jazzu

**enthusiastic** [ɪnθuːzɪˈæstɪk] *adj* (*person, response*) pełen entuzjazmu; (*reception*) entuzjastyczny; (*crowds*) rozentuzjazmowany; **to be ~ about** entuzjazmować się *+instr*

**entice** [ɪnˈtaɪs] *vt* wabić (zwabić *perf*)

**enticing** [ɪnˈtaɪsɪŋ] *adj* (*person*) ponętny; (*offer*) kuszący

**entire** [ɪnˈtaɪəʳ] *adj* cały

**entirely** [ɪnˈtaɪəlɪ] *adv* (*exclusively*) wyłącznie; (*completely*) całkowicie

**entirety** [ɪnˈtaɪərətɪ] *n*: **in its ~** w całości

**entitle** [ɪnˈtaɪtl] *vt*: **to be ~d to do sth** mieć prawo coś (z)robić; **to ~ sb to sth/to do sth** uprawniać kogoś do czegoś/do (z)robienia czegoś

**entitled** [ɪnˈtaɪtld] *adj* zatytułowany, pod tytułem

**entity** [ˈɛntɪtɪ] *n* jednostka *f*

**entourage** [ɔntuˈrɑːʒ] *n* świta *f*

**entrails** [ˈɛntreɪlz] *npl* wnętrzności *pl*

**entrance** [*n* ˈɛntrns, *vb* ɪnˈtrɑːns] *n* wejście *nt* ▷ *vt* oczarowywać (oczarować *perf*); **to gain ~ to** (*university*) dostawać się (dostać się *perf*) na *+acc*; (*profession*) uzyskiwać (uzyskać *perf*) wstęp do *+gen*

**entrance examination** *n* egzamin *m* wstępny

**entrance fee** *n* (*to museum etc*) opłata *f* za wstęp; (*to organization*) wpisowe *nt*

**entrance ramp** (*US*) *n* wjazd *m* (na autostradę)

**entrancing** [ɪnˈtrɑːnsɪŋ] *adj* czarujący

**entrant** [ˈɛntrnt] *n* uczestnik(-iczka) *m(f)*

**entreat** [ɛnˈtriːt] *vt*: **to ~ sb to do sth** błagać kogoś, żeby coś zrobił

**entreaty** [ɛnˈtriːtɪ] *n* błaganie *nt*, usilna prośba *f*

**entrée** [ˈɔntreɪ] (*Culin*) *n* danie *nt* główne

**entrenched** [ɛnˈtrɛntʃt] *adj* (*ideas*) zakorzeniony; (*power*) utrwalony

**entrepreneur** [ˈɔntrəprəˈnəːʳ] *n* przedsiębiorca *m*

**entrepreneurial** [ˈɔntrəprəˈnəːrɪəl] *adj* (*capitalism*) inwestycyjny; **the ~ spirit** duch przedsiębiorczości

**entrust** [ɪnˈtrʌst] *vt*: **to ~ sth to sb, sb with sth** powierzać (powierzyć *perf*) coś komuś

**entry** [ˈɛntrɪ] *n* (*way in, arrival*) wejście *nt*; (*in competition: story, drawing*) praca *f* (konkursowa); (*: taking part*) udział *m*; (*in register, account book*) pozycja *f*, zapis *m*; (*in reference book*) hasło *nt*; (*to country*) wjazd *m*; **"no ~"** „zakaz wstępu"; (*Aut*) „zakaz wjazdu"; **single/double ~ book-keeping** księgowanie pojedyncze/podwójne

**entry form** *n* kwestionariusz *m*

**entry phone** (*Brit*) *n* domofon *m*

**entwine** [ɪnˈtwaɪn] *vt* splatać (spleść *perf*)

**E-number** [iːˈnʌmbəʳ] *n poprzedzona literą „E" liczba identyfikująca substancje dodawane w Europie do artykułów żywnościowych*

**enumerate** [ɪˈnjuːməreɪt] *vt* wyliczać (wyliczyć *perf*)

**enunciate** [ɪˈnʌnsɪeɪt] *vt* (*word*) (starannie) wymawiać (wymówić *perf*); (*principle, plan*) ogłaszać (ogłosić *perf*)

**envelop** [ɪnˈvɛləp] *vt* okrywać (okryć *perf*)

**envelope** [ˈɛnvələup] *n* koperta *f*

**enviable** [ˈɛnvɪəbl] *adj* godny pozazdroszczenia

**envious** [ˈɛnvɪəs] *adj* zazdrosny; **to be ~ of sth/sb** być zazdrosnym o coś/kogoś

**environment** [ɪnˈvaɪərnmənt] *n* (*surroundings*) środowisko *nt*, otoczenie *nt*; **the ~** środowisko

(naturalne); **Department of the E~** (*Brit*) ≈ Ministerstwo Ochrony Środowiska
**environmental** [ɪnvaɪərn'mɛntl] *adj* (*studies*) środowiskowy; **~ conditions** warunki otoczenia; **~ contamination** skażenie środowiska
**environmentalist** [ɪnvaɪərn'mɛntlɪst] *n* działacz(ka) *m(f)* na rzecz ochrony środowiska, ekolog *m*
**environmentally** [ɪnvaɪərn'mɛntlɪ] *adv*: **~ sound/friendly** ekologiczny
**Environmental Protection Agency** (*US*) *n* Agencja *f* Ochrony Środowiska
**envisage** [ɪn'vɪzɪdʒ] *vt* przewidywać (przewidzieć *perf*)
**envision** [ɪn'vɪʒən] (*US*) *vt* = **envisage**
**envoy** ['ɛnvɔɪ] *n* wysłannik(-iczka) *m(f)*
**envy** ['ɛnvɪ] *n* zawiść *f*, zazdrość *f* ▷ *vt*: **to ~ sb (sth)** zazdrościć komuś (czegoś)
**enzyme** ['ɛnzaɪm] *n* enzym *m*
**EPA** (*US*) *n abbr* (= *Environmental Protection Agency*) *agencja rządowa sprawująca kontrolę nad ochroną środowiska*
**ephemeral** [ɪ'fɛmərl] *adj* ulotny, efemeryczny
**epic** ['ɛpɪk] *n* epos *m*, epopeja *f* ▷ *adj* (*great*) imponujący
**epicentre**, (*US*) **epicenter** ['ɛpɪsɛntəʳ] *n* epicentrum *nt*
**epidemic** [ɛpɪ'dɛmɪk] *n* epidemia *f*
**epigram** ['ɛpɪgræm] *n* epigram(at) *m*
**epilepsy** ['ɛpɪlɛpsɪ] *n* padaczka *f*, epilepsja *f*
**epileptic** [ɛpɪ'lɛptɪk] *adj* epileptyczny ▷ *n* epileptyk(-yczka) *m(f)*
**epilogue** ['ɛpɪlɔg] *n* epilog *m*
**Epiphany** [ɪ'pɪfənɪ] *n* Objawienie *nt* Pańskie, święto *nt* Trzech Króli
**episcopal** [ɪ'pɪskəpl] *adj* biskupi; **the E~ Church** Kościół Episkopalny
**episode** ['ɛpɪsəud] *n* (*period, event*) epizod *m*; (*TV, Radio*) odcinek *m*
**epistle** [ɪ'pɪsl] *n* list *m*; (*long, boring*) epistoła *f*
**epitaph** ['ɛpɪtɑːf] *n* epitafium *nt*
**epithet** ['ɛpɪθɛt] *n* epitet *m*
**epitome** [ɪ'pɪtəmɪ] *n* (*person*) uosobienie *nt*; (*thing*) typowy przykład *m*
**epitomize** [ɪ'pɪtəmaɪz] *vt* (*person*) uosabiać; (*thing, quality*) zawierać w sobie
**epoch** ['iːpɔk] *n* epoka *f*
**epoch-making** ['iːpɔkmeɪkɪŋ] *adj* epokowy
**eponymous** [ɪ'pɔnɪməs] *adj*: **~ hero** tytułowy bohater *m*
**equable** ['ɛkwəbl] *adj* (*climate*) łagodny; (*temperatures*) wyrównany; (*temper*) zrównoważony
**equal** ['iːkwl] *adj* równy; (*intensity, quality*) jednakowy ▷ *n* równy *m* ▷ *vt* (*number, amount*) równać się; (*match, rival*) dorównywać (dorównać *perf*) +*dat*; **they are roughly ~ in size** są mniej więcej równej wielkości; **the number of exports should be ~ to imports** eksport powinien równać się importowi; **to be ~ to the task** stawać (stanąć *perf*) na wysokości zadania
**equality** [iː'kwɔlɪtɪ] *n* równość *f*; **~ of opportunity** równouprawnienie
**equalize** ['iːkwəlaɪz] *vi* (*Sport*) wyrównywać (wyrównać *perf*) ▷ *vt* (*wealth, opportunities*) zrównywać (zrównać *perf*); (*society*) znosić (znieść *perf*) różnice w +*loc*
**equally** ['iːkwəlɪ] *adv* (*share, divide*) równo; (*good, bad*) równie; **they are ~ clever** są tak samo *or* jednakowo inteligentni
**Equal Opportunities Commission**, (*US*) **Equal Employment Opportunity Commission** *n komisja do spraw równouprawnienia zawodowego*
**equals sign** *n* znak *m* równości
**equanimity** [ɛkwə'nɪmɪtɪ] *n* opanowanie *nt*, spokój *m*
**equate** [ɪ'kweɪt] *vt*: **to ~ sth with** identyfikować coś z +*instr*; **to ~ A to B** przyrównywać (przyrównać *perf*) A do B
**equation** [ɪ'kweɪʃən] *n* równanie *nt*
**equator** [ɪ'kweɪtəʳ] *n*: **the ~** równik *m*
**equatorial** [ɛkwə'tɔːrɪəl] *adj* równikowy
**Equatorial Guinea** *n* Gwinea *f* Równikowa
**equestrian** [ɪ'kwɛstrɪən] *adj* (*competition*) hipiczny; (*club*) jeździecki; (*outfit*) do jazdy konnej *post* ▷ *n* jeździec *m*
**equilibrium** [iːkwɪ'lɪbrɪəm] *n* równowaga *f*
**equinox** ['iːkwɪnɔks] *n* równonoc *f*; **the spring/autumn ~** równonoc wiosenna/jesienna
**equip** [ɪ'kwɪp] *vt*: **to ~ (with)** wyposażać (wyposażyć *perf*) (w +*acc*); **they were well ~ped for the negotiations** byli dobrze przygotowani do negocjacji
**equipment** [ɪ'kwɪpmənt] *n* wyposażenie *nt*, sprzęt *m*
**equitable** ['ɛkwɪtəbl] *adj* sprawiedliwy
**equities** ['ɛkwɪtɪz] (*Brit*) *npl* akcje *pl* zwykłe *or* nieuprzywilejowane
**equity** ['ɛkwɪtɪ] *n* sprawiedliwość *f*
**equity capital** *n* kapitał *m* własny
**equivalent** [ɪ'kwɪvələnt] *adj*: **~ (to)** równoważny (+*dat*); (*in meaning*) równoznaczny (z +*instr*) ▷ *n* (*counterpart*) odpowiednik *m*; (*sth of equal value*) równoważnik *m*, ekwiwalent *m*
**equivocal** [ɪ'kwɪvəkl] *adj* dwuznaczny, niejednoznaczny
**equivocate** [ɪ'kwɪvəkeɪt] *vi* wyrażać się dwuznacznie
**equivocation** [ɪkwɪvə'keɪʃən] *n* dwuznaczność *f*

**ER** (*Brit*) *abbr* (= *Elizabeth Regina*) Królowa *f* Elżbieta
**ERA** (*US*) *n abbr* (*Pol:* = *Equal Rights Amendment*) *poprawka do konstytucji amerykańskiej gwarantująca równouprawnienie kobiet*
**era** ['ɪərə] *n* era *f*; **the post-war era** okres powojenny
**eradicate** [ɪ'rædɪkeɪt] *vt* (*prejudice, bad habits*) wykorzeniać (wykorzenić *perf*); (*problems*) eliminować (wyeliminować *perf*)
**erase** [ɪ'reɪz] *vt* (*lit, fig*) wymazywać (wymazać *perf*); (*recording*) kasować (skasować *perf*)
**eraser** [ɪ'reɪzə^r] *n* gumka *f*
**erect** [ɪ'rɛkt] *adj* (*posture*) wyprostowany, prosty; (*tail, ears*) podniesiony ▷ *vt* (*build*) wznosić (wznieść *perf*); (*assemble*) montować (zmontować *perf*)
**erection** [ɪ'rɛkʃən] *n* (*of monument*) wzniesienie *nt*; (*of tent*) postawienie *nt*; (*of machine*) montaż *m*; (*Physiol*) wzwód *m*, erekcja *f*
**ergonomics** [ə:gə'nɔmɪks] *n* ergonomia *f*
**ERISA** (*US*) *n abbr* = **Employee Retirement Income Security Act**
**ERM** *n abbr* (= *Exchange Rate Mechanism*) *dopuszczalne odchylenia kursu centralnego walut krajów należących do Europejskiego Systemu Walutowego*
**ermine** ['ə:mɪn] *n* gronostaje *pl*
**ERNIE** ['ə:nɪ] (*Brit*) *n abbr* (= *Electronic Random Number Indicator Equipment*) *urządzenie do elektronicznego wybierania numerów wygrywających bonów*
**erode** [ɪ'rəud] *vt* powodować (spowodować *perf*) erozję *+gen*; (*fig: freedom*) ograniczać (ograniczyć *perf*); (*: authority*) podrywać (poderwać *perf*); (*: confidence*) podkopywać (podkopać *perf*)
**erosion** [ɪ'rəuʒən] *n* erozja *f*; (*fig: of freedom*) ograniczenie *nt*
**erotic** [ɪ'rɔtɪk] *adj* erotyczny
**eroticism** [ɪ'rɔtɪsɪzəm] *n* (*of book, picture*) erotyka *f*; (*of person*) erotyzm *m*
**err** [ə:^r] (*fml*) *vi* błądzić (zbłądzić *perf*); **to err on the side of caution** grzeszyć nadmiarem ostrożności
**errand** ['ɛrənd] *n* polecenie *nt*; **to run ~s** załatwiać sprawy; **an ~ of mercy** misja dobroci
**erratic** [ɪ'rætɪk] *adj* (*behaviour, attempts*) niekonsekwentny; (*noise*) nieregularny
**erroneous** [ɪ'rəunɪəs] *adj* błędny, mylny
**error** ['ɛrə^r] *n* błąd *m*; **spelling ~** błąd ortograficzny; **typing ~** błąd maszynowy; **in ~** przez pomyłkę; **~s and omissions excepted** z zastrzeżeniem omyłki (*na rachunkach*)
**error message** (*Comput*) *n* komunikat *m* błędu
**erstwhile** ['ə:stwaɪl] *adj* były, niegdysiejszy (*old*)
**erudite** ['ɛrjudaɪt] *adj* uczony
**erupt** [ɪ'rʌpt] *vi* wybuchać (wybuchnąć *perf*)
**eruption** [ɪ'rʌpʃən] *n* (*of volcano*) erupcja *f*, wybuch *m*; (*of fighting*) wybuch *m*
**ESA** *n abbr* (= *European Space Agency*) ESA *f inv*, Europejska Agencja *f* Przestrzeni Kosmicznej
**escalate** ['ɛskəleɪt] *vi* nasilać się (nasilić się *perf*)
**escalation** [ɛskə'leɪʃən] *n* nasilanie się *nt*, eskalacja *f*
**escalation clause** (*Comm*) *n* klauzula *f* o warunkach zmiany cen; (*in employment contract*) klauzula *f* regulująca warunki indeksacji płac
**escalator** ['ɛskəleɪtə^r] *n* schody *pl* ruchome
**escapade** [ɛskə'peɪd] *n* eskapada *f*
**escape** [ɪs'keɪp] *n* ucieczka *f*; (*of liquid*) wyciek *m*; (*of gas*) ulatnianie się *nt* ▷ *vi* (*person*) uciekać (uciec *perf*); (*liquid*) wyciekać (wyciec *perf*); (*gas*) uchodzić, ulatniać się ▷ *vt* (*consequences, responsibility*) unikać (uniknąć *perf*) *+gen*; **his name ~s me** nie mogę sobie przypomnieć jego nazwiska; **to ~ from** (*place*) uciekać (uciec *perf*) z *+gen*; (*person*) uciekać (uciec *perf*) od *+gen*; **to ~ to safety** chronić się (schronić się *perf*) w bezpieczne miejsce; **to ~ notice** umykać (umknąć *perf*) uwadze
**escape artist** *n magik uwalniający się z więzów lub zamknięcia*
**escape clause** *n* (*Comm*) klauzula *f* uprawniająca do uwolnienia od zobowiązania
**escape hatch** *n* luk *m* ratunkowy
**escape key** (*Comput*) *n* klawisz *m* „escape"
**escape route** *n* (*from fire*) droga *f* ewakuacyjna; (*of prisoners*) droga *f* ucieczki
**escapism** [ɪs'keɪpɪzəm] *n* eskapizm *m*
**escapist** [ɪs'keɪpɪst] *adj* eskapistyczny
**escapologist** [ɛskə'pɔlədʒɪst] (*Brit*) *n* = **escape artist**
**escarpment** [ɪs'kɑ:pmənt] *n* skarpa *f*
**eschew** [ɪs'tʃu:] *vt* wystrzegać się *+gen*
**escort** [*n* 'ɛskɔ:t, *vb* ɪs'kɔ:t] *n* (*companion*) osoba *f* towarzysząca; (*Mil, Police*) eskorta *f* ▷ *vt* towarzyszyć *+dat*; (*Mil, Police*) eskortować (odeskortować *perf*)
**escort agency** *n* agencja *f* towarzyska
**Eskimo** ['ɛskɪməu] *n* Eskimos(ka) *m(f)*
**ESL** (*Scol*) *n abbr* = **English as a Second Language**
**esophagus** [i:'sɔfəgəs] (*US*) *n* = **oesophagus**
**esoteric** [ɛsə'tɛrɪk] *adj* ezoteryczny
**ESP** *n abbr* = **extrasensory perception**; (*Scol*) = **English for Special Purposes**
**esp.** *abbr* (= *especially*) szczeg.

**especially** [ɪs'pɛʃlɪ] *adv* (*above all, particularly*) szczególnie, zwłaszcza; (*more than normally*) szczególnie
**espionage** ['ɛspɪənɑːʒ] *n* szpiegostwo *nt*
**esplanade** [ɛsplə'neɪd] *n* promenada *f*, esplanada *f*
**espouse** [ɪs'pauz] *vt* opowiadać się za *+instr*
**espresso** [ɪ'sprɛsəu] *n* kawa z ekspresu *f*
**Esquire** [ɪs'kwaɪə[r]] *n*: **J. Brown, ~** *or* **Esq.** Wielmożny Pan *or* W.P. J. Brown
**essay** ['ɛseɪ] *n* (*Scol*) wypracowanie *nt*; (*Literature*) esej *m*
**essence** ['ɛsns] *n* (*soul, spirit*) istota *f*; (*Culin*) esencja *f*, olejek *m*; **in ~** w gruncie rzeczy; **speed is of the ~** konieczny jest pośpiech
**essential** [ɪ'sɛnʃl] *adj* (*necessary, vital*) niezbędny; (*basic*) istotny, zasadniczy ▷ *n* rzecz *f* niezbędna; **it is ~ that ...** jest niezmiernie ważne, żeby ...; **the ~s of English grammar** najważniejsze zasady gramatyki angielskiej
**essentially** [ɪ'sɛnʃəlɪ] *adv* (*broadly, basically*) zasadniczo; (*really*) w gruncie rzeczy
**EST** (*US*) *abbr* = **Eastern Standard Time**
**est.** *abbr* (= *established*) zał.; (= *estimate*) ocena; (= *estimated*) szacunkowy
**establish** [ɪs'tæblɪʃ] *vt* (*organization, firm*) zakładać (założyć *perf*); (*facts, cause*) ustalać (ustalić *perf*); (*relations, contact*) nawiązywać (nawiązać *perf*); **to ~ one's reputation as** wyrabiać (wyrobić *perf*) sobie reputację *+gen*
**established** [ɪs'tæblɪʃt] *adj* (*business*) o ustalonej reputacji *post*; (*custom, practice*) ustalony, przyjęty
**establishment** [ɪs'tæblɪʃmənt] *n* (*of organization, firm*) założenie *nt*; (*shop etc*) placówka *f*; **the E~** establishment
**estate** [ɪs'teɪt] *n* (*land*) posiadłość *f*, majątek *m* (ziemski); (*Brit*: *also*: **housing estate**) osiedle *nt* (mieszkaniowe); (*Jur*) majątek *m*
**estate agency** (*Brit*) *n* biuro *nt* pośrednictwa handlu nieruchomościami
**estate agent** (*Brit*) *n* pośrednik(-iczka) *m(f)* w handlu nieruchomościami
**estate car** (*Brit*) *n* samochód *m* kombi, kombi *nt inv*
**esteem** [ɪs'tiːm] *n*: **to hold sb in high ~** darzyć kogoś wielkim szacunkiem
**esthetic** [ɪs'θɛtɪk] (*US*) *adj* = **aesthetic**
**estimate** [*n* 'ɛstɪmət, *vb* 'ɛstɪmeɪt] *n* (*calculation*) szacunkowe *or* przybliżone obliczenie *nt*, szacunek *m*; (*assessment*) ocena *f*; (*of builder etc*) kosztorys *m* ▷ *vt* szacować (oszacować *perf*); **to give sb an ~ of** przedstawiać (przedstawić *perf*) komuś kosztorys *+gen*; **at a rough ~** w przybliżeniu; **I ~ that ...** według moich szacunków, ...
**estimation** [ɛstɪ'meɪʃən] *n* (*of person, situation*) opinia *f*; (*of amount, value*) szacunkowe obliczenie *nt*; **in my ~** w moim odczuciu
**Estonia** [ɛs'təunɪə] *n* Estonia *f*
**estranged** [ɪs'treɪndʒd] *adj*: **to be ~ from** (*spouse*) pozostawać w separacji z *+instr*; (*family*) nie mieszkać z *+instr*; **~ couple** para pozostająca w separacji
**estrangement** [ɪs'treɪndʒmənt] *n* separacja *f*
**estrogen** ['iːstrəudʒən] (*US*) *n* = **oestrogen**
**estuary** ['ɛstjuərɪ] *n* ujście *nt* (rzeki)
**ET** *n abbr* (*Brit*: = *Employment Training*) szkolenie *nt* zawodowe ▷ *abbr* (*US*) = **Eastern Time**
**ETA** *n abbr* (= *estimated time of arrival*) przewidywany czas *m* przylotu
**et al.** *abbr* (= *et alii*) i in.
**etc.** *abbr* (= *et cetera*) itd.
**etch** [ɛtʃ] *vi* robić (zrobić *perf*) kwasoryt ▷ *vt*: **to ~ (on)** ryć (w *+loc*)
**etching** ['ɛtʃɪŋ] *n* kwasoryt *m*
**ETD** *n abbr* (= *estimated time of departure*) przewidywany czas *m* odlotu
**eternal** [ɪ'təːnl] *adj* (*everlasting*) wieczny; (*unchanging*) niezmienny
**eternity** [ɪ'təːnɪtɪ] *n* wieczność *f*
**ether** ['iːθə[r]] (*Chem*) *n* eter *m*
**ethereal** [ɪ'θɪərɪəl] *adj* eteryczny
**ethical** ['ɛθɪkl] *adj* etyczny
**ethics** ['ɛθɪks] *n* etyka *f* (*nauka*) ▷ *npl* etyka *f* (*moralność*)
**Ethiopia** [iːθɪ'əupɪə] *n* Etiopia *f*
**Ethiopian** [iːθɪ'əupɪən] *adj* etiopski ▷ *n* Etiopczyk(-pka) *m(f)*
**ethnic** ['ɛθnɪk] *adj* etniczny
**ethnology** [ɛθ'nɔlədʒɪ] *n* etnologia *f*, etnografia *f*
**ethos** ['iːθɔs] *n* etos *m*
**etiquette** ['ɛtɪkɛt] *n* etykieta *f*
**ETV** (*US*) *n abbr* = **Educational Television**
**etymology** [ɛtɪ'mɔlədʒɪ] *n* etymologia *f*
**EU** *n abbr* (= *European Union*) UE
**eucalyptus** [juːkə'lɪptəs] *n* eukaliptus *m*
**Eucharist** ['juːkərɪst] *n*: **the ~** Eucharystia *f*
**eulogy** ['juːlədʒɪ] *n* (*written*) panegiryk *m*; (*spoken*) mowa *f* pochwalna
**euphemism** ['juːfəmɪzəm] *n* eufemizm *m*
**euphemistic** [juːfə'mɪstɪk] *adj* eufemistyczny
**euphoria** [juː'fɔːrɪə] *n* euforia *f*
**Eurasia** [juə'reɪʃə] *n* Eurazja *f*
**Eurasian** [juə'reɪʃən] *adj* eurazjatycki ▷ *n* Eurazjata(-tka) *m(f)*
**Euratom** [juə'rætəm] *n abbr* (= *European Atomic Energy Community*) Euratom *m*, Europejska Wspólnota *f* Energii Atomowej
**Euro** ['juərəu] *n* euro *nt inv*
**Eurocheque** ['juərəutʃɛk] *n* euroczek *m*
**Eurocrat** ['juərəukræt] *n* eurokrata(-tka) *m(f)*

**Eurodollar** ['juərəudɔləʳ] *n* eurodolar *m*
**Europe** ['juərəp] *n* Europa *f*
**European** [juərə'pi:ən] *adj* europejski ▷ *n* Europejczyk(-jka) *m(f)*
**European Community** *n*: **the ~** Wspólnota *f* Europejska
**European Court of Justice** *n*: **the ~** Europejski Trybunał *m* Sprawiedliwości
**European Economic Community** *n*: **the ~** Europejska Wspólnota *f* Gospodarcza
**European Union** *n* Unia *f* Europejska
**euthanasia** [ju:θə'neɪzɪə] *n* eutanazja *f*
**evacuate** [ɪ'vækjueɪt] *vt* ewakuować (ewakuować *perf*)
**evacuation** [ɪvækju'eɪʃən] *n* ewakuacja *f*
**evade** [ɪ'veɪd] *vt* (*tax, duty, responsibility*) uchylać się (uchylić się *perf*) od *+gen*; (*question*) uchylać się (uchylić się *perf*) od odpowiedzi na *+acc*; (*person: avoid meeting*) unikać (uniknąć *perf*) *+gen*; (*: escape from*) umykać (umknąć *perf*) *or* wymykać się (wymknąć się *perf*) *+dat*
**evaluate** [ɪ'væljueɪt] *vt* oceniać (ocenić *perf*)
**evangelical** [i:væn'dʒɛlɪkl] *adj* ewangelicki
**evangelist** [ɪ'vændʒəlɪst] *n* (wędrowny) kaznodzieja *m* (*głoszący ewangelię na wielkich zgromadzeniach*)
**evangelize** [ɪ'vændʒəlaɪz] *vi* głosić ewangelię
**evaporate** [ɪ'væpəreɪt] *vi* wyparowywać (wyparować *perf*); (*fig*) ulatniać się (ulotnić się *perf*)
**evaporated milk** [ɪ'væpəreɪtɪd-] *n* mleko *nt* skondensowane
**evaporation** [ɪvæpə'reɪʃən] *n* parowanie *nt*
**evasion** [ɪ'veɪʒən] *n* (*of responsibility, tax etc*) uchylanie się *nt*
**evasive** [ɪ'veɪsɪv] *adj* (*reply*) wymijający; **to take ~ action** stosować (zastosować *perf*) unik
**eve** [i:v] *n*: **on the eve of** w przeddzień *or* przededniu *+gen*; **Christmas Eve** Wigilia; **New Year's Eve** sylwester
**even** ['i:vn] *adj* (*level, equal*) równy; (*smooth*) gładki; (*distribution, breathing*) równomierny; (*number*) parzysty ▷ *adv* (*showing surprise*) nawet; (*introducing a comparison*) jeszcze; **~ if** nawet jeśli; **~ though** (po)mimo że, chociaż; **there were ~ more people yesterday** wczoraj było jeszcze więcej ludzi; **he loved her ~ more** kochał ją jeszcze bardziej; **the work is going ~ faster now** praca idzie teraz jeszcze szybciej; **~ so** mimo to; **not ~** nawet nie; **~ he was there** nawet on tam był; **~ on Sundays** nawet w niedzielę; **to break ~** wychodzić (wyjść *perf*) na czysto *or* na zero; **I'll get ~ with you!** jeszcze ci się odpłacę *or* odwdzięczę!
▸ **even out** *vi* wyrównywać się (wyrównać się *perf*)
**evening** ['i:vnɪŋ] *n* wieczór *m*; **in the ~** wieczorem; **this ~** dziś wieczorem *or* wieczór; **tomorrow/yesterday ~** jutro/wczoraj wieczorem
**evening class** *n* kurs *m* wieczorowy
**evening dress** *n* (*no pl: formal clothes*) strój *m* wieczorowy; (*woman's gown*) suknia *f* wieczorowa
**evenly** ['i:vnlɪ] *adv* (*distribute, space, spread*) równomiernie, równo; (*divide*) równo; (*breathe*) równomiernie
**evensong** ['i:vnsɔŋ] *n* wieczorne nabożeństwo *nt* (*w kościele anglikańskim*)
**event** [ɪ'vɛnt] *n* (*occurrence*) wydarzenie *nt*; (*Sport*) konkurencja *f*; **in the normal course of ~s** w normalnych okolicznościach; **in the ~ of** w przypadku *or* razie *+gen*; **in the ~** ostatecznie; **at all ~s** (*Brit*), **in any ~** w każdym razie
**eventful** [ɪ'vɛntful] *adj* obfitujący *or* bogaty w wydarzenia *post*
**eventing** [ɪ'vɛntɪŋ] *n* udział *m* w konkursie hipicznym
**eventual** [ɪ'vɛntʃuəl] *adj* ostateczny, końcowy
**eventuality** [ɪvɛntʃu'ælɪtɪ] *n* ewentualność *f*
**eventually** [ɪ'vɛntʃuəlɪ] *adv* ostatecznie, koniec końców
**ever** ['ɛvəʳ] *adv* (*always*) zawsze; (*at any time*) kiedykolwiek; **I'd rather not go — why ~ not?** wolałabym nie iść — ale dlaczego (nie)?; **you cannot do that — why ~ not?** nie możesz tego zrobić — (a) dlaczegóż by nie?; **have you ~ been to Poland?** (czy) byłeś kiedyś w Polsce?; **where ~ have you been?** gdzieś ty był?; **the best kid ~** najlepszy dzieciak pod słońcem; **the best movie ~** najlepszy film wszech czasów; **for ~** na zawsze; **hardly ~** prawie nigdy; **better than ~ (before)** lepszy niż kiedykolwiek (przedtem); **~ since** *adv* od tego czasu, od tej pory ▷ *conj* już od *+gen*; **she's ~ so pretty** jest prześliczna; **thank you ~ so much** ogromnie ci dziękuję; **yours ~** (*Brit: in letter*) uściski
**Everest** ['ɛvərɪst] *n* (*also*: **Mount Everest**) Mount Everest *m*, Czomolungma *f*
**evergreen** ['ɛvəgri:n] *n* (*Bot*) roślina *f* zimozielona
**everlasting** [ɛvə'lɑ:stɪŋ] *adj* wieczny

 KEYWORD

**every** ['ɛvrɪ] *adj* **1** (*each*) każdy; **every time** za każdym razem; **every one of them** (*persons*) (oni) wszyscy *vir pl*, (one) wszystkie *nvir pl*; (*objects*) wszystkie *pl*; **every shop in the**

**town was closed** wszystkie sklepy w mieście były zamknięte
**2** (*all possible*): **we wish you every success** życzymy ci wszelkich sukcesów; **I have every confidence in him** mam do niego pełne zaufanie
**3** (*showing recurrence*) co *+acc*; **every day** codziennie; **every week** co tydzień; **every other/third day** co drugi/trzeci dzień; **every now and then** co jakiś czas

**everybody** [ˈɛvrɪbɔdɪ] *pron* (*each*) każdy *m*; (*all*) wszyscy *vir pl*; **~ knows about it** wszyscy o tym wiedzą, każdy o tym wie; **~ else** wszyscy inni
**everyday** [ˈɛvrɪdeɪ] *adj* codzienny
**everyone** [ˈɛvrɪwʌn] *pron* = **everybody**
**everything** [ˈɛvrɪθɪŋ] *pron* wszystko *nt*; **~ is ready** wszystko gotowe; **he did ~ possible** zrobił wszystko, co było możliwe
**everywhere** [ˈɛvrɪwɛəʳ] *adv* wszędzie; **~ you go you meet ...** gdziekolwiek pójdziesz, spotykasz *+acc*
**evict** [ɪˈvɪkt] *vt* eksmitować (eksmitować *or* wyeksmitować *perf*)
**eviction** [ɪˈvɪkʃən] *n* eksmisja *f*
**eviction notice** *n* zawiadomienie *nt* o eksmisji
**eviction order** *n* nakaz *m* eksmisji
**evidence** [ˈɛvɪdns] *n* (*proof*) dowód *m*; (*Jur: information*) dowody *pl*; (*: testimony*) zeznania *pl*; (*signs, indications*) oznaki *pl*, dowody *pl*; **to give ~** składać (złożyć *perf*) zeznania; **to show ~ of** zdradzać oznaki *+gen*; **the servants were never in ~** służących nigdy nie było widać
**evident** [ˈɛvɪdnt] *adj* widoczny; **~ to** oczywisty dla *+gen*
**evidently** [ˈɛvɪdntlɪ] *adv* (*obviously*) ewidentnie; (*apparently*) najwyraźniej
**evil** [ˈiːvl] *adj* zły ▷ *n* zło *nt*
**evocative** [ɪˈvɔkətɪv] *adj* (*description, music*) poruszający
**evoke** [ɪˈvəuk] *vt* wywoływać (wywołać *perf*)
**evolution** [iːvəˈluːʃən] *n* ewolucja *f*
**evolve** [ɪˈvɔlv] *vt* rozwijać (rozwinąć *perf*) ▷ *vi* rozwijać się (rozwinąć się *perf*), ewoluować (*literary*); **to ~ into** przekształcać się (przekształcić się *perf*) w *+acc*
**ewe** [juː] *n* owca *f*
**ewer** [ˈjuːəʳ] *n* dzban *m*
**ex-** [ɛks] *pref* eks-, były (*adj*)
**exacerbate** [ɛksˈæsəbeɪt] *vt* (*situation, pain*) zaostrzać (zaostrzyć *perf*)
**exact** [ɪgˈzækt] *adj* dokładny ▷ *vt*: **to ~ sth (from)** egzekwować (wyegzekwować *perf*) coś (od *+gen*)
**exacting** [ɪgˈzæktɪŋ] *adj* (*master, boss*) wymagający; (*task*) pracochłonny
**exactly** [ɪgˈzæktlɪ] *adv* dokładnie; **~!** dokładnie!
**exaggerate** [ɪgˈzædʒəreɪt] *vt* wyolbrzymiać (wyolbrzymić *perf*) ▷ *vi* przesadzać (przesadzić *perf*)
**exaggerated** [ɪgˈzædʒəreɪtɪd] *adj* (*politeness*) przesadny; (*remark*) przesadzony; (*idea of o.s.*) wygórowany
**exaggeration** [ɪgzædʒəˈreɪʃən] *n* przesada *f*
**exalt** [ɪgˈzɔːlt] *vt* (*praise*) wychwalać
**exalted** [ɪgˈzɔːltɪd] *adj* (*prominent*) wysoko postawiony; (*elated*) wniebowzięty
**exam** [ɪgˈzæm] *n abbr* = **examination**
**examination** [ɪgzæmɪˈneɪʃən] *n* (*of object*) oględziny *pl*; (*of plan*) analiza *f*; (*of accounts*) kontrola *f*; (*Scol*) egzamin *m*; (*Jur*) przesłuchanie *nt*; (*Med*) badanie *nt*; **to take** *or* (*Brit*) **sit an ~** przystępować (przystąpić *perf*) do egzaminu; **the matter is under ~** sprawa jest rozpatrywana
**examine** [ɪgˈzæmɪn] *vt* (*object*) oglądać (obejrzeć *perf*); (*plan*) analizować (przeanalizować *perf*); (*accounts*) kontrolować (skontrolować *perf*); (*Scol*) egzaminować (przeegzaminować *perf*); (*Jur*) przesłuchiwać (przesłuchać *perf*); (*Med*) badać (zbadać *perf*)
**examiner** [ɪgˈzæmɪnəʳ] *n* (*Scol*) egzaminator(ka) *m(f)*
**example** [ɪgˈzɑːmpl] *n* (*illustration*) przykład *m*; (*model*) wzór *m*; **for ~** na przykład; **to set a good/bad ~** dawać (dać *perf*) dobry/zły przykład
**exasperate** [ɪgˈzɑːspəreɪt] *vt* doprowadzać (doprowadzić *perf*) do rozpaczy; **I was ~d by** *or* **with her stubbornness** jej upór doprowadzał mnie do rozpaczy
**exasperating** [ɪgˈzɑːspəreɪtɪŋ] *adj* doprowadzający do rozpaczy
**exasperation** [ɪgzɑːspəˈreɪʃən] *n* rozdrażnienie *nt*, złość *f*; **I was almost crying from ~** prawie płakałam ze złości
**excavate** [ˈɛkskəveɪt] *vt* wykopywać (wykopać *perf*) ▷ *vi* (*archeologists*) prowadzić wykopaliska; (*builders*) kopać
**excavation** [ɛkskəˈveɪʃən] *n* wykop *m*
**excavator** [ˈɛkskəveɪtəʳ] *n* koparka *f*
**exceed** [ɪkˈsiːd] *vt* przekraczać (przekroczyć *perf*)
**exceedingly** [ɪkˈsiːdɪŋlɪ] *adv* niezmiernie
**excel** [ɪkˈsɛl] *vi* być najlepszym; **to ~ in** *or* **at** celować w *+loc*; **to ~ o.s.** (*Brit*) przechodzić (przejść *perf*) samego siebie
**excellence** [ˈɛksələns] *n* doskonałość *f*
**Excellency** [ˈɛksələnsɪ] *n*: **His ~** Jego Ekscelencja *m*
**excellent** [ˈɛksələnt] *adj* doskonały ▷ *excl* doskonale

**except** [ɪk'sɛpt] *prep* (*also*: **except for**) oprócz *+gen*, poza *+instr* ▷ *vt*: **to ~ sb (from)** wyłączać (wyłączyć *perf*) kogoś (spod *+gen*); **~ if/when** chyba, że; **~ that** (tyle) tylko, że; **present company ~ed** z wyjątkiem tu obecnych
**excepting** [ɪk'sɛptɪŋ] *prep* z wyjątkiem *+gen*
**exception** [ɪk'sɛpʃən] *n* wyjątek *m*; **to take ~ to** (*be offended*) czuć się (poczuć się *perf*) urażonym *+instr*; (*complain*) protestować (zaprotestować *perf*) przeciw *+dat*; **with the ~ of** z wyjątkiem *+gen*
**exceptional** [ɪk'sɛpʃənl] *adj* wyjątkowy
**excerpt** ['ɛksə:pt] *n* (*from text, symphony*) wyjątek *m*, ustęp *m*; (*from film*) urywek *m*
**excess** [ɪk'sɛs] *n* (*surfeit*) nadmiar *m*; (*amount by which sth is greater*) nadwyżka *f*; (*: of money paid*) nadpłata *f*; (*Insurance*) udział *m* własny ▷ *adj* zbędny; **excesses** *npl* (*irresponsible, stupid*) wybryki *pl*, ekscesy *pl*; (*cruel*) okrucieństwa *pl*; **in ~ of** powyżej *+gen*
**excess baggage** *n* dodatkowy bagaż *m*
**excess fare** (*Brit*) *n* dopłata *f* (*do biletu*)
**excessive** [ɪk'sɛsɪv] *adj* nadmierny
**excess supply** *n* nadwyżka *f* podaży
**exchange** [ɪks'tʃeɪndʒ] *n* (*of prisoners, infomation, students*) wymiana *f*; (*conversation*) wymiana *f* zdań; (*also*: **telephone exchange**) centrala *f* (telefoniczna) ▷ *vt*: **to ~ (for)** wymieniać (wymienić *perf*) (na *+acc*); **in ~ for** w zamian za *+acc*; **foreign ~** waluta obca, dewizy
**exchange control** *n* kontrola *f* rynku dewizowego
**exchange market** *n* rynek *m* dewizowy *or* walutowy
**exchange rate** *n* kurs *m* dewizowy
**Exchequer** [ɪks'tʃɛkə^r] (*Brit*) *n*: **the ~** Ministerstwo *nt* Skarbu
**excisable** [ɪk'saɪzəbl] *adj* podlegający akcyzie
**excise** [*n* 'ɛksaɪz, *vb* ɛk'saɪz] *n* akcyza *f* ▷ *vt* wycinać (wyciąć *perf*)
**excise duties** *npl* opłaty *pl* akcyzowe
**excitable** [ɪk'saɪtəbl] *adj* pobudliwy
**excite** [ɪk'saɪt] *vt* (*stimulate*) ekscytować; (*arouse*) podniecać (podniecić *perf*); **to get ~d** podniecać się (podniecić się *perf*)
**excitement** [ɪk'saɪtmənt] *n* (*agitation*) podniecenie *nt*; (*exhilaration*) podniecenie *nt*, podekscytowanie *nt*
**exciting** [ɪk'saɪtɪŋ] *adj* (*place*) ekscytujący; (*event, period*) pasjonujący
**excl.** *abbr* (= *excluding, exclusive (of)*) wył.
**exclaim** [ɪks'kleɪm] *vi* zawołać (*perf*), wykrzyknąć (*perf*)
**exclamation** [ɛksklə'meɪʃən] *n* okrzyk *m*
**exclamation mark** (*Ling*) *n* wykrzyknik *m*
**exclude** [ɪks'klu:d] *vt* (*person, fact*) wyłączać (wyłączyć *perf*), wykluczać (wykluczyć *perf*); (*possibility*) wykluczać (wykluczyć *perf*)
**excluding** [ɪks'klu:dɪŋ] *prep*: **~ VAT** wyłączając VAT
**exclusion** [ɪks'klu:ʒən] *n* (*of person, fact*) wyłączenie *nt*, wykluczenie *nt*; (*of possibility*) wykluczenie *nt*; **to the ~ of** z wyłączeniem *+gen*
**exclusion clause** *n* klauzula *f* wyłączająca
**exclusive** [ɪks'klu:sɪv] *adj* (*club, district*) ekskluzywny; (*use, property*) wyłączny; (*story, interview*) zastrzeżony ▷ *n* (*Press*) wyłączna własność *f*; **~ of postage/tax** wyłączając opłatę pocztową/podatek; **from 1st to 15th March ~** od 1 do 15 marca wyłącznie; **mutually ~ statements** wzajemnie wykluczające się stwierdzenia
**exclusively** [ɪks'klu:sɪvlɪ] *adv* wyłącznie
**exclusive rights** (*Comm*) *npl* wyłączne prawa *pl*
**excommunicate** [ɛkskə'mju:nɪkeɪt] (*Rel*) *vt* ekskomunikować (ekskomunikować *perf*)
**excrement** ['ɛkskrəmənt] *n* odchody *pl*
**excruciating** [ɪks'kru:ʃɪeɪtɪŋ] *adj* nieznośny, straszliwy
**excursion** [ɪks'kə:ʃən] *n* wycieczka *f*
**excursion ticket** *n* bilet *m* wycieczkowy
**excusable** [ɪks'kju:zəbl] *adj* wybaczalny
**excuse** [*n* ɪks'kju:s, *vb* ɪks'kju:z] *n* (*justification*) usprawiedliwienie *nt*, wytłumaczenie *nt*; (*: untrue*) wymówka *f*; (*reason (not) to do sth*) pretekst *m* ▷ *vt* (*justify*) usprawiedliwiać (usprawiedliwić *perf*), tłumaczyć (wytłumaczyć *perf*); (*forgive*) wybaczać (wybaczyć *perf*); **to ~ sb from doing sth** zwalniać (zwolnić *perf*) kogoś z robienia czegoś; **~ me!** przepraszam!; **if you will ~ me** jeśli Pan/Pani pozwoli; **to ~ o.s. for sth/for doing sth** tłumaczyć się (wytłumaczyć się *perf*) z czegoś/ze zrobienia czegoś; **to make ~s for sb** usprawiedliwiać kogoś; **that's no ~!** to żadne usprawiedliwienie!
**ex-directory** ['ɛksdɪ'rɛktərɪ] (*Brit: Tel*) *adj* zastrzeżony; **she's ~** ma zastrzeżony numer
**execrable** ['ɛksɪkrəbl] *adj* (*accent*) okropny; (*food, taste*) ohydny, wstrętny
**execute** ['ɛksɪkju:t] *vt* (*person*) wykonywać (wykonać *perf*) egzekucję na *+loc*, stracić (*perf*) (*literary*); (*order, movement, manoeuvre*) wykonywać (wykonać *perf*); (*plan*) przeprowadzać (przeprowadzić *perf*), wprowadzać (wprowadzić *perf*) w życie
**execution** [ɛksɪ'kju:ʃən] *n* (*of person*) egzekucja *f*; (*of order, movement, manoeuvre*) wykonanie *nt*; (*of plan*) przeprowadzenie *nt*, wprowadzenie *nt* w życie
**executioner** [ɛksɪ'kju:ʃnə^r] *n* kat *m*

**executive** [ɪg'zɛkjutɪv] *n* (*of company*) pracownik *m* szczebla kierowniczego; (*of political party*) komitet *m* wykonawczy, egzekutywa *f*; (*Pol*) władza *f* wykonawcza, egzekutywa *f* ▷ *adj* (*role*) wykonawczy, kierowniczy; (*car, chair*) dyrektorski; **~ board** zarząd; **~ secretary** sekretarka dyrektora; **~ toys** *maskotki charakterystyczne dla gabinetów pracowników szczebla kierowniczego*

**executive director** *n* dyrektor *m* wykonawczy

**executor** [ɪg'zɛkjutə<sup>r</sup>] (*Jur*) *n* wykonawca *m* testamentu

**exemplary** [ɪg'zɛmplərɪ] *adj* przykładny

**exemplify** [ɪg'zɛmplɪfaɪ] *vt* (*typify*) stanowić przykład *+gen*; (*illustrate*) ilustrować (zilustrować *perf*)

**exempt** [ɪg'zɛmpt] *adj*: **~ from** zwolniony z *+gen* ▷ *vt*: **to ~ sb from** zwalniać (zwolnić *perf*) kogoś z *+gen*

**exemption** [ɪg'zɛmpʃən] *n* zwolnienie *nt* (*z obowiązku itp*)

**exercise** ['ɛksəsaɪz] *n* (*no pl: keep-fit*) ćwiczenia *pl* fizyczne; (*piece of work, practice*) ćwiczenie *nt*; (*Mil*) ćwiczenia *pl*, manewry *pl* ▷ *vt* (*right*) korzystać (skorzystać *perf*) z *+gen*; (*patience*) wykazywać (wykazać *perf*); (*dog*) ćwiczyć; (*problem: mind*) zaprzątać ▷ *vi* (*also*: **to take exercise**) uprawiać sport; **the ~ of one's rights** korzystanie z przysługujących praw

**exercise bike** *n* rower *m* treningowy

**exercise book** *n* zeszyt *m*

**exert** [ɪg'zə:t] *vt* (*influence*) wywierać (wywrzeć *perf*); (*authority*) używać (użyć *perf*) *+gen*; **to ~ o.s.** wytężać się, wysilać się

**exertion** [ɪg'zə:ʃən] *n* wysiłek *m*

**ex gratia** ['ɛks'greɪʃə] *adj*: **~ payment** płatność *f* dobrowolna

**exhale** [ɛks'heɪl] *vt* wydychać ▷ *vi* wypuszczać (wypuścić *perf*) powietrze

**exhaust** [ɪg'zɔ:st] *n* (*also*: **exhaust pipe**) rura *f* wydechowa; (*fumes*) spaliny *pl* ▷ *vt* wyczerpywać (wyczerpać *perf*); **to ~ o.s.** przemęczać się (przemęczyć się *perf*)

**exhausted** [ɪg'zɔ:stɪd] *adj* wyczerpany

**exhausting** [ɪg'zɔ:stɪŋ] *adj* wyczerpujący

**exhaustion** [ɪg'zɔ:stʃən] *n* wyczerpanie *nt*, przemęczenie *nt*; **nervous ~** wyczerpanie nerwowe

**exhaustive** [ɪg'zɔ:stɪv] *adj* wyczerpujący

**exhibit** [ɪg'zɪbɪt] *n* (*Art*) eksponat *m*; (*Jur*) dowód *m* (rzeczowy) ▷ *vt* (*quality, ability*) wykazywać (wykazać *perf*); (*emotion*) okazywać (okazać *perf*); (*paintings*) wystawiać (wystawić *perf*)

**exhibition** [ɛksɪ'bɪʃən] *n* (*of paintings etc*) wystawa *f*; (*of ill-temper, talent*) pokaz *m*; **to make an ~ of o.s.** robić (zrobić *perf*) z siebie widowisko

**exhibitionist** [ɛksɪ'bɪʃənɪst] *n* (*show-off*) osoba *f* lubiąca się popisywać; (*Psych*) ekshibicjonista *m*

**exhibitor** [ɪg'zɪbɪtə<sup>r</sup>] (*Art*) *n* wystawca(-wczyni) *m(f)*

**exhilarating** [ɪg'zɪləreɪtɪŋ] *adj* radosny

**exhilaration** [ɪgzɪlə'reɪʃən] *n* radosne podniecenie *nt*, rozradowanie *nt*

**exhort** [ɪg'zɔ:t] *vt*: **to ~ sb to do sth** nawoływać kogoś do (z)robienia czegoś

**exile** ['ɛksaɪl] *n* (*state*) wygnanie *nt*, emigracja *f*; (*person*) wygnaniec *m*, emigrant *m* ▷ *vt* skazywać (skazać *perf*) na wygnanie; **in ~** na wygnaniu *or* emigracji

**exist** [ɪg'zɪst] *vi* (*be present*) istnieć; (*live*) egzystować, utrzymywać się przy życiu

**existence** [ɪg'zɪstəns] *n* (*reality*) istnienie *nt*; (*life*) egzystencja *f*; **to be in ~** istnieć

**existentialism** [ɛgzɪs'tɛnʃlɪzəm] *n* egzystencjalizm *m*

**existing** [ɪg'zɪstɪŋ] *adj* istniejący

**exit** ['ɛksɪt] *n* wyjście *nt*; (*from motorway*) zjazd *m*, wylot *m* ▷ *vi* wychodzić (wyjść *perf*); **to ~ from** opuszczać (opuścić *perf*) *+acc*

**exit ramp** (*US: Aut*) *n* zjazd *f* z autostrady

**exit visa** *n* wiza *f* wyjazdowa

**exodus** ['ɛksədəs] *n* exodus *m*; **the ~ to the cities** migracja do miast

**ex officio** ['ɛksə'fɪʃɪəu] *adj* z urzędu *post*, ex officio *post* ▷ *adv* z urzędu, ex officio

**exonerate** [ɪg'zɔnəreɪt] *vt*: **to ~ from** (*guilt etc*) oczyszczać (oczyścić *perf*) z *+gen*

**exorbitant** [ɪg'zɔ:bɪtnt] *adj* (*prices*) niebotyczny; (*demands*) wygórowany

**exorcize** ['ɛksɔ:saɪz] *vt* egzorcyzmować

**exotic** [ɪg'zɔtɪk] *adj* egzotyczny

**expand** [ɪks'pænd] *vt* (*business*) rozwijać (rozwinąć *perf*); (*area, staff*) powiększać (powiększyć *perf*); (*influence*) rozszerzać (rozszerzyć *perf*) ▷ *vi* (*population, business*) rozrastać się (rozrosnąć się *perf*); (*gas, metal*) roszerzać się (rozszerzyć się *perf*); **to ~ on** omawiać (omówić *perf*) szerzej *+acc*

**expanse** [ɪks'pæns] *n* obszar *m*, przestrzeń *f*

**expansion** [ɪks'pænʃən] *n* (*of business, economy etc*) rozwój *m*, wzrost *m*; (*of gas, metal*) rozszerzanie się *nt*

**expansionism** [ɪks'pænʃənɪzəm] *n* espansjonizm *m*

**expansionist** [ɪks'pænʃənɪst] *adj* ekspansjonistyczny

**expatriate** [ɛks'pætrɪət] *n*: **~ Poles** Polacy *vir pl* (żyjący) na emigracji

**expect** [ɪks'pɛkt] *vt* (*anticipate, hope for*) spodziewać się *+gen*; (*await, require, count on*) oczekiwać *+gen*; (*suppose*): **to ~ that …** przypuszczać, że … ▷ *vi*: **to be ~ing** spodziewać się dziecka; **to ~ sb to do sth** (*anticipate*) spodziewać się, że ktoś coś zrobi; (*demand*) oczekiwać od kogoś zrobienia czegoś; **as ~ed** zgodnie z oczekiwaniami; **I ~ so** tak przypuszczam

**expectancy** [ɪks'pɛktənsɪ] *n* wyczekiwanie *nt*, nadzieja *f*; **life ~** średnia długość życia

**expectant** [ɪks'pɛktənt] *adj* (*crowd, silence*) wyczekujący

**expectantly** [ɪks'pɛktəntlɪ] *adv* wyczekująco

**expectant mother** *n* przyszła matka *f*

**expectation** [ɛkspɛk'teɪʃən] *n* oczekiwanie *nt*; **against** *or* **contrary to all ~(s)** wbrew (wszelkim) oczekiwaniom; **to come** *or* **live up to sb's ~s** spełniać (spełnić *perf*) czyjeś oczekiwania

**expedience** [ɪks'piːdɪəns] *n* = **expediency**

**expediency** [ɪks'piːdɪənsɪ] *n* doraźne cele *pl*; **for the sake of ~** ze względów praktycznych

**expedient** [ɪks'piːdɪənt] *adj* celowy, wskazany ▷ *n* doraźny środek *m*

**expedite** ['ɛkspədaɪt] *vt* przyspieszać (przyspieszyć *perf*)

**expedition** [ɛkspə'dɪʃən] *n* wyprawa *f*, ekspedycja *f*; **a shopping ~** wyprawa po zakupy

**expeditionary force** [ɛkspə'dɪʃənrɪ-] (*Mil*) *n* ekspedycja *f*

**expeditious** [ɛkspə'dɪʃəs] *adj* szybki

**expel** [ɪks'pɛl] *vt* (*person: from school, organization*) wydalać (wydalić *perf*), usuwać (usunąć *perf*); (*: from place*) wypędzać (wypędzić *perf*); (*gas, liquid*) wyrzucać (wyrzucić *perf*)

**expend** [ɪks'pɛnd] *vt* wydatkować (wydatkować *perf*)

**expendable** [ɪks'pɛndəbl] *adj* zbędny, zbyteczny

**expenditure** [ɪks'pɛndɪtʃə[r]] *n* (*of money*) wydatki *pl*; (*of energy, time*) wydatkowanie *nt*, nakład *m*

**expense** [ɪks'pɛns] *n* (*cost*) koszt *m*; (*expenditure*) wydatek *m*; **expenses** *npl* wydatki *pl*, koszty *pl*; **at the ~ of** kosztem *+gen*; **he's gone to the ~ of buying a car** wykosztował się na samochód; **at great/little ~** wielkim/małym kosztem

**expense account** *n* rachunek *m* wydatków *or* kosztów

**expensive** [ɪks'pɛnsɪv] *adj* (*article*) drogi, kosztowny; (*mistake, tastes*) kosztowny

**experience** [ɪks'pɪərɪəns] *n* (*knowledge, skill*) doświadczenie *nt*; (*event, activity*) przeżycie *nt* ▷ *vt* (*situation, problem*) doświadczać (doświadczyć *perf*) *+gen*; (*feeling*) doznawać (doznać *perf*) *+gen*; **to know sth by** *or* **from ~** znać coś z własnego doświadczenia *or* z autopsji; **to learn by ~** uczyć się przez doświadczenie

**experienced** [ɪks'pɪərɪənst] *adj* doświadczony

**experiment** [ɪks'pɛrɪmənt] *n* (*Science*) eksperyment *m*, doświadczenie *nt*; (*trial*) eksperyment *m*, próba *f* ▷ *vi* (*Science*): **to ~ (with/on)** eksperymentować *or* prowadzić doświadczenia (z *+instr*/na *+loc*); (*fig*) eksperymentować; **to perform** *or* **carry out an ~** wykonywać (wykonać *perf*) *or* przeprowadzać (przeprowadzić *perf*) eksperyment; **as an ~** tytułem próby

**experimental** [ɪkspɛrɪ'mɛntl] *adj* (*methods*) eksperymentalny; (*ideas*) eksperymentatorski; (*tests*) doświadczalny; **at the ~ stage** w fazie prób

**expert** ['ɛkspəːt] *adj* (*driver etc*) wytrawny; (*help, advice*) specjalistyczny ▷ *n* ekspert *m*; **~ in** *or* **at sth** biegły w czymś; **an ~ on sth** znawca czegoś; **~ witness** (*Jur*) rzeczoznawca, biegły; **~ opinion** opinia specjalisty

**expertise** [ɛkspəː'tiːz] *n* wiedza *f* (specjalistyczna), umiejętności *pl* (specjalistyczne)

**expire** [ɪks'paɪə[r]] *vi* wygasać (wygasnąć *perf*), tracić (stracić *perf*) ważność

**expiry** [ɪks'paɪərɪ] *n* wygaśnięcie *nt*, utrata *f* ważności

**expiry date** *n* data *f* ważności

**explain** [ɪks'pleɪn] *vt* wyjaśniać (wyjaśnić *perf*), tłumaczyć (wytłumaczyć *perf*)

▸ **explain away** *vt* (*mistake etc*) znajdować (znaleźć *perf*) wytłumaczenie *or* usprawiedliwienie dla *+gen*

**explanation** [ɛksplə'neɪʃən] *n* (*reason*) wyjaśnienie *nt*, wytłumaczenie *nt*; (*description*) objaśnienie *nt*; **to find an ~ for sth** znajdować (znaleźć *perf*) wytłumaczenie dla czegoś

**explanatory** [ɪks'plænətrɪ] *adj* (*statement*) wyjaśniający; (*leaflet, note*) objaśniający

**explicable** [ɪks'plɪkəbl] *adj* wytłumaczalny; **for no ~ reason** z niewyjaśnionych *or* niezrozumiałych powodów

**explicit** [ɪks'plɪsɪt] *adj* wyraźny; **to be ~ (about sth)** mówić (o czymś) otwarcie *or* jasno

**explode** [ɪks'pləud] *vi* (*bomb*) wybuchać (wybuchnąć *perf*), eksplodować (eksplodować *perf*); (*person*) wybuchać (wybuchnąć *perf*) ▷ *vt* (*bomb*) powodować (spowodować *perf*) wybuch *+gen*, dokonywać (dokonać *perf*) eksplozji *+gen*; (*myth, theory*) obalać (obalić *perf*); **the population was still**

**exploding** liczba ludności nadal gwałtownie rosła

**exploit** [*n* 'ɛksplɔɪt, *vb* ɪks'plɔɪt] *n* wyczyn *m* ▷ *vt* (*person*) wyzyskiwać (wyzyskać *perf*); (*idea, opportunity*) wykorzystywać (wykorzystać *perf*); (*resources*) eksploatować (wyeksploatować *perf*)

**exploitation** [ɛksplɔɪ'teɪʃən] *n* (*of person*) wyzysk *m*; (*of idea, opportunity*) wykorzystanie *nt*; (*of resources*) eksploatacja *f*

**exploration** [ɛksplə'reɪʃən] *n* (*of place, space*) badanie *nt*, eksploracja *f* (*fml*); (*of idea, suggestion*) zgłębianie *nt*

**exploratory** [ɪks'plɔrətrɪ] *adj* (*expedition*) badawczy; (*talks*) przygotowawczy, wstępny; (*operation*) rozpoznawczy; **~ operation** (*Med*) eksploracja chirurgiczna

**explore** [ɪks'plɔːʳ] *vt* (*place, space*) badać (zbadać *perf*); (*idea, suggestion*) zgłębiać (zgłębić *perf*)

**explorer** [ɪks'plɔːrəʳ] *n* badacz(ka) *m(f)*

**explosion** [ɪks'pləuʒən] *n* (*of bomb*) wybuch *m*, eksplozja *f*; (*of population*) eksplozja *f*; (*of rage, laughter*) wybuch *m*

**explosive** [ɪks'pləusɪv] *adj* (*material, temper*) wybuchowy; (*situation*) zapalny ▷ *n* materiał *m* wybuchowy

**exponent** [ɪks'pəunənt] *n* (*of idea, theory*) propagator(ka) *m(f)*; (*of skill, activity*) przedstawiciel(ka) *m(f)*, reprezentant(ka) *m(f)*; (*Math*) wykładnik *m* (potęgi)

**exponential** [ɛkspəu'nɛnʃl] *adj* (*growth, increase*) gwałtowny; (*Math*) wykładniczy

**export** [*vb* ɛks'pɔːt, *n, cpd* 'ɛkspɔːt] *vt* eksportować (eksportować *perf*) ▷ *n* (*process*) eksport *m*; (*product*) towar *m or* produkt *m* eksportowy ▷ *cpd*: **~ duty** cło *nt* eksportowe *or* wywozowe; **~ permit** pozwolenie na eksport *or* wywóz

**exportation** [ɛkspɔː'teɪʃən] *n* wywóz *m*, eksport *m*

**exporter** [ɛks'pɔːtəʳ] *n* eksporter *m*

**expose** [ɪks'pəuz] *vt* (*object*) odsłaniać (odsłonić *perf*); (*person*) demaskować (zdemaskować *perf*); (*situation*) ujawniać (ujawnić *perf*); **to ~ o.s.** (*Jur*) obnażać się (obnażyć się *perf*) (w miejscu publicznym)

**exposé** [ɛks'pəuzeɪ] *n* eksposé *nt inv*

**exposed** [ɪks'pəuzd] *adj* nie osłonięty, odkryty; (*Elec*) nieizolowany, nie zabezpieczony

**exposition** [ɛkspə'zɪʃən] *n* (*explanation*) przedstawienie *nt*; (*exhibition*) ekspozycja *f*, wystawa *f*

**exposure** [ɪks'pəuʒəʳ] *n* (*publicity*) nagłośnienie *nt*; (*of truth*) ujawnienie *nt*; (*of person*) zdemaskowanie *nt*; (*Phot*: *amount of light*) naświetlenie *nt*; (*: shot*) klatka *f*; **~ to** (*heat, radiation etc*) wystawienie na *+acc or* na działanie *+gen*; **death from ~** śmierć na skutek nadmiernego ochłodzenia organizmu

**exposure meter** *n* światłomierz *m*

**expound** [ɪks'paund] *vt* (*theory, opinion*) wykładać (wyłożyć *perf*)

**express** [ɪks'prɛs] *adj* (*command, intention*) wyraźny; (*letter, train, bus*) ekspresowy ▷ *n* (*Rail*) ekspres *m* ▷ *adv*: **to send sth ~** wysyłać (wysłać *perf*) coś ekspresem ▷ *vt* wyrażać (wyrazić *perf*); **to ~ o.s.** wyrażać się (wyrazić się *perf*), wysławiać się (wysłowić się *perf*)

**expression** [ɪks'prɛʃən] *n* (*word, phrase*) wyrażenie *nt*, zwrot *m*; (*of welcome, support*) wyraz *m*; (*on face*) wyraz *m* twarzy; (*of actor, singer*) ekspresja *f*; **freedom of ~** wolność słowa

**expressionism** [ɪks'prɛʃənɪzəm] *n* ekspresjonizm *m*

**expressive** [ɪks'prɛsɪv] *adj* pełen wyrazu; **~ ability** umiejętność wysławiania się

**expressly** [ɪks'prɛslɪ] *adv* wyraźnie

**expressway** [ɪks'prɛsweɪ] (*US*) *n* ≈ autostrada *f*

**expropriate** [ɛks'prəuprɪeɪt] *vt* (*government etc*) konfiskować (skonfiskować *perf*), przejmować (przejąć *perf*); (*person*) przywłaszczać (przywłaszczyć *perf*) sobie

**expulsion** [ɪks'pʌlʃən] *n* (*Scol, Pol*) wydalenie *nt*; (*of gas, liquid*) wypuszczenie *nt*

**expurgate** ['ɛkspəːgeɪt] *vt* okrawać (okroić *perf*); **the ~d version** okrojona wersja

**exquisite** [ɛks'kwɪzɪt] *adj* (*beautiful*) przepiękny; (*perfect*) znakomity, wyśmienity; (*pain*) dojmujący; (*pleasure, relief*) wyraźny

**exquisitely** [ɛks'kwɪzɪtlɪ] *adv* (*beautifully*) przepięknie; (*perfectly*) znakomicie, wyśmienicie; (*polite, sensitive*) nienagannie

**ex-serviceman** ['ɛks'səːvɪsmən] *n* były wojskowy *m*

**ext.** (*Tel*) *abbr* (= *extension*) w., wew., wewn.

**extemporize** [ɪks'tɛmpəraɪz] *vi* improwizować

**extend** [ɪks'tɛnd] *vt* (*make longer*) przedłużać (przedłużyć *perf*); (*make larger*) powiększać (powiększyć *perf*); (*offer*) składać (złożyć *perf*); (*invitation*) wystosowywać (wystosować *perf*); (*arm, hand*) wyciągać (wyciągnąć *perf*); (*deadline, visa*) przedłużać (przedłużyć *perf*); (*credit*) udzielać (udzielić *perf*) *+gen* ▷ *vi* (*land, road*) rozciągać się, ciągnąć się; (*period*) trwać, ciągnąć się

**extension** [ɪks'tɛnʃən] *n* (*of building*) dobudówka *f*; (*of time, road, table*) przedłużenie *nt*; (*of campaign, rights*) rozszerzenie *nt*; (*Elec*) przedłużacz *m*; (*Tel*: *in private house*) dodatkowy aparat *m*; (: *in office*) numer *m* wewnętrzny; ~ **3718** wewnętrzny 3718

**extension cable** *n* przedłużacz *m*

**extension lead** *n* = **extension cable**

**extensive** [ɪks'tɛnsɪv] *adj* (*area, knowledge, damage*) rozległy; (*coverage, discussion, inquiries*) szczegółowy; (*quotation*) obszerny; **to make ~ use of** korzystać w znacznym stopniu z *+gen*

**extensively** [ɪks'tɛnsɪvlɪ] *adv*: **he's travelled ~** wiele podróżował

**extent** [ɪks'tɛnt] *n* (*of area, land*) rozmiary *pl*; (*of problem*) zakres *m*, zasięg *m*; (*of damage, loss*) stopień *m*, rozmiary *pl*; **to some ~, to a certain ~** do pewnego stopnia, w pewnej mierze; **to a large ~** w dużym stopniu, w dużej mierze; **to the ~ of ...** aż po *+acc*; **to such an ~ that ...** do tego stopnia, że ...

**extenuating** [ɪks'tɛnjueɪtɪŋ] *adj*: **~ circumstances** okoliczności *pl* łagodzące

**exterior** [ɛks'tɪərɪə^r] *adj* zewnętrzny ▷ *n* (*outside*) zewnętrzna *f* strona; (*appearance*) powierzchowność *f*

**exterminate** [ɪks'tə:mɪneɪt] *vt* (*animals*) tępić (wytępić *perf*); (*people*) eksterminować

**extermination** [ɪkstə:mɪ'neɪʃən] *n* (*of animals*) wytępienie *nt*; (*of people*) eksterminacja *f*

**external** [ɛks'tə:nl] *adj* (*walls, use*) zewnętrzny; (*examiner, auditor*) z zewnątrz *post*; **externals** *npl* trywia *pl*; **for ~ use only** (wyłącznie) do użytku zewnętrznego; **~ affairs** sprawy zagraniczne

**externally** [ɛks'tə:nəlɪ] *adv* zewnętrznie

**extinct** [ɪks'tɪŋkt] *adj* (*animal, plant*) wymarły; (*volcano*) wygasły

**extinction** [ɪks'tɪŋkʃən] *n* wyginięcie *nt*, wymarcie *nt*

**extinguish** [ɪks'tɪŋgwɪʃ] *vt* (*fire*) gasić (ugasić *perf*); (*light, cigarette*) gasić (zgasić *perf*); (*memory*) wymazywać (wymazać *perf*); (*hope*) niweczyć (zniweczyć *perf*)

**extinguisher** [ɪks'tɪŋgwɪʃə^r] *n* (*also*: **fire extinguisher**) gaśnica *f*

**extol**, (*US*) **extoll** [ɪks'təul] *vt* wychwalać

**extort** [ɪks'tɔ:t] *vt*: **to ~ from sb** (*money etc*) wydzierać (wydrzeć *perf*) komuś; (*confession, promise*) wymuszać (wymusić *perf*) na kimś

**extortion** [ɪks'tɔ:ʃən] *n* (*crime*) wymuszenie *nt*; (*exorbitant charge*) zdzierstwo *nt*

**extortionate** [ɪks'tɔ:ʃnɪt] *adj* wygórowany

**extra** ['ɛkstrə] *adj* dodatkowy ▷ *adv* dodatkowo, ekstra (*inf*) ▷ *n* (*luxury*) dodatek *m*; (*surcharge*) dopłata *f*; (*Film, Theat*) statysta(-tka) *m(f)*; **wine will cost ~** za wino trzeba będzie zapłacić osobno

**extra...** ['ɛkstrə] *pref* (*very*): **~-large** bardzo duży; (*from outside*): **~-parliamentary** pozaparlamentarny

**extract** [*vb* ɪks'trækt, *n* 'ɛkstrækt] *vt* (*object*) wyciągać (wyciągnąć *perf*); (*tooth*) usuwać (usunąć *perf*), wyrywać (wyrwać *perf*); (*mineral*: *from ground*) wydobywać (wydobyć *perf*); (: *from another substance*) uzyskiwać (uzyskać *perf*); (*promise, confession*) wymuszać (wymusić *perf*); (*money*) wyłudzać (wyłudzić *perf*) ▷ *n* (*of novel*) wyjątek *m*, urywek *m*; (*of recording*) fragment *m*; (*from plant etc*) wyciąg *m*, ekstrakt *m*

**extraction** [ɪks'trækʃən] *n* (*of tooth*) usunięcie *nt*, wyrwanie *nt*, ekstrakcja *f* (*fml*); (*descent*) pochodzenie *nt*; (*of mineral*: *from ground*) wydobycie *nt*; (: *from another substance*) uzyskanie *nt*; (*of promise, confession*) wymuszenie *nt*; (*of money*) wyłudzenie *nt*; **he is of Scottish ~, he is Scottish by ~** jest z pochodzenia Szkotem

**extracurricular** ['ɛkstrəkə'rɪkjulə^r] *adj* ponadprogramowy

**extradite** ['ɛkstrədaɪt] *vt* ekstradować (*perf*)

**extradition** [ɛkstrə'dɪʃən] *n* ekstradycja *f* ▷ *cpd*: **~ order** nakaz *m* ekstradycji; **~ treaty** umowa o ekstradycji

**extramarital** ['ɛkstrə'mærɪtl] *adj* pozamałżeński

**extramural** ['ɛkstrə'mjuərl] *adj* (*studies, course*) zaoczny; (*activities*) dodatkowy

**extraneous** [ɛks'treɪnɪəs] *adj* uboczny

**extraordinary** [ɪks'trɔ:dnrɪ] *adj* nadzwyczajny, niezwykły; (*meeting*) nadzwyczajny; **the ~ thing is that ...** niezwykłe jest to, że ...

**extraordinary general meeting** *n* nadzwyczajne walne zebranie *nt*

**extrapolation** [ɛkstræpə'leɪʃən] *n* ekstrapolacja *f*

**extra-sensory perception** *n* percepcja *f* pozazmysłowa

**extra time** (*Football*) *n* dogrywka *f*

**extravagance** [ɪks'trævəgəns] *n* (*no pl*: *quality*) rozrzutność *f*; (*instance*) ekstrawagancja *f*

**extravagant** [ɪks'trævəgənt] *adj* (*person*) rozrzutny; (*gift*) (przesadnie) kosztowny; (*tastes, ideas*) ekstrawagancki; (*praise*) przesadny

**extreme** [ɪks'tri:m] *adj* (*conditions, opinions, methods*) ekstremalny; (*poverty, example*) skrajny; (*caution*) największy ▷ *n* ekstremalność *f*, skrajność *f*; **~ point/tip** czubek, koniec; **~ edge** skraj, kraniec; **the ~ right/left** (*Pol*) skrajna prawica/lewica; **~s of temperature** ekstremalne *or* skrajne temperatury

**extremely** [ɪks'tri:mlɪ] *adv* niezmiernie, nadzwyczajnie

**extremist** [ɪks'tri:mɪst] *n* ekstremista(-tka) *m(f)* ▷ *adj* ekstremistyczny
**extremity** [ɪks'trɛmɪtɪ] *n* (*edge, end*) kraniec *m*, skraj *m*; (*of situation*) skrajność *f*; **extremities** *npl* (*Anat*) kończyny *pl*
**extricate** ['ɛkstrɪkeɪt] *vt*: **to ~ sb/sth from** (*trap*) wyswobadzać (wyswobodzić *perf*) kogoś/coś z *+gen*; (*difficult situation*) wyplątywać (wyplątać *perf*) kogoś/coś z *+gen*
**extrovert** ['ɛkstrəvə:t] *n* ekstrawertyk(-yczka) *m(f)*
**exuberance** [ɪg'zju:bərns] *n* entuzjazm *m*
**exuberant** [ɪg'zju:bərnt] *adj* (*person*) tryskający energią *or* entuzjazmem; (*imagination, foliage*) bujny, wybujały
**exude** [ɪg'zju:d] *vt* (*confidence, enthusiasm*) tryskać *+instr*; (*liquid, smell*) wydzielać
**exult** [ɪg'zʌlt] *vi* nie posiadać się z radości; **he ~ed in the title of ...** chlubił się tytułem *+gen*
**exultant** [ɪg'zʌltənt] *adj* rozradowany
**exultation** [ɛgzʌl'teɪʃən] *n* rozradowanie *nt*
**eye** [aɪ] *n* (*Anat*) oko *nt*; (*of needle*) ucho *nt* ▷ *vt* przypatrywać się (przypatrzyć się *perf*) *+dat*; **to keep an eye on** mieć na oku *+acc*; **as far as the eye can see** jak okiem sięgnąć; **in the public eye** w centrum uwagi publicznej; **to see eye to eye with sb** całkowicie się z kimś zgadzać; **to have an eye for** mieć (doskonałe) wyczucie *+gen*; **there's more to this than meets the eye** kryje się za tym coś więcej
**eyeball** ['aɪbɔ:l] *n* gałka *f* oczna
**eyebath** ['aɪbɑ:θ] (*Brit*) *n* kieliszek *m* do przemywania oczu
**eyebrow** ['aɪbrau] *n* brew *f*
**eyebrow pencil** *n* ołówek *m* do brwi
**eye-catching** ['aɪkætʃɪŋ] *adj* przyciągający wzrok
**eye cup** (*US*) *n* = **eyebath**
**eyedrops** ['aɪdrɔps] *npl* krople *pl* do oczu
**eyeglass** ['aɪglɑ:s] *n* monokl *m*
**eyelash** ['aɪlæʃ] *n* rzęsa *f*
**eyelet** ['aɪlɪt] *n* (*on belt, shoes*) dziurka *f*
**eye-level** ['aɪlɛvl] *adj* na wysokości oczu *post*
**eyelid** ['aɪlɪd] *n* powieka *f*
**eyeliner** ['aɪlaɪnəʳ] *n* ołówek *m* do oczu, eyeliner *m*
**eye-opener** ['aɪəupnəʳ] *n* objawienie *nt*
**eyeshadow** ['aɪʃædəu] *n* cień *m* do powiek
**eyesight** ['aɪsaɪt] *n* wzrok *m*
**eyesore** ['aɪsɔ:ʳ] *n* (*fig*) szkaradzieństwo *nt*, brzydactwo *nt*
**eyestrain** ['aɪstreɪn] *n*: **to get ~** przemęczyć (*perf*) oczy *or* wzrok
**eyetooth** ['aɪtu:θ] (*pl* **eyeteeth**) *n* (górny) kieł *m* (*ludzki*); **I would give my eyeteeth for/to** wiele bym dał za *+acc*/, żeby móc *+infin*
**eyewash** ['aɪwɔʃ] *n* płyn *m* do przemywania oczu; (*fig*) mydlenie *nt* oczu
**eye witness** *n* naoczny świadek *m*
**eyrie** ['ɪərɪ] *n* niedostępne gniazdo *nt* (*orle itp*)

# Ff

**F¹, f** [ɛf] *n* (*letter*) F *nt*, f *nt*; **F for Frederick,** (*US*) **F for Fox** ≈ F jak Franciszek
**F²** [ɛf] *n* (*Mus*) F *nt*, f *nt*
**F³** *abbr* (= *Fahrenheit*) °F
**FA** (*Brit*) *n abbr* (= *Football Association*) ≈ PZPN *m*
**FAA** (*US*) *n abbr* (= *Federal Aviation Administration*) *urząd federalny sprawujący kontrolę nad lotnictwem*
**fable** ['feɪbl] *n* bajka *f*
**fabric** ['fæbrɪk] *n* (*cloth*) tkanina *f*; (*of society*) struktura *f*; (*of building*) konstrukcja *f*
**fabricate** ['fæbrɪkeɪt] *vt* (*evidence, story*) fabrykować (sfabrykować *perf*); (*parts, equipment*) produkować (wyprodukować *perf*)
**fabrication** [fæbrɪ'keɪʃən] *n* (*lie*) wymysł *m*; (*manufacturing*) produkcja *f*
**fabric ribbon** *n* taśma *f* do maszyny (do pisania)
**fabulous** ['fæbjuləs] *adj* (*person, looks, mood*) fantastyczny; (*beauty, wealth, luxury*) bajeczny; (*mythical*) baśniowy, bajkowy
**facade** *n* (*lit, fig*) fasada *f*
**face** [feɪs] *n* (*Anat*) twarz *f*; (*expression*) mina *f*; (*of clock*) tarcza *f*; (*of mountain, cliff*) ściana *f*; (*of cube, dice*) ścianka *f*; (*fig*) oblicze *nt* ▷ *vt* (*person: direction, object*) zwracać się (zwrócić się *perf*) twarzą do *+gen*; (*: unpleasant situation*) stawiać (stawić *perf*) czoło *+dat*; (*building, seat*) być zwróconym w kierunku *+gen*; **~ down/up** (*person*) (leżący) na brzuchu/plecach; (*card*) zakryty/odkryty; **to lose/save ~** stracić (*perf*)/ zachować (*perf*) twarz; **to make** *or* **pull a ~** robić (zrobić *perf*) minę; **to make ~s** robić *or* stroić miny; **in the ~ of** w obliczu *+gen*; **on the ~ of it** na pierwszy rzut oka; **~ to ~ (with)** twarzą w twarz (z *+instr*); **to be facing sb/sth** (*person*) być zwróconym twarzą do kogoś/ czegoś; **to ~ the fact that ...** przyjmować (przyjąć *perf*) do wiadomości (fakt), że ...
▸ **face up to** *vt fus* (*problems, obstacles*) stawiać (stawić *perf*) czoło *+dat*; (*one's responsibilities, duties*) uznawać (uznać *perf*) *+acc*
**face cloth** (*Brit*) *n* myjka *f* do twarzy
**face cream** *n* krem *m* do twarzy
**faceless** ['feɪslɪs] *adj* bezimienny, anonimowy
**face lift** *n* (*of person*) lifting *m* twarzy; (*of building, room, furniture*) odnowienie *nt*
**face powder** *n* puder *m* (kosmetyczny)
**face-saving** ['feɪs'seɪvɪŋ] *adj* (*compromise, gesture*) pozwalający zachować twarz
**facet** ['fæsɪt] *n* (*of question, personality*) strona *f*, aspekt *m*; (*of gem*) faseta *f*
**facetious** [fə'si:ʃəs] *adj* (*comment, remark*) żartobliwy; (*person*) frywolny
**face-to-face** ['feɪstə'feɪs] *adv* twarzą w twarz *post*
**face value** *n* wartość *f* nominalna; **to take sth at ~** (*fig*) brać (wziąć *perf*) coś za dobrą monetę
**facia** ['feɪʃə] *n* = **fascia**
**facial** ['feɪʃl] *adj*: **~ expression** wyraz *m* twarzy; **~ hair** owłosienie *nt* twarzy, zarost *m* ▷ *n* zabieg *m* kosmetyczny (twarzy)
**facile** ['fæsaɪl] *adj* płytki, powierzchowny
**facilitate** [fə'sɪlɪteɪt] *vt* ułatwiać (ułatwić *perf*)
**facilities** [fə'sɪlɪtɪz] *npl* (*buildings*) pomieszczenia *pl*; (*equipment*) urządzenia *pl*; **credit ~** możliwość zaciągnięcia kredytu; **she had no cooking ~ in her room** nie miała w swoim pokoju warunków do gotowania
**facility** [fə'sɪlɪtɪ] *n* (*service*) udogodnienie *nt*; (*feature*) (dodatkowa) funkcja *f*; (*aptitude*): **to have a ~ for** (*languages etc*) mieć zdolności do *+gen*
**facing** ['feɪsɪŋ] *n* fliselina *f*, materiał *m* usztywniający
**facsimile** [fæk'sɪmɪlɪ] *n* faksymile *nt*
**fact** [fækt] *n* fakt *m*; **in ~** (*expressing emphasis*) faktycznie; (*disagreeing*) w rzeczywistości; (*qualifying statement*) właściwie; **I know for a ~ (that ...)** wiem na pewno (, że ...); **the ~ (of the matter) is (that) ...** rzecz w tym, że ...; **have you told your son the ~s of life yet?** czy uświadomiłeś już syna?; **the service fell victim to the economic ~s of life** usługi padły ofiarą naturalnych praw rozwoju ekonomicznego
**fact-finding** ['fæktfaɪndɪŋ] *adj* (*mission, trip*) dla zebrania informacji *post*

**faction** ['fækʃən] *n* odłam *m*, frakcja *f*
**factor** ['fæktə^r] *n* czynnik *m*; (*Math*) współczynnik *m*
**factory** ['fæktərɪ] *n* fabryka *f*
**factory farming** (*Brit*) *n* chów *m* przemysłowy; (*of pigs*) tucz *m* przemysłowy
**factory ship** *n* statek *m* przetwórnia *f*
**factual** ['fæktjuəl] *adj* (*analysis, information*) rzeczowy
**faculty** ['fækəltɪ] *n* (*sense, ability*) zdolność *f*; (*of university*) wydział *m*; (*US: teaching staff*) wykładowcy *vir pl*
**fad** [fæd] *n* przelotna *or* chwilowa moda *f*
**fade** [feɪd] *vi* (*colour, wallpaper, photograph*) blaknąć (wyblaknąć *perf*); (*sound*) cichnąć, ucichać (ucichnąć *perf*); (*hope, memory, smile*) gasnąć (zgasnąć *perf*); **the light was fading** ściemniało się
▸ **fade in** *vt* (*picture*) rozjaśniać (rozjaśnić *perf*); (*sound*) wzmacniać (wzmocnić *perf*)
▸ **fade out** *vt* (*picture*) ściemniać (ściemnić *perf*); (*sound*) wyciszać (wyciszyć *perf*)
**faeces**, (US) **feces** ['fi:si:z] *npl* kał *m*, odchody *pl*
**fag** [fæg] *n* (*Brit: inf: cigarette*) fajka *f* (*inf*); (*: chore*) mordęga *f*; (*US: inf!*) pedał *m* (*inf!*)
**fail** [feɪl] *vt* (*person: exam*) nie zdawać (nie zdać *perf*) *+gen*, oblewać (oblać *perf*); (*examiner: candidate*) oblewać (oblać *perf*); (*leader, memory*) zawodzić (zawieść *perf*); (*courage*) opuszczać (opuścić *perf*) ▹ *vi* (*candidate*) nie zdawać (nie zdać *perf*), oblewać (oblać *perf*); (*attempt*) nie powieść się (*perf*); (*brakes*) zawodzić (zawieść *perf*); (*eyesight, health*) pogarszać się (pogorszyć się *perf*); (*light*) gasnąć (zgasnąć *perf*); **to ~ to do sth** (*not succeed*) nie zdołać (*perf*) czegoś zrobić; (*neglect*) nie zrobić (*perf*) czegoś; **without ~** (*always, religiously*) obowiązkowo; (*definitely*) na pewno
**failing** ['feɪlɪŋ] *n* wada *f* ▹ *prep* jeżeli nie będzie *+gen*; **~ that** ewentualnie
**failsafe** ['feɪlseɪf] *adj* (*machine, system*) bezpieczny w razie uszkodzenia; (*device, mechanism*) zabezpieczający
**failure** ['feɪljə^r] *n* (*lack of success*) niepowodzenie *nt*; (*person*) ofiara *f* (życiowa), nieudacznik *m*; (*of engine*) uszkodzenie *nt*; (*of heart*) niedomoga *f*, niewydolność *f*; (*of crops*) nieurodzaj *m*; **his ~ to turn up** jego niestawienie się; **it was a complete ~** to była kompletna klęska
**faint** [feɪnt] *adj* nikły, słaby; (*smell, breeze*) lekki ▹ *vi* (*Med*) mdleć (zemdleć *perf*) ▹ *n* (*Med*) omdlenie *nt*; **I feel ~** słabo mi
**faint-hearted** ['feɪnt'hɑ:tɪd] *adj* (*attempt*) nieśmiały; (*person*) bojaźliwy
**faintly** ['feɪntlɪ] *adv* (*slightly*) z lekka; (*weakly*) słabo
**fair** [fɛə^r] *adj* (*just, impartial*) sprawiedliwy; (*honest, honourable*) uczciwy; (*size, number, chance*) spory; (*guess, assessment*) trafny; (*complexion, hair*) jasny; (*weather*) ładny ▹ *adv*: **to play ~** (*Sport*) grać fair; (*fig*) postępować uczciwie ▹ *n* (*also*: **trade fair**) targi *pl*; (*Brit: also*: **funfair**) wesołe miasteczko *nt*; **it's not ~!** to nie fair!; **a ~ amount of money** spora suma pieniędzy; **a ~ amount of success** spory sukces
**fair copy** *n* czystopis *m*
**fair-haired** [fɛə'hɛəd] *adj* jasnowłosy
**fairly** ['fɛəlɪ] *adv* (*justly*) sprawiedliwie; (*quite*) dość, dosyć
**fair-minded** [fɛə'maɪndɪd] *adj* bezstronny
**fairness** ['fɛənɪs] *n* sprawiedliwość *f*; **in all ~** gwoli sprawiedliwości
**fair play** *n* fair play *nt inv*
**fairway** ['fɛəweɪ] *n* (*Golf*) bieżnia *f*
**fairy** ['fɛərɪ] *n* wróżka *f* (*z bajki*)
**fairy godmother** *n* (*fig*) dobra *f* wróżka
**fairy lights** (*Brit*) *npl* kolorowe światełka *pl or* lampki *pl*
**fairy tale** *n* bajka *f*, baśń *f*
**faith** [feɪθ] *n* wiara *f*; **to have ~ in sb/sth** wierzyć w kogoś/coś
**faithful** ['feɪθful] *adj* wierny; **to be ~ to** (*spouse*) być wiernym *+dat*; (*book, original*) wiernie oddawać (oddać *perf*) *+acc*
**faithfully** ['feɪθfəlɪ] *adv* wiernie; **Yours ~** Z poważaniem
**faith healer** *n* uzdrowiciel(ka) *m(f)*, uzdrawiacz(ka) *m(f)* (*pej*)
**fake** [feɪk] *n* falsyfikat *m*, podróbka *f* (*inf*) ▹ *adj* (*antique*) podrabiany; (*passport*) fałszywy; (*laugh*) udawany ▹ *vt* (*painting, document, signature*) podrabiać (podrobić *perf*); (*accounts, results*) fałszować (sfałszować *perf*); (*illness, emotion*) udawać (udać *perf*); **he's a ~** nie jest tym, za kogo się podaje
**falcon** ['fɔ:lkən] *n* sokół *m*
**Falkland Islands** ['fɔ:lklənd-] *npl*: **the ~** Wyspy *pl* Falklandzkie
**fall** [fɔ:l] (*pt* **fell**, *pp* **~en**) *n* (*of person, object, government*) upadek *m*; (*in price, temperature*) spadek *m*; (*of snow*) opady *pl*; (*US: autumn*) jesień *f* ▹ *vi* (*person, object, government*) upadać (upaść *perf*); (*snow, rain*) padać, spadać (spaść *perf*); (*price, temperature, dollar*) spadać (spaść *perf*); (*night, darkness, silence*) zapadać (zapaść *perf*); (*light, shadow*) padać (paść *perf*); (*sadness*) zapanowywać (zapanować *perf*); **falls** *npl* wodospad *m*; **to ~ flat** nie udawać się (nie udać się *perf*), nie wychodzić (nie wyjść *perf*); **to ~ in love (with sb/sth)** zakochiwać się (zakochać się *perf*) (w kimś/czymś); **to ~ short of sb's expectations** nie spełniać (nie

spełnić *perf*) czyichś oczekiwań

▸ **fall apart** *vi* rozpadać się (rozpaść się *perf*), rozlatywać się (rozlecieć się *perf*); (*inf: emotionally*) rozklejać się (rozkleić się *perf*)

▸ **fall back** *vt fus* (*Mil*) wycofywać się (wycofać się *perf*); (*in fear, disgust*) cofać się (cofnąć się *perf*)

▸ **fall back on** *vt fus* zdawać się (zdać się *perf*) na *+acc*, uciekać się (uciec się *perf*) do *+gen*

▸ **fall behind** *vi* pozostawać (pozostać *perf*) w tyle; (*fig: with payment*) zalegać

▸ **fall down** *vi* (*person*) upadać (upaść *perf*); (*building*) walić się (zawalić się *perf*)

▸ **fall for** *vt fus* (*trick, story*) dawać (dać *perf*) się nabrać na *+acc*; (*person*) zakochiwać się (zakochać się *perf*) w *+loc*

▸ **fall in** *vi* (*roof*) zapadać się (zapaść się *perf*); (*Mil*) formować (sformować *perf*) szereg

▸ **fall in with** *vt fus* (*plan, suggestion*) zgadzać się (zgodzić się *perf*) na *+acc*; (*remark*) zgadzać się (zgodzić się *perf*) z *+instr*

▸ **fall off** *vi* (*person, object*) odpadać (odpaść *perf*); (*takings, attendance*) spadać (spaść *perf*)

▸ **fall out** *vi* (*hair, teeth*) wypadać (wypaść *perf*); (*friends etc*): **to ~ out (with sb)** poróżnić się (*perf*) (z kimś)

▸ **fall over** *vi* przewracać się (przewrócić się *perf*) ▹ *vt* (*object*) przewracać (przewrócić *perf*); **to ~ over o.s. to do sth** stawać (stanąć *perf*) na głowie, żeby coś zrobić

▸ **fall through** *vi* nie dochodzić (nie dojść *perf*) do skutku

**fallacy** ['fæləsɪ] *n* (*misconception*) mit *m*; (*in reasoning, argument*) błąd *m* (logiczny)

**fallback** ['fɔːlbæk] *n* odwrót *m* ▹ *cpd*: **~ position** upatrzona pozycja *f*

**fallen** ['fɔːlən] *pp of* **fall**

**fallible** ['fæləbl] *adj* (*person*) omylny; (*memory*) zawodny

**falling** ['fɔːlɪŋ] *adj*: **~ market** załamujący się rynek *m*

**falling-off** ['fɔːlɪŋ'ɔf] *n* (*of business, interest*) spadek *m*

**fallopian tube** [fə'ləupɪən-] *n* jajowód *m*

**fallout** ['fɔːlaut] *n* opad *m* radioaktywny

**fallout shelter** *n* schron *m* przeciwatomowy

**fallow** ['fæləu] *adj*: **~ land/field** ugór *m*

**false** [fɔːls] *adj* fałszywy; **~ imprisonment** bezprawne pozbawienie wolności

**false alarm** *n* fałszywy alarm *m*

**falsehood** ['fɔːlshud] *n* fałsz *m*

**falsely** ['fɔːlslɪ] *adv* (*accuse*) bezpodstawnie

**false pretences** *npl*: **under ~** pod fałszywym pretekstem

**false teeth** (*Brit*) *npl* sztuczna szczęka *f*

**falsify** ['fɔːlsɪfaɪ] *vt* fałszować (sfałszować *perf*)

**falter** ['fɔːltəʳ] *vi* (*engine*) przerywać; (*voice*) łamać się, załamywać się (załamać się *perf*); (*weaken: person*) wahać się (zawahać się *perf*); (*: demand, interest*) słabnąć (osłabnąć *perf*); **he ~ed, his steps ~ed** zachwiał się

**fame** [feɪm] *n* sława *f*

**familiar** [fə'mɪlɪəʳ] *adj* (*well-known*) (dobrze) znany, znajomy; (*too intimate*) poufały; **I am ~ with her work** znam jej prace; **to be on ~ terms with sb** być z kimś w zażyłych stosunkach

**familiarity** [fəmɪlɪ'ærɪtɪ] *n* (*of place*) znajomy wygląd *m or* charakter *m*; (*excessive intimacy*) poufałość *f*; (*knowledge*): **~ with** znajomość *f +gen*

**familiarize** [fə'mɪlɪəraɪz] *vt*: **to ~ o.s. with sth** zaznajamiać się (zaznajomić się *perf*) z czymś

**family** ['fæmɪlɪ] *n* rodzina *f*; **mothers with large families** matki z licznym potomstwem; **after raising a ~** po odchowaniu dzieci

**family business** *n* firma *f* rodzinna

**family doctor** *n* lekarz *m* domowy

**family life** *n* życie *nt* rodzinne

**family planning** *n* planowanie *nt* rodziny; **~ clinic** poradnia rodzinna

**family tree** *n* drzewo *nt* genealogiczne

**famine** ['fæmɪn] *n* głód *m*, klęska *f* głodu

**famished** ['fæmɪʃt] (*inf*) *adj* wygłodniały; **I'm ~** umieram z głodu

**famous** ['feɪməs] *adj* sławny, znany; **~ for** słynny *or* słynący z *+gen*

**famously** ['feɪməslɪ] *adv*: **to get on ~ (with sb)** bardzo dobrze się (z kimś) zgadzać

**fan** [fæn] *n* (*folding*) wachlarz *m*; (*Elec*) wentylator *m*; (*of pop star*) fan(ka) *m(f)*; (*of sports team*) kibic *m* ▹ *vt* (*face, person*) wachlować (powachlować *perf*); (*fire, fear, anger*) podsycać (podsycić *perf*)

▸ **fan out** *vi* (*spread out*) rozbiegać się (rozbiec się *perf*) (półkoliście)

**fanatic** [fə'nætɪk] *n* fanatyk(-yczka) *m(f)*

**fanatical** [fə'nætɪkl] *adj* fanatyczny

**fan belt** *n* pasek *m* klinowy wentylatora

**fanciful** ['fænsɪful] *adj* (*notion, idea*) dziwaczny; (*design, name*) udziwniony, wymyślny

**fancy** ['fænsɪ] *n* (*liking*) upodobanie *nt*; (*imagination*) wyobraźnia *f*, fantazja *f*; (*fantasy*) marzenie *nt*, mrzonka *f* ▹ *adj* (*clothes, hat*) wymyślny, fantazyjny; (*hotel*) wytworny, luksusowy ▹ *vt* (*feel like, want*) mieć ochotę na *+acc*; (*imagine*) wyobrażać (wyobrazić *perf*) sobie; **I fancied (that) ...** wydawało mi się, że ...; **I took a ~ to him** przypadł mi do gustu; **when the ~ takes him** kiedy mu przyjdzie ochota; **the vase immediately took** *or* **caught her ~** wazon natychmiast wpadł jej w oko; **he fancies himself** jest zakochany w sobie; **he fancies himself as an intellectual** wyobraża sobie, że jest intelektualistą; **she fancies you** (*inf*) podobasz jej się; **well, ~ that!** a to dopiero!, coś takiego!

**fancy dress** *n* przebranie *nt*, kostium *m*

**fancy-dress ball** ['fænsɪdrɛs-] *n* bal *m* kostiumowy *or* przebierańców

**fancy goods** *npl* luksusowe towary *pl*

**fanfare** ['fænfɛəʳ] *n* fanfara *f*

**fang** [fæŋ] *n* kieł *m*

**fan heater** (*Brit*) *n* termowentylator *m*

**fanlight** ['fænlaɪt] *n* naświetle *nt* (*półkoliste okienko nad drzwiami*)

**fantasize** ['fæntəsaɪz] *vi* marzyć

**fantastic** [fæn'tæstɪk] *adj* fantastyczny; (*strange, incredible*) niezwykły

**fantasy** ['fæntəsɪ] *n* (*dream*) marzenie *nt*; (*unreality*) fikcja *f*; (*imagination*) wyobraźnia *f*; (*Literature*) fantastyka *f* baśniowa

**FAO** *n abbr* (= *Food and Agriculture Organization*) FAO *nt inv*

**FAQ** (*Comput*) *abbr* (= *frequently asked questions*) często zadawane pytania

**f.a.q.** *abbr* (= *free alongside quay*) franco nabrzeże

**far** [fɑːʳ] *adj* daleki ▷ *adv* (*a long way*) daleko; (*much, greatly*) w dużym stopniu; **at the far side** na drugiej stronie; **at the far end** na drugim końcu; **far away** daleko; **far off** daleko; **far better** daleko lepiej; **he was far from poor** nie był bynajmniej biedny; **far from speeding up, the car stopped** zamiast przyspieszyć, samochód zatrzymał się; **by far** zdecydowanie; **is it far to London?** czy daleko do Londynu?; **it's not far from here** to niedaleko stąd; **go as far as the farm** idź (aż) do farmy; **as far back as the thirteenth century** już w trzynastym wieku; **as far as I know** o ile wiem; **as far as possible** na tyle, na ile (to) możliwe, w miarę możliwości; **he went too far** posunął się zbyt daleko; **he went so far as to resign** posunął się aż do złożenia rezygnacji; **far and away** zdecydowanie; **from far and wide** zewsząd; **far from it** bynajmniej; **far be it from me to criticise** daleki jestem od tego, by krytykować; **so far** (jak) dotąd *or* do tej pory, dotychczas; **how far?** (*in distance, progress*) jak daleko?; (*in degree*) na ile?, do jakiego stopnia?; **the far left/right** (*Pol*) skrajna lewica/prawica

**faraway** ['fɑːrəweɪ] *adj* (*place*) odległy, daleki; (*sound*) daleki; (*look, thought*) oddalony

**farce** [fɑːs] *n* (*lit, fig*) farsa *f*

**farcical** ['fɑːsɪkl] *adj* absurdalny, niedorzeczny

**fare** [fɛəʳ] *n* (*on train, bus*) opłata *f* (za przejazd); (*food*) strawa *f*; (*in taxi*) klient(ka) *m(f)*; **he ~s well/badly** dobrze/źle mu się powodzi *or* wiedzie; **how did you ~?** jak ci poszło?; **they ~d badly in the recent elections** nie powiodło im się w ostatnich wyborach; **half/full ~** opłata ulgowa/normalna

**Far East** *n*: **the ~** Daleki Wschód *m*

**farewell** [fɛə'wɛl] *excl.* żegnaj(cie) ▷ *n* pożegnanie *nt*; **to bid sb ~** żegnać się (pożegnać się *perf*) z kimś ▷ *cpd* pożegnalny

**far-fetched** ['fɑː'fɛtʃt] *adj* (*argument*) naciągany (*inf*); (*conclusion*) zbyt daleko idący

**farm** [fɑːm] *n* gospodarstwo *nt* (rolne); (*specialist*) farma *f* ▷ *vt* (*land*) uprawiać
▶ **farm out** *vt* (*work etc*) zlecać (zlecić *perf*)

**farmer** ['fɑːməʳ] *n* rolnik *m*; (*on specialist farm*) farmer *m*

**farmhand** ['fɑːmhænd] *n* robotnik(-ica) *m(f)* rolny(-na) *m(f)*

**farmhouse** ['fɑːmhaus] *n* dom *m* w gospodarstwie rolnym

**farming** ['fɑːmɪŋ] *n* (*agriculture*) gospodarka *f* rolna; (*of crops*) uprawa *f*; (*of animals*) hodowla *f*; **sheep ~** hodowla owiec; **intensive ~** intensywna gospodarka rolna

**farm labourer** *n* = **farmhand**

**farmland** ['fɑːmlænd] *n* pole *nt* uprawne

**farm produce** *n* produkty *pl* rolne

**farm worker** *n* = **farmhand**

**farmyard** ['fɑːmjɑːd] *n* podwórze *nt*

**Faroe Islands** ['fɛərəu-] *npl*: **the ~** Wyspy *pl* Owcze

**Faroes** ['fɛərəuz] *npl* = **Faroe Islands**

**far-reaching** ['fɑː'riːtʃɪŋ] *adj* dalekosiężny

**far-sighted** ['fɑː'saɪtɪd] *adj* (*US*) dalekowzroczny

**fart** [fɑːt] (*inf!*) *vi* pierdzieć (pierdnąć *perf*) (*inf!*) ▷ *n* pierdnięcie *nt* (*inf!*)

**farther** ['fɑːðəʳ] *adv* dalej ▷ *adj* (*shore, side*) drugi

**farthest** ['fɑːðɪst] *adv* najdalej

**f.a.s.** (*Brit*) *abbr* (= *free alongside ship*) franco wzdłuż burty statku

**fascia** ['feɪʃə] *n* (*Aut*) deska *f* rozdzielcza

**fascinate** ['fæsɪneɪt] *vt* fascynować (zafascynować *perf*)

**fascinating** ['fæsɪneɪtɪŋ] *adj* fascynujący

**fascination** [fæsɪ'neɪʃən] *n* fascynacja *f*, zafascynowanie *nt*; **to hold** *or* **exercise a ~ for sb** być dla kogoś źródłem fascynacji

**fascism** ['fæʃɪzəm] *n* faszyzm *m*

**fascist** ['fæʃɪst] *adj* faszystowski ▷ *n* faszysta(-tka) *m(f)*

**fashion** ['fæʃən] *n* (*trend, clothes*) moda *f*; (*manner*) sposób *m* ▷ *vt* (*out of clay etc*)

f

modelować (wymodelować *perf*); **in ~** w modzie; **to go out of ~** wychodzić (wyjść *perf*) z mody; **after a ~** jako tako
**fashionable** ['fæʃnəbl] *adj* modny
**fashion designer** *n* projektant(ka) *m(f)* mody
**fashion show** *n* pokaz *m* mody
**fast** [fɑːst] *adj* (*runner, car, progress*) szybki; (*dye, colour*) trwały ▷ *adv* (*run, act, think*) szybko; (*stuck, held*) mocno ▷ *n* post *m* ▷ *vi* pościć; **my watch is (5 minutes) ~** mój zegarek śpieszy się (o 5 minut); **to be ~ asleep** spać głęboko; **as ~ as I can** najszybciej jak mogę; **to make a boat ~** (*Brit*) cumować (zacumować *perf*) łódź
**fasten** ['fɑːsn] *vt* (*one thing to another*) przymocowywać (przymocować *perf*); (*coat, dress, seat-belt*) zapinać (zapiąć *perf*) ▷ *vi* (*dress etc*) zapinać się (zapiąć się *perf*)
▸ **fasten (up)on** *vt fus* (*idea, scheme*) uchwycić się (*perf*) *+gen*
**fastener** ['fɑːsnəʳ] *n* zapięcie *nt*
**fastening** ['fɑːsnɪŋ] *n* = **fastener**
**fast food** *n* szybkie dania *pl*; **~ restaurant** bar szybkiej obsługi; **~ chain** sieć barów szybkiej obsługi
**fast-forward** *vt* przewijać (przewinąć *perf*) ▷ *vi* (*tape*) przewijać (przewinąć *perf*) się (*do przodu*)
**fastidious** [fæs'tɪdɪəs] *adj* (*fussy*) wybredny; (*attentive to detail*) drobiazgowy, skrupulatny
**fast lane** *n*: **the ~** pas *m* szybkiego ruchu
**fat** [fæt] *adj* (*animal*) tłusty; (*person, book, wallet*) gruby; (*profit*) pokaźny ▷ *n* tłuszcz *m*; **to live off the fat of the land** opływać w dostatki; **that's a fat lot of use** *or* **good to us** (*inf*) strasznie dużo nam z tego przyjdzie!
**fatal** ['feɪtl] *adj* (*injury, illness, accident*) śmiertelny; (*mistake*) fatalny
**fatalistic** [feɪtə'lɪstɪk] *adj* fatalistyczny
**fatality** [fə'tælɪtɪ] *n* (*death*) wypadek *m* śmiertelny
**fatally** ['feɪtəlɪ] *adv* (*wounded, injured*) śmiertelnie
**fate** [feɪt] *n* los *m*; **to meet one's ~** spotykać (spotkać *perf*) swoje przeznaczenie
**fated** ['feɪtɪd] *adj*: **we were ~ to meet, it was ~ that we should meet** było nam przeznaczone *or* sądzone się spotkać
**fateful** ['feɪtful] *adj* brzemienny w skutki
**fat-free** *adj* beztłuszczowy
**father** ['fɑːðəʳ] *n* (*lit, fig*) ojciec *m*
**Father Christmas** *n* ≈ Święty Mikołaj *m*
**fatherhood** ['fɑːðəhud] *n* ojcostwo *nt*
**father-in-law** ['fɑːðərənlɔː] *n* teść *m*
**fatherland** ['fɑːðəlænd] *n* ojczyzna *f*
**fatherly** ['fɑːðəlɪ] *adj* ojcowski
**fathom** ['fæðəm] *n* (*Naut*) sążeń *m* (angielski) ▷ *vt* (*mystery*) zgłębiać (zgłębić *perf*); (*meaning, reason*) pojmować (pojąć *perf*)
**fatigue** [fə'tiːg] *n* (*tiredness*) zmęczenie *nt*; **fatigues** *npl* (*Mil*) mundur *m* polowy; **metal ~** zmęczenie metalu
**fatness** ['fætnɪs] *n* tusza *f*
**fatten** ['fætn] *vt* tuczyć (utuczyć *perf*); **chocolate is ~ing** czekolada jest tucząca
**fatty** ['fætɪ] *adj* (*food*) tłusty ▷ *n* (*inf*) grubas(ka) *m(f)*
**fatuous** ['fætjuəs] *adj* niedorzeczny
**faucet** ['fɔːsɪt] (*US*) *n* kran *m*
**fault** [fɔːlt] *n* (*mistake*) błąd *m*; (*defect: in person*) wada *f*; (*: in machine*) usterka *f*; (*Geol*) uskok *m*; (*Tennis*) błąd *m* serwisowy ▷ *vt*: **I couldn't ~ him** nie mogłem mu nic zarzucić; **it's my ~** to moja wina; **if my memory is not at ~** jeśli mnie pamięć nie myli; **to find ~ with sb/sth** czepiać się kogoś/czegoś; **to be at ~** ponosić winę; **generous to a ~** hojny (aż) do przesady
**faultless** ['fɔːltlɪs] *adj* bezbłędny
**faulty** ['fɔːltɪ] *adj* wadliwy
**fauna** ['fɔːnə] *n* fauna *f*
**faux pas** *n inv* faux pas *nt inv*
**favour**, (*US*) **favor** ['feɪvəʳ] *n* (*approval*) przychylność *f*; (*act of kindness*) przysługa *f* ▷ *vt* (*prefer: solution, view*) preferować; (*: person*) faworyzować; (*be advantageous to*) sprzyjać *+dat*; **to ask a ~ of sb** prosić (poprosić *perf*) kogoś o przysługę; **to do sb a ~** wyświadczać (wyświadczyć *perf*) komuś przysługę; **in ~ of** na korzyść *+gen*; **to be in ~ of sth/doing sth** być zwolennikiem czegoś/(z)robienia czegoś; **to find ~ with sb** przypadać (przypaść *perf*) komuś do gustu
**favourable** ['feɪvrəbl] *adj* (*reaction, review*) przychylny; (*terms, conditions, impression*) korzystny; **to be ~ to** być przychylnie nastawionym do *+gen*
**favourably** ['feɪvrəblɪ] *adv* (*react, speak, review*) przychylnie; (*placed*) korzystnie; **to compare ~ with** wypadać (wypaść *perf*) korzystnie w porównaniu z *+instr*
**favourite** ['feɪvrɪt] *adj* ulubiony ▷ *n* (*of teacher, parent*) ulubieniec(-ica) *m(f)*; (*in race*) faworyt(ka) *m(f)*
**favouritism** ['feɪvrɪtɪzəm] *n* protekcja *f*
**fawn** [fɔːn] *n* jelonek *m* ▷ *adj* (*also*: **fawn-coloured**) płowy ▷ *vi*: **to ~ (up)on** nadskakiwać *+dat*
**fax** [fæks] *n* faks *m* ▷ *vt* faksować (przefaksować *perf*)
**FBI** (*US*) *n abbr* (= *Federal Bureau of Investigation*) FBI *nt inv*
**FCC** (*US*) *n abbr* (= *Federal Communications Commission*) *federalny urząd łączności*
**FCO** (*Brit*) *n abbr* (= *Foreign and Commonwealth Office*) Ministerstwo *nt* Spraw Zagranicznych i Stosunków z Krajami Wspólnoty Narodów

**FD** (US) *n abbr* (= *fire department*) SP *f inv* (= *Straż Pożarna*)
**FDA** (US) *n abbr* (= *Food and Drug Administration*) *urząd federalny sprawujący kontrolę nad jakością żywności i lekarstw*
**fear** [fɪəʳ] *n* (*dread*) strach *m*; (: *indefinite, irrational*) lęk *m*; (*anxiety*) obawa *f* ▷ *vt* (*be scared of*) bać się *+gen*; (*be worried about*) obawiać się *+gen* ▷ *vi*: **to ~ for** lękać się *or* obawiać się o *+acc*; **to ~ that ...** obawiać się, że ...; **~ of heights** lęk wysokości; **for ~ of offending him** (w obawie,) żeby go nie urazić
**fearful** ['fɪəful] *adj* (*person*) bojaźliwy; (*sight, consequences*) przerażający, straszny; (*scream, racket*) przeraźliwy, straszliwy; **to be ~ of sth/doing sth** bać się czegoś/coś (z)robić
**fearfully** ['fɪəfəlɪ] *adv* (*timidly*) bojaźliwie; (*fml: very*) przeraźliwie, straszliwie
**fearless** ['fɪəlɪs] *adj* nieustraszony
**fearsome** ['fɪəsəm] *adj* przerażający
**feasibility** [fiːzə'bɪlɪtɪ] *n* wykonalność *f*
**feasibility study** *n* techniczno-ekonomiczne badanie *nt* wykonalności
**feasible** ['fiːzəbl] *adj* wykonalny
**feast** [fiːst] *n* (*banquet*) uczta *f*; (*Rel: also*: **feast day**) święto *nt* ▷ *vi* ucztować; **to ~ on** zajadać się *+instr*; **to ~ one's eyes (up)on sb/sth** sycić wzrok widokiem kogoś/czegoś
**feat** [fiːt] *n* wyczyn *m*
**feather** ['fɛðəʳ] *n* pióro *nt* ▷ *cpd* (*mattress, pillow*) puchowy ▷ *vt*: **to ~ one's nest** (*fig*) nabijać (nabić *perf*) kabzę; **a ~ in one's cap** powód do dumy
**featherweight** ['fɛðəweɪt] *n* bokser *m* wagi piórkowej; (*fig*) płotka *f*
**feature** ['fiːtʃəʳ] *n* cecha *f*; (*Press, TV, Radio*) (obszerny) reportaż *m* (*na poważny temat nie związany bezpośrednio z najświeższymi wiadomościami*) ▷ *vt*: **the film ~s two famous actors** w filmie występują dwaj znani aktorzy ▷ *vi*: **to ~ in** (*film*) grać (zagrać *perf*) pierwszoplanową rolę w *+loc*; (*situation*) odgrywać (odegrać *perf*) ważną rolę w *+loc*; **features** *npl* rysy *pl* (twarzy)
**feature film** *n* film *m* fabularny
**featureless** ['fiːtʃəlɪs] *adj* niczym się nie wyróżniający
**Feb.** *abbr* (= *February*) lut.
**February** ['fɛbruərɪ] *n* luty *m*; *see also* **July**
**feces** ['fiːsiːz] (US) *npl* = **faeces**
**feckless** ['fɛklɪs] *adj* nieodpowiedzialny
**fed** [fɛd] *pt, pp of* **feed**
**Fed** (US) *abbr* = **federal**; **federation**
**Fed.** [fɛd] (US: *inf*) *n abbr* (= *Federal Reserve Board*) *rada banków rezerwy federalnej, tworzących bank centralny Stanów Zjednoczonych*
**federal** ['fɛdərəl] *adj* federalny
**Federal Republic of Germany** *n* Republika *f* Federalna Niemiec
**Federal Reserve Board** (US) *n* Federalny Bank *m* Rezerw
**Federal Trade Commission** (US) *n* Federalna Komisja *f* do Spraw Handlowych
**federation** [fɛdə'reɪʃən] *n* federacja *f*
**fed up** *adj*: **to be ~ (with)** mieć dość (*+gen*)
**fee** [fiː] *n* opłata *f*; (*of doctor, lawyer*) honorarium *nt*; **school fees** czesne; **entrance fee** (*to organization*) wpisowe; **membership fee** składka członkowska; **for a small fee** za niewielką opłatą
**feeble** ['fiːbl] *adj* słaby; (*joke, excuse*) kiepski
**feeble-minded** ['fiːbl'maɪndɪd] *adj* słaby na umyśle
**feed** [fiːd] (*pt, pp* **fed**) *n* (*feeding*) karmienie *nt*; (*fodder*) pasza *f*; (*on printer*) dane *pl* wejściowe ▷ *vt* (*baby, invalid, dog*) karmić (nakarmić *perf*); (*family*) żywić (wyżywić *perf*); (*data, information: into computer*) wprowadzać (wprowadzić *perf*); (*coins: into meter, payphone*) wrzucać (wrzucić *perf*)
▸ **feed on** *vt fus* żywić się *+instr*; **anger ~s on disappointment** rozczarowanie stanowi pożywkę dla gniewu
**feedback** ['fiːdbæk] *n* (*noise*) sprzężenie *nt*; (*from person*) reakcja *f*
**feeder** ['fiːdəʳ] *n*: **the baby is a slow/sleepy ~** niemowlę je wolno/zasypia przy jedzeniu
**feeding bottle** ['fiːdɪŋ-] (*Brit*) *n* butelka *f* dla niemowląt
**feel** [fiːl] (*pt, pp* **felt**) *n*: **it has a smooth/prickly ~** to jest gładkie/kłujące w dotyku ▷ *vt* (*touch*) dotykać (dotknąć *perf*) *+gen*; (*experience*) czuć (poczuć *perf*); (*think, believe*): **to ~ that ...** uważać, że ...; **the place had a completely different ~** to miejsce miało zupełnie inną atmosferę; **I ~ I'm neglecting him** czuję, że go zaniedbuję; **she knew how I felt about it** wiedziała, co sądzę na ten temat; **we didn't ~ hungry** nie odczuwaliśmy głodu; **I ~ cold/hot** jest mi zimno/gorąco; **to ~ lonely/better** czuć się samotnie/lepiej; **I don't ~ well** nie czuję się dobrze; **I ~ sorry for her** żal mi jej; **the cloth ~s soft** tkanina jest miękka w dotyku; **it ~s like velvet** przypomina (w dotyku) aksamit; **it ~s colder here** tu jest zimniej; **to ~ like sth** mieć ochotę na coś; **I felt like a criminal** czułem się jak przestępca; **I'm still ~ing my way** nadal poruszam się po omacku; **you'll soon get the ~ of it** wkrótce się przyzwyczaisz
▸ **feel about** *vi* szukać po omacku; **to ~ about** *or* **around in one's pocket for** szperać *or* grzebać w kieszeni w poszukiwaniu *+gen*
▸ **feel around** *vi* = **feel about**

**feeler** ['fiːləʳ] *n* (*of insect*) czułek *m*; **to put out a ~** *or* **~s** (*fig*) badać (zbadać *perf*) grunt
**feeling** ['fiːlɪŋ] *n* uczucie *nt*; **~s were running high** rozgorzały namiętności; **what are your ~s about the matter?** co sądzisz na ten temat?; **I have a ~ (that) we are being followed** mam uczucie, że ktoś nas śledzi; **my ~ is that ...** mam wrażenie, że ...; **I didn't want to hurt his ~s** nie chciałam go urazić
**feet** [fiːt] *npl of* **foot**
**feign** [feɪn] *vt* (*illness*) symulować; (*interest, surprise*) udawać (udać *perf*)
**feigned** [feɪnd] *adj*: **~ surprise** udawane zdziwienie *nt*
**feint** [feɪnt] *n* papier *m* w linie
**felicitous** [fɪ'lɪsɪtəs] *adj* (*combination*) udany, szczęśliwy; (*word, remark*) trafny
**feline** ['fiːlaɪn] *adj* koci
**fell** [fɛl] *pt of* **fall** ▷ *vt* (*tree*) ścinać (ściąć *perf*); (*opponent*) powalić (*perf*) ▷ *n* (*Brit*) *góra, wzgórze lub wrzosowisko w dzikim krajobrazie północnej Anglii* ▷ *adj*: **in one ~ swoop** za jednym zamachem
**fellow** ['fɛləu] *n* (*chap*) gość *m* (*inf*), facet *m* (*inf*); (*comrade*) towarzysz *m*; (*of learned society*) ≈ członek *m* (rzeczywisty); (*of university*) *nauczyciel akademicki będący członkiem kolegium uniwersytetu* ▷ *cpd*: **their ~ prisoners** ich współwięźniowie *vir pl*; **a ~ passenger** towarzysz podróży; **his ~ workers** jego koledzy z pracy; **with some of his ~ students** z kilkoma innymi studentami
**fellow citizen** *n* współobywatel(ka) *m(f)*
**fellow countryman** (*irreg*: *like* **man**) *n* rodak/rodaczka *m/f*
**fellow men** *npl* bliźni *vir pl*
**fellowship** ['fɛləuʃɪp] *n* (*comradeship*) koleżeństwo *nt*; (*society*) towarzystwo *nt*; (*Scol*) *członkostwo kolegium uniwersytetu*
**fell-walking** ['fɛlwɔːkɪŋ] (*Brit*) *n* górska turystyka *f* piesza
**felon** ['fɛlən] *n* (*Jur*) zbrodniarz(-arka) *m(f)*
**felony** ['fɛlənɪ] *n* ciężkie przestępstwo *nt*
**felt** [fɛlt] *pt, pp of* **feel** ▷ *n* filc *m*
**felt-tip pen** ['fɛlttɪp-] *n* pisak *m*
**female** ['fiːmeɪl] *n* (*Zool*) samica *f*; (*woman*) kobieta *f* ▷ *adj* (*child*) płci żeńskiej *post*; (*sex, plant, plug*) żeński; (*Zool*: *instincts*) samiczy; (: *animal*): **~ whale** samica *f* wieloryba; **the ~ body** ciało kobiety; **~ equality** równouprawnienie kobiet; **~ suffrage** prawo wyborcze dla kobiet; **male and ~ students** studenci obojga płci, studenci i studentki
**female impersonator** *n* (*Theat*) odtwórca *m* ról żeńskich
**feminine** ['fɛmɪnɪn] *adj* kobiecy; (*Ling*: *gender*) żeński; (: *noun, pronoun*) rodzaju żeńskiego *post*
**femininity** [fɛmɪ'nɪnɪtɪ] *n* kobiecość *f*
**feminism** ['fɛmɪnɪzəm] *n* feminizm *m*
**feminist** ['fɛmɪnɪst] *n* feminista(-tka) *m(f)*
**fen** [fɛn] (*Brit*) *n*: **the Fens** *nisko położone, błotniste tereny we wschodniej Anglii*
**fence** [fɛns] *n* płot *m* ▷ *vt* (*also*: **fence in**) ogradzać (ogrodzić *perf*) ▷ *vi* (*Sport*) uprawiać szermierkę; **to sit on the ~** (*fig*) zachowywać (zachować *perf*) neutralność
**fencing** ['fɛnsɪŋ] *n* (*Sport*) szermierka *f*
**fend** [fɛnd] *vi*: **grown-up children should ~ for themselves** dorosłe dzieci powinny radzić sobie same
▸ **fend off** *vt* (*attack, attacker, blow*) odpierać (odeprzeć *perf*); (*unwanted questions etc*) bronić się (obronić się *perf*) przed *+instr*
**fender** ['fɛndəʳ] *n* (*of fireplace*) osłona *f* zabezpieczająca; (*on boat*) odbijacz *m*; (*US*: *of car*) błotnik *m*
**fennel** ['fɛnl] *n* (*as herb*) koper *m* włoski; (*as vegetable*) fenkuł *m*
**ferment** [*vb* fə'mɛnt, *n* 'fəːmɛnt] *vi* fermentować (sfermentować *perf*) ▷ *n* (*fig*) wrzenie *nt*, ferment *m*
**fermentation** [fəːmɛn'teɪʃən] *n* fermentacja *f*
**fern** [fəːn] *n* paproć *f*
**ferocious** [fə'rəuʃəs] *adj* (*animal, yell*) dziki; (*assault, fighting, heat*) okrutny; (*climate, expression, criticism*) srogi; (*competition, opposition*) ostry
**ferocity** [fə'rɔsɪtɪ] *n* (*of animal*) dzikość *f*; (*of assault*) okrucieństwo *nt*; (*of climate*) srogość *f*; (*of competition*) ostrość *f*
**ferret** ['fɛrɪt] *n* fretka *f*
▸ **ferret about** *vi* myszkować
▸ **ferret around** *vi* = **ferret about**
▸ **ferret out** *vt* (*information*) wyszperać (*perf*)
**ferry** ['fɛrɪ] *n* prom *m* ▷ *vt* (*by sea, air, road*) przewozić (przewieźć *perf*); **to ~ sth/sb across** *or* **over** przewozić (przewieźć *perf*) kogoś/coś
**ferryman** ['fɛrɪmən] *n* przewoźnik *m*
**fertile** ['fəːtaɪl] *adj* (*soil*) żyzny, urodzajny; (*imagination, woman*) płodny
**fertility** [fə'tɪlɪtɪ] *n* (*of soil*) żyzność *f*; (*of imagination, woman*) płodność *f*
**fertility drug** *n* środek *m* *or* lekarstwo *nt* na bezpłodność
**fertilization** [fəːtɪlaɪ'zeɪʃən] *n* zapłodnienie *nt*
**fertilize** ['fəːtɪlaɪz] *vt* (*land*) nawozić (nawieźć *perf*), użyźniać (użyźnić *perf*); (*Bio*) zapładniać (zapłodnić *perf*)
**fertilizer** ['fəːtɪlaɪzəʳ] *n* nawóz *m*
**fervent** ['fəːvənt] *adj* (*admirer, supporter*) zagorzały; (*belief*) żarliwy
**fervour**, (*US*) **fervor** ['fəːvəʳ] *n* zapał *m*, gorliwość *f*

**fester** ['fɛstəʳ] *vi* (*wound*) ropieć, jątrzyć się (rozjątrzyć się *perf*); (*row*) zaogniać się (zaognić się *perf*)
**festival** ['fɛstɪvəl] *n* (*Rel*) święto *nt*; (*Art, Mus*) festiwal *m*
**festive** ['fɛstɪv] *adj* świąteczny, odświętny; **the ~ season** (*Brit*) okres gwiazdkowy
**festivities** [fɛs'tɪvɪtɪz] *npl* uroczystości *pl*, obchody *pl*
**festoon** [fɛs'tu:n] *vt*: **to ~ sth with** przystrajać (przystroić *perf*) coś *+instr*
**fetch** [fɛtʃ] *vt* przynosić (przynieść *perf*); **~ me a jug of water** przynieś mi dzbanek wody; **how much did it ~?** ile to przyniosło?
▸ **fetch up** *vi* lądować (wylądować *perf*) (*fig*)
**fetching** ['fɛtʃɪŋ] *adj* (*woman*) ponętny; (*dress*) twarzowy
**fete** [feɪt] *n* (*at school*) festyn *m*; (*at church*) odpust *m*
**fetid** ['fɛtɪd] *adj* cuchnący
**fetish** ['fɛtɪʃ] *n* (*object*) fetysz *m*; (*obsession*) fiksacja *f*
**fetter** ['fɛtəʳ] *vt* krępować (skrępować *perf*), pętać (spętać *perf*)
**fetters** ['fɛtəz] *npl* (*lit*) kajdany *pl*; (*fig*) pęta *pl*, okowy *pl*
**fettle** ['fɛtl] (*Brit*) *n*: **in fine ~** w świetnej formie
**fetus** ['fi:təs] (*US*) *n* = **foetus**
**feud** [fju:d] *n* waśń *f* ▹ *vi* być zwaśnionym; **a family ~** waśń rodzinna
**feudal** ['fju:dl] *adj* feudalny
**feudalism** ['fju:dlɪzəm] *n* feudalizm *m*
**fever** ['fi:vəʳ] *n* gorączka *f*
**feverish** ['fi:vərɪʃ] *adj* (*child, face*) rozpalony; (*fig: emotion, activity*) gorączkowy; (*: person*) rozgorączkowany
**few** [fju:] *adj* niewiele (*+gen*), mało (*+gen*); (*of groups of people including at least one male*) niewielu (*+gen*) ▹ *pron* niewiele; (*of groups of people including at least one male*) niewielu; **a few** *adj* kilka (*+gen*), parę (*+gen*); (*of groups of people including at least one male*) kilku (*+gen*), paru (*+gen*); (*of children, groups of people of both sexes*) kilkoro (*+gen*) ▹ *pron* kilka, parę; (*of groups of people including at least one male*) kilku, paru; **very few survived** bardzo niewielu przeżyło; **a good few, quite a few** (całkiem) sporo; **as few as** zaledwie, tylko; **no fewer than** nie mniej niż, aż; **her visits are few and far between** jej wizyty są bardzo rzadkie; **in the next/past few days** w ciągu kilku najbliższych/ostatnich dni; **every few days/months** co kilka dni/miesięcy
**fewer** ['fju:əʳ] *adj* mniej (*+gen*); **they are ~** jest ich mniej; **there are ~ buses on Sundays** w niedzielę jeździ mniej autobusów
**fewest** ['fju:ɪst] *adj* najmniej (*+gen*)
**FFA** *n abbr* = **Future Farmers of America**
**FH** (*Brit*) *n abbr* = **fire hydrant**
**FHA** (*US*) *n abbr* = **Federal Housing Administration**
**fiancé** [fɪ'ɑ̃:ŋseɪ] *n* narzeczony *m*
**fiancée** [fɪ'ɑ̃:ŋseɪ] *n* narzeczona *f*
**fiasco** [fɪ'æskəu] *n* fiasko *nt*
**fib** [fɪb] *n* bajka *f*, bujda *f* (*inf*); **to tell fibs** bujać (*inf*)
**fibre**, (*US*) **fiber** ['faɪbəʳ] *n* włókno *nt*; (*roughage*) błonnik *m*
**fibreboard** ['faɪbəbɔ:d], (*US*) **fiberboard** *n* płyta *f* pilśniowa
**fibre-glass** ['faɪbəglɑ:s], (*US*) **fiber-glass** *n* włókno *nt* szklane
**fibrositis** [faɪbrə'saɪtɪs] *n* gościec *m* mięśniowo-ścięgnisty
**FICA** (*US*) *n abbr* = **Federal Insurance Contributions Act**
**fickle** ['fɪkl] *adj* kapryśny, zmienny
**fiction** ['fɪkʃən] *n* (*Literature*) beletrystyka *f*, literatura *f* piękna; (*invention, lie*) fikcja *f*
**fictional** ['fɪkʃənl] *adj* fikcyjny
**fictionalize** ['fɪkʃnəlaɪz] *vt* fabularyzować (sfabularyzować *perf*)
**fictitious** [fɪk'tɪʃəs] *adj* fikcyjny, zmyślony
**fiddle** ['fɪdl] *n* (*Mus*) skrzypki *pl*, skrzypce *pl*; (*fraud*) szwindel *m* (*inf*) ▹ *vt* (*Brit: accounts*) fałszować (sfałszować *perf*); **tax ~** oszustwo podatkowe; **to work a ~** dopuścić się (*perf*) szwindlu (*inf*)
▸ **fiddle with** *vt fus* bawić się *+instr*
**fiddler** ['fɪdləʳ] *n* skrzypek(-paczka) *m*(*f*)
**fiddly** ['fɪdlɪ] *adj* (*task*) delikatny; (*object*) fikuśny (*inf*)
**fidelity** [fɪ'dɛlɪtɪ] *n* wierność *f*
**fidget** ['fɪdʒɪt] *vi* wiercić się
**fidgety** ['fɪdʒɪtɪ] *adj* niespokojny
**fiduciary** [fɪ'dju:ʃɪərɪ] *n* (*Jur*) powiernik *m*
**field** [fi:ld] *n* (*also Elec, Comput*) pole *nt*; (*Sport*) boisko *nt*; (*fig*) dziedzina *f*, pole *nt*; **~ study** badania terenowe; **the ~** (*competitors*) stawka; **to lead the ~** (*Sport*) prowadzić stawkę; (*fig*) przodować
**field day** *n*: **to have a ~** mieć używanie
**field glasses** *npl* lornetka *f* (*polowa*)
**field marshal** *n* marszałek *m* (polny), feldmarszałek *m*
**fieldwork** ['fi:ldwə:k] *n* badania *pl* terenowe
**fiend** [fi:nd] *n* potwór *m*
**fiendish** ['fi:ndɪʃ] *adj* (*person*) okrutny; (*problem*) piekielnie trudny; (*plan*) szatański
**fierce** [fɪəs] *adj* (*animal*) dziki; (*warrior*) zaciekły, zawzięty; (*look*) surowy; (*loyalty*) niezłomny; (*resistance, competition*) zaciekły; (*storm*) gwałtowny

**fiery** ['faɪərɪ] *adj* *(sun)* ognisty; *(fig)* ognisty, płomienny
**FIFA** ['fi:fə] *n abbr (= Fédération Internationale de Football Association)* FIFA *f inv*
**fifteen** [fɪf'ti:n] *num* piętnaście
**fifteenth** [fɪf'ti:nθ] *num* piętnasty
**fifth** [fɪfθ] *num* piąty
**fiftieth** ['fɪftɪɪθ] *num* pięćdziesiąty
**fifty** ['fɪftɪ] *num* pięćdziesiąt
**fifty-fifty** ['fɪftɪ'fɪftɪ] *adj* *(deal etc)* pół na pół *post* ▷ *adv* pół na pół, po połowie; **to go ~ with sb** dzielić się (podzielić się *perf*) z kimś pół na pół; **to have a ~ chance (of success)** mieć pięćdziesiąt procent szans (na sukces)
**fig** [fɪg] *n* *(fruit)* figa *f*; *(tree)* drzewo *nt* figowe
**fight** [faɪt] *n* walka *f*; *(brawl)* bójka *f*; *(row)* kłótnia *f*, sprzeczka *f* ▷ *vt* *(pt, pp* **fought***)* *(person, urge)* walczyć z *+instr*; *(cancer, prejudice etc)* walczyć z *+instr*, zwalczać (zwalczyć *perf*); *(Boxing)* walczyć przeciwko *+dat or* z *+instr*; **to ~ an election** prowadzić walkę (przed) wyborczą; **to ~ a case** *(Jur)* bronić sprawy ▷ *vi* walczyć, bić się; **to put up a ~** dzielnie się bronić; **to ~ with sb** walczyć z kimś; **to ~ for/against sth** walczyć o coś/z czymś; **to ~ one's way through a crowd/the undergrowth** przedzierać się (przedrzeć się *perf*) przez tłum/zarośla
▸ **fight back** *vi* bronić się, odpowiadać (odpowiedzieć *perf*) na atak ▷ *vt fus* *(tears etc)* walczyć z *+instr*
▸ **fight down** *vt* zwalczać (zwalczyć *perf*) w sobie
▸ **fight off** *vt* *(attack)* odpierać (odeprzeć *perf*); *(disease, urge)* walczyć z *+instr*, zwalczać (zwalczyć *perf*); *(sleep)* walczyć *or* zmagać się z *+instr*
▸ **fight out** *vt*: **to ~ it out** rozstrzygać (rozstrzygnąć *perf*) to między sobą
**fighter** ['faɪtə^r] *n* *(combatant)* walczący *m*; *(plane)* samolot *m* myśliwski, myśliwiec *m*; *(fig)* bojownik(-iczka) *m(f)*
**fighter pilot** *n* pilot *m* myśliwca
**fighting** ['faɪtɪŋ] *n* *(battle)* walka *f*, bitwa *f*; *(brawl)* bójka *f*, bijatyka *f*
**figment** ['fɪgmənt] *n*: **a ~ of sb's imagination** wytwór *m* czyjejś wyobraźni
**figurative** ['fɪgjurətɪv] *adj* *(expression)* przenośny, metaforyczny; *(style)* obfitujący w przenośnie; *(art)* figuratywny; **in a ~ sense** w znaczeniu przenośnym, w przenośni
**figure** ['fɪgə^r] *n* *(Geom)* figura *f*; *(number)* liczba *f*, cyfra *f*; *(body)* figura *f*; *(person)* postać *f*; *(personality)* postać *f*, figura *f* ▷ *vt* *(esp US)* dojść *(perf)* do wniosku ▷ *vi* figurować, pojawiać się (pojawić się *perf*); **I couldn't put a ~ on it** nie potrafiłem podać dokładnej liczby; **public ~** osoba publiczna; **that ~s** to było do przewidzenia, można się (było) tego spodziewać
▸ **figure out** *vt* wymyślić *(perf)*, wykombinować *(perf) (inf)*; **to ~ out sb/a problem** rozpracować *(perf) or* rozgryźć *(perf)* kogoś/problem
**figurehead** ['fɪgəhɛd] *n* *(Naut)* galion *m*; *(Pol)* marionetkowy przywódca *m*
**figure of speech** *n* figura *f* retoryczna
**figure skating** *n* jazda *f* figurowa na lodzie, łyżwiarstwo *nt* figurowe
**Fiji (Islands)** ['fi:dʒi:-] *n(pl)* (wyspy *pl*) Fidżi
**filament** ['fɪləmənt] *n* *(Elec)* włókno *nt* *(żarówki itp)*; *(Bio)* nitka *f* pyłkowa
**filch** [fɪltʃ] *(inf) vt* zwędzić *(perf) (inf)*
**file** [faɪl] *n* *(dossier)* akta *pl*, dossier *nt inv*; *(folder)* kartoteka *f*, teczka *f*; *(for loose leaf)* segregator *m*, skoroszyt *m*; *(Comput)* plik *m*; *(tool)* pilnik *m* ▷ *vt* *(document)* włączać (włączyć *perf*) do dokumentacji; *(lawsuit)* wnosić (wnieść *perf*); *(metal, fingernails)* piłować (spiłować *perf*); **to ~ in** wchodzić (wejść *perf*) jeden za drugim *or* gęsiego; **to ~ out** wychodzić (wyjść *perf*) jeden za drugim *or* gęsiego; **to ~ past** przechodzić (przejść *perf*) obok jeden za drugim *or* gęsiego, przedefilować *(perf)* obok; **to ~ for divorce** wnosić (wnieść *perf*) sprawę o rozwód
**file name** *n* *(Comput)* nazwa *f* pliku
**filibuster** ['fɪlɪbʌstə^r] *(esp US: Pol) n* ≈ obstrukcja *f* parlamentarna ▷ *vi* ≈ stosować obstrukcję parlamentarną
**filing** ['faɪlɪŋ] *n* segregowanie *nt*
**filing cabinet** *n* szafka *f* na akta
**filing clerk** *n* urzędnik(-iczka) *m(f)* prowadzący(-ca) *m(f)* dokumentację
**Filipino** [fɪlɪ'pi:nəu] *n* Filipińczyk(-inka) *m(f)* ▷ *adj* filipiński
**fill** [fɪl] *vt* *(container)* napełniać (napełnić *perf*); *(space, time, gap)* wypełniać (wypełnić *perf*); *(tooth)* wypełniać (wypełnić *perf*), plombować (zaplombować *perf*); *(vacancy)* zapełniać (zapełnić *perf*) ▷ *vi* wypełniać się (wypełnić się *perf*), zapełniać się (zapełnić się *perf*) ▷ *n*: **to eat/drink one's ~** najeść się *(perf)*/napić się *(perf)* do syta; **to have one's ~ of sth** mieć czegoś dosyć; **to ~ sth with sth** napełniać (napełnić *perf*) *or* wypełniać (wypełnić *perf*) coś czymś; **~ed with anger/resentment** pełen gniewu/urazy
▸ **fill in** *vt* wypełniać (wypełnić *perf*); **to ~ in for sb** zastępować (zastąpić *perf*) kogoś; **to ~ sb in on sth** *(inf)* wprowadzać (wprowadzić *perf*) kogoś w coś
▸ **fill out** *vt* *(form)* wypełniać (wypełnić *perf*); *(receipt)* wypisywać (wypisać *perf*)

▸ **fill up** *vt* (*container*) napełniać (napełnić *perf*); (*space*) wypełniać (wypełnić *perf*) ▷ *vi* wypełniać się (wypełnić się *perf*), zapełniać się (zapełnić się *perf*); **~ it** *or* **her up, please** (*Aut*) do pełna, proszę!
**fillet** ['fɪlɪt] *n* filet *m* ▷ *vt* filetować
**fillet steak** *n* stek *m* z polędwicy
**filling** ['fɪlɪŋ] *n* (*for tooth*) wypełnienie *nt*, plomba *f*; (*of cake*) nadzienie *nt*
**filling station** *n* stacja *f* paliw
**fillip** ['fɪlɪp] *n* ożywienie *nt*; **to give a ~ to sth** ożywiać (ożywić *perf*) coś
**filly** ['fɪlɪ] *n* klaczka *f*, młoda klacz *f*
**film** [fɪlm] *n* (*Film, TV, Phot*) film *m*; (*of dust etc*) cienka warstwa *f*, warstewka *f*; (*of tears*) mgiełka *f*; (*for wrapping*) folia *f* ▷ *vt* filmować (sfilmować *perf*) ▷ *vi* filmować, kręcić (*inf*)
**film star** *n* gwiazda *f* filmowa
**filmstrip** ['fɪlmstrɪp] *n* diapozytyw *m*
**film studio** *n* studio *nt* filmowe
**filter** ['fɪltəʳ] *n* (*also Phot*) filtr *m* ▷ *vt* filtrować (przefiltrować *perf*)
▸ **filter in** *vi* (*sound, light*) sączyć się
▸ **filter through** *vi* (*news*) rozchodzić się (rozejść się *perf*)
**filter coffee** *n* kawa *f* do parzenia w ekspresie
**filter lane** (*Brit*) *n pas jezdni wymuszający ograniczenie prędkości*
**filter tip** *n* filtr *m* (*papierosa*), ustnik *m*
**filter-tipped** ['fɪltə'tɪpt] *adj* z filtrem *post*
**filth** [fɪlθ] *n* (*dirt*) brud *m*; (*smut*) brudy *pl*
**filthy** ['fɪlθɪ] *adj* (*object, person*) bardzo brudny; (*language*) sprośny, plugawy; (*behaviour*) obrzydliwy, ohydny
**fin** [fɪn] *n* płetwa *f*
**final** ['faɪnl] *adj* (*last*) ostatni, końcowy; (*penalty*) najwyższy; (*irony*) największy; (*decision, offer*) ostateczny ▷ *n* (*Sport*) finał *m*; **finals** *npl* (*Scol*) egzaminy *pl* końcowe
**final demand** *n* (*on invoice etc*) ostatnie ponaglenie *nt*
**finale** [fɪ'nɑːlɪ] *n* finał *m*
**finalist** ['faɪnəlɪst] *n* finalista(-tka) *m(f)*
**finality** [faɪ'nælɪtɪ] *n* ostateczność *f*, nieodwołalność *f*; **with an air of ~** stanowczo
**finalize** ['faɪnəlaɪz] *vt* finalizować (sfinalizować *perf*)
**finally** ['faɪnəlɪ] *adv* (*eventually*) w końcu, ostatecznie; (*lastly*) na koniec; (*irrevocably*) ostatecznie
**finance** [faɪ'næns] *n* (*backing*) środki *pl* finansowe, finanse *pl*; (*management*) gospodarka *f* finansowa ▷ *vt* finansować (sfinansować *perf*); **finances** *npl* fundusze *pl*
**financial** [faɪ'nænʃəl] *adj* finansowy
**financially** [faɪ'nænʃəlɪ] *adv* finansowo
**financial year** *n* rok *m* finansowy
**financier** [faɪ'nænsɪəʳ] *n* (*backer*) sponsor *m*; (*expert*) finansista *m*
**find** [faɪnd] (*pt, pp* **found**) *vt* (*locate*) znajdować (znaleźć *perf*), odnajdywać (odnaleźć *perf*) (*fml*); (*discover: answer, solution*) znajdować (znaleźć *perf*); (*: object, person*) odkryć (*perf*); (*consider*) uznać (*perf*) za *+acc*, uważać za *+acc*; (*get: work, time*) znajdować (znaleźć *perf*) ▷ *n* (*discovery*) odkrycie *nt*; (*object found*) znalezisko *nt*; **to ~ sb guilty** (*Jur*) uznawać (uznać *perf*) kogoś za winnego; **to ~ that...** przekonać się (*perf*), że..., odkryć (*perf*), że...; **I ~ it easy/difficult** przychodzi mi to z łatwością/trudnością
▸ **find out** *vt* (*fact*) dowiadywać się (dowiedzieć się *perf*) *+gen*; (*truth*) odkrywać (odkryć *perf*), poznawać (poznać *perf*); (*person*) poznać się *perf* na *+loc* ▷ *vi*: **to ~ out about sth** dowiadywać się (dowiedzieć się *perf*) o czymś
**findings** ['faɪndɪŋz] *npl* (*of committee*) wyniki *pl* badań; (*of report*) wnioski *pl*
**fine** [faɪn] *adj* (*quality etc*) świetny; (*thread*) cienki; (*sand etc*) drobny, miałki; (*detail etc*) drobny; (*weather*) piękny; (*satisfactory*) w porządku *post*, w sam raz *post* ▷ *adv* (*well*) świetnie; (*thinly*) drobno ▷ *n* grzywna *f* ▷ *vt* karać (ukarać *perf*) grzywną; **(I'm) ~** (mam się) dobrze; **(that's) ~** dobrze; **don't cut it ~** nie rób tego na styk (*inf*); **you're doing ~** świetnie ci idzie; **a speeding/parking ~** mandat za przekroczenie prędkości/niewłaściwe parkowanie
**fine arts** *npl* sztuki *pl* piękne
**finely** ['faɪnlɪ] *adv* (*constructed*) świetnie; (*chopped*) drobno; (*sliced*) cienko; (*tuned*) precyzyjnie
**finery** ['faɪnərɪ] *n* (*clothing*) wytworny *or* wyszukany strój *m*; (*jewellery*) kosztowności *pl*; **in (all) one's ~** (cały) wystrojony
**finesse** [fɪ'nɛs] *n* finezja *f*
**fine-tooth comb** ['faɪntuːθ-] *n*: **to go through sth with a ~** (*fig*) gruntownie coś badać (zbadać *perf*)
**finger** ['fɪŋgəʳ] *n* palec *m* ▷ *vt* dotykać (dotknąć *perf*) palcem *+gen*; **little/index ~** mały/wskazujący palec
**fingernail** ['fɪŋgəneɪl] *n* paznokieć *m* (*u ręki*)
**fingerprint** ['fɪŋgəprɪnt] *n* odcisk *m* palca ▷ *vt* zdejmować (zdjąć *perf*) odciski palców *+gen*
**fingertip** ['fɪŋgətɪp] *n* koniuszek *m* palca; **to have sth at one's ~s** (*at one's disposal*) mieć coś w zasięgu ręki; (*know well*) mieć coś w małym palcu
**finicky** ['fɪnɪkɪ] *adj* wybredny
**finish** ['fɪnɪʃ] *n* (*end*) koniec *m*, zakończenie *nt*; (*Sport*) końcówka *f*, finisz *m*; (*polish etc*)

wykończenie *nt* ▷ *vt* kończyć (skończyć *perf*) ▷ *vi* (*person*) kończyć (skończyć *perf*); (*course*) kończyć się (skończyć się *perf*); **let me ~** pozwól mi skończyć; **to ~ doing sth** kończyć (skończyć *perf*) coś robić; **to ~ third** zająć (*perf*) trzecie miejsce; **she's ~ed with him** skończyła z nim; **a close ~** zacięty finisz, zacięta końcówka
▸ **finish off** *vt* (*job*) dokończyć (*perf*), skończyć (*perf*); (*dinner*) dokończyć (*perf*); (*kill*) wykończyć (*perf*) (*inf*)
▸ **finish up** *vt* dokończyć (*perf*), skończyć (*perf*)
▸ **finish up (as/in)** *vi* kończyć (skończyć *perf*) (jako +*nom*/w +*loc*) (*pej*)

**finished** ['fɪnɪʃt] *adj* (*product*) gotowy; (*event, activity*) zakończony, skończony; (*inf: person*) skończony

**finishing line** ['fɪnɪʃɪŋ-] *n* meta *f*, linia *f* mety

**finishing school** *n szkoła dobrych manier dla dziewcząt z wyższych sfer*

**finishing touches** *npl*: **to put the ~ to sth** wykańczać (wykończyć *perf*) coś

**finite** ['faɪnaɪt] *adj* (*number, amount*) skończony; **~ verb** odmienna forma czasownika

**Finland** ['fɪnlənd] *n* Finlandia *f*

**Finn** [fɪn] *n* Fin(ka) *m(f)*

**Finnish** ['fɪnɪʃ] *adj* fiński ▷ *n* (język *m*) fiński

**fiord** [fjɔ:d] *n* = **fjord**

**fir** [fə:ʳ] *n* jodła *f*

**fire** ['faɪəʳ] *n* ogień *m*; (*accidental*) pożar *m* ▷ *vt* (*shoot: gun*) strzelać (strzelić *perf*) z +*gen*; (*: arrow*) wystrzeliwać (wystrzelić *perf*); (*stimulate*) rozpalać (rozpalić *perf*); (*inf*) wyrzucać (wyrzucić *perf*) z pracy, wylać (*perf*) (*inf*) ▷ *vi* strzelać (strzelić *perf*); **to catch ~** zapalać się (zapalić się *perf*), zajmować się (zająć się *perf*); **to be on ~** palić się, płonąć; **to set ~ to sth, set sth on ~** podkładać (podłożyć *perf*) ogień pod coś, podpalać (podpalić *perf*) coś; **insured against ~** ubezpieczony na wypadek pożaru; **electric/gas ~** grzejnik elektryczny/gazowy; **to come/be under ~ (from)** znaleźć się (*perf*)/być pod ostrzałem (+*gen*); **to open ~** otwierać (otworzyć *perf*) ogień; **to ~ a shot** oddawać (oddać *perf*) strzał

**fire alarm** *n* alarm *m* pożarowy

**firearm** ['faɪərɑ:m] *n* broń *f* palna

**fire brigade** *n* straż *f* pożarna

**fire chief** *n* komendant *m* straży pożarnej

**fire department** (US) *n* = **fire brigade**

**fire drill** *n* ćwiczenia *pl* przeciwpożarowe

**fire engine** *n* wóz *m* strażacki

**fire escape** *n* schody *pl* pożarowe

**fire extinguisher** ['faɪərɪk'stɪŋgwɪʃəʳ] *n* gaśnica *f*

**fireguard** ['faɪəgɑ:d] (*Brit*) *n* osłona *f* zabezpieczająca kominek

**fire hazard** *n*: **that's a ~** to grozi pożarem

**fire hydrant** *n* hydrant *m* pożarowy

**fire insurance** *n* ubezpieczenie *nt* od ognia

**fireman** ['faɪəmən] (*irreg: like* **man**) *n* strażak *m*

**fireplace** ['faɪəpleɪs] *n* kominek *m*

**fireplug** ['faɪəplʌg] (US) *n* = **fire hydrant**

**fireproof** ['faɪəpru:f] *adj* ognioodporny, ogniotrwały

**fire regulations** *npl* przepisy *pl* przeciwpożarowe

**fireside** ['faɪəsaɪd] *n*: **to sit by the ~** siedzieć przy kominku

**fire station** *n* posterunek *m* straży pożarnej

**firewood** ['faɪəwud] *n* drewno *nt* opałowe

**fireworks** ['faɪəwə:ks] *npl* fajerwerki *pl*, sztuczne ognie *pl*

**firing line** ['faɪərɪŋ-] *n*: **to be in the ~** (*fig*) być obiektem ataków

**firing squad** *n* pluton *m* egzekucyjny

**firm** [fə:m] *adj* (*mattress*) twardy; (*ground*) ubity; (*grasp, hold*) mocny, pewny; (*: fig*) gruntowny, solidny; (*views*) niewzruszony; (*leadership*) nieugięty; (*offer, date*) wiążący; (*decision*) stanowczy; (*evidence*) niezbity; (*voice*) pewny ▷ *n* przedsiębiorstwo *nt*, firma *f*; **to be a ~ believer in sth** mocno w coś wierzyć

**firmly** ['fə:mlɪ] *adv* (*strongly*) mocno; (*securely*) pewnie; (*say, tell*) stanowczo

**firmness** ['fə:mnɪs] *n* (*of mattress, cake etc*) twardość *f*; (*of decision etc*) stanowczość *f*, kategoryczność *f*

**first** [fə:st] *adj* pierwszy ▷ *adv* (*before anyone else*) (jako) pierwszy; (*before other things*) najpierw; (*when listing reasons*) po pierwsze; (*for the first time*) po raz pierwszy ▷ *n* (*Aut*) pierwszy bieg *m*, jedynka *f* (*inf*); (Brit: *Scol*) *dyplom ukończenia studiów z najwyższą oceną*; **the ~ of January** pierwszy stycznia; **at ~** najpierw, z początku; **~ of all** przede wszystkim; **in the ~ instance** w pierwszej kolejności; **I'll do it ~ thing (tomorrow)** zrobię to (jutro) z samego rana; **from the very ~** od samego początku; **to put sb/sth ~** stawiać (postawić *perf*) kogoś/coś na pierwszym miejscu; **at ~ hand** z pierwszej ręki

**first aid** *n* pierwsza pomoc *f*

**first-aid kit** [fə:st'eɪd-] *n* apteczka *f* (pierwszej pomocy)

**first-class** ['fə:st'klɑ:s] *adj* pierwszorzędny; **a ~ carriage/ticket** wagon/bilet pierwszej klasy ▷ *adv* pierwszą klasą

**first-hand** ['fə:st'hænd] *adj* z pierwszej ręki *post*

**first lady** (US) *n* pierwsza dama *f* (*żona prezydenta*); **the ~ of jazz** pierwsza dama jazzu

**firstly** ['fə:stlɪ] *adv* po pierwsze
**first name** *n* imię *nt*; **to be on first-name terms (with sb)** być (z kimś) na „ty"
**first night** *n* premiera *f*
**first-rate** ['fə:st'reɪt] *adj* pierwszorzędny
**fir tree** *n* jodła *f*
**FIS** (*Brit*) *n abbr* (= *Family Income Supplement*) *pomoc finansowa dla rodzin o niskich dochodach*
**fiscal** ['fɪskl] *adj* fiskalny, podatkowy
**fish** [fɪʃ] *n inv* ryba *f* ▷ *vi* (*commercially*) poławiać ryby; (*as sport, hobby*) łowić ryby, wędkować; **to go ~ing** iść (pójść *perf*) na ryby
▸ **fish out** *vt* wyławiać (wyłowić *perf*)
**fishbone** ['fɪʃbəun] *n* ość *f*
**fishcake** ['fɪʃkeɪk] *n* kotlet *m* rybny
**fisherman** ['fɪʃəmən] (*irreg: like* **man**) *n* rybak *m*; (*amateur*) wędkarz *m*
**fishery** ['fɪʃərɪ] *n* (*area*) łowisko *nt*; (*industry*) rybołówstwo *nt*
**fish farm** *n* gospodarstwo *nt* rybne
**fish fingers** (*Brit*) *npl* paluszki *pl* rybne
**fish hook** *n* haczyk *m*
**fishing boat** ['fɪʃɪŋ-] *n* łódź *f* rybacka
**fishing line** *n* żyłka *f* (*do wędki*)
**fishing net** *n* sieć *f* rybacka
**fishing rod** *n* wędka *f*
**fishing tackle** *n* sprzęt *m* wędkarski
**fish market** *n* targ *m* rybny
**fishmonger** ['fɪʃmʌŋgə^r] *n* handlarz *m* ryb
**fishmonger's (shop)** ['fɪʃmʌŋgəz-] *n* sklep *m* rybny
**fish slice** (*Brit*) *n* łopatka *f* do ryb
**fish sticks** (*US*) *npl* = **fish fingers**
**fishy** ['fɪʃɪ] (*inf*) *adj* (*suspicious*) podejrzany
**fission** ['fɪʃən] *n*: **atomic** *or* **nuclear ~** rozszczepienie *nt* jądra atomowego
**fissure** ['fɪʃə^r] *n* szczelina *f*
**fist** [fɪst] *n* pięść *f*
**fistfight** ['fɪstfaɪt] *n* walka *f* na pięści
**fit** [fɪt] *adj* (*suitable*) odpowiedni; (*healthy*) sprawny (fizycznie), w dobrej kondycji *or* formie *post* ▷ *vt* (*be the right size for*) pasować na *+acc*; (*match*) pasować do *+gen*; (*attach*) zakładać (założyć *perf*), montować (zamontować *perf*); (*suit*) odpowiadać *+dat*, pasować do *+gen* ▷ *vi* pasować ▷ *n* (*Med*) napad *m*, atak *m*; **he looked fit to explode** wyglądał, jakby miał zaraz wybuchnąć; **to be fit for sth** nadawać się do czegoś; **to keep fit** utrzymywać dobrą kondycję; **to see fit to do sth** uznawać (uznać *perf*) za stosowne coś zrobić; **to fit sth with sth** wyposażać (wyposażyć *perf*) coś w coś; **a fit of rage/pride** przypływ gniewu/dumy; **a fit of giggles/hysterics** atak śmiechu/histerii; **to have a fit** dostać (*perf*) szału; **this dress is a good fit** ta sukienka dobrze leży; **by fits and starts** zrywami
▸ **fit in** *vi* mieścić się (zmieścić się *perf*); (*fig*) pasować ▷ *vt* (*fig: appointment, visitor*) wcisnąć (*perf*) (*inf*); **to fit in with sb's plans** pasować do czyichś planów
▸ **fit into** *vt fus* (*hole etc*) pasować do *+gen*; (*suitcase etc*) mieścić się w *+loc*
**fitful** ['fɪtful] *adj* (*sleep*) niespokojny
**fitment** ['fɪtmənt] *n* mebel *m* zamontowany na stałe
**fitness** ['fɪtnɪs] *n* sprawność *f* fizyczna, kondycja *f*
**fitted carpet** ['fɪtɪd-] *n* wykładzina *f* dywanowa
**fitted cupboards** *npl* szafki *pl* umocowane na stałe
**fitted kitchen** (*Brit*) *n* kuchnia *f* na wymiar
**fitter** ['fɪtə^r] *n* monter *m*
**fitting** ['fɪtɪŋ] *adj* stosowny ▷ *n* przymiarka *f*; **fittings** *npl* armatura *f*
**fitting room** *n* przymierzalnia *f*, kabina *f*
**five** [faɪv] *num* pięć
**five-day week** ['faɪvdeɪ-] *n* pięciodniowy tydzień *m* pracy
**fiver** ['faɪvə^r] (*inf*) *n* (*Brit*) banknot *m* pięciofuntowy, piątka *f* (*inf*)
**fix** [fɪks] *vt* (*date, amount*) ustalać (ustalić *perf*), wyznaczać (wyznaczyć *perf*); (*leak, radio*) naprawiać (naprawić *perf*); (*meal*) przygotowywać (przygotować *perf*); (*inf: game, election*) fingować (sfingować *perf*); (*: result*) fałszować (sfałszować *perf*) ▷ *n*: **to be in a fix** (*inf*) być w tarapatach; **the fight was a fix** (*inf*) walka została sfingowana; **to fix sth to/on sth** (*attach*) przymocowywać (przymocować *perf*) coś do czegoś; (*pin*) przypinać (przypiąć (*perf*)) coś do czegoś; **to fix one's eyes/gaze on sb** utkwić (*perf*) w kimś oczy/wzrok
▸ **fix up** *vt* (*meeting etc*) organizować (zorganizować *perf*); **to fix sb up with sth** załatwiać (załatwić *perf*) komuś coś
**fixation** [fɪk'seɪʃən] *n* fiksacja *f*
**fixative** ['fɪksətɪv] *n* utrwalacz *m*
**fixed** [fɪkst] *adj* (*price, intervals etc*) stały, niezmienny; (*ideas*) (głęboko) zakorzeniony; (*smile*) przylepiony; **there's a ~ charge** pobiera się stałą opłatę; **how are you ~ for money?** (*inf*) jak wyglądasz z pieniędzmi?; **of no ~ abode** bez stałego miejsca zamieszkania
**fixture** ['fɪkstʃə^r] *n* element *m* instalacji (*wanna, zlew itp*); (*Sport*) impreza *f*
**fizz** [fɪz] *vi* (*drink*) musować; (*firework*) skwierczeć
**fizzle out** ['fɪzl-] *vi* (*plan*) spalić (*perf*) na panewce; (*interest*) wygasać (wygasnąć *perf*)
**fizzy** ['fɪzɪ] *adj* gazowany, musujący
**fjord** [fjɔ:d] *n* fiord *m*

**FL** (*US: Post*) *abbr* = **Florida**
**flabbergasted** ['flæbəgɑːstɪd] *adj* osłupiały
**flabby** ['flæbɪ] *adj* sflaczały
**flag** [flæg] *n* (*of country, for signalling*) flaga *f*; (*of organization*) sztandar *m*, chorągiew *f*; (*also:* **flagstone**) płyta *f* chodnikowa ▷ *vi* słabnąć (osłabnąć *perf*); ~ **of convenience** tania bandera; **to ~ down** (*taxi etc*) zatrzymywać (zatrzymać *perf*)
**flagon** ['flægən] *n* dzban *m* (*na wino itp*)
**flagpole** ['flægpəul] *n* maszt *m*
**flagrant** ['fleɪgrənt] *adj* (*injustice etc*) rażący
**flagship** ['flægʃɪp] *n* (*Naut*) okręt *m* flagowy; (*fig*) produkt *m* sztandarowy
**flagstone** ['flægstəun] *n* płyta *f* chodnikowa
**flag stop** (*US*) *n* przystanek *m* na żądanie
**flair** [flɛəʳ] *n* styl *m*; **to have a ~ for sth** mieć smykałkę do czegoś
**flak** [flæk] *n* ogień *m* przeciwlotniczy; (*inf*) ogień *m* krytyki
**flake** [fleɪk] *n* płatek *m* ▷ *vi* (*also:* **flake off**) złuszczać się (złuszczyć się *perf*)
▸ **flake out** (*inf*) *vi* padać (paść *perf*) ze zmęczenia
**flaky** ['fleɪkɪ] *adj* złuszczający się
**flaky pastry** *n* ciasto *nt* francuskie
**flamboyant** [flæm'bɔɪənt] *adj* (*brightly coloured*) krzykliwy (*pej*); (*showy, confident*) ekstrawagancki
**flame** [fleɪm] *n* płomień *m*; **to burst into ~s** stawać (stanąć *perf*) w płomieniach; **in ~s** w płomieniach; **an old ~** (*inf*) stara miłość
**flaming** ['fleɪmɪŋ] (*inf!*) *adj* cholerny (*inf*)
**flamingo** [flə'mɪŋgəu] *n* flaming *m*
**flammable** ['flæməbl] *adj* łatwopalny
**flan** [flæn] (*Brit*) *n* tarta *f*
**Flanders** ['flɑːndəz] *n* Flandria *f*
**flank** [flæŋk] *n* (*of animal*) bok *m*; (*of army*) skrzydło *nt* ▷ *vt*: **~ed by** (po)między *+instr*
**flannel** ['flænl] *n* (*fabric*) flanela *f*; (*Brit: also:* **face flannel**) myjka *f*; (*: inf*): **he gave us no ~** nie owijał w bawełnę; **flannels** *npl* spodnie *pl* flanelowe
**flannelette** [flænə'lɛt] *n* flaneleta *f* (*bawełniana imitacja flaneli*)
**flap** [flæp] *n* klapa *f*; (*small*) klapka *f* ▷ *vt* machać (machnąć *perf*) *+instr* ▷ *vi* łopotać (załopotać *perf*); **to get in a ~ (about sth)** (*inf*) wpaść (*perf*) w panikę (z powodu czegoś)
**flapjack** ['flæpdʒæk] *n* (*US*) naleśnik *m*; (*Brit*) *herbatnik z płatków owsianych*
**flare** [flɛəʳ] *n* rakieta *f* świetlna, raca *f*
▸ **flare up** *vi* (*fire*) zapłonąć (*perf*); (*fighting*) wybuchać (wybuchnąć *perf*); **flares** *npl* (*trousers*) dzwony *pl*
**flared** ['flɛəd] *adj* kloszowy, rozszerzany ku dołowi
**flash** [flæʃ] *n* (*of light*) błysk *m*; (*Phot*) flesz *m*, lampa *f* błyskowa; (*US*) latarka *f* ▷ *adj* (*inf*) wystrzałowy (*inf*) ▷ *vt* (*light*) błyskać (błysnąć *perf*) *+instr*; (*news, message*) przesyłać (przesłać *perf*); (*look, smile*) posyłać (posłać *perf*) ▷ *vi* (*lightning, light*) błyskać (błysnąć *perf*); (*eyes*) miotać błyskawice; **in a ~** w okamgnieniu; **quick as a ~** szybki jak błyskawica; **~ of inspiration/anger** przypływ natchnienia/gniewu; **to ~ one's headlights** dawać (dać *perf*) znak światłami drogowymi; **the thought ~ed through his mind** przemknęło mu to przez myśl; **to ~ by** *or* **past** przemykać (przemknąć *perf*) obok *+gen*
**flashback** ['flæʃbæk] *n* (*Film*) retrospekcja *f*
**flashbulb** ['flæʃbʌlb] *n* żarówka *f* błyskowa
**flashcard** ['flæʃkɑːd] *n karta tekturowa używana jako pomoc dydaktyczna*
**flashcube** ['flæʃkjuːb] *n* (*Phot*) *kostka zawierająca cztery żarówki błyskowe*
**flasher** ['flæʃəʳ] *n* (*Aut*) migacz *m*; (*inf!*) ekshibicjonista *m*
**flashlight** ['flæʃlaɪt] *n* latarka *f*
**flashpoint** ['flæʃpɔɪnt] *n* (*fig: moment*) punkt *m* krytyczny; (*place*) punkt *m* zapalny
**flashy** ['flæʃɪ] *adj* (*pej*) krzykliwy (*pej*)
**flask** [flɑːsk] *n* płaska butelka *f*, piersiówka *f* (*inf*); (*Chem*) kolba *f*; (*also:* **vacuum flask**) termos *m*
**flat** [flæt] *adj* (*surface*) płaski; (*tyre*) bez powietrza *post*; (*battery*) rozładowany; (*beer*) zwietrzały; (*refusal*) stanowczy; (*Mus*) za niski; (*rate, fee*) ryczałtowy ▷ *n* (*Brit*) mieszkanie *nt*; (*Aut*) guma *f* (*inf*); (*Mus*) bemol *m* ▷ *adv* płasko ▷ *n*: **the ~ of one's hand** otwarta dłoń *f*; **to work ~ out** pracować na wysokich obrotach; **in 10 minutes ~** dokładnie za 10 minut
**flat-footed** ['flæt'futɪd] *adj*: **to be ~** mieć płaskostopie
**flatly** ['flætlɪ] *adv* (*refuse etc*) stanowczo
**flatmate** ['flætmeɪt] (*Brit*) *n* współlokator(ka) *m(f)*
**flatness** ['flætnɪs] *n* płaskość *f*
**flatten** ['flætn] *vt* (*also:* **flatten out**) spłaszczać (spłaszczyć *perf*); (*terrain*) wyrównywać (wyrównać *perf*); (*building, city*) zrównywać (zrównać *perf*) z ziemią; **to ~ o.s. against a wall/door** przywierać (przywrzeć *perf*) do ściany/drzwi
**flatter** ['flætəʳ] *vt* schlebiać *or* pochlebiać *+dat*; **that dress doesn't ~ her** w tej sukience jej nie do twarzy; **I was ~ed that...** pochlebiało mi, że...; **to ~ o.s. on sth** szczycić się czymś
**flatterer** ['flætərəʳ] *n* pochlebca *m*
**flattering** ['flætərɪŋ] *adj* (*comment*) pochlebny; (*dress*) twarzowy; (*photograph*) udany

**flattery** ['flætərɪ] *n* pochlebstwo *nt*
**flatulence** ['flætjuləns] *n* wzdęcie *nt*
**flaunt** [flɔːnt] *vt* obnosić się *or* afiszować się z *+instr*
**flavour**, (*US*) **flavor** ['fleɪvəʳ] *n* smak *m* ▷ *vt* (*food*) przyprawiać (przyprawić *perf*), doprawiać (doprawić *perf*); (*drink*) aromatyzować; **strawberry-~ed** o smaku truskawkowym; **music with an African ~** muzyka o afrykańskim brzmieniu
**flavouring** ['fleɪvərɪŋ] *n* dodatek *m* smakowy
**flaw** [flɔː] *n* skaza *f*; (*in argument, policy*) słaby punkt *m*
**flawless** ['flɔːlɪs] *adj* nieskazitelny, bez skazy *post*
**flax** [flæks] *n* len *m*
**flaxen** ['flæksən] *adj* (*hair*) płowy, lniany
**flea** [fliː] *n* pchła *f*
**flea market** *n* pchli targ *m*
**fleck** [flɛk] *n* plamka *f* ▷ *vt*: **~ed with mud/blood** poplamiony błotem/krwią; **brown ~ed with white** brązowy w białe plamki; **~s of dust** drobinki kurzu
**fled** [flɛd] *pt, pp of* **flee**
**fledg(e)ling** ['flɛdʒlɪŋ] *n* świeżo opierzone pisklę *nt*
**flee** [fliː] (*pt, pp* **fled**) *vt* (*danger, famine*) uciekać (uciec *perf*) przed *+instr*; (*country*) uciekać (uciec *perf*) z *+gen* ▷ *vi* uciekać (uciec *perf*)
**fleece** [fliːs] *n* (*of sheep*) runo *nt*, wełna *f*; (*to wear*) polar *m* ▷ *vt* (*inf: cheat*) oskubać (*perf*) (*inf*)
**fleecy** ['fliːsɪ] *adj* wełnisty
**fleet** [fliːt] *n* (*of ships*) flota *f*; (*of lorries etc*) park *m* (*samochodowy*)
**fleeting** ['fliːtɪŋ] *adj* przelotny
**Flemish** ['flɛmɪʃ] *adj* flamandzki ▷ *n* (język *m*) flamandzki
**flesh** [flɛʃ] *n* (*of pig etc*) mięso *nt*; (*of fruit*) miąższ *m*; (*skin*) ciało *nt*; **in the ~** we własnej osobie
▸ **flesh out** *vt* (*idea*) rozwijać (rozwinąć *perf*)
**flesh wound** [-wuːnd] *n* rana *f* powierzchowna
**flew** [fluː] *pt of* **fly**
**flex** [flɛks] *n* sznur *m* sieciowy ▷ *vt* (*muscles*) napinać (napiąć *perf*); (*fingers*) wyginać (wygiąć *perf*)
**flexibility** [flɛksɪ'bɪlɪtɪ] *n* giętkość *f*, elastyczność *f*
**flexible** ['flɛksəbl] *adj* (*adaptable*) elastyczny; (*bending easily*) giętki, elastyczny; **~ working hours** ruchomy czas pracy
**flick** [flɪk] *n* (*of hand, arm*) wyrzut *m*; (*of finger*) prztyczek *m*; (*of towel, whip*) trzaśnięcie *nt*, smagnięcie *nt*; (*through book, pages*) kartkowanie *nt* ▷ *vt* (*with finger, hand*) strzepywać (strzepnąć *perf*); (*whip*) strzelać (strzelić *perf*) z *+gen*; (*ash*) strząsać (strząsnąć *perf*); (*switch*) pstrykać (pstryknąć *perf*) *+instr*; **the flicks** (*Brit: inf*) *npl* kino *nt*
▸ **flick through** *vt fus* kartkować
**flicker** ['flɪkəʳ] *vi* migotać (zamigotać *perf*) ▷ *n* (*of light*) migotanie *nt*; (*of pain, fear, smile*) cień *m*; **he didn't ~ an eyelid** nawet nie mrugnął okiem
**flick knife** (*Brit*) *n* nóż *m* sprężynowy
**flier** ['flaɪəʳ] *n* lotnik *m*
**flight** [flaɪt] *n* lot *m*; (*escape*) ucieczka *f*; (*also:* **flight of stairs**) kondygnacja *f*, piętro *nt*; **to take ~** uciekać (uciec *perf*); **a ~ of fancy** wybryk fantazji
**flight attendant** (*US*) *n* steward(essa) *m(f)*
**flight crew** *n* załoga *f* samolotu
**flight deck** *n* (*Aviat*) kabina *f* pilota; (*Naut*) pokład *m* lotniskowca
**flight recorder** *n* czarna skrzynka *f*
**flimsy** ['flɪmzɪ] *adj* (*clothes*) cienki; (*hut*) lichy; (*excuse, evidence*) marny
**flinch** [flɪntʃ] *vi* wzdrygać się (wzdrygnąć się *perf*); **to ~ from** wzdragać się przed *+instr*
**fling** [flɪŋ] (*pt, pp* **flung**) *vt* ciskać (cisnąć *perf*), rzucać (rzucić *perf*) ▷ *n* romans *m*; **to ~ o.s.** rzucać się (rzucić się *perf*); **to ~ one's arms around someone** obejmować (objąć *perf*) kogoś (ramionami)
**flint** [flɪnt] *n* (*stone*) krzemień *m*; (*in lighter*) kamień *m* do zapalniczki
**flip** [flɪp] *vt* (*switch*) pstrykać (pstryknąć *perf*) *+instr*; (*coin*) rzucać (rzucić *perf*); (*pancake, page*) przewracać (przewrócić *perf*) ▷ *vi*: **let's ~ for it** rzućmy monetę
▸ **flip through** *vt fus* (*book*) kartkować (przekartkować *perf*); (*pages*) przerzucać (przerzucić *perf*)
**flippant** ['flɪpənt] *adj* nonszalancki
**flipper** ['flɪpəʳ] *n* płetwa *f*
**flip side** *n* strona *f* B (*płyty*)
**flirt** [fləːt] *vi* flirtować ▷ *n* flirt *m*; **to ~ with** (*idea etc*) zabawiać się *+instr*
**flirtation** [fləː'teɪʃən] *n* flirt *m*
**flit** [flɪt] *vi* (*birds, insects*) polatywać; (*expression, smile*) przemykać (przemknąć *perf*)
**float** [fləut] *n* (*for swimming*) pływak *m*; (*for fishing*) spławik *m*; (*money*) drobne *pl*; (*in carnival*) ruchoma platforma *f* (*na której odgrywane są sceny rodzajowe*) ▷ *vi* (*on water, through air*) unosić się; (*currency*) mieć płynny kurs ▷ *vt* (*currency*) upłynniać (upłynnić *perf*) kurs *+gen*; (*company*) zakładać (założyć *perf*); (*idea, plan*) wprowadzać (wprowadzić *perf*) w życie
▸ **float around** *vi* krążyć
**flock** [flɔk] *n* (*of sheep etc*) stado *nt*; (*Rel*) parafia *f*

▸ **flock to** *vt fus* *(gather)* gromadzić się (zgromadzić się *perf*) (tłumnie) przy *+instr*; *(go)* podążać (podążyć *perf*) (tłumnie) do *+gen*
**floe** [fləu] *n* *(also:* **ice floe***)* kra *f (na morzu)*
**flog** [flɔg] *vt* chłostać (wychłostać *perf*); *(inf: sell)* wciskać (wcisnąć *perf*) *(inf)*
**flood** [flʌd] *n* *(of water)* powódź *f*; *(of letters, imports)* zalew *m*; *(Rel)*: **the F~** potop *m* ▹ *vt* zalewać (zalać *perf*); **to ~ into** napływać (napłynąć *perf*) do *+gen*; **the river is in ~** rzeka wylała; **the kitchen was ~ed** zalało kuchnię
**flooding** ['flʌdɪŋ] *n* wylew *m* (rzeki)
**floodlight** ['flʌdlaɪt] *n* reflektor *m* ▹ *vt* oświetlać (oświetlić *perf*) reflektorami
**floodlit** ['flʌdlɪt] *pt, pp of* **floodlight** ▹ *adj* oświetlony reflektorami
**flood tide** *n* przypływ *m*
**floor** [flɔː[r]] *n* *(of room)* podłoga *f*; *(storey)* piętro *nt*; *(of sea, valley)* dno *nt*; *(for dancing)* parkiet *m*; *(fig: at meeting)* prawo *nt* głosu ▹ *vt* powalać (powalić *perf*) (na ziemię); *(fig)* zbijać (zbić *perf*) z tropu; **ground ~**, (US) **first ~** parter; **first ~**, (US) **second ~** pierwsze piętro; **top ~** ostatnie piętro; **to have/take the ~** mieć/zabierać (zabrać *perf*) głos; **questions from the ~** pytania z sali
**floorboard** ['flɔːbɔːd] *n* deska *f* podłogowa
**flooring** ['flɔːrɪŋ] *n* materiał *m* podłogowy
**floor lamp** (US) *n* lampa *f* stojąca
**floor show** *n* występy *pl* artystyczne *(w nocnym klubie itp)*
**floorwalker** ['flɔːwɔːkə[r]] *n* *(esp US)* kierownik(-iczka) *m(f)* piętra w domu towarowym
**flop** [flɔp] *n* klapa *f (inf)* ▹ *vi* *(fail)* robić (zrobić *perf*) klapę *(inf)*; *(into chair, onto floor)* klapnąć *(perf)*
**floppy** ['flɔpɪ] *adj* (miękko) opadający
**floppy disk** *n* *(Comput)* dyskietka *f*
**flora** ['flɔːrə] *n* flora *f*
**floral** ['flɔːrl] *adj* kwiecisty
**Florence** ['flɔrəns] *n* Florencja *f*
**Florentine** ['flɔrəntaɪn] *adj* florencki
**florid** ['flɔrɪd] *adj* *(style, verse)* kwiecisty; *(complexion)* rumiany
**florist** ['flɔrɪst] *n* kwiaciarz(-arka) *m(f)*
**florist's (shop)** ['flɔrɪsts-] *n* kwiaciarnia *f*
**flotation** [fləu'teɪʃən] *n* *(of shares)* emisja *f*; *(of company)* uruchomienie *nt*
**flotsam** ['flɔtsəm] *n* *(also:* **flotsam and jetsam***: of ship, plane)* szczątki *pl* (wraku); *(: rubbish)* rupiecie *pl*; *(: people)* życiowi rozbitkowie *vir pl*
**flounce** [flauns] *n* falbana *f*
▸ **flounce out** *or* **off** *vi* wybiegać (wybiec *perf*) jak szalony
**flounder** ['flaundə[r]] *vi* *(swimmer)* miotać się, rzucać się; *(fig: speaker)* plątać się; *(: economy)* kuleć ▹ *n* flądra *f*
**flour** ['flauə[r]] *n* mąka *f*
**flourish** ['flʌrɪʃ] *vi* kwitnąć ▹ *vt* wymachiwać *+instr* ▹ *n* *(in writing)* zawijas *m*; *(bold gesture)*: **with a ~** z rozmachem
**flourishing** ['flʌrɪʃɪŋ] *adj* kwitnący
**flout** [flaut] *vt* *(law, convention)* (świadomie) łamać (złamać *perf*), lekceważyć (zlekceważyć *perf*)
**flow** [fləu] *n* *(of blood, river, information)* przepływ *m*; *(of traffic)* strumień *m*; *(of tide)* przypływ *m*; *(of thought, speech)* potok *m* ▹ *vi* płynąć; *(clothes, hair)* spływać
**flow chart** *n* (blokowy) schemat *m* działania, organigram *m*
**flow diagram** *n* = **flow chart**
**flower** ['flauə[r]] *n* kwiat *m* ▹ *vi* kwitnąć; **to be in ~** kwitnąć
**flower bed** *n* klomb *m*
**flowerpot** ['flauəpɔt] *n* doniczka *f*
**flowery** ['flauərɪ] *adj* *(pattern, speech)* kwiecisty; *(perfume)* kwiatowy
**flown** [fləun] *pp of* **fly**
**flu** [fluː] *n* grypa *f*
**fluctuate** ['flʌktjueɪt] *vi* zmieniać się (nieregularnie), wahać się
**fluctuation** [flʌktju'eɪʃən] *n* zmiany *pl*, wahania *pl*
**flue** [fluː] *n* przewód *m* kominowy
**fluency** ['fluːənsɪ] *n* biegłość *f*, płynność *f*; **his ~ in French** jego biegła znajomość francuskiego
**fluent** ['fluːənt] *adj* *(linguist)* biegły; *(speech, writing)* płynny; **he's a ~ speaker/reader** płynnie mówi/czyta; **he speaks ~ French, he's ~ in French** biegle mówi po francusku
**fluently** ['fluːəntlɪ] *adv* biegle, płynnie
**fluff** [flʌf] *n* *(on jacket, carpet)* meszek *m*, kłaczki *pl*; *(of young animal)* puch *m* ▹ *vt* *(inf: exam etc)* zawalać (zawalić *perf*) *(inf)*; *(also:* **fluff out***: hair)* wzburzać (wzburzyć *perf*); *(: feathers)* napuszać (napuszyć *perf*)
**fluffy** ['flʌfɪ] *adj* puszysty, puchaty
**fluid** ['fluːɪd] *adj* płynny ▹ *n* płyn *m*
**fluid ounce** *(Brit)* *n* *(= 0.028l)* uncja *f* objętości (płynu)
**fluke** [fluːk] *(inf)* *n* fuks *m (inf)*
**flummox** ['flʌməks] *vt* peszyć (speszyć *perf*)
**flung** [flʌŋ] *pt, pp of* **fling**
**fluorescent** [fluə'rɛsnt] *adj* *(dial, paint)* fluorescencyjny; *(light)* jarzeniowy, fluorescencyjny
**fluoride** ['fluəraɪd] *n* fluorek *m*
**fluorine** ['fluəriːn] *n* fluor *m*
**flurry** ['flʌrɪ] *n* śnieżyca *f*; **a ~ of activity/excitement** przypływ ożywienia/podniecenia

**flush** [flʌʃ] *n* (*on face*) rumieniec *m*, wypieki *pl*; (*Cards*) sekwens *m* ▷ *vt* przepłukiwać (przepłukać *perf*) ▷ *vi* rumienić się (zarumienić się *perf*), czerwienić się (zaczerwienić się *perf*) ▷ *adv*: **~ with** równo z *+instr*; **~ against** tuż przy *+loc*; **in the first ~ of youth/freedom** w pierwszym porywie młodości/wolności; **hot ~es** (*Med*) uderzenia gorąca; **to ~ the toilet** spuszczać (spuścić *perf*) wodę (w toalecie)
▸ **flush out** *vt* płoszyć (spłoszyć *perf*)

**flushed** ['flʌʃt] *adj* zarumieniony, zaczerwieniony; **~ with success/victory** promieniejący sukcesem/zwycięstwem

**fluster** ['flʌstə^r] *n*: **in a ~** podenerwowany ▷ *vt* denerwować (podenerwować *perf*)

**flustered** ['flʌstəd] *adj* podenerwowany

**flute** [flu:t] *n* flet *m*

**fluted** ['flu:tɪd] *adj* żłobiony

**flutter** ['flʌtə^r] *n* (*of wings*) trzepot *m*, trzepotanie *nt*; (*of panic, excitement*) przypływ *m* ▷ *vi* trzepotać (zatrzepotać *perf*) ▷ *vt* trzepotać (zatrzepotać *perf*) *+instr*

**flux** [flʌks] *n*: **to be in a state of ~** nieustannie się zmieniać

**fly** [flaɪ] (*pt* **flew**, *pp* **flown**) *n* (*insect*) mucha *f*; (*also*: **flies**) rozporek *m* ▷ *vt* (*plane*) pilotować; (*passengers, cargo*) przewozić (przewieźć *perf*) samolotem; (*distances*) przelatywać (przelecieć *perf*); (*kite*) puszczać (puścić *perf*) ▷ *vi* (*plane, passengers*) lecieć (polecieć *perf*); (*: habitually*) latać; (*bird, insect*) lecieć (polecieć *perf*), frunąć (pofrunąć *perf*); (*: habitually*) latać, fruwać; (*prisoner*) uciekać (uciec *perf*); (*flags*) fruwać; **to fly open** gwałtownie się otwierać (otworzyć *perf*); **to fly off the handle** tracić (stracić *perf*) panowanie nad sobą; **pieces of metal went flying everywhere** kawałki metalu fruwały dookoła; **she came flying into the room** wpadła do pokoju; **her glasses flew off** zleciały jej okulary; **he flew into a rage** wpadł we wściekłość; **sorry, I must fly** przepraszam, muszę lecieć
▸ **fly away** *vi* odlatywać (odlecieć *perf*)
▸ **fly in** *vi* przylatywać (przylecieć *perf*)
▸ **fly off** *vi* = **fly away**
▸ **fly out** *vi* wylatywać (wylecieć *perf*)

**fly-fishing** ['flaɪfɪʃɪŋ] *n* łowienie *nt* ryb na muchę

**flying** ['flaɪɪŋ] *n* latanie *nt* ▷ *adj*: **a ~ visit** krótka wizyta *f*; **with ~ colours** z honorami; **he doesn't like ~** nie lubi latać

**flying buttress** *n* łuk *m* przyporowy

**flying saucer** *n* latający talerz *m*

**flying start** *n*: **to get off to a ~** brawurowo zaczynać (zacząć *perf*)

**flyleaf** ['flaɪli:f] *n* strona *f* przedtytułowa

**flyover** ['flaɪəuvə^r] (*Brit*) *n* wiadukt *m*, estakada *f*

**flysheet** ['flaɪʃi:t] *n* tropik *m* (*namiotu*)

**flywheel** ['flaɪwi:l] *n* koło *nt* zamachowe

**FM** *abbr* (*Brit*: *Mil*) = **field marshal**; (*Radio*: *= frequency modulation*) FM, ≈ UKF

**FMB** (*US*) *n abbr* (*= Federal Maritime Board*) *instytucja rządowa sprawująca kontrolę nad marynarką handlową*

**FMCS** (*US*) *n abbr* (*= Federal Mediation and Conciliation Services*) *federalna komisja mediacyjna i pojednawcza*

**FO** (*Brit*) *n abbr* (*= Foreign Office*) ≈ MSZ *m*

**foal** [fəul] *n* źrebię *nt*, źrebak *m*

**foam** [fəum] *n* (*surf, soapy water*) piana *f*; (*on beer, coffee*) pianka *f*; (*also*: **foam rubber**) guma *f* piankowa ▷ *vi* pienić się; **he was ~ing at the mouth** toczył pianę z ust

**f.o.b.** (*Comm*) *abbr* (*= free on board*) franco statek

**fob** [fɔb] *vt*: **to fob sb off** zbywać (zbyć *perf*) kogoś ▷ *n* (*also*: **watch fob**) dewizka *f*

**foc** (*Comm*: *Brit*) *abbr* (*= free of charge*) bezpłatnie, bez ponoszenia kosztów

**focal point** ['fəukl-] *n* punkt *m* centralny; (*of lens, mirror*) ognisko *nt*

**focus** ['fəukəs] (*pl* **~es**) *n* (*Phot*) ostrość *f*; (*fig*) skupienie *nt* uwagi ▷ *vt* (*telescope etc*) ustawiać (ustawić *perf*) ostrość *+gen*; (*light rays, one's eyes, attention*) skupiać (skupić *perf*) ▷ *vi*: **to ~ (on)** (*with camera*) nastawiać (nastawić *perf*) ostrość (na *+acc*); (*person*) skupiać się (skupić się *perf*) (na *+loc*); **in/out of ~** ostry/nieostry; **to be the ~ of attention** stanowić centrum zainteresowania

**fodder** ['fɔdə^r] *n* pasza *f*

**FOE** *n abbr* (*= Friends of the Earth*) *organizacja propagująca ochronę środowiska*

**foe** [fəu] *n* wróg *m*, nieprzyjaciel *m*

**foetus**, (*US*) **fetus** ['fi:təs] *n* płód *m*

**fog** [fɔg] *n* mgła *f*

**fogbound** ['fɔgbaund] *adj* unieruchomiony przez mgłę

**foggy** ['fɔgɪ] *adj* mglisty; **it's ~** jest mgła; **I haven't the foggiest (idea)** (*inf*) nie mam zielonego pojęcia (*inf*)

**fog lamp**, (*US*) **fog light** *n* (*Aut*) reflektor *m* przeciwmgłowy *or* przeciwmgielny

**foible** ['fɔɪbl] *n* słabostka *f*

**foil** [fɔɪl] *vt* (*attack, attempt*) udaremniać (udaremnić *perf*); (*plans*) krzyżować (pokrzyżować *perf*) ▷ *n* (*for wrapping food*) folia *f*; (*complement*) dodatek *m*; (*Fencing*) floret *m*; **to act as a ~ to** (*fig*) uwydatniać *or* podkreślać *+acc*

**foist** [fɔɪst] *vt*: **to ~ sth on sb** narzucać (narzucić *perf*) coś komuś

**fold** [fəuld] *n* (*in paper*) zagięcie *nt*; (*in dress, of skin*) fałda *f*; (*for sheep*) koszara *f*; (*fig*) owczarnia *f* ▷ *vt* (*clothes*) składać (złożyć *perf*);

f

(*paper*) składać (złożyć *perf*), zaginać (zagiąć *perf*); (*one's arms*) krzyżować (skrzyżować *perf*) ▷ *vi* (*business, organization*) upadać (upaść *perf*)
▸ **fold up** *vi* (*map, bed, table*) składać się (złożyć się *perf*); (*business*) upadać (upaść *perf*) ▷ *vt* składać (złożyć *perf*)

**folder** ['fəuldəʳ] *n* teczka *f* (papierowa)

**folding** ['fəuldɪŋ] *adj* składany

**foliage** ['fəulɪɪdʒ] *n* listowie *nt*

**folk** [fəuk] *npl* (*people*) ludzie *vir pl*; (*ethnic group*) lud *m* ▷ *cpd* ludowy; **~s** (*inf*) *npl* (*parents*) starzy *vir pl* (*inf*)

**folklore** ['fəuklɔːʳ] *n* folklor *m*

**folk music** *n* muzyka *f* ludowa

**folk song** *n* piosenka *f* ludowa

**follow** ['fɔləu] *vt* (*person: on foot*) iść (pójść *perf*) za *+instr*, podążać (podążyć *perf*) za *+instr* (*fml*); (*: by vehicle*) jechać (pojechać *perf*) za *+instr*; (*suspect, event, story*) śledzić; (*route, path: on foot*) iść (pójść *perf*) *+instr*; (*: by vehicle*) jechać (pojechać *perf*) *+instr*; (*advice, instructions*) stosować się (zastosować się *perf*) do *+gen*; (*example*) iść (pójść *perf*) za *+instr*; (*with eyes*) wodzić (powieść *perf*) wzrokiem po *+loc* ▷ *vi* (*person*): **she made for the stairs and he ~ed** skierowała się ku schodom, a on podążył *or* poszedł za nią; (*period of time*) następować (nastąpić *perf*); (*result, conclusion*) wynikać (wyniknąć *perf*); **to ~ in sb's footsteps** iść (pójść *perf*) w czyjeś ślady; **I don't quite ~ you** nie całkiem cię rozumiem; **it ~s that ...** wynika z tego, że ...; **as ~s** jak następuje; **to ~ suit** (*fig*) iść (pójść *perf*) za czyimś przykładem
▸ **follow on** *vi* następować (nastąpić *perf*) po *+loc*
▸ **follow out** *vt* (*idea, plan*) realizować (zrealizować *perf*); (*advice, instructions*) stosować się (zastosować się *perf*) do *+gen*
▸ **follow through** *vt* = **follow out**
▸ **follow up** *vt* (*offer*) sprawdzać (sprawdzić *perf*); (*idea, suggestion*) badać (zbadać *perf*)

**follower** ['fɔləuəʳ] *n* zwolennik(-iczka) *m*(*f*)

**following** ['fɔləuɪŋ] *adj* (*next*) następny; (*next-mentioned*) następujący ▷ *n* zwolennicy *vir pl*

**follow-up** ['fɔləuʌp] *n* ciąg *m* dalszy, kontynuacja *f* ▷ *adj* dalszy, uzupełniający

**folly** ['fɔlɪ] *n* (*foolishness*) szaleństwo *nt*; (*building*) *imitacja zamku, świątyni itp ustawiona w parku w celach dekoracyjnych*

**fond** [fɔnd] *adj* (*smile, look*) czuły; (*hopes, dreams*) naiwny; **to be ~ of sb/sth** lubić kogoś/coś; **to be ~ of doing sth** lubić coś robić

**fondle** ['fɔndl] *vt* pieścić

**fondly** ['fɔndlɪ] *adv* czule, z czułością; **he ~ imagined that ...** naiwnie wyobrażał sobie, że...

**fondness** ['fɔndnɪs] *n* czułość *f*; **a special ~ for** szczególne upodobanie do *+gen*

**font** [fɔnt] *n* (*in church*) chrzcielnica *f*; (*Typ*) czcionka *f*

**food** [fuːd] *n* żywność *f*, pokarm *m*

**food mixer** *n* mikser *m*

**food poisoning** *n* zatrucie *nt* pokarmowe

**food processor** *n* robot *m* kuchenny

**foodstuffs** ['fuːdstʌfs] *npl* artykuły *pl* żywnościowe

**fool** [fuːl] *n* (*person*) głupiec *m*, idiota(-tka) *m*(*f*); (*Culin*) *mus owocowy z dodatkiem cukru, jajek i śmietany* ▷ *vt* oszukiwać (oszukać *perf*), nabierać (nabrać *perf*) ▷ *vi* wygłupiać się; **to make a ~ of sb** (*ridicule*) ośmieszać (ośmieszyć *perf*) kogoś; (*trick*) wystrychnąć (*perf*) kogoś na dudka; **to make a ~ of o.s.** zbłaźnić się (*perf*); **you can't ~ me** mnie nie nabierzesz
▸ **fool about** (*pej*) *vi* (*waste time*) obijać się; (*behave foolishly*) wygłupiać się, błaznować
▸ **fool around** *vi* = **fool about**

**foolhardy** ['fuːlhɑːdɪ] *adj* ryzykancki

**foolish** ['fuːlɪʃ] *adj* (*stupid*) głupi; (*rash*) pochopny

**foolishly** ['fuːlɪʃlɪ] *adv* (*stupidly*) głupio; (*rashly*) pochopnie

**foolishness** ['fuːlɪʃnɪs] *n* głupota *f*

**foolproof** ['fuːlpruːf] *adj* niezawodny

**foolscap** ['fuːlskæp] *n papier formatu 34 x 43 cm*

**foot** [fut] (*pl* **feet**) *n* (*of person, as measure*) stopa *f*; (*of animal*) łapa *f*; (*of cliff*) podnóże *nt*; (*of page, stairs*) dół *m*; **at the ~ of the bed** w nogach łóżka; **on ~** pieszo, piechotą; **to find one's feet** (*fig*) czuć (poczuć *perf*) grunt pod nogami; **to put one's ~ down** (*Aut*) dodawać (dodać *perf*) gazu; (*say no*) stawiać się (postawić się *perf*); **to ~ the bill (for sth)** płacić (zapłacić *perf*) (za coś)

**footage** ['futɪdʒ] *n* materiał *m* filmowy

**foot and mouth (disease)** *n* pryszczyca *f*

**football** ['futbɔːl] *n* (*ball*) piłka *f* nożna; (*Sport: Brit*) piłka *f* nożna, futbol *m*; (*: US*) futbol *m* amerykański

**football ground** *n* boisko *nt* do gry w piłkę nożną

**football match** (*Brit*) *n* mecz *m* piłki nożnej

**football player** *n* (*Brit: also*: **footballer**) piłkarz *m*; (*US*) futbolista *m*

**footbrake** ['futbreɪk] *n* hamulec *m* nożny

**footbridge** ['futbrɪdʒ] *n* kładka *f*

**foothills** ['futhɪlz] *npl* pogórze *nt*

**foothold** ['futhəuld] *n* oparcie *nt* dla stóp; **to get a ~** (*fig*) znajdować (znaleźć *perf*) punkt zaczepienia

**footing** ['futɪŋ] *n* (*fig*) stopa *f*; **to lose one's ~** tracić (stracić *perf*) równowagę; **on an equal ~ with** na równi z *+instr*

**footlights** ['futlaɪts] *npl (Theat)* rampa *f*
**footman** ['futmən] *(irreg: like* **man***) n* lokaj *m*
**footnote** ['futnəut] *n* przypis *m*
**footpath** ['futpɑːθ] *n* ścieżka *f*
**footprint** ['futprɪnt] *n (of person)* odcisk *m* stopy; *(of animal)* odcisk *m* łapy
**footrest** ['futrɛst] *n* podnóżek *m*
**footstep** ['futstɛp] *n* krok *m*
**footwear** ['futwɛəʳ] *n* obuwie *nt*
**f.o.r.** *(Comm) abbr (= free on rail)* franco wagon

KEYWORD

**for** [fɔːʳ] *prep* **1** *(indicating recipient)* dla *+gen*
**2** *(indicating destination, application)* do *+gen*; **the train for London** pociąg do Londynu; **what's it for?** do czego to jest?
**3** *(indicating intention)* po *+acc*; **he went for the paper** wyszedł po gazetę
**4** *(indicating purpose)*: **give it to me — what for?** daj mi to — po co?; **it's time for lunch** czas na obiad; **clothes for children** ubrania dla dzieci; **to pray for peace** modlić się o pokój
**5** *(representing)*: **the MP for Hove** poseł/posłanka *m/f* z Hove; **he works for the government** pracuje na rządowej posadzie; **I'll ask him for you** zapytam go w twoim imieniu; **N for Nan** ≈ N jak Natalia
**6** *(because of)* z *+gen*; **for this reason** z tego powodu; **the town is famous for its canals** miasto słynie ze swoich kanałów
**7** *(with regard to)*: **he's mature for his age** jest dojrzały (jak) na swój wiek; **a gift for languages** talent do języków
**8** *(in exchange for)* za *+acc*; **I sold it for 5 pounds** sprzedałam to za 5 funtów
**9** *(in favour of)* za *+instr*; **are you for or against us?** jesteś za nami, czy przeciwko nam?; **vote for X** głosuj na X
**10** *(referring to distance)* (przez) *+acc*; **there are roadworks for 5 km** przez 5 km ciągną się roboty drogowe; **we walked for miles** szliśmy wiele mil
**11** *(referring to time)*: **he was away for two years** nie było go (przez) dwa lata; **it hasn't rained for 3 weeks** nie padało od trzech tygodni; **can you do it for tomorrow?** czy możesz to zrobić na jutro?
**12** *(with infinitive clause)*: **it would be best for you to leave** byłoby najlepiej, gdybyś wyjechał; **it is not for me to decide** ja nie mogę tu decydować; **for this to be possible** aby to było możliwe
**13** *(in spite of)* (po)mimo *+gen*; **for all his complaints, he is very fond of her** (po)mimo wszystkich zastrzeżeń, bardzo ją lubi
▷ *conj (fml)* ponieważ, gdyż; **she was very angry, for he was late again** była bardzo zła, ponieważ *or* gdyż znów się spóźnił

**forage** ['fɔrɪdʒ] *n* pasza *f* ▷ *vi (for food)* szukać pożywienia; *(for interesting objects)* szperać
**forage cap** *n* furażerka *f*
**foray** ['fɔreɪ] *n* najazd *m*
**forbad(e)** [fə'bæd] *pt of* **forbid**
**forbearing** [fɔː'bɛərɪŋ] *adj* wyrozumiały
**forbid** [fə'bɪd] *(pt* **forbad(e)**, *pp* **~den***) vt* zakazywać (zakazać *perf*) *+gen*; **to ~ sb to do sth** zabraniać (zabronić *perf*) komuś coś robić
**forbidden** [fə'bɪdn] *pp of* **forbid** ▷ *adj* zakazany, tabu *post*
**forbidding** [fə'bɪdɪŋ] *adj (prospect)* posępny; *(look, person)* posępny, odpychający
**force** [fɔːs] *n (also Phys)* siła *f*; *(power, influence)* siła *f*, moc *f* ▷ *vt (person)* zmuszać (zmusić *perf*); *(confession etc)* wymuszać (wymusić *perf*); *(push)* pchnąć *(perf)*; *(lock, door)* wyłamywać (wyłamać *perf*); **the Forces** *(Brit) npl* Siły *pl* Zbrojne; **in ~** licznie, masowo; **to come into ~** wchodzić (wejść *perf*) w życie; **to join ~s** łączyć (połączyć *perf*) siły; **a ~ 5 wind** wiatr o sile 5 stopni; **the sales ~** *(Comm)* agenci handlowi; **through** *or* **from ~ of habit** siłą nawyku; **to ~ o.s. to do sth** zmuszać się (zmusić się *perf*) do (z)robienia czegoś; **to ~ sb to do sth** zmuszać (zmusić *perf*) kogoś do (z)robienia czegoś; **to ~ sb's hand** zmuszać (zmusić *perf*) kogoś do ujawnienia zamiarów; **to ~ sth (up)on sb** narzucać (narzucić *perf*) coś komuś; **to ~ o.s. (up)on sb** narzucać się komuś; **they ~d him into a small room** wepchnęli go do małego pokoiku
▸ **force back** *vt (tears, urge)* powstrzymywać (powstrzymać *perf*)
**forced** [fɔːst] *adj (labour, landing)* przymusowy; *(smile)* wymuszony
**force-feed** ['fɔːsfiːd] *vt* karmić (nakarmić *perf*) siłą
**forceful** ['fɔːsful] *adj (person, point)* przekonujący; *(attack)* silny
**forceps** ['fɔːsɛps] *npl* kleszcze *pl*, szczypce *pl*
**forcible** ['fɔːsəbl] *adj (entry, imposition)* bezprawny, dokonany przemocą; *(reminder)* ostry; *(lesson)* porządny
**forcibly** ['fɔːsəblɪ] *adv (remove)* siłą; *(express)* dobitnie, dosadnie
**ford** [fɔːd] *n* bród *m*; **to ~ the river** przebyć *(perf)* rzekę w bród
**fore** [fɔːʳ] *n*: **to come to the ~** wysuwać się (wysunąć się *perf*) na czoło
**forearm** ['fɔːrɑːm] *n* przedramię *nt*
**forebear** ['fɔːbɛəʳ] *n* przodek *m*
**foreboding** [fɔː'bəudɪŋ] *n* złe przeczucie *nt*

**forecast** ['fɔ:kɑ:st] (*irreg: like* **cast**) *n* przewidywanie *nt*, prognoza *f* ▷ *vt* przewidywać (przewidzieć *perf*); **the weather ~** prognoza pogody
**foreclose** [fɔ:'kləuz] *vt* (*also:* **foreclose on:** *property*) orzekać (orzec *perf*) przepadek *+gen*; (*: person*) przejmować (przejąć *perf*) mienie *+gen*
**foreclosure** [fɔ:'kləuʒə^r] *n* egzekucja *f* (mienia)
**forecourt** ['fɔ:kɔ:t] *n* podjazd *m*
**forefathers** ['fɔ:fɑ:ðəz] *npl* przodkowie *vir pl*, ojcowie *vir pl*
**forefinger** ['fɔ:fɪŋgə^r] *n* palec *m* wskazujący
**forefront** ['fɔ:frʌnt] *n*: **in the ~ of** na czele *+gen*
**forego** [fɔ:'gəu] (*irreg: like* **go**) *vt* (*give up*) zrzekać się (zrzec się *perf*) *+gen*, rezygnować (zrezygnować *perf*) z *+gen*; (*go without*) obywać się (obyć się *perf*) bez *+gen*
**foregoing** ['fɔ:gəuɪŋ] *adj* powyższy ▷ *n*: **the ~** powyższe *nt*
**foregone** ['fɔ:gɔn] *pp of* **forego** ▷ *adj*: **it's a ~ conclusion** to sprawa przesądzona
**foreground** ['fɔ:graund] *n* pierwszy plan *m*; **a ~ program** (*Comput*) program pierwszoplanowy
**forehand** ['fɔ:hænd] *n* forhend *m*
**forehead** ['fɔrɪd] *n* czoło *nt*
**foreign** ['fɔrɪn] *adj* (*country, matter*) obcy; (*trade, student*) zagraniczny; **~ holidays** wakacje za granicą
**foreign body** *n* obce ciało *nt*
**foreign currency** *n* waluta *f* obca
**foreigner** ['fɔrɪnə^r] *n* cudzoziemiec(-mka) *m(f)*
**foreign exchange** *n* (*system*) wymiana *f* walut; (*money*) waluty *pl* obce
**foreign exchange market** *n* rynek *m* dewizowy
**foreign exchange rate** *n* kurs *m* walutowy
**foreign minister** *n* Minister *m* Spraw Zagranicznych
**Foreign Office** (*Brit*) *n* Ministerstwo *nt* Spraw Zagranicznych
**Foreign Secretary** (*Brit*) *n* Minister *m* Spraw Zagranicznych
**foreleg** ['fɔ:lɛg] *n* (*of animal*) przednia noga *f*
**foreman** ['fɔ:mən] (*irreg: like* **man**) *n* (*in factory*) brygadzista *m*; (*on building site*) kierownik *m* (robót); (*of jury*) przewodniczący *m*
**foremost** ['fɔ:məust] *adj* główny ▷ *adv*: **first and ~** przede wszystkim
**forename** ['fɔ:neɪm] *n* imię *nt*
**forensic** [fə'rɛnsɪk] *adj* (*medicine*) sądowy; (*skill*) prawniczy
**forerunner** ['fɔ:rʌnə^r] *n* prekursor *m*
**foresaw** *pt of* **foresee**
**foresee** [fɔ:'si:] (*irreg: like* **see**) *vt* przewidywać (przewidzieć *perf*)
**foreseeable** [fɔ:'si:əbl] *adj* dający się przewidzieć, przewidywalny; **in the ~ future** w najbliższej przyszłości
**foreseen** [fɔ:'si:n] *pp of* **foresee**
**foreshadow** [fɔ:'ʃædəu] *vt* (*event*) zapowiadać (zapowiedzieć *perf*)
**foreshore** ['fɔ'ʃɔ:^r] *n* przedbrzeże *nt*
**foreshorten** [fɔ:'ʃɔ:tn] *vt* przedstawiać (przedstawić *perf*) w rzucie perspektywicznym
**foresight** ['fɔ:saɪt] *n* zdolność *f* przewidywania, przezorność *f*
**foreskin** ['fɔ:skɪn] *n* napletek *m*
**forest** ['fɔrɪst] *n* las *m*
**forestall** [fɔ:'stɔ:l] *vt* ubiegać (ubiec *perf*)
**forestry** ['fɔrɪstrɪ] *n* leśnictwo *nt*
**foretaste** ['fɔ:teɪst] *n*: **a ~ of** przedsmak *m +gen*
**foretell** [fɔ:'tɛl] (*irreg: like* **tell**) *vt* przepowiadać (przepowiedzieć *perf*)
**forethought** ['fɔ:θɔ:t] *n* przezorność *f*, zapobiegliwość *f*
**foretold** [fɔ:'təuld] *pt, pp of* **foretell**
**forever** [fə'rɛvə^r] *adv* (*permanently*) trwale, na trwałe; (*always*) (na) zawsze, wiecznie; (*continually*) ciągle, bezustannie; **it has gone ~** (to) minęło bezpowrotnie; **it will last ~** to będzie trwać wiecznie; **you're ~ finding difficulties** ty ciągle wynajdujesz problemy
**forewarn** [fɔ:'wɔ:n] *vt* przestrzegać (przestrzec *perf*)
**forewent** [fɔ:'wɛnt] *pt of* **forego**
**foreword** ['fɔ:wə:d] *n* przedmowa *f*
**forfeit** ['fɔ:fɪt] *n* grzywna *f* ▷ *vt* (*right, chance etc*) tracić (stracić *perf*); (*one's happiness, health*) poświęcać (poświęcić *perf*); (*one's income*) zrzekać się (zrzec się *perf*) *+gen*
**forgave** [fə'geɪv] *pt of* **forgive**
**forge** [fɔ:dʒ] *n* kuźnia *f* ▷ *vt* (*signature, money etc*) fałszować (sfałszować *perf*); (*wrought iron*) kuć (wykuć *perf*); (*alliance*) zawierać (zawrzeć *perf*)
▸ **forge ahead** *vi* iść (pójść *perf*) do przodu
**forger** ['fɔ:dʒə^r] *n* fałszerz *m*
**forgery** ['fɔ:dʒərɪ] *n* (*crime*) fałszerstwo *nt*; (*document, painting etc*) falsyfikat *m*
**forget** [fə'gɛt] (*pt* **forgot**, *pp* **forgotten**) *vt* zapominać (zapomnieć *perf*) *+gen*; (*birthday, appointment, person*) zapominać (zapomnieć *perf*) o *+loc* ▷ *vi* zapominać (zapomnieć *perf*); **his fourth or fifth play, I ~ which** jego czwarta czy piąta sztuka, nie pamiętam; **to ~ o.s.** zapominać się (zapomnieć się *perf*)
**forgetful** [fə'gɛtful] *adj*: **to be ~** mieć słabą pamięć; **~ of** nie zważający na *+acc*

**forgetfulness** [fəˈgɛtfulnɪs] *n* słaba pamięć *f*
**forget-me-not** [fəˈgɛtmɪnɔt] *n* niezapominajka *f*
**forgive** [fəˈgɪv] (*pt* **forgave**, *pp* **~n**) *vt* wybaczać (wybaczyć *perf*) *or* przebaczać (przebaczyć *perf*) *+dat*; **to ~ sb for sth** wybaczyć (*perf*) komuś coś; **to ~ sb for doing sth** wybaczyć (*perf*) komuś, że coś zrobił; **~ my ignorance, but ...** proszę wybaczyć moją niewiedzę, lecz ...; **they could be ~n for thinking that ...** można im wybaczyć, iż myśleli, że...; **let's ~ and forget** puśćmy to w niepamięć
**forgiveness** [fəˈgɪvnɪs] *n* przebaczenie *nt*; **to ask** *or* **beg sb's ~** prosić *or* błagać kogoś o wybaczenie
**forgiving** [fəˈgɪvɪŋ] *adj* wyrozumiały
**forgo** [fɔːˈgəu] (*pt* **forwent**, *pp* **~ne**) *vt* = **forego**
**forgot** [fəˈgɔt] *pt of* **forget**
**forgotten** [fəˈgɔtn] *pp of* **forget**
**fork** [fɔːk] *n* (*for eating*) widelec *m*; (*for gardening*) widły *pl*; (*in road, river*) rozwidlenie *nt* ▷ *vi* (*road*) rozwidlać się
▸ **fork out** (*inf*) *vt* bulić (wybulić *perf*) (*inf*) ▷ *vi* bulić (zabulić *perf*) (*inf*)
**forked** [fɔːkt] *adj*: **~ lightning** błyskawica *f* zygzakowata
**fork-lift truck** [ˈfɔːklɪft-] *n* podnośnik *m* widłowy
**forlorn** [fəˈlɔːn] *adj* (*person*) opuszczony; (*cry, voice*) żałosny; (*place*) wymarły; (*attempt, hope*) rozpaczliwy
**form** [fɔːm] *n* (*type*) forma *f*; (*shape*) postać *f*; (*Scol*) klasa *f*; (*questionnaire*) formularz *m* ▷ *vt* (*shape, organization*) tworzyć (utworzyć *perf*); (*idea, impression*) wyrabiać (wyrobić *perf*) sobie; (*relationship*) zawierać (zawrzeć *perf*); (*habit*) nabierać (nabrać *perf*) *+gen* ▷ *vi* tworzyć się (utworzyć się *perf*); **in the ~ of** w formie *+gen*; **to take the ~ of** mieć *or* przybierać (przybrać *perf*) formę *+gen*; **to ~ part of sth** stanowić część czegoś; **to be in good** *or* **top ~** (*Sport*) być w dobrej *or* szczytowej formie; (*fig*) być w dobrej *or* wspaniałej formie; **to be on ~** być w formie
**formal** [ˈfɔːməl] *adj* (*education, style*) formalny; (*statement, behaviour*) formalny, oficjalny; (*occasion, dinner*) uroczysty; (*gardens*) tradycyjny, typowy; **~ dress** strój oficjalny *or* wizytowy
**formality** [fɔːˈmælɪtɪ] *n* (*procedure*) formalność *f*; (*politeness*) formalna uprzejmość *f*; **formalities** *npl* formalności *pl*
**formalize** [ˈfɔːməlaɪz] *vt* nadawać (nadać *perf*) formalny wyraz *+dat*
**formally** [ˈfɔːməlɪ] *adv* (*announce, approve*) formalnie, oficjalnie; (*dress, behave*) formalnie; **to be ~ invited** otrzymać (*perf*) oficjalne zaproszenie
**format** [ˈfɔːmæt] *n* forma *f* ▷ *vt* (*Comput*) formatować (sformatować *perf*)
**formation** [fɔːˈmeɪʃən] *n* (*of organization, business*) utworzenie *nt*; (*of theory, ideas*) powstawanie *nt*, formowanie się *nt*; (*pattern*) formacja *f*; (*of rocks, clouds*) tworzenie się *nt*, powstawanie *nt*
**formative** [ˈfɔːmətɪv] *adj*: **~ years** okres kształtujący osobowość
**former** [ˈfɔːməʳ] *adj* (*one-time*) były; (*earlier*) dawny ▷ *n*: **the ~** ten pierwszy *m*/ta pierwsza *f*/to pierwsze *nt*; **in ~ times** w dawnych czasach, niegdyś
**formerly** [ˈfɔːməlɪ] *adv* uprzednio
**Formica** [fɔːˈmaɪkə]® *n* formika *f*
**formidable** [ˈfɔːmɪdəbl] *adj* (*opponent*) budzący grozę; (*task*) ogromny
**formula** [ˈfɔːmjulə] (*pl* **~e** *or* **~s**) *n* (*Math, Chem*) wzór *m*, formuła *f*; (*plan*) recepta *f*, przepis *m*; **F~ One** (*Aut*) Formuła I
**formulate** [ˈfɔːmjuleɪt] *vt* (*plan, strategy*) opracowywać (opracować *perf*); (*thought, opinion*) formułować (sformułować *perf*)
**fornicate** [ˈfɔːnɪkeɪt] *vi* cudzołożyć
**forsake** [fəˈseɪk] (*pt* **forsook**, *pp* **~n**) *vt* porzucać (porzucić *perf*)
**forsook** [fəˈsuk] *pt of* **forsake**
**fort** [fɔːt] *n* (*Mil*) fort *m*; **to hold the ~** (*fig*) sprawować pieczę (*pod czyjąś nieobecność*)
**forte** [ˈfɔːtɪ] *n* mocna strona *f*
**forth** [fɔːθ] *adv*: **to set ~** wyruszać (wyruszyć *perf*); **back and ~** tam i z powrotem; **to bring ~** (*child*) wydać (*perf*) na świat; (*revulsion, discussion etc*) wywoływać (wywołać *perf*); **and so ~** i tak dalej
**forthcoming** [fɔːθˈkʌmɪŋ] *adj* (*event*) nadchodzący, zbliżający się; (*book*) mający się ukazać; (*help, money*) dostępny; (*person*) rozmowny
**forthright** [ˈfɔːθraɪt] *adj* otwarty, jawny
**forthwith** [ˈfɔːθˈwɪθ] *adv* niezwłocznie
**fortieth** [ˈfɔːtɪɪθ] *num* czterdziesty
**fortification** [fɔːtɪfɪˈkeɪʃən] *n* fortyfikacja *f*
**fortified wine** [ˈfɔːtɪfaɪd-] *n* wino *nt* alkoholizowane
**fortify** [ˈfɔːtɪfaɪ] *vt* (*city*) obwarowywać (obwarować *perf*); (*person*) umacniać (umocnić *perf*)
**fortitude** [ˈfɔːtɪtjuːd] *n* hart *m* ducha
**fortnight** [ˈfɔːtnaɪt] (*Brit*) *n* dwa tygodnie *pl*; **it's a ~ since ...** minęły dwa tygodnie od (czasu, gdy) ...
**fortnightly** [ˈfɔːtnaɪtlɪ] *adj* (*lasting two weeks*) dwutygodniowy; (*happening every two weeks*) odbywający się co dwa tygodnie ▷ *adv* co dwa tygodnie; **a ~ magazine** dwutygodnik
**FORTRAN** [ˈfɔːtræn] *n* (język *m*) FORTRAN

**fortress** [ˈfɔːtrɪs] *n* twierdza *f*, forteca *f*

**fortuitous** [fɔːˈtjuːɪtəs] *adj* przypadkowy

**fortunate** [ˈfɔːtʃənɪt] *adj* (*person*) szczęśliwy; (*event*) pomyślny; **to be ~** mieć szczęście; **he is ~ to have ...** on ma szczęście, że ma *+acc*; **it is ~ that ...** dobrze się składa, że ...

**fortunately** [ˈfɔːtʃənɪtlɪ] *adv* na szczęście, szczęśliwie

**fortune** [ˈfɔːtʃən] *n* (*luck*) szczęście *nt*, powodzenie *nt*; (*wealth*) fortuna *f*, majątek *m*; **to make a ~** zbijać (zbić *perf*) majątek; **to tell sb's ~** przepowiadać (przepowiedzieć *perf*) komuś przyszłość

**fortune-teller** [ˈfɔːtʃəntɛləʳ] *n* wróżka *f*

**forty** [ˈfɔːtɪ] *num* czterdzieści

**forum** [ˈfɔːrəm] *n* forum *nt*

**forward** [ˈfɔːwəd] *adj* (*movement*) do przodu *post*; (*part*) przedni; (*not shy*) śmiały ▷ *n* (*Sport*) napastnik(-iczka) *m(f)* ▷ *vt* (*letter, parcel*) przesyłać (przesłać *perf*) (dalej); (*career, plans*) posuwać (posunąć *perf*) do przodu; **"please ~"** „proszę przesłać na nowy adres"; **~ planning** planowanie perspektywiczne

**forward(s)** [ˈfɔːwəd(z)] *adv* (*in space*) do przodu; (*in development, time*) naprzód; **to look forward** patrzeć w przyszłość

**fossil** [ˈfɔsl] *n* skamielina *f*

**fossil fuel** *n* paliwo *nt* kopalniane

**foster** [ˈfɔstəʳ] *vt* (*child*) wychowywać, brać (wziąć *perf*) na wychowanie; (*idea, activity*) rozwijać (rozwinąć *perf*), popierać (poprzeć *perf*)

**foster child** *n* przybrane dziecko *nt*

**foster mother** *n* przybrana matka *f*

**fought** [fɔːt] *pt, pp of* **fight**

**foul** [faul] *adj* (*place, taste*) wstrętny, paskudny; (*smell*) cuchnący; (*temper, weather*) okropny; (*language*) sprośny, plugawy ▷ *n* (*Sport*) faul *m* ▷ *vt* brudzić (zabrudzić *perf*), zanieczyszczać (zanieczyścić *perf*); (*Sport*) faulować (sfaulować *perf*); (*anchor, propeller*) blokować (zablokować *perf*); (*fishing net*) uszkadzać (uszkodzić *perf*)

**foul play** *n* przestępstwo *nt*; **~ is not suspected** nie podejrzewa się przestępstwa

**found** [faund] *pt, pp of* **find** ▷ *vt* zakładać (założyć *perf*)

**foundation** [faunˈdeɪʃən] *n* (*of business, theatre etc*) założenie *nt*; (*basis*) podstawa *f*; (*fig*) oparcie *nt*; (*organization*) fundacja *f*; (*also*: **foundation cream**) podkład *m* (pod makijaż); **foundations** *npl* fundamenty *pl*; **the rumours are without ~** te plotki są bezpodstawne; **to lay the ~s of sth** (*fig*) kłaść (położyć *perf*) podwaliny pod coś

**foundation stone** *n* kamień *m* węgielny

**founder** [ˈfaundəʳ] *n* założyciel(ka) *m(f)* ▷ *vi* (*ship*) tonąć (zatonąć *perf*)

**founder member** *n* członek *m* — założyciel *m*

**founding** [ˈfaundɪŋ] *adj*: **~ father** (*fig*) ojciec *m*; **the F~ Fathers** (*US*) Ojcowie Założyciele (*członkowie Federalnej Konwencji Konstytucyjnej z 1787 r.*)

**foundry** [ˈfaundrɪ] *n* odlewnia *f*

**fount** [faunt] *n* (*of knowledge etc*) (ważne) źródło *nt*; (*Typ*) czcionka *f*

**fountain** [ˈfauntɪn] *n* fontanna *f*

**fountain pen** *n* wieczne pióro *nt*

**four** [fɔːʳ] *num* cztery; **on all ~s** na czworakach

**four-letter word** [ˈfɔːlɛtə-] *n* brzydki wyraz *m*

**four-poster** [ˈfɔːˈpəustəʳ] *n* (*also*: **four-poster bed**) łoże *nt* z baldachimem

**foursome** [ˈfɔːsəm] *n* czwórka *f* (*grupa*)

**fourteen** [ˈfɔːˈtiːn] *num* czternaście

**fourteenth** [ˈfɔːˈtiːnθ] *num* czternasty

**fourth** [ˈfɔːθ] *num* czwarty ▷ *n* (*Aut*: *also*: **fourth gear**) czwarty bieg *m*, czwórka *f* (*inf*)

**four-wheel drive** [ˈfɔːwiːl-] *n*: **with ~** z napędem na cztery koła

**fowl** [faul] *n* (*bird*) ptak *m*; (*birds*) ptactwo *nt*; (*: domestic*) drób *m*

**fox** [fɔks] *n* lis *m* ▷ *vt* dezorientować (zdezorientować *perf*)

**foxglove** [ˈfɔksglʌv] *n* (*Bot*) naparstnica *f*

**fox-hunting** [ˈfɔkshʌntɪŋ] *n* polowanie *nt* na lisa

**foxtrot** [ˈfɔkstrɔt] *n* fokstrot *m*

**foyer** [ˈfɔɪeɪ] *n* foyer *nt inv*

**FPA** (*Brit*) *n abbr* (= *Family Planning Association*) *stowarzyszenie propagujące planowanie rodziny*

**Fr.** (*Rel*) *abbr* = **father**; (*priest*) ks.; (*friar*) o.

**fr.** *abbr* (= *franc*) F (= *frank*)

**fracas** [ˈfrækɑː] *n* awantura *f*

**fraction** [ˈfrækʃən] *n* (*portion*) odrobina *f*; (*Math*) ułamek *m*; **for a ~ of a second** przez ułamek sekundy

**fractionally** [ˈfrækʃnəlɪ] *adv*: **~ smaller** *etc* odrobinę mniejszy *etc*

**fractious** [ˈfrækʃəs] *adj* marudny

**fracture** [ˈfræktʃəʳ] *n* (*of bone*) złamanie *nt*, pęknięcie *nt* ▷ *vt* (*bone*) powodować (spowodować *perf*) pęknięcie *+gen*

**fragile** [ˈfrædʒaɪl] *adj* (*object, structure*) kruchy; (*person*) delikatny; (*economy*) wątły

**fragment** [ˈfrægmənt] *n* część *f*, kawałek *m*; (*of bone, cup*) odłamek *m*; (*of conversation, poem*) fragment *m*, urywek *m*; (*of paper, fabric*) skrawek *m* ▷ *vi* rozpadać się (rozpaść się *perf*)

**fragmentary** [ˈfrægməntərɪ] *adj* fragmentaryczny

**fragrance** [ˈfreɪgrəns] *n* zapach *m*

**fragrant** [ˈfreɪgrənt] *adj* pachnący

**frail** [freɪl] *adj* (*person*) słabowity, wątły; (*structure*) kruchy

**frame** [freɪm] *n* (*of picture, bicycle*) rama *f*; (*of door, window*) framuga *f*, rama *f*; (*of building, structure*) szkielet *m*; (*of human, animal*) sylwetka *f*, ciało *nt*; (*of spectacles: also*: **frames**) oprawka *f*; (*Phot*) klatka *f* ▷ *vt* (*picture*) oprawiać (oprawić *perf*); (*law, theory*) formułować (sformułować *perf*); **to ~ sb** (*inf*) wrabiać (wrobić *perf*) kogoś (*inf*)

**frame of mind** *n* nastrój *m*

**framework** ['freɪmwəːk] *n* (*structure*) struktura *f*, szkielet *m*; (*fig*) podstawa *f*, ramy *pl*

**France** [frɑːns] *n* Francja *f*

**franchise** ['fræntʃaɪz] *n* (*Pol*) prawo *nt* wyborcze; (*Comm*) franszyza *f* (*koncesja na autoryzowaną dystrybucję*)

**frank** [fræŋk] *adj* szczery ▷ *vt* (*letter*) frankować (ofrankować *perf*)

**Frankfurt** ['fræŋkfəːt] *n* Frankfurt *m*

**frankfurter** ['fræŋkfəːtə[r]] *n* cienka parówka *f*

**franking machine** ['fræŋkɪŋ-] *n* maszyna *f* do frankowania listów

**frankly** ['fræŋklɪ] *adv* (*honestly*) szczerze; (*candidly*) otwarcie; **~, ...** szczerze mówiąc, ...

**frankness** ['fræŋknɪs] *n* szczerość *f*

**frantic** ['fræntɪk] *adj* (*person*) oszalały; (*rush, pace*) szalony; (*search*) gorączkowy; (*need*) palący; **we were ~ with worry** szaleliśmy ze zmartwienia

**frantically** ['fræntɪklɪ] *adv* gorączkowo

**fraternal** [frə'təːnl] *adj* braterski

**fraternity** [frə'təːnɪtɪ] *n* (*feeling*) braterstwo *nt*; (*group of people*) bractwo *nt*

**fraternize** ['frætənaɪz] *vi* bratać się

**fraud** [frɔːd] *n* (*crime*) oszustwo *nt*; (*person*) oszust(ka) *m(f)*

**fraudulent** ['frɔːdjulənt] *adj* oszukańczy

**fraught** [frɔːt] *adj* (*person*) spięty; (*evening, meeting*) pełen napięcia; **to be ~ with danger/problems** obfitować w niebezpieczeństwa/problemy

**fray** [freɪ] *vi* strzępić się (postrzępić się *perf*) ▷ *n*: **to return to the ~** wracać (wrócić *perf*) w ogień walki; **tempers were ~ed** nerwy zawodziły; **her nerves were ~ed** była kłębkiem nerwów

**FRB** (*US*) *n abbr* (*= Federal Reserve Board*) *rada banków rezerwy federalnej, tworzących bank centralny Stanów Zjednoczonych*

**FRCM** (*Brit*) *n abbr* = **Fellow of the Royal College of Music**

**FRCO** (*Brit*) *n abbr* = **Fellow of the Royal College of Organists**

**FRCP** (*Brit*) *n abbr* = **Fellow of the Royal College of Physicians**

**FRCS** (*Brit*) *n abbr* = **Fellow of the Royal College of Surgeons**

**freak** [friːk] *n* (*in attitude, behaviour*) dziwak(-aczka) *m(f)*; (*in appearance*) dziwoląg *m*, wybryk *m* natury; (*pej*): **health ~** maniak(-aczka) *m(f)* na punkcie zdrowia ▷ *adj* dziwaczny
▶ **freak out** (*inf*) *vi* bzikować (zbzikować *perf*), głupieć (zgłupieć *perf*); **I was ~ed out** wyszedłem z siebie (*inf*)

**freakish** ['friːkɪʃ] *adj* dziwaczny, cudaczny

**freckle** ['frɛkl] *n* pieg *m*

**freckled** ['frɛkld] *adj* piegowaty

**free** [friː] *adj* wolny; (*meal, ticket*) bezpłatny ▷ *vt* (*prisoner, colony*) uwalniać (uwolnić *perf*); (*jammed object*) zwalniać (zwolnić *perf*); (*person: from responsibility, duty*) zwalniać (zwolnić *perf*); **to give sb a ~ hand** dawać (dać *perf*) komuś wolną rękę; **~ and easy** na luzie; **"admission ~", "~ admission"** „wstęp wolny"; **to be ~ of sth** być wolnym od czegoś; **we are ~ to do it** wolno nam to robić; **~ (of charge), for ~** za darmo

**free agent** *n*: **to be a ~** mieć całkowitą swobodę działania

**freebie** ['friːbɪ] (*inf*) *n* podarunek *m* (*od firmy, instytucji itp w celach reklamowych*)

**freedom** ['friːdəm] *n* wolność *f*; (*of movement*) swoboda *f*; **~ from hunger/poverty/disease** wolność od głodu/ubóstwa/chorób

**freedom fighter** *n* bojownik(-iczka) *m(f)* o wolność

**free enterprise** *n* wolny rynek *m*

**free-for-all** ['friːfərɔːl] *n*: **it's a ~** wszystkie chwyty (są) dozwolone

**free gift** *n* bezpłatny podarunek *m*

**freehold** ['friːhəuld] *n* tytuł *m* nieograniczonej własności

**free kick** *n* rzut *m* wolny

**freelance** ['friːlɑːns] *adj* (*journalist, photographer*) niezależny ▷ *n* wolny strzelec *m*

**freeloader** ['friːləudə[r]] (*pej*) *n* naciągacz(ka) *m(f)* (*pej*)

**freely** ['friːlɪ] *adv* (*talk, move*) swobodnie; (*perspire, donate*) obficie; (*spend*) lekką ręką; **drugs are ~ available** narkotyki są łatwo dostępne

**Freemason** ['friːmeɪsn] *n* mason *m*, wolnomularz *m*

**freemasonry** ['friːmeɪsnrɪ] *n* masoneria *f*, wolnomularstwo *nt*

**Freepost®** ['friːpəust] *n przesyłka na koszt adresata*

**free-range** ['friː'reɪndʒ] *adj* (*eggs, chickens*) wiejski

**free sample** *n* bezpłatna próbka *f*

**freesia** ['friːzɪə] *n* frezja *f*

**free speech** *n* wolność *f* słowa

**freestyle** ['friːstaɪl] *n* (*Sport*) styl *m* wolny

**free trade** *n* wolny handel *m*
**freeway** ['fri:weɪ] (US) *n* autostrada *f*
**freewheel** [fri:'wi:l] *vi* jechać na wolnym biegu
**free will** *n* wolna wola *f*; **of one's own ~** z własnej woli
**freeze** [fri:z] (*pt* **froze**, *pp* **frozen**) *vi* (*weather*) mrozić (przymrozić *perf*); (*liquid, pipe*) zamarzać (zamarznąć *perf*); (*person: with cold*) marznąć (zmarznąć *perf*); (*: from fear*) zastygać (zastygnąć *perf*) (w bezruchu) ▷ *vt* (*water, lake*) skuwać (skuć *perf*) lodem; (*food, prices*) zamrażać (zamrozić *perf*) ▷ *n* (*cold weather*) przymrozek *m*; (*on arms, wages*) zamrożenie *nt*; **it'll ~ tonight** dziś wieczorem będzie mróz
▶ **freeze over** *vi* (*river, windows*) zamarzać (zamarznąć *perf*)
**freeze-dried** ['fri:zdraɪd] *adj* liofilizowany
**freezer** ['fri:zə^r] *n* zamrażarka *f*
**freezing** ['fri:zɪŋ] *adj* (*also*: **freezing cold**) lodowaty; **3 degrees below ~** 3 stopnie poniżej zera; **I'm ~** jest mi bardzo zimno; **it's ~ outside** na zewnątrz jest bardzo zimno
**freezing point** *n* punkt *m* zamarzania
**freight** [freɪt] *n* fracht *m*; **to send sth by air/sea ~** przesyłać (przesłać *perf*) coś drogą powietrzną/morską
**freight car** (US) *n* wagon *m* towarowy
**freighter** ['freɪtə^r] *n* (*Naut*) frachtowiec *m*, transportowiec *m*; (*Aviat*) transportowiec *m*
**freight train** (US) *n* pociąg *m* towarowy
**French** [frɛntʃ] *adj* francuski; **the French** *npl* Francuzi *vir pl*
**French bean** (*Brit*) *n* fasola *f* zwyczajna
**French Canadian** [frɛntʃkə'neɪdjən] *n* Kanadyjczyk(-jka) *m(f)* francuskojęzyczny(-na) *m(f)*
**French dressing** *n* sos *m* francuski
**French fries** [-fraɪz] (*esp US*) *npl* frytki *pl*
**French Guiana** [-gaɪ'ænə] *n* Gujana *f* Francuska
**Frenchman** ['frɛntʃmən] (*irreg*: *like* **man**) *n* Francuz *m*
**French Riviera** *n*: **the ~** Riwiera *f* Francuska
**French window** *n* oszklone drzwi *pl*
**Frenchwoman** ['frɛntʃwumən] (*irreg*: *like* **woman**) *n* Francuzka *f*
**frenetic** [frə'nɛtɪk] *adj* gorączkowy
**frenzied** ['frɛnzɪd] *adj* szalony
**frenzy** ['frɛnzɪ] *n* (*of violence*) szał *m*; (*of joy, excitement*) szał *m*, szaleństwo *nt*; **to drive sb into a ~** doprowadzać (doprowadzić *perf*) kogoś do szału *or* szaleństwa; **to be in a ~** szaleć
**frequency** ['fri:kwənsɪ] *n* (*of event*) częstość *f*, częstotliwość *f*; (*Radio*) częstotliwość *f*; **to increase in ~** występować z większą częstotliwością
**frequency modulation** *n* modulacja *f* częstotliwości
**frequent** [*adj* 'fri:kwənt, *vb* frɪ'kwɛnt] *adj* częsty ▷ *vt* często bywać w *+loc*
**frequently** ['fri:kwəntlɪ] *adv* często
**fresco** ['frɛskəu] *n* fresk *m*
**fresh** [frɛʃ] *adj* świeży; (*approach*) nowatorski; (*water*) słodki; (*person*) bezczelny; **to make a ~ start** zaczynać (zacząć *perf*) od nowa; **he's ~ from university** on jest świeżo po studiach; **we're ~ out of bread** właśnie skończył nam się chleb
**freshen** ['frɛʃən] *vi* (*wind*) wzmagać się (wzmóc się *perf*), przybierać (przybrać *perf*) na sile
▶ **freshen up** *vi* odświeżać się (odświeżyć się *perf*)
**freshener** ['frɛʃnə^r] *n*: **skin ~** płyn *m* tonizujący; **air ~** odświeżacz powietrza
**fresher** ['frɛʃə^r] (*Brit*: *inf*) *n* student(ka) *m(f)* pierwszego roku
**freshly** ['frɛʃlɪ] *adv* świeżo
**freshman** ['frɛʃmən] (US) (*irreg*: *like* **man**) *n* = **fresher**
**freshness** ['frɛʃnɪs] *n* świeżość *f*
**freshwater** ['frɛʃwɔ:tə^r] *adj* słodkowodny
**fret** [frɛt] *vi* gryźć się, trapić się (*literary*)
**fretful** ['frɛtful] *adj* płaczliwy
**Freudian** ['frɔɪdɪən] *adj* freudowski; **~ slip** freudowskie przejęzyczenie
**FRG** *n abbr* (= *Federal Republic of Germany*) RFN *nt inv*
**Fri.** *abbr* (= *Friday*) pt.
**friar** ['fraɪə^r] *n* zakonnik *m*, brat *m* zakonny
**friction** ['frɪkʃən] *n* (*resistance*) tarcie *nt*; (*rubbing*) ocieranie *nt*; (*conflict*) tarcia *pl*
**Friday** ['fraɪdɪ] *n* piątek *m*; *see also* **Tuesday**
**fridge** [frɪdʒ] (*Brit*) *n* lodówka *f*
**fried** [fraɪd] *pt, pp of* **fry** ▷ *adj* smażony
**friend** [frɛnd] *n* przyjaciel(-ciółka) *m(f)*; (*not close*) kolega/koleżanka *m/f*; **to make ~s (with)** zaprzyjaźniać się (zaprzyjaźnić się *perf*) (z *+instr*)
**friendliness** ['frɛndlɪnɪs] *n* (*hospitality*) przyjazne nastawienie *nt*; (*of voice, manner*) życzliwość *f*
**friendly** ['frɛndlɪ] *adj* (*person, smile, country*) przyjazny, życzliwy; (*place, restaurant*) przyjemny; (*game, match, argument*) towarzyski ▷ *n* (*Sport*) spotkanie *nt* towarzyskie; **to be ~ with** przyjaźnić się z *+instr*; **to be ~ to** być przyjaźnie nastawionym do *+gen*
**friendly society** *n* towarzystwo *nt* wzajemnej asekuracji
**friendship** ['frɛndʃɪp] *n* przyjaźń *f*
**frieze** [fri:z] *n* fryz *m*
**frigate** ['frɪgɪt] *n* fregata *f*

**fright** [fraɪt] *n* (*terror*) przerażenie *nt*; (*shock*) strach *m*, przestrach *m*; **to get a ~** przestraszyć się (*perf*); **to take ~** przestraszyć się (*perf*); **to give sb a ~** przestraszyć (*perf*) *or* nastraszyć (*perf*) kogoś; **she looks a ~** wygląda jak straszydło
**frighten** ['fraɪtn] *vt* przestraszać (przestraszyć *perf*), przerażać (przerazić *perf*)
▸ **frighten away** *vt* odstraszać (odstraszyć *perf*)
▸ **frighten off** *vt* = **frighten away**
**frightened** ['fraɪtnd] *adj* (*afraid*) przestraszony, przerażony; (*anxious*) wylękniony; **to be ~ (that/to...)** bać się (, że/+*infin*); **to be ~ of sth/doing sth** bać się czegoś/zrobić coś
**frightening** ['fraɪtnɪŋ] *adj* przerażający
**frightful** ['fraɪtful] *adj* przeraźliwy
**frightfully** ['fraɪtfəlɪ] *adv* strasznie, straszliwie; **I'm ~ sorry** jest mi strasznie przykro
**frigid** ['frɪdʒɪd] *adj* oziębły
**frigidity** [frɪ'dʒɪdɪtɪ] *n* oziębłość *f*
**frill** [frɪl] *n* falbanka *f*; **without** *or* **with no ~s** (*fig*) bez dodatków
**fringe** [frɪndʒ] *n* (*Brit*: *of hair*) grzywka *f*; (*on shawl, lampshade*) frędzle *pl*; (*of forest*) skraj *m*; (*fig*: *of organization*) (skrajne) skrzydło *nt*; (: *of activity*) obrzeża *pl*
**fringe benefits** *npl* dodatkowe świadczenia *pl*
**fringe theatre** *n* teatr *m* awangardowy
**frisk** [frɪsk] *vt* przeszukiwać (przeszukać *perf*) (*podejrzanego*) ▷ *vi* brykać
**frisky** ['frɪskɪ] *adj* rozbrykany
**fritter** ['frɪtə[r]] *n kawałek owocu lub warzywa zapiekany w cieście*
▸ **fritter away** *vt* trwonić (roztrwonić *perf*)
**frivolity** [frɪ'vɔlɪtɪ] *n* frywolność *f*; **frivolities** *npl* głupstwa *pl*
**frivolous** ['frɪvələs] *adj* (*flippant*) frywolny; (*unimportant*) błahy
**frizzy** ['frɪzɪ] *adj* (*hair*) kręcony
**fro** [frəu] *adv*: **to and fro** tam i z powrotem
**frock** [frɔk] *n* sukienka *f*
**frog** [frɔg] *n* żaba *f*; **to have a ~ in one's throat** mieć chrypkę
**frogman** ['frɔgmən] (*irreg*: *like* **man**) *n* płetwonurek *m*
**frogmarch** ['frɔgmɑːtʃ] (*Brit*) *vt*: **to ~ sb in/out** doprowadzić (*perf*)/wyprowadzić (*perf*) kogoś siłą
**frolic** ['frɔlɪk] *vi* baraszkować ▷ *n* igraszki *pl*

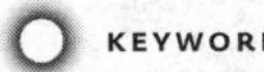
KEYWORD

**from** [frɔm] *prep* **1** (*indicating starting place, origin etc*): **from London to Glasgow** z Londynu do Glasgow; **a letter/telephone call from my sister** list/telefon od mojej siostry; **a quotation from Dickens** cytat z Dickensa; **where do you come from?** skąd Pan/Pani pochodzi?
**2** (*indicating time, distance, range of price, number etc*) od +*gen*; **from one o'clock to** *or* **until** *or* **till two** od (godziny) pierwszej do drugiej; **from January (on)** (począwszy) od stycznia; **we're still a long way from home** wciąż jesteśmy daleko od domu; **prices from 10 to 50 pounds** ceny od 10 do 50 funtów
**3** (*indicating change of price, number etc*) z +*gen*; **the interest rate was increased from 9% to 10%** oprocentowanie zostało podniesione z 9% na 10%
**4** (*indicating difference*) od +*gen*; **he can't tell red from green** nie odróżnia czerwonego od zielonego; **to be different from sb/sth** być różnym od kogoś/czegoś *or* innym niż ktoś/coś
**5** (*because of, on the basis of*) z +*gen*; **from what he says** z tego, co (on) mówi; **weak from hunger** słaby z głodu

**frond** [frɔnd] *n* liść *m* (*palmy, paproci itp*)
**front** [frʌnt] *n* przód *m*; (*also*: **sea front**) brzeg *m* morza; (*Mil, Meteor*) front *m*; (*fig*: *pretence*) pozory *pl* ▷ *adj* przedni ▷ *vi*: **to ~ onto** (*house etc*) wychodzić na +*acc*; **in ~** przodem, z przodu; **in ~ of** przed +*instr*; (*in the presence of*) przy +*loc*; **on the political ~** na froncie politycznym
**frontage** ['frʌntɪdʒ] *n* fronton *m*
**frontal** ['frʌntl] *adj* (*attack*) czołowy, frontalny; (*view*) od przodu *post*
**front bench** (*Brit*) *n członkowie Parlamentu zajmujący stanowiska w rządzie lub w gabinecie cieni*
**front desk** (*US*) *n* (*in hotel*) recepcja *f*
**front door** *n* drzwi *pl* frontowe *or* wejściowe
**frontier** ['frʌntɪə[r]] *n* granica *f*; (*between settled and wild country*) kresy *pl*
**frontispiece** ['frʌntɪspiːs] *n* frontyspis *m*
**front page** *n* strona *f* tytułowa
**front room** (*Brit*) *n* pokój *m* od ulicy
**front-runner** ['frʌntrʌnə[r]] *n* (*fig*) faworyt(ka) *m(f)*
**front-wheel drive** ['frʌntwiːl-] *n* (*Aut*) napęd *m* przedni
**frost** [frɔst] *n* (*weather*) mróz *m*; (*substance*) szron *m*
**frostbite** ['frɔstbaɪt] *n* odmrożenie *nt*
**frosted** ['frɔstɪd] *adj* (*glass*) matowy; (*esp US*: *cake*) lukrowany
**frosting** ['frɔstɪŋ] *n* (*esp US*) lukier *m*
**frosty** ['frɔstɪ] *adj* (*weather, night*) mroźny; (*welcome, look*) lodowaty; (*grass, window*) oszroniony

f

**froth** ['frɔθ] *n* piana *f*
**frothy** ['frɔθɪ] *adj* pienisty
**frown** [fraun] *n* zmarszczenie *nt* brwi ▷ *vi* marszczyć (zmarszczyć *perf*) brwi
▸ **frown on** *vt fus* (*fig*) patrzeć z dezaprobatą na *+acc*
**froze** [frəuz] *pt of* **freeze**
**frozen** ['frəuzn] *pp of* **freeze** ▷ *adj* (*food*) mrożony; (*lake*) zamarznięty; (*fingers*) zmarznięty; (*Comm: assets*) zamrożony
**FRS** *n abbr* (*Brit*) = **Fellow of the Royal Society**; (*US: = Federal Reserve System*) *bank centralny Stanów Zjednoczonych*
**frugal** ['fru:gl] *adj* (*person*) oszczędny; (*meal*) skromny
**fruit** [fru:t] *n inv* owoc *m*; (*fig: results*) owoce *pl*
**fruiterer** ['fru:tərə^r^] *n* handlarz(-arka) *m(f)* owoców
**fruitful** ['fru:tful] *adj* owocny
**fruition** [fru:'ɪʃən] *n*: **to come to ~** (*actions, efforts*) owocować (zaowocować *perf*); (*plan, hope*) ziszczać się (ziścić się *perf*)
**fruit juice** *n* sok *m* owocowy
**fruitless** ['fru:tlɪs] *adj* (*fig*) bezowocny
**fruit machine** (*Brit*) *n* automat *m* do gry
**fruit salad** *n* sałatka *f* owocowa
**fruity** ['fru:tɪ] *adj* owocowy; (*laugh etc*) soczysty
**frump** [frʌmp] (*pej*) *n* czupiradło *nt* (*pej*)
**frustrate** [frʌs'treɪt] *vt* (*person*) frustrować (sfrustrować *perf*); (*plan, attempt*) udaremniać (udaremnić *perf*)
**frustrated** [frʌs'treɪtɪd] *adj* sfrustrowany
**frustrating** [frʌs'treɪtɪŋ] *adj* frustrujący
**frustration** [frʌs'treɪʃən] *n* (*irritation*) frustracja *f*, złość *f*; (*of hope, plan*) fiasko *nt*
**fry** [fraɪ] (*pt, pp* **fried**) *vt* smażyć (usmażyć *perf*); *see also* **small**
**frying pan** ['fraɪɪŋ-] *n* patelnia *f*
**FT** (*Brit*) *n abbr* (*= Financial Times*) *gazeta finansowa*; **the FT index** indeks *or* wskaźnik FT (*wskaźnik kursów giełdy londyńskiej publikowany przez The Financial Times*)
**ft.** *abbr* = **foot, feet**
**FTC** (*US*) *n abbr* (*= Federal Trade Commission*) *Federalna Komisja do Spraw Handlu*
**fuchsia** ['fju:ʃə] *n* fuksja *f*
**fuck** [fʌk] (*inf!*) *vt* pierdolić (*inf!*) ▷ *vi* pierdolić się (*inf!*); **~ off!** odpierdol się (*inf!*)
**fuddled** ['fʌdld] *adj* zamroczony
**fuddy-duddy** ['fʌdɪdʌdɪ] (*pej*) *n* (stary) nudziarz *m* (*pej*)
**fudge** [fʌdʒ] *n* krówka *f* (*cukierek*) ▷ *vt* (*issue, problem*) omijać (ominąć *perf*)
**fuel** ['fjuəl] *n* opał *m*; (*for vehicles, industry*) paliwo *nt* ▷ *vt* (*furnace etc*) dostarczać paliwa do *+gen*; (*fig: rumours, dispute*) podsycać (podsycić *perf*); **to ~ an aircraft/ship etc** tankować (zatankować *perf*)
**fuel oil** *n* (*for engines*) olej *m* napędowy; (*for heating*) olej *m* opałowy
**fuel pump** *n* pompa *f* paliwowa
**fuel tank** *n* zbiornik *m* paliwowy
**fug** [fʌg] (*Brit*) *n* zaduch *m*
**fugitive** ['fju:dʒɪtɪv] *n* zbieg *m*, uciekinier(ka) *m(f)*
**fulfil**, (*US*) **fulfill** [ful'fɪl] *vt* spełniać (spełnić *perf*)
**fulfilled** [ful'fɪld] *adj* (*person*) zaspokojony; (*life*) spełniony
**fulfilment** [ful'fɪlmənt], (*US*) **fulfillment** *n* satysfakcja *f*, zaspokojenie *nt*; (*of promise, desire*) spełnienie *nt*
**full** [ful] *adj* pełny; (*skirt, sleeve*) szeroki ▷ *adv*: **to know ~ well that ...** w pełni zdawać sobie sprawę (z tego), że ...; **~ up** (*hotel etc*) wypełniony; **I'm ~ (up)** jestem najedzony; **a ~ week** okrągły tydzień; **in ~ view of sb** na czyichś oczach; **~ marks** maksymalna liczba punktów; **at ~ speed** z pełną *or* maksymalną prędkością; **~ of** pełen *+gen*; **in ~** w całości; **to write one's name in ~** podpisywać się (podpisać się *perf*) pełnym imieniem i nazwiskiem; **~ in the face** prosto w twarz; **to the ~** w (całej) pełni
**fullback** ['fulbæk] *n* (*Rugby, Football*) cofnięty obrońca *m*
**full-blooded** ['ful'blʌdɪd] *adj* (*attack, support*) pełen zaangażowania; (*person, animal*) czystej krwi *post*; (*virile: man*) z krwi i kości *post*, prawdziwy
**full board** *n* pełne wyżywienie *nt*
**full-cream** ['ful'kri:m] *adj*: **~ milk** (*Brit*) mleko *nt* pełne *or* pełnotłuste
**full employment** *n* pełne zatrudnienie *nt*
**full grown** *adj* dorosły
**full-length** ['ful'lɛŋθ] *adj* (*film*) pełnometrażowy; (*coat*) długi; (*portrait, mirror*) obejmujący całą postać
**full moon** *n* pełnia *f* księżyca
**fullness** ['fulnɪs] *n*: **in the ~ of time** w swoim czasie
**full-page** ['fulpeɪdʒ] *adj* całostronicowy
**full-scale** ['fulskeɪl] *adj* (*attack, war*) totalny; (*model*) naturalnej wielkości; (*negotiations*) na pełną skalę *post*
**full-sized** ['ful'saɪzd] *adj* naturalnej wielkości
**full stop** *n* kropka *f*; **to come to a ~** (*fig*) zatrzymać się (*perf*)
**full-time** ['ful'taɪm] *adj* pełnoetatowy, na pełen etat *post* ▷ *adv* (*work*) na pełen etat; (*study*) w pełnym wymiarze godzin; **a full time student** ≈ student stacjonarny

**fully** ['fulɪ] *adv* (*completely*) w pełni; (*in full*) dokładnie, wyczerpująco; (*as many as*) aż
**fully-fledged** ['fulɪ'flɛdʒd] *adj* (*teacher, doctor*) wykwalifikowany; (*member, partner*) pełnoprawny; (*atheist*) stuprocentowy; (*bird*) wypierzony
**fulsome** ['fulsəm] (*pej*) *adj* (*praise, apologies*) przesadny; (*manner*) wylewny
**fumble** ['fʌmbl] *vt* (*ball*) nieczysto zatrzymywać (zatrzymać *perf*); **to ~ a catch** zepsuć (*perf*) podanie
▸ **fumble for** *vt fus* grzebać w poszukiwaniu *+gen*
▸ **fumble with** *vt fus* (*key, pen*) bawić się *+instr*
**fume** [fju:m] *vi* wściekać się
**fumes** [fju:mz] *npl* (*of fire*) dymy *pl*; (*of fuel, alcohol*) opary *pl*; (*of factories*) wyziewy *pl*; (*of car*) spaliny *pl*
**fumigate** ['fju:mɪgeɪt] *vt* odkażać (odkazić *perf*)
**fun** [fʌn] *n* zabawa *f*; **to have fun** dobrze się bawić; **to get a lot of fun out of** czerpać wiele przyjemności z *+gen*; **he's good fun (to be with)** jest świetnym kumplem; **for fun** dla przyjemności; **in fun** w żartach; **it's not much fun** to nie jest zbyt zabawne; **to make fun of** wyśmiewać *+acc*; **to poke fun at** stroić sobie żarty z *+gen*
**function** ['fʌŋkʃən] *n* funkcja *f*; (*social occasion*) uroczystość *f* ▹ *vi* działać, funkcjonować; **to ~ as** pełnić rolę *+gen*
**functional** ['fʌŋkʃənl] *adj* (*operational*) na chodzie *post*; (*practical*) funkcjonalny
**function key** *n* (*Comput*) klawisz *m* funkcyjny
**fund** [fʌnd] *n* (*of money*) fundusz *m*; (*source, store*) zapas *m* ▹ *vt* finansować (sfinansować *perf*); **funds** *npl* fundusze *pl*
**fundamental** [fʌndə'mɛntl] *adj* (*essential*) podstawowy; (*basic, elementary*) zasadniczy, fundamentalny
**fundamentalist** [fʌndə'mɛntəlɪst] *n* fundamentalista(-tka) *m(f)*
**fundamentally** [fʌndə'mɛntəlɪ] *adv* (*basically*) w zasadzie; (*radically*) zasadniczo
**fundamentals** [fʌndə'mɛntlz] *npl* podstawowe zasady *pl*
**fund-raising** ['fʌndreɪzɪŋ] *n* zbiórka *f* pieniędzy, zdobywanie *f* funduszy
**funeral** ['fju:nərəl] *n* pogrzeb *m*
**funeral director** *n* przedsiębiorca *m* pogrzebowy
**funeral parlour** *n* dom *m* pogrzebowy
**funeral service** *n* uroczystość *f* pogrzebowa
**funereal** [fju:'nɪərɪəl] *adj* (*atmosphere*) pogrzebowy; (*pace*) ślimaczy
**funfair** ['fʌnfɛə^r] (*Brit*) *n* wesołe miasteczko *nt*
**fungi** ['fʌŋgaɪ] *npl of* **fungus**
**fungus** ['fʌŋgəs] (*pl* **fungi**) *n* grzyb *m*
**funicular** [fju:'nɪkjulə^r] *n* (*also*: **funicular railway**) kolejka *f* linowo-terenowa
**funnel** ['fʌnl] *n* (*for pouring*) lejek *m*; (*of ship*) komin *m*
**funnily** ['fʌnɪlɪ] *adv* dziwnie; **~ enough** dziwnym trafem
**funny** ['fʌnɪ] *adj* (*amusing*) zabawny; (*strange*) dziwny
**funny bone** (*inf*) *n* czułe miejsce *nt* (*w łokciu*)
**fur** [fə:^r] *n* (*of animal*) futro *nt*, sierść *f*; (*garment*) futro *nt*; (*Brit: in kettle etc*) osad *m*, kamień *m* kotłowy
**fur coat** *n* futro *nt*
**furious** ['fjuərɪəs] *adj* (*person*) wściekły; (*row, argument*) zażarty; (*effort, speed*) szaleńczy, szalony; **to be ~ with sb** wściekać się na kogoś
**furiously** ['fjuərɪəslɪ] *adv* (*angrily*) wściekle; (*vigorously*) gwałtownie
**furl** [fə:l] *vt* (*sails, flag*) zwijać (zwinąć *perf*); (*umbrella*) składać (złożyć *perf*)
**furlong** ['fə:lɔŋ] *n* (*Horse-racing*) 220 jardów (*201,2m*)
**furlough** ['fə:ləu] *n* (*Mil*) urlop *m*
**furnace** ['fə:nɪs] *n* (*in foundry, power plant*) piec *m*
**furnish** ['fə:nɪʃ] *vt* (*room, building*) meblować (umeblować *perf*); (*supply*) dostarczać (dostarczyć *perf*); **to ~ sb with sth** dostarczać (dostarczyć *perf*) komuś czegoś, wyposażać (wyposażyć *perf*) kogoś w coś; **~ed flat** *or* (*US*) **apartment** umeblowane mieszkanie
**furnishings** ['fə:nɪʃɪŋz] *npl* wyposażenie *nt*
**furniture** ['fə:nɪtʃə^r] *n* meble *pl*; **a piece of ~** mebel
**furniture polish** *n* politura *f*
**furore** [fjuə'rɔ:rɪ] *n* wrzawa *f*
**furrier** ['fʌrɪə^r] *n* kuśnierz *m*
**furrow** ['fʌrəu] *n* bruzda *f* ▹ *vt* (*brow*) marszczyć (zmarszczyć *perf*)
**furry** ['fə:rɪ] *adj* (*tail, animal*) puszysty; (*coat, toy*) futrzany
**further** ['fə:ðə^r] *adj* dalszy ▹ *adv* (*in distance, time*) dalej; (*in degree*) dalej, jeszcze bardziej; (*in addition*) ponadto, w dodatku ▹ *vt* (*project, cause*) popierać (poprzeć *perf*), wspierać (wesprzeć *perf*); **I have nothing ~ to say** nie mam nic więcej do powiedzenia; **to ~ one's interests/one's career** troszczyć się o swoje sprawy/swoją karierę; **until ~ notice** (aż) do odwołania; **how much ~ is it?** jak daleko jeszcze?; **~ to your letter of ...** (*Comm*) w nawiązaniu do Pana/Pani listu z ...
**further education** (*Brit*) *n* ≈ kształcenie pomaturalne
**furthermore** [fə:ðə'mɔ:^r] *adv* ponadto, co więcej
**furthermost** ['fə:ðəməust] *adj* najdalszy

**furthest** ['fə:ðɪst] *adv* (*in distance, time*) najdalej; (*in degree*) najdalej, najbardziej ▷ *adj* najdalszy
**furtive** ['fə:tɪv] *adj* potajemny, ukradkowy
**furtively** ['fə:tɪvlɪ] *adv* potajemnie, ukradkiem
**fury** ['fjuərɪ] *n* furia *f*; **in a ~** w furii
**fuse**, (*US*) **fuze** [fju:z] *n* (*in plug, circuit*) bezpiecznik *m*; (*for bomb etc*) zapalnik *m* ▷ *vt* (*metal*) topić (stopić *perf*); (*fig: ideas, systems*) łączyć (połączyć *perf*) ▷ *vi* (*metal*) topić się (stopić się *perf*); (*fig: ideas, systems*) łączyć się (połączyć się *perf*); **to ~ the lights** (*Brit*) robić (zrobić *perf*) zwarcie; **the lights have ~d** (*Brit*) światło wysiadło (*inf*); **a ~ has blown** bezpiecznik się przepalił
**fuse box** *n* skrzynka *f* bezpiecznikowa
**fuselage** ['fju:zəlɑ:ʒ] *n* kadłub *m* samolotu
**fuse wire** *n* drut *m* topikowy
**fusillade** [fju:zɪ'leɪd] *n* strzelanina *f*; (*fig*) ostrzał *m*
**fusion** ['fju:ʒən] *n* połączenie *nt*; (*also*: **nuclear fusion**) synteza *f* jądrowa
**fuss** [fʌs] *n* (*bother*) zamieszanie *nt*; (*annoyance*) awantura *f* ▷ *vi* panikować (*inf*) ▷ *vt* zawracać głowę *+dat*; **to make a ~ (about sth)** robić (zrobić *perf*) zamieszanie (z powodu *or* wokół czegoś); **to make a ~ of sb** nadskakiwać komuś, robić dużo hałasu wokół kogoś
▶ **fuss over** *vt fus* trząść się nad *+instr* (*inf*)
**fussy** ['fʌsɪ] *adj* (*person*) grymaśny, wybredny; (*clothes, curtains*) przeładowany ozdobami; **I'm not ~** nie jestem wybredny
**futile** ['fju:taɪl] *adj* (*attempt*) daremny; (*remark*) płytki, powierzchowny
**futility** [fju:'tɪlɪtɪ] *n* (*of attempt*) daremność *f*; (*remark*) płytkość *f*, powierzchowność *f*
**future** ['fju:tʃə[r]] *adj* przyszły ▷ *n* przyszłość *f*; (*Ling*) czas *m* przyszły; **futures** *npl* (*Comm*) sprzedaż *f* terminowa; **in (the) ~** w przyszłości; **in the near/foreseeable ~** w najbliższej/przewidywalnej przyszłości
**futuristic** [fju:tʃə'rɪstɪk] *adj* futurystyczny
**fuze** (*US*) *n, vt, vi* = **fuse**
**fuzz** [fʌz] *n* (*on face, arms etc*) meszek *m*; **the ~** (*inf*) gliny *pl* (*inf*)
**fuzzy** ['fʌzɪ] *adj* (*photo, image*) zamazany, nieostry; (*hair*) kędzierzawy; (*thoughts, ideas*) mętny
**fwd.** *abbr* = **forward**
**fwy** (*US*) *abbr* = **freeway**
**FY** *abbr* (= *fiscal year*) rok *m* budżetowy
**FYI** *abbr* = **for your information**

# Gg

**G¹, g¹** [dʒiː] *n* (*letter*) G *nt*, g *nt*; **G for George** ≈ G jak Genowefa

**G²** [dʒiː] *n* (*Mus*) G *nt*, g *nt*

**G³** *n abbr* (*Brit*: *Scol*: = *good*) db; (*US*: *Film*: = *general* (*audience*)) b.o.; (*Phys*): **G-force** siła ciężkości

**g²** *abbr* (= *gram*) g; (*Phys*) = **gravity**

**G8** *n abbr* (*Pol*: = *Group of Eight*) Grupa *f* Ośmiu, Wielka Ósemka *f*

**GA** (*US*: *Post*) *n abbr* = **Georgia**

**gab** [gæb] (*inf*) *n*: **to have the gift of the gab** mieć gadane (*inf*)

**gabble** ['gæbl] *vi* trajkotać

**gaberdine** [gæbə'diːn] *n* gabardyna *f*

**gable** ['geɪbl] *n* szczyt *m* (*domu*)

**Gabon** [gə'bɔn] *n* Gabon *m*

**gad about** [gæd-] (*inf*) *vi* szwendać się (*inf*)

**gadget** ['gædʒɪt] *n* urządzenie *nt*, gadżet *m* (*inf*)

**gadgetry** ['gædʒɪtrɪ] *n* sprzęty *pl* mechaniczne

**Gaelic** ['geɪlɪk] *adj* celtycki ▷ *n* (język *m*) galijski (*używany w Irlandii i Szkocji*)

**gaffe** [gæf] *n* gafa *f*

**gag** [gæg] *n* (*on mouth*) knebel *m*; (*joke*) gag *m* ▷ *vt* kneblować (zakneblować *perf*) ▷ *vi* krztusić się (zakrztusić się *perf*)

**gaga** ['gɑːgɑː] (*inf*) *adj*: **to go ~** (*old person*) ramoleć (zramoleć *perf*) (*inf*); **to be/go ~ over sb** mieć/dostawać (dostać *perf*) fioła na czyimś punkcie (*inf*)

**gage** [geɪdʒ] (*US*) *n*, *vt* = **gauge**

**gaiety** ['geɪɪtɪ] *n* wesołość *f*

**gaily** ['geɪlɪ] *adv* wesoło; **~ coloured** bardzo kolorowy

**gain** [geɪn] *n* (*increase, improvement*) przyrost *m*; (*profit*) korzyść *f* ▷ *vt* (*speed, confidence*) nabierać (nabrać *perf*) +*gen*; (*weight*) przybierać (przybrać *perf*) na +*loc* ▷ *vi* (*clock, watch*) śpieszyć się; (*benefit*): **to ~ from sth** zyskiwać (zyskać *perf*) na czymś; **to ~ in** zyskiwać (zyskać *perf*) na +*loc*; **to ~ ground** zyskiwać (zyskać *perf*) popularność; **to ~ on sb** doganiać (dogonić *perf*) kogoś; **to ~ 3lbs (in weight)** przybierać (przybrać *perf*) 3 funty (na wadze); **to do sth for ~** robić (zrobić *perf*) coś dla zysku

**gainful** ['geɪnful] *adj*: **~ employment** praca *f* zarobkowa

**gainsay** [geɪn'seɪ] (*irreg*: *like* **say**) *vt* polemizować z +*instr*, kwestionować (zakwestionować *perf*)

**gait** [geɪt] *n* chód *m*, sposób *m* chodzenia; **to walk with a slow/confident ~** chodzić powolnym/pewnym krokiem

**gala** ['gɑːlə] *n* gala *f*; **swimming ~** pokaz pływacki

**Galapagos (Islands)** *npl*: **(the) ~** Galapagos *nt inv*, Wyspy *pl* Żółwie

**galaxy** ['gæləksɪ] *n* galaktyka *f*

**gale** [geɪl] *n* wichura *f*; **~ force 10** siła wiatru 10 stopni

**gall** [gɔːl] *n* (*Anat*) żółć *f*; (*fig*) tupet *m*, czelność *f* ▷ *vt* irytować, drażnić

**gall.** *abbr* = **gallon**

**gallant** ['gælənt] *adj* (*brave*) waleczny; (*polite*) szarmancki

**gallantry** ['gæləntrɪ] *n* (*bravery*) waleczność *f*; (*politeness*) galanteria *f*

**gall bladder** *n* pęcherzyk *m or* woreczek *m* żółciowy

**galleon** ['gælɪən] *n* galeon *m*

**gallery** ['gælərɪ] *n* (*of art, at Parliament*) galeria *f*; (*in theatre*) balkon *m*, galeria *f*; (*in church*) chór *m*, balkon *m*

**galley** ['gælɪ] *n* (*ship's kitchen*) kuchnia *f* okrętowa, kambuz *m* (*inf*); (*ship*) galera *f*; (*also*: **galley proof**) korekta *f* (szpaltowa)

**Gallic** ['gælɪk] *adj* (*of Gaul*) galijski; (*French*) francuski

**galling** ['gɔːlɪŋ] *adj* irytujący, drażniący

**gallon** ['gæln] *n* (*Brit = 4.5l, US = 3.8l*) galon *m*

**gallop** ['gæləp] *n* galop *m* ▷ *vi* galopować; **~ing inflation** galopująca inflacja

**gallows** ['gæləuz] *n* szubienica *f*

**gallstone** ['gɔːlstəun] *n* kamień *m* żółciowy

**galore** [gə'lɔːʳ] *adv* w bród; **there were restaurants and night clubs ~** restauracji i nocnych lokali było tam w bród

**galvanize** ['gælvənaɪz] *vt* (*fig*) elektryzować (zelektryzować *perf*); **to ~ sb into action** zdopingować (*perf*) kogoś do

działania, porwać *(perf)* kogoś do czynu *(literary)*
**Gambia** ['gæmbɪə] *n* Gambia *f*
**gambit** ['gæmbɪt] *n* *(fig)*: **(opening) ~** zagrywka *f*
**gamble** ['gæmbl] *n* ryzyko *nt* ▷ *vt*: **to ~ away** *(money, profits)* przegrywać (przegrać *perf*), przepuszczać (przepuścić *perf*) *(inf)* ▷ *vi* *(risk)* ryzykować (zaryzykować *perf*); *(bet)* uprawiać hazard; **to ~ on** stawiać (postawić *perf*) na *+acc*; **to ~ on the Stock Exchange** spekulować na giełdzie papierów wartościowych; **he used to ~ on the horses** grywał na wyścigach
**gambler** ['gæmbləʳ] *n* hazardzista(-tka) *m(f)*
**gambling** ['gæmblɪŋ] *n* hazard *m*
**gambol** ['gæmbl] *vi* hasać
**game** [geɪm] *n* *(lit, fig)* gra *f*; *(of football etc)* mecz *m*; *(part of tennis match)* gem *m*; *(Hunting)* zwierzyna *f*; *(Culin)* dziczyzna *f* ▷ *adj* odważny; **games** *npl* *(Scol)* ≈ wychowanie *nt* fizyczne; **big ~** gruba zwierzyna; **I'm ~ to try/for anything** jestem gotów spróbować/ na wszystko; **who's ~ for ...?** kto ma ochotę na *+acc*?
**gamebird** ['geɪmbə:d] *n* ptak *m* łowny
**gamekeeper** ['geɪmki:pəʳ] *n* łowczy *m*
**gamely** ['geɪmlɪ] *adv* odważnie
**game reserve** *n* łowisko *nt*, teren *m* łowiecki
**game show** *n* teleturniej *m*
**gamesmanship** ['geɪmzmənʃɪp] *n* nieczysta gra *f*
**gammon** ['gæmən] *n* *(bacon)* bekon *m*; *(ham)* szynka *f*
**gamut** ['gæmət] *n* gama *f*; **to run the ~ of** *(experience)* przechodzić (przejść *perf*) (przez) wszystkie stadia *+gen*; *(express)* wyrażać (wyrazić *perf*) wszystkie odcienie *+gen*; **she ran the ~ of all baby illnesses** przeszła wszystkie choroby wieku niemowlęcego
**gander** ['gændəʳ] *n* gąsior *m* *(ptak)*
**gang** [gæŋ] *n* *(of criminals)* gang *m*; *(of hooligans)* banda *f*; *(of friends)* paczka *f*; *(of workmen)* brygada *f*; **~ warfare** wojna między gangami
▶ **gang up** *vi*: **to ~ up on sb** sprzysięgać się (sprzysiąc się *perf*) przeciwko komuś
**Ganges** ['gændʒi:z] *n*: **the ~** Ganges *m*
**gangling** ['gæŋglɪŋ] *adj* patykowaty
**gangplank** ['gæŋplæŋk] *n* trap *m*
**gangrene** ['gæŋgri:n] *n* gangrena *f*, zgorzel *m*
**gangster** ['gæŋstəʳ] *n* gangster *m*
**gangway** ['gæŋweɪ] *n* *(from ship)* trap *m*; *(Brit: in cinema, bus, plane)* przejście *nt*
**gantry** ['gæntrɪ] *n* *(for crane, railway signal)* portal *m*; *(for rocket)* wyrzutnia *f*
**GAO** *(US)* *n abbr (= General Accounting Office) rządowe biuro rewidentów ksiąg handlowych*
**gaol** [dʒeɪl] *(Brit)* *n, vt* = **jail**
**gap** [gæp] *n* *(in mountains)* szczelina *f*; *(in teeth)* szpara *f*; *(in time)* przerwa *f*; *(in market, records)* luka *f*; *(fig)* przepaść *f*
**gape** [geɪp] *vi* *(person)* gapić się *(inf)*; *(shirt, lips)* rozchylać się; *(hole)* ziać
**gaping** ['geɪpɪŋ] *adj* *(hole)* ziejący; *(wound)* otwarty; *(mouth)* rozdziawiony *(inf)*
**gap year** *n* *(Scol)* roczna przerwa *f* *(przed podjęciem studiów)*
**garage** ['gærɑ:ʒ] *n* *(of private house)* garaż *m*; *(for car repairs)* warsztat *m*; *(petrol station)* stacja *f* benzynowa
**garb** [gɑ:b] *n* ubiór *m*, strój *m*
**garbage** ['gɑ:bɪdʒ] *n* *(US: rubbish)* śmieci *pl*; *(inf: nonsense)* bzdury *pl* *(inf)*; *(fig: film, book)* szmira *f*
**garbage can** *(US)* *n* pojemnik *m* na śmieci
**garbage disposal (unit)** *n* młynek *m* zlewozmywakowy, kuchenny rozdrabniacz *m* odpadków
**garbled** ['gɑ:bld] *adj* przekręcony, przeinaczony
**garden** ['gɑ:dn] *n* ogród *m* ▷ *vi* pracować w ogrodzie; **gardens** *npl* *(public)* park *m*; *(botanical, private)* ogród *m*; **she was busy ~ing** pracowała w ogrodzie
**garden centre** *n* centrum *m* ogrodnicze
**gardener** ['gɑ:dnəʳ] *n* ogrodnik *m*
**gardening** ['gɑ:dnɪŋ] *n* ogrodnictwo *nt*
**gargle** ['gɑ:gl] *vi* płukać gardło ▷ *n* płyn *m* do płukania gardła
**gargoyle** ['gɑ:gɔɪl] *n* *(Archit)* gargulec *m*, rzygacz *m*
**garish** ['gɛərɪʃ] *adj* jaskrawy
**garland** ['gɑ:lənd] *n* *(on head)* wianek *m*; *(round neck)* girlanda *f*
**garlic** ['gɑ:lɪk] *n* czosnek *m*
**garment** ['gɑ:mənt] *n* część *m* garderoby
**garner** ['gɑ:nəʳ] *vt* *(information)* zbierać (zebrać *perf*)
**garnish** ['gɑ:nɪʃ] *vt* *(Culin)* przybierać (przybrać *perf*), garnirować
**garret** ['gærɪt] *n* pokój *m* na poddaszu
**garrison** ['gærɪsn] *n* garnizon *m*
**garrulous** ['gærjuləs] *adj* gadatliwy
**garter** ['gɑ:təʳ] *n* *(Brit)* podwiązka *f* *(opaska podtrzymująca pończochę lub skarpetkę)*; *(US)* podwiązka *f* *(część pasa do pończoch)*
**garter belt** *(US)* *n* pas *m* do pończoch
**gas** [gæs] *n* gaz *m*; *(US: gasoline)* benzyna *f*; *(Med)* gaz *m* rozweselający ▷ *vt* *(kill)* zagazowywać (zagazować *perf*); *(Mil)* przeprowadzać (przeprowadzić *perf*) atak gazowy
**gas chamber** *n* komora *f* gazowa
**Gascony** ['gæskənɪ] *n* Gaskonia *f*

**gas cooker** *n* kuchenka *f* gazowa
**gas cylinder** *n* butla *f* gazowa
**gaseous** ['gæsɪəs] *adj* lotny
**gas fire** (*Brit*) *n* piecyk *m* gazowy
**gash** [gæʃ] *n* (*wound*) (głęboka) rana *f* cięta; (*tear*) rozdarcie *nt* ▷ *vt* (*arm etc*) rozciąć (*perf*)
**gasket** ['gæskɪt] *n* uszczelka *f*
**gas mask** *n* maska *f* gazowa
**gas meter** *n* licznik *m* gazowy
**gasoline** ['gæsəli:n] (*US*) *n* benzyna *f*
**gasp** [gɑ:sp] *n*: **to breathe in ~s** mieć przerywany oddech ▷ *vi* (*pant*) łapać (złapać *perf*) (z trudem) powietrze; (*say while panting*) wykrztusić (*perf*); **she let out a ~ of amazement** zachłysnęła się ze zdumienia; **I am ~ing for a drink** umieram z pragnienia
**gas ring** *n* palnik *m* gazowy
**gas station** (*US*) *n* stacja *f* benzynowa
**gas stove** *n* kuchnia *f* gazowa
**gassy** ['gæsɪ] *adj* (*beer etc*) gazowany
**gas tank** *n* zbiornik *m* gazowy
**gastric** ['gæstrɪk] *adj* żołądkowy, gastryczny
**gastric ulcer** *n* wrzód *m* żołądka
**gastroenteritis** ['gæstrəuɛntə'raɪtɪs] *n* zapalenie *nt* żołądka i jelit
**gastronomy** [gæs'trɔnəmɪ] *n* gastronomia *f*
**gasworks** ['gæswə:ks] *n* gazownia *f*
**gate** [geɪt] *n* (*of building*) brama *f*; (*of garden, field*) furtka *f*; (*at airport*) wyjście *nt*; (*of level-crossing etc*) bariera *f*, szlaban *m*
**gateau** ['gætəu] (*pl* **~x**) *n* torcik *m*
**gatecrash** ['geɪtkræʃ] (*Brit*) *vt* wchodzić (wejść *perf*) bez zaproszenia na *+acc* ▷ *vi* wchodzić (wejść *perf*) bez zaproszenia
**gatecrasher** ['geɪtkræʃə^r] *n* nieproszony gość *m*
**gateway** ['geɪtweɪ] *n* brama *f*; (*fig*) droga *f*; **the ~ to the city** wjazd do miasta
**gather** ['gæðə^r] *vt* zbierać (zebrać *perf*), gromadzić (zgromadzić *perf*); (*Sewing*) marszczyć (zmarszczyć *perf*) ▷ *vi* (*people, clouds*) zbierać się (zebrać się *perf*), gromadzić się (zgromadzić się *perf*); (*dust*) zbierać się; **to ~ (from/that)** wnioskować (wywnioskować *perf*) (z *+gen*/, że); **as far as I can ~** o ile się orientuję; **to ~ speed** nabierać (nabrać *perf*) prędkości
**gathering** ['gæðərɪŋ] *n* zgromadzenie *nt*
**GATT** [gæt] *n abbr* (*= General Agreement on Tariffs and Trade*) GATT *m inv*, Układ *m* Ogólny w Sprawie Taryf Celnych i Handlu
**gauche** [gəuʃ] *adj* niezdarny
**gaudy** ['gɔ:dɪ] *adj* (*clothes etc*) krzykliwy
**gauge** [geɪdʒ] *n* (*instrument*) przyrząd *m* pomiarowy; (*Rail*) szerokość *m* toru ▷ *vt* (*amount, quantity*) określać (określić *perf*); (*fig: feelings, character*) oceniać (ocenić *perf*); **petrol ~, fuel ~,** (*US*) **gas ~** wskaźnik poziomu paliwa
**Gaul** [gɔ:l] *n* (*country*) Galia *f*; (*person*) Galijczyk(-jka) *m(f)*
**gaunt** [gɔ:nt] *adj* (*haggard*) wymizerowany; (*stark*) nagi
**gauntlet** ['gɔ:ntlɪt] *n* rękawica *f*; **to run the ~ of** być wystawionym *or* narażonym na *+acc*; **to throw down the ~** rzucać (rzucić *perf*) wyzwanie *or* rękawicę
**gauze** [gɔ:z] *n* gaza *f*
**gave** [geɪv] *pt of* **give**
**gavel** ['gævl] *n* młotek *m* (*sędziego, przewodniczącego itp*)
**gawk** [gɔ:k] (*inf*) *vi* gapić się (*inf*)
**gawky** ['gɔ:kɪ] *adj* niezdarny, niezgrabny
**gawp** [gɔ:p] *vi*: **to ~ at** gapić się na *+acc*
**gay** [geɪ] *adj* (*person*): **he's gay** on jest homoseksualistą; (*organization, rights*) homoseksualistów *post*; (*bar, magazine*) gejowski, dla homoseksualistów *or* gejów *post*; (*old: cheerful*) wesoły; (*colour, music*) żywy; (*dress*) barwny ▷ *n* gej *m*
**gaze** [geɪz] *n* wzrok *m*, spojrzenie *nt* ▷ *vi*: **to ~ at sth** wpatrywać się w coś
**gazelle** [gə'zɛl] *n* gazela *f*
**gazette** [gə'zɛt] *n* (*newspaper*) gazeta *f*; (*official publication*) dziennik *m* urzędowy
**gazetteer** [gæzə'tɪə^r] *n* (*index*) wykaz *m or* indeks *m* nazw geograficznych; (*book*) słownik *m* nazw geograficznych
**gazumping** [gə'zʌmpɪŋ] (*Brit*) *n odmowa sprzedaży domu pomimo wcześniejszych uzgodnień, ponieważ pojawił się klient oferujący wyższą cenę*
**GB** *abbr* = **Great Britain**
**GBH** (*Brit: Jur*) *n abbr* (*= grievous bodily harm*) ciężkie uszkodzenie *nt* ciała
**GC** (*Brit*) *n abbr* (*= George Cross*) *brytyjski order za odwagę*
**GCE** (*Brit*) *n abbr* (*= General Certificate of Education*) *świadectwo ukończenia szkoły średniej*, ≈ świadectwo dojrzałości, ≈ matura
**GCHQ** (*Brit*) *n abbr* = **Government Communications Headquarters**
**GCSE** (*Brit*) *n abbr* (*= General Certificate of Secondary Education*) *świadectwo ukończenia szkoły średniej, nie uprawniające do podjęcia studiów wyższych*
**Gdns.** *abbr* (*in street names*) = **Gardens**
**GDP** *n abbr* (*= gross domestic product*) PKB *m inv* (*= produkt krajowy brutto*)
**GDR** (*old*) *n abbr* (*= German Democratic Republic*) NRD *nt inv*
**gear** [gɪə^r] *n* (*equipment*) sprzęt *m*; (*clothing*) strój *m*; (*belongings*) rzeczy *pl*; (*Tech*) przekładnia *f*; (*Aut*) bieg *m* ▷ *vt*: **to be ~ed to** *or* **for** być nastawionym na *+acc*; **top** *or* (*US*) **high/low/bottom ~** wysokie/niskie/

najniższe obroty; **in ~** na biegu; **our service is ~ed to meet the needs of the disabled** jesteśmy nastawieni na zaspokajanie potrzeb osób niepełnosprawnych
▸ **gear up** *vi*: **to ~ up (to sth/to do sth)** szykować się (do czegoś/zrobienia czegoś) ▹ *vt*: **to ~ o.s. up (to sth/to do sth)** szykować się (do czegoś/zrobienia czegoś)

**gearbox** ['gɪəbɔks] *n* skrzynia *f* biegów

**gear lever**, (*US*) **gear shift** *n* dźwignia *f* zmiany biegów

**GED** (*US*: *Scol*) *n abbr* = **general educational development**

**geese** [gi:s] *npl of* **goose**

**Geiger counter** ['gaɪgə-] *n* licznik *m* geigerowski *or* Geigera-Müllera

**gel** [dʒɛl] *n* żel *m* ▹ *vi* (*liquid*) tężeć (stężeć *perf*); (*fig*: *thought, idea*) krystalizować się (wykrystalizować się *perf*)

**gelatin(e)** ['dʒɛləti:n] *n* żelatyna *f*

**gelignite** ['dʒɛlɪgnaɪt] *n silny materiał wybuchowy*

**gem** [dʒɛm] *n* kamień *m* szlachetny, klejnot *m*; (*fig*: *person*) skarb *m*; (: *idea, house*) klejnot *m*, perła *f*

**Gemini** ['dʒɛmɪnaɪ] *n* Bliźnięta *pl*; **to be ~** być spod znaku Bliźniąt

**gen** [dʒɛn] (*Brit*: *inf*) *n*: **to give sb the gen on sth** wprowadzać (wprowadzić *perf*) kogoś w szczegóły czegoś

**Gen.** (*Mil*) *abbr* (= *general*) gen.

**gen.** *abbr* (= *general, generally*) og.

**gender** ['dʒɛndə^r] *n* (*sex*) płeć *f*; (*Ling*) rodzaj *m*

**gene** [dʒi:n] *n* gen *m*

**genealogy** [dʒi:nɪ'ælədʒɪ] *n* genealogia *f*

**general** ['dʒɛnərl] *n* generał *m* ▹ *adj* ogólny; (*secretary etc*) generalny; **in ~** (*on the whole*) ogólnie *or* generalnie (rzecz) biorąc; (*as a whole*) w ogóle; (*ordinarily*) na ogół; **the ~ public** ogół społeczeństwa; **~ audit** (*Comm*) kontrola ogólna

**general anaesthetic** *n* znieczulenie *nt* ogólne

**general delivery** (*US*) *n* poste restante *nt inv*

**general election** *n* wybory *pl* powszechne

**generalization** ['dʒɛnrəlaɪ'zeɪʃən] *n* uogólnienie *nt*, generalizacja *f*

**generalize** ['dʒɛnrəlaɪz] *vi* uogólniać (uogólnić *perf*), generalizować

**generally** ['dʒɛnrəlɪ] *adv* ogólnie *or* generalnie (rzecz) biorąc

**general manager** *n* dyrektor *m* naczelny *or* generalny

**general practitioner** *n* lekarz *m* ogólny

**general strike** *n* strajk *m* generalny

**generate** ['dʒɛnəreɪt] *vt* (*energy, electricity*) wytwarzać (wytworzyć *perf*); (*jobs*) stwarzać (stworzyć *perf*); (*profits*) przynosić (przynieść *perf*)

**generation** [dʒɛnə'reɪʃən] *n* (*people*) pokolenie *nt*, generacja *f*; (*period of time*) pokolenie *nt*; (*of electricity etc*) wytwarzanie *nt*

**generator** ['dʒɛnəreɪtə^r] *n* generator *m*

**generic** [dʒɪ'nɛrɪk] *adj* ogólny; (*Bio*) gatunkowy

**generosity** [dʒɛnə'rɔsɪtɪ] *n* (*of spirit*) wspaniałomyślność *f*, wielkoduszność *f*; (*with money, gifts*) hojność *f*, szczodrość *f*

**generous** ['dʒɛnərəs] *adj* (*magnanimous*) wspaniałomyślny, wielkoduszny; (*lavish, liberal*) hojny, szczodry

**genesis** ['dʒɛnɪsɪs] *n* geneza *f*

**genetic** [dʒɪ'nɛtɪk] *adj* genetyczny

**genetic engineering** *n* inżynieria *f* genetyczna

**genetics** [dʒɪ'nɛtɪks] *n* genetyka *f*

**Geneva** [dʒɪ'ni:və] *n* Genewa *f*

**genial** ['dʒi:nɪəl] *adj* miły, przyjazny

**genitals** ['dʒɛnɪtlz] *npl* genitalia *pl*

**genitive** ['dʒɛnɪtɪv] *n* (*Ling*) dopełniacz *m*

**genius** ['dʒi:nɪəs] *n* (*person*) geniusz *m*; (*ability, skill*): **a ~ for (doing) sth** (wielki) talent do (robienia) czegoś

**Genoa** ['dʒɛnəuə] *n* Genua *f*

**genocide** ['dʒɛnəusaɪd] *n* ludobójstwo *nt*

**Genoese** [dʒɛnəu'i:z] *adj* genueński ▹ *n inv* genueńczyk(-enka) *m*(*f*)

**gent** [dʒɛnt] (*Brit*: *inf*) *n abbr* = **gentleman**

**genteel** [dʒɛn'ti:l] *adj* dystyngowany; (*pej*) afektowany, z pretensjami *post*

**gentle** ['dʒɛntl] *adj* łagodny; **a ~ hint** delikatna aluzja

**gentleman** ['dʒɛntlmən] (*irreg*: *like* **man**) *n* (*man*) pan *m*; (*referring to social position*) człowiek *m* szlachetnie *or* wysoko urodzony, ≈ szlachcic *m* (*old*); (*well-mannered man*) dżentelmen *m*; **~'s agreement** dżentelmeńska umowa

**gentlemanly** ['dʒɛntlmənlɪ] *adj* (*person*) dobrze wychowany; (*behaviour*) dżentelmeński

**gentleness** ['dʒɛntlnɪs] *n* łagodność *f*

**gently** ['dʒɛntlɪ] *adv* łagodnie; (*lightly*) delikatnie

**gentry** *n inv*: **the ~** ≈ szlachta *f*

**gents** [dʒɛnts] *n*: **the ~** męska toaleta *f*

**genuine** ['dʒɛnjuɪn] *adj* (*real*) prawdziwy; (*sincere*) szczery

**genuinely** ['dʒɛnjuɪnlɪ] *adv* prawdziwie

**geographer** [dʒɪ'ɔgrəfə^r] *n* geograf *m*

**geographic(al)** [dʒɪə'græfɪk(l)] *adj* geograficzny

**geography** [dʒɪ'ɔgrəfɪ] *n* geografia *f*

**geological** [dʒɪə'lɔdʒɪkl] *adj* geologiczny

**geologist** [dʒɪ'ɔlədʒɪst] *n* geolog *m*
**geology** [dʒɪ'ɔlədʒɪ] *n* geologia *f*
**geometric(al)** [dʒɪə'mɛtrɪk(l)] *adj* geometryczny
**geometry** [dʒɪ'ɔmətrɪ] *n* geometria *f*
**Geordie** ['dʒɔːdɪ] (*Brit: inf*) *n osoba lub akcent z Newcastle*
**geranium** [dʒɪ'reɪnɪəm] *n* pelargonia *f*
**geriatric** [dʒɛrɪ'ætrɪk] *adj* geriatryczny ▷ *n* osoba *f* w podeszłym wieku
**germ** [dʒəːm] *n* (*Med*) zarazek *m*; (*fig*): **the ~ of an idea** zalążek *m* pomysłu
**German** ['dʒəːmən] *adj* niemiecki ▷ *n* (*person*) Niemiec(-mka) *m(f)*; (*Ling*) (język *m*) niemiecki
**German Democratic Republic** *n* Niemiecka Republika *f* Demokratyczna
**German measles** (*Brit*) *n* różyczka *f*
**Germany** ['dʒəːmənɪ] *n* Niemcy *pl*
**germinate** ['dʒəːmɪneɪt] *vi* kiełkować (zakiełkować *perf*)
**germination** [dʒəːmɪ'neɪʃən] *n* kiełkowanie *nt*
**germ warfare** *n* broń *f* biologiczna
**gerrymandering** ['dʒɛrɪmændərɪŋ] *n przedwyborcza manipulacja podziałem na okręgi wyborcze*
**gestation** [dʒɛs'teɪʃən] *n* ciąża *f*
**gesticulate** [dʒɛs'tɪkjuleɪt] *vi* gestykulować
**gesture** ['dʒɛstjəʳ] *n* (*movement*) gest *m*; (*symbol, token*) gest *m*, akt *m*; **as a ~ of friendship** na znak przyjaźni

KEYWORD

**get** [gɛt] (*pt, pp* **got**, *US pp* **gotten**) *vi* **1** (*become, be*) stawać się (stać się *perf*), robić się (zrobić się *perf*); (*+past participle*) zostać (*perf*); **this is getting more and more difficult** to się staje coraz trudniejsze; **it's getting late** robi się późno; **to get elected** zostać (*perf*) wybranym
**2** (*go*): **to get from/to** dostawać się (dostać się *perf*) z *+gen*/do *+gen*; **to get home** docierać (dotrzeć *perf*) do domu
**3** (*begin*) zaczynać (zacząć *perf*); **I'm getting to like him** zaczynam go lubić; **to get to know sb** poznawać (poznać *perf*) kogoś (bliżej); **let's get going** *or* **started** zaczynajmy
▷ *modal aux vb*: **you've got to do it** musisz to zrobić
▷ *vt* **1**: **to get sth done** (*do oneself*) zrobić (*perf*) coś; (*have done*) (od)dać (*perf*) coś do zrobienia; **to get the washing done** zrobić (*perf*) pranie; **to get one's hair cut** obcinać (obciąć *perf*) sobie włosy; **to get sb to do sth** nakłonić (*perf*) kogoś, żeby coś zrobił; **to get sb into trouble** wpakować (*perf*) kogoś w tarapaty
**2** (*obtain, find, receive, acquire*) dostawać (dostać *perf*); **how much did you get for the painting?** ile dostałeś za ten obraz?
**3** (*fetch: person, doctor*) sprowadzać (sprowadzić *perf*); (*: object*) przynosić (przynieść *perf*); **to get sth for sb** (*obtain*) zdobyć (*perf*) coś dla kogoś; (*fetch*) przynieść (*perf*) coś komuś
**4** (*catch*) łapać (złapać *perf*); **get him!** łapać go!
**5** (*hit*) trafić (*perf*); **the bullet got him in the leg** kula trafiła go w nogę
**6** (*take, move*): **to get sth to sb** dostarczyć (*perf*) coś komuś
**7** (*take: plane, bus etc*): **we got a plane to London and then a train to Colchester** do Londynu polecieliśmy samolotem, a potem pojechaliśmy pociągiem do Colchester
**8** (*understand*) rozumieć (zrozumieć *perf*); **I get it** rozumiem
**9** (*have, possess*): **how many have you got?** ile (ich) masz?
▸ **get about** *vi* (*person*) przenosić się z miejsca na miejsce; (*news, rumour*) rozchodzić się (rozejść się *perf*)
▸ **get across** *vi* (*meaning, message*) docierać (dotrzeć *perf*)
▷ *vt*: **to get sth across (to sb)** znaleźć (*perf*) zrozumienie dla czegoś (u kogoś)
▸ **get along** *vi* (*be friends*) być w dobrych stosunkach; (*depart*) pójść (*perf*) (sobie)
▸ **get around** = **get round**
▸ **get at** *vt fus* (*attack, criticize*) naskakiwać (naskoczyć *perf*) na *+acc*; (*reach*) dosięgać (dosięgnąć *perf*) *+gen*; **what are you getting at?** do czego zmierzasz?
▸ **get away** *vi* (*leave*) odchodzić (odejść *perf*), wyrywać się (wyrwać się *perf*) (*inf*); (*on holiday*) wyjeżdżać (wyjechać *perf*); (*escape*) uciekać (uciec *perf*)
▸ **get away with** *vt fus*: **he'll never get away with it!** nie ujdzie mu to na sucho!
▸ **get back** *vi* wracać (wrócić *perf*)
▷ *vt* odzyskiwać (odzyskać *perf*); **get back!** odsuń się!
▸ **get back at** (*inf*) *vt fus*: **to get back at sb (for sth)** odpłacić się (*perf*) komuś (za coś)
▸ **get back to** *vt fus* powracać (powrócić *perf*) do *+gen*; **to get back to sb on sth** skontaktować się (*perf*) z kimś ponownie w jakiejś sprawie; **to get back to sleep** zasypiać (zasnąć *perf*) ponownie *or* z powrotem
▸ **get by** *vi* (*pass*) przechodzić (przejść *perf*); (*manage*) radzić (poradzić *perf*) sobie (jakoś), dawać (dać *perf*) sobie (jakoś) radę; **I can get**

**by in Dutch** potrafię się dogadać po holendersku
▸ **get down** *vi* (*descend*) schodzić (zejść *perf*); (*on floor, ground*) siadać (siąść *perf*), usiąść (*perf*)
▹ *vt* (*depress*) przygnębiać (przygnębić *perf*); (*write*) notować (zanotować *perf*), zapisywać (zapisać *perf*)
▸ **get down to** *vt fus* zabierać się (zabrać się *perf*) do *+gen*; **to get down to business** (*fig*) przechodzić (przejść *perf*) do rzeczy
▸ **get in** *vi* (*be elected*) wchodzić (wejść *perf*) (*do parlamentu itp*); (*train*) wjeżdżać (wjechać *perf*) (na stację), przyjeżdżać (przyjechać *perf*) (na miejsce); (*arrive home*) wchodzić (wejść *perf*) do domu
▹ *vt* (*harvest*) zbierać (zebrać *perf*); (*supplies*) gromadzić (zgromadzić *perf*)
▸ **get into** *vt fus* (*conversation, fight*) wdawać się (wdać się *perf*) w *+acc*; (*vehicle*) wsiadać (wsiąść *perf*) do *+gen*; (*clothes*) wchodzić (wejść *perf*) w *+acc*; **to get into the habit of doing sth** przyzwyczajać się (przyzwyczaić się *perf*) do robienia czegoś
▸ **get off** *vi* (*from train etc*) wysiadać (wysiąść *perf*); (*escape*) wykpić się (*perf*); **he got off with a 50-pound fine** wykpił się 50-funtową grzywną; **to get off to a good start** (*fig: person*) dobrze zaczynać (zacząć *perf*); (*event*) dobrze się zaczynać (zacząć *perf*)
▹ *vt* (*clothes*) zdejmować (zdjąć *perf*); (*stain*) wywabiać (wywabić *perf*); **we get three days off at Christmas** na Boże Narodzenie mamy trzy dni wolnego
▹ *vt fus* (*train, bus*) wysiadać (wysiąść *perf*) z *+gen*
▸ **get on** *vi* (*be friends*) być w dobrych stosunkach
▹ *vt fus* (*bus, train*) wsiadać (wsiąść *perf*) do *+gen*; **how are you getting on?** jak ci idzie?; **time is getting on** czas nagli
▸ **get on to** (*Brit*) *vt fus* (*subject*) przechodzić (przejść *perf*) do *+gen*; (*person*) skontaktować się (*perf*) z *+instr*
▸ **get on with** *vt fus* (*person*) być w dobrych stosunkach z *+instr*; (*meeting, work*) kontynuować *+acc*
▸ **get out** *vi* (*of place*) wychodzić (wyjść *perf*); (: *with effort*) wydostawać się (wydostać się *perf*); (*of vehicle*) wysiadać (wysiąść *perf*); (*news etc*) wychodzić (wyjść *perf*) na jaw
▹ *vt* (*object*) wyciągać (wyciągnąć *perf*), wyjmować (wyjąć *perf*); (*stain*) wywabiać (wywabić *perf*)
▸ **get out of** *vt fus* (*duty etc*) wymigiwać się (wymigać się *perf*) od *+gen*; **to get money out of the bank** podejmować (podjąć *perf*) pieniądze z banku
▹ *vt* (*confession etc*) wydobywać (wydobyć *perf*); (*pleasure, benefit*) czerpać
▸ **get over** *vt fus* (*illness, shock*) wychodzić (wyjść *perf*) z *+gen*; (*idea etc*) przekazywać (przekazać *perf*)
▹ *vt*: **to get it over with** raz z tym skończyć (*perf*)
▸ **get round** *vt fus* (*law, rule*) obchodzić (obejść *perf*); (*person*) przekonać (*perf*)
▸ **get round to** *vt fus* (w końcu) zabrać się (*perf*) za *+acc*
▸ **get through** *vi* (*Tel*) uzyskiwać (uzyskać *perf*) połączenie
▹ *vt fus* (*work*) uporać się (*perf*) z *+instr*; (*book*) przebrnąć (*perf*) przez *+acc*
▸ **get through to** (*Tel*) *vt fus* dodzwonić się (*perf*) do *+gen*
▸ **get together** *vi* spotykać się (spotkać się *perf*)
▹ *vt* (*people*) zbierać (zebrać *perf*); (*project, plan etc*) sporządzać (sporządzić *perf*)
▸ **get up** *vi* wstawać (wstać *perf*)
▹ *vt*: **to get up enthusiasm for sth** rozbudzać (rozbudzić *perf*) entuzjazm dla czegoś
▸ **get up to** *vt fus* wyprawiać *or* wyrabiać *+acc*

**getaway** [ˈgɛtəweɪ] *n*: **to make a** *or* **one's ~** zbiec (*perf*), uciec (*perf*)
**getaway car** *n samochód, którym sprawcy uciekają z miejsca przestępstwa*
**get-together** [ˈgɛttəgɛðə^r] *n* spotkanie *nt*
**get-up** [ˈgɛtʌp] (*inf*) *n* strój *m* (*zwłaszcza dziwaczny lub nieodpowiedni na daną okazję*)
**get-well card** [gɛtˈwɛl-] *n* kartka *f* z życzeniami powrotu do zdrowia
**geyser** [ˈgiːzə^r] *n* (*Geol*) gejzer *m*; (*Brit: water heater*) bojler *m*
**Ghana** [ˈgɑːnə] *n* Ghana *f*
**Ghanaian** [gɑːˈneɪən] *adj* ghański ▹ *n* Ghańczyk/Ghanka *m/f*
**ghastly** [ˈgɑːstlɪ] *adj* koszmarny; (*complexion, whiteness*) upiorny; **you look ~!** wyglądasz okropnie *or* strasznie!
**gherkin** [ˈgəːkɪn] *n* korniszon *m*
**ghetto** [ˈgɛtəu] *n* getto *nt*
**ghetto blaster** [-ˈblɑːstə^r] (*inf*) *n* przenośny radiomagnetofon *m*
**ghost** [gəust] *n* duch *m* ▹ *vt*: **to ~ sb's books** pisać za kogoś książki; **to give up the ~** (*fig*) wyzionąć (*perf*) ducha; **~ story** historia o duchach
**ghost town** *n* wymarłe miasto *nt*
**ghostwriter** [ˈgəustraɪtə^r] *n* autor *f* piszący za kogoś, murzyn *m* (*inf*)
**ghoul** [guːl] *n* (*ghost*) upiór *m*
**ghoulish** [ˈguːlɪʃ] *adj* makabryczny

**GHQ** (*Mil*) *n abbr* (= *general headquarters*) KG (= *Kwatera Główna*)
**GI** (*US: inf*) *n abbr* (= *government issue*) *popularny skrót oznaczający żołnierza armii amerykańskiej*
**giant** ['dʒaɪənt] *n* (*in stories*) olbrzym *m*, wielkolud *m*; (*fig: large company*) gigant *m*, potentat *m* ▷ *adj* gigantyczny; **~ (size) packet** wielkie opakowanie
**gibber** ['dʒɪbəʳ] *vi* bełkotać (wybełkotać *perf*)
**gibberish** ['dʒɪbərɪʃ] *n* bełkot *m*, bzdury *pl*; **to talk ~** gadać od rzeczy
**gibe** [dʒaɪb] *n* przycinek *m*, docinek *m* ▷ *vi*: **to ~ at** przycinać (przyciąć *+dat*)
**giblets** ['dʒɪblɪts] *npl* podroby *pl* drobiowe
**Gibraltar** [dʒɪ'brɔːltəʳ] *n* Gibraltar *m*
**giddiness** ['gɪdɪnɪs] *n* zawroty *pl* głowy
**giddy** ['gɪdɪ] *adj* (*dizzy*): **to be/feel ~** mieć/odczuwać zawroty głowy; (*fig*) przyprawiający o zawrót głowy; **~ with success** oszołomiony *or* upojony powodzeniem
**gift** [gɪft] *n* (*present*) prezent *m*, upominek *m*; (*Comm: also*: **free gift**) darmowy *or* gratisowy upominek *m*; **~ of** dar *+gen*; **~ for** talent do *+gen*
**gifted** ['gɪftɪd] *adj* utalentowany
**gift token** *n* talon *m or* bon *m* na zakupy (*dawany w prezencie*)
**gift voucher** *n* = **gift token**
**gig** [gɪg] (*inf*) *n* koncert *m*
**gigabyte** ['gɪgəbaɪt] *n* (*Comput*) gigabajt *m*
**gigantic** [dʒaɪ'gæntɪk] *adj* gigantyczny
**giggle** ['gɪgl] *vi* chichotać (zachichotać *perf*) ▷ *n* chichot *m*; **a fit of the ~s** atak wesołości; **to do sth for a ~** robić (zrobić *perf*) coś dla śmiechu
**GIGO** ['gaɪgəu] (*Comput: inf*) *abbr* (= *garbage in, garbage out*) błędne dane *pl* — błędne wyniki *pl*
**gild** [gɪld] *vt* złocić, pozłacać (pozłocić *perf*)
**gill** [dʒɪl] *n* (*Brit* = *0.14l, US* = *0.12l*) ćwierć *f* kwarty
**gills** [gɪlz] *npl* skrzela *pl*
**gilt** [gɪlt] *adj* złocony, pozłacany ▷ *n* złocenie *nt*, pozłota *f*; **gilts** *npl* (*Comm*) obligacje *pl* państwowe
**gilt-edged** ['gɪltɛdʒd] (*Comm*) *adj*: **~ stocks/securities** obligacje *pl* państwowe
**gimlet** ['gɪmlɪt] *n* świder *m* ręczny
**gimmick** ['gɪmɪk] *n* sztuczka *f*
**gin** [dʒɪn] *n* dżin *m*
**ginger** ['dʒɪndʒəʳ] *n* imbir *m* ▷ *adj* rudy
**ginger ale** *n* napój *m* imbirowy
**ginger beer** *n* napój *m* imbirowy; (*alcoholic*) piwo *nt* imbirowe
**gingerbread** ['dʒɪndʒəbrɛd] *n* (*cake*) piernik *m*; (*biscuit*) pierniczek *m*
**ginger group** (*Brit*) *n* grupa *f* nacisku
**gingerly** ['dʒɪndʒəlɪ] *adv* ostrożnie
**gingham** ['gɪŋəm] *n tkanina bawełniana w drobną białą kratkę*
**gipsy** ['dʒɪpsɪ] *n* Cygan(ka) *m(f)*
**gipsy caravan** *n* wóz *m* cygański
**giraffe** [dʒɪ'rɑːf] *n* żyrafa *f*
**girder** ['gəːdəʳ] *n* dźwigar *m*
**girdle** ['gəːdl] *n* (*corset*) gorset *m*; (*belt*) pasek *m* ▷ *vt* opasywać (opasać *perf*)
**girl** [gəːl] *n* (*child, daughter*) dziewczynka *f*; (*young woman*) dziewczyna *f*; **this is my little ~** to moja córeczka; **an English ~** (młoda) Angielka; **a ~s' school** szkoła dla dziewcząt
**girlfriend** ['gəːlfrɛnd] *n* (*of girl*) koleżanka *f*; (*: close*) przyjaciółka *f*; (*of boy*) dziewczyna *f*
**Girl Guide** *n* ≈ harcerka *f*
**girlish** ['gəːlɪʃ] *adj* dziewczęcy
**Girl Scout** (*US*) *n* ≈ harcerka *f*
**Giro** ['dʒaɪrəu] *n*: **the National ~** *brytyjski system pocztowych rachunków czekowych*
**giro** ['dʒaɪrəu] *n* (*bank giro*) bankowy system *m* przelewowy; (*post office giro*) pocztowy system *m* przelewowy; (*Brit: welfare cheque*) *przekaz pocztowy z zasiłkiem*
**girth** [gəːθ] *n* (*circumference*) obwód *m*; (*of horse*) popręg *m*
**gist** [dʒɪst] *n* (*general meaning*) esencja *f*, sedno *nt*; (*main points*) najważniejsze *pl* punkty

KEYWORD

**give** [gɪv] (*pt* **gave**, *pt* **given**) *vt* **1**: **to give sb sth, give sth to sb** dawać (dać *perf*) komuś coś
**2** (*used with noun to replace verb*): **to give a sigh** westchnąć (*perf*); **to give a cry** zapłakać (*perf*)
**3** (*deliver: news, message etc*) podawać (podać *perf*), przekazywać (przekazać *perf*); (*: advice*) dawać (dać *perf*); **to give the right/wrong answer** udzielać (udzielić *perf*) prawidłowej/nieprawidłowej odpowiedzi
**4** (*provide: opportunity, job etc*) dawać (dać *perf*); (*: surprise*) sprawiać (sprawić *perf*)
**5** (*bestow: title, honour*) nadawać (nadać *perf*); (*: right*) dawać (dać *perf*); **that's given me an idea** to podsunęło mi (pewien) pomysł
**6** (*devote: time, attention*) poświęcać (poświęcić *perf*); (*: one's life*) oddawać (oddać *perf*)
**7** (*organize*): **to give a party/dinner** wydawać (wydać *perf*) przyjęcie/obiad
▷ *vi* **1** (*also*: **give way**) załamywać się (załamać się *perf*); **the roof gave as I stepped on it** dach załamał się, gdy na nim stanąłem; **his legs gave beneath him** nogi się pod nim ugięły
**2** (*stretch*) rozciągać się (rozciągnąć się *perf*)
▸ **give away** *vt* (*money, prizes*) rozdawać (rozdać *perf*); (*opportunity*) pozbawiać się

g

(pozbawić się *perf*) *+gen*; (*secret, information*) wyjawiać (wyjawić *perf*); (*bride*) poprowadzić (*perf*) do ołtarza (*do pana młodego*); **that immediately gave him away** to go natychmiast zdradziło
▸ **give back** *vt* oddawać (oddać *perf*)
▸ **give in** *vi* poddawać się (poddać się *perf*), ustępować (ustąpić *perf*)
▷ *vt* (*essay etc*) składać (złożyć *perf*), oddawać (oddać *perf*)
▸ **give off** *vt* (*heat, smoke*) wydzielać (wydzielić *perf*)
▸ **give out** *vt* rozdawać (rozdać *perf*)
▷ *vi* (*be exhausted: supplies*) wyczerpywać się (wyczerpać się *perf*), kończyć się (skończyć się *perf*); (*fail*) psuć się (popsuć się *perf*)
▸ **give up** *vi* poddawać się (poddać się *perf*), rezygnować (zrezygnować *perf*)
▷ *vt* (*job, boyfriend, habit*) rzucać (rzucić *perf*); (*idea, hope*) porzucać (porzucić *perf*); **to give o.s. up to** oddawać się (oddać się *perf*) *+dat*
▸ **give way** *vi* (*yield*) ustępować (ustąpić *perf*) (miejsca); (*rope, ladder etc*) nie wytrzymać (*perf*), puścić (*perf*) (*inf*); (*Brit: Aut*) ustępować (ustąpić *perf*) pierwszeństwa przejazdu

**give-and-take** ['gɪvənd'teɪk] *n* kompromis *m*, (wzajemne) ustępstwa *pl*
**giveaway** (*inf*) *n*: **her expression was a ~** wyraz twarzy zdradzał ją; **~ prices** śmiesznie niskie ceny
**given** ['gɪvn] *pp of* **give** ▷ *adj* dany ▷ *conj*: **~ the circumstances, ...** wziąwszy pod uwagę okoliczności, ...; **~ that...** zważywszy, że...
**glacial** ['gleɪsɪəl] *adj* (*period*) lodowcowy; (*landscape*) polodowcowy; (*fig: person*) oziębły; (*: smile, stare*) lodowaty
**glacier** ['glæsɪə^r] *n* lodowiec *m*
**glad** [glæd] *adj* zadowolony; **to be ~ about sth/that ...** cieszyć się z czegoś/, że ...; **I was ~ of his help** byłem mu wdzięczny za pomoc
**gladden** ['glædn] *vt* cieszyć (ucieszyć *perf*), radować (uradować *perf*); **it ~ed his heart to see her well again** serce mu się radowało, że znów widzi ją w dobrym zdrowiu
**glade** [gleɪd] *n* polana *f*; (*small*) polanka *f*
**gladioli** [glædɪ'əulaɪ] *npl* gladiole *pl*, mieczyki *pl*
**gladly** ['glædlɪ] *adv* chętnie
**glamorous** ['glæmərəs] *adj* olśniewający
**glamour** ['glæmə^r] *n* blask *m*, świetność *f*
**glance** [glɑ:ns] *n* zerknięcie *nt*, rzut *m* oka ▷ *vi*: **to ~ at** zerkać (zerknąć *perf*) na *+acc*, rzucać (rzucić *perf*) okiem na *+acc*
▸ **glance off** *vt fus* odbijać się (odbić się *perf*) od *+gen*
**glancing** ['glɑ:nsɪŋ] *adj* (*blow*) ukośny, z boku *post*
**gland** [glænd] *n* gruczoł *m*
**glandular** ['glændjulə^r] *adj*: **~ fever** (*Brit*) mononukleoza *f* zakaźna
**glare** [glɛə^r] *n* (*look*) piorunujące spojrzenie *nt*; (*light*) oślepiające światło *nt*; (*fig: of publicity*) blask *m* ▷ *vi* świecić oślepiającym blaskiem; **to ~ at** patrzyć z wściekłością na *+acc*
**glaring** ['glɛərɪŋ] *adj* (*mistake*) rażący
**glass** [glɑ:s] *n* (*substance*) szkło *nt*; (*for/of milk, water etc*) szklanka *f*; (*for/of beer*) kufel *m*; (*for/of wine, champagne*) lampka *f*; (*for/of other alcoholic drink*) kieliszek *m*; **glasses** *npl* okulary *pl*
**glass-blowing** ['glɑ:sbləuɪŋ] *n* dmuchanie *nt* szkła
**glass fibre** *n* włókno *nt* szklane
**glasshouse** ['glɑ:shaus] *n* szklarnia *f*
**glassware** ['glɑ:swɛə^r] *n* wyroby *pl* szklane, szkło *nt*
**glassy** ['glɑ:sɪ] *adj* (*eyes, stare*) szklisty, szklany
**Glaswegian** [glæs'wi:dʒən] *adj* z Glasgow *post* ▷ *n* mieszkaniec(-nka) *m(f)* Glasgow
**glaze** [gleɪz] *vt* (*window etc*) szklić (oszklić *perf*); (*pottery*) glazurować ▷ *n* glazura *f*
**glazed** [gleɪzd] *adj* (*eyes*) szklisty, szklany; (*pottery*) glazurowany
**glazier** ['gleɪzɪə^r] *n* szklarz *m*
**gleam** [gli:m] *vi* błyszczeć, świecić się; **a ~ of hope** promyk nadziei
**gleaming** ['gli:mɪŋ] *adj* błyszczący, świecący
**glean** [gli:n] *vt* (*information*) z trudem gromadzić (zgromadzić *perf*)
**glee** [gli:] *n* radość *f*
**gleeful** ['gli:ful] *adj* rozradowany
**glen** [glɛn] *n* dolina *f* (górska)
**glib** [glɪb] *adj* (*person*) wygadany; (*promise*) (zbyt) łatwy; (*response*) bez zająknienia *post*
**glibly** ['glɪblɪ] *adv* gładko, bez zająknienia
**glide** [glaɪd] *vi* (*snake*) ślizgać się, sunąć; (*dancer, boat*) sunąć; (*bird, aeroplane*) szybować ▷ *n* ślizg *m*
**glider** ['glaɪdə^r] *n* szybowiec *m*
**gliding** ['glaɪdɪŋ] *n* (*sport*) szybownictwo *nt*; (*activity*) szybowanie *nt*
**glimmer** ['glɪmə^r] *n* (*of light*) (wątły) promyk *m*, migotanie *nt*; (*fig*) przebłysk *m* ▷ *vi* świecić (zaświecić *perf*) słabym światłem, migotać (zamigotać *perf*); **not a ~ of hope/interest** ani odrobiny nadziei/zainteresowania
**glimpse** [glɪmps] *n* mignięcie *nt* ▷ *vt* ujrzeć (*perf*) przelotnie; **to catch a ~ of** ujrzeć (*perf*) przelotnie *+acc*; **a village they had ~d through the trees** wioska, która mignęła im między drzewami
**glint** [glɪnt] *vi* błyskać, iskrzyć się ▷ *n* (*of light, metal*) błysk *m*; (*in eyes*) błysk *m*, iskra *f*
**glisten** ['glɪsn] *vi* lśnić, połyskiwać

**glitch** ['glɪtʃ] *(inf)* *n* usterka *f (inf)*; *(Comput)* błąd *m*
**glitter** ['glɪtəʳ] *vi* błyszczeć, skrzyć się ▷ *n* blask *m*
**glittering** ['glɪtərɪŋ] *adj* błyszczący, skrzący się; *(career)* błyskotliwy
**glitz** [glɪts] *(inf)* *n* blichtr *m*
**gloat** [gləut] *vi* tryumfować; **to ~ over** *(one's own success)* napawać się *+instr*; *(sb else's failure)* cieszyć się z *+gen*
**global** ['gləubl] *adj* *(worldwide)* (ogólno) światowy; *(overall)* globalny
**globalization** [gləubəlaɪ'zeɪʃən] *n* globalizacja *f*
**global warming** *n* globalne ocieplenie *nt*
**globe** [gləub] *n* *(world)* kula *f* ziemska, świat *m*; *(model)* globus *m*; *(shape)* kula *f*
**globetrotter** ['gləubtrɔtəʳ] *n* globtroter *m*, obieżyświat *m*
**globule** ['glɔbju:l] *n* *(of blood, water)* kropelka *f*; *(of gold)* kuleczka *f*
**gloom** [glu:m] *n* *(dark)* mrok *m*; *(sadness)* ponurość *f*, posępność *f*
**gloomily** ['glu:mɪlɪ] *adv* ponuro, posępnie
**gloomy** ['glu:mɪ] *adj* *(dark: place)* mroczny; *(: sky, day)* pochmurny; *(sad: person, place)* ponury, posępny; *(: situation)* przygnębiający
**glorification** [glɔ:rɪfɪ'keɪʃən] *n* wysławianie *nt*, gloryfikacja *f*
**glorify** ['glɔ:rɪfaɪ] *vt* wysławiać, gloryfikować
**glorious** ['glɔ:rɪəs] *adj* wspaniały
**glory** ['glɔ:rɪ] *n* *(prestige)* sława *f*, chwała *f*; *(splendour)* wspaniałość *f* ▷ *vi*: **to ~ in** rozkoszować się *+instr*
**glory hole** *(inf)* *n* rupieciarnia *f*
**Glos** *(Brit: Post)* *abbr* = **Gloucestershire**
**gloss** [glɔs] *n* *(shine)* połysk *m*; *(also:* **gloss paint***)* emalia *f*
▸ **gloss over** *vt fus* *(error)* tuszować *+acc*, zatuszowywać (zatuszować *perf*) *+acc*; *(problem)* przechodzić (przejść *perf*) do porządku dziennego nad *+instr*
**glossary** ['glɔsərɪ] *n* słowniczek *m* *(w książce)*
**glossy** ['glɔsɪ] *adj* *(hair)* lśniący; *(photograph)* z połyskiem *post* ▷ *n*: **~ magazine** ilustrowane czasopismo *nt* *(drukowane na lśniącym papierze)*
**glove** [glʌv] *n* rękawiczka *f*; *(boxer's, surgeon's)* rękawica *f*
**glove compartment** *(Aut)* *n* schowek *m* na rękawiczki
**glow** [gləu] *vi* *(embers)* żarzyć się, jarzyć się; *(stars)* jarzyć się; *(eyes)* błyszczeć; *(face)* różowić się ▷ *n* *(of embers)* żar *m*; *(of stars)* poświata *f*; *(of eyes)* blask *m*; *(of face)* zaróżowienie *nt*
**glower** ['glauəʳ] *vi*: **to ~ (at sb)** patrzyć (popatrzyć *perf*) wilkiem (na kogoś)
**glowing** ['gləuɪŋ] *adj* *(fire)* żarzący się; *(complexion)* zaróżowiony; *(fig)* pochlebny, pochwalny
**glow-worm** ['gləuwə:m] *n* świetlik *m*, robaczek *m* świętojański
**glucose** ['glu:kəus] *n* glukoza *f*
**glue** [glu:] *n* klej *m* ▷ *vt*: **to ~ sth onto sth** naklejać (nakleić *perf*) coś na coś; **to ~ sth into place** przyklejać (przykleić *perf*) coś
**glue-sniffing** ['glu:snɪfɪŋ] *n* wąchanie *nt* kleju
**glum** [glʌm] *adj* przybity
**glut** [glʌt] *n* przesycenie *nt* ▷ *vt* przesycony; **to be ~ted with** *(market etc)* być zalanym *+instr*
**glutinous** ['glu:tɪnəs] *adj* kleisty, lepki
**glutton** ['glʌtn] *n* żarłok *m*, obżartuch *m (inf)*; **a ~ for work** tytan pracy; **a ~ for punishment** masochista
**gluttonous** ['glʌtənəs] *adj* żarłoczny
**gluttony** ['glʌtənɪ] *n* *(act)* obżarstwo *nt*; *(habit)* żarłoczność *f*
**glycerin(e)** ['glɪsəri:n] *n* gliceryna *f*
**gm** *abbr* (= *gram*) g
**GMAT** *(US)* *n abbr* (= *Graduate Management Admissions Test*) *egzamin, którego zdanie uprawnia do podjęcia studiów magisterskich w dziedzinie handlu i zarządzania*
**GMB** *(Brit)* *n abbr* = **General Municipal and Boilermakers (Union)**
**GMT** *abbr* (= *Greenwich Mean Time*) (czas *m*) GMT, czas *m* Greenwich
**gnarled** [nɑ:ld] *adj* sękaty
**gnash** [næʃ] *vt*: **to ~ one's teeth** zgrzytać zębami
**gnat** [næt] *n* komar *m*
**gnaw** [nɔ:] *vt* o(b)gryzać (o(b)gryźć *perf*); *(fig)*: **to ~ at** *(desires, doubts etc)* szarpać *+instr*, targać *+instr*
**gnome** [nəum] *n* krasnal *m*, krasnoludek *m*
**GNP** *n abbr* (= *gross national product*) PNB *m inv* (= *produkt narodowy brutto*)

 KEYWORD

**go** [gəu] (*pt* **went**, *pp* **gone**, *pl* **goes**) *vi* **1** *(on foot)* iść (pójść *perf*); *(: habitually, regularly)* chodzić; *(by car etc)* jechać (pojechać *perf*); *(: habitually, regularly)* jeździć; **she went to the kitchen** poszła do kuchni; **I go to see her whenever I can** chodzę do niej, kiedy tylko mogę; **shall we go by car or by train?** pojedziemy samochodem czy pociągiem?; **they go to Tunisia every winter** co roku w zimie jeżdżą do Tunezji
**2** *(depart: on foot)* wychodzić (wyjść *perf*), iść (pójść *perf*); *(: by car etc)* odjeżdżać (odjechać *perf*), wyjeżdżać (wyjechać *perf*)



g

**3** (*attend*) chodzić; **she goes to her dancing class on Tuesdays** we wtorki chodzi na swój kurs tańca
**4** (*take part in an activity*) iść (pójść *perf*); (: *habitually, regularly*) chodzić; **to go for a walk** iść (pójść *perf*) na spacer; **we go dancing on Saturdays** w soboty chodzimy potańczyć
**5** (*work*) chodzić; **the tape recorder was still going** magnetofon ciągle chodził; **the bell went just then** właśnie wtedy zadzwonił dzwonek
**6** (*become*): **to go pale** blednąć (zblednąć *perf*); **to go mouldy** pleśnieć (spleśnieć *perf*)
**7** (*be sold*): **to go for 10 pounds** pójść (*perf*) za 10 funtów
**8** (*intend to*): **we're going to leave in an hour** wyjdziemy za godzinę
**9** (*be about to*): **it's going to rain** będzie padać
**10** (*time*) mijać (minąć *perf*), płynąć; **time went very slowly** czas mijał *or* płynął bardzo wolno
**11** (*event, activity*) iść (pójść *perf*); **how did it go?** jak poszło?
**12** (*be given*): **to go to sb** dostać się (*perf*) komuś
**13** (*break etc*) pójść (*perf*) (*inf*); **the fuse went** poszedł bezpiecznik
**14** (*be placed*): **the milk goes in the fridge** mleko trzymamy w lodówce
▷ *n* **1** (*try*): **to have a go (at)** próbować (spróbować *perf*) (+*gen*); **I'll have a go at mending it** spróbuję to zreperować
**2** (*turn*) kolej *f*; **whose go is it?** czyja (teraz) kolej?
**3** (*move*): **to be on the go** być w ruchu
▸ **go about** *vi* (*also*: **go around**) krążyć
▷ *vt fus*: **how do I go about this?** jak (mam) się za to zabrać?; **to go about one's business** zajmować się swoimi sprawami
▸ **go after** *vt fus* (*person*) ruszać (ruszyć *perf*) w pogoń za +*instr*; (*job*) szukać +*gen*; (*record*) próbować (spróbować *perf*) pobić +*acc*
▸ **go against** *vt fus* (*advice, sb's wishes*) postępować (postąpić *perf*) wbrew +*dat*; (*be unfavourable to*): **when things go against me, ...** kiedy sprawy nie idą po mojej myśli, ...
▸ **go ahead** *vi* (*proceed*) przebiegać (przebiec *perf*); **to go ahead (with)** przystępować (przystąpić *perf*) (do +*gen*); **do you mind if I smoke? — go ahead!** czy mogę zapalić? — proszę (bardzo)!
▸ **go along** *vi* przechodzić (przejść *perf*)
▸ **go along with** *vt fus* (*agree with*: *plan, decision*) postępować (postąpić *perf*) zgodnie z +*instr*; (: *person, idea*) zgadzać się (zgodzić się *perf*) z +*instr*; (*accompany*) towarzyszyć +*dat*
▸ **go away** *vi* odchodzić (odejść *perf*); **"go away!"** „idź sobie!"
▸ **go back** *vi* wracać (wrócić *perf*)
▸ **go back on** *vt fus* (*promise etc*) nie dotrzymywać (nie dotrzymać *perf*) +*gen*
▸ **go by** *vi* płynąć *or* upływać (upłynąć *perf*), mijać (minąć *perf*)
▷ *vt fus* (*rule etc*) kierować się +*instr*
▸ **go down** *vi* (*descend*: *on foot*) schodzić (zejść *perf*) (na dół); (: *in lift etc*) zjeżdżać (zjechać *perf*); (*ship*) iść (pójść *perf*) na dno; (*sun*) zachodzić (zajść *perf*); (*price, level*) obniżać się (obniżyć się *perf*)
▷ *vt fus* (*stairs, ladder*) schodzić (zejść *perf*) po +*loc*; **the speech went down well** przemówienie zostało dobrze przyjęte
▸ **go for** *vt fus* (*fetch*) iść (pójść *perf*) po +*acc*; (*favour*) woleć +*acc*; (*attack*) rzucać się (rzucić się *perf*) na +*acc*; (*apply to*) dotyczyć +*gen*
▸ **go in** *vi* wchodzić (wejść *perf*) (do środka)
▸ **go in for** *vt fus* (*competition*) startować (wystartować *perf*) w +*loc*; (*activity*) uprawiać +*acc*
▸ **go into** *vt fus* (*enter*) wchodzić (wejść *perf*) do +*gen*; (*investigate*) zagłębiać się (zagłębić się *perf*) w +*acc*; (*career*) zająć się (*perf*) +*instr*
▸ **go off** *vi* (*person*) wychodzić (wyjść *perf*); (*food*) psuć się (zepsuć się *perf*); (*bomb*) eksplodować (eksplodować *perf*); (*gun*) wypalić (*perf*); (*event*) przebiegać (przebiec *perf*), iść (pójść *perf*) (*inf*); (*lights etc*) gasnąć (zgasnąć *perf*); **to go off to sleep** zasypiać (zasnąć *perf*); **the party went off well** przyjęcie się udało
▷ *vt fus* (*inf*: *person, place, food*) przestawać (przestać *perf*) lubić +*acc*; **she's gone off the idea** przestał jej się podobać ten pomysł
▸ **go on** *vi* (*continue*: *on foot*) iść (pójść *perf*) dalej; (: *in a vehicle*) jechać (pojechać *perf*) dalej; (*happen*) dziać się, odbywać się; (*lights*) zapalać się (zapalić się *perf*)
▷ *vt fus* (*evidence etc*) opierać się (oprzeć się *perf*) na +*loc*; **to go on doing sth** robić coś dalej; **what's going on here?** co się tu dzieje?
▸ **go on at** (*inf*) *vt fus* marudzić +*dat* (*inf*)
▸ **go on with** *vt fus* kontynuować +*acc*
▸ **go out** *vt fus* wychodzić (wyjść *perf*)
▷ *vi* (*fire, light*) gasnąć (zgasnąć *perf*); (*for entertainment*): **are you going out tonight?** wychodzisz dziś wieczorem?; (*couple*): **they went out for 3 years** chodzili ze sobą (przez) trzy lata
▸ **go over** *vi* przechodzić (przejść *perf*); **go over and help him** idź tam i pomóż mu
▷ *vt* sprawdzać (sprawdzić *perf*); **to go over sth in one's mind** rozważać (rozważyć *perf*) coś w myślach
▸ **go round** *vi* (*circulate*) krążyć; (*revolve*) obracać się; (*visit*): **to go round (to sb's**

**house)** zachodzić (zajść *perf*) (do kogoś); **there was never enough food to go round** nigdy nie starczało jedzenia dla wszystkich
▸ **go through** *vt fus* (*undergo*) przechodzić (przejść *perf*) (przez *+acc*); (*search through*) przeszukiwać (przeszukać *perf*) *+acc*; (*discuss*) omawiać (omówić *perf*) *+acc*; (*perform*) wykonywać (wykonać *perf*) (po kolei) *+acc*; **could you go through the names again?** czy mógłbyś jeszcze raz wymienić wszystkie nazwiska?
▸ **go through with** *vt fus* przeprowadzić (*perf*), doprowadzić (*perf*) do końca; **I couldn't go through with it** nie mogłem się na to zdobyć
▸ **go under** *vi* iść (pójść *perf*) na dno; (*fig: business, project*) padać (paść *perf*)
▸ **go up** *vi* (*on foot*) iść (pójść *perf*) na górę; (*in lift etc*) wjeżdżać (wjechać *perf*) (na górę); (*price, level*) iść (pójść *perf*) w górę; **to go up in flames** stawać (stanąć *perf*) w płomieniach
▸ **go with** *vt fus* (*suit*) pasować do *+gen*
▸ **go without** *vt fus* (*food*) nie mieć *+gen*; (*treats, luxury*) obywać się (obyć się *perf*) bez *+gen*

**goad** [gəud] *vt* podjudzać (podjudzić *perf*)
▸ **goad on** *vt fus* pobudzać (pobudzić *perf*) do działania *+acc*
**go-ahead** ['gəuəhɛd] *adj* (*person*) przedsiębiorczy, rzutki; (*organization*) postępowy ▹ *n* zgoda *f*; **to give sb the ~ (for sth)** dawać (dać *perf*) komuś zgodę (na coś)
**goal** [gəul] *n* (*Sport: point gained*) bramka *f*, gol *m*; (*: space*) bramka *f*; (*aim*) cel *m*; **to score a ~** zdobywać (zdobyć *perf*) bramkę
**goalie** ['gəulɪ] (*inf*) *n* bramkarz(-arka) *m(f)*
**goalkeeper** ['gəulki:pə^r] *n* bramkarz *m*
**goalpost** ['gəulpəust] *n* słupek *m* (bramki)
**goat** [gəut] *n* koza *f*; (*male*) kozioł *m*
**gobble** ['gɔbl] *vt* (*also:* **gobble down, gobble up**) pożerać (pożreć *perf*)
**go-between** ['gəubɪtwi:n] *n* (*intermediary*) pośrednik(-iczka) *m(f)*; (*messenger*) posłaniec *m*
**Gobi Desert** ['gəubɪ-] *n*: **the ~** Pustynia *f* Gobi
**goblet** ['gɔblɪt] *n* kielich *m*
**goblin** ['gɔblɪn] *n* chochlik *m*
**go-cart** ['gəukɑ:t] *n* wózek *m*
**God** [gɔd] *n* Bóg *m* ▹ *excl* Boże (*voc*)
**god** [gɔd] *n* (*Myth, Rel*) bóg *m*, bóstwo *nt*; (*: less important*) bożek *m*; (*fig*) bóstwo *nt*, bożyszcze *nt*
**godchild** ['gɔdtʃaɪld] (*irreg: like* **child**) *n* chrześniak(-aczka) *m(f)*
**goddaughter** ['gɔddɔ:tə^r] *n* chrześniaczka *f*
**goddess** ['gɔdɪs] *n* bogini *f*
**godfather** ['gɔdfɑ:ðə^r] *n* ojciec *m* chrzestny
**god-forsaken** ['gɔdfəseɪkən] *adj* (*place*) opuszczony
**godmother** ['gɔdmʌðə^r] *n* matka *f* chrzestna
**godparent** ['gɔdpɛərənt] *n* (*godmother*) matka *f* chrzestna; (*godfather*) ojciec *m* chrzestny
**godsend** ['gɔdsɛnd] *n* dar *m* niebios
**godson** ['gɔdsʌn] *n* chrześniak *m*
**goes** [gəuz] *vb see* **go**
**go-getter** ['gəugɛtə^r] *n* osoba *f* przebojowa
**goggle** ['gɔgl] *vi* (*inf*): **to ~ at** wybałuszać (wybałuszyć *perf*) oczy na *+acc*
**goggles** ['gɔglz] *npl* gogle *pl*
**going** ['gəuɪŋ] *n* sytuacja *f*, warunki *pl* ▹ *adj*: **the ~ rate** aktualna stawka *f*; **a ~ concern** prosperujące przedsiębiorstwo; **it was slow ~** szło opornie
**goings-on** ['gəuɪŋz'ɔn] (*inf*) *npl*: **the ~ at that bar** to, co się wyprawia w tym barze (*inf*)
**go-kart** ['gəukɑ:t] *n* gokart *m*
**gold** [gəuld] *n* złoto *nt* ▹ *adj* złoty; **~ reserves** rezerwy w złocie
**golden** ['gəuldən] *adj* (*gold*) złoty; (*in colour*) złoty, złocisty; (*fig: opportunity, future*) wielki
**golden age** *n* złoty wiek *m*
**golden handshake** (*Brit*) *n* ≈ odprawa *f*
**golden rule** *n* najważniejsze przykazanie *nt*
**goldfish** ['gəuldfɪʃ] *n* złota rybka *f*
**gold leaf** *n* folia *f* złota
**gold medal** *n* złoty medal *m*
**goldmine** ['gəuldmaɪn] *n* kopalnia *f* złota
**gold-plated** ['gəuld'pleɪtɪd] *adj* pozłacany, złocony
**goldsmith** ['gəuldsmɪθ] *n* złotnik *m*
**gold standard** *n*: **the ~** waluta *f or* standard *m* złota
**golf** [gɔlf] *n* golf *m*
**golf ball** *n* piłka *f* do golfa; (*on typewriter*) głowica *f* kulista
**golf club** *n* (*organization*) klub *m* golfowy; (*stick*) kij *m* do golfa
**golf course** *n* pole *nt* golfowe
**golfer** ['gɔlfə^r] *n* gracz *m* w golfa
**gondola** ['gɔndələ] *n* gondola *f*
**gondolier** [gɔndə'lɪə^r] *n* gondolier *m*
**gone** [gɔn] *pp of* **go** ▹ *adj* miniony
**gong** [gɔŋ] *n* gong *m*
**good** [gud] *adj* dobry; (*valid*) ważny; (*well-behaved*) grzeczny ▹ *n* dobro *nt*; **goods** *npl* towary *pl*, towar *m*; **~!** dobrze!; **to be ~ at** być dobrym w *+loc*; **to be ~ for sth/sb** być dobrym do czegoś/dla kogoś; **it's ~ for you** to (jest) zdrowe; **it's a ~ thing you were there** dobrze, że tam byłeś; **she is ~ with children** dobrze sobie radzi z dziećmi; **to feel ~** czuć się dobrze; **it's ~ to see you** miło cię widzieć; **he's up to no ~** nie ma dobrych zamiarów; **for the common ~** dla wspólnego dobra, dla dobra ogółu; **would you be ~ enough to ...?** czy zechciałbyś *+infin*?; **that's very ~ of you**

to bardzo uprzejmie z twojej strony; **is this any ~?** (*will it do?*) czy to będzie dobre?; (*what's it like?*) czy to coś dobrego?; **a ~ deal (of)** dużo (*+gen*); **a ~ many** bardzo wiele; **take a ~ look** przyjrzyj się dobrze; **a ~ while ago** dość dawno (temu); **to make ~** (*damage*) naprawiać (naprawić *perf*); (*loss*) rekompensować (zrekompensować *perf*); **it's no ~ complaining** nie ma co narzekać; **for ~** na dobre; **~ morning/afternoon!** dzień dobry!; **~ evening!** dobry wieczór!; **~ night!** dobranoc!; **~s and chattels** dobytek

**goodbye** [gud'baɪ] *excl* do widzenia; **to say ~** żegnać się (pożegnać się *perf*)

**good-for-nothing** ['gudfənʌθɪŋ] *n* nicpoń *m*

**Good Friday** *n* Wielki Piątek *m*

**good-humoured** ['gud'hju:məd] *adj* dobroduszny

**good-looking** ['gud'lukɪŋ] *adj* atrakcyjny

**good-natured** ['gud'neɪtʃəd] *adj* (*person, pet*) o łagodnym usposobieniu *post*; (*discussion*) uprzejmy

**goodness** ['gudnɪs] *n* dobroć *f*; **for ~ sake!** na litość *or* miłość boską!; **~ gracious!** Boże (drogi)!; **out of the ~ of one's heart** z dobrego serca

**goods train** (*Brit*) *n* pociąg *m* towarowy

**goodwill** [gud'wɪl] *n* dobra wola *f*; (*Comm*) reputacja *f* przedsiębiorstwa

**goody-goody** ['gudɪgudɪ] (*inf, pej*) *n* świętoszek(-szka) *m(f)* (*pej*)

**Google®** ['gu:gl] *vt* (*Comput*) googlować *imperf*

**goose** [gu:s] (*pl* **geese**) *n* gęś *f*

**gooseberry** ['guzbərɪ] *n* agrest *m*; **to play ~** (*Brit*) służyć za przyzwoitkę

**gooseflesh** ['gu:sflɛʃ] *n* = **goose pimples**

**goose pimples** *npl* gęsia skórka *f*

**goose step** *n* krok *m* defiladowy

**GOP** (*US: Pol: inf*) *n abbr* (= *Grand Old Party*) Partia *f* Republikańska

**gopher** ['gəufə^r^] *n* (*Zool*) suseł *m*; (*Comput*) gopher *m*

**gore** [gɔ:^r^] *vt* brać (wziąć *perf*) na rogi ▷ *n* (rozlana) krew *f*

**gorge** [gɔ:dʒ] *n* wąwóz *m* ▷ *vt*: **to ~ o.s. (on)** objadać się (objeść się *perf*) (*+instr*)

**gorgeous** ['gɔ:dʒəs] *adj* wspaniały, cudowny

**gorilla** [gə'rɪlə] (*Zool*) *n* goryl *m*

**gormless** ['gɔ:mlɪs] (*Brit: inf*) *adj* ciężko myślący

**gorse** [gɔ:s] (*Bot*) *n* janowiec *m*

**gory** ['gɔ:rɪ] *adj* krwawy

**gosh** [gɔʃ] *excl* ojej

**go-slow** ['gəu'sləu] (*Brit*) *n strajk polegający na obniżeniu wydajności pracy*

**gospel** ['gɔspl] *n* (*Rel*) ewangelia *f*; (*doctrine*) doktryna *f*

**gossamer** ['gɔsəmə^r^] *n* babie lato *nt*; (*fabric*) cienka gaza *f*

**gossip** ['gɔsɪp] *n* (*rumours, chat*) plotki *pl*; (*person*) plotkarz(-arka) *m(f)* ▷ *vi* plotkować (poplotkować *perf*); **a piece of ~** plotka

**gossip column** (*Press*) *n* kronika *f* towarzyska

**got** [gɔt] *pt, pp of* **get**

**Gothic** ['gɔθɪk] *adj* gotycki

**gotten** ['gɔtn] (*US*) *pp of* **get**

**gouge** [gaudʒ] *vt* (*also*: **gouge out**) dłubać (wydłubać *perf*); **to ~ sb's eyes out** wyłupiać (wyłupić *perf*) komuś oczy

**gourd** [guəd] *n* tykwa *f*

**gourmet** ['guəmeɪ] *n* smakosz *m*

**gout** [gaut] (*Med*) *n* dna *f*, skaza *f* moczanowa

**govern** ['gʌvən] *vt* rządzić *+instr*

**governess** ['gʌvənɪs] *n* guwernantka *f*

**governing** ['gʌvənɪŋ] *adj* rządzący

**governing body** *n* ciało *nt* zarządzające, zarząd *m*

**government** ['gʌvnmənt] *n* (*act*) rządzenie *nt*, zarządzanie *nt*; (*body*) rząd *m*; (*Brit: ministers*) rada *f* ministrów, rząd *m* ▷ *cpd* rządowy; **local ~** samorząd terytorialny

**governmental** [gʌvn'mɛntl] *adj* rządowy

**government housing** (*US*) *n* ≈ mieszkania *pl* komunalne *or* kwaterunkowe

**government stock** *n* państwowe papiery *pl* wartościowe

**governor** ['gʌvənə^r^] *n* (*of state, colony*) gubernator *m*; (*of bank, school etc*) członek(-nkini) *m(f)* zarządu; (*Brit: of prison*) naczelnik *m*; **the Board of G~s** zarząd

**Govt** *abbr* = **government**

**gown** [gaun] *n* (*dress*) suknia *f*; (*Brit: of teacher, judge*) toga *f*

**GP** *n abbr* = **general practitioner**

**GPMU** (*Brit*) *n abbr* = **Graphical Media and Paper Union**

**GPO** *n abbr* (*Brit: formerly*) = **General Post Office**; (*US*: = *Government Printing Office*) *drukarnia rządowa*

**gr.** (*Comm*) *abbr* = **gross**

**grab** [græb] *vt* chwytać (chwycić *perf*); (*chance, opportunity*) korzystać (skorzystać *perf*) z *+gen*; **I ~bed some sleep/food** udało mi się trochę przespać/coś zjeść ▷ *vi*: **to ~ at** porywać (porwać *perf*) *+acc*, rzucać się (rzucić się *perf*) na *+acc*

**grace** [greɪs] *n* (*Rel*) łaska *f*; (*gracefulness*) gracja *f* ▷ *vt* (*honour*) zaszczycać (zaszczycić *perf*); (*adorn*) zdobić, ozdabiać (ozdobić *perf*); **5 days' ~** 5 dni wytchnienia; **with (a) good ~** nie okazując niechęci; **with (a) bad ~** nie kryjąc niechęci; **his sense of humour is his saving ~** ratuje go poczucie humoru; **to say ~** odmawiać (odmówić *perf*) modlitwę (*przed posiłkiem*)

**graceful** ['greɪsful] *adj* pełen wdzięku; (*refusal*) taktowny
**gracious** ['greɪʃəs] *adj* (*person, smile*) łaskawy; (*living etc*) wytworny ▷ *excl*: **(good) ~!** Boże (drogi)!
**gradation** [grə'deɪʃən] *n* stopniowanie *nt*, gradacja *f*
**grade** [greɪd] *n* (*Comm*) jakość *f*; (*in hierarchy*) ranga *f*; (*mark*) stopień *m*, ocena *f*; (*US: Scol*) klasa *f*; (*: gradient*) pochyłość *f*, nachylenie *nt* ▷ *vt* klasyfikować (sklasyfikować *perf*); **to make the ~** (*fig*) radzić (poradzić *perf*) sobie
**grade crossing** (*US*) *n* przejazd *m* kolejowy
**grade school** (*US*) *n* ≈ szkoła *f* podstawowa
**gradient** ['greɪdɪənt] *n* (*of road, slope*) nachylenie *nt*; (*Math*) gradient *m*
**gradual** ['grædjuəl] *adj* stopniowy
**gradually** ['grædjuəlɪ] *adv* stopniowo
**graduate** [*n* 'grædjuɪt, *vb* 'grædjueɪt] *n* absolwent(ka) *m(f)* ▷ *vi* kończyć (skończyć *perf*) studia; (*US*) kończyć (skończyć *perf*) szkołę średnią
**graduated pension** ['grædjueɪtɪd-] *n* emerytura *f* krocząca *or* progresywna
**graduation** [grædju'eɪʃən] *n* uroczystość *f* wręczenia świadectw
**graffiti** [grə'fi:tɪ] *n, npl* graffiti *pl*
**graft** [grɑ:ft] *n* (*Agr*) szczep *m*; (*Med*) przeszczep *m*; (*Brit: inf*) harówka *f* (*inf*); (*US*) łapówka *f* ▷ *vt*: **to ~ (onto)** (*Agr*) zaszczepiać (zaszczepić *perf*) (na +*loc*); (*Med*) przeszczepiać (przeszczepić *perf*) (na +*acc*), wszczepiać (wszczepić *perf*) (do +*gen*); (*fig*) doczepiać (doczepić *perf*) (na siłę) (do +*gen*)
**grain** [greɪn] *n* (*seed*) ziarno *nt*; (*no pl: cereals*) zboże *nt*; (*of sand, salt*) ziar(e)nko *nt*; (*of wood*) słoje *pl*; **it goes against the ~** (*fig*) to się kłóci z zasadami
**gram** [græm] *n* gram *m*
**grammar** ['græmə<sup>r</sup>] *n* gramatyka *f*
**grammar school** (*Brit*) *n* ≈ liceum *nt* (ogólnokształcące)
**grammatical** [grə'mætɪkl] *adj* gramatyczny
**gramme** [græm] *n* = **gram**
**gramophone** ['græməfəun] (*Brit: old*) *n* gramofon *m*, adapter *m*
**granary** ['grænərɪ] *n* spichlerz *m*; **~ bread** *or* **loaf**® chleb pełnoziarnisty
**grand** [grænd] *adj* (*splendid, impressive*) okazały; (*inf: great, wonderful*) świetny; (*gesture*) wielkopański; (*scale, plans*) wielki ▷ *n* (*inf*) tysiąc *m* (*dolarów lub funtów*)
**grandchild** ['græntʃaɪld] (*irreg: like* **child**) *n* wnuk *m*
**granddad** ['grændæd] (*inf*) *n* dziadek *m*, dziadzio *m*
**granddaughter** ['grændɔ:tə<sup>r</sup>] *n* wnuczka *f*
**grandeur** ['grændjə<sup>r</sup>] *n* okazałość *f*, wspaniałość *f*
**grandfather** ['grændfɑ:ðə<sup>r</sup>] *n* dziadek *m*
**grandiose** ['grændɪəus] (*pej*) *adj* (*scheme*) wielce ambitny; (*building*) pretensjonalny
**grand jury** (*US*) *n sąd przysięgłych decydujący, czy sprawa ma być skierowana do dalszego rozpatrywania*
**grandma** ['grænmɑ:] (*inf*) *n* babcia *f*
**grandmother** ['grænmʌðə<sup>r</sup>] *n* babka *f*
**grandpa** ['grænpɑ:] (*inf*) *n* = **granddad**
**grandparents** ['grændpɛərənts] *npl* dziadkowie *vir pl*
**grand piano** *n* fortepian *m*
**Grand Prix** ['grɑ̃:'pri:] (*Aut*) *n* Grand Prix *nt inv*
**grandson** ['grænsʌn] *n* wnuk *m*
**grandstand** ['grændstænd] (*Sport*) *n* trybuna *f* główna
**grand total** *n* (całkowita) suma *f*
**granite** ['grænɪt] *n* granit *m*
**granny** ['grænɪ] (*inf*) *n* babcia *f*, babunia *f*
**grant** [grɑ:nt] *vt* (*money*) przyznawać (przyznać *perf*); (*request*) spełniać (spełnić *perf*); (*visa*) udzielać (udzielić *perf*) +*gen* ▷ *n* (*Scol*) stypendium *m*; (*Admin*) dotacja *f*; **to take sb for ~ed** zaniedbywać kogoś; **to take sth for ~ed** przyjmować (przyjąć *perf*) coś za pewnik; **to ~ that ...** przyznawać (przyznać *perf*), że ...; **it was silly, I ~ you** to było głupie, przyznaję
**granulated sugar** ['grænjuleɪtɪd-] *n* cukier *m* kryształ *m*
**granule** ['grænju:l] *n* ziar(e)nko *nt*
**grape** [greɪp] *n* (*fruit*) winogrono *nt*; (*plant*) winorośl *f*; **a bunch of ~s** kiść winogron
**grapefruit** ['greɪpfru:t] (*pl* **~** *or* **~s**) *n* grejpfrut *m*
**grapevine** ['greɪpvaɪn] *n* winorośl *f*; **I heard it on the ~** doszło to do mnie pocztą pantoflową
**graph** [grɑ:f] *n* wykres *m*
**graphic** ['græfɪk] *adj* (*account, description*) obrazowy; (*: of sth unpleasant*) drastyczny; (*art, design*) graficzny; *see also* **graphics**
**graphic designer** *n* grafik *m*
**graphics** ['græfɪks] *n* (*art*) grafika *f* ▷ *npl* (*drawings*) grafika *f*
**graphite** ['græfaɪt] *n* grafit *m*
**graph paper** *n* papier *m* milimetrowy
**grapple** ['græpl] *vi*: **to ~ with sb/sth** mocować się z kimś/czymś; (*fig*) zmagać się z kimś/czymś
**grasp** [grɑ:sp] *vt* (*hold, seize*) chwytać (chwycić *perf*); (*understand*) pojmować (pojąć *perf*) ▷ *n* (*grip*) (u)chwyt *m*; (*understanding*) pojmowanie *nt*; **it slipped from my ~** wyślizgnęło mi się (z ręki); **to have sth within one's ~** mieć coś w zasięgu ręki; **to have a good ~ of sth** (*fig*) dobrze się w czymś orientować

▶ **grasp at** *vt fus* chwytać (chwycić *perf*) (za) *+acc*; (*fig: opportunity*) nie przepuszczać (nie przepuścić *perf*) *+gen*
**grasping** ['grɑːspɪŋ] *adj* zachłanny
**grass** [grɑːs] *n* trawa *f*; (*Brit: inf: informer*) kapuś *m* (*inf*)
**grasshopper** ['grɑːshɔpə<sup>r</sup>] *n* konik *m* polny, pasikonik *m*
**grass-roots** ['grɑːsruːts] *cpd*: **~ support** poparcie *nt* zwykłych ludzi
**grass snake** *n* zaskroniec *m*
**grassy** ['grɑːsɪ] *adj* trawiasty
**grate** [greɪt] *n* palenisko *nt* (*w kominku*) ▷ *vi*: **to ~ (on)** (*metal, chalk*) zgrzytać (zazgrzytać *perf*) (na *+loc*); (*fig: noise, laughter*) działać na nerwy (*+dat*) ▷ *vt* (*Culin*) trzeć (zetrzeć *perf*)
**grateful** ['greɪtful] *adj* (*person*) wdzięczny; (*thanks*) pełen wdzięczności
**gratefully** ['greɪtfəlɪ] *adv* z wdzięcznością
**grater** ['greɪtə<sup>r</sup>] *n* tarka *f*
**gratification** [grætɪfɪ'keɪʃən] *n* zadowolenie *nt*, satysfakcja *f*; (*of desire, appetite*) zaspokojenie *nt*
**gratify** ['grætɪfaɪ] *vt* (*person*) zadowalać (zadowolić *perf*), satysfakcjonować (usatysfakcjonować *perf*); (*desire, appetite*) zaspokajać (zaspokoić *perf*)
**gratifying** ['grætɪfaɪɪŋ] *adj* zadowalający, satysfakcjonujący
**grating** ['greɪtɪŋ] *n* krata *f* ▷ *adj* zgrzytliwy
**gratitude** ['grætɪtjuːd] *n* wdzięczność *f*
**gratuitous** [grə'tjuːɪtəs] *adj* niepotrzebny, nieuzasadniony
**gratuity** [grə'tjuːɪtɪ] *n* napiwek *m*
**grave** [greɪv] *n* grób *m* ▷ *adj* poważny
**gravedigger** ['greɪvdɪgə<sup>r</sup>] *n* grabarz *m*
**gravel** ['grævl] *n* żwir *m*
**gravely** ['greɪvlɪ] *adv* poważnie
**gravestone** ['greɪvstəun] *n* nagrobek *m*
**graveyard** ['greɪvjɑːd] *n* cmentarz *m*
**gravitate** ['grævɪteɪt] *vi*: **to ~ towards** ciążyć ku *+dat*; (*fig*) skłaniać się ku *+dat*
**gravity** ['grævɪtɪ] *n* (*Phys*) ciążenie *nt*, grawitacja *f*; (*seriousness*) powaga *f*
**gravy** ['greɪvɪ] *n* sos *m* (mięsny)
**gravy boat** *n* sosjerka *f*
**gravy train** (*inf*) *n*: **to ride the ~** zbijać łatwe pieniądze
**gray** [greɪ] (*US*) *adj* = **grey**
**graze** [greɪz] *vi* paść się ▷ *vt* (*scrape*) otrzeć (*perf*) (do krwi); (*touch lightly*) muskać (musnąć *perf*) ▷ *n* otarcie *nt* naskórka
**grazing** ['greɪzɪŋ] *n* pastwisko *nt*
**grease** [griːs] *n* (*lubricant*) smar *m*; (*fat*) tłuszcz *m* ▷ *vt* (*lubricate*) smarować (nasmarować *perf*); (*Culin*) smarować (posmarować *perf*) tłuszczem, natłuszczać (natłuścić *perf*); **to ~ the skids** (*US: fig*) posmarować (*perf*) (*inf*)
**grease gun** *n* smarownica *f*
**greasepaint** ['griːspeɪnt] *n* szminka *f* (aktorska)
**greaseproof paper** ['griːspruːf-] (*Brit*) *n* papier *m* woskowany
**greasy** ['griːsɪ] *adj* (*full of grease*) tłusty; (*covered with grease*) zatłuszczony; (*Brit: slippery*) śliski; (*hair*) tłusty, przetłuszczający się
**great** [greɪt] *adj* wielki; (*idea*) świetny; **they're ~ friends** są wielkimi przyjaciółmi; **we had a ~ time** świetnie się bawiliśmy; **it was ~!** było świetnie!; **the ~ thing is that ...** najlepsze jest to, że ...
**Great Barrier Reef** *n*: **the ~** Wielka Rafa *f* Koralowa
**Great Britain** *n* Wielka Brytania *f*
**greater** ['greɪtə<sup>r</sup>] *adj*: **G~ London/ Manchester** Wielki Londyn/Manchester, konurbacja *f* londyńska/manchesterska
**great-grandchild** [greɪt'græntʃaɪld] (*irreg: like* **child**) *n* (*male*) prawnuk *m*; (*female*) prawnuczka *f*
**great-grandfather** [greɪt'grænfɑːðə<sup>r</sup>] *n* pradziadek *m*, pradziad *m* (*fml*)
**great-grandmother** [greɪt'grænmʌðə<sup>r</sup>] *n* prababka *f*
**Great Lakes** *npl*: **the ~** Wielkie Jeziora *pl*
**greatly** ['greɪtlɪ] *adv* wielce
**greatness** ['greɪtnɪs] *n* wielkość *f*
**Grecian** ['griːʃən] *adj* grecki
**Greece** [griːs] *n* Grecja *f*
**greed** [griːd] *n* (*also*: **greediness**) chciwość *f*, zachłanność *f*; (*for power, wealth*) żądza *f*
**greedily** ['griːdɪlɪ] *adv* chciwie, zachłannie
**greedy** ['griːdɪ] *adj* chciwy, zachłanny; **~ for power/wealth** żądny władzy/bogactw
**Greek** [griːk] *adj* grecki ▷ *n* (*person*) Grek/ Greczynka *m/f*; (*Ling*) (język *m*) grecki; **ancient/modern ~** greka starożytna/ współczesna
**green** [griːn] *adj* zielony ▷ *n* (*colour*) (kolor *m*) zielony, zieleń *f*; (*grass*) zieleń *f*; (*Golf*) pole *nt* puttingowe; (*also*: **village green**) błonia *pl* wiejskie; **greens** *npl* warzywa *pl* zielone; (*Pol*): **the Greens** zieloni *vir pl*; **to have ~ fingers** *or* (*US*) **a ~ thumb** (*fig*) mieć dobrą rękę do roślin; **to give sb the ~ light** zapalać (zapalić *perf*) komuś zielone światło
**green belt** *n* pas *m or* pierścień *m* zieleni
**green card** *n* (*Aut*) ubezpieczenie *nt* międzynarodowe; (*US: Admin*) zielona karta *f*
**greenery** ['griːnərɪ] *n* zieleń *f*
**greenfly** ['griːnflaɪ] (*Brit*) *n* mszyca *f*
**greengage** ['griːngeɪdʒ] *n* renkloda *f*

**greengrocer** ['gri:ngrəusə$^r$] *(Brit)* *n* *(person)* kupiec *m* warzywny, zieleniarz(-arka) *m(f)*; *(shop)* sklep *m* warzywny, warzywniak *m* *(inf)*

**greenhouse** ['gri:nhaus] *n* szklarnia *f*, cieplarnia *f*

**greenhouse effect** *n*: **the ~** efekt *m* cieplarniany

**greenhouse gas** *n jeden z gazów powodujących efekt cieplarniany*

**greenish** ['gri:nɪʃ] *adj* zielonkawy

**Greenland** ['gri:nlənd] *n* Grenlandia *f*

**Greenlander** ['gri:nləndə$^r$] *n* Grenlandczyk(-dka) *m(f)*

**green pepper** *n* zielona papryka *f*

**greet** [gri:t] *vt* *(in the street etc)* pozdrawiać (pozdrowić *perf*); *(welcome)* witać (powitać *perf*); *(receive: news)* przyjmować (przyjąć *perf*)

**greeting** ['gri:tɪŋ] *n* *(salutation)* pozdrowienie *nt*; *(welcome)* powitanie *nt*; **Christmas/ birthday ~s** życzenia świąteczne/ urodzinowe; **Season's ~s** ≈ (życzenia) Wesołych Świąt i Szczęśliwego Nowego Roku

**greetings card** *n* kartka *f* z życzeniami, kartka *f* okolicznościowa

**gregarious** [grə'gɛərɪəs] *adj* *(person)* towarzyski; *(animal)* stadny

**grenade** [grə'neɪd] *n* *(also:* **hand grenade***)* granat *m*

**grew** [gru:] *pt of* **grow**

**grey** [greɪ], (US) **gray** *adj* *(colour)* szary, popielaty; *(hair)* siwy; *(dismal)* szary ▷ *n* (kolor *m*) szary *or* popielaty, popiel *m*; **to go ~** *(person)* siwieć (osiwieć *perf*); *(hair)* siwieć (posiwieć *perf*)

**grey-haired** [greɪ'hɛəd] *adj* siwy

**greyhound** ['greɪhaund] *n* chart *m* angielski

**grid** [grɪd] *n* *(pattern)* kratka *f*, siatka *f*; *(Elec)* sieć *f*; (US) pasy *pl* *(dla pieszych)*

**griddle** [grɪdl] *n okrągła blacha do pieczenia ciastek na wolnym ogniu*

**gridiron** ['grɪdaɪən] *n* ruszt *m*

**grief** [gri:f] *n* *(distress)* zmartwienie *nt*, zgryzota *f*; *(sorrow)* żal *m*; **to come to ~** *(plan)* spełzać (spełznąć *perf*) na niczym; *(person)*: **I ran away once but came to ~** raz uciekłem, ale źle się to dla mnie skończyło; **good ~!** Boże drogi!

**grievance** ['gri:vəns] *n* *(feeling)* żal *m*, pretensja *f*; *(complaint)* skarga *f*; *(cause for complaint)* krzywda *f*

**grieve** [gri:v] *vi* martwić się, smucić się ▷ *vt* martwić (zmartwić *perf*), zasmucać (zasmucić *perf*); **to ~ for sb** opłakiwać kogoś; **it ~s me to say this, but ...** przykro mi to mówić, ale ...

**grievous** ['gri:vəs] *adj* *(mistake)* poważny; *(shock, situation)* ciężki; *(injury)* ciężki, poważny; **~ bodily harm** *(Jur)* ciężkie uszkodzenie ciała

**grill** [grɪl] *n* *(on cooker)* ruszt *m*, grill *m*; *(also:* **mixed grill***)* mięso *nt* z rusztu ▷ *vt* *(Brit: food)* piec (upiec *perf*) (na ruszcie); *(inf: person)* maglować (wymaglować *perf*) *(inf)*

**grille** [grɪl] *n* *(screen: on window, counter)* krata *f*; *(Aut)* osłona *f*

**grill(room)** ['grɪl(rum)] *n* grill *m* *(restauracja)*

**grim** [grɪm] *adj* *(unpleasant)* ponury; *(serious, stern)* groźny, surowy

**grimace** [grɪ'meɪs] *n* grymas *m* ▷ *vi* wykrzywiać się (wykrzywić się *perf*)

**grime** [graɪm] *n* brud *m*

**grimy** ['graɪmɪ] *adj* brudny

**grin** [grɪn] *n* szeroki uśmiech *m* ▷ *vi*: **to ~ (at)** uśmiechać się (uśmiechnąć się *perf*) szeroko (do *+gen*), szczerzyć się *or* szczerzyć zęby (do *+gen*) *(inf)*

**grind** [graɪnd] *(pt, pp* **ground***)* *vt* *(tablet etc)* kruszyć (rozkruszyć *perf*); *(coffee, pepper, meat)* mielić (zmielić *perf*); *(knife)* ostrzyć (naostrzyć *perf*); *(gem, lens)* szlifować (oszlifować *perf*) ▷ *vi* zgrzytać (zazgrzytać *perf*) ▷ *n* harówka *f* *(inf)*; **to ~ one's teeth** zgrzytać (zazgrzytać *perf*) zębami; **to ~ to a halt** *(vehicle)* zatrzymać się *(perf)* powoli; *(talks, scheme)* zabrnąć *(perf)* w ślepy zaułek; *(work, production)* stawać (stanąć *perf*) w miejscu; **the daily ~** *(inf)* codzienna harówka *(inf)*

**grinder** ['graɪndə$^r$] *n* *(for coffee)* młynek *m*; *(for sharpening)* szlifierka *f*; *(for waste disposal)* kuchenny rozdrabniacz *m* odpadków

**grindstone** ['graɪndstəun] *n*: **to keep one's nose to the ~** harować bez wytchnienia

**grip** [grɪp] *n* *(hold)* (u)chwyt *m*, uścisk *m*; *(control, grasp)* kontrola *f*, panowanie *nt*; *(of tyre, shoe)* przyczepność *f*; *(handle)* rękojeść *f*, uchwyt *m*; *(holdall)* torba *f* (podróżna) ▷ *vt* *(object)* chwytać (chwycić *perf*); *(person)* pasjonować, fascynować; *(attention)* przyciągać (przyciągnąć *perf*); **to come to ~s with** zmierzyć się *(perf)* z *+instr*; **to ~ the road** *(car)* trzymać się szosy; **to lose one's ~** *(fig)* tracić (stracić *perf*) kontrolę

**gripe** [graɪp] *n* *(inf)* bolączka *f* ▷ *vi* *(inf)* biadolić *(inf)*; **the ~s** *(Med)* kolka *f*

**gripping** ['grɪpɪŋ] *adj* pasjonujący, fascynujący

**grisly** ['grɪzlɪ] *adj* makabryczny, potworny

**grist** [grɪst] *n*: **it's all ~ to his mill** wszystko to (jest) woda na jego młyn

**gristle** ['grɪsl] *n* chrząstka *f*

**grit** [grɪt] *n* *(stone)* żwirek *m*, grys *m*; *(of person)* zacięcie *nt*, determinacja *f* ▷ *vt* posypywać

(posypać *perf*) żwirkiem; **grits** *npl* (*US*) kasza *f*; **to ~ one's teeth** zaciskać (zacisnąć *perf*) zęby; **I've got a piece of ~ in my eye** wpadł mi do oka (jakiś) pyłek
**grizzle** ['grɪzl] (*Brit*) *vi* popłakiwać
**grizzly** ['grɪzlɪ] *n* (*also*: **grizzly bear**) niedźwiedź *m* północnoamerykański *or* siwy
**groan** [grəun] *n* (*of pain*) jęk *m*; (*of disapproval*) pomruk *m* ▷ *vi* (*in pain*) jęczeć (jęknąć *perf or* zajęczeć *perf*); (*in disapproval*) mruczeć (zamruczeć *perf*); (*tree, floorboard*) trzeszczeć (zatrzeszczeć *perf*)
**grocer** ['grəusəʳ] *n* właściciel(ka) *m(f)* sklepu spożywczego
**groceries** ['grəusərɪz] *npl* artykuły *pl* spożywcze
**grocer's (shop)** *n* sklep *m* spożywczy
**grog** [grɔg] *n* grog *m*
**groggy** ['grɔgɪ] *adj* oszołomiony, odurzony
**groin** [grɔɪn] *n* pachwina *f*
**groom** [gru:m] *n* (*for horse*) stajenny *m*; (*also*: **bridegroom**) pan *m* młody ▷ *vt* (*horse*) oporządzać (oporządzić *perf*); **to ~ sb for** sposobić *or* przysposabiać (przysposobić *perf*) kogoś do *+gen*; **well-~ed** zadbany
**groove** [gru:v] *n* (*in record etc*) rowek *m*
**grope** [grəup] *vi*: **to ~ for** szukać po omacku *+gen*; (*fig*: *words*) szukać *+gen*
**gross** [grəus] *adj* (*neglect, injustice*) rażący; (*behaviour*) grubiański, ordynarny; (*income, weight*) brutto *post*; (*earrings etc*) toporny ▷ *n inv* gros *m* (*dwanaście tuzinów*) ▷ *vt*: **to ~ 500,000 pounds** zarabiać (zarobić *perf*) 500.000 funtów brutto
**gross domestic product** *n* produkt *m* krajowy brutto
**grossly** ['grəuslɪ] *adv* rażąco
**gross national product** *n* produkt *m* narodowy brutto
**grotesque** [grə'tɛsk] *adj* groteskowy
**grotto** ['grɔtəu] *n* grota *f*
**grotty** ['grɔtɪ] (*inf*) *adj* okropny
**grouch** [grautʃ] (*inf*) *vi* gderać, zrzędzić ▷ *n* zrzęda *m/f*
**ground** [graund] *pt, pp of* **grind** ▷ *n* (*earth, soil*) ziemia *f*; (*floor*) podłoga *f*; (*land*) grunt *m*; (*area*) teren *m*; (*US*: *also*: **ground wire**) uziemienie *nt*; (*usu pl*: *reason*) podstawa *f* ▷ *vt* (*plane, pilot*) odmawiać (odmówić *perf*) zgody na start *+dat*; (*US*: *Elec*) uziemiać (uziemić *perf*) ▷ *adj* mielony ▷ *vi* (*ship*) osiadać (osiąść *perf*) (*na mieliźnie, skałach*); **grounds** *npl* (*of coffee etc*) fusy *pl*; (*gardens etc*) teren *m*; **football ~s** tereny do gry w piłkę nożną; **on the ~** na ziemi; **to the ~** na ziemię; **below ~** pod ziemią; **to gain/lose ~** zyskiwać (zyskać *perf*)/ tracić (stracić *perf*) poparcie; **common ~** (*fig*) punkty wspólne; **he declined on the ~s of ill health** *or* **on the ~s that he was ill** odmówił, podając jako powód zły stan zdrowia
**ground cloth** (*US*) *n* = **groundsheet**
**ground control** *n* (*Aviat, Space*) kontrola *f* naziemna
**ground floor** *n* parter *m*
**grounding** ['graundɪŋ] *n*: **~ (in)** (podstawowe) przygotowanie *nt* (z zakresu *+gen*)
**groundless** ['graundlɪs] *adj* bezpodstawny
**groundnut** ['graundnʌt] *n* orzeszek *m* ziemny
**ground rent** (*Brit*) *n* opłata *f* za dzierżawę gruntu
**groundsheet** ['graundʃi:t] (*Brit*) *n* *nieprzemakalny podkład pod namiot*
**groundskeeper** ['graundzki:pəʳ] (*US*) *n* = **groundsman**
**groundsman** ['graundzmən] (*Sport*) *n* dozorca *m or* opiekun *m* terenów sportowych
**ground staff** (*Sport*) *n* *personel zajmujący się utrzymaniem obiektu sportowego*
**groundswell** ['graundswɛl] *n*: **~ of opinion against/in favour of** narastająca fala *f* sprzeciwu wobec *+gen*/poparcia dla *+gen*
**ground-to-ground** ['grauntə'graund] *adj*: **~ missile** pocisk *m* (klasy) ziemia-ziemia
**groundwork** ['graundwə:k] *n* podwaliny *pl*
**group** [gru:p] *n* grupa *f*; (*also*: **pop-group**) zespół *m* ▷ *vt* (*also*: **group together**) grupować (zgrupować *perf*) ▷ *vi* (*also*: **group together**) łączyć się (połączyć się *perf*) w grupy; **newspaper ~** koncern prasowy
**grouse** [graus] *n inv* pardwa *f* ▷ *vi* gderać
**grove** [grəuv] *n* gaj *m*
**grovel** ['grɔvl] *vi* (*be humble*) płaszczyć się; (*crawl*) czołgać się
**grow** [grəu] (*pt* **grew**, *pp* **~n**) *vi* (*plant, tree*) rosnąć (wyrosnąć *perf*); (*person, animal*) rosnąć (urosnąć *perf*); (*increase*) rosnąć (wzrosnąć *perf*) ▷ *vt* (*roses, vegetables*) hodować; (*crops*) uprawiać; (*beard*) zapuszczać (zapuścić *perf*); **to ~ rich** bogacić się (wzbogacić się *perf*); **to ~ weak** słabnąć (osłabnąć *perf*); **to ~ out of/ from** brać się (wziąć się *perf*) z *+gen*; **she grew tired of waiting** zmęczyło ją czekanie
▸ **grow apart** *vi* (*fig*) oddalać się (oddalić się *perf*) od siebie
▸ **grow away from** *vt fus* (*fig*) oddalać się (oddalić się *perf*) od *+gen*
▸ **grow on** *vt fus*: **that painting is ~ing on me** ten obraz coraz bardziej mi się podoba
▸ **grow out of** *vt fus* wyrastać (wyrosnąć *perf*) z *+gen*; **he'll ~ out of it** wyrośnie z tego
▸ **grow up** *vi* (*child*) dorastać (dorosnąć *perf*); (*idea, friendship*) rozwijać się (rozwinąć się *perf*)

**grower** ['grəuəʳ] *n* hodowca *m*
**growing** ['grəuɪŋ] *adj* rosnący; **~ pains** (*Med*) bóle wzrostowe; (*fig*) początkowe trudności
**growl** [graul] *vi* warczeć (warknąć *perf*)
**grown** [grəun] *pp of* **grow**
**grown-up** [grəun'ʌp] *n* dorosły *m*
**growth** [grəuθ] *n* (*growing, development*) wzrost *m*; (*increase in amount*) przyrost *m*; (*Med*) narośl *f*; **a week's ~ of beard** tygodniowy zarost
**growth rate** *n* tempo *nt* wzrostu
**grub** [grʌb] *n* larwa *f*; (*inf: food*) żarcie *nt* (*inf*) ▷ *vi*: **to ~ about** *or* **around (for)** grzebać (w poszukiwaniu *+gen*)
**grubby** ['grʌbɪ] *adj* niechlujny; (*fig*) odrażający
**grudge** [grʌdʒ] *n* uraza *f* ▷ *vt*: **to ~ sb sth** zazdrościć komuś czegoś; **to bear sb a ~** żywić do kogoś urazę
**grudging** ['grʌdʒɪŋ] *adj* (*action*) niechętny; (*respect, praise*) wymuszony
**grudgingly** ['grʌdʒɪŋlɪ] *adv* niechętnie
**gruelling** ['gruəlɪŋ], (US) **grueling** *adj* wyczerpujący
**gruesome** ['gru:səm] *adj* makabryczny
**gruff** [grʌf] *adj* szorstki
**grumble** ['grʌmbl] *vi* zrzędzić
**grumpy** ['grʌmpɪ] *adj* zrzędliwy
**grunt** [grʌnt] *vi* (*pig*) chrząkać (chrząknąć *perf*); (*person*) burknąć (*perf*) ▷ *n* (*of pig*) chrząknięcie *nt*; (*of person*) burknięcie *nt*
**G-string** ['dʒi:strɪŋ] *n* stringi *pl*
**GSUSA** *n abbr* (*= Girl Scouts of the United States of America*) *dziewczęca organizacja skautowska*
**GT** (*Aut*) *abbr* (*= gran turismo*) GT
**GU** (*US: Post*) *abbr* = **Guam**
**guarantee** [gærən'ti:] *n* gwarancja *f* ▷ *vt* (*assure*) gwarantować (zagwarantować *perf*); (*Comm*) dawać (dać *perf*) gwarancję na *+acc*; **he can't ~ (that) he'll come** nie może zagwarantować, że przyjdzie
**guarantor** [gærən'tɔ:ʳ] (*Comm*) *n* gwarant *m*
**guard** [gɑ:d] *n* (*one person*) strażnik *m*; (*squad*) straż *f*; (*on machine*) osłona *f*; (*also*: **fireguard**) krata *f* przed kominkiem; (*Brit: Rail*) konduktor(ka) *m(f)*; (*Boxing, Fencing*) garda *f* ▷ *vt* strzec *+gen*; **to be on one's ~** mieć się na baczności
▸ **guard against** *vt fus* chronić od *+gen*
**guard dog** *n* pies *m* obronny
**guarded** ['gɑ:dɪd] *adj* ostrożny
**guardian** ['gɑ:dɪən] *n* (*Jur*) opiekun(ka) *m(f)*; (*defender*) stróż *m*, obrońca *m*
**guardian angel** *n* anioł *m* stróż *m*
**guard-rail** ['gɑ:dreɪl] *n* (*along road*) bariera *f* (ochronna); (*on staircase*) poręcz *f*, balustrada *f*
**guard's van** (*Brit: Rail*) *n* ≈ wagon *m* służbowy
**Guatemala** [gwɑ:tɪ'mɑ:lə] *n* Gwatemala *f*
**Guatemalan** [gwɑ:tɪ'mɑ:lən] *adj* gwatemalski
**Guernsey** ['gə:nzɪ] *n* wyspa *f* Guernsey
**guerrilla** [gə'rɪlə] *n* partyzant(ka) *m(f)*
**guerrilla warfare** *n* wojna *f* partyzancka, partyzantka *f*
**guess** [gɛs] *vt* (*number, distance etc*) zgadywać (zgadnąć *perf*); (*correct answer*) odgadywać (odgadnąć *perf*) ▷ *vi* domyślać się (domyślić się *perf*) ▷ *n*: **I'll give you three ~es** możesz zgadywać trzy razy; **to take** *or* **have a ~** zgadywać; **my ~ is that ...** sądzę *or* przypuszczam, że...; **I ~...** (*esp US*) sądzę *or* przypuszczam, że ...; **I ~ so** chyba tak; **I ~ you're right** chyba masz rację; **to keep sb ~ing** trzymać kogoś w niewiedzy
**guesstimate** ['gɛstɪmɪt] (*inf*) *n* szacunkowe określenie *nt* (*zwłaszcza ilości*)
**guesswork** ['gɛswə:k] *n* domysły *pl*, spekulacje *pl*; **I got the answer by ~** (przypadkowo) odgadłem odpowiedź
**guest** [gɛst] *n* gość *m*; **be my ~** (*inf*) proszę bardzo, nie krępuj się
**guest-house** ['gɛsthaus] *n* pensjonat *m*
**guest room** *n* pokój *m* gościnny
**guffaw** [gʌ'fɔ:] *vi* śmiać się (roześmiać się *perf*) głośno ▷ *n* głośny śmiech *m*
**guidance** ['gaɪdəns] *n* porada *f*; **under the ~ of** pod przewodnictwem *+gen*; **vocational/marriage ~** poradnictwo zawodowe/małżeńskie
**guide** [gaɪd] *n* (*person*) przewodnik(-iczka) *m(f)*; (*book*) przewodnik *m*; (*Brit: also*: **girl guide**) ≈ harcerka *f* ▷ *vt* (*round city, museum*) oprowadzać (oprowadzić *perf*); (*lead, direct*) prowadzić (poprowadzić *perf*); **to be ~d by sth** kierować się czymś
**guidebook** ['gaɪdbuk] *n* przewodnik *m*
**guided missile** *n* pocisk *m* zdalnie sterowany
**guide dog** *n* pies *m* przewodnik *m*
**guidelines** ['gaɪdlaɪnz] *npl* wskazówki *pl*
**guild** [gɪld] *n* cech *m*
**guildhall** ['gɪldhɔ:l] (*Brit*) *n* siedziba *f* cechu
**guile** [gaɪl] *n* przebiegłość *f*
**guileless** ['gaɪllɪs] *adj* prostoduszny
**guillotine** ['gɪləti:n] *n* (*for execution*) gilotyna *f*; (*for paper*) gilotynka *f*
**guilt** [gɪlt] *n* wina *f*
**guilty** ['gɪltɪ] *adj* (*to blame*) winny; (*expression*) zmieszany; (*secret, conscience*) nieczysty; **to plead ~/not ~** przyznawać się (przyznać się *perf*)/nie przyznawać się (nie przyznać się *perf*) do winy; **to feel ~ about doing sth** czuć się (poczuć się *perf*) winnym z powodu zrobienia czegoś
**Guinea** ['gɪnɪ] *n*: **Republic of ~** Republika *f* Gwinei

g

**guinea** ['gɪnɪ] (*Brit: old*) *n* gwinea *f*
**guinea pig** *n* świnka *f* morska; (*fig*) królik *m* doświadczalny
**guise** [gaɪz] *n*: **in** *or* **under the ~ of** pod płaszczykiem *+gen*
**guitar** [gɪ'tɑːʳ] *n* gitara *f*
**guitarist** [gɪ'tɑːrɪst] *n* gitarzysta(-tka) *m(f)*
**gulch** [gʌltʃ] (US) *n* parów *m*
**gulf** [gʌlf] *n* (*bay*) zatoka *f*; (*abyss, difference*) przepaść *f*; **the (Persian) G~** Zatoka Perska
**Gulf States** *npl*: **the ~** kraje *pl* Zatoki Perskiej
**Gulf Stream** *n*: **the ~** Prąd *m* Zatokowy, Golfsztrom *m*
**gull** [gʌl] *n* mewa *f*
**gullet** ['gʌlɪt] *n* przełyk *m*
**gullibility** [gʌlɪ'bɪlɪtɪ] *n* łatwowierność *f*
**gullible** ['gʌlɪbl] *adj* łatwowierny
**gully** ['gʌlɪ] *n* (*ravine*) wąwóz *m* (*bardzo stromy i wąski*)
**gulp** [gʌlp] *vt* (*also*: **gulp down**) (w pośpiechu) połykać (połknąć *perf*) ▹ *vi* (*from nerves, excitement*) przełykać (przełknąć *perf*) ślinę; **at** *or* **in one ~** jednym haustem
**gum** [gʌm] *n* (*Anat*) dziąsło *nt*; (*glue*) klej *m*; (*also*: **gumdrop**) żelatynka *f* (*cukierek*); (*also*: **chewing-gum**) guma *f* (do żucia) ▹ *vt*: **to gum together** sklejać (skleić *perf*)
▸ **gum up** *vt*: **to gum up the works** (*inf*) powodować (spowodować *perf*) zastój w pracy
**gumboots** ['gʌmbuːts] (*Brit*) *npl* gumowce *pl*
**gumption** ['gʌmpʃən] (*inf*) *n* olej *m* w głowie
**gum tree** *n*: **to be up a ~** (*fig: inf*) znajdować się (znaleźć się *perf*) w kropce
**gun** [gʌn] *n* (*revolver, pistol*) pistolet *m*; (*rifle, airgun*) strzelba *f*; (*cannon*) działo *nt* ▹ *vt* (*also*: **gun down**: *kill*) zastrzelić (*perf*); **to stick to one's guns** (*fig*) upierać się przy swoim; **they have guns** mają broń
**gunboat** ['gʌnbəut] *n* kanonierka *f*
**gun dog** *n* pies *m* myśliwski
**gunfire** ['gʌnfaɪəʳ] *n* ogień *m* armatni *or* z broni palnej
**gung-ho** ['gʌŋhəu] (*inf*) *adj* nadgorliwy, napalony (*inf*)
**gunk** [gʌŋk] (*inf*) *n* maź *f*
**gunman** ['gʌnmən] (*irreg: like* **man**) *n* uzbrojony bandyta *m*
**gunner** ['gʌnəʳ] *n* artylerzysta *m*
**gunpoint** ['gʌnpɔɪnt] *n*: **to hold sb at ~** trzymać kogoś na muszce
**gunpowder** ['gʌnpaudəʳ] *n* proch *m* (strzelniczy)
**gunrunner** ['gʌnrʌnəʳ] *n* przemytnik *m* broni
**gunrunning** ['gʌnrʌnɪŋ] *n* przemyt *m* broni
**gunshot** ['gʌnʃɔt] *n* wystrzał *m*
**gunsmith** ['gʌnsmɪθ] *n* rusznikarz *m*
**gurgle** ['gəːgl] *vi* (*baby*) gaworzyć; (*water*) bulgotać (zabulgotać *perf*)
**guru** ['guruː] *n* guru *m inv*
**gush** [gʌʃ] *vi* tryskać (trysnąć *perf*) ▹ *n* (*of water etc*) wytrysk *m*; **to ~ over** rozpływać się nad *+instr*
**gusset** ['gʌsɪt] *n* (*Sewing*) klin *m*, wstawka *f*
**gust** [gʌst] *n* podmuch *m*, powiew *m*
**gusto** ['gʌstəu] *n*: **with ~** z zapałem *or* upodobaniem
**gut** [gʌt] *n* (*Anat*) jelito *nt*; (*also*: **catgut**: *Mus*) struna *f*; (: *Tennis*) naciąg *m* ▹ *vt* (*poultry, fish*) patroszyć (wypatroszyć *perf*); **guts** *npl* (*Anat*) wnętrzności *pl*, trzewia *pl*; (*fig: inf*) odwaga *f*; **to hate sb's guts** serdecznie kogoś nienawidzić; **the whole house was gutted by fire** ogień strawił cały dom
**gut reaction** *n* instynktowna reakcja *f*
**gutted** ['gʌtɪd] (*inf*) *adj*: **I was ~** byłem załamany
**gutter** ['gʌtəʳ] *n* (*in street*) rynsztok *m*; (*of roof*) rynna *f*
**guttural** ['gʌtərl] *adj* gardłowy
**guy** [gaɪ] *n* (*inf: man*) gość *m* (*inf*), facet *m* (*inf*); (*also*: **guyrope**) naciąg *m* (namiotu); (*also*: **Guy Fawkes**) *kukła Guya Fawkesa, palona 5. listopada na pamiątkę nieudanej próby podpalenia Parlamentu*
**Guyana** [gaɪ'ænə] *n* Gujana *f*
**guzzle** ['gʌzl] *vt* (*drink*) żłopać (wyżłopać *perf*) (*inf*); (*food*) żreć (zeżreć *perf*) (*inf*)
**gym** [dʒɪm] *n* (*also*: **gymnasium**) sala *f* gimnastyczna; (*also*: **gymnastics**) gimnastyka *f*
**gymkhana** [dʒɪm'kɑːnə] *n* zawody *pl* hipiczne
**gymnasium** [dʒɪm'neɪzɪəm] *n* sala *f* gimnastyczna
**gymnast** ['dʒɪmnæst] *n* gimnastyk(-yczka) *m(f)*
**gymnastics** [dʒɪm'næstɪks] *n* gimnastyka *f*
**gym shoes** *npl* tenisówki *pl*
**gym slip** (*Brit*) *n* mundurek *m* szkolny (*dziewczęcy, bez rękawów*)
**gynaecologist** [gaɪnɪ'kɔlədʒɪst], (*US*) **gynecologist** *n* ginekolog *m*
**gynaecology** [gaɪnə'kɔlədʒɪ], (*US*) **gynecology** *n* ginekologia *f*
**gypsy** ['dʒɪpsɪ] *n* = **gipsy**
**gyrate** [dʒaɪ'reɪt] *vi* wirować
**gyroscope** ['dʒaɪərəskəup] *n* żyroskop *m*

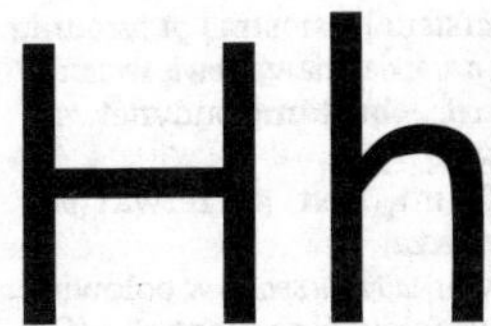

**H, h** [eɪtʃ] *n* (*letter*) H *nt*, h *nt*; **H for Harry,** (*US*) **H for How** ≈ H jak Henryk
**habeas corpus** ['heɪbɪəs'kɔ:pəs] *n ustawa zabraniająca aresztowania obywatela bez zgody sądu*
**haberdashery** [hæbə'dæʃərɪ] (*Brit*) *n* pasmanteria *f*
**habit** ['hæbɪt] *n* (*custom*) zwyczaj *m*; (*addiction*) nałóg *m*; (*Rel*) habit *m*; **a marijuana/cocaine ~** uzależnienie od marihuany/kokainy; **to get into the ~ of doing sth** przyzwyczajać się (przyzwyczaić się *perf*) do robienia czegoś; **to get out of the ~ of doing sth** odzwyczajać się (odzwyczaić się *perf*) od robienia czegoś; **to be in the ~ of doing sth** mieć w zwyczaju robić coś
**habitable** ['hæbɪtəbl] *adj* nadający się do zamieszkania
**habitat** ['hæbɪtæt] *n* (naturalne) środowisko *nt*
**habitation** [hæbɪ'teɪʃən] *n* domostwo *nt*; **fit for human ~** nadający się do zamieszkania przez ludzi
**habitual** [hə'bɪtjuəl] *adj* (*action*) charakterystyczny; (*drinker, smoker*) nałogowy; (*liar, criminal*) notoryczny
**habitually** [hə'bɪtjuəlɪ] *adv* stale, notorycznie
**hack** [hæk] *vt* rąbać (porąbać *perf*) ▷ *n* (*pej: writer*) pismak *m* (*pej*); (*horse*) wynajmowany koń *m* ▷ *vi* przesiadywać przy komputerze
▸ **hack into** *vt fus* (*Comput*) włamywać się (włamać się *perf*) do *+gen*
**hacker** ['hækə^r] (*Comput*) *n* maniak *m* komputerowy, haker *m* (*pej*)
**hackles** ['hæklz] *npl*: **to make sb's ~ rise** (*fig*) doprowadzać (doprowadzić *perf*) kogoś do szału
**hackney cab** ['hæknɪ-] *n* taksówka *f* (*zwłaszcza tradycyjna londyńska*)
**hackneyed** ['hæknɪd] *adj* (*phrase*) wyświechtany, wytarty
**had** [hæd] *pt, pp of* **have**
**haddock** ['hædək] (*pl* **~** *or* **~s**) *n* łupacz *m*
**hadn't** ['hædnt] = **had not**
**haematology**, (US) **hematology** ['hi:mə'tɔlədʒɪ] *n* hematologia *f*
**haemoglobin**, (US) **hemoglobin** ['hi:mə'gləubɪn] *n* hemoglobina *f*
**haemophilia**, (US) **hemophilia** ['hi:mə'fɪlɪə] *n* hemofilia *f*
**haemorrhage**, (US) **hemorrhage** ['hɛmərɪdʒ] *n* krwotok *m*
**haemorroids**, (US) **hemorrhoids** ['hɛmərɔɪdz] *npl* hemoroidy *pl*
**hag** [hæg] *n* wiedźma *f*
**haggard** ['hægəd] *adj* zabiedzony, wymizerowany
**haggis** ['hægɪs] (*Scottish*) *n podobna do kaszanki potrawa z podróbek baranich, łoju i owsa*
**haggle** ['hægl] *vi* targować się; **to ~ over** targować się o *+acc*
**haggling** ['hæglɪŋ] *n* targowanie się *nt*
**Hague** [heɪg] *n*: **The ~** Haga *f*
**hail** [heɪl] *n* grad *m* ▷ *vt* (*call*) przywoływać (przywołać *perf*); (*acclaim*): **to ~ sb/sth as** okrzykiwać (okrzyknąć *perf*) *or* obwoływać (obwołać *perf*) kogoś/coś *+instr* ▷ *vi*: **it ~ed** padał grad; **he ~s from Scotland** on pochodzi ze Szkocji
**hailstone** ['heɪlstəun] *n* kulka *f* gradu
**hailstorm** ['heɪlstɔ:m] *n* burza *f* gradowa, gradobicie *nt*
**hair** [hɛə^r] *n* (*of person*) włosy *pl*; (*of animal*) sierść *f*; (*single hair*) włos *m*, włosek *m*; **to do one's ~** układać (ułożyć *perf*) sobie włosy; **by a ~'s breadth** (*fig*) (dosłownie) o włos
**hairbrush** ['hɛəbrʌʃ] *n* szczotka *f* do włosów
**haircut** ['hɛəkʌt] *n* (*action*) strzyżenie *nt*, obcięcie *nt* włosów; (*style*) fryzura *f*; **to have/get a ~** dać (*perf*) sobie obciąć *or* ostrzyc włosy
**hairdo** ['hɛədu:] *n* fryzura *f*, uczesanie *nt*
**hairdresser** ['hɛədrɛsə^r] *n* fryzjer(ka) *m(f)*
**hairdresser's** ['hɛədrɛsəz] *n* zakład *m* fryzjerski, fryzjer *m*
**hair dryer** *n* suszarka *f* do włosów
**-haired** [hɛəd] *suff*: **fair-/long~** jasno-/długowłosy, o jasnych/długich włosach *post*
**hairgrip** ['hɛəgrɪp] *n* klamra *f* do włosów
**hairline** ['hɛəlaɪn] *n* linia *f or* granica *f* włosów (*z przodu*); **his ~ was receding** robiły mu się zakola

**hairline fracture** *n* włoskowate pęknięcie *nt*
**hairnet** ['hɛənɛt] *n* siatka *f* na włosy
**hair oil** *n* brylantyna *f*
**hairpiece** ['hɛəpi:s] *n* peruka *f*
**hairpin** ['hɛəpɪn] *n* wsuwka *f or* spinka *f* do włosów
**hairpin bend**, (*US*) **hairpin curve** *n* zakręt *m* o 180 stopni
**hair-raising** ['hɛəreɪzɪŋ] *adj* jeżący włos na głowie
**hair remover** *n* depilator *m*
**hair slide** *n* klamra *f* do włosów
**hair spray** *n* lakier *m* do włosów
**hairstyle** ['hɛəstaɪl] *n* fryzura *f*, uczesanie *nt*
**hairy** ['hɛərɪ] *adj* (*person, arms*) owłosiony; (*animal*) włochaty, kosmaty; (*inf*: *situation*) gorący (*inf*)
**Haiti** ['heɪtɪ] *n* Haiti *nt inv*
**hake** [heɪk] (*pl* **~** *or* **~s**) *n* morszczuk *m*
**halcyon** ['hælsɪən] *adj* błogi
**hale** [heɪl] *adj*: **~ and hearty** krzepki
**half** [hɑ:f] (*pl* **halves**) *n* (*of amount, object*) połowa *f*; (*Travel*) połówka *f* (*inf*) ▷ *adj*: **~ bottle** pół *nt inv* butelki; **~ pay** połowa zapłaty ▷ *adv* do połowy, w połowie; **first/second ~** (*Sport*) pierwsza/druga połowa; **a ~ of beer** pół kufla piwa; **two and a ~** dwa i pół; **~-an-hour** pół godziny; **~ a dozen** sześć, pół tuzina (*fml*); **a week and a ~** półtora tygodnia; **~ (of it)** połowa (z tego); **~ (of)** połowa (*+gen*); **~ as much** o połowę mniej; **to cut sth in ~** przecinać (przeciąć *perf*) coś na pół; **~ past three** (w)pół do czwartej; **~ empty** w połowie opróżniony; **~ closed** (w) półprzymknięty; **to go halves (with sb)** dzielić się (podzielić się *perf*) (z kimś) po połowie; **she never does things by halves** (ona) nigdy niczego nie robi połowicznie; **he's too clever by ~** jest o wiele za sprytny
**half-baked** ['hɑ:f'beɪkt] *adj* nie w pełni przemyślany, niedopracowany
**half board** *n* zakwaterowanie *nt* ze śniadaniem i kolacją
**half-brother** ['hɑ:fbrʌðəʳ] *n* brat *m* przyrodni
**half-caste** ['hɑ:fkɑ:st] (*pej*) *n* mieszaniec *m*
**half day** *n* dzień *m* pracy skrócony o połowę
**half-hearted** ['hɑ:f'hɑ:tɪd] *adj* wymuszony, bez przekonania *or* entuzjazmu *post*
**half-hour** [hɑ:f'auəʳ] *n* pół *nt inv* godziny
**half-life** ['hɑ:flaɪf] *n* (*Tech*) okres *m* połowicznego rozpadu
**half-mast** ['hɑ:f'mɑ:st] *adv*: **to fly at ~** być opuszczonym do połowy masztu
**halfpenny** ['heɪpnɪ] (*Brit*) *n dawna moneta półpensowa*
**half-price** ['hɑ:f'praɪs] *adj* o połowę tańszy ▷ *adv* za pół ceny
**half-sister** ['hɑ:fsɪstəʳ] *n* siostra *f* przyrodnia
**half term** (*Brit*) *n krótkie ferie w połowie semestru*
**half-timbered** *adj*: **~ building** budynek *m* z muru pruskiego
**half-time** [hɑ:f'taɪm] (*Sport*) *n* przerwa *f* (*po pierwszej połowie meczu*)
**halfway** ['hɑ:f'weɪ] *adv* (*in space*) w połowie drogi; (*in time*) w połowie; **to meet sb ~** (*fig*) wychodzić (wyjść *perf*) komuś naprzeciw
**half-yearly** [hɑ:f'jɪəlɪ] *adj* półroczny
**halibut** ['hælɪbət] *n inv* halibut *m*
**halitosis** [hælɪ'təusɪs] *n* cuchnący oddech *m*
**hall** [hɔ:l] *n* (*of flat*) przedpokój *m*; (*of building*) hall *m*, hol *m*; (*town/city hall*) ratusz *m*; (*mansion*) dwór *m*; (*for concerts*) sala *f*; (*for meetings*) aula *f*, sala *f*; **to live in ~** (*Brit*) ≈ mieszkać w akademiku
**hallmark** ['hɔ:lmɑ:k] *n* (*on metal*) próba *f*, znak *m* stempla probierczego (*fml*); (*of writer, artist*) cecha *f* charakterystyczna
**hallo** [hə'ləu] *excl* = **hello**
**hall of residence** (*Brit pl* **halls of residence**) *n* ≈ dom *m* studencki, ≈ akademik *m* (*inf*)
**hallowed** ['hæləud] *adj* (*Rel*: *ground*) święty; (*fig*: *old building etc*) otaczany (wielkim) szacunkiem
**Hallowe'en** ['hæləu'i:n] *n* wigilia *f* Wszystkich Świętych, Halloween *nt*
**hallucination** [həlu:sɪ'neɪʃən] *n* halucynacja *f*
**hallway** ['hɔ:lweɪ] *n* hall *m*, hol *m*
**halo** ['heɪləu] *n* aureola *f*
**halt** [hɔ:lt] *n*: **to come to a ~** zatrzymać się (*perf*) ▷ *vt* powstrzymać (*perf*), zatrzymać (*perf*) ▷ *vi* przystanąć (*perf*), zatrzymać się (*perf*); **to call a ~ to sth** zarzucić (*perf*) coś, zaniechać (*perf*) czegoś
**halter** ['hɔ:ltəʳ] *n* uździenica *f*
**halterneck** ['hɔ:ltənɛk] *adj*: **~ dress** suknia *f* bez ramion i pleców
**halve** [hɑ:v] *vt* (*reduce*) zmniejszać (zmniejszyć *perf*) o połowę; (*divide*) dzielić (podzielić *perf*) na pół, przepoławiać (przepołowić *perf*)
**halves** [hɑ:vz] *pl of* **half**
**ham** [hæm] *n* (*meat*) szynka *f*; (*inf*: *also*: **radio ham**) radioamator(ka) *m(f)*; (: *actor*) szmirus(ka) *m(f)* (*inf*) ▷ *vt*: **to ham it up** zgrywać się (*o aktorze*)
**Hamburg** ['hæmbə:g] *n* Hamburg *m*
**hamburger** ['hæmbə:gəʳ] *n* hamburger *m*
**ham-fisted** ['hæm'fɪstɪd], (*US*) **ham-handed** *adj* niezręczny
**hamlet** ['hæmlɪt] *n* wioska *f*, sioło *nt* (*old*)
**hammer** ['hæməʳ] *n* młot *m*; (*small*) młotek *m* ▷ *vt* (*nail*) wbijać (wbić *perf*); (*fig*: *criticize*) gromić (zgromić *perf*) ▷ *vi* walić; **to ~ sth into**

**sb** wbijać (wbić *perf*) coś komuś do głowy
▸ **hammer out** *vt* (*dent etc*) wyklepywać (wyklepać *perf*); (*fig: agreement etc*) dopracować się (*perf*) *+gen*, wynegocjować (*perf*)
**hammock** ['hæmək] *n* hamak *m*
**hamper** ['hæmpəʳ] *vt* (*person*) przeszkadzać *+dat*; (*movement, effort*) utrudniać ▹ *n* kosz(yk) *m* (z przykrywką)
**hamster** ['hæmstəʳ] *n* chomik *m*
**hamstring** ['hæmstrɪŋ] *n* (*Anat*) ścięgno *nt* podkolanowe ▹ *vt* (*fig*) paraliżować (sparaliżować *perf*)
**hand** [hænd] *n* (*Anat*) ręka *f*; (*of clock*) wskazówka *f*; (*handwriting*) pismo *nt*, charakter *m* pisma; (*worker*) robotnik(-ica) *m(f)*; (*deal of cards*) rozdanie *nt*; (*cards held in hand*) karty *pl*; (*of horse*) *jednostka pomiaru wysokości konia w kłębie* ▹ *vt* podawać (podać *perf*); **to give** *or* **lend sb a ~** pomóc (*perf*) komuś; **at ~** pod ręką; **by ~** ręcznie; **time in ~** czas do dyspozycji; **the job in ~** praca do wykonania *or* zrobienia; **we have the matter in ~** panujemy nad sytuacją; **to be on ~** być *or* pozostawać do dyspozycji; **out of ~** z miejsca; **to have sth to ~** mieć coś pod ręką *or* na podorędziu; **on the one ~ ..., on the other ~ ...** z jednej strony ..., z drugiej strony ...; **to force sb's ~** zmuszać (zmusić *perf*) kogoś do ujawnienia zamiarów; **to give sb a free ~** dawać (dać *perf*) komuś wolną rękę; **to change ~s** zmieniać (zmienić *perf*) właściciela; **~s-on experience** doświadczenie praktyczne; **"~s off!"** „ręce przy sobie!"
▸ **hand down** *vt* przekazywać (przekazać *perf*)
▸ **hand in** *vt* (*essay, work*) oddawać (oddać *perf*)
▸ **hand out** *vt* (*things*) wydawać (wydać *perf*), rozdawać (rozdać *perf*); (*information*) udzielać (udzielić *perf*) *+gen*; (*punishment*) wymierzać (wymierzyć *perf*)
▸ **hand over** *vt* przekazywać (przekazać *perf*)
▸ **hand round** *vt* (*distribute*) rozdawać (rozdać *perf*); (*cakes etc*) częstować (poczęstować *perf*) wszystkich *+instr*
**handbag** ['hændbæg] *n* torebka *f* (damska)
**handball** ['hændbɔːl] *n* piłka *f* ręczna
**handbasin** ['hændbeɪsn] *n* umywalka *f*
**handbook** ['hændbuk] *n* (*for school*) podręcznik *m*; (*of practical advice*) poradnik *m*
**handbrake** ['hændbreɪk] *n* ręczny hamulec *m*
**h & c** (*Brit*) *abbr* (*= hot and cold (water)*) gorąca i zimna woda *f*
**hand cream** *n* krem *m* do rąk
**handcuff** ['hændkʌf] *vt* zakładać (założyć *perf*) kajdanki *+dat*
**handcuffs** ['hændkʌfs] *npl* kajdanki *pl*
**handful** ['hændful] *n* (*of soil, stones*) garść *f*; (*of people*) garstka *f*
**handicap** ['hændɪkæp] *n* (*disability*) ułomność *f*, upośledzenie *nt*; (*disadvantage*) przeszkoda *f*, utrudnienie *nt*; (*horse racing, golf*) handicap *m*, wyrównanie *nt* ▹ *vt* utrudniać (utrudnić *perf*); **mentally/physically ~ped** umysłowo/fizycznie niepełnosprawny; **people with ~s, ~ped people** (ludzie) niepełnosprawni
**handicraft** ['hændɪkrɑːft] *n* (*activity*) rękodzielnictwo *nt*, rękodzieło *nt*; (*object*) wyrób *m* rękodzielniczy, rękodzieło *nt*
**handiwork** ['hændɪwəːk] *n* własne *or* własnoręczne dzieło *nt*
**handkerchief** ['hæŋkətʃɪf] *n* chusteczka *f* (do nosa)
**handle** ['hændl] *n* rączka *f*; (*of door*) klamka *f*; (*of drawer*) uchwyt *m*; (*of cup, mug*) ucho *nt*; (*CB Radio: name*) ksywa *f* ▹ *vt* (*touch*) dotykać (dotknąć *perf*) *+gen*; (*deal with*) obchodzić się (obejść się *perf*) z *+instr*; (*: successfully*) radzić (poradzić *perf*) sobie z *+instr*; **"~ with care"** „ostrożnie"; **to fly off the ~** tracić (stracić *perf*) panowanie nad sobą; **I couldn't get a ~ on it** (*inf*) nie wiedziałem, z której strony się do tego zabrać (*inf*)
**handlebar(s)** ['hændlbɑː(z)] *n(pl)* kierownica *f* (roweru)
**handling charges** *npl* opłaty *pl* manipulacyjne
**hand luggage** *n* bagaż *m* ręczny
**handmade** ['hænd'meɪd] *adj* robiony ręcznie; **it's ~** to ręczna robota
**handout** ['hændaut] *n* (*money, food etc*) jałmużna *f*; (*publicity leaflet*) ulotka *f* reklamowa; (*at lecture, meeting*) konspekt *m*
**hand-picked** ['hænd'pɪkt] *adj* (*fruit*) ręcznie zbierany; (*staff*) starannie wyselekcjonowany
**handrail** ['hændreɪl] *n* (*on stair, ledge*) poręcz *f*
**handset** ['hændsɛt] (*Tel*) *n* słuchawka *f*
**handshake** ['hændʃeɪk] *n* uścisk *m* dłoni
**handsome** ['hænsəm] *adj* (*person*) przystojny; (*building, garden*) ładny; (*fig: profit*) pokaźny
**handstand** ['hændstænd] *n*: **to do a ~** stawać (stanąć *perf*) na rękach
**hand-to-mouth** ['hændtə'mauθ] *adj* (*existence*) nędzny ▹ *adv* (*live*) z dnia na dzień
**handwriting** ['hændraɪtɪŋ] *n* charakter *m* pisma, pismo *nt*
**handwritten** ['hændrɪtn] *adj* napisany ręcznie
**handy** ['hændɪ] *adj* (*useful*) przydatny; (*easy to use*) poręczny; (*skilful*) zręczny; (*close at hand*) pod ręką *post*; **to come in ~** przydawać się (przydać się *perf*)
**handyman** ['hændɪmæn] (*irreg: like* **man**) *n* majster *m* do wszystkiego, złota rączka *f*
**hang** [hæŋ] (*pt, pp* **hung**) *vt* (*painting*) zawieszać (zawiesić *perf*); (*head*) zwieszać

h

(zwiesić *perf*); (*criminal*) (*pt, pp* **~ed**) wieszać (powiesić *perf*) ▷ *vi* (*painting, coat*) wisieć; (*drapery*) zwisać; (*hair*) opadać; **once you have got the ~ of it, ...** (*inf*) jak już raz chwycisz, o co chodzi, ... (*inf*)
▸ **hang about** *vi* pałętać się (*inf*)
▸ **hang around** *vi* = **hang about**
▸ **hang back** *vi* (*hesitate*) ociągać się
▸ **hang on** *vi* poczekać (*perf*) ▷ *vt fus* (*depend on*) zależeć od *+gen*
▸ **hang onto** *vt fus* (*grasp*) kurczowo ściskać *+acc* (w ręce); (*keep*) przechowywać *+acc*
▸ **hang out** *vt* (*washing*) rozwieszać (rozwiesić *perf*) ▷ *vi*: **the sheets are ~ing out to dry** prześcieradła się suszą; (*inf*): **where do they usually ~ out?** gdzie zwykle spędzają czas?
▸ **hang together** *vi* trzymać się kupy (*inf*)
▸ **hang up** *vi*: **to ~ up (on sb)** odkładać (odłożyć *perf*) słuchawkę ▷ *vt* (*coat*) wieszać (powiesić *perf*); (*painting*) zawieszać (zawiesić *perf*)
**hangar** ['hæŋəʳ] *n* hangar *m*
**hangdog** ['hæŋdɔg] *adj* (*look, expression*) winny
**hanger** ['hæŋəʳ] *n* (*also*: **coat hanger**) wieszak *m*
**hanger-on** [hæŋər'ɔn] (*pl* **hangers-on**) *n* pieczeniarz *m*
**hang-gliding** ['hæŋglaɪdɪŋ] *n* lotniarstwo *nt*
**hanging** ['hæŋɪŋ] *n* (*execution*) powieszenie *nt*; (*for wall*) draperia *f*
**hangman** ['hæŋmən] (*irreg*: *like* **man**) *n* kat *m*
**hangover** ['hæŋəuvəʳ] *n* (*after drinking*) kac *m*; (*from past*) przeżytek *m*
**hang-up** ['hæŋʌp] *n* zahamowanie *nt*
**hank** [hæŋk] *n* motek *m*
**hanker** ['hæŋkəʳ] *vi*: **to ~ after** wzdychać do *+gen*
**hankie** ['hæŋkɪ] *n abbr* = **handkerchief**
**hanky** ['hæŋkɪ] *n abbr* = **hankie**
**Hants** [hænts] (*Brit*: *Post*) *abbr* = **Hampshire**
**haphazard** [hæp'hæzəd] *adj* przypadkowy, niesystematyczny; **in a ~ way** na chybił trafił
**hapless** ['hæplɪs] *adj* nieszczęsny
**happen** ['hæpən] *vi* zdarzać się (zdarzyć się *perf*), wydarzać się (wydarzyć się *perf*); **if you ~ to see Jane, ...** gdybyś przypadkiem zobaczył Jane, ...; **as it ~s, ...** tak się (akurat) składa, że ...; **what's ~ing?** co się dzieje?; **what ~ed?** co się stało?; **she ~ed to be free** akurat była wolna; **if anything ~ed to him ...** gdyby coś mu się stało, ...
▸ **happen (up)on** *vt fus* natrafić (*perf*) *or* natknąć się (*perf*) na *+acc*
**happening** ['hæpnɪŋ] *n* wydarzenie *nt*
**happily** ['hæpɪlɪ] *adv* (*luckily*) na szczęście, szczęśliwie; (*cheerfully*) wesoło
**happiness** ['hæpɪnɪs] *n* szczęście *nt*
**happy** ['hæpɪ] *adj* szczęśliwy; **to be ~ with** być zadowolonym z *+gen*; **we'll be ~ to help you** chętnie *or* z przyjemnością ci pomożemy; **~ birthday!** wszystkiego najlepszego w dniu urodzin!
**happy-go-lucky** ['hæpɪgəu'lʌkɪ] *adj* niefrasobliwy
**harangue** [hə'ræŋ] *vt* prawić kazanie *+dat*
**harass** ['hærəs] *vt* nękać
**harassed** ['hærəst] *adj* znękany
**harassment** ['hærəsmənt] *n* nękanie *nt*; **sexual ~** napastowanie (seksualne)
**harbour**, (*US*) **harbor** ['hɑːbəʳ] *n* port *m* ▷ *vt* (*hope, fear*) żywić; (*criminal, fugitive*) dawać (dać *perf*) schronienie *+dat*; **to ~ a grudge against sb** żywić do kogoś urazę
**harbo(u)r dues** *npl* opłaty *pl* portowe
**harbo(u)r master** *n* komendant *m* portu
**hard** [hɑːd] *adj* (*object, surface, drugs*) twardy; (*question, problem*) trudny; (*work, life*) ciężki; (*person*) surowy; (*evidence*) niepodważalny, niezbity; (*drink*) mocny ▷ *adv* (*work*) ciężko; (*think*) intensywnie; (*try*) mocno; **to look ~ at** poważnie przyglądać się (przyjrzeć się *perf*) *+dat*; **~ luck!** a to pech!; **no ~ feelings!** bez urazy!; **to be ~ of hearing** mieć słaby słuch; **to feel ~ done by** czuć się oszukanym; **I find it ~ to believe that ...** trudno mi uwierzyć, że ...
**hard-and-fast** ['hɑːdən'fɑːst] *adj* (*rule*) żelazny; (*information*) pewny
**hardback** ['hɑːdbæk] *n* książka *f* w twardej *or* sztywnej oprawie
**hardboard** ['hɑːdbɔːd] *n* płyta *f* pilśniowa twarda
**hard-boiled egg** ['hɑːd'bɔɪld-] *n* jajko *nt* na twardo
**hard cash** *n* gotówka *f*
**hard copy** (*Comput*) *n* wydruk *m*
**hard core** *n* (*of group*) trzon *m*
**hard-core** ['hɑːd'kɔːʳ] *adj* (*pornography*) twardy (*inf*); (*supporters*) najzagorzalszy
**hard court** *n* twardy kort *m*
**hard disk** *n* dysk *m* twardy *or* stały
**harden** ['hɑːdn] *vt* (*wax, glue*) utwardzać (utwardzić *perf*); (*person*) hartować (zahartować *perf*) ▷ *vi* (*wax, glue*) twardnieć (stwardnieć *perf*)
**hardened** ['hɑːdnd] *adj* (*criminal*) zatwardziały; **to get** *or* **become ~ to sth** uodparniać się (uodpornić się *perf*) na coś
**hardening** ['hɑːdnɪŋ] *n* (*of attitude*) usztywnienie *nt*; (*of opposition*) nasilenie *nt*
**hard graft** *n*: **by sheer ~** tylko dzięki wytężonej pracy
**hard-headed** ['hɑːd'hɛdɪd] *adj* wyrachowany

**hard-hearted** ['hɑ:d'hɑ:tɪd] *adj* bezwzględny
**hard labour** *n* ciężkie roboty *pl*
**hardliner** [hɑ:d'laɪnəʳ] (*Pol*) *n* dogmatyk *m*
**hardly** ['hɑ:dlɪ] *adv* ledwie, ledwo; **~ anywhere/ever** prawie nigdzie/nigdy; **~ anyone knows that ...** mało kto wie, że ...; **it's ~ likely** to mało prawdopodobne; **I can ~ believe it** ledwie mogę w to uwierzyć
**hard sell** *n* nachalna reklama *f*
**hardship** ['hɑ:dʃɪp] *n* trudności *pl*
**hard shoulder** (*Brit*: *Aut*) *n* pobocze *nt* (drogi)
**hard up** (*inf*) *adj* spłukany (*inf*)
**hardware** ['hɑ:dwɛəʳ] *n* (*ironmongery*) towary *pl* żelazne; (*Comput*) hardware *m*; (*Mil*) ciężkie uzbrojenie *nt*
**hardware shop** *n* sklep *m* żelazny
**hard-wearing** [hɑ:d'wɛərɪŋ] *adj* (*shoes etc*) mocny, nie do zdarcia *post*
**hard-working** [hɑ:d'wə:kɪŋ] *adj* pracowity
**hardy** ['hɑ:dɪ] *adj* odporny
**hare** [hɛəʳ] *n* zając *m*
**hare-brained** ['hɛəbreɪnd] *adj* (*person*) postrzelony; (*scheme, idea*) niedorzeczny
**harelip** ['hɛəlɪp] *n* zajęcza warga *f*
**harem** [hɑ:'ri:m] *n* harem *m*
**hark back** [hɑ:k-] *vt fus*: **to ~ to** nawiązywać (nawiązać *perf*) do *+gen*
**harm** [hɑ:m] *n* (*physical*) uszkodzenie *nt* ciała; (*damage*) szkoda *f*; (*: to person*) krzywda *f* ▷ *vt* (*person*) krzywdzić (skrzywdzić *perf*); (*object*) uszkadzać (uszkodzić *perf*); **to mean no ~** nie mieć złych zamiarów; **out of ~'s way** w bezpiecznym miejscu; **there's no ~ in trying** nie zaszkodzi spróbować
**harmful** ['hɑ:mful] *adj* szkodliwy
**harmless** [hɑ:mlɪs] *adj* (*person, animal*) nieszkodliwy; (*joke, pleasure*) niewinny
**harmonic** [hɑ:'mɔnɪk] *adj* harmoniczny
**harmonica** [hɑ:'mɔnɪkə] *n* harmonijka *f* (ustna), organki *pl*
**harmonics** [hɑ:'mɔnɪks] *npl* harmonika *f*
**harmonious** [hɑ:'məunɪəs] *adj* harmonijny
**harmonium** [hɑ:'məunɪəm] *n* fisharmonia *f*
**harmonize** ['hɑ:mənaɪz], **harmonise** *vi* (*Mus*) harmonizować; **to ~ (with)** harmonizować (z *+instr*)
**harmony** ['hɑ:mənɪ] *n* (*accord*) zgoda *f*; (*Mus*) harmonia *f*; **in ~** (*live*) w zgodzie; (*work*) zgodnie; (*sing*) na głosy
**harness** ['hɑ:nɪs] *n* (*for horse*) uprząż *f*; (*for child*) szelki *pl*; (*also*: **safety harness**) pas *m* bezpieczeństwa (*np. do pracy na wysokości*) ▷ *vt* (*resources, energy*) wykorzystywać (wykorzystać *perf*); (*horse, dog*) zaprzęgać (zaprząc *perf*)
**harp** [hɑ:p] *n* harfa *f* ▷ *vi*: **to ~ on (about)** (*pej*) nudzić (o *+loc*) (*pej, inf*)
**harpist** ['hɑ:pɪst] *n* harfista(-tka) *m(f)*
**harpoon** [hɑ:'pu:n] *n* harpun *m*
**harpsichord** ['hɑ:psɪkɔ:d] *n* klawesyn *m*
**harried** ['hærɪd] *adj* udręczony
**harrow** ['hærəu] *n* brona *f*
**harrowing** ['hærəuɪŋ] *adj* wstrząsający
**harry** ['hærɪ] *vt* zadręczać
**harsh** [hɑ:ʃ] *adj* (*judge, criticism, winter*) surowy; (*sound, light, colour*) ostry
**harshly** ['hɑ:ʃlɪ] *adv* surowo
**harshness** ['hɑ:ʃnɪs] *n* (*of judge, criticism, winter*) surowość *f*; (*of sound, light, colour*) ostrość *f*
**harvest** ['hɑ:vɪst] *n* (*harvest time*) żniwa *pl*; (*crops*) zbiory *pl* ▷ *vt* zbierać (zebrać *perf*)
**harvester** ['hɑ:vɪstəʳ] *n* (*also*: **combine harvester**) kombajn *m* (żniwny)
**has** [hæz] *vb see* **have**
**has-been** ['hæzbi:n] (*inf*) *n*: **he's/she's a ~** jego/jej czas (już) minął
**hash** [hæʃ] *n* (*fig*): **to make a ~ of sth** zawalić (*perf*) coś (*inf*); (*Culin*) *potrawa z siekanego mięsa zasmażanego z cebulą, ziemniakami itp* ▷ *n abbr* (*inf*) = **hashish**
**hashish** ['hæʃɪʃ] *n* haszysz *m*
**hasn't** ['hæznt] = **has not**
**hassle** ['hæsl] (*inf*) *n* (*bother*) kłopot *m*, zawracanie *nt* głowy (*inf*) ▷ *vt* dokuczać *+dat*
**haste** [heɪst] *n* pośpiech *m*; **in ~** w pośpiechu; **to make ~ (to)** śpieszyć się (pośpieszyć się *perf*) (, żeby *+infin*)
**hasten** ['heɪsn] *vt* przyśpieszać (przyśpieszyć *perf*) ▷ *vi*: **I ~ to add** od razu dodam, śpieszę dodać (*literary*); **he ~ed to increase the prize** pośpiesznie zwiększył wysokość nagrody; **she ~ed back to the house** pośpieszyła z powrotem do domu
**hastily** ['heɪstɪlɪ] *adv* (*hurriedly*) pośpiesznie; (*rashly*) pochopnie
**hasty** ['heɪstɪ] *adj* pośpieszny; (*rash*) pochopny
**hat** [hæt] *n* kapelusz *m*; **to keep sth under one's hat** zachowywać (zachować *perf*) coś dla siebie
**hatbox** ['hætbɔks] *n* pudło *nt* na kapelusze
**hatch** [hætʃ] *n* (*Naut*) luk *m*, właz *m*; (*also*: **service hatch**) okienko *nt* ▷ *vi* wylęgać się (wylęgnąć się *perf*), wykluwać się (wykluć się *perf*) ▷ *vt* (*plot etc*) knuć (uknuć *perf*); **after ten days, the eggs ~** po dziesięciu dniach (z jaj) wykluwają się pisklęta; **we've ~ed fourteen birds in the incubator** wyhodowaliśmy w inkubatorze czternaście piskląt
**hatchback** ['hætʃbæk] *n* (*Aut*) hatchback *m*
**hatchet** ['hætʃɪt] *n* topór *m*; **to bury the ~** (*fig*) zakopywać (zakopać *perf*) topór wojenny
**hate** [heɪt] *vt* nienawidzić (znienawidzić *perf*) ▷ *n* nienawiść *f*; **to ~ to do/doing sth** bardzo

niechętnie coś (z)robić; **I ~ to trouble you, but ...** przepraszam, że cię niepokoję, ale ...
**hateful** ['heɪtful] *adj (person)* pełen nienawiści; *(week etc)* okropny
**hatred** ['heɪtrɪd] *n* nienawiść *f*
**hat trick** *(Sport) n trzy punkty (np. bramki) zdobyte w meczu przez jednego zawodnika*
**haughty** ['hɔːtɪ] *adj* wyniosły
**haul** [hɔːl] *vt (pull)* ciągnąć, wyciągać (wyciągnąć *perf*); *(by lorry)* przewozić (przewieźć *perf*); *(Naut)* holować ▷ *n (stolen goods etc)* łup *m*, zdobycz *f*; *(of fish)* połów *m*; **he ~ed himself out of the pool** wygramolił się z basenu
**haulage** ['hɔːlɪdʒ] *n* przewóz *m*
**haulage contractor** *(Brit) n* przedsiębiorca *m* przewozowy, przewoźnik *m*
**hauler** ['hɔːlə^r] *(US) n* = **haulier**
**haulier** ['hɔːlɪə^r] *(Brit) n* przewoźnik *m*
**haunch** [hɔːntʃ] *n (Anat)* pośladek *m (razem z biodrem i górną częścią uda)*; *(of meat)* udziec *m*, comber *m*; **to sit on one's ~es** przykucać (przykucnąć *perf*)
**haunt** [hɔːnt] *vt (ghost, spirit)* straszyć, nawiedzać; *(fig: mystery, memory)* nie dawać spokoju *+dat*, prześladować; *(problem, fear)* nękać ▷ *n* (ulubione) miejsce *nt* spotkań
**haunted** ['hɔːntɪd] *adj (expression, look)* udręczony, znękany; **~ house** dom, w którym straszy
**haunting** ['hɔːntɪŋ] *adj* zapadający w pamięć, nie dający spokoju
**Havana** [hə'vænə] *n* Hawana *f*

 KEYWORD

**have** [hæv] *(pt, pp* **had***) aux vb* **1** *(usu)*: **to have arrived** przybyć *(perf)*; **to have gone** odejść *(perf)*; **she has been promoted** dostała awans; **has he told you?** powiedział ci?; **having finished** *or* **when he had finished, he left** skończywszy *or* kiedy skończył, wyszedł
**2** *(in tag questions)* prawda; **you've done it, haven't you?** zrobiłeś to, prawda?
**3** *(in short answers and questions)*: **you've made a mistake — no I haven't/so I have** pomyliłeś się — nie/tak (, rzeczywiście); **we haven't paid — yes we have!** nie zapłaciliśmy — ależ tak!; **I've been there before — have you?** już kiedyś tam byłem — naprawdę?
▷ *modal aux vb*: **to have (got) to do sth** musieć coś (z)robić; **I haven't got** *or* **I don't have to wear glasses** nie muszę nosić okularów
▷ *vt* **1** *(possess)* mieć; **he has (got) blue eyes** ma niebieskie oczy; **do you have** *or* **have you got a car?** (czy) masz samochód?
**2** *(eat)* jeść (zjeść *perf*); *(drink)* pić (wypić *perf*); **to have breakfast** jeść (zjeść *perf*) śniadanie
**3** *(receive, obtain etc)* mieć, dostawać (dostać *perf*); **you can have it for 5 pounds** możesz to dostać *or* mieć za pięć funtów
**4** *(allow)* pozwalać (pozwolić *perf*) na *+acc*; **I won't have it!** nie pozwolę na to!
**5**: **to have sth done** dawać (dać *perf*) *or* oddawać (oddać *perf*) coś do zrobienia, kazać (kazać *perf*) (sobie) coś zrobić; **to have one's hair cut** obcinać (obciąć *perf*) włosy; **I must have my jacket cleaned** muszę oddać marynarkę do czyszczenia; **to have sb doing sth** sprawiać (sprawić *perf*), że ktoś coś robi; **he soon had them all laughing** wkrótce sprawił, że wszyscy się śmiali
**6** *(experience, suffer)* mieć; **to have a cold** być przeziębionym; **to have flu** mieć grypę; **he had his arm broken** złamali mu rękę; **she had her bag stolen** ukradli jej torebkę
**7** *(+noun)*: **to have a swim** popływać *(perf)*; **to have a walk** przespacerować się *(perf)*; **to have a rest** odpocząć *(perf)*; **to have a baby** urodzić *(perf)* dziecko; **let's have a look** spójrzmy, popatrzmy; **let me have a try** daj mi spróbować
**8** *(inf)*: **you've been had** dałeś się nabrać *(inf)*
▶ **have in** *(inf) vt*: **to have it in for sb** uwziąć się *(perf)* na kogoś
▶ **have on** *vt (Brit: inf: tease)* nabierać (nabrać *perf*) *(inf)*; *(wear)* mieć na sobie; **I don't have any money on me** nie mam przy sobie (żadnych) pieniędzy; **have you anything on tomorrow?** masz coś jutro w planie?
▶ **have out** *vt*: **to have it out with sb** zagrać *(perf)* z kimś w otwarte karty

**haven** ['heɪvn] *n* schronienie *nt*, przystań *f*
**haven't** ['hævnt] = **have not**
**haversack** ['hævəsæk] *n* chlebak *m*
**haves** [hævz] *(inf) npl*: **the ~ and have-nots** bogaci i biedni
**havoc** ['hævək] *n (devastation)* spustoszenia *pl*; *(confusion)* zamęt *m*, zamieszanie *nt*; **to play ~ with** wprowadzać (wprowadzić *perf*) zamęt w *+loc*; **to wreak ~ (with)** siać (posiać *perf*) spustoszenie (w *+loc*)
**Hawaii** [hə'waɪiː] *n* Hawaje *pl*
**Hawaiian** [hə'waɪjən] *adj* hawajski ▷ *n (person)* Hawajczyk(-jka) *m(f)*; *(Ling)* (język *m*) hawajski
**hawk** [hɔːk] *n* jastrząb *m*
**hawker** ['hɔːkə^r] *n* domokrążca *m*
**hawthorn** ['hɔːθɔːn] *n* głóg *m*
**hay** [heɪ] *n* siano *nt*
**hay fever** *n* katar *m* sienny

**haystack** ['heɪstæk] *n* stóg *m* siana; **it's like looking for a needle in a ~** to (jest) jak szukanie igły w stogu siana
**haywire** ['heɪwaɪə^r] (*inf*) *adj*: **to go ~** (*computer, watch*) fiksować (sfiksować *perf*) (*inf*); (*plans*) brać (wziąć *perf*) w łeb (*inf*)
**hazard** ['hæzəd] *n* zagrożenie *nt*, niebezpieczeństwo *nt* ▷ *vt* ryzykować (zaryzykować *perf*); **to be a fire/health ~** stanowić zagrożenie pożarowe/dla zdrowia; **I will ~ a guess that ...** zaryzykuję twierdzenie, że ...
**hazardous** ['hæzədəs] *adj* (*dangerous*) niebezpieczny; (*risky*) ryzykowny
**hazard pay** (*US*) *n* dodatek *m* za pracę w niebezpiecznych warunkach
**hazard (warning) lights** (*Aut*) *npl* światła *pl* awaryjne
**haze** [heɪz] *n* (*light mist*) mgiełka *f*; (*of smoke, fumes*) opary *pl*
**hazel** [heɪzl] *n* leszczyna *f* ▷ *adj* (*eyes*) piwny
**hazelnut** ['heɪzlnʌt] *n* orzech *m* laskowy
**hazy** ['heɪzɪ] *adj* (*sky, view*) zamglony; (*idea, memory*) mglisty; **I'm rather ~ about the details** mam dość mgliste pojęcie o szczegółach
**H-bomb** ['eɪtʃbɔm] *n* bomba *f* wodorowa
**HE** *abbr* (*Rel, Diplomacy*: = *His (or Her) Excellency*) JE (= *Jego (or Jej) Ekscelencja*); (*Rel*: = *His Eminence*) JE (= *Jego Eminencja*); = **high explosive**
**he** [hiː] *pron* on; **he who ...** ten, kto ...; **here he is** oto (i) on; **he-bear** samiec niedźwiedzia
**head** [hɛd] *n* (*lit, fig*) głowa *f*; (*of table*) szczyt *m*; (*of company*) dyrektor *m*; (*of country, organization*) przywódca(-dczyni) *m(f)*; (*of school*) dyrektor(ka) *m(f)*; (*of list, queue*) czoło *nt*; (*on coin*) reszka *f*; (*on tape recorder, computer*) głowica *f* ▷ *vt* (*list, group*) znajdować się na czele *+gen*; (*company*) prowadzić, kierować *+instr*; (*ball*) odbijać (odbić *perf*) głową; **~s or tails?** orzeł czy reszka?; **~ first** (*fall*) głową naprzód *or* do przodu; (*dive*) na główkę; **~ over heels in love** zakochany po uszy; **10 pounds a** *or* **per ~** 10 funtów na głowę; **to sit at the ~ of the table** siedzieć u szczytu stołu; **to have a ~ for business** mieć głowę do interesu; **to have no ~ for heights** mieć lęk wysokości; **to come to a ~** (*fig*: *situation etc*) osiągać (osiągnąć *perf*) punkt krytyczny; **let's put our ~s together** zastanówmy się wspólnie; **off the top of my ~** (tak) z głowy; **on your own ~ be it!** na twoją odpowiedzialność!; **to bite** *or* **snap sb's ~ off** warczeć (warknąć *perf*) na kogoś (*inf*); **the brandy/success went to his ~** koniak/sukces uderzył mu do głowy; **to keep one's ~** nie tracić (nie stracić *perf*) głowy; **to lose one's ~** tracić (stracić *perf*) głowę; **I can't make ~ nor tail of this** nie mogę się w tym połapać; **he's off his ~!** (*inf*) odbiło mu! (*inf*)
▸ **head for** *vt fus* (*place*) zmierzać *or* kierować się do *+gen or* ku *+dat*; (*disaster*) zmierzać (prosto) do *+gen or* ku *+dat*
▸ **head off** *vt* zażegnywać (zażegnać *perf*)
**headache** ['hɛdeɪk] *n* ból *m* głowy; (*fig*) utrapienie *nt*; **I have a ~** boli mnie głowa
**head cold** *n* katar *m*
**headdress** ['hɛddrɛs] (*Brit*) *n* przybranie *nt* głowy (*np. pióropusz*)
**header** ['hɛdə^r] (*Brit*: *Football*) *n* główka *f*
**headgear** ['hɛdgɪə^r] *n* nakrycie *nt* głowy
**head-hunter** ['hɛdhʌntə^r] *n* łowca *m* głów
**heading** ['hɛdɪŋ] *n* nagłówek *m*
**headlamp** ['hɛdlæmp] (*Brit*) *n* = **headlight**
**headland** ['hɛdlənd] *n* cypel *m*, przylądek *m*
**headlight** ['hɛdlaɪt] *n* reflektor *m*
**headline** ['hɛdlaɪn] *n* (*Press*) nagłówek *m*; (*Radio, TV*): **(news) ~s** skrót *m* (najważniejszych) wiadomości; **to hit** *or* **make the ~s** trafić na pierwsze strony gazet
**headlong** ['hɛdlɔŋ] *adv* (*fall*) głową naprzód; (*run*) na łeb, na szyję; (*rush*) na oślep, bez namysłu
**headmaster** [hɛd'mɑːstə^r] *n* dyrektor *m* (szkoły)
**headmistress** [hɛd'mɪstrɪs] *n* dyrektorka *f* (szkoły)
**head office** *n* centrala *f*, siedziba *f* główna
**head of state** (*pl* **heads of state**) *n* głowa *f* państwa
**head-on** [hɛd'ɔn] *adj* (*collision*) czołowy; (*confrontation*) twarzą w twarz *post*
**headphones** ['hɛdfəunz] *npl* słuchawki *pl*
**headquarters** ['hɛdkwɔːtəz] *npl* (*of company, organization*) centrala *f*, siedziba *f* główna; (*Mil*) kwatera *f* główna, punkt *m* dowodzenia
**headrest** ['hɛdrɛst] *n* zagłówek *m*
**headroom** ['hɛdrum] *n* (*under bridge etc*) prześwit *m*; **"max. ~: 3.4 metres"** „dopuszczalna wysokość pojazdu: 3,4 metra"
**headscarf** ['hɛdskɑːf] *n* chustka *f* na głowę
**headset** ['hɛdsɛt] *n* = **headphones**
**head start** *n*: **to give sb a ~** (*in race*) dawać (dać *perf*) komuś fory; (*fig*) zapewniać (zapewnić *perf*) komuś przewagę
**headstone** ['hɛdstəun] *n* nagrobek *m*, płyta *f* nagrobkowa
**headstrong** ['hɛdstrɔŋ] *adj* zawzięty, nieustępliwy
**head waiter** *n* kierownik *m* sali (*w restauracji*)
**headway** ['hɛdweɪ] *n*: **to make ~** robić (zrobić *perf*) postępy, posuwać się (posunąć się *perf*) naprzód
**headwind** ['hɛdwɪnd] *n* wiatr *m* przeciwny

h

**heady** ['hɛdɪ] *adj (experience, time)* ekscytujący, podniecający; *(drink, atmosphere)* idący *or* uderzający do głowy

**heal** [hi:l] *vt* leczyć (wyleczyć *perf*); *(esp miraculously)* uzdrawiać (uzdrowić *perf*) ▷ *vi* goić się (zagoić się *perf*)

**health** [hɛlθ] *n* zdrowie *nt*

**health centre** *(Brit) n* ośrodek *m* zdrowia

**health food** *n* zdrowa *f* żywność

**health food shop** *n* sklep *m* ze zdrową żywnością

**health hazard** *n* zagrożenie *nt* dla zdrowia

**the (National) Health Service** *(Brit) n* ≈ służba *f* zdrowia

**healthy** ['hɛlθɪ] *adj* zdrowy; *(fig: profit, majority)* znaczny, pokaźny

**heap** [hi:p] *n* stos *m*, sterta *f* ▷ *vt*: **to ~ (up)** *(sand etc)* usypywać (usypać *perf*) stos z *+gen*; *(stones etc)* układać (ułożyć *perf*) w stos ▷ *vt*: **to ~ sth on sth** układać (ułożyć *perf*) coś w stos na czymś; **my plate was ~ed with food** na talerzu miałam górę jedzenia; **we've got ~s of time/money** *(inf)* mamy kupę czasu/pieniędzy *(inf)*; **to ~ praises/gifts on sb** obsypywać (obsypać *perf*) kogoś pochwałami/prezentami

**hear** [hɪəʳ] *(pt, pp* **~d**) *vt (sound, information)* słyszeć (usłyszeć *perf*); *(lecture, concert)* słuchać (wysłuchać *perf*) *+gen*; *(orchestra, player)* słuchać (posłuchać *perf*) *+gen*; *(Jur: case)* rozpoznawać (rozpoznać *perf*); **have you ~d about ...?** (czy) słyszałeś o *+loc*?; **to ~ from sb** mieć wiadomości od kogoś; **I can't ~ you** nie słyszę cię; **I've never ~d of that book** nigdy nie słyszałam o tej książce; **I wouldn't ~ of it!** (nawet) nie chcę o tym słyszeć!

▸ **hear out** *vt* wysłuchiwać (wysłuchać *perf*) *+gen* (do końca)

**heard** [hə:d] *pt, pp of* **hear**

**hearing** ['hɪərɪŋ] *n (sense)* słuch *m*; *(Jur)* rozprawa *f*; **to say sth within sb's ~** mówić (powiedzieć *perf*) coś przy kimś; **to give sb a (fair) ~** *(Brit)* wysłuchać *(perf)* kogoś (bezstronnie)

**hearing aid** *n* aparat *m* słuchowy

**hearsay** ['hɪəseɪ] *n* pogłoski *pl*

**hearse** [hə:s] *n* karawan *m*

**heart** [hɑ:t] *n (lit, fig)* serce *nt*; *(of lettuce etc)* środek *m*; **hearts** *npl* kiery *pl*; **to lose ~** tracić (stracić *perf*) ducha; **to take ~** nabierać (nabrać *perf*) otuchy; **at ~** w głębi serca; **by ~** na pamięć; **to have a weak ~** mieć słabe serce; **to set one's ~ on sth** pragnąć (zapragnąć *perf*) czegoś z całej duszy; **the ~ of the matter** sedno sprawy

**heart attack** *n* atak *m* serca, zawał *m*

**heartbeat** ['hɑ:tbi:t] *n* bicie *nt* serca; *(single)* uderzenie *nt* serca

**heartbreak** ['hɑ:tbreɪk] *n* zawód *m* miłosny

**heartbreaking** ['hɑ:tbreɪkɪŋ] *adj* rozdzierający serce

**heartbroken** ['hɑ:tbrəukən] *adj*: **to be ~** mieć złamane serce

**heartburn** ['hɑ:tbə:n] *n* zgaga *f*

**-hearted** ['hɑ:tɪd] *suff*: **kind~** dobrotliwy, z sercem *post*

**heartening** ['hɑ:tnɪŋ] *adj* podnoszący na duchu

**heart failure** *n* niewydolność *f* serca

**heartfelt** ['hɑ:tfɛlt] *adj* (płynący) z głębi serca

**hearth** [hɑ:θ] *n* palenisko *nt*

**heartily** ['hɑ:tɪlɪ] *adv* serdecznie; *(eat)* z apetytem

**heartland** ['hɑ:tlænd] *n* centrum *nt*; **Britain's industrial ~** centrum przemysłowe Wielkiej Brytanii

**heartless** ['hɑ:tlɪs] *adj* bez serca *post*, nieczuły

**heart-to-heart** ['hɑ:t'tə'hɑ:t] *n* szczera rozmowa *f* ▷ *adj* szczery

**heart transplant** *n* przeszczep *m* serca

**heartwarming** ['hɑ:twɔ:mɪŋ] *adj* podnoszący na duchu, radujący serce

**hearty** ['hɑ:tɪ] *adj* serdeczny; *(appetite)* zdrowy

**heat** [hi:t] *n (warmth)* gorąco *nt*, ciepło *nt*; *(temperature)* ciepło *nt*, temperatura *f*; *(weather)* upał *m*; *(excitement)* gorączka *f*; *(also:* **qualifying heat**) wyścig *m* eliminacyjny; **in** *or (Brit)* **on ~** w okresie rui ▷ *vt (food)* podgrzewać (podgrzać *perf*); *(water)* zagrzewać (zagrzać *perf*); *(room)* ogrzewać (ogrzać *perf*)

▸ **heat up** *vi (water)* zagrzewać się (zagrzać się *perf*); *(room)* ogrzewać się (ogrzać się *perf*) ▷ *vt* podgrzewać (podgrzać *perf*)

**heated** ['hi:tɪd] *adj (room)* ogrzewany; *(pool)* podgrzewany; *(argument)* gorący

**heater** ['hi:təʳ] *n (electric, gas etc)* grzejnik *m*; *(in car)* ogrzewanie *nt*

**heath** [hi:θ] *n* wrzosowisko *nt*

**heathen** ['hi:ðn] *n* poganin(-anka) *m(f)*

**heather** ['hɛðəʳ] *n* wrzos *m*

**heating** ['hi:tɪŋ] *n* ogrzewanie *nt*

**heat-resistant** ['hi:trɪzɪstənt] *adj* żaroodporny, termoodporny

**heat-stroke** *n* udar *m* cieplny

**heatwave** ['hi:tweɪv] *n* fala *f* upałów

**heave** [hi:v] *vt (pull)* przeciągać (przeciągnąć *perf*); *(push)* przepychać (przepchnąć *perf*); *(lift)* podźwignąć *(perf)* ▷ *vi (chest)* falować; *(person)* mieć torsje ▷ *n (pull)* przeciągnięcie *nt*; *(push)* pchnięcie *nt*; *(lift)* dźwignięcie *nt*; **to ~ a sigh** westchnąć *(perf)* ciężko

▸ **heave to** *(pt, pp* **hove**) *(Naut) vi* dobić *(perf)* do brzegu

**heaven** ['hɛvn] *n* niebo *nt*, raj *m*; **thank ~!** dzięki Bogu!; **~ forbid!** niech (Pan) Bóg broni!; **for ~'s sake!** na miłość *or* litość boską!
**heavenly** ['hɛvnlɪ] *adj* (*Rel*) niebiański, boski; (*body*) niebieski; (*fig*) boski
**heaven-sent** [hɛvn'sɛnt] *adj* opatrznościowy, zesłany przez los
**heavily** ['hɛvɪlɪ] *adv* ciężko; (*drink, smoke*) dużo; (*depend*) w dużym stopniu
**heavy** ['hɛvɪ] *adj* ciężki; (*rain, snow*) obfity; (*responsibility*) wielki; (*drinker, smoker*) nałogowy; (*schedule*) obciążony, przeciążony; (*food*) ciężko strawny; **~ casualties** duże straty (w ludziach); **how ~ are you?** ile ważysz?; **the conversation was ~ going** rozmowa nie kleiła się
**heavy cream** (*US*) *n* kremówka *f* (*śmietana*)
**heavy duty** *adj* trwały, wytrzymały
**heavy goods vehicle** *n* ciężarówka *f*
**heavy-handed** ['hɛvɪ'hændɪd] *adj* (*fig*) grubo ciosany
**heavy industry** *n* przemysł *m* ciężki
**heavyweight** ['hɛvɪweɪt] (*Boxing*) *n* waga *f* ciężka
**Hebrew** ['hi:bru:] *adj* hebrajski ▷ *n* (język *m*) hebrajski
**Hebrides** ['hɛbrɪdi:z] *npl*: **the ~** Hebrydy *pl*
**heckle** ['hɛkl] *vt* (*speaker, performer*) przeszkadzać (przeszkodzić *perf*) *+dat* (*w wystąpieniu*)
**heckler** ['hɛklə^r] *n* warchoł *m* (*przerywający wystąpienie*)
**hectare** ['hɛkta:^r] (*Brit*) *n* hektar *m*
**hectic** ['hɛktɪk] *adj* gorączkowy
**hector** ['hɛktə^r] *vt* napastować
**he'd** [hi:d] = **he would; he had**
**hedge** [hɛdʒ] *n* żywopłot *m* ▷ *vi* wykręcać się (wykręcić się *perf*); **to ~ one's bets** (*fig*) zabezpieczać się (zabezpieczyć się *perf*) na dwie strony; **as a ~ against inflation** jako zabezpieczenie przeciwko inflacji
▸ **hedge in** *vt* paraliżować (sparaliżować *perf*)
**hedgehog** ['hɛdʒhɔg] *n* jeż *m*
**hedgerow** ['hɛdʒrəu] *n* rząd *m* krzewów *or* drzew
**hedonism** ['hi:dənɪzəm] *n* hedonizm *m*
**heed** [hi:d] *vt* (*also*: **take heed of**) brać (wziąć *perf*) pod uwagę ▷ *n*: **to pay (no) ~ to, take (no) ~ of** (nie) zważać na *+acc*
**heedless** ['hi:dlɪs] *adj*: **to be ~ of** nie zważać na *+acc*, nie dbać o *+acc*
**heel** [hi:l] *n* (*of foot*) pięta *f*; (*of shoe*) obcas *m* ▷ *vt* dorabiać (dorobić *perf*) obcas *or* obcasy do *+gen*; **to bring to ~** przywoływać (przywoływać *perf*) do nogi; (*fig*) zmuszać (zmusić *perf*) do posłuszeństwa; **to take to one's ~s** (*inf*) brać (wziąć *perf*) nogi za pas, dawać (dać *perf*) nogę (*inf*)
**hefty** ['hɛftɪ] *adj* (*person*) masywny, zwalisty; (*parcel*) ciężki; (*profit*) ogromny
**heifer** ['hɛfə^r] *n* jałówka *f*
**height** [haɪt] *n* (*of person*) wzrost *m*; (*of building, plane*) wysokość *f*; (*of terrain*) wzniesienie *nt*; (*fig*) szczyt *m*; **what ~ are you?** ile masz wzrostu?, ile mierzysz?; **of average ~** średniego wzrostu; **to be afraid of ~s** mieć lęk wysokości; **it's the ~ of fashion** to jest szczyt mody; **at the ~ of the tourist season** w szczycie sezonu turystycznego
**heighten** ['haɪtn] *vt* wzmagać (wzmóc *perf*), potęgować (spotęgować *perf*)
**heinous** ['heɪnəs] *adj* haniebny, ohydny
**heir** [ɛə^r] *n* (*to throne*) następca *m*; (*to fortune*) spadkobierca *m*
**heir apparent** *n* prawowity następca *m or* spadkobierca *m*
**heiress** ['ɛərɛs] *n* (*to throne*) następczyni *f*; (*to fortune*) spadkobierczyni *f*
**heirloom** ['ɛəlu:m] *n* pamiątka *f* rodowa
**heist** [haɪst] (*US*: *inf*) *n* skok *m* (*inf*)
**held** [hɛld] *pt, pp of* **hold**
**helicopter** ['hɛlɪkɔptə^r] *n* helikopter *m*
**heliport** ['hɛlɪpɔ:t] *n* lądowisko *nt* dla helikopterów
**helium** ['hi:lɪəm] *n* hel *m*
**hell** [hɛl] *n* piekło *nt*; **~!** (*inf!*) do diabła! (*inf*); **a ~ of a mess/noise** (*inf*) piekielny *or* potworny bałagan/hałas; **a ~ of a player/writer** (*inf*) świetny gracz/pisarz
**he'll** [hi:l] = **he will; he shall**
**hellish** ['hɛlɪʃ] (*inf*) *adj* piekielny
**hello** [hə'ləu] *excl* (*as greeting*) cześć, witam; (*to attract attention*) halo; (*expressing surprise*) no no
**helm** [hɛlm] *n* koło *nt* sterowe, ster *m*; **at the ~** (*fig*) u steru
**helmet** ['hɛlmɪt] *n* kask *m*; (*of soldier*) hełm *m*
**helmsman** ['hɛlmzmən] *n* sternik *m*
**help** [hɛlp] *n* pomoc *f*; (*charwoman*) pomoc *f* domowa ▷ *vt* pomagać (pomóc *perf*) *+dat*; **with the ~ of** (*person*) przy pomocy *+gen*; (*tool etc*) za pomocą *+gen*; **to be of ~ to sb** być komuś pomocnym; **~!** pomocy!, ratunku!; **can I ~ you?** czym mogę służyć?; **~ yourself** poczęstuj się; **he can't ~ it** nie może nic na to poradzić; **I can't ~ thinking that ...** coś mi się zdaje, że ...; **she couldn't ~ laughing** nie mogła powstrzymać (się od) śmiechu
**helper** ['hɛlpə^r] *n* pomocnik(-ica) *m(f)*
**helpful** ['hɛlpful] *adj* pomocny, przydatny
**helping** ['hɛlpɪŋ] *n* porcja *f*
**helpless** ['hɛlplɪs] *adj* (*incapable*) bezradny; (*defenceless*) bezbronny
**helplessly** ['hɛlplɪslɪ] *adv* bezradnie
**helpline** ['hɛlplaɪn] *n* infolinia *f*
**Helsinki** ['hɛlsɪŋkɪ] *n* Helsinki *pl*

h

**helter-skelter** ['hɛltə'skɛltə^r] (*Brit*) *n* zjeżdżalnia *f* (*w wesołym miasteczku*)
**hem** [hɛm] *n* rąbek *m*, brzeg *m* ▷ *vt* obrębiać (obrębić *perf*), obszywać (obszyć *perf*)
▶ **hem in** *vt* otaczać (otoczyć *perf*), okrążać (okrążyć *perf*); **to feel hemmed in** (*fig*) czuć się (poczuć się *perf*) osaczonym
**hematology** ['hi:mə'tɔlədʒɪ] (*US*) *n* = **haematology**
**hemisphere** ['hɛmɪsfɪə^r] *n* półkula *f*
**hemlock** ['hɛmlɔk] *n* cykuta *f*
**hemoglobin** ['hi:mə'gləubɪn] (*US*) *n* = **haemoglobin**
**hemophilia** ['hi:mə'fɪlɪə] (*US*) *n* = **haemophilia**
**hemorrhage** ['hɛmərɪdʒ] (*US*) *n* = **haemorrhage**
**hemorrhoids** ['hɛmərɔɪdz] (*US*) *npl* = **haemorrhoids**
**hemp** [hɛmp] *n* konopie *pl*
**hen** [hɛn] *n* (*female chicken*) kura *f*; (*female bird*) samica *f* (*ptaka*)
**hence** [hɛns] *adv* stąd, w związku z tym; **2 years ~** za 2 lata
**henceforth** [hɛns'fɔ:θ] *adv* odtąd
**henchman** ['hɛntʃmən] (*pej*) (*irreg: like* **man**) *n* poplecznik *m*
**henna** ['hɛnə] *n* henna *f*
**hen party** (*inf*) *n* babski wieczór *m* (*inf*)
**henpecked** ['hɛnpɛkt] *adj* (*husband*) pod pantoflem *post*
**hepatitis** [hɛpə'taɪtɪs] *n* zapalenie *nt* wątroby
**her** [hə:^r] *adj* jej ▷ *pron* (*direct*) ją; (*indirect*) jej; **not her again!** tylko nie ona!; **I saw her** widziałem ją; **give her a book** daj jej książkę; **after/with her** za/z nią; **about/to her** o/do niej; *see also* **my; me**
**herald** ['hɛrəld] *n* zwiastun *m* ▷ *vt* zwiastować
**heraldic** [hɛ'rældɪk] *adj* heraldyczny
**heraldry** ['hɛrəldrɪ] *n* heraldyka *f*
**herb** [hə:b] *n* ziele *nt*, zioło *nt*
**herbaceous** [hə:'beɪʃəs] *adj* zielny
**herbal** ['hə:bl] *adj* ziołowy; **~ tea** herbata ziołowa
**herbicide** ['hə:bɪsaɪd] *n* środek *m* chwastobójczy, herbicyd *m*
**herd** [hə:d] *n* stado *nt* ▷ *vt* spędzać (spędzić *perf*), zaganiać (zagonić *perf*); **~ed together** stłoczeni
**here** [hɪə^r] *adv* tu(taj); **she left ~ yesterday** wyjechała stąd wczoraj; **"~!"** „obecny(-na)!" *m(f)*; **~ is the news** oto wiadomości; **~ you are** proszę bardzo *or* uprzejmie; **~ we are!** (*finding*) o, tu(taj) (jest/są)!; **~ she is!** otóż i ona!; **~'s my sister** oto moja siostra; **~ she comes** właśnie nadchodzi; **come ~!** chodź tu(taj)!; **~ and t~** tu i tam; **"~'s to ..."** (*toast*) „za *+acc*"
**hereabouts** ['hɪərə'bauts] *adv* gdzieś tutaj, w okolicy *or* pobliżu
**hereafter** [hɪər'ɑ:ftə^r] *adv* odtąd ▷ *n* (*Rel*): **the ~** życie *nt* przyszłe
**hereby** [hɪə'baɪ] (*fml*) *adv* niniejszym
**hereditary** [hɪ'rɛdɪtrɪ] *adj* dziedziczny
**heredity** [hɪ'rɛdɪtɪ] *n* dziedziczność *f*
**heresy** ['hɛrəsɪ] *n* herezja *f*
**heretic** ['hɛrətɪk] *n* heretyk(-yczka) *m(f)*
**heretical** [hɪ'rɛtɪkl] *adj* (*unorthodox*) nieprawomyślny; (*Rel*) heretycki
**herewith** [hɪə'wɪð] (*fml*) *adv* (*in letter*) w załączeniu
**heritage** ['hɛrɪtɪdʒ] *n* dziedzictwo *nt*, spuścizna *f* ▷ *cpd*: **~ trail** szlak *m* historyczny; **our national ~** nasze narodowe dziedzictwo
**hermetically** [hə:'mɛtɪklɪ] *adv* hermetycznie
**hermit** ['hə:mɪt] *n* pustelnik(-ica) *m(f)*
**hernia** ['hə:nɪə] *n* przepuklina *f*
**hero** ['hɪərəu] (*pl* **~es**) *n* bohater *m*; (*idol*) idol *m*
**heroic** [hɪ'rəuɪk] *adj* bohaterski, heroiczny
**heroin** ['hɛrəuɪn] *n* heroina *f* (*narkotyk*)
**heroin addict** *n* uzależniony(-na) *m(f)* od heroiny
**heroine** ['hɛrəuɪn] *n* (*in book, film*) bohaterka *f*, heroina *f* (*literary*); (*of battle, struggle*) bohaterka *f*; (*idol*) idol *m*
**heroism** ['hɛrəuɪzəm] *n* bohaterstwo *nt*, heroizm *m*
**heron** ['hɛrən] *n* czapla *f*
**hero worship** *n* kult *m* idola
**herring** ['hɛrɪŋ] *n* śledź *m*
**hers** [hə:z] *pron* jej; **a friend of ~** (pewien) jej znajomy; **this is ~** to jest jej; *see also* **mine**
**herself** [hə:'sɛlf] *pron* (*reflexive*) się; (*after prep*) siebie (*gen, acc*), sobie (*dat, loc*), sobą (*instr*); (*after conj*) ona; (*emphatic*) sama; *see also* **oneself**
**Herts** [hɑ:ts] (*Brit: Post*) *abbr* = **Hertfordshire**
**he's** [hi:z] = **he is; he has**
**hesitant** ['hɛzɪtənt] *adj* (*smile*) niepewny; (*reaction*) niezdecydowany; **to be ~ about doing sth** nie móc się zdecydować na zrobienie czegoś
**hesitate** ['hɛzɪteɪt] *vi* wahać się (zawahać się *perf*); **don't ~ to ask** nie wahaj się pytać; **don't ~ to see a doctor if you are worried** nie zwlekaj z wizytą u lekarza, jeśli coś cię niepokoi
**hesitation** [hɛzɪ'teɪʃən] *n* wahanie *nt*; **I have no ~ in saying (that) ...** bez wahania mogę powiedzieć (, że) ...
**hessian** ['hɛsɪən] *n* juta *f* (*tkanina*)
**heterogenous** [hɛtə'rɔdʒɪnəs] *adj* niejednorodny, heterogeniczny

**heterosexual** ['hɛtərəu'sɛksjuəl] *adj* heteroseksualny ▷ *n* heteroseksualista(-tka) *m(f)*
**het up** [hɛt-] (*inf*) *adj*: **to get ~ (about)** przejmować się (przejąć się *perf*) (*+instr*)
**HEW** (*US*) *n abbr* (= *Department of Health, Education and Welfare*) Ministerstwo *nt* Zdrowia, Edukacji i Opieki Społecznej
**hew** [hju:] (*pp* **hewed** *or* **hewn**) *vt* rąbać (porąbać *perf*), ciosać
**hex** [hɛks] (*US*) *n* (zły) urok *m or* czar *m* ▷ *vt* rzucać (rzucić *perf*) urok na *+acc*
**hexagon** ['hɛksəgən] *n* sześciokąt *m*
**hexagonal** [hɛk'sægənl] *adj* sześciokątny
**hey** [heɪ] *excl* hej
**heyday** ['heɪdeɪ] *n*: **the ~ of** okres *m* rozkwitu *+gen*
**HF** *n abbr* (= *high frequency*) w. cz. (= *wysoka częstotliwość*)
**HGV** (*Brit*) *n abbr* (= *heavy goods vehicle*) samochód *m* ciężarowy
**HI** (*US: Post*) *abbr* = **Hawaii**
**hi** [haɪ] *excl* (*as greeting*) cześć, witam; (*to attract attention*) hej
**hiatus** [haɪ'eɪtəs] *n* przerwa *f*; (*Ling*) rozziew *m*
**hibernate** ['haɪbəneɪt] *vi* (*animal*) zapadać (zapaść *perf*) w sen zimowy
**hibernation** [haɪbə'neɪʃən] *n* hibernacja *f*, sen *m* zimowy
**hiccough** ['hɪkʌp] *vi* mieć czkawkę, czkać (czknąć *perf*) ▷ *n* (*fig*) (drobna) przeszkoda *f*
**hiccoughs** ['hɪkʌps] *npl* czkawka *f*; **to have (the) ~** mieć czkawkę
**hiccup** ['hɪkʌp] *vi* = **hiccough**
**hiccups** ['hɪkʌps] *npl* = **hiccoughs**
**hid** [hɪd] *pt of* **hide**
**hidden** ['hɪdn] *pp of* **hide** ▷ *adj*: **there are no ~ extras** nie ma żadnych ukrytych kosztów dodatkowych; **~ agenda** ukryte motywy
**hide** [haɪd] (*pt* **hid**, *pp* **hidden**) *n* skóra *f* (*zwierzęca*); (*of birdwatcher etc*) stanowisko *nt* (obserwacyjne) ▷ *vt* (*object, person*) ukrywać (ukryć *perf*), chować (schować *perf*); (*feeling*) ukrywać (ukryć *perf*), skrywać; (*sun, view*) zasłaniać (zasłonić *perf*) ▷ *vi*: **to ~ (from sb)** ukrywać się (ukryć się *perf*) *or* chować się (schować się *perf*) (przed kimś); **to ~ sth (from sb)** ukrywać (ukryć *perf*) coś (przed kimś)
**hide-and-seek** ['haɪdən'si:k] *n* zabawa *f* w chowanego
**hideaway** ['haɪdəweɪ] *n* kryjówka *f*
**hideous** ['hɪdɪəs] *adj* (*painting, face*) ohydny, szkaradny; (*conditions*) okropny; (*mistake*) paskudny
**hideously** ['hɪdɪəslɪ] *adv* (*ugly*) ohydnie, szkaradnie; (*difficult*) okropnie, paskudnie
**hideout** ['haɪdaut] *n* kryjówka *f*
**hiding** ['haɪdɪŋ] *n* (*beating*) lanie *nt*; (*seclusion*): **to be in ~** pozostawać w ukryciu, ukrywać się
**hiding place** *n* (*for person*) kryjówka *f*; (*for money etc*) schowek *m*
**hierarchy** ['haɪərɑ:kɪ] *n* (*system*) hierarchia *f*; (*people*) władze *pl*
**hieroglyphic** [haɪərə'glɪfɪk] *adj* hieroglificzny
**hieroglyphics** [haɪərə'glɪfɪks] *npl* hieroglify *pl*
**hi-fi** ['haɪfaɪ] *n abbr* (= *high fidelity*) hi-fi ▷ *n* zestaw *m* hi-fi ▷ *cpd*: **~ equipment/system** sprzęt *m*/system *m* hi-fi
**higgledy-piggledy** ['hɪgldɪ'pɪgldɪ] *adj* w nieładzie *post* ▷ *adv* bezładnie
**high** [haɪ] *adj* wysoki; (*speed*) duży; (*wind*) silny; (*inf: on drugs*) na haju *post* (*inf*); (*: on drink*) pod gazem *post* (*inf*); (*Culin: meat, game*) skruszały; (*: cheese etc*) zbyt dojrzały, nadpsuty ▷ *adv* wysoko ▷ *n*: **exports have reached a new ~** eksport osiągnął nie notowany dotąd poziom; **it is 20 m ~** ma 20 metrów wysokości; **~ in the air** wysoko w powietrzu; **to pay a ~ price for sth** płacić (zapłacić *perf*) za coś wysoką cenę; **it's ~ time you learned how to do it** najwyższy czas, żebyś nauczył się to robić
**highball** ['haɪbɔ:l] (*US*) *n* whisky *f inv* z wodą (*w wysokiej szklance*)
**highboy** ['haɪbɔɪ] (*US*) *n* (wysoka) komoda *f* (*na nóżkach*)
**highbrow** ['haɪbrau] *n* intelektualista(-tka) *m(f)* ▷ *adj* intelektualny; (*pej*) przeintelektualizowany (*pej*)
**high chair** *n* wysokie krzesełko *nt* (*do sadzania dziecka podczas posiłków*)
**high-class** ['haɪ'klɑ:s] *adj* ekskluzywny
**High Court** *n*: **the ~** Wysoki Trybunał *m*
**higher** ['haɪə^r] *adj* wyższy ▷ *adv* wyżej
**higher education** *n* wyższe wykształcenie *nt*
**high finance** *n* wielka finansjera *f*
**high-flier** [haɪ'flaɪə^r] *n*: **to be a ~** wysoko mierzyć
**high-flying** [haɪ'flaɪɪŋ] *adj* mierzący wysoko
**high-handed** [haɪ'hændɪd] *adj* władczy
**high-heeled** [haɪ'hi:ld] *adj* na wysokim obcasie *post*
**high heels** *npl* buty *pl* na wysokim obcasie
**high jump** *n* skok *m* wzwyż; **you'll be for the ~** (*fig*) dostaniesz za swoje
**Highlands** ['haɪləndz] *npl*: **the ~** *pogórze w północnej Szkocji*
**high-level** ['haɪlɛvl] *adj* (*talks etc*) na wysokim szczeblu *post*; **~ language** (*Comput*) język wysokiego poziomu

h

**highlight** ['haılaıt] *n* (*fig*) główna atrakcja *f* ▷ *vt* (*problem, need*) zwracać (zwrócić *perf*) uwagę na *+acc*; (*piece of text*) zakreślać (zakreślić *perf*); **highlights** *npl* (*in hair*) pasemka *pl*
**highlighter** ['haılaıtəʳ] *n* marker *m*, zakreślacz *m*
**highly** ['haılı] *adv* (*placed, skilled*) wysoko; (*improbable, complex*) wysoce, wielce; (*paid*) bardzo dobrze; (*critical*) bardzo; (*confidential*) ściśle; **to speak ~ of** wyrażać się (bardzo) pochlebnie o *+loc*; **to think ~ of** mieć wysokie mniemanie o *+loc*
**highly strung** *adj* nerwowy
**High Mass** *n* suma *f*
**highness** ['haınıs] *n*: **Her/His H~** Jego/Jej Wysokość
**high-pitched** [haı'pıtʃt] *adj* (*tone*) wysoki; (*voice*) cienki
**high-powered** ['haı'pauəd] *adj* (*rifle*) o dużym zasięgu *post*; (*microscope*) (o) dużej mocy *post*; (*fig: course*) zaawansowany; (*: businessman, advertising*) dynamiczny
**high-pressure** ['haıprɛʃəʳ] *adj* pod wysokim ciśnieniem *post*
**high-rise** ['haıraız] *adj* (*building*) wielopiętrowy; (*flats*) w wieżowcu *post* ▷ *n* wieżowiec *m*, wysokościowiec *m*
**high school** *n* ≈ szkoła *f* średnia
**high season** (*Brit*) *n*: **the ~** szczyt *m* *or* środek *m* sezonu
**high spirits** *npl* świetny *or* doskonały humor *m*; **to be in ~** być w świetnym *or* doskonałym humorze
**high street** (*Brit*) *n* główna ulica *f*
**high tide** *n* przypływ *m*
**highway** ['haıweı] *n* (*US*) autostrada *f*; (*public road*) szosa *f*
**Highway Code** (*Brit*) *n*: **the ~** kodeks *m* drogowy
**highwayman** ['haıweımən] (*irreg: like* **man**) *n* rozbójnik *m*
**hijack** ['haıdʒæk] *vt* (*plane etc*) porywać (porwać *perf*) ▷ *n* (*also:* **hijacking**) porwanie *nt*
**hijacker** ['haıdʒækəʳ] *n* porywacz(ka) *m(f)*
**hike** [haık] *vi* wędrować (pieszo) ▷ *n* piesza wycieczka *f*; (*inf: in prices*) podwyżka *f*
▸ **hike up** *vt* (*inf: trousers etc*) podciągać (podciągnąć *perf*)
**hiker** ['haıkəʳ] *n* turysta(-tka) *m(f)* pieszy(-sza) *m(f)*
**hiking** ['haıkıŋ] *n* wycieczki *pl* piesze
**hilarious** [hı'lɛərıəs] *adj* komiczny
**hilarity** [hı'lærıtı] *n* wesołość *f*
**hill** [hıl] *n* (*small*) pagórek *m*, wzniesienie *nt*; (*fairly high*) wzgórze *nt*; **up/down the ~** pod górę/z góry
**hillbilly** ['hılbılı] (*US: pej*) *n niewykształcony farmer z południowo-wschodnich Stanów*
**hillock** ['hılək] *n* górka *f*
**hillside** ['hılsaıd] *n* stok *m*
**hill start** (*Aut*) *n* start *m* pod górkę
**hilltop** ['hıltɔp] *n* szczyt *m*
**hilly** ['hılı] *adj* pagórkowaty
**hilt** [hılt] *n* rękojeść *f*; **to back sb to the ~** (*fig*) dawać (dać *perf*) komuś pełne poparcie
**him** [hım] *pron* (*direct*) (je)go; (*indirect*) (je)mu; (*after prep*) niego (*gen*), nim (*instr, loc*); (*after conj*) on; **not him!** (tylko) nie on!; *see also* **me**
**Himalayas** [hımə'leıəz] *npl*: **the ~** Himalaje *pl*
**himself** [hım'sɛlf] *pron* (*reflexive*) się; (*after prep*) siebie (*gen, acc*), sobie (*dat, loc*), sobą (*instr*); (*after conj*) on; (*emphatic*) sam; **it was easy for a man like ~ to...** człowiekowi takiemu jak on łatwo było *+infin*; *see also* **oneself**
**hind** [haınd] *adj* tylny, zadni ▷ *n* łania *f*
**hinder** ['hındəʳ] *vt* utrudniać; **to ~ sb from doing sth** przeszkadzać (przeszkodzić *perf*) komuś coś robić
**hindquarters** ['haınd'kwɔːtəz] *npl* zad *m*
**hindrance** ['hındrəns] *n* przeszkoda *f*
**hindsight** ['haındsaıt] *n*: **with ~** po fakcie
**Hindu** ['hınduː] *adj* hinduski
**hinge** [hındʒ] *n* zawias *m* ▷ *vi*: **to ~ on** (*fig*) zależeć (całkowicie) od *+gen*
**hint** [hınt] *n* (*indirect suggestion*) aluzja *f*; (*advice*) wskazówka *f*; (*sign, glimmer*) cień *m*, ślad *m* ▷ *vt*: **to ~ that ...** sugerować (zasugerować *perf*), że ... ▷ *vi*: **to ~ at** dawać (dać *perf*) do zrozumienia *+acc*; **to drop a ~** napomykać (napomknąć *perf*), robić (zrobić *perf*) aluzję; **give me a ~** naprowadź mnie; **white with a ~ of pink** biały z odcieniem różu
**hip** [hıp] *n* biodro *nt*
**hip flask** *n* piersiówka *f*
**hippie** ['hıpı] *n* hipis(ka) *m(f)*
**hippo** ['hıpəu] *n* hipopotam *m*
**hip pocket** *n* tylna kieszeń *f* (spodni)
**hippopotamus** [hıpə'pɔtəməs] (*pl* **~es** *or* **hippopotami**) *n* hipopotam *m*
**hippy** ['hıpı] *n* = **hippie**
**hire** ['haıəʳ] *vt* (*Brit: car, equipment, hall*) wynajmować (wynająć *perf*) (*od kogoś*); (*worker*) najmować (nająć *perf*) ▷ *n* (*Brit*) wynajęcie *nt*; **for ~** (*boat etc*) do wynajęcia; (*taxi*) wolny; **on ~** wynajęty
▸ **hire out** *vt* wynajmować (wynająć *perf*) (*komuś*)
**hire(d) car** (*Brit*) *n* wynajmowany samochód *m*
**hire purchase** (*Brit*) *n* sprzedaż *f* ratalna; **to buy sth on ~** kupować (kupić *perf*) coś na raty
**his** [hız] *pron* jego ▷ *adj* jego; **he sold his house** sprzedał (swój) dom; *see also* **my**; **mine**

**hiss** [hɪs] *vi* (*snake, gas, fat*) syczeć (zasyczeć *perf*); (*person*) syczeć (syknąć *perf*); (*audience*) syczeć ▷ *n* syk *m*, syczenie *nt*

**histogram** ['hɪstəgræm] *n* histogram *m*

**historian** [hɪ'stɔːrɪən] *n* historyk(-yczka) *m(f)*

**historic** [hɪ'stɔrɪk] *adj* historyczny, wiekopomny

**historic(al)** [hɪ'stɔrɪk(əl)] *adj* (*person, novel*) historyczny

**history** ['hɪstərɪ] *n* historia *f*; **medical ~** wywiad chorobowy; **there's a long ~ of asthma in his family** wiele osób w jego rodzinie chorowało na astmę

**hit** [hɪt] (*pt, pp* **hit**) *vt* (*strike*) uderzać (uderzyć *perf*); (*reach*) trafiać (trafić *perf*) w *+acc*; (*collide with, affect*) uderzać (uderzyć *perf*) w *+acc* ▷ *n* (*knock, blow*) uderzenie *nt*; (*shot*) trafienie *nt*; (*play, film, song*) hit *m*, przebój *m*; **to hit it off with sb** zaprzyjaźnić się (*perf*) kimś; **to hit the headlines** trafiać (trafić *perf*) na pierwsze strony gazet; **to hit the road** (*inf*) (wy)ruszyć (*perf*) w drogę; **to hit the roof** (*inf*) wściec się (*perf*) (*inf*); **to give sb a hit on the head** uderzyć (*perf*) kogoś w głowę
▸ **hit back** *vi*: **to hit back (at sb)** oddawać (oddać *perf*) (komuś) cios *or* uderzenie, oddawać (oddać *perf*) (komuś) (*inf*)
▸ **hit out at** *vt fus* walić (walnąć *perf*) na oślep w *+acc*; (*fig*) (ostro) atakować (zaatakować *perf*)
▸ **hit (up)on** *vt fus* (*answer, solution*) wpadać (wpaść *perf*) na *+acc*

**hit-and-run driver** ['hɪtən'rʌn-] *n* kierowca *m* zbiegły z miejsca wypadku

**hitch** [hɪtʃ] *vt* (*fasten*) przyczepiać (przyczepić *perf*); (*also*: **hitch up**: *trousers, skirt*) podciągać (podciągnąć *perf*) ▷ *n* komplikacja *f*; **to ~ a lift** łapać (złapać *perf*) okazję (*inf*); **a technical ~** problem natury technicznej
▸ **hitch up** *vt* zaprzęgać (zaprząc *perf or* zaprzęgnąć *perf*); *see also* **hitch**

**hitch-hike** ['hɪtʃhaɪk] *vi* (*travel around*) jeździć *or* podróżować autostopem; (*to a place*) jechać (pojechać *perf*) autostopem

**hitch-hiker** ['hɪtʃhaɪkə^r] *n* autostopowicz(ka) *m(f)*

**hi-tech** ['haɪ'tɛk] *adj* supernowoczesny

**hitherto** [hɪðə'tuː] *adv* dotychczas

**hitman** ['hɪtmæn] (*irreg*: *like* **man**) *n* płatny morderca *m*

**hit-or-miss** ['hɪtə'mɪs] *adj* na oślep *post*, na chybił trafił *post*; **it's ~ whether ...** trudno przewidzieć, czy ...

**hit parade** (*old*) *n* lista *f* przebojów

**HIV** *n abbr* (= *human immunodeficiency virus*) (wirus *m*) HIV; **HIV-negative** nie zarażony wirusem HIV; **HIV-positive** zarażony wirusem HIV

**hive** [haɪv] *n* ul *m*; (*fig*) dynamiczny *or* prężny ośrodek *m*
▸ **hive off** (*inf*) *vt* przesuwać (przesunąć *perf*) (*zwłaszcza do sektora prywatnego*)

**hl** *abbr* (= *hectolitre*) hl

**HM** *abbr* (= *His (or Her) Majesty*) JKM

**HMG** (*Brit*) *abbr* (= *His (or Her) Majesty's Government*) Rząd *m* Jego (*or* Jej) Królewskiej Mości

**HMI** (*Brit*: *Scol*) *n abbr* (= *His (or Her) Majesty's Inspector*) rządowy wizytator *m* szkolny

**HMO** (*US*) *n abbr* = **health maintenance organization**

**HMS** (*Brit*) *abbr* (= *His (or Her) Majesty's Ship*) *skrót stanowiący część nazwy brytyjskich okrętów wojennych*

**HMSO** (*Brit*) *n abbr* (= *His (or Her) Majesty's Stationery Office*) *drukarnia rządowa*

**HNC** (*Brit*) *n abbr* (= *Higher National Certificate*) *rodzaj uprawnień zawodowych*

**HND** (*Brit*) *n abbr* (= *Higher National Diploma*) *rodzaj uprawnień zawodowych*

**hoard** [hɔːd] *n* zapasy *pl*, zasoby *pl* ▷ *vt* gromadzić (zgromadzić *perf*)

**hoarding** ['hɔːdɪŋ] (*Brit*) *n* billboard *m*

**hoarfrost** ['hɔːfrɔst] *n* szron *m*

**hoarse** [hɔːs] *adj* zachrypły, ochrypły

**hoax** [həuks] *n* (głupi) żart *m or* kawał *m* (*zwykle w celu wywołania fałszywego alarmu*)

**hob** [hɔb] *n* płyta *f* grzejna (*kuchenki*)

**hobble** ['hɔbl] *vi* kuśtykać

**hobby** ['hɔbɪ] *n* hobby *nt inv*

**hobby-horse** ['hɔbɪhɔːs] *n* (*fig*) konik *m*

**hobnob** ['hɔbnɔb] *vt*: **to ~ with** zadawać się z *+instr*

**hobo** ['həubəu] (*US*) *n* włóczęga *m*

**hock** [hɔk] *n* (*Brit*: *drink*) (wino *nt*) reńskie; (*of horse*) staw *m* skokowy; (*Culin*) golonka *f*; (*inf*): **in ~** (*person*) zadłużony; (*object*) zastawiony, oddany w zastaw

**hockey** ['hɔkɪ] *n* hokej *m*

**hocus-pocus** ['həukəs'pəukəs] *n* (*trickery*) sztuczki *pl*; (*of magician*) czary-mary *pl*, hokus-pokus *nt inv*; (*jargon*) bełkot *m*

**hodgepodge** ['hɔdʒpɔdʒ] (*US*) *n* = **hotchpotch**

**hoe** [həu] *n* motyka *f* ▷ *vt* okopywać (okopać *perf*)

**hog** [hɔg] *n* wieprz *m* ▷ *vt* (*fig*: *telephone, bathroom*) okupować; **to hog the road** blokować jezdnię; **to go the whole hog** iść (pójść *perf*) na całego

**hoist** [hɔɪst] *n* dźwig *m*, wyciąg *m* ▷ *vt* (*heavy object*) podnosić (podnieść *perf*); (*flag, sail*) wciągać (wciągnąć *perf*) (na maszt); **he ~ed the rope over the branch** przerzucił linę nad gałęzią

**hold** [həuld] (*pt, pp* **held**) *vt* (*in hand*) trzymać; (*contain*) mieścić (pomieścić *perf*);

(*qualifications*) posiadać; (*power, permit, opinion*) mieć; (*meeting, conversation*) odbywać (odbyć *perf*); (*prisoner, hostage*) przetrzymywać (przetrzymać *perf*) ▷ *vi* (*glue etc*) trzymać (mocno); (*argument etc*) zachowywać (zachować *perf*) ważność, pozostawać w mocy; (*offer, invitation*) być aktualnym; (*luck, weather*) utrzymywać się (utrzymać się *perf*); (*Tel*) czekać (zaczekać *perf*) ▷ *n* (*grasp*) chwyt *m*; (*of ship, plane*) ładownia *f*; **to ~ sb responsible/liable** obarczać (obarczyć *perf*) kogoś odpowiedzialnością; **to ~ one's head up** trzymać *or* nosić głowę wysoko; **to have a ~ over sb** trzymać kogoś w garści; **to get ~ of** (*fig: object, information*) zdobywać (zdobyć *perf*) *+acc*; (*person*) łapać (złapać *perf*) *+acc* (*inf*); **to get ~ of o.s.** brać (wziąć *perf*) się w garść; **~ the line!** proszę nie odkładać słuchawki!; **to ~ one's own** (*fig*) nie poddawać się; **to catch** *or* **get (a) ~ of** chwycić się (*perf*) *+gen*, złapać (*perf*) za *+acc* (*inf*); **to ~ firm** *or* **fast** trzymać się mocno; **he ~s the view that ...** jest zdania, że ...; **I don't ~ with ...** nie popieram *+gen*; **~ it!** zaczekaj!; **~ still, ~ steady** nie ruszaj się

▸ **hold back** *vt* (*person, thing*) powstrzymywać (powstrzymać *perf*); (*information*) zatajać (zataić *perf*)

▸ **hold down** *vt* (*person*) przytrzymywać (przytrzymać *perf*); (*job*) utrzymywać (utrzymać *perf*)

▸ **hold forth** *vi* rozwodzić się (*na jakiś temat*)

▸ **hold off** *vt* (*enemy*) powstrzymywać (powstrzymać *perf*); (*decision*) wstrzymywać się (wstrzymać się *perf*) z *+instr* ▷ *vi*: **if the rain ~s off** jeżeli nie zacznie padać

▸ **hold on** *vi* (*hang on*) przytrzymywać się (przytrzymać się *perf*); (*wait*) czekać (poczekać *perf or* zaczekać *perf*)

▸ **hold on to** *vt fus* (*for support*) przytrzymywać się (przytrzymać się *perf*) *+gen*; (*keep: for o.s.*) nie oddawać (nie oddać *perf*) *+gen*; (*: for sb*) przechowywać (przechować *perf*) *+acc*

▸ **hold out** *vt* (*hand*) wyciągać (wyciągnąć *perf*); (*hope*) dawać (dać *perf*) ▷ *vi*: **to ~ out for** domagać się *or* żądać *+gen*

▸ **hold over** *vt* (*meeting etc*) odkładać (odłożyć *perf*), odraczać (odroczyć *perf*)

▸ **hold up** *vt* (*raise*) unosić (unieść *perf*); (*support*) podtrzymywać (podtrzymać *perf*), podpierać (podeprzeć *perf*); (*delay*) zatrzymywać (zatrzymać *perf*); (*bank etc*) napadać (napaść *perf*) na *+acc* (*przy użyciu broni palnej*)

**holdall** ['həuldɔːl] (*Brit*) *n* (duża) torba *f* podróżna

**holder** ['həuldəʳ] *n* (*of lamp etc*) uchwyt *m*; (*person*) posiadacz *m*

**holding** ['həuldɪŋ] *n* (*share*) udziały *pl*; (*small farm*) gospodarstwo *nt* rolne ▷ *adj* (*operation, tactic*) mający na celu utrzymanie istniejącego stanu rzeczy

**holding company** *n* towarzystwo *nt* holdingowe, holding *m*

**hold-up** ['həuldʌp] *n* (*robbery*) napad *m* rabunkowy; (*delay*) komplikacje *pl*; (*Brit: in traffic*) zator *m* (drogowy), korek *m* (uliczny)

**hole** [həul] *n* (*lit, fig*) dziura *f* ▷ *vt* (*make holes*) dziurawić (podziurawić *perf*); (*make a hole*) dziurawić (przedziurawić *perf*); **~ in the heart** (*Med*) ubytek w przegrodzie; **to pick ~s in** (*fig*) wyszukiwać słabe punkty w *+loc*

▸ **hole up** *vi* zaszywać się (zaszyć się *perf*)

**holiday** ['hɔlɪdeɪ] *n* (*Brit: vacation*) wakacje *pl*; (*leave*) urlop *m*; (*public holiday*) święto *nt*; **to be/go on ~** być na wakacjach/wyjeżdżać (wyjechać *perf*) na wakacje; **tomorrow is a ~** jutro jest święto

**holiday camp** (*Brit*) *n* ośrodek *m* wypoczynkowy *or* wczasowy

**holidaymaker** ['hɔlɪdeɪmeɪkəʳ] (*Brit*) *n* wczasowicz(ka) *m(f)*

**holiday pay** *n* wynagrodzenie *nt* w okresie urlopu

**holiday resort** *n* miejscowość *f* wypoczynkowa *or* wczasowa

**holiday season** *n* sezon *m* wakacyjny

**holiness** ['həulɪnɪs] *n* świętość *f*; **His H~** Jego Świątobliwość

**Holland** ['hɔlənd] *n* Holandia *f*

**hollow** ['hɔləu] *adj* (*container, log, tree*) pusty, wydrążony; (*cheeks, eyes*) zapadnięty; (*claim, promise, laugh*) pusty; (*sound*) głuchy; (*doctrine, opinion*) płytki ▷ *n* wgłębienie *nt*, zagłębienie *nt* ▷ *vt*: **to ~ out** wydrążać (wydrążyć *perf*)

**holly** ['hɔlɪ] *n* (*Bot*) ostrokrzew *m*

**hollyhock** ['hɔlɪhɔk] *n* malwa *f*

**holocaust** ['hɔləkɔːst] *n* zagłada *f*; **the H~** Holocaust

**hologram** ['hɔləgræm] *n* hologram *m*

**holster** ['həulstəʳ] *n* kabura *f*

**holy** ['həulɪ] *adj* (*picture, place*) święty; (*water*) święcony; (*person*) świątobliwy

**Holy Communion** *n* Komunia *f* Święta

**Holy Father** *n* Ojciec *m* Święty

**Holy Ghost** *n* Duch *m* Święty

**Holy Land** *n*: **the ~** Ziemia *f* Święta

**holy orders** *npl* święcenia *pl*

**Holy Spirit** *n* = **Holy Ghost**

**homage** ['hɔmɪdʒ] *n* hołd *m*, cześć *f*; **to pay ~ to** składać (złożyć *perf*) hołd *or* oddawać (oddać *perf*) cześć *+dat*

**home** [həum] *n* dom *m* ▷ *cpd* (*employment*) chałupniczy; (*Econ, Pol*) wewnętrzny, krajowy; (*Sport: team*) miejscowy;

(: *game, win*) na własnym boisku *post*, u siebie *post* ▷ *adv* (*be*) w domu; (*go, travel*) do domu; (*press, push*) do środka, na swoje miejsce; **at ~** (*in house*) w domu; (*in country*) w kraju; (*comfortable*) swojsko, jak u siebie; **make yourself at ~** czuj się jak u siebie (w domu); **to make one's ~ somewhere** zamieszkać (*perf*) gdzieś; **the ~ of free enterprise/jazz** kolebka wolnej przedsiębiorczości/jazzu; **we're ~ and dry** udało (nam) się; **a ~ from ~** drugi dom; **to bring sth ~ to sb** uświadamiać (uświadomić *perf*) coś komuś
▶ **home in on** *vt fus* namierzać (namierzyć *perf*) +*acc*

**home address** *n* adres *m* domowy
**home-brew** [həum'bru:] *n* piwo *nt* domowej roboty, podpiwek *m*
**homecoming** ['həumkʌmɪŋ] *n* powrót *m* do domu; (*Scol, Univ*) zjazd *m* absolwentów
**home computer** *n* komputer *m* domowy
**Home Counties** (*Brit*) *npl*: **the ~** *hrabstwa położone wokół Londynu*
**home economics** *n* (*Scol*) *zajęcia z gospodarstwa domowego*
**home-grown** ['həumgrəun] *adj* (*not foreign*) hodowany w kraju, krajowy; (*from garden*) z własnego ogródka *post*
**homeland** ['həumlænd] *n* ziemia *f* ojczysta *or* rodzinna
**homeless** ['həumlɪs] *adj* bezdomny
**home loan** *n* ≈ kredyt *m* mieszkaniowy
**homely** ['həumlɪ] *adj* prosty, skromny
**home-made** [həum'meɪd] *adj* (*bread*) domowej roboty *post*; (*bomb*) wykonany domowym sposobem
**homemaker** ['həum'meɪkə^r] (*US*) *n* gospodyni *f* domowa
**Home Office** (*Brit*) *n*: **the ~** ≈ Ministerstwo *nt* Spraw Wewnętrznych
**homeopathy** [həumɪ'ɔpəθɪ] (*US*) *n* = **homoeopathy**
**home page** (*Comput*) *n* strona *f* główna
**home rule** *n* (*Pol*) samorządność *f*
**Home Secretary** (*Brit*) *n*: **the ~** ≈ Minister *m* Spraw Wewnętrznych
**homesick** ['həumsɪk] *adj*: **to be** *or* **feel ~** tęsknić za domem
**homestead** ['həumstɛd] *n* gospodarstwo *nt* rolne
**home town** *n* miasto *nt* rodzinne
**homeward** ['həumwəd] *adj*: **~ journey** droga *f* powrotna *or* do domu
**homeward(s)** ['həumwəd(z)] *adv* do domu
**homework** ['həumwə:k] *n* zadanie *nt* domowe, praca *f* domowa; **he never did any ~** nigdy nie odrabiał zadań domowych
**homicidal** [hɔmɪ'saɪdl] *adj* (*maniac*) niebezpieczny dla otoczenia; (*instincts*) morderczy
**homicide** ['hɔmɪsaɪd] (*US*) *n* zabójstwo *nt*
**homily** ['hɔmɪlɪ] *n* kazanie *nt*
**homing** ['həumɪŋ] *adj* (*device*) (samo) naprowadzający; (*missile*) samosterujący; (*pigeon*) pocztowy
**homoeopath**, (*US*) **homeopath** ['həumɪəupæθ] *n* homeopata(-tka) *m(f)*
**homoeopathy**, (*US*) **homeopathy** [həumɪ'ɔpəθɪ] *n* homeopatia *f*
**homogeneous** [hɔməu'dʒi:nɪəs] *adj* jednorodny, homogeniczny
**homogenized** [hə'mɔdʒənaɪzd] *adj*: **~ milk** mleko *nt* homogenizowane
**homophobia** [həumɔə'fəubɪə] *n* homofobia *f*
**homosexual** [hɔməu'sɛksjuəl] *adj* homoseksualny ▷ *n* homoseksualista(-tka) *m(f)*; **to be ~** być homoseksualistą
**Hon.** *abbr* = **honourable; honorary**
**Honduras** [hɔn'djuərəs] *n* Honduras *m*
**hone** [həun] *vt* ostrzyć (zaostrzyć *perf*)
**honest** ['ɔnɪst] *adj* (*truthful, trustworthy*) uczciwy; (*sincere*) szczery; **to be quite ~ with you ...** jeśli mam być z tobą zupełnie szczery, ...
**honestly** ['ɔnɪstlɪ] *adv* (*truthfully*) uczciwie; (*sincerely*) szczerze
**honesty** ['ɔnɪstɪ] *n* (*truthfulness*) uczciwość *f*; (*sincerity*) szczerość *f*
**honey** ['hʌnɪ] *n* miód *m*; (*US*: *inf*: *form of address*) kochanie *nt*
**honeycomb** ['hʌnɪkəum] *n* plaster *m* miodu ▷ *vt* (*fig*): **~ed with** (*passages etc*) poprzecinany +*instr*; (*holes etc*) usiany +*instr*
**honeymoon** ['hʌnɪmu:n] *n* (*trip*) podróż *f* poślubna; (*period*) miodowy miesiąc *m*
**honeysuckle** ['hʌnɪsʌkl] *n* kapryfolium *nt*, przewiercień *m*
**Hong Kong** ['hɔŋ'kɔŋ] *n* Hongkong *m*
**honk** [hɔŋk] *vi* (*Aut*) trąbić (zatrąbić *perf*) ▷ *vt*: **to ~ the horn** trąbić (zatrąbić *perf*), dawać (dać *perf*) znak klaksonem
**Honolulu** [hɔnə'lu:lu:] *n* Honolulu *nt inv*
**honor** ['ɔnə^r] (*US*) *vt, n* = **honour**
**honorary** ['ɔnərərɪ] *adj* (*job, title*) honorowy
**honour**, (*US*) **honor** ['ɔnə^r] *vt* (*person*) uhonorować (*perf*); (*commitment, agreement*) honorować; (*promise*) dotrzymywać (dotrzymać *perf*) +*gen* ▷ *n* (*pride, self-respect*) honor *m*; (*tribute*) zaszczyt *m*; **in ~ of** na cześć +*gen*
**hono(u)rable** ['ɔnərəbl] *adj* (*person, action*) honorowy
**hono(u)r-bound** ['ɔnə'baund] *adj*: **to be ~ to** czuć się moralnie zobowiązanym do +*gen*

**hono(u)rs degree** *n* ≈ dyplom *m* z wyróżnieniem
**Hons.** *(Univ) abbr* = **hono(u)rs degree**
**hood** [hud] *n (of coat)* kaptur *m*; *(of cooker)* pokrywa *f*; *(Aut: Brit)* składany dach *m*; *(: US)* maska *f*
**hooded** ['hudɪd] *adj (robber)* zakapturzony; *(jacket)* z kapturem *post*
**hoodlum** ['hu:dləm] *n* bandzior *m (inf)*
**hoodwink** ['hudwɪŋk] *vt* nabierać (nabrać *perf)*
**hoof** [hu:f] *(pl* **hooves***) n* kopyto *nt*
**hook** [huk] *n (for coats, curtains)* hak *m*; *(for fishing)* haczyk *m*; *(on dress)* haftka *f (jej haczykowata część)* ▷ *vt (fasten)* przyczepiać (przyczepić *perf)*; *(fish)* łapać (złapać *perf)* (na haczyk); **by ~ or by crook** nie przebierając w środkach; **to be ~ed on** *(inf: addicted)* być uzależnionym od *+gen*; *(attracted)* przepadać za *+instr*
▶ **hook up** *vt (Radio, TV etc)* podłączać (podłączyć *perf)*
**hook and eye** *(pl* **hooks and eyes***) n* haftka *f*
**hooligan** ['hu:lɪgən] *n* chuligan *m*
**hooliganism** ['hu:lɪgənɪzəm] *n* chuligaństwo *nt*
**hoop** [hu:p] *n* obręcz *f*; *(Croquet) jeden z metalowych łuków, przez które przeprowadza się piłkę w grze w krokieta*
**hooray** [hu:'reɪ] *excl* = **hurrah**
**hoot** [hu:t] *vi (Aut)* trąbić (zatrąbić *perf)*; *(siren)* wyć (zawyć *perf)*; *(owl)* hukać (zahukać *perf)*; *(jeer)* wyć (zawyć *perf)* ▷ *vt (Aut)* trąbić (zatrąbić *perf) +instr* ▷ *n (Aut)* trąbienie *nt*, klakson *m*; *(of owl)* hukanie *nt*; **to ~ with laughter** zanosić się od śmiechu; **to give a ~ of laughter** parsknąć *(perf)* śmiechem
**hooter** ['hu:təʳ] *n (Aut)* klakson *m*; *(Naut, Industry)* syrena *f*
**hoover**® ['hu:vəʳ] *(Brit) n* odkurzacz *m* ▷ *vt* odkurzać (odkurzyć *perf)*
**hooves** [hu:vz] *npl of* **hoof**
**hop** [hɔp] *vi (person)* podskakiwać *or* skakać na jednej nodze; *(bird)* skakać, podskakiwać ▷ *n (of person)* podskok *m* (na jednej nodze); *(of animal)* skok *m*
**hope** [həup] *n* nadzieja *f* ▷ *vi* mieć nadzieję ▷ *vt:* **to ~ that ...** mieć nadzieję, że ...; **to ~ to do sth** mieć nadzieję, że się coś zrobi; **I ~ so/not** mam nadzieję, że tak/nie; **to ~ for the best** być dobrej myśli; **to have no ~ of sth/doing sth** nie liczyć na coś/zrobienie czegoś; **in the ~ that/of** w nadziei, że/na *+acc*
**hopeful** ['həupful] *adj (person)* pełen nadziei; *(situation)* napawający nadzieją, rokujący nadzieje; **I'm ~ that...** żywię nadzieję, że ...
**hopefully** ['həupfulɪ] *adv (expectantly)* z nadzieją; *(one hopes)* o ile szczęście dopisze; **~, he'll come back** miejmy nadzieję, że wróci
**hopeless** ['həuplɪs] *adj (desperate: situation)* beznadziejny; *(: person)* zrozpaczony; *(: grief)* rozpaczliwy; *(useless)* beznadziejny
**hopper** ['hɔpəʳ] *n* zsypnia *f*
**hops** [hɔps] *npl* chmiel *m*
**horde** [hɔ:d] *n* horda *f*
**horizon** [hə'raɪzn] *n* horyzont *m*
**horizontal** [hɔrɪ'zɔntl] *adj* poziomy
**hormone** ['hɔ:məun] *n* hormon *m*
**horn** [hɔ:n] *n* róg *m*; *(also:* **French horn***)* waltornia *f*, róg *m*; *(Aut)* klakson *m*
**horned** [hɔ:nd] *adj* rogaty
**hornet** ['hɔ:nɪt] *n* szerszeń *m*
**horn-rimmed** ['hɔ:n'rɪmd] *adj*: **~ spectacles** okulary *pl* w rogowych oprawkach
**horny** ['hɔ:nɪ] *(inf) adj* napalony *(inf)*
**horoscope** ['hɔrəskəup] *n* horoskop *m*
**horrendous** [hə'rɛndəs] *adj (crime, error)* straszliwy; *(price, cost)* horrendalny
**horrible** ['hɔrɪbl] *adj (colour, food, mess)* okropny; *(scream, dream)* straszny
**horrid** ['hɔrɪd] *adj* obrzydliwy, wstrętny
**horrific** [hɔ'rɪfɪk] *adj* przerażający
**horrify** ['hɔrɪfaɪ] *vt* przerażać (przerazić *perf)*
**horrifying** ['hɔrɪfaɪɪŋ] *adj* przerażający
**horror** ['hɔrəʳ] *n (alarm)* przerażenie *nt*; *(of battle, warfare)* groza *f*; *(abhorrence)*: **~ of** wstręt *m* do *+gen*
**horror film** *n* film *m* grozy, horror *m*
**horror-stricken** ['hɔrəstrɪkn] *adj* = **horror-struck**
**horror-struck** ['hɔrəstrʌk] *adj* struchlały z przerażenia, zdjęty grozą
**hors d'oeuvre** [ɔ:'də:vrə] *n* przystawka *f*
**horse** [hɔ:s] *n* koń *m*
**horseback** ['hɔ:sbæk] *adv* konno, wierzchem *(old)*; **on ~** na koniu
**horse box** *n* wóz *m* do przewozu koni
**horse chestnut** *n (tree)* kasztan(owiec) *m*; *(nut)* kasztan *m*
**horse-drawn** ['hɔ:sdrɔ:n] *adj* konny
**horsefly** ['hɔ:sflaɪ] *n* giez *m* (koński), mucha *f* końska
**horseman** ['hɔ:smən] *(irreg: like* **man***) n* jeździec *m*
**horsemanship** ['hɔ:smənʃɪp] *n* umiejętności *pl* jeździeckie
**horseplay** ['hɔ:spleɪ] *n* (dzikie) harce *pl*
**horsepower** ['hɔ:spauəʳ] *n* ≈ koń *m* mechaniczny
**horse-racing** ['hɔ:sreɪsɪŋ] *n* wyścigi *pl* konne
**horseradish** ['hɔ:srædɪʃ] *n* chrzan *m*
**horseshoe** ['hɔ:sʃu:] *n* podkowa *f*

**horse show** *n* zawody *pl* jeździeckie *or* hipiczne

**horse-trading** ['hɔːstreɪdɪŋ] *n* przetargi *pl*

**horse trials** *npl* = **horse show**

**horsewhip** ['hɔːswɪp] *n* szpicruta *f* ▷ *vt* bić (zbić *perf*) szpicrutą

**horsewoman** ['hɔːswumən] (*irreg: like* **woman**) *n* amazonka *f*

**horsey** ['hɔːsɪ] *adj* (*person*) kochający konie; (*face*) koński

**horticulture** ['hɔːtɪkʌltʃə[r]] *n* ogrodnictwo *nt*

**hose** [həuz] *n* (*also*: **hosepipe**) wąż *m*; (*Tech*) wężyk *m*; (*also*: **garden hose**) wąż *m* (ogrodowy)

▸ **hose down** *vt* polewać (polać *perf*) wężem

**hosiery** ['həuzɪərɪ] *n* wyroby *pl* pończosznicze

**hospice** ['hɔspɪs] *n* hospicjum *nt*

**hospitable** ['hɔspɪtəbl] *adj* (*person*) gościnny; (*invitation, welcome*) serdeczny; (*climate*) przyjazny

**hospital** ['hɔspɪtl] *n* szpital *m*; **in ~,** (*US*) **in the ~** w szpitalu

**hospitality** [hɔspɪ'tælɪtɪ] *n* (*of person*) gościnność *f*; (*of welcome*) serdeczność *f*

**hospitalize** ['hɔspɪtəlaɪz] *vt* umieszczać (umieścić *perf*) w szpitalu, hospitalizować

**host** [həust] *n* (*at party, dinner*) gospodarz *m*; (*TV, Radio*) gospodarz *m* (programu); (*Rel*) hostia *f* ▷ *adj* (*organization*) pełniący rolę gospodarza; (*country, community*): **his ~ country** goszczący go kraj ▷ *vt* (*TV programme*) prowadzić, być gospodarzem *+gen*; **a ~ of** mnóstwo *+gen*

**hostage** ['hɔstɪdʒ] *n* zakładnik(-iczka) *m(f)*; **he was taken/held ~** wzięto/trzymano go jako zakładnika

**hostel** ['hɔstl] *n* (*for homeless*) schronisko *nt*; (*also*: **youth hostel**) schronisko *nt* (młodzieżowe)

**hostelling** ['hɔstlɪŋ] *n*: **we went (youth) ~ round England** podróżowaliśmy po Anglii, zatrzymując się w schroniskach (młodzieżowych)

**hostess** ['həustɪs] *n* (*at party, dinner*) gospodyni *f*; (*Brit*: *also*: **air hostess**) stewardessa *f*; (*TV, Radio*) gospodyni *f* (programu); (*in night-club*) fordanserka *f*

**hostile** ['hɔstaɪl] *adj* (*person*) nieprzyjazny, wrogo nastawiony *or* usposobiony; (*attitude*) wrogi; (*conditions, environment*) niesprzyjający; **~ to** *or* **towards** wrogo nastawiony do *+gen or* w stosunku do *+gen*

**hostility** [hɔ'stɪlɪtɪ] *n* wrogość *f*; **hostilities** *npl* działania *pl* wojenne

**hot** [hɔt] *adj* gorący; (*spicy*) ostry, pikantny; (*contest, argument*) zawzięty; (*temper*) porywczy; **I am hot** jest mi gorąco; **it was terribly hot yesterday** wczoraj było okropnie gorąco; **to be hot on sth** (*inf*: *knowledgable, skilful*) być świetnym w czymś; (*interested*) pasjonować się czymś; **not so hot** (*inf*) nieszczególny

▸ **hot up** (*Brit*: *inf*) *vi* (*party*) rozkręcać się (rozkręcić się *perf*) (*inf*); (*situation, events*): **the situation was hotting up** robiło się gorąco (*inf*) ▷ *vt* (*pace*) podkręcać (podkręcić *perf*) (*inf*); (*engine*) podrasowywać (podrasować *perf*) (*inf*)

**hot air** *n* czcza gadanina *f*

**hot-air balloon** [hɔt'ɛə-] *n* balon *m* na gorące powietrze

**hotbed** ['hɔtbɛd] *n* (*fig*: *of evil*) siedlisko *nt*; (*of criminals*) wylęgarnia *f*

**hot-blooded** [hɔt'blʌdɪd] *adj* krewki

**hotchpotch** ['hɔtʃpɔtʃ] (*Brit*) *n* mieszanina *f*, miszmasz *m* (*inf*)

**hot dog** *n* hot dog *m*

**hotel** [həu'tɛl] *n* hotel *m*

**hotelier** [həu'tɛlɪə[r]] *n* hotelarz(-arka) *m(f)*

**hotel industry** *n* hotelarstwo *nt*

**hotel room** *n* pokój *m* hotelowy

**hotfoot** ['hɔtfut] *adv* ochoczo, żwawo

**hot-headed** [hɔt'hɛdɪd] *adj* w gorącej wodzie kąpany

**hothouse** ['hɔthaus] *n* cieplarnia *f*

**hot line** *n* gorąca linia *f*

**hotly** ['hɔtlɪ] *adv* (*contest*) ostro, zawzięcie; (*speak, deny*) stanowczo, kategorycznie

**hotplate** ['hɔtpleɪt] *n* płytka *f* grzejna (*kuchenki elektrycznej*)

**hotpot** ['hɔtpɔt] (*Brit*) *n* potrawka *f* z jarzynami

**hot seat** *n* (*fig*): **in the ~** na cenzurowanym

**hot spot** (*Pol*) *n* punkt *m* zapalny

**hot spring** *n* gorące źródło *nt*

**hot stuff** (*inf*) *n* (*woman*) laska *f* (*inf*); (*activity*): **skateboarding is ~ now** jest teraz szał na jazdę na deskorolce

**hot-tempered** ['hɔt'tɛmpəd] *adj* porywczy

**hot-water bottle** [hɔt'wɔːtə-] *n* termofor *m*

**hound** [haund] *vt* napastować ▷ *n* pies *m* gończy, ogar *m*

**hour** ['auə[r]] *n* godzina *f*; **60 miles an ~** 60 mil na godzinę; **lunch ~** ≈ przerwa obiadowa; **to pay sb by the ~** płacić komuś od godziny

**hourly** ['auəlɪ] *adj* (*service*) cogodzinny; (*rate*) godzinny ▷ *adv* (*each hour*) co godzinę; (*soon*) w każdej chwili

**house** [*n* haus, *vb* hauz] *n* dom *m*; (*Pol*) izba *f*; (*Theat*) sala *f*, widownia *f*; (*of Windsor etc*) dynastia *f* ▷ *vt* (*person*) przydzielać (przydzielić *perf*) mieszkanie *+dat*; (*collection, library*) mieścić; **at my ~** u mnie w domu; **publishing ~** wydawnictwo; **fashion ~** dom mody; **royal ~** rodzina królewska; **the H~ of**

h

**Commons** (*Brit*) Izba Gmin; **the H~ of Representatives** (*US*) Izba Reprezentantów; **on the ~** (*fig*) na koszt firmy
**house arrest** *n* areszt *m* domowy
**houseboat** ['hausbəut] *n* łódź *f* mieszkalna
**housebound** ['hausbaund] *adj*: **to be ~** nie móc wychodzić (z domu)
**housebreaking** ['hausbreɪkɪŋ] *n* włamanie *nt*
**house-broken** ['hausbrəukn] (*US*) *adj* = **house-trained**
**housecoat** ['hauskəut] *n* podomka *f*
**household** ['haushəuld] *n* (*people*) rodzina *f*; (*home*) gospodarstwo *nt* (domowe); **~ name** powszechnie znane nazwisko
**householder** ['haushəuldə^r] *n* (*owner*) właściciel(ka) *m(f)*; (*tenant*) lokator(ka) *m(f)*
**househunting** ['haushʌntɪŋ] *n* szukanie *nt* mieszkania
**housekeeper** ['hauski:pə^r] *n* gosposia *f*
**housekeeping** ['hauski:pɪŋ] *n* (*work*) prowadzenie *nt* gospodarstwa (domowego); (*money*) pieniądze *pl* na życie
**houseman** ['hausmən] (*Brit*) (*irreg*: *like* **man**) *n* lekarz *m* stażysta *m*
**houseplant** ['hausplɑ:nt] *n* roślina *f* domowa *or* doniczkowa
**house-proud** ['hauspraud] *adj*: **to be ~** pedantycznie dbać o wygląd domu
**house-to-house** ['haustə'haus] *adj* (*enquiries*) po domach *post*; (*selling*) obwoźny, domokrążny
**house-trained** ['haustreɪnd] (*Brit*) *adj*: **my dog is ~** mój pies nie brudzi (w domu)
**house-warming (party)** ['hauswɔ:mɪŋ-] *n* oblewanie *nt* nowego mieszkania/domu, parapetówa *f* (*inf*)
**housewife** ['hauswaɪf] (*irreg*: *like* **wife**) *n* gospodyni *f* domowa
**housework** ['hauswə:k] *n* prace *pl* domowe
**housing** ['hauzɪŋ] *n* (*buildings*) zakwaterowanie *nt*; (*conditions*) warunki *pl* mieszkaniowe; (*provision*) gospodarka *f* mieszkaniowa ▷ *cpd* (*problem*) mieszkaniowy; **~ shortage** brak mieszkań
**housing association** *n* ≈ spółdzielnia *f* mieszkaniowa
**housing conditions** *npl* warunki *pl* mieszkaniowe
**housing development** (*Brit*) *n* = **housing estate**
**housing estate** *n* osiedle *nt* (mieszkaniowe)
**hovel** ['hɔvl] *n* (nędzna) chałupa *f*; (*fig*) nora *f*
**hover** ['hɔvə^r] *vi* (*bird, insect*) wisieć *or* unosić się w powietrzu; (*person*) stać wyczekująco, ociągać się; **to ~ round sb** kręcić się koło kogoś
**hovercraft** ['hɔvəkrɑ:ft] *n* poduszkowiec *m*
**hoverport** ['hɔvəpɔ:t] *n* przystań *f* dla poduszkowców
**how** [hau] *adv* jak; **how are you?** jak się masz?; **how is school?** jak tam szkoła *or* w szkole?; **how long have you been here?** jak długo (już) tu jesteś?; **how lovely/awful!** jak cudownie/okropnie!; **how many people?** ilu ludzi?; **how much milk?** ile mleka?
**however** [hau'ɛvə^r] *conj* jednak(że) ▷ *adv* jakkolwiek; (*in questions*) jakże(ż)
**howl** [haul] *vi* (*animal, person*) wyć; (*baby*) głośno płakać; (*wind*) wyć, zawodzić ▷ *n* wycie *nt*; (*of baby*) głośny płacz *m*
**howler** ['haulə^r] (*inf*) *n* wsypa *f* (*inf*)
**HP** (*Brit*) *n abbr* = **hire purchase**
**h.p.** (*Aut*) *abbr* (= *horsepower*) KM
**HQ** *abbr* (= *headquarters*) KG
**HR** (*US*: *Pol*) *n abbr* (= *House of Representatives*) Izba *f* Reprezentantów
**HRH** (*Brit*) *abbr* (= *His (or Her) Royal Highness*) JKW
**hr(s)** *abbr* (= *hour(s)*) godz.
**HS** (*US*) *abbr* = **high school**
**HST** (*US*) *abbr* = **Hawaiian Standard Time**
**HTML** (*Comput*) *n abbr* (= *Hyper-Text Mark-up Language*) HTML *nt*, język *m* znaczników hipertekstowych
**hub** [hʌb] *n* (*of wheel*) piasta *f*; (*fig*) centrum *nt* **to be the hub of the universe** być najważniejszym na świecie
**hubbub** ['hʌbʌb] *n* wrzawa *f*, zgiełk *m*
**hubcap** ['hʌbkæp] *n* (*Aut*) kołpak *m*
**HUD** (*US*) *n abbr* (= *Department of Housing and Urban Development*) Ministerstwo *nt* Gospodarki Mieszkaniowej i Rozwoju Miast
**huddle** ['hʌdl] *vi*: **to ~ together** skupiać się (skupić się *perf*), ścieśniać się (ścieśnić się *perf*) ▷ *n* bezładna masa *f*, kupa *f* (*inf*)
**hue** [hju:] *n* (*colour*) barwa *f*; (*shade*) odcień *m*
**hue and cry** *n* wrzawa *f*, krzyk *m* (*protestu*)
**huff** [hʌf] *n*: **in a ~** wzburzony ▷ *vi*: **to ~ and puff** ciężko dyszeć
**hug** [hʌg] *vt* (*person*) ściskać (uściskać *perf*), przytulać (przytulić *perf*) (do siebie); (*thing*) obejmować (objąć *perf*) (rękoma), przyciskać (przycisnąć *perf*) (do siebie) ▷ *n* uścisk *m*; **to give sb a hug** przytulić (*perf*) *or* uściskać (*perf*) kogoś
**huge** [hju:dʒ] *adj* ogromny
**hugely** ['hju:dʒlɪ] *adv* ogromnie
**hulk** [hʌlk] *n* (*ship*) kadłub *m* rozbitego statku (*person, building etc*) kolos *m*
**hulking** ['hʌlkɪŋ] *adj*: **~ great** olbrzymi
**hull** [hʌl] *n* (*of ship*) kadłub *m*; (*of nut*) łupina *f*; (*of strawberry*) szypułka *f* ▷ *vt* (*strawberries etc*) obierać (obrać *perf*)
**hullaballoo** ['hʌləbə'lu:] (*inf*) *n* harmider *m*

**hullo** [həˈləu] *excl* = **hello**
**hum** [hʌm] *vt* nucić (zanucić *perf*) ▷ *vi* (*person*) nucić (sobie); (*machine*) (głośno) buczeć; (*insect*) bzykać, bzyczeć ▷ *n* (*of traffic*) szum *m*; (*of machines*) buczenie *nt*; (*of voices*) szmer *m*
**human** [ˈhju:mən] *adj* ludzki ▷ *n* (*also*: **human being**) człowiek *m*, istota *f* ludzka; **the ~ race** rodzaj ludzki
**humane** [hju:ˈmeɪn] *adj* (*treatment*) humanitarny, ludzki; (*slaughter*) humanitarny
**humanism** [ˈhju:mənɪzəm] *n* humanizm *m*
**humanitarian** [hju:mænɪˈtɛərɪən] *adj* humanitarny
**humanity** [hju:ˈmænɪtɪ] *n* (*mankind*) ludzkość *f*; (*condition*) człowieczeństwo *nt*; (*humaneness, kindness*) człowieczeństwo *nt*, humanitaryzm *m*; **humanities** *npl*: **(the) humanities** nauki *pl* humanistyczne; (*Scol*) przedmioty *pl* humanistyczne
**humanly** [ˈhju:mənlɪ] *adv*: **~ possible** w ludzkiej mocy
**humanoid** [ˈhju:mənɔɪd] *adj* człekopodobny, humanoidalny ▷ *n* humanoid *m*
**humble** [ˈhʌmbl] *adj* (*modest*) skromny; (*deferential*) pokorny; (*background, birth*) niski ▷ *vt* upokarzać (upokorzyć *perf*)
**humbly** [ˈhʌmblɪ] *adv* (*modestly*) skromnie; (*deferentially*) pokornie
**humbug** [ˈhʌmbʌg] *n* blaga *f*; (*Brit*: *sweet*) *twardy, czarno-biały cukierek o smaku miętowym*
**humdrum** [ˈhʌmdrʌm] *adj* nudny, monotonny
**humid** [ˈhju:mɪd] *adj* wilgotny
**humidifier** [hju:ˈmɪdɪfaɪəʳ] *n* nawilżacz *m* (powietrza)
**humidity** [hju:ˈmɪdɪtɪ] *n* wilgotność *f*
**humiliate** [hju:ˈmɪlɪeɪt] *vt* poniżać (poniżyć *perf*), upokarzać (upokorzyć *perf*)
**humiliating** [hju:ˈmɪlɪeɪtɪŋ] *adj* poniżający, upokarzający
**humiliation** [hju:mɪlɪˈeɪʃən] *n* poniżenie *nt*, upokorzenie *nt*
**humility** [hju:ˈmɪlɪtɪ] *n* (*modesty*) skromność *f*; (*deference*) pokora *f*
**humor** [ˈhju:məʳ] (US) *n* = **humour**
**humorist** [ˈhju:mərɪst] *n* (*writer*) humorysta(-tka) *m(f)*; (*performer*) komik(-iczka) *m(f)*
**humorous** [ˈhju:mərəs] *adj* (*book*) humorystyczny; (*person, remark*) dowcipny
**humour**, (US) **humor** [ˈhju:məʳ] *n* humor *m* ▷ *vt* spełniać (spełnić *perf*) zachcianki *+gen*; **sense of ~** poczucie humoru; **to be in good/bad ~** być w dobrym/złym humorze
**humo(u)rless** [ˈhju:məlɪs] *adj* pozbawiony poczucia humoru
**hump** [hʌmp] *n* garb *m*
**humpbacked** [ˈhʌmpbækt] *adj*: **~ bridge** mostek *m* w kształcie łuku
**humus** [ˈhju:məs] *n* humus *m*, próchnica *f*
**hunch** [hʌntʃ] *n* przeczucie *nt*; **I have a ~ that …** mam przeczucie, że …
**hunchback** [ˈhʌntʃbæk] *n* garbus *m*
**hunched** [hʌntʃt] *adj* zgarbiony
**hundred** [ˈhʌndrəd] *num* sto; **~s of** setki *+gen*; **I'm a ~ per cent sure** jestem w stu procentach pewny
**hundredth** [ˈhʌndrədθ] *num* setny
**hundredweight** [ˈhʌndrɪdweɪt] *n* cetnar *m* (*Brit* = *50.8 kg; 112 lb; US* = *45.3 kg; 100 lb*)
**hung** [hʌŋ] *pt, pp of* **hang**
**Hungarian** [hʌŋˈgɛərɪən] *adj* węgierski ▷ *n* (*person*) Węgier(ka) *m(f)*; (*Ling*) (język *m*) węgierski
**Hungary** [ˈhʌŋgərɪ] *n* Węgry *pl*
**hunger** [ˈhʌŋgəʳ] *n* głód *m* ▷ *vi*: **to ~ for** łaknąć *or* być złaknionym *+gen*
**hunger strike** *n* strajk *m* głodowy
**hungrily** [ˈhʌŋgrəlɪ] *adv* łapczywie
**hungry** [ˈhʌŋgrɪ] *adj* głodny; **~ for** złakniony *+gen*; **to go ~** głodować
**hung up** (*inf*) *adj*: **to be ~ on** *or* **about** być przeczulonym na punkcie *+gen*
**hunk** [hʌŋk] *n* (*of bread etc*) kawał *m*; (*inf*: *man*) (wielkie) chłopisko *nt* (*inf*)
**hunt** [hʌnt] *vt* (*animals*) polować na *+acc*; (*criminal*) ścigać, tropić ▷ *vi* polować ▷ *n* (*for animals*) polowanie *nt*; (*search*) poszukiwanie *nt*; (*Sport*) *klub myśliwych polujących na lisa*; **to ~ for** (*right word etc*) szukać *+gen*
▸ **hunt down** *vt* ścigać
**hunter** [ˈhʌntəʳ] *n* myśliwy *m*
**hunting** [ˈhʌntɪŋ] *n* myślistwo *nt*; (*Sport*) polowanie *nt* na lisa
**hurdle** [ˈhə:dl] *n* przeszkoda *f*; (*Sport*) płotek *m*
**hurl** [hə:l] *vt* ciskać (cisnąć *perf*)
**hurrah** [huˈrɑ:] *excl* hur(r)a
**hurray** [huˈreɪ] *n* = **hurrah**
**hurricane** [ˈhʌrɪkən] *n* huragan *m*
**hurried** [ˈhʌrɪd] *adj* pośpieszny
**hurriedly** [ˈhʌrɪdlɪ] *adv* pośpiesznie, w pośpiechu
**hurry** [ˈhʌrɪ] *n* pośpiech *m* ▷ *vi* śpieszyć się (pośpieszyć się *perf*) ▷ *vt* (*person*) popędzać (popędzić *perf*); (*work*) wykonywać (wykonać *perf*) w pośpiechu; **to be in a ~** śpieszyć się; **to do sth in a ~** robić (zrobić *perf*) coś w pośpiechu; **to ~ in/out** wchodzić (wejść *perf*)/wychodzić (wyjść *perf*) pośpiesznie; **they hurried to help him** pośpieszyli mu z pomocą; **to ~ home** śpieszyć się do domu; **there's no ~** nie ma pośpiechu; **what's the ~?** po co ten pośpiech?

h

▸ **hurry along** *vi* śpieszyć się (pośpieszyć się *perf*)
▸ **hurry away** *vi* odchodzić (odejść *perf*) pośpiesznie
▸ **hurry off** *vi* = **hurry away**
▸ **hurry up** *vt* popędzać (popędzić *perf*) ▹ *vi* śpieszyć się (pośpieszyć się *perf*)

**hurt** [həːt] (*pt, pp* **~**) *vt* (*cause pain to*) sprawiać (sprawić *perf*) ból *+dat*; (*injure: lit, fig*) ranić (zranić *perf*) ▹ *vi* boleć (zaboleć *perf*) ▹ *adj* ranny; **I've ~ my arm** zraniłem się w rękę; **where does it ~?** gdzie (Pana/Panią) boli?
**hurtful** ['həːtful] *adj* bolesny
**hurtle** ['həːtl] *vi*: **to ~ past** przemknąć (*perf*) (obok); **the plane ~d down the runway** samolot popędził po pasie startowym
**husband** ['hʌzbənd] *n* mąż *m* ▹ *vt* (*resources etc*) gospodarować oszczędnie *+instr*
**hush** [hʌʃ] *n* cisza *f* ▹ *vi* uciszać się (uciszyć się *perf*); **~!** sza!
▸ **hush up** *vt* (*scandal etc*) tuszować (zatuszować *perf*)
**hushed** [hʌʃt] *adj* (*place*) cichy; (*voice*) przyciszony, przytłumiony
**hush-hush** [hʌʃ'hʌʃ] (*inf*) *adj* poufny
**husk** [hʌsk] *n* łuska *f*
**husky** ['hʌskɪ] *adj* (*voice*) chrypiący, chrapliwy ▹ *n* (*dog*) husky *m*
**hustings** ['hʌstɪŋz] (*Brit*) *npl* kampania *f* wyborcza
**hustle** ['hʌsl] *vt* wypychać (wypchnąć *perf*) ▹ *n*: **~ and bustle** zgiełk *m*
**hut** [hʌt] *n* (*house*) chata *f*; (*shed*) szopa *f*
**hutch** [hʌtʃ] *n* klatka *f*
**hyacinth** ['haɪəsɪnθ] *n* hiacynt *m*
**hybrid** ['haɪbrɪd] *n* (*plant, animal*) mieszaniec *m*, hybryd *m*; (*fig*) skrzyżowanie *nt* ▹ *adj* hybrydowy
**hydrant** ['haɪdrənt] *n* (*also:* **fire hydrant**) hydrant *m*
**hydraulic** [haɪ'drɔːlɪk] *adj* hydrauliczny
**hydraulics** [haɪ'drɔːlɪks] *n* hydromechanika *f* techniczna
**hydrochloric** ['haɪdrəu'klɔrɪk] *adj*: **~ acid** kwas *m* chlorowodorowy *or* solny
**hydro-electric** *adj* (*power*) hydroelektryczny; **~ power station** elektrownia wodna, hydroelektrownia
**hydrofoil** ['haɪdrəfɔɪl] *n* wodolot *m*
**hydrogen** ['haɪdrədʒən] *n* wodór *m*
**hydrogen bomb** *n* bomba *f* wodorowa
**hydrophobia** ['haɪdrə'fəubɪə] *n* wodowstręt *m*
**hydroplane** ['haɪdrəpleɪn] *n* ślizgacz *m* ▹ *vi* ślizgać się (po wodzie)
**hyena** [haɪ'iːnə] *n* hiena *f*
**hygiene** ['haɪdʒiːn] *n* higiena *f*
**hygienic** [haɪ'dʒiːnɪk] *adj* higieniczny
**hymn** [hɪm] *n* hymn *m*
**hype** [haɪp] (*inf*) *n* szum *m* ▹ *vt* robić szum (narobić *perf* szumu) wokół *+gen*
**hyped up** (*inf*) *adj* nakręcony (*inf*) (*podekscytowany*)
**hyperactive** ['haɪpər'æktɪv] *adj* nadczynny, nadmiernie ruchliwy
**hypermarket** ['haɪpəmɑːkɪt] *n olbrzymi supermarket*
**hypertension** ['haɪpə'tɛnʃən] *n* nadciśnienie *nt*
**hyphen** ['haɪfn] *n* łącznik *m*
**hyphenated** ['haɪfəneɪtɪd] *adj* pisany z łącznikiem
**hypnosis** [hɪp'nəusɪs] *n* hipnoza *f*
**hypnotic** [hɪp'nɔtɪk] *adj* hipnotyczny
**hypnotism** ['hɪpnətɪzəm] *n* hipnoza *f*
**hypnotist** ['hɪpnətɪst] *n* hipnotyzer(ka) *m(f)*
**hypnotize** ['hɪpnətaɪz] *vt* hipnotyzować (zahipnotyzować *perf*); (*fig*) fascynować (zafascynować *perf*)
**hypoallergenic** ['haɪpəuælə'dʒɛnɪk] *adj* hipoalergiczny
**hypochondriac** [haɪpə'kɔndrɪæk] *n* hipochondryk(-yczka) *m(f)*
**hypocrisy** [hɪ'pɔkrɪsɪ] *n* hipokryzja *f*, obłuda *f*
**hypocrite** ['hɪpəkrɪt] *n* hipokryta(-tka) *m(f)*, obłudnik(-ica) *m(f)*
**hypocritical** [hɪpə'krɪtɪkl] *adj* obłudny
**hypodermic** [haɪpə'dəːmɪk] *adj* podskórny ▹ *n* strzykawka *f* podskórna
**hypothermia** [haɪpə'θəːmɪə] *n* hipotermia *f*
**hypothesis** [haɪ'pɔθɪsɪs] (*pl* **hypotheses**) *n* hipoteza *f*
**hypothetical** [haɪpəu'θɛtɪk(l)] *adj* hipotetyczny
**hysterectomy** [hɪstə'rɛktəmɪ] *n* wycięcie *nt* macicy, histerektomia *f*
**hysteria** [hɪ'stɪərɪə] *n* histeria *f*
**hysterical** [hɪ'stɛrɪkl] *adj* histeryczny; (*inf: hilarious*) komiczny
**hysterically** [hɪ'stɛrɪklɪ] *adv* histerycznie; **~ funny** komiczny
**hysterics** [hɪ'stɛrɪks] (*inf*) *npl*: **to be in/have ~** (*panic, get angry*) histeryzować/wpadać (wpaść *perf*) w histerię; (*laugh loudly*) zaśmiewać się, zanosić się od śmiechu
**Hz** *abbr* (= *hertz*) Hz

**I¹, i** [aɪ] *n* (*letter*) I *nt*, i *nt*; **I for Isaac,** (*US*) **I for Item** ≈ I jak Irena

**I²** [aɪ] *pron* ja

**I.** *abbr* (= *island, isle*) w.

**IA** (*US: Post*) *abbr* = **Iowa**

**IAEA** *n abbr* = **International Atomic Energy Agency**

**IBA** (*Brit*) *n abbr* = **Independent Broadcasting Authority**

**Iberian** [aɪ'bɪərɪən] *adj*: **the ~ Peninsula** Półwysep *m* Iberyjski

**IBEW** (*US*) *n abbr* (= *International Brotherhood of Electrical Workers*) *związek zawodowy elektryków*

**ib(id)** *abbr* (= *ibidem*) tamże

**i/c** (*Brit*) *abbr* = **in charge** *see* **charge**

**ICBM** *n abbr* (= *intercontinental ballistic missile*) międzykontynentalny pocisk *m* balistyczny

**ICC** *n abbr* = **International Chamber of Commerce**; (*US*: = *Interstate Commerce Commission*) *komisja sprawująca kontrolę nad transportem towarów między stanami USA*

**ice** [aɪs] *n* lód *m* ▷ *vt* (*cake*) lukrować (polukrować *perf*) ▷ *vi* (*also*: **ice over, ice up**) pokrywać się (pokryć się *perf*) lodem; **to put sth on ice** (*fig*) odkładać (odłożyć *perf*) coś na później

**Ice Age** *n* epoka *f* lodowa *or* lodowcowa

**ice axe** *n* czekan *m*

**iceberg** ['aɪsbə:g] *n* góra *f* lodowa; **the tip of the ~** (*fig*) wierzchołek góry lodowej

**icebox** ['aɪsbɔks] *n* (*US*) lodówka *f*; (*Brit*) zamrażalnik *m*; (*insulated box*) lodówka *f* turystyczna

**icebreaker** ['aɪsbreɪkə^r] *n* lodołamacz *m*

**ice bucket** *n* wiaderko *nt* z lodem

**ice-cold** [aɪs'kəuld] *adj* lodowato zimny

**ice cream** *n* lody *pl*

**ice-cream soda** ['aɪskri:m-] *n lody z syropem owocowym i wodą sodową*

**ice cube** *n* kostka *f* lodu

**iced** [aɪst] *adj* (*cake*) lukrowany; (*beer*) schłodzony; (*tea*) mrożony

**ice hockey** *n* hokej *m* (na lodzie)

**Iceland** ['aɪslənd] *n* Islandia *f*

**Icelander** ['aɪsləndə^r] *n* Islandczyk(-dka) *m(f)*

**Icelandic** [aɪs'lændɪk] *adj* islandzki ▷ *n* (język *m*) islandzki

**ice lolly** (*Brit*) *n lizak z mrożonej wody z sokiem owocowym*

**ice pick** *n* szpikulec *m* do lodu

**ice rink** *n* lodowisko *nt*

**ice-skate** ['aɪsskeɪt] *n* łyżwa *f* ▷ *vi* jeździć na łyżwach

**ice-skating** ['aɪsskeɪtɪŋ] *n* łyżwiarstwo *nt*

**icicle** ['aɪsɪkl] *n* sopel *m*

**icing** ['aɪsɪŋ] *n* (*Culin*) lukier *m*; (*Aviat etc*) oblodzenie *nt*

**icing sugar** (*Brit*) *n* ≈ cukier *m* puder *m*

**ICJ** *n abbr* = **International Court of Justice**

**icon** ['aɪkɔn] *n* ikona *f*

**ICR** (*US*) *n abbr* = **Institute for Cancer Research**

**ICU** (*Med*) *n abbr* (= *intensive care unit*) IOM *m*, oddział *m* intensywnej opieki medycznej

**icy** ['aɪsɪ] *adj* (*water*) lodowaty; (*road*) oblodzony

**ID** (*US: Post*) *abbr* = **Idaho**

**I'd** [aɪd] = **I would; I had**

**ID card** *n* = **identity card**

**IDD** (*Brit: Tel*) *n abbr* (= *international direct dialling*) międzynarodowe połączenie *nt* automatyczne

**idea** [aɪ'dɪə] *n* (*scheme*) pomysł *m*; (*opinion*) pogląd *m*; (*notion*) pojęcie *nt*; (*objective*) założenie *nt*, idea *f*; **good ~!** dobry pomysł!; **to have a good ~ of** mieć dobre pojęcie o *+loc*; **I haven't the least** *or* **faintest ~** nie mam najmniejszego *or* zielonego pojęcia; **that's not my ~ of ...** nie tak wyobrażam sobie *+acc*

**ideal** [aɪ'dɪəl] *n* ideał *m* ▷ *adj* idealny

**idealist** [aɪ'dɪəlɪst] *n* idealista(-tka) *m(f)*

**ideally** [aɪ'dɪəlɪ] *adv* idealnie; **~ the book should have ...** najlepiej (byłoby), gdyby książka miała ...; **she's ~ suited for the job** ona się idealnie nadaje do tej pracy

**identical** [aɪ'dɛntɪkl] *adj* identyczny

**identification** [aɪdɛntɪfɪ'keɪʃən] *n* rozpoznanie *nt*; (*of person, dead body*) identyfikacja *f*; **(means of) ~** dowód tożsamości

**identify** [aɪ'dɛntɪfaɪ] *vt* rozpoznawać (rozpoznać *perf*); (*suspect, dead body*)

identyfikować (zidentyfikować *perf*); **this will ~ him** po tym będzie można go rozpoznać; **to ~ sb/sth with** utożsamiać (utożsamić *perf*) kogoś/coś z *+instr*
**Identikit**® [aɪ'dɛntɪkɪt] *n*: **~ (picture)** portret *m* pamięciowy
**identity** [aɪ'dɛntɪtɪ] *n* tożsamość *f*
**identity card** *n* ≈ dowód *m* osobisty
**identity papers** *npl* dowód *m* tożsamości, dokumenty *pl*
**identity parade** (*Brit*) *n* konfrontacja *f* (*mająca na celu zidentyfikowanie podejrzanego*)
**identity theft** *n* kradzież *f* tożsamości
**ideological** [aɪdɪə'lɔdʒɪkl] *adj* ideologiczny
**ideology** [aɪdɪ'ɔlədʒɪ] *n* ideologia *f*
**idiocy** ['ɪdɪəsɪ] *n* idiotyzm *m*
**idiom** ['ɪdɪəm] *n* (*in architecture, music*) styl *m*; (*Ling*) idiom *m*
**idiomatic** [ɪdɪə'mætɪk] *adj* idiomatyczny
**idiosyncrasy** [ɪdɪəu'sɪŋkrəsɪ] *n* dziwactwo *nt*
**idiosyncratic** [ɪdɪəusɪŋ'krætɪk] *adj* specyficzny
**idiot** ['ɪdɪət] *n* idiota(-tka) *m(f)*
**idiotic** [ɪdɪ'ɔtɪk] *adj* idiotyczny
**idle** ['aɪdl] *adj* (*inactive*) bezczynny; (*lazy*) leniwy; (*unemployed*) bezrobotny; (*machinery, factory*) nieczynny; (*conversation*) jałowy; (*threat, boast*) pusty ▷ *vi* (*machine, engine*) pracować na wolnych obrotach; **to be ~** próżnować; **to lie ~** być nieczynnym
▸ **idle away** *vt*: **to ~ away the time** trwonić czas
**idleness** ['aɪdlnɪs] *n* (*inactivity*) bezczynność *f*; (*laziness*) próżniactwo *nt*
**idler** ['aɪdlə^r] *n* próżniak *m*
**idle time** (*Comm*) *n* przestój *m*
**idly** ['aɪdlɪ] *adv* (*sit*) bezczynnie, z założonymi rękami; (*glance*) nieuważnie
**idol** ['aɪdl] *n* idol *m*
**idolize** ['aɪdəlaɪz] *vt* ubóstwiać
**idyllic** [ɪ'dɪlɪk] *adj* idylliczny, sielankowy
**i.e.** *abbr* (= *id est*) tj.

KEYWORD

**if** [ɪf] *conj* **1** (*conditional use*) jeżeli, jeśli; (*: with unreal or unlikely conditions, in polite requests*) gdyby; **I'll go if you come with me** pójdę, jeśli *or* jeżeli pójdziesz ze mną; **if we had known** gdybyśmy wiedzieli; **if only I could** gdybym tylko mógł; **I'd be pleased if you could do it** cieszyłbym się, gdybyś mógł to zrobić; **if necessary** jeśli to konieczne, jeśli trzeba; **if I were you ...** (ja) na twoim miejscu ...
**2** (*whenever*) gdy tylko, zawsze gdy *or* kiedy; **if we are in Scotland, we always go to see her** gdy tylko jesteśmy w Szkocji, zawsze ją odwiedzamy
**3** (*although*): **(even) if** choćby (nawet); **I am determined to finish it, (even) if it takes all week** zamierzam to skończyć, choćby (nawet) miało to zabrać cały tydzień
**4** (*whether*) czy; **ask him if he can come** zapytaj go, czy może przyjść
**5**: **if so/not** jeśli tak/nie; **if only to** choćby po to, (że)by *+infin*; *see also* **as**

**igloo** ['ɪglu:] *n* igloo *nt inv*
**ignite** [ɪg'naɪt] *vt* zapalać (zapalić *perf*) ▷ *vi* zapalać się (zapalić się *perf*)
**ignition** [ɪg'nɪʃən] *n* (*Aut*) zapłon *m*; **to switch on/off the ~** włączać (włączyć *perf*)/wyłączać (wyłączyć *perf*) zapłon
**ignition key** (*Aut*) *n* kluczyk *m* zapłonu
**ignoble** [ɪg'nəubl] *adj* niegodziwy
**ignominious** [ɪgnə'mɪnɪəs] *adj* haniebny
**ignoramus** [ɪgnə'reɪməs] *n* ignorant(ka) *m(f)*
**ignorance** ['ɪgnərəns] *n* niewiedza *f*, ignorancja *f*; **to keep sb in ~ of sth** utrzymywać kogoś w nieświadomości czegoś
**ignorant** ['ɪgnərənt] *adj* niedouczony; **to be ~ of** (*subject*) nie znać *+gen*; (*events*) nie wiedzieć o *+loc*
**ignore** [ɪg'nɔ:^r] *vt* (*pay no attention to*) ignorować (zignorować *perf*); (*fail to take into account*) nie brać (nie wziąć *perf*) pod uwagę *+gen*
**ikon** ['aɪkɔn] *n* = **icon**
**IL** (*US: Post*) *abbr* = **Illinois**
**ILA** (*US*) *n abbr* (= *International Longshore Association*) *związek zawodowy dokerów*
**I'll** [aɪl] = **I will; I shall**
**ill** [ɪl] *adj* (*person*) chory; (*effects*) szkodliwy ▷ *n* (*evil*) zło *nt*; (*trouble*) dolegliwość *f* ▷ *adv*: **to speak/think ill of sb** źle o kimś mówić/myśleć; **to be taken ill** (nagle) zachorować (*perf*)
**ill-advised** [ɪləd'vaɪzd] *adj* nierozważny, nierozsądny
**ill-at-ease** [ɪlət'i:z] *adj* skrępowany
**ill-considered** [ɪlkən'sɪdəd] *adj* nie przemyślany
**ill-disposed** [ɪldɪs'pəuzd] *adj*: **~ toward sb/sth** nieprzychylnie nastawiony do kogoś/czegoś
**illegal** [ɪ'li:gl] *adj* (*activity*) sprzeczny z prawem, nielegalny; (*immigrant, organization*) nielegalny
**illegally** [ɪ'li:gəlɪ] *adv* (*in breach of law*) nielegalnie; (*in breach of rules*) nieprzepisowo
**illegible** [ɪ'lɛdʒɪbl] *adj* nieczytelny
**illegitimate** [ɪlɪ'dʒɪtɪmət] *adj* (*child*) nieślubny; (*activity*) bezprawny
**ill-fated** [ɪl'feɪtɪd] *adj* fatalny

**ill-favoured**, (*US*) **ill-favored** [ɪl'feɪvəd] *adj* niezbyt urodziwy
**ill feeling** *n* uraza *f*
**ill-gotten** ['ɪlgɔtn] *adj*: **~ gains** nieuczciwie osiągnięte zyski *pl*
**illicit** [ɪ'lɪsɪt] *adj* (*sale*) nielegalny; (*substance*) zakazany, niedozwolony; **an ~ association** romans
**ill-informed** [ɪlɪn'fɔ:md] *adj* (*judgement*) mylny; (*person*) źle poinformowany
**illiterate** [ɪ'lɪtərət] *adj* niepiśmienny; **he's ~** jest analfabetą
**ill-mannered** [ɪl'mænəd] *adj* źle wychowany
**illness** ['ɪlnɪs] *n* choroba *f*
**illogical** [ɪ'lɔdʒɪkl] *adj* (*argument*) nielogiczny; (*fear*) niedorzeczny
**ill-suited** [ɪl'su:tɪd] *adj* (*couple*) niedobrany; **he is ~ to the job** on się nie nadaje do tej pracy
**ill-timed** [ɪl'taɪmd] *adj* nie w porę *post*
**ill-treat** [ɪl'tri:t] *vt* (*treat badly*) źle traktować; (*treat cruelly*) maltretować, znęcać się nad *+instr*
**ill-treatment** [ɪl'tri:tmənt] *n* (*bad treatment*) złe traktowanie *nt*; (*cruelty*) maltretowanie *nt*, znęcanie się *nt*
**illuminate** [ɪ'lu:mɪneɪt] *vt* oświetlać (oświetlić *perf*)
**illuminated sign** [ɪ'lu:mɪneɪtɪd-] *n* podświetlony znak *m*
**illuminating** [ɪ'lu:mɪneɪtɪŋ] *adj* pouczający
**illumination** [ɪlu:mɪ'neɪʃən] *n* (*lighting*) oświetlenie *nt*; (*illustration*) iluminacja *f*; **illuminations** *npl* dekoracje *pl* świetlne
**illusion** [ɪ'lu:ʒən] *n* (*false idea, belief*) złudzenie *nt*, iluzja *f*; (*trick*) sztuczka *f* magiczna; **to be under the ~ that ...** łudzić się, że ...
**illusive** [ɪ'lu:sɪv] *adj* = **illusory**
**illusory** [ɪ'lu:sərɪ] *adj* złudny, iluzoryczny
**illustrate** ['ɪləstreɪt] *vt* ilustrować (zilustrować *perf*)
**illustration** [ɪlə'streɪʃən] *n* (*picture, example*) ilustracja *f*; (*act of illustrating*) ilustrowanie *nt*
**illustrator** ['ɪləstreɪtə^r] *n* ilustrator(ka) *m(f)*
**illustrious** [ɪ'lʌstrɪəs] *adj* znakomity
**ill will** *n* wrogość *f*
**ILO** *n abbr* = **International Labour Organization**
**ILWU** (*US*) *n abbr* = **International Longshoremen's and Warehousemen's Union**
**I'm** [aɪm] = **I am**
**image** ['ɪmɪdʒ] *n* (*picture, public face*) wizerunek *m*; (*reflection*) odbicie *nt*
**imagery** ['ɪmɪdʒərɪ] *n* (*in writing, painting*) symbolika *f*
**imaginable** [ɪ'mædʒɪnəbl] *adj* wyobrażalny; **we've tried every ~ solution** próbowaliśmy wszystkich rozwiązań, jakie można sobie wyobrazić; **she had the prettiest hair ~** miała prześliczne włosy
**imaginary** [ɪ'mædʒɪnərɪ] *adj* wyimaginowany
**imagination** [ɪmædʒɪ'neɪʃən] *n* (*inventiveness, part of mind*) wyobraźnia *f*; (*illusion*) urojenie *nt*; **it's just your ~** to tylko wytwór twojej wyobraźni
**imaginative** [ɪ'mædʒɪnətɪv] *adj* (*person*) twórczy; (*solution*) pomysłowy
**imagine** [ɪ'mædʒɪn] *vt* (*visualize*) wyobrażać (wyobrazić *perf*) sobie; (*suppose*): **I ~ that ...** zdaje mi się, że ...; **you must have ~d it** zdawało ci się
**imbalance** [ɪm'bæləns] *n* brak *m* równowagi
**imbecile** ['ɪmbəsi:l] *n* imbecyl *m*
**imbue** [ɪm'bju:] *vt*: **to be ~d with** być przepojonym *+instr*
**IMF** *n abbr* (*= International Monetary Fund*) MFW *m inv* (*= Międzynarodowy Fundusz Walutowy*)
**imitate** ['ɪmɪteɪt] *vt* (*copy*) naśladować; (*mimic*) naśladować, imitować
**imitation** [ɪmɪ'teɪʃən] *n* (*act*) naśladowanie *nt*; (*instance*) imitacja *f*
**imitator** ['ɪmɪteɪtə^r] *n* naśladowca(-wczyni) *m(f)*, imitator(ka) *m(f)*
**immaculate** [ɪ'mækjulət] *adj* (*spotless*) nieskazitelnie czysty; (*flawless*) nieskazitelny; (*Rel*) niepokalany
**immaterial** [ɪmə'tɪərɪəl] *adj* nieistotny
**immature** [ɪmə'tjuə^r] *adj* niedojrzały
**immaturity** [ɪmə'tjuərɪtɪ] *n* niedojrzałość *f*
**immeasurable** [ɪ'mɛʒrəbl] *adj* niezmierzony
**immediacy** [ɪ'mi:dɪəsɪ] *n* (*of events*) bezpośredniość *f*; (*of reaction*) natychmiastowość *f*
**immediate** [ɪ'mi:dɪət] *adj* (*reaction, answer*) natychmiastowy; (*need*) pilny; (*vicinity, predecessor*) bezpośredni; (*family, neighbourhood*) najbliższy
**immediately** [ɪ'mi:dɪətlɪ] *adv* (*at once*) natychmiast; (*directly*) bezpośrednio; **~ behind/next to** tuż za *+instr*/przy *+loc*
**immense** [ɪ'mɛns] *adj* ogromny
**immensely** [ɪ'mɛnslɪ] *adv* ogromnie, niezmiernie
**immensity** [ɪ'mɛnsɪtɪ] *n* ogrom *m*
**immerse** [ɪ'mə:s] *vt*: **to ~ sth (in)** zanurzać (zanurzyć *perf*) coś (w *+loc*); **to be ~d in thought/work** (*fig*) być zatopionym w myślach/pochłoniętym pracą
**immersion heater** [ɪ'mə:ʃən-] (*Brit*) *n* grzejnik *m* nurkowy
**immigrant** ['ɪmɪgrənt] *n* imigrant(ka) *m(f)*
**immigration** [ɪmɪ'greɪʃən] *n* (*process*) imigracja *f*; (*also*: **immigration control**) kontrola *f* paszportowa *or* graniczna ▷ *cpd*:

~ **officer** przedstawiciel(ka) *m(f)* urzędu imigracyjnego; ~ **laws** prawo przesiedleńcze
**imminent** ['ɪmɪnənt] *adj* (*war, disaster*) nieuchronny; (*arrival*) bliski
**immobile** [ɪ'məubaɪl] *adj* nieruchomy
**immobilize** [ɪ'məubɪlaɪz] *vt* unieruchamiać (unieruchomić *perf*)
**immoderate** [ɪ'mɔdərət] *adj* nieumiarkowany
**immodest** [ɪ'mɔdɪst] *adj* nieskromny
**immoral** [ɪ'mɔrl] *adj* niemoralny
**immorality** [ɪmɔ'rælɪtɪ] *n* niemoralność *f*
**immortal** [ɪ'mɔ:tl] *adj* nieśmiertelny
**immortality** [ɪmɔ:'tælɪtɪ] *n* nieśmiertelność *f*
**immortalize** [ɪ'mɔ:tlaɪz] *vt* uwieczniać (uwiecznić *perf*), unieśmiertelniać (unieśmiertelnić *perf*)
**immovable** [ɪ'mu:vəbl] *adj* (*object*) nieruchomy; (*opinion*) niewzruszony, niezachwiany
**immune** [ɪ'mju:n] *adj*: ~ **(to)** (*disease*) odporny (na *+acc*); (*flattery, criticism*) nieczuły (na *+acc*)
**immunity** [ɪ'mju:nɪtɪ] *n* (*to disease*) odporność *f*; (*of diplomat etc*) immunitet *m*, nietykalność *f*
**immunization** [ɪmjunaɪ'zeɪʃən] *n* (*Med*) uodpornienie *nt*
**immunize** ['ɪmjunaɪz] *vt* (*Med*): **to ~ (against)** uodparniać (uodpornić *perf*) (przeciwko *+dat*)
**imp** [ɪmp] *n* diabełek *m*
**impact** ['ɪmpækt] *n* (*of bullet, crash: contact*) uderzenie *nt*; (*: force*) siła *f* uderzenia; (*of law, measure*) wpływ *m*; **on ~** przy uderzeniu
**impair** [ɪm'pɛə[r]] *vt* osłabiać (osłabić *perf*)
**impale** [ɪm'peɪl] *vt*: **to ~ sth (on)** nadziewać (nadziać *perf*) coś (na *+acc*)
**impart** [ɪm'pɑ:t] *vt*: **to ~ (to)** (*information*) przekazywać (przekazać *perf*) (*+dat*); (*flavour*) nadawać (nadać *perf*) (*+dat*)
**impartial** [ɪm'pɑ:ʃl] *adj* bezstronny
**impartiality** [ɪmpɑ:ʃɪ'ælɪtɪ] *n* bezstronność *f*
**impassable** [ɪm'pɑ:səbl] *adj* (*road*) nieprzejezdny; (*river*) nieżeglowny
**impasse** [æm'pɑ:s] *n* impas *m*
**impassive** [ɪm'pæsɪv] *adj* beznamiętny
**impatience** [ɪm'peɪʃəns] *n* (*annoyance, irritation*) zniecierpliwienie *nt*; (*eagerness*) niecierpliwość *f*
**impatient** [ɪm'peɪʃənt] *adj* (*annoyed*) zniecierpliwiony; (*irritable, eager, in a hurry*) niecierpliwy; **to be ~ to do sth** niecierpliwić się, żeby coś zrobić; **to get** *or* **grow ~** zaczynać (zacząć *perf*) się niecierpliwić
**impatiently** [ɪm'peɪʃəntlɪ] *adv* niecierpliwie
**impeach** [ɪm'pi:tʃ] *vt* stawiać (postawić *perf*) w stan oskarżenia
**impeachment** [ɪm'pi:tʃmənt] *n* postawienie *nt* w stan oskarżenia
**impeccable** [ɪm'pɛkəbl] *adj* nienaganny
**impecunious** [ɪmpɪ'kju:nɪəs] *adj* (*fml*) ubogi
**impede** [ɪm'pi:d] *vt* utrudniać (utrudnić *perf*)
**impediment** [ɪm'pɛdɪmənt] *n* utrudnienie *nt*, przeszkoda *f*; **speech ~** wada wymowy
**impel** [ɪm'pɛl] *vt*: **to ~ sb to do sth** zmuszać (zmusić *perf*) kogoś do zrobienia czegoś
**impending** [ɪm'pɛndɪŋ] *adj* zbliżający się
**impenetrable** [ɪm'pɛnɪtrəbl] *adj* (*jungle*) niedostępny, nie do przebycia *post*; (*fortress*) nie do zdobycia *post*; (*fig: text*) nieprzystępny; (*: look, expression*) nieprzenikniony; (*: mystery*) niezgłębiony
**imperative** [ɪm'pɛrətɪv] *adj*: **it's ~ that you (should) call him immediately** koniecznie musisz natychmiast do niego zadzwonić ▷ *n* (*Ling*) tryb *m* rozkazujący; (*moral*) imperatyw *m*
**imperceptible** [ɪmpə'sɛptɪbl] *adj* niezauważalny
**imperfect** [ɪm'pə:fɪkt] *adj* wadliwy ▷ *n* (*Ling: also*: **imperfect tense**) czas *m* przeszły o aspekcie niedokonanym
**imperfection** [ɪmpə:'fɛkʃən] *n* (*failing*) wada *f* (*blemish*) skaza *f*
**imperial** [ɪm'pɪərɪəl] *adj* imperialny; (*Brit*): ~ **system** *tradycyjny brytyjski system miar i wag*
**imperialism** [ɪm'pɪərɪəlɪzəm] *n* imperializm *m*
**imperil** [ɪm'pɛrɪl] *vt* narażać (narazić *perf*) na niebezpieczeństwo
**imperious** [ɪm'pɪərɪəs] *adj* władczy
**impersonal** [ɪm'pə:sənl] *adj* bezosobowy
**impersonate** [ɪm'pə:səneɪt] *vt* (*pass o.s. off as*) podawać się (podać się *perf*) za *+acc*; (*Theat*) wcielać się (wcielić się *perf*) w postać *+gen*
**impersonation** [ɪmpə:sə'neɪʃən] *n*: **~ of** (*Jur*) podawanie się *nt* za *+acc*; (*Theat*) wcielenie się *nt* w postać *+gen*
**impertinent** [ɪm'pə:tɪnənt] *adj* impertynencki
**imperturbable** [ɪmpə'tə:bəbl] *adj* niewzruszony
**impervious** [ɪm'pə:vɪəs] *adj* (*fig*): **~ to** nieczuły na *+acc*
**impetuous** [ɪm'pɛtjuəs] *adj* porywczy
**impetus** ['ɪmpətəs] *n* (*of runner*) rozpęd *m*, impet *m*; (*fig*) bodziec *m*
**impinge** [ɪm'pɪndʒ] *vt fus*: **to ~ on** (*sb's life*) rzutować na *+acc*; (*sb's rights*) naruszać *+acc*
**implacable** [ɪm'plækəbl] *adj* (*hatred*) zaciekły; (*opposition*) nieprzejednany
**implant** [ɪm'plɑ:nt] *vt* (*Med*) wszczepiać (wszczepić *perf*); (*fig*) zaszczepiać (zaszczepić *perf*)
**implausible** [ɪm'plɔ:zɪbl] *adj* mało prawdopodobny
**implement** [*n* 'ɪmplɪmənt, *vb* 'ɪmplɪmɛnt] *n* narzędzie *nt* ▷ *vt* wprowadzać (wprowadzić *perf*) w życie

**implicate** ['ɪmplɪkeɪt] *vt*: **to be ~d in** być zamieszanym w *+acc*
**implication** [ɪmplɪ'keɪʃən] *n* (*inference*) implikacja *f*; (*involvement*): **~ in** zamieszanie *nt* w *+acc*; **by ~** tym samym
**implicit** [ɪm'plɪsɪt] *adj* (*threat, meaning*) ukryty; (*belief, trust*) bezgraniczny
**implicitly** [ɪm'plɪsɪtlɪ] *adv* (*indirectly*) pośrednio; (*totally*) bezgranicznie, bez zastrzeżeń
**implore** [ɪm'plɔːʳ] *vt*: **to ~ sb (to do sth)** błagać kogoś (, żeby coś zrobił); **to ~ sth (from sb)** błagać (kogoś) o coś
**imply** [ɪm'plaɪ] *vt* (*hint*) sugerować (zasugerować *perf*), dawać (dać *perf*) do zrozumienia; (*mean*) implikować
**impolite** [ɪmpə'laɪt] *adj* niegrzeczny
**imponderable** [ɪm'pɔndərəbl] *adj* nieogarniony ▷ *n* imponderabilia *pl* (*no sg*)
**import** [*vb* ɪm'pɔːt, *n, cpd* 'ɪmpɔːt] *vt* importować (importować *perf*) ▷ *n* (*article*) towar *m* importowany; (*importation*) import *m*, przywóz *m* ▷ *cpd*: **~ duty** cło *nt* przywozowe; **~ licence** licencja importowa
**importance** [ɪm'pɔːtns] *n* znaczenie *nt*, waga *f*; **to be of great/little ~** mieć duże/małe znaczenie; **a person/position of ~** ważna osoba/pozycja
**important** [ɪm'pɔːtnt] *adj* ważny; **it's not ~** to nieważne, to nie ma znaczenia
**importantly** [ɪm'pɔːtntlɪ] *adv* znacznie; **more ~, ...** co ważniejsze, ...
**importation** [ɪmpɔː'teɪʃən] *n* import *m*, przywóz *m*
**imported** [ɪm'pɔːtɪd] *adj* importowany
**importer** [ɪm'pɔːtəʳ] *n* importer *m*
**impose** [ɪm'pəuz] *vt* (*sanctions, restrictions*) nakładać (nałożyć *perf*); (*discipline*) narzucać (narzucić *perf*) ▷ *vi*: **to ~ on sb** nadużywać czyjejś uprzejmości
**imposing** [ɪm'pəuzɪŋ] *adj* imponujący
**imposition** [ɪmpə'zɪʃən] *n* (*of tax, sanctions*) nałożenie *nt*; (*of discipline*) narzucenie *nt*; **it would be an ~ to ask him that** proszenie go o to byłoby nadużywaniem jego uprzejmości
**impossibility** [ɪmpɔsə'bɪlɪtɪ] *n* niemożliwość *f*
**impossible** [ɪm'pɔsɪbl] *adj* niemożliwy; (*situation*) beznadziejny; **it's ~ for me to leave now** nie mogę teraz wyjść
**impossibly** [ɪm'pɔsɪblɪ] *adj* niemożliwie
**imposter** [ɪm'pɔstəʳ] *n* = **impostor**
**impostor** [ɪm'pɔstəʳ] *n* oszust(ka) *m(f)* (*podający się za kogoś*)
**impotence** ['ɪmpətns] *n* niemoc *f*; (*Med*) impotencja *f*
**impotent** ['ɪmpətnt] *adj* (*powerless*) bezsilny; (*Med*): **he's ~** jest impotentem
**impound** [ɪm'paund] *vt* konfiskować (skonfiskować *perf*)
**impoverished** [ɪm'pɔvərɪʃt] *adj* zubożały
**impracticable** [ɪm'præktɪkəbl] *adj* niewykonalny (w praktyce)
**impractical** [ɪm'præktɪkl] *adj* (*plan, expectation*) nierealny; (*person*) niepraktyczny
**imprecise** [ɪmprɪ'saɪs] *adj* nieścisły, nieprecyzyjny
**impregnable** [ɪm'prɛgnəbl] *adj* (*castle, fortress*) nie do zdobycia *post*; (*fig: person*) niewzruszony
**impregnate** ['ɪmprɛgneɪt] *vt* (*saturate*) nasączać (nasączyć *perf*); (*fertilize*) zapładniać (zapłodnić *perf*)
**impresario** [ɪmprɪ'sɑːrɪəu] (*Theat*) *n* impresario *m*
**impress** [ɪm'prɛs] *vt* (*person*) wywierać (wywrzeć *perf*) wrażenie na *+loc*, imponować (zaimponować *perf*) *+dat*; (*imprint*) odciskać (odcisnąć *perf*); **to ~ sth on sb** uzmysłowić (*perf*) coś komuś
**impression** [ɪm'prɛʃən] *n* (*of situation, person*) wrażenie *nt*; (*of stamp, seal*) odcisk *m*; (*idea*) wrażenie *nt*, impresja *f*; (*imitation*) parodia *f*; **to make a good/bad ~ on sb** wywierać (wywrzeć *perf*) na kimś dobre/złe wrażenie; **to be under the ~ that ...** mieć wrażenie, że ...
**impressionable** [ɪm'prɛʃnəbl] *adj* łatwowierny, bezkrytyczny
**impressionist** [ɪm'prɛʃənɪst] *n* (*Art*) impresjonista(-tka) *m(f)*; (*entertainer*) parodysta(-tka) *m(f)*
**impressive** [ɪm'prɛsɪv] *adj* imponujący, robiący wrażenie
**imprint** ['ɪmprɪnt] *n* (*of hand etc*) odcisk *m*; (*fig*) piętno *nt*; (*Typ*) metryczka *f* (*książki*)
**imprinted** [ɪm'prɪntɪd] *adj*: **to be ~ on** (*fig*) tkwić głęboko w *+loc*
**imprison** [ɪm'prɪzn] *vt* zamykać (zamknąć *perf*) w więzieniu, wtrącać (wtrącić *perf*) do więzienia
**imprisonment** [ɪm'prɪznmənt] *n* (*form of punishment*) kara *f* więzienia, więzienie *nt*; (*act*) uwięzienie *nt*, wtrącenie *nt* do więzienia
**improbable** [ɪm'prɔbəbl] *adj* nieprawdopodobny
**impromptu** [ɪm'prɔmptjuː] *adj* improwizowany, zaimprowizowany
**improper** [ɪm'prɔpəʳ] *adj* (*conduct, procedure*) niestosowny, niewłaściwy; (*activities*) niedozwolony
**impropriety** [ɪmprə'praɪətɪ] *n* niestosowność *f*
**improve** [ɪm'pruːv] *vt* poprawiać (poprawić *perf*), ulepszać (ulepszyć *perf*) ▷ *vi* poprawiać się (poprawić się *perf*), polepszać się

(polepszyć się *perf*); **she may ~ with treatment** po leczeniu stan jej zdrowia może się poprawić
▸ **improve (up)on** *vt fus* (*one's own achievement*) robić (zrobić *perf*) postęp(y) w *+loc*; (*sb's achievement*) przewyższać (przewyższyć *perf*)
**improvement** [ɪm'pru:vmənt] *n*: **~ (in)** poprawa *f* (*+gen*); **to make ~s to** ulepszać (ulepszyć *perf*) *or* udoskonalać (udoskonalić *perf*) *+acc*
**improvisation** [ɪmprəvaɪ'zeɪʃən] *n* (*of meal, bed*) prowizorka *f* (*pej*); (*Theat, Mus*) improwizacja *f*
**improvise** ['ɪmprəvaɪz] *vt* robić (zrobić *perf*) naprędce *or* prowizorycznie ▹ *vi* improwizować (zaimprowizować *perf*)
**imprudence** [ɪm'pru:dns] *n* nieroztropność *f*
**imprudent** [ɪm'pru:dnt] *adj* nieroztropny
**impudent** ['ɪmpjudnt] *adj* zuchwały
**impugn** [ɪm'pju:n] (*fml*) *vt* kwestionować (zakwestionować *perf*), podawać (podać *perf*) w wątpliwość
**impulse** ['ɪmpʌls] *n* (*urge*) (nagła) ochota *f or* chęć *f*, poryw *m*; (*Elec*) impuls *m*; **to act on ~** działać pod wpływem impulsu
**impulse buy** *n* nie planowany zakup *m*
**impulsive** [ɪm'pʌlsɪv] *adj* (*purchase*) nie planowany; (*gesture*) odruchowy; (*person*) impulsywny, porywczy
**impunity** [ɪm'pju:nɪtɪ] *n*: **with ~** bezkarnie
**impure** [ɪm'pjuə^r] *adj* (*substance*) zanieczyszczony; (*thoughts*) nieczysty
**impurity** [ɪm'pjuərɪtɪ] *n* zanieczyszczenie *nt*
**IN** (*US*: *Post*) *abbr* = **Indiana**

 KEYWORD

**in** [ɪn] *prep* **1** (*indicating place*) w *+loc*; **in town** w mieście; **in the country** na wsi; **in here/there** tu/tam (wewnątrz); **in London** w Londynie
**2** (*indicating time*: *during*) w *+loc*; **in winter/summer** w zimie/lecie, zimą/latem; **in the afternoon** po południu
**3** (*indicating time*: *in the space of*) w *+acc*; **I did it in three hours/days** zrobiłem to w trzy godziny/dni
**4** (*indicating time*: *after*) za *+acc*; **I'll see you in 2 weeks** *or* **in 2 weeks' time** do zobaczenia za 2 tygodnie
**5** (*indicating manner etc*): **in a loud voice** głośno; **in pencil** ołówkiem; **in English/French** po angielsku/francusku
**6** (*indicating circumstances, mood, state*) w *+loc*; **in the sun/rain** w słońcu/deszczu; **in anger/despair/haste** w gniewie/rozpaczy/pośpiechu; **a change in policy** zmiana polityki
**7** (*with ratios, numbers*) na *+acc*; **one in ten men** jeden mężczyzna na dziesięciu; **you can save up to 20 pence in the pound** można zaoszczędzić do 20 pensów na (każdym) funcie
**8** (*referring to people, works*) u *+gen*; **the disease is common in children** ta choroba często występuje u dzieci; **in Dickens** u Dickensa; **in the works of Dickens** w dziełach Dickensa
**9** (*indicating profession etc*): **to be in teaching/publishing** zajmować się nauczaniem/działalnością wydawniczą
**10** (*with present participle*): **in saying this** mówiąc to
▹ *adv*: **to be in** (*person*: *at home*) być w domu; (: *at work*) być w pracy, być obecnym; (*train*) przyjechać (*perf*); (*ship*) przypłynąć (*perf*); (*plane*) przylecieć (*perf*); (*in fashion*) być popularnym *or* w modzie; **to ask sb in** prosić (poprosić *perf*) kogoś do środka; **to march in** wmaszerowywać (wmaszerować *perf*) (do środka)
▹ *n*: **the ins and outs** szczegóły *pl*, zawiłości *pl*

**in.** *abbr* = **inch**
**inability** [ɪnə'bɪlɪtɪ] *n*: **~ (to do sth)** niemożność *f* (zrobienia czegoś)
**inaccessible** [ɪnək'sɛsɪbl] *adj* (*place*) niedostępny; (*fig*: *text etc*) nieprzystępny
**inaccuracy** [ɪn'ækjurəsɪ] *n* (*quality*) niedokładność *f*; (*mistake*) nieścisłość *f*
**inaccurate** [ɪn'ækjurət] *adj* niedokładny, nieścisły
**inaction** [ɪn'ækʃən] *n* bezczynność *f*
**inactive** [ɪn'æktɪv] *adj* (*person*) bezczynny; (*volcano*) nieczynny
**inactivity** [ɪnæk'tɪvɪtɪ] *n* bezczynność *f*
**inadequacy** [ɪn'ædɪkwəsɪ] *n* (*of preparations etc*) niedostateczność *f*; (*of person*) niedociągnięcie *nt*
**inadequate** [ɪn'ædɪkwət] *adj* (*amount*) niedostateczny, niewystarczający; (*reply*) niepełny, niezadowalający; (*person*) nieodpowiedni
**inadmissible** [ɪnəd'mɪsəbl] *adj* niedopuszczalny
**inadvertently** [ɪnəd'və:tntlɪ] *adv* nieumyślnie
**inadvisable** [ɪnəd'vaɪzəbl] *adj* niewskazany, nie zalecany; **it is ~ to ring him too early** zbyt wczesne telefonowanie do niego nie jest wskazane
**inane** [ɪ'neɪn] *adj* bezmyślny
**inanimate** [ɪn'ænɪmət] *adj* nieożywiony; (*Ling*) nieżywotny

**inapplicable** [ɪn'æplɪkəbl] *adj (description, comment)* nieadekwatny; **to be ~ to sb/sth** nie stosować się do kogoś/czegoś
**inappropriate** [ɪnə'prəuprɪət] *adj (unsuitable)* nieodpowiedni; *(improper)* niewłaściwy, niestosowny
**inapt** [ɪn'æpt] *adj* niestosowny, niewłaściwy
**inarticulate** [ɪnɑː'tɪkjulət] *adj (person)* nie potrafiący się wysłowić; *(speech)* niewyraźny, nieartykułowany
**inasmuch as** [ɪnəz'mʌtʃ-] *adv (in that)* przez to, że ...; *(insofar as)* o tyle, o ile ..., w (takim) stopniu, w jakim ...
**inattention** [ɪnə'tɛnʃən] *n (lack of attention)* nieuwaga *f*; *(neglect)* niedbałość *f*
**inattentive** [ɪnə'tɛntɪv] *adj* nieuważny
**inaudible** [ɪn'ɔːdɪbl] *adj* niesłyszalny
**inaugural** [ɪ'nɔːgjurəl] *adj* inauguracyjny
**inaugurate** [ɪ'nɔːgjureɪt] *vt (official)* wprowadzać (wprowadzić *perf*) na stanowisko *or* urząd; *(system)* wprowadzać (wprowadzić *perf*); *(festival)* inaugurować (zainaugurować *perf*)
**inauguration** [ɪnɔːgju'reɪʃən] *n* (uroczyste) wprowadzenie *nt* na stanowisko *or* urząd
**inauspicious** [ɪnɔːs'pɪʃəs] *adj* nie wróżący sukcesu
**in-between** [ɪnbɪ'twiːn] *adj* przejściowy, pośredni
**inborn** [ɪn'bɔːn] *adj* wrodzony
**inbred** [ɪn'brɛd] *adj (quality)* wrodzony, przyrodzony; *(family: of people)* endogamiczny, wewnętrznie skoligacony; *(: of animals)* wsobny
**inbreeding** [ɪn'briːdɪŋ] *n (of people)* endogamia *f*; *(of animals)* rozmnażanie *nt* wsobne
**inbuilt** [ɪn'bɪlt] *adj* wrodzony, właściwy z natury
**Inc.** *abbr* = **incorporated**
**Inca** ['ɪŋkə] *adj (also:* **Incan**) Inków *post*, inkaski ▷ *n* Inka *m/f*, Inkas(ka) *m(f)*
**incalculable** [ɪn'kælkjuləbl] *adj* nieobliczalny, nieoszacowany
**incapable** [ɪn'keɪpəbl] *adj* nieporadny; **to be ~ of sth/doing sth** *(incompetent)* nie potrafić czegoś/(z)robić czegoś; *(too nice)* nie być zdolnym do czegoś/zrobienia czegoś
**incapacitate** [ɪnkə'pæsɪteɪt] *vt*: **to ~ sb** czynić (uczynić *perf*) kogoś niesprawnym; *(Jur)* ubezwłasnowolniać (ubezwłasnowolnić *perf*) kogoś
**incapacitated** [ɪnkə'pæsɪteɪtɪd] *(Jur) adj* ubezwłasnowolniony
**incapacity** [ɪnkə'pæsɪtɪ] *n (weakness)* niesprawność *f*, niemoc *f*; *(inability)* nieumiejętność *f*
**incarcerate** [ɪn'kɑːsəreɪt] *vt* więzić (uwięzić *perf*)
**incarnate** [ɪn'kɑːnɪt] *adj* wcielony, ucieleśniony; **evil ~** ucieleśnienie zła
**incarnation** [ɪnkɑː'neɪʃən] *n (of beauty, evil)* ucieleśnienie *nt*; *(Rel)* wcielenie *nt*
**incendiary** [ɪn'sɛndɪərɪ] *adj* zapalający
**incense** [*n* 'ɪnsɛns, *vb* ɪn'sɛns] *n* kadzidło *nt* ▷ *vt* rozwścieczać (rozwścieczyć *perf*)
**incense burner** *n* kadzielnica *f*
**incentive** [ɪn'sɛntɪv] *n* bodziec *m*, zachęta *f* ▷ *cpd (Comm: bonus etc)* motywacyjny
**inception** [ɪn'sɛpʃən] *n (of institution)* powstanie *nt*; *(of activity)* rozpoczęcie *nt*
**incessant** [ɪn'sɛsnt] *adj* ustawiczny, nieustający
**incessantly** [ɪn'sɛsntlɪ] *adv* nieprzerwanie, bez przerwy
**incest** ['ɪnsɛst] *n* kazirodztwo *nt*
**inch** [ɪntʃ] *n* cal *m*; **he didn't give an ~** *(fig)* nie ustąpił ani trochę
▸ **inch forward** *vi* posuwać się powoli (do przodu)
**incidence** ['ɪnsɪdns] *n (frequency)* częstość *f or* częstotliwość *f* (występowania); *(extent)* zasięg *m* (występowania)
**incident** ['ɪnsɪdnt] *n* wydarzenie *nt*; *(involving violence etc)* incydent *m*, zajście *nt*
**incidental** [ɪnsɪ'dɛntl] *adj* uboczny; **to be ~ to** wiązać się z *+instr*; **~ expenses** wydatki uboczne
**incidentally** [ɪnsɪ'dɛntəlɪ] *adv* nawiasem mówiąc
**incidental music** *n* podkład *m* muzyczny *(do filmu itp)*
**incinerate** [ɪn'sɪnəreɪt] *vt* spalać (spalić *perf*)
**incinerator** [ɪn'sɪnəreɪtəʳ] *n* piec *m* do spalania śmieci
**incipient** [ɪn'sɪpɪənt] *adj* w stadium początkowym *post*, rozpoczynający się
**incision** [ɪn'sɪʒən] *(Med) n* cięcie *nt*, nacięcie *nt*
**incisive** [ɪn'saɪsɪv] *adj* cięty, zjadliwy
**incisor** [ɪn'saɪzəʳ] *(Anat) n* siekacz *m*
**incite** [ɪn'saɪt] *vt (rioters)* podburzać (podburzyć *perf*); *(hatred)* wzniecać (wzniecić *perf*)
**incl.** *abbr (= including, inclusive (of))* wł.
**inclement** [ɪn'klɛmənt] *adj*: **~ weather** niepogoda *f*
**inclination** [ɪnklɪ'neɪʃən] *n (tendency)* skłonność *f*; *(disposition)* upodobanie *nt*, inklinacja *f*
**incline** [*n* 'ɪnklaɪn, *vb* ɪn'klaɪn] *n (of terrain)* pochyłość *f*, spadek *m*; *(of mountain)* zbocze *nt* ▷ *vt* pochylać (pochylić *perf*) ▷ *vi* być nachylonym; **to be ~d to do sth** mieć skłonność *or* skłonności do robienia czegoś;

**to be well ~d towards sb** być przyjaźnie nastawionym do kogoś
**include** [ɪn'klu:d] *vt* zawierać (zawrzeć *perf*), obejmować (objąć *perf*); **the crew ~d two Britons** w skład załogi wchodziło dwóch Brytyjczyków; **the tip is not ~d in the price** napiwek nie jest wliczony w cenę
**including** [ɪn'klu:dɪŋ] *prep* w tym *+acc*, wliczając (w to) *+acc*; **~ service charge** łącznie z opłatą za obsługę
**inclusion** [ɪn'klu:ʒən] *n* włączenie *nt*
**inclusive** [ɪn'klu:sɪv] *adj* globalny, łączny; **~ of** z wliczeniem *or* włączeniem *+gen*; **Monday to Friday ~** od poniedziałku do piątku włącznie
**incognito** [ɪnkɔg'ni:təu] *adv* incognito
**incoherent** [ɪnkəu'hɪərənt] *adj* (*argument*) niespójny; (*speech*) nieskładny, nie trzymający się kupy (*inf*); (*person*): **he was ~** mówił bez ładu i składu (*inf*)
**income** ['ɪnkʌm] *n* (*earned*) dochód *m*; (*from property, investment, pension*) dochody *pl*; **gross/net ~** dochód brutto/netto; **~ and expenditure account** rachunek przychodów i rozchodów; **~ bracket** przedział *or* grupa dochodu
**income tax** *n* podatek *m* dochodowy ▷ *cpd* (*Comm: inspector, return*) podatkowy
**incoming** ['ɪnkʌmɪŋ] *adj* (*passengers*) przybywający; (*: by air*) przylatujący; (*call*) z zewnątrz *post*; (*mail*) przychodzący, napływający; (*official*) obejmujący urząd; (*government*) nowy; (*wave*) nadciągający, nadchodzący; **~ flights** przyloty; **~ tide** przypływ
**incommunicado** ['ɪnkəmjunɪ'kɑ:dəu] *adj*: **to hold sb ~** izolować kogoś
**incomparable** [ɪn'kɔmpərəbl] *adj* niezrównany
**incompatible** [ɪnkəm'pætɪbl] *adj* (*aims*) nie do pogodzenia (ze sobą) *post*; (*Comput*) niekompatybilny
**incompetence** [ɪn'kɔmpɪtns] *n* brak *m* kompetencji, nieudolność *f*
**incompetent** [ɪn'kɔmpɪtnt] *adj* nieudolny
**incomplete** [ɪnkəm'pli:t] *adj* (*unfinished*) niedokończony, nie skończony; (*partial*) niepełny, niekompletny
**incomprehensible** [ɪnkɔmprɪ'hɛnsɪbl] *adj* niezrozumiały
**inconceivable** [ɪnkən'si:vəbl] *adj* niepojęty, nie do pomyślenia *post*; **it is ~ that ...** jest nie do pomyślenia, żeby ...
**inconclusive** [ɪnkən'klu:sɪv] *adj* (*experiment*) nie dowodzący niczego; (*evidence*) nieprzekonujący; (*discussion*) nie prowadzący do niczego, nie przynoszący rozstrzygnięcia
**incongruous** [ɪn'kɔŋgruəs] *adj* (*situation, figure*) osobliwy, absurdalny; (*remark, act*) niestosowny, nie na miejscu *post*
**inconsequential** [ɪnkɔnsɪ'kwɛnʃl] *adj* mało ważny, błahy
**inconsiderable** [ɪnkən'sɪdərəbl] *adj*: **not ~** niemały, pokaźny
**inconsiderate** [ɪnkən'sɪdərət] *adj* nie liczący się z innymi
**inconsistency** [ɪnkən'sɪstənsɪ] *n* brak *m* konsekwencji, niekonsekwencja *f*
**inconsistent** [ɪnkən'sɪstnt] *adj* (*behaviour, person*) niekonsekwentny; (*work*) nierówny; (*statement*) wewnętrznie sprzeczny; **~ with** niezgodny z *+instr*
**inconsolable** [ɪnkən'səuləbl] *adj* niepocieszony
**inconspicuous** [ɪnkən'spɪkjuəs] *adj* niepozorny, nie rzucający się w oczy; **to make o.s. ~** starać się (postarać się *perf*) nie zwracać na siebie uwagi
**incontinence** [ɪn'kɔntɪnəns] *n* nietrzymanie *nt* moczu/stolca
**incontinent** [ɪn'kɔntɪnənt] *adj* nie trzymający moczu/stolca
**inconvenience** [ɪnkən'vi:njəns] *n* (*problem*) niedogodność *f*; (*trouble*) kłopot *m* ▷ *vt* przysparzać (przysporzyć *perf*) kłopotu *+dat*; **don't ~ yourself** nie rób sobie kłopotu
**inconvenient** [ɪnkən'vi:njənt] *adj* (*time, place*) niedogodny; (*visitor*) uciążliwy, kłopotliwy; **that time is very ~ for me** to bardzo niedogodna dla mnie pora
**incorporate** [ɪn'kɔ:pəreɪt] *vt* (*include*) włączać (włączyć *perf*); (*contain*) zawierać (w sobie); **safety features have been ~d in the design** w projekcie uwzględniono wymogi bezpieczeństwa
**incorporated company** [ɪn'kɔ:pəreɪtɪd-] (*US*) *n* spółka *f* posiadająca osobowość prawną
**incorrect** [ɪnkə'rɛkt] *adj* (*information, predictions*) błędny; (*answer*) nieprawidłowy, błędny; (*behaviour*) niestosowny; (*attitude*) niewłaściwy
**incorrigible** [ɪn'kɔrɪdʒɪbl] *adj* niepoprawny
**incorruptible** [ɪnkə'rʌptɪbl] *adj* nieprzekupny
**increase** [*n* 'ɪnkri:s, *vb* ɪn'kri:s] *n*: **~ (in/of)** wzrost *m* (*+gen*) ▷ *vi* wzrastać (wzrosnąć *perf*), zwiększać się (zwiększyć się *perf*) ▷ *vt* (*number, size*) zwiększać (zwiększyć *perf*); (*prices, wages*) podwyższać (podwyższyć *perf*); **an ~ of 5%** wzrost o 5%; **to be on the ~** wzrastać
**increasing** [ɪn'kri:sɪŋ] *adj* rosnący
**increasingly** [ɪn'kri:sɪŋlɪ] *adv* (*more and more*): **~ strong/difficult** coraz mocniejszy/trudniejszy; (*more often*) coraz częściej

**incredible** [ɪn'krɛdɪbl] *adj* niewiarygodny
**incredulity** [ɪnkrɪ'dju:lɪtɪ] *n* niedowierzanie *nt*
**incredulous** [ɪn'krɛdjuləs] *adj* (*person*) nie dowierzający; (*tone, expression*) pełen niedowierzania *post*
**increment** ['ɪnkrɪmənt] *n* przyrost *m*
**incriminate** [ɪn'krɪmɪneɪt] *vt* (*Jur*) obciążać (obciążyć *perf*)
**incriminating** [ɪn'krɪmɪneɪtɪŋ] (*Jur*) *adj* obciążający
**incrust** [ɪn'krʌst] *vt* = **encrust**
**incubate** ['ɪnkjubeɪt] *vt* wysiadywać ▷ *vi* (*eggs*) dojrzewać (*do momentu wylęgu*); (*disease*) rozwijać się
**incubation** [ɪnkju'beɪʃən] *n* wylęganie *nt*, inkubacja *f*
**incubation period** *n* okres *m* wylęgania *or* inkubacyjny
**incubator** ['ɪnkjubeɪtə^r] *n* inkubator *m*
**inculcate** ['ɪnkʌlkeɪt] (*fml*) *vt*: **to ~ sth in sb** wpajać (wpoić *perf*) coś komuś
**incumbent** [ɪn'kʌmbənt] *n* osoba *f* sprawująca urząd ▷ *adj*: **it is ~ on him to ...** jest zobowiązany *+infin*
**incur** [ɪn'kə:^r] *vt* (*expenses, loss*) ponosić (ponieść *perf*); (*debt*) zaciągać (zaciągnąć *perf*); (*disapproval, anger*) wywoływać (wywołać *perf*)
**incurable** [ɪn'kjuərəbl] *adj* nieuleczalny
**incursion** [ɪn'kə:ʃən] (*Mil*) *n* wtargnięcie *nt*
**indebted** [ɪn'dɛtɪd] *adj*: **to be ~ to sb** być komuś wdzięcznym *or* zobowiązanym
**indecency** [ɪn'di:snsɪ] *n* nieprzyzwoitość *f*
**indecent** [ɪn'di:snt] *adj* nieprzyzwoity, gorszący
**indecent assault** (*Brit*) *n* czyn *m* nierządny
**indecent exposure** *n* obnażenie się *nt* w miejscu publicznym
**indecipherable** [ɪndɪ'saɪfərəbl] *adj* (*writing*) nie do odcyfrowania *post*; (*expression, glance*) nieodgadniony
**indecision** [ɪndɪ'sɪʒən] *n* niezdecydowanie *nt*
**indecisive** [ɪndɪ'saɪsɪv] *adj* niezdecydowany
**indeed** [ɪn'di:d] *adv* (*certainly, in fact*) istotnie; (*furthermore*) wręcz, (a) nawet; **yes ~!** ależ oczywiście!; **thank you very much ~** dziękuję bardzo; **we have very little information ~** mamy naprawdę bardzo mało informacji
**indefatigable** [ɪndɪ'fætɪgəbl] *adj* (*person*) niestrudzony, niezmordowany; (*rhythm, pulse*) nie słabnący
**indefensible** [ɪndɪ'fɛnsɪbl] *adj* niewybaczalny
**indefinable** [ɪndɪ'faɪnəbl] *adj* nieuchwytny, nieokreślony
**indefinite** [ɪn'dɛfɪnɪt] *adj* (*answer, view*) niejasny; (*period, number*) nieokreślony
**indefinite article** (*Ling*) *n* przedimek *m or* rodzajnik *m* nieokreślony
**indefinitely** [ɪn'dɛfɪnɪtlɪ] *adv* (*continue, wait*) bez końca; (*closed, postponed*) na czas nieokreślony
**indelible** [ɪn'dɛlɪbl] *adj* (*mark, stain*) nieusuwalny, nie dający się usunąć; (*pen*) kopiowy, chemiczny; (*impression*) niezatarty
**indelicate** [ɪn'dɛlɪkɪt] *adj* nietaktowny
**indemnify** [ɪn'dɛmnɪfaɪ] (*Comm*) *vt* gwarantować (zagwarantować *perf*) rekompensatę *+dat*
**indemnity** [ɪn'dɛmnɪtɪ] *n* (*insurance*) gwarancja *f* rekompensaty; (*compensation*) odszkodowanie *nt*, (re)kompensata *f*; **~ fund** fundusz kompensacyjny
**indent** [ɪn'dɛnt] *vt* (*text*) zaczynać (zacząć *perf*) akapitem *or* od akapitu
**indentation** [ɪndɛn'teɪʃən] *n* (*Typ*) **akapit** *m*; (*in surface*) wgłębienie *nt*
**indenture** [ɪn'dɛntʃə^r] *n* umowa *f* terminatorska
**independence** [ɪndɪ'pɛndns] *n* (*of country*) niepodległość *f*; (*of person, thinking*) niezależność *f*, samodzielność *f*
**independent** [ɪndɪ'pɛndnt] *adj* (*country*) niepodległy; (*person, thought*) niezależny, samodzielny; (*business, inquiry*) niezależny; (*school, broadcasting company*) ≈ prywatny
**independently** [ɪndɪ'pɛndntlɪ] *adv*: **~ (of)** niezależnie (od *+gen*)
**indescribable** [ɪndɪs'kraɪbəbl] *adj* nieopisany
**indestructible** [ɪndɪs'trʌktəbl] *adj* niezniszczalny
**indeterminate** [ɪndɪ'tə:mɪnɪt] *adj* nieokreślony
**index** ['ɪndɛks] (*pl* **~es**) *n* (*in book*) indeks *m*, skorowidz *m*; (*in library*) katalog *m* (alfabetyczny); (*pl* **indices**: *ratio, sign*) wskaźnik *m*
**index card** *n* karta *f* katalogowa, fiszka *f*
**indexed** ['ɪndɛkst] (*US*) *adj* = **index-linked**
**index finger** *n* palec *m* wskazujący
**index-linked** ['ɪndɛks'lɪŋkt] *adj* indeksowany
**India** ['ɪndɪə] *n* Indie *pl*
**Indian** ['ɪndɪən] *adj* (*of India*) indyjski; (*American Indian*) indiański ▷ *n* (*from India*) Hindus(ka) *m*(*f*); (*American Indian*) Indianin(anka) *m*(*f*); **Red ~** czerwonoskóry
**Indian Ocean** *n*: **the ~** Ocean *m* Indyjski
**Indian Summer** *n* (*fig*) babie lato *nt*
**India paper** *n* papier *m* biblijny
**India rubber** *n* kauczuk *m*
**indicate** ['ɪndɪkeɪt] *vt* (*show, point to*) wskazywać (wskazać *perf*); (*mention*) sygnalizować (zasygnalizować *perf*) ▷ *vi* (*Brit: Aut*): **to ~ left/right** sygnalizować (zasygnalizować *perf*) skręt w lewo/prawo

**indication** [ɪndɪ'keɪʃən] *n* znak *m*
**indicative** [ɪn'dɪkətɪv] *adj*: **to be ~ of** być przejawem *+gen* ▷ *n* (*Ling*) tryb *m* oznajmujący
**indicator** ['ɪndɪkeɪtə[r]] *n* (*marker, signal*) oznaka *f*; (*Aut*) kierunkowskaz *m*; (*device, gauge*) wskaźnik *m*
**indices** ['ɪndɪsi:z] *npl of* **index**
**indict** [ɪn'daɪt]: **to ~ sb (for)** *vt* stawiać (postawić *perf*) kogoś w stan oskarżenia (pod zarzutem *+gen*)
**indictable** [ɪn'daɪtəbl] *adj* (*offence*) podlegający formalnemu oskarżeniu
**indictment** [ɪn'daɪtmənt] *n* (*Jur*) akt *m* oskarżenia; **to be an ~ of** wystawiać złe świadectwo *+dat*
**indifference** [ɪn'dɪfrəns] *n* obojętność *f*
**indifferent** [ɪn'dɪfrənt] *adj* (*uninterested*) obojętny; (*mediocre*) mierny
**indigenous** [ɪn'dɪdʒɪnəs] *adj* (*population*) rdzenny; **animals ~ to Africa** zwierzęta zamieszkujące Afrykę
**indigestible** [ɪndɪ'dʒɛstɪbl] *adj* niestrawny
**indigestion** [ɪndɪ'dʒɛstʃən] *n* niestrawność *f*
**indignant** [ɪn'dɪgnənt] *adj*: **to be ~ at sth/ with sb** być oburzonym na coś/na kogoś
**indignation** [ɪndɪg'neɪʃən] *n* oburzenie *nt*
**indignity** [ɪn'dɪgnɪtɪ] *n* upokorzenie *nt*
**indigo** ['ɪndɪgəu] *n* kolor *m* indygo
**indirect** [ɪndɪ'rɛkt] *adj* (*way, effect*) pośredni; (*answer*) wymijający; (*flight*) z przesiadką *post*
**indirectly** [ɪndɪ'rɛktlɪ] *adv* pośrednio
**indiscreet** [ɪndɪs'kri:t] *adj* niedyskretny
**indiscretion** [ɪndɪs'krɛʃən] *n* niedyskrecja *f*
**indiscriminate** [ɪndɪs'krɪmɪnət] *adj* (*bombing*) masowy; (*taste, person*) niewybredny
**indispensable** [ɪndɪs'pɛnsəbl] *adj* (*tool*) nieodzowny, niezbędny; (*worker*) niezastąpiony
**indisposed** [ɪndɪs'pəuzd] *adj* niedysponowany
**indisputable** [ɪndɪs'pju:təbl] *adj* niezaprzeczalny, bezsprzeczny
**indistinct** [ɪndɪs'tɪŋkt] *adj* niewyraźny
**indistinguishable** [ɪndɪs'tɪŋgwɪʃəbl] *adj*: **~ from** nie dający się odróżnić od *+gen*
**individual** [ɪndɪ'vɪdjuəl] *n* osoba *f*; (*as opposed to group, society*) jednostka *f* ▷ *adj* (*personal*) osobisty; (*single*) pojedynczy; (*unique*) indywidualny
**individualist** [ɪndɪ'vɪdjuəlɪst] *n* indywidualista(-tka) *m(f)*
**individuality** [ɪndɪvɪdju'ælɪtɪ] *n* indywidualność *f*
**individually** [ɪndɪ'vɪdjuəlɪ] *adv* (*work*) indywidualnie; (*packed, wrapped*) osobno
**indivisible** [ɪndɪ'vɪzɪbl] *adj* niepodzielny
**Indo-China** ['ɪndəu'tʃaɪnə] *n* Indochiny *pl*
**indoctrinate** [ɪn'dɔktrɪneɪt] *vt* indoktrynować
**indoctrination** [ɪndɔktrɪ'neɪʃən] *n* indoktrynacja *f*
**indolence** ['ɪndələns] *n* lenistwo *nt*
**indolent** ['ɪndələnt] *adj* leniwy
**Indonesia** [ɪndə'ni:zɪə] *n* Indonezja *f*
**Indonesian** [ɪndə'ni:zɪən] *adj* indonezyjski ▷ *n* (*person*) Indonezyjczyk(-jka) *m(f)*; (*Ling*) (język *m*) indonezyjski
**indoor** ['ɪndɔ:[r]] *adj* (*plant*) pokojowy; (*swimming pool*) kryty; (*games, sport*) halowy
**indoors** [ɪn'dɔ:z] *adv* (*be*) wewnątrz; (*go*) do środka; **she stayed ~ all day** przez cały dzień nie wychodziła z domu
**indubitable** [ɪn'dju:bɪtəbl] *adj* niewątpliwy
**indubitably** [ɪn'dju:bɪtəblɪ] *adv* niewątpliwie
**induce** [ɪn'dju:s] *vt* (*feeling, birth*) wywoływać (wywołać *perf*); **to ~ sb to do sth** nakłaniać (nakłonić *perf*) kogoś do zrobienia czegoś
**inducement** [ɪn'dju:smənt] *n* (*incentive*) bodziec *m*; (*pej*: *bribe*) łapówka *f*
**induct** [ɪn'dʌkt] *vt* powierzać (powierzyć *perf*) stanowisko *+dat*; (*US*: *Mil*) powoływać (powołać *perf*) (do wojska)
**induction** [ɪn'dʌkʃən] *n* (*of birth*) wywołanie *nt*
**induction course** (*Brit*) *n* kurs *m* wprowadzający (*dla nowo przyjętych studentów itp*)
**indulge** [ɪn'dʌldʒ] *vt* (*desire, whim*) zaspokajać (zaspokoić *perf*); (*person, child*) spełniać zachcianki (spełnić zachciankę *perf*) *+gen*; (*also*: **indulge in**: *vice, hobby*) oddawać się *+dat*
**indulgence** [ɪn'dʌldʒəns] *n* (*pleasure*) słabostka *f*; (*leniency*) pobłażliwość *f*
**indulgent** [ɪn'dʌldʒənt] *adj* pobłażliwy
**industrial** [ɪn'dʌstrɪəl] *adj* przemysłowy; **~ accident** wypadek w miejscu pracy
**industrial action** *n* akcja *f* protestacyjna *or* strajkowa
**industrial design** *n* wzór *m* przemysłowy
**industrial estate** (*Brit*) *n* teren *m* fabryczny *or* przemysłowy
**industrialist** [ɪn'dʌstrɪəlɪst] *n* przemysłowiec *m*
**industrialize** [ɪn'dʌstrɪəlaɪz] *vt* uprzemysławiać (uprzemysłowić *perf*), industrializować (zindustrializować *perf*)
**industrial park** (*US*) *n* = **industrial estate**
**industrial relations** *npl* stosunki *pl* między pracownikami a pracodawcą
**industrial tribunal** (*Brit*) *n* ≈ sąd *m* pracy
**industrial unrest** (*Brit*) *n* zagrożenie *nt* akcją strajkową
**industrious** [ɪn'dʌstrɪəs] *adj* pracowity
**industry** ['ɪndəstrɪ] *n* (*Comm*) przemysł *m*; (*diligence*) pracowitość *f*
**inebriated** [ɪ'ni:brɪeɪtɪd] (*fml*) *adj* nietrzeźwy
**inedible** [ɪn'ɛdɪbl] *adj* niejadalny

**ineffective** [ɪnɪ'fɛktɪv] *adj* nieskuteczny
**ineffectual** [ɪnɪ'fɛktʃuəl] *adj* = **ineffective**
**inefficiency** [ɪnɪ'fɪʃənsɪ] *n* (*of person*) nieudolność *f*; (*of machine, system*) niewydolność *f*
**inefficient** [ɪnɪ'fɪʃənt] *adj* (*person*) nieudolny; (*machine, system*) niewydolny
**inelegant** [ɪn'ɛlɪgənt] *adj* mało elegancki
**ineligible** [ɪn'ɛlɪdʒɪbl] *adj* (*candidate*) nie spełniający wymogów *or* warunków; **he's ~ for ...** nie przysługuje mu prawo do *+gen*
**inept** [ɪ'nɛpt] *adj* niekompetentny
**ineptitude** [ɪ'nɛptɪtju:d] *n* niekompetencja *f*
**inequality** [ɪnɪ'kwɔlɪtɪ] *n* nierówność *f*
**inequitable** [ɪn'ɛkwɪtəbl] *adj* niesprawiedliwy
**inert** [ɪ'nə:t] *adj* bezwładny; (*gas*) obojętny
**inertia** [ɪ'nə:ʃə] *n* bezwład *m*, inercja *f*
**inertia-reel seat belt** [ɪ'nə:ʃə'ri:l-] *n* pas *m* bezwładnościowy
**inescapable** [ɪnɪ'skeɪpəbl] *adj* nieunikniony
**inessential** [ɪnɪ'sɛnʃl] *adj* niepotrzebny
**inessentials** [ɪnɪ'sɛnʃlz] *npl* rzeczy *pl* nieważne
**inestimable** [ɪn'ɛstɪməbl] *adj* nieoceniony
**inevitability** [ɪnɛvɪtə'bɪlɪtɪ] *n* nieuchronność *f*; **it is an ~** jest to nieuchronne
**inevitable** [ɪn'ɛvɪtəbl] *adj* nieuchronny, nieunikniony
**inevitably** [ɪn'ɛvɪtəblɪ] *adv* nieuchronnie; **as ~ happens ...** jak to zwykle (w takich wypadkach) bywa, ...
**inexact** [ɪnɪg'zækt] *adj* niedokładny
**inexcusable** [ɪnɪks'kju:zəbl] *adj* niewybaczalny
**inexhaustible** [ɪnɪg'zɔ:stɪbl] *adj* niewyczerpany
**inexorable** [ɪn'ɛksərəbl] *adj* nieuchronny
**inexpensive** [ɪnɪk'spɛnsɪv] *adj* niedrogi
**inexperience** [ɪnɪk'spɪərɪəns] *n* brak *m* doświadczenia
**inexperienced** [ɪnɪk'spɪərɪənst] *adj* niedoświadczony; **to be ~ in** nie mieć doświadczenia w *+loc*
**inexplicable** [ɪnɪk'splɪkəbl] *adj* niewytłumaczalny
**inexpressible** [ɪnɪk'sprɛsɪbl] *adj* niewysłowiony
**inextricable** [ɪnɪk'strɪkəbl] *adj* (*union*) nierozerwalny; (*knot*) nie do rozwiązania *post*
**inextricably** [ɪnɪk'strɪkəblɪ] *adv* nierozerwalnie
**infallibility** [ɪnfælə'bɪlɪtɪ] *n* nieomylność *f*
**infallible** [ɪn'fælɪbl] *adj* nieomylny
**infamous** ['ɪnfəməs] *adj* niesławny
**infamy** ['ɪnfəmɪ] *n* niesława *f*
**infancy** ['ɪnfənsɪ] *n* (*of person*) wczesne dzieciństwo *nt*; (*of movement, firm*) stadium *m* początkowe
**infant** ['ɪnfənt] *n* (*baby*) niemowlę *nt*; (*young child*) małe dziecko *nt* ▷ *cpd*: **~ mortality** śmiertelność *m* noworodków; **~ foods** odżywki dla niemowląt
**infantile** ['ɪnfəntaɪl] *adj* (*disease etc*) dziecięcy; (*childish*) dziecinny, infantylny
**infantry** ['ɪnfəntrɪ] *n* piechota *f*
**infantryman** ['ɪnfəntrɪmən] (*irreg: like* **man**) *n* żołnierz *m* piechoty
**infant school** (*Brit*) *n szkoła dla dzieci w wieku 5-7 lat*
**infatuated** [ɪn'fætjueɪtɪd] *adj*: **~ with** zadurzony w *+loc*; **to become ~ with** zadurzyć się (*perf*) w *+loc*
**infatuation** [ɪnfætju'eɪʃən] *n* zadurzenie *nt*
**infect** [ɪn'fɛkt] *vt* (*lit, fig*) zarażać (zarazić *perf*); (*food*) zakażać (zakazić *perf*); **to become ~ed** (*wound*) ulegać (ulec *perf*) zakażeniu; **her pessimism ~ed everyone** jej pesymizm udzielił się wszystkim
**infection** [ɪn'fɛkʃən] (*Med*) *n* (*disease*) infekcja *f*; (*contagion*) zakażenie *nt*
**infectious** [ɪn'fɛkʃəs] *adj* (*disease*) zaraźliwy, zakaźny; (*fig*) zaraźliwy; **to be ~** (*person, animal*) roznosić zarazki
**infer** [ɪn'fə:ʳ] *vt* (*deduce*) wnioskować (wywnioskować *perf*); (*imply*) dawać (dać *perf*) do zrozumienia
**inference** ['ɪnfərəns] *n* (*result*) wniosek *m*; (*process*) wnioskowanie *nt*
**inferior** [ɪn'fɪərɪəʳ] *adj* (*in rank*) niższy; (*in quality*) gorszy, pośledniejszy ▷ *n* (*subordinate*) podwładny(-na) *m*(*f*); (*junior*) młodszy(-sza) *m*(*f*) rangą; **to feel ~ (to)** czuć się gorszym (od *+gen*)
**inferiority** [ɪnfɪərɪ'ɔrətɪ] *n* (*in rank*) niższość *f*; (*in quality*) pośledniość *f*
**inferiority complex** *n* kompleks *m* niższości
**infernal** [ɪn'fə:nl] *adj* piekielny
**inferno** [ɪn'fə:nəu] *n* piekło *nt*
**infertile** [ɪn'fə:taɪl] *adj* (*soil*) nieurodzajny; (*person, animal*) niepłodny, bezpłodny
**infertility** [ɪnfə:'tɪlɪtɪ] *n* (*of soil*) nieurodzajność *f*; (*of person, animal*) niepłodność *f*, bezpłodność *f*
**infested** [ɪn'fɛstɪd] *adj*: **~ (with vermin)** zaatakowany (przez szkodniki)
**infidelity** [ɪnfɪ'dɛlɪtɪ] *n* niewierność *f*
**in-fighting** ['ɪnfaɪtɪŋ] *n* walki *pl or* konflikty *pl* wewnętrzne (*w ramach partii politycznej itp*)
**infiltrate** ['ɪnfɪltreɪt] *vt* infiltrować
**infinite** ['ɪnfɪnɪt] *adj* (*without limits*) nieskończony; (*very great*) ogromny
**infinitely** ['ɪnfɪnɪtlɪ] *adv* nieskończenie
**infinitesimal** [ɪnfɪnɪ'tɛsɪməl] *adj* znikomy
**infinitive** [ɪn'fɪnɪtɪv] *n* (*Ling*) bezokolicznik *m*

**infinity** [ɪn'fɪnɪtɪ] *n* nieskończoność *f*; (*infinite number*) nieskończona liczba *f*
**infirm** [ɪn'fə:m] *adj* (*weak*) niedołężny; (*: from old age*) zniedołężniały; (*ill*) chory
**infirmary** [ɪn'fə:mərɪ] *n* szpital *m*
**infirmity** [ɪn'fə:mɪtɪ] *n* (*weakness*) niedołęstwo *nt*; (*: from old age*) zniedołężnienie *nt*; (*illness*) choroba *f*
**inflame** [ɪn'fleɪm] *vt* (*person*) wzburzać (wzburzyć *perf*); (*emotions*) rozpalać (rozpalić *perf*)
**inflamed** [ɪn'fleɪmd] *adj* (*throat, appendix*) w stanie zapalnym *post*
**inflammable** [ɪn'flæməbl] *adj* łatwopalny
**inflammation** [ɪnflə'meɪʃən] *n* (*Med*) zapalenie *nt*
**inflammatory** [ɪn'flæmətərɪ] *adj* (*speech*) podburzający
**inflatable** [ɪn'fleɪtəbl] *adj* nadmuchiwany
**inflate** [ɪn'fleɪt] *vt* (*tyre*) pompować (napompować *perf*); (*balloon*) nadmuchiwać (nadmuchać *perf*); (*price*) (sztucznie) zawyżać (zawyżyć *perf*); (*expectations*) rozdmuchiwać (rozdmuchać *perf*)
**inflated** [ɪn'fleɪtɪd] *adj* (*price, statistics*) (sztucznie) zawyżony; (*expectations, opinion of o.s.*) wygórowany; (*style, language*) nadęty, napuszony
**inflation** [ɪn'fleɪʃən] *n* inflacja *f*
**inflationary** [ɪn'fleɪʃənərɪ] *adj* inflacyjny
**inflexible** [ɪn'flɛksɪbl] *adj* (*rules, hours*) sztywny; (*person*) mało elastyczny; (*: in particular matter*) nieugięty
**inflict** [ɪn'flɪkt] *vt*: **to ~ on sb** (*damage*) wyrządzać (wyrządzić *perf*) komuś; (*pain*) zadawać (zadać *perf*) komuś; (*punishment*) wymierzać (wymierzyć *perf*) komuś
**infliction** [ɪn'flɪkʃən] *n* (*of damage*) wyrządzanie *nt*; (*of pain*) zadawanie *nt*
**in-flight** ['ɪnflaɪt] *adj* (*refuelling*) w powietrzu *post*; (*entertainment*) podczas lotu *post*
**inflow** ['ɪnfləu] *n* napływ *m*
**influence** ['ɪnfluəns] *n* wpływ *m* ▷ *vt* wpływać (wpłynąć *perf*) na *+acc*; **under the ~ of alcohol** pod wpływem alkoholu
**influential** [ɪnflu'ɛnʃl] *adj* wpływowy
**influenza** [ɪnflu'ɛnzə] *n* grypa *f*
**influx** ['ɪnflʌks] *n* (*of refugees*) napływ *m*; (*of funds*) dopływ *m*
**infomercial** ['ɪnfəumə:ʃəl] (*US: TV*) *n* klip *m* informacyjno-reklamowy
**inform** [ɪn'fɔ:m] *vt*: **to ~ sb of sth** powiadamiać (powiadomić *perf*) *or* informować (poinformować *perf*) kogoś o czymś ▷ *vi*: **to ~ on sb** donosić (donieść *perf*) na kogoś
**informal** [ɪn'fɔ:ml] *adj* (*manner*) bezpośredni; (*language*) potoczny; (*discussion, clothes*) swobodny; (*visit, invitation, announcement*) nieoficjalny
**informality** [ɪnfɔ:'mælɪtɪ] *n* (*of manner*) bezpośredniość *f*; (*of language*) potoczność *f*; (*of discussion*) swoboda *f*; (*of clothes*) swobodny styl *m*; (*of visit, gathering*) nieoficjalny charakter *m*
**informally** [ɪn'fɔ:məlɪ] *adv* (*talk, dress*) swobodnie; (*invite, agree*) nieoficjalnie
**informant** [ɪn'fɔ:mənt] *n* informator(ka) *m(f)*
**information** [ɪnfə'meɪʃən] *n* informacja *f*; **to get ~ on** otrzymywać (otrzymać *perf*) informacje o *+loc*; **a piece of ~** informacja; **for your ~, ...** jeśli chcesz wiedzieć, ...; **for your ~ only** wyłącznie do twojej wiadomości
**information bureau** *n* = **information office**
**information office** *n* biuro *nt* informacji
**information processing** *n* przetwarzanie *nt* informacji
**information retrieval** *n* wyszukiwanie *nt* informacji
**information science** *n* informatyka *f*
**information technology** *n* technika *f* informacyjna
**informative** [ɪn'fɔ:mətɪv] *adj* (*providing useful facts*) zawierający dużo informacji; (*providing useful ideas*) pouczający
**informed** [ɪn'fɔ:md] *adj* (*guess, opinion*) uzasadniony; (*person*): **to be well ~** być dobrze zorientowanym
**informer** [ɪn'fɔ:mə^r] *n* (*also*: **police informer**) informator(ka) *m(f)*
**infra dig** ['ɪnfrə'dɪg] (*inf*) *adj abbr* (= *infra dignitatem*) poniżej mojej/twojej *etc* godności
**infra-red** [ɪnfrə'rɛd] *adj* podczerwony
**infrastructure** ['ɪnfrəstrʌktʃə^r] *n* infrastruktura *f*
**infrequent** [ɪn'fri:kwənt] *adj* rzadki
**infringe** [ɪn'frɪndʒ] *vt* naruszać (naruszyć *perf*) ▷ *vi*: **to ~ on** naruszać (naruszyć *perf*) *+acc*
**infringement** [ɪn'frɪndʒmənt] *n* naruszenie *nt*
**infuriate** [ɪn'fjuərɪeɪt] *vt* rozwścieczać (rozwścieczyć *perf*)
**infuriating** [ɪn'fjuərɪeɪtɪŋ] *adj* (*habit, noise*) denerwujący
**infuse** [ɪn'fju:z] *vt* parzyć (zaparzyć *perf*); **to ~ sb with sth** (*fig*) natchnąć (*perf*) kogoś czymś
**infusion** [ɪn'fju:ʒən] *n* napar *m*
**ingenious** [ɪn'dʒi:njəs] *adj* pomysłowy
**ingenuity** [ɪndʒɪ'nju:ɪtɪ] *n* pomysłowość *f*
**ingenuous** [ɪn'dʒɛnjuəs] *adj* prostoduszny
**ingot** ['ɪŋgət] *n* sztaba *f*
**ingrained** [ɪn'greɪnd] *adj* zakorzeniony
**ingratiate** [ɪn'greɪʃɪeɪt] *vt*: **to ~ o.s. with** przypochlebiać się *or* przymilać się *+dat*
**ingratiating** [ɪn'greɪʃɪeɪtɪŋ] *adj* przypochlebny, przymilny

**ingratitude** [ɪn'grætɪtju:d] *n* niewdzięczność *f*
**ingredient** [ɪn'gri:dɪənt] *n* (*of cake*) składnik *m*; (*of situation*) element *m*
**ingrowing** ['ɪngrəuɪŋ] *adj*: **~ toenail** wrastający paznokieć *m* (u nogi)
**inhabit** [ɪn'hæbɪt] *vt* zamieszkiwać
**inhabitant** [ɪn'hæbɪtnt] *n* mieszkaniec(-nka) *m(f)*
**inhale** [ɪn'heɪl] *vt* wdychać ▷ *vi* (*breathe in*) robić (zrobić *perf*) wdech; (*when smoking*) zaciągać się (zaciągnąć się *perf*)
**inherent** [ɪn'hɪərənt] *adj* (*innate*) wrodzony; **~ in/to** właściwy *+dat*/dla *+gen*
**inherently** [ɪn'hɪərəntlɪ] *adv* z natury
**inherit** [ɪn'herɪt] *vt* dziedziczyć (odziedziczyć *perf*)
**inheritance** [ɪn'herɪtəns] *n* spadek *m*; (*cultural, political*) dziedzictwo *nt*, spuścizna *f*; (*genetic*) dziedziczenie *nt*
**inhibit** [ɪn'hɪbɪt] *vt* (*growth*) hamować (zahamować *perf*); (*person*): **to ~ sb from** powstrzymywać (powstrzymać *perf*) kogoś przed *+instr*
**inhibited** [ɪn'hɪbɪtɪd] (*Psych*) *adj* cierpiący na zahamowania
**inhibiting** [ɪn'hɪbɪtɪŋ] *adj* (*factor*) hamujący; (*situation*) powodujący zahamowania
**inhibition** [ɪnhɪ'bɪʃən] *n* zahamowanie *nt*
**inhospitable** [ɪnhɔs'pɪtəbl] *adj* (*person*) niegościnny; (*place, climate*) nieprzyjazny; (*weather*) niesprzyjający
**inhuman** [ɪn'hju:mən] *adj* nieludzki
**inhumane** [ɪnhju:'meɪn] *adj* niehumanitarny
**inimitable** [ɪ'nɪmɪtəbl] *adj* niepowtarzalny, nie do podrobienia *post* (*inf*)
**iniquitous** [ɪ'nɪkwɪtəs] (*fml*) *adj* niesprawiedliwy
**iniquity** [ɪ'nɪkwɪtɪ] (*fml*) *n* (*wickedness*) niegodziwość *f*; (*injustice*) niesprawiedliwość *f*
**initial** [ɪ'nɪʃl] *adj* początkowy ▷ *n* pierwsza litera *f* ▷ *vt* parafować (parafować *perf*); **initials** *npl* inicjały *pl*; **can I have your ~, Mrs Jones?** poproszę o pierwszą literę Pani imienia, Pani Jones
**initialize** [ɪ'nɪʃəlaɪz] (*Comput*) *vt* inicjować
**initially** [ɪ'nɪʃəlɪ] *adv* (*at first*) początkowo; (*originally*) pierwotnie
**initiate** [ɪ'nɪʃɪeɪt] *vt* (*talks, process*) zapoczątkowywać (zapoczątkować *perf*), inicjować (zainicjować *perf*); **to ~ sb into** (*club, society*) wprowadzać (wprowadzić *perf*) kogoś do *+gen*; (*new skill*) zapoznawać (zapoznać *perf*) kogoś z *+instr*; **to ~ proceedings against sb** (*Jur*) wszczynać (wszcząć *perf*) przeciw(ko) komuś postępowanie
**initiation** [ɪnɪʃɪ'eɪʃən] *n* (*beginning*) zapoczątkowanie *nt*; (*into secret*) wtajemniczenie *nt*; (*into adulthood*) inicjacja *f*
**initiative** [ɪ'nɪʃətɪv] *n* inicjatywa *f*; **to take the ~** podejmować (podjąć *perf*) inicjatywę
**inject** [ɪn'dʒɛkt] *vt* wstrzykiwać (wstrzyknąć *perf*); **to ~ sb with sth** robić (zrobić *perf*) komuś zastrzyk z czegoś, wstrzykiwać (wstrzyknąć *perf*) komuś coś; **to ~ money into** pompować pieniądze w *+acc*
**injection** [ɪn'dʒɛkʃən] *n* (*lit, fig*) zastrzyk *m*; **to give/have an ~** robić (zrobić *perf*)/dostawać (dostać *perf*) zastrzyk
**injudicious** [ɪndʒu'dɪʃəs] *adj* nieroztropny
**injunction** [ɪn'dʒʌŋkʃən] (*Jur*) *n* nakaz *m* sądowy
**injure** ['ɪndʒə<sup>r</sup>] *vt* (*person, feelings*) ranić (zranić *perf*); (*reputation*) szargać (zszargać *perf*); **to ~ o.s.** zranić się (*perf*); **to ~ one's arm** zranić się (*perf*) w ramię
**injured** ['ɪndʒəd] *adj* (*person*) ranny; (*arm, feelings*) zraniony; (*tone*) urażony; **~ party** (*Jur*) poszkodowany
**injurious** [ɪn'dʒuərɪəs] *adj*: **~ to** szkodliwy dla *+gen*
**injury** ['ɪndʒərɪ] *n* uraz *m*; (*Sport*) kontuzja *f*; **severe injuries** ciężkie obrażenia; **to escape without ~** wychodzić (wyjść *perf*) bez szwanku
**injury time** *n dodatkowy czas gry dla wyrównania przerw spowodowanych kontuzjami zawodników*
**injustice** [ɪn'dʒʌstɪs] *n* niesprawiedliwość *f*; **you do me an ~** jesteś wobec mnie niesprawiedliwy
**ink** [ɪŋk] *n* atrament *m*
**ink-jet printer** ['ɪŋkdʒɛt-] *n* drukarka *f* atramentowa
**inkling** ['ɪŋklɪŋ] *n*: **to have an ~ of** mieć pojęcie o *+loc*
**ink-pad** ['ɪŋkpæd] *n* poduszka *f* do pieczątek
**inky** ['ɪŋkɪ] *adj* (*blackness, sky*) atramentowy; (*object*) poplamiony atramentem
**inlaid** ['ɪnleɪd] *adj*: **~ (with)** inkrustowany (*+instr*)
**inland** [*adj* 'ɪnlənd, *adv* ɪn'lænd] *adj* śródlądowy ▷ *adv* w głąb lądu
**Inland Revenue** (*Brit*) *n* ≈ Urząd *m* Skarbowy
**in-laws** ['ɪnlɔ:z] *npl* teściowie *vir pl*
**inlet** ['ɪnlɛt] *n* (wąska) zatoczka *f*
**inlet pipe** *n* rura *f* wlotowa
**inmate** ['ɪnmeɪt] *n* (*of prison*) więzień/więźniarka *m/f*; (*of asylum*) pacjent(ka) *m(f)*
**inmost** ['ɪnməust] *adj* najskrytszy
**inn** [ɪn] *n* gospoda *f*
**innards** ['ɪnədz] (*inf*) *npl* wnętrzności *pl*
**innate** [ɪ'neɪt] *adj* wrodzony
**inner** ['ɪnə<sup>r</sup>] *adj* wewnętrzny

**inner city** *n zamieszkana przez ubogich część śródmieścia, borykająca się z problemami ekonomicznymi i społecznymi*
**innermost** ['ɪnəməust] *adj* = **inmost**
**inner tube** *n* dętka *f*
**innings** ['ɪnɪŋz] *n runda meczu krykietowego, w której gracze jednej drużyny bronią po kolei swojej bramki*; **he's had a good ~** (*fig*) dobrze przeżył życie
**innocence** ['ɪnəsns] *n* niewinność *f*
**innocent** ['ɪnəsnt] *adj* niewinny
**innocuous** [ɪ'nɔkjuəs] *adj* nieszkodliwy
**innovation** [ɪnəu'veɪʃən] *n* innowacja *f*
**innuendo** [ɪnju'ɛndəu] (*pl* **~es**) *n* insynuacja *f*
**innumerable** [ɪ'nju:mrəbl] *adj* niezliczony
**inoculate** [ɪ'nɔkjuleɪt] *vt*: **to ~ sb against sth** szczepić (zaszczepić *perf*) kogoś przeciwko czemuś; **to ~ sb with sth** zaszczepiać (zaszczepić *perf*) komuś coś
**inoculation** [ɪnɔkju'leɪʃən] *n* szczepienie *nt*
**inoffensive** [ɪnə'fɛnsɪv] *adj* nieszkodliwy
**inopportune** [ɪn'ɔpətju:n] *adj* niefortunny
**inordinate** [ɪ'nɔ:dɪnət] *adj* (*pleasure*) niezwykły; (*amount*) nadmierny
**inordinately** [ɪ'nɔ:dɪnətlɪ] *adv* (*pleasant*) niezwykle; (*large*) nadmiernie
**inorganic** [ɪnɔ:'gænɪk] *adj* nieorganiczny
**in-patient** ['ɪnpeɪʃənt] *n* chory(ra) *m(f)* hospitalizowany(-na) *m(f)*
**input** ['ɪnput] *n* (*of resources*) wkład *m*; (*Comput*) dane *pl* wejściowe
**inquest** ['ɪnkwɛst] *n* dochodzenie *nt* (*zwłaszcza mające na celu ustalenie przyczyny zgonu*)
**inquire** [ɪn'kwaɪə^r] *vi* pytać (zapytać *perf or* spytać *perf*) ▷ *vt*: **to ~ (about)** pytać (zapytać *perf or* spytać *perf*) o *+acc*; **to ~ when/where/whether** dowiadywać się, kiedy/gdzie/czy
▸ **inquire after** *vt fus* pytać (zapytać *perf*) o *+acc*
▸ **inquire into** *vt fus* badać (zbadać *perf*) *+acc*
**inquiring** [ɪn'kwaɪərɪŋ] *adj* dociekliwy
**inquiry** [ɪn'kwaɪərɪ] *n* (*question*) zapytanie *nt*; (*investigation*) dochodzenie *nt*; **to hold an ~ into** przeprowadzać (przeprowadzić *perf*) dochodzenie w sprawie *+gen*
**inquiry desk** (*Brit*) *n* punkt *m* informacyjny
**inquiry office** (*Brit*) *n* biuro *nt* informacji
**inquisition** [ɪnkwɪ'zɪʃən] *n* (*interrogation*) przesłuchanie *nt*; (*Rel*): **the I~** inkwizycja *f*
**inquisitive** [ɪn'kwɪzɪtɪv] *adj* dociekliwy
**inroads** ['ɪnrəudz] *npl*: **to make ~ into** (*savings, supplies*) naruszać (naruszyć *perf*) *+acc*
**ins** *abbr* = **inches**
**insane** [ɪn'seɪn] *adj* (*Med*) chory umysłowo; (*foolish, crazy*) szalony
**insanitary** [ɪn'sænɪtərɪ] *adj* niehigieniczny
**insanity** [ɪn'sænɪtɪ] *n* (*Med*) choroba *f* umysłowa; (*of idea etc*) niedorzeczność *f*
**insatiable** [ɪn'seɪʃəbl] *adj* nienasycony
**inscribe** [ɪn'skraɪb] *vt*: **to ~ sth on a wall, to ~ a wall with sth** (*write*) pisać (napisać *perf*) coś na ścianie; (*carve*) ryć (wyryć *perf*) coś na ścianie; **to ~ a book** pisać (napisać *perf*) dedykację w książce; **to ~ a ring/monogram** grawerować (wygrawerować *perf*) pierścionek/monogram
**inscription** [ɪn'skrɪpʃən] *n* (*on gravestone, memorial*) napis *m*, inskrypcja *f*; (*in book*) dedykacja *f*
**inscrutable** [ɪn'skru:təbl] *adj* (*comment*) zagadkowy; (*expression*) nieodgadniony
**inseam** ['ɪnsi:m] (*US*) *n*: **~ measurement** wewnętrzna długość *f* nogawki
**insect** ['ɪnsɛkt] *n* owad *m*
**insect bite** *n* ukąszenie *nt* owada
**insecticide** [ɪn'sɛktɪsaɪd] *n* środek *m* owadobójczy
**insect repellent** *n* środek *m* odstraszający owady
**insecure** [ɪnsɪ'kjuə^r] *adj* (*structure, job*) niepewny; **to be ~** (*person*) nie wierzyć w siebie; **to feel ~** nie czuć się pewnie
**insecurity** [ɪnsɪ'kjuərɪtɪ] *n* niepewność *f*; **job ~** niebezpieczeństwo utraty pracy
**insemination** [ɪnsɛmɪ'neɪʃən] *n*: **artificial ~** sztuczne zapłodnienie *nt*, inseminacja *f*
**insensible** [ɪn'sɛnsɪbl] *adj* (*unconscious*) nieprzytomny; (*unaffected*): **~ to** obojętny *or* niewrażliwy na *+acc*; (*unaware*): **~ of** nieświadomy *+gen*; **to render a patient ~** usypiać (uśpić *perf*) pacjenta
**insensitive** [ɪn'sɛnsɪtɪv] *adj* (*uncaring*) nieczuły; (*to pain etc*) niewrażliwy
**insensitivity** [ɪnsɛnsɪ'tɪvɪtɪ] *n* (*of person*) nieczułość *f*, brak *m* wrażliwości; (*to pain etc*) niewrażliwość *f*
**inseparable** [ɪn'sɛprəbl] *adj* (*friends*) nierozłączny; (*ideas etc*): **to be ~ from** być nierozłącznie *or* nierozerwalnie związanym z *+instr*
**insert** [*vb* ɪn'sə:t, *n* 'ɪnsə:t] *vt* wkładać (włożyć *perf*) ▷ *n* wkładka *f*
**insertion** [ɪn'sə:ʃən] *n* (*of needle*) wprowadzenie *nt*; (*of peg etc*) włożenie *nt*; (*of comment*) wtrącenie *nt*
**in-service** ['ɪn'sə:vɪs] *adj*: **~ training** doskonalenie *nt* zawodowe; **~ course** kurs doskonalenia zawodowego
**inshore** [ɪn'ʃɔ:^r] *adj* przybrzeżny ▷ *adv* (*be*) przy brzegu; (*move*) ku brzegowi
**inside** ['ɪn'saɪd] *n* (*interior*) wnętrze *nt*; (*of road: Brit*) lewa strona *f*; (*: US, Europe*) prawa strona *f* ▷ *adj* wewnętrzny ▷ *adv* (*go*) do środka; (*be*) w środku, wewnątrz ▷ *prep* (*location*) wewnątrz *+gen*; (*time*) w ciągu *+gen*; **insides** *npl* (*inf*) wnętrzności *pl*
**inside forward** *n* środkowy napastnik *m*

**inside information** *n* informacja *f* z pierwszej ręki
**inside lane** (*Aut*) *n* (*Brit*) lewy pas *m*; (*US, Europe*) prawy pas *m*
**inside leg measurement** (*Brit*) *n* wewnętrzna długość *f* nogawki
**inside out** *adv* na lewą stronę; (*fig: know*) na wylot
**insider** [ɪn'saɪdəʳ] *n* osoba *f* dobrze poinformowana
**insider dealing** *or* **trading** *n handel akcjami w oparciu o nielegalne wykorzystanie informacji posiadanych z racji zajmowanego stanowiska*
**inside story** *n* relacja *f* z pierwszej ręki
**insidious** [ɪn'sɪdɪəs] *adj* zdradziecki, podstępny
**insight** ['ɪnsaɪt] *n* (*Psych*) wgląd *m*; **to gain (an) ~ into sth** zgłębić (*perf*) coś; **a flash of ~** olśnienie; **a number of interesting ~s** szereg interesujących spostrzeżeń
**insignia** [ɪn'sɪgnɪə] *n inv* insygnia *pl*
**insignificant** [ɪnsɪg'nɪfɪknt] *adj* (*unimportant*) mało znaczący, bez znaczenia *post*; (*small*) nieznaczny
**insincere** [ɪnsɪn'sɪəʳ] *adj* nieszczery
**insincerity** [ɪnsɪn'sɛrɪtɪ] *n* nieszczerość *f*
**insinuate** [ɪn'sɪnjueɪt] *vt* (*imply*) insynuować
**insinuation** [ɪnsɪnju'eɪʃən] *n* insynuacja *f*
**insipid** [ɪn'sɪpɪd] *adj* mdły, bez smaku *post*; (*fig: person, style*) bezbarwny
**insist** [ɪn'sɪst] *vi* upierać się, nalegać; **to ~ on sth** upierać się przy czymś; **to ~ that ...** (*demand*) upierać się *or* nalegać, żeby ...; (*claim*) utrzymywać *or* uparcie twierdzić, że ...
**insistence** [ɪn'sɪstəns] *n* nalegania *pl*; **~ on** upieranie się przy *+loc*
**insistent** [ɪn'sɪstənt] *adj* (*resolute*) stanowczy; (*continual*) uporczywy; **he was ~ that we should have a drink** nalegał, żebyśmy się napili
**insole** ['ɪnsəul] *n* brandzel *m*
**insolence** ['ɪnsələns] *n* bezczelność *f*
**insolent** ['ɪnsələnt] *adj* bezczelny
**insoluble** [ɪn'sɔljubl] *adj* nierozwiąz(yw)alny, nie do rozwiązania *post*
**insolvency** [ɪn'sɔlvənsɪ] *n* niewypłacalność *f*
**insolvent** [ɪn'sɔlvənt] *adj* niewypłacalny
**insomnia** [ɪn'sɔmnɪə] *n* bezsenność *f*
**insomniac** [ɪn'sɔmnɪæk] *n* osoba *f* cierpiąca na bezsenność
**inspect** [ɪn'spɛkt] *vt* (*examine*) badać (zbadać *perf*); (*premises, equipment*) kontrolować (skontrolować *perf*), robić (zrobić *perf*) przegląd *or* inspekcję *+gen*; (*troops*) dokonywać (dokonać *perf*) przeglądu *or* inspekcji *+gen*
**inspection** [ɪn'spɛkʃən] *n* (*examination*) badanie *nt*; (*of premises, equipment, troops*) przegląd *m*, inspekcja *f*
**inspector** [ɪn'spɛktəʳ] *n* (*Admin, Police*) inspektor *m*; (*Brit: on bus, train*) kontroler(ka) *m(f)* (biletów)
**inspiration** [ɪnspə'reɪʃən] *n* (*encouragement*) inspiracja *f*; (*influence, source*) źródło *nt* inspiracji; (*idea*) natchnienie *nt*
**inspire** [ɪn'spaɪəʳ] *vt* (*person*) inspirować (zainspirować *perf*); (*confidence, hope*) wzbudzać (wzbudzić *perf*)
**inspired** [ɪn'spaɪəd] *adj* (*writer, book etc*) natchniony; **in an ~ moment** w chwili natchnienia
**inspiring** [ɪn'spaɪərɪŋ] *adj* porywający; (*for artist*) inspirujący, budzący natchnienie
**inst.** (*Brit: Comm*) *abbr* (= *instant*): **of the 16th ~** 16 bm. (= *16 bieżącego miesiąca*)
**instability** [ɪnstə'bɪlɪtɪ] *n* brak *m* stabilności, chwiejność *f*
**install** [ɪn'stɔːl] *vt* (*machine*) instalować (zainstalować *perf*); (*official*) wprowadzać (wprowadzić *perf*) na stanowisko
**installation** [ɪnstə'leɪʃən] *n* instalacja *f*; **military/industrial ~s** obiekty militarne/przemysłowe
**installment plan** (*US*) *n* system *m* ratalny
**instalment**, (*US*) **installment** [ɪn'stɔːlmənt] *n* (*of payment*) rata *f*; (*of story, TV serial*) odcinek *m*; **in ~s** w ratach
**instance** ['ɪnstəns] *n* przypadek *m*; **for ~** na przykład; **in that ~** w tym przypadku *or* wypadku; **in many ~s** w wielu wypadkach; **in the first ~** w pierwszej kolejności
**instant** ['ɪnstənt] *n* chwila *f*, moment *m* ▷ *adj* (*reaction, success*) natychmiastowy; (*coffee*) rozpuszczalny, instant *post*; (*potatoes, rice*) błyskawiczny; **the 10th ~** dziesiątego bieżącego miesiąca
**instantaneous** [ɪnstən'teɪnɪəs] *adj* natychmiastowy
**instantly** ['ɪnstəntlɪ] *adv* natychmiast; **he was killed ~** zginął na miejscu
**instant replay** (*TV*) *n* powtórka *f*
**instead** [ɪn'stɛd] *adv* zamiast tego; **~ of** zamiast *+gen*
**instep** ['ɪnstɛp] *n* podbicie *nt*
**instigate** ['ɪnstɪgeɪt] *vt* (*rebellion*) wzniecać (wzniecić *perf*); (*search*) wszczynać (wszcząć *perf*); (*talks*) doprowadzać (doprowadzić *perf*) do *+gen*
**instigation** [ɪnstɪ'geɪʃən] *n* namowa *f*; **at sb's ~** za czyjąś namową
**instil** [ɪn'stɪl] *vt*: **to ~ fear** *etc* **into sb** wzbudzać (wzbudzić *perf*) w kimś strach *etc*
**instinct** ['ɪnstɪŋkt] *n* (*Bio*) instynkt *m*; (*reaction*) odruch *m*

**instinctive** [ɪn'stɪŋktɪv] *adj* instynktowny, odruchowy
**instinctively** [ɪn'stɪŋktɪvlɪ] *adv* instynktownie, odruchowo
**institute** ['ɪnstɪtju:t] *n* instytut *m* ▷ *vt* (*system, rule*) ustanawiać (ustanowić *perf*); (*scheme, course of action*) wprowadzać (wprowadzić *perf*); (*proceedings, inquiry*) wszczynać (wszcząć *perf*)
**institution** [ɪnstɪ'tju:ʃən] *n* (*establishment*) ustanowienie *nt*; (*custom, tradition, organization*) instytucja *f*; (*mental home etc*) zakład *m*
**institutional** [ɪnstɪ'tju:ʃənl] *adj* (*education*) formalny; (*value, quality*) tradycyjny; **to be in ~ care** (*mental patient, child*) przebywać w zakładzie
**instruct** [ɪn'strʌkt] *vt* (*teach*): **to ~ sb in sth** szkolić (wyszkolić *perf*) kogoś w czymś; (*order*): **to ~ sb to do sth** instruować (poinstruować *perf*) kogoś, żeby coś zrobił
**instruction** [ɪn'strʌkʃən] *n* szkolenie *nt*, instruktaż *m* ▷ *cpd*: **~ manual/leaflet** instrukcja *f*; **instructions** *npl* instrukcje *pl*; **~s (for use)** instrukcja (obsługi)
**instructive** [ɪn'strʌktɪv] *adj* pouczający
**instructor** [ɪn'strʌktəʳ] *n* instruktor(ka) *m(f)*
**instrument** ['ɪnstrumənt] *n* narzędzie *nt*; (*Mus*) instrument *m*
**instrumental** [ɪnstru'mɛntl] *adj* (*Mus*) instrumentalny; **to be ~ in** odgrywać (odegrać *perf*) znaczącą rolę w *+loc*
**instrumentalist** [ɪnstru'mɛntəlɪst] *n* instrumentalista(-tka) *m(f)*
**instrument panel** *n* tablica *f* rozdzielcza
**insubordination** [ɪnsəbɔ:də'neɪʃən] *n* niesubordynacja *f*
**insufferable** [ɪn'sʌfrəbl] *adj* nieznośny, nie do zniesienia *post*
**insufficient** [ɪnsə'fɪʃənt] *adj* niewystarczający
**insufficiently** [ɪnsə'fɪʃəntlɪ] *adv* niewystarczająco
**insular** ['ɪnsjuləʳ] *adj* (*outlook*) ciasny; (*person*) zasklepiony w sobie
**insulate** ['ɪnsjuleɪt] *vt* izolować (odizolować *perf*); (*against electricity*) izolować (zaizolować *perf*)
**insulating tape** ['ɪnsjuleɪtɪŋ-] *n* taśma *f* izolacyjna
**insulation** [ɪnsju'leɪʃən] *n* izolacja *f*
**insulator** ['ɪnsjuleɪtəʳ] *n* izolator *m*
**insulin** ['ɪnsjulɪn] *n* insulina *f*
**insult** [*n* 'ɪnsʌlt, *vb* ɪn'sʌlt] *n* zniewaga *f*, obelga *f* ▷ *vt* znieważać (znieważyć *perf*), obrażać (obrazić *perf*)
**insulting** [ɪn'sʌltɪŋ] *adj* obelżywy
**insuperable** [ɪn'sju:prəbl] *adj* nie do pokonania *post*
**insurance** [ɪn'ʃuərəns] *n* ubezpieczenie *nt*; **fire/life ~** ubezpieczenie na wypadek pożaru/na życie; **to take out ~ (against)** ubezpieczać się (ubezpieczyć się *perf*) (od *+gen*)
**insurance agent** *n* agent(ka) *m(f)* ubezpieczeniowy(-wa) *m(f)*
**insurance broker** *n* makler *m or* broker *m* ubezpieczeniowy
**insurance policy** *n* polisa *f* ubezpieczeniowa
**insurance premium** *n* składka *f* ubezpieczeniowa
**insure** [ɪn'ʃuəʳ] *vt*: **to ~ (against)** ubezpieczać (ubezpieczyć *perf*) (od *+gen*); **to ~ (o.s.) against sth** (*to prevent it from happening*) zabezpieczać się (zabezpieczyć się *perf*) przed czymś; (*in case it happens*) zabezpieczać się (zabezpieczyć się *perf*) na wypadek czegoś; **to be ~d for 5,000 pounds** być ubezpieczonym na 5,000 funtów
**insured** [ɪn'ʃuəd] *n*: **the ~** ubezpieczony(-na) *m(f)*
**insurer** [ɪn'ʃuərəʳ] *n* ubezpieczyciel *m*
**insurgent** [ɪn'sə:dʒənt] *adj* rebeliancki ▷ *n* powstaniec *m*, rebeliant *m*
**insurmountable** [ɪnsə'mauntəbl] *adj* nie do pokonania *post*
**insurrection** [ɪnsə'rɛkʃən] *n* powstanie *nt*
**intact** [ɪn'tækt] *adj* nietknięty, nienaruszony
**intake** ['ɪnteɪk] *n* (*of food, drink*) spożycie *nt*; (*of air, oxygen*) zużycie *nt*; (*Brit: Scol*) nabór *m*
**intangible** [ɪn'tændʒɪbl] *adj* (*idea, quality*) nieuchwytny; (*benefit*) nienamacalny
**integer** ['ɪntɪdʒəʳ] *n* liczba *f* całkowita
**integral** ['ɪntɪgrəl] *adj* integralny
**integrate** ['ɪntɪgreɪt] *vt* (*newcomer*) wprowadzać (wprowadzić *perf*); (*ideas, systems*) łączyć (połączyć *perf*) (w jedną całość), integrować (zintegrować *perf*) ▷ *vi* integrować się (zintegrować się *perf*)
**integrated circuit** ['ɪntɪgreɪtɪd-] *n* układ *m or* obwód *m* scalony
**integration** [ɪntɪ'greɪʃən] *n* integracja *f*
**integrity** [ɪn'tɛgrɪtɪ] *n* (*of person*) prawość *f*; (*of culture, group*) integralność *f*
**intellect** ['ɪntəlɛkt] *n* (*intelligence*) inteligencja *f*; (*cleverness*) intelekt *m*
**intellectual** [ɪntə'lɛktjuəl] *adj* intelektualny ▷ *n* intelektualista(-tka) *m(f)*
**intelligence** [ɪn'tɛlɪdʒəns] *n* inteligencja *f*; (*Mil etc*) wywiad *m*
**intelligence quotient** *n* iloraz *m* inteligencji
**intelligence service** *n* służba *f* wywiadowcza
**intelligence test** *n* test *m* na inteligencję
**intelligent** [ɪn'tɛlɪdʒənt] *adj* inteligentny
**intelligently** [ɪn'tɛlɪdʒəntlɪ] *adv* inteligentnie
**intelligentsia** [ɪntɛlɪ'dʒɛntsɪə] *n*: **the ~** inteligencja *f*, inteligenci *vir pl*

**intelligible** [ɪn'tɛlɪdʒɪbl] *adj* zrozumiały
**intemperate** [ɪn'tɛmpərət] *adj* nieumiarkowany, przesadny
**intend** [ɪn'tɛnd] *vt*: **to ~ sth for sb** przeznaczać (przeznaczyć *perf*) coś dla kogoś; **to ~ to do sth** zamierzać coś (z)robić
**intended** [ɪn'tɛndɪd] *adj (effect, insult)* zamierzony; *(journey)* planowany
**intense** [ɪn'tɛns] *adj (heat)* wielki; *(effort, activity)* intensywny; *(effect, emotion, experience)* silny, głęboki; *(person: serious)* poważny; *(: emotional)* uczuciowy
**intensely** [ɪn'tɛnslɪ] *adv (extremely)* wielce; *(feel, experience)* silnie, głęboko
**intensify** [ɪn'tɛnsɪfaɪ] *vt* nasilać (nasilić *perf*)
**intensity** [ɪn'tɛnsɪtɪ] *n (of heat, anger)* nasilenie *nt*; *(of effort)* intensywność *f*
**intensive** [ɪn'tɛnsɪv] *adj* intensywny
**intensive care** *n*: **to be in ~** przebywać na oddziale intensywnej opieki medycznej
**intensive care unit** *n* oddział *m* intensywnej opieki medycznej
**intent** [ɪn'tɛnt] *n (fml)* intencja *f* ▷ *adj* skupiony; **~ on** skupiony na *+loc*; **to be ~ on doing sth** być zdecydowanym coś (z)robić; **to all ~s and purposes** praktycznie rzecz biorąc
**intention** [ɪn'tɛnʃən] *n* zamiar *m*
**intentional** [ɪn'tɛnʃənl] *adj* zamierzony, celowy
**intentionally** [ɪn'tɛnʃnəlɪ] *adv* celowo
**intently** [ɪn'tɛntlɪ] *adv* w skupieniu, uważnie
**inter** [ɪn'təːʳ] *vt* chować (pochować *perf*)
**interact** [ɪntər'ækt] *vi* oddziaływać na siebie (wzajemnie); **to ~ (with sb)** *(co-operate)* współdziałać (z kimś)
**interaction** [ɪntər'ækʃən] *n* wzajemne oddziaływanie *nt*; *(co-operation)* współdziałanie *nt*; *(social)* interakcja *f*
**interactive** [ɪntər'æktɪv] *adj* interakcyjny
**intercede** [ɪntə'siːd] *vi*: **to ~ with sb on behalf of sb** *or* **for sb** wstawiać się (wstawić się *perf*) u kogoś za kimś
**intercept** [ɪntə'sɛpt] *vt (message)* przechwytywać (przechwycić *perf*); *(person, car)* zatrzymywać (zatrzymać *perf*)
**interception** [ɪntə'sɛpʃən] *n (of message)* przechwycenie *nt*
**interchange** ['ɪntətʃeɪndʒ] *n (of information etc)* wymiana *f*; *(Aut)* rozjazd *m (na autostradzie)*
**interchangeable** [ɪntə'tʃeɪndʒəbl] *adj* zamienny
**intercity** [ɪntə'sɪtɪ] *adj*: **~ train** pociąg *m* InterCity
**intercom** ['ɪntəkɔm] *n* telefon *m* komunikacji wewnętrznej, intercom *m*
**interconnect** [ɪntəkə'nɛkt] *vi* łączyć się (ze sobą)
**intercontinental** ['ɪntəkɔntɪ'nɛntl] *adj* międzykontynentalny
**intercourse** ['ɪntəkɔːs] *n (sexual)* stosunek *m*, zbliżenie *nt*; *(verbal)* kontakty *pl*; **social ~** współżycie społeczne
**interdependence** [ɪntədɪ'pɛndəns] *n* współzależność *f*
**interdependent** [ɪntədɪ'pɛndənt] *adj* współzależny
**interest** ['ɪntrɪst] *n (desire to know, pastime)*: **~ (in)** zainteresowanie *nt (+instr)*; *(advantage, profit)* interes *m*; *(Comm: in company)* udział *m*; *(: sum of money)* odsetki *pl*, procent *m* ▷ *vt* interesować (zainteresować *perf*); **controlling ~** pakiet kontrolny; **compound/simple ~** procent składany/zwykły; **British ~s in the Middle East** interesy brytyjskie na Bliskim Wschodzie; **his main ~ is ...** interesuje się głównie *+instr*; **it is in our ~ to ...** jest *or* leży w naszym interesie, żeby *+infin*
**interested** ['ɪntrɪstɪd] *adj* zainteresowany; **to be ~ in sth/sb** interesować się czymś/kimś; **to be ~ in doing sth** być zainteresowanym robieniem czegoś
**interest-free** ['ɪntrɪst'friː] *adj* bezprocentowy, nie oprocentowany ▷ *adv* bezprocentowo, bez oprocentowania
**interesting** ['ɪntrɪstɪŋ] *adj* interesujący, ciekawy
**interest rate** *n* stopa *f* procentowa
**interface** ['ɪntəfeɪs] *n (Comput)* interfejs *m*; *(fig)* obszar *m* wzajemnego oddziaływania
**interfere** [ɪntə'fɪəʳ] *vi*: **to ~ in** wtrącać się (wtrącić się *perf*) do *+gen or* w *+acc*; **to ~ with** *(object)* majstrować przy *+loc*; *(career)* przeszkadzać (przeszkodzić *perf*) w *+loc*; *(plans)* kolidować z *+instr*; **don't ~** nie wtrącaj się
**interference** [ɪntə'fɪərəns] *n (in sb's affairs)* wtrącanie się *nt*, ingerencja *f*; *(Radio, TV)* interferencja *f*
**interfering** [ɪntə'fɪərɪŋ] *adj* wścibski
**interim** ['ɪntərɪm] *adj* tymczasowy ▷ *n*: **in the ~** w międzyczasie
**interim dividend** *n* dywidenda *f* tymczasowa
**interior** [ɪn'tɪərɪəʳ] *n* wnętrze *nt* ▷ *adj* wewnętrzny; **(in)to/in the ~ of** *(country, continent)* w głąb/w głębi *+gen*; **~ minister/department** Minister/Departament Spraw Wewnętrznych
**interior decorator** *n* dekorator(ka) *m(f)* wnętrz
**interior designer** *n* projektant(ka) *m(f)* wnętrz
**interjection** [ɪntə'dʒɛkʃən] *n (interruption)* wtrącenie *nt*; *(Ling)* wykrzyknik *m*
**interlock** [ɪntə'lɔk] *vi* łączyć się (ze sobą), zazębiać się (o siebie)

i

**interloper** ['ɪntələupəʳ] *n* intruz *m*
**interlude** ['ɪntəlu:d] *n* (*break*) przerwa *f*; (*Theat*) antrakt *m*
**intermarry** [ɪntə'mærɪ] *vi* żenić się między sobą
**intermediary** [ɪntə'mi:dɪərɪ] *n* pośrednik(-iczka) *m(f)*
**intermediate** [ɪntə'mi:dɪət] *adj* (*stage*) pośredni; (*student*) średniozaawansowany
**interminable** [ɪn'tə:mɪnəbl] *adj* nie kończący się, bez końca *post*
**intermission** [ɪntə'mɪʃən] *n* przerwa *f*; (*Theat*) antrakt *m*
**intermittent** [ɪntə'mɪtnt] *adj* (*noise*) przerywany; (*publication*) nieregularny
**intermittently** [ɪntə'mɪtntlɪ] *adv* nieregularnie
**intern** [*vb* ɪn'tə:n, *n* 'ɪntə:n] *vt* internować (internować *perf*) ▷ *n* (*US*) lekarz *m* stażysta *m*
**internal** [ɪn'tə:nl] *adj* wewnętrzny
**internally** [ɪn'tə:nəlɪ] *adv*: **"not to be taken ~"** „do użytku zewnętrznego"
**Internal Revenue Service** (*US*) *n* ≈ Izba *f* Skarbowa
**international** [ɪntə'næʃənl] *adj* międzynarodowy ▷ *n* (*Brit*: *Sport*) mecz *m* międzypaństwowy
**International Atomic Energy Agency** *n* Międzynarodowa Agencja *f* Energii Atomowej
**International Chamber of Commerce** *n* Międzynarodowa Izba *f* Handlowa
**International Court of Justice** *n* Międzynarodowy Trybunał *m* Sprawiedliwości
**international date line** *n* linia *f* zmiany daty
**International Labour Organization** *n* Międzynarodowa Organizacja *f* Pracy
**internationally** [ɪntə'næʃnəlɪ] *adv* na arenie międzynarodowej
**International Monetary Fund** *n* Międzynarodowy Fundusz *m* Walutowy
**internecine** [ɪntə'ni:saɪn] *adj* (*war, quarrel*) wyniszczający dla obu stron
**internee** [ɪntə:'ni:] *n* internowany(-na) *m(f)*
**Internet** ['ɪntə:nɛt] (*Comput*) *n*: **the ~** Internet *m*
**Internet café** *n* (*Comput*) kawiarenka *f* internetowa
**internment** [ɪn'tə:nmənt] *n* internowanie *nt*
**interpersonal** [ɪntə:'pə:sənəl] *adj* międzyludzki
**interplay** ['ɪntəpleɪ] *n*: **~ (of/between)** (wzajemne) oddziaływanie *nt* (*+gen*/między *+instr*)
**Interpol** ['ɪntəpɔl] *n* Interpol *m*
**interpret** [ɪn'tə:prɪt] *vt* (*explain, understand*) interpretować (zinterpretować *perf*); (*translate*) tłumaczyć (przetłumaczyć *perf*) (*ustnie*) ▷ *vi* tłumaczyć (*ustnie*)
**interpretation** [ɪntə:prɪ'teɪʃən] *n* interpretacja *f*
**interpreter** [ɪn'tə:prɪtəʳ] *n* tłumacz(ka) *m(f)*
**interpreting** [ɪn'tə:prɪtɪŋ] *n* tłumaczenie *nt*
**interrelated** [ɪntərɪ'leɪtɪd] *adj* powiązany (ze sobą)
**interrogate** [ɪn'tɛrəugeɪt] *vt* przesłuchiwać (przesłuchać *perf*)
**interrogation** [ɪntɛrəu'geɪʃən] *n* przesłuchanie *nt*
**interrogative** [ɪntə'rɔgətɪv] (*Ling*) *adj* pytajny
**interrogator** [ɪn'tɛrəgeɪtəʳ] *n* przesłuchujący(-ca) *m(f)*, śledczy *m*
**interrupt** [ɪntə'rʌpt] *vt* (*speaker*) przerywać (przerwać *perf*) *+dat*; (*conversation*) przerywać (przerwać *perf*) ▷ *vi* przerywać (przerwać *perf*)
**interruption** [ɪntə'rʌpʃən] *n*: **there were several ~s** kilka razy przerywano; **she hates ~s** nie znosi, kiedy się jej przerywa
**intersect** [ɪntə'sɛkt] *vi* przecinać się (przeciąć się *perf*) ▷ *vt* przecinać (przeciąć *perf*)
**intersection** [ɪntə'sɛkʃən] *n* (*of roads*) przecięcie *nt*, skrzyżowanie *nt*; (*Math*: *point*) punkt *m* przecięcia; (: *set*) część *f* wspólna (zbiorów)
**intersperse** [ɪntə'spə:s] *vt*: **to ~ sth with** urozmaicać (urozmaicić *perf*) coś *+instr*
**intertwine** [ɪntə'twaɪn] *vi* splatać się (spleść się *perf*)
**interval** ['ɪntəvl] *n* przerwa *f*; (*Mus*) interwał *m*; **sunny ~s** przejaśnienia; **at six-month ~s** w sześciomiesięcznych odstępach
**intervene** [ɪntə'vi:n] *vi* (*in situation*) interweniować (zainterweniować *perf*); (*in speech*) wtrącać się (wtrącić się *perf*); (*event*) przeszkadzać (przeszkodzić *perf*); (*years, months*) upływać (upłynąć *perf*)
**intervening** [ɪntə'vi:nɪŋ] *adj*: **in the ~ period/years** od tamtego czasu
**intervention** [ɪntə'vɛnʃən] *n* interwencja *f*
**interview** ['ɪntəvju:] *n* (*for job*) rozmowa *f* kwalifikacyjna; (*Radio, TV*) wywiad *m* ▷ *vt* (*for job*) przeprowadzać (przeprowadzić *perf*) rozmowę kwalifikacyjną z *+instr*; (*Radio, TV*) przeprowadzać (przeprowadzić *perf*) wywiad z *+instr*
**interviewer** ['ɪntəvjuəʳ] *n* (*of candidate, job applicant*) przeprowadzający(-ca) *m(f)* rozmowę kwalifikacyjną; (*Radio, TV*) dziennikarz(-arka) *m(f)* przeprowadzający(-ca) *m(f)* wywiad
**intestate** [ɪn'tɛsteɪt] *adv*: **to die ~** umrzeć (*perf*) nie pozostawiwszy testamentu
**intestinal** [ɪn'tɛstɪnl] *adj* jelitowy
**intestine** [ɪn'tɛstɪn] *n* jelito *nt*

**intimacy** ['ɪntɪməsɪ] *n* bliskość *f*
**intimate** [*adj* 'ɪntɪmət, *vb* 'ɪntɪmeɪt] *adj* (*friend*) bliski; (*relations, matter, detail*) intymny; (*restaurant, atmosphere*) kameralny; (*knowledge*) gruntowny ▷ *vt* napomykać (napomknąć *perf*) o *+loc*; **to ~ that ...** dawać (dać *perf*) do zrozumienia, że...
**intimately** ['ɪntɪmətlɪ] *adv* (*acquainted*) blisko; (*inside out*) gruntownie; (*sexually*) intymnie; **to talk ~ about** zwierzać się sobie z *+gen*
**intimation** [ɪntɪ'meɪʃən] *n*: **to feel** *or* **have an ~ of** mieć przeczucie *+gen*
**intimidate** [ɪn'tɪmɪdeɪt] *vt* zastraszać (zastraszyć *perf*)
**intimidation** [ɪntɪmɪ'deɪʃən] *n* zastraszenie *nt*

 KEYWORD

**into** ['ɪntu] *prep* **1** (*indicating motion or direction*) do *+gen*; **to go into town** iść (pójść *perf*) do miasta; **throw it into the fire** wrzuć to do ognia *or* w ogień; **research into cancer** badania nad rakiem
**2** (*indicating change of condition, result*): **the vase broke into pieces** wazon rozbił się na kawałki; **she burst into tears** wybuchła płaczem; **they got into trouble** wpadli w tarapaty

**intolerable** [ɪn'tɔlərəbl] *adj* (*life, situation*) nieznośny, nie do zniesienia *post*; (*quality, methods*) nie do przyjęcia *post*
**intolerance** [ɪn'tɔlərns] *n* nietolerancja *f*
**intolerant** [ɪn'tɔlərnt] *adj*: **~ (of)** nietolerancyjny (wobec *or* w stosunku do *+gen*)
**intonation** [ɪntəu'neɪʃən] *n* intonacja *f*
**intoxicated** [ɪn'tɔksɪkeɪtɪd] *adj* odurzony *or* upojony (alkoholem)
**intoxication** [ɪntɔksɪ'keɪʃən] *n* upojenie *nt* alkoholowe, odurzenie *nt* alkoholem
**intractable** [ɪn'træktəbl] *adj* (*person*) nieustępliwy; (*problem*) trudny do rozwiązania
**intransigence** [ɪn'trænsɪdʒəns] *n* nieprzejednanie *nt*
**intransigent** [ɪn'trænsɪdʒənt] *adj* nieprzejednany
**intransitive** [ɪn'trænsɪtɪv] *adj* (*Ling*) nieprzechodni
**intra-uterine device** ['ɪntrə'ju:təraɪn-] *n* wkładka *f* domaciczna *or* wewnątrzmaciczna
**intravenous** [ɪntrə'vi:nəs] *adj* dożylny
**in-tray** ['ɪntreɪ] *n* tacka *f* na korespondencję przychodzącą
**intrepid** [ɪn'trɛpɪd] *adj* nieustraszony
**intricacy** ['ɪntrɪkəsɪ] *n* zawiłość *f*
**intricate** ['ɪntrɪkət] *adj* zawiły
**intrigue** [ɪn'tri:g] *n* (*plotting*) intrygi *pl*; (*instance*) intryga *f* ▷ *vt* intrygować (zaintrygować *perf*)
**intriguing** [ɪn'tri:gɪŋ] *adj* intrygujący
**intrinsic** [ɪn'trɪnsɪk] *adj* (*goodness, superiority*) wrodzony; (*part*) nieodłączny; **these objects have no ~ value** przedmioty te nie przedstawiają sobą żadnej wartości; **it is a problem of great ~ interest** jest to problem wielce interesujący sam w sobie
**introduce** [ɪntrə'dju:s] *vt* (*new idea, method*) wprowadzać (wprowadzić *perf*); (*speaker*) przedstawiać (przedstawić *perf*); **to ~ sb (to sb)** przedstawiać (przedstawić *perf*) kogoś (komuś); **to ~ sb to sth** zaznajamiać (zaznajomić *perf*) kogoś z czymś; **may I ~ ...?** Pan/Pani pozwoli, że przedstawię ...
**introduction** [ɪntrə'dʌkʃən] *n* (*of new idea, measure*) wprowadzenie *nt*; (*of person*) przedstawienie *nt*, prezentacja *f*; (*to new experience*) zapoznanie *nt*, zaznajomienie *nt*; (*in book*) wstęp *m*, wprowadzenie *nt*; **a letter of ~** list polecający
**introductory** [ɪntrə'dʌktərɪ] *adj* wstępny; **~ remarks** uwagi wstępne; **an ~ offer** oferta wstępna
**introspection** [ɪntrəu'spɛkʃən] *n* introspekcja *f*
**introspective** [ɪntrəu'spɛktɪv] *adj* introspekcyjny
**introvert** ['ɪntrəuvə:t] *n* introwertyk(-yczka) *m(f)* ▷ *adj* (*also*: **introverted**: *behaviour*) introwersyjny; (*child*) introwertyczny
**intrude** [ɪn'tru:d] *vi* przeszkadzać (przeszkodzić *perf*); **to ~ on** zakłócać (zakłócić *perf*) *+acc*; **am I intruding?** czy nie przeszkadzam?
**intruder** [ɪn'tru:dəʳ] *n* intruz *m*
**intrusion** [ɪn'tru:ʒən] *n* (*of person*) wtargnięcie *nt*; (*of outside influences*) wpływ *m*
**intrusive** [ɪn'tru:sɪv] *adj* niepożądany
**intuition** [ɪntju:'ɪʃən] *n* intuicja *f*; **an ~** przeczucie *nt*
**intuitive** [ɪn'tju:ɪtɪv] *adj* intuicyjny
**inundate** ['ɪnʌndeɪt] *vt*: **to ~ sb/sth with** zasypywać (zasypać *perf*) kogoś/coś *+instr*
**inure** [ɪn'juəʳ] *vt*: **to ~ o.s. to** przyzwyczajać się (przyzwyczaić się *perf*) do *+gen*, uodparniać się (uodpornić się *perf*) na *+acc*
**invade** [ɪn'veɪd] *vt* (*Mil*) najeżdżać (najechać *perf*); (*fig*: *people*) robić (zrobić *perf*) najazd na *+acc*; (*pests etc*) atakować (zaatakować *perf*)
**invader** [ɪn'veɪdəʳ] *n* (*Mil*) najeźdźca *m*
**invalid** [*n* 'ɪnvəlɪd, *adj* ɪn'vælɪd] *n* inwalida(-dka) *m(f)* ▷ *adj* (*ticket*) nieważny; (*argument*) oparty na błędnych przesłankach

**invalidate** [ɪn'vælɪdeɪt] *vt (law, marriage)* unieważniać (unieważnić *perf*); *(argument)* obalać (obalić *perf*)
**invaluable** [ɪn'væljuəbl] *adj* nieoceniony
**invariable** [ɪn'vɛərɪəbl] *adj* niezmienny
**invariably** [ɪn'vɛərɪəblɪ] *adv* niezmiennie; **she is ~ late** ona zawsze się spóźnia
**invasion** [ɪn'veɪʒən] *n (lit, fig)* najazd *m*, inwazja *f*; **an ~ of privacy** naruszenie prywatności
**invective** [ɪn'vɛktɪv] *n* obelga *f*, inwektywa *f*
**inveigle** [ɪn'vi:gl] *vt*: **to ~ sb into (doing) sth** nakłaniać (nakłonić *perf*) kogoś do (zrobienia) czegoś
**invent** [ɪn'vɛnt] *vt (machine, system)* wynajdywać (wynaleźć *perf*); *(game, phrase)* wymyślać (wymyślić *perf*); *(fabricate)* zmyślać (zmyślić *perf*), wymyślać (wymyślić *perf*)
**invention** [ɪn'vɛnʃən] *n (machine, system)* wynalazek *m*; *(untrue story)* wymysł *m*; *(act of inventing)* wynalezienie *nt*
**inventive** [ɪn'vɛntɪv] *adj* pomysłowy
**inventiveness** [ɪn'vɛntɪvnɪs] *n* pomysłowość *f*
**inventor** [ɪn'vɛntə<sup>r</sup>] *n* wynalazca(-zczyni) *m(f)*
**inventory** ['ɪnvəntrɪ] *n* spis *m* inwentarza
**inventory control** *n* kontrola *f* zapasów
**inverse** [ɪn'və:s] *adj* odwrotny; **to vary in ~ proportion to** być odwrotnie proporcjonalnym do *+gen*
**invert** [ɪn'və:t] *vt* odwracać (odwrócić *perf*)
**invertebrate** [ɪn'və:tɪbrət] *n* bezkręgowiec *m*
**inverted commas** [ɪn'və:tɪd-] *(Brit) npl* cudzysłów *m*
**invest** [ɪn'vɛst] *vt* inwestować (zainwestować *perf*) ▷ *vi*: **~ in** inwestować (zainwestować *perf*) w *+acc*; **to ~ sb with sth** obdarzać (obdarzyć *perf*) kogoś czymś
**investigate** [ɪn'vɛstɪgeɪt] *vt* badać (zbadać *perf*); *(Police)* prowadzić (poprowadzić *perf*) dochodzenie w sprawie *+gen*
**investigation** [ɪnvɛstɪ'geɪʃən] *n* dochodzenie *nt*
**investigative** [ɪn'vɛstɪgeɪtɪv] *adj*: **~ journalism** dziennikarstwo *nt* dochodzeniowe
**investigator** [ɪn'vɛstɪgeɪtə<sup>r</sup>] *n* badacz(ka) *m(f)*; *(Police)* oficer *m* śledczy; **private ~** prywatny detektyw
**investiture** [ɪn'vɛstɪtʃə<sup>r</sup>] *n (of chancellor)* mianowanie *nt*; *(of prince)* nadanie *nt* tytułu
**investment** [ɪn'vɛstmənt] *n (activity)* inwestowanie *pl*; *(amount of money)* inwestycja *f*
**investment income** *n* dochód *m* z inwestycji kapitałowych
**investment trust** *n* spółka *f* inwestycyjna
**investor** [ɪn'vɛstə<sup>r</sup>] *n* inwestor *m*
**inveterate** [ɪn'vɛtərət] *adj* niepoprawny, zatwardziały
**invidious** [ɪn'vɪdɪəs] *adj (task)* niewdzięczny; *(comparison, decision)* krzywdzący
**invigilator** [ɪn'vɪdʒɪleɪtə<sup>r</sup>] *n osoba nadzorująca przebieg egzaminu*
**invigorating** [ɪn'vɪgəreɪtɪŋ] *adj* orzeźwiający; *(fig)* ożywczy
**invincible** [ɪn'vɪnsɪbl] *adj (army)* niepokonany, niezwyciężony; *(belief)* niezachwiany
**inviolate** [ɪn'vaɪələt] *(fml) adj* nietknięty
**invisible** [ɪn'vɪzɪbl] *adj* niewidoczny; *(in fairy tales etc)* niewidzialny; **~ earnings** *(Comm)* wpływy z eksportu niewidocznego
**invisible mending** *n* cerowanie *nt* artystyczne
**invitation** [ɪnvɪ'teɪʃən] *n* zaproszenie *nt*; **by ~ only** wyłącznie za okazaniem zaproszenia; **at sb's ~** na czyjeś zaproszenie
**invite** [ɪn'vaɪt] *vt* zapraszać (zaprosić *perf*); *(discussion, criticism)* zachęcać (zachęcić *perf*) do *+gen*; **to ~ sb to do sth** poprosić *(perf)* kogoś, żeby coś zrobił; **to ~ sb to dinner** zapraszać (zaprosić *perf*) kogoś na obiad
▸ **invite out** *vt* umawiać się (umówić się *perf*) z *+instr*
**inviting** [ɪn'vaɪtɪŋ] *adj* kuszący
**invoice** ['ɪnvɔɪs] *n (Comm)* faktura *f* ▷ *vt* fakturować (zafakturować *perf*); **to ~ sb for goods** wystawiać (wystawić *perf*) komuś fakturę na towar
**invoke** [ɪn'vəuk] *vt (law)* powoływać się (powołać się *perf*) na *+acc*; *(memories)* wywoływać (wywołać *perf*)
**involuntary** [ɪn'vɔləntrɪ] *adj* mimowolny
**involve** [ɪn'vɔlv] *vt (entail)* wymagać *+gen*; *(concern, affect)* dotyczyć *+gen*; **to ~ sb (in sth)** angażować (zaangażować *perf*) kogoś (w coś)
**involved** [ɪn'vɔlvd] *adj (complicated)* zawiły; *(required)* wymagany; **to be ~ in** być zaangażowanym w *+acc*; **to become ~ with sb** wiązać się (związać się *perf*) z kimś
**involvement** [ɪn'vɔlvmənt] *n* zaangażowanie *nt*
**invulnerable** [ɪn'vʌlnərəbl] *adj (person)* niewrażliwy *(na ciosy, krytykę itp)*; *(ship, building)* niezniszczalny
**inward** ['ɪnwəd] *adj (thought, feeling)* skryty; *(concentration)* wewnętrzny; *(movement)* do wewnątrz *post*
**inwardly** ['ɪnwədlɪ] *adv* wewnętrznie, w duchu
**inward(s)** ['ɪnwəd(z)] *adv* do wewnątrz, do środka
**I/O** *(Comput) abbr (= input/output)* we/wy

**IOC** *n abbr (= International Olympic Committee)* MKOl *m (= Międzynarodowy Komitet Olimpijski)*
**iodine** ['aɪəudi:n] *n* jodyna *f*
**IOM** *(Brit: Post) abbr* = **Isle of Man**
**ion** ['aɪən] *n* jon *m*
**Ionian Sea** [aɪ'əunɪən-] *n*: **the ~** Morze *nt* Jońskie
**iota** [aɪ'əutə] *n* odrobina *f*, jota *f*
**IOU** *n abbr (= I owe you)* rewers *m*, skrypt *m* dłużny
**IOW** *(Brit: Post) abbr* = **Isle of Wight**
**IPA** *n abbr (= International Phonetic Alphabet)* międzynarodowy alfabet *m* fonetyczny, alfabet *m* IPA
**IQ** *n abbr (= intelligence quotient)* IQ *nt inv*, iloraz *m* inteligencji
**IRA** *n abbr (= Irish Republican Army)* IRA *f inv*; *(US)* = **individual retirement account**
**Iran** [ɪ'rɑ:n] *n* Iran *m*
**Iranian** [ɪ'reɪnɪən] *adj* irański ▷ *n (person)* Irańczyk(-anka) *m(f)*; *(Ling)* (język *m*) irański
**Iraq** [ɪ'rɑ:k] *n* Irak *m*
**Iraqi** [ɪ'rɑ:kɪ] *adj* iracki ▷ *n* Irakijczyk(-jka) *m(f)*
**irascible** [ɪ'ræsɪbl] *adj* wybuchowy
**irate** [aɪ'reɪt] *adj* gniewny
**Ireland** ['aɪələnd] *n* Irlandia *f*; **the Republic of ~** Republika Irlandii
**iris** ['aɪrɪs] *(pl* **~es**) *n (Anat)* tęczówka *f*; *(Bot)* irys *m*
**Irish** ['aɪrɪʃ] *adj* irlandzki ▷ *npl*: **the ~** Irlandczycy *vir pl*
**Irishman** ['aɪrɪʃmən] *(irreg: like* **man**) *n* Irlandczyk *m*
**Irish Sea** *n*: **the ~** Morze *nt* Irlandzkie
**Irishwoman** ['aɪrɪʃwumən] *(irreg: like* **woman**) *n* Irlandka *f*
**irk** [ə:k] *vt* drażnić
**irksome** ['ə:ksəm] *adj* drażniący
**IRN** *n abbr* = **Independent Radio News**
**IRO** *(US) n abbr* = **International Refugee Organization**
**iron** ['aɪən] *n* żelazo *nt*; *(for clothes)* żelazko *nt* ▷ *cpd* żelazny ▷ *vt* prasować (wyprasować *perf*) ▶ **iron out** *vt (fig)* rozwiązywać (rozwiązać *perf*)
**Iron Curtain** *n*: **the ~** żelazna kurtyna *f*
**iron foundry** *n* odlewnia *f* żeliwa
**ironic(al)** [aɪ'rɔnɪk(l)] *adj* ironiczny; *(situation)* paradoksalny
**ironically** [aɪ'rɔnɪklɪ] *adv* ironicznie; **~, the intelligence chief was the last to find out** jak na ironię, szef wywiadu dowiedział się ostatni
**ironing** ['aɪənɪŋ] *n* prasowanie *nt*
**ironing board** *n* deska *f* do prasowania
**iron lung** *(Med) n* żelazne płuco *nt*
**ironmonger** ['aɪənmʌŋgəʳ] *(Brit) n* właściciel(ka) *m(f)* sklepu z wyrobami żelaznymi
**ironmonger's (shop)** ['aɪənmʌŋgəz-] *n* sklep *m* z wyrobami żelaznymi
**iron ore** *n* ruda *f* żelaza
**irons** ['aɪəns] *npl* kajdany *pl*; **to clap sb in ~** zakuwać (zakuć *perf*) kogoś w kajdany
**ironworks** ['aɪənwə:ks] *n* huta *f* stali
**irony** ['aɪrənɪ] *n* ironia *f*
**irrational** [ɪ'ræʃənl] *adj* irracjonalny
**irreconcilable** [ɪrɛkən'saɪləbl] *adj (ideas, views)* nie do pogodzenia *post*; *(conflict)* nierozwiązywalny
**irredeemable** [ɪrɪ'di:məbl] *adj (selfishness etc)* nieuleczalny
**irrefutable** [ɪrɪ'fju:təbl] *adj* niepodważalny, niezbity
**irregular** [ɪ'rɛgjuləʳ] *adj (action, pattern, verb)* nieregularny; *(surface)* nierówny; *(behaviour)* nieodpowiedni
**irregularity** [ɪrɛgju'lærɪtɪ] *n (of action, pattern, verb)* nieregularność *f*; *(of surface)* nierówność *f*; *(anomaly)* nieprawidłowość *f*
**irrelevance** [ɪ'rɛləvəns] *n* brak *m* związku (z tematem); **an ~** rzecz nieistotna
**irrelevant** [ɪ'rɛləvənt] *adj (remark)* nie na temat *post*; *(detail)* nieistotny
**irreligious** [ɪrɪ'lɪdʒəs] *adj* niewierzący
**irreparable** [ɪ'rɛprəbl] *adj* nieodwracalny
**irreplaceable** [ɪrɪ'pleɪsəbl] *adj* niezastąpiony
**irrepressible** [ɪrɪ'prɛsəbl] *adj (good humour)* wieczny; *(laughter)* niepohamowany; *(person)*: **to be ~** być niepoprawnym optymistą
**irreproachable** [ɪrɪ'prəutʃəbl] *adj* nienaganny
**irresistible** [ɪrɪ'zɪstɪbl] *adj* nieodparty
**irresolute** [ɪ'rɛzəlu:t] *adj* niezdecydowany
**irrespective** [ɪrɪ'spɛktɪv]: **~ of** *prep* bez względu na *+acc*
**irresponsible** [ɪrɪ'spɔnsɪbl] *adj* nieodpowiedzialny
**irretrievable** [ɪrɪ'tri:vəbl] *adj* nieodwracalny
**irreverent** [ɪ'rɛvərnt] *adj* lekceważący
**irrevocable** [ɪ'rɛvəkəbl] *adj* nieodwołalny
**irrigate** ['ɪrɪgeɪt] *vt* nawadniać (nawodnić *perf*)
**irrigation** [ɪrɪ'geɪʃən] *n* nawadnianie *nt*
**irritable** ['ɪrɪtəbl] *adj* drażliwy
**irritant** ['ɪrɪtənt] *n* czynnik *m* drażniący
**irritate** ['ɪrɪteɪt] *vt* drażnić (rozdrażnić *perf*), irytować (zirytować *perf*); *(Med)* drażnić (podrażnić *perf*)
**irritating** ['ɪrɪteɪtɪŋ] *adj* drażniący, irytujący
**irritation** [ɪrɪ'teɪʃən] *n (feeling)* rozdrażnienie *nt*, irytacja *f*; *(Med)* podrażnienie *nt*; *(thing)* utrapienie *nt*

**IRS** (US) *n abbr* = **Internal Revenue Service**
**is** [ɪz] *vb see* **be**
**ISBN** *n abbr (= International Standard Book Number)* ISBN *m inv*, numer *m* ISBN
**Islam** ['ɪzlɑːm] *n* islam *m*
**Islamic** [ɪz'læmɪk] *adj* islamski
**island** ['aɪlənd] *n* wyspa *f*; (*also*: **traffic island**) wysepka *f*
**islander** ['aɪləndə^r] *n* wyspiarz(-arka) *m(f)*
**isle** [aɪl] *n* wyspa *f*
**isn't** ['ɪznt] = **is not**
**isobar** ['aɪsəubɑː^r] *n* izobara *f*
**isolate** ['aɪsəleɪt] *vt* izolować (izolować *perf*), odizolowywać (odizolować *perf*); (*substance*) izolować (wyizolować *perf*)
**isolated** ['aɪsəleɪtɪd] *adj* (*place, incident*) odosobniony; (*person*) wyobcowany
**isolation** [aɪsə'leɪʃən] *n* izolacja *f*, odosobnienie *nt*
**isolationism** [aɪsə'leɪʃənɪzəm] *n* izolacjonizm *m*
**isotope** ['aɪsəutəup] *n* izotop *m*
**Israel** ['ɪzreɪl] *n* Izrael *m*
**Israeli** [ɪz'reɪlɪ] *adj* izraelski ▷ *n* Izraelczyk(-lka) *m(f)*
**issue** ['ɪʃuː] *n* (*problem*) sprawa *f*, kwestia *f*; (*of magazine*: *edition*) wydanie *nt*; (*: number*) numer *m*; (*old*: *offspring*) potomstwo *nt* ▷ *vt* wydawać (wydać *perf*) ▷ *vi*: **to ~ from** wypływać z *+gen*; **that's just not the ~** po prostu nie o to chodzi; **the point at ~ is ...** chodzi o *+acc*; **he avoided the** ~ unikał tego tematu; **to confuse** *or* **cloud the ~** zaciemniać (zaciemnić *perf*) sprawę; **to ~ sth to sb, ~ sb with sth** wydawać (wydać *perf*) coś komuś; **to take ~ with sb (over)** nie zgadzać się (nie zgodzić się *perf*) z kimś (w kwestii *+gen*); **to make an ~ of sth** robić (zrobić *perf*) z czegoś (wielką) sprawę
**Istanbul** [ɪstæn'buːl] *n* Stambuł *m*, Istambuł *m*
**isthmus** ['ɪsməs] *n* przesmyk *m*
**IT** *n abbr* = **Information Technology**

 KEYWORD

**it** [ɪt] *pron* **1** (*specific*) ono *nt* (*also: on, ona, depending on grammatical gender of replaced noun*), to *nt*; **give it to me** daj mi to; **I can't find it** nie mogę go znaleźć; **about/in/on/with it** o/w/na/z tym; **from/to/without it** z/do/bez tego
**2** (*impersonal*): **it's raining** pada (deszcz); **it's six o'clock/the 10th of August** jest szósta/dziesiąty sierpnia; **how far is it?** jak to daleko?; **who is it? — it's me** kto tam? — (to) ja

**ITA** (Brit) *n abbr (= initial teaching alphabet) uproszczony, częściowo fonetyczny alfabet używany w nauce czytania w języku angielskim*
**Italian** [ɪ'tæljən] *adj* włoski ▷ *n* (*person*) Włoch/Włoszka *m/f*; (*Ling*) (język *m*) włoski; **the ~s** Włosi *vir pl*
**italics** [ɪ'tælɪks] *npl* kursywa *f*
**Italy** ['ɪtəlɪ] *n* Włochy *pl*
**ITC** (Brit) *n abbr (= Independent Televison Commission) komisja sprawująca kontrolę nad sektorem prywatnym telewizji brytyjskiej*
**itch** [ɪtʃ] *n* swędzenie *nt* ▷ *vi*: **I ~** swędzi mnie; **my toes are ~ing** swędzą mnie palce u nóg; **to be ~ing to do sth** mieć chętkę coś zrobić
**itchy** ['ɪtʃɪ] *adj* swędzący; **my back is ~** swędzą mnie plecy; **I'm all ~** wszystko mnie swędzi; **to have ~ feet** (*fig*) nie móc usiedzieć na miejscu
**it'd** ['ɪtd] = **it would; it had**
**item** ['aɪtəm] *n* rzecz *f*; (*on list, agenda*) punkt *m*, pozycja *f*; (*also*: **news item**) wiadomość *f*; **~s of clothing** rzeczy
**itemize** ['aɪtəmaɪz] *vt* wyszczególniać (wyszczególnić *perf*)
**itinerant** [ɪ'tɪnərənt] *adj* wędrowny
**itinerary** [aɪ'tɪnərərɪ] *n* plan *m* podróży
**it'll** ['ɪtl] = **it will; it shall**
**ITN** (Brit: TV) *n abbr* = **Independent Television News**
**its** [ɪts] *adj* swój, jego; **the baby was lying in its room** dziecko leżało w swoim pokoju; **he liked London for its exotic quality** lubił Londyn za jego egzotykę; **the creature lifted its head** stworzenie uniosło głowę ▷ *pron* swój
**it's** [ɪts] = **it is; it has**
**itself** [ɪt'sɛlf] *pron* (*reflexive*) się; (*after prep*) siebie (*gen, acc*), sobie (*dat, loc*), sobą (*instr*); (*emphatic*) samo
**ITV** (Brit: TV) *n abbr* = **Independent Television**
**IUD** *n abbr (= intra-uterine device)* wkładka *f* domaciczna *or* wewnątrzmaciczna
**I've** [aɪv] = **I have**
**ivory** ['aɪvərɪ] *n* kość *f* słoniowa
**Ivory Coast** *n*: **the ~** Wybrzeże *nt* Kości Słoniowej
**ivory tower** *n* (*fig*) wieża *f* z kości słoniowej
**ivy** ['aɪvɪ] *n* bluszcz *m*
**Ivy League** *n grupa ośmiu prestiżowych uniwersytetów we wschodniej części Stanów Zjednoczonych*

**J, j** [dʒeɪ] *n (letter)* J *nt*, j *nt*; **J for Jack,** *(US)* **J for Jig** ≈ J jak Jadwiga
**JA** *n abbr* = **judge advocate**
**J/A** *abbr* = **joint account**
**jab** [dʒæb] *vt (person)* dźgać (dźgnąć *perf*); *(finger, stick etc)*: **to jab a finger at sb** dźgać (dźgnąć *perf*) kogoś palcem ▷ *n (inf: injection)* szczepienie *nt*; *(poke)* dźgnięcie *nt*; **to jab at** stukać w *+acc*; **to jab sth into sth** wbijać (wbić *perf*) coś w coś
**jack** [dʒæk] *n (Aut)* podnośnik *m*, lewarek *m*; *(Cards)* walet *m*; *(Bowls) biała kula, do której celują grający*
▸ **jack in** *(inf) vt* rzucać (rzucić *perf*) w diabły *(inf)*
▸ **jack up** *vt (Aut)* podnosić (podnieść *perf*) (lewarkiem *or* na podnośniku)
**jackal** ['dʒækl] *n* szakal *m*
**jackass** ['dʒækæs] *(inf) n* osioł *m (inf)*
**jackdaw** ['dʒækdɔː] *n* kawka *f*
**jacket** ['dʒækɪt] *n (men's)* marynarka *f*; *(women's)* żakiet *m*; *(coat)* kurtka *f*; *(of book)* obwoluta *f*; **potatoes in their ~s, ~ potatoes** ziemniaki w mundurkach
**jack-in-the-box** ['dʒækɪnðəbɔks] *n zabawka w formie pudełka, z którego po otwarciu wyskakuje figurka na sprężynie*
**jack-knife** ['dʒæknaɪf] *vi* składać się (złożyć się *perf*) jak scyzoryk ▷ *n* (duży) składany nóż *m*
**jack-of-all-trades** ['dʒækəv'ɔːltreɪdz] *n* majster *m* do wszystkiego
**jack plug** *n* wtyczka *f* typu jack
**jackpot** ['dʒækpɔt] *n* najwyższa stawka *f*, cała pula *f*; **to hit the ~** *(fig)* wygrać *(perf)* los na loterii
**jacuzzi** [dʒə'kuːzɪ] *n* wanna *f* z masażem wodnym, jacuzzi *nt inv*
**jade** [dʒeɪd] *n* nefryt *m*
**jaded** ['dʒeɪdɪd] *adj* znudzony
**JAG** *n abbr (= Judge Advocate General) zwierzchnik wojskowego wymiaru sprawiedliwości*
**jagged** ['dʒægɪd] *adj (outline, edge)* postrzępiony; *(blade)* wyszczerbiony
**jaguar** ['dʒægjuəʳ] *n* jaguar *m*
**jail** [dʒeɪl] *n* więzienie *nt* ▷ *vt* wsadzać (wsadzić *perf*) do więzienia
**jailbird** ['dʒeɪlbəːd] *n* kryminalista(-tka) *m(f)*
**jailbreak** ['dʒeɪlbreɪk] *n* ucieczka *f* z więzienia
**jalopy** [dʒə'lɔpɪ] *(inf) n* gruchot *m (inf)*
**jam** [dʒæm] *n (food)* dżem *m*; *(also:* **traffic jam)** korek *m*; *(inf: difficulty)* tarapaty *pl* ▷ *vt (passage, road)* tarasować (zatarasować *perf*); *(mechanism, drawer)* zablokowywać (zablokować *perf*); *(Radio)* zagłuszać (zagłuszyć *perf*) ▷ *vi (mechanism, drawer etc)* zacinać się (zaciąć się *perf*), zablokowywać się (zablokować się *perf*); *(Mus)* improwizować; **to be in a jam** *(inf)* być w tarapatach; **to get sb out of a jam** *(inf)* wyciągać (wyciągnąć *perf*) kogoś z tarapatów; **the switchboard was jammed** centrala (telefoniczna) się zablokowała; **to jam sth into sth** wpychać (wepchnąć *perf*) coś do czegoś
**Jamaica** [dʒə'meɪkə] *n* Jamajka *f*
**Jamaican** [dʒə'meɪkən] *adj* jamajski ▷ *n* Jamajczyk(-jka) *m(f)*
**jamb** ['dʒæm] *n (Archit)* węgar *m*
**jamboree** [dʒæmbə'riː] *n* wielka zabawa *f*
**jam-packed** [dʒæm'pækt] *adj*: **~ (with)** zapchany *(+instr)*
**jam session** *n* jam session *nt inv*
**Jan.** *abbr (= January)* stycz.
**jangle** ['dʒæŋgl] *vi* pobrzękiwać
**janitor** ['dʒænɪtəʳ] *n (esp US)* stróż *m*; *(Scol)* woźny(-na) *m(f)*
**January** ['dʒænjuərɪ] *n* styczeń *m*; *see also* **July**
**Japan** [dʒə'pæn] *n* Japonia *f*
**Japanese** [dʒæpə'niːz] *adj* japoński ▷ *n inv (person)* Japończyk(-onka) *m(f)*; *(Ling)* (język *m*) japoński
**jar** [dʒɑːʳ] *n* słoik *m*; *(large)* słój *m* ▷ *vi (sound)* drażnić ▷ *vt*: **to jar one's bones** poobijać *(perf)* sobie kości
**jargon** ['dʒɑːgən] *n* żargon *m*
**jarring** ['dʒɑːrɪŋ] *adj (sound)* drażniący; *(colour, contradiction)* rażący
**Jas.** *abbr* = **James**
**jasmine** ['dʒæzmɪn] *n* jaśmin *m*
**jaundice** ['dʒɔːndɪs] *n* żółtaczka *f*

**jaundiced** ['dʒɔːndɪst] *adj (fig: attitude)* cyniczny
**jaunt** [dʒɔːnt] *n* wypad *m*
**jaunty** ['dʒɔːntɪ] *adj* raźny
**Java** ['dʒɑːvə] *n* Jawa *f*
**javelin** ['dʒævlɪn] *n* oszczep *m*
**jaw** [dʒɔː] *n* szczęka *f*; **the panther held a snake in its jaws** pantera trzymała w zębach węża
**jawbone** ['dʒɔːbəun] *n* kość *f* szczękowa (dolna), żuchwa *f*
**jay** [dʒeɪ] *n* sójka *f*
**jaywalker** ['dʒeɪwɔːkə^r] *n* pieszy *m* nieprawidłowo przechodzący przez jezdnię
**jazz** [dʒæz] *n* jazz *m*; **and all that ~** *(inf)* i cała reszta
▸**jazz up** *vt (inf)* ożywiać (ożywić *perf)*
**jazz band** *n* orkiestra *f* jazzowa
**JCS** *(US) n abbr (= Joint Chiefs of Staff)* Kolegium *nt* Szefów Sztabów
**JD** *(US) n abbr (= Doctor of Laws) stopień naukowy,* ≈ dr; *(= Justice Department)* ≈ Ministerstwo *nt* Sprawiedliwości
**jealous** ['dʒɛləs] *adj*: **~ (of)** zazdrosny (o *+acc*); **they may feel ~ of your success** mogą ci zazdrościć sukcesu
**jealously** ['dʒɛləslɪ] *adv* zazdrośnie
**jealousy** ['dʒɛləsɪ] *n* zazdrość *f*, zawiść *f*
**jeans** [dʒiːnz] *npl* dżinsy *pl*
**jeep®** [dʒiːp] *n* jeep *m*
**jeer** [dʒɪə^r] *vi*: **to ~ (at)** wyszydzać (wyszydzić *perf) (+acc)*, drwić (z *+gen*); **jeers** *npl* gwizdy *pl*
**jeering** ['dʒɪərɪŋ] *adj (remark)* szyderczy, drwiący; *(crowd)* szydzący ▹ *n* gwizdy *pl*
**jelly** ['dʒɛlɪ] *n* galaretka *f*
**jellyfish** ['dʒɛlɪfɪʃ] *n* meduza *f*
**jeopardize** ['dʒɛpədaɪz] *vt (circumstances, opinion)* zagrażać (zagrozić *perf) +dat*; *(person)* narażać (narazić *perf)* na szwank; **to ~ sb's/one's job** narażać (narazić *perf)* kogoś/się na utratę pracy
**jeopardy** ['dʒɛpədɪ] *n*: **to be in ~** być zagrożonym *or* w niebezpieczeństwie
**jerk** [dʒəːk] *n* szarpnięcie *nt*; *(inf: idiot)* palant *m (inf)* ▹ *vt* szarpać (szarpnąć *perf)* ▹ *vi* szarpać (szarpnąć *perf)*; **to give sth a ~** szarpnąć *(perf)* coś
**jerkin** ['dʒəːkɪn] *n* kabat *m*
**jerky** ['dʒəːkɪ] *adj* szarpany, urywany
**jerry-built** ['dʒɛrɪbɪlt] *adj* zbudowany byle jak
**jerry can** ['dʒɛrɪ-] *n* kanister *m*
**Jersey** ['dʒəːzɪ] *n* Jersey *nt (wyspa)*
**jersey** ['dʒəːzɪ] *n (garment)* pulower *m*; *(fabric)* dżersej *m*
**Jerusalem** [dʒə'ruːsləm] *n* Jerozolima *f*
**jest** [dʒɛst] *n* żart *m*; **in ~** żartem
**jester** ['dʒɛstə^r] *n*: **(court) ~** błazen *m* (królewski)
**Jesus** ['dʒiːzəs] *n* Jezus *m*; **~ Christ** Jezus Chrystus
**jet** [dʒɛt] *n (of gas, liquid)* silny strumień *m*; *(Aviat)* odrzutowiec *m*; *(stone)* gagat *m*
**jet-black** ['dʒɛt'blæk] *adj* czarny jak węgiel; *(hair)* kruczoczarny
**jet engine** *n* silnik *m* odrzutowy
**jet lag** *n zmęczenie po podróży samolotem spowodowane różnicą czasu*
**jet-propelled** ['dʒɛtprəpɛld] *adj* odrzutowy
**jetsam** ['dʒɛtsəm] *n see* **flotsam**
**jettison** ['dʒɛtɪsn] *vt (fuel, cargo)* wyrzucać (wyrzucić *perf)* za burtę; *(fig: idea, chance)* odrzucać (odrzucić *perf)*
**jetty** ['dʒɛtɪ] *n* pirs *m*
**Jew** [dʒuː] *n* Żyd *m*
**jewel** ['dʒuːəl] *n (lit, fig)* klejnot *m*; *(in watch)* kamień *m*
**jeweller** ['dʒuːələ^r], *(US)* **jeweler** *n* jubiler *m*
**jeweller's (shop)** *n* sklep *m* jubilerski, jubiler *m*
**jewellery** ['dʒuːəlrɪ], *(US)* **jewelry** *n* biżuteria *f*
**Jewess** ['dʒuːɪs] *n* Żydówka *f*
**Jewish** ['dʒuːɪʃ] *adj* żydowski
**JFK** *(US) n abbr (= John Fitzgerald Kennedy International Airport)* lotnisko *nt* im. Johna F. Kennedy'ego *(w Nowym Jorku)*
**jib** [dʒɪb] *n (Naut)* kliwer *m*; *(of crane)* ramię *nt*, wysięgnik *m* ▹ *vi* zapierać się (zaprzeć się *perf)*; **to jib at sth/doing sth** wzdragać się przed czymś/zrobieniem czegoś
**jibe** [dʒaɪb] *n* = **gibe**
**jiffy** ['dʒɪfɪ] *(inf) n*: **in a ~** za sekundkę *or* momencik
**jig** [dʒɪg] *n (dance)* giga *f*
**jigsaw** ['dʒɪgsɔː] *n (also:* **jigsaw puzzle***)* układanka *f*; *(: fig)* łamigłówka *f*; *(tool)* wyrzynarka *f*, laubzega *f*
**jilt** [dʒɪlt] *vt* porzucać (porzucić *perf)*
**jingle** ['dʒɪŋgl] *n (for advert)* dżingiel *m* ▹ *vi (bells)* dzwonić; *(bracelets, keys)* pobrzękiwać
**jingoism** ['dʒɪŋgəuɪzəm] *n* dżingoizm *m*, szowinizm *m*
**jinx** [dʒɪŋks] *(inf) n* (złe) fatum *nt* ▹ *vt*: **that car is ~ed** ten samochód jest pechowy
**jitters** ['dʒɪtəz] *(inf) npl*: **to get the ~** dostawać (dostać *perf)* trzęsiączki *(inf)*
**jittery** ['dʒɪtərɪ] *(inf) adj* roztrzęsiony
**jiujitsu** [dʒuː'dʒɪtsuː] *n* dżiu-dżitsu *or* ju-jitsu *nt inv*
**job** [dʒɔb] *n* praca *f*; **it's a good job that ...** (to) dobrze, że ...; **it's not my job** to nie należy do mnie; **I had a job finding it** miałem trudności ze znalezieniem go; **a part-time/full-time job** praca na pół etatu/cały etat; **he's only doing his job** on tylko robi, co do

niego należy; **just the job!** (*inf*) o to właśnie chodziło!
**jobber** ['dʒɔbə^r] (*Brit*) *n* makler *m*
**jobbing** ['dʒɔbɪŋ] (*Brit*) *adj* (*builder, plumber*) pracujący na zlecenie
**job centre** (*Brit*) *n* ≈ biuro *nt* pośrednictwa pracy
**job creation scheme** *n* program *m* tworzenia nowych miejsc pracy
**job description** *n* zakres *m* obowiązków
**jobless** ['dʒɔblɪs] *adj* bez pracy *post* ▷ *npl*: **the ~** bezrobotni *vir pl*
**job lot** *n* partia *f* (*taniego, używanego towaru, np. na aukcji*)
**job satisfaction** *n* satysfakcja *f* z pracy
**job security** *n* gwarancja *f* stałego zatrudnienia
**job sharing** *n* dzielenie się *nt* etatem (*przez dwóch półetatowych pracowników*)
**jockey** ['dʒɔkɪ] *n* dżokej *m* ▷ *vi*: **to ~ for position** walczyć (o pierwszeństwo) nie przebierając w środkach
**jockey box** *n* (*US*: *Aut*) schowek *m* na rękawiczki
**jocular** ['dʒɔkjulə^r] *adj* (*person*) dowcipny; (*remark*) żartobliwy
**jog** [dʒɔg] *vt* trącać (trącić *perf*), potrącać (potrącić *perf*) ▷ *vi* uprawiać jogging; **to jog your memory** żeby ci pomóc sobie przypomnieć
▸ **jog along** *vi* biec (przebiec *perf*)
**jogger** ['dʒɔgə^r] *n* osoba *f* uprawiająca jogging
**jogging** ['dʒɔgɪŋ] *n* jogging *m*
**join** [dʒɔɪn] *vt* (*queue*) dołączać (dołączyć *perf*) do *+gen*; (*club, organization*) wstępować (wstąpić *perf*) do *+gen*; (*things, places*) łączyć (połączyć *perf*); (*person*: *meet*) spotykać się (spotkać się *perf*) z *+instr*; (*: in an activity*) przyłączać się (przyłączyć się *perf*) do *+gen*; (*road, river*) łączyć się z *+instr* ▷ *vi* (*roads, rivers*) łączyć się ▷ *n* złączenie *nt*; **to ~ forces (with)** (*fig*) połączyć (*perf*) siły (z *+instr*); **will you ~ us for dinner?** (czy) zjesz z nami obiad?; **I'll ~ you later** dołączę do was później
▸ **join in** *vi* włączać się (włączyć się *perf*) ▷ *vt fus* (*work, discussion*) włączać się (włączyć się *perf*) do *+gen*
▸ **join up** *vi* (*Mil*) wstępować (wstąpić *perf*) do wojska; **they all ~ed up in X for the rest of the holiday** wszyscy spotkali się w X, gdzie razem spędzili resztę wakacji
**joiner** ['dʒɔɪnə^r] (*Brit*) *n* stolarz *m* (*robiący drzwi, framugi itp*)
**joinery** ['dʒɔɪnərɪ] (*Brit*) *n* stolarka *f*
**joint** [dʒɔɪnt] *n* (*Tech*) złącze *nt*, spoina *f*; (*Anat*) staw *m*; (*Brit*: *Culin*) sztuka *f* mięsa; (*inf*: *place*) lokal *m*; (*: of cannabis*) skręt *m* (*inf*) ▷ *adj* wspólny; **~ owners** współwłaściciele
**joint account** *n* (*Banking*) wspólny rachunek *m*
**jointly** ['dʒɔɪntlɪ] *adj* wspólnie
**joint ownership** *n* współwłasność *f*
**joint-stock company** *n* spółka *f* akcyjna
**joint venture** *n* spółka *f* joint venture
**joist** [dʒɔɪst] *n* (*in ceiling*) belka *f* stropowa; (*in floor*) legar *m* podłogowy
**joke** [dʒəuk] *n* (*gag*) dowcip *m*, kawał *m* (*inf*); (*sth not serious*) żart *m*; (*also*: **practical joke**) psikus *m*, kawał *m* (*inf*) ▷ *vi* żartować; **to play a ~ on sb** robić (zrobić *perf*) komuś kawał; **you must be joking!** (*inf*) chyba żartujesz!
**joker** ['dʒəukə^r] *n* (*Cards*) joker *m*, dżoker *m*
**joking** ['dʒəukɪŋ] *n* żarty *pl*
**jokingly** ['dʒəukɪŋlɪ] *adv* żartem, w żartach
**jollity** ['dʒɔlɪtɪ] *n* wesołość *f*
**jolly** ['dʒɔlɪ] *adj* wesoły ▷ *adv* (*Brit*: *inf*) naprawdę ▷ *vt* (*Brit*): **to ~ sb along** podbudowywać (podbudować *perf*) kogoś; **~ good!** świetnie!
**jolt** [dʒəult] *n* (*jerk*) szarpnięcie *nt*; (*shock*) wstrząs *m* ▷ *vt* (*physically*) szarpnąć (*perf*), potrząsnąć (*perf*) *+instr*; (*emotionally*) wstrząsnąć (*perf*) *+instr*; **with a ~** gwałtownie; **to give sb a ~** wstrząsnąć (*perf*) kimś
**Jordan** [dʒɔ:dən] *n* Jordania *f*; **the (river) ~** Jordan *m*
**Jordanian** [dʒɔ:'deɪnɪən] *adj* jordański ▷ *n* Jordańczyk(-anka) *m(f)*
**joss stick** ['dʒɔs-] *n* kadzidełko *nt*
**jostle** ['dʒɔsl] *vt* potrącać, popychać ▷ *vi* rozpychać się
**jot** [dʒɔt] *n*: **not a jot** ani trochę
▸ **jot down** *vt* notować (zanotować *perf*)
**jotter** ['dʒɔtə^r] (*Brit*) *n* notes *m*
**journal** ['dʒə:nl] *n* (*magazine*) czasopismo *nt*; (*: in titles*) magazyn *m*; (*diary*) dziennik *m*
**journalese** [dʒə:nə'li:z] (*pej*) *n* żargon *m* dziennikarski
**journalism** ['dʒə:nəlɪzəm] *n* dziennikarstwo *nt*
**journalist** ['dʒə:nəlɪst] *n* dziennikarz(-arka) *m(f)*
**journey** ['dʒə:nɪ] *n* podróż *f* ▷ *vi* podróżować; **as they ~ed north ...** w miarę jak posuwali się na północ, ...; **a five-hour/six-mile ~** pięciogodzinna/sześciomilowa podróż; **it's a five-hour ~** to pięć godzin drogi; **return ~** droga powrotna
**jovial** ['dʒəuvɪəl] *adj* jowialny
**jowls** [dʒaulz] *npl* policzki *pl* (*część przykrywająca żuchwę*)
**joy** [dʒɔɪ] *n* radość *f*
**joyful** ['dʒɔɪful] *adj* (*mood, laugh*) radosny; (*person*) uradowany
**joyrider** ['dʒɔɪraɪdə^r] *n amator przejażdżek kradzionymi samochodami*

j

**joystick** ['dʒɔɪstɪk] *n* (*Aviat*) drążek *m* sterowy; (*Comput*) joystick *m*, dżojstik *m*

**JP** *n abbr* = **Justice of the Peace**

**Jr** *abbr* (*in names*: = *junior*) jr

**JTPA** (*US*) *n abbr* = **Job Training Partnership Act**

**jubilant** ['dʒu:bɪlnt] *adj* rozradowany

**jubilation** [dʒu:bɪ'leɪʃən] *n* rozradowanie *nt*

**jubilee** ['dʒu:bɪli:] *n* jubileusz *m*; **silver/golden ~** srebrny/złoty jubileusz

**judge** [dʒʌdʒ] *n* (*Jur*) sędzia(-ina) *m(f)*; (*in competition*) sędzia(-ina) *m(f)*, juror(ka) *m(f)*; (*fig*) ekspert *m* ▷ *vt* (*competition, match*) sędziować; (*estimate*) określać (określić *perf*), oceniać (ocenić *perf*); (*evaluate*) oceniać; (*consider*) uznawać (uznać *perf*) za *+acc* ▷ *vi* wydawać (wydać *perf*) opinię; **she's a good ~ of character** ona zna się na ludziach; **I'll be the ~ of that** ja to ocenię; **judging** *or* **to ~ by his expression** sądząc z jego wyrazu twarzy; **as far as I can ~** o ile się orientuję; **I ~d it necessary to inform him** uznałem za konieczne poinformować go

**judge advocate** *n* (*Brit*) asesor *m* sądu; (*US*) prokurator *m* wojskowy

**judg(e)ment** ['dʒʌdʒmənt] *n* (*Jur*) orzeczenie *nt*, wyrok *m*; (*view, opinion*) pogląd *m*, opinia *f*; (*discernment*) ocena *f* sytuacji; (*Rel*) kara *f*; **in my ~** w moim mniemaniu *or* odczuciu; **to pass ~ (on)** (*Jur*) wydawać (wydać *perf*) wyrok (na *+acc*); (*fig*) wydawać opinię (na temat *+gen*)

**judicial** [dʒu:'dɪʃl] *adj* sądowy; **~ review** rewizja (procesu)

**judiciary** [dʒu:'dɪʃɪərɪ] *n*: **the ~** sądownictwo *nt*, władza *f* sądownicza

**judicious** [dʒu:'dɪʃəs] *adj* rozważny, rozsądny

**judo** ['dʒu:dəu] *n* judo *nt inv*, dżudo *nt inv*

**jug** [dʒʌg] *n* dzbanek *m*

**jugged hare** ['dʒʌgd-] (*Brit*) *n* potrawka *f* z zająca

**juggernaut** ['dʒʌgənɔ:t] (*Brit*) *n* wielka ciężarówka *f*

**juggle** ['dʒʌgl] *vi* żonglować ▷ *vt* (*fig*) zmieniać (zmienić *perf*), przesuwać (przesunąć *perf*); **to ~ with sth** żonglować czymś

**juggler** ['dʒʌgləʳ] *n* żongler(ka) *m(f)*

**Jugoslav** *etc* = **Yugoslav** *etc*

**jugular** ['dʒʌgjuləʳ] *n* żyła *f* szyjna; **to go for the ~** (*fig*) uderzać (uderzyć *perf*) w najsłabszy punkt

**juice** [dʒu:s] *n* sok *m*; (*inf*: *petrol*) benzyna *f*

**juicy** ['dʒu:sɪ] *adj* soczysty; (*inf*: *scandalous*) pikantny

**jukebox** ['dʒu:kbɔks] *n* szafa *f* grająca

**Jul.** *abbr* (= *July*) lip.

**July** [dʒu:'laɪ] *n* lipiec *m*; **the first of ~** pierwszy lipca; **on the eleventh of ~** jedenastego lipca; **in the month of ~** w miesiącu lipcu; **at the beginning/end of ~** na początku/pod koniec lipca; **in the middle of ~** w środku lipca; **during ~** w lipcu, przez lipiec; **in ~ of next year** w lipcu przyszłego roku; **each** *or* **every ~** co roku w lipcu; **~ was wet this year** lipiec był w tym roku deszczowy

**jumble** ['dʒʌmbl] *n* (*of things, colours, qualities*) (bezładna) mieszanina *f*; (*Brit*: *items for sale*) rzeczy *pl* używane (*przeznaczone na wyprzedaż*) ▷ *vt* (*also*: **jumble up**) mieszać (pomieszać *perf*)

**jumble sale** (*Brit*) *n* wyprzedaż *f* rzeczy używanych (*zwykle na cele dobroczynne*)

**jumbo** ['dʒʌmbəu] *n* (*also*: **jumbo jet**) wielki odrzutowiec *m*, Jumbo Jet *m* ▷ *adj* (*also*: **jumbo-sized**) olbrzymi

**jump** [dʒʌmp] *vi* skakać (skoczyć *perf*); (*with fear, surprise*) wzdrygnąć się (*perf*) ▷ *vt* przeskakiwać (przeskoczyć *perf*) (przez) ▷ *n* (*leap*) skok *m*; (*increase*) skok *m* (w górę); **to ~ the queue** (*Brit*) wpychać się (wepchnąć się *perf*) poza kolejką *or* kolejnością

▸ **jump at** *vt fus* skwapliwie skorzystać (*perf*) z *+gen*

▸ **jump down** *vi* zeskakiwać (zeskoczyć *perf*)

▸ **jump up** *vi* zrywać się (zerwać się *perf*)

**jumped-up** ['dʒʌmptʌp] (*Brit*: *pej*) *adj* nadęty (*pej*), napuszony (*pej*)

**jumper** ['dʒʌmpəʳ] *n* (*Brit*) pulower *m*; (*US*) bezrękawnik *m*; (*person, animal*) skoczek *m*

**jumper cables** (*US*) *npl* = **jump leads**

**jump leads** (*Brit*) *npl* (*Aut*) przewody *pl* rozruchowe

**jump suit** *n* kombinezon *m*

**jumpy** ['dʒʌmpɪ] *adj* zdenerwowany

**Jun.** *abbr* (= *June*) czerw.

**junction** ['dʒʌŋkʃən] (*Brit*) *n* (*of roads*) skrzyżowanie *nt*; (*Rail*) rozjazd *m*, stacja *f* węzłowa

**junction box** *n* (*Elec*) skrzynka *f* przyłączeniowa

**juncture** ['dʒʌŋktʃəʳ] *n*: **at this ~** w tym momencie *or* punkcie

**June** [dʒu:n] *n* czerwiec *m*; *see also* **July**

**jungle** ['dʒʌŋgl] *n* dżungla *f*, puszcza *f*; (*fig*) dżungla *f*

**junior** ['dʒu:nɪəʳ] *adj* niższy rangą, młodszy ▷ *n* (*subordinate*) podwładny(-na) *m(f)*; (*Brit*) ≈ uczeń/uczennica *m/f* szkoły podstawowej (*w wieku 7-11 lat*); **he's my ~ by 2 years, he's 2 years my ~** jest ode mnie o 2 lata młodszy; **he's ~ to me** jest ode mnie niższy rangą; **Douglas Fairbanks J~** Douglas Fairbanks junior *or* młodszy

**junior executive** *n* samodzielny pracownik *m* niższego szczebla
**junior high school** (*US*) *n szkoła średnia obejmująca siódmą, ósmą i czasami dziewiątą klasę*
**junior minister** (*Brit*) *n* ≈ podsekretarz *m* stanu
**junior partner** *n* młodszy wspólnik *m*
**junior school** (*Brit*) *n czteroletnia szkoła podstawowa*
**juniper** ['dʒu:nɪpəʳ] *n* jałowiec *m*
**juniper berry** *n* owoc *m* jałowca
**junk** [dʒʌŋk] *n* (*rubbish*) graty *pl*, rupiecie *pl*; (*cheap goods*) starzyzna *f*; (*ship*) dżonka *f* ▷ *vt* (*inf*) wyrzucać (wyrzucić *perf*) (na śmietnik)
**junket** ['dʒʌŋkɪt] *n* (*Culin*) *słodki deser mleczny*; **to go on a ~** (*inf*) przejechać się (*perf*) za pieniądze podatników
**junk food** *n* niezdrowe jedzenie *nt*
**junkie** ['dʒʌŋkɪ] (*inf*) *n* ćpun(ka) *m(f)* (*inf*)
**junk mail** *n* przesyłki *pl* reklamowe
**junk shop** *n* sklep *m* ze starzyzną
**Junr** *abbr* (*in names*: = *junior*) jr
**junta** ['dʒʌntə] *n* junta *f*
**Jupiter** ['dʒu:pɪtəʳ] *n* Jowisz *m*
**jurisdiction** [dʒuərɪs'dɪkʃən] *n* jurysdykcja *f*; **it falls** *or* **comes within/outside my ~** to leży/nie leży w moich kompetencjach
**jurisprudence** [dʒuərɪs'pru:dəns] *n* prawoznawstwo *nt*
**juror** ['dʒuərəʳ] *n* (*Jur*) przysięgły(-ła) *m(f)*; (*in competition*) juror(ka) *m(f)*
**jury** ['dʒuərɪ] *n* (*Jur*) sąd *m or* ława *f* przysięgłych; (*in competition*) jury *nt inv*
**jury box** *n* ława *f* przysięgłych (*miejsce*)
**juryman** ['dʒuərɪmən] (*irreg*: *like* **man**) *n* = **juror**
**just** [dʒʌst] *adj* (*decision, person, society*) sprawiedliwy; (*reward*) zasłużony; (*cause*) słuszny ▷ *adv* (*exactly*) właśnie, dokładnie; (*merely*) tylko, jedynie; **he's ~ left** właśnie wyszedł; **~ as I expected** dokładnie tak, jak się spodziewałem; **~ right** w sam raz; **~ now** (*a moment ago*) dopiero co; (*at the present time*) w tej chwili; **we were ~ going** właśnie wychodziliśmy; **I was ~ about to phone** właśnie miałem zatelefonować *or* zadzwonić; **she's ~ as clever as you** jest nie mniej inteligentna niż ty; **it's ~ as well (that ...)** no i dobrze (, że ...); **~ as he was leaving** w chwili, gdy wychodził; **~ before/after** krótko przed *+instr*/po *+loc*; **~ after you called** krótko po tym, jak zadzwoniłeś; **~ enough** akurat tyle, ile potrzeba; **there was ~ enough petrol** ledwo starczyło benzyny; **~ here** o tutaj; **he ~ missed** minimalnie chybił; **it's ~ me** to tylko ja; **it's ~ a mistake** to zwykła pomyłka; **~ listen** posłuchaj tylko; **~ ask someone the way** po prostu zapytaj kogoś o drogę; **not ~ now** nie w tej chwili; **~ a minute!, ~ one moment!** chwileczkę!, momencik!
**justice** ['dʒʌstɪs] *n* (*Jur*) sprawiedliwość *f*, wymiar *m* sprawiedliwości; (*of cause*) słuszność *f*; (*of complaint*) zasadność *f*; (*fairness*) sprawiedliwość *f*; (*US*: *judge*) sędzia *m*; **Lord Chief J~** (*Brit*: *Jur*) *przewodniczący Ławy Królewskiej Sądu Najwyższego i Prezes (Wydziału Kryminalnego) Sądu Apelacyjnego.*; **to do ~ to** (*fig*: *represent, capture*) dobrze oddawać (oddać *perf*) *+acc*; (*deal properly with*) dawać (dać *perf*) sobie radę z *+instr*, uporać się (*perf*) z *+instr*; **she didn't do herself ~** nie pokazała, na co ją stać; **to bring sb to ~** oddawać (oddać *perf*) kogoś w ręce sprawiedliwości
**Justice of the Peace** *n* sędzia *m* pokoju
**justifiable** [dʒʌstɪ'faɪəbl] *adj* uzasadniony, słuszny
**justifiably** [dʒʌstɪ'faɪəblɪ] *adv* słusznie, ze słusznych względów
**justification** [dʒʌstɪfɪ'keɪʃən] *n* (*reason*) uzasadnienie *nt*; (*Typ*) justowanie *nt*
**justify** ['dʒʌstɪfaɪ] *vt* (*action, decision*) uzasadniać (uzasadnić *perf*), tłumaczyć (wytłumaczyć *perf*); (*Typ*: *text*) justować; **to be justified in doing sth** mieć słuszne powody, żeby coś (z)robić
**justly** ['dʒʌstlɪ] *adv* (*fairly*) sprawiedliwie; (*deservedly*) słusznie
**jut** [dʒʌt] *vi* (*also*: **jut out**) wystawać, sterczeć
**jute** [dʒu:t] *n* juta *f*
**juvenile** ['dʒu:vənaɪl] *adj* (*offender*) nieletni, młodociany; (*mentality, person*) dziecinny ▷ *n* nieletni(a) *m(f)*; **~ crime** przestępczość nieletnich; **~ court** sąd dla nieletnich
**juvenile delinquency** *n* przestępczość *f* nieletnich
**juvenile delinquent** *n* młodociany przestępca *m*
**juxtapose** ['dʒʌkstəpəuz] *vt* zestawiać (zestawić *perf*) (ze sobą)
**juxtaposition** ['dʒʌkstəpə'zɪʃən] *n* zestawienie *nt*

J

# Kk

**K¹, k** [keɪ] *n* (*letter*) K *nt*, k *nt*; **K for King** ≈ K jak Karol

**K²** *abbr* = **one thousand**; (*Comput*: = *kilobyte*) kB; (*Brit*: *in titles*) = **Knight**

**kaftan** [ˈkæftæn] *n* kaftan *m*

**Kalahari Desert** [kælәˈhɑːrɪ-] *n*: **the ~** pustynia *f* Kalahari

**kale** [keɪl] *n* jarmuż *m*

**kaleidoscope** [kәˈlaɪdәskәup] *n* kalejdoskop *m*

**Kampala** [kæmˈpɑːlә] *n* Kampala *f*

**Kampuchea** [kæmpuˈtʃɪә] *n* Kampucza *f*

**Kampuchean** [kæmpuˈtʃɪәn] *adj* kampuczański

**kangaroo** [kæŋgәˈruː] *n* kangur(-urzyca) *m(f)*

**kaput** [kәˈput] (*inf*) *adj* zepsuty

**karate** [kәˈrɑːtɪ] *n* karate *nt inv*

**Kashmir** [kæʃˈmɪә$^r$] *n* Kaszmir *m*

**kayak** [ˈkaɪæk] *n* kajak *m* eskimoski

**KC** (*Brit*: *Jur*) *n abbr* (= *King's Counsel*) *stopień w hierarchii sądowej*

**kd** (*US*: *Comm*) *abbr* (= *knocked down*) zdemontowany

**kebab** [kәˈbæb] *n* kebab *m*

**keel** [kiːl] *n* kil *m*; **on an even ~** (*fig*) w stanie równowagi

▸ **keel over** *vi* (*Naut*) przewracać się (przewrócić się *perf*) na burtę; (*person*) przewracać się (przewrócić się *perf*), przekręcić się (*perf*) (*inf*)

**keen** [kiːn] *adj* (*person*) zapalony, gorliwy; (*interest, desire*) żywy; (*eye, intelligence*) bystry, przenikliwy; (*competition*) zawzięty; (*edge, blade*) ostry; **to be ~ to do** *or* **on doing sth** palić się do (robienia) czegoś; **to be ~ on sth/sb** interesować się czymś/kimś; **I'm not ~ on going** nie mam ochoty iść

**keenly** [ˈkiːnlɪ] *adv* (*interested*) żywo; (*feel*) dotkliwie; (*watch*) bacznie; (*compete*) zawzięcie

**keenness** [ˈkiːnnɪs] *n* zapał *m*, gorliwość *f*

**keep** [kiːp] (*pt, pp* **kept**) *vt* (*retain*: *receipt*) zachowywać (zachować *perf*); (: *money*) zatrzymywać (zatrzymać *perf*); (: *job*) utrzymywać (utrzymać *perf*); (*preserve, store*) przechowywać (przechować *perf*), trzymać; (*detain*) zatrzymywać (zatrzymać *perf*); (*hold back*) powstrzymywać (powstrzymać *perf*); (*shop, accounts, notes*) prowadzić; (*chickens etc*) hodować, trzymać (*inf*); (*family*) utrzymywać; (*promise*) dotrzymywać (dotrzymać *perf*) *+gen* ▹ *vi* trzymać się ▹ *n* (*expenses*) utrzymanie *nt*; (*of castle*) baszta *f*; **I ~ thinking about it** ciągle o tym myślę; **~ walking** idź dalej; **we try to ~ her happy** staramy się, żeby była zadowolona; **~ the kitchen tidy** utrzymuj kuchnię w czystości; **to ~ sb waiting** kazać (kazać *perf*) komuś czekać; **to ~ an appointment** przychodzić (przyjść *perf*) na (umówione) spotkanie; **to ~ a record of** rejestrować *or* notować *+acc*; **to ~ sth to o.s.** zachowywać (zachować *perf*) coś dla siebie; **to ~ sth (back) from sb** zatajać (zataić *perf*) coś przed kimś; **to ~ sb from doing sth** powstrzymywać (powstrzymać *perf*) kogoś od (z)robienia czegoś; **to ~ sth from happening** zapobiegać (zapobiec *perf*) czemuś; **to ~ time** (*clock*) wskazywać czas; **to ~ warm** trzymać się ciepło; **~ to the path** trzymaj się ścieżki; **how are you ~ing?** (*inf*) jak (ci) leci? (*inf*)

▸ **keep away** *vt*: **to ~ sth/sb away from sth/sb** trzymać coś/kogoś z dala *or* daleka od czegoś/kogoś

▸ **keep away** *vi*: **to ~ away (from)** trzymać się z dala *or* daleka (od *+gen*)

▸ **keep back** *vt* (*crowds, tears*) powstrzymywać (powstrzymać *perf*); (*money*) zostawiać (zostawić *perf*) sobie; (*information*) zatajać (zataić *perf*) ▹ *vi* nie zbliżać się

▸ **keep down** *vt* (*costs, spending*) ograniczać (ograniczyć *perf*); (*food*) nie zwymiotować (*perf*) *+gen* ▹ *vi* nie podnosić się

▸ **keep in** *vt* (*invalid, child*) zatrzymywać (zatrzymać *perf*) w domu; **to ~ sb in at school** zostawiać (zostawić *perf*) kogoś po lekcjach

▸ **keep in with** *vt* utrzymywać dobre stosunki z *+instr*

▸ **keep off** *vt* zabraniać (zabronić *perf*) wstępu *+dat*, nie wpuszczać (nie wpuścić *perf*) *+gen* ▹ *vi* (*rain, snow*) nie zaczynać (nie zacząć *perf*) padać; **"~ off the grass"** „nie deptać trawy";

"~ your hands off" „ręce przy sobie"
▸ **keep on** *vi*: **to ~ on doing sth** nadal coś robić; **to ~ on (about sth)** nudzić (o czymś)
▸ **keep out** *vt* (*intruder etc*) trzymać z daleka; **"~ out"** (*do not enter*) „wstęp wzbroniony"; (*stay away*) „nie zbliżać się"
▸ **keep up** *vt* (*standards etc*) utrzymywać (utrzymać *perf*); (*person*) nie pozwalać (nie pozwolić *perf*) spać +*dat* ▷ *vi*: **to ~ up (with)** nadążać (nadążyć *perf*) (za +*instr*)

**keeper** ['ki:pə^r] *n* (*in zoo, park*) dozorca *m*
**keep fit** *n* zajęcia *pl* sportowe
**keeping** ['ki:pɪŋ] *n* opieka *f*; **in ~ with** zgodnie z +*instr*; **to be in/out of ~ with** harmonizować/nie harmonizować z +*instr*; **I'll leave this in your ~** zostawię to pod twoją opieką.
**keeps** [ki:ps] *n*: **for ~** (*inf*) na zawsze
**keepsake** ['ki:pseɪk] *n* pamiątka *f*
**keg** [kɛg] *n* (*barrel*) beczułka *f*; (*also*: **keg beer**) piwo *nt* beczkowe
**kennel** ['kɛnl] *n* psia buda *f*
**kennels** ['kɛnlz] *npl* schronisko *nt* dla psów
**Kenya** ['kɛnjə] *n* Kenia *f*
**Kenyan** ['kɛnjən] *adj* kenijski ▷ *n* Kenijczyk(-jka) *m(f)*
**kept** *pt, pp of* **keep**
**kerb** [kə:b] (*Brit*) *n* krawężnik *m*
**kernel** ['kə:nl] *n* (*of nut*) jądro *nt*; (*fig*: *of idea*) sedno *nt*, istota *f*
**kerosene** ['kɛrəsi:n] (*US*) *n* nafta *f*
**kestrel** ['kɛstrəl] *n* pustułka *f*
**ketchup** ['kɛtʃəp] *n* keczup *m*
**kettle** ['kɛtl] *n* czajnik *m*
**kettledrum** ['kɛtldrʌm] *n* (*Mus*) kotły *pl*
**key** [ki:] *n* (*lit, fig*) klucz *m*; (*Mus*) tonacja *f*; (*of piano, computer*) klawisz *m* ▷ *adj* kluczowy ▷ *vt* (*also*: **key in**) wpisywać (wpisać *perf*) (*za pomocą klawiatury*)
**keyboard** ['ki:bɔ:d] *n* klawiatura *f*; **keyboards** *npl* instrumenty *pl* klawiszowe
**keyed up** [ki:d-'] *adj* (*person*) spięty
**keyhole** ['ki:həul] *n* dziurka *f* od klucza
**keynote** ['ki:nəut] *n* (*of speech*) myśl *f* przewodnia; (*Mus*) tonika *f*
**keypad** ['ki:pæd] (*Comput, Elec*) *n* klawiatura *f* pomocnicza
**key ring** *n* kółko *nt* na klucze, breloczek *m*
**keystroke** ['ki:strəuk] *n* uderzenie *nt* w klawisz
**kg** *abbr* (= *kilogram*) kg
**KGB** (*Pol*) *n abbr* (*formerly*) KGB *nt inv*
**khaki** ['kɑ:kɪ] *n* khaki *nt inv*
**kHz** *abbr* (= *kilohertz*) kHz
**kibbutz** [kɪ'buts] *n* kibuc *m*
**kick** [kɪk] *vt* kopać (kopnąć *perf*); (*inf*: *addiction*) rzucać (rzucić *perf*) ▷ *vi* wierzgać (wierzgnąć *perf*) ▷ *n* (*of person*) kopnięcie *nt*, kopniak *m*; (*of animal*) wierzgnięcie *nt*, kopnięcie *nt*; (*of ball*) rzut *m* wolny; (*thrill*) frajda *f* (*inf*); (*of rifle*) odrzut *m*; **to do sth for ~s** (*inf*) robić (zrobić *perf*) coś dla frajdy (*inf*); **I could ~ myself** (*inf*) pluję sobie w brodę (*inf*)
▸ **kick around** (*inf*) *vi* poniewierać się ▷ *vt* (*ideas*) obgadywać (obgadać *perf*)
▸ **kick off** (*Sport*) *vi* rozpoczynać (rozpocząć *perf*) mecz

**kick-off** ['kɪkɔf] (*Sport*) *n* rozpoczęcie *nt* meczu
**kick start** (*Aut*) *n* (*also*: **kick starter**) rozrusznik *m* nożny
**kid** [kɪd] *n* (*inf*: *child*) dzieciak *m*, dziecko *nt*; (*goat*) koźlę *nt*; (*leather*) kozia skóra *f* ▷ *vi* (*inf*) żartować; **kid brother** (*inf*) młodszy brat
**kidnap** ['kɪdnæp] *vt* porywać (porwać *perf*)
**kidnapper** ['kɪdnæpə^r] *n* porywacz(ka) *m(f)*
**kidnapping** ['kɪdnæpɪŋ] *n* porwanie *nt*
**kidney** ['kɪdnɪ] *n* (*Anat*) nerka *f*; (*Culin*) cynaderka *f*
**kidney bean** *n* fasola *f* kidney
**kidney machine** *n* dializator *m*
**Kilimanjaro** [kɪlɪmən'dʒɑ:rəu] *n*: **Mount ~** Kilimandżaro *nt inv*
**kill** [kɪl] *vt* zabijać (zabić *perf*); (*fig*: *conversation*) ucinać (uciąć *perf*); (: *inf*: *lights, motor*) gasić (zgasić *perf*); (: *pain*) uśmierzać (uśmierzyć *perf*) ▷ *n* (*animal killed*) zdobycz *f*; (*act of killing*) zabicie *nt*; **to ~ time** zabijać (zabić *perf*) czas; **to ~ o.s. to do sth** (*inf*) wypruwać sobie żyły, żeby coś zrobić (*inf*); **to ~ o.s. laughing** *or* **with laughter** (*inf*) umierać (umrzeć *perf*) ze śmiechu; **my back's ~ing me** (*inf*) plecy bardzo mi dokuczają; **to be in at the ~** (*fig*) być świadkiem zajścia
▸ **kill off** *vt* (*bacteria, rats*) tępić (wytępić *perf*); (*fig*: *characters in book etc*) wykańczać (wykończyć *perf*) (*inf*)

**killer** ['kɪlə^r] *n* zabójca(-jczyni) *m(f)*
**killing** ['kɪlɪŋ] *n* zabójstwo *nt*; **to make a ~** (*inf*) obławiać się (obłowić się *perf*) (*inf*)
**killjoy** ['kɪldʒɔɪ] *n*: **to be a ~** psuć innym zabawę
**kiln** [kɪln] *n* piec *m* do wypalania
**kilo** ['ki:ləu] *n* kilo *nt inv*
**kilobyte** ['ki:ləubaɪt] *n* kilobajt *m*
**kilogram(me)** ['kɪləugræm] *n* kilogram *m*
**kilohertz** ['kɪləuhə:ts] *n inv* kiloherc *m*
**kilometre**, (*US*) **kilometer** ['kɪləmi:tə^r] *n* kilometr *m*
**kilowatt** ['kɪləuwɔt] *n* kilowat *m*
**kilt** [kɪlt] *n* spódnica *f* szkocka
**kilter** ['kɪltə^r] *n*: **to be out of ~** nie działać
**kimono** [kɪ'məunəu] *n* kimono *nt*
**kin** [kɪn] *n see* **kith**; **next**
**kind** [kaɪnd] *adj* uprzejmy, życzliwy ▷ *n* rodzaj *m*; **of some ~** jakiś; **that ~ of thing** coś w tym

K

rodzaju; **in ~** (*Comm*) w towarze; **I'm a ~ of anarchist** jestem swego rodzaju anarchistą; **they're two of a ~** (obaj) są ulepieni z tej samej gliny; **would you be ~ enough to ...?** czy byłbyś uprzejmy *+infin?*; **would you be so ~ as to help me?** czy byłbyś tak miły i pomógł mi?; **it's very ~ of you** (to) bardzo miło z twojej strony

**kindergarten** ['kɪndəgɑ:tn] *n* przedszkole *nt*

**kind-hearted** [kaɪnd'hɑ:tɪd] *adj* życzliwy

**kindle** ['kɪndl] *vt* rozpalać (rozpalić *perf*)

**kindling** ['kɪndlɪŋ] *n* drewno *nt* na rozpałkę

**kindly** ['kaɪndlɪ] *adj* (*person*) dobrotliwy; (*tone, interest*) życzliwy ▷ *adv* uprzejmie, życzliwie; **will you ~ ...** czy mógłbyś łaskawie *+infin?*; **he didn't take ~ to being criticized** źle znosił krytykę

**kindness** ['kaɪndnɪs] *n* (*quality*) uprzejmość *f*, życzliwość *f*; (*act*) uprzejmość *f*, przysługa *f*

**kindred** ['kɪndrɪd] *adj*: **~ spirit** bratnia dusza *f*

**kinetic** [kɪ'nɛtɪk] *adj* (*energy*) kinetyczny; (*art*) ruchomy

**king** [kɪŋ] *n* król *m*

**kingdom** ['kɪŋdəm] *n* królestwo *nt*

**kingfisher** ['kɪŋfɪʃə^r] *n* zimorodek *m*

**kingpin** ['kɪŋpɪn] *n* (*Tech*) sworzeń *m*; (*fig*) oś *f*

**king-size(d)** ['kɪŋsaɪz(d)] *adj* olbrzymi; (*cigarette*) długi

**kink** [kɪŋk] *n* (*in rope*) supeł *m*; (*in wire*) skręt *m*; (*fig*) dziwactwo *nt*; (*: sexual*) perwersja *f*, zboczenie *nt*

**kinky** ['kɪŋkɪ] (*inf, pej*) *adj* (*person*) zboczony (*inf, pej*); (*underwear, tastes*) perwersyjny

**kinship** ['kɪnʃɪp] *n* (*relations*) pokrewieństwo *nt*; (*affinity*) więź *f*

**kinsman** ['kɪnzmən] (*irreg: like* **man**) *n* krewniak *m*, krewny *m*

**kinswoman** ['kɪnzwumən] (*irreg: like* **woman**) *n* krewniaczka *f*, krewna *f*

**kiosk** ['ki:ɔsk] *n* (*shop*) kiosk *m* spożywczy; (*Brit: Tel*) budka *f* (telefoniczna); (*also:* **newspaper kiosk**) kiosk *m* (z gazetami)

**kipper** ['kɪpə^r] *n* śledź *m* wędzony

**kiss** [kɪs] *n* pocałunek *m*, całus *m* ▷ *vt* całować (pocałować *perf*) ▷ *vi* całować się (pocałować się *perf*); **to ~ sb goodbye** całować (pocałować *perf*) kogoś na pożegnanie

**kiss of life** (*Brit*) *n*: **the ~** usta – usta *nt inv*

**kit** [kɪt] *n* (*sports kit etc*) strój *m*, kostium *m*; (*Mil*) ekwipunek *m*; (*of tools etc*) komplet *m*, zestaw *m*; (*for assembly*) zestaw *m*
▸ **kit out** (*Brit*) *vt* wyposażać (wyposażyć *perf*), wyekwipować (*perf*)

**kitbag** ['kɪtbæg] *n* (*Mil*) plecak *m* wojskowy; (*Naut*) worek *m* marynarski

**kitchen** ['kɪtʃɪn] *n* kuchnia *f*

**kitchen garden** *n* ogród *m* warzywny

**kitchen sink** *n* zlewozmywak *m*

**kitchen unit** (*Brit*) *n* szafka *f* kuchenna

**kitchenware** ['kɪtʃɪnwεə^r] *n* naczynia *pl* kuchenne

**kite** [kaɪt] *n* (*toy*) latawiec *m*; (*Zool*) kania *f*

**kith** [kɪθ] *n*: **~ and kin** przyjaciele *vir pl* i krewni *vir pl*

**kitten** ['kɪtn] *n* kotek *m*, kociątko *nt*

**kitty** ['kɪtɪ] *n* wspólna kasa *f*

**KKK** (*US*) *n abbr* (*= Ku Klux Klan*) Ku Klux Klan *m*

**Kleenex**® ['kli:nεks] *n* chusteczka *f* higieniczna

**kleptomaniac** [klεptəu'meɪnɪæk] *n* kleptoman(ka) *m(f)*

**km** *abbr* (*= kilometre*) km

**km/h** *abbr* (*= kilometres per hour*) km/h *or* km/godz

**knack** [næk] *n*: **to have the ~ of/for** mieć talent do *+gen*; **there's a ~ to doing this** potrzeba talentu, żeby to zrobić

**knapsack** ['næpsæk] *n* chlebak *m*

**knead** [ni:d] *vt* (*dough, clay*) wyrabiać (wyrobić *perf*)

**knee** [ni:] *n* kolano *nt*

**kneecap** ['ni:kæp] *n* (*Anat*) rzepka *f*

**knee-deep** ['ni:'di:p] *adj, adv*: **the water was ~** wody było po kolana; **~ in mud** po kolana w błocie

**kneel** [ni:l] (*pt, pp* **knelt**) *vi* (*also:* **kneel down**) klękać (klęknąć *perf or* uklęknąć *perf*)

**kneepad** ['ni:pæd] *n* nakolannik *m*

**knell** [nεl] *n*: **death ~** ostatnia godzina *f*

**knelt** [nεlt] *pt, pp of* **kneel**

**knew** [nju:] *pt of* **know**

**knickers** ['nɪkəz] (*Brit*) *npl* figi *pl*

**knick-knacks** ['nɪknæks] *npl* bibeloty *pl*

**knife** [naɪf] (*pl* **knives**) *n* nóż *m* ▷ *vt* pchnąć (*perf*) nożem; **~, fork and spoon** sztućce

**knight** [naɪt] *n* rycerz *m*; (*Chess*) skoczek *m*, konik *m* ▷ *vt* nadawać (nadać *perf*) tytuł szlachecki *+dat*

**knighthood** ['naɪthud] (*Brit*) *n*: **to be given a ~** otrzymywać (otrzymać *perf*) tytuł szlachecki

**knit** [nɪt] *vt* robić (zrobić *perf*) na drutach ▷ *vi* robić na drutach; (*bones*) zrastać się (zrosnąć się *perf*); **to ~ one's brows** marszczyć (zmarszczyć *perf*) brwi

**knitted** ['nɪtɪd] *adj* (z)robiony na drutach *post*, dziany

**knitting** ['nɪtɪŋ] *n* (*activity*) robienie *nt* na drutach; (*garment being knitted*) robótka *f*

**knitting machine** *n* maszyna *f* dziewiarska

**knitting needle** *n* drut *m* (do robót dzianych)

**knitting pattern** *n* wzór *m* dzianiny

**knitwear** ['nɪtwεə^r] *n* wyroby *pl* z dzianiny

**knives** [naɪvz] *npl of* **knife**

**knob** [nɔb] *n* gałka *f*; **a ~ of butter** (*Brit*) ≈ odrobina masła
**knobbly** ['nɔblɪ], (*US*) **knobby** *adj* guz(k) owaty
**knock** [nɔk] *vt* (*strike*) uderzać (uderzyć *perf*); (*hole*) wybijać (wybić *perf*); (*inf: criticize*) najeżdżać (najechać *perf*) na *+acc* (*inf*) ▷ *vi* (*at door etc*) pukać (zapukać *perf*), stukać (zastukać *perf*); (*engine*) stukać ▷ *n* (*blow, bump*) uderzenie *nt*; (*on door*) pukanie *nt*, stukanie *nt*; **to ~ sb to the ground** powalić (*perf*) kogoś na ziemię; **she ~ed at the door** zapukała do drzwi; **he ~ed the drink out of my hand** wytrącił mi drinka z ręki; **to ~ a nail into sth** wbijać (wbić *perf*) gwóźdź w coś; **to ~ some sense into sb** wbić (*perf*) komuś trochę rozumu do głowy
▶ **knock about** (*inf*) *vt* poniewierać ▷ *vi*: **~ about with** włóczyć się z *+instr*
▶ **knock around** *vt, vi* = **knock about**
▶ **knock back** (*inf*) *vt* (*drink*) obciągać (obciągnąć *perf*) (*inf*)
▶ **knock down** *vt* (*Aut*) potrącić (*perf*); (*: fatally*) przejechać (*perf*); (*building*) burzyć (zburzyć *perf*); (*wall*) wyburzać (wyburzyć *perf*); (*price*) obniżać (obniżyć *perf*)
▶ **knock off** *vi* (*inf*) kończyć (skończyć *perf*) (pracę) ▷ *vt* (*from price*) spuszczać (spuścić *perf*); (*inf: steal*) podprowadzać (podprowadzić *perf*) (*inf*); (*: murder*) sprzątnąć (*perf*) (*inf*); **~ it off!** (*inf*) przestań!
▶ **knock out** *vt* (*person*) pozbawiać (pozbawić *perf*) przytomności; (*drug*) zwalać (zwalić *perf*) z nóg; (*Boxing*) nokautować (znokautować *perf*); (*in game, competition*) eliminować (wyeliminować *perf*)
▶ **knock over** *vt* przewracać (przewrócić *perf*); (*Aut*) potrącić (*perf*)
**knockdown** ['nɔkdaun] *adj* (*price*) śmiesznie niski
**knocker** ['nɔkə^r] *n* kołatka *f*
**knocking** ['nɔkɪŋ] *n* pukanie *nt*, stukanie *nt*
**knock-kneed** [nɔk'ni:d] *adj*: **to be ~** mieć iksowate nogi
**knockout** ['nɔkaut] *n* nokaut *m* ▷ *adj* (*competition etc*) rozgrywany systemem pucharowym
**knock-up** ['nɔkʌp] (*Tennis*) *n*: **to have a ~** rozgrywać (rozegrać *perf*) parę wolnych
**knot** [nɔt] *n* (*in rope*) węzeł *m*, supeł *m*; (*in wood*) sęk *m*; (*Naut*) węzeł *m* ▷ *vt* związywać (związać *perf*); **to tie a ~** zawiązywać (zawiązać *perf*) węzeł *or* supeł
**knotty** ['nɔtɪ] *adj* zawiły
**know** [nəu] (*pt* **knew**, *pp* **~n**) *vt* (*be aware of/that/how etc*) wiedzieć; (*be acquainted with, have experience of*) znać; (*recognize*) poznawać (poznać *perf*); **to ~ how to swim** umieć pływać; **to ~ English** znać angielski; **to ~ about** *or* **of sth/sb** wiedzieć o czymś/kimś; **to get to ~ sb** poznawać (poznać *perf*) kogoś bliżej; **I don't ~ him** nie znam go; **to ~ right from wrong** odróżniać dobro od zła; **as far as I ~** o ile wiem; **yes, I ~** tak, wiem; **I don't ~** nie wiem
**know-all** ['nəuɔ:l] (*Brit: inf, pej*) *n* mądrala *m/f*
**know-how** ['nəuhau] *n* wiedza *f* (technologiczna)
**knowing** ['nəuɪŋ] *adj* (*look*) porozumiewawczy
**knowingly** ['nəuɪŋlɪ] *adv* (*intentionally*) świadomie; (*smile, look*) porozumiewawczo
**know-it-all** ['nəuɪtɔ:l] (*US*) *n* = **know-all**
**knowledge** ['nɔlɪdʒ] *n* wiedza *f*; (*of language etc*) znajomość *f*; **to have no ~ of** nic nie wiedzieć na temat *+gen*; **not to my ~** nic mi o tym nie wiadomo; **without my ~** bez mojej wiedzy; **she has a working ~ of French** potrafi się porozumieć po francusku; **it is common ~ that ...** powszechnie wiadomo, że ...
**knowledgeable** ['nɔlɪdʒəbl] *adj*: **to be ~ about** dobrze znać się na *+loc*
**known** [nəun] *pp of* **know** ▷ *adj* znany
**knuckle** ['nʌkl] *n* kostka *f* (*u ręki*)
▶ **knuckle under** (*inf*) *vi* podporządkowywać się (podporządkować się *perf*)
**knuckle-duster** ['nʌkldʌstə^r] *n* kastet *m*
**KO** *n abbr* (= *knockout*) KO *nt inv*, nokaut *m* ▷ *vt* nokautować (znokautować *perf*)
**koala** [kəu'ɑ:lə] *n* (*also*: **koala bear**) (niedźwiadek *m*) koala *m*
**kook** [ku:k] (*US: inf*) *n* czubek *m* (*inf*)
**Koran** [kɔ'rɑ:n] *n*: **the ~** Koran *m*
**Korea** [kə'rɪə] *n* Korea *f*; **North/South ~** Korea Północna/Południowa
**Korean** [kə'rɪən] *adj* koreański ▷ *n* (*person*) Koreańczyk(-anka) *m(f)*; (*Ling*) (język *m*) koreański
**kosher** ['kəuʃə^r] *adj* koszerny
**kowtow** ['kau'tau] *vi*: **to ~ to sb** płaszczyć się przed kimś
**Kremlin** ['krɛmlɪn] *n*: **the ~** Kreml *m*
**KS** (*US: Post*) *abbr* = **Kansas**
**Kuala Lumpur** ['kwɑ:lə'lumpuə^r] *n* Kuala Lumpur *nt inv*
**kudos** ['kju:dɔs] *n* prestiż *m*
**Kuwait** [ku'weɪt] *n* Kuwejt *m*
**Kuwaiti** [ku'weɪtɪ] *adj* kuwejcki ▷ *n* Kuwejtczyk(-tka) *m(f)*
**kW** *abbr* (= *kilowatt*) kW
**KY** (*US: Post*) *abbr* = **Kentucky**

k

# Ll

**L¹, l¹** [ɛl] *n* (*letter*) L *nt*, l *nt*; **L for Lucy, (US) L for Love** ≈ L jak Leon

**L²** *abbr* (*Brit: Aut*: = *learner*) L; (= *lake*) jez.; = **large**; (= *left*) l.

**l²** *abbr* (= *litre*) l

**LA** (US) *n abbr* = **Los Angeles** ▷ *abbr* (*Post*) = **Louisiana**

**lab** [læb] *n abbr* (= *laboratory*) lab.

**label** ['leɪbl] *n* (*adhesive*) etykieta *f*, nalepka *f*; (*tie-on*) etykieta *f*, przywieszka *f*; (*of record*) znak *m* wytwórni płytowej ▷ *vt* etykietować; (*fig: person*) określać (określić *perf*) mianem *+gen*

**labor** *etc* (US) *n* = **labour** *etc*

**laboratory** [lə'bɔrətərɪ] *n* (*scientific*) laboratorium *nt*; (*school*) pracownia *f*

**Labor Day** (US) *n święto pracy obchodzone w pierwszy poniedziałek września*

**laborious** [lə'bɔːrɪəs] *adj* mozolny, żmudny

**labor union** (US) *n* związek *m* zawodowy

**labour**, (US) **labor** ['leɪbəʳ] *n* (*hard work*) ciężka praca *f*; (*work force*) siła *f* robocza; (*work done by work force*) praca *f*; (*Med*): **to be in ~** rodzić ▷ *vi*: **to ~ (at sth)** mozolić się (nad czymś) ▷ *vt*: **to ~ a point** (zbytnio) rozwodzić się nad zagadnieniem; **L~, the L~ Party** (*Brit*) Partia Pracy; **hard ~** (*toil*) harówka (*inf*); (*punishment*) ciężkie roboty

**labo(u)r camp** *n* obóz *m* pracy

**labo(u)r cost** *n* koszt *m* robocizny

**labo(u)r dispute** *n* spór *m* o warunki pracy

**labo(u)red** ['leɪbəd] *adj* (*breathing*) ciężki; (*movement*) ciężki, ociężały; (*style, writing*) niezdarny, wymęczony; **his breathing was laboured** oddychał z trudem

**labo(u)rer** ['leɪbərəʳ] *n* robotnik(-ica) *m(f)*; **farm labourer** robotnik rolny

**labo(u)r force** *n* siła *f* robocza

**labo(u)r intensive** *adj* pracochłonny

**labo(u)r market** *n* rynek *m* pracy

**labo(u)r pains** *npl* bóle *pl* porodowe

**labo(u)r relations** *npl* stosunki *pl* pracy (*między kierownictwem a pracownikami*)

**labo(u)r-saving** ['leɪbəseɪvɪŋ] *adj* usprawniający *or* ułatwiający pracę

**laburnum** [lə'bəːnəm] (*Bot*) *n* złotokap *m* zwyczajny

**labyrinth** ['læbɪrɪnθ] *n* labirynt *m*

**lace** [leɪs] *n* (*fabric*) koronka *f*; (*of shoe etc*) sznurowadło *nt* ▷ *vt* (*also*: **lace up**: *shoe etc*) sznurować (zasznurować *perf*); (*coffee*) wzmacniać (wzmocnić *perf*) (*alkoholem*)

**lacemaking** ['leɪsmeɪkɪŋ] *n* koronkarstwo *nt*

**lacerate** ['læsəreɪt] *vt* poranić (*perf*), pokaleczyć (*perf*)

**laceration** [læsə'reɪʃən] *n* rana *f* (*darta lub szarpana*)

**lace-up** ['leɪsʌp] *adj* (*shoes etc*) sznurowany, wiązany

**lack** [læk] *n* brak *m* ▷ *vt*: **he ~s money/confidence** brak(uje) mu pieniędzy/pewności siebie; **through** *or* **for ~ of** ze względu na brak *+gen*; **something is ~ing here** czegoś tu brak(uje); **to be ~ing in** być pozbawionym *+gen*

**lackadaisical** [lækə'deɪzɪkl] *adj* nieobecny duchem, bujający w obłokach

**lackey** ['lækɪ] (*pej*) *n* lokaj *m* (*pej*)

**lacklustre** ['læklʌstəʳ], (US) **lackluster** *adj* bezbarwny, bez życia *post*

**laconic** [lə'kɔnɪk] *adj* lakoniczny

**lacquer** ['lækəʳ] *n* (*paint*) lakier *m*; (*also*: **hair lacquer**) lakier *m* (do włosów)

**lacrosse** [lə'krɔs] *n gra zespołowa, w której do odbijania piłeczki i strzelania bramek służą zakończone siatką kijki*

**lacy** ['leɪsɪ] *adj* koronkowy

**lad** [læd] *n* (*boy*) chłopak *m*; (*young man*) młodzieniec *m*

**ladder** ['lædəʳ] *n* (*metal, wood*) drabina *f*; (*rope*) drabinka *f*; (*Brit: in tights*) oczko *nt*; (*fig*) drabina *f* społeczna ▷ *vt fus* (*Brit*): **I ~ed my tights, my tights ~ed** poszło *or* poleciało mi oczko w rajstopach

**laden** ['leɪdn] *adj*: **to be ~ (with)** uginać się (od *+gen*); **fully ~** z pełnym ładunkiem

**ladle** ['leɪdl] *n* chochla *f*, łyżka *f* wazowa ▷ *vt* (*soup*) nalewać (nalać *perf*) (chochlą); (*stew*) nakładać (nałożyć *perf*)

▸ **ladle out** *vt* (*fig: money*) rozdawać (rozdać *perf*) (na prawo i lewo); (*advice, information*) serwować (zaserwować *perf*) (*inf*); (*compliments, praise*) szafować *+instr*

**lady** ['leɪdɪ] *n* kobieta *f*, pani *f* (*polite*); (*dignified etc*) dama *f*; (*Brit: title*) lady *f inv*; **ladies and gentlemen, …** Panie i Panowie, …, Szanowni Państwo, …; **young ~** młoda dama; **the ladies' (room)** toaleta damska

**ladybird** ['leɪdɪbə:d] *n* biedronka *f*

**ladybug** ['leɪdɪbʌg] (*US*) *n* = **ladybird**

**lady-in-waiting** ['leɪdɪɪn'weɪtɪŋ] *n* dama *f* dworu

**ladykiller** ['leɪdɪkɪlə^r] *n* pożeracz *m or* pogromca *m* serc (niewieścich)

**ladylike** ['leɪdɪlaɪk] *adj* (*behaviour*) dystyngowany, wytworny; **she's ~** zachowuje się jak (prawdziwa) dama

**ladyship** ['leɪdɪʃɪp] *n*: **your ~** ≈ jaśnie pani *f*

**lag** [læg] *n* opóźnienie *nt* ▹ *vi* (*also*: **lag behind**) pozostawać (pozostać *perf*) w tyle; (*trade etc*) podupadać (podupaść *perf*) ▹ *vt* (*pipes etc*) izolować (izolować *perf*); **old lag** (*inf: prisoner*) recydywa (*inf, pej*)

**lager** ['lɑ:gə^r] *n* piwo *nt* pełne jasne

**lagging** ['lægɪŋ] *n* izolacja *f*, otulina *f*

**lagoon** [lə'gu:n] *n* laguna *f*

**Lagos** ['leɪgɔs] *n* Lagos *nt inv*

**laid** [leɪd] *pt, pp of* **lay**

**laid-back** [leɪd'bæk] (*inf*) *adj* (*person*) na luzie *post* (*inf*), wyluzowany (*inf*); (*atmosphere*) swobodny

**laid up** *adj*: **to be ~ with** być złożonym *+instr*

**lain** [leɪn] *pp of* **lie**

**lair** [lɛə^r] (*Zool*) *n* matecznik *m*, legowisko *nt*

**laissez-faire** [lɛseɪ'fɛə^r] *n* (*Comm*) polityka *f* nieinterwencji *or* wolnej ręki

**laity** ['leɪətɪ] *n or npl* świeccy *vir pl*, laikat *m* (*fml*)

**lake** [leɪk] *n* jezioro *nt*

**Lake District** (*Brit*) *n*: **the ~** ≈ Kraina *f* Jezior (*w północno-zachodniej Anglii*)

**lamb** [læm] *n* (*Zool*) jagnię *nt*; (*Rel: fig*) baranek *m*; (*in nursery rhymes etc*) owieczka *f*; (*Culin*) jagnięcina *f*

**lambada** [læm'bɑ:də] *n* lambada *f*

**lamb chop** *n* kotlet *m* z jagnięcia

**lambskin** ['læmskɪn] *n* skóra *f* jagnięca

**lambswool** ['læmzwul] *n* wełna *f* jagnięca

**lame** [leɪm] *adj* (*person, animal*) kulawy, chromy (*literary*); (*excuse, argument*) lichy, kiepski; **to be ~** kuleć

**lame duck** *n* (*person*) nieudacznik *m* (*pej*); (*business*) bankrut *m*

**lamely** ['leɪmlɪ] *adv* (*explain, apologize*) nieprzekonująco

**lament** [lə'mɛnt] *n* (*mourning*) opłakiwanie *nt*; (*complaining*) lament *m*, biadanie *nt* ▹ *vt* (*mourn*) opłakiwać; (*complain about*) lamentować *or* biadać nad *+instr*

**lamentable** ['læməntəbl] *adj* opłakany, pożałowania godny

**laminated** ['læmɪneɪtɪd] *adj* (*metal, wood*) wielowarstwowy; (*book cover*) laminowany

**lamp** [læmp] *n* lampa *f*

**lamplight** ['læmplaɪt] *n*: **by ~** przy (zapalonej) lampie

**lampoon** [læm'pu:n] *n* satyra *f* ▹ *vt* ośmieszać (ośmieszyć *perf*) (*zwykle za pomocą satyry w prasie*)

**lamppost** ['læmppəust] (*Brit*) *n* latarnia *f* (uliczna)

**lampshade** ['læmpʃeɪd] *n* abażur *m*; (*glass*) klosz *m*

**lance** [lɑ:ns] *n* lanca *f* ▹ *vt* (*Med*) nacinać (naciąć *perf*) (*ropień itp*)

**lance corporal** (*Brit*) *n* ≈ starszy szeregowy *m*

**lancet** ['lɑ:nsɪt] *n* lancet *m*

**Lancs** [læŋks] (*Brit: Post*) *abbr* = **Lancashire**

**land** [lænd] *n* (*area of open ground*) ziemia *f*; (*property, estate*) ziemia *f*, grunty *pl*; (*as opposed to sea*) ląd *m*; (*country*) kraj *m*, ziemia *f* (*literary*) ▹ *vi* (*lit, fig*) lądować (wylądować *perf*) ▹ *vt* (*passengers*) wysadzać (wysadzić *perf*); (*goods*) wyładowywać (wyładować *perf*); **to own ~** być właścicielem ziemskim; **to go/travel by ~** jechać (pojechać *perf*)/podróżować lądem; **to ~ on one's feet** (*fig*) spadać (spaść *perf*) na cztery łapy (*inf*); **to ~ sb with sth** (*inf*) zwalać (zwalić *perf*) komuś coś na głowę (*inf*)

▸ **land up** *vi*: **to ~ up in** lądować (wylądować *perf*) w *+loc*

**landed gentry** ['lændɪd-] *n* ziemiaństwo *nt*, ziemianie *vir pl*

**landfill site** ['lændfɪl-] *n* ≈ wysypisko *nt* (śmieci)

**landing** ['lændɪŋ] *n* (*of house*) półpiętro *nt*, podest *m*; (*Aviat*) lądowanie *nt*

**landing card** *n* (*Aviat*) karta *f* lądowania; (*Naut*) karta *f* zejścia na ląd

**landing craft** *n inv* okręt *m* desantowy

**landing gear** (*Aviat*) *n* podwozie *nt*

**landing stage** *n* pomost *m*

**landing strip** *n* lądowisko *nt*, pas *m* do lądowania

**landlady** ['lændleɪdɪ] *n* (*of rented house, flat*) właścicielka *f*; (*of rented room*) gospodyni *f*; (*of pub: owner*) właścicielka *f*; (*: manageress*) kierowniczka *f*

**landline** ['lændlaɪn] *n* (*phone*) linia *f* stacjonarna

**landlocked** ['lændlɔkt] *adj* nie posiadający dostępu do morza, bez dostępu do morza *post*

**landlord** ['lændlɔ:d] *n* (*of rented house, flat*) właściciel *m*; (*of rented room*) gospodarz *m*; (*of*

l

*pub: owner)* właściciel *m*; *(: manager)* kierownik *m*
**landlubber** ['lændlʌbəʳ] *(old) n* szczur *m* lądowy
**landmark** ['lændmɑːk] *n* punkt *m* orientacyjny; *(fig)* kamień *m* milowy
**landowner** ['lændəunəʳ] *n* właściciel(ka) *m(f)* ziemski(-ka) *m(f)*
**landscape** ['lænskeɪp] *n* krajobraz *m*; *(Art)* pejzaż *m* ▷ *vt (park, garden)* projektować (zaprojektować *perf*)
**landscape architect** *n* architekt *m* krajobrazu, projektant(ka) *m(f)* terenów zielonych
**landscape gardener** *n* = **landscape architect**
**landscape painting** *n* malarstwo *nt* pejzażowe
**landslide** ['lændslaɪd] *n* osunięcie się *nt* ziemi; *(fig)*: **a ~ victory** przygniatające zwycięstwo *nt*
**lane** [leɪn] *n (in country)* dróżka *f*; *(in town)* uliczka *f*; *(Aut)* pas *m* (ruchu); *(of race course, swimming pool)* tor *m*; **shipping ~** szlak żeglugowy
**language** ['læŋgwɪdʒ] *n* język *m*; **bad ~** wulgarny język
**language laboratory** *n* laboratorium *nt* językowe
**languid** ['læŋgwɪd] *adj (person)* powolny; *(movement)* leniwy, ociężały
**languish** ['læŋgwɪʃ] *vi (person)* marnieć, usychać; *(project, case)* wlec się
**lank** [læŋk] *adj (hair)* w strąkach *post*
**lanky** ['læŋkɪ] *adj* tyczkowaty, patykowaty
**lanolin(e)** ['lænəlɪn] *n* lanolina *f*
**lantern** ['læntən] *n* lampion *m*
**Laos** [laus] *n* Laos *m*
**lap** [læp] *n (in race)* okrążenie *nt*; *(of person)*: **in his/my lap** u niego/u mnie na kolanach ▷ *vt (also*: **lap up**) chłeptać (wychłeptać *perf*) ▷ *vi (water)* pluskać
▸ **lap up** *vt (fig)* przyjmować (przyjąć *perf*) za dobrą monetę
**La Paz** [læ'pæz] *n* La Paz *nt inv*
**lapdog** ['læpdɔg] *(pej) n (lit, fig)* piesek *m* salonowy
**lapel** [lə'pɛl] *n* klapa *f*, wyłóg *m*
**Lapland** ['læplænd] *n* Laponia *f*
**Lapp** [læp] *adj* lapoński ▷ *n (person)* Lapończyk(-onka) *m(f)*; *(Ling)* (język *m*) lapoński
**lapse** [læps] *n (bad behaviour)* uchybienie *nt*; *(of time)* upływ *m* ▷ *vi (contract, membership)* wygasać (wygasnąć *perf*); *(passport)* tracić (stracić *perf*) ważność; **a ~ of attention/concentration** chwila nieuwagi; **I had a memory ~** chwilowo zawiodła mnie pamięć; **to ~ into bad habits** popadać (popaść *perf*) w złe nawyki
**laptop** ['læptɔp] *(Comput) n* laptop *m*
**larceny** ['lɑːsənɪ] *n* kradzież *f*
**larch** [lɑːtʃ] *n* modrzew *m*
**lard** [lɑːd] *n* smalec *m*
**larder** ['lɑːdəʳ] *n* spiżarnia *f*
**large** [lɑːdʒ] *adj* duży, wielki; **to make ~r** powiększać (powiększyć *perf*); **a ~ number of people** wielu ludzi; **on a ~ scale** na dużą *or* wielką skalę; **at ~** *(at liberty)* na wolności; **people at ~** ogół (ludzi); **the country at ~** cały kraj; **by and ~** ogólnie (rzecz) biorąc
**largely** ['lɑːdʒlɪ] *adv* w dużej mierze
**large-scale** ['lɑːdʒ'skeɪl] *adj (event)* na dużą skalę *post*; *(map)* w dużej skali *post*
**largesse** [lɑː'ʒɛs] *n* szczodrość *f*
**lark** [lɑːk] *n (bird)* skowronek *m*; *(joke)* kawał *m*
▸ **lark about** *vi* dokazywać
**larva** ['lɑːvə] *(pl* **~e**) *n* larwa *f*
**laryngitis** [lærɪn'dʒaɪtɪs] *n* zapalenie *nt* krtani
**larynx** ['lærɪŋks] *n* krtań *f*
**lasagne**, *(US)* **lasagna** [lə'sænjə] *n (Culin)* lazanie *f*
**lascivious** [lə'sɪvɪəs] *adj* lubieżny
**laser** ['leɪzəʳ] *n* laser *m*
**laser beam** *n* wiązka *f* laserowa
**laser printer** *n* drukarka *f* laserowa
**lash** [læʃ] *n (also*: **eyelash**) rzęsa *f*; *(of whip)* uderzenie *nt (batem)* ▷ *vt (whip)* chłostać (wychłostać *perf*); *(wind)* smagać; *(rain)* zacinać; **to ~ to** przywiązywać (przywiązać *perf*) do *+gen*; **to ~ together** związywać (związać *perf*)
▸ **lash down** *vt* przywiązywać (przywiązać *perf*) ▷ *vi (rain)* lać
▸ **lash out** *vi*: **to ~ out (at sb)** *(with weapon, hands)* bić (kogoś) na oślep; *(with feet)* kopać (kogoś) na oślep; **to ~ out at** *or* **against sb** *(criticize)* naskakiwać (naskoczyć *perf*) na kogoś
**lashing** ['læʃɪŋ] *n*: **~s of** *(Brit: inf)* masa *+gen (inf)*
**lass** [læs] *(Brit) n* dziewczyna *f*
**lasso** [læ'suː] *n* lasso *nt* ▷ *vt* chwytać (schwytać *perf*) na lasso
**last** [lɑːst] *adj* ostatni ▷ *adv (most recently)* ostatnio, ostatni raz; *(finally)* na końcu ▷ *vi (continue)* trwać; *(food)* zachowywać (zachować *perf*) świeżość; *(money, commodity)* wystarczać (wystarczyć *perf*), starczać (starczyć *perf*); **~ week** w zeszłym tygodniu; **~ night** zeszłej nocy; **at ~** wreszcie, w końcu; **~ but one** przedostatni; **the ~ time** ostatni raz; **the film ~s (for) two hours** film trwa dwie godziny

**last-ditch** ['lɑ:st'dɪtʃ] *adj* (*attempt*) ostatni, ostateczny
**lasting** ['lɑ:stɪŋ] *adj* trwały
**lastly** ['lɑ:stlɪ] *adv* na koniec
**last-minute** ['lɑ:stmɪnɪt] *adj* (*decision etc*) w ostatniej chwili *post*
**latch** [lætʃ] *n* (*metal bar*) zasuwa *f*; (*automatic lock*) zatrzask *m*; **the door was on the ~** drzwi nie były zatrzaśnięte, drzwi były zamknięte (tylko) na klamkę
▸ **latch on to** *vt fus* uczepić się (*perf*) *+gen*
**latchkey** ['lætʃki:] *n* klucz *m* (od drzwi wejściowych)
**latchkey child** *n* dziecko *nt* z kluczem (na szyi)
**late** [leɪt] *adj* (*far on in time*) późny; (*not on time*) spóźniony; (*deceased*) świętej pamięci ▹ *adv* (*far on in time*) późno; (*behind time*) z opóźnieniem; **to be (10 minutes) ~** spóźniać się (spóźnić się *perf*) (o 10 minut); **to work ~** pracować do późna; **~ in life** w późnym wieku; **of ~** ostatnio; **in ~ May** pod koniec maja; **Jane Smith, ~ of X** Jane Smith, do niedawna zamieszkała w X
**latecomer** ['leɪtkʌməʳ] *n* spóźnialski(-ka) *m(f)*
**lately** ['leɪtlɪ] *adv* ostatnio
**lateness** ['leɪtnɪs] *n* (*of person*) spóźnienie *nt*; (*of event, train*) opóźnienie *nt*; **owing to the ~ of the hour** ze względu na późną porę
**latent** ['leɪtnt] *adj* ukryty, utajony
**later** ['leɪtəʳ] *adj* późniejszy ▹ *adv* później; **~ on** później
**lateral** ['lætərl] *adj* boczny; **~ thinking** myślenie lateralne
**latest** ['leɪtɪst] *adj* ostatni, najnowszy; **at the ~** najpóźniej
**latex** ['leɪtɛks] *n* lateks *m*
**lathe** [leɪð] *n* tokarka *f*
**lather** ['lɑ:ðəʳ] *n* piana *f* ▹ *vt* namydlać (namydlić *perf*)
**Latin** ['lætɪn] *n* (*Ling*) łacina *f*; (*person*) *osoba pochodząca z Hiszpanii, Włoch lub południowej Francji* ▹ *adj* łaciński
**Latin America** *n* Ameryka *f* Łacińska
**Latin American** *adj* latynoamerykański, latynoski ▹ *n* Latynos(ka) *m(f)*
**latitude** ['lætɪtju:d] *n* szerokość *f* geograficzna; (*fig*) swoboda *f*
**latrine** [lə'tri:n] *n* latryna *f*
**latter** ['lætəʳ] *adj* (*of two*) drugi; (*recent*) ostatni ▹ *n*: **the ~** ten ostatni *m*/ta ostatnia *f*/to ostatnie *nt*; **the ~ part of the week** druga połowa tygodnia; **in the ~ years of his life** na starość
**latter-day** ['lætədeɪ] *adj* dzisiejszy, współczesny
**latterly** ['lætəlɪ] *adv* ostatnio
**lattice** ['lætɪs] *n* kratownica *f*
**lattice window** *n okno z szybkami osadzonymi w kratownicy z ołowiu*
**Latvia** ['lætvɪə] *n* Łotwa *f*
**laudable** ['lɔ:dəbl] *adj* chwalebny, godny pochwały
**laudatory** ['lɔ:dətrɪ] *adj* pochwalny
**laugh** [lɑ:f] *n* śmiech *m* ▹ *vi* śmiać się (zaśmiać się *perf*); **for a ~** dla śmiechu
▸ **laugh at** *vt fus* śmiać się z *+gen*
▸ **laugh off** *vt* obracać (obrócić *perf*) w żart
**laughable** ['lɑ:fəbl] *adj* śmieszny
**laughing gas** ['lɑ:fɪŋ-] *n* gaz *m* rozweselający
**laughing matter** *n*: **this is no ~** to nie (są) żarty
**laughing stock** *n*: **to be the ~ of** być pośmiewiskiem *+gen*
**laughter** ['lɑ:ftəʳ] *n* śmiech *m*
**launch** [lɔ:ntʃ] *n* (*of ship*) wodowanie *nt*; (*of rocket, satellite*) wystrzelenie *nt*; (*Comm*) wprowadzenie *nt or* wypuszczenie *nt* na rynek; (*motorboat*) motorówka *f* ▹ *vt* (*ship*) wodować (zwodować *perf*); (*rocket, satellite*) wystrzeliwać (wystrzelić *perf*); (*Comm*) wprowadzać (wprowadzić *perf*) *or* wypuszczać (wypuścić *perf*) na rynek; (*fig*) zapoczątkowywać (zapoczątkować *perf*)
▸ **launch into** *vt fus* (*activity*) angażować się (zaangażować się *perf*) w *+acc*; (*description*) wdawać się (wdać się *perf*) w *+acc*
▸ **launch out** *vi*: **to ~ out (into)** (*new activity, job*) angażować się (zaangażować się *perf*) (w *+acc*)
**launching** ['lɔ:ntʃɪŋ] *n* (*of rocket, satellite*) wystrzelenie *nt*; (*of ship*) wodowanie *nt*; (*Comm*) wprowadzenie *nt or* wypuszczenie *nt* na rynek; (*fig*) zapoczątkowanie *nt*
**launch(ing) pad** *n* płyta *f* wyrzutni rakietowej
**launder** ['lɔ:ndəʳ] *vt* (*clothes, sheets*) prać i prasować (wyprać *perf* i wyprasować *perf*); (*pej*: *money*) prać (wyprać *perf*)
**laundrette, launderette** [lɔ:n'drɛt] (*Brit*) *n* pralnia *f* samoobsługowa
**Laundromat**® ['lɔ:ndrəmæt] (*US*) *n* = **laundrette**
**laundry** ['lɔ:ndrɪ] *n* (*clothes, linen*) pranie *nt*; (*place*) pralnia *f*; **to do the ~** robić (zrobić *perf*) pranie
**laureate** ['lɔ:rɪət] *adj* see **poet laureate**
**laurel** ['lɔrl] *n* laur *m*, wawrzyn *m*; **to rest on one's ~s** spoczywać (spocząć *perf*) na laurach
**Lausanne** [ləu'zæn] *n* Lozanna *f*
**lava** ['lɑ:və] *n* lawa *f*
**lavatory** ['lævətərɪ] *n* toaleta *f*
**lavatory paper** *n* papier *m* toaletowy
**lavender** ['lævəndəʳ] *n* lawenda *f*

**lavish** ['lævɪʃ] *adj* (*amount, hospitality*) szczodry; (*person*) szczodry, hojny; (*surroundings*) urządzony z przepychem ▷ *vt*: **to ~ gifts/ praise on sb** obsypywać (obsypać *perf*) kogoś prezentami/pochwałami; **to ~ time/ attention on sb** poświęcać (poświęcić *perf*) komuś wiele czasu/uwagi; **to be ~ with** nie skąpić *+gen*
**lavishly** ['lævɪʃlɪ] *adv* (*generously*) szczodrze, hojnie; (*sumptuously*) z przepychem
**law** [lɔː] *n* prawo *nt*; **against the law** niezgodny z prawem; **to go to law** iść (pójść *perf*) do sądu; **to break the law** łamać (złamać *perf*) prawo
**law-abiding** ['lɔːəbaɪdɪŋ] *adj* prawomyślny, praworządny
**law and order** *n* prawo *nt* i porządek *m*
**lawbreaker** ['lɔːbreɪkəʳ] *n*: **to be a ~** łamać prawo
**law court** *n* sąd *m*
**lawful** ['lɔːful] *adj* legalny
**lawfully** ['lɔːfəlɪ] *adv* legalnie
**lawless** ['lɔːlɪs] *adj* bezprawny
**lawn** [lɔːn] *n* trawnik *m*
**lawnmower** ['lɔːnməuəʳ] *n* kosiarka *f* (do trawy)
**lawn tennis** *n* tenis *m* ziemny
**law school** (*US*) *n* wydział *m* prawa
**law student** *n* student(ka) *m(f)* prawa
**lawsuit** ['lɔːsuːt] *n* proces *m* (sądowy)
**lawyer** ['lɔːjəʳ] *n* (*solicitor*) prawnik(-iczka) *m(f)*, radca *m* prawny; (*barrister*) adwokat *m*
**lax** [læks] *adj* (*behaviour*) zbyt swobodny, niedbały; (*discipline, security*) rozluźniony
**laxative** ['læksətɪv] *n* środek *m* przeczyszczający
**laxity** ['læksɪtɪ] *n* (*of laws, rules*) nieprecyzyjność *f*; (*moral*) rozprzężenie *nt*
**lay** [leɪ] (*pt, pp* **laid**) *pt of* **lie** ▷ *adj* (*Rel*) świecki; (*not expert*): **lay person** laik *m* ▷ *vt* (*put*) kłaść (położyć *perf*); (*table*) nakrywać (nakryć *perf*), nakrywać (nakryć *perf*) do *+gen*; (*plans*) układać (ułożyć *perf*); (*trap*) zastawiać (zastawić *perf*); (*egg: insect, frog*) składać (złożyć *perf*); (*: bird*) znosić (znieść *perf*); **to lay facts/proposals before sb** przedstawiać (przedstawić *perf*) komuś fakty/propozycje; **she reads anything she can lay her hands on** czyta wszystko, co wpadnie jej w ręce; **to get laid** (*inf!*) przelecieć (*perf*) kogoś (*inf!*)
▶ **lay aside** *vt* odkładać (odłożyć *perf*) (na bok)
▶ **lay by** *vt* (*money*) odkładać (odłożyć *perf*)
▶ **lay down** *vt* (*pen, book*) odkładać (odłożyć *perf*); (*rules etc*) ustanawiać (ustanowić *perf*); (*arms*) składać (złożyć *perf*); **to lay down the law** rządzić się (*pej*); **to lay down one's life (for)** oddawać (oddać *perf*) życie (za *+acc*)
▶ **lay in** *vt* robić (zrobić *perf*) zapasy *+gen*
▶ **lay into** *vt fus* (*lit, fig*) rzucać się (rzucić się *perf*) na *+acc*
▶ **lay off** *vt* zwalniać (zwolnić *perf*) (z pracy)
▶ **lay on** *vt* (*meal, entertainment*) zadbać (*perf*) *or* zatroszczyć się (*perf*) o *+acc*; (*water, gas*) doprowadzać (doprowadzić *perf*); (*paint*) kłaść (położyć *perf*)
▶ **lay out** *vt* wykładać (wyłożyć *perf*)
▶ **lay up** *vt* (*illness: person*) złożyć (*perf*), rozkładać (rozłożyć *perf*) (*inf*)
**layabout** ['leɪəbaut] (*inf, pej*) *n* obibok *m* (*pej*), leser(ka) *m(f)* (*pej*)
**lay-by** ['leɪbaɪ] (*Brit: Aut*) *n* zato(cz)ka *f*
**lay-days** ['leɪdeɪz] (*Naut*) *npl* dni *pl* postoju w porcie
**layer** ['leɪəʳ] *n* warstwa *f*
**layette** [leɪ'ɛt] *n* wyprawka *f* niemowlęca
**layman** ['leɪmən] (*irreg: like* **man**) *n* laik *m*
**lay-off** ['leɪɔf] *n* zwolnienie *nt* (z pracy)
**layout** ['leɪaut] *n* (*of garden, building*) rozkład *m*; (*of piece of writing*) układ *m* (graficzny)
**laze** [leɪz] *vi* (*also*: **laze about**) leniuchować
**laziness** ['leɪzɪnɪs] *n* lenistwo *nt*
**lazy** ['leɪzɪ] *adj* leniwy
**LB** (*Canada*) *abbr* = **Labrador**
**lb.** *abbr* (= *pound (weight)*) funt *m* (*jednostka wagi*)
**lbw** (*Cricket*) *abbr* (= *leg before wicket*) *rodzaj błędu w grze*
**LC** (*US*) *n abbr* (= *Library of Congress*) Biblioteka *f* Kongresu
**lc** (*Typ*) *abbr* = **lower case**
**L/C** *abbr* (= *letter of credit*) akredytywa *f*
**LCD** *n abbr* = **liquid crystal display**
**Ld** (*Brit*) *abbr* (*in titles*) = **lord**
**LDS** *n abbr* (*Brit*: = *Licentiate in Dental Surgery*) *stopień naukowy* ▷ *abbr* (= *Latter-day Saints*) Kościół *m* Jezusa Chrystusa Świętych Dni Ostatnich
**LEA** (*Brit*) *n abbr* (= *Local Education Authority*) ≈ Kuratorium *nt* Oświaty i Wychowania
**lead¹** [liːd] (*pt, pp* **led**) *n* (*Sport*) prowadzenie *nt*; (*fig*) przywództwo *nt*; (*piece of information, clue*) trop *m*; (*in play, film*) główna rola *f*; (*for dog*) smycz *f*; (*Elec*) przewód *m* ▷ *vt* (*walk in front, guide*) prowadzić (poprowadzić *perf*); (*organization, activity*) kierować (pokierować *perf*) *+instr*; (*Brit*): **to ~ the orchestra** grać (zagrać *perf*) partię pierwszych skrzypiec (w orkiestrze) ▷ *vi* prowadzić; **one-minute ~** jednominutowa przewaga; **in the ~** na prowadzeniu; **to take the ~** obejmować (objąć *perf*) prowadzenie; **to ~ the way** prowadzić, wskazywać drogę; **to ~ sb astray** (*mislead*) zwieść (*perf*) kogoś; (*corrupt*) sprowadzić (*perf*) kogoś na manowce *or* złą drogę; **to ~ sb to believe that ...** dawać (dać

*perf)* komuś powody sądzić, że...; **to ~ sb to do sth** sprawić *(perf)*, że ktoś coś zrobi
▸ **lead away** *vt*: **to be led away** dać *(perf)* się poprowadzić (bezmyślnie)
▸ **lead back** *vt* prowadzić (zaprowadzić *perf)* z powrotem
▸ **lead off** *vi (in game, conversation)*: **to ~ off with** rozpoczynać (rozpocząć *perf) +instr or* od *+gen*; *(road)*: **to ~ off from** odchodzić od *+gen* ▷ *vt fus (room)* wychodzić na *+acc*; *(corridor)* prowadzić do *+gen*
▸ **lead on** *vt* zwodzić
▸ **lead to** *vt fus* prowadzić (doprowadzić *perf)* do *+gen*
▸ **lead up to** *vt fus (events)* prowadzić (doprowadzić *perf)* do *+gen*; *(person)* starać się skierować rozmowę na *+acc*

**lead²** [lɛd] *n (metal)* ołów *m*; *(in pencil)* grafit *m* ▷ *cpd* ołowiany

**leaded** ['lɛdɪd] *adj (window)* witrażowy; *(petrol)* ołowiowy

**leaden** ['lɛdn] *adj (sky, sea)* ołowiany; *(fig: steps etc)* ciężki, jak z ołowiu *post*

**leader** ['li:dəʳ] *n (of group, organization)* przywódca(-dczyni) *m(f)*, lider(ka) *m(f)*; *(Sport)* lider(ka) *m(f)*, prowadzący(-ca) *m(f)*; *(in newspaper)* artykuł *m* wstępny, wstępniak *m (inf)*; **the L~ of the House** *(Brit)* Przewodniczący Izby

**leadership** ['li:dəʃɪp] *n (group)* kierownictwo *nt*; *(position)* stanowisko *nt* przywódcy; *(quality)* umiejętność *f* przewodzenia

**lead-free** ['lɛdfri:] *(old) adj* bezołowiowy

**leading** ['li:dɪŋ] *adj (most important)* czołowy; *(first, front)* prowadzący, znajdujący się na czele; *(role)* główny

**leading lady** *(Theat) n* odtwórczyni *f* głównej roli

**leading light** *n* czołowa postać *f*

**leading man** *(irreg: like* **man***)* *(Theat) n* odtwórca *m* głównej roli

**leading question** *n (pej)* pytanie *nt* sugerujące odpowiedź *(np. w sądzie)*

**lead pencil** [lɛd-] *n* ołówek *m*

**lead poisoning** [lɛd-] *n* zatrucie *nt* ołowiem

**lead singer** [li:d-] *n* główny(-na) *m(f)* wokalista(-tka) *m(f)*

**lead time** [li:d-] *(Comm) n okres projektowania i wdrażania towaru do produkcji*

**leaf** [li:f] *(pl* **leaves***)* *n* liść *m*; *(of table)* dodatkowy blat *m*; **to turn over a new ~** rozpoczynać (rozpocząć *perf)* nowe życie; **to take a ~ out of sb's book** brać (wziąć *perf)* z kogoś przykład
▸ **leaf through** *vt fus* kartkować (przekartkować *perf)*

**leaflet** ['li:flɪt] *n* ulotka *f*

**leafy** ['li:fɪ] *adj (branch)* pokryty liśćmi; *(suburb)* zielony

**league** [li:g] *n* liga *f*; **to be in ~ with sb** być w zmowie z kimś

**leak** [li:k] *n (of liquid, gas)* wyciek *m*; *(in pipe etc)* dziura *f*; *(piece of information)* przeciek *m* ▷ *vi (ship, roof)* przeciekać; *(shoes)* przemakać; *(liquid)* wyciekać (wyciec *perf)*, przeciekać (przeciec *perf)*; *(gas)* ulatniać się (ulotnić się *perf)* ▷ *vt (information)* ujawniać (ujawnić *perf)*
▸ **leak out** *vi (liquid)* wyciekać (wyciec *perf)*; *(information)* wychodzić (wyjść *perf)* na jaw

**leakage** ['li:kɪdʒ] *n* wyciek *m*

**leaky** ['li:kɪ] *adj* nieszczelny

**lean** [li:n] *(pt, pp* **~ed** *or* **~t***)* *adj (person)* szczupły; *(meat, year)* chudy ▷ *vt*: **to ~ sth on sth** opierać (oprzeć *perf)* coś na czymś ▷ *vi* pochylać się (pochylić się *perf)*; **to ~ against** opierać się (oprzeć się *perf)* o *+acc*; **to ~ on** *(rely on)* polegać na *+loc*; *(pressurize)* wywierać nacisk na *+acc*; **to ~ forward/back** pochylać się (pochylić się *perf)* do przodu/do tyłu; **to ~ towards** skłaniać się ku *+dat*
▸ **lean out** *vi* wychylać się (wychylić się *perf)*
▸ **lean over** *vi* przechylać się (przechylić się *perf)*

**leaning** ['li:nɪŋ] *n* skłonności *pl* ▷ *adj*: **the ~ Tower of Pisa** krzywa wieża *f* w Pizie

**leant** [lɛnt] *pt, pp of* **lean**

**lean-to** ['li:ntu:] *n* przybudówka *f (gospodarcza)*

**leap** [li:p] *(pt, pp* **~ed** *or* **~t***)* *n (lit, fig)* skok *m* ▷ *vi (jump)* skakać (skoczyć *perf)*; *(move)*: **to ~ into/out of** wskakiwać (wskoczyć *perf)* do *+gen*/wyskakiwać (wyskoczyć *perf)* z *+gen*; *(price, number etc)* skakać (skoczyć *perf)*, podskoczyć *(perf)*
▸ **leap at** *vt fus* skwapliwie skorzystać *(perf)* z *+gen*
▸ **leap up** *vi* zrywać się (zerwać się *perf)*, skoczyć *(perf)* na równe nogi

**leapfrog** ['li:pfrɔg] *n zabawa, w której osoby stojące w rzędzie po kolei przeskakują przez siebie jak przez kozioł*

**leapt** [lɛpt] *pt, pp of* **leap**

**leap year** *n* rok *m* przestępny

**learn** [lə:n] *(pt, pp* **~ed** *or* **~t***)* *vt* uczyć się (nauczyć się *perf) +gen* ▷ *vi* uczyć się; **to ~ about** *or* **of sth** *(hear, read)* dowiadywać się (dowiedzieć się *perf)* o czymś; **to ~ about sth** *(study)* uczyć się o czymś; **to ~ that ...** dowiedzieć się *(perf)*, że ...; **to ~ to do sth** uczyć się (nauczyć się *perf)* coś robić

**learned** ['lə:nɪd] *adj* uczony

**learner** ['lə:nəʳ] *(Brit) n* uczący(-ca) *m(f)* się; *(also:* **learner driver***)* zdający(-ca) *m(f)* na prawo jazdy; **to be a slow ~** wolno się uczyć

**learning** ['lə:nɪŋ] *n (knowledge)* wiedza *f*

**learnt** [lə:nt] *pt, pp of* **learn**
**lease** [li:s] *n* umowa *f* o dzierżawę *or* najem ▷ *vt* dzierżawić (wydzierżawić *perf*); **on ~ (to)** wydzierżawiony (*+dat*)
▸ **lease back** *vt dzierżawić dobra inwestycyjne od firmy, której wcześniej się te dobra sprzedało*
**leaseback** ['li:sbæk] *n dzierżawa dóbr od firmy, której wcześniej się te dobra sprzedało*
**leasehold** ['li:shəuld] *n* dzierżawa *f* ▷ *adj* (wy) dzierżawiony
**leash** [li:ʃ] *n* smycz *f*
**least** [li:st] *adj*: **the ~** (*smallest amount of*) najmniej (*+gen*); (*slightest*) najmniejszy ▷ *adv* (*+verb*) najmniej; (*+adjective*): **the ~** najmniej; **at ~** (*in expressions of quantity, comparisons*) co najmniej, przynajmniej; (*still, or rather*) przynajmniej; **you could at ~ have written** mogłeś przynajmniej napisać; **I do not mind in the ~** absolutnie mi to nie przeszkadza; **it was the ~ I could do** przynajmniej to mogłem zrobić
**leather** ['lɛðəʳ] *n* skóra *f* (*zwierzęca, wyprawiona*)
**leather goods** *npl* wyroby *pl* skórzane *or* ze skóry
**leave** [li:v] (*pt, pp* **left**) *vt* (*place: on foot*) wychodzić (wyjść *perf*) z *+gen*; (*: in vehicle*) wyjeżdżać (wyjechać *perf*) z *+gen*; (*place, institution: permanently*) opuszczać (opuścić *perf*), odchodzić (odejść *perf*) z *+gen*; (*person, thing, space, time*) zostawiać (zostawić *perf*); (*mark, stain*) zostawiać (zostawić *perf*), pozostawiać (pozostawić *perf*); (*husband, wife*) opuszczać (opuścić *perf*), odchodzić (odejść *perf*) od *+gen*, zostawiać (zostawić *perf*) (*inf*) ▷ *vi* (*person: on foot*) odchodzić (odejść *perf*); (*: in vehicle*) wyjeżdżać (wyjechać *perf*); (*: permanently*) odchodzić (odejść *perf*); (*bus, train*) odjeżdżać (odjechać *perf*), odchodzić (odejść *perf*); (*plane*) odlatywać (odlecieć *perf*) ▷ *n* urlop *m*; **to ~ sth to sb** zostawiać (zostawić *perf*) coś komuś; **they were left with nothing** nic im nie zostało; **you have/there was ten minutes left** zostało ci/zostało (jeszcze) dziesięć minut; **to be left over** (*food, drink*) zostawać (zostać *perf*); **to take one's ~ of sb** żegnać się (pożegnać się *perf*) z kimś; **on ~** na urlopie; **on sick ~** na zwolnieniu (lekarskim)
▸ **leave behind** *vt* zostawiać (zostawić *perf*)
▸ **leave off** *vt*: **to ~ the heating/lights off** zostawiać (zostawić *perf*) wyłączone ogrzewanie/światła; **she left the saucepan lid off** nie przykryła rondla (pokrywką) ▷ *vi* (*inf: stop*) przestać (*perf*)
▸ **leave on** *vt*: **to ~ the heating/lights on** zostawiać (zostawić *perf*) włączone ogrzewanie/światła
▸ **leave out** *vt* opuszczać (opuścić *perf*), pomijać (pominąć *perf*)
**leave of absence** *n* urlop *m*
**leaves** [li:vz] *npl of* **leaf**
**Lebanese** [lɛbə'ni:z] *adj* libański ▷ *n inv* Libańczyk(-anka) *m(f)*
**Lebanon** ['lɛbənən] *n* Liban *m*
**lecherous** ['lɛtʃərəs] (*pej*) *adj* lubieżny
**lectern** ['lɛktə:n] *n* pulpit *m*
**lecture** ['lɛktʃəʳ] *n* wykład *m* ▷ *vi* prowadzić wykłady, wykładać ▷ *vt*: **to ~ sb on** *or* **about sth** robić komuś uwagi na temat czegoś; **to give a ~ on** wygłaszać (wygłosić *perf*) wykład na temat *+gen*
**lecture hall** *n* sala *f* wykładowa
**lecturer** ['lɛktʃərəʳ] (*Brit*) *n* (*at university*) wykładowca *m*; (*speaker*) mówca *m*
**LED** (*Elec*) *n abbr* (*= light-emitting diode*) LED *m inv*
**led** [lɛd] *pt, pp of* **lead¹**
**ledge** [lɛdʒ] *n* (*of mountain*) występ *m* skalny, półka *f* skalna; (*of window*) parapet *m*; (*on wall*) półka *f*
**ledger** ['lɛdʒəʳ] (*Comm*) *n* księga *f* główna
**lee** [li:] *n* osłona *f*
**leech** [li:tʃ] *n* pijawka *f*; (*fig*) pasożyt *m*
**leek** [li:k] *n* por *m*
**leer** [lɪəʳ] *vi*: **to ~ at sb** uśmiechać się (uśmiechnąć się *perf*) lubieżnie do kogoś
**leeward** ['li:wəd] (*Naut*) *adj* zawietrzny ▷ *adv* na zawietrzną ▷ *n*: **to ~** na zawietrzną
**leeway** ['li:weɪ] *n* (*fig*): **to have some ~** mieć pewną swobodę działania; **there's a lot of ~ to make up** jest mnóstwo zaległości do odrobienia
**left** [lɛft] *pt, pp of* **leave** ▷ *adj* (*of direction, position*) lewy; (*remaining*) pozostawiony, pozostały; **to be ~** zostawać (zostać *perf*), pozostawać (pozostać *perf*) ▷ *n*: **the ~** lewa strona *f* ▷ *adv* (*turn, look etc*) w lewo; **on/to the ~** na lewo; **the L~** (*Pol*) lewica
**left-hand drive** ['lɛfthænd-] *adj* z lewostronnym układem kierowniczym *post*
**left-handed** [lɛft'hændɪd] *adj* leworęczny
**left-hand side** *n* lewa strona *f*
**leftist** ['lɛftɪst] *n* lewicowiec *m* ▷ *adj* lewicowy
**left-luggage (office)** [lɛft'lʌgɪdʒ(-)] (*Brit*) *n* przechowalnia *f* bagażu
**leftovers** ['lɛftəuvəz] *npl* resztki *pl*
**left-wing** ['lɛft'wɪŋ] *adj* lewicowy
**left-winger** ['lɛft'wɪŋəʳ] *n* lewicowiec *m*
**leg** [lɛg] *n* (*of person, animal, table*) noga *f*; (*of trousers*) nogawka *f*; (*Culin: of lamb, pork*) udziec *m*; (*: of chicken*) udko *nt*; (*of journey etc*) etap *m*; **1st/2nd/final leg** (*Sport*) pierwsza/druga/ostatnia runda; **to stretch one's legs** rozprostowywać (rozprostować *perf*) nogi;

**to get one's leg over** (*inf*) zaliczyć (*perf*) dziewczynę/chłopaka (*inf*)
**legacy** ['lɛgəsɪ] *n* spadek *m*; (*fig*) spuścizna *f*, dziedzictwo *nt*
**legal** ['li:gl] *adj* (*of the law*) prawny; (*allowed by law*) legalny, zgodny z prawem; **to take ~ action/proceedings against sb** wytaczać (wytoczyć *perf*) komuś sprawę
**legal adviser** *n* radca *m* prawny
**legal holiday** (*US*) *n* święto *nt* państwowe
**legality** [lɪ'gælɪtɪ] *n* legalność *f*
**legalize** ['li:gəlaɪz] *vt* legalizować (zalegalizować *perf*)
**legally** ['li:gəlɪ] *adv* (*with regard to the law*) prawnie; (*in accordance with the law*) legalnie, prawnie; **~ binding** prawnie wiążący
**legal tender** *n* prawny środek *m* płatniczy
**legation** [lɪ'geɪʃən] *n* poselstwo *nt*
**legend** ['lɛdʒənd] *n* legenda *f*; (*fig: person*) (żywa) legenda *f*
**legendary** ['lɛdʒəndərɪ] *adj* legendarny
**-legged** ['lɛgɪd] *suff* -nożny
**leggings** ['lɛgɪŋz] *npl* (*woman's*) legginsy *pl*; (*protective*) getry *pl* (*ze skóry, grubej tkaniny itp*)
**legibility** [lɛdʒɪ'bɪlɪtɪ] *n* czytelność *f*
**legible** ['lɛdʒəbl] *adj* czytelny
**legibly** ['lɛdʒəblɪ] *adv* czytelnie
**legion** ['li:dʒən] *n* legion *m*, legia *f*; **stories about him are ~** krążą o nim niezliczone opowieści
**legionnaire** [li:dʒə'nɛə<sup>r</sup>] *n* legionista *m*
**legionnaire's disease** *n* choroba *f* legionistów
**legislate** ['lɛdʒɪsleɪt] *vi* uchwalać (uchwalić *perf*) ustawę
**legislation** [lɛdʒɪs'leɪʃən] *n* legislacja *f*, ustawodawstwo *nt*
**legislative** ['lɛdʒɪslətɪv] *adj* legislacyjny, ustawodawczy
**legislator** ['lɛdʒɪsleɪtə[r]] *n* członek(-nkini) *m(f)* ciała ustawodawczego
**legislature** ['lɛdʒɪslətʃə[r]] *n* ciało *nt* ustawodawcze
**legitimacy** [lɪ'dʒɪtɪməsɪ] *n* (*validity*) zasadność *f*; (*legality*) legalność *f*
**legitimate** [lɪ'dʒɪtɪmət] *adj* (*valid*) uzasadniony; (*legal*) legalny
**legitimize** [lɪ'dʒɪtɪmaɪz] *vt* sankcjonować (usankcjonować *perf*) prawnie
**leg-room** ['lɛgru:m] *n* (*on plane etc*) miejsce *nt* na nogi
**Leics** (*Brit: Post*) *abbr* = **Leicestershire**
**leisure** ['lɛʒə[r]] *n* wolny czas *m*; **at ~** bez pośpiechu, w spokoju
**leisure centre** *n* kompleks *m* rekreacyjny (*mieszczący halę sportową, sale konferencyjne, kawiarnię itp*)
**leisurely** ['lɛʒəlɪ] *adj* spokojny, zrelaksowany
**leisure suit** *n* dres *m*
**lemon** ['lɛmən] *n* cytryna *f* ▷ *adj* cytrynowy
**lemonade** [lɛmə'neɪd] *n* lemoniada *f*
**lemon cheese** *n* = **lemon curd**
**lemon curd** *n* krem *m* cytrynowy
**lemon juice** *n* sok *m* cytrynowy
**lemon squeezer** *n* wyciskacz *m* do cytryn
**lemon tea** *n* herbata *f* cytrynowa
**lend** [lɛnd] (*pt, pp* **lent**) *vt*: **to ~ sth to sb** pożyczać (pożyczyć *perf*) coś komuś; **it ~s itself to ...** to nadaje się do *+gen*; **the problem doesn't ~ itself to simple solutions** tego problemu nie da się rozwiązać w prosty sposób; **to ~ sb a hand (with sth)** pomagać (pomóc *perf*) komuś (przy czymś)
**lender** ['lɛndə[r]] *n* pożyczkodawca *m*
**lending library** ['lɛndɪŋ-] *n* wypożyczalnia *f* (*książek*)
**length** [lɛŋθ] *n* długość *f*; (*piece of wood, string etc*) kawałek *m*; **2 metres in ~** 2 metry długości; **at ~** (*at last*) wreszcie; (*fully*) obszernie; (*for a long time*) długo; **they travelled the ~ of the island** przejechali wzdłuż całą wyspę; **he fell/was lying full-~** przewrócił się/leżał jak długi; **they went to great ~s to please us** nie szczędzili starań, by nas zadowolić
**lengthen** ['lɛŋθn] *vt* (*workday*) wydłużać (wydłużyć *perf*); (*tramline, cord*) przedłużać (przedłużyć *perf*); (*dress*) podłużać (podłużyć *perf*) ▷ *vi* (*queue, waiting list*) wydłużać się (wydłużyć się *perf*); (*silence*) przedłużać się (przedłużyć się *perf*)
**lengthways** ['lɛŋθweɪz] *adv* wzdłuż
**lengthy** ['lɛŋθɪ] *adj* przydługi, rozwlekły
**leniency** ['li:nɪənsɪ] *n* łagodność *f*, pobłażliwość *f*
**lenient** ['li:nɪənt] *adj* (*person, attitude*) pobłażliwy; (*judge's sentence*) łagodny
**leniently** ['li:nɪəntlɪ] *adv* łagodnie, pobłażliwie
**lens** [lɛnz] *n* (*of spectacles*) soczewka *f*; (*of camera, telescope*) obiektyw *m*
**Lent** [lɛnt] *n* wielki post *m*
**lent** [lɛnt] *pt, pp of* **lend**
**lentil** ['lɛntl] *n* soczewica *f*
**Leo** ['li:əu] *n* Lew *m*; **to be Leo** być spod znaku Lwa
**leopard** ['lɛpəd] *n* lampart *m*
**leotard** ['li:ətɑ:d] *n* trykot *m*
**leper** ['lɛpə[r]] *n* trędowaty(-ta) *m(f)*
**leper colony** *n* osada *f* trędowatych
**leprosy** ['lɛprəsɪ] *n* trąd *m*
**lesbian** ['lɛzbɪən] *adj* lesbijski ▷ *n* lesbijka *f*
**lesion** ['li:ʒən] (*Med*) *n* uszkodzenie *nt*
**Lesotho** [lɪ'su:tu:] *n* Lesoto *nt inv*

L

**less** [lɛs] *adj* mniej *(+gen)* ▷ *pron* mniej ▷ *adv* mniej ▷ *prep*: **~ tax/10% discount** minus podatek/10% rabatu; **~ than half** mniej niż połowa; **~ than ever** mniej niż kiedykolwiek; **~ and ~** coraz mniej; **the ~ he works ...** im mniej pracuje, ...; **the Prime Minister, no ~** ni mniej, ni więcej, tylko premier
**lessee** [lɛ'si:] *n* *(of land)* dzierżawca *m*; *(of flat)* najemca *m*
**lessen** ['lɛsn] *vi* zmniejszać się (zmniejszyć się *perf*), maleć (zmaleć *perf*) ▷ *vt* zmniejszać (zmniejszyć *perf*)
**lesser** ['lɛsəʳ] *adj* *(in degree, amount)* mniejszy; *(in importance)* pomniejszy; **to a ~ extent** w mniejszym stopniu
**lesson** ['lɛsn] *n* *(class)* lekcja *f*; *(example, warning)* nauka *f*, nauczka *f*; **to teach sb a ~** *(fig)* dawać (dać *perf*) komuś nauczkę
**lessor** ['lɛsəʳ] *n* *(of land)* wydzierżawiający *m*; *(of flat)* wynajmujący *m*
**lest** [lɛst] *conj* żeby nie
**let** [lɛt] *(pt, pp* **let***)* *vt* *(allow)* pozwalać (pozwolić *perf*); *(Brit: lease)* wynajmować (wynająć *perf*); **to let sb do sth** pozwalać (pozwolić *perf*) komuś coś robić; **to let sb know sth** powiadamiać (powiadomić *perf*) kogoś o czymś; **let's go** chodźmy; **let him come** niech przyjdzie; **"to let"** „do wynajęcia"; **to let go** *vi* *(release one's grip)* puszczać się (puścić się *perf*) ▷ *vt* wypuszczać (wypuścić *perf*); **to let go of sth** puszczać (puścić *perf*) coś; **to let o.s. go** *(relax)* rozluźniać się (rozluźnić się *perf*); *(neglect o.s.)* zaniedbywać się (zaniedbać się *perf*)
▸ **let down** *vt* *(tyre)* spuszczać (spuścić *perf*) powietrze z *+gen*; *(person)* zawodzić (zawieść *perf*); *(dress)* podłużać (podłużyć *perf*); **to let one's hair down** *(fig)* wyluzowywać się (wyluzować się *perf*) *(inf)*
▸ **let in** *vt* *(water, air)* przepuszczać (przepuścić *perf*); *(person)* wpuszczać (wpuścić *perf*)
▸ **let off** *vt* *(culprit)* puszczać (puścić *perf*) wolno; *(gun)* wystrzelić *(perf)* z *+gen*; *(bomb)* detonować (zdetonować *perf*); *(firework)* puszczać (puścić *perf*); **to let sb off housework** *etc* zwalniać (zwolnić *perf*) kogoś z prac domowych *etc*; **to let off steam** *(inf: fig)* wyładowywać się (wyładować się *perf*)
▸ **let on** *vi* wygadywać się (wygadać się *perf*)
▸ **let out** *vt* *(person, air, water)* wypuszczać (wypuścić *perf*); *(sound)* wydawać (wydać *perf*); *(house, room)* wynajmować (wynająć *perf*)
▸ **let up** *vi* *(cease)* ustawać (ustać *perf*); *(diminish)* zelżeć *(perf)*
**letdown** ['lɛtdaun] *n* zawód *m*, rozczarowanie *nt*
**lethal** ['li:θl] *adj* śmiercionośny
**lethargic** [lɛ'θɑ:dʒɪk] *adj* *(sleep)* letargiczny; *(person)* ospały
**lethargy** ['lɛθədʒɪ] *n* letarg *m*
**letter** ['lɛtəʳ] *n* *(correspondence)* list *m*; *(of alphabet)* litera *f*; **small/capital ~** mała/wielka litera
**letter bomb** *n* przesyłka *f* z bombą
**letterbox** ['lɛtəbɔks] *(Brit)* *n* *(on door, at entrance)* skrzynka *f* na listy; *(mailbox)* skrzynka *f* pocztowa *or* na listy
**letterhead** ['lɛtəhɛd] *n* nagłówek *m* *(na papierze firmowym)*
**lettering** ['lɛtərɪŋ] *n* liternictwo *nt*, krój *m* liter
**letter of credit** *n* akredytywa *f*
**letter-opener** ['lɛtə'əupnəʳ] *n* nóż *m* do (rozcinania) listów
**letterpress** ['lɛtəprɛs] *n* typografia *f* *(technika)*
**letter-quality printer** ['lɛtəkwɔlɪtɪ-] *(Comput)* *n* drukarka *f* wysokiej jakości druku
**letters patent** *npl* zaświadczenie *nt* patentowe o wynalazku
**lettuce** ['lɛtɪs] *n* sałata *f*
**let-up** ['lɛtʌp] *n* *(in violence etc)* spadek *m*
**leukaemia**, *(US)* **leukemia** [lu:'ki:mɪə] *n* białaczka *f*
**level** ['lɛvl] *adj* równy ▷ *adv*: **to draw ~ with** zrównywać się (zrównać się *perf*) z *+instr* ▷ *n* *(lit, fig)* poziom *m*; *(also:* **spirit level***)* poziomnica *f* ▷ *vt* zrównywać (zrównać *perf*) z ziemią ▷ *vi*: **to ~ with sb** *(inf)* być z kimś szczerym; **to be/keep ~ with** być/utrzymywać się na tym samym poziomie co *+nom*; **on the ~** *(fig)* uczciwy; **to ~ a gun at sb** celować (wycelować *perf*) do kogoś z pistoletu; **to ~ an accusation/a criticism at** *or* **against sb** kierować (skierować *perf*) oskarżenie/krytykę pod czyimś adresem; **to do one's ~ best** dokładać (dołożyć *perf*) wszelkich starań; **'A' ~s** *(Brit)* *egzaminy końcowe z poszczególnych przedmiotów w szkole średniej na poziomie zaawansowanym*; **'O' ~s** *(Brit)* *egzaminy z poszczególnych przedmiotów na poziomie średnio zaawansowanym, do których uczniowie przystępują w wieku 15-16 lat*
▸ **level off** *vi* stabilizować się (ustabilizować się *perf*)
▸ **level out** *vi* = **level off**
**level crossing** *(Brit)* *n* przejazd *m* kolejowy
**level-headed** [lɛvl'hɛdɪd] *adj* zrównoważony
**levelling** ['lɛvlɪŋ] *n* wyrównanie *nt*
**lever** ['li:vəʳ] *n* dźwignia *f*; *(fig)* środek *m* nacisku ▷ *vt*: **to ~ up** podważać (podważyć *perf*); **to ~ out** wyważać (wyważyć *perf*); **to ~ o.s. up** podźwignąć się *(perf)*
**leverage** ['li:vərɪdʒ] *n* nacisk *m*; *(fig)* wpływ *m*

**levity** ['lɛvɪtɪ] *n* beztroska *f*
**levy** ['lɛvɪ] *n* pobór *m* ▷ *vt* (*tax: impose*) nakładać (nałożyć *perf*); (*: collect*) pobierać (pobrać *perf*), ściągać (ściągnąć *perf*)
**lewd** [lu:d] *adj* lubieżny
**LI** (*US*) *abbr* = **Long Island**
**liability** [laɪə'bɪlətɪ] *n* (*person, thing*) ciężar *m*, kłopot *m*; (*Jur*) odpowiedzialność *f* (karna); **liabilities** *npl* (*Comm*) pasywa *pl*
**liable** ['laɪəbl] *adj* (*prone*): **~ to** podatny na *+acc*; (*responsible*): **~ for** odpowiedzialny za *+acc*; (*likely*): **she's ~ to cry when she gets upset** ma tendencję do płaczu, kiedy się zdenerwuje; **these houses are ~ to collapse** te domy narażone są na zawalenie
**liaise** [li:'eɪz] *vi*: **to ~ (with)** współpracować *or* współdziałać (z *+instr*)
**liaison** [li:'eɪzɔn] *n* (*cooperation*) współpraca *f*, współdziałanie *nt*; (*sexual*) związek *m*, romans *m*
**liar** ['laɪə^r] *n* kłamca *m*, łgarz *m*; (*in small matters*) kłamczuch(a) *m(f)*
**libel** ['laɪbl] *n* zniesławienie *nt* ▷ *vt* zniesławiać (zniesławić *perf*)
**libellous** ['laɪbləs], (*US*) **libelous** *adj* zniesławiający
**liberal** ['lɪbərl] *adj* (*open-minded*) liberalny; (*generous*) hojny, szczodry ▷ *n* liberał *m*; **to be ~ with** (*generous*) nie żałować *+gen*
**liberalize** ['lɪbərəlaɪz] *vt* liberalizować (zliberalizować *perf*)
**Liberal Democrat** *n*: **the ~s** (*Brit*) Partia Liberalnych Demokratów
**liberally** ['lɪbrəlɪ] *adv* (*generously*) hojnie, suto
**liberal-minded** ['lɪbərl'maɪndɪd] *adj* o liberalnych poglądach *post*
**liberate** ['lɪbəreɪt] *vt* (*people, country*) wyzwalać (wyzwolić *perf*); (*hostage, prisoner*) uwalniać (uwolnić *perf*)
**liberation** [lɪbə'reɪʃən] *n* wyzwolenie *nt*
**Liberia** [laɪ'bɪərɪə] *n* Liberia *f*
**Liberian** [laɪ'bɪərɪən] *adj* liberyjski ▷ *n* Liberyjczyk(-jka) *m(f)*
**liberty** ['lɪbətɪ] *n* (*of individual*) wolność *f*; (*of movement*) swoboda *f*; **to be at ~** być *or* przebywać na wolności; **to be at ~ to do sth** mieć przyzwolenie na (z)robienie czegoś; **to take the ~ of doing sth** pozwalać (pozwolić *perf*) sobie zrobić coś
**libido** [lɪ'bi:dəu] *n* libido *nt inv*
**Libra** ['li:brə] *n* Waga *f*; **to be ~** być spod znaku Wagi
**librarian** [laɪ'brɛərɪən] *n* bibliotekarz(-arka) *m(f)*
**library** ['laɪbrərɪ] *n* (*institution, collection of books*) biblioteka *f*; (*of gramophone records*) płytoteka *f*
**library book** *n* książka *f* z biblioteki
**libretto** [lɪ'brɛtəu] *n* libretto *nt*
**Libya** ['lɪbɪə] *n* Libia *f*
**Libyan** ['lɪbɪən] *adj* libijski ▷ *n* Libijczyk(-jka) *m(f)*
**lice** [laɪs] *npl of* **louse**
**licence**, (*US*) **license** ['laɪsns] *n* (*official document*) pozwolenie *nt*, zezwolenie *nt*; (*Comm*) licencja *f*, koncesja *f*; (*excessive freedom*) rozpusta *f*, rozwiązłość *f*; **a driving** *or* **driver's ~** prawo jazdy; **to manufacture sth under ~** wytwarzać *or* produkować coś na licencji
**license** ['laɪsns] *n* (*US*) = **licence** ▷ *vt* udzielać (udzielić *perf*) pozwolenia *or* zezwolenia *+dat*
**licensed** ['laɪsnst] *adj* (*car etc*) zarejestrowany; (*hotel, restaurant*) posiadający koncesję na sprzedaż alkoholu
**licensee** [laɪsən'si:] *n* licencjobiorca(-rczyni) *m(f)*, koncesjonariusz(ka) *m(f)*
**license plate** (*US*) *n* tablica *f* rejestracyjna
**licensing hours** ['laɪsnsɪŋ] (*Brit*) *npl* godziny *pl* otwarcia pubu
**licentious** [laɪ'sɛnʃəs] *adj* rozpustny, rozwiązły
**lichen** ['laɪkən] *n* (*Bot*) porost *m*, porosty *pl*
**lick** [lɪk] *vt* lizać (polizać *perf*) ▷ *n* liźnięcie *nt*; **to get ~ed** (*inf*) dostawać (dostać *perf*) cięgi; **a ~ of paint** odrobina farby; **to ~ one's lips** oblizywać się (oblizać się *perf*); (*fig*) zacierać ręce
**licorice** ['lɪkərɪs] (*US*) *n* = **liquorice**
**lid** [lɪd] *n* (*of case, large box*) wieko *nt*; (*of jar, small box*) wieczko *nt*; (*of pan*) pokrywka *f*; (*of large container*) pokrywa *f*; (*eyelid*) powieka *f*; **to take the lid off sth** (*fig*) demaskować (zdemaskować *perf*) coś
**lido** ['laɪdəu] (*Brit*) *n* kąpielisko *nt*
**lie** [laɪ] (*pt* **lay**, *pp* **lain**) *vi* (*lit, fig*) leżeć; (*pt, pp* **lied**) kłamać (skłamać *perf*) ▷ *n* kłamstwo *nt*; **to tell lies** kłamać; **France and Britain lie third and fourth respectively** Francja i Wielka Brytania plasują się odpowiednio na trzeciej i czwartej pozycji; **to lie low** (*fig*) przeczekiwać (przeczekać *perf*) (w ukryciu)
▸ **lie about** *vi* (*things*) poniewierać się; (*people*) rozkładać się, rozwalać się (*inf*)
▸ **lie around** *vi* = **lie about**
▸ **lie back** *vi* kłaść się (położyć się *perf*) na plecach; (*fig*) dawać (dać *perf*) sobie luz (*inf*)
▸ **lie up** *vi* zostawać (zostać *perf*) w łóżku
**Liechtenstein** ['lɪktənstaɪn] *n* Liechtenstein *m*, Księstwo *nt* Liechtenstein
**lie detector** *n* wykrywacz *m* kłamstw
**lie-down** ['laɪdaun] (*Brit*) *n*: **to have a ~** położyć się (*perf*) (do łóżka)
**lie-in** ['laɪɪn] (*Brit*) *n*: **to have a ~** poleżeć (*perf*) sobie (w łóżku)

**lieu** [lu:]: **in ~ of** *prep* zamiast *or* w miejsce *+gen*
**Lieut.** (*Mil*) *abbr* (= *lieutenant*) por.
**lieutenant** [lɛf'tɛnənt] *n* porucznik *m*
**lieutenant-colonel** *n* podpułkownik *m*
**life** [laɪf] (*pl* **lives**) *n* życie *nt*; **true to ~** realistyczny; **to paint from ~** malować z natury; **to be sent to prison for ~** zostać (*perf*) skazanym na dożywocie; **to come to ~** (*fig*) ożywiać się (ożywić się *perf*)
**life annuity** *n* renta *f* dożywotnia
**life assurance** (*Brit*) *n* = **life insurance**
**lifebelt** ['laɪfbɛlt] (*Brit*) *n* koło *nt* ratunkowe
**lifeblood** ['laɪfblʌd] *n* (*fig*) siła *f* napędowa
**lifeboat** ['laɪfbəut] *n* łódź *f* ratunkowa
**lifebuoy** ['laɪfbɔɪ] *n* koło *nt* ratunkowe
**life expectancy** *n* średnia długość *f* życia
**lifeguard** ['laɪfgɑ:d] *n* ratownik(-iczka) *m(f)* (*na plaży, basenie*)
**life imprisonment** *n* dożywocie *nt*
**life insurance** *n* ubezpieczenie *nt* na życie
**life jacket** *n* kamizelka *f* ratunkowa
**lifeless** ['laɪflɪs] *adj* martwy; (*fig*) bez życia *post*
**lifelike** ['laɪflaɪk] *adj* (*model etc*) jak żywy *post*; (*painting, performance*) realistyczny
**lifeline** ['laɪflaɪn] *n* lina *f* ratunkowa
**lifelong** ['laɪflɔŋ] *adj* (*friend*) na całe życie *post*; (*ambition*) życiowy
**life preserver** (*US*) *n* = **lifebelt**; **life jacket**
**life raft** *n* tratwa *f* ratunkowa
**life-saver** ['laɪfseɪvə^r] *n* ratownik(-iczka) *m(f)*
**life science** *n* nauki *pl* biologiczne
**life sentence** *n* kara *f* dożywocia *or* dożywotniego więzienia
**life-size(d)** ['laɪfsaɪz(d)] *adj* naturalnych rozmiarów *post*, naturalnej wielkości *post*
**life-span** ['laɪfspæn] *n* długość *f* życia; (*fig: of product etc*) żywotność *f*
**life style** ['laɪfstaɪl] *n* styl *m* życia
**life support system** (*Med*) *n* respirator *m*
**lifetime** ['laɪftaɪm] *n* (*of person*) życie *nt*; (*of thing*) okres *m* istnienia; **once in a ~** raz w życiu; **the chance of a ~** życiowa szansa
**lift** [lɪft] *vt* (*thing, part of body*) ponosić (podnieść *perf*), unosić (unieść *perf*); (*ban, requirement*) znosić (znieść *perf*); (*plagiarize*) przepisywać (przepisać *perf*), zwalać (zwalić *perf*) (*inf*); (*inf: steal*) podwędzić (*perf*) (*inf*), gwizdnąć (*perf*) (*inf*) ▷ *vi* (*fog*) podnosić się (podnieść się *perf*) ▷ *n* (*Brit*) winda *f*; **to give sb a ~** (*Brit*) podwozić (podwieźć *perf*) kogoś, podrzucać (podrzucić *perf*) kogoś (*inf*)
▸ **lift off** *vi* (*rocket*) startować (wystartować *perf*)
▸ **lift up** *vt* podnosić (podnieść *perf*)
**lift-off** ['lɪftɔf] *n* start *m* (*samolotu lub rakiety*)
**ligament** ['lɪgəmənt] *n* (*Anat*) wiązadło *nt*
**light** [laɪt] (*pt, pp* **lit**) *n* światło *nt*; (*for cigarette etc*) ogień *m* ▷ *vt* (*candle, cigarette*) zapalać (zapalić *perf*); (*fire*) rozpalać (rozpalić *perf*); (*room*) oświetlać (oświetlić *perf*); (*sky*) rozświetlać (rozświetlić *perf*) ▷ *adj* lekki; (*pale, bright*) jasny; **lights** *npl* (*also*: **traffic lights**) światła *pl*; **to turn the ~ on/off** zapalać (zapalić *perf*)/gasić (zgasić *perf*) światło; **to come to ~** wychodzić (wyjść *perf*) na jaw; **to cast** *or* **shed** *or* **throw ~ on** (*fig*) rzucać (rzucić *perf*) światło na *+acc*; **in the ~ of** w świetle *+gen*; **to make ~ of sth** (*fig*) bagatelizować (zbagatelizować *perf*) coś; **to travel ~** podróżować z małą ilością bagażu
▸ **light up** *vi* rozjaśniać się (rozjaśnić się *perf*)
**light bulb** *n* żarówka *f*
**lighten** ['laɪtn] *vt* zmniejszać (zmniejszyć *perf*) ▷ *vi* przejaśniać się (przejaśnić się *perf*)
**lighter** ['laɪtə^r] *n* (*also*: **cigarette lighter**) zapalniczka *f*
**light-fingered** [laɪt'fɪŋgəd] (*inf*) *adj*: **to be ~** mieć długie *or* lepkie palce (*inf*)
**light-headed** [laɪt'hɛdɪd] *adj* (*excited*) beztroski; (*dizzy*): **to be/feel ~** mieć zawroty głowy
**light-hearted** [laɪt'hɑ:tɪd] *adj* (*person*) beztroski; (*question, remark*) niefrasobliwy
**lighthouse** ['laɪthaus] *n* latarnia *f* morska
**lighting** ['laɪtɪŋ] *n* oświetlenie *nt*
**lighting-up time** [laɪtɪŋ'ʌp-] *n czas włączania oświetlenia ulicznego*
**lightly** ['laɪtlɪ] *adv* lekko; **to get off ~** wykręcić się (*perf*) sianem
**light meter** *n* światłomierz *m*
**lightness** ['laɪtnɪs] *n* lekkość *f*
**lightning** ['laɪtnɪŋ] *n* błyskawica *f* ▷ *adj* błyskawiczny
**lightning conductor** *n* piorunochron *m*
**lightning rod** (*US*) *n* = **lightning conductor**
**light pen** *n* pióro *nt* świetlne
**lightship** ['laɪtʃɪp] *n* latarniowiec *m*
**lightweight** ['laɪtweɪt] *adj* lekki ▷ *n* bokser *m* wagi lekkiej
**light year** *n* rok *m* świetlny
**like** [laɪk] *vt* lubić (polubić *perf*) ▷ *prep* (taki) jak *+nom* ▷ *n*: **and the ~** i tym podobne; **I would ~, I'd ~** chciał(a)bym; **if you ~** jeśli chcesz; **to be/look ~ sb/sth** być/wyglądać jak ktoś/coś; **something ~ that** coś w tym rodzaju; **what does it look/taste/sound ~?** jak to wygląda/smakuje/brzmi?; **what's he ~?** jaki on jest?; **what's the weather ~?** jaka jest pogoda?; **I feel ~ a drink** mam ochotę się napić; **there's nothing ~ ...** nie ma (to) jak...; **that's just ~ him** to do niego pasuje; **do it ~ this** (z)rób to tak *or* w ten sposób; **it is nothing ~ ...** to zupełnie nie to (samo), co...;

**his ~s and dislikes** jego sympatie i antypatie
**likeable** ['laɪkəbl] *adj* przyjemny
**likelihood** ['laɪklɪhud] *n* prawdopodobieństwo *nt*; **there is every ~ that ...** istnieje wszelkie prawdopodobieństwo, że...; **in all ~** najprawdopodobniej
**likely** ['laɪklɪ] *adj* prawdopodobny; **he is ~ to do it** on prawdopodobnie to zrobi; **not ~!** (*inf*) na pewno nie!, jeszcze czego!
**like-minded** ['laɪk'maɪndɪd] *adj*: **to be ~** mieć podobne zapatrywania
**liken** ['laɪkən] *vt*: **to ~ sth to sth** porównywać (porównać *perf*) coś do czegoś
**likeness** ['laɪknɪs] *n* podobieństwo *nt*; **that's a good ~** podobieństwo zostało dobrze uchwycone
**likewise** ['laɪkwaɪz] *adv* podobnie; **to do ~** robić (zrobić *perf*) to samo
**liking** ['laɪkɪŋ] *n*: **~ (for)** (*thing*) upodobanie *nt* (do *+gen*); (*person*) sympatia *f* (do *+gen*); **to be to sb's ~** odpowiadać komuś; **to take a ~ to sb** polubić (*perf*) kogoś
**lilac** ['laɪlək] *n* bez *m* ▷ *adj* liliowy
**lilt** [lɪlt] *n* melodyjna intonacja *f*
**lilting** ['lɪltɪŋ] *adj* melodyjny, śpiewny
**lily** ['lɪlɪ] *n* lilia *f*
**lily of the valley** *n* konwalia *f*
**Lima** ['li:mə] *n* Lima *f*
**limb** [lɪm] *n* (*Anat*) kończyna *f*; (*of tree*) konar *m*; **to go out on a ~** (*fig*) wychylać się (wychylić się *perf*)
**limber up** ['lɪmbəʳ-] (*Sport*) *vi* przygotowywać się (przygotować się *perf*) (*przed startem*)
**limbo** ['lɪmbəu] *n*: **in ~** (*fig*) w stanie zawieszenia
**lime** [laɪm] *n* (*citrus fruit*) limona *f*; (*also*: **lime juice**) sok *m* z limony; (*linden*) lipa *f*; (*for soil*) wapno *nt*; (*rock*) wapień *m*
**limelight** ['laɪmlaɪt] *n*: **to be in the ~** znajdować się w centrum zainteresowania
**limerick** ['lɪmərɪk] *n* limeryk *m*
**limestone** ['laɪmstəun] *n* wapień *m*
**limit** ['lɪmɪt] *n* (*greatest amount, extent*) granica *f*, kres *m*; (*on time, money etc*) ograniczenie *nt*, limit *m*; (*of area*) granica *f*, kraniec *m* ▷ *vt* ograniczać (ograniczyć *perf*); **within ~s** w pewnych granicach
**limitation** [lɪmɪ'teɪʃən] *n* ograniczenie *nt*; **limitations** *npl* ograniczenia *pl*
**limited** ['lɪmɪtɪd] *adj* ograniczony; **to be ~ to** być ograniczonym do *+gen*
**limited edition** *n* ograniczony nakład *m*
**limited (liability) company** (*Brit*) *n* spółka *f* z ograniczoną odpowiedzialnością
**limitless** ['lɪmɪtlɪs] *adj* (*resources etc*) nieograniczony; (*fascination etc*) bezgraniczny
**limousine** ['lɪməzi:n] *n* limuzyna *f*
**limp** [lɪmp] *n*: **to have a ~** utykać, kuleć ▷ *vi* utykać, kuleć ▷ *adj* bezwładny
**limpet** ['lɪmpɪt] *n* (*Zool*) skałoczep *m*; (*fig*) rzep *m*
**limpid** ['lɪmpɪd] *adj* przezroczysty, przejrzysty
**limply** ['lɪmplɪ] *adv* bezwładnie
**linchpin, lynchpin** ['lɪntʃpɪn] *n* (*fig*) podpora *f*
**Lincs** [lɪŋks] (*Brit*: *Post*) *abbr* = **Lincolnshire**
**line** [laɪn] *n* (*mark*) linia *f*, kreska *f*; (*wrinkle*) zmarszczka *f*; (*of people*) kolejka *f*; (*of things*) rząd *m*, szpaler *m*; (*of writing, song*) linijka *f*, wiersz *m*; (*rope*) lina *f*, sznur *m*; (*for fishing*) żyłka *f*; (*wire*) przewód *m*; (*Tel*) linia *f*, połączenie *nt*; (*railway track*) tor *m*; (*bus, train route*) linia *f*; (*fig*: *attitude, policy*) linia *f*, kurs *m*; (: *business, work*) dziedzina *f*, branża *f*; (*Comm*: *of product(s)*) typ *m*, model *m* ▷ *vt* (*road*) ustawiać się (ustawić się *perf*) wzdłuż *+gen*, tworzyć (utworzyć *perf*) szpaler wzdłuż *+gen*; (*clothing*) podszywać (podszyć *perf*); (*container*) wykładać (wyłożyć *perf*); **to ~ sth with sth** wykładać (wyłożyć *perf*) coś czymś; **to ~ the streets** wypełniać (wypełnić *perf*) ulice; **hold the ~ please!** (*Tel*) proszę nie odkładać słuchawki!; **to cut in ~** (*US*) wpychać się (wepchnąć się *perf*) do kolejki; **in ~** rzędem, w szeregu; **in ~ with** w zgodzie z *+instr*; **to be in ~ for sth** być następnym w kolejce do czegoś; **to bring sth into ~ with sth** dostosowywać (dostosować *perf*) coś do czegoś; **on the right ~s** na właściwej drodze; **to draw the ~ at doing sth** stanowczo sprzeciwiać się (sprzeciwić się *perf*) robieniu czegoś
▸ **line up** *vi* ustawiać się (ustawić się *perf*) w rzędzie *or* rzędem ▷ *vt* (*people*) zbierać (zebrać *perf*); (*event*) przygotowywać (przygotować *perf*); **to have sth ~d up** mieć coś (starannie) zaplanowane
**linear** ['lɪnɪəʳ] *adj* (*process, sequence*) liniowy, linearny; (*shape, form*) linearny
**lined** [laɪnd] *adj* (*face*) pomarszczony, pokryty zmarszczkami; (*paper*) w linie *post*, liniowany; (*jacket*) na podszewce *post*
**line editing** (*Comput*) *n* edycja *f* wierszowa
**line feed** (*Comput*) *n* znak *m* wysuwu wiersza
**linen** ['lɪnɪn] *n* (*cloth*) płótno *nt*; (*sheets etc*) bielizna *f* (*pościelowa lub stołowa*)
**line printer** (*Comput*) *n* drukarka *f* wierszowa
**liner** ['laɪnəʳ] *n* (*ship*) liniowiec *m*; (*also*: **bin liner**) worek *m* na śmieci (*wkładany do kosza*)
**linesman** ['laɪnzmən] (*irreg*: *like* **man**) (*Sport*) *n* sędzia *m* liniowy
**line-up** ['laɪnʌp] *n* (*US*) kolejka *f*; (*Sport*) skład *m* (*zespołu*); (*at concert, festival*) obsada *f*, lista *f* wykonawców; (*identity parade*) konfrontacja *f*

**linger** ['lɪŋgəʳ] *vi* (*smell, tradition*) utrzymywać się (utrzymać się *perf*); (*person: remain long*) zasiedzieć się (*perf*); (*: tarry*) zwlekać, ociągać się
**lingerie** ['lænʒəri:] *n* bielizna *f* damska
**lingering** ['lɪŋgərɪŋ] *adj* (*sense, feeling*) uporczywy
**lingo** ['lɪŋgəu] (*pl* **~es**) (*inf*) *n* mowa *f*
**linguist** ['lɪŋgwɪst] *n* (*specialist*) językoznawca *m*, lingwista(-tka) *m(f)*; **she's a good ~** (*speaks several languages*) zna (obce) języki
**linguistic** [lɪŋ'gwɪstɪk] *adj* językoznawczy, lingwistyczny
**linguistics** [lɪŋ'gwɪstɪks] *n* językoznawstwo *nt*, lingwistyka *f*
**liniment** ['lɪnɪmənt] *n* mazidło *nt*
**lining** ['laɪnɪŋ] *n* (*cloth*) podszewka *f*; (*Anat*) wyściółka *f*; (*Tech, Aut*) okładzina *f*
**link** [lɪŋk] *n* więź *f*, związek *m*; (*communications link*) połączenie *nt*; (*of chain*) ogniwo *nt*; (*Comput*) link *m*, łącze *nt* ▷ *vt* łączyć (połączyć *perf*); **links** *npl* pole *nt* golfowe (*nad morzem*); **rail ~** połączenie kolejowe
▸ **link up** *vt* podłączać (podłączyć *perf*) ▷ *vi* łączyć się (połączyć się *perf*)
**link-up** ['lɪŋkʌp] *n* (*also Radio, TV*) połączenie *nt*
**lino** ['laɪnəu] *n* = **linoleum**
**linoleum** [lɪ'nəulɪəm] *n* linoleum *nt*
**linseed oil** ['lɪnsi:d-] *n* olej *m* lniany
**lint** [lɪnt] *n* płótno *nt* opatrunkowe
**lintel** ['lɪntl] *n* nadproże *nt*
**lion** ['laɪən] *n* lew *m*
**lion cub** *n* lwiątko *nt*
**lioness** ['laɪənɪs] *n* lwica *f*
**lip** [lɪp] *n* (*Anat*) warga *f*; (*of cup etc*) brzeg *m*, krawędź *f*; (*inf*) pyskowanie *nt* (*inf*)
**lip-read** ['lɪpri:d] *vi* czytać z (ruchu) warg
**lip salve** *n* maść *f* do warg
**lip service** (*pej*) *n*: **to pay ~ to sth** składać gołosłowne deklaracje poparcia dla czegoś
**lipstick** ['lɪpstɪk] *n* pomadka *f* (do ust), szminka *f*
**liquefy** ['lɪkwɪfaɪ] *vt* skraplać (skroplić *perf*) ▷ *vi* skraplać się (skroplić się *perf*)
**liqueur** [lɪ'kjuəʳ] *n* likier *m*
**liquid** ['lɪkwɪd] *adj* płynny ▷ *n* płyn *m*, ciecz *f*
**liquid assets** *npl* środki *pl* płynne
**liquidate** ['lɪkwɪdeɪt] *vt* likwidować (zlikwidować *perf*)
**liquidation** [lɪkwɪ'deɪʃən] (*Comm*) *n* likwidacja *f*
**liquidation sale** (*US*) *n* wyprzedaż *f* likwidacyjna
**liquidator** ['lɪkwɪdeɪtəʳ] *n* likwidator *m*
**liquid crystal display** *n* wyświetlacz *m* ciekłokrystaliczny
**liquidity** [lɪ'kwɪdɪtɪ] *n* płynność *f*
**liquidize** ['lɪkwɪdaɪz] *vt* miksować (zmiksować *perf*)
**liquidizer** ['lɪkwɪdaɪzəʳ] *n* mikser *m*
**liquor** ['lɪkəʳ] *n* wysokoprocentowy napój *m* alkoholowy, (silny) trunek *m*
**liquorice** ['lɪkərɪs] (*Brit*) *n* lukrecja *f*
**liquor store** (*US*) *n* (sklep *m*) monopolowy
**Lisbon** ['lɪzbən] *n* Lizbona *f*
**lisp** [lɪsp] *n* seplenienie *nt* ▷ *vi* seplenić
**lissom(e)** ['lɪsəm] *adj* smukły
**list** [lɪst] *n* lista *f*, spis *m* ▷ *vt* (*record*) wyliczać (wyliczyć *perf*), wymieniać (wymienić *perf*); (*Comput*) listować (wylistować *perf*); (*write down*) robić (zrobić *perf*) listę *+gen*, spisywać (spisać *perf*); (*put down on list*) umieszczać (umieścić *perf*) na liście ▷ *vi* (*ship*) mieć przechył
**listed building** ['lɪstɪd-] (*Brit*) *n zabytkowy budynek znajdujący się w rejestrze obiektów prawnie chronionych*
**listed company** *n* przedsiębiorstwo *nt* notowane na giełdzie
**listen** ['lɪsn] *vi* słuchać; **to ~ (out) for** nasłuchiwać *+gen*; **to ~ to sb/sth** słuchać kogoś/czegoś; **~!** posłuchaj!
**listener** ['lɪsnəʳ] *n* słuchacz(ka) *m(f)*; (*Radio*) (radio)słuchacz(ka) *m(f)*
**listing** [lɪstɪŋ] *n* (*entry*) pozycja *f*, hasło *nt*; (*list*) lista *f*, wykaz *m*
**listless** ['lɪstlɪs] *adj* apatyczny
**listlessly** ['lɪstlɪslɪ] *adv* apatycznie
**list price** *n* cena *f* według cennika
**lit** [lɪt] *pt, pp of* **light**
**litany** ['lɪtənɪ] *n* litania *f*
**liter** ['li:təʳ] (*US*) *n* = **litre**
**literacy** ['lɪtərəsɪ] *n* umiejętność *f* czytania i pisania
**literacy campaign** *n* akcja *f* walki z analfabetyzmem
**literal** ['lɪtərl] *adj* dosłowny
**literally** ['lɪtrəlɪ] *adv* dosłownie
**literary** ['lɪtərərɪ] *adj* literacki
**literate** ['lɪtərət] *adj* (*able to read etc*) piśmienny, umiejący czytać i pisać; (*educated*) oczytany
**literature** ['lɪtrɪtʃəʳ] *n* literatura *f*
**lithe** [laɪð] *adj* gibki, giętki
**lithograph** ['lɪθəgrɑ:f] *n* litografia *f* (*odbitka*)
**lithography** [lɪ'θɔgrəfɪ] *n* litografia *f* (*technika*)
**Lithuania** [lɪθju'eɪnɪə] *n* Litwa *f*
**litigation** [lɪtɪ'geɪʃən] *n* (*Jur*) spór *m*
**litmus** ['lɪtməs] *n*: **~ paper** papierek *m* lakmusowy
**litre**, (*US*) **liter** ['li:təʳ] *n* litr *m*
**litter** ['lɪtəʳ] *n* (*rubbish*) śmieci *pl*; (*young animals*) miot *m*
**litter bin** (*Brit*) *n* kosz *m* na śmieci

**litterbug** ['lɪtəbʌg] *n osoba zaśmiecająca miejsca publiczne*
**littered** ['lɪtəd] *adj*: **~ with** zawalony *+instr*
**litter lout** *n* = **litterbug**
**little** ['lɪtl] *adj* mały; (*brother etc*) młodszy; (*distance, time*) krótki ▷ *adv* mało, niewiele; **a ~** trochę, troszkę; **a ~ bit** troszkę, troszeczkę; **~ by ~** po trochu; **to have ~ time/money** mieć mało czasu/pieniędzy
**little finger** *n* mały palec *m*
**liturgy** ['lɪtədʒɪ] *n* liturgia *f*
**live** [*vb* lɪv, *adj* laɪv] *vi* żyć; (*reside*) mieszkać ▷ *adj* żywy; (*performance etc*) na żywo *post*; (*Elec*) pod napięciem *post*; (*bullet, bomb*) ostry; **to ~ with sb** żyć z kimś
▶ **live down** *vt* odkupywać (odkupić *perf*), zmazywać (zmazać *perf*); **you'd never ~ it down** nigdy by ci tego nie zapomniano
▶ **live for** *vt* żyć dla *+gen*
▶ **live in** *vi* mieszkać na miejscu
▶ **live off** *vt fus* (*food*) żyć na *+loc*; (*land*) żyć z *+gen*; (*parents etc*) pasożytować *or* żerować na *+loc*
▶ **live on** *vt fus* (*food*) żyć na *+loc*; (*salary*) żyć z *+gen*
▶ **live out** *vi* (*Brit*) mieszkać poza miejscem nauki/pracy ▷ *vt*: **to ~ out one's days** *or* **life** przeżywać (przeżyć *perf*) swoje dni *or* życie
▶ **live together** *vi* mieszkać (zamieszkać *perf*) ze sobą
▶ **live up** *vt*: **to ~ it up** używać sobie, żyć na całego
▶ **live up to** *vt fus* spełniać (spełnić *perf*) *+acc*
**livelihood** ['laɪvlɪhud] *n* środki *pl* egzystencji *or* do życia
**liveliness** ['laɪvlɪnɪs] *n* żwawość *f*, ożywienie *nt*
**lively** ['laɪvlɪ] *adj* (*person*) żwawy, pełen życia; (*place*) tętniący życiem, pełen życia; (*interest*) żywy; (*conversation*) ożywiony; (*book*) zajmujący
**liven up** ['laɪvn-] *vt* ożywiać (ożywić *perf*) ▷ *vi* ożywiać się (ożywić się *perf*)
**liver** ['lɪvəʳ] *n* (*Anat*) wątroba *f*; (*Culin*) wątróbka *f*
**liverish** ['lɪvərɪʃ] *adj* niedysponowany (*zwłaszcza z przejedzenia lub przepicia*)
**Liverpudlian** [lɪvə'pʌdlɪən] *adj* liverpoolski ▷ *n* mieszkaniec(-nka) *m(f)* Liverpoolu
**livery** ['lɪvərɪ] *n* liberia *f*
**lives** [laɪvz] *npl of* **life**
**livestock** ['laɪvstɔk] *n* żywy inwentarz *m*
**livid** ['lɪvɪd] *adj* (*colour*) siny; (*inf*: *person*) wściekły
**living** ['lɪvɪŋ] *adj* żyjący ▷ *n*: **to earn** *or* **make a ~** zarabiać (zarobić *perf*) na życie; **within ~ memory** za ludzkiej pamięci; **the cost of ~** koszty utrzymania
**living conditions** *npl* warunki *pl* życia
**living expenses** *npl* wydatki *pl* na życie *or* utrzymanie
**living room** *n* salon *m*
**living standards** *npl* stopa *f* życiowa
**living wage** *n* płaca *f* wystarczająca na utrzymanie
**lizard** ['lɪzəd] *n* jaszczurka *f*
**llama** ['lɑːmə] *n* lama *f*
**LLB** *n abbr* (= *Bachelor of Laws*) *stopień naukowy*
**LLD** *n abbr* (= *Doctor of Laws*) *stopień naukowy*, ≈ dr hab.
**LMT** (*US*) *abbr* (= *Local Mean Time*) *czas lokalny*
**load** [ləud] *n* (*thing carried*) ładunek *m*; (*weight*) obciążenie *nt* ▷ *vt* ładować, załadowywać (załadować *perf*); **a ~ of rubbish** (*inf*) stek bzdur; **~s of** *or* **a ~ of** (*fig*) mnóstwo *+gen*
**loaded** ['ləudɪd] *adj* (*vehicle*) załadowany; (*question*) podchwytliwy; (*inf*: *person*) nadziany (*inf*); (*dice*) fałszowany
**loading bay** ['ləudɪŋ-] *n* hala *f* wsadowa
**loaf** [ləuf] (*pl* **loaves**) *n* bochenek *m* ▷ *vi* (*also*: **loaf about, loaf around**) obijać się, byczyć się (*inf*); **use your ~!** (*inf*) rusz łbem! (*inf*)
**loam** [ləum] *n* ił *m*, gleba *f* ilasta
**loan** [ləun] *n* pożyczka *f*; (*from bank*) kredyt *m* ▷ *vt* pożyczać (pożyczyć *perf*); **on ~** pożyczony, wypożyczony
**loan account** *n* rachunek *m* kredytowy
**loan capital** *n* kapitał *m* pożyczkowy
**loath** [ləuθ], **loth** *adj*: **to be ~ to do sth** nie mieć ochoty czegoś (z)robić
**loathe** [ləuð] *vt* nie cierpieć *+gen*
**loathing** ['ləuðɪŋ] *n* odraza *f*, obrzydzenie *nt*
**loathsome** ['ləuðsəm] *adj* wstrętny, obmierzły
**loaves** [ləuvz] *npl of* **loaf**
**lob** [lɔb] *vt* (*ball*) lobować
**lobby** ['lɔbɪ] *n* (*of building*) westybul *m*, hall *m*; (*Pol*) lobby *nt inv* ▷ *vt* (*MP etc*) wywierać nacisk na *+acc*
**lobbyist** ['lɔbɪɪst] *n* członek(-nkini) *m(f)* lobby
**lobe** [ləub] *n* (*of ear*) płatek *m*; (*of brain, lung*) płat *m*
**lobster** ['lɔbstəʳ] *n* homar *m*
**lobster pot** *n* sieć *f* na homary
**local** ['ləukl] *adj* lokalny, miejscowy ▷ *n* pub *m* (*pobliski, często odwiedzany*); **the locals** *npl* miejscowi *vir pl*
**local anaesthetic** *n* znieczulenie *nt* miejscowe
**local authority** *n* władze *pl* lokalne
**local call** *n* (*Tel*) rozmowa *f* miejscowa
**local government** *n* samorząd *m* terytorialny
**locality** [ləu'kælɪtɪ] *n* rejon *m*

**localize** ['ləukəlaɪz] *vt* lokalizować (zlokalizować *perf*), umiejscawiać (umiejscowić *perf*)
**locally** ['ləukəlɪ] *adv* lokalnie, miejscowo
**locate** [ləu'keɪt] *vt* lokalizować (zlokalizować *perf*), umiejscawiać (umiejscowić *perf*); **~d in** umiejscowiony *or* położony w *+loc*
**location** [ləu'keɪʃən] *n* położenie *nt*; **on ~** (*Film*) w plenerach
**loch** [lɔx] *n* jezioro *nt*
**lock** [lɔk] *n* (*of door, suitcase*) zamek *m*; (*on canal*) śluza *f*; (*of hair*) lok *m*, loczek *m* ▷ *vt* (*door etc*) zamykać (zamknąć *perf*) na klucz; (*immobilize*) unieruchamiać (unieruchomić *perf*) ▷ *vi* (*door etc*) zamykać się (zamknąć się *perf*) na klucz; (*knee, mechanism*) blokować się (zablokować się *perf*); **the battery ~ed into place** bateria wskoczyła na miejsce; **(on) full ~** (*Aut*) pełen promień skrętu; **~, stock and barrel** w całości
▸ **lock away** *vt* trzymać pod kluczem
▸ **lock in** *vt* zamykać (zamknąć *perf*) na klucz, brać (wziąć *perf*) pod klucz
▸ **lock out** *vt* (*person*) zamykać (zamknąć *perf*) drzwi na klucz przed *+instr*/za *+instr*; (*Industry*) stosować (zastosować *perf*) lokaut wobec *+gen*
▸ **lock up** *vt* (*criminal, mental patient*) zamykać (zamknąć *perf*) ▷ *vi* pozamykać (*perf*)
**locker** ['lɔkə^r] *n* (*in school*) szafka *f*; (*at railway station*) schowek *m* na bagaż
**locker room** *n* (*in sports club etc*) szatnia *f*
**locket** ['lɔkɪt] *n* medalion *m*
**lockjaw** ['lɔkdʒɔ:] *n* szczękościsk *m*
**lockout** ['lɔkaut] *n* lokaut *m*
**locksmith** ['lɔksmɪθ] *n* ślusarz *m*
**lockup** ['lɔkʌp] *n* (*US: inf*) areszt *m*, paka *f* (*inf*); (*also*: **lock-up garage**) (wynajęty) garaż *m*
**locomotive** [ləukə'məutɪv] *n* lokomotywa *f*
**locum** ['ləukəm] (*Med*) *n* zastępstwo *nt*
**locust** ['ləukəst] *n* szarańcza *f*
**lodge** [lɔdʒ] *n* (*small house*) stróżówka *f*; (*hunting lodge*) domek *m* myśliwski; (*masons' lodge*) loża *f* ▷ *vi* (*bullet*) utkwić (*perf*); (*person*): **to ~ (with)** mieszkać (zamieszkać *perf*) (u *+gen*) ▷ *vt* (*complaint etc*) wnosić (wnieść *perf*)
**lodger** ['lɔdʒə^r] *n* lokator(ka) *m(f)*
**lodging** ['lɔdʒɪŋ] *n* zakwaterowanie *nt*
**lodging house** *n* pensjonat *m*
**lodgings** ['lɔdʒɪŋz] *npl* wynajęte mieszkanie *nt*
**loft** [lɔft] *n* strych *m*
**lofty** ['lɔftɪ] *adj* (*ideal, aim*) wzniosły; (*manner*) wyniosły; (*position*) wysoki
**log** [lɔg] *n* (*piece of wood*) kłoda *f*; (*written account*) dziennik *m* ▷ *n abbr* (*Math*: = *logarithm*) log, lg ▷ *vt* zapisywać (zapisać *perf*) w dzienniku
▸ **log in, log on** *vi* (*Comput*) logować się (zalogować się *perf*)
▸ **log into** (*Comput*) *vt fus* logować się (zalogować się *perf*) do *+gen*
▸ **log out, log off** (*Comput*) *vi* wylogowywać się (wylogować się *perf*)
**logarithm** ['lɔgərɪðm] *n* logarytm *m*
**logbook** ['lɔgbuk] *n* (*Naut*) dziennik *m* okrętowy; (*Aviat*) dziennik *m* pokładowy; (*of car*) dowód *m* rejestracyjny; (*of lorry driver*) książka *f* pracy kierowcy; (*of events*) dziennik *m*
**log fire** *n* kominek *m*
**loggerheads** ['lɔgəhɛdz] *npl*: **to be at ~ (with)** drzeć koty (z *+instr*)
**logic** ['lɔdʒɪk] *n* logika *f*
**logical** ['lɔdʒɪkl] *adj* logiczny
**logically** ['lɔdʒɪkəlɪ] *adv* logicznie
**login** ['lɔgɪn] (*Comput*) *n* logowanie (się) *nt*
**logistics** [lɔ'dʒɪstɪks] *n* logistyka *f*
**logo** ['ləugəu] *n* logo *nt inv*
**loin** [lɔɪn] *n* polędwica *f*; **loins** *npl* (*old: Anat*) lędźwie *pl*
**loincloth** ['lɔɪnklɔθ] *n* przepaska *f* na biodra
**loiter** ['lɔɪtə^r] *vi* wałęsać się
**loll** [lɔl] *vi* (*also*: **loll about**: *person*) rozkładać się (rozłożyć się *perf*), rozwalać się (rozwalić się *perf*) (*inf*); (*head*) zwisać (zwisnąć *perf*); **the dog's tongue ~ed out** pies miał wywieszony język
**lollipop** ['lɔlɪpɔp] *n* lizak *m* ▷ *cpd*: **~ lady/man** (*Brit*) *osoba zaopatrzona w duży znak w kształcie lizaka, pomagająca dzieciom w przejściu przez ruchliwe skrzyżowanie*
**lollop** ['lɔləp] *vi* podskakiwać (podskoczyć *perf*)
**Lombardy** ['lɔmbədɪ] *n* Lombardia *f*
**London** ['lʌndən] *n* Londyn *m*
**Londoner** ['lʌndənə^r] *n* londyńczyk *m*, mieszkaniec(-nka) *m(f)* Londynu
**lone** [ləun] *adj* samotny
**loneliness** ['ləunlɪnɪs] *n* samotność *f*
**lonely** ['ləunlɪ] *adj* (*person, period of time*) samotny; (*place*) odludny
**loner** ['ləunə^r] *n* samotnik(-iczka) *m(f)*
**lonesome** ['ləunsəm] *adj* samotny
**long** [lɔŋ] *adj* długi ▷ *adv* długo ▷ *vi*: **to ~ for sth** tęsknić do czegoś; **in the ~ run** na dłuższą metę; **so** *or* **as ~ as** (*on condition that*) pod warunkiem, że; (*while*) jak długo, dopóki; **don't be ~!** pośpiesz się!; **to be 6 metres ~** mieć 6 metrów długości; **to be 6 months ~** trwać 6 miesięcy; **all night ~** (przez) całą noc; **he no ~er comes** już nie przychodzi; **~ ago** dawno temu; **~ before** na długo przed *+instr*; **~ after** długo po *+loc*; **they'll catch him before ~** niedługo go złapią; **before ~ we were back home** niedługo potem byliśmy z powrotem w domu; **at ~ last** wreszcie; **the ~**

**and the short of it is that ...** krótko mówiąc, ...

**long-distance** [lɔŋ'dɪstəns] *adj* (*travel*) daleki; (*race*) długodystansowy; (*phone call: within same country*) zamiejscowy; (*: international*) międzynarodowy

**longevity** [lɔn'dʒɛvɪtɪ] *n* długowieczność *f*

**long-haired** ['lɔŋ'hɛəd] *adj* długowłosy

**longhand** ['lɔŋhænd] *n* pismo *nt* ręczne

**longing** ['lɔŋɪŋ] *n* tęsknota *f*

**longingly** ['lɔŋɪŋlɪ] *adv* tęsknie

**longitude** ['lɔŋgɪtju:d] *n* długość *f* geograficzna

**long johns** [-dʒɔnz] *npl* kalesony *pl*

**long jump** *n* skok *m* w dal

**long-life** ['lɔŋlaɪf] *adj* o przedłużonej trwałości *post*

**long-lost** ['lɔŋlɔst] *adj* (*relative, friend*) dawno nie widziany

**long-playing record** ['lɔŋpleɪɪŋ-] *n* płyta *f* długogrająca

**long-range** ['lɔŋ'reɪndʒ] *adj* (*plan*) długookresowy; (*forecast*) długoterminowy; (*missile*) dalekiego zasięgu *post*

**longshoreman** ['lɔŋʃɔ:mən] (*US*) (*irreg: like* **man**) *n* doker *m*

**long-sighted** ['lɔŋ'saɪtɪd] *adj*: **to be ~** być dalekowidzem

**long-standing** ['lɔŋ'stændɪŋ] *adj* (*offer, invitation*) dawny; (*reputation*) (dawno) ugruntowany

**long-suffering** [lɔŋ'sʌfərɪŋ] *adj* anielsko cierpliwy

**long-term** ['lɔŋtə:m] *adj* długoterminowy

**long wave** *n* fale *pl* długie

**long-winded** [lɔŋ'wɪndɪd] *adj* rozwlekły

**loo** [lu:] (*Brit: inf*) *n* ubikacja *f*

**loofah** ['lu:fə] *n* gąbka *f* (z luffy)

**look** [luk] *vi* patrzeć (popatrzeć *perf*) ▷ *n* (*glance*) spojrzenie *nt*; (*appearance, expression*) wygląd *m*; **looks** *npl* uroda *f*; **he ~ed scared** wyglądał na przestraszonego; **to ~ south/(out) onto the sea** (*building etc*) wychodzić na południe/na morze; **~!** patrz!; **~ (here)!** słuchaj (no)!; **to ~ like sb/sth** wyglądać jak ktoś/coś; **it ~s like** *or* **as if he's not coming** wygląda na to, że nie przyjdzie; **it ~s about 4 metres long** na oko ma ze 4 metry (długości); **everything ~s all right to me** moim zdaniem wszystko jest w porządku; **let's have a ~** spójrzmy, popatrzmy; **to have a ~ at sth** przyglądać się (przyjrzeć się *perf*) czemuś; **to have a ~ for sth** szukać (poszukać *perf*) czegoś; **to ~ ahead** patrzeć (popatrzeć *perf*) przed siebie; (*fig*) patrzeć (popatrzeć *perf*) w przyszłość

▸ **look after** *vt fus* (*care for*) opiekować się (zaopiekować się *perf*) +*instr*; (*deal with*) zajmować się (zająć się *perf*) +*instr*

▸ **look at** *vt fus* patrzeć (popatrzeć *perf*) na +*acc*; (*read quickly*) przeglądać (przejrzeć *perf*) +*acc*; (*study, consider*) przyglądać się (przyjrzeć się *perf*) +*dat*

▸ **look back** *vi* patrzeć (popatrzeć *perf*) *or* spoglądać (spojrzeć *perf*) wstecz; **to ~ back at sth/sb** oglądać się (obejrzeć się *perf*) na coś/kogoś; **to ~ back on** wspominać (wspomnieć *perf*) +*acc*

▸ **look down on** *vt fus* (*fig*) spoglądać z góry na +*acc*

▸ **look for** *vt fus* szukać (poszukać *perf*) +*gen*

▸ **look forward to** *vt fus* z niecierpliwością czekać na +*acc or* oczekiwać +*gen*, cieszyć się na +*acc*; **we ~ forward to hearing from you** (*in letter*) czekamy na wiadomości od was

▸ **look in** *vi*: **to ~ in on sb** zaglądać (zajrzeć *perf*) do kogoś

▸ **look into** *vt fus* (*investigate*) badać (zbadać *perf*) +*acc*

▸ **look on** *vi* przyglądać się

▸ **look out** *vi* uważać

▸ **look out for** *vt fus* wypatrywać +*gen*

▸ **look over** *vt* (*essay*) przeglądać (przejrzeć *perf*); (*person*) lustrować (zlustrować *perf*); (*view, window: town, sea etc*) wychodzić na +*acc*

▸ **look round** *vi* rozglądać się (rozejrzeć się *perf*)

▸ **look through** *vt fus* przeglądać (przejrzeć *perf*)

▸ **look to** *vt fus*: **to ~ to sb for sth** oczekiwać od kogoś czegoś

▸ **look up** *vi* podnosić (podnieść *perf*) wzrok, spoglądać (spojrzeć *perf*) w górę; **things are ~ing up** idzie ku lepszemu ▷ *vt* (*in dictionary, timetable etc*) sprawdzać (sprawdzić *perf*)

▸ **look up to** *vt fus* (*hero, idol*) podziwiać

**look-alike** ['lukəlaɪk] *n* sobowtór *m*

**look-in** ['lukɪn] *n*: **to get a ~** (*inf*) mieć okazję się odezwać

**lookout** ['lukaut] *n* (*tower etc*) punkt *m* obserwacyjny; (*person*) obserwator *m*; **to be on the ~ for** (*work*) rozglądać się za +*instr*; (*mistakes, explosives*) uważać na +*acc*

**loom** [lu:m] *vi* (*also:* **loom up**: *object, shape*) wyłaniać się (wyłonić się *perf*); (*event*) zbliżać się, nadchodzić ▷ *n* krosno *nt*

**loony** ['lu:nɪ] (*inf*) *adj* pomylony (*inf*) ▷ *n* pomyleniec *m* (*inf*)

**loop** [lu:p] *n* pętla *f* ▷ *vt*: **to ~ sth around sth** obwiązywać (obwiązać *perf*) czymś coś

**loophole** ['lu:phəul] *n* luka *f* (*prawna*)

**loose** [lu:s] *adj* luźny; (*hair*) rozpuszczony; (*life*) rozwiązły ▷ *n*: **to be on the ~** być na wolności ▷ *vt* (*free*) uwalniać (uwolnić *perf*); (*set off, unleash*) wywoływać (wywołać *perf*)

**loose change** *n* drobne *pl*

**loose chippings** *npl* sypki żwir *m*
**loose end** *n*: **to be at a ~** *or (US)* **at ~s** nie mieć nic do roboty; **to tie up ~s** wyjaśniać (wyjaśnić *perf*) szczegóły
**loose-fitting** ['lu:sfɪtɪŋ] *adj* luźny
**loose-leaf** ['lu:sli:f] *adj* z luźnymi kartkami *post*
**loose-limbed** [lu:s'lɪmd] *adj* gibki
**loosely** ['lu:slɪ] *adv* luźno
**loosen** ['lu:sn] *vt* (*screw etc*) poluzowywać (poluzować *perf*); (*clothing, belt*) rozluźniać (rozluźnić *perf*)
**loosen up** *vi* rozluźniać się (rozluźnić się *perf*)
**loot** [lu:t] *n* (*inf*) łup *m* ▷ *vt* grabić (ograbić *perf*), plądrować (splądrować *perf*)
**looter** ['lu:tə^r] *n* (*during war*) grabieżca *m*; (*during riot*) złodziej(ka) *m(f)*
**looting** ['lu:tɪŋ] *n* grabież *m*
**lop off** [lɔp-] *vt* obcinać (obciąć *perf*)
**lopsided** ['lɔp'saɪdɪd] *adj* krzywy
**lord** [lɔ:d] *n* (*Brit*) lord *m*; **the L~** (*Rel*) Pan (Bóg); **my ~** (*to noble*) milordzie; (*to bishop, judge*) ekscelencjo; **good L~!** dobry Boże!; **the (House of) L~s** (*Brit*) Izba Lordów
**lordly** ['lɔ:dlɪ] *adj* wielkopański
**lordship** ['lɔ:dʃɪp] *n*: **your L~** wasza lordowska mość
**lore** [lɔ:^r] *n* tradycja *f* (ustna)
**lorry** ['lɔrɪ] (*Brit*) *n* ciężarówka *f*
**lorry driver** (*Brit*) *n* kierowca *m* ciężarówki
**lose** [lu:z] (*pt, pp* **lost**) *vt* (*object, pursuers*) gubić (zgubić *perf*); (*job, money, patience, voice, father*) tracić (stracić *perf*); (*game, election*) przegrywać (przegrać *perf*) ▷ *vi* przegrywać (przegrać *perf*); **my watch ~s about 5 minutes a day** mój zegarek spóźnia się jakieś 5 minut dziennie; **to ~ sight of** (*person, object*) tracić (stracić *perf*) z oczu *+acc*; (*moral values etc*) zatracać (zatracić *perf*) *+acc*
**loser** ['lu:zə^r] *n* (*in contest*) przegrywający(-ca) *m(f)*; (*inf: failure*) ofiara *f* (życiowa); **to be a good/bad ~** umieć/nie umieć przegrywać
**loss** [lɔs] *n* (*no pl: of memory, blood, consciousness*) utrata *f*; (*of time, money, person through death*) strata *f*; (*Comm*): **to make a ~** (*business*) przynosić (przynieść *perf*) straty; (*company*) ponosić (ponieść *perf*) straty; **to sell sth at a ~** sprzedawać (sprzedać *perf*) coś ze stratą; **heavy ~es** (*Mil*) ciężkie straty; **to cut one's ~es** zapobiegać (zapobiec *perf*) dalszym stratom; **I'm at a ~** nie wiem, co robić; **I'm at a ~ for words** nie wiem, co powiedzieć
**loss adjuster** (*Insurance*) *n* likwidator *m* szkód
**loss leader** (*Comm*) *n towar sprzedawany tanio, aby przyciągnąć klientów*
**lost** [lɔst] *pt, pp of* **lose** ▷ *adj* (*person, animal*) zaginiony; (*object*) zgubiony; **to get ~** gubić się (zgubić się *perf*); **we're ~** zgubiliśmy się; **get ~!** (*inf*) spadaj! (*inf*); **~ in thought** zatopiony w myślach
**lost and found** (*US*) *n* = **lost property**
**lost cause** *n* przegrana *or* beznadziejna sprawa *f*
**lost property** *n* biuro *nt* rzeczy znalezionych
**lot** [lɔt] *n* (*of things*) zestaw *m*; (*of people*) grupa *f*; (*of merchandise*) partia *f*; (*at auctions*) artykuł *m*; (*destiny*) los *m*; **the (whole) lot** wszystko; **a lot (of)** dużo (*+gen*); **quite a lot (of)** sporo (*+gen*); **lots of** mnóstwo *+gen*; **a lot bigger/more expensive** dużo większy/droższy; **this happens a lot** to się często zdarza; **have you been seeing a lot of each other?** (czy) często się widujecie?; **thanks a lot!** dziękuję bardzo!; **to draw lots** ciągnąć losy
**lotion** ['ləuʃən] *n* płyn *m* kosmetyczny
**lottery** ['lɔtərɪ] *n* loteria *f*
**loud** [laud] *adj* (*noise, voice*) głośny; (*clothes*) krzykliwy ▷ *adv* głośno; **out ~** na głos; **to be ~ in one's support/disapproval of** głośno wyrażać swoje poparcie/dezaprobatę dla *+gen*
**loudhailer** [laud'heɪlə^r] (*Brit*) *n* megafon *m*
**loudly** ['laudlɪ] *adv* głośno
**loud-mouthed** ['laudmauðd] *adj* głośny
**loudspeaker** [laud'spi:kə^r] *n* głośnik *m*
**lounge** [laundʒ] *n* (*in house*) salon *m*; (*in hotel*) hall *m*; (*at station*) poczekalnia *f*; (*Brit: also:* **lounge bar**) bar *m* (*w hotelu lub pubie*) ▷ *vi* rozpierać się; **arrivals/departures ~** (*at airport*) hala przylotów/odlotów
▸ **lounge about** *vi* próżnować
▸ **lounge around** *vi* = **lounge about**
**lounge suit** (*Brit*) *n* garnitur *m*
**louse** [laus] (*pl* **lice**) *n* wesz *f*
▸ **louse up** (*inf*) *vt* paprać (spaprać *perf*) (*inf*)
**lousy** ['lauzɪ] (*inf*) *adj* (*show, meal*) nędzny; (*person, behaviour*) podły, wstrętny; **to feel ~** czuć się (poczuć się *perf*) podle
**lout** [laut] *n* cham *m*, prostak *m*
**louvre**, (*US*) **louver** ['lu:və^r] *n* (*window*) okno *nt* żaluzjowe
**lovable** ['lʌvəbl] *adj* miły, sympatyczny
**love** [lʌv] *n* miłość *f*; (*for sport, activity*) zamiłowanie *nt* ▷ *vt* kochać (pokochać *perf*); **"~ (from) Anne"** „uściski *or* ściskam, Anna"; **I'd ~ to come** przyszedłbym z przyjemnością; **I ~ chocolate** uwielbiam czekoladę; **to be in ~ with sb** być w kimś zakochanym; **to fall in ~ with sb** zakochiwać się (zakochać się *perf*) w kimś; **to make ~** kochać się; **~ at first sight** miłość od pierwszego wejrzenia; **to send one's ~ to sb** przesyłać (przesłać *perf*) komuś pozdrowienia; **"15 ~"** (*Tennis*) „15:0"
**love affair** *n* romans *m*

**ove letter** *n* list *m* miłosny

**ove life** *n* życie *nt* intymne

**ovely** ['lʌvlɪ] *adj* (*place, person*) śliczny, uroczy; (*meal, holiday*) cudowny

**over** ['lʌvə^r] *n* (*sexual partner*) kochanek(-nka) *m(f)*; (*person in love*) zakochany(-na) *m(f)*; **a ~ of art/music** miłośnik(-iczka) *m(f)* sztuki/muzyki

**ovesick** ['lʌvsɪk] *adj* chory z miłości

**ove song** *n* pieśń *f* miłosna

**oving** ['lʌvɪŋ] *adj* (*person*) kochający; (*action*) pełen miłości

**ow** [ləu] *adj* niski; (*quiet*) cichy; (*depressed*) przygnębiony ▷ *adv* (*speak*) cicho; (*fly*) nisko ▷ *n* (*Meteor*) niż *m*; **we're running low on milk** kończy nam się mleko; **to reach a new** *or* **an all-time low** spadać (spaść *perf*) do rekordowo niskiego poziomu

**ow-alcohol** ['ləu'ælkəhɔl] *adj* o niskiej zawartości alkoholu *post*

**owbrow** ['ləubrau] *adj* niewyszukany

**ow-calorie** ['ləu'kælərɪ] *adj* niskokaloryczny

**ow-cut** ['ləukʌt] *adj* głęboko wycięty, z dużym dekoltem *post*

**owdown** ['ləudaun] *n* (*inf*): **he gave me the ~ on it** podał mi wszystkie szczegóły na ten temat

**ower** ['ləuə^r] *adj* (*bottom*) dolny; (*less important*) niższy ▷ *vt* (*object*) opuszczać (opuścić *perf*); (*prices, level*) obniżać (obniżyć *perf*); (*voice*) zniżać (zniżyć *perf*); (*eyes*) spuszczać (spuścić *perf*)

**ow-fat** ['ləu'fæt] *adj* o niskiej zawartości tłuszczu *post*

**ow-key** ['ləu'ki:] *adj* (*manner*) powściągliwy; (*speech*) stonowany

**owlands** ['ləuləndz] *npl* niziny *pl*

**ow-level language** ['ləulɛvl-] (*Comput*) *n* język *m* niskiego poziomu

**ow-loader** ['ləuləudə^r] *n* pojazd *m* niskopodwoziowy

**owly** ['ləulɪ] *adj* skromny

**ow-lying** [ləu'laɪɪŋ] *adj* nizinny

**ow-paid** [ləu'peɪd] *adj* (*worker*) nisko opłacany; (*job*) źle płatny

**oyal** ['lɔɪəl] *adj* lojalny

**oyalist** ['lɔɪəlɪst] *n* lojalista(-tka) *m(f)*

**oyalty** ['lɔɪəltɪ] *n* lojalność *f*

**ozenge** ['lɔzɪndʒ] *n* (*tablet*) tabletka *f* do ssania; (*shape*) romb *m*

**LP** *n abbr* = **long-playing record**

**L-plates** ['ɛlpleɪts] (*Brit*) *npl tablice z literą „L" umieszczane na samochodach osób uczących się jeździć*

**LPN** (*US*) *n abbr* (= *Licensed Practical Nurse*) ≈ pielęgniarka(-arz) *f(m)* dyplomowana(-ny) *f(m)*

**LRAM** (*Brit*) *n abbr* = **Licentiate of the Royal Academy of Music**

**LSAT** (*US*) *n abbr* (= *Law School Admissions Test*) *egzamin, którego zdanie umożliwia podjęcie magisterskich studiów prawniczych*

**LSD** *n abbr* (= *lysergic acid diethylamide*) LSD *nt inv*; (*Brit*: = *pounds, shillings and pence*) *system monetarny w Wielkiej Brytanii do roku 1971*

**LSE** (*Brit*) *n abbr* = **London School of Economics**

**LT** (*Elec*) *abbr* (= *low tension*) niskie napięcie *nt*

**Lt** (*Mil*) *abbr* (= *lieutenant*) por.

**Ltd** (*Comm*) *abbr* (= *limited company*) ≈ Sp. z o.o.

**lubricant** ['lu:brɪkənt] *n* smar *m*

**lubricate** ['lu:brɪkeɪt] *vt* smarować (nasmarować *perf*)

**lucid** ['lu:sɪd] *adj* (*writing, speech*) klarowny; (*person, mind*) przytomny

**lucidity** [lu:'sɪdɪtɪ] *n* (*of writing, speech*) klarowność *f*; (*of person, mind*) przytomność *f*

**luck** [lʌk] *n* szczęście *nt*; **good ~** szczęście; **bad ~** pech; **good ~!** powodzenia!; **bad** *or* **hard** *or* **tough ~!** a to pech!; **to be in ~** mieć szczęście; **to be out of ~** nie mieć szczęścia

**luckily** ['lʌkɪlɪ] *adv* na szczęście

**lucky** ['lʌkɪ] *adj* szczęśliwy; **she's ~** ma szczęście

**lucrative** ['lu:krətɪv] *adj* intratny, lukratywny

**ludicrous** ['lu:dɪkrəs] *adj* śmieszny, śmiechu warty

**ludo** ['lu:dəu] (*game*) *n* chińczyk *m*

**lug** [lʌg] (*inf*) *vt* taszczyć (zataszczyć *perf*) (*inf*)

**luggage** ['lʌgɪdʒ] *n* bagaż *m*

**luggage car** (*US*) *n* wagon *m* bagażowy

**luggage rack** *n* (*Aut*) bagażnik *m* na dach; (*in train*) półka *f* (na bagaż)

**luggage van** *n* wagon *m* bagażowy

**lugubrious** [lu'gu:brɪəs] *adj* smętny

**lukewarm** ['lu:kwɔ:m] *adj* (*lit, fig*) letni

**lull** [lʌl] *n* okres *m* ciszy ▷ *vt*: **to ~ sb (to sleep)** kołysać (ukołysać *perf*) kogoś (do snu); **they were ~ed into a false sense of security** ich czujność została uśpiona

**lullaby** ['lʌləbaɪ] *n* kołysanka *f*

**lumbago** [lʌm'beɪgəu] *n* lumbago *nt inv*

**lumber** ['lʌmbə^r] *n* (*wood*) tarcica *f*; (*junk*) rupiecie *pl* ▷ *vi*: **to ~ about/along** wlec się (powlec się *perf*)

▸ **lumber with** *vt*: **to be/get ~ed with sth** być/zostawać (zostać *perf*) czymś obarczonym

**lumberjack** ['lʌmbədʒæk] *n* drwal *m*

**lumber room** (*Brit*) *n* rupieciarnia *f*

**lumberyard** ['lʌmbəjɑ:d] (*US*) *n* skład *m* drzewny

**luminous** ['lu:mɪnəs] *adj* (*fabric*) świecący; (*dial*) fosforyzujący

**lump** [lʌmp] *n* (*of clay etc*) bryła *f*; (*on body*) guzek *m*; (*also*: **sugar lump**) kostka *f* (cukru)

▷ *vt*: **to ~ together** traktować (potraktować *perf*) jednakowo, wrzucać (wrzucić *perf*) do jednego worka (*inf*); **a ~ sum** jednorazowa wypłata
**lumpy** [ˈlʌmpɪ] *adj* (*sauce*) grudkowaty; (*bed*) nierówny
**lunacy** [ˈlu:nəsɪ] *n* (*strange behaviour*) szaleństwo *nt*; (*old*: *mental illness*) obłęd *m*
**lunar** [ˈlu:nə^r] *adj* księżycowy
**lunatic** [ˈlu:nətɪk] *adj* szalony ▷ *n* (*foolish person*) szaleniec *m*; (*old*: *mad person*) obłąkany(-na) *m(f)*
**lunatic asylum** *n* zakład *m* dla umysłowo chorych
**lunatic fringe** *n*: **the ~** (*of organization*) skrajne elementy *pl*
**lunch** [lʌntʃ] *n* lunch *m* ▷ *vi* jeść (zjeść *perf*) lunch
**lunch break** *n* przerwa *f* na lunch
**luncheon** [ˈlʌntʃən] *n* uroczysty lunch *m*
**luncheon meat** *n* mielonka *f* (*konserwa*)
**luncheon voucher** (*Brit*) *n* kupon *m* na lunch
**lunch hour** *n* przerwa *f* na lunch
**lunchtime** [ˈlʌntʃtaɪm] *n* pora *f* lunchu
**lung** [lʌŋ] *n* płuco *nt*
**lunge** [lʌndʒ] *vi* (*also*: **lunge forward**) rzucać się (rzucić się *perf*) naprzód; **to ~ at** rzucać się (rzucić się *perf*) na *+acc*
**lupin** [ˈlu:pɪn] *n* łubin *m*
**lurch** [lə:tʃ] *vi* (*vehicle*) szarpnąć (*perf*); (*person*) zatoczyć się (*perf*) ▷ *n* szarpnięcie *nt*; **to leave sb in the ~** zostawiać (zostawić *perf*) kogoś na lodzie (*inf*); **he fell with a ~** zatoczywszy się, upadł
**lure** [luə^r] *n* powab *m* ▷ *vt* wabić (zwabić *perf*)
**lurid** [ˈluərɪd] *adj* (*violent, graphic*) brutalny, drastyczny; (*brightly coloured*) krzykliwy
**lurk** [lə:k] *vi* czaić się (zaczaić się *perf*)
**luscious** [ˈlʌʃəs] *adj* (*person*) pociągający; (*food*) soczysty
**lush** [lʌʃ] *adj* (*vegetation*) bujny; (*restaurant*) luksusowy
**lust** [lʌst] (*pej*) *n* (*sexual*) pożądanie *nt*, żądza *f*; (*for money, power*) żądza *f*
▶ **lust after** *vt fus* (*desire sexually*) pożądać *+gen*; (*crave*) pragnąć *+gen*
▶ **lust for** *vt fus* = **lust after**
**lustful** [ˈlʌstful] *adj* pożądliwy
**lustre**, (*US*) **luster** [ˈlʌstə^r] *n* połysk *m*
**lusty** [ˈlʌstɪ] *adj* krzepki
**lute** [lu:t] *n* lutnia *f*
**Luxembourg** [ˈlʌksəmbə:g] *n* Luksemburg *m*
**luxuriant** [lʌgˈzjuərɪənt] *adj* bujny
**luxuriate** [lʌgˈzjuərɪeɪt] *vi*: **to ~ in sth** rozkoszować się czymś
**luxurious** [lʌgˈzjuərɪəs] *adj* luksusowy
**luxury** [ˈlʌkʃərɪ] *n* luksus *m* ▷ *cpd* luksusowy
**LV** *n abbr* = **luncheon voucher**
**LW** (*Radio*) *abbr* (= *long wave*) f.dł.
**lying** [ˈlaɪɪŋ] *n* kłamstwo *nt* ▷ *adj* kłamliwy
**lynch** [lɪntʃ] *vt* linczować (zlinczować *perf*)
**lynx** [lɪŋks] *n* ryś *m*
**lyric** [ˈlɪrɪk] *adj* liryczny
**lyrical** [ˈlɪrɪkl] *adj* liryczny; (*fig*): **to grow/wax ~ about** rozpływać się nad *+instr*
**lyricism** [ˈlɪrɪsɪzəm] *n* liryzm *m*
**lyrics** [ˈlɪrɪks] *npl* (*of song*) słowa *pl*, tekst *m*

# Mm

**M¹, m** [ɛm] *n* (*letter*) M *nt*, m *nt*; **M for Mary,** (*US*) **M for Mike** ≈ M jak Maria
**M²** *n abbr* (*Brit*: = *motorway*): **the M8** autostrada *f* M8 ▷ *abbr* = **medium**
**m.** *abbr* (= *metre*) m; = **mile**; (= *million*) mln
**MA** *n abbr* (= *Master of Arts*) *stopień naukowy*, ≈ mgr; (= *military academy*) akademia *f* wojskowa ▷ *abbr* (*US*: *Post*) = **Massachusetts**
**mac** [mæk] (*Brit*) *n* płaszcz *m* nieprzemakalny
**macabre** [mə'kɑːbrə] *adj* makabryczny
**macaroni** [mækə'rəunɪ] *n* makaron *m* rurki
**macaroon** [mækə'ruːn] *n* makaronik *m*
**mace** [meɪs] *n* (*weapon*) maczuga *f*; (*ceremonial*) buława *f*; (*spice*) gałka *f* muszkatołowa
**machinations** [mækɪ'neɪʃənz] *npl* knowania *pl*, machinacje *pl*
**machine** [mə'ʃiːn] *n* maszyna *f*; (*fig*) machina *f* ▷ *vt* (*Tech*) obrabiać (obrobić *perf*); (*dress etc*) szyć (uszyć *perf*) na maszynie
**machine code** *n* (*Comput*) kod *m* maszynowy
**machine gun** *n* karabin *m* maszynowy
**machine language** *n* (*Comput*) język *m* maszynowy
**machine-readable** [mə'ʃiːnriːdəbl] *adj* (*Comput*) nadający się do przetwarzania automatycznego
**machinery** [mə'ʃiːnərɪ] *n* (*equipment*) maszyny *pl*; (*fig*: *of government etc*) mechanizm *m* (funkcjonowania *+gen*)
**machine shop** *n* warsztat *m* mechaniczny
**machine tool** *n* obrabiarka *f*
**machine washable** *adj* nadający się do prania w pralce
**machinist** [mə'ʃiːnɪst] *n* operator *m* (*maszyny*)
**macho** ['mætʃəu] *adj*: **~ man** macho *m inv*
**mackerel** ['mækrl] *n inv* makrela *f*
**mackintosh** ['mækɪntɔʃ] (*Brit*) *n* płaszcz *m* nieprzemakalny
**macro...** ['mækrəu] *pref* makro...
**macro-economics** ['mækrəuiːkə'nɔmɪks] *npl* makroekonomia *f*
**mad** [mæd] *adj* (*insane*) szalony, obłąkany; (*foolish*) szalony, pomylony; (*angry*) wściekły; **to be mad about** szaleć za *+instr*; **to go mad** (*insane*) szaleć (oszaleć *perf*), wariować (zwariować *perf*); (*angry*) wściekać się (wściec się *perf*)
**madam** ['mædəm] *n* (*form of address*) proszę pani (*voc*); **yes, ~** tak, proszę pani; **M~ Chairman** pani przewodnicząca; **Dear M~,** Szanowna Pani!
**madden** ['mædn] *vt* rozwścieczać (rozwścieczyć *perf*)
**maddening** ['mædnɪŋ] *adj* nieznośny, doprowadzający do szału
**made** [meɪd] *pt, pp of* **make**
**Madeira** [mə'dɪərə] *n* (*Geog*) Madera *f*; (*wine*) madera *f*
**made-to-measure** ['meɪdtə'mɛʒəʳ] (*Brit*) *adj* szyty na miarę
**madly** ['mædlɪ] *adv* (*frantically*) jak szalony; (*very*) szalenie; **~ in love** zakochany do szaleństwa
**madman** ['mædmən] (*irreg*: *like* **man**) *n* szaleniec *m*
**madness** ['mædnɪs] *n* (*insanity*) szaleństwo *nt*, obłęd *m*; (*foolishness*) szaleństwo *nt*
**Madrid** [mə'drɪd] *n* Madryt *m*
**Mafia** ['mæfɪə] *n*: **the ~** mafia *f*
**mag** [mæg] (*Brit*: *inf*) *n abbr* = **magazine**
**magazine** [mægə'ziːn] *n* (*Press*) (czaso)pismo *nt*; (*Radio, TV*) magazyn *m*; (*of firearm*) magazynek *m*; (*Mil*) skład *m*
**maggot** ['mægət] *n* larwa *f* muchy
**magic** ['mædʒɪk] *n* (*supernatural power*) magia *f*, czary *pl*; (*conjuring*) sztu(cz)ki *pl* magiczne ▷ *adj* (*powers, ritual, formula*) magiczny; (*fig*: *place, moment, experience*) cudowny
**magical** ['mædʒɪkl] *adj* (*powers, ritual*) magiczny; (*experience, evening*) cudowny
**magician** [mə'dʒɪʃən] *n* (*wizard*) czarodziej *m*, czarnoksiężnik *m*; (*conjurer*) magik *m*, sztukmistrz *m*
**magistrate** ['mædʒɪstreɪt] *n* (*Jur*) sędzia *m* pokoju
**magnanimous** [mæg'nænɪməs] *adj* wspaniałomyślny
**magnate** ['mægneɪt] *n* magnat *m*
**magnesium** [mæg'niːzɪəm] *n* magnez *m*

**magnet** ['mægnɪt] *n* magnes *m*
**magnetic** [mæg'nɛtɪk] *adj (Phys)* magnetyczny; *(personality, appeal)* zniewalający
**magnetic disk** *n* dysk *m* magnetyczny
**magnetic tape** *n* taśma *f* magnetyczna
**magnetism** ['mægnɪtɪzəm] *n* magnetyzm *m*
**magnification** [mægnɪfɪ'keɪʃən] *n* powiększenie *nt*
**magnificence** [mæg'nɪfɪsns] *n* wspaniałość *f*
**magnificent** [mæg'nɪfɪsnt] *adj* wspaniały
**magnify** ['mægnɪfaɪ] *vt (enlarge)* powiększać (powiększyć *perf*); *(increase: sound)* wzmacniać (wzmocnić *perf*); *(fig: exaggerate)* wyolbrzymiać (wyolbrzymić *perf*)
**magnifying glass** ['mægnɪfaɪɪŋ-] *n* szkło *nt* powiększające.
**magnitude** ['mægnɪtju:d] *n (size)* rozmiary *pl*; *(importance)* waga *f*
**magnolia** [mæg'nəulɪə] *n* magnolia *f*
**magpie** ['mægpaɪ] *n* sroka *f*
**mahogany** [mə'hɔgənɪ] *n* mahoń *m* ▷ *cpd* mahoniowy
**maid** [meɪd] *n* pokojówka *f*; **old ~** *(pej)* stara panna
**maiden** ['meɪdn] *n (literary)* panna *f*, dziewica *f (old, literary)* ▷ *adj (aunt)* niezamężny; *(voyage)* dziewiczy; *(speech)* pierwszy
**maiden name** *n* nazwisko *nt* panieńskie
**mail** [meɪl] *n* poczta *f* ▷ *vt* wysyłać (wysłać *perf*) (pocztą); **by ~** pocztą
**mailbox** ['meɪlbɔks] *n (US)* skrzynka *f* pocztowa *(przed domem)*; *(Comput)* skrzynka *f*
**mailing list** ['meɪlɪŋ-] *n* lista *f* adresowa
**mailman** ['meɪlmæn] *(US) (irreg: like* **man***) n* listonosz *m*
**mail order** *n* sprzedaż *f* wysyłkowa ▷ *cpd*: **mail-order** wysyłkowy
**mailshot** ['meɪlʃɔt] *(Brit) n* przesyłki *pl* reklamowe
**mail train** *n* pociąg *m* pocztowy
**mail truck** *(US) n* furgonetka *f* pocztowa
**mail van** *(Brit) n (Aut)* furgonetka *f* pocztowa; *(Rail)* wagon *m* pocztowy
**maim** [meɪm] *vt* okaleczać (okaleczyć *perf*)
**main** [meɪn] *adj* główny ▷ *n*: **gas/water ~** magistrala *f* gazowa/wodna; **the mains** *npl (Elec etc)* sieć *f*; **in the ~** na ogół
**main course** *n* danie *nt* główne
**mainframe** ['meɪnfreɪm] *n* komputer *m* dużej mocy
**mainland** ['meɪnlənd] *n*: **the ~** ląd *m* stały
**mainline** ['meɪnlaɪn] *adj* położony przy magistrali (kolejowej) *post* ▷ *vt, vi (drugs slang)* wstrzykiwać (wstrzyknąć *perf*) sobie
**main line** *n* magistrala *f* (kolejowa)
**mainly** ['meɪnlɪ] *adv* głównie
**main road** *n* droga *f* główna
**mainstay** ['meɪnsteɪ] *n* podstawa *f*
**mainstream** ['meɪnstri:m] *n* główny *or* dominujący nurt *m* ▷ *adj*: **~ cinema** *etc* główny nurt *m* kinematografii *etc*
**maintain** [meɪn'teɪn] *vt* utrzymywać (utrzymać *perf*); *(friendship, good relations)* podtrzymywać (podtrzymać *perf*); **to ~ one's innocence** zapewniać o swej niewinności; **to ~ that ...** utrzymywać, że ...
**maintenance** ['meɪntənəns] *n* utrzymanie *nt*; *(Jur)* alimenty *pl*
**maintenance contract** *n* umowa *f* serwisowa
**maintenance order** *n (Jur)* nakaz *m* alimentacji
**maisonette** [meɪzə'nɛt] *(Brit) n* mieszkanie *nt* dwupoziomowe
**maize** [meɪz] *n* kukurydza *f*
**Maj.** *(Mil) abbr (= major)* mjr.
**majestic** [mə'dʒɛstɪk] *adj* majestatyczny
**majesty** ['mædʒɪstɪ] *n (splendour)* majestatyczność *f*; **Your M~** *(form of address)* Wasza Królewska Mość
**major** ['meɪdʒə<sup>r</sup>] *n (Mil)* major *m* ▷ *adj* ważny, znaczący; *(Mus)* dur *post* ▷ *vi (US: Scol)*: **to ~ in** studiować *+acc (jako główny kierunek)*; **a ~ operation** *(Med)* duża *or* rozległa operacja; *(fig)* poważna operacja
**Majorca** [mə'jɔ:kə] *n* Majorka *f*
**major general** *n (Brit)* ≈ generał *m* brygady; *(US)* ≈ generał *m* dywizji
**majority** [mə'dʒɔrɪtɪ] *n* większość *f* ▷ *cpd*: **~ verdict** orzeczenie *nt* podjęte większością głosów; **~ (share)holding** kontrolny pakiet akcji
**make** [meɪk] *(pt, pp* **made***) vt (object, mistake, remark)* robić (zrobić *perf*); *(clothes)* szyć (uszyć *perf*); *(cake)* piec (upiec *perf*); *(noise)* robić, narobić *(perf) +gen*; *(speech)* wygłaszać (wygłosić *perf*); *(goods)* produkować (wyprodukować *perf*), wytwarzać; *(money)* zarabiać (zarobić *perf*); *(cause to be)*: **to ~ sb sad/happy** zasmucać (zasmucić *perf*)/uszczęśliwiać (uszczęśliwić *perf*) kogoś; *(force)*: **to ~ sb do sth** zmuszać (zmusić *perf*) kogoś do (z)robienia czegoś; *(equal)*: **2 and 2 ~ 4** dwa i dwa jest cztery ▷ *n* marka *f*; **to ~ the bed** słać (posłać *perf*) łóżko; **to ~ a fool of sb** ośmieszać (ośmieszyć *perf*) kogoś; **to ~ a profit** osiągać (osiągnąć *perf*) zysk, zarabiać (zarobić *perf*); **to ~ a loss** *(business)* przynosić (przynieść *perf*) straty; *(company)* ponosić (ponieść *perf*) straty; **may I ~ a suggestion?** czy mogę coś zaproponować?; **he made it** *(arrived)* dotarł na miejsce; *(arrived in time)* zdążył; *(succeeded)* udało mu się; **what time do you ~ it?** którą masz godzinę?; **to ~ good** *vt (threat, promise)* spełniać (spełnić *perf*);

(*damage*) naprawiać (naprawić *perf*); (*loss*) nadrabiać (nadrobić *perf*); **he has made good** powiodło mu się, odniósł sukces; **to ~ do with** zadowalać się (zadowolić się *perf*) *+instr*

▸ **make for** *vt fus* kierować się (skierować się *perf*) do *+gen or* ku *+dat*

▸ **make off** *vi* umykać (umknąć *perf*)

▸ **make out** *vt* (*decipher*) odczytać (*perf*); (*understand*) zorientować się (*perf*) w *+loc*; (*see*) dostrzegać (dostrzec *perf*); (*write: cheque*) wypisywać (wypisać *perf*); (*claim, imply*) twierdzić; (*pretend*) udawać; **to ~ out a case for sth** znajdować (znaleźć *perf*) uzasadnienie dla czegoś

▸ **make over** *vt*: **to ~ over (to)** przekazywać (przekazać *perf*) (prawnie) (*+dat*)

▸ **make up** *vt* (*constitute*) stanowić; (*invent*) wymyślać (wymyślić *perf*); (*prepare*) przygotowywać (przygotować *perf*) ▹ *vi* (*after quarrel*) godzić się (pogodzić się *perf*); (*with cosmetics*) robić (zrobić *perf*) (sobie) makijaż, malować się (umalować się *perf*); **to ~ up one's mind** zdecydować się (*perf*); **to be made up of** składać się z *+gen*

▸ **make up for** *vt fus* nadrabiać (nadrobić *perf*) *+acc*

**make-believe** ['meɪkbɪliːv] *n* pozory *pl*; **a world of ~** świat iluzji *or* fantazji; **it's just ~** to zwykła fikcja

**maker** ['meɪkəʳ] *n* producent *m*

**makeshift** ['meɪkʃɪft] *adj* prowizoryczny

**make-up** ['meɪkʌp] *n* (*cosmetics*) kosmetyki *pl* upiększające; (*on sb*) makijaż *m*; (*also*: **stage make-up**) charakteryzacja *f*

**make-up bag** *n* kosmetyczka *f*

**make-up remover** *n* płyn *m* do demakijażu

**making** ['meɪkɪŋ] *n* (*fig*): **he's a linguist in the ~** będzie z niego językoznawca; **to have the ~s of** mieć (wszelkie) zadatki na *+acc*

**maladjusted** [mælə'dʒʌstɪd] *adj* (społecznie) nieprzystosowany

**maladroit** [mælə'drɔɪt] *adj* niezręczny

**malaise** [mæ'leɪz] *n* (*Med*) (ogólne) złe samopoczucie *nt*; (*fig*) niemoc *f*, apatia *f*

**malaria** [mə'lɛərɪə] *n* malaria *f*

**Malawi** [mə'lɑːwɪ] *n* Malawi *nt inv*

**Malay** [mə'leɪ] *adj* malajski ▹ *n* Malaj(ka) *m(f)*; (*Ling*) (język *m*) malajski

**Malaya** [mə'leɪə] *n* Malaje *pl*

**Malayan** [mə'leɪən] *adj, n* = **Malay**

**Malaysia** [mə'leɪzɪə] *n* Malezja *f*

**Malaysian** [mə'leɪzɪən] *adj* malezyjski ▹ *n* Malezyjczyk(-jka) *m(f)*

**Maldives** ['mɔːldaɪvz] *npl*: **the ~** Malediwy *pl*

**male** [meɪl] *n* (*Bio*) samiec *m*; (*man*) mężczyzna *m* ▹ *adj* (*sex, attitude*) męski; (*child*) płci męskiej *post*; (*Elec*): **~ plug** wtyczka *f* z bolcem *or* męska; **~ and female students** studenci obojga płci, studenci i studentki

**male chauvinist** *n* męski szowinista *m*

**male nurse** *n* pielęgniarz *m*

**malevolence** [mə'lɛvələns] *n* wrogość *f*

**malevolent** [mə'lɛvələnt] *adj* wrogi

**malfunction** [mæl'fʌŋkʃən] *n* (*of computer, machine*) niesprawność ▹ *vi* nie działać

**malice** ['mælɪs] *n* złośliwość *f*

**malicious** [mə'lɪʃəs] *adj* (*person, gossip, accusation*) złośliwy; **~ intent** (*Jur*) zły zamiar

**malign** [mə'laɪn] *vt* rzucać oszczerstwa na *+acc* ▹ *adj* (*influence*) szkodliwy, zły; (*interpretation*) wrogi, pełen złej woli

**malignant** [mə'lɪgnənt] *adj* (*tumour, growth*) złośliwy; (*behaviour, intention*) wrogi

**malingerer** [mə'lɪŋgərəʳ] *n* symulant(ka) *m(f)*

**mall** [mɔːl] *n* (*also*: **shopping mall**) centrum *nt* handlowe

**malleable** ['mælɪəbl] *adj* (*substance*) plastyczny; (*person*) podatny na wpływy

**mallet** ['mælɪt] *n* drewniany młotek *m*, pobijak *m*

**malnutrition** [mælnjuː'trɪʃən] *n* (*eating too little*) niedożywienie *nt*; (*eating wrong food*) niewłaściwe *or* złe odżywianie *nt*

**malpractice** [mæl'præktɪs] *n* postępowanie *nt* niezgodne z etyką zawodową

**malt** [mɔːlt] *n* (*grain*) słód *m*; (*also*: **malt whisky**) whisky *f inv* słodowa

**Malta** ['mɔːltə] *n* Malta *f*

**Maltese** [mɔːl'tiːz] *adj* maltański ▹ *n inv* (*person*) Maltańczyk(-anka) *m(f)*; (*Ling*) (język *m*) maltański

**maltreat** [mæl'triːt] *vt* maltretować

**mammal** ['mæml] *n* ssak *m*

**mammoth** ['mæməθ] *n* mamut *m* ▹ *adj* gigantyczny

**man** [mæn] (*pl* **men**) *n* (*male*) mężczyzna *m*; (*human being, mankind*) człowiek *m*; (*Chess*) pionek *m* ▹ *vt* (*post*) obsadzać (obsadzić *perf*); (*machine*) obsługiwać; **man and wife** mąż i żona

**manage** ['mænɪdʒ] *vi* (*get by financially*) dawać (dać *perf*) sobie radę; (*succeed*): **he ~d to find her** udało mu się ją odnaleźć ▹ *vt* (*business, organization*) zarządzać *+instr*; (*object, device, person*) radzić (poradzić *perf*) sobie z *+instr*; **to ~ without sb/sth** radzić (poradzić *perf*) sobie *or* dawać (dać *perf*) sobie radę bez kogoś/czegoś

**manageable** ['mænɪdʒəbl] *adj* (*task*) wykonalny; **documents are ~ in small numbers** z dokumentami w małych ilościach można sobie poradzić

**management** ['mænɪdʒmənt] *n* (*control, organization*) zarządzanie *nt*; (*persons*) zarząd *m*, dyrekcja *f*; **"under new ~"** *napis informujący o zmianie dyrekcji*

**management accounting** *n* księgowość *f*
**management consultant** *n* konsultant *m* do spraw zarządzania
**manager** ['mænɪdʒəʳ] *n* (*of large business, institution, department*) dyrektor *m*; (*of smaller business, unit, institution*) kierownik *m*; (*of pop star, sports team*) menażer *m*; **sales ~** dyrektor handlowy; **an educated class of ~s and bureaucrats** wykształcona klasa menedżerów i biurokratów
**manageress** [mænɪdʒə'rɛs] *n* kierowniczka *f*
**managerial** [mænɪ'dʒɪərɪəl] *adj* (*role, post, staff*) kierowniczy; (*skills*) menedżerski; (*decisions*) dotyczący zarządzania
**managing director** ['mænɪdʒɪŋ-] *n* dyrektor *m* (główny *or* naczelny)
**Mancunian** [mæŋ'kju:nɪən] *n* mieszkaniec(-nka) *m(f)* Manchesteru
**mandarin** ['mændərɪn] *n* (*also*: **mandarin orange**) mandarynka *f*; (*official*) szycha *f* (*inf*); (*: Chinese*) mandaryn *m*
**mandate** ['mændeɪt] *n* (*Pol*) mandat *m*; (*task*) zadanie *nt*
**mandatory** ['mændətərɪ] *adj* obowiązkowy
**mandolin(e)** ['mændəlɪn] *n* mandolina *f*
**mane** [meɪn] *n* grzywa *f*
**maneuver** [mə'nu:vəʳ] (*US*) = **manoeuvre**
**manfully** ['mænfəlɪ] *adv* mężnie
**manganese** [mæŋgə'ni:z] *n* mangan *m*
**mangle** ['mæŋgl] *vt* zniekształcać (zniekształcić *perf*) ▷ *n* magiel *m* (*przyrząd*)
**mango** ['mæŋgəu] (*pl* **~es**) *n* mango *nt inv*
**mangrove** ['mæŋgrəuv] *n* namorzyn *m*, mangrowe *nt inv*
**mangy** ['meɪndʒɪ] *adj* wyliniały
**manhandle** ['mænhændl] *vt* (*mistreat*) poniewierać *+instr*; (*move by hand*) przenosić (przenieść *perf*)
**manhole** ['mænhəul] *n* właz *m* (kanalizacyjny)
**manhood** ['mænhud] *n* (*age*) wiek *m* męski (*fml*); (*state*) męskość *f*; **in his early ~** we wczesnej młodości
**man-hour** ['mænauəʳ] *n* roboczogodzina *f*
**manhunt** ['mænhʌnt] *n* obława *f*
**mania** ['meɪnɪə] *n* mania *f*
**maniac** ['meɪnɪæk] *n* (*lunatic*) maniak *m*, szaleniec *m*; (*fig*) maniak(-aczka) *m(f)*
**manic** ['mænɪk] *adj* szaleńczy
**manic-depressive** ['mænɪkdɪ'prɛsɪv] *n* chory(-ra) *m(f)* z zespołem maniakalno-depresyjnym ▷ *adj* maniakalno-depresyjny
**manicure** ['mænɪkjuəʳ] *n* manicure *m* ▷ *vt* robić (zrobić *perf*) manicure *+dat*
**manicure set** *n* zestaw *m* (przyborów) do manicure'u
**manifest** ['mænɪfɛst] *vt* manifestować (zamanifestować *perf*) ▷ *adj* oczywisty, wyraźny ▷ *n* (*Aviat, Naut*) manifest *m*, wykaz *m* ładunków
**manifestation** [mænɪfɛs'teɪʃən] *n* przejaw *m*, oznaka *f*
**manifesto** [mænɪ'fɛstəu] *n* manifest *m*
**manifold** ['mænɪfəuld] *adj* różnoraki, różnorodny ▷ *n*: **exhaust ~** rura *f* wydechowa
**Manila** [mə'nɪlə] *n* Manila *f*
**manila** [mə'nɪlə] *adj*: **~ envelope** szara koperta *f*
**manipulate** [mə'nɪpjuleɪt] *vt* manipulować *+instr*
**manipulation** [mənɪpju'leɪʃən] *n* manipulacja *f*, manipulowanie *nt*
**mankind** [mæn'kaɪnd] *n* ludzkość *f*
**manliness** ['mænlɪnɪs] *n* męskość *f*
**manly** ['mænlɪ] *adj* męski
**man-made** ['mæn'meɪd] *adj* sztuczny
**manna** ['mænə] *n* manna *f*
**mannequin** ['mænɪkɪn] *n* (*dummy*) manekin *m*; (*old: fashion model*) model(ka) *m(f)*
**manner** ['mænəʳ] *n* (*way*) sposób *m*; (*behaviour*) zachowanie *nt*; (*type, sort*): **all ~ of things/ people** wszelkiego rodzaju rzeczy/ludzie; **manners** *npl* maniery *pl*
**mannerism** ['mænərɪzəm] *n* maniera *f*
**mannerly** ['mænəlɪ] *adj* dobrze ułożony *or* wychowany
**manoeuvrable**, (*US*) **maneuverable** [mə'nu:vrəbl] *adj* ruchomy
**manoeuvre**, (*US*) **maneuver** [mə'nu:vəʳ] *vt* (*car etc*) manewrować (wymanewrować *perf*) *+instr* ▷ *n* (*fig*) manewr *m*; **manoeuvres** *npl* manewry *pl*; **to ~ sth into** ulokować (*perf*) coś w *+loc*; **to ~ sth out of** wydostać (*perf*) *or* wydobyć (*perf*) coś z *+gen*; **to ~ sb into doing sth** pokierować (*perf*) kimś tak, żeby coś zrobił
**manor** ['mænəʳ] *n* (*also*: **manor house**) rezydencja *f* ziemska, dwór *m*
**manpower** ['mænpauəʳ] *n* siła *f* robocza
**Manpower Services Commission** (*Brit*) *n* *urząd d/s tworzenia nowych miejsc pracy, pośrednictwa i kształcenia zawodowego*
**manservant** ['mænsə:vənt] (*pl* **menservants**) *n* służący *m*
**mansion** ['mænʃən] *n* rezydencja *f*
**manslaughter** ['mænslɔ:təʳ] (*Jur*) *n* nieumyślne spowodowanie *nt* śmierci
**mantelpiece** ['mæntlpi:s] *n* gzyms *m* kominka
**mantle** ['mæntl] *n* (*layer*) powłoka *f*; (*garment*) opończa *f*; (*fig*) obowiązki *pl*
**man-to-man** ['mæntə'mæn] *adj* otwarty, szczery ▷ *adv* otwarcie, szczerze
**mantra** ['mæntrə] *n* mantra *f*

**manual** ['mænjuəl] *adj* (*work, worker*) fizyczny; (*controls*) ręczny ▷ *n* podręcznik *m*
**manufacture** [mænju'fæktʃəʳ] *vt* produkować (wyprodukować *perf*) ▷ *n* produkcja *f*
**manufactured goods** *npl* wyroby *pl* gotowe, produkty *pl*
**manufacturer** [mænju'fæktʃərəʳ] *n* wytwórca *m*, producent *m*
**manufacturing** [mænju'fæktʃərɪŋ] *n* wytwarzanie *nt*, produkcja *f* (przemysłowa)
**manure** [mə'njuəʳ] *n* nawóz *m* naturalny, obornik *m*
**manuscript** ['mænjuskrɪpt] *n* rękopis *m*; (*ancient*) manuskrypt *m*
**many** ['mɛnɪ] *adj* wiele (*+gen nvir pl*), wielu (*+gen vir pl*), dużo (*+gen pl*) ▷ *pron* wiele *nvir*, wielu *vir*; **a great ~ men/women** bardzo wielu mężczyzn/wiele kobiet; **how ~?** ile?; **too ~ difficulties** zbyt wiele trudności; **twice as ~** dwa razy tyle; **~ a time** niejeden raz
**map** [mæp] *n* mapa *f* ▷ *vt* sporządzać (sporządzić *perf*) mapę *+gen*
▸ **map out** *vt* (*plan, task*) nakreślać (nakreślić *perf*); (*career, holiday*) planować (zaplanować *perf*)
**maple** ['meɪpl] *n* klon *m*
**mar** [mɑːʳ] *vt* (*appearance*) szpecić (zeszpecić *perf or* oszpecić *perf*); (*day, event*) psuć (zepsuć *perf*)
**Mar.** *abbr* (= *March*) marz.
**marathon** ['mærəθən] *n* maraton *m* ▷ *adj* długi i wyczerpujący
**marathon runner** *n* maratończyk *m*
**marauder** [mə'rɔːdəʳ] *n* (*robber*) rabuś *m*; (*killer*) bandyta *m*; (*animal*) drapieżnik *m*
**marble** ['mɑːbl] *n* (*stone*) marmur *m*; (*toy*) kulka *f* (*do gry*)
**marbles** ['mɑːblz] *n* (*game*) kulki *pl*
**March** [mɑːtʃ] *n* marzec *m*; *see also* **July**
**march** [mɑːtʃ] *vi* (*soldiers, protesters*) maszerować (przemaszerować *perf*); (*walk briskly*) maszerować (pomaszerować *perf*) ▷ *n* marsz *m*; **to ~ out of** wymaszerowywać (wymaszerować *perf*) z *+gen*; **to ~ into** wmaszerowywać (wmaszerować *perf*) do *+gen*
**marcher** ['mɑːtʃəʳ] *n* maszerujący(-ca) *m(f)*
**marching orders** ['mɑːtʃɪŋ-] *npl*: **to give sb his ~** (*fig*) odprawić (*perf*) kogoś
**march past** *n* defilada *f*
**mare** [mɛəʳ] *n* klacz *f*
**margarine** [mɑːdʒə'riːn] *n* margaryna *f*
**marge** [mɑːdʒ] (*Brit: inf*) *n abbr* = **margarine**
**margin** ['mɑːdʒɪn] *n* (*on page, of society, for error, safety*) margines *m*; (*of votes*) różnica *f*; (*of wood etc*) skraj *m*; (*Comm*) marża *f*
**marginal** ['mɑːdʒɪnl] *adj* marginesowy, marginalny
**marginally** ['mɑːdʒɪnəlɪ] *adv* (*different*) (tylko) nieznacznie; (*kinder etc*) (tylko) trochę
**marginal (seat)** (*Pol*) *n mandat wyborczy, o którym decyduje minimalna większość głosów*
**marigold** ['mærɪgəuld] *n* nagietek *m*
**marijuana** [mærɪ'wɑːnə] *n* marihuana *f*
**marina** [mə'riːnə] *n* przystań *f*
**marinade** [*n* mærɪ'neɪd, *vb* 'mærɪneɪd] *n* zalewa *f* octowa, marynata *f* ▷ *vt* = **marinate**
**marinate** ['mærɪneɪt] *vt* marynować (zamarynować *perf*)
**marine** [mə'riːn] *adj* (*life, plant*) morski; (*engineering*) okrętowy ▷ *n* (*Brit*) żołnierz *m* służący w marynarce; (*also*: **US marine**) żołnierz *m* piechoty morskiej
**marine insurance** *n* ubezpieczenie *nt* morskie
**marital** ['mærɪtl] *adj* małżeński; **~ status** stan cywilny
**maritime** ['mærɪtaɪm] *adj* morski; **~ nation** naród żeglarzy
**marjoram** ['mɑːdʒərəm] *n* majeranek *m*
**mark** [mɑːk] *n* (*sign*) znak *m*; (*: of friendship, respect*) oznaka *f*; (*trace*) ślad *m*; (*stain*) plama *f*; (*point*) punkt *m*; (*level*) poziom *m*; (*Brit: Scol: grade*) stopień *m*, ocena *f*; (*Brit: Tech*) wersja *f*; (*formerly: currency*): **the German M~** marka *f* niemiecka ▷ *vt* (*label*) znakować (oznakować *perf*), oznaczać (oznaczyć *perf*); (*stain*) plamić (poplamić *perf*); (*characterise*) cechować; (*with shoes, tyres*) zostawiać (zostawić *perf*) ślad(y) na *+loc*; (*passage, page in book*) zaznaczać (zaznaczyć *perf*); (*place, time*) wyznaczać (wyznaczyć *perf*); (*event, occasion*) upamiętniać (upamiętnić *perf*); (*Brit: Scol*) oceniać (ocenić *perf*); (*Sport: player*) kryć; **punctuation ~s** znaki przestankowe; **to ~ time** (*Mil*) maszerować w miejscu; (*fig*) dreptać w miejscu; **to be quick off the ~ (in doing sth)** (*fig*) nie zwlekać (ze zrobieniem czegoś); **up to the ~** na poziomie
▸ **mark down** *vt* (*prices*) obniżać (obniżyć *perf*); (*goods*) przeceniać (przecenić *perf*)
▸ **mark off** *vt* odhaczać (odhaczyć *perf*) (*inf*), odfajkowywać (odfajkować *perf*) (*inf*)
▸ **mark out** *vt* (*area, land*) wytyczać (wytyczyć *perf*) granice *+gen*; (*person*) wyróżniać (wyróżnić *perf*)
▸ **mark up** *vt* (*price*) podnosić (podnieść *perf*); (*goods*) podnosić (podnieść *perf*) cenę *+gen*
**marked** [mɑːkt] *adj* wyraźny
**markedly** ['mɑːkɪdlɪ] *adv* wyraźnie
**marker** ['mɑːkəʳ] *n* (*sign*) znak *m*; (*bookmark*) zakładka *f*; (*pen*) zakreślacz *m*
**market** ['mɑːkɪt] *n* (*for vegetables etc*) targ *m*; (*Comm*) rynek *m* (zbytu) ▷ *vt* sprzedawać; (*new product*) wprowadzać (wprowadzić *perf*)

na rynek; **on the ~** dostępny na rynku, w sprzedaży; **on the open ~** na wolnym rynku; **to play the ~** grać na giełdzie
**marketable** ['mɑ:kɪtəbl] *adj* znajdujący zbyt
**market analysis** (*Comm*) *n* analiza *f or* badanie *nt* rynku
**market day** *n* dzień *m* targowy
**market demand** (*Comm*) *n* popyt *m* rynkowy
**market forces** *npl* siły *pl* rynkowe
**market garden** (*Brit*) *n ogród, w którym uprawia się warzywa i owoce na sprzedaż*
**marketing** ['mɑ:kɪtɪŋ] *n* marketing *m*
**marketing manager** *n* dyrektor *m* do spraw marketingu
**marketplace** ['mɑ:kɪtpleɪs] *n* rynek *m*, plac *m* targowy; (*Comm*) rynek *m*
**market price** (*Comm*) *n* cena *f* rynkowa
**market research** *n* badanie *nt* rynku
**market value** *n* wartość *f* rynkowa
**marking** ['mɑ:kɪŋ] *n* (*on animal*) plam(k)a *f*; (*for identification*) oznakowanie *nt*; (*on road*) znakowanie *nt* poziome
**marksman** ['mɑ:ksmən] (*irreg: like* **man**) *n* strzelec *m* wyborowy
**marksmanship** ['mɑ:ksmənʃɪp] *n* umiejętności *pl* strzeleckie
**mark-up** ['mɑ:kʌp] *n* (*margin*) narzut *m*, marża *f*; (*increase*) podwyżka *f*
**marmalade** ['mɑ:məleɪd] *n* marmolada *f*
**maroon** [mə'ru:n] *adj* bordowy ▷ *vt*: **~ed** wyrzucony (na brzeg) (*np. bezludnej wyspy*); (*fig*) pozostawiony sam(emu) sobie
**marquee** [mɑ:'ki:] *n* (duży) namiot *m* (*na festynie itp*)
**marquess** ['mɑ:kwɪs] *n* markiz *m*
**marquis** ['mɑ:kwɪs] *n* = **marquess**
**Marrakech, Marrakesh** [mærə'kɛʃ] *n* Marrakesz *m*
**marriage** ['mærɪdʒ] *n* (*relationship, institution*) małżeństwo *nt*; (*wedding*) ślub *m*
**marriage bureau** *n* biuro *nt* matrymonialne
**marriage certificate** *n* akt *m* małżeństwa *or* ślubu
**marriage guidance**, (*US*) **marriage counseling** *n* poradnictwo *nt* małżeńskie
**married** ['mærɪd] *adj* (*man*) żonaty; (*woman*) zamężny; (*life, love*) małżeński; **to get ~** (*man*) żenić się (ożenić się *perf*); (*woman*) wychodzić (wyjść *perf*) za mąż; (*couple*) pobierać się (pobrać się *perf*), brać (wziąć *perf*) ślub
**marrow** ['mærəu] *n* (*vegetable*) kabaczek *m*; (*also*: **bone marrow**) szpik *m* kostny
**marry** ['mærɪ] *vt* (*man*) żenić się (ożenić się *perf*) z *+instr*; (*woman*) wychodzić (wyjść *perf*) (za mąż) za *+acc*; (*registrar, priest*) udzielać (udzielić *perf*) ślubu *+dat* ▷ *vi* (*couple*) pobierać się (pobrać się *perf*), brać (wziąć *perf*) ślub
**Mars** [mɑ:z] *n* Mars *m*
**Marseilles** [mɑ:'seɪ] *n* Marsylia *f*
**marsh** [mɑ:ʃ] *n* bagna *pl*, moczary *pl*
**marshal** ['mɑ:ʃl] *n* (*Mil*) marszałek *m*; (*US: of police, fire department*) ≈ komendant *m*; (*at sports meeting etc*) organizator *m* ▷ *vt* (*thoughts, soldiers*) zbierać (zebrać *perf*); (*support*) zdobywać (zdobyć *perf*)
**marshalling yard** ['mɑ:ʃlɪŋ-] (*Rail*) *n* stacja *f* rozrządowa
**marshmallow** [mɑ:ʃ'mæləu] *n* (*Bot*) prawoślaz *m* lekarski; (*sweet*) cukierek *m* ślazowy
**marshy** ['mɑ:ʃɪ] *adj* bagnisty, grząski
**marsupial** [mɑ:'su:pɪəl] (*Zool*) *n* torbacz *m*
**martial** ['mɑ:ʃl] *adj* (*music*) wojskowy; (*behaviour*) żołnierski
**martial arts** *npl* (wschodnie) sztuki *pl* walki
**martial law** *n* stan *m* wojenny
**Martian** ['mɑ:ʃən] *n* Marsjanin(-anka) *m(f)*
**martin** ['mɑ:tɪn] *n* (*also*: **house martin**) jaskółka *f* (oknówka)
**martyr** ['mɑ:tə^r] *n* męczennik(-ica) *m(f)* ▷ *vt* męczyć, zamęczać (zamęczyć *perf*)
**martyrdom** ['mɑ:tədəm] *n* męczeństwo *nt*
**marvel** ['mɑ:vl] *n* cud *m* ▷ *vi*: **to ~ (at)** (*in admiration*) zachwycać się (*+instr*); (*in surprise*) zdumiewać się (*+instr*)
**marvellous** ['mɑ:vləs], (*US*) **marvelous** *adj* cudowny
**Marxism** ['mɑ:ksɪzəm] *n* marksizm *m*
**Marxist** ['mɑ:ksɪst] *adj* marksistowski ▷ *n* marksista(-tka) *m(f)*
**marzipan** ['mɑ:zɪpæn] *n* marcepan *m*
**mascara** [mæs'kɑ:rə] *n* tusz *m* do rzęs
**mascot** ['mæskət] *n* maskotka *f*
**masculine** ['mæskjulɪn] *adj* (*characteristics, pride, gender*) męski; (*noun, pronoun*) rodzaju męskiego *post*; **she looks ~** wygląda jak mężczyzna
**masculinity** [mæskju'lɪnɪtɪ] *n* męskość *f*
**MASH** [mæʃ] (*US*) *n abbr* (= *mobile army surgical hospital*) szpital *m* polowy
**mash** [mæʃ] (*Culin*) *vt* tłuc (utłuc *perf*)
**mashed potatoes** [mæʃt-] *npl* ziemniaki *pl* purée
**mask** [mɑ:sk] *n* maska *f* ▷ *vt* (*face*) zakrywać (zakryć *perf*), zasłaniać (zasłonić *perf*); (*feelings*) maskować (zamaskować *perf*)
**masking tape** ['mɑ:skɪŋ-] *n* taśma *f* maskująca
**masochism** ['mæsəukɪzəm] *n* masochizm *m*
**masochist** ['mæsəukɪst] *n* masochista(-tka) *m(f)*
**mason** ['meɪsn] *n* (*also*: **stone mason**) kamieniarz *m*; (*also*: **freemason**) mason(ka) *m(f)*
**masonic** [mə'sɔnɪk] *adj* masoński

**masonry** ['meɪsnrɪ] *n* konstrukcje *pl* z kamienia
**masquerade** [mæskə'reɪd] *vi*: **to ~ as** udawać *+acc* ▷ *n* maskarada *f*
**mass** [mæs] *n* masa *f*; (*of air*) masy *pl*; (*of land*) połacie *pl*; (*Rel*): **M~** msza *f* ▷ *cpd* masowy ▷ *vi* gromadzić się (zgromadzić się *perf*) masowo *or* licznie; **the masses** *npl* masy *pl*; **to go to M~** iść (pójść *perf*) na mszę; **~es of** (*inf*) (cała) masa *f* *+gen* (*inf*)
**massacre** ['mæsəkə^r] *n* masakra *f* ▷ *vt* urządzać (urządzić *perf*) masakrę *+gen*
**massage** ['mæsɑːʒ] *n* masaż *m* ▷ *vt* masować (wymasować *perf*)
**masseur** [mæ'səː^r] *n* masażysta *m*
**masseuse** [mæ'səːz] *n* masażystka *f*
**massive** ['mæsɪv] *adj* masywny; (*fig*: *changes, increase etc*) ogromny
**mass market** *n* rynek *m* masowego odbiorcy
**mass media** *n inv*: **the ~** mass media *pl*, środki *pl* masowego przekazu
**mass meeting** *n* wiec *m*
**mass-produce** ['mæsprə'djuːs] *vt* produkować na skalę masową
**mass-production** ['mæsprə'dʌkʃən] *n* produkcja *f* masowa
**mast** [mɑːst] *n* maszt *m*
**master** ['mɑːstə^r] *n* (*of servant, animal, situation*) pan *m*; (*secondary school teacher*) ≈ profesor *m*; (*title for boys*): **M~ X** panicz *m* X; (*artist, craftsman*) mistrz *m* ▷ *cpd*: **~ carpenter/builder** mistrz *m* stolarski/murarski ▷ *vt* (*overcome*) przezwyciężać (przezwyciężyć *perf*); (*learn, understand*) opanowywać (opanować *perf*); **M~'s degree** tytuł magistra
**master disk** (*Comput*) *n* dysk *m* główny
**masterful** ['mɑːstəful] *adj* władczy
**master key** *n* klucz *m* uniwersalny
**masterly** ['mɑːstəlɪ] *adj* mistrzowski
**mastermind** ['mɑːstəmaɪnd] *n* mózg *m* (*fig*) ▷ *vt* sterować *+instr*; (*robbery etc*) zaplanować (*perf*)
**Master of Arts** *n* (*degree*) ≈ stopień *m* magistra (nauk humanistycznych); (*person*) ≈ magister *m* (nauk humanistycznych)
**Master of Ceremonies** *n* mistrz *m* ceremonii
**Master of Science** *n* (*degree*) ≈ tytuł *m* magistra (nauk ścisłych lub przyrodniczych); (*person*) ≈ magister *m* (nauk ścisłych lub przyrodniczych)
**masterpiece** ['mɑːstəpiːs] *n* arcydzieło *nt*
**master plan** *n* wielki plan *m*
**masterstroke** ['mɑːstəstrəuk] *n* majsterszyk *m*
**mastery** ['mɑːstərɪ] *n*: **~ of** biegłe opanowanie *nt* *+gen*
**mastiff** ['mæstɪf] *n* mastif *m*
**masturbate** ['mæstəbeɪt] *vi* onanizować się
**masturbation** [mæstə'beɪʃən] *n* onanizm *m*, masturbacja *f*
**mat** [mæt] *n* (*on floor*) dywanik *m*; (*also*: **doormat**) wycieraczka *f*; (*also*: **table mat**) podkładka *f* (*pod nakrycie*) ▷ *adj* = **matt**
**match** [mætʃ] *n* (*game*) mecz *m*; (*for lighting fire*) zapałka *f*; (*equivalent*): **to be a good** *etc* **~** dobrze *etc* pasować ▷ *vt* (*go well with*) pasować do *+gen*; (*equal*) dorównywać (dorównać *perf*) *+dat*; (*correspond to*) odpowiadać *+dat*; (*also*: **match up**) dopasowywać (dopasować *perf*) (do siebie) ▷ *vi* pasować (do siebie); **they are a good ~** tworzą dobraną parę; **to be no ~ for** nie móc się równać z *+instr*; **she had on a yellow dress with yellow shoes to ~** miała na sobie żółtą sukienkę i buty pod kolor
▶ **match up** *vi* pasować (do siebie)
**matchbox** ['mætʃbɔks] *n* pudełko *nt* od zapałek
**matching** ['mætʃɪŋ] *adj* dobrze dobrany; (*in colour*) pod kolor *post*
**matchless** ['mætʃlɪs] *adj* niezrównany
**mate** [meɪt] *n* (*inf*: *friend*) kumpel *m* (*inf*); (*assistant*) pomocnik *m*; (*Naut*) oficer *m* (*na statku handlowym*); (*animal, spouse*) partner(ka) *m(f)*; (*in chess*) mat *m* ▷ *vi* (*animals*) łączyć się *or* kojarzyć się w pary
**material** [mə'tɪərɪəl] *n* materiał *m* ▷ *adj* (*possessions, existence*) materialny; (*evidence*) istotny, mający znaczenie dla sprawy; **materials** *npl* materiały *pl*; **writing ~s** przybory do pisania
**materialistic** [mətɪərɪə'lɪstɪk] *adj* materialistyczny
**materialize** [mə'tɪərɪəlaɪz] *vi* (*event*) zaistnieć (*perf*); (*person*) pojawiać się (pojawić się *perf*); (*hopes, plans*) materializować się (zmaterializować się *perf*)
**maternal** [mə'təːnl] *adj* macierzyński
**maternity** [mə'təːnɪtɪ] *n* macierzyństwo *nt* ▷ *cpd* (*ward etc*) położniczy
**maternity benefit** *n* zasiłek *m* macierzyński
**maternity dress** *n* suknia *f* ciążowa
**maternity hospital** *n* szpital *m* położniczy
**maternity leave** *n* urlop *m* macierzyński
**matey** ['meɪtɪ] (*Brit*: *inf*) *adj* koleżeński, równy (*inf*)
**math** [mæθ] (*US*) *n abbr* = **mathematics**
**mathematical** [mæθə'mætɪkl] *adj* matematyczny
**mathematician** [mæθəmə'tɪʃən] *n* matematyk(-yczka) *m(f)*
**mathematics** [mæθə'mætɪks] *n* matematyka *f*
**maths** [mæθs], (*US*) **math** *n abbr* = **mathematics**
**matinée** ['mætɪneɪ] *n* (*Film*) seans *m* popołudniowy; (*Theat*) spektakl *m* popołudniowy, popołudniówka *f* (*inf*)

m

**mating** ['meɪtɪŋ] *n* łączenie się *nt* w pary, parzenie się *nt*
**mating call** *n* godowe wołanie *nt* samca
**mating season** *n* okres *m* godowy, pora *f* godowa
**matriarchal** [meɪtrɪ'ɑ:kl] *adj* matriarchalny
**matrices** ['meɪtrɪsi:z] *npl of* **matrix**
**matriculation** [mətrɪkju'leɪʃən] *n* immatrykulacja *f*
**matrimonial** [mætrɪ'məunɪəl] *adj* małżeński
**matrimony** ['mætrɪmənɪ] *n* małżeństwo *nt*
**matrix** ['meɪtrɪks] (*pl* **matrices**) *n* (*social, cultural etc*) kontekst *m*; (*Tech*) matryca *f*; (*Math*) macierz *f*
**matron** ['meɪtrən] *n* (*in hospital*) przełożona *f* pielęgniarek; (*in school*) pielęgniarka *f* (szkolna)
**matronly** ['meɪtrənlɪ] *adj* przy kości *post*
**matt** [mæt], **mat** *adj* matowy
**matted** ['mætɪd] *adj* splątany
**matter** ['mætə^r] *n* (*situation, problem*) sprawa *f*; (*Phys*) materia *f*; (*substance*) substancja *f*; (*Med: pus*) ropa *f* ▷ *vi* liczyć się, mieć znaczenie; **matters** *npl* sytuacja *f*; **it doesn't ~** (*is not important, makes no difference*) to nie ma znaczenia; (*never mind*) (nic) nie szkodzi; **what's the ~?** o co chodzi?; **no ~ what** bez względu na to, co się stanie; **that's another ~** to inna sprawa; **as a ~ of course** automatycznie; **as a ~ of fact** właściwie; **it's a ~ of habit** to kwestia przyzwyczajenia; **printed ~** druki; **reading ~** (*Brit*) lektura
**matter-of-fact** ['mætərəv'fækt] *adj* rzeczowy
**matting** ['mætɪŋ] *n* mata *f* (podłogowa)
**mattress** ['mætrɪs] *n* materac *m*
**mature** [mə'tjuə^r] *adj* dojrzały ▷ *vi* dojrzewać (dojrzeć *perf*); **this policy is due to ~ next year** płatności z tytułu tej polisy rozpoczną się w przyszłym roku
**maturity** [mə'tjuərɪtɪ] *n* dojrzałość *f*
**maudlin** ['mɔ:dlɪn] *adj* (*voice*) płaczliwy, rzewny; **to get ~** rozklejać się (rozkleić się *perf*) (*zwłaszcza pod wpływem alkoholu*)
**maul** [mɔ:l] *vt* poturbować (*perf*), pokiereszować (*perf*)
**Mauritania** [mɔ:rɪ'teɪnɪə] *n* Mauretania *f*
**Mauritius** [mə'rɪʃəs] *n* Mauritius *m*
**mausoleum** [mɔ:sə'lɪəm] *n* mauzoleum *nt*
**mauve** [məuv] *adj* jasnofioletowy
**maverick** ['mævrɪk] *n* (*fig*) indywidualista(-tka) *m(f)*
**mawkish** ['mɔ:kɪʃ] *adj* ckliwy, czułostkowy
**max.** *abbr* (= *maximum*) maks.
**maxim** ['mæksɪm] *n* maksyma *f*
**maxima** ['mæksɪmə] *npl of* **maximum**
**maximize** ['mæksɪmaɪz] *vt* maksymalnie zwiększać (zwiększyć *perf*), maksymalizować (zmaksymalizować *perf*)
**maximum** ['mæksɪməm] (*pl* **maxima** *or* **~s**) *adj* maksymalny ▷ *n* maksimum *nt*
**May** [meɪ] *n* maj *m*; *see also* **July**
**may** [meɪ] (*conditional* **might**) *vi* (*indicating possibility, permission*) móc; (*indicating wishes*): **may he justify our hopes** oby spełnił nasze nadzieje; **may I smoke?** czy mogę zapalić?; **he might be there** (on) może tam być; **you might like to try** może chciałbyś spróbować; **you may as well go** (właściwie) możesz iść; **may God bless you!** niech cię Bóg błogosławi!
**maybe** ['meɪbi:] *adv* (być) może
**May Day** *n* 1 Maja
**mayhem** ['meɪhɛm] *n* chaos *m*
**mayonnaise** [meɪə'neɪz] *n* majonez *m*
**mayor** [mɛə^r] *n* burmistrz *m*
**mayoress** ['mɛərɛs] *n* (*also*: **lady mayor**) pani *f* burmistrz; (*wife*) żona *f* burmistrza, burmistrzowa *f*
**maypole** ['meɪpəul] *n* ≈ gaik *m* (*zwyczaj ludowy*)
**maze** [meɪz] *n* labirynt *m*
**MB** *abbr* (*Comput*: = *megabyte*) MB; (*Canada*) = **Manitoba**
**MBA** *n abbr* (= *Master of Business Administration*) *stopień naukowy*, ≈ mgr
**MBBS** (*Brit*) *n abbr* (= *Bachelor of Medicine and Surgery*) *stopień naukowy*
**MBChB** (*Brit*) *n abbr* (= *Bachelor of Medicine and Surgery*) *stopień naukowy*
**MBE** (*Brit*) *n abbr* (= *Member of the Order of the British Empire*) *order brytyjski*
**MC** *n abbr* = **Master of Ceremonies**
**MCAT** (*US*) *n abbr* (= *Medical College Admissions Test*) *egzamin, którego zdanie uprawnia do podjęcia studiów medycznych*
**MCP** (*Brit*: *inf*) *n abbr* = **male chauvinist pig**
**MD** *n abbr* (= *Doctor of Medicine*) *stopień naukowy*, ≈ dr; (*Comm*) = **managing director** ▷ *abbr* (*US*: *Post*) = **Maryland**
**MDT** (*US*) *abbr* = **Mountain Daylight Time**
**ME** *n abbr* (*US*: = *medical examiner*) ekspert *m* medycyny sądowej; (*Med*: = *myalgic encephalomyelitis*) zapalenie *nt* mózgu i rdzenia z mialgią ▷ *abbr* (*US*: *Post*) = **Maine**

 KEYWORD

**me** [mi:] *pron* **1** (*direct object*) mnie; **can you hear me?** słyszysz mnie?; **it's me** to ja
**2** (*indirect object*) mi; (: *stressed*) mnie; **he gave me the money** dał mi pieniądze; **he gave the money to me, not to her** dał pieniądze mnie, nie jej; **give them to me** daj mi je
**3** (*after prep*): **it's for me** to dla mnie; **without me** beze mnie; **with me** ze mną; **about me** o mnie

**meadow** ['mɛdəu] *n* łąka *f*

**meagre**, (*US*) **meager** ['mi:gəʳ] *adj* skąpy, skromny

**meal** [mi:l] *n* (*occasion, food*) posiłek *m*; (*flour*) mąka *f* razowa; **to go out for a ~** wychodzić (wyjść *perf*) do restauracji; **to make a ~ of sth** (*fig*) robić (zrobić *perf*) z czegoś problem

**mealtime** ['mi:ltaɪm] *n* pora *f* posiłku

**mealy-mouthed** ['mi:lɪmauðd] *adj* (*person*) mówiący półsłówkami

**mean** [mi:n] (*pt, pp* **~t**) *adj* (*with money*) skąpy; (*unkind: person, trick*) podły; (*US: inf: vicious: person, animal*) złośliwy; (*shabby*) nędzny; (*average*) średni ▷ *vt* (*signify*) znaczyć, oznaczać; (*refer to*): **I thought you ~t her** sądziłem, że miałeś na myśli ją; (*intend*): **to ~ to do sth** zamierzać *or* mieć zamiar coś zrobić ▷ *n* (*average*) średnia *f*; **means** (*pl* **~s**) *n* środek *m*, sposób *m* ▷ *npl* środki *pl*; **by ~s of sth** za pomocą czegoś; **by all ~s!** jak najbardziej!; **do you ~ it?** mówisz poważnie?; **what do you ~?** co masz na myśli?; **to be ~t for sb** być przeznaczonym dla kogoś; **to be ~t for sth** być stworzonym do czegoś

**meander** [mɪ'ændəʳ] *vi* (*river*) meandrować, wić się; (*person*) błąkać się, włóczyć się

**meaning** ['mi:nɪŋ] *n* (*of word, gesture, book*) znaczenie *nt*; (*purpose, value*) sens *m*

**meaningful** ['mi:nɪŋful] *adj* (*result, explanation*) sensowny; (*glance, remark*) znaczący; (*relationship, experience*) głęboki

**meaningless** ['mi:nɪŋlɪs] *adj* (*incomprehensible*) niezrozumiały; (*of no importance or relevance*) bez znaczenia *post*; (*futile*) bezsensowny

**meanness** ['mi:nnɪs] *n* (*with money*) skąpstwo *nt*; (*unkindness*) podłość *f*; (*shabbiness*) nędza *f*

**means test** [mi:nz-] *n* ocena *f* dochodów (*dla ustalenia prawa do zasiłku*)

**means-tested** ['mi:nztɛstɪd] *adj*: **~ benefit** zasiłek *m* o wysokości uzależnionej od dochodu

**meant** [mɛnt] *pt, pp of* **mean**

**meantime** ['mi:ntaɪm] *adv* (*also*: **in the meantime**) tymczasem

**meanwhile** ['mi:nwaɪl] *adv* = **meantime**

**measles** ['mi:zlz] *n* odra *f*

**measly** ['mi:zlɪ] (*inf*) *adj* marny, nędzny

**measurable** ['mɛʒərəbl] *adj* wymierny

**measure** ['mɛʒəʳ] *vt* mierzyć (zmierzyć *perf*) ▷ *vi* mierzyć ▷ *n* (*degree*) stopień *m*; (*portion*) porcja *f*; (*ruler*) miar(k)a *f*; (*standard*) miara *f*; (*action*) środek *m* (zaradczy); **a litre ~** miarka litrowa; **~s have been taken to limit the economic decline** podjęto kroki mające na celu ograniczenie spadku gospodarczego
▸ **measure up** *vi*: **to ~ up to** (*standards, expectations*) spełniać (spełnić *perf*) *+acc*

**measured** ['mɛʒəd] *adj* (*tone*) wyważony; (*step*) miarowy

**measurement** ['mɛʒəmənt] *n* pomiar *m*; **chest/hip ~** obwód klatki piersiowej/bioder

**measurements** ['mɛʒəmənts] *npl* wymiary *pl*; **to take sb's ~** brać (wziąć *perf*) *or* zdejmować (zdjąć *perf*) z kogoś miarę

**meat** [mi:t] *n* mięso *nt*; **cold ~s** (*Brit*) wędliny

**meatball** ['mi:tbɔ:l] *n* klopsik *m*

**meat pie** *n mięso zapiekane w cieście*

**Mecca** ['mɛkə] *n* (*Geog*) Mekka *f*; (*fig*) mekka *f*

**mechanic** [mɪ'kænɪk] *n* mechanik *m*

**mechanical** [mɪ'kænɪkl] *adj* mechaniczny

**mechanical engineering** *n* budowa *f* maszyn

**mechanics** [mɪ'kænɪks] *n* (*Phys*) mechanika *f* ▷ *npl*: **the ~ of the market** mechanizmy *pl* rynkowe; **the ~ of reading** przebieg procesu czytania

**mechanism** ['mɛkənɪzəm] *n* (*device, automatic reaction*) mechanizm *m*; (*procedure*) tryb *m*

**mechanization** [mɛkənaɪ'zeɪʃən] *n* mechanizacja *f*

**mechanize** ['mɛkənaɪz] *vt* mechanizować (zmechanizować *perf*) ▷ *vi* wprowadzać (wprowadzić *perf*) mechanizację

**MEd** *n abbr* (= *Master of Education*) *stopień naukowy*, ≈ mgr

**medal** ['mɛdl] *n* medal *m*

**medallion** [mɪ'dælɪən] *n* medalion *m*

**medallist** ['mɛdlɪst], (*US*) **medalist** *n* medalista(-tka) *m(f)*

**meddle** ['mɛdl] *vi*: **to ~ in** *or* **with** mieszać się w *+acc or* do *+gen*

**meddlesome** ['mɛdlsəm] *adj* wścibski

**media** ['mi:dɪə] *npl* (mass) media *pl*, środki *pl* (masowego) przekazu

**mediaeval** [mɛdɪ'i:vl] *adj* = **medieval**

**median** ['mi:dɪən] (*US*) *n* (*also*: **median strip**) pas *m* zieleni

**mediate** ['mi:dɪeɪt] *vi* pośredniczyć, występować (wystąpić *perf*) w roli mediatora

**mediation** [mi:dɪ'eɪʃən] *n* mediacja *f*

**mediator** ['mi:dɪeɪtəʳ] *n* mediator(ka) *m(f)*

**Medicaid** ['mɛdɪkeɪd] (*US*) *n rządowy program pomagający osobom o niskich dochodach pokryć koszty leczenia*

**medical** ['mɛdɪkl] *adj* medyczny ▷ *n* badania *pl* (*kontrolne lub okresowe*)

**medical certificate** *n* zaświadczenie *nt* lekarskie

**medical examiner** (*US*) *n* (*Jur*) ekspert *m* medycyny sądowej

**medical student** *n* student(ka) *m(f)* medycyny

**Medicare** ['mɛdɪkɛəʳ] (*US*) *n rządowy program pomagający osobom w podeszłym wieku w pokryciu kosztów leczenia*

**medicated** ['mɛdɪkeɪtɪd] *adj* leczniczy

**medication** [mɛdɪˈkeɪʃən] *n* leki *pl*
**medicinal** [mɛˈdɪsɪnl] *adj* leczniczy
**medicine** [ˈmɛdsɪn] *n* (*science*) medycyna *f*; (*drug*) lek *m*
**medicine ball** *n* piłka *f* lekarska
**medicine chest** *n* apteczka *f*
**medicine man** *n* czarownik *m*, szaman *m*
**medieval** [mɛdɪˈi:vl] *adj* średniowieczny
**mediocre** [mi:dɪˈəukəʳ] *adj* mierny, pośledni
**mediocrity** [mi:dɪˈɔkrɪtɪ] *n* (*quality*) mierność *f*; (*person*) miernota *f*
**meditate** [ˈmɛdɪteɪt] *vi* (*think carefully*): **to ~ (on)** rozmyślać *or* medytować (nad *+instr or* o *+loc*); (*Rel*) oddawać się medytacji
**meditation** [mɛdɪˈteɪʃən] *n* rozmyślania *pl*, medytacja *f*; (*Rel*) medytacja *f*
**Mediterranean** [mɛdɪtəˈreɪnɪən] *adj* śródziemnomorski; **the ~ (Sea)** Morze Śródziemne
**medium** [ˈmi:dɪəm] (*pl* **media** *or* **~s**) *adj* (*size, level*) średni; (*colour*) pośredni ▷ *n* (*of communication*) środek *m* przekazu; (*Art*) forma *f* przekazu; (*environment*) ośrodek *m*, środowisko *nt*; (*pl* **mediums**: *person*) medium *nt*; **English is the ~ of instruction** językiem wykładowym jest angielski; **to strike a happy ~** znajdować (znaleźć *perf*) złoty środek
**medium-sized** [ˈmi:dɪəmˈsaɪzd] *adj* (*object*) średniej wielkości *post*; (*clothes*) w średnich rozmiarach *post*; (*person*) średniej postury *post*
**medium wave** (*Radio*) *n* fale *pl* średnie
**medley** [ˈmɛdlɪ] *n* mieszanka *f*; (*Mus*) składanka *f*
**meek** [mi:k] *adj* potulny
**meet** [mi:t] (*pt, pp* **met**) *vt* (*accidentally*) spotykać (spotkać *perf*); (*by arrangement*) spotykać się (spotkać się *perf*) z *+instr*; (*for the first time*) poznawać (poznać *perf*); (*condition*) spełniać (spełnić *perf*); (*need*) zaspokajać (zaspokoić *perf*); (*problem, challenge*) sprostać (*perf*) *+dat*; (*expenses*) ponosić (ponieść *perf*); (*bill*) płacić (zapłacić *perf*); (*join*: *line, road*) łączyć się (połączyć się *perf*) z *+instr* ▷ *vi* spotykać się (spotkać się *perf*); (*for the first time*) poznawać się (poznać się *perf*) ▷ *n* (*Brit*: *Hunting*) zbiórka *f* (*przed rozpoczęciem polowania*); (*US*: *Sport*) mityng *m*; **pleased to ~ you!** miło mi Pana/Panią poznać; **he came to the station to ~ me** (*on foot*) wyszedł po mnie na stację; (*by car*) wyjechał po mnie na stację
▸ **meet up** *vi*: **to ~ up (with sb)** spotykać się (spotkać się *perf*) (z kimś)
▸ **meet with** *vt fus* (*difficulties*) napotykać (napotkać *perf*); (*success*) odnosić (odnieść *perf*)
**meeting** [ˈmi:tɪŋ] *n* spotkanie *nt*; (*Comm*) zebranie *nt*; (*Sport*) mityng *m*; **she's at a ~** (*Comm*) jest na zebraniu; **to call a ~** zwoływać (zwołać *perf*) zebranie
**meeting-place** [ˈmi:tɪŋpleɪs] *n* miejsce *nt* spotkania
**megabyte** [ˈmɛgəbaɪt] *n* megabajt *m*
**megalomaniac** [mɛgələˈmeɪnɪæk] *n* megaloman(ka) *m(f)*
**megaphone** [ˈmɛgəfəun] *n* megafon *m*
**melancholy** [ˈmɛlənkəlɪ] *n* melancholia *f* ▷ *adj* melancholijny
**mellow** [ˈmɛləu] *adj* (*sound, light, person*) łagodny; (*voice*) aksamitny; (*colour*) spokojny; (*stone, building*) pokryty patyną wieków; (*wine*) dojrzały ▷ *vi* (*person*) łagodnieć (złagodnieć *perf*)
**melodious** [mɪˈləudɪəs] *adj* melodyjny
**melodrama** [ˈmɛləudrɑ:mə] *n* melodramat *m*
**melodramatic** [mɛlədrəˈmætɪk] *adj* melodramatyczny
**melody** [ˈmɛlədɪ] *n* melodia *f*
**melon** [ˈmɛlən] *n* melon *m*
**melt** [mɛlt] *vi* (*metal*) topić się (stopić się *perf*); (*snow*) topnieć (stopnieć *perf*) ▷ *vt* (*metal*) topić (stopić *perf*); (*snow, butter*) roztapiać (roztopić *perf*); **my heart ~ed as he told his tale** jego opowieść chwyciła mnie za serce
▸ **melt down** *vt* (*metal*) przetapiać (przetopić *perf*)
**meltdown** [ˈmɛltdaun] *n* topnienie *nt* (*rdzenia reaktora atomowego*)
**melting point** [ˈmɛltɪŋ-] *n* temperatura *f* topnienia
**melting pot** *n* (*fig*) tygiel *m*; **to be in the ~** (*plans etc*) być w stadium krystalizacji
**member** [ˈmɛmbəʳ] *n* członek *m* ▷ *cpd*: **~ country** kraj *m* członkowski; **M~ of Parliament** (*Brit*) poseł/posłanka *m/f*
**membership** [ˈmɛmbəʃɪp] *n* (*state*) członkostwo *nt*; (*members*) członkowie *vir pl*; (*number of members*) liczba *f* członków
**membership card** *n* legitymacja *f* członkowska
**membrane** [ˈmɛmbreɪn] (*Anat, Bio*) *n* błona *f*
**memento** [məˈmɛntəu] *n* pamiątka *f*
**memo** [ˈmɛməu] *n* notatka *f* (*zwłaszcza służbowa*)
**memoir** [ˈmɛmwɑ:ʳ] *n* wspomnienie *nt* (*artykuł itp*)
**memoirs** [ˈmɛmwɑ:z] *npl* wspomnienia *pl*, pamiętniki *pl*
**memo pad** *n* notatnik *m*
**memorable** [ˈmɛmərəbl] *adj* pamiętny
**memorandum** [mɛməˈrændəm] (*pl* **memoranda**) *n* (*memo*) notatka *f* (*zwłaszcza służbowa*); (*Pol*) memorandum *nt*
**memorial** [mɪˈmɔ:rɪəl] *n* pomnik *m* ▷ *adj* (*plaque etc*) pamiątkowy; **~ service** nabożeństwo żałobne

**memorize** ['mɛməraɪz] *vt* uczyć się (nauczyć się *perf*) na pamięć *+gen*
**memory** ['mɛmərɪ] *n* (*also Comput*) pamięć *f*; (*recollection*) wspomnienie *nt*; **in ~ of** ku pamięci *+gen*; **to have a good/bad ~** mieć dobrą/złą pamięć; **loss of ~** utrata pamięci
**men** [mɛn] *npl of* **man**
**menace** ['mɛnɪs] *n* (*threat*) groźba *f*; (*nuisance*) zmora *f* ▷ *vt* zagrażać *+dat*; **a public ~** zagrożenie dla społeczeństwa; **a ~ to democracy** zagrożenie dla demokracji
**menacing** ['mɛnɪsɪŋ] *adj* groźny
**menagerie** [mɪ'nædʒərɪ] *n* menażeria *f*
**mend** [mɛnd] *vt* (*repair*) naprawiać (naprawić *perf*); (*darn*) cerować (zacerować *perf*) ▷ *n*: **to be on the ~** wracać do zdrowia; **to ~ one's ways** poprawiać się (poprawić się *perf*)
**mending** ['mɛndɪŋ] *n* (*repairing*) naprawa *f*; (*clothes*) cerowanie *nt*
**menial** ['mi:nɪəl] (*often pej*) *adj* (*work*) służebny, czarny (*pej*)
**meningitis** [mɛnɪn'dʒaɪtɪs] *n* zapalenie *nt* opon mózgowych
**menopause** ['mɛnəupɔ:z] (*Med*) *n*: **the ~** menopauza *f*, klimakterium *nt*
**menservants** ['mɛnsə:vənts] *npl of* **manservant**
**menstrual** ['mɛnstruəl] *adj* miesiączkowy, menstruacyjny
**menstruate** ['mɛnstrueɪt] *vi* miesiączkować
**menstruation** [mɛnstru'eɪʃən] *n* miesiączka *f*, menstruacja *f*
**mental** ['mɛntl] *adj* umysłowy; **~ arithmetic** rachunek pamięciowy
**mentality** [mɛn'tælɪtɪ] *n* mentalność *f*
**mentally** ['mɛntlɪ] *adv*: **~ handicapped** upośledzony umysłowo
**menthol** ['mɛnθɔl] *n* mentol *m*
**mention** ['mɛnʃən] *n* wzmianka *f* ▷ *vt* wspominać (wspomnieć *perf*) o *+loc*; **thank you — don't ~ it!** dziękuję — nie ma za co!; **she ~ed that ...** wspomniała, że ...; **not to ~ ...** nie mówiąc (już) o *+loc*
**mentor** ['mɛntɔ:ʳ] *n* mentor(ka) *m(f)*
**menu** ['mɛnju:] *n* (*selection of dishes*) zestaw *m*; (*printed*) menu *nt inv*, karta *f* (dań *or* potraw); (*Comput*) menu *nt inv*
**menu-driven** ['mɛnju:drɪvn] (*Comput*) *adj* sterowany za pomocą menu
**MEP** (*Brit*) *n abbr* (= *Member of the European Parliament*) poseł/posłanka *m/f* do Parlamentu Europejskiego
**mercantile** ['mə:kəntaɪl] *adj* (*class, society*) kupiecki; (*law*) handlowy
**mercenary** ['mə:sɪnərɪ] *adj* wyrachowany, interesowny ▷ *n* najemnik *m* (*żołnierz*)
**merchandise** ['mə:tʃəndaɪz] *n* towar *m*, towary *pl*
**merchandiser** ['mə:tʃəndaɪzəʳ] *n* handlowiec *m*
**merchant** ['mə:tʃənt] *n* kupiec *m*; **timber/wine ~** kupiec drewnem/winem
**merchant bank** (*Brit*) *n* bank *m* handlowy
**merchantman** ['mə:tʃəntmən] (*irreg: like* **man**) *n* statek *m* handlowy
**merchant navy**, (*US*) **merchant marine** *n* marynarka *f* handlowa
**merciful** ['mə:sɪful] *adj* litościwy, miłosierny; **a ~ release** wybawienie
**mercifully** ['mə:sɪflɪ] *adv* (*fortunately*) na szczęście
**merciless** ['mə:sɪlɪs] *adj* bezlitosny
**mercurial** [mə:'kjuərɪəl] *adj* (*unpredictable*) zmienny, nieprzewidywalny; (*lively*) żywy
**mercury** ['mə:kjurɪ] *n* rtęć *f*
**mercy** ['mə:sɪ] *n* litość *f*; **to have ~ on sb** mieć litość nad kimś; **to be at the ~ of** być zdanym na łaskę *+gen*
**mercy killing** *n* eutanazja *f*
**mere** [mɪəʳ] *adj* zwykły; **his ~ presence irritates her** sama jego obecność denerwuje ją; **by ~ chance** przez czysty przypadek; **she's a ~ child** jest tylko dzieckiem; **a ~ one hundred metres** zaledwie sto metrów
**merely** ['mɪəlɪ] *adv* tylko, jedynie
**merge** [mə:dʒ] *vt* łączyć (połączyć *perf*); (*Comput: files*) scalać (scalić *perf*) ▷ *vi* (*roads, companies*) łączyć się (połączyć się *perf*); (*colours, sounds*) zlewać się (zlać się *perf*)
**merger** ['mə:dʒəʳ] (*Comm*) *n* fuzja *f*
**meridian** [mə'rɪdɪən] *n* południk *m*
**meringue** [mə'ræŋ] *n* beza *f*
**merit** ['mɛrɪt] *n* (*worth, value*) wartość *f*; (*advantage*) zaleta *f* ▷ *vt* zasługiwać (zasłużyć *perf*) na *+acc*
**meritocracy** [mɛrɪ'tɔkrəsɪ] *n* merytrokracja *f*
**mermaid** ['mə:meɪd] *n* syrena *f*
**merrily** ['mɛrɪlɪ] *adv* wesoło
**merriment** ['mɛrɪmənt] *n* wesołość *f*
**merry** ['mɛrɪ] *adj* wesoły; **M~ Christmas!** Wesołych Świąt!
**merry-go-round** ['mɛrɪgəuraund] *n* karuzela *f*
**mesh** [mɛʃ] *n* (*net*) siatka *f*; **wire ~** siatka druciana
**mesmerize** ['mɛzməraɪz] *vt* hipnotyzować (zahipnotyzować *perf*)
**mess** [mɛs] *n* (*in room*) bałagan *m*; (*dirt*) brud *m*; (*Mil*) kantyna *f*; (*: officers'*) kasyno *nt*; (*Naut*) mesa *f*; **in a ~** (*untidy*) w nieładzie; (*in difficulty*) w kłopotach; **my life is a dreadful ~** moje życie jest straszliwie pogmatwane; **to get o.s. in a ~** pakować się (wpakować się *perf*) w kłopoty

m

▸ **mess about** (*inf*) *vi* (*waste time*) obijać się; (*fool around*) wygłupiać się
▸ **mess about with** (*inf*) *vt fus* (*thing*) grzebać przy *+loc*; (*person*) nie traktować poważnie *+gen*
▸ **mess around** (*inf*) *vi* = **mess about**
▸ **mess around with** (*inf*) *vt fus* = **mess about with**
▸ **mess up** (*inf*) *vt* (*spoil*) spaprać (*perf*) (*inf*); (*dirty*) zapaprać (*perf*) (*inf*)
**message** ['mɛsɪdʒ] *n* (*piece of information*) wiadomość *f*; (*meaning*) przesłanie *nt*; (*Comput*) wiadomość *f* ▹ *vt* (*Comput*) wysyłać (wysłać *perf*) wiadomość do *+gen*; **he finally got the ~** (*inf*: *fig*) wreszcie do niego dotarło (*inf*)
**message switching** [-'swɪtʃɪŋ] (*Comput*) *n* rozsyłanie *nt* komunikatów w sieci
**messenger** ['mɛsɪndʒə^r] *n* posłaniec *m*
**Messiah** [mɪ'saɪə] *n* Mesjasz *m*
**Messrs** ['mɛsəz] *abbr* (*on letters*: = *messieurs*) Panowie
**messy** ['mɛsɪ] *adj* (*dirty*) brudny; (*untidy*) niechlujny
**Met** [mɛt] *n abbr* (*US*) = **Metropolitan Opera** ▹ *adj abbr* (= *meteorological*): **the Met Office** ≈ IMGW *m inv*
**met** [mɛt] *pt, pp of* **meet**
**metabolism** [mɛ'tæbəlɪzəm] *n* przemiana *f* materii, metabolizm *m*
**metal** ['mɛtl] *n* metal *m*
**metalled** ['mɛtld] *adj* (*road*) tłuczniowy
**metallic** [mɪ'tælɪk] *adj* metaliczny
**metallurgy** [mɛ'tælədʒɪ] *n* metalurgia *f*
**metalwork** ['mɛtlwəːk] *n* (*craft*) obróbka *f* metali
**metamorphosis** [mɛtə'mɔːfəsɪs] (*pl* **metamorphoses**) *n* metamorfoza *f*
**metaphor** ['mɛtəfə^r] *n* przenośnia *f*, metafora *f*
**metaphorical** [mɛtə'fɔrɪkl] *adj* przenośny, metaforyczny
**metaphysics** [mɛtə'fɪzɪks] *n* metafizyka *f*
**meteor** ['miːtɪə^r] *n* meteor *m*
**meteoric** [miːtɪ'ɔrɪk] *adj* (*fig*) błyskawiczny
**meteorite** ['miːtɪəraɪt] *n* meteoryt *m*
**meteorological** [miːtɪərə'lɔdʒɪkl] *adj* meteorologiczny
**meteorology** [miːtɪə'rɔlədʒɪ] *n* meteorologia *f*
**mete out** [miːt-] *vt* wymierzać (wymierzyć *perf*)
**meter** ['miːtə^r] *n* licznik *m*; (*parking meter*) parkometr *m*; (*US*) = **metre**
**methane** ['miːθeɪn] *n* metan *m*
**method** ['mɛθəd] *n* metoda *f*; **~ of payment** sposób zapłaty
**methodical** [mɪ'θɔdɪkl] *adj* metodyczny
**Methodist** ['mɛθədɪst] *n* metodysta(-tka) *m(f)*
**methodology** [mɛθə'dɔlədʒɪ] *n* (*of research*) metodologia *f*; (*of teaching*) metodyka *f*
**meths** [mɛθs] (*Brit*) *n* = **methylated spirit**
**methylated spirit** ['mɛθɪleɪtɪd-] (*Brit*) *n* denaturat *m*
**meticulous** [mɪ'tɪkjuləs] *adj* skrupulatny
**metre**, (*US*) **meter** ['miːtə^r] *n* metr *m*
**metric** ['mɛtrɪk] *adj* metryczny; **to go ~** przechodzić (przejść *perf*) na system metryczny
**metrical** ['mɛtrɪkl] *adj* metryczny
**metrication** [mɛtrɪ'keɪʃən] *n* przechodzenie *nt* na system metryczny
**metric system** *n* system *m* metryczny
**metric ton** *n* tona *f*
**metronome** ['mɛtrənəum] *n* metronom *m*
**metropolis** [mɪ'trɔpəlɪs] *n* metropolia *f*
**metropolitan** [mɛtrə'pɔlɪtn] *adj* wielkomiejski; (*Pol*) metropolitalny
**Metropolitan Police** (*Brit*) *n*: **the ~** *policja londyńska*
**mettle** ['mɛtl] *n*: **to be on one's ~** chcieć się jak najlepiej zaprezentować; **to show/prove one's ~** wykazać się (*perf*)
**mew** [mjuː] *vi* miauczeć (zamiauczeć *perf*)
**mews** [mjuːz] (*Brit*) *n*: **~ flat** *mieszkanie w budynku przerobionym z dawnych stajni*
**Mexican** ['mɛksɪkən] *adj* meksykański ▹ *n* Meksykanin(-anka) *m(f)*
**Mexico** ['mɛksɪkəu] *n* Meksyk *m*
**Mexico City** *n* Meksyk *m*
**mezzanine** ['mɛtsəniːn] *n* antresola *f*
**MFA** (*US*) *n abbr* (= *Master of Fine Arts*) *stopień naukowy*, ≈ mgr
**mfr** *abbr* = **manufacture; manufacturer**
**mg** *abbr* (= *milligram*) mg
**Mgr** *abbr* (= *Monseigneur, Monsignor*) *tytuł przysługujący wysokim dostojnikom kościelnym*; (*Comm*: = *manager*) ≈ dyr.
**MHR** (*US*) *n abbr* (= *Member of the House of Representatives*) członek *m* Izby Reprezentantów
**MHz** *abbr* (= *megahertz*) MHz
**MI** (*US*: *Post*) *abbr* = **Michigan**
**MI5** (*Brit*) *n abbr* (= *Military Intelligence 5*) *kontrwywiad brytyjski*
**MI6** (*Brit*) *n abbr* (= *Military Intelligence 6*) *wywiad brytyjski*
**MIA** (*Mil*) *abbr* (= *missing in action*) zaginiony(-na) *m(f)* w toku działań
**miaow** [miː'au] *vi* miauczeć (zamiauczeć *perf*)
**mice** [maɪs] *npl of* **mouse**
**micro...** ['maɪkrəu] *pref* mikro...
**microbe** ['maɪkrəub] *n* mikrob *m*
**microbiology** [maɪkrəbaɪ'ɔlədʒɪ] *n* mikrobiologia *f*
**microchip** ['maɪkrəutʃɪp] *n* układ *m* scalony

**micro(computer)** ['maɪkrəu(kəm'pju:təʳ)] *n* (mikro)komputer *m*
**microcosm** ['maɪkrəukɔzəm] *n* mikrokosmos *m*
**microeconomics** ['maɪkrəui:kə'nɔmɪks] *n* mikroekonomia *f*
**microelectronics** ['maɪkrəuɪlɛk'trɔnɪks] *n* mikroelektronika *f*
**microfiche** ['maɪkrəufi:ʃ] *n* mikrofisza *f*
**microfilm** ['maɪkrəufɪlm] *n* mikrofilm *m*
**microlight** ['maɪkrəulaɪt] *n mały, lekki samolot silnikowy dla dwóch osób*
**micrometer** [maɪ'krɔmɪtəʳ] *n* mikrometr *m*
**microphone** ['maɪkrəfəun] *n* mikrofon *m*
**microprocessor** ['maɪkrəu'prəusesəʳ] *n* mikroprocesor *m*
**microscope** ['maɪkrəskəup] *n* mikroskop *m*; **under the ~** pod mikroskopem
**microscopic** [maɪkrə'skɔpɪk] *adj* mikroskopijny
**microwave** ['maɪkrəuweɪv] *n* (*also*: **microwave oven**) kuchenka *f* mikrofalowa, mikrofalówka *f* (*inf*)
**mid-** [mɪd] *adj*: **in ~May** w połowie maja; **in ~afternoon** po południu; **in ~air** w powietrzu; **he's in his ~thirties** ma około trzydziestu pięciu lat
**midday** [mɪd'deɪ] *n* południe *nt*
**middle** ['mɪdl] *n* (*centre*) środek *m*; (*half-way point*) połowa *f*; (*midriff*) brzuch *m* ▷ *adj* (*place, position*) środkowy; (*course*) pośredni; **in the ~ of the night** w środku nocy; **I'm in the ~ of...** jestem w trakcie *+gen*
**middle age** *n* wiek *m* średni
**middle-aged** [mɪdl'eɪdʒd] *adj* w średnim wieku *post*
**Middle Ages** *npl*: **the ~** średniowiecze *nt*, wieki *pl* średnie
**middle-class** [mɪdl'klɑ:s] *adj* z klasy średniej *post*
**middle class(es)** *n(pl)*: **the ~** klasa *f or* warstwa *f* średnia, (klasy *pl or* warstwy *pl* średnie)
**Middle East** *n*: **the ~** Bliski Wschód *m*
**middleman** ['mɪdlmæn] (*irreg*: *like* **man**) *n* pośrednik *m*
**middle management** *n* kadra *f* kierownicza średniego szczebla
**middle name** *n* drugie imię *nt*
**middle-of-the-road** ['mɪdləvðə'rəud] *adj* (*Pol*) umiarkowany; **~ music** muzyka środka
**middleweight** ['mɪdlweɪt] (*Boxing*) *n* waga *f* średnia
**middling** ['mɪdlɪŋ] *adj* przeciętny
**Middx** (*Brit*: *Post*) *abbr* = **Middlesex**
**midge** [mɪdʒ] *n* komar *f*
**midget** ['mɪdʒɪt] *n* karzeł/karlica *m/f*
**Midlands** ['mɪdləndz] (*Brit*) *npl*: **the ~** *środkowa Anglia*
**midlife crisis** ['mɪdlaɪf'kraɪsɪs] *n* kryzys *m* wieku średniego
**midnight** ['mɪdnaɪt] *n* północ *f* ▷ *cpd*: **~ party** *etc* nocne przyjęcie *nt etc*; **at ~** o północy
**midriff** ['mɪdrɪf] *n* talia *f*
**midst** [mɪdst] *n*: **in the ~ of** (*crowd*) wśród *or* pośród *+gen*; (*event*) w (samym) środku *+gen*; (*action*) w trakcie *+gen*
**midsummer** [mɪd'sʌməʳ] *n* pełnia *f or* środek *m* lata; **M~('s) Day** dzień św. Jana
**midway** [mɪd'weɪ] *adj* w połowie drogi *post* ▷ *adv*: **~ (between)** (*in space*) w połowie drogi (między *+instr*); **~ through** (*in time*) w połowie *+gen*
**midweek** [mɪd'wi:k] *adv* w środku *or* połowie tygodnia ▷ *adj* w środku *or* połowie tygodnia *post*
**midwife** ['mɪdwaɪf] (*pl* **midwives**) *n* położna *f*, akuszerka *f*
**midwifery** ['mɪdwɪfərɪ] *n* położnictwo *nt*
**midwinter** [mɪd'wɪntəʳ] *n*: **in ~** w środku zimy
**might** [maɪt] *vb see* **may** ▷ *n* moc *f*, potęga *f*; **with all one's ~** z całej siły, z całych sił
**mighty** ['maɪtɪ] *adj* potężny
**migraine** ['mi:greɪn] *n* migrena *f*
**migrant** ['maɪgrənt] *adj* wędrowny ▷ *n* (*bird*) ptak *m* wędrowny; (*person*) tułacz *m*
**migrate** [maɪ'greɪt] *vi* migrować
**migration** [maɪ'greɪʃən] *n* migracja *f*
**mike** [maɪk] *n abbr* = **microphone**
**Milan** [mɪ'læn] *n* Mediolan *m*
**mild** [maɪld] *adj* (*gentle*) łagodny; (*slight*) umiarkowany
**mildew** ['mɪldju:] *n* pleśń *f*
**mildly** ['maɪldlɪ] *adv* (*gently*) łagodnie; (*slightly*) umiarkowanie, w miarę; **to put it ~** delikatnie mówiąc
**mildness** ['maɪldnɪs] *n* łagodność *f*
**mile** [maɪl] *n* mila *f*; **how many ~s per gallon does your car do?** ile spala *or* pali twój samochód?
**mileage** ['maɪlɪdʒ] *n* (przebyta) odległość *f or* droga *f* (*w milach*); (*fig*) (potencjalna) przydatność *f*
**mileage allowance** *n* zwrot *m* kosztów podróży (*na podstawie ilości przebytych mil*)
**mileometer** [maɪ'lɔmɪtəʳ] *n* szybkościomierz *m*
**milestone** ['maɪlstəun] *n* kamień *m* milowy
**milieu** ['mi:ljə:] *n* środowisko *nt*
**militant** ['mɪlɪtnt] *adj* wojowniczy, wojujący ▷ *n* bojownik(-iczka) *m(f)*
**militarism** ['mɪlɪtərɪzəm] *n* militaryzm *m*
**militaristic** [mɪlɪtə'rɪstɪk] *adj* militarystyczny
**military** ['mɪlɪtərɪ] *adj* militarny, wojskowy ▷ *n*: **the ~** wojsko *nt*

m

**military police** *n* żandarmeria *f* wojskowa
**militate** ['mɪlɪteɪt] *vi*: **to ~ against** stawać (stanąć *perf*) na przeszkodzie *+dat*
**militia** [mɪ'lɪʃə] *n* milicja *f*
**milk** [mɪlk] *n* mleko *nt* ▷ *vt* doić (wydoić *perf*); (*fig*) eksploatować (wyeksploatować *perf*)
**milk chocolate** *n* czekolada *f* mleczna
**milk float** (*Brit*) *n* pojazd *m* rozwożący mleko
**milking** ['mɪlkɪŋ] *n* dojenie *nt*
**milkman** ['mɪlkmən] (*irreg: like* **man**) *n* mleczarz *m*
**milkshake** ['mɪlkʃeɪk] *n* koktajl *m* mleczny
**milk tooth** *n* ząb *m* mleczny
**milk truck** (*US*) *n* = **milk float**
**milky** ['mɪlkɪ] *adj* (*colour*) mleczny; (*drink*) z mlekiem *post*
**Milky Way** *n*: **the ~** Droga *f* Mleczna
**mill** [mɪl] *n* (*for grain*) młyn *m*; (*also*: **coffee mill**) młynek *m* (do kawy); (*also*: **pepper mill**) młynek *f* (do pieprzu); (*factory*) zakład *m* (przemysłowy) ▷ *vt* mielić (zmielić *perf*) ▷ *vi* (*also*: **mill about**: *crowd etc*) falować
**millennium** [mɪ'lɛnɪəm] (*pl* **~s** *or* **millennia**) *n* tysiąclecie *nt*, mil(l)en(n)ium *nt*
**miller** ['mɪlə^r] *n* młynarz *m*
**millet** ['mɪlɪt] *n* proso *nt*
**milli...** ['mɪlɪ] *pref* mili...
**milligram(me)** ['mɪlɪgræm] *n* miligram *m*
**millilitre** ['mɪlɪli:tə^r], (*US*) **milliliter** *n* mililitr *m*
**millimetre** ['mɪlɪmi:tə^r], (*US*) **millimeter** *n* milimetr *m*
**millinery** ['mɪlɪnərɪ] *n* damskie kapelusze *pl*
**million** ['mɪljən] *n* milion *m*; **a ~ times** (*fig*) setki razy
**millionaire** [mɪljə'nɛə^r] *n* milioner(ka) *m(f)*
**millipede** ['mɪlɪpi:d] *n* (*Zool*) krocionóg *m*
**millstone** ['mɪlstəun] *n* (*fig*): **to be a ~ round sb's neck** być komuś kamieniem u szyi
**millwheel** ['mɪlwi:l] *n* koło *nt* młyńskie
**milometer** [maɪ'lɔmɪtə^r] *n* = **mileometer**
**mime** [maɪm] *n* (*Art*) pantomima *f*; (*actor*) mim *m* ▷ *vt* pokazywać (pokazać *perf*) na migi; **in ~** na migi
**mimic** ['mɪmɪk] *n* imitator *m* ▷ *vt* imitować, naśladować
**mimicry** ['mɪmɪkrɪ] *n* imitowanie *nt*, naśladowanie *nt*; (*Bio*) mimikra *f*
**Min.** (*Brit: Pol*) *abbr* (= *ministry*) Min.
**min.** *abbr* (= *minute*) min.; (= *minimum*) min.
**minaret** [mɪnə'rɛt] *n* minaret *m*
**mince** [mɪns] *vt* (*in mincer*) mielić (zmielić *perf*); (*with knife*) siekać (posiekać *perf*) ▷ *vi* dreptać ▷ *n* (*Brit*) (mięso *nt*) mielone; **he does not ~ (his) words** (on) nie przebiera w słowach
**mincemeat** ['mɪnsmi:t] *n* (*Brit*) *słodkie nadzienie z bakalii, tłuszczu i przypraw korzennych*; (*US*) (mięso *nt*) mielone; **to make ~ of sb** rozbić (*perf*) *or* zgnieść (*perf*) kogoś na miazgę
**mince pie** *n rodzaj okrągłego pierożka z nadzieniem z bakalii spożywanego tradycyjnie w okresie Świąt Bożego Narodzenia*
**mincer** ['mɪnsə^r] *n* maszynka *f* do (mielenia) mięsa
**mincing** ['mɪnsɪŋ] *adj* (*steps*) drobny; (*way of talking*) zmanierowany
**mind** [maɪnd] *n* (*intellect*) umysł *m*; (*thoughts*) myśli *pl*; (*head*) głowa *f* ▷ *vt* (*attend to, look after*) doglądać *+gen*; (*be careful of*) uważać na *+acc*; (*object to*) mieć coś przeciwko *+dat*; **do you ~ if I smoke?** czy nie będzie Panu/Pani przeszkadzało, jeżeli zapalę?; **to my ~** według mnie; **he must be out of his ~** chyba postradał zmysły; **it's constantly on my ~** ciągle mi to chodzi po głowie; **to keep** *or* **bear sth in ~** pamiętać o czymś; **to make up one's ~** zdecydować się (*perf*); **to change one's ~** zmieniać (zmienić *perf*) zdanie, rozmyślić się (*perf*); **I'm in two ~s (about it)** nie mogę się zdecydować; **to have it in ~ to do sth** nosić się z zamiarem zrobienia czegoś; **to have sb/sth in ~** mieć kogoś/coś na myśli; **it completely slipped my ~** całkiem mi to wyleciało z głowy; **to bring** *or* **call sth to ~** przywodzić (przywieść *perf*) coś na myśl; **I don't ~** (*when choosing*) wszystko jedno; (*when offered drink etc*) chętnie; **~ you, ...** zwróć uwagę, że ...; **never ~!** (nic) nie szkodzi!; **"~ the step"** „uwaga stopień"
**-minded** ['maɪndɪd] *adj*: **marriage-/career~** nastawiony na małżeństwo/karierę; **liberally~** liberalnie nastawiony
**minder** ['maɪndə^r] *n* (*also*: **childminder**) opiekun(ka) *m(f)* do dziecka; (*inf: bodyguard*) goryl *m* (*inf*)
**mindful** ['maɪndful] *adj*: **to be ~ of** mieć na względzie *+acc*
**mindless** ['maɪndlɪs] *adj* bezmyślny
**mine**[1] *pron* mój; **that book is ~** ta(mta) książka jest moja; **a friend of ~** (pewien) (mój) kolega *m*/(pewna) (moja) koleżanka *f*
**mine**[2] *n* (*coal etc*) kopalnia *f*; (*bomb*) mina *f* ▷ *vt* (*coal*) wydobywać (wydobyć *perf*); (*beach*) minować (zaminować *perf*)
**mine detector** *n* wykrywacz *m* min
**minefield** ['maɪnfi:ld] *n* pole *nt* minowe; (*fig*) niebezpieczny grunt *m*
**miner** ['maɪnə^r] *n* górnik *m*
**mineral** ['mɪnərəl] *adj* mineralny ▷ *n* minerał *m*; **minerals** *npl* (*Brit*) napoje *pl* gazowane
**mineralogy** [mɪnə'rælədʒɪ] *n* mineralogia *f*
**mineral water** *n* woda *f* mineralna
**minesweeper** ['maɪnswi:pə^r] *n* trałowiec *m*

**mingle** ['mɪŋgl] *vi* bywać wśród ludzi; **to ~ with** *(people)* obracać się wśród *+gen*; *(sounds, smells)* mieszać się z *+instr*
**mingy** ['mɪndʒɪ] *(inf) adj* skąpy
**mini...** ['mɪnɪ] *pref* mini...
**miniature** ['mɪnətʃəʳ] *adj* miniaturowy ▷ *n* miniatura *f*
**minibus** ['mɪnɪbʌs] *n* mikrobus *m*
**minicab** ['mɪnɪkæb] *(Aut) n* taksówka *f (prywatna, wzywana przez telefon)*
**minicomputer** ['mɪnɪkəm'pju:təʳ] *n* minikomputer *m*
**minim** ['mɪnɪm] *n (Mus)* półnuta *f*
**minima** ['mɪnɪmə] *npl of* **minimum**
**minimal** ['mɪnɪml] *adj* minimalny
**minimize** ['mɪnɪmaɪz] *vt (reduce)* minimalizować (zminimalizować *perf*); *(play down)* umniejszać (umniejszyć *perf*)
**minimum** ['mɪnɪməm] *(pl* **minima**) *n* minimum *nt* ▷ *adj* minimalny; **to reduce sth to a ~** redukować (zredukować *perf*) coś do minimum; **~ wage** płaca minimalna
**minimum lending rate** *n* minimalne oprocentowanie *nt* kredytu
**mining** ['maɪnɪŋ] *n* górnictwo *nt* ▷ *cpd (town)* górniczy; *(industry)* wydobywczy
**minion** ['mɪnjən] *(pej) n* sługus *m (inf)*
**miniskirt** ['mɪnɪskə:t] *n* minispódniczka *f*
**minister** ['mɪnɪstəʳ] *n (Brit: Pol)* minister *m*; *(Rel)* duchowny *m (protestancki)* ▷ *vi*: **to ~ to sb/sb's needs** służyć komuś
**ministerial** [mɪnɪs'tɪərɪəl] *(Brit) adj* ministerialny
**ministry** ['mɪnɪstrɪ] *n (Brit: Pol)* ministerstwo *nt*; *(Rel)* stan *m* duchowny
**Ministry of Defence** *(Brit) n* ≈ Ministerstwo *nt* Obrony Narodowej
**mink** [mɪŋk] *(pl* **~s** *or* **~**) *n (fur)* norki *pl*; *(animal)* norka *f*
**mink coat** *n* futro *nt* z norek
**minnow** ['mɪnəu] *n nazwa wspólna dla wielu gatunków małych rybek z rodziny karpiowatych*; *(fig: person)* płotka *f*
**minor** ['maɪnəʳ] *adj (repairs, injuries)* drobny; *(poet)* pomniejszy; *(Med: operation)* mały; *(Mus)* moll *post* ▷ *n* nieletni(a) *m(f)*
**Minorca** [mɪ'nɔ:kə] *n* Minorka *f*
**minority** [maɪ'nɔrɪtɪ] *n* mniejszość *f*; **to be in a ~** być w mniejszości
**minster** ['mɪnstəʳ] *n* kościół *m* katedralny
**minstrel** ['mɪnstrəl] *n* minstrel *m*
**mint** [mɪnt] *n (Bot, Culin)* mięta *f*; *(sweet)* miętówka *f*; *(factory)* mennica *f* ▷ *vt (coins)* bić, wybijać (wybić *perf*); **in ~ condition** w idealnym stanie
**mint sauce** *n* sos *m* miętowy
**minuet** [mɪnju'ɛt] *n* menuet *m*
**minus** ['maɪnəs] *n (also:* **minus sign**) minus *m* ▷ *prep*: **12 ~ 6 equals 6** 12 minus 6 równa się 6; **~ 24 (degrees)** minus 24 (stopnie Celsjusza)
**minuscule** ['mɪnəskju:l] *adj* maluteńki, malusieńki
**minute¹** [maɪ'nju:t] *adj (search)* drobiazgowy; *(amount)* minimalny; **in ~ detail** z najdrobniejszymi szczegółami
**minute²** ['mɪnɪt] *n* minuta *f*; *(fig)* minu(t)ka *f*; **minutes** *npl (of meeting)* protokół *m*; **it is five ~s past three** jest pięć (minut) po trzeciej; **wait a ~!, just a ~!** chwileczkę!; **up-to-the-~** *(news)* najświeższy; *(machine, technology)* najnowszy, najnowocześniejszy; **at the last ~** w ostatniej chwili
**minute book** *n* księga *f* protokołów
**minute hand** *n* wskazówka *f* minutowa
**minutely** [maɪ'nju:tlɪ] *adv (in detail)* drobiazgowo; *(by a small amount)* (bardzo) nieznacznie
**miracle** ['mɪrəkl] *n* cud *m*
**miraculous** [mɪ'rækjuləs] *adj* cudowny
**mirage** ['mɪrɑ:ʒ] *n* miraż *m*
**mire** ['maɪəʳ] *n* bagno *nt*, grzęzawisko *nt*
**mirror** ['mɪrəʳ] *n (in bedroom, bathroom)* lustro *nt*; *(in car)* lusterko *nt* ▷ *vt (fig)* odzwierciedlać
**mirror image** *n* lustrzane odbicie *nt*
**mirth** [mə:θ] *n* rozbawienie *nt*, wesołość *f*
**misadventure** [mɪsəd'vɛntʃəʳ] *n* nieszczęśliwy wypadek *m*, nieszczęście *nt*; **death by ~** *(Brit)* śmierć na skutek nieszczęśliwego wypadku
**misanthropist** [mɪ'zænθrəpɪst] *n* mizantrop *m*
**misapply** [mɪsə'plaɪ] *vt* źle *or* niewłaściwie stosować (zastosować *perf*)
**misapprehension** ['mɪsæprɪ'hɛnʃən] *n (wrong idea)* błędne mniemanie *nt*; *(misunderstanding)* nieporozumienie *nt*
**misappropriate** [mɪsə'prəuprɪeɪt] *vt* sprzeniewierzać (sprzeniewierzyć *perf*)
**misappropriation** ['mɪsəprəuprɪ'eɪʃən] *n* sprzeniewierzenie *nt*
**misbehave** [mɪsbɪ'heɪv] *vi* źle się zachowywać
**misbehaviour** [mɪsbɪ'heɪvjəʳ], *(US)* **misbehavior** *n* złe zachowanie *nt*
**misc.** *abbr* = **miscellaneous**
**miscalculate** [mɪs'kælkjuleɪt] *vt* źle *or* błędnie ocenić *(perf)* ▷ *vi* przeliczyć się *(perf)*
**miscalculation** ['mɪskælkju'leɪʃən] *n* błędna ocena *f*
**miscarriage** ['mɪskærɪdʒ] *n* poronienie *nt*; **~ of justice** pomyłka sądowa
**miscarry** [mɪs'kærɪ] *vi (Med)* ronić (poronić *perf*); *(plans)* nie powieść się *(perf)*
**miscellaneous** [mɪsɪ'leɪnɪəs] *adj* różny, rozmaity; **~ expenses** wydatki różne *or* inne

**mischance** [mɪs'tʃɑːns] *n* (*bad luck*) pech *m*; (*misfortune*) nieszczęście *nt*

**mischief** ['mɪstʃɪf] *n* (*naughtiness: of child*) psoty *pl*; (*playfulness*) figlarność *f*; (*maliciousness*) intrygi *pl*; **to get into ~** psocić (napsocić *perf*); **to do sb/o.s. a ~** robić (zrobić *perf*) komuś/sobie krzywdę

**mischievous** ['mɪstʃɪvəs] *adj* (*naughty*) psotny; (*playful*) figlarny

**misconception** ['mɪskən'sɛpʃən] *n* błędne mniemanie *nt or* przekonanie *nt*

**misconduct** [mɪs'kɔndʌkt] *n* (*bad behaviour*) złe prowadzenie się *nt*; (*instance*) występek *m*; **professional ~** zachowanie niezgodne z etyką zawodową

**misconstrue** [mɪskən'struː] *vt* błędnie interpretować (zinterpretować *perf*)

**miscount** [mɪs'kaunt] *vt* źle policzyć (*perf*) ▷ *vi* mylić się (pomylić się *perf*) w liczeniu

**misdemeanour**, (*US*) **misdemeanor** [mɪsdɪ'miːnə[r]] *n* występek *m*, wykroczenie *nt*

**misdirect** [mɪsdɪ'rɛkt] *vt* (*person*) źle *or* mylnie kierować (skierować *perf*); (*talent*) niewłaściwie wykorzystywać (wykorzystać *perf*)

**miser** ['maɪzə[r]] *n* skąpiec *m*, sknera *m/f* (*inf*)

**miserable** ['mɪzərəbl] *adj* (*unhappy*) nieszczęśliwy; (*unpleasant: weather*) ponury; (*: person*) nieprzyjemny; (*wretched: conditions*) nędzny; (*contemptible: donation etc*) nędzny, marny; (*: failure*) sromotny; **to feel ~** być bardzo przygnębionym

**miserably** ['mɪzərəblɪ] *adv* (*fail*) sromotnie; (*live*) nędznie; (*smile, say*) ponuro; (*small*) żałośnie

**miserly** ['maɪzəlɪ] *adj* skąpy

**misery** ['mɪzərɪ] *n* (*unhappiness*) nieszczęście *nt*; (*wretchedness*) nędza *f*; (*inf: person*) maruda *m/f* (*inf*)

**misfire** [mɪs'faɪə[r]] *vi* (*plan*) spełznąć (*perf*) na niczym, nie wypalić (*perf*) (*inf*); (*car engine*) nie zapalać (nie zapalić *perf*)

**misfit** ['mɪsfɪt] *n* odmieniec *m*

**misfortune** [mɪs'fɔːtʃən] *n* nieszczęście *nt*

**misgiving** [mɪs'gɪvɪŋ] *n* (*often pl*) obawy *pl*, złe przeczucia *pl*

**misguided** [mɪs'gaɪdɪd] *adj* (*opinion*) błędny, mylny

**mishandle** [mɪs'hændl] *vt* (*instrument*) nieumiejętnie obchodzić się z *+instr*; (*situation*) źle rozgrywać (rozegrać *perf*); (*case, negotiations*) źle prowadzić (poprowadzić *perf*)

**mishap** ['mɪshæp] *n* niefortunny wypadek *m*

**mishear** [mɪs'hɪə[r]] (*irreg: like* **hear**) *vt* źle usłyszeć (*perf*) ▷ *vi* przesłyszeć się (*perf*)

**misheard** [mɪs'həːd] *pt, pp of* **mishear**

**mishmash** ['mɪʃmæʃ] (*inf*) *n* bezładna mieszanina *f*, miszmasz *m* (*inf*)

**misinform** [mɪsɪn'fɔːm] *vt* wprowadzać (wprowadzić *perf*) w błąd

**misinterpret** [mɪsɪn'təːprɪt] *vt* źle *or* błędnie interpretować (zinterpretować *perf*)

**misinterpretation** ['mɪsɪntəːprɪ'teɪʃən] *n* błędna interpretacja *f*

**misjudge** [mɪs'dʒʌdʒ] *vt* (*person*) źle osądzić (*perf*); (*situation, action*) źle *or* niewłaściwie ocenić (*perf*)

**mislay** [mɪs'leɪ] (*irreg: like* **lay**) *vt* zapodziać (*perf*), zawieruszyć (*perf*)

**mislead** [mɪs'liːd] (*irreg: like* **lead**) *vt* wprowadzać (wprowadzić *perf*) w błąd, zmylić (*perf*)

**misleading** [mɪs'liːdɪŋ] *adj* mylący, wprowadzający w błąd

**misled** *pt, pp of* **mislead**

**mismanage** [mɪs'mænɪdʒ] *vt* źle *or* niewłaściwie zarządzać *+instr*

**mismanagement** [mɪs'mænɪdʒmənt] *n* niewłaściwe zarządzanie *nt*, niegospodarność *f*

**misnomer** [mɪs'nəumə[r]] *n* błędna *or* niewłaściwa nazwa *f*

**misogynist** [mɪ'sɔdʒɪnɪst] *n* mizogin(ista) *m*

**misplaced** [mɪs'pleɪst] *adj* (*feeling: inappropriate*) nie na miejscu *post*; (*: directed towards wrong person*) źle *or* niewłaściwie ulokowany; (*accent etc*) źle *or* niewłaściwie umieszczony

**misprint** ['mɪsprɪnt] *n* literówka *f*

**mispronounce** *vt* źle *or* niewłaściwie wymawiać (wymówić *perf*)

**misquote** ['mɪs'kwəut] *vt* błędnie cytować (zacytować *perf*)

**misread** [mɪs'riːd] (*irreg: like* **read**) *vt* błędnie odczytywać (odczytać *perf*)

**misrepresent** [mɪsrɛprɪ'zɛnt] *vt* przeinaczać (przeinaczyć *perf*)

**Miss** [mɪs] *n* (*with surname*) pani *f*, panna *f* (*old*); (*Scol: as form of address*) proszę pani (*voc*); (*beauty queen*) miss *f inv*; **Dear ~ Smith** Droga Pani Smith

**miss** [mɪs] *vt* (*train etc*) spóźniać się (spóźnić się *perf*) na *+acc*; (*target*) nie trafiać (nie trafić *perf*) w *+acc*; (*chance*) tracić (stracić *perf*); (*meeting*) opuszczać (opuścić *perf*); (*notice loss of*) zauważać (zauważyć *perf*) brak *+gen*; (*regret absence of*) tęsknić za *+instr* ▷ *vi* chybiać (chybić *perf*), nie trafiać (nie trafić *perf*), pudłować (spudłować *perf*) (*inf*) ▷ *n* chybienie *nt*, pudło *nt* (*inf*); **you can't ~ it** nie można tego przeoczyć *or* nie zauważyć; **the bus just ~ed the wall** autobus omal nie wpadł na mur; **you're ~ing the point** nie rozumiesz istoty sprawy

▸ **miss out** (*Brit*) *vt* opuszczać (opuścić *perf*)

▸ **miss out on** *vt fus* tracić (stracić *perf*) *+acc*, nie załapać się (*perf*) na *+acc* (*inf*)
**missal** ['mɪsl] *n* mszał *m*
**misshapen** [mɪs'ʃeɪpən] *adj* zniekształcony
**missile** ['mɪsaɪl] *n* pocisk *m*; **~s** (*objects thrown*) amunicja
**missile base** *n* baza *f* rakietowa
**missile launcher** [-'lɔːntʃəʳ] *n* wyrzutnia *f* pocisków rakietowych
**missing** ['mɪsɪŋ] *adj* (*lost*) zaginiony; (*removed: tooth, wheel*) brakujący; (*Mil*): **~ in action** zaginiony w toku działań; **sb/sth is ~** kogoś/czegoś brakuje; **to go ~** (*object*) zginąć (*perf*); (*person*) zaginąć (*perf*); **~ person** osoba zaginiona
**mission** ['mɪʃən] *n* misja *f*; (*Mil*) lot *m* bojowy; **to be on a secret ~** odbywać (odbyć *perf*) tajną misję
**missionary** ['mɪʃənrɪ] *n* misjonarz(-arka) *m(f)*
**missive** ['mɪsɪv] (*fml*) *n* pismo *nt*, list *m*
**misspell** ['mɪs'spɛl] (*irreg: like* **spell**) *vt* źle *or* błędnie pisać (napisać *perf*)
**misspent** ['mɪs'spɛnt] *adj*: **his ~ youth** jego zmarnowana młodość *f*
**mist** [mɪst] *n* mgła *f*; (*light*) mgiełka *f* ▷ *vi* (*also*: **mist over**: *eyes*) zachodzić (zajść *perf*) mgłą, zamglić się (*perf*); (*Brit*: *also*: **mist over, mist up**: *windows*) zaparowywać (zaparować *perf*)
**mistake** [mɪs'teɪk] (*irreg: like* **take**) *n* (*error*) błąd *m*; (*misunderstanding*) pomyłka *f* ▷ *vt* (*address etc*) pomylić (*perf*); (*intentions*) źle rozumieć (zrozumieć *perf*); **by ~** przez pomyłkę, omyłkowo; **to make a ~** (*in writing, calculation*) popełniać (popełnić *perf*) *or* robić (zrobić *perf*) błąd, mylić się (pomylić się *perf*); **to make a ~ about sb/sth** mylić się (pomylić się *perf*) co do kogoś/czegoś; **to ~ sb/sth for** mylić (pomylić *perf*) kogoś/coś z *+instr*, brać (wziąć *perf*) kogoś/coś za *+acc*
**mistaken** [mɪs'teɪkən] *pp of* **mistake** ▷ *adj* mylny, błędny; **to be ~** mylić się, być w błędzie
**mistaken identity** *n*: **it was a case of ~** wzięto go/ją za kogo innego
**mistakenly** [mɪs'teɪkənlɪ] *adv* mylnie, błędnie
**mister** ['mɪstəʳ] *n* (*inf*) proszę pana (*voc*); *see* **Mr**
**mistletoe** ['mɪsltəu] *n* jemioła *f*
**mistook** [mɪs'tuk] *pt of* **mistake**
**mistranslation** [mɪstræns'leɪʃən] *n* błędne tłumaczenie *nt*
**mistreat** [mɪs'triːt] *vt* znęcać się nad *+instr*
**mistress** ['mɪstrɪs] *n* (*lover*) kochanka *f*; (*of servant, dog, situation*) pani *f*; (*Brit*: *Scol*) nauczycielka *f*
**mistrust** [mɪs'trʌst] *vt* nie ufać *+dat*, nie dowierzać *+dat* ▷ *n*: **~ of** nieufność *f* (w stosunku) do *+gen*
**mistrustful** [mɪs'trʌstful] *adj*: **~ (of)** nieufny (w stosunku do *+gen*)
**misty** ['mɪstɪ] *adj* (*day*) mglisty; (*glasses, windows*) zamglony
**misty-eyed** ['mɪstɪ'aɪd] *adj* (*fig*): **she goes ~ at the sight/thought of ...** oczy zachodzą jej mgłą na widok *+gen*/myśl o *+loc*
**misunderstand** [mɪsʌndə'stænd] (*irreg: like* **stand**) *vt* źle rozumieć (zrozumieć *perf*) ▷ *vi* nie rozumieć (nie zrozumieć *perf*)
**misunderstanding** ['mɪsʌndə'stændɪŋ] *n* nieporozumienie *nt*
**misunderstood** [mɪsʌndə'stud] *pt, pp of* **misunderstand**
**misuse** [*n* mɪs'juːs, *vb* mɪs'juːz] *n* (*of power, funds*) nadużywanie *nt*; (*of tool, word*) niewłaściwe używanie *nt* ▷ *vt* (*power*) nadużywać (nadużyć *perf*) *+gen*; (*word*) niewłaściwie używać (użyć *perf*) *+gen*
**MIT** (*US*) *n abbr* = **Massachusetts Institute of Technology**
**mite** [maɪt] *n* (*small quantity*) ździebko *nt*; (*Brit*: *small child*) kruszyn(k)a *f*
**miter** ['maɪtəʳ] (*US*) *n* = **mitre**
**mitigate** ['mɪtɪgeɪt] *vt* łagodzić (złagodzić *perf*); **mitigating circumstances** okoliczności łagodzące
**mitigation** [mɪtɪ'geɪʃən] *n* złagodzenie *nt*
**mitre**, (*US*) **miter** ['maɪtəʳ] *n* (*Rel*) mitra *f*, infuła *f*; (*also*: **mitre joint**) połączenie *nt* narożnikowe (na ucios)
**mitt(en)** ['mɪt(n)] *n* rękawiczka *f* (z jednym palcem)
**mix** [mɪks] *vt* (*ingredients, colours*) mieszać (zmieszać *perf*); (*drink, sauce*) przyrządzać (przyrządzić *perf*); (*cake*) kręcić (ukręcić *perf*); (*cement*) mieszać (wymieszać *perf*) ▷ *vi*: **to mix (with)** utrzymywać kontakty towarzyskie (z *+instr*) ▷ *n* (*combination*) połączenie *nt*; (*powder*) mieszanka *f*; **to mix business with pleasure** łączyć (połączyć *perf*) przyjemne z pożytecznym; **cake mix** ciasto w proszku
▸ **mix in** (*Culin*) *vt* dodawać (dodać *perf*)
▸ **mix up** *vt* (*confuse*) mylić (pomylić *perf*) (ze sobą); (*muddle up*) mieszać (pomieszać *perf*); **to be mixed up in sth** być w coś zamieszanym; **I got (all) mixed up** wszystko mi się pomieszało
**mixed** [mɪkst] *adj* mieszany
**mixed doubles** *npl* gra *f* mieszana, mikst *m*
**mixed economy** *n* gospodarka *f* mieszana
**mixed grill** (*Brit*) *n danie z rusztu złożone z różnych gatunków mięsa i wędlin*

m

**mixed-up** [mɪkst'ʌp] *adj* *(person)* zagubiony; *(papers)* pomieszany
**mixer** ['mɪksəʳ] *n* *(machine)* mikser *m*; *(tonic, juice etc)* dodatek *m* do drinków; **he's a good ~** łatwo nawiązuje (nowe) znajomości
**mixture** ['mɪkstʃəʳ] *n* mieszanka *f*; *(Med)* mikstura *f (old)*
**mix-up** ['mɪksʌp] *n* zamieszanie *nt*, nieporozumienie *nt*
**MK** *(Brit: Tech) abbr* = **mark**
**mk** *(Fin) abbr* = **mark**
**mkt** *abbr* = **market**
**MLitt** *n abbr (= Master of Literature, Master of Letters) stopień naukowy*, ≈ mgr
**MLR** *(Brit) n abbr (= minimum lending rate)* stopa *f* dyskontowa Banku Anglii
**mm** *abbr (= millimetre)* mm
**MN** *abbr (Brit)* = **Merchant Navy**; *(US: Post)* = **Minnesota**
**MO** *n abbr* = **medical officer**; *(US: inf: = modus operandi)* modus *m* operandi ▷ *abbr (US: Post)* = **Missouri**
**m.o.** *abbr* = **money order**
**moan** [məun] *n* jęk *m* ▷ *vi (inf)*: **to ~ (about)** jęczeć (z powodu *+gen*) *(inf)*
**moat** [məut] *n* fosa *f*
**mob** [mɔb] *n* *(disorderly)* tłum *m*, motłoch *m* *(pej)*; *(orderly)* paczka *f (inf)* ▷ *vt* oblegać (oblec *perf*) (tłumnie)
**mobile** ['məubaɪl] *adj* *(workforce, social group)* mobilny; *(able to move)*: **to be ~** móc się poruszać ▷ *n* *(phone)* komórka *f*; *(decoration)* mobile *pl*; **applicants must be ~** kandydat musi posiadać samochód
**mobile home** *n* dom *f* na kółkach
**mobile phone** *n* przenośny aparat *m* telefoniczny
**mobility** [məu'bɪlɪtɪ] *n* *(physical)* możliwość *f* poruszania się; *(social)* mobilność *f*
**mobility allowance** *n* *(Brit) zapomoga dla niepełnosprawnych na pokrycie wydatków związanych z transportem*
**mobilize** ['məubɪlaɪz] *vt* *(work force)* organizować (zorganizować *perf*); *(country, army, organization)* mobilizować (zmobilizować *perf*) ▷ *vi* *(Mil)* mobilizować się (zmobilizować się *perf*)
**moccasin** ['mɔkəsɪn] *n* mokasyn *m*
**mock** [mɔk] *vt* kpić z *+gen*; *(by imitating)* przedrzeźniać ▷ *adj* *(exam, battle)* próbny; *(terror, disbelief)* udawany; **~ crystal** *etc* imitacja kryształu *etc*
**mockery** ['mɔkərɪ] *n* kpina *f*; **to make a ~ of** wystawiać (wystawić *perf*) na pośmiewisko *+acc*
**mocking** ['mɔkɪŋ] *adj* kpiący
**mockingbird** ['mɔkɪŋbəːd] *n* przedrzeźniacz *m (ptak)*
**mock-up** ['mɔkʌp] *n* makieta *f*
**MOD** *(Brit) n abbr (= Ministry of Defence)* Ministerstwo *nt* Obrony, ≈ MON *m*
**mod cons** ['mɔd'kɔnz] *(Brit) npl abbr (= modern conveniences)* wygody *pl*
**mode** [məud] *n* *(of life)* tryb *m*; *(of action)* sposób *m*; *(of transport)* forma *f*; *(Comput)* tryb *m*
**model** ['mɔdl] *n* *(of boat, building etc)* model *m*; *(fashion model, artist's model)* model(ka) *m(f)*; *(example)* wzór *m*, model *m* ▷ *adj* *(excellent)* wzorowy; *(small scale)* miniaturowy ▷ *vt* *(clothes)* prezentować; *(object)* wykonywać (wykonać *perf*) model *+gen* ▷ *vi* *(for designer)* pracować jako model(ka) *m(f)*; *(for painter, photographer)* pozować; **to ~ o.s. on** wzorować się na *+loc*
**modeller** ['mɔdləʳ], *(US)* **modeler** *n* modelarz *m*
**model railway** *n* miniaturowa kolejka *f*
**modem** ['məudɛm] *n* modem *m*
**moderate** [*adj, n* 'mɔdərət, *vb* 'mɔdəreɪt] *adj* umiarkowany; *(change)* nieznaczny ▷ *n* osoba *f* o umiarkowanych poglądach ▷ *vi* *(wind etc)* słabnąć (osłabnąć *perf*) ▷ *vt* łagodzić (złagodzić *perf*)
**moderately** ['mɔdərətlɪ] *adv* *(difficult etc)* umiarkowanie; *(pleased)* w miarę; *(drink etc)* z umiarem; **~ priced goods** towary po przystępnych cenach
**moderation** [mɔdə'reɪʃən] *n* umiar *m*; **in ~** z umiarem
**modern** ['mɔdən] *adj* *(contemporary)* współczesny; *(up-to-date)* nowoczesny; **~ languages** języki nowożytne
**modernization** [mɔdənaɪ'zeɪʃən] *n* modernizacja *f*, unowocześnianie *nt*
**modernize** ['mɔdənaɪz] *vt* modernizować (zmodernizować *perf*), unowocześniać (unowocześnić *perf*)
**modest** ['mɔdɪst] *adj* skromny
**modestly** ['mɔdɪstlɪ] *adv* skromnie
**modesty** ['mɔdɪstɪ] *n* skromność *f*
**modicum** ['mɔdɪkəm] *n*: **a ~ of** odrobina *f +gen*
**modification** [mɔdɪfɪ'keɪʃən] *n* modyfikacja *f*; **to make ~s to** modyfikować (zmodyfikować *perf*) *+acc*
**modify** ['mɔdɪfaɪ] *vt* modyfikować (zmodyfikować *perf*)
**Mods** [mɔdz] *(Brit: Scol) n abbr (= (Honour) Moderations) egzamin na Uniwersytecie Oksfordzkim*
**modular** ['mɔdjuləʳ] *adj* modularny
**modulate** ['mɔdjuleɪt] *vt* *(voice)* modulować; *(process, activity)* przekształcać (przekształcić *perf*)
**modulation** [mɔdju'leɪʃən] *n* modulacja *f*; *(of process, activity)* modyfikacja *f*, przekształcenie *nt*

**module** ['mɔdju:l] *n* moduł *m*; (*Space*) człon *m* (statku kosmicznego)
**modus operandi** ['məudəsɔpə'rændi:] *n* sposób *m* działania
**Mogadishu** [mɔgə'dɪʃu:] *n* Mogadiszu *nt inv*
**mogul** ['məugl] *n* (*fig*) magnat *m*
**MOH** (*Brit*) *n abbr* (*formerly*) = **Medical Officer of Health**
**mohair** ['məuhɛəʳ] *n* moher *m*
**Mohammed** [mə'hæmɛd] (*Rel*) *n* Mahomet *m*
**moist** [mɔɪst] *adj* wilgotny
**moisten** ['mɔɪsn] *vt* zwilżać (zwilżyć *perf*)
**moisture** ['mɔɪstʃəʳ] *n* wilgoć *f*; (*on glass*) para *f*
**moisturize** ['mɔɪstʃəraɪz] *vt* nawilżać (nawilżyć *perf*)
**moisturizer** ['mɔɪstʃəraɪzəʳ] *n* krem *m* nawilżający
**molar** ['məuləʳ] *n* ząb *m* trzonowy
**molasses** [məu'læsɪz] *n* melasa *f*
**mold** [məuld] (*US*) *n*, *vt* = **mould**
**mole** [məul] *n* (*on skin*) pieprzyk *m*; (*Zool*) kret *m*; (*fig*: *spy*) wtyczka *f* (*inf*)
**molecular** [məu'lɛkjuləʳ] *adj* molekularny
**molecule** ['mɔlɪkju:l] *n* cząsteczka *f*, molekuła *f*
**molehill** ['məulhɪl] *n* kretowisko *nt*
**molest** [mə'lɛst] *vt* napastować
**mollusc** ['mɔləsk] (*Zool*) *n* mięczak *m*
**mollycoddle** ['mɔlɪkɔdl] *vt* rozpieszczać (rozpieścić *perf*)
**molt** [məult] (*US*) *vi* = **moult**
**molten** ['məultən] *adj* roztopiony
**mom** [mɔm] (*US*) *n* = **mum**
**moment** ['məumənt] *n* chwila *f*, moment *m*; **at the ~** w tej chwili; **for a ~** (*go out*) na chwilę; (*hesitate*) przez chwilę; **for the ~** na razie, chwilowo; **in a ~** za chwilę; **"one ~ please"** (*Tel*) „chwileczkę"; **a matter of great ~** sprawa wielkiej wagi
**momentarily** ['məuməntrɪlɪ] *adv* przez chwilę *or* moment; (*US*: *very soon*) lada chwila *or* moment; **I had ~ forgotten** przez chwilę nie mogłem sobie przypomnieć
**momentary** ['məuməntərɪ] *adj* chwilowy
**momentous** [məu'mɛntəs] *adj* doniosły, wielkiej wagi *post*
**momentum** [məu'mɛntəm] *n* (*Phys*) pęd *m*; (*fig*: *of change*) tempo *nt*; **to gather ~** nabierać (nabrać *perf*) rozpędu; (*fig*: *change*) nabierać (nabrać *perf*) impetu; (: *movement*, *struggle*) przybierać (przybrać *perf*) na sile
**mommy** ['mɔmɪ] (*US*) *n* = **mummy**
**Mon.** *abbr* (= *Monday*) pon.
**Monaco** ['mɔnəkəu] *n* Monako *nt inv*
**monarch** ['mɔnək] *n* monarcha *m*
**monarchist** ['mɔnəkɪst] *n* monarchista(-tka) *m*(*f*)
**monarchy** ['mɔnəkɪ] *n* monarchia *f*
**monastery** ['mɔnəstərɪ] *n* klasztor *m*
**monastic** [mə'næstɪk] *adj* klasztorny; **a ~ life** (*fig*) żywot mnicha/mniszki
**Monday** ['mʌndɪ] *n* poniedziałek *m*; *see also* **Tuesday**
**Monegasque** [mɔnə'gæsk] *adj*: **~ casinos** kasyna *pl* Monte Carlo ▷ *n* mieszkaniec(-nka) *m*(*f*) Monte Carlo
**monetarist** ['mʌnɪtərɪst] *n* monetarysta(-tka) *m*(*f*) ▷ *adj* monetarystyczny
**monetary** ['mʌnɪtərɪ] *adj* (*system*) walutowy, pieniężny; (*policy*) walutowy, monetarny; (*control*) dewizowy
**money** ['mʌnɪ] *n* pieniądze *pl*; **to make ~** (*person*) zarabiać (zarobić *perf*); (*business*) przynosić (przynieść *perf*) zysk; **danger ~** (*Brit*) ≈ dodatek za pracę w szkodliwych warunkach; **I've got no ~ left** nie mam już pieniędzy
**moneyed** ['mʌnɪd] (*fml*) *adj* majętny
**moneylender** ['mʌnɪlɛndəʳ] *n* lichwiarz(-arka) *m*(*f*)
**moneymaking** ['mʌnɪmeɪkɪŋ] *adj* dochodowy, zyskowny
**money market** *n* rynek *m* pieniężny
**money order** *n* przekaz *m* (pieniężny)
**money-spinner** ['mʌnɪspɪnəʳ] (*inf*) *n*: **this business is a real ~** to bardzo dochodowy interes
**money supply** *n* podaż *f* pieniądza
**Mongol** ['mɔŋgəl] *n* (*person*) Mongoł(ka) *m*(*f*); (*Ling*) (język *m*) mongolski
**mongol** ['mɔŋgəl] (*inf!*) *n* mongoł *m* (*inf!*)
**Mongolia** [mɔŋ'gəulɪə] *n* Mongolia *f*
**Mongolian** [mɔŋ'gəulɪən] *adj* mongolski ▷ *n* (*person*) Mongoł(ka) *m*(*f*); (*Ling*) (język *m*) mongolski
**mongoose** ['mɔŋgu:s] *n* mangusta *f*
**mongrel** ['mʌŋgrəl] *n* kundel *m*
**monitor** ['mɔnɪtəʳ] *n* monitor *m* ▷ *vt* (*heartbeat*, *progress*) monitorować; (*broadcasts*) wsłuchiwać się w *+acc*
**monk** [mʌŋk] *n* mnich *m*, zakonnik *m*
**monkey** ['mʌŋkɪ] *n* małpa *f*
**monkey business** (*inf*) *n* machlojki *pl* (*inf*)
**monkey nut** (*Brit*) *n* orzeszek *m* ziemny
**monkey tricks** *npl* = **monkey business**
**monkey wrench** *n* klucz *m* nastawny
**mono** ['mɔnəu] *adj* monofoniczy, mono *post*
**monochrome** ['mɔnəkrəum] *adj* monochromatyczny
**monogamy** [mə'nɔgəmɪ] *n* monogamia *f*
**monogram** ['mɔnəgræm] *n* monogram *m*
**monolingual** [mɔnə'lɪŋgwəl] *adj* jednojęzyczny

m

**monolith** ['mɔnəlɪθ] *n* monolit *m*
**monolithic** [mɔnə'lɪθɪk] *adj* monolityczny
**monologue** ['mɔnələg] *n* monolog *m*
**monoplane** ['mɔnəpleɪn] *n* jednopłatowiec *m*, jednopłat *m*
**monopolize** [mə'nɔpəlaɪz] *vt* monopolizować (zmonopolizować *perf*)
**monopoly** [mə'nɔpəlɪ] *n* monopol *m*; **Monopolies and Mergers Commission** (*Brit*) ≈ Urząd Antymonopolowy
**monorail** ['mɔnəureɪl] *n* kolej *f* jednoszynowa
**monosodium glutamate** ['mɔnəsəudɪəm 'glutameɪt] *n* glutaminian *m* sodowy
**monosyllabic** [mɔnəsɪ'læbɪk] *adj* (*word*) monosylabiczny, jednozgłoskowy; (*person, reply*) burkliwy
**monosyllable** ['mɔnəsɪləbl] *n* monosylaba *f*
**monotone** ['mɔnətəun] *n*: **to speak in a ~** mówić monotonnie
**monotonous** [mə'nɔtənəs] *adj* monotonny
**monotony** [mə'nɔtənɪ] *n* monotonia *f*
**monsoon** [mɔn'su:n] *n* monsun *m*
**monster** ['mɔnstə^r] *n* (*animal, person, imaginary creature*) potwór *m*; (*monstrosity*) monstrum *nt*
**monstrosity** [mɔn'strɔsɪtɪ] *n* monstrum *nt*
**monstrous** ['mɔnstrəs] *adj* (*ugly, atrocious*) potworny, monstrualny; (*huge*) monstrualnie wielki
**montage** [mɔn'tɑ:ʒ] (*Film, Art, Mus*) *n* montaż *m*
**Mont Blanc** [mɔ̃ 'blɑ̃] *n* Mont Blanc *m inv*
**month** [mʌnθ] *n* miesiąc *m*; **every ~** co miesiąc; **300 dollars a ~** 300 dolarów na miesiąc *or* miesięcznie
**monthly** ['mʌnθlɪ] *adj* (*ticket, installment, income*) miesięczny; (*meeting*) comiesięczny ▷ *adv* co miesiąc; (*paid*) miesięcznie; **twice ~** dwa razy w miesiącu
**Montreal** [mɔntrɪ'ɔ:l] *n* Montreal *m*
**monument** ['mɔnjumənt] *n* pomnik *m*, monument *m* (*literary*)
**monumental** [mɔnju'mɛntl] *adj* (*building, work*) monumentalny; (*storm, row*) straszny
**moo** [mu:] *vi* ryczeć (zaryczeć *perf*)
**mood** [mu:d] *n* (*of person*) nastrój *m*, humor *m*; (*of crowd, group*) nastrój *m*; **to be in a good/bad ~** być w dobrym/złym nastroju *or* humorze; **I'm not in the ~ for** nie jestem w nastroju do *+gen*; **I'm in the ~ for a drink/to watch TV** mam ochotę się napić/pooglądać telewizję
**moodily** ['mu:dɪlɪ] *adv* (*sit*) ponuro, markotnie; (*behave*) kapryśnie
**moody** ['mu:dɪ] *adj* (*temperamental*) kapryśny, humorzasty (*inf*); (*sullen*) markotny, w złym humorze *post*
**moon** [mu:n] *n* księżyc *m*
**moonlight** ['mu:nlaɪt] *n* światło *nt* księżyca ▷ *vi* (*inf*) dorabiać na boku (*inf*)
**moonlighting** ['mu:nlaɪtɪŋ] (*inf*) *n* dorabianie *nt* na boku (*inf*)
**moonlit** ['mu:nlɪt] *adj*: **a ~ night** księżycowa noc *f*
**moonshot** ['mu:nʃɔt] *n* lot *m* na Księżyc
**moor** [muə^r] *n* wrzosowisko *nt* ▷ *vt* cumować (zacumować *perf or* przycumować *perf*) ▷ *vi* cumować (zacumować *perf*)
**mooring** ['muərɪŋ] *n* (*place*) miejsce *nt* cumowania; **moorings** *npl* cumy *pl*
**Moorish** ['muərɪʃ] *adj* mauretański
**moorland** ['muələnd] *n* wrzosowisko *nt*
**moose** [mu:s] *n inv* łoś *m* (amerykański)
**moot** [mu:t] *vt*: **to be ~ed** zostawać (zostać *perf*) poddanym pod dyskusję ▷ *adj*: **~ point** punkt *m* sporny
**mop** [mɔp] *n* (*for floor*) mop *m*; (*for dishes*) zmywak *m* (*na rączce*); (*of hair*) czupryna *f* ▷ *vt* (*floor*) myć (umyć *perf*), zmywać (zmyć *perf*); (*eyes, face*) ocierać (otrzeć *perf*)
▶ **mop up** *vt* (*liquid*) ścierać (zetrzeć *perf*)
**mope** [məup] *vi* rozczulać się nad sobą
▶ **mope about** *vi* snuć się z nieszczęśliwą miną
▶ **mope around** *vi* = **mope about**
**moped** ['məupɛd] *n* motorower *m*
**moquette** [mɔ'kɛt] *n* tkanina *f* pluszowa (*stosowana zwłaszcza w tapicerce*)
**MOR** *adj abbr* (*Mus*) = **middle-of-the-road**
**moral** ['mɔrl] *adj* moralny ▷ *n* morał *m*; **morals** *npl* moralność *f*; **~ support** wsparcie moralne
**morale** [mɔ'rɑ:l] *n* morale *nt inv*
**morality** [mə'rælɪtɪ] *n* moralność *f*
**moralize** ['mɔrəlaɪz] *vi*: **to ~ (about)** moralizować (na temat *+gen*)
**morally** ['mɔrəlɪ] *adv* moralnie
**morass** [mə'ræs] *n* bagno *nt*, mokradło *nt*; (*fig*) gąszcz *m*
**moratorium** [mɔrə'tɔ:rɪəm] *n* moratorium *nt*
**morbid** ['mɔ:bɪd] *adj* (*imagination, interest*) niezdrowy, chorobliwy; (*subject, joke*) makabryczny

 KEYWORD

**more** [mɔ:^r] *adj* **1** (*greater in number etc*) więcej (*+gen*); **more people/work than we expected** więcej ludzi/pracy niż się spodziewaliśmy; **more and more problems** coraz więcej kłopotów
**2** (*additional*) jeszcze; (*: in negatives*) już; **do you want (some) more tea?** chcesz jeszcze (trochę) herbaty?; **I have no** *or* **I don't have any more money** nie mam już więcej pieniędzy

▷ *pron* **1** (*greater amount*) więcej; **more than 10** więcej niż dziesięć; **it cost more than we expected** kosztowało więcej, niż się spodziewaliśmy
**2** (*further or additional amount*) jeszcze (trochę); (*: in negatives*) już; **is there any more?** czy jest jeszcze trochę?; **there's no more** nie ma już (ani trochę); **this cost much more** to kosztowało znacznie więcej; **you can take this pen; I have many more** możesz wziąć ten długopis — mam (ich) jeszcze dużo
▷ *adv* bardziej; **more lonely (than you)** bardziej samotny (niż ty *or* od ciebie); **more difficult** trudniejszy; **more easily** łatwiej; **more economically** oszczędniej; **more and more** coraz bardziej; **more and more excited** coraz bardziej podniecony; **more or less** mniej więcej; **more beautiful than ever** piękniejsza niż kiedykolwiek

**moreover** [mɔːˈrəuvəʳ] *adv* ponadto, poza tym
**morgue** [mɔːg] *n* kostnica *f*
**MORI** [ˈmɔːrɪ] (*Brit*) *n abbr* (*= Market & Opinion Research Institute*) *ośrodek badania rynku i opinii społecznej*
**moribund** [ˈmɔrɪbʌnd] *adj* chylący się ku upadkowi
**Mormon** [ˈmɔːmən] *n* mormon(ka) *m(f)*
**morning** [ˈmɔːnɪŋ] *n* poranek *m*, ranek *m* ▷ *cpd* (*sun, walk*) ranny, poranny; (*paper*) poranny; **this ~** dziś rano; **in the early hours of this ~** (dziś) we wczesnych godzinach rannych; **in the ~** (*between midnight and 3 o'clock*) w nocy; (*shortly before dawn*) nad ranem; (*around waking time*) rano; (*before noon*) przed południem; **three o'clock in the ~** trzecia w nocy; **seven o'clock in the ~** siódma rano
**morning sickness** *n* mdłości *pl* poranne
**Moroccan** [məˈrɔkən] *adj* marokański ▷ *n* Marokańczyk(-anka) *m(f)*
**Morocco** [məˈrɔkəu] *n* Maroko *nt*
**moron** [ˈmɔːrɔn] (*inf*) *n* debil(ka) *m(f)* (*inf*)
**moronic** [məˈrɔnɪk] (*inf*) *adj* (*person*) psychiczny (*inf*); (*behaviour*) kretyński (*inf*)
**morose** [məˈrəus] *adj* posępny, ponury
**morphine** [ˈmɔːfiːn] *n* morfina *f*
**Morse** [mɔːs] *n* (*also*: **Morse code**) alfabet *m* Morse'a, mors *m* (*inf*)
**morsel** [ˈmɔːsl] *n* (*tasty piece of food*) kąsek *m*; (*small piece or quantity*) odrobina *f*
**mortal** [ˈmɔːtl] *adj* śmiertelny ▷ *n* śmiertelnik *m*; **~ combat** walka na śmierć i życie
**mortality** [mɔːˈtælɪtɪ] *n* (*being mortal*) śmiertelność *f*; (*number of deaths*) umieralność *f*, śmiertelność *f*
**mortality rate** *n* współczynnik *m* umieralności
**mortar** [ˈmɔːtəʳ] *n* (*Mil, Culin*) moździerz *m*; (*Constr*) zaprawa *f* (murarska)
**mortgage** [ˈmɔːgɪdʒ] *n* (*loan*) kredyt *m* hipoteczny (*na budowę lub zakup domu*) ▷ *vt* zastawiać (zastawić *perf*), oddawać (oddać *perf*) w zastaw hipoteczny (*fml*); **to take out a ~** zaciągać (zaciągnąć *perf*) kredyt hipoteczny
**mortgage company** (*US*) *n towarzystwo udzielające kredytów hipotecznych*
**mortgagee** [mɔːgəˈdʒiː] *n* wierzyciel *m* hipoteczny
**mortgagor** [ˈmɔːgədʒəʳ] *n* dłużnik *m* hipoteczny
**mortician** [mɔːˈtɪʃən] (*US*) *n* pracownik *m* zakładu pogrzebowego
**mortified** [ˈmɔːtɪfaɪd] *adj*: **to be ~** czuć się potwornie zawstydzonym *or* zażenowanym
**mortify** [ˈmɔːtɪfaɪ] *vt* zawstydzać (zawstydzić *perf*)
**mortise lock** [ˈmɔːtɪs-] *n* zamek *m* (drzwiowy) wpuszczany
**mortuary** [ˈmɔːtjuərɪ] *n* kostnica *f*
**mosaic** [məuˈzeɪɪk] *n* mozaika *f*
**Moscow** [ˈmɔskəu] *n* Moskwa *f*
**Moslem** [ˈmɔzləm] *adj, n* = **Muslim**
**mosque** [mɔsk] *n* meczet *m*
**mosquito** [mɔsˈkiːtəu] (*pl* **~es**) *n* (*in damp places*) komar *m*; (*in tropics*) moskit *m*
**mosquito net** *n* moskitiera *f*
**moss** [mɔs] *n* mech *m*
**mossy** [ˈmɔsɪ] *adj* omszały

 KEYWORD

**most** [məust] *adj* **1** (*people, things*) większość *f* (*+gen*); **most men behave like that** większość mężczyzn tak się zachowuje
**2** (*interest, money etc*) najwięcej *+gen*; **he derived the most pleasure from her visit** jej wizyta sprawiła mu najwięcej przyjemności
▷ *pron* większość; **most of it/them** większość (tego)/z nich; **the most** najwięcej; **to make the most of sth** maksymalnie coś wykorzystywać (wykorzystać *perf*); **at the (very) most** (co) najwyżej
▷ *adv* (*+verb: spend, eat, work etc*) najwięcej; (*+adjective*): **the most expensive** najbardziej kosztowny, najkosztowniejszy; (*+adverb: carefully, easily etc*) najbardziej; (*very: polite, interesting etc*) wysoce, wielce

**mostly** [ˈməustlɪ] *adv* (*chiefly*) głównie; (*for the most part*) przeważnie

**MOT** (Brit) *n abbr* (= *Ministry of Transport*): **MOT (test)** ≈ przegląd *m* techniczny (*pojazdu samochodowego*)
**motel** [məu'tɛl] *n* motel *m*
**moth** [mɔθ] *n* ćma *f*; (*also*: **clothes moth**) mól *m*
**mothball** ['mɔθbɔ:l] *n* kulka *f* naftalinowa
**moth-eaten** ['mɔθi:tn] (*pej*) *adj* zniszczony przez mole
**mother** ['mʌðə^r] *n* matka *f* ▷ *cpd* (*country*) ojczysty; (*company*) macierzysty ▷ *vt* (*act as mother to*) wychowywać; (*pamper, protect*) matkować *+dat*
**mother board** ['mʌðəbɔ:d] (*Comput*) *n* płyta *f* główna
**motherhood** ['mʌðəhud] *n* macierzyństwo *nt*
**mother-in-law** ['mʌðərɪnlɔ:] *n* teściowa *f*
**motherly** ['mʌðəlɪ] *adj* (*attitude*) macierzyński; (*hands, care*) matczyny
**mother-of-pearl** ['mʌðərəv'pə:l] *n* macica *f* perłowa
**mother's help** *n* pomoc *f* domowa
**mother-to-be** ['mʌðətə'bi:] *n* przyszła matka *f*
**mother tongue** *n* język *m* ojczysty
**mothproof** ['mɔθpru:f] *adj* moloodporny
**motif** [məu'ti:f] *n* (*design*) wzór *m*; (*theme*) motyw *m*
**motion** ['məuʃən] *n* (*movement, gesture*) ruch *m*; (*proposal*) wniosek *m*; (Brit: *also*: **bowel motion**: *act*) wypróżnienie *nt*; (: *faeces*) stolec *m* ▷ *vt, vi*: **to ~ (to) sb to do sth** skinąć (*perf*) na kogoś, żeby coś zrobił; **to be in ~** (*vehicle*) być w ruchu; **to set in ~** (*machine*) uruchamiać (uruchomić *perf*); (*process*) nadawać (nadać *perf*) bieg *+dat*; **he went through the ~s of clapping** udawał, że klaszcze
**motionless** ['məuʃənlɪs] *adj* nieruchomy, w bezruchu *post*
**motion picture** *n* film *m*
**motivate** ['məutɪveɪt] *vt* (*act, decision*) powodować (spowodować *perf*); (*person*) zwiększać (zwiększyć *perf*) motywację *+gen*
**motivated** ['məutɪveɪtɪd] *adj*: **to be (highly) ~** mieć (silną) motywację; **~ by** (*envy, desire*) powodowany *+instr*; **he was ~ by envy** powodowała nim zawiść
**motivation** [məutɪ'veɪʃən] *n* motywacja *f*
**motive** ['məutɪv] *n* motyw *m*, pobudka *f* ▷ *adj* (*force*) napędowy; **from the best (of) ~s** w najlepszej wierze
**motley** ['mɔtlɪ] *adj*: **~ collection/crew** *etc* zbieranina *f*
**motor** ['məutə^r] *n* (*of machine, vehicle*) silnik *m*; (Brit: *inf*: *car*) maszyna *f* (*inf*) ▷ *cpd* (*industry*) motoryzacyjny; (*mechanic, accident*) samochodowy
**motorbike** ['məutəbaɪk] *n* motor *m*
**motorboat** ['məutəbəut] *n* motorówka *f*
**motorcar** ['məutəkɑ:] (Brit) *n* samochód *m*
**motorcoach** ['məutəkəutʃ] (Brit) *n* autokar *m*
**motorcycle** ['məutəsaɪkl] *n* motocykl *m*
**motorcycle racing** *n* wyścigi *pl* motocyklowe
**motorcyclist** ['məutəsaɪklɪst] *n* motocyklista(-tka) *m(f)*
**motoring** ['məutərɪŋ] (Brit) *n* jazda *f* or kierowanie *nt* samochodem ▷ *cpd* (*accident*) samochodowy, drogowy; (*offence*) drogowy
**motorist** ['məutərɪst] *n* kierowca *m*
**motorized** ['məutəraɪzd] *adj* (*transport*) samochodowy; (*barge etc*) motorowy; (*regiment*) zmotoryzowany
**motor oil** *n* olej *m* silnikowy
**motor racing** (Brit) *n* wyścigi *pl* samochodowe
**motor scooter** *n* skuter *m*
**motor vehicle** *n* pojazd *m* mechaniczny
**motorway** ['məutəweɪ] (Brit) *n* autostrada *f*
**mottled** ['mɔtld] *adj* cętkowany, w cętki *post*
**motto** ['mɔtəu] (*pl* **~es**) *n* (*of school, in book*) motto *nt*; (*watchword*) motto *nt* (życiowe), dewiza *f*
**mould**, (US) **mold** [məuld] *n* (*cast*) forma *f*; (*mildew*) pleśń *f* ▷ *vt* (*plastic, clay etc*) modelować; (*fig*: *public opinion, character*) kształtować, urabiać; **clay ~ed into battleships** okręty wojenne wymodelowane z gliny
**mo(u)lder** ['məuldə^r] *vi* rozkładać się, gnić
**mo(u)lding** ['məuldɪŋ] (*Archit*) *n* sztukateria *f*
**mo(u)ldy** ['məuldɪ] *adj* (*bread, cheese*) spleśniały; (*smell*) stęchły
**moult**, (US) **molt** [məult] *vi* linieć (wylinieć *perf*)
**mound** [maund] *n* (*of earth*) kopiec *m*; (*of blankets, leaves*) stos *m*
**mount** [maunt] *n* (*in proper names*): **M~ Carmel** Mount *m inv* Carmel; (*horse*) wierzchowiec *m*; (*for picture, jewel*) oprawa *f* ▷ *vt* (*horse*) dosiadać (dosiąść *perf*) *+gen*; (*exhibition, display*) urządzać (urządzić *perf*); (*machine, engine*) mocować (zamocować *perf*), montować (zamontować *perf*); (*jewel, picture*) oprawiać (oprawić *perf*); (*staircase*) wspinać się (wspiąć się *perf*) na *+acc*; (*stamp*) umieszczać (umieścić *perf*); (*attack, campaign*) przeprowadzać (przeprowadzić *perf*) ▷ *vi* (*inflation, tension, problems*) nasilać się (nasilić się *perf*), narastać (narosnąć *perf*); (*person*) dosiadać (dosiąść *perf*) konia
▶ **mount up** *vi* (*costs*) rosnąć, wzrastać (wzrosnąć *perf*); (*savings*) rosnąć (urosnąć *perf*)
**mountain** ['mauntɪn] *n* góra *f* ▷ *cpd* górski; **a ~ of** (*papers*) góra *+gen*; (*work*) nawał *+gen*; **to make a ~ out of a molehill** robić z igły widły

**mountain bike** *n* rower *m* górski
**mountaineer** [mauntɪ'nɪəʳ] *n* alpinista(-tka) *m(f)*, ≈ taternik(-iczka) *m(f)*
**mountaineering** [mauntɪ'nɪərɪŋ] *n* wspinaczka *f* górska; **to go ~** wybierać się (wybrać się *perf*) na wspinaczkę
**mountainous** ['mauntɪnəs] *adj* górzysty
**mountain rescue team** *n* górskie pogotowie *nt* ratunkowe
**mountainside** ['mauntɪnsaɪd] *n* stok *m* (górski), zbocze *nt* (górskie)
**mounted** ['mauntɪd] *adj* (*police*) konny; (*soldiers*) na koniach *post*
**Mount Everest** *n* Mount Everest *m inv*
**mourn** [mɔːn] *vt* opłakiwać ▷ *vi*: **to ~ for sb** opłakiwać kogoś; **to ~ for** *or* **over sth** żałować czegoś
**mourner** ['mɔːnəʳ] *n* żałobnik *m*
**mournful** ['mɔːnful] *adj* zasmucony, (bardzo) smutny
**mourning** ['mɔːnɪŋ] *n* żałoba *f*; **in ~** w żałobie
**mouse** [maus] (*pl* **mice**) *n* (*Zool, Comput*) mysz *f*; (*fig*: *person*) tchórz *m*
**mousetrap** ['maustræp] *n* (pu)łapka *f* na myszy
**mousse** [muːs] *n* (*Culin*) mus *m*; (*cosmetic*) pianka *f*
**moustache**, (*US*) **mustache** [məs'tɑːʃ] *n* wąsy *pl*
**mousy** ['mausɪ] *adj* (*hair*) mysi
**mouth** [mauθ] (*pl* **~s**) *n* (*Anat*) usta *pl*; (*of cave, hole*) wylot *m*; (*of river*) ujście *nt*; (*of bottle*) otwór *m*
**mouthful** ['mauθful] *n* (*of drink*) łyk *m*; (*of food*) kęs *m*
**mouth organ** *n* harmonijka *f* ustna, organki *pl*
**mouthpiece** ['mauθpiːs] *n* (*of musical instrument*) ustnik *m*; (*spokesperson*) rzecznik(-iczka) *m(f)*
**mouth-to-mouth** ['mauθtə'mauθ] *adj*: **~ resuscitation** oddychanie *nt* metodą usta-usta, sztuczne oddychanie *nt*
**mouthwash** ['mauθwɔʃ] *n* płyn *m* do płukania jamy ustnej
**mouth-watering** ['mauθwɔːtərɪŋ] *adj* apetyczny, smakowity
**movable** ['muːvəbl] *adj* ruchomy; **~ feast** święto ruchome
**move** [muːv] *n* (*movement*) ruch *m*; (*action*) posunięcie *nt*; (*of house*) przeprowadzka *f*; (*of employee*) przesunięcie *nt* ▷ *vt* (*furniture, car*) przesuwać (przesunąć *perf*); (*in game*) przesuwać (przesunąć *perf*), ruszać (ruszyć *perf*); (*emotionally*) wzruszać (wzruszyć *perf*), poruszać (poruszyć *perf*) ▷ *vi* (*person, animal*) ruszać się (ruszyć się *perf*); (*traffic*) posuwać się (posunąć się *perf*); (*in game*) wykonywać (wykonać *perf*) ruch; (*also*: **move house**) przeprowadzać się (przeprowadzić się *perf*); (*develop*: *events*) biec; (: *situation*) rozwijać się; **to ~ towards** zbliżać się (zbliżyć się *perf*) do *+gen*; **to ~ sb to do sth** skłaniać (skłonić *perf*) kogoś do zrobienia czegoś; **she ~d that the meeting be adjourned** zgłosiła wniosek o odroczenie posiedzenia; **get a ~ on!** rusz się!
▸ **move about** *vi* (*change position*) ruszać się; (*travel*) jeździć; (*change residence, job*) przenosić się
▸ **move along** *vi* przesuwać się (przesunąć się *perf*)
▸ **move around** *vi* = **move about**
▸ **move away** *vi* (*leave*) wyprowadzać się (wyprowadzić się *perf*); (*step away*) odsuwać się (odsunąć się *perf*)
▸ **move back** *vi* (*return*) wracać (wrócić *perf*); (*to the rear*) cofać się (cofnąć się *perf*)
▸ **move forward** *vi* posuwać się (posunąć się *perf*) naprzód *or* do przodu
▸ **move in** *vi* (*to house*) wprowadzać się (wprowadzić się *perf*); (*police, soldiers*) wkraczać (wkroczyć *perf*)
▸ **move off** *vi* (*car*) odjeżdżać (odjechać *perf*)
▸ **move on** *vi* ruszać (ruszyć *perf*) ▷ *vt* (*police*: *onlookers etc*) usuwać (usunąć *perf*)
▸ **move out** *vi* wyprowadzać się (wyprowadzić się *perf*)
▸ **move over** *vi* (*to make room*) przesuwać się (przesunąć się *perf*)
▸ **move up** *vi* (*employee*) awansować (awansować *perf*)
**moveable** ['muːvəbl] *adj* = **movable**
**movement** ['muːvmənt] *n* ruch *m*; (*of goods*) przewóz *m*; (*in attitude, policy*) tendencja *f*; (*of symphony etc*) część *f*; (*also*: **bowel movement**) wypróżnienie *nt*
**mover** ['muːvəʳ] *n* (*proposer*) wnioskodawca(-wczyni) *m(f)*
**movie** ['muːvɪ] *n* film *m*; **to go to the ~s** iść (pójść *perf*) do kina
**movie camera** *n* kamera *f* filmowa
**moviegoer** ['muːvɪgəuəʳ] (*US*) *n* kinoman(ka) *m(f)*
**moving** ['muːvɪŋ] *adj* (*emotional*) wzruszający; (*mobile*) ruchomy; (*force*) sprawczy, napędowy; (*spirit*) przewodni
**mow** [məu] (*pt* **mowed**, *pp* **mowed** *or* **mown**) *vt* kosić (skosić *perf*)
▸ **mow down** *vt* (*kill*) skosić (*perf*) (*inf*), wykosić (*perf*) (*inf*)
**mower** ['məuəʳ] *n* (*also*: **lawnmower**) kosiarka *f* (do trawy)
**Mozambique** [məuzəm'biːk] *n* Mozambik *m*
**MP** *n abbr* (= *Member of Parliament*) poseł/posłanka *m/f*; (= *Military Police*) ≈ ŻW; (*Canada*: = *Mounted Police*) policja *f* konna

**mpg** *n abbr* = **miles per gallon**
**mph** *abbr* = **miles per hour**
**MPhil** *n abbr (= Master of Philosophy) stopień naukowy*, ≈ mgr
**MPS** (*Brit*) *n abbr* = **Member of the Pharmaceutical Society**
**Mr**, (*US*) **Mr.** [ˈmɪstəʳ] *n*: **Mr Smith** pan *m* Smith
**MRC** (*Brit*) *n abbr* = **Medical Research Council**
**MRCP** (*Brit*) *n abbr* = **Member of the Royal College of Physicians**
**MRCS** (*Brit*) *n abbr* = **Member of the Royal College of Surgeons**
**MRCVS** (*Brit*) *n abbr* = **Member of the Royal College of Veterinary Surgeons**
**Mrs**, (*US*) **Mrs.** [ˈmɪsɪz] *n*: **Mrs Smith** pani *f* Smith
**Ms**, (*US*) **Ms.** [mɪz] *n*: **Ms Smith** pani *f* Smith
**MS** *n abbr* = **multiple sclerosis**; (*US*: = *Master of Science*) *stopień naukowy*, ≈ mgr ▷ *abbr* (*US*: *Post*) = **Mississippi**
**MS.** *n abbr* = **manuscript**
**MSA** (*US*) *n abbr (= Master of Science in Agriculture) stopień naukowy*, ≈ mgr
**MSc** *n abbr (= Master of Science) stopień naukowy*, ≈ mgr
**MSG** *n abbr* = **monosodium glutamate**
**MST** (*US*) *abbr* = **Mountain Standard Time**
**MSW** (*US*) *n abbr (= Master of Social Work) stopień naukowy*, ≈ mgr
**MT** *n abbr* (*Comput, Ling*: = *machine translation*) tłumaczenie *nt* maszynowe *or* automatyczne ▷ *abbr* (*US*: *Post*) = **Montana**
**Mt** (*Geog*) *abbr* (= *mount*) G.
**MTV** (*US*) *n abbr* (= *music television*) MTV *f inv*

 KEYWORD

**much** [mʌtʃ] *adj* (*time, money, effort*) dużo (*+gen*), wiele (*+gen*); **we haven't got much time/money** nie mamy dużo *or* wiele czasu/pieniędzy; **I have as much money/intelligence as you** mam tyle samo pieniędzy/rozumu co ty; **as much as 50 pounds** aż 50 funtów
▷ *pron* dużo, wiele; **there isn't much to do** nie ma dużo *or* wiele do zrobienia; **how much is it?** ile to kosztuje?
▷ *adv* **1** (*greatly, a great deal*) bardzo; **thank you very much** dziękuję bardzo; **I read as much as possible/as ever** czytam tyle, ile to możliwe/co zawsze; **he is as much a part of the community as you** jest w takim samym stopniu częścią tej społeczności, co i ty
**2** (*by far*: *+comparative*) znacznie; (: *+superlative*) zdecydowanie; **I'm much better now** czuję się teraz znacznie lepiej; **it's much the biggest publishing company in Europe** jest to zdecydowanie największe wydawnictwo w Europie
**3** (*almost*): **the view is much as it was ten years ago** widok jest w dużym stopniu taki, jak dziesięć lat temu; **how are you feeling? — much the same** jak się czujesz? — prawie tak samo

**muck** [mʌk] *n* (*dirt*) brud *m*; (*manure*) gnój *m*
▸ **muck about** (*inf*) *vi* wygłupiać się ▷ *vt*: **to ~ sb about** traktować kogoś niepoważnie
▸ **muck around** *vi* = **muck about**
▸ **muck in** (*Brit*: *inf*) *vi*: **to ~ in (with)** przyłączać się (przyłączyć się *perf*) (do *+gen*)
▸ **muck out** *vt* (*stable etc*) wyrzucać (wyrzucić *perf*) gnój z *+gen*
▸ **muck up** (*inf*) *vt* (*test, exam*) zawalać (zawalić *perf*) (*inf*)
**muckraking** [ˈmʌkreɪkɪŋ] (*inf*) *n* (*fig*) pranie *nt* brudów ▷ *adj* (*fig*: *reporters etc*) szukający sensacji
**mucky** [ˈmʌkɪ] *adj* (*boots*) bardzo brudny; (*field*) błotnisty
**mucus** [ˈmjuːkəs] *n* śluz *m*
**mud** [mʌd] *n* błoto *nt*
**muddle** [ˈmʌdl] *n* (*mess*) bałagan *m*; (*confusion*) zamieszanie *nt*, zamęt *m* ▷ *vt* (*person*) mieszać (namieszać *perf*) w głowie *+dat*; (*also*: **muddle up**: *things*) mieszać (pomieszać *perf*); (: *names etc*) mylić (pomylić *perf*); **I'm in a ~** mam zamęt w głowie; **to get in a ~** (*while explaining etc*) plątać się (zaplątać się *perf*)
▸ **muddle along** *vi* brnąć na oślep
▸ **muddle through** *vi* jakoś sobie radzić (poradzić *perf*)
**muddle-headed** [mʌdlˈhɛdɪd] *adj* nierozgarnięty
**muddy** [ˈmʌdɪ] *adj* (*field*) błotnisty; (*floor*) zabłocony
**mud flats** *npl tereny przybrzeżne zalewane podczas przypływów*
**mudguard** [ˈmʌdgɑːd] *n* błotnik *m*
**mudpack** [ˈmʌdpæk] *n* maseczka *f* błotna
**mud-slinging** [ˈmʌdslɪŋɪŋ] *n* (*fig*) obrzucanie się *nt* błotem
**muesli** [ˈmjuːzlɪ] *n* muesli *nt inv*
**muffin** [ˈmʌfɪn] *n rodzaj bułeczki jadanej na ciepło*
**muffle** [ˈmʌfl] *vt* (*sound*) tłumić (stłumić *perf*); (*against cold*) opatulać (opatulić *perf*)
**muffled** [ˈmʌfld] *adj* (*sound*) stłumiony; (*against cold*) opatulony
**muffler** [ˈmʌfləʳ] *n* (*US*: *Aut*) tłumik *m*; (*scarf*) szalik *m*
**mufti** [ˈmʌftɪ] *n*: **in ~** po cywilnemu
**mug** [mʌg] *n* (*cup*) kubek *m*; (*for beer*) kufel *m*; (*inf*: *face*) gęba *f* (*inf*); (: *fool*) frajer *m* (*inf*) ▷ *vt*

napadać (napaść *perf*) (*na ulicy*); **it's a mug's game** (*Brit*) to robota dla frajerów
▶ **mug up** (*Brit: inf*) *vt* (*also*: **mug up on**) wkuwać *or* zakuwać *+acc* (*inf*)
**mugger** ['mʌgəʳ] *n* (uliczny) bandyta *m*
**mugging** ['mʌgɪŋ] *n* napad *m* (uliczny)
**muggy** ['mʌgɪ] *adj* parny
**mulatto** [mju:'lætəu] (*pl* **~es**) *n* mulat(ka) *m(f)*
**mulberry** ['mʌlbrɪ] *n* morwa *f*
**mule** [mju:l] *n* muł *m*
**mullah** ['mʌlə] (*Rel*) *n* mułła *m*
**mulled** [mʌld] *adj*: **~ wine** grzane wino *nt*
**mullioned** ['mʌlɪənd] *adj*: **~ window** okno *nt* wielodzielne
**mull over** [mʌl-] *vt* przetrawić *perf +acc* (*fig*)
**multi...** ['mʌltɪ] *pref* wielo..., multi...
**multi-access** ['mʌltɪ'æksɛs] (*Comput*) *adj* wielodostępny
**multicoloured** ['mʌltɪkʌləd], (*US*) **multicolored** *adj* wielobarwny, różnokolorowy
**multifarious** [mʌltɪ'fɛərɪəs] *adj* różnoraki
**multilateral** [mʌltɪ'lætərl] *adj* wielostronny
**multi-level** ['mʌltɪlɛvl] (*US*) *adj* wielopoziomowy
**multimedia** ['mʌltɪ'mi:dɪə] *adj* multimedialny ▷ *n* multimedia *pl*
**multimillionaire** [mʌltɪmɪljə'nɛəʳ] *n* multimilioner(ka) *m(f)*
**multinational** [mʌltɪ'næʃənl] *adj* (*company*) międzynarodowy; (*state*) wielonarodowościowy ▷ *n* (wielkie) przedsiębiorstwo *nt* międzynarodowe
**multiple** ['mʌltɪpl] *adj* (*collision*) zbiorowy; (*injuries*) wielokrotny; (*interests, causes*) wieloraki ▷ *n* wielokrotność *f*
**multiple-choice** ['mʌltɪpltʃɔɪs] *adj*: **~ test** test *m* wielokrotnego wyboru
**multiple sclerosis** *n* stwardnienie *nt* rozsiane
**multiplex** ['mʌltɪplɛks] *n* multipleks *m*
**multiplication** [mʌltɪplɪ'keɪʃən] *n* (*Math*) mnożenie *nt*; (*increase*) pomnożenie się *nt*
**multiplication table** *n* tabliczka *f* mnożenia
**multiplicity** [mʌltɪ'plɪsɪtɪ] *n*: **a ~ of** mnogość *f +gen*
**multiply** ['mʌltɪplaɪ] *vt* mnożyć (pomnożyć *perf*) ▷ *vi* (*animals*) rozmnażać się; (*problems*) mnożyć się
**multiracial** [mʌltɪ'reɪʃl] *adj* wielorasowy
**multi-storey** (*Brit*) *adj* wielopiętrowy
**multitude** ['mʌltɪtju:d] *n* (*crowd*) rzesza *f*; **a ~ of** mnóstwo *+gen*; **for a ~ of reasons** z wielu (różnych) powodów
**mum** [mʌm] (*Brit: inf*) *n* mama *f* ▷ *adj*: **to keep mum** nie puszczać (nie puścić *perf*) pary z ust; **mum's the word!** ani mru-mru! (*inf*)
**mumble** ['mʌmbl] *vt* mamrotać (wymamrotać *perf*) ▷ *vi* mamrotać (wymamrotać *perf*)
**mummify** ['mʌmɪfaɪ] *vt* mumifikować (zmumifikować *perf*)
**mummy** ['mʌmɪ] *n* (*Brit: mother*) mamusia *f*; (*corpse*) mumia *f*
**mumps** [mʌmps] (*Med*) *n* świnka *f*
**munch** [mʌntʃ] *vt* żuć ▷ *vi* żuć
**mundane** [mʌn'deɪn] *adj* przyziemny
**Munich** ['mju:nɪk] *n* Monachium *nt inv*
**municipal** [mju:'nɪsɪpl] *adj* miejski, municypalny (*fml*)
**municipality** [mju:nɪsɪ'pælɪtɪ] *n* (*city, town*) miasto *nt*
**munitions** [mju:'nɪʃənz] *npl amunicja i sprzęt bojowy*
**mural** ['mjuərl] *n* malowidło *nt* ścienne
**murder** ['mə:dəʳ] *n* morderstwo *nt* ▷ *vt* mordować (zamordować *perf*); **to commit ~** popełniać (popełnić *perf*) morderstwo
**murderer** ['mə:dərəʳ] *n* morderca *m*
**murderess** ['mə:dərɪs] *n* morderczyni *f*
**murderous** ['mə:dərəs] *adj* (*tendencies*) zbrodniczy; (*attack, instinct*) morderczy
**murk** [mə:k] *n* mrok *m*
**murky** ['mə:kɪ] *adj* (*street*) mroczny; (*water*) mętny
**murmur** ['mə:məʳ] *n* szmer *m* ▷ *vt* mruczeć (mruknąć *perf*) ▷ *vi* mruczeć (mruknąć *perf*); **heart ~** (*Med*) szmer w sercu
**MusB(ac)** *n abbr* (= *Bachelor of Music*) *stopień naukowy*
**muscle** ['mʌsl] *n* (*Anat*) mięsień *m*; (*fig*) siła *f*
▶ **muscle in** *vi* pchać się (wepchać się *perf*) (na siłę)
**muscular** ['mʌskjuləʳ] *adj* (*pain*) mięśniowy; (*person*) umięśniony, muskularny; (*build*) muskularny
**MusD(oc)** *n abbr* (= *Doctor of Music*) *stopień naukowy*, ≈ dr
**muse** [mju:z] *vi* dumać ▷ *n* muza *f*
**museum** [mju:'zɪəm] *n* muzeum *nt*
**mush** [mʌʃ] *n* breja *f*; (*fig: pej*) ckliwe bzdury *pl*
**mushroom** ['mʌʃrum] *n* grzyb *m* ▷ *vi* (*fig: town, organization*) szybko się rozrastać (rozrosnąć *perf*)
**music** ['mju:zɪk] *n* muzyka *f*
**musical** ['mju:zɪkl] *adj* (*career, skills*) muzyczny; (*person*) muzykalny; (*sound, tune*) melodyjny ▷ *n* musical *m*
**music(al) box** *n* pozytywka *f*
**musical instrument** *n* instrument *m* muzyczny
**music hall** *n* wodewil *m*

**musician** [mju:'zɪʃən] *n* muzyk *m*
**music stand** *n* pulpit *m* do nut
**musk** [mʌsk] *n* piżmo *nt*
**musket** ['mʌskɪt] *n* muszkiet *m*
**muskrat** ['mʌskræt] *n* piżmak *m*, szczur *m* piżmowy
**musk rose** (*Bot*) *n* róża *f* piżmowa
**Muslim** ['mʌzlɪm] *adj* muzułmański ▷ *n* muzułmanin(-anka) *m(f)*
**muslin** ['mʌzlɪn] *n* muślin *m*
**musquash** ['mʌskwɔʃ] *n* (*Zool*) = **muskrat**; (*fur*) futro *nt* z piżmaków
**mussel** ['mʌsl] *n* małż *m* (jadalny)
**must** [mʌst] *aux vb* (*necessity, obligation*): **I ~ do it** muszę to zrobić; (*prohibition*): **you ~n't do it** nie wolno ci tego robić; (*probability*): **he ~ be there by now** musi już tam być, pewnie już tam jest; (*suggestion, invitation*): **you ~ come and see me** (koniecznie) musisz mnie odwiedzić; (*guess, assumption*): **I ~ have made a mistake** musiałam się pomylić; (*indicating sth unwelcome*): **why ~ he always call so late?** dlaczego zawsze musi dzwonić tak późno? ▷ *n* konieczność *f*; **it's a ~** to konieczne
**mustache** ['mʌstæʃ] (*US*) *n* = **moustache**
**mustard** ['mʌstəd] *n* musztarda *f*
**mustard gas** *n* iperyt *m*, gaz *m* musztardowy
**muster** ['mʌstə^r] *vt* (*energy, troops*) zbierać (zebrać *perf*); (*support*) uzyskiwać (uzyskać *perf*); (*also*: **muster up**: *enthusiasm etc*) wykrzesać (*perf*) z siebie; (: *courage*) zdobywać się (zdobyć się *perf*) na *+acc* ▷ *n*: **to pass ~** sprostać (*perf*) wymaganiom
**mustiness** ['mʌstɪnɪs] *n* stęchlizna *f*
**mustn't** ['mʌsnt] = **must not**
**musty** ['mʌstɪ] *adj* (*smell*) stęchły; (*place*) pachnący stęchlizną
**mutant** ['mju:tənt] *n* mutant *m*
**mutate** [mju:'teɪt] *vi* mutować, ulegać (ulec *perf*) mutacji
**mutation** [mju:'teɪʃən] *n* (*Bio*) mutacja *f*; (*alteration*) zmiana *f*
**mute** [mju:t] *adj* niemy
**muted** ['mju:tɪd] *adj* przytłumiony; **~ trumpet** trąbka z tłumikiem
**mutilate** ['mju:tɪleɪt] *vt* (*person*) okaleczać (okaleczyć *perf*); (*thing*) uszkadzać (uszkodzić *perf*)
**mutilation** [mju:tɪ'leɪʃən] *n* okaleczenie *nt*
**mutinous** ['mju:tɪnəs] *adj* (*troops*) zbuntowany; (*attitude*) buntowniczy
**mutiny** ['mju:tɪnɪ] *n* bunt *m* ▷ *vi* buntować się (zbuntować się *perf*)
**mutter** ['mʌtə^r] *vt* mamrotać (wymamrotać *perf*) ▷ *vi* mamrotać (wymamrotać *perf*)
**mutton** ['mʌtn] *n* baranina *f*
**mutual** ['mju:tʃuəl] *adj* (*help, respect*) wzajemny; (*friend, interest*) wspólny
**mutually** ['mju:tʃuəlɪ] *adv* (*exclusive, respectful*) wzajemnie; **~ beneficial** korzystny dla obu stron
**muzzle** ['mʌzl] *n* (*of dog*) pysk *m*; (*of gun*) wylot *m* lufy; (*for dog*) kaganiec *m* ▷ *vt* zakładać (założyć *perf*) kaganiec *+dat*; (*fig*) ograniczać (ograniczyć *perf*) swobodę wypowiedzi *+gen*
**MV** *abbr* = **motor vessel**
**MVP** (*US*: *Sport*) *n abbr* = **most valuable player**
**MW** (*Radio*) *abbr* (= *medium wave*) f.śr.
**my** [maɪ] *adj* mój; **this is my house/brother** to (jest) mój dom/brat; **I've washed my hair** umyłem włosy; **I've cut my finger** skaleczyłam się w palec
**myopic** [maɪ'ɔpɪk] *adj* (*person*): **to be ~** być krótkowidzem; (*fig*) krótkowzroczny
**myriad** ['mɪrɪəd] *n* miriady *pl*
**myrrh** [mə:^r] *n* mirra *f*
**myself** [maɪ'sɛlf] *pron* (*reflexive*) się; (*emphatic*): **I dealt with it ~** sam sobie z tym poradziłem; (*after prep*) siebie (*gen, acc*), sobie (*dat, loc*), sobą (*instr*); **he's a Pole, like ~** jest Polakiem, podobnie jak ja; *see also* **oneself**
**mysterious** [mɪs'tɪərɪəs] *adj* tajemniczy
**mysteriously** [mɪs'tɪərɪəslɪ] *adv* (*smile*) tajemniczo; (*disappear*) w tajemniczy sposób; (*die*) w tajemniczych okolicznościach
**mystery** ['mɪstərɪ] *n* (*puzzle*) tajemnica *f*; (*strangeness*) tajemniczość *f* ▷ *cpd* tajemniczy
**mystery story** *n opowiadanie, w którym niezwykłe wydarzenia znajdują wytłumaczenie dopiero w zakończeniu*
**mystic** ['mɪstɪk] *n* mistyk(-yczka) *m(f)*
**mystic(al)** ['mɪstɪk(l)] *adj* mistyczny
**mystify** ['mɪstɪfaɪ] *vt* zadziwiać (zadziwić *perf*)
**mystique** [mɪs'ti:k] *n*: **the ~ surrounding sb/sth** aura *f* tajemniczości otaczająca kogoś/coś
**myth** [mɪθ] *n* mit *f*
**mythical** ['mɪθɪkl] *adj* mityczny
**mythological** [mɪθə'lɔdʒɪkl] *adj* mitologiczny
**mythology** [mɪ'θɔlədʒɪ] *n* mitologia *f*

# Nn

**N[1], n** [ɛn] *n* (*letter*) N *nt*, n *nt*; **N for Nellie,** (*US*) **N for Nan** ≈ N jak Natalia
**N[2]** *abbr* (= *north*) płn.
**NA** (*US*) *n abbr* (= *Narcotics Anonymous*) *organizacja niosąca pomoc osobom uzależnionym od narkotyków*; = **National Academy**
**n/a** *abbr* (= *not applicable*) nie dot.; (*Comm etc*: = *no account*) brak rachunku (*bieżącego*)
**NAACP** (*US*) *n abbr* = **National Association for the Advancement of Colored People**
**NAAFI** ['næfɪ] (*Brit*) *n abbr* (= *Navy, Army & Air Force Institute*) *instytucja prowadząca sklepy, stołówki itp dla żołnierzy brytyjskich*
**NACU** (*US*) *n abbr* = **National Association of Colleges and Universities**
**nadir** ['neɪdɪə$^r$] *n* (*Astron*) nadir *m*; (*fig*) najniższy punkt *m*
**nag** [næg] *vt* strofować ▷ *vi* zrzędzić ▷ *n* (*pej*: *horse*) szkapa *f* (*pej*); (: *person*) zrzęda *f* (*pej*); **to nag at sb** dręczyć kogoś
**nagging** ['nægɪŋ] *adj* (*doubt, suspicion*) dręczący; (*pain*) dokuczliwy; **I have a ~ suspicion/doubt that...** dręczy mnie podejrzenie/wątpliwość, że...
**nail** [neɪl] *n* (*on finger*) paznokieć *m*; (*metal*) gwóźdź *m* ▷ *vt* (*inf*: *thief etc*) nakryć (*perf*) (*inf*); **to ~ sth to sth** przybijać (przybić *perf*) coś do czegoś; **to ~ sb down (to sth)** przyciskać (przycisnąć *perf*) kogoś (w jakiejś sprawie)
**nailbrush** ['neɪlbrʌʃ] *n* szczoteczka *f* do paznokci
**nailfile** ['neɪlfaɪl] *n* pilnik *m* do paznokci
**nail polish** *n* lakier *m* do paznokci
**nail polish remover** *n* zmywacz *m* do paznokci
**nail scissors** *npl* nożyczki *pl* do paznokci
**nail varnish** (*Brit*) *n* = **nail polish**
**Nairobi** [naɪ'rəubɪ] *n* Nairobi *nt inv*
**naïve** [naɪ'i:v] *adj* naiwny
**naïveté** [naɪ'i:vteɪ] *n* = **naivety**
**naivety** [naɪ'i:vteɪ] *n* naiwność *f*
**naked** ['neɪkɪd] *adj* (*person*) nagi; (*flame*) odkryty; **with/to the ~ eye** gołym okiem
**nakedness** ['neɪkɪdnɪs] *n* nagość *f*
**NAM** (*US*) *n abbr* = **National Association of Manufacturers**
**name** [neɪm] *n* (*first name*) imię *nt*; (*surname*) nazwisko *nt*; (*of animal, place, illness*) nazwa *f*; (*of pet*) imię *nt*; (*reputation*) reputacja *f*, dobre imię *nt* ▷ *vt* (*baby*) dawać (dać *perf*) na imię *+dat*; (*ship etc*) nadawać (nadać *perf*) imię *+dat*; (*criminal etc*) wymieniać (wymienić *perf*) z nazwiska; (*price, date etc*) podawać (podać *perf*); **what's your ~?** (*surname*) jak się Pan/Pani nazywa?; (*first name*) jak masz na imię?, jak ci na imię?; **by ~** z nazwiska; **in the ~ of** na nazwisko *+nom*; (*fig*) w imię *+gen*; **in sb's ~** na czyjeś nazwisko; **my ~ is Peter** mam na imię Peter; **to give one's ~ and address** podać (*perf*) (swoje) nazwisko i adres; **to make a ~ for o.s.** zdobyć (*perf*) sławę; **to give sb a bad ~** psuć (popsuć *perf*) komuś opinię *or* reputację; **to call sb ~s** obrzucać (obrzucić *perf*) kogoś wyzwiskami; **the college is ~d after her** kolegium nazwano jej imieniem
**name-dropping** ['neɪmdrɔpɪŋ] *n* rzucanie *nt* znanymi nazwiskami (*żeby zrobić na kimś wrażenie*)
**nameless** ['neɪmlɪs] *adj* (*anonymous*) nieznany, bezimienny; (*vague*) nieokreślony; **who/which shall remain ~** którego nie wymienię
**namely** ['neɪmlɪ] *adv* (a) mianowicie
**nameplate** ['neɪmpleɪt] *n* tabliczka *f* z nazwiskiem
**namesake** ['neɪmseɪk] *n* imiennik(-iczka) *m(f)*
**nanny** ['nænɪ] *n* niania *f*
**nanny-goat** ['nænɪgəut] *n* koza *f*
**nap** [næp] *n* (*sleep*) drzemka *f*; (*of fabric*) włos *m* ▷ *vi*: **to be caught napping** (*fig*) dać (*perf*) się zaskoczyć; **to have a nap** ucinać (uciąć *perf*) sobie drzemkę
**NAPA** (*US*) *n abbr* (= *National Association of Performing Artists*) ≈ ZASP
**napalm** ['neɪpɑ:m] *n* napalm *m*
**nape** [neɪp] *n*: **the ~ of the neck** kark *m*
**napkin** ['næpkɪn] *n* serwetka *f*
**Naples** ['neɪplz] *n* Neapol *m*
**Napoleonic** [nəpəulɪ'ɔnɪk] *adj* napoleoński
**nappy** ['næpɪ] (*Brit*) *n* pieluszka *f*

**nappy liner** (*Brit*) *n wkładka wchłaniająca do tetrowej pieluszki*
**nappy rash** *n* odparzenie *nt* (*od pieluszki*)
**narcissistic** [nɑːsɪˈsɪstɪk] *adj* narcystyczny
**narcissus** [nɑːˈsɪsəs] (*pl* **narcissi**) *n* (*Bot*) narcyz *m*
**narcotic** [nɑːˈkɔtɪk] *adj* narkotyczny ▷ *n* narkotyk *m*; **narcotics** *npl* narkotyki *pl*
**nark** [nɑːk] (*Brit*: *inf*) *vt*: **to be ~ed at sth** być czymś wkurzonym (*inf*)
**narrate** [nəˈreɪt] *vt* (*story*) opowiadać; (*film, programme*) występować w roli narratora *+gen*
**narration** [nəˈreɪʃən] *n* (*in novel etc*) narracja *f*; (*to film etc*) komentarz *m*
**narrative** [ˈnærətɪv] *n* (*in novel etc*) narracja *f*; (*of journey etc*) relacja *f*
**narrator** [nəˈreɪtəʳ] *n* narrator(ka) *m(f)*
**narrow** [ˈnærəu] *adj* (*space, sense*) wąski; (*majority, defeat*) nieznaczny; (*ideas, view*) ograniczony ▷ *vi* (*road*) zwężać się (zwężyć się *perf*); (*gap*) zmniejszać się (zmniejszyć się *perf*) ▷ *vt* (*gap*) zmniejszać (zmniejszyć *perf*); (*eyes*) mrużyć (zmrużyć *perf*); **to have a ~ escape** ledwo ujść (*perf*) cało; **to ~ sth down (to sth)** zawężać (zawęzić *perf*) coś (do czegoś)
**narrow-gauge** *adj* (*Rail*) wąskotorowy
**narrowly** [ˈnærəulɪ] *adv* ledwo, z ledwością; **he ~ missed the target** minimalnie chybił
**narrow-minded** [nærəuˈmaɪndɪd] *adj* (*person*) ograniczony, o wąskich horyzontach (umysłowych) *post*; (*attitude*) pełen uprzedzeń
**NAS** (*US*) *n abbr* = **National Academy of Sciences**
**NASA** [ˈnæsə] (*US*) *n abbr* (= *National Aeronautics and Space Administration*) NASA *f inv*
**nasal** [ˈneɪzl] *adj* nosowy
**Nassau** [ˈnæsɔː] *n* Nassau *nt inv*
**nastily** [ˈnɑːstɪlɪ] *adv* złośliwie
**nastiness** [ˈnɑːstɪnɪs] *n* (*of person, remark*) złośliwość *f*
**nasturtium** [nəsˈtəːʃəm] *n* (*Bot*) nasturcja *f*
**nasty** [ˈnɑːstɪ] *adj* (*remark*) złośliwy; (*person*) złośliwy, niemiły; (*taste, smell*) nieprzyjemny; (*wound, accident, weather*) paskudny; (*shock*) niemiły, przykry; (*problem*) trudny; (*question*) podstępny, podchwytliwy; **to turn ~** stawać się (stać się *perf*) nieprzyjemnym; **it's a ~ business** to paskudna sprawa
**NAS/UWT** (*Brit*) *n abbr* (= *National Association of Schoolmasters/Union of Women Teachers*) *związek zawodowy nauczycieli*
**nation** [ˈneɪʃən] *n* (*people*) naród *m*; (*country*) państwo *nt*
**national** [ˈnæʃənl] *adj* (*newspaper*) (ogólno) krajowy; (*monument, characteristic*) narodowy; (*interests*) państwowy ▷ *n* obywatel(ka) *m(f)*
**national anthem** *n* hymn *m* państwowy
**national debt** *n* (*Econ*) dług *m* publiczny
**national dress** *n* strój *m* narodowy
**National Guard** (*US*) *n* Gwardia *f* Narodowa
**National Health Service** (*Brit*) *n* ≈ służba *f* zdrowia
**National Insurance** (*Brit*) *n* ≈ Zakład *m* Ubezpieczeń Społecznych
**nationalism** [ˈnæʃnəlɪzəm] *n* nacjonalizm *m*
**nationalist** [ˈnæʃnəlɪst] *adj* nacjonalistyczny ▷ *n* nacjonalista(-tka) *m(f)*
**nationality** [næʃəˈnælɪtɪ] *n* narodowość *f*; (*dual etc*) obywatelstwo *nt*
**nationalization** [næʃnəlaɪˈzeɪʃən] *n* nacjonalizacja *f*, upaństwowienie *nt*
**nationalize** [ˈnæʃnəlaɪz] *vt* nacjonalizować (znacjonalizować *perf*), upaństwawiać (upaństwowić *perf*)
**nationally** [ˈnæʃnəlɪ] *adv* na szczeblu centralnym
**national park** *n* park *m* narodowy
**national press** *n* prasa *f* krajowa
**National Security Council** (*US*) *n* Rada *f* Bezpieczeństwa Narodowego
**national service** *n* obowiązkowa służba *f* wojskowa
**nationwide** [ˈneɪʃənwaɪd] *adj* ogólnokrajowy ▷ *adv* w całym kraju
**native** [ˈneɪtɪv] *n* tubylec *m*, krajowiec *m* ▷ *adj* (*population*) rodowity; (*country, language*) ojczysty; (*ability*) wrodzony; **a ~ of Ireland** rodowity Irlandczyk; **~ to** rodem z *+gen*
**native speaker** *n* rodzimy użytkownik *m* języka
**Nativity** [nəˈtɪvɪtɪ] *n* (*Rel*): **the ~** narodzenie *nt* Chrystusa
**NATO** [ˈneɪtəu] *n abbr* (= *North Atlantic Treaty Organization*) NATO *nt inv*
**natter** [ˈnætəʳ] (*Brit*) *vi* paplać ▷ *n*: **to have a ~** ucinać (uciąć *perf*) sobie pogawędkę, plotkować (poplotkować *perf*)
**natural** [ˈnætʃrəl] *adj* naturalny; (*disaster*) żywiołowy; (*performer, hostess etc*) urodzony; (*Mus*) niealterowany; **to die of ~ causes** umierać (umrzeć *perf*) śmiercią naturalną
**natural childbirth** *n* poród *m* naturalny
**natural gas** *n* gaz *m* ziemny
**naturalist** [ˈnætʃrəlɪst] *n* przyrodnik(-iczka) *m(f)*
**naturalize** [ˈnætʃrəlaɪz] *vt*: **to become ~d** naturalizować się (*perf*)
**naturally** [ˈnætʃrəlɪ] *adv* naturalnie; (*result, happen*) w sposób naturalny; (*die*) śmiercią naturalną; (*cheerful, talented*) z natury; **she is ~ blonde** jest naturalną blondynką
**naturalness** [ˈnætʃrəlnɪs] *n* naturalność *f*
**natural resources** *npl* bogactwa *pl* naturalne

**natural wastage** *n* (*Industry*) odpady *pl* naturalne
**nature** ['neɪtʃəʳ] *n* (*also*: **Nature**) natura *f*, przyroda *f*; (*kind, sort*) natura *f*; (*character*: *of thing*) istota *f*, właściwość *f*; (: *of person*) usposobienie *nt*, natura *f*; **by ~** z natury; **by its (very) ~** z natury rzeczy; **documents of a confidential ~** dokumenty o charakterze poufnym; **something of that ~** coś w tym rodzaju
**-natured** ['neɪtʃəd] *suff*: **ill~** złośliwy; **good~** dobroduszny
**nature reserve** (*Brit*) *n* rezerwat *m* przyrody
**nature trail** *n* szlak *m* przyrodoznawczy
**naturist** ['neɪtʃərɪst] *n* naturysta(-tka) *m(f)*
**naught** [nɔːt] *n* = **nought**
**naughtiness** ['nɔːtɪnɪs] *n* (*of child*) niegrzeczne zachowanie *nt*, krnąbrność *f*; (*of story etc*) nieprzyzwoitość *f*
**naughty** ['nɔːtɪ] *adj* (*child*) niegrzeczny, krnąbrny; (*story*) nieprzyzwoity
**nausea** ['nɔːsɪə] *n* mdłości *pl*
**nauseate** ['nɔːsɪeɪt] *vt* przyprawiać (przyprawić *perf*) o mdłości; (*fig*) budzić wstręt *or* obrzydzenie w *+loc*
**nauseating** ['nɔːsɪeɪtɪŋ] *adj* (*smell, sight*) przyprawiający o mdłości; (*fig*) budzący *or* wzbudzający obrzydzenie
**nauseous** ['nɔːsɪəs] *adj* przyprawiający o mdłości; **to feel ~** mieć mdłości
**nautical** ['nɔːtɪkl] *adj* żeglarski; **a ~ man** człowiek morza
**nautical mile** *n* mila *f* morska (= *1853 m*)
**naval** ['neɪvl] *adj* (*uniform*) marynarski; (*battle, forces*) morski
**naval officer** *n* oficer *m* marynarki
**nave** [neɪv] *n* (*Archit*) nawa *f* główna
**navel** ['neɪvl] *n* (*Anat*) pępek *m*
**navigable** ['nævɪgəbl] *adj* żeglowny, spławny
**navigate** ['nævɪgeɪt] *vt* (*river, path*) pokonywać (pokonać *perf*) ▹ *vi* (*birds etc*) odnajdywać drogę; (*Naut, Aviat*) nawigować; (*Aut*) pilotować
**navigation** [nævɪ'geɪʃən] *n* (*activity*) nawigowanie *nt*, pilotowanie *nt*; (*science*) nawigacja *f*
**navigator** ['nævɪgeɪtəʳ] *n* (*Naut, Aviat*) nawigator *m*; (*Aut*) pilot *m*
**navvy** ['nævɪ] (*Brit*) *n* robotnik *m* niewykwalifikowany
**navy** ['neɪvɪ] *n* (*branch of military*) marynarka *f* (wojenna); (*ships*) flota *f* (wojenna); **Department of the N~** (*US*) Departament *m* Marynarki Wojennej
**navy(-blue)** ['neɪvɪ('bluː)] *adj* granatowy
**Nazareth** ['næzərɪθ] *n* Nazaret *m*
**Nazi** ['nɑːtsɪ] *n* nazista(-tka) *m(f)*
**NB** *abbr* (= *nota bene*) nb.; (*Canada*) = **New Brunswick**
**NBA** (*US*) *n abbr* = **National Basketball Association; National Boxing Association**
**NBC** (*US*) *n abbr* = **National Broadcasting Company**
**NBS** (*US*) *n abbr* (= *National Bureau of Standards*) *urząd normalizacyjny*
**NC** *abbr* (*Comm etc*: = *no charge*) bezpł.; (*US*: *Post*) = **North Carolina**
**NCC** *n abbr* (*Brit*) = **Nature Conservancy Council**; (*US*) = **National Council of Churches**
**NCCL** (*Brit*) *n abbr* (= *National Council for Civil Liberties*) *organizacja występująca w obronie praw obywatelskich*
**NCO** (*Mil*) *n abbr* = **non-commissioned officer**
**ND** (*US*: *Post*) *abbr* = **North Dakota**
**NE** (*US*: *Post*) *abbr* = **New England; Nebraska**
**NEA** (*US*) *n abbr* = **National Education Association**
**neap** [niːp] *n* (*also*: **neap tide**) pływ *m* mały *or* kwadrowy
**Neapolitan** [nɪə'pɔlɪtən] *adj* neapolitański ▹ *n* neapolitańczyk(-anka) *m(f)*
**near** [nɪəʳ] *adj* (*in space, time*) bliski, niedaleki; (*relative*) bliski; (*darkness*) prawie zupełny ▹ *adv* (*in space*) blisko; (*perfect, impossible*) prawie, niemal ▹ *prep* (*also*: **near to**: *in space*) blisko *+gen*; (: *in time*) około *+gen*; (: *in situation, intimacy*) bliski *+gen* ▹ *vt* zbliżać się (zbliżyć się *perf*) do *+gen*; **Christmas is quite ~ now** już niedaleko do Świąt Bożego Narodzenia; **25,000 pounds or ~est offer** (*Brit*) 25.000 funtów lub oferta najbliższa tej sumie; **in the ~ future** w niedalekiej przyszłości; **~ the beginning of the play** krótko po rozpoczęciu sztuki; **~ the end of the year** (na) krótko przed końcem roku; **~ here/there** tutaj/tam niedaleko, niedaleko stąd/stamtąd; **none of us could really get ~ her** nikt z nas nie mógł się naprawdę do niej zbliżyć; **this has brought her ~er to me** to zbliżyło nas do siebie; **the building is ~ing completion** budowa jest na ukończeniu *or* dobiega końca; **confusion ~ing hysteria** zamieszanie graniczące z histerią
**nearby** [nɪə'baɪ] *adj* pobliski ▹ *adv* w pobliżu
**Near East** *n*: **the ~** Bliski Wschód *m*
**nearer** ['nɪərəʳ] *adj, adv comp of* **near**
**nearest** ['nɪərɛst] *adj, adv superl of* **near**
**nearly** ['nɪəlɪ] *adv* prawie; **I ~ fell** o mało nie upadłem; **it's not ~ big enough** jest o wiele za mały; **she was ~ crying** była bliska płaczu
**near miss** *n* (*shot*) minimalnie chybiony strzał *m*; **it was a ~** (*accident avoided*) o mało (co) nie doszło do wypadku
**nearness** ['nɪənɪs] *n* bliskość *f*

n

**nearside** ['nɪəsaɪd] *(Aut) n (with left-hand drive)* prawa strona *f (pojazdu)*; *(with right-hand drive)* lewa strona *f (pojazdu)*
**near-sighted** [nɪə'saɪtɪd] *adj* krótkowzroczny
**neat** [ni:t] *adj (person, room)* schludny; *(handwriting)* staranny; *(plan)* zgrabny; *(solution, description)* elegancki; *(spirits)* czysty; **I drink it ~** piję to bez rozcieńczania
**neatly** ['ni:tlɪ] *adv (tidily)* starannie; *(conveniently)* zgrabnie
**neatness** ['ni:tnɪs] *n (of person, place)* schludność *f*; *(of solution)* elegancja *f*
**nebulous** ['nɛbjuləs] *adj* mglisty
**necessarily** ['nɛsɪsrɪlɪ] *adv* z konieczności; **not ~** niekoniecznie
**necessary** ['nɛsɪsrɪ] *adj (skill, item)* niezbędny; *(effect)* nieunikniony; *(connection, condition)* konieczny; **if ~** jeśli to konieczne, jeśli trzeba; **it is ~ to examine this** *or* **that we examine this** trzeba to zbadać
**necessitate** [nɪ'sɛsɪteɪt] *vt* wymagać *+gen*
**necessity** [nɪ'sɛsɪtɪ] *n (inevitability)* konieczność *f*; *(compelling need)* potrzeba *f*, konieczność *f*; *(essential item)* artykuł *m* pierwszej potrzeby; **of ~** z konieczności; **out of ~** z konieczności
**neck** [nɛk] *n* szyja *f*; *(of shirt, dress)* wykończenie *nt* przy szyi; *(of bottle)* szyjka *f* ▷ *vi (inf)* całować się; **~ and ~** łeb w łeb; **to stick one's ~ out** *(inf)* wychylać się (wychylić się *perf*) *(inf)*
**necklace** ['nɛklɪs] *n* naszyjnik *m*
**neckline** ['nɛklaɪn] *n* dekolt *m*
**necktie** ['nɛktaɪ] *(esp US) n* krawat *m*
**nectar** ['nɛktə[r]] *n* nektar *m*
**nectarine** ['nɛktərɪn] *n* nektarynka *f*
**NEDC** *(Brit) n abbr (formerly)* = **National Economic Development Council**
**Neddy** ['nɛdɪ] *(Brit: inf, formerly) n abbr* = **NEDC**
**née** [neɪ] *prep*: **~ Scott** z domu Scott
**need** [ni:d] *n (necessity)* potrzeba *f*, konieczność *f*; *(demand)* potrzeba *f*, zapotrzebowanie *nt*; *(poverty)* ubóstwo *nt*, bieda *f* ▷ *vt (want)* potrzebować *+gen*; *(could do with)* wymagać *+gen*; **in ~** w potrzebie; **to be in ~ of** wymagać *or* potrzebować *+gen*; **ten pounds will meet my immediate ~s** dziesięć funtów zaspokoi moje najpilniejsze potrzeby; **(there's) no ~** nie trzeba; **there's no ~ to ...** nie ma potrzeby *+infin*; **he had no ~ to...** nie musiał *+infin*; **you ~ a haircut** powinieneś iść do fryzjera; **I ~ to do it** muszę to zrobić; **you don't ~ to go, you ~n't go** nie musisz iść; **a signature is ~ed** potrzebny jest podpis
**needle** ['ni:dl] *n* igła *f*; *(for knitting)* drut *m* ▷ *vt (fig: inf)* dokuczać *+dat*
**needless** ['ni:dlɪs] *adj* niepotrzebny; **~ to say** rzecz jasna
**needlessly** ['ni:dlɪslɪ] *adv* niepotrzebnie
**needlework** ['ni:dlwə:k] *n (object)* robótka *f*; *(activity)* robótki *pl* ręczne
**needn't** ['ni:dnt] = **need not**
**needy** ['ni:dɪ] *adj* ubogi ▷ *npl*: **the ~** ubodzy *vir pl*
**negation** [nɪ'geɪʃən] *n* negowanie *nt*; *(Ling)* negacja *f*, przeczenie *nt*
**negative** ['nɛgətɪv] *adj (answer)* odmowny, negatywny; *(attitude, experience)* negatywny; *(pregnancy test, electrical charge)* ujemny ▷ *n (Phot)* negatyw *m*; *(Ling)* przeczenie *nt*, negacja *f*; **to answer in the ~** odpowiadać (odpowiedzieć *perf*) przecząco
**neglect** [nɪ'glɛkt] *vt (leave undone)* zaniedbywać (zaniedbać *perf*); *(ignore)* nie dostrzegać (nie dostrzec *perf*) *+gen*, lekceważyć (zlekceważyć *perf*) ▷ *n* zaniedbanie *nt*
**neglected** [nɪ'glɛktɪd] *adj (child, garden)* zaniedbany; *(artist)* niedostrzegany, niedoceniany
**neglectful** [nɪ'glɛktful] *adj* zaniedbujący (swoje) obowiązki; **to be ~ of** zaniedbywać *+acc*
**negligee** ['nɛglɪʒeɪ] *n* negliż *m*
**negligence** ['nɛglɪdʒəns] *n* niedbalstwo *nt*
**negligent** ['nɛglɪdʒənt] *adj (person)* niedbały; *(attitude)* nonszalancki; **to be ~ of sb** zaniedbywać kogoś
**negligently** ['nɛglɪdʒəntlɪ] *adv* nonszalancko, od niechcenia
**negligible** ['nɛglɪdʒɪbl] *adj* nieistotny
**negotiable** [nɪ'gəuʃɪəbl] *adj (salary)* do uzgodnienia *post*; *(path)* przejezdny; *(river)* spławny; **not ~** *(cheque etc)* nie podlegający realizacji w gotówce
**negotiate** [nɪ'gəuʃɪeɪt] *vi* negocjować ▷ *vt (treaty etc)* negocjować (wynegocjować *perf*); *(obstacle, bend)* pokonywać (pokonać *perf*); **to ~ with sb (for sth)** pertraktować z kimś (w sprawie czegoś)
**negotiation** [nɪgəuʃɪ'eɪʃən] *n* negocjacje *pl*; **under ~** w fazie negocjacji
**negotiator** [nɪ'gəuʃɪeɪtə[r]] *n* negocjator(ka) *m(f)*
**Negress** ['ni:grɪs] *n* Murzynka *f*
**Negro** ['ni:grəu] *n (pl* **~es***)* Murzyn *m* ▷ *adj* murzyński
**neigh** [neɪ] *vi* rżeć (zarżeć *perf*)
**neighbour**, *(US)* **neighbor** ['neɪbə[r]] *n* sąsiad(ka) *m(f)*; *(Rel)* bliźni *m*
**neighbourhood** ['neɪbəhud] *n (place)* okolice *pl*; *(part of town)* dzielnica *f*; *(people)* sąsiedzi *vir pl*; **in the ~ of** *(place)* w sąsiedztwie *+gen*; *(sum of money)* około *+gen*
**neighbouring** ['neɪbərɪŋ] *adj* sąsiedni

**neighbourly** ['neɪbəlɪ] *adj* życzliwy, przyjazny
**neither** ['naɪðə^r] *conj*: **I didn't move and ~ did John** nie ruszyłem się i John też nie ▷ *pron* żaden (*z dwóch*), ani jeden, ani drugi ▷ *adv*: **~ ... nor ...** ani ..., ani ...; **~ story is true** żadna z tych dwóch historii nie jest prawdziwa; **~ is true** ani jedno, ani drugie nie jest prawdą; **~ do I/have I** ja też nie
**neo...** ['ni:əu] *pref* neo...
**neolithic** [ni:əu'lɪθɪk] *adj* neolityczny
**neologism** [nɪ'ɔlədʒɪzəm] *n* neologizm *m*
**neon** ['ni:ɔn] *n* neon *m*
**neon light** *n* neonówka *f*
**neon sign** *n* neon *m*
**Nepal** [nɪ'pɔ:l] *n* Nepal *m*
**nephew** ['nɛvju:] *n* (*sister's son*) siostrzeniec *m*; (*brother's son*) bratanek *m*
**nepotism** ['nɛpətɪzəm] *n* nepotyzm *m*
**nerve** [nə:v] *n* (*Anat*) nerw *m*; (*courage*) odwaga *f*; (*impudence*) czelność *f*; **nerves** *npl* nerwy *pl*; **he gets on my ~s** on działa mi na nerwy; **to lose one's ~** tracić (stracić *perf*) zimną krew
**nerve-centre** ['nə:vsɛntə^r] *n* (*fig*) ośrodek *m* decyzyjny
**nerve gas** *n* gaz *m* paraliżujący
**nerve-racking** ['nə:vrækɪŋ] *adj* wykańczający nerwowo (*inf*)
**nervous** ['nə:vəs] *adj* (*also Med*) nerwowy; (*anxious*) zdenerwowany; **to be ~ of/about** obawiać się *+gen*
**nervous breakdown** *n* załamanie *nt* nerwowe
**nervously** ['nə:vəslɪ] *adv* nerwowo
**nervousness** ['nə:vəsnɪs] *n* zdenerwowanie *nt*, niepokój *m*
**nervous system** *n* układ *m* nerwowy
**nest** [nɛst] *n* gniazdo *nt* ▷ *vi* gnieździć się; **~ of tables** *zestaw stolików wsuwanych jeden pod drugi*
**nest egg** *n* oszczędności *pl* (*gromadzone z zamiarem przeznaczenia na konkretny cel*)
**nestle** ['nɛsl] *vi* przytulać się (przytulić się *perf*); **a house nestling in the hills** dom wtulony we wzgórza
**nestling** ['nɛstlɪŋ] *n* pisklę *nt*
**net** [nɛt] *n* siatka *f*; (*for fish*) podbierak *m*; (*also*: **fishing net**) sieć *f* (rybacka); (*fabric*) tiul *m*; (*fig*) sieć *f* ▷ *adj* (*Comm*) netto *post*; (*result*) ostateczny, końcowy ▷ *vt* (*fish, butterfly*) łapać (złapać *perf*) (*w sieć, siatkę*); (*profit*) przynosić (przynieść *perf*) na czysto; (*deal, sale*) zdobywać (zdobyć *perf*); (*fortune*) zbijać (zbić *perf*); **net of tax** po odliczeniu podatku; **he earns ten thousand pounds net per year** zarabia na czysto dziesięć tysięcy funtów rocznie; **it weighs 250g net** to waży 250g netto; **the Net** (*Comput*) net *m*
**netball** ['nɛtbɔ:l] *n gra podobna do koszykówki*
**net curtains** *npl* firanki *pl*
**Netherlands** ['nɛðələndz] *npl*: **the ~** Holandia *f*
**nett** [nɛt] *adj* = **net**
**netting** ['nɛtɪŋ] *n* siatka *f*
**nettle** ['nɛtl] *n* pokrzywa *f*; **to grasp the ~** (*fig*) brać (wziąć *perf*) byka za rogi
**network** ['nɛtwə:k] *n* sieć *f*; (*of veins*) siateczka *f* ▷ *vt* (*TV, Radio*) transmitować jednocześnie (przez różne stacje); (*computers*) łączyć (połączyć *perf*) w sieć
**neuralgia** [njuə'rældʒə] *n* nerwoból *m*
**neurosis** [njuə'rəusɪs] (*pl* **neuroses**) (*Psych: fig*) *n* nerwica *f*
**neurotic** [njuə'rɔtɪk] *adj* przewrażliwiony; (*Med*) neurotyczny ▷ *n* neurotyk(-yczka) *m(f)*
**neuter** ['nju:tə^r] *adj* (*Ling*) nijaki ▷ *vt* (*animal*) sterylizować (wysterylizować *perf*)
**neutral** ['nju:trəl] *adj* (*country*) neutralny; (*view, person*) neutralny, bezstronny; (*colour*) niezdecydowany, bliżej nieokreślony; (*shoe cream*) bezbarwny; (*Elec: wire*) zerowy ▷ *n* (*Aut*) bieg *m* jałowy
**neutrality** [nju:'trælɪtɪ] *n* (*of country*) neutralność *f*; (*of view, person*) neutralność *f*, bezstronność *f*
**neutralize** ['nju:trəlaɪz] *vt* neutralizować (zneutralizować *perf*)
**neutron** ['nju:trɔn] *n* neutron *m*
**neutron bomb** *n* bomba *f* neutronowa
**never** ['nɛvə^r] *adv* (*not at any time*) nigdy; (*not*) wcale nie; **~ in my life** nigdy w życiu; **~ again** nigdy więcej; **well I ~!** nie do wiary!; *see also* **mind**
**never-ending** [nɛvər'ɛndɪŋ] *adj* nie kończący się
**nevertheless** [nɛvəðə'lɛs] *adv* pomimo to, niemniej jednak
**new** [nju:] *adj* nowy; (*country, parent*) młody; **as good as new** jak nowy; **to be new to sb** być nowym dla kogoś
**newborn** ['nju:bɔ:n] *adj* nowo narodzony
**newcomer** ['nju:kʌmə^r] *n* przybysz *m*, nowy(-wa) *m(f)* (*inf*)
**new-fangled** ['nju:fæŋgld] *adj* nowomodny
**new-found** ['nju:faund] *adj* świeżo odkryty
**Newfoundland** ['nju:fənlənd] *n* Nowa Fundlandia *f*
**New Guinea** *n* Nowa Gwinea *f*
**newly** ['nju:lɪ] *adv* nowo
**newly-weds** ['nju:lɪwɛdz] *npl* nowożeńcy *vir pl*, państwo *vir pl* młodzi
**new moon** *n* nów *m*
**newness** ['nju:nɪs] *n* nowość *f*
**New Orleans** [-'ɔ:li:ənz] *n* Nowy Orlean *m*
**news** [nju:z] *n* wiadomość *f*, wiadomości *pl*; **a piece of ~** wiadomość; **the ~** (*Radio, TV*) wiadomości; **good/bad ~** dobra/zła wiadomość

**news agency** *n* agencja *f* prasowa
**newsagent** ['nju:zeɪdʒənt] (*Brit*) *n* (*person*) kioskarz(-arka) *m(f)*; (*shop*) kiosk *m* z gazetami
**news bulletin** *n* serwis *m* informacyjny
**newscaster** ['nju:zkɑ:stəʳ] *n* prezenter(ka) *m(f)* wiadomości
**newsdealer** ['nju:zdi:ləʳ] (*US*) *n* = **newsagent**
**newsflash** ['nju:zflæʃ] *n* wiadomości *pl* z ostatniej chwili
**newsletter** ['nju:zlɛtəʳ] *n* biuletyn *m*
**newspaper** ['nju:zpeɪpəʳ] *n* gazeta *f*; **daily ~** dziennik; **weekly ~** tygodnik
**newsprint** ['nju:zprɪnt] *n* papier *m* gazetowy
**newsreader** ['nju:zri:dəʳ] *n* = **newscaster**
**newsreel** ['nju:zri:l] *n* kronika *f* filmowa
**newsroom** ['nju:zru:m] *n* (*Press, Radio, TV*) pokój *m* redakcji informacyjnej
**news stand** ['nju:zstænd] *n* stoisko *nt* z gazetami
**newt** [nju:t] *n* traszka *f*
**New Year** *n* Nowy Rok *m*; **Happy ~!** Szczęśliwego Nowego Roku!; **to wish sb a happy new year** życzyć komuś szczęśliwego nowego roku
**New Year's Day** *n* Nowy Rok *m*
**New Year's Eve** *n* sylwester *m*
**New York** [-'jɔ:k] *n* Nowy Jork *m*; (*also*: **New York State**) stan *m* Nowy Jork
**New Zealand** [-'zi:lənd] *n* Nowa Zelandia *f* ▷ *adj* nowozelandzki
**New Zealander** [-'zi:ləndəʳ] *n* Nowozelandczyk(-dka) *m(f)*
**next** [nɛkst] *adj* (*in space*) sąsiedni, znajdujący się obok; (*in time*) następny, najbliższy ▷ *adv* (*in space*) obok; (*in time*) następnie, potem; **the ~ day** następnego dnia, nazajutrz (*literary*); **~ time** następnym razem; **~ year** w przyszłym roku; **~ to** obok *+gen*; **~ to nothing** tyle co nic; **~ please!** następny, proszę!; **who's ~?** kto następny?; **"turn to the ~ page"** „proszę przewrócić stronę"; **the week after ~** za dwa tygodnie; **the ~ on the right/left** pierwsza (ulica) w prawo/lewo; **the ~ best** drugi w kolejności; **the ~ thing I knew** nim się spostrzegłem; **when do we meet ~?** kiedy się spotykamy następnym razem?
**next door** *adv* obok ▷ *adj* (*flat*) sąsiedni; (*neighbour*) najbliższy, zza ściany *post*
**next-of-kin** ['nɛkstəv'kɪn] *n* najbliższa rodzina *f*
**NF** *n abbr* (*Brit*: *Pol*: = *National Front*) *radykalna partia prawicowa* ▷ *abbr* (*Canada*) = **Newfoundland**
**NFL** (*US*) *n abbr* = **National Football League**
**NG** (*US*) *abbr* = **National Guard**
**NGO** (*US*) *n abbr* (= *non-governmental organization*) organizacja *f* pozarządowa
**NH** (*US*: *Post*) *abbr* = **New Hampshire**
**NHL** (*US*) *n abbr* = **National Hockey League**
**NHS** (*Brit*) *n abbr* = **National Health Service**
**NI** *abbr* = **Northern Ireland**; (*Brit*) = **National Insurance**
**Niagara Falls** [naɪ'ægərə-] *npl* wodospad *m* Niagara
**nib** [nɪb] *n* stalówka *f*
**nibble** ['nɪbl] *vt* (*eat*) skubać (skubnąć *perf or* poskubać *perf*); (*bite*) przygryzać (przygryźć *perf*) ▷ *vi*: **to ~ at** skubać (skubnąć *perf*) *+acc*
**Nicaragua** [nɪkə'rægjuə] *n* Nikaragua *f*
**Nicaraguan** [nɪkə'rægjuən] *adj* nikaraguański ▷ *n* Nikaraguańczyk(-anka) *m(f)*
**Nice** [ni:s] *n* Nicea *f*
**nice** [naɪs] *adj* (*kind, friendly*) miły; (*pleasant*) przyjemny; (*attractive*) ładny
**nicely** ['naɪslɪ] *adv* (*attractively*) ładnie; (*satisfactorily*) dobrze; **that will do ~** to w zupełności wystarczy
**niceties** ['naɪsɪtɪz] *npl*: **the ~** subtelności *pl*
**niche** [ni:ʃ] *n* nisza *f*; **to find one's ~ in** znajdować (znaleźć *perf*) swoje miejsce w *+loc*
**nick** [nɪk] *n* (*on face etc*) zadraśnięcie *nt*; (*in metal, wood*) nacięcie *nt* ▷ *vt* (*Brit*: *inf*: *steal*) zwędzić (*perf*) (*inf*); (: *arrest*) przymykać (przymknąć *perf*) (*inf*); (*cut*): **to ~ o.s.** zacinać się (zaciąć się *perf*); **in good ~** (*Brit*: *inf*) w dobrej formie; **in the ~** (*Brit*: *inf*) w pace (*inf*); **in the ~ of time** w samą porę
**nickel** ['nɪkl] *n* (*metal*) nikiel *m*; (*US*) pięciocentówka *f*
**nickname** ['nɪkneɪm] *n* przezwisko *nt*, przydomek *m* ▷ *vt* przezywać, nadawać przydomek *+dat*
**Nicosia** [nɪkə'si:ə] *n* Nikozja *f*
**nicotine** ['nɪkəti:n] *n* nikotyna *f*
**nicotine patch** *n* plaster *m* nikotynowy
**niece** [ni:s] *n* (*sister's daughter*) siostrzenica *f*; (*brother's daughter*) bratanica *f*
**nifty** ['nɪftɪ] (*inf*) *adj* (*car, jacket*) świetny; (*gadget, tool*) zmyślny (*inf*)
**Niger** ['naɪdʒəʳ] *n* Niger *m*
**Nigeria** [naɪ'dʒɪərɪə] *n* Nigeria *f*
**Nigerian** [naɪ'dʒɪərɪən] *adj* nigeryjski ▷ *n* Nigeryjczyk(-jka) *m(f)*
**niggardly** ['nɪgədlɪ] *adj* skąpy
**nigger** [nɪgəʳ] (*inf!*) *n* czarnuch *m* (*inf!*)
**niggle** ['nɪgl] *vt* męczyć ▷ *vi* czepiać się (*inf*)
**niggling** ['nɪglɪŋ] *adj* (*doubt, anxiety*) dręczący; (*pain*) uporczywy
**night** [naɪt] *n* noc *f*; (*evening*) wieczór *m*; **the ~ before last** przedwczoraj w nocy; **at ~** w nocy; **by ~** nocą; **nine o'clock at ~** dziewiąta

wieczór; **we didn't go out last ~** wczoraj wieczorem nigdzie nie wychodziliśmy; **in the ~, during the ~** w nocy; **~ and day** dzień i noc
**nightcap** ['naɪtkæp] *n* kieliszek *m* przed snem
**nightclub** ['naɪtklʌb] *n* nocny lokal *m*
**nightdress** ['naɪtdrɛs] *n* koszula *f* nocna
**nightfall** ['naɪtfɔːl] *n* zmrok *m*
**nightgown** ['naɪtgaun] *n* = **nightdress**
**nightie** ['naɪtɪ] *n* = **nightdress**
**nightingale** ['naɪtɪŋgeɪl] *n* słowik *m*
**nightlife** ['naɪtlaɪf] *n* nocne życie *nt*
**nightly** ['naɪtlɪ] *adj* wieczorny ▷ *adv* (*every night*) co noc; (*every evening*) co wieczór
**nightmare** ['naɪtmɛə[r]] *n* koszmarny sen *m*; (*fig*) koszmar *m*
**night porter** *n* nocny portier *m* (*w hotelu*)
**night safe** *n* (*Comm*) trezor *m*, wrzutnia *f*
**night school** *n* szkoła *f* wieczorowa
**nightshade** ['naɪtʃeɪd] *n*: **deadly ~** (*Bot*) wilcza jagoda *f*
**night shift** *n* nocna zmiana *f*
**night-time** ['naɪttaɪm] *n* noc *f*
**night watchman** (*irreg: like* **man**) *n* nocny stróż *m*
**nihilism** ['naɪɪlɪzəm] *n* nihilizm *m*
**nil** [nɪl] *n* nic *nt*; (*Brit: Sport*) zero *nt*
**Nile** [naɪl] *n*: **the ~** Nil *m*
**nimble** ['nɪmbl] *adj* (*person, movements*) zwinny; (*mind*) bystry
**nine** [naɪn] *num* dziewięć
**nineteen** ['naɪn'tiːn] *num* dziewiętnaście
**nineteenth** ['naɪn'tiːnθ] *num* dziewiętnasty
**ninety** ['naɪntɪ] *num* dziewięćdziesiąt
**ninth** [naɪnθ] *num* dziewiąty
**nip** [nɪp] *vt* szczypać (szczypnąć *perf or* uszczypnąć *perf*) ▷ *n* (*bite*) uszczypnięcie *nt*; (*drink*) łyk *m*; **to nip out** (*Brit: inf*) wyskakiwać (wyskoczyć *perf*) (*inf*); **to nip downstairs/upstairs** (*Brit: inf*) wyskoczyć (*perf*) na dół/na górę (*inf*); **to nip into a shop** (*Brit: inf*) wskoczyć (*perf*) do sklepu (*inf*)
**nipple** ['nɪpl] *n* (*Anat*) brodawka *f* sutkowa
**nippy** ['nɪpɪ] (*Brit*) *adj* (*person*) żwawy; (*car*) szybki; (*air*) mroźny
**nit** [nɪt] *n* (*in hair*) gnida *f*; (*inf: idiot*) dureń *m* (*inf*)
**nitpicking** ['nɪtpɪkɪŋ] (*inf*) *n* szukanie *nt* dziury w całym
**nitrogen** ['naɪtrədʒən] *n* azot *m*
**nitroglycerin(e)** ['naɪtrəu'glɪsəriːn] *n* nitrogliceryna *f*
**nitty-gritty** ['nɪtɪ'grɪtɪ] (*inf*) *n*: **to get down to the ~** przechodzić (przejść *perf*) do konkretów
**nitwit** ['nɪtwɪt] (*inf*) *n* przygłup *m* (*inf*)
**NJ** (*US: Post*) *abbr* = **New Jersey**
**NLF** *n abbr* (= *National Liberation Front*) FWN *m* (= *Front Wyzwolenia Narodowego*)
**NLQ** (*Comput, Typ*) *abbr* (= *near letter quality*) NLQ
**NLRB** (*US*) *n abbr* (= *National Labor Relations Board*) *rada regulująca stosunki między pracodawcami a pracobiorcami*
**NM** (*US: Post*) *abbr* = **New Mexico**

 KEYWORD

**no** [nəu] *adv* nie
▷ *adj*: **I have no money/books** nie mam (żadnych) pieniędzy/książek; **there is no time/bread left** nie zostało ani trochę czasu/chleba; **"no entry"** „wstęp wzbroniony"; **"no smoking"** „palenie wzbronione"
▷ *n* (*pl* **noes**) (*in voting*) głos *m* przeciw; (*refusal*) odmowa *f*; **I won't take no for an answer** nie przyjmę odmowy

**no.** *abbr* = **number**
**nobble** [nɔbl] (*Brit: inf*) *vt* (*bribe*) dawać (dać *perf*) w łapę +*dat* (*inf*); (*buttonhole*) łapać (złapać *perf*); (*Racing: horse, dog*) podtruć (*perf*)
**Nobel Prize** [nəu'bɛl-] *n* Nagroda *f* Nobla
**nobility** [nəu'bɪlɪtɪ] *n* (*aristocracy*) szlachta *f*; (*dignity*) godność *f*; (*virtue*) szlachetność *f*
**noble** ['nəubl] *adj* (*admirable*) szlachetny; (*aristocratic*) szlachecki; (*impressive*) wspaniały, imponujący; **of ~ birth** szlachetnie urodzony
**nobleman** ['nəublmən] (*irreg: like* **man**) *n* szlachcic *m*
**nobly** ['nəublɪ] *adv* szlachetnie
**nobody** ['nəubədɪ] *pron* nikt ▷ *n*: **he's a ~** on nic nie znaczy
**no-claims bonus** ['nəukleɪmz-] *n* (*Insurance*) zniżka *f* za bezszkodowość
**nocturnal** [nɔk'təːnl] *adj* nocny
**nod** [nɔd] *vi* (*in agreement*) przytakiwać (przytaknąć *perf*); (*as greeting*) kłaniać się (ukłonić się *perf*); (*gesture*) wskazywać (wskazać *perf*) ruchem głowy; (*fig: flowers etc*) kołysać się ▷ *vt*: **to nod one's head** skinąć (*perf*) głową ▷ *n* kiwnięcie *nt*, skinienie *nt*; **to give sb a nod** kiwać (kiwnąć *perf*) do kogoś głową; **they nodded their agreement** kiwnęli głowami na znak zgody
▸ **nod off** *vi* przysypiać (przysnąć *perf*) (*inf*)
**noise** [nɔɪz] *n* (*sound*) dźwięk *m*, odgłos *m*; (*din*) hałas *m*
**noiseless** ['nɔɪzlɪs] *adj* bezgłośny
**noisily** ['nɔɪzɪlɪ] *adv* hałaśliwie
**noisy** ['nɔɪzɪ] *adj* (*audience, machine*) hałaśliwy; (*place*) pełen zgiełku

**nomad** ['nəumæd] *n* koczownik(-iczka) *m(f)*
**nomadic** [nəu'mædɪk] *adj* koczowniczy
**no-man's-land** ['nəumænzlænd] *n* ziemia *f* niczyja
**nominal** ['nɔmɪnl] *adj* (*leader*) tytularny; (*price*) nominalny
**nominate** ['nɔmɪneɪt] *vt* (*propose*) wysuwać kandydaturę *+gen*, nominować *+acc*; (*appoint*) mianować
**nomination** [nɔmɪ'neɪʃən] *n* (*proposal*) kandydatura *f*; (*appointment*) mianowanie *nt*
**nominee** [nɔmɪ'ni:] *n* kandydat(ka) *m(f)*
**non...** [nɔn] *pref* nie..., bez...
**non-alcoholic** [nɔnælkə'hɔlɪk] *adj* bezalkoholowy
**non-aligned** [nɔnə'laɪnd] *adj* niezaangażowany, neutralny
**non-breakable** [nɔn'breɪkəbl] *adj* nietłukący
**nonce word** ['nɔns-] *n słowo wymyślone na daną okazję*
**nonchalant** ['nɔnʃələnt] *adj* nonszalancki
**non-commissioned officer** *n* (*Mil*) podoficer *m*
**non-committal** [nɔnkə'mɪtl] *adj* (*person*) nie zajmujący zdecydowanego stanowiska; (*answer*) wymijający
**nonconformist** [nɔnkən'fɔ:mɪst] *n* nonkonformista(-tka) *m(f)* ▷ *adj* nonkonformistyczny
**non-cooperation** ['nɔnkəuɔpə'reɪʃən] *n* odmowa *f* współpracy
**nondescript** ['nɔndɪskrɪpt] *adj* (*person, clothes*) nijaki; (*colour*) nieokreślony, nijaki
**none** [nʌn] *pron* (*not one*) żaden, ani jeden; (*not any*) ani trochę; **~ of sth** ani trochę z czegoś; **~ of us** żaden z nas; **I've ~ left** (*not any*) nie zostało mi ani trochę; (*not one*) nie został mi ani jeden; **~ at all** (*not any*) ani trochę; (*not one*) absolutnie żaden; **I was ~ the wiser** nadal nic nie rozumiałem; **she would have ~ of it** nie chciała o tym słyszeć; **it was ~ other than X** był to nie kto inny tylko X
**nonentity** [nɔ'nɛntɪtɪ] *n* (*person*) miernota *f*
**non-essential** [nɔnɪ'sɛnʃl] *adj* zbędny ▷ *n*: **~s** rzeczy *pl* zbędne
**nonetheless** ['nʌnðə'lɛs] *adv* pomimo to
**non-existent** [nɔnɪg'zɪstənt] *adj* nie istniejący
**non-fiction** [nɔn'fɪkʃən] *n* literatura *f* faktu ▷ *adj* niebeletrystyczny
**non-flammable** [nɔn'flæməbl] *adj* niepalny
**non-intervention** ['nɔnɪntə'vɛnʃən] *n* nieinterwencja *f*, nieingerencja *f*
**non obst.** *abbr* (*= non obstante*) pomimo
**non-payment** [nɔn'peɪmənt] *n* niepłacenie *nt*
**nonplussed** [nɔn'plʌst] *adj* skonsternowany
**non-profit making** *adj* niedochodowy
**nonsense** ['nɔnsəns] *n* nonsens *m*; **~!** nonsens!, bzdura!; **it is ~ to say that ...** to nonsens twierdzić, że ...; **to make (a) ~ of sth** odbierać (odebrać *perf*) czemuś sens, czynić (uczynić *perf*) coś bezsensownym
**non-shrink** [nɔn'ʃrɪŋk] (*Brit*) *adj* niekurczliwy
**non-smoker** ['nɔn'sməukə^r] *n* niepalący(-ca) *m(f)*
**non-stick** ['nɔn'stɪk] *adj* teflonowy
**non-stop** ['nɔn'stɔp] *adj* (*unceasing*) nie kończący się; (*without pauses*) nieprzerwany; (*flight*) bezpośredni ▷ *adv* (*speak*) bez przerwy; (*fly*) bezpośrednio
**non-taxable** [nɔn'tæksəbl] *adj* (*Comm*) nie podlegający opodatkowaniu
**non-U** ['nɔnju:] (*Brit: inf*) *adj abbr* (*= non-upper class*) pospolity
**non-white** ['nɔn'waɪt] *adj* kolorowy ▷ *n* kolorowy(-wa) *m(f)*
**noodles** ['nu:dlz] *npl* makaron *m*
**nook** [nuk] *n*: **every ~ and cranny** każdy kąt *m*, wszystkie zakamarki *pl*
**noon** [nu:n] *n* południe *nt*
**no-one** ['nəuwʌn] *pron* = **nobody**
**noose** [nu:s] *n* pętla *f*
**nor** [nɔ:^r] *conj* = **neither** ▷ *adv see* **neither**
**Norf** (*Brit: Post*) *abbr* = **Norfolk**
**norm** [nɔ:m] *n* norma *f*; **to be the ~** być regułą
**normal** ['nɔ:ml] *adj* normalny ▷ *n*: **to return to ~** wracać (wrócić *perf*) do normy
**normality** [nɔ:'mælɪtɪ] *n* normalność *f*
**normally** ['nɔ:məlɪ] *adv* normalnie
**Normandy** ['nɔ:məndɪ] *n* Normandia *f*
**north** [nɔ:θ] *n* północ *f* ▷ *adj* północny ▷ *adv* na północ; **~ of** na północ od *+gen*
**North Africa** *n* Afryka *f* Północna
**North African** *adj* północnoafrykański ▷ *n* mieszkaniec(-nka) *m(f)* Afryki Północnej
**North America** *n* Ameryka *f* Północna
**North American** *adj* północnoamerykański ▷ *n* mieszkaniec(-nka) *m(f)* Ameryki Północnej
**Northants** [nɔ:'θænts] (*Brit: Post*) *abbr* = **Northamptonshire**
**northbound** ['nɔ:θbaund] *adj* (*traffic*) zdążający na północ; (*carriageway*) prowadzący na północ
**Northd** (*Brit: Post*) *abbr* = **Northumberland**
**north-east** [nɔ:θ'i:st] *n* północny wschód *m* ▷ *adj* północno-wschodni ▷ *adv* na północny wschód; **~ of** na północny wschód od *+gen*
**northerly** ['nɔ:ðəlɪ] *adj* północny
**northern** ['nɔ:ðən] *adj* północny
**Northern Ireland** *n* Irlandia *f* Północna
**North Korea** *n* Korea *f* Północna
**North Pole** *n*: **the ~** biegun *m* północny

**North Sea** *n*: **the ~** Morze *nt* Północne
**North Sea oil** *n* ropa *f* z Morza Północnego
**northward(s)** ['nɔ:θwəd(z)] *adv* na północ
**north-west** [nɔ:θ'wɛst] *n* północny zachód *m* ▷ *adj* północno-zachodni ▷ *adv* na północny zachód; **~ of** na północny zachód od *+gen*
**Norway** ['nɔ:weɪ] *n* Norwegia *f*
**Norwegian** [nɔ:'wi:dʒən] *adj* norweski ▷ *n* (*person*) Norweg(-eżka) *m(f)*; (*Ling*) (język *m*) norweski
**nos.** *abbr* (= *numbers*) nry (= *numery*)
**nose** [nəuz] *n* nos *m*; (*of aircraft*) dziób *m*; (*of car*) przód *m* ▷ *vi* (*also*: **nose one's way**) sunąć powoli; **to follow one's ~** (*go straight ahead*) iść (pójść *perf*) prosto przed siebie; (*be guided by instinct*) zdawać się (zdać *perf*) się na wyczucie; **it gets up my ~** (*inf*) to mnie wkurza (*inf*); **to have a (good) ~ for sth** mieć (dobrego) nosa do czegoś; **to keep one's ~ clean** (*inf*) nie mieszać się w nic; **to look down one's ~ at sb/sth** (*inf*) nie mieć o kimś/czymś wysokiego mniemania; **to pay through the ~ (for sth)** (*inf*) zapłacić (*perf*) kupę pieniędzy (za coś) (*inf*); **to rub sb's ~ in sth** (*inf*) wypominać komuś coś; **to turn one's ~ up at sth** (*inf*) gardzić (wzgardzić *perf*) czymś; **under sb's ~** pod czyimś nosem
▸ **nose about** *vi* węszyć
▸ **nose around** *vi* = **nose about**
**nosebleed** ['nəuzbli:d] *n* krwawienie *nt* z nosa
**nose-dive** ['nəuzdaɪv] *n* (*of plane*) lot *m* nurkowy; (*of prices*) gwałtowny spadek *m* ▷ *vi* (*plane*) pikować; (*prices*) gwałtownie spadać (spaść *perf*)
**nose drops** *npl* krople *pl* do nosa
**nose job** (*inf*) *n* korekta *f* (plastyczna) nosa
**nosey** ['nəuzɪ] (*inf*) *adj* = **nosy**
**nostalgia** [nɔs'tældʒɪə] *n* nostalgia *f*
**nostalgic** [nɔs'tældʒɪk] *adj* nostalgiczny
**nostril** ['nɔstrɪl] *n* nozdrze *nt*
**nosy** ['nəuzɪ] (*inf*) *adj* wścibski
**not** [nɔt] *adv* nie; **he is not** *or* **isn't here** nie ma go tu(taj); **you must not** *or* **you mustn't do that** nie wolno (ci) tego robić; **he asked me not to do it** (po)prosił, żebym tego nie robił; **it's not that I don't like him ...** nie, żebym go nie lubił ...; **not yet** jeszcze nie; **not now** nie teraz; *see also* **all**; **only**
**notable** ['nəutəbl] *adj* godny uwagi
**notably** ['nəutəblɪ] *adv* (*particularly*) w szczególności, zwłaszcza; (*markedly*) wyraźnie
**notary** ['nəutərɪ] *n* (*Jur*: *also*: **notary public**) notariusz *m*
**notation** [nəu'teɪʃən] *n* (*Mus, Math*) zapis *m*, notacja *f*
**notch** [nɔtʃ] *n* nacięcie *nt*, karb *m*; **to be several ~es above sth** znacznie coś przewyższać
▸ **notch up** *vt* (*score, votes*) zdobyć (*perf*); (*victory*) osiągnąć (*perf*)
**note** [nəut] *n* (*Mus*) nuta *f*; (*of lecturer, secretary*) notatka *f*; (*in book*) przypis *m*; (*letter*) wiadomość *f* (*na piśmie*); (*banknote*) banknot *m* ▷ *vt* (*notice*) zauważyć (*perf*); (*also*: **note down**) notować (zanotować *perf*), zapisywać (zapisać *perf*); (*fact*) odnotowywać (odnotować *perf*); **of ~** znaczący; **to make a ~ of sth** zapamiętywać (zapamiętać *perf*) coś; **to take ~s** robić (zrobić *perf*) notatki; **to take ~ of sth** brać (wziąć *perf*) coś pod uwagę
**notebook** ['nəutbuk] *n* notatnik *m*, notes *m*
**noted** ['nəutɪd] *adj* znany
**notepad** ['nəutpæd] *n* (*for letters*) blok *m* listowy; (*for notes*) blok *m* biurowy
**notepaper** ['nəutpeɪpə$^r$] *n* papier *m* listowy
**noteworthy** ['nəutwə:ðɪ] *adj* znaczący, godny uwagi
**nothing** ['nʌθɪŋ] *n* nic *nt*; **~ new/much** *etc* nic nowego/wielkiego *etc*; **~ else** nic innego; **for ~** (*free*) za darmo, za nic; (*in vain*) na próżno; **~ at all** absolutnie nic
**notice** ['nəutɪs] *n* (*announcement*) ogłoszenie *nt*; (*dismissal*) wymówienie *nt*; (*Brit*: *review*) recenzja *f* ▷ *vt* zauważać (zauważyć *perf*); **to bring sth to sb's ~** zwrócić (zwracać *perf*) na coś czyjąś uwagę; **to take no ~ of** nie zwracać (nie zwrócić *perf*) uwagi na *+acc*; **to escape sb's ~** umykać (umknąć *perf*) czyjejś uwadze; **it has come to my ~ that ...** (*I have been told*) dotarło do mnie, że...; (*I have noticed*) zwróciło moją uwagę, że...; **to give sb ~ of sth** powiadamiać (powiadomić *perf*) kogoś o czymś z wyprzedzeniem; **without ~** bez uprzedzenia *or* ostrzeżenia; **advance ~** wcześniejsze powiadomienie; **at short ~** (*leave etc*) bezzwłocznie; **at a moment's ~** natychmiast; **until further ~** (aż) do odwołania; **to hand in one's ~** składać (złożyć *perf*) wymówienie; **to be given one's ~** dostawać (dostać *perf*) wymówienie
**noticeable** ['nəutɪsəbl] *adj* zauważalny, widoczny
**noticeboard** ['nəutɪsbɔ:d] (*Brit*) *n* tablica *f* ogłoszeń
**notification** [nəutɪfɪ'keɪʃən] *n* zawiadomienie *nt*
**notify** ['nəutɪfaɪ] *vt*: **to ~ sb (of sth)** powiadamiać (powiadomić *perf*) kogoś (o czymś)
**notion** ['nəuʃən] *n* (*idea*) pojęcie *nt*; (*belief*) pogląd *m*; **notions** (*US*) *npl* galanteria *f*
**notoriety** [nəutə'raɪətɪ] *n* zła sława *f*

**notorious** [nəu'tɔ:rɪəs] *adj (liar etc)* notoryczny; *(place)* cieszący się złą sławą
**notoriously** [nəu'tɔ:rɪəslɪ] *adv* notorycznie
**Notts** [nɔts] *(Brit: Post) abbr* = **Nottinghamshire**
**notwithstanding** [nɔtwɪθ'stændɪŋ] *adv* jednak, mimo wszystko ▷ *prep* pomimo *+gen*
**nougat** ['nu:gɑ:] *n* nugat *m*
**nought** [nɔ:t] *n* zero *nt*
**noun** [naun] *n* rzeczownik *m*
**nourish** ['nʌrɪʃ] *vt (feed)* odżywiać; *(fig: foster)* żywić
**nourishing** ['nʌrɪʃɪŋ] *adj* pożywny
**nourishment** ['nʌrɪʃmənt] *n* pożywienie *nt*
**Nov.** *abbr (= November)* list., listop.
**Nova Scotia** ['nəuvə'skəuʃə] *n* Nowa Szkocja *f*
**novel** ['nɔvl] *n* powieść *f* ▷ *adj* nowatorski
**novelist** ['nɔvəlɪst] *n* powieściopisarz(-arka) *m(f)*
**novelty** ['nɔvəltɪ] *n* nowość *f*
**November** [nəu'vɛmbə^r] *n* listopad *m*; *see also* **July**
**novice** ['nɔvɪs] *n* nowicjusz(ka) *m(f)*
**NOW** [nau] *(US) n abbr* = **National Organization for Women**
**now** [nau] *adv* teraz ▷ *conj*: **now (that)** teraz, gdy; **right now** w tej chwili; **by now** teraz, w tej chwili; **that's the fashion just now** to jest aktualnie w modzie; **I saw her just now** widziałem ją przed chwilą; **(every) now and then, (every) now and again** od czasu do czasu, co jakiś czas; **from now on** od tej pory; **in three days from now** za trzy dni; **between now and Monday** do poniedziałku; **that's all for now** to wszystko na teraz; **any day now** lada dzień; **now then** a więc, a zatem
**nowadays** ['nauədeɪz] *adv* obecnie, dzisiaj
**nowhere** ['nəuwɛə^r] *adv (be)* nigdzie; *(go)* donikąd; **there was ~ to hide** nie było się gdzie schować; **~ else** nigdzie indziej; **she had ~ to go** nie miała dokąd pójść
**noxious** ['nɔkʃəs] *adj (gas)* trujący; *(smell)* obrzydliwy
**nozzle** ['nɔzl] *n* końcówka *f* wylotowa, dysza *f*
**NP** *(Jur) n abbr* = **notary public**
**NS** *(Canada) abbr* = **Nova Scotia**
**NSC** *(US) n abbr (= National Security Council) rada wchodząca w skład w skład biura prezydenta i zajmująca się sprawami bezpieczeństwa państwa*
**NSF** *(US) n abbr* = **National Science Foundation**
**NSPCC** *(Brit) n abbr* = **National Society for the Prevention of Cruelty to Children**
**NSW** *(Australia) abbr* = **New South Wales**
**NT** *(Bible) n abbr (= New Testament)* NT
**nth** [ɛnθ] *(inf) adj*: **to the nth degree** do entej potęgi
**nuance** ['nju:ɑ̃:ns] *n* niuans *m*
**nubile** ['nju:baɪl] *adj* na wydaniu *post*
**nuclear** ['nju:klɪə^r] *adj* jądrowy
**nuclear disarmament** *n* rozbrojenie *nt* nuklearne
**nuclear family** *n* rodzina *f* elementarna
**nuclei** ['nju:klɪaɪ] *npl of* **nucleus**
**nucleus** ['nju:klɪəs] *(pl* **nuclei***) n (of atom, cell)* jądro *nt*; *(fig: of group)* zaczątek *m*
**NUCPS** *(Brit) n abbr (formerly)* = **National Union of Civil and Public Servants**
**nude** [nju:d] *adj* nagi ▷ *n (Art)* akt *m*; **in the ~** nago
**nudge** [nʌdʒ] *vt* szturchać (szturchnąć *perf*)
**nudist** ['nju:dɪst] *n* nudysta(-tka) *m(f)*
**nudist colony** *n* kolonia *f* nudystów
**nudity** ['nju:dɪtɪ] *n* nagość *f*
**nugget** ['nʌgɪt] *n (of gold)* bryłka *f*; *(fig)* cenna informacja *f*
**nuisance** ['nju:sns] *n (situation)* niedogodność *f*; *(thing, person)* utrapienie *nt*; **it's a ~** to prawdziwe utrapienie; **to be a ~** sprawiać kłopot; **what a ~!** a niech to! *(inf)*
**NUJ** *(Brit) n abbr* = **National Union of Journalists**
**null** [nʌl] *adj*: **~ and void** nieważny, nie posiadający mocy prawnej
**nullify** ['nʌlɪfaɪ] *vt (advantage, power)* odbierać (odebrać *perf*); *(law)* unieważniać (unieważnić *perf*)
**NUM** *(Brit) n abbr* = **National Union of Mineworkers**
**numb** [nʌm] *adj* zdrętwiały ▷ *vt (fingers etc)* powodować drętwienie *+gen*; *(pain)* uśmierzać (uśmierzyć *perf*); *(fig: mind)* paraliżować (sparaliżować *perf*)
**number** ['nʌmbə^r] *n* liczba *f*; *(of house, bus etc)* numer *m* ▷ *vt (pages etc)* numerować (ponumerować *perf*); *(amount to)* liczyć; **a ~ of** kilka *+gen*; **any ~ of** wiele (różnych) *+gen*; **wrong ~** *(Tel)* pomyłka; **to be ~ed among** zaliczać się do *+gen*
**number plate** ['nʌmbəpleɪt] *(Brit) n* tablica *f* rejestracyjna
**Number Ten** *(Brit) n siedziba premiera Wielkiej Brytanii*
**numbness** ['nʌmnɪs] *n* drętwienie *nt*; *(fig)* odrętwienie *nt*, otępienie *nt*
**numeral** ['nju:mərəl] *n* liczebnik *m*
**numerate** ['nju:mərɪt] *(Brit) adj*: **to be ~** umieć liczyć
**numerical** [nju:'mɛrɪkl] *adj* liczbowy
**numerous** ['nju:mərəs] *adj* liczny
**nun** [nʌn] *n* zakonnica *f*
**nuptial** ['nʌpʃəl] *adj (ceremony)* ślubny; *(bliss)* małżeński

**nurse** [nə:s] *n* (*in hospital*) pielęgniarka(-arz) *f*(*m*); (*also*: **nursemaid**) opiekunka *f* do dzieci ▷ *vt* (*patient*) opiekować się *+instr*, pielęgnować; (*cold, toothache etc*) odleżeć (*perf*); (*baby*) karmić (piersią); (*fig*: *desire, grudge*) żywić

**nursery** ['nə:sərɪ] *n* (*institution*) żłobek *m*; (*room*) pokój *m* dziecięcy; (*for plants*) szkółka *f*

**nursery rhyme** *n* wierszyk *m* dla dzieci, rymowanka *f*

**nursery school** *n* przedszkole *nt*

**nursery slope** (*Brit*) *n* ośla łączka *f*

**nursing** ['nə:sɪŋ] *n* (*profession*) pielęgniarstwo *nt*; (*care*) opieka *f* pielęgniarska

**nursing home** *n* (*hospital*) klinika *f* prywatna; (*residential home*) ≈ dom *m* pogodnej starości

**nursing mother** *n* matka *f* karmiąca

**nurture** ['nə:tʃə^r] *vt* (*child*) wychowywać; (*plant*) hodować; (*fig*: *ideas, creativity*) kultywować

**NUS** (*Brit*) *n abbr* = **National Union of Students**

**NUT** (*Brit*) *n abbr* = **National Union of Teachers**

**nut** [nʌt] *n* (*Tech*) nakrętka *f*; (*Bot*) orzech *m*; (*inf*: *lunatic*) świr *m* (*inf*)

**nutcase** ['nʌtkeɪs] (*inf*) *n* świr *m* (*inf*)

**nutcrackers** ['nʌtkrækəz] *npl* dziadek *m* do orzechów

**nutmeg** ['nʌtmɛg] *n* gałka *f* muszkatołowa

**nutrient** ['nju:trɪənt] *n* składnik *m* pokarmowy

**nutrition** [nju:'trɪʃən] *n* (*diet*) odżywianie *nt*; (*nourishment*) wartość *f* odżywcza

**nutritionist** [nju:'trɪʃənɪst] *n* dietetyk(-yczka) *m*(*f*)

**nutritious** [nju:'trɪʃəs] *adj* pożywny

**nuts** [nʌts] (*inf*) *adj* świrnięty (*inf*)

**nutshell** ['nʌtʃɛl] *n* łupina *f* orzecha; **in a ~** (*fig*) w (dużym) skrócie

**nuzzle** ['nʌzl] *vi*: **to ~ up to** łasić się do *+gen*

**NV** (*US*: *Post*) *abbr* = **Nevada**

**NWT** (*Canada*) *abbr* = **Northwest Territories**

**NY** (*US*: *Post*) *abbr* = **New York**

**NYC** (*US*: *Post*) *abbr* = **New York City**

**nylon** ['naɪlɔn] *n* nylon *m* ▷ *adj* nylonowy; **nylons** *npl* (*stockings*) nylony *pl*

**nymph** [nɪmf] *n* (*Myth*) nimfa *f*; (*Bio*) poczwarka *f*

**nymphomaniac** ['nɪmfəu'meɪnɪæk] *n* nimfomanka *f*

**NYSE** (*US*) *n abbr* = **New York Stock Exchange**

**NZ** *abbr* = **New Zealand**

# Oo

**O, o** [əu] *n* *(letter)* O *nt*, o *nt*; *(US: Scol)* celujący *m*; *(Tel etc)* zero *nt*; **O for Olive,** *(US)* **O for oboe** ≈ O jak Olga

**oaf** [əuf] *n* *(stupid person)* prostak *m*; *(clumsy person)* niezdara *m/f*

**oak** [əuk] *n* *(tree)* dąb *m*; *(wood)* dąb *m*, dębina *f* ▷ *adj* dębowy

**O & M** *n abbr* = **organization and method**

**OAP** *(Brit)* *n abbr* = **old-age pensioner**

**oar** [ɔ:ʳ] *n* wiosło *nt*; **to put** *or* **shove one's oar in** *(inf: fig)* wtrącać (wtrącić *perf*) swoje trzy grosze

**OAS** *n abbr* = **Organization of American States**

**oasis** [əu'eɪsɪs] *(pl* **oases***)* *n* oaza *f*

**oath** [əuθ] *n* *(promise)* przysięga *f*; *(swear word)* przekleństwo *nt*; **on** *(Brit)* *or* **under ~** pod przysięgą; **to take the ~** składać (złożyć *perf*) przysięgę

**oatmeal** ['əutmi:l] *n* płatki *pl* owsiane ▷ *adj* *(colour)* jasnokremowy

**oats** [əuts] *n* owies *m*

**OAU** *n abbr* = **Organization of African Unity**

**obdurate** ['ɔbdjurɪt] *adj* *(person)* uparty; *(leadership)* nieugięty

**OBE** *(Brit)* *n abbr* *(= Order of the British Empire)* *order brytyjski*

**obedience** [ə'bi:dɪəns] *n* posłuszeństwo *nt*; **in ~ to** zgodnie z *+instr*

**obedient** [ə'bi:dɪənt] *adj* posłuszny; **to be ~ to sb/sth** być posłusznym komuś/czemuś

**obelisk** ['ɔbɪlɪsk] *n* obelisk *m*

**obese** [əu'bi:s] *adj* otyły

**obesity** [əu'bi:sɪtɪ] *n* otyłość *f*

**obey** [ə'beɪ] *vt* *(person)* słuchać (usłuchać *perf* *or* posłuchać *perf*) *+gen*; *(order)* wykonywać (wykonać *perf*); *(instructions, law)* przestrzegać *+gen* ▷ *vi* być posłusznym

**obituary** [ə'bɪtjuərɪ] *n* nekrolog *m*

**object** [*n* 'ɔbdʒɪkt, *vb* əb'dʒɛkt] *n* *(thing)* przedmiot *m*, obiekt *m*; *(aim, purpose)* cel *m*; *(Ling)* dopełnienie *nt* ▷ *vi*: **to ~ (to)** sprzeciwiać się (sprzeciwić się *perf*) *(+dat)*; **money is no ~** pieniądze nie grają roli; **he ~ed that ...** wysunął zarzut, że ...; **I ~!** sprzeciw!, protestuję!; **do you ~ to my smoking?** czy nie przeszkadza ci, że palę?

**objection** [əb'dʒɛkʃən] *n* *(expression of opposition)* sprzeciw *m*; *(argument)* zarzut *m*; **I have no ~ to** nie mam nic przeciwko *+dat*; **if you have no ~** jeśli nie masz nic przeciwk temu; **to raise** *or* **voice an ~** zgłaszać (zgłosi *perf*) *or* wyrażać (wyrazić *perf*) sprzeciw

**objectionable** [əb'dʒɛkʃənəbl] *adj* nie do przyjęcia *post*

**objective** [əb'dʒɛktɪv] *adj* obiektywny ▷ *n* cel

**objectively** [əb'dʒɛktɪvlɪ] *adv* obiektywnie

**objectivity** [ɔbdʒɪk'tɪvɪtɪ] *n* obiektywność *f*, obiektywizm *m*

**object lesson** *n* *(fig)* pokazowa lekcja *f*

**objector** [əb'dʒɛktəʳ] *n* przeciwnik(-iczka) *m(f)*

**obligation** [ɔblɪ'geɪʃən] *n* obowiązek *m*; **to be under an ~ to sb** być komuś zobowiązanym; **to be under an ~ to do sth** być zobowiązanym coś (z)robić; **"no ~ to buy"** *(Comm)* „bez obowiązku kupna"

**obligatory** [ə'blɪgətərɪ] *adj* obowiązkowy

**oblige** [ə'blaɪdʒ] *vt*: **to ~ sb to do sth** zobowiązywać (zobowiązać *perf*) kogoś do zrobienia czegoś; **to ~ sb** wyświadczać (wyświadczyć *perf*) komuś przysługę; **to be ~d to sb for sth** być zobowiązanym komuś za coś; **anything to ~!** *(inf)* zawsze do usług! *(inf)*; **I'd be very ~d** byłbym Panu/Pani bard wdzięczny *or* zobowiązany

**obliging** [ə'blaɪdʒɪŋ] *adj* uczynny

**oblique** [ə'bli:k] *adj* *(line)* ukośny, pochyły; *(compliment)* ukryty; *(reference)* niewyraźny ▷ *n* *(Brit: Typ: also:* **oblique stroke***)* kreska *f* pochyła

**obliterate** [ə'blɪtəreɪt] *vt* *(village)* zrównywa (zrównać *perf*) z ziemią; *(traces)* zacierać (zatrzeć *perf*); *(fig: thought, error)* wymazywać (wymazać *perf*) z pamięci

**oblivion** [ə'blɪvɪən] *n* *(unconsciousness)* stan *m* nieświadomości; *(being forgotten)* niepamięć zapomnienie *nt*; **to sink into ~** odchodzić (odejść *perf*) w niepamięć *or* zapomnienie

**oblivious** [ə'blɪvɪəs] *adj*: **~ of** *or* **to** nieświadomy *+gen*

**oblong** ['ɔblɔŋ] *adj* prostokątny ▷ *n* prostokąt *m*
**obnoxious** [əb'nɔkʃəs] *adj (behaviour, person)* okropny; *(smell)* ohydny
**o.b.o.** *(US) abbr (in classified adds: = or best offer)* lub najwyższa oferta
**oboe** ['əubəu] *n* obój *m*
**obscene** [əb'si:n] *adj* nieprzyzwoity
**obscenity** [əb'sɛnɪtɪ] *n* nieprzyzwoitość *f*
**obscure** [əb'skjuəʳ] *adj (place, author etc)* mało znany; *(point, issue)* niejasny; *(shape)* niewyraźny, słabo widoczny ▷ *vt* przysłaniać (przysłonić *perf*)
**obscurity** [əb'skjuərɪtɪ] *n* niejasność *f*; **to rise from ~** zyskiwać (zyskać *perf*) rozgłos, wypływać (wypłynąć *perf*) *(inf)*
**obsequious** [əb'si:kwɪəs] *adj* służalczy
**observable** [əb'zə:vəbl] *adj* widoczny, zauważalny
**observance** [əb'zə:vns] *n* przestrzeganie *nt (prawa, zwyczajów itp)*; **religious ~s** obrzędy religijne
**observant** [əb'zə:vnt] *adj* spostrzegawczy
**observation** [ɔbzə'veɪʃən] *n* obserwacja *f*; *(remark)* uwaga *f*; **she's under ~** *(Med)* jest pod obserwacją
**observation post** *n* punkt *m* obserwacyjny
**observatory** [əb'zə:vətrɪ] *n* obserwatorium *nt*
**observe** [əb'zə:v] *vt (watch)* obserwować; *(notice)* zauważyć *(perf)*, spostrzec *(perf)*; *(remark)* zauważać (zauważyć *perf*); *(rule, convention)* przestrzegać *+gen*
**observer** [əb'zə:vəʳ] *n* obserwator(ka) *m(f)*
**obsess** [əb'sɛs] *vt* prześladować, dręczyć; **to be ~ed by** *or* **with sb/sth** mieć obsesję na punkcie kogoś/czegoś
**obsession** [əb'sɛʃən] *n* obsesja *f*
**obsessive** [əb'sɛsɪv] *adj* obsesyjny, chorobliwy; *(person)*: **to be ~ about** mieć obsesję na punkcie *+gen*
**obsolescence** [ɔbsə'lɛsns] *n* starzenie się *nt*; **built-in** *or* **planned ~** *(Comm)* żywotność
**obsolete** ['ɔbsəli:t] *adj* przestarzały
**obstacle** ['ɔbstəkl] *n* przeszkoda *f*
**obstacle race** *n* bieg *m* z przeszkodami
**obstetrics** [ɔb'stɛtrɪks] *n* położnictwo *nt*
**obstinacy** ['ɔbstɪnəsɪ] *n* upór *m*
**obstinate** ['ɔbstɪnɪt] *adj* uparty; *(cough)* uporczywy
**obstruct** [əb'strʌkt] *vt (road, path, traffic)* blokować (zablokować *perf*); *(fig)* utrudniać (utrudnić *perf*)
**obstruction** [əb'strʌkʃən] *n* przeszkoda *f*; *(Pol)* obstrukcja *f*
**obstructive** [əb'strʌktɪv] *adj*: **to be ~** stwarzać trudności
**obtain** [əb'teɪn] *vt (book etc)* dostawać (dostać *perf*), nabywać (nabyć *perf*) *(fml)*; *(degree, information)* uzyskiwać (uzyskać *perf*), otrzymywać (otrzymać *perf*) ▷ *vi (fml: situation, custom)* istnieć, panować; *(: regulations)* obowiązywać
**obtainable** [əb'teɪnəbl] *adj* osiągalny
**obtrusive** [əb'tru:sɪv] *adj* natrętny
**obtuse** [əb'tju:s] *adj (person)* tępy, ograniczony; *(Math)* rozwarty
**obverse** ['ɔbvə:s] *n* odwrotność *f*, przeciwieństwo *nt*
**obviate** ['ɔbvɪeɪt] *vt* usuwać (usunąć *perf*), eliminować (wyeliminować *perf*)
**obvious** ['ɔbvɪəs] *adj* oczywisty
**obviously** ['ɔbvɪəslɪ] *adv (clearly)* wyraźnie; *(of course)* oczywiście; **~!** (ależ) oczywiście!; **~ not** najwyraźniej nie; **he was ~ not drunk** najwyraźniej nie był pijany; **he was not ~ drunk** nie był wyraźnie pijany
**OCAS** *n abbr* = **Organization of Central American States**
**occasion** [ə'keɪʒən] *n (point in time)* sytuacja *f*; *(event, celebration etc)* wydarzenie *nt*; *(opportunity)* okazja *f* ▷ *vt (fml)* powodować (spowodować *perf*); **on ~** czasami; **on that ~** tym razem; **to rise to the ~** stawać (stanąć *perf*) na wysokości zadania
**occasional** [ə'keɪʒənl] *adj* sporadyczny; *(rain, showers)* przelotny; **architects, planners, and the ~ sociologist** architekci, planiści i niektórzy socjologowie
**occasionally** [ə'keɪʒənəlɪ] *adv* czasami; **very ~** (bardzo) rzadko
**occasional table** *n* stolik *m*, stoliczek *m*
**occult** [ɔ'kʌlt] *n*: **the ~** okultyzm *m* ▷ *adj (subject)* okultystyczny; *(powers)* tajemny
**occupancy** ['ɔkjupənsɪ] *n* zajmowanie *nt (pomieszczenia, budynku)*
**occupant** ['ɔkjupənt] *n (of house)* mieszkaniec(-nka) *m(f)*, lokator(ka) *m(f)*; *(of room)* sublokator(ka) *m(f)*; *(of office)* użytkownik(-iczka) *m(f)*; *(of vehicle)* pasażer(ka) *m(f)*
**occupation** [ɔkju'peɪʃən] *n (job)* zawód *m*; *(pastime)* zajęcie *nt*; *(of building, country)* okupacja *f*
**occupational guidance** [ɔkju'peɪʃənl-] *(Brit) n* poradnictwo *nt* zawodowe
**occupational hazard** *n* ryzyko *nt* zawodowe
**occupational pension scheme** *n* zawodowy system *m* emerytalny
**occupational therapy** *n (Med)* terapia *f* zajęciowa
**occupier** ['ɔkjupaɪəʳ] *n (of house, flat)* najemca *m*; *(of land etc)* dzierżawca *m*; **"to the ~"** „do najemcy lokalu"
**occupy** ['ɔkjupaɪ] *vt* zajmować (zająć *perf*); **to ~ o.s. in** *or* **with sth/doing sth** zajmować się

O

czymś/robieniem czegoś; **to be occupied in** *or* **with sth/doing sth** być zajętym czymś/robieniem czegoś
**occur** [ə'kə:ʳ] *vi* (*event*) zdarzać się (zdarzyć się *perf*), wydarzać się (wydarzyć się *perf*), mieć miejsce; (*phenomenon*) występować (wystąpić *perf*); **to ~ to sb** przychodzić (przyjść *perf*) komuś do głowy
**occurrence** [ə'kʌrəns] *n* (*event*) wydarzenie *nt*; (*incidence*) występowanie *nt*
**ocean** ['əuʃən] *n* ocean *m*; **~s of** (*inf*) morze *+gen*
**ocean bed** *n* dno *nt* oceanu
**ocean-going** ['əuʃəngəuɪŋ] *adj* (*ship, vessel*) pełnomorski
**Oceania** [əuʃɪ'eɪnɪə] *n* Oceania *f*
**ocean liner** *n* liniowiec *m*
**ochre**, (*US*) **ocher** ['əukəʳ] *adj* żółtobrunatny, w kolorze ochry *post*
**o'clock** [ə'klɔk] *adv*: **it is five ~** jest (godzina) piąta
**OCR** (*Comput*) *n abbr* = **optical character recogniton**; (= *optical character reader*) OCR *nt*
**Oct.** *abbr* (= *October*) paźdz.
**octagonal** [ɔk'tægənl] *adj* ośmiokątny
**octane** ['ɔkteɪn] *n* oktan *m*; **high-~ petrol** *or* (*US*) **gas** benzyna wysokooktanowa
**octave** ['ɔktɪv] *n* oktawa *f*
**October** [ɔk'təubəʳ] *n* październik *m*; *see also* **July**
**octogenarian** ['ɔktəudʒɪ'nεərɪən] *n* osiemdziesięciolatek(-tka) *m(f)*
**octopus** ['ɔktəpəs] *n* ośmiornica *f*
**odd** [ɔd] *adj* (*strange*) dziwny; (*uneven*) nieparzysty; (*not paired*) nie do pary *post*; (*some*) jakiś; (*miscellaneous*) różne (*+pl*); **we had the odd sunny day** czasem trafił się słoneczny dzień; **sixty-odd** sześćdziesiąt kilka *or* parę; **at odd times** co jakiś czas; **to be the odd one out** wyróżniać się
**oddball** ['ɔdbɔ:l] (*inf*) *n* dziwak *m*
**oddity** ['ɔdɪtɪ] *n* osobliwość *f*
**odd-job man** [ɔd'dʒɔb-] *n* złota rączka *f*
**odd jobs** *npl* prace *pl* dorywcze
**oddly** ['ɔdlɪ] *adv* dziwnie; *see also* **enough**
**oddments** ['ɔdmənts] *npl* resztki *pl* (*pojedyncze egzemplarze pozostałe z większej partii towaru*)
**odds** [ɔdz] *npl* (*in betting*) szanse *pl* wygranej; (*fig*) szanse *pl* powodzenia; **the ~ are that...** wszystko wskazuje na to, że...; **the ~ are in favour of/against his coming** wszystko wskazuje na to, że przyjdzie/nie przyjdzie; **to succeed against all the ~** odnieść (*perf*) sukces mimo wszelkich przeciwności; **it makes no ~** (to) nie ma znaczenia, bez różnicy; **to be at ~ (with)** (*in disagreement*) nie zgadzać się (z *+instr*); (*at variance*) nie pasować (do *+gen*), kłócić się (z *+instr*)
**odds and ends** *npl* różności *pl*
**ode** [əud] *n* oda *f*
**odious** ['əudɪəs] *adj* wstrętny
**odometer** [ɔ'dɔmɪtəʳ] (*US*) *n* hodometr *m*, drogomierz *m*
**odour**, (*US*) **odor** ['əudəʳ] *n* zapach *m*
**odo(u)rless** ['əudəlɪs] *adj* bez zapachu *post*, bezwonny
**OECD** *n abbr* (= *Organization for Economic Cooperation and Development*) OECD *f inv*, Organizacja *f* Współpracy Gospodarczej i Rozwoju
**oesophagus**, (*US*) **esophagus** [i:'sɔfəgəs] *n* przełyk *m*
**oestrogen**, (*US*) **estrogen** ['i:strəudʒən] *n* estrogen *m*

 KEYWORD

**of** [ɔv, əv] *prep* **1** (*usu*): **the history of Europe** historia Europy; **the winter of 1987** zima roku 1987; **the 5th of July** 5 lipca; **the four of us** nas czworo; **a friend of ours** (pewien nasz) kolega; **a boy of 10** dziesięcioletni chłopiec; **that was kind of you** to było uprzejme z twojej strony; **the city of New York** (miasto) Nowy Jork
**2** (*from, out of*) z *+gen*; **a bracelet of solid gold** bransoletka ze szczerego złota; **made of wood** zrobiony z drewna
**3** (*about*) o *+loc*; **I've never heard of him** nigdy o nim nie słyszałam
**4** (*indicating source, direction*) od *+gen*; **don't expect too much of him** nie oczekuj od niego zbyt wiele; **south of London** na południe od Londynu

 KEYWORD

**off** [ɔf] *adv* **1** (*referring to distance*): **it's a long way off** to daleko (stąd)
**2** (*referring to time*) za *+acc*; **the game is 3 days off** mecz jest za trzy dni
**3** (*departure*): **I must be off** muszę (już) iść; **to go off to Paris** wyjeżdżać (wyjechać *perf*) do Paryża
**4** (*removal*): **to take off one's hat/clothes** zdejmować (zdjąć *perf*) kapelusz/ubranie; **the button came off** guzik odpadł; **10% off** (*Comm*) 10% zniżki *or* rabatu
**5**: **to be off** (*not at work*: *on holiday*) mieć wolne *or* urlop; (: *due to sickness*) być na zwolnieniu (lekarskim); **to have a day off** mieć dzień wolny; **to be off sick** być na zwolnieniu (lekarskim); **to be well off** być dobrze sytuowanym
▷ *adj* **1** (*not turned on*: *machine, light, engine*)

wyłączony; (: *water, gas, tap*) zakręcony
**2** (*cancelled*: *meeting, match*) odwołany; (: *agreement, negotiations*) zerwany
**3** (*Brit*: *not fresh*) nieświeży, zepsuty
**4**: **on the off chance** na wypadek, gdyby; **to have an off day** mieć gorszy dzień
▷ *prep* **1** (*indicating motion, removal etc*): **he fell off a cliff** spadł ze skały; **a button came off my coat** guzik mi odpadł od płaszcza
**2** (*distant from*) (w bok) od *+gen*; **it's 5 km off the main road** to pięć kilometrów (w bok) od głównej drogi
**3**: **I am off meat/beer** (już) nie lubię mięsa/piwa

**offal** ['ɔfl] *n* podroby *pl*

**off-beat** ['ɔfbi:t] *adj* ekscentryczny

**off-centre**, (US) **off-center** [ɔf'sɛntə^r] *adj* skrzywiony; (*Tech*) niewspółosiowy, mimośrodowy ▷ *adv* nie pośrodku; (*Tech*) niewspółosiowo, mimośrodowo

**off-colour** ['ɔf'kʌlə^r] (*Brit*) *adj* nie w formie *post*, niedysponowany

**offence**, (US) **offense** [ə'fɛns] *n* (*crime*) przestępstwo *nt*, wykroczenie *nt*; (*insult*) obraza *f*; **to commit an ~** popełnić (*perf*) przestępstwo; **to take ~ (at)** obrażać się (obrazić się *perf*) (na *+acc*); **to give ~ (to)** obrażać (obrazić *perf*) *or* urażać (urazić *perf*) (*+acc*); **no ~** bez obrazy

**offend** [ə'fɛnd] *vt* obrażać (obrazić *perf*), urażać (urazić *perf*); **to ~ against** (*law, rule*) naruszać (naruszyć *perf*) *+acc*

**offender** [ə'fɛndə^r] *n* przestępca(-pczyni) *m(f)*

**offense** [ə'fɛns] (US) *n* = **offence**

**offensive** [ə'fɛnsɪv] *adj* (*remark, behaviour*) obraźliwy; (*smell etc*) wstrętny, ohydny; (*weapon*) zaczepny ▷ *n* ofensywa *f*

**offer** ['ɔfə^r] *n* oferta *f*; (*of assistance etc*) propozycja *f* ▷ *vt* (*cigarette, seat etc*) proponować (zaproponować *perf*); (*service, product*) oferować (zaoferować *perf*); (*help, friendship*) ofiarować (zaofiarować *perf*); (*advice, praise*) udzielać (udzielić *perf*) *+gen*; (*congratulations*) składać (złożyć *perf*); (*opportunity, prospect*) dawać (dać *perf*), stwarzać (stworzyć *perf*); **to make an ~ for sth** składać (złożyć *perf*) ofertę na coś; **to ~ sth to sb** proponować (zaproponować *perf*) coś komuś; **he ~ed to take us...** zaofiarował się zabrać nas...; **"on ~"** (*Comm*: *available*) oferowany; (: *cheaper*) przeceniony

**offering** ['ɔfərɪŋ] *n* propozycja *f*, oferta *f*; (*Rel*) ofiara *f*

**off-hand** [ɔf'hænd] *adj* bezceremonialny, obcesowy ▷ *adv* (tak) od razu *or* od ręki; **I can't tell you ~** nie umiem odpowiedzieć ci na poczekaniu

**office** ['ɔfɪs] *n* (*room, workplace*) biuro *nt*; (*position*) urząd *m*; **doctor's ~** (US) gabinet lekarski; **to take ~** (*government*) obejmować (objąć *perf*) władzę; (*minister*) obejmować (objąć *perf*) urząd; **in ~** (*government, party*) u władzy; (*minister*) na stanowisku *or* urzędzie; **through his good ~s** dzięki jego uprzejmości; **O~ of Fair Trading** (*Brit*) *departament rządu kontrolujący uczciwość handlu i reklamy*

**office block**, (US) **office building** *n* budynek *m* biurowy, biurowiec *m*

**office boy** *n* goniec *m*

**office holder** *n* osoba *f* piastująca urząd

**office hours** *npl* (*Comm*) godziny *pl* urzędowania; (*US*: *Med*) godziny *pl* przyjęć

**office manager** *n* kierownik(-iczka) *m(f)* biura

**officer** ['ɔfɪsə^r] *n* (*Mil*) oficer *m*; (*also*: **police officer**) policjant(ka) *m(f)*; (*of organization*) przedstawiciel(ka) *m(f)*; **regional ~** przedstawiciel regionalny

**office work** *n* praca *f* biurowa

**office worker** *n* urzędnik(-iczka) *m(f)*

**official** [ə'fɪʃl] *adj* oficjalny ▷ *n* urzędnik *m* (*w rządzie, związkach zawodowych itp*)

**officialdom** [ə'fɪʃldəm] (*pej*) *n* biurokracja *f* (*pej*)

**officially** [ə'fɪʃəlɪ] *adv* oficjalnie

**official receiver** *n* (*Comm*) niezależny likwidator *m*

**officiate** [ə'fɪʃɪeɪt] *vi* pełnić obowiązki gospodarza; (*Rel*) odprawiać *or* celebrować nabożeństwo *or* mszę

**officious** [ə'fɪʃəs] *adj* nadgorliwy

**offing** ['ɔfɪŋ] *n*: **in the ~** bliski

**off-key** [ɔf'ki:] *adj* (*Mus*) fałszywy

**off-licence** ['ɔflaɪsns] (*Brit*) *n* ≈ (sklep *m*) monopolowy

**off-limits** [ɔf'lɪmɪts] *adj* niedostępny, zakazany

**off-line** [ɔf'laɪn] *adj* (*Comput*) autonomiczny, rozłączny; (*switched off*) odłączony

**off-load** ['ɔfləud] *vt* (*work, duties*) przerzucać (przerzucić *perf*) (*na kogoś*)

**off-peak** ['ɔf'pi:k] *adj* poza godzinami szczytu *post*

**off-putting** ['ɔfputɪŋ] (*Brit*) *adj* odpychający

**off-season** ['ɔf'si:zn] *adj* poza sezonem *post* ▷ *adv* poza sezonem

**offset** ['ɔfsɛt] (*irreg*: *like* **set**) *vt* równoważyć (zrównoważyć *perf*)

**offshoot** ['ɔfʃu:t] *n* (*of organization etc*) gałąź *f*, odgałęzienie *nt*

**offshore** [ɔf'ʃɔ:^r] *adj* (*breeze*) od lądu *post*; (*oilrig, fishing*) przybrzeżny

**offside** [ˈɔfˈsaɪd] *adj* (*Aut: with right-hand drive*) prawy; (*: with left-hand drive*) lewy; (*Sport*): **to be ~** być na spalonym ▷ *n*: **the ~** (*Aut: with right-hand drive*) prawa strona *f*; (*: with left-hand drive*) lewa strona *f*
**offspring** [ˈɔfsprɪŋ] *n inv* potomstwo *nt*
**offstage** [ɔfˈsteɪdʒ] *adv* za sceną; (*of actors' behaviour*) prywatnie
**off-the-cuff** [ɔfðəˈkʌf] *adj* (*remark*) spontaniczny
**off-the-job** [ˈɔfðəˈdʒɔb] *adj*: **~ training** szkolenie *nt* zawodowe poza miejscem pracy
**off-the-peg** [ˈɔfðəˈpɛg], (*US*) **off-the-rack** [ˈɔfðəˈræk] *adj* gotowy ▷ *adv*: **to buy clothes ~** kupować gotową odzież
**off-the-record** [ˈɔfðəˈrɛkɔːd] *adj* nieoficjalny, poza protokołem *post* ▷ *adv* nieoficjalnie, między nami (mówiąc)
**off-white** [ˈɔfwaɪt] *adj* w kolorze złamanej bieli *post*
**often** [ˈɔfn] *adv* często; **how ~ have you been there?** jak często tam bywasz?; **more ~ than not** najczęściej; **as ~ as not** dość często; **every so ~** co jakiś czas
**ogle** [ˈəugl] *vt* przyglądać się pożądliwie *+dat*
**ogre** [ˈəugəʳ] *n* (*in fairy tales*) ludojad *m*
**OH** (*US: Post*) *abbr* = **Ohio**
**oh** [əu] *excl* ach
**ohm** [əum] *n* (*Elec*) om *m*
**OHMS** (*Brit*) *abbr* (*= On His (or Her) Majesty's Service*) *napis na przesyłkach urzędowych*
**oil** [ɔɪl] *n* (*Culin*) olej *m*, oliwa *f*; (*petroleum*) ropa *f* (naftowa); (*for heating*) paliwo *nt* olejowe ▷ *vt* oliwić (naoliwić *perf*)
**oilcan** [ˈɔɪlkæn] *n* oliwiarka *f*
**oil change** *n* (*Aut*) zmiana *f* oleju
**oilcloth** [ˈɔɪlklɔθ] *n* cerata *f*
**oilfield** [ˈɔɪlfiːld] *n* pole *nt* naftowe
**oil filter** *n* (*Aut*) filtr *m* oleju
**oil-fired** [ˈɔɪlfaɪəd] *adj* opalany paliwem olejowym
**oil gauge** *n* (*Aut*) wskaźnik *m* oleju
**oil painting** *n* obraz *m* olejny
**oil refinery** *n* rafineria *f* (ropy naftowej)
**oil rig** *n* szyb *m* naftowy; (*at sea*) platforma *f* wiertnicza
**oilskins** [ˈɔɪlskɪnz] *npl* ubranie *nt* sztormowe
**oil slick** *n* plama *f* ropy naftowej
**oil tanker** *n* (*ship*) tankowiec *m*, zbiornikowiec *m*; (*truck*) cysterna *f*
**oil well** *n* szyb *m* naftowy
**oily** [ˈɔɪlɪ] *adj* (*substance*) oleisty; (*rag*) zatłuszczony; (*food*) tłusty
**ointment** [ˈɔɪntmənt] *n* maść *f*
**OK** (*US: Post*) *abbr* = **Oklahoma**
**O.K.** [ˈəuˈkeɪ] (*inf*) *excl* (*showing agreement*) w porządku; (*in questions*) dobrze?, zgoda?; (*granted*) zgoda ▷ *adj* (*average*) w porządku p[...] (*acceptable*) do przyjęcia *post* ▷ *vt* zgadzać się (zgodzić się *perf*) na *+acc* ▷ *n*: **to give sb the ~ (to ...)** pozwalać (pozwolić *perf*) komuś (*+infin*); **to give sth the ~** wyrażać (wyrazić *perf*) zgodę na coś; **if that's okay** jeśli możn[...] **is it ~?** może być?; **are you ~?** (czy) wszystk[...] w porządku?; **are you ~ for money?** (czy) masz dosyć pieniędzy?; **it's ~ with** *or* **by m[...]** mnie to nie przeszkadza
**okay** [ˈəuˈkeɪ] = **O.K.**
**old** [əuld] *adj* stary; (*former*) stary, dawny; **h[...] old are you?** ile masz lat?; **he's ten years old** ma dziesięć lat; **older brother** starszy brat; **any old thing will do** wystarczy byle[...]
**old age** *n* starość *f*
**old age pension** *n* emerytura *f*
**old age pensioner** (*Brit*) *n* emeryt(ka) *m(f)*
**old-fashioned** [ˈəuldˈfæʃnd] *adj* (*style, design[...] clothes*) staromodny, niemodny; (*person, values*) staroświecki
**old hand** *n* stary wyga *m*
**old hat** *adj* już niemodny
**old maid** *n* stara panna *f*
**old people's home** *n* ≈ dom *m* starców *or* spokojnej starości
**old-time dancing** [ˈəuldˈtaɪm-] *n* przedwojenne tańce *pl* (*walce, fokstroty itp*)
**old-timer** [əuldˈtaɪməʳ] (*esp US*) *n* weteran(k[...] *m(f)*
**old wives' tale** *n* przesąd *m*, babskie gadanie[...]
**oleander** [əulɪˈændəʳ] *n* oleander *m*
**olive** [ˈɔlɪv] *n* (*fruit*) oliwka *f*; (*tree*) drzewo *nt* oliwne ▷ *adj* (*also*: **olive-green**) oliwkowy; **t[...] offer an ~ branch to sb** (*fig*) przyjść (*perf*) d[...] kogoś z gałązką oliwną
**olive oil** *n* oliwa *f* z oliwek
**Olympic** [əuˈlɪmpɪk] *adj* olimpijski
**Olympic Games** *npl*: **the ~** (*also*: **the Olympics**) igrzyska *pl* olimpijskie, olimpiada *f*
**OM** (*Brit*) *n abbr* (*= Order of Merit*) *order brytyjski*
**Oman** [əuˈmɑːn] *n* Oman *m*
**OMB** (*US*) *n abbr* = **Office of Management an[...] Budget**
**ombudsman** [ˈɔmbudzmən] *n* rzecznik *m* praw obywatelskich
**omelette**, (*US*) **omelet** [ˈɔmlɪt] *n* omlet *m*; **ham/cheese ~** omlet z szynką/serem
**omen** [ˈəumən] *n* omen *m*
**ominous** [ˈɔmɪnəs] *adj* (*silence*) złowrogi, złowieszczy; (*clouds, smoke*) złowróżbny, złowieszczy
**omission** [əuˈmɪʃən] *n* (*thing omitted*) przeoczenie *nt*; (*act of omitting*) pominięcie *n[...]*
**omit** [əuˈmɪt] *vt* pomijać (pominąć *perf*) ▷ *vi*: **to ~ to do sth** nie zrobić (*perf*) czegoś

**omnivorous** [ɔm'nɪvrəs] *adj* wszystkożerny
**ON** (*Canada*) *abbr* = **Ontario**

KEYWORD

**on** [ɔn] *prep* **1** (*indicating position*) na *+loc*; **on the wall** na ścianie; **on the left** na lewo; **the house is on the main road** dom stoi przy głównej drodze
**2** (*indicating means, method, condition etc*): **on foot** pieszo, piechotą; **on the train/plane** (*go*) pociągiem/samolotem; (*be*) w pociągu/samolocie; **she's on the telephone** rozmawia przez telefon; **on television/the radio** w telewizji/radiu; **to be on tranquillizers** brać leki uspokajające; **to be on holiday** być na wakacjach
**3** (*referring to time*) w *+acc*; **on Friday** w piątek; **on June 20th** dwudziestego czerwca; **a week on Friday** od piątku za tydzień; **on arrival** po przyjeździe; **on seeing this** widząc *or* ujrzawszy to
**4** (*about, concerning*) o *+loc*, na temat *+gen*; **books on philosophy** książki o *or* na temat filozofii; **information on train services** informacja kolejowa
▷ *adv* **1** (*referring to clothes*) na sobie; **to have one's coat on** mieć na sobie płaszcz; **she put her hat on** założyła kapelusz
**2** (*referring to covering*): **screw the lid on tightly** przykręć mocno pokrywę
**3** (*further, continuously*) dalej; **to walk on** iść (pójść *perf*) dalej
▷ *adj* **1** (*in operation: machine, radio, TV, light*) włączony; (*: tap*) odkręcony; (*: handbrake*) zaciągnięty; (*: meeting*) w toku *post*
**2** (*not cancelled*) aktualny; **is the meeting still on?** czy (to) zebranie jest nadal aktualne?
**3**: **that's not on!** (*inf*) to (jest) nie do przyjęcia!

**ONC** (*Brit*) *n abbr* (= *Ordinary National Certificate*) *świadectwo odpowiadające w przybliżeniu GCE A level*
**once** [wʌns] *adv* (*on one occasion*) (jeden) raz; (*formerly*) dawniej, kiedyś; (*a long time ago*) kiedyś, swego czasu ▷ *conj* zaraz po tym, jak, gdy tylko; **at ~** (*immediately*) od razu; (*simultaneously*) na raz; **~ a week** raz w tygodniu *or* na tydzień; **~ more** *or* **again** jeszcze raz; **~ and for all** raz na zawsze; **~ upon a time** pewnego razu; **~ in a while** raz na jakiś czas; **all at ~** naraz, ni z tego, ni z owego; **for ~ she was able to relax** chociaż raz mogła odpocząć; **for ~ I am completely lost** tym razem jestem całkowicie zagubiony; **~ or twice** raz czy dwa
**oncoming** ['ɔnkʌmɪŋ] *adj* (*traffic*) (nadjeżdżający) z przeciwka; (*winter*) nadchodzący
**OND** (*Brit*) *n abbr* (= *Ordinary National Diploma*) *uprawnienia zawodowe uzyskiwane po dwuletnim kursie*

KEYWORD

**one** [wʌn] *num* jeden; **I asked for two coffees, not one** prosiłam o dwie kawy, nie jedną; **one hundred and fifty** sto pięćdziesiąt; **one day there was a knock at the door** któregoś *or* pewnego dnia rozległo się pukanie do drzwi; **one by one** pojedynczo
▷ *adj* **1** (*sole*) jedyny; **that is my one worry** to moje jedyne zmartwienie
**2** (*same*) (ten) jeden; **they came in the one car** przyjechali (tym) jednym samochodem
▷ *pron* **1**: **this one** ten *m*/ta *f*/to *nt*; **that one** (tam)ten *m*/(tam)ta *f*/(tam)to *nt*; **she chose the black dress, though I liked the red one** wybrała tę czarną sukienkę, choć mnie podobała się ta czerwona
**2**: **one another** się; **do you two ever see one another?** czy wy dwoje w ogóle się widujecie?; **the boys didn't dare look at one another** chłopcy nie mieli odwagi spojrzeć na siebie
**3** (*impersonal*): **one never knows** nigdy nie wiadomo; **to cut one's finger** skaleczyć się (*perf*) w palec

**one-day excursion** ['wʌndeɪ-] (*US*) *n* bilet *m* powrotny jednodniowy
**one-man** ['wʌn'mæn] *adj* (*show*) jednoosobowy; (*business*) indywidualny
**one-man band** *n* człowiek *m* orkiestra *f*
**one-off** [wʌn'ɔf] (*Brit: inf*) *n* fuks *m* (*inf*)
**one-piece** ['wʌnpiːs] *adj*: **~ swimsuit** strój *m* (kąpielowy) jednoczęściowy
**onerous** ['ɔnərəs] *adj* uciążliwy

KEYWORD

**oneself** [wʌn'sɛlf] *pron* (*reflexive*) się; (*after prep*) siebie (*gen, acc*), sobie (*dat, loc*), sobą (*instr*); (*emphatic*) samemu; **to hurt oneself** ranić (zranić *perf*) się; **to talk to oneself** mówić do siebie; **to talk about oneself** mówić o sobie; **to be oneself** być sobą; **others might find odd what one finds normal oneself** to, co samemu uważa się za normalne, inni mogą uznać za dziwne

**one-shot** ['wʌnʃɔt] (*US*) *n* = **one-off**

O

**one-sided** [wʌn'saɪdɪd] *adj* jednostronny; (*contest*) nierówny
**one-time** ['wʌntaɪm] *adj* były
**one-to-one** ['wʌntəwʌn] *adj* (*tuition etc*) indywidualny
**one-upmanship** [wʌn'ʌpmənʃɪp] *n*: **the art of ~** umiejętność *f* zdobywania i utrzymywania przewagi
**one-way** ['wʌnweɪ] *adj* (*street, traffic*) jednokierunkowy; (*ticket, trip*) w jedną stronę *post*
**ongoing** ['ɔngəuɪŋ] *adj* (*discussion*) toczący się; (*crisis*) trwający
**onion** ['ʌnjən] *n* cebula *f*
**on-line** ['ɔnlaɪn] (*Comput*) *adj* (*mode, processing*) bezpośredni; (*database*) dostępny bezpośrednio; (*switched on*) włączony ▷ *adv* w trybie bezpośrednim
**onlooker** ['ɔnlukə^r] *n* widz *m*, obserwator(ka) *m(f)*
**only** ['əunlɪ] *adv* (*solely*) jedynie; (*merely, just*) tylko ▷ *adj* jedyny ▷ *conj* tylko; **an ~ child** jedynak(-aczka) *m(f)*; **I ~ took one** wziąłem tylko jedno; **I saw her ~ yesterday** widziałam ją dopiero wczoraj; **I'd be ~ too pleased to help** z przyjemnością pomógłbym; **I would come, ~ I'm busy** przyszedłbym, tylko (że) jestem zajęty; **not ~ ... but (also)** nie tylko..., lecz (także)
**ono** (*Brit*) *abbr* (*in classified ads*) = **or near(est) offer**; *see* **near**
**onset** ['ɔnsɛt] *n* początek *m*
**onshore** ['ɔnʃɔː^r] *adj* (*wind*) od morza *post*
**onslaught** ['ɔnslɔːt] *n* szturm *m*
**on-the-job** ['ɔnðə'dʒɔb] *adj*: **~ training** szkolenie *nt* w czasie pracy
**onto** ['ɔntu] *prep* = **on to**
**onus** ['əunəs] *n* ciężar *m*, brzemię *nt*; **the ~ is on him to prove it** na nim spoczywa ciężar udowodnienia tego
**onward(s)** ['ɔnwəd(z)] *adv* (*move, travel*) dalej ▷ *adj* postępujący; **from that time ~** od tego czasu
**onyx** ['ɔnɪks] *n* onyks *m*
**ooze** [uːz] *vi* wyciekać, sączyć się
**opacity** [əu'pæsɪtɪ] *n* nieprzezroczystość *f*
**opal** ['əupl] *n* opal *m*
**opaque** [əu'peɪk] *adj* nieprzezroczysty
**OPEC** ['əupɛk] *n abbr* (= *Organization of Petroleum-Exporting Countries*) OPEC *f inv*, Organizacja *f* Państw-Eksporterów Ropy Naftowej
**open** ['əupn] *adj* otwarty; (*vacancy*) wolny ▷ *vt* otwierać (otworzyć *perf*) ▷ *vi* otwierać się (otworzyć się *perf*); (*debate etc*) rozpoczynać się (rozpocząć się *perf*); **in the ~ (air)** na wolnym powietrzu; **the ~ sea** otwarte morze; **I have an ~ mind on that** nie mam wyrobionego zdania na ten temat; **he didn't ~ his mouth once** ani razu nie otworzył ust; **to be ~ to** (*suggestions*) być otwartym na *+acc*; (*criticism*) być narażonym na *+acc*; **the palace is ~ to the public** pałac jest otwarty dla publiczności; **the film/play has recently ~ed in New York** niedawno odbyła się premiera filmu/sztuki w Nowym Jorku
▸ **open on to** *vt fus* (*room, door*) wychodzić na *+acc*
▸ **open up** *vi* otwierać (otworzyć *perf*); **he never ~s up** nigdy nie mówi, co czuje
**open-air** [əupn'ɛə^r] *adj* na wolnym powietrzu *post*
**open-and-shut** ['əupnən'ʃʌt] *adj*: **~ case** oczywisty przypadek *m*
**open day** *n* dzień *m* otwarty
**open-ended** [əupn'ɛndɪd] *adj* (*discussion*) luźny
**opener** ['əupnə^r] *n* (*also*: **tin opener, can opener**) otwieracz *m* (do puszek)
**open-heart** [əupn'hɑːt] *adj*: **~ surgery** operacja *f* na otwartym sercu
**opening** ['əupnɪŋ] *adj* początkowy ▷ *n* (*gap, hole*) otwór *m*; (*of play, book*) początek *m*; (*of new building*) otwarcie *nt*; (*job*) wakat *m*; **the ~ ceremony** uroczystość *or* ceremonia otwarcia
**opening hours** *npl* (*of shop, library, pub*) godziny *pl* otwarcia; (*of office, bank*) godziny *pl* urzędowania
**opening night** *n* (*Theat*) premiera *f*
**openly** ['əupnlɪ] *adv* otwarcie
**open-minded** [əupn'maɪndɪd] *adj* (*person*) otwarty; (*approach*) wolny od uprzedzeń
**open-necked** ['əupnnɛkt] *adj* nie zapięty pod szyją
**openness** ['əupnnɪs] *n* otwartość *f*
**open-plan** ['əupn'plæn] *adj* (*office*) bez ścianek działowych *post*
**open sandwich** *n* kanapka *f*
**open shop** *n przedsiębiorstwo zatrudniające robotników bez względu na przynależność do związków zawodowych*
**Open University** (*Brit*) *n* uniwersytet *m* otwarty
**open verdict** *n* (*Jur*) *orzeczenie stwierdzające, że nie wykryto sprawcy lub że zgon mógł nastąpić w wyniku nieszczęśliwego wypadku*
**opera** ['ɔpərə] *n* opera *f*
**opera glasses** *npl* lornetka *f* teatralna
**opera house** *n* opera *f*
**opera singer** *n* śpiewak(-aczka) *m(f)* operowy(-wa) *m(f)*
**operate** ['ɔpəreɪt] *vt* (*machine*) obsługiwać; (*tool, method*) posługiwać się *+instr* ▷ *vi* działa

(*Med*) operować; **to ~ on sb** operować (zoperować *perf*) kogoś
**operatic** [ɔpəˈrætɪk] *adj* operowy
**operating system** [ˈɔpəreɪtɪŋ-] *n* (*Comput*) system *m* operacyjny
**operating table** *n* stół *m* operacyjny
**operating theatre** *n* sala *f* operacyjna
**operation** [ɔpəˈreɪʃən] *n* operacja *f*; (*of machine, vehicle*) obsługa *f*; (*of company*) działanie *nt*; **to be in ~** (*scheme, regulation*) być stosowanym; **I had an ~ on my spine** miałem operację kręgosłupa; **to perform an ~** (*Med*) przeprowadzać (przeprowadzić *perf*) operację
**operational** [ɔpəˈreɪʃənl] *adj* sprawny
**operative** [ˈɔpərətɪv] *adj* działający ▷ *n* (*in factory*) operator *m*; **"if" being the ~ word** z akcentem na (słowo) „jeżeli"
**operator** [ˈɔpəreɪtə[r]] *n* (*Tel*) telefonista(-tka) *m(f)*; (*of machine*) operator(ka) *m(f)*
**operetta** [ɔpəˈrɛtə] *n* operetka *f*
**ophthalmic** [ɔfˈθælmɪk] *adj* okulistyczny
**ophthalmic optician** *n* optyk *m* — okulista *m*
**ophthalmologist** [ɔfθælˈmɔlədʒɪst] *n* okulista(-tka) *m(f)*
**opinion** [əˈpɪnjən] *n* opinia *f*, zdanie *nt*; **in my ~** moim zdaniem; **to have a good** *or* **high ~ of sb** mieć dobrą opinię o kimś; **to have a good** *or* **high ~ of o.s.** mieć wysokie mniemanie o sobie; **to be of the ~ that ...** być zdania, że...; **to get a second ~** zasięgać (zasięgnąć *perf*) opinii innego specjalisty
**opinionated** [əˈpɪnjəneɪtɪd] (*pej*) *adj* zadufany (w sobie) (*pej*)
**opinion poll** *n* badanie *nt* opinii publicznej
**opium** [ˈəupɪəm] *n* opium *nt inv*
**opponent** [əˈpəunənt] *n* przeciwnik(-iczka) *m(f)*
**opportune** [ˈɔpətjuːn] *adj* dogodny
**opportunism** [ɔpəˈtjuːnɪsəm] *n* oportunizm *m*
**opportunist** [ɔpəˈtjuːnɪst] *n* oportunista(-tka) *m(f)*
**opportunity** [ɔpəˈtjuːnɪtɪ] *n* (*chance*) okazja *f*, sposobność *f*; (*prospects*) możliwości *pl*; **I took the ~ of visiting her** skorzystałem z okazji i odwiedziłem ją
**oppose** [əˈpəuz] *vt* sprzeciwiać się (sprzeciwić się *perf*) +*dat*; **to be ~d to sth** być przeciwnym czemuś; **(there is a need for) X as ~d to Y** (potrzebne jest) X, a nie Y
**opposing** [əˈpəuzɪŋ] *adj* (*side, team*) przeciwny; (*ideas, tendencies*) przeciwstawny
**opposite** [ˈɔpəzɪt] *adj* (*house, door*) naprzeciw(ko) *post*; (*end*) przeciwległy; (*direction, point of view, effect*) przeciwny ▷ *adv* naprzeciw(ko) ▷ *prep* (*in front of*) naprzeciw(ko) +*gen*; (*next to: on list etc*) przy +*loc* ▷ *n*: **the ~** przeciwieństwo *nt*; **he says one thing and does the ~** on mówi jedno, a robi coś (wręcz) odwrotnego; **the ~ sex** płeć przeciwna; **"see ~ page"** „patrz sąsiednia strona"
**opposite number** *n* odpowiednik(-iczka) *m(f)*
**opposition** [ɔpəˈzɪʃən] *n* (*resistance*) opozycja *f*, opór *m*; (*Sport*) przeciwnik *m*; **the O~** (*Pol*) opozycja
**oppress** [əˈprɛs] *vt* uciskać, gnębić
**oppressed** [əˈprɛst] *adj* uciskany, gnębiony
**oppression** [əˈprɛʃən] *n* ucisk *m*
**oppressive** [əˈprɛsɪv] *adj* (*weather, heat*) przytłaczający; (*political regime*) oparty na ucisku
**opprobrium** [əˈprəubrɪəm] *n* (*fml*) potępienie *nt*
**opt** [ɔpt] *vi*: **to opt for** optować za +*instr*; **he opted to fight** zdecydował się walczyć
▸ **opt out (of)** *vi* (*not participate*) wycofywać się (wycofać się *perf*) (z +*gen*); (*Pol: hospital, school*) uniezależniać się (uniezależnić się *perf*) (od +*gen*)
**optical** [ˈɔptɪkl] *adj* optyczny
**optical character reader** *n* (*Comput*) optyczny czytnik *m* znaków
**optical character recognition** *n* (*Comput*) optyczne rozpoznawanie *nt* znaków
**optical illusion** *n* złudzenie *nt* optyczne
**optician** [ɔpˈtɪʃən] *n* optyk(-yczka) *m(f)*
**optics** [ˈɔptɪks] *n* optyka *f*
**optimism** [ˈɔptɪmɪzəm] *n* optymizm *m*
**optimist** [ˈɔptɪmɪst] *n* optymista(-tka) *m(f)*
**optimistic** [ɔptɪˈmɪstɪk] *adj* optymistyczny
**optimum** [ˈɔptɪməm] *adj* optymalny
**option** [ˈɔpʃən] *n* opcja *f*; (*Scol*) kurs *m* (*z wybranego przedmiotu*); **they have no ~** nie mają wyboru; **keep your ~s open** nie podejmuj (jeszcze) ostatecznej decyzji
**optional** [ˈɔpʃənl] *adj* nadobowiązkowy, fakultatywny; **~ extras** (*Comm*) dodatki
**opulence** [ˈɔpjuləns] *n* bogactwo *nt*
**opulent** [ˈɔpjulənt] *adj* bardzo bogaty
**OR** (*US: Post*) *abbr* = **Oregon**
**or** [ɔː[r]] *conj* (*linking alternatives*) czy; (*also:* **or else**) bo inaczej; (*qualifying previous statement*) albo; **he hasn't seen or heard anything** niczego nie widział ani nie słyszał; **fifty or sixty people** pięćdziesiąt czy sześćdziesiąt osób
**oracle** [ˈɔrəkl] *n* wyrocznia *f*
**oral** [ˈɔːrəl] *adj* (*spoken*) ustny; (*Med*) doustny ▷ *n* (*Scol*) egzamin *m* ustny
**orange** [ˈɔrɪndʒ] *n* pomarańcza *f* ▷ *adj* pomarańczowy
**orangeade** [ɔrɪndʒˈeɪd] *n* oranżada *f*

O

**oration** [ɔːˈreɪʃən] *n* mowa *f*, oracja *f*
**orator** [ˈɔrətəʳ] *n* mówca(-wczyni) *m(f)*, orator *m*
**oratorio** [ɔrəˈtɔːrɪəu] *n* oratorium *nt*
**orb** [ɔːb] *n* (*sphere*) kula *f*; (*of monarch*) jabłko *nt*
**orbit** [ˈɔːbɪt] *n* orbita *f* ▷ *vt* okrążać (okrążyć *perf*)
**orchard** [ˈɔːtʃəd] *n* sad *m*; **apple ~** sad jabłkowy
**orchestra** [ˈɔːkɪstrə] *n* orkiestra *f*; (*US: seating*) parter *m*
**orchestral** [ɔːˈkɛstrəl] *adj* orkiestralny
**orchestrate** [ˈɔːkɪstreɪt] *vt* (*Mus*) orkiestrować, aranżować (zaaranżować *perf*) na orkiestrę; (*campaign etc*) wyreżyserować (*perf*)
**orchid** [ˈɔːkɪd] *n* orchidea *f*, storczyk *m*
**ordain** [ɔːˈdeɪn] *vt* (*Rel*) wyświęcać (wyświęcić *perf*); (*decree*) zarządzać (zarządzić *perf*)
**ordeal** [ɔːˈdiːl] *n* przeprawa *f*, gehenna *f*
**order** [ˈɔːdəʳ] *n* (*command*) rozkaz *m*; (*from shop, company, in restaurant*) zamówienie *nt*; (*sequence, organization, discipline*) porządek *m*; (*Rel*) zakon *m* ▷ *vt* (*command*) nakazywać (nakazać *perf*), rozkazywać (rozkazać *perf*); (*from shop, company, in restaurant*) zamawiać (zamówić *perf*); (*also*: **put in order**) porządkować (uporządkować *perf*); **in ~** w porządku; **in (working) ~** na chodzie; **in ~ to/that** żeby *+infin*; **in ~ of size** według wielkości; **the equipment is already on ~** (*Comm*) sprzęt jest już zamówiony; **out of ~** (*not working*) niesprawny; (*in wrong sequence*) nie po kolei; (*resolution, behaviour*) niezgodny z przepisami; **to ~ sb to do sth** kazać (kazać *perf*) komuś coś zrobić; **to place an ~ for sth with sb** składać (złożyć *perf*) u kogoś zamówienie na coś; **made to ~** wykonany na zamówienie; **to be under ~s to do sth** mieć rozkaz coś (z)robić; **to take ~s from sb** wykonywać czyjeś rozkazy; **I'd like to raise a point of ~** chciałabym zabrać głos w kwestii formalnej; **a cheque to the ~ of** czek (opiewający) na kwotę *+gen*; **of** *or* **in the ~ of** rzędu *+gen*
▸ **order around** *vt* (*also*: **order about**) pomiatać *+instr*
**order book** *n* (*Comm*) księga *f* zamówień
**order form** *n* (*Comm*) formularz *m* zamówieniowy
**orderly** [ˈɔːdəlɪ] *n* (*Mil*) ordynans *m*; (*Med*) sanitariusz *m* ▷ *adj* (*sequence*) uporządkowany; (*system*) sprawny; (*manner*) zorganizowany
**order number** *n* (*Comm*) numer *m* zamówienia
**ordinal** [ˈɔːdɪnl] *adj*: **~ number** liczebnik *m* porządkowy
**ordinarily** [ˈɔːdnrɪlɪ] *adv* zazwyczaj, zwykle
**ordinary** [ˈɔːdnrɪ] *adj* zwyczajny, zwykły; (*pej*) pospolity; **out of the ~** niezwykły, niepospolity
**ordinary seaman** (*Brit*) *n* marynarz *m* drugiej klasy
**ordinary shares** *npl* akcje *pl* zwyczajne
**ordination** [ɔːdɪˈneɪʃən] *n* święcenia *pl* (kapłańskie)
**ordnance** [ˈɔːdnəns] *n* (*Mil*) zaopatrzenie *nt* ▷ *adj* zaopatrzeniowy
**Ordnance Survey** (*Brit*) *n brytyjski urząd kartograficzny*
**ore** [ɔːʳ] *n* ruda *f*
**organ** [ˈɔːgən] *n* (*Anat*) narząd *m*, organ *m*; (*Mus*) organy *pl*
**organic** [ɔːˈgænɪk] *adj* organiczny
**organism** [ˈɔːgənɪzəm] *n* organizm *m*
**organist** [ˈɔːgənɪst] *n* organista *m*
**organization** [ɔːgənaɪˈzeɪʃən] *n* organizacja *f*
**organization chart** *n* schemat *m* organizacyjny
**organize** [ˈɔːgənaɪz] *vt* organizować (zorganizować *perf*); **get ~d, we're leaving in five minutes** zbierajcie się, za pięć minut wychodzimy
**organized crime** *n* przestępczość *f* zorganizowana
**organized labour** *n* związki *pl* zawodowe
**organizer** [ˈɔːgənaɪzəʳ] *n* organizator(ka) *m(f)*
**orgasm** [ˈɔːgæzəm] *n* orgazm *m*
**orgy** [ˈɔːdʒɪ] *n* orgia *f*; **an ~ of destruction** szał niszczycielski
**Orient** [ˈɔːrɪənt] *n*: **the ~** Orient *m*
**orient** [ˈɔːrɪənt] *vt*: **to ~ o.s.** nabierać (nabrać *perf*) orientacji *or* rozeznania; **to be ~ed towards** być nastawionym na *+acc*
**oriental** [ɔːrɪˈɛntl] *adj* orientalny, dalekowschodni
**orientate** [ˈɔːrɪənteɪt] *vt*: **to ~ o.s.** (*with map, compass etc*) orientować się (zorientować *perf* się) w swoim położeniu; (*fig*) nabierać (nabrać *perf*) orientacji *or* rozeznania; **to be ~d towards** być nastawionym na *+acc*
**orifice** [ˈɔrɪfɪs] *n* (*Anat*) otwór *m*
**origin** [ˈɔrɪdʒɪn] *n* początek *m*, źródło *nt*; (*of person*) pochodzenie *nt*; **country of ~** kraj pochodzenia
**original** [əˈrɪdʒɪnl] *adj* (*first*) pierwotny, pierwszy; (*genuine*) oryginalny, autentyczny; (*imaginative*) oryginalny ▷ *n* oryginał *m*, autentyk *m*
**originality** [ərɪdʒɪˈnælɪtɪ] *n* oryginalność *f*
**originally** [əˈrɪdʒɪnəlɪ] *adv* pierwotnie, początkowo
**originate** [əˈrɪdʒɪneɪt] *vi*: **to ~ in** powstawać (powstać *perf*) w *+loc*, pochodzić z *+gen*; **to ~ with** *or* **from sb** pochodzić od kogoś

**originator** [əˈrɪdʒɪneɪtəʳ] *n* twórca(-rczyni) *m(f)*, pomysłodawca(-wczyni) *m(f)*
**Orkneys** [ˈɔːknɪz] *npl*: **the ~** (*also*: **the Orkney Islands**) Orkady *pl*
**ornament** [ˈɔːnəmənt] *n* (*object*) ozdoba *f*; (*decoration*) ornament *m*
**ornamental** [ɔːnəˈmɛntl] *adj* ozdobny
**ornamentation** [ɔːnəmɛnˈteɪʃən] *n* ornamentacja *f*
**ornate** [ɔːˈneɪt] *adj* ozdobny
**ornithologist** [ɔːnɪˈθɔlədʒɪst] *n* ornitolog *m*
**ornithology** [ɔːnɪˈθɔlədʒɪ] *n* ornitologia *f*
**orphan** [ˈɔːfn] *n* sierota *f* ▷ *vt*: **to be ~ed** zostawać (zostać *perf*) sierotą
**orphanage** [ˈɔːfənɪdʒ] *n* sierociniec *m*
**orthodox** [ˈɔːθədɔks] *adj* ortodoksyjny; **~ medicine** medycyna konwencjonalna
**orthodoxy** [ˈɔːθədɔksɪ] *n* (*view*) dominujący pogląd *m*; (*trend*) dominujący kierunek *m*; (*in ideology, religion*) ortodoksja *f*
**orthopaedic**, (*US*) **orthopedic** [ɔːθəˈpiːdɪk] *adj* ortopedyczny
**OS** *abbr* (*Brit*) = **Ordnance Survey**; (*Naut*) = **ordinary seaman**; (*Dress*) = **outsize**
**O/S** (*Comm*) *abbr* (= *out of stock*) brak na składzie, zapas towaru wyczerpany
**oscillate** [ˈɔsɪleɪt] *vi* oscylować
**OSHA** (*US*) *n abbr* = **Occupational Safety and Health Administration**
**Oslo** [ˈɔzləu] *n* Oslo *nt inv*
**ostensible** [ɔsˈtɛnsɪbl] *adj* rzekomy
**ostensibly** [ɔsˈtɛnsɪblɪ] *adv* rzekomo
**ostentation** [ɔstɛnˈteɪʃən] *n* ostentacja *f*, zbytek *m*
**ostentatious** [ɔstɛnˈteɪʃəs] *adj* (*showy*) wystawny; (*deliberately conspicuous*) ostentacyjny; (*person*) chełpliwy
**osteopath** [ˈɔstɪəpæθ] *n* kręgarz *m*
**ostracize** [ˈɔstrəsaɪz] *vt* bojkotować (towarzysko)
**ostrich** [ˈɔstrɪtʃ] *n* struś *m*
**OT** (*Bible*) *abbr* (= *Old Testament*) ST
**OTB** (*US*) *n abbr* (= *off-track betting*) *zakłady zawierane poza terenem wyścigów konnych*
**OTE** (*Comm*) *abbr* (= *on-target earnings*) osiągalne zarobki *pl*
**other** [ˈʌðəʳ] *adj* inny; (*opposite*) przeciwny, drugi ▷ *pron*: **the ~ (one)** (ten) drugi; **~s** (*other people*) inni; (*other ones*) inne; **the ~s** (*the other people*) pozostali; (*the other ones*) pozostałe; **there is no choice ~ than to...** nie ma innego wyjścia jak tylko *+infin*; **she never discussed it with anyone ~ than Tom** nie rozmawiała o tym z nikim oprócz Toma; **the ~ day** parę dni temu; **some actor or ~** jakiś (tam) aktor; **somebody or ~** ktoś (tam); **it was none ~ than Robert** był to nie kto inny jak Robert
**otherwise** [ˈʌðəwaɪz] *adv* (*differently*) inaczej; (*apart from that*) poza tym; (*if not*) w przeciwnym razie; **in an ~ good piece of work** w skądinąd dobrej pracy
**OTT** (*inf*) *abbr* = **over the top** *see* **top**
**otter** [ˈɔtəʳ] *n* (*Zool*) wydra *f*
**OU** (*Brit*) *n abbr* = **Open University**
**ouch** [autʃ] *excl* au
**ought** [ɔːt] (*pt* **~**) *aux vb*: **I ~ to do it** powinienem to zrobić; **this ~ to have been corrected** to powinno było zostać poprawione; **he ~ to win** powinien wygrać; **you ~ to go and see it** powinieneś pójść to zobaczyć
**ounce** [auns] *n* uncja *f*; (*fig*) odrobina *f*
**our** [ˈauəʳ] *adj* nasz; *see also* **my**
**ours** [auəz] *pron* nasz; *see also* **mine¹**
**ourselves** *pron pl* (*reflexive*) się; (*after prep*) siebie (*gen, acc*), sobie (*dat, loc*), sobą (*instr*); (*emphatic*) sami; **we did it (all) by ~** zrobiliśmy to (zupełnie) sami; **with the exception of a few tourists and ~** z wyjątkiem kilku turystów i nas; *see also* **oneself**
**oust** [aust] *vt* usuwać (usunąć *perf*)

KEYWORD

**out** [aut] *adv* **1** (*not in*) na zewnątrz, na dworze; **(to stand) out in the rain/snow** (stać) (na dworze *or* na zewnątrz) w deszczu/śniegu; **they're out in the garden** są w ogrodzie; **it's hot out here** gorąco tutaj; **to go/come out** wychodzić (wyjść *perf*) (na zewnątrz); **out loud** głośno, na głos
**2** (*not at home, absent*): **she's out at the moment** nie ma jej w tej chwili; **to have a day/night out** spędzać (spędzić *perf*) dzień/wieczór poza domem
**3** (*indicating distance*) (o) *+acc* dalej; **the boat was 10 km out** łódź była (o) dziesięć kilometrów dalej; **three days out from Plymouth** trzy dni drogi z Plymouth
**4** (*Sport*) na aut; **the ball is/has gone out** piłka jest na aucie/wyszła na aut
▷ *adj* **1**: **to be out** (*unconscious*) być nieprzytomnym; (*of game*) wypaść (*perf*) z gry; (*of fashion*) wyjść (*perf*) z mody; (*have appeared*: *flowers*) zakwitnąć (*perf*); (: *news, secret*) wyjść (*perf*) na jaw; (*extinguished*: *fire, light, gas*) nie palić się
**2** (*finished*): **before the week was out** zanim tydzień się skończył
**3**: **to be out to do sth** mieć zamiar coś (z)robić
**4**: **to be out in one's calculations** mylić się (pomylić się *perf*) w obliczeniach

O

**outage** ['autɪdʒ] *n* (*esp US*) przerwa *f* w dopływie energii elektrycznej
**out-and-out** ['autəndaut] *adj* absolutny
**outback** ['autbæk] *n* (*in Australia*): **in the ~** w głębi kraju
**outbid** [aut'bɪd] *vt* przelicytowywać (przelicytować *perf*)
**outboard** ['autbɔ:d] *n* (*also*: **outboard motor**) silnik *m* przyczepny (*na łodzi motorowej*)
**outbreak** ['autbreɪk] *n* (*of war*) wybuch *m*; (*of disease*) epidemia *f*
**outbuilding** ['autbɪldɪŋ] *n* budynek *m* gospodarczy
**outburst** ['autbə:st] *n* wybuch *m*
**outcast** ['autkɑ:st] *n* wyrzutek *m*
**outclass** [aut'klɑ:s] *vt* przewyższać (przewyższyć *perf*) o klasę
**outcome** ['autkʌm] *n* wynik *m*
**outcrop** ['autkrɔp] *n* odsłonięta skała *f*
**outcry** ['autkraɪ] *n* głosy *pl* protestu
**outdated** [aut'deɪtɪd] *adj* przestarzały
**outdo** [aut'du:] (*irreg*: *like* **do**) *vt* prześcigać (prześcignąć *perf*), przewyższać (przewyższyć *perf*)
**outdoor** [aut'dɔ:ʳ] *adj* (*activities, work*) na świeżym powietrzu *post*; (*swimming pool*) odkryty; (*clothes*) wierzchni; **I'm an ~ person** lubię przebywać na świeżym powietrzu
**outdoors** [aut'dɔ:z] *adv* na dworze *or* (świeżym) powietrzu
**outer** ['autəʳ] *adj* zewnętrzny; **~ suburbs** odległe przedmieścia
**outer space** *n* przestrzeń *f* kosmiczna, kosmos *m*
**outfit** ['autfɪt] *n* (*clothes*) strój *m*; (*inf*: *team*) ekipa *f* (*inf*)
**outfitter's** ['autfɪtəz] (*Brit*) *n* sklep *m* z odzieżą męską
**outgoing** ['autgəuɪŋ] *adj* (*extrovert*) otwarty; (*retiring*) ustępujący; (*mail*) wychodzący
**outgoings** ['autgəuɪŋz] (*Brit*) *npl* wydatki *pl*
**outgrow** [aut'grəu] (*irreg*: *like* **grow**) *vt* (*lit, fig*) wyrastać (wyrosnąć *perf*) z *+gen*
**outhouse** ['authaus] *n* (*outbuilding*) budynek *m* gospodarczy; (*US*: *outer toilet*) ubikacja *f* na dworze
**outing** ['autɪŋ] *n* wycieczka *f*
**outlandish** [aut'lændɪʃ] *adj* dziwaczny
**outlast** [aut'lɑ:st] *vt* przeżyć (*perf*)
**outlaw** ['autlɔ:] *n* osoba *f* wyjęta spod prawa, banita *m* (*old*) ▷ *vt* (*person, organization*) wyjmować (wyjąć *perf*) spod prawa; (*activity*) zakazywać (zakazać *perf*) *+gen*
**outlay** ['autleɪ] *n* nakład *m* (finansowy)
**outlet** ['autlɛt] *n* (*hole*) wylot *m*; (*pipe*) odpływ *m*; (*US*: *Elec*) gniazdo *nt* wtykowe; (*also*: **retail outlet**) punkt *m* sprzedaży detalicznej; (*fig*: *for grief, anger*) ujście *nt*
**outline** ['autlaɪn] *n* (*lit, fig*) zarys *m*; (*rough sketch*) szkic *m* ▷ *vt* (*fig*) szkicować (naszkicować *perf*), przedstawiać (przedstawić *perf*) w zarysie
**outlive** [aut'lɪv] *vt* przeżyć (*perf*)
**outlook** ['autluk] *n* (*view, attitude*) pogląd *m*; (*prospects*) perspektywy *pl*; (*for weather*) prognoza *f*
**outlying** ['autlaɪɪŋ] *adj* oddalony
**outmanoeuvre**, (*US*) **outmaneuver** [autmə'nu:vəʳ] *vt* przechytrzać (przechytrzyć *perf*), wymanewrowywać (wymanewrować *perf*) (*inf*)
**outmoded** [aut'məudɪd] *adj* przestarzały
**outnumber** [aut'nʌmbəʳ] *vt* przewyższać (przewyższyć *f*) liczebnie; **we were ~ed (by) 5 to 1** było nas 5 razy mniej

 **KEYWORD**

**out of** *prep* **1** (*outside*) z *+gen*; **to go out of the house** wychodzić (wyjść *perf*) z domu
**2** (*beyond*): **out of town** za miastem; **out of reach** nieosiągalny; **she is out of danger** nie zagraża jej już niebezpieczeństwo
**3** (*indicating cause, motive, origin, material*) z *+gen*; **out of curiosity/greed** z ciekawości/chciwości; **to drink out of a cup** pić z filiżanki; **made out of glass** zrobiony ze szkła
**4** (*from among*) na *+acc*; **one out of three** jeden na trzech
**5** (*without*) bez *+gen*; **out of breath** bez tchu; **to be out of milk/sugar** nie mieć mleka/cukru

**out of bounds** *adj*: **this area is ~** to jest teren zakazany
**out-of-date** [autəv'deɪt] *adj* (*passport, ticket*) nieważny; (*dictionary, concept*) przestarzały; (*clothes*) niemodny
**out-of-doors** [autəv'dɔ:z] *adv* na dworze *or* (świeżym) powietrzu
**out-of-the-way** ['autəvðə'weɪ] *adj* (*place*) odległy; (*pub, restaurant*) mało znany
**out-of-work** ['autəvwə:k] *adj* bezrobotny
**outpatient** ['autpeɪʃənt] *n* pacjent(ka) *m(f)* ambulatoryjny(-na) *m(f)*
**outpost** ['autpəust] *n* placówka *f*
**output** ['autput] *n* (*of factory*) produkcja *f*; (*of writer*) twórczość *f*, dorobek *m*; (*Comput*) dane *pl* wyjściowe ▷ *vt* (*Comput*) przetwarzać (przetworzyć *perf*)
**outrage** ['autreɪdʒ] *n* (*anger*) oburzenie *nt*; (*atrocity*) akt *m* przemocy; (*scandal*) skandal *m*

▷ *vt* oburzać (oburzyć *perf*); **bomb ~** zamach bombowy; **to be an ~ against** stanowić obrazę *+gen*
**outrageous** [aut'reɪdʒəs] *adj* oburzający
**outrider** ['autraɪdəʳ] *n* członek *m* eskorty (*motocyklowej lub konnej*)
**outright** [*adv* aut'raɪt, *adj* 'autraɪt] *adv* (*win*) bezapelacyjnie; (*ban*) całkowicie; (*buy*) za gotówkę; (*ask*) wprost; (*deny*) otwarcie ▷ *adj* (*winner, victory*) bezapelacyjny; (*denial, hostility*) otwarty; **he was killed ~** zginął na miejscu
**outrun** [aut'rʌn] (*irreg: like* **run**) *vt* prześcigać (prześcignąć *perf*)
**outset** ['autsɛt] *n* początek *m*; **from the ~** od (samego) początku; **at the ~** na (samym) początku
**outshine** [aut'ʃaɪn] (*irreg: like* **shine**) *vt* (*fig*) zaćmiewać (zaćmić *perf*)
**outside** [aut'saɪd] *n* zewnętrzna strona *f* ▷ *adj* (*wall*) zewnętrzny; (*lavatory*) na zewnątrz *post* ▷ *adv* na zewnątrz ▷ *prep* (*building*) przed *+instr*; (*door*) za *+instr*; (*office hours, organization, country*) poza *+instr*; **a village ~ Birmingham** wioska pod Birmingham; **an ~ chance** niewielkie szanse; **at the ~** (*at the most*) najwyżej; (*at the latest*) najdalej; **you're wearing your shirt-tails ~ your trousers** tył koszuli wystaje ci ze spodni
**outside broadcast** *n* (*Radio, TV*) transmisja *f*
**outside lane** *n* zewnętrzny pas *m* ruchu
**outside line** *n* (*Tel*): **dial o for an ~** wyjście na miasto przez o
**outsider** [aut'saɪdəʳ] *n* (*person not involved*) osoba *f* postronna; (*in race etc*) autsajder *m*; **they felt like ~s** czuli się obco
**outsize** ['autsaɪz] *adj*: **~ clothes** odzież *f* ponadrozmiarowa
**outskirts** ['autskə:ts] *npl* peryferie *pl*
**outsmart** [aut'smɑ:t] *vt* przechytrzać (przechytrzyć *perf*)
**outsourcing** ['autsɔ:sɪŋ] (*Econ*) *n* outsourcing *m*
**outspoken** [aut'spəukən] *adj* otwarty
**outspread** [aut'sprɛd] *adj* rozpostarty
**outstanding** [aut'stændɪŋ] *adj* (*actor, work*) wybitny; (*debt, problem*) zaległy; **your account is still ~** do tej pory nie uregulował/a Pan/Pani rachunku
**outstay** [aut'steɪ] *vt*: **to ~ one's welcome** nadużywać (nadużyć *perf*) czyjejś gościnności
**outstretched** [aut'strɛtʃt] *adj* (*hand*) wyciągnięty; (*arms*) wyciągnięty, rozpostarty; (*body*) rozciągnięty; (*wings*) rozpostarty
**outstrip** [aut'strɪp] *vt* przewyższać (przewyższyć *perf*)
**out tray** *n* tacka *f* na korespondencję wychodzącą
**outvote** [aut'vəut] *vt* (*person*) przegłosowywać (przegłosować *perf*); (*proposal*) odrzucać (odrzucić *perf*) (w głosowaniu)
**outward** ['autwəd] *adj* (*sign, appearances*) zewnętrzny; (*journey*) w tamtą stronę *post*
**outwardly** ['autwədlɪ] *adv* pozornie, na pozór
**outward(s)** *adv* na zewnątrz
**outweigh** [aut'weɪ] *vt* przeważać (przeważyć *perf*)
**outwit** [aut'wɪt] *vt* przechytrzać (przechytrzyć *perf*)
**ova** ['əuvə] *npl of* **ovum**
**oval** ['əuvl] *adj* owalny ▷ *n* owal *m*
**ovary** ['əuvərɪ] *n* jajnik *m*
**ovation** [əu'veɪʃən] *n* owacja *f*
**oven** ['ʌvn] *n* piekarnik *m*
**ovenproof** ['ʌvnpru:f] *adj* żaroodporny
**oven-ready** ['ʌvnrɛdɪ] *adj* do podgrzania w piekarniku *post*
**ovenware** ['ʌvnwɛəʳ] *n* naczynia *pl* żaroodporne

 KEYWORD

**over** ['əuvəʳ] *adv* **1** (*across*): **to cross over to the other side** przechodzić (przejść *perf*) na drugą stronę; **you can come over tonight** możesz przyjść dziś wieczorem; **to ask sb over** zapraszać (zaprosić *perf*) kogoś (do domu *or* do siebie); **over here/there** tu/tam
**2** (*indicating movement from upright*): **to fall over** przewracać się (przewrócić się *perf*)
**3** (*finished*): **to be over** skończyć się (*perf*)
**4** (*excessively*) zbyt, nadmiernie; **she's not over intelligent, is she?** nie jest zbyt *or* nadmiernie inteligentna, prawda?
**5** (*remaining*): **there are three over** zostały (jeszcze) trzy
**6**: **all over** wszędzie; **over and over (again)** wielokrotnie, w kółko (*inf*)
▷ *prep* **1** (*above*) nad *+instr*; (*on top of*) na *+loc*; **a canopy over the bed** baldachim nad łóżkiem; **to spread a sheet over sth** rozkładać (rozłożyć *perf*) na czymś prześcieradło
**2** (*on the other side of*) po drugiej stronie *+gen*; (*to the other side of*) przez *+acc*, na drugą stronę *+gen*; **the pub over the road** pub po drugiej stronie ulicy; **he jumped over the wall** przeskoczył przez mur *or* na drugą stronę muru
**3** (*more than*) ponad *+acc*; **over 200 people came** przyszło ponad dwieście osób; **over and above** poza *+instr*, w dodatku do *+gen*

O

**4** *(during)* przez *+acc*, podczas *+gen*; **over the last few years** przez parę ostatnich lat; **over the winter** podczas zimy; **let's discuss it over dinner** porozmawiajmy o tym przy obiedzie

**over...** ['əuvəʳ] *pref przedrostek, któremu w języku polskim odpowiada prze..., nad... lub zbyt*
**overact** [əuvər'ækt] *vi* *(Theat)* szarżować (przeszarżować *perf*)
**overall** [*adj, n* 'əuvərɔ:l, *adv* əuvər'ɔ:l] *adj* *(length, cost)* całkowity; *(impression, view)* ogólny ▷ *adv* *(measure, cost)* w sumie; *(generally)* ogólnie (biorąc) ▷ *n* *(Brit)* kitel *m*; **overalls** *npl* kombinezon *m* *(roboczy)*
**overanxious** [əuvər'æŋkʃəs] *adj*: **to be ~** zbytnio się przejmować
**overawe** [əuvər'ɔ:] *vt*: **to be ~d (by)** być onieśmielonym *(+instr)*
**overbalance** [əuvə'bæləns] *vi* tracić (stracić *perf*) równowagę
**overbearing** [əuvə'bɛərɪŋ] *adj* władczy
**overboard** ['əuvəbɔ:d] *adv* *(be)* za burtą; *(fall)* za burtę; **to go ~** *(fig)* popadać (popaść *perf*) w przesadę
**overbook** [əuvə'buk] *vt*: **to ~ a show** sprzedać *(perf)* więcej biletów na przedstawienie, niż jest miejsc
**overcame** [əuvə'keɪm] *pt of* **overcome**
**overcapitalize** [əuvə'kæpɪtəlaɪz] *vt* przeinwestować *(perf)*
**overcast** ['əuvəkɑ:st] *adj* pochmurny
**overcharge** [əuvə'tʃɑ:dʒ] *vt* liczyć (policzyć *perf*) za dużo *+dat*
**overcoat** ['əuvəkəut] *n* płaszcz *m*
**overcome** [əuvə'kʌm] *(irreg: like* **come***)* *vt* przezwyciężać (przezwyciężyć *perf*) ▷ *adj*: **~ with** ogarnięty *or* owładnięty *+instr*; **~ with grief** pogrążony w smutku; **I was ~ by a sense of failure** ogarnęło mnie poczucie klęski
**overconfident** [əuvə'kɔnfɪdənt] *adj* zbyt pewny siebie
**overcrowded** [əuvə'kraudɪd] *adj* przepełniony
**overcrowding** [əuvə'kraudɪŋ] *n* przepełnienie *f*
**overdo** [əuvə'du:] *(irreg: like* **do***)* *vt* przesadzać (przesadzić *perf*) z *+instr*; **don't ~ it** *(don't exaggerate)* nie przesadzaj; *(when ill, weak etc)* nie przemęczaj się
**overdose** ['əuvədəus] *n* przedawkowanie *nt*; **to take an ~** przedawkowywać (przedawkować *perf*)
**overdraft** ['əuvədrɑ:ft] *n* przekroczenie *nt* stanu konta, debet *m*
**overdrawn** [əuvə'drɔ:n] *adj*: **he is** *or* **his account is ~** przekroczył stan konta, ma debet
**overdrive** ['əuvədraɪv] *n* najwyższy bieg *m*
**overdue** [əuvə'dju:] *adj* *(bill, library book)* zaległy; **to be ~** *(person, bus, train)* spóźniać się; *(change, reform)* opóźniać się; **that change was long ~** tę zmianę należało przeprowadzić o wiele wcześniej
**overestimate** [əuvər'ɛstɪmeɪt] *vt* przeceniać (przecenić *perf*)
**overexcited** [əuvərɪk'saɪtɪd] *adj* zbyt *or* nadmiernie podniecony
**overexertion** [əuvərɪg'zə:ʃən] *n* nadmierny wysiłek *m*
**overexpose** [əuvərɪk'spəuz] *vt* *(Phot)* prześwietlać (prześwietlić *perf*)
**overflow** [əuvə'fləu] *vi* *(river)* wylewać (wylać *perf*); *(sink, bath)* przelewać się (przelać się *perf*) ▷ *n* *(also:* **overflow pipe***)* rurka *f* przelewowa
**overgenerous** [əuvə'dʒɛnərəs] *adj* zbyt hojny
**overgrown** [əuvə'grəun] *adj* *(garden)* zarośnięty; **he's just an ~ schoolboy** *(fig)* to taki duży dzieciak
**overhang** ['əuvə'hæŋ] *(irreg: like* **hang***)* *vt* wisieć nad *+instr* ▷ *vi* zwisać ▷ *n* nawis *m*
**overhaul** [*vb* əuvə'hɔ:l, *n* 'əuvəhɔ:l] *vt* dokonywać (dokonać *perf*) przeglądu i remontu kapitalnego *+gen* ▷ *n* przegląd *m* i remont *m* kapitalny
**overhead** [*adv* əuvə'hɛd, *adj, n* 'əuvəhɛd] *adv* *(above)* na górze, nad głową; *(in the sky)* w górze ▷ *adj* *(light, lighting)* górny; *(cables, wires)* napowietrzny ▷ *n* *(US)* = **overheads**; **overheads** *npl* koszty *pl* stałe
**overhear** [əuvə'hɪəʳ] *(irreg: like* **hear***)* *vt* podsłuchać *(perf)*, przypadkiem usłyszeć *(perf)*
**overheat** [əuvə'hi:t] *vi* *(engine)* przegrzewać się (przegrzać się *perf*)
**overjoyed** [əuvə'dʒɔɪd] *adj* uradowany, zachwycony; **to be ~ (at)** być zachwyconym *(+instr)*
**overkill** ['əuvəkɪl] *n* *(fig)*: **it would be ~** to by była przesada
**overland** ['əuvəlænd] *adj* *(journey)* lądowy ▷ *adv*: **to travel ~** podróżować lądem *or* drogą lądową
**overlap** [əuvə'læp] *vi* *(edges, figures)* zachodzić (zajść *perf*) na siebie; *(fig: ideas, activities)* zazębiać się (zazębić się *perf*) (o siebie)
**overleaf** [əuvə'li:f] *adv* na odwrocie (strony)
**overload** [əuvə'ləud] *vt* przeładowywać (przeładować *perf*), przeciążać (przeciążyć *perf*)
**overlook** [əuvə'luk] *vt* *(building, hill)* wznosić się *or* górować nad *+instr*; *(window)* wychodzić na *+acc*; *(fail to notice)* nie zauważać (nie zauważyć *perf*) *+gen*, przeoczyć *(perf)*; *(excuse, forgive)* przymykać (przymknąć *perf*) oczy na

+*acc*, nie zwracać (nie zwrócić *perf*) uwagi na +*acc*
**overlord** ['əuvəlɔːd] *n* suweren *m*, pan *m*
**overmanning** [əuvə'mænɪŋ] *n* nadmiar *m* siły roboczej
**overnight** [əuvə'naɪt] *adv* na *or* przez (całą) noc; (*fig*) z dnia na dzień; **~ stay/stop** nocleg; **to travel ~** podróżować nocą; **he'll be away ~** nie wróci na noc; **to stay ~** zostawać (zostać *perf*) na noc
**overnight bag** *n* torba *f* podróżna
**overpass** ['əuvəpɑːs] *n* (*esp US*) estakada *f*
**overpay** [əuvə'peɪ] *vt*: **to ~ sb by 50 pounds** wypłacić (*perf*) komuś o 50 funtów za dużo
**overpower** [əuvə'pauə<sup>r</sup>] *vt* obezwładniać (obezwładnić *perf*)
**overpowering** [əuvə'pauərɪŋ] *adj* (*heat, smell*) obezwładniający; (*feeling*) przytłaczający; (*desire*) przemożny
**overproduction** ['əuvəprə'dʌkʃən] *n* nadprodukcja *f*
**overrate** [əuvə'reɪt] *vt* przeceniać (przecenić *perf*), przereklamowywać (przereklamować *perf*)
**overreach** [əuvə'riːtʃ] *vt*: **to ~ o.s.** przeliczyć się (*perf*), przecenić (*perf*) swoje siły *or* możliwości
**overreact** [əuvəriː'ækt] *vi* reagować (zareagować *perf*) zbyt mocno
**override** [əuvə'raɪd] (*irreg: like* **ride**) *vt* unieważniać (unieważnić *perf*), uchylać (uchylić *perf*)
**overriding** [əuvə'raɪdɪŋ] *adj* nadrzędny
**overrule** [əuvə'ruːl] *vt* (*decision*) unieważniać (unieważnić *perf*); (*claim*) odrzucać (odrzucić *perf*); (*Jur: objection*) uchylać (uchylić *perf*)
**overrun** [əuvə'rʌn] (*irreg: like* **run**) *vt* (*country etc*) opanowywać (opanować *perf*) ▷ *vi* (*meeting etc*) przedłużać się (przedłużyć się *perf*); **the town is ~ with tourists** miasto zostało opanowane przez turystów
**overseas** [əuvə'siːz] *adv* (*live, work*) za granicą; (*travel*) za granicę ▷ *adj* zagraniczny
**overseer** ['əuvəsɪə<sup>r</sup>] *n* nadzorca *m*
**overshadow** [əuvə'ʃædəu] *vt* wznosić się *or* górować nad +*instr*; (*fig*) usuwać (usunąć *perf*) w cień
**overshoot** [əuvə'ʃuːt] (*irreg: like* **shoot**) *vt* minąć (*perf*), przejechać (*perf*)
**oversight** ['əuvəsaɪt] *n* niedopatrzenie *nt*; **due to an ~** z powodu niedopatrzenia
**oversimplify** [əuvə'sɪmplɪfaɪ] *vt* nadmiernie upraszczać (uprościć *perf*)
**oversleep** [əuvə'sliːp] (*irreg: like* **sleep**) *vi* zaspać (*perf*)
**overspend** [əuvə'spɛnd] (*irreg: like* **spend**) *vi* wydawać (wydać *perf*) za dużo; **we have overspent by 5,000 dollars** przekroczyliśmy budżet o 5.000 dolarów
**overspill** ['əuvəspɪl] *n* *odpływ ludności z przeludnionego miasta na peryferie*
**overstaffed** [əuvə'stɑːft] *adj*: **to be ~** mieć zbyt wielu pracowników
**overstate** [əuvə'steɪt] *vt* wyolbrzymiać (wyolbrzymić *perf*), przeceniać (przecenić *perf*); **to ~ the case** przesadzać (przesadzić *perf*)
**overstatement** [əuvə'steɪtmənt] *n* przesada *f*
**overstep** [əuvə'stɛp] *vt*: **to ~ the mark** przeciągać (przeciągnąć *perf*) strunę
**overstock** [əuvə'stɔk] *vt* zaopatrywać (zaopatrzyć *perf*) zbyt obficie
**overstrike** [*n* 'əuvəstraɪk, *vb* əuvə'straɪk] (*irreg: like* **strike**) *n* (*on printer*) nadrukowywanie *nt* ▷ *vt* nadrukowywać (nadrukować *perf*)
**oversubscribed** [əuvəsəb'skraɪbd] *adj*: **the shares are ~** popyt na akcje przekracza podaż
**overt** [əu'vəːt] *adj* otwarty, jawny
**overtake** [əuvə'teɪk] (*irreg: like* **take**) *vt* (*Aut*) wyprzedzać (wyprzedzić *perf*); (*event, change*) zaskakiwać (zaskoczyć *perf*); (*emotion, weakness*) ogarniać (ogarnąć *perf*) ▷ *vi* (*Aut*) wyprzedzać
**overtaking** [əuvə'teɪkɪŋ] *n* (*Aut*) wyprzedzanie *nt*
**overtax** [əuvə'tæks] *vt* (*Econ*) nadmiernie obkładać (obłożyć *perf*) podatkami; (*strength, patience*) nadwerężać (nadwerężyć *perf*); **to ~ o.s.** przeforsowywać się (przeforsować się *perf*)
**overthrow** [əuvə'θrəu] (*irreg: like* **throw**) *vt* obalać (obalić *perf*)
**overtime** ['əuvətaɪm] *n* nadgodziny *pl*; **to do** *or* **work ~** pracować w nadgodzinach
**overtime ban** *n* zakaz *m* pracy w nadgodzinach
**overtone** ['əuvətəun] *n* (*also:* **overtones**) zabarwienie *nt*, podtekst *m*
**overture** ['əuvətʃuə<sup>r</sup>] *n* (*Mus*) uwertura *f*; (*fig*) wstęp *m*; **~s of friendship** przyjazne gesty
**overturn** [əuvə'təːn] *vt* przewracać (przewrócić *perf*); (*fig: decision*) unieważniać (unieważnić *perf*); (*: government*) obalać (obalić *perf*) ▷ *vi* wywracać się (wywrócić się *perf*)
**overweight** [əuvə'weɪt] *adj*: **to be ~** mieć nadwagę
**overwhelm** [əuvə'wɛlm] *vt* (*defeat*) obezwładniać (obezwładnić *perf*); (*affect deeply*) przytłaczać (przytłoczyć *perf*)
**overwhelming** [əuvə'wɛlmɪŋ] *adj* (*majority, feeling*) przytłaczający; (*heat*)

O

obezwładniający; (*desire*) przemożny; **one's ~ impression is of heat** dominuje wrażenie gorąca

**overwhelmingly** [əuvəˈwɛlmɪŋlɪ] *adv* (*decide*) przytłaczającą *or* miażdżącą większością głosów; (*generous etc*) ogromnie; (*predominantly*) w przeważającej części

**overwork** [əuvəˈwəːk] *n* przepracowanie *nt* ▷ *vt* (*person*) przeciążać (przeciążyć *perf*) pracą; (*word*) nadużywać *+gen* ▷ *vi* przepracowywać się (przepracować się *perf*)

**overwrite** [əuvəˈraɪt] *vt* (*Comput*) kasować (skasować *perf*) przez wpisanie nowego tekstu

**overwrought** [əuvəˈrɔːt] *adj* wyczerpany nerwowo

**ovulate** [ˈɔvjuleɪt] *vi* (*Bio*) przechodzić owulację, jajeczkować

**ovulation** [ɔvjuˈleɪʃən] *n* owulacja *f*, jajeczkowanie *nt*

**ovum** [ˈəuvəm] (*pl* **ova**) *n* (*Med, Anat*) jajo *nt*

**owe** [əu] *vt*: **to owe sb sth, to owe sth to sb** (*money, explanation*) być komuś coś winnym; (*life, talent*) zawdzięczać coś komuś

**owing to** [ˈəuɪŋ-] *prep* z powodu *+gen*

**owl** [aul] *n* (*Zool*) sowa *f*

**own** [əun] *vt* posiadać ▷ *vi* (*Brit*: *fml*): **to own to sth** przyznawać się (przyznać się *perf*) do czegoś ▷ *adj* własny; **a room of my/his** *etc* **own** (swój) własny pokój; **to make one's own bed** słać (posłać *perf*) sobie łóżko; **to get one's own back on sb** odpłacić się (*perf*) komuś; **to live on one's own** mieszkać samotnie; **to do sth on one's own** robić (zrobić *perf*) coś samemu; **from now on, you're on your own** od tej chwili jesteś zdany na własne siły; **he'll come into his own** pokaże, na co go stać

▶ **own up** *vi* przyznać się (*perf*)

**own brand** *n* (*Comm*) produkt *m* firmowy

**owner** [ˈəunəʳ] *n* właściciel(ka) *m(f)*

**owner-occupier** [ˈəunərˈɔkjupaɪəʳ] *n* lokator(ka) *m(f)* mieszkania własnościowego

**ownership** [ˈəunəʃɪp] *n* posiadanie *nt*, własność *f*; **to be under new ~** mieć nowego właściciela

**ox** [ɔks] (*pl* **oxen**) *n* wół *m*

**OXFAM** (*Brit*) *n abbr* (= *Oxford Committee for Famine Relief*) *organizacja dobroczynna*

**oxide** [ˈɔksaɪd] *n* tlenek *m*

**oxidize** [ˈɔksɪdaɪz] *vi* utleniać się (utlenić się *perf*)

**Oxon.** [ˈɔksn] (*Brit*) *abbr* (*Post*) = **Oxfordshire**; (*in degree titles*: = *Oxoniensis*) Uniwersytetu Oxfordzkiego

**oxtail** [ˈɔksteɪl] *n*: **~ soup** zupa *f* ogonowa

**oxyacetylene** [ˈɔksɪəˈsɛtɪliːn] *adj* acetylenowo-tlenowy

**oxygen** [ˈɔksɪdʒən] *n* tlen *m*

**oxygen mask** *n* maska *f* tlenowa

**oxygen tent** *n* namiot *m* tlenowy

**oyster** [ˈɔɪstəʳ] *n* ostryga *f*

**oz.** *abbr* = **ounce**

**ozone** [ˈəuzəun] *n* ozon *m*

**ozone layer** *n*: **the ~** powłoka *f or* warstwa *f* ozonowa

# Pp

**P, p**[1] [pi:] *n* (*letter*) P *nt*, p *nt*; **P for Peter** ≈ P jak Paweł
**P.** *abbr* (= *president*) prez.; (= *prince*) ks.
**p**[2] (*Brit*) *abbr* = **penny, pence**
**p.** *abbr* (= *page*) s.
**PA** *n abbr* = **personal assistant; public address system** ▷ *abbr* (*US*: *Post*) = **Pennsylvania**
**pa** [pɑ:] (*inf*) *n* tata *m*
**p.a.** *abbr* (= *per annum*) roczn.
**PAC** (*US*) *n abbr* = **political action committee**
**pace** [peɪs] *n* (*step, manner of walking*) krok *m*; (*speed*) tempo *nt* ▷ *vi*: **to ~ up and down** chodzić tam i z powrotem; **to keep ~ with** (*person*) dotrzymywać (dotrzymać *perf*) kroku *+dat*; (*events*) nadążać (nadążyć *perf*) za *+instr*; **to set the ~** narzucać (narzucić *perf*) tempo; **we put him through his ~s** (*fig*) kazaliśmy mu pokazać, co potrafi
**pacemaker** ['peɪsmeɪkə<sup>r</sup>] *n* (*Med*) stymulator *m* serca; (*Sport*) nadający(-ca) *m(f)* tempo
**Pacific** [pə'sɪfɪk] *n*: **the ~ (Ocean)** Ocean *m* Spokojny, Pacyfik *m*
**pacific** [pə'sɪfɪk] *adj* (*intentions etc*) pokojowy
**pacifier** ['pæsɪfaɪə<sup>r</sup>] (*US*) *n* smoczek *m*
**pacifist** ['pæsɪfɪst] *n* pacyfista(-tka) *m(f)*
**pacify** ['pæsɪfaɪ] *vt* uspokajać (uspokoić *perf*)
**pack** [pæk] *n* (*packet*) paczka *f*; (*back pack*) plecak *m*; (*of hounds*) sfora *f*; (*of people*) paczka *f* (*inf*); (*of cards*) talia *f* ▷ *vt* pakować (spakować *perf*); (*press down*) przyciskać (przycisnąć *perf*); (*Comput*) upakowywać (upakować *perf*) ▷ *vi* pakować się (spakować się *perf*); **to ~ into** wpakowywać (wpakować *perf*) do *+gen* (*inf*); **to send sb ~ing** (*inf*) odprawiać (odprawić *perf*) kogoś, przeganiać (przegonić *perf*) kogoś (*inf*)
▸ **pack in** (*Brit*: *inf*) *vt* (*boyfriend, job*) rzucać (rzucić *perf*); **~ it in!** przestań!
▸ **pack off** *vt* (*person*: *to school etc*) wyprawiać (wyprawić *perf*); (: *to bed*) pakować (zapakować *perf*)
▸ **pack up** *vi* (*Brit*: *inf*: *machine*) nawalać (nawalić *perf*) (*inf*); (: *person*) zbierać się (zebrać się *perf*) ▷ *vt* spakować (*perf*)
**package** ['pækɪdʒ] *n* (*parcel*) paczka *f*; (*also*: **package deal**) umowa *f* wiązana; (*Comput*) pakiet *m* ▷ *vt* (*goods*) pakować
**package holiday** (*Brit*) *n* wczasy *pl* zorganizowane
**package tour** (*Brit*) *n* wycieczka *f* zorganizowana
**packaging** ['pækɪdʒɪŋ] *n* opakowania *pl*
**packed** [pækt] *adj*: **~ (with)** wypełniony (*+instr*), pełen (*+gen*)
**packed lunch** (*Brit*) *n* (*taken to school*) drugie śniadanie *nt*; (*taken on outing*) suchy prowiant *m*
**packer** ['pækə<sup>r</sup>] *n* pakowacz(ka) *m(f)*
**packet** ['pækɪt] *n* (*of cigarettes, crisps*) paczka *f*; (*of washing powder etc*) opakowanie *nt*; **to make a ~ (out of)** (*Brit*: *inf*) robić (zrobić *perf*) duże pieniądze (na *+loc*) (*inf*)
**packet switching** (*Comput*) *n* komutacja *f* pakietów
**pack ice** ['pækaɪs] *n* lód *m* spiętrzony, pak *m* polarny
**packing** ['pækɪŋ] *n* (*act*) pakowanie *nt*; (*paper, plastic etc*) opakowanie *nt*
**packing case** *n* skrzynia *f*
**pact** [pækt] *n* pakt *m*, układ *m*
**pad** [pæd] *n* (*of paper*) blok *m*, bloczek *m*; (*of cotton wool*) tampon *m*; (*shoulder pad*: *in jacket, dress*) poduszka *f*; (*Sport*) ochraniacz *m*; (*inf*: *home*) cztery ściany *pl* ▷ *vt* (*upholster*) obijać (obić *perf*); (*stuff*) wypychać (wypchać *perf*) ▷ *vi*: **to pad about/in/out** chodzić/wchodzić (wejść *perf*)/wychodzić (wyjść *perf*) po cichu
**padding** ['pædɪŋ] *n* (*of coat etc*) podszycie *nt*; (*of door*) obicie *nt*; (*fig*) wodolejstwo *nt* (*inf*)
**paddle** ['pædl] *n* wiosło *nt*; (*US*: *for table tennis*) rakietka *f* ▷ *vi* (*at seaside*) brodzić; (*row*) wiosłować ▷ *vt*: **to ~ a boat** płynąć (popłynąć *perf*) łódką
**paddle steamer** *n* parowiec *m* (rzeczny)
**paddling pool** ['pædlɪŋ-] (*Brit*) *n* brodzik *m*
**paddock** ['pædək] *n* wybieg *m* (dla koni); (*at race course*) padok *m*
**paddy field** ['pædɪ-] *n* pole *nt* ryżowe
**padlock** ['pædlɔk] *n* kłódka *f* ▷ *vt* zamykać (zamknąć *perf*) na kłódkę
**padre** ['pɑ:drɪ] *n* kapelan *m*; (*as form of address*) ojcze (*voc*)

**Padua** ['pædʒuə] *n* Padwa *f*
**paediatrics**, (*US*) **pediatrics** [pi:dɪ'ætrɪks] *n* pediatria *f*
**paedophile**, (*US*) **pedophile** ['pi:dəufaɪl] *n* pedofil(ka) *m(f)*
**pagan** ['peɪgən] *adj* pogański ▷ *n* poganin(-anka) *m(f)*
**page** [peɪdʒ] *n* (*of book etc*) strona *f*; (*knight's servant*) paź *m*; (*also*: **page boy**: *in hotel*) boy *m* *or* chłopiec *m* hotelowy; (: *at wedding*) *jeden z chłopców usługujących pannie młodej* ▷ *vt* wzywać (wezwać *perf*) (*przez głośnik itp*); **Paging Peter Smith. Would you please go to ...** Pan Peter Smith proszony jest o zgłoszenie się do *+gen*
**pageant** ['pædʒənt] *n* (*historical procession*) widowisko *nt* historyczne (*w formie parady, żywych obrazów itp na świeżym powietrzu*); (*show*) pokaz *m*
**pageantry** ['pædʒəntrɪ] *n* (wielka) gala *f*
**pager** ['peɪdʒə^r] *n* pager *m*
**paginate** ['pædʒɪneɪt] *vt* numerować (ponumerować *perf*) strony *+gen*
**pagination** [pædʒɪ'neɪʃən] *n* numeracja *f* stron
**pagoda** [pə'gəudə] *n* pagoda *f*
**paid** [peɪd] *pt, pp of* **pay** ▷ *adj* (*work, holiday*) płatny; (*staff*) opłacany; **to put ~ to** (*Brit*) niweczyć (zniweczyć *perf*) *+acc*
**paid-up** ['peɪdʌp], (*US*) **paid-in** *adj* (*member*) płacący składki; (*Comm*: *shares*) spłacony; **~ capital** kapitał wpłacony
**pail** [peɪl] *n* wiadro *nt*
**pain** [peɪn] *n* ból *m*; (*inf*: *nuisance*) utrapienie *nt*; **I have a ~ in the chest/arm** mam bóle w klatce piersiowej/ramieniu; **to be in ~** cierpieć (ból); **to take ~s to do sth** zadawać (zadać *perf*) sobie trud, żeby coś zrobić; **on ~ of death** pod karą *or* groźbą śmierci
**pained** [peɪnd] *adj* (*look etc*) urażony
**painful** ['peɪnful] *adj* (*sore*) obolały; (*causing pain*) bolesny; (*laborious*) żmudny, mozolny
**painfully** ['peɪnfəlɪ] *adv* (*fig*) boleśnie, dotkliwie
**painkiller** ['peɪnkɪlə^r] *n* środek *m* przeciwbólowy
**painless** ['peɪnlɪs] *adj* bezbolesny
**painstaking** ['peɪnzteɪkɪŋ] *adj* staranny, skrupulatny
**paint** [peɪnt] *n* farba *f* ▷ *vt* (*wall etc*) malować (pomalować *perf*); (*person, picture*) malować (namalować *perf*); **to ~ the door blue** malować (pomalować *perf*) drzwi na niebiesko; **to ~ in oils** malować farbami olejnymi; **to ~ a gloomy picture of sth** malować (namalować *perf*) coś w czarnych barwach
**paint box** *n* pudełko *nt* z farbami
**paintbrush** ['peɪntbrʌʃ] *n* pędzel *m*
**painter** ['peɪntə^r] *n* (*artist*) malarz(-arka) *m(f)*; (*decorator*) malarz *m* (pokojowy)
**painting** ['peɪntɪŋ] *n* (*activity*) malowanie *nt*; (*art*) malarstwo *nt*; (*picture*) obraz *m*
**paint-stripper** ['peɪntstrɪpə^r] *n* zmywacz *m* do farby
**paintwork** ['peɪntwə:k] *n* farba *f*; (*of car*) lakier *m*
**pair** [pɛə^r] *n* para *f*; **a ~ of scissors** nożyczki; **a ~ of trousers** para spodni
▸ **pair off** *vi*: **to ~ off with sb** tworzyć (utworzyć *perf*) z kimś parę
**pajamas** [pə'dʒɑ:məz] (*US*) *npl* piżama *f*
**Pakistan** [pɑ:kɪ'stɑ:n] *n* Pakistan *m*
**Pakistani** [pɑ:kɪ'stɑ:nɪ] *adj* pakistański ▷ *n* Pakistańczyk(-anka) *m(f)*
**PAL** (TV) *n abbr* (= *phase alternation line*) PAL *m*
**pal** [pæl] (*inf*) *n* kumpel *m* (*inf*)
**palace** ['pæləs] *n* pałac *m*
**palatable** ['pælɪtəbl] *adj* (*food*) smaczny; (*fig*: *truth etc*) miły
**palate** ['pælɪt] *n* podniebienie *nt*
**palatial** [pə'leɪʃəl] *adj* (*residence etc*) wspaniały, imponujący
**palaver** [pə'lɑ:və^r] (*inf*) *n* zawracanie *nt* głowy (*inf*)
**pale** [peɪl] *adj* blady ▷ *n*: **beyond the ~** nie do przyjęcia ▷ *vi* pobladnąć (*perf*); **to grow** *or* **turn ~** blednąć (zblednąć *perf*); **~ blue** bladoniebieski; **to ~ into insignificance (beside)** schodzić (zejść *perf*) na dalszy plan (wobec *+gen*)
**paleness** ['peɪlnɪs] *n* bladość *f*
**Palestine** ['pælɪstaɪn] *n* Palestyna *f*
**Palestinian** [pælɪs'tɪnɪən] *adj* palestyński ▷ *n* Palestyńczyk(-tynka) *m(f)*
**palette** ['pælɪt] *n* paleta *f*
**palings** ['peɪlɪŋz] *npl* parkan *m*, płot *m*
**palisade** [pælɪ'seɪd] *n* palisada *f*
**pall** [pɔ:l] *n* obłok *m* dymu ▷ *vi* przykrzyć się (sprzykrzyć się *perf*)
**pallet** ['pælɪt] *n* paleta *f* (*rodzaj platformy*)
**palliative** ['pælɪətɪv] *n* (*Med*) środek *m* uśmierzający; (*fig*) półśrodek *m*
**pallid** ['pælɪd] *adj* blady; (*fig*) bezbarwny
**pallor** ['pælə^r] *n* bladość *f* (*niezdrowa*)
**pally** ['pælɪ] *adj*: **to be ~ with sb** być z kimś w zażyłych stosunkach
**palm** [pɑ:m] *n* (*also*: **palm tree**) palma *f*; (*of hand*) dłoń *f* ▷ *vt*: **to ~ sth off on sb** (*inf*) wcisnąć (*perf*) *or* opchnąć (*perf*) coś komuś (*inf*)
**palmistry** ['pɑ:mɪstrɪ] *n* wróżenie *nt* z ręki
**Palm Sunday** *n* Niedziela *f* Palmowa
**palpable** ['pælpəbl] *adj* ewidentny
**palpitations** [pælpɪ'teɪʃənz] *npl* palpitacje *pl*, kołatanie *nt* serca
**paltry** ['pɔ:ltrɪ] *adj* marny

**pamper** ['pæmpə^r] *vt* rozpieszczać (rozpieścić *perf*)
**pamphlet** ['pæmflət] *n* broszur(k)a *f*
**pan** [pæn] *n* (*also*: **saucepan**) rondel *m*; (*also*: **frying pan**) patelnia *f* ▷ *vi* (*film camera*) panoramować ▷ *vt* (*inf*: *criticize*) zjechać (*perf*) (*inf*); **to pan for gold** wypłukiwać złoto
**panacea** [pænə'sɪə] *n* panaceum *nt*
**panache** [pə'næʃ] *n* szyk *f*
**Panama** ['pænəmɑ:] *n* Panama *f*
**panama** *n* (*also*: **panama hat**) panama *f*
**Panama Canal** *n*: **the ~** Kanał *m* Panamski
**Panamanian** [pænə'meɪnɪən] *adj* panamski ▷ *n* Panamczyk(-mka) *m(f)*
**pancake** ['pænkeɪk] *n* naleśnik *m*
**Pancake Day** (*Brit*) *n* ≈ ostatki *pl* (*ostatni dzień karnawału*)
**pancreas** ['pæŋkrɪəs] *n* trzustka *f*
**panda** ['pændə] *n* panda *f*
**panda car** (*Brit*) *n* radiowóz *m* (policyjny)
**pandemonium** [pændɪ'məunɪəm] *n* zamieszanie *nt*, wrzawa *f*
**pander** ['pændə^r] *vi*: **to ~ to** (*person*) hołubić *+acc*; (*sb's whim*) folgować *+dat*
**p & h** (*US*) *abbr* (= *postage and handling*) wysyłka *f*
**P & L** *abbr* (= *profit and loss*) rachunek *m* zysków i strat
**p & p** (*Brit*) *abbr* (= *postage and packing*) pakowanie *nt* i wysyłka *f*
**pane** [peɪn] *n* szyba *f*
**panel** ['pænl] *n* (*of wood, glass etc*) płycina *f*; (*of experts*) zespół *m* ekspertów; (*of judges*) komisja *f*
**panel game** (*Brit*: *TV, Radio*) *n* quiz *m*
**panelling** ['pænəlɪŋ], (*US*) **paneling** *n* boazeria *f*
**panellist** ['pænəlɪst], (*US*) **panelist** (*TV, Radio*) *n* uczestnik(-iczka) *m(f)* dyskusji
**pang** [pæŋ] *n*: **a ~ of regret** ukłucie *nt* żalu; **hunger ~s** skurcze głodowe (żołądka)
**panic** ['pænɪk] *n* panika *f* ▷ *vi* wpadać (wpaść *perf*) w panikę
**panic attack** (*Psych*) *n* atak *m* paniki
**panicky** ['pænɪkɪ] *adj* (*behaviour*) panikarski (*pej*); **a ~ feeling** uczucie paniki
**panic-stricken** ['pænɪkstrɪkən] *adj* ogarnięty (panicznym) strachem
**pannier** ['pænɪə^r] *n* (*on bicycle*) sakwa *f*; (*on animal*) kosz *m* (*juczny*)
**panorama** [pænə'rɑ:mə] *n* panorama *f*
**panoramic** [pænə'ræmɪk] *adj* panoramiczny
**pansy** ['pænzɪ] *n* (*Bot*) bratek *m*; (*inf*: *pej*) mięczak *m* (*inf, pej*)
**pant** [pænt] *vi* (*person*) dyszeć; (*dog*) ziajać
**pantechnicon** [pæn'tɛknɪkən] (*Brit*) *n* meblowóz *m*
**panther** ['pænθə^r] *n* pantera *f*
**panties** ['pæntɪz] *npl* majtki *pl*, figi *pl*
**pantomime** ['pæntəmaɪm] *n* (*also*: **mime**) pantomima *f*; (*Brit*) *bajka muzyczna dla dzieci wystawiana w okresie Gwiazdki*
**pantry** ['pæntrɪ] *n* spiżarnia *f*
**pants** [pænts] *npl* (*Brit*: *woman's*) majtki *pl*; (: *man's*) slipy *pl*; (*US*) spodnie *pl*
**panty hose** *n* rajstopy *pl*
**papacy** ['peɪpəsɪ] *n* papiestwo *nt*
**papal** ['peɪpəl] *adj* papieski
**paparazzi** [pæpə'rætsi:] *npl* paparazzi *vir pl*
**paper** ['peɪpə^r] *n* papier *m*; (*also*: **newspaper**) gazeta *f*; (*exam*) egzamin *m*; (*academic essay*) referat *m*; (*wallpaper*) tapeta *f* ▷ *adj* papierowy, z papieru *post* ▷ *vt* tapetować (wytapetować *perf*); **papers** *npl* (*documents, identity papers*) papiery *pl*; **a piece of ~** (*odd bit*) kawałek *m* papieru; (*sheet*) kartka *f* (papieru); **to put sth down on ~** zapisywać (zapisać *perf*) coś
**paper advance** *n* (*Comput*) przesuw *m* papieru
**paperback** ['peɪpəbæk] *n* książka *f* w miękkiej okładce ▷ *adj*: **~ edition** wydanie *nt* w miękkiej okładce
**paper bag** *n* torebka *f* papierowa
**paperboy** ['peɪpəbɔɪ] *n* gazeciarz *m*
**paper clip** *n* spinacz *m*
**paper hankie** *n* chusteczka *f* higieniczna
**paper mill** *n* papiernia *f*
**paper money** *n* pieniądze *pl* papierowe
**paperweight** ['peɪpəweɪt] *n* przycisk *m* (do papieru)
**paperwork** ['peɪpəwə:k] *n* papierkowa robota *f*
**papier-mâché** ['pæpɪeɪ'mæʃeɪ] *n* masa *f* papierowa, papier mâché *nt inv*
**paprika** ['pæprɪkə] *n* papryka *f* (*przyprawa*)
**Pap Smear** *n* wymaz *m* z szyjki macicy
**Pap Test** (*Med*) *n* = **Pap Smear**
**par** [pɑ:^r] *n* (*Golf*) norma *f*; **to be on a par with** stać na równi z *+instr*; **at/above/below par** (*Comm*) według/powyżej/poniżej parytetu *or* nominału; **above** *or* **over par/ below** *or* **under par** (*Golf*) powyżej/poniżej normy; **to feel below** *or* **under par** nie czuć się w formie; **it's par for the course** (*fig*) to było do przewidzenia
**parable** ['pærəbl] *n* przypowieść *f*
**parabola** [pə'ræbələ] *n* parabola *f*
**parachute** ['pærəʃu:t] *n* spadochron *m*
**parachute jump** *n* skok *m* spadochronowy
**parachutist** ['pærəʃu:tɪst] *n* spadochroniarz(-arka) *m(f)*
**parade** [pə'reɪd] *n* (*public procession*) (uroczysty) pochód *m*; (*Mil*) parada *f* ▷ *vt* (*troops etc*) przeprowadzać (przeprowadzić *perf*); (*wealth etc*) afiszować się z *+instr* ▷ *vi* defilować (przedefilować *perf*); **fashion ~** rewia mody
**parade ground** *n* plac *m* apelowy

P

**paradise** ['pærədaɪs] *n* raj *m*
**paradox** ['pærədɔks] *n* paradoks *m*
**paradoxical** [pærə'dɔksɪkl] *adj* paradoksalny
**paradoxically** [pærə'dɔksɪklɪ] *adv* paradoksalnie
**paraffin** ['pærəfɪn] (*Brit*) *n* (*also*: **paraffin oil**) nafta *f*; **liquid** ~ parafina płynna
**paraffin heater** (*Brit*) *n* grzejnik *m* naftowy
**paraffin lamp** (*Brit*) *n* lampa *f* naftowa
**paragon** ['pærəgən] *n* (niedościgniony) wzór *m*
**paragraph** ['pærəgrɑːf] *n* akapit *m*, ustęp *m*; **to begin a new** ~ rozpoczynać (rozpocząć *perf*) od nowego akapitu
**Paraguay** ['pærəgwaɪ] *n* Paragwaj *m*
**Paraguayan** [pærə'gwaɪən] *adj* paragwajski ▷ *n* Paragwajczyk(-jka) *m(f)*
**parallel** ['pærəlɛl] *adj* (*also Comput*) równoległy; (*fig*) zbliżony, podobny ▷ *n* (*similarity*) podobieństwo *nt*, paralela *f* (*fml*); (*sth similar*) odpowiednik *m*; (*Geog*) równoleżnik *m*; **to draw ~s between/with** wykazywać (wykazać *perf*) podobieństwa między *+instr*/z *+instr*; **to run ~ (with** *or* **to)** biec równolegle (do *+gen*); (*fig*) występować (wystąpić *perf*) równolegle (z *+instr*); **in ~** (*Elec*) równolegle
**paralyse** ['pærəlaɪz] (*Brit*) *vt* paraliżować (sparaliżować *perf*)
**paralysis** [pə'rælɪsɪs] (*pl* **paralyses**) *n* paraliż *m*
**paralytic** [pærə'lɪtɪk] *adj* sparaliżowany; (*Brit*: *inf*: *drunk*) ululany (*inf*)
**paralyze** ['pærəlaɪz] (*US*) *vt* = **paralyse**
**parameter** [pə'ræmɪtə^r] *n* parametr *m*
**paramilitary** [pærə'mɪlɪtərɪ] *adj* paramilitarny
**paramount** ['pærəmaunt] *adj* najważniejszy; **of ~ importance** pierwszorzędnej *or* najwyższej wagi
**paranoia** [pærə'nɔɪə] *n* paranoja *f*
**paranoid** ['pærənɔɪd] *adj* paranoidalny, paranoiczny; (*person*): **he's** ~ to paranoik
**paranormal** [pærə'nɔːml] *adj* paranormalny ▷ *n*: **the** ~ zjawiska *pl* paranormalne
**parapet** ['pærəpɪt] *n* gzyms *m*
**paraphernalia** [pærəfə'neɪlɪə] *n* akcesoria *pl*
**paraphrase** ['pærəfreɪz] *vt* parafrazować (sparafrazować *perf*)
**paraplegic** [pærə'pliːdʒɪk] *n*: **to be** ~ cierpieć na porażenie kończyn dolnych
**parapsychology** [pærəsaɪ'kɔlədʒɪ] *n* parapsychologia *f*
**parasite** ['pærəsaɪt] *n* (*lit, fig*) pasożyt *m*
**parasol** ['pærəsɔl] *n* parasolka *f* (*od słońca*); (*at café etc*) parasol *m*
**paratrooper** ['pærətruːpə^r] (*Mil*) *n* spadochroniarz *m*
**parcel** ['pɑːsl] *n* paczka *f* ▷ *vt* (*also*: **parcel up**) pakować, zapakowywać (zapakować *perf*) ▶ **parcel out** *vt* rozparcelowywać (rozparcelować *perf*)
**parcel bomb** (*Brit*) *n przesyłka zawierająca ładunek wybuchowy*
**parcel post** *n*: **to send sth by** ~ wysyłać (wysłać *perf*) coś jako paczkę
**parch** [pɑːtʃ] *vt* spiekać (spiec *perf*)
**parched** [pɑːtʃt] *adj* (*lips, skin*) spieczony; **I'm** ~ (*inf*) zaschło mi w gardle
**parchment** ['pɑːtʃmənt] *n* pergamin *m*
**pardon** ['pɑːdn] *n* (*Jur*) ułaskawienie *nt* ▷ *vt* (*person*) wybaczać (wybaczyć *perf*) *+dat*; (*sin, error*) wybaczać (wybaczyć *perf*); (*Jur*) ułaskawiać (ułaskawić *perf*); **~ me!, I beg your ~!** przepraszam!; **(I beg your) ~?**, (*US*) **~ me?** słucham?
**pare** [pɛə^r] *vt* (*Brit*: *nails*) obcinać (obciąć *perf*); (*fruit*) obierać (obrać *perf*); (*fig*: *costs, expenses*) redukować (zredukować *perf*)
**parent** ['pɛərənt] *n* (*mother*) matka *f*; (*father*) ojciec *m*; **parents** *npl* rodzice *vir pl*
**parentage** ['pɛərəntɪdʒ] *n* pochodzenie *nt*; **of unknown** ~ nieznanego pochodzenia
**parental** [pə'rɛntl] *adj* rodzicielski
**parent company** (*Comm*) *n* firma *f* macierzysta
**parentheses** [pə'rɛnθɪsiːz] *npl of* **parenthesis**
**parenthesis** [pə'rɛnθɪsɪs] (*pl* **parentheses**) *n* (*phrase*) zdanie *nt* wtrącone; (*word*) wyraz *m* wtrącony; **parentheses** *npl* (*brackets*) nawiasy *pl*; **in** ~ (*say, add*) w nawiasie
**parenthood** ['pɛərənthud] *n* rodzicielstwo *nt*
**parenting** ['pɛərəntɪŋ] *n* wychowanie *nt*
**Paris** ['pærɪs] *n* Paryż *m*
**parish** ['pærɪʃ] *n* (*Rel*) parafia *f*; (*Brit*: *civil*) ≈ gmina *f*
**parish council** (*Brit*) *n* rada *f* gminy
**parishioner** [pə'rɪʃənə^r] *n* parafianin(-anka) *m(f)*
**Parisian** [pə'rɪzɪən] *adj* paryski ▷ *n* Paryżanin(-anka) *m(f)*
**parity** ['pærɪtɪ] *n* równość *f*; (*Econ*) parytet *m*
**park** [pɑːk] *n* park *m* ▷ *vt* parkować (zaparkować *perf*) ▷ *vi* parkować (zaparkować *perf*)
**parka** ['pɑːkə] *n długa kurtka z kapturem, zwykle na futrze*
**parking** ['pɑːkɪŋ] *n* (*action*) parkowanie *nt*; **"no ~"** „zakaz parkowania"
**parking lights** *npl* światła *pl* postojowe
**parking lot** (*US*) *n* parking *m*
**parking meter** *n* parkometr *m*
**parking offence** (*Brit*) *n* niedozwolone parkowanie *nt*
**parking place** *n* miejsce *nt* do parkowania

**parking ticket** *n* mandat *m* za niedozwolone parkowanie
**parking violation** (*US*) *n* = **parking offence**
**parkway** ['pɑ:kweɪ] (*US*) *n* aleja *f*
**parlance** ['pɑ:ləns] *n*: **in common ~** w mowie potocznej
**parliament** ['pɑ:ləmənt] *n* parlament *m*
**parliamentary** [pɑ:lə'mɛntərɪ] *adj* parlamentarny
**parlour**, (*US*) **parlor** ['pɑ:lə$^r$] *n* salon *m*
**parlous** ['pɑ:ləs] *adj* (*state*) opłakany
**Parmesan** [pɑ:mɪ'zæn] *n* (*also*: **Parmesan cheese**) parmezan *m*
**parochial** [pə'rəukɪəl] (*pej*) *adj* zaściankowy
**parody** ['pærədɪ] *n* parodia *f* ▷ *vt* parodiować (sparodiować *perf*)
**parole** [pə'rəul] (*Jur*) *n* zwolnienie *nt* warunkowe; **he was released on ~** został zwolniony warunkowo
**paroxysm** ['pærəksɪzəm] *n* paroksyzm *m*
**parquet** ['pɑ:keɪ] *n*: **~ floor(ing)** parkiet *m*
**parrot** ['pærət] *n* papuga *f*
**parrot fashion** *adv* jak papuga
**parry** ['pærɪ] *vt* (*blow*) odparowywać (odparować *perf*); (*argument*) odpierać (odeprzeć *perf*)
**parsimonious** [pɑ:sɪ'məunɪəs] *adj* skąpy
**parsley** ['pɑ:slɪ] *n* pietruszka *f*
**parsnip** ['pɑ:snɪp] *n* pasternak *m*
**parson** ['pɑ:sn] *n* duchowny *m*; (*Church of England*) pastor *m*
**part** [pɑ:t] *n* (*section, division, component*) część *f*; (*role*) rola *f*; (*episode*) odcinek *m*; (*US*: *in hair*) przedziałek *m*; (*Mus*) partia *f* ▷ *adv* = **partly** ▷ *vt* rozdzielać (rozdzielić *perf*) ▷ *vi* (*two people*) rozstawać się (rozstać się *perf*); (*crowd*) rozstępować się (rozstąpić się *perf*); (*fig*: *roads*) rozchodzić się (rozejść się *perf*); **to take ~ in** brać (wziąć *perf*) udział w *+loc*; **to take sth in good ~** przyjmować (przyjąć *perf*) coś w dobrej wierze; **to take sb's ~** stawać (stanąć *perf*) po czyjejś stronie; **on his ~** z jego strony; **for my ~** jeśli o mnie chodzi; **for the most ~** (*usually*) przeważnie; (*generally*) w przeważającej części; **for the better** *or* **best ~ of the day** przez większą część dnia; **to be ~ and parcel of** stanowić nieodłączną część *+gen*; **~ of speech** część mowy
▶ **part with** *vt fus* rozstawać się (rozstać się *perf*) z *+instr*
**partake** [pɑ:'teɪk] (*irreg*: *like* **take**); (*fml*) *vi*: **to ~ of** (*food, drink*) spożywać (spożyć *perf*) *+acc*; (*activity*) brać (wziąć *perf*) udział w *+loc*
**part exchange** (*Brit*: *Comm*) *n*: **in ~** w rozliczeniu
**partial** ['pɑ:ʃl] *adj* (*not complete*) częściowy; (*unjust*) stronniczy; **to be ~ to** mieć słabość do *+gen*
**partially** ['pɑ:ʃəlɪ] *adv* częściowo
**participant** [pɑ:'tɪsɪpənt] *n* uczestnik(-iczka) *m(f)*
**participate** [pɑ:'tɪsɪpeɪt] *vi* udzielać się; **to ~ in** uczestniczyć w *+loc*
**participation** [pɑ:tɪsɪ'peɪʃən] *n* udział *m*, uczestnictwo *nt*
**participle** ['pɑ:tɪsɪpl] *n* imiesłów *m*
**particle** ['pɑ:tɪkl] *n* cząsteczka *f*
**particular** [pə'tɪkjulə$^r$] *adj* szczególny; **particulars** *npl* (*details*) szczegóły *pl*; (*name, address etc*) dane *pl* osobiste; **in ~** w szczególności; **to be very ~ about** być bardzo wymagającym, jeśli chodzi o *+acc*
**particularly** [pə'tɪkjuləlɪ] *adv* szczególnie
**parting** ['pɑ:tɪŋ] *n* (*farewell*) rozstanie *nt*; (*of crowd etc*) rozstąpienie się *nt*; (*of roads*) rozejście się *nt*; (*Brit*: *in hair*) przedziałek *m* ▷ *adj* pożegnalny; **his ~ shot was ...** (*fig*) na odchodnym rzucił ...
**partisan** [pɑ:tɪ'zæn] *adj* (*politics, views*) stronniczy ▷ *n* (*fighter*) partyzant *m*; (*supporter*) zwolennik(-iczka) *m(f)*
**partition** [pɑ:'tɪʃən] *n* (*wall, screen*) przepierzenie *nt*; (*of country*) podział *m*; (: *among foreign powers*) rozbiór *m* ▷ *vt* dzielić (podzielić *perf*)
**partly** ['pɑ:tlɪ] *adv* częściowo
**partner** ['pɑ:tnə$^r$] *n* partner(ka) *m(f)*; (*Comm*) wspólnik(-iczka) *m(f)* ▷ *vt* być partnerem *+gen*, partnerować *+dat*
**partnership** ['pɑ:tnəʃɪp] *n* partnerstwo *nt*; (*Comm*) spółka *f*; **to go into ~ (with), form a ~ (with)** wchodzić (wejść *perf*) w spółkę (z *+instr*)
**part payment** *n* (*Comm*) częściowe rozliczenie *nt* płatności
**partridge** ['pɑ:trɪdʒ] *n* kuropatwa *f*
**part-time** ['pɑ:t'taɪm] *adj* niepełnoetatowy ▷ *adv* na niepełen etat
**part-timer** [pɑ:t'taɪmə$^r$] *n* (*also*: **part-time worker**) pracownik *m* niepełnoetatowy
**party** ['pɑ:tɪ] *n* (*Pol*) partia *f*; (*celebration, social event*) przyjęcie *nt*; (*of people*) grupa *f*; (*Jur*) strona *f* ▷ *cpd* (*Pol*) partyjny; **dinner ~** proszony obiad; **to give** *or* **throw a ~** wydawać (wydać *perf*) przyjęcie; **we're having a ~ next Saturday** w przyszłą sobotę urządzamy przyjęcie; **our son's birthday ~** przyjęcie urodzinowe naszego syna; **to be (a) ~ to a crime** być zamieszanym w przestępstwo
**party dress** *n* suknia *f* wieczorowa
**party line** *n* (*Tel*) wspólna linia *f* telefoniczna; (*Pol*) linia *f* partyjna
**par value** (*Comm*) *n* (*of share, bond*) wartość *f* pierwotna
**pass** [pɑ:s] *vt* (*time*) spędzać (spędzić *perf*); (*salt, glass etc*) podawać (podać *perf*); (*place,*

*person*) mijać (minąć *perf*); (*car*) wyprzedzać (wyprzedzić *perf*); (*exam*) zdawać (zdać *perf*); (*law*) uchwalać (uchwalić *perf*); (*proposal*) przyjmować (przyjąć *perf*); (*fig: limit, mark*) przekraczać (przekroczyć *perf*) ▷ *vi* (*person*) przechodzić (przejść *perf*); (: *in exam etc*) zdawać (zdać *perf*); (*time*) mijać (minąć *perf*); (*vehicle*) przejeżdżać (przejechać *perf*) ▷ *n* (*permit*) przepustka *f*; (*in mountains*) przełęcz *f*; (*Sport*) podanie *nt*; **to get a ~ in** (*Scol*) otrzymywać (otrzymać *perf*) zaliczenie z *+gen*; **~ the thread through the needle** nawlecz igłę; **could you ~ the vegetables round?** czy mógłbyś podać warzywa?; **things have come to a pretty ~** (*Brit: inf*) sprawy mają się kiepsko (*inf*); **to make a ~ at sb** (*inf*) przystawiać się do kogoś (*inf*)

▸ **pass away** *vi* umrzeć (*perf*)

▸ **pass by** *vi* przechodzić (przejść *perf*) ▷ *vt* (*lit, fig*) przechodzić (przejść *perf*) obok *+gen*

▸ **pass down** *vt* (*traditions etc*) przekazywać (przekazać *perf*)

▸ **pass for** *vt* uchodzić za *+acc*

▸ **pass on (to)** *vt* (*news, object*) przekazywać (przekazać *perf*) (*+dat*); (*illness*) zarażać (zarazić *perf*) *+instr* (*+acc*); (*costs, price rises*) przerzucać (przerzucić *perf*) (na *+acc*) ▷ *vi* umrzeć (*perf*)

▸ **pass out** *vi* mdleć (zemdleć *perf*); (*Brit: Mil*) zostawać (zostać *perf*) promowanym

▸ **pass over** *vt* (*ignore*) pomijać (pominąć *perf*) ▷ *vi* umrzeć (*perf*)

▸ **pass up** *vt* (*opportunity*) przepuszczać (przepuścić *perf*)

**passable** ['pɑːsəbl] *adj* (*road*) przejezdny; (*acceptable*) znośny

**passage** ['pæsɪdʒ] *n* (*also:* **passageway**) korytarz *m*; (*in book*) fragment *m*, ustęp *m*; (*way through crowd etc*) przejście *nt*; (*Anat*) przewód *m*; (*act of passing*) przejazd *m*; (*journey*) przeprawa *f*

**passenger** ['pæsɪndʒəʳ] *n* pasażer(ka) *m(f)*

**passer-by** [pɑːsə'baɪ] (*pl* **passers-by**) *n* przechodzień *m*

**passing** ['pɑːsɪŋ] *adj* przelotny; **in ~** mimochodem; **to mention sth in ~** napomykać (napomknąć *perf*) o czymś mimochodem

**passing place** (*Aut*) *n* mijanka *f*

**passion** ['pæʃən] *n* namiętność *f*; (*fig*) pasja *f*; **to have a ~ for sth** mieć zamiłowanie do czegoś

**passionate** ['pæʃənɪt] *adj* namiętny

**passive** ['pæsɪv] *adj* bierny ▷ *n* (*Ling*) strona *f* bierna

**passive smoking** *n* bierne palenie *nt*

**passkey** ['pɑːskiː] *n* klucz *m* uniwersalny

**Passover** ['pɑːsəuvəʳ] *n* Pascha *f*

**passport** ['pɑːspɔːt] *n* paszport *m*; (*fig*) klucz *m*, przepustka *f*

**passport control** *n* kontrola *f* paszportowa

**password** ['pɑːswəːd] *n* hasło *nt*

**past** [pɑːst] *prep* (*in front of*) obok *+gen*; (*beyond: be*) za *or* poza *+instr*; (: *go*) za *or* poza *+acc*; (*later than*) po *+loc* ▷ *adj* (*previous: government*) poprzedni; (: *week, month*) ubiegły, miniony; (*experience*) wcześniejszy; (*Ling*) przeszły ▷ *n* przeszłość *f*; **he's ~ forty** jest po czterdziestce; **ten/quarter ~ eight/midnight** dziesięć/kwadrans po ósmej/północy; **for the ~ few days** przez ostatnich kilka dni; **to run ~ (sb/sth)** przebiegać (przebiec *perf*) obok (kogoś/czegoś); **in the ~** w przeszłości; (*Ling*) w czasie przeszłym; **I'm ~ caring** przestało mi zależeć; **he's ~ it** (*Brit: inf*) to już nie te lata

**pasta** ['pæstə] *n* makaron *m*

**paste** [peɪst] *n* (*wet mixture*) papka *f*; (*glue*) klej *m* mączny, klajster *m*; (*jewellery*) stras *m*; (*Culin*) pasta *f* ▷ *vt* smarować (posmarować *perf*) klejem; **to ~ sth on sth** naklejać (nakleić *perf*) coś na coś; **to ~ together** sklejać (skleić *perf*); **~ emeralds** sztuczne szmaragdy

**pastel** ['pæstl] *adj* pastelowy

**pasteurized** ['pæstʃəraɪzd] *adj* pasteryzowany

**pastille** ['pæstl] *n* pastylka *f* (*cukierek*)

**pastime** ['pɑːstaɪm] *n* hobby *nt inv*

**past master** (*Brit*) *n*: **to be a ~ at** być mistrzem w *+loc*

**pastor** ['pɑːstəʳ] *n* pastor *m*

**pastoral** ['pɑːstərl] (*Rel*) *adj* duszpasterski

**pastry** ['peɪstrɪ] *n* (*dough*) ciasto *nt*; (*cake*) ciastko *nt*

**pasture** ['pɑːstʃəʳ] *n* pastwisko *nt*

**pasty** [*n* 'pæstɪ, *adj* 'peɪstɪ] *n* pasztecik *m* ▷ *adj* niezdrowo blady

**pat** [pæt] *vt* klepać (klepnąć *perf*), poklepywać (poklepać *perf*) ▷ *adj* (*answer etc*) bez zająknienia *post*; **to give sb/o.s. a pat on the back** (*fig*) chwalić (pochwalić *perf*) kogoś/się; **he knows it off pat,** (*US*) **he has it down pat** zna to na wyrywki

**patch** [pætʃ] *n* (*piece of material*) łata *f*; (*also:* **eye patch**) przepaska *f* na oko; (*damp, black etc*) plama *f*; (*of land*) zagon *m* ▷ *vt* łatać (załatać *perf or* połatać *perf*); **a bald ~** łysina; **to go through a bad ~** przechodzić zły okres

▸ **patch up** *vt* (*clothes*) łatać (załatać *perf or* połatać *perf*); (*quarrel*) łagodzić (załagodzić *perf*); (*relationship*) naprawiać (naprawić *perf*)

**patchwork** ['pætʃwəːk] *n* patchwork *m*

**patchy** ['pætʃɪ] *adj* (*colour*) niejednolity; (*information, knowledge*) wyrywkowy

**pate** [peɪt] *n*: **a bald ~** łysina *f*

**pâté** ['pæteɪ] *n* pasztet *m*
**patent** ['peɪtnt] *n* patent *m* ▷ *vt* opatentowywać (opatentować *perf*) ▷ *adj* oczywisty, ewidentny
**patent leather** *n* skóra *f* lakierowana; **~ shoes** lakierki
**patently** ['peɪtntlɪ] *adv* ewidentnie
**patent medicine** *n* (*produced by one firm*) specyfik *m*; (*cure-all*) cudowny lek *m*
**patent office** *n* urząd *m* patentowy
**paternal** [pə'tə:nl] *adj* (*love, duty*) ojcowski; (*grandmother*) ze strony ojca *post*
**paternalistic** [pətə:nə'lɪstɪk] *adj* paternalistyczny
**paternity** [pə'tə:nɪtɪ] *n* ojcostwo *nt*
**paternity leave** *n urlop przysługujący ojcu z tytułu narodzin dziecka*
**paternity suit** *n* postępowanie *nt* o ustalenie ojcostwa
**path** [pɑ:θ] *n* ścieżka *f*, dróżka *f*; (*trajectory*) tor *m*; (*fig*) droga *f*
**pathetic** [pə'θɛtɪk] *adj* żałosny
**pathological** [pæθə'lɔdʒɪkl] *adj* patologiczny
**pathologist** [pə'θɔlədʒɪst] *n* patolog *m*
**pathology** [pə'θɔlədʒɪ] *n* patologia *f*
**pathos** ['peɪθɔs] *n* patos *m*
**pathway** ['pɑ:θweɪ] *n* ścieżka *f*; (*fig*) droga *f*
**patience** ['peɪʃns] *n* cierpliwość *f*; (*Brit: Cards*) pasjans *m*; **to lose (one's) ~** tracić (stracić *perf*) cierpliwość
**patient** ['peɪʃnt] *n* pacjent(ka) *m(f)* ▷ *adj* cierpliwy; **to be ~ with sb** mieć do kogoś cierpliwość
**patiently** ['peɪʃntlɪ] *adv* cierpliwie
**patio** ['pætɪəu] *n* patio *nt*
**patriot** ['peɪtrɪət] *n* patriota(-tka) *m(f)*
**patriotic** [pætrɪ'ɔtɪk] *adj* (*song, speech*) patriotyczny; (*person*): **he/she is ~** jest patriotą/patriotką
**patriotism** ['pætrɪətɪzəm] *n* patriotyzm *m*
**patrol** [pə'trəul] *n* patrol *m* ▷ *vt* patrolować; **to be on ~** odbywać patrol
**patrol boat** *n* łódź *f* patrolowa
**patrol car** *n* wóz *m* patrolowy
**patrolman** [pə'trəulmən] (*US*) (*irreg: like* **man**) *n* policjant *m* na patrolu
**patron** ['peɪtrən] *n* (*of shop*) (stały(-ła) *m(f)*) klient(ka) *m(f)*; (*of hotel, restaurant*) gość *m* (*zwłaszcza częsty*); (*benefactor*) patron *m*; **~ of the arts** mecenas sztuki
**patronage** ['pætrənɪdʒ] *n*: **~ (of)** (*artist, charity etc*) patronat *m* (nad *+instr*)
**patronize** ['pætrənaɪz] *vt* (*pej: look down on*) traktować protekcjonalnie; (*artist*) być patronem *+gen*; (*shop*) kupować w *+loc*; (*restaurant etc*) (często) bywać w *+loc*; (*firm*) korzystać z usług *+gen*
**patronizing** ['pætrənaɪzɪŋ] *adj* protekcjonalny
**patron saint** (*Rel*) *n* patron(ka) *m(f)*
**patter** ['pætə^r] *n* (*of feet*) tupot *m*; (*of rain*) bębnienie *nt*; (*sales talk etc*) gadka *f* (*inf*) ▷ *vi* (*footsteps*) tupać (zatupać *perf*); (*rain*) bębnić (zabębnić *perf*)
**pattern** ['pætən] *n* (*design*) wzór *m*; (*sample*) próbka *f*; **behaviour ~s** wzory zachowań
**patterned** ['pætənd] *adj* wzorzysty; **~ with flowers** (z wzorem) w kwiatki
**paucity** ['pɔ:sɪtɪ] *n* niedostatek *m*
**paunch** [pɔ:ntʃ] *n* brzuch *m*
**pauper** ['pɔ:pə^r] *n* nędzarz(-arka) *m(f)*; **~'s grave** grób komunalny
**pause** [pɔ:z] *n* przerwa *f*; (*Mus*) fermata *f* ▷ *vi* (*stop temporarily*) zatrzymywać się (zatrzymać się *perf*); (*: while speaking*) przerywać (przerwać *perf*); **to ~ for breath** zatrzymywać się (zatrzymać się *perf*) dla nabrania oddechu; **without pausing for breath** (*fig*) bez wytchnienia
**pave** [peɪv] *vt* (*with stone*) brukować (wybrukować *perf*); (*with concrete*) betonować (wybetonować *perf*); **to ~ the way for** (*fig*) torować (utorować *perf*) drogę *+dat or* dla *+gen*
**pavement** ['peɪvmənt] *n* (*Brit*) chodnik *m*; (*US*) nawierzchnia *f* drogi
**pavilion** [pə'vɪlɪən] *n* (*Sport*) szatnia *f*; (*at exhibition*) pawilon *m*
**paving** ['peɪvɪŋ] *n* nawierzchnia *f*
**paving stone** *n* płyta *f* chodnikowa
**paw** [pɔ:] *n* łapa *f* ▷ *vt* (*cat etc*) skrobać (łapą *or* łapami) w *+acc*; (*pej: person*) obłapywać, obmacywać; **the horse was pawing the ground** koń darł kopytami ziemię
**pawn** [pɔ:n] *n* pionek *m* ▷ *vt* zastawiać (zastawić *perf*)
**pawnbroker** ['pɔ:nbrəukə^r] *n* właściciel(ka) *m(f)* lombardu
**pawnshop** ['pɔ:nʃɔp] *n* lombard *m*
**pay** [peɪ] (*pt, pp* **paid**) *n* płaca *f* ▷ *vt* (*sum of money, bill*) płacić (zapłacić *perf*); (*person*) płacić (zapłacić *perf*) *+dat* ▷ *vi* opłacać się (opłacić się *perf*); (*fig*) opłacać się (opłacić się *perf*), popłacać; **how much did you pay for it?** ile za to zapłaciłaś?; **to pay one's way** płacić (zapłacić *perf*) za siebie; **to pay dividends** (*fig*) procentować (zaprocentować *perf*); **to pay a high price for sth** (*fig*) płacić (zapłacić *perf*) za coś wysoką cenę; **to pay the penalty for sth** ponosić (ponieść *perf*) karę za coś; **to pay sb a compliment** powiedzieć (*perf*) komuś komplement; **to pay attention (to)** zwracać (zwrócić *perf*) uwagę (na *+acc*); **to pay sb a visit** składać (złożyć *perf*) komuś wizytę; **to pay one's respects to sb** składać (złożyć *perf*) komuś wyrazy szacunku

P

▶ **pay back** *vt* (*money*) zwracać (zwrócić *perf*), oddawać (oddać *perf*); (*loan*) spłacać (spłacić *perf*); (*person*) zwracać (zwrócić *perf*) *or* oddawać (oddać *perf*) pieniądze *+dat*
▶ **pay for** *vt fus* (*lit, fig*) płacić (zapłacić *perf*) za *+acc*
▶ **pay in** *vt* wpłacać (wpłacić *perf*)
▶ **pay off** *vt* (*debt, creditor*) spłacać (spłacić *perf*); (*person: before dismissing*) dać (dawać *perf*) odprawę *+dat*; (*person: bribe*) przekupywać (przekupić *perf*) ▷ *vi* opłacać się (opłacić się *perf*); **to pay sth off in instalments** spłacać (spłacić *perf*) coś w ratach
▶ **pay out** *vt* (*money*) wydawać (wydać *perf*); (*rope*) popuszczać (popuścić *perf*)
▶ **pay up** *vi* oddawać (oddać *perf*) pieniądze (*zwłaszcza niechętnie lub po terminie*)

**payable** ['peɪəbl] *adj* (*tax etc*) do zapłaty *post*; **cheques should be made ~ to** czeki powinny być wystawione na *+acc*
**pay day** *n* dzień *m* wypłaty
**PAYE** (*Brit*) *n abbr* (*= pay as you earn*) *płacenie podatku dochodowego przy otrzymywaniu płacy*
**payee** [peɪ'iː] *n* (*of postal order*) odbiorca *m*; (*of cheque*) beneficjant *m*, remitent *m*
**pay envelope** (*US*) *n* = **pay packet**
**paying guest** ['peɪɪŋ-] *n* sublokator(ka) *m(f)*
**payload** ['peɪləud] *n* ładunek *m* handlowy *or* użyteczny
**payment** ['peɪmənt] *n* (*act*) zapłata *f*; (*of bill*) płatność *f*; (*sum of money*) wypłata *f*; **advance ~** (*part sum*) zaliczka; (*total sum*) wypłata z góry; **deferred ~** zaległa wypłata; **~ by installments** wypłata w ratach; **monthly ~** miesięczna wypłata; **on ~ of** po opłaceniu *+gen*
**pay packet** (*Brit*) *n* koperta *f* z wypłatą
**pay phone** *n* automat *m* telefoniczny (*na monety*)
**payroll** ['peɪrəul] *n* lista *f* płac; **to be on a firm's ~** być na liście płac przedsiębiorstwa
**pay slip** (*Brit*) *n* odcinek *m* (od) wypłaty
**pay station** (*US*) *n* = **pay phone**
**PBS** (*US*) *n abbr* = **Public Broadcasting Service**
**PC** *n abbr* (*= personal computer*) pecet *m* (*inf*); (*Brit*) = **police constable** ▷ *adj abbr* = **politically correct** ▷ *abbr* (*Brit*) = **Privy Councillor**
**pc** *abbr* (*= per cent*) proc.; = **postcard**
**p/c** *abbr* = **petty cash**
**PCB** *n abbr* (*Elec, Comput: = printed circuit board*) płytka *f* drukowana; (*= polychlorinated biphenyl*) dwufenyl *m* polichlorowany (*ciecz izolacyjna*)
**pcm** *abbr* (*= per calendar month*) za miesiąc kalendarzowy
**PD** (*US*) *n abbr* = **police department**
**pd** *abbr* (*= paid*) zapł.
**pdq** (*inf*) *adv abbr* (*= pretty damn quick*) cholernie szybko (*inf*)
**PDSA** (*Brit*) *n abbr* (*= People's Dispensary for Sick Animals*) *darmowa lecznica dla zwierząt domowych*
**PDT** (*US*) *abbr* = **Pacific Daylight Time**
**PE** *n abbr* (*Scol: = physical education*) WF *m* ▷ *abbr* (*Canada*) = **Prince Edward Island**
**pea** [piː] *n* groch *m*, groszek *m*
**peace** [piːs] *n* (*not war*) pokój *m*; (*calm*) spokój *m*; **to be at ~ with sb/sth** żyć w przyjaźni z kimś/czymś; **to keep the ~** utrzymywać spokój
**peaceable** ['piːsəbl] *adj* (*person*) pokojowo nastawiony; (*attitude*) pokojowy
**peaceful** ['piːsful] *adj* (*calm*) spokojny; (*without violence*) pokojowy
**peace offering** *n* (*fig*) pojednawczy gest *m*
**peach** [piːtʃ] *n* brzoskwinia *f*
**peacock** ['piːkɔk] *n* paw *m*
**peak** [piːk] *n* (*lit, fig*) szczyt *m*; (*of cap*) daszek *m*
**peak hours** *npl* godziny *pl* szczytu
**peak period** *n* okres *m* szczytowy
**peaky** ['piːkɪ] (*Brit: inf*) *adj* mizerny
**peal** [piːl] *n* (*of bells*) bicie *nt*; **~s of laughter** salwy śmiechu
**peanut** ['piːnʌt] *n* orzeszek *m* ziemny
**peanut butter** *n* masło *nt* orzechowe
**pear** [pɛəʳ] *n* gruszka *f*
**pearl** [pəːl] *n* perła *f*
**peasant** ['pɛznt] *n* chłop(ka) *m(f)*
**peat** [piːt] *n* torf *m*
**pebble** ['pɛbl] *n* kamyk *m*, otoczak *m*
**peck** [pɛk] *vt* dziobać (dziobnąć *perf*); (*also:* **peck at**) dziobać (podziobać *perf*) ▷ *n* (*of bird*) dziobnięcie *nt*; (*kiss*) muśnięcie *nt* (wargami); **to ~ a hole in sth** wydziobywać (wydziobać *perf*) w czymś dziurę
**pecking order** ['pɛkɪŋ-] *n* (*fig*) hierarchia *f* (*w obrębie danej grupy*)
**peckish** ['pɛkɪʃ] (*Brit: inf*) *adj* głodnawy
**peculiar** [pɪ'kjuːlɪəʳ] *adj* osobliwy; **~ to** właściwy (szczególnie) *+dat*
**peculiarity** [pɪkjuːlɪ'ærɪtɪ] *n* (*strange habit, characteristic*) osobliwość *f*; (*distinctive feature*) cecha *f* szczególna
**peculiarly** [pɪ'kjuːlɪəlɪ] *adv* (*oddly*) osobliwie; (*distinctively*) szczególnie
**pecuniary** [pɪ'kjuːnɪərɪ] *adj* pieniężny
**pedal** ['pɛdl] *n* pedał *m* ▷ *vi* pedałować
**pedal bin** (*Brit*) *n* kosz *m* na śmieci (*z pedałem*)
**pedant** ['pɛdənt] *n* pedant(ka) *m(f)*
**pedantic** [pɪ'dæntɪk] *adj* pedantyczny
**peddle** ['pɛdl] *vt* (*goods, drugs*) handlować *+instr*; (*gossip*) rozpowszechniać
**peddler** ['pɛdləʳ] *n* (*also:* **drug peddler**) handlarz(-arka) *m(f)* narkotyków
**pedestal** ['pɛdəstl] *n* piedestał *m*

**pedestrian** [pɪˈdɛstrɪən] *n* pieszy(-sza) *m(f)* ▷ *adj* pieszy; (*fig*) przeciętny
**pedestrian crossing** (*Brit*) *n* przejście *nt* dla pieszych
**pedestrian precinct** (*Brit*) *n* strefa *f* ruchu pieszego
**pediatrics** [piːdɪˈætrɪks] (*US*) *n* = **paediatrics**
**pedigree** [ˈpɛdɪgriː] *n* (*lit, fig*) rodowód *m* ▷ *cpd*: ~ **dog** pies *m* z rodowodem
**pedophile** [ˈpiːdəufaɪl] (*US*) *n* = **paedophile**
**pee** [piː] (*inf*) *vi* siusiać (*inf*)
**peek** [piːk] *vi*: **to ~ at/over** zerkać (zerknąć *perf*) na *+acc*/ponad *+instr* ▷ *n*: **to have** *or* **take a ~ (at)** rzucać (rzucić *perf*) okiem (na *+acc*)
**peel** [piːl] *n* (*of orange etc*) skórka *f* ▷ *vt* obierać (obrać *perf*) ▷ *vi* (*paint*) łuszczyć się; (*wallpaper*) odpadać (płatami); (*skin*) schodzić; **my back's ~ing** schodzi mi skóra z pleców
▶ **peel back** *vt* odrywać (oderwać *perf*)
**peeler** [ˈpiːlə^r] *n nożyk do obierania warzyw i owoców*
**peelings** [ˈpiːlɪŋz] *npl* obierki *pl*
**peep** [piːp] *n* (*look*) zerknięcie *nt*; (*sound*) pisk *m* ▷ *vi* (*look*) zerkać (zerknąć *perf*); **to have** *or* **take a ~ (at)** zerkać (zerknąć *perf*) (na *+acc*)
▶ **peep out** *vi* wyglądać (wyjrzeć *perf*)
**peephole** [ˈpiːphəul] *n* wizjer *m*, judasz *m* (*inf*)
**peer** [pɪə^r] *n* (*noble*) par *m*; (*equal*) równy(-na) *m(f)*; (*contemporary*) rówieśnik(-iczka) *m(f)* ▷ *vi*: **to ~ at** przyglądać się (przyjrzeć się *perf*) *+dat*
**peerage** [ˈpɪərɪdʒ] *n*: **a ~** godność *f* para; **the ~** parowie *vir pl*
**peerless** [ˈpɪəlɪs] *adj* nie mający sobie równych
**peeved** [piːvd] *adj* (*inf*) wkurzony (*inf*)
**peevish** [ˈpiːvɪʃ] *adj* drażliwy
**peg** [pɛg] *n* (*for coat*) wieszak *m*; (*Brit*: *also*: **clothes peg**) klamerka *f*; (*also*: **tent peg**) śledź *m* ▷ *vt* (*washing*) wieszać; (*prices*) ustalać (ustalić *perf*); **off the peg** (*clothes*) gotowy
**pejorative** [pɪˈdʒɔrətɪv] *adj* pejoratywny
**Pekin** [piːˈkɪn] *n* = **Peking**
**Peking** [piːˈkɪŋ] *n* Pekin *m*
**Pekin(g)ese** [piːkɪˈniːz] *n* pekińczyk *m*
**pelican** [ˈpɛlɪkən] *n* pelikan *m*
**pelican crossing** (*Brit*) *n* przejście *nt* dla pieszych (*z ręczną obsługą sygnalizacji świetlnej*)
**pellet** [ˈpɛlɪt] *n* (*of paper*) kulka *f*; (*of mud*) grudka *f*; (*for shotgun*) ziarno *nt or* kulka *f* śrutu
**pell-mell** [ˈpɛlˈmɛl] *adv* (*without order*) bezładnie; (*hurriedly*) pośpiesznie
**pelmet** [ˈpɛlmɪt] *n* lambrekin *m*
**pelt** [pɛlt] *vt*: **to ~ sb with sth** obrzucać (obrzucić *perf*) kogoś czymś ▷ *vi* (*rain*: *also*: **pelt down**) lać; (*inf*: *run*) pędzić (popędzić *perf*) ▷ *n* skóra *f* (zwierzęca)
**pelvis** [ˈpɛlvɪs] (*Anat*) *n* miednica *f*
**pen** [pɛn] *n* (*also*: **fountain pen**) wieczne pióro *nt*; (*also*: **ballpoint pen**) długopis *m*; (*also*: **felt-tip pen**) pisak *m*; (*for sheep etc*) zagroda *f*; (*US*: *inf*: *prison*) pudło *nt* (*inf*); **to put pen to paper** (*start to write*) zabrać się (*perf*) do pisania; (*write sth*) napisać (*perf*) coś
**penal** [ˈpiːnl] *adj* karny
**penalize** [ˈpiːnəlaɪz] *vt* karać (ukarać *perf*); (*fig*) pokrzywdzić (*perf*)
**penal servitude** [-ˈsəːvɪtjuːd] (*Jur*) *n* ciężkie roboty *pl*
**penalty** [ˈpɛnltɪ] *n* (*punishment*) kara *f*; (*fine*) grzywna *f*; (*Sport*: *disadvantage*) kara *f*; (: *penalty kick*) rzut *m* karny
**penalty area** (*Brit*: *Sport*) *n* pole *nt* karne
**penalty clause** (*Comm*) *n* klauzula *f* dotycząca kar umownych
**penalty kick** *n* rzut *m* karny
**penance** [ˈpɛnəns] (*Rel*) *n* pokuta *f*; **to do ~ for one's sins** odprawiać (odprawić *perf*) pokutę za grzechy
**pence** [pɛns] *npl of* **penny**
**penchant** [ˈpɑ̃ːʃɑ̃ːŋ] *n* skłonność *f*; **to have a ~ for** mieć skłonność do *+gen*
**pencil** [ˈpɛnsl] *n* ołówek *m* ▷ *vt*: **to ~ sb/sth in** wpisywać (wpisać *perf*) kogoś/coś wstępnie
**pencil case** *n* piórnik *m*
**pencil sharpener** *n* temperówka *f*
**pendant** [ˈpɛndnt] *n* wisiorek *m*
**pending** [ˈpɛndɪŋ] *prep* (*until*) do czasu *+gen*; (*during*) podczas *+gen* ▷ *adj* (*exam*) zbliżający się; (*lawsuit*) w toku *post*; (*question etc*) nie rozstrzygnięty; (*business*) do załatwienia *post*
**pendulum** [ˈpɛndjuləm] *n* wahadło *nt*
**penetrate** [ˈpɛnɪtreɪt] *vt* (*person*: *territory*) przedostawać się (przedostać się *perf*) na *+acc*; (*light, water*) przenikać (przeniknąć *perf*) przez *+acc*
**penetrating** [ˈpɛnɪtreɪtɪŋ] *adj* (*sound, gaze*) przenikliwy; (*observation*) wnikliwy
**penetration** [pɛnɪˈtreɪʃən] *n* przedostanie się *nt*, przeniknięcie *nt*
**penfriend** [ˈpɛnfrɛnd] (*Brit*) *n* korespondencyjny(-na) przyjaciel(-iółka) *m(f)*
**penguin** [ˈpɛŋgwɪn] *n* pingwin *m*
**penicillin** [pɛnɪˈsɪlɪn] *n* penicylina *f*
**peninsula** [pəˈnɪnsjulə] *n* półwysep *m*
**penis** [ˈpiːnɪs] *n* członek *m*, prącie *nt*
**penitence** [ˈpɛnɪtns] *n* skrucha *f*; (*Rel*) żal *m* za grzechy
**penitent** [ˈpɛnɪtnt] *adj* skruszony
**penitentiary** [pɛnɪˈtɛnʃərɪ] (*US*) *n* więzienie *nt*
**penknife** [ˈpɛnnaɪf] *n* scyzoryk *m*
**pen name** *n* pseudonim *m* literacki

**pennant** ['pɛnənt] *n* proporczyk *m*
**penniless** ['pɛnɪlɪs] *adj* bez grosza *post*
**Pennines** ['pɛnaɪnz] *npl*: **the ~** Góry *pl* Pennińskie
**penny** ['pɛnɪ] (*pl* **pennies** *or Brit* **pence**) *n* (*Brit*) pens *m*; (*US*) moneta *f* jednocentowa, jednocentówka *f*; **it was worth every ~** to było warte swojej ceny; **it won't cost you a ~** nie będzie cię to kosztowało ani pensa/grosza
**pen pal** *n* = **penfriend**
**pension** ['pɛnʃən] *n* (*when retired*) emerytura *f*; (*when disabled*) renta *f*
▸ **pension off** *vt* przenosić (przenieść *perf*) na emeryturę
**pensionable** ['pɛnʃnəbl] *adj* (*age*) emerytalny; (*job*) uprawniający do emerytury *post*
**pensioner** ['pɛnʃənə^r] (*Brit*) *n* emeryt(ka) *m(f)*
**pension fund** *n* fundusz *m* emerytalny
**pensive** ['pɛnsɪv] *adj* zamyślony
**pentagon** ['pɛntəgən] (*US*) *n*: **the P~** Pentagon *m*
**Pentecost** ['pɛntɪkɔst] *n* (*in Judaism*) Święto *nt* Pierwszych Płodów, Święto *nt* Koszenia; (*in Christianity*) Zielone Świątki *pl*, Zesłanie *nt* Ducha Świętego
**penthouse** ['pɛnthaus] *n* apartament *m* na ostatnim piętrze
**pent-up** ['pɛntʌp] *adj* (*feelings*) zdławiony
**penultimate** [pɛ'nʌltɪmət] *adj* przedostatni
**penury** ['pɛnjurɪ] *n* nędza *f*
**people** ['pi:pl] *npl* ludzie *vir pl* ▹ *n* (*tribe, race*) lud *m*; (*nation*) naród *m*; **the ~** (*Pol*) lud *m*; **old ~** starzy ludzie, starcy; **young ~** młodzież; **a man of the ~** człowiek ludu; **the room was full of ~** pokój był pełen ludzi; **~ say that ...** mówią *or* mówi się, że...
**pep** [pɛp] (*inf*) *n* werwa *f*, wigor *m*
▸ **pep up** *vt* (*person*) ożywiać (ożywić *perf*); (*food*) dodawać (dodać *perf*) smaku *+dat*
**pepper** ['pɛpə^r] *n* (*spice*) pieprz *m*; (*green, red etc*) papryka *f* ▹ *vt*: **to ~ with** (*fig: bullets, questions*) zasypywać (zasypać *perf*) *+instr*
**peppercorn** ['pɛpəkɔ:n] *n* ziarno *nt* pieprzu
**pepper mill** *n* młynek *m* do pieprzu
**peppermint** ['pɛpəmɪnt] *n* (*sweet*) miętówka *f*; (*plant*) mięta *f* pieprzowa
**pepperpot** ['pɛpəpɔt] *n* pieprzniczka *f*
**pep talk** (*inf*) *n* przemówienie *nt* podnoszące na duchu
**per** [pə:^r] *prep* na *+acc*; **per day/person** na dzień/osobę; **per hour** (*miles etc*) na godzinę; (*fee*) za godzinę; **per kilo** za kilogram; **as per your instructions** według twoich instrukcji; **per annum** na rok
**per capita** *adj* na głowę *post*, na jednego mieszkańca *post* ▹ *adv* na głowę, na jednego mieszkańca
**perceive** [pə'si:v] *vt* (*sound, light*) postrzegać; (*difference*) dostrzegać (dostrzec *perf*); (*view, understand*) widzieć, postrzegać
**per cent** *n* procent *m*; **a 20 ~ discount** dwudziestoprocentowa zniżka
**percentage** [pə'sɛntɪdʒ] *n* procent *m*; **on a ~ basis** procentowo
**perceptible** [pə'sɛptɪbl] *adj* dostrzegalny
**perception** [pə'sɛpʃən] *n* (*insight*) wnikliwość *f*; (*impression*) wrażenie *nt*; (*opinion, belief*) opinia *f*; (*observation*) spostrzeżenie *nt*; (*understanding*) rozumienie *nt*; (*faculty*) postrzeganie *nt*, percepcja *f*
**perceptive** [pə'sɛptɪv] *adj* (*person*) spostrzegawczy; (*analysis*) wnikliwy
**perch** [pə:tʃ] *n* (*for bird*) grzęda *f*; (*fish*) okoń *m* ▹ *vi*: **to ~ (on)** przysiadać (przysiąść *perf*) (na *+loc*)
**percolate** ['pə:kəleɪt] *vt* (*coffee*) zaparzać (zaparzyć *perf*) ▹ *vi* (*coffee*) zaparzać się (zaparzyć się *perf*); **to ~ through/into** *etc* (*idea*) rozpowszechniać się (rozpowszechnić się *perf*) powoli w *+loc*; (*light*) sączyć się przez *+acc* /do *+gen*, przesączać się (przesączyć się *perf*) przez *+acc* /do *+gen*
**percolator** ['pə:kəleɪtə^r] *n* dzbanek *m* do parzenia kawy
**percussion** [pə'kʌʃən] *n* perkusja *f*, instrumenty *pl* perkusyjne
**peremptory** [pə'rɛmptərɪ] (*pej*) *adj* nie znoszący sprzeciwu
**perennial** [pə'rɛnɪəl] *adj* (*Bot: plant*) wieloletni; (*fig: problem*) wieczny; (*: feature*) nieodłączny ▹ *n* (*Bot*) bylina *f*
**perfect** [*adj, n* 'pə:fɪkt, *vb* pə'fɛkt] *adj* (*faultless, ideal*) doskonały; (*utter*) zupełny ▹ *vt* doskonalić (udoskonalić *perf*) ▹ *n*: **the ~** (*also*: **the perfect tense**) czas *m* dokonany; **he's a ~ stranger to me** w ogóle go nie znam
**perfection** [pə'fɛkʃən] *n* perfekcja *f*, doskonałość *f*
**perfectionist** [pə'fɛkʃənɪst] *n* perfekcjonista(-tka) *m(f)*
**perfectly** ['pə:fɪktlɪ] *adv* (*honest etc*) zupełnie; (*perform, do etc*) doskonale; (*agree*) całkowicie, w zupełności; **I'm ~ happy with the situation** jestem całkowicie zadowolony z sytuacji; **you know ~ well** doskonale wiesz; **I understood it ~** rozumiałem to doskonale
**perforate** ['pə:fəreɪt] *vt* perforować
**perforated ulcer** ['pə:fəreɪtəd-] (*Med*) *n* pęknięty wrzód *m*
**perforation** [pə:fə'reɪʃən] *n* (*small hole*) otwór *m*; (*line of holes*) perforacja *f*
**perform** [pə'fɔ:m] *vt* (*task, piece of music etc*) wykonywać (wykonać *perf*); (*ceremony*) prowadzić (poprowadzić *perf*); (*: Rel*)

odprawiać (odprawić *perf*) ▷ *vi* (*well, badly*) wypadać (wypaść *perf*); **the ceremony will be ~ed next week** ceremonia odbędzie się w przyszłym tygodniu

**performance** [pəˈfɔːməns] *n* (*of actor, athlete*) występ *m*; (*of play*) przedstawienie *nt*; (*of car, engine*) osiągi *pl*; (*of company*) wyniki *pl* działalności; **~ of the economy** stan gospodarki; **the team put up a good ~** zespół dobrze się spisał

**performer** [pəˈfɔːməʳ] *n* wykonawca(-wczyni) *m(f)*

**performing** [pəˈfɔːmɪŋ] *adj* (*animal*) tresowany

**perfume** [ˈpəːfjuːm] *n* (*cologne etc*) perfumy *pl*; (*fragrance*) woń *f*, zapach *m* ▷ *vt* (*air, room etc*) przesycać (przesycić *perf*) zapachem *+gen*; (*apply perfume*) perfumować

**perfunctory** [pəˈfʌŋktərɪ] *adj* (*search*) pobieżny; (*kiss, remark*) niedbały

**perhaps** [pəˈhæps] *adv* (być) może; **~ not** może nie

**peril** [ˈpɛrɪl] *n* niebezpieczeństwo *nt*

**perilous** [ˈpɛrɪləs] *adj* niebezpieczny

**perilously** [ˈpɛrɪləslɪ] *adv* niebezpiecznie

**perimeter** [pəˈrɪmɪtəʳ] *n* (*length of edge*) obwód *m*; (*of camp, clearing*) granice *pl*

**perimeter fence** *n* ogrodzenie *nt*

**period** [ˈpɪərɪəd] *n* (*length of time*) okres *m*, czas *m*; (*era*) okres *m*; (*Scol*) lekcja *f*; (*esp US: full stop*) kropka *f*; (*Med*) okres *m*, miesiączka *f* ▷ *adj* stylowy, z epoki *post*; **for a ~ of three weeks** na okres trzech tygodni; **the holiday ~** (*Brit*) okres urlopowy; **I won't do it. P~.** nie zrobię tego i kropka.

**periodic** [pɪərɪˈɔdɪk] *adj* okresowy

**periodical** [pɪərɪˈɔdɪkl] *n* czasopismo *nt* ▷ *adj* okresowy

**periodically** [pɪərɪˈɔdɪklɪ] *adv* okresowo

**period pains** (*Brit: Med*) *npl* bóle *pl* miesiączkowe

**peripatetic** [pɛrɪpəˈtɛtɪk] *adj* wędrowny; **~ teacher** (*Brit*) *nauczyciel zatrudniony w dwu lub więcej szkołach i podróżujący między nimi*

**peripheral** [pəˈrɪfərəl] *adj* uboczny; **~ vision** widzenie obwodowe ▷ *n* (*Comput*) urządzenie *nt* peryferyjne

**periphery** [pəˈrɪfərɪ] *n* skraj *m*

**periscope** [ˈpɛrɪskəup] *n* peryskop *m*

**perish** [ˈpɛrɪʃ] *vi* (*die*) ginąć (zginąć *perf*); (*rubber, leather*) rozpadać się (rozpaść się *perf*)

**perishable** [ˈpɛrɪʃəbl] *adj* (*food*) łatwo psujący się

**perishables** [ˈpɛrɪʃəblz] *npl* produkty *pl* łatwo psujące się

**perishing** [ˈpɛrɪʃɪŋ] *adj*: **it's ~ cold** jest przeraźliwie zimno

**peritonitis** [pɛrɪtəˈnaɪtɪs] *n* zapalenie *nt* otrzewnej

**perjure** [ˈpəːdʒəʳ] (*Jur*) *vt*: **to ~ o.s.** krzywoprzysięgać (krzywoprzysiąc *perf*)

**perjury** [ˈpəːdʒərɪ] (*Jur*) *n* krzywoprzysięstwo *nt*

**perks** [pəːks] (*inf*) *npl* korzyści *pl* uboczne

**perk up** *vi* ożywiać się (ożywić się *perf*)

**perky** [ˈpəːkɪ] *adj* żwawy

**perm** [pəːm] *n* trwała *f* ▷ *vt*: **to have one's hair ~ed** robić (zrobić *perf*) sobie trwałą (ondulację)

**permanence** [ˈpəːmənəns] *n* trwałość *f*

**permanent** [ˈpəːmənənt] *adj* (*lasting forever*) trwały; (*present all the time*) ciągły; (*job, address*) stały; **I'm not ~ here** nie jestem tu na stałe

**permanently** [ˈpəːmənəntlɪ] *adv* (*damage*) trwale; (*stay, live*) na stałe; (*locked etc*) stale

**permeable** [ˈpəːmɪəbl] *adj* przepuszczalny

**permeate** [ˈpəːmɪeɪt] *vt* przenikać (przeniknąć *perf*) ▷ *vi*: **to ~ through** (*liquid*) przesiąkać (przesiąknąć *perf*) przez *+acc*; (*idea*) przenikać (przeniknąć *perf*) do *+gen*

**permissible** [pəˈmɪsɪbl] *adj* dopuszczalny, dozwolony

**permission** [pəˈmɪʃən] *n* (*consent*) pozwolenie *nt*; (*authorization*) zezwolenie *nt*; **to give sb ~ to do sth** dawać (dać *perf*) komuś zezwolenie na zrobienie czegoś

**permissive** [pəˈmɪsɪv] *adj* pobłażliwy, permisywny (*fml*)

**permit** [*n* ˈpəːmɪt, *vb* pəˈmɪt] *n* (*authorization*) zezwolenie *nt*; (*entrance pass*) przepustka *f* ▷ *vt* pozwalać (pozwolić *perf*) na *+acc*; **to ~ sb to do sth** pozwalać (pozwolić *perf*) komuś coś (z)robić; **weather ~ting** jeśli pogoda dopisze; **fishing ~** (*for a year*) karta wędkarska; (*for a week etc*) zezwolenie wędkarskie

**permutation** [pəːmjuˈteɪʃən] *n* (*Math*) permutacja *f*; (*fig*) kombinacja *f*

**pernicious** [pəːˈnɪʃəs] *adj* (*lie, nonsense*) szkodliwy; (*effect*) zgubny

**pernickety** [pəˈnɪkɪtɪ] (*inf*) *adj* drobiazgowy

**perpendicular** [pəːpənˈdɪkjuləʳ] *adj* pionowy ▷ *n*: **the ~** pion *m*; **~ to** prostopadły do *+gen*

**perpetrate** [ˈpəːpɪtreɪt] *vt* popełniać (popełnić *perf*)

**perpetual** [pəˈpɛtjuəl] *adj* (*motion, darkness*) wieczny; (*noise, questions*) nieustanny

**perpetuate** [pəˈpɛtjueɪt] *vt* zachowywać (zachować *perf*)

**perpetuity** [pəːpɪˈtjuːɪtɪ] *n*: **in ~** po wieczne czasy

**perplex** [pəˈplɛks] *vt* wprawiać (wprawić *perf*) w zakłopotanie

**perplexing** [pəːˈplɛksɪŋ] *adj* wprawiający w zakłopotanie

P

**perquisites** ['pə:kwɪzɪts] (*fml*) *npl* uboczne korzyści *pl*
**per se** [-seɪ] *adv* jako taki
**persecute** ['pə:sɪkju:t] *vt* prześladować
**persecution** [pə:sɪ'kju:ʃən] *n* prześladowanie *nt*
**perseverance** [pə:sɪ'vɪərns] *n* wytrwałość *f*
**persevere** [pə:sɪ'vɪəʳ] *vi* wytrwać (*perf*), nie ustawać
**Persia** ['pə:ʃə] *n* Persja *f*
**Persian** ['pə:ʃən] *adj* perski ▷ *n* (język *m*) perski; **the ~ Gulf** Zatoka Perska
**persist** [pə'sɪst] *vi* (*pain, weather etc*) utrzymywać się; (*person*) upierać się; **to ~ with sth** obstawać przy czymś; **to ~ in doing sth** wciąż coś robić, nie przestawać czegoś robić
**persistence** [pə'sɪstəns] *n* wytrwałość *f*
**persistent** [pə'sɪstənt] *adj* (*noise, smell, cough*) uporczywy; (*person*) wytrwały; (*lateness, rain*) bezustanny; **~ offender** (*Jur*) recydywista(-tka) *m(f)*
**persnickety** [pə'snɪkɪtɪ] (*US: inf*) *adj* = **pernickety**
**person** ['pə:sn] *n* osoba *f*; **in ~** osobiście; **on** *or* **about one's ~** przy sobie; **~ to ~ call** (*Tel*) ≈ rozmowa z przywołaniem
**personable** ['pə:snəbl] *adj* przystojny
**personal** ['pə:snl] *adj* (*belongings, account, appeal etc*) osobisty; (*opinion, life, habits*) prywatny; **to be/get ~** robić osobiste wycieczki; **nothing ~!** bez obrazy!
**personal allowance** *n* kwota *f* dochodu osobistego nie podlegająca opodatkowaniu
**personal assistant** *n* osobisty(-ta) *m(f)* asystent(ka) *m(f)*
**personal column** *n* ogłoszenia *pl* drobne
**personal computer** *n* komputer *m* osobisty
**personal details** *npl* dane *pl* osobowe
**personal hygiene** *n* higiena *f* osobista
**personal identification number** *n* numer *m* PIN (*używany przy elektronicznych przelewach płatności i przy poborze pieniędzy z bankomatów*)
**personality** [pə:sə'nælɪtɪ] *n* (*character*) osobowość *f*; (*famous person*) osobistość *f*
**personal loan** (*Banking*) *n* kredyt *m* konsumpcyjny
**personally** ['pə:snəlɪ] *adv* osobiście; **to take sth ~** brać (wziąć *perf*) coś do siebie
**personal organizer** *n* terminarz *m*
**personal stereo** *n* walkman *m*
**personify** [pə:'sɔnɪfaɪ] *vt* (*Literature*) personifikować; (*embody*) uosabiać (uosobić *perf*)
**personnel** [pə:sə'nɛl] *n* personel *m*, pracownicy *vir pl*
**personnel department** *n* dział *m* kadr
**personnel manager** *n* kierownik(-iczka) *m(f)* działu kadr
**perspective** [pə'spɛktɪv] *n* (*Archit, Art*) perspektywa *f*; (*way of thinking*) punkt *m* widzenia, pogląd *m*; **to get sth into ~** (*fig*) spojrzeć (*perf*) na coś z właściwej perspektywy
**Perspex®** ['pə:spɛks] *n* pleksiglas *m*
**perspicacity** [pə:spɪ'kæsɪtɪ] *n* bystrość *f*
**perspiration** [pə:spɪ'reɪʃən] *n* (*sweat*) pot *m*; (*act of sweating*) pocenie się *nt*
**perspire** [pə'spaɪəʳ] *vi* pocić się (spocić się *perf*)
**persuade** [pə'sweɪd] *vt*: **to ~ sb to do sth** przekonywać (przekonać *perf*) kogoś, by coś zrobił; **to ~ sb that** przekonywać (przekonać *perf*) kogoś, że; **to be ~d of sth** być przekonanym o czymś
**persuasion** [pə'sweɪʒən] *n* (*act*) perswazja *f*; (*creed*) wyznanie *nt*
**persuasive** [pə'sweɪsɪv] *adj* przekonujący
**pert** [pə:t] *adj* (*person*) zuchwały; (*nose*) zadarty; (*buttocks*) jędrny; (*hat*) zawadiacki
**pertaining** [pə:'teɪnɪŋ]: **~ to** *prep* odnoszący się do *+gen*
**pertinent** ['pə:tɪnənt] *adj* adekwatny, na temat *post*
**perturb** [pə'tə:b] *vt* niepokoić (zaniepokoić *perf*)
**Peru** [pə'ru:] *n* Peru *nt inv*
**perusal** [pə'ru:zl] *n* przejrzenie *nt*
**peruse** [pə'ru:z] *vt* przeglądać (przejrzeć *perf*)
**Peruvian** [pə'ru:vjən] *adj* peruwiański ▷ *n* Peruwiańczyk(-anka) *m(f)*
**pervade** [pə'veɪd] *vt* przenikać (przeniknąć *perf*)
**pervasive** [pə'veɪzɪv] *adj* (*smell*) wszechobecny; (*influence*) szeroki; (*atmosphere*) szerzący się
**perverse** [pə'və:s] *adj* (*wayward*) przekorny, przewrotny; (*devious*) perwersyjny
**perversion** [pə'və:ʃən] *n* (*sexual*) zboczenie *nt*, perwersja *f*; (*of truth, justice*) wypaczenie *nt*
**perversity** [pə'və:sɪtɪ] *n* przekora *f*
**pervert** [*n* 'pə:və:t, *vb* pə'və:t] *n* zboczeniec *m* ▷ *vt* (*person, mind*) deprawować (zdeprawować *perf*); (*truth, sb's words*) wypaczać (wypaczyć *perf*)
**pessimism** ['pɛsɪmɪzəm] *n* pesymizm *m*
**pessimist** ['pɛsɪmɪst] *n* pesymista(-tka) *m(f)*
**pessimistic** [pɛsɪ'mɪstɪk] *adj* pesymistyczny
**pest** [pɛst] *n* (*insect*) szkodnik *m*; (*fig: nuisance*) utrapienie *nt*
**pest control** *n* zwalczanie *nt* szkodników
**pester** ['pɛstəʳ] *vt* męczyć
**pesticide** ['pɛstɪsaɪd] *n* pestycyd *m*
**pestilence** ['pɛstɪləns] *n* zaraza *f*
**pestle** ['pɛsl] *n* tłuczek *m*
**pet** [pɛt] *n* zwierzę *nt* domowe ▷ *adj* ulubiony

▷ *vt* pieścić ▷ *vi* (*inf: sexually*) pieścić się; **pet rabbit** *etc* domowy *or* oswojony królik *etc*; **teacher's pet** pupilek(-lka) *m(f)* nauczyciela

**petal** ['pɛtl] *n* płatek *m*

**peter out** ['pi:tə-] *vi* (stopniowo) kończyć się (skończyć się *perf*)

**petite** [pə'ti:t] *adj* drobny

**petition** [pə'tɪʃən] *n* (*signed document*) petycja *f*; (*Jur*) pozew *m* ▷ *vt* wnosić (wnieść *perf*) petycję do *+gen* ▷ *vi*: **to ~ for divorce** wnosić (wnieść *perf*) pozew o rozwód

**pet name** (*Brit*) *n* pieszczotliwe przezwisko *nt*

**petrified** ['pɛtrɪfaɪd] *adj* skamieniały

**petrify** ['pɛtrɪfaɪ] *vt* paraliżować (sparaliżować *perf*), przerażać (przerazić *perf*)

**petrochemical** [pɛtrə'kɛmɪkl] *adj* petrochemiczny

**petrodollars** ['pɛtrəudɔləz] *npl* petrodolary *pl*

**petrol** ['pɛtrəl] (*Brit*) *n* benzyna *f*; **two/four-star** ~ benzyna niebieska/żółta; **unleaded** ~ benzyna bezołowiowa

**petrol can** *n* kanister *m*

**petrol engine** (*Brit*) *n* silnik *m* benzynowy

**petroleum** [pə'trəulɪəm] *n* ropa *f* naftowa

**petroleum jelly** *n* wazelina *f*

**petrol pump** (*Brit*) *n* (*in garage*) dystrybutor *m*; (*in engine*) pompa *f* paliwowa

**petrol station** (*Brit*) *n* stacja *f* benzynowa

**petrol tank** (*Brit*) *n* zbiornik *m* paliwa

**petticoat** ['pɛtɪkəut] *n* (*full length*) halka *f*; (*waist*) półhalka *f*

**pettifogging** ['pɛtɪfɔgɪŋ] *adj* drobnostkowy

**pettiness** ['pɛtɪnɪs] *n* drobnostkowość *f*, małostkowość *f*

**petty** ['pɛtɪ] *adj* (*detail, problem*) drobny, nieistotny; (*crime*) drobny; (*person*) małostkowy

**petty cash** *n* kasa *f* podręczna

**petty officer** *n* podoficer *m* (*w marynarce wojennej*)

**petulant** ['pɛtjulənt] *adj* (*person*) nieznośny; (*expression*) nadąsany

**pew** [pju:] *n* ławka *f* (kościelna)

**pewter** ['pju:tə^r] *n* stop *m* cyny z ołowiem; ~ **plate** talerz cynowy

**Pfc** (*US: Mil*) *abbr* (= *private first class*) ≈ st. szer.

**PG** (*Film*) *n abbr* (= *parental guidance*) *kategoria filmów, które dzieci mogą oglądać za zgodą rodziców*

**PGA** *n abbr* = **Professional Golfers Association**

**PH** (*US: Mil*) *n abbr* (= *Purple Heart*) *amerykańskie odznaczenie wojskowe nadawane za rany odniesione w walce*

**pH** *n abbr* (= *potential of hydrogen*) pH *nt inv*

**PHA** (*US*) *n abbr* = **Public Housing Administration**

**phallic** ['fælɪk] *adj* falliczny

**phantom** ['fæntəm] *n* zjawa *f*, widmo *nt*, fantom *m* ▷ *adj* (*fig*) tajemniczy

**Pharaoh** ['fɛərəu] *n* faraon *m*

**pharmaceutical** [fɑ:mə'sju:tɪkl] *adj* farmaceutyczny; **pharmaceuticals** *npl* środki *pl* farmaceutyczne

**pharmacist** ['fɑ:məsɪst] *n* farmaceuta(-tka) *m(f)*

**pharmacy** ['fɑ:məsɪ] *n* (*shop*) apteka *f*; (*science*) farmacja *f*

**phase** [feɪz] *n* faza *f* ▷ *vt*: **to ~ sth in** wprowadzać (wprowadzić *perf*) coś; **to ~ sth out** wycofywać (wycofać *perf*) coś

**PhD** *n abbr* (= *Doctor of Philosophy*) *stopień naukowy*, ≈ dr

**pheasant** ['fɛznt] *n* bażant *m*

**phenomena** [fə'nɔmɪnə] *npl of* **phenomenon**

**phenomenal** [fə'nɔmɪnl] *adj* fenomenalny

**phenomenon** [fə'nɔmɪnən] (*pl* **phenomena**) *n* zjawisko *nt*

**phew** [fju:] *excl* uff

**phial** ['faɪəl] *n* fiolka *f*

**philanderer** [fɪ'lændərə^r] *n* flirciarz *m*

**philanthropic** [fɪlən'θrɔpɪk] *adj* filantropijny

**philanthropist** [fɪ'lænθrəpɪst] *n* filantrop(ka) *m(f)*

**philatelist** [fɪ'lætəlɪst] *n* filatelista(-tka) *m(f)*

**philately** [fɪ'lætəlɪ] *n* filatelistyka *f*

**Philippines** ['fɪlɪpi:nz] *npl*: **the** ~ Filipiny *pl*

**Philistine** ['fɪlɪstaɪn] *n* filister *m*

**philosopher** [fɪ'lɔsəfə^r] *n* filozof *m*

**philosophical** [fɪlə'sɔfɪkl] *adj* filozoficzny

**philosophize** [fɪ'lɔsəfaɪz] *vi* filozofować

**philosophy** [fɪ'lɔsəfɪ] *n* filozofia *f*

**phlegm** [flɛm] *n* flegma *f*

**phlegmatic** [flɛg'mætɪk] *adj* flegmatyczny

**phobia** ['fəubjə] *n* fobia *f*, chorobliwy lęk *m*

**phone** [fəun] *n* telefon *m* ▷ *vt* dzwonić (zadzwonić *perf*) *or* telefonować (zatelefonować *perf*) do *+gen*; **to be on the ~** (*possess phone*) mieć telefon; (*be calling*) rozmawiać przez telefon

▸ **phone back** *vt* zadzwonić (*perf*) później do *+gen* ▷ *vi* zadzwonić (*perf*) później, oddzwonić (*perf*)

▸ **phone up** *vt* dzwonić (zadzwonić *perf*) do *+gen* ▷ *vi* dzwonić (zadzwonić *perf*)

**phone book** *n* książka *f* telefoniczna

**phone booth** *n* kabina *f* telefoniczna

**phone box** (*Brit*) *n* budka *f* telefoniczna

**phone call** *n* rozmowa *f* telefoniczna

**phonecard** ['fəunkɑ:d] *n* karta *f* telefoniczna

**phone-in** ['fəunɪn] (*Brit*) *n program z telefonicznym udziałem słuchaczy/widzów*

**phonetic** [fə'nɛtɪk] *adj* fonetyczny

**phonetics** [fə'nɛtɪks] *n* fonetyka *f*

**phoney** ['fəunɪ] *adj* (*address, person*) fałszywy; (*accent*) sztuczny

P

**phonograph** ['fəunəgrɑ:f] (US) *n* gramofon *m*
**phony** ['fəunɪ] *adj* = **phoney**
**phosphate** ['fɔsfeɪt] *n* fosforan *m*
**phosphorus** ['fɔsfərəs] *n* fosfor *m*
**photo** ['fəutəu] *n* fotografia *f*, zdjęcie *nt*
**photo...** ['fəutəu] *pref* foto...
**photocopier** ['fəutəukɔpɪəʳ] *n* fotokopiarka *f*
**photocopy** ['fəutəukɔpɪ] *n* fotokopia *f* ▷ *vt* robić (zrobić *perf*) fotokopię *+gen*
**photoelectric** [fəutəuɪ'lɛktrɪk] *adj* fotoelektryczny
**photo finish** (*Racing*) *n sytuacja, gdy dla ustalenia kolejności zawodników na mecie konieczne jest odwołanie się do fotokomórki*
**photogenic** [fəutəu'dʒɛnɪk] *adj* fotogeniczny
**photograph** ['fəutəgræf] *n* fotografia *f*, zdjęcie *nt* ▷ *vt* fotografować (sfotografować *perf*); **to take a ~ of sb** robić (zrobić *perf*) komuś zdjęcie
**photographer** [fə'tɔgrəfəʳ] *n* fotograf *m*
**photographic** [fəutə'græfɪk] *adj* fotograficzny
**photography** [fə'tɔgrəfɪ] *n* (*subject*) fotografia *f*; (*art*) fotografika *f*
**photostat** ['fəutəustæt] *n* fotokopia *f*
**photosynthesis** [fəutəu'sɪnθəsɪs] (*Bio*) *n* fotosynteza *f*
**phrase** [freɪz] *n* (*group of words, expression*) zwrot *m*, określenie *nt*; (*Ling*) zwrot *m*; (*Mus*) fraza *f* ▷ *vt* (*thought, idea*) wyrażać (wyrazić *perf*); (*letter*) układać (ułożyć *perf*)
**phrase book** *n* rozmówki *pl*
**physical** ['fɪzɪkl] *adj* (*geography, properties*) fizyczny; (*world, universe, object*) materialny; (*law, explanation*) naukowy; **~ examination** badanie lekarskie; **the ~ sciences** nauki fizyczne
**physical education** *n* wychowanie *nt* fizyczne
**physically** ['fɪzɪklɪ] *adv* fizycznie
**physician** [fɪ'zɪʃən] *n* lekarz(-arka) *m(f)*
**physicist** ['fɪzɪsɪst] *n* fizyk *m*
**physics** ['fɪzɪks] *n* fizyka *f*
**physiological** ['fɪzɪə'lɔdʒɪkl] *adj* fizjologiczny
**physiology** [fɪzɪ'ɔlədʒɪ] *n* fizjologia *f*
**physiotherapist** [fɪzɪəu'θɛrəpɪst] *n* fizjoterapeuta(-tka) *m(f)*
**physiotherapy** [fɪzɪəu'θɛrəpɪ] *n* fizjoterapia *f*
**physique** [fɪ'zi:k] *n* budowa *f* (ciała), konstytucja *f*
**pianist** ['pi:ənɪst] *n* pianista(-tka) *m(f)*
**piano** [pɪ'ænəu] *n* pianino *nt*; **grand ~** fortepian
**piano accordion** (*Brit*) *n* akordeon *m*
**Picardy** ['pɪkədɪ] *n* Pikardia *f*
**piccolo** ['pɪkələu] *n* pikolo *nt*
**pick** [pɪk] *n* kilof *m*, oskard *m* ▷ *vt* (*select*) wybierać (wybrać *perf*); (*fruit, flowers*) zrywać (zerwać *perf*); (*mushrooms*) zbierać (zebrać *perf*); (*book from shelf etc*) zdejmować (zdjąć *perf*); (*lock*) otwierać (otworzyć *perf*); (*spot*) wyciskać (wycisnąć *perf*); (*scab*) zrywać (zerwać *perf*); **take your ~** wybieraj; **the ~ of** najlepsza część *+gen*; **to ~ one's nose/teeth** dłubać w nosie/zębach; **to ~ sb's brains** radzić się (poradzić się *perf*) kogoś; **to ~ sb's pocket** dobierać się (dobrać się *perf*) komuś do kieszeni; **to ~ a quarrel (with sb)** wywoływać (wywołać *perf*) kłótnię (z kimś)
▸ **pick at** *vt fus* (*food*) dziobać (dziobnąć *perf*)
▸ **pick off** *vt* wystrzelać (*perf*)
▸ **pick on** *vt fus* czepiać się *+gen*
▸ **pick out** *vt* (*distinguish*) dostrzegać (dostrzec *perf*); (*select*) wybierać (wybrać *perf*)
▸ **pick up** *vi* (*health*) poprawiać się (poprawić się *perf*); (*economy, trade*) polepszać się (polepszyć się *perf*) ▷ *vt* (*lift*) podnosić (podnieść *perf*); (*arrest*) przymykać (przymknąć *perf*) (*inf*); (*collect: person, parcel*) odbierać (odebrać *perf*); (*hitchhiker*) zabierać (zabrać *perf*); (*girl*) podrywać (poderwać *perf*); (*language, skill*) nauczyć się (*perf*) *+gen*; (*Radio*) łapać (złapać *perf*) (*inf*); **to ~ up speed** nabierać (nabrać *perf*) szybkości; **to ~ o.s. up** zbierać się (pozbierać się *perf*), podnieść się (*perf*); **let's ~ up where we left off** zacznijmy tam, gdzie przerwaliśmy
**pickaxe**, (US) **pickax** ['pɪkæks] *n* kilof *m*, oskard *m*
**picket** ['pɪkɪt] *n* pikieta *f* ▷ *vt* pikietować
**picketing** ['pɪkɪtɪŋ] *n* pikietowanie *nt*
**picket line** *n* linia *f* pikiety
**pickings** ['pɪkɪŋz] *npl*: **there are rich ~ to be had here** można się tu nieźle obłowić (*inf*)
**pickle** ['pɪkl] *n* (*also*: **pickles**) pikle *pl* ▷ *vt* (*in vinegar*) marynować (zamarynować *perf*); (*in salt water*) kwasić (zakwasić *perf*), kisić (zakisić *perf*); **to get in a ~** urządzić się (*perf*) (*inf*)
**pick-me-up** ['pɪkmi:ʌp] *n* (*nonalcoholic*) napój *m* orzeźwiający; (*alcoholic*) kieliszek *m* na wzmocnienie
**pickpocket** ['pɪkpɔkɪt] *n* złodziej *m* kieszonkowy, kieszonkowiec *m*
**pick-up** ['pɪkʌp] *n* (*also*: **pick-up truck**) furgonetka *f*; (*Brit*: *on record player*) ramię *nt* gramofonu
**picnic** ['pɪknɪk] *n* piknik *m* ▷ *vi* urządzać (urządzić *perf*) piknik
**picnicker** ['pɪknɪkəʳ] *n* uczestnik(-iczka) *m(f)* pikniku
**pictorial** [pɪk'tɔ:rɪəl] *adj* obrazkowy
**picture** ['pɪktʃəʳ] *n* (*lit, fig*) obraz *m*; (*photo*) zdjęcie *nt*; (*film*) film *m*, obraz *m* (*fml*); **the**

**economic ~** sytuacja gospodarcza ▷ *vt* wyobrażać (wyobrazić *perf*) sobie; **the ~s** (*Brit: inf*) kino *nt*; **to take a ~ of sb/sth** robić (zrobić *perf*) komuś/czemuś zdjęcie; **to put sb in the ~** wprowadzać (wprowadzić *perf*) kogoś w sytuację

**picture book** *n* książeczka *f* obrazkowa

**picturesque** [pɪktʃə'rɛsk] *adj* malowniczy

**picture window** *n* okno *nt* panoramiczne

**piddling** ['pɪdlɪŋ] (*inf*) *adj* błahy

**pidgin** ['pɪdʒɪn] *n* (język) pidgin *m*

**pie** [paɪ] *n* placek *m* (*z nadzieniem mięsnym, warzywnym lub owocowym*)

**piebald** ['paɪbɔːld] *adj* (*horse*) srokaty

**piece** [piːs] *n* (*bit*) kawałek *m*; (*part*) część *f*; (*Chess etc*) figura *f*; **in ~s** w kawałkach *or* częściach; **a ~ of clothing** część garderoby; **a ~ of furniture** mebel; **a ~ of advice** rada; **a ~ of music** utwór; **to take sth to ~s** rozkładać (rozłożyć *perf*) *or* rozbierać (rozebrać *perf*) coś na części; **in one ~** cały; **a 10p ~** (*Brit*) moneta dziesięciopensowa; **~ by ~** kawałek po kawałku, część po części; **a six-~ band** sześcioosobowy zespół; **I've said my ~** powiedziałem, co miałem do powiedzenia
▸ **piece together** *vt* układać (ułożyć *perf*) w całość, poskładać (*perf*)

**piecemeal** ['piːsmiːl] *adv* po kawałku

**piecework** ['piːswəːk] *n* praca *f* na akord

**pie chart** (*Math*) *n* diagram *m* kołowy

**Piedmont** ['piːdmɔnt] *n* Piemont *m*

**pier** [pɪəʳ] *n* molo *nt*, pomost *m*

**pierce** [pɪəs] *vt* przebijać (przebić *perf*), przekłuwać (przekłuć *perf*); **to have one's ears ~d** przekłuwać (przekłuć *perf*) sobie uszy

**piercing** ['pɪəsɪŋ] *adj* (*fig*) przeszywający

**piety** ['paɪətɪ] *n* pobożność *f*

**piffling** ['pɪflɪŋ] (*inf*) *adj* śmiesznie błahy

**pig** [pɪg] *n* (*lit, fig*) świnia *f*

**pigeon** ['pɪdʒən] *n* gołąb *m*

**pigeonhole** ['pɪdʒənhəul] *n* (*for letters, messages*) przegródka *f*, dziupla *f* (*inf*); (*fig*) przypisane miejsce *nt* ▷ *vt* szufladkować (zaszufladkować *perf*)

**piggy bank** ['pɪgɪ-] *n* skarbonka *f*

**pig-headed** ['pɪg'hɛdɪd] (*pej*) *adj* (głupio) uparty

**piglet** ['pɪglɪt] *n* prosię *nt*, prosiak *m*

**pigment** ['pɪgmənt] *n* barwnik *m*, pigment *m*

**pigmentation** [pɪgmən'teɪʃən] *n* ubarwienie *nt*, pigmentacja *f*

**pigmy** ['pɪgmɪ] *n* = **pygmy**

**pigskin** ['pɪgskɪn] *n* świńska skóra *f*

**pigsty** ['pɪgstaɪ] *n* (*lit, fig*) chlew *m*

**pigtail** ['pɪgteɪl] *n* warkoczyk *m*

**pike** [paɪk] *n* (*fish*) szczupak *m*; (*spear*) pika *f*

**pilchard** ['pɪltʃəd] *n* sardynka *f* (europejska)

**pile** [paɪl] *n* (*heap, stack*) stos *m*, sterta *f*; (*of carpet, velvet*) włos *m*; (*pillar*) pal *m* ▷ *vt* (*also*: **pile up**) układać (ułożyć *perf*) w stos; **arranged in a ~** ułożone w stos; **to ~ into** ładować się (władować się *perf*) do *+gen*; **to ~ out of** wylewać się *or* wysypywać się z *+gen*
▸ **pile on** *vt*: **to ~ it on** (*inf*) przesadzać (przesadzić *perf*)
▸ **pile up** *vi* gromadzić się (nagromadzić się *perf*)

**piles** [paɪlz] (*Med*) *npl* hemoroidy *pl*

**pile-up** ['paɪlʌp] (*Aut*) *n* karambol *m*

**pilfer** ['pɪlfəʳ] *vt* kraść (ukraść *perf*) (*rzecz drobną lub mało wartościową*) ▷ *vi* kraść

**pilfering** ['pɪlfərɪŋ] *n* drobne kradzieże *pl*

**pilgrim** ['pɪlgrɪm] *n* pielgrzym *m*

**pilgrimage** ['pɪlgrɪmɪdʒ] *n* pielgrzymka *f*

**pill** [pɪl] *n* pigułka *f*; **the ~** pigułka antykoncepcyjna; **to be on the ~** stosować pigułkę antykoncepcyjną *or* antykoncepcję doustną

**pillage** ['pɪlɪdʒ] *n* grabież *f* ▷ *vt* grabić (ograbić *perf*)

**pillar** ['pɪləʳ] *n* (*lit, fig*) filar *m*

**pillar box** (*Brit*) *n* skrzynka *f* pocztowa

**pillion** ['pɪljən] *n*: **to ride ~** (*on motorcycle*) jechać na tylnym siodełku; (*on horse*) *jechać na koniu, siedząc za plecami jeźdźca*

**pillory** ['pɪlərɪ] *vt* stawiać (postawić *perf*) pod pręgierzem ▷ *n* pręgierz *m*

**pillow** ['pɪləu] *n* poduszka *f*

**pillowcase** ['pɪləukeɪs] *n* poszewka *f* (*na poduszkę*)

**pillowslip** ['pɪləuslɪp] *n* = **pillowcase**

**pilot** ['paɪlət] *n* pilot(ka) *m*(*f*) ▷ *adj* pilotażowy ▷ *vt* pilotować; (*fig*: *new law, scheme*) nadzorować wprowadzenie w życie *+gen*

**pilot boat** *n* łódź *f* pilota portowego

**pilot light** *n* (*on cooker, boiler*) płomyk *m* zapalacza

**pimento** [pɪ'mɛntəu] *n* piment *m*, ziele *nt* angielskie

**pimp** [pɪmp] *n* sutener *m*, alfons *m* (*inf*)

**pimple** ['pɪmpl] *n* pryszcz *m*

**pimply** ['pɪmplɪ] *adj* pryszczaty

**PIN** *n abbr* = **personal identification number**

**pin** [pɪn] *n* (*for clothes, papers*) szpilka *f*; (*in engine, machine*) zatyczka *f*, sworzeń *m*; (*Brit*: *also*: **drawing pin**) pinezka *f*; (: *Elec*) bolec *m*; (*in grenade*) zawleczka *f* ▷ *vt* przypinać (przypiąć *perf*); **pins and needles** mrowienie; **to pin sb against/to** przyciskać (przycisnąć *perf*) kogoś do *+gen*; **to pin the blame on sb** (*fig*) zrzucać (zrzucić *perf*) winę na kogoś
▸ **pin down** *vt* (*fig*): **to pin sb down (to sth)** zmuszać (zmusić *perf*) kogoś do zajęcia stanowiska (w jakiejś sprawie); **there's**

P

**something strange here but I can't quite pin it down** coś tu jest dziwnego, ale nie potrafię (dokładnie) powiedzieć, co
**pinafore** ['pɪnəfɔːʳ] *n* (*also*: **pinafore dress**) bezrękawnik *m*
**pinball** ['pɪnbɔːl] *n* bilard *m* (elektryczny)
**pincers** ['pɪnsəz] *npl* (*tool*) obcęgi *pl*, szczypce *pl*; (*of crab, lobster*) szczypce *pl*
**pinch** [pɪntʃ] *n* szczypta *f* ▷ *vt* szczypać (uszczypnąć *perf*); (*inf*: *thing, money*) zwędzić (*perf*), zwinąć (*perf*) (*inf*); (*idea*) podkradać (podkraść *perf*) ▷ *vi* (*shoe*) cisnąć, uwierać; **at a ~** w ostateczności; **he feels the ~** (*fig*) brak pieniędzy daje mu się we znaki
**pinched** [pɪntʃt] *adj* (*face*) ściągnięty; **~ with cold** ściągnięty z zimna
**pincushion** ['pɪnkuʃən] *n* poduszeczka *f* na igły
**pine** [paɪn] *n* sosna *f* ▷ *vi*: **to ~ for** usychać z tęsknoty za *+instr*
▸ **pine away** *vi* marnieć (zmarnieć *perf*) (z żalu)
**pineapple** ['paɪnæpl] *n* ananas *m*
**pine-cone** ['paɪnkəun] *n* szyszka *f* sosnowa
**pine-needles** ['paɪnniːdlz] *npl* igliwie *nt* sosnowe
**ping** [pɪŋ] *n* (*of bell*) brzęk *m*; (*of bullet*) świst *m*, gwizd *m*
**ping-pong**® ['pɪŋpɔŋ] *n* ping-pong *m*
**pink** [pɪŋk] *adj* różowy ▷ *n* (*colour*) (kolor *m*) różowy, róż *m*; (*Bot*) goździk *m*
**pinking shears** *npl* nożyce *pl* ząbkowane
**pin money** (*Brit*: *inf*) *n* pieniądze *pl* na drobne wydatki
**pinnacle** ['pɪnəkl] *n* (*of building, mountain*) iglica *f*; (*fig*) szczyt *m*
**pinpoint** ['pɪnpɔɪnt] *vt* wskazywać (wskazać *perf*) (dokładnie)
**pinstripe** ['pɪnstraɪp] *adj*: **~ suit** garnitur *m* w prążki
**pint** [paɪnt] *n* (*measure*) pół *nt inv* kwarty (*Brit* = *0,568 l*, *US* = *0,473 l*); (*Brit*: *inf*) ≈ duże piwo *nt*
**pin-up** ['pɪnʌp] *n* plakat *m* ze zdjęciem idola
**pioneer** [paɪə'nɪəʳ] *n* pionier(ka) *m(f)* ▷ *vt* być pionierem *+gen*
**pious** ['paɪəs] *adj* pobożny
**pip** [pɪp] *n* pestka *f* ▷ *vt*: **to be pipped at the post** (*Brit*: *fig*) zostać (*perf*) pokonanym w ostatniej chwili; **the pips** *npl* (*Brit*: *Radio*) sygnał *m* czasu
**pipe** [paɪp] *n* (*for water, gas*) rura *f*; (*for smoking*) fajka *f*; (*Mus*) piszczałka *f*, fujarka *f* ▷ *vt* doprowadzać (doprowadzić *perf*) (rurami); **pipes** *npl* (*also*: **bagpipes**) dudy *pl*
▸ **pipe down** (*inf*) *vi* przymykać się (przymknąć się *perf*) (*inf*)
**pipe cleaner** *n* wycior *m* do fajki
**piped music** [paɪpt-] *n* muzyka *f* z głośników (*w supermarkecie, na dworcu itp*)
**pipe dream** *n* marzenie *nt* ściętej głowy
**pipeline** ['paɪplaɪn] *n* (*for oil*) rurociąg *m*; (*for gas*) gazociąg *m*; **to be in the ~** (*fig*) być w przygotowaniu
**piper** ['paɪpəʳ] *n* dudziarz *m*
**pipe tobacco** *n* tytoń *m* fajkowy
**piping** ['paɪpɪŋ] *adv*: **~ hot** wrzący
**piquant** ['piːkənt] *adj* pikantny; (*fig*) intrygujący
**pique** ['piːk] *n*: **in a fit of ~** w poczuciu urażonej dumy
**piracy** ['paɪərəsɪ] *n* piractwo *nt*
**pirate** ['paɪərət] *n* pirat *m* ▷ *vt* nielegalnie kopiować (skopiować *perf*); **~d video tapes** pirackie kasety wideo
**pirate radio** (*Brit*) *n* radiostacja *f* piracka
**pirouette** [pɪru'ɛt] *n* piruet *m* ▷ *vi* robić (zrobić *perf*) piruet
**Pisces** ['paɪsiːz] *n* Ryby *pl*; **to be ~** być spod znaku Ryb
**piss** [pɪs] (*inf!*) *vi* sikać (*inf*) ▷ *n* siki *pl* (*inf*); **~ off!** odpieprz się! (*inf!*); **to be ~ed off with sb/sth** mieć kogoś/czegoś po dziurki w nosie; **to take the ~ (out of sb)** (*Brit*) robić sobie jaja (z kogoś) (*inf!*); **it's ~ing down** (*Brit*) leje
**pissed** [pɪst] (*inf!*) *adj* zalany (*inf*)
**pistol** ['pɪstl] *n* pistolet *m*
**piston** ['pɪstən] *n* tłok *m*
**pit** [pɪt] *n* (*hole dug*) dół *m*, wykop *m*; (*in road, face*) dziura *f*; (*coal mine*) kopalnia *f*; (*also*: **orchestra pit**) kanał *m* dla orkiestry ▷ *vt*: **to pit one's wits against sb** mierzyć się (zmierzyć się *perf*) (intelektualnie) z kimś; **the pits** *npl* (*Aut*) boks *m*, kanał *m*; **the pit of one's stomach** dołek; **to pit o.s. against** mierzyć się (zmierzyć się *perf*) z *+instr*; **to pit sb against sb** rzucać (rzucić *perf*) kogoś przeciw komuś
**pit-a-pat** ['pɪtə'pæt] (*Brit*) *adv*: **to go ~** (*heart*) kołatać; (*rain*) bębnić
**pitch** [pɪtʃ] *n* (*Brit*: *Sport*) boisko *nt*; (*of note, voice*) wysokość *f*; (*fig*) poziom *m*; (*tar*) smoła *f*; (*of boat*) rzucanie *nt*, kiwanie *nt*; (*also*: **sales pitch**) nawijka *f* (*inf*) ▷ *vt* (*throw*) rzucać (rzucić *perf*); (*set*) ustawiać (ustawić *perf*) poziom *or* wysokość *+gen* ▷ *vi* (*person*) upaść (*perf*) *or* runąć (*perf*) (głową do przodu); (*Naut*) rzucać (rzucić *perf*); **to ~ a tent** rozbijać (rozbić *perf*) namiot
**pitch-black** ['pɪtʃ'blæk] *adj* czarny jak smoła
**pitched battle** [pɪtʃt-] *n* zażarty bój *m*
**pitcher** ['pɪtʃəʳ] *n* dzban *m*; (*US*: *Baseball*) zawodnik *m* rzucający piłkę
**pitchfork** ['pɪtʃfɔːk] *n* widły *pl*

**piteous** ['pɪtɪəs] *adj* żałosny
**pitfall** ['pɪtfɔ:l] *n* pułapka *f*
**pith** [pɪθ] *n (of orange, lemon)* miękisz *m* (skórki); *(of plant)* rdzeń *m*; *(fig)* sedno *nt*, istota *f*
**pithead** ['pɪthɛd] *n* nadszybie *nt*
**pithy** ['pɪθɪ] *adj* zwięzły, treściwy
**pitiable** ['pɪtɪəbl] *adj* żałosny, godny pożałowania *or* politowania
**pitiful** ['pɪtɪful] *adj* żałosny
**pitifully** ['pɪtɪfəlɪ] *adv* żałośnie
**pitiless** ['pɪtɪlɪs] *adj* bezlitosny
**pittance** ['pɪtns] *n* grosze *pl*, psie pieniądze *pl*
**pitted** ['pɪtɪd] *adj*: **~ with** *(chicken pox)* podziobany *+instr*; *(craters, caves)* usiany *+instr*; *(rust)* przeżarty *+instr*
**pity** ['pɪtɪ] *n* litość *f*, współczucie *nt* ▷ *vt* współczuć *+dat*, żałować *+gen*; **I ~ you** żal mi cię; **what a ~!** jaka szkoda!; **it is a ~ that you can't come** szkoda, że nie możesz przyjść; **to take ~ on sb** litować się (zlitować się *perf*) nad kimś
**pitying** ['pɪtɪɪŋ] *adj* współczujący
**pivot** ['pɪvət] *n (Tech)* sworzeń *m*, oś *f*; *(fig)* oś *f* ▷ *vi* obracać się (obrócić się *perf*) wokół osi
▸ **pivot on** *vt fus* zależeć od *+gen*
**pixel** ['pɪksl] *(Comput) n* piksel *m*
**pixie** ['pɪksɪ] *n* elf *m*, skrzat *m*
**pizza** ['pi:tsə] *n* pizza *f*
**placard** ['plækɑ:d] *n (outside newsagent's)* afisz *m*; *(in march)* transparent *m*
**placate** [plə'keɪt] *vt (person)* udobruchać *(perf)*; *(anger)* załagodzić *(perf)*
**placatory** [plə'keɪtərɪ] *adj* łagodzący, uspokajający
**place** [pleɪs] *n* miejsce *nt*; *(in street names)* ≈ ulica *f* ▷ *vt (put)* umieszczać (umieścić *perf*); *(identify: person)* przypominać (przypomnieć *perf*) sobie; **to take ~** mieć miejsce; **at his ~** u niego (w domu); **to his ~** do niego (do domu); **from ~ to ~** z miejsca na miejsce; **all over the ~** wszędzie; **in ~s** miejscami; **in sb's ~** na czyimś miejscu; **in sth's ~** na miejscu czegoś; **to take sb's/sth's ~** zajmować (zająć *perf*) czyjeś miejsce/miejsce czegoś; **to get a ~ at college/university** dostawać się (dostać się *perf*) do kolegium/na uniwersytet; **out of ~** nie na miejscu; **I feel out of ~ here** zupełnie tu nie pasuję; **in the first ~** po pierwsze; **to be ~d first/third** plasować się (uplasować się *perf*) na pierwszym/trzecim miejscu; **to change ~s with sb** zamieniać się (zamienić się *perf*) (miejscami) z kimś; **to put sb in their ~** *(fig)* pokazywać (pokazać *perf*) komuś, gdzie jest jego miejsce; **he's going ~s** on daleko zajdzie; **it was not my ~ to say so** nie wypadało mi tego powiedzieć; **to ~ an order with sb (for sth)** składać (złożyć *perf*) u kogoś zamówienie (na coś); **how are you ~d next week?** jak wyglądasz w przyszłym tygodniu (z czasem)?
**placebo** [plə'si:bəu] *n (Med)* placebo *nt inv*; *(fig)* coś *nt* na pocieszenie
**place mat** *n* podkładka *f* pod nakrycie
**placement** ['pleɪsmənt] *n (job)* posada *f*
**place name** *n* nazwa *f* miejscowa
**placenta** [plə'sɛntə] *n (Anat)* łożysko *nt*
**place of birth** *n* miejsce *nt* urodzenia
**place setting** *n* nakrycie *nt (stołowe)*
**placid** ['plæsɪd] *adj* spokojny
**plagiarism** ['pleɪdʒjərɪzəm] *n (activity)* plagiatorstwo *nt*; *(instance)* plagiat *m*
**plagiarist** ['pleɪdʒjərɪst] *n* plagiator(ka) *m(f)*
**plagiarize** ['pleɪdʒjəraɪz] *vt* dokonywać (dokonać *perf*) plagiatu *+gen*
**plague** [pleɪg] *n (disease)* dżuma *f*; *(epidemic)* zaraza *f*; *(fig: of locusts etc)* plaga *f* ▷ *vt (fig: problems etc)* nękać; **to ~ sb with questions** męczyć *or* zamęczać kogoś pytaniami
**plaice** [pleɪs] *n inv* płastuga *f*
**plaid** [plæd] *n* materiał *m* w kratę
**plain** [pleɪn] *adj (unpatterned)* gładki; *(simple)* prosty; *(clear, easily understood)* jasny; *(not beautiful)* niełądny; *(frank)* otwarty ▷ *adv* po prostu ▷ *n (area of land)* równina *f*; *(Knitting)* prawe oczko *nt*; **to make sth ~ to sb** dawać (dać *perf*) coś komuś jasno do zrozumienia
**plain chocolate** *n* ≈ czekolada *f* deserowa
**plain-clothes** ['pleɪnkləuðz] *adj (police officer)* ubrany po cywilnemu
**plainly** ['pleɪnlɪ] *adv* wyraźnie
**plainness** ['pleɪnnɪs] *n* prostota *f*
**plaintiff** ['pleɪntɪf] *n (Jur)* powód(ka) *m(f)*
**plaintive** ['pleɪntɪv] *adj (cry, voice)* zawodzący, żałosny; *(song, look)* tęskny
**plait** [plæt] *n (hair)* warkocz *m*; *(rope)* (pleciona) lina *f* ▷ *vt (hair)* pleść, zaplatać (zapleść *perf*); *(rope)* pleść, splatać (spleść *perf*)
**plan** [plæn] *n* plan *m* ▷ *vt* planować (zaplanować *perf*) ▷ *vi* planować; **to ~ to do sth/on doing sth** planować coś (z)robić; **how long do you ~ to stay?** jak długo planujesz zostać?; **to ~ for** *or* **on** spodziewać się *+gen*
**plane** [pleɪn] *n (Aviat)* samolot *m*; *(Math)* płaszczyzna *f*; *(tool)* strug *m*, hebel *m*; *(also:* **plane tree)** platan *m*; *(fig)* poziom *m* ▷ *vt (wood)* heblować (oheblować *perf*) ▷ *vi*: **to ~ across water** ślizgać się po wodzie
**planet** ['plænɪt] *n* planeta *f*
**planetarium** [plænɪ'tɛərɪəm] *n* planetarium *nt*
**plank** [plæŋk] *n (of wood)* deska *f*; *(fig: of policy, campaign)* punkt *m* (programowy)

P

**plankton** ['plæŋktən] *n* plankton *m*
**planner** ['plænəʳ] *n* (*town planner*) urbanista(-tka) *m(f)*; (*of project etc*) planista(-tka) *m(f)*
**planning** ['plænɪŋ] *n* planowanie *nt*; (*also*: **town planning**) planowanie *nt* przestrzenne, urbanistyka *f*
**planning permission** (*Brit*) *n* zezwolenie *nt* na budowę
**plant** [plɑ:nt] *n* (*Bot*) roślina *f*; (*machinery*) maszyny *pl*; (*factory*) fabryka *f*; (*also*: **power plant**) elektrownia *f* ▷ *vt* (*plants, trees*) sadzić (zasadzić *perf*); (*seed, crops*) siać (zasiać *perf*); (*field, garden*: *with plants*) obsadzać (obsadzić *perf*); (: *with crops*) obsiewać (obsiać *perf*); (*microphone, bomb, incriminating evidence*) podkładać (podłożyć *perf*); (*fig*: *object*) lokować (ulokować *perf*); (: *kiss*) składać (złożyć *perf*)
**plantation** [plæn'teɪʃən] *n* plantacja *f*
**plant pot** (*Brit*) *n* doniczka *f*
**plaque** [plæk] *n* (*on building*) tablica *f* (pamiątkowa); (*on teeth*) płytka *f* nazębna
**plasma** ['plæzmə] *n* plazma *f*
**plaster** ['plɑ:stəʳ] *n* (*for walls*) tynk *m*; (*also*: **plaster of Paris**) gips *m*; (*Brit*: *also*: **sticking plaster**) plaster *m*, przylepiec *m* ▷ *vt* tynkować (otynkować *perf*); **in ~** (*Brit*) w gipsie; **the walls were ~ed with posters** ściany były oblepione plakatami.
**plaster cast** *n* (*Med*) opatrunek *m* gipsowy, gips *m*; (*model, statue*) odlew *m* gipsowy
**plastered** ['plɑ:stəd] *adj* (*inf*: *drunk*) zaprawiony (*inf*)
**plasterer** ['plɑ:stərəʳ] *n* tynkarz *m*
**plastic** ['plæstɪk] *n* plastik *m* ▷ *adj* (*made of plastic*) plastikowy; (*flexible*) plastyczny; **the ~ arts** sztuki plastyczne
**plastic bag** *n* (*shopping bag*) torba *f* plastikowa; (*lunch bag*) woreczek *m* plastikowy *or* foliowy
**plastic explosive** *n* plastik *m*
**Plasticine**® ['plæstɪsi:n] *n* plastelina *f*
**plastic surgery** *n* (*branch of medicine*) chirurgia *f* plastyczna; (*operation*) operacja *f* plastyczna
**plate** [pleɪt] *n* (*dish, plateful*) talerz *m*; (*metal cover*) płyta *f*, pokrywa *f*; (*gold plate, silver plate*) platery *pl*; (*Typ*) płyta *f* drukująca; (*Aut*) tablica *f* (rejestracyjna); (*in book*) rycina *f*; (*dental plate*) proteza *f* (stomatologiczna); (*on door*) tabliczka *f*; **a car with Irish ~s** samochód z irlandzką rejestracją
**plateau** ['plætəu] (*pl* **~s** *or* **~x**) *n* (*Geog*) plateau *nt inv*; (*fig*): **to reach a ~** stawać (stanąć *perf*) w miejscu
**plateful** ['pleɪtful] *n* (pełen) talerz *m*
**plate glass** *n* szkło *nt* płaskie walcowane
**platen** ['plætən] *n* (*Typ*) wałek *m*
**plate rack** *n* suszarka *f* (do naczyń)
**platform** ['plætfɔ:m] *n* (*for speaker*) podium *nt*, trybuna *f*; (*for landing, loading*) platforma *f*; (*Rail*) peron *m*; (*Brit*: *of bus*) pomost *m*, platforma *f*; (*Pol*) program *m*; **the train leaves from ~ seven** pociąg odjeżdża z peronu siódmego
**platform ticket** (*Brit*: *Rail*) *n* bilet *m* peronowy, peronówka *f*
**platinum** ['plætɪnəm] *n* platyna *f*
**platitude** ['plætɪtju:d] *n* frazes *m*
**platonic** [plə'tɔnɪk] *adj* platoniczny
**platoon** [plə'tu:n] *n* (*Mil*) pluton *m*
**platter** ['plætəʳ] *n* półmisek *m*
**plaudits** ['plɔ:dɪts] *npl* uznanie *nt*, aplauz *m*
**plausible** ['plɔ:zɪbl] *adj* (*theory, excuse, statement*) prawdopodobny; (*person*) budzący zaufanie
**play** [pleɪ] *n* (*Theat etc*) sztuka *f*; (*activity*) zabawa *f* ▷ *vt* (*hide-and-seek etc*) bawić się w *+acc*; (*football, chess*) grać (zagrać *perf*) w *+acc*; (*team, opponent*) grać (zagrać *perf*) z *+instr*; (*role, piece of music, note*) grać (zagrać *perf*); (*instrument*) grać (zagrać *perf*) na *+loc*; (*tape, record*) puszczać (puścić *perf*) ▷ *vi* (*children*) bawić się (pobawić się *perf*); (*orchestra, band*) grać (zagrać *perf*); (*record, tape, radio*) grać; **to bring sth into ~** posłużyć się (*perf*) czymś; **a ~ on words** gra słów; **he ~ed a trick on us** zrobił nam kawał; **to ~ for time** (*fig*) grać na zwłokę *or* czas; **to ~ a part/role in** (*fig*) odgrywać (odegrać *perf*) rolę w *+loc*; **to ~ safe** nie ryzykować; **to ~ into sb's hands** podkładać się (podłożyć się *perf*) komuś (*inf*)
▸ **play about with** *vt fus* = **play around with**
▸ **play along with** *vt fus* (*person*) iść (pójść *perf*) na rękę *+dat*; (*plan*) (chwilowo) przystać (*perf*) na *+acc*
▸ **play around with** *vt fus* bawić się *+instr*
▸ **play at** *vt fus* (*politics etc*) bawić się w *+acc*; **they ~ed at being soldiers** bawili się w żołnierzy
▸ **play back** *vt* (*recording*) odtwarzać (odtworzyć *perf*)
▸ **play down** *vt* pomniejszać (pomniejszyć *perf*) znaczenie *+gen*
▸ **play on** *vt fus* (*sb's feelings*) grać (zagrać *perf*) na *+loc*; (*sb's credulity, prejudices*) wykorzystywać (wykorzystać *perf*) *+acc*; **to ~ on sb's mind** zatruwać komuś spokój
▸ **play up** *vi* (*machine, knee*) nawalać (*inf*); (*children*) szaleć
**play-act** ['pleɪækt] *vi* udawać
**playboy** ['pleɪbɔɪ] *n* playboy *m*
**player** ['pleɪəʳ] *n* (*in sport, game*) gracz *m*; (*Theat*) aktor(ka) *m(f)*; (*Mus*): **guitar** *etc* **~** gitarzysta(-tka) *m(f)* *etc*

**playful** ['pleɪful] *adj (remark, gesture)* żartobliwy; *(person)* figlarny; *(animal)* rozbrykany
**playgoer** ['pleɪgəuəʳ] *n* teatroman(ka) *m(f)*
**playground** ['pleɪgraund] *n (in park)* plac *m* zabaw; *(in school)* boisko *nt*
**playgroup** ['pleɪgru:p] *n rodzaj środowiskowego przedszkola organizowanego przez grupę zaprzyjaźnionych rodziców*
**playing card** ['pleɪɪŋ-] *n* karta *f* do gry
**playing field** *n* boisko *nt* sportowe
**playmate** ['pleɪmeɪt] *n* towarzysz(ka) *m(f)* zabaw
**play-off** ['pleɪɔf] *n* baraż *m*
**playpen** ['pleɪpɛn] *n* kojec *m*
**playroom** ['pleɪru:m] *n* pokój *m* do zabawy
**playschool** ['pleɪsku:l] *n* = **playgroup**
**plaything** ['pleɪθɪŋ] *n* zabawka *f*; *(fig)*: **we are the ~s of fate** jesteśmy igraszką losu
**playtime** ['pleɪtaɪm] *n* przerwa *f (w szkole)*
**playwright** ['pleɪraɪt] *n* dramaturg *m*, dramatopisarz(-arka) *m(f)*
**plc** *(Brit) abbr (= public limited company) duża spółka akcyjna, której akcje mogą być kupowane na giełdzie,* ≈ S.A.
**plea** [pli:] *n (request)* błaganie *nt*, apel *m*; *(excuse)* usprawiedliwienie *nt*; *(Jur)*: **~ of (not) guilty** (nie)przyznanie się *nt* do winy
**plead** [pli:d] *vt (ignorance, ill health)* tłumaczyć się *+instr*; *(Jur)*: **to ~ sb's case** bronić czyjejś sprawy ▷ *vi (Jur) odpowiadać na zarzuty przedstawione w akcie oskarżenia*; **to ~ with sb to do sth** błagać kogoś, żeby coś (z)robił; **to ~ for sth** apelować o coś; **to ~ (not) guilty** (nie) przyznawać się ((nie) przyznać się *perf*) do winy
**pleasant** ['plɛznt] *adj* przyjemny; *(person)* miły, sympatyczny
**pleasantly** ['plɛzntlɪ] *adv (surprised)* mile, przyjemnie; *(say, behave)* uprzejmie
**pleasantries** ['plɛzntrɪz] *npl* uprzejmości *pl*
**please** [pli:z] *excl* proszę ▷ *vt (satisfy)* zadowalać (zadowolić *perf*); *(give pleasure)* sprawiać (sprawić *perf*) przyjemność *+dat* ▷ *vi*: **to be eager/anxious to ~** bardzo się starać; **yes, ~** tak, poproszę; **could I speak to Sue, ~?** czy mógłbym rozmawiać z Sue?, czy mogę prosić Sue?; **~ miss, ...** *(to teacher)* proszę pani, ...; **he's difficult/impossible to ~** trudno/ nie sposób mu dogodzić; **do as you ~** rób, jak uważasz; **my bill, ~** poproszę o rachunek; **~ don't cry!** proszę, nie płacz!; **~ yourself!** *(inf)* rób, jak chcesz! *(inf)*
**pleased** [pli:zd] *adj*: **~ (with/about)** zadowolony (z *+gen*); **~ to meet you** bardzo mi miło; **we are ~ to inform you that ...** miło nam poinformować Pana/Panią, że ...
**pleasing** ['pli:zɪŋ] *adj* przyjemny
**pleasurable** ['plɛʒərəbl] *adj* przyjemny
**pleasure** ['plɛʒəʳ] *n (happiness, satisfaction)* zadowolenie *nt*; *(fun, enjoyable experience)* przyjemność *f*; **it's a ~, my ~** cała przyjemność po mojej stronie; **with ~** z przyjemnością; **to take ~ in** *(activity)* znajdować przyjemność w *+loc*; *(sb's progress, success)* czerpać zadowolenie *or* cieszyć się z *+gen*; **is this trip for business or ~?** czy to podróż służbowa, czy dla przyjemności?
**pleasure boat** *n* statek *f* spacerowy
**pleasure cruise** *n* wycieczka *f* statkiem
**pleat** [pli:t] *n* plisa *f*
**pleb** [plɛb] *(inf, pej) n* prostak(-aczka) *m(f)*; **plebs** *npl* plebs *m*
**plebiscite** ['plɛbɪsɪt] *n* plebiscyt *m*
**plectrum** ['plɛktrəm] *n* kostka *f (do gry na gitarze itp)*
**pledge** [plɛdʒ] *n* przyrzeczenie *nt*, zobowiązanie *nt* ▷ *vt* przyrzekać (przyrzec *perf*); **to ~ sb to secrecy** zobowiązywać (zobowiązać *perf*) kogoś do zachowania tajemnicy
**plenary** ['pli:nərɪ] *adj* plenarny; **~ powers** pełnomocnictwo
**plentiful** ['plɛntɪful] *adj (abundant, copious)* obfity; *(amount)* olbrzymi; **food was ~** jedzenia było w bród
**plenty** ['plɛntɪ] *n*: **~ of** *(food, people)* pełno *or* dużo *+gen*; *(money, jobs, houses)* dużo *+gen*; **there had been ~ going on** bardzo dużo się działo; **we've got ~ of time to get there** mamy dużo czasu (na to), żeby tam dotrzeć; **five should be ~** pięć powinno (w zupełności) wystarczyć
**plethora** ['plɛθərə] *n*: **a ~ of** mrowie *nt +gen*
**pleurisy** ['pluərɪsɪ] *n* zapalenie *nt* opłucnej
**Plexiglas®** ['plɛksɪglɑ:s] *(US) n* pleksiglas *m*
**pliable** ['plaɪəbl] *adj* giętki; *(fig: easily controlled)* uległy; *(: easily influenced)* podatny na wpływy
**pliant** ['plaɪənt] *adj* = **pliable**
**pliers** ['plaɪəz] *npl* szczypce *pl*, kombinerki *pl*
**plight** [plaɪt] *n* ciężkie położenie *nt*
**plimsolls** ['plɪmsəlz] *(Brit) npl* tenisówki *pl*
**plinth** [plɪnθ] *n* cokół *m*, postument *m*
**PLO** *n abbr (= Palestine Liberation Organization)* OWP *nt inv*
**plod** [plɔd] *vi* wlec się (powlec się *perf*); *(fig)* harować
**plodder** ['plɔdəʳ] *(pej) n*: **to be a ~** guzdrać się (z robotą)
**plonk** [plɔŋk] *(inf) n (Brit: wine)* bełt *m (inf)* ▷ *vt*: **he ~ed himself down on the sofa** walnął się na kanapę *(inf)*; **just ~ it down here** rzuć to gdzieś tutaj

P

**plot** [plɔt] *n* (*secret plan*) spisek *m*; (*of story, play, film*) fabuła *f*; (*of land*) działka *f* ▷ *vt* knuć (uknuć *perf*); (*Aviat, Naut*) nanosić (nanieść *perf*) na mapę; (*Math*) nanosić (nanieść *perf*) (*na wykres itp*) ▷ *vi* spiskować; **vegetable ~** (*Brit*) działka (warzywna)
**plotter** ['plɔtəʳ] *n* (*instrument*) koordynatograf *m*; (*Comput*) ploter *m*
**plough**, (*US*) **plow** [plau] *n* pług *m* ▷ *vt* orać (zaorać *perf*); **to ~ money into** wkładać (włożyć *perf*) pieniądze w *+acc*
▸ **plough back** *vt* (*Comm*) reinwestować
▸ **plough into** *vt fus* (*car: crowd*) wjeżdżać (wjechać *perf*) w *+acc*
**ploughman** ['plaumən], (*US*) **plowman** *n* oracz *m*
**ploughman's lunch** ['plaumənz-] (*Brit*) *n* *posiłek składający się z chleba, sera i marynowanych warzyw*
**plow** (*US*) = **plough**
**ploy** [plɔɪ] *n* chwyt *m*, sztuczka *f*
**pluck** [plʌk] *vt* (*fruit, flower, leaf*) zrywać (zerwać *perf*); (*bird*) skubać (oskubać *perf*); (*eyebrows*) wyskubywać (wyskubać *perf*); (*strings*) uderzać (uderzyć *perf*) w *+acc* ▷ *n* odwaga *f*; **to ~ up courage** zbierać się (zebrać się *perf*) na odwagę
**plucky** ['plʌkɪ] (*inf*) *adj* odważny
**plug** [plʌg] *n* (*Elec*) wtyczka *f*; (*in sink, bath*) korek *m*; (*Aut: also:* **spark(ing) plug**) świeca *f* ▷ *vt* zatykać (zatkać *perf*); (*inf*) zachwalać; **to give sb/sth a ~** reklamować (zareklamować *perf*) kogoś/coś
▸ **plug in** *vt* (*Elec*) włączać (włączyć *perf*) (do kontaktu) ▷ *vi*: **where does this ~ in?** gdzie to się włącza?
**plughole** ['plʌghəul] (*Brit*) *n* otwór *m* odpływowy, odpływ *m*
**plug-in** ['plʌgɪn] (*Comput*) *n* wtyczka *f* programowa
**plum** [plʌm] *n* śliwka *f* ▷ *adj* (*inf*): **a ~ job/part** wymarzona praca *f*/rola *f*
**plumage** ['plu:mɪdʒ] *n* (*of bird*) upierzenie *nt*
**plumb** [plʌm] *vt*: **to ~ the depths of bad taste** być skrajnym przykładem złego smaku
▸ **plumb in** *vt* przyłączać (przyłączyć *perf*) do instalacji wodociągowej
**plumber** ['plʌməʳ] *n* hydraulik *m*, instalator *m*
**plumbing** ['plʌmɪŋ] *n* (*piping*) instalacja *f or* sieć *f* wodno-kanalizacyjna; (*trade*) instalatorstwo *nt*
**plumb line** *n* pion *m* (*przyrząd*)
**plume** [plu:m] *n* (*of bird*) pióro *nt*; (*on helmet, horse's head*) pióropusz *m*; **~ of smoke** słup dymu
**plummet** ['plʌmɪt] *vi* (*bird*) spadać (spaść *perf*); (*aircraft*) runąć (*perf*); (*price etc*) gwałtownie zniżkować
**plump** [plʌmp] *adj* pulchny
▸ **plump for** (*inf*) *vt fus* wybierać (wybrać *perf*) *+acc*
▸ **plump up** *vt* (*cushion, pillow*) poprawiać (poprawić *perf*)
**plunder** ['plʌndəʳ] *n* (*activity*) grabież *f*; (*stolen things*) łup *m* ▷ *vt* plądrować (splądrować *perf*)
**plunge** [plʌndʒ] *n* (*of bird*) nurkowanie *nt*; (*of person*) skok *m* (*do morza itp*); (*fig: of prices, rates*) gwałtowny spadek *m* ▷ *vt* (*hand: into pocket*) wkładać (włożyć *perf*); (*knife*) zatapiać (zatopić *perf*) ▷ *vi* (*fall*) wpadać (wpaść *perf*); (*dive: bird*) nurkować (zanurkować *perf*); (*: person*) wskakiwać (wskoczyć *perf*); (*fig: prices, rates*) spadać (spaść *perf*) (gwałtownie); **to take the ~** (*fig*) podejmować (podjąć *perf*) życiową decyzję; **the room was ~d into darkness** pokój ogarnęły ciemności
**plunger** ['plʌndʒəʳ] *n* (*for sink*) przepychacz *m*
**plunging** ['plʌndʒɪŋ] *adj*: **~ neckline** głęboki dekolt *m*
**pluperfect** [plu:'pə:fɪkt] *n*: **the ~** czas *m* zaprzeszły
**plural** ['pluərl] *n* liczba *f* mnoga ▷ *adj* (*number*) mnogi *m*; **the ~ form of the noun** rzeczownik w liczbie mnogiej; **the first person ~** pierwsza osoba liczby mnogiej
**plus** [plʌs] *n* (*lit, fig*) plus *m* ▷ *prep* plus *+nom*; (*Math*): **two ~ three** dwa dodać *or* plus trzy; **ten/twenty ~** ponad dziesięć/dwadzieścia, powyżej dziesięciu/dwudziestu; **B ~** (*Scol*) ≈ dobry plus
**plus fours** *npl rodzaj bryczesów do gry w golfa*
**plush** [plʌʃ] *adj* (*hotel etc*) luksusowy ▷ *n* plusz *m*
**plutonium** [plu:'təunɪəm] *n* (*Chem*) pluton *m*
**ply** [plaɪ] *vt* (*trade*) uprawiać; (*tool*) posługiwać się *+instr* ▷ *vi* (*ship*) kursować ▷ *n* (*of wool, rope*) grubość *f*; (*also:* **plywood**) sklejka *f*; **to ply sb with questions** zasypywać (zasypać *perf*) kogoś pytaniami; **to ply sb with drink** wlewać w kogoś alkohol
**plywood** ['plaɪwud] *n* sklejka *f*
**PM** (*Brit*) *abbr* = **Prime Minister**
**p.m.** *adv abbr* (= *post meridiem*) po południu
**PMT** *abbr* = **premenstrual tension**
**pneumatic** [nju:'mætɪk] *adj* pneumatyczny
**pneumatic drill** *n* młot *m* pneumatyczny
**pneumonia** [nju:'məunɪə] *n* zapalenie *nt* płuc
**PO** *n abbr* = **Post Office**; (*Mil*) = **petty officer**
**p.o.** *abbr* = **postal order**
**POA** (*Brit*) *n abbr* (= *Prison Officers' Association*) *związek zawodowy pracowników więziennictwa*

**poach** [pəutʃ] *vt* (*steal*) kłusować na *+acc*; (*cook: egg*) gotować (ugotować *perf*) bez skorupki; (*: fish etc*) gotować (ugotować *perf*) we wrzątku ▷ *vi* kłusować

**poached** [pəutʃt] *adj* (*egg*) w koszulce *post*; (*fish*) gotowany we wrzątku

**poacher** ['pəutʃəʳ] *n* kłusownik(-iczka) *m(f)*

**PO Box** *n abbr* (= *Post Office Box*) skr. poczt.

**pocket** ['pɔkɪt] *n* kieszeń *f*; (*fig: small area*) ognisko *nt* (*fig*) ▷ *vt* wkładać (włożyć *perf*) do kieszeni; (*steal*) przywłaszczać (przywłaszczyć *perf*) sobie; **to be out of ~** (*Brit*) ponieść (*perf*) stratę

**pocketbook** ['pɔkɪtbuk] *n* (*US: wallet*) portfel *m*; (*notebook*) notes *m* kieszonkowy; (*US: handbag*) kopertówka *f*

**pocket calculator** *n* kalkulator *m* kieszonkowy

**pocket knife** *n* scyzoryk *m*

**pocket money** *n* kieszonkowe *nt*

**pocket-sized** ['pɔkɪtsaɪzd] *adj* kieszonkowy

**pockmarked** ['pɔkmɑːkt] *adj* ospowaty, dziobaty

**pod** [pɔd] *n* strączek *m*

**podcast** ['pɔdkɑːst] *n* (*Comput*) podcast *m*

**podgy** ['pɔdʒɪ] (*inf*) *adj* pękaty, tłusty

**podiatrist** [pɔ'diːətrɪst] (*US*) *n* podiatra *m* (*lekarz leczący choroby stóp*)

**podiatry** [pɔ'diːətrɪ] (*US*) *n* podiatria *f* (*leczenie chorób stóp*)

**podium** ['pəudɪəm] *n* podium *nt*

**POE** *n abbr* (= *port of embarkation*) port *m* załadunku; (= *port of entry*) port *m* przywozowy

**poem** ['pəuɪm] *n* wiersz *m*

**poet** ['pəuɪt] *n* poeta(-tka) *m(f)*

**poetic** [pəu'ɛtɪk] *adj* poetycki; (*fig*) poetyczny

**poetic justice** *n*: **it was ~** sprawiedliwości stało się zadość

**poetic licence** *n* licencja *f* poetycka, licentia *f* poetica

**poet laureate** *n* poeta *m* narodowy

**poetry** ['pəuɪtrɪ] *n* poezja *f*

**poignant** ['pɔɪnjənt] *adj* (*emotion*) przejmujący; (*pain*) dojmujący; (*moment*) wzruszający; (*taste, remark*) cierpki; (*smell*) ostry

**point** [pɔɪnt] *n* (*also Geom*) punkt *m*; (*sharpened tip*) czubek *m*, szpic *m*; (*purpose*) sens *m*; (*significant part*) cecha *f*, istota *f*; (*subject, idea*) kwestia *f*; (*Elec: also*: **power point**) gniazdko *nt*; (*also*: **decimal point**) przecinek *m* ▷ *vt* wskazywać (wskazać *perf*) ▷ *vi* (*with finger etc*) wskazywać (wskazać *perf*); **points** *npl* (*Aut*) styki *pl*; (*Rail*) zwrotnica *f*; **at this ~** w tym momencie; **to ~ at** wskazywać (wskazać *perf*) na *+acc*; **to ~ sth at sb** celować (wycelować *perf*) czymś w kogoś, kierować (skierować *perf*) coś w stronę kogoś; **two ~ five (= 2.5)** dwa przecinek pięć (= 2,5); **good/bad ~s** mocne/słabe punkty; **to be on the ~ of doing sth** mieć właśnie coś zrobić; **to make a ~ of doing sth** dokładać (dołożyć *perf*) starań, aby coś zrobić; **to get the ~** pojmować (pojąć *perf*) istotę sprawy; **to miss the ~** nie dostrzegać (nie dostrzec *perf*) istoty sprawy; **to come/get to the ~** przechodzić (przejść *perf*) do sedna sprawy; **to make one's ~** przedstawiać (przedstawić *perf*) swoje argumenty; **that's the whole ~!** w tym cały problem!; **to be beside the ~** nie mieć nic do rzeczy; **there's no ~ (in doing it)** nie ma sensu (tego robić); **you've got a ~ there!** tu się z tobą zgadzam!; **in ~ of fact** właściwie, w rzeczy samej; **~ of sale** (*Comm*) punkt sprzedaży

▸ **point out** *vt* (*person, object*) wskazywać (wskazać *perf*); (*in debate etc*) wykazywać (wykazać *perf*), zwracać (zwrócić *perf*) uwagę na *+acc*

▸ **point to** *vt fus* wskazywać (wskazać *perf*) na *+acc*

**point-blank** ['pɔɪnt'blæŋk] *adv* (*ask*) wprost, bez ogródek; (*refuse*) kategorycznie; (*also*: **at point-blank range**) z bliska

**point duty** (*Brit*) *n*: **to be on ~** kierować ruchem drogowym

**pointed** ['pɔɪntɪd] *adj* (*chin, nose*) spiczasty; (*stick, pencil*) ostry, zaostrzony; (*fig: remark*) uszczypliwy; (*: look*) znaczący

**pointedly** ['pɔɪntɪdlɪ] *adv* (*remark*) uszczypliwie; (*look*) znacząco

**pointer** ['pɔɪntəʳ] *n* (*on machine, scale*) wskaźnik *m*, strzałka *f*; (*fig: advice*) wskazówka *f*; (*stick*) wskaźnik *m*; (*dog*) pointer *m*

**pointing** ['pɔɪntɪŋ] *n* spoinowanie *nt*

**pointless** ['pɔɪntlɪs] *adj* bezcelowy

**point of view** *n* punkt *m* widzenia; **from a practical ~** z praktycznego punktu widzenia

**poise** [pɔɪz] *n* (*composure*) opanowanie *nt*, pewność *f* siebie; (*balance*) równowaga *f*, postawa *f* ▷ *vt*: **to be ~d for** (*fig*) być gotowym *or* przygotowanym do *+gen*

**poison** ['pɔɪzn] *n* trucizna *f* ▷ *vt* truć (otruć *perf*)

**poisoning** ['pɔɪznɪŋ] *n* zatrucie *nt*

**poisonous** ['pɔɪznəs] *adj* (*substance*) trujący; (*snake*) jadowity; (*fig: rumours*) obrzydliwy

**poison-pen letter** [pɔɪzn'pɛn] *n* obrzydliwy anonim *m*

**poke** [pəuk] *vt* szturchać (szturchnąć *perf*) ▷ *n* szturchnięcie *nt*; **to ~ sth in(to)** wtykać (wetknąć *perf*) coś do *+gen*; **to ~ the fire** grzebać w piecu; **to ~ one's head out of the**

P

**window** wystawiać (wystawić *perf*) głowę przez okno; **to ~ fun at sb** stroić sobie z kogoś żarty
▸ **poke about** *vi* myszkować
▸ **poke out** *vi* wystawać
**poker** ['pəukə[r]] *n* pogrzebacz *m*; (*Cards*) poker *m*
**poker-faced** ['pəukə'feɪst] *adj* z kamienną twarzą *post*
**poky** ['pəukɪ] (*pej*) *adj* (*room etc*) przyciasny (*inf*)
**Poland** ['pəulənd] *n* Polska *f*
**polar** ['pəulə[r]] *adj* polarny
**polar bear** *n* niedźwiedź *m* polarny
**polarize** ['pəuləraɪz] *vt* polaryzować (spolaryzować *perf*)
**Pole** [pəul] *n* Polak(-lka) *m(f)*
**pole** [pəul] *n* (*post*) słup *m*; (*stick*) drąg *m*; (*also*: **flag pole**) maszt *m*; (*Geog, Elec*) biegun *m*; **to be ~s apart** (*fig*) znajdować się na przeciwstawnych biegunach
**pole bean** (*US*) *n* fasola *f* tyczkowa
**polecat** ['pəulkæt] *n* (*Zool*) tchórz *m*
**Pol. Econ.** ['pɔlɪkɔn] *n abbr* (= *political economy*) ekon. polit.
**polemic** [pɔ'lɛmɪk] *n* polemika *f*
**pole star** ['pəulstɑː[r]] *n* Gwiazda *f* Polarna
**pole vault** ['pəulvɔːlt] *n* skok *m* o tyczce
**police** [pə'liːs] *npl* policja *f* ▹ *vt* patrolować; **a large number of ~ were hurt** wielu policjantów odniosło obrażenia
**police car** *n* samochód *m or* radiowóz *m* policyjny
**police constable** (*Brit*) *n* policjant *m* (*szeregowy*)
**police department** (*US*) *n* wydział *m* policji
**police force** *n* policja *f*
**policeman** [pə'liːsmən] (*irreg*: *like* **man**) *n* policjant *m*
**police officer** *n* = **police constable**
**police record** *n*: **to have a ~** być notowanym (w kartotece policyjnej)
**police state** *n* państwo *nt* policyjne
**police station** *n* komisariat *m* policji
**policewoman** [pə'liːswumən] (*irreg*: *like* **woman**) *n* policjantka *f*
**policy** ['pɔlɪsɪ] *n* (*Pol, Econ*) polityka *f*; (*also*: **insurance policy**) polisa *f* ubezpieczeniowa; **to take out a ~** ubezpieczać się (ubezpieczyć się *perf*)
**policy holder** *n* ubezpieczony(-na) *m(f)*, posiadacz(ka) *m(f)* polisy ubezpieczeniowej
**polio** ['pəulɪəu] *n* choroba *f* Heinego-Medina, polio *nt inv*
**Polish** ['pəulɪʃ] *adj* polski ▹ *n* (język *m*) polski
**polish** ['pɔlɪʃ] *n* (*for shoes, floors*) pasta *f*; (*for furniture*) środek *m* do polerowania; (*shine*) połysk *m*; (*fig*) polor *m*, blask *m* ▹ *vt* (*shoes, furniture*) polerować (wypolerować *perf*); (*floor etc*) froterować (wyfroterować *perf*)
▸ **polish off** *vt* (*work*) wygładzać (wygładzić *perf*); (*food*) pałaszować (spałaszować *perf*)
**polished** ['pɔlɪʃt] *adj* (*fig*) wytworny
**polite** [pə'laɪt] *adj* (*person*) uprzejmy, grzeczny; (*company*) kulturalny; **it's not ~ to do that** to niegrzecznie robić coś takiego
**politely** [pə'laɪtlɪ] *adv* uprzejmie, grzecznie
**politeness** [pə'laɪtnɪs] *n* uprzejmość *f*, grzeczność
**politic** ['pɔlɪtɪk] *adj*: **it would be ~ to ...** byłoby rozsądnie *+infin*
**political** [pə'lɪtɪkl] *adj* polityczny; (*person*) rozpolitykowany
**political asylum** *n* azyl *m* polityczny
**politically** [pə'lɪtɪklɪ] *adv* politycznie; **~ correct** politycznie poprawny
**politician** [pɔlɪ'tɪʃən] *n* polityk *m*
**politics** ['pɔlɪtɪks] *n* polityka *f* ▹ *npl* przekonania *pl* polityczne
**polka** ['pɔlkə] *n* polka *f*
**poll** [pəul] *n* (*also*: **opinion poll**) ankieta *f*, badanie *nt* opinii publicznej; (*election*) głosowanie *nt*, wybory *pl* ▹ *vt* (*people*) ankietować; (*votes*) zdobywać (zdobyć *perf*); **to go to the ~s** (*voters*) iść (pójść *perf*) do urn wyborczych; (*government*) stawać (stanąć *perf*) do wyborów
**pollen** ['pɔlən] *n* pyłek *m* kwiatowy
**pollen count** *n* stężenie *nt* pyłków w powietrzu
**pollinate** ['pɔlɪneɪt] *vt* zapylać (zapylić *perf*)
**polling booth** ['pəulɪŋ-] (*Brit*) *n* kabina *f* do głosowania
**polling day** (*Brit*) *n* dzień *m* wyborów
**polling station** (*Brit*) *n* lokal *m* wyborczy
**pollute** [pə'luːt] *vt* zanieczyszczać (zanieczyścić *perf*)
**pollution** [pə'luːʃən] *n* (*contamination*) zanieczyszczenie *nt*; (*substances*) zanieczyszczenia *pl*
**polo** ['pəuləu] *n* polo *nt inv*
**polo neck** *n* golf *m* (*sweter*)
**polo-necked** ['pəuləunɛkt] *adj* z golfem *post*
**poltergeist** ['pɔːltəgaɪst] *n* złośliwy duch *m*
**poly** ['pɔlɪ] (*Brit*) *n abbr* = **polytechnic**
**poly...** ['pɔlɪ] *pref* poli..., wielo...
**polyester** [pɔlɪ'ɛstə[r]] *n* poliester *m*
**polygamy** [pə'lɪgəmɪ] *n* poligamia *f*, wielożeństwo *nt*
**Polynesia** [pɔlɪ'niːzɪə] *n* Polinezja *f*
**Polynesian** [pɔlɪ'niːzɪən] *adj* polinezyjski ▹ *n* Polinezyjczyk(-jka) *m(f)*
**polyp** ['pɔlɪp] (*Med*) *n* polip *m*
**polystyrene** [pɔlɪ'staɪriːn] *n* polistyren *m*
**polytechnic** [pɔlɪ'tɛknɪk] *n* politechnika *f*
**polythene** ['pɔlɪθiːn] *n* polietylen *m*

**polythene bag** *n* torba *f* polietylenowa
**polyurethane** [pɔlɪ'juərɪθeɪn] *n* poliuretan *m*
**pomegranate** ['pɔmɪgrænɪt] *n* granat *m* (*owoc*)
**pommel** ['pɔml] *n* kula *f* (*wzniesiony łęk siodła*) ▷ *vt* (*US*) = **pummel**
**pomp** [pɔmp] *n* pompa *f*, przepych *m*
**pompom** ['pɔmpɔm] *n* pompon *m*
**pompous** ['pɔmpəs] (*pej*) *adj* pompatyczny (*pej*)
**pond** [pɔnd] *n* staw *m*
**ponder** ['pɔndə$^r$] *vt* rozważać ▷ *vi* rozmyślać
**ponderous** ['pɔndərəs] *adj* (*style*) ciężki
**pong** [pɔŋ] (*Brit*: *inf*) *n* smród *m*, fetor *m* (*inf*) ▷ *vi* cuchnąć
**pontiff** ['pɔntɪf] *n*: **the ~** papież *m*
**pontificate** [pɔn'tɪfɪkeɪt] *vi* perorować
**pontoon** [pɔn'tu:n] *n* ponton *m*; (*Cards*) oko *nt*
**pony** ['pəunɪ] *n* kucyk *m*
**ponytail** ['pəunɪteɪl] *n* (*hairstyle*) koński ogon *m*; **she had her hair in a ~** była uczesana w koński ogon
**pony trekking** (*Brit*) *n* wycieczka *f* konna
**poodle** ['pu:dl] *n* pudel *m*
**pooh-pooh** [pu:'pu:] *vt* wyśmiewać (wyśmiać *perf*)
**pool** [pu:l] *n* (*pond*) sadzawka *f*; (*also*: **swimming pool**) basen *m*; (*of light*) krąg *m*; (*of blood etc*) kałuża *f*; (*Sport*) bilard *m*; (*of cash*) wspólny fundusz *m*; (*of labour*) zasoby *pl*, rezerwy *pl*; (*Cards*) pula *f*; (*Comm*) kartel *m* ▷ *vt* (*money*) składać (złożyć *perf*) do wspólnego funduszu; (*knowledge, resources*) tworzyć (stworzyć *perf*) (wspólny) bank *+gen*; **pools** *npl* totalizator *m* sportowy; **typing ~, (US) secretary ~** hala maszyn; **to do the (football) ~s** grać (zagrać *perf*) w totalizatora
**poor** [puə$^r$] *adj* (*not rich*) biedny, ubogi; (*bad*) słaby, kiepski ▷ *npl*: **the ~** biedni *vir pl*; **~ in** ubogi w *+acc*; **~ thing** biedactwo
**poorly** ['puəlɪ] *adj* chory ▷ *adv* słabo, kiepsko
**pop** [pɔp] *n* (*Mus*) pop *m*; (*drink*) napój *m* gazowany *or* musujący; (*US*: *inf*: *father*) tata *m*; (*sound*) huk *m*, trzask *m* ▷ *vi* (*balloon*) pękać (pęknąć *perf*); (*cork*) strzelać (strzelić *perf*); (*eyes*) wychodzić (wyjść *perf*) na wierzch ▷ *vt*: **to pop sth into/onto/on** *etc* wsuwać (wsunąć *perf*) coś do *+gen*/na *+acc*; **she popped her head out of the window** wystawiła głowę przez okno
▸ **pop in** *vi* wpadać (wpaść *perf*)
▸ **pop out** *vi* wyskakiwać (wyskoczyć *perf*)
▸ **pop up** *vi* pojawiać się (pojawić się *perf*)
**popcorn** ['pɔpkɔ:n] *n* prażona kukurydza *f*
**pope** [pəup] *n* papież *m*
**poplar** ['pɔplə$^r$] *n* topola *f*
**poplin** ['pɔplɪn] *n* popelina *f*
**popper** ['pɔpə$^r$] (*Brit*: *inf*) *n* zatrzask *m* (*przy ubraniu, torebce itp*)
**poppy** ['pɔpɪ] *n* mak *m*
**poppycock** ['pɔpɪkɔk] (*inf*) *n* banialuki *pl*
**Popsicle**® ['pɔpsɪkl] (*US*) *n lizak z mrożonej wody z sokiem owocowym*
**pop star** *n* gwiazda *f* muzyki pop
**populace** ['pɔpjuləs] *n*: **the ~** społeczeństwo *nt*
**popular** ['pɔpjulə$^r$] *adj* (*well-liked, fashionable, non-specialist*) popularny; (*general*) powszechny; (*Pol*: *movement, cause*) (ogólno) społeczny; **to be ~ with** cieszyć się popularnością wśród *or* u *+gen*
**popularity** [pɔpju'lærɪtɪ] *n* popularność *f*
**popularize** ['pɔpjuləraɪz] *vt* popularyzować (spopularyzować *perf*)
**popularly** ['pɔpjuləlɪ] *adv* (*believed, held*) powszechnie; (*called, known as*) potocznie
**population** [pɔpju'leɪʃən] *n* (*inhabitants*) ludność *f*; (*number of people*) liczba *f* ludności *or* mieszkańców; (*of species*) populacja *f*; **the civilian ~** ludność cywilna; **a prison ~ of 44,000** 44 tysiące osób przebywających w więzieniach
**population explosion** *n* eksplozja *f* demograficzna
**populous** ['pɔpjuləs] *adj* gęsto zaludniony
**porcelain** ['pɔ:slɪn] *n* porcelana *f*
**porch** [pɔ:tʃ] *n* ganek *m*; (*US*) weranda *f*
**porcupine** ['pɔ:kjupaɪn] *n* jeżozwierz *m*
**pore** [pɔ:$^r$] *n* por *m* ▷ *vi*: **to ~ over** (*book, article*) zagłębiać się w *+acc*; (*map, chart*) studiować *+acc*
**pork** [pɔ:k] *n* wieprzowina *f*
**pork chop** *n* kotlet *m* schabowy
**pornographic** [pɔ:nə'græfɪk] *adj* pornograficzny
**pornography** [pɔ:'nɔgrəfɪ] *n* pornografia *f*
**porous** ['pɔ:rəs] *adj* porowaty
**porpoise** ['pɔ:pəs] *n* morświn *m*
**porridge** ['pɔrɪdʒ] *n* owsianka *f*
**port** [pɔ:t] *n* (*harbour*) port *m*; (*Naut*) lewa burta *f*; (*wine*) porto *nt inv*; (*Comput*) port *m*, gniazdo *nt* wejściowe ▷ *adj* portowy; **to ~** (*Naut*) z lewej; **~ of call** (*Naut*) port zawinięcia *or* pośredni
**portable** ['pɔ:təbl] *adj* przenośny
**portal** ['pɔ:tl] *n* portal *m*
**portcullis** [pɔ:t'kʌlɪs] *n* (spuszczana) krata *f* (*w bramie twierdzy*)
**portend** [pɔ:'tɛnd] *vt* zwiastować
**portent** ['pɔ:tɛnt] *n* zwiastun *m*
**porter** ['pɔ:tə$^r$] *n* (*for luggage*) bagażowy *m*, tragarz *m*; (*doorkeeper*) portier(ka) *m*(*f*); (*US*) *pracownik kolei obsługujący pasażerów w wagonie z miejscówkami lub sypialnym*

P

**portfolio** [pɔːtˈfəulɪəu] *n (for papers, drawings)* teczka *f*; *(Pol)* teka *f*; *(Fin)* portfel *m*
**porthole** [ˈpɔːthəul] *n* luk *m*
**portico** [ˈpɔːtɪkəu] *n* portyk *m*
**portion** [ˈpɔːʃən] *n (part)* część *f*; *(helping)* porcja *f*
**portly** [ˈpɔːtlɪ] *adj* korpulentny
**portrait** [ˈpɔːtreɪt] *n* portret *m*
**portray** [pɔːˈtreɪ] *vt (depict)* przedstawiać (przedstawić *perf*), portretować (sportretować *perf*); *(actor)* odtwarzać (odtworzyć *perf*) rolę *+gen*
**portrayal** [pɔːˈtreɪəl] *n (depiction)* przedstawienie *nt*, portret *m*; *(actor's)* odtworzenie *nt* roli
**Portugal** [ˈpɔːtjugl] *n* Portugalia *f*
**Portuguese** [pɔːtjuˈgiːz] *adj* portugalski ▷ *n inv (person)* Portugalczyk(-lka) *m(f)*; *(Ling)* (język *m*) portugalski
**Portuguese man-of-war** [-mænəvˈwɔːʳ] *n (Zool)* żeglarz *m* portugalski
**pose** [pəuz] *n* poza *f* ▷ *vt (question)* stawiać (postawić *perf*); *(problem, danger)* stanowić ▷ *vi*: **to ~ as** podawać się za *+acc*; **to ~ for** *(painting etc)* pozować do *+gen*; **to strike a ~** przybierać (przybrać *perf*) pozę
**poser** [ˈpəuzəʳ] *n (problem, puzzle)* łamigłówka *f*; *(person)* = **poseur**
**poseur** [pəuˈzəːʳ] *(pej) n* pozer(ka) *m(f) (pej)*
**posh** [pɔʃ] *(inf) adj (smart)* elegancki; *(upper-class)* z wyższych sfer *post*; **to talk ~** *mówić z akcentem charakterystycznym dla wyższych sfer*
**position** [pəˈzɪʃən] *n (place, situation)* położenie *nt*; *(of body, in competition, society)* pozycja *f*; *(job, attitude)* stanowisko *nt* ▷ *vt* umieszczać (umieścić *perf*); **to ~ o.s.** lokować się (ulokować się *perf*); **to be in a ~ to do sth** być w stanie coś (z)robić
**positive** [ˈpɔzɪtɪv] *adj (certain)* pewny; *(hopeful, confident, affirmative)* pozytywny; *(decisive)* stanowczy; *(Math, Elec)* dodatni; **the current flows from ~ to negative** prąd płynie od plusa do minusa
**positively** [ˈpɔzɪtɪvlɪ] *adv (expressing emphasis)* wręcz; *(encouragingly)* pozytywnie; *(definitely)* stanowczo; *(Elec)* dodatnio; **the body has been ~ identified** ciało zostało zidentyfikowane
**posse** [ˈpɔsɪ] *(US) n* oddział *m* pościgowy
**possess** [pəˈzɛs] *vt (have, own)* posiadać; *(obsess)* opętywać (opętać *perf*); **like a man ~ed** jak opętany; **whatever ~ed you to do it?** co cię napadło, żeby to zrobić?
**possession** [pəˈzɛʃən] *n (state of possessing)* posiadanie *nt*; **possessions** *npl* dobytek *m*; **to take ~ of** brać (wziąć *perf*) w posiadanie *+acc*
**possessive** [pəˈzɛsɪv] *adj (of another person)* zaborczy; *(of things)* zazdrosny; *(Ling)* dzierżawczy
**possessiveness** [pəˈzɛsɪvnɪs] *n* zaborczość *f*
**possessor** [pəˈzɛsəʳ] *n* posiadacz(ka) *m(f)*
**possibility** [pɔsɪˈbɪlɪtɪ] *n* możliwość *f*
**possible** [ˈpɔsɪbl] *adj* możliwy; **it's ~** (to jest) możliwe; **it's ~ to do it** to się da zrobić; **as far as ~** na tyle, na ile (to) możliwe, w miarę możliwości; **if ~** jeśli to możliwe; **as soon as ~** (możliwie) jak najszybciej
**possibly** [ˈpɔsɪblɪ] *adv (perhaps)* być może; **what could they ~ want?** czegóż mogą chcieć?; **if you ~ can** jeśli tylko możesz; **he will do everything he ~ can** zrobi wszystko, co tylko możliwe; **I couldn't ~ afford it** w żaden sposób nie mogłabym sobie na to pozwolić
**post** [pəust] *n (Brit)* poczta *f*; *(pole)* słup *m*, pal *m*; *(job)* stanowisko *nt*; *(Mil)* posterunek *m*; *(also*: **trading post**) faktoria *f*; *(also*: **goalpost**) słupek *m* ▷ *vt (Brit: letter)* wysyłać (wysłać *perf*); *(Mil: guards)* wystawiać (wystawić *perf*); **to ~ sb to** oddelegowywać (oddelegować *perf*) kogoś do *+gen*; **by ~** *(Brit)* pocztą; **by return of ~** *(Brit)* odwrotną pocztą; **I'll keep you ~ed** będę cię informować na bieżąco
▸ **post up** *vt* wywieszać (wywiesić *perf*)
**post...** [pəust] *pref* po...
**postage** [ˈpəustɪdʒ] *n* opłata *f* pocztowa
**postage stamp** *n* znaczek *m* pocztowy
**postal** [ˈpəustl] *adj* pocztowy
**postal order** *(Brit) n* przekaz *m* pocztowy
**postbag** [ˈpəustbæg] *(Brit) n* listy *pl*, korespondencja *f*; *(postman's)* torba *f* (listonosza)
**postbox** [ˈpəustbɔks] *(Brit) n* skrzynka *f* pocztowa
**postcard** [ˈpəustkɑːd] *n* pocztówka *f*, widokówka *f*
**postcode** [ˈpəustkəud] *(Brit) n* kod *m* pocztowy
**postdate** [ˈpəustˈdeɪt] *vt* postdatować *(perf)*
**poster** [ˈpəustəʳ] *n* plakat *m*, afisz *m*
**poste restante** [pəustˈrɛstɑ̃ːnt] *(Brit) n* poste restante *nt inv*
**posterior** [pɔsˈtɪərɪəʳ] *(humorous) n* siedzenie *nt*, tyłek *m (inf)*
**posterity** [pɔsˈtɛrɪtɪ] *n* potomność *f*
**poster paint** *n* farba *f* plakatowa
**post exchange** *(US) n sklep na terenie jednostki wojskowej*
**post-free** [pəustˈfriː] *(Brit) adj* wolny od opłaty pocztowej ▷ *adv* bez opłaty pocztowej
**postgraduate** [ˈpəustˈgrædjuət] *n (working for MA etc)* ≈ magistrant(ka) *m(f)*; *(working for PhD etc)* ≈ doktorant(ka) *m(f)*

**posthumous** ['pɔstjuməs] *adj* pośmiertny
**posthumously** ['pɔstjuməslɪ] *adv* pośmiertnie
**posting** ['pəustɪŋ] *n* posada *f* (*na którą jest się oddelegowanym, np. za granicę*)
**postman** ['pəustmən] (*irreg: like* **man**) *n* listonosz *m*
**postmark** ['pəustmɑːk] *n* stempel *m* pocztowy
**postmaster** ['pəustmɑːstəʳ] *n* naczelnik *m* poczty
**Postmaster General** *n* ≈ Minister *m* Łączności
**postmistress** ['pəustmɪstrɪs] *n* naczelniczka *f* poczty
**postmortem** [pəust'mɔːtəm] *n* (*Med*) sekcja *f* zwłok; (*fig*) analiza *f or* badanie *m* (*przyczyn niepowodzenia*)
**postnatal** ['pəust'neɪtl] *adj* poporodowy
**post office** *n* urząd *m* pocztowy; **the Post Office** ≈ Poczta Polska
**Post Office Box** *n* skrytka *f* pocztowa
**post-paid** ['pəust'peɪd] (*US*) *adj, adv* = **post-free**
**postpone** [pəus'pəun] *vt* odraczać (odroczyć *perf*), odkładać (odłożyć *perf*)
**postscript** ['pəustskrɪpt] *n* postscriptum *nt*
**postulate** ['pɔstjuleɪt] *vt* postulować
**posture** ['pɔstʃəʳ] *n* postura *f*, postawa *f*; (*fig*) postawa *f* ▷ *vi* (*pej*) pozować
**postwar** [pəust'wɔːʳ] *adj* powojenny
**posy** ['pəuzɪ] *n* bukiecik *m*
**pot** [pɔt] *n* (*for cooking*) garnek *m*; (*teapot, coffee pot, potful*) dzbanek *m*; (*for jam etc*) słoik *m*; (*flowerpot*) doniczka *f*; (*inf: marijuana*) traw(k)a *f* (*inf*) ▷ *vt* sadzić (posadzić *perf*) w doniczce; **to go to pot** (*inf*) schodzić (zejść *perf*) na psy; **pots of** (*Brit: inf*) kupa *+gen* (*inf*)
**potash** ['pɔtæʃ] *n* potaż *m*
**potassium** [pə'tæsɪəm] *n* potas *m*
**potato** [pə'teɪtəu] (*pl* **~es**) *n* ziemniak *m*
**potato chips** (*US*) *npl* = **potato crisps**
**potato crisps** *npl* chipsy *pl* ziemniaczane
**potato flour** *n* mąka *f* ziemniaczana
**potato peeler** *n* nóż *m* do obierania ziemniaków
**potbellied** ['pɔtbɛlɪd] *adj* (*from overeating*) brzuchaty; (*from malnutrition*) z rozdętym brzuchem *post*
**potency** ['pəutnsɪ] *n* (*sexual*) potencja *f*; (*of drink, drug*) moc *f*
**potent** ['pəutnt] *adj* (*weapon*) potężny; (*argument*) przekonujący; (*drink*) mocny; (*man*) sprawny seksualnie
**potentate** ['pəutnteɪt] *n* potentat(ka) *m(f)*
**potential** [pə'tɛnʃl] *adj* potencjalny ▷ *n* (*talent, ability*) potencjał *m*; (*promise, possibilities*) zadatki *pl*; **has she got executive ~?** czy ma zdolności kierownicze?; **many children do not achieve their full ~** wiele dzieci nie osiąga pełni swoich możliwości
**potentially** [pə'tɛnʃəlɪ] *adv* potencjalnie; **it's ~ dangerous** to jest potencjalnie niebezpieczne
**pothole** ['pɔthəul] *n* (*in road*) wybój *m*; (*cave*) jaskinia *f*
**potholing** ['pɔthəulɪŋ] *n*: **to go ~** chodzić po jaskiniach
**potion** ['pəuʃən] *n* (*medicine*) płynny lek *m*; (*poison*) trujący napój *m*; (*charm*) napój *m* magiczny, eliksir *m*
**potluck** [pɔt'lʌk] *n*: **to take ~** zadowalać się (zadowolić się *perf*) tym, co jest
**potpourri** [pəu'puriː] *n aromatyczna mieszanka suszonych płatków kwiatów, liści i ziół*; (*fig*) mieszanina *f*, zbieranina *f*
**pot roast** *n* duszone mięso *nt*
**pot shot** *n*: **to take a ~ at** strzelać (strzelić *perf*) na chybił trafił do *+gen*
**potted** ['pɔtɪd] *adj* (*food*) wekowany; (*plant*) doniczkowy; (*history, biography*) skrócony
**potter** ['pɔtəʳ] *n* garncarz(-arka) *m(f)* ▷ *vi*: **to ~ around, ~ about** (*Brit*) pałętać się; **to ~ around the house** kręcić się po domu
**potter's wheel** *n* koło *nt* garncarskie
**pottery** ['pɔtərɪ] *n* (*pots, dishes*) wyroby *pl* garncarskie; (*work, hobby*) garncarstwo *nt*; (*factory, workshop*) garncarnia *f*; **a piece of ~** naczynie gliniane
**potty** ['pɔtɪ] *adj* (*inf*) stuknięty (*inf*) ▷ *n* nocniczek *m*
**potty-training** ['pɔtɪtreɪnɪŋ] *n przyzwyczajanie dziecka do korzystania z nocniczka*
**pouch** [pautʃ] *n* (*for tobacco*) kapciuch *m*; (*for coins*) sakiewka *f*; (*Zool*) torba *f*
**pouf(fe)** [puːf] *n* puf *m*
**poultice** ['pəultɪs] *n* gorący okład *m*
**poultry** ['pəultrɪ] *n* drób *m*
**poultry farm** *n* ferma *f* drobiarska
**poultry farmer** *n* hodowca *m* drobiu
**pounce** [pauns] *vi*: **to ~ on** rzucać się (rzucić się *perf*) na *+acc*; (*fig: mistakes*) wytykać (wytknąć *perf*) *+acc*
**pound** [paund] *n* (*unit of money, weight*) funt *m*; (*for cars*) *miejsce odholowywania nieprawidłowo zaparkowanych samochodów*; (*for dogs etc*) *schronisko, w którym zwierzęta są przechowywane przez określony czas, a następnie usypiane, jeśli nie znajdą właściciela* ▷ *vt* (*beat*) walić w *+acc*; (*crush*) tłuc (utłuc *perf*); (*with guns*) ostrzeliwać (ostrzelać *perf*) ▷ *vi* (*heart*) walić; **half a ~ of** pół funta *+gen*; **a five-~ note** banknot pięciofuntowy; **my head is ~ing** w głowie mi huczy

P

**pounding** ['paundɪŋ] *n*: **to take a ~** *(fig)* dostawać (dostać *perf*) lanie
**pound sterling** *n* funt *m* szterling
**pour** [pɔːʳ] *vt* lać, nalewać (nalać *perf*) ▷ *vi* *(water, blood, sweat)* lać się; *(rain)* lać; **to ~ sb some tea** nalewać (nalać *perf*) komuś herbaty; **it is ~ing with rain** leje jak z cebra
▸ **pour away** *vt* wylewać (wylać *perf*)
▸ **pour in** *vi* *(people, crowd)* wlewać się; *(letters)* (masowo) napływać
▸ **pour out** *vi* *(people, crowd)* wylewać się ▷ *vt* nalewać (nalać *perf*); *(fig: thoughts, feelings)* wylewać (wylać *perf*) z siebie
**pouring** ['pɔːrɪŋ] *adj*: **~ rain** ulewny deszcz *m*
**pout** [paut] *vi* wydymać (wydąć *perf*) wargi
**poverty** ['pɔvətɪ] *n* bieda *f*, ubóstwo *nt*
**poverty-stricken** ['pɔvətɪstrɪkn] *adj* dotknięty biedą *or* ubóstwem
**poverty trap** *(Brit)* *n* zamknięte *or* zaklęte koło *nt* ubóstwa
**POW** *n abbr* = **prisoner of war**
**powder** ['paudəʳ] *n* *(granules)* proszek *m*; *(face powder)* puder *m* (kosmetyczny) ▷ *vt*: **to ~ one's face** pudrować (upudrować *perf or* przypudrować *perf*) twarz; **I must ~ my nose** *(euphemism)* ≈ muszę umyć ręce
**powder compact** *n* puderniczka *f*
**powdered milk** ['paudəd-] *n* mleko *nt* w proszku
**powder puff** *n* puszek *m* do pudru
**powder room** *(euphemism)* *n* damska toaleta *f*
**power** ['pauəʳ] *n* *(control)* władza *f*; *(ability: of speech etc)* zdolność *f*; *(legal right)* uprawnienie *nt*; *(of engine, electricity)* moc *f*; *(strength: lit, fig)* siła *f*; **two to the ~ of three** dwa do potęgi trzeciej; **she did everything in her ~ to help** zrobiła wszystko, co było w jej mocy, by pomóc; **a world ~** światowe mocarstwo; **the ~s that be** ci na górze *(inf)*; **to be in ~** być u władzy; **to turn the ~ on** włączać (włączyć *perf*) zasilanie
**powerboat** ['pauəbəut] *n* szybka łódź *f* motorowa
**power cut** *n* przerwa *f* w dopływie energii elektrycznej
**powered** ['pauəd] *adj*: **~ by** napędzany *+instr*; **nuclear-~ submarine** atomowa łódź podwodna
**power failure** *n* przerwa *f* w dopływie energii elektrycznej
**powerful** ['pauəful] *adj* *(strong)* mocny, silny; *(influential)* wpływowy; *(ruler)* potężny
**powerhouse** ['pauəhaus] *n*: **to be a ~ of ideas** być niewyczerpanym w pomysłach
**powerless** ['pauəlɪs] *adj* bezsilny; **to be ~ to do sth** nie być w stanie czegoś zrobić
**power line** *n* linia *f* elektroenergetyczna
**power point** *(Brit)* *n* gniazdo *nt* sieciowe
**power station** *n* elektrownia *f*
**power steering** *n* *(Aut)* kierowanie *nt* ze wspomaganiem
**powwow** ['pauwau] *n* narada *f*
**pp** *abbr* (= *per procurationem*) z up., w/z
**pp.** *abbr* (= *pages*) s.
**PPE** *(Brit: Univ)* *n abbr* = **philosophy, politics and economics**
**PPS** *n abbr* (= *post postscriptum*) PPS; *(Brit: = parliamentary private secretary) poseł-pomocnik ministra*
**PQ** *(Canada)* *abbr* = **Province of Quebec**
**PR** *n abbr* = **public relations**; *(Pol)* = **proportional representation** ▷ *abbr* *(US: Post)* = **Puerto Rico**
**Pr.** *abbr* (= *prince*) ks.
**practicability** [præktɪkə'bɪlɪtɪ] *n* wykonalność *f*; *(of legislation etc)* możliwość *f* wprowadzenia w życie
**practicable** ['præktɪkəbl] *adj* wykonalny; **as far as is ~** w takim stopniu, w jakim jest to możliwe
**practical** ['præktɪkl] *adj* praktyczny; *(good with hands)* sprawny manualnie; *(ideas, methods)* możliwy (do zastosowania) w praktyce
**practicality** [præktɪ'kælɪtɪ] *n* praktyczność *f*; **practicalities** *npl* strona *f* praktyczna
**practical joke** *n* psikus *m*, figiel *m*
**practically** ['præktɪklɪ] *adv* praktycznie
**practice** ['præktɪs] *n* praktyka *f*; *(custom)* zwyczaj *m*; *(exercise, training)* wprawa *f* ▷ *vt, vi* *(US)* = **practise**; **in ~** w praktyce; **I am out of ~** wyszedłem z wprawy; **2 hours' piano ~** dwugodzinne ćwiczenie gry na pianinie; **it's common** *or* **standard ~** (jest) to powszechna *or* typowa praktyka; **to put sth into ~** stosować (zastosować *perf*) coś w praktyce; **target ~** ćwiczenia na strzelnicy
**practice match** *(Sport)* *n* spotkanie *nt* kontrolne
**practise**, *(US)* **practice** ['præktɪs] *vt* ćwiczyć; *(Sport)* trenować; *(custom, activity)* praktykować; *(profession)* wykonywać ▷ *vi* ćwiczyć; *(sportsman)* trenować; *(lawyer, doctor)* praktykować, prowadzić praktykę
**practised** ['præktɪst] *(Brit)* *adj* *(person)* doświadczony; *(performance)* przećwiczony, wyćwiczony; **with a ~ eye** wprawnym okiem
**practising** ['præktɪsɪŋ] *adj* *(Christian, lawyer)* praktykujący; *(homosexual)* aktywny
**practitioner** [præk'tɪʃənəʳ] *n*: **medical ~** terapeuta(-tka) *m(f)*
**pragmatic** [præg'mætɪk] *adj* pragmatyczny
**pragmatism** ['prægmətɪzəm] *n* pragmatyzm *m*

**Prague** [prɑ:g] *n* Praga *f*
**prairie** ['prɛərɪ] *n* preria *f*; **the ~s** (*US*) preria
**praise** [preɪz] *n* pochwała *f* ▷ *vt* chwalić (pochwalić *perf*); (*Rel*) chwalić
**praiseworthy** ['preɪzwə:ðɪ] *adj* (*behaviour*) godny pochwały; (*attempt*) chwalebny
**pram** [præm] (*Brit*) *n* wózek *m* dziecięcy
**prance** [prɑ:ns] *vi* (*horse*) tańczyć; **to ~ along/ up and down/about** (*person*) paradować
**prank** [præŋk] *n* psikus *m*
**prattle** ['prætl] *vi* paplać
**prawn** [prɔ:n] *n* krewetka *f*; **~ cocktail** koktajl z krewetek
**pray** [preɪ] *vi* modlić się (pomodlić się *perf*); **to ~ for/that** (*Rel*) modlić się (pomodlić się *perf*) o *+acc*/, żeby; (*fig*) błagać o *+acc*/, żeby
**prayer** [prɛə^r] *n* modlitwa *f*; **to say one's ~s** modlić się (pomodlić się *perf*)
**prayer book** *n* modlitewnik *m*
**pre...** ['pri:] *pref* pre..., przed...; **~70** sprzed 1970 roku
**preach** [pri:tʃ] *vi* wygłaszać (wygłosić *perf*) kazanie ▷ *vt* (*sermon*) wygłaszać (wygłosić *perf*); (*ideology etc*) propagować; **to ~ (at sb)** (*fig*) prawić (komuś) kazanie; **to ~ to the converted** (*fig*) nawracać nawróconych; **don't ~!** nie truj! (*inf*)
**preacher** ['pri:tʃə^r] *n* kaznodzieja *m*
**preamble** [prɪ'æmbl] *n* wstęp *m*; (*in document*) preambuła *f* (*fml*)
**prearranged** [pri:ə'reɪndʒd] *adj* umówiony
**precarious** [prɪ'kɛərɪəs] *adj* niebezpieczny; (*position*) niepewny
**precaution** [prɪ'kɔ:ʃən] *n* zabezpieczenie *nt*; **to take ~s** przedsiębrać (przedsięwziąć *perf*) środki ostrożności
**precautionary** [prɪ'kɔ:ʃənrɪ] *adj*: **~ measure** środek *m* ostrożności
**precede** [prɪ'si:d] *vt* (*event, words*) poprzedzać (poprzedzić *perf*); (*person*) iść przed *+instr*; **she ~d us, we were ~d by her** szła przed nami
**precedence** ['prɛsɪdəns] *n* pierwszeństwo *nt*; **to take ~ over** mieć pierwszeństwo przed *+instr*
**precedent** ['prɛsɪdənt] *n* precedens *m*; **to establish** *or* **set a ~** ustanawiać (ustanowić *perf*) *or* stwarzać (stworzyć *perf*) precedens
**preceding** [prɪ'si:dɪŋ] *adj* poprzedni
**precept** ['pri:sɛpt] *n* zasada *f*
**precinct** ['pri:sɪŋkt] *n* (*US*) dzielnica *f*; **precincts** *npl* (*of cathedral, palace*) teren *m*; **pedestrian ~** (*Brit*) strefa ruchu pieszego; **shopping ~** (*Brit*) centrum handlowe (*zamknięte dla ruchu samochodowego*)
**precious** ['prɛʃəs] *adj* cenny; (*pej*) afektowany; (*ironic*): **your ~ brother** twój kochany braciszek ▷ *adv* (*inf*): **~ little/few** bardzo niewiele/niewielu
**precious stone** *n* kamień *m* szlachetny
**precipice** ['prɛsɪpɪs] *n* urwisko *nt*, przepaść *f*; (*fig*): **at the edge of an economic ~** na skraju katastrofy ekonomicznej
**precipitate** [*vb* prɪ'sɪpɪteɪt, *adj* prɪ'sɪpɪtɪt] *vt* przyśpieszać (przyśpieszyć *perf*) ▷ *adj* pośpieszny
**precipitation** [prɪsɪpɪ'teɪʃən] *n* opad *m* atmosferyczny
**precipitous** [prɪ'sɪpɪtəs] *adj* (*steep*) urwisty; (*hasty*) pośpieszny
**précis** ['preɪsi:] *n inv* streszczenie *nt*
**precise** [prɪ'saɪs] *adj* (*nature, position*) dokładny; (*instructions, definition*) precyzyjny, dokładny; **to be ~** ściśle(j) mówiąc
**precisely** [prɪ'saɪslɪ] *adv* dokładnie; **~!** (no) właśnie!, dokładnie!
**precision** [prɪ'sɪʒən] *n* precyzja *f*, dokładność *f*
**preclude** [prɪ'klu:d] *vt* wykluczać (wykluczyć *perf*); **to ~ sb from doing sth** uniemożliwiać (uniemożliwić *perf*) komuś (z)robienie czegoś
**precocious** [prɪ'kəuʃəs] *adj* (*child*) rozwinięty nad wiek; (*talent*) wcześnie rozwinięty
**preconceived** [pri:kən'si:vd] *adj* z góry przyjęty *or* założony
**preconception** ['pri:kən'sɛpʃən] *n* z góry przyjęta opinia *f*; (*negative*) uprzedzenie *nt*
**precondition** ['pri:kən'dɪʃən] *n* warunek *m* wstępny
**precursor** [pri:'kə:sə^r] *n* prekursor *m*
**predate** ['pri:'deɪt] *vt* poprzedzać (poprzedzić *perf*), być wcześniejszym od *+gen*
**predator** ['prɛdətə^r] *n* drapieżnik *m*; (*fig*) sęp *m*
**predatory** ['prɛdətərɪ] *adj* drapieżny
**predecessor** ['pri:dɪsɛsə^r] *n* poprzednik(-iczka) *m(f)*
**predestination** [pri:dɛstɪ'neɪʃən] *n* predestynacja *f*
**predetermine** [pri:dɪ'tə:mɪn] *vt* ustalać (ustalić *perf*) z góry
**predicament** [prɪ'dɪkəmənt] *n* kłopotliwe położenie *nt*
**predicate** ['prɛdɪkɪt] *n* (*Ling*) orzeczenie *nt*
**predict** [prɪ'dɪkt] *vt* przewidywać (przewidzieć *perf*)
**predictable** [prɪ'dɪktəbl] *adj* przewidywalny, do przewidzenia *post*
**predictably** [prɪ'dɪktəblɪ] *adv* w sposób możliwy do przewidzenia; **~ she didn't arrive** jak można było przewidzieć, nie przyjechała
**prediction** [prɪ'dɪkʃən] *n* przewidywanie *nt*
**predispose** ['pri:dɪs'pəuz] *vt* usposabiać (usposobić *perf*)

P

**predominance** [prɪˈdɔmɪnəns] *n* przewaga *f*
**predominant** [prɪˈdɔmɪnənt] *adj* dominujący; **to become ~** zaczynać (zacząć *perf*) dominować
**predominantly** [prɪˈdɔmɪnəntlɪ] *adv* w przeważającej mierze *or* części, przeważnie
**predominate** [prɪˈdɔmɪneɪt] *vi* przeważać
**pre-eminent** [pri:ˈɛmɪnənt] *adj* wyróżniający się
**pre-empt** [pri:ˈɛmt] *vt* (*plan*) udaremniać (udaremnić *perf*); (*decision*) uprzedzać (uprzedzić *perf*)
**pre-emptive** [pri:ˈɛmtɪv] *adj*: **~ strike** uderzenie *nt* wyprzedzające
**preen** [pri:n] *vt*: **to ~ o.s.** (*bird*) muskać się; (*person*) stroić się
**prefab** [ˈpri:fæb] *n* dom *m* z prefabrykatów
**prefabricated** [pri:ˈfæbrɪkeɪtɪd] *adj* prefabrykowany
**preface** [ˈprɛfəs] *n* przedmowa *f* ▷ *vt*: **to ~ with/by** poprzedzać (poprzedzić *perf*) *+instr*
**prefect** [ˈpri:fɛkt] (*Brit*) *n starszy uczeń pomagający nauczycielowi w utrzymaniu porządku*
**prefer** [prɪˈfə:ʳ] *vt* woleć, preferować (*fml*); **to ~ charges** (*Jur*) stawiać (postawić *perf*) zarzut; **to ~ doing sth** *or* **to do sth** woleć coś robić; **I ~ coffee to tea** wolę kawę od herbaty
**preferable** [ˈprɛfrəbl] *adj* bardziej pożądany
**preferably** [ˈprɛfrəblɪ] *adv* najlepiej
**preference** [ˈprɛfrəns] *n* preferencja *f*; **to have a ~ for** woleć *or* preferować *+acc*; **in ~ to sth** zamiast czegoś; **to give ~ to** dawać (dać *perf*) preferencje *+dat*; **by ~** z wyboru
**preference shares** (*Brit*) *npl* akcje *pl* uprzywilejowane
**preferential** [prɛfəˈrɛnʃəl] *adj*: **~ treatment** traktowanie *nt* preferencyjne
**preferred stock** [prɪˈfəd-] (*US*) *npl* = **preference shares**
**prefix** [ˈpri:fɪks] *n* przedrostek *m*
**pregnancy** [ˈprɛgnənsɪ] *n* ciąża *f*
**pregnancy test** *n* test *m* ciążowy
**pregnant** [ˈprɛgnənt] *adj* w ciąży *post*, ciężarny; (*pause etc*) znaczący; **~ with** (*fig*) nabrzmiały *+instr*; **three months ~** w trzecim miesiącu ciąży
**prehistoric** [ˈpri:hɪsˈtɔrɪk] *adj* prehistoryczny
**prehistory** [pri:ˈhɪstərɪ] *n* prehistoria *f*
**prejudge** [pri:ˈdʒʌdʒ] *vt* przedwcześnie osądzać (osądzić *perf*)
**prejudice** [ˈprɛdʒudɪs] *n* (*against*) uprzedzenie *nt*; (*in favour*) przychylne nastawienie *nt* ▷ *vt* (*sb's chances*) pogarszać (pogorszyć *perf*); **without ~ to** (*fml*) bez szkody dla *+gen*; **to ~ sb in favour of** nastawiać (nastawiać *perf*) kogoś przychylnie do *+gen*; **to ~ sb against** uprzedzać (uprzedzić *perf*) kogoś do *+gen*
**prejudiced** [ˈprɛdʒudɪst] *adj* (*person*: *against*) uprzedzony; (: *in favour*) przychylnie nastawiony; (*view*) stronniczy
**prelate** [ˈprɛlət] *n* prałat *m*
**preliminaries** [prɪˈlɪmɪnərɪz] *npl* wstęp *m*
**preliminary** [prɪˈlɪmɪnərɪ] *adj* wstępny
**prelude** [ˈprɛlju:d] *n* preludium *nt*; **a ~ to** (*fig*) przygrywka do *+gen*
**premarital** [ˈpri:ˈmærɪtl] *adj* przedmałżeński
**premature** [ˈprɛmətʃuəʳ] *adj* przedwczesny; **you are being a little ~** działasz nieco zbyt pochopnie; **~ baby** wcześniak
**premeditated** [pri:ˈmɛdɪteɪtɪd] *adj* (*act*) przemyślany; (*crime*) z premedytacją *post*
**premeditation** [pri:mɛdɪˈteɪʃən] *n* premedytacja *f*
**premenstrual tension** [pri:ˈmɛnstruəl-] *n* napięcie *nt* przedmiesiączkowe
**premier** [ˈprɛmɪəʳ] *adj* główny ▷ *n* premier *m*
**première** [ˈprɛmɪɛəʳ] *n* premiera *f*
**premise** [ˈprɛmɪs] *n* (*of argument*) przesłanka *f*; **premises** *npl* teren *m*, siedziba *f*; **on the ~s** na miejscu
**premium** [ˈpri:mɪəm] *n* (*extra money*) premia *f*; (*Insurance*) składka *f* ubezpieczeniowa; **at a ~** (*expensive*) sprzedawany po wyższej cenie; (*hard to get*) poszukiwany
**premium bond** (*Brit*) *n* obligacja *f* pożyczki premiowej
**premium deal** *n* oferta *f* specjalna
**premium gasoline** (*US*) *n* etylina *f* super
**premonition** [prɛməˈnɪʃən] *n* przeczucie *nt*
**preoccupation** [pri:ɔkjuˈpeɪʃən] *n*: **~ with** zaabsorbowanie *nt* *+instr*
**preoccupied** [pri:ˈɔkjupaɪd] *adj* zaabsorbowany
**prep** [prɛp] (*Brit*: *Scol*) *adj abbr*: **~ school** (= *preparatory school*) *prywatna szkoła podstawowa* ▷ *n abbr* (= *preparation*) przygotowanie *nt*
**prepaid** [pri:ˈpeɪd] *adj* opłacony; **pre-paid envelope** koperta zwrotna (*ze znaczkiem*)
**preparation** [prɛpəˈreɪʃən] *n* (*activity*) przygotowanie *nt*; (*medicine, cosmetic*) preparat *m*; (*food*) przetwór *m*; **preparations** *npl* przygotowania *pl*; **in ~ for sth** w przygotowaniu na *+acc*
**preparatory** [prɪˈpærətərɪ] *adj* przygotowawczy; **~ to sth/to doing sth** przed *+instr*
**preparatory school** *n* (*Brit*) *prywatna szkoła podstawowa*; (*US*) *prywatna szkoła średnia przygotowująca do studiów wyższych*
**prepare** [prɪˈpɛəʳ] *vt* przygotowywać (przygotować *perf*) ▷ *vi*: **to ~ for** (*action, exam*) przygotowywać się (przygotować się *perf*) do *+gen*; (*sth new or unpleasant*) przygotowywać się (przygotować się *perf*) na *+acc*

**prepared** [prɪ'pɛəd] *adj*: **~ to** gotowy *+infin*; **~ for** *(action, exam)* przygotowany do *+gen*; *(sth new or unpleasant)* przygotowany na *+acc*
**preponderance** [prɪ'pɔndərns] *n* przewaga *f*
**preposition** [prɛpə'zɪʃən] *n* przyimek *m*
**prepossessing** [pri:pə'zɛsɪŋ] *adj* ujmujący
**preposterous** [prɪ'pɔstərəs] *adj* niedorzeczny
**prep school** *n* = **preparatory school**
**prerecorded** ['pri:rɪ'kɔ:dɪd] *adj (broadcast)* nagrany wcześniej; *(cassette)* nagrany
**prerequisite** [pri:'rɛkwɪzɪt] *n* warunek *m* wstępny
**prerogative** [prɪ'rɔgətɪv] *n* przywilej *m*, prerogatywa *f (fml)*
**Presbyterian** [prɛzbɪ'tɪərɪən] *adj* prezbiteriański ▷ *n* prezbiterianin(-anka) *m(f)*
**presbytery** ['prɛzbɪtərɪ] *n* prezbiterium *nt*
**preschool** ['pri:'sku:l] *adj (age)* przedszkolny; *(child)* w wieku przedszkolnym *post*
**prescribe** [prɪ'skraɪb] *vt (Med)* przepisywać (przepisać *perf*); *(demand)* nakazywać (nakazać *perf*)
**prescribed** [prɪ'skraɪbd] *adj* nakazany
**prescription** [prɪ'skrɪpʃən] *n (slip of paper)* recepta *f*; *(medicine)* przepisane lekarstwo *nt*; **to make up** *or (US)* **fill a ~** realizować (zrealizować *perf*) receptę; **"only available on ~"** „wydaje się z przepisu lekarza"
**prescription charges** *(Brit) npl* opłata *f* za realizację recepty
**prescriptive** [prɪ'skrɪptɪv] *adj (system)* nakazowy; *(Ling)* preskryptywny
**presence** ['prɛzns] *n (being somewhere)* obecność *f*; *(personality)* prezencja *f*; *(spirit)* istota *f*; **in sb's ~** w czyjejś obecności
**presence of mind** *n* przytomność *f* umysłu
**present** ['prɛznt] *adj* obecny ▷ *n (gift)* prezent *m*; *(Ling: also:* **present tense***)* czas *m* teraźniejszy; *(actuality)*: **the ~** teraźniejszość *f* ▷ *vt (prize)* wręczać (wręczyć *perf*); *(difficulty, threat)* stanowić; *(person, information)* przedstawiać (przedstawić *perf*); *(radio/tv programme)* prowadzić (poprowadzić *perf*); **to ~ sth to sb, to ~ sb with sth** wręczać (wręczyć *perf*) coś komuś; **to ~ sb to** przedstawiać (przedstawić *perf*) kogoś *+dat*; **to give sb a ~** dawać (dać *perf*) komuś prezent; **to be ~ at** być obecnym na *+loc*; **those ~** obecni; **if an opportunity ~ed itself** gdyby nadarzyła się okazja; **at ~** obecnie
**presentable** [prɪ'zɛntəbl] *adj (person)* o dobrej prezencji *post*; **to be/look ~** dobrze się prezentować
**presentation** [prɛzn'teɪʃən] *n (of plan etc)* przedstawienie *nt*, prezentacja *f*; *(appearance)* wygląd *m*; *(lecture)* wystąpienie *nt*; **on ~ of** za okazaniem *+gen*
**present-day** ['prɛzntdeɪ] *adj* dzisiejszy, współczesny
**presenter** [prɪ'zɛntə[r]] *n* prezenter(ka) *m(f)*
**presently** ['prɛzntlɪ] *adv (soon, soon after)* wkrótce; *(currently)* obecnie
**present participle** *n* imiesłów *m* czynny
**preservation** [prɛzə'veɪʃən] *n (of peace)* zachowanie *nt*; *(of standards)* utrzymanie *nt*
**preservative** [prɪ'zə:vətɪv] *n (for food)* konserwant *m*; *(for wood, metal)* środek *m* konserwujący
**preserve** [prɪ'zə:v] *vt (customs, independence etc)* zachowywać (zachować *perf*); *(building, manuscript, food)* konserwować (zakonserwować *perf*) ▷ *n (often pl: jam etc)* zaprawy *pl*; *(for game, fish)* rezerwat *m*; **a male/ working class ~** *(fig)* dziedzina zdominowana przez mężczyzn/klasę robotniczą
**preshrunk** ['pri:'ʃrʌŋk] *adj (jeans etc)* zdekatyzowany
**preside** [prɪ'zaɪd] *vi*: **to ~ over** *(meeting)* przewodniczyć *+dat*; *(event)* kierować (pokierować *perf*) *+instr*
**presidency** ['prɛzɪdənsɪ] *n (Pol: position)* urząd *m* prezydenta; *(: function, period of time)* prezydentura *f*; *(US: of company)* prezesura *f*
**president** ['prɛzɪdənt] *n (Pol)* prezydent *m*; *(of organization)* prezes *m*, przewodniczący(ca) *m(f)*
**presidential** [prɛzɪ'dɛnʃl] *adj (election, campaign)* prezydencki; **~ adviser/ representative** doradca/przedstawiciel prezydenta; **~ candidate** kandydat na prezydenta
**press** [prɛs] *n (also:* **printing press***)* prasa *f* (drukarska); *(of switch, bell)* naciśnięcie *nt*; *(for wine)* prasa *f* ▷ *vt (one thing against another)* przyciskać (przycisnąć *perf*); *(button, switch)* naciskać (nacisnąć *perf*); *(clothes)* prasować (wyprasować *perf*); *(person)* naciskać (nacisnąć *perf*) (na *+acc*); *(idea, demand)* forsować (przeforsować *perf*); *(squeeze)* ściskać (ścisnąć *perf*) ▷ *vi* przeciskać się (przecisnąć się *perf*); **the P~** prasa; **to ~ sth (up)on sb** wciskać (wcisnąć *perf*) coś komuś; **to ~ for** domagać się *+gen*; **we are ~ed for time/ money** mamy mało czasu/pieniędzy; **to ~ sb for an answer** żądać (zażądać *perf*) od kogoś odpowiedzi; **to ~ sb to do** *or* **into doing sth** *(urge)* zmuszać (zmusić *perf*) kogoś do zrobienia czegoś; **to ~ charges (against sb)** wnosić (wnieść *perf*) oskarżenie (przeciwko komuś); **to go to ~** iść (pójść *perf*) do druku; **to be in ~** być w druku; **to be in the ~** być w gazetach
▶ **press on** *vi* nie ustawać w wysiłkach

P

**press agency** *n* agencja *f* prasowa
**press clipping** *n* wycinek *m* prasowy
**press conference** *n* konferencja *f* prasowa
**press cutting** *n* = **press clipping**
**press-gang** ['prɛsgæŋ] *vt*: **to ~ sb into doing sth** zmuszać (zmusić *perf*) kogoś do zrobienia czegoś
**pressing** ['prɛsɪŋ] *adj* pilny, nie cierpiący zwłoki
**press release** *n* oświadczenie *nt* prasowe
**press stud** (*Brit*) *n* zatrzask *m*
**press-up** ['prɛsʌp] (*Brit*) *n* pompka *f* (*ćwiczenie*)
**pressure** ['prɛʃə^r] *n* (*physical force*) nacisk *m*, ucisk *m*; (*of air, water*) ciśnienie *nt*; (*fig: demand*) naciski *pl*; (*: stress*) napięcie *nt* ▷ *vt*: **to ~ sb (to do sth)** zmuszać (zmusić *perf*) kogoś (do zrobienia czegoś); **to put ~ on sb (to do sth)** wywierać (wywrzeć *perf*) presję na kogoś (, by coś zrobił); **high/low ~** wysokie/niskie ciśnienie
**pressure cooker** *n* szybkowar *m*
**pressure gauge** *n* ciśnieniomierz *m*
**pressure group** *n* grupa *f* nacisku
**pressurize** ['prɛʃəraɪz] *vt*: **to ~ sb (to do/into doing sth)** wywierać (wywrzeć *perf*) nacisk(i) na kogoś (, by coś zrobił)
**pressurized** ['prɛʃəraɪzd] *adj* ciśnieniowy
**prestige** [prɛs'tiːʒ] *n* prestiż *m*
**prestigious** [prɛs'tɪdʒəs] *adj* prestiżowy
**presumably** [prɪ'zjuːməblɪ] *adv* przypuszczalnie; **~ he did it** prawdopodobnie to zrobił
**presume** [prɪ'zjuːm] *vt*: **to ~ that ...** przyjmować (przyjąć *perf*), że ...; **to ~ to** odważać się (odważyć się *perf*) *+infin*; **I ~ so** tak przypuszczam, przypuszczam, że tak
**presumption** [prɪ'zʌmpʃən] *n* (*supposition*) założenie *nt*, domniemanie *nt*; (*audacity*) arogancja *f*
**presumptuous** [prɪ'zʌmpʃəs] *adj* arogancki
**presuppose** [priːsə'pəuz] *vt* zakładać
**presupposition** [priːsʌpə'zɪʃən] *n* założenie *nt*, presupozycja *f* (*fml*)
**pre-tax** [priː'tæks] *adj* przed opodatkowaniem *post*
**pretence**, (*US*) **pretense** [prɪ'tɛns] *n* pozory *pl*; **under false ~s** pod fałszywym pretekstem; **she is devoid of all ~** jest całkowicie bezpretensjonalna; **to make a ~ of doing sth** udawać (udać *perf*), że się coś robi
**pretend** [prɪ'tɛnd] *vt* udawać (udać *perf*) ▷ *vi* udawać; **I don't ~ to understand it** nie twierdzę, że to rozumiem
**pretense** [prɪ'tɛns] (*US*) *n* = **pretence**
**pretentious** [prɪ'tɛnʃəs] *adj* pretensjonalny
**preterite** ['prɛtərɪt] (*Ling*) *n* czas *m* przeszły
**pretext** ['priːtɛkst] *n* pretekst *m*; **on** *or* **under the ~ of doing sth** pod pretekstem robienia czegoś
**pretty** ['prɪtɪ] *adj* ładny ▷ *adv*: **~ clever/good** całkiem bystry/niezły
**prevail** [prɪ'veɪl] *vi* (*be current*) przeważać, dominować; (*triumph*) brać (wziąć *perf*) górę; **to ~ (up)on sb to do sth** nakłonić (*perf*) kogoś, żeby coś zrobił
**prevailing** [prɪ'veɪlɪŋ] *adj* (*wind*) przeważający; (*fashion, view*) panujący, powszechny
**prevalent** ['prɛvələnt] *adj* powszechny
**prevaricate** [prɪ'værɪkeɪt] *vi* lawirować
**prevarication** [prɪværɪ'keɪʃən] *n* lawirowanie *nt*, wykręty *pl*
**prevent** [prɪ'vɛnt] *vt* zapobiegać (zapobiec *perf*) *+dat*; **to ~ sb from doing sth** uniemożliwiać (uniemożliwić *perf*) komuś zrobienie czegoś; **to ~ sth from happening** zapobiegać (zapobiec *perf*) czemuś, nie dopuszczać (nie dopuścić *perf*) do czegoś
**preventable** [prɪ'vɛntəbl] *adj* do uniknięcia *post*; **~ diseases** choroby, którym można zapobiegać
**preventative** [prɪ'vɛntətɪv] *adj* = **preventive**
**prevention** [prɪ'vɛnʃən] *n* zapobieganie *nt*, profilaktyka *f*
**preventive** [prɪ'vɛntɪv] *adj* zapobiegawczy, profilaktyczny
**preview** ['priːvjuː] *n* pokaz *m* przedpremierowy
**previous** ['priːvɪəs] *adj* poprzedni; **~ to** przed *+instr*
**previously** ['priːvɪəslɪ] *adv* (*before*) wcześniej; (*formerly*) poprzednio
**prewar** [priː'wɔː^r] *adj* przedwojenny
**prey** [preɪ] *n* zdobycz *f*; **to fall ~ to** (*fig*) padać (paść *perf*) ofiarą *+gen*
▶ **prey on** *vt fus* polować na *+acc*; **it was ~ing on his mind** nie dawało mu to spokoju
**price** [praɪs] *n* cena *f* ▷ *vt* wyceniać (wycenić *perf*); **what is the ~ of...?** ile kosztuje *+nom*?; **to go up** *or* **rise in ~** drożeć (zdrożeć *perf*); **to put a ~ on sth** (*fig*) przeliczać (przeliczyć *perf*) coś na pieniądze; **to ~ o.s. out of the market** nie utrzymać się (*perf*) na rynku ze względu na zawyżone ceny; **what ~ his promises now?** cóż są teraz warte jego obietnice?; **he regained his freedom, but at a ~** odzyskał wolność, ale drogo za to zapłacił
**price control** *n* regulacja *f* cen
**price-cutting** ['praɪskʌtɪŋ] *n* obniżanie *nt* cen
**priceless** ['praɪslɪs] *adj* bezcenny; (*inf: amusing*) kapitalny (*inf*)
**price list** *n* cennik *m*

**price range** *n* rozpiętość *f* cen; **it's within my ~** stać mnie na to
**price tag** *n* metka *f*; (*fig*) cena *f*
**price war** *n* wojna *f* cenowa
**pricey** ['praɪsɪ] (*inf*) *adj* drogawy (*inf*)
**prick** [prɪk] *n* ukłucie *nt*; (*inf!*) kutas *m* (*inf!*) ▷ *vt* (*make hole in*) nakłuwać (nakłuć *perf*); (*scratch*) kłuć (pokłuć *perf*); **to ~ up one's ears** nadstawiać (nadstawić *perf*) uszu
**prickle** ['prɪkl] *n* (*of plant*) kolec *m*; (*sensation*) ciarki *pl*
**prickly** ['prɪklɪ] *adj* (*plant*) kłujący, kolczasty; (*fabric*) kłujący, szorstki
**prickly heat** *n* potówki *pl*
**prickly pear** *n* opuncja *f*
**pride** [praɪd] *n* duma *f*; (*pej*) pycha *f* ▷ *vt*: **to ~ o.s. on** szczycić się *+instr*; **to take (a) ~ in** być dumnym z *+gen*; **to have** *or* **take ~ of place** (*Brit*) znajdować się (znaleźć się *perf*) na honorowym miejscu
**priest** [pri:st] *n* (*Christian*) ksiądz *m*, kapłan *m*; (*non-Christian*) kapłan *m*
**priestess** ['pri:stɪs] *n* kapłanka *f*
**priesthood** ['pri:sthud] *n* (*position, office*) kapłaństwo *nt*; (*clergy*) duchowieństwo *nt*
**prig** [prɪg] *n* zarozumialec *m*
**prim** [prɪm] (*pej*) *adj* (*person, avoidance of issue*) pruderyjny (*pej*); (*voice*) afektowany; (*manner*) wymuszony, sztywny
**prima facie** ['praɪmə'feɪʃɪ] *adj* (*Jur*) oparty na domniemaniu faktycznym
**primarily** ['praɪmərɪlɪ] *adv* w pierwszym rzędzie, głównie
**primary** ['praɪmərɪ] *adj* podstawowy ▷ *n* (*US*) wybory *pl* wstępne
**primary colour** *n* barwa *f* podstawowa
**primary school** (*Brit*) *n* szkoła *f* podstawowa
**primate** ['praɪmɪt] *n* (*Zool*) naczelny *m*, ssak *m* z rzędu naczelnych; (*Rel*) prymas *m*
**prime** [praɪm] *adj* pierwszorzędny ▷ *n* najlepsze lata *pl* ▷ *vt* (*wood*) zagruntowywać (zagruntować *perf*); (*fig*: *person*) instruować (poinstruować (*perf*)); (*gun*) uzbrajać (uzbroić *perf*); (*pump*) zalewać (zalać *perf*); **in the ~ of life** w kwiecie wieku; **a ~ example of** klasyczny przykład *+gen*
**Prime Minister** *n* premier *m*, Prezes *m* Rady Ministrów
**prime time** (*Radio, TV*) *n* najlepszy czas *m* antenowy
**primeval** [praɪ'mi:vl] *adj* (*forest, beast*) pradawny; (*fig*: *feelings*) odwieczny
**primitive** ['prɪmɪtɪv] *adj* prymitywny
**primrose** ['prɪmrəuz] *n* pierwiosnek *m*
**primula** ['prɪmjulə] *n* prymul(k)a *f*
**primus (stove)**® ['praɪməs-] (*Brit*) *n* kuchenka *f* turystyczna
**prince** [prɪns] *n* książę *m*, królewicz *m*
**Prince Charming** (*humorous*) *n* książę *m or* królewicz *m* z bajki
**princess** [prɪn'sɛs] *n* (*king's daughter*) księżniczka *f*, królewna *f*; (*prince's wife*) księżna *f*
**principal** ['prɪnsɪpl] *adj* główny ▷ *n* (*Scol*) dyrektor(ka) *m(f)*; (*Theat*) odtwórca(-rczyni) *m(f)* głównej roli; (*Fin*) suma *f* główna, kapitał *m*
**principality** [prɪnsɪ'pælɪtɪ] *n* księstwo *nt*
**principally** ['prɪnsɪplɪ] *adv* głównie
**principle** ['prɪnsɪpl] *n* zasada *f*; **in ~** w zasadzie; **on ~** z *or* dla zasady
**print** [prɪnt] *n* (*Typ*) druk *m*; (*Art*) sztych *m*, rycina *f*; (*Phot*) odbitka *f*; (*fabric*) tkanina *f* drukowana ▷ *vt* (*books etc*) drukować (wydrukować *perf*); (*cloth, pattern*) drukować; (*write in capitals*) pisać (napisać *perf*) drukowanymi literami; **prints** *npl* odciski *pl* palców; **the book is out of ~** nakład książki jest wyczerpany; **in ~** w sprzedaży (*o książce itp*); **the fine** *or* **small ~** adnotacje drobnym drukiem
▶ **print out** *vt* (*Comput*) drukować (wydrukować *perf*)
**printed circuit** *n* obwód *m* drukowany
**printed matter** *n* druki *pl*
**printer** ['prɪntə$^r$] *n* (*person*) drukarz *m*; (*firm*) drukarnia *f*; (*machine*) drukarka *f*
**printhead** ['prɪnthɛd] (*Comput*) *n* głowica *f* drukująca
**printing** ['prɪntɪŋ] *n* (*activity*) drukowanie *nt*; (*profession*) drukarstwo *nt*
**printing press** *n* prasa *f* drukarska
**printout** ['prɪntaut] (*Comput*) *n* wydruk *m*
**print wheel** (*Comput*) *n* głowica *f* wirująca drukarki
**prior** ['praɪə$^r$] *adj* (*previous*) uprzedni, wcześniejszy; (*more important*) ważniejszy ▷ *n* (*Rel*) przeor *m*; **without ~ notice** bez wcześniejszego powiadomienia; **to have a ~ claim on sth** mieć większe prawo do czegoś; **~ to** przed *+instr*
**priority** [praɪ'ɔrɪtɪ] *n* sprawa *f* nadrzędna; **priorities** *npl* priorytety *pl*, hierarchia *f* ważności; **to take** *or* **have ~ (over)** być nadrzędnym (w stosunku do *+gen*); **to give ~ to sb/sth** dawać (dać *perf*) pierwszeństwo komuś/czemuś
**priory** ['praɪərɪ] *n* (mały) klasztor *m*
**prise** [praɪz] (*Brit*) *vt*: **to ~ open** wyważać (wyważyć *perf*)
**prism** ['prɪzəm] *n* pryzmat *m*
**prison** ['prɪzn] *n* (*lit, fig*) więzienie *nt*; (*imprisonment*) kara *f* więzienia ▷ *cpd* więzienny

**prison camp** *n* obóz *m* jeniecki
**prisoner** ['prɪznəʳ] *n* (*in prison*) więzień/więźniarka *m/f*; (*during war etc*) jeniec *m*; **the ~ at the bar** oskarżony przed sądem; **to take sb ~** brać (wziąć *perf*) kogoś do niewoli
**prisoner of war** *n* jeniec *m* wojenny
**prissy** ['prɪsɪ] (*pej*) *adj* afektowany (*pej*)
**pristine** ['prɪsti:n] *adj* nieskazitelny; **in ~ condition** w nienaruszonym stanie
**privacy** ['prɪvəsɪ] *n* prywatność *f*; **in the ~ of one's own home** w zaciszu własnego domu
**private** ['praɪvɪt] *adj* (*personal, confidential, not public*) prywatny; (*secluded*) ustronny; (*secretive*) skryty ▷ *n* (*Mil*) szeregowy(-wa) *m(f)*; **"~"** (*on envelope*) „poufne", „do rąk własnych"; (*on door*) „obcym wstęp wzbroniony"; **in ~** na osobności, bez świadków; **in (his) ~ life** w życiu prywatnym, prywatnie; **to be in ~ practice** (*Med*) prowadzić prywatną praktykę; **~ hearing** (*Jur*) przesłuchanie niejawne
**private enterprise** *n* prywatna przedsiębiorczość *f*
**private eye** *n* prywatny detektyw *m*
**private limited company** (*Brit*) *n* prywatna spółka *f* z ograniczoną odpowiedzialnością
**privately** ['praɪvɪtlɪ] *adv* (*in private*) prywatnie; (*secretly*) w głębi duszy; **to be ~ owned** mieć prywatnego właściciela
**private parts** *npl* intymne części *pl* ciała
**private property** *n* własność *f* prywatna
**private school** *n* szkoła *f* prywatna
**privation** [praɪ'veɪʃən] *n* niedostatek *m*
**privatize** ['praɪvɪtaɪz] *vt* prywatyzować (sprywatyzować *perf*)
**privet** ['prɪvɪt] *n* ligustr *m*
**privilege** ['prɪvɪlɪdʒ] *n* (*advantage*) przywilej *m*; (*honour*) zaszczyt *m*
**privileged** ['prɪvɪlɪdʒd] *adj* uprzywilejowany; **to be ~ to do sth** mieć zaszczyt coś (z)robić
**privy** ['prɪvɪ] *adj*: **to be ~ to** być wtajemniczonym w *+acc*
**Privy Council** (*Brit*) *n* Tajna Rada *f*
**Privy Councillor** (*Brit*) *n* członek *m* Tajnej Rady
**prize** [praɪz] *n* (*in competition, sports*) nagroda *f*; (*at lottery*) wygrana *f* ▷ *adj* (*first-class*) pierwszorzędny, przedni; (*example*) klasyczny; (*inf: idiot*) wyjątkowy ▷ *vt* wysoko (sobie) cenić
**prize-fighter** ['praɪzfaɪtəʳ] *n* bokser *m* zawodowy
**prize-giving** ['praɪzgɪvɪŋ] *n* rozdanie *nt* nagród
**prize money** *n* wygrana *f* pieniężna
**prizewinner** ['praɪzwɪnəʳ] *n* zdobywca(-wczyni) *m(f)* nagrody, laureat(ka) *m(f)*
**prizewinning** ['praɪzwɪnɪŋ] *adj* nagrodzony
**PRO** *n abbr* = **public relations officer**
**pro** [prəu] *n* (*Sport*) zawodowiec *m* ▷ *prep* za *+instr*; **the pros and cons** za i przeciw
**pro-** [prəu] *pref* pro...; **~Soviet** prosowiecki
**probability** [prɔbə'bɪlɪtɪ] *n*: **the ~ that/of** prawdopodobieństwo *nt*, że/*+gen*; **in all ~** według wszelkiego prawdopodobieństwa
**probable** ['prɔbəbl] *adj* prawdopodobny; **it seems ~ that ...** wydaje się prawdopodobne, że ...
**probably** ['prɔbəblɪ] *adv* prawdopodobnie
**probate** ['prəubɪt] (*Jur*) *n* poświadczenie *nt* autentyczności testamentu
**probation** [prə'beɪʃən] *n*: **to be on ~** (*lawbreaker*) odbywać wyrok w zawieszeniu; (*employee*) odbywać staż
**probationary** [prə'beɪʃənrɪ] *adj* (*period*) próbny
**probationer** [prə'beɪʃənəʳ] *n* (*nurse*) praktykant(ka) *m(f)*
**probation officer** *n* opiekun(ka) *m(f)* sądowy(-wa) *m(f)*, kurator(ka) *m(f)*
**probe** [prəub] *n* (*Med*) sonda *f*, zgłębnik *m*; (*Space*) sonda *f* kosmiczna; (*enquiry*) dochodzenie *nt* ▷ *vt* badać (zbadać *perf*)
**probity** ['prəubɪtɪ] *n* prawość *f*
**problem** ['prɔbləm] *n* problem *m*; (*Math*) zadanie *nt*; **to have ~s with the car** mieć kłopoty z samochodem; **what's the ~?** w czym problem?; **I had no ~ finding her** znalazłem ją bez problemu; **no ~!** nie ma sprawy! (*inf*)
**problematic(al)** [prɔblə'mætɪk(l)] *adj* skomplikowany
**procedural** [prə'si:djurəl] *adj* (*agreement*) formalny; (*obstacle*) formalny, proceduralny
**procedure** [prə'si:dʒəʳ] *n* procedura *f*
**proceed** [prə'si:d] *vi* (*carry on*) kontynuować; (*go*) iść; **to ~ to do sth** przystępować (przystąpić *perf*) do robienia czegoś; **to ~ with sth** kontynuować coś; **I am not sure how to ~** nie jestem pewien, co (mam) robić dalej; **to ~ against sb** (*Jur*) wszczynać (wszcząć *perf*) postępowanie przeciwko komuś
**proceedings** [prə'si:dɪŋz] *npl* (*organized events*) przebieg *m* (*uroczystości, obchodów itp*); (*Jur*) postępowanie *nt* prawne; (*written records*) sprawozdanie *nt*, protokół *m*
**proceeds** ['prəusi:dz] *npl* dochód *m*
**process** ['prəusɛs] *n* proces *m* ▷ *vt* (*raw materials, food*) przerabiać (przerobić *perf*), przetwarzać (przetworzyć *perf*); (*application*) rozpatrywać (rozpatrzyć *perf*); (*data*) przetwarzać (przetworzyć *perf*); **in the ~** w tym samym czasie, równocześnie; **to be in the ~ of doing sth** być w trakcie robienia czegoś

**processed cheese** ['prəusɛst-], (*US*) **process cheese** *n* ≈ ser *m* topiony
**processing** ['prəusɛsɪŋ] (*Phot*) *n* obróbka *f* (fotograficzna)
**procession** [prə'sɛʃən] *n* pochód *m*; (*Rel*) procesja *f*; **wedding ~** orszak ślubny; **funeral ~** kondukt żałobny
**proclaim** [prə'kleɪm] *vt* proklamować, ogłaszać (ogłosić *perf*)
**proclamation** [prɔklə'meɪʃən] *n* proklamacja *f*
**proclivity** [prə'klɪvɪtɪ] (*fml*) *n* skłonność *f*
**procrastinate** [prəu'kræstɪneɪt] *vi* zwlekać
**procrastination** [prəukræstɪ'neɪʃən] *n* zwłoka *f*
**procreation** [prəukrɪ'eɪʃən] *n* prokreacja *f*
**procure** [prə'kjuə$^r$] *vt* zdobywać (zdobyć *perf*)
**procurement** [prə'kjuəmənt] (*Comm*) *n* zaopatrzenie *nt*
**prod** [prɔd] *vt* szturchać (szturchnąć *perf*); (*with sth sharp*) dźgać (dźgnąć *perf*); (*fig*) popychać (popchnąć *perf*) ▷ *n* szturchnięcie *nt*; (*with sth sharp*) dźgnięcie *nt*; (*fig*) przypomnienie *nt*
**prodigal** ['prɔdɪgl] *adj*: **~ son** syn *m* marnotrawny
**prodigious** [prə'dɪdʒəs] *adj* kolosalny
**prodigy** ['prɔdɪdʒɪ] *n* cudowne dziecko *nt*
**produce** [*n* 'prɔdju:s, *vb* prə'dju:s] *n* płody *pl* rolne ▷ *vt* (*effect etc*) przynosić (przynieść *perf*); (*goods*) produkować (wyprodukować *perf*); (*Bio, Chem*) wytwarzać (wytworzyć *perf*); (*fig: evidence etc*) przedstawiać (przedstawić *perf*); (*play*) wystawiać (wystawić *perf*); (*film, programme*) być producentem *+gen*; (*bring or take out*) wyjmować (wyjąć *perf*)
**producer** [prə'dju:sə$^r$] *n* producent *m*
**product** ['prɔdʌkt] *n* (*goods*) produkt *m*; (*result*) wytwór *m*
**production** [prə'dʌkʃən] *n* produkcja *f*; (*Theat*) wystawienie *nt* (sztuki), inscenizacja *f*; **to go into ~** zostawać (zostać *perf*) wdrożonym do produkcji; **on ~ of** za okazaniem *+gen*
**production agreement** (*US*) *n* umowa *f* w sprawie premii za wydajność
**production line** *n* linia *f* produkcyjna
**production manager** *n* kierownik *m* produkcji
**productive** [prə'dʌktɪv] *adj* wydajny; (*fig*) owocny
**productivity** [prɔdʌk'tɪvɪtɪ] *n* wydajność *f*
**productivity agreement** (*Brit*) *n* umowa *f* w sprawie premii za wydajność
**productivity bonus** *n* premia *f* za wydajność
**product placement** *n* kryptoreklama *f* (*polegająca na umieszczeniu danego produktu w filmie itp*)
**Prof.** *n abbr* (= *professor*) prof.
**profane** [prə'feɪn] *adj* (*language etc*) bluźnierczy; (*secular*) świecki
**profess** [prə'fɛs] *vt* (*feelings, opinions*) wyrażać (wyrazić *perf*); **I do not ~ to be an expert** nie twierdzę, że jestem znawcą; **he ~ed ignorance, he ~ed not to know anything** utrzymywał, że nic nie wie
**professed** [prə'fɛst] *adj* zdeklarowany
**profession** [prə'fɛʃən] *n* zawód *m*; **the ~s** wolne zawody; **the medical/teaching ~** (*occupation*) zawód lekarza/nauczyciela; (*people*) lekarze/nauczyciele
**professional** [prə'fɛʃənl] *adj* (*not amateur*) zawodowy; (*skilful*) fachowy, profesjonalny ▷ *n* (*not amateur*) zawodowiec *m*; (*skilled person*) fachowiec *m*, profesjonalista(-tka) *m(f)*; **to seek ~ advice** szukać fachowej porady
**professionalism** [prə'fɛʃnəlɪzəm] *n* fachowość *f*, profesjonalizm *m*
**professionally** [prə'fɛʃnəlɪ] *adv* (*qualified*) zawodowo; (*Sport, Mus*) profesjonalnie; **I only know him ~** znam go jedynie z pracy
**professor** [prə'fɛsə$^r$] *n* (*Brit*) profesor *m*; (*US, Canada*) nauczyciel *m* akademicki
**professorship** [prə'fɛsəʃɪp] *n* profesura *f*
**proffer** ['prɔfə$^r$] *vt* (*help, drink*) oferować (zaoferować *perf*); (*apologies, resignation*) składać (złożyć *perf*); (*one's hand*) wyciągać (wyciągnąć *perf*)
**PR officer** *n* piarowiec *m*
**proficiency** [prə'fɪʃənsɪ] *n* biegłość *f*, wprawa *f*
**proficient** [prə'fɪʃənt] *adj* biegły, wprawny; **to be ~ at** *or* **in** być biegłym w *+loc*
**profile** ['prəufaɪl] *n* profil *m*; (*fig*) rys *m* biograficzny; **to keep a low ~** (*fig*) starać się nie zwracać na siebie uwagi; **to have a high ~** (*fig*) być bardzo widocznym
**profit** ['prɔfɪt] *n* zysk *m* ▷ *vi*: **to ~ by** *or* **from** (*fig*) odnosić (odnieść *perf*) korzyść *or* korzyści z *+gen*, mieć pożytek z *+gen*; **~ and loss** zyski i straty; **to make a ~** osiągać (osiągnąć *perf*) zysk, zarabiać (zarobić *perf*); **to sell (sth) at a ~** sprzedawać (sprzedać *perf*) (coś) z zyskiem
**profitability** [prɔfɪtə'bɪlɪtɪ] *n* opłacalność *f*
**profitable** ['prɔfɪtəbl] *adj* opłacalny, dochodowy; (*fig*) korzystny, pożyteczny
**profit centre** *n* centrum *nt* zysku *or* zysków
**profiteering** [prɔfɪ'tɪərɪŋ] (*pej*) *n* paskarstwo *nt* (*pej*)
**profit-making** ['prɔfɪtmeɪkɪŋ] *adj* dochodowy
**profit margin** *n* marża *f*
**profit-sharing** ['prɔfɪtʃɛərɪŋ] *n* udział *m* w zysku
**profits tax** (*Brit*) *n* podatek *m* od zysku

P

**profligate** ['prɔflɪgɪt] *adj* rozrzutny; **to be ~ with** nie liczyć się z *+instr*
**pro forma** ['prəu'fɔːmə] *adj*: **~ invoice** faktura *f* tymczasowa *or* pro forma
**profound** [prə'faund] *adj* głęboki
**profuse** [prə'fjuːs] *adj* wylewny
**profusely** [prə'fjuːslɪ] *adv* wylewnie
**profusion** [prə'fjuːʒən] *n* obfitość *f*
**progeny** ['prɔdʒɪnɪ] *n* potomstwo *nt*
**prognoses** [prɔg'nəusiːz] *npl of* **prognosis**
**prognosis** [prɔg'nəusɪs] (*pl* **prognoses**) *n* (*Med*) rokowanie *nt*; (*fig*) prognoza *f*
**programme** ['prəugræm] *n* program *m* ▷ *vt* programować (zaprogramować *perf*)
**programmer** ['prəugræmə^r] (*Comput*) *n* programista(-tka) *m(f)*
**programming** ['prəugræmɪŋ], (*US*) **programing** (*Comput*) *n* programowanie *nt*
**programming language** *n* język *m* programowania
**progress** [*n* 'prəugrɛs, *vb* prə'grɛs] *n* (*improvement, advances*) postęp *m*; (*development*) rozwój *m* ▷ *vi* (*advance*) robić (zrobić *perf*) postęp(y); (*become higher in rank*) awansować (awansować *perf*); (*continue*) postępować *or* posuwać się naprzód; **in ~** w toku; **to make ~** robić (zrobić *perf*) postęp(y)
**progression** [prə'grɛʃən] *n* (*development*) postęp *m*; (*series*) ciąg *m*
**progressive** [prə'grɛsɪv] *adj* (*enlightened*) postępowy; (*gradual*) postępujący
**progressively** [prə'grɛsɪvlɪ] *adv* (stopniowo) coraz (to)
**progress report** *n* (*Med*) karta *f* choroby; (*Admin*) sprawozdanie *nt*, raport *m*
**prohibit** [prə'hɪbɪt] *vt* zakazywać (zakazać *perf*) *+gen*; **to ~ sb from doing sth** zakazywać (zakazać *perf*) komuś robienia czegoś; **"smoking ~ed"** „palenie wzbronione"
**prohibition** [prəuɪ'bɪʃən] *n* zakaz *m*; **P~** (*US*) prohibicja *f*
**prohibitive** [prə'hɪbɪtɪv] *adj* (*cost etc*) wygórowany
**project** [*n* 'prɔdʒɛkt, *vb* prə'dʒɛkt] *n* projekt *m*; (*Scol*) referat *m* ▷ *vt* (*plan*) projektować (zaprojektować *perf*); (*estimate*) przewidywać (przewidzieć *perf*); (*film*) wyświetlać (wyświetlić *perf*) ▷ *vi* wystawać
**projectile** [prə'dʒɛktaɪl] *n* pocisk *m*
**projection** [prə'dʒɛkʃən] *n* (*estimate*) przewidywanie *nt*; (*overhang*) występ *m*; (*Film*) projekcja *f*
**projectionist** [prə'dʒɛkʃənɪst] *n* kinooperator(ka) *m(f)*
**projection room** *n* kabina *f* projekcyjna
**projector** [prə'dʒɛktə^r] *n* rzutnik *m*
**proletarian** [prəulɪ'tɛərɪən] *adj* proletariacki
**proletariat** [prəulɪ'tɛərɪət] *n*: **the ~** proletariat *m*
**proliferate** [prə'lɪfəreɪt] *vi* mnożyć się
**proliferation** [prəlɪfə'reɪʃən] *n* rozprzestrzenianie *nt*
**prolific** [prə'lɪfɪk] *adj* (*writer etc*) płodny
**prologue**, (*US*) **prolog** ['prəulɔg] *n* prolog *m*
**prolong** [prə'lɔŋ] *vt* przedłużać (przedłużyć *perf*)
**prom** [prɔm] *n abbr* = **promenade**; (*Mus*) = **promenade concert**; (*US*) *bal w szkole średniej lub college'u*
**promenade** [prɔmə'nɑːd] *n* promenada *f*
**promenade concert** (*Brit*) *n* koncert *m* na świeżym powietrzu
**promenade deck** (*Naut*) *n* pokład *m* spacerowy
**prominence** ['prɔmɪnəns] *n* ważność *f*; **to rise to ~** osiągać (osiągnąć *perf*) znaczącą pozycję
**prominent** ['prɔmɪnənt] *adj* (*important*) wybitny; (*very noticeable*) widoczny; **he is ~ in the field of ...** jest wybitny w dziedzinie *+gen*
**prominently** ['prɔmɪnəntlɪ] *adv* na widocznym miejscu; **he figured ~ in the case** odegrał znaczącą rolę w tej sprawie
**promiscuity** [prɔmɪs'kjuːɪtɪ] *n* rozwiązłość *f*
**promiscuous** [prə'mɪskjuəs] *adj* rozwiązły
**promise** ['prɔmɪs] *n* (*vow*) przyrzeczenie *nt*, obietnica *f*; (*potential*) zadatki *pl*; (*hope*) nadzieja *f* ▷ *vi* przyrzekać (przyrzec *perf*), obiecywać (obiecać *perf*) ▷ *vt*: **to ~ sb sth, ~ sth to sb** przyrzekać (przyrzec *perf*) *or* obiecywać (obiecać *perf*) coś komuś; **to ~ (sb) to do sth** obiecywać (obiecać *perf*) (komuś) coś zrobić; **to ~ (sb) that ...** dawać (dać *perf*) (komuś) słowo, że ...; **to make a ~** składać (złożyć *perf*) obietnicę; **to break a ~** łamać (złamać *perf*) obietnicę; **to keep a ~** dotrzymywać (dotrzymać *perf*) obietnicy; **a young man of ~** dobrze zapowiadający się młody człowiek; **she shows ~** ona się dobrze zapowiada; **it ~s to be lively** zapowiada się ciekawie
**promising** ['prɔmɪsɪŋ] *adj* obiecujący
**promissory note** ['prɔmɪsərɪ-] (*Comm*) *n* skrypt *m* dłużny
**promontory** ['prɔməntrɪ] *n* cypel *m*
**promote** [prə'məut] *vt* (*employee*) awansować (awansować *perf*), dawać (dać *perf*) awans *+dat*; (*product*) promować (wypromować *perf*), lansować (wylansować *perf*); (*understanding, peace*) przyczyniać się (przyczynić się *perf*) do *+gen*; **the team was ~d to the first division** (*Brit*) zespół awansował do pierwszej ligi

**promoter** [prə'məutə^r] *n* (*of concert, sporting event*) sponsor *m*; (*of cause, idea*) rzecznik(-iczka) *m(f)*
**promotion** [prə'məuʃən] *n* (*at work*) awans *m*; (*of product*) reklama *f*; (*of idea*) propagowanie *nt*; (*publicity campaign*) promocja *f*
**prompt** [prɔmpt] *adj* natychmiastowy ▷ *adv* punktualnie ▷ *n* (*Comput*) znak *m* zachęty *or* systemu ▷ *vt* (*cause*) powodować (spowodować *perf*); (*when talking*) zachęcać (zachęcić *perf*) (do kontynuowania wypowiedzi); (*Theat*) podpowiadać (podpowiedzieć *perf*) *+dat*; **they're very ~** są bardzo punktualni; **at eight o'clock ~** punktualnie o ósmej; **he was ~ to accept it** przyjął to natychmiast; **to ~ sb to do sth** skłonić (*perf*) *or* nakłonić (*perf*) kogoś do zrobienia czegoś
**prompter** ['prɔmptə^r] (*Theat*) *n* sufler(ka) *m(f)*
**promptly** ['prɔmptlɪ] *adv* (*immediately*) natychmiast; (*exactly*) punktualnie
**promptness** ['prɔmptnɪs] *n* szybkość *f*; **with ~** szybko
**promulgate** ['prɔməlgeɪt] *vt* obwieszczać (obwieścić *perf*)
**prone** [prəun] *adj* leżący twarzą w dół *or* na brzuchu; **to be ~ to** mieć skłonność do *+gen*; **she is ~ to burst into tears** ma skłonność do wybuchania płaczem
**prong** [prɔŋ] *n* (*of fork*) ząb *m*
**pronoun** ['prəunaun] *n* zaimek *m*
**pronounce** [prə'nauns] *vt* (*word*) wymawiać (wymówić *perf*); (*verdict, opinion*) ogłaszać (ogłosić *perf*) ▷ *vi*: **to ~ (up)on** wydawać (wydać *perf*) opinię na temat *+gen*; **to ~ sb guilty/dead** uznawać (uznać *perf*) kogoś za winnego/zmarłego; **they ~d him unfit to drive** uznali go za niezdolnego do prowadzenia pojazdu
**pronounced** [prə'naunst] *adj* wyraźny
**pronouncement** [prə'naunsmənt] *n* oświadczenie *nt*
**pronto** ['prɔntəu] (*inf*) *adv* migiem (*inf*)
**pronunciation** [prənʌnsɪ'eɪʃən] *n* wymowa *f*
**proof** [pru:f] *n* dowód *m*; (*Typ*) korekta *f* ▷ *adj*: **~ against** odporny na *+acc*; **to be 70% ~** (*alcohol*) zawierać 40% alkoholu
**proofreader** ['pru:fri:də^r] *n* korektor(ka) *m(f)*
**prop** [prɔp] *n* podpora *f*; (*fig*) podpora *f*, ostoja *f* ▷ *vt*: **to ~ sth against** opierać (oprzeć *perf*) coś o *+acc*
▸ **prop up** *vt* podpierać (podeprzeć *perf*), podtrzymywać (podtrzymać *perf*); (*fig*) wspierać (wesprzeć *perf*), wspomagać (wspomóc *perf*)
**Prop.** (*Comm*) *abbr* (= *proprietor*) wł. (= *właściciel*)
**propaganda** [prɔpə'gændə] *n* propaganda *f*
**propagate** ['prɔpəgeɪt] *vt* (*ideas*) propagować, szerzyć; (*plants*) rozmnażać (rozmnożyć *perf*)
**propagation** [prɔpə'geɪʃən] *n* (*of ideas*) propagowanie *nt*, szerzenie *nt*; (*of plants*) rozmnażanie *nt*
**propel** [prə'pɛl] *vt* (*machine*) napędzać; (*fig: person*) popychać (popchnąć *perf*)
**propeller** [prə'pɛlə^r] *n* śmigło *nt*
**propelling pencil** [prə'pɛlɪŋ-] (*Brit*) *n* ołówek *m* automatyczny
**propensity** [prə'pɛnsɪtɪ] *n*: **a ~ for** *or* **to sth** skłonność *f* do czegoś; **a ~ to do sth** skłonność do robienia czegoś
**proper** ['prɔpə^r] *adj* (*genuine*) prawdziwy; (*correct*) właściwy; (*socially acceptable*) stosowny; **in the town/city ~** w samym mieście; **a ~ fool** (*inf*) skończony idiota (*inf*); **to go through the ~ channels** przechodzić (przejść *perf*) właściwymi kanałami
**properly** ['prɔpəlɪ] *adv* (*eat, work*) odpowiednio, właściwie; (*behave*) stosownie
**proper noun** *n* nazwa *f* własna
**property** ['prɔpətɪ] *n* (*possessions*) własność *f*, mienie *nt*; (*building and its land*) posiadłość *f*, nieruchomość *f*; (*quality*) własność *f* ▷ *cpd*: **~ market** handel *m* nieruchomościami; **~ owner** właściciel nieruchomości
**prophecy** ['prɔfɪsɪ] *n* proroctwo *nt*, przepowiednia *f*
**prophesy** ['prɔfɪsaɪ] *vt* prorokować (wyprorokować *perf*), przepowiadać (przepowiedzieć *perf*) ▷ *vi* prorokować
**prophet** ['prɔfɪt] *n* prorok *m*; **a ~ of doom** czarnowidz
**prophetic** [prə'fɛtɪk] *adj* proroczy
**proportion** [prə'pɔ:ʃən] *n* (*part*) odsetek *m*; (*quantity*) liczba *f*, ilość *f*; (*ratio*) stosunek *m*; (*Math*) proporcja *f*; **in ~ to** (*at the same rate as*) proporcjonalnie do *+gen*; (*in relation to*) w stosunku do *+gen*; **to be out of all ~ to** być niewspółmiernym do *+gen*; **to get sth out of ~** wyolbrzymiać (wyolbrzymić *perf*) coś; **a sense of ~** wyczucie proporcji
**proportional** [prə'pɔ:ʃənl] *adj*: **~ to** proporcjonalny do *+gen*
**proportional representation** *n* przedstawicielstwo *nt* proporcjonalne
**proportionate** [prə'pɔ:ʃənɪt] *adj* = **proportional**
**proposal** [prə'pəuzl] *n* propozycja *f*; (*of marriage*) oświadczyny *pl*
**propose** [prə'pəuz] *vt* (*plan*) proponować (zaproponować *perf*); (*motion*) składać (złożyć *perf*), przedkładać (przedłożyć *perf*); (*toast*) wznosić (wznieść *perf*) ▷ *vi* oświadczać się (oświadczyć się *perf*); **to ~ to do** *or* **doing sth** zamierzać coś (z)robić

P

**proposer** [prəˈpəuzəʳ] *n* wnioskodawca(-wczyni) *m(f)*
**proposition** [prɔpəˈzɪʃən] *n* (*statement*) twierdzenie *nt*; (*offer*) propozycja *f*; **to make sb a ~** składać (złożyć *perf*) komuś propozycję
**propound** [prəˈpaund] *vt* przedkładać (przedłożyć *perf*)
**proprietary** [prəˈpraɪətərɪ] *adj* (*brand*) firmowy, (prawnie) zastrzeżony; (*tone*) władczy
**proprietor** [prəˈpraɪətəʳ] *n* właściciel(ka) *m(f)*
**propriety** [prəˈpraɪətɪ] *n* stosowność *f*
**propulsion** [prəˈpʌlʃən] *n* napęd *m*
**pro rata** [prəuˈrɑːtə] *adv* proporcjonalnie ▷ *adj* proporcjonalny
**prosaic** [prəuˈzeɪɪk] *adj* prozaiczny
**Pros. Atty.** (*US*) *abbr* (= *prosecuting attorney*) prok.
**proscribe** [prəˈskraɪb] (*fml*) *vt* zakazywać (zakazać *perf*) *+gen*
**prose** [prəuz] *n* proza *f*; (*Brit: Scol*) praca *f* pisemna w języku obcym
**prosecute** [ˈprɔsɪkjuːt] *vt* podawać (podać *perf*) do sądu, wnosić (wnieść *perf*) oskarżenie przeciwko *+dat*; **who ~d the case?** kto oskarżał w tej sprawie?
**prosecuting attorney** [ˈprɔsɪkjuːtɪŋ-] (*US*) *n* oskarżyciel *m* publiczny, prokurator *m*
**prosecution** [prɔsɪˈkjuːʃən] *n* (*action*) zaskarżenie *nt*, wniesienie *nt* oskarżenia; (*accusing side*) oskarżenie *nt*
**prosecutor** [ˈprɔsɪkjuːtəʳ] *n* oskarżyciel *m*, prokurator *m*; (*also*: **public prosecutor**) oskarżyciel *m* publiczny, prokurator *m*
**prospect** [*n* ˈprɔspɛkt, *vt* prəˈspɛkt] *n* (*likelihood*) perspektywa *f*; (*thought*) myśl *f* ▷ *vi*: **to ~ for** poszukiwać *+gen*; **prospects** *npl* perspektywy *pl*; **we are faced with the ~ of having to leave** stoimy przed perspektywą przymusowego wyjazdu
**prospecting** [ˈprɔspɛktɪŋ] *n* (*for gold, oil*) poszukiwanie *nt*
**prospective** [prəˈspɛktɪv] *adj* (*son-in-law, legislation*) przyszły; (*customer*) potencjalny
**prospectus** [prəˈspɛktəs] *n* prospekt *m* (*informator*)
**prosper** [ˈprɔspəʳ] *vi* prosperować
**prosperity** [prɔˈspɛrɪtɪ] *n* (*of business*) (dobra) koniunktura *f*; (*of person*) powodzenie *nt*
**prosperous** [ˈprɔspərəs] *adj* (*business*) (dobrze) prosperujący; **is he ~?** czy dobrze mu się powodzi?
**prostate** [ˈprɔsteɪt] *n* (*also*: **prostate gland**) gruczoł *m* krokowy, prostata *f*
**prostitute** [ˈprɔstɪtjuːt] *n* prostytutka *f*
**prostitution** [prɔstɪˈtjuːʃən] *n* prostytucja *f* ▷ *vt*: **to prostitute o.s.** (*fig*) prostytuować się
**prostrate** [*adj* ˈprɔstreɪt, *vb* prɔˈstreɪt] *adj* leżący twarzą ku ziemi; (*fig*) załamany ▷ *vt*: **to ~ o.s. before** padać (paść *perf*) na twarz przed *+instr*; **~ with grief** pogrążony w smutku
**protagonist** [prəˈtægənɪst] *n* (*of idea*) szermierz *m*; (*Literature*) protagonista *m*
**protect** [prəˈtɛkt] *vt* chronić, ochraniać (ochronić *perf*)
**protection** [prəˈtɛkʃən] *n* ochrona *f*; **to offer police ~** proponować (zaproponować *perf*) ochronę policyjną
**protectionism** [prəˈtɛkʃənɪzəm] *n* protekcjonizm *m*
**protection racket** *n* wyłudzanie *nt* pieniędzy w zamian za ochronę
**protective** [prəˈtɛktɪv] *adj* ochronny; (*person*) opiekuńczy; **~ custody** areszt zapobiegawczy *or* prewencyjny
**protector** [prəˈtɛktəʳ] *n* (*person*) opiekun(ka) *m(f)*; (*device*) ochraniacz *m*
**protégé** [ˈprəutɛʒeɪ] *n* protegowany *m*
**protégée** [ˈprəutɛʒeɪ] *n* protegowana *f*
**protein** [ˈprəutiːn] *n* białko *nt*, proteina *f*
**pro tem** [prəuˈtɛm] *adv abbr* (= *pro tempore*) tymczasowo
**protest** [*n* ˈprəutɛst, *vb* prəˈtɛst] *n* protest *m* ▷ *vi*: **to ~ about/against/at** protestować przeciw(ko) *+dat* ▷ *vt*: **to ~ (that ...)** zapewniać (zapewnić *perf*) (, że ...)
**Protestant** [ˈprɔtɪstənt] *adj* protestancki ▷ *n* protestant(ka) *m(f)*
**protester** [prəˈtɛstəʳ] *n* protestujący(-ca) *m(f)*
**protest march** *n* marsz *m* protestacyjny
**protestor** [prəˈtɛstəʳ] *n* = **protester**
**protocol** [ˈprəutəkɔl] *n* protokół *m*
**proton** [ˈprəutɔn] *n* proton *m*
**prototype** [ˈprəutətaɪp] *n* prototyp *m*
**protracted** [prəˈtræktɪd] *adj* przedłużający się
**protractor** [prəˈtræktəʳ] *n* kątomierz *m*
**protrude** [prəˈtruːd] *vi* wystawać, sterczeć
**protuberance** [prəˈtjuːbərəns] *n* wypukłość *f*
**proud** [praud] *adj* dumny; (*pej*) pyszny, hardy; **~ of sb/sth** dumny z kogoś/czegoś; **to be ~ to do sth** robić (zrobić *perf*) coś z dumą; **to do sb ~** (*inf*) ugaszczać (ugościć *perf*) kogoś po królewsku; **to do o.s. ~** (*inf*) niczego sobie nie odmawiać
**proudly** [ˈpraudlɪ] *adv* dumnie
**prove** [pruːv] *vt* udowadniać (udowodnić *perf*), dowodzić (dowieść *perf*) *+gen* ▷ *vi*: **to ~ (to be) correct/useful** okazywać się (okazać się *perf*) słusznym/użytecznym; **he was ~d right in the end** ostatecznie okazało się, że miał rację
**Provençal** [prɔvɔnˈsɑːl] *adj* prowansalski

**rovence** [prɔ'vɑ̃:s] *n* Prowansja *f*
**roverb** ['prɔvə:b] *n* przysłowie *nt*
**roverbial** [prə'və:bɪəl] *adj* przysłowiowy
**rovide** [prə'vaɪd] *vt* dostarczać (dostarczyć *perf*) *+gen*; **to ~ sb with** (*food*) zaopatrywać (zaopatrzyć *perf*) kogoś w *+acc*; (*information*) dostarczać (dostarczyć *perf*) komuś *+gen*; (*job*) zapewniać (zapewnić *perf*) komuś *+acc*; **to be ~d with** (*person*) mieć do dyspozycji *+acc*; (*thing*) być wyposażonym w *+acc*
▸ **provide for** *vt fus* (*person*) utrzymywać (utrzymać *perf*) *+acc*; (*future event*) uwzględniać (uwzględnić *perf*) *+acc*
**rovided** [prə'vaɪdɪd] *conj*: **~ that** pod warunkiem, że
**rovidence** ['prɔvɪdəns] *n* opatrzność *f*
**roviding** [prə'vaɪdɪŋ] *conj*: **~ (that)** = **provided (that)**
**rovince** ['prɔvɪns] *n* (*Admin*) prowincja *f*; (*of person*) kompetencje *pl*; **provinces** *npl*: **the provinces** prowincja *f*
**rovincial** [prə'vɪnʃəl] *adj* prowincjonalny
**rovision** [prə'vɪʒən] *n* (*supplying*) zaopatrywanie *nt*; (*preparation*) zabezpieczenie *nt*; (*of contract, agreement*) warunek *m*, klauzula *f*; **provisions** *npl* zapasy *pl*; **~ of services** świadczenie usług; **to make ~ for** (*the future*) zabezpieczać się (zabezpieczyć się *perf*) na *+acc*; (*one's family*) zabezpieczać (zabezpieczyć *perf*) *+acc*; **there's no ~ for this in the contract** umowa tego nie przewiduje
**rovisional** [prə'vɪʒənl] *adj* tymczasowy ▹ *n*: **P~** *członek radykalnego skrzydła Irlandzkiej Armii Republikańskiej*
**rovisional licence** (*Brit*) *n* tymczasowe prawo *nt* jazdy
**rovisionally** [prə'vɪʒnəlɪ] *adv* tymczasowo
**roviso** [prə'vaɪzəu] *n* zastrzeżenie *nt*; **with the ~ that ...** pod warunkiem, że...
**rovo** ['prɔvəu] (*Irish: Pol: inf*) *n abbr* = **Provisional**
**rovocation** [prɔvə'keɪʃən] *n* prowokacja *f*; **to do sth under ~** zostać (*perf*) sprowokowanym do zrobienia czegoś
**rovocative** [prə'vɔkətɪv] *adj* prowokacyjny; (*sexually*) prowokujący; (*thought-provoking*) skłaniający do zastanowienia
**rovoke** [prə'vəuk] *vt* (*person, fight*) prowokować (sprowokować *perf*); (*reaction, criticism*) wywoływać (wywołać *perf*); **to ~ sb to do** *or* **into doing sth** prowokować (sprowokować *perf*) kogoś do zrobienia czegoś
**rovost** ['prɔvəst] *n* (*Brit: of university*) rektor *m*; (*Scottish*) burmistrz *m*
**row** [prau] *n* (*of boat*) dziób *m*

**prowess** ['prauɪs] *n* (wyjątkowa) biegłość *f*; (*in battle*) męstwo *nt*; (*sexual*) sprawność *f*; **his ~ as a footballer** jego wyjątkowe umiejętności piłkarskie
**prowl** [praul] *vi* (*also*: **prowl about, prowl around**) grasować ▹ *n*: **to be on the ~** (*animal*) polować; (*fig: person*) czaić się
**prowler** ['praulə[r]] *n*: **there's a ~ outside** ktoś podejrzany kręci się koło domu
**proximity** [prɔk'sɪmɪtɪ] *n* bliskość *f*
**proxy** ['prɔksɪ] *n*: **by ~** przez pełnomocnika
**prude** [pru:d] *n* świętoszek(-szka) *m(f)*
**prudence** ['pru:dns] *n* rozwaga *f*, roztropność *f*
**prudent** ['pru:dnt] *adj* rozważny, roztropny
**prudish** ['pru:dɪʃ] *adj* pruderyjny, świętoszkowaty
**prune** [pru:n] *n* suszona śliwka *f* ▹ *vt* (*tree*) przycinać (przyciąć *perf*)
**pry** [praɪ] *vi* węszyć; **to pry into** wścibiać nos w *+acc*
**PS** *abbr* (= *postscript*) PS
**psalm** [sɑ:m] *n* psalm *m*
**PSAT** (*US*) *n abbr* = **Preliminary Scholastic Aptitude Test**
**PSBR** (*Brit: Econ*) *n abbr* (= *public sector borrowing requirement*) zapotrzebowanie *nt* na kredyty ze strony sektora państwowego
**pseud** [sju:d] (*Brit: inf, pej*) *n* pozer(ka) *m(f)* (*pej*)
**pseudo-** ['sju:dəu] *pref* pseudo...
**pseudonym** ['sju:dənɪm] *n* pseudonim *m*
**PST** (*US*) *abbr* = **Pacific Standard Time**
**PSV** (*Brit*) *n abbr* = **public service vehicle**
**psyche** ['saɪkɪ] *n* psychika *f*
**psychedelic** [saɪkə'dɛlɪk] *adj* psychodeliczny
**psychiatric** [saɪkɪ'ætrɪk] *adj* psychiatryczny
**psychiatrist** [saɪ'kaɪətrɪst] *n* psychiatra *m*
**psychiatry** [saɪ'kaɪətrɪ] *n* psychiatria *f*
**psychic** ['saɪkɪk] *adj* (*disorder*) psychiczny; (*person*) mający zdolności parapsychiczne ▹ *n* medium *nt*
**psycho** ['saɪkəu] (*inf*) *n* psychol *m* (*inf*), świr *m* (*inf*)
**psychoanalyse** [saɪkəu'ænəlaɪz] *vt* poddawać (poddać *perf*) psychoanalizie
**psychoanalysis** [saɪkəuə'nælɪsɪs] (*pl* **psychoanalyses**) *n* psychoanaliza *f*
**psychoanalyst** [saɪkəu'ænəlɪst] *n* psychoanalityk(-yczka) *m(f)*
**psychological** [saɪkə'lɔdʒɪkl] *adj* (*mental*) psychiczny; (*relating to psychology*) psychologiczny
**psychologist** [saɪ'kɔlədʒɪst] *n* psycholog *m*
**psychology** [saɪ'kɔlədʒɪ] *n* (*science*) psychologia *f*; (*character*) psychika *f*
**psychopath** ['saɪkəupæθ] *n* psychopata(-tka) *m(f)*

P

**psychosis** [saɪ'kəusɪs] (*pl* **psychoses**) *n* psychoza *f*
**psychosomatic** ['saɪkəusə'mætɪk] *adj* psychosomatyczny
**psychotherapy** [saɪkəu'θɛrəpɪ] *n* psychoterapia *f*
**psychotic** [saɪ'kɔtɪk] *adj* psychotyczny
**PT** (*Brit: Scol*) *n abbr* (= *physical training*) WF *m*
**Pt** *abbr* (*in place names*) = **Point**
**pt** *abbr* = **pint**; (= *point*) p.
**PTA** *n abbr* (= *Parent-Teacher Association*) ≈ komitet rodzicielski
**Pte** (*Brit: Mil*) *abbr* (= *private*) szer.
**PTO** *abbr* (= *please turn over*) verte
**PTV** (*US*) *n abbr* (= *pay television*) *telewizja płatna*; (= *public television*) *telewizja publiczna*
**pub** [pʌb] *n* = **public house**
**puberty** ['pju:bətɪ] *n* dojrzewanie *nt* płciowe, pokwitanie *nt*
**pubic** ['pju:bɪk] *adj* łonowy
**public** ['pʌblɪk] *adj* publiczny; (*support, interest*) społeczny; (*spending, official*) państwowy ▷ *n*: **the ~** (*people in general*) społeczeństwo *nt*; (*particular set of people*) publiczność *f*; **in ~** publicznie; **the general ~** (*society*) ogół społeczeństwa; (*readers, viewers etc*) szeroka publiczność; **to be ~ knowledge** być powszechnie wiadomym; **to make sth ~** ujawniać (ujawnić *perf*) coś; **to go ~** (*Comm*) wystawiać (wystawić *perf*) akcje na sprzedaż
**public address system** *n* system *m* nagłaśniający
**publican** ['pʌblɪkən] *n* właściciel(ka) *m(f)* pubu
**publication** [pʌblɪ'keɪʃən] *n* (*act*) wydanie *nt*, publikacja *f*; (*book, magazine*) publikacja *f*
**public company** *n* spółka *f* akcyjna
**public convenience** (*Brit*) *n* toaleta *f* publiczna
**public holiday** *n* święto *nt* urzędowe *or* państwowe
**public house** (*Brit*) *n* pub *m*
**publicity** [pʌb'lɪsɪtɪ] *n* (*information*) reklama *f*; (*attention*) rozgłos *m*
**publicize** ['pʌblɪsaɪz] *vt* podawać (podać *perf*) do publicznej wiadomości
**public limited company** *n* = **public company**
**publicly** ['pʌblɪklɪ] *adv* publicznie; **~ owned** w rękach publicznych akcjonariuszy
**public opinion** *n* opinia *f* publiczna
**public ownership** *n*: **taken into ~** upaństwowiony
**Public Prosecutor** *n* oskarżyciel *m* publiczny, prokurator *m*
**public relations** *n* kreowanie *nt* wizerunku firmy
**public relations officer** *n* specjalista *m* od kreowania wizerunku firmy
**public school** *n* (*Brit*) szkoła *f* prywatna (średniego stopnia); (*US*) szkoła *f* państwow
**public sector** *n*: **the ~** sektor *m* państwowy
**public service vehicle** (*Brit*) *n* pojazd *m* komunikacji miejskiej
**public-spirited** [pʌblɪk'spɪrɪtɪd] *adj* społecznikowski
**public transport** *n* komunikacja *f* publiczna
**public utility** *n* zakład *m* użyteczności publicznej *or* usług komunalnych
**public works** *npl* roboty *pl* publiczne
**publish** ['pʌblɪʃ] *vt* (*book, magazine, newspaper*) wydawać (wydać *perf*); (*letter, article*) publikować (opublikować *perf*)
**publisher** ['pʌblɪʃə^r] *n* wydawca *m*
**publishing** ['pʌblɪʃɪŋ] *n* działalność *f* wydawnicza
**publishing company** *n* wydawnictwo *nt*
**puce** [pju:s] *adj* fioletowobrązowy
**puck** [pʌk] *n* krążek *m* (*do gry w hokeja*)
**pucker** ['pʌkə^r] *vi* (*mouth, face*) wykrzywiać się (wykrzywić się *perf*); (*fabric etc*) marszczyć się (pomarszczyć się *perf*) ▷ *vt* (*mouth, face*) wykrzywiać (wykrzywić *perf*); (*fabric etc*) marszczyć (pomarszczyć *perf*)
**pudding** ['pudɪŋ] *n* pudding *m*; (*Brit: dessert*) deser *m*; **black ~**, (*US*) **blood ~** ≈ kaszanka
**puddle** ['pʌdl] *n* kałuża *f*
**puerile** ['pjuəraɪl] *adj* infantylny
**Puerto Rico** ['pwə:təu'ri:kəu] *n* Porto Rico *nt inv*
**puff** [pʌf] *n* (*of cigarette, pipe*) zaciągnięcie się *nt*; (*gasp*) sapnięcie *nt*; (*of air*) podmuch *m* ▷ *vt* (*also*: **puff on, puff at**: *pipe*) pykać (pyknąć *perf*) +*acc*; (*cigarette*) zaciągnąć się (zaciągać się *perf*) +*instr* ▷ *vi* sapać
▸ **puff out** *vt* (*one's chest*) wypinać (wypiąć *perf*); (*one's cheeks*) nadymać (nadąć *perf*)
**puffed** [pʌft] (*inf*) *adj* zasapany
**puffin** ['pʌfɪn] *n* maskonur *m* (*ptak*)
**puff pastry**, (*US*) **puff paste** *n* ciasto *nt* francuskie
**puffy** ['pʌfɪ] *adj* (*face*) spuchnięty; (*eye*) podpuchnięty
**pugnacious** [pʌg'neɪʃəs] *adj* zaczepny, kłótliwy
**pull** [pul] *vt* (*rope, hair etc*) ciągnąć (pociągnąć *perf*) za +*acc*; (*handle*) pociągać (pociągnąć *perf*) za +*acc*; (*trigger*) naciskać (nacisnąć *perf*) (na +*acc*); (*cart etc*) ciągnąć; (*curtain, blind*) zaciąga (zaciągnąć *perf*); (*inf: people*) przyciągać (przyciągnąć *perf*); (*: sexual partner*) podrywać (poderwać *perf*) (*inf*); (*pint of beer*) nalewać (nalać *perf*) (*z beczki*) ▷ *vi* ciągnąć (pociągnąć *perf*) ▷ *n* (*of moon, magnet*) przyciąganie *nt*; (*fig*) wpływ *m*; **to give sth a ~** pociągnąć (*perf*) (za) coś; **to ~ a face** robić (zrobić *perf*) minę; **to ~**

**a muscle** naciągnąć *(perf)* mięsień; **not to ~ one's** *or* **any punches** *(fig)* walić prosto z mostu *(inf)*; **to ~ sth to pieces** *(fig)* nie zostawiać (nie zostawić *perf*) na czymś suchej nitki; **to ~ one's weight** *(fig)* przykładać się (przyłożyć się *perf*) (do pracy); **to ~ o.s. together** brać się (wziąć się *perf*) w garść; **to ~ sb's leg** *(fig)* nabierać (nabrać *perf*) kogoś; **to ~ strings (for sb)** używać (użyć *perf*) swoich wpływów (by komuś pomóc)
▸ **pull apart** *vt* rozdzielać (rozdzielić *perf*)
▸ **pull away** *vi (Aut)* odholowywać (odholować *perf*)
▸ **pull back** *vi* wycofywać się (wycofać się *perf*); *(fig)* hamować się (pohamować się *perf*)
▸ **pull down** *vt (building)* rozbierać (rozebrać *perf*)
▸ **pull in** *vi (Aut: at the kerb)* zatrzymywać się (zatrzymać się *perf*); *(Rail)* wjeżdżać (wjechać *perf*) (na peron *or* stację) ▷ *vt (inf: crowds)* przyciągać (przyciągnąć *perf*); *(inf: money, suspect)* zgarniać (zgarnąć *perf*) *(inf)*
▸ **pull off** *vt (clothes)* ściągać (ściągnąć *perf*); *(fig: difficult thing)* dokonywać (dokonać *perf*) *+gen*
▸ **pull out** *vi (Aut: from kerb)* odjeżdżać (odjechać *perf*); *(: when overtaking)* zmieniać (zmienić *perf*) pas ruchu; *(Rail)* odjeżdżać (odjechać *perf*) (z peronu *or* stacji); *(withdraw)* wycofywać się (wycofać się *perf*) ▷ *vt* wyciągać (wyciągnąć *perf*)
▸ **pull over** *vi (Aut)* zjeżdżać (zjechać *perf*) na bok
▸ **pull through** *vi* wyzdrowieć *(perf)*, wylizać się *(perf) (inf)*
▸ **pull up** *vi (Aut, Rail)* zatrzymywać się (zatrzymać się *perf*) ▷ *vt (object, clothing)* podciągać (podciągnąć *perf*); *(weeds)* wyrywać (wyrwać *perf*); *(chair)* przysuwać (przysunąć *perf*) (sobie)

**pulley** ['pulɪ] *n* blok *m*, wielokrążek *m*
**pull-out** ['pulaut] *n (in magazine)* wkładka *f*
**pullover** ['puləuvə^r] *n* pulower *m*
**pulp** [pʌlp] *n (of fruit)* miąższ *m*; *(for paper)* miazga *f*; *(Literature: pej)* czytadła *pl* ▷ *adj*: **~ fiction** tandetna powieść *f* sensacyjna; **to reduce sth to a ~** ścierać (zetrzeć *perf*) coś na miazgę
**pulpit** ['pulpɪt] *n* ambona *f*
**pulsate** [pʌl'seɪt] *vi (heart)* bić; *(music)* tętnić, pulsować
**pulse** [pʌls] *n (lit, fig)* tętno *nt*, puls *m*; *(Tech)* impuls *m* ▷ *vi* pulsować; **pulses** *npl* nasiona *pl* roślin strączkowych; **to take sb's ~** mierzyć (zmierzyć *(perf)*) komuś tętno; **to have one's finger on the ~** *(fig)* trzymać rękę na pulsie
**pulverize** ['pʌlvəraɪz] *vt* proszkować (sproszkować *perf*); *(fig)* ścierać (zetrzeć *perf*) na proch
**puma** ['pju:mə] *n* puma *f*
**pumice** ['pʌmɪs] *n (also:* **pumice stone***)* pumeks *m*
**pummel** ['pʌml] *vt* okładać pięściami
**pump** [pʌmp] *n* pompa *f*; *(for bicycle)* pompka *f*; *(petrol pump)* dystrybutor *m* (paliwa), pompa *f* benzynowa; *(shoe)* czółenko *nt* ▷ *vt* pompować; **to ~ sb for information** podpytywać (podpytać *perf*) kogoś; **he had his stomach ~ed** zrobili mu płukanie żołądka
▸ **pump up** *vt* pompować (napompować *perf*)
**pumpkin** ['pʌmpkɪn] *n* dynia *f*
**pun** [pʌn] *n* kalambur *m*, gra *f* słów
**punch** [pʌntʃ] *n (blow)* uderzenie *nt* pięścią; *(fig)* siła *f*; *(tool)* dziurkacz *m*; *(drink)* poncz *m* ▷ *vt (person)* uderzać (uderzyć *perf*) pięścią; *(ticket)* kasować (skasować *perf*); **to ~ a hole in** dziurawić (przedziurawić *perf*) *+acc*
▸ **punch in** *(US) vi* odbijać (odbić *perf*) kartę (po przyjściu do pracy)
▸ **punch out** *(US) vi* odbijać (odbić *perf*) kartę (przy wyjściu z pracy)
**Punch and Judy show** *n przedstawienie kukiełkowe z parą stałych bohaterów, Punchem i Judy*
**punch-drunk** ['pʌntʃdrʌŋk] *(Brit) adj (Med)* cierpiący na encefalopatię bokserską; *(fig)* zamroczony, skołowany
**punch(ed) card** *(Comput) n* karta *f* perforowana
**punchline** ['pʌntʃlaɪn] *n* puenta *f*
**punch-up** ['pʌntʃʌp] *(Brit: inf) n* bijatyka *f*
**punctual** ['pʌŋktjuəl] *adj* punktualny
**punctuality** [pʌŋktju'ælɪtɪ] *n* punktualność *f*
**punctually** ['pʌŋktjuəlɪ] *adv* punktualnie; **it will start ~ at six** zacznie się punktualnie o szóstej
**punctuation** [pʌŋktju'eɪʃən] *n* interpunkcja *f*
**punctuation mark** *n* znak *m* przestankowy
**puncture** ['pʌŋktʃə^r] *(Aut) n* przebicie *nt* dętki ▷ *vt* przebijać (przebić *perf*); **I have a ~** złapałem gumę *(inf)*
**pundit** ['pʌndɪt] *n* mędrzec *m* hinduski
**pungent** ['pʌndʒənt] *adj (smell)* gryzący; *(taste)* cierpki; *(fig: article, speech)* ostry; *(: remark)* cierpki
**punish** ['pʌnɪʃ] *vt* karać (ukarać *perf*); **to ~ sb for sth/for doing sth** karać (ukarać *perf*) kogoś za coś/za (z)robienie czegoś
**punishable** ['pʌnɪʃəbl] *adj (offence)* karalny
**punishing** ['pʌnɪʃɪŋ] *adj (fig: exercise, ordeal)* wyczerpujący
**punishment** ['pʌnɪʃmənt] *n* kara *f*; **he took a lot of ~** *(fig)* porządnie mu się dostało

P

**punitive** ['pju:nıtıv] *adj* (*action, measure*) karny
**punk** [pʌŋk] *n* (*also*: **punk rocker**) punk *m*; (*also*: **punk rock**) punk-rock *m*; (*US*: *inf*: *hoodlum*) chuligan *m*
**punnet** ['pʌnıt] *n* kobiałka *f*
**punt** [pʌnt] *n* łódź *f* płaskodenna ▷ *vi* płynąć łodzią płaskodenną
**punter** ['pʌntə^r] (*Brit*) *n* gracz *m* na wyścigach konnych; (*inf*) klient(ka) *m(f)*
**puny** ['pju:nı] *adj* mizerny
**pup** [pʌp] *n* (*young dog*) szczenię *nt*; (*young seal etc*) młode *nt*
**pupil** ['pju:pl] *n* (*Scol*) uczeń/uczennica *m/f*; (*of eye*) źrenica *f*
**puppet** ['pʌpıt] *n* kukiełka *f*; (*fig*) marionetka *f*
**puppet government** *n* rząd *m* marionetkowy
**puppy** ['pʌpı] *n* szczenię *nt*, szczeniak *m*
**purchase** ['pə:tʃıs] *n* (*act*) zakup *m*, kupno *nt*; (*item*) zakup *m*, nabytek *m* ▷ *vt* nabywać (nabyć *perf*), zakupywać (zakupić *perf*); **to get** *or* **gain (a) ~** znajdować (znaleźć *perf*) punkt podparcia *or* oparcia
**purchase order** *n* zamówienie *nt*
**purchase price** *n* cena *f* kupna
**purchaser** ['pə:tʃısə^r] *n* nabywca *m*, kupujący *m*
**purchase tax** *n* podatek *m* od wartości dodanej (*przy zakupie*)
**purchasing power** ['pə:tʃısıŋ-] *n* siła *f* nabywcza
**pure** [pjuə^r] *adj* (*lit, fig*) czysty; **a ~ wool jumper** sweter z czystej wełny; **it's laziness ~ and simple** to (jest) czyste lenistwo
**purebred** ['pjuəbrɛd] *adj* czystej krwi *post*
**purée** ['pjuəreı] *n* przecier *m*
**purely** ['pjuəlı] *adv* (*wholly*) całkowicie
**purgatory** ['pə:gətərı] *n* czyściec *m*
**purge** [pə:dʒ] *n* czystka *f* ▷ *vt* (*organization, party*) przeprowadzać (przeprowadzić *perf*) czystkę w *+loc*; **to ~ sth of** (*lit, fig*) oczyszczać (oczyścić *perf*) coś z *+gen*; **they ~d extremists from the party** oczyścili partię z ekstremistów; **she wanted to ~ her heart of that love** pragnęła usunąć z serca tę miłość
**purification** [pjuərıfı'keıʃən] *n* oczyszczenie *nt*
**purify** ['pjuərıfaı] *vt* oczyszczać (oczyścić *perf*)
**purist** ['pjuərıst] *n* purysta(-tka) *m(f)*
**puritan** ['pjuərıtən] *n* purytanin(-anka) *m(f)*
**puritanical** [pjuərı'tænıkl] *adj* purytański
**purity** ['pjuərıtı] *n* czystość *f*
**purl** [pə:l] (*Knitting*) *n* lewe oczko *nt*
**purloin** [pə:'lɔın] (*fml*) *vt* przywłaszczać (przywłaszczyć *perf*) sobie
**purple** ['pə:pl] *adj* fioletowy
**purport** [pə:'pɔ:t] *vi*: **they ~ to be objective** utrzymują, że są obiektywni; **he ~s not to care** twierdzi, że jakoby mu nie zależy
**purpose** ['pə:pəs] *n* cel *m*; **on ~** celowo; **for illustrative ~s** dla ilustracji; **for all practical ~s** z praktycznego punktu widzenia; **for the ~s of this meeting** dla celów tego spotkania; **to no ~** na próżno; **it was all to little ~** wszystko to nie na wiele się zdało; **a sense of ~** poczucie celu
**purpose-built** ['pə:pəs'bılt] (*Brit*) *adj* specjalnie zbudowany
**purposeful** ['pə:pəsful] *adj* celowy
**purposely** ['pə:pəslı] *adv* celowo
**purr** [pə:^r] *vi* (*cat*) mruczeć
**purse** [pə:s] *n* (*Brit*) portmonetka *f*; (*US*) (damska) torebka *f* ▷ *vt* (*lips*) zaciskać (zacisnąć *perf*)
**purser** ['pə:sə^r] *n* (*Naut*) ochmistrz *m*; (*Mil*) *n* oficer *m* płatnik *m*
**purse-snatcher** ['pə:ssnætʃə^r] (*US*) *n* złodziej(ka) *m(f)* torebek
**pursue** [pə'sju:] *vt* ścigać; (*fig*: *policy, interest, plan*) realizować; (: *aim, objective*) dążyć do osiągnięcia *+gen*
**pursuer** [pə'sju:ə^r] *n* ścigający *m*
**pursuit** [pə'sju:t] *n* (*pastime*) zajęcie *nt*; (*chase*) pościg *m*; (: *fig*) pogoń *f*; **in ~ of** w pościgu za *+instr*; (*fig*: *happiness, pleasure*) w pogoni za *+instr*
**purveyor** [pə'veıə^r] (*fml*) *n* dostarczyciel(ka) *m(f)*
**pus** [pʌs] (*Med*) *n* ropa *f*
**push** [puʃ] *n* (*of button etc*) naciśnięcie *nt*; (*of door*) pchnięcie *nt*; (*of car, person*) popchnięcie *nt* ▷ *vt* (*button, knob*) naciskać (nacisnąć *perf*); (*door*) pchać (pchnąć *perf*); (*car, person*) popychać (popchnąć *perf*); (*fig*: *person*: *to work harder*) dopingować; (: *to reveal information*) naciskać; (: *product*) reklamować; (*inf*: *drugs*) handlować *+instr* ▷ *vi* (*press*) naciskać (nacisnąć *perf*); (*shove*) pchać (pchnąć *perf*); **to ~ for** domagać się *+gen*; **to ~ a door open/shut** otwierać (otworzyć *perf*)/zamykać (zamknąć *perf*) drzwi; **"~"** (*on door*) „pchać"; (*on bell*) „dzwonić"; **to be ~ed for time/money** (*inf*) mieć mało czasu/pieniędzy; **she is ~ing fifty** (*inf*) idzie jej piąty krzyżyk (*inf*); **at a ~** (*Brit*: *inf*) na siłę
▸ **push around** *vt* pomiatać *+instr*
▸ **push aside** *vt* odpychać (odepchnąć *perf*); (*fig*) odsuwać (odsunąć *perf*) na bok
▸ **push in** *vi* wpychać się (wepchnąć się *perf*)
▸ **push off** (*inf*) *vi* spływać (spłynąć *perf*) (*inf*)
▸ **push on** *vi* ciągnąć *or* jechać dalej (*fig*)
▸ **push over** *vt* przewracać (przewrócić *perf*)
▸ **push through** *vt* (*measure, scheme*) przeprowadzać (przeprowadzić *perf*)
▸ **push up** *vt* (*prices etc*) podnosić (podnieść *perf*)

**ush-bike** ['puʃbaɪk] (*Brit*) *n* rower *m*

**ush-button** ['puʃbʌtn] *adj* obsługiwany przez naciskanie przycisków

**ushchair** ['puʃtʃɛə$^{r}$] (*Brit*) *n* spacerówka *f*

**usher** ['puʃə$^{r}$] *n* handlarz *m* narkotykami

**ushover** ['puʃəuvə$^{r}$] (*inf*) *n*: **it's a ~** to łatwizna (*inf*)

**ush-up** ['puʃʌp] (*US*) *n* pompka *f* (*ćwiczenie*)

**ushy** ['puʃɪ] (*pej*) *adj* natarczywy, natrętny

**uss** [pus] (*inf*) *n* kiciuś *m*

**ussy(cat)** ['pusɪ(kæt)] (*inf*) *n* = **puss**

**ut** [put] (*pt, pp* **put**) *vt* (*thing*) kłaść (położyć *perf*); (*person: in room, institution*) umieszczać (umieścić *perf*); (*: in position, situation*) stawiać (postawić *perf*); (*idea, view, case*) przedstawiać (przedstawić *perf*); (*question*) stawiać (postawić *perf*); (*in class, category*) zaliczać (zaliczyć *perf*); (*word, sentence*) zapisywać (zapisać *perf*); **to put sb in a good/bad mood** wprawiać (wprawić *perf*) kogoś w dobry/zły nastrój; **to put sb to bed** kłaść (położyć *perf*) kogoś do łóżka; **to put sb to a lot of trouble** sprawiać (sprawić *perf*) komuś wiele kłopotu; **how shall I put it?** jak by to powiedzieć?; **to put a lot of time into sth** poświęcać (poświęcić *perf*) czemuś wiele czasu; **to put money on a horse** obstawiać (obstawić *perf*) konia; **the cost is now put at 2 billion pounds** koszt szacuje się obecnie na 2 miliardy funtów; **I put it to you that ...** (*Brit*) mówię ci, że...; **to stay put** nie ruszać się (z miejsca)

▸ **put about** *vi* (*Naut*) zmieniać (zmienić *perf*) kurs na przeciwny ▹ *vt* (*rumour*) rozpuszczać (rozpuścić *perf*)

▸ **put across** *vt* (*ideas etc*) wyjaśniać (wyjaśnić *perf*)

▸ **put around** *vt* = **put about**

▸ **put aside** *vt* (*work, money*) odkładać (odłożyć *perf*); (*idea, problem*) pomijać (pominąć *perf*)

▸ **put away** *vt* (*shopping etc*) chować (pochować *perf*); (*money*) odkładać (odłożyć *perf*); (*imprison*) zamykać (zamknąć *perf*); (*inf: consume*) sprzątnąć (*perf*) (*inf*)

▸ **put back** *vt* (*replace*) odkładać (odłożyć *perf*); (*postpone*) przekładać (przełożyć *perf*); (*delay*) opóźniać (opóźnić *perf*)

▸ **put by** *vt* (*money, supplies*) odkładać (odłożyć *perf*)

▸ **put down** *vt* (*book, spectacles*) odkładać (odłożyć *perf*); (*cup, chair*) odstawiać (odstawić *perf*); (*in writing*) zapisywać (zapisać *perf*); (*riot, rebellion*) tłumić (stłumić *perf*); (*humiliate*) poniżać (poniżyć *perf*); (*kill: animal*) usypiać (uśpić *perf*)

▸ **put down to** *vt* przypisywać (przypisać *perf*) +*dat*

▸ **put forward** *vt* (*proposal*) wysuwać (wysunąć *perf*), przedstawiać (przedstawić *perf*); (*ideas, argument*) przedstawiać (przedstawić *perf*); (*watch, clock*) przesuwać (przesunąć *perf*) do przodu; (*date, meeting*) przesuwać (przesunąć *perf*)

▸ **put in** *vt* (*application, complaint*) składać (złożyć *perf*); (*time, effort*) wkładać (włożyć *perf*); (*gas, electricity*) instalować (zainstalować *perf*) ▹ *vi* (*Naut*) zawijać (zawinąć *perf*) do portu

▸ **put in for** *vt fus* (*promotion, leave*) składać (złożyć *perf*) podanie o +*acc*

▸ **put off** *vt* (*postpone*) odkładać (odłożyć *perf*); (*discourage*) zniechęcać (zniechęcić *perf*); (*distract*) rozpraszać

▸ **put on** *vt* (*clothes, glasses*) zakładać (założyć *perf*); (*make-up, ointment*) nakładać (nałożyć *perf*); (*light, TV, record*) włączać (włączyć *perf*); (*play*) wystawiać (wystawić *perf*); (*brake*) naciskać (nacisnąć *perf*) na +*acc*; (*kettle, dinner*) wstawiać (wstawić *perf*); (*accent etc*) udawać; (*extra bus, train*) puszczać (puścić *perf*); (*inf: tease*) podpuszczać (podpuścić *perf*) (*inf*); **to put on airs** wynosić się, wywyższać się; **to put on weight** przybierać (przybrać *perf*) na wadze, tyć (przytyć *perf*)

▸ **put onto** *vt*: **could you put me onto a good lawyer/doctor?** czy mógłbyś mi wskazać dobrego adwokata/lekarza?

▸ **put out** *vt* (*fire*) gasić (ugasić *perf*); (*candle, cigarette, light*) gasić (zgasić *perf*); (*rubbish*) wystawiać (wystawić *perf*) (*przed dom, do zabrania przez służby oczyszczania miasta*); (*cat*) wypuszczać (wypuścić *perf*); (*one's hand*) wyciągać (wyciągnąć *perf*); (*one's tongue*) wystawiać (wystawić *perf*); (*statement etc*) ogłaszać (ogłosić *perf*); (*Brit: shoulder etc*) przemieszczać (przemieścić *perf*); (*inf: inconvenience*) fatygować ▹ *vi*: **to put out to sea** wychodzić (wyjść *perf*) w morze; **to put out from Plymouth** wypływać (wypłynąć *perf*) z Plymouth

▸ **put through** *vt* (*Tel*) łączyć (połączyć *perf*); (*plan, agreement*) przyjmować (przyjąć *perf*); **put me through to Miss Blair** połącz mnie z panną Blair

▸ **put together** *vt* (*furniture, toy*) składać (złożyć *perf*); (*plan, campaign*) organizować (zorganizować *perf*); **more than the rest of them put together** bardziej niż wszyscy pozostali razem wzięci

▸ **put up** *vt* (*fence, building, tent*) stawiać (postawić *perf*); (*umbrella*) rozkładać (rozłożyć *perf*); (*poster, sign*) wywieszać (wywiesić *perf*); (*price, cost*) podnosić (podnieść *perf*); (*person*) przenocowywać (przenocować *perf*);

(*resistance*) stawiać (stawić *perf*); **to put sb up to sth/doing sth** namawiać (namówić *perf*) kogoś do czegoś/(z)robienia czegoś; **to put sth up for sale** wystawiać (wystawić *perf*) coś na sprzedaż

▸ **put upon** *vt fus* nadużywać uprzejmości *+gen*

▸ **put up with** *vt fus* znosić (znieść *perf*) *+acc*

**putative** ['pju:tətɪv] *adj* domniemany

**putrid** ['pju:trɪd] *adj* gnijący

**putt** [pʌt] (*Golf*) *n* uderzenie *nt* piłki

**putter** ['pʌtəʳ] *n* (*Golf*) putter *m* ▹ *vi* (*US*) = **potter**

**putting green** ['pʌtɪŋ-] *n* pole *f* puttingowe

**putty** ['pʌtɪ] *n* kit *m*

**put-up** ['putʌp] *n*: **it was a ~ job** to było wcześniej ukartowane

**puzzle** ['pʌzl] *n* (*mystery*) zagadka *f*; (*game, toy*) układanka *f* ▹ *vt* stanowić zagadkę dla *+gen* ▹ *vi*: **to ~ over sth** głowić się nad czymś; **I'm ~d as to why ...** nie pojmuję, dlaczego...

**puzzling** ['pʌzlɪŋ] *adj* zagadkowy

**PVC** *n abbr* (= *polyvinyl chloride*) PCW *nt inv*

**Pvt.** (*US: Mil*) *abbr* (= *private*) szer.

**PW** (*US*) *n abbr* = **prisoner of war**

**p.w.** *abbr* (= *per week*) tyg.

**PX** (*US: Mil*) *n abbr* = **post exchange**

**pygmy** ['pɪgmɪ] *n* Pigmej(ka) *m(f)*

**pyjamas**, (*US*) **pajamas** [pə'dʒɑ:məz] *npl*: **(a pair of) ~** piżama *f*

**pylon** ['paɪlən] *n* pylon *m*

**pyramid** ['pɪrəmɪd] *n* (*Archit*) piramida *f*; (*Geom*) ostrosłup *m*; (*pile*) stos *m*

**Pyrenean** [pɪrə'ni:ən] *adj* pirenejski

**Pyrenees** [pɪrə'ni:z] *npl*: **the ~** Pireneje *pl*

**Pyrex®** ['paɪrɛks] *n* pyreks *m* (*szkło żaroodporne*) ▹ *adj* żaroodporny

**python** ['paɪθən] *n* pyton *m*

# Qq

**, q** [kjuː] *n* (*letter*) Q *nt*, q *nt*; **Q for Queen** ≈ Q jak Quebec

**atar** [kæ'tɑːʳ] (*Geog*) *n* Katar *m*

**C** (*Brit*: *Jur*) *n abbr* (= *Queen's Counsel*) *stopień w hierarchii sądowej*

**ED** *abbr* (= *quod erat demonstrandum*) c.b.d.o. (= *co było do okazania*), c.n.d. (= *co należało dowieść*)

**M** *n abbr* (*Mil*) = **quartermaster**

**.t.** (*inf*) *n abbr* (= *quiet*): **on the ~** cichcem (*inf*), cichaczem (*inf*)

**ty** *abbr* = **quantity**

**uack** [kwæk] *n* (*of duck*) kwaknięcie *nt*; (*inf, pej*: *doctor*) konował *m* (*inf, pej*) ▷ *vi* kwakać (kwaknąć *perf or* zakwakać *perf*)

**uad** [kwɔd] *abbr* = **quadrangle**; **quadruplet**

**uadrangle** ['kwɔdræŋgl] *n* (*courtyard*) czworokątny dziedziniec *m*

**uadrilateral** [kwɔdrɪ'lætərəl] (*Geom*) *n* czworobok *m*

**uadruped** ['kwɔdrupɛd] *n* czworonóg *m*

**uadruple** [kwɔ'druːpl] *vt* czterokrotnie zwiększać (zwiększyć *perf*) ▷ *vi* wzrastać (wzrosnąć *perf*) czterokrotnie

**uadruplets** [kwɔ'druːplɪts] *npl* czworaczki *pl*

**uagmire** ['kwægmaɪəʳ] *n* trzęsawisko *nt*; (*fig*) gąszcz *m*

**uail** [kweɪl] *n* (*bird*) przepiórka *f* ▷ *vi*: **to ~ at the thought of** drżeć (zadrżeć *perf*) na myśl o *+loc*

**uaint** [kweɪnt] *adj* oryginalny, ciekawy (*najczęściej także staromodny*)

**uake** [kweɪk] *vi* trząść się, dygotać ▷ *n* = **earthquake**

**uaker** ['kweɪkəʳ] *n* kwakier(ka) *m(f)*

**ualification** [kwɔlɪfɪ'keɪʃən] *n* (*often pl*: *degree, diploma*) kwalifikacje *pl*; (*attribute*) zdolność *f*; (*reservation*) zastrzeżenie *nt*; **what are your ~s?** jakie ma Pan/Pani kwalifikacje?

**ualified** ['kwɔlɪfaɪd] *adj* (*doctor, engineer*) dyplomowany; (*worker*) wykwalifikowany; (*agreement, success*) połowiczny; (*praise*) powściągliwy; **to be/feel ~ to do sth** być/czuć się kompetentnym, by coś (z)robić; **he's not ~ for the job** on nie ma kwalifikacji do tej pracy

**qualify** ['kwɔlɪfaɪ] *vt* (*entitle*) upoważniać (upoważnić *perf*); (*modify*) uściślać (uściślić *perf*) ▷ *vi* zdobywać (zdobyć *perf*) dyplom; **to ~ for** (*be eligible*) móc ubiegać się o *+acc*; (*in competition*) kwalifikować się (zakwalifikować się *perf*) do *+gen*; **to ~ as an engineer** zdobywać (zdobyć *perf*) dyplom inżyniera

**qualifying** ['kwɔlɪfaɪɪŋ] *adj*: **~ exam** egzamin *m* kwalifikacyjny; **~ round** eliminacje

**qualitative** ['kwɔlɪtətɪv] *adj* jakościowy

**quality** ['kwɔlɪtɪ] *n* (*standard*) jakość *f*; (*characteristic*: *of person*) cecha *f* (charakteru), przymiot *m* (*usu pl*); (: *of wood, stone*) właściwość *f* ▷ *cpd* dobry jakościowo; **of good/poor ~** dobrej/złej jakości

**quality control** *n* kontrola *f* jakości

**quality papers** (*Brit*) *npl*: **the ~** poważne gazety *pl*

**qualm** [kwɑːm] *n* niepokój *m*; **to have ~s about sth** mieć skrupuły w związku z czymś

**quandary** ['kwɔndrɪ] *n*: **to be in a ~** być w rozterce

**quango** ['kwæŋgəu] (*Brit*) *n abbr* = **quasi-autonomous non-governmental organization**

**quantitative** ['kwɔntɪtətɪv] *adj* ilościowy

**quantity** ['kwɔntɪtɪ] *n* ilość *f*; **in large/small quantities** w dużych/małych ilościach; **in ~** w dużych ilościach; **an unknown ~** (*fig*) niewiadoma

**quantity surveyor** *n* kosztorysant(ka) *m(f)*

**quarantine** ['kwɔrntiːn] *n* kwarantanna *f*; **to be in ~** przechodzić (przejść *perf*) kwarantannę

**quarrel** ['kwɔrl] *n* kłótnia *f* ▷ *vi* kłócić się; **we had a ~ with them** pokłóciliśmy się z nimi; **I've no ~ with him** nic do niego nie mam; **I can't ~ with that** nie mogę się z tym nie zgodzić

**quarrelsome** ['kwɔrəlsəm] *adj* kłótliwy

**quarry** ['kwɔrɪ] *n* (*for stone*) kamieniołom *m*; (*animal being hunted*) zwierzyna *f* ▷ *vt* wydobywać (wydobyć *perf*)

q

**quart** [kwɔ:t] *n* kwarta *f* (1.137 l)
**quarter** ['kwɔ:tə^r] *n* (*fourth part*) ćwierć *f*; (*US: coin*) ćwierć *f* dolara; (*of year*) kwartał *m*; (*of city*) dzielnica *f* ▷ *vt* ćwiartować (poćwiartować *perf*); (*Mil: lodge*) zakwaterowywać (zakwaterować *perf*); **quarters** *npl* (*Mil*) kwatery *pl*; (*for servants, for sleeping etc*) pomieszczenia *pl*; **he had to leave his previous ~s** musiał opuścić (swoje) poprzednie miejsce zamieszkania; **a ~ of an hour** kwadrans; **it's a ~ to 3,** (*US*) **it's a ~ of 3** jest za kwadrans trzecia; **it's a ~ past 3,** (*US*) **it's a ~ after 3** jest kwadrans po trzeciej; **from all ~s** ze wszystkich stron; **at close ~s** z bliska
**quarterdeck** ['kwɔ:tədɛk] (*Naut*) *n* tylny pokład *m*
**quarterfinal** ['kwɔ:tə'faɪnl] *n* ćwierćfinał *m*
**quarterly** ['kwɔ:təlɪ] *adj* kwartalny ▷ *adv* kwartalnie ▷ *n* kwartalnik *m*
**quartermaster** ['kwɔ:təmɑ:stə^r] *n* kwatermistrz *m*
**quartet** [kwɔ:'tɛt] *n* kwartet *m*
**quarto** ['kwɔ:təu] *n* (*size of paper*) kwarto *nt* (*arkusz o wymiarach 20 na 26 cm*); (*book*) *książka formatu kwarto*
**quartz** [kwɔ:ts] *n* kwarc *m* ▷ *cpd* kwarcowy
**quash** [kwɔʃ] *vt* (*verdict etc*) unieważniać (unieważnić *perf*)
**quasi-** ['kweɪzaɪ] *pref* quasi-, niby
**quaver** ['kweɪvə^r] *n* (*Brit: Mus*) ósemka *f* ▷ *vi* (*voice*) drżeć
**quay** [ki:] *n* nabrzeże *nt*
**quayside** ['ki:saɪd] *n* nabrzeże *nt*
**queasiness** ['kwi:zɪnɪs] *n* mdłości *pl*
**queasy** ['kwi:zɪ] *adj*: **to feel ~** mieć mdłości; (*fig*) czuć się niewyraźnie
**Quebec** [kwɪ'bɛk] *n* Quebec *m*
**queen** [kwi:n] *n* królowa *f*; (*Cards*) dama *f*; (*Chess*) hetman *m*, królowa *f*
**queen mother** *n* królowa *f* matka *f*
**queer** [kwɪə^r] *adj* dziwny ▷ *n* (*inf!*) pedał *m* (*inf!*); **I feel ~** (*Brit*) trochę źle się czuję
**quell** [kwɛl] *vt* tłumić (stłumić *perf*)
**quench** [kwɛntʃ] *vt*: **to ~ one's thirst** gasić (ugasić *perf*) pragnienie
**querulous** ['kwɛruləs] *adj* (*person*) kwękający; (*voice*) płaczliwy
**query** ['kwɪərɪ] *n* zapytanie *nt* ▷ *vt* kwestionować (zakwestionować *perf*)
**quest** [kwɛst] *n* poszukiwanie *nt*
**question** ['kwɛstʃən] *n* (*query, problem in exam*) pytanie *nt*; (*doubt*) wątpliwość *f*; (*issue*) kwestia *f* ▷ *vt* (*interrogate*) pytać; (*doubt*) wątpić; **to ask sb a ~, put a ~ to sb** zadawać (zadać *perf*) komuś pytanie; **to bring** *or* **call sth into ~** podawać (podać *perf*) coś w wątpliwość; **the ~ is, ...** problem w tym, ...; **there's no ~ of** nie ma mowy o *+loc*; **the person/night in ~** osoba/noc, o której mowa **it's beyond ~** to nie ulega wątpliwości; **it's out of the ~** (to) wykluczone
**questionable** ['kwɛstʃənəbl] *adj* wątpliwy
**questioner** ['kwɛstʃənə^r] *n* osoba *f* zadająca pytanie
**questioning** ['kwɛstʃənɪŋ] *adj* (*look, expression*) pytający; (*mind*) dociekliwy ▷ *n* (*Police*) przesłuchanie *nt*
**question mark** *n* znak *m* zapytania, pytajnik *m*
**questionnaire** [kwɛstʃə'nɛə^r] *n* kwestionariusz *m*, ankieta *f*
**queue** [kju:] (*Brit*) *n* kolejka *f* ▷ *vi* (*also*: **queue up**) stać w kolejce; **to jump the ~** wpychać się (wepchnąć się *perf*) poza kolejką *or* kolejnością
**quibble** ['kwɪbl] *vi*: **to ~ about** *or* **over sth/with sb** sprzeczać się (posprzeczać się *perf*) o coś/z kimś ▷ *n* drobne zastrzeżenie *nt*
**quiche** [ki:ʃ] *n* tarta *f* (*z nadzieniem z jajek, sera, boczku itp*)
**quick** [kwɪk] *adj* (*fast, swift*) szybki; (*sharp: mind*) bystry; (*: wit*) cięty; (*brief*) krótki ▷ *adv* szybko ▷ *n*: **to cut sb to the ~** (*fig*) dotykać (dotknąć *perf*) kogoś do żywego; **be ~!** szybko!, pospiesz się!; **to be ~ to act** działać szybko; **she was ~ to see that ...** szybko zauważyła, że...; **she has a ~ temper** ma porywcze usposobienie
**quicken** ['kwɪkən] *vt* (*pace, step*) przyśpieszać (przyśpieszyć *perf*) *+gen* ▷ *vi*: **his pace ~ed** przyśpieszył kroku; **her heart would ~ when ...** serce zaczynało jej szybciej bić, gdy ...
**quick-fire** ['kwɪkfaɪə^r] *adj*: **~ questions** grad *m* pytań
**quicklime** ['kwɪklaɪm] *n* wapno *nt* niegaszone
**quickly** ['kwɪklɪ] *adv* szybko
**quickness** ['kwɪknɪs] *n* szybkość *f*; **~ of mind** bystrość umysłu
**quicksand** ['kwɪksænd] *n* ruchomy piasek *m*
**quickstep** ['kwɪkstɛp] *n* szybki fokstrot *m*
**quick-tempered** [kwɪk'tɛmpəd] *adj* porywczy, zapalczywy
**quick-witted** [kwɪk'wɪtɪd] *adj* bystry
**quid** [kwɪd] (*Brit: inf*) *n inv* funciak *m* (*inf*)
**quid pro quo** ['kwɪdprəu'kwəu] *n* usługa *f* za usługę
**quiet** ['kwaɪət] *adj* (*lit, fig*) cichy; (*peaceful, not busy*) spokojny; (*not speaking*) milczący; (*engine, aircraft*) cichobieżny ▷ *n* (*silence*) cisza *f*; (*peacefulness*) spokój *m* ▷ *vt, vi* (*US*) = **quieten**; **keep** *or* **be ~!** bądź *or* siedź cicho!;

**on the ~** cichcem (*inf*), cichaczem (*inf*); **I'll have a ~ word with him** pomówię z nim na osobności
**quieten** ['kwaɪətn] (*Brit*: *also*: **quieten down**) *vi* (*grow calm*) uspokajać się (uspokoić się *perf*); (*grow silent*) cichnąć, ucichać (ucichnąć *perf*) ▷ *vt* (*make less active*) uspokajać (uspokoić *perf*); (*make less noisy*) uciszać (uciszyć *perf*)
**quietly** ['kwaɪətlɪ] *adv* (*not loudly*) cicho; (*without speaking*) w milczeniu; (*calmly*) spokojnie; **she's ~ confident** jest pewna siebie bez okazywania tego
**quietness** ['kwaɪətnɪs] *n* (*peacefulness*) spokój *m*; (*silence*) cisza *f*
**quill** [kwɪl] *n* (*pen*) gęsie pióro *nt*; (*of porcupine*) kolec *m*
**quilt** [kwɪlt] *n* narzuta *f* (*na łóżko*); (*also*: **continental quilt**) kołdra *f*
**quin** [kwɪn] (*Brit*) *n abbr* = **quintuplet**
**quince** [kwɪns] *n* pigwa *f*
**quinine** [kwɪ'ni:n] *n* chinina *f*
**quintet** [kwɪn'tɛt] *n* kwintet *m*
**quintuplets** [kwɪn'tju:plɪts] *npl* pięcioraczki *pl*
**quip** [kwɪp] *n* dowcipna uwaga *f* ▷ *vi*: **..., he ~ped.** ... — zażartował
**quire** ['kwaɪəʳ] *n* libra *f* (*miara papieru*)
**quirk** [kwə:k] *n* dziwactwo *nt*; **a ~ of fate** kaprys losu
**quit** [kwɪt] (*pt, pp* **~** *or* **~ted**) *vt* (*smoking, job*) rzucać (rzucić *perf*); (*premises*) opuszczać (opuścić *perf*) ▷ *vi* rezygnować (zrezygnować *perf*); **to ~ doing sth** przestawać (przestać *perf*) coś robić; **~ stalling!** (*US*: *inf*) przestań kręcić! (*inf*); **notice to ~** (*Brit*) wymówienie
**quite** [kwaɪt] *adv* (*rather*) całkiem, dosyć *or* dość; (*entirely*) całkowicie, zupełnie; **it's not ~ big enough** jest odrobinę za mały; **I ~ like it** całkiem mi się podoba; **I ~ understand** całkowicie rozumiem; **I don't ~ remember** niezupełnie pamiętam; **not ~ as many as the last time** trochę mniej niż ostatnio; **that dinner was ~ something!** co to był za obiad!; **it was ~ a sight** był to niezły widok; **~ a few** sporo; **~ (so)!** (no) właśnie!
**Quito** ['ki:təu] *n* Quito *nt inv*
**quits** [kwɪts] *adj*: **we're ~** jesteśmy kwita; **let's call it ~** niech będzie kwita
**quiver** ['kwɪvəʳ] *vi* drżeć
**quiz** [kwɪz] *n* (*game*) kwiz *m*, quiz *m* ▷ *vt* przepytywać (przepytać *perf*)
**quizzical** ['kwɪzɪkl] *adj* zagadkowy
**quoits** [kwɔɪts] *npl gra polegająca na zarzucaniu pierścieni na słupek*
**quorum** ['kwɔ:rəm] *n* kworum *nt*
**quota** ['kwəutə] *n* (*of imported goods*) kontyngent *m*; (*ration*) przydział *m*
**quotation** [kwəu'teɪʃən] *n* (*from book etc*) cytat *m*; (*estimate*) wycena *f*; (*of shares*) notowanie *nt*
**quotation marks** *npl* cudzysłów *m*
**quote** [kwəut] *n* (*from book etc*) cytat *m*; (*estimate*) wycena *f* ▷ *vt* cytować (zacytować *perf*); (*price*) podawać (podać *perf*); **quotes** *npl* cudzysłów *m*; **in ~s** w cudzysłowie; **~ ... un~** cytuję ... koniec cytatu
**quotient** ['kwəuʃənt] *n* współczynnik *m*
**qv** *abbr* (= *quod vide*) zob.
**qwerty keyboard** ['kwə:tɪ-] *n* klawiatura *f* QWERTY

q

# Rr

**R**[1], **r** [ɑːʳ] *n* (*letter*) R *nt*, r *nt*; **R for Robert,** (*US*) **R for Roger** ≈ R jak Roman

**R**[2] *abbr* (= *Réaumur (scale)*) R; (*US*: *Film*: = *restricted*) (od lat) 18

**R.** *abbr* (= *right*) pr.; (= *river*) rz.; (*US*: *Pol*) = **republican**; (*Brit*: = *Rex*) Król *m*; (: = *Regina*) Królowa *f*

**RA** *abbr* (*Mil*) = **rear admiral** ▷ *n abbr* (*Brit*) = **Royal Academy**; = **Royal Academician**

**RAAF** *n abbr* (*Mil*) = **Royal Australian Air Force**

**Rabat** [rə'bɑːt] *n* Rabat *m*

**rabbi** ['ræbaɪ] *n* rabin *m*

**rabbit** ['ræbɪt] *n* królik *m* ▷ *vi* (*Brit*: *inf*: *also*: **to rabbit on**) ględzić (*inf*)

**rabbit hole** *n* nora *f* królicza

**rabbit hutch** *n* klatka *f* dla królików

**rabble** ['ræbl] (*pej*) *n* motłoch *m* (*pej*)

**rabid** ['ræbɪd] *adj* wściekły; (*fig*) fanatyczny

**rabies** ['reɪbiːz] *n* wścieklizna *f*

**RAC** (*Brit*) *n abbr* = **Royal Automobile Club**

**raccoon** [rə'kuːn] *n* szop *m* (pracz *m*)

**race** [reɪs] *n* (*species*) rasa *f*; (*competition*) wyścig *m* ▷ *vt*: **to ~ horses/cars** *etc* brać udział w wyścigach konnych/ samochodowych *etc* ▷ *vi* (*compete*) ścigać się; (*hurry*) pędzić (popędzić *perf*), gnać (pognać *perf*); (*heart*) bić szybko; (*engine*) pracować na podwyższonych obrotach; **the human ~** rodzaj ludzki; **the arms ~** wyścig zbrojeń; **a ~ against time** wyścig z czasem; **to ~ sb** *or* **against sb** ścigać się z kimś; **his pulse ~d** miał mocno przyśpieszony puls; **to ~ in/out** wpadać (wpaść *perf*)/wypadać (wypaść *perf*)

**race car** (*US*) *n* = **racing car**

**race car driver** (*US*) *n* = **racing driver**

**racecourse** ['reɪskɔːs] *n* tor *m* wyścigowy

**racehorse** ['reɪshɔːs] *n* koń *m* wyścigowy

**race meeting** *n* wyścigi *pl* konne

**race relations** *npl* stosunki *pl* rasowe

**racetrack** ['reɪstræk] *n* (*for people*) bieżnia *f*; (*for cars*) tor *m* wyścigowy; (*US*) = **racecourse**

**racial** ['reɪʃl] *adj* (*discrimination, prejudice*) rasowy; **~ equality** równouprawnienie ras

**racialism** ['reɪʃlɪzəm] *n* rasizm *m*

**racialist** ['reɪʃlɪst] *adj* rasistowski ▷ *n* rasista(-tka) *m(f)*

**racing** ['reɪsɪŋ] *n* wyścigi *pl*

**racing car** (*Brit*) *n* samochód *m* wyścigowy

**racing driver** (*Brit*) *n* kierowca *m* wyścigowy

**racism** ['reɪsɪzəm] *n* rasizm *m*

**racist** ['reɪsɪst] *adj* rasistowski ▷ *n* rasista(-tka) *m(f)*

**rack** [ræk] *n* (*also*: **luggage rack**) półka *f* (na bagaż); (*also*: **roof rack**) bagażnik *m* na dach; (*for dresses*) wieszak *m*; (*for dishes*) suszarka *f* ▷ *vt*: **~ed by** (*pain, anxiety*) dręczony +*instr*; (*doubts*) nękany +*instr*; **to ~ one's brains** łamać sobie głowę; **magazine ~** stojak na czasopisma; **toast ~** stojak na grzanki; **to go to ~ and ruin** (*building*) zamieniać się (zamienić się *perf*) w ruinę; (*business*) podupadać (podupaść *perf*)

**racket** ['rækɪt] *n* (*for tennis etc*) rakieta *f*; (*noise*) hałas *m*; (*swindle*) kant *m*

**racketeer** [rækɪ'tɪəʳ] (*esp US*) *n* kanciarz *m*

**racoon** [rə'kuːn] *n* = **raccoon**

**racquet** ['rækɪt] *n* (*for tennis etc*) rakieta *f*

**racy** ['reɪsɪ] *adj* (*story etc*) pikantny

**RADA** [rɑːdə] (*Brit*) *n abbr* = **Royal Academy of Dramatic Art**

**radar** ['reɪdɑːʳ] *n* radar *m* ▷ *cpd* radarowy

**radar trap** *n* kontrola *f* radarowa

**radial** ['reɪdɪəl] *adj* promienisty ▷ *n* (*Aut*: *also*: **radial tyre**) opona *f* radialna; **~ roads** drogi rozchodzące się promieniście

**radiance** ['reɪdɪəns] *n* blask *m*

**radiant** ['reɪdɪənt] *adj* (*smile*) promienny; (*person*) rozpromieniony; (*Phys*: *energy*) promienisty; (: *element*) promieniujący

**radiate** ['reɪdɪeɪt] *vt* promieniować, wypromieniowywać (wypromieniować *perf*) (*fig*) promieniować +*instr* ▷ *vi* (*lines, roads*) rozchodzić się promieniście

**radiation** [reɪdɪ'eɪʃən] *n* promieniowanie *nt*

**radiation sickness** *n* choroba *f* popromienna

**radiator** ['reɪdɪeɪtəʳ] *n* (*heater*) kaloryfer *m*; (*Aut*) chłodnica *f*

**radiator cap** *n* korek *m* chłodnicy

**radiator grill** *n* okratowanie *nt* wlotu chłodnicy
**radical** ['rædɪkl] *adj* radykalny ▷ *n* radykał *m*
**radii** ['reɪdɪaɪ] *npl of* **radius**
**radio** ['reɪdɪəu] *n* (*broadcasting*) radio *nt*; (*device: for receiving broadcasts*) radioodbiornik *m*, radio *nt*; (*: for transmitting and receiving*) radiostacja *f* ▷ *vi*: **to ~ to sb** łączyć się (połączyć się *perf*) z kimś przez radio ▷ *vt* (*person*) łączyć się (połączyć się *perf*) przez radio z *+instr*; (*information, message*) nadawać (nadać *perf*) przez radio; (*one's position*) podawać (podać *perf*) przez radio; **on the ~** w radiu
**radio...** ['reɪdɪəu] *pref* radio...
**radioactive** ['reɪdɪəu'æktɪv] *adj* promieniotwórczy, radioaktywny
**radioactivity** ['reɪdɪəuæk'tɪvɪtɪ] *n* (*of substance*) promieniotwórczość *f*, radioaktywność *f*; (*radiation*) promieniowanie *nt*
**radio announcer** *n* spiker(ka) *m(f)* radiowy(-wa) *m(f)*
**radio-controlled** ['reɪdɪəukən'trəuld] *adj* sterowany radiowo
**radiographer** [reɪdɪ'ɔgrəfəʳ] *n* technik *m* rentgenowski
**radiography** [reɪdɪ'ɔgrəfɪ] *n* radiografia *f*
**radiologist** [reɪdɪ'ɔlədʒɪst] *n* radiolog *m*, rentgenolog *m*
**radiology** [reɪdɪ'ɔlədʒɪ] *n* radiologia *f*, rentgenologia *f*
**radio station** *n* stacja *f* radiowa
**radio taxi** *n* radio-taxi *nt inv*
**radiotelephone** ['reɪdɪəu'tɛlɪfəun] *n* radiotelefon *m*
**radio telescope** *n* radioteleskop *m*
**radiotherapist** ['reɪdɪəu'θɛrəpɪst] *n* radioterapeuta(-tka) *m(f)*
**radiotherapy** ['reɪdɪəu'θɛrəpɪ] *n* radioterapia *f*
**radish** ['rædɪʃ] *n* rzodkiewka *f*
**radium** ['reɪdɪəm] *n* rad *m*
**radius** ['reɪdɪəs] (*pl* **radii**) *n* promień *m*; **within a ~ of 50 miles** w promieniu 50 mil; **from a 25-mile ~** z terenów w promieniu 25 mil
**RAF** (*Brit*) *n abbr* = **Royal Air Force**
**raffia** ['ræfɪə] *n* rafia *f*
**raffish** ['ræfɪʃ] *adj* rozhukany
**raffle** ['ræfl] *n* loteria *f* fantowa ▷ *vt* wystawiać (wystawić *perf*) jako fant na loterii; **~ ticket** los loterii fantowej
**raft** [rɑ:ft] *n* (*craft*) tratwa *f*; (*also*: **life raft**) tratwa *f* ratunkowa
**rafter** ['rɑ:ftəʳ] *n* krokiew *f*
**rag** [ræg] *n* (*piece of cloth*) szmata *f*; (*: small*) szmatka *f*; (*pej: newspaper*) szmatławiec *m* (*pej*); (*Brit: Scol*) *seria imprez studenckich, z których dochód przeznaczony jest na cele dobroczynne* ▷ *vt* (*Brit*) dokuczać *+dat*; **rags** *npl* łachmany *pl*; **in rags** (*person*) w łachmanach; (*clothes*) w strzępach; **a rags-to-riches story** historia zawrotnej kariery
**rag-and-bone man** [rægən'bəun-] (*Brit*) *n* handlarz *m* starzyzną, szmaciarz *m* (*inf*)
**ragbag** ['rægbæg] *n* miszmasz *m* (*inf*)
**rag doll** *n* szmaciana lalka *f*
**rage** [reɪdʒ] *n* wściekłość *f* ▷ *vi* (*person*) wściekać się; (*storm*) szaleć; (*debate*) wrzeć; **it's all the ~** to (jest) ostatni krzyk mody; **to fly into a ~** wpadać (wpaść *perf*) we wściekłość
**ragged** ['rægɪd] *adj* (*edge, line*) nierówny; (*clothes*) podarty; (*person*) obdarty; (*beard*) postrzępiony
**raging** ['reɪdʒɪŋ] *adj* (*sea*) wzburzony; (*storm*) szalejący; (*fever*) bardzo wysoki; (*thirst*) dokuczliwy; (*toothache*) dotkliwy
**rag trade** (*inf*) *n*: **the ~** przemysł *m* odzieżowy
**raid** [reɪd] *n* (*Mil*) atak *m*; (*by aircraft, police*) nalot *m*; (*by criminal*) napad *m* ▷ *vt* (*Mil*) atakować; (*by aircraft*) dokonywać (dokonać *perf*) nalotu na *+acc*; (*police*) robić (zrobić *perf*) nalot na *+acc*; (*criminal*) napadać (napaść *perf*) na *+acc*
**rail** [reɪl] *n* (*on stairs, bridge*) poręcz *f*; (*on deck of ship*) reling *m*; **rails** *npl* szyny *pl*; **by ~** koleją
**railcard** ['reɪlkɑ:d] (*Brit*) *n legitymacja uprawniająca młodzież i emerytów do ulgowych przejazdów kolejowych*
**railing(s)** ['reɪlɪŋ(z)] *n(pl)* płot *m* (*z metalowych prętów*)
**railroad** ['reɪlrəud] (*US*) *n* = **railway**
**railway** ['reɪlweɪ] (*Brit*) *n* (*system, company*) kolej *f*; (*track*) linia *f* kolejowa
**railway engine** (*Brit*) *n* lokomotywa *f*
**railway line** (*Brit*) *n* linia *f* kolejowa
**railwayman** ['reɪlweɪmən] (*Brit: irreg*) *n* kolejarz *m*
**railway station** (*Brit*) *n* dworzec *m* kolejowy
**rain** [reɪn] *n* deszcz *m* ▷ *vi*: **it's ~ing** pada (deszcz); **in the ~** w *or* na deszczu; **it's ~ing cats and dogs** leje jak z cebra; **as right as ~** zdrów jak ryba
**rainbow** ['reɪnbəu] *n* tęcza *f*
**rain check** (*US*) *n*: **I'll take a ~ (on it)** może później skorzystam
**raincoat** ['reɪnkəut] *n* płaszcz *m* przeciwdeszczowy
**raindrop** ['reɪndrɔp] *n* kropla *f* deszczu
**rainfall** ['reɪnfɔ:l] *n* opad *m or* opady *pl* deszczu
**rainforest** ['reɪnfɔrɪst] *n* tropikalny las *m* deszczowy
**rainproof** ['reɪnpru:f] *adj* nieprzemakalny

r

**rainstorm** ['reɪnstɔːm] *n* ulewa *f*
**rainwater** ['reɪnwɔːtəʳ] *n* deszczówka *f*
**rainy** ['reɪnɪ] *adj* (*day, season*) deszczowy; (*area*) z dużą ilością opadów *post*; **to save sth for a ~ day** odkładać (odłożyć *perf*) coś na czarną godzinę
**raise** [reɪz] *n* (*esp US: payrise*) podwyżka *f* ▷ *vt* (*hand, one's voice, salary, question*) podnosić (podnieść *perf*); (*siege*) zakańczać (zakończyć *perf*); (*embargo*) znosić (znieść *perf*); (*objection*) wnosić (wnieść *perf*); (*doubts, hopes*) wzbudzać (wzbudzić *perf*); (*cattle, plant*) hodować (wyhodować *perf*); (*crop*) uprawiać; (*child*) wychowywać (wychować *perf*); (*funds, army*) zbierać (zebrać *perf*); (*loan*) zaciągać (zaciągnąć *perf*); **to ~ a glass to sb/sth** wznosić (wznieść *perf*) toast za kogoś/coś; **to ~ a laugh/smile** wywoływać (wywołać *perf*) śmiech/uśmiech
**raisin** ['reɪzn] *n* rodzynek *m*, rodzynka *f*
**Raj** [rɑːdʒ] *n*: **the Raj** *okres panowania brytyjskiego w Indiach*
**rajah** ['rɑːdʒə] *n* radża *m*
**rake** [reɪk] *n* (*tool*) grabie *pl*; (*old: person*) hulaka *m* ▷ *vt* (*person: soil, lawn*) grabić (zagrabić *perf*); (*: leaves*) grabić (zgrabić *perf*); (*gun*) ostrzeliwać (ostrzelać *perf*); (*searchlight*) przeczesywać (przeczesać *perf*); **he's raking it in** (*inf*) robi duże pieniądze (*inf*)
**rake-off** ['reɪkɔf] (*inf*) *n* działka *f* (*inf*), dola *f* (*inf*)
**rally** ['rælɪ] *n* (*Pol*) wiec *m*; (*Aut*) rajd *m*; (*Tennis etc*) wymiana *f* piłek ▷ *vt* (*support*) pozyskiwać (pozyskać *perf*); (*public opinion, supporters*) mobilizować (zmobilizować *perf*) ▷ *vi* (*sick person*) dochodzić (dojść *perf*) do siebie; (*Stock Exchange*) zwyżkować, ożywiać się (ożywić się *perf*)
▸ **rally round** *vi* łączyć (połączyć *perf*) siły ▷ *vt fus* skupiać się (skupić się *perf*) wokół *+gen*
**rallying point** ['rælɪɪŋ-] *n* punkt *m* zborny
**RAM** [ræm] (*Comput*) *n abbr* (= *random access memory*) RAM *m*
**ram** [ræm] *n* baran *m* ▷ *vt* (*crash into*) taranować (staranować *perf*); (*force into place: post, stick*) wbijać (wbić *perf*); (*: bolt*) zasuwać (zasunąć *perf*)
**Ramadan** ['ræmədæn] (*Rel*) *n* ramadan *m*
**ramble** ['ræmbl] *n* wędrówka *f*, (piesza) wycieczka *f* ▷ *vi* (*walk*) wędrować; (*also:* **ramble on**) mówić bez ładu i składu
**rambler** ['ræmbləʳ] *n* (*walker*) turysta(-tka) *m(f)* pieszy(-sza) *m(f)*; (*Bot*) pnącze *nt*
**rambling** ['ræmblɪŋ] *adj* (*speech, letter*) bezładny, chaotyczny; (*house*) chaotycznie zbudowany; (*Bot*) pnący
**rambunctious** [ræm'bʌŋkʃəs] (*US*) *adj* = **rumbustious**

**RAMC** (*Brit*) *n abbr* = **Royal Army Medical Corps**
**ramifications** [ræmɪfɪ'keɪʃənz] *npl* konsekwencje *pl*, implikacje *pl*
**ramp** [ræmp] *n* podjazd *m*; **on ~** (*US*) wjazd na autostradę; **off ~** (*US*) zjazd z autostrady
**rampage** [ræm'peɪdʒ] *n*: **to be/go on the ~** siać zniszczenie ▷ *vi*: **they went rampaging through the town** przeszli przez miasto, siejąc zniszczenie
**rampant** ['ræmpənt] *adj*: **to be ~** szerzyć się
**rampart** ['ræmpɑːt] *n* wał *m* obronny
**ramshackle** ['ræmʃækl] *adj* (*house*) walący się; (*cart, table*) rozklekotany
**RAN** *n abbr* = **Royal Australian Navy**
**ran** [ræn] *pt of* **run**
**ranch** [rɑːntʃ] *n* ranczo *nt*, rancho *nt*
**rancher** ['rɑːntʃəʳ] *n* (*owner*) ranczer *m*; (*worker*) pomocnik *m* (na ranczo)
**rancid** ['rænsɪd] *adj* zjełczały
**rancour**, (*US*) **rancor** ['ræŋkəʳ] *n* nienawiść *f*
**random** ['rændəm] *adj* (*arrangement, selection*) przypadkowy; (*Comput, Math*) losowy ▷ *n*: **at ~** na chybił trafił
**random access** (*Comput*) *n* dostęp *m* swobodny
**random access memory** (*Comput*) *n* pamięć *f* o dostępie swobodnym
**randy** ['rændɪ] (*Brit: inf*) *adj* napalony (*inf*)
**rang** [ræŋ] *pt of* **ring**
**range** [reɪndʒ] *n* (*of mountains*) łańcuch *m*; (*of missile*) zasięg *m*; (*of voice*) skala *f*; (*of subjects, possibilities*) zakres *m*; (*of products*) asortyment *m*; (*also:* **rifle range**) strzelnica *f*; (*also:* **kitchen range**) piec *m* (kuchenny) ▷ *vt* ustawiać (ustawić *perf*) w rzędzie ▷ *vi*: **to ~ over** obejmować *+acc*; **to ~ from ... to ...** wahać się od *+gen* do *+gen*; **do you have anything else in this price ~?** czy ma Pan/Pani coś jeszcze w tym przedziale cenowym?; **within (firing) ~** w zasięgu strzału; **~d right/left** (*text*) wysunięty w prawo/lewo; **at close ~** z bliska
**ranger** ['reɪndʒəʳ] *n* strażnik *m* leśny
**Rangoon** [ræŋ'guːn] *n* Rangun *m*
**rank** [ræŋk] *n* (*row*) szereg *m*; (*status*) ranga *f*; (*Mil*) stopień *m*; (*of society*) warstwa *f*; (*Brit: also:* **taxi rank**) postój *m* (taksówek) ▷ *vi*: **to ~ as/among** zaliczać się do *+gen* ▷ *vt*: **he is ~ed third** jest klasyfikowany na trzecim miejscu ▷ *adj* (*stinking*) cuchnący; (*sheer*) czysty; **the ranks** *npl* (*Mil*) szeregowi (żołnierze) *pl*; **the ~ and file** (*of organization*) szeregowi członkowie; **to close ~s** (*fig*) zwierać (zewrzeć *perf*) szeregi
**rankle** ['ræŋkl] *vi*: **to ~ with sb** napełniać kogoś goryczą

**ansack** ['rænsæk] *vt* (*search*) przetrząsać (przetrząsnąć *perf*); (*plunder*) plądrować (splądrować *perf*)
**ansom** ['rænsəm] *n* okup *m*; **to hold to ~** trzymać *or* przetrzymywać w charakterze zakładnika; (*fig*) stawiać (postawić *perf*) w przymusowej sytuacji
**ant** [rænt] *vi*: **to ~ (and rave)** wygłaszać (wygłosić *perf*) tyradę; (*angrily*) rzucać gromy
**anting** ['ræntɪŋ] *n* tyrada *f*
**ap** [ræp] *vi* (*on door, table*) pukać (zapukać *perf*), stukać (zastukać *perf*) ▷ *n* (*at door*) pukanie *nt*, stukanie *nt*; (*also*: **rap music**) rap *m*; **to receive a rap on** *or* **over the knuckles** dostawać (dostać *perf*) po łapach (*fig*)
**ape** [reɪp] *n* (*crime*) gwałt *m*; (*Bot*) rzepak *m* ▷ *vt* gwałcić (zgwałcić *perf*)
**ape(seed) oil** ['reɪp(si:d)-] *n* olej *m* rzepakowy
**apid** ['ræpɪd] *adj* (*growth, change*) gwałtowny; (*heartbeat, steps*) bardzo szybki
**apidity** [rə'pɪdɪtɪ] *n* (*of growth, change*) gwałtowność *f*; (*of movement*) szybkość *f*
**apidly** ['ræpɪdlɪ] *adv* (*grow, increase*) gwałtownie; (*walk, move*) bardzo szybko
**apids** ['ræpɪdz] *npl* progi *pl* (*rzeczne*)
**apist** ['reɪpɪst] *n* gwałciciel *m*
**apport** [ræ'pɔː[r]] *n* porozumienie *nt*, wzajemne zrozumienie *nt*
**approchement** [ræ'prɔʃmɑ̃:ŋ] *n* zbliżenie *nt*
**apt** [ræpt] *adj* (*attention*) wytężony, napięty; **she was ~ in contemplation** była pogrążona w myślach
**apture** ['ræptʃə[r]] *n* zachwyt *m*; **to go into ~s over** unosić się z zachwytu nad *+instr*
**apturous** ['ræptʃərəs] *adj* (*applause*) pełen zachwytu *or* uniesienia; (*welcome*) entuzjastyczny
**are** [rɛə[r]] *adj* rzadki; (*steak*) krwisty; **it is ~ to** .. rzadko udaje się *+infin*
**arebit** ['rɛəbɪt] *n see* **Welsh rarebit**
**arefied** ['rɛərɪfaɪd] *adj* rozrzedzony; (*fig*) elitarny, ekskluzywny
**arely** ['rɛəlɪ] *adv* rzadko
**aring** ['rɛərɪŋ] *adj*: **they are ~ to go** (*inf*) palą się, żeby zacząć
**arity** ['rɛərɪtɪ] *n* rzadkość *f*
**ascal** ['rɑ:skl] *n* (*child*) łobuz *m*; (*rogue*) łajdak *m*
**ash** [ræʃ] *adj* pochopny ▷ *n* (*Med*) wysypka *f*; (*of events, robberies*) seria *f*; **to come out in a ~** dostawać (dostać *perf*) wysypki
**asher** ['ræʃə[r]] *n* (*of bacon*) plasterek *m*
**ashly** ['ræʃlɪ] *adv* pochopnie
**asp** [rɑ:sp] *n* (*tool*) tarnik *m*, raszpla *f*; (*sound*) zgrzyt *m*, zgrzytanie *nt* ▷ *vt* chrypieć (wychrypieć *perf*)
**raspberry** ['rɑ:zbərɪ] *n* malina *f*; **to blow a ~** (*inf*) prychnąć (*perf*)
**rasping** ['rɑ:spɪŋ] *adj* zgrzytliwy
**rat** [ræt] *n* szczur *m*
**ratable** ['reɪtəbl] *adj* = **rateable**
**ratchet** ['rætʃɪt] *n* mechanizm *m* zapadkowy; **~ wheel** koło zapadkowe
**rate** [reɪt] *n* (*pace*) tempo *nt*; (*ratio*) współczynnik *m* ▷ *vt* (*value*) cenić; (*estimate*) oceniać (ocenić *perf*); **rates** *npl* (*Brit*: *property tax*) podatek *m* od nieruchomości; (*fees*) składki *pl*; (*prices*) ceny *pl*; **to ~ sb/sth as** uważać kogoś/coś za *+acc*; **to ~ sb/sth among** zaliczać (zaliczyć *perf*) kogoś/coś do *+gen*; **at a ~ of 60 kph** z szybkością 60 km/h; **~ of taxation/interest** stopa podatkowa/ procentowa; **an eight per cent inflation ~** ośmioprocentowa stopa inflacji; **~ of growth** (*Econ*) tempo wzrostu gospodarczego; **~ of return** stopa zysku; **mortgage ~** oprocentowanie kredytu hipotecznego; **birth ~** współczynnik urodzeń; **pulse ~** częstość tętna; **at this/that ~** w tym tempie; (*fig*) w ten sposób; **at any ~** w każdym razie
**rateable value** ['reɪtəbl-] (*Brit*) *n* wartość *f* opodatkowana (*nieruchomości*)
**ratepayer** ['reɪtpeɪə[r]] (*Brit*) *n* osoba *f* płacąca podatek od nieruchomości
**rather** ['rɑ:ðə[r]] *adv* dość, dosyć; **~ a lot** trochę (za) dużo; **it's ~ expensive** to (jest) trochę (zbyt) drogie; **it's ~ a pity** trochę szkoda; **I would ~ go** wolałabym pójść; **I'd ~ not say** wolałbym nie mówić; **~ than** zamiast *+gen*; **or ~** czy (też) raczej; **I ~ think he won't come** mam wrażenie, że (raczej) nie przyjdzie
**ratification** [rætɪfɪ'keɪʃən] *n* ratyfikacja *f*
**ratify** ['rætɪfaɪ] *vt* ratyfikować (ratyfikować *perf*)
**rating** ['reɪtɪŋ] *n* (*score*) wskaźnik *m*; (*assessment*) ocena *f*; (*Naut*: *Brit*) marynarz *m*; **ratings** *npl* (*Radio, TV*) notowania *pl*
**ratio** ['reɪʃɪəu] *n* stosunek *m*; **in the ~ of five to one** w stosunku pięć do jednego; **a high pupil/teacher ~** duża liczba uczniów przypadających na jednego nauczyciela
**ration** ['ræʃən] *n* przydział *m*, racja *f* ▷ *vt* racjonować, wydzielać; **rations** *npl* (*Mil*) racje *pl* żywnościowe
**rational** ['ræʃənl] *adj* racjonalny
**rationale** [ræʃə'nɑ:l] *n* racjonalna podstawa *f*
**rationalization** [ræʃnəlaɪ'zeɪʃən] *n* racjonalizacja *f*
**rationalize** ['ræʃnəlaɪz] *vt* racjonalizować (zracjonalizować *perf*)
**rationally** ['ræʃnəlɪ] *adv* racjonalnie
**rationing** ['ræʃnɪŋ] *n* reglamentacja *f*

**rat poison** *n* trutka *f* na szczury
**rat race** *n*: **the ~** wyścig *m* szczurów (*bezkompromisowa walka o sukces*)
**rattan** [ræ'tæn] *n* rattan *m*
**rattle** ['rætl] *n* (*of window*) stukanie *nt*; (*of train*) turkot *m*; (*of engine*) stukot *m*; (*of coins*) brzęk *m*; (*of chain*) szczęk *m*; (*for baby*) grzechotka *f*; (*of snake*) grzechotanie *nt* ▷ *vi* (*window, engine*) stukać; (*train*) turkotać (zaturkotać *perf*); (*coins, bottles*) brzęczeć (zabrzęczeć *perf*); (*chains*) szczękać (szczęknąć *perf*) ▷ *vt* trząść (zatrząść *perf*) +*instr*; (*fig*) wytrącać (wytrącić *perf*) z równowagi; **to ~ along** przejeżdżać (przejechać *perf*) z turkotem
**rattlesnake** ['rætlsneɪk] *n* grzechotnik *m*
**ratty** ['rætɪ] (*inf*) *adj* nerwowy, popędliwy
**raucous** ['rɔ:kəs] *adj* (*voice, laughter*) chrapliwy; (*party*) hałaśliwy
**raucously** ['rɔ:kəslɪ] *adv* hałaśliwie
**raunchy** ['rɔ:ntʃɪ] *adj* seksowny (*inf*)
**ravage** ['rævɪdʒ] *vt* pustoszyć (spustoszyć *perf*)
**ravages** ['rævɪdʒɪz] *npl* spustoszenia *pl*
**rave** [reɪv] *vi* (*in anger*) wrzeszczeć ▷ *adj* (*inf: review*) entuzjastyczny ▷ *n* (*Brit: inf: dance*) impreza *f* (*inf*)
▸ **rave about** *vt fus* zachwycać się +*instr*
**raven** ['reɪvən] *n* kruk *m*
**ravenous** ['rævənəs] *adj* (*person*) wygłodniały; (*appetite*) wilczy
**ravine** [rə'vi:n] *n* wąwóz *m*
**raving** ['reɪvɪŋ] *adj*: **~ lunatic** skończony wariat *m*
**ravings** ['reɪvɪŋz] *npl* bełkot *m*
**ravioli** [rævɪ'əulɪ] *n* ravioli *nt inv*
**ravishing** ['rævɪʃɪŋ] *adj* olśniewający
**raw** [rɔ:] *adj* (*meat, cotton*) surowy; (*sugar*) nierafinowany; (*wound*) otwarty; (*skin*) obtarty; (*: from sun*) spalony; (*person: inexperienced*) zielony (*inf*); (*day*) przenikliwie zimny; **to get a raw deal** zostać (*perf*) źle potraktowanym
**Rawalpindi** [rɔ:l'pɪndɪ] *n* Rawalpindi *nt inv*
**raw material** *n* surowiec *m*
**ray** [reɪ] *n* promień *m*; **ray of hope** promyk nadziei
**rayon** ['reɪɔn] *n* sztuczny jedwab *m*
**raze** [reɪz] *vt* (*also*: **raze to the ground**) zrównywać (zrównać *perf*) z ziemią
**razor** ['reɪzə^r] *n* brzytwa *f*; (*safety razor*) maszynka *f* do golenia; (*electric*) golarka *f* elektryczna, elektryczna maszynka *f* do golenia
**razor blade** *n* żyletka *f*
**razzle** ['ræzl] (*Brit: inf*) *n*: **to go on the ~** iść (pójść *perf*) się zabawić
**razzmatazz** ['ræzmə'tæz] (*inf*) *n* pompa *f*
**R & B** *n abbr* = **rhythm and blues**
**R & D** *n abbr* (= *research and development*) prace *pl* badawczo-rozwojowe
**R & R** (*US: Mil*) *n abbr* = **rest and recreation**
**RC** *abbr* (= *Roman Catholic*) rz.-kat.
**RCAF** *n abbr* = **Royal Canadian Air Force**
**RCMP** *n abbr* = **Royal Canadian Mounted Police**
**RCN** *n abbr* = **Royal Canadian Navy**
**RD** (*US: Post*) *abbr* = **rural delivery**
**Rd** *abbr* (= *road*) ul.
**RDC** (*Brit*) *n abbr* (*formerly*) = **rural district council**
**RE** (*Brit*) *n abbr* (*Scol*: = *religious education*) religia *f*; (*Mil*: = *Royal Engineers*) *królewscy saperzy*
**re** [ri:] *prep* (*in letter*) dotyczy +*gen*, w sprawie +*gen*
**reach** [ri:tʃ] *n* zasięg *m* ▷ *vt* (*destination*) docierać (dotrzeć *perf*) do +*gen*; (*conclusion*) dochodzić (dojść *perf*) do +*gen*; (*decision*) podejmować (podjąć *perf*); (*age, agreement*) osiągać (osiągnąć *perf*); (*extend to*) sięgać (sięgnąć *perf*) do +*gen*, dochodzić (dojść *perf*) do +*gen*; (*be able to touch*) dosięgać (dosięgnąć *perf*) (do) +*gen*; (*by telephone*) kontaktować się (skontaktować się *perf*) (telefonicznie) z +*instr* ▷ *vi* wyciągać (wyciągnąć *perf*) rękę; **reaches** *npl* (*of river*) dorzecze *nt*; **within ~** osiągalny; **out of ~** nieosiągalny; **within (easy) ~ of the shops/station** (bardzo) blisko sklepów/ dworca; **beyond the ~ of** (*fig*) poza zasięgiem +*gen*; **"keep out of the ~ of children"** „chronić przed dziećmi"; **can I ~ you at your hotel?** czy można się z tobą skontaktować w hotelu?
▸ **reach out** *vt* wyciągać (wyciągnąć *perf*) ▷ *vi* wyciągać (wyciągnąć *perf*) rękę; **to ~ out for sth** sięgać (sięgnąć *perf*) po coś
**react** [ri:'ækt] *vi* (*respond*): **to ~ (to)** reagować (zareagować *perf*) (na +*acc*); (*rebel*): **to ~ (against)** buntować się (zbuntować się *perf*) (przeciwko +*dat*); (*Chem*): **to ~ (with)** reagować (z +*instr*)
**reaction** [ri:'ækʃən] *n* reakcja *f*; **reactions** *npl* (*reflexes*) reakcje *pl*; **a ~ against sth** bunt przeciwko czemuś
**reactionary** [ri:'ækʃənrɪ] *adj* reakcyjny ▷ *n* reakcjonista(-tka) *m(f)*
**reactor** [ri:'æktə^r] *n* (*also*: **nuclear reactor**) reaktor *m* (jądrowy)
**read** [ri:d] (*pt, pp* ~) *vi* (*person*) czytać; (*piece of writing*) brzmieć ▷ *vt* (*book*) czytać (przeczytać *perf*); (*sb's mood*) odgadywać (odgadnąć *perf*); (*sb's thoughts*) czytać w +*loc*; (*sb's lips*) czytać z +*gen*; (*meter etc*) odczytywać (odczytać *perf*); (*subject at university*) studiować; **do you ~ music?** czy umiesz czytać nuty?; **to ~ sb's mind** czytać w czyichś myślach; **to ~**

**between the lines** czytać między wierszami; **thermometers are ~ing 108 degrees in the shade** termometry wskazują czterdzieści dwa stopnie w cieniu; **to take sth as ~** brać (wziąć *perf*) coś za pewnik; **do you ~ me?** (*Tel*) słyszysz mnie?; **to ~ sth into sb's remarks** doszukiwać się (doszukać się *perf*) czegoś w czyichś uwagach
▸ **read out** *vt* odczytywać (odczytać *perf*) (na głos)
▸ **read over** *vt* czytać (przeczytać *perf*) jeszcze raz
▸ **read through** *vt* (*quickly*) czytać (przeczytać *perf*) pobieżnie; (*thoroughly*) czytać (przeczytać *perf*) uważnie
▸ **read up on** *vt fus* poczytać (*perf*) na temat *+gen*

**readable** ['ri:dəbl] *adj* (*legible*) czytelny; (*worth reading*) wart przeczytania

**reader** ['ri:dəʳ] *n* (*person*) czytelnik(-iczka) *m(f)*; (*book*) wypisy *pl*; (*: for children*) czytanka *f*; (*Brit: at university*) *starszy wykładowca, niższy o stopień od profesora*; **he is an avid ~** bardzo lubi czytać

**readership** ['ri:dəʃɪp] *n* czytelnicy *vir pl*

**readily** ['rɛdɪlɪ] *adv* (*accept, agree*) ochoczo; (*available*) łatwo

**readiness** ['rɛdɪnɪs] *n* gotowość *f*; **in ~ for** gotowy do *+gen*

**reading** ['ri:dɪŋ] *n* (*of books etc*) czytanie *nt*, lektura *f*; (*understanding*) rozumienie *nt*; (*literary event*) czytanie *nt*; (*on meter etc*) odczyt *m*

**reading lamp** *n* lampka *f* na biurko

**reading matter** *n* materiały *pl* do czytania

**reading room** *n* czytelnia *f*

**readjust** [ri:ə'dʒʌst] *vt* (*knob, focus*) ustawiać (ustawić *perf*); (*instrument*) regulować (wyregulować *perf*) ▹ *vi*: **to ~ (to)** przystosowywać się (przystosować się *perf*) (do *+gen*)

**readjustment** [ri:ə'dʒʌstmənt] *n* aklimatyzacja *f*

**ready** ['rɛdɪ] *adj* gotowy; (*easy*) łatwy ▹ *n*: **at the ~** (*Mil*) gotowy do strzału; (*fig*) w pogotowiu; **~ for use** gotowy do użycia; **to get ~** *vi* przygotowywać się (przygotować się *perf*) ▹ *vt* przygotowywać (przygotować *perf*)

**ready cash** *n* gotówka *f*

**ready-cooked** ['rɛdɪkukt] *adj* gotowy

**ready-made** ['rɛdɪ'meɪd] *adj* (*clothes*) gotowy

**ready-mix** ['rɛdɪmɪks] *n* (*for cakes*) ciasto *nt* w proszku; (*concrete*) masa *f* betonowa prefabrykowana

**ready money** *n* = **ready cash**

**ready reckoner** [-'rɛkənəʳ] (*Brit*) *n* tablice *pl* obliczeniowe *or* przeliczeniowe

**ready-to-wear** ['rɛdɪtə'wɛəʳ] *adj*: **~ clothes** konfekcja *f*

**reaffirm** [ri:ə'fə:m] *vt* potwierdzać (potwierdzić *perf*)

**reagent** [ri:'eɪdʒənt] *n*: **chemical ~** odczynnik *m* (chemiczny)

**real** [rɪəl] *adj* prawdziwy ▹ *adv* (*US: inf*) naprawdę; **in ~ life** w rzeczywistości; **in ~ terms** faktycznie

**real estate** *n* nieruchomość *f* ▹ *cpd* (*US*): **~ business** handel *m* nieruchomościami

**realism** ['rɪəlɪzəm] *n* realizm *m*

**realist** ['rɪəlɪst] *n* realista(-tka) *m(f)*

**realistic** [rɪə'lɪstɪk] *adj* realistyczny

**reality** [ri:'ælɪtɪ] *n* rzeczywistość *f*; **in ~** w rzeczywistości

**reality TV** *n* telewizja *f* reality

**realization** [rɪəlaɪ'zeɪʃən] *n* (*understanding*) uświadomienie *nt* sobie, zrozumienie *nt*; (*of dreams, hopes*) spełnienie *nt*; (*Fin: of asset*) upłynnienie *nt*

**realize** ['rɪəlaɪz] *vt* (*understand*) uświadamiać (uświadomić *perf*) sobie, zdawać (zdać *perf*) sobie sprawę z *+gen*; (*dreams, hopes*) spełniać (spełnić *perf*); (*ambition, project*) realizować (zrealizować *perf*); (*amount, profit*) przynosić (przynieść *perf*); **I ~ that ...** zdaję sobie sprawę (z tego), że ...

**really** ['rɪəlɪ] *adv* naprawdę, rzeczywiście; **~?** naprawdę?; **~!** coś podobnego!

**realm** [rɛlm] *n* (*fig: field*) dziedzina *f*, sfera *f*; (*kingdom*) królestwo *nt*

**real-time** ['ri:ltaɪm] (*Comput*) *adj*: **~ processing** przetwarzanie *nt* w czasie rzeczywistym

**realtor** ['rɪəltɔ:ʳ] (*US*) *n* pośrednik *m* handlu nieruchomościami

**ream** [ri:m] *n* (*of paper*) ryza *f*; **reams** (*inf: fig*) (całe) masy *pl*, stosy *pl*

**reap** [ri:p] *vt* (*crop, rewards*) zbierać (zebrać *perf*); (*benefits*) czerpać

**reaper** ['ri:pəʳ] *n* (*machine*) żniwiarka *f*

**reappear** [ri:ə'pɪəʳ] *vi* pojawiać się (pojawić się *perf*) ponownie

**reappearance** [ri:ə'pɪərəns] *n* ponowne pojawienie się *nt*

**reapply** [ri:ə'plaɪ] *vi*: **to ~ for** ponownie ubiegać się o *+acc*

**reappoint** [ri:ə'pɔɪnt] *vt* ponownie mianować (mianować *perf*)

**reappraisal** [ri:ə'preɪzl] *n* ponowna analiza *f* *or* ocena *f*

**rear** [rɪəʳ] *adj* tylny ▹ *n* (*back*) tył *m*; (*buttocks*) tyłek *m* (*inf*) ▹ *vt* (*cattle, chickens*) hodować; (*children*) wychowywać (wychować *perf*) ▹ *vi* (*also*: **rear up**) stawać (stanąć *perf*) dęba

**rear admiral** *n* kontradmirał *m*

r

**rear-engined** ['rɪər'ɛndʒɪnd] (*Aut*) *adj* z silnikiem z tyłu *post*
**rearguard** ['rɪəgɑ:d] *n* straż *f* tylna; **to fight a ~ action** (*fig*) bronić straconych pozycji
**rearm** [ri:'ɑ:m] *vt* (*country*) remilitaryzować (zremilitaryzować *perf*) ▷ *vi* remilitaryzować się (zremilitaryzować się *perf*)
**rearmament** [ri:'ɑ:məmənt] *n* remilitaryzacja *f*
**rearrange** [ri:ə'reɪndʒ] *vt* (*furniture*) przestawiać (przestawić *perf*); (*meeting*) przekładać (przełożyć *perf*)
**rear-view mirror** ['rɪəvju:-] (*Aut*) *n* lusterko *nt* wsteczne
**reason** ['ri:zn] *n* (*cause*) powód *m*, przyczyna *f*; (*rationality*) rozum *m*; (*common sense*) rozsądek *m* ▷ *vi*: **to ~ with sb** przemawiać (przemówić *perf*) komuś do rozsądku; **the ~ for** przyczyna *or* powód *+gen*; **the ~ why ...** przyczyna, dla której ..., powód, dla którego ...; **to have ~ to believe that ...** mieć powód przypuszczać, że ...; **it stands to ~ that ...** jest zrozumiałe, że ...; **she claims with good ~ that ...** twierdzi, nie bez powodu, że ...; **all the more ~ why you should go** tym bardziej powinieneś pójść; **within ~** w granicach (zdrowego) rozsądku
**reasonable** ['ri:znəbl] *adj* (*person*) rozsądny; (*explanation, request*) sensowny; (*amount, price*) umiarkowany; (*not bad*) znośny; **be ~!** bądź rozsądny!
**reasonably** ['ri:znəblɪ] *adv* (*fairly*) dość, dosyć; (*sensibly*) rozsądnie
**reasoned** ['ri:znd] *adj* racjonalny
**reasoning** ['ri:znɪŋ] *n* rozumowanie *nt*
**reassemble** [ri:ə'sɛmbl] *vt* ponownie montować (zmontować *perf*) ▷ *vi* zbierać się (zebrać się *perf*) ponownie
**reassert** [ri:ə'sə:t] *vt* (*one's authority*) ponownie zaznaczać (zaznaczyć *perf*); **he will ~ himself as soon as he gets back** jak tylko wróci, znowu da nam odczuć swoją władzę
**reassurance** [ri:ə'ʃuərəns] *n* (*comfort*) wsparcie *nt* (duchowe), otucha *f*; (*guarantee*) zapewnienie *nt*
**reassure** [ri:ə'ʃuə^r] *vt* dodawać (dodać *perf*) otuchy *+dat*
**reassuring** [ri:ə'ʃuərɪŋ] *adj* dodający otuchy
**reawakening** [ri:ə'weɪknɪŋ] *n* (*of feeling, idea*) odrodzenie się *nt*
**rebate** ['ri:beɪt] *n* zwrot *m* nadpłaty
**rebel** [*n* 'rɛbl, *vb* rɪ'bɛl] *n* (*Pol*) rebeliant(ka) *m(f)*; (*against society, parents*) buntownik(-iczka) *m(f)* ▷ *vi* buntować się (zbuntować się *perf*)
**rebellion** [rɪ'bɛljən] *n* (*Pol*) rebelia *f*; (*against society, parents*) bunt *m*
**rebellious** [rɪ'bɛljəs] *adj* (*subject, child*) nieposłuszny; (*behaviour*) buntowniczy
**rebirth** [ri:'bə:θ] *n* odrodzenie się *nt*
**rebound** [*vb* rɪ'baund, *n* 'ri:baund] *vi* odbijać się (odbić się *perf*) ▷ *n*: **on the ~** (*ball*) odbity; **she married him on the ~** wyszła za niego po przeżyciu zawodu miłosnego
**rebuff** [rɪ'bʌf] *n* odtrącenie *nt* ▷ *vt* (*person*) odtrącać (odtrącić *perf*); (*offer*) odrzucać (odrzucić *perf*)
**rebuild** [ri:'bɪld] (*irreg: like* **build**) *vt* odbudowywać (odbudować *perf*)
**rebuke** [rɪ'bju:k] *vt* karcić (skarcić *perf*), upominać (upomnieć *perf*) ▷ *n* upomnienie *nt*
**rebut** [rɪ'bʌt] (*fml*) *vt* (*criticism*) odpierać (odeprzeć *perf*); (*theory*) obalać (obalić *perf*)
**rebuttal** [rɪ'bʌtl] (*fml*) *n* (*of charges, criticism*) odparcie *nt*
**recalcitrant** [rɪ'kælsɪtrənt] *adj* krnąbrny
**recall** [*vb* rɪ'kɔ:l, *n* 'ri:kɔl] *vt* (*remember*) przypominać (przypomnieć *perf*) sobie; (*ambassador*) odwoływać (odwołać *perf*); (*product*) wycofywać (wycofać *perf*) (ze sprzedaży) ▷ *n* (*of past event*) przypomnienie *nt* (sobie), przywołanie *nt*; (*of ambassador etc*) odwołanie *nt*; **parliament was ~ed from recess** odwołano parlament z wakacji; **beyond ~** nieodwołalny
**recant** [rɪ'kænt] *vi* kajać się (pokajać się *perf*); (*Rel*) wypierać się (wyprzeć się *perf*) swojej wiary
**recap** ['ri:kæp] *vt* rekapitulować (zrekapitulować *perf*), reasumować (zreasumować *perf*) ▷ *vi* rekapitulować, reasumować ▷ *n* rekapitulacja *f*
**recapitulate** [ri:kə'pɪtjuleɪt] *vt, vi* = **recap**
**recapture** [ri:'kæptʃə^r] *vt* (*town*) odbijać (odbić *perf*); (*escaped prisoner*) ponownie ująć (*perf*); (*atmosphere, mood*) odtwarzać (odtworzyć *perf*)
**rec'd** (*Comm*) *abbr* = **received**
**recede** [rɪ'si:d] *vi* (*tide*) cofać się (cofnąć się *perf*); (*lights*) oddalać się (oddalić się *perf*); (*hope*) wygasać (wygasnąć *perf*); (*memory*) słabnąć (osłabnąć *perf*); (*hair*) rzednąć (*na skroniach*)
**receding** [rɪ'si:dɪŋ] *adj* cofnięty
**receipt** [rɪ'si:t] *n* (*for goods purchased*) pokwitowanie *nt*, paragon *m*; (*for parcel etc*) dowód *m* nadania; (*act of receiving*) odbiór *m*; **receipts** *npl* (*Comm*) wpływy *pl*; **on ~ of** po otrzymaniu *+gen*; **in ~ of** otrzymujący *+acc*
**receivable** [rɪ'si:vəbl] *adj* należny, przypadający do zapłaty
**receive** [rɪ'si:v] *vt* (*money, letter*) otrzymywać (otrzymać *perf*); (*injury*) odnosić (odnieść *perf*);

(*criticism, acclaim*) spotykać się (spotkać się *perf*) z *+instr*; (*visitor*) przyjmować (przyjąć *perf*); **to ~ treatment** być leczonym; **on the receiving end (of)** narażony (na *+acc*); **"~d with thanks"** (*Comm*) ≈ „potwierdzam odbiór"

**receiver** [rɪ'siːvə^r] *n* (*Tel*) słuchawka *f*; (*Radio, TV*) odbiornik *m*; (*of stolen goods*) paser *m*; (*Comm*) syndyk *m*, zarządca *m* masy upadłościowej

**recent** ['riːsnt] *adj* niedawny, ostatni; **in ~ years** w ostatnich latach

**recently** ['riːsntlɪ] *adv* (*not long ago*) niedawno; (*lately*) ostatnio; **as ~ as yesterday** zaledwie wczoraj; **it was discovered as ~ as 1903** odkryto go dopiero w roku 1903; **until ~** do niedawna

**receptacle** [rɪ'sɛptɪkl] *n* pojemnik *m*

**reception** [rɪ'sɛpʃən] *n* (*in hotel*) recepcja *f*; (*in office*) portiernia *f*; (*in hospital*) rejestracja *f*; (*party, welcome*) przyjęcie *nt*; (*Radio, TV*) odbiór *m*

**reception centre** (*Brit*) *n* schronisko *nt* dla bezdomnych

**reception desk** *n* (*in hotel*) recepcja *f*; (*in hospital, at doctor's*) rejestracja *f*; (*in large building, offices*) portiernia *f*

**receptionist** [rɪ'sɛpʃənɪst] *n* (*in hotel*) recepcjonista(-tka) *m(f)*; (*in doctor's surgery*) rejestrator(ka) *m(f)*

**receptive** [rɪ'sɛptɪv] *adj* (*person, attitude*) otwarty

**recess** [rɪ'sɛs] *n* (*in room*) nisza *f*, wnęka *f*; (*secret place*) zakamarek *m*; (*of parliament*) wakacje *pl*, przerwa *f* (między sesjami); (*US: Jur, Scol*) przerwa *f*

**recession** [rɪ'sɛʃən] *n* recesja *f*

**recharge** [riː'tʃɑːdʒ] *vt* (*battery*) ponownie ładować (naładować *perf*)

**rechargeable** [riː'tʃɑːdʒəbl] *adj*: **~ battery** akumulatorek *m*

**recipe** ['rɛsɪpɪ] *n* (*Culin*) przepis *m*; **a ~ for success** recepta na sukces

**recipient** [rɪ'sɪpɪənt] *n* odbiorca(-rczyni) *m(f)*

**reciprocal** [rɪ'sɪprəkl] *adj* obustronny, obopólny

**reciprocate** [rɪ'sɪprəkeɪt] *vt* odwzajemniać (odwzajemnić *perf*) ▷ *vi* odwzajemniać się (odwzajemnić się *perf*)

**recital** [rɪ'saɪtl] *n* recital *m*

**recitation** [rɛsɪ'teɪʃən] *n* recytacja *f*

**recite** [rɪ'saɪt] *vt* (*poem*) recytować (wyrecytować *perf*), deklamować (zadeklamować *perf*); (*complaints, grievances*) wyliczać (wyliczyć *perf*)

**reckless** ['rɛkləs] *adj* lekkomyślny; (*driver, driving*) nieostrożny

**recklessly** ['rɛkləslɪ] *adv* lekkomyślnie; (*drive*) nieostrożnie

**reckon** ['rɛkən] *vt* (*consider*): **to ~ sb/sth to be** uznawać (uznać *perf*) kogoś/coś za *+acc*; (*calculate*) obliczać (obliczyć *perf*) ▷ *vi*: **he is somebody to be ~ed with** z nim trzeba się liczyć; **to ~ without sth** nie przewidzieć (*perf*) czegoś; **I ~ that ...** myślę, że ...
▸ **reckon on** *vt fus* liczyć na *+acc*

**reckoning** ['rɛknɪŋ] *n* obliczenia *pl*, kalkulacje *pl*; **the day of ~** czas porachunków

**reclaim** [rɪ'kleɪm] *vt* (*luggage: at airport etc*) odbierać (odebrać *perf*); (*money*) żądać (zażądać *perf*) zwrotu *+gen*; (*land: from sea, forest*) rekultywować (zrekultywować *perf*); (*waste materials*) utylizować (zutylizować *perf*)

**reclamation** [rɛklə'meɪʃən] *n* (*of land*) rekultywacja *f*

**recline** [rɪ'klaɪn] *vi* układać się (ułożyć się *perf*) w pozycji półleżącej

**reclining** [rɪ'klaɪnɪŋ] *adj* (*seat*) z opuszczanym oparciem *post*

**recluse** [rɪ'kluːs] *n* odludek *m*

**recognition** [rɛkəg'nɪʃən] *n* (*of person, place*) rozpoznanie *nt*; (*of fact, achievement*) uznanie *nt*; **in ~ of** w uznaniu (dla) *+gen*; **to gain ~** zdobywać (zdobyć *perf*) (sobie) uznanie; **to change beyond ~** zmieniać się (zmienić się *perf*) nie do poznania

**recognizable** ['rɛkəgnaɪzəbl] *adj* rozpoznawalny

**recognize** ['rɛkəgnaɪz] *vt* (*person, place, voice*) rozpoznawać (rozpoznać *perf*), poznawać (poznać *perf*); (*sign, symptom*) rozpoznawać (rozpoznać *perf*); (*problem, need*) uznawać (uznać *perf*) istnienie *+gen*; (*achievement, government*) uznawać (uznać *perf*); (*qualifications*) honorować; **to ~ sb by/as** rozpoznawać (rozpoznać *perf*) kogoś po *+loc*/jako *+acc*

**recoil** [*vb* rɪ'kɔɪl, *n* 'riːkɔɪl] *vi*: **to ~ (from)** odsuwać się (odsunąć się *perf*) (od *+gen*); (*fig*) wzdrygać się (wzdrygnąć się *perf*) (na widok *+gen*) ▷ *n* (*of gun*) odrzut *m*

**recollect** [rɛkə'lɛkt] *vt* przypominać (przypomnieć *perf*) sobie

**recollection** [rɛkə'lɛkʃən] *n* wspomnienie *nt*; **she had a flash of ~** nagle sobie przypomniała; **to the best of my ~** o ile sobie przypominam

**recommend** [rɛkə'mɛnd] *vt* (*book, person*) polecać (polecić *perf*); (*course of action*) zalecać (zalecić *perf*); **she has a lot to ~ her** wiele przemawia na jej korzyść

**recommendation** [rɛkəmɛn'deɪʃən] *n* (*act of recommending*) rekomendacja *f*; (*suggestion to follow*) zalecenie *nt*; **on the ~ of** na wniosek *+gen*

r

**recommended retail price** (*Brit*: *Comm*) *n* sugerowana cena *f* detaliczna
**recompense** ['rɛkəmpɛns] *n* rekompensata *f*
**reconcilable** ['rɛkənsaɪləbl] *adj*: **to be ~** dawać (dać *perf*) się pogodzić
**reconcile** ['rɛkənsaɪl] *vt* godzić (pogodzić *perf*); **to ~ o.s. to sth** godzić się (pogodzić się *perf*) z czymś
**reconciliation** [rɛkənsɪlɪ'eɪʃən] *n* (*of people*) pojednanie *nt*; (*of facts, beliefs*) pogodzenie *nt*
**recondite** [rɪ'kɔndaɪt] *adj* (*knowledge*) tajemny, ezoteryczny; (*style*) zawiły
**recondition** [ri:kən'dɪʃən] *vt* (*machine*) remontować (wyremontować *perf*)
**reconditioned** [ri:kən'dɪʃənd] *adj* wyremontowany
**reconnaissance** [rɪ'kɔnɪsns] *n* rozpoznanie *nt*, rekonesans *m*
**reconnoitre** [rɛkə'nɔɪtə^r], (*US*) **reconnoiter** *vt* przeprowadzać (przeprowadzić *perf*) rozpoznanie *or* rekonesans *+gen*
**reconsider** [ri:kən'sɪdə^r] *vt* (*decision*) rozważać (rozważyć *perf*) ponownie; (*opinion*) rewidować (zrewidować *perf*) ▷ *vi* zastanawiać się (zastanowić się *perf*) ponownie
**reconstitute** [ri:'kɔnstɪtju:t] *vt* (*organization*) zawiązywać (zawiązać *perf*) ponownie; (*committee, board*) ukonstytuować (*perf*) ponownie; (*dried food*) *doprowadzać do pierwotnej postaci przez dodanie wody*
**reconstruct** [ri:kən'strʌkt] *vt* (*building, policy*) odbudowywać (odbudować *perf*); (*event, crime*) rekonstruować (zrekonstruować *perf*), odtwarzać (odtworzyć *perf*)
**reconstruction** [ri:kən'strʌkʃən] *n* (*of building, country*) odbudowa *f*; (*of crime*) rekonstrukcja *f*
**record** [*n* 'rɛkɔ:d, *vb* rɪ'kɔ:d] *n* (*written account*) zapis *m*; (*of meeting*) protokół *m*; (*of attendance*) lista *f*; (*file*) akta *pl*; (*Comput, Sport*) rekord *m*; (*Mus*) płyta *f*; (*history*: *of person, company*) przeszłość *f* ▷ *vt* (*events etc*) zapisywać (zapisać *perf*); (*temperature, speed, time*) wskazywać; (*voice, song*) nagrywać (nagrać *perf*) ▷ *adj* rekordowy; **he has a criminal ~** był wcześniej karany; **I need to have a ~ of this decision** muszę mieć tę decyzję na piśmie; **public ~s** archiwum państwowe; **to keep a ~ of** zapisywać *or* notować *+acc*; **to set** *or* **put the ~ straight** (*fig*) prostować (sprostować *perf*) nieścisłości; **he is on ~ as saying that ...** stwierdził publicznie, że...; **off the ~** (*statement*) nieoficjalny; (*speak*) nieoficjalnie
**recorded delivery** [rɪ'kɔ:dɪd-] (*Brit*) *n*: **send the letter (by) ~** wyślij list jako polecony
**recorder** [rɪ'kɔ:də^r] *n* (*Mus*) flet *m* prosty; (*Jur*) *sędzia z określonymi uprawnieniami do orzekania w sprawach cywilnych i karnych*
**record holder** *n* rekordzista(-tka) *m(f)*
**recording** [rɪ'kɔ:dɪŋ] *n* nagranie *nt*
**recording studio** *n* studio *nt* nagrań
**record library** *n* płytoteka *f*
**record player** *n* gramofon *m*
**recount** [rɪ'kaunt] *vt* (*story*) opowiadać (opowiedzieć *perf*); (*event*) opowiadać (opowiedzieć *perf*) o *+loc*
**re-count** [*n* 'ri:kaunt, *vb* ri:'kaunt] *n* ponowne przeliczenie *nt* ▷ *vt* przeliczać (przeliczyć *perf*) ponownie
**recoup** [rɪ'ku:p] *vt* odzyskiwać (odzyskać *perf*); **to ~ one's losses** wynagradzać (wynagrodzić *perf*) sobie straty, powetować (*perf*) sobie szkody
**recourse** [rɪ'kɔ:s] *n*: **to have ~ to** uciekać się (uciec się *perf*) do *+gen*
**recover** [rɪ'kʌvə^r] *vt* odzyskiwać (odzyskać *perf*); (*from dangerous place etc*) wydobywać (wydobyć *perf*) ▷ *vi* (*from illness*) zdrowieć (wyzdrowieć *perf*); (*from shock, experience*) dochodzić (dojść *perf*) do siebie; (*economy, country*) wychodzić (wyjść *perf*) z kryzysu
**re-cover** [ri:'kʌvə^r] *vt* (*chair etc*) zmieniać (zmienić *perf*) obicie *+gen*
**recovery** [rɪ'kʌvərɪ] *n* (*from illness*) wyzdrowienie *nt*; (*in economy*) ożywienie *nt*; (*of sth stolen*) odzyskanie *nt*
**recreate** [ri:krɪ'eɪt] *vt* odtwarzać (odtworzyć *perf*)
**recreation** [rɛkrɪ'eɪʃən] *n* rekreacja *f*
**recreational** [rɛkrɪ'eɪʃənl] *adj* rekreacyjny
**recreational drug** *n* *narkotyk używany dla wprowadzenia się w stan odprężenia i nie powodujący uzależnienia*
**recreational vehicle** (*US*) *n* samochód *m* kempingowy
**recrimination** [rɪkrɪmɪ'neɪʃən] *n* (*also pl*) wzajemne oskarżenia *pl*
**recruit** [rɪ'kru:t] *n* (*Mil*) rekrut *m*; (*in company*) nowicjusz(ka) *m(f)* ▷ *vt* (*Mil*) rekrutować; (*staff*) przyjmować (przyjąć *perf*) (do pracy); (*new members*) werbować (zwerbować *perf*)
**recruiting office** [rɪ'kru:tɪŋ-] (*Mil*) *n* ≈ wojskowa komenda *f* uzupełnień
**recruitment** [rɪ'kru:tmənt] *n* nabór *m*
**rectangle** ['rɛktæŋgl] *n* prostokąt *m*
**rectangular** [rɛk'tæŋgjulə^r] *adj* prostokątny
**rectify** ['rɛktɪfaɪ] *vt* naprawiać (naprawić *perf*)
**rector** ['rɛktə^r] (*Rel*) *n* proboszcz *m* (*w kościele anglikańskim*)
**rectory** ['rɛktərɪ] *n* probostwo *nt* (*w kościele anglikańskim*)
**rectum** ['rɛktəm] *n* odbytnica *f*
**recuperate** [rɪ'kju:pəreɪt] *vi* wracać (wrócić *perf*) do zdrowia

**recur** [rɪ'kəːʳ] *vi (error, event)* powtarzać się (powtórzyć się *perf*); *(illness, pain)* nawracać
**recurrence** [rɪ'kʌrəns] *n (of error, event)* powtórzenie się *nt*; *(of illness, pain)* nawrót *m*
**recurrent** [rɪ'kʌrnt] *adj (error, event)* powtarzający się; *(illness, pain)* nawracający
**recurring** [rɪ'kʌrɪŋ] *adj (problem)* powracający; *(dream)* powtarzający się; *(Math)* okresowy
**recycle** [riː'saɪkl] *vt* utylizować
**red** [rɛd] *n (colour)* (kolor *m*) czerwony, czerwień *f*; *(pej: Pol)* czerwony(-na) *m(f)* ▷ *adj* czerwony; *(hair)* rudy; **I'm** *or* **my bank account is in the red** mam debet na koncie; **his business is in the red** jego firma ma deficyt
**red carpet treatment** *n*: **to give sb the ~** przyjmować (przyjąć *perf*) kogoś z (wielkimi) honorami
**Red Cross** *n* Czerwony Krzyż *m*
**redcurrant** ['rɛdkʌrənt] *n* czerwona porzeczka *f*
**redden** ['rɛdn] *vt* zabarwiać (zabarwić *perf*) na czerwono ▷ *vi* czerwienić się (zaczerwienić się *perf*), czerwienieć (poczerwienieć *perf*)
**reddish** ['rɛdɪʃ] *adj* czerwonawy; *(hair)* rudawy
**redecorate** [riː'dɛkəreɪt] *vt (building)* remontować (wyremontować *perf*); *(room)* odnawiać (odnowić *perf*) ▷ *vi* robić (zrobić *perf*) remont
**redecoration** [riːdɛkə'reɪʃən] *n (of building)* remont *m*; *(of room)* odnowienie *nt*
**redeem** [rɪ'diːm] *vt (situation, reputation)* ratować (uratować *perf*); *(sth in pawn)* wykupywać (wykupić *perf*); *(loan)* spłacać (spłacić *perf*); *(Rel)* odkupić *(perf)*; **to ~ o.s.** zrehabilitować się *(perf)*
**redeemable** [rɪ'diːməbl] *adj (voucher, gift certificate) wymienialny na gotówkę lub towar o określonej wartości*
**redeeming** [rɪ'diːmɪŋ] *adj*: **~ feature** *or* **quality** jedyna zaleta *f*; **with no ~ qualities** pozbawiony jakichkolwiek zalet
**redemption** [rɪ'dɛmʃən] *n (Rel)* odkupienie *nt*; **past** *or* **beyond ~** nie do uratowania, stracony
**redeploy** [riːdɪ'plɔɪ] *vt (staff)* przegrupowywać (przegrupować *perf*); *(resources)* przerzucać (przerzucić *perf*)
**redeployment** [riːdɪ'plɔɪmənt] *n (of staff)* przegrupowanie *nt*; *(of resources)* przerzucenie *nt*
**redevelop** [riːdɪ'vɛləp] *vt* modernizować (zmodernizować *perf*)
**redevelopment** [riːdɪ'vɛləpmənt] *n* modernizacja *f*
**red-handed** [rɛd'hændɪd] *adj*: **to be caught ~** zostać *(perf)* złapanym *or* przyłapanym na gorącym uczynku
**redhead** ['rɛdhɛd] *n* rudzielec *m (inf)*, rudy(-da) *m(f)*
**red herring** *n (fig)* manewr *m* dla odwrócenia uwagi
**red-hot** [rɛd'hɔt] *adj* rozgrzany do czerwoności
**redirect** [riːdaɪ'rɛkt] *vt (mail)* przeadresowywać (przeadresować *perf*); *(traffic)* skierowywać (skierować *perf*) inną trasą
**rediscover** [riːdɪs'kʌvəʳ] *vt* odkrywać (odkryć *perf*) na nowo
**redistribute** [riːdɪs'trɪbjuːt] *vt* dokonywać (dokonać *perf*) redystrybucji *+gen*
**red-letter day** ['rɛdlɛtə-] *n* pamiętny dzień *m*
**red light** *(Aut) n*: **to go through a ~** przejeżdżać (przejechać *perf*) na czerwonym świetle
**red-light district** ['rɛdlaɪt-] *n* dzielnica *f* domów publicznych
**red meat** *n mięso, które po ugotowaniu staje się ciemnobrązowe, np. wołowina lub baranina*
**redneck** ['rɛdnɛk] *(US: inf) n* wsiok *m (inf)*, burak *n (inf)*
**redness** ['rɛdnɪs] *n (of rose)* czerwień *f*; *(of face, eyes)* zaczerwienienie *nt*; *(of hair)* rudość *f*
**redo** [riː'duː] *(irreg: like* **do***) vt* przerabiać (przerobić *perf*)
**redolent** ['rɛdələnt] *adj*: **~ of** *(sth pleasant)* (intensywnie) pachnący *+instr*; *(sth unpleasant)* cuchnący *+instr*; *(fig)* przywodzący na myśl *+acc*
**redouble** [riː'dʌbl] *vt* podwajać (podwoić *perf*)
**redraft** [riː'drɑːft] *vt* przeredagowywać (przeredagować *perf*)
**redress** [rɪ'drɛs] *n* zadośćuczynienie *nt* ▷ *vt (error, wrong)* naprawiać (naprawić *perf*); **to ~ the balance** przywracać (przywrócić *perf*) równowagę
**Red Sea** *n*: **the ~** Morze *nt* Czerwone
**redskin** ['rɛdskɪn] *(old: offensive) n* czerwonoskóry *m*
**red tape** *n (fig)* biurokracja *f*
**reduce** [rɪ'djuːs] *vt* zmniejszać (zmniejszyć *perf*), redukować (zredukować *perf*); **to ~ sth by/to** redukować (zredukować *perf*) coś o *+acc*/do *+gen*; **to ~ sb to** *(tears)* doprowadzać (doprowadzić *perf*) kogoś do *+gen*; *(begging, stealing, silence)* zmuszać (zmusić *perf*) kogoś do *+gen*; **"~ speed now"** ≈ ograniczenie prędkości
**reduced** [rɪ'djuːst] *adj (goods)* przeceniony; **"greatly ~ prices"** „wielka obniżka cen"
**reduction** [rɪ'dʌkʃən] *n (in price, cost)* obniżka *f*; *(in numbers)* obniżenie *nt*, redukcja *f*
**redundancy** [rɪ'dʌndənsɪ] *(Brit) n (dismissal)* zwolnienie *nt* z pracy (*w sytuacji nadmiaru*

r

*zatrudnienia*); (*unemployment*) bezrobocie *nt*; **compulsory/voluntary** ~ przymusowe zwolnienie/dobrowolne zwolnienie się z pracy (*w sytuacji nadmiaru zatrudnienia*)
**redundancy payment** (*Brit*) *n* odprawa *f* (*przy zwolnieniu z pracy*)
**redundant** [rɪ'dʌndnt] *adj* (*Brit: worker*) zwolniony; (*superfluous*) zbędny, zbyteczny; **he was made** ~ zwolnili go (z pracy)
**reed** [ri:d] *n* (*Bot*) trzcina *f*; (*Mus*) stroik *m*
**reedy** ['ri:dɪ] *adj* (*voice*) piskliwy
**reef** [ri:f] *n* rafa *f*
**reek** [ri:k] *vi* (*smell*): **to ~ (of)** cuchnąć (*+instr*); (*fig*): **to ~ of** trącić *or* zalatywać *+instr*
**reel** [ri:l] *n* (*of thread*) szpulka *f*; (*of film, tape*) szpula *f*; (*Phot*) rolka *f*; (*on fishing-rod*) kołowrotek *m*; (*dance*) *skoczny taniec szkocki lub irlandzki* ▷ *vi* (*person*) zataczać się (zatoczyć się *perf*); **my head is ~ing** w głowie mi się kręci
▸ **reel in** *vt* (*fish*) wyciągać (wyciągnąć *perf*) (*za pomocą kołowrotka*); (*line*) wybierać (wybrać *perf*) (*za pomocą kołowrotka*)
▸ **reel off** *vt* recytować (wyrecytować *perf*) (na zawołanie)
**re-election** [ri:ɪ'lɛkʃən] *n* ponowny wybór *m*
**re-enter** [ri:'ɛntə^r] *vt* (*country*) powtórnie przekraczać (przekroczyć *perf*) granicę *+gen*; (*earth's atmosphere*) wchodzić (wejść *perf*) (powtórnie) w *+acc*
**re-entry** [ri:'ɛntrɪ] *n* powtórne przekroczenie *nt* granicy; (*Space*) (powtórne) wejście *nt* w atmosferę
**re-examine** [ri:ɪg'zæmɪn] *vt* (*possibility, proposal*) ponownie badać (zbadać *perf*); (*witness*) ponownie przesłuchiwać (przesłuchać *perf*)
**re-export** [*vb* 'ri:ɪks'pɔ:t, *n* ri:'ɛkspɔ:t] (*Comm*) *vt* reeksportować (reeksportować *perf*) ▷ *n* reeksport *m*
**ref** [rɛf] (*Sport: inf*) *n abbr* = **referee**
**ref.** (*Comm*) *abbr* (= *with reference to*) dot.
**refectory** [rɪ'fɛktərɪ] *n* refektarz *m*
**refer** [rɪ'fə:^r] *vt*: **to ~ sb to** (*book*) odsyłać (odesłać *perf*) kogoś do *+gen*; (*doctor, hospital, manager*) kierować (skierować *perf*) kogoś do *+gen*; **to ~ the matter to** kierować (skierować *perf*) sprawę do *+gen*; **to ~ the task to** przekazywać (przekazać *perf*) zadanie *+dat*
▸ **refer to** *vt fus* (*mention*) wspominać (wspomnieć *perf*) o *+loc*; (*relate to: name, number*) oznaczać *+acc*; (*: remark*) odnosić się do *+gen*; (*consult: dictionary etc*) korzystać (skorzystać *perf*) z *+gen*
**referee** [rɛfə'ri:] *n* (*Sport*) sędzia *m*; (*Brit: for job application*) osoba *f* polecająca ▷ *vt* sędziować
**reference** ['rɛfrəns] *n* (*mention*) wzmianka *f*; (*idea, phrase*) odniesienie *nt*; (*for job application: letter*) list *m* polecający; (*: person*) osoba *f* polecająca; **references** *npl* (*list of books*) bibliografia *f*; (*for job application*) referencje *pl*; **with ~ to** (*in letter*) w nawiązaniu do *+gen*; **"please quote this ~"** (*Comm*) „proszę powoływać się na ten numer"
**reference book** *n encyklopedia, słownik, leksykon itp.*
**reference library** *n* księgozbiór *m* podręczny
**reference number** *n* numer *m* porządkowy
**referenda** [rɛfə'rɛndə] *npl of* **referendum**
**referendum** [rɛfə'rɛndəm] (*pl* **referenda**) *n* referendum *nt*
**refill** [*vb* ri:'fɪl, *n* 'ri:fɪl] *vt* powtórnie napełniać (napełnić *perf*) ▷ *n* (*for pen etc*) wkład *m*; **would you like a ~?** (*another drink*) czy mogę Panu/ Pani dolać?
**refine** [rɪ'faɪn] *vt* (*sugar, oil*) rafinować; (*theory*) udoskonalać (udoskonalić *perf*)
**refined** [rɪ'faɪnd] *adj* (*person, taste*) wytworny, wykwintny; (*sugar, oil*) rafinowany
**refinement** [rɪ'faɪnmənt] *n* (*of person*) wytworność *f*, wykwintność *f*; (*of system, ideas*) udoskonalenie *nt*
**refinery** [rɪ'faɪnərɪ] *n* rafineria *f*
**refit** [*n* ri:'fɪt, *vb* 'ri:fɪt] (*Naut*) *n* remont *m* ▷ *vt* (*ship*) remontować (wyremontować *perf*)
**reflate** [ri:'fleɪt] *vt*: **to ~ the economy** powodować (spowodować *perf*) reflację, zwiększać (zwiększyć *perf*) podaż pieniądza
**reflation** [ri:'fleɪʃən] *n* reflacja *f*, zwiększenie *nt* podaży pieniądza
**reflationary** [ri:'fleɪʃənrɪ] *adj* powodujący reflację, zwiększający podaż pieniądza
**reflect** [rɪ'flɛkt] *vt* (*light, image*) odbijać (odbić *perf*); (*fig: situation, attitude*) odzwierciedlać (odzwierciedlić *perf*) ▷ *vi* zastanawiać się (zastanowić się *perf*)
▸ **reflect on** *vt fus* (*discredit*) stawiać (postawić *perf*) w złym świetle *+acc*
**reflection** [rɪ'flɛkʃən] *n* odbicie *nt*; (*fig: of situation, attitude*) odzwierciedlenie *nt*; (*: thought*) zastanawianie się *nt*, refleksja *f*; **on** ~ po zastanowieniu; ~ **on** refleksja nad *+instr*
**reflector** [rɪ'flɛktə^r] *n* (*on car, bicycle*) światło *nt* odblaskowe; (*for light, heat*) reflektor *m*
**reflex** ['ri:flɛks] *adj* odruch *m*; **reflexes** *npl* odruchy *pl*; **to have slow/quick ~es** mieć słaby/szybki refleks
**reflexive** [rɪ'flɛksɪv] (*Ling*) *adj* zwrotny
**reform** [rɪ'fɔ:m] *n* reforma *f* ▷ *vt* reformować (zreformować *perf*) ▷ *vi* poprawiać się (poprawić się *perf*)
**reformat** [ri:'fɔ:mæt] (*Comput*) *vt* ponownie formatować (sformatować *perf*)
**Reformation** [rɛfə'meɪʃən] *n*: **the ~** reformacja *f*

**reformatory** [rɪ'fɔ:mətərɪ] (US) *n* zakład *m* poprawczy
**reformed** [rɪ'fɔ:md] *adj* nawrócony ze złej drogi
**refrain** [rɪ'freɪn] *vi*: **to ~ from doing sth** powstrzymywać się (powstrzymać się *perf*) od (z)robienia czegoś ▷ *n* refren *m*
**refresh** [rɪ'frɛʃ] *vt* (*drink*) orzeźwiać (orzeźwić *perf*); (*swim*) odświeżać (odświeżyć *perf*); (*sleep, rest*) pokrzepiać (pokrzepić *perf*); **to ~ sb's memory** odświeżać (odświeżyć *perf*) komuś pamięć
**refresher course** [rɪ'frɛʃə-] *n* ≈ kurs *m* doskonalenia zawodowego
**refreshing** [rɪ'frɛʃɪŋ] *adj* (*drink*) orzeźwiający; (*swim*) odświeżający; (*sleep, rest*) pokrzepiający; (*fact, idea etc*) pokrzepiający, krzepiący
**refreshment** [rɪ'frɛʃmənt] *n* (*resting*) odpoczynek *m*
**refreshments** [rɪ'frɛʃmənts] *npl* przekąski *pl* i napoje *pl*
**refrigeration** [rɪfrɪdʒə'reɪʃən] *n* chłodzenie *nt*
**refrigerator** [rɪ'frɪdʒəreɪtə^r] *n* lodówka *f*, chłodziarka *f*
**refuel** [ri:'fjuəl] *vt, vi* tankować (zatankować *perf*)
**refuelling** [ri:'fjuəlɪŋ] *n* tankowanie *nt*
**refuge** ['rɛfju:dʒ] *n* schronienie *nt*; (*fig*) ucieczka *f*; **to take ~ in** chronić się (schronić się *perf*) w *+loc*; **he sought ~ in silence** szukał ucieczki w milczeniu
**refugee** [rɛfju'dʒi:] *n* uchodźca *m*; **a political ~** uchodźca polityczny
**refugee camp** *n* obóz *m* dla uchodźców
**refund** [*n* 'ri:fʌnd, *vb* rɪ'fʌnd] *n* zwrot *m* pieniędzy ▷ *vt* zwracać (zwrócić *perf*); **tax ~** zwrot nadpłaconego podatku
**refurbish** [ri:'fə:bɪʃ] *vt* odnawiać (odnowić *perf*)
**refurnish** [ri:'fə:nɪʃ] *vt* zmieniać (zmienić *perf*) umeblowanie *+gen*
**refusal** [rɪ'fju:zəl] *n* odmowa *f*; **first ~** prawo pierwokupu
**refuse**[1] [rɪ'fju:z] *vt* (*permission, consent*) odmawiać (odmówić *perf*) *+gen*; (*request*) odmawiać (odmówić *perf*) *+dat*; (*invitation, gift, offer*) odrzucać (odrzucić *perf*) ▷ *vi* odmawiać (odmówić *perf*); (*horse*) zatrzymywać się (zatrzymać się *perf*) przed przeszkodą; **to ~ to do sth** odmawiać (odmówić *perf*) zrobienia czegoś
**refuse**[2] ['rɛfju:s] *n* odpadki *pl*, śmieci *pl*
**refuse collection** *n* wywóz *m* śmieci
**refuse disposal** *n* usuwanie *nt* odpadków
**refute** [rɪ'fju:t] *vt* obalać (obalić *perf*)
**regain** [rɪ'geɪn] *vt* odzyskiwać (odzyskać *perf*)
**regal** ['ri:gl] *adj* królewski
**regale** [rɪ'geɪl] *vt*: **to ~ sb with sth** raczyć (uraczyć *perf*) kogoś czymś
**regalia** [rɪ'geɪlɪə] *n* insygnia *pl*
**regard** [rɪ'gɑ:d] *n* szacunek *m* ▷ *vt* (*consider*) uważać; (*view*) patrzeć na *+acc*; **to give one's ~s to** przekazywać (przekazać *perf*) pozdrowienia *+dat*; **"with kindest ~s"** „łączę najserdeczniejsze pozdrowienia"; **as ~s, with ~ to** co do *+gen*, jeśli chodzi o *+acc*
**regarding** [rɪ'gɑ:dɪŋ] *prep* odnośnie do *+gen*
**regardless** [rɪ'gɑ:dlɪs] *adv* mimo to; **~ of** bez względu na *+acc*
**regatta** [rɪ'gætə] *n* regaty *pl*
**regency** ['ri:dʒənsɪ] *n* regencja *f* ▷ *adj*: **R~ chair/building** krzesło *nt*/budynek *m* z okresu Regencji (*w przypadku Anglii z lat 1811-20*)
**regenerate** [rɪ'dʒɛnəreɪt] *vt* (*inner cities, feelings*) ożywiać (ożywić *perf*); (*arts, democracy*) odradzać (odrodzić *perf*) ▷ *vi* (*Bio*) regenerować się (zregenerować się *perf*)
**regent** ['ri:dʒənt] *n* regent(ka) *m(f)*
**reggae** ['regeɪ] *n* reggae *nt inv*
**regime** [reɪ'ʒi:m] *n* reżim *m*
**regiment** [*n* 'rɛdʒɪmənt, *vb* 'rɛdʒɪmɛnt] *n* (*Mil*) pułk *m* ▷ *vt* (*people*) poddawać (poddać *perf*) surowej dyscyplinie; (*system*) sprawować ścisłą kontrolę nad *+instr*
**regimental** [rɛdʒɪ'mɛntl] *adj* pułkowy
**regimentation** [rɛdʒɪmɛn'teɪʃən] *n* surowa dyscyplina *f*
**region** ['ri:dʒən] *n* (*of land*) okolica *f*, rejon *m*; (*: geographical*) region *m*; (*: administrative*) okręg *m*; (*of body*) okolica *f*; **in the ~ of** około *+gen*
**regional** ['ri:dʒənl] *adj* (*committee etc*) okręgowy; (*accent, foods*) regionalny
**regional development** *n* rozwój *m* regionalny
**register** ['rɛdʒɪstə^r] *n* (*Admin, Mus, Ling*) rejestr *m*; (*also*: **electoral register**) spis *m* wyborców; (*Scol*) dziennik *m* ▷ *vt* rejestrować (zarejestrować *perf*); (*letter*) nadawać (nadać *perf*) jako polecony ▷ *vi* (*person*: *at hotel, for work*) meldować się (zameldować się *perf*); (*: at doctor's*) rejestrować się (zarejestrować się *perf*); (*amount, measurement*) zostać (*perf*) zarejestrowanym; **to ~ a protest** zgłaszać (zgłosić *perf*) sprzeciw; **I told them, but I don't think it ~ed** mówiłam im, ale chyba (do nich) nie dotarło
**registered** ['rɛdʒɪstəd] *adj* (*letter*) polecony; (*drug addict, childminder*) zarejestrowany
**registered company** (*Comm*) *n* spółka *f* akcyjna wpisana do rejestru
**registered nurse** (US) *n* ≈ pielęgniarka(-arz) *f(m)* dyplomowana(-ny) *f(m)*

r

**registered trademark** *n* znak *m* handlowy prawnie zastrzeżony
**register office** *n* = **registry office**
**registrar** [ˈrɛdʒɪstrɑːʳ] *n* (*in registry office*) urzędnik(-iczka) *m(f)* stanu cywilnego; (*in college, university*) sekretarz *m* uniwersytetu; (*Brit: in hospital*) ≈ lekarz *m* specjalista *m*
**registration** [rɛdʒɪsˈtreɪʃən] *n* rejestracja *f*
**registration number** (*Brit: Aut*) *n* numer *m* rejestracyjny
**registry** [ˈrɛdʒɪstrɪ] *n* archiwum *nt*
**registry office** (*Brit*) *n* urząd *m* stanu cywilnego; **to get married in a ~** brać (wziąć *perf*) ślub cywilny
**regret** [rɪˈgrɛt] *n* żal *m* ▷ *vt* (*decision, action*) żałować *+gen*; (*loss, death*) opłakiwać; (*inconvenience*) wyrażać (wyrazić *perf*) ubolewanie z powodu *+gen*; **with ~** z żalem; **to have no ~s (about)** wcale nie żałować (*+gen*); **to ~ that ...** żałować, że ...; **we ~ to inform you that ...** z żalem zawiadamiamy, że ...
**regretfully** [rɪˈgrɛtfəlɪ] *adv* z żalem
**regrettable** [rɪˈgrɛtəbl] *adj* (*causing sadness*) godny ubolewania; (*causing disapproval*) pożałowania godny, żałosny
**regrettably** [rɪˈgrɛtəblɪ] *adv* (*drunk, late*) bardzo mocno; **~**, ... niestety, ...
**Regt** (*Mil*) *abbr* = **regiment**
**regular** [ˈrɛgjuləʳ] *adj* (*breathing, features, exercise, verb*) regularny; (*time, doctor, customer*) stały; (*soldier*) zawodowy; (*size*) normalny ▷ *n* (*in shop*) stały(-ła) *m(f)* klient(ka) *m(f)*; (*in pub etc*) stały(-ła) *m(f)* bywalec(-lczyni) *m(f)*
**regularity** [rɛgjuˈlærɪtɪ] *n* regularność *f*
**regularly** [ˈrɛgjuləlɪ] *adv* regularnie
**regulate** [ˈrɛgjuleɪt] *vt* (*control*) kontrolować; (*adjust*) regulować
**regulation** [rɛgjuˈleɪʃən] *n* (*control*) kontrola *f*; (*rule*) przepis *m*
**rehab** [ˈriːˈhæb] (*US: inf*) *n* odwyk *m* (*inf*)
**rehabilitate** [riːəˈbɪlɪteɪt] *vt* (*criminal*) resocjalizować (zresocjalizować *perf*); (*invalid, drug addict*) poddawać (poddać *perf*) rehabilitacji; (*politician, dissident*) rehabilitować (zrehabilitować *perf*)
**rehabilitation** [ˈriːəbɪlɪˈteɪʃən] *n* (*of criminal*) resocjalizacja *f*; (*of invalid, drug addict, politician*) rehabilitacja *f*
**rehash** [riːˈhæʃ] (*inf*) *vt* (*old ideas etc*) odgrzewać (*inf, pej*)
**rehearsal** [rɪˈhəːsəl] *n* próba *f*; **dress ~** próba generalna
**rehearse** [rɪˈhəːs] *vt* (*play*) robić (zrobić *perf*) próbę *+gen*, próbować (*inf*); (*dance, speech*) ćwiczyć
**rehouse** [riːˈhauz] *vt* przesiedlać (przesiedlić *perf*)
**reign** [reɪn] *n* (*of monarch*) panowanie *nt*; (*fig: of terror etc*) rządy *pl* ▷ *vi* (*lit, fig*) panować, rządzić
**reigning** [ˈreɪnɪŋ] *adj* (*monarch*) panujący; (*champion*) aktualny
**reimburse** [riːɪmˈbəːs] *vt*: **to ~ sb for sth** zwracać (zwrócić *perf*) komuś koszty czegoś, refundować (zrefundować *perf*) komuś coś
**rein** [reɪn] *n*: **~s** (*for horse*) lejce *pl*; (*for toddler*) szelki *pl*; **to give sb free ~** (*fig*) dawać (dać *perf*) komuś wolną rękę; **to keep a tight ~ on** (*fig*) trzymać krótko *+acc*
**reincarnation** [riːɪnkɑːˈneɪʃən] *n* (*belief*) reinkarnacja *f*; (*person, animal*) (ponowne) wcielenie *nt*
**reindeer** [ˈreɪndɪəʳ] *n inv* renifer *m*
**reinforce** [riːɪnˈfɔːs] *vt* (*object*) wzmacniać (wzmocnić *perf*); (*belief, prejudice*) umacniać (umocnić *perf*)
**reinforced concrete** *n* żelazobeton *m*
**reinforcement** [riːɪnˈfɔːsmənt] *n* (*of object*) wzmocnienie *nt*; (*of attitude, prejudice*) umocnienie *nt*; **reinforcements** *pl* (*Mil*) posiłki *pl*
**reinstate** [riːɪnˈsteɪt] *vt* (*employee*) przywracać (przywrócić *perf*) do pracy; (*tax, law*) przywracać (przywrócić *perf*)
**reinstatement** [riːɪnˈsteɪtmənt] *n* (*of employee*) przywrócenie *nt* do pracy
**reissue** [riːˈɪʃjuː] *vt* (*book etc*) wznawiać (wznowić *perf*)
**reiterate** [riːˈɪtəreɪt] *vt* (wielokrotnie) powtarzać (powtórzyć *perf*)
**reject** [*n* ˈriːdʒɛkt, *vb* rɪˈdʒɛkt] *n* (*Comm*) odrzut *m* ▷ *vt* odrzucać (odrzucić *perf*); (*machine: coin*) nie przyjmować (nie przyjąć *perf*) *+gen*
**rejection** [rɪˈdʒɛkʃən] *n* odrzucenie *nt*
**rejoice** [rɪˈdʒɔɪs] *vi*: **to ~ at** *or* **over** radować się *+instr or* z *+gen*
**rejoinder** [rɪˈdʒɔɪndəʳ] *n* replika *f*, riposta *f*
**rejuvenate** [rɪˈdʒuːvəneɪt] *vt* (*person*) odmładzać (odmłodzić *perf*); (*organization, economy*) ożywiać (ożywić *perf*)
**rekindle** [riːˈkɪndl] *vt* (*interest, emotion*) rozpalać (rozpalić *perf*) na nowo
**relapse** [rɪˈlæps] *n* (*Med*) nawrót *m* ▷ *vi*: **to ~ into** (*depression etc*) popadać (popaść *perf*) w *+acc*; **to ~ into silence** (ponownie) zamilknąć (*perf*)
**relate** [rɪˈleɪt] *vt* (*tell*) relacjonować (zrelacjonować *perf*); (*connect*) wiązać (powiązać *perf*) ▷ *vi*: **to ~ to** (*other people*) nawiązywać (nawiązać *perf*) kontakt z *+instr*, znajdować (znaleźć *perf*) wspólny język z

*+instr*; (*idea*) identyfikować się z *+instr*; (*subject, thing*) odnosić się do *+gen*

**elated** [rɪ'leɪtɪd] *adj* (*people, species*) spokrewniony; (*languages, words*) pokrewny; (*questions, issues*) powiązany

**elating to** [rɪ'leɪtɪŋ-] *prep* odnośnie do *+gen*

**elation** [rɪ'leɪʃən] *n* (*member of family*) krewny(na) *m(f)*; (*connection*) relacja *f*, związek *m*; **relations** *npl* (*dealings*) relacje *pl*, stosunki *pl*; (*relatives*) krewni *vir pl*; **diplomatic/international ~s** stosunki dyplomatyczne/międzynarodowe; **in ~ to** w stosunku do *+gen*; **to bear no ~ to** nie mieć żadnego związku z *+instr*

**elationship** [rɪ'leɪʃənʃɪp] *n* (*between two people*) stosunek *m*; (*between two countries*) stosunki *pl*; (*between two things*) związek *m*, powiązanie *nt*; (*affair*) związek *m*; **they have a good ~** stosunki między nimi układają się dobrze

**elative** ['rɛlətɪv] *n* krewny(na) *m(f)* ▷ *adj* (*not absolute*) względny; (*comparative*) względny, stosunkowy; **~ to** w stosunku do *+gen*; **it's all ~** to wszystko jest względne

**elatively** ['rɛlətɪvlɪ] *adv* względnie, stosunkowo

**elative pronoun** *n* zaimek *m* względny

**elax** [rɪ'læks] *vi* (*unwind*) odprężać się (odprężyć się *perf*), relaksować się (zrelaksować się *perf*); (*calm down*) uspokajać się (uspokoić się *perf*); (*muscle*) rozluźniać się (rozluźnić się *perf*) ▷ *vt* (*one's grip*) rozluźniać (rozluźnić *perf*); (*mind, person*) relaksować (zrelaksować *perf*); (*rule, control*) łagodzić (złagodzić *perf*)

**elaxation** [ri:læk'seɪʃən] *n* (*rest, recreation*) odprężenie *nt*, relaks *m*; (*of rule, control*) złagodzenie *nt*

**elaxed** [rɪ'lækst] *adj* (*person*) odprężony, rozluźniony; (*atmosphere*) spokojny

**elaxing** [rɪ'læksɪŋ] *adj* odprężający, relaksujący

**elay** [*n* 'ri:leɪ, *vb* rɪ'leɪ] *n* sztafeta *f* ▷ *vt* (*message, news*) przekazywać (przekazać *perf*); (*programme, broadcast*) transmitować

**elease** [rɪ'li:s] *n* (*from prison, obligation*) zwolnienie *nt*; (*of documents*) udostępnienie *nt*; (*of funds*) uruchomienie *nt*; (*of gas, water*) spuszczenie *nt*; (*of book, record*) wydanie *nt*; (*of film*) wejście *nt* na ekrany; (*Tech*) mechanizm *m* wyzwalający ▷ *vt* (*from prison, obligation, responsibility*) zwalniać (zwolnić *perf*); (*from wreckage etc*) uwalniać (uwolnić *perf*), wyswobadzać (wyswobodzić *perf*); (*gas etc*) spuszczać (spuścić *perf*); (*catch, brake*) zwalniać (zwolnić *perf*); (*film, record*) wypuszczać (wypuścić *perf*); (*report, news, figures*) publikować (opublikować *perf*); **a new ~** (*record*) nowa płyta, nowy album; (*film*) nowy film; **on general ~** na ekranach kin; *see also* **press release**

**relegate** ['rɛləgeɪt] *vt* degradować (zdegradować *perf*); (*Brit: Sport*): **to be ~d** spadać (spaść *perf*) do niższej ligi; **part of the text can be ~d to the footnotes** część tekstu można przenieść do przypisów

**relent** [rɪ'lɛnt] *vi* ustępować (ustąpić *perf*)

**relentless** [rɪ'lɛntlɪs] *adj* (*heat, noise*) bezustanny; (*person*) nieustępliwy

**relevance** ['rɛləvəns] *n* (*of remarks, information*) odniesienie *nt*; (*of action, question*) doniosłość *f*; **the ~ of sth to** znaczenie czegoś dla *+gen*

**relevant** ['rɛləvənt] *adj* (*information, question*) istotny; (*chapter*) odnośny; (*area*) dany; **to be ~ to** mieć związek z *+instr*

**reliability** [rɪlaɪə'bɪlɪtɪ] *n* (*of person, firm*) solidność *f*; (*of method, machine*) niezawodność *f*

**reliable** [rɪ'laɪəbl] *adj* (*person, firm*) solidny; (*method, machine*) niezawodny; (*information, source*) wiarygodny, pewny

**reliably** [rɪ'laɪəblɪ] *adv*: **we are ~ informed that ...** posiadamy pewne informacje, że...

**reliance** [rɪ'laɪəns] *n*: **~ on** (*person*) poleganie *nt* na *+loc*; (*drugs, financial support*) uzależnienie *nt* od *+gen*

**reliant** [rɪ'laɪənt] *adj*: **to be ~ on sth/sb** być zależnym od czegoś/kogoś

**relic** ['rɛlɪk] *n* (*Rel*) relikwia *f*; (*of the past*) relikt *m*

**relief** [rɪ'li:f] *n* (*feeling*) ulga *f*; (*aid*) pomoc *f*; (*Art*) relief *m*, płaskorzeźba *f*; (*Geol*) rzeźba *f* terenu; **~ driver** zmiennik(-iczka) *m(f)*; **light ~** (*Theat*) lekki przerywnik; **a globe of the world in ~** globus plastyczny

**relief map** *n* mapa *f* plastyczna

**relief road** (*Brit*) *n* objazd *m*

**relieve** [rɪ'li:v] *vt* (*pain, fear*) łagodzić (złagodzić *perf*), uśmierzać (uśmierzyć *perf*); (*colleague, guard*) zmieniać (zmienić *perf*), zluzowywać (zluzować *perf*) (*inf*); **to ~ sb of** (*load*) uwalniać (uwolnić *perf*) kogoś od *+gen*; (*duties, post*) zwalniać (zwolnić *perf*) kogoś z *+gen*; **to ~ o.s.** załatwiać się (załatwić się *perf*) (*inf*)

**relieved** [rɪ'li:vd] *adj*: **to be** *or* **feel ~** odczuwać (odczuć *perf*) ulgę; **he was ~ that ...** ulżyło mu, że...; **I'm ~ to hear it** kamień spadł mi z serca

**religion** [rɪ'lɪdʒən] *n* religia *f*

**religious** [rɪ'lɪdʒəs] *adj* religijny

**religiously** [rɪ'lɪdʒəslɪ] *adv* sumiennie, skrupulatnie

**relinquish** [rɪˈlɪŋkwɪʃ] *vt* (*authority*) zrzekać się (zrzec się *perf*) *+gen*; (*claim*) zaniechać (*perf*) *+gen*, rezygnować (zrezygnować *perf*) z *+gen*
**relish** [ˈrɛlɪʃ] *n* (*Culin*) przyprawa *f* smakowa (*sos, marynata itp.*); (*enjoyment*) rozkosz *f* ▷ *vt* rozkoszować się *+instr*; **to ~ doing sth** rozkoszować się robieniem czegoś; **she didn't ~ the prospect of** nie była zachwycona perspektywą *+gen*
**relive** [riːˈlɪv] *vt* przeżywać (przeżyć *perf*) na nowo
**reload** [riːˈləud] *vt* (*gun*) załadować (*perf*)
**relocate** [riːləuˈkeɪt] *vt* przenosić (przenieść *perf*) ▷ *vi*: **to ~ (in)** przenosić się (przenieść się *perf*) (do *+gen*)
**reluctance** [rɪˈlʌktəns] *n* niechęć *f*
**reluctant** [rɪˈlʌktənt] *adj* niechętny; **he was ~ to go** nie miał ochoty iść
**reluctantly** [rɪˈlʌktəntlɪ] *adv* niechętnie
**rely on** [rɪˈlaɪ-] *vt fus* (*be dependent on*) zależeć od *+gen*; (*trust*) polegać na *+loc*
**remain** [rɪˈmeɪn] *vi* (*stay*) zostawać (zostać *perf*); (*survive, continue to be*) pozostawać (pozostać *perf*); **to ~ silent** zachowywać (zachować *perf*) milczenie; **much ~s to be done** wiele pozostaje do zrobienia; **the fact ~s that ...** nie zmienia to faktu, że...; **that ~s to be seen** to się dopiero okaże
**remainder** [rɪˈmeɪndəʳ] *n* reszta *f* ▷ *vt* wyprzedawać po bardzo niskiej cenie (*zwłaszcza ostatnie egzemplarze źle sprzedającej się książki*)
**remaining** [rɪˈmeɪnɪŋ] *adj* pozostały
**remains** [rɪˈmeɪnz] *npl* (*of meal*) resztki *pl*; (*of building etc*) pozostałości *pl*; (*of body, corpse*) szczątki *pl*
**remake** [ˈriːmeɪk] (*Film*) *n* remake *m*
**remand** [rɪˈmɑːnd] *n*: **to be on ~** przebywać w areszcie śledczym ▷ *vt*: **to be ~ed in custody** przebywać w areszcie śledczym
**remand home** (*Brit*) *n* ≈ izba *f* zatrzymań dla nieletnich
**remark** [rɪˈmɑːk] *n* uwaga *f* ▷ *vi*: **to ~ (that ...)** zauważać (zauważyć *perf*) (, że ...); **to ~ on sth** robić (zrobić *perf*) uwagę na temat czegoś
**remarkable** [rɪˈmɑːkəbl] *adj* nadzwyczajny, niezwykły
**remarry** [riːˈmærɪ] *vi* (*woman*) ponownie wychodzić (wyjść *perf*) za mąż; (*man*) ponownie się żenić (ożenić *perf*)
**remedial** [rɪˈmiːdɪəl] *adj* (*tuition, classes*) wyrównawczy; (*exercise*) rehabilitacyjny, korekcyjny
**remedy** [ˈrɛmədɪ] *n* lekarstwo *nt*; (*fig*) środek *m* ▷ *vt* (*situation*) zaradzić (*perf*) *+dat*; (*mistake*) naprawiać (naprawić *perf*)
**remember** [rɪˈmɛmbəʳ] *vt* (*recall*) przypominać (przypomnieć *perf*) sobie; (*bear in mind*) pamiętać (zapamiętać *perf*); **~ me to him** pozdrów go ode mnie; **I ~ seeing it, I ~ having seen it** pamiętam, że to widziałem; **she ~ed to call me** pamiętała, żeby do mnie zadzwonić
**remembrance** [rɪˈmɛmbrəns] *n* (*memory*) pamięć *f*; (*souvenir*) pamiątka *f*; **in ~ of sb** dla uczczenia czyjejś pamięci; **in ~ of sth** na pamiątkę czegoś
**remind** [rɪˈmaɪnd] *vt*: **to ~ sb of sth/to do sth** przypominać (przypomnieć *perf*) komuś o czymś/, żeby coś zrobił; **to ~ sb that ...** przypominać (przypomnieć *perf*) komuś, że...; **she ~s me of my mother** przypomina mi moją matkę; **that ~s me!** à propos!
**reminder** [rɪˈmaɪndəʳ] *n* (*of person, event*) przypomnienie *nt*; (*letter*) upomnienie *nt*
**reminisce** [rɛmɪˈnɪs] *vi*: **to ~ (about)** wspominać (*+acc*)
**reminiscences** [rɛmɪˈnɪsnsɪz] *npl* wspomnienia *pl*
**reminiscent** [rɛmɪˈnɪsnt] *adj*: **to be ~ of sth** przypominać coś
**remiss** [rɪˈmɪs] *adj* niedbały; **it was ~ of him** było to niedbalstwo z jego strony
**remission** [rɪˈmɪʃən] *n* (*of prison sentence*) zmniejszenie *nt* kary; (*Med*) remisja *f*; (*Rel: of sins*) odpuszczenie *nt*
**remit** [rɪˈmɪt] *vt* (*money*) przesyłać (przesłać *perf*) ▷ *n* kompetencje *pl*, zakres *m* obowiązków
**remittance** [rɪˈmɪtns] *n* przekaz *m* (pocztowy)
**remnant** [ˈrɛmnənt] *n* pozostałość *f*; (*of cloth*) resztka *f*
**remonstrate** [ˈrɛmənstreɪt] *vi*: **to ~ (with sb about sth)** protestować (zaprotestować *perf*) (u kogoś z powodu czegoś)
**remorse** [rɪˈmɔːs] *n* wyrzuty *pl* sumienia
**remorseful** [rɪˈmɔːsful] *adj* skruszony
**remorseless** [rɪˈmɔːslɪs] *adj* (*noise, pain*) niemiłosierny
**remote** [rɪˈməut] *adj* (*place, time*) odległy; (*person*) nieprzystępny; (*possibility, chance*) niewielki; **there is a ~ possibility that ...** istnieją niewielkie szanse (na to), że...
**remote control** *n* zdalne sterowanie *nt*; (*TV etc*) pilot *m*
**remote-controlled** [rɪˈməutkənˈtrəuld] *adj* zdalnie sterowany
**remotely** [rɪˈməutlɪ] *adv*: **I'm not even ~ interested** nie jestem w najmniejszym stopniu zainteresowany
**remoteness** [rɪˈməutnɪs] *n* (*of place*) oddalenie *nt*; (*of person*) nieprzystępność *f*

**mould** ['ri:məuld] (*Brit: Aut*) *n* opona *f* powtórnie bieżnikowana
**movable** [rɪ'mu:vəbl] *adj* ruchomy
**moval** [rɪ'mu:vəl] *n* (*of object, stain, kidney*) usunięcie *nt*; (*from office*) zwolnienie *nt*; (*Brit*) przewóz *m* mebli
**moval man** (*irreg: Brit*) *n pracownik firmy najmującej się przewozem mebli*
**moval van** (*Brit*) *n* meblowóz *m*
**move** [rɪ'mu:v] *vt* (*obstacle, stain, kidney*) usuwać (usunąć *perf*); (*employee*) zwalniać (zwolnić *perf*); (*plates, debris*) uprzątać (uprzątnąć *perf*); (*clothing, bandage*) zdejmować (zdjąć *perf*); **he's my first cousin once ~d** on jest synem mojego kuzyna
**mover** [rɪ'mu:vəʳ] *n* (*for paint*) rozpuszczalnik *m*; (*for varnish*) zmywacz *m*; **stain ~** odplamiacz; **make-up ~** płyn do demakijażu
**munerate** [rɪ'mju:nəreɪt] *vt* wynagradzać (wynagrodzić *perf*)
**muneration** [rɪmju:nə'reɪʃən] *n* wynagrodzenie *nt*
**enaissance** [rɪ'neɪsɑ̃:s] *n*: **the ~** Renesans *m*, Odrodzenie *nt*
**nal** ['ri:nl] (*Med*) *adj* nerkowy
**nal failure** *n* niewydolność *f* nerek
**name** [ri:'neɪm] *vt* przemianowywać (przemianować *perf*)
**nd** [rɛnd] (*pt, pp* **rent**) *vt* rozdzierać (rozedrzeć *perf*)
**nder** ['rɛndəʳ] *vt* (*assistance, aid*) udzielać (udzielić *perf*) *+gen*; (*account, bill*) przedkładać (przedłożyć *perf*); **to ~ sth possible/invisible** czynić (uczynić *perf*) coś możliwym/niewidzialnym; **to ~ sb/sth harmless** unieszkodliwiać (unieszkodliwić *perf*) kogoś/coś; **the blow ~ed him unconscious** od uderzenia stracił przytomność
**ndering** ['rɛndərɪŋ] (*Brit*) *n* = **rendition**
**ndezvous** ['rɔndɪvu:] *n* (*meeting*) spotkanie *nt* (*zwłaszcza potajemne*); (*: of lovers*) schadzka *f*; (*haunt*) (ulubione) miejsce *nt* spotkań ▷ *vi*: **to ~ (with sb)** spotykać się (spotkać się *perf*) (z kimś) w umówionym miejscu
**ndition** [rɛn'dɪʃən] *n* wykonanie *nt*, interpretacja *f*
**enegade** ['rɛnɪgeɪd] *n* renegat *m*, odstępca *m*
**new** [rɪ'nju:] *vt* (*efforts, attack*) ponawiać (ponowić *perf*); (*loan*) przedłużać (przedłużyć *perf*) (termin płatności *+gen*); (*negotiations*) podejmować (podjąć *perf*) na nowo; (*acquaintance, contract*) odnawiać (odnowić *perf*)
**enewable** [rɪ'nuəbl] *adj* odnawialny
**enewal** [rɪ'nju:əl] *n* (*of hostilities etc*) wznowienie *nt*; (*of licence etc*) odnowienie *nt*, przedłużenie *nt* ważności

**renounce** [rɪ'nauns] *vt* (*belief, course of action*) wyrzekać się (wyrzec się *perf*) *+gen*; (*right, title*) zrzekać się (zrzec się *perf*) *+gen*
**renovate** ['rɛnəveɪt] *vt* odnawiać (odnowić *perf*), przeprowadzać (przeprowadzić *perf*) renowację *+gen*
**renovation** [rɛnə'veɪʃən] *n* renowacja *f*
**renown** [rɪ'naun] *n* sława *f*
**renowned** [rɪ'naund] *adj* sławny
**rent** [rɛnt] *pt, pp of* **rend** ▷ *n* czynsz *m* ▷ *vt* (*house, room*) wynajmować (wynająć *perf*); (*television, car*) wypożyczać (wypożyczyć *perf*)
**rental** ['rɛntl] *n* (*for television, car*) opłata *f* (*kwartalna, miesięczna*)
**renunciation** [rɪnʌnsɪ'eɪʃən] *n* (*of belief, course of action*) wyrzeczenie się *nt*; (*of right, title*) zrzeczenie się *nt*; (*self-denial*) umartwianie się *nt*
**reopen** [ri:'əupən] *vt* (*shop etc*) otwierać (otworzyć *perf*) ponownie; (*negotiations etc*) wznawiać (wznowić *perf*)
**reopening** [ri:'əupnɪŋ] *n* (*of shop*) ponowne otwarcie *nt*; (*of negotiations*) wznowienie *nt*
**reorder** [ri:'ɔ:dəʳ] *vt* (*papers*) przekładać (przełożyć *perf*); (*furniture*) przestawiać (przestawić *perf*)
**reorganization** ['ri:ɔ:gənaɪ'zeɪʃən] *n* reorganizacja *f*
**reorganize** [ri:'ɔ:gənaɪz] *vt* reorganizować (zreorganizować *perf*)
**Rep.** (*US: Pol*) *abbr* = **representative**; **republican**
**rep** [rɛp] *n abbr* (*Comm*) = **representative**; (*Theat*) = **repertory**
**repair** [rɪ'pɛəʳ] *n* naprawa *f* ▷ *vt* naprawiać (naprawić *perf*), reperować (zreperować *perf*); (*building*) remontować (wyremontować *perf*); **in good/bad ~** w dobrym/złym stanie; **beyond ~** nie do naprawy; **under ~** w naprawie
**repair kit** *n* zestaw *m* naprawczy
**repair man** (*irreg: like* **man**) *n* mechanik *m*
**repair shop** (*Aut, Elec*) *n* warsztat *m* naprawczy
**repartee** [rɛpɑ:'ti:] *n* (*banter*) przekomarzanie się *nt*; (*answer*) riposta *f*
**repast** [rɪ'pɑ:st] (*fml*) *n* posiłek *m*
**repatriate** [ri:'pætrɪeɪt] *vt* repatriować
**repay** [ri:'peɪ] (*irreg: like* **pay**) *vt* (*money*) oddawać (oddać *perf*), zwracać (zwrócić *perf*); (*person*) zwracać (zwrócić *perf*) pieniądze *+dat*; (*sb's efforts*) być wartym *+gen*; (*favour*) odwdzięczać się (odwdzięczyć się *perf*) *or* rewanżować się (zrewanżować się *perf*) za *+acc*
**repayment** [ri:'peɪmənt] *n* spłata *f*
**repeal** [rɪ'pi:l] *n* uchylenie *nt*, zniesienie *nt* ▷ *vt* uchylać (uchylić *perf*), znosić (znieść *perf*)

**repeat** [rɪ'pi:t] *n* (*Radio, TV*) powtórka *f* ▷ *vt* powtarzać (powtórzyć *perf*); (*order*) ponawiać (ponowić *perf*) ▷ *vi* powtarzać (powtórzyć *perf*); **~ performance** powtórka; **~ order** ponowne zamówienie; **to ~ o.s.** powtarzać się; **to ~ itself** powtarzać się (powtórzyć się *perf*)
**repeatedly** [rɪ'pi:tɪdlɪ] *adv* wielokrotnie
**repel** [rɪ'pɛl] *vt* (*drive away*) odpierać (odeprzeć *perf*); (*disgust*) odpychać
**repellent** [rɪ'pɛlənt] *adj* (*appearance, smell*) odpychający, odrażający; (*idea, thought*) odrażający, wstrętny ▷ *n*: **insect ~** (*also*: **insect repellent**) środek *m* odstraszający owady
**repent** [rɪ'pɛnt] *vi*: **to ~ (of)** żałować (*+gen*)
**repentance** [rɪ'pɛntəns] *n* żal *m*, skrucha *f*
**repercussions** [ri:pə'kʌʃənz] *npl* reperkusje *pl*
**repertoire** ['rɛpətwɑ:ʳ] *n* (*Mus, Theat*) repertuar *m*; (*fig*) repertuar *m*, zakres *m*
**repertory** ['rɛpətərɪ] *n* (*also*: **repertory theatre**) teatr *m* stały
**repertory company** *n zespół aktorów zatrudnionych w teatrze stałym*
**repetition** [rɛpɪ'tɪʃən] *n* (*repeat*) powtórzenie *nt*, powtórka *f*; (*Comm*: *of order etc*) ponowienie *nt*
**repetitious** [rɛpɪ'tɪʃəs] *adj* zawierający powtórzenia
**repetitive** [rɪ'pɛtɪtɪv] *adj* (*movement*) powtarzający się; (*noise, work*) monotonny; (*speech*) zawierający powtórzenia
**replace** [rɪ'pleɪs] *vt* (*put back*) odkładać (odłożyć *perf*) (na miejsce); (*take the place of*) zastępować (zastąpić *perf*); **to ~ sth with sth else** zastępować (zastąpić *perf*) coś czymś innym; **"~ the receiver"** (*Tel*) „odłóż słuchawkę"
**replacement** [rɪ'pleɪsmənt] *n* (*substitution*) zastąpienie *nt*; (*substitute*) zastępca(-pczyni) *m(f)*
**replacement part** *n* część *f* zamienna
**replay** [*n* 'ri:pleɪ, *vb* ri:'pleɪ] *n* powtórny mecz *m* ▷ *vt* (*game*) rozgrywać (rozegrać *perf*) powtórnie; (*track, song*) odtwarzać (odtworzyć *perf*)
**replenish** [rɪ'plɛnɪʃ] *vt* (*glass*) dopełniać (dopełnić *perf*); (*stock etc*) uzupełniać (uzupełnić *perf*)
**replete** [rɪ'pli:t] *adj* syty; **~ with** pełen *+gen*
**replica** ['rɛplɪkə] *n* kopia *f*, replika *f*
**reply** [rɪ'plaɪ] *n* odpowiedź *f* ▷ *vi* odpowiadać (odpowiedzieć *perf*); **in ~ to** w odpowiedzi na *+acc*; **there's no ~** (*Tel*) nikt nie odpowiada
**reply coupon** *n* odcinek *m* na odpowiedź
**report** [rɪ'pɔ:t] *n* (*account*) sprawozdanie *nt*, raport *m*; (*Press, TV etc*) doniesienie *nt*, relacja *f*; (*Brit*: *also*: **school report**) świadectwo *nt* (szkolne); (*of gun*) huk *m* ▷ *vt* (*state*) komunikować (zakomunikować *perf*); (*Press, TV etc*) relacjonować (zrelacjonować *perf*); (*casualties, damage etc*) donosić (donieść *perf*) o *+loc*, odnotowywać (odnotować *perf*); (*bring to notice*: *theft, accident*) zgłaszać (zgłosić *perf*); (: *person*) donosić (donieść *perf*) na *+acc* ▷ *vi* sporządzać (sporządzić *perf*) raport; **to ~ to sb** (*present o.s. to*) zgłaszać się (zgłosić się *perf*) do kogoś; (*be responsible to*) podlegać komuś; **to ~ on sth** składać (złożyć *perf*) raport z czegoś; **to ~ sick** zgłaszać (zgłosić *perf*) niezdolność do pracy z powodu choroby; **it is ~ed that ...** mówi się, że ...
**report card** (*US, Scottish*) *n* świadectwo *nt* szkolne
**reportedly** [rɪ'pɔ:tɪdlɪ] *adv* podobno; **he ~ ordered them to ...** podobno kazał im *+infin*
**reported speech** (*Ling*) *n* mowa *f* zależna
**reporter** [rɪ'pɔ:təʳ] *n* reporter(ka) *m(f)*
**repose** [rɪ'pəuz] *n*: **in ~** (*face, mouth*) podczas spoczynku
**repository** [rɪ'pɔzɪtərɪ] *n* (*person*: *of knowledge*) kopalnia *f*; (: *of secrets*) powiernik(-iczka) *m(f)*; (*place*) składnica *f*
**repossess** ['ri:pə'zɛs] *vt* (*goods, building*) przejmować (przejąć *perf*)
**reprehensible** [rɛprɪ'hɛnsɪbl] *adj* naganny
**represent** [rɛprɪ'zɛnt] *vt* (*person, nation, view*) reprezentować; (*symbolize*: *word, object*) przedstawiać; (: *idea, emotion*) być symbolem *+gen*; (*constitute*) stanowić; **to ~ sth as** przedstawiać (przedstawić *perf*) coś jako *+acc*
**representation** [rɛprɪzɛn'teɪʃən] *n* (*state of being represented*) reprezentacja *f*; (*picture, statue*) przedstawienie *nt*; **representations** *npl* zażalenia *pl*
**representative** [rɛprɪ'zɛntətɪv] *n* przedstawiciel(ka) *m(f)*; (*US*: *Pol*) *członek izby niższej Kongresu federalnego lub jednego z kongresów stanowych* ▷ *adj* reprezentatywny; **~ of** reprezentatywny dla *+gen*
**repress** [rɪ'prɛs] *vt* (*people*) utrzymywać (utrzymać *perf*) w ryzach, poskramiać (poskromić *perf*); (*revolt*) tłumić (stłumić *perf*); (*feeling, impulse*) tłumić (stłumić *perf*), pohamowywać (pohamować *perf*); (*desire*) powstrzymywać (powstrzymać *perf*), pohamowywać (pohamować *perf*)
**repression** [rɪ'prɛʃən] *n* (*of people, country*) ucisk *m*; (*of feelings*) tłumienie *nt*
**repressive** [rɪ'prɛsɪv] *adj* represyjny
**reprieve** [rɪ'pri:v] *n* (*Jur*) ułaskawienie *nt*; (*fig*) ulga *f* ▷ *vt* (*Jur*) ułaskawiać (ułaskawić *perf*)
**reprimand** ['rɛprɪmɑ:nd] *n* nagana *f*, reprymenda *f* ▷ *vt* ganić (zganić *perf*), udzielać (udzielić *perf*) nagany *+dat*

**reprint** [*n* 'ri:prɪnt, *vb* ri:'prɪnt] *n* przedruk *m*, wznowienie *nt* ▷ *vt* przedrukowywać (przedrukować *perf*), wznawiać (wznowić *perf*)
**reprisal** [rɪ'praɪzl] *n* odwet *m*; **reprisals** *npl* czyny *pl or* środki *pl* odwetowe; **to take ~s** stosować (zastosować *perf*) środki odwetowe
**reproach** [rɪ'prəutʃ] *n* wyrzut *m* ▷ *vt*: **to ~ sb for sth** wyrzucać komuś coś; **beyond ~** bez zarzutu; **to ~ sb with sth** zarzucać (zarzucić *perf*) komuś coś
**reproachful** [rɪ'prəutʃful] *adj* pełen wyrzutu
**reproduce** [ri:prə'dju:s] *vt* (*copy*) powielać (powielić *perf*); (*in newspaper etc*) publikować (opublikować *perf*); (*sound*) naśladować ▷ *vi* rozmnażać się (rozmnożyć się *perf*)
**reproduction** [ri:prə'dʌkʃən] *n* (*copy*) powielenie *nt*; (*in newspaper*) opublikowanie *nt*; (*of sound*) odtwarzanie *nt*; (*of painting*) reprodukcja *f*; (*Bio*) rozmnażanie się *nt*
**reproductive** [ri:prə'dʌktɪv] *adj* rozrodczy
**reproof** [rɪ'pru:f] *n* nagana *f*; **with ~** z naganą
**reprove** [rɪ'pru:v] *vt*: **to ~ (sb for sth)** ganić (zganić *perf*) (kogoś za coś)
**reproving** [rɪ'pru:vɪŋ] *adj* pełen wyrzutu
**reptile** ['rɛptaɪl] *n* gad *m*
**Repub.** (*US*: *Pol*) *abbr* = **republican**
**republic** [rɪ'pʌblɪk] *n* republika *f*
**republican** [rɪ'pʌblɪkən] *adj* republikański ▷ *n* republikanin(-anka) *m(f)*; (*US*: *Pol*): **R~** Republikanin(-anka) *m(f)*
**repudiate** [rɪ'pju:dɪeɪt] *vt* (*accusation*) odrzucać (odrzucić *perf*); (*violence*) wyrzekać się (wyrzec się *perf*) *+gen*, odcinać się (odciąć się *perf*) od *+gen*; (*friend, wife etc*) wypierać się (wyprzeć się *perf*) *+gen*
**repugnance** [rɪ'pʌgnəns] *n* wstręt *m*, odraza *f*
**repugnant** [rɪ'pʌgnənt] *adj* wstrętny, odrażający
**repulse** [rɪ'pʌls] *vt* (*drive back*) odpierać (odeprzeć *perf*); (*repel*) napełniać (napełnić *perf*) odrazą
**repulsion** [rɪ'pʌlʃən] *n* wstręt *m*, odraza *f*
**repulsive** [rɪ'pʌlsɪv] *adj* odpychający
**reputable** ['rɛpjutəbl] *adj* szanowany, cieszący się poważaniem
**reputation** [rɛpju'teɪʃən] *n* reputacja *f*, renoma *f*; **to have a ~ for** być znanym z *+gen*; **he has a ~ for being awkward** jest znany ze swej niezdarności
**repute** [rɪ'pju:t] *n*: **of ~** renomowany; **to be held in high ~** cieszyć się znakomitą renomą
**reputed** [rɪ'pju:tɪd] *adj* rzekomy; **he is ~ to be rich** podobno jest bogaty
**reputedly** [rɪ'pju:tɪdlɪ] *adv* rzekomo
**request** [rɪ'kwɛst] *n* (*polite*) prośba *f*; (*formal*) wniosek *m*; (*Radio*) życzenie *nt* ▷ *vt* prosić (poprosić *perf*) o *+acc*; **Mr and Mrs Oliver Barrett ~ the pleasure of your company** Państwo Barrettowie mają przyjemność zaprosić Pana/Panią; **at the ~ of** na prośbę *+gen*; **"you are ~ed not to smoke"** „prosimy o niepalenie"
**request stop** (*Brit*) *n* przystanek *m* na żądanie
**requiem** ['rɛkwɪəm] *n* (*Rel*: *also*: **requiem mass**) msza *f* żałobna; (*Mus*) requiem *nt inv*, rekwiem *nt inv*
**require** [rɪ'kwaɪə$^r$] *vt* (*need*: *person*) potrzebować *+gen*, życzyć (zażyczyć *perf*) sobie *+gen*; (: *thing, situation*) wymagać *+gen*; (*demand*) wymagać *+gen*; **to ~ sb to do sth** wymagać od kogoś, by coś robił; **if ~d** w razie potrzeby; **what qualifications are ~d?** jakie kwalifikacje są wymagane?
**required** [rɪ'kwaɪəd] *adj* wymagany; **~ by law** wymagany przez prawo
**requirement** [rɪ'kwaɪəmənt] *n* (*need*) potrzeba *f*; (*condition*) wymaganie *nt*; **to meet sb's ~s** odpowiadać czyimś wymaganiom
**requisite** ['rɛkwɪzɪt] *adj* wymagany; **requisites** *npl* (*Comm*): **toilet/travel ~s** przybory *pl* toaletowe/do podróży
**requisition** [rɛkwɪ'zɪʃən] *n*: **~ (for)** zapotrzebowanie *nt* (na *+acc*) ▷ *vt* (*Mil*) rekwirować (zarekwirować *perf*)
**reroute** [ri:'ru:t] *vt* kierować (skierować *perf*) inną trasą
**resale** [ri:'seɪl] *n* odsprzedaż *f*; **"not for ~"** „egzemplarz bezpłatny"
**resale price maintenance** (*Comm*) *n* utrzymanie *nt* ceny przy odsprzedaży
**rescind** [rɪ'sɪnd] *vt* (*law*) uchylać (uchylić *perf*); (*decision, agreement*) unieważniać (unieważnić *perf*); (*order*) odwoływać (odwołać *perf*)
**rescue** ['rɛskju:] *n* (*help*) ratunek *m*; (*from drowning etc*) akcja *f* ratownicza ▷ *vt* ratować (uratować *perf*); **to come to sb's ~** przychodzić (przyjść *perf*) komuś na ratunek
**rescue party** *n* ekipa *f* ratownicza
**rescuer** ['rɛskjuə$^r$] *n* ratownik(-iczka) *m(f)*
**research** [rɪ'sə:tʃ] *n* badanie *nt or* badania *pl* (naukowe) ▷ *vt* badać (zbadać *perf*) ▷ *vi*: **to ~ (into sth)** prowadzić badania (czegoś); **to do ~** prowadzić badania; **a piece of ~** praca badawcza; **~ and development** prace badawczo-rozwojowe
**researcher** [rɪ'sə:tʃə$^r$] *n* badacz(ka) *m(f)*
**research work** *n* praca *f* naukowo-badawcza
**research worker** *n* pracownik *m* naukowy
**resell** [ri:'sɛl] (*irreg*: *like* **sell**) *vt* odsprzedawać (odsprzedać *perf*)
**resemblance** [rɪ'zɛmbləns] *n* podobieństwo *nt*; **to bear a strong ~ to** być bardzo

r

podobnym do *+gen*, bardzo przypominać *+acc*; **it bears no ~ to ...** to w ogóle nie przypomina *+gen*

**resemble** [rɪ'zɛmbl] *vt* przypominać, być podobnym do *+gen*

**resent** [rɪ'zɛnt] *vt* (*attitude, treatment*) czuć się urażonym *+instr*, oburzać się na *+acc*; (*person*) mieć pretensje do *+gen*

**resentful** [rɪ'zɛntful] *adj* urażony, pełen urazy

**resentment** [rɪ'zɛntmənt] *n* uraza *f*

**reservation** [rɛzə'veɪʃən] *n* (*booking*) rezerwacja *f*; (*doubt*) zastrzez˙enie *nt*; (*land*) rezerwat *m*; **to make a ~** robić (zrobić *perf*) rezerwację; **with ~(s)** z (pewnymi) zastrzeżeniami

**reservation desk** (*US*) *n* recepcja *f*

**reserve** [rɪ'zə:v] *n* zapas *m*, rezerwa *f*; (*fig: of energy, talent etc*) rezerwa *f*; (*Sport*) rezerwowy(-wa) *m(f)*; (*nature reserve*) rezerwat *m* przyrody; (*restraint*) powściągliwość *f*, rezerwa *f* ▷ *vt* rezerwować (zarezerwować *perf*); **reserves** *npl* (*Mil*) rezerwy *pl*; **in ~** w rezerwie

**reserve currency** *n* rezerwy *pl* dewizowe

**reserved** [rɪ'zə:vd] *adj* (*person*) powściągliwy; (*seat*) zarezerwowany

**reserve price** (*Brit*) *n* cena *f* wywoławcza

**reserve team** (*Brit: Sport*) *n* drużyna *f* rezerwowa

**reservist** [rɪ'zə:vɪst] (*Mil*) *n* rezerwista *m*

**reservoir** ['rɛzəvwɑ:ʳ] *n* (*of water*) rezerwuar *m*, zbiornik *m*; (*fig: of talent etc*) kopalnia *f*, skarbnica *f*

**reset** [ri:'sɛt] (*irreg: like* **set**) *vt* (*clock, watch*) przestawiać (przestawić *perf*); (*broken bone*) nastawiać (nastawić *perf*); (*Comput*) zerować (wyzerować *perf*), resetować (zresetować *perf*) (*inf*)

**reshape** [ri:'ʃeɪp] *vt* (*policy, view*) zmieniać (zmienić *perf*) kształt *+gen*

**reshuffle** [ri:'ʃʌfl] *n*: **Cabinet ~** (*Pol*) przetasowanie *nt* w gabinecie

**reside** [rɪ'zaɪd] *vi* zamieszkiwać
▸ **reside in** *vt fus* tkwić w *+loc*

**residence** ['rɛzɪdəns] *n* (*fml: home*) rezydencja *f*; (*length of stay*) pobyt *m*; **to take up ~** zamieszkać (*perf*); **to be in ~** (*queen etc*) rezydować; **in ~** (*writer, artist etc*) *związany z daną instytucją lub uczelnią*

**residence permit** (*Brit*) *n* pozwolenie *nt* na pobyt

**resident** ['rɛzɪdənt] *n* (*of country, town*) mieszkaniec(-nka) *m(f)*; (*in hotel*) gość *m* ▷ *adj* (*population*) stały; (*doctor, landlord*) mieszkający na miejscu; **to be ~ in** mieszkać w *+loc*

**residential** [rɛzɪ'dɛnʃəl] *adj* (*area*) mieszkaniowy; (*staff*) mieszkający w miejscu pracy; **~ course** ≈ kurs wyjazdowy

**residue** ['rɛzɪdju:] *n* (*Chem*) pozostałość *f*; (*fig*) posmak *m*

**resign** [rɪ'zaɪn] *vt* rezygnować (zrezygnować *perf*) z *+gen* ▷ *vi* ustępować (ustąpić *perf*); **to ~ o.s. to** pogodzić się (*perf*) z *+instr*

**resignation** [rɛzɪg'neɪʃən] *n* rezygnacja *f*; **to tender one's ~** składać (złożyć *perf*) (swoją) rezygnację

**resigned** [rɪ'zaɪnd] *adj*: **~ to** (*situation etc*) pogodzony z *+instr*

**resilience** [rɪ'zɪlɪəns] *n* (*of material*) sprężystość *f*; (*of person*) prężność *f*

**resilient** [rɪ'zɪlɪənt] *adj* (*material*) sprężysty; (*person*) prężny

**resin** ['rɛzɪn] *n* żywica *f*

**resist** [rɪ'zɪst] *vt* opierać się (oprzeć się *perf*) *+dat*; **I couldn't ~ it** nie mogłem się temu oprzeć; **I couldn't ~ doing it** nie mogłem się powstrzymać, żeby tego nie zrobić

**resistance** [rɪ'zɪstəns] *n* (*to change, attack*) opór *m*; (*to illness*) odporność *f*; (*Elec*) oporność *f*

**resistant** [rɪ'zɪstənt] *adj*: **~ (to)** (*change etc*) przeciwny (*+dat*); (*antibiotics etc*) odporny (na *+acc*)

**resit** (*Brit: Univ, Scol*) ['ri:sɪt] *n* poprawka (*f*) [ri:'sɪt] *vt* zdawać ponownie (*egzamin, test*), ponownie podchodzić do *+gen*

**resolute** ['rɛzəlu:t] *adj* zdecydowany, stanowczy

**resolution** [rɛzə'lu:ʃən] *n* (*decision*) rezolucja *f*; (*determination*) zdecydowanie *nt*, stanowczość *f*; (*of problem*) rozwiązanie *nt*; **to make a ~** zrobić (*perf*) postanowienie

**resolve** [rɪ'zɔlv] *n* (*determination*) zdecydowanie *nt*; (*intention*) postanowienie *nt* ▷ *vt* rozwiązywać (rozwiązać *perf*) ▷ *vi*: **to ~ to do sth** postanawiać (postanowić *perf*) coś zrobić

**resolved** [rɪ'zɔlvd] *adj* zdecydowany

**resonance** ['rɛzənəns] (*Tech*) *n* rezonans *m*

**resonant** ['rɛzənənt] *adj* (*voice*) donośny; (*place*) z (dużym) pogłosem *post*

**resort** [rɪ'zɔ:t] *n* (*town*) miejscowość *f* wypoczynkowa; (*recourse*) uciekanie się *nt* ▷ *vi*: **to ~ to** uciekać się (uciec się *perf*) do *+gen*; **seaside/winter sports ~** ośrodek sportów wodnych/zimowych; **as a last ~** w ostateczności; **in the last ~** koniec końców

**resound** [rɪ'zaund] *vi*: **to ~ (with)** rozbrzmiewać (*+instr*)

**resounding** [rɪ'zaundɪŋ] *adj* (*voice*) głośny; (*fig: success etc*) oszałamiający

**resource** [rɪ'sɔ:s] *n* surowiec *m*; **resources** *npl* (*coal, oil etc*) zasoby *pl*; (*money*) zasoby *pl or* środki *pl* (pieniężne); **natural ~s** bogactwa naturalne

**resourceful** [rɪ'sɔːsful] *adj* pomysłowy, zaradny
**resourcefulness** [rɪ'sɔːsfəlnɪs] *n* pomysłowość *f*, zaradność *f*
**respect** [rɪs'pɛkt] *n* szacunek *m* ▷ *vt* szanować (uszanować *perf*); **respects** *npl* wyrazy *pl* uszanowania; **to have ~ for sb/sth** mieć szacunek dla kogoś/czegoś; **to show sb/sth ~** okazywać (okazać *perf*) komuś/czemuś szacunek; **out of ~ for** z szacunku dla *+gen*, dla uszanowania *+gen*; **with ~ to, in ~ of** pod względem *+gen*, w związku z *+instr*; **in this ~** pod tym względem; **in some/many ~s** pod kilkoma/wieloma względami; **with (all due) ~** z całym szacunkiem
**respectability** [rɪspɛktə'bɪlɪtɪ] *n* (*repute*) poważanie *nt*; (*decency*) poczucie *nt* przyzwoitości
**respectable** [rɪs'pɛktəbl] *adj* (*reputable*) poważany, szanowany; (*decent, adequate*) przyzwoity, porządny
**respected** [rɪs'pɛktɪd] *adj* poważany
**respectful** [rɪs'pɛktful] *adj* pełen szacunku *or* uszanowania
**respectfully** [rɪs'pɛktfəlɪ] *adv* z szacunkiem *or* uszanowaniem
**respective** [rɪs'pɛktɪv] *adj*: **they returned to their ~ homes** wrócili każdy do swego domu
**respectively** [rɪs'pɛktɪvlɪ] *adv* odpowiednio; **France and Britain were third and fourth ~** Francja i Wielka Brytania zajęły odpowiednio trzecie i czwarte miejsce
**respiration** [rɛspɪ'reɪʃən] *n* *see* **artificial**
**respirator** ['rɛspɪreɪtə$^r$] (*Med*) *n* respirator *m*
**respiratory** ['rɛspərətərɪ] *adj* oddechowy
**respite** ['rɛspaɪt] *n* wytchnienie *nt*
**resplendent** [rɪs'plɛndənt] *adj* oszałamiający
**respond** [rɪs'pɔnd] *vi* (*answer*) odpowiadać (odpowiedzieć *perf*); (*react*) reagować (zareagować *perf*)
**respondent** [rɪs'pɔndənt] (*Jur*) *n* pozwany(-na) *m(f)*
**response** [rɪs'pɔns] *n* (*to question*) odpowiedź *f*; (*to situation, event*) reakcja *f*; **in ~ to** w odpowiedzi na *+acc*
**responsibility** [rɪspɔnsɪ'bɪlɪtɪ] *n* odpowiedzialność *f*; (*duty*) obowiązek *m*; **to have a ~ to sb** być odpowiedzialnym przed kimś; **to take ~ for** przyjmować (przyjąć *perf*) (na siebie) odpowiedzialność za *+acc*
**responsible** [rɪs'pɔnsɪbl] *adj* odpowiedzialny; **to be ~ for sth** odpowiadać za coś; **to be ~ to sb** być odpowiedzialnym przed kimś
**responsibly** [rɪs'pɔnsɪblɪ] *adv* opowiedzialnie
**responsive** [rɪs'pɔnsɪv] *adj*: **to be ~ (to)** (żywo) reagować (na *+acc*)
**rest** [rɛst] *n* (*relaxation, pause*) odpoczynek *m*; (*remainder*) reszta *f*; (*Mus*) pauza *f* ▷ *vi* odpoczywać (odpocząć *perf*) ▷ *vt* (*eyes, legs*) dawać (dać *perf*) odpoczynek *+dat*; **to ~ sth on/against sth** opierać (oprzeć *perf*) coś na czymś/o coś; **to ~ on sth** (*lit, fig*) opierać się (oprzeć się *perf*) na czymś; **foot ~** podnóżek; **the ~ of them** reszta; **to put** *or* **set sb's mind at ~** uspokoić (*perf*) kogoś; **to come to ~** zatrzymać się (*perf*), znieruchomieć (*perf*); **to lay sb to ~** składać (złożyć *perf*) kogoś na wieczny spoczynek; **to ~ one's eyes** *or* **gaze on sth** zatrzymywać (zatrzymać *perf*) wzrok na czymś; **to let the matter ~** dawać (dać *perf*) sprawie spokój; **~ assured that ...** bądź pewny *or* spokojny, że...; **I won't ~ until ...** nie spocznę, dopóki...; **I ~ my case** na tym chciałbym skończyć; **may he/she ~ in peace** niech spoczywa w pokoju
**restart** [riː'stɑːt] *vt* (*engine*) uruchamiać (uruchomić *perf*) ponownie; (*work*) wznawiać (wznowić *perf*)
**restaurant** ['rɛstərɔŋ] *n* restauracja *f*
**restaurant car** (*Brit*) *n* wagon *m* restauracyjny
**rest cure** *n* leczenie *nt* odpoczynkiem
**restful** ['rɛstful] *adj* (*lighting, music*) kojący; (*place*) spokojny
**rest home** *n* ≈ dom *m* spokojnej starości
**restitution** [rɛstɪ'tjuːʃən] *n*: **to make ~ to sb for sth** rekompensować (zrekompensować *perf*) komuś coś
**restive** ['rɛstɪv] *adj* (*person, crew*) zniecierpliwiony, niezadowolony; (*horse*) narowisty
**restless** ['rɛstlɪs] *adj* niespokojny; **to feel ~** nie móc sobie znaleźć miejsca; **to get ~** zaczynać (zacząć *perf*) się niecierpliwić
**restlessly** ['rɛstlɪslɪ] *adv* niespokojnie
**restock** [riː'stɔk] *vt* (*shop, freezer*) uzupełniać (uzupełnić *perf*) zapasy w *+loc*; (*lake, river*) zarybiać (zarybić *perf*) na nowo
**restoration** [rɛstə'reɪʃən] *n* (*of painting, church*) restauracja *f*; (*of health, rights, order*) przywrócenie *nt*; (*of land, stolen property*) zwrot *m*; **the R~** restauracja *f* (Stuartów)
**restorative** [rɪ'stɔrətɪv] *adj* wzmacniający ▷ *n* (*old*) kieliszek *m* (czegoś) na wzmocnienie
**restore** [rɪ'stɔː$^r$] *vt* (*painting, building*) odrestaurowywać (odrestaurować *perf*); (*order, health, faith*) przywracać (przywrócić *perf*); (*land, stolen property*) zwracać (zwrócić *perf*); **to ~ sb to power** przywracać (przywrócić *perf*) komuś władzę; **to ~ sth to its former state** przywracać (przywrócić *perf*) czemuś (jego) dawny kształt
**restorer** [rɪ'stɔːrə$^r$] (*Art etc*) *n* restaurator(ka) *m(f)*

r

**restrain** [rɪs'treɪn] *vt* (*person, feeling*) hamować (pohamować *perf*); (*growth, inflation*) hamować (zahamować *perf*); **to ~ sb/o.s. from doing sth** powstrzymywać (powstrzymać *perf*) kogoś/się od zrobienia czegoś
**restrained** [rɪs'treɪnd] *adj* (*person, behaviour*) powściągliwy; (*style*) surowy; (*colours*) spokojny
**restraint** [rɪs'treɪnt] *n* (*restriction*) ograniczenie *nt*; (*moderation*) umiar *m*, powściągliwość *f*; **wage ~** powstrzymywanie wzrostu płac
**restrict** [rɪs'trɪkt] *vt* ograniczać (ograniczyć *perf*)
**restricted area** (*Brit*: *Aut*) *n* strefa *f* ograniczonego ruchu
**restriction** [rɪs'trɪkʃən] *n* ograniczenie *nt*
**restrictive** [rɪs'trɪktɪv] *adj* (*law, policy*) restrykcyjny; (*clothing*) krępujący
**restrictive practices** (*Brit*: *Industry*) *npl* praktyki *pl* restrykcyjne
**rest room** (US) *n* toaleta *f*
**restructure** [ri:'strʌktʃə^r] *vt* restrukturyzować (zrestrukturyzować *perf*)
**result** [rɪ'zʌlt] *n* (*consequence*) skutek *m*, rezultat *m*; (*of exam, competition, calculation*) wynik *m* ▹ *vi*: **to ~ in** prowadzić (doprowadzić *perf*) do *+gen*; **as a ~ of** na skutek *or* w wyniku *+gen*; **to ~ (from)** wynikać (wyniknąć *perf*) (z *+gen*); **as a ~ it is too expensive** w rezultacie jest zbyt drogi
**resultant** [rɪ'zʌltənt] *adj*: **the ~ savings** powstałe w ten sposób oszczędności *pl*; **the ~ problems** wynikające stąd problemy
**resume** [rɪ'zju:m] *vt* (*work, journey*) podejmować (podjąć *perf*) na nowo, kontynuować (*po przerwie*); (*efforts*) wznawiać (wznowić *perf*) ▹ *vi* rozpoczynać się (rozpocząć się *perf*) na nowo; **to ~ one's seat** wracać (wrócić *perf*) na miejsce
**résumé** ['reɪzju:meɪ] *n* streszczenie *nt*; (US: *curriculum vitae*) życiorys *m*
**resumption** [rɪ'zʌmpʃən] *n* (ponowne) podjęcie *nt*, wznowienie *nt*
**resurgence** [rɪ'sə:dʒəns] *n* (*of energy*) (ponowny) przypływ *m*; (*of activity*) odrodzenie się *nt*
**resurrection** [rɛzə'rɛkʃən] *n* (*of fears, customs*) wskrzeszenie *nt*; (*of hopes*) (ponowne) rozbudzenie *nt*; (*of event, practice*) wznowienie *nt*; (*Rel*): **the R~** Zmartwychwstanie *nt*
**resuscitate** [rɪ'sʌsɪteɪt] *vt* (*Med*) reanimować; (*fig*) przywracać (przywrócić *perf*) do życia
**resuscitation** [rɪsʌsɪ'teɪʃən] (*Med*) *n* reanimacja *f*
**retail** ['ri:teɪl] *adj* detaliczny ▹ *adv* detalicznie, w detalu ▹ *vt* sprzedawać (sprzedać *perf*) detalicznie ▹ *vi*: **this product ~s at 25 pounds** cena detaliczna tego artykułu wynosi 25 funtów
**retailer** ['ri:teɪlə^r] *n* kupiec *m* detaliczny, detalista(-tka) *m*(*f*)
**retail outlet** *n* punkt *m* sprzedaży detalicznej
**retail price** *n* cena *f* detaliczna
**retail price index** *n* wskaźnik *m* cen detalicznych
**retain** [rɪ'teɪn] *vt* (*independence, souvenir, ticket*) zachowywać (zachować *perf*); (*heat, moisture*) zatrzymywać (zatrzymać *perf*)
**retainer** [rɪ'teɪnə^r] *n* zaliczka *f* dla adwokata
**retaliate** [rɪ'tælɪeɪt] *vi* brać (wziąć *perf*) odwet
**retaliation** [rɪtælɪ'eɪʃən] *n* odwet *m*; **in ~ for** w odwecie za *+acc*
**retaliatory** [rɪ'tælɪətərɪ] *adj* odwetowy
**retarded** [rɪ'tɑ:dɪd] *adj* (*also*: **mentally retarded**) opóźniony w rozwoju, upośledzony psychicznie
**retch** [rɛtʃ] *vi* mieć torsje
**retention** [rɪ'tɛnʃən] *n* (*of organization, land*) utrzymanie *nt*; (*of traditions*) podtrzymywanie *nt*; (*of memories*) przechowywanie *nt*; (*of heat, fluid*) zatrzymywanie *nt*
**retentive** [rɪ'tɛntɪv] *adj* (*memory*) trwały
**rethink** ['ri:'θɪŋk] *vt* przemyśliwać (przemyśleć *perf*) (na nowo)
**reticence** ['rɛtɪsns] *n* małomówność *f*
**reticent** ['rɛtɪsnt] *adj* małomówny
**retina** ['rɛtɪnə] *n* (*Anat*) siatkówka *f*
**retinue** ['rɛtɪnju:] *n* świta *f*
**retire** [rɪ'taɪə^r] *vi* (*give up work*) przechodzić (przejść *perf*) na emeryturę; (*withdraw*) oddalać się (oddalić się *perf*); (*go to bed*) udawać się (udać się *perf*) na spoczynek
**retired** [rɪ'taɪəd] *adj* emerytowany
**retirement** [rɪ'taɪəmənt] *n* (*state*) emerytura *f*; (*act*) przejście *nt* na emeryturę
**retirement age** *n* wiek *m* emerytalny
**retiring** [rɪ'taɪərɪŋ] *adj* (*shy*) nieśmiały; (*official, MP*) ustępujący
**retort** [rɪ'tɔ:t] *vi* ripostować (zripostować *perf*) ▹ *n* riposta *f*
**retrace** [ri:'treɪs] *vt*: **to ~ one's steps** wracać (wrócić *perf*) tą samą drogą; (*fig*) odtwarzać (odtworzyć *perf*) tok rozumowania
**retract** [rɪ'trækt] *vt* (*promise, confession*) cofać (cofnąć *perf*); (*claws*) chować (schować *perf*); (*undercarriage*) wciągać (wciągnąć *perf*)
**retractable** [rɪ'træktəbl] *adj* (*undercarriage*) wciągany; (*aerial*) wysuwany
**retrain** [ri:'treɪn] *vt* przekwalifikowywać (przekwalifikować *perf*) ▹ *vi* przekwalifikowywać się (przekwalifikować się *perf*)

**retraining** [riːˈtreɪnɪŋ] *n* przekwalifikowanie *nt*
**retread** [ˈriːtrɛd] *n* opona *f* powtórnie bieżnikowana
**retreat** [rɪˈtriːt] *n* (*place*) ustronie *nt*; (*withdrawal*) ucieczka *f*; (*Mil*) odwrót *m* ▷ *vi* wycofywać się (wycofać się *perf*); **to beat a hasty ~** pośpiesznie się wycofywać (wycofać *perf*)
**retrial** [riːˈtraɪəl] (*Jur*) *n* rewizja *f* procesu
**retribution** [rɛtrɪˈbjuːʃən] *n* kara *f*
**retrieval** [rɪˈtriːvəl] *n* (*of object: regaining*) odzyskanie *nt*; (*: finding*) odnalezienie *nt*; (*Comput*) wyszukiwanie *nt*
**retrieve** [rɪˈtriːv] *vt* (*person: object*) odzyskiwać (odzyskać *perf*); (*: situation*) ratować (uratować *perf*); (*dog*) aportować; (*Comput*) wyszukiwać (wyszukać *perf*); **to ~ sth from somewhere** wydobyć (*perf*) *or* wydostać (*perf*) coś skądś
**retriever** [rɪˈtriːvəʳ] *n* pies *m* myśliwski
**retroactive** [rɛtrəuˈæktɪv] *adj* działający wstecz
**retrograde** [ˈrɛtrəgreɪd] *adj* wsteczny; **a ~ step** krok do tyłu *or* wstecz
**retrospect** [ˈrɛtrəspɛkt] *n*: **in ~** z perspektywy czasu
**retrospective** [rɛtrəˈspɛktɪv] *adj* (*exhibition*) retrospektywny; (*law, tax*) działający wstecz; (*opinion*) z perspektywy czasu *post* ▷ *n* (*Art*) wystawa *f* retrospektywna, retrospektywa *f*; **I'm in a ~ mood** mam ochotę powspominać
**return** [rɪˈtəːn] *n* (*going or coming back*) powrót *m*; (*of sth stolen, borrowed, bought*) zwrot *m*; (*from land, shares, investment*) dochód *m*; (*tax etc*) zeznanie *nt* ▷ *cpd* (*journey, ticket*) powrotny; (*match*) rewanżowy ▷ *vi* (*person*) wracać (wrócić *perf*); (*feelings*) powracać (powrócić *perf*); (*illness, symptoms etc*): **if the illness/pain ~s, …** jeśli wystąpi nawrót choroby/bólu, … ▷ *vt* (*greetings, sentiment*) odwzajemniać (odwzajemnić *perf*); (*sth borrowed, stolen, bought*) zwracać (zwrócić *perf*); (*verdict*) wydawać (wydać *perf*); (*ball: during game*) odsyłać (odesłać *perf*); (*Pol*) wybierać (wybrać *perf*) (do parlamentu); **returns** *npl* (*Comm*) dochody *pl*; **in ~ (for)** w zamian (za *+acc*); **by ~ of post** odwrotną pocztą; **many happy ~s (of the day)!** wszystkiego najlepszego (z okazji urodzin)!; **I promise I'll ~ the favour some day** obiecuję, że kiedyś się odwdzięczę
▶ **return to** *vt fus* powracać (powrócić *perf*) do *+gen*
**returnable** [rɪˈtəːnəbl] *adj* (*bottle etc*) do zwrotu *post*
**return key** (*Comput*) *n* klawisz *m* powrotu karetki
**reunion** [riːˈjuːnɪən] *n* (*of school, class, family*) zjazd *m*; (*of two people*) spotkanie *nt* (po latach)
**reunite** [riːjuːˈnaɪt] *vt* (*country*) (ponownie) jednoczyć (zjednoczyć *perf*); (*organization, movement*) przywracać (przywrócić *perf*) jedność w *+loc*; **to be ~d** (*friends etc*) spotykać się (spotkać się *perf*) (po latach); (*families*) łączyć się (połączyć się *perf*)
**rev** [rɛv] (*Aut*) *n abbr* (= *revolution*) obr. ▷ *vt* (*also:* **rev up**) rozgrzewać (*na wysokich obrotach*)
**revaluation** [riːvæljuˈeɪʃən] *n* (*of property*) rewaloryzacja *f*; (*of currency*) rewaluacja *f*; (*of attitudes*) przewartościowanie *nt*
**revamp** [riːˈvæmp] *vt* reformować (zreformować *perf*)
**rev counter** (*Brit: Aut*) *n* obrotomierz *m*
**Rev(d).** (*Rel*) *abbr* = **reverend**
**reveal** [rɪˈviːl] *vt* (*make known*) ujawniać (ujawnić *perf*); (*make visible*) odsłaniać (odsłonić *perf*)
**revealing** [rɪˈviːlɪŋ] *adj* odkrywczy; **she wore a ~ dress** miała na sobie sukienkę, która niewiele zakrywała
**reveille** [rɪˈvælɪ] (*Mil*) *n* pobudka *f*
**revel** [ˈrɛvl] *vi*: **to ~ in sth/in doing sth** rozkoszować się czymś/robieniem czegoś
**revelation** [rɛvəˈleɪʃən] *n* rewelacja *f*; (*Rel*) objawienie *nt*
**reveller** [ˈrɛvləʳ] *n* hałaśliwy biesiadnik *m*
**revelry** [ˈrɛvlrɪ] *n* hulanka *f*
**revenge** [rɪˈvɛndʒ] *n* zemsta *f* ▷ *vt* mścić (pomścić *perf*); **to get one's ~ (for sth)** mścić się (zemścić się *perf*) (za coś); **to take (one's) ~ (on sb)** dokonywać (dokonać *perf*) zemsty (na kimś); **to ~ o.s. (on sb)** mścić się (zemścić się *perf*) (na kimś)
**revengeful** [rɪˈvɛndʒful] *adj* mściwy
**revenue** [ˈrɛvənjuː] *n* dochody *pl*
**reverberate** [rɪˈvəːbəreɪt] *vi* (*sound*) rozlegać się (rozlec się *perf*); (*fig: ideas etc*) odbijać się (odbić się *perf*) szerokim echem; (*place*): **to ~ with** rozbrzmiewać *+instr*
**reverberation** [rɪvəːbəˈreɪʃən] *n* pogłos *m*, echo *nt*; (*fig*) reperkusje *pl*
**revere** [rɪˈvɪəʳ] *vt* czcić
**reverence** [ˈrɛvərəns] *n* cześć *f*
**Reverend** [ˈrɛvərənd] *adj* wielebny; **the ~ John Smith** Wielebny John Smith
**reverent** [ˈrɛvərənt] *adj* pełen czci
**reverie** [ˈrɛvərɪ] *n* marzenia *pl*; **I fell into a ~** pogrążyłem się w marzeniach
**reversal** [rɪˈvəːsl] *n* (*of decision, policy*) (radykalna) zmiana *f*; (*of roles*) odwrócenie *nt*
**reverse** [rɪˈvəːs] *n* (*opposite*) przeciwieństwo *nt*; (*of paper*) odwrotna strona *f*; (*of cloth*) lewa strona *f*; (*of coin, medal*) rewers *m*; (*also:* **reverse gear**) (bieg *m*) wsteczny; (*setback*) niepowodzenie *nt*; (*defeat*) porażka *f* ▷ *adj* (*side*) odwrotny; (*process*) przeciwny; (*direction*)

r

przeciwny, odwrotny ▷ *vt* (*order, roles*) odwracać (odwrócić *perf*); (*decision, verdict*) unieważniać (unieważnić *perf*); (*car*) cofać (cofnąć *perf*) ▷ *vi* (*Brit: Aut*) cofać się (cofnąć się *perf*); **they may do quite the ~ (of what you want)** mogą postąpić dokładnie odwrotnie (niż chcesz); **in ~ order** w odwrotnej kolejności; **in ~** zaczynając od końca; **their fortunes went into ~** szczęście odwróciło się od nich

**reverse-charge call** [rɪ'vəːstʃɑːdʒ-] (*Brit: Tel*) *n* rozmowa *f* „R" (*płatna przez wzywanego*)

**reverse video** (*Comput*) *n* obraz *m* negatywowy

**reversible** [rɪ'vəːsəbl] *adj* (*garment*) dwustronny; (*decision, surgery*) odwracalny

**reversing lights** [rɪ'vəːsɪŋ-] (*Brit: Aut*) *npl* światła *pl* cofania

**reversion** [rɪ'vəːʃən] *n* (*Zool*) atawizm *m*; **~ to** powrót do *+gen*

**revert** [rɪ'vəːt] *vi*: **to ~ to** (*previous owner, topic, state*) powracać (powrócić *perf*) do *+gen*; (*less advanced state*) cofać się (cofnąć się *perf*) do *+gen*

**review** [rɪ'vjuː] *n* przegląd *m*; (*of book, play etc*) recenzja *f*; (*of policy etc*) rewizja *f* ▷ *vt* (*Mil: troops*) dokonywać (dokonać *perf*) przeglądu *+gen*; (*book, play*) recenzować (zrecenzować *perf*); (*policy*) rewidować (zrewidować *perf*); **to be under ~** być ocenianym *or* poddawanym ocenie; **to come under ~** zostawać (zostać *perf*) poddanym ocenie

**reviewer** [rɪ'vjuːəʳ] *n* recenzent(ka) *m(f)*

**revile** [rɪ'vaɪl] *vt* obrzucać (obrzucić *perf*) obelgami

**revise** [rɪ'vaɪz] *vt* (*manuscript*) poprawiać (poprawić *perf*); (*opinion, attitude*) rewidować (zrewidować *perf*); (*price, procedure*) korygować (skorygować *perf*) ▷ *vi* (*for exam etc*) powtarzać (materiał); **~d edition** wydanie poprawione

**revision** [rɪ'vɪʒən] *n* (*of manuscript*) korekta *f*; (*of schedule*) zmiana *f*; (*of law*) rewizja *f*; (*for exam*) powtórka *f*

**revitalize** [riː'vaɪtəlaɪz] *vt* ożywiać (ożywić *perf*)

**revival** [rɪ'vaɪvəl] *n* (*Econ*) ożywienie *nt*; (*Theat*) wznowienie *nt*

**revive** [rɪ'vaɪv] *vt* (*person*) cucić (ocucić *perf*); (*economy*) ożywiać (ożywić *perf*); (*custom*) wskrzeszać (wskrzesić *perf*); (*hope, interest*) (ponownie) rozbudzać (rozbudzić *perf*); (*play*) wznawiać (wznowić *perf*) ▷ *vi* (*person*) odzyskiwać (odzyskać *perf*) przytomność; (*activity, economy*) ożywiać się (ożywić się *perf*); (*hope, faith, interest*) odradzać się (odrodzić się *perf*)

**revoke** [rɪ'vəuk] *vt* (*treaty*) unieważniać (unieważnić *perf*); (*law*) uchylać (uchylić *perf*); (*promise, decision*) cofać (cofnąć *perf*)

**revolt** [rɪ'vəult] *n* bunt *m*, rewolta *f* ▷ *vi* buntować się (zbuntować się *perf*) ▷ *vt* budzić (wzbudzić *perf*) odrazę w *+loc*; **to ~ against sb/sth** buntować się przeciwko komuś/czemuś

**revolting** [rɪ'vəultɪŋ] *adj* odrażający, budzący odrazę

**revolution** [rɛvə'luːʃən] *n* (*in politics, industry, education*) rewolucja *f*; (*of wheel, earth*) obrót *m*

**revolutionary** [rɛvə'luːʃənrɪ] *adj* rewolucyjny ▷ *n* rewolucjonista(-tka) *m(f)*

**revolutionize** [rɛvə'luːʃənaɪz] *vt* rewolucjonizować (zrewolucjonizować *perf*)

**revolve** [rɪ'vɔlv] *vi* obracać się (obrócić się *perf*); **to ~ (a)round** obracać się wokół *+gen*

**revolver** [rɪ'vɔlvəʳ] *n* rewolwer *m*

**revolving** [rɪ'vɔlvɪŋ] *adj* obrotowy

**revolving door** *n* drzwi *pl* obrotowe

**revue** [rɪ'vjuː] (*Theat*) *n* rewia *f*

**revulsion** [rɪ'vʌlʃən] *n* odraza *f*, wstręt *m*

**reward** [rɪ'wɔːd] *n* nagroda *f* ▷ *vt* nagradzać (nagrodzić *perf*); **the ~s of parenthood** satysfakcja z posiadania dzieci

**rewarding** [rɪ'wɔːdɪŋ] *adj* (*job*) przynoszący satysfakcję; (*experience*) cenny; **financially ~** opłacający się

**rewind** [riː'waɪnd] (*irreg: like* **wind**) *vt* (*tape, cassette*) przewijać (przewinąć *perf*)

**rewire** [riː'waɪəʳ] *vt* (*house*) wymieniać (wymienić *perf*) instalację elektryczną w *+loc*

**reword** [riː'wəːd] *vt* przeredagowywać (przeredagować *perf*)

**rewrite** [riː'raɪt] (*irreg: like* **write**) *vt* przerabiać (przerobić *perf*); (*completely*) pisać (napisać *perf*) od nowa

**Reykjavik** ['reɪkjəviːk] *n* Rejkiawik *m*

**RFD** (*US: Post*) *abbr* = **rural free delivery**

**Rh** *abbr* (= *rhesus*) Rh *nt inv*

**rhapsody** ['ræpsədɪ] *n* rapsodia *f*

**rhesus negative** ['riːsəs-] *adj*: **to be ~** mieć ujemne Rh

**rhesus positive** *adj*: **to be ~** mieć dodatnie Rh

**rhetoric** ['rɛtərɪk] *n* retoryka *f*

**rhetorical** [rɪ'tɔrɪkl] *adj* retoryczny

**rheumatic** [ruː'mætɪk] *adj* (*changes, pain*) reumatyczny; (*person*): **to be ~** mieć reumatyzm; **~ fingers** palce zniekształcone reumatyzmem

**rheumatism** ['ruːmətɪzəm] *n* reumatyzm *m*

**rheumatoid arthritis** ['ruːmətɔɪd-] *n* reumatoidalne zapalenie *nt* stawów

**Rhine** [raɪn] *n*: **the ~** Ren *m*

**rhinestone** ['raɪnstəun] *n* kryształ *m* górski (*stosowany w jubilerstwie*)

**rhinoceros** [raɪ'nɔsərəs] *n* nosorożec *m*

**Rhodes** [rəudz] *n* Rodos *nt inv*

**Rhodesia** [rəu'di:ʒə] *n* Rodezja *f*
**Rhodesian** [rəu'di:ʒən] *adj* rodezyjski ▷ *n* Rodezyjczyk(-jka) *m(f)*
**rhododendron** [rəudə'dɛndrn] *n* rododendron *m*
**Rhone** [rəun] *n*: **the ~** Rodan *m*
**rhubarb** ['ru:bɑ:b] *n* rabarbar *m*
**rhyme** [raɪm] *n* (*rhyming words*) rym *m*; (*verse*) wierszyk *m*, rymowanka *f*; (*technique*) rymowanie *nt* ▷ *vi*: **to ~ (with)** rymować się (z +*instr*); **without ~ or reason** ni stąd ni zowąd
**rhythm** ['rɪðm] *n* rytm *m*
**rhythmic(al)** ['rɪðmɪk(l)] *adj* rytmiczny
**rhythmically** ['rɪðmɪklɪ] *adv* rytmicznie
**RI** *n abbr* (*Brit*: *Scol*: = *religious instruction*) religia *f* ▷ *abbr* (*US*: *Post*) = **Rhode Island**
**rib** [rɪb] *n* (*Anat*) żebro *nt* ▷ *vt* (*inf*): **to rib sb (about sth)** przekomarzać się z kimś (z jakiegoś powodu)
**ribald** ['rɪbəld] *adj* sprośny
**ribbed** [rɪbd] *adj* prążkowany, w prążki *post*
**ribbon** ['rɪbən] *n* (*for hair, decoration*) wstążka *f*; (*of typewriter*) taśma *f*; **in ~s** w strzępach
**rice** [raɪs] *n* ryż *m*
**ricefield** ['raɪsfi:ld] *n* pole *nt* ryżowe
**rice pudding** *n* pudding *m* ryżowy
**rich** [rɪtʃ] *adj* (*person*) bogaty; (*life*) urozmaicony; (*soil*) żyzny; (*colour*) nasycony; (*voice*) głęboki; (*tapestries, silks*) kosztowny; (*food, diet*) *bogaty w tłuszcze i węglowodany* ▷ *npl*: **the ~** bogaci *vir pl*; **~ in** bogaty w +*acc*
**riches** ['rɪtʃɪz] *npl* bogactwo *nt*, bogactwa *pl*
**richly** ['rɪtʃlɪ] *adv* (*decorated*) bogato; (*deserved, earned*) w pełni; (*rewarded*) sowicie
**richness** ['rɪtʃnɪs] *n* (*of person*) bogactwo *nt*; (*of soil*) żyzność *f*; (*of costumes, furnishings*) bogactwo *nt*, przepych *m*
**rickets** ['rɪkɪts] *n* krzywica *f*
**rickety** ['rɪkɪtɪ] *adj* chybotliwy
**rickshaw** ['rɪkʃɔ:] *n* riksza *f*
**ricochet** ['rɪkəʃeɪ] *vi* odbijać się (odbić się *perf*) rykoszetem ▷ *n* rykoszet *m*
**rid** [rɪd] (*pt, pp* **rid**) *vt*: **to rid sb/sth of** uwalniać (uwolnić *perf*) kogoś/coś od +*gen*; **to get rid of** pozbywać się (pozbyć się *perf*) +*gen*
**riddance** ['rɪdns] *n*: **good ~!** krzyżyk na drogę!
**ridden** ['rɪdn] *pp of* **ride**
**riddle** ['rɪdl] *n* zagadka *f* ▷ *vt*: **~d with** (*guilt, doubts*) pełen +*gen*; (*corruption*) przesiąknięty +*instr*; **~d with holes** podziurawiony
**ride** [raɪd] (*pt* **rode**, *pp* **ridden**) *n* jazda *f*; (*path*) leśna droga *f* (*po której można przejechać konno*) ▷ *vi* (*as sport*) jeździć konno; (*go somewhere, travel*) jechać (pojechać *perf*) ▷ *vt* (*horse, bicycle*) jeździć na +*loc*; (*distance*) przejeżdżać (przejechać *perf*); **we rode all day** jechaliśmy cały dzień; **we rode all the way** całą drogę jechaliśmy; **can you ~ a bike?** (czy) umiesz jeździć na rowerze?; **(horse/car) ~** przejażdżka (konna/samochodem); **let's go for a ~** przejedźmy się; **to take sb for a ~** zabierać (zabrać *perf*) kogoś na przejażdżkę; (*fig*) nabierać (nabrać *perf*) kogoś; **to give sb a ~** podwozić (podwieźć *perf*) kogoś; **to ~ at anchor** stać na kotwicy
▸ **ride out** *vt*: **to ~ out the storm/recession** (*fig*) przetrzymywać (przetrzymać *perf*) burzę/recesję
**rider** ['raɪdəʳ] *n* (*on horse*) jeździec *m*; (*on bicycle*) rowerzysta(-tka) *m(f)*; (*on motorcycle*) motocyklista(-tka) *m(f)*; (*in document etc*) uzupełnienie *nt*, poprawka *f*
**ridge** [rɪdʒ] *n* (*of hill*) grzbiet *m*; (*of roof*) kalenica *f*; (*in ploughed land*) skiba *f*
**ridicule** ['rɪdɪkju:l] *n* kpiny *pl* ▷ *vt* wyśmiewać (wyśmiać *perf*); **to be the object of ~** być przedmiotem kpin
**ridiculous** [rɪ'dɪkjuləs] *adj* śmieszny
**riding** ['raɪdɪŋ] *n* jazda *f* konna
**riding school** *n* szkółka *f* jeździecka
**rife** [raɪf] *adj*: **to be ~** (*corruption, superstition*) kwitnąć; (*disease*) srożyć się; **the office was ~ with rumours** w biurze huczało od plotek
**riffraff** ['rɪfræf] *n* hołota *f*
**rifle** ['raɪfl] *n* karabin *m*; (*for hunting*) strzelba *f* ▷ *vt* (*sb's wallet, pocket*) opróżniać (opróżnić *perf*)
▸ **rifle through** *vt fus* przetrząsać (przetrząsnąć *perf*) +*acc*
**rifle range** *n* strzelnica *f*
**rift** [rɪft] *n* szczelina *f*; (*fig*) rozdźwięk *m*
**rig** [rɪg] *n* (*also*: **oil rig**: *at sea*) platforma *f* wiertnicza; (*: on land*) szyb *m* wiertniczy ▷ *vt* (*election, cards*) fałszować (sfałszować *perf*)
▸ **rig out** (*Brit*) *vt*: **to rig sb out as/in** przebierać (przebrać *perf*) kogoś za +*acc*/w +*acc*
▸ **rig up** *vt* (*device, net*) (naprędce) łatać (połatać *perf*)
**rigging** ['rɪgɪŋ] *n* olinowanie *nt*
**right** [raɪt] *adj* (*correct*) dobry, poprawny; (*suitable*) właściwy, odpowiedni; (*morally good*) dobry; (*not left*) prawy ▷ *n* (*what is morally right*) dobro *nt*; (*entitlement*) prawo *nt*; (*not left*): **the ~** prawa strona *f* ▷ *adv* dobrze; (*turn*) w prawo; (*swerve*) na prawo ▷ *vt* naprawiać (naprawić *perf*) ▷ *excl* dobrze; **the ~ time** (*exact*) dokładny czas; (*most suitable*) odpowiedni czas; **the R~** (*Pol*) prawica; **you're ~** masz rację; **you are French, is that ~?** jesteś Francuzem, prawda?; **is that clock ~?** czy ten zegar dobrze chodzi?; **let's get it ~ this time!** tym razem zróbmy to jak należy!; **I got the first question ~** odpowiedziałam

r

dobrze na pierwsze pytanie; **you did the ~ thing** postąpiłeś właściwie; **to put a mistake ~** naprawiać (naprawić *perf*) błąd; **~ now** w tej chwili; **~ before/after** tuż przed *+instr*/po *+loc*; **~ ahead** (*walk etc*) prosto przed siebie; **by ~s** na dobrą sprawę; **he's in the ~** słuszność jest po jego stronie; **~ away** natychmiast; **~ in the middle** w samym środku; **~ against the wall** przy samej ścianie, tuż przy ścianie; **I'll be ~ back** zaraz wracam; **to be within one's ~s to do sth** mieć (pełne) prawo coś (z)robić; **(as) ~ as rain** zdrów jak ryba; **film ~s** prawo do ekranizacji; **on the ~** z prawej (strony); **from left to ~** z lewa na prawo; **to ~ oneself** (*ship*) wyprostowywać się (wyprostować się *perf*); **it's interesting in its own ~** to jest ciekawe samo w sobie

**right angle** *n* kąt *m* prosty

**righteous** ['raɪtʃəs] *adj* (*person*) prawy; (*indignation*) słuszny

**righteousness** ['raɪtʃəsnɪs] *n* prawość *f*

**rightful** ['raɪtful] *adj* (*heir, owner*) prawowity, prawny; (*place, share*) należny

**rightfully** ['raɪtfəlɪ] *adv* prawowicie, prawnie

**right-hand drive** ['raɪthænd-] *n* układ *m* kierowniczy prawostronny ▷ *adj* z prawostronnym układem kierowniczym *post*

**right-handed** [raɪt'hændɪd] *adj* praworęczny

**right-hand man** *n* prawa ręka *f*

**right-hand side** *n* prawa strona *f*

**rightly** ['raɪtlɪ] *adv* (*with reason*) słusznie; **if I remember ~** (*Brit*) jeśli dobrze pamiętam

**right-minded** [raɪt'maɪndɪd] *adj* rozsądny

**right of way** *n* (*Aut*) pierwszeństwo *nt* przejazdu; (*on path etc*) *prawo przechodzenia przez teren prywatny*

**rights issue** (*Stock Exchange*) *n* emisja *f* praw poboru

**right wing** *n* prawe skrzydło *nt*

**right-wing** [raɪt'wɪŋ] *adj* (*Pol*) prawicowy

**right-winger** [raɪt'wɪŋə^r] *n* (*Pol*) prawicowiec *m*; (*Sport*) prawoskrzydłowy(-wa) *m(f)*

**rigid** ['rɪdʒɪd] *adj* (*structure, back*) sztywny; (*attitude, views*) skostniały; (*control, censorship*) ścisły; (*methods*) surowy

**rigidity** [rɪ'dʒɪdɪtɪ] *n* sztywność *f*

**rigidly** ['rɪdʒɪdlɪ] *adv* (*tightly*) sztywno; (*closely*) ściśle

**rigmarole** ['rɪgmərəul] *n* (*complicated procedure*) korowody *pl* (*inf*)

**rigor** ['rɪgə^r] (US) *n* = **rigour**

**rigor mortis** ['rɪgə'mɔ:tɪs] *n* stężenie *nt* pośmiertne

**rigorous** ['rɪgərəs] *adj* rygorystyczny; (*training*) wymagający

**rigorously** ['rɪgərəslɪ] *adv* rygorystycznie

**rigour**, (US) **rigor** ['rɪgə^r] *n* (*of law, punishment*) surowość *f*; (*of argument*) dyscyplina *f* logiczna; (*of research, methods*) dokładność *f*, ścisłość *f*; **the ~s of life** trudy życia

**rig-out** ['rɪgaut] (*Brit: inf*) *n* strój *m*

**rile** [raɪl] *vt* drażnić (rozdrażnić *perf*)

**rim** [rɪm] *n* (*of glass, dish*) brzeg *m*; (*of spectacles*) obwódka *f*; (*of wheel*) obręcz *f*

**rimless** ['rɪmlɪs] *adj* (*spectacles*) bezobwódkowy

**rimmed** [rɪmd] *adj*: **~ with black/red** z czarnymi/czerwonymi obwódkami

**rind** [raɪnd] *n* skórka *f*

**ring** [rɪŋ] (*pt* **rang**, *pp* **rung**) *n* (*on finger*) pierścionek *m*; (*: large*) pierścień *m*; (*also*: **wedding ring**) obrączka *f*; (*for keys, of smoke*) kółko *nt*; (*of people, objects*) krąg *m*, koło *nt*; (*of spies*) siatka *f*; (*of drug-dealers*) gang *m*; (*for boxing*) ring *m*; (*of circus, for bullfighting*) arena *f*; (*on cooker*) palnik *m*; (*sound of bell*) dzwonek *m* ▷ *vi* dzwonić (zadzwonić *perf*); (*also*: **ring out**) rozbrzmiewać (rozbrzmieć *perf*) ▷ *vt* (*Brit: Tel*) dzwonić (zadzwonić *perf*) do *+gen*; (*mark*) zakreślać (zakreślić *perf*), brać (wziąć *perf*) w kółeczko (*inf*); **to give sb a ~** (*Brit*) dzwonić (zadzwonić *perf*) do kogoś; **that has a ~ of truth about it** to brzmi wiarygodnie; **to ~ the bell** dzwonić (zadzwonić *perf*); **the name doesn't ~ a bell (with me)** to nazwisko nic mi nie mówi; **my ears are ~ing** dzwoni mi w uszach; **to ~ true/false** brzmieć szczerze/fałszywie; **to run ~s round sb** (*inf: fig*) bić kogoś na głowę (*inf*)

▸ **ring back** (*Brit*) *vt* oddzwaniać (oddzwonić *perf*) *+dat* ▷ *vi* oddzwaniać (oddzwonić *perf*)

▸ **ring off** (*Brit*) *vi* odkładać (odłożyć *perf*) słuchawkę

▸ **ring up** (*Brit*) *vt* dzwonić (zadzwonić *perf*) do *+gen*

**ring binder** *n* segregator *m*

**ring finger** *n* palec *m* serdeczny

**ringing** ['rɪŋɪŋ] *n* dzwonienie *nt*

**ringing tone** (*Brit: Tel*) *n* sygnał *m* wołania

**ringleader** ['rɪŋli:də^r] *n* prowodyr *m*

**ringlets** ['rɪŋlɪts] *npl* loki *pl*

**ring road** (*Brit*) *n* obwodnica *f*

**ringtone** ['rɪŋtəun] *n* dzwonek *m* do telefonu

**rink** [rɪŋk] *n* (*also*: **ice rink**) lodowisko *nt*; (*also*: **roller skating rink**) tor *m* do jazdy na wrotkach

**rinse** [rɪns] *n* (*act*) płukanie *nt*; (*hair dye*) płukanka *f* do włosów ▷ *vt* (*dishes*) płukać (opłukać *perf*); (*hands*) opłukiwać (opłukać *perf*); (*hair*) płukać (spłukać *perf*); (*also*: **rinse out**: *clothes*) płukać (wypłukać *perf*); (*: mouth*) przepłukiwać (przepłukać *perf*)

**io (de Janeiro)** ['ri:əu(dədʒə'nɪərəu)] *n* Rio de Janeiro *nt inv*

**iot** ['raɪət] *n* rozruchy *pl* ▹ *vi* burzyć się; **to be a ~ of colours** mienić się wszystkimi kolorami; **to run ~** szaleć

**ioter** ['raɪətə^r] *n* uczestnik(-iczka) *m(f)* rozruchów

**iotous** ['raɪətəs] *adj* (*mob, crowd*) wzburzony; (*living*) hulaszczy; (*party, welcome*) hałaśliwy

**iotously** ['raɪətəslɪ] *adv*: **~ funny/comic** prześmieszny/przekomiczny

**iot police** *n* ≈ oddziały *pl* prewencji; **hundreds of ~** setki policjantów z oddziałów prewencji

**IP** *abbr* (= *rest in peace*) RIP

**ip** [rɪp] *n* rozdarcie *nt* ▹ *vt* drzeć (podrzeć *perf*) ▹ *vi* drzeć się (podrzeć się *perf*); **I ripped open the envelope** rozdarłem *or* rozerwałem kopertę

▸ **rip off** *vt* (*shirt etc*) zdzierać (zedrzeć *perf*); (*inf: person*) zdzierać (zedrzeć *perf*) skórę z *+gen* (*inf*)

▸ **rip up** *vt* drzeć (podrzeć *perf*) (na kawałki)

**ipcord** ['rɪpkɔ:d] *n* (*on parachute*) linka *f* wyzwalająca

**ipe** [raɪp] *adj* dojrzały; **to be ~ for sth** (*fig*) dojrzeć (*perf*) do czegoś; **he lived to a ~ old age** dożył sędziwego wieku

**ipen** ['raɪpn] *vi* dojrzewać (dojrzeć *perf*) ▹ *vt* (*fruit, crop etc*): **the sun will ~ them soon** na słońcu szybko dojrzeją

**ipeness** ['raɪpnɪs] *n* dojrzałość *perf*

**ip-off** ['rɪpɔf] (*inf*) *n*: **it's a ~!** to zdzierstwo! (*inf*)

**iposte** [rɪ'pɔst] *n* riposta *f*

**ipple** ['rɪpl] *n* (*wave*) zmarszczka *f*; (*of applause*) szmer *m* ▹ *vi* (*water*) marszczyć się (zmarszczyć się *perf*); (*muscles*) prężyć się, drgać ▹ *vt* marszczyć (zmarszczyć *perf*)

**ise** [raɪz] (*pt* **rose**, *pp* **~n**) *n* (*incline*) wzniesienie *nt*; (*Brit: salary increase*) podwyżka *f*; (*in prices, temperature*) wzrost *m*; (*fig*): **~ to power** dojście *nt* do władzy ▹ *vi* (*prices, numbers*) rosnąć, wzrastać (wzrosnąć *perf*); (*waters, voice, level*) podnosić się (podnieść się *perf*); (*sun, moon*) wschodzić (wzejść *perf*); (*wind*) przybierać (przybrać *perf*) na sile; (*sound*) wznosić się (wznieść się *perf*); (*from bed, knees*) wstawać (wstać *perf*); (*also*: **rise up**: *tower, building*) wznosić się; (*: rebel*) powstawać (powstać *perf*); **to ~ in rank** awansować (awansować *perf*); **to ~ to power** dochodzić (dojść *perf*) do władzy; **to give ~ to** (*discussion, misunderstandings*) wywoływać (wywołać *perf*); (*life*) dawać (dać *perf*) początek *+dat*; **to ~ to the occasion** stawać (stanąć *perf*) na wysokości zadania

**risen** [rɪzn] *pp of* **rise**

**rising** ['raɪzɪŋ] *adj* (*number, prices*) rosnący; (*sun, film star*) wschodzący; (*politician, musician*) dobrze się zapowiadający; **~ tide** przypływ

**rising damp** *n* wilgoć *f* (*przesuwająca się wzwyż po zewnętrznych ścianach budynku*)

**risk** [rɪsk] *n* ryzyko *nt*; (*danger*) niebezpieczeństwo *nt* ▹ *vt* ryzykować (zaryzykować *perf*); **to take a ~** podejmować (podjąć *perf*) ryzyko; **to run the ~ of** narażać się na *+acc*; **at ~** w niebezpieczeństwie; **at one's own ~** na (swoje) własne ryzyko; **at the ~ of sounding rude, I propose ...** być może zabrzmi to niegrzecznie, ale proponuję ...; **to be a fire/health ~** stanowić zagrożenie pożarowe/dla zdrowia; **I'll ~ it** zaryzykuję

**risk capital** *n* kapitał *m* spekulacyjny (*narażony za szczególne ryzyko*)

**risky** ['rɪskɪ] *adj* ryzykowny

**risqué** ['ri:skeɪ] *adj* (*joke, story*) nieprzyzwoity

**rissole** ['rɪsəul] *n* kotlet *m* siekany (*z mięsa, ryb lub warzyw*)

**rite** [raɪt] *n* obrządek *m*, obrzęd *m*; **last ~s** (*Rel*) ostatnie namaszczenie

**ritual** ['rɪtjuəl] *adj* rytualny ▹ *n* rytuał *m*

**rival** ['raɪvl] *n* (*in competition, love*) rywal(ka) *m(f)*; (*in business*) konkurent(ka) *m(f)* ▹ *adj* (*firm, newspaper*) konkurencyjny; (*team*) przeciwny ▹ *vt* równać się z *+instr*; **to ~ sb/sth in** konkurować z kimś/czymś *+instr*

**rivalry** ['raɪvlrɪ] *n* rywalizacja *f*, współzawodnictwo *nt*

**river** ['rɪvə^r] *n* (*lit, fig*) rzeka *f* ▹ *cpd* rzeczny; **up/down ~** w górę/dół rzeki

**river bank** *n* brzeg *m* rzeki

**river bed** *n* koryto *nt* rzeki

**riverside** ['rɪvəsaɪd] *n* brzeg *m* rzeki

**rivet** ['rɪvɪt] *n* nit *m* ▹ *vt* (*fig: eyes, attention*) przykuwać (przykuć *perf*)

**riveting** ['rɪvɪtɪŋ] *adj* (*fig*) pasjonujący, fascynujący

**Riviera** [rɪvɪ'ɛərə] *n*: **the (French) ~** Riwiera *f* (Francuska); **the Italian ~** Riwiera Włoska

**Riyadh** [rɪ'jɑ:d] *n* Rijad *m*

**RN** *n abbr* (*Brit*) = **Royal Navy**; (*US: = registered nurse*) ≈ pielęgniarka(-arz) *f(m)* dyplomowana(-ny) *f(m)*

**RNA** *n abbr* (= *ribonucleic acid*) RNA *m inv*

**RNLI** (*Brit*) *n abbr* (= *Royal National Lifeboat Institution*) *organizacja zajmująca się ratownictwem wodnym*

**RNZAF** *n abbr* = **Royal New Zealand Air Force**

**RNZN** *n abbr* = **Royal New Zealand Navy**

**road** [rəud] *n* (*lit, fig*) droga *f*; (*motorway etc*) szosa *f*, autostrada *f*; (*in town*) ulica *f* ▹ *cpd* drogowy; **main ~** szosa główna; **it takes four hours by ~** samochodem jedzie się tam cztery godziny; **let's hit the ~** ruszajmy (w drogę); **to be on the ~** być w trasie; **on the ~ to success** na drodze do sukcesu; **major/ minor ~** droga główna/boczna

**roadblock** ['rəudblɔk] *n* blokada *f* drogi

**road haulage** *n* transport *m* drogowy

**roadhog** ['rəudhɔg] *n* zawalidroga *m*

**road map** *n* mapa *f* samochodowa

**road safety** *n* bezpieczeństwo *nt* na drodze

**roadside** ['rəudsaɪd] *n* pobocze *nt* (drogi) ▷ *cpd* przydrożny; **by the ~** na poboczu

**road sign** *n* znak *m* drogowy

**roadsweeper** ['rəudswiːpə^r] (*Brit*) *n* (*person*) zamiatacz *m* ulic; (*vehicle*) maszyna *f* do zamiatania ulic

**road user** *n* użytkownik *m* drogi

**roadway** ['rəudweɪ] *n* jezdnia *f*

**road works** *npl* roboty *pl* drogowe

**roadworthy** ['rəudwəːðɪ] *adj* (*car*) zdatny do jazdy

**roam** [rəum] *vi* wędrować, włóczyć się ▷ *vt* (*streets*) włóczyć się *+instr*; (*countryside*) wędrować *or* włóczyć się po *+loc*

**roar** [rɔː^r] *n* ryk *m* ▷ *vi* ryczeć (zaryczeć *perf*); **to ~ with laughter** ryczeć (ryknąć *perf*) śmiechem

**roaring** ['rɔːrɪŋ] *adj* (*fire*) buzujący; (*success*) oszałamiający; **to do a ~ trade (in sth)** robić (zrobić *perf*) (na czymś) świetny interes

**roast** [rəust] *n* pieczeń *f* ▷ *vt* (*meat, potatoes*) piec (upiec *perf*); (*coffee*) palić

**roast beef** *n* rostbef *m*, pieczeń *f* wołowa

**rob** [rɔb] *vt* rabować (obrabować *perf*), okradać (okraść *perf*); **to rob sb of sth** okradać (okraść *perf*) kogoś z czegoś; (*fig*) pozbawiać (pozbawić *perf*) kogoś czegoś

**robber** ['rɔbə^r] *n* rabuś *m*, bandyta *m*

**robbery** ['rɔbərɪ] *n* rabunek *m*; (*using force or threats*) napad *m*

**robe** [rəub] *n* (*for ceremony*) toga *f*; (*also*: **bath robe**) płaszcz *m* kąpielowy; (US) szlafrok *m*, podomka *f* ▷ *vt*: **to be ~d in** (*fml*) być odzianym w *+acc* (*fml*)

**robin** ['rɔbɪn] *n* (*European*) rudzik *m*; (*North American*) drozd *m* wędrowny

**robot** ['rəubɔt] *n* robot *m*

**robotics** [rə'bɔtɪks] *n* robotyka *f*

**robust** [rəu'bʌst] *adj* (*person*) krzepki; (*appetite*) zdrowy, tęgi; (*economy*) silny; **to be in ~ health** cieszyć się wyśmienitym zdrowiem

**rock** [rɔk] *n* (*substance*) skała *f*; (*boulder*) skała *f*, głaz *m*; (US: *small stone*) kamień *m*; (*also*: **rock music**) rock *m*; (*Brit*: *sweet*) *twardy cukierek w kształcie spiralnej laseczki* ▷ *vt* (*person*: *baby, cradle*) kołysać; (*waves*: *ship*) kołysać *+instr*; (*explosion, news*) wstrząsać (wstrząsnąć *perf*) *+instr* ▷ *vi* kołysać się (zakołysać się *perf*); **on the ~s** (*drink*) z lodem *post*; (*ship*) na skałach *post*; (*marriage etc*) w rozsypce *post*; **to ~ the boat** (*fig*) wprowadzać (wprowadzić *perf*) zamieszanie

**rock and roll** *n* rock and roll *m*

**rock-bottom** ['rɔk'bɔtəm] *adj* najniższy ▷ *n*: **to reach** *or* **touch** *or* **hit ~** upaść (*perf*) *or* stoczyć się (*perf*) na samo dno

**rock cake** *n* ≈ brukowiec *m* (*pierniczek*)

**rock climber** *n* alpinista(-tka) *m(f)*

**rock climbing** *n* wspinaczka *f* (górska), alpinistyka *f*

**rockery** ['rɔkərɪ] *n* ogród(ek) *m* skalny, alpinarium *nt*

**rocket** ['rɔkɪt] *n* rakieta *f* ▷ *vi* (*prices, sales*) skakać (skoczyć *perf*) w górę

**rocket launcher** *n* wyrzutnia *f* rakietowa

**rock face** *n* ściana *f* skalna

**rock fall** *n* obryw *m* skalny

**rocking chair** ['rɔkɪŋ-] *n* fotel *m* bujany

**rocking horse** *n* koń *m* na biegunach

**rocky** ['rɔkɪ] *adj* skalisty; (*fig*) chwiejny, niepewny

**Rocky Mountains** *npl*: **the ~** Góry *pl* Skaliste

**rod** [rɔd] *n* (*bar*) pręt *m*; (*stick*) rózga *f*; (*also*: **fishing rod**) wędka *f*

**rode** [rəud] *pt of* **ride**

**rodent** ['rəudnt] *n* gryzoń *m*

**rodeo** ['rəudɪəu] (US) *n* rodeo *nt*

**roe** [rəu] *n*: **hard roe** ikra *f*; **soft roe** mlecz *m* (rybi)

**roe deer** *n inv* sarna *f*

**rogue** [rəug] *n* łobuz *m*

**roguish** ['rəugɪʃ] *adj* łobuzerski

**role** [rəul] *n* rola *f*

**roll** [rəul] *n* (*of paper*) rolka *f*; (*of cloth*) bela *f*; (*of banknotes*) zwitek *m*; (*of members etc*) lista *f*, wykaz *m*; (*in parish etc*) rejestr *m*, archiwum *nt*; (*of drums*) werbel *m*; (*also*: **bread roll**) bułka *f* ▷ *vt* (*ball, dice*) toczyć, kulać; (*also*: **roll up**: *string*) zwijać (zwinąć *perf*); (: *sleeves*) podwijać (podwinąć *perf*); (*cigarette*) skręcać (skręcić *perf*); (*eyes*) przewracać *+instr*; (*also*: **roll out**: *pastry*) wałkować, rozwałkowywać (rozwałkować *perf*); (*road, lawn*) walcować ▷ *vi* (*ball, stone, tears*) toczyć się (potoczyć się *perf*); (*thunder*) przetaczać się (przetoczyć się *perf*); (*ship*) kołysać się; (*sweat*) spływać; (*camera, printing press*) chodzić; **cheese/ham ~** bułka z serem/szynką; **he's ~ing in it** (*inf*) on leży *or* siedzi *or* śpi na pieniądzach (*inf*)

▸ **roll about** *vi* turlać się, tarzać się

▸ **roll around** *vi* = **roll about**

▸ **roll in** *vi* (*money, invitations*) napływać (napłynąć *perf*)

▸ **roll over** *vi*: **to ~ over (on one's stomach)** przewracać się (przewrócić się *perf*) (na brzuch)

▸ **roll up** *vi* (*inf*) nadciągać (nadciągnąć *perf*), napływać (napłynąć *perf*) ▷ *vt* zwijać (zwinąć *perf*); **to ~ o.s. up into a ball** zwijać się (zwinąć się *perf*) w kłębek
**roll call** *n* odczytanie *nt* listy obecności
**rolled gold** [rəuld-] *adj*: **the watch is ~** zegarek jest platerowany złotem
**roller** ['rəulə^r] *n* (*in machine*) wałek *m*, rolka *f*; (*for lawn, road*) walec *m*; (*for hair*) wałek *m*
**roller blind** *n* roleta *f*
**roller coaster** *n* (*at funfair*) kolejka *f* górska
**roller skates** *npl* wrotki *pl*
**rollicking** ['rɔlıkıŋ] *adj* swawolny, rozhukany; **to have a ~ time** hucznie się bawić
**rolling** ['rəulıŋ] *adj* (*hills*) falisty
**rolling mill** *n* walcownia *f*
**rolling pin** *n* wałek *m* do ciasta
**rolling stock** *n* tabor *m* kolejowy
**roll-on-roll-off** ['rəulɔn'rəulɔf] (*Brit*) *adj* statek *m* typu „ro-ro"
**roly-poly** ['rəulı'pəulı] (*Brit*: *Culin*) *n rolada z nadzieniem z konfitur*
**ROM** [rɔm] (*Comput*) *n abbr* (= *read-only memory*) ROM *m*
**Roman** ['rəumən] *adj* rzymski ▷ *n* Rzymianin(-anka) *m(f)*
**Roman Catholic** *adj* rzymskokatolicki ▷ *n* katolik(-iczka) *m(f)*
**romance** [rə'mæns] *n* (*love affair, novel*) romans *m*; (*charm*) urok *m*, czar *m*
**Romanesque** [rəumə'nɛsk] (*Archit*) *adj* romański
**Romania** [rəu'meınıə] *n* Rumunia *f*
**Romanian** [rəu'meınıən] *adj* rumuński ▷ *n* (*person*) Rumun(ka) *m(f)*; (*Ling*) (język *m*) rumuński
**Roman numeral** *n* cyfra *f* rzymska
**romantic** [rə'mæntık] *adj* romantyczny
**romanticism** [rə'mæntısızəm] *n* romantyzm *m*
**Romany** ['rɔmənı] *adj* cygański, Romów *post* ▷ *n* Rom/Romni *m/f inv*; (*Ling*) (język *m*) cygański *or* romani
**Rome** [rəum] *n* Rzym *m*
**romp** [rɔmp] *n* igraszki *pl* ▷ *vi* (*also*: **romp about**) dokazywać, baraszkować; **to ~ home** (*horse*) wygrywać (wygrać *perf*) bez wysiłku
**rompers** ['rɔmpəz] *npl* pajacyk *m* (*ubranko*)
**rondo** ['rɔndəu] (*Mus*) *n* rondo *nt*
**roof** [ru:f] (*pl* **~s**) *n* dach *m* ▷ *vt* pokrywać (pokryć *perf*) dachem, zadaszać (zadaszyć *perf*); **the ~ of the mouth** podniebienie
**roof garden** *n* ogród *m* na dachu
**roofing** ['ru:fıŋ] *n* pokrycie *nt* dachowe; **~ felt** papa *f*
**roof rack** (*Aut*) *n* bagażnik *m* na dach
**rook** [ruk] *n* (*Zool*) gawron *m*; (*Chess*) wieża *f*
**room** [ru:m] *n* (*in house, hotel*) pokój *m*; (*in school etc*) sala *f*, pomieszczenie *nt*; (*space*) miejsce *nt*; (*for change, manoeuvre*) pole *nt* ▷ *vi*: **to ~ with sb** (*esp US*) wynajmować wspólnie z kimś pokój; **rooms** *npl* mieszkanie *nt*; **"~s to let"**, (*US*) **"~s for rent"** „pokoje do wynajęcia"; **single/double ~** pokój jednoosobowy/dwuosobowy; **is there ~ for this?** czy jest na to miejsce?; **to make ~ for sb** robić (zrobić *perf*) miejsce dla kogoś; **there is plenty of ~ for improvement here** (jeszcze) wiele można tu ulepszyć
**rooming house** ['ru:mıŋ-] (*US*) *n* blok *m* mieszkalny (*z mieszkaniami lub pokojami do wynajęcia*)
**roommate** ['ru:mmeıt] *n* współlokator(ka) *m(f)*, współmieszkaniec(-nka) *m(f)*
**room service** *n* obsługa *f* kelnerska do pokojów; **to call ~** dzwonić (zadzwonić *perf*) po kelnera
**room temperature** *n* temperatura *f* pokojowa; **"serve at ~"** „podawać w temperaturze pokojowej"
**roomy** ['ru:mı] *adj* przestronny
**roost** [ru:st] *vi* siedzieć na grzędzie
**rooster** ['ru:stə^r] (*esp US*) *n* kogut *m*
**root** [ru:t] *n* (*of plant, tooth*) korzeń *m*; (*Math*) pierwiastek *m*; (*of hair*) cebulka *f*; (*of problem, belief*) źródło *nt* ▷ *vi* ukorzeniać się (ukorzenić się *perf*), wypuszczać (wypuścić *perf*) korzenie ▷ *vt*: **to be ~ed in** być zakorzenionym w *+loc*; **roots** *npl* korzenie *pl*; **to take ~** (*lit, fig*) zakorzeniać się (zakorzenić się *perf*); **the ~ cause of the problem** podstawowa przyczyna problemu
▸ **root about** *vi* (*fig*) szperać
▸ **root for** *vt fus* kibicować *+dat*, dopingować *+acc*
▸ **root out** *vt* wykorzeniać (wykorzenić *perf*)
**rope** [rəup] *n* (*thick string*) sznur *m*, powróz *m*; (*Naut*) cuma *f*, lina *f*; (*for climbing*) lina *f* ▷ *vt* (*also*: **rope together**) związywać (związać *perf*), powiązać (*perf*); (*tie*): **to ~ sth (to)** przywiązywać (przywiązać *perf*) coś (do *+gen*); **to know the ~s** (*fig*) znać się na rzeczy
▸ **rope in** *vt* (*fig*) werbować (zwerbować *perf*)
▸ **rope off** *vt* (*area*) odgradzać (odgrodzić *perf*) (liną)
**rope ladder** *n* drabina *f* sznurowa
**rosary** ['rəuzərı] *n* różaniec *m*
**rose** [rəuz] *pt of* **rise** ▷ *n* róża *f*; (*on watering can*) sitko *nt* ▷ *adj* różowy
**rosé** ['rəuzeı] *n* różowe wino *nt*
**rosebed** ['rəuzbɛd] *n* klomb *m* róż
**rosebud** ['rəuzbʌd] *n* pączek *m* róży
**rosebush** ['rəuzbuʃ] *n* krzew *m* różany
**rosemary** ['rəuzmərı] *n* rozmaryn *m*

r

**rosette** [rəu'zɛt] *n* rozetka *f*
**ROSPA** ['rɔspə] *(Brit) n abbr* = **Royal Society for the Prevention of Accidents**
**roster** ['rɔstə^r] *n*: **duty ~** harmonogram *m* dyżurów
**rostrum** ['rɔstrəm] *n* mównica *f*
**rosy** ['rəuzɪ] *adj (colour)* różowy; *(cheeks)* zaróżowiony; *(situation)* obiecujący; **a ~ future** świetlana przyszłość
**rot** [rɔt] *n (decay)* gnicie *nt*; *(fig: rubbish)* bzdury *pl* ▷ *vt* psuć (zepsuć *perf*), niszczyć (zniszczyć *perf*) ▷ *vi (teeth)* psuć się (popsuć się *perf*); *(wood, fruit, etc)* gnić (zgnić *perf*); **to stop the rot** *(Brit: fig)* powstrzymywać (powstrzymać *perf*) proces rozkładu; **dry rot** mursz; **wet rot** zgnilizna
**rota** ['rəutə] *n* rozkład *m or* harmonogram *m* dyżurów; **on a ~ basis** według harmonogramu
**rotary** ['rəutərɪ] *adj (motion)* obrotowy, rotacyjny; *(cutter)* krążkowy
**rotate** [rəu'teɪt] *vt (spin)* obracać (obrócić *perf*) ▷ *vi* obracać się (obrócić się *perf*); **to ~ crops** stosować płodozmian; **to ~ jobs** zmieniać się na stanowiskach pracy
**rotating** [rəu'teɪtɪŋ] *adj* obrotowy
**rotation** [rəu'teɪʃən] *n (of planet, drum)* obrót *m*; *(of crops)* płodozmian *m*; *(of jobs)* rotacja *f*; **in ~** w określonej kolejności
**rote** [rəut] *n*: **by ~** na pamięć
**rotor** ['rəutə^r] *n (also:* **rotor blade***)* wirnik *m*
**rotten** ['rɔtn] *adj (fruit)* zgniły; *(meat, eggs, teeth)* zepsuty; *(wood)* spróchniały, zmurszały; *(inf: unpleasant)* paskudny; *(: bad)* kiepski, marny; **to feel ~** czuć się podle
**rottweiler** ['rɔtvaɪlə^r] *n* rottweiler *m*
**rotund** [rəu'tʌnd] *adj* pulchny
**rouble** ['ru:bl], *(US)* **ruble** *n* rubel *m*
**rouge** [ru:ʒ] *n* róż *m*
**rough** [rʌf] *adj (surface)* szorstki, chropowaty; *(terrain)* nierówny, wyboisty; *(person, manner)* grubiański, obcesowy; *(town, area)* niespokojny; *(treatment)* brutalny; *(conditions, journey)* ciężki; *(sea)* wzburzony; *(sketch, plan)* schematyczny; *(estimate)* przybliżony ▷ *n (Golf)*: **in the ~** w zaroślach ▷ *vt*: **to ~ it** żyć w prymitywnych warunkach, obywać się bez wygód; **to have a ~ time** przeżywać ciężkie chwile; **to play ~** *(fig)* grać (zagrać *perf*) brutalnie; **can you give me a ~ idea of the cost?** czy może mi Pan/Pani podać orientacyjny koszt?; **to sleep ~** *(Brit)* spać pod gołym niebem; **to feel ~** *(Brit)* czuć się źle
▸ **rough out** *vt* szkicować (naszkicować *perf*)
**roughage** ['rʌfɪdʒ] *n* nietrawiona część *f* pożywienia
**rough-and-ready** ['rʌfən'rɛdɪ] *adj* prymitywny, prowizoryczny
**rough-and-tumble** ['rʌfən'tʌmbl] *n (fighting)* bijatyka *f*, szamotanina *f*; *(fig)* przepychanki *pl*
**roughcast** ['rʌfkɑ:st] *n* tynk *m* kamyczkowy
**rough copy** *n* brudnopis *m*
**rough draft** *n* szkic *m*
**rough justice** *n* surowy, ale sprawiedliwy wyrok *m*
**roughly** ['rʌflɪ] *adv (push, grab)* gwałtownie; *(make)* niestarannie; *(answer)* pobieżnie; *(approximately)* z grubsza, mniej więcej; **~ speaking** mniej więcej
**roughness** ['rʌfnɪs] *n (of surface)* szorstkość *f*, chropowatość *f*; *(of manner)* grubiaństwo *nt*
**roughshod** ['rʌfʃɔd] *adv*: **to ride ~ over** *(person)* poniewierać *+instr*; *(objections)* ignorować (zignorować *perf*) *+acc*
**roulette** [ru:'lɛt] *n* ruletka *f*
**Roumania** [ru:'meɪnɪə] *n* = **Rumania**
**round** [raund] *adj* okrągły ▷ *n (by policeman, doctor)* obchód *m*; *(of competition, talks)* runda *f*; *(of golf)* partia *f*; *(of ammunition)* nabój *m*, pocisk *m*; *(of drinks)* kolejka *f*; *(of sandwiches)* porcja *f* ▷ *vt (lake etc)* okrążać (okrążyć *perf*); *(cape)* opływać (opłynąć *perf*) ▷ *prep*: **~ his neck/the table** wokół jego szyi/stołu; **to sail ~ the world** płynąć (popłynąć *perf*) dookoła świata; **to move ~ a room** chodzić po pokoju; **~ about 300** około 300 ▷ *adv*: **all ~** dookoła; **the long way ~** okrężną drogą; **all (the) year ~** przez cały rok; **the wrong way ~** odwrotnie, na odwrót; **in ~ figures** w zaokrągleniu; **it's just ~ the corner** to jest tuż za rogiem; **to ask sb ~** zapraszać (zaprosić *perf*) kogoś do siebie; **I'll be ~ at six o'clock** będę o szóstej; **to go ~** obracać się; **to go ~ to sb's (house)** zachodzić (zajść *perf*) do kogoś; **to go ~ the back** wchodzić (wejść *perf*) od tyłu; **to go ~ an obstacle** obchodzić (obejść *perf*) przeszkodę; **there is enough to go ~** wystarczy dla wszystkich; **~ the clock** (przez) całą dobę, na okrągło *(inf)*; **the daily ~** *(fig)* dzienny przydział; **a ~ of applause** owacja; **to ~ the corner** skręcać (skręcić *perf*) za róg
▸ **round off** *vt* zakańczać (zakończyć *perf*)
▸ **round up** *vt (cattle)* spędzać (spędzić *perf*), zaganiać (zagonić *perf*); *(people)* spędzać (spędzić *perf*); *(price, figure)* zaokrąglać (zaokrąglić *perf*)
**roundabout** ['raundəbaut] *(Brit) n (Aut)* rondo *nt*; *(at fair)* karuzela *f* ▷ *adj* okrężny; *(fig: way, means)* zawoalowany
**rounded** ['raundɪd] *adj (hill)* łagodny; *(body, figure)* zaokrąglony
**rounders** ['raundəz] *n odmiana palanta*
**roundly** ['raundlɪ] *adv (fig)* otwarcie

**und-shouldered** ['raund'ʃəuldəd] *adj* ɪrzygarbiony
**und trip** *n* podróż *f* w obie strony
**undup** ['raundʌp] *n* (*of news*) przegląd *m*; (*of* *nimals*) spęd *m*; (*of criminals*) obława *f*; **a ~ of** **he latest news** przegląd najświeższych viadomości
**use** [rauz] *vt* (*wake up*) budzić (obudzić *perf*); *stir up*) wzbudzać (wzbudzić *perf*)
**using** ['rauzɪŋ] *adj* porywający
**ut** [raut] (*Mil*) *n* pogrom *m* ▷ *vt* rozgromić *perf*)
**ute** [ru:t] *n* (*way*) szlak *m*, droga *f*; (*of bus,* *rocession*) trasa *f*; (*of shipping*) szlak *m*; (*fig*) lroga *f*; **"all ~s"** (*Aut*) „wszystkie kierunki"; **he best ~ to London** najlepsza droga do ondynu; **en ~ for** po *or* w drodze do *+gen*; **en ~** **rom ... to ...** na *or* w drodze z *+gen* do *+gen*
**ute map** (Brit) *n* (*for journey*) mapa *f* lrogowa; (*for trains etc*) plan *m* trasy
**utine** [ru:'ti:n] *adj* rutynowy ▷ *n* *organization*) rozkład *m* zajęć; (*drudgery*) nonotonna harówka *f*; (*Theat*) układ *m*; **~** **rocedure** postępowanie rutynowe
**ve** [rəuv] *vt* włóczyć się po *+loc*
**ving reporter** *n* wędrowny reporter *m*
**w¹** [rəu] *n* rząd *m*; (*Knitting*) rządek *m* ▷ *vi* viosłować ▷ *vt*: **to row a boat** wiosłować; **in** **row** (*fig*) z rzędu
**w²** [rau] *n* (*din*) zgiełk *m*; (*dispute*) awantura ; (*quarrel*) kłótnia *f* ▷ *vi* kłócić się (pokłócić się *erf*); **to have a row** kłócić się (pokłócić się *erf*)
**wboat** ['rəubəut] (US) *n* łódź *f* (wiosłowa)
**wdiness** ['raudɪnɪs] *n* awanturnictwo *nt*
**wdy** ['raudɪ] *adj* awanturniczy
**wdyism** ['raudɪɪzəm] *n* awanturnictwo *nt*
**wing** ['rəuɪŋ] *n* wioślarstwo *nt*
**wing boat** (Brit) *n* łódź *f* (wiosłowa)
**wlock** ['rɔlək] (Brit) *n* dulka *f*
**yal** ['rɔɪəl] *adj* królewski
**ɔyal Air Force** (Brit) *n*: **the ~** Królewskie Siły l Powietrzne
**yal blue** *adj* błękit *m* kobaltowy
**yalist** ['rɔɪəlɪst] *n* rojalista(-tka) *m(f)* ▷ *adj* ojalistyczny
**ɔyal Navy** (Brit) *n*: **the ~** Królewska Marynarka *f* Wojenna
**yalty** ['rɔɪəltɪ] *n* członkowie *vir pl* rodziny królewskiej; **royalties** *npl* tantiemy *pl*
**P** (Brit) *n abbr* (= *received pronunciation*) *standard* *vymowy brytyjskiej*
**m** *abbr* (= *revolutions per minute*) obr/min
**R** (US) *abbr* = **railroad**
**RP** (Brit) *n abbr* = **recommended retail price**
**SA** (Brit) *n abbr* = **Royal Society of Arts**; **Royal** **Scottish Academy**
**RSI** (*Med*) *n abbr* (= *repetitive strain injury*) uszkodzenie *nt* przeciążeniowe
**RSPB** (Brit) *n abbr* = **Royal Society for the Protection of Birds**
**RSPCA** (Brit) *n abbr* = **Royal Society for the Prevention of Cruelty to Animals**
**RSVP** *abbr* (= *répondez s'il vous plaît*) uprasza się o odpowiedź
**RTA** *n abbr* = **road traffic accident**
**Rt Hon.** (Brit) *abbr* (= *Right Honourable*) *tytuł przysługujący niektórym sędziom i członkom Privy Council*
**Rt Rev.** (Rel) *abbr* (= *Right Reverend*) *tytuł przysługujący biskupowi*
**rub** [rʌb] *vt* (*part of body*) pocierać (potrzeć *perf*); (*object*) przecierać (przetrzeć *perf*); (*hands*) zacierać (zatrzeć *perf*) ▷ *n*: **to give sth a rub** przecierać (przetrzeć *perf*) coś; **to rub sb up** *or* (*US*) **rub sb the wrong way** działać komuś na nerwy
▸**rub down** *vt* wycierać (wytrzeć *perf*)
▸**rub in** *vt* wcierać (wetrzeć *perf*); **don't rub it in!** (*fig*) nie wypominaj mi tego bez końca!
▸**rub off** *vi* (*paint*) ścierać się (zetrzeć się *perf*)
▸**rub off on** *vt fus* udzielać się (udzielić się *perf*) *+dat*
▸**rub out** *vt* wymazywać (wymazać *perf*), zmazywać (zmazać *perf*)
**rubber** ['rʌbə^r] *n* (*substance*) guma *f*; (*Brit: eraser*) gumka *f*; (*US: inf*) kondom *m* (*inf*)
**rubber band** *n* gumka *f*, recepturka *f*
**rubber plant** *n* drzewo *nt* kauczukowe
**rubber ring** *n* (nadmuchiwane) koło *nt* do pływania
**rubber stamp** *n* pieczątka *f*
**rubber-stamp** [rʌbə'stæmp] *vt* (*fig*) mechanicznie zatwierdzać (zatwierdzić *perf*)
**rubbery** ['rʌbərɪ] *adj* (*material*) gumowy; (*food*) gumowaty
**rubbish** ['rʌbɪʃ] (Brit) *n* śmieci *pl*, odpadki *pl*; (*fig: junk*) szmira *f*; (*: nonsense*) bzdury *pl*, brednie *pl* ▷ *vt* (*inf*) mieszać (zmieszać *perf*) z błotem (*inf*); **~!** bzdura!
**rubbish bin** (Brit) *n* pojemnik *m* na śmieci *or* odpadki
**rubbish dump** (Brit) *n* wysypisko *nt* śmieci
**rubbishy** ['rʌbɪʃɪ] (Brit: *inf*) *adj* tandetny, szmirowaty
**rubble** ['rʌbl] *n* (*debris*) gruz *m*; (*of house*) gruzy *pl*; (*Constr*) tłuczeń *m*
**ruble** ['ru:bl] (US) *n* = **rouble**
**ruby** ['ru:bɪ] *n* rubin *m* ▷ *adj* rubinowy
**RUC** (Brit) *n abbr* (= *Royal Ulster Constabulary*) *policja północnoirlandzka*
**rucksack** ['rʌksæk] *n* plecak *m*
**ructions** ['rʌkʃənz] (*inf*) *npl* afera *f* (*inf*)
**rudder** ['rʌdə^r] *n* ster *m*

r

**ruddy** ['rʌdɪ] *adj* (*face*) rumiany; (*glow*) czerwonawy; **~!** (*inf*) do licha!
**rude** [ru:d] *adj* (*person, behaviour*) niegrzeczny; (*word, joke*) nieprzyzwoity; (*shock*) gwałtowny; (*shelter etc*) prymitywny; **to be ~ to sb** być niegrzecznym wobec kogoś; **a ~ awakening** gwałtowne przebudzenie
**rudely** ['ru:dlɪ] *adv* niegrzecznie
**rudeness** ['ru:dnɪs] *n* niegrzeczność *f*
**rudimentary** [ru:dɪ'mɛntərɪ] *adj* elementarny, podstawowy
**rudiments** ['ru:dɪmənts] *npl* podstawy *pl*
**rueful** ['ru:ful] *adj* smutny
**ruff** [rʌf] *n* kreza *f*
**ruffian** ['rʌfɪən] *n* zbój *m*
**ruffle** ['rʌfl] *vt* (*hair*) mierzwić (zmierzwić *perf*), wichrzyć (zwichrzyć *perf*); (*water*) marszczyć (zmarszczyć *perf*); (*bird: feathers*) stroszyć (nastroszyć *perf*); (*fig: person*) poruszać (poruszyć *perf*)
**rug** [rʌg] *n* (*on floor*) dywanik *m*; (*Brit: blanket*) pled *m*
**rugby** ['rʌgbɪ] *n* (*also:* **rugby football**) rugby *nt inv*
**rugged** ['rʌgɪd] *adj* (*landscape, features, face*) surowy; (*character*) szorstki; (*man, determination*) twardy
**rugger** ['rʌgə^r] (*Brit: inf*) *n* rugby *nt inv*
**ruin** ['ru:ɪn] *n* (*destruction, remains*) ruina *f*; (*downfall*) upadek *m*; (*bankruptcy*) upadek *m*, ruina *f* ▷ *vt* (*building, person, health*) rujnować (zrujnować *perf*); (*plans*) niweczyć (zniweczyć *perf*); (*prospects, relations*) psuć (popsuć *perf*); (*clothes, carpet*) niszczyć (zniszczyć *perf*); (*hopes*) pogrzebać (*perf*); **ruins** *npl* ruiny *pl*; **in ~s** w gruzach
**ruination** [ru:ɪ'neɪʃən] *n* (*of building, place*) zniszczenie *nt*; (*of person, life, career*) zrujnowanie *nt*
**ruinous** ['ru:ɪnəs] *adj* rujnujący
**rule** [ru:l] *n* (*norm*) reguła *f*; (*regulation*) przepis *m*; (*government*) rządy *pl*, panowanie *nt* ▷ *vt* rządzić *+instr* ▷ *vi*: **to ~ (over sb/sth)** rządzić (kimś/czymś); **to ~ in favour of/against/on** wydawać (wydać *perf*) orzeczenie na korzyść *+gen*/na niekorzyść *+gen*/w sprawie *+gen*; **to ~ that ...** orzekać (orzec *perf*), że ...; **it's against the ~s** to niezgodne z przepisami *or* niedozwolone; **as a ~ of thumb, ...** można przyjąć, że ...; **under British ~** pod panowaniem brytyjskim; **as a ~** z reguły
▸ **rule out** *vt* wykluczać (wykluczyć *perf*); **murder cannot be ~d out** nie można wykluczyć morderstwa
**ruled** [ru:ld] *adj* (*paper*) liniowany, w linię *post*
**ruler** ['ru:lə^r] *n* (*sovereign*) władca(-dczyni) *m(f)*; (*for measuring*) linijka *f*
**ruling** ['ru:lɪŋ] *adj* rządzący ▷ *n* (*Jur*) orzeczenie *nt*
**rum** [rʌm] *n* rum *m* ▷ *adj* (*Brit: inf*) dziwaczny
**Rumania** *etc n* = **Romania** *etc*
**rumble** ['rʌmbl] *n* (*of thunder, guns*) dudnienie *nt*; (*of voices*) gwar *m* ▷ *vi* dudnić (zadudnić *perf*); (*also:* **rumble along**) toczyć się (potoczyć się *perf*) z łoskotem; **my stomach was rumbling** burczało mi w brzuchu
**rumbustious** [rʌm'bʌstʃəs] *adj* rubaszny
**ruminate** ['ru:mɪneɪt] *vi* (*person*) zastanawiać się; (*cow, sheep*) przeżuwać
**rummage** ['rʌmɪdʒ] *vi* grzebać, szperać
**rummage sale** (US) *n* wyprzedaż *f* rzeczy używanych (*na cele dobroczynne*)
**rumour**, (US) **rumor** ['ru:mə^r] *n* pogłoska *f* ▷ *vt*: **it is ~ed that ...** chodzą słuchy, że ...
**rump** [rʌmp] *n* (*of animal*) zad *m*; (*of group, political party*) niedobitki *pl* (*najwierniejsi członkowie*)
**rumple** ['rʌmpl] *vt* (*clothes, sheets*) miąć (pomiąć *perf*)
**rump steak** *n* wołowina *f* krzyżowa
**rumpus** ['rʌmpəs] *n* wrzawa *f*, szum *m*; **to kick up a ~** podnosić (podnieść *perf*) wrzawę, robić szum (narobić *perf* szumu)
**run** [rʌn] (*pt* **ran**, *pp* **run**) *n* (*fast pace, race*) bieg *m*; (*in car*) przejażdżka *f*; (*of train, bus, for skiing*) trasa *f*; (*of victories, defeats*) seria *f*; (*in tights, stockings*) oczko *nt*; (*Cricket, Baseball*) *punkt za przebiegnięcie między oznaczonymi miejscami po uderzeniu piłki* ▷ *vt* (*distance*) biec (przebiec *perf*); (*business, shop, hotel*) prowadzić; (*competition, course*) przeprowadzać (przeprowadzić *perf*); (*Comput: program*) uruchamiać (uruchomić *perf*); (*hand, fingers*) przesuwać (przesunąć *perf*); (*water*) puszczać (puścić *perf*); (*Press: article*) zamieszczać (zamieścić *perf*) ▷ *vi* (*move quickly*) biec (pobiec *perf*); (*: habitually, regularly*) biegać; (*flee*) uciekać (uciec *perf*); (*bus, train: operate*) kursować, jeździć; (*: travel*) jechać (pojechać *perf*); (*play, show*) być granym, iść (*inf*); (*contract*) być ważnym; (*river, tears*) płynąć (popłynąć *perf*); (*colours, washing*) farbować, puszczać; (*road, railway*) biec; (*horse: in race*) ścigać się; **to go for a run** iść (pójść *perf*) pobiegać; **to break into a run** zaczynać (zacząć *perf*) biec; **it's a 50-minute run from Glasgow to Edinburgh** z Glasgow do Edynburga jedzie się 50 minut; **the play had a 6 week run at the Apollo Theatre** sztuka szła w Teatrze Apollo przez 6 tygodni; **a run of good/bad luck** dobra/zła passa; **to have the run of sb's house** móc korzystać z czyjegoś domu; **there was a run on ...** był run na *+acc*; **in the long/short run** na dłuższą/krótką metę; **we'll have to make a**

**run for it** będziemy musieli szybko (stąd) uciekać; **to be on the run** (*fugitive*) ukrywać się; **I'll run you to the station** zawiozę cię na dworzec; **to run the risk of** narażać się na *+acc*; **the baby's nose was running** niemowlę miało katar; **to run errands** załatwiać sprawy; **my car is very cheap to run** mój samochód jest bardzo tani w eksploatacji; **to run on petrol** jeździć na benzynę; **to run off batteries** działać na baterie; **the engine/computer is running** silnik/komputer jest włączony; **to run for president/in an election** kandydować na prezydenta/w wyborach; **the well has run dry** studnia wyschła; **tempers were running high** panowała nerwowa atmosfera; **unemployment is running at twenty per cent** bezrobocie kształtuje się na poziomie dwudziestu procent; **to run a bath** przygotowywać (przygotować *perf*) kąpiel; **blonde hair runs in the family** jasne włosy są cechą rodzinną; **to be run off one's feet** (*Brit*) być bardzo zabieganym

▸ **run across** *vt fus* (*find*) natykać się (natknąć się *perf*) na *+acc*

▸ **run after** *vt fus* biec (pobiec *perf*) za *+instr*

▸ **run away** *vi* uciekać (uciec *perf*)

▸ **run down** *vt* (*production*) ograniczać (ograniczyć *perf*); (*company*) ograniczać (ograniczyć *perf*) działalność *+gen*; (*Aut*: *person*) potrącać (potrącić *perf*); (*criticize*) źle mówić o *+loc* ▹ *vi* (*battery*) wyczerpywać się (wyczerpać się *perf*); **she's run down** jest wyczerpana

▸ **run in** (*Brit*) *vt* (*car*) docierać (dotrzeć *perf*)

▸ **run into** *vt fus* (*person, fence, post*) wpadać (wpaść *perf*) na *+acc*; (*problems*) napotykać (napotkać *perf*); (*another vehicle*) zderzać się (zderzyć się *perf*) z *+instr*; **to run into debt/trouble** wpadać (wpaść *perf*) w długi/kłopoty; **their losses ran into millions** ich straty sięgały milionów

▸ **run off** *vt* (*liquid*) wylewać (wylać *perf*); (*copies*) robić (zrobić *perf*) ▹ *vi* uciekać (uciec *perf*)

▸ **run out** *vi* (*time, money*) kończyć się (skończyć się *perf*); (*passport*) tracić (stracić *perf*) ważność

▸ **run out of** *vt fus*: **we're running out of money/ideas/matches** kończą nam się pieniądze/pomysły/zapałki

▸ **run over** *vt* (*Aut*: *person*) przejechać (*perf*) ▹ *vt fus* (*repeat*) powtarzać (powtórzyć *perf*) ▹ *vi* (*bath, water*) przelewać się (przelać się *perf*)

▸ **run through** *vt fus* (*discuss*) omawiać (omówić *perf*); (*examine*) przeglądać (przejrzeć *perf*); (*rehearse*) ćwiczyć (przećwiczyć *perf*)

▸ **run up** *vt* (*debt*) zaciągać (zaciągnąć *perf*)

▸ **run up against** *vt fus* (*difficulties*) napotykać (napotkać *perf*)

**runabout** [ˈrʌnəbaut] (*Aut*) *n* samochód *m* miejski

**runaway** [ˈrʌnəweɪ] *adj* (*slave, prisoner*) zbiegły; (*inflation*) nie dający się opanować; (*success*) spektakularny; **~ child** mały uciekinier; **~ horse** koń, który poniósł

**rundown** [ˈrʌndaun] *n* (*of company*) ograniczenie *nt* działalności ▹ *adj*: **run-down** (*person*) wyczerpany; (*building, area*) zaniedbany, zapuszczony

**rung** [rʌŋ] *pp of* **ring** ▹ *n* (*lit, fig*) szczebel *m*

**run-in** [ˈrʌnɪn] (*inf*) *n* starcie *nt*

**runner** [ˈrʌnə^r] *n* (*in race*: *person*) biegacz(ka) *m(f)*; (: *horse*) koń *m* wyścigowy; (*on sledge*) płoza *f*; (*on drawer*) prowadnica *f*

**runner bean** (*Brit*) *n* fasolka *f* szparagowa

**runner-up** [rʌnərˈʌp] *n* zdobywca(-wczyni) *m(f)* drugiego miejsca

**running** [ˈrʌnɪŋ] *n* (*sport*) bieganie *nt*; (*of business, organization*) prowadzenie *nt*; (*of machine*) eksploatacja *f*; (*of event*) organizacja *f* ▹ *adj* (*stream*) płynący; (*water*) bieżący; **to be in/out of the ~ for sth** mieć szansę/nie mieć szansy na coś; **six days ~** sześć dni z rzędu; **to have a ~ battle with sb** być z kimś w stanie ciągłej wojny; **to give a ~ commentary on sth** komentować coś na bieżąco; **a ~ sore** jątrzący wrzód; **to make the ~** (*in race*) prowadzić; (*fig*) przewodzić, wieść prym

**running costs** *npl* koszty *pl* eksploatacji *or* użytkowania

**running head** (*Typ*) *n* żywa pagina *f*

**running mate** (*US*: *Pol*) *n* kandydat(ka) *m(f)* na wiceprezydenta

**runny** [ˈrʌnɪ] *adj* (*honey, omelette*) (zbyt) rzadki; (*eyes*) załzawiony; **his nose is ~** cieknie mu z nosa

**run-off** [ˈrʌnɔf] *n* (*in contest*) dogrywka *f*; (*in election*) druga tura *f*; (*extra race*) dodatkowy bieg *m*

**run-of-the-mill** [ˈrʌnəvðəˈmɪl] *adj* tuzinkowy

**runt** [rʌnt] *n* (*animal*) *najsłabszy z miotu*; (*pej*: *person*) cherlak *m* (*pej*)

**run-through** [ˈrʌnθruː] *n* próba *f*

**run-up** [ˈrʌnʌp] *n*: **the ~ to** okres *m* poprzedzający *+acc*

**runway** [ˈrʌnweɪ] *n* pas *m* startowy

**rupee** [ruːˈpiː] *n* rupia *f*

**rupture** [ˈrʌptʃə^r] *n* (*Med*: *hernia*) przepuklina *f*; (: *of blood vessel, appendix*) pęknięcie *nt*; (*between people, groups*) zerwanie *nt* ▹ *vt*: **to ~ o.s.** (*Med*) dostać (*perf*) przepukliny

**rural** [ˈruərl] *adj* (*area*) wiejski; (*economy*) rolny; (*country*) rolniczy

**rural district council** (*Brit*) *n rada okręgu wiejskiego*
**ruse** [ru:z] *n* podstęp *m*
**rush** [rʌʃ] *n* (*hurry*) pośpiech *m*; (*Comm*) nagły popyt *m*; (*of air*) podmuch *m*; (*of feeling, emotion*) przypływ *m* ▷ *vt* (*lunch, job*) śpieszyć się (pośpieszyć się *perf*) z *+instr*; (*supplies*) natychmiast wysyłać (wysłać *perf*) ▷ *vi* (*person*) pędzić (popędzić *perf*); (*air, water*): **to ~ in(to)** wdzierać się (wedrzeć się *perf*) (do *+gen*); **rushes** *npl* (*Bot*) sitowie *nt*; **is there any ~ for this?** czy to pilne?; **I'm in a ~ (to)** śpieszę się (, żeby *+infin*); **we've had a ~ of orders** mieliśmy mnóstwo zamówień; **don't ~ me!** nie poganiaj mnie!; **to ~ sth off** wysyłać (wysłać *perf*) coś natychmiast; **they ~ed her to hospital** natychmiast zawieźli ją do szpitala; **she ~ed to book a seat** pośpieszyła zarezerwować miejsce; **to ~ sb into doing sth** przynaglać kogoś do zrobienia czegoś; **gold ~** gorączka złota
▸ **rush through** *vt* (*order, application*) szybko załatwiać (załatwić *perf*)
**rush hour** *n* godzina *f* szczytu
**rush job** *n*: **it was a ~** to było robione w pośpiechu
**rush matting** *n* mata *f*
**rusk** [rʌsk] *n* sucharek *m*
**Russia** ['rʌʃə] *n* Rosja *f*
**Russian** ['rʌʃən] *adj* rosyjski ▷ *n* (*person*) Rosjanin(-anka) *m*(*f*); (*Ling*) (język *m*) rosyjski
**rust** [rʌst] *n* rdza *f* ▷ *vi* rdzewieć (zardzewieć *perf*)
**rustic** ['rʌstɪk] *adj* wiejski; (*style, furniture*) rustykalny ▷ *n* (*pej*) prostak(-aczka) *m*(*f*)
**rustle** ['rʌsl] *vi* szeleścić (zaszeleścić *perf*) ▷ *vt* (*paper etc*) szeleścić (zaszeleścić *perf*) *+instr*; (*US: cattle*) kraść (ukraść *perf*)
**rustproof** ['rʌstpru:f] *adj* odporny na rdzę
**rustproofing** ['rʌstpru:fɪŋ] *n* ochrona *f* przed rdzą
**rusty** ['rʌstɪ] *adj* zardzewiały; (*fig: skill*): **my German is pretty ~** dużo zapomniałem z niemieckiego
**rut** [rʌt] *n* (*in path, ground*) koleina *f*; (*Zool*) okres *m* godowy; **he is in a rut** (*fig*) popadł w rutynę
**rutabaga** [ru:tə'beɪgə] (*US*) *n* brukiew *f*
**ruthless** ['ru:θlɪs] *adj* bezwzględny
**ruthlessness** ['ru:θlɪsnɪs] *n* bezwzględność *f*
**RV** *abbr* (*Bible: = revised version*) *angielskie tłumaczenie Biblii z roku 1885* ▷ *n abbr* (*US*) = **recreational vehicle**
**rye** [raɪ] *n* żyto *nt*
**rye bread** *n* chleb *m* żytni

# Ss

**S¹, s** [ɛs] *n* (*letter*) S *nt*, s *nt*; (*US*: *Scol*) ≈ dostateczny *nt inv*; **S for sugar** ≈ S jak Stanisław
**S²** *abbr* (= *south*) płd.; = **small**; (= *saint*) św.
**SA** *abbr* = **South Africa**; **South America**
**Sabbath** ['sæbəθ] *n* (*Jewish*) sabat *m*, szabas *m*; (*Christian*) Dzień *m* Pański
**sabbatical** [sə'bætɪkl] *n* (*also*: **sabbatical year**) urlop *m* naukowy
**sabotage** ['sæbətɑ:ʒ] *n* sabotaż *m* ▷ *vt* (*machine, building*) niszczyć (zniszczyć *perf*) (*w akcie sabotażu*); (*plan, meeting*) sabotować
**sabre** ['seɪbə^r] *n* szabla *f*
**saccharin(e)** ['sækərɪn] *n* sacharyna *f* ▷ *adj* (*fig*) cukierkowy
**sachet** ['sæʃeɪ] *n* torebeczka *f*
**sack** [sæk] *n* worek *m* ▷ *vt* (*dismiss*) zwalniać (zwolnić *perf*), wylewać (wylać *perf*) (*inf*); (*plunder*) łupić (złupić *perf*); **he got the ~** zwolnili *or* wylali (*inf*) go
**sackful** ['sækful] *n*: **a ~ of** worek *+gen*
**sacking** ['sækɪŋ] *n* (*dismissal*) zwolnienie *nt*; (*material*) płótno *nt* workowe
**sacrament** ['sækrəmənt] *n* sakrament *m*
**sacred** ['seɪkrɪd] *adj* (*music, writings*) sakralny; (*animal, calling, duty*) święty
**sacred cow** *n* (*fig*) święta krowa *f*
**sacrifice** ['sækrɪfaɪs] *n* (*offering*) składanie *nt* ofiary; (*animal etc offered*) ofiara *f*; (*fig*) poświęcenie *nt*, wyrzeczenie *nt* ▷ *vt* składać (złożyć *perf*) w ofierze, składać (złożyć *perf*) ofiarę z *+gen*; (*fig*) poświęcać (poświęcić *perf*); **to make ~s (for sb)** poświęcać się (dla kogoś)
**sacrilege** ['sækrɪlɪdʒ] *n* świętokradztwo *nt*
**sacrosanct** ['sækrəusæŋkt] *adj* (*fig*: *custom*) uświęcony (tradycją); (*law*) święty, nienaruszalny; (*place, person*) święty, nietykalny
**sad** [sæd] *adj* smutny
**sadden** ['sædn] *vt* smucić, zasmucać (zasmucić *perf*)
**saddle** ['sædl] *n* (*for horse*) siodło *nt*; (*of bicycle*) siodełko *nt* ▷ *vt* (*horse*) siodłać (osiodłać *perf*); **to be ~d with** (*inf*) być obarczonym *+instr*
**saddlebag** ['sædlbæg] *n* sakwa *f* (*przy siodle, rowerowa itp*)
**sadism** ['seɪdɪzəm] *n* sadyzm *m*
**sadist** ['seɪdɪst] *n* sadysta(-tka) *m(f)*
**sadistic** [sə'dɪstɪk] *adj* sadystyczny
**sadly** ['sædlɪ] *adv* (*unhappily*) smutno, ze smutkiem; (*unfortunately*) niestety; (*mistaken, neglected*) poważnie; **the school is ~ lacking in equipment** szkoła odczuwa dotkliwe braki w wyposażeniu
**sadness** ['sædnɪs] *n* smutek *m*
**sae** (*Brit*) *abbr* = **stamped addressed envelope** *see* **stamp**
**safari** [sə'fɑ:rɪ] *n* safari *nt inv*
**safari park** *n* park *m* safari
**safe** [seɪf] *adj* bezpieczny; (*Pol*: *seat*) pewny ▷ *n* sejf *m*; **they are ~ from attack** nie grozi im atak; **~ and sound** cały i zdrowy; **(just) to be on the ~ side** (tak) na wszelki wypadek; **to play ~** nie ryzykować; **it is ~ to say that ...** śmiało można powiedzieć, że ...; **~ journey!** szczęśliwej podróży!
**safe-breaker** ['seɪfbreɪkə^r] (*Brit*) *n* kasiarz *m* (*inf*)
**safe-conduct** [seɪf'kɔndʌkt] *n* (*document*) list *m* żelazny, glejt *m*
**safe-cracker** ['seɪfkrækə^r] *n* = **safe-breaker**
**safe-deposit** ['seɪfdɪpɔzɪt] *n* (*vault*) skarbiec *m* pancerny, sejf *m* bankowy; (*also*: **safe-deposit box**) skrytka *f* depozytowa *or* sejfowa *or* bankowa
**safeguard** ['seɪfgɑ:d] *n* zabezpieczenie *nt* ▷ *vt* (*future*) zabezpieczać (zabezpieczyć *perf*); (*life, interests*) ochraniać, chronić
**safe house** *n* lokal *m* kontaktowy
**safekeeping** ['seɪf'ki:pɪŋ] *n* przechowanie *nt*
**safely** ['seɪflɪ] *adv* (*assume, say*) spokojnie, śmiało; (*drive, arrive*) bezpiecznie; (*shut, lock*) dokładnie
**safe sex** *n* bezpieczny seks *m*
**safety** ['seɪftɪ] *n* bezpieczeństwo *nt*; **~ first!** bezpieczeństwo przede wszystkim!
**safety belt** *n* pas *m* bezpieczeństwa
**safety catch** *n* (*on gun*) bezpiecznik *m*; (*on window, door*) zapornica *f*
**safety net** *n* siatka *f* asekuracyjna; (*fig*) zabezpieczenie *nt*

**safety pin** *n* agrafka *f*
**safety valve** *n* zawór *m* bezpieczeństwa
**saffron** ['sæfrən] *n* szafran *m*
**sag** [sæg] *vi* (*bed*) zapadać się; (*breasts*) obwisać; (*fig*: *demand*) spadać (spaść *perf*); **his spirits sagged** upadł na duchu
**saga** ['sɑːgə] *n* saga *f*
**sage** [seɪdʒ] *n* (*Bot*) szałwia *f*; (*person*) mędrzec *m*
**Sagittarius** [sædʒɪ'tɛərɪəs] *n* Strzelec *m*; **to be ~** być spod znaku Strzelca
**sago** ['seɪgəu] (*Culin*) *n* sago *nt inv*
**Sahara** [sə'hɑːrə] *n*: **the ~ (Desert)** Sahara *f*
**Sahel** [sæ'hɛl] *n* Sahel *m*
**said** [sɛd] *pt, pp of* **say**
**Saigon** [saɪ'gɔn] *n* Sajgon *m*
**sail** [seɪl] *n* żagiel *m* ▷ *vt* (*ship, boat*) płynąć (popłynąć *perf*) *+instr*; (*: regularly, as job*) pływać na *+loc*; (*ocean*) przepływać (przepłynąć *perf*) ▷ *vi* (*travel*) płynąć (popłynąć *perf*); (*Sport*) uprawiać żeglarstwo, żeglować; (*also*: **set sail**) wypływać (wypłynąć *perf*); (*fig*: *ball etc*) szybować (poszybować *perf*); **to go for a ~** wybierać się (wybrać się *perf*) na żagle
▶ **sail through** *vt fus* (*fig*): **she ~ed through the exam** śpiewająco zdała egzamin
**sailboat** ['seɪlbəut] (*US*) *n* żaglówka *f*
**sailing** ['seɪlɪŋ] *n* (*Sport*) żeglarstwo *nt*; (*voyage*) rejs *m*; **to go ~** wybierać się (wybrać się *perf*) na żagle
**sailing boat** *n* żaglówka *f*
**sailing ship** *n* żaglowiec *m*
**sailor** ['seɪlə[r]] *n* marynarz *m*; (*on sailing boat/ship*) żeglarz(-arka) *m(f)*
**saint** [seɪnt] *n* święty(-ta) *m(f)*
**saintly** ['seɪntlɪ] *adj* świątobliwy
**sake** [seɪk] *n*: **for the ~ of sb/sth, for sb's/sth's ~** ze względu *or* przez wzgląd na kogoś/coś; **he enjoys talking for talking's ~** lubi mówić dla samego mówienia; **for the ~ of argument** (czysto) teoretycznie; **art for art's ~** sztuka dla sztuki; **for heaven's ~!** na miłość *or* litość boską!
**salad** ['sæləd] *n* sałatka *f*; **tomato ~** sałatka z pomidorów; **green ~** (zielona) sałata (*często z dodatkiem innych zielonych warzyw*)
**salad bowl** *n* salaterka *f*
**salad cream** (*Brit*) *n* sos *m* do sałatek (*na bazie majonezu*)
**salad dressing** *n* sos *m* do sałatek (*typu vinaigrette*)
**salami** [sə'lɑːmɪ] *n* salami *nt inv*
**salaried** ['sælərɪd] *adj* otrzymujący pensję
**salary** ['sælərɪ] *n* pensja *f*, pobory *pl*
**salary scale** *n* skala *f* płac
**sale** [seɪl] *n* (*selling*) sprzedaż *f*; (*at reduced prices*) wyprzedaż *f*; (*auction*) aukcja *f*, licytacja *f*; **sales** *npl* obroty *pl*, ogół *m* transakcji ▷ *cpd* (*campaign*) reklamowy, promocyjny; (*conference*) handlowy; **~s figures** wysokość sprzedaży; **~s target** zakładana wysokość sprzedaży; **"for ~"** „na sprzedaż"; **on ~** (*available in shops*) w sprzedaży; **these goods are on ~ or return** w razie niesprzedania towary te podlegają zwrotowi; **closing-down** *or* (*US*) **liquidation ~** wyprzedaż końcowa *or* likwidacyjna
**sale and lease back** *n sprzedaż dóbr z zastrzeżeniem możliwości dalszego ich użytkowania na zasadzie wynajmu*
**saleroom** ['seɪlruːm] *n* sala *f or* hala *f* aukcyjna
**sales assistant** [seɪlz-], (*US*) **sales clerk** *n* sprzedawca(-wczyni) *m(f)*, ekspedient(ka) *m(f)*
**sales force** *n* agenci *pl* handlowi
**salesman** ['seɪlzmən] (*irreg*: *like* **man**) *n* (*in shop*) sprzedawca *m*, ekspedient *m*; (*representative*) akwizytor *m*
**sales manager** *n* kierownik *m* działu sprzedaży *or* zbytu; (*in big company*) dyrektor *m* handlowy
**salesmanship** ['seɪlzmənʃɪp] *n* sztuka *f* pozyskiwania klienta
**sales representative** *n* przedstawiciel *m* handlowy
**sales tax** (*US*) *n* podatek *m* od wartości dodanej (*przy zakupie*)
**saleswoman** ['seɪlzwumən] (*irreg*: *like* **woman**) *n* (*in shop*) sprzedawczyni *f*, ekspedientka *f*; (*representative*) akwizytorka *f*
**salient** ['seɪlɪənt] *adj* (*points*) najistotniejszy; (*features*) (najbardziej) rzucający się w oczy
**saline** ['seɪlaɪn] *adj* (*deposits*) solny; **~ solution** roztwór soli
**saliva** [sə'laɪvə] *n* ślina *f*
**sallow** ['sæləu] *adj* ziemisty
**sally forth** ['sælɪ-] (*old*) *vi* wyruszać (wyruszyć *perf*)
**sally out** *vi* = **sally forth**
**salmon** ['sæmən] *n inv* łosoś *m*
**salmon trout** *n* pstrąg *m* potokowy, troć *f*
**salon** ['sælɔn] *n*: **beauty ~** gabinet *m* kosmetyczny, salon *m* piękności; **hairdressing ~** salon fryzjerski
**saloon** [sə'luːn] *n* (*US*) bar *m*; (*Brit*: *Aut*) sedan *m*; (*ship's lounge*) salon *m*
**salsa** ['sælsə] *n* (*Mus*) salsa *f*; (*Culin*) salsa *f*
**SALT** [sɔːlt] *n abbr* (= *Strategic Arms Limitation Talks/Treaty*) rokowania *pl*/układ *m* SALT
**salt** [sɔːlt] *n* sól *f* ▷ *vt* (*preserve*) solić, zasalać (zasolić *perf*); (*potatoes, soup*) solić (posolić *perf*); (*road*) posypywać (posypać *perf*) solą ▷ *cpd* (*lake*) słony; (*deposits*) solny, soli *post*;

(*Culin*) solony; **the ~ of the earth** (*fig*) sól ziemi; **to take sth with a pinch** *or* **grain of ~** (*fig*) podchodzić (podejść *perf*) do czegoś z rezerwą
**salt cellar** *n* solniczka *f*
**salt-free** ['sɔ:lt'fri:] *adj* nie zawierający soli
**salt mine** *n* kopalnia *f* soli
**saltwater** ['sɔ:lt'wɔ:tə^r] *adj* słonowodny
**salty** ['sɔ:ltɪ] *adj* słony
**salubrious** [sə'lu:brɪəs] *adj* (*air, living conditions*) zdrowy; (*district etc*) porządny
**salutary** ['sæljutərɪ] *adj* pożyteczny
**salute** [sə'lu:t] *n* (*Mil*) honory *pl* (wojskowe); (: *with guns*) salut *m*, salwa *f* (honorowa); (*greeting*) pozdrowienie *nt* ▷ *vt* (*officer*) salutować (zasalutować *perf*) *+dat*; (*flag*) oddawać (oddać *perf*) honory (wojskowe) *+dat*; (*fig*) oddawać (oddać *perf*) cześć *or* hołd *+dat*
**salvage** ['sælvɪdʒ] *n* (*saving*) ocalenie *nt*; (*things saved*) ocalone mienie *nt* ▷ *vt* (*lit, fig*) ratować (uratować *perf*), ocalać (ocalić *perf*); **~ operation** akcja ratunkowa *or* ratownicza
**salvage vessel** *n* statek *m or* okręt *m* ratowniczy
**salvation** [sæl'veɪʃən] *n* (*Rel*) zbawienie *nt*; (*fig*) ratunek *m*, wybawienie *nt*
**Salvation Army** *n* Armia *f* Zbawienia
**salver** ['sælvə^r] *n* taca *f* (*ozdobna, najczęściej srebrna*)
**salvo** ['sælvəu] (*pl* **~es**) *n* salwa *f*
**Samaritan** [sə'mærɪtən] *n*: **the ~s** Samarytanie *vir pl* (*organizacja niosąca pomoc osobom znajdującym się w kryzysie życiowym*)
**same** [seɪm] *adj* ten sam; (*identical*) taki sam ▷ *pron*: **the ~ (is true of art)** to samo (dotyczy sztuki); **(he will never be) the ~ (again)** (już nigdy nie będzie) taki sam; **on the ~ day** tego samego dnia; **at the ~ time** (*simultaneously*) w tym samym momencie, równocześnie; (*yet*) jednocześnie, zarazem; **all** *or* **just the ~** (po) mimo to, niemniej jednak; **to do the ~ (as sb)** robić (zrobić *perf*) to samo (co ktoś); **happy New Year! — ~ to you!** szczęśliwego Nowego Roku! — nawzajem!; **you're a fool! — ~ to you!** głupi jesteś! — sam jesteś głupi!; **I hate him — ~ here!** nienawidzę go — ja też!; **they're one and the ~ (person)** to jedna i ta sama osoba; **they're one and the ~ (thing)** to jedno i to samo; **~ again!** (*in bar etc*) jeszcze raz to samo!; **(no, but) thanks all the ~** (nie, ale) mimo to dziękuję
**sample** ['sɑ:mpl] *n* próbka *f* ▷ *vt* (*food, wine*) próbować (spróbować *perf*) *+gen*; **to take a ~** brać (wziąć *perf*) próbkę; **free ~** darmowa próbka
**sanatorium** [sænə'tɔ:rɪəm] (*pl* **sanatoria**) *n* sanatorium *nt*
**sanctify** ['sæŋktɪfaɪ] *vt* uświęcać (uświęcić *perf*)
**sanctimonious** [sæŋktɪ'məunɪəs] *adj* świętoszkowaty
**sanction** ['sæŋkʃən] *n* (*approval*) poparcie *nt* ▷ *vt* sankcjonować (usankcjonować *perf*); **sanctions** *npl* sankcje *pl*; **to impose economic ~s on** *or* **against** nakładać (nałożyć *perf*) sankcje ekonomiczne na *+acc*
**sanctity** ['sæŋktɪtɪ] *n* świętość *f*
**sanctuary** ['sæŋktjuərɪ] *n* (*for birds, animals*) rezerwat *m*; (*for person*) (bezpieczne) schronienie *nt*, azyl *m*; (*in church*) prezbiterium *nt*
**sand** [sænd] *n* piasek *m* ▷ *vt* (*also*: **sand down**) wygładzać (wygładzić *perf*) papierem ściernym; *see also* **sands**
**sandal** ['sændl] *n* sandał *m*
**sandbag** ['sændbæg] *n* worek *m* z piaskiem
**sandblast** ['sændblɑ:st] *vt* piaskować
**sandbox** ['sændbɔks] (US) *n* = **sandpit**
**sandcastle** ['sændkɑ:sl] *n* zamek *m* z piasku
**sand dune** *n* wydma *f* (piaszczysta)
**S & M** *n abbr* (= *sadomasochism*) sadomasochizm *m*
**sandpaper** ['sændpeɪpə^r] *n* papier *m* ścierny
**sandpit** ['sændpɪt] *n* piaskownica *f*
**sands** [sændz] *npl* piaski *pl*
**sandstone** ['sændstəun] *n* piaskowiec *m*
**sandstorm** ['sændstɔ:m] *n* burza *f* piaskowa
**sandwich** ['sændwɪtʃ] *n* kanapka *f* ▷ *vt*: **~ed between** wciśnięty (po)między *+acc*; **cheese/ham ~** kanapka z serem/szynką
**sandwich board** *n* tablica *f* reklamowa (*noszona na piersiach i plecach przez człowieka-reklamę*)
**sandwich course** (*Brit*) *n kurs, w którym okresy nauki przeplatają się z okresami praktyki zawodowej*
**sandwich man** (*irreg*: *like* **man**) *n* człowiek *m* — reklama *f*
**sandy** ['sændɪ] *adj* (*beach*) piaszczysty; (*hair*) rudoblond
**sane** [seɪn] *adj* (*person*: *Med*) zdrowy psychicznie; (: *fig*) zdrowy na umyśle, przy zdrowych zmysłach *post*; (*decision, action*) rozumny, rozsądny
**sang** [sæŋ] *pt of* **sing**
**sanguine** ['sæŋgwɪn] *adj* (*person*) ufny, pełen optymizmu; (*attitude*) optymistyczny; **to be ~ of** *or* **about** ufać w *+acc*
**sanitarium** [sænɪ'tɛərɪəm] (*US pl* **sanitaria**) *n* = **sanatorium**
**sanitary** ['sænɪtərɪ] *adj* (*inspector, conditions, facilities*) sanitarny; (*clean*) higieniczny
**sanitary towel**, (*US*) **sanitary napkin** *n* podpaska *f* (higieniczna)

S

**sanitation** [sænɪ'teɪʃən] *n* (*conditions*) warunki *f* sanitarne; (*facilities*) urządzenia *pl* sanitarne
**sanitation department** (*US*) *n* ≈ przedsiębiorstwo *nt* oczyszczania miasta
**sanity** ['sænɪtɪ] *n* (*of person*) zdrowie *nt* psychiczne; (*common sense*) (zdrowy) rozsądek *m*
**sank** [sæŋk] *pt of* **sink**
**San Marino** ['sænmə'ri:nəu] *n* San Marino *nt inv*
**Santa Claus** [sæntə'klɔ:z] *n* Święty Mikołaj *m*
**Santiago** [sæntɪ'ɑ:gəu] *n* (*also*: **Santiago de Chile**) Santiago *nt inv*
**sap** [sæp] *n* sok *m* (*z rośliny*) ▷ *vt* nadwątlać (nadwątlić *perf*)
**sapling** ['sæplɪŋ] *n* młode drzewko *nt*
**sapphire** ['sæfaɪə^r] *n* szafir *m*
**sarcasm** ['sɑ:kæzm] *n* sarkazm *m*
**sarcastic** [sɑ:'kæstɪk] *adj* sarkastyczny
**sarcophagus** [sɑ:'kɔfəgəs] (*pl* **sarcophagi**) *n* sarkofag *m*
**sardine** [sɑ:'di:n] *n* sardynka *f*
**Sardinia** [sɑ:'dɪnɪə] *n* Sardynia *f*
**Sardinian** [sɑ:'dɪnɪən] *adj* sardyński ▷ *n* (*person*) Sardyńczyk(-ynka) *m(f)*; (*Ling*) (język *m*) sardyński
**sardonic** [sɑ:'dɔnɪk] *adj* sardoniczny
**sari** ['sɑ:rɪ] *n* sari *nt inv*
**sartorial** [sɑ:'tɔ:rɪəl] *adj*: **he was a man of great ~ elegance** odznaczał się wielką elegancją stroju
**SAS** (*Brit*: *Mil*) *n abbr* (= *Special Air Service*) *jednostka wojskowa do zadań specjalnych*
**SASE** (*US*) *n abbr* (= *self-addressed stamped envelope*) koperta *f* zwrotna ze znaczkiem
**sash** [sæʃ] *n* (*of garment*) szarfa *f*; (*of window*) skrzydło *nt*
**sash window** *n* okno *nt* otwierane pionowo (*przez przesuwanie do góry jednego ze skrzydeł*)
**SAT** (*US*) *n abbr* (= *Scholastic Aptitude Test*) *egzamin sprawdzający zdolności naukowe kandydata na studia wyższe*
**sat** [sæt] *pt, pp of* **sit**
**Sat.** *abbr* (= *Saturday*) so., sob.
**Satan** ['seɪtn] *n* szatan *m*
**satanic** [sə'tænɪk] *adj* (*cult, rites*) sataniczny; (*smile*) szatański
**satchel** ['sætʃl] *n* tornister *m*
**sated** ['seɪtɪd] *adj* (*person*) nasycony; (*appetite*) zaspokojony; **to be ~ with sth** (*fig*) mieć przesyt czegoś
**satellite** ['sætəlaɪt] *n* satelita *m*; (*Pol*: *also*: **satellite state**) państwo *nt* satelitarne, satelita *m*
**satellite dish** *n* antena *f* satelitarna
**satellite television** *n* telewizja *f* satelitarna
**satiate** ['seɪʃɪeɪt] *vt* sycić (nasycić *perf*); (*fig*) zaspokajać (zaspokoić *perf*)
**satin** ['sætɪn] *n* atłas *m*, satyna *f* ▷ *adj* atłasowy, satynowy; **with a ~ finish** (*wood etc*) z połyskiem
**satire** ['sætaɪə^r] *n* satyra *f*
**satirical** [sə'tɪrɪkl] *adj* satyryczny
**satirist** ['sætɪrɪst] *n* satyryk(-yczka) *m(f)*
**satirize** ['sætɪraɪz] *vt* ośmieszać (ośmieszyć *perf*) (*posługując się satyrą*)
**satisfaction** [sætɪs'fækʃən] *n* (*contentment*) zadowolenie *nt*, satysfakcja *f*; (*apology*) zadośćuczynienie *nt*; (*refund*) rekompensata *f*; **has it been done to your ~?** czy wszystko zostało zrobione tak, jak Pan/Pani sobie życzył/a?
**satisfactorily** [sætɪs'fæktərɪlɪ] *adv* (*perform*) zadowalająco; (*recover*) dostatecznie
**satisfactory** [sætɪs'fæktərɪ] *adj* zadowalający; (*Scol*: *grade*) dostateczny
**satisfied** ['sætɪsfaɪd] *adj* (*customer*) zadowolony; **to be ~ (with sth)** być zadowolonym (z czegoś)
**satisfy** ['sætɪsfaɪ] *vt* (*person*) zadowalać (zadowolić *perf*); (*needs, demand*) zaspokajać (zaspokoić *perf*); (*conditions*) spełniać (spełnić *perf*); **to ~ sb that ...** przekonać (*perf*) kogoś, że...; **to ~ o.s. that ...** upewniać się (upewnić się *perf*), że...
**satisfying** ['sætɪsfaɪɪŋ] *adj* (*meal*) suty; (*feeling*) przyjemny; (*job*) dający zadowolenie *or* satysfakcję
**satnav** ['sætnæv] *n* (*Aut*) GPS *m*
**satsuma** [sæt'su:mə] *n rodzaj mandarynki*
**saturate** ['sætʃəreɪt] *vt*: **to ~ (with)** nasycać (nasycić *perf*) (+*instr*); (*fig*) zarzucać (zarzucić *perf*) *or* zasypywać (zasypać *perf*) (+*instr*); **his shirt was ~d with blood/sweat** koszulę miał przesiąkniętą krwią/potem
**saturation** [sætʃə'reɪʃən] *n* nasycenie *nt* ▷ *cpd* (*bombing*) zmasowany; **~ point** punkt nasycenia
**Saturday** ['sætədɪ] *n* sobota *f*; *see also* **Tuesday**
**sauce** [sɔ:s] *n* sos *m*
**saucepan** ['sɔ:spən] *n* rondel *m*
**saucer** ['sɔ:sə^r] *n* spodek *m*, spodeczek *m*
**saucy** ['sɔ:sɪ] *adj* bezczelny
**Saudi** ['saudi-] *adj* (*also*: **Saudi Arabian**) saudyjski
**Saudi Arabia** ['saudɪ-] *n* Arabia *f* Saudyjska
**sauna** ['sɔ:nə] *n* sauna *f*
**saunter** ['sɔ:ntə^r] *vi* (*about a place*) przechadzać się; (*somewhere*) przespacerować się (*perf*)
**sausage** ['sɔsɪdʒ] *n* kiełbasa *f*
**sausage roll** *n rodzaj pasztecika z kiełbaską*
**sauté** ['səuteɪ] *vt* smażyć (usmażyć *perf*) (*bez panierowania*) ▷ *adj*: **~ *or* ~ed potatoes**

ziemniaki *pl* sauté; **~ the onions until golden brown** (*in recipe*) podsmażać cebulę (aż) do zrumienienia

**savage** ['sævɪdʒ] *adj* (*animal, tribe*) dziki; (*attack*) wściekły, brutalny; (*voice, criticism*) srogi, ostry ▷ *n* (*old, pej*) dzikus(ka) *m(f)* ▷ *vt* (mocno) pokiereszować (*perf*) *or* poturbować (*perf*); (*fig*) nie zostawiać (nie zostawić *perf*) suchej nitki na *+loc*

**savagely** ['sævɪdʒlɪ] *adv* (*attack, beat*) brutalnie; (*criticize*) ostro

**savagery** ['sævɪdʒrɪ] *n* brutalność *f*, okrucieństwo *nt*

**save** [seɪv] *vt* (*person, sb's life, marriage*) ratować (uratować *perf*), ocalać (ocalić *perf*); (*food, wine*) zachowywać (zachować *perf*) (na później); (*money, time*) oszczędzać (oszczędzić *perf or* zaoszczędzić *perf*); (*work, trouble*) oszczędzać (oszczędzić *perf*) *or* zaoszczędzać (zaoszczędzić *perf*) *+gen*; (*receipt etc*) zachowywać (zachować *perf*); (*seat: for sb*) zajmować (zająć *perf*); (*Sport*) bronić (obronić *perf*); (*Comput*) zapisywać (zapisać *perf*) ▷ *vi* (*also*: **save up**) oszczędzać ▷ *n* (*Sport*): **he made a brilliant ~** znakomicie obronił (piłkę) ▷ *prep* (*fml*) z wyjątkiem *+gen*, wyjąwszy *+acc* (*fml*); **it will ~ me an hour** dzięki temu zaoszczędzę godzinę; **to ~ face** ratować (uratować *perf*) twarz; **God ~ the Queen!** Boże zachowaj Królową!

**saving** ['seɪvɪŋ] *n* oszczędność *f* ▷ *adj*: **the ~ grace of sth** jedyny plus *m* czegoś; **the play's ~ grace was good acting** sztukę (u)ratowało dobre aktorstwo; **savings** *npl* oszczędności *pl*; **to make ~s** robić (porobić *perf*) oszczędności

**savings account** *n* rachunek *m* oszczędnościowy

**savings bank** *n* ≈ kasa *f* oszczędności

**saviour**, (*US*) **savior** ['seɪvjəʳ] *n* zbawca *m*; (*Rel*) Zbawiciel *m*

**savoir-faire** ['sævwɑːfɛəʳ] *n* ogłada *f*

**savour**, (*US*) **savor** ['seɪvəʳ] *vt* delektować się *+instr* ▷ *n* aromat *m*

**savoury**, (*US*) **savory** ['seɪvərɪ] *adj* (*food, dish*) pikantny

**savvy** ['sævɪ] (*inf*) *n* (*political etc*) zmysł *m*

**saw** [sɔː] (*pt* **sawed**, *pp* **sawed** *or* **sawn**) *vt* piłować, przepiłowywać (przepiłować *perf*) ▷ *n* piła *f* ▷ *pt of* **see**; **to saw sth up** ciąć (pociąć *perf*) coś (piłą) na kawałki

**sawdust** ['sɔːdʌst] *n* trociny *pl*

**sawmill** ['sɔːmɪl] *n* tartak *m*

**sawn** [sɔːn] *pp of* **saw**

**sawn-off** ['sɔːnɔf], (*US*) **sawed-off** *adj*: **~ shotgun** obrzynek *m*

**saxophone** ['sæksəfəun] *n* saksofon *m*

**say** [seɪ] (*pt, pp* **said**) *vt* mówić (powiedzieć *perf*) ▷ *n*: **to have one's say** wypowiadać się (wypowiedzieć się *perf*); **to have a** *or* **some say in sth** mieć coś do powiedzenia w jakiejś sprawie, mieć na coś (pewien) wpływ; **to say yes** zgadzać się (zgodzić się *perf*); **to say no** odmawiać (odmówić *perf*); **could you say that again?** czy mógłbyś powtórzyć?; **you can say that again!** zgadza się!; **she said (that) I was to give you this** powiedziała, że mam ci to dać; **my watch says three o'clock** mój zegarek wskazuje trzecią; **it says on the sign "No Smoking"** na znaku napisane jest „Palenie wzbronione"; **(shall we) say 8 o'clock?** powiedzmy o 8-ej?; **that doesn't say much for him** to niezbyt dobrze o nim świadczy; **when all is said and done** koniec końców; **there is something/a lot to be said for this description** ten opis ma parę/wiele zalet; **that is to say** to znaczy *or* jest; **it goes without saying that ...** to oczywiste, że ...; **to say nothing of** nie mówiąc (już) o *+loc*; **say (that) you won a million pounds** powiedzmy, że wygrałeś milion funtów

**saying** ['seɪɪŋ] *n* powiedzenie *nt*

**say-so** ['seɪsəu] *n* zgoda *f*, zezwolenie *nt*; **to do sth on sb's ~** robić (zrobić *perf*) coś za czyjąś zgodą

**SBA** (*US*) *n abbr* (= *Small Business Administration*) *urząd federalny udzielający pomocy małym i średnim przedsiębiorstwom*

**SC** (*US*) *n abbr* (= *supreme court*) ≈ SN ▷ *abbr* (*Post*) = **South Carolina**

**s/c** *abbr* = **self-contained**

**scab** [skæb] *n* (*on wound*) strup *m*; (*pej: person*) łamistrajk *m*

**scabby** ['skæbɪ] (*pej*) *adj* pokryty strupami

**scaffold** ['skæfəld] *n* (*for execution*) szafot *m*

**scaffolding** ['skæfəldɪŋ] *n* rusztowanie *nt*

**scald** [skɔːld] *n* poparzenie *nt* (*wrzątkiem*) ▷ *vt* parzyć (poparzyć *perf*) (*wrzątkiem*)

**scalding** ['skɔːldɪŋ] *adj* (*also*: **scalding hot**) bardzo gorący

**scale** [skeɪl] *n* (*of numbers, salaries, model*) skala *f*; (*of map*) skala *f*, podziałka *f*; (*of fish*) łuska *f*; (*Mus*) gama *f*; (*size, extent*) rozmiary *pl*, wielkość *f* ▷ *vt* wdrapywać się (wdrapać się *perf*) na *+acc*; **scales** *npl* waga *f*; **pay ~** skala *or* tabela płac; **~ of charges** tabela *or* taryfa opłat; **to draw sth to ~** rysować (narysować *perf*) coś w skali; **a small-~ model** model małych rozmiarów; **on a large ~** na dużą *or* wielką skalę

▸ **scale down** *vt* (proporcjonalnie) zmniejszać (zmniejszyć *perf*)

**scale drawing** *n* rysunek *m* w skali zmniejszonej

S

**scallion** ['skæljən] (*Culin, Bot*) *n* cebulka *f*; (*US*: *shallot*) szalotka *f*; (: *leek*) por *m*
**scallop** ['skɔləp] *n* (*Zool*) przegrzebek *m* (*małż morski*); (*Sewing*) (ozdobny) obrębek *m*
**scalp** [skælp] *n* skóra *f* głowy; (*removed from dead body*) skalp *m* ▷ *vt* skalpować (oskalpować *perf*)
**scalpel** ['skælpl] (*Med*) *n* skalpel *m*
**scalper** ['skælpə[r]] (*US*: *inf*) *n* (*ticket tout*) konik *m* (*inf*)
**scamp** [skæmp] (*inf*) *n* urwis *m*, łobuziak *m*
**scamper** ['skæmpə[r]] *vi*: **to ~ away** *or* **off** czmychać (czmychnąć *perf*)
**scampi** ['skæmpɪ] (*Brit*) *npl* panierowane krewetki *pl*
**scan** [skæn] *vt* (*scrutinize*) badawczo przyglądać się (przyjrzeć się *perf*) *+dat*; (*look through*) przeglądać (przejrzeć *perf*); (*Radar*) badać, penetrować; (*TV*) składać ▷ *vi* (*poetry*) mieć rytm ▷ *n* (*Med*): **brain** *etc* **~** obrazowanie *nt* mózgu *etc* (*za pomocą tomografii, magnetycznego rezonansu jądrowego itp.*)
**scandal** ['skændl] *n* (*shocking event, disgrace*) skandal *m*; (*gossip*) plotki *pl*
**scandalize** ['skændəlaɪz] *vt* gorszyć (zgorszyć *perf*), oburzać (oburzyć *perf*)
**scandalous** ['skændələs] *adj* skandaliczny
**Scandinavia** [skændɪ'neɪvɪə] *n* Skandynawia *f*
**Scandinavian** [skændɪ'neɪvɪən] *adj* skandynawski ▷ *n* Skandynaw(ka) *m(f)*
**scanner** ['skænə[r]] *n* (*Med*) skaner *m*; (*Radar*) antena *f* radarowa *or* przeszukująca
**scant** [skænt] *adj* niewielki
**scantily** ['skæntɪlɪ] *adv*: **~ clad** *or* **dressed** skąpo odziany
**scanty** ['skæntɪ] *adj* skąpy
**scapegoat** ['skeɪpgəut] *n* kozioł *m* ofiarny
**scar** [skɑː] *n* (*on skin*) blizna *f*, szrama *f*; (*fig*) piętno *nt* ▷ *vt* pokrywać (pokryć *perf*) bliznami; (*fig*) wywoływać (wywołać *perf*) (trwały) uraz u *+gen*
**scarce** [skɛəs] *adj*: **water/food was ~** brakowało *or* było za mało wody/jedzenia; **to make o.s. ~** (*inf*) ulatniać się (ulotnić się *perf*) (*inf*)
**scarcely** ['skɛəslɪ] *adv* ledwo, (za)ledwie; **~ anybody** prawie nikt; **I can ~ believe it** ledwo *or* z ledwością mogę w to uwierzyć; **there could ~ be a worse environment for children** trudno o gorsze środowisko dla dzieci
**scarcity** ['skɛəsɪtɪ] *n* niedobór *m*; (*Comm*): **their ~ value makes them expensive** ich rzadkość sprawia, że są drogie
**scare** [skɛə[r]] *n* (*fright*): **to give sb a ~** napędzać (napędzić *perf*) komuś strachu *or* stracha; (*public fear*) panika *f* ▷ *vt* przestraszać (przestraszyć *perf*); **bomb ~** panika wywołana informacją o podłożeniu bomby
▸ **scare away** *vt* (*animal*) płoszyć (spłoszyć *perf*); (*investor, buyer*) odstraszać (odstraszyć *perf*)
▸ **scare off** *vt* = **scare away**
**scarecrow** ['skɛəkrəu] *n* strach *m* na wróble
**scared** [skɛəd] *adj* przestraszony, wystraszony; **to be ~ (to do sth** *or* **of doing sth)** bać się (coś zrobić); **I was ~ stiff** śmiertelnie się bałam
**scaremonger** ['skɛəmʌŋgə[r]] *n* panikarz(-ara) *m(f)* (*pej*)
**scarf** [skɑːf] (*pl* **~s** *or* **scarves**) *n* (*long*) szal *m*, szalik *m*; (*square, triangular*) chusta *f*
**scarlet** ['skɑːlɪt] *adj* jasnoczerwony
**scarlet fever** *n* szkarlatyna *f*
**scarred** [skɑːd] *adj* pokryty bliznami; (*fig*) naznaczony, napiętnowany
**scarves** [skɑːvz] *npl of* **scarf**
**scary** ['skɛərɪ] (*inf*) *adj* straszny
**scathing** ['skeɪðɪŋ] *adj* (*comment ect*) cięty, zjadliwy; **to be ~ about sth** odnosić się do czegoś pogardliwie *or* z pogardą
**scatter** ['skætə[r]] *vt* (*seeds, papers*) rozrzucać (rozrzucić *or* porozrzucać *perf*); (*flock of birds, crowd*) rozpędzać (rozpędzić *perf*) ▷ *vi* (*crowd*) rozpraszać się (rozproszyć się *perf*)
**scatterbrained** ['skætəbreɪnd] (*inf*) *adj* roztrzepany
**scattered** ['skætəd] *adj* rozproszony, rozsiany; **~ showers** przelotne opady
**scatty** ['skætɪ] (*Brit*: *inf*) *adj* roztrzepany
**scavenge** ['skævəndʒ] *vi*: **to ~ (for food)** grzebać w odpadkach (w poszukiwaniu jedzenia)
**scavenger** ['skævəndʒə[r]] *n* (*person*) *osoba grzebiąca w odpadkach*; (*animal, bird*) padlinożerca *m*
**SCE** *n abbr* (= *Scottish Certificate of Education*) *szkockie świadectwo ukończenia szkoły*
**scenario** [sɪ'nɑːrɪəu] *n* (*lit, fig*) scenariusz *m*
**scene** [siːn] *n* (*lit, fig*) scena *f*; (*of crime, accident*) miejsce *nt*; (*sight*) obraz *m*; **behind the ~s** (*lit, fig*) za kulisami; **to make a ~** (*inf*) urządzać (urządzić *perf*) scenę; **to appear on the ~** (*fig*) pojawiać się (pojawić się *perf*); **the political ~** scena polityczna
**scenery** ['siːnərɪ] *n* (*Theat*) dekoracje *pl*; (*landscape*) krajobraz *m*
**scenic** ['siːnɪk] *adj* (*route, location*) malowniczy
**scent** [sɛnt] *n* (*fragrance*) woń *f*, zapach *m*; (*perfume*) perfumy *pl*; (*track*: *lit, fig*) trop *m*; **to put** *or* **throw sb off the ~** (*fig*) zmylić (*perf*) kogoś
**sceptic**, (*US*) **skeptic** ['skɛptɪk] *n* sceptyk(-yczka) *m(f)*

**sceptical**, (*US*) **skeptical** ['skɛptɪkl] *adj* sceptyczny
**scepticism**, (*US*) **skepticism** ['skɛptɪsɪzəm] *n* sceptycyzm *m*
**sceptre**, (*US*) **scepter** ['sɛptə[r]] *n* berło *nt*
**schedule** ['ʃɛdju:l] *n* (*of trains, buses*) rozkład *m* jazdy; (*of events and times*) harmonogram *m*, rozkład *m* (zajęć); (*of prices, details etc*) wykaz *m*, zestawienie *nt* ▷ *vt* planować (zaplanować *perf*); **he was ~d to leave yesterday** (zgodnie z planem) miał wyjechać wczoraj; **on ~** (dokładnie) według planu; **we are working to a very tight ~** pracujemy według bardzo napiętego planu; **everything went according to ~** wszystko poszło zgodnie z planem; **they arrived ahead of ~** przybyli przed czasem; **we are behind ~** mamy opóźnienie
**scheduled** ['ʃɛdju:ld] *adj* (*date, time*) wyznaczony; (*visit, event*) zaplanowany; (*train, bus*) figurujący w rozkładzie
**scheduled flight** *n* lot *m* rejsowy
**schematic** [skɪ'mætɪk] *adj* schematyczny
**scheme** [ski:m] *n* plan *m*; (*of government etc*) program *m* ▷ *vi* spiskować, knuć *or* snuć intrygi; **colour ~** kolorystyka
**scheming** ['ski:mɪŋ] *adj* intrygancki ▷ *n* intrygi *pl*
**schism** ['skɪzəm] *n* schizma *f*
**schizophrenia** [skɪtsə'fri:nɪə] *n* schizofrenia *f*
**schizophrenic** [skɪtsə'frɛnɪk] *adj* schizofreniczny ▷ *n* schizofrenik(-iczka) *m(f)*
**scholar** ['skɔlə[r]] *n* (*learned person*) naukowiec *m*; (*scholarship holder*) stypendysta(-tka) *m(f)*
**scholarly** ['skɔləlɪ] *adj* (*text, approach*) naukowy; (*person*) uczony
**scholarship** ['skɔləʃɪp] *n* (*knowledge: of person*) uczoność *f*, erudycja *f*; (*: of period, area*) nauka *f*; (*grant*) stypendium *nt*
**school** [sku:l] *n* (*primary, secondary*) szkoła *f*; (*faculty, college*) ≈ instytut *m*; (*US: inf*) uniwersytet *m*; (*of whales, fish*) ławica *f* ▷ *cpd* szkolny
**school age** *n* wiek *m* szkolny
**schoolbook** ['sku:lbuk] *n* podręcznik *m* (szkolny)
**schoolboy** ['sku:lbɔɪ] *n* uczeń *m*
**schoolchildren** ['sku:ltʃɪldrən] *npl* uczniowie *vir pl*
**schooldays** ['sku:ldeɪz] *npl* szkolne lata *pl*
**schoolgirl** ['sku:lgə:l] *n* uczennica *f*
**schooling** ['sku:lɪŋ] *n* nauka *f* szkolna; **they had no ~ at all** nie mieli żadnego wykształcenia
**school-leaver** [sku:l'li:və[r]] (*Brit*) *n* absolwent(ka) *m(f)* (szkoły)
**schoolmaster** ['sku:lma:stə[r]] *n* (*old*) nauczyciel *m*
**schoolmistress** ['sku:lmɪstrɪs] *n* (*old*) nauczycielka *f*
**school report** (*Brit*) *n* świadectwo *nt* szkolne
**schoolroom** ['sku:lru:m] *n* sala *f* lekcyjna
**schoolteacher** ['sku:lti:tʃə[r]] *n* nauczyciel(ka) *m(f)*
**schooner** ['sku:nə[r]] *n* (*ship*) szkuner *m*; (*glass*) *duży, pękaty kieliszek do sherry lub piwa*
**sciatica** [saɪ'ætɪkə] *n* rwa *f* kulszowa
**science** ['saɪəns] *n* nauka *f*; **the ~s** nauki przyrodnicze; (*Scol*) przedmioty ścisłe
**science fiction** *n* fantastyka *f* naukowa, science fiction *f inv*
**scientific** [saɪən'tɪfɪk] *adj* naukowy
**scientist** ['saɪəntɪst] *n* naukowiec *m*; (*eminent*) uczony(-na) *m(f)*
**sci-fi** ['saɪfaɪ] (*inf*) *n abbr* (= *science fiction*) SF
**Scillies** ['sɪlɪz] *npl* = **Scilly Isles**
**Scilly Isles** ['sɪlɪ'aɪlz] *npl*: **the ~** Wyspy *pl* Scilly
**scintillating** ['sɪntɪleɪtɪŋ] *adj* (*fig*) błyskotliwy
**scissors** ['sɪzəz] *npl*: **(a pair of) ~** nożyczki *pl*; (*large*) nożyce *pl*
**sclerosis** [sklɪ'rəusɪs] *n* skleroza *f*
**scoff** [skɔf] *vt* (*Brit: inf: eat*) wsuwać (wsunąć *perf*) (*inf*) ▷ *vi*: **to ~ (at)** naśmiewać się (z *+gen*)
**scold** [skəuld] *vt* besztać (zbesztać *perf*), krzyczeć (nakrzyczeć *perf*) na *+acc*
**scolding** ['skəuldɪŋ] *n* bura *f*
**scone** [skɔn] *n rodzaj babeczki jadanej z masłem na podwieczorek*
**scoop** [sku:p] *n* (*for flour etc*) łopatka *f*; (*for ice cream*) łyżka *f*; (*of ice cream*) gałka *f*, kulka *f*; (*Press*) sensacyjna wiadomość *f* (*opublikowana wcześniej niż w konkurencyjnych gazetach*)
▸ **scoop out** *vt* wybierać (wybrać *perf*), wyskrobywać (wyskrobać *perf*)
▸ **scoop up** *vt* nabierać (nabrać *perf*)
**scooter** ['sku:tə[r]] *n* (*also*: **motor scooter**) skuter *m*; (*toy*) hulajnoga *f*
**scope** [skəup] *n* (*opportunity*) miejsce *nt*; (*range: of plan, undertaking*) zasięg *m*, zakres *m*; (*: of person*) możliwości *pl* (działania); **within the ~ of** w ramach *+gen*; **there is plenty of ~ for improvement** (*Brit*) dużo (jeszcze) można poprawić
**scorch** [skɔ:tʃ] *vt* (*iron: clothes*) przypalać (przypalić *perf*); (*sun: earth, grass*) wypalać (wypalić *perf*)
**scorched earth policy** (*Mil*) *n* taktyka *f* spalonej ziemi
**scorcher** ['skɔ:tʃə[r]] (*inf*) *n* skwarny dzień *m*
**scorching** ['skɔ:tʃɪŋ] *adj* skwarny
**score** [skɔ:[r]] *n* (*total number of points*) wynik *m*; (*Mus*) partytura *f*; (*to film, play*) muzyka *f*; (*twenty*) dwudziestka *f* ▷ *vt* (*goal, point*)

zdobywać (zdobyć *perf*); (*mark*) wydrapywać (wydrapać *perf*), wyryć (*perf*); (*leather, wood, card*) robić (zrobić *perf*) nacięcie w *+loc*; (*success*) odnosić (odnieść *perf*) ▷ *vi* (*in game*) zdobyć (*perf*) punkt; (*Football etc*) zdobyć (*perf*) bramkę; (*keep score*) notować wyniki, liczyć punkty; **to settle an old ~ with sb** (*fig*) wyrównać (*perf*) z kimś stare porachunki; **~s of** dziesiątki *+gen*; **on that ~** w tej mierze, w tym względzie; **to ~ well** osiągnąć (*perf*) dobry wynik; **to ~ six out of ten** uzyskać (*perf*) sześć punktów na dziesięć (możliwych); **to ~ (a point) over sb** (*fig*) zdobyć (*perf*) przewagę nad kimś
▸ **score out** *vt* wykreślać (wykreślić *perf*)
**scoreboard** ['skɔ:bɔ:d] *n* tablica *f* wyników
**scorecard** ['skɔ:kɑ:d] (*Sport*) *n* karta *f* wyników *or* punktowa
**scorer** ['skɔ:rəʳ] *n* (*Football etc*) strzelec *m*, zdobywca(-wczyni) *m(f)* bramki; (*person keeping score*) *osoba notująca punkty w czasie gry*
**scorn** [skɔ:n] *n* pogarda *f* ▷ *vt* (*despise*) gardzić (wzgardzić *perf*) *+instr*, pogardzać *+instr*; (*reject*) gardzić *+instr*
**scornful** ['skɔ:nful] *adj* pogardliwy
**Scorpio** ['skɔ:pɪəu] *n* Skorpion *m*; **to be ~** być spod znaku Skorpiona
**scorpion** ['skɔ:pɪən] *n* skorpion *m*
**Scot** [skɔt] *n* Szkot(ka) *m(f)*
**Scotch** [skɔtʃ] *n* (*whisky*) szkocka *f*
**scotch** [skɔtʃ] *vt* zdusić (*perf*) w zarodku
**Scotch tape**® *n* ≈ taśma *f* klejąca
**scot-free** ['skɔt'fri:] *adv*: **he got off ~** uszło mu to płazem *or* na sucho
**Scotland** ['skɔtlənd] *n* Szkocja *f*
**Scots** [skɔts] *adj* (*accent*) szkocki
**Scotsman** ['skɔtsmən] (*irreg: like* **man**) *n* Szkot *m*
**Scotswoman** ['skɔtswumən] (*irreg: like* **woman**) *n* Szkotka *f*
**Scottish** ['skɔtɪʃ] *adj* (*history, clans*) szkocki
**scoundrel** ['skaundrl] *n* łajdak *m*
**scour** ['skauəʳ] *vt* (*countryside etc*) przetrząsać (przetrząsnąć *perf*), przeszukiwać (przeszukać *perf*); (*book etc*) wertować (przewertować *perf*); (*floor, pan etc*) szorować (wyszorować *perf*)
**scourer** ['skauərəʳ] *n* druciak *m* (*do szorowania garnków*)
**scourge** [skə:dʒ] *n* (*thing*) plaga *f*, zmora *f*; (*person*) utrapienie *nt*
**scout** [skaut] *n* (*Mil*) zwiadowca *m*; (*also*: **boy scout**) skaut *m*, ≈ harcerz *m*; **girl ~** (*US*) ≈ harcerka *f*
▸ **scout around** *vi* rozglądać się (rozejrzeć się *perf*)
**scowl** [skaul] *vi* krzywić się (skrzywić się *perf*), nachmurzyć się (*perf*) ▷ *n* nachmurzona mina *f*; **to ~ at sb** krzywić się (skrzywić się *perf*) na kogoś
**scrabble** ['skræbl] *vi* macać rękami dokoła ▷ *n*: **S~**® Scrabble *nt inv*; **to ~ at sth** próbować dosięgnąć *or* uczepić się czegoś; **to ~ about** *or* **around for sth** szukać czegoś po omacku
**scraggy** ['skrægɪ] *adj* chudy
**scram** [skræm] (*inf*) *vi* zwiewać (zwiać *perf*) (*inf*)
**scramble** ['skræmbl] *n* (*climb*) wdrapanie się *nt*; (*struggle, rush*) szamotanina *f*; (*Sport*) motocross *m* ▷ *vi*: **to ~ up** wdrapywać się (wdrapać się *perf*); **to ~ over** przedzierać się (przedrzeć się *perf*) przez *+acc*; **to ~ for** rzucać się (rzucić się *perf*) na *+acc*, wydzierać sobie *+acc*
**scrambled eggs** ['skræmbld-] *n* jajecznica *f*
**scrap** [skræp] *n* (*of paper, material*) skrawek *m*; (*fig: of truth, evidence*) odrobina *f*, krzt(yn)a *f*; (*fight*) utarczka *f*, starcie *nt*; (*also*: **scrap metal**) złom *m* ▷ *vt* (*machines etc*) przeznaczać (przeznaczyć *perf*) na złom; (*fig: plans etc*) skasować (*perf*) (*inf*) ▷ *vi* gryźć się (pogryźć się *perf*) (*fig*); **scraps** *npl* (*of food*) resztki *pl*; (*of material*) skrawki *pl*, resztki *pl*; **to sell sth for ~** sprzedawać (sprzedać *perf*) coś na złom
**scrapbook** ['skræpbuk] *n* album *m* z wycinkami
**scrap dealer** *n* handlarz *m* złomem
**scrape** [skreɪp] *vt* (*mud, paint, etc*) zeskrobywać (zeskrobać *perf*), zdrapywać (zdrapać *perf*); (*potato, carrot*) skrobać (oskrobać *perf*); (*hand, car*) zadrapać (*perf*), zadrasnąć (*perf*) ▷ *n*: **to get into a ~** wpaść (*perf*) w tarapaty
▸ **scrape through** *vt* (*exam etc*) przebrnąć (*perf*) przez *+acc*
▸ **scrape together** *vt* uciułać (*perf*)
**scraper** ['skreɪpəʳ] *n* skrobaczka *f* do butów
**scrap heap** *n* (*fig*): **to throw sb on the ~** odstawić (*perf*) kogoś na bocznicę; **to throw sth on the ~** wyrzucić (*perf*) coś do lamusa
**scrap merchant** (*Brit*) *n* handlarz *m* złomem
**scrap metal** *n* złom *m*
**scrap paper** *n* papier *m* do pisania na brudno
**scrappy** ['skræpɪ] *adj* chaotyczny, nieprzemyślany
**scrap yard** *n* skład *m* złomu; (*for cars*) złomowisko *nt*
**scratch** [skrætʃ] *n* (*on furniture, record*) rysa *f*; (*on body*) zadrapanie *nt*, zadraśnięcie *nt* ▷ *vt* (*body*) drapać (podrapać *perf*); (*paint, car, record*) porysować (*perf*); (*with claw, nail*) zadrapać (*perf*), zadrasnąć (*perf*); (*Comput*) wymazywać (wymazać *perf*) (*z dysku*) ▷ *vi* drapać się (podrapać się *perf*) ▷ *cpd* naprędce sklecony; **to ~ one's nose/head** drapać się (podrapać się *perf*) w nos/głowę; **to start from ~** zaczynać (zacząć *perf*) od zera; **to be up to ~**

spełniać wymogi; **to ~ the surface** (*fig*) ślizgać się po powierzchni
**scratch pad** (*US*) *n* notatnik *m*
**scrawl** [skrɔ:l] *n* bazgroły *pl*, gryzmoły *pl* ▷ *vt* bazgrać (nabazgrać *perf*), gryzmolić (nagryzmolić *perf*)
**scrawny** ['skrɔ:nɪ] *adj* kościsty
**scream** [skri:m] *n* krzyk *m*, wrzask *m*; (*of tyres, brakes*) pisk *m*; (*of siren*) wycie *nt*, buczenie *nt* ▷ *vi* wrzeszczeć (wrzasnąć *perf*), krzyczeć (krzyknąć *perf*); **he's a ~** on jest pocieszny *or* komiczny; **to ~ at sb (to do sth)** wrzeszczeć (wrzasnąć *perf*) na kogoś (, żeby coś zrobił)
**scree** [skri:] *n* osypisko *nt* (kamieni)
**screech** [skri:tʃ] *vi* (*person, bird*) skrzeczeć (zaskrzeczeć *perf*); (*tyres, brakes*) piszczeć (zapiszczeć *perf*) ▷ *n* pisk *m*
**screen** [skri:n] *n* (*Film, TV, Comput*) ekran *m*; (*movable barrier*) parawan *m*; (*fig: cover*) zasłona *f*, przykrywka *f*; (*also:* **windscreen**) przednia szyba *f* ▷ *vt* (*protect, conceal*) zasłaniać (zasłonić *perf*); (*from wind etc*) osłaniać (osłonić *perf*); (*film, programme*) wyświetlać (wyświetlić *perf*), emitować (wyemitować *perf*) (*w TV*); (*candidates*) sprawdzać (sprawdzić *perf*), badać (zbadać *perf*); (*for illness*) poddawać (poddać *perf*) badaniom przesiewowym
**screen editing** (*Comput*) *n* edycja *f* ekranowa
**screening** ['skri:nɪŋ] *n* (*Med*) badania *pl* przesiewowe; (*of film*) emisja *f* (*w TV*), projekcja *f*; (*for security*) badanie *nt*
**screen memory** (*Comput*) *n* pamięć *f* obrazu
**screenplay** ['skri:npleɪ] *n* scenariusz *m*
**screen test** *n* zdjęcia *pl* próbne
**screw** [skru:] *n* śruba *f*, wkręt *m* ▷ *vt* (*fasten*) przykręcać (przykręcić *perf*); (*inf!: have sex with*) pieprzyć (*inf!*); **to ~ sth in** wkręcać (wkręcić *perf*) coś; **to ~ sth to the wall** przykręcać (przykręcić *perf*) coś do ściany; **to have one's head ~ed on** (*fig*) mieć głowę na karku
▸ **screw up** *vt* (*paper etc*) zmiąć (*perf*), zgnieść (*perf*); (*inf: ruin*) spieprzyć (*perf*) (*inf*); **to ~ up one's eyes** mrużyć (zmrużyć *perf*) oczy
**screwdriver** ['skru:draɪvə<sup>r</sup>] *n* śrubokręt *m*
**screwy** ['skru:ɪ] (*inf*) *adj* (*person*) pokręcony (*inf*)
**scribble** ['skrɪbl] *n* gryzmoły *pl* ▷ *vt* (*note, letter etc*) skrobać (skrobnąć *perf*) ▷ *vi* bazgrać (nabazgrać *perf*); **to ~ sth down** (szybko) coś zapisać (*perf*)
**scribe** [skraɪb] *n* skryba *m/f*, kopista(-tka) *m(f)*
**script** [skrɪpt] *n* (*Film etc*) scenariusz *m*; (*alphabet*) pismo *nt*; (*in exam*) arkusz *m* egzaminacyjny
**scripted** ['skrɪptɪd] (*Radio, TV*) *adj* (*dialogue, interview*) wcześniej przygotowany
**scripture(s)** *n(pl)* święte pisma *pl or* księgi *pl*; **the Scriptures** Biblia
**scriptwriter** ['skrɪptraɪtə<sup>r</sup>] *n* autor(ka) *m(f)* scenariusza
**scroll** [skrəul] *n* zwój *m* ▷ *vt* (*Comput*) przeglądać, przewijać (przewinąć *perf*)
**scrotum** ['skrəutəm] *n* moszna *f*
**scrounge** [skraundʒ] (*inf*) *vt*: **to ~ sth off sb** wyłudzać (wyłudzić *perf*) coś od kogoś, naciągać (naciągnąć *perf*) kogoś na coś (*inf*) ▷ *vi* żyć cudzym kosztem ▷ *n*: **on the ~** po prośbie
**scrounger** ['skraundʒə<sup>r</sup>] (*inf*) *n* pasożyt *m*
**scrub** [skrʌb] *n obszar porośnięty karłowatą roślinnością* ▷ *vt* (*floor, hands, washing*) szorować (wyszorować *perf*); (*inf: idea, plan*) odrzucić (*perf*)
**scrubbing brush** ['skrʌbɪŋ-] *n* szczotka *f* ryżowa
**scruff** [skrʌf] *n*: **by the ~ of the neck** za kark
**scruffy** ['skrʌfɪ] *adj* niechlujny
**scrum(mage)** ['skrʌm(ɪdʒ)] (*Rugby*) *n* młyn *m*
**scruple** ['skru:pl] *n* (*usu pl*) skrupuły *pl*; **to have no ~s about sth** nie mieć skrupułów odnośnie czegoś
**scrupulous** ['skru:pjuləs] *adj* (*painstaking*) sumienny, skrupulatny; (*fair-minded*) uczciwy
**scrupulously** ['skru:pjuləslɪ] *adv* (*behave, act*) uczciwie; (*honest, fair, clean*) nienagannie
**scrutinize** ['skru:tɪnaɪz] *vt* (*face*) przypatrywać się (przypatrzeć się *perf*) +*dat*; (*data, records*) analizować (przeanalizować *perf*)
**scrutiny** ['skru:tɪnɪ] *n* badanie *nt*, analiza *f*; **under the ~ of sb** pod czyjąś obserwacją
**scuba** ['sku:bə] *n* akwalung *m*, aparat *m* tlenowy
**scuba diving** *n* nurkowanie *nt* z akwalungiem *or* aparatem tlenowym
**scuff** [skʌf] *vt* (*shoes*) zdzierać (zedrzeć *perf*); (*floor*) rysować (porysować *perf*)
**scuffle** ['skʌfl] *n* starcie *nt*
**scull** [skʌl] *n* wiosło *nt* jednopiórowe
**scullery** ['skʌlərɪ] *n* (*old*) *pomieszczenie przylegające do kuchni, w którym odbywało się pranie, zmywanie itp*
**sculptor** ['skʌlptə<sup>r</sup>] *n* rzeźbiarz(-arka) *m(f)*
**sculpture** ['skʌlptʃə<sup>r</sup>] *n* (*art*) rzeźba *f*, rzeźbiarstwo *nt*; (*object*) rzeźba *f*
**scum** [skʌm] *n* (*on liquid*) piana *f*; (*pej: people*) szumowiny *pl* (*pej*)
**scupper** ['skʌpə<sup>r</sup>] (*Brit: inf*) *vt* sknocić (*perf*) (*inf*)
**scurrilous** ['skʌrɪləs] *adj* obelżywy
**scurry** ['skʌrɪ] *vi* mknąć (pomknąć *perf*), pędzić (popędzić *perf*)

S

▸ **scurry off** *vi* rzucać się (rzucić się *perf*) do ucieczki

**scurvy** ['skə:vɪ] *n* szkorbut *m*

**scuttle** ['skʌtl] *n* (*also*: **coal scuttle**) wiadro *nt* na węgiel ▷ *vt* dokonywać (dokonać *perf*) samozatopienia +*gen* ▷ *vi*: **to ~ away** *or* **off** oddalić się (*perf*) drobnymi kroczkami

**scythe** [saɪð] *n* kosa *f*

**SD** (*US*: *Post*) *abbr* = **South Dakota**

**SDI** (*US*: *Mil*) *n abbr* (= *Strategic Defense Initiative*) Inicjatywa *f* Obrony Strategicznej, SDI *f inv*

**SDLP** (*Brit*: *Pol*) *n abbr* (= *Social Democratic and Labour Party*) *partia północnoirlandzka*

**SDP** (*Brit*: *Pol*) *n abbr* = **Social Democratic Party**

**sea** [si:] *n* morze *nt* ▷ *cpd* (*breeze, bird etc*) morski; **by sea** morzem; **beside** *or* **by the sea** (*holiday*) nad morzem; (*village*) nadmorski; **on the sea** na morzu; **to be all at sea** (*fig*) być zupełnie zdezorientowanym; **at sea** na (pełnym) morzu; **out to sea** na (pełne) morze; **to look out to sea** spoglądać (spojrzeć *perf*) daleko w morze; **heavy** *or* **rough sea(s)** wzburzone morze

**sea anemone** *n* ukwiał *m*

**sea bed** *n* dno *nt* morskie

**seaboard** ['si:bɔ:d] *n* wybrzeże *nt*

**seafarer** ['si:fɛərə^r] *n* żeglarz *m*

**seafaring** ['si:fɛərɪŋ] *adj* żeglarski

**seafood** ['si:fu:d] *n* owoce *pl* morza

**seafront** ['si:frʌnt] *n* ulica *f* nadbrzeżna

**seagoing** ['si:gəuɪŋ] *adj* (*ship*) dalekomorski

**seagull** ['si:gʌl] *n* mewa *f*

**seal** [si:l] *n* (*animal*) foka *f*; (*official stamp*) pieczęć *f*; (*in machine etc*) plomba *f*, uszczelnienie *nt* ▷ *vt* (*envelope, opening*) zaklejać (zakleić *perf*); (*with seal*) pieczętować (zapieczętować *perf*); (*sb's fate*) pieczętować (przypieczętować *perf*); (*agreement*) przypieczętować (*perf*); **to give sth one's ~ of approval** aprobować (zaaprobować *perf*) coś

▸ **seal off** *vt* odcinać (odciąć *perf*) dostęp do +*gen*

**sea level** *n* poziom *m* morza; **2,000 ft above/below ~** 610 m nad poziomem morza *or* n.p.m./poniżej poziomu morza

**sealing wax** ['si:lɪŋ-] *n* lak *m*

**sea lion** *n* lew *m* morski

**sealskin** ['si:lskɪn] *n* futro *nt* z fok

**seam** [si:m] *n* (*line of stitches*) szew *m*; (*where edges meet*) łączenie *nt*; (*of coal etc*) pokład *m*; **the hall was bursting at the ~s** sala pękała w szwach

**seaman** ['si:mən] (*irreg*: *like* **man**) *n* marynarz *m*

**seamanship** ['si:mənʃɪp] *n* umiejętności *pl* żeglarskie

**seamless** ['si:mlɪs] *adj* (*stockings, tights*) bez szwu *post*; (*fig*) jednolity

**seamy** ['si:mɪ] *adj* przykry, nieprzyjemny

**séance** ['seɪɔns] *n* seans *m* (spirytystyczny)

**seaplane** ['si:pleɪn] *n* hydroplan *m*

**seaport** ['si:pɔ:t] *n* port *m* morski

**search** [sə:tʃ] *n* (*for person, thing*) poszukiwani *pl*; (*Comput*) szukanie *nt* (*w dokumencie*); (*of sb' home*) rewizja *f* ▷ *vt* (*place*) przeszukiwać (przeszukać *perf*); (*mind, memory*) szukać w +*loc*; (*person, luggage*) przeszukiwać (przeszukać *perf*), rewidować (zrewidować *perf*) ▷ *vi*: **to ~ for** poszukiwać +*gen*; **"~ and replace"** (*Comput*) funkcja szukania i zamiany; **in ~ of** w poszukiwaniu +*gen*

▸ **search through** *vt fus* przeszukiwać (przeszukać *perf*), przetrząsać (przetrząsnąć *perf*)

**search engine** (*Comput*) *n* wyszukiwarka *f*

**searcher** ['sə:tʃə^r] *n* poszukiwacz(ka) *m(f)*

**searching** ['sə:tʃɪŋ] *adj* (*look*) dociekliwy, badawczy; (*question*) dociekliwy, wnikliwy; (*examination, inquiry*) wnikliwy, drobiazgowy

**searchlight** ['sə:tʃlaɪt] *n* reflektor *m*

**search party** *n* ekipa *f* poszukiwawcza; **to send out a ~** wysyłać (wysłać *perf*) ekipę poszukiwawczą

**search warrant** *n* nakaz *m* rewizji

**searing** ['sɪərɪŋ] *adj* (*pain*) piekący; **~ heat** spiekota

**seashore** ['si:ʃɔ:^r] *n* brzeg *m* morza; **on the ~** nad brzegiem morza

**seasick** ['si:sɪk] *adj*: **to be ~** dostać (*perf*) choroby morskiej

**seasickness** ['si:sɪknɪs] *n* choroba *f* morska

**seaside** ['si:saɪd] *n* wybrzeże *nt*; **to go to the ~** jechać (pojechać *perf*) nad morze; **at the ~** nad morzem

**seaside resort** *n* nadmorski ośrodek *m* wypoczynkowy

**season** ['si:zn] *n* (*of year*) pora *f* roku; (*Agr*) sezon *m*, pora *f*; (*Sport*) sezon *m*; (*of films etc*) przegląd *m*, cykl *m* ▷ *vt* (*food*) doprawiać (doprawić *perf*); **the planting ~** pora sadzenia; **oysters are out of ~ now** sezon na ostrygi już minął, sezon na ostrygi jeszcze się nie rozpoczął; **raspberries are in ~ now** jest teraz sezon na maliny; **the busy ~** (*for shops*) okres wzmożonych zakupów, szczyt; (*for hotels etc*) sezon (turystyczny/letni); **the open ~** (otwarty) sezon łowiecki

**seasonal** ['si:znl] *adj* (*work*) sezonowy

**seasoned** ['si:znd] *adj* (*fig*: *traveller*) wytrawny; (*wood*) wysuszony; **a ~ campaigner** weteran, kombatant

**seasoning** ['si:znɪŋ] *n* (*condiment*) przyprawa *f*; (*spices*) przyprawy *pl*

**season ticket** *n* (*Rail*) bilet *m* okresowy; (*Sport, Theat*) abonament *m*
**seat** [si:t] *n* miejsce *nt*; (*Parl*) miejsce *nt*, mandat *m*; (*buttocks, of trousers*) siedzenie *nt*; (*of government, learning etc*) siedziba *f* ▷ *vt* (*place: guests etc*) sadzać (posadzić *perf*); (*have room for*) móc pomieścić; **the driver's ~** siedzenie kierowcy; **the table ~s eight** to stół na osiem osób; **are there any ~s left?** czy są jakieś wolne miejsca?; **to take one's ~** zajmować (zająć *perf*) (swoje) miejsce; **please be ~ed** proszę usiąść *or* spocząć; **to be ~ed** siedzieć
**seat belt** (*Aut*) *n* pas *m* (bezpieczeństwa)
**seating arrangements** ['si:tɪŋ-] *npl* rozmieszczenie *nt* (przy stole)
**seating capacity** *n* liczba *f* miejsc siedzących
**SEATO** ['si:təu] *n abbr* (= *Southeast Asia Treaty Organization*) SEATO *nt inv*
**sea urchin** *n* jeżowiec *m*
**sea water** *n* woda *f* morska
**seaweed** ['si:wi:d] *n* wodorosty *pl*
**seaworthy** ['si:wə:ðɪ] *adj* zdatny do żeglugi
**SEC** (*US*) *n abbr* (= *Securities and Exchange Commission*) *komisja nadzorująca działalność giełdy papierów wartościowych*
**sec.** *abbr* = **second**
**secateurs** [sɛkə'tə:z] *npl* sekator *m*
**secede** [sɪ'si:d] *vi* (*Pol*): **to ~ (from)** odłączać się (odłączyć się *perf*) (od *+gen*)
**secluded** [sɪ'klu:dɪd] *adj* odosobniony, zaciszny
**seclusion** [sɪ'klu:ʒən] *n* (*place*) zacisze *nt*, ustronie *nt*; (*state*) odosobnienie *nt*, osamotnienie *nt*
**second**[1] [sɪ'kɔnd] (*Brit*) *vt* (*employee*) przesuwać (przesunąć *perf*), oddelegowywać (oddelegować *perf*)
**second**[2] ['sɛkənd] *adj* drugi ▷ *adv* (*in race etc*) jako drugi; (*when listing*) po drugie ▷ *n* (*unit of time*) sekunda *f*; (*Aut*: *also*: **second gear**) drugi bieg *m*, dwójka *f* (*inf*); (*Comm*) towar *m* wybrakowany ▷ *vt* (*motion*) popierać (poprzeć *perf*); **upper/lower ~** (*Brit*) *dyplom ukończenia studiów z wynikiem dobrym/zadowalającym*; **Charles the S~** Karol II; **~ floor** (*Brit*) drugie piętro; (*US*) pierwsze piętro; **to ask for a ~ opinion** zasięgać (zasięgnąć *perf*) drugiej opinii; **just a ~!** chwileczkę!
**secondary** ['sɛkəndərɪ] *adj* drugorzędny
**secondary education** *n* szkolnictwo *nt* średnie *or* ponadpodstawowe
**secondary school** *n* szkoła *f* średnia
**second-best** [sɛkənd'bɛst] *adj* zastępczy ▷ *n* namiastka *f*; **as a ~** z braku lepszej możliwości
**second-class** ['sɛkənd'kla:s] *adj* (*citizen, standard etc*) drugiej kategorii *post*; (*Rail: ticket, carriage*) drugiej klasy *post* ▷ *adv*: **to send sth ~** wysyłać (wysłać *perf*) coś drugą klasą; **a ~ stamp/letter** znaczek/list drugiej klasy; **to travel ~** podróżować drugą klasą
**second cousin** *n* kuzyn(ka) *m(f)* w drugiej linii
**seconder** ['sɛkəndə<sup>r</sup>] *n* osoba *f* popierająca wniosek
**secondhand** ['sɛkənd'hænd] *adj* używany, z drugiej ręki *post* ▷ *adv*: **I bought this car ~** to używany samochód; **to hear sth ~** słyszeć (usłyszeć *perf*) o czymś z drugiej ręki
**second hand** *n* wskazówka *f* sekundowa, sekundnik *m*
**second-in-command** ['sɛkəndɪnkə'ma:nd] *n* (*Mil*) zastępca *m* głównodowodzącego; (*Admin*) zastępca *m* kierownika
**secondly** ['sɛkəndlɪ] *adv* po drugie, po wtóre (*fml*)
**secondment** [sɪ'kɔndmənt] (*Brit*) *n*: **he's on ~ to** został czasowo oddelegowany do *+gen*
**second-rate** ['sɛkənd'reɪt] *adj* podrzędny
**second thoughts** *npl*: **on ~** *or* (*US*) **thought** po namyśle; **to have ~ (about sth)** mieć wątpliwości (co do czegoś)
**secrecy** ['si:krəsɪ] *n* (*state of being kept secret*) tajemnica *f*; (*act of keeping sth secret*) dyskrecja *f*; **surrounded by ~** otoczony tajemnicą; **in ~** w tajemnicy
**secret** ['si:krɪt] *adj* (*plan*) tajny; (*passage*) tajemny, potajemny; (*admirer*) cichy ▷ *n* sekret *m*, tajemnica *f*; **in ~** potajemnie, w sekrecie; **to keep sth ~ from sb** trzymać coś przed kimś w tajemnicy; **can you keep a ~?** czy potrafisz dochować tajemnicy?; **to make no ~ of sth** nie robić z czegoś tajemnicy, nie ukrywać czegoś
**secret agent** *n* tajny(-na) *m(f)* agent(ka) *m(f)*
**secretarial** [sɛkrɪ'tɛərɪəl] *adj*: **~ course** kurs dla sekretarek; **~ work** praca *f* sekretarki; **~ staff** pracownicy sekretariatu
**secretariat** [sɛkrɪ'tɛərɪət] *n* sekretariat *m*
**secretary** ['sɛkrətərɪ] *n* (*Comm*) sekretarz(-arka) *m(f)*; (*of club*) sekretarz *m*; **S~ of State (for)** (*Brit*) ≈ minister (do spraw *+gen*); **S~ of State** (*US*) Sekretarz Stanu
**secrete** [sɪ'kri:t] *vt* (*Bio, Med*) wydzielać; (*hide*) ukrywać (ukryć *perf*)
**secretion** [sɪ'kri:ʃən] *n* wydzielina *f*
**secretive** ['si:krətɪv] *adj* tajemniczy
**secretly** ['si:krɪtlɪ] *adv* potajemnie, po cichu; **to hope ~** mieć cichą nadzieję
**secret service** *n* tajne służby *pl*
**sect** [sɛkt] *n* sekta *f*
**sectarian** [sɛk'tɛərɪən] *adj* (*views*) sekciarski; (*violence*) na tle różnic między sektami *post*

S

**section** ['sɛkʃən] *n (of society, exam)* część *f*; *(of road etc)* odcinek *m*; *(of company)* dział *m*; *(of orchestra, sports club)* sekcja *f*; *(of document)* paragraf *m*; *(cross-section)* przekrój *m* ▷ *vt* dzielić (podzielić *perf*) (na części); **the business ~** *(Press)* dział gospodarczy
**sectional** ['sɛkʃənl] *adj (drawing)* przekrojowy
**sector** ['sɛktə^r] *n* sektor *m*; *(Mil)* sektor *m*, strefa *f*
**secular** ['sɛkjulə^r] *adj* świecki
**secure** [sɪ'kjuə^r] *adj (safe)* bezpieczny; *(free from anxiety)* spokojny; *(job, investment)* pewny; *(building, windows)* zabezpieczony; *(rope, shelf)* dobrze umocowany ▷ *vt (shelf etc)* mocować (umocować *perf*); *(votes etc)* uzyskiwać (uzyskać *perf*); **to feel financially ~** czuć się zabezpieczonym finansowo; **to make sth ~** zabezpieczać (zabezpieczyć *perf*) coś; **to ~ sth for sb** uzyskiwać (uzyskać *perf*) coś dla kogoś; **to ~ a loan** dawać (dać *perf*) zabezpieczenie pod pożyczkę
**secured creditor** [sɪ'kjuəd-] *(Comm) n* wierzyciel *m* zabezpieczony
**securely** [sɪ'kjuəlɪ] *adv (firmly)* mocno; *(safely)* pewnie
**security** [sɪ'kjuərɪtɪ] *n (freedom from anxiety)* bezpieczeństwo *nt*, poczucie *nt* bezpieczeństwa; *(security measures)* środki *pl* bezpieczeństwa; *(Fin)* zabezpieczenie *nt*; **securities** *npl* papiery *pl* wartościowe; **to increase** *or* **tighten ~** wzmacniać (wzmocnić *perf*) środki bezpieczeństwa; **~ of tenure** zagwarantowane miejsce pracy *(na uniwersytecie)*
**security forces** *npl* siły *pl* bezpieczeństwa
**security guard** *n* strażnik *m*
**security risk** *n (thing)* zagrożenie *nt*; *(person)* osoba *f* niepewna *(pod względem lojalności)*
**secy.** *abbr (= secretary)* sekr.
**sedan** [sə'dæn] *(US) n* sedan *m*
**sedate** [sɪ'deɪt] *adj (person, life)* stateczny; *(pace)* powolny ▷ *vt (Med)* podawać (podać *perf*) środek uspokajający *+dat*
**sedation** [sɪ'deɪʃən] *n*: **to be under ~** być pod wpływem środka uspokajającego
**sedative** ['sɛdɪtɪv] *n* środek *m* uspokajający
**sedentary** ['sɛdntrɪ] *adj (work)* siedzący; *(population)* osiadły
**sediment** ['sɛdɪmənt] *n* osad *m*
**sedimentary** [sɛdɪ'mɛntərɪ] *adj* osadowy
**sedition** [sɪ'dɪʃən] *n* działalność *f* wywrotowa
**seduce** [sɪ'dju:s] *vt (entice)* kusić (skusić *perf*), nęcić (znęcić *perf*); *(beguile)* mamić (omamić *perf*), zwodzić (zwieść *perf*); *(sexually)* uwodzić (uwieść *perf*)
**seduction** [sɪ'dʌkʃən] *n (attraction)* pokusa *f*; *(act of seducing)* uwiedzenie *nt*
**seductive** [sɪ'dʌktɪv] *adj (look)* uwodzicielski; *(fig: offer)* kuszący
**see** [si:] *(pt* **saw**, *pp* **seen**) *vt (perceive)* widzieć; *(look at)* zobaczyć *(perf)*; *(understand)* rozumieć (zrozumieć *perf*); *(notice)* zauważać (zauważyć *perf*), spostrzegać (spostrzec *perf*); *(doctor etc)* iść (pójść *perf*) do *+gen*; *(film)* oglądać (obejrzeć *perf*), zobaczyć *(perf)* ▷ *vi* widzieć; *(find out: by searching)* sprawdzić *(perf)*; *(: by inquiring)* dowiedzieć się *(perf)* ▷ *n (Rel)* biskupstwo *nt*; **to see that ...** dopilnować *(perf)*, żeby ...; **I've seen** *or* **I saw this play** widziałem tę sztukę; **to see sb to the door** odprowadzać (odprowadzić *perf*) kogoś do drzwi; **there was nobody to be seen** nie było nikogo widać; **let me see** *(show me)* pokaż; *(let me think)* niech pomyślę; **I see** rozumiem; **you see** widzisz; **to go and see sb** odwiedzać kogoś; **see for yourself** zobacz sam; **I don't know what she sees in him** nie wiem, co ona w nim widzi; **as far as I can see** o ile się orientuję; **see you!** do zobaczenia!, cześć! *(inf)*; **see you soon!** do zobaczenia wkrótce!
▸ **see about** *vt fus* zajmować się (zająć się *perf*) *+instr*, załatwiać (załatwić *perf*) *+acc*
▸ **see off** *vt* odprowadzać (odprowadzić *perf*)
▸ **see through** *vt* wspierać (wesprzeć *perf*) ▷ *vt fus* przejrzeć *(perf)*
▸ **see to** *vt fus* zajmować się (zająć się *perf*) *+instr*
**seed** [si:d] *n* nasienie *nt*; *(fig: usu pl)* ziarno *nt*; **the number two ~** *(Tennis)* gracz rozstawiony z numerem dwa; **to go to ~** *(plant)* wydawać (wydać *perf*) nasiona; *(fig: person)* niedołężnieć (zniedołężnieć *perf*)
**seedless** ['si:dlɪs] *adj* bezpestkowy
**seedling** ['si:dlɪŋ] *n* sadzonka *f*
**seedy** ['si:dɪ] *adj* zapuszczony *(pej)*
**seeing** ['si:ɪŋ] *conj*: **~ as** *or* **that** skoro, jako że
**seek** [si:k] *(pt, pp* **sought**) *vt* szukać (poszukać *perf*) *+gen*; **to ~ advice/help from sb** szukać rady/pomocy u kogoś
▸ **seek out** *vt* odszukiwać (odszukać *perf*)
**seem** [si:m] *vi* wydawać się (wydać się *perf*) (być); **there ~s to be ...** zdaje się, że jest ...; **it ~s (that)** wydaje się, że; **what ~s to be the trouble?** w czym kłopot?; *(to child)* co się stało?; *(to patient)* co Panu/Pani dolega?
**seemingly** ['si:mɪŋlɪ] *adv* pozornie
**seemly** ['si:mlɪ] *adj* właściwy, odpowiedni
**seen** [si:n] *pp of* **see**
**seep** [si:p] *vi (liquid)* przeciekać (przeciec *perf*), przesączać się (przesączyć się *perf*); *(gas)* przenikać (przeniknąć *perf*), przedostawać się (przedostać się *perf*); *(fig: information)* przeciekać (przeciec *perf*)
**seersucker** ['sɪəsʌkə^r] *n* kora *f (tkanina)*

**seesaw** ['si:sɔ:] *n* huśtawka *f*
**seethe** [si:ð] *vi*: **the street ~d with people/ isects** na ulicy roiło się od ludzi/owadów; **the ship ~d with activity/noise** na statku wrzało od krzątaniny/hałasu; **to ~ with anger** wrzeć (zawrzeć *perf*) gniewem
**see-through** ['si:θru:] *adj* przejrzysty, przezroczysty
**segment** ['sɛgmənt] *n* część *f*; (*Geom*) odcinek *m*; (*of orange*) cząstka *f*
**segregate** ['sɛgrɪgeɪt] *vt* rozdzielać (rozdzielić *perf*)
**segregation** [sɛgrɪ'geɪʃən] *n* segregacja *f*, rozdział *m*
**Seine** [seɪn] *n*: **the ~** Sekwana *f*
**seismic** ['saɪzmɪk] *adj* sejsmiczny
**seize** [si:z] *vt* (*person, object*) chwytać (chwycić *perf*); (*fig: opportunity*) korzystać (skorzystać *perf*) z *+gen*; (*power*) przechwytywać (przechwycić *perf*), przejmować (przejąć *perf*); (*territory*) zajmować (zająć *perf*), zdobywać (zdobyć *perf*); (*criminal*) chwytać (schwytać *perf*); (*hostage*) brać (wziąć *perf*); (*Jur*) zajmować (zająć *perf*)
▸ **seize up** *vi* (*engine*) zacierać się (zatrzeć się *perf*)
▸ **seize (up)on** *vt fus* wykorzystywać (wykorzystać *perf*) *+acc*
**seizure** ['si:ʒə^r] *n* (*Med*) napad *m*; (*of power*) przechwycenie *nt*, przejęcie *nt*; (*Jur: of property*) zajęcie *nt*, konfiskata *f*
**seldom** ['sɛldəm] *adv* rzadko
**select** [sɪ'lɛkt] *adj* (*school, district*) ekskluzywny; (*group*) doborowy ▷ *vt* wybierać (wybrać *perf*); (*Sport*) selekcjonować (wyselekcjonować *perf*); **a ~ few** garstka wybrańców
**selection** [sɪ'lɛkʃən] *n* wybór *m*
**selection committee** *n* komisja *f* kwalifikacyjna
**selective** [sɪ'lɛktɪv] *adj* (*discriminating*) wybiórczy, selektywny; (*strike etc*) ograniczony; (*education etc*) elitarny
**selector** [sɪ'lɛktə^r] *n* (*person*) selekcjoner(ka) *m(f)*; (*Tech*) przełącznik *m*
**self** [sɛlf] (*pl* **selves**) *n* (swoje) ja *nt inv*; **to have no thought of ~** nie myśleć o sobie; **to be/ become one's normal ~** być/stawać się (stać się *perf*) sobą
**self...** [sɛlf] *pref* samo...
**self-addressed** ['sɛlfə'drɛst] *adj*: **~ envelope** zaadresowana koperta *f* zwrotna
**self-adhesive** [sɛlfəd'hi:zɪv] *adj* samoprzylepny
**self-appointed** [sɛlfə'pɔɪntɪd] *adj* samozwańczy
**self-assertive** [sɛlfə'sə:tɪv] *adj* pewny siebie
**self-assurance** [sɛlfə'ʃuərəns] *n* pewność *f* siebie
**self-assured** [sɛlfə'ʃuəd] *adj* pewny siebie
**self-catering** [sɛlf'keɪtərɪŋ] (*Brit*) *adj* z wyżywieniem we własnym zakresie *post*
**self-centred**, (*US*) **self-centered** [sɛlf'sɛntəd] *adj* egocentryczny
**self-cleaning** [sɛlf'kli:nɪŋ] *adj* samooczyszczający się
**self-confessed** [sɛlfkən'fɛst] *adj*: **~ alcoholic** alkoholik *m* przyznający się do nałogu
**self-confidence** [sɛlf'kɔnfɪdns] *n* wiara *f* w siebie
**self-confident** [sɛlf'kɔnfɪdənt] *adj* ufny we własne siły, wierzący w siebie
**self-conscious** [sɛlf'kɔnʃəs] *adj* skrępowany
**self-contained** [sɛlfkən'teɪnd] (*Brit*) *adj* (*flat etc*) samodzielny; (*society*) samowystarczalny; (*person*) zamknięty (w sobie)
**self-control** [sɛlfkən'trəul] *n* opanowanie *nt*
**self-defeating** [sɛlfdɪ'fi:tɪŋ] *adj* daremny, bezskuteczny
**self-defence**, (*US*) **self-defense** [sɛlfdɪ'fɛns] *n* samoobrona *f*; **to act in ~** działać w obronie własnej
**self-discipline** [sɛlf'dɪsɪplɪn] *n* samodyscyplina *f*
**self-employed** [sɛlfɪm'plɔɪd] *adj* niezależny (*pracujący dla siebie*)
**self-esteem** [sɛlfɪs'ti:m] *n* poczucie *nt* własnej wartości
**self-evident** [sɛlf'ɛvɪdnt] *adj* oczywisty
**self-explanatory** [sɛlfɪks'plænətrɪ] *adj* oczywisty
**self-financing** [sɛlffaɪ'nænsɪŋ] *adj* samofinansujący się
**self-governing** [sɛlf'gʌvənɪŋ] *adj* samorządny
**self-help** ['sɛlf'hɛlp] *n* samopomoc *f*
**self-importance** [sɛlfɪm'pɔ:tns] *n* zarozumiałość *f*
**self-indulgent** [sɛlfɪn'dʌldʒənt] *adj*: **to be ~** nie stronić od przyjemności
**self-inflicted** [sɛlfɪn'flɪktɪd] *adj*: **~ wound** rana *f* zadana samemu sobie
**self-interest** [sɛlf'ɪntrɪst] *n* korzyść *f* własna
**selfish** ['sɛlfɪʃ] *adj* samolubny
**selfishly** ['sɛlfɪʃlɪ] *adv* samolubnie
**selfishness** ['sɛlfɪʃnɪs] *n* samolubstwo *nt*, egoizm *m*
**selfless** ['sɛlflɪs] *adj* bezinteresowny
**selflessly** ['sɛlflɪslɪ] *adv* bezinteresownie
**selflessness** ['sɛlflɪsnɪs] *n* bezinteresowność *f*
**self-made** ['sɛlfmeɪd] *adj*: **~ man** człowiek *m*, który wszystko zawdzięcza sobie
**self-pity** [sɛlf'pɪtɪ] *n* rozczulanie się *nt* nad sobą

**self-portrait** [sɛlfˈpɔːtreɪt] *n* autoportret *m*
**self-possessed** [sɛlfpəˈzɛst] *adj* opanowany
**self-preservation** [ˈsɛlfprɛzəˈveɪʃən] *n*: **the instinct of** *or* **for ~** instynkt *m* samozachowawczy
**self-raising** [sɛlfˈreɪzɪŋ], (*US*) **self-rising** *adj*: **~ flour** *mąka zmieszana z proszkiem do pieczenia*
**self-reliant** [sɛlfrɪˈlaɪənt] *adj* samodzielny, niezależny
**self-respect** [sɛlfrɪsˈpɛkt] *n* szacunek *m* dla samego siebie
**self-respecting** [sɛlfrɪsˈpɛktɪŋ] *adj* szanujący się
**self-righteous** [sɛlfˈraɪtʃəs] *adj* zadufany (w sobie)
**self-rising** [sɛlfˈraɪzɪŋ] (*US*) *adj* = **self-raising**
**self-sacrifice** [sɛlfˈsækrɪfaɪs] *n* wyrzeczenie *nt*, poświęcenie *nt*
**self-same** [ˈsɛlfseɪm] *adj* (dokładnie) ten sam
**self-satisfied** [sɛlfˈsætɪsfaɪd] *adj* (*person*) zadowolony z siebie; (*smile*) pełen samozadowolenia
**self-sealing** [sɛlfˈsiːlɪŋ] *adj*: **~ envelope** koperta *f* samoklejąca
**self-service** [sɛlfˈsəːvɪs] *adj* samoobsługowy
**self-styled** [ˈsɛlfstaɪld] *adj* samozwańczy
**self-sufficient** [sɛlfsəˈfɪʃənt] *adj* samowystarczalny; **to be ~ in coal** być samowystarczalnym pod względem węgla
**self-supporting** [sɛlfsəˈpɔːtɪŋ] *adj* samofinansujący się
**self-taught** [sɛlfˈtɔːt] *adj*: **~ pianist** pianista *m* samouk *m*
**self-test** [ˈsɛlftɛst] (*Comput*) *n* autotest *m*
**sell** [sɛl] (*pt, pp* **sold**) *vt* sprzedawać (sprzedać *perf*); (*fig*): **to ~ sth to sb** przekonywać (przekonać *perf*) kogoś do czegoś ▷ *vi* sprzedawać się (sprzedać się *perf*); **to ~ at** *or* **for 10 pounds** kosztować 10 funtów; **to ~ sb sth** sprzedawać (sprzedać *perf*) komuś coś; **to ~ o.s.** prezentować się (zaprezentować się *perf*) dobrze
▸ **sell off** *vt* wyprzedawać (wyprzedać *perf*)
▸ **sell out** *vi*: **to ~ out (of sth)** wyprzedać (*perf*) (coś); **that shop is never sold out of bread** w tym sklepie nigdy nie brakuje chleba; **the tickets are sold out** bilety zostały wyprzedane; **sorry, we're sold out** niestety, już nie ma
▸ **sell up** *vi* sprzedać (*perf*) wszystko
**sell-by date** [ˈsɛlbaɪ-] *n* data *f* ważności
**seller** [ˈsɛləʳ] *n* sprzedawca(-wczyni) *m(f)*; **the ~ and the buyer** sprzedający i kupujący; **~'s market** rynek sprzedawcy
**selling price** [ˈsɛlɪŋ-] *n* cena *f* zbytu
**sellotape®** [ˈsɛləuteɪp] (*Brit*) *n* ≈ taśma *f* klejąca
**sellout** [ˈsɛlaut] *n* (*inf*) zaprzedanie się *nt*; **th… match was a ~** wykupiono wszystkie bilety na ten mecz; (*fig*) mecz został kupiony
**selves** [sɛlvz] *pl of* **self**
**semantic** [sɪˈmæntɪk] *adj* semantyczny
**semantics** [sɪˈmæntɪks] *n* semantyka *f*
**semaphore** [ˈsɛməfɔːʳ] *n* semafor *m* (*system sygnalizacji morskiej*)
**semblance** [ˈsɛmblns] *n* pozory *pl*
**semen** [ˈsiːmən] *n* nasienie *nt*
**semester** [sɪˈmɛstəʳ] (*esp US*) *n* semestr *m*
**semi** [ˈsɛmɪ] *n* = **semidetached (house)**
**semi...** [ˈsɛmɪ] *pref* pół...
**semibreve** [ˈsɛmɪbriːv] (*Brit: Mus*) *n* cała nuta *f*
**semicircle** [ˈsɛmɪsəːkl] *n* półkole *nt*
**semicircular** [ˈsɛmɪˈsəːkjuləʳ] *adj* półkolisty
**semicolon** [sɛmɪˈkəulən] *n* średnik *m*
**semiconductor** [sɛmɪkənˈdʌktəʳ] *n* półprzewodnik *m*
**semiconscious** [sɛmɪˈkɔnʃəs] *adj* półprzytomny
**semidetached (house)** (*Brit*) *n* dom *m* bliźniaczy, bliźniak *m* (*inf*)
**semifinal** [sɛmɪˈfaɪnl] *n* półfinał *m*
**seminar** [ˈsɛmɪnɑːʳ] *n* seminarium *nt*
**seminary** [ˈsɛmɪnərɪ] (*Rel*) *n* seminarium *nt*
**semi-precious** [sɛmɪˈprɛʃəs] *adj* półszlachetny
**semiquaver** [ˈsɛmɪkweɪvəʳ] (*Brit: Mus*) *n* szesnastka *f*
**semiskilled** [sɛmɪˈskɪld] *adj*: **~ worker** pracownik *m* nie w pełni wykwalifikowany; **~ work** praca nie wymagająca pełnych kwalifikacji
**semi-skimmed** [sɛmɪˈskɪmd] *adj* (*milk*) półtłusty
**Semitic** [sɪˈmɪtɪk] *adj* semicki
**semitone** [ˈsɛmɪtəun] (*Mus*) *n* półton *m*
**semolina** [sɛməˈliːnə] *n* kasza *f* manna *f*
**SEN** (*Brit*) *n abbr* (= *State Enrolled Nurse*) ≈ pielęgniarka(-arz) *f(m)* dyplomowana(-ny) *f(m)*
**Sen.** *abbr* (*US:* = *senator*) sen.; (*in names:* = *senior*) sen., sr.
**sen.** *abbr* = **Sen.**
**senate** [ˈsɛnɪt] *n* senat *m*
**senator** [ˈsɛnɪtəʳ] *n* senator *m*
**send** [sɛnd] (*pt, pp* **sent**) *vt* (*letter etc*) wysyłać (wysłać *perf*); (*signal, picture*) przesyłać (przesłać *perf*); **to ~ sth by post** *or* (*US*) **mail** wysyłać (wysłać *perf*) coś pocztą; **to ~ sb for sth** wysyłać (wysłać *perf*) kogoś po coś; **to ~ s… for a check-up** wysłać (*perf*) kogoś na badania kontrolne; **to ~ word that ...** przysłać (*perf*) wiadomość, że ...; **she ~s (you… her love** przesyła (ci) pozdrowienia; **to ~ sb**

**to Coventry** (*Brit*) bojkotować (zbojkotować *perf*) kogoś; **to ~ sb to sleep** usypiać (uśpić *perf*) kogoś; **to ~ sth flying** ciskać (cisnąć *perf*) czymś

▸ **send away** *vt* (*visitor*) odprawiać (odprawić *perf*)

▸ **send away for** *vt fus* zamawiać (zamówić *perf*) pocztą

▸ **send back** *vt* odsyłać (odesłać *perf*)

▸ **send for** *vt fus* (*by post*) zamawiać (zamówić *perf*) (pocztą); (*doctor, police*) wzywać (wezwać *perf*)

▸ **send in** *vt* nadsyłać (nadesłać *perf*)

▸ **send off** *vt* (*goods*) wysyłać (wysłać *perf*); (*Brit: Sport*) usuwać (usunąć *perf*) z boiska

▸ **send on** *vt* (*Brit: letter*) przesyłać (przesłać *perf*) (na nowy adres); (*luggage etc*) nadawać (nadać *perf*)

▸ **send out** *vt* (*invitation, signal*) wysyłać (wysłać *perf*); (*heat*) wydzielać (wydzielić *perf*)

▸ **send round** *vt* (*by post*) rozsyłać (rozesłać *perf*); (*at meeting*) puszczać (puścić *perf*) w obieg

▸ **send up** *vt* (*price, blood pressure*) podnosić (podnieść *perf*); (*astronaut*) wysyłać (wysłać *perf*); (*Brit*) parodiować (sparodiować *perf*)

**sender** ['sɛndəʳ] *n* nadawca(-wczyni) *m(f)*

**send-off** *n*: **a good ~** ładne pożegnanie *nt*

**send-up** ['sɛndʌp] *n* parodia *f*

**Senegal** [sɛnɪ'gɔːl] *n* Senegal *m*

**Senegalese** ['sɛnɪgə'liːz] *adj* senegalski ▹ *n inv* Senegalczyk(-lka) *m(f)*

**senile** ['siːnaɪl] *adj* zniedołężniały

**senility** [sɪ'nɪlɪtɪ] *n* zniedołężnienie *nt* starcze

**senior** ['siːnɪəʳ] *adj* (*staff, officer*) starszy *or* wysoki rangą; (*manager*) wysoki rangą; (*post, position*) wysoki ▹ *n* (*Scol*): **the ~s** (*at school*) uczniowie *vir pl* starszych klas; (*at college or university*) studenci *vir pl* wyższych lat; **to be ~ to sb** być od kogoś starszym rangą; **she is 15 years his ~** jest (od niego) starsza o 15 lat; **P. Jones ~** P. Jones senior *or* starszy

**senior citizen** *n* emeryt(ka) *m(f)*

**senior high school** (*US*) *n szkoła średnia, zwykle obejmująca dziesiątą, jedenastą i dwunastą klasę*

**seniority** [siːnɪ'ɔrɪtɪ] *n* (*degree of importance*) starszeństwo *nt*; (*length of work*) staż *m* pracy, wysługa *f* lat

**sensation** [sɛn'seɪʃən] *n* (*feeling*) uczucie *nt*; (*ability to feel*) czucie *nt*; (*great success*) wydarzenie *nt*, sensacja *f*; **to cause a ~** wzbudzać (wzbudzić *perf*) sensację

**sensational** [sɛn'seɪʃənl] *adj* (*wonderful*) wspaniały, fantastyczny; (*surprising, exaggerated*) sensacyjny

**sense** [sɛns] *n* (*physical*) zmysł *m*; (*of guilt*) poczucie *nt*; (*of shame, pleasure*) uczucie *nt*; (*good sense*) rozsądek *m*; (*of word*) sens *m*, znaczenie *nt*; (*of letter, conversation*) sens *m* ▹ *vt* wyczuwać (wyczuć *perf*); **it makes ~** to ma sens; **there is no ~ in that/doing that** to/robienie tego nie ma (żadnego) sensu; **to come to one's ~s** opamiętać się (*perf*); **to take leave of one's ~s** postradać (*perf*) zmysły

**senseless** ['sɛnslɪs] *adj* (*pointless*) bezsensowny; (*unconscious*) nieprzytomny

**sense of humour** *n* poczucie *nt* humoru

**sensibility** [sɛnsɪ'bɪlɪtɪ] *n* wrażliwość *f*

**sensible** ['sɛnsɪbl] *adj* (*person, advice*) rozsądny; (*shoes, clothes*) praktyczny; **to be ~ for** nadawać się do *+gen*

**sensitive** ['sɛnsɪtɪv] *adj* (*person, skin*) wrażliwy; (*instrument*) czuły; (*fig: touchy*) drażliwy; **~ to** wrażliwy *or* czuły na *+acc*; **he is very ~ about it** jest bardzo wrażliwy *or* czuły na tym punkcie

**sensitivity** [sɛnsɪ'tɪvɪtɪ] *n* (*of person, skin*) wrażliwość *f*; (*to touch etc*) czułość *f*; (*of issue etc*) delikatna natura *f*

**sensual** ['sɛnsjuəl] *adj* (*of the senses*) zmysłowy; (*life*) pełen zmysłowych przyjemności *post*

**sensuous** ['sɛnsjuəs] *adj* (*lips*) zmysłowy; (*material*) przyjemny w dotyku

**sent** [sɛnt] *pt, pp of* **send**

**sentence** ['sɛntns] *n* (*Ling*) zdanie *nt*; (*Jur: judgement*) wyrok *m*; (*: punishment*) kara *f* ▹ *vt*: **to ~ sb to death/to five years in prison** skazywać (skazać *perf*) kogoś na karę śmierci/na karę pięciu lat więzienia; **to pass ~ on sb** wydawać (wydać *perf*) wyrok na kogoś

**sentiment** ['sɛntɪmənt] *n* (*tender feelings*) tkliwość *f*, sentyment *m*; (*also pl: opinion*) odczucie *nt*, zapatrywanie *nt*

**sentimental** [sɛntɪ'mɛntl] *adj* sentymentalny; **to get ~** roztkliwiać się (roztkliwić się *perf*)

**sentimentality** ['sɛntɪmɛn'tælɪtɪ] *n* sentymentalność *f*; (*exaggerated*) sentymentalizm *m*, czułostkowość *f*

**sentry** ['sɛntrɪ] *n* wartownik *m*

**sentry duty** *n*: **to be on ~** stać na warcie

**Seoul** [səul] *n* Seul *m*

**separable** ['sɛprəbl] *adj*: **to be ~ from** dawać (dać *perf*) się oddzielić od *+gen*

**separate** [*adj* 'sɛprɪt, *vb* 'sɛpəreɪt] *adj* (*piles*) osobny; (*occasions, reasons, ways*) różny; (*rooms*) oddzielny ▹ *vt* (*people, things*) rozdzielać (rozdzielić *perf*); (*ideas*) oddzielać (oddzielić *perf*) (od siebie) ▹ *vi* (*part*) rozstawać się (rozstać się *perf*); (*move apart*) rozchodzić się (rozejść się *perf*), rozdzielać się (rozdzielić się *perf*); (*split up: couple*) rozstawać się (rozstać się *perf*); (: *parents, married couple*) brać (wziąć *perf*) separację; **to keep sth ~** trzymać coś oddzielnie; **she kept** *or* **remained ~ from us** trzymała się oddzielnie; **under ~ cover** (*Comm*) osobną pocztą; **to ~ into** dzielić (podzielić *perf*) *or* rozdzielać (rozdzielić *perf*) na *+acc*; *see also* **separates**

**separately** ['sɛprɪtlɪ] *adv* osobno, oddzielnie

**separates** ['sɛprɪts] *npl części ubrania, które można nosić w różnych zestawach*

**separation** [sɛpə'reɪʃən] *n* (*being apart*) oddzielenie *nt*; (*time spent apart*) rozłąka *f*; (*Jur*) separacja *f*

**sepia** ['siːpjə] *adj* sepiowy, w kolorze sepii *post*

**Sept.** *abbr* (= *September*) wrzes.

**September** [sɛp'tɛmbəʳ] *n* wrzesień *m*; *see also* **July**

**septic** ['sɛptɪk] *adj* (*Med*) septyczny, zakaźny; (*wound, finger*) zakażony; **the wound is going ~** w ranie rozwija się zakażenie

**septicaemia**, (*US*) **septicemia** [sɛptɪ'siːmɪə] (*Med*) *n* posocznica *f*

**septic tank** *n* szambo *nt*, dół *m* gnilny

**sequel** ['siːkwl] *n* (*follow-up*) dalszy ciąg *m*; (*consequence*) następstwo *nt*

**sequence** ['siːkwəns] *n* (*order*) kolejność *f*, porządek *m*; (*ordered chain*) seria *f*; (*in dance, film*) sekwencja *f*; **~ of events** łańcuch zdarzeń; **in ~** w *or* według kolejności

**sequential** [sɪ'kwɛnʃəl] *adj*: **~ link** ogniwo *nt* łączące; **~ access** (*Comput*) dostęp sekwencyjny

**sequestrate** [sɪ'kwɛstreɪt] (*Jur, Comm*) *vt* nakładać (nałożyć *perf*) sekwestr na *+acc*

**sequin** ['siːkwɪn] *n* cekin *m*

**Serbo-Croat** ['səːbəu'krəuæt] *n* (język *m*) serbsko-chorwacki

**serenade** [sɛrə'neɪd] *n* serenada *f* ▷ *vt* śpiewać (zaśpiewać *perf*) serenadę *+dat*

**serene** [sɪ'riːn] *adj* spokojny

**serenity** [sə'rɛnɪtɪ] *n* spokój *m*

**sergeant** ['sɑːdʒənt] *n* sierżant *m*

**sergeant-major** ['sɑːdʒənt'meɪdʒəʳ] *n* starszy sierżant *m*

**serial** ['sɪərɪəl] *n* serial *m* ▷ *adj* (*Comput*) szeregowy

**serialize** ['sɪərɪəlaɪz] *vt* (*on radio, TV*) nadawać w odcinkach; (*in newspaper*) publikować w odcinkach

**serial killer** *n* seryjny morderca *m*

**serial number** *n* (*of machine*) numer *m* seryjny; (*of banknote*) numer *m* serii

**series** *n inv* seria *f*; (*TV*: *of shows, talks*) cykl *m*, seria *f*; (: *of films*) serial *m*

**serious** ['sɪərɪəs] *adj* poważny; **to be ~** nie żartować; **are you ~ (about it)?** mówisz (to) poważnie?

**seriously** ['sɪərɪəslɪ] *adv* poważnie; **to take sb/sth ~** brać (wziąć *perf*) kogoś/coś (na) poważnie *or* serio

**seriousness** ['sɪərɪəsnɪs] *n* (*of person, situation*) powaga *f*; (*of problem*) waga *f*

**sermon** ['səːmən] *n* kazanie *nt*

**serrated** [sɪ'reɪtɪd] *adj* ząbkowany

**serum** ['sɪərəm] *n* surowica *f*

**servant** ['səːvənt] *n* służący(-ca) *m(f)*; (*fig*) sługa *m*

**serve** [səːv] *vt* (*country, purpose*) służyć *+dat*; (*guest, customer*) obsługiwać (obsłużyć *perf*); (*food*) podawać (podać *perf*); (*apprenticeship, prison term*) odbywać (odbyć *perf*) ▷ *vi* (*at table*) podawać (podać *perf*); (*Tennis*) serwować (zaserwować *perf*); (*in army*) służyć ▷ *n* (*Tennis*) serwis *m*, serw *m*; **to ~ as** (*minister, governor*) sprawować urząd *+gen*; (*delegate, representative*) pełnić funkcję *+gen*; **the delegates ~ for five years** delegaci pełnią swoją funkcję przez pięć lat; **to ~ as/for** służyć (posłużyć *perf*) za *+acc*; **are you being ~d?** czy ktoś Pana/Panią obsługuje?; **to ~ on a committee/jury** zasiadać w komisji/na ławie przysięgłych; **it ~s him right** dobrze mu tak

▸ **serve out** *vt* serwować, podawać (podać *perf*)

▸ **serve up** *vt* = **serve out**

**service** ['səːvɪs] *n* usługa *f*; (*in hotel, restaurant*) obsługa *f*; (*also*: **train service**) połączenie *nt* kolejowe; (*Rel*) nabożeństwo *nt*; (*Aut*) przegląd *m*; (*Tennis*) serwis *m*, podanie *nt*; (*plates, etc*) serwis *m*; **the Services** *npl* siły *pl* zbrojne ▷ *vt* dokonywać (dokonać *perf*) przeglądu *+gen*; **~s (to)** usługi (dla *+gen*); (*extraordinary*) zasługi *pl* (dla *+gen*); **military ~** służba wojskowa; **national ~** powszechna służba wojskowa; **to be of ~ to sb** przydawać się (przydać się *perf*) komuś; **to do sb a ~** wyświadczyć (*perf*) komuś przysługę; **to put one's car in for a ~** oddawać (oddać *perf*) samochód do przeglądu

**serviceable** ['səːvɪsəbl] *adj* (*useful*) użyteczny, przydatny; (*able to be used*) zdatny do użycia, sprawny; (*durable*) mocny

**service area** *n punkt usługowy przy autostradzie*

**service charge** (*Brit*) *n* dodatek *m* za obsługę

**service industry** *n*: **service industries** usługi *pl*

**serviceman** ['səːvɪsmən] *n* (*irreg*: *like* **man**) żołnierz *m*

**service station** *n* stacja *f* obsługi

**serviette** [səːvɪ'ɛt] (*Brit*) *n* serwetka *f*

**servile** ['səːvaɪl] *adj* służalczy

**session** ['sɛʃən] *n* (*period of activity*) sesja *f*; (*sitting*) posiedzenie *nt*, sesja *f*; (*US, Scottish*: *Scol*) semestr *m*; **to be in ~** (*court etc*) obradować

**set** [sɛt] (*pt, pp* **set**) *n* (*of problems*) zespół *m*; (*of saucepans, books*) komplet *m*; (*of people*) grupa *f*; (*also*: **radio set**) radio *nt*, odbiornik *m* radiowy; (*also*: **TV set**) telewizor *m*, odbiornik *m* telewizyjny; (*Tennis*) set *m*; (*Math*) zbiór *m*; (*Film*) plan *m*; (*Theat*) dekoracje *pl*; (*of hair*) ułożenie *nt*, modelowanie *nt* ▷ *adj* (*fixed*) ustalony, stały; (*ready*) gotowy ▷ *vt* (*place, stage*) przygotowywać (przygotować *perf*); (*time, rules*) ustalać (ustalić *perf*); (*record*) ustanawiać (ustanowić *perf*); (*alarm, watch*) nastawiać (nastawić *perf*); (*task, exercise*) zadawać (zadać *perf*); (*exam*) układać (ułożyć *perf*); (*Typ*) składać (złożyć *perf*) ▷ *vi* (*sun*) zachodzić (zajść *perf*); (*jelly, concrete*) tężeć (stężeć *perf*); (*glue*) wysychać (wyschnąć *perf*); (*bone*) zrastać się (zrosnąć się *perf*); **a set of false teeth** sztuczna szczęka; **a set of dining-room furniture** komplet mebli stołowych; **a chess set** szachy; **a set phrase** utarty zwrot; **to be set on doing sth** być zdeterminowanym coś zrobić; **to be all set to do sth** być gotowym do (zrobienia) czegoś; **he's set in his ways** on jest mało elastyczny; **the novel is set in Rome** akcja powieści rozgrywa się w Rzymie; **to set the table** nakrywać (nakryć *perf*) do stołu; **to set sth to music** komponować (skomponować *perf*) muzykę do czegoś; **to set on fire** podpalać (podpalić *perf*); **to set free** uwalniać (uwolnić *perf*), zwalniać (zwolnić *perf*); **to set sail** podnosić (podnieść *perf*) żagle

▸ **set about** *vt fus* przystępować (przystąpić *perf*) do *+gen*; **to set about doing sth** zabierać się (zabrać się *perf*) do czegoś

▸ **set aside** *vt* (*money etc*) odkładać (odłożyć *perf*); (*time*) rezerwować (zarezerwować *perf*)

▸ **set back** *vt*: **to set sb back 5 pounds** kosztować kogoś 5 funtów; **to set sb back (by)** opóźniać (opóźnić *perf*) kogoś (o *+acc*); **a house set back from the road** dom z dala od szosy

▸ **set in** *vi* (*bad weather*) nadchodzić (nadejść *perf*); (*infection*) wdawać się (wdać się *perf*); **the rain has set in for the day** rozpadało się na dobre

▸ **set off** *vi* wyruszać (wyruszyć *perf*) ▷ *vt* (*bomb*) detonować (zdetonować *perf*); (*alarm*) uruchamiać (uruchomić *perf*); (*chain of events*) wywoływać (wywołać *perf*); (*jewels*) uwydatniać (uwydatnić *perf*); (*tan, complexion*) podkreślać (podkreślić *perf*)

▸ **set out** *vi* wyruszać (wyruszyć *perf*) ▷ *vt* (*goods etc*) wystawiać (wystawić *perf*); (*arguments*) wykładać (wyłożyć *perf*); **to set out to do sth** przystępować (przystąpić *perf*) do robienia czegoś; **to set out from home** wyruszać (wyruszyć *perf*) z domu

▸ **set up** *vt* (*organization*) zakładać (założyć *perf*); (*monument*) wznosić (wznieść *perf*); **to set up shop** (*fig*) zakładać (założyć *perf*) interes

**setback** ['sɛtbæk] *n* (*hitch*) komplikacja *f*; (*in health*) pogorszenie *nt*

**set menu** *n* ustalone menu *nt inv*

**set square** *n* ekierka *f*

**settee** [sɛ'ti:] *n* sofa *f*

**setting** ['sɛtɪŋ] *n* (*background*) miejsce *nt*, otoczenie *nt*; (*of controls*) nastawa *f*; (*of jewel*) oprawa *f*

**setting lotion** *n* płyn *m* do układania włosów

**settle** ['sɛtl] *vt* (*argument*) rozstrzygać (rozstrzygnąć *perf*); (*accounts*) regulować (uregulować *perf*); (*affairs*) porządkować (uporządkować *perf*); (*land*) zasiedlać (zasiedlić *perf*) ▷ *vi* (*also*: **settle down**) sadowić się (usadowić się *perf*); (*calm down*) uspokajać się (uspokoić się *perf*); (*bird, insect*) siadać (siąść *perf or* usiąść *perf*); (*dust, sediment*) osiadać (osiąść *perf*), osadzać się (osadzić się *perf*); **to ~ down to sth** zasiadać (zasiąść *perf*) do czegoś; **it'll ~ your stomach** to ci dobrze zrobi na żołądek; **that's ~d then!** no to załatwione!

▸ **settle for** *vt fus* zadowalać się (zadowolić się *perf*) *+instr*

▸ **settle in** *vi* przyzwyczajać się (przyzwyczaić się *perf*) (do nowego miejsca)

▸ **settle on** *vt fus* decydować się (zdecydować się *perf*) na *+acc*

▸ **settle up** *vi*: **to ~ up with sb** rozliczać się (rozliczyć się *perf*) z kimś

**settlement** ['sɛtlmənt] *n* (*payment: of debt*) spłata *f*; (*: in compensation*) odszkodowanie *nt*; (*agreement*) rozstrzygnięcie *nt*, porozumienie *nt*; (*village etc*) osada *f*; (*colonization*) zasiedlanie *nt*, osadnictwo *nt*; **in ~ of our account** (*Comm*) na pokrycie należności.

**settler** ['sɛtlə[r]] *n* osadnik(-iczka) *m(f)*

**setup** ['sɛtʌp], **set-up** *n* układ *m*

**seven** ['sɛvn] *num* siedem

**seventeen** [sɛvn'ti:n] *num* siedemnaście

**seventh** ['sɛvnθ] *num* siódmy

**seventy** ['sɛvntɪ] *num* siedemdziesiąt

**sever** ['sɛvə[r]] *vt* (*artery, pipe*) przerywać (przerwać *perf*); (*fig: relations*) zrywać (zerwać *perf*)

**several** ['sɛvərl] *adj* kilka (*+gen*); (*of groups of people including at least one male*) kilku (*+gen*) ▷ *pron* kilka; (*of groups of people including at least one male*) kilku; **~ of us** kilkoro z nas; **~ times** kilka razy

S

**severance** ['sɛvərəns] *n* (*of relations*) zerwanie *nt*
**severance pay** *n* odprawa *f* (pieniężna)
**severe** [sɪ'vɪəʳ] *adj* (*pain*) ostry; (*damage, shortage*) poważny; (*winter, person, expression*) surowy
**severely** [sɪ'vɪəlɪ] *adv* (*damage*) poważnie; (*punish*) surowo; (*wounded, ill*) ciężko, poważnie
**severity** [sɪ'vɛrɪtɪ] *n* surowość *f*; (*of pain, attacks*) ostrość *f*
**sew** [səu] (*pt* **sewed**, *pp* **sewn**) *vt* (*dress etc*) szyć (uszyć *perf*); (*edges*) zszywać (zszyć *perf*) ▷ *vi* szyć
▶ **sew up** *vt* (*pieces of cloth*) zszywać (zszyć *perf*); (*tear*) zaszywać (zaszyć *perf*); **the deal was sewn up** (*fig*) sprawa została zapięta na ostatni guzik
**sewage** ['suːɪdʒ] *n* ścieki *pl*
**sewer** ['suːəʳ] *n* ściek *m*
**sewing** ['səuɪŋ] *n* szycie *nt*
**sewing machine** *n* maszyna *f* do szycia
**sewn** [səun] *pp of* **sew**
**sex** [sɛks] *n* (*gender*) płeć *f*; (*lovemaking*) seks *m*; **to have sex with sb** mieć z kimś stosunek
**sex act** *n* stosunek *m* płciowy
**sexism** ['sɛksɪzəm] *n* seksizm *m*
**sexist** ['sɛksɪst] *adj* seksistowski
**sextet** [sɛks'tɛt] *n* sekstet *m*
**sexual** ['sɛksjuəl] *adj* płciowy; **~ equality** równouprawnienie płci
**sexual assault** *n* napad *m* na tle seksualnym
**sexual harassment** *n* molestowanie *nt* seksualne (*zwłaszcza w miejscu pracy*)
**sexual intercourse** *n* stosunek *m* płciowy
**sexuality** [sɛkʃu'ælɪtɪ] *n* seksualność *f*
**sexually** ['sɛksjuəlɪ] *adv* (*attractive*) seksualnie; (*segregate*) według płci; (*reproduce*) płciowo
**sexy** ['sɛksɪ] *adj* seksowny
**Seychelles** [seɪ'ʃɛl(z)] *npl*: **the ~** Seszele *pl*
**SF** *n abbr* (= *science fiction*) SF
**SG** (US) *n abbr* (= *Surgeon General*) (*Med*) ≈ Naczelny Lekarz *m* Kraju; (*Mil*) ≈ Naczelny Lekarz *m* Wojskowy
**Sgt** (*Police, Mil*) *abbr* (= *sergeant*) sierż.
**shabbiness** ['ʃæbɪnɪs] *n* nędzny stan *m*
**shabby** ['ʃæbɪ] *adj* (*person*) obdarty; (*clothes*) wytarty, wyświechtany; (*trick, behaviour*) podły; (*building*) odrapany
**shack** [ʃæk] *n* chałupa *f*
▶ **shack up** (*inf*) *vi*: **to ~ up (with sb)** żyć (z kimś) na kocią łapę (*inf*)
**shackles** ['ʃæklz] *npl* kajdany *pl*; (*fig*) pęta *pl*
**shade** [ʃeɪd] *n* (*shelter*) cień *m*; (*for lamp*) abażur *m*, klosz *m*; (*of colour*) odcień *m*; (US: *also*: **window shade**) roleta *f* ▷ *vt* (*shelter*) ocieniać (ocienić *perf*); (*eyes*) osłaniać (osłonić *perf*); **shades** *npl* (*inf*) okulary *pl* słoneczne; **in the ~** w cieniu; **a ~ (too large/more)** odrobinę (za duży/więcej)
**shadow** ['ʃædəu] *n* cień *m* ▷ *vt* śledzić; **without** *or* **beyond a ~ of a doubt** bez cienia wątpliwości
**shadow cabinet** (*Brit*) *n* gabinet *m* cieni
**shadowy** ['ʃædəuɪ] *adj* (*in shadow*) cienisty, zacieniony; (*dim*) niewyraźny
**shady** ['ʃeɪdɪ] *adj* cienisty; (*fig*) podejrzany
**shaft** [ʃɑːft] *n* (*of arrow, spear*) drzewce *nt*; (*Aut, Tech*) wał(ek) *m*; (*of mine, lift*) szyb *m*; (*of light*) snop *m*; **ventilation ~** szyb wentylacyjny
**shaggy** ['ʃægɪ] *adj* (*beard*) zmierzwiony; (*man*) zarośnięty; (*dog, sheep*) kudłaty
**shake** [ʃeɪk] (*pt* **shook**, *pp* **~n**) *vt* trząść *+instr*, potrząsać (potrząsnąć *perf*) *+instr*; (*bottle, person*) wstrząsać (wstrząsnąć *perf*) *+instr*; (*cocktail*) mieszać (zmieszać *perf*); (*beliefs, resolve*) zachwiać (*perf*) *+instr* ▷ *vi* trząść się (zatrząść się *perf*), drżeć (zadrżeć *perf*) ▷ *n* potrząśnięcie *nt*; **to ~ one's head** kręcić (pokręcić *perf*) głową; **to ~ hands with sb** uścisnąć (*perf*) czyjąś dłoń, podawać (podać *perf*) komuś rękę; **to ~ one's fist (at sb)** wygrażać (komuś) pięścią; **give it a good ~** dobrze potrząśnij
▶ **shake off** *vt* strząsać (strząsnąć *perf*), strącać (strącić *perf*); (*fig*: *pursuer*) zgubić (*perf*)
▶ **shake up** *vt* (*ingredients*) mieszać (zmieszać *perf*); (*fig*: *person*) wstrząsać (wstrząsnąć *perf*) *+instr*
**shake-up** ['ʃeɪkʌp] *n* przebudowa *f*
**shakily** ['ʃeɪkɪlɪ] *adv* (*reply*) drżącym głosem; (*walk, stand*) chwiejnie, na drżących nogach
**shaky** ['ʃeɪkɪ] *adj* (*hand, voice*) trzęsący się, drżący; (*memory*) mglisty, niewyraźny; (*knowledge*) słaby; (*prospects, future*) chwiejny, niepewny; (*start*) niepewny, nieśmiały
**shale** [ʃeɪl] *n* łupek *m*
**shall** [ʃæl] *aux vb*: **I ~ go** pójdę; **~ I open the door?** czy mam otworzyć drzwi?; **I'll get some, ~ I?** przyniosę kilka, dobrze?
**shallot** [ʃə'lɔt] (*Brit*) *n* szalotka *f*
**shallow** ['ʃæləu] *adj* (*lit, fig*) płytki; **the shallows** *npl* mielizna *f*, płycizna *f*
**sham** [ʃæm] *n* pozór *m* ▷ *adj* (*jewellery*) sztuczny; (*antique furniture*) podrabiany; (*fight*) udawany, pozorowany ▷ *vt* udawać (udać *perf*)
**shambles** ['ʃæmblz] *n* bałagan *m*; **the economy is (in) a complete ~** gospodarka jest w stanie kompletnego chaosu
**shame** [ʃeɪm] *n* wstyd *m* ▷ *vt* zawstydzać (zawstydzić *perf*); **it is a ~ to ...** szkoda *+infin*; **it is a ~ that ...** szkoda, że ...; **what a ~!** co za

wstyd!; **to put sb to ~** zawstydzać (zawstydzić *perf*) kogoś; **to put sth to ~** przyćmiewać (przyćmić *perf*) coś

**shamefaced** [ˈʃeɪmfeɪst] *adj* zawstydzony

**shameful** [ˈʃeɪmful] *adj* haniebny

**shameless** [ˈʃeɪmlɪs] *adj* bezwstydny

**shampoo** [ʃæmˈpuː] *n* szampon *m* ▷ *vt* myć (umyć *perf*) (szamponem)

**shampoo and set** *n* mycie *nt* i modelowanie *nt*

**shamrock** [ˈʃæmrɔk] *n* koniczyna *f* biała

**shandy** [ˈʃændɪ] *n drink składający się z piwa i lemoniady*

**shan't** [ʃɑːnt] = **shall not**

**shanty town** [ˈʃæntɪ-] *n* dzielnica *f* slumsów

**SHAPE** [ʃeɪp] (*Mil*) *n abbr* (= *Supreme Headquarters Allied Powers, Europe*) *naczelne dowództwo sił alianckich w Europie podczas drugiej wojny światowej*

**shape** [ʃeɪp] *n* kształt *m* ▷ *vt* (*with one's hands*) formować (uformować *perf*); (*sb's ideas, sb's life*) kształtować (ukształtować *perf*); **to take ~** nabierać (nabrać *perf*) kształtu; **in the ~ of a heart** w kształcie serca; **I can't bear gardening in any ~ or form** nie znoszę pracy w ogrodzie w żadnej postaci; **to get (o.s.) into ~** dochodzić (dojść *perf*) do formy
▸ **shape up** *vi* (*events*) dobrze się układać (ułożyć *perf*); (*person*) radzić sobie

**-shaped** [ʃeɪpt] *suff*: **heart~** w kształcie serca

**shapeless** [ˈʃeɪplɪs] *adj* bezkształtny, nieforemny

**shapely** [ˈʃeɪplɪ] *adj* (*woman, legs*) zgrabny

**share** [ʃɛəʳ] *n* (*part*) część *f*; (*contribution*) udział *m*; (*Comm*) akcja *f*, udział *m* ▷ *vt* (*books, cost*) dzielić (podzielić *perf*); (*room, taxi*) dzielić; **China and Japan ~ many characteristics** Chiny i Japonia mają wiele cech wspólnych; **to ~ in** (*joy, sorrow*) dzielić *+acc*; (*profits*) partycypować *or* mieć (swój) udział w *+loc*; (*work*) uczestniczyć w *+gen*
▸ **share out** *vt* rozdzielać (rozdzielić *perf*)

**share capital** *n* kapitał *m* akcyjny

**share certificate** *n* certyfikat *m* akcji

**shareholder** [ˈʃɛəhəuldəʳ] *n* akcjonariusz(ka) *m(f)*

**share index** *n* wskaźnik *m* kursów akcji

**share issue** *n* emisja *f* akcji

**shark** [ʃɑːk] *n* rekin *m*

**sharp** [ʃɑːp] *adj* ostry; (*Mus*) podwyższony o pół tonu; (*person, eye*) bystry ▷ *n* (*Mus*) nuta *f* z krzyżykiem; (*: symbol*) krzyżyk *m* ▷ *adv*: **at 2 o'clock ~** punktualnie o drugiej; **turn ~ left** skręć ostro w lewo; **to be ~ with sb** postępować (postąpić *perf*) z kimś ostro; **look ~!** pośpiesz się!; **C ~** (*Mus*) cis; **~ practices** (*Comm*) nieuczciwe praktyki

**sharpen** [ˈʃɑːpn] *vt* ostrzyć (zaostrzyć *perf*)

**sharpener** [ˈʃɑːpnəʳ] *n* (*also*: **pencil sharpener**) temperówka *f*; (*also*: **knife sharpener**) ostrzarka *f*

**sharp-eyed** [ʃɑːpˈaɪd] *adj* (*person*) bystrooki

**sharply** [ˈʃɑːplɪ] *adv* ostro

**sharp-tempered** [ʃɑːpˈtɛmpəd] *adj* porywczy, wybuchowy

**sharp-witted** [ʃɑːpˈwɪtɪd] *adj* bystry, rozgarnięty

**shatter** [ˈʃætəʳ] *vt* roztrzaskiwać (roztrzaskać *perf*); (*fig*) rujnować (zrujnować *perf*) ▷ *vi* roztrzaskiwać się (roztrzaskać się *perf*); **my dreams have been ~ed** moje marzenia legły w gruzach

**shattered** [ˈʃætəd] *adj* (*overwhelmed*) zdruzgotany; (*inf*: *exhausted*) wykończony (*inf*)

**shattering** [ˈʃætərɪŋ] *adj* (*experience*) wstrząsający; (*effect*) druzgocący; (*exhausting*) wyczerpujący

**shatterproof** [ˈʃætəpruːf] *adj* (*glass*) nietłukący

**shave** [ʃeɪv] *vt* (*person, face, legs*) golić (ogolić *perf*); (*beard*) golić (zgolić *perf*) ▷ *vi* golić się (ogolić się *perf*) ▷ *n*: **to have a ~** golić się (ogolić się *perf*)

**shaven** [ˈʃeɪvn] *adj* (*head*) ogolony, wygolony

**shaver** [ˈʃeɪvəʳ] *n* (*also*: **electric shaver**) golarka *f* elektryczna, (elektryczna) maszynka *f* do golenia

**shaving** [ˈʃeɪvɪŋ] *n* golenie *nt*; **shavings** *npl* strużyny *pl*, wióry *pl*

**shaving brush** *n* pędzel *m* do golenia

**shaving cream** *n* krem *m* do golenia

**shaving foam** *n* pianka *f* do golenia

**shaving point** *n* gniazdko *nt* do maszynki do golenia

**shaving soap** *n* mydło *nt* do golenia

**shawl** [ʃɔːl] *n* szal *m*

**she** [ʃiː] *pron* ona *f* ▷ *pref*: **she-cat** kotka *f*, kocica *f*; **there she is** otóż i ona

**sheaf** [ʃiːf] (*pl* **sheaves**) *n* (*of corn*) snop *m*; (*of papers*) plik *m*

**shear** [ʃɪəʳ] (*pt* **~ed**, *pp* **shorn**) *vt* (*sheep*) strzyc (ostrzyc *perf*)
▸ **shear off** *vi* (*bolt etc*) urywać się (urwać się *perf*)

**shears** [ˈʃɪəz] *npl* nożyce *pl* ogrodnicze, sekator *m*

**sheath** [ʃiːθ] *n* (*of knife*) pochwa *f*; (*contraceptive*) prezerwatywa *f*

**sheathe** [ʃiːð] *vt* powlekać (powlec *perf*); (*sword*) chować (schować *perf*) do pochwy

**sheath knife** *n* nóż *m* fiński

**sheaves** [ʃiːvz] *npl of* **sheaf**

**shed** [ʃɛd] (*pt, pp* **~**) *n* (*for bicycles, tools*) szopa *f*; (*Rail*) zajezdnia *f*; (*Aviat, Naut*) hangar *m* ▷ *vt*

S

(*skin*) zrzucać (zrzucić *perf*); (*tears*) wylewać (wylać *perf*); (*blood*) przelewać (przelać *perf*); (*load*) gubić (zgubić *perf*); (*workers*) pozbywać się (pozbyć się *perf*) *+gen*; **to ~ light on** rzucać (rzucić *perf*) światło na *+acc*

**she'd** [ʃi:d] = **she had; she would**

**sheen** [ʃi:n] *n* połysk *m*

**sheep** [ʃi:p] *n inv* owca *f*

**sheepdog** ['ʃi:pdɔg] *n* owczarek *m*

**sheep farmer** *n* hodowca *m* owiec

**sheepish** ['ʃi:pɪʃ] *adj* zmieszany

**sheepskin** ['ʃi:pskɪn] *n* barania skóra *f*, kożuch *m* ▷ *cpd*: **~ coat/jacket** kożuch *m*/ kożuszek *m*

**sheer** [ʃɪəʳ] *adj* (*utter*) czysty, najzwyklejszy; (*steep*) stromy, pionowy; (*almost transparent*) przejrzysty ▷ *adv* stromo, pionowo; **by ~ chance** przez czysty przypadek

**sheet** [ʃi:t] *n* (*on bed*) prześcieradło *nt*; (*of paper*) kartka *f*; (*of glass*) płyta *f*; (*of metal*) arkusz *m*, płyta *f*; (*of ice*) tafla *f*

**sheet feed** *n* (*on printer*) podawanie *nt* pojedynczych arkuszy papieru

**sheet lightning** *n* błyskawica *f* rozświetlająca całe niebo

**sheet metal** *n* blacha *f* cienka

**sheet music** *n* nuty *pl*

**sheik(h)** [ʃeɪk] *n* szejk *m*

**shelf** [ʃɛlf] (*pl* **shelves**) *n* półka *f*; **set of shelves** regał

**shelf life** *n* okres *m* przechowywania

**shell** [ʃɛl] *n* (*on beach*) muszla *f*; (*: small*) muszelka *f*; (*of egg*) skorupka *f*; (*of nut etc*) łupina *f*; (*of tortoise*) skorupa *f*; (*explosive*) pocisk *m*; (*of building*) szkielet *m* ▷ *vt* (*peas*) łuskać; (*egg*) obierać (obrać *perf*) ze skorupki; (*Mil*) ostrzeliwać (ostrzelać *perf*)

▶ **shell out** (*inf*) *vt*: **to ~ out (for)** bulić (wybulić *perf*) (za *+acc*) (*inf*)

**she'll** [ʃi:l] = **she will; she shall**

**shellfish** ['ʃɛlfɪʃ] *n inv* skorupiak *m*; (*as food*) małż *m*

**shelter** ['ʃɛltəʳ] *n* (*refuge*) schronienie *nt*; (*protection*) osłona *f*, ochrona *f*; (*also*: **air-raid shelter**) schron *m* ▷ *vt* (*protect*) osłaniać (osłonić *perf*); (*give lodging to*) udzielać (udzielić *perf*) schronienia *+dat* ▷ *vi* (*from rain etc*) chronić się (schronić się *perf*); **to take ~ (from)** znajdować (znaleźć *perf*) schronienie (przed *+instr*)

**sheltered** ['ʃɛltəd] *adj* (*life*) pod kloszem *post*; (*spot*) osłonięty; **~ housing** *dom z całodobową opieką dla osób starszych lub niepełnosprawnych*

**shelve** [ʃɛlv] *vt* (*fig: plan*) odkładać (odłożyć *perf*) do szuflady

**shelves** [ʃɛlvz] *npl of* **shelf**

**shelving** ['ʃɛlvɪŋ] *n* półki *pl*

**shepherd** ['ʃɛpəd] *n* pasterz *m* ▷ *vt* prowadzić (poprowadzić *perf*)

**shepherdess** ['ʃɛpədɪs] *n* pasterka *f*

**shepherd's pie** (*Brit*) *n zapiekanka z mielonego mięsa i ziemniaków*

**sherbet** ['ʃə:bət] *n* (*Brit*) oranżada *f* w proszku; (*US*) sorbet *m*

**sheriff** ['ʃɛrɪf] (*US*) *n* szeryf *m*

**sherry** ['ʃɛrɪ] *n* sherry *f inv*

**she's** [ʃi:z] = **she is; she has**

**Shetland** ['ʃɛtlənd] *n* (*also*: **the Shetland Islands**) Szetlandy *pl*

**shield** [ʃi:ld] *n* (*Mil*) tarcza *f*; (*Sport*) odznaka *f*; (*fig*) osłona *f* ▷ *vt*: **to ~ (from)** osłaniać (osłonić *perf*) (przed *+instr*)

**shift** [ʃɪft] *n* zmiana *f* ▷ *vt* (*move*) przesuwać (przesunąć *perf*); (*remove*) usuwać (usunąć *perf*) ▷ *vi* przesuwać się (przesunąć się *perf*); **the wind has ~ed to the south** wiatr zmienił się na południowy; **a ~ in demand** (*Comm*) zmiana charakteru popytu

**shift key** *n* klawisz *m* „shift"

**shiftless** ['ʃɪftlɪs] *adj* niemrawy

**shift work** *n* praca *f* zmianowa; **to do ~** pracować na zmiany

**shifty** ['ʃɪftɪ] *adj* chytry, przebiegły

**shilling** ['ʃɪlɪŋ] (*Brit: old*) *n* szyling *m*

**shilly-shally** ['ʃɪlɪʃælɪ] *vi* wahać się

**shimmer** ['ʃɪməʳ] *vi* migotać, skrzyć się

**shimmering** ['ʃɪmərɪŋ] *adj* migotliwy

**shin** [ʃɪn] *n* goleń *f* ▷ *vi*: **to ~ up a tree** wdrapywać się (wdrapać się *perf*) na drzewo

**shindig** ['ʃɪndɪg] (*inf*) *n* ubaw *m* (*inf*)

**shine** [ʃaɪn] (*pt, pp* **shone**) *n* połysk *m* ▷ *vi* (*sun, light*) świecić; (*eyes, hair*) błyszczeć, lśnić; (*fig: person*) błyszczeć ▷ *vt* (*shoes etc: pt, pp shined*) czyścić (wyczyścić *perf*) (do połysku), pucować (wypucować *perf*) (*inf*); **to ~ a torch on sth** oświetlać (oświetlić *perf*) coś latarką

**shingle** ['ʃɪŋgl] *n* (*on beach*) kamyk *m*; (*on roof*) gont *m*

**shingles** ['ʃɪŋglz] (*Med*) *npl* półpasiec *m*

**shining** ['ʃaɪnɪŋ] *adj* (*surface*) lśniący, błyszczący; (*example*) godny naśladowania; (*achievement*) godny podziwu

**shiny** ['ʃaɪnɪ] *adj* (*coin, hair*) błyszczący, lśniący; (*shoes*) wypolerowany

**ship** [ʃɪp] *n* statek *m*, okręt *m* ▷ *vt* (*transport: by ship*) przewozić (przewieźć *perf*) drogą morską; (*: by rail etc*) przewozić (przewieźć *perf*); (*water*) nabierać (nabrać *perf*) *+gen*; **on board ~** na pokładzie statku

**shipbuilder** ['ʃɪpbɪldəʳ] *n* (*person*) budowniczy *m* okrętów; (*company*) stocznia *f*

**shipbuilding** ['ʃɪpbɪldɪŋ] *n* budownictwo *nt* okrętowe

**ship canal** *n* kanał *m* morski

**ship chandler** [-'tʃɑːndləʳ] *n* dostawca *m* okrętowy
**shipment** ['ʃɪpmənt] *n* (*of goods*) transport *m*
**shipowner** ['ʃɪpəunəʳ] *n* armator *m*
**shipper** ['ʃɪpəʳ] *n* spedytor *m*
**shipping** ['ʃɪpɪŋ] *n* (*of cargo*) transport *m* morski; (*ships*) flota *f* handlowa
**shipping agent** *n* agent *m* okrętowy, spedytor *m* portowy
**shipping company** *n* towarzystwo *nt* żeglugowe, linia *f* żeglugowa
**shipping lane** *n* szlak *m* żeglugowy
**shipping line** *n* = **shipping company**
**shipshape** ['ʃɪpʃeɪp] *adj*: **I got the house all ~** wysprzątałem dom na tip-top
**shipwreck** ['ʃɪprɛk] *n* (*event*) katastrofa *f* morska; (*ship*) wrak *m* (statku) ▷ *vt*: **to be ~ed** ocaleć (*perf*) z katastrofy morskiej
**shipyard** ['ʃɪpjɑːd] *n* stocznia *f*
**shire** ['ʃaɪəʳ] (*Brit*) *n* hrabstwo *nt*
**shirk** [ʃəːk] *vt* wymigiwać się od *+gen*
**shirt** [ʃəːt] *n* (*man's*) koszula *f*; (*woman's*) bluzka *f* (koszulowa); **in (one's) ~ sleeves** w samej koszuli, bez marynarki
**shirty** ['ʃəːtɪ] (*Brit*: *inf*) *adj* wkurzony (*inf*)
**shit** [ʃɪt] (*inf!*) *excl* cholera! (*inf*)
**shiver** ['ʃɪvəʳ] *n* drżenie *nt* ▷ *vi* drżeć (zadrżeć *perf*)
**shoal** [ʃəul] *n* (*of fish*) ławica *f*; (*also*: **shoals**: *fig*) tłumy *pl*
**shock** [ʃɔk] *n* wstrząs *m*, szok *m*; (*also*: **electric shock**) porażenie *nt* (prądem) ▷ *vt* (*upset*) wstrząsać (wstrząsnąć *perf*) *+instr*; (*offend*) szokować (zaszokować *perf*); **to be suffering from ~** (*Med*) być w szoku; **it gave us a ~** to nami wstrząsnęło; **it came as a ~ to hear that ...** zaszokowała nas wiadomość, że ...
**shock absorber** (*Aut*) *n* amortyzator *m*
**shocking** ['ʃɔkɪŋ] *adj* (*very bad*) fatalny; (*outrageous*) szokujący
**shockproof** ['ʃɔkpruːf] *adj* odporny na wstrząsy
**shock therapy** *n* terapia *f* wstrząsowa, leczenie *nt* wstrząsowe
**shock treatment** *n* = **shock therapy**
**shod** [ʃɔd] *pt, pp of* **shoe**
**shoddy** ['ʃɔdɪ] *adj* lichy
**shoe** [ʃuː] (*pt, pp* **shod**) *n* (*for person*) but *m*; (*for horse*) podkowa *f*; (*also*: **brake shoe**) klocek *m* hamulcowy, szczęka *f* hamulcowa ▷ *vt* (*horse*) podkuwać (podkuć *perf*)
**shoebrush** ['ʃuːbrʌʃ] *n* szczotka *f* do butów
**shoehorn** ['ʃuːhɔːn] *n* łyżka *f* do butów
**shoelace** ['ʃuːleɪs] *n* sznurowadło *nt*
**shoemaker** ['ʃuːmeɪkəʳ] *n* szewc *m*
**shoe polish** *n* pasta *f* do butów
**shoe shop** *n* sklep *m* obuwniczy
**shoestring** ['ʃuːstrɪŋ] *n* (*fig*): **on a ~** małym nakładem (środków)
**shoetree** ['ʃuːtriː] *n* prawidło *nt*
**shone** [ʃɔn] *pt, pp of* **shine**
**shoo** [ʃuː] *excl* sio, a kysz ▷ *vt* (*also*: **shoo away, shoo off,** *etc*: *birds*) płoszyć (wypłoszyć *perf*); (*person*) przeganiać (przegonić *perf*)
**shook** [ʃuk] *pt of* **shake**
**shoot** [ʃuːt] (*pt, pp* **shot**) *n* (*on branch*) pęd *m*; (*on seedling*) kiełek *m*; (*Sport*) polowanie *nt* ▷ *vt* (*arrow*) wystrzelić (*perf*); (*gun*) (wy)strzelić (*perf*) z *+gen*; (*kill*) zastrzelić (*perf*); (*wound*) postrzelić (*perf*); (*execute*) rozstrzeliwać (rozstrzelać *perf*); (*Brit*: *game birds*) polować na *+acc*; (*film*) kręcić (nakręcić *perf*) ▷ *vi*: **to ~ (at)** strzelać (strzelić *perf*) (do *+gen*); **to ~ past/through** przemykać (przemknąć *perf*) obok *+gen*/przez *+acc*; **to ~ into** wpadać (wpaść *perf*) do *+gen*
▸ **shoot down** *vt* zestrzeliwać (zestrzelić *perf*)
▸ **shoot in** *vi* wpadać (wpaść *perf*)
▸ **shoot out** *vi* wypadać (wypaść *perf*)
▸ **shoot up** *vi* (*fig*: *inflation etc*) skakać (skoczyć *perf*), podskakiwać (podskoczyć *perf*)
**shooting** ['ʃuːtɪŋ] *n* (*shots*) strzelanina *f*; (*murder*) zastrzelenie *nt*; (*wounding*) postrzelenie *nt*; (*Film*) zdjęcia *pl*, kręcenie *nt* zdjęć; (*Hunting*) polowanie *nt*
**shooting range** *n* strzelnica *f*
**shooting star** *n* spadająca gwiazda *f*
**shop** [ʃɔp] *n* (*selling goods*) sklep *m*; (*workshop*) warsztat *m* ▷ *vi* (*also*: **go shopping**) robić (zrobić *perf*) zakupy; **repair ~** warsztat naprawczy; **to talk ~** (*fig*) rozmawiać o sprawach zawodowych
▸ **shop around** *vi*: **to ~ around (for)** (*lit, fig*) rozglądać się (rozejrzeć się *perf*) (za *+instr*)
**shop assistant** (*Brit*) *n* sprzedawca(-wczyni) *m(f)*
**shop floor** (*Brit*: *Industry*) *n* załoga *f*
**shopkeeper** ['ʃɔpkiːpəʳ] *n* sklepikarz(-arka) *m(f)*
**shoplifter** ['ʃɔplɪftəʳ] *n* złodziej(ka) *m(f)* sklepowy(-wa) *m(f)*
**shoplifting** ['ʃɔplɪftɪŋ] *n* kradzież *f* sklepowa
**shopper** ['ʃɔpəʳ] *n* kupujący(-ca) *m(f)*, klient(ka) *m(f)*
**shopping** ['ʃɔpɪŋ] *n* zakupy *pl*
**shopping bag** *n* torba *f* na zakupy
**shopping centre**, (*US*) **shopping center** *n* centrum *nt* handlowe
**shopping mall** *n* centrum *nt* handlowe
**shop-soiled** ['ʃɔpsɔɪld] *adj* (*goods*) *niepełnowartościowy wskutek długiego leżenia na wystawie, wielokrotnego przymierzania itp.*
**shop steward** (*Brit*: *Industry*) *n* mąż *m* zaufania (*związku zawodowego*)

S

**shop window** *n* witryna *f*, wystawa *f* sklepowa

**shore** [ʃɔːʳ] *n* (*of sea*) brzeg *m*, wybrzeże *nt*; (*of lake*) brzeg *m* ▷ *vt*: **to ~ (up)** podpierać (podeprzeć *perf*); **on ~** na lądzie

**shore leave** (*Naut*) *n* przepustka *f* (na ląd)

**shorn** [ʃɔːn] *pp of* **shear**; **to be ~ of** zostać (*perf*) pozbawionym *+gen*

**short** [ʃɔːt] *adj* (*not long*) krótki; (*not tall*) niski; (*curt*) szorstki ▷ *n* film *m* krótkometrażowy; **money is ~** brakuje pieniędzy; **we are ~ of staff** brakuje nam personelu; **I'm three pounds ~** mam o trzy funty za mało, brakuje mi trzech funtów; **in ~** jednym słowem; **meat/petrol is in ~ supply** brakuje mięsa/benzyny; **~ of sth/doing sth** bez posuwania się do *+gen*; **it is ~ for ...** to skrót od *+gen*; **a ~ time ago** niedawno (temu); **in the ~ term** na krótką metę; **to cut ~** (*speech*) ucinać (uciąć *perf*); (*visit*) skracać (skrócić *perf*); **everything ~ of ...** wszystko z wyjątkiem *+gen*; **to fall ~ of expectations** zawodzić (zawieść *perf*) oczekiwania; **we were running ~ of food** zaczynało nam brakować żywności; **to stop ~** (nagle) przestać (*perf*) *or* przerwać (*perf*); **to stop ~ of** powstrzymywać się (powstrzymać się *perf*) przed *+instr*; *see also* **shorts**

**shortage** ['ʃɔːtɪdʒ] *n*: **a ~ of** niedobór *m +gen*

**shortbread** ['ʃɔːtbrɛd] *n* herbatnik *m* maślany

**short-change** [ʃɔːt'tʃeɪndʒ] *vt*: **to ~ sb** wydawać (wydać *perf*) komuś za mało (reszty)

**short circuit** *n* zwarcie *nt*

**shortcoming** ['ʃɔːtkʌmɪŋ] *n* niedostatek *m*, mankament *m*

**shortcrust pastry** (*Brit*) *n* kruche ciasto *nt*

**short cut** *n* skrót *m*; (*fig*) ułatwienie *nt*; **to take a ~** iść (pójść *perf*) na skróty.

**shorten** ['ʃɔːtn] *vt* skracać (skrócić *perf*)

**shortening** ['ʃɔːtnɪŋ] *n* tłuszcz *m* piekarniczy

**shortfall** ['ʃɔːtfɔːl] *n* niedobór *m*

**shorthand** ['ʃɔːthænd] *n* (*Brit*) stenografia *f*; (*fig*) skrót *m*; **to take sth down in ~** stenografować coś

**shorthand notebook** (*Brit*) *n* notes *m* stenograficzny

**shorthand typist** (*Brit*) *n* stenotypista(-tka) *m(f)*

**short list** (*Brit*) *n* (ostateczna) lista *f* kandydatów

**short-lived** ['ʃɔːt'lɪvd] *adj* krótkotrwały

**shortly** ['ʃɔːtlɪ] *adv* wkrótce

**shorts** [ʃɔːts] *npl* szorty *pl*

**short-sighted** [ʃɔːt'saɪtɪd] *adj* (*lit, fig*) krótkowzroczny

**short-sightedness** [ʃɔːt'saɪtɪdnɪs] *n* krótkowzroczność *f*

**short-staffed** [ʃɔːt'stɑːft] *adj*: **to be ~** mieć niedobory personalne *or* kadrowe

**short story** *n* opowiadanie *nt*, nowela *f*

**short-tempered** [ʃɔːt'tɛmpəd] *adj* zapalczywy, wybuchowy

**short-term** ['ʃɔːttəːm] *adj* krótkoterminowy

**short time** *n*: **to work ~, to be on ~** pracować w niepełnym wymiarze godzin

**short-wave** ['ʃɔːtweɪv] (*Radio*) *adj* krótkofalowy

**shot** [ʃɔt] *pt, pp of* **shoot** ▷ *n* (*of gun*) wystrzał *m*, strzał *m*; (*shotgun pellets*) śrut *m*; (*Football etc*) strzał *m*; (*injection*) zastrzyk *m*; (*Phot*) ujęcie *nt*; **to fire a ~ at sb/sth** strzelać (strzelić *perf*) do kogoś/czegoś; **to have a ~ at sth/doing sth** próbować (spróbować *perf*) czegoś/zrobić coś; **to get ~ of sb/sth** (*inf*) pozbywać się (pozbyć się *perf*) kogoś/czegoś; **a big ~** (*inf*) gruba ryba *f* (*inf*), szycha *f* (*inf*); **a good/poor ~** dobry/zły strzelec; **like a ~** migiem

**shotgun** ['ʃɔtgʌn] *n* śrutówka *f*

**should** [ʃud] *aux vb*: **I ~ go now** powinienem już iść; **he ~ be there now** powinien tam teraz być; **I ~ go if I were you** na twoim miejscu poszłabym; **I ~ like to** chciałbym; **~ he phone ...** gdyby (przypadkiem) dzwonił, ...

**shoulder** ['ʃəuldəʳ] *n* (*Anat*) bark *m* ▷ *vt* (*fig: burden*) brać (wziąć *perf*) na swoje barki; (*responsibility*) brać (wziąć *perf*) na siebie; **to look over one's ~** spoglądać (spojrzeć *perf*) przez ramię; **to rub ~s with sb** (*fig*) ocierać się (otrzeć się *perf*) o kogoś; **to give sb the cold ~** (*fig*) traktować (potraktować *perf*) kogoś ozięble

**shoulder bag** *n* torba *f* na ramię

**shoulder blade** *n* (*Anat*) łopatka *f*

**shoulder strap** *n* (*on clothing*) ramiączko *nt*; (*on bag*) pasek *m*

**shouldn't** ['ʃudnt] = **should not**

**shout** [ʃaut] *n* okrzyk *m* ▷ *vt* krzyczeć (krzyknąć *perf*) ▷ *vi* (*also*: **shout out**) krzyczeć (krzyknąć *perf*), wykrzykiwać (wykrzyknąć *perf*); **to give sb a ~** wołać (zawołać *perf*) kogoś

▸ **shout down** *vt* zakrzykiwać (zakrzyczeć *perf*)

**shouting** ['ʃautɪŋ] *n* krzyki *pl*

**shove** [ʃʌv] *vt* pchać (pchnąć *perf*) ▷ *n*: **to give sb/sth a ~** popychać (popchnąć *perf*) kogoś/coś; **to ~ sth in** (*inf*) wpychać (wepchnąć *perf*) coś; **he ~d me out of the way** zepchnął mnie z drogi

▸ **shove off** (*inf*) *vi* spływać (spłynąć *perf*) (*inf*)

**shovel** ['ʃʌvl] *n* szufla *f*, łopata *f*; (*mechanical*) koparka *f* ▷ *vt* szuflować

**show** [ʃəu] (*pt* **~ed**, *pp* **~n**) *n* (*of emotion*) wyraz *m*, przejaw *m*; (*flower show etc*) wystawa *f*;

(*Theat*) spektakl *m*, przedstawienie *nt*; (*Film*) seans *m*; (*TV*) program *m* rozrywkowy, show *m* ▷ *vt* (*indicate*) pokazywać (pokazać *perf*), wykazywać (wykazać *perf*); (*exhibit*) wystawiać (wystawić *perf*); (*illustrate, depict*) pokazywać (pokazać *perf*), przedstawiać (przedstawić *perf*); (*courage, ability*) wykazywać (wykazać *perf*); (*programme, film*) pokazywać (pokazać *perf*) ▷ *vi* być widocznym; **to ~ sb to his seat/ to the door** odprowadzać (odprowadzić *perf*) kogoś na miejsce/do drzwi; **to ~ a profit/loss** (*Comm*) wykazywać (wykazać *perf*) zyski/ straty; **it ~s** to widać; **it just goes to ~ that ...** to tylko świadczy o tym, że...; **to ask for a ~ of hands** prosić (poprosić *perf*) o głosowanie przez podniesienie ręki; **for ~** na pokaz; **on ~** wystawiony; **who's running the ~ here?** (*inf*) kto tu jest szefem?

▸ **show in** *vt* wprowadzać (wprowadzić *perf*), wpuszczać (wpuścić *perf*)

▸ **show off** *vi* (*pej*) popisywać się ▷ *vt* popisywać się *+instr*

▸ **show out** *vt* odprowadzać (odprowadzić *perf*) do wyjścia

▸ **show up** *vi* (*stand out*) być widocznym; (*inf*: *turn up*) pokazywać się (pokazać się *perf*), pojawiać się (pojawić się *perf*) ▷ *vt* uwidaczniać (uwidocznić *perf*), odsłaniać (odsłonić *perf*)

**show business** *n* przemysł *m* rozrywkowy

**showcase** ['ʃəukeɪs] *n* gablota *f*; (*fig*) wizytówka *f*

**showdown** ['ʃəudaun] *n* ostateczna rozgrywka *f*

**shower** ['ʃauə^r] *n* (*rain*) przelotny deszcz *m*; (*of stones etc*) grad *m*; (*for bathing*) prysznic *m*; (*US*: *party*) *przyjęcie, na którym obdarowuje się prezentami honorowego gościa — zwykle kobietę wychodzącą za mąż lub spodziewającą się dziecka* ▷ *vi* brać (wziąć *perf*) prysznic ▷ *vt*: **to ~ sb with** (*gifts, kisses*) obsypywać (obsypać *perf*) kogoś *+instr*; (*stones, abuse*) obrzucać (obrzucić *perf*) kogoś *+instr*; (*questions*) zasypywać (zasypać *perf*) kogoś *+instr*; **to have** *or* **take a ~** brać (wziąć *perf*) prysznic

**showercap** ['ʃauəkæp] *n* czepek *m* kąpielowy

**showerproof** ['ʃauəpru:f] *adj* przeciwdeszczowy

**showery** ['ʃauərɪ] *adj* deszczowy

**showground** ['ʃəugraund] *n* teren *m* wystawowy

**showing** ['ʃəuɪŋ] *n* (*of film*) projekcja *f*, pokaz *m*

**show jumping** *n* konkurs *m* hipiczny

**showman** ['ʃəumən] (*irreg*: *like* **man**) *n* (*at circus*) artysta *m* cyrkowy; (*at fair*) kuglarz *m*; (*fig*) showman *m*

**showmanship** ['ʃəumənʃɪp] *n* talent *m* showmana

**shown** [ʃəun] *pp of* **show**

**show-off** ['ʃəuɔf] (*inf*) *n*: **he's a ~** lubi się popisywać

**showpiece** ['ʃəupi:s] *n* eksponat *m*; **that hospital is a ~** to (jest) pokazowy szpital

**showroom** ['ʃəurum] *n* salon *m* wystawowy *or* sprzedaży

**showy** ['ʃəuɪ] *adj* ostentacyjny, krzykliwy

**shrank** [ʃræŋk] *pt of* **shrink**

**shrapnel** ['ʃræpnl] *n* szrapnel *m*

**shred** [ʃrɛd] *n* (*usu pl*) strzęp *m*; (*fig*: *of truth*) krzt(yn)a *f*; (: *of evidence*) cień *m* ▷ *vt* (*paper, cloth*) strzępić (postrzępić *perf*); (*Culin*) szatkować (poszatkować *perf*)

**shredder** ['ʃrɛdə^r] *n* (*vegetable shredder*) szatkownica *f*; (*document shredder*) niszczarka *f* dokumentów

**shrew** [ʃru:] *n* (*Zool*) sorek *m*, ryjówka *f*; (*fig*: *pej*) złośnica *f*, jędza *f*

**shrewd** [ʃru:d] *adj* przebiegły, sprytny

**shrewdness** ['ʃru:dnɪs] *n* przebiegłość *f*, spryt *m*

**shriek** [ʃri:k] *n* pisk *m* ▷ *vi* piszczeć (zapiszczeć *perf*)

**shrift** [ʃrɪft] *n*: **to give sb short ~** rozprawiać się (rozprawić się *perf*) z kimś krótko

**shrill** [ʃrɪl] *adj* piskliwy

**shrimp** [ʃrɪmp] *n* krewetka *f*

**shrine** [ʃraɪn] *n* (*Rel*: *place*) miejsce *nt* kultu (*np. grób świętego będący celem pielgrzymek*); (: *container*) relikwiarz *m*; (*fig*) kaplica *f*

**shrink** [ʃrɪŋk] (*pt* **shrank**, *pp* **shrunk**) *vi* kurczyć się (skurczyć się *perf*); (*also*: **shrink away**) wzdrygać się (wzdrygnąć się *perf*) ▷ *n* (*inf*: *pej*) psychiatra *m*; **to ~ from (doing) sth** wzbraniać się od (robienia) czegoś *or* przed robieniem czegoś

**shrinkage** ['ʃrɪŋkɪdʒ] *n* skurczenie się *nt*, zbiegnięcie się *nt*

**shrink-wrap** ['ʃrɪŋkræp] *vt* pakować w folię termokórczliwą

**shrivel** ['ʃrɪvl] (*also*: **shrivel up**) *vt* wysuszać (wysuszyć *perf*) ▷ *vi* wysychać (wyschnąć *perf*)

**shroud** [ʃraud] *n* całun *m* ▷ *vt*: **~ed in mystery** okryty tajemnicą

**Shrove Tuesday** ['ʃrəuv-] *n* ostatki *pl*

**shrub** [ʃrʌb] *n* krzew *m*, krzak *m*

**shrubbery** ['ʃrʌbərɪ] *n* krzewy *pl*, krzaki *pl*

**shrug** [ʃrʌg] *n* wzruszenie *nt* ramion ▷ *vi* wzruszać (wzruszyć *perf*) ramionami ▷ *vt*: **to ~ one's shoulders** wzruszać (wzruszyć *perf*) ramionami

▸ **shrug off** *vt* bagatelizować (zbagatelizować *perf*), nic sobie nie robić z *+gen*

**shrunk** [ʃrʌŋk] *pp of* **shrink**

S

**shrunken** ['ʃrʌŋkn] *adj* skurczony
**shudder** ['ʃʌdəʳ] *n* dreszcz *m* ▷ *vi* dygotać (zadygotać *perf*), wzdrygać się (wzdrygnąć się *perf*); **I ~ to think of it** (*fig*) drżę na (samą) myśl o tym
**shuffle** ['ʃʌfl] *vt* tasować (potasować *perf*) ▷ *vi* iść powłócząc nogami; **to ~ (one's feet)** przestępować (przestąpić *perf*) z nogi na nogę
**shun** [ʃʌn] *vt* (*publicity*) unikać *+gen*; (*neighbours*) stronić od *+gen*
**shunt** [ʃʌnt] *vt* (*train*) przetaczać (przetoczyć *perf*)
**shunting yard** ['ʃʌntɪŋ-] *n* (*Rail*) stacja *f* rozrządowa
**shush** [ʃuʃ] *excl* sza
**shut** [ʃʌt] (*pt, pp* **~**) *vt* zamykać (zamknąć *perf*) ▷ *vi* zamykać się (zamknąć się *perf*); **the shops ~ at six** sklepy zamyka się o szóstej
▶ **shut down** *vt* (*factory etc*) zamykać (zamknąć *perf*); (*machine*) wyłączać (wyłączyć *perf*) ▷ *vi* zostać (*perf*) zamkniętym
▶ **shut off** *vt* (*supply etc*) odcinać (odciąć *perf*); (*view*) zasłaniać (zasłonić *perf*)
▶ **shut out** *vt* (*person, cold*) nie wpuszczać (nie wpuścić *perf*) *+gen* (do środka); (*noise*) tłumić (stłumić *perf*); (*thought*) nie dopuszczać (nie dopuścić *perf*) *+gen* (do siebie)
▶ **shut up** *vi* (*inf*) uciszyć się (*perf*), zamknąć się (*perf*) (*inf*) ▷ *vt* uciszać (uciszyć *perf*)
**shutdown** ['ʃʌtdaun] *n* (*temporary*) przerwa *f* (w pracy); (*permanent*) zamknięcie *nt*
**shutter** ['ʃʌtəʳ] *n* (*on window*) okiennica *f*; (*Phot*) migawka *f*
**shuttle** ['ʃʌtl] *n* (*plane etc*) *środek transportu kursujący tam i z powrotem (wahadłowo)*; (*space shuttle*) prom *m* kosmiczny; (*also*: **shuttle service**) linia *f* lokalna; (*for weaving*) czółenko *nt* ▷ *vi*: **to ~ to and fro/between** kursować tam i z powrotem/pomiędzy *+instr* ▷ *vt* (*passengers*) transportować (przetransportować *perf*); (*troops*) przerzucać (przerzucić *perf*)
**shuttlecock** ['ʃʌtlkɔk] *n* lotka *f*
**shy** [ʃaɪ] *adj* (*person*) nieśmiały; (*animal*) płochliwy ▷ *vi*: **to shy away from doing sth** (*fig*) wzbraniać się przed robieniem czegoś; **to fight shy of** starać się unikać *+gen*; **to be shy of doing sth** wstydzić się coś (z)robić (*perf*)
**shyly** ['ʃaɪlɪ] *adv* nieśmiało
**shyness** ['ʃaɪnɪs] *n* nieśmiałość *f*
**Siam** [saɪ'æm] *n* Syjam *m*
**Siamese** [saɪə'mi:z] *adj*: **~ cat** kot *m* syjamski; **~ twins** bliźnięta syjamskie
**Siberia** [saɪ'bɪərɪə] *n* Syberia *f*
**sibling** ['sɪblɪŋ] *n* (*brother*) brat *nt*; (*sister*) siostra *nt*; **~s** rodzeństwo *nt*
**Sicilian** [sɪ'sɪlɪən] *adj* sycylijski ▷ *n* Sycylijczyk(-jka) *m(f)*
**Sicily** ['sɪsɪlɪ] *n* Sycylia *f*
**sick** [sɪk] *adj* chory; (*humour*) niesmaczny; **to be ~** wymiotować (zwymiotować *perf*); **I feel ~** jest mi niedobrze; **to fall ~** zachorować (*perf*); **to be (off) ~** być na zwolnieniu (lekarskim); **a ~ person** chory(-ra) *m(f)*; **I am ~ of** (*fig*) niedobrze mi się robi od *+gen*
**sickbag** ['sɪkbæg] *n* (*on airplane*) torebka *f* higieniczna
**sickbay** ['sɪkbeɪ] *n* izba *f* chorych; (*on ship*) szpital *m* pokładowy
**sickbed** ['sɪkbɛd] *n* łóżko *nt* (chorego)
**sicken** ['sɪkn] *vt* napawać obrzydzeniem ▷ *vi*: **to be ~ing for a cold/flu** mieć pierwsze objawy przeziębienia/grypy
**sickening** ['sɪknɪŋ] *adj* (*fig*) obrzydliwy
**sickle** ['sɪkl] *n* sierp *m*
**sick leave** *n* zwolnienie *nt* (lekarskie)
**sick list** *n* lista *f* chorych
**sickly** ['sɪklɪ] *adj* chorowity; (*smell*) mdły
**sickness** ['sɪknɪs] *n* (*illness*) choroba *f*; (*vomiting*) wymioty *pl*
**sickness benefit** *n* zasiłek *m* chorobowy
**sick pay** *n* zasiłek *m* chorobowy
**sickroom** ['sɪkru:m] *n* pokój *m* chorego
**side** [saɪd] *n* strona *f*; (*of body*) bok *m*; (*team*) przeciwnik *m*; (*of hill*) zbocze *nt* ▷ *adj* boczny ▷ *vi*: **to ~ with sb** stawać (stanąć *perf*) po czyjejś stronie; **by the ~ of** przy *+instr*; **~ by ~** (*work*) wspólnie; (*stand*) obok siebie; **the right/wrong ~** właściwa/niewłaściwa strona; **they are on our ~** są po naszej stronie; **she never left my ~** zawsze była przy moim boku; **to put sth to one ~** odkładać (odłożyć *perf*) coś na bok; **from ~ to ~** z boku na bok; **I'm not going to take ~s** nie stanę po niczyjej stronie; **a ~ of beef** pół tuszy wołowej
**sideboard** ['saɪdbɔ:d] *n* (niski) kredens *m* (*w jadalni*); **sideboards** (*Brit*) *npl* = **sideburns**
**sideburns** ['saɪdbə:nz] *npl* baczki *pl*
**sidecar** ['saɪdkɑ:ʳ] *n* przyczepa *f* (motocykla)
**side dish** *n sałatka lub inny dodatek do dania głównego*
**side drum** *n* werbel *m*
**side effect** *n* (*Med*) działanie *nt* uboczne; (*fig*) skutek *m* uboczny
**sidekick** ['saɪdkɪk] (*inf*) *n* pomagier *m* (*inf*)
**sidelight** ['saɪdlaɪt] *n* światło *nt* boczne
**sideline** ['saɪdlaɪn] *n* (*Sport*) linia *f* boczna; (*fig*) dodatkowy etat *m*; **to wait/stand on the ~s** (*fig*) stać z boku
**sidelong** ['saɪdlɔŋ] *adj*: **to give sb a ~ glance** spoglądać (spojrzeć *perf*) na kogoś ukradkiem; **to exchange ~ glances**

wymieniać (wymienić *perf*) porozumiewawcze spojrzenia
**side plate** *n* talerzyk *m* na sałatkę
**side road** *n* boczna droga *f*
**side-saddle** ['saɪdsædl] *adv* siodło *nt* damskie
**sideshow** ['saɪdʃəu] *n jedna z pomniejszych atrakcji w wesołym miasteczku lub towarzysząca występom cyrku, np. strzelnica lub teatrzyk kukiełkowy*
**sidestep** ['saɪdstɛp] *vt* (*fig*) omijać (ominąć *perf*) ▷ *vi* robić (zrobić *perf*) unik
**side street** *n* boczna uliczka *f*
**sidetrack** ['saɪdtræk] *vt* (*fig*) odwracać (odwrócić *perf*) uwagę *+gen*
**sidewalk** ['saɪdwɔːk] (*US*) *n* chodnik *m*
**sideways** ['saɪdweɪz] *adv* (*lean*) na bok; (*go in, move*) bokiem; (*look*) z ukosa
**siding** ['saɪdɪŋ] *n* bocznica *f*
**sidle** ['saɪdl] *vi*: **to ~ up (to)** podchodzić (podejść *perf*) ukradkiem *or* chyłkiem (do *+gen*)
**SIDS** (*Med*) *n abbr* (= *sudden infant death syndrome*) zespół *m* nagłej śmierci niemowląt
**siege** [siːdʒ] *n* oblężenie *nt*; **to be under ~** być oblężonym; **to lay ~ to** oblegać (oblec *perf*) *+acc*
**siege economy** *n* antyimportowa polityka *f* gospodarcza
**Sierra Leone** [sɪ'ɛrəlɪ'əun] *n* Sierra Leone *nt inv*
**siesta** [sɪ'ɛstə] *n* sjesta *f*
**sieve** [sɪv] *n* sito *nt*; (*small*) sitko *nt* ▷ *vt* przesiewać (przesiać *perf*)
**sift** [sɪft] *vt* (*flour etc*) przesiewać (przesiać *perf*); (*also*: **sift through**: *documents etc*) segregować (posegregować *perf*)
**sigh** [saɪ] *n* westchnienie *nt* ▷ *vi* wzdychać (westchnąć *perf*); **to breathe a ~ of relief** odetchnąć (*perf*) z ulgą
**sight** [saɪt] *n* (*faculty*) wzrok *m*; (*spectacle*) widok *m*; (*on gun*) celownik *m* ▷ *vt* widzieć, zobaczyć (*perf*); **in ~** w zasięgu wzroku; **on ~** (*shoot*) bez uprzedzenia; **out of ~** poza zasięgiem wzroku; **payable at ~** płatny za okazaniem *or* awista; **at first ~** na pierwszy rzut oka; **love at first ~** miłość od pierwszego wejrzenia; **I know her by ~** znam ją z widzenia; **to catch ~ of sb/sth** dostrzegać (dostrzec *perf*) kogoś/coś; **to lose ~ of sth** (*fig*) tracić (stracić *perf*) coś z oczu; **to set one's ~s on sth** stawiać (postawić *perf*) sobie coś za cel
**sighted** ['saɪtɪd] *adj* widzący; **partially ~** niedowidzący
**sightseeing** ['saɪtsiːɪŋ] *n* zwiedzanie *nt*; **to go ~** udawać się (udać się *perf*) na zwiedzanie
**sightseer** ['saɪtsiːəʳ] *n* zwiedzający(-ca) *m(f)*
**sign** [saɪn] *n* (*symbol*) znak *m*; (*notice*) napis *m*; (*with hand*) gest *m*; (*indication, evidence*) oznaka *f* (*usu pl*); (*also*: **road sign**) znak *m* drogowy ▷ *vt* (*document*) podpisywać (podpisać *perf*); (*Football etc*: *player*) pozyskiwać (pozyskać *perf*); **a ~ of the times** znak czasu; **it's a good/bad ~** to dobry/zły znak; **plus/minus ~** znak dodawania/odejmowania; **there's no ~ of her changing her mind** nic nie wskazuje na to, by miała zmienić zdanie; **he was showing ~s of improvement** wykazywał oznaki poprawy; **to ~ one's name** podpisywać się (podpisać się *perf*); **to ~ sth over to sb** przepisywać (przepisać *perf*) coś na kogoś
▸ **sign away** *vt* (*independence*) wyrzekać się (wyrzec się *perf*) *+gen*; (*rights, property*) zrzekać się (zrzec się *perf*) *+gen*
▸ **sign in** *vi* (*in hotel*) meldować się (zameldować się *perf*); (*in club etc*) wpisywać się (wpisać się *perf*) (*do księgi gości*)
▸ **sign off** *vi* (*Radio, TV*) kończyć (zakończyć *perf*) emisję; (*in letter*) kończyć (skończyć *perf*)
▸ **sign on** *vi* (*Mil*) zaciągać się (zaciągnąć się *perf*); (*for course*) zapisywać się (zapisać się *perf*); (*Brit*: *as unemployed*) zgłaszać się (zgłosić się *perf*) (*w urzędzie d/s bezrobotnych*) ▷ *vt* (*Mil*) wcielać (wcielić *perf*) do służby wojskowej; (*employee*) przyjmować (przyjąć *perf*)
▸ **sign out** *vi* (*from hotel etc*) wymeldowywać się (wymeldować się *perf*)
▸ **sign up** *vi* (*Mil*) wstępować (wstąpić *perf*) do wojska; (*for course*) zapisywać się (zapisać się *perf*) ▷ *vt* werbować (zwerbować *perf*)
**signal** ['sɪgnl] *n* sygnał *m*; (*Rail*) semafor *m* ▷ *vi* (*Aut*) włączać (włączyć *perf*) migacz *or* kierunkowskaz ▷ *vt* dawać (dać *perf*) znak *+dat*; **to ~ a right/left turn** włączać (włączyć *perf*) prawy/lewy migacz *or* kierunkowskaz
**signal box** *n* (*Rail*) nastawnia *f*
**signalman** [sɪgnlmən] (*irreg*: *like* **man**) *n* nastawniczy *m*
**signatory** ['sɪgnətərɪ] *n* sygnatariusz *m*
**signature** ['sɪgnətʃəʳ] *n* podpis *m*
**signature tune** *n* sygnał *m* programu
**signet ring** ['sɪgnət-] *n* sygnet *m*
**significance** [sɪg'nɪfɪkəns] *n* znaczenie *nt*; **that is of no ~** to jest bez znaczenia
**significant** [sɪg'nɪfɪkənt] *adj* znaczący; **it is ~ that ...** znamienne jest, że...
**significantly** [sɪg'nɪfɪkəntlɪ] *adv* (*improve, increase*) znacznie; (*smile*) znacząco
**signify** ['sɪgnɪfaɪ] *vt* oznaczać; (*person*) dawać (dać *perf*) do zrozumienia
**sign language** *n* język *m* migowy
**signpost** ['saɪnpəust] *n* drogowskaz *m*; (*fig*) wskazówka *f*

S

**Sikh** [si:k] *n* Sikh(ijka) *m(f)* ▷ *adj* sikhijski
**silage** ['saılıdʒ] *n* kiszonka *f*
**silence** ['saıləns] *n* cisza *f*; (*someone's*) milczenie *nt* ▷ *vt* uciszać (uciszyć *perf*); (*fig*) zamykać (zamknąć *perf*) usta *+dat*
**silencer** ['saılənsəʳ] *n* tłumik *m*
**silent** ['saılənt] *adj* (*quiet*) cichy; (*taciturn*) małomówny; (*film*) niemy; **to remain ~** zachowywać (zachować *perf*) milczenie
**silently** ['saıləntlı] *adv* (*quietly*) cicho; (*without speaking*) w milczeniu
**silent partner** *n* cichy wspólnik *m*
**silhouette** [sılu:'ɛt] *n* zarys *m*, sylwetka *f* ▷ *vt*: **~d against** rysujący się na tle *+gen*
**silicon** ['sılıkən] *n* krzem *m*
**silicon chip** *n* (krzemowy) obwód *m* scalony
**silicone** ['sılıkəun] *n* silikon *m*
**Silicon Valley** *n* Dolina *f* Krzemowa
**silk** [sılk] *n* jedwab *m* ▷ *adj* jedwabny
**silky** ['sılkı] *adj* jedwabisty
**sill** [sıl] *n* (*also*: **window sill**) parapet *m* (okienny); (*of door*) próg *m*
**silly** ['sılı] *adj* głupi, niemądry; **to do something ~** robić (zrobić *perf*) coś głupiego
**silo** ['saıləu] *n* (*on farm*) silos *m*; (*for missile*) podziemna wyrzutnia *f* rakietowa
**silt** [sılt] *n* muł *m*
▸ **silt up** *vi* zamulać się (zamulić się *perf*) ▷ *vt* zamulać (zamulić *perf*)
**silver** ['sılvəʳ] *n* (*metal*) srebro *nt*; (*coins*) bilon *m*; (*items made of silver*) srebra *pl* ▷ *adj* srebrny
**silver foil** (*Brit*) *n* (*kitchen*) folia *f* aluminiowa; (*wrapping*) cynfolia *f*
**silver paper** (*Brit*) *n* cynfolia *f*
**silver-plated** [sılvə'pleıtıd] *adj* posrebrzany
**silversmith** ['sılvəsmıθ] *n* złotnik *m*
**silverware** ['sılvəwɛəʳ] *n* srebra *pl* stołowe
**silver wedding (anniversary)** *n* srebrne wesele *nt*
**silvery** ['sılvrı] *adj* srebrzysty
**similar** ['sımıləʳ] *adj*: **~ (to)** podobny (do *+gen*)
**similarity** [sımı'lærıtı] *n* podobieństwo *nt*
**similarly** ['sımıləlı] *adv* podobnie
**simile** ['sımılı] *n* (*Ling*) porównanie *nt*
**simmer** ['sıməʳ] (*Culin*) *vi* gotować się (na wolnym ogniu)
▸ **simmer down** (*inf*) *vi* (*fig*) ochłonąć (*perf*)
**simper** ['sımpəʳ] *vi* uśmiechać się niemądrze
**simpering** ['sımprıŋ] *adj* (*person*) uśmiechający się niemądrze; (*smile*) niemądry
**simple** ['sımpl] *adj* (*easy, plain*) prosty; (*foolish*) ograniczony
**simple interest** (*Comm*) *n* odsetki *pl* proste *or* zwykłe
**simple-minded** [sımpl'maındıd] (*pej*) *adj* naiwny
**simpleton** ['sımpltən] (*pej*) *n* prostak(-aczka) *m(f)* (*pej*)
**simplicity** [sım'plısıtı] *n* prostota *f*
**simplification** [sımplıfı'keıʃən] *n* uproszczenie *nt*
**simplify** ['sımplıfaı] *vt* upraszczać (uprościć *perf*)
**simply** ['sımplı] *adv* (*just, merely*) po prostu; (*in a simple way*) prosto
**simulate** ['sımjuleıt] *vt* (*enthusiasm, innocence*) udawać; (*illness*) symulować, pozorować
**simulated** ['sımjuleıtıd] *adj* (*pleasure*) udawany; (*nuclear explosion*) symulowany; (*fur, hair*) sztuczny
**simulation** [sımju'leıʃən] *n* udawanie *nt*; (*Tech*) symulacja *f*
**simultaneous** [sıməl'teınıəs] *adj* (*broadcast*) równoczesny; (*translation*) symultaniczny, równoległy
**simultaneously** [sıməl'teınıəslı] *adv* równocześnie
**sin** [sın] *n* grzech *m* ▷ *vi* grzeszyć (zgrzeszyć *perf*)
**Sinai** ['saıneıaı] *n* Synaj *m*
**since** [sıns] *adv* od tego czasu ▷ *prep* od *+gen* ▷ *conj* (*time*) odkąd; (*because*) ponieważ; **~ then, ever ~** od tego czasu
**sincere** [sın'sıəʳ] *adj* szczery
**sincerely** [sın'sıəlı] *adv* szczerze; **Yours ~** Z poważaniem
**sincerity** [sın'sɛrıtı] *n* szczerość *f*
**sine** [saın] (*Math*) *n* sinus *m*
**sine qua non** [sınıkwɑ:'nɔn] *n* warunek *m* sine qua non *or* konieczny
**sinew** ['sınju:] *n* ścięgno *nt*
**sinful** ['sınful] *adj* grzeszny
**sing** [sıŋ] (*pt* **sang**, *pp* **sung**) *vt* śpiewać (zaśpiewać *perf*) ▷ *vi* śpiewać (zaśpiewać *perf*)
**Singapore** [sıŋgə'pɔ:ʳ] *n* Singapur *m*
**singe** [sındʒ] *vt* przypalać (przypalić *perf*)
**singer** ['sıŋəʳ] *n* (*in opera etc*) śpiewak(-aczka) *m(f)*; (*pop, rock etc*) piosenkarz(-arka) *m(f)*
**Singhalese** [sıŋə'li:z] *adj* = **Sinhalese**
**singing** ['sıŋıŋ] *n* śpiew *m*; **a ~ in the ears** dzwonienie w uszach
**single** ['sıŋgl] *adj* (*solitary*) jeden; (*individual, not double*) pojedynczy; (*unmarried: man*) nieżonaty; (*: woman*) niezamężny ▷ *n* (*Brit: also*: **single ticket**) bilet *m* (w jedną stronę); (*record*) singel *m*; **not a ~ one was left** nie pozostał ani jeden; **every ~ day** każdego dnia; **~ spacing** (*Typ*) pojedynczy odstęp (*między wierszami*)
▸ **single out** *vt* wybierać (wybrać *perf*)
**single bed** *n* łóżko *nt* pojedyncze
**single-breasted** ['sıŋglbrɛstıd] *adj* (*jacket*) jednorzędowy

**single file** *n*: **in ~** gęsiego
**single-handed** [sɪŋgl'hændɪd] *adv* bez niczyjej pomocy; *(sail)* samotnie
**single-minded** [sɪŋgl'maɪndɪd] *adj*: **to be ~** mieć (tylko) jeden cel
**single parent** *n (mother)* samotna matka *f*; *(father)* samotny ojciec *m*
**single room** *n* pokój *m* pojedynczy
**singles** ['sɪŋglz] *npl (Tennis)* singel *m*, gra *f* singlowa *or* pojedyncza
**singles bar** *n* bar *m* dla samotnych
**singly** ['sɪŋglɪ] *adv* pojedynczo
**singsong** ['sɪŋsɔŋ] *adj (intonation etc)* jednostajnie wznoszący się i opadający ▷ *n* wspólne śpiewanie *nt*
**singular** ['sɪŋgjuləʳ] *adj (outstanding)* wyjątkowy; *(Ling)* pojedynczy; *(odd)* szczególny ▷ *n (Ling)* liczba *f* pojedyncza; **in the feminine ~** w liczbie pojedynczej rodzaju żeńskiego
**singularly** ['sɪŋgjuləlɪ] *adv* wyjątkowo
**Sinhalese** [sɪnhə'li:z] *adj* syngaleski
**sinister** ['sɪnɪstəʳ] *adj (event, implications)* złowróżbny, złowieszczy; *(figure)* złowrogi, groźny
**sink** [sɪŋk] *(pt* **sank**, *pp* **sunk***) n* zlew *m*, zlewozmywak *m* ▷ *vt (ship)* zatapiać (zatopić *perf*); *(well, foundations)* wykopywać (wykopać *perf*) ▷ *vi (ship)* tonąć (zatonąć *perf*); *(heart)* zamierać (zamrzeć *perf*); *(ground)* zapadać się (zapaść się *perf*); *(also:* **sink down***: in exhaustion)* osuwać się (osunąć się *perf*); **to ~ one's teeth/claws into** zatapiać (zatopić *perf*) zęby/pazury w *+loc*; **he sank (back) into a chair** *(in exhaustion)* opadł na fotel; *(getting comfortable)* zagłębił się w fotelu; **he sank into the mud** wpadł w błoto; **I had that ~ing feeling** poczułem się niewyraźnie
▸ **sink in** *vi (fig)*: **it took a moment for her words to ~ in** dopiero po chwili dotarło do mnie, co powiedziała
**sinking fund** *n* fundusz *m* amortyzacyjny
**sink unit** *n* zlewozmywak *m (z obudową)*
**sinner** ['sɪnəʳ] *n* grzesznik(-ica) *m(f)*
**Sino-** ['saɪnəu] *pref* sino-
**sinuous** ['sɪnjuəs] *adj (snake)* wijący się
**sinus** ['saɪnəs] *(Anat) n* zatoka *f*
**sip** [sɪp] *n* łyk *m*, łyczek *m* ▷ *vt* popijać *(małymi łykami)*
**siphon** ['saɪfən] *n* syfon *m*
▸ **siphon off** *vt (liquid)* ociągać (odciągnąć *perf*); *(money)* odprowadzać (odprowadzić *perf*) *(niezgodnie z pierwotnym przeznaczeniem)*
**sir** [səʳ] *n uprzejma forma zwracania się do mężczyzn, zwłaszcza w sytuacjach formalnych*; **what would you like, sir?** czego Pan sobie życzy?; **yes, sir** tak, proszę Pana; *(Mil)* tak jest; **Sir John Smith** Sir John Smith *(tytuł szlachecki)*; **Dear Sir** Szanowny Panie
**siren** ['saɪərn] *n* syrena *f*
**sirloin** ['sə:lɔɪn] *n (also:* **sirloin steak***)* befsztyk *m* z polędwicy
**sirocco** [sɪ'rɔkəu] *n* sirocco *m or nt*
**sisal** ['saɪsəl] *n* sizal *m*
**sissy** ['sɪsɪ] *(inf, pej) n (boy, man)* baba *f (inf, pej)*
**sister** ['sɪstəʳ] *n (relation, nun)* siostra *f*; *(Brit: nurse)* siostra *f* oddziałowa ▷ *cpd (ship, city)* siostrzany
**sister-in-law** ['sɪstərɪnlɔ:] *n (husband's sister, wife's sister)* szwagierka *f*; *(brother's wife)* bratowa *f*, szwagierka *f*
**sit** [sɪt] *(pt, pp* **sat***) vi (sit down)* siadać (usiąść *perf*); *(be sitting)* siedzieć; *(for painter)* pozować; *(assembly)* obradować ▷ *vt (exam)* zdawać, przystępować (przystąpić *perf*) do *+gen*; **to sit on** *(committee etc)* zasiadać (zasiąść *perf*) w *+loc*; **to sit tight** nie podejmować żadnych działań
▸ **sit about** *vi* przesiadywać
▸ **sit around** *vi* = **sit about**
▸ **sit back** *vi* rozsiadać się (rozsiąść się *perf*), siadać (usiąść *perf*) wygodnie
▸ **sit down** *vi* siadać (usiąść *perf*); **to be sitting down** siedzieć
▸ **sit in on** *vt fus* być obecnym na *+loc*
▸ **sit up** *vi (after lying)* podnosić się (podnieść się *perf*); *(straight)* wyprostowywać się (wyprostować się *perf*); *(stay up)* nie kłaść się (spać)
**sitcom** ['sɪtkɔm] *(TV) n abbr* = **situation comedy**
**sit-down** ['sɪtdaun] *adj*: **a ~ strike** strajk *m* okupacyjny; **a ~ meal** posiłek spożywany przy stole
**site** [saɪt] *n* miejsce *nt*; *(also:* **building site***)* plac *m* budowy; *(Comput)* witryna *f* internetowa ▷ *vt (factory)* lokalizować (zlokalizować *perf*); *(missiles)* rozmieszczać (rozmieścić *perf*)
**sit-in** ['sɪtɪn] *n* okupacja *f* (budynku) *(na znak protestu)*
**siting** ['saɪtɪŋ] *n* lokalizacja *f*
**sitter** ['sɪtəʳ] *n (for painter)* model(ka) *m(f)*; *(also:* **baby-sitter***)* opiekun(ka) *m(f)* do dziecka
**sitting** ['sɪtɪŋ] *n (of assembly)* posiedzenie *nt*; *(in canteen)* zmiana *f (osób jedzących posiłek)*; **at a single ~** za jednym posiedzeniem
**sitting member** *(Pol) n* poseł/posłanka *m/f* bieżącej kadencji
**sitting room** *n* salon *m*
**sitting tenant** *(Brit) n* lokator(ka) *m(f) (wynajmujący dom lub mieszkanie na stałe)*
**situate** ['sɪtjueɪt] *vt* umieszczać (umieścić *perf*) *(w kontekście)*

S

**situated** ['sɪtjueɪtɪd] *adj* położony; **to be ~** znajdować się; (*town etc*) być położonym
**situation** [sɪtju'eɪʃən] *n* (*state*) sytuacja *f*; (*job*) posada *f*; (*location*) położenie *nt*; **"~s vacant"** (*Brit*) ≈ „Praca" (*rubryka w ogłoszeniach gazetowych*)
**situation comedy** *n* (*TV*) komedia *f* sytuacyjna
**six** [sɪks] *num* sześć
**sixteen** [sɪks'ti:n] *num* szesnaście
**sixth** ['sɪksθ] *num* szósty; **the upper/lower ~** (*Brit*) *ostatni/przedostatni rok nauki w szkole średniej*
**sixth sense** *n* szósty zmysł *m*
**sixty** ['sɪkstɪ] *num* sześćdziesiąt
**size** [saɪz] *n* wielkość *f*; (*of project etc*) rozmiary *pl*; (*of clothing, shoes*) rozmiar *m*, numer *m*; **I take ~ 14** (*dress etc*) ≈ noszę rozmiar 42; **the small/large ~** (*of soap powder etc*) małe/duże opakowanie; **it's the ~ of** jest wielkości *+gen*; **cut to ~** przycięty na miarę
▸ **size up** *vt* (*person*) mierzyć (zmierzyć *perf*) wzrokiem; (*situation*) oceniać (ocenić *perf*)
**sizeable** ['saɪzəbl] *adj* spory, pokaźny
**sizzle** ['sɪzl] *vi* skwierczeć
**SK** (*Canada*) *abbr* = **Saskatchewan**
**skate** [skeɪt] *n* (*ice skate*) łyżwa *f*; (*roller skate*) wrotka *f*; (*fish*) płaszczka *f* ▹ *vi* (*on ice*) jeździć na łyżwach; (*roller skate*) jeździć na wrotkach
▸ **skate around, skate over** *vt fus* (*avoid dealing with*) prześlizgiwać się (prześlizgnąć się *perf*) nad *+instr*; (*deal with superficially*) prześlizgiwać się (prześlizgnąć się *perf*) po *+loc*
**skateboard** ['skeɪtbɔ:d] *n* deskorolka *f*
**skater** ['skeɪtə^r] *n* (*on ice*) łyżwiarz(-arka) *m(f)*; (*on roller skates*) wrotkarz(-arka) *m(f)*
**skating** ['skeɪtɪŋ] *n* jazda *f* na łyżwach; (*Sport*) łyżwiarstwo *nt*; **figure ~** łyżwiarstwo figurowe, jazda figurowa na lodzie
**skating rink** *n* lodowisko *nt*
**skeleton** ['skɛlɪtn] *n* (*Anat, Tech*) szkielet *m*; (*outline*) zarys *m*
**skeleton key** *n* klucz *m* uniwersalny
**skeleton staff** *n* niezbędny personel *m*
**skeptic** *etc* (*US*) = **sceptic** *etc*
**sketch** [skɛtʃ] *n* (*drawing, outline*) szkic *m*; (*Theat, TV*) skecz *m* ▹ *vt* szkicować (naszkicować *perf*); (*also*: **sketch out**) nakreślać (nakreślić *perf*), zarysowywać (zarysować *perf*)
**sketchbook** ['skɛtʃbuk] *n* szkicownik *m*
**sketchpad** ['skɛtʃpæd] *n* blok *m* rysunkowy
**sketchy** ['skɛtʃɪ] *adj* pobieżny
**skew** [skju:] *adj* przekrzywiony
**skewed** [skju:d] *adj* wypaczony
**skewer** ['skju:ə^r] *n* (*Culin*) szpikulec *m* (*do zrazów, szaszłyków itp*)

**ski** [ski:] *n* narta *f* ▹ *vi* jeździć na nartach
**ski boot** *n* but *m* narciarski
**skid** [skɪd] *n* (*Aut*) poślizg *m* ▹ *vi*: **the car ~ded** samochód zarzuciło; **we ~ded** zarzuciło nas; **to go into a ~** wpadać (wpaść *perf*) w poślizg
**skid marks** *npl* ślady *pl* poślizgu
**skier** ['ski:ə^r] *n* narciarz(-arka) *m(f)*
**skiing** ['ski:ɪŋ] *n* jazda *f* na nartach; (*Sport*) narciarstwo *nt*; **to go ~** wybierać się (wybrać się *perf*) na narty
**ski instructor** *n* instruktor *m* narciarski
**ski jump** *n* (*event*) skoki *pl* (narciarskie); (*ramp*) skocznia *f* (narciarska)
**skilful**, (*US*) **skillful** ['skɪlful] *adj* (*negotiator etc*) wprawny; (*handling of situation*) umiejętny, zręczny
**ski lift** *n* wyciąg *m* narciarski
**skill** [skɪl] *n* (*dexterity*) wprawa *f*, zręczność *f*; (*expertise*) umiejętności *pl*; (*work or art requiring training*) umiejętność *f*
**skilled** [skɪld] *adj* (*worker*) wykwalifikowany; **~ and semi-~ work** praca dla osób w pełni i częściowo wykwalifikowanych
**skillet** ['skɪlɪt] *n* patelnia *f*
**skillful** ['skɪlful] (*US*) *adj* = **skilful**
**skil(l)fully** ['skɪlfəlɪ] *adv* umiejętnie, zręcznie
**skim** [skɪm] *vt* (*also*: **skim off**: *cream, fat*) zbierać (zebrać *perf*); (*glide over*) prześlizgiwać się (prześlizgnąć się *perf*) po *+loc*; (*also*: **skim through**) przeglądać (przejrzeć *perf*) (pobieżnie)
**skimmed milk** [skɪmd-] *n* ≈ chude mleko *nt*
**skimp** [skɪmp] (*also*: **skimp on**) *vt* żałować *or* skąpić *+gen*
**skimpy** ['skɪmpɪ] *adj* (*meal*) skąpy; (*skirt*) kusy
**skin** [skɪn] *n* (*of person, animal*) skóra *f*; (*of fruit*) skórka *f*; (*complexion*) cera *f* ▹ *vt* (*animal*) zdejmować (zdjąć *perf*) skórę z *+gen*; **wet** *or* **soaked to the ~** przemoczony *or* przemoknięty do suchej nitki
**skin cancer** *n* rak *m* skóry
**skin-deep** ['skɪn'di:p] *adj* powierzchowny
**skin diver** *n* płetwonurek *m*
**skin diving** *n* płetwonurkowanie *nt*
**skinflint** ['skɪnflɪnt] *n* kutwa *m/f*, sknera *m/f*
**skin graft** *n* przeszczep *m* skóry
**skinhead** ['skɪnhɛd] *n* skinhead *m*, skin *m*
**skinny** ['skɪnɪ] *adj* chudy
**skin test** *n* (*Med*) próba *f* skórna
**skintight** ['skɪntaɪt] *adj* obcisły
**skip** [skɪp] *n* (*movement*) podskok *m*; (*Brit*: *for rubbish, debris*) kontener *m* ▹ *vi* (*jump*) podskakiwać (podskoczyć *perf*); (*with rope*) skakać przez skakankę ▹ *vt* (*pass over*) opuszczać (opuścić *perf*), pomijać (pominąć *perf*); (*miss*: *lunch etc*) nie jeść *+gen*; (: *lecture etc*)

nie iść (nie pójść *perf*) na *+acc*; **to ~ school** (*esp US*) nie iść (nie pójść *perf*) do szkoły
**ski pants** *npl* spodnie *pl* narciarskie
**ski pole** *n* kijek *m* do nart
**skipper** ['skɪpəʳ] *n* (*Naut*) szyper *m*; (*inf: Sport*) kapitan *m* ▷ *vt* być kapitanem *+gen*
**skipping rope** ['skɪpɪŋ-] *n* skakanka *f*
**ski resort** *n* ośrodek *m* narciarski
**skirmish** ['skəːmɪʃ] *n* (*Mil*) potyczka *f*; (*political etc*) utarczka *f*
**skirt** [skəːt] *n* spódnica *f* ▷ *vt* (*fig: issue etc*) unikać podjęcia *+gen*
**skirting board** ['skəːtɪŋ-] *n* listwa *f* przypodłogowa
**ski run** *n* trasa *f* narciarska
**ski slope** *n* stok *m* narciarski
**ski suit** *n* kombinezon *m* narciarski
**skit** [skɪt] *n* skecz *m*
**ski tow** *n* wyciąg *m* narciarski
**skittle** ['skɪtl] *n* kręgiel *m*
**skittles** ['skɪtlz] *n* kręgle *pl*
**skive** [skaɪv] (*Brit: inf*) *vi* obijać się (*inf*)
**skulk** [skʌlk] *vi* przyczaić się (*perf*), przycupnąć (*perf*)
**skull** [skʌl] *n* czaszka *f*
**skullcap** ['skʌlkæp] *n* (*of Catholic priest*) piuska *f*; (*of Jew*) jarmułka *f*, mycka *f*
**skunk** [skʌŋk] *n* skunks *m*
**sky** [skaɪ] *n* niebo *nt*; **to praise sb to the skies** wychwalać kogoś pod niebiosa
**sky-blue** [skaɪ'bluː] *adj* błękitny
**skylark** ['skaɪlɑːk] *n* skowronek *m*
**skylight** ['skaɪlaɪt] *n* świetlik *m* (*okno*)
**skyline** ['skaɪlaɪn] *n* linia *f* horyzontu; (*of city*) sylwetka *f*
**skyscraper** ['skaɪskreɪpəʳ] *n* drapacz *m* chmur
**slab** [slæb] *n* (*of stone, wood*) płyta *f*; (*of cake, cheese*) kawał *m*
**slack** [slæk] *adj* (*trousers, skin*) obwisły; (*security, discipline*) rozluźniony; (*period, season*) martwy ▷ *n* (*in rope etc*) luźny kawałek *m*; **slacks** *npl* spodnie *pl*; **the business/market is ~** panuje zastój w interesach/na rynku
**slacken** ['slækn] *vi* (*also:* **slacken off**: *speed, demand*) maleć (zmaleć *perf*); (*: depression, effort*) tracić (stracić *perf*) na sile; (*: rain*) słabnąć (osłabnąć *perf*) ▷ *vt* zwalniać (zwolnić *perf*)
**slag heap** [slæg-] *n* hałda *f*
**slag off** (*Brit: inf*) *vt* przygadywać (przygadać *perf*) *+dat* (*inf*)
**slain** [sleɪn] *pp of* **slay**
**slake** [sleɪk] *vt*: **to ~ one's thirst** gasić (ugasić *perf*) pragnienie
**slalom** ['slɑːləm] *n* slalom *m*
**slam** [slæm] *vt* (*door*) trzaskać (trzasnąć *perf*) *+instr*; (*money, papers*) ciskać (cisnąć *perf*); (*person, proposal*) zjechać (*perf*) (*inf*) ▷ *vi* (*door*) trzaskać (trzasnąć *perf*); **I ~med the phone down** rzuciłem *or* trzasnąłem słuchawką; **to ~ on the brakes** (*Aut*) gwałtownie nacisnąć (*perf*) na hamulce
**slander** ['slɑːndəʳ] *n* (*Jur*) zniesławienie *nt*; (*insult*) oszczerstwo *nt*, pomówienie *nt* ▷ *vt* rzucać oszczerstwa na *+acc*
**slanderous** ['slɑːndrəs] *adj* oszczerczy
**slang** [slæŋ] *n* (*informal language*) slang *m*; (*prison slang etc*) gwara *f*
**slant** [slɑːnt] *n* (*position*) nachylenie *nt*; (*fig*) punkt *m* widzenia ▷ *vi* być nachylonym
**slanted** ['slɑːntɪd] *adj* skośny
**slanting** ['slɑːntɪŋ] *adj* = **slanted**
**slap** [slæp] *n* klaps *m* ▷ *vt* dawać (dać *perf*) klapsa *+dat* ▷ *adv* (*inf*) prosto; **to ~ sb in** *or* **across the face** uderzyć (*perf*) kogoś w twarz; **to ~ some paint on the wall** pacnąć (*perf*) trochę farby na ścianę (*inf*); **it fell ~(-bang) in the middle** wylądowało w samym środku
**slapdash** ['slæpdæʃ] *adj* (*person*) niedbały; (*work*) byle jaki, na odczepnego *post*
**slapstick** ['slæpstɪk] *n* komedia *f* slapstickowa
**slap-up** ['slæpʌp] *adj*: **a ~ meal** (*Brit*) wystawne żarcie *nt* (*inf*)
**slash** [slæʃ] *vt* (*upholstery etc*) ciąć (pociąć *perf*); (*fig: prices*) drastycznie obniżać (obniżyć *perf*)
**slat** [slæt] *n* listewka *f* (*np. w żaluzji*)
**slate** [sleɪt] *n* (*material*) łupki *pl*; (*for roof*) płytka *f* łupkowa ▷ *vt* (*fig: criticize*) zjechać (*perf*) (*inf*)
**slaughter** ['slɔːtəʳ] *n* rzeź *f* ▷ *vt* (*animals*) ubijać (ubić *perf*); (*people*) dokonywać (dokonać *perf*) rzezi na *+loc*
**slaughterhouse** ['slɔːtəhaus] *n* rzeźnia *f*
**Slav** [slɑːv] *adj* słowiański ▷ *n* Słowianin(-anka) *m(f)*
**slave** [sleɪv] *n* niewolnik(-ica) *m(f)* ▷ *vi* (*also:* **slave away**) harować; **to ~ (away) at** męczyć się nad *+instr*
**slave labour** *n* praca *f* niewolników; **it's just ~** (*fig*) to po prostu katorżnicza robota
**slaver** ['slævəʳ] *vi* ślinić się
**slavery** ['sleɪvərɪ] *n* (*system*) niewolnictwo *nt*; (*condition*) niewola *f*
**Slavic** ['slævɪk] *adj* słowiański
**slavish** ['sleɪvɪʃ] *adj* (*obedience*) niewolniczy; (*imitation*) dosłowny
**Slavonic** [slə'vɔnɪk] *adj* słowiański; **~ people** Słowianie
**slay** [sleɪ] (*pt* **slew**, *pp* **slain**) *vt* (*literary*) zgładzić (*perf*), uśmiercać (uśmiercić *perf*)
**sleazy** ['sliːzɪ] *adj* obskurny
**sledge** [slɛdʒ] *n* (*for travelling*) sanie *pl*; (*child's*) sanki *pl*, saneczki *pl*; (*Sport*) saneczki *pl*

S

**sledgehammer** ['slɛdʒhæməʳ] *n* młot *m* (oburęczny)
**sleek** [sli:k] *adj* (*hair, fur*) lśniący; (*car, boat*) elegancki
**sleep** [sli:p] (*pt, pp* **slept**) *n* sen *m* ▷ *vi* spać ▷ *vt* (*person*): **we can ~ four** możemy przenocować cztery osoby; (*place*): **the cottage ~s six** w domku jest sześć miejsc do spania; **to go to ~** zasypiać (zasnąć *perf*); **to have a good night's ~** dobrze się wyspać (*perf*); **to put to ~** (*animal*) usypiać (uśpić *perf*); **to ~ lightly** mieć lekki sen; **to ~ with sb** (*have sex*) spać *or* sypiać z kimś
▸ **sleep around** *vi* sypiać z wszystkimi dookoła
▸ **sleep in** *vi* (*oversleep*) zaspać (*perf*); (*rise late*) spać (pospać *perf*) dłużej
**sleeper** ['sli:pəʳ] *n* (*train*) pociąg *m* sypialny; (*berth*) miejsce *nt* w wagonie sypialnym; (*Brit: on track*) podkład *m* kolejowy; **to be a light/heavy ~** mieć lekki/mocny *or* twardy sen
**sleepily** ['sli:pɪlɪ] *adv* sennie
**sleeping** ['sli:pɪŋ] *adj*: **~ accommodation** miejsca *pl* do spania
**sleeping bag** *n* śpiwór *m*
**sleeping car** *n* wagon *m* sypialny
**sleeping partner** (*Brit: Comm*) *n* = **silent partner**
**sleeping pill** *n* tabletka *f* nasenna
**sleepless** ['sli:plɪs] *adj* (*night*) bezsenny
**sleeplessness** ['sli:plɪsnɪs] *n* bezsenność *f*
**sleepwalker** ['sli:pwɔ:kəʳ] *n* lunatyk(-yczka) *m(f)*
**sleepy** ['sli:pɪ] *adj* (*person*) śpiący, senny; (*fig: town etc*) senny; **I am** *or* **feel ~** chce mi się spać, jestem śpiący
**sleet** [sli:t] *n* deszcz *m* ze śniegiem
**sleeve** [sli:v] *n* (*of jacket etc*) rękaw *m*; (*of record*) okładka *f*; **to have sth up one's ~** (*fig*) mieć coś w zanadrzu
**sleeveless** ['sli:vlɪs] *adj* bez rękawów *post*
**sleigh** [sleɪ] *n* sanie *pl*
**sleight** [slaɪt] *n*: **by ~ of hand** zręcznym *or* wprawnym ruchem
**slender** ['slɛndəʳ] *adj* (*figure*) smukły, szczupły; (*means*) skromny; (*majority*) niewielki, nieznaczny; (*prospects*) nikły
**slept** [slɛpt] *pt, pp of* **sleep**
**sleuth** [slu:θ] *n* detektyw *m*
**slew** [slu:] *vi* (*also:* **slew round**) (gwałtownie) skręcić (*perf*) *or* obrócić się (*perf*) (*np. na skutek poślizgu*) ▷ *pt of* **slay**
**slice** [slaɪs] *n* (*of ham, lemon*) plasterek *m*; (*of bread*) kromka *f*; (*cake slice, fish slice*) łopatka *f* ▷ *vt* kroić (pokroić *perf*) w plasterki; (*bread*) kroić (pokroić *perf*); **she thinks he's the best thing since ~d bread** jest nim zachwycona
**slick** [slɪk] *adj* (*film etc*) sprawnie zrobiony; (*pej: salesman, answer*) sprytny ▷ *n* (*also:* **oil slick**) plama *f* ropy
**slid** [slɪd] *pt, pp of* **slide**
**slide** [slaɪd] (*pt, pp* **slid**) *n* (*downward movement*) obniżanie się *nt*; (*: moral etc*) staczanie się *nt*; (*in playground*) zjeżdżalnia *f*; (*Phot*) przeźrocze *nt*, slajd *m*; (*Comm: in prices*) spadek *m* cen; (*: currency*) spadek *m* kursu; (*also:* **microscope slide**) preparat *m*; (*Brit: also:* **hair slide**) klamra *f* do włosów ▷ *vt*: **to ~ sth into sth** wsuwać (wsunąć *perf*) coś do czegoś ▷ *vi* przesuwać się (przesunąć się *perf*), sunąć; **to ~ out** wysuwać się (wysunąć się *perf*); **to let things ~** (*fig*) zaniedbywać (zaniedbać *perf*) sprawy
**slide projector** *n* rzutnik *m*
**slide rule** *n* suwak *m* (logarytmiczny)
**sliding door** ['slaɪdɪŋ-] *n* drzwi *pl* rozsuwane
**sliding roof** *n* (*Aut*) szyberdach *m*
**sliding scale** *n* ruchoma skala *f*
**slight** [slaɪt] *adj* (*person, error*) drobny; (*accent, pain*) lekki; (*increase, difference*) nieznaczny, niewielki; (*book etc*) mało znaczący ▷ *n* afront *m*; **the ~est noise/problem** najmniejszy hałas/problem; **I haven't the ~est idea** nie mam najmniejszego pojęcia; **not in the ~est** ani trochę, zupełnie nie
**slightly** ['slaɪtlɪ] *adv* odrobinę; **~ built** drobnej budowy *post*
**slim** [slɪm] *adj* (*figure*) szczupły; (*chance*) znikomy, nikły ▷ *vi* odchudzać się
**slime** [slaɪm] *n* (*in pond*) szlam *m*, muł *m*; (*on tub*) (brudny) osad *m*; (*of snail*) śluz *m*
**slimming** [slɪmɪŋ] *n* odchudzanie *nt*
**slimy** ['slaɪmɪ] *adj* (*pond*) mulisty, zamulony; (*pej: fig: person*) oślizgły (*inf, pej*)
**sling** [slɪŋ] (*pt, pp* **slung**) *n* (*Med*) temblak *m*; (*for baby*) nosidełko *nt*; (*weapon*) proca *f* ▷ *vt* (*throw*) ciskać (cisnąć *perf*); **to have one's arm in a ~** mieć rękę na temblaku
**slink** [slɪŋk] (*pt, pp* **slunk**) *vi*: **to ~ away** *or* **off** oddalać się (oddalić się *perf*) chyłkiem
**slip** [slɪp] *n* (*fall*) poślizgnięcie (się) *nt*; (*mistake*) pomyłka *f*; (*underskirt*) halka *f*; (*of paper*) kawałek *m* ▷ *vt* wsuwać (wsunąć *perf*) ▷ *vi* (*person*) poślizgnąć się (*perf*); (*production, profits*) spadać (spaść *perf*); **to ~ into the room** wślizgiwać się (wślizgnąć się *perf*) do pokoju; **to ~ out of the house** wymykać się (wymknąć się *perf*) z domu; **to let a chance ~ by** przepuścić (*perf*) okazję; **the cup ~ped from her hand** filiżanka wyślizgnęła się jej z ręki; **a ~ of the tongue** przejęzyczenie; **to give sb the ~** zwiać (*perf*) komuś (*inf*); **to ~ on one's jacket** narzucać (narzucić *perf*) marynarkę; **to ~ on one's shoes** wciągać (wciągnąć *perf*) buty

▸ **slip away** *vi* wymykać się (wymknąć się *perf*)
▸ **slip in** *vt* wsuwać (wsunąć *perf*) *or* wrzucać (wrzucić *perf*) do *+gen*
▸ **slip out** *vi* *(go out)* wyskakiwać (wyskoczyć *perf*)
▸ **slip up** *vi* pomylić się *(perf)*

**slip-on** ['slɪpɔn] *adj* *(garment)* wciągany (przez głowę); **~ shoes** buty wsuwane
**slipped disc** [slɪpt-] *n* przesunięty *or* wypadnięty dysk *m*
**slipper** ['slɪpə^r] *n* pantofel *m* (domowy), kapeć *m*
**slippery** ['slɪpərɪ] *adj* śliski; *(fig)* szczwany
**slip road** *n* *(Brit: onto motorway)* wjazd *m*; *(: off motorway)* zjazd *m*
**slipshod** ['slɪpʃɔd] *adj* byle jaki
**slipstream** ['slɪpstri:m] *n strumień powietrza powstający za szybko poruszającym się pojazdem*
**slip-up** ['slɪpʌp] *n* potknięcie *nt* *(fig)*, wpadka *f* *(inf)*
**slipway** ['slɪpweɪ] *(Naut)* *n* pochylnia *f*
**slit** [slɪt] *(pt, pp* **~**) *n* *(cut)* nacięcie *nt*; *(opening)* szpara *f*; *(tear)* rozdarcie *nt* ▹ *vt* rozcinać (rozciąć *perf*); **to ~ sb's throat** poderżnąć *(perf)* komuś gardło
**slither** ['slɪðə^r] *vi* *(person)* ślizgać się; *(snake)* pełzać (zygzakiem)
**sliver** ['slɪvə^r] *n* *(of wood, glass)* drzazga *f*; *(of cheese etc)* skrawek *m*
**slob** [slɔb] *(inf)* *n* niechluj *m* *(inf)*
**slog** [slɔg] *(Brit)* *vi* mozolić się ▹ *n*: **it was a hard ~** to była ciężka robota
**slogan** ['sləugən] *n* hasło *nt*, slogan *m*
**slop** [slɔp] *vi* wylewać się (wylać się *perf*) ▹ *vt* rozlewać (rozlać *perf*)
▸ **slop out** *vi* *(in prison etc)* opróżniać (opróżnić *perf*) kubeł
**slope** [sləup] *n* *(gentle hill)* wzniesienie *nt*; *(side of mountain)* zbocze *nt*, stok *m*; *(ski slope)* stok *m* narciarski; *(slant)* nachylenie *nt* ▹ *vi*: **to ~ down** opadać; **to ~ up** wznosić się
**sloping** ['sləupɪŋ] *adj* pochyły
**sloppy** ['slɔpɪ] *adj* *(work)* byle jaki; *(appearance)* niechlujny; *(film, letter)* ckliwy, łzawy
**slops** [slɔps] *npl* zlewki *pl*
**slosh** [slɔʃ] *(inf)* *vi*: **to ~ around** *or* **about** *(person)* taplać się; *(liquid)* rozchlapywać się (rozchlapać się *perf*)
**sloshed** [slɔʃt] *(inf)* *adj* zalany *(inf)*
**slot** [slɔt] *n* otwór *m* *(automatu, telefonu itp)*; *(fig: in timetable, TV)* okienko *nt* ▹ *vt*: **to ~ sth in** wrzucać (wrzucić *perf*) coś ▹ *vi*: **to ~ into** wchodzić *or* pasować do *+gen*
**sloth** [sləuθ] *n* *(laziness)* opieszałość *f*; *(Zool)* leniwiec *m*
**slot machine** *n* *(Brit)* automat *m* *(ze słodyczami, napojami itp)*; *(for gambling)* automat *m* do gry
**slot meter** *(Brit)* *n* licznik *m* samoinkasujący
**slouch** [slautʃ] *vi* garbić się ▹ *n*: **he's no ~ (when it comes to)** nie leni się (jeśli chodzi o *+acc*); **to ~ about** *or* **around** snuć się; **she was ~ed in a chair** siedziała oklapnięta w fotelu *(inf)*
**slovenly** ['slʌvənlɪ] *adj* niechlujny
**slow** [sləu] *adj* wolny, powolny ▹ *adv* wolno, powoli ▹ *vt* *(also:* **slow down, slow up***: speed)* zmniejszać (zmniejszyć *perf*); *(: business etc)* przyhamowywać (przyhamować *perf*) ▹ *vi* *(also:* **slow down, slow up**) zwalniać (zwolnić *perf*); **to ~ down** *or* **up the car** zwalniać (zwolnić *perf*); **"~"** *znak ograniczenia prędkości*; **at a ~ speed** powoli; **to be ~ to act/decide** zbyt wolno działać/podejmować decyzje; **my watch is 20 minutes ~** mój zegarek spóźnia się o dwadzieścia minut; **business is ~** w interesach panuje zastój; **to go ~** *(driver)* jechać wolno *or* powoli; *(Brit: workers)* zwalniać (zwolnić *perf*) tempo pracy *(w ramach akcji protestacyjnej)*
**slow-acting** [sləu'æktɪŋ] *adj* *(chemical etc)* o powolnym działaniu *post*
**slowly** ['sləulɪ] *adv* *(not quickly)* wolno, powoli; *(gradually)* powoli; **to drive ~** jechać wolno
**slow motion** *n*: **in ~** w zwolnionym tempie
**slow-moving** [sləu'mu:vɪŋ] *adj* poruszający się wolno
**slowness** ['sləunɪs] *n* wolne tempo *nt*, powolność *f*
**sludge** [slʌdʒ] *n* *(mud)* muł *m*; *(sewage)* ścieki *pl*
**slue** [slu:] *(US)* *vi* = **slew**
**slug** [slʌg] *n* ślimak *m* nagi; *(US: inf: bullet)* kula *f*
**sluggish** ['slʌgɪʃ] *adj* *(person)* ociężały, ospały; *(engine)* powolny; *(Comm: business)* w zastoju *post*
**sluice** [slu:s] *n* *(gate)* śluza *f*; *(channel)* kanał *m* ▹ *vt*: **to ~ down/out** spłukiwać (spłukać *perf*)/ wypłukiwać (wypłukać *perf*)
**slum** [slʌm] *n* slumsy *pl*
**slumber** ['slʌmbə^r] *n* sen *m*
**slump** [slʌmp] *n* *(economic)* załamanie *nt*, kryzys *m* ▹ *vi* *(prices)* (gwałtownie) spadać (spaść *perf*); **he ~ed into his chair** ciężko opadł na krzesło; **he was ~ed over the wheel** leżał bezwładnie na kierownicy
**slung** [slʌŋ] *pt, pp of* **sling**
**slunk** *pt, pp of* **slink**
**slur** [slə:^r] *n* *(fig)* obelga *f* ▹ *vt*: **to ~ one's words** mówić niewyraźnie; **to cast a ~ on** rzucać (rzucić *perf*) obelgę na *+acc*
**slurred** [slə:d] *adj* niewyraźny
**slush** [slʌʃ] *n* rozmokły śnieg *m*
**slush fund** *n* pieniądze *pl* na łapówki

S

**slushy** ['slʌʃɪ] *adj* (*snow*) rozmokły; (*street*) pokryty rozmokłym śniegiem; (*Brit: fig*) ckliwy
**slut** [slʌt] (*pej*) *n* dziwka *f* (*pej*)
**sly** [slaɪ] *adj* przebiegły; **on the sly** po kryjomu
**smack** [smæk] *n* klaps *m*; (*on face*) policzek *m* ▷ *vt* (*hit*) klepać (klepnąć *perf*); (*: child*) dawać (dać *perf*) klapsa *+dat*; (*: on face*) uderzać (uderzyć *perf*) ▷ *vi*: **to ~ of** trącić *+instr* ▷ *adv*: **it fell ~ in the middle** (*inf*) upadło w sam środek; **to ~ one's lips** cmokać (cmoknąć *perf*)
**smacker** ['smækə^r] (*inf*) *n* całus *m*
**small** [smɔːl] *adj* mały ▷ *n*: **the ~ of the back** krzyż *m*; **to get** *or* **grow ~er** maleć (zmaleć *perf*), zmniejszać się (zmniejszyć się *perf*); **to make ~er** zmniejszać (zmniejszyć *perf*); **a ~ shopkeeper** drobny sklepikarz
**small ads** (*Brit*) *npl* ogłoszenia *pl* drobne
**small arms** (*Mil*) *n* broń *f* małokalibrowa *or* ręczna
**small change** *n* drobne *pl*
**small fry** *npl* (*people*) płotki *pl*
**smallholder** ['smɔːlhəuldə^r] (*Brit*) *n* chłop *m* małorolny
**smallholding** ['smɔːlhəuldɪŋ] (*Brit*) *n* małe gospodarstwo *nt* rolne
**small hours** *npl*: **in the ~** wczesnym ran(ki)em, we wczesnych godzinach rannych
**smallish** ['smɔːlɪʃ] *adj* przymały (*inf*)
**small-minded** [smɔːl'maɪndɪd] *adj* małostkowy
**smallpox** ['smɔːlpɔks] *n* ospa *f*
**small print** *n* (*in contract etc*) adnotacje *pl* drobnym drukiem
**small-scale** ['smɔːlskeɪl] *adj* (*map, model*) w małej skali *post*; (*business, farming*) na małą skalę *post*
**small talk** *n* rozmowa *f* towarzyska
**small-time** ['smɔːltaɪm] *adj* drobny; **a ~ thief** drobny złodziejaszek
**smarmy** ['smɑːmɪ] (*Brit: pej*) *adj* wazeliniarski (*pej*)
**smart** [smɑːt] *adj* (*neat, fashionable*) elegancki; (*clever: person*) bystry, rozgarnięty; (*: idea*) chytry, sprytny; (*pace*) żwawy; (*blow*) silny ▷ *vi* (*eyes, wound*) piec, szczypać; **she was ~ing from a guilty conscience** dręczyły ją wyrzuty sumienia; **the ~ set** eleganckie towarzystwo; **to look ~** wyglądać elegancko
**smart card** (*Banking*) *n* karta *f* magnetyczna
**smarten up** ['smɑːtn-] *vi* ogarniać się (ogarnąć się *perf*) ▷ *vt* (*room etc*) odświeżać (odświeżyć *perf*)
**smartphone** ['smɑːtfəun] *n* smartphone *m*
**smash** [smæʃ] *n* (*also*: **smash-up**) kraksa *f*; (*sound*) trzask *m*; (*song, play, film*) przebój *m*; (*Tennis*) ścięcie *nt* ▷ *vt* roztrzaskiwać (roztrzaskać *perf*); (*fig: sb's career*) rujnować (zrujnować *perf*); (*: political system*) obalać (obalić *perf*); (*: record*) bić (pobić *perf*) ▷ *vi* (*break*) roztrzaskiwać się (roztrzaskać się *perf*); (*against wall/into sth*) walnąć (*perf*)
▸ **smash up** *vt* (*car*) rozwalać (rozwalić *perf*) (*inf*), roztrzaskiwać (roztrzaskać *perf*); (*room*) rujnować (zrujnować *perf*)
**smash hit** *n* przebój *m*
**smashing** ['smæʃɪŋ] (*inf*) *adj* kapitalny, fantastyczny
**smattering** ['smætərɪŋ] *n*: **a ~ of** odrobina *+gen*
**smear** [smɪə^r] *n* (*trace*) smuga *f*; (*insult*) potwarz *f*, oszczerstwo *nt*; (*Med*) wymaz *m*, rozmaz *m* ▷ *vt* (*spread*) rozmazywać (rozmazać *perf*); (*make dirty*) usmarować (*perf*), umazać (*perf*); **his hands were ~ed with oil/ink** ręce miał usmarowane olejem/ powalane atramentem
**smear campaign** *n* kampania *f* oszczerstw
**smear test** *n* badanie *nt* cytologiczne, wymaz *m* z szyjki macicy
**smell** [smɛl] (*pt, pp* **smelt** *or* **~ed**) *n* (*odour*) zapach *m*; (*sense*) węch *m*, powonienie *nt* ▷ *vt* wyczuwać (wyczuć *perf*) ▷ *vi* pachnieć; (*pej*) śmierdzieć; **to ~ of** pachnieć *+instr*; (*pej*) śmierdzieć *+instr*
**smelly** ['smɛlɪ] (*pej*) *adj* śmierdzący
**smelt** [smɛlt] *pt, pp of* **smell** ▷ *vt* wytapiać (wytopić *perf*)
**smile** [smaɪl] *n* uśmiech *m* ▷ *vi* uśmiechać się (uśmiechnąć się *perf*)
**smiling** ['smaɪlɪŋ] *adj* uśmiechnięty
**smirk** [smɔːk] (*pej*) *n* uśmiech *m* wyższości, uśmieszek *m*
**smithy** ['smɪðɪ] *n* kuźnia *f*
**smitten** ['smɪtn] *adj*: **~ with** oczarowany *+instr*
**smock** [smɔk] *n* (*woman's*) bluzka *f* koszulowa (*długa i luźna*); (*artist's, doctor's*) kitel *m*
**smog** [smɔg] *n* smog *m*
**smoke** [sməuk] *n* dym *m* ▷ *vi* (*person*) palić; (*chimney*) dymić ▷ *vt* palić (wypalić *perf*); **to have a ~** zapalić (*perf*); **do you ~?** (czy) palisz?; **to go up in ~** iść (pójść *perf*) z dymem; (*fig*) spalić (*perf*) na panewce
**smoked** ['sməukt] *adj* (*bacon, salmon*) wędzony; (*glass*) zadymiony, przyciemniony
**smokeless fuel** ['sməuklɪs-] *n* paliwo *nt* bezdymne
**smokeless zone** (*Brit*) *n* strefa *f* bezdymna
**smoker** ['sməukə^r] *n* (*person*) palacz(ka) *m*(*f*); (*Rail*) wagon *m* dla palących
**smokescreen** ['sməukskriːn] *n* (*lit, fig*) zasłona *f* dymna

**smoke shop** (*US*) *n* sklep *m* z wyrobami tytoniowymi
**smoking** ['sməukɪŋ] *n* palenie *nt*; **"no ~"** „palenie wzbronione"
**smoking compartment**, (*US*) **smoking car** *n* wagon *m* dla palących
**smoking room** *n* palarnia *f*
**smoky** ['sməukɪ] *adj* zadymiony; (*whisky*) pachnący dymem
**smolder** ['sməuldə^r] (*US*) *vi* = **smoulder**
**smooth** [smu:ð] *adj* gładki; (*flavour, landing, take-off*) łagodny; (*movement*) płynny; (*flight*) spokojny; (*pej: person*) ugrzeczniony
▸ **smooth out** *vt* (*skirt, piece of paper*) wygładzać (wygładzić *perf*); (*fig: difficulties*) usuwać (usunąć *perf*)
▸ **smooth over** *vt*: **to ~ things over** (*fig*) łagodzić (załagodzić *perf*) sytuację
**smoothly** ['smu:ðlɪ] *adv* gładko; (*peacefully*) spokojnie; **everything went ~** wszystko poszło gładko
**smoothness** ['smu:ðnɪs] *n* gładkość *f*; (*steadiness*) spokój *m*
**smother** ['smʌðə^r] *vt* (*fire, emotions*) tłumić (stłumić *perf*), dusić (zdusić *perf*); (*person*) dusić (udusić *perf*)
**smoulder**, (*US*) **smolder** ['sməuldə^r] *vi* (*lit, fig*) tlić się
**smudge** [smʌdʒ] *n* smuga *f* ▹ *vt* rozmazywać (rozmazać *perf*)
**smug** [smʌg] (*pej*) *adj* zadowolony z siebie
**smuggle** ['smʌgl] *vt* przemycać (przemycić *perf*), szmuglować (przeszmuglować *perf*); **to ~ sth in/out** przemycać (przemycić *perf*) coś do *+gen*/z *+gen*
**smuggler** ['smʌglə^r] *n* przemytnik(-iczka) *m(f)*, szmugler *m*
**smuggling** ['smʌglɪŋ] *n* przemyt *m*
**smut** [smʌt] *n* pyłek *m* sadzy; (*fig*) nieprzyzwoitość *f*
**smutty** ['smʌtɪ] *adj* (*fig*) nieprzyzwoity, sprośny
**snack** [snæk] *n* przekąska *f*; **to have a ~** przekąsić (*perf*) coś
**snack bar** *n* bar *m* szybkiej obsługi
**snag** [snæg] *n* (drobny) problem *m*
**snail** [sneɪl] *n* ślimak *m*
**snake** [sneɪk] *n* wąż *m*
**snap** [snæp] *n* (*sound*) trzask *m*; (*photograph*) zdjęcie *nt*, fotka *f* (*inf*); (*Cards*) *rodzaj gry w karty* ▹ *adj* (*decision etc*) nagły ▹ *vt* łamać (złamać *perf*) ▹ *vi* pękać (pęknąć *perf*); (*fig*) tracić (stracić *perf*) panowanie nad sobą; **to ~ one's fingers** pstrykać (pstryknąć *perf*) *or* strzelać (strzelić *perf*) palcami; **a cold ~** nagłe ochłodzenie; **to ~ open** otwierać się (otworzyć *perf* się) z trzaskiem; **to ~ shut** zamykać się (zamknąć się *perf*) z trzaskiem
▸ **snap at** *vt fus* (*dog*) kłapać (kłapnąć *perf*) zębami na *+acc*; (*person*) warczeć (warknąć *perf*) na *+acc*
▸ **snap off** *vt* odłamywać (odłamać *perf*)
▸ **snap up** *vt* rzucać się (rzucić się *perf*) na *+acc*
**snap fastener** *n* zatrzask *m*, napa *f*
**snappy** ['snæpɪ] (*inf*) *adj* zgryźliwy; **make it ~** pośpiesz się; **a ~ dresser** elegant(ka) *m(f)*
**snapshot** ['snæpʃɔt] *n* zdjęcie *nt*, fotka *f* (*inf*)
**snare** [snɛə^r] *n* sidła *pl*, wnyki *pl* ▹ *vt* (*animal*) łapać (złapać *perf*) w sidła; (*fig: person*) chwytać (schwytać *perf*) w pułapkę
**snarl** [snɑ:l] *vi* warczeć (warknąć *perf*) ▹ *vt*: **~ed up** (*plans*) wstrzymany; (*traffic*) zablokowany
**snarl-up** ['snɑ:lʌp] *n* blokada *f*
**snatch** [snætʃ] *n* strzęp *m*, urywek *m* ▹ *vt* porywać (porwać *perf*); (*fig: opportunity*) (skwapliwie) korzystać (skorzystać *perf*) z *+gen*; (*: time*) urywać (urwać *perf*) (*inf*) ▹ *vi*: **don't ~!** nie zabieraj!; **to ~ a sandwich** szybko coś przegryźć (*perf*); **to ~ some sleep** przespać się (*perf*) trochę; **to ~ a look at** rzucać (rzucić *perf*) ukradkowe spojrzenie na *+acc*
▸ **snatch up** *vt* złapać (*perf*)
**sneak** [sni:k] (*pt* (*US*) *also* **snuck**) *vi*: **to ~ in** zakradać się (zakraść się *perf*); **to ~ out** wymykać się (wymknąć się *perf*) ▹ *vt*: **to ~ a look at sth** rzucać (rzucić *perf*) ukradkowe spojrzenie na coś ▹ *n* (*inf, pej*) donosiciel(ka) *m(f)* (*inf, pej*)
▸ **sneak up** *vi*: **to ~ up on sb** donosić (donieść *perf*) na kogoś
**sneakers** ['sni:kəz] *npl* tenisówki *pl*
**sneaking** ['sni:kɪŋ] *adj*: **I have a ~ feeling** *or* **suspicion that ...** dręczy mnie podejrzenie, że...
**sneaky** ['sni:kɪ] *adj* (*pej*) podstępny
**sneer** [snɪə^r] *vi* uśmiechać się (uśmiechnąć się *perf*) szyderczo; **to ~ at** szydzić z *+gen* ▹ *n* (*remark*) drwina *f*, szyderstwo *nt*; (*expression*) szyderczy uśmiech *m*
**sneeze** [sni:z] *n* kichnięcie *nt* ▹ *vi* kichać (kichnąć *perf*)
▸ **sneeze at** *vt fus*: **not to be ~d at** nie do pogardzenia
**snide** [snaɪd] (*pej*) *adj* (*remark*) złośliwy
**sniff** [snɪf] *n* (*sound*) pociągnięcie *nt* nosem; (*smell*) obwąchanie *nt* ▹ *vi* pociągać (pociągnąć *perf*) nosem ▹ *vt* wąchać (powąchać *perf*); (*glue*) wąchać
**sniffer dog** ['snɪfə-] *n* pies *m* policyjny
**snigger** ['snɪgə^r] *vi* chichotać (zachichotać *perf*)

S

**snip** [snɪp] *n* cięcie *nt*, ciachnięcie *nt* (*inf*); (*Brit*: *inf*: *bargain*) okazja *f* ▷ *vt* przecinać (przeciąć *perf*), ciachać (ciachnąć *perf*) (*inf*)
**sniper** [ˈsnaɪpəʳ] *n* snajper *m*
**snippet** [ˈsnɪpɪt] *n* (*of information, news*) strzęp *m*
**snivelling**, (US) **sniveling** [ˈsnɪvlɪŋ] *adj* mazgajowaty
**snob** [snɔb] *n* snob(ka) *m(f)*
**snobbery** [ˈsnɔbərɪ] *n* snobizm *m*
**snobbish** [ˈsnɔbɪʃ] *adj* snobistyczny
**snooker** [ˈsnu:kəʳ] *n* (*Sport*) snooker *m* ▷ *vt* (*Brit*: *inf*): **to be ~ed** mieć związane ręce
**snoop** [ˈsnu:p] *vi*: **to ~ about** węszyć; **to ~ on sb** wtykać nos w czyjeś sprawy
**snooper** [ˈsnu:pəʳ] *n* osoba *f* wtykająca nos w cudze sprawy
**snooty** [ˈsnu:tɪ] *adj* przemądrzały
**snooze** [snu:z] *n* drzemka *f* ▷ *vi* drzemać
**snore** [snɔ:ʳ] *n* chrapanie *nt* ▷ *vi* chrapać
**snoring** [ˈsnɔ:rɪŋ] *n* chrapanie *nt*
**snorkel** [ˈsnɔ:kl] *n* fajka *f* (*do nurkowania*)
**snort** [snɔ:t] *n* prychnięcie *nt*, parsknięcie *nt* ▷ *vi* prychać (prychnąć *perf*), parskać (parsknąć *perf*) ▷ *vt* (*inf*: *cocaine*) wdychać
**snotty** [ˈsnɔtɪ] *adj* (*inf*) zasmarkany; (*pej*: *proud*) zadzierający nosa
**snout** [snaut] *n* (*of pig*) ryj *m*; (*of dog*) pysk *m*
**snow** [snəu] *n* śnieg *m* ▷ *vi*: **it ~ed/is ~ing** padał/pada śnieg ▷ *vt*: **to be ~ed under with work** być zawalonym pracą
**snowball** [ˈsnəubɔ:l] *n* śnieżka *f* ▷ *vi* (*fig*: *campaign, business*) rozkręcać się (rozkręcić się *perf*); (: *problem*) narastać (narosnąć *perf*) (w szybkim tempie)
**snowbound** [ˈsnəubaund] *adj* zasypany śniegiem
**snow-capped** [ˈsnəukæpt] *adj* ośnieżony
**snowdrift** [ˈsnəudrɪft] *n* zaspa *f* (śnieżna)
**snowdrop** [ˈsnəudrɔp] *n* przebiśnieg *m*
**snowfall** [ˈsnəufɔ:l] *n* opad *m* śniegu
**snowflake** [ˈsnəufleɪk] *n* płatek *m* śniegu, śnieżynka *f*
**snowline** [ˈsnəulaɪn] *n* linia *f* wiecznego śniegu
**snowman** [ˈsnəumæn] *n* (*irreg*: *like* **man**) bałwan *m*
**snowplough**, (US) **snowplow** [ˈsnəuplau] *n* pług *m* śnieżny
**snowshoe** [ˈsnəuʃu:] *n* rakieta *f* śnieżna
**snowstorm** [ˈsnəustɔ:m] *n* zamieć *f* śnieżna, śnieżyca *f*
**snowy** [ˈsnəuɪ] *adj* (*hair*) biały jak śnieg; (*peak*) ośnieżony
**SNP** (*Brit*: *Pol*) *n abbr* = **Scottish National Party**
**snub** [snʌb] *vt* robić (zrobić *perf*) afront *+dat* ▷ *n* afront *m*
**snub-nosed** [snʌbˈnəuzd] *adj* z zadartym nosem *post*
**snuff** [snʌf] *n* tabaka *f* ▷ *vt* (*also*: **snuff out**: *candle*) gasić (zgasić *perf*) (*nakrywając płomień albo palcami*)
**snuff movie** *n film porno zawierający autentyczne sceny tortur lub śmierci*
**snug** [snʌg] *adj* (*place*) przytulny; (*garment*) (dobrze) dopasowany; **I'm very ~ here** jest mi tu bardzo wygodnie; **the dress is a ~ fit** suknia jest dobrze dopasowana
**snuggle** [ˈsnʌgl] *vi*: **to ~ up to sb** przytulać się (przytulić się *perf*) do kogoś; **to ~ down (in bed)** opatulać się (opatulić się *perf*) kołdrą
**snugly** [ˈsnʌglɪ] *adv*: **~ wrapped** ciepło opatulony; **to fit ~** (*object in pocket etc*) wygodnie się mieścić (zmieścić *perf*); (*garment*) być dobrze dopasowanym
**SO** (*Banking*) *n abbr* = **standing order**

KEYWORD

**so** [səu] *adv* **1** (*thus, likewise*) tak; **if so** jeśli tak; **I didn't do it — you did so!** ja tego nie zrobiłem — a właśnie, że zrobiłeś!; **so do I, so am I** *etc* ja też; **I've got work to do — so has Paul** mam robotę — Paul też; **it's five o'clock — so it is!** jest piąta — rzeczywiście!; **I hope so** mam nadzieję, że tak; **so far** (jak) dotąd *or* do tej pory, dotychczas
**2** (*to such a degree*: *+adjective*) tak *or* taki; (: *+adverb*) tak; **so big (that)** tak(i) duży (, że); **she's not so clever as her brother** nie jest tak bystra jak jej brat; **so quickly (that)** tak szybko (, że)
**3**: **so much** *adj* tyle *+gen*, tak dużo *or* wiele *+gen*; **I've got so much work** mam tyle *or* tak dużo pracy
▷ *adv* tak bardzo; **I love you so much** tak bardzo cię kocham; **so many** tyle *+gen*, tak wiele *or* dużo *+gen*; **there are so many things to do** jest tyle *or* tak wiele rzeczy do zrobienia
**4** (*phrases*): **ten or so** z dziesięć; **so long!** (*inf*) tymczasem! (*inf*), na razie! (*inf*)
▷ *conj* **1** (*expressing purpose*): **so as to** żeby *+infin*; **we hurried so as not to be late** popędziliśmy, żeby się nie spóźnić; **so (that)** żeby; **I brought it so (that) you could see it** przyniosłem, żebyś mógł to zobaczyć
**2** (*expressing result*) więc; **he didn't arrive so I left** nie przyjechał, więc wyszedłem; **so I was right after all** (a) więc jednak miałam rację

**soak** [səuk] *vt* (*drench*) przemoczyć (*perf*); (*steep in water*) namaczać (namoczyć *perf*) ▷ *vi*

moczyć się; **to be ~ed through** być (doszczętnie *or* na wskroś) przemoczonym
▸ **soak in** *vi* wsiąkać (wsiąknąć *perf*)
▸ **soak up** *vt* wchłaniać (wchłonąć *perf*)
**oaking** ['səukɪŋ] *adj* (*also*: **soaking wet**) przemoczony
**o-and-so** ['səuənsəu] *n*: **(Mr/Dr) ~** (Pan/Dr) taki *m* a taki *m*; **you ~!** (*pej*) ty taki owaki!
**oap** [səup] *n* mydło *nt*; (TV: *also*: **soap opera**) telenowela *f*, powieść *f* telewizyjna
**oapflakes** ['səupfleɪks] *npl* płatki *pl* mydlane
**oap opera** *n* telenowela *f*, powieść *f* telewizyjna
**oap powder** *n* proszek *m* do prania
**oapsuds** ['səupsʌds] *npl* mydliny *pl*
**oapy** ['səupɪ] *adj* (*water*) mydlany; (*hands*) namydlony
**oar** [sɔːʳ] *vi* (*bird, plane*) wzbijać się (wzbić się *perf*) (wysoko); (*buildings, trees*) wznosić się (wysoko); (*price, production, temperature*) gwałtownie wzrastać (wzrosnąć *perf*) *or* iść (pójść *perf*) w górę
**oaring** ['sɔːrɪŋ] *adj* (*prices etc*) gwałtownie rosnący
**ob** [sɔb] *n* szloch *m* ▹ *vi* szlochać
**.o.b.** (*US*: *inf!*) *n abbr* (= *son of a bitch*) sukinsyn *m* (*inf!*)
**ober** ['səubəʳ] *adj* (*not drunk, realistic, practical*) trzeźwy; (*serious*) poważny; (*colour etc*) spokojny, stonowany
▸ **sober up** *vt* otrzeźwiać (otrzeźwić *perf*) ▹ *vi* trzeźwieć (wytrzeźwieć *perf*)
**obriety** [sə'braɪətɪ] *n* trzeźwość *f*; (*seriousness*) powaga *f*
**oc.** *abbr* = **society**
**o-called** ['səu'kɔːld] *adj* tak zwany
**occer** ['sɔkəʳ] *n* piłka *f* nożna
**occer pitch** *n* boisko *nt* piłkarskie
**occer player** *n* piłkarz *m*
**ociable** ['səuʃəbl] *adj* towarzyski
**ocial** ['səuʃl] *adj* (*history, structure, background*) społeczny; (*policy, benefit*) socjalny; (*event, contact*) towarzyski; (*animal*) stadny ▹ *n* spotkanie *nt* towarzyskie; **~ life** życie towarzyskie
**ocial class** *n* klasa *f* społeczna
**ocial climber** (*pej*) *n* snob(ka) *m(f)* (*pej*)
**ocial club** *n* klub *m* towarzyski
**ocial democrat** *n* socjaldemokrata(-tka) *m(f)*
**ocial insurance** (*US*) *n* ubezpieczenia *pl* społeczne
**ocialism** ['səuʃəlɪzəm] *n* socjalizm *m*
**ocialist** ['səuʃəlɪst] *adj* socjalistyczny ▹ *n* socjalista(-tka) *m(f)*
**ocialite** ['səuʃəlaɪt] *n* osoba *f* z towarzystwa
**socialize** ['səuʃəlaɪz] *vi* udzielać się towarzysko; **to ~ with** utrzymywać stosunki (towarzyskie) z +*instr*
**socially** ['səuʃəlɪ] *adv* (*visit*) towarzysko, w celach towarzyskich; (*acceptable*) społecznie
**social networking site** [-'nɛtwəːkɪŋ-] *n* (*Comput*) serwis *m* społecznościowy
**social science** *n* nauki *pl* społeczne
**social security** (*Brit*) *n* ubezpieczenia *pl* społeczne; **Department of Social Security** Ministerstwo Ubezpieczeń Społecznych
**social services** *npl* opieka *f* społeczna
**social welfare** *n* ubezpieczenia *pl* społeczne
**social work** *n* praca *f* w opiece społecznej
**social worker** *n* pracownik(-ica) *m(f)* opieki społecznej
**society** [sə'saɪətɪ] *n* społeczeństwo *nt*; (*local*) społeczność *f*; (*club*) towarzystwo *nt*; (*also*: **high society**) wytworne towarzystwo *nt* ▹ *cpd*: **~ lady** dama *f* z towarzystwa
**socioeconomic** ['səusɪəuiːkə'nɔmɪk] *adj* społeczno-ekonomiczny
**sociological** [səusɪə'lɔdʒɪkl] *adj* socjologiczny
**sociologist** [səusɪ'ɔlədʒɪst] *n* socjolog *m*
**sociology** [səusɪ'ɔlədʒɪ] *n* socjologia *f*
**sock** [sɔk] *n* skarpeta *f*, skarpetka *f* ▹ *vt* (*inf*) walnąć (*perf*) (pięścią) (*inf*); **to pull one's ~s up** (*fig*) brać (wziąć *perf*) się w garść
**socket** ['sɔkɪt] *n* (*Anat*: *of eye*) oczodół *m*; (: *of tooth*) zębodół *m*; (: *of hip etc*) panewka *f* (stawu); (*Brit*: *in wall*) gniazdko *nt*; (: *for light bulb*) oprawka *f*; **her eyes popped out of their ~s** oczy wyszły jej z orbit
**sod** [sɔd] *n* (*earth*) darń *f*; (*Brit*: *inf!*: *person*) gnojek *m* (*inf!*)
**soda** ['səudə] *n* (*Chem*) soda *f*; (*also*: **soda water**) woda *f* sodowa; (*US*: *also*: **soda pop**) napój *m* gazowany
**sodden** ['sɔdn] *adj* (*clothes*) przemoczony; (*ground*) rozmokły
**sodium** ['səudɪəm] *n* sód *m*
**sodium chloride** *n* chlorek *m* sodu *or* sodowy
**sofa** ['səufə] *n* kanapa *f*
**Sofia** ['səufɪə] *n* Sofia *f*
**soft** [sɔft] *adj* (*lit, fig*) miękki; (*voice, music, light*) łagodny; (*skin*) delikatny; **~ in the head** (*inf*) przygłupi (*inf*)
**soft-boiled** ['sɔftbɔɪld] *adj*: **~ egg** jajko *nt* na miękko
**soft drink** *n* napój *m* bezalkoholowy
**soft drugs** *npl* narkotyki *pl* miękkie
**soften** ['sɔfn] *vt* zmiękczać (zmiękczyć *perf*); (*effect, blow*) łagodzić (złagodzić *perf*) ▹ *vi* mięknąć (zmięknąć *perf*); (*voice, expression*) łagodnieć (złagodnieć *perf*); **the memory of that meeting ~ed her face** na wspomnienie tego spotkania twarz jej złagodniała

S

**softener** ['sɔfnə^r] *n* (*water softener*) środek *m* do zmiękczania wody; (*fabric softener*) środek *m* do zmiękczania tkanin
**soft fruit** (*Brit*) *n* owoce *pl* miękkie
**soft furnishings** *npl zasłony, obicia i inne elementy wystroju wnętrz wykonane z materiału*
**soft-hearted** [sɔft'hɑːtɪd] *adj*: **to be ~** mieć miękkie serce
**softly** ['sɔftlɪ] *adv* miękko, łagodnie
**softness** ['sɔftnɪs] *n* miękkość *f*; (*gentleness*) łagodność *f*, delikatność *f*
**soft sell** *n* nienachalna reklama *f*
**soft spot** *n*: **to have a ~ for sb** mieć do kogoś słabość
**soft toy** *n* pluszowa zabawka *f*
**software** ['sɔftwɛə^r] *n* oprogramowanie *nt*
**software package** (*Comput*) *n* pakiet *m* programowy
**soft water** *n* miękka woda *f*
**soggy** ['sɔgɪ] *adj* rozmokły
**soil** [sɔɪl] *n* (*earth*) gleba *f*, ziemia *f*; (*territory*) ziemia *f* ▷ *vt* brudzić (pobrudzić *perf*); (*fig*) plamić (splamić *perf*)
**soiled** [sɔɪld] *adj* (*handkerchief, nappy*) brudny
**sojourn** ['sɔdʒəːn] (*fml*) *n* pobyt *m*
**solace** ['sɔlɪs] *n* pocieszenie *nt*
**solar** ['səulə^r] *adj* słoneczny
**solarium** [sə'lɛərɪəm] (*pl* **solaria**) *n* solarium *nt*
**solar panel** *n* bateria *f* słoneczna
**solar plexus** [-'plɛksəs] *n* splot *m* słoneczny
**solar power** *n* energia *f* słoneczna
**solar system** *n* układ *m* słoneczny
**sold** [səuld] *pt, pp of* **sell**
**solder** ['səuldə^r] *vt* lutować (zlutować *perf*) ▷ *n* lut *m*
**soldier** ['səuldʒə^r] *n* żołnierz *m* ▷ *vi*: **to ~ on** nie poddawać się; **to ~ on doing sth** nadal (wytrwale) coś robić; **toy ~** żołnierzyk
**sold out** *adj* (*goods, tickets*) wyprzedany; **the concert was ~** (wszystkie) bilety na koncert zostały wyprzedane; **we're ~ (of bread)** (chleba) (już) nie ma
**sole** [səul] *n* (*of foot, shoe*) podeszwa *f*; (*fish*: *pl inv*) sola *f* ▷ *adj* (*unique*) jedyny; (*exclusive*) wyłączny; **the ~ reason** jedyny powód
**solely** ['səullɪ] *adv* jedynie, wyłącznie; **I will hold you ~ responsible** cała odpowiedzialność spoczywa na tobie
**solemn** ['sɔləm] *adj* uroczysty
**sole trader** (*Comm*) *n* firma *f* jednoosobowa
**solicit** [sə'lɪsɪt] *vt* zabiegać o *+acc* ▷ *vi* (*prostitute*) nagabywać klientów
**solicitor** [sə'lɪsɪtə^r] (*Brit*) *n* ≈ notariusz *m*
**solid** ['sɔlɪd] *adj* (*not hollow*) lity; (*not liquid*) stały; (*reliable, strong*) solidny; (*substantial*: *advice etc*) konkretny; (*unbroken*: *hours etc*) bity; (*pure*: *gold etc*) szczery, czysty ▷ *n* ciało *nt* stałe; **solids** *npl* pokarmy *pl* stałe; **to be on ~ ground** (*fig*) mieć solidne podstawy; **I read for two hours ~** czytałem przez bite dwie godziny
**solidarity** [sɔlɪ'dærɪtɪ] *n* solidarność *f*
**solidify** [sə'lɪdɪfaɪ] *vi* krzepnąć (skrzepnąć *perf*), tężeć (stężeć *perf*); (*fig*) krzepnąć (okrzepnąć *perf*), utrwalać się (utrwalić się *perf*) ▷ *vt* utrwalać (utrwalić *perf*)
**solidity** [sə'lɪdɪtɪ] *n* solidność *f*
**solidly** ['sɔlɪdlɪ] *adv* (*built*) solidnie; (*respectable*) z gruntu; (*in favour*) twardo
**solid-state** ['sɔlɪdsteɪt] (*Elec*) *adj* półprzewodnikowy
**soliloquy** [sə'lɪləkwɪ] *n* monolog *m*
**solitaire** [sɔlɪ'tɛə^r] *n* (*gem*) soliter *m*; (*game*) samotnik *m*; (*card game*) pasjans *m*
**solitary** ['sɔlɪtərɪ] *adj* (*lonely, single*) samotny; (*empty*) pusty, opustoszały
**solitary confinement** *n* więzienna izolatka *f*; **to be in ~** przebywać w izolatce
**solitude** ['sɔlɪtjuːd] *n* samotność *f*; **to live in ~** żyć w odosobnieniu
**solo** ['səuləu] *n* solo *nt inv* ▷ *adv* w pojedynkę, solo; **~ flight** samotny lot
**soloist** ['səuləuɪst] *n* solista(-tka) *m(f)*
**Solomon Islands** ['sɔləmən-] *npl*: **the ~** Wyspy *pl* Salomona
**solstice** ['sɔlstɪs] *n* przesilenie *nt* (*letnie lub zimowe*)
**soluble** ['sɔljubl] *adj* rozpuszczalny
**solution** [sə'luːʃən] *n* (*answer*) rozwiązanie *nt*; (*liquid*) roztwór *m*, mieszanina *f*
**solve** [sɔlv] *vt* rozwiązywać (rozwiązać *perf*)
**solvency** ['sɔlvənsɪ] *n* wypłacalność *f*
**solvent** ['sɔlvənt] *adj* wypłacalny ▷ *n* (*Chem*) rozpuszczalnik *m*
**solvent abuse** *n* odurzanie się *nt* chemikaliami
**Som.** (*Brit*: *Post*) *abbr* = **Somerset**
**Somali** [sə'mɑːlɪ] *adj* somalijski ▷ *n* Somalijczyk(-jka) *m(f)*
**Somalia** [sə'mɑːlɪə] *n* Somalia *f*
**sombre**, (*US*) **somber** ['sɔmbə^r] *adj* (*dark*) ciemny, mroczny; (*grave*) ponury, posępny

KEYWORD

**some** [sʌm] *adj* **1** (*a certain amount of*) trochę *+gen*; (*a certain number of*) parę *+gen nvir pl*, paru *+gen vir pl*, kilka *+gen nvir pl*, kilku *+gen vir pl*; **some tea/water** trochę herbaty/wody; **some biscuits** parę *or* kilka herbatników; **some policemen** paru *or* kilku policjantów
**2** (*certain*: *in contrasts*) niektóre *+nvir pl*, niektórzy *+vir pl*; **some people say that ...** niektórzy (ludzie) mówią, że ...; **some films**

**were excellent** niektóre filmy były świetne
**3** *(unspecified)*: **some woman was asking for you** jakaś kobieta pytała o ciebie; **some day** pewnego dnia
▷ *pron* **1** *(a certain number)* parę *nvir pl*, paru *vir pl*, kilka *nvir pl*, kilku *vir pl*; **have you got any friends? — yes, I've got some** (czy) masz jakichś przyjaciół? — tak, mam paru *or* kilku; **have you got any stamps? — yes, I've got some** (czy) masz jakieś znaczki? — tak, mam parę *or* kilka
**2** *(a certain amount)* trochę; **have we got any money? — yes, we've got some** (czy) mamy jakieś pieniądze? — tak, mamy trochę; **some was left** trochę zostało
▷ *adv*: **some ten people** jakieś dziesięć osób

**omebody** ['sʌmbədɪ] *pron* = **someone**
**omeday** ['sʌmdeɪ] *adv* pewnego dnia
**omehow** ['sʌmhau] *adv* jakoś
**omeone** ['sʌmwʌn] *pron* ktoś *m*
**omeplace** ['sʌmpleɪs] (US) *adv* = **somewhere**
**omersault** ['sʌməsɔːlt] *n* koziołek *m*, fikołek *m*; *(Sport)* salto *nt* ▷ *vi* koziołkować (przekoziołkować *perf*)
**omething** ['sʌmθɪŋ] *pron* coś *nt*; **~ nice** coś miłego; **~ to do** coś do zrobienia; **there's ~ wrong** coś tu jest nie tak, coś tu nie gra *(inf)*
**ometime** ['sʌmtaɪm] *adv* kiedyś; **I'll finish it ~** kiedyś to skończę
**ometimes** ['sʌmtaɪmz] *adv* czasami, czasem
**omewhat** ['sʌmwɔt] *adv* w pewnym stopniu, nieco; **~ to my surprise** ku memu niejakiemu zdziwieniu
**omewhere** ['sʌmwɛə$^r$] *adv* gdzieś; **it's ~ or other in Scotland** to (jest) gdzieś w Szkocji; **~ else** gdzie(ś) indziej
**on** [sʌn] *n* syn *m*
**onar** ['səunɑː$^r$] *(Naut)* *n* sonar *m*, hydrolokator *m*
**onata** [sə'nɑːtə] *n* sonata *f*
**ong** [sɔŋ] *n* *(Mus)* pieśń *f*; *(: popular)* piosenka *f*; *(of bird)* śpiew *m*
**ongbook** ['sɔŋbuk] *n* śpiewnik *m*
**ongwriter** ['sɔŋraɪtə$^r$] *n* autor(ka) *m(f)* piosenek
**onic** ['sɔnɪk] *adj* dźwiękowy; **~ boom** uderzenie dźwiękowe
**on-in-law** ['sʌnɪnlɔː] *n* zięć *m*
**onnet** ['sɔnɪt] *n* sonet *m*
**onny** ['sʌnɪ] *(inf)* *n* synu *(voc)* *(inf)*
**oon** [suːn] *adv* *(before long)* wkrótce, niebawem; *(early)* wcześnie; **~ afterwards** wkrótce *or* niedługo potem; **quite ~** już wkrótce; **how ~ can you do it?** kiedy (najwcześniej) możesz to zrobić?; **see you ~!** do zobaczenia wkrótce!; *see also* **as**

**sooner** ['suːnə$^r$] *adv* *(time)* prędzej; *(preference)*: **I would ~ read than watch TV** wolałbym poczytać, niż oglądać telewizję; **~ or later** prędzej czy później; **the ~ the better** im prędzej, tym lepiej; **it was no ~ said than done** zostało to zrobione natychmiast; **no ~ had we left than ...** ledwie wyszliśmy, gdy ...
**soot** [sut] *n* sadza *f*
**soothe** [suːð] *vt* *(person, animal)* uspokajać (uspokoić *perf*); *(pain)* koić (ukoić *perf*), łagodzić (złagodzić *perf*)
**soothing** ['suːðɪŋ] *adj* kojący
**SOP** *n abbr* = **standard operating procedure**
**sop** [sɔp] *n*: **that's only a sop** to tylko coś na odczepnego
**sophisticated** [sə'fɪstɪkeɪtɪd] *adj* *(person, audience)* wyrobiony, bywały; *(fashion, dish)* wyrafinowany, wyszukany, wymyślny; *(machinery, arguments)* skomplikowany
**sophistication** [səfɪstɪ'keɪʃən] *n* *(of person)* wyrobienie *nt*; *(of machine, argument)* stopień *m* złożoności *or* skomplikowania
**sophomore** ['sɔfəmɔː$^r$] *(US: Scol)* *n student drugiego roku college'u*
**soporific** [sɔpə'rɪfɪk] *adj* *(drug)* nasenny; *(lecture etc)* usypiający ▷ *n* środek *m* nasenny
**sopping** ['sɔpɪŋ] *adj*: **~ (wet)** ociekający wodą
**soppy** ['sɔpɪ] *(pej)* *adj* ckliwy *(pej)*
**soprano** [sə'prɑːnəu] *n* sopran *m*, sopranista(-tka) *m(f)*
**sorbet** ['sɔːbeɪ] *n* sorbet *m*
**sorcerer** ['sɔːsərə$^r$] *n* czarnoksiężnik *m*
**sordid** ['sɔːdɪd] *adj* *(dirty)* obskurny; *(wretched)* paskudny, ohydny
**sore** [sɔː$^r$] *adj* *(painful)* bolesny, obolały; *(esp US: offended)* dotknięty ▷ *n* owrzodzenie *nt*; **I have a ~ throat** boli mnie gardło; **a ~ point** *(fig)* czułe miejsce
**sorely** ['sɔːlɪ] *adv*: **I am ~ tempted (to)** mam wielką ochotę *(+infin)*
**soreness** ['sɔːnɪs] *n* bolesność *f*
**sorrel** ['sɔrəl] *n* szczaw *m*
**sorrow** ['sɔrəu] *n* smutek *m*, żal *m*; **sorrows** *npl* smutki *pl*, żale *pl*
**sorrowful** ['sɔrəuful] *adj* *(day)* przygnębiający; *(smile)* przygnębiony
**sorry** ['sɔrɪ] *adj* *(condition)* opłakany; *(sight)* pożałowania godny; **to be ~** żałować; **~!** przepraszam!; **~?** słucham?; **to feel ~ for sb** współczuć komuś; **I'm ~ to hear that** przykro mi to słyszeć; **to be ~ about sth** przepraszać (przeprosić *perf*) za coś; **what a ~ sight you are!** wyglądasz jak półtora nieszczęścia!
**sort** [sɔːt] *n* *(type)* rodzaj *m*; *(make: of coffee)* gatunek *m*; *(: of car)* marka *f* ▷ *vt* *(also:* **sort out**: *papers, belongings)* segregować

S

(posegregować *perf*); (: *problems*) rozwiązywać (rozwiązać *perf*); (*Comput*) sortować (posortować *perf*); **what ~ do you want?** jaki rodzaj Pan/Pani sobie życzy?; **what ~ of car?** samochód jakiej marki?; **I'll do nothing of the ~!** nic podobnego nie zrobię!; **all ~s of reasons** najróżniejsze powody; **it's ~ of awkward** (*inf*) to tak jakoś niezręcznie

**sortie** ['sɔːtɪ] *n* wypad *m*

**sorting office** ['sɔːtɪŋ-] (*Post*) *n* oddział *m* rozdzielni przesyłek

**SOS** *n abbr* (= *save our souls*) SOS *nt inv*

**so-so** ['səusəu] *adv* tak sobie ▷ *adj* taki sobie

**soufflé** ['suːfleɪ] *n* suflet *m*

**sought** [sɔːt] *pt, pp of* **seek**

**sought-after** ['sɔːtɑːftə[r]] *adj* poszukiwany; **a much ~ item** bardzo poszukiwana pozycja

**soul** [səul] *n* dusza *f*; (*Mus*) soul *m*; **the poor ~ had nowhere to sleep** biedactwo nie miało gdzie spać; **I didn't see a ~** nie widziałem żywej duszy

**soul-destroying** ['səuldɪstrɔɪɪŋ] *adj* przygnębiający, przytłaczający

**soulful** ['səulful] *adj* (*eyes, music*) pełen wyrazu

**soulless** ['səullɪs] *adj* (*place*) bez życia *post*; (*job*) monotonny

**soul mate** *n* przyjaciel(-ciółka) *m(f)* od serca

**soul-searching** ['səulsəːtʃɪŋ] *n*: **after much ~, I decided ...** po głębokim namyśle zdecydowałam ...

**sound** [saund] *adj* (*healthy*) zdrowy; (*not damaged*) nietknięty; (*reliable, thorough*) solidny, dogłębny; (*investment*) pewny, bezpieczny; (*advice*) rozsądny; (*argument, policy*) słuszny ▷ *adv*: **to be ~ asleep** spać głęboko ▷ *n* (*noise*) dźwięk *m*, odgłos *m*; (*volume*: *on TV etc*) dźwięk *m*, głośność *f*; (*Geog*) przesmyk *m* ▷ *vt* (*alarm, horn*) włączać (włączyć *perf*) ▷ *vi* (*alarm, horn*) dźwięczeć (zadźwięczeć *perf*); (*fig*: *seem*) wydawać się; **to ~ like sb** mówić *or* brzmieć jak ktoś; **it ~s like French** to wygląda na francuski; **that ~s like them returning** wygląda na to, że wracają; **to be of ~ mind** być przy zdrowych zmysłach; **I don't like the ~ of it** nie podoba mi się to; **to ~ one's horn** (*Aut*) trąbić (zatrąbić *perf*); **it ~s as if ...** wygląda na to, że ...

▸ **sound off** (*inf*) *vi*: **to ~ off (about)** wygłaszać opinie (o *+loc*)

▸ **sound out** *vt* badać (wybadać *perf*), sondować (wysondować *perf*)

**sound barrier** *n* bariera *f* dźwięku

**soundbite** ['saundbaɪt] *n* sformułowanie *nt* łatwo wpadające w ucho (*wycięte z dłuższej wypowiedzi i prezentowane w mediach*)

**sound effects** *npl* efekty *pl* dźwiękowe

**sound engineer** (*Radio, TV etc*) *n* realizator(ka) *m(f)* dźwięku

**sounding** ['saundɪŋ] (*Naut*) *n* sondowanie *nt*

**sounding board** (*Mus*) *n* płyta *f* rezonująca; (*fig*): **to use sb as a ~ for one's ideas** omawiać z kimś swoje pomysły

**soundly** ['saundlɪ] *adv* (*sleep*) głęboko, mocno; (*beat*) dotkliwie

**soundproof** ['saundpruːf] *adj* dźwiękoszczelny ▷ *vt* izolować (wyizolować *perf*) akustycznie

**soundtrack** ['saundtræk] *n* ścieżka *f* dźwiękowa

**sound wave** *n* fala *f* akustyczna

**soup** [suːp] *n* zupa *f*; **in the ~** (*fig*) w opałach

**soup course** *n* zupa *f*

**soup kitchen** *n* ≈ garkuchnia *f*

**soup plate** *n* głęboki talerz *m*

**soupspoon** ['suːpspuːn] *n* łyżka *f* do zupy

**sour** ['sauə[r]] *adj* kwaśny; (*milk*) kwaśny, skwaśniały; (*fig*) cierpki; **to go** *or* **turn ~** kwaśnieć (skwaśnieć *perf*); (*fig*: *relationship*) psuć się (popsuć się *perf*); **~ grapes** (*fig*) kwaśne winogrona

**source** [sɔːs] *n* źródło *nt*; **I have it from a reliable ~ that ...** wiem z wiarygodnego źródła, że ...

**south** [sauθ] *n* południe *nt* ▷ *adj* południowy ▷ *adv* na południe; **(to the) ~ of** na południe od *+gen*; **to travel ~** jechać na południe; **the S~ of France** południe Francji

**South Africa** *n* Republika *f* Południowej Afryki

**South African** *adj* południowoafrykański ▷ *n* Południowoafrykańczyk(-anka) *m(f)*

**South America** *n* Ameryka *f* Południowa

**South American** *adj* południowoamerykański ▷ *n* mieszkaniec(-nka) *m(f)* Ameryki Południowej

**southbound** ['sauθbaund] *adj* (*traffic*) zdążający na południe; (*carriageway*) prowadzący na południe

**south-east** [sauθ'iːst] *n* południowy wschód *m*

**South-East Asia** *n* południowo-wschodnia Azja *f*

**southerly** ['sʌðəlɪ] *adj* południowy

**southern** ['sʌðən] *adj* południowy; **the ~ hemisphere** półkula południowa

**South Korea** *n* Korea *f* Południowa

**South Pole** *n*: **the ~** biegun *m* południowy

**South Sea Islands** *npl* Oceania *f*

**South Seas** *npl*: **the ~** Południowy Pacyfik *m*

**southward(s)** ['sauθwəd(z)] *adv* na południe

**south-west** [sauθ'wɛst] *n* południowy zachód *m*

**souvenir** [su:və'nɪəʳ] *n* pamiątka *f*, souvenir *m*
**sovereign** ['sɔvrɪn] *n* monarcha *m*
**sovereignty** ['sɔvrɪntɪ] *n* suwerenność *f*
**Soviet** ['səuvɪət] *adj* radziecki ▷ *n* mieszkaniec(-nka) *m(f)* Związku Radzieckiego; **the ~ Union** Związek Radziecki
**sow**[1] [sau] *n* locha *f*, maciora *f*
**sow**[2] [səu] (*pt* **sowed**, *pp* **sown**) *vt* siać (posiać *perf*), wysiewać (wysiać *perf*); (*fig*: *suspicion etc*) siać (zasiać *perf*)
**soya** ['sɔɪə], (*US*) **soy** *n*: **~ bean** soja *f*; **~ sauce** sos sojowy
**spa** [spɑ:] *n* (*town*) uzdrowisko *nt*; (*US*: *also*: **health spa**) ≈ centrum *m* odnowy biologicznej
**space** [speɪs] *n* (*gap*) szpara *f*; (*room*) miejsce *nt*; (*beyond Earth*) przestrzeń *f* kosmiczna, kosmos *m*; (*period*): **(with)in the ~ of** na przestrzeni *or* w przeciągu *+gen* ▷ *cpd*: **~ research** badania *pl* kosmosu ▷ *vt* (*also*: **space out**: *text*) rozmieszczać (rozmieścić *perf*); (*: payments, visits*) rozkładać (rozłożyć *perf*); **to clear a ~ for sth** przygotowywać (przygotować *perf*) miejsce pod *or* na coś; **in a confined ~** w zamkniętej przestrzeni; **in a short ~ of time** w krótkim czasie
**space bar** *n* klawisz *m* odstępów, odstępnik *m*
**spacecraft** ['speɪskrɑ:ft] *n* statek *m* kosmiczny
**spaceman** ['speɪsmæn] *n* (*irreg*: *like* **man**) kosmonauta *m*
**spaceship** ['speɪsʃɪp] *n* = **spacecraft**
**space shuttle** *n* prom *m* kosmiczny, wahadłowiec *m*
**spacesuit** ['speɪssu:t] *n* skafander *m or* kombinezon *m* kosmiczny
**spacewoman** ['speɪswumən] *n* (*irreg*: *like* **woman**) kosmonautka *f*
**spacing** ['speɪsɪŋ] *n* odstęp *m*; **single/double ~** (*Typ etc*) jednopunktowa/dwupunktowa interlinia
**spacious** ['speɪʃəs] *adj* przestronny
**spade** [speɪd] *n* łopata *f*; (*child's*) łopatka *f*; **spades** *npl* (*Cards*) piki *pl*
**spadework** ['speɪdwə:k] *n* (*fig*) czarna robota *f*
**spaghetti** [spə'gɛtɪ] *n* spaghetti *nt inv*
**Spain** [speɪn] *n* Hiszpania *f*
**spam** [spæm] *n* (*Comput*) spam *m*
**span** [spæn] *n* (*of wings, arch*) rozpiętość *f*; (*in time*) okres *m* ▷ *vt* (*river*) łączyć (połączyć *perf*) brzegi *+gen*; (*fig*: *time*) obejmować (objąć *perf*)
**Spaniard** ['spænjəd] *n* Hiszpan(ka) *m(f)*
**spaniel** ['spænjəl] *n* spaniel *m*
**Spanish** ['spænɪʃ] *adj* hiszpański ▷ *n* (*język m*) hiszpański; **the Spanish** *npl* Hiszpanie *vir pl*; **~ omelette** omlet po hiszpańsku (*z pomidorami, papryką i zielem angielskim*)
**spank** [spæŋk] *vt* dawać (dać *perf*) klapsa *+dat*
**spanner** ['spænəʳ] (*Brit*) *n* klucz *m* (*maszynowy*)
**spar** [spɑ:ʳ] *n* (*Naut*) drzewce *nt* ▷ *vi* (*Boxing*) odbywać (odbyć *perf*) sparing
**spare** [spɛəʳ] *adj* (*free*) wolny; (*extra*) zapasowy ▷ *n* = **spare part** ▷ *vt* (*save*: *trouble etc*) oszczędzać (oszczędzić *perf*) *+gen*; (*make available*) przeznaczać (przeznaczyć *perf*); (*afford to give*) użyczać (użyczyć *perf*) *+gen*; (*refrain from hurting*) oszczędzać (oszczędzić *perf*); **to ~** w zapasie; **these two are going ~** tych dwoje dostaje szału; **to ~ no expense** nie szczędzić kosztów; **can you ~ the time?** czy możesz poświęcić trochę czasu?; **I've a few minutes to ~** mam kilka wolnych minut; **there is no time to ~** nie ma chwili do stracenia; **~ me the details** oszczędź mi szczegółów
**spare part** *n* część *f* zamienna *or* zapasowa
**spare room** *n* pokój *m* gościnny
**spare time** *n* wolny czas *m*
**spare tyre** *n* zapasowa opona *f*
**spare wheel** *n* zapasowe koło *nt*
**sparing** ['spɛərɪŋ] *adj*: **to be ~ with** oszczędzać na *+loc*
**sparingly** ['spɛərɪŋlɪ] *adv* oszczędnie
**spark** [spɑ:k] *n* iskra *f*; (*fig*: *of wit etc*) przebłysk *m*
**spark(ing) plug** ['spɑ:k(ɪŋ)-] *n* świeca *f* zapłonowa
**sparkle** ['spɑ:kl] *n* połysk *m* ▷ *vi* mienić się, skrzyć się
**sparkling** ['spɑ:klɪŋ] *adj* (*water*) gazowany; (*wine*) musujący; (*fig*: *conversation, performance*) błyskotliwy
**sparrow** ['spærəu] *n* wróbel *m*
**sparse** [spɑ:s] *adj* (*hair*) rzadki; (*rainfall*) skąpy; (*population*) nieliczny
**spartan** ['spɑ:tən] *adj* (*fig*) spartański
**spasm** ['spæzəm] *n* (*Med*) skurcz *m*, spazm *m*; (*fig*: *of anger etc*) paroksyzm *m*
**spasmodic** [spæz'mɔdɪk] *adj* (*fig*) nerwowy
**spastic** ['spæstɪk] (*Med*) *n* (*old*) osoba *f* z porażeniem kurczowym ▷ *adj* spastyczny, kurczowy
**spat** [spæt] *pt, pp of* **spit** ▷ *n* (*US*) sprzeczka *f*
**spate** [speɪt] *n* (*fig*): **a ~ of** (*letters etc*) nawał *m or* powódź *f +gen*; **a river in ~** wezbrana rzeka
**spatial** ['speɪʃl] *adj* przestrzenny
**spatter** ['spætəʳ] *vt* (*liquid*) rozpryskiwać (rozpryskać *perf*); (*surface*) opryskiwać (opryskać *perf*) ▷ *vi* rozpryskiwać się (rozpryskać się *perf*)
**spatula** ['spætjulə] *n* (*Culin*) łopatka *f*; (*Med*) szpatułka *f*

S

**spawn** [spɔːn] *vi* (*fish*) składać (złożyć *perf*) ikrę; (*frog*) składać (złożyć *perf*) skrzek ▷ *vt* (*group, problem etc*) dawać (dać *perf*) początek *+dat* ▷ *n* (*of fish*) ikra *f*; (*of frog*) skrzek *m*
**SPCA** (*US*) *n abbr* = **Society for the Prevention of Cruelty to Animals**
**SPCC** (*US*) *n abbr* = **Society for the Prevention of Cruelty to Children**
**speak** [spiːk] (*pt* **spoke**, *pp* **spoken**) *vi* (*use voice*) mówić; (*make a speech*) przemawiać (przemówić *perf*); (*truth*) mówić (powiedzieć *perf*); **to ~ to sb/of** *or* **about sth** rozmawiać (porozmawiać *perf*) z kimś/o czymś; **~ up!** mów głośniej!; **to ~ English** mówić po angielsku; **to ~ at a conference/in a debate** zabierać (zabrać *perf*) głos na konferencji/w debacie; **to ~ one's mind** wyrażać (wyrazić *perf*) swoje zdanie; **he has no money to ~ of** on nie ma praktycznie żadnych pieniędzy; **so to ~** że tak powiem, że się tak wyrażę
▸ **speak for** *vt fus*: **to ~ for sb** mówić za kogoś *or* w czyimś imieniu; **that picture is already spoken for** ten obraz jest już sprzedany; **~ for yourself!** mów za siebie!
**speaker** ['spiːkə$^r$] *n* (*person*) mówca *m*; (*also*: **loudspeaker**) głośnik *m*; **the S~** (*Brit, US*) *przewodniczący jednej z izb Parlamentu/Kongresu*; **are you a Welsh ~?** czy mówisz po walijsku?
**speaking** ['spiːkɪŋ] *adj* mówiący; **a ~ clock** zegarynka; **Italian-~ people** ludzie mówiący po włosku; **they are not on ~ terms** oni ze sobą nie rozmawiają
**spear** [spɪə$^r$] *n* włócznia *f* ▷ *vt* dźgać (dźgnąć *perf*) włócznią
**spearhead** ['spɪəhɛd] *vt* stać (stanąć *perf*) na czele *+gen*
**spearmint** ['spɪəmɪnt] *n* mięta *f* kędzierzawa
**spec** [spɛk] (*inf*) *n*: **on ~** w ciemno (*inf*); **to buy/go on ~** kupować/iść w ciemno (*inf*)
**spec.** (*Tech*) *n abbr* (= *specification*) specyfikacja *f*
**special** ['spɛʃl] *adj* (*effort, help, occasion*) specjalny, szczególny; (*adviser, permission, school*) specjalny ▷ *n* pociąg *m* specjalny *or* dodatkowy; **take ~ care** bądź szczególnie ostrożny; **nothing ~** nic szczególnego *or* specjalnego; **today's ~ is ...** dziś polecamy *+acc*
**special agent** *n* agent *m* specjalny
**special correspondent** *n* specjalny korespondent *m or* wysłannik *m*
**special delivery** (*Post*) *n*: **by ~** przesyłką ekspresową
**special effects** *npl* efekty *pl* specjalne
**specialist** ['spɛʃəlɪst] *n* specjalista(-tka) *m(f)*; **heart ~** specjalista kardiolog *or* chorób serca
**speciality** [spɛʃɪ'ælɪtɪ] *n* specjalność *f*
**specialize** ['spɛʃəlaɪz] *vi*: **to ~ (in)** specjalizować się (w *+loc*)
**specially** ['spɛʃlɪ] *adv* specjalnie
**special offer** (*Comm*) *n* oferta *f* specjalna, okazja *f*
**specialty** ['spɛʃəltɪ] (*esp US*) *n* = **speciality**
**species** ['spiːʃiːz] *n inv* gatunek *m*
**specific** [spə'sɪfɪk] *adj* (*fixed*) określony; (*exact*) ścisły; **~ to** specyficzny dla *+gen*
**specifically** [spə'sɪfɪklɪ] *adv* (*specially*) specjalnie; (*exactly*) ściśle
**specification** [spɛsɪfɪ'keɪʃən] *n* (*Tech*) opis *m* techniczny; (*requirement*) wymóg *m*; **specifications** *npl* (*Tech*) parametry *pl*
**specify** ['spɛsɪfaɪ] *vt* wyszczególniać (wyszczególnić *perf*); **unless otherwise specified** przy braku innych wskazań
**specimen** ['spɛsɪmən] *n* (*single example*) okaz *m*; (*Med*) próbka *f*
**specimen copy** *n* egzemplarz *m* próbny
**specimen signature** *n* wzór *m* podpisu
**speck** [spɛk] *n* drobinka *f*, pyłek *m*
**speckled** ['spɛkld] *adj* (*hen, eggs*) nakrapiany
**specs** [spɛks] (*inf*) *npl* okulary *pl*
**spectacle** ['spɛktəkl] *n* widowisko *nt*; **spectacles** *npl* okulary *pl*
**spectacle case** (*Brit*) *n* etui *nt inv* do okularów
**spectacular** [spɛk'tækjulə$^r$] *adj* (*rise etc*) dramatyczny; (*success*) spektakularny ▷ *n* (*Theat*) gala *f*
**spectator** [spɛk'teɪtə$^r$] *n* widz *m*; **a ~ sport** sport widowiskowy
**spectra** ['spɛktrə] *npl of* **spectrum**
**spectre**, (*US*) **specter** ['spɛktə$^r$] *n* widmo *nt*
**spectrum** ['spɛktrəm] (*pl* **spectra**) *n* widmo *nt*; (*fig*: *of opinion etc*) spektrum *m*
**speculate** ['spɛkjuleɪt] *vi* (*Fin*) spekulować, grać (*na giełdzie*); **to ~ about** snuć domysły na temat *+gen*
**speculation** [spɛkju'leɪʃən] *n* (*Fin*) spekulacja *f*; (*guesswork*) domysły *pl*, spekulacje *pl*
**speculative** ['spɛkjulətɪv] *adj* oparty na domysłach
**speculator** ['spɛkjuleɪtə$^r$] *n* spekulant(ka) *m(f)*
**sped** [spɛd] *pt, pp of* **speed**
**speech** [spiːtʃ] *n* (*faculty, act, part of play*) mowa *f*; (*manner of speaking, enunciation*) wymowa *f*; (*formal talk*) przemówienie *nt*, przemowa *f*
**speech day** (*Brit*: *Scol*) *n dzień, w którym uczniom rozdaje się nagrody, zaprasza się do szkoły rodziców i wygłasza przemówienia*
**speech impediment** *n* zaburzenie *nt* mowy
**speechless** ['spiːtʃlɪs] *adj* oniemiały; **he was ~** zaniemówił, oniemiał
**speech therapist** *n* logopeda *m*
**speech therapy** *n* leczenie *nt* logopedyczne
**speed** [spiːd] (*pt, pp* **sped**) *n* (*rate*) prędkość *f*, szybkość *f*; (*fast travel, promptness, haste*)

szybkość *f* ▷ *vi*: **to ~ (along/by)** pędzić (popędzić *perf*) (wzdłuż *+gen*/obok *+gen*); (*Aut*) jechać z nadmierną prędkością, przekraczać (przekroczyć *perf*) dozwoloną prędkość; **at ~** (*Brit*) z dużą prędkością; **at full** *or* **top ~** z maksymalną prędkością; **at a ~ of 70km/h** z prędkością siedemdziesięciu kilometrów na godzinę; **shorthand/typing ~** szybkość stenografowania/pisania na maszynie; **a five-~ gearbox** pięciobiegowa skrzynia biegów
▸ **speed up** (*pt, pp* **~ed up**) *vi* przyspieszać (przyspieszyć *perf*) ▷ *vt* przyspieszać (przyspieszyć *perf*)

**speedboat** ['spi:dbəut] *n* ślizgacz *m* (*łódź motorowa*)

**speedily** ['spi:dɪlɪ] *adv* szybko, pośpiesznie

**speeding** ['spi:dɪŋ] (*Aut*) *n* jazda *f* z nadmierną prędkością, przekroczenie *nt* dozwolonej prędkości

**speed limit** (*Aut*) *n* ograniczenie *nt* prędkości

**speedometer** [spɪ'dɔmɪtə^r] (*Aut*) *n* szybkościomierz *m*

**speed trap** (*Aut*) *n miejsce, w którym prowadzi się radarową kontrolę prędkości przejeżdżających pojazdów*

**speedway** ['spi:dweɪ] *n* (*also*: **speedway racing**) wyścigi *pl* na żużlu

**speedy** [spi:dɪ] *adj* (*fast*) szybki, prędki; (*prompt*) szybki, rychły

**speleologist** [spɛlɪ'ɔlədʒɪst] *n* speleolog *m*

**spell** [spɛl] (*pt, pp* **spelt** (*Brit*) *or* **~ed**) *n* (*also*: **magic spell**) zaklęcie *nt*, urok *m*; (*period*) okres *m* ▷ *vt* (*in writing*) pisać (napisać *perf*); (*also*: **spell out**) literować (przeliterować *perf*); (*signify*: *danger etc*) oznaczać; **to cast a ~ on sb** rzucać (rzucić *perf*) na kogoś czar *or* urok; **cold/hot ~** fala chłodów/upałów; **he can't ~** on robi błędy ortograficzne; **how do you ~ your name?** jak się pisze Pana/Pani nazwisko?; **can you ~ it for me?** czy może mi Pan/Pani to przeliterować?

**spellbound** ['spɛlbaund] *adj* oczarowany

**spelling** ['spɛlɪŋ] *n* (*word form*) pisownia *f*; (*ability*) ortografia *f*; **~ mistake** błąd ortograficzny

**spelt** [spɛlt] *pt, pp of* **spell**

**spend** [spɛnd] (*pt, pp* **spent**) *vt* (*money*) wydawać (wydać *perf*); (*time, life*) spędzać (spędzić *perf*); (*devote*): **to ~ time/money/effort on sth** poświęcać (poświęcić *perf*) czas/pieniądze/wysiłek na coś

**spending** ['spɛndɪŋ] *n* wydatki *pl*; **government ~** wydatki publiczne

**spending money** *n* kieszonkowe *nt*

**spending power** *n* siła *f or* zdolność *f* nabywcza

**spendthrift** ['spɛndθrɪft] *n* rozrzutnik *m*

**spent** [spɛnt] *pt, pp of* **spend** ▷ *adj* (*patience*) wyczerpany; (*cartridge, matches*) zużyty; (*bullets*) wystrzelony

**sperm** [spə:m] *n* nasienie *nt*, sperma *f*; (*single*) plemnik *m*

**sperm whale** *n* kaszalot *m*

**spew** [spju:] *vt* wypluwać (wypluć *perf*), wyrzucać (wyrzucić *perf*) (z siebie)

**sphere** [sfɪə^r] *n* (*round object*) kula *f*; (*area*) sfera *f*

**spherical** ['sfɛrɪkl] *adj* kulisty, sferyczny

**sphinx** [sfɪŋks] *n* sfinks *m*

**spice** [spaɪs] *n* przyprawa *f* ▷ *vt* przyprawiać (przyprawić *perf*)

**spick-and-span** ['spɪkən'spæn] *adj* (*house etc*) lśniący czystością, wychuchany (*inf*)

**spicy** ['spaɪsɪ] *adj* mocno przyprawiony, ostry

**spider** ['spaɪdə^r] *n* pająk *m*; **~'s web** pajęczyna

**spidery** ['spaɪdərɪ] *adj* przypominający pajęczynę

**spiel** [spi:l] (*inf*) *n* gadka *f* (*inf, pej*)

**spike** [spaɪk] *n* (*point*) kolec *m*; (*Bot*) kwiatostan *f* stożkowaty; (*Elec*) impuls *m*; **spikes** *npl* (*Sport*) kolce *pl*

**spike heel** (*US*) *n* szpilka *f* (*obcas lub but*)

**spiky** ['spaɪkɪ] *adj* kolczasty

**spill** [spɪl] (*pt, pp* **spilt** *or* **~ed**) *vt* rozlewać (rozlać *perf*) ▷ *vi* rozlewać się (rozlać się *perf*), wylewać się (wylać się *perf*); **to ~ the beans** (*inf*: *fig*) wygadać się (*perf*), puszczać (puścić *perf*) farbę (*inf*)
▸ **spill out** *vi* (*people*) wysypywać się (wysypać się *perf*)
▸ **spill over** *vi* (*liquid*) przelewać się (przelać się *perf*); (*fig*: *conflict*) rozszerzać się (rozszerzyć się *perf*)

**spin** [spɪn] (*pt* **spun, span**, *pp* **spun**) *n* (*in car*) przejażdżka *f*; (*revolution of wheel*) wirowanie *nt*; (*: single*) obrót *m*; (*Aviat*) korkociąg *m* ▷ *vt* (*wool etc*) prząść (uprząść *perf*); (*wheel*) obracać (obrócić *perf*) *+instr*; (*Brit*: *also*: **spin-dry**) odwirowywać (odwirować *perf*) ▷ *vi* (*make thread*) prząść; (*turn round*) okręcać się (okręcić się *perf*), obracać się (obrócić się *perf*); **to put ~ on a ball** podkręcać (podkręcić *perf*) piłkę (*inf*); **to ~ a yarn** opowiadać niestworzone historie; **to ~ a coin** (*Brit*) rzucać (rzucić *perf*) monetą; **my head is ~ning** kręci mi się w głowie
▸ **spin out** *vt* (*talk, holiday*) przeciągać (przeciągnąć *perf*); (*money*) gospodarować oszczędnie *+instr*

**spinach** ['spɪnɪtʃ] *n* szpinak *m*

**spinal** ['spaɪnl] *adj*: **~ injury** uraz *m* kręgosłupa

**spinal column** *n* kręgosłup *m*

S

**spinal cord** *n* rdzeń *m* kręgowy
**spindly** ['spɪndlɪ] *adj* wrzecionowaty
**spin-dry** ['spɪn'draɪ] *vt* odwirowywać (odwirować *perf*)
**spin-dryer** [spɪn'draɪəʳ] (*Brit*) *n* wirówka *f*
**spine** [spaɪn] *n* (*Anat*) kręgosłup *m*; (*thorn*) kolec *m*
**spine-chilling** ['spaɪntʃɪlɪŋ] *adj* mrożący krew w żyłach
**spineless** ['spaɪnlɪs] *adj* (*fig: person*) bez kręgosłupa *post*
**spinner** ['spɪnəʳ] *n* prządzarz/prządka *m/f*
**spinning** ['spɪnɪŋ] *n* przędzenie *nt*
**spinning top** *n* (*toy*) bąk *m*
**spinning wheel** *n* kołowrotek *m*
**spin-off** ['spɪnɔf] *n* (*fig*) efekt *m* uboczny
**spinster** ['spɪnstəʳ] *n* stara panna *f*
**spiral** ['spaɪərl] *n* spirala *f* ▷ *vi* (*fig: prices etc*) wzrastać (wzrosnąć *perf*) gwałtownie; **the inflationary ~** spirala inflacyjna
**spiral staircase** *n* schody *pl* kręcone
**spire** ['spaɪəʳ] *n* iglica *f*
**spirit** ['spɪrɪt] *n* (*soul*) dusza *f*; (*ghost, sense*) duch *m*; (*courage*) odwaga *f*; (*frame of mind*) nastrój *m*; **spirits** *npl* napoje *pl* alkoholowe; **in good ~s** w dobrym humorze *or* nastroju; **community ~** poczucie *or* duch wspólnoty
**spirited** ['spɪrɪtɪd] *adj* (*resistance*) żarliwy, zagorzały; (*performance*) porywający
**spirit level** *n* poziomnica *f*
**spiritual** ['spɪrɪtjuəl] *adj* duchowy ▷ *n* (*also:* **Negro spiritual**) *utwór chóralny o charakterze religijnym wywodzący się z kultury Murzynów północnoamerykańskich*
**spiritualism** ['spɪrɪtjuəlɪzəm] *n* spirytyzm *m*
**spit** [spɪt] (*pt, pp* **spat**) *n* (*for roasting*) rożen *m*; (*saliva*) plwocina *f* ▷ *vi* (*person*) pluć (plunąć *perf*), spluwać (splunąć *perf*); (*cooking*) skwierczeć (zaskwierczeć *perf*); (*fire*) trzaskać (trzasnąć *perf*); (*inf: rain*) siąpić
**spite** [spaɪt] *n* złośliwość *f* ▷ *vt* robić (zrobić *perf*) na złość *+dat*; **in ~ of** (po)mimo *+gen*
**spiteful** ['spaɪtful] *adj* złośliwy, zawzięty
**spitroast** ['spɪt'rəust] *n* pieczeń *f* z rożna
**spitting** ['spɪtɪŋ] *n*: **"~ prohibited"** „nie pluć" ▷ *adj*: **to be the ~ image of sb** być podobnym do kogoś jak dwie krople wody
**spittle** ['spɪtl] *n* ślina *f*
**spiv** [spɪv] (*Brit: inf, pej*) *n* kombinator *m* (*inf, pej*)
**splash** [splæʃ] *n* (*sound*) plusk *m*, pluśnięcie *nt*; (*of colour*) plama *f* ▷ *excl* plusk, chlup ▷ *vt* ochlapywać (ochlapać *perf*) ▷ *vi* (*also:* **splash about**) pluskać się; (*water*) chlapać; **to ~ paint on the floor** chlapać (pochlapać *perf*) podłogę farbą
**splashdown** ['splæʃdaun] *n* wodowanie *nt* statku kosmicznego
**splayfooted** ['spleɪfutɪd] *adj* platfusowaty
**spleen** [spliːn] *n* śledziona *f*
**splendid** ['splɛndɪd] *adj* (*excellent*) doskonały, świetny; (*impressive*) okazały, wspaniały
**splendour**, (*US*) **splendor** ['splɛndəʳ] *n* wspaniałość *f*; **splendours** *npl* wspaniałości *pl*
**splice** [splaɪs] *vt* kleić (skleić *perf*)
**splint** [splɪnt] *n* szyna *f* (usztywniająca), łubek *m*
**splinter** ['splɪntəʳ] *n* (*of wood*) drzazga *f*; (*of glass*) odłamek *m* ▷ *vi* rozszczepiać się (rozszczepić się *perf*), rozłupywać się (rozłupać się *perf*)
**splinter group** *n* odłam *m*
**split** [splɪt] (*pt, pp* **~**) *n* (*crack, tear*) pęknięcie *nt*; (*fig*) podział *m*; (*Pol*) rozłam *m* ▷ *vt* (*divide*) dzielić (podzielić *perf*); (*party*) powodować (spowodować *perf*) podział *or* rozłam w *+loc*; (*work, profits*) dzielić (podzielić *perf*) ▷ *vi* (*divide*) dzielić się (podzielić się *perf*); (*crack*) pękać (pęknąć *perf*); (*tear*) rozdzierać się (rozedrzeć się *perf*); **let's ~ the difference** (*with money*) podzielmy resztę na połowę; (*fig: in argument*) pójdźmy na kompromis; **to do the ~s** robić (zrobić *perf*) szpagat
▸ **split up** *vi* (*couple*) zrywać (zerwać *perf*) (ze sobą), rozstawać się (rozstać się *perf*); (*group*) rozdzielać się (rozdzielić się *perf*)
**split-level** ['splɪtlɛvl] *adj* (*house*) wielopoziomowy
**split peas** *npl* groch *m or* groszek *m* łuskany
**split personality** *n* rozdwojenie *nt* jaźni
**split second** *n* ułamek *m* sekundy
**splitting** ['splɪtɪŋ] *adj*: **I have a ~ headache** głowa mi pęka
**splutter** ['splʌtəʳ] *vi* prychać (prychnąć *perf*), parskać (parsknąć *perf*)
**spoil** [spɔɪl] (*pt, pp* **~t** *or* **~ed**) *vt* (*thing*) uszkadzać (uszkodzić *perf*); (*enjoyment*) psuć (zepsuć *perf*); (*child*) rozpieszczać (rozpieścić *perf*), psuć ▷ *vi*: **to be ~ing for a fight** rwać się do walki; **to ~ a vote** oddawać (oddać *perf*) nieważny głos
**spoils** [spɔɪlz] *npl* łupy *pl*
**spoilsport** ['spɔɪlspɔːt] (*pej*) *n*: **don't be a ~** nie psuj ludziom zabawy
**spoilt** [spɔɪlt] *pt, pp of* **spoil** ▷ *adj* (*child*) rozpieszczony; (*ballot paper*) nieważny
**spoke** [spəuk] *pt of* **speak** ▷ *n* szprycha *f*
**spoken** ['spəukn] *pp of* **speak**
**spokesman** ['spəuksmən] (*irreg: like* **man**) *n* rzecznik *m*
**spokesperson** ['spəukspəːsn] *n* (*irreg: like* **person**) rzecznik(-iczka) *m(f)*
**spokeswoman** ['spəukswumən] *n* (*irreg: like* **woman**) rzeczniczka *f*

**sponge** [spʌndʒ] *n* gąbka *f*; (*also*: **sponge cake**) biszkopt *m* ▷ *vt* przecierać (przetrzeć *perf*) gąbką ▷ *vi*: **to ~ off** *or* **on sb** wyciągać od kogoś pieniądze
**sponge bag** (*Brit*) *n* kosmetyczka *f*
**sponger** ['spʌndʒəʳ] *n* (*pej*) pasożyt *m* (*pej*)
**spongy** ['spʌndʒɪ] *adj* gąbczasty
**sponsor** ['spɔnsəʳ] *n* (*of player, programme, event*) sponsor(ka) *m(f)*; (*for application*) poręczyciel(ka) *m(f)*; (*for bill in parliament*) inicjator(ka) *m(f)* ▷ *vt* (*player, programme, event*) sponsorować; (*proposal*) przedkładać (przedłożyć *perf*); **I ~ed him at 3p a mile** (*in fund-raising race*) sponsorowałem go w kwocie 3 pensów za milę
**sponsorship** ['spɔnsəʃɪp] *n* sponsorowanie *nt*
**spontaneity** [spɔntə'neɪɪtɪ] *n* spontaniczność *f*
**spontaneous** [spɔn'teɪnɪəs] *adj* spontaniczny; **~ combustion** samozapłon
**spooky** ['spu:kɪ] (*inf*) *adj* straszny
**spool** [spu:l] *n* (*for thread*) szpulka *f*; (*for film, tape*) szpula *f*
**spoon** [spu:n] *n* łyżka *f*; (*small*) łyżeczka *f*
**spoon-feed** ['spu:nfi:d] *vt* (*baby*) karmić łyżeczką; (*patient*) karmić łyżką; (*fig*: *students*) podawać (podać *perf*) wszystko na tacy *+dat*
**spoonful** ['spu:nful] *n* (pełna) łyżka *f*
**sporadic** [spə'rædɪk] *adj* sporadyczny
**sport** [spɔ:t] *n* (*game*) sport *m*; (*also*: **good sport**) świetny kumpel *m* ▷ *vt* (*piece of clothing, jewellery*) paradować w *+loc*; (*purse, umbrella*) paradować z *+instr*; **indoor/outdoor ~s** sporty halowe/rozgrywane na wolnym powietrzu
**sporting** ['spɔ:tɪŋ] *adj* (*event*) sportowy; (*gesture*) szlachetny; **a ~ chance** realna szansa
**sport jacket** (*US*) *n* = **sports jacket**
**sports car** *n* samochód *m* sportowy
**sports centre** *n* ośrodek *m* sportowy
**sports ground** *n* boisko *nt* (sportowe)
**sports jacket** (*Brit*) *n* sportowa marynarka *f*
**sportsman** ['spɔ:tsmən] *n* (*irreg*: *like* **man**) sportowiec *m*
**sportsmanship** ['spɔ:tsmənʃɪp] *n* sportowe zachowanie *nt*
**sports page** (*Press*) *n* dział *m* sportowy
**sportswear** ['spɔ:tswɛəʳ] *n* odzież *f* sportowa
**sportswoman** ['spɔ:tswumən] *n* (*irreg*: *like* **woman**) sportsmenka *f*
**sporty** ['spɔ:tɪ] *adj* wysportowany
**spot** [spɔt] *n* (*dot*) kropka *f*; (*mark*: *dirty, unwanted*) plama *f*; (: *on animal*) cętka *f*; (*on skin*) pryszcz *m*; (*place*) miejsce *nt*; (*also*: **spot advertisement**) reklama *f* (*między programami*); (*Radio, TV*) *część programu zarezerwowana dla konkretnego artysty lub określonego typu rozrywki* ▷ *vt* zauważać (zauważyć *perf*); **on the ~** (*in that place*) na miejscu; (*immediately*) z miejsca; **a ~ of trouble** mały kłopot; **I'll do a ~ of gardening** popracuję trochę w ogrodzie; **in a ~** w kropce; **to put sb on the ~** stawiać (postawić *perf*) kogoś w trudnej sytuacji; **to come out in ~s** dostawać (dostać *perf*) wysypki
**spot check** *n* wyrywkowa kontrola *f*
**spotless** ['spɔtlɪs] *adj* nieskazitelny
**spotlight** ['spɔtlaɪt] *n* jupiter *m*
**spot-on** [spɔt'ɔn] (*Brit*: *inf*) *adj*: **to be ~** trafiać (trafić *perf*) w dziesiątkę
**spot price** (*Comm*) *n* cena *f* loco
**spotted** ['spɔtɪd] *adj* (*bird*) nakrapiany; (*animal*) cętkowany; (*garment*) w kropki *post*; **~ with** poplamiony *+instr*
**spotty** ['spɔtɪ] *adj* pryszczaty
**spouse** [spaus] *n* małżonek(-nka) *m(f)*
**spout** [spaut] *n* (*of jug, teapot*) dziobek *m*; (*of pipe*) wylot *m*; (*of liquid*) struga *f* ▷ *vi* chlustać (chlusnąć *perf*), bluzgać (bluznąć *perf*)
**sprain** [spreɪn] *n* (*Med*) skręcenie *nt* ▷ *vt*: **to ~ one's ankle/wrist** skręcić (*perf*) nogę w kostce/rękę w nadgarstku
**sprang** [spræŋ] *pt of* **spring**
**sprawl** [sprɔ:l] *vi* rozciągać się (rozciągnąć się *perf*) ▷ *n*: **urban ~** rozrastanie się *nt* miasta (*w sposób nadmierny i/lub niekontrolowany*); **to send sb ~ing** zwalać (zwalić *perf*) kogoś z nóg
**spray** [spreɪ] *n* (*small drops*) rozpylona ciecz *f*; (: *of water*) pył *m* wodny; (*sea spray*) mgiełka *f* od wody; (*container*) spray *m*, aerozol *m*; (*garden spray*) spryskiwacz *m* ogrodowy; (*of flowers*) gałązka *f* ▷ *vt* (*liquid*) rozpryskiwać (rozpryskać *perf*); (*crops*) opryskiwać (opryskać *perf*) ▷ *cpd*: **~ deodorant** dezodorant *m* w sprayu *or* aerozolu; **~ can** spray, aerozol; **to ~ water on sth, to ~ sth with water** opryskiwać (opryskać *perf*) coś wodą
**spread** [sprɛd] (*pt, pp* **~**) *n* (*area covered*) zasięg *m*; (*span, variety*) rozpiętość *f*; (*distribution*) rozkład *m*; (*expansion*) rozprzestrzenianie się *nt*; (*Culin*) pasta *f* (*do smarowania pieczywa*); (*inf*: *food*) uczta *f*; (*Press*) rozkładówka *f* ▷ *vt* (*objects, one's arms, repayments*) rozkładać (rozłożyć *perf*); (*dirt, rumour, disease*) roznosić (roznieść *perf*) ▷ *vi* (*disease*) rozprzestrzeniać się (rozprzestrzenić się *perf*); (*news*) rozchodzić się (rozejść się *perf*); (*stain*) rozlewać się (rozlać się *perf*); **middle-age ~** zaokrąglanie się figury w średnim wieku; **to ~ butter on, to ~ with butter** smarować (posmarować *perf*) masłem *+acc*
▶ **spread out** *vi* (*move apart*) rozchodzić się (rozejść się *perf*), rozdzielać się (rozdzielić się *perf*); (*extend*) rozciągać się

S

**spread-eagled** ['sprɛdi:gld] *adj*: **he was (lying)** ~ leżał z rozrzuconymi kończynami
**spreadsheet** ['sprɛdʃi:t] (*Comput*) *n* arkusz *m* kalkulacyjny
**spree** [spri:] *n*: **let's go on a** ~ chodźmy zaszaleć
**sprig** [sprɪg] *n* gałązka *f*
**sprightly** ['spraɪtlɪ] *adj* dziarski, żwawy
**spring** [sprɪŋ] (*pt* **sprang**, *pp* **sprung**) *n* (*coiled metal*) sprężyna *f*; (*season*) wiosna *f*; (*of water*) źródło *nt*; (: *small*) źródełko *nt* ▷ *vi* (*leap*) skakać (skoczyć *perf*) ▷ *vt*: **the pipe/boat had sprung a leak** rura/łódka zaczęła przeciekać; **in** ~ wiosną, na wiosnę; **to walk with a ~ in one's step** chodzić sprężystym krokiem; **to ~ from** wynikać (wyniknąć *perf*) z *+gen*; **to ~ into action** zaczynać (zacząć *perf*) działać; **he sprang the news on me** zaskoczył mnie tą wiadomością
▸ **spring up** *vi* wyrastać (wyrosnąć *perf*) (jak grzyby po deszczu)
**springboard** ['sprɪŋbɔ:d] *n* (*Sport*) trampolina *f*; (*fig*): **to be the ~ for** stanowić odskocznię dla *+gen*
**spring-clean(ing)** [sprɪŋ'kli:n(ɪŋ)] *n* wiosenne porządki *pl*
**spring onion** (*Brit*) *n* zielona cebulka *f*
**springtime** ['sprɪŋtaɪm] *n* wiosenna pora *f*; **in** ~ wiosną, na wiosnę
**springy** ['sprɪŋɪ] *adj* sprężysty
**sprinkle** ['sprɪŋkl] *vt*: **to ~ water on sth, to ~ sth with water** skrapiać (skropić *perf*) *or* zraszać (zrosić *perf*) coś wodą; **to ~ salt/sugar on sth, to ~ sth with salt/sugar** posypywać (posypać *perf*) coś solą/cukrem
**sprinkler** ['sprɪŋklə^r] *n* (*for lawn*) spryskiwacz *m*, zraszacz *m*; (*to put out fire*) instalacja *f* tryskaczowa *or* sprinklerowa
**sprinkling** ['sprɪŋklɪŋ] *n* (*of water*) kilka *pl* kropli; (*of salt, sugar*) szczypta *f*; (*fig*) odrobina *f*
**sprint** [sprɪnt] *n* sprint *m* ▷ *vi* biec (pobiec *perf*) sprintem; **the 200 metres** ~ bieg na 200 metrów
**sprinter** ['sprɪntə^r] *n* sprinter(ka) *m(f)*
**sprite** [spraɪt] *n* chochlik *m*
**sprocket** ['sprɔkɪt] *n* koło *nt* łańcuchowe
**sprout** [spraut] *vi* kiełkować (wykiełkować *perf*)
**sprouts** [sprauts] *npl* (*also*: **Brussels sprouts**) brukselka *f*
**spruce** [spru:s] *n inv* świerk *m* ▷ *adj* elegancki
▸ **spruce up** *vt* (*room, car*) wyszykować (*perf*); **to ~ o.s. up** stroić się (wystroić się *perf*)
**sprung** [sprʌŋ] *pp of* **spring**
**spry** [spraɪ] *adj* dziarski, żwawy
**SPUC** *n abbr* = **Society for the Protection of Unborn Children**
**spud** [spʌd] (*inf*) *n* kartofel *m*
**spun** [spʌn] *pt, pp of* **spin**
**spur** [spə:^r] *n* ostroga *f*; (*fig*) bodziec *m*, zachęta *f* ▷ *vt* (*also*: **spur on**) zachęcać (zachęcić *perf*); **on the ~ of the moment** pod wpływem chwilowego impulsu
**spurious** ['spjuərɪəs] *adj* (*attraction*) złudny; (*argument*) błędny; (*sympathy*) fałszywy, udawany
**spurn** [spə:n] *vt* (*proposal, idea*) odrzucać (odrzucić *perf*); (*person*) odtrącać (odtrącić *perf*)
**spurt** [spə:t] *n* (*of blood etc*) struga *f*; (*of emotion*) poryw *m* ▷ *vi* (*blood*) tryskać (trysnąć *perf*); (*flame*) strzelać (strzelić *perf*); **to put on a ~** (*runner*) przyśpieszać (przyśpieszyć *perf*)
**sputter** ['spʌtə^r] *vi* = **splutter**
**spy** [spaɪ] *n* szpieg *m* ▷ *vi*: **to spy on** szpiegować *+acc* ▷ *vt* ujrzeć (*perf*), spostrzec (*perf*) ▷ *cpd* szpiegowski
**spying** ['spaɪɪŋ] *n* szpiegostwo *nt*
**Sq.** *abbr* (*in address*: = *square*) pl.
**sq.** *abbr* (= *square*) kw.
**squabble** ['skwɔbl] *vi* sprzeczać się (posprzeczać się *perf*) ▷ *n* sprzeczka *f*
**squad** [skwɔd] *n* (*Mil, Police*) oddział *m*; (*Sport*) ekipa *f*; **flying** ~ (*Police*) lotna brygada
**squad car** (*Brit*) *n* samochód *m or* wóz *m* patrolowy
**squadron** ['skwɔdrn] *n* (*Mil*) eskadra *f*; (*Aviat, Naut*) dywizjon *m*
**squalid** ['skwɔlɪd] *adj* (*conditions, house*) nędzny; (*story*) plugawy
**squall** [skwɔ:l] *n* szkwał *m*
**squalor** ['skwɔlə^r] *n* nędza *f*
**squander** ['skwɔndə^r] *vt* (*money*) trwonić (roztrwonić *perf*); (*chances*) trwonić (strwonić *perf*)
**square** [skwɛə^r] *n* (*shape*) kwadrat *m*; (*in town*) plac *m*; (*US*: *block of houses*) kwartał *m*; (*also*: **set square**) ekierka *f* ▷ *adj* (*in shape*) kwadratowy; (*meal*) solidny; (*inf*: *ideas, person*) staromodny, staroświecki ▷ *vt* (*arrange*) układać (ułożyć *perf*); (*Math*) podnosić (podnieść *perf*) do kwadratu; (*reconcile*) godzić (pogodzić *perf*) ▷ *vi*: **to ~ with** przystawać *or* pasować do *+gen*; **don't be such a ~** (*inf*) nie bądź taki nie na czasie; **the match was all ~** wynik meczu był remisowy; **two metres ~** kwadrat o boku dwóch metrów; **two ~ metres** dwa metry kwadratowe; **I'll ~ it with him** (*inf*) załatwię to z nim; **can you ~ it with your conscience?** czy pozwala ci na to sumienie?; **we're back to ~ one** wróciliśmy do punktu wyjścia
▸ **square up** (*Brit*) *vi* wyrównywać (wyrównać *perf*) rachunki; **to ~ up with sb** rozliczać się (rozliczyć się *perf*) z kimś

**square bracket** *n* nawias *m* kwadratowy
**squarely** ['skwɛəlɪ] *adv* (*fall etc*) prosto; (*confront, look*) odważnie, wprost
**square root** *n* pierwiastek *m* kwadratowy
**squash** [skwɔʃ] *n* (*US*) kabaczek *m*; (*Sport*) squash *m*; (*Brit*): **lemon/orange ~** sok *m* cytrynowy/pomarańczowy (*z koncentratu*) ▷ *vt* zgniatać (zgnieść *perf*)
**squat** [skwɔt] *adj* przysadzisty ▷ *vi* (*also*: **squat down**) przykucać (przykucnąć *perf*); (*on property*) mieszkać nielegalnie
**squatter** ['skwɔtə^r] *n* dziki(-ka) *m*(*f*) lokator(ka) *m*(*f*)
**squawk** [skwɔ:k] *vi* skrzeczeć (zaskrzeczeć *perf*)
**squeak** [skwi:k] *vi* (*door*) skrzypieć (zaskrzypieć *perf*); (*mouse*) piszczeć (zapiszczeć *perf*) ▷ *n* (*of hinge*) skrzypienie *nt*; (*of mouse*) pisk *m*
**squeal** [skwi:l] *vi* piszczeć (zapiszczeć *perf*)
**squeamish** ['skwi:mɪʃ] *adj* przewrażliwiony, przeczulony
**squeeze** [skwi:z] *n* (*of hand etc*) uścisk *m*; (*Econ*) ograniczenie *nt*; (*also*: **credit squeeze**) ograniczenie *nt* kredytu ▷ *vt* ściskać (ścisnąć *perf*) ▷ *vi*: **to ~ past/under sth** przeciskać się (przecisnąć się *perf*) obok czegoś/pod czymś; **a ~ of lemon** odrobina soku z cytryny
▶ **squeeze out** *vt* (*juice etc*) wyciskać (wycisnąć *perf*); (*fig*: *person*) wykluczać (wykluczyć *perf*), wykolegowywać (wykolegować *perf*) (*inf*)
**squelch** [skwɛltʃ] *vi* chlupać (chlupnąć *perf*), chlupotać (zachlupotać *perf*)
**squib** [skwɪb] *n* petarda *f*
**squid** [skwɪd] *n* kałamarnica *f*, mątwa *f*
**squiggle** ['skwɪgl] *n* zakrętas *m*, zawijas *m*
**squint** [skwɪnt] *vi*: **to ~ (at)** patrzeć (popatrzeć *perf*) przez zmrużone oczy (na *+acc*) ▷ *n* zez *m*; **he has a ~** on ma zeza
**squire** ['skwaɪə^r] (*Brit*) *n* ≈ dziedzic *m*, ≈ ziemianin *m*; (*inf*) szefie (*voc*) (*inf*)
**squirm** [skwə:m] *vi* wiercić się; (*fig*: *with embarassment*) skręcać się (*inf*)
**squirrel** ['skwɪrəl] *n* wiewiórka *f*
**squirt** [skwə:t] *vi* tryskać (trysnąć *perf*), sikać (siknąć *perf*) (*inf*) ▷ *vt* strzykać (strzyknąć *perf*) *+instr*
**Sr** *abbr* (*in names*: *= senior*) sen., sr.; (*Rel*: *= sister*) s.
**SRC** (*Brit*) *n abbr* = **Students' Representative Council**
**Sri Lanka** [srɪ'læŋkə] *n* Sri Lanka *f*
**SRN** (*Brit*) *n abbr* (*= State Registered Nurse*) ≈ pielęgniarka(-arz) *f*(*m*) dyplomowana(-ny) *f*(*m*)
**SRO** (*US*) *abbr* (*= standing room only*) tylko miejsca stojące
**SS** *abbr* = **steamship**
**SSA** (*US*) *n abbr* (*= Social Security Administration*) *agencja rządowa sprawująca kontrolę nad systemem ubezpieczeń społecznych*
**SST** (*US*) *n abbr* (*= supersonic transport*) transport *m* ponaddźwiękowy
**ST** (*US*) *abbr* = **Standard Time**
**St** *abbr* (*= saint*) św.; (*= street*) ul.
**stab** [stæb] *n* (*with knife etc*) pchnięcie *nt*, dźgnięcie *nt*; (*of pain*) ukłucie *nt*; (*inf*): **to have a ~ at sth/doing sth** próbować (spróbować *perf*) czegoś/zrobić coś ▷ *vt* pchnąć (*perf*) *or* dźgnąć (*perf*) nożem; **to ~ sb to death** zadźgać (*perf*) kogoś
**stabbing** ['stæbɪŋ] *n* napad *m* z nożem ▷ *adj* kłujący
**stability** [stə'bɪlɪtɪ] *n* stabilność *f*
**stabilization** [steɪbəlaɪ'zeɪʃən] *n* stabilizacja *f*
**stabilize** ['steɪbəlaɪz] *vt* stabilizować (ustabilizować *perf*) ▷ *vi* stabilizować się (ustabilizować się *perf*)
**stabilizer** ['steɪbəlaɪzə^r] *n* (*Aviat, Naut*) stabilizator *m*; (*food additive*) środek *m* stabilizujący
**stable** ['steɪbl] *adj* (*prices, patient's condition*) stabilny; (*marriage*) trwały ▷ *n* (*for horse*) stajnia *f*; (*for cattle*) obora *f*; **riding ~s** ujeżdżalnia
**staccato** [stə'kɑ:təu] *adv* staccato ▷ *adj* przerywany
**stack** [stæk] *n* stos *m* ▷ *vt* (*also*: **stack up**) układać (ułożyć *perf*) w stos, gromadzić (nagromadzić *perf*); **to ~ a room/table with** zastawiać (zastawić *perf*) pokój/stół *+instr*; **there's ~s of time** (*Brit*: *inf*) jest mnóstwo czasu
**stadia** ['steɪdɪə] *npl of* **stadium**
**stadium** ['steɪdɪəm] (*pl* **stadia** *or* **~s**) *n* stadion *m*
**staff** [stɑ:f] *n* (*workforce*) pracownicy *vir pl*, personel *m*; (*Brit*: *also*: **teaching staff**) grono *nt* nauczycielskie *or* pedagogiczne; (*servants*) służba *f*; (*Mil*) sztab *m*; (*stick*) laska *f* ▷ *vt* obsadzać (obsadzić *perf*)
**staffroom** ['stɑ:fru:m] *n* pokój *m* nauczycielski
**Staffs** (*Brit*: *Post*) *abbr* = **Staffordshire**
**stag** [stæg] *n* rogacz *m*; (*Brit*) *gracz spekulujący nowo emitowanymi akcjami*; **~ market** (*Brit*) *spekulacja nowo emitowanymi akcjami*
**stage** [steɪdʒ] *n* (*in theatre etc*) scena *f*; (*platform*) podium *nt*, estrada *f*; (*point, period*) etap *m*, okres *m* ▷ *vt* (*play*) wystawiać (wystawić *perf*); (*demonstration*) organizować (zorganizować *perf*); (*perform for effect*) inscenizować (zainscenizować *perf*); **the ~** (*Theat*) scena; **in ~s** stopniowo; **to go**

S

**through a difficult ~** przechodzić trudny okres; **in the early ~s** we wczesnych stadiach; **in the final ~s** w końcowych stadiach
**stagecoach** ['steɪdʒkəutʃ] *n* dyliżans *m*
**stage door** *n* wejście *nt* dla aktorów
**stage fright** *n* trema *f*
**stagehand** ['steɪdʒhænd] *n* inspicjent(ka) *m(f)*
**stage-manage** ['steɪdʒmænɪdʒ] *vt (fig)* wyreżyserować *(perf)*
**stage manager** *(Theat) n* reżyser *m*
**stagger** ['stægəʳ] *vi* zataczać się (zatoczyć się *perf*), iść (pójść *perf*) zataczając się ▷ *vt* wstrząsać (wstrząsnąć *perf*) *+instr*; *(hours, holidays)* układać (ułożyć *perf*) naprzemiennie
**staggering** ['stægərɪŋ] *adj (sum, price)* zawrotny
**stagnant** ['stægnənt] *adj (water)* stojący; *(economy)* martwy, w zastoju *post*
**stagnate** [stæg'neɪt] *vi* trwać w zastoju
**stagnation** [stæg'neɪʃən] *n* stagnacja *f*, zastój *m*
**stag party** *n* wieczór *m* kawalerski
**staid** [steɪd] *adj* stateczny
**stain** [steɪn] *n (mark)* plama *f*; *(colouring)* bejca *f* ▷ *vt (mark)* plamić (poplamić *perf*); *(: fig)* plamić (splamić *perf*); *(wood)* bejcować (zabejcować *perf*)
**stained glass window** [steɪnd-] *n* witraż *m*
**stainless steel** ['steɪnlɪs-] *n* stal *f* nierdzewna
**stain remover** *n* odplamiacz *m*, wywabiacz *m* plam
**stair** [stɛəʳ] *n* stopień *m*; **stairs** *npl* schody *pl*; **on the ~s** na schodach
**staircase** ['stɛəkeɪs] *n* klatka *f* schodowa
**stairway** ['stɛəweɪ] *n* = **staircase**
**stairwell** ['stɛəwɛl] *n* klatka *f* schodowa
**stake** [steɪk] *n (post)* słup *m*; *(Comm)* udział *m*; *(Betting: usu pl)* stawka *f* ▷ *vt (money)* stawiać (postawić *perf*); *(life, reputation)* ryzykować (zaryzykować *perf*); *(also:* **stake out***)* ogradzać (ogrodzić *perf*); **to ~ a claim (to sth)** rościć sobie prawo (do czegoś); **to be at ~** wchodzić w grę; **to have a ~ in sth** być zainteresowanym czymś
**stalactite** ['stæləktaɪt] *n* stalaktyt *m*
**stalagmite** ['stæləgmaɪt] *n* stalagmit *m*
**stale** [steɪl] *adj (bread)* czerstwy; *(food)* nieświeży; *(smell, air)* stęchły; *(beer)* zwietrzały
**stalemate** ['steɪlmeɪt] *n (Chess)* pat *m*; *(fig)* sytuacja *f* patowa
**stalk** [stɔːk] *n (of flower)* łodyga *f*; *(of fruit)* szypułka *f* ▷ *vt* śledzić, podchodzić ▷ *vi*: **to ~ out/off** oddalać się (oddalić się *perf*)
**stall** [stɔːl] *n (Brit)* stoisko *nt*, stragan *m*; *(in stable)* przegroda *f* ▷ *vt (Aut)*: **I ~ed the car** zgasł mi silnik; *(fig: decision etc)* opóźniać (opóźnić *perf*), przeciągać (przeciągnąć *perf*); *(: person)* zwodzić (zwieść *perf*), zbywać (zbyć *perf*) ▷ *vi (engine, car)* gasnąć (zgasnąć *perf*); *(fig: person)* grać na zwłokę *or* czas; **stalls** *npl (Brit: in cinema, theatre)* parter *m*; **a seat in the ~s** miejsce na parterze; **a clothes/flower ~** stoisko *or* budka z odzieżą/kwiatami
**stallholder** ['stɔːlhəuldəʳ] *(Brit) n* straganiarz(-arka) *m(f)*
**stallion** ['stæljən] *n* ogier *m*
**stalwart** ['stɔːlwət] *adj* lojalny, oddany
**stamen** ['steɪmɛn] *(Bot) n* pręcik *m*
**stamina** ['stæmɪnə] *n* wytrzymałość *f*, wytrwałość *f*
**stammer** ['stæməʳ] *n* jąkanie (się) *nt* ▷ *vi* jąkać się, zająkiwać się (zająknąć się *perf*); **to have a ~** jąkać się
**stamp** [stæmp] *n (postage stamp)* znaczek *m* (pocztowy); *(rubber stamp, mark)* pieczątka *f*, stempel *m*; *(fig)* piętno *nt* ▷ *vi (also:* **stamp one's foot***)* tupać (tupnąć *perf*) ▷ *vt (letter)* naklejać (nakleić *perf*) znaczek na *+acc*; *(mark)* znaczyć (oznaczyć *perf*), znakować (oznakować *perf*); *(with rubber stamp)* stemplować (ostemplować *perf*); **~ed addressed envelope** zaadresowana koperta ze znaczkiem
▸ **stamp out** *vt* tłumić (stłumić *perf*); *(fig: crime)* wypleniać (wyplenić *perf*)
**stamp album** *n* album *m* na znaczki *or* filatelistyczny
**stamp collecting** *n* filatelistyka *f*, zbieranie *nt* znaczków
**stamp duty** *(Brit) n* opłata *f* stemplowa
**stampede** [stæm'piːd] *n* paniczna ucieczka *f*; *(fig)* panika *f*, popłoch *m*; **a ~ for tickets** pogoń za biletami
**stamp machine** *n* automat *m* do sprzedaży znaczków
**stance** [stæns] *n* pozycja *f*; *(fig)* postawa *f*, stanowisko *nt*
**stand** [stænd] *(pt, pp* **stood***) n (Comm: stall)* stoisko *nt*, budka *f*; *(: at exhibition)* stoisko *nt*; *(Sport)* trybuna *f*; *(piece of furniture)* wieszak *m*, stojak *m* ▷ *vi (be on foot, be placed)* stać; *(rise)* wstawać (wstać *perf*), powstawać (powstać *perf*); *(remain)* pozostawać (pozostać *perf*) ważnym, zachowywać (zachować *perf*) aktualność; *(in election etc)* kandydować ▷ *vt (object)* stawiać (postawić *perf*); *(person, situation)* znosić (znieść *perf*); **to ~ at** *(level, score etc)* wynosić (wynieść *perf*); **to make a ~ against sth** dawać (dać *perf*) odpór czemuś; **to take a ~ on sth** zajmować (zająć *perf*) stanowisko w jakiejś sprawie; **to take the ~** *(US)* zajmować (zająć *perf*) miejsce dla

świadków; **to ~ for parliament** (*Brit*) kandydować do parlamentu; **to ~ to gain/ lose sth** móc coś zyskać/stracić; **to ~ sb a drink/meal** stawiać (postawić *perf*) komuś drinka/obiad; **it ~s to reason** to jest logiczne; **as things ~** w obecnym stanie rzeczy; **I can't ~ him** nie mogę go znieść; **we don't ~ a chance** nie mamy (najmniejszej) szansy; **to ~ trial** stawać (stanąć *perf*) przed sądem

▸ **stand by** *vi* (*be ready*) być gotowym *or* przygotowanym, stać w pogotowiu; (*fig*) stać (bezczynnie) ▹ *vt fus* (*opinion*) podtrzymywać (podtrzymać *perf*); (*person*) stawać (stanąć *perf*) po stronie *+gen*

▸ **stand down** *vi* ustępować (ustąpić *perf*), wycofywać się (wycofać się *perf*)

▸ **stand for** *vt fus* (*signify*) znaczyć, oznaczać; (*represent*) reprezentować (sobą), przedstawiać (sobą); (*tolerate*) znosić (znieść *perf*)

▸ **stand in for** *vt fus* zastępować (zastąpić *perf*)

▸ **stand out** *vi* wyróżniać się, rzucać się w oczy

▸ **stand up** *vi* wstawać (wstać *perf*), powstawać (powstać *perf*)

▸ **stand up for** *vt fus* stawać (stanąć *perf*) w obronie *+gen*

▸ **stand up to** *vt fus* (*pressure etc*) (dobrze) wytrzymywać *or* znosić *+acc*; (*person*) stawiać (stawić *perf*) czoło *+dat*

**stand-alone** ['stændələun] (*Comput*) *adj* autonomiczny

**standard** ['stændəd] *n* (*level*) poziom *m*; (*norm, criterion*) norma *f*, standard *m*; (*flag*) sztandar *m* ▹ *adj* (*size etc*) typowy; (*textbook*) klasyczny; (*practice*) znormalizowany, standardowy; (*model, feature*) standardowy, podstawowy; **standards** *npl* obyczaje *pl*; **to be** *or* **to come up to ~** być na odpowiednim poziomie; **to apply a double ~** stosować (zastosować *perf*) podwójną miarę

**standardization** [stændədaɪ'zeɪʃən] *n* standaryzacja *f*, ujednolicenie *nt*

**standardize** ['stændədaɪz] *vt* standaryzować, ujednolicać (ujednolicić *perf*)

**standard lamp** (*Brit*) *n* lampa *f* stojąca

**standard of living** *n* stopa *f* życiowa

**standard time** *n* czas *m* urzędowy

**stand-by** ['stændbaɪ], **standby** *n* rezerwa *f*, środek *m* awaryjny ▹ *adj* rezerwowy, awaryjny; **on ~** w pogotowiu

**stand-by ticket** *n* *tani bilet kupowany tuż przed rozpoczęciem spektaklu, odlotem samolotu itp.*

**stand-in** ['stændɪn] *n* zastępca(-pczyni) *m(f)*

**standing** ['stændɪŋ] *adj* stały ▹ *n* pozycja *f* (społeczna); **~ ovation** owacja na stojąco; **of many years' ~** długoletni, wieloletni; **he received/was given a ~ ovation** sprawiono mu owację na stojąco; **of 6 months' ~** sześciomiesięczny; **a man of some ~** człowiek o pewnej pozycji

**standing committee** *n* stała komisja *f*

**standing joke** *n* pośmiewisko *nt*

**standing order** (*Brit*) *n* (*at bank*) zlecenie *nt* stałe

**standing room** *n* miejsca *pl* stojące

**stand-offish** [stænd'ɔfɪʃ] *adj* sztywny

**standpat** ['stændpæt] (*US*) *adj* konserwatywny

**standpipe** ['stændpaɪp] *n* hydrant *m*

**standpoint** ['stændpɔɪnt] *n* punkt *m* widzenia, stanowisko *nt*

**standstill** ['stændstɪl] *n*: **at a ~** zablokowany; (*fig*) w martwym punkcie; **to come to a ~** (*traffic*) stanąć (*perf*)

**stank** [stæŋk] *pt of* **stink**

**stanza** ['stænzə] *n* zwrotka *f*

**staple** ['steɪpl] *n* (*for papers*) zszywka *f*; (*chief product*) główny artykuł *m* (handlowy) ▹ *adj* (*food etc*) podstawowy, główny ▹ *vt* zszywać (zszyć *perf*)

**stapler** ['steɪplə$^r$] *n* zszywacz *m*

**star** [stɑː$^r$] *n* gwiazda *f* ▹ *vt*: **the movie ~red Lana Turner** główną rolę w filmie grała Lana Turner ▹ *vi*: **to ~ in** grać (zagrać *perf*) (jedną z głównych ról) w *+loc*; **the stars** *npl* (*horoscope*) gwiazdy *pl*; **4-~ hotel** hotel czterogwiazdkowy; **2-~ petrol** (*Brit*) benzyna średniooktanowa; **4-~ petrol** (*Brit*) benzyna wysokooktanowa

**star attraction** *n* główna atrakcja *f*

**starboard** ['stɑːbəd] *adj* (*Naut, Aviat*) po prawej stronie *post*; **to ~** na sterburtę

**starch** [stɑːtʃ] *n* (*for clothes*) krochmal *m*; (*Culin*) skrobia *f*

**starched** ['stɑːtʃt] *adj* wykrochmalony

**starchy** ['stɑːtʃɪ] *adj* bogaty w skrobię; (*pej: person*) sztywny (*pej*)

**stardom** ['stɑːdəm] *n* sława *f*

**stare** [stɛə$^r$] *n* spojrzenie *nt* ▹ *vi*: **to ~ at** wpatrywać się w *+acc*, gapić się na *+acc* (*pej*)

**starfish** ['stɑːfɪʃ] *n* rozgwiazda *f*

**stark** [stɑːk] *adj* (*landscape, simplicity*) surowy; (*reality, facts*) nagi; (*poverty*) skrajny ▹ *adv*: **~ naked** zupełnie nagi

**starlet** ['stɑːlɪt] *n* gwiazdka *f*

**starlight** ['stɑːlaɪt] *n* światło *nt* gwiazd; **by ~** przy świetle gwiazd

**starling** ['stɑːlɪŋ] *n* szpak *m*

**starlit** ['stɑːlɪt] *adj* rozświetlony gwiazdami

**starry** ['stɑːrɪ] *adj* gwiaździsty

**starry-eyed** [stɑːrɪ'aɪd] *adj* naiwny; **to be ~** (*from wonder*) robić wielkie oczy (*inf*)

S

**star sign** *n* znak *m* Zodiaku
**star-studded** ['stɑːstʌdɪd] *adj*: **a ~ cast** obsada *f* pełna gwiazd
**START** (*Mil*) *n abbr* (= *Strategic Arms Reduction Talks*) rokowania *pl* START
**start** [stɑːt] *n* (*beginning*) początek *m*; (*Sport*) start *m*; (*sudden movement*) poderwanie się *nt*; (*advantage*) fory *pl* ▷ *vt* (*begin*) rozpoczynać (rozpocząć *perf*), zaczynać (zacząć *perf*); (*panic etc*) powodować (spowodować *perf*); (*business etc*) zakładać (założyć *perf*); (*engine*) uruchamiać (uruchomić *perf*) ▷ *vi* (*begin*) rozpoczynać się (rozpocząć się *perf*), zaczynać się (zacząć się *perf*); (*with fright*) wzdrygać się (wzdrygnąć się *perf*); (*engine etc*) zaskakiwać (zaskoczyć *perf*); **at the ~** na *or* z początku; **for a ~** po pierwsze; **to make an early ~** wcześnie wyruszać (wyruszyć *perf*); **to ~ (off) with ...** (*firstly*) po pierwsze ...; (*at the beginning*) na (samym) początku; **to ~ a fire** rozpalać (rozpalić *perf*) ogień; **to ~ doing** *or* **to do sth** zaczynać (zacząć *perf*) coś robić
▸ **start off** *vi* (*begin*) zaczynać (zacząć *perf*) działać; (*leave*) wyruszać (wyruszyć *perf*)
▸ **start over** (*US*) *vi* zaczynać (zacząć *perf*) od początku
▸ **start up** *vt* (*business etc*) zakładać (założyć *perf*); (*engine, car*) uruchamiać (uruchomić *perf*)
**starter** ['stɑːtə[r]] *n* (*Aut*) rozrusznik *m*; (*Sport: official*) starter *m*; (*: runner, horse*) startujący *m*; (*Brit: Culin*) przystawka *f*
**starting point** ['stɑːtɪŋ-] *n* punkt *m* wyjścia
**starting price** *n* cena *f* wywoławcza *or* wyjściowa
**startle** ['stɑːtl] *vt* zaskakiwać (zaskoczyć *perf*), przestraszać (przestraszyć *perf*)
**startling** ['stɑːtlɪŋ] *adj* (*news etc*) zaskakujący
**star turn** (*Brit*) *n* główna atrakcja *f*
**starvation** [stɑː'veɪʃən] *n* głód *m*; **to die of/from ~** umierać (umrzeć *perf*) z głodu
**starve** [stɑːv] *vi* (*be very hungry*) być wygłodzonym; (*to death*) umierać (umrzeć *perf*) *or* ginąć (zginąć *perf*) z głodu ▷ *vt* głodzić (zagłodzić *perf*), morzyć (zamorzyć *perf*) głodem; (*fig*): **to ~ sb of sth** pozbawiać (pozbawić *perf*) kogoś czegoś; **I'm starving** umieram z głodu
**state** [steɪt] *n* (*condition*) stan *m*; (*government*) państwo *nt* ▷ *vt* oświadczać (oświadczyć *perf*), stwierdzać (stwierdzić *perf*); **the States** *npl* Stany *pl* (Zjednoczone); **to be in a ~** być zdenerwowanym; **to get into a ~** denerwować się (zdenerwować się *perf*); **in ~** uroczyście; **to lie in ~** być wystawionym na widok publiczny (*o zwłokach*); **~ of emergency** stan wyjątkowy; **~ of mind** nastrój
**state control** *n* nadzór *m* państwowy
**stated** ['steɪtɪd] *adj* (*purpose etc*) podany
**State Department** (*US*) *n* Departament *m* Stanu
**state education** (*Brit*) *n* oświata *f* państwowa
**stateless** ['steɪtlɪs] *adj* bezpaństwowy, bez obywatelstwa *post*
**stately** ['steɪtlɪ] *adj* majestatyczny; **~ home** rezydencja
**statement** ['steɪtmənt] *n* oświadczenie *nt*, wypowiedź *f*; (*Fin*) bilans *m*; **official ~** oficjalne oświadczenie; **bank ~** wyciąg (z konta)
**state of the art** *n*: **the ~** współczesny stan *m* wiedzy (*w określonej dziedzinie*) ▷ *adj*: **state-of-the-art** najnowocześniejszy
**state-owned** ['steɪtəund] *adj* państwowy
**state secret** *n* tajemnica *f* państwowa
**statesman** ['steɪtsmən] (*irreg: like* **man**) *n* mąż *m* stanu
**statesmanship** ['steɪtsmənʃɪp] *n* zalety *pl* właściwe mężowi stanu
**static** ['stætɪk] *n* (*Radio, TV*) zakłócenia *pl* ▷ *adj* statyczny, nieruchomy
**static electricity** *n* ładunek *m* elektrostatyczny
**station** ['steɪʃən] *n* (*Rail*) dworzec *m*; (*: small*) stacja *f*; (*also*: **bus station**) dworzec *m* autobusowy; (*also*: **police station**) posterunek *m* (policji); (*Radio*) stacja *f* ▷ *vt* (*guards etc*) wystawiać (wystawić *perf*); **to be ~ed in/at** (*Mil*) stacjonować w *+loc*; **action ~s** (*Mil*) posterunki bojowe; **above one's ~** ponad stan
**stationary** ['steɪʃnərɪ] *adj* nieruchomy, stały
**stationer** ['steɪʃənə[r]] *n* sprzedawca *m* artykułów piśmiennych *or* papierniczych
**stationer's (shop)** *n* sklep *m* papierniczy *or* z artykułami piśmiennymi
**stationery** ['steɪʃnərɪ] *n* artykuły *pl* piśmienne
**stationmaster** ['steɪʃənmɑːstə[r]] *n* naczelnik *m* stacji
**station wagon** (*US*) *n* kombi *nt inv*
**statistic** [stə'tɪstɪk] *n* dana *f* statystyczna (*usu pl*)
**statistical** [stə'tɪstɪkl] *adj* statystyczny
**statistics** [stə'tɪstɪks] *n* statystyka *f*
**statue** ['stætjuː] *n* posąg *m*, statua *f*
**statuesque** [stætju'ɛsk] *adj* posągowy
**statuette** [stætju'ɛt] *n* posążek *m*, statuetka *f*
**stature** ['stætʃə[r]] *n* postura *f*; (*fig*) renoma *f*
**status** ['steɪtəs] *n* pozycja *f*, status *m*; **the ~ quo** (istniejący) stan rzeczy, status quo
**status line** (*Comput*) *n* wiersz *m* stanu *or* statusu
**status symbol** *n* symbol *m* statusu (społecznego)

**statute** ['stætju:t] *n* ustawa *f*; **statutes** *npl* statut *m*
**statute book** *n*: **on the ~** w kodeksie
**statutory** ['stætjutrɪ] *adj* ustawowy, statutowy; **~ meeting** zgromadzenie założycielskie
**staunch** [stɔ:ntʃ] *adj* zagorzały ▷ *vt* tamować (zatamować *perf*)
**stave** [steɪv] *n* pięciolinia *f*
▸ **stave off** *vt* (*attack*) odpierać (odeprzeć *perf*); (*threat*) powstrzymywać (powstrzymać *perf*)
**stay** [steɪ] *n* pobyt *m* ▷ *vi* pozostawać (pozostać *perf*), zostawać (zostać *perf*); **to ~ put** nie ruszać się (z miejsca); **~ of execution** (*Jur*) zawieszenie wykonania wyroku; **to ~ with friends** mieszkać u przyjaciół *or* znajomych; **to ~ the night** zostawać (zostać *perf*) na noc
▸ **stay behind** *vi* zostawać (zostać *perf*), zaczekać (*perf*)
▸ **stay in** *vi* zostawać (zostać *perf*) w domu
▸ **stay on** *vi* pozostawać (pozostać *perf*)
▸ **stay out** *vi* (*of house*) pozostawać (pozostać *perf*) *or* być poza domem; (*on strike*) kontynuować strajk
▸ **stay up** *vi* nie kłaść się (spać)
**staying power** ['steɪɪŋ-] *n* wytrzymałość *f*
**STD** *n abbr* (*Brit*: *Tel*: = *subscriber trunk dialling*) automatyczne połączenie *nt* międzymiastowe; (*Med*: = *sexually transmitted disease*) choroba *f* przenoszona drogą płciową
**stead** [stɛd] *n*: **in sb's ~** zamiast kogoś; **to stand sb in good ~** (bardzo) przydawać się (przydać się *perf*) komuś
**steadfast** ['stɛdfɑ:st] *adj* (*person*) niezachwiany; (*refusal, support*) zdecydowany
**steadily** ['stɛdɪlɪ] *adv* (*breathe*) równomiernie, miarowo; (*rise, grow*) stale; (*look*) bacznie
**steady** ['stɛdɪ] *adj* (*constant*) stały; (*regular*) równomierny, miarowy; (*firm*) pewny; (*calm*: *look*) baczny; (: *voice*) opanowany; (*person, character*) solidny ▷ *vt* (*stabilize*) podtrzymywać (podtrzymać *perf*); (*nerves*) uspokajać (uspokoić *perf*); **to ~ o.s. on** *or* **against sth** oprzeć się (*perf*) o coś
**steak** [steɪk] *n* stek *m*
**steakhouse** ['steɪkhaus] *n restauracja specjalizująca się w podawaniu steków*
**steal** [sti:l] (*pt* **stole**, *pp* **stolen**) *vt* kraść (ukraść *perf*) ▷ *vi* kraść; (*move secretly*) skradać się
▸ **steal away** *vi* wykradać się (wykraść się *perf*)
**stealth** [stɛlθ] *n*: **by ~** po kryjomu, ukradkiem
**stealthy** ['stɛlθɪ] *adj* ukradkowy
**steam** [sti:m] *n* para *f* (wodna) ▷ *vt* gotować (ugotować *perf*) na parze ▷ *vi* parować; **under one's own ~** (*fig*) o własnych siłach; **I ran out of ~** (*fig*) zabrakło mi energii *or* sił; **to let off ~** (*inf*: *fig*) wyładowywać się (wyładować się *perf*)
▸ **steam up** *vi* zachodzić (zajść *perf*) parą; **to get ~ed up about sth** (*inf*: *fig*) podniecać się (podniecić się *perf*) czymś (*inf*)
**steam engine** *n* (*Rail*) parowóz *m*
**steamer** ['sti:mə[r]] *n* (*ship*) parowiec *m*; (*Culin*) garnek *m* do gotowania na parze
**steam iron** *n* żelazko *nt* z nawilżaczem
**steamroller** ['sti:mrəulə[r]] *n* walec *m* parowy
**steamship** ['sti:mʃɪp] *n* = **steamer**
**steamy** ['sti:mɪ] *adj* (*window*) zaparowany; (*book, film*) pikantny
**steed** [sti:d] *n* rumak *m*
**steel** [sti:l] *n* stal *f* ▷ *adj* stalowy
**steel band** *n zespół muzyków grających na metalowych bębnach.*
**steel industry** *n* przemysł *m* stalowy
**steel mill** *n* walcownia *f* stali
**steelworks** ['sti:lwə:ks] *n* stalownia *f*
**steely** ['sti:lɪ] *adj* (*determination*) żelazny; (*eyes, gaze*) stalowy
**steep** [sti:p] *adj* (*stair, slope*) stromy; (*increase*) gwałtowny; (*price*) wygórowany ▷ *vt* zamaczać (zamoczyć *perf*); **to be ~ed in history** (*fig*) być przesiąkniętym historią
**steeple** ['sti:pl] *n* (*Archit*) wieża *f* strzelista
**steeplechase** ['sti:pltʃeɪs] *n* (*on horse*) długodystansowy wyścig *m* z przeszkodami; (*on foot*) bieg *m* z przeszkodami
**steeplejack** ['sti:pldʒæk] *n robotnik wykonujący prace remontowe na dużej wysokości*
**steeply** ['sti:plɪ] *adv* (*rise, fall*: *mountains*) stromo; (: *prices*) gwałtownie
**steer** [stɪə[r]] *vt* (*vehicle*) kierować *+instr*; (*boat*) sterować *+instr*; (*person*) prowadzić (poprowadzić *perf*) ▷ *vi*: **the ship ~ed out of Santiago Bay** statek wypłynął z Santiago Bay; **to ~ clear of sb/sth** (*fig*) trzymać się z daleka od kogoś/czegoś
**steering** ['stɪərɪŋ] (*Aut*) *n* układ *m* kierowniczy
**steering column** (*Aut*) *n* kolumna *f* kierownicy
**steering committee** *n* komisja *f* koordynacyjna *or* kontroli
**steering wheel** *n* kierownica *f*
**stellar** ['stɛlə[r]] *adj* gwiezdny
**stem** [stɛm] *n* (*of plant*) łodyga *f*; (*of leaf, fruit*) szypułka *f*, ogonek *m*; (*of glass*) nóżka *f*; (*of pipe*) trzon *m* ▷ *vt* tamować (zatamować *perf*)
▸ **stem from** *vt fus* mieć swoje źródło w *+loc*, brać się z *+gen*

S

**stench** [stɛntʃ] *(pej)* *n* smród *m* *(pej)*
**stencil** ['stɛnsl] *n* *(lettering, design)* szablon *m*; *(pattern used)* matryca *f* ▷ *vt* malować (namalować *perf*) przez szablon
**stenographer** [stɛ'nɔgrəfə<sup>r</sup>] *(US)* *n* stenografista(-tka) *m(f)*
**stenography** [stɛ'nɔgrəfɪ] *(US)* *n* stenografia *f*
**step** [stɛp] *n* krok *m*; *(of stairs)* stopień *m* ▷ *vi*: **to ~ forward/back** występować (wystąpić *perf*) w przód/w tył; **steps** *npl* *(Brit)* = **stepladder**; **~ by ~** *(fig)* krok po kroku; **to march in/out of ~ (with)** maszerować w takt/nie w takt *(+gen)*; **to be in/out of ~ with** *(fig)* być/nie być zgodnym z *+instr*
▸ **step down** *vi* *(fig)* ustępować (ustąpić *perf*)
▸ **step in** *vi* *(fig)* wkraczać (wkroczyć *perf*)
▸ **step off** *vt fus* wysiadać (wysiąść *perf*) (z *+gen*)
▸ **step on** *vt fus* następować (nastąpić *perf*) na *+acc*
▸ **step over** *vt fus* przestępować (przestąpić *perf*) *+acc*
▸ **step up** *vt* *(efforts)* wzmagać (wzmóc *perf*); *(pace)* przyśpieszać (przyśpieszyć *perf*)
**stepbrother** ['stɛpbrʌðə<sup>r</sup>] *n* brat *m* przyrodni
**stepchild** ['stɛptʃaɪld] *n* pasierb(ica) *m(f)*
**stepdaughter** ['stɛpdɔːtə<sup>r</sup>] *n* pasierbica *f*
**stepfather** ['stɛpfɑːðə<sup>r</sup>] *n* ojczym *m*
**stepladder** ['stɛplædə<sup>r</sup>] *(Brit)* *n* składane schodki *pl*
**stepmother** ['stɛpmʌðə<sup>r</sup>] *n* macocha *f*
**stepping stone** ['stɛpɪŋ-] *n* *(fig)* odskocznia *f*; **~s** *kamienie, po których można przejść przez rzekę itp*
**stepsister** ['stɛpsɪstə<sup>r</sup>] *n* siostra *f* przyrodnia
**stepson** ['stɛpsʌn] *n* pasierb *m*
**stereo** ['stɛrɪəu] *n* zestaw *m* stereo ▷ *adj* stereofoniczny; **in ~** (w) stereo
**stereotype** ['stɪərɪətaɪp] *n* stereotyp *m* ▷ *vt* szufladkować (zaszufladkować *perf*)
**sterile** ['stɛraɪl] *adj* *(free from germs)* sterylny, wyjałowiony; *(barren)* bezpłodny; *(fig)* jałowy
**sterility** [stɛ'rɪlɪtɪ] *n* bezpłodność *f*
**sterilization** [stɛrɪlaɪ'zeɪʃən] *n* sterylizacja *f*
**sterilize** ['stɛrɪlaɪz] *vt* *(thing, place)* wyjaławiać (wyjałowić *perf*), sterylizować (wysterylizować *perf*); *(person, animal)* sterylizować (wysterylizować *perf*)
**sterling** ['stəːlɪŋ] *adj* *(silver)* standardowy; *(fig: character, work)* najwyższej próby *post* ▷ *n* funt *m* szterling; **one pound ~** jeden funt szterling
**sterling area** *n* strefa *f* szterlingowa
**stern** [stəːn] *adj* surowy ▷ *n* rufa *f*
**sternum** ['stəːnəm] *n* *(Anat)* mostek *m*
**steroid** ['stɪərɔɪd] *n* steroid *m*, steryd *m*
**stethoscope** ['stɛθəskəup] *n* słuchawka *f* lekarska, stetoskop *m*
**stevedore** ['stiːvədɔː<sup>r</sup>] *n* doker *m*
**stew** [stjuː] *n* gulasz *m* ▷ *vt* *(meat, vegetables)* dusić (udusić *perf*); *(fruit)* robić (zrobić *perf*) kompot z *+gen* ▷ *vi* dusić się (udusić się *perf*); **~ed tea** zbyt mocna herbata; **~ed fruit** kompot
**steward** ['stjuːəd] *n* *(on ship, plane etc)* steward *m*; *(in club etc)* gospodarz *m*; *(also*: **shop steward**) mąż *m* zaufania *(związku zawodowego)*
**stewardess** ['stjuədɛs] *n* stewardessa *f*
**stewing steak** ['stjuːɪŋ-], *(US)* **stew meat** *n* wołowina *f* na gulasz
**St. Ex.** *abbr (= stock exchange)* GPW *f inv (= Giełda Papierów Wartościowych)*
**stg** *abbr* = **sterling**
**stick** [stɪk] *(pt, pp* **stuck**) *n* *(of wood)* kij *m*; *(: smaller)* patyk *m*, kijek *m*; *(of dynamite, for walking)* laska *f*; *(of chalk etc)* kawałek *m* ▷ *vt* *(with glue etc)* przyklejać (przykleić *perf*); *(inf: put)* wtykać (wetknąć *perf*); *(: tolerate)* wytrzymywać (wytrzymać *perf*); *(thrust)*: **to ~ sth into** wbijać (wbić *perf*) coś w *+acc* ▷ *vi* *(dough etc)* kleić się, lepić się; *(thought: in mind)* tkwić (utkwić *perf*); *(drawer etc)* zacinać się (zaciąć się *perf*); **to get hold of the wrong end of the ~** *(Brit: fig)* zrozumieć *(perf)* coś opacznie *or* na opak; **I nicknamed him "Fingers", and the name stuck** przezwałem go „Fingers" i przezwisko to przylgnęło do niego
▸ **stick around** *(inf)* *vi* kręcić się (pokręcić się *perf*) *(inf)*
▸ **stick out** *vi* wystawać ▷ *vt*: **to ~ it out** *(inf)* wytrzymywać (wytrzymać *perf*) do końca
▸ **stick to** *vt fus* *(one's word)* pozostawać (pozostać *perf*) wiernym *+dat*; *(agreement)* przestrzegać *+gen*; *(the truth, facts)* trzymać się *+gen*
▸ **stick up** *vi* sterczeć
▸ **stick up for** *vt fus* stawać (stanąć *perf*) w obronie *+gen*
**sticker** ['stɪkə<sup>r</sup>] *n* naklejka *f*
**sticking plaster** ['stɪkɪŋ-] *n* przylepiec *m*, plaster *m*
**stickleback** ['stɪklbæk] *(Zool)* *n* ciernik *m*
**stickler** ['stɪklə<sup>r</sup>] *n*: **to be a ~ for** być pedantem na punkcie *+gen*
**stick-up** ['stɪkʌp] *(inf)* *n* napad *m* z bronią w ręku
**sticky** ['stɪkɪ] *adj* *(hands)* lepki; *(tape)* klejący; *(day)* parny
**stiff** [stɪf] *adj* sztywny; *(competition)* zacięty; *(penalty)* ciężki; *(drink)* mocny; *(breeze)* silny ▷ *adv*: **bored/scared ~** śmiertelnie znudzony/przestraszony; **the door was rather ~** drzwi chodziły dość opornie; **I am/**

**feel too ~ to move** jestem/czuję się zbyt obolały, żeby się ruszyć; **to have a ~ neck/ back** nie móc zgiąć karku/pleców; **to keep a ~ upper lip** (*Brit: fig*) nie okazywać emocji

**stiffen** ['stɪfn] *vi* sztywnieć (zesztywnieć *perf*)

**stiffness** ['stɪfnɪs] *n* sztywność *f*

**stifle** ['staɪfl] *vt* tłumić (stłumić *perf*); (*heat, scent*) dławić, dusić

**stifling** ['staɪflɪŋ] *adj* duszący

**stigma** ['stɪgmə] *n* (*of failure etc*) piętno *nt*; (*Bot*) znamię *nt*; **stigmata** *npl* stygmaty *pl*

**stile** [staɪl] *n* przełaz *m*

**stiletto** [stɪ'lɛtəu] (*Brit*) *n* (*also*: **stiletto heel**) szpilka *f* (*but lub obcas*)

**still** [stɪl] *adj* (*motionless*) nieruchomy; (*tranquil*) spokojny; (*Brit: drink*) niegazowany ▷ *adv* (*up to this time*) nadal, ciągle; (*even, yet*) jeszcze; (*nonetheless*) mimo to ▷ *n* (*Film*) fotos *m*; **to stand ~** stać nieruchomo *or* w bezruchu; **keep ~!** nie ruszaj się!; **he ~ hasn't arrived** ciągle (jeszcze) go nie ma

**stillborn** ['stɪlbɔːn] *adj* martwo urodzony

**still life** *n* martwa natura *f*

**stilt** [stɪlt] *n* (*pile*) pal *m*; (*for walking on*) szczudło *nt*

**stilted** ['stɪltɪd] *adj* sztywny, wymuszony

**stimulant** ['stɪmjulənt] *n* środek *m* pobudzający, stymulant *m*

**stimulate** ['stɪmjuleɪt] *vt* (*demand*) pobudzać (pobudzić *perf*), stymulować; (*person*) pobudzać (pobudzić *perf*) do działania, inspirować (zainspirować *perf*)

**stimulating** ['stɪmjuleɪtɪŋ] *adj* inspirujący, stymulujący

**stimulation** [stɪmju'leɪʃən] *n* stymulacja *f*

**stimuli** ['stɪmjulaɪ] *npl of* **stimulus**

**stimulus** ['stɪmjuləs] (*pl* **stimuli**) *n* bodziec *m*

**sting** [stɪŋ] (*pt, pp* **stung**) *n* (*wound: of mosquito, snake*) ukąszenie *nt*; (*: of bee, wasp*) użądlenie *nt*; (*: of nettle, jellyfish*) oparzenie *nt*; (*organ*) żądło *nt*; (*inf*) kant *m* (*inf*) ▷ *vt* kłuć (ukłuć *perf*); (*fig*) dotykać (dotknąć *perf*), urazić (*perf*)) ▷ *vi* (*bee, wasp*) żądlić; (*mosquito, snake*) kąsać; (*plant, hedgehog*) kłuć; (*nettle, jellyfish*) parzyć; (*eyes, ointment*) szczypać, piec; **my eyes are ~ing** oczy mnie szczypią *or* pieką

**stingy** ['stɪndʒɪ] (*pej*) *adj* skąpy, sknerowaty

**stink** [stɪŋk] (*pt* **stank**, *pp* **stunk**) *n* smród *m* ▷ *vi* śmierdzieć

**stinker** ['stɪŋkə^r] (*inf*) *n* (*person*) drań *m*; **it's a real ~** (*problem, exam*) to naprawdę cholernie trudne (*inf*)

**stinking** ['stɪŋkɪŋ] (*inf*) *adj* (*fig*) parszywy (*inf*); **a ~ cold** paskudne przeziębienie; **he's ~ rich** jest nadziany (*inf*)

**stint** [stɪnt] *n*: **I've done my ~** wykonałem swoją część pracy ▷ *vi*: **to ~ on** skąpić (poskąpić *perf*) *or* żałować (pożałować *perf*) *+gen*; **during his ~ in Washington/as a lecturer** w okresie, gdy pracował w Waszyngtonie/jako wykładowca

**stipend** ['staɪpɛnd] *n* pensja *f* (*zwłaszcza duchownego*)

**stipendiary** [staɪ'pɛndɪərɪ] *adj*: **~ magistrate** *sędzia niższej instancji otrzymujący pensję*

**stipulate** ['stɪpjuleɪt] *vt* (*conditions, amount*) określać (określić *perf*), ustalać (ustalić *perf*)

**stipulation** [stɪpju'leɪʃən] *n* warunek *m*

**stir** [stəː^r] *n* (*fig*) poruszenie *nt* ▷ *vt* (*tea etc*) mieszać (zamieszać *perf*); (*fig: emotions, person*) poruszać (poruszyć *perf*) ▷ *vi* drgać (drgnąć *perf*); **to give sth a ~** zamieszać (*perf*) coś; **to cause a ~** wywoływać (wywołać *perf*) poruszenie

▸ **stir up** *vt* (*trouble*) wywoływać (wywołać *perf*)

**stirring** ['stəːrɪŋ] *adj* poruszający

**stirrup** ['stɪrəp] *n* strzemię *nt*

**stitch** [stɪtʃ] *n* (*Sewing*) ścieg *m*; (*Knitting*) oczko *nt*; (*Med*) szew *m*; (*pain*) kolka *f* ▷ *vt* zszywać (zszyć *perf*)

**stoat** [stəut] *n* gronostaj *m*

**stock** [stɔk] *n* (*supply*) zapas *m*; (*Comm*) zapas *m* towaru; (*Agr*) (żywy) inwentarz *m*; (*Culin*) wywar *m*; (*descent, origin*) ród *m*; (*Fin*) papiery *pl* wartościowe; (*Rail: also*: **rolling stock**) tabor *m* (kolejowy) ▷ *adj* (*reply, excuse*) szablonowy ▷ *vt* mieć na składzie; **~s and shares** akcje i obligacje; **in ~** na składzie; **out of ~** wyprzedany; **well-~ed** dobrze zaopatrzony; **to take ~ of** (*fig*) oceniać (ocenić *perf*) *+acc*; **government ~** obligacje rządowe

▸ **stock up** *vi*: **to ~ up (with)** robić (zrobić *perf*) zapasy (*+gen*)

**stockade** [stɔ'keɪd] *n* częstokół *m*

**stockbroker** ['stɔkbrəukə^r] *n* makler *m* giełdowy

**stock control** *n* inwentaryzacja *f* zapasów

**stock cube** (*Brit*) *n* kostka *f* bulionowa *or* rosołowa

**stock exchange** *n* giełda *f* papierów wartościowych

**stockholder** ['stɔkhəuldə^r] (*esp US*) *n* akcjonariusz(ka) *m(f)*

**Stockholm** ['stɔkhəum] *n* Sztokholm *m*

**stocking** ['stɔkɪŋ] *n* pończocha *f*

**stock-in-trade** ['stɔkɪn'treɪd] *n* (*fig*): **it's his ~** (*usual job*) to dla niego chleb powszedni; (*typical behaviour*) to jego specjalność

**stockist** ['stɔkɪst] (*Brit*) *n* sklep *m* firmowy

**stock market** (*Brit*) *n* rynek *m* papierów wartościowych

**stock phrase** *n* utarty zwrot *m*

**stockpile** ['stɔkpaɪl] *n* (*of weapons, food*) skład *m* ▷ *vt* składować

S

**stockroom** ['stɔkru:m] *n* skład *m*, magazyn *m*
**stocktaking** ['stɔkteɪkɪŋ] (*Brit*) *n* inwentaryzacja *f*, remanent *m*
**stocky** ['stɔkɪ] *adj* krępy
**stodgy** ['stɔdʒɪ] *adj* (*food*) ciężki
**stoic** ['stəuɪk] *n* stoik *m*
**stoic(al)** ['stəuɪk(l)] *adj* stoicki
**stoke** [stəuk] *vt* (*fire, furnace*) dorzucać do *+gen*
**stoker** ['stəukə[r]] *n* palacz *m* (*zawód*)
**stole** [stəul] *pt of* **steal** ▷ *n* (*silk*) szal *m*; (*fur*) etola *f*; (*priest's*) stuła *f*
**stolen** ['stəuln] *pp of* **steal**
**stolid** ['stɔlɪd] *adj* beznamiętny
**stomach** ['stʌmək] *n* (*Anat*) żołądek *m*; (*belly*) brzuch *m* ▷ *vt* (*fig*) trawić (strawić *perf*)
**stomach ache** *n* ból *m* żołądka *or* brzucha
**stomach pump** *n* odsysacz *m* treści żołądka
**stomach ulcer** *n* wrzód *m* żołądka
**stomp** [stɔmp] *vi*: **to ~ in/out** wchodzić (wejść *perf*)/wychodzić (wyjść *perf*) ciężkim krokiem
**stone** [stəun] *n* (*also Med*) kamień *m*; (*pebble*) kamyk *m*, kamyczek *m*; (*in fruit*) pestka *f*; (*Brit: weight*) *6,35 kg* ▷ *adj* kamienny ▷ *vt* (*person*) kamienować (ukamienować *perf*); (*fruit*) drylować (wydrylować *perf*); **within a ~'s throw of the station** o dwa kroki od stacji
**Stone Age** *n*: **the ~** epoka *f* kamienna
**stone-cold** ['stəun'kəuld] *adj* lodowato zimny
**stoned** [stəund] (*inf*) *adj* (*on drugs*) naćpany (*inf*); (*drunk*) urżnięty (*inf*)
**stone-deaf** ['stəun'dɛf] *adj* głuchy jak pień
**stonemason** ['stəunmeɪsn] *n* kamieniarz *m*
**stonework** ['stəunwə:k] *n* kamieniarka *f*
**stony** ['stəunɪ] *adj* (*ground*) kamienisty; (*fig: silence, face*) kamienny; (*: glance*) lodowaty
**stood** [stud] *pt, pp of* **stand**
**stool** [stu:l] *n* taboret *m*
**stoop** [stu:p] *vi* (*also*: **stoop down**) schylać się (schylić się *perf*); (*walk with a stoop*) garbić się; **to ~ to sth/doing sth** (*fig*) zniżać się (zniżyć się *perf*) do czegoś/robienia czegoś
**stop** [stɔp] *n* przystanek *m*; (*also*: **full stop**) kropka *f* ▷ *vt* (*person*) powstrzymywać (powstrzymać *perf*); (*car*) zatrzymywać (zatrzymać *perf*); (*pay*) wstrzymywać (wstrzymać *perf*); (*crime*) zapobiegać (zapobiec *perf*) *+dat* ▷ *vi* (*person*) zatrzymywać się (zatrzymać się *perf*); (*watch, clock*) stawać (stanąć *perf*); (*rain, noise*) ustawać (ustać *perf*); **to come to a ~** zatrzymywać się (zatrzymać się *perf*); **to ~ a cheque** wstrzymywać (wstrzymać *perf*) wypłatę z czeku; **to ~ doing sth** przestawać (przestać *perf*) coś robić; **to put a ~ to** kłaść (położyć *perf*) kres *+dat*; **to ~ sb (from) doing sth** powstrzymywać (powstrzymać *perf*) kogoś od zrobienia czegoś; **~ it!** przestań!
▸ **stop by** *vi* zachodzić (zajść *perf*), wpadać (wpaść *perf*)
▸ **stop off** *vi* zatrzymywać się (zatrzymać się *perf*) (*podczas podróży*)
▸ **stop up** *vt* (*hole*) zatykać (zatkać *perf*)
**stopcock** ['stɔpkɔk] *n* zawór *m* odcinający
**stopgap** ['stɔpgæp] *n* (*person*) (tymczasowe) zastępstwo *nt*; (*thing*) substytut *m*; **~ measure** środek tymczasowy
**stoplights** ['stɔplaɪts] (*Aut*) *npl* światła *pl* stopu
**stopover** ['stɔpəuvə[r]] *n* przerwa *f* (w podróży)
**stoppage** ['stɔpɪdʒ] *n* (*strike*) przestój *m*; (*blockage*) zablokowanie *nt*, blokada *f*; (*of pay*) potrącenie *nt*
**stopper** ['stɔpə[r]] *n* korek *m*, zatyczka *f*
**stop press** *n* wiadomości *pl* z ostatniej chwili (*w gazecie*)
**stopwatch** ['stɔpwɔtʃ] *n* stoper *m*
**storage** ['stɔ:rɪdʒ] *n* przechowywanie *nt*, składowanie *nt*; (*of nuclear waste etc*) składowanie *nt*; (*Comput*) pamięć *f*; (*in house*): **~ space** schowki *pl*
**storage capacity** (*Comput*) *n* pojemność *f* pamięci
**storage heater** (*Brit*) *n* grzejnik *m* akumulacyjny
**store** [stɔ:[r]] *n* (*stock*) zapasy *pl*; (*depot*) schowek *m*; (*shop*: US) sklep *m*; (: Brit) dom *m* towarowy; (*fig: of patience, understanding*) pokłady *pl* ▷ *vt* (*information, medicines, files*) przechowywać; (*goods*) magazynować; (*nuclear waste*) składować; **stores** *npl* (*provisions*) zapasy *pl* żywności (*podczas ekspedycji, operacji wojskowej itp*); **in ~** na przechowaniu; **who knows what's in ~ for us?** kto wie, co nas czeka?; **to set great/little ~ by sth** przywiązywać wielką/małą wagę do czegoś
▸ **store up** *vt* (*food*) trzymać *or* mieć w zapasie; (*fig: memories*) (pieczołowicie) przechowywać (przechować *perf*)
**storehouse** ['stɔ:haus] *n* (US) magazyn *m*; (*fig*) skarbnica *f*
**storekeeper** ['stɔ:ki:pə[r]] (US) *n* sklepikarz(-arka) *m(f)*
**storeroom** ['stɔ:ru:m] *n* schowek *m*
**storey**, (US) **story** ['stɔ:rɪ] *n* piętro *nt*
**stork** [stɔ:k] *n* bocian *m*
**storm** [stɔ:m] *n* (*lit, fig*) burza *f*; (*at sea*) sztorm *m* ▷ *vi* (*fig: speak angrily*) grzmieć (zagrzmieć *perf*) ▷ *vt* szturmować, przypuszczać (przypuścić *perf*) szturm na *+acc*; **to take by ~** brać (wziąć *perf*) szturmem
**storm cloud** *n* chmura *f* burzowa

**orm door** *n* zewnętrzne drzwi *pl* werandowe
**ormy** ['stɔ:mɪ] *adj* (*weather*) burzowy; (: *at* *ea*) sztormowy; (*fig*) burzliwy
**ory** ['stɔ:rɪ] *n* (*history*) historia *f*; (*account*) ›powieść *f*; (*tale*) opowiadanie *nt*; (*Press*) ɪrtykuł *m*; (*lie*) historyjka *f*, bajka *f*; (*US*) = **storey**
**orybook** ['stɔ:rɪbuk] *n* książeczka *f* z ›powiadaniami *or* bajkami
**out** [staut] *adj* (*branch*) gruby; (*person*) tęgi, korpulentny; (*supporter, resistance*) niezłomny › *n* porter *m*
**ove** [stəuv] *n* (*for cooking*) kuchenka *f*; (*for* *heating*) piec *m*, piecyk *m*; **gas/electric ~** kuchenka gazowa/elektryczna
**ow** [stəu] *vt* (*also*: **stow away**) składać złożyć *perf*)
**owaway** ['stəuəweɪ] *n* pasażer(ka) *m(f)* na gapę
**raddle** ['strædl] *vt* (*sit*) siedzieć (usiąść *perf*) okrakiem na *+loc*; (*stand*) stać (stanąć *perf*) okrakiem nad *+instr*; (*fig*) obejmować (objąć *perf*)
**rafe** [strɑ:f] *vt* (*with bullets*) ostrzeliwać ostrzelać *perf*); (*with bombs*) bombardować zbombardować *perf*)
**raggle** ['strægl] *vi* (*person*) odłączać się odłączyć się *perf*); **the houses ~d down the hillside** domy były rozsiane *or* rozrzucone po zboczu
**raggler** [stræglə$^r$] *n* maruder *m*
**raggly** ['stræglɪ] *adj* (*hair*) rozwichrzony
**raight** [streɪt] *adj* (*line, back, hair*) prosty; *answer*) jasny; (*choice, fight*) bezpośredni; *Theat*: *part, play*) dramatyczny; (*whisky etc*) czysty; (*inf*: *heterosexual*) normalny ▷ *adv* prosto ▷ *n*: **the ~** (*Sport*) prosta *f*; **to put** *or* **get sth ~** (*make clear*) wyjaśniać (wyjaśnić *perf*) coś; (*make tidy*) doprowadzać (doprowadzić *perf*) coś do porządku; **let's get this ~** ustalmy fakty; **10 ~ wins** 10 wygranych z rzędu; **I like my whisky ~** lubię czystą whisky; **to go ~ home** iść (pójść *perf*) prosto do domu; **to tell sb ~ out** powiedzieć (*perf*) komuś prosto z mostu; **~ away, ~ off** od razu
**raighten** ['streɪtn] *vt* (*skirt, bed*) poprawiać poprawić *perf*)
▸ **straighten out** *vt* (*fig*: *problem*) wyjaśniać wyjaśnić *perf*); (*matters*) porządkować uporządkować *perf*)
**raight-faced** [streɪt'feɪst] *adj*: **to be ~** zachowywać (zachować *perf*) poważną minę ▷ *adv* z poważną miną
**raightforward** [streɪt'fɔ:wəd] *adj* (*simple*) prosty; (*honest*) prostolinijny
**rain** [streɪn] *n* (*pressure*) obciążenie *nt*; (*Med*: *physical*) nadwerężenie *nt*; (: *mental*) stres *m*; (*of virus*) szczep *m*; (*breed*) odmiana *f* ▷ *vt* (*one's back, resources*) nadwerężać (nadwerężyć *perf*); (*potatoes etc*) cedzić (odcedzić *perf*) ▷ *vi*: **to ~ to hear/see** wytężać (wytężyć *perf*) słuch/wzrok; **strains** *npl* (*Mus*) dźwięki *pl*; **he's been under a lot of ~ recently** ostatnio żyje w ciągłym stresie
**strained** [streɪnd] *adj* (*back, muscle*) nadwerężony; (*laugh*) wymuszony; (*relations*) napięty
**strainer** ['streɪnə$^r$] *n* cedzak *m*, durszlak *m*
**strait** [streɪt] *n* cieśnina *f*; **straits** *npl* (*fig*): **to be in dire straits** znajdować się w ciężkich tarapatach
**straitjacket** ['streɪtdʒækɪt] *n* kaftan *m* bezpieczeństwa
**strait-laced** [streɪt'leɪst] *adj* purytański
**strand** [strænd] *n* (*of thread, wool*) włókno *nt*; (*of wire*) żyła *f*; (*of hair*) kosmyk *m*; (*fig*) element *m*
**stranded** ['strændɪd] *adj*: **to be ~** (*ship*) osiąść (*perf*) na mieliźnie; (*sea creature*) zostać (*perf*) wyrzuconym na brzeg; (*traveller, holidaymaker*) znaleźć się (*perf*) w tarapatach (*bez pieniędzy, paszportu itp.*)
**strange** [streɪndʒ] *adj* (*unfamiliar*) obcy; (*odd*) dziwny
**strangely** ['streɪndʒlɪ] *adv* dziwnie; *see also* **enough**
**stranger** ['streɪndʒə$^r$] *n* (*unknown person*) nieznajomy(-ma) *m(f)*; (*from another area*) obcy(-ca) *m(f)*; **I'm a ~ here** (*in company*) nikogo tu nie znam; (*in town, country*) jestem nietutejszy
**strangle** ['stræŋgl] *vt* (*victim*) dusić (udusić *perf*); (*fig*: *creativity etc*) tłamsić (stłamsić *perf*)
**stranglehold** ['stræŋglhəuld] *n* (*fig*) ucisk *m*
**strangulation** [stræŋgju'leɪʃən] *n* uduszenie *nt*
**strap** [stræp] *n* (*of watch, bag*) pasek *m*; (*of slip, dress*) ramiączko *nt* ▷ *vt* (*also*: **strap in, strap on**) przypinać (przypiąć *perf*)
**straphanging** ['stræphæŋɪŋ] *n* jazda *f* na stojąco (*w autobusie itp*)
**strapless** ['stræplɪs] *adj* bez ramiączek *post*
**strapping** ['stræpɪŋ] *adj* rosły, postawny
**Strasbourg** ['stræzbə:g] *n* Strasburg *m*
**strata** ['strɑ:tə] *npl of* **stratum**
**stratagem** ['strætɪdʒəm] *n* fortel *m*
**strategic** [strə'ti:dʒɪk] *adj* strategiczny
**strategist** ['strætɪdʒɪst] *n* strateg *m*
**strategy** ['strætɪdʒɪ] *n* strategia *f*
**stratosphere** ['strætəsfɪə$^r$] *n* stratosfera *f*
**stratum** ['strɑ:təm] (*pl* **strata**) *n* warstwa *f*
**straw** [strɔ:] *n* (*dried stalks*) słoma *f*; (*for drinking*) słomka *f*; **that's the last ~!** tego już za wiele!

S

**strawberry** ['strɔːbərɪ] *n* truskawka *f*
**stray** [streɪ] *adj* (*animal*) bezpański; (*bullet*) z(a)błąkany; (*pieces of information*) nie powiązany (ze sobą) ▷ *vi* (*animals*) uciekać (uciec *perf*); (*children*) błąkać się (zabłąkać się *perf*); (*thoughts*) błądzić
**streak** [striːk] *n* smuga *f*, pasmo *nt*; (*in hair*) pasemko *nt*; (*fig: of madness etc*) pierwiastek *m*, element *m* ▷ *vt* tworzyć smugi na *+loc* ▷ *vi*: **to ~ past** przemykać (przemknąć *perf*); **to have ~s in one's hair** mieć pasemka we włosach; **a winning/losing ~** dobra/zła passa
**streaky** ['striːkɪ] *adj* (*bacon*) przerośnięty *or* poprzerastany (tłuszczem)
**stream** [striːm] *n* (*small river*) strumień *m*, potok *m*; (*current*) prąd *m*; (*of people, vehicles, insults*) strumień *m*, potok *m*; (*of smoke*) warkocz *m*; (*of questions*) seria *f*; (*Scol*) *klasa utworzona z uczniów o zbliżonym poziomie* ▷ *vt* (*Scol*) *dzielić na klasy według poziomu*
▸ **stream down** *vi* spływać (spłynąć *perf*)
▸ **stream out** *vi* wypływać (wypłynąć *perf*); **the audience began to ~ in/out** publiczność zaczęła tłoczyć się do wejścia/wyjścia; **against the ~** pod prąd; **to come on ~** (*new power plant etc*) zostać (*perf*) uruchomionym
**streamer** ['striːmə^r] *n* (papierowa) serpentyna *f*
**stream feed** *n* (*on photocopier etc*) podawanie *nt* ciągłe (*papieru*)
**streamline** ['striːmlaɪn] *vt* nadawać (nadać *perf*) opływowy kształt *+dat*; (*fig: text*) okroić (*perf*); (*: organization*) usprawnić (*perf*) działanie *+gen* (*np. przez zmniejszenie zatrudnienia*)
**streamlined** ['striːmlaɪnd] *adj* opływowy; (*Aviat*) aerodynamiczny; (*fig: text, account*) okrojony
**street** [striːt] *n* ulica *f*; **the back ~s** biedniejsze ulice; **to be on the ~s** (*homeless*) być na bruku; (*as prostitute*) pracować na ulicy, stać pod latarnią (*inf*)
**streetcar** ['striːtkɑː^r] (*US*) *n* tramwaj *m*
**street lamp** *n* latarnia *f* uliczna
**street lighting** *n* oświetlenie *nt* uliczne
**street map** *n* plan *m* miasta
**street market** *n* targ *m* uliczny
**street plan** *n* plan *m* miasta
**streetwise** ['striːtwaɪz] (*inf*) *adj* cwany (*inf*)
**strength** [strɛŋθ] *n* (*lit, fig*) siła *f*; (*of knot etc*) wytrzymałość *f*; (*of chemical solution, wine*) moc *f*; **on the ~ of** pod wpływem *+gen*; **at full ~** w pełnym składzie; **below ~** w niepełnym składzie
**strengthen** ['strɛŋθn] *vt* (*lit, fig*) wzmacniać (wzmocnić *perf*), umacniać (umocnić *perf*)
**strenuous** ['strɛnjuəs] *adj* (*walk, exercise*) forsowny; (*efforts*) wytężony, uparty
**strenuously** ['strɛnjuəslɪ] *adv*: **she ~ denied the rumour** z uporem zaprzeczała plotce
**stress** [strɛs] *n* (*applied to object*) nacisk *m*; (*internal to object*) naprężenie *nt*; (*mental strain*) stres *m*; (*Ling*) akcent *m*; (*emphasis*) nacisk *m*, akcent *m* ▷ *vt* akcentować (zaakcentować *perf*); **to lay great ~ on sth** kłaść (położyć *perf*) wielki nacisk na coś; **to be under ~** przeżywać stres
**stressful** ['strɛsful] *adj* (*job*) stresujący; (*situation*) stresowy
**stretch** [strɛtʃ] *n* (*of ocean, forest*) obszar *m*; (*of water*) akwen *m*; (*of road, river, beach*) odcinek *m*; (*of time*) okres *m* ▷ *vi* (*person, animal*) przeciągać się (przeciągnąć się *perf*); (*land, area*) rozciągać się, ciągnąć się ▷ *vt* rozciągać (rozciągnąć *perf*); (*fig: job, task*) zmuszać (zmusić *perf*) do wysiłku; **to ~ to/as far as** ciągnąć się do *+gen* /aż po *+acc*; **it ~es as far as the eye can see** ciągnie się tak daleko, jak okiem sięgnąć; **at a ~** jednym ciągiem, bez przerwy; **to ~ one's legs** rozprostowywać (rozprostować *perf*) nogi; **by no ~ of the imagination** w żaden sposób
▸ **stretch out** *vi* wyciągać się (wyciągnąć się *perf*) ▷ *vt* (*arm etc*) wyciągać (wyciągnąć *perf*)
▸ **stretch to** *vt fus* (*money, food*) wystarczać (wystarczyć *perf*) na *+acc*
**stretcher** ['strɛtʃə^r] *n* nosze *pl*
**stretcher-bearer** ['strɛtʃəbɛərə^r] *n* noszowy(-wa) *m*(*f*)
**stretch marks** *npl* rozstępy *pl*
**strewn** [struːn] *adj*: **the carpet was ~ with broken glass** na dywanie porozrzucane były kawałki szkła
**stricken** ['strɪkən] *adj* (*industry, city*) dotknięty *or* ogarnięty kryzysem; **~ by** (*fear, doubts*) ogarnięty *+instr*; **~ with** (*disease*) dotknięty *+instr*
**strict** [strɪkt] *adj* (*severe, firm*) surowy; (*precise*) ścisły; **she told me about it in the ~est confidence** powiedziała mi o tym w najgłębszej tajemnicy
**strictly** ['strɪktlɪ] *adv* (*severely*) surowo; (*exactly*) ściśle; (*solely*) wyłącznie; **~ confidential** ściśle poufne; **~ speaking** ściśle(j) mówiąc; **~ between ourselves** wyłącznie między nami
**strictness** ['strɪktnɪs] *n* surowość *f*
**stridden** ['strɪdn] *pp of* **stride**
**stride** [straɪd] (*pt* **strode**, *pp* **stridden**) *n* krok *m* ▷ *vi* kroczyć; **to take sth in one's ~** (*fig*) spokojnie podchodzić (podejść *perf*) do czegoś, podchodzić (podejść *perf*) do czegoś z marszu (*inf*)
**strident** ['straɪdnt] *adj* (*voice, sound*) ostry, przenikliwy; (*demands*) natarczywy

**rife** [straɪf] *n* spór *m*
**rike** [straɪk] (*pt, pp* **struck**) *n* (*of workers*) ,trajk *m*; (*attack*) uderzenie *nt* ▷ *vt* (*person, hing*) uderzać (uderzyć *perf*); (*oil etc*) natrafiać natrafić *perf*) na *+acc*; (*deal*) zawierać zawrzeć *perf*); (*coin, medal*) wybijać (wybić erf); (*fig: occur to*) uderzać (uderzyć *perf*) ▷ *vi workers*) strajkować (zastrajkować *perf*); *illness, snake*) atakować (zaatakować *perf*); *clock*) bić, wybijać (wybić *perf*) godzinę; *killer*) uderzać (uderzyć *perf*); **to be on ~** strajkować; **to ~ a balance** zachowywać zachować *perf*) proporcje; **to ~ a bargain with sb** ubijać (ubić *perf*) z kimś interes; **the ree was struck by lightning** w drzewo ıderzył piorun; **the clock struck eleven** egar wybił (godzinę) jedenastą; **when personal disaster ~s ...** gdy kogoś dotknie osobiste nieszczęście, ...; **to ~ a match** zapalać (zapalić *perf*) zapałkę
▸ **strike back** *vi* (*Mil*) kontratakować; (*fig*) odgrywać się (odegrać się *perf*)
▸ **strike down** *vt* powalać (powalić *perf*)
▸ **strike off** *vt* (*name from list*) skreślać skreślić *perf*); (*doctor, lawyer*) pozbawiać pozbawić *perf*) prawa wykonywania zawodu
▸ **strike out** *vi*: **to ~ out on one's own** ıniezależnić się (*perf*) ▷ *vt* skreślać (skreślić erf)
▸ **strike up** *vt* (*Mus*) zaczynać (zacząć *perf*) grać; (*conversation*) zagajać (zagaić *perf*); *friendship*) zawierać (zawrzeć *perf*)
**rikebreaker** ['straɪkbreɪkə^r] *n* łamistrajk *m*
**rike pay** *n* zasiłek *m* z funduszu strajkowego (*wypłacany stajkującym przez związki zawodowe*)
**riker** ['straɪkə^r] *n* (*worker*) strajkujący(-ca) *m(f)*; (*Sport*) napastnik(-iczka) *m(f)*
**riking** ['straɪkɪŋ] *adj* (*remarkable*) uderzający; *stunning*) uderzająco piękny, zachwycający
**ring** [strɪŋ] (*pt, pp* **strung**) *n* (*thin rope*) sznurek *m*; (*of beads, cars, islands*) sznur *m*; (*of disasters, excuses*) seria *f*; (*Comput*) ciąg *m* znaków; (*Mus*) struna *f* ▷ *vt*: **to ~ together** związywać (związać *perf*) (ze sobą); **the strings** *npl* (*Mus*) smyczki *pl*; **to pull ~s** (*fig*) pociągać za sznurki; **with no ~s attached** *(fig)* bez dodatkowych zobowiązań; **villages strung out along dirt roads** wsie ciągnące się wzdłuż polnych dróg
**ring bean** *n* fasolka *f* szparagowa
**ringed instrument** *n* instrument *m* strunowy
**ringent** ['strɪndʒənt] *adj* surowy
**ring quartet** *n* kwartet *m* smyczkowy
**rip** [strɪp] *n* (*of paper, cloth*) pasek *m*; (*of land, water*) pas *m*; (*Sport*) stroje *pl*, kostiumy *pl* ▷ *vt* (*person*) rozbierać (rozebrać *perf*); (*paint*) zdrapywać (zdrapać *perf*); (*also*: **strip down**: *machine*) rozbierać (rozebrać *perf*) na części ▷ *vi* rozbierać się (rozebrać się *perf*)
**strip cartoon** *n* komiks *m*
**stripe** [straɪp] *n* pasek *m*; **stripes** *npl* (*Mil, Police*) ≈ belki *pl*
**striped** [straɪpt] *adj* w paski *post*
**strip lighting** (*Brit*) *n* oświetlenie *nt* jarzeniowe
**stripper** ['strɪpə^r] *n* striptizerka *f*
**strip-tease** ['strɪpti:z] *n* striptiz *m*, striptease *m*
**strive** [straɪv] (*pt* **strove**, *pp* **~n**) *vi*: **to ~ for sth** dążyć do czegoś, starać się coś osiągnąć; **to ~ to ...** starać się *+infin*
**striven** ['strɪvn] *pp of* **strive**
**strode** [strəud] *pt of* **stride**
**stroke** [strəuk] *n* (*blow*) raz *m*, uderzenie *nt*; (*Swimming*) styl *m*; (*Med*) udar *m*, wylew *m*; (*of clock*) uderzenie *nt*; (*of paintbrush*) pociągnięcie *nt* ▷ *vt* głaskać (pogłaskać *perf*); **at a ~** za jednym zamachem *or* pociągnięciem; **on the ~ of five** punktualnie o piątej; **a ~ of luck** uśmiech losu, łut szczęścia; **a two-~ engine** silnik dwusuwowy
**stroll** [strəul] *n* spacer *m*, przechadzka *f* ▷ *vi* spacerować, przechadzać się; **to go for a ~, have** *or* **take a ~** iść (pójść *perf*) na spacer, przejść się (*perf*) *or* przespacerować się (*perf*)
**stroller** ['strəulə^r] (*US*) *n* spacerówka *f*
**strong** [strɔŋ] *adj* silny, mocny; (*material, drink, point, language*) mocny ▷ *adv*: **to be going ~** świetnie się trzymać; **50 ~** w sile *or* liczbie 50 ludzi
**strong-arm** ['strɔŋɑ:m] *adj*: **~ method/tactics** metoda *f*/taktyka *f* silnej *or* twardej ręki
**strongbox** ['strɔŋbɔks] *n* kasa *f* ogniotrwała
**stronghold** ['strɔŋhəuld] *n* forteca *f*; (*fig*) bastion *m*
**strongly** ['strɔŋlɪ] *adv* silnie, mocno; (*defend, advise, argue*) zdecydowanie; **I feel ~ about it** (*deeply*) to mi bardzo leży na sercu; (*negatively*) jestem temu zdecydowanie przeciwny
**strongman** ['strɔŋmæn] (*irreg: like* **man**) *n* siłacz *m*; **the ~ of British politics** najbardziej wpływowy polityk brytyjski
**strongroom** ['strɔŋru:m] *n* skarbiec *m*
**strove** [strəuv] *pt of* **strive**
**struck** *pt, pp of* **strike**
**structural** ['strʌktʃrəl] *adj* (*changes, similarities*) strukturalny; (*defect*) konstrukcyjny
**structurally** ['strʌktʃrəlɪ] *adv* strukturalnie
**structure** ['strʌktʃə^r] *n* struktura *f*; (*building*) konstrukcja *f*
**struggle** ['strʌgl] *n* (*fight*) walka *f*; (*effort*) zmaganie się *nt*, borykanie się *nt* ▷ *vi*

S

walczyć; **to ~ to do sth** usiłować coś zrobić; **to have a ~ to do sth** wkładać (włożyć *perf*) w coś wiele wysiłku
**strum** [strʌm] *vt* (*guitar*) brzdąkać na *+instr*
**strung** *pt, pp of* **string**
**strut** [strʌt] *n* rozpórka *f* ▷ *vi* kroczyć dumnie
**strychnine** ['strɪkni:n] *n* strychnina *f*
**stub** [stʌb] *n* (*of cheque, ticket*) odcinek *m* (kontrolny); (*of cigarette*) niedopałek *m* ▷ *vt*: **to ~ one's toe** uderzyć się (*perf*) w palec u nogi
▸ **stub out** *vt* (*cigarette*) gasić (zgasić *perf*)
**stubble** ['stʌbl] *n* (*on field*) ściernisko *nt*; (*on chin*) szczecina *f*
**stubborn** ['stʌbən] *adj* (*child*) uparty; (*stain*) oporny; (*pain, illness*) uporczywy
**stubby** ['stʌbɪ] *adj* krótki i gruby
**stucco** ['stʌkəu] *n* tynk *m* szlachetny, stiuk *m*
**stuck** [stʌk] *pt, pp of* **stick** ▷ *adj* zablokowany; **to be/get ~** utknąć (*perf*); (*fig*) napotykać (napotkać *perf*) trudności
**stuck-up** [stʌk'ʌp] (*inf*) *adj* zadzierający nosa
**stud** [stʌd] *n* (*on clothing*) ćwiek *m*; (*collar stud*) spinka *f*; (*jewellery*) kolczyk *m* (*tzw. wkrętka*); (*on sole of boot*) korek *m*; (*also*: **stud farm**) stadnina *f*; (*also*: **stud horse**) ogier *m* rozpłodowy ▷ *vt*: **~ded with** (*precious stones*) nabijany *+instr*; (*stars*) usiany *+instr*
**student** ['stju:dənt] *n* (*at university*) student(ka) *m(f)*, słuchacz(ka) *m(f)*; (*at school*) uczeń/uczennica *m/f* ▷ *cpd* studencki; **law/medical ~** student(ka) *m(f)* prawa/medycyny; **~ nurse/teacher** słuchacz(ka) *m(f)* szkoły pielęgniarskiej/pedagogicznej
**student driver** (*US*) *n* uczestnik(-iczka) *m(f)* kursu prawa jazdy
**students' union** ['stju:dənts-] (*Brit*) *n* (*association*) zrzeszenie *nt* studentów; (*building*) klub *m* studencki
**studied** ['stʌdɪd] *adj* (*expression etc*) wystudiowany
**studio** ['stju:dɪəu] *n* (*TV etc*) studio *nt*; (*sculptor's etc*) pracownia *f*, atelier *nt inv*
**studio flat**, (*US*) **studio apartment** *n* ≈ kawalerka *f*
**studious** ['stju:dɪəs] *adj* pilny, staranny
**studiously** ['stju:dɪəslɪ] *adv* pilnie, starannie
**study** ['stʌdɪ] *n* (*activity*) nauka *f*; (*room*) gabinet *m* ▷ *vt* (*subject*) studiować, uczyć się *+gen*; (*face, evidence*) studiować (przestudiować *perf*) ▷ *vi* studiować, uczyć się; **studies** *npl* studia *pl*; **to make a ~ of sth** studiować (przestudiować *perf*) coś; **to ~ for an exam** uczyć się do egzaminu
**stuff** [stʌf] *n* (*thing(s)*) rzeczy *pl*; (*substance*) coś *nt* ▷ *vt* (*soft toy, dead animals*) wypychać (wypchać *perf*); (*Culin*) faszerować (nafaszerować *perf*), nadziewać (nadziać *per*; (*inf*: *push*) upychać (upchnąć *perf*); **my nose i ~ed up** mam zapchany nos; **get ~ed!** (*inf!*) wypchaj się! (*inf!*)
**stuffed toy** [stʌft-] *n* pluszowa zabawka *f*
**stuffing** ['stʌfɪŋ] *n* (*in sofa, pillow*) wypełnien *nt*; (*Culin*) farsz *m*, nadzienie *nt*
**stuffy** ['stʌfɪ] *adj* (*room*) duszny; (*person, ideas*) staroświecki
**stumble** ['stʌmbl] *vi* potykać się (potknąć si *perf*); **to ~ across** *or* **on** (*fig*) natykać się (natknąć się *perf*) na *+acc*
**stumbling block** ['stʌmblɪŋ-] *n* przeszkoda; zawada *f*
**stump** [stʌmp] *n* (*of tree*) pniak *m*; (*of limb*) kikut *m* ▷ *vt*: **~ed** zbity z tropu
**stun** [stʌn] *vt* (*news*) oszałamiać (oszołomić *perf*); (*blow on head*) ogłuszać (ogłuszyć *perf*)
**stung** [stʌŋ] *pt, pp of* **sting**
**stunk** [stʌŋk] *pp of* **stink**
**stunning** ['stʌnɪŋ] *adj* (*victory*) oszałamiając (*girl, dress*) uderzająco piękny, zachwycający
**stunt** [stʌnt] *n* (*in film*) wyczyn *m* kaskadersk (*also*: **publicity stunt**) chwyt *m* reklamowy
**stunted** ['stʌntɪd] *adj* (*trees*) skarłowaciały; (*growth*) zahamowany
**stuntman** ['stʌntmæn] (*irreg*: *like* **man**) *n* kaskader *m*
**stupefaction** [stju:pɪ'fækʃən] *n* (*daze*) otępienie *nt*; (*amazement*) oszołomienie *nt*
**stupefy** ['stju:pɪfaɪ] *vt* wprawiać (wprawić *perf*) w otępienie; (*fig*) oszałamiać (oszołomi *perf*)
**stupendous** [stju:'pɛndəs] *adj* zdumiewając wielki
**stupid** ['stju:pɪd] *adj* głupi
**stupidity** [stju:'pɪdɪtɪ] *n* głupota *f*
**stupidly** ['stju:pɪdlɪ] *adv* głupio
**stupor** ['stju:pər] *n* osłupienie *nt*, zamroczenie *nt*; **in a ~** w stanie zamroczeni
**sturdily** ['stə:dɪlɪ] *adv* (*built*) mocno, solidnie
**sturdy** ['stə:dɪ] *adj* mocny
**sturgeon** ['stə:dʒən] *n* jesiotr *m*
**stutter** ['stʌtər] *n* jąkanie (się) *nt* ▷ *vi* jąkać się; **to have a ~** jąkać się
**Stuttgart** ['stutgɑ:t] *n* Stuttgart *m*
**sty** [staɪ] *n* chlew *m*
**stye** [staɪ] (*Med*) *n* jęczmień *m*
**style** [staɪl] *n* (*way, attitude*) styl *m*; (*elegance*) styl *m*, szyk *m*; (*design*) fason *m*; **in the latest ~** w najnowszym fasonie; **hair ~** fryzura
**styli** ['staɪlaɪ] *npl of* **stylus**
**stylish** ['staɪlɪʃ] *adj* szykowny
**stylist** ['staɪlɪst] *n* (*hair stylist*) fryzjer(ka) *m(f)*; (*writer*) stylista(-tka) *m(f)*
**stylistic** [staɪ'lɪstɪk] *adj* stylistyczny
**stylized** ['staɪlaɪzd] *adj* stylizowany

**ylus** ['staɪləs] (*pl* **styli** *or* **~es**) *n* igła *f* gramofonowa)
**ave** [swɑːv] *adj* uprzedzająco grzeczny
**b** [sʌb] *n abbr* (*Naut*) = **submarine**; (*Admin*) **subscription**; (*Press*) = **sub-editor**
**b...** [sʌb] *pref* pod...
**bcommittee** ['sʌbkəmɪtɪ] *n* podkomitet *m*, odkomisja *f*
**bconscious** [sʌb'kɔnʃəs] *adj* podświadomy
**bcontinent** [sʌb'kɔntɪnənt] *n*: **the Indian)** ~ subkontynent *m* indyjski
**bcontract** [*vb* sʌbkən'trækt, *n* ʌb'kɔntrækt] *vt* zlecać (zlecić *perf*) odwykonawcy ▷ *n* podkontrakt *m*, ubkontrakt *m*
**bcontractor** ['sʌbkən'træktəʳ] *n* odwykonawca *m*
**bculture** ['sʌbkʌltʃəʳ] *n* subkultura *f*
**bdivide** [sʌbdɪ'vaɪd] *vt* dzielić (podzielić *erf*) (dalej)
**bdivision** ['sʌbdɪvɪʒən] *n* (dalszy) podział *m*
**bdue** [səb'djuː] *vt* (*rebels etc*) ujarzmiać ujarzmić *perf*); (*emotions*) tłumić (stłumić *erf*)
**bdued** [səb'djuːd] *adj* (*light*) przyćmiony, rzytłumiony; (*person*) przygnębiony
**b-editor** ['sʌb'ɛdɪtəʳ] (*Brit*: *Press*) *n* zastępca redaktora naczelnego
**bject** [*n* 'sʌbdʒɪkt, *vb* səb'dʒɛkt] *n* (*matter*) emat *m*; (*Scol*) przedmiot *m*; (*of kingdom*) oddany(-na) *m(f)*; (*Ling*) podmiot *m* ▷ *vt*: **to sb to sth** poddawać (poddać *perf*) kogoś zemuś; **to be ~ to** (*law, tax*) podlegać *+dat*; *heart attacks*) być narażonym na *+acc*; **~ to onfirmation in writing** podlegający atwierdzeniu na piśmie; **to change the ~** mieniać (zmienić *perf*) temat
**bjection** [səb'dʒɛkʃən] *n* odporządkowanie *nt*
**bjective** [səb'dʒɛktɪv] *adj* subiektywny
**bject matter** *n* tematyka *f*, temat *m*
**b judice** [sʌb'dʒuːdɪsɪ] (*Jur*) *adj* w trakcie ostępowania sądowego *post*
**bjugate** ['sʌbdʒugeɪt] *vt* (*people*) podbijać podbić *perf*); (*wishes, desires*) odporządkowywać (podporządkować *perf*)
**bjunctive** [səb'dʒʌŋktɪv] (*Ling*) *n* tryb *m* łączący
**blet** [sʌb'lɛt] *vt* podnajmować (podnająć *erf*)
**blime** [sə'blaɪm] *adj* wzniosły, ysublimowany; **from the ~ to the idiculous** od wzniosłości do śmieszności
**bliminal** [sʌb'lɪmɪnl] *adj* podświadomy
**bmachine gun** ['sʌbmə'ʃiːn-] *n* pistolet *m* naszynowy
**bmarine** [sʌbmə'riːn] *n* łódź *f* podwodna

**submerge** [səb'məːdʒ] *vt* zanurzać (zanurzyć *perf*) ▷ *vi* zanurzać się (zanurzyć się *perf*)
**submersion** [səb'məːʃən] *n* zanurzenie *nt*
**submission** [səb'mɪʃən] *n* (*subjection*) uległość *f*, posłuszeństwo *nt*; (*of plan, proposal*) przedłożenie *nt*; (*of application*) złożenie *nt*; (*proposal*) propozycja *f*
**submissive** [səb'mɪsɪv] *adj* uległy, posłuszny
**submit** [səb'mɪt] *vt* (*proposal*) przedkładać (przedłożyć *perf*); (*application, resignation*) składać (złożyć *perf*) ▷ *vi*: **to ~ to sth** poddawać się (poddać się *perf*) czemuś
**subnormal** [sʌb'nɔːml] *adj* (*temperatures*) poniżej normy *post*; (*old*: *child*) opóźniony w rozwoju
**subordinate** [sə'bɔːdɪnət] *n* podwładny(-na) *m(f)* ▷ *adj* (*also Ling*) podrzędny; **to be ~ to sb** podlegać komuś
**subpoena** [səb'piːnə] (*Jur*) *n* wezwanie *nt* do sądu *or* stawienia się przed sądem ▷ *vt* wzywać (wezwać *perf*) do stawienia się przed sądem
**subroutine** [sʌbruː'tiːn] (*Comput*) *n* podprogram *m*
**subscribe** [səb'skraɪb] *vi*: **to ~ to** (*theory, values*) wyznawać *+acc*; (*opinion*) podpisywać się pod *+instr*; (*fund, charity*) wspierać finansowo *+acc*, łożyć na *+acc*; (*magazine etc*) prenumerować *+acc*
**subscriber** [səb'skraɪbəʳ] *n* (*to magazine*) prenumerator *m*; (*Tel*) abonent *m*
**subscript** ['sʌbskrɪpt] (*Typ*) *n* indeks *m* dolny
**subscription** [səb'skrɪpʃən] *n* (*to magazine etc*) prenumerata *f*; (*membership dues*) składka *f* (członkowska); **to take out a ~ to** (*organization*) zapisać się (*perf*) do *+gen*; (*magazine*) zaprenumerować (*perf*) *+acc*
**subsequent** ['sʌbsɪkwənt] *adj* późniejszy; **~ to** w następstwie *+gen*
**subsequently** ['sʌbsɪkwəntlɪ] *adv* później
**subservient** [səb'səːvɪənt] *adj* (*person, behaviour*) służalczy; (*policy, goals*) drugorzędny; **to be ~ to** być podporządkowanym *+dat*
**subside** [səb'saɪd] *vi* (*feeling, pain*) ustępować (ustąpić *perf*); (*earth*) obsuwać się (obsunąć się *perf*); **the flood ~d** wody powodziowe opadły
**subsidence** [səb'saɪdns] *n* obsuwanie się *nt* gruntu
**subsidiarity** [səbsɪdɪ'ærɪtɪ] (*Pol*) *n* subsydiarność *f*
**subsidiary** [səb'sɪdɪərɪ] *adj* (*question, role*) drugorzędny; (*Brit*: *Scol*: *subject*) dodatkowy ▷ *n* (*also*: **subsidiary company**) przedsiębiorstwo *nt* filialne, filia *f*
**subsidize** ['sʌbsɪdaɪz] *vt* dotować, subsydiować

S

**subsidy** ['sʌbsɪdɪ] *n* dotacja *f*
**subsist** [səb'sɪst] *vi*: **to ~ on sth** utrzymywać się przy życiu dzięki czemuś
**subsistence** [səb'sɪstəns] *n* utrzymanie się *nt* przy życiu, przetrwanie *nt*
**subsistence allowance** *n* (*for poor person*) zapomoga *f*; (*for traveller*) dieta *f*
**subsistence level** *n* ≈ poziom *m* minimum socjalnego
**substance** ['sʌbstəns] *n* substancja *f*; (*fig*) istota *f*; **a man of ~** wpływowy człowiek; **to lack ~** (*argument*) być pozbawionym (solidnych) podstaw; (*book, film*) być pozbawionym treści
**substandard** [sʌb'stændəd] *adj* (*goods*) niskiej jakości *post*; (*housing*) o niskim standardzie *post*
**substantial** [səb'stænʃl] *adj* (*building, meal*) solidny; (*amount*) pokaźny
**substantially** [səb'stænʃəlɪ] *adv* (*by a large amount*) znacznie; (*in essence*) z gruntu, zasadniczo; **~ bigger** znacznie większy
**substantiate** [səb'stænʃɪeɪt] *vt* (*confirm*) potwierdzać (potwierdzić *perf*); (*prove*) udowadniać (udowodnić *perf*)
**substitute** ['sʌbstɪtju:t] *n* (*thing*) substytut *m*; (*person*): **to be a ~ for** zastępować (zastąpić *perf*) *+acc* ▷ *vt*: **to ~ sth for sth** zastępować (zastąpić *perf*) coś czymś
**substitute teacher** (*US*) *n* nauczyciel(ka) *m(f)* na zastępstwie
**substitution** [sʌbstɪ'tju:ʃən] *n* zastąpienie *nt*; (*Football*) zmiana *f*
**subterfuge** ['sʌbtəfju:dʒ] *n* wybieg *m*, podstęp *m*
**subterranean** [sʌbtə'reɪnɪən] *adj* podziemny
**subtitles** ['sʌbtaɪtlz] (*Film*) *npl* napisy *pl*
**subtle** ['sʌtl] *adj* subtelny
**subtlety** ['sʌtltɪ] *n* subtelność *f*; **subtleties** *npl* subtelności *pl*
**subtly** ['sʌtlɪ] *adv* (*change, vary*) nieznacznie; (*criticize, persuade*) w subtelny sposób; (*flavoured etc*) subtelnie; (*different*) nieco
**subtotal** [sʌb'təutl] *n* suma *f* częściowa
**subtract** [səb'trækt] *vt* odejmować (odjąć *perf*)
**subtraction** [səb'trækʃən] *n* odejmowanie *nt*
**subtropical** [sʌb'trɔpɪkl] *adj* podzwrotnikowy, subtropikalny
**suburb** ['sʌbə:b] *n* przedmieście *nt*; **the suburbs** *npl* przedmieścia *pl*, peryferie *pl*
**suburban** [sə'bə:bən] *adj* (*train*) podmiejski; (*lifestyle*) zaściankowy (*pej*)
**suburbia** [sə'bə:bɪə] *n* przedmieścia *pl*, peryferie *pl*
**subvention** [səb'vɛnʃən] *n* subwencja *f*
**subversion** [səb'və:ʃən] *n* działalność *f* wywrotowa
**subversive** [səb'və:sɪv] *adj* wywrotowy
**subway** ['sʌbweɪ] *n* (*US*) metro *nt*; (*Brit*) przejście *nt* podziemne
**sub-zero** [sʌb'zɪərəu] *adj*: **~ temperatures** temperatury *pl* poniżej zera *or* ujemne
**succeed** [sək'si:d] *vi* (*plan*) powieść się (*perf*); (*person*) odnieść (*perf*) sukces ▷ *vt* (*in job*) przejmować (przejąć *perf*) obowiązki po *+loc*; (*in order*) następować (nastąpić *perf*) po *+loc*; **did you ~ in finding them?** czy udało ci się ich znaleźć?
**succeeding** [sək'si:dɪŋ] *adj* następny; **~ generations** następne pokolenia
**success** [sək'sɛs] *n* (*achievement*) sukces *m*, powodzenie *nt*; (*hit*) przebój *m*; **to be a ~** odnieść (*perf*) sukces; **without ~** bez powodzenia
**successful** [sək'sɛsful] *adj* (*venture, attempt*) udany, pomyślny; (*writer*) wzięty; (*business*) dobrze prosperujący; (*Pol: candidate*) zwycięski; **to be ~ as** odnosić sukcesy jako *+nom*; **I was ~ in getting the job** udało mi się zdobyć tę pracę
**successfully** [sək'sɛsfəlɪ] *adv* pomyślnie
**succession** [sək'sɛʃən] *n* (*of things, events*) seria *f*; (*to throne, peerage*) sukcesja *f*; **three years in ~** przez trzy kolejne lata
**successive** [sək'sɛsɪv] *adj* następujący po sobie, kolejny; **on three ~ days** przez trzy kolejne dni
**successor** [sək'sɛsə^r] *n* następca(-pczyni) *m(f)*
**succinct** [sək'sɪŋkt] *adj* zwięzły
**succulent** ['sʌkjulənt] *adj* soczysty ▷ *n* (*Bot*) sukulent *m*
**succumb** [sə'kʌm] *vi* (*to temptation*) ulegać (ulec *perf*) *+dat*; (*to illness*) poddawać się (poddać się *perf*) *+dat*
**such** [sʌtʃ] *adj* taki; **~ a book** taka książka; **~ courage** taka odwaga; **~ a lovely day** taki piękny dzień; **~ a lot of** tyle *or* tak dużo *+gen*; **~ a long time ago** tak dawno (temu); **in Brighton or some ~ place** w Brighton, czy w jakimś takim miejscu; **she made ~ a noise that ...** narobiła tyle hałasu, że ...; **~ as** taki jak *+nom*; **~ books as I have** takie książki, jakie mam; **I said no ~ thing** nic takiego *or* podobnego nie powiedziałam; **as ~** jako taki
**such-and-such** ['sʌtʃənsʌtʃ] *adj* taki a taki
**suchlike** ['sʌtʃlaɪk] (*inf*) *pron*: **and ~** i temu podobne
**suck** [sʌk] *vt* ssać; (*pump etc*) zasysać
**sucker** ['sʌkə^r] *n* (*Zool, Tech*) przyssawka *f*; (*Bot*) odrost *m*; (*inf*) frajer *m* (*inf*)
**suckle** ['sʌkl] *vt* (*baby*) karmić piersią; (*young animal*) karmić własnym mlekiem
**suction** ['sʌkʃən] *n* ssanie *nt*
**suction pump** *n* pompa *f* ssąca

**dan** [su'dɑ:n] *n* Sudan *m*
**danese** [su:də'ni:z] *adj* sudański ▷ *n* *person)* Sudańczyk(-anka) *m(f)*
**dden** ['sʌdn] *adj* nagły; **all of a ~** nagle
**ddenly** ['sʌdnlɪ] *adv* nagle
**ds** [sʌdz] *npl* mydliny *pl*
**e** [su:] *vt* podawać (podać *perf*) do sądu, askarżać (zaskarżyć *perf*) ▷ *vi* procesować ię; **to sue for divorce** występować wystąpić *perf*) o rozwód; **to sue sb for lamages** zaskarżać (zaskarżyć *perf*) kogoś o dszkodowanie
**ede** [sweɪd] *n* zamsz *m* ▷ *cpd* zamszowy
**et** ['suɪt] *(Culin)* *n* łój *m*
**ez** ['su:ɪz] *n*: **the ~ Canal** Kanał *m* Sueski
**ff.** *(Brit: Post)* *abbr* = **Suffolk**
**ffer** ['sʌfəʳ] *vt* *(undergo)* doznawać (doznać *erf)* *+gen*, doświadczać (doświadczyć *perf)* *gen*; *(old: bear, allow)* cierpieć (ścierpieć *perf)* *vi*: **your studies are ~ing** cierpią na tym woje studia; **he would be the first to ~** on ierwszy by na tym ucierpiał; **to ~ from** *llness)* cierpieć na *+acc*; *(shock)* doznawać doznać *perf) +gen*; **to ~ the effects of lcohol/a fall** cierpieć z powodu *or* na skutek vypicia alkoholu/upadku
**fferance** ['sʌfərns] *n*: **he was only there n ~** był tam zaledwie tolerowany
**fferer** ['sʌfərəʳ] *n* *(Med)* cierpiący(-ca) *m(f)*
**ffering** ['sʌfərɪŋ] *n* cierpienie *nt*
**ffice** [sə'faɪs] *vi* wystarczać (wystarczyć *perf)*
**fficient** [sə'fɪʃənt] *adj* wystarczający, lostateczny; **~ money** wystarczająco dużo ieniędzy
**fficiently** [sə'fɪʃəntlɪ] *adv* wystarczająco, lostatecznie
**ffix** ['sʌfɪks] *n* *(Ling)* przyrostek *m*
**ffocate** ['sʌfəkeɪt] *vi* *(have difficulty reathing)* dusić się; *(die from lack of air)* udusić ię *(perf)*
**ffocation** [sʌfə'keɪʃən] *n* uduszenie *nt*
**ffrage** ['sʌfrɪdʒ] *n* prawo *nt* wyborcze
**ffragette** [sʌfrə'dʒɛt] *n* sufrażystka *f*
**ffused** [sə'fju:zd] *adj*: **~ with** *(light)* skąpany v *+loc*; *(tears)* zalany *+instr*; *(colour)* nasycony *instr*
**gar** ['ʃugəʳ] *n* cukier *m* ▷ *vt* słodzić posłodzić *perf)*
**gar beet** *n* burak *m* cukrowy
**gar bowl** *n* cukierniczka *f*
**gar cane** *n* trzcina *f* cukrowa
**gar-coated** ['ʃugə'kəutɪd] *adj*: **~ pill/sweet** rażetka *f*
**gar lump** *n* kostka *f* cukru
**gar refinery** *n* rafineria *f* cukru
**gary** ['ʃugərɪ] *adj* bogaty w cukier; *(fig)* ukierkowy

**suggest** [sə'dʒɛst] *vt* *(propose)* proponować (zaproponować *perf*); *(indicate)* wskazywać na *+acc*; **what do you ~ I do?** co według ciebie powinienem zrobić?
**suggestion** [sə'dʒɛstʃən] *n* *(proposal)* propozycja *f*; *(indication)* oznaka *f*
**suggestive** [sə'dʒɛstɪv] *(pej)* *adj* niedwuznaczny
**suicidal** [suɪ'saɪdl] *adj* *(act)* samobójczy; *(person)*: **to be** *or* **feel ~** być w nastroju samobójczym
**suicide** ['suɪsaɪd] *n* *(act)* samobójstwo *nt*; *(person)* samobójca(-jczyni) *m(f)*; *see also* **commit**
**suicide attempt** *n* próba *f* samobójstwa
**suicide bid** *n* = **suicide attempt**
**suit** [su:t] *n* *(man's)* garnitur *m*, ubranie *nt*; *(woman's)* kostium *m*, garsonka *m*; *(Jur)* proces *m*; *(Cards)* kolor *m* ▷ *vt* odpowiadać *+dat*; **to ~ sth to** dostosowywać (dostosować *perf)* coś do *+gen*; **that colour/hat doesn't ~ you** w tym kolorze/kapeluszu nie jest ci do twarzy; **to be ~ed to** nadawać się do *+gen*; **to bring a ~ against sb** wytaczać (wytoczyć *perf)* komuś proces; **he bowed his head; I followed ~** skłonił głowę — poszłam za jego przykładem; **~ yourself!** rób, jak chcesz!; **a well ~ed couple** dobrana para
**suitability** [su:tə'bɪlɪtɪ] *n* odpowiedniość *f*
**suitable** ['su:təbl] *adj* odpowiedni; **would tomorrow be ~?** czy jutrzejszy dzień byłby odpowiedni?; **we found somebody ~** znaleźliśmy kogoś odpowiedniego
**suitably** ['su:təblɪ] *adv* odpowiednio
**suitcase** ['su:tkeɪs] *n* walizka *f*
**suite** [swi:t] *n* *(in hotel)* apartament *m*; *(Mus)* suita *f*; **bedroom/dining room ~** komplet mebli do sypialni/jadalni; **a three-piece ~** zestaw wypoczynkowy
**suitor** ['su:təʳ] *n* starający się *m* *(o rękę)*
**sulfate** ['sʌlfeɪt] *(US)* *n* = **sulphate**
**sulfur** ['sʌlfəʳ] *(US)* *n* = **sulphur**
**sulfuric** [sʌl'fjuərɪk] *(US)* *adj* = **sulphuric**
**sulk** [sʌlk] *vi* dąsać się
**sulky** ['sʌlkɪ] *adj* *(child, face)* nadąsany; **to be in a ~ mood** być nadąsanym, dąsać się
**sullen** ['sʌlən] *adj* ponury
**sulphate**, *(US)* **sulfate** ['sʌlfeɪt] *n* siarczan *m*; *see also* **copper sulphate**
**sulphur**, *(US)* **sulfur** ['sʌlfəʳ] *n* siarka *f*
**sulphuric**, *(US)* **sulfuric** [sʌl'fjuərɪk] *adj*: **~ acid** kwas *m* siarkowy
**sultan** ['sʌltən] *n* sułtan *m*
**sultana** [sʌl'tɑ:nə] *n* rodzynka *f* sułtańska, sułtanka *f*
**sultry** ['sʌltrɪ] *adj* duszny, parny

S

**sum** [sʌm] *n* (*calculation*) obliczenie *nt*; (*result of addition*) suma *f*; (*amount*) suma *f*, kwota *f* ▶ **sum up** *vt* (*describe*) podsumowywać (podsumować *perf*); (*size up*) oceniać (ocenić *perf*) ▷ *vi* podsumowywać (podsumować *perf*)
**Sumatra** [su'mɑːtrə] *n* Sumatra *f*
**summarize** ['sʌməraɪz] *vt* streszczać (streścić *perf*)
**summary** ['sʌmərɪ] *n* streszczenie *nt*, skrót *m* ▷ *adj* doraźny, natychmiastowy
**summer** ['sʌmə^r] *n* lato *nt* ▷ *cpd* (*dress, school*) letni; **in ~** w lecie, latem
**summer camp** (*US*) *n* obóz *m* letni, kolonie *pl* letnie
**summer holidays** *npl* wakacje *pl* letnie
**summerhouse** ['sʌməhaus] *n* altana *f*
**summertime** ['sʌmətaɪm] *n* lato *nt*, pora *f* letnia
**summer time** *n* czas *m* letni
**summery** ['sʌmərɪ] *adj* letni
**summing-up** [sʌmɪŋ'ʌp] *n* mowa *f* podsumowująca (*skierowana do przysięgłych*)
**summit** ['sʌmɪt] *n* (*of mountain*) szczyt *m*, wierzchołek *m*; (*also*: **summit conference/meeting**) szczyt *m*
**summon** ['sʌmən] *vt* (*police, witness*) wzywać (wezwać *perf*); (*meeting*) zwoływać (zwołać *perf*) ▶ **summon up** *vt* (*strength, energy*) zbierać (zebrać *perf*); (*courage*) zebrać się (*perf*) *or* zdobyć się (*perf*) na *+acc*
**summons** ['sʌmənz] *n* (*also Jur*) wezwanie *nt* ▷ *vt* wzywać (wezwać *perf*) do sądu; **to serve a ~ on sb** doręczać (doręczyć *perf*) komuś urzędowe wezwanie
**sump** [sʌmp] (*Brit*: *Aut*) *n* miska *f* olejowa
**sumptuous** ['sʌmptjuəs] *adj* wspaniały, okazały
**sun** [sʌn] *n* słońce *nt*; **in the sun** w *or* na słońcu; **to catch the sun** lekko się opalić (*perf*); **everything under the sun** wszystko, co można sobie wyobrazić
**Sun.** *abbr* (= *Sunday*) nd., niedz.
**sunbathe** ['sʌnbeɪð] *vi* opalać się
**sunbeam** ['sʌnbiːm] *n* promień *m* słońca
**sunbed** ['sʌnbɛd] *n* łóżko *nt* z kwarcówką
**sunburn** ['sʌnbəːn] *n* oparzenie *nt* słoneczne
**sunburned** ['sʌnbəːnd] *adj* = **sunburnt**
**sunburnt** ['sʌnbəːnt] *adj* (*tanned*) opalony; (*painfully*) spalony (słońcem)
**sun-cream** ['sʌnkriːm] *n* krem *m* do opalania
**sundae** ['sʌndeɪ] *n* deser *m* lodowy
**Sunday** ['sʌndɪ] *n* niedziela *f*; *see also* **Tuesday**
**Sunday school** *n* szkółka *f* niedzielna
**sundial** ['sʌndaɪəl] *n* zegar *m* słoneczny
**sundown** ['sʌndaun] (*esp US*) *n* zachód *m* (słońca)
**sundries** ['sʌndrɪz] *npl* różności *pl*, inne *pl* (drobiazgi)
**sundry** ['sʌndrɪ] *adj* różny, rozmaity; **all and** wszyscy bez wyjątku
**sunflower** ['sʌnflauə^r] *n* słonecznik *m*
**sunflower oil** *n* olej *m* słonecznikowy
**sung** [sʌŋ] *pp of* **sing**
**sunglasses** ['sʌnglɑːsɪz] *npl* okulary *pl* (przeciw)słoneczne
**sunk** [sʌŋk] *pp of* **sink**
**sunken** ['sʌŋkn] *adj* (*rock*) podwodny; (*ship*) zatopiony; (*eyes, cheeks*) zapadnięty; (*bath*) wpuszczony (w podłogę)
**sunlamp** ['sʌnlæmp] *n* lampa *f* kwarcowa, kwarcówka *f*
**sunlight** ['sʌnlaɪt] *n* światło *nt* słoneczne, słońce *nt*
**sunlit** ['sʌnlɪt] *adj* nasłoneczniony
**sunny** ['sʌnɪ] *adj* (*weather, day, place*) słoneczn (*fig*: *disposition, person*) pogodny; **it is ~** jest słonecznie
**sunrise** ['sʌnraɪz] *n* wschód *m* (słońca)
**sun roof** *n* (*Aut*) szyberdach *m*; (*on building*) taras *m*
**sunscreen** ['sʌnskriːn] *n* krem *m* z filtrem ochronnym
**sunset** ['sʌnsɛt] *n* zachód *m* (słońca)
**sunshade** ['sʌnʃeɪd] *n* (*over table*) parasol *m* (przeciw)słoneczny; (*US*: *over window*) markiza *f*; (*lady's*) parasolka *f* (przeciw) słoneczna
**sunshine** ['sʌnʃaɪn] *n* słońce *nt*, (piękna) pogoda *f*
**sunspot** ['sʌnspɔt] (*Astron*) *n* plama *f* słoneczn
**sunstroke** ['sʌnstrəuk] *n* porażenie *nt* słoneczne, udar *m* słoneczny
**suntan** ['sʌntæn] *n* opalenizna *f*
**suntan lotion** *n* emulsja *f* do opalania
**suntanned** ['sʌntænd] *adj* opalony
**suntan oil** *n* olejek *m* do opalania
**suntrap** ['sʌntræp] *n bardzo nasłonecznione miejsce*
**super** ['suːpə^r] (*inf*) *adj* super (*inf*)
**superannuation** [suːpərænju'eɪʃən] *n* składka *f* na fundusz emerytalny
**superb** [suː'pəːb] *adj* pierwszorzędny, znakomity
**supercilious** [suːpə'sɪlɪəs] *adj* wyniosły
**superficial** [suːpə'fɪʃəl] *adj* powierzchowny
**superficially** [suːpə'fɪʃəlɪ] *adv* powierzchownie, z wierzchu
**superfluous** [su'pəːfluəs] *adj* zbyteczny
**superhuman** [suːpə'hjuːmən] *adj* nadludzki
**superimpose** ['suːpərɪm'pəuz] *vt* nakładać (nałożyć *perf*)
**superintend** [suːpərɪn'tɛnd] *vt* nadzorować, kierować (pokierować *perf*) *+instr*

**superintendent** [su:pərɪn'tɛndənt] *n (of place, activity)* kierownik *m*; *(Police)* inspektor *m*
**superior** [su'pɪərɪə^r] *adj (better)* lepszy; *(more senior)* starszy (rangą); *(smug)* wyniosły ▷ *n* przełożony(-na) *m(f)*; **Mother S~** matka *or* siostra przełożona
**superiority** [supɪərɪ'ɔrɪtɪ] *n* wyższość *f*, przewaga *f*
**superlative** [su'pə:lətɪv] *n (Ling)* stopień *m* najwyższy ▷ *adj* doskonały
**superman** ['su:pəmæn] *(irreg: like* **man**) *n* superman *m*
**supermarket** ['su:pəma:kɪt] *n* supermarket *m*, supersam *m*
**supermodel** ['su:pəmɔdəl] *n* supermodel(ka) *m(f)*
**supernatural** [su:pə'nætʃərəl] *adj* nadprzyrodzony ▷ *n*: **the ~** siły *pl or* zjawiska *pl* nadprzyrodzone
**superpower** ['su:pəpauə^r] *n* supermocarstwo *nt*
**superscript** ['su:pəskrɪpt] *(Typ) n* indeks *m* górny
**supersede** [su:pə'si:d] *vt* wypierać (wyprzeć *perf*)
**supersonic** ['su:pə'sɔnɪk] *adj* (po) naddźwiękowy
**superstar** ['su:pəsta:^r] *n* supergwiazda *f*
**superstition** [su:pə'stɪʃən] *n* przesąd *m*, zabobon *m*
**superstitious** [su:pə'stɪʃəs] *adj (person)* przesądny, zabobonny; *(practices)* zabobonny
**superstore** ['su:pəstɔ:^r] *(Brit) n* megasam *m*
**supertanker** ['su:pətæŋkə^r] *n* supertankowiec *m*
**supertax** ['su:pətæks] *n* domiar *m* podatkowy
**supervise** ['su:pəvaɪz] *vt (person, activity)* nadzorować; *(children)* pilnować *+gen*
**supervision** [su:pə'vɪʒən] *n* nadzór *m*; **under medical ~** pod kontrolą lekarza
**supervisor** ['su:pəvaɪzə^r] *n (of workers)* kierownik(-iczka) *m(f)*; *(of students)* opiekun(ka) *m(f)*, promotor(ka) *m(f)*
**supervisory** ['su:pəvaɪzərɪ] *adj* nadzorujący, nadzorczy
**supine** ['su:paɪn] *adj* leżący na wznak *or* na plecach ▷ *adv* na wznak, na plecach
**supper** ['sʌpə^r] *n* kolacja *f*; **to have ~** jeść (zjeść *perf*) kolację
**supplant** [sə'pla:nt] *vt* wypierać (wyprzeć *perf*), zastępować (zastąpić *perf*)
**supple** ['sʌpl] *adj (person, body)* gibki, giętki; *(leather etc)* miękki, elastyczny
**supplement** ['sʌplɪmənt] *n (of vitamins etc)* uzupełnienie *nt*, dawka *f* uzupełniająca; *(of book)* suplement *m*; *(of newspaper, magazine)* dodatek *m* ▷ *vt* uzupełniać (uzupełnić *perf*)
**supplementary** [sʌplɪ'mɛntərɪ] *adj* dodatkowy, uzupełniający
**supplementary benefit** *(Brit: old) n* zasiłek *m*
**supplier** [sə'plaɪə^r] *n* dostawca *m*
**supply** [sə'plaɪ] *vt (provide, deliver)* dostarczać (dostarczyć *perf*); *(satisfy)* zaspokajać (zaspokoić *perf*) ▷ *n (stock)* zapas *m*; *(supplying)* dostawa *f*; **supplies** *npl* dostawy *pl*; **to ~ sth to sb** dostarczać (dostarczyć *perf*) coś komuś; **to ~ sth with sth** zaopatrywać (zaopatrzyć *perf*) coś w coś; **office supplies** materiały biurowe; **petrol is in short ~** brakuje benzyny; **the electricity/water/gas ~** dostawy prądu/wody/gazu; **~ and demand** podaż i popyt; **it comes supplied with an adaptor** dołączony jest do niego zasilacz
**supply teacher** *(Brit) n nauczyciel zastępujący nieobecnych nauczycieli w kilku szkołach*
**support** [sə'pɔ:t] *n (moral)* poparcie *m*, wsparcie *nt*; *(financial)* wsparcie *nt*; *(Tech)* podpora *f* ▷ *vt (policy)* popierać (poprzeć *perf*); *(family)* utrzymywać (utrzymać *perf*); *(Tech)* podtrzymywać (podtrzymać *perf*), podpierać (podeprzeć *perf*); *(theory)* potwierdzać (potwierdzić *perf*); *(football team etc)* kibicować *+dat*; **they stopped work in ~ of ...** przerwali pracę na znak poparcia dla *+gen*; **to ~ o.s.** utrzymywać się (utrzymać się *perf*), zarabiać (zarobić *perf*) na siebie
**supporter** [sə'pɔ:tə^r] *n (Pol etc)* stronnik(-iczka) *m(f)*; *(Sport)* kibic *m*
**supporting** [sə'pɔ:tɪŋ] *adj (role, actor)* drugoplanowy
**suppose** [sə'pəuz] *vt (think likely)* sądzić; *(imagine)* przypuszczać; **he is ~d to do it** ma *or* powinien to zrobić; **it was worse than she'd ~d** było gorzej, niż przypuszczała; **I don't ~ she'll come** nie sądzę, żeby przyszła; **he's about sixty, I ~** ma chyba około sześćdziesiątki; **he's ~d to be an expert** on jest podobno specjalistą; **I ~ so/not** sądzę, że tak/nie
**supposedly** [sə'pəuzɪdlɪ] *adv* podobno
**supposing** [sə'pəuzɪŋ] *conj* (a) jeśli *or* gdyby, przypuśćmy, że
**supposition** [sʌpə'zɪʃən] *n* przypuszczenie *nt*
**suppository** [sə'pɔzɪtrɪ] *(Med) n* czopek *m*
**suppress** [sə'prɛs] *vt (revolt, feeling, yawn)* tłumić (stłumić *perf*); *(activities)* zakazywać (zakazać *perf*) *+gen*; *(information)* zatajać (zataić *perf*); *(publication)* zakazywać (zakazać *perf*) rozpowszechniania *+gen*; *(scandal)* tuszować (zatuszować *perf*)
**suppression** [sə'prɛʃən] *n (of rights)* odebranie *nt*; *(of activities)* zakaz *m*; *(of information)*

S

zatajenie *nt*; (*of feelings, yawn, revolt*) (s) tłumienie *nt*
**suppressor** [sə'prɛsə^r] (*Elec etc*) *n* tłumik *m*
**supremacy** [su'prɛməsɪ] *n* supremacja *f*
**supreme** [su'pri:m] *adj* (*in titles*) najwyższy, naczelny; (*effort, achievement*) niezwykły, olbrzymi
**Supreme Court** (*US*) *n* Sąd *m* Najwyższy
**Supt.** (*Police*) *abbr* = **superintendent**
**surcharge** ['sə:tʃɑ:dʒ] *n* opłata *f* dodatkowa
**sure** [ʃuə^r] *adj* (*convinced*) pewny; (*reliable*) niezawodny ▷ *adv* (*inf*: *esp US*): **that ~ is pretty, that's ~ pretty** to jest faktycznie ładne; **to make ~ that** upewniać się (upewnić się *perf*), że *or* czy; **to make ~ of sth** upewniać się (upewnić się *perf*) co do czegoś; **~!** jasne!, pewnie!; **~ enough** rzeczywiście; **I'm ~ of it** jestem tego pewna; **I'm not ~ how/why/when** nie jestem pewien jak/dlaczego/kiedy; **to be ~ of o.s.** być pewnym siebie
**sure-footed** [ʃuə'futɪd] *adj* trzymający się pewnie na nogach
**surely** ['ʃuəlɪ] *adv* z pewnością, na pewno; **~ you don't mean that!** chyba nie mówisz tego poważnie!
**surety** ['ʃuərətɪ] *n* (*money*) gwarancja *f*, poręczenie *nt*; (*person*) poręczyciel(ka) *m(f)*; **to go** *or* **stand ~ for sb** ręczyć (poręczyć *perf*) za kogoś
**surf** [sə:f] *n* morska piana *f* (*z fal rozbijających się o brzeg lub skały*)
**surface** ['sə:fɪs] *n* powierzchnia *f*; (*of lake, pond*) tafla *f* ▷ *vt* (*road*) pokrywać (pokryć *perf*) (nową) nawierzchnią ▷ *vi* wynurzać się (wynurzyć się *perf*), wypływać (wypłynąć *perf*) (na powierzchnię); (*fig*: *news, feeling*) pojawiać się (pojawić się *perf*); (: *person*: *inf*) zwlekać się (zwlec się *perf*) z łóżka (*inf*); **on the ~** (*fig*) na pozór, na pierwszy rzut oka
**surface area** *n* pole *nt* (powierzchni), powierzchnia *f*
**surface mail** *n* poczta *f* zwykła (*lądowa lub morska*)
**surfboard** ['sə:fbɔ:d] *n* deska *f* surfingowa
**surfeit** ['sə:fɪt] *n*: **a ~ of** nadmiar *m* +*gen*
**surfer** ['sə:fə^r] *n osoba uprawiająca surfing*
**surfing** ['sə:fɪŋ] *n* surfing *m*, pływanie *nt* na desce
**surge** [sə:dʒ] *n* (*increase*) skok *m*, nagły wzrost *m*; (*fig*: *of emotion*) przypływ *m*; (*Elec*) skok *m* napięcia ▷ *vi* (*water*) przelewać się; (*people*) rzucać się (rzucić się *perf*); (*emotion*) wzbierać (wezbrać *perf*); (*Elec*: *power*) skakać (skoczyć *perf*); **to ~ forward** ruszać (ruszyć *perf*) naprzód
**surgeon** ['sə:dʒən] *n* chirurg *m*
**Surgeon General** (*US*) *n* ≈ Naczelny Lekarz *m* Kraju
**surgery** ['sə:dʒərɪ] *n* (*practice*) chirurgia *f*; (*operation*) operacja *f*; (: *minor*) zabieg *m* (chirurgiczny); (*Brit*) gabinet *m* (lekarski); (*also*: **surgery hours**) godziny *pl* przyjęć; (: *of MP etc*) godziny *pl* przyjęć; **to undergo ~** przechodzić (przejść *perf*) operację
**surgical** ['sə:dʒɪkl] *adj* (*instrument, mask*) chirurgiczny; (*treatment*) chirurgiczny, operacyjny
**surgical spirit** (*Brit*) *n* spirytus *m* skażony
**surly** ['sə:lɪ] *adj* opryskliwy
**surmise** [sə:'maɪz] *vt*: **to ~ that ...** domyślać się, że ...
**surmount** [sə:'maunt] *vt* (*fig*: *obstacle*) przezwyciężać (przezwyciężyć *perf*)
**surname** ['sə:neɪm] *n* nazwisko *nt*
**surpass** [sə:'pɑ:s] *vt* (*fig*) przewyższać (przewyższyć *perf*)
**surplus** ['sə:pləs] *n* nadwyżka *f* ▷ *adj*: **~ stock/grain** nadwyżka zapasów/ziarna; **it is ~ to our requirements** to wykracza poza nasze potrzeby
**surprise** [sə'praɪz] *n* (*unexpected event*) niespodzianka *f*, zaskoczenie *nt*; (*astonishment*) zdziwienie *nt* ▷ *vt* (*astonish*) dziwić (zdziwić *perf*); (*catch unawares*) zaskakiwać (zaskoczyć *perf*); **to take sb by ~** zaskakiwać (zaskoczyć *perf*) kogoś
**surprising** [sə'praɪzɪŋ] *adj* zaskakujący, niespodziewany; **it is ~ how/that** (to) zaskakujące, jak/że
**surprisingly** [sə'praɪzɪŋlɪ] *adv* zaskakująco, niespodziewanie; **(somewhat) ~, he agreed** (dość) nieoczekiwanie zgodził się
**surrealism** [sə'rɪəlɪzəm] *n* surrealizm *m*
**surrealist** [sə'rɪəlɪst] *adj* surrealistyczny
**surrender** [sə'rɛndə^r] *n* poddanie się *nt* ▷ *vi* poddawać się (poddać się *perf*) ▷ *vt* zrzekać się (zrzec się *perf*) +*gen*
**surrender value** *n* suma *f* wykupu (*polisy ubezpieczeniowej*)
**surreptitious** [sʌrəp'tɪʃəs] *adj* potajemny, ukradkowy
**surrogate** ['sʌrəgɪt] *n* namiastka *f*, surogat *m* ▷ *adj* zastępczy
**surrogate mother** *n* matka *f* zastępcza (*rodząca dziecko dla innej kobiety*)
**surround** [sə'raund] *vt* otaczać (otoczyć *perf*)
**surrounding** [sə'raundɪŋ] *adj* otaczający, okoliczny
**surroundings** [sə'raundɪŋz] *npl* otoczenie *nt*, okolica *f*
**surtax** ['sə:tæks] *n* podatek *m* wyrównawczy
**surveillance** [sə:'veɪləns] *n* inwigilacja *f*; **to be under ~** być inwigilowanym

**survey** [*n* 'sə:veɪ, *vb* sə:'veɪ] *n* (*examination: of land*) pomiar *m*; (*: of house*) oględziny *pl*, ekspertyza *f*; (*comprehensive view*) przegląd *m* ▷ *vt* (*land*) dokonywać (dokonać *perf*) pomiarów *+gen*; (*house*) poddawać (poddać *perf*) ekspertyzie *or* oględzinom; (*scene, prospects etc*) oceniać (ocenić *perf*), przyglądać się (przyjrzeć się *perf*) *+dat*
**surveying** [sə'veɪɪŋ] *n* (*of land*) pomiar *m* (geodezyjny)
**surveyor** [sə'veɪə^r] *n* (*of land*) mierniczy *m*; (*of house*) rzeczoznawca *m* budowlany
**survival** [sə'vaɪvl] *n* (*state*) przetrwanie *nt*, przeżycie *nt*; (*object*) relikt *m* ▷ *cpd*: **~ kit** zestaw *m* ratunkowy; **~ course** kurs *or* szkoła przetrwania
**survive** [sə'vaɪv] *vi* (*person, animal*) przeżyć (*perf*); (*custom etc*) przetrwać (*perf*) ▷ *vt* przeżyć (*perf*)
**survivor** [sə'vaɪvə^r] *n* ocalały *m*, pozostały *m* przy życiu
**susceptible** [sə'sɛptəbl] *adj*: **~ (to)** (*injury, pressure*) podatny (na *+acc*); (*heat*) wrażliwy (na *+acc*)
**suspect** [*adj, n* 'sʌspɛkt, *vb* səs'pɛkt] *adj* podejrzany ▷ *n* podejrzany(-na) *m(f)* ▷ *vt* podejrzewać; (*doubt*) powątpiewać w *+acc*
**suspend** [səs'pɛnd] *vt* (*lit, fig*) zawieszać (zawiesić *perf*)
**suspended sentence** *n* wyrok *m* w zawieszeniu
**suspender belt** [səs'pɛndə^r-] *n* pas *m* do pończoch
**suspenders** [səs'pɛndəz] *npl* (*Brit*) podwiązki *pl*; (*US*) szelki *pl*
**suspense** [səs'pɛns] *n* (*uncertainty*) niepewność *f*; (*in film etc*) napięcie *nt*; **to keep sb in ~** trzymać kogoś w niepewności
**suspension** [səs'pɛnʃən] *n* zawieszenie *nt*; (*liquid*) zawiesina *f*
**suspension bridge** *n* most *m* wiszący
**suspicion** [səs'pɪʃən] *n* (*distrust*) podejrzenie *nt*; (*idea*) myśl *f*; (*trace*): **a ~ of danger** cień *m* niebezpieczeństwa; **to be under ~** być podejrzanym; **arrested on ~ of murder** aresztowany pod zarzutem morderstwa
**suspicious** [səs'pɪʃəs] *adj* (*suspecting*) podejrzliwy; (*causing suspicion*) podejrzany; **to be ~ of** *or* **about sb/sth** mieć podejrzenia co do kogoś/czegoś
**suss out** [sʌs-] (*Brit: inf*) *vt* rozpracować (*perf*) (*inf*)
**sustain** [səs'teɪn] *vt* (*interest etc*) podtrzymywać (podtrzymać *perf*); (*injury*) odnosić (odnieść *perf*); (*give energy*) krzepić (pokrzepić *perf*)
**sustained** [səs'teɪnd] *adj* ciągły, nieprzerwany
**sustenance** ['sʌstɪnəns] *n* pożywienie *nt*
**suture** ['su:tʃə^r] (*Med*) *n* szew *m*
**SW** (*Radio*) *abbr* (= *short wave*) f.kr.
**swab** [swɔb] *n* (*Med*) wacik *m* ▷ *vt* (*Naut: also*: **swab down**) szorować (wyszorować *perf*)
**swagger** ['swægə^r] *vi* chodzić *or* iść dumnie
**swallow** ['swɔləu] *n* (*bird*) jaskółka *f*; (*of food*) kęs *m*; (*of drink*) łyk *m*, haust *m* ▷ *vt* przełykać (przełknąć *perf*), połykać (połknąć *perf*); (*fig: story, insult*) przełykać (przełknąć *perf*); (*: one's words*) odwoływać (odwołać *perf*); (*: one's pride*) przezwyciężać (przezwyciężyć *perf*)
▸ **swallow up** *vt* (*savings*) pochłaniać (pochłonąć *perf*); (*business*) wchłaniać (wchłonąć *perf*)
**swam** [swæm] *pt of* **swim**
**swamp** [swɔmp] *n* bagno *nt*, mokradło *nt* ▷ *vt* (*ship etc*) zatapiać (zatopić *perf*); (*fig: with complaints etc*) zalewać (zalać *perf*)
**swampy** ['swɔmpɪ] *adj* bagnisty, podmokły
**swan** [swɔn] *n* łabędź *m*
**swank** [swæŋk] (*inf*) *vi* szpanować (*inf*)
**swansong** ['swɔnsɔŋ] *n* (*fig*) łabędzi śpiew *m*
**swap** [swɔp] *n* zamiana *f*, wymiana *f* ▷ *vt*: **to ~ (for)** (*exchange*) zamieniać (zamienić *perf*) (na *+acc*); (*replace*) wymieniać (wymienić *perf*) (na *+acc*)
**swarm** [swɔ:m] *n* (*of bees*) rój *m*; (*of people*) mrowie *nt* ▷ *vi* (*bees*) roić się; (*people*) tłoczyć się, iść tłumem; **the garden was ~ing with security men** w ogrodzie roiło się od agentów obstawy
**swarthy** ['swɔ:ðɪ] *adj* ogorzały, smagły
**swashbuckling** ['swɔʃbʌklɪŋ] *adj* (*look, behaviour*) zawadiacki
**swastika** ['swɔstɪkə] *n* swastyka *f*
**swat** [swɔt] *vt* (*insect*) pacnąć (*perf*) w *+acc* ▷ *n* (*Brit: also*: **fly swat**) packa *f* na muchy
**swathe** [sweɪð] *vt*: **to ~ sth in** (*silk etc*) spowijać (spowić *perf*) coś w *+acc*; (*warm blanket etc*) opatulać (opatulić *perf*) coś *+instr*
**swatter** ['swɔtə^r] *n* (*also*: **fly swatter**) packa *f* na muchy
**sway** [sweɪ] *vi* chwiać się (zachwiać się *perf*), kołysać się (zakołysać się *perf*) ▷ *vt* sterować *+instr* ▷ *n*: **to hold ~ (over sb)** rządzić (kimś)
**Swaziland** ['swɑ:zɪlænd] *n* Suazi *nt inv*
**swear** [swɛə^r] (*pt* **swore**, *pp* **sworn**) *vi* (*curse*) kląć (zakląć *perf*), przeklinać ▷ *vt* (*promise*) przysięgać (przysiąc *perf*); **to ~ an oath** składać (złożyć *perf*) przysięgę
▸ **swear in** *vt* zaprzysięgać (zaprzysiąc *perf*)
**swearword** ['swɛəwə:d] *n* przekleństwo *nt*
**sweat** [swɛt] *n* pot *m* ▷ *vi* pocić się (spocić się *perf*); **in a ~** spocony

S

**sweatband** ['swɛtbænd] *(Sport)* *n* opaska *f* (na czoło)
**sweater** ['swɛtəʳ] *n* sweter *m*
**sweatshirt** ['swɛtʃəːt] *n* bluza *f*
**sweatshop** ['swɛtʃɔp] *(pej)* *n fabryka lub warsztat wyzyskujący robotników*
**sweaty** ['swɛtɪ] *adj* *(clothes)* przepocony; *(hands)* spocony
**Swede** [swiːd] *n* Szwed(ka) *m(f)*
**swede** [swiːd] *(Brit)* *n* brukiew *f*
**Sweden** ['swiːdn] *n* Szwecja *f*
**Swedish** ['swiːdɪʃ] *adj* szwedzki ▷ *n* (język *m*) szwedzki
**sweep** [swiːp] *(pt, pp* **swept**) *n* *(act)* zamiecenie *nt*; *(curve)* łuk *m*, krzywizna *f*; *(range)* krąg *m*; *(also:* **chimney sweep**) kominiarz *m* ▷ *vt* *(brush)* zamiatać (zamieść *perf*); *(with hand)* zgarniać (zgarnąć *perf*); *(current)* znosić (znieść *perf*) ▷ *vi* *(wind)* wiać; *(hand, arm)* machnąć *(perf)*
▸ **sweep away** *vt* *(restrictions etc)* znosić (znieść *perf*)
▸ **sweep past** *vi* przemykać (przemknąć *perf*) (obok)
▸ **sweep up** *vi* zamiatać (pozamiatać *perf*)
**sweeping** ['swiːpɪŋ] *adj* *(gesture)* zamaszysty; *(changes)* daleko idący *or* posunięty; *(statement)* pochopny
**sweepstake** ['swiːpsteɪk] *n* zakłady *pl*, totalizator *m*
**sweet** [swiːt] *n* *(candy)* cukierek *m*; *(Brit: pudding)* deser *m* ▷ *adj* *(lit, fig)* słodki; *(kind)* dobry ▷ *adv*: **to smell ~** pachnieć słodko; **this tastes ~** to jest słodkie; **~ and sour** słodko-kwaśny
**sweetbread** ['swiːtbrɛd] *n potrawa z grasicy jagnięcej lub cielęcej*
**sweetcorn** ['swiːtkɔːn] *n* (słodka) kukurydza *f*
**sweeten** ['swiːtn] *vt* słodzić (posłodzić *perf*); **he bought her lunch to ~ her before telling her the bad news** postawił jej obiad, żeby osłodzić złą wiadomość, którą miał jej przekazać
**sweetener** ['swiːtnəʳ] *n* *(Culin)* słodzik *m*; *(fig)* zachęta *f*
**sweetheart** ['swiːthɑːt] *n* ukochany(-na) *m(f)*; *(as form of address)* kochanie *nt*
**sweetness** ['swiːtnɪs] *n* *(amount of sugar)* słodkość *f*, słodycz *f*; *(kindness)* słodycz *f*, dobroć *f*
**sweet pea** *(Bot)* *n* groszek *m* pachnący
**sweet potato** *(Bot)* *n* batat *m*, patat *m*
**sweetshop** ['swiːtʃɔp] *(Brit)* *n* kiosk *m or* sklepik *m* ze słodyczami
**sweet tooth** *n*: **to have a ~** przepadać za słodyczami
**swell** [swɛl] *(pt* **~ed**, *pp* **swollen** *or* **~ed**) *n* *(of sea)* fala *f* ▷ *adj* *(US: inf)* kapitalny ▷ *vi* *(increase)* wzrastać (wzrosnąć *perf*); *(get stronger)* narastać (narosnąć *perf*), wzmagać się (wzmóc się *perf*); *(also:* **swell up**) puchnąć (spuchnąć *perf or* opuchnąć *perf*)
**swelling** ['swɛlɪŋ] *n* opuchlizna *f*, obrzęk *m*
**sweltering** ['swɛltərɪŋ] *adj* upalny, skwarny
**swept** [swɛpt] *pt, pp of* **sweep**
**swerve** [swəːv] *vi* (gwałtownie) skręcać (skręcić *perf*)
**swift** [swɪft] *n* jerzyk *m* ▷ *adj* szybki; *(stream)* wartki, bystry
**swiftly** ['swɪftlɪ] *adv* szybko
**swiftness** ['swɪftnɪs] *n* szybkość *f*
**swig** [swɪg] *(inf)* *n* łyk *m*, haust *m* ▷ *vt* pociągać (pociągnąć *perf*) *(inf)*
**swill** [swɪl] *(inf)* *vt* *(also:* **swill down**) trąbić (wytrąbić *perf*) *(inf)*; *(also:* **swill out**) płukać (wypłukać *perf*) ▷ *n* pomyje *pl*
**swim** [swɪm] *(pt* **swam**, *pp* **swum**) *vi* płynąć (popłynąć *perf*); *(regularly etc)* pływać; *(shimmer)* latać przed oczami ▷ *vt* przepływać (przepłynąć *perf*) ▷ *n*: **to go for a ~, to go ~ming** iść (pójść *perf*) popływać; **my head is ~ming** kręci mi się w głowie
**swimmer** ['swɪməʳ] *n* pływak(-aczka) *m(f)*
**swimming** ['swɪmɪŋ] *n* pływanie *nt*
**swimming baths** *(Brit)* *npl* kryty basen *m*, kryta pływalnia *f*
**swimming cap** *n* czepek *m* (kąpielowy)
**swimming costume** *(Brit)* *n* kostium *m or* strój *m* kąpielowy
**swimming pool** *n* basen *m*, pływalnia *f*
**swimming trunks** *npl* kąpielówki *pl*
**swimsuit** ['swɪmsuːt] *n* = **swimming costume**
**swindle** ['swɪndl] *n* szwindel *m* *(inf)*, kant *m* *(inf)* ▷ *vt* kantować (okantować *perf*) *(inf)*
**swindler** ['swɪndləʳ] *n* kanciarz *m* *(inf)*
**swine** [swaɪn] *(inf!)* *n* świnia *f* *(inf)*
**swing** [swɪŋ] *(pt, pp* **swung**) *n* *(in playground)* huśtawka *f*; *(movement)* kołysanie *nt*; *(in opinions etc)* zwrot *m*; *(Mus)* swing *m* ▷ *vt* machać *or* wymachiwać *+instr* ▷ *vi* kołysać się, huśtać się; *(also:* **swing round**: *person)* obracać się (obrócić się *perf*); (: *vehicle)* zawracać (zawrócić *perf*); **a ~ to the left** *(Pol)* zwrot w lewo; **to get into the ~ of things** wciągać się (wciągnąć się *perf*) (w coś); **the party was in full ~** przyjęcie rozkręciło się na dobre; **to ~ the car (round)** zawracać (zawrócić *perf*); **the door swung open** drzwi otworzyły się na oścież
**swing bridge** *n* most *m* obrotowy
**swing door**, *(US)* **swinging door** *n* drzwi *pl* wahadłowe

**swingeing** ['swɪndʒɪŋ] (*Brit*) *adj* druzgocący, miażdżący

**swinging** ['swɪŋɪŋ] *adj* wahadłowy; (*old*: *fig*) tętniący życiem

**swipe** [swaɪp] *vt* (*also*: **swipe at**) zamachnąć się (*perf*) na *+acc*; (*inf*: *steal*) zakosić (*perf*) (*inf*) ▷ *n*: **to take a ~ (at)** zamachnąć się (*perf*) (na *+acc*)

**swipecard** ['swaɪpkɑ:d] *n* karta *f* magnetyczna

**swirl** [swə:l] *vi* wirować (zawirować *perf*) ▷ *n* wirowanie *nt*

**swish** [swɪʃ] *vi* (*tail*) świsnąć (*perf*); (*curtains*) szeleścić (zaszeleścić *perf*) ▷ *n* (*of tail*) świst *m*; (*of curtains*) szelest *m* ▷ *adj* (*inf*) szykowny

**Swiss** [swɪs] *adj* szwajcarski ▷ *n inv* Szwajcar(ka) *m(f)*

**Swiss French** *adj dotyczący francuskojęzycznej części Szwajcarii*

**Swiss German** *adj dotyczący niemieckojęzycznej części Szwajcarii*

**Swiss roll** *n* rożek *m* (*z dżemem lub kremem*)

**switch** [swɪtʃ] *n* (*for light, radio etc*) przełącznik *m*, wyłącznik *m*; (*change*) zmiana *f*, zwrot *m* ▷ *vt* (*change*) zmieniać (zmienić *perf*); (*exchange*) wymieniać (wymienić *perf*), zamieniać (zamienić *perf*); **to ~ round** *or* **over** zamieniać (zamienić *perf*) miejscami
▸ **switch off** *vt* wyłączać (wyłączyć *perf*) ▷ *vi* (*fig*) wyłączać się (wyłączyć się *perf*)
▸ **switch on** *vt* włączać (włączyć *perf*)

**witchback** ['swɪtʃbæk] (*Brit*) *n* serpentyna *f*, kręta droga *f*

**witchblade** ['swɪtʃbleɪd] *n* nóż *m* sprężynowy

**witchboard** ['swɪtʃbɔ:d] *n* centrala *f or* łącznica *f* (telefoniczna)

**witchboard operator** *n* telefonista(-tka) *m(f)*

**witzerland** ['swɪtsələnd] *n* Szwajcaria *f*

**wivel** ['swɪvl] *vi* (*also*: **swivel round**) obracać się (obrócić się *perf*), okręcać się (okręcić się *perf*)

**wollen** ['swəulən] *pp of* **swell** ▷ *adj* (*ankle etc*) spuchnięty, opuchnięty; (*lake etc*) wezbrany

**woon** [swu:n] *vi* omdlewać ▷ *n* omdlenie *nt*

**woop** [swu:p] *n* (*by police etc*) nalot *m*; (*of bird*) lot *m* nurkowy ▷ *vi* (*also*: **swoop down**) nurkować (zanurkować *perf*), pikować

**wop** [swɔp] = **swap**

**word** [sɔ:d] *n* miecz *m*

**wordfish** ['sɔ:dfɪʃ] *n* miecznik *m*

**wore** [swɔ:ʳ] *pt of* **swear**

**worn** [swɔ:n] *pp of* **swear** ▷ *adj* (*statement, evidence*) pod przysięgą *post*; (*enemy*) zaprzysięgły

**swot** [swɔt] *vi* (*inf*) wkuwać (*inf*), zakuwać (*inf*) ▷ *n* (*pej*: *inf*) kujon *m* (*pej, inf*)
▸ **swot up** *vt* (*inf*): **to ~ up (on)** wkuwać (wkuć *perf*) *or* zakuwać (zakuć *perf*) (*+acc*) (*inf*)

**swum** [swʌm] *pp of* **swim**

**swung** [swʌŋ] *pt, pp of* **swing**

**sycamore** ['sɪkəmɔ:ʳ] *n* (*US*) platan *m*; (*Brit*) jawor *m*; (*in the Near East*) sykomora *f*

**sycophant** ['sɪkəfænt] *n* pochlebca *m*

**sycophantic** [sɪkə'fæntɪk] *adj* służalczy, podlizujący się

**Sydney** ['sɪdnɪ] *n* Sydney *nt inv*

**syllable** ['sɪləbl] *n* sylaba *f*, zgłoska *f*

**syllabus** ['sɪləbəs] *n* program *m or* plan *m* zajęć; **on the ~** w programie *or* planie (zajęć)

**symbol** ['sɪmbl] *n* symbol *m*

**symbolic(al)** [sɪm'bɔlɪk(l)] *adj* symboliczny; **to be symbolic of sth** symbolizować coś

**symbolism** ['sɪmbəlɪzəm] *n* symbolizm *m*

**symbolize** ['sɪmbəlaɪz] *vt* symbolizować

**symmetrical** [sɪ'mɛtrɪkl] *adj* symetryczny

**symmetry** ['sɪmɪtrɪ] *n* symetria *f*

**sympathetic** [sɪmpə'θɛtɪk] *adj* (*understanding*) współczujący; (*likeable*) sympatyczny; (*supportive*) życzliwy; **to be ~ to a cause** sympatyzować ze sprawą

**sympathetically** [sɪmpə'θɛtɪklɪ] *adv* (*with understanding*) współczująco; (*with support*) życzliwie

**sympathize** ['sɪmpəθaɪz] *vi*: **to ~ with** (*person*) współczuć *+dat*; (*feelings*) podzielać *+acc*; (*cause*) sympatyzować z *+instr*

**sympathizer** ['sɪmpəθaɪzəʳ] (*Pol*) *n* sympatyk(-yczka) *m(f)*

**sympathy** ['sɪmpəθɪ] *n* współczucie *nt*; **sympathies** *npl* sympatie *pl*; **with our deepest ~** z wyrazami najgłębszego współczucia; **to come out in ~** przeprowadzać (przeprowadzić *perf*) strajk solidarnościowy

**symphonic** [sɪm'fɔnɪk] *adj* symfoniczny

**symphony** ['sɪmfənɪ] *n* symfonia *f*

**symphony orchestra** *n* orkiestra *f* symfoniczna

**symposia** [sɪm'pəuzɪə] *npl of* **symposium**

**symposium** [sɪm'pəuzɪəm] (*pl* **~s** *or* **symposia**) *n* sympozjum *nt*

**symptom** ['sɪmptəm] *n* objaw *m*, symptom *m*; (*fig*) oznaka *f*

**symptomatic** [sɪmptə'mætɪk] *adj*: **to be ~ of** być przejawem *+gen*

**synagogue** ['sɪnəgɔg] *n* synagoga *f*, bóżnica *f*

**synchromesh** [sɪŋkrəu'mɛʃ] *n* synchronizator *f* (skrzyni biegów)

**synchronize** ['sɪŋkrənaɪz] *vt* synchronizować (zsynchronizować *perf*) ▷ *vi*: **to ~ with** być zsynchronizowanym z *+instr*

S

**syncopated** ['sɪŋkəpeɪtɪd] *adj* synkopowany
**syndicate** ['sɪndɪkɪt] *n* syndykat *m*
**syndrome** ['sɪndrəum] *n* syndrom *m*
**synonym** ['sɪnənɪm] *n* synonim *m*
**synonymous** [sɪ'nɔnɪməs] *adj* (*fig*): ~ **(with)** równoznaczny (z *+instr*)
**synopses** [sɪ'nɔpsi:z] *npl of* **synopsis**
**synopsis** [sɪ'nɔpsɪs] (*pl* **synopses**) *n* streszczenie *nt*
**syntactic** [sɪn'tæktɪk] *adj* składniowy, syntaktyczny
**syntax** ['sɪntæks] *n* składnia *f*, syntaksa *f*
**syntax error** *n* błąd *m* składniowy *or* syntaktyczny
**syntheses** ['sɪnθəsi:z] *npl of* **synthesis**
**synthesis** ['sɪnθəsɪs] (*pl* **syntheses**) *n* synteza *f*
**synthesizer** ['sɪnθəsaɪzə^r] *n* syntezator *m*
**synthetic** [sɪn'θɛtɪk] *adj* syntetyczny; **synthetics** *npl* włókna *pl* syntetyczne *or* sztuczne
**syphilis** ['sɪfɪlɪs] *n* kiła *f*, syfilis *m*
**syphon** ['saɪfən] = **siphon**
**Syria** ['sɪrɪə] *n* Syria *f*
**Syrian** ['sɪrɪən] *adj* syryjski ▷ *n* Syryjczyk(-jka) *m(f)*
**syringe** [sɪ'rɪndʒ] *n* strzykawka *f*
**syrup** ['sɪrəp] *n* syrop *m*; (*also*: **golden syrup**) *przesycony roztwór cukrów używany do celów spożywczych*
**syrupy** ['sɪrəpɪ] *adj* lepki; (*pej*: *fig*) ckliwy
**system** ['sɪstəm] *n* (*organization, method*) system *m*; (*body*) organizm *m*; (*Anat*) układ *m*; **it was a shock to his ~** był to wstrząs dla jego organizmu
**systematic** [sɪstə'mætɪk] *adj* systematyczny
**system disk** (*Comput*) *n* dysk *m* systemowy
**systems analyst** ['sɪstəmz-] (*Comput*) *n* analityk *m* systemów

# Tt

**T, t** [ti:] *n* (*letter*) T *nt*, t *nt*; **T for Tommy** ≈ T jak Tadeusz
**TA** (*Brit*) *n abbr* = **Territorial Army**
**ta** [tɑ:] (*Brit: inf*) *excl* dzięki (*inf*)
**tab** [tæb] *n abbr* = **tabulator; to keep tabs on sb/sth** (*fig*) mieć kogoś/coś na oku
**tabby** ['tæbɪ] *n* (*also*: **tabby cat**) pręgowany kot *m*
**tabernacle** ['tæbənækl] *n* tabernakulum *nt*
**table** ['teɪbl] *n* (*furniture*) stół *m*; (*Math, Chem etc*) tabela *f*, tablica *f* ▷ *vt* (*Brit: motion etc*) przedstawiać (przedstawić *perf*); **to lay** *or* **set the ~** nakrywać (nakryć *perf*) do stołu; **to clear the ~** sprzątać (sprzątnąć *perf*) ze stołu; **league ~** (*Brit*) tabela ligowa
**tablecloth** ['teɪblklɔθ] *n* obrus *m*
**table d'hôte** [tɑ:bl'dəut] *adj* (*menu, meal*) *składający się z ograniczonej liczby dań o ustalonej cenie*
**table lamp** *n* lampka *f* na stolik
**tablemat** ['teɪblmæt] *n* (*for plate*) serwetka *f*; (*for hot dish*) podkładka *f*
**table of contents** *n* spis *m* treści
**table salt** *n* sól *f* kuchenna
**tablespoon** ['teɪblspu:n] *n* łyżka *f* stołowa
**tablet** ['tæblɪt] *n* (*Med*) tabletka *f*; (*for writing*) tabliczka *f*; (*plaque*) tablica *f*; **a ~ of soap** (*Brit: fml*) kostka mydła
**table tennis** *n* tenis *m* stołowy
**table wine** *n* wino *nt* stołowe
**tabloid** ['tæblɔɪd] *n* ≈ brukowiec *m* (*pej*); **the ~s** ≈ prasa brukowa
**taboo** [tə'bu:] *n* tabu *nt* ▷ *adj* zakazany, tabu *post*
**tabulate** ['tæbjuleɪt] *vt* układać (ułożyć *perf*) w tabelę
**abulator** ['tæbjuleɪtə$^{r}$] *n* (*on typewriter*) tabulator *m*
**achograph** ['tækəgrɑ:f] (*Aut*) *n* tachograf *m*
**achometer** [tæ'kɔmɪtə$^{r}$] (*Aut*) *n* obrotomierz *m*
**acit** ['tæsɪt] *adj* milczący
**aciturn** ['tæsɪtə:n] *adj* małomówny
**ack** [tæk] *n* pinezka *f* ▷ *vt* (*nail*) przypinać (przypiąć *perf*) (pinezkami); (*stitch*) fastrygować (sfastrygować *perf*) ▷ *vi* (*Naut*) halsować; **to change ~** (*fig*) zmieniać (zmienić *perf*) kurs; **to ~ sth on to (the end of) sth** dołączać (dołączyć *perf*) coś do czegoś
**tackle** ['tækl] *n* (*for fishing*) sprzęt *m* wędkarski; (*for lifting*) wyciąg *m* (wielokrążkowy); (*Football, Rugby*) zablokowanie *nt* ▷ *vt* (*deal with, challenge*) stawiać (stawić *perf*) czoło *+dat*; (*grapple with*) podejmować (podjąć *perf*) walkę z *+instr*; (*Football, Rugby*) blokować (zablokować *perf*)
**tacky** ['tækɪ] *adj* (*sticky*) lepki; (*pej*) tandetny (*pej*)
**tact** [tækt] *n* takt *m*
**tactful** ['tæktful] *adj* taktowny
**tactfully** ['tæktfəlɪ] *adv* taktownie
**tactical** ['tæktɪkl] *adj* taktyczny; **~ error** błąd taktyczny
**tactics** ['tæktɪks] *npl* taktyka *f*
**tactless** ['tæktlɪs] *adj* nietaktowny
**tactlessly** ['tæktlɪslɪ] *adv* nietaktownie
**tadpole** ['tædpəul] *n* kijanka *f*
**taffy** ['tæfɪ] (*US*) *n* toffi *nt inv*
**tag** [tæg] *n* (*price*) metka *f*; (*airline*) przywieszka *f*; **name tag** identyfikator
▸ **tag along** *vi* (*person*) przyczepić się (*perf*)
**Tahiti** [tɑ:'hi:tɪ] *n* Tahiti *nt inv*
**tail** [teɪl] *n* (*of animal, plane*) ogon *m*; (*of shirt, coat*) poła *f* ▷ *vt* śledzić; **tails** *npl* frak *m*; **to turn ~** dawać (dać *perf*) nogę (*inf*); *see also* **head**
▸ **tail off** *vi* stopniowo maleć (zmaleć *perf*); (*voice*) zamierać (zamrzeć *perf*)
**tailback** ['teɪlbæk] (*Brit*) *n* korek *m* (*uliczny*)
**tail coat** *n* = **tails**
**tail end** *n* końcówka *f*
**tailgate** ['teɪlgeɪt] *n* (*Aut*) tylna klapa *f*
**tail light** (*Aut*) *n* tylne światło *nt*
**tailor** ['teɪlə$^{r}$] *n* krawiec *m* męski ▷ *vt*: **to ~ sth (to)** dopasowywać (dopasować *perf*) coś (do *+gen*); **~'s shop** zakład krawiecki
**tailoring** ['teɪlərɪŋ] *n* (*craft*) krawiectwo *nt*; (*cut*) krój *m*
**tailor-made** ['teɪlə'meɪd] *adj* (*suit*) (szyty) na miarę; (*fig: part in play, person for job*) wymarzony

**tailwind** ['teɪlwɪnd] *n* wiatr *m* w plecy
**taint** [teɪnt] *vt* (*food, water*) zanieczyszczać (zanieczyścić *perf*); (*fig: reputation*) brukać (zbrukać *perf*), nadszarpywać (nadszarpnąć *perf*)
**tainted** ['teɪntɪd] *adj* (*food, air*) skażony, zanieczyszczony; (*fig: reputation*) zbrukany, nadszarpnięty
**Taiwan** ['taɪ'wɑːn] *n* Tajwan *m*
**take** [teɪk] (*pt* **took**, *pp* **~n**) *vt* (*shower, holiday*) brać (wziąć *perf*); (*photo*) robić (zrobić *perf*); (*decision*) podejmować (podjąć *perf*); (*steal*) zabierać (zabrać *perf*); (*courage, time*) wymagać *+gen*; (*pain etc*) znosić (znieść *perf*); (*passengers, spectators etc*) mieścić (pomieścić *perf*); (*accompany: person*) zabierać (zabrać *perf*); (*carry, bring: object*) brać (wziąć *perf*), zabierać (zabrać *perf*); (*exam, test*) zdawać, podchodzić (podejść *perf*) do *+gen*; (*drug, pill etc*) brać (wziąć *perf*), zażywać (zażyć *perf*) ▷ *vi* (*drug*) działać (zadziałać *perf*); (*dye*) przyjmować się (przyjąć się *perf*), chwytać (chwycić *perf*) (*inf*) ▷ *n* (*Film*) ujęcie *nt*; **to ~ sth from** wyjmować (wyjąć *perf*) coś z *+gen*; **I ~ it (that)** zakładam (, że); **I took him for a doctor** wziąłem go za lekarza; **she took them for geography** uczyła ich geografii; **to ~ sb's hand** brać (wziąć *perf*) kogoś za rękę; **to ~ sb for a walk** brać (zabrać *perf*) kogoś na spacer; **to be ~n ill** (nagle) zachorować (*perf*); **to ~ it upon o.s. to do sth** brać (wziąć *perf*) na siebie zrobienie czegoś; **~ the first (street) on the left** skręć w pierwszą ulicę w lewo; **to ~ Russian at university** mieć na uniwersytecie zajęcia z języka rosyjskiego; **it won't ~ long** to nie potrwa długo; **I was quite ~n with her** bardzo mi się spodobała
▸ **take after** *vt fus* przypominać *+acc*, być podobnym do *+gen*
▸ **take apart** *vt* rozbierać (rozebrać *perf*) (na części)
▸ **take away** *vt* (*remove*) odbierać (odebrać *perf*); (*carry off*) wynosić (wynieść *perf*); (*Math*) odejmować (odjąć *perf*) ▷ *vi*: **to ~ away from** umniejszać (umniejszyć *perf*) *+acc*
▸ **take back** *vt* (*goods*) zwracać (zwrócić *perf*); (*one's words*) cofać (cofnąć *perf*), odwoływać (odwołać *perf*)
▸ **take down** *vt* (*write down*) notować (zanotować *perf*), zapisywać (zapisać *perf*); (*dismantle*) rozbierać (rozebrać *perf*)
▸ **take in** *vt* (*deceive*) oszukiwać (oszukać *perf*); (*understand*) przyjmować (przyjąć *perf*) do wiadomości; (*include*) wchłaniać (wchłonąć *perf*); (*lodger*) brać (wziąć *perf*); (*orphan*) przygarniać (przygarnąć *perf*); (*dress*) zwężać (zwęzić *perf*)
▸ **take off** *vi* (*Aviat*) startować (wystartować *perf*); (*go away*) wybrać się (*perf*) ▷ *vt* (*clothes*) zdejmować (zdjąć *perf*); (*make-up*) usuwać (usunąć *perf*); (*person*) naśladować
▸ **take on** *vt* (*work, responsibility, employee*) przyjmować (przyjąć *perf*); (*competitor*) stawać (stanąć *perf*) do współzawodnictwa z *+instr*
▸ **take out** *vt* (*person*) zapraszać (zaprosić *perf*) (*do lokalu*); (*tooth*) usuwać (usunąć *perf*); (*licence*) uzyskiwać (uzyskać *perf*); **to ~ sth out of sth** wyjmować (wyjąć *perf*) coś z czegoś; **don't ~ it out on me!** nie odgrywaj się na mnie!
▸ **take over** *vt* (*business*) przejmować (przejąć *perf*); (*country*) zajmować (zająć *perf*) ▷ *vi*: **to ~ over from sb** przejmować (przejąć *perf*) od kogoś obowiązki, zastępować (zastąpić *perf*) kogoś
▸ **take to** *vt fus* polubić (*perf*); **to ~ to doing sth** zacząć (*perf*) coś robić
▸ **take up** *vt* (*hobby, sport*) zainteresować się (*perf*) *or* zająć się (*perf*) *+instr*; (*post*) obejmować (objąć *perf*); (*idea, suggestion*) podejmować (podjąć *perf*), podchwytywać (podchwycić *perf*); (*time, space*) zajmować (zająć *perf*), zabierać (zabrać *perf*); (*task, story*) podejmować (podjąć *perf*); (*garment*) skracać (skrócić *perf*) ▷ *vi*: **to ~ up with sb** zaprzyjaźnić się (*perf*) z kimś; **to ~ sb up on an offer/invitation** skorzystać (*perf*) z czyjejś propozycji/czyjegoś zaproszenia
**takeaway** ['teɪkəweɪ] (*Brit*) *n* (*food*) dania *pl* na wynos; (*shop, restaurant*) *restauracja specjalizująca się w daniach na wynos*
**take-home pay** ['teɪkhəum-] *n* płaca *f* na rękę
**taken** ['teɪkən] *pp of* **take**
**takeoff** ['teɪkɔf] (*Aviat*) *n* start *m*
**takeout** ['teɪkaut] (*US*) *n* = **takeaway**
**takeover** ['teɪkəuvə[r]] *n* (*Comm*) przejęcie *nt*; (*of country*) zajęcie *nt*
**takeover bid** (*Comm*) *n* oferta *f* przejęcia
**takings** ['teɪkɪŋz] (*Comm*) *npl* wpływy *pl*
**talc** [tælk] *n* talk *m*
**tale** [teɪl] *n* (*story*) baśń *f*, opowieść *f*; (*account*) historia *f*; **to tell ~s** skarżyć
**talent** ['tælnt] *n* talent *m*
**talented** ['tæləntɪd] *adj* utalentowany, uzdolniony
**talent scout** *n* łowca *m* talentów
**talk** [tɔːk] *n* (*prepared speech*) wykład *m*; (*: non-academic*) pogadanka *f*; (*conversation*) rozmowa *f*; (*gossip*) plotki *pl* ▷ *vi* (*speak*) mówić; (*gossip*) gadać (*inf*); (*chat*) rozmawiać; **talks** *npl* (*Pol etc*) rozmowy *pl*; **to give a ~** wygłaszać (wygłosić *perf*) wykład *or* pogadankę; **to ~ about** mówić *or* rozmawiać o *+loc*; **~ing of**

**films, have you seen ...?** à propos filmów, czy widziałaś *+acc*?; **to ~ sb into doing sth** namówić *(perf)* kogoś do zrobienia czegoś; **to ~ sb out of doing sth** wyperswadować *(perf)* komuś zrobienie czegoś; **to ~ shop** rozmawiać o sprawach zawodowych
▶ **talk over** *vt* omawiać (omówić *perf*)
**talkative** ['tɔ:kətɪv] *adj* rozmowny
**talker** ['tɔ:kə^r] *n*: **a good/entertaining** *etc* **~** dobry/zajmujący *etc* mówca *m*
**talking point** ['tɔ:kɪŋ-] *n* przedmiot *m* rozmów
**talking-to** ['tɔ:kɪŋtu] *n*: **to give sb a (good) ~** (ostro) kogoś zbesztać *(perf)*
**talk show** *n* talk show *m*
**tall** [tɔ:l] *adj* wysoki; **to be 6 feet ~** mieć 6 stóp (wzrostu); **how ~ are you?** ile masz wzrostu?
**tallboy** ['tɔ:lbɔɪ] *(Brit) n* (wysoka) komoda *f*
**tallness** ['tɔ:lnɪs] *n (of person)* wzrost *m*; *(of object)* wysokość *f*
**tall story** *n* nieprawdopodobna historia *f*
**tally** ['tælɪ] *n (of marks, amounts of money etc)* rejestr *m* ▷ *vi*: **to ~ (with)** *(figures, stories etc)* zgadzać się (z *+instr*); **to keep a ~ of sth** prowadzić rejestr czegoś
**talon** ['tælən] *n* pazur *m*, szpon *m*
**tambourine** [tæmbə'ri:n] *n* tamburyn *m*
**tame** [teɪm] *adj (animal)* oswojony; *(fig: story, performance)* ugłaskany
**tamper** ['tæmpə^r] *vi*: **to ~ with sth** majstrować przy czymś
**tampon** ['tæmpɔn] *n* tampon *m*
**tan** [tæn] *n (also:* **suntan**) opalenizna *f* ▷ *vi* opalać się (opalić się *perf*) ▷ *vt* garbować (wygarbować *perf*) ▷ *adj* jasnobrązowy; **to get a tan** opalić się *(perf)*
**tandem** ['tændəm] *n (cycle)* tandem *m*; **in ~ (with)** w parze (z *+instr*)
**tang** [tæŋ] *n (flavour)* posmak *m*; *(smell)* intensywny zapach *m*
**tangent** ['tændʒənt] *n* tangens *m*; **to go off at a ~** *(fig)* odbiegać (odbiec *perf*) od tematu
**tangerine** [tændʒə'ri:n] *n (fruit)* mandarynka *f*; *(colour)* pomarańczowy
**tangible** ['tændʒəbl] *adj* namacalny; **~ assets** majątek rzeczowy
**Tangier** [tæn'dʒɪə^r] *n* Tanger *m*
**tangle** ['tæŋgl] *n* plątanina *f*, gąszcz *m*; *(fig)* mętlik *m*; **to be/get in a ~** plątać się/zaplątać się *(perf)*
**tango** ['tæŋgəu] *n* tango *nt*
**tank** [tæŋk] *n (for water, petrol)* zbiornik *m*; *(for photographic processing)* kuweta *f*; *(also:* **fish tank**) akwarium *nt*; *(Mil)* czołg *m*
**tankard** ['tæŋkəd] *n* kufel *m*
**tanker** ['tæŋkə^r] *n (ship)* tankowiec *m*; *(truck)* samochód *m* cysterna *f*; *(Rail)* wagon *m* cysterna *f*
**tanned** [tænd] *adj* opalony
**tannin** ['tænɪn] *n* tanina *f*
**tanning** ['tænɪŋ] *n* garbowanie *nt*
**tannoy** ['tænɔɪ], **Tannoy**® *(Brit) n* system *m* nagłaśniający; **over the ~** przez megafony
**tantalizing** ['tæntəlaɪzɪŋ] *adj* zwodniczy
**tantamount** ['tæntəmaunt] *adj*: **~ to** równoznaczny z *+instr*
**tantrum** ['tæntrəm] *n* napad *m* złości; **to throw a ~** wpadać (wpaść *perf*) w złość
**Tanzania** [tænzə'nɪə] *n* Tanzania *f*
**Tanzanian** [tænzə'nɪən] *adj* tanzański ▷ *n* Tanzańczyk(-anka) *m(f)*
**tap** [tæp] *n (on sink)* kran *m*; *(gas tap)* zawór *m*, kurek *m*; *(gentle blow)* klepnięcie *nt* ▷ *vt (hit gently)* klepać (klepnąć *perf*); *(exploit: resources etc)* wykorzystywać (wykorzystać *perf*); **on tap** *(fig: resources, information)* dostępny; *(beer)* z beczki; **to tap sb's telephone** zakładać (założyć *perf*) u kogoś podsłuch
**tap-dancing** ['tæpdɑ:nsɪŋ] *n* stepowanie *nt*
**tape** [teɪp] *n (also:* **magnetic tape**) taśma *f* (magnetyczna); *(cassette)* kaseta *f*; *(also:* **sticky tape**) taśma *f* klejąca; *(for tying)* tasiemka *f* ▷ *vt (record, conversation)* nagrywać (nagrać *perf*); *(stick)* przyklejać (przykleić *perf*) *(taśmą)*; **on ~** nagrany (na taśmie)
**tape deck** *n* magnetofon *m (bez wzmacniacza)*
**tape measure** *n* centymetr *m (miara)*
**taper** ['teɪpə^r] *n* długa cienka świeca *f* ▷ *vi* zwężać się (ku dołowi)
**tape recorder** *n* magnetofon *m*
**tape recording** *n* nagranie *nt*
**tapered** ['teɪpəd] *adj (skirt etc)* zwężany
**tapering** ['teɪpərɪŋ] *adj (fingers)* cienki
**tapestry** ['tæpɪstrɪ] *n* gobelin *m*; *(fig)* (wielowątkowy) obraz *m*
**tapeworm** ['teɪpwə:m] *n* tasiemiec *m*
**tapioca** [tæpɪ'əukə] *n* tapioka *f*
**tappet** ['tæpɪt] *(Aut) n* popychacz *m*
**tar** [tɑ:] *n* smoła *f*; **low/middle tar cigarettes** papierosy o niskiej/średniej zawartości substancji smolistych
**tarantula** [tə'ræntjulə] *n* tarantula *f*
**tardy** ['tɑ:dɪ] *adj (reply, letter)* spóźniony; *(progress)* powolny
**target** ['tɑ:gɪt] *n* cel *m*; *(fig)* obiekt *m*; **on ~** *(work, sales)* zgodny z planem
**target practice** *n* ćwiczenia *pl* na strzelnicy
**tariff** ['tærɪf] *n (on goods)* taryfa *f* celna; *(Brit: in hotel etc)* cennik *m*
**tariff barrier** *n* bariera *f* celna
**tarmac**® ['tɑ:mæk] *n (Brit)* ≈ asfalt *m*; *(Aviat)*: **on the ~** w kolejce do startu ▷ *vt (Brit)* pokrywać (pokryć *perf*) asfaltem
**tarn** [tɑ:n] *n* staw *m* (górski)
**tarnish** ['tɑ:nɪʃ] *vt (silver etc)* powodować

t

matowienie *+gen*; (*fig: reputation*) brukać (zbrukać *perf*), szargać (zszargać *perf*)
**tarpaulin** [tɑːˈpɔːlɪn] *n* brezent *m*
**tarragon** [ˈtærəgən] *n* estragon *m*
**tart** [tɑːt] *n* tarta *f* (*z owocami, dżemem itp*); (*small*) ciastko *nt* z owocami; (*Brit: inf*) dziwka *f* (*inf, pej*) ▹ *adj* cierpki
▸ **tart up** (*Brit: inf*) *vt* (*place, room*) odstawiać (odstawić *perf*) (*inf*); **to ~ o.s. up** stroić się (wystroić się *perf*); (*pej*) odstawiać się (odstawić się *perf*) (*inf*)
**tartan** [ˈtɑːtn] *n* tartan *m* ▹ *adj* w szkocką kratę *post*
**tartar** [ˈtɑːtəʳ] *n* kamień *m* (nazębny); (*pej*) herod-baba *f* (*inf, pej*)
**tartar(e) sauce** [ˈtɑːtə-] *n* sos *m* tatarski
**task** [tɑːsk] *n* zadanie *nt*; **to take sb to ~** udzielać (udzielić *perf*) komuś nagany
**task force** *n* oddział *m* specjalny
**taskmaster** [ˈtɑːskmɑːstəʳ] *n*: **he's a hard ~** jest bardzo wymagający
**Tasmania** [tæzˈmeɪnɪə] *n* Tasmania *f*
**tassel** [ˈtæsl] *n* frędzel *m*
**taste** [teɪst] *n* (*lit, fig: flavour*) smak *m*; (*sense*) smak *m*, zmysł *m* smaku; (*sample*) odrobina *f* na spróbowanie ▹ *vt* (*get flavour of*) czuć (poczuć *perf*) smak *+gen*; (*test*) próbować (spróbować *perf*) *or* kosztować (skosztować *perf*) *+gen* ▹ *vi*: **to ~ of** *or* **like sth** smakować jak coś; **what does it ~ like?** jak to smakuje?; **you can ~ the garlic (in it)** czuć w tym czosnek; **to have a ~ of sth** próbować (spróbować *perf*) czegoś; (*fig*) zakosztować (*perf*) czegoś; **to acquire a ~ for sth** zasmakować (*perf*) w czymś; **to be in good/bad ~** być w dobrym/złym guście
**taste buds** *npl* kubki *pl* smakowe
**tasteful** [ˈteɪstful] *adj* gustowny
**tastefully** [ˈteɪstfəlɪ] *adv* gustownie
**tasteless** [ˈteɪstlɪs] *adj* (*food*) bez smaku *post*; (*remark, joke*) niesmaczny; (*furnishings*) niegustowny
**tasty** [ˈteɪstɪ] *adj* smaczny
**tattered** [ˈtætəd] *adj* (*clothes*) podarty, wystrzępiony; (*paper*) porwany, porozrywany; (*fig: hopes*) zrujnowany
**tatters** [ˈtætəz] *npl*: **in ~** w strzępach
**tattoo** [təˈtuː] *n* (*on skin*) tatuaż *m*; (*spectacle*) capstrzyk *m* ▹ *vt*: **to ~ sth on sth** tatuować (wytatuować *perf*) coś na czymś
**tatty** [ˈtætɪ] (*Brit: inf*) *adj* (*clothes*) niechlujny; (*furniture, room*) zapuszczony
**taught** [tɔːt] *pt, pp of* **teach**
**taunt** [tɔːnt] *n* drwina *f* ▹ *vt* szydzić *or* drwić z *+gen*; **to ~ sb with cowardice** zarzucać (zarzucić *perf*) komuś tchórzostwo
**Taurus** [ˈtɔːrəs] *n* Byk *m*; **to be ~** być spod znaku Byka
**taut** [tɔːt] *adj* napięty, naprężony
**tavern** [ˈtævən] *n* tawerna *f*
**tawdry** [ˈtɔːdrɪ] *adj* tandetny
**tawny** [ˈtɔːnɪ] *adj* śniady, ogorzały
**tawny owl** *n* puszczyk *m*
**tax** [tæks] *n* podatek *m* ▹ *vt* opodatkowywać (opodatkować *perf*); (*fig*) wystawiać (wystawić *perf*) na próbę; **before tax** przed opodatkowaniem; **after tax** po opodatkowaniu; **free of tax** wolny od podatku
**taxable** [ˈtæksəbl] *adj* podlegający opodatkowaniu
**tax allowance** *n* ulga *f* podatkowa
**taxation** [tækˈseɪʃən] *n* (*system*) opodatkowanie *nt*; (*money paid*) podatki *pl*
**tax avoidance** *n* obchodzenie *nt* przepisów podatkowych
**tax collector** *n* poborca *m* podatkowy
**tax disc** (*Brit: Aut*) *n nalepka na szybę samochodu świadcząca o opłaceniu podatku*
**tax evasion** *n* uchylanie się *nt* od podatków
**tax exemption** *n* zwolnienie *nt* od podatku
**tax exile** *n* wychodźca *m* podatkowy
**tax-free** [ˈtæksfriː] *adj* wolny od podatku
**tax haven** *n* raj *m* podatkowy
**taxi** [ˈtæksɪ] *n* taksówka *f*, taxi *nt inv* ▹ *vi* (*Aviat*) kołować
**taxidermist** [ˈtæksɪdəːmɪst] *n* wypychacz *m* zwierząt
**taxi driver** *n* taksówkarz *m*
**tax inspector** (*Brit*) *n* inspektor *m* podatkowy
**taxi rank** (*Brit*) *n* postój *m* taksówek
**taxi stand** *n* = **taxi rank**
**taxpayer** [ˈtækspeɪəʳ] *n* podatnik(-iczka) *m(f)*
**tax rebate** *n* zwrot *m* nadpłaconego podatku
**tax relief** *n* ulga *f* podatkowa
**tax return** *n* zeznanie *nt* podatkowe, deklaracja *f* podatkowa
**tax shelter** (*Comm*) *n możliwość uzyskania ulgi podatkowej dzięki inwestycjom itp*
**tax year** *n* rok *m* podatkowy
**TB** *n abbr* = **tuberculosis**
**TD** (*US*) *n abbr* = **Treasury Department**; (*Football*) = **touchdown**
**tea** [tiː] *n* (*drink, plant*) herbata *f*; (*Brit: also:* **high tea**) (późny) obiad *m*, obiadokolacja *f*; (*also: afternoon tea*) podwieczorek *m*
**tea bag** *n* torebka *f* herbaty ekspresowej
**tea break** (*Brit*) *n* przerwa *f* na herbatę
**teacake** [ˈtiːkeɪk] (*Brit*) *n słodka bułka z rodzynkami, jedzona najczęściej w postaci grzanek z masłem*
**teach** [tiːtʃ] (*pt, pp* **taught**) *vt* (*pupils*) uczyć; (*subject*) uczyć *or* nauczać *+gen*; (*instruct*):

**to ~ sb sth, ~ sth to sb** uczyć (nauczyć *perf*) kogoś czegoś ▷ *vi* uczyć; **it taught him a lesson** (*fig*) była to dla niego nauczka
**eacher** ['ti:tʃə^r] *n* nauczyciel(ka) *m(f)*; **French ~** nauczyciel(ka) *m(f)* francuskiego
**eacher training college** *n* kolegium *nt* nauczycielskie
**eaching** ['ti:tʃɪŋ] *n* nauczanie *nt*, uczenie *nt*
**eaching aids** *npl* pomoce *pl* naukowe
**eaching hospital** (*Brit*) *n* ≈ klinika *f* (Akademii Medycznej)
**eaching staff** (*Brit*) *n* personel *m* dydaktyczny
**ea cosy** *n okrycie na dzbanek zapobiegające stygnięciu herbaty*
**eacup** ['ti:kʌp] *n* filiżanka *f* do herbaty
**eak** [ti:k] *n* tik *m*, tek *m*
**ea leaves** *npl* fusy *pl* (herbaciane)
**eam** [ti:m] *n* (*of people, experts*) zespół *m*; (*Sport*) drużyna *f*; (*of horses, oxen*) zaprzęg *m*
▸ **team up** *vi*: **to ~ up (with)** łączyć (połączyć *perf*) siły (z *+instr*)
**eam games** *npl* gry *pl* zespołowe
**eam spirit** *n* duch *m* zespołowy
**eamwork** ['ti:mwə:k] *n* praca *f* zespołowa
**ea party** *n* herbatka *f* (towarzyska)
**eapot** ['ti:pɔt] *n* dzbanek *m* do herbaty
**ear**[1] [tɛə^r] (*pt* **tore**, *pp* **torn**) *n* rozdarcie *nt*, dziura *f* ▷ *vt* drzeć (podrzeć *perf*) ▷ *vi* drzeć się (podrzeć się *perf*); **to ~ to pieces** *or* **to bits** *or* **to shreds** (*paper, letter, clothes*) drzeć (podrzeć *perf*) na kawałki *or* na strzępy; (*fig: person, work*) nie zostawić (*perf*) suchej nitki na *+loc*; **to ~ each other to pieces** niszczyć się (zniszczyć się *perf*) nawzajem
▸ **tear along** *vi* pędzić (popędzić *perf*)
▸ **tear apart** *vt* (*book, clothes*) rozrywać (rozerwać *perf*), rozdzierać (rozedrzeć *perf*); (*people*) rozdzielać (rozdzielić *perf*); **to be torn apart (by)** (*fig*) być rozdartym wewnętrznie (przez *+acc*)
▸ **tear away** *vt*: **to ~ o.s. away from sth** (*fig*) odrywać się (oderwać się *perf*) od czegoś
▸ **tear out** *vt* wyrywać (wyrwać *perf*)
▸ **tear up** *vt* (*sheet of paper, cheque*) drzeć (podrzeć *perf*)
**ear**[2] [tɪə^r] *n* łza *f*; **in ~s** we łzach; **to burst into ~s** wybuchać (wybuchnąć *perf*) płaczem
**earaway** ['tɛərəweɪ] (*Brit: inf*) *n* narwaniec *m* (*inf*)
**eardrop** ['tɪədrɔp] *n* łza *f*
**earful** ['tɪəful] *adj* zapłakany
**ear gas** *n* gaz *m* łzawiący
**earing** ['tɛərɪŋ] *adj*: **to be in a ~ hurry** strasznie się spieszyć
**earoom** ['ti:ru:m] *n* = **teashop**
**ease** [ti:z] *vt* dokuczać *+dat* ▷ *n* kpiarz *m*
**tea set** *n* serwis *m* do herbaty
**teashop** ['ti:ʃɔp] (*Brit*) *n* herbaciarnia *f*
**teaspoon** ['ti:spu:n] *n* łyżeczka *f* (do herbaty)
**tea strainer** *n* sitko *nt* do herbaty
**teat** [ti:t] *n* (*on bottle*) smoczek *m*
**teatime** ['ti:taɪm] *n* pora *f* podwieczorku
**tea towel** (*Brit*) *n* ścier(ecz)ka *f* do naczyń
**tea urn** *n* termos *m* bufetowy
**tech** [tɛk] (*inf*) *n abbr* = **technology**; **technical college**
**technical** ['tɛknɪkl] *adj* (*advances*) techniczny; (*terms, language*) techniczny, fachowy
**technical college** (*Brit*) *n* ≈ technikum *nt*
**technicality** [tɛknɪ'kælɪtɪ] *n* (*detail*) szczegół *m* techniczny; (*point of law*) szczegół *m* (prawny); **on a ~, the judge dismissed the case** z powodu uchybienia formalnego sędzia oddalił sprawę
**technically** ['tɛknɪklɪ] *adv* (*strictly speaking*) formalnie rzecz biorąc; (*regarding technique: of dancer, musician*) technicznie, z technicznego punktu widzenia; (*: of painter, actor*) warsztatowo, pod względem warsztatu
**technician** [tɛk'nɪʃən] *n* technik *m*
**technique** [tɛk'ni:k] *n* technika *f*
**technocrat** ['tɛknəkræt] *n* technokrata(-tka) *m(f)*
**technological** [tɛknə'lɔdʒɪkl] *adj* techniczny
**technologist** [tɛk'nɔlədʒɪst] *n* technolog *m*
**technology** [tɛk'nɔlədʒɪ] *n* technika *f*
**teddy (bear)** ['tɛdɪ(-)] *n* (pluszowy) miś *m*
**tedious** ['ti:dɪəs] *adj* nużący
**tedium** ['ti:dɪəm] *n* nuda *f*
**tee** [ti:] (*Golf*) *n* (*peg*) podstawka *f*; (*area*) rzutnia *f*
▸ **tee off** (*Golf*) *vi* rozpoczynać (rozpocząć *perf*) grę
**teem** [ti:m] *vi*: **the museum was ~ing with tourists/visitors** w muzeum roiło się od turystów/zwiedzających; **it is ~ing down** leje jak z cebra
**teenage** ['ti:neɪdʒ] *adj* (*fashions*) młodzieżowy; (*children*) nastoletni
**teenager** ['ti:neɪdʒə^r] *n* nastolatek(-tka) *m(f)*
**teens** [ti:nz] *npl*: **to be in one's ~** być nastolatkiem(-ką) *m(f)*
**tee-shirt** ['ti:ʃə:t] *n* = **T-shirt**
**teeter** ['ti:tə^r] *vi* chwiać się (zachwiać się *perf*); (*fig*): **to ~ on the edge/brink of** stać na krawędzi *+gen*
**teeth** [ti:θ] *npl of* **tooth**
**teethe** [ti:ð] *vi*: **she's teething** ząbkuje, wyrzynają jej się ząbki
**teething ring** ['ti:ðɪŋ-] *n* gryzak *m*
**teething troubles** *npl* (*fig*) początkowe trudności *pl*
**teetotal** ['ti:'təutl] *adj* niepijący

t

**teetotaller**, (*US*) **teetotaler** ['ti:'təutlə[r]] *n* abstynent(ka) *m(f)*, niepijący(-ca) *m(f)*
**TEFL** ['tɛfl] *n abbr* = **Teaching of English as a Foreign Language**
**Teheran** [tɛə'rɑ:n] *n* Teheran *m*
**tel.** *abbr* (= *telephone*) tel.
**Tel Aviv** ['tɛlə'vi:v] *n* Tel-Awiw *m*
**telecast** ['tɛlɪkɑ:st] *n* transmisja *f* telewizyjna
**telecommunications** ['tɛlɪkəmju:nɪ'keɪʃənz] *n* telekomunikacja *f*
**telegram** ['tɛlɪgræm] *n* telegram *m*
**telegraph** ['tɛlɪgrɑ:f] *n* telegraf *m*
**telegraphic** [tɛlɪ'græfɪk] *adj* telegraficzny
**telegraph pole** *n* słup *m* telegraficzny
**telegraph wire** *n* drut *m* telegraficzny
**telepathic** [tɛlɪ'pæθɪk] *adj* (*power, communication*) telepatyczny; (*person*): **to be ~** mieć zdolności telepatyczne
**telepathy** [tə'lɛpəθɪ] *n* telepatia *f*
**telephone** ['tɛlɪfəun] *n* telefon *m* ▷ *vt* telefonować (zatelefonować *perf*) *or* dzwonić (zadzwonić *perf*) do *+gen* ▷ *vi* telefonować (zatelefonować *perf*), dzwonić (zadzwonić *perf*); **to be on the ~** (*talking*) rozmawiać przez telefon; (*possess phone*) mieć telefon
**telephone booth**, (*Brit*) **telephone box** *n* budka *f* telefoniczna
**telephone call** *n* rozmowa *f* telefoniczna; **there was a ~ for you** był do ciebie telefon; **can I make a ~?** czy mogę zatelefonować?
**telephone directory** *n* książka *f* telefoniczna
**telephone exchange** *n* centrala *f* telefoniczna
**telephone number** *n* numer *m* telefonu
**telephone operator** *n* telefonista(-tka) *m(f)*
**telephone tapping** *n* podsłuch *m* telefoniczny
**telephonist** [tə'lɛfənɪst] (*Brit*) *n* telefonista(-tka) *m(f)*
**telephoto** ['tɛlɪ'fəutəu] *adj*: **~ lens** teleobiektyw *m*
**teleprinter** ['tɛlɪprɪntə[r]] *n* dalekopis *m*
**Teleprompter** ['tɛlɪprɔmptə[r]]® (*US*) *n* czytnik *m* telewizyjny
**telescope** ['tɛlɪskəup] *n* teleskop *m* ▷ *vi* (*fig: bus, lorry*) składać się (złożyć się *perf*) w harmonijkę ▷ *vt* (*instrument etc*) składać (złożyć *perf*) (*teleskopowo*)
**telescopic** [tɛlɪ'skɔpɪk] *adj* (*aerial*) teleskopowy; (*legs*) składany; **a 400 mm ~ lense** teleobiektyw o ogniskowej 400 mm
**Teletext**® ['tɛlɪtɛkst] *n* teletekst *m*, telegazeta *f*
**televise** ['tɛlɪvaɪz] *vt* transmitować w telewizji
**television** ['tɛlɪvɪʒən] *n* (*set*) telewizor *m*; (*system, business*) telewizja *f*; **to be on ~** (*person*) występować (wystąpić *perf*) w telewizji; **what's on ~ tonight?** co jest dziś wieczorem w telewizji?
**television licence** (*Brit*) *n* abonament *m* telewizyjny
**television programme** *n* program *m* telewizyjny
**television set** *n* telewizor *m*
**telex** ['tɛlɛks] *n* teleks *m* ▷ *vt* (*message*) przesyłać (przesłać *perf*) teleksem; (*company*) teleksować (zateleksować *perf*) do *+gen* ▷ *vi* teleksować (zateleksować *perf*)
**tell** [tɛl] (*pt, pp* **told**) *vt* (*say*) mówić (powiedzieć *perf*); (*relate*) opowiadać (opowiedzieć *perf*); (*distinguish*): **to ~ sth from sth** odróżniać (odróżnić *perf*) coś od czegoś ▷ *vi*: **to ~ on** (*affect*) odbijać się (odbić się *perf*) na *+loc*; **to ~ sb to do sth** kazać (kazać *perf*) komuś coś zrobić; **to ~ sb of** *or* **about sth** (*inform*) mówić (powiedzieć *perf*) komuś o czymś; (*at length*) opowiadać (opowiedzieć *perf*) komuś o czymś; **I couldn't ~ what they were thinking** nie miałem pojęcia, co myślą; **to be able to ~ the time** znać się na zegarze; **can you ~ me the time?** czy może mi Pan/Pani powiedzieć, która (jest) godzina?; **(I) ~ you what ...** wiesz co, ...; **I can't ~ them apart** nie rozróżniam ich
▸ **tell off** *vt* besztać (zbesztać *perf*)
▸ **tell on** *vt fus* skarżyć (naskarżyć *perf*) na *+acc*
**teller** ['tɛlə[r]] *n* (*in bank*) kasjer(ka) *m(f)*
**telling** ['tɛlɪŋ] *adj* (*revealing*) wymowny, wiele mówiący; (*significant*) znaczący
**telltale** ['tɛlteɪl] *adj* (*sign*) charakterystyczny ▷ *n* (*pej*) skarżypyta *m/f* (*pej*)
**telly** ['tɛlɪ] (*Brit: inf*) *n abbr* = **television**
**temerity** [tə'mɛrɪtɪ] *n*: **to have the ~ to ...** mieć czelność *+infin*
**temp** [tɛmp] (*Brit: inf*) *n abbr* (= *temporary office worker*) tymczasowa pomoc *f* biurowa ▷ *vi* pracować jako tymczasowa pomoc biurowa
**temper** ['tɛmpə[r]] *n* (*nature*) usposobienie *nt*; (*mood*) nastrój *m*, humor *m*; (*fit of anger*) gniew *m* ▷ *vt* (*moderate*) łagodzić (złagodzić *perf*); **to be in a ~** być rozdrażnionym; **to lose one's ~** tracić (stracić *perf*) panowanie nad sobą
**temperament** ['tɛmprəmənt] *n* temperament *m*, usposobienie *nt*
**temperamental** [tɛmprə'mɛntl] *adj* (*person*) zmienny, (łatwo) ulegający nastrojom; (*fig: car, machine*) kapryśny
**temperate** ['tɛmprət] *adj* umiarkowany
**temperature** ['tɛmprətʃə[r]] *n* temperatura *f*; **to have** *or* **run a ~** mieć gorączkę; **to take**

**sb's ~** mierzyć (zmierzyć *perf*) komuś temperaturę
**temperature chart** (*Med*) *n* karta *f* gorączkowa
**tempered** ['tɛmpəd] *adj* (*steel*) hartowany
**tempest** ['tɛmpɪst] *n* burza *f*
**tempestuous** [tɛm'pɛstjuəs] *adj* (*time, relationship*) burzliwy; (*person*) gwałtowny, porywczy
**tempi** ['tɛmpi:] *npl of* **tempo**
**template** ['tɛmplɪt] *n* szablon *m*
**temple** ['tɛmpl] *n* (*building*) świątynia *f*; (*Anat*) skroń *f*
**tempo** ['tɛmpəu] (*pl* **~s** *or* **tempi**) *n* tempo *nt*
**temporal** ['tɛmpərl] *adj* (*secular*) świecki; (*earthly*) doczesny; (*relating to time*) czasowy
**temporarily** ['tɛmpərərɪlɪ] *adv* (*stay, accommodate*) tymczasowo, chwilowo; (*closed, unavailable, alone*) chwilowo
**temporary** ['tɛmpərərɪ] *adj* tymczasowy
**temporize** ['tɛmpəraɪz] *vi* grać na zwłokę *or* na czas
**tempt** [tɛmpt] *vt* (*attract*) kusić (skusić *perf*); (*: client, customer*) przyciągać (przyciągnąć *perf*); (*persuade*): **to ~ sb to do sth/into doing sth** nakłaniać (nakłonić *perf*) kogoś do zrobienia czegoś; **to be ~ed to do sth** mieć (wielką) ochotę coś (z)robić
**temptation** [tɛmp'teɪʃən] *n* pokusa *f*
**tempting** ['tɛmptɪŋ] *adj* kuszący
**ten** [tɛn] *num* dziesięć ▷ *n*: **tens of thousands** dziesiątki *pl* tysięcy
**tenable** ['tɛnəbl] *adj* (*argument*) dający się obronić; **the position of Chairman is ~ for a maximum of 3 years** kadencja przewodniczącego trwa maksimum 3 lata
**tenacious** [tə'neɪʃəs] *adj* (*person*) uparty, nieustępliwy; (*idea*) (głęboko) zakorzeniony
**tenacity** [tə'næsɪtɪ] *n* upór *m*, nieustępliwość *f*
**tenancy** ['tɛnənsɪ] *n* dzierżawa *f*, najem *m*
**tenant** ['tɛnənt] *n* (*of land, property*) dzierżawca *m*, najemca *m*; (*of flat*) najemca *m*, lokator(ka) *m(f)*; (*of room*) sublokator(ka) *m(f)*
**tend** [tɛnd] *vt* (*crops*) uprawiać; (*sick person*) doglądać *+gen* ▷ *vt*: **I ~ to wake up early** mam zwyczaj budzić się *or* zwykle budzę się wcześnie
**tendency** ['tɛndənsɪ] *n* (*inclination*) skłonność *f*; (*habit*) zwyczaj *m*; (*trend*) tendencja *f*
**tender** ['tɛndə^r] *adj* (*affectionate*) czuły; (*sore*) obolały; (*meat*) miękki, kruchy; (*age*): **he's at a ~ age, he's of ~ years** jest (jeszcze) bardzo młody ▷ *n* (*Comm*) oferta *f*; (*money*): **legal ~** środek *m* płatniczy ▷ *vt* (*offer, resignation*) składać (złożyć *perf*); **to put in a ~ (for)** składać (złożyć *perf*) ofertę (na *+acc*); **to put work out to ~** (*Brit*) ogłaszać (ogłosić *perf*) przetarg na wykonanie prac
**tenderize** ['tɛndəraɪz] (*Culin*) *vt* (*meat*) zmiękczać (zmiękczyć *perf*)
**tenderly** ['tɛndəlɪ] *adv* czule
**tenderness** ['tɛndənɪs] *n* (*affection*) czułość *f*; (*of meat*) miękkość *f*, kruchość *f*
**tendon** ['tɛndən] *n* ścięgno *nt*
**tendril** ['tɛndrɪl] *n* (*Bot*) wąs *m* (*pnącza*); (*of hair*) kosmyk *m*
**tenement** ['tɛnəmənt] *n* kamienica *f* czynszowa
**Tenerife** [tɛnə'ri:f] *n* Teneryfa *f*
**tenet** ['tɛnət] *n* zasada *f*
**tenner** ['tɛnə^r] *n* (*Brit: inf: ten pounds*) dycha *f* (*inf*)
**tennis** ['tɛnɪs] *n* tenis *m*
**tennis ball** *n* piłka *f* tenisowa
**tennis club** *n* klub *m* tenisowy
**tennis court** *n* kort *m* tenisowy
**tennis elbow** (*Med*) *n* łokieć *m* tenisisty
**tennis match** *n* mecz *m* tenisowy
**tennis player** *n* tenisista(-tka) *m(f)*
**tennis racket** *n* rakieta *f* tenisowa
**tennis shoes** *npl* tenisówki *pl*
**tenor** ['tɛnə^r] *n* (*Mus*) tenor *m*; (*of speech, reply*) wydźwięk *m*
**tenpin bowling** ['tɛnpɪn-] (*Brit: Sport*) *n* kręgle *pl*
**tense** [tɛns] *adj* (*person*) spięty; (*situation, atmosphere*) napięty; (*muscle*) napięty, naprężony; (*smile*) nerwowy ▷ *n* (*Ling*) czas *m* ▷ *vt* napinać (napiąć *perf*), naprężać (naprężyć *perf*)
**tenseness** ['tɛnsnɪs] *n* napięcie *nt*
**tension** ['tɛnʃən] *n* (*nervousness*) napięcie *nt*; (*between ropes etc*) naprężenie *nt*, napięcie *nt*
**tent** [tɛnt] *n* namiot *m*
**tentacle** ['tɛntəkl] *n* (*Zool: of octopus*) macka *f*; (*: of snail*) czułek *m*; (*fig: of organization*) macka *f*; (*: of idea, class background*) okowa *f* (*usu pl*)
**tentative** ['tɛntətɪv] *adj* (*conclusion, plans*) wstępny; (*person, step, smile*) niepewny
**tentatively** ['tɛntətɪvlɪ] *adv* (*suggest*) wstępnie; (*wave, smile*) niepewnie
**tenterhooks** ['tɛntəhuks] *npl*: **on ~** jak na szpilkach
**tenth** [tɛnθ] *num* dziesiąty
**tent peg** *n* kołek *m* namiotowy *or* do namiotu, śledź *m*
**tent pole** *n* maszt *m* namiotowy
**tenuous** ['tɛnjuəs] *adj* (*hold, links etc*) słaby
**tenure** ['tɛnjuə^r] *n* (*of land, buildings*) tytuł *m* własności; (*holding of office*) urzędowanie *nt*; (*period in office*) kadencja *f*; (*Univ*): **to have ~** mieć dożywotnią posadę

**tepid** ['tɛpɪd] *adj* letni; (*fig*: *reaction*) chłodny; (: *applause*) wstrzemięźliwy

**term** [tə:m] *n* (*word*) termin *m*; (*expression*) określenie *nt*; (*period in power*) kadencja *f*; (*Scol*) ≈ semestr *m* ▷ *vt* nazywać (nazwać *perf*); **terms** *npl* warunki *pl*; **in economic/political ~s** w kategoriach ekonomicznych/politycznych; **in ~s of** (*as regards*) pod względem *+gen*; **~ of imprisonment** okres pozbawienia wolności; **easy ~s** (*Comm*) dogodne warunki; **in the short/long ~** na krótką/dłuższą metę; **to be on good ~s with sb** być z kimś w dobrych stosunkach; **to come to ~s with** godzić się (pogodzić się *perf*) z *+instr*

**terminal** ['tə:mɪnl] *adj* (*disease*) nieuleczalny; (*patient*) nieuleczalnie chory ▷ *n* (*Elec*) końcówka *f*, przyłącze *nt*; (*Comput*) terminal *m*; (*also*: **air terminal**) terminal *m* lotniczy; (*Brit*: *also*: **bus terminal**) pętla *f* autobusowa

**terminate** ['tə:mɪneɪt] *vt* (*discussion*) zakańczać (zakończyć *perf*); (*pregnancy*) przerywać (przerwać *perf*); (*contract*) rozwiązywać (rozwiązać *perf*) ▷ *vi*: **to ~ in** kończyć się (skończyć się *perf*) *+instr*

**termination** [tə:mɪ'neɪʃən] *n* (*of discussion*) zakończenie *nt*; (*of links, contacts*) zerwanie *nt*; (*of contract*) wygaśnięcie *nt*; (: *before time*) rozwiązanie *nt*; (*Med*) przerwanie *nt* ciąży

**termini** ['tə:mɪnaɪ] *npl of* **terminus**

**terminology** [tə:mɪ'nɔlədʒɪ] *n* terminologia *f*

**terminus** ['tə:mɪnəs] (*pl* **termini**) *n* (*for buses*) przystanek *m* końcowy; (*for trains*) stacja *f* końcowa

**termite** ['tə:maɪt] *n* termit *m*

**Ter(r).** *abbr* (*in street names*) = **terrace**

**terrace** ['tɛrəs] *n* (*on roof, of garden*) taras *m*; (*next to house*) patio *nt*; (*Brit*: *houses*) *szereg przylegających do siebie domków jednorodzinnych*; **the terraces** (*Brit*: *Sport*) *npl* trybuny *pl* stojące

**terraced** ['tɛrəst] *adj* (*house*) szeregowy; (*garden*) tarasowy

**terracotta** ['tɛrə'kɔtə] *n* terakota *f* ▷ *adj* z terakoty *post*

**terrain** [tɛ'reɪn] *n* teren *m*

**terrible** ['tɛrɪbl] *adj* straszny, okropny; (*inf*: *awful*) okropny

**terribly** ['tɛrɪblɪ] *adv* strasznie, okropnie

**terrier** ['tɛrɪə^r] *n* terier *m*

**terrific** [tə'rɪfɪk] *adj* (*very great*: *thunderstorm*) straszny, okropny; (: *speed etc*) zawrotny; (*wonderful*) wspaniały

**terrify** ['tɛrɪfaɪ] *vt* przerażać (przerazić *perf*); **to be terrified** być przerażonym

**terrifying** ['tɛrɪfaɪɪŋ] *adj* przerażający

**territorial** [tɛrɪ'tɔ:rɪəl] *adj* terytorialny; (*Brit*) *n członek ochotniczej rezerwy Królewskich Sił Zbrojnych*

**Territorial Army** (*Brit*) *n*: **the ~** *ochotnicza rezerwa Królewskich Sił Zbrojnych*

**territorial waters** *npl* wody *pl* terytorialne

**territory** ['tɛrɪtərɪ] *n* terytorium *nt*; (*fig*) teren *m*

**terror** ['tɛrə^r] *n* przerażenie *nt*, paniczny strach *m*

**terrorism** ['tɛrərɪzəm] *n* terroryzm *m*

**terrorist** ['tɛrərɪst] *n* terrorysta(-tka) *m(f)*

**terrorize** ['tɛrəraɪz] *vt* terroryzować (sterroryzować *perf*)

**terse** [tə:s] *adj* (*statement*) zwięzły, lakoniczny; (*style*) lapidarny

**tertiary** ['tə:ʃərɪ] *adj* trzeciorzędny; **~ education** (*Brit*) szkolnictwo wyższe

**Terylene**® ['tɛrɪli:n] *n* torlen *m* ▷ *adj* torlenowy

**TESL** ['tɛsl] *n abbr* = **Teaching of English as a Second Language**

**test** [tɛst] *n* (*trial, check*) próba *f*; (*Med*) badanie *nt*, analiza *f*; (*Scol*) sprawdzian *m*, test *m*; (*Psych*) test *m*; (*also*: **driving test**) egzamin *m* na prawo jazdy ▷ *vt* (*try out*) testować (przetestować *perf*); (*examine*) badać (zbadać *perf*); (*Scol*: *pupil*) testować (przetestować *perf*) (: *knowledge*) sprawdzać (sprawdzić *perf*); **to put sth to the ~** poddawać (poddać *perf*) coś próbie; **to ~ sth for sth** badać (zbadać *perf*) coś na zawartość czegoś

**testament** ['tɛstəmənt] *n* (*testimony*) świadectwo *nt*; (*also*: **last will and testament**) testament *m*; **the Old/New T~** Stary/Nowy Testament

**test ban** *n* (*also*: **nuclear test ban**) zakaz *m* prób jądrowych

**test card** (*TV*) *n* plansza *f* kontrolna

**test case** *n* (*Jur*) precedens *m* sądowy; **to be a ~ for** (*fig*) mieć precedensowe znaczenie dla *+gen*

**test flight** *n* lot *m* próbny

**testicle** ['tɛstɪkl] (*Med*) *n* jądro *nt*

**testify** ['tɛstɪfaɪ] *vi* zeznawać (zeznać *perf*); **to ~ to sth** (*Jur*) poświadczać (poświadczyć *perf*) coś; (*be sign of*) świadczyć o *+loc*

**testimonial** [tɛstɪ'məunɪəl] *n* (*Brit*) referencje *pl*

**testimony** ['tɛstɪmənɪ] *n* zeznanie *nt*; **to be (a) ~ to** być świadectwem *+gen*

**testing** ['tɛstɪŋ] *adj* (*situation, period*) trudny

**test match** (*Cricket, Rugby*) *n* mecz *m* reprezentacji narodowych

**test paper** *n* (pisemna) praca *f* klasowa

**test pilot** *n* oblatywacz *m*

**test tube** *n* probówka *f*

**est-tube baby** ['tɛsttju:b-] *n* dziecko *nt* z probówki
**esty** ['tɛstɪ] *adj* (*person*) drażliwy; (*comment*) złośliwy
**etanus** ['tɛtənəs] *n* tężec *m*
**etchy** ['tɛtʃɪ] *adj* popędliwy
**ether** ['tɛðəʳ] *n*: **at the end of one's ~** u kresu wytrzymałości ▷ *vt* pętać (spętać *perf*)
**ext** [tɛkst] *n* tekst *m*; (*also*: **text message**) wiadomość *f* tekstowa, SMS *m* ▷ *vt* wysyłać (wysłać *perf*) SMS-a *+dat*, SMS-ować do *+gen*
**extbook** ['tɛkstbuk] *n* podręcznik *m*
**extiles** ['tɛkstaɪlz] *npl* (*fabrics*) tekstylia *pl*, wyroby *pl* włókiennicze; (*industry*) włókiennictwo *nt*, przemysł *m* włókienniczy
**exture** ['tɛkstʃəʳ] *n* (*of cloth, paper*) faktura *f*; (*of rock*) tekstura *f*; (*of soil*) struktura *f*
**GWU** (*Brit*) *n abbr* = **Transport and General Workers' Union**
**hai** [taɪ] *adj* tajski, tajlandzki ▷ *n* (*person*) Tajlandczyk(-dka) *m*(*f*); (*Ling*) (język *m*) syjamski
**hailand** ['taɪlænd] *n* Tajlandia *f*
**halidomide**® [θə'lɪdəmaɪd] (*Med*) *n* thalidomid *m*
**hames** [tɛmz] *n*: **the ~** Tamiza *f*
**han** [ðæn, ðən] *conj* niż; **I have more ~ you** mam więcej niż ty; **we have more wine ~ beer** mamy więcej wina niż piwa; **she is older ~ you think** jest starsza, niż przypuszczasz; **it's more ~ likely** to więcej niż prawdopodobne; **more ~ once** nie raz
**hank** [θæŋk] *vt* dziękować (podziękować *perf*) *+dat*; **~ you (very much)** dziękuję (bardzo); **~ God!** dzięki Bogu!
**hankful** ['θæŋkful] *adj*: **~ (for)** wdzięczny (za *+acc*); **we were ~ that it was all over** byliśmy wdzięczni (za to), że było już po wszystkim
**hankfully** ['θæŋkfəlɪ] *adv* z wdzięcznością; **~ there were few victims** na szczęście było niewiele ofiar
**thankless** ['θæŋklɪs] *adj* niewdzięczny
**thanks** [θæŋks] *npl* podziękowanie *nt*, podziękowania *pl* ▷ *excl* (*also*: **many thanks, thanks a lot**) (stokrotne) dzięki; **~ to** dzięki *+dat*
**Thanksgiving (Day)** ['θæŋksgɪvɪŋ(-)] (US) *n* Święto *nt* Dziękczynienia

KEYWORD

**that** [ðæt, ðət] (*pl* **those**) *adj* (*demonstrative*) ten; (*: in contrast to 'this' or to indicate (greater) distance*) tamten; **that man/woman/chair** ten mężczyzna/ta kobieta/to krzesło; **that one** (tam)ten *m*/(tam)ta *f*/(tam)to *nt*; **that one over there** tamten, ten tam (*inf*)
▷ *pron* **1** (*demonstrative*) to *nt*; (*: in contrast to 'this' or referring to something (more) distant*) tamto *nt*; **who's/what's that?** kto/co to (jest)?; **is that you?** czy to ty?; **I prefer this to that** wolę to od tamtego; **that's what he said** to właśnie powiedział; **what happened after that?** co się stało potem?; **that is (to say)** to jest *or* znaczy
**2** (*relative*) który; (*: after 'all', 'anything' etc*) co; **the man (that) I saw** człowiek, którego widziałem; **the people (that) I spoke to** ludzie, z którymi rozmawiałem; **all (that) I have** wszystko, co mam
**3** (*relative: of time*) kiedy, gdy; **the day (that) he came** tego dnia, kiedy *or* gdy przyszedł
▷ *conj* że, iż (*fml*); **he thought that I was ill** myślał, że jestem chory; **she suggested that I phone you** poradziła mi, żebym do ciebie zadzwonił
▷ *adv* (*+adjective*) (aż) tak *or* taki; (*+adverb*) (aż) tak; **I can't work that much** nie mogę (aż) tyle pracować; **I didn't realize it was that bad** nie zdawałam sobie sprawy, że jest (aż) tak źle

**thatched** [θætʃt] *adj* kryty strzechą
**thaw** [θɔ:] *n* odwilż *f* ▷ *vi* (*ice*) topić się (stopić się *perf*), tająć (stajać *perf*); (*food*) rozmrażać się (rozmrozić się *perf*) ▷ *vt* (*also*: **thaw out**) rozmrażać (rozmrozić *perf*); **it's ~ing** jest odwilż

 KEYWORD

**the** [ðə, ði:] *def art* **1** (*usu*): **the history of Poland** historia Polski; **the books/children are in the library** książki/dzieci są w bibliotece; **the rich and the poor** bogaci i biedni; **to attempt the impossible** porywać się z motyką na słońce
**2** (*in titles*): **Elizabeth the First** Elżbieta I; **Peter the Great** Piotr Wielki
**3** (*in comparisons*): **the more he works the more he earns** im więcej pracuje, tym więcej zarabia

**theatre**, (US) **theater** ['θɪətəʳ] *n* teatr *m*; (*also*: **lecture theatre**) sala *f* wykładowa; (*also*: **operating theatre**) sala *f* operacyjna
**theatre-goer** ['θɪətəgəuəʳ] *n* teatroman(ka) *m*(*f*)
**theatrical** [θɪ'ætrɪkl] *adj* teatralny
**theft** [θɛft] *n* kradzież *f*
**their** [ðɛəʳ] *adj* ich, swój; **companies and ~ workers** przedsiębiorstwa i ich pracownicy; **they never left ~ village** nigdy nie wyjeżdżali ze swojej wioski
**theirs** [ðɛəz] *pron* ich; **it is ~** to (jest) ich; **a friend of ~** (pewien) ich znajomy; *see also* **my**; **mine**¹

t

**them** [ðɛm, ðəm] *pron* (*direct*) ich *vir*, je *nvir*; (*indirect*) im; (*stressed, after prep*) nich; **I see ~** widzę ich/je; **give ~ the book** daj im książkę; **give me a few of ~** daj mi kilka z nich; *see also* **me**
**theme** [θi:m] *n* temat *m*
**theme park** *n park rozrywki, w którym atrakcje pogrupowane są wg tematu i dotyczą konkretnej dziedziny lub epoki*
**theme song** *n* melodia *f* przewodnia, motyw *f* przewodni
**theme tune** *n* = **theme song**
**themselves** [ðəm'sɛlvz] *pl pron* (*reflexive*) się; (*after prep*) siebie (*gen, acc*), sobie (*dat, loc*), sobą (*instr*); (*emphatic*) sami *vir*, same *nvir*; **between ~** między sobą
**then** [ðɛn] *adv* (*at that time*) wtedy, wówczas; (*next*) następnie, potem ▷ *conj* tak więc ▷ *adj*: **the ~ president** ówczesny prezydent; **by ~** (*past*) do tego czasu; (*future*) do tej pory, do tego czasu; **from ~ on** od tego czasu, od tamtej chwili *or* pory; **before ~** przedtem; **until ~** do tego czasu; **and ~ what?** i co wtedy?; **what do you want me to do ~?** (*afterwards*) co chcesz, żebym zrobił potem?; (*in that case*) co w takim razie chcesz, żebym zrobił?; **the importance of education, ~, ...** tak więc, znaczenie wykształcenia ...; **but ~** z drugiej strony (jednak)
**theologian** [θɪə'ləudʒən] *n* teolog *m*
**theological** [θɪə'lɔdʒɪkl] *adj* teologiczny; **~ college** akademia teologiczna
**theology** [θɪ'ɔlədʒɪ] *n* teologia *f*
**theorem** ['θɪərəm] *n* twierdzenie *nt*
**theoretical** [θɪə'rɛtɪkl] *adj* teoretyczny
**theorize** ['θɪəraɪz] *vi* teoretyzować
**theory** ['θɪərɪ] *n* teoria *f*; **in ~** teoretycznie
**therapeutic** [θɛrə'pju:tɪk] *adj* terapeutyczny, leczniczy
**therapist** ['θɛrəpɪst] *n* terapeuta(-tka) *m(f)*
**therapy** ['θɛrəpɪ] *n* terapia *f*, leczenie *nt*

KEYWORD

**there** [ðɛə^r] *adv* **1**: **there is/there are** jest/są; **there are 3 of them** jest ich 3; **there has been an accident** wydarzył się wypadek; **there will be a meeting tomorrow** jutro odbędzie się zebranie
**2** (*referring to place*) tam; **up/down there** tam na górze/na dole; **there he is!** oto i on!
**3**: **there, there** (no) już dobrze

**thereabouts** ['ðɛərə'bauts] *adv* (*place*) gdzieś tam (w pobliżu), w okolicy; (*amount*) coś koło tego
**thereafter** [ðɛər'ɑ:ftə^r] *adv* od tego czasu
**thereby** ['ðɛəbaɪ] *adv* przez to, tym samym
**therefore** ['ðɛəfɔ:^r] *adv* dlatego (też), zatem
**there's** ['ðɛəz] = **there is**; **there has**
**thereupon** [ðɛərə'pɔn] *adv* następnie
**thermal** ['θə:ml] *adj* (*energy*) cieplny; (*underwear*) ocieplany; (*paper, printer*) termiczny; **~ springs** cieplice
**thermodynamics** ['θə:mədaɪ'næmɪks] *n* termodynamika *f*
**thermometer** [θə'mɔmɪtə^r] *n* termometr
**thermonuclear** ['θə:məu'nju:klɪə^r] *adj* termojądrowy
**Thermos**® ['θə:məs] *n* (*also*: **Thermos flask**) termos *m*
**thermostat** ['θə:məustæt] *n* termostat *m*
**thesaurus** [θɪ'sɔ:rəs] *n* tezaurus *m*, ≈ słownik *m* wyrazów bliskoznacznych
**these** [ði:z] *pl adj* ci (*+vir pl*), te (*+nvir pl*) ▷ *pl pron* ci *vir*, te *nvir*
**theses** ['θi:si:z] *npl of* **thesis**
**thesis** ['θi:sɪs] (*pl* **theses**) *n* (*for doctorate etc*) rozprawa *f*, praca *f*
**they** [ðeɪ] *pl pron* oni; **~ say that ...** mówią, że ..., mówi się, że...
**they'd** = **they had**; **they would**
**they'll** = **they shall**; **they will**
**they're** = **they are**
**they've** [ðeɪv] = **they have**
**thick** [θɪk] *adj* (*slice, line, socks*) gruby; (*sauce, forest, hair*) gęsty; (*inf*: *person*) tępy ▷ *n*: **in the ~ of the battle** w wirze walki; **it's 20 cm ~** ma 20 cm grubości
**thicken** ['θɪkn] *vi* gęstnieć (zgęstnieć *perf*) ▷ *vt* zagęszczać (zagęścić *perf*); **the plot ~s** akcja się komplikuje
**thicket** ['θɪkɪt] *n* gąszcz *m*, zarośla *pl*
**thickly** ['θɪklɪ] *adv* (*spread, cut*) grubo; (*populated*) gęsto
**thickness** ['θɪknɪs] *n* grubość *f*; (*layer*) warstwa *f*
**thickset** [θɪk'sɛt] *adj* przysadzisty
**thick-skinned** [θɪk'skɪnd] *adj* (*fig*) gruboskórny
**thief** [θi:f] (*pl* **thieves**) *n* złodziej *m*
**thieves** [θi:vz] *npl of* **thief**
**thieving** ['θi:vɪŋ] *n* złodziejstwo *nt*
**thigh** [θaɪ] *n* udo *nt*
**thighbone** ['θaɪbəun] *n* kość *f* udowa
**thimble** ['θɪmbl] *n* naparstek *m*
**thin** [θɪn] *adj* (*slice, line, book*) cienki; (*person, animal*) chudy; (*soup, fog, hair*) rzadki ▷ *vt*: **t**[illegible] **(down)** rozrzedzać (rozrzedzić *perf*), rozcieńczać (rozcieńczyć *perf*) ▷ *vi* przerzedzać się (przerzedzić się *perf*); **his h**[illegible] **is ~ning** włosy mu rzedną
**thing** [θɪŋ] *n* rzecz *f*; **things** *npl* rzeczy *pl*; **d**[illegible] **you know how to drive this ~?** czy wiesz,

jak się tym kieruje?; **he has a ~ about blondes** (*inf*) ma słabość do blondynek; **first ~ in the morning** z samego rana; **last ~ at night** przed (samym) pójściem spać; **the ~ is ...** rzecz w tym, że ...; **for one ~** przede wszystkim; **don't worry about a ~** (o) nic się nie martw; **you'll do no such ~!** nic takiego nie zrobisz!; **poor ~** biedactwo; **the best ~ would be to ...** najlepiej byłoby *+infin*; **how are ~s?** co słychać?

**hink** [θɪŋk] (*pt, pp* **thought**) *vi* (*reflect*) myśleć (pomyśleć *perf*); (*reason*) myśleć ▷ *vt* myśleć (pomyśleć *perf*); **to ~ of** (*reflect upon, show consideration for*) myśleć (pomyśleć *perf*) o *+loc*; (*recall*) przypominać (przypomnieć *perf*) sobie *+acc*; (*conceive*) pomyśleć (*perf*) o *+loc*; **what did you ~ of them?** jakie zrobili na tobie wrażenie?; **to ~ about sth/sb** myśleć (pomyśleć *perf*) o czymś/kimś; **I'll ~ about it** zastanowię się nad tym; **she ~s of going away to Italy** myśli o wyjeździe do Włoch; **I ~ so/not** myślę, że tak/nie; **to ~ highly of sb** być wysokiego mniemania o kimś; **to ~ aloud** myśleć głośno *or* na głos; **~ again!** zastanów się!

▸ **think over** *vt* przemyśliwać (przemyśleć *perf*), rozważać (rozważyć *perf*); **I'd like to ~ things over** chciałabym (to) wszystko przemyśleć

▸ **think through** *vt* przemyśliwać (przemyśleć *perf*)

▸ **think up** *vt* (*excuse*) wymyślać (wymyślić *perf*); (*plan*) obmyślać (obmyślić *perf*)

**hinking** ['θɪŋkɪŋ] *n* myślenie *nt*; **to my (way of) ~** w moim pojęciu

**hink tank** *n* sztab *m* ekspertów

**hinly** ['θɪnlɪ] *adv* (*spread, cut*) cienko; (*disguised*) ledwie

**hinness** ['θɪnnɪs] *n* cienkość *f*

**hird** [θə:d] *num* trzeci ▷ *n* (*fraction*) jedna trzecia *f*; (*Aut*) trzeci bieg *m*, trójka *f* (*inf*); (*Brit: Scol*) *dyplom ukończenia studiów z najniższą oceną*; **a ~ of** trzecia część *+gen*

**hird-degree burns** ['θə:ddɪgri:-] *npl* poparzenia *pl* trzeciego stopnia

**hirdly** ['θə:dlɪ] *adv* po trzecie

**hird party insurance** (*Brit*) *n* ubezpieczenie *nt* od odpowiedzialności cywilnej

**hird-rate** ['θə:d'reɪt] (*pej*) *adj* trzeciorzędny

**hird World** *n*: **the ~** Trzeci Świat *m* ▷ *adj*: **~ countries** kraje *pl* Trzeciego Świata

**hirst** [θə:st] *n* pragnienie *nt*

**hirsty** ['θə:stɪ] *adj* spragniony; **I am ~** chce mi się pić; **gardening is ~ work** przy pracy w ogrodzie chce się pić

**hirteen** [θə:'ti:n] *num* trzynaście

**hirteenth** [θə:'ti:nθ] *num* trzynasty

**thirtieth** ['θə:tɪɪθ] *num* trzydziesty

**thirty** ['θə:tɪ] *num* trzydzieści

 KEYWORD

**this** [ðɪs] (*pl* **these**) *adj* (*demonstrative*) ten; **this man/woman/child** ten mężczyzna/ta kobieta/to dziecko; **these people** ci ludzie; **these children** te dzieci; **this one** ten *m*/ta *f*/to *nt*

▷ *pron* to; **who/what is this?** co/kto to jest?; **this is where I live** tutaj (właśnie) mieszkam; **this is Mr Brown** (*in introductions*) (to) pan Brown; (*in photo*) to (jest) pan Brown; (*on telephone*) mówi Brown, tu Brown

▷ *adv* (*+adjective*) tak *or* taki; (*+adverb*) tak; **it was about this big** to było mniej więcej takie duże; **now we've gone this far** teraz, gdy zaszliśmy (już) tak daleko

**thistle** ['θɪsl] *n* oset *m*

**thong** [θɔŋ] *n* pasek *m*, rzemień *m*

**thongs** (*US*) *n* japonki *pl* (*klapki*)

**thorn** [θɔ:n] *n* cierń *m*, kolec *m*

**thorny** ['θɔ:nɪ] *adj* ciernisty; (*fig*) najeżony trudnościami

**thorough** ['θʌrə] *adj* gruntowny; (*person*) sumienny, skrupulatny

**thoroughbred** ['θʌrəbrɛd] *n* koń *m* czystej krwi

**thoroughfare** ['θʌrəfɛə^r] *n* główna arteria *f* komunikacyjna; **"no ~"** (*Brit*) „przejazd wzbroniony"

**thoroughly** ['θʌrəlɪ] *adv* gruntownie; **I was ~ ashamed** było mi bardzo wstyd; **I ~ agree** całkowicie się zgadzam

**thoroughness** ['θʌrənɪs] *n* gruntowność *f*

**those** [ðəuz] *pl adj* (tam)ci (*+vir pl*), (tam)te (*+nvir pl*) ▷ *pl pron* (tam)ci *vir*, (tam)te *nvir*

**though** [ðəu] *conj* chociaż, mimo że ▷ *adv* jednak; **even ~** (po)mimo że, chociaż; **it's not easy, ~** nie jest to jednak łatwe

**thought** [θɔ:t] *pt, pp of* **think** ▷ *n* (*idea, intention*) myśl *f*; (*reflection*) namysł *m*; **thoughts** *npl* zdanie *nt*, opinia *f*; **after much ~** po długim namyśle; **I've just had a ~** właśnie przyszedł mi do głowy pewien pomysł; **I'll give it some ~** pomyślę o tym, zastanowię się nad tym

**thoughtful** ['θɔ:tful] *adj* (*pensive*) zamyślony; (*considerate*) troskliwy

**thoughtfully** ['θɔ:tfəlɪ] *adv* (*pensively*) w zamyśleniu; (*considerately*) troskliwie

**thoughtless** ['θɔ:tlɪs] *adj* bezmyślny

**thoughtlessly** ['θɔ:tlɪslɪ] *adv* bezmyślnie

**thoughtlessness** ['θɔ:tlɪsnɪs] *n* bezmyślność *f*

**thousand** ['θauzənd] *num* tysiąc; **two ~** dwa tysiące; **~s of** tysiące *+gen*

t

**thousandth** [ˈθauzəntθ] *num* tysięczny
**thrash** [θræʃ] *vt* (*beat*) bić (zbić *perf*), lać (zlać *perf*) (*inf*); (*defeat*) pobić (*perf*) na głowę
▸ **thrash about** *vi* rzucać się
▸ **thrash around** *vi* = **thrash about**
▸ **thrash out** *vt* (*problem*) rozpracowywać (rozpracować *perf*)
**thrashing** [ˈθræʃɪŋ] *n*: **to give sb a ~** sprawić (*perf*) komuś lanie
**thread** [θrɛd] *n* (*yarn*) nić *f*, nitka *f*; (*of screw*) gwint *m* ▷ *vt* (*needle*) nawlekać (nawlec *perf*); **to ~ one's way between** przemykać (przemknąć *perf*) pomiędzy *+instr*
**threadbare** [ˈθrɛdbɛə^r] *adj* wytarty, przetarty
**threat** [θrɛt] *n* groźba *f*, pogróżka *f*; (*fig*) zagrożenie *nt*; **we are under ~ of** grozi nam *+nom*
**threaten** [ˈθrɛtn] *vi* grozić, zagrażać ▷ *vt*: **to ~ sb with sth** grozić (zagrozić *perf*) komuś czymś; **the riots ~ed to get out of hand** istniało niebezpieczeństwo, że rozruchy wymkną się spod kontroli
**threatening** [ˈθrɛtnɪŋ] *adj* groźny
**three** [θriː] *num* trzy
**three-dimensional** [θriːdɪˈmɛnʃənl] *adj* trójwymiarowy
**threefold** [ˈθriːfəuld] *adv*: **to increase ~** wzrastać (wzrosnąć *perf*) trzykrotnie
**three-piece suit** [ˈθriːpiːs-] *n* garnitur *m* trzyczęściowy
**three-piece suite** *n* zestaw *m* wypoczynkowy
**three-ply** [θriːˈplaɪ] *adj* (*wool*) potrójny; (*wood*) trójwarstwowy
**three-quarters** [θriːˈkwɔːtəz] *npl* trzy czwarte *pl*; **~ full** napełniony w trzech czwartych
**three-wheeler** [θriːˈwiːlə^r] *n* samochód *m* na trzech kołach
**thresh** [θrɛʃ] *vt* młócić (wymłócić *perf*)
**threshing machine** [ˈθrɛʃɪŋ-] *n* młocarnia *f*
**threshold** [ˈθrɛʃhəuld] *n* próg *m*; **to be on the ~ of** (*fig*) być u progu *+gen*
**threshold agreement** (*Econ*) *n* porozumienie *nt* progowe
**threw** [θruː] *pt of* **throw**
**thrift** [θrɪft] *n* oszczędność *f*, zapobiegliwość *f*
**thrifty** [ˈθrɪftɪ] *adj* oszczędny, zapobiegliwy
**thrill** [θrɪl] *n* (*excitement*) dreszcz(yk) *m* emocji, emocje *pl*; (*shudder*) dreszcz *m* ▷ *vi*: **to ~ to sth** ekscytować się czymś ▷ *vt* ekscytować; **to be ~ed** być podekscytowanym
**thriller** [ˈθrɪlə^r] *n* dreszczowiec *m*
**thrilling** [ˈθrɪlɪŋ] *adj* podniecający, ekscytujący
**thrive** [θraɪv] (*pt* **~d** *or* **throve**, *pp* **~d**) *vi* dobrze się rozwijać; **he ~s on hard work** ciężka praca mu służy
**thriving** [ˈθraɪvɪŋ] *adj* kwitnący, (dobrze) prosperujący
**throat** [θrəut] *n* gardło *nt*; **I have a sore ~** boli mnie gardło
**throb** [θrɔb] *n* (*of heart*) (silne) bicie *nt*; (*of pain*) rwanie *nt*, pulsowanie *nt*; (*of engine*) warkot *m* ▷ *vi* (*heart*) walić; (*arm etc*) rwać; (*machine*) warczeć; **my head is ~bing** głowa mi pęka
**throes** [θrəuz] *npl*: **in the ~ of** w wirze *or* ferworze *+gen*; **death ~** drgawki przedśmiertne; (*fig*) ostatnie podrygi
**thrombosis** [θrɔmˈbəusɪs] (*Med*) *n* zakrzepica *f*
**throne** [θrəun] *n* tron *m*
**throng** [ˈθrɔŋ] *n* tłum *m* ▷ *vt* (*streets etc*) wypełniać (wypełnić *perf*) ▷ *vi*: **to ~ to** ciągnąć do *+gen*, walić do *+gen* (*inf*)
**throttle** [ˈθrɔtl] *n* przepustnica *f*, zawór *m* dławiący ▷ *vt* dusić (udusić *perf*)
**through** [θruː] *prep* przez *+acc* ▷ *adj* (*train etc*) bezpośredni ▷ *adv* bezpośrednio, prosto; **(from) Monday ~ Friday** (*US*) od poniedziałku do piątku; **to let sb ~** przepuszczać (przepuścić *perf*) kogoś; **to put sb ~ to sb** (*Tel*) łączyć (połączyć *perf*) kogoś z kimś; **to be ~** (*Tel*) mieć połączenie; **to be ~ with sb/sth** skończyć (*perf*) z kimś/czymś; **"no ~ road"** (*Brit*) *ślepa uliczka*; **"no ~ traffic"** (*US*) *ślepa uliczka*
**throughout** [θruːˈaut] *prep* (*place*) w całym *+loc*; (*time*) przez cały *+acc* ▷ *adv* (*everywhere*) wszędzie; (*the whole time*) od początku do końca, przez cały czas; **the pictures can be transmitted by satellite ~ the world** zdjęcia te można transmitować przez satelitę na cały świat
**throughput** [ˈθruːput] *n* (*of materials*) przerób *m*; (*of information*) przepustowość *f*
**throve** [θrəuv] *pt of* **thrive**
**throw** [θrəu] (*pt* **threw**, *pp* **~n**) *n* rzut *m* ▷ *vt* (*object*) rzucać (rzucić *perf*); (*rider*) zrzucać (zrzucić *perf*); (*pottery*) toczyć; (*fig*) zbić (*perf*) z tropu; **to ~ a party** urządzać (urządzić *perf*) przyjęcie; **to ~ open** (*doors*) otwierać (otworzyć *perf*) na oścież; (*debate*) zapraszać (zaprosić *perf*) wszystkich do udziału w *+instr*
▸ **throw about** *vt* trwonić (roztrwonić *perf*)
▸ **throw around** *vt* = **throw about**
▸ **throw away** *vt* (*rubbish*) wyrzucać (wyrzucić *perf*); (*money*) trwonić (roztrwonić *perf*), przepuszczać (przepuścić *perf*) (*inf*)
▸ **throw off** *vt* zrzucać (zrzucić *perf*)
▸ **throw out** *vt* (*rubbish, person*) wyrzucać (wyrzucić *perf*); (*idea*) odrzucać (odrzucić *perf*)
▸ **throw together** *vt* (*meal*) pichcić (upichcić *perf*) (*inf*), pitrasić (upitrasić *perf*) (*inf*); (*costume, essay*) klecić (sklecić *perf*)

▸ **throw up** *vi* wymiotować (zwymiotować *perf*)

**throwaway** ['θrəuəweɪ] *adj* (*toothbrush etc*) jednorazowy; (*remark*) rzucony od niechcenia

**throwback** ['θrəubæk] *n*: **it's a ~ to** to przejaw powrotu do *+gen*

**throw-in** ['θrəuɪn] (*Football*) *n* wrzut *m* z autu

**thrown** [θrəun] *pp of* **throw**

**thru** [θru:] (*US*) = **through**

**thrush** [θrʌʃ] *n* (*bird*) drozd *m*; (*Med: esp in children*) pleśniawka *f*; (*: Brit: in women*) grzybica *f* pochwy

**thrust** [θrʌst] (*pt, pp* **~**) *n* (*Tech*) ciąg *m*, siła *f* ciągu; (*push*) pchnięcie *nt*; (*fig*) kierunek *m* ▹ *vt* pchać (pchnąć *perf*); **to ~ sth into sth** wpychać (wepchnąć *perf*) coś do czegoś

**thud** [θʌd] *n* łomot *m*

**thug** [θʌg] *n* opryszek *m*, zbir *m*

**thumb** [θʌm] *n* kciuk *m* ▹ *vt*: **to ~ a lift** zatrzymywać (zatrzymać *perf*) autostop; **to give sb/sth the ~s up** zapalać (zapalić *perf*) dla kogoś/czegoś zielone światło

▸ **thumb through** *vt fus* kartkować (przekartkować *perf*), przerzucać (przerzucić *perf*) strony *+gen*

**thumb index** *n zaokrąglone wcięcia z brzegu książki, z których każde oznacza początek sekcji (np. danej litery w słowniku)*

**thumbnail** ['θʌmneɪl] *n* paznokieć *m* kciuka

**thumbnail sketch** *n* zarys *m*

**thumbtack** ['θʌmtæk] (*US*) *n* pluskiewka *f*, pinezka *f*

**thump** [θʌmp] *n* grzmotnięcie *nt* ▹ *vt* grzmocić (grzmotnąć *perf*) (*inf*), walić (walnąć *perf*) (*inf*) ▹ *vi* (*heart etc*) walić

**thumping** ['θʌmpɪŋ] *adj* (*majority, victory*) miażdżący; (*headache*) potężny

**thunder** ['θʌndə$^r$] *n* grzmot *m* ▹ *vi* grzmieć (zagrzmieć *perf*); **~ and lightning** piorun; **to ~ past** (*train etc*) przelatywać (przelecieć *perf*) z hukiem

**thunderbolt** ['θʌndəbəult] *n* piorun *m*

**thunderclap** ['θʌndəklæp] *n* trzask *m* pioruna

**thunderous** ['θʌndrəs] *adj* (*crash*) ogłuszający; (*applause*) gromki

**thunderstorm** ['θʌndəstɔ:m] *n* burza *f* z piorunami

**thunderstruck** ['θʌndəstrʌk] *adj* jak rażony piorunem *or* gromem

**thundery** ['θʌndərɪ] *adj* burzowy

**Thur(s).** *abbr* (= *Thursday*) cz., czw.

**Thursday** ['θə:zdɪ] *n* czwartek *m*; *see also* **Tuesday**

**thus** [ðʌs] *adv* (*in this way*) tak, w ten sposób; (*consequently*) tak więc, a zatem

**thwart** [θwɔ:t] *vt* (*plans*) krzyżować (pokrzyżować *perf*); (*person*) psuć (popsuć *perf*) szyki *+dat*

**thyme** [taɪm] *n* tymianek *m*

**thyroid** ['θaɪrɔɪd] *n* (*also:* **thyroid gland**) tarczyca *f*

**tiara** [tɪ'ɑ:rə] *n* (*woman's jewellery*) diadem *m*; (*papal crown*) tiara *f*

**Tiber** ['taɪbə$^r$] *n*: **the ~** Tyber *m*

**Tibet** [tɪ'bɛt] *n* Tybet *m*

**Tibetan** [tɪ'bɛtən] *adj* tybetański ▹ *n* (*person*) Tybetańczyk(-anka) *m(f)*; (*Ling*) (język *m*) tybetański

**tibia** ['tɪbɪə] *n* piszczel *f*

**tic** [tɪk] *n* tik *m*

**tick** [tɪk] *n* (*sound*) tykanie *nt*; (*mark*) fajka *f* (*inf*), ptaszek *m* (*inf*); (*Zool*) kleszcz *m*; (*Brit: inf*) momencik *m*, chwileczka *f* ▹ *vi* tykać ▹ *vt* (*item on list*) odfajkowywać (odfajkować *perf*) (*inf*), odhaczać (odhaczyć *perf*) (*inf*); **what makes him ~?** co jest motorem jego działania?; **to put a ~ against sth** stawiać (postawić *perf*) przy czymś ptaszek; **to buy sth on ~** (*Brit: inf*) kupować (kupić *perf*) coś na kredyt

▸ **tick off** *vt* (*item on list*) odfajkowywać (odfajkować *perf*) (*inf*), odhaczać (odhaczyć *perf*) (*inf*); (*person*) besztać (zbesztać *perf*)

▸ **tick over** *vi* (*engine*) chodzić na jałowym biegu; (*fig: business etc*) funkcjonować na zwolnionych obrotach

**ticker tape** ['tɪkəteɪp] *n* taśma *f* perforowana; (*US: in celebrations*) serpentyna *f*

**ticket** ['tɪkɪt] *n* bilet *m*; (*in shop: on goods*) metka *f*, etykieta *f*; (*: from cash register*) paragon *m*; (*for library*) karta *f*; (*also:* **parking ticket**) mandat *m* (za złe parkowanie); (*US: Pol*) mandat *m*

**ticket agency** (*Theat*) *n* biuro *nt* sprzedaży biletów

**ticket collector** (*Rail*) *n pracownik odbierający od wysiadających wykorzystane bilety*

**ticket holder** *n* posiadacz(ka) *m(f)* biletu

**ticket inspector** *n* (*on bus*) kontroler(ka) *m(f)* biletów

**ticket office** *n* (*Rail*) kasa *f* biletowa; (*Theat*) kasa *f*

**tickle** ['tɪkl] *vt* łaskotać (połaskotać *perf*); (*fig*) bawić (ubawić *perf*) ▹ *vi* łaskotać; **it ~s!** to łaskocze!

**ticklish** ['tɪklɪʃ] *adj* (*problem etc*) delikatny, drażliwy; (*person*): **to be ~** mieć łaskotki

**tidal** ['taɪdl] *adj* pływowy

**tidal wave** *n* fala *f* pływowa

**tidbit** ['tɪdbɪt] (*US*) *n* = **titbit**

**tiddlywinks** ['tɪdlɪwɪŋks] *n* pchełki *pl* (*gra*)

**tide** [taɪd] *n* (*in sea*) pływ *m*; (*fig: of events, opinion*) fala *f*; **high ~** przypływ; **low ~** odpływ;

t

**the ~ was coming in** nadchodził przypływ
▸ **tide over** *vt*: **this money will ~ me over till Monday** dzięki tym pieniądzom przeżyję do poniedziałku
**tidily** ['taɪdɪlɪ] *adv* starannie, schludnie
**tidiness** ['taɪdɪnɪs] *n* staranność *f*, schludność *f*
**tidy** ['taɪdɪ] *adj* (*room*) czysty, schludny; (*person*) staranny, schludny; (*sum*) spory, pokaźny ▷ *vt* (*also*: **tidy up**) porządkować (uporządkować *perf*), sprzątać (posprzątać *perf*)
**tie** [taɪ] *n* (*Brit*: *also*: **necktie**) krawat *m*; (*string etc*) wiązanie *nt*, wiązadło *nt*; (*fig*) więź *f*; (*match*) spotkanie *nt*, mecz *m*; (*draw*) remis *m* ▷ *vt* (*parcel*) związywać (związać *perf*); (*shoelaces*) zawiązywać (zawiązać *perf*) ▷ *vi* remisować (zremisować *perf*); **"black/white tie"** *uwaga na zaproszeniu, oznaczająca, że wymaganym na przyjęciu strojem jest smoking/frak*; **family ties** więzi *or* więzy rodzinne; **to tie sth in a bow** zawiązywać (zawiązać *perf*) coś na kokardkę; **to tie a knot in sth** zawiązywać (zawiązać *perf*) na czymś węzeł
▸ **tie down** *vt* (*fig*: *person*) krępować (skrępować *perf*); **to tie sb down (to a date etc)** wiązać (związać *perf*) kogoś (terminem *etc*)
▸ **tie in** *vi*: **to tie in with** pozostawać (pozostać *perf*) w związku z *+instr*
▸ **tie on** *vt* (*Brit*: *label etc*) przywiązywać (przywiązać *perf*), przyczepiać (przyczepić *perf*)
▸ **tie up** *vt* (*parcel*) związywać (związać *perf*); (*dog, boat*) wiązać (uwiązać *perf*); (*person*) związywać (związać *perf*), krępować (skrępować *perf*); (*arrangements*) finalizować (sfinalizować *perf*); **to be tied up** być zajętym
**tie-break(er)** ['taɪbreɪk(əʳ)] *n* (*Tennis*) tie-break *m*; (*in quiz*) *dogrywka mająca wyłonić zwycięzcę konkursu w przypadku remisu*
**tie-on** ['taɪɔn] (*Brit*) *adj* (*label*) przywiązywany
**tie-pin** ['taɪpɪn] (*Brit*) *n* spinka *f* do krawata
**tier** [tɪəʳ] *n* (*of stadium etc*) rząd *m*, kondygnacja *f*; (*of cake*) warstwa *f*
**Tierra del Fuego** [tɪ'ɛrədɛl'fweɪgəu] *n* Ziemia *f* Ognista
**tie tack** (*US*) *n* = **tie-pin**
**tiff** [tɪf] *n* sprzeczka *f*
**tiger** ['taɪgəʳ] *n* tygrys *m*
**tight** [taɪt] *adj* (*screw*) dokręcony; (*knot*) zaciśnięty; (*grip*) mocny; (*clothes*) obcisły; (*shoes*) ciasny; (*budget, schedule*) napięty; (*bend, security*) ostry; (*inf*: *drunk*) wstawiony (*inf*); (: *stingy*) skąpy ▷ *adv* (*hold, squeeze*) mocno; (*shut*: *window*) szczelnie; (: *eyes*) mocno; **money is ~** krucho z pieniędzmi; **the suitcase was packed ~** walizka była mocno wypakowana; **people were packed ~** ludzie byli stłoczeni; **hold ~!** trzymaj się mocno!
**tighten** ['taɪtn] *vt* (*rope*) napinać (napiąć *perf*), naprężać (naprężyć *perf*); (*screw*) dokręcać (dokręcić *perf*); (*grip*) zacieśniać (zacieśnić *perf*); (*security*) zaostrzać (zaostrzyć *perf*) ▷ *vi* (*fingers*) zaciskać się (zacisnąć się *perf*); (*rope, chain*) napinać się (napiąć się *perf*), naprężać się (naprężyć się *perf*)
**tightfisted** [taɪt'fɪstɪd] *adj* skąpy
**tightly** ['taɪtlɪ] *adv* (*grasp, cling*) mocno; (*pack*) ciasno
**tightrope** ['taɪtrəup] *n* lina *f* (*do akrobacji*); **to be on** *or* **walking a ~** (*fig*) balansować na linie
**tightrope walker** *n* linoskoczek *m*
**tights** [taɪts] (*Brit*) *npl* rajstopy *pl*
**tigress** ['taɪgrɪs] *n* tygrysica *f*
**tilde** ['tɪldə] *n* tylda *f*
**tile** [taɪl] *n* (*on roof*) dachówka *f*; (*on floor, wall*) kafelek *m* ▷ *vt* (*wall, bathroom etc*) wykładać (wyłożyć *perf*) kafelkami, kafelkować (wykafelkować *perf*) (*inf*)
**tiled** [taɪld] *adj* (*wall, bathroom*) wykafelkowany
**till** [tɪl] *n* kasa *f* (*sklepowa*) ▷ *vt* (*land*) uprawiać ▷ *prep, conj* = **until**
**tiller** ['tɪləʳ] (*Naut*) *n* rumpel *m*
**tilt** [tɪlt] *vt* przechylać (przechylić *perf*) ▷ *vi* przechylać się (przechylić się *perf*) ▷ *n*: **with a ~ of her head** przechylając głowę; **to wear one's hat at a ~** nosić czapkę na bakier; **she was running at full ~** pędziła co sił
**timber** ['tɪmbəʳ] *n* (*material*) drewno *nt*; (*trees*) drzewa *pl* na budulec
**time** [taɪm] *n* czas *m*; (*often pl*: *epoch*) czasy *pl*; (*moment*) chwila *f*; (*occasion*) raz *m*; (*Mus*): **in 3/4 ~** w rytmie na 3/4 ▷ *vt* (*measure time of*) mierzyć (zmierzyć *perf*) czas *+gen*; (*fix moment for*) ustalać (ustalić *perf*) czas *+gen*; **to ~ sth well/badly** wybierać (wybrać *perf*) dobry/zły czas na coś; **I will see you at the same ~ next week** do zobaczenia w przyszłym tygodniu o tej samej porze; **for a long ~** przez długi czas; **for the ~ being** na razie; **four at a ~** (po) cztery na raz; **from ~ to ~** od czasu do czasu; **~ after ~, ~ and again** wielokrotnie, wiele razy; **at ~s** czasami, czasem; **in ~** (*soon enough*) na czas, w porę; (*eventually*) z czasem; (*Mus*) w takt, do taktu; **in a week's ~** za tydzień; **in no ~** w mgnieniu oka, w mig; **any ~** obojętnie kiedy; **any ~ you want** kiedy tylko zechcesz; **on ~** na czas; **to be 30 mins behind/ahead of ~** być 30 minut po czasie/przed czasem; **by the ~ he arrived** zanim przyjechał; **5 ~s 5** 5 razy 5; **what ~ is it?** która (jest) godzina?; **to have a good ~** dobrze się

bawić; **we had a hard ~** było nam ciężko; **~'s up!** czas minął!; **I've no ~ for it** *(fig)* szkoda mi na to czasu; **he'll do it in his own (good) ~** *(without being hurried)* zrobi to w swoim czasie; **he'll do it in** *or (US)* **on his own ~** *(after hours)* zrobi to po godzinach; **to be behind the ~s** być nie na czasie; **the bomb was ~d to go off five minutes later** bombę nastawiono na wybuch po pięciu minutach

**time-and-motion study** ['taɪmənd'məuʃən-] *n* badanie *nt* efektywności pracy

**time bomb** *n* bomba *f* zegarowa; *(fig)* bomba *f* z opóźnionym zapłonem

**time card** *n* karta *f* kontrolna *(pracownika)*

**time clock** *n* zegar *m* kontrolny

**time-consuming** ['taɪmkənsju:mɪŋ] *adj* czasochłonny

**time difference** *n* różnica *f* czasu

**time-honoured**, *(US)* **time-honored** ['taɪmɔnəd] *adj* uświęcony tradycją *or* zwyczajem

**timekeeper** ['taɪmki:pə^r] *n*: **she's a good/poor ~** punktualnie przychodzi/spóźnia się do pracy

**time lag** *n* zwłoka *f*, opóźnienie *nt*

**timeless** ['taɪmlɪs] *adj* ponadczasowy

**time limit** *n* termin *m*

**timely** ['taɪmlɪ] *adj* w (samą) porę *post*

**time off** *n* wolne *nt*

**timer** ['taɪmə^r] *n* regulator *m* czasowy

**time-saving** ['taɪmseɪvɪŋ] *adj* czasooszczędny

**timescale** ['taɪmskeɪl] *(Brit)* *n* okres *m*

**time-share** ['taɪmʃɛə^r] *n prawo użytkowania wspólnego domku letniskowego przez określony okres każdego roku*

**time-sharing** ['taɪmʃɛərɪŋ] *n (Comput) system umożliwiający wielu osobom jednoczesne korzystanie z tego samego komputera*

**time sheet** *n* = **time card**

**time signal** *(Radio)* *n* sygnał *m* czasu

**time switch** *n* wyłącznik *m* zegarowy

**timetable** ['taɪmteɪbl] *n* *(Rail)* rozkład *m* jazdy; *(Scol)* plan *m* zajęć; *(of events)* program *m*

**time zone** *n* strefa *f* czasu

**timid** ['tɪmɪd] *adj* *(person)* nieśmiały; *(animal)* bojaźliwy

**timidity** [tɪ'mɪdɪtɪ] *n* *(of person)* nieśmiałość *f*; *(of animal)* bojaźliwość *f*

**timing** ['taɪmɪŋ] *n* *(Sport)* wyczucie *nt* czasu; **the ~ of his resignation was completely wrong** wybrał fatalny moment na złożenie rezygnacji

**timing device** *n* *(on bomb)* urządzenie *nt* zegarowe

**timpani** ['tɪmpənɪ] *npl* *(Mus)* kotły *pl*

**tin** [tɪn] *n* *(metal)* cyna *f*; *(for biscuits etc)* (blaszane) pudełko *nt*; *(for baking)* forma *f* do pieczenia *or* ciasta; *(Brit: can)* puszka *f*; **we'll need 2 tins of paint** będziemy potrzebować 2 puszki farby

**tinfoil** ['tɪnfɔɪl] *n* folia *f* aluminiowa

**tinge** [tɪndʒ] *n* *(of colour)* odcień *m*; *(fig: of emotion)* domieszka *f* ▷ *vt*: **~d with** *(fig: emotion etc)* zabarwiony *+instr*; **her eyes were ~d with red** miała zaczerwienione oczy

**tingle** ['tɪŋgl] *vi*: **my leg was tingling** czułem mrowienie w nodze; **he was tingling with excitement** drżał z podniecenia

**tinker** ['tɪŋkə^r] *n* druciarz *m*

▸ **tinker with** *vt fus* majstrować przy *+loc*

**tinkle** ['tɪŋkl] *vi* dzwonić (zadzwonić *perf*), brzęczeć (zabrzęczeć *perf*) ▷ *n* *(inf)*: **to give sb a ~** *(Tel)* zadzwonić *(perf)* do kogoś

**tin mine** *n* kopalnia *f* cyny

**tinned** [tɪnd] *(Brit)* *adj* *(food)* puszkowany; *(salmon, peas)* konserwowy

**tinny** ['tɪnɪ] *(pej)* *adj* *(sound)* metaliczny; *(car etc)* lichy, byle jaki

**tin opener** [-əupnə^r] *(Brit)* *n* otwieracz *m* do puszek *or* konserw

**tinsel** ['tɪnsl] *n* lameta *f*

**tint** [tɪnt] *n* *(colour)* odcień *m*, zabarwienie *nt*; *(for hair)* płukanka *f* koloryzująca ▷ *vt* *(hair)* farbować (ufarbować *perf*)

**tinted** ['tɪntɪd] *adj* *(glass)* barwiony; *(hair)* farbowany

**tiny** ['taɪnɪ] *adj* malutki, maleńki

**tip** [tɪp] *n* *(of paintbrush, tree)* czubek *m*; *(of tongue)* koniec *m*; *(gratuity)* napiwek *m*; *(Brit: for rubbish)* wysypisko *nt*; *(: for coal)* hałda *f*; *(advice)* rada *f*, wskazówka *f* ▷ *vt* *(waiter)* dawać (dać *perf*) napiwek *+dat*; *(bowl, bottle)* przechylać (przechylić *perf*); *(also:* **tip over***)* przewracać (przewrócić *perf*); *(also:* **tip out***)* wysypywać (wysypać *perf*); *(predict)* typować (wytypować *perf*)

▸ **tip off** *vt* udzielać (udzielić *perf*) poufnych informacji *+dat*, dawać (dać *perf*) cynk *+dat* *(inf)*

**tip-off** ['tɪpɔf] *n* poufna informacja *f*, cynk *m* *(inf)*

**tipped** ['tɪpt] *adj* *(Brit)*: **~ cigarette** papieros *m* z filtrem; **steel-~** ze stalowym czubkiem

**Tipp-Ex**® ['tɪpɛks] *n* korektor *m*

**tipple** ['tɪpl] *(Brit)* *vi* popijać *(alkohol)* ▷ *n*: **what's your ~?** co pijesz? *(inf)*

**tipsy** ['tɪpsɪ] *(inf)* *adj* wstawiony *(inf)*

**tiptoe** ['tɪptəu] *n*: **on ~** na palcach *or* paluszkach

**tip-top** ['tɪptɔp] *adj*: **in ~ condition** w pierwszorzędnym stanie

**tire** ['taɪə^r] *n* *(US)* = **tyre** ▷ *vt* męczyć (zmęczyć *perf*) ▷ *vi* męczyć się (zmęczyć się *perf*); **to ~ of** męczyć się (zmęczyć się *perf*) *+instr*

▸ **tire out** *vt* wyczerpywać (wyczerpać *perf*)

**tired** ['taɪəd] *adj* zmęczony; **to be/feel ~** być/ czuć się zmęczonym; **to look ~** wyglądać na zmęczonego; **to be ~ of sth/of doing sth** mieć dosyć czegoś/robienia czegoś
**tiredness** ['taɪədnɪs] *n* zmęczenie *nt*
**tireless** ['taɪəlɪs] *adj* niestrudzony
**tiresome** ['taɪsəm] *adj* dokuczliwy
**tiring** ['taɪərɪŋ] *adj* męczący
**tissue** ['tɪʃu:] *n* (*Anat, Bio*) tkanka *f*; (*paper handkerchief*) chusteczka *f* higieniczna
**tissue paper** *n* bibułka *f*
**tit** [tɪt] *n* (*Zool*) sikora *f*; (*inf*) cycek *m* (*inf*); **tit for tat** wet za wet
**titanium** [tɪ'teɪnɪəm] *n* tytan *m* (*metal*)
**titbit**, (*US*) **tidbit** ['tɪtbɪt] *n* smaczny kąsek *m*; (*fig*) łakomy *or* pikantny kąsek *m*
**titillate** ['tɪtɪleɪt] *vt* podniecać (podniecić *perf*)
**titivate** ['tɪtɪveɪt] *vt* upiększać (upiększyć *perf*)
**title** ['taɪtl] *n* tytuł *m*; (*Jur*): **~ to** tytuł *m or* prawo *nt* do *+gen*
**title deed** *n* tytuł *m* własności
**title page** *n* strona *f* tytułowa
**title role** *n* rola *f* tytułowa
**titter** ['tɪtə^r] *vi* chichotać (zachichotać *perf*)
**tittle-tattle** ['tɪtltætl] (*inf*) *n* gadanina *f*
**tizzy** ['tɪzɪ] *n*: **to be/get in a ~** denerwować się (zdenerwować się *perf*) (bez powodu)
**T-junction** ['ti:'dʒʌŋkʃən] *n* skrzyżowanie *nt* w kształcie litery T
**TM** *abbr* = **trademark**; **transcendental meditation**
**TN** (*US: Post*) *abbr* = **Tennessee**
**TNT** *n abbr* (= *trinitrotoluene*) trotyl *m*

 **KEYWORD**

**to** [tu:, tə] *prep* **1** (*usu*) do *+gen*; **to go to Germany** jechać (pojechać *perf*) do Niemiec; **to count to ten** liczyć (policzyć *perf*) do dziesięciu; **the key to the front door** klucz do drzwi frontowych; **A is to B as C is to D** A ma się do B tak jak C do D; **three goals to two** trzy do dwóch; **to the left/right** na lewo/prawo; **she is secretary to the director** jest sekretarką dyrektora; **30 miles to the gallon** 1 galon na 30 mil
**2** (*with expressions of time*) za *+acc*; **a quarter to five** za kwadrans *or* za piętnaście piąta
**3** (*introducing indirect object*): **to give sth to sb** dawać (dać *perf*) coś komuś; **to talk to sb** rozmawiać (porozmawiać *perf*) z kimś; **to cause damage to sth** uszkadzać (uszkodzić *perf*) coś; **to be a danger to sb/sth** stanowić zagrożenie dla kogoś/czegoś; **to carry out repairs to sth** wykonywać naprawy czegoś
**4** (*purpose, result*): **to come to sb's aid** przychodzić (przyjść *perf*) komuś z pomocą; **to sentence sb to death** skazywać (skazać *perf*) kogoś na śmierć; **to my surprise** ku m(oj)emu zdziwieniu
▷ *with verb* **1** (*simple infinitive*): **to eat** jeść (zjeść *perf*); **to want to sleep** chcieć spać
**2** (*with verb omitted*): **I don't want to** nie chcę; **you ought to** powinieneś
**3** (*purpose, result*) żeby, (a)by; **I did it to help you** zrobiłem to, żeby *or* aby ci pomóc; **he came to see you** przyszedł (, żeby) się z tobą zobaczyć
**4** (*equivalent to relative clause*): **he has a lot to lose** ma wiele do stracenia; **I have things to do** jestem zajęta; **the main thing is to try** najważniejsza rzecz to spróbować
**5** (*after adjective etc*) żeby, (a)by; **too old/young to ...** za stary/młody, żeby *+infin*; **ready to go** gotowy do drogi
▷ *adv*: **to push/pull the door to** przymykać (przymknąć *perf*) drzwi

**toad** [təud] *n* ropucha *f*
**toadstool** ['təudstu:l] *n* muchomor *m*
**toady** ['təudɪ] (*pej*) *vi*: **to ~ to sb** podlizywać się komuś (*pej*)
**toast** [təust] *n* (*Culin*) grzanka *f*, tost *m*; (*drink*) toast *m* ▷ *vt* (*Culin*) opiekać (opiec *perf*); (*drink to*) wznosić (wznieść *perf*) toast za *+acc*; **a piece** *or* **slice of ~** grzanka, tost
**toaster** ['təustə^r] *n* opiekacz *m*, toster *m*
**toastmaster** ['təustmɑ:stə^r] *n osoba kierująca porządkiem wznoszonych toastów*
**toast rack** *n* stojak *m* na grzanki
**tobacco** [tə'bækəu] *n* tytoń *m*; **pipe ~** tytoń fajkowy
**tobacconist** [tə'bækənɪst] *n* właściciel *m* sklepu z wyrobami tytoniowymi
**tobacconist's (shop)** [tə'bækənɪsts-] *n* sklep *m* z wyrobami tytoniowymi
**Tobago** [tə'beɪgəu] *n see* **Trinidad**
**toboggan** [tə'bɔgən] *n* tobogan *m*; (*child's*) sanki *pl*
**today** [tə'deɪ] *adv* dzisiaj, dziś ▷ *n* dzisiaj *nt inv*, dziś *nt inv*; **the writers of ~** dzisiejsi pisarze; **what day is it ~?** jaki jest dzisiaj dzień?; **what date is it ~?** którego dzisiaj mamy?; **~ is the 4th of March** dzisiaj jest 4 marca; **a week ago ~** (dokładnie) tydzień temu; **~'s paper** dzisiejsza gazeta
**toddle** ['tɔdl] (*inf*) *vi*: **to ~ along** dreptać (podreptać *perf*)
**toddler** ['tɔdlə^r] *n* maluch *m*, szkrab *m*
**to-do** [tə'du:] *n* zamieszanie *nt*
**toe** [təu] *n* (*of foot*) palec *m* (u nogi); (*of shoe, sock*) palce *pl*; **to toe the line** (*fig*) podporządkowywać się (podporządkować *perf*); **big/little toe** duży/mały palec u nogi

**ɔehold** ['təuhəuld] *n* (*in climbing*) oparcie *nt* dla stopy; (*fig*): **to get/gain a ~ (in)** zaczepić się (*perf*) (w *+loc*)
**ɔenail** ['təuneɪl] *n* paznokieć *m* u nogi
**ɔffee** ['tɔfɪ] *n* toffi *nt inv*
**ɔffee apple** (*Brit*) *n jabłko na patyku w polewie z toffi*
**ɔga** ['təugə] *n* toga *f*
**ɔgether** [tə'gɛðə^r] *adv* razem; **~ with** razem *or* wraz z *+instr*
**ɔgetherness** [tə'gɛðənɪs] *n* poczucie *nt* wspólnoty
**ɔggle switch** ['tɔgl-] (*Comput*) *n* przełącznik *m* dwustabilny
**ogo** ['təugəu] *n* Togo *nt inv*
**ɔgs** [tɔgz] (*inf*) *npl* ciuchy *pl* (*inf*)
**ɔil** [tɔɪl] *n* trud *m* ▷ *vi* trudzić się
**ɔilet** ['tɔɪlət] *n* toaleta *f* ▷ *cpd* toaletowy; **to go to the ~** iść (pójść (*perf*)) do toalety
**ɔilet bag** (*Brit*) *n* kosmetyczka *f*
**ɔilet bowl** *n* muszla *f* klozetowa
**ɔilet paper** *n* papier *m* toaletowy
**ɔiletries** ['tɔɪlətrɪz] *npl* przybory *pl* toaletowe
**ɔilet roll** *n* rolka *f* papieru toaletowego
**ɔilet soap** *n* mydło *nt* toaletowe
**ɔilet water** *n* woda *f* toaletowa
**ɔ-ing and fro-ing** ['tu:ɪŋən'frəuɪŋ] (*Brit*) *n* kursowanie *nt* w tę i z powrotem
**ɔken** ['təukən] *n* (*sign*) znak *m*; (*souvenir*) pamiątka *f*; (*substitute coin*) żeton *m* ▷ *adj* symboliczny; **by the same ~** (*for the same reasons*) z tych samych powodów; (*in the same way*) tak samo; (*thereby*) tym samym; **~ strike** strajk manifestacyjny; **gift ~** (*Brit*) talon *or* bon na zakupy (*dawany w prezencie*)
**okyo** ['təukjəu] *n* Tokio *nt inv*
**ɔld** [təuld] *pt, pp of* **tell**
**olerable** ['tɔlərəbl] *adj* znośny
**ɔlerably** ['tɔlərəblɪ] *adv*: **~ good** dość dobry
**olerance** ['tɔlərns] *n* tolerancja *f*
**olerant** ['tɔlərnt] *adj* tolerancyjny; **to be ~ of** być wytrzymałym na *+acc*
**olerate** ['tɔləreɪt] *vt* znosić (znieść *perf*)
**ɔleration** [tɔlə'reɪʃən] *n* tolerancja *f*; **~ of** (*person*) tolerancja w stosunku do *+gen*; (*pain, noise*) wytrzymałość na *+acc*
**oll** [təul] *n* (*casualties*) liczba *f* ofiar; (*charge*) opłata *f* (za przejazd) ▷ *vi* (*bell*) bić; **death ~** liczba ofiar śmiertelnych; **the work took its ~ on us** praca dała nam się we znaki
**ollbridge** ['təulbrɪdʒ] *n* most *m* z płatnym przejazdem
**oll road** *n* droga *f* z płatnym przejazdem
**omato** [tə'mɑ:təu] (*pl* **~es**) *n* pomidor *m*
**omato purée** *n* przecier *m* pomidorowy
**omb** [tu:m] *n* grobowiec *m*
**ombola** [tɔm'bəulə] *n* loteria *f*
**tomboy** ['tɔmbɔɪ] *n* chłopczyca *f*
**tombstone** ['tu:mstəun] *n* nagrobek *m*
**tomcat** ['tɔmkæt] *n* kocur *m*
**tome** [təum] (*fml*) *n* tom *m*
**tomorrow** [tə'mɔrəu] *adv* jutro ▷ *n* jutro *nt*; **a week ~** od jutra za tydzień; **~ morning** jutro rano; **the day after ~** pojutrze; **~'s performance** jutrzejsze przedstawienie
**ton** [tʌn] *n* (*metric ton*) tona *f*; (*Brit*) *1016 kg*; (*US*: *also*: **short ton**) *907,18 kg*; **I've got tons of books** (*inf*) mam masę książek (*inf*)
**tonal** ['təunl] *adj* tonalny
**tone** [təun] *n* ton *m*; (*Tel*) sygnał *m* ▷ *vi*: **to ~ in with** pasować do *+gen*, harmonizować z *+instr*
▸ **tone down** *vt* tonować (stonować *perf*)
▸ **tone up** *vt* (*muscles*) wyrabiać (wyrobić *perf*)
**tone-deaf** [təun'dɛf] *adj* pozbawiony słuchu
**toner** ['təunə^r] *n* (*for photocopier*) toner *m*
**Tonga** [tɔŋə] *n* Tonga *nt inv*
**tongs** [tɔŋz] *npl* szczypce *pl*; (*also*: **curling tongs**) lokówka *f* (nożycowa)
**tongue** [tʌŋ] *n* język *m*; (*Culin*) ozór *m*, ozorek *m*; **~ in cheek** (*speak, say*) żartem
**tongue-tied** ['tʌŋtaɪd] *adj* (*fig*): **he was ~** język stanął mu kołkiem
**tongue-twister** ['tʌŋtwɪstə^r] *n* łamaniec *m* językowy
**tonic** ['tɔnɪk] *n* (*Med*) lek *m* tonizujący; (*also*: **tonic water**) tonik *m*; (*Mus*) tonika *f*; (*fig*) pokrzepienie *nt*
**tonight** [tə'naɪt] *adv* (*this evening*) dzisiaj *or* dziś wieczorem; (*this night*) dzisiejszej nocy ▷ *n* (*this evening*) dzisiejszy wieczór *m*; (*this night*) dzisiejsza noc *f*; **(I'll) see you ~!** do zobaczenia wieczorem!; **in ~'s programme** w dzisiejszym programie
**tonnage** ['tʌnɪdʒ] *n* tonaż *m*
**tonne** [tʌn] (*Brit*) *n* tona *f* (metryczna)
**tonsil** ['tɔnsl] *n* migdałek *m*; **he had to have his ~s out** trzeba mu było wyciąć migdałki
**tonsillitis** [tɔnsɪ'laɪtɪs] *n* zapalenie *nt* migdałków, angina *f*
**too** [tu:] *adv* (*excessively*) zbyt, za; (*also*) też, także ▷ *adj*: **there's too much water** jest za dużo wody; **there are too many people** jest za dużo ludzi; **it's too sweet** to zbyt słodkie; **I went there too** ja też tam poszedłem; **she loves him too much to ...** zbyt *or* zanadto go kocha, żeby *+infin*; **too bad!** (wielka) szkoda!
**took** [tuk] *pt of* **take**
**tool** [tu:l] *n* narzędzie *nt*
**tool box** *n* skrzynka *f* narzędziowa
**tool kit** *n* zestaw *m* narzędzi
**toot** [tu:t] *n* (*of horn*) trąbienie *nt*; (*of whistle*) gwizd *m* ▷ *vi* (*with car-horn*) trąbić (zatrąbić *perf*)

t

**tooth** [tu:θ] (*pl* **teeth**) *n* ząb *m*; **to have a ~ out** *or (US)* **pulled** mieć wyrwany ząb; **to brush one's teeth** myć (umyć *perf*) zęby; **by the skin of one's teeth** (*fig*) o mały włos
**toothache** ['tu:θeɪk] *n* ból *m* zęba; **she has ~** boli ją ząb
**toothbrush** ['tu:θbrʌʃ] *n* szczoteczka *f* do zębów
**toothpaste** ['tu:θpeɪst] *n* pasta *f* do zębów
**toothpick** ['tu:θpɪk] *n* wykałaczka *f*
**toothpowder** ['tu:θpaudə^r] *n* proszek *m* do czyszczenia zębów
**top** [tɔp] *n* (*of mountain, ladder*) szczyt *m*; (*of tree*) wierzchołek *m*; (*of cupboard, table*) blat *m*; (*of page, pyjamas*) góra *f*; (*of bottle*) zakrętka *f*; (*of jar, box*) wieczko *nt*; (*also*: **top gear**) najwyższy bieg *m*; (*also*: **spinning top**) bąk *m*; (*blouse etc*) góra *f* ▷ *adj* najwyższy ▷ *vt* (*be first in*) znajdować się (znaleźć się *perf*) na czele *+gen*; (*exceed*) przewyższać (przewyższyć *perf*); **at the top of the stairs** u szczytu schodów; **at the top of the street** na (drugim) końcu ulicy; **on top of** (*on*) na *+loc*; (*in addition to*) w dodatku do *+gen*; **on top of that** na dodatek; **from top to bottom** od góry do dołu; **from top to toe** (*Brit*) od stóp do głów; **at the top of the list** na początku listy; **at the top of one's voice** na cały głos; **a top player** jeden z najlepszych graczy; **at top speed** z maksymalną prędkością; **to go over the top** (*inf*) przeholować (*perf*) (*inf*)
▸ **top up**, (*US*) **top off** *vt* (*salary*) podnosić (podnieść *perf*); (*phone*) doładowywać (doładować *perf*); **to top up sb's drink** *or* **glass** dolewać (dolać *perf*) komuś
**topaz** ['təupæz] *n* topaz *m*
**topcoat** ['tɔpkəut] *n* (*of paint*) warstwa *f* zewnętrzna
**top floor** *n* najwyższe piętro *nt*
**top hat** *n* cylinder *m*
**top-heavy** [tɔp'hɛvɪ] *adj* (*object*) przeciążony u góry; (*fig: organization*) z przerostem kierownictwa *post*
**topic** ['tɔpɪk] *n* temat *m*
**topical** ['tɔpɪkl] *adj* aktualny
**topless** ['tɔplɪs] *adj* (*bather*) rozebrany do pasa; (*waitress*) w toplesie *post* (*inf*)
**top-level** ['tɔplɛvl] *adj* na najwyższym szczeblu *post*
**topmost** ['tɔpməust] *adj* najwyższy
**topography** [tə'pɔgrəfɪ] *n* topografia *f*
**topping** ['tɔpɪŋ] *n* (*on dessert*) przybranie *nt*; (*on pizza*) dodatek *m*
**topple** ['tɔpl] *vt* (*government, leader*) obalać (obalić *perf*) ▷ *vi* przewracać się (przewrócić się *perf*)
**top-ranking** ['tɔpræŋkɪŋ] *adj* wysoko postawiony
**top-secret** ['tɔp'si:krɪt] *adj* ściśle tajny
**top-security** ['tɔpsə'kjuərɪtɪ] (*Brit*) *adj*: **~ prison** więzienie *nt* o zaostrzonych środkach bezpieczeństwa
**topsy-turvy** ['tɔpsɪ'tə:vɪ] *adj* postawiony na głowie, przewrócony do góry nogami ▷ *adv* do góry nogami
**top-up** ['tɔpʌp] *n*: **would you like a ~?** dolać Panu/Pani?
**torch** [tɔ:tʃ] *n* (*with flame*) pochodnia *f*; (*Brit: electric*) latarka *f*
**tore** [tɔ:^r] *pt of* **tear**
**torment** [*n* 'tɔ:mɛnt, *vb* tɔ:'mɛnt] *n* męczarnie *pl* ▷ *vt* dręczyć
**torn** [tɔ:n] *pp of* **tear¹** ▷ *adj*: **~ between** (*fig*) rozdarty pomiędzy *+instr*
**tornado** [tɔ:'neɪdəu] (*pl* **~es**) *n* tornado *nt*
**torpedo** [tɔ:'pi:dəu] (*pl* **~es**) *n* torpeda *f*
**torpedo boat** *n* kuter *m* torpedowy
**torpor** ['tɔ:pə^r] *n* odrętwienie *nt*
**torrent** ['tɔrnt] *n* (*lit, fig*) potok *m*
**torrential** [tɔ'rɛnʃl] *adj* ulewny
**torrid** ['tɔrɪd] *adj* (*weather*) skwarny; (*love affair*) gorący
**torso** ['tɔ:səu] *n* tułów *m*
**tortoise** ['tɔ:təs] *n* żółw *m* (*lądowy lub słodkowodny*)
**tortoiseshell** ['tɔ:təʃɛl] *adj* (*jewellery, ornaments*) szylkretowy; (*cat*) brązowo-czarno-żółty
**tortuous** ['tɔ:tjuəs] *adj* (*path*) kręty; (*argument, essay*) zawiły
**torture** ['tɔ:tʃə^r] *n* tortury *pl*; (*fig*) tortura *f*, męczarnia *f* ▷ *vt* torturować; (*fig*) zadręczać
**torturer** ['tɔ:tʃərə^r] *n* oprawca *m*, kat *m*
**Tory** ['tɔ:rɪ] (*Brit*) *adj* torysowski ▷ *n* torys *m*
**toss** [tɔs] *vt* (*object*) rzucać (rzucić *perf*); (*salad*) mieszać (wymieszać *perf*); (*pancake*) przewracać (przewrócić *perf*) (w locie); (*one's head*) odrzucać (odrzucić *perf*) do tyłu ▷ *n*: **with a ~ of her head** (gwałtownie) odrzucając głowę do tyłu; **to ~ a coin** rzucać (rzucić *perf*) monetę; **to ~ up for sth** grać (zagrać *perf*) o coś w orła i reszkę; **to ~ and turn** (*in bed*) przewracać się (z boku na bok), rzucać się; **to win/lose the ~** wygrywać (wygrać *perf*)/przegrywać (przegrać *perf*) losowanie
**tot** [tɔt] *n* (*Brit: drink*) kropelka *f*, kapka *f*; (*child*) szkrab *m*, brzdąc *m*
▸ **tot up** (*Brit*) *vt* sumować (zsumować *perf*)
**total** ['təutl] *adj* (*number, cost*) całkowity; (*failure, wreck, stranger*) zupełny ▷ *n* (*of figures*) suma *f*; (*of things, people*) ogólna liczba *f* ▷ *vt* (*add up*) sumować (zsumować *perf*), dodawać (dodać *perf*); (*add up to*) wynosić (wynieść *perf*); **in ~** w sumie

**totalitarian** [təutælɪ'tɛərɪən] *adj* totalitarny
**totality** [təu'tælɪtɪ] *n* całość *f*
**totally** ['təutəlɪ] *adv* całkowicie, zupełnie
**totem pole** ['təutəm-] *n* słup *m* totemiczny
**totter** ['tɔtə^r] *vi* (*person*) zataczać się (zatoczyć się *perf*), chwiać się (zachwiać się *perf*) (na nogach); (*fig*: *government*) chwiać się
**touch** [tʌtʃ] *n* (*sense*) dotyk *m*; (*contact*) dotknięcie *nt*; (*skill*) ręka *f* ▷ *vt* dotykać (dotknąć *perf*) *+gen*; (*tamper with*) tykać (tknąć *perf*); (*emotionally*: *move*) wzruszać (wzruszyć *perf*); (: *stir*) poruszać (poruszyć *perf*) ▷ *vi* dotykać się (dotknąć się *perf*), stykać się (zetknąć się *perf*); **the personal ~** indywidualne podejście; **to put the finishing ~es to sth** wykańczać (wykończyć *perf*) coś; **a ~ of** (*fig*) odrobina *+gen*; **in ~ with** w kontakcie z *+instr*; **to put sb in ~ with** kontaktować (skontaktować *perf*) kogoś z *+instr*; **to get in ~ with sb** kontaktować się (skontaktować się *perf*) z kimś; **I'll be in ~** odezwę się; **we've lost ~** straciliśmy (ze sobą) kontakt; **to be out of ~ with events** nie nadążać za biegiem wypadków, nie być na bieżąco; **~ wood!** odpukać (w niemalowane drewno)!
▸ **touch on** *vt fus* (*topic*) poruszać (poruszyć *perf*) *+acc*
▸ **touch up** *vt* retuszować (podretuszować *perf*)
**touch-and-go** ['tʌtʃən'gəu] *adj* niepewny; **it was ~ whether we'd succeed** nie było pewne, czy nam się uda
**touchdown** ['tʌtʃdaun] *n* (*of rocket, plane*) lądowanie *nt*; (*US*: *Football*) przyłożenie *nt*
**touched** [tʌtʃt] *adj* (*moved*) wzruszony; (*inf*: *mad*) szurnięty (*inf*)
**touching** ['tʌtʃɪŋ] *adj* wzruszający
**touchline** ['tʌtʃlaɪn] (*Sport*) *n* linia *f* autowa *or* boczna
**touch-type** ['tʌtʃtaɪp] *vi* pisać (na maszynie) bez patrzenia na klawiaturę
**touchy** ['tʌtʃɪ] *adj* (*person*) przewrażliwiony; (*subject*) drażliwy
**tough** [tʌf] *adj* (*material, meat, policy*) twardy; (*shoes, rope*) mocny; (*person, animal*) wytrzymały; (*choice, task*) trudny, ciężki; (*neighbourhood*) niebezpieczny; **~ luck!** trudno!; **they're having a ~ time** jest im ciężko
**toughen** ['tʌfn] *vt* (*sb's character*) hartować (zahartować *perf*); (*glass etc*) utwardzać (utwardzić *perf*), hartować
**toughness** ['tʌfnɪs] *n* (*of person*) wytrzymałość *f*, hart *m* (ducha); (*of glass etc*) twardość *f*
**toupee** ['tu:peɪ] *n* tupecik *m*, peruczka *f*

**tour** ['tuə^r] *n*: **a ~ (of)** (*country, region*) podróż *f* (po *+loc*); (*town, museum*) wycieczka *f* (po *+loc*); (*by pop group etc*) tournée *nt inv* (po *+loc*) ▷ *vt* (*in vehicle*) objeżdżać (objechać *perf*); (*on foot*) obchodzić (obejść *perf*), zwiedzać (zwiedzić *perf*); **to go on a ~ of** wybierać się (wybrać się *perf*) na wycieczkę po *+loc*; **to be on ~** być w trasie; **to go on ~** wyjeżdżać (wyjechać *perf*) w trasę
**touring** ['tuərɪŋ] *n* zwiedzanie *nt*; (*of pop group etc*) tournée *nt inv*
**tourism** ['tuərɪzm] *n* turystyka *f*
**tourist** ['tuərɪst] *n* turysta(-tka) *m(f)* ▷ *cpd* turystyczny; **the ~ trade** przemysł turystyczny
**tourist class** (*Naut, Aviat*) *n* klasa *f* turystyczna
**tourist information centre** (*Brit*) *n* biuro *nt* informacji turystycznej
**tourist office** *n* biuro *nt* turystyczne
**tournament** ['tuənəmənt] *n* turniej *m*
**tourniquet** ['tuənɪkeɪ] *n* opaska *f* uciskowa
**tour operator** (*Brit*) *n* organizator *m* wycieczki
**tousled** ['tauzld] *adj* potargany, rozczochrany
**tout** [taut] *vi*: **to ~ for business/custom** nagabywać (potencjalnych) klientów ▷ *n* (*also*: **ticket tout**) konik *m*
**tow** [təu] *vt* holować ▷ *n*: **to give sb a tow** (*Aut*) brać (wziąć *perf*) kogoś na hol; **"on** *or* (*US*) **in tow"** (*Aut*) „pojazd na holu"
**toward(s)** [tə'wɔ:d(z)] *prep* (*to*) do *+gen*, ku *+dat* (*fml*); (*in direction of*) w kierunku *or* stronę *+gen*; (*in relation to*) do *+gen*, wobec *+gen*; (*as conribution to*) na *+acc*, na rzecz *+gen*; **towards noon** około południa; **towards the end (of the year)** pod koniec (roku); **to feel friendly ~ sb** czuć do kogoś sympatię
**tow away** *vt* odholowywać (odholować *perf*)
**towel** ['tauəl] *n*: **(hand/bath) ~** ręcznik *m* (do rąk/kąpielowy); **to throw in the ~** (*fig*) poddawać się (poddać się *perf*)
**towelling** ['tauəlɪŋ] *n* tkanina *f* frotté
**towel rail**, (*US*) **towel rack** *n* wieszak *m* na ręczniki
**tower** ['tauə^r] *n* wieża *f* ▷ *vi*: **to ~ (above** *or* **over sb/sth)** wznosić się (nad kimś/czymś)
**tower block** (*Brit*) *n* wieżowiec *m*
**towering** ['tauərɪŋ] *adj* gigantyczny
**towline** ['təulaɪn] *n* (*Naut*) lina *f* holownicza
**town** [taun] *n* miasto *nt*; **to go to ~** iść (pójść *perf*) do miasta; (*fig*) zaszaleć (*perf*) (*inf*); **I had lunch in ~** zjadłem obiad na mieście; **I'll be out of ~** nie będzie mnie w mieście
**town centre** *n* centrum *nt* (miasta)
**town clerk** *n* urzędnik *m* miejski
**town council** *n* rada *f* miejska

**town hall** *n* ratusz *m*
**town plan** *n* plan *m* miasta
**town planner** *n* urbanista(-tka) *m(f)*
**town planning** *n* urbanistyka *f*
**townspeople** ['taunzpi:pl] *npl* mieszkańcy *pl* miasta
**towpath** ['təupɑ:θ] *n ścieżka wzdłuż kanału lub rzeki, którą chodziły konie holujące barki*
**towrope** ['təurəup] *n* (*Aut*) linka *f* holownicza, hol *m*
**tow truck** (*US*) *n* holownik *m* (*pojazd serwisowy*)
**toxic** ['tɔksɪk] *adj* toksyczny, trujący
**toxin** ['tɔksɪn] *n* toksyna *f*, substancja *f* trująca
**toy** [tɔɪ] *n* zabawka *f*
▸ **toy with** *vt fus* (*object, food*) bawić się *+instr*; (*idea*) rozważać
**toyshop** ['tɔɪʃɔp] *n* sklep *m* z zabawkami
**trace** [treɪs] *n* (*sign, small amount*) ślad *m*; (*of emotion*) cień *m* ▹ *vt* (*draw*) odrysowywać (odrysować *perf*) przez kalkę, kalkować (przekalkować *perf*); (*locate*) odszukiwać (odszukać *perf*); (*: cause*) odkrywać (odkryć *perf*); **without ~** bez śladu; **there was no ~ of him** zniknął bez śladu; **empiricism can be ~d back to Hume and Locke** empiryzm wywodzi się od Hume'a i Locke'a
**trace element** *n* pierwiastek *m* śladowy
**trachea** [trə'kɪə] *n* tchawica *f*
**tracing paper** ['treɪsɪŋ-] *n* kalka *f* techniczna
**track** [træk] *n* (*road*) droga *f* (*gruntowa*); (*path*) ścieżka *f*; (*of bullet, planet, for train*) tor *m*; (*of suspect, animal*) ślad *m*; (*on tape, record*) utwór *m*; (*Sport*) bieżnia *f* ▹ *vt* tropić (wytropić *perf*); **to keep ~ of** (*fig*) śledzić *+acc*; **to be on the right ~** (*fig*) zmierzać we właściwym kierunku
▸ **track down** *vt* tropić (wytropić *perf*)
**tracker dog** ['trækə-] (*Brit*) *n* pies *m* gończy
**track events** *npl* biegi *pl* lekkoatletyczne
**tracking station** ['trækɪŋ-] *n* stacja *f* śledzenia (*lotu obiektów kosmicznych*)
**track record** *n*: **to have a good ~** mieć na swoim koncie osiągnięcia
**tracksuit** ['træksu:t] *n* dres *m*
**tract** [trækt] *n* (*of land*) przestrzeń *f*; (*pamphlet*) traktat *m*; **respiratory ~** drogi oddechowe
**traction** ['trækʃən] *n* (*power*) trakcja *f*; (*Aut*) przyczepność *f*; (*Med*): **in ~** na wyciągu
**traction engine** *n* lokomobila *f*
**tractor** ['træktə^r] *n* traktor *m*, ciągnik *m*
**trade** [treɪd] *n* (*exchanging goods*) handel *m*; (*business*) branża *f*; (*skill, job*) fach *m* ▹ *vi* handlować ▹ *vt*: **to ~ sth (for sth)** wymieniać (wymienić *perf*) coś (na coś); **to ~ in/with** prowadzić handel *+instr*/z *+instr*; **foreign ~** handel zagraniczny; **Department of T~ and Industry** (*Brit*) Ministerstwo Handlu i Przemysłu
▸ **trade in** *vt* wymieniać (wymienić *perf*) na nowy za dopłatą
**trade barrier** *n* bariera *f* handlowa
**trade deficit** *n* deficyt *m* handlowy
**Trade Descriptions Act** (*Brit*) *n ustawa regulująca zasady opisu i reklamy produktów*
**trade discount** *n* rabat *m* hurtowy
**trade fair** *n* targi *pl* handlowe
**trade-in** ['treɪdɪn] *n*: **to take sth as a ~** *przyjąć coś, najczęściej używanego, w rozliczeniu za nowy artykuł*
**trade-in value** *n* wartość *f* wymienna
**trademark** ['treɪdmɑ:k] *n* znak *m* fabryczny towarowy
**trade mission** *n* przedstawicielstwo *nt* handlowe
**trade name** *n* nazwa *f* handlowa *or* firmowa
**trader** ['treɪdə^r] *n* handlowiec *m*
**trade secret** *n* tajemnica *f* handlowa; (*fig*) tajemnica *f*
**tradesman** ['treɪdzmən] *n* (*irreg: like* **man**); (*shopkeeper*) handlowiec *m*
**trade union** *n* związek *m* zawodowy
**trade unionist** [-'ju:njənɪst] *n* działacz(ka) *m(f)* związkowy(wa) *m(f)*
**trade wind** *n* pasat *m*
**trading** ['treɪdɪŋ] *n* handel *m*
**trading estate** (*Brit*) *n* teren *m* przemysłowy
**trading stamp** *n* kupon *m* premiowy (*w handlu detalicznym*)
**tradition** [trə'dɪʃən] *n* tradycja *f*
**traditional** [trə'dɪʃənl] *adj* tradycyjny
**traditionally** [trə'dɪʃnəlɪ] *adv* tradycyjnie
**traffic** ['træfɪk] *n* (*Aut, Aviat etc*) ruch *m*; (*in drugs, stolen goods*) handel *m* ▹ *vi*: **to ~ in** handlować *+instr*
**traffic circle** (*US*) *n* rondo *nt*
**traffic island** (*Aut*) *n* wysepka *f*
**traffic jam** *n* korek *m* (uliczny)
**trafficker** ['træfɪkə^r] *n* handlarz(-arka) *m(f)* (*nielegalnym towarem*)
**traffic lights** *npl* sygnalizacja *f* świetlna, światła *pl*
**traffic offence** (*Brit*) *n* wykroczenie *nt* drogowe
**traffic sign** *n* znak *m* drogowy
**traffic violation** (*US*) *n* = **traffic offence**
**traffic warden** *n funkcjonariusz kontrolujący prawidłowość parkowania pojazdów*
**tragedy** ['trædʒədɪ] *n* tragedia *f*
**tragic** ['trædʒɪk] *adj* tragiczny
**tragically** ['trædʒɪkəlɪ] *adv* tragicznie
**trail** [treɪl] *n* (*path*) szlak *m*; (*of smoke*) smuga *f* ▹ *vt* (*drag*) ciągnąć; (*follow*) tropić ▹ *vi* (*hang loosely*) ciągnąć się; (*in game, contest*) przegrywać; **a ~ of footprints** ślady; **to be**

**on sb's ~** podążać czyimś tropem *or* śladem
**trail away** *vi* (*sound, voice*) zamierać
zamrzeć *perf*)
**trail behind** *vi* ciągnąć się (z tyłu)
**trail off** *vi* = **trail away**

**ailer** ['treɪlə<sup>r</sup>] *n* (*Aut*) przyczepa *f*; (*US*: *aravan*) przyczepa *f* kempingowa; (*Film, TV*) ;wiastun *m*

**ailer truck** *n* (*US*) ciężarówka *f* z naczepą

**ain** [treɪn] *n* (*Rail*) pociąg *m*; (*underground rain*) kolejka *f* (podziemna); (*of dress*) tren *m* ▷ *vt* (*apprentice, doctor*) szkolić (wyszkolić *perf*); *dog*) tresować (wytresować *perf*); (*athlete*) renować (wytrenować *perf*); (*mind*) ćwiczyć wyćwiczyć *perf*); (*plant*): **to ~ along** puszczać puścić *perf*) wzdłuż *+gen*; (*camera, gun*): **to ~ on** :elować (wycelować *perf*) w *+acc* ▷ *vi* (*learn a kill*) szkolić się; (*Sport*) trenować; **my ~ of thought** tok moich myśli; **~ of events** bieg wydarzeń; **to go by ~** jechać (pojechać *perf*) pociągiem; **to ~ sb to do sth** szkolić wyszkolić *perf*) kogoś w robieniu czegoś

**ain attendant** (*US*) *n* ≈ konduktor *m*

**ained** [treɪnd] *adj* (*worker, manpower*) wykwalifikowany; (*animal*) tresowany; (*eye*) wprawny

**ainee** [treɪ'ni:] *n* praktykant(ka) *m(f)*, stażysta(-tka) *m(f)*

**ainer** ['treɪnə<sup>r</sup>] *n* (*coach*) trener(ka) *m(f)*; *shoe*) but *m* sportowy; (*of animals*) treser(ka) *n(f)*

**aining** ['treɪnɪŋ] *n* (*for occupation*) szkolenie *it*; (*Sport*) trening *m*; **to be in ~ for** (*Sport*) trenować do *+gen*

**aining college** *n* (*for teachers*) kolegium *nt* nauczycielskie

**aining course** *n* kurs *m* szkoleniowy

**aipse** [treɪps] *vi*: **to ~ (a)round** włóczyć się po *+loc*

**ait** [treɪt] *n* cecha *f*

**aitor** ['treɪtə<sup>r</sup>] *n* zdrajca(-jczyni) *m(f)*

**ajectory** [trə'dʒɛktərɪ] *n* tor *m*

**am** [træm] (*Brit*) *n* (*also*: **tramcar**) tramwaj *m*

**amline** ['træmlaɪn] *n* szyny *pl or* tory *pl* tramwajowe

**amp** [træmp] *n* włóczęga *m*, tramp *m*; (*inf, pej*) dziwka *f* (*inf, pej*) ▷ *vi* brnąć ▷ *vt* (*town, streets*) przemierzać

**ample** ['træmpl] *vt*: **to ~ (underfoot)** deptać (podeptać *perf*) ▷ *vi*: **to ~ on** (*sb's feelings, rights*) deptać (podeptać *perf*)

**ampoline** ['træmpəli:n] *n* trampolina *f*

**ance** [trɑ:ns] *n* trans *m*; **to go into a ~** wpadać (wpaść *perf*) w trans

**anquil** ['træŋkwɪl] *adj* spokojny

**anquillity**, (*US*) **tranquility** [træŋ'kwɪlɪtɪ] *n* spokój *m*

**tranquillizer**, (*US*) **tranquilizer** ['træŋkwɪlaɪzə<sup>r</sup>] *n* środek *m* uspokajający

**transact** [træn'zækt] *vt* (*business*) załatwiać (załatwić *perf*); (*deal*) zawierać (zawrzeć *perf*)

**transaction** [træn'zækʃən] *n* transakcja *f*; **cash ~** transakcja gotówkowa

**transatlantic** ['trænzət'læntɪk] *adj* transatlantycki

**transcend** [træn'sɛnd] *vt* wykraczać poza *+acc*

**transcendental** [trænsɛn'dɛntl] *adj* transcendentalny

**transcribe** [træn'skraɪb] *vt* transkrybować (przetranskrybować *perf*)

**transcript** ['trænskrɪpt] *n* zapis *m*, transkrypt *m*

**transcription** [træn'skrɪpʃən] *n* transkrypcja *f*

**transept** ['trænsɛpt] *n* transept *m*, nawa *f* poprzeczna

**transfer** [*n* 'trænsfə<sup>r</sup>, *vb* træns'fə:<sup>r</sup>] *n* (*of employee*) przeniesienie *nt*; (*of money*) przelew *m*; (*of power*) przekazanie *nt*; (*Sport*) transfer *m*; (*picture etc*) kalkomania *f* ▷ *vt* (*employee*) przenosić (przenieść *perf*); (*money*) przelewać (przelać *perf*); (*power, ownership*) przekazywać (przekazać *perf*); **to ~ the charges** (*Brit*) telefonować (zatelefonować *perf*) na koszt przyjmującego rozmowę; **by bank ~** przelewem bankowym

**transferable** [træns'fə:rəbl] *adj* (*Jur*) zbywalny; **"not ~"** (*on ticket*) ≈ „bilet nie może być odstępowany"

**transfix** [træns'fɪks] *vt* przebijać (przebić *perf*), przeszywać (przeszyć *perf*); **~ed with fear** skamieniały ze strachu

**transform** [træns'fɔ:m] *vt* odmieniać (odmienić *perf*); **to ~ into** przekształcać (przekształcić *perf*) w *+acc*

**transformation** [trænsfə'meɪʃən] *n* przemiana *f*, transformacja *f*

**transformer** [træns'fɔ:mə<sup>r</sup>] (*Elec*) *n* transformator *m*

**transfusion** [træns'fju:ʒən] *n* (*also*: **blood transfusion**) transfuzja *f* (krwi)

**transgress** [træns'grɛs] *vt* przekraczać (przekroczyć *perf*)

**transient** ['trænzɪənt] *adj* przelotny

**transistor** [træn'zɪstə<sup>r</sup>] *n* tranzystor *m*

**transit** ['trænzɪt] *n*: **in ~** (*things*) podczas transportu; (*people*) w podróży

**transit camp** *n* obóz *m* przejściowy

**transition** [træn'zɪʃən] *n* przejście *nt*

**transitional** [træn'zɪʃənl] *adj* przejściowy

**transitive** ['trænzɪtɪv] *adj* (*Ling*) przechodni

**transit lounge** *n* (*at airport etc*) hala *f* tranzytowa

**transitory** ['trænzɪtərɪ] *adj* (*emotion*) przemijający, krótkotrwały; (*arrangement, character*) przejściowy

t

**transit visa** *n* wiza *f* tranzytowa
**translate** [trænz'leɪt] *vt*: **to ~ (from/into)** tłumaczyć (przetłumaczyć *perf*) *or* przekładać (przełożyć *perf*) (z *+gen*/na *+acc*)
**translation** [trænz'leɪʃən] *n* tłumaczenie *nt*, przekład *m*; **in ~** w tłumaczeniu *or* przekładzie
**translator** [trænz'leɪtə^r] *n* tłumacz(ka) *m(f)*
**translucent** [trænz'lu:snt] *adj* półprzezroczysty
**transmission** [trænz'mɪʃən] *n* (*of information, energy, data*) przesyłanie *nt*; (*of disease*) przenoszenie *nt*; (*TV*) transmisja *f*; (*Aut*) przekładnia *f*
**transmit** [trænz'mɪt] *vt* (*message, signal*) przesyłać (przesłać *perf*), transmitować; (*disease*) przenosić (przenieść *perf*); (*Radio, TV*) nadawać (nadać *perf*), transmitować; (*knowledge, ideas*) przekazywać (przekazać *perf*)
**transmitter** [trænz'mɪtə^r] *n* przekaźnik *m*
**transparency** [træns'pɛərnsɪ] *n* (*quality*) przezroczystość *f*; (*Brit*: *Phot*) przezrocze *nt*
**transparent** [træns'pærnt] *adj* przezroczysty; (*fig*) jawny, oczywisty
**transpire** [træns'paɪə^r] *vi* (*become known*): **it finally ~d that ...** w końcu okazało się *or* wyszło na jaw, że ...; (*happen*): **nobody knows what ~d at the meeting** nikt nie wie, co się wydarzyło na zebraniu
**transplant** [*vb* træns'plɑ:nt, *n* 'trænsplɑ:nt] *vt* (*Med*) przeszczepiać (przeszczepić *perf*); (*seedlings*) przesadzać (przesadzić *perf*) ▷ *n* (*Med*) przeszczep *m*; **to have a heart ~** mieć przeszczepione serce
**transport** [*n* 'trænspɔ:t, *vb* træns'pɔ:t] *n* transport *m* ▷ *vt* przewozić (przewieźć *perf*); **public ~** ≈ komunikacja miejska; **Department of T~** (*Brit*) ≈ Ministerstwo Transportu
**transportation** ['trænspɔ:'teɪʃən] *n* (*moving*) przewóz *m*, transport *m*; (*means of transport*) środek *m* transportu; **Department of T~** (*US*) ≈ Ministerstwo Transportu
**transport café** (*Brit*) *n* bar *m* przydrożny
**transpose** [træns'pəuz] *vt* transponować (przetransponować *perf*)
**transverse** ['trænzvə:s] *adj* (*beam etc*) poprzeczny
**transvestite** [trænz'vɛstaɪt] *n* transwestyta(-tka) *m(f)*
**trap** [træp] *n* (*for mice, rats*) pułapka *f*; (*for larger animals*) sidła *pl*, wnyki *pl*; (*carriage*) dwukółka *f*; (*fig*) pułapka *f*, zasadzka *f* ▷ *vt* (*mouse*) łapać (złapać *perf*) w pułapkę; (*hare etc*) łapać (złapać *perf*) w sidła *or* we wnyki; (*energy*) pozyskiwać; (*fig*: *trick*) łapać (złapać *perf*) w pułapkę; **to set** *or* **lay a ~ (for sb)** zastawiać (zastawić *perf*) (na kogoś) pułapkę; **to be ~ped** (*in bad marriage, under rubble etc*) być uwięzionym; **he ~ped his finger in the door** przytrzasnął sobie palec drzwiami; **shut your ~!** (*inf!*) stul gębę! (*inf!*)
**trap door, trapdoor** *n* drzwi *pl* spustowe; (*in stage*) zapadnia *f*; (*in mine*) drzwi *pl* zapadowe
**trapeze** [trə'pi:z] *n* trapez *m* (*przyrząd*)
**trapper** ['træpə^r] *n* traper *m*
**trappings** ['træpɪŋz] *npl* przywileje *pl*
**trash** [træʃ] *n* (*rubbish*) śmieci *pl*; (*pej*: *books etc*) chłam *m* (*pej*)
**trash can** (*US*) *n* kosz *m* na śmieci
**trashy** ['træʃɪ] *adj* szmirowaty
**trauma** ['trɔ:mə] *n* bolesne przeżycie *nt*; (*Med, Psych*) uraz *m*, trauma *f*
**traumatic** [trɔ:'mætɪk] *adj* traumatyczny
**travel** ['trævl] *n* podróż *f* ▷ *vi* (*person*) podróżować; (*car, aeroplane*) poruszać się; (*news, sound*) rozchodzić się (rozejść się *perf*) ▷ *vt* (*distance*) przejeżdżać (przejechać *perf*); **travels** *npl* podróże *pl*; **I ~ to work by train** jeżdżę do pracy pociągiem; **this wine doesn't ~ well** to wino źle znosi transport
**travel agency** *n* biuro *nt* podróży
**travel agent** *n* pracownik(-ica) *m(f)* biura podróży
**travel brochure** *n* prospekt *m* turystyczny
**traveller**, (*US*) **traveler** ['trævlə^r] *n* podróżnik(-iczka) *m(f)*; (*Comm*) komiwojażer(ka) *m(f)*
**traveller's cheque**, (*US*) **traveler's check** *n* czek *m* podróżny
**travelling**, (*US*) **traveling** ['trævlɪŋ] *n* podróżowanie *nt* ▷ *cpd* (*circus*) wędrowny; (*exhibition*) objazdowy; (*bag, clock*) podróżny; ~ **expenses** koszty podróży
**travel(l)ing salesman** *n* komiwojażer *m*
**travelogue** ['trævəlɔg] *n* (*book*) książka *f* podróżnicza; (*talk*) odczyt *m* o podróżach; (*film*) film *m* podróżniczy
**travel sickness** *n* choroba *f* lokomocyjna
**traverse** ['trævəs] *vt* przemierzać (przemierzyć *perf*)
**travesty** ['trævəstɪ] *n* parodia *f*
**trawler** ['trɔ:lə^r] *n* trawler *m*
**tray** [treɪ] *n* taca *f*; (*also*: **in-tray/out-tray**) tacka *f* (na korespondencję)
**treacherous** ['trɛtʃərəs] *adj* (*person, look*) zdradziecki; (*ground, tide*) zdradliwy; **road conditions are ~** warunki drogowe są niebezpieczne
**treachery** ['trɛtʃərɪ] *n* zdrada *f*
**treacle** ['tri:kl] *n* (*black treacle*) melasa *f*
**tread** [trɛd] (*pt* **trod**, *pp* **trodden**) *n* (*of tyre*) bieżnik *m*; (*step*) chód *m*; (*of stair*) stopień *m* ▷ *vi* stąpać

▸ **tread on** *vt fus* nadeptywać (nadepnąć *perf*) na *+acc*
**eadle** ['trɛdl] *n* (*on sewing machine etc*) pedał *m*
**eas.** *abbr* = **treasurer**
**eason** ['tri:zn] *n* zdrada *f*
**easure** ['trɛʒə^r] *n* (*lit, fig*) skarb *m* ▷ *vt* (*object*) być bardzo przywiązanym do *+gen*; (*memory, thought*) (pieczołowicie) przechowywać w pamięci; (*friendship*) pielęgnować; **treasures** *npl* skarby *pl*
**easure hunt** *n* poszukiwanie *nt* skarbów
**easurer** ['trɛʒərə^r] *n* skarbnik(-iczka) *m(f)*
**easury** ['trɛʒərɪ] *n*: **the T~,** (*US*) **the T~ Department** ≈ Ministerstwo *nt* Finansów
**easury bill** *n* bilet *m* skarbowy
**eat** [tri:t] *n* uczta *f* (*fig*) ▷ *vt* (*handle, regard*) traktować (potraktować *perf*); (*Med*) leczyć; (*Tech*) impregnować (zaimpregnować *perf*); **it came as a real ~** to była prawdziwa przyjemność; **this is my ~** ja stawiam; **to ~ sth as a joke** traktować (potraktować *perf*) coś jako żart; **she ~ed us to dinner** poczęstowała nas obiadem
**eatment** ['tri:tmənt] *n* (*attention, handling*) traktowanie *nt*; (*Med*) leczenie *nt*; **to have ~ for sth** poddawać się (poddać się *perf*) leczeniu na coś
**eaty** ['tri:tɪ] *n* traktat *m*
**eble** ['trɛbl] *adj* (*triple*) potrójny; (*Mus: part, instrument*) sopranowy; (*voice*) dyszkantowy, sopranowy ▷ *n* (*singer*) sopranista(-tka) *m(f)*; (*on radio etc*) wysokie tony *pl* ▷ *vt* potrajać (potroić *perf*) ▷ *vi* potrajać się (potroić się *perf*); **to be ~ the amount/size of** być trzykrotnie większym od *+gen*
**eble clef** *n* klucz *m* wiolinowy
**ee** [tri:] *n* drzewo *nt*
**ee-lined** ['tri:laɪnd] *adj* wysadzany drzewami
**eetop** ['tri:tɔp] *n* wierzchołek *m or* korona *f* drzewa
**ee trunk** *n* pień *m* drzewa
**ek** [trɛk] *n* (*long difficult journey*) wyprawa *f*; (*tiring walk*) wędrówka *f* ▷ *vi* wędrować
**ellis** ['trɛlɪs] *n* trejaż *m*, treliaż *m*
**emble** ['trɛmbl] *vi* drżeć (zadrżeć *perf*)
**embling** ['trɛmblɪŋ] *n* drżenie *nt* ▷ *adj* drżący
**emendous** [trɪ'mɛndəs] *adj* (*enormous*) olbrzymi, ogromny; (*excellent*) wspaniały
**emendously** [trɪ'mɛndəslɪ] *adv* ogromnie; **he enjoyed it ~** sprawiło mu to ogromną przyjemność
**emor** ['trɛmə^r] *n* (*of excitement, fear*) dreszcz *m*; (*in voice*) drżenie *nt*; (*also*: **earth tremor**) wstrząs *m* (podziemny)
**ench** [trɛntʃ] *n* rów *m*; (*Mil*) okop *m*
**trench coat** *n* trencz *m*
**trench warfare** *n* wojna *f* okopowa
**trend** [trɛnd] *n* (*in attitudes, fashion*) trend *m*; (*of events*) kierunek *m*; **~ towards** tendencja w kierunku *+gen*; **~ away from** odejście od *+gen*; **to set a/the ~** nadawać (nadać *perf*) kierunek *or* ton
**trendy** ['trɛndɪ] *adj* modny
**trepidation** [trɛpɪ'deɪʃən] *n* trwoga *f*; **in ~** zatrwożony
**trespass** ['trɛspəs] *vi*: **to ~ on** (*private property*) wkraczać (wkroczyć *perf*) na *+acc*; **"no ~ing"** „teren prywatny — wstęp wzbroniony"
**trespasser** ['trɛspəsə^r] *n osoba wkraczająca na teren prywatny bez zgody właściciela*; **"~s will be prosecuted"** „wstęp pod karą wzbroniony"
**tress** [trɛs] *n* pukiel *m*
**trestle** ['trɛsl] *n* kozioł *m* (*podpora*)
**trestle table** *n* stół *m* na kozłach
**trial** ['traɪəl] *n* (*Jur*) proces *m*; (*of machine, drug etc*) próba *f*; (*worry*) utrapienie *nt*; **trials** *npl* (*unpleasant*) przykre przejścia *pl*; (*difficult*) perypetie *pl*; **horse ~s** gonitwa próbna *or* przygotowawcza; **~ by jury** rozprawa przed ławą przysięgłych; **the case was sent for ~** sprawa została skierowana do sądu; **he went on ~ for larceny** był sądzony za kradzież; **by ~ and error** metodą prób i błędów
**trial balance** *n* (*Comm*) bilans *m* próbny
**trial basis** *n*: **on a ~** tytułem próby
**trial period** *n* okres *m* próbny
**trial run** *n* próba *f*
**triangle** ['traɪæŋgl] *n* trójkąt *m*
**triangular** [traɪ'æŋgjulə^r] *adj* trójkątny
**tribal** ['traɪbl] *adj* plemienny
**tribe** [traɪb] *n* plemię *nt*
**tribesman** ['traɪbzmən] *n* (*irreg: like* **man**) członek *m* plemienia
**tribulations** [trɪbju'leɪʃənz] *npl* troski *pl*
**tribunal** [traɪ'bju:nl] *n* trybunał *m*; **industrial (relations) ~** sąd pracy
**tributary** ['trɪbjutərɪ] *n* dopływ *m*
**tribute** ['trɪbju:t] *n* (*compliment*) wyrazy *pl* uznania; **to pay ~ to** wyrażać (wyrazić *perf*) uznanie dla *+gen*
**trice** [traɪs] *n*: **in a ~** w okamgnieniu
**trick** [trɪk] *n* sztuczka *f*; (*Cards*) lewa *f* ▷ *vt* oszukiwać (oszukać *perf*); **the ~ is to ...** (cała) sztuka polega na tym, żeby *+infin*; **to play a ~ on sb** spłatać (*perf*) komuś figla; **to ~ sb into doing sth** podstępem zmusić (*perf*) kogoś do zrobienia czegoś; **to ~ sb out of sth** podstępem pozbawić (*perf*) kogoś czegoś; **it's a ~ of the light** to złudzenie optyczne; **that should do the ~** to powinno załatwić sprawę
**trickery** ['trɪkərɪ] *n* oszustwo *nt*

t

**trickle** ['trɪkl] *n* strużka *f* ▷ *vi* (*water*) sączyć się, kapać; (*rain, tears*) kapać; (*people*) iść małymi grupkami
**trick photography** *n* fotografia *f* trikowa
**trick question** *n* podchwytliwe pytanie *nt*
**trickster** ['trɪkstəʳ] *n* oszust(ka) *m(f)*, naciągacz(ka) *m(f)* (*inf*)
**tricky** ['trɪkɪ] *adj* (*problem etc*) skomplikowany
**tricycle** ['traɪsɪkl] *n* rower *m* trójkołowy
**trifle** ['traɪfl] *n* błahostka *f*, drobnostka *f*; (*Culin*) *ciasto biszkoptowe przekładane owocami, galaretką lub kremem* ▷ *adv*: **a ~ long** (nieco) przydługi ▷ *vi*: **to ~ with sb/sth** stroić sobie żarty z kogoś/czegoś
**trifling** ['traɪflɪŋ] *adj* błahy
**trigger** ['trɪgəʳ] *n* spust *m*, cyngiel *m*
▸ **trigger off** *vt fus* wywoływać (wywołać *perf*)
**trigonometry** [trɪgə'nɔmətrɪ] *n* trygonometria *f*
**trilby** ['trɪlbɪ] (*Brit*) *n* (*also*: **trilby hat**) kapelusz *m* filcowy
**trill** [trɪl] *n* (*Mus*) tryl *m*; (*of birds*) trele *pl*
**trilogy** ['trɪlədʒɪ] *n* trylogia *f*
**trim** [trɪm] *adj* (*house, garden*) starannie utrzymany; (*figure, person*) szczupły ▷ *n* (*haircut*) podstrzyżenie *nt*, podcięcie *nt*; (*on clothes*) lamówka *f*, wykończenie *nt*; (*on car*) elementy *pl* ozdobne karoserii ▷ *vt* (*cut*) przycinać (przyciąć *perf*), przystrzygać (przystrzyc *perf*); (*decorate*): **to ~ (with)** ozdabiać (ozdobić *perf*) (*+instr*); (*Naut*: *sail*) ustawiać (ustawić *perf*); **to keep in (good) ~** utrzymywać (dobrą) formę, dobrze się trzymać (*inf*)
**trimmings** ['trɪmɪŋz] *npl* (*Culin*) garnirunek *m*; (*cuttings*) skrawki *pl*
**Trinidad and Tobago** ['trɪnɪdæd-] *n* Trynidad *m* i Tobago *nt inv*
**trinity** ['trɪnɪtɪ] *n* (*Rel*): **the (Holy) T~** Trójca *f* Święta
**trinket** ['trɪŋkɪt] *n* (*ornament*) ozdóbka *f*; (*piece of jewellery*) błyskotka *f*, świecidełko *nt*
**trio** ['tri:əu] *n* trójka *f*; (*Mus*: *musicians*) trio *nt*, tercet *m*; (: *composition*) trio *nt*
**trip** [trɪp] *n* (*journey*) podróż *f*; (*outing*) wycieczka *f* ▷ *vi* (*stumble*) potykać się (potknąć się *perf*); (*go lightly*) iść lekkim krokiem; **to go on a (business) ~** wyjeżdżać (wyjechać *perf*) w podróż (służbową)
▸ **trip over** *vt fus* potykać się (potknąć się *perf*) o *+acc*
▸ **trip up** *vi* potykać się (potknąć się *perf*) ▷ *vt* podstawiać (podstawić *perf*) nogę *+dat*
**tripartite** [traɪ'pɑ:taɪt] *adj* trójstronny
**tripe** [traɪp] *n* (*Culin*) flaczki *pl*, flaki *pl*; (*pej*) bzdury *pl*
**triple** ['trɪpl] *adj* potrójny ▷ *adv*: **~ the distance/speed** trzy razy dalej/szybciej
**triplets** ['trɪplɪts] *npl* trojaczki *pl*
**triplicate** ['trɪplɪkət] *n*: **in ~** w trzech egzemplarzach
**tripod** ['traɪpɔd] *n* trójnóg *m*
**Tripoli** ['trɪpəlɪ] *n* Trypolis *m*
**tripper** ['trɪpəʳ] (*Brit*) *n* wycieczkowicz(ka) *m(f)*
**tripwire** ['trɪpwaɪəʳ] *n* linka *f* turbulencyjna, turbilizator *m*
**trite** [traɪt] (*pej*) *adj* wyświechtany, oklepany
**triumph** ['traɪʌmf] *n* tryumf *m or* triumf *m* ▷ *vi* tryumfować (zatryumfować *perf*); **to ~ over** (*opponent*) odnosić (odnieść *perf*) zwycięstwo nad *+instr*; (*disabilities, adversities*) przezwyciężać (przezwyciężyć *perf*) *+acc*
**triumphal** [traɪ'ʌmfl] *adj* tryumfalny *or* triumfalny
**triumphant** [traɪ'ʌmfənt] *adj* (*team*) zwycięski, tryumfujący *or* triumfujący; (*return*) tryumfalny *or* triumfalny; (*smile, expression*) tryumfalny *or* triumfalny, tryumfujący *or* triumfujący
**triumphantly** [traɪ'ʌmfəntlɪ] *adv* tryumfalnie *or* triumfalnie, tryumfująco *or* triumfująco
**trivia** ['trɪvɪə] (*pej*) *npl* błahostki *pl*
**trivial** ['trɪvɪəl] *adj* (*unimportant*) błahy; (*commonplace*) trywialny, banalny
**triviality** [trɪvɪ'ælɪtɪ] *n* (*state of being trivial*) błahość *f*; (*sth trivial*) rzecz *f* błaha
**trivialize** ['trɪvɪəlaɪz] *vt* bagatelizować (zbagatelizować *perf*)
**trod** [trɔd] *pt of* **tread**
**trodden** [trɔdn] *pp of* **tread**
**trolley** ['trɔlɪ] *n* (*for luggage, shopping*) wózek *m*; (*table*) stolik *m* na kółkach; (*also*: **trolley bus**) trolejbus *m*
**trollop** ['trɔləp] (*pej*) *n* flądra *f* (*pej, inf*)
**trombone** [trɔm'bəun] *n* puzon *m*
**troop** [tru:p] *n* (*of people*) gromada *f*; (*of monkeys*) stado *nt* ▷ *vi*: **to ~ in/out** wchodzić (wejść *perf*)/wychodzić (wyjść *perf*) gromadnie; **troops** *npl* wojsko *nt*, żołnierze *p*
**troop carrier** *n* transportowiec *m* (*samolot lub okręt*)
**trooper** ['tru:pəʳ] *n* (*Mil*) żołnierz *m* (*niższej rangi, w kawalerii i w wojskach pancernych*); (*US*) policjant(ka) *m(f)*
**trooping the colour** ['tru:pɪŋ-] (*Brit*) *n* parad *f* wojskowa
**troopship** ['tru:pʃɪp] *n* transportowiec *m*
**trophy** ['trəufɪ] *n* trofeum *m*
**tropic** ['trɔpɪk] *n* zwrotnik *m*; **the tropics** *npl* tropik *m*, tropiki *pl*; **T~ of Cancer/Capricorn** zwrotnik Raka/Koziorożca
**tropical** ['trɔpɪkl] *adj* tropikalny, zwrotnikowy

**rot** [trɔt] *n* (*fast pace*) trucht *m*; (*of horse*) kłus *m* ▷ *vi* (*horse*) kłusować (pokłusować *perf*); (*person*) biec (pobiec *perf*) truchtem; **on the ~** (*Brit: one after another*) z rzędu
▸ **trot out** *vt* (*excuse, reason*) recytować (wyrecytować *perf*); (*names, facts*) wyciągać (wyciągnąć *perf*) z lamusa

**rouble** [ˈtrʌbl] *n* (*difficulty, bother*) kłopot *m*; (*unrest*) zamieszki *pl* ▷ *vt* (*worry*) martwić (zmartwić *perf*); (*disturb*) niepokoić ▷ *vi*: **to ~ to do sth** zadawać (zadać *perf*) sobie trud zrobienia czegoś; **troubles** *npl* kłopoty *pl*; **to be in ~** mieć kłopoty *or* nieprzyjemności; (*ship, climber etc*) być w tarapatach *or* opałach; **to go to the ~ of doing sth** zadawać (zadać *perf*) sobie trud, żeby coś zrobić; **it's no ~!** to żaden kłopot!; **please don't ~ yourself** proszę się nie fatygować; **the ~ is ...** kłopot w tym, że ...; **did you have any ~ finding your way here?** czy miałaś jakieś kłopoty z trafieniem tutaj?; **what's the ~?** co się stało?; (*to patient*) co Panu/Pani dolega?; **stomach ~** dolegliwości żołądkowe

**roubled** [trʌbld] *adj* (*person*) zmartwiony; (*era, life*) burzliwy; (*water*) wzburzony; (*country*) targany konfliktami

**rouble-free** [ˈtrʌblfriː] *adj* bezproblemowy

**roublemaker** [ˈtrʌblmeɪkəʳ] *n* wichrzyciel *m*

**roubleshooter** [ˈtrʌblʃuːtəʳ] *n* mediator *m*, rozjemca *m*

**roublesome** [ˈtrʌblsəm] *adj* (*child*) nieznośny; (*cough, stammer*) dokuczliwy

**rouble spot** *n* punkt *m* zapalny

**rough** [trɔf] *n* (*also*: **drinking/feeding trough**) koryto *nt*; (*channel*) rów *m*; (*low point*) spadek *m*; **a ~ of low pressure** klin niskiego ciśnienia

**rounce** [trauns] *vt* sprawić (*perf*) sążniste lanie *+dat* (*np. drużynie przeciwnika*)

**roupe** [truːp] *n* trupa *f*

**rouser press** [ˈtrauzə-] *n* prasownica *f* do spodni

**rousers** [ˈtrauzəz] *npl* spodnie *pl*; **short ~** krótkie spodenki; **a pair of ~** para spodni

**rouser suit** (*Brit*) *n* kostium *m* ze spodniami

**rousseau** [ˈtruːsəu] (*pl* **~x** *or* **~s**) *n* wyprawa *f* (ślubna)

**rout** [traut] *n inv* pstrąg *m*

**rowel** [ˈtrauəl] *n* (*garden tool*) rydel *m*; (*builder's tool*) kielnia *f*

**ruant** [ˈtruənt] (*Brit*) *n*: **to play ~** iść (pójść *perf*) na wagary; (*frequently*) chodzić na wagary, wagarować

**ruce** [truːs] *n* rozejm *m*, zawieszenie *nt* broni

**ruck** [trʌk] *n* (*lorry*) ciężarówka *f*, samochód *m* ciężarowy; (*Rail*) platforma *f*; (*for luggage*) wózek *m*; **I will have no ~ with them** nie chcę mieć z nimi do czynienia

**truck driver** *n* kierowca *m* ciężarówki

**trucker** [ˈtrʌkəʳ] (*US*) *n* = **truck driver**

**truck farm** (*US*) *n* gospodarstwo *nt* warzywnicze

**trucking** [ˈtrʌkɪŋ] (*US*) *n* transport *m* samochodowy, przewóz *m* samochodami ciężarowymi

**trucking company** (*US*) *n* przedsiębiorstwo *nt* przewozowe

**truculent** [ˈtrʌkjulənt] *adj* zaczepny, zadziorny

**trudge** [trʌdʒ] *vi* (*also*: **trudge along**) iść powłócząc nogami, wlec się

**true** [truː] *adj* (*not false, real, genuine*) prawdziwy; (*accurate, faithful*) wierny; (*wall etc*) dobrze wypionowany; **it's ~** to prawda; **to come ~** (*dreams*) spełniać się (spełnić się *perf*); (*predictions*) sprawdzać się (sprawdzić się *perf*); **to be ~ to life** wiernie oddawać rzeczywistość

**truffle** [ˈtrʌfl] *n* trufla *f*

**truism** [ˈtruɪzəm] *n* truizm *m*

**truly** [ˈtruːlɪ] *adv* (*genuinely, truthfully*) naprawdę; (*really*) doprawdy; **yours ~** (*in letter*) z poważaniem

**trump** [trʌmp] *n* (*lit, fig*) karta *f* atutowa; **to turn up ~s** (*fig: help*) poratować (*perf*) kogoś w potrzebie

**trumped up** *adj*: **a trumped-up charge** sfabrykowane oskarżenie *nt*

**trumpet** [ˈtrʌmpɪt] *n* trąbka *f*

**truncated** [trʌŋˈkeɪtɪd] *adj* (*object*) skrócony, przycięty; (*message*) okrojony

**truncheon** [ˈtrʌntʃən] (*Brit: Police*) *n* pałka *f*

**trundle** [ˈtrʌndl] *vt* (*trolley etc*) pchać *or* popychać (powoli) ▷ *vi*: **to ~ along** (*vehicle*) toczyć się (potoczyć się *perf*); (*person*) iść (pójść *perf*) powoli

**trunk** [trʌŋk] *n* (*of tree*) pień *m*; (*of person*) tułów *m*; (*of elephant*) trąba *f*; (*case*) kufer *m*; (*US: Aut*) bagażnik *m*; **trunks** *npl* (*also*: **swimming trunks**) kąpielówki *pl*

**trunk call** (*Brit*) *n* rozmowa *f* międzymiastowa

**trunk road** (*Brit*) *n* magistrala *f*

**truss** [trʌs] *n* (*Med*) pas *m* przepuklinowy
▸ **truss (up)** *vt* (*Culin*) związywać (związać *perf*) nogi i skrzydła *+dat*; (*person*) związywać (związać *perf*) mocno

**trust** [trʌst] *n* zaufanie *nt*; (*in bright future, human goodness etc*) ufność *f*; (*Comm*) trust *m* ▷ *vt* ufać (zaufać *perf*) *+dat*; **to take sth on ~** przyjmować (przyjąć *perf*) coś na słowo; **to have ~ in** pokładać ufność w *+loc*; **to ~ sth to sb** powierzać (powierzyć *perf*) coś komuś; **in ~** (*Jur*) pod zarządem powierniczym; **to ~ (that)** mieć nadzieję(, że)

t

**trust company** *n* spółka *f* powiernicza
**trusted** ['trʌstɪd] *adj* zaufany
**trustee** [trʌs'ti:] *n* (*Jur*) powiernik(-iczka) *m(f)*; (*of school etc*) członek *m* zarządu
**trustful** ['trʌstful] *adj* ufny
**trust fund** *n* fundusz *m* powierniczy
**trusting** ['trʌstɪŋ] *adj* ufny
**trustworthy** ['trʌstwə:ðɪ] *adj* godny zaufania
**trusty** ['trʌstɪ] *adj* (*horse*) wierny; (*pen etc*) sprawdzony
**truth** [tru:θ] (*pl* **~s**) *n* prawda *f*
**truthful** ['tru:θful] *adj* (*person*) prawdomówny; (*answer, account*) zgodny z prawdą *post*
**truthfully** ['tru:θfəlɪ] *adv* zgodnie z prawdą
**truthfulness** ['tru:θfəlnɪs] *n* (*of person*) prawdomówność *f*; (*of account*) prawdziwość *f*
**try** [traɪ] *n* próba *f*; (*Rugby*) przyłożenie *nt* ▷ *vt* (*attempt, experience*) próbować (spróbować *perf*) *+gen*; (*Jur*) sądzić; (*patience*) wystawiać (wystawić *perf*) na próbę ▷ *vi* (*attempt*) próbować (spróbować *perf*); (*make effort*) starać się (postarać się *perf*); **to have a try** próbować (spróbować *perf*); **to try to do sth** próbować (spróbować *perf*) coś zrobić; **to try one's (very) best** *or* **one's (very) hardest** starać się ze wszystkich sił
▸ **try on** *vt* przymierzać (przymierzyć *perf*); **to try it on (with sb)** (*fig*) próbować (spróbować *perf*) (na kimś) swoich sztuczek
▸ **try out** *vt* wypróbowywać (wypróbować *perf*)
**trying** ['traɪɪŋ] *adj* męczący
**tsar** [zɑ:ʳ] *n* car *m*
**T-shirt** ['ti:ʃə:t] *n* koszulka *f* (z krótkim rękawem)
**T-square** ['ti:skwɛəʳ] *n* przykładnica *f*
**TT** *adj abbr* (*Brit: inf*) = **teetotal** ▷ *abbr* (*US: Post*) = **Trust Territory**
**tub** [tʌb] *n* (*container*) kadź *f*; (*bath*) wanna *f*
**tuba** ['tju:bə] *n* tuba *f*
**tubby** ['tʌbɪ] *adj* pulchny
**tube** [tju:b] *n* (*pipe*) rurka *f*; (*: wide*) rura *f*; (*container*) tubka *f*; (*Brit: underground*) metro *nt*; (*US: inf*): **the ~** telewizja *f*
**tubeless** ['tju:blɪs] *adj* (*tyre*) bezdętkowy
**tuber** ['tju:bəʳ] (*Bot*) *n* bulwa *f*
**tuberculosis** [tjubə:kju'ləusɪs] *n* gruźlica *f*
**tube station** (*Brit*) *n* stacja *f* metra
**tubing** ['tju:bɪŋ] *n* rurka *f*; (*wide*) rura *f*
**tubular** ['tju:bjuləʳ] *adj* (*scaffolding, furniture*) rurowy; (*container*) cylindryczny; **~ steel** rury stalowe
**TUC** (*Brit*) *n abbr* (= *Trades Union Congress*) *federacja brytyjskich związków zawodowych*
**tuck** [tʌk] *vt* wsuwać (wsunąć *perf*) ▷ *n* (*Sewing*) zakładka *f*
▸ **tuck away** *vt* (*money*) odkładać (odłożyć *perf*); **~ed away** ukryty (głęboko)
▸ **tuck in** *vt* (*shirt etc*) wkładać (włożyć *perf*) w spodnie/spódnicę; (*child*) otulać (otulić *perf*) (*do snu*) ▷ *vi* zajadać, wcinać (*inf*)
▸ **tuck up** *vt* otulać (otulić *perf*) (*do snu*)
**tuck shop** *n* sklepik *m* ze słodyczami
**Tue(s).** *abbr* (= *Tuesday*) wt.
**Tuesday** ['tju:zdɪ] *n* wtorek *m*; **it is ~ 23rd March** (dziś) jest wtorek, 23 marca; **on ~** we wtorek; **on ~s** we wtorki; **every ~** w każdy wtorek; **every other ~** w co drugi wtorek; **last/next ~** w zeszły/przyszły wtorek; **the following ~** w następny wtorek; **~'s newspaper** wtorkowa gazeta; **a week/fortnight on ~** od wtorku za tydzień/dwa tygodnie; **the ~ before last** we wtorek dwa tygodnie temu; **the ~ after next** we wtorek za dwa tygodnie; **~ morning/afternoon/evening** we wtorek rano/po południu/wieczorem; **we spent ~ night in Leeds** wtorkową noc spędziliśmy w Leeds
**tuft** [tʌft] *n* kępka *f*
**tug** [tʌg] *n* holownik *m* ▷ *vt* pociągać (pociągnąć *perf*) (mocno)
**tug-of-war** [tʌgəv'wɔ:ʳ] *n* zawody *pl* w przeciąganiu liny; (*fig*) rywalizacja *f*
**tuition** [tju:'ɪʃən] *n* (*Brit: instruction*) nauka *f*, lekcje *pl*; (*US: school fees*) czesne *nt*; **to have private ~** mieć prywatne lekcje
**tulip** ['tju:lɪp] *n* tulipan *m*
**tumble** ['tʌmbl] *n* upadek *m* ▷ *vi* spadać (spaść *perf*), staczać się (stoczyć się *perf*)
▸ **tumble to** (*inf*) *vt fus*: **to ~ to the fact that ...** pokapować się (*perf*), że ... (*inf*)
**tumbledown** ['tʌmbldaun] *adj* walący się
**tumble dryer** (*Brit*) *n* suszarka *f* (bębnowa)
**tumbler** ['tʌmbləʳ] *n* (*glass*) szklaneczka *f*; (*: tall*) szklanka *f*
**tummy** ['tʌmɪ] (*inf*) *n* brzuch *m*
**tumour**, (*US*) **tumor** ['tju:məʳ] (*Med*) *n* guz *m*
**tumult** ['tju:mʌlt] *n* (*uproar*) zgiełk *m*, tumult *m*
**tumultuous** [tju:'mʌltjuəs] *adj* burzliwy
**tuna** ['tju:nə] *n inv* (*also:* **tuna fish**) tuńczyk *m*
**tune** [tju:n] *n* melodia *f* ▷ *vt* (*Mus*) stroić (nastroić *perf*); (*Radio, TV*) nastawiać (nastawić *perf*); (*Aut*) regulować (wyregulować *perf*); **to be in ~** (*instrument*) być nastrojonym; (*singer*) śpiewać czysto; **to be out of ~** (*instrument*) być nie nastrojonym; (*singer*) fałszować; **to be in/out of ~ with** (*fig*) harmonizować/nie harmonizować z *+instr*; **she was robbed to the ~ of 10,000 pounds** obrabowano ją na kwotę 10.000 funtów
▸ **tune in** *vi* (*Radio, TV*): **to ~ in (to)** nastawiać (nastawić *perf*) odbiornik (na *+acc*)

▸ **tune up** *vi* stroić (nastroić *perf*) instrumenty
**tuneful** ['tju:nful] *adj* melodyjny
**tuner** ['tju:nəʳ] *n* (*radio set*) tuner *m*; **piano ~** stroiciel fortepianów
**tuner amplifier** *n* tuner *m* ze wzmacniaczem
**tungsten** ['tʌŋstn] *n* wolfram *m*
**tunic** ['tju:nɪk] *n* tunika *f*
**tuning fork** ['tju:nɪŋ-] *n* kamerton *m*
**Tunis** ['tju:nɪs] *n* Tunis *m*
**Tunisia** [tju:'nɪzɪə] *n* Tunezja *f*
**Tunisian** [tju:'nɪzɪən] *adj* tunezyjski ▹ *n* Tunezyjczyk(-jka) *m(f)*
**tunnel** ['tʌnl] *n* (*passage*) tunel *m*; (*in mine*) sztolnia *f* ▹ *vi* przekopywać (przekopać *perf*) tunel
**tunny** ['tʌnɪ] *n* tuńczyk *m*
**turban** ['tə:bən] *n* turban *m*
**turbid** ['tə:bɪd] *adj* (*water*) mętny; (*air*) zapylony
**turbine** ['tə:baɪn] *n* turbina *f*
**turbojet** [tə:bəu'dʒɛt] *n* (*engine*) silnik *m* turboodrzutowy; (*plane*) samolot *m* turboodrzutowy
**turboprop** [tə:bəu'prɔp] *n* (*engine*) silnik *m* turbośmigłowy; (*plane*) samolot *m* turbośmigłowy
**turbot** ['tə:bət] *n inv* (*Zool*) turbot *m*
**turbulence** ['tə:bjuləns] *n* turbulencja *f*
**turbulent** ['tə:bjulənt] *adj* (*lit, fig*) burzliwy
**tureen** [tə'ri:n] *n* waza *f*
**turf** [tə:f] *n* (*grass*) darń *f*; (*clod*) bryła *f* darni ▹ *vt* pokrywać (pokryć *perf*) darnią; **the T~** (*horse-racing*) wyścigi konne
▸ **turf out** (*inf*) *vt* wyrzucać (wyrzucić *perf*)
**turf accountant** (*Brit*) *n* bukmacher *m*
**turgid** ['tə:dʒɪd] *adj* (*speech, style*) napuszony; (*verse, film*) ciężki
**Turin** ['tjuə'rɪn] *n* Turyn *m*
**Turk** [tə:k] *n* Turek/Turczynka *m/f*
**Turkey** ['tə:kɪ] *n* Turcja *f*
**turkey** ['tə:kɪ] *n* indyk *m*
**Turkish** ['tə:kɪʃ] *adj* turecki ▹ *n* (język *m*) turecki
**Turkish bath** *n* łaźnia *f* turecka
**Turkish delight** *n* rachatłukum *nt inv*
**turmeric** ['tə:mərɪk] *n* (*Culin*) kurkuma *f*
**turmoil** ['tə:mɔɪl] *n* zgiełk *m*, wrzawa *f*; **in ~** wzburzony
**turn** [tə:n] *n* (*rotation*) obrót *m*; (*in road*) zakręt *m*; (*change*) zmiana *f*; (*chance*) kolej *f*; (*performance*) występ *m*; (*inf: of illness*) napad *m* ▹ *vt* (*handle*) przekręcać (przekręcić *perf*); (*key*) przekręcać (przekręcić *perf*), obracać (obrócić *perf*); (*steak, page*) przewracać (przewrócić *perf*); (*wood, metal*) toczyć ▹ *vi* (*rotate*) obracać się (obrócić się *perf*); (*change direction*) skręcać (skręcić *perf*); (*face in different direction*) odwracać się (odwrócić się *perf*); (*milk*) kwaśnieć (skwaśnieć *perf*); **her hair is ~ing grey** włosy jej siwieją; **he has ~ed forty** skończył czterdzieści lat; **I did him a good ~** wyświadczyłam mu przysługę; **a ~ of events** obrót spraw; **it gave me quite a ~** (*inf*) to mnie nieźle zaszokowało (*inf*); **"no left ~"** „zakaz skrętu w lewo"; **it's your ~** twoja kolej; **in ~** (*in succession*) po kolei; (*indicating consequence, cause etc*) z kolei; **to take ~s (at)** zmieniać się (zmienić się *perf*) (przy *+loc*); **at the ~ of the century** u schyłku wieku, na przełomie wieków; **at the ~ of the year** pod koniec roku; **to take a ~ for the worse** przybierać (przybrać *perf*) zły obrót; **his health** *or* **he has taken a ~ for the worse** jego stan pogorszył się, pogorszyło mu się (*inf*)
▸ **turn against** *vt fus* zwracać się (zwrócić się *perf*) przeciw(ko) *+dat*
▸ **turn around** *vi* odwracać się (odwrócić się *perf*)
▸ **turn away** *vi* odwracać się (odwrócić się *perf*) ▹ *vt* (*applicants*) odprawiać (odprawić *perf*) (z niczym *or* z kwitkiem); **one should never ~ away business** nigdy nie należy gardzić możliwością zrobienia interesu
▸ **turn back** *vi* zawracać (zawrócić *perf*) ▹ *vt* zawracać (zawrócić *perf*)
▸ **turn down** *vt* (*offer*) odrzucać (odrzucić *perf*); (*person, request*) odmawiać (odmówić *perf*) *+dat*; (*heater*) przykręcać (przykręcić *perf*); (*radio*) przyciszać (przyciszyć *perf*), ściszać (ściszyć *perf*); (*bedclothes*) odwijać (odwinąć *perf*)
▸ **turn in** *vi* (*inf*) iść (pójść *perf*) spać ▹ *vt* (*to police*) wydawać (wydać *perf*)
▸ **turn into** *vt fus* zamieniać się (zamienić się *perf*) w *+acc*
▸ **turn off** *vi* (*from road*) skręcać (skręcić *perf*) ▹ *vt* (*light, engine, radio*) wyłączać (wyłączyć *perf*); (*tap*) zakręcać (zakręcić *perf*)
▸ **turn on** *vt* (*light, engine, radio*) włączać (włączyć *perf*); (*tap*) odkręcać (odkręcić *perf*)
▸ **turn out** *vt* (*light, gas*) wyłączać (wyłączyć *perf*) ▹ *vi* (*people*) przybywać (przybyć *perf*); **the house ~ed out to be a ruin** dom okazał się (być) ruiną; **how did the cake ~ out?** jak się udało ciasto?
▸ **turn over** *vi* (*person*) przewracać się (przewrócić się *perf*) na drugi bok ▹ *vt* (*object*) odwracać (odwrócić *perf*); (*page*) przewracać (przewrócić *perf*); **to ~ sth over to** (*different function*) przestawiać (przestawić *perf*) coś na *+acc*; (*rightful owner*) zwracać (zwrócić *perf*) coś *+dat*

▸ **turn round** *vi* (*person*) odwracać się (odwrócić się *perf*); (*vehicle*) zawracać (zawrócić *perf*); (*rotate*) obracać się (obrócić się *perf*)
▸ **turn up** *vi* (*person*) pojawiać się (pojawić się *perf*); (*lost object*) znajdować się (znaleźć się *perf*) ▹ *vt* (*collar*) stawiać (postawić *perf*); (*radio*) podgłaśniać (podgłośnić *perf*); (*heater*) podkręcać (podkręcić *perf*)
**turnabout** ['tə:nəbaut] *n* (*fig*) zwrot *m* o 180 stopni
**turnaround** ['tə:nəraund] *n* (*fig*) = **turnabout**
**turncoat** ['tə:nkəut] *n* renegat *m*
**turned-up** ['tə:ndʌp] *adj* (*nose*) zadarty
**turning** ['tə:nɪŋ] *n* (*in road*) zakręt *m*; **the first ~ on the right** pierwszy zakręt w prawo
**turning circle** (*Brit*: *Aut*) *n* promień *m* skrętu
**turning point** *n* (*fig*) punkt *m* zwrotny
**turning radius** (*US*) *n* = **turning circle**
**turnip** ['tə:nɪp] *n* rzepa *f*
**turnout** ['tə:naut] *n* (*of voters etc*) frekwencja *f*
**turnover** ['tə:nəuvəʳ] *n* (*Comm*) obrót *m*, obroty *pl*; (*Culin*) *zawijane ciastko z owocami lub dżemem*; **~ of staff** fluktuacja kadr
**turnpike** ['tə:npaɪk] (*US*) *n* autostrada *f* (*zwykle płatna*)
**turnstile** ['tə:nstaɪl] *n* kołowrót *m* (*przy wejściu na stadion itp*)
**turntable** ['tə:nteɪbl] *n* (*on record player*) talerz *m* obrotowy
**turn-up** ['tə:nʌp] (*Brit*) *n* (*on trousers*) mankiet *m*; **that's a ~ for the books!** (*inf*) a to ci dopiero! (*inf*)
**turpentine** ['tə:pəntaɪn] *n* (*also*: **turps**) terpentyna *f*
**turquoise** ['tə:kwɔɪz] *n* turkus *m* ▹ *adj* turkusowy
**turret** ['tʌrɪt] *n* wieżyczka *f*
**turtle** ['tə:tl] *n* żółw *m*
**turtleneck (sweater)** ['tə:tlnɛk(-)] *n* golf *m*
**Tuscan** ['tʌskən] *adj* toskański ▹ *n* Toskańczyk(-anka) *m(f)*
**Tuscany** ['tʌskənɪ] *n* Toskania *f*
**tusk** [tʌsk] *n* kieł *m*
**tussle** ['tʌsl] *n* bójka *f*
**tutor** ['tju:təʳ] *n* (*Brit*) *wykładowca prowadzący zajęcia z małą grupą studentów lub opiekujący się indywidualnymi studentami*; (*private tutor*) prywatny(na) *m(f)* nauczyciel(-ka) *m(f)*
**tutorial** [tju:'tɔ:rɪəl] *n* zajęcia *pl* (*dla małej grupy studentów*)
**tuxedo** [tʌk'si:dəu] (*US*) *n* smoking *m*
**TV** [ti:'vi:] *n abbr* = **television**
**twaddle** ['twɔdl] (*inf*) *n* bzdury *pl*
**twang** [twæŋ] *n* (*of tight wire*) brzdęk *m*; (*of voice*) nosowe brzmienie *nt* ▹ *vi* (*springs etc*) brzęczeć (brzęknąć *perf*) ▹ *vt* (*guitar*) brzdąkać na *+loc*
**tweak** [twi:k] *vt* (*ear*) wykręcać (wykręcić *perf*); (*nose*) szczypać (uszczypnąć *perf*) w *+acc*; (*tail*) ciągnąć (pociągnąć *perf*) za *+acc*
**tweed** [twi:d] *n* tweed *m* ▹ *adj* tweedowy
**tweet** [twi:t] *n* (*on Twitter*) tweet *m* ▹ *vt* tweetować *imperf*
**tweezers** ['twi:zəz] *npl* pinceta *f*
**twelfth** [twɛlfθ] *num* dwunasty
**Twelfth Night** *n* wigilia *f* Trzech Króli
**twelve** [twɛlv] *num* dwanaście; **at ~ (o'clock)** o (godzinie) dwunastej
**twentieth** ['twɛntɪɪθ] *num* dwudziesty
**twenty** ['twɛntɪ] *num* dwadzieścia
**twerp** [twə:p] (*inf*) *n* przygłup *m* (*inf*)
**twice** [twaɪs] *adv* dwa razy, dwukrotnie; **~ as much** dwa razy tyle; **~ a week** dwa razy w tygodniu; **she is ~ your age** jest od ciebie dwa razy starsza
**twiddle** ['twɪdl] *vt* kręcić *+instr* ▹ *vi*: **to ~ with sth** kręcić czymś; **to ~ one's thumbs** (*fig*) zbijać bąki
**twig** [twɪg] *n* gałązka *f* ▹ *vi* (*Brit*: *inf*) skapować (się) (*perf*) (*inf*)
**twilight** ['twaɪlaɪt] *n* (*evening*) zmierzch *m*; (*morning*) brzask *m*; **in the ~ of his career** u schyłku (swej) kariery
**twill** [twɪl] *n* diagonal *m* (*tkanina*)
**twin** [twɪn] *n* bliźniak(-aczka) *m(f)*; (*in hotel*) pokój *m* z dwoma łóżkami ▹ *adj* (*towers, pregnancy*) bliźniaczy ▹ *vt*: **Nottingham is ~ned with Poznań** Nottingham i Poznań to miasta bliźniacze; **~ brother** (brat) bliźniak; **~ sister** (siostra) bliźniaczka; **~s** bliźniaki, bliźnięta
**twin-bedded room** ['twɪn'bɛdɪd-] *n* pokój *m* z dwoma łóżkami
**twin beds** *npl* dwa pojedyncze łóżka *pl* (*w jednym pokoju*)
**twin-carburettor** ['twɪnkɑ:bju'rɛtəʳ] *adj* dwugaźnikowy
**twine** [twaɪn] *n* szpagat *m* (*sznurek*) ▹ *vi* (*plant*) wić się
**twin-engined** [twɪn'ɛndʒɪnd] *adj* dwusilnikowy
**twinge** [twɪndʒ] *n* (*of pain, regret*) ukłucie *nt*; (*of conscience*) wyrzut *m*
**twinkle** ['twɪŋkl] *vi* (*star, light*) migotać (zamigotać *perf*); (*eyes*) skrzyć się ▹ *n* (*in eye*) błysk *m*, iskra *f*
**twin town** *n* miasto *nt* bliźniacze
**twirl** [twə:l] *vt* (*umbrella etc*) kręcić *+instr* ▹ *vi* kręcić się, wirować ▹ *n* obrót *m*
**twist** [twɪst] *n* (*of body*) skręt *m*; (*of coil*) zwój *m*; (*in road*) (ostry) zakręt *m*; (*in attitudes, story*) zwrot *m* ▹ *vt* (*head*) odwracać (odwrócić *perf*); (*ankle etc*) skręcać (skręcić *perf*); (*scarf etc*) owijać (owinąć *perf*); (*fig*: *words*) przekręcać

(przekręcić *perf*); (: *meaning*) wypaczać (wypaczyć *perf*) ▷ *vi* (*road, river*) wić się; **to ~ sb's arm** (*fig*) przyciskać (przycisnąć *perf*) kogoś

**twisted** ['twɪstɪd] *adj* (*rope*) poskręcany; (*ankle, wrist*) skręcony; (*fig: logic*) pokrętny; (: *personality*) skrzywiony

**twit** [twɪt] (*inf*) *n* przygłup *m* (*inf*)

**twitch** [twɪtʃ] *n* (*nervous*) drgnięcie *nt*; (*at sleeve*) szarpnięcie *nt* ▷ *vi* drgać

**two** [tu:] *num* dwa; **two by two, in twos** dwójkami; **to put two and two together** (*fig*) kojarzyć (skojarzyć *perf*) fakty

**two-door** [tu:'dɔ:ʳ] *adj* dwudrzwiowy

**two-faced** [tu:'feɪst] *adj* (*pej*) dwulicowy

**twofold** ['tu:fəuld] *adv* (*increase*) dwukrotnie ▷ *adj* (*increase*) dwukrotny; (*aim, value*) dwojaki

**two-piece (suit)** ['tu:pi:s-] *n* kostium *m*

**two-piece (swimsuit)** *n* kostium *m* (kąpielowy) dwuczęściowy

**two-ply** ['tu:plaɪ] *adj* (*tissues*) dwuwarstwowy; (*wool*) dwuniciowy

**two-seater** [tu:'si:təʳ] *n* samochód *m* dwumiejscowy

**twosome** ['tu:səm] *n* dwójka *f*

**two-stroke** ['tu:strəuk] *n* (*also*: **two-stroke engine**) silnik *m* dwusuwowy ▷ *adj* dwusuwowy

**two-tone** ['tu:'təun] *adj* (*shoes etc*) w dwóch odcieniach *post*

**two-way** ['tu:weɪ] *adj* (*traffic, street*) dwukierunkowy; **~ radio** urządzenie nadawczo-odbiorcze, krótkofalówka

**TX** (*US: Post*) *abbr* = **Texas**

**tycoon** [taɪ'ku:n] *n* magnat *m*

**type** [taɪp] *n* typ *m*; (*Typ*) czcionka *f* ▷ *vt* pisać (napisać *perf*) na maszynie; **what ~ do you want?** jaki rodzaj Pan/Pani sobie życzy?; **in bold ~** tłustym drukiem; **in italic ~** kursywą

**typecast** ['taɪpkɑ:st] (*irreg: like* **cast**) *vt* (*actor*) szufladkować (zaszufladkować *perf*)

**typeface** ['taɪpfeɪs] *n* krój *m* pisma

**typescript** ['taɪpskrɪpt] *n* maszynopis *m*

**typeset** ['taɪpsɛt] *vt* (*Typ*) składać (złożyć *perf*)

**typesetter** ['taɪpsɛtəʳ] *n* składacz *m*, zecer *m*

**typewriter** ['taɪpraɪtəʳ] *n* maszyna *f* do pisania

**typewritten** ['taɪprɪtn] *adj* napisany na maszynie

**typhoid** ['taɪfɔɪd] *n* tyfus *m or* dur *m* brzuszny

**typhoon** [taɪ'fu:n] *n* tajfun *m*

**typhus** ['taɪfəs] *n* tyfus *m or* dur *m* plamisty

**typical** ['tɪpɪkl] *adj*: **~ (of)** typowy (dla *+gen*)

**typify** ['tɪpɪfaɪ] *vt* (*person*) być uosobieniem *+gen*

**typing** ['taɪpɪŋ] *n* pisanie *nt* na maszynie

**typing error** *n* błąd *m* maszynowy

**typing pool** *n* hala *f* maszyn

**typist** ['taɪpɪst] *n* maszynistka *f*

**typo** ['taɪpəu] (*inf*) *n abbr* (= *typographical error*) (*in typing*) błąd *m* maszynowy; (*in typesetting*) błąd *m* drukarski

**typography** [tɪ'pɔgrəfɪ] *n* typografia *f*

**tyranny** ['tɪrənɪ] *n* tyrania *f*

**tyrant** ['taɪərnt] *n* tyran *m*

**tyre**, (*US*) **tire** ['taɪəʳ] *n* opona *f*

**tyre pressure** *n* ciśnienie *nt* w ogumieniu

**Tyrol** [tɪ'rəul] *n* Tyrol *m*

**Tyrolean** [tɪrə'li:ən] *adj* tyrolski ▷ *n* Tyrolczyk(-lka) *m(f)*

**Tyrolese** [tɪrə'li:z] = **Tyrolean**

**Tyrrhenian Sea** [tɪ'ri:nɪən-] *n*: **the ~** Morze *nt* Tyrreńskie

**tzar** [zɑ:ʳ] *n* = **tsar**

t

# Uu

**U[1], u** [juː] *n* (*letter*) U *nt*, u *nt*; **U for Uncle** ≈ U jak Urszula
**U[2]** (*Brit*: *Film*) *n abbr* (= *universal*) b.o.
**UAW** (*US*) *n abbr* (= *United Automobile Workers*) *związek zawodowy pracowników przemysłu motoryzacyjnego*
**UB40** (*Brit*) *n abbr* (= *unemployment benefit form 40*) *karta rejestracyjna bezrobotnego*
**U-bend** [ˈjuːbɛnd] *n* (*in pipe*) syfon *m*
**ubiquitous** [juːˈbɪkwɪtəs] *adj* wszechobecny
**UCCA** [ˈʌkə] (*Brit*) *n abbr* (= *Universities Central Council on Admissions*) *rada koordynująca przyjęcia na uniwersyteckie studia wyższe*
**UDA** (*Brit*) *n abbr* (= *Ulster Defence Association*) *protestancka organizacja paramilitarna w Irlandii Północnej*
**UDC** (*Brit*) *n abbr* (*formerly*) = **Urban District Council**
**udder** [ˈʌdəʳ] *n* wymię *nt*
**UDI** (*Brit*: *Pol*) *n abbr* = **unilateral declaration of independence**
**UDR** (*Brit*) *n abbr* (= *Ulster Defence Regiment*) *część armii brytyjskiej w Irlandii Północnej składająca się z mieszkańców Ulsteru*
**UEFA** [juːˈeɪfə] *n abbr* (= *Union of European Football Associations*) UEFA *f inv*
**UFO** [ˈjuːfəu] *n abbr* (= *unidentified flying object*) UFO *nt inv*, NOL *m* (= *Niezidentyfikowany Obiekt Latający*)
**Uganda** [juːˈgændə] *n* Uganda *f*
**Ugandan** [juːˈgændən] *adj* ugandyjski ▷ *n* Ugandyjczyk(-jka) *m*(*f*)
**UGC** (*Brit*) *n abbr* (= *University Grants Committee*) *komisja koordynująca finansowanie uniwersytetów*
**ugh** [əːh] *excl* fu(j)
**ugliness** [ˈʌglɪnɪs] *n* brzydota *f*
**ugly** [ˈʌglɪ] *adj* brzydki; (*situation, incident*) paskudny
**UHF** *abbr* (= *ultra-high frequency*) UHF *nt inv*
**UHT** *abbr* (= *ultra-heat treated*) UHT; **UHT milk** mleko UHT
**UK** *n abbr* = **United Kingdom**
**ulcer** [ˈʌlsəʳ] *n* (*also*: **stomach** *etc* **ulcer**) wrzód *m*; (*also*: **mouth ulcer**) afta *f*
**Ulster** [ˈʌlstəʳ] *n* Ulster *m*
**ulterior** [ʌlˈtɪərɪəʳ] *adj*: **~ motive** ukryty motyw *m*
**ultimata** [ʌltɪˈmeɪtə] *npl of* **ultimatum**
**ultimate** [ˈʌltɪmət] *adj* (*final*) ostateczny; (*greatest*: *insult, deterrent*) największy; (: *authority*) najwyższy ▷ *n*: **the ~ in luxury** szczyt *m* luksusu
**ultimately** [ˈʌltɪmətlɪ] *adv* ostatecznie
**ultimatum** [ʌltɪˈmeɪtəm] (*pl* **~s** *or* **ultimata**) ultimatum *nt*
**ultrasonic** [ʌltrəˈsɔnɪk] *adj* ultradźwiękowy, (po)naddźwiękowy
**ultrasound** [ˈʌltrəsaund] *n* ultradźwięk *m*
**ultraviolet** [ˈʌltrəˈvaɪəlɪt] *adj* ultrafioletowy nadfioletowy
**umbilical cord** [ʌmˈbɪlɪkl-] *n* pępowina *f*
**umbrage** [ˈʌmbrɪdʒ] *n*: **to take ~** poczuć się (*perf*) urażonym
**umbrella** [ʌmˈbrɛlə] *n* parasol *m*; (*lady's*) parasolka *f*; (*fig*): **under the ~ of** pod egidą c patronatem *+gen*
**umpire** [ˈʌmpaɪəʳ] *n* arbiter *m*, sędzia *m* ▷ *vt*, sędziować
**umpteen** [ʌmpˈtiːn] *adj* ileś tam *+gen*, en *+ger*
**umpteenth** [ʌmpˈtiːnθ] *adj*: **for the ~ time** po raz któryś *or* enty (z rzędu)
**UMW** *n abbr* = **United Mineworkers of America**
**UN** *n abbr* = **United Nations**
**unabashed** [ʌnəˈbæʃt] *adj*: **to be/seem ~** nie być/nie wydawać się zbitym z tropu
**unabated** [ʌnəˈbeɪtɪd] *adv*: **to continue ~** n słabnąć ▷ *adj* niesłabnący
**unable** [ʌnˈeɪbl] *adj*: **to be ~ to do sth** nie by w stanie czegoś (z)robić
**unabridged** [ʌnəˈbrɪdʒd] *adj* (*novel, article*) ni skrócony
**unacceptable** [ʌnəkˈsɛptəbl] *adj* (*behaviour*) niedopuszczalny; (*price, proposal*) nie do przyjęcia *post*
**unaccompanied** [ʌnəˈkʌmpənɪd] *adj* (*child, luggage*) bez opieki *post*; (*song*) bez akompaniamentu *post*
**unaccountably** [ʌnəˈkauntəblɪ] *adv* z niewyjaśnionych przyczyn

**naccounted** [ʌnə'kauntɪd] *adj*: **thirty per cent were ~ for** brakowało trzydziestu procent
**naccustomed** [ʌnə'kʌstəmd] *adj*: **to be ~ to** nie być przyzwyczajonym do *+gen*
**nacquainted** [ʌnə'kweɪntɪd] *adj*: **to be ~ with** nie być zaznajomionym z *+instr*
**nadulterated** [ʌnə'dʌltəreɪtɪd] *adj* (*nonsense, misery*) czysty; (*food, water*) nie skażony
**naffected** [ʌnə'fɛktɪd] *adj* bezpretensjonalny; **he was ~ by it** nie wpłynęło to na niego
**nafraid** [ʌnə'freɪd] *adj*: **to be ~ (of)** nie obawiać się (*+gen*)
**naided** [ʌn'eɪdɪd] *adv* bez (niczyjej) pomocy
**nanimity** [ju:nə'nɪmɪtɪ] *n* jednomyślność *f*
**nanimous** [ju:'nænɪməs] *adj* jednomyślny, jednogłośny
**nanimously** [ju:'nænɪməslɪ] *adv* jednomyślnie, jednogłośnie
**nanswered** [ʌn'ɑ:nsəd] *adj* bez odpowiedzi *post*
**nappetizing** [ʌn'æpɪtaɪzɪŋ] *adj* nieapetyczny
**nappreciative** [ʌnə'pri:ʃɪətɪv] *adj* niewdzięczny
**narmed** [ʌn'ɑ:md] *adj* nie uzbrojony; **~ combat** walka wręcz
**nashamed** [ʌnə'ʃeɪmd] *adj* bezwstydny
**nassisted** [ʌnə'sɪstɪd] *adv* bez (niczyjej) pomocy
**nassuming** [ʌnə'sju:mɪŋ] *adj* (*person*) skromny; (*manner*) nie narzucający się
**nattached** [ʌnə'tætʃt] *adj* (*single*) samotny; (*unconnected*): **~ to** nie związany z *+instr*
**nattended** [ʌnə'tɛndɪd] *adj* pozostawiony bez opieki
**nattractive** [ʌnə'træktɪv] *adj* (*person, appearance*) nieatrakcyjny; (*character, idea*) nieciekawy
**nauthorized** [ʌn'ɔ:θəraɪzd] *adj* (*visit, use*) bezprawny, bez pozwolenia *post*; (*version*) nie autoryzowany
**navailable** [ʌnə'veɪləbl] *adj* nieosiągalny
**navoidable** [ʌnə'vɔɪdəbl] *adj* nieunikniony
**navoidably** [ʌnə'vɔɪdəblɪ] *adv* (*delayed etc*) z przyczyn obiektywnych *post*
**naware** [ʌnə'wɛə^r] *adj*: **to be ~ of** być nieświadomym *+gen*
**nawares** [ʌnə'wɛəz] *adv* znienacka
**nbalanced** [ʌn'bælənst] *adj* (*report etc*) nie wyważony; (*person, mind*) niezrównoważony
**nbearable** [ʌn'bɛərəbl] *adj* nieznośny, nie do zniesienia *or* wytrzymania *post*
**nbeatable** [ʌn'bi:təbl] *adj* bezkonkurencyjny
**nbeaten** [ʌn'bi:tn] *adj* (*record*) nie pobity; (*team, army*) nie pokonany, nie zwyciężony

**unbecoming** [ʌnbɪ'kʌmɪŋ] *adj* (*language, behaviour*) niestosowny; (*garment, colour*) nietwarzowy; **~ to** niegodny *+gen*
**unbeknown(st)** [ʌnbɪ'nəun(st)] *adv*: **~ to me** bez mojej wiedzy
**unbelief** [ʌnbɪ'li:f] *n* niewiara *f*
**unbelievable** [ʌnbɪ'li:vəbl] *adj* niewiarygodny
**unbelievably** [ʌnbɪ'li:vəblɪ] *adv* niewiarygodnie
**unbend** [ʌn'bɛnd] (*irreg: like* **bend**) *vi* (*become less tense*) rozluźniać się (rozluźnić się *perf*); (*become less strict*) mięknąć (zmięknąć *perf*) (*inf*) ▷ *vt* odginać (odgiąć *perf*), prostować (wyprostować *perf*)
**unbending** [ʌn'bɛndɪŋ] *adj* nieugięty
**unbiased** [ʌn'baɪəst] *adj* bezstronny
**unblemished** [ʌn'blɛmɪʃt] *adj* nieskalany; (*fig: reputation*) nieposzlakowany
**unblock** [ʌn'blɔk] *vt* (*pipe*) przetykać (przetkać *perf*)
**unborn** [ʌn'bɔ:n] *adj* nie narodzony
**unbounded** [ʌn'baundɪd] *adj* bezgraniczny
**unbreakable** [ʌn'breɪkəbl] *adj* (*glass, china*) nietłukący; (*plastic*) niełamliwy
**unbridled** [ʌn'braɪdld] *adj* (*emotion, behaviour*) nieokiełznany; (*gluttony*) niepohamowany
**unbroken** [ʌn'brəukən] *adj* (*seal*) nie uszkodzony; (*silence*) niezmącony; (*record*) nie pobity; (*series*) nieprzerwany
**unbuckle** [ʌn'bʌkl] *vt* rozpinać (rozpiąć *perf*) (z klamry)
**unburden** [ʌn'bə:dn] *vt*: **to ~ o.s. (to sb)** wywnętrzać się (wywnętrzyć się *perf*) (przed *+instr*)
**unbusinesslike** [ʌn'bɪznɪslaɪk] *adj* nieprofesjonalny
**unbutton** [ʌn'bʌtn] *vt* rozpinać (rozpiąć *perf*)
**uncalled-for** [ʌn'kɔ:ldfɔ:^r] *adj* (*remark*) nie na miejscu *post*; (*rudeness*) (niczym) nie usprawiedliwiony
**uncanny** [ʌn'kænɪ] *adj* (*resemblance, silence*) niesamowity; (*knack*) osobliwy
**unceasing** [ʌn'si:sɪŋ] *adj* nieustający
**unceremonious** [ʌnsɛrɪ'məunɪəs] *adj* bezceremonialny, obcesowy
**uncertain** [ʌn'sə:tn] *adj* niepewny; **to be ~ about** nie być pewnym *+gen*; **in no ~ terms** dosadnie, bez ogródek
**uncertainty** [ʌn'sə:tntɪ] *n* niepewność *f*; **uncertainties** *npl* niewiadome *pl*
**unchallenged** [ʌn'tʃælɪndʒd] *adj* nie kwestionowany ▷ *adv*: **he walked, ~, past a stewardess** nie zatrzymywany (przez nikogo) przeszedł koło stewardesy; **her decisions always went ~** nigdy nie kwestionowano jej decyzji

U

**unchanged** [ʌn'tʃeɪndʒd] *adj* nie zmieniony
**uncharitable** [ʌn'tʃærɪtəbl] *adj* nieżyczliwy
**uncharted** [ʌn'tʃɑ:tɪd] *adj* nieznany
**unchecked** [ʌn'tʃɛkt] *adv* w niekontrolowany sposób
**uncivil** [ʌn'sɪvɪl] *adj* nieuprzejmy, niegrzeczny
**uncivilized** [ʌn'sɪvɪlaɪzd] *adj* niecywilizowany; (*fig: behaviour, hour*) barbarzyński
**uncle** ['ʌŋkl] *n* wujek *m*, wuj *m*
**unclear** [ʌn'klɪə^r] *adj* niejasny; **I'm still ~ about what I'm supposed to do** wciąż nie jestem pewna, czego się ode mnie wymaga
**uncoil** [ʌn'kɔɪl] *vt* rozwijać (rozwinąć *perf*) ▷ *vi* (*snake*) rozwijać się (rozwinąć się *perf*)
**uncomfortable** [ʌn'kʌmfətəbl] *adj* (*chair, situation, fact*) niewygodny; (*person: nervous*) nieswój; **I am ~ here** jest mi tu niewygodnie; **to feel ~** czuć się (poczuć się *perf*) niezręcznie *or* nieswojo
**uncomfortably** [ʌn'kʌmfətəblɪ] *adv* (*sit*) niewygodnie; (*smile*) niewyraźnie
**uncommitted** [ʌnkə'mɪtɪd] *adj* niezaangażowany
**uncommon** [ʌn'kɔmən] *adj* niezwykły
**uncommunicative** [ʌnkə'mju:nɪkətɪv] *adj* niekomunikatywny
**uncomplicated** [ʌn'kɔmplɪkeɪtɪd] *adj* nieskomplikowany
**uncompromising** [ʌn'kɔmprəmaɪzɪŋ] *adj* bezkompromisowy
**unconcerned** [ʌnkən'sə:nd] *adj* nie zainteresowany; **to be ~ about sth** nie przejmować się czymś
**unconditional** [ʌnkən'dɪʃənl] *adj* bezwarunkowy
**uncongenial** [ʌnkən'dʒi:nɪəl] *adj* nieprzyjazny
**unconnected** [ʌnkə'nɛktɪd] *adj* nie związany, nie powiązany; **to be ~ with sth** nie mieć związku z czymś
**unconscious** [ʌn'kɔnʃəs] *adj* nieprzytomny; **~ of** nieświadomy *+gen* ▷ *n*: **the ~** podświadomość *f*; **to knock sb ~** pozbawić (*perf*) kogoś przytomności
**unconsciously** [ʌn'kɔnʃəslɪ] *adv* nieświadomie, bezwiednie
**unconsciousness** [ʌn'kɔnʃəsnɪs] *n* nieprzytomność *f*
**unconstitutional** ['ʌnkɔnstɪ'tju:ʃənl] *adj* niezgodny z konstytucją, niekonstytucyjny
**uncontested** [ʌnkən'tɛstɪd] *adj* (*victory*) bezsporny; (*divorce*) za zgodą obu stron *post*; (*Pol: seat, election*) bez kontrkandydatur *post*
**uncontrollable** [ʌnkən'trəuləbl] *adj* (*person, animal*) nieokiełznany, nieposkromiony; (*temper, laughter*) niepohamowany
**uncontrolled** [ʌnkən'trəuld] *adj* niekontrolowany
**unconventional** [ʌnkən'vɛnʃənl] *adj* niekonwencjonalny
**unconvinced** [ʌnkən'vɪnst] *adj*: **to be** *or* **remain ~** nie być *or* nie zostać (*perf*) przekonanym
**unconvincing** [ʌnkən'vɪnsɪŋ] *adj* nieprzekonujący
**uncork** [ʌn'kɔ:k] *vt* odkorkowywać (odkorkować *perf*)
**uncorroborated** [ʌnkə'rɔbəreɪtɪd] *adj* nie potwierdzony
**uncouth** [ʌn'ku:θ] *adj* nieokrzesany
**uncover** [ʌn'kʌvə^r] *vt* odkrywać (odkryć *perf*)
**unctuous** ['ʌŋktjuəs] (*fml*) *adj* obłudny
**undamaged** [ʌn'dæmɪdʒd] *adj* nie uszkodzony
**undaunted** [ʌn'dɔ:ntɪd] *adj* nie zrażony; **~, she struggled on** nie zrażona walczyła dalej
**undecided** [ʌndɪ'saɪdɪd] *adj* (*person*) niezdecydowany; (*question*) nie rozstrzygnięty
**undelivered** [ʌndɪ'lɪvəd] *adj* nie dostarczony; **if ~ return to sender** w przypadku niedostarczenia odesłać na adres zwrotny
**undeniable** [ʌndɪ'naɪəbl] *adj* niezaprzeczalny
**undeniably** [ʌndɪ'naɪəblɪ] *adv* niezaprzeczalnie
**under** ['ʌndə^r] *prep* (*in space*) pod *+instr*; (*in age, price*) poniżej *+gen*; (*law, agreement etc*) w myśl *+gen*, zgodnie z *+instr*; (*sb's leadership*) pod rządami *+gen* ▷ *adv* pod spodem; **from ~ sth** spod czegoś; **~ there** tam (na dole); **in ~ 2 hours** w niecałe dwie godziny; **~ anaesthetic** pod narkozą, w znieczuleniu; **~ repair** w naprawie; **~ the circumstances** w tej sytuacji; **the project ~ discussion** omawiany projekt
**under...** ['ʌndə^r] *pref przedrostek, któremu w języku polskim odpowiadają najczęściej przedrostki pod..., nie... lub niedo...*
**under-age** [ʌndər'eɪdʒ] *adj* niepełnoletni, nieletni; **~ drinking** picie alkoholu przez nieletnich
**underarm** ['ʌndərɑ:m] *adv* spod ramienia ▷ *adj* (*throw etc*) spod ramienia *post*; **~ deodorant** ≈ dezodorant do ciała
**undercapitalized** ['ʌndə'kæpɪtəlaɪzd] *adj* niedoinwestowany
**undercarriage** ['ʌndəkærɪdʒ] (*Aviat*) *n* podwozie *nt*
**undercharge** [ʌndə'tʃɑ:dʒ] *vt* liczyć (policzyć *perf*) za mało *+dat*
**underclothes** ['ʌndəkləuðz] *npl* bielizna *f*
**undercoat** ['ʌndəkəut] *n* podkład *m* (*farby*)

**undercover** [ʌndə'kʌvə^r] *adj* tajny ▷ *adv* w przebraniu

**undercurrent** ['ʌndəkʌrnt] *n* (*fig: of feeling*) ukryta nuta *f*

**undercut** [ʌndə'kʌt] (*irreg: like* **cut**) *vt* konkurować cenami z *+instr*

**underdeveloped** ['ʌndədɪ'vɛləpt] *adj* nierozwinięty, zacofany

**underdog** ['ʌndədɔg] *n*: **the ~** (*in society*) słabsi *vir pl*; (*in team competition*) słabsza drużyna *f*

**underdone** [ʌndə'dʌn] *adj* nie dogotowany

**under-employment** ['ʌndərɪm'plɔɪmənt] *n* częściowe bezrobocie *nt*

**underestimate** ['ʌndər'ɛstɪmeɪt] *vt* nie doceniać (nie docenić *perf*) *+gen*

**underexposed** ['ʌndərɪks'pəuzd] (*Phot*) *adj* niedoświetlony

**underfed** [ʌndə'fɛd] *adj* niedożywiony

**underfoot** [ʌndə'fut] *adv* pod stopami

**undergo** [ʌndə'gəu] (*irreg: like* **go**) *vt* (*change*) ulegać (ulec *perf*) *+dat*; (*test, operation*) zostawać (zostać *perf*) poddanym *+dat*, przechodzić (przejść *perf*); **the car is ~ing repairs** samochód jest w naprawie

**undergraduate** [ʌndə'grædjuɪt] *n student, który nie zdobył jeszcze stopnia BA* ▷ *cpd*: **~ courses** *kursy akademickie prowadzące do stopnia BA*

**underground** ['ʌndəgraund] *n*: **the ~** (*Brit*) metro *nt*; (*Pol*) podziemie *nt* ▷ *adj* podziemny ▷ *adv* pod ziemią; **to go ~** (*Pol*) schodzić (zejść *perf*) do podziemia

**undergrowth** ['ʌndəgrəuθ] *n* podszycie *nt* (leśne)

**underhand(ed)** [ʌndə'hænd(ɪd)] *adj* (*fig*) podstępny

**underinsured** [ʌndərɪn'ʃuəd] *adj* niedostatecznie ubezpieczony

**underlay** [ʌndə'leɪ] *n* warstwa *f* izolująca (*między dywanem a podłogą*)

**underlie** [ʌndə'laɪ] (*irreg: like* **go**) *vt* (*fig*) leżeć *or* tkwić u podstaw *+gen*; **the underlying cause** właściwa przyczyna

**underline** [ʌndə'laɪn] *vt* podkreślać (podkreślić *perf*)

**underling** ['ʌndəlɪŋ] (*pej*) *n* podwładny(-na) *m(f)*

**undermanning** [ʌndə'mænɪŋ] *n* niedobory *pl* personelu *or* kadrowe

**undermentioned** [ʌndə'mɛnʃənd] *adj* wymieniony (po)niżej

**undermine** [ʌndə'maɪn] *vt* podkopywać (podkopać *perf*)

**underneath** [ʌndə'ni:θ] *adv* pod spodem ▷ *prep* pod *+instr*

**undernourished** [ʌndə'nʌrɪʃt] *adj* niedożywiony

**underpaid** [ʌndə'peɪd] *adj* źle opłacany

**underpants** ['ʌndəpænts] *npl* slipy *pl*

**underpass** ['ʌndəpɑ:s] (*Brit*) *n* przejście *nt* podziemne; (*on motorway*) przejazd *m* podziemny

**underpin** [ʌndə'pɪn] *vt* podtrzymywać (podtrzymać *perf*)

**underplay** [ʌndə'pleɪ] (*Brit*) *vt* pomniejszać (pomniejszyć *perf*) znaczenie *+gen*

**underpopulated** [ʌndə'pɔpjuleɪtɪd] *adj* słabo zaludniony

**underprice** [ʌndə'praɪs] *vt* zaniżać (zaniżyć *perf*) ceny *+gen*

**underprivileged** [ʌndə'prɪvɪlɪdʒd] *adj* społecznie upośledzony

**underrate** [ʌndə'reɪt] *vt* nie doceniać (nie docenić *perf*) *+gen*

**underscore** [ʌndə'skɔ:^r] *vt* podkreślać (podkreślić *perf*)

**underseal** [ʌndə'si:l] (*Brit*) *vt* zabezpieczać (zabezpieczyć *perf*) przed korozją ▷ *n* powłoka *f* antykorozyjna

**undersecretary** ['ʌndə'sɛkrətərɪ] *n* podsekretarz *m*

**undersell** [ʌndə'sɛl] (*irreg: like* **sell**) *vt* konkurować cenami z *+instr*

**undershirt** ['ʌndəʃə:t] (*US*) *n* podkoszulek *m*

**undershorts** ['ʌndəʃɔ:ts] (*US*) *npl* kalesonki *pl*

**underside** ['ʌndəsaɪd] *n* (*of object*) spód *m*; (*of animal*) podbrzusze *nt*

**undersigned** ['ʌndə'saɪnd] *adj* niżej podpisany ▷ *n*: **the ~** niżej podpisany(-na) *m(f)*; **we the ~ agree that ...** my, niżej podpisani, uzgadniamy, że ...

**underskirt** ['ʌndəskə:t] (*Brit*) *n* (pół)halka *f*

**understaffed** [ʌndə'stɑ:ft] *adj* cierpiący na niedobory kadrowe

**understand** [ʌndə'stænd] (*irreg: like* **stand**) *vt* rozumieć (zrozumieć *perf*); **I ~ (that) ...** rozumiem, że ...; **to make o.s. understood** porozumieć się (*perf*) (*nie znając dobrze języka*), dogadać się (*perf*) (*inf*)

**understandable** [ʌndə'stændəbl] *adj* zrozumiały

**understanding** [ʌndə'stændɪŋ] *adj* wyrozumiały ▷ *n* (*of subject, language*) znajomość *f*; (*sympathy*) wyrozumiałość *f*, zrozumienie *nt*; (*co-operation*) porozumienie *nt*; **to come to an ~ with sb** dochodzić (dojść *perf*) z kimś do porozumienia; **on the ~ that ...** przy założeniu, że ...

**understate** [ʌndə'steɪt] *vt* (*seriousness*) pomniejszać (pomniejszyć *perf*); (*amount*) zaniżać (zaniżyć *perf*)

**understatement** ['ʌndəsteɪtmənt] *n* niedopowiedzenie *nt*, niedomówienie *nt*; **that's an ~!** to mało powiedziane!

**understood** [ʌndəˈstud] *pt, pp of* **understand** ▷ *adj* (*agreed*) ustalony; (*implied*) zrozumiały sam przez się
**understudy** [ˈʌndəstʌdɪ] *n* dubler(ka) *m(f)* (*w teatrze*)
**undertake** [ʌndəˈteɪk] (*irreg: like* **take**) *vt* podejmować się (podjąć się *perf*) *+gen* ▷ *vi*: **to ~ to do sth** podejmować się (podjąć się *perf*) zrobienia czegoś
**undertaker** [ˈʌndəteɪkəʳ] *n* przedsiębiorca *m* pogrzebowy
**undertaking** [ˈʌndəteɪkɪŋ] *n* (*job*) przedsięwzięcie *nt*; (*promise*) zobowiązanie *nt*
**undertone** [ˈʌndətəun] *n* (*of criticism etc*) zabarwienie *nt*; **in an ~** półgłosem
**undervalue** [ʌndəˈvælju:] *vt* nie doceniać (nie docenić *perf*) *+gen*
**underwater** [ʌndəˈwɔ:təʳ] *adv* pod wodą ▷ *adj* podwodny
**underwear** [ˈʌndəwɛəʳ] *n* bielizna *f*
**underweight** [ʌndəˈweɪt] *adj*: **to be ~** mieć niedowagę
**underworld** [ˈʌndəwə:ld] *n* świat *m* przestępczy
**underwrite** [ʌndəˈraɪt] *vt* (*Fin*) poręczać (poręczyć *perf*); (*Insurance*) przyjmować (przyjąć *perf*) do ubezpieczenia
**underwriter** [ˈʌndəraɪtəʳ] (*Insurance*) *n* agent(ka) *m(f)* ubezpieczeniowy(-wa) *m(f)*
**undeserved** [ʌndɪˈzə:vd] *adj* niezasłużony
**undesirable** [ʌndɪˈzaɪərəbl] *adj* (*objectionable*) nieodpowiedni; (*unwanted*) niepożądany
**undeveloped** [ʌndɪˈvɛləpt] *adj* (*land, resources*) nie zagospodarowany; (*countries*) nie rozwinięty
**undies** [ˈʌndɪz] (*inf*) *npl* bielizna *f* (*zwłaszcza damska*)
**undiluted** [ˈʌndaɪˈlu:tɪd] *adj* (*substance, liquid*) nie rozcieńczony; (*emotion*) silny
**undiplomatic** [ˈʌndɪpləˈmætɪk] *adj* niedyplomatyczny
**undischarged** [ˈʌndɪsˈtʃɑ:dʒd] *adj*: **~ bankrupt** *dłużnik, w stosunku do którego nie uchylono upadłości*
**undisciplined** [ʌnˈdɪsɪplɪnd] *adj* niezdyscyplinowany
**undiscovered** [ˈʌndɪsˈkʌvəd] *adj* nie odkryty
**undisguised** [ˈʌndɪsˈgaɪzd] *adj* nie skrywany
**undisputed** [ˈʌndɪsˈpju:tɪd] *adj* bezdyskusyjny, bezsporny
**undistinguished** [ˈʌndɪsˈtɪŋgwɪʃt] *adj* nie wyróżniający się (niczym)
**undisturbed** [ʌndɪsˈtə:bd] *adj* niezakłócony; **to leave sth ~** pozostawiać (pozostawić *perf*) coś w nienaruszonym stanie
**undivided** [ʌndɪˈvaɪdɪd] *adj*: **you have my ~ attention** słucham cię z całą uwagą
**undo** [ʌnˈdu:] (*irreg: like* **do**) *vt* (*shoelaces, string*) rozwiązywać (rozwiązać *perf*); (*buttons*) rozpinać (rozpiąć *perf*); (*fig: work, hopes*) niweczyć (zniweczyć *perf*); (*: person*) gubić (zgubić *perf*)
**undoing** [ʌnˈdu:ɪŋ] *n* (*downfall*) zguba *f*
**undone** [ʌnˈdʌn] *pp of* **undo**; **to come ~** (*shoelaces, string*) rozwiązywać się (rozwiązać się *perf*); (*button*) rozpinać się (rozpiąć się *perf*)
**undoubted** [ʌnˈdautɪd] *adj* niewątpliwy
**undoubtedly** [ʌnˈdautɪdlɪ] *adv* niewątpliwie, bez wątpienia
**undress** [ʌnˈdrɛs] *vi* rozbierać się (rozebrać się *perf*) ▷ *vt* rozbierać (rozebrać *perf*)
**undrinkable** [ʌnˈdrɪŋkəbl] *adj*: **to be ~** nie nadawać się do picia
**undue** [ʌnˈdju:] *adj* nadmierny, zbytni
**undulating** [ˈʌndjuleɪtɪŋ] *adj* (*landscape*) pofalowany, falisty; (*movement*) falujący
**unduly** [ʌnˈdju:lɪ] *adv* nadmiernie, zbytnio
**undying** [ʌnˈdaɪɪŋ] *adj* (*love, loyalty*) dozgonny; (*fame*) nieśmiertelny
**unearned** [ʌnˈə:nd] *adj* niezasłużony; **~ income** dochód nie pochodzący z pracy
**unearth** [ʌnˈə:θ] *vt* (*skeleton etc*) wykopywać (wykopać *perf*); (*ruins*) odkopywać (odkopać *perf*); (*fig: secrets etc*) wydobywać (wydobyć *perf*) na światło dzienne
**unearthly** [ʌnˈə:θlɪ] *adj* niesamowity, nie z tej ziemi *post*; **at some ~ hour** o nieprzyzwoitej porze
**unease** [ʌnˈi:z] *n* niepokój *m*
**uneasy** [ʌnˈi:zɪ] *adj* (*person*) zaniepokojony; (*feeling*) nieprzyjemny, nie dający spokoju; (*peace*) niepewny; **I am** *or* **I feel ~ about taking his money** niechętnie biorę od niego pieniądze
**uneconomic** [ˈʌni:kəˈnɔmɪk] *adj* nierentowny
**uneconomical** [ˈʌni:kəˈnɔmɪkl] *adj* nieekonomiczny
**uneducated** [ʌnˈɛdjukeɪtɪd] *adj* niewykształcony, bez wykształcenia *post*
**unemployed** [ʌnɪmˈplɔɪd] *adj* bezrobotny ▷ *npl*: **the ~** bezrobotni *vir pl*
**unemployment** [ʌnɪmˈplɔɪmənt] *n* bezrobocie *nt*
**unemployment benefit** (*Brit*) *n* zasiłek *m* dla bezrobotnych
**unemployment compensation** (*US*) *n* = **unemployment benefit**
**unending** [ʌnˈɛndɪŋ] *adj* nie kończący się
**unenviable** [ʌnˈɛnvɪəbl] *adj* nie do pozazdroszczenia *post*
**unequal** [ʌnˈi:kwəl] *adj* nierówny; **to feel/be ~ to** nie być w stanie sprostać *+dat*; **~ pay** zróżnicowanie płac

**unequalled**, (*US*) **unequaled** [ʌn'i:kwəld] *adj* niezrównany, niedościgniony
**unequivocal** [ʌnɪ'kwɪvəkl] *adj* niedwuznaczny, jednoznaczny; **he was ~ about it** powiedział wprost, co o tym myśli
**unerring** [ʌn'ə:rɪŋ] *adj* nieomylny, niezawodny
**UNESCO** [ju:'nɛskəu] *n abbr* (= *United Nations Educational, Scientific and Cultural Organization*) UNESCO *nt inv*
**unethical** [ʌn'ɛθɪkl] *adj* (*methods*) nieetyczny; (*doctor's behaviour*) niezgodny z etyką zawodową *post*
**uneven** [ʌn'i:vn] *adj* nierówny
**uneventful** [ʌnɪ'vɛntful] *adj* spokojny
**unexceptional** [ʌnɪk'sɛpʃənl] *adj* zwyczajny, przeciętny
**unexciting** [ʌnɪk'saɪtɪŋ] *adj* nieciekawy
**unexpected** [ʌnɪks'pɛktɪd] *adj* nieoczekiwany, niespodziewany
**unexpectedly** [ʌnɪks'pɛktɪdlɪ] *adv* nieoczekiwanie, niespodziewanie
**unexplained** [ʌnɪks'pleɪnd] *adj* nie wyjaśniony
**unexploded** [ʌnɪks'pləudɪd] *adj*: **~ bomb/shell** niewybuch *m*
**unfailing** [ʌn'feɪlɪŋ] *adj* (*support*) niezawodny; (*energy*) niewyczerpany
**unfair** [ʌn'fɛə^r] *adj* (*system*) niesprawiedliwy; (*advantage*) nieuczciwy; **~ to** niesprawiedliwy w stosunku do *+gen*; **it's ~ that ...** to niesprawiedliwe, że ...
**unfair dismissal** *n* nieuzasadnione zwolnienie *nt* (z pracy)
**unfairly** [ʌn'fɛəlɪ] *adv* (*treat*) niesprawiedliwie; (*dismiss*) niesłusznie
**unfaithful** [ʌn'feɪθful] *adj* niewierny
**unfamiliar** [ʌnfə'mɪlɪə^r] *adj* nieznany; **to be ~ with** nie znać *+gen*
**unfashionable** [ʌn'fæʃnəbl] *adj* niemodny
**unfasten** [ʌn'fɑ:sn] *vt* rozpinać (rozpiąć *perf*)
**unfathomable** [ʌn'fæðəməbl] *adj* niezgłębiony
**unfavourable**, (*US*) **unfavorable** [ʌn'feɪvrəbl] *adj* (*circumstances, weather*) niesprzyjający; (*opinion*) nieprzychylny
**unfavo(u)rably** [ʌn'feɪvrəblɪ] *adv* (*review*) niekorzystnie; **to compare unfavourably with** wypadać (wypaść *perf*) niekorzystnie w porównaniu z *+instr*; **to look unfavourably on** ustosunkowywać się (ustosunkować się *perf*) nieprzychylnie do *+gen*
**unfeeling** [ʌn'fi:lɪŋ] *adj* bezduszny
**unfinished** [ʌn'fɪnɪʃt] *adj* nie dokończony
**unfit** [ʌn'fɪt] *adj* (*physically*) mało sprawny, w słabej kondycji *post*; (*incompetent*) niezdolny; **~ for work** niezdolny do pracy; **~ for human consumption** nie nadający się do spożycia
**unflagging** [ʌn'flægɪŋ] *adj* nie słabnący
**unflappable** [ʌn'flæpəbl] *adj*: **he's ~** nie można go wyprowadzić z równowagi
**unflattering** [ʌn'flætərɪŋ] *adj* (*dress, hairstyle*) nietwarzowy; (*remark*) niepochlebny
**unflinching** [ʌn'flɪntʃɪŋ] *adj* niezachwiany
**unfold** [ʌn'fəuld] *vt* rozkładać (rozłożyć *perf*) ▷ *vi* rozwijać się (rozwinąć się *perf*)
**unforeseeable** [ʌnfɔ:'si:əbl] *adj* nieprzewidywalny, nie do przewidzenia *post*
**unforeseen** ['ʌnfɔ:'si:n] *adj* nieprzewidziany
**unforgettable** [ʌnfə'gɛtəbl] *adj* niezapomniany
**unforgivable** [ʌnfə'gɪvəbl] *adj* niewybaczalny
**unformatted** [ʌn'fɔ:mætɪd] (*Comput*) *adj* nie sformatowany
**unfortunate** [ʌn'fɔ:tʃənət] *adj* (*person*) pechowy; (*accident*) nieszczęśliwy; (*event, remark*) niefortunny; **it is ~ that ...** szkoda, że ...
**unfortunately** [ʌn'fɔ:tʃənətlɪ] *adv* niestety
**unfounded** [ʌn'faundɪd] *adj* bezpodstawny, nieuzasadniony
**unfriendly** [ʌn'frɛndlɪ] *adj* (*person*) nieprzyjazny; (*behaviour, remark*) nieprzyjemny
**unfulfilled** [ʌnful'fɪld] *adj* (*ambition, prophecy*) nie spełniony; (*person*) niespełniony
**unfurl** [ʌn'fə:l] *vt* (*flag*) rozpościerać (rozpostrzeć *perf*); (*umbrella*) rozkładać (rozłożyć *perf*)
**unfurnished** [ʌn'fə:nɪʃt] *adj* nie umeblowany
**ungainly** [ʌn'geɪnlɪ] *adj* niezgrabny
**ungodly** [ʌn'gɔdlɪ] *adj* piekielny; **at some ~ hour** o nieprzyzwoitej porze
**ungrammatical** [ʌngrə'mætɪkəl] *adj* niegramatyczny
**ungrateful** [ʌn'greɪtful] *adj* niewdzięczny
**unguarded** [ʌn'gɑ:dɪd] *adj*: **in an ~ moment** w chwili nieuwagi
**unhappily** [ʌn'hæpɪlɪ] *adv* (*sadly*) nieszczęśliwie; (*unfortunately*) niestety
**unhappiness** [ʌn'hæpɪnɪs] *n* nieszczęście *nt*, zgryzota *f*
**unhappy** [ʌn'hæpɪ] *adj* nieszczęśliwy; **~ about/with** niezadowolony z *+gen*
**unharmed** [ʌn'hɑ:md] *adj* bez szwanku *post*
**UNHCR** *n abbr* (= *United Nations High Commission for Refugees*) Wysoka Komisja *f* ONZ do spraw Uchodźców
**unhealthy** [ʌn'hɛlθɪ] *adj* (*person*) chory; (*place*) niezdrowy; (*fig: interest*) chorobliwy, niezdrowy
**unheard-of** [ʌn'hə:dɔv] *adj* niespotykany, nieznany

U

**unhelpful** [ʌn'hɛlpful] *adj* (*person*) niezbyt pomocny; (*advice*) nieprzydatny
**unhesitating** [ʌn'hɛzɪteɪtɪŋ] *adj* (*loyalty*) niezachwiany; (*reply*) zdecydowany, stanowczy
**unhook** [ʌn'huk] *vt* rozpinać (rozpiąć *perf*)
**unhurt** [ʌn'hə:t] *adj* bez szwanku *post*; **to be ~** nie doznać (*perf*) (żadnych) obrażeń
**unhygienic** ['ʌnhaɪ'dʒi:nɪk] *adj* (*room*) urągający higienie; (*conditions*) niehigieniczny
**UNICEF** ['ju:nɪsɛf] *n abbr* (= *United Nations International Children's Emergency Fund*) UNICEF *m*
**unicorn** ['ju:nɪkɔ:n] *n* jednorożec *m*
**unidentified** [ʌnaɪ'dɛntɪfaɪd] *adj* (*unfamiliar*) niezidentyfikowany; (*unnamed*) (bliżej) nieokreślony; *see also* **UFO**
**unification** [ju:nɪfɪ'keɪʃən] *n* zjednoczenie *nt*
**uniform** ['ju:nɪfɔ:m] *n* mundur *m* ▷ *adj* jednolity
**uniformity** [ju:nɪ'fɔ:mɪtɪ] *n* jednolitość *f*
**unify** ['ju:nɪfaɪ] *vt* jednoczyć się (zjednoczyć się *perf*)
**unilateral** [ju:nɪ'lætərəl] *adj* jednostronny
**unimaginable** [ʌnɪ'mædʒɪnəbl] *adj* niewyobrażalny
**unimaginative** [ʌnɪ'mædʒɪnətɪv] *adj* (*person*) pozbawiony wyobraźni, bez wyobraźni *post*; (*design*) niewyszukany
**unimpaired** [ʌnɪm'pɛəd] *adj* nienaruszony, nie osłabiony
**unimportant** [ʌnɪm'pɔ:tənt] *adj* nieważny, nieistotny
**unimpressed** [ʌnɪm'prɛst] *adj* niewzruszony
**uninhabited** [ʌnɪn'hæbɪtɪd] *adj* (*house*) niezamieszkały; (*island*) bezludny
**uninhibited** [ʌnɪn'hɪbɪtɪd] *adj* (*person*) bez zahamowań *post*; (*behaviour*) swobodny
**uninjured** [ʌn'ɪndʒəd] *adj* bez szwanku *or* szkody *post*
**unintelligent** [ʌnɪn'tɛlɪdʒənt] *adj* nieinteligentny
**unintentional** [ʌnɪn'tɛnʃənəl] *adj* nie zamierzony
**unintentionally** [ʌnɪn'tɛnʃnəlɪ] *adv* niechcący
**uninterested** [ʌn'ɪntrəstɪd] *adj* niezainteresowany
**uninvited** [ʌnɪn'vaɪtɪd] *adj* nieproszony
**uninviting** [ʌnɪn'vaɪtɪŋ] *adj* (*food*) nieapetyczny; (*place*) niezbyt zachęcający
**union** ['ju:njən] *n* (*unification*) zjednoczenie *nt*, unia *f*; (*also*: **trade union**) związek *m* zawodowy ▷ *cpd* (*activities, leader*) związkowy; **~ president** przewodniczący związku; **the U~** (*US*) Unia (*Stany Zjednoczone*)
**unionize** ['ju:njənaɪz] *vt* organizować (zorganizować *perf*) w związek zawodowy
**Union Jack** *n flaga brytyjska*
**Union of Soviet Socialist Republics** *n* (*formerly*) Związek *m* Socjalistycznych Republik Radzieckich
**union shop** *n zakład pracy zatrudniający wyłącznie członków związku zawodowego*
**unique** [ju:'ni:k] *adj* (*object*) unikalny; (*performance*) jedyny w swoim rodzaju, niepowtarzalny; (*number*) nie powtarzający się; (*ability, skill*) wyjątkowy; **to be ~ to** być wyłączną cechą *+gen*
**unisex** ['ju:nɪsɛks] *adj* (*hairdresser*) damsko-męski; **~ clothes** odzież uniseks
**unison** ['ju:nɪsn] *n*: **in ~** (*say, act*) zgodnie; (*sing*) unisono
**UNISON** *n federacja wolnych związków zawodowych w Wielkiej Brytanii*
**unit** ['ju:nɪt] *n* jednostka *f*; **production ~** jednostka produkcyjna; **kitchen ~** szafka kuchenna
**unit cost** (*Comm*) *n* koszt *m* jednostkowy
**unite** [ju:'naɪt] *vt* jednoczyć (zjednoczyć *perf*) ▷ *vi* jednoczyć się (zjednoczyć się *perf*)
**united** [ju:'naɪtɪd] *adj* (*agreed*) zgodny; (*country, party*) zjednoczony
**United Arab Emirates** *npl*: **the ~** Zjednoczone Emiraty *pl* Arabskie
**United Kingdom** *n*: **the ~** Zjednoczone Królestwo *nt* (Wielkiej Brytanii)
**United Nations** *n*: **the ~** Narody *pl* Zjednoczone, Organizacja *f* Narodów Zjednoczonych
**United States (of America)** *n*: **the United States** Stany *pl* Zjednoczone (Ameryki Północnej)
**unit price** (*Comm*) *n* cena *f* jednostkowa
**unit trust** (*Brit*: *Comm*) *n* fundusz *m* powierniczy
**unity** ['ju:nɪtɪ] *n* jedność *f*
**Univ.** *abbr* (= *university*) uniw.
**universal** [ju:nɪ'və:sl] *adj* powszechny, uniwersalny
**universe** ['ju:nɪvə:s] *n* wszechświat *m*
**university** [ju:nɪ'və:sɪtɪ] *n* uniwersytet *m* ▷ *cpd* (*year*) akademicki; (*education*) uniwersytecki; **~ student/professor** student/profesor uniwersytetu
**university degree** *n* stopień *m* naukowy
**unjust** [ʌn'dʒʌst] *adj* niesprawiedliwy
**unjustifiable** ['ʌndʒʌstɪ'faɪəbl] *adj* nieuzasadniony, nie dający się usprawiedliwić
**unjustified** [ʌn'dʒʌstɪfaɪd] *adj* (*belief, action*) bezpodstawny, nieuzasadniony; (*text*) niejustowany

**unkempt** [ʌn'kɛmpt] *adj* (*appearance*) zaniedbany; (*hair, beard*) rozczochrany
**unkind** [ʌn'kaɪnd] *adj* niegrzeczny, nieżyczliwy
**unkindly** [ʌn'kaɪndlɪ] *adv* niegrzecznie, nieżyczliwie
**unknown** [ʌn'nəun] *adj* (*fact*) nieznany, niewiadomy; (*person*) nieznajomy, nieznany; **~ to me** bez mojej wiedzy; **~ quantity** (*Math*) niewiadoma
**unladen** [ʌn'leɪdn] *adj* (*ship*) bez ładunku *post*; (*weight*) wyładowany, rozładowany
**unlawful** [ʌn'lɔ:ful] *adj* bezprawny, nielegalny
**unleaded** ['ʌn'lɛdɪd] *adj* bezołowiowy
**unleash** [ʌn'li:ʃ] *vt* (*fig: feeling, forces etc*) uwalniać (uwolnić *perf*)
**unleavened** [ʌn'lɛvnd] *adj* przaśny, bezdrożdżowy
**unless** [ʌn'lɛs] *conj* jeżeli nie, o ile nie, chyba że; **... ~ he comes ...** jeżeli nie przyjdzie, ... chyba że przyjdzie; **U~ he comes, ...** Jeżeli nie przyjdzie, ...; **~ otherwise stated** o ile nie określono inaczej; **~ I am mistaken** o ile się nie mylę
**unlicensed** [ʌn'laɪsnst] (*Brit*) *adj* (*restaurant*) nie posiadający koncesji na sprzedaż alkoholu
**unlike** [ʌn'laɪk] *adj* niepodobny ▷ *prep* (*not like*) w odróżnieniu od *+gen*; (*different from*) niepodobny do *+gen*
**unlikelihood** [ʌn'laɪklɪhud] *n* małe prawdopodobieństwo *nt*, nieprawdopodobieństwo *nt*
**unlikely** [ʌn'laɪklɪ] *adj* (*not likely*) nieprawdopodobny, mało prawdopodobny; (*unexpected*) nieoczekiwany; **in the ~ event of any trouble, ...** gdyby były jakieś kłopoty, co (jest) mało prawdopodobne, ...; **in the ~ event that they give you any trouble, ...** gdyby sprawiali wam jakieś kłopoty, co (jest) mało prawdopodobne, ...
**unlimited** [ʌn'lɪmɪtɪd] *adj* nieograniczony, bez ograniczeń *post*
**unlisted** ['ʌn'lɪstɪd] *adj* (*US: telephone number*) zastrzeżony; (*company*) nie notowany na giełdzie
**unlit** [ʌn'lɪt] *adj* nie oświetlony
**unload** [ʌn'ləud] *vt* wyładowywać (wyładować *perf*), rozładowywać (rozładować *perf*)
**unlock** [ʌn'lɔk] *vt* otwierać (otworzyć *perf*) (*kluczem*)
**unlucky** [ʌn'lʌkɪ] *adj* (*person*) nieszczęśliwy, pechowy; (*object, number*) pechowy; **to be ~** mieć pecha
**unmanageable** [ʌn'mænɪdʒəbl] *adj* (*tool, book*) nieporęczny; (*situation*) wymykający się spod kontroli, nie do opanowania *post*
**unmanned** [ʌn'mænd] *adj* bezzałogowy
**unmarked** [ʌn'mɑ:kt] *adj* bez skazy *post*; **~ police car** samochód policyjny bez oznakowań
**unmarried** [ʌn'mærɪd] *adj* (*man*) nieżonaty; (*woman*) niezamężna
**unmarried mother** *n* samotna matka *f*
**unmask** [ʌn'mɑ:sk] *vt* demaskować (zdemaskować *perf*)
**unmatched** [ʌn'mætʃt] *adj* niezrównany
**unmentionable** [ʌn'mɛnʃnəbl] *adj* (*topic*) zakazany, tabu *post*; (*word*) niecenzuralny
**unmerciful** [ʌn'mə:sɪful] *adj* bezlitosny
**unmistak(e)able** [ʌnmɪs'teɪkəbl] *adj* wyraźny, niewątpliwy
**unmistak(e)ably** [ʌnmɪs'teɪkəblɪ] *adv* wyraźnie, niewątpliwie
**unmitigated** [ʌn'mɪtɪgeɪtɪd] *adj* totalny, absolutny
**unnamed** [ʌn'neɪmd] *adj* (*nameless*) nie nazwany; (*anonymous*) nie wymieniony z nazwiska
**unnatural** [ʌn'nætʃrəl] *adj* nienaturalny
**unnecessarily** [ʌn'nɛsəsərɪlɪ] *adv* (*worry etc*) niepotrzebnie, zbytecznie; (*severe etc*) nadmiernie
**unnecessary** [ʌn'nɛsəsərɪ] *adj* niepotrzebny, zbyteczny
**unnerve** [ʌn'nə:v] *vt* wytrącać (wytrącić *perf*) z równowagi
**unnoticed** [ʌn'nəutɪst] *adj*: **to go** *or* **pass ~** pozostawać (pozostać *perf*) nie zauważonym
**UNO** ['ju:nəu] *n abbr* (= *United Nations Organization*) ONZ *m*
**unobservant** [ʌnəb'zə:vnt] *adj* mało spostrzegawczy
**unobtainable** [ʌnəb'teɪnəbl] *adj* (*item*) niedostępny; (*Tel*) nieosiągalny
**unobtrusive** [ʌnəb'tru:sɪv] *adj* nie rzucający się w oczy, dyskretny
**unoccupied** [ʌn'ɔkjupaɪd] *adj* (*seat*) nie zajęty; (*house*) niezamieszkały
**unofficial** [ʌnə'fɪʃl] *adj* (*news*) nie potwierdzony; (*strike*) nieoficjalny
**unopened** [ʌn'əupənd] *adj* nie otwarty
**unopposed** [ʌnə'pəuzd] *adj* nie napotykający oporu *or* sprzeciwu
**unorthodox** [ʌn'ɔ:θədɔks] *adj* (*treatment*) niekonwencjonalny; (*Rel*) nieortodoksyjny
**unpack** [ʌn'pæk] *vi* rozpakowywać się (rozpakować się *perf*) ▷ *vt* rozpakowywać (rozpakować *perf*)
**unpaid** [ʌn'peɪd] *adj* (*bill*) nie zapłacony; (*holiday, leave*) bezpłatny; (*work*) niepłatny; (*worker*) nie opłacany

U

**unpalatable** [ʌn'pælətəbl] *adj* (*meal*) niesmaczny; (*truth*) trudny do przełknięcia
**unparalleled** [ʌn'pærəlɛld] *adj* niezrównany
**unpatriotic** ['ʌnpætrɪ'ɔtɪk] *adj* niepatriotyczny
**unplanned** [ʌn'plænd] *adj* nie zaplanowany
**unpleasant** [ʌn'plɛznt] *adj* nieprzyjemny, niemiły
**unplug** [ʌn'plʌg] *vt* wyłączać (wyłączyć *perf*) z sieci
**unpolluted** [ʌnpə'lu:tɪd] *adj* nie zanieczyszczony, nie skażony
**unpopular** [ʌn'pɔpjuləʳ] *adj* niepopularny; **to make o.s. ~ (with)** narażać się (narazić się *perf*) (*+dat*), podpadać (podpaść *perf*) (*+dat*) (*inf*)
**unprecedented** [ʌn'prɛsɪdəntɪd] *adj* (*decision, event*) bezprecedensowy; (*wealth, scale*) niespotykany
**unpredictable** [ʌnprɪ'dɪktəbl] *adj* nieprzewidywalny
**unprejudiced** [ʌn'prɛdʒudɪst] *adj* nieuprzedzony
**unprepared** [ʌnprɪ'pɛəd] *adj* (*person*) nie przygotowany; (*speech*) (za)improwizowany
**unprepossessing** ['ʌnpri:pə'zɛsɪŋ] *adj* nieatrakcyjny, nieciekawy
**unpretentious** [ʌnprɪ'tɛnʃəs] *adj* bezpretensjonalny
**unprincipled** [ʌn'prɪnsɪpld] *adj* bez zasad *post*
**unproductive** [ʌnprə'dʌktɪv] *adj* (*land*) jałowy; (*discussion*) jałowy, bezproduktywny
**unprofessional** [ʌnprə'fɛʃənl] *adj* (*attitude*) nieprofesjonalny; (*conduct*) sprzeczny z etyką zawodową
**unprofitable** [ʌn'prɔfɪtəbl] *adj* nieopłacalny, nierentowny
**unprovoked** [ʌnprə'vəukt] *adj* nieuzasadniony, bezpodstawny
**unpunished** [ʌn'pʌnɪʃt] *adj*: **to go ~** nie zostać (*perf*) ukaranym
**unqualified** [ʌn'kwɔlɪfaɪd] *adj* (*nurse etc*) niewykwalifikowany; (*disaster*) kompletny; (*success*) pełen
**unquestionably** [ʌn'kwɛstʃənəblɪ] *adv* niewątpliwie, bezsprzecznie
**unquestioning** [ʌn'kwɛstʃənɪŋ] *adj* (*obedience etc*) ślepy, bezwarunkowy
**unravel** [ʌn'rævl] *vt* rozwijać (rozwinąć *perf*), rozplątywać (rozplątać *perf*); (*fig*) rozwiązywać (rozwiązać *perf*), rozwikływać (rozwikłać *perf*)
**unreal** [ʌn'rɪəl] *adj* (*artificial*) sztuczny; (*peculiar*) nierzeczywisty, nierealny
**unrealistic** ['ʌnrɪə'lɪstɪk] *adj* nierealistyczny
**unreasonable** [ʌn'ri:znəbl] *adj* (*person*) nierozsądny; (*idea*) niedorzeczny; (*demand*) wygórowany; (*length of time*) nadmierny
**unrecognizable** [ʌn'rɛkəgnaɪzəbl] *adj* nie do poznania *post*
**unrecognized** [ʌn'rɛkəgnaɪzd] *adj* (*talent, genius*) nie rozpoznany; (*Pol*: *regime*) nie uznawany
**unrecorded** [ʌnrə'kɔ:dɪd] *adj* (*piece of music etc*) nie nagrany; (*incident, statement*) nie odnotowany
**unrefined** [ʌnrə'faɪnd] *adj* nie rafinowany, nie oczyszczony
**unrehearsed** [ʌnrɪ'hə:st] *adj* (*Theat etc*) bez prób(y) *post*; (*spontaneous*) (za) improwizowany, spontaniczny
**unrelated** [ʌnrɪ'leɪtɪd] *adj* (*incident*) nie powiązany, nie związany; (*family*) nie spokrewniony
**unrelenting** [ʌnrɪ'lɛntɪŋ] *adj* (*person*) bezlitosny, nieubłagany; (*activity*) nie słabnący, uporczywy
**unreliable** [ʌnrɪ'laɪəbl] *adj* (*person, firm*) niesolidny; (*machine, method*) zawodny
**unrelieved** [ʌnrɪ'li:vd] *adj* (*monotony, misery*) beznadziejny
**unremitting** [ʌnrɪ'mɪtɪŋ] *adj* nieustający, nieustanny
**unrepeatable** [ʌnrɪ'pi:təbl] *adj* nie nadający się do powtórzenia
**unrepentant** [ʌnrɪ'pɛntənt] *adj* nie skruszony
**unrepresentative** ['ʌnrɛprɪ'zɛntətɪv] *adj*: **~ (of)** niereprezentatywny (dla *+gen*)
**unrequited** [ʌnrɪ'kwaɪtɪd] *adj* nieodwzajemniony
**unreserved** [ʌnrɪ'zə:vd] *adj* (*seat*) nie zarezerwowany; (*approval*) całkowity; (*admiration*) szczery
**unreservedly** [ʌnrɪ'zə:vɪdlɪ] *adv* (*approve*) całkowicie, w pełni; (*admire*) szczerze
**unresponsive** [ʌnrɪs'pɔnsɪv] *adj* obojętny; **to be ~ to** nie reagować na *+acc*
**unrest** [ʌn'rɛst] *n* niepokój *m*
**unrestricted** [ʌnrɪ'strɪktɪd] *adj* nieograniczony; **to have ~ access to** mieć nieograniczony dostęp do *+gen*
**unrewarded** [ʌnrɪ'wɔ:dɪd] *adj*: **his efforts went ~** jego wysiłki nie zostały nagrodzone
**unripe** [ʌn'raɪp] *adj* niedojrzały
**unrivalled**, (US) **unrivaled** [ʌn'raɪvəld] *adj* niezrównany
**unroll** [ʌn'rəul] *vt* rozwijać (rozwinąć *perf*)
**unruffled** [ʌn'rʌfld] *adj* (*person*) nie poruszony; (*hair, surface*) gładki
**unruly** [ʌn'ru:lɪ] *adj* niesforny
**unsafe** [ʌn'seɪf] *adj* (*in danger*) zagrożony; (*dangerous*) niebezpieczny; **~ to eat/drink** niezdatny do spożycia/picia
**unsaid** [ʌn'sɛd] *adj*: **to leave sth ~** przemilczeć (*perf*) coś

**unsaleable**, (*US*) **unsalable** [ʌn'seɪləbl] *adj* niechodliwy; **it's practically ~** tego praktycznie nie da się sprzedać
**unsatisfactory** ['ʌnsætɪs'fæktərɪ] *adj* niezadowalający
**unsatisfied** [ʌn'sætɪsfaɪd] *adj* nie usatysfakcjonowany, niezadowolony
**unsavoury**, (*US*) **unsavory** [ʌn'seɪvərɪ] *adj* (*fig*) podejrzany
**unscathed** [ʌn'skeɪðd] *adj* nietknięty
**unscientific** ['ʌnsaɪən'tɪfɪk] *adj* nienaukowy
**unscrew** [ʌn'skru:] *vt* odkręcać (odkręcić *perf*)
**unscrupulous** [ʌn'skru:pjuləs] *adj* pozbawiony skrupułów
**unsecured** ['ʌnsɪ'kjuəd] *adj* (*creditor*) bez zabezpieczenia *post*; (*loan*) nie zabezpieczony
**unseemly** [ʌn'si:mlɪ] *adj* niewłaściwy, niestosowny
**unseen** [ʌn'si:n] *adj* (*hidden object*) niewidoczny; (*forces, hand*) niewidzialny; (*danger*) ukryty
**unselfish** [ʌn'sɛlfɪʃ] *adj* bezinteresowny
**ınsettled** [ʌn'sɛtld] *adj* (*person*) niespokojny; (*future, weather*) niepewny; (*question*) nie rozstrzygnięty
**ınsettling** [ʌn'sɛtlɪŋ] *adj* niepokojący
**ınshak(e)able** [ʌn'ʃeɪkəbl] *adj* niewzruszony, niezachwiany
**ınshaven** [ʌn'ʃeɪvn] *adj* nie ogolony
**ınsightly** [ʌn'saɪtlɪ] *adj* szpetny
**ınskilled** [ʌn'skɪld] *adj* niewykwalifikowany
**ınsociable** [ʌn'səuʃəbl] *adj* nietowarzyski
**ınsocial** [ʌn'səuʃl] *adj*: **to work ~ hours** pracować w nietypowych godzinach
**ınsold** [ʌn'səuld] *adj* nie sprzedany
**nsolicited** [ʌnsə'lɪsɪtɪd] *adj* (*goods, manuscripts*) nie zamówiony; **she was given much ~ advice** dostała dużo rad, o które nie prosiła
**ınsophisticated** [ʌnsə'fɪstɪkeɪtɪd] *adj* (*person*) prosty; (*method, device*) nieskomplikowany
**ınsound** [ʌn'saund] *adj* (*floor, foundations*) słaby; (*policy, advice*) oparty na błędnych przesłankach; **of ~ mind** nie w pełni władz umysłowych
**ıspeakable** [ʌn'spi:kəbl] *adj* (*indescribable*) niewymowny, niewypowiedziany; (*awful*) okropny
**ıspoken** [ʌn'spəukn] *adj* (*word*) nie wypowiedziany; (*agreement*) milczący
**ıstable** [ʌn'steɪbl] *adj* (*piece of furniture*) chwiejny; (*government*) niestabilny; (*person: mentally*) niezrównoważony
**ısteady** [ʌn'stɛdɪ] *adj* niepewny
**ıstinting** [ʌn'stɪntɪŋ] *adj* hojny, szczodry

**unstuck** [ʌn'stʌk] *adj*: **to come ~** (*label etc*) odklejać się (odkleić się *perf*); (*fig: plan, system*) zawodzić (zawieść *perf*)
**unsubstantiated** ['ʌnsəb'stænʃɪeɪtɪd] *adj* (*rumour*) nie potwierdzony; (*accusation*) bezpodstawny
**unsuccessful** [ʌnsək'sɛsful] *adj* (*attempt, marriage*) nieudany; **her application was ~** jej podanie zostało odrzucone; **he was ~** (*in attempting sth*) nie udało mu się; (*in examination*) nie powiodło mu się; (*as writer etc*) nie miał powodzenia
**unsuccessfully** [ʌnsək'sɛsfəlɪ] *adv* bez powodzenia
**unsuitable** [ʌn'su:təbl] *adj* nieodpowiedni
**unsuited** [ʌn'su:tɪd] *adj*: **to be ~ for** *or* **to sth** nie nadawać się do czegoś; **he is ~ to be leader of a party** nie nadaje się na lidera partii
**unsure** [ʌn'ʃuə^r] *adj* niepewny; **to be ~ of o.s.** nie być pewnym siebie
**unsuspecting** [ʌnsəs'pɛktɪŋ] *adj* niczego nie podejrzewający
**unsweetened** [ʌn'swi:tnd] *adj* nie słodzony
**unswerving** [ʌn'swə:vɪŋ] *adj* niezachwiany
**unsympathetic** ['ʌnsɪmpə'θɛtɪk] *adj* (*showing no understanding*) obojętny; (*unlikeable*) niesympatyczny, antypatyczny; **~ to(wards)** nieprzychylny *+dat*
**untangle** [ʌn'tæŋgl] *vt* (*string*) rozplątywać (rozplątać *perf*); (*mystery*) rozwikływać (rozwikłać *perf*)
**untapped** [ʌn'tæpt] *adj* (*resources*) nie wykorzystany
**untaxed** [ʌn'tækst] *adj* nie opodatkowany
**unthinkable** [ʌn'θɪŋkəbl] *adj* nie do pomyślenia *post*
**untidy** [ʌn'taɪdɪ] *adj* (*room*) nie posprzątany; (*person*) nieporządny
**untie** [ʌn'taɪ] *vt* (*knot, parcel, prisoner*) rozwiązywać (rozwiązać *perf*); (*dog, horse*) odwiązywać (odwiązać *perf*)
**until** [ən'tɪl] *prep* (aż) do *+gen* ▷ *conj* aż; (*after negative*) dopóki nie; **they didn't find her ~ the next day** znaleźli ją dopiero następnego dnia; **she waited ~ he had gone** poczekała, aż wyszedł; **~ he comes** dopóki nie przyjdzie; **~ now** dotychczas; **~ then** do tego czasu; **from morning ~ night** od rana do wieczora *or* nocy
**untimely** [ʌn'taɪmlɪ] *adj* (*arrival*) nie w porę *post*; (*moment*) niedogodny; (*death*) przedwczesny
**untold** [ʌn'təuld] *adj* (*suffering, wealth*) nieopisany; **the ~ story** kulisy, tło
**untouched** [ʌn'tʌtʃt] *adj* nietknięty; **~ by** (*unaffected*) obojętny *or* nieczuły na *+acc*

U

**untoward** [ʌntəˈwɔ:d] *adj* (*unforeseen*) nieprzewidziany; (*adverse*) niefortunny
**untrammelled** [ʌnˈtræmld] *adj* nieskrępowany
**untranslatable** [ʌntrænzˈleɪtəbl] *adj* nieprzetłumaczalny
**untried** [ʌnˈtraɪd] *adj* (*policy, remedy*) nie wypróbowany; (*prisoner*) nie sądzony
**untrue** [ʌnˈtru:] *adj* nieprawdziwy
**untrustworthy** [ʌnˈtrʌstwə:ðɪ] *adj* niegodny zaufania
**unusable** [ʌnˈju:zəbl] *adj* nie nadający się do użytku
**unused**[1] [ʌnˈju:zd] *adj* (*clothes*) nie używany; (*land*) nie wykorzystany
**unused**[2] [ʌnˈju:st] *adj*: **to be ~ to sth/to doing sth** nie być przyzwyczajonym do czegoś/do robienia czegoś
**unusual** [ʌnˈju:ʒuəl] *adj* niezwykły, niecodzienny; **it was not ~ to come home at three in the morning** powroty do domu o trzeciej nad ranem nie należały do rzadkości
**unusually** [ʌnˈju:ʒuəlɪ] *adv* niezwykle
**unveil** [ʌnˈveɪl] *vt* odsłaniać (odsłonić *perf*)
**unwanted** [ʌnˈwɔntɪd] *adj* (*clothing*) niepotrzebny; (*child, pregnancy*) nie chciany
**unwarranted** [ʌnˈwɔrəntɪd] *adj* nieuzasadniony
**unwary** [ʌnˈwɛərɪ] *adj* nieświadomy
**unwavering** [ʌnˈweɪvərɪŋ] *adj* (*faith, support*) niezłomny, niezachwiany; (*gaze*) uporczywy
**unwelcome** [ʌnˈwɛlkəm] *adj* (*guest*) niepożądany, niemile widziany; (*facts, situation*) niewygodny; **I felt ~** czułem się jak intruz
**unwell** [ʌnˈwɛl] *adj*: **I feel ~** źle się czuję; **she's ~** jest chora
**unwieldy** [ʌnˈwi:ldɪ] *adj* (*object*) nieporęczny; (*system*) niesprawny
**unwilling** [ʌnˈwɪlɪŋ] *adj*: **to be ~ to do sth** nie chcieć czegoś (z)robić
**unwillingly** [ʌnˈwɪlɪŋlɪ] *adv* niechętnie
**unwind** [ʌnˈwaɪnd] (*irreg: like* **wind**) *vt* (*bandage*) odwijać (odwinąć *perf*); (*ball of string*) rozwijać (rozwinąć *perf*) ▷ *vi* odprężać się (odprężyć się *perf*), relaksować się (zrelaksować się *perf*)
**unwise** [ʌnˈwaɪz] *adj* niemądry
**unwitting** [ʌnˈwɪtɪŋ] *adj* bezwiedny
**unwittingly** [ʌnˈwɪtɪŋlɪ] *adv* niechcący
**unworkable** [ʌnˈwə:kəbl] *adj* niewykonalny
**unworthy** [ʌnˈwə:ðɪ] *adj*: **~ of** niegodny *or* niewart *+gen*; **to be ~ of sth/to do sth** nie zasługiwać na coś/, by coś (z)robić; **that kind of behaviour is ~ of you** takie zachowanie ci nie przystoi

**unwrap** [ʌnˈræp] *vt* rozwijać (rozwinąć *perf*, rozpakowywać (rozpakować *perf*)
**unwritten** [ʌnˈrɪtn] *adj* niepisany
**unzip** [ʌnˈzɪp] *vt* rozpinać (rozpiąć *perf*)

 KEYWORD

**up** [ʌp] *prep*: **to go up the stairs** wchodzić (wejść *perf*) po schodach; **he wen up the hill** wszedł na wzgórze; **the cat wa up a tree** kot był na drzewie; **they live further up the street** mieszkają dalej na tej ulicy
▷ *adv* **1** (*upwards, higher*): **up in the sky/the mountains** wysoko na niebie/w górach; **put it a bit higher up** połóż to troszkę wyżej; **up there** tam w *or* na górze; **up abo** wysoko
**2**: **to be up** (*out of bed*) być na nogach; (*prices level*) wzrosnąć (*perf*); (*building, tent*) stać
**3**: **up to** do *+gen*; **I've read up to page 60** przeczytałem do strony 60.; **the water can up to his knees** woda podeszła mu do kola **up to now** do tej pory
**4**: **to be up to** (*depend on*) zależeć od *+gen*; **it' up to you** to zależy od ciebie; **it's not up t me to decide** decyzja nie należy do mnie
**5**: **to be up to** (*equal to: person*) podołać (*perf*, sprostać (*perf*) *+dat*; (*: work etc*) spełniać (spełnić *perf*) *+acc*, odpowiadać *+dat*; **he's nc up to it** nie podoła temu; **their work is no up to the required standard** ich praca ni spełnia wymaganych norm
**6**: **to be up to** (*inf: be doing*) porabiać; **what he up to?** co on porabia?; (*showing disapprov suspicion*) co on kombinuje? (*inf*)
▷ *n*: **ups and downs** wzloty *pl* i upadki *pl*

**up-and-coming** [ʌpəndˈkʌmɪŋ] *adj* dobrze się zapowiadający
**upbeat** [ˈʌpbi:t] *n* (*Mus*) nieakcentowana miara *f* taktu; (*in economy, prosperity*) boom *m* wzrost *m* ▷ *adj* (*person*) w dobrym nastroju *post*; (*mood, ending*) optymistyczny
**upbraid** [ʌpˈbreɪd] *vt* karcić (skarcić *perf*)
**upbringing** [ˈʌpbrɪŋɪŋ] *n* wychowanie *nt*
**update** [ʌpˈdeɪt] *vt* uaktualniać (uaktualni *perf*)
**upend** [ʌpˈɛnd] *vt* stawiać (postawić *perf*) pionowo
**upgrade** [ʌpˈgreɪd] *vt* (*house*) podnosić (podnieść *perf*) standard *+gen*; (*pay, status*) podnosić (podnieść *perf*); (*employee*) awansować (awansować *perf*); (*Comput*) zastępować (zastąpić *perf*) nowszą wersją
**upheaval** [ʌpˈhi:vl] *n* (*emotional*) wstrząs *m*; (*Pol*) wstrząsy *pl*, wrzenie *nt*

**uphill** [ʌp'hɪl] *adj* (*climb*) pod górę *post*; (*fig*: *task*) żmudny ▷ *adv* pod górę; **to go ~** wspinać się (w górę)
**uphold** [ʌp'həuld] (*irreg*: *like* **hold**) *vt* (*law*, *principle*) przestrzegać *+gen*; (*decision*, *conviction*) podtrzymywać (podtrzymać *perf*)
**upholstery** [ʌp'həulstərɪ] *n* tapicerka *f*, obicie *nt*
**upkeep** ['ʌpki:p] *n* utrzymanie *nt*, koszty *pl* utrzymania
**up-market** [ʌp'mɑ:kɪt] *adj* ekskluzywny
**upon** [ə'pɔn] *prep* na *+loc*
**upper** ['ʌpə$^{r}$] *adj* górny, wyższy ▷ *n* (*of shoe*) wierzch *m*, cholewka *f*
**upper class** *n*: **the ~** warstwa *f or* klasa *f* wyższa
**upper-class** ['ʌpə'klɑ:s] *adj* (*families*, *accent*) arystokratyczny; (*district*) ekskluzywny
**upper hand** *n*: **to have the ~** mieć przewagę
**uppermost** ['ʌpəməust] *adj* najwyższy, znajdujący się na (samej) górze; **there were two thoughts ~ in my mind** myślałam przede wszystkim o dwóch rzeczach
**Upper Volta** [-'vɔltə] *n* Górna Wolta *f*
**upright** ['ʌpraɪt] *adj* (*vertical*) pionowy; (*erect*) wyprostowany; (*fig*: *honest*) prawy ▷ *adv* prosto ▷ *n* wspornik *m* pionowy, belka *f* pionowa
**uprising** ['ʌpraɪzɪŋ] *n* powstanie *nt*
**uproar** ['ʌprɔ:$^{r}$] *n* (*shouts*) hałas *m*; (*protest*) poruszenie *nt*, wrzawa *f*
**uproot** [ʌp'ru:t] *vt* (*tree*) wyrywać (wyrwać *perf*) z korzeniami; (*fig*: *family*) wysiedlać (wysiedlić *perf*)
**upset** [*vb*, *adj* ʌp'sɛt, *n* 'ʌpsɛt] (*irreg*: *like* **set**) *vt* (*knock over*) przewracać (przewrócić *perf*); (*make sad*) martwić (zmartwić *perf*); (*make angry or nervous*) denerwować (zdenerwować *perf*); (*routine*, *plan*) dezorganizować (zdezorganizować *perf*) ▷ *adj* (*person*: *worried*) zmartwiony; (: *angry*) zdenerwowany; (*stomach*) rozstrojony ▷ *n*: **to have a stomach ~** (*Brit*) mieć rozstrój żołądka; **I get ~ when...** (*sad*) jest mi przykro, gdy...; (*angry*) denerwuję się, gdy...
**upset price** ['ʌpsɛt-] (*US*, *Scottish*) *n* cena *f* wywoławcza
**upsetting** [ʌp'sɛtɪŋ] *adj* przykry
**upshot** ['ʌpʃɔt] *n* wynik *m*, rezultat *m*; **the ~ of it all was that ...** skończyło się na tym, że ...
**upside down** ['ʌpsaɪd-] *adv* do góry nogami; **to turn a place ~** (*fig*) przetrząsać (przetrząsnąć *perf*) wszystkie kąty
**upstairs** [ʌp'stɛəz] *adv* (*be*) na piętrze, na górze; (*go*) na piętro, na górę ▷ *adj* na piętrze *post* ▷ *n* piętro *nt*, góra *f*; **there's no ~** jest tylko parter *or* jedno piętro
**upstart** ['ʌpstɑ:t] (*pej*) *n* ważniak(-aczka) *m*(*f*) (*pej*)
**upstream** [ʌp'stri:m] *adv* pod prąd ▷ *adj*: **to be ~** znajdować się (dalej) w górę rzeki
**upsurge** ['ʌpsə:dʒ] *n* (*of enthusiasm etc*) przypływ *m*
**uptake** ['ʌpteɪk] *n*: **to be quick/slow on the ~** szybko/wolno się orientować
**uptight** [ʌp'taɪt] (*inf*) *adj* spięty
**up-to-date** ['ʌptə'deɪt] *adj* (*modern*) nowoczesny; (*having latest information*: *map etc*) aktualny; (: *person*) dobrze poinformowany
**upturn** ['ʌptə:n] *n* zmiana *f* na lepsze
**upturned** ['ʌptə:nd] *adj* (*nose*) zadarty
**upward** ['ʌpwəd] *adj* (*movement*) w górę *post*
**upwards** ['ʌpwədz] *adv* w górę; **upward(s) of 200,000 people** z górą 200 tysięcy osób
**URA** (*US*) *n abbr* = **Urban Renewal Administration**
**Ural Mountains** *n*: **the ~** (*also*: **the Urals**) Ural *m*
**uranium** [juə'reɪnɪəm] *n* uran *m*
**Uranus** [juə'reɪnəs] *n* Uran *m*
**urban** ['ə:bən] *adj* (wielko)miejski
**urbane** [ə:'beɪn] *adj* grzeczny, dobrze wychowany
**urbanization** [ə:bənaɪ'zeɪʃən] *n* urbanizacja *f*
**urchin** ['ə:tʃɪn] *n* urwis *m*
**urge** [ə:dʒ] *n* pragnienie *nt*, chęć *f* ▷ *vt*: **to ~ sb to do sth** namawiać (namówić *perf*) kogoś, żeby coś zrobił *or* do zrobienia czegoś; **to ~ caution** zalecać (zalecić *perf*) ostrożność
▶ **urge on** *vt* zachęcać
**urgency** ['ə:dʒənsɪ] *n* (*need to act quickly*) pośpiech *m*; (*of tone*) zaniepokojenie *nt*; **a matter of ~** (bardzo) pilna sprawa
**urgent** ['ə:dʒənt] *adj* (*need*) naglący; (*message*) pilny; (*voice*) natarczywy
**urgently** ['ə:dʒəntlɪ] *adv* pilnie
**urinal** ['juərɪnl] *n* (*building*) toaleta *f* męska; (*vessel*) pisuar *m*
**urinate** ['juərɪneɪt] *vi* oddawać (oddać *perf*) mocz
**urine** ['juərɪn] *n* mocz *m*
**urn** [ə:n] *n* (*container*) urna *f*; (*also*: **tea urn**) termos *m* bufetowy
**Uruguay** ['juərəgwaɪ] *n* Urugwaj *m*
**Uruguayan** [juərə'gwaɪən] *adj* urugwajski ▷ *n* Urugwajczyk(-jka) *m*(*f*)
**US** *n abbr* = **United States**
**us** [ʌs] *pron* nas (*gen*, *acc*, *loc*), nam (*dat*), nami (*instr*); *see also* **me**
**USA** *n abbr* = **United States of America**; (*Mil*) = **United States Army**
**usable** ['ju:zəbl] *adj* (*information*) użyteczny, przydatny; (*tool etc*) nadający się do użytku
**USAF** *n abbr* = **United States Air Force**

**usage** ['ju:zɪdʒ] (*Ling*) *n* użycie *nt*

**USCG** *n abbr* = **United States Coast Guard**

**USDA** *n abbr* (= *United States Department of Agriculture*) Ministerstwo *nt* Rolnictwa

**USDAW** ['ʌzdɔ:] (*Brit*) *n abbr* = **Union of Shop, Distributive and Allied Workers**

**USDI** *n abbr* (= *United States Department of the Interior*) Ministerstwo *nt* Ochrony Środowiska, Zasobów Naturalnych i Leśnictwa

**use** [*n* ju:s, *vb* ju:z] *n* (*using*) użycie *nt*, stosowanie *nt*; (*usefulness*) użytek *m*, zastosowanie *nt* ▷ *vt* używać (użyć *perf*) +*gen*, posługiwać się (posłużyć się *perf*) +*instr*; **in use** w użyciu; **to go out of use** wychodzić (wyjść *perf*) z użycia; **to be of use** przydawać się (przydać się *perf*); **to make use of sth** stosować (zastosować *perf*) *or* wykorzystywać (wykorzystać *perf*) coś; **it's no use!** nic z tego!; **it's no use arguing with you** dyskusja z tobą nie ma sensu; **she used to live in this street** mieszkała kiedyś na tej ulicy; **to have the use of** móc korzystać z +*gen*; **what's this used for?** do czego to służy?; **to be used to** być przyzwyczajonym do +*gen*; **to get used to** przyzwyczajać się (przyzwyczaić się *perf*) *or* przywykać (przywyknąć *perf*) do +*gen*
▸ **use up** *vt* (*food, leftovers*) zużywać (zużyć *perf*); (*money*) wydawać (wydać *perf*)

**used** [ju:zd] *adj* używany

**useful** ['ju:sful] *adj* użyteczny, przydatny; **to come in ~** przydawać się (przydać się *perf*)

**usefulness** ['ju:sfəlnɪs] *n* użyteczność *f*, przydatność *f*

**useless** ['ju:slɪs] *adj* (*unusable*) bezużyteczny, nieprzydatny; (*pointless*) bezcelowy; (*bad, hopeless*) beznadziejny

**user** ['ju:zə^r] *n* użytkownik(-iczka) *m*(*f*); (*of gas etc*) odbiorca *m*

**user-friendly** ['ju:zə'frɛndlɪ] *adj* łatwy w użyciu *or* zastosowaniu

**USES** *n abbr* = **United States Employment Service**

**usher** ['ʌʃə^r] *n osoba usadzająca gości na weselu, widzów w teatrze itp* ▷ *vt*: **to ~ sb in** wprowadzać (wprowadzić *perf*) kogoś

**usherette** [ʌʃə'rɛt] *n* (*in cinema*) bileterka *f*

**USIA** *n abbr* (= *United States Information Agency*) *Ministerstwo Informacji USA*

**USM** *n abbr* (= *United States Mint*) *mennica państwowa*; = **United States Mail**

**USN** *n abbr* = **United States Navy**

**USPHS** *n abbr* = **United States Public Health Service**

**USPO** *n abbr* = **United States Post Office**

**USS** *abbr* (= *United States Ship*) *skrót stanowiący część nazwy amerykańskich okrętów wojennych*

**USSR** *n abbr* (*formerly*: = *Union of Soviet Socialist Republics*) ZSRR *nt inv*

**usu.** *abbr* = **usually**

**usual** ['ju:ʒuəl] *adj* zwykły; **as ~** jak zwykle

**usually** ['ju:ʒuəlɪ] *adv* zwykle, zazwyczaj

**usurer** ['ju:ʒərə^r] *n* lichwiarz(-arka) *m*(*f*)

**usurp** [ju:'zə:p] *vt* uzurpować (uzurpować *perf*) sobie

**usury** ['ju:ʒurɪ] *n* lichwa *f*

**UT** (*US: Post*) *abbr* = **Utah**

**utensil** [ju:'tɛnsl] *n*: **kitchen ~s** przybory *pl* kuchenne

**uterus** ['ju:tərəs] (*Anat*) *n* macica *f*

**utilitarian** [ju:tɪlɪ'tɛərɪən] *adj* (*object*) funkcjonalny; (*Philosophy*) utylitarystyczny

**utility** [ju:'tɪlɪtɪ] *n* użyteczność *f*, przydatność *f*; **public utilities** usługi komunalne

**utility room** *n* pomieszczenie *nt* gospodarcze

**utilization** [ju:tɪlaɪ'zeɪʃən] *n* wykorzystanie *n*

**utilize** ['ju:tɪlaɪz] *vt* wykorzystywać (wykorzystać *perf*), użytkować (zużytkować *perf*)

**utmost** ['ʌtməust] *adj* najwyższy ▷ *n*: **we wil do our ~ to ...** zrobimy wszystko, co w nasze mocy, by +*infin*; **to be of the ~ importance** być sprawą najwyższej wagi

**utter** ['ʌtə^r] *adj* (*conviction*) pełny, całkowity; (*amazement*) kompletny; (*rubbish, fool*) zupełn skończony ▷ *vt* (*sounds*) wydawać (wydać *per* (z siebie); (*words*) wypowiadać (wypowiedzieć *perf*)

**utterance** ['ʌtrns] *n* wypowiedź *f*

**utterly** ['ʌtəlɪ] *adv* zupełnie

**U-turn** ['ju:'tə:n] *n* (*Aut*) zawracanie *nt*; (*fig*) zwrot *m* o 180 stopni

# Vv

**V¹, v** [vi:] *n* (*letter*) V *nt*, v *nt*; **V for Victor** ≈ V jak Violetta
**V²** *abbr* (= *volt*) V
**v.** *abbr* (= *verse*) w.; = **versus**; (= *vide*) zob.
**VA** (*US: Post*) *abbr* = **Virginia**
**vac** [væk] (*Brit: inf*) *n abbr* = **vacation**
**vacancy** ['veɪkənsɪ] *n* (*Brit: job*) wakat *m*, wolny etat *m*; (*in hotel*) wolny pokój *m*; **"no vacancies"** „wolnych miejsc brak"; **have you any vacancies?** (*hotel*) czy mają Państwo (jakieś) wolne pokoje?; (*office*) czy mają Państwo (jakieś) wolne etaty?
**vacant** ['veɪkənt] *adj* (*room, post*) wolny; (*look, expression*) nieobecny
**vacant lot** (*US*) *n* wolna działka *f*
**vacate** [və'keɪt] *vt* (*house*) wyprowadzać się (wyprowadzić się *perf*) z *+gen*; (*post, seat*) zwalniać (zwolnić *perf*)
**vacation** [və'keɪʃən] *n* (*esp US*) urlop *m*; (*Scol*) wakacje *pl*; **to take a ~** brać (wziąć *perf*) urlop; **on ~** na urlopie
**vacation course** *n* kurs *m* wakacyjny
**vaccinate** ['væksɪneɪt] *vt*: **to ~ sb (against sth)** szczepić (zaszczepić *perf*) kogoś (przeciwko czemuś)
**vaccination** [væksɪ'neɪʃən] *n* (*no pl: act of vaccinating*) szczepienia *pl*; (*instance*) szczepienie *nt*
**vaccine** ['væksi:n] *n* szczepionka *f*
**vacuum** ['vækjum] *n* próżnia *f*
**vacuum cleaner** *n* odkurzacz *m*
**vacuum flask** (*Brit*) *n* termos *m*
**vacuum-packed** ['vækjum'pækt] *adj* pakowany próżniowo
**vagabond** ['vægəbɔnd] *n* włóczęga *m*, wagabunda *m*
**vagary** ['veɪgərɪ] *n*: **the vagaries of** kaprysy *+gen*
**vagina** [və'dʒaɪnə] (*Anat*) *n* pochwa *f*
**vagrancy** ['veɪgrənsɪ] *n* włóczęgostwo *nt*
**vagrant** ['veɪgrənt] *n* włóczęga *m*
**vague** [veɪg] *adj* (*blurred*) niewyraźny; (*unclear*) niejasny; (*not precise*) ogólnikowy; (*evasive*) wymijający; **he was ~** wyrażał się mało konkretnie; **I haven't the ~st idea** nie mam najmniejszego pojęcia
**vaguely** ['veɪglɪ] *adv* (*not precisely*) ogólnikowo; (*evasively*) wymijająco; (*slightly*) trochę
**vagueness** ['veɪgnɪs] *n* ogólnikowość *f*
**vain** [veɪn] *adj* (*person*) próżny; (*attempt*) daremny; **in ~** na próżno, (na)daremnie
**vainly** ['veɪnlɪ] *adv* na próżno, (na)daremnie
**valance** ['væləns] *n ozdobna falbanka zwisająca z ramy łóżka*
**valedictory** [vælɪ'dɪktərɪ] *adj* pożegnalny
**valentine** ['væləntaɪn] *n* (*also*: **valentine card**) walentynka *f*; (*person*) *osoba, której wysyła się walentynkę*
**Valentine's Day** *n* Walentynki *pl*
**valet** ['vælɪt] *n* służący *m*
**valet parking** *n parkowanie samochodów gości przez obsługę hotelu, restauracji itp*
**valet service** *n* usługi *pl* (*hotelowe itp*)
**valiant** ['vælɪənt] *adj* mężny
**valid** ['vælɪd] *adj* (*ticket, document*) ważny; (*argument*) przekonujący; (*reason, criticism*) uzasadniony
**validate** ['vælɪdeɪt] *vt* (*contract*) zatwierdzać (zatwierdzić *perf*); (*document*) nadawać (nadać *perf*) ważność *+dat*; (*argument, claim*) uzasadniać (uzasadnić *perf*)
**validity** [və'lɪdɪtɪ] *n* (*of argument, reason*) zasadność *f*; (*of figures, data*) wiarygodność *f*, prawdziwość *f*
**valise** [və'li:z] *n* (mała) walizka *f*
**valley** ['vælɪ] *n* dolina *f*
**valour**, (*US*) **valor** ['vælə^r] *n* męstwo *nt*
**valuable** ['væljuəbl] *adj* (*jewel etc*) wartościowy, cenny; (*advice, time*) cenny
**valuables** ['væljuəblz] *npl* kosztowności *pl*
**valuation** [vælju'eɪʃən] *n* (*of house etc*) wycena *f*; (*judgement of quality*) ocena *f*
**value** ['vælju:] *n* (*financial worth*) wartość *f*; (*importance*) znaczenie *nt* ▷ *vt* (*fix price of*) wyceniać (wycenić *perf*); (*appreciate*) doceniać (docenić *perf*); **values** *npl* wartości *pl*; **it's good ~ for money** to jest warte swej ceny; **you get good ~ for money in that shop** opłaca się robić zakupy w tym sklepie; **to lose/gain (in) ~** tracić (stracić *perf*)/zyskiwać

(zyskać *perf*) na wartości; **to be of great ~ (to sb)** (*fig*) mieć (dla kogoś) wielką wartość
**value added tax** (*Brit*) *n* podatek *m* od wartości dodanej
**valued** ['vælju:d] *adj* (*advice*) cenny; (*specialist, customer*) ceniony
**valuer** ['væljuəʳ] *n* rzeczoznawca *m*, taksator *m*
**valve** [vælv] *n* (*Tech*) zawór *m*; (*Med*) zastawka *f*
**vampire** ['væmpaɪəʳ] *n* (*lit*) wampir(-irzyca) *m(f)*
**van** [væn] *n* (*Aut*) furgonetka *f*, półciężarówka *f*; (*Brit: Rail*) ≈ wagon *m* kryty
**V and A** (*Brit*) *n abbr* = **Victoria and Albert Museum**
**vandal** ['vændl] *n* wandal *m*
**vandalism** ['vændəlɪzəm] *n* wandalizm *m*
**vandalize** ['vændəlaɪz] *vt* dewastować (zdewastować *perf*)
**vanguard** ['vængɑ:d] *n* (*fig*): **in the ~ of** na czele *+gen*, w awangardzie *+gen* (*literary*)
**vanilla** [və'nɪlə] *n* wanilia *f*
**vanilla ice cream** *n* lody *pl* waniliowe
**vanish** ['vænɪʃ] *vi* znikać (zniknąć *perf*)
**vanity** ['vænɪtɪ] *n* próżność *f*
**vanity case** *n walizeczka na kosmetyki*
**vantage point** ['vɑ:ntɪdʒ-] *n* dogodny punkt *m* (obserwacyjny); (*fig*) punkt *m* widzenia
**vaporize** ['veɪpəraɪz] *vt* odparowywać (odparować *perf*) ▷ *vi* parować
**vapour**, (*US*) **vapor** ['veɪpəʳ] *n* (*gas*) para *f*; (*mist, steam*) opary *pl*
**vapo(u)r trail** (*Aviat*) *n* smuga *f* kondensacyjna
**variable** ['vɛərɪəbl] *adj* (*likely to change*) zmienny; (*able to be changed*) regulowany ▷ *n* czynnik *m*; (*Math*) zmienna *f*
**variance** ['vɛərɪəns] *n*: **to be at ~ (with)** różnić się (od *+gen*); **to be at ~ with** (*facts etc*) być sprzecznym z *+instr*
**variant** ['vɛərɪənt] *n* odmiana *f*, wariant *m*
**variation** [vɛərɪ'eɪʃən] *n* (*fluctuation*) zmiany *pl*; (*different form*) odmiana *f*; (*Mus*) wariacja *f*
**varicose** ['værɪkəus] *adj*: **~ veins** żylaki *pl*
**varied** ['vɛərɪd] *adj* (*diverse*) różnorodny; (*full of changes*) urozmaicony
**variety** [və'raɪətɪ] *n* (*degree of choice*) wybór *m*; (*diversity*) zróżnicowanie *nt*, urozmaicenie *nt*; (*type*) rodzaj *m*; **a ~ of people** rozmaici ludzie; **a ~ of noises** rozmaite odgłosy; **the library had a wide ~ of books** biblioteka miała duży wybór książek; **for a ~ of reasons** z wielu różnych powodów
**variety show** *n* variétés *nt inv*
**various** ['vɛərɪəs] *adj* (*different, diverse*) różny; (*several*) kilku (*+gen vir pl*), kilka (*+gen nvir pl*); **at ~ times** (*at different times*) o różnych porach; (*several times*) kilka razy
**varnish** ['vɑ:nɪʃ] *n* lakier *m* ▷ *vt* (*wood etc*) lakierować (polakierować *perf*); (*nails*) malować (pomalować *perf*)
**vary** ['vɛərɪ] *vt* urozmaicać (urozmaicić *perf*) ▷ *vi* różnić się; **to ~ with** zmieniać się w zależności od *+gen*
**varying** ['vɛərɪɪŋ] *adj* różny
**vase** [vɑ:z] *n* wazon *m*
**vasectomy** [væ'sɛktəmɪ] (*Med*) *n* wycięcie *nt* nasieniowodu, wazektomia *f*
**Vaseline**® ['væsɪli:n] *n* wazelina *f*
**vast** [vɑ:st] *adj* (*knowledge*) rozległy; (*expense, area*) olbrzymi, ogromny
**vastly** ['vɑ:stlɪ] *adv* znacznie
**vastness** ['vɑ:stnɪs] *n* ogrom *m*
**VAT** [væt] (*Brit*) *n abbr* (= *value added tax*) VAT *m*
**vat** [væt] *n* kadź *f*
**Vatican** ['vætɪkən] *n*: **the ~** Watykan *m*
**vaudeville** ['vəudəvɪl] *n* wodewil *m*
**vault** [vɔ:lt] *n* (*of roof*) sklepienie *nt*; (*in church*) krypta *f*; (*in cemetery*) grobowiec *m*; (*in bank*) skarbiec *m*; (*jump*) skok *m* ▷ *vt* (*also*: **vault over**) przeskakiwać (przeskoczyć *perf*) (przez)
**vaunted** ['vɔ:ntɪd] *adj*: **much-~** wychwalany
**VC** *n abbr* = **vice-chairman**; (*Brit*: = *Victoria Cross*) *brytyjski order za odwagę*
**VCR** *n abbr* = **video cassette recorder**
**VD** *n abbr* = **venereal disease**
**VDU** (*Comput*) *n abbr* = **visual display unit**
**veal** [vi:l] *n* cielęcina *f*
**veer** [vɪəʳ] *vi* skręcać (skręcić *perf*) gwałtownie
**veg.** [vɛdʒ] (*Brit: inf*) *n abbr* = **vegetable(s)**
**vegan** ['vi:gən] *n* weganin(-anka) *m(f)*
**vegetable** ['vɛdʒtəbl] *n* warzywo *nt* ▷ *cpd* (*oil, matter*) roślinny; (*garden, plot*) warzywny; **the ~ kingdom** królestwo roślin
**vegetarian** [vɛdʒɪ'tɛərɪən] *n* wegetarianin(-anka) *m(f)*, jarosz *m* ▷ *adj* (*diet, dish*) wegetariański, jarski; (*restaurant*) wegetariański
**vegetate** ['vɛdʒɪteɪt] *vi* wegetować
**vegetation** [vɛdʒɪ'teɪʃən] *n* roślinność *f*
**vehemence** ['vi:ɪməns] *n* pasja *f*
**vehement** ['vi:ɪmənt] *adj* gwałtowny
**vehicle** ['vi:ɪkl] *n* pojazd *m*; (*fig: means*) narzędzie *nt*
**vehicular** [vɪ'hɪkjuləʳ] (*Aut*) *adj*: **"no ~ traffic"** „zakaz *m* ruchu wszelkich pojazdów"
**veil** [veɪl] *n* woalka *f*; (*long*) welon *m* ▷ *vt* (*fig*) ukrywać (ukryć *perf*); **under a ~ of secrecy** (*fig*) w sekrecie *or* tajemnicy
**veiled** [veɪld] *adj* (*fig*) zawoalowany
**vein** [veɪn] *n* (*blood vessel, mineral deposit*) żyła *f*; (*of leaf*) żyłka *f*; (*fig*) ton *m*

**llum** ['vɛləm] *n* welin *m*, papier *m* velinowy
**locity** [vɪ'lɔsɪtɪ] *n* prędkość *f*, szybkość *f*
**lvet** ['vɛlvɪt] *n* aksamit *m* ▷ *adj* aksamitny
**ndetta** [vɛn'dɛtə] *n* wendeta *f*
**nding machine** ['vɛndɪŋ-] *n* automat *m* (*do przedaży papierosów, kawy itp*)
**ndor** ['vɛndəʳ] *n* (*of house, land*) sprzedający *n*; **street ~** handlarz uliczny
**neer** [və'nɪəʳ] *n* okleina *f*, fornir *m*; (*fig*) pozory *pl*, fasada *f*
**nerable** ['vɛnərəbl] *adj* (*person*) czcigodny, zacowny; (*building etc*) szacowny; (*Rel: Anglican*) *tytuł przysługujący archidiakonowi*; *: Roman Catholic*) sługa *m* Boży (*określenie osoby, w stosunku do której rozpoczęto proces beatyfikacyjny*)
**nereal** [vɪ'nɪərɪəl] *adj*: **~ disease** choroba *f* weneryczna
**netian** [vɪ'ni:ʃən] *adj* wenecki ▷ *n* Wenecjanin(-anka) *m(f)*
**netian blind** *n* żaluzja *f*
**nezuela** [vɛnɛ'zweɪlə] *n* Wenezuela *f*
**nezuelan** [vɛnɛ'zweɪlən] *adj* wenezuelski ▷ *n* Wenezuelczyk(-lka) *m(f)*
**ngeance** ['vɛndʒəns] *n* zemsta *f*; **with a ~** *fig*) zapamiętale, zawzięcie
**ngeful** ['vɛndʒful] *adj* mściwy
**nice** ['vɛnɪs] *n* Wenecja *f*
**nison** ['vɛnɪsn] *n* dziczyzna *f*
**nom** ['vɛnəm] *n* (*of snake, insect*) jad *m*; (*of erson, remark*) jadowitość *f*
**nomous** ['vɛnəməs] *adj* (*lit, fig*) jadowity
**nt** [vɛnt] *n* (*also*: **air vent**) otwór *m* wentylacyjny; (*in jacket*) rozcięcie *nt* ▷ *vt* (*fig*) dawać (dać *perf*) upust *+dat*; **to ~ one's anger on sb/sth** wyładowywać (wyładować *perf*) swoją) złość na kimś/czymś
**ntilate** ['vɛntɪleɪt] *vt* wietrzyć (wywietrzyć *perf*)
**ntilation** [vɛntɪ'leɪʃən] *n* wentylacja *f*
**ntilation shaft** *n* szyb *m* wentylacyjny
**ntilator** ['vɛntɪleɪtəʳ] *n* (*Tech*) wentylator *m*; (*Med*) respirator *m*
**ntriloquist** [vɛn'trɪləkwɪst] *n* brzuchomówca *m*
**nture** ['vɛntʃəʳ] *n* przedsięwzięcie *nt* ▷ *vt*: **to ~ an opinion** nieśmiało wyrażać (wyrazić *perf*) swoje zdanie ▷ *vi* odważyć się (*perf*) *or* ośmielić się (*perf*) pójść; **business ~** przedsięwzięcie handlowe, interes; **to ~ to do sth** odważyć się (*perf*) *or* ośmielić się (*perf*) coś zrobić
**nture capital** *n* kapitał *m* zainwestowany *z ryzykiem*)
**nue** ['vɛnju:] *n* miejsce *nt* (*konferencji, występu itp*)
**nus** ['vi:nəs] *n* Wenus *f*

**veracity** [və'ræsɪtɪ] *n* (*of person*) prawdomówność *f*; (*of documents*) prawdziwość *f*
**veranda(h)** [və'rændə] *n* weranda *f*
**verb** [və:b] *n* czasownik *m*
**verbal** ['və:bl] *adj* (*skills*) werbalny; (*translation*) ustny; (*attack*) słowny; (*of a verb*) czasownikowy, werbalny
**verbally** ['və:bəlɪ] *adv* słownie
**verbatim** [və:'beɪtɪm] *adj* dosłowny ▷ *adv* słowo w słowo, dosłownie
**verbose** [və:'bəus] *adj* (*style*) rozwlekły; (*piece of writing*) przegadany (*inf*); (*person*) gadatliwy
**verdict** ['və:dɪkt] *n* (*Jur*) orzeczenie *nt*, werdykt *m*; (*fig*) opinia *f*, zdanie *nt*; **~ of guilty/not guilty** wyrok skazujący/uniewinniający
**verge** [və:dʒ] *n* (*Brit: of road*) pobocze *nt*; **he was on the ~ of giving up** już miał zrezygnować; **"soft ~s"** (*Brit*) *napis informujący o niebezpiecznym miękkim poboczu*
▶ **verge on** *vt fus* graniczyć z *+instr*
**verger** ['və:dʒəʳ] *n* kościelny *m* (*w kościele anglikańskim*)
**verification** [vɛrɪfɪ'keɪʃən] *n* weryfikacja *f*
**verify** ['vɛrɪfaɪ] *vt* weryfikować (zweryfikować *perf*)
**veritable** ['vɛrɪtəbl] *adj* prawdziwy, istny
**vermin** ['və:mɪn] *npl* (*mice, rats etc*) szkodniki *pl*; (*fleas, lice etc*) robactwo *nt*
**vermouth** ['və:məθ] *n* wermut *m*
**vernacular** [və'nækjuləʳ] *n* (*of country*) miejscowy język *m*; (*of region*) miejscowy dialekt *m*
**versatile** ['və:sətaɪl] *adj* (*person*) wszechstronny; (*substance, tool*) mający wiele zastosowań
**versatility** [və:sə'tɪlɪtɪ] *n* (*of person*) wszechstronność *f*
**verse** [və:s] *n* (*poetry*) poezja *f*, wiersze *pl*; (*part of poem or song*) strofa *f*, zwrotka *f*; (*in Bible*) werset *m*; **in ~** wierszem
**versed** [və:st] *adj*: **to be (well-)~ in** (dobrze) znać się na *+loc*
**version** ['və:ʃən] *n* wersja *f*
**versus** ['və:səs] *prep* (*in contrast to*) a *+nom*; (*against*) kontra *+nom*, przeciw *+dat*
**vertebra** ['və:tɪbrə] (*pl* **~e**) *n* kręg *m*
**vertebrae** ['və:tɪbri:] *npl of* **vertebra**
**vertebrate** ['və:tɪbrɪt] *n* kręgowiec *m*
**vertical** ['və:tɪkl] *adj* pionowy ▷ *n* linia *f* pionu
**vertically** ['və:tɪklɪ] *adv* pionowo
**vertigo** ['və:tɪgəu] *n* zawroty *pl* głowy; **to suffer from ~** cierpieć na zawroty głowy
**verve** [və:v] *n* werwa *f*

V

**very** ['vɛrɪ] *adv* bardzo ▷ *adj*: **the ~ book which...** właśnie ta książka, która...; **the ~ thought (of it) alarms me** sama myśl (o tym) mnie przeraża; **at the ~ end** na samym końcu; **the ~ last** (zupełnie) ostatni; **at the ~ least** przynajmniej; **~ much** bardzo
**vespers** ['vɛspəz] *npl* nieszpory *pl*
**vessel** ['vɛsl] *n* (*military*) okręt *m*; (*fishing*) statek *m*; (*container, vein*) naczynie *nt*; *see* **blood**
**vest** [vɛst] *n* (*Brit*) podkoszulek *m*; (*US*) kamizelka *f* ▷ *vt*: **to ~ sb with sth, to ~ sth in sb** powierzać (powierzyć *perf*) coś komuś
**vested interest** ['vɛstɪd-] *n* (*Comm*) ulokowany *or* włożony kapitał *m*; **to have a ~ in** być żywotnie *or* osobiście zainteresowanym *+instr*
**vestibule** ['vɛstɪbju:l] *n* przedsionek *m*, westybul *m*
**vestige** ['vɛstɪdʒ] *n* pozostałość *f*, ślad *m*
**vestment** ['vɛstmənt] *n* ornat *m*
**vestry** ['vɛstrɪ] *n* zakrystia *f*
**Vesuvius** [vɪ'su:vɪəs] *n* Wezuwiusz *m*
**vet** [vɛt] *n abbr* = **veterinary surgeon** ▷ *vt* (*Brit: candidate*) weryfikować (zweryfikować *perf*); (*text*) sprawdzać (sprawdzić *perf*)
**veteran** ['vɛtərn] *n* kombatant(ka) *m(f)*, weteran(ka) *m(f)* ▷ *adj*: **she's a ~ campaigner for ...** jest zasłużoną orędowniczką *+gen*
**veteran car** *n samochód wyprodukowany przed rokiem 1919*
**veterinarian** [vɛtrɪ'nɛərɪən] (*US*) *n* weterynarz *m*
**veterinary** ['vɛtrɪnərɪ] *adj* weterynaryjny
**veterinary surgeon** (*Brit*) *n* weterynarz *m*
**veto** ['vi:təu] (*pl* **~es**) *n* (*right*) prawo *nt* weta; (*act*) weto *nt* ▷ *vt* wetować (zawetować *perf*); **to put a ~ on** zakładać (założyć *perf*) *or* stawiać (postawić *perf*) weto wobec *+gen*
**vetting** ['vɛtɪŋ] *n* (*of person*) weryfikacja *f*; (*Pol*) lustracja *f*
**vex** [vɛks] *vt* drażnić, irytować
**vexed** [vɛkst] *adj* (*question*) stale powracający
**VFD** (*US*) *n abbr* (= *voluntary fire department*) OSP *f inv* (= *Ochotnicza Straż Pożarna*)
**VG** (*Brit: Scol etc*) *n abbr* (= *very good*) bdb
**VHF** (*Radio*) *abbr* = **very high frequency**
**VI** (*US: Post*) *abbr* = **Virgin Islands**
**via** ['vaɪə] *prep* przez *+acc*
**viability** [vaɪə'bɪlɪtɪ] *n* (*of project*) wykonalność *f*; (*of product*) możliwość *f* utrzymania się na rynku; (*of organism*) zdolność *f* utrzymania się przy życiu
**viable** ['vaɪəbl] *adj* (*project*) wykonalny; (*alternative*) realny; (*company*) rentowny
**viaduct** ['vaɪədʌkt] *n* wiadukt *m*
**vibrant** ['vaɪbrnt] *adj* (*lively*) żywy; (*colour, light*) jaskrawy; (*voice*) dźwięczny
**vibrate** [vaɪ'breɪt] *vi* (*house, machine*) drżeć (zadrżeć *perf*); (*sound*) rozbrzmiewać (rozbrzmieć *perf*)
**vibration** [vaɪ'breɪʃən] *n* wibracja *f*, drganie *nt*; (*single*) drgnięcie *nt*, drgnienie *nt*
**vicar** ['vɪkə[r]] *n* pastor *m* (*kościoła anglikańskiego*)
**vicarage** ['vɪkərɪdʒ] *n* plebania *f* (*w kościele anglikańskim*)
**vicarious** [vɪ'kɛərɪəs] *adj* pośrednio doznawany
**vice** [vaɪs] *n* (*moral fault*) wada *f*, przywara *f*; (*Tech*) imadło *nt*
**vice-** [vaɪs] *pref* wice...
**vice-chairman** [vaɪs'tʃɛəmən] *n* wiceprzewodniczący *m*, wiceprezes *m*
**vice chancellor** (*Brit*) *n* rektor *m* (uniwersytetu)
**vice president** *n* wiceprezydent *m*
**vice squad** *n* (*Police*) ≈ obyczajówka *f* (*inf*)
**vice versa** ['vaɪsɪ'və:sə] *adv* na odwrót, vice versa
**vicinity** [vɪ'sɪnɪtɪ] *n*: **in the ~ (of)** w pobliżu *or* sąsiedztwie (*+gen*)
**vicious** ['vɪʃəs] *adj* (*attack, blow*) wściekły; (*words*) zjadliwy; (*look*) nienawistny; (*horse*) narowisty; (*dog*) zły
**vicious circle** *n* błędne koło *nt*
**viciousness** ['vɪʃəsnɪs] *n* nienawiść *f*
**vicissitudes** [vɪ'sɪsɪtju:dz] *npl* (zmienne) koleje *pl*
**victim** ['vɪktɪm] *n* ofiara *f*; **to be the ~ of** padać (paść *perf*) ofiarą *+gen*
**victimization** ['vɪktɪmaɪ'zeɪʃən] *n* represjonowanie *nt*
**victimize** ['vɪktɪmaɪz] *vt* represjonować, stosować represje wobec *+gen*
**victor** ['vɪktə[r]] *n* zwycięzca *m*
**Victorian** [vɪk'tɔ:rɪən] *adj* wiktoriański
**victorious** [vɪk'tɔ:rɪəs] *adj* zwycięski
**victory** ['vɪktərɪ] *n* zwycięstwo *nt*; **to win a ~ over sb** odnosić (odnieść *perf*) zwycięstwo nad kimś
**video** ['vɪdɪəu] *n* (*film*) film *m* wideo, wideo *nt* (*also*: **video cassette**) kaseta *f* wideo; (*also*: **video cassette recorder**) magnetowid *m*, wideo *nt*
**video game** *n* gra *f* wideo
**video recording** *n* nagranie *nt* wideo
**video tape** *n* taśma *f* wideo
**vie** [vaɪ] *vi*: **to vie (with sb) (for sth)** rywalizować (z kimś) (o coś)
**Vienna** [vɪ'ɛnə] *n* Wiedeń *m*
**Viennese** [vɪə'ni:z] *adj* wiedeński
**Vietnam** ['vjɛt'næm] *n* Wietnam *m*
**Viet Nam** ['vjɛt'næm] *n* = **Vietnam**

**·tnamese** [vjɛtnə'mi:z] *adj* wietnamski
*n inv (person)* Wietnamczyk(-mka) *m(f)*;
*.ing)* (język *m*) wietnamski
**·w** [vju:] *n (sight)* widok *m*; *(outlook)*
ɔojrzenie *nt*; *(opinion)* pogląd *m* ▷ *vt (look at)*
glądać (obejrzeć *perf*), przyglądać się
ɔrzyjrzeć się *perf*) *+dat*; *(fig)* ustosunkowywać
.ę (ustosunkować się *perf*) do *+gen*; *(situation)*
'idzieć, zapatrywać się na *+acc*; **to ~ (sth) as**
ważać (coś) za *+acc*; **the exhibition on ~**
ystawiona ekspozycja; **in full ~ of** na
czach *+gen*; **he takes the ~ that ...** stoi na
:anowisku, że ...; **in ~ of ...** zważywszy na
*ıcc*; **in my ~** w moim mniemaniu; **an**
**verall ~ of the situation** ogólne spojrzenie
a sytuację; **with a ~ to doing sth** z myślą o
ym, żeby coś zrobić
**·wer** ['vju:əʳ] *n (person)* (tele)widz *m*;
*iewfinder)* wizjer *m*, celownik *m*; *(for slides)*
rzeglądarka *f*
**·wfinder** ['vju:faɪndəʳ] *n* wizjer *m*,
elownik *m*
**·wpoint** ['vju:pɔɪnt] *n (attitude)* punkt *m*
idzenia; *(place)* punkt *m* widokowy
**gil** ['vɪdʒɪl] *n* czuwanie *nt*; **to keep ~** czuwać
**gilance** ['vɪdʒɪləns] *n* czujność *f*
**gilant** ['vɪdʒɪlənt] *adj* czujny
**gorous** ['vɪgərəs] *adj (action)* energiczny;
*lant)* żywotny
**gour**, (US) **vigor** ['vɪgəʳ] *n (of person)* wigor
:, energia *f*; *(of campaign, democracy)*
rężność *f*
**e** [vaɪl] *adj (evil)* nikczemny, podły;
*npleasant)* obrzydliwy, wstrętny
**ify** ['vɪlɪfaɪ] *vt* szkalować (oszkalować *perf*)
**la** ['vɪlə] *n* willa *f*
**lage** ['vɪlɪdʒ] *n* wieś *f*, wioska *f*
**lager** ['vɪlɪdʒəʳ] *n* mieszkaniec(-nka) *m(f)*
/si
**lain** ['vɪlən] *n (scoundrel)* łajdak *m*, łotr *m*; *(in*
*ɔvel, film)* czarny charakter *m*; *(Brit: criminal)*
:oczyńca *f*
**N** (US) *n abbr* = **vehicle identification**
**umber**
**ıdicate** ['vɪndɪkeɪt] *vt (person)*
ehabilitować (zrehabilitować *perf*); *(action)*
otwierdzać (potwierdzić *perf*) słuszność *+gen*
**ıdication** [vɪndɪ'keɪʃən] *n (of person)*
ehabilitacja *f*; *(of action)* potwierdzenie *nt*
łuszności
**ıdictive** [vɪn'dɪktɪv] *adj* mściwy
**ıe** [vaɪn] *n* winorośl *f*
**ıegar** ['vɪnɪgəʳ] *n* ocet *m*
**ıe grower** *n* hodowca *m* winorośli
**ıe-growing** ['vaɪngrəuɪŋ] *adj*: **~ region**
egion *m* uprawy winorośli ▷ *n* uprawa *f*
/inorośli

**vineyard** ['vɪnjɑ:d] *n* winnica *f*
**vintage** ['vɪntɪdʒ] *n (of wine)* dobry rocznik *m* ▷ *cpd (comedy, performance etc)* klasyczny; **the 1970 ~** *(of wine)* rocznik 1970
**vintage car** *n samochód wyprodukowany w latach 1919-1930*
**vintage wine** *n* wino *nt* z dobrego rocznika
**vinyl** ['vaɪnl] *n (material)* winyl *m*; *(records)* płyty *pl* winylowe
**viola** [vɪ'əulə] *n* altówka *f*
**violate** ['vaɪəleɪt] *vt (agreement)* naruszać (naruszyć *perf*); *(peace)* zakłócać (zakłócić *perf*); *(graveyard)* bezcześcić (zbezcześcić *perf*)
**violation** [vaɪə'leɪʃən] *n (of agreement etc)* naruszenie *nt*; **in ~ of** z naruszeniem *+gen*
**violence** ['vaɪələns] *n* przemoc *f*; *(strength)* gwałtowność *f*
**violent** ['vaɪələnt] *adj* gwałtowny; **a ~ dislike of sb/sth** silna niechęć do kogoś/czegoś
**violently** ['vaɪələntlɪ] *adv* gwałtownie; *(ill, angry)* bardzo
**violet** ['vaɪələt] *adj* fioletowy ▷ *n (colour)* (kolor *m*) fioletowy, fiolet *m*; *(plant)* fiołek *m*
**violin** [vaɪə'lɪn] *n* skrzypce *pl*
**violinist** [vaɪə'lɪnɪst] *n* skrzypek(-paczka) *m(f)*
**VIP** *n abbr (= very important person)* VIP *m*
**viper** ['vaɪpəʳ] *(Zool) n* żmija *f*
**virgin** ['və:dʒɪn] *n (woman)* dziewica *f*; *(man)* prawiczek *m* ▷ *adj* dziewiczy; **the Blessed V~** Najświętsza Panna
**virginity** [və:'dʒɪnɪtɪ] *n* dziewictwo *nt*
**Virgo** ['və:gəu] *n* Panna *f*; **to be ~** być spod znaku Panny
**virile** ['vɪraɪl] *adj* męski
**virility** [vɪ'rɪlɪtɪ] *n* męskość *f*
**virtual** ['və:tjuəl] *adj (Comput, Phys)* wirtualny; **it's a ~ impossibility** to praktycznie niemożliwe; **the ~ leader** rzeczywisty *or* faktyczny przywódca
**virtually** ['və:tjuəlɪ] *adv* praktycznie
**virtual reality** *n* rzeczywistość *f* wirtualna
**virtue** ['və:tju:] *n (moral correctness)* moralność *f*; *(good quality)* cnota *f*; *(advantage)* zaleta *f*; **by ~ of** z racji *+gen*
**virtuosi** [və:tju'əuzɪ] *npl of* **virtuoso**
**virtuoso** [və:tju'əuzəu] *(pl* **~s** *or* **virtuosi***) n* wirtuoz(ka) *m(f)*
**virtuous** ['və:tjuəs] *adj* cnotliwy
**virulence** ['vɪruləns] *n (of disease)* złośliwość *f*; *(hatred)* zjadliwość *f*
**virulent** ['vɪrulənt] *adj (disease)* złośliwy; *(attack, loathing)* zajadły; *(speech)* jadowity
**virus** ['vaɪərəs] *n* wirus *m*
**visa** ['vi:zə] *n* wiza *f*
**vis-à-vis** [vi:zə'vi:] *prep* w porównaniu z *+instr*, względem *+gen*
**viscose** ['vɪskəus] *n* wiskoza *f*

V

**viscount** ['vaɪkaunt] *n* wicehrabia *m*
**viscous** ['vɪskəs] *adj* lepki
**vise** [vaɪs] (*US*: *Tech*) *n* = **vice**
**visibility** [vɪzɪ'bɪlɪtɪ] *n* widoczność *f*, widzialność *f*
**visible** ['vɪzəbl] *adj* widoczny; (*fig*) wyraźny, dostrzegalny; ~ **exports/imports** eksport/import widzialny
**visibly** ['vɪzəblɪ] *adv* (*nervous etc*) wyraźnie
**vision** ['vɪʒən] *n* (*sight*) wzrok *m*; (*foresight*) zdolność *f or* dar *m* przewidywania; (*in dream etc*) wizja *f*, widzenie *nt*
**visionary** ['vɪʒənrɪ] *adj* wizjonerski
**visit** ['vɪzɪt] *n* (*to person*) wizyta *f*, odwiedziny *pl*; (*to place*) pobyt *m*, wizyta *f* ▷ *vt* odwiedzać (odwiedzić *perf*); **on a private/an official** ~ z wizytą prywatną/oficjalną
**visiting** ['vɪzɪtɪŋ] *adj*: ~ **speaker** gościnny mówca *m*; ~ **team** drużyna gości
**visiting card** *n* bilet *m* wizytowy, wizytówka *f*
**visiting hours** *npl* godziny *pl* odwiedzin
**visiting professor** *n* profesor *m* na gościnnych wykładach
**visitor** ['vɪzɪtə$^{r}$] *n* gość *m*
**visitors' book** ['vɪzɪtəz-] *n* księga *f* gości
**visor** ['vaɪzə$^{r}$] *n* (*of helmet*) osłona *f*; (*of cap*) daszek *m*
**VISTA** ['vɪstə] *n abbr* (= *Volunteers in Service to America*) *ochotnicza organizacja udzielająca pomocy najuboższym mieszkańcom USA*
**vista** ['vɪstə] *n* perspektywa *f*
**visual** ['vɪzjuəl] *adj* (*image*) wizualny; (*memory*) wzrokowy; ~ **arts** sztuki plastyczne
**visual aid** (*Scol*) *n* wizualna pomoc *f* naukowa
**visual display unit** (*Comput*) *n* monitor *m* ekranowy
**visualize** ['vɪzjuəlaɪz] *vt* wyobrażać (wyobrazić *perf*) sobie
**visually** ['vɪzjuəlɪ] *adv* wizualnie; ~ **appealing** atrakcyjny z wyglądu; ~ **handicapped** (*with impaired vision*) niedowidzący; (*blind*) niewidomy
**vital** ['vaɪtl] *adj* (*essential*) zasadniczy, istotny; (*full of life*) pełen życia; (*necessary for life*) żywotny; **of ~ importance (to sb/sth)** najwyższej wagi (dla kogoś/czegoś)
**vitality** [vaɪ'tælɪtɪ] *n* witalność *f*
**vitally** ['vaɪtəlɪ] *adv*: ~ **important** niezwykle ważny
**vital statistics** *npl* (*fig*: *of woman*) wymiary *pl*; (*of population*) dane *pl* demograficzne
**vitamin** ['vɪtəmɪn] *n* witamina *f* ▷ *cpd*: ~ **deficiencies** niedobory *pl* witamin
**vitiate** ['vɪʃɪeɪt] *vt* (*spoil*) psuć (zepsuć *perf*)
**vitreous** ['vɪtrɪəs] *adj* (*china*) nieporowaty; (*enamel*) szklisty
**vitriolic** [vɪtrɪ'ɔlɪk] *adj* (*criticism*) zjadliwy, jadowity; (*behaviour*) złośliwy
**viva** ['vaɪvə] *n* (*also*: **viva voce**) egzamin *m* ustny
**vivacious** [vɪ'veɪʃəs] *adj* żywotny
**vivacity** [vɪ'væsɪtɪ] *n* żywotność *f*
**vivid** ['vɪvɪd] *adj* (*imagination, memory, colour*) żywy; (*light*) jaskrawy
**vividly** ['vɪvɪdlɪ] *adv* żywo
**vivisection** [vɪvɪ'sɛkʃən] *n* wiwisekcja *f*
**vixen** ['vɪksn] *n* lisica *f*; (*pej*: *woman*) jędza *f* (*pej*)
**viz** [vɪz] *abbr* (= *videlicet*) mianowicie
**VLF** (*Radio*) *abbr* = **very low frequency**
**V-neck** ['vi:nɛk] *n* (*also*: **V-neck jumper** *or* **pullover**) sweter *m* z dekoltem w szpic
**VOA** *n abbr* (= *Voice of America*) Głos *m* Ameryki
**vocabulary** [vəu'kæbjulərɪ] *n* słownictwo *n*
**vocal** ['vəukl] *adj* (*of the voice*) głosowy; (: *in singing*) wokalny; (*articulate*): **to be ~ (on)** zabierać głos *or* wypowiadać się (w sprawie +*gen*)
**vocal cords** *npl* wiązadła *pl* głosowe
**vocalist** ['vəukəlɪst] *n* wokalista(-tka) *m*(*f*)
**vocals** ['vəuklz] *npl* śpiew *m*, partie *pl* wokal
**vocation** [vəu'keɪʃən] *n* powołanie *nt*
**vocational** [vəu'keɪʃənl] *adj* zawodowy
**vociferous** [və'sɪfərəs] *adj* głośny, hałaśliwy
**vodka** ['vɔdkə] *n* wódka *f*
**vogue** [vəug] *n* (*fashion*) moda *f*; (*popularity*) powodzenie *nt*; **in** ~ w modzie
**voice** [vɔɪs] *n* głos *m* ▷ *vt* wyrażać (wyrazić *perf*); **in a loud/soft** ~ głośno/cicho; **to give ~ to** dawać (dać *perf*) wyraz +*dat*
**voicemail** ['vɔɪsmeɪl] (*Tel*) *n* poczta *f* głosow
**void** [vɔɪd] *n* (*hole*) przepaść *f*; (*fig*: *emptiness*) próżnia *f*, pustka *f* ▷ *adj* nieważny; ~ **of** pozbawiony +*gen*
**voile** [vɔɪl] *n* woal *m* (*tkanina*)
**vol.** *abbr* (= *volume*) t.
**volatile** ['vɔlətaɪl] *adj* (*situation*) niestabilny; (*person*) zmienny; (*substance*) lotny
**volcanic** [vɔl'kænɪk] *adj* wulkaniczny
**volcano** [vɔl'keɪnəu] (*pl* **~es**) *n* wulkan *m*
**volition** [və'lɪʃən] *n*: **of one's own** ~ z własn woli
**volley** ['vɔlɪ] *n* (*of gunfire*) salwa *f*; (*of stones*) grad *m*; (*of questions*) potok *m*; (*Tennis etc*) wol *m*; **a ~ of abuse** stek przekleństw
**volleyball** ['vɔlɪbɔ:l] *n* siatkówka *f*
**volt** [vəult] *n* wolt *m*
**voltage** ['vəultɪdʒ] *n* napięcie *nt*; **high/low ~** wysokie/niskie napięcie
**volte-face** ['vɔlt'fɑ:s] *n* (całkowita) zmiana frontu, zwrot *m* o 180 stopni
**voluble** ['vɔljubl] *adj* (*person*) gadatliwy; (*speech*) potoczysty

**olume** ['vɔlju:m] *n* (*space*) objętość *f*; *amount*: *of exports, trade*) wolumen *m*, ozmiary *pl*; (: *of traffic*) natężenie *nt*; (*of book*) om *m*; (*sound level*) głośność *f*; **~ one/two** tom ierwszy/drugi; **his expression spoke ~s** z ego wyrazu twarzy wiele można było vyczytać
**olume control** (*Radio, TV*) *n* regulacja *f* łośności
**olume discount** (*Comm*) *n* rabat *m* przy użym zamówieniu
**luminous** [və'lu:mɪnəs] *adj* (*clothes, notes*) bszerny; (*correspondence*) obfity
**luntarily** ['vɔləntrɪlɪ] *adv* dobrowolnie
**luntary** ['vɔləntərɪ] *adj* (*done willingly*) lobrowolny; (*unpaid*) ochotniczy
**luntary liquidation** (*Comm*) *n* likwidacja *f* lobrowolna
**luntary redundancy** (*Brit*) *n* dobrowolne wolnienie się *nt* z pracy (*w sytuacji nadmiaru atrudnienia*)
**lunteer** [vɔlən'tɪə^r] *n* ochotnik(-iczka) *m*(*f*) ▷ *vt* (*information*) (dobrowolnie) udzielać udzielić *perf*) *+gen* ▷ *vi* zgłaszać się (zgłosić się erf) na ochotnika; **to ~ to do sth** ofiarować się (zaofiarować się *perf*) coś zrobić
**luptuous** [və'lʌptjuəs] *adj* zmysłowy
**mit** ['vɔmɪt] *n* wymiociny *pl* ▷ *vt, vi* vymiotować (zwymiotować *perf*)
**te** [vəut] *n* (*indication of choice*) głos *m*; (*votes ast*) głosy *pl*; (*right to vote*) prawo *nt* do łosowania, czynne prawo *nt* wyborcze ▷ *vt* *elect*): **he was ~d chairman** wybrano go na rzewodniczącego; (*propose*): **to ~ that** roponować (zaproponować *perf*), żeby ▷ *vi* łosować (zagłosować *perf*); **to ~ to do sth** powiadać się *or* głosować za zrobieniem zegoś; **to put sth to the ~, take a ~ on sth** oddawać (poddać *perf*) coś pod głosowanie; **to ~ for** *or* **in favour of/against** głosować za *instr*/przeciw(ko) *+dat*; **to ~ on sth** poddawać poddać *perf*) coś pod głosowanie; **to ~ yes to** rzyjmować (przyjąć *perf*) *+acc*; **to ~ no to** odrzucać (odrzucić *perf*) *+acc*; **she ~d Labour** łosowała na Partię Pracy; **to pass a ~ of confidence/no confidence** uchwalać uchwalić *perf*) wotum zaufania/nieufności; **they passed a ~ of censure on** przyjęli wniosek potępiający *+acc*
**vote of thanks** *n* oficjalne podziękowanie *nt* (*w formie przemówienia*)
**voter** ['vəutə^r] *n* głosujący *m*, wyborca *m*
**voting** ['vəutɪŋ] *n* głosowanie *nt*
**voting paper** (*Brit*) *n* karta *f* wyborcza *or* do głosowania
**voting right** *n* prawo *nt* wyborcze
**vouch** [vautʃ]: **~ for** *vt fus* ręczyć *or* zaręczać (zaręczyć *perf*) za *+acc*
**voucher** ['vautʃə^r] *n* (*with petrol etc*) kupon *m*, talon *m*; (*receipt*) kwit *m*; **luncheon ~** bon obiadowy; **travel ~** bon na (darmowy) przejazd; **gift ~** talon *or* bon na zakupy (*dawany w prezencie*)
**vow** [vau] *n* przyrzeczenie *nt* ▷ *vt*: **to vow that/to do sth** przyrzekać (przyrzec *perf*) (uroczyście), że/, że się coś zrobi; **she took** *or* **made a vow to give up smoking** postanowiła uroczyście, że rzuci palenie
**vowel** ['vauəl] *n* samogłoska *f*
**voyage** ['vɔɪɪdʒ] *n* podróż *m*
**VP** *n abbr* = **vice-president**
**vs** *abbr* = **versus**
**V-sign** ['vi:saɪn] *n* znak *m* zwycięstwa; (*Brit*) *wulgarny gest, w którym palce ułożone są jak do znaku zwycięstwa, a dłoń zwrócona do wewnątrz*
**VSO** (*Brit*) *n abbr* (= *Voluntary Service Overseas*) *organizacja kierująca ochotników do pracy w krajach słabo rozwiniętych*
**VT** (*US: Post*) *abbr* = **Vermont**
**vulgar** ['vʌlgə^r] *adj* (*rude*) wulgarny, ordynarny; (*in bad taste*) ordynarny
**vulgarity** [vʌl'gærɪtɪ] *n* (*rudeness*) wulgarność *f*; (*ostentation*) ordynarność *f*
**vulnerability** [vʌlnərə'bɪlɪtɪ] *n* (*to illness, bad influence etc*) podatność *f*; (*being easily hurt*) wrażliwość *f*; (*weakness*) słabość *f*
**vulnerable** ['vʌlnərəbl] *adj* (*position*) trudny do obrony; (*point*) czuły; (*person*): **~ (to)** (*influences, depression, infection*) podatny (na *+acc*); (*danger*) narażony (na *+acc*); **she's very ~** (*sensitive*) bardzo łatwo ją zranić
**vulture** ['vʌltʃə^r] *n* sęp *m*; (*fig*: *pej*: *person*) szakal *m*
**vulva** ['vʌlvə] (*Anat*) *n* srom *m*

V

**W¹, w** ['dʌblju:] *n (letter)* W *nt*, w *nt*; **W for William** ≈ W jak Wacław
**W²** *abbr (= west)* zach.; *(Elec: = watt)* W
**WA** *(US: Post) abbr* = **Washington**
**wad** [wɔd] *n (of cotton wool)* tampon *m*; *(of paper, banknotes)* zwitek *m*
**wadding** ['wɔdɪŋ] *n* watowanie *nt*, watolina *f*
**waddle** ['wɔdl] *vi* człapać
**wade** [weɪd] *vi* brodzić; **to ~ across** *(river etc)* przechodzić (przejść *perf*) (w bród) przez *+acc*; **to ~ through** *(fig: a book)* brnąć (przebrnąć *perf*) przez *+acc*
**wafer** ['weɪfə^r] *n (biscuit)* wafelek *m*; *(Rel)* opłatek *m*
**wafer-thin** ['weɪfə'θɪn] *adj* cieniutki
**waffle** ['wɔfl] *n (Culin)* gofr *m*; *(empty talk)* ględzenie *nt* ▷ *vi* ględzić
**waffle iron** *n* gofrownica *f*
**waft** [wɔft] *vt (sound, scent)* nieść, unosić (unieść *perf*) ▷ *vi (sound, scent)* nieść się, unosić się (unieść się *perf*)
**wag** [wæg] *vt (tail)* merdać (zamerdać *perf*) *+instr*; *(finger)* kiwać (pokiwać *perf*) *+instr* ▷ *vi* kiwać się; **the dog wagged its tail** pies zamerdał ogonem
**wage** [weɪdʒ] *n (also: **wages**)* zarobki *pl*, płaca *f* ▷ *vt*: **to ~ war** toczyć *or* prowadzić wojnę; **a day's ~s** dniówka
**wage claim** *n* roszczenia *pl* płacowe
**wage differential** *n* rozpiętość *f* płac
**wage earner** [-ə:nə^r] *n* zarabiający(-ca) *m(f)*
**wage freeze** *n* zamrożenie *nt* płac
**wage packet** *n* wypłata *f*
**wager** ['weɪdʒə^r] *n* zakład *m* ▷ *vt* stawiać (postawić *perf*), zakładać się (założyć się *perf*) o *+acc*
**waggle** ['wægl] *vt (ears etc)* ruszać *+instr* ▷ *vi* ruszać się
**wag(g)on** ['wægən] *n (horse-drawn)* wóz *m* (zaprzęgowy); *(Brit: Rail)* wagon *m*
**wail** [weɪl] *n (of person)* płacz *m*, zawodzenie *nt*; *(of siren)* wycie *nt* ▷ *vi (person)* zawodzić, płakać (zapłakać *perf*); *(siren)* wyć (zawyć *perf*)
**waist** [weɪst] *n (Anat)* talia *f*, pas *m*; *(of clothing)* talia *f*, pas(ek) *m*
**waistcoat** ['weɪskəut] *(Brit) n* kamizelka *f*
**waistline** ['weɪstlaɪn] *n* talia *f*
**wait** [weɪt] *n (interval)* przerwa *f*; *(act of waiting)* oczekiwanie *nt* ▷ *vi* czekać (poczekać *perf or* zaczekać *perf*); **to keep sb ~ing** kazać (kazać *perf*) komuś czekać; **I can't ~ to tell her** nie mogę się doczekać, kiedy jej powiem; **to ~ for sb/sth** czekać (poczekać *perf*) na kogoś/coś; **~ a minute!** zaraz, zaraz!, chwileczkę!; **"repairs while you ~"** „naprawy na poczekaniu"; **to lie in ~ for sb** czaić się (zaczaić się *perf*) na kogoś
▶ **wait behind** *vi* zostawać (zostać *perf*), zaczekać *(perf)*
▶ **wait on** *vt fus* obsługiwać (obsłużyć *perf*) *+acc*
▶ **wait up** *vi*: **don't ~ up for me** nie czekaj na mnie, idź spać
**waiter** ['weɪtə^r] *n* kelner *m*
**waiting** ['weɪtɪŋ] *n*: **"no ~"** *(Brit)* „zakaz *m* postoju"
**waiting list** *n* lista *f* oczekujących
**waiting room** *n* poczekalnia *f*
**waitress** ['weɪtrɪs] *n* kelnerka *f*
**waive** [weɪv] *vt* odstępować (odstąpić *perf*) od *+gen*
**waiver** ['weɪvə^r] *n* zrzeczenie się *nt*
**wake** [weɪk] *(pt* **woke, ~d**, *pp* **woken, ~d**) *vt (also:* **wake up**) budzić (obudzić *perf*) ▷ *vi (also:* **wake up**) budzić się (obudzić się *perf*) ▷ *n (for dead)* stypa *f*; *(Naut)* kilwater *m*; **to ~ up to sth** *(fig)* uświadamiać (uświadomić *perf*) sobie coś; **in the ~ of** *(fig)* w ślad za *+instr*; **to follow in sb's ~** *(fig)* podążać (podążyć *perf*) za kimś *or* czyimś śladem
**waken** ['weɪkn] *vt, vi* = **wake**
**Wales** [weɪlz] *n* Walia *f*; **the Prince of ~** książę Walii
**walk** [wɔ:k] *n (hike)* wycieczka *f*; *(shorter)* spacer *m*; *(gait)* chód *m*; *(path)* alej(k)a *f*, ścieżka *f*; *(along coast etc)* promenada *f* ▷ *vi (go on foot)* chodzić, iść (pójść *perf*); *(for pleasure, exercise)* chodzić piechotą *or* pieszo *or* na piechotę, iść (pójść *perf*) piechotą, przechadzać się (przejść się *perf*) ▷ *vt*

(*distance*) przechodzić (przejść *perf*); (*dog*) wyprowadzać (wyprowadzić *perf*) (na spacer); **it's ten minutes' ~ from here** to jest piechotą dziesięć minut stąd; **to go for a ~** iść (pójść *perf*) na spacer; **to slow to a ~** zwalniać (zwolnić *perf*) do marszu; **people from all ~s of life** ludzie (ze) wszystkich sfer; **to ~ in one's sleep** chodzić we śnie; **I'll ~ you home** odprowadzę cię do domu
▸ **walk out** *vi* (*audience*) wychodzić (wyjść *perf*) przed końcem (przedstawienia); (*workers*) strajkować (zastrajkować *perf*)
▸ **walk out on** (*inf*) *vt fus* (*boyfriend etc*) odchodzić (odejść *perf*) od *+gen*
**walker** ['wɔːkəʳ] *n* piechur *m*
**walkie-talkie** ['wɔːkɪ'tɔːkɪ] *n* walkie-talkie *nt inv*, krótkofalówka *f*
**walking** ['wɔːkɪŋ] *n* chodzenie *nt*, wycieczki *pl* piesze; **it's within ~ distance** można tam dojść pieszo *or* piechotą
**walking holiday** *n* wczasy *pl* wędrowne
**walking shoes** *npl* buty *pl* turystyczne
**walking stick** *n* laska *f*
**Walkman®** ['wɔːkmən] *n* walkman *m*
**walk-on** ['wɔːkɔn] (*Theat*) *adj* (*part*) epizodyczny
**walkout** ['wɔːkaut] *n* strajk *m*
**walkover** ['wɔːkəuvəʳ] (*inf*) *n* łatwe zwycięstwo *nt*
**walkway** ['wɔːkweɪ] *n* pasaż *m*, przejście *nt*
**wall** [wɔːl] *n* (*interior*) ściana *f*; (*exterior*) mur *m*, ściana *f*; (*of tunnel, cave*) ściana *f*, ścianka *f*; (*city wall etc*) mur *m*; **to go to the ~** (*fig*) podupadać (podupaść *perf*)
▸ **wall in** *vt* otaczać (otoczyć *perf*) murem
**wall cupboard** *n* szafka *f* ścienna
**walled** [wɔːld] *adj* otoczony murem
**wallet** ['wɔlɪt] *n* portfel *m*
**wallflower** ['wɔːlflauəʳ] *n* (*Bot*) lak *m* wonny; **to be a ~** (*fig*) podpierać ściany
**wall hanging** *n* draperia *f*
**wallop** ['wɔləp] (*Brit: inf*) *vt* tłuc (stłuc *perf*), przywalić (*perf*) *+dat* (*inf*)
**wallow** ['wɔləu] *vi* (*in mud*) tarzać się; (*in water*) pławić się; (*in grief etc*) pogrążać się (pogrążyć się *perf*)
**wallpaper** ['wɔːlpeɪpəʳ] *n* tapeta *f* ▹ *vt* tapetować (wytapetować *perf*)
**wall-to-wall** ['wɔːltə'wɔːl] *adj* na całą podłogę *post*
**wally** [wɔlɪ] (*inf*) *n* tuman *m* (*inf*)
**walnut** ['wɔːlnʌt] *n* (*nut, tree*) orzech *m* włoski; (*wood*) orzech *m*
**walrus** ['wɔːlrəs] (*pl* **~** *or* **~es**) *n* mors *m*
**waltz** [wɔːlts] *n* walc *m* ▹ *vi* tańczyć (zatańczyć *perf*) walca
**wan** [wɔn] *adj* blady, mizerny
**wand** [wɔnd] *n* (*also*: **magic wand**) (czarodziejska) różdżka *f*
**wander** ['wɔndəʳ] *vi* (*person*) wędrować, włóczyć się; (*mind*) błądzić ▹ *vt* przemierzać, przechadzać się po *+loc*; **my thoughts kept wondering back to that night** myślami wracałam ciągle do tamtej nocy
**wanderer** ['wɔndərəʳ] *n* wędrowiec *m*
**wandering** ['wɔndrɪŋ] *adj* wędrowny
**wane** [weɪn] *vi* zmniejszać się (zmniejszyć się *perf*), maleć (zmaleć *perf*); **the moon is waning** ubywa księżyca
**wangle** ['wæŋgl] (*Brit: inf*) *vt* załatwiać (załatwić *perf*) sobie
**want** [wɔnt] *vt* (*wish for*) chcieć *+gen or +acc*; (*need, require*) wymagać *+gen* ▹ *n*: **for ~ of** z braku *+gen*; **wants** *pl* potrzeby *pl*; **to ~ to do sth** chcieć coś (z)robić; **to ~ sb to do sth** chcieć, żeby ktoś coś (z)robił; **to ~ in/out** (*US, Scottish*) chcieć wejść/wyjść; (*fig*) chcieć się przyłączyć/wycofać; **you're ~ed on the phone** jest do ciebie telefon; **he is ~ed by the police** poszukuje go policja; **a ~ of foresight** brak umiejętności przewidywania
**want ads** (*US*) *npl* ogłoszenia *pl* drobne
**wanted** ['wɔntɪd] *adj* poszukiwany; **"cook ~"** „zatrudnię kucharza"
**wanting** ['wɔntɪŋ] *adj* niedoskonały, nie spełniający wymogów
**wanton** ['wɔntn] *adj* (*violence*) nieusprawiedliwiony, niepotrzebny; (*woman*) rozwiązły
**war** [wɔːʳ] *n* wojna *f*; **to go to war** wszczynać (wszcząć *perf*) wojnę; **to be at war (with)** prowadzić *or* toczyć wojnę *or* wojny (z *+instr*); **to make war (on)** prowadzić *or* toczyć wojnę *or* wojny (z *+instr*); **a war on drugs/crime** walka z narkotykami/przestępczością
**warble** ['wɔːbl] *n* świergot *m*, ćwierkanie *nt* ▹ *vi* ćwierkać
**war cry** *n* okrzyk *m* bojowy; (*fig*) hasło *nt*
**ward** [wɔːd] *n* (*in hospital*) oddział *m*; (*Pol*) okręg *m*, dzielnica *f*; (*also*: **ward of court**) *osoba niepełnoletnia pod kuratelą sądu*
▸ **ward off** *vt* (*attack*) odpierać (odeprzeć *perf*); (*danger, illness*) zapobiegać (zapobiec *perf*) *+dat*; (*evil spirits*) odpędzać (odpędzić *perf*)
**warden** ['wɔːdn] *n* (*of game reserve etc*) ≈ gajowy *m*; (*of jail*) naczelnik *m*; (*Brit: of youth hostel, in university*) ≈ dyrektor *m* (administracyjny); (*also: traffic warden*) *funkcjonariusz nadzorujący poprawność parkowania pojazdów*
**warder** ['wɔːdəʳ] (*Brit*) *n* strażnik *m* (więzienny)
**wardrobe** ['wɔːdrəub] *n* (*for clothes*) szafa *f*; (*collection of clothes*) garderoba *f*, odzież *f*; (*Film, Theat*) garderoba *f*

W

**warehouse** ['wɛəhaus] *n* magazyn *m*, hurtownia *f*
**wares** [wɛəz] *npl* towary *pl*
**warfare** ['wɔːfɛə<sup>r</sup>] *n* działania *pl* wojenne, wojna *f*
**war game** *n* gra *f* wojenna
**warhead** ['wɔːhɛd] *n* głowica *f* bojowa
**warily** ['wɛərɪlɪ] *adv* ostrożnie, z rezerwą
**Warks** (*Brit*: *Post*) *abbr* = **Warwickshire**
**warlike** ['wɔːlaɪk] *adj* (*nation*) wojowniczy; (*appearance*) zawadiacki
**warm** [wɔːm] *adj* ciepły; (*thanks, applause*) gorący, serdeczny; (*person, heart*) czuły; **it's ~** jest ciepło; **I'm ~** ciepło mi; **to keep a room** *etc* **~** utrzymywać (utrzymać *perf*) ciepło w pokoju *etc*; **with my ~est thanks/ congratulations** załączam najserdeczniejsze podziękowania/gratulacje ▸ **warm up** *vi* (*weather*) ocieplać się (ocieplić się *perf*); (*water*) zagrzewać się (zagrzać się *perf*); (*athlete*) rozgrzewać się (rozgrzać się *perf*); (*engine*) nagrzewać się (nagrzać się *perf*) ▷ *vt* (*food*) podgrzewać (podgrzać *perf*), odgrzewać (odgrzać *perf*); (*person*) rozgrzewać (rozgrzać *perf*), ogrzewać (ogrzać *perf*)
**warm-blooded** ['wɔːm'blʌdɪd] *adj* stałocieplny
**war memorial** *n* pomnik *m* poległych (na wojnie)
**warm-hearted** [wɔːm'hɑːtɪd] *adj* serdeczny
**warmly** ['wɔːmlɪ] *adv* ciepło
**warmonger** ['wɔːmʌŋgə<sup>r</sup>] (*pej*) *n* podżegacz *m* wojenny (*pej*)
**warmongering** ['wɔːmʌŋgrɪŋ] (*pej*) *n* podżeganie *nt* do wojny (*pej*)
**warmth** [wɔːmθ] *n* (*heat*) ciepło *nt*; (*friendliness*) serdeczność *f*
**warm-up** ['wɔːmʌp] *n* (*also*: **warm-up exercise**) rozgrzewka *f*
**warn** [wɔːn] *vt*: **to ~ sb that ...** przestrzegać (przestrzec *perf*) *or* ostrzegać (ostrzec *perf*) kogoś, że ...; **to ~ sb of/against sth** przestrzegać (przestrzec *perf*) *or* ostrzegać (ostrzec *perf*) kogoś przed czymś; **to ~ sb not to do sth** *or* **against doing sth** ostrzegać (ostrzec *perf*) kogoś, żeby czegoś nie robił
**warning** ['wɔːnɪŋ] *n* ostrzeżenie *nt*; (*signal*) uprzedzenie *nt*; **without (any) ~** (*suddenly*) bez (najmniejszego) ostrzeżenia; (*without notifying*) bez (żadnego) uprzedzenia; **gale ~** ostrzeżenie przed sztormem
**warning light** *n* światło *nt* ostrzegawcze
**warning triangle** *n* (*Aut*) trójkąt *m* odblaskowy *or* ostrzegawczy
**warp** [wɔːp] *vi* wypaczać się (wypaczyć się *perf*) ▷ *vt* (*fig*) wypaczać (wypaczyć *perf*) ▷ *n* osnowa *f*
**warpath** ['wɔːpɑːθ] *n*: **to be on the ~** (*fig*) być na wojennej ścieżce
**warped** [wɔːpt] *adj* wypaczony
**warrant** ['wɔrnt] *n* (*for arrest*) nakaz *m*; (*also*: **search warrant**) nakaz *m* rewizji ▷ *vt* dawać (dać *perf*) podstawy do *+gen*
**warrant officer** *n* (*Mil*) chorąży *m*; (*Naut*) ≈ bosman *m*
**warranty** ['wɔrəntɪ] *n* gwarancja *f*; **under ~** (*Comm*) na gwarancji
**warren** ['wɔrən] *n* (*of rabbits*) kolonia *f*; (*fig*: *of streets etc*) labirynt *m*; **the ~s of** (*city*) zaułki *+gen*
**warring** ['wɔːrɪŋ] *adj* (*nations, factions*) walczący, wojujący; (*interests*) sprzeczny
**warrior** ['wɔrɪə<sup>r</sup>] *n* wojownik *m*
**Warsaw** ['wɔːsɔː] *n* Warszawa *f*
**warship** ['wɔːʃɪp] *n* okręt *m* wojenny
**wart** [wɔːt] *n* brodawka *f*
**wartime** ['wɔːtaɪm] *n*: **in ~** w czasie wojny
**wary** ['wɛərɪ] *adj* nieufny; **to be ~ about** *or* **of doing sth** nieufnie podchodzić (podejść *perf*) do (robienia) czegoś
**was** [wɔz] *pt of* **be**
**wash** [wɔʃ] *vt* (*clothes*) prać (wyprać *perf*); (*objects, face, hair*) myć (umyć *perf*); (*dishes, grease, paint*) zmywać (zmyć *perf*) ▷ *vi* myć się (umyć się *perf*) ▷ *n* pranie *nt*; (*of ship*) kilwater *m*; **to ~ over/against sth** (*sea etc*) obmywać (obmyć *perf*) coś; **he was ~ed overboard** zmyło go z pokładu; **to have a ~** myć się (umyć się *perf*); **to give sth a ~** myć (umyć *perf*) coś
▸ **wash away** *vt* (*flood etc*) zmywać (zmyć *perf*)
▸ **wash down** *vt* (*wall*) zmywać (zmyć *perf*); (*path, car*) spłukiwać (spłukać *perf*); (*food*) popijać (popić *perf*)
▸ **wash off** *vi* zmywać się (zmyć się *perf*); (*in the wash*) spierać się (sprać się *perf*) ▷ *vt* zmywać (zmyć *perf*)
▸ **wash out** *vt* spierać (sprać *perf*)
▸ **wash up** *vi* (*Brit*) zmywać (zmyć *perf or* pozmywać *perf*) (naczynia); (*US*) myć się (umyć się *perf*)
**washable** ['wɔʃəbl] *adj* (*fabric*) nadający się do prania; (*wallpaper*) zmywalny
**washbasin** ['wɔʃbeɪsn] *n* umywalka *f*
**washbowl** ['wɔʃbəul] (*US*) *n* umywalka *f*
**washcloth** ['wɔʃklɔθ] (*US*) *n* myjka *f*
**washer** ['wɔʃə<sup>r</sup>] *n* (*on tap etc*) podkładka *f*
**washing** ['wɔʃɪŋ] *n* pranie *nt*
**washing line** (*Brit*) *n* sznur *m* do prania *or* bielizny
**washing machine** *n* pralka *f* (automatyczna)
**washing powder** (*Brit*) *n* proszek *m* do prania
**Washington** ['wɔʃɪŋtən] *n* Waszyngton *m*

**washing-up** [wɔʃɪŋ'ʌp] *n* mycie *nt* naczyń, zmywanie *nt*; **to do the ~** zmywać (pozmywać *perf*) (naczynia)
**washing-up liquid** (*Brit*) *n* płyn *m* do (mycia) naczyń
**wash-out** ['wɔʃaut] (*inf*) *n* klapa *f* (*inf*)
**washroom** ['wɔʃrum] (*US*) *n* toaleta *f*
**wasn't** ['wɔznt] = **was not**
**WASP** [wɔsp] (*US: inf*) *n abbr* (= *White Anglo-Saxon Protestant*) *określenie, mające często negatywne zabarwienie, oznaczające białego Amerykanina o anglosaskim rodowodzie*
**Wasp** [wɔsp] *n abbr* = **WASP**
**wasp** [wɔsp] *n* osa *f*
**waspish** ['wɔspɪʃ] *adj* (*remark*) cięty; (*person*) zły jak osa
**wastage** ['weɪstɪdʒ] *n* (*amount wasted*) straty *pl*; (*loss: in manufacturing etc*) marnotrawstwo *nt*, marnowanie *nt*; **natural ~** ubytek naturalny
**waste** [weɪst] *n* (*of life, energy*) marnowanie *nt*; (*of money, time*) strata *f*; (*act of wasting*) marnotrawstwo *nt*; (*rubbish*) odpady *pl* ▷ *adj* (*by-product*) odpadowy; (*left over*) nie wykorzystany ▷ *vt* (*time, money*) tracić (stracić *perf*); (*opportunity, life, energy*) marnować (zmarnować *perf*); **wastes** *npl* pustkowie *nt*; **it's a ~ of money** to strata pieniędzy; **to go to ~** marnować się (zmarnować się *perf*); **to lay ~** obracać (obrócić *perf*) w perzynę
▶ **waste away** *vi* marnieć (zmarnieć *perf*)
**wastebasket** ['weɪstbɑ:skɪt] (*US*) *n* = **wastepaper basket**
**waste disposal unit** (*Brit*) *n* młynek *m* zlewozmywakowy, kuchenny rozdrabniacz *m* odpadków
**wasteful** ['weɪstful] *adj* (*person*) rozrzutny; (*process*) nieekonomiczny
**waste ground** (*Brit*) *n* nieużytki *pl*
**wasteland** ['weɪstlənd] *n* nieużytki *pl*; (*in town*) teren *m* nie zagospodarowany; (*fig*) pustynia *f*
**wastepaper basket** ['weɪstpeɪpə-] (*Brit*) *n* kosz *m* na śmieci
**waste pipe** *n* rura *f* ściekowa
**waste products** *npl* odpady *pl* produkcyjne
**watch** [wɔtʃ] *n* (*also:* **wristwatch**) zegarek *m*; (*surveillance*) obserwacja *f*; (*group of guards*) warta *f*; (*Naut: spell of duty*) wachta *f* ▷ *vt* (*people, objects*) przyglądać się *+dat*, patrzeć *or* patrzyć na *+acc*; (*match, TV*) oglądać (obejrzeć *perf*); (*spy on, guard*) obserwować; (*be careful of*) uważać na *+acc* ▷ *vi* patrzyć, przyglądać się; **on ~** na warcie; **to keep a close ~ on sb/sth** bacznie kogoś/coś obserwować; **~ what you're doing/how you drive** uważaj, co robisz/jak jedziesz
▶ **watch out** *vi* uważać; **~ out!** uważaj!
**watchband** ['wɔtʃbænd] (*US*) *n* pasek *m* do zegarka
**watchdog** ['wɔtʃdɔg] *n* pies *m* podwórzowy; (*fig*) jednostka *f* nadzorująca
**watchful** ['wɔtʃful] *adj* czujny
**watchmaker** ['wɔtʃmeɪkə<sup>r</sup>] *n* zegarmistrz *m*
**watchman** ['wɔtʃmən] (*irreg: like* **man**) *n see* **night watchman**
**watch stem** (*US*) *n* pokrętło *nt* (zegarka)
**watchstrap** ['wɔtʃstræp] *n* pasek *m* do zegarka
**watchword** ['wɔtʃwə:d] *n* hasło *nt* (wywoławcze)
**water** ['wɔ:tə<sup>r</sup>] *n* woda *f* ▷ *vt* podlewać (podlać *perf*) ▷ *vi* łzawić; **my mouth's ~ing** cieknie mi ślinka; **a drink of ~** szklanka wody; **in British ~s** na brytyjskich wodach (terytorialnych); **to pass ~** oddawać (oddać *perf*) mocz; **to make sb's mouth ~** robić komuś apetyt (narobić *perf* komuś apetytu)
▶ **water down** *vt* rozwadniać (rozwodnić *perf*); (*fig*) tonować (stonować *perf*)
**water biscuit** *n* krakers *m*
**water cannon** *n* armatka *f* wodna
**water closet** (*Brit*) *n* ustęp *m*, WC *nt inv*
**watercolour**, (*US*) **watercolor** ['wɔ:təkʌlə<sup>r</sup>] *n* akwarela *f*; **watercolours** *npl* akwarele *pl*, farby *pl* wodne
**water-cooled** ['wɔ:təku:ld] *adj* chłodzony wodą
**watercress** ['wɔ:təkrɛs] *n* rzeżucha *f*
**waterfall** ['wɔ:təfɔ:l] *n* wodospad *m*
**waterfront** ['wɔ:təfrʌnt] *n* (*at seaside*) wybrzeże *nt*; (*at docks*) nabrzeże *nt*
**water heater** *n* podgrzewacz *m* wody
**water hole** *n* źródełko *nt*
**water ice** *n* sorbet *m*
**watering can** ['wɔ:tərɪŋ-] *n* konewka *f*
**water level** *n* poziom *m* wody
**water lily** *n* lilia *f* wodna, nenufar *m*
**waterline** ['wɔ:təlaɪn] *n* linia *f* wodna
**waterlogged** ['wɔ:təlɔgd] *adj* (*ground*) zalany (wodą); (*wood*) przesiąknięty wodą
**water main** *n* magistrala *f* wodna
**watermark** ['wɔ:təmɑ:k] *n* znak *m* wodny
**watermelon** ['wɔ:təmɛlən] *n* arbuz *m*
**waterproof** ['wɔ:təpru:f] *adj* (*clothes*) nieprzemakalny; (*watch*) wodoodporny
**water-repellent** ['wɔ:tərɪ'pɛlnt] *adj* impregnowany
**watershed** ['wɔ:təʃɛd] *n* (*Geog*) dział *m* wodny; (*fig*) punkt *m* zwrotny
**water-skiing** ['wɔ:təski:ɪŋ] *n* narciarstwo *nt* wodne
**water softener** *n* środek *m* do zmiękczania wody

W

**water tank** *n* zbiornik *m* wody
**watertight** ['wɔ:tətaɪt] *adj* (*seal, door*) wodoszczelny; (*fig: excuse etc*) niepodważalny
**water vapour** *n* para *f* wodna
**waterway** ['wɔ:təweɪ] *n* (*canal, river*) droga *f* wodna; (*sea channel*) kanał *m*
**waterworks** ['wɔ:təwə:ks] *n* zakład *m* wodociągowy; (*inf: fig*) pęcherz *m*
**watery** ['wɔ:tərɪ] *adj* (*soup etc*) wodnisty; (*eyes*) załzawiony
**watt** [wɔt] *n* wat *m*
**wattage** ['wɔtɪdʒ] *n* moc *f* (znamionowa)
**wattle** ['wɔtl] *n* wiklina *f*
**wattle and daub** *n*: **a house of wattle-and-daub** lepianka *f*
**wave** [weɪv] *n* fala *f*; (*of hand*) machnięcie *nt* ▷ *vi* (*move in the air*) falować (zafalować *perf*); (*signal*) machać (pomachać *perf*) ▷ *vt* (*hand, handkerchief*) machać (pomachać *perf*) *+instr*; (*flag*) powiewać *+instr*; (*gun, stick*) wymachiwać *+instr*; (*hair*) kręcić (zakręcić *perf*); **short/medium/long ~** fale krótkie/średnie/długie; **the new ~** nowa fala; **he ~d us over to his table** skinieniem dłoni przywołał nas do swojego stolika; **to ~ goodbye to sb** machać (pomachać *perf*) komuś na pożegnanie
▶ **wave aside** *vt* (*fig*) przechodzić (przejść *perf*) do porządku (dziennego) nad *+instr*
**waveband** ['weɪvbænd] *n* zakres *m* or pasmo *nt* częstotliwości
**wavelength** ['weɪvlɛŋθ] *n* (*size*) długość *f* fali; (*frequency*) częstotliwość *f*; **to be on the same ~** (*fig*) świetnie się rozumieć
**waver** ['weɪvə[r]] *vi* (*voice*) drżeć (zadrżeć *perf*); (*eyes*) mrugać (mrugnąć *perf*); (*love*) chwiać się (zachwiać się *perf*); (*person*) wahać się (zawahać się *perf*)
**wavy** ['weɪvɪ] *adj* (*line*) falisty; (*hair*) falujący
**wax** [wæks] *n* wosk *m*; (*for skis*) parafina *f*; (*in ear*) woskowina *f* ▷ *vt* (*floor, car*) woskować (nawoskować *perf*); (*skis*) smarować (nasmarować *perf*); **the moon is waxing** przybywa księżyca
**waxed** [wækst] *adj* woskowany
**waxen** [wæksn] *adj* woskowo blady
**waxworks** ['wækswə:ks] *npl* figury *pl* woskowe ▷ *n* gabinet *m* figur woskowych
**way** [weɪ] *n* (*route*) droga *f*; (*access*) przejście *nt*; (*distance*) kawał(ek) *m* (drogi); (*direction*) strona *f*; (*manner, method*) sposób *m*; (*habit*) zwyczaj *m*, przyzwyczajenie *nt*; **a way of life** styl życia; **which way? — this way** którędy? — tędy; **on the way** po drodze; **to be on one's way** być w drodze; **to fight one's way through a crowd** torować (utorować *perf*) sobie drogę przez tłum; **to lie one's way out of sth** wyłgać się (*perf*) od czegoś; **to keep out of sb's way** trzymać się z dala od kogoś, nie wchodzić komuś w drogę; **it's a long way away** to daleko stąd; **the village is rather out of the way** wieś położona jest raczej na uboczu; **to go out of one's way to do sth** zadawać (zadać *perf*) sobie wiele trudu, żeby coś zrobić; **to be in the way** zawadzać; **to lose one's way** błądzić (zabłądzić *perf*), gubić (zgubić *perf*) drogę; **under way** w toku; **the way back** droga powrotna; **to make way (for sb/sth)** robić (zrobić *perf*) miejsce (dla kogoś/czegoś); **to get one's own way** stawiać (postawić *perf*) na swoim; **put it the right way up** (*Brit*) postaw to właściwą stroną ku górze; **the wrong way round** odwrotnie, na odwrót; **he's in a bad way** kiepsko z nim; **in a way** w pewnym sensie; **in some ways** pod pewnymi względami; **no way!** (*inf*) ani mi się śni! (*inf*); **by the way** à propos, nawiasem mówiąc; **"way in"** (*Brit*) „wejście"; **"way out"** (*Brit*) „wyjście"; **"give way"** (*Brit: Aut*) „ustąp pierwszeństwa przejazdu"
**waybill** ['weɪbɪl] *n* list *m* przewozowy
**waylay** [weɪ'leɪ] (*irreg: like* **lay**) *vt* zasadzać się (zasadzić się *perf*) na *+acc*; **to get waylaid** (*fig*) zostać (*perf*) zatrzymanym
**wayside** ['weɪsaɪd] *n*: **~ inn** zajazd *m*, przydrożna gospoda *f*; **to fall by the ~** (*fig*) nie dawać (nie dać *perf*) (sobie) rady
**way station** (*US*) *n* (*Rail*) przystanek *m*; (*fig*) etap *m* pośredni
**wayward** ['weɪwəd] *adj* krnąbrny
**WC** (*Brit*) *n abbr* = **water closet**
**WCC** *n abbr* = **World Council of Churches**
**we** [wi:] *pl pron* my; **here we are** (*arriving*) jesteśmy na miejscu; (*finding*) (już) jest, (już) mam
**weak** [wi:k] *adj* słaby; **to grow ~(er)** słabnąć (osłabnąć *perf*)
**weaken** ['wi:kn] *vi* słabnąć (osłabnąć *perf*) ▷ *vt* osłabiać (osłabić *perf*)
**weak-kneed** ['wi:k'ni:d] *adj* (*fig*) bez charakteru *post*
**weakling** ['wi:klɪŋ] *n* słabeusz *m*
**weakly** ['wi:klɪ] *adv* (*stand*) niepewnie; (*say*) nieśmiało; (*protest*) słabo
**weakness** ['wi:knɪs] *n* (*frailty*) osłabienie *nt*; (*of system etc*) słabość *f*; (*of signal etc*) niski poziom *m*; **to have a ~ for** mieć słabość do *+gen*
**wealth** [wɛlθ] *n* bogactwo *nt*; (*of knowledge*) (duży) zasób *m*
**wealth tax** *n* podatek *m* majątkowy
**wealthy** ['wɛlθɪ] *adj* bogaty, zamożny (*fml*)

**wean** [wi:n] *vt* odstawiać (odstawić *perf*) od piersi; (*fig*) odzwyczajać (odzwyczaić *perf*)
**weapon** ['wɛpən] *n* broń *f*
**wear** [wɛəʳ] (*pt* **wore**, *pp* **worn**) *n* (*use*) noszenie *nt* (*odzieży, butów itp*); (*damage through use*) zużycie *nt* ▷ *vt* (*clothes, shoes*) mieć na sobie, być ubranym w *+acc*; (: *habitually*) nosić, ubierać się w *+acc*; (*spectacles, beard*) nosić; (*put on*) ubierać się (ubrać się *perf*) w *+acc* ▷ *vi* (*last*) być trwałym; (*become old*) zużywać się (zużyć się *perf*); (: *clothes, shoes etc*) wycierać się (wytrzeć się *perf*), zdzierać się (zedrzeć się *perf*); **sports/baby~** odzież sportowa/niemowlęca; **town/evening ~** strój wyjściowy/wieczorowy; **to ~ a hole in sth** przetrzeć (*perf*) coś na wylot
▸ **wear away** *vt* wycierać (wytrzeć *perf*) ▷ *vi* zacierać się (zatrzeć się *perf*)
▸ **wear down** *vt* (*heels*) ścierać (zetrzeć *perf*); (*person, strength*) wyczerpywać (wyczerpać *perf*); (*resistance*) łamać (złamać *perf*)
▸ **wear off** *vi* (*pain etc*) mijać (minąć *perf*), przechodzić (przejść *perf*)
▸ **wear on** *vi* ciągnąć się, wlec się
▸ **wear out** *vt* (*shoes, clothing*) zdzierać (zedrzeć *perf*); (*person, strength*) wyczerpywać (wyczerpać *perf*)
**wearable** ['wɛərəbl] *adj* nadający się do noszenia
**wear and tear** [-tɛəʳ] *n* zużycie *nt* (eksploatacyjne)
**wearer** ['wɛərəʳ] *n* posiadacz(ka) *m(f)*
**wearily** ['wɪərɪlɪ] *adv* ze znużeniem
**weariness** ['wɪərɪnɪs] *n* znużenie *nt*
**wearisome** ['wɪərɪsəm] *adj* nużący
**weary** ['wɪərɪ] *adj* (*tired*) znużony; (*dispirited*) bezbarwny ▷ *vi*: **I'm beginning to ~ of it** zaczyna mnie to nużyć
**weasel** ['wi:zl] *n* łasica *f*
**weather** ['wɛðəʳ] *n* pogoda *f* ▷ *vt* (*crisis etc*) przetrwać (*perf*); (*wood etc*) powodować (spowodować *perf*) niszczenie *or* rozkład *+gen* ▷ *vi* (*rock etc*) wietrzeć (zwietrzeć *perf*); **what's the ~ like?** jaka jest pogoda?; **under the ~** (*fig*) chory
**weather-beaten** ['wɛðəbi:tn] *adj* (*face*) ogorzały; (*building*) sponiewierany przez burze
**weathercock** ['wɛðəkɔk] *n* wiatrowskaz *m* (*na dachu*)
**weather forecast** *n* prognoza *f* pogody
**weatherman** ['wɛðəmæn] (*irreg*: *like* **man**) *n* synoptyk *m*
**weatherproof** ['wɛðəpru:f] *adj* (*garment*) nieprzemakalny; (*building*) odporny na działanie czynników atmosferycznych
**weather report** *n* komunikat *m* o pogodzie *or* meteorologiczny
**weather vane** [-veɪn] *n* = **weathercock**
**weave** [wi:v] (*pt* **wove**, *pp* **woven**) *vt* (*cloth*) tkać (utkać *perf*); (*basket*) pleść (upleść *perf*) ▷ *vi* (*fig*: *pt, pp weaved*) przemykać się (przemknąć się *perf*)
**weaver** ['wi:vəʳ] *n* tkacz(ka) *m(f)*
**weaving** ['wi:vɪŋ] *n* tkactwo *nt*
**web** [wɛb] *n* (*of spider*) pajęczyna *f*; (*on duck's foot*) błona *f* pławna; (*network*) sieć *f*; (*fig*: *of reasons etc*) splot *m*
**webbed** ['wɛbd] *adj* płetwiasty
**webbing** ['wɛbɪŋ] *n*: **a belt of ~** pas *m* parciany
**webmaster** ['wɛbma:stəʳ] (*Comput*) *n* administrator(ka) *m(f)* strony WWW
**website** ['wɛbsaɪt] (*Comput*) *n* strona *f* internetowa
**wed** [wɛd] (*pt, pp* **wedded**) *vt* poślubiać (poślubić *perf*) ▷ *vi* pobierać się (pobrać się *perf*), brać (wziąć *perf*) ślub ▷ *n*: **the newly-weds** nowożeńcy *vir pl*, młoda para *f*
**Wed.** *abbr* (= *Wednesday*) śr.
**we'd** [wi:d] = **we had**; **we would**
**wedded** ['wɛdɪd] *pt, pp of* **wed** ▷ *adj*: **to be ~ to** (*fig*) być oddanym *+dat*
**wedding** [wɛdɪŋ] *n* (*ceremony*) ślub *m*; (*party*) wesele *nt*; **silver/golden ~** srebrne/złote gody *or* wesele
**wedding day** *n* dzień *m* ślubu
**wedding dress** *n* suknia *f* ślubna
**wedding present** *n* prezent *m* ślubny
**wedding ring** *n* obrączka *f*
**wedge** [wɛdʒ] *n* klin *m*; (*of cake*) kawałek *m* ▷ *vt* (*fasten*) klinować (zaklinować *perf*); (*pack tightly*) wciskać (wcisnąć *perf*)
**wedge-heeled shoes** ['wɛdʒhi:ld-] *npl* buty *pl* na koturnie
**wedlock** ['wɛdlɔk] *n* związek *m* małżeński
**Wednesday** ['wɛdnzdɪ] *n* środa *f*; *see also* **Tuesday**
**wee** [wi:] (*Scottish*) *adj* mały
**weed** [wi:d] *n* (*Bot*) chwast *m*; (*pej*) wymoczek *m* (*pej*), cherlak *m* (*pej*) ▷ *vt* pielić (wypielić *perf*)
**weedkiller** ['wi:dkɪləʳ] *n* środek *m* chwastobójczy
**weedy** ['wi:dɪ] *adj* (*pej*) cherlawy (*pej*)
**week** [wi:k] *n* tydzień *m*; **once/twice a ~** raz/dwa razy w tygodniu; **in two ~s' time** za dwa tygodnie; **a ~ today/on Friday** od dziś/od piątku za tydzień
**weekday** ['wi:kdeɪ] *n* (*Monday to Friday*) dzień *m* roboczy; (*Monday to Saturday*) dzień *m* powszedni
**weekend** [wi:k'ɛnd] *n* weekend *m*; **this/next/last ~** w ten/zeszły/przyszły weekend; **what are you doing at the ~?** co robisz w ten

W

weekend?; **open at ~s** otwarte w soboty i niedziele

**weekly** ['wi:klɪ] *adv* (*once a week*) raz w tygodniu; (*every week*) co tydzień ▷ *adj* (co) tygodniowy ▷ *n* tygodnik *m*

**weep** [wi:p] (*pt, pp* **wept**) *vi* płakać (zapłakać *perf*), łkać (załkać *perf*) (*literary*); **the wound is ~ing** sączy się z rany

**weeping willow** ['wi:pɪŋ-] *n* wierzba *f* płacząca

**weft** [wɛft] *n* wątek *m* (*układ nici*)

**weigh** [weɪ] *vt* ważyć (zważyć *perf*); (*fig: evidence, risks*) rozważać (rozważyć *perf*) ▷ *vi* ważyć; **to ~ anchor** podnosić (podnieść *perf*) kotwicę

▸ **weigh down** *vt* obciążać (obciążyć *perf*); (*fig*): **to be ~ed down by** *or* **with** być przytłoczonym *+instr*

▸ **weigh out** *vt* odważać (odważyć *perf*)

▸ **weigh up** *vt* (*person*) oceniać (ocenić *perf*); (*offer, pros and cons*) rozważać (rozważyć *perf*)

**weighbridge** ['weɪbrɪdʒ] *n* waga *f* pomostowa

**weighing machine** ['weɪɪŋ-] *n* waga *f* automatyczna

**weight** [weɪt] *n* (*metal object*) odważnik *m*; (*heaviness*) waga *f* ▷ *vt* (*fig*): **to be ~ed in favour of** działać na korzyść *+gen*; **sold by ~** sprzedawany na wagę; **to lose/put on ~** tracić (stracić *perf*)/przybierać (przybrać *perf*) na wadze; **~s and measures** miary i wagi

**weighting** ['weɪtɪŋ] *n* dodatek *m* specjalny (*rekompensujący wyższe koszty utrzymania*)

**weightlessness** ['weɪtlɪsnɪs] *n* nieważkość *f*

**weightlifter** ['weɪtlɪftə^r] *n* ciężarowiec *m*

**weight limit** *n* limit *m* wagowy

**weighty** ['weɪtɪ] *adj* (*heavy*) ciężki; (*important*) ważki

**weir** [wɪə^r] *n* jaz *m*

**weird** [wɪəd] *adj* (*strange*) dziwny, dziwaczny; (*eerie*) przedziwny, niesamowity

**welcome** ['wɛlkəm] *adj* mile widziany ▷ *n* powitanie *nt* ▷ *vt* (*bid welcome to*) witać (powitać *perf*); (*be glad of*) witać (powitać *perf*) z zadowoleniem; **~ to Szczecin** witamy w Szczecinie; **to make sb ~** życzliwie kogoś przyjmować (przyjąć *perf*); **you're ~ to try** możesz spróbować; **thank you — you're ~!** dziękuję — proszę bardzo!

**welcoming** ['wɛlkəmɪŋ] *adj* (*person, smile*) serdeczny; (*room*) przyjemny; (*speech*) powitalny

**weld** [wɛld] *n* spaw *m* ▷ *vt* spawać (zespawać *perf*)

**welder** ['wɛldə^r] *n* spawacz *m*

**welding** ['wɛldɪŋ] *n* spawanie *nt*

**welfare** ['wɛlfɛə^r] *n* (*well-being*) dobro *nt*; (*US: social aid*) opieka *f* społeczna; (*: supplementary benefit*) zasiłek *m* (*z opieki społecznej*)

**welfare state** *n* państwo *nt* opiekuńcze

**welfare work** *n* praca *f* w opiece społecznej

**well** [wɛl] *n* (*for water*) studnia *f*; (*oil well*) szyb *m* naftowy ▷ *adv* dobrze ▷ *adj*: **she's ~** (*healthy*) jest zdrowa ▷ *excl* (no) cóż; **I don't feel ~** nie czuję się dobrze; **I woke ~ before dawn** obudziłam się (na) długo przed świtem; **the film is ~ worth seeing** film jest zdecydowanie wart obejrzenia; **as ~** również; **you might as ~ tell me** lepiej mi powiedz; **he played as ~ as he could** grał najlepiej jak potrafił; **X as ~ as Y** zarówno X, jak i Y; **~, as I was saying ...** a więc, jak mówiłem, ...; **~ done!** brawo!, bardzo dobrze!; **get ~ soon!** wracaj szybko do zdrowia!; **to do ~** dobrze sobie radzić (poradzić *perf*)

▸ **well up** *vi* wzbierać (wezbrać *perf*)

**we'll = we will; we shall**

**well-behaved** ['wɛlbɪ'heɪvd] *adj* dobrze wychowany

**well-being** ['wɛl'bi:ɪŋ] *n* dobro *nt*, pomyślność *f*

**well-bred** ['wɛl'brɛd] *adj* dobrze wychowany

**well-built** ['wɛl'bɪlt] *adj* dobrze zbudowany

**well-chosen** ['wɛl'tʃəuzn] *adj* (*remark*) trafny

**well-deserved** ['wɛldɪ'zə:vd] *adj* zasłużony

**well-developed** ['wɛldɪ'vɛləpt] *adj* dobrze rozwinięty

**well-disposed** ['wɛl'dɪspəuzd] *adj*: **~ to(wards)** życzliwie usposobiony do *+gen*

**well-dressed** ['wɛl'drɛst] *adj* dobrze ubrany

**well-earned** ['wɛl'ə:nd] *adj* zasłużony

**well-groomed** ['wɛl'gru:md] *adj* zadbany

**well-heeled** ['wɛl'hi:ld] (*inf*) *adj* nadziany (*inf*)

**well-informed** ['wɛlɪn'fɔ:md] *adj* (*having knowledge of sth*) dobrze poinformowany; (*having general knowledge*) wykształcony

**Wellington** ['wɛlɪŋtən] (*Geog*) *n* Wellington *nt inv*

**wellingtons** ['wɛlɪŋtənz] *npl* gumowce *pl*

**well-kept** ['wɛl'kɛpt] *adj* (*house*) dobrze utrzymany; (*secret*) pilnie strzeżony

**well-known** ['wɛl'nəun] *adj* dobrze znany

**well-mannered** ['wɛl'mænəd] *adj* dobrze wychowany

**well-meaning** ['wɛl'mi:nɪŋ] *adj* (*person*) mający dobre intencje; (*offer, effort*) w dobrej wierze *post*

**well-nigh** ['wɛl'naɪ] *adv*: **it's ~ impossible** to prawie niemożliwie

**well-off** ['wɛl'ɔf] *adj* dobrze sytuowany, zamożny

**well-read** ['wɛl'rɛd] *adj* oczytany

**well-spoken** ['wɛl'spəukn] *adj*: **to be ~** mówić poprawnie *or* poprawnym językiem

**well-stocked** ['wɛl'stɔkt] *adj* dobrze zaopatrzony
**well-timed** ['wɛl'taɪmd] *adj* na czasie *post*
**well-to-do** ['wɛltə'du:] *adj* dobrze sytuowany, zamożny
**well-wisher** ['wɛlwɪʃə^r] *n* sympatyk(-yczka) *m(f)*
**Welsh** [wɛlʃ] *adj* walijski ▷ *n* (język *m*) walijski; **the Welsh** *npl* Walijczycy *vir pl*
**Welshman** ['wɛlʃmən] (*irreg: like* **man**) *n* Walijczyk *m*
**Welsh rarebit** *n* grzanka *f* z serem
**Welshwoman** ['wɛlʃwumən] (*irreg: like* **woman**) *n* Walijka *f*
**welter** ['wɛltə^r] *n* zamęt *m*
**went** [wɛnt] *pt of* **go**
**wept** [wɛpt] *pt, pp of* **weep**
**were** [wə:^r] *pt of* **be**
**we're** [wɪə^r] = **we are**
**weren't** [wə:nt] = **were not**
**werewolf** ['wɪəwulf] (*pl* **werewolves**) *n* wilkołak *m*
**werewolves** ['wɪəwulvz] *npl of* **werewolf**
**west** [wɛst] *n* zachód *m* ▷ *adj* zachodni ▷ *adv* na zachód; ~ **of** na zachód od *+gen*
**West** [wɛst]: **the** ~ *n* Zachód *m*
**westbound** ['wɛstbaund] *adj* (*traffic*) zdążający na zachód; (*carriageway*) prowadzący na zachód
**West Country** (*Brit*): **the** ~ *n południowo-zachodnia Anglia*
**westerly** ['wɛstəlɪ] *adj* zachodni
**western** ['wɛstən] zachodni *n* (*Film*) western *m*
**westernized** ['wɛstənaɪzd] *adj* zeuropeizowany (*przyjmujący wartości i styl życia charakterystyczny dla Europy Zachodniej*)
**West German** *adj* zachodnioniemiecki ▷ *n* Niemiec(-mka) *m(f)* z RFN
**West Germany** *n* Niemcy *pl* Zachodnie
**West Indian** *adj* z Indii Zachodnich *post* ▷ *n* mieszkaniec(-nka) *m(f)* Indii Zachodnich
**West Indies** [-'ɪndɪz] *npl*: **the** ~ Indie *pl* Zachodnie
**westward(s)** ['wɛstwəd(z)] *adv* na zachód
**wet** [wɛt] *adj* mokry; (*weather, day*) deszczowy; (*climate*) wilgotny ▷ *n* (*Brit: Pol*): **Tory Wets** umiarkowani torysi *vir pl*; **to wet o.s.** moczyć się (zmoczyć się *perf*); **to wet one's pants** siusiać (zsiusiać się *perf*) w majtki (*inf*); **to get wet** moknąć (zmoknąć *perf*); **"wet paint"** „świeżo malowane"; **to be a wet blanket** (*pej*) odbierać innym ochotę do zabawy
**wetness** ['wɛtnɪs] *n* wilgotność *f*
**wetsuit** ['wɛtsu:t] *n* strój *m* piankowy
**we've** [wi:v] = **we have**
**whack** [wæk] *vt* walić (walnąć *perf*) (*inf*)
**whacked** [wækt] (*Brit: inf*) *adj* wykończony (*inf*), skonany (*inf*)
**whale** [weɪl] *n* wieloryb *m*
**whaler** ['weɪlə^r] *n* (*ship*) statek *m* wielorybniczy
**wharf** [wɔ:f] (*pl* **wharves**) *n* nabrzeże *nt*
**wharves** [wɔ:vz] *npl of* **wharf**

KEYWORD

**what** [wɔt] *adj* **1** (*in questions*) jaki; **what colour/shape is it?** jakiego to jest koloru/kształtu?
**2** (*in exclamations*) co za, ale(ż); **what a mess!** co za bałagan!; **what a fool I am!** ale głupiec ze mnie!
▷ *pron* **1** (*interrogative*) co; **what are you doing?** co robisz?; **what about me?** (a) co ze mną?; **what is it called?** jak to się nazywa?; **what about having something to eat?** (a) może byśmy coś zjedli?
**2** (*relative*) (to,) co; **I saw what you did** widziałam, co zrobiłeś
▷ *excl* (*disbelieving*) co?!

**whatever** [wɔt'ɛvə^r] *adj* jakikolwiek ▷ *pron*: **do ~ is necessary/you want** rób, co konieczne/co chcesz; ~ **happens** cokolwiek się stanie; **for no reason ~** *or* **whatsoever** zupełnie *or* absolutnie bez powodu; **nothing ~** *or* **whatsoever** zupełnie *or* absolutnie nic
**whatsoever** [wɔtsəu'ɛvə^r] *adj* = **whatever**
**wheat** [wi:t] *n* pszenica *f*
**wheatgerm** ['wi:tdʒə:m] *n* kiełki *pl* pszenicy
**wheatmeal** ['wi:tmi:l] *n rodzaj mąki pszennej*
**wheedle** ['wi:dl] *vt*: **to ~ sth out of sb** wyłudzać (wyłudzić *perf*) coś od kogoś; **to ~ sb into doing sth** nakłaniać (nakłonić *perf*) kogoś do zrobienia czegoś (*pochlebstwami itp*)
**wheel** [wi:l] *n* koło *nt*; (*also*: **steering wheel**) kierownica *f*; (*Naut*) koło *nt* sterowe, ster *m* ▷ *vt* (*pram, cart*) pchać; (*bicycle*) prowadzić ▷ *vi* (*birds*) krążyć; (*also*: **wheel round**: *person*) odwracać się (odwrócić się *perf*)
**wheelbarrow** ['wi:lbærəu] *n* taczki *pl*
**wheelbase** ['wi:lbeɪs] *n* rozstaw *m* osi
**wheelchair** ['wi:ltʃɛə^r] *n* wózek *m* (inwalidzki)
**wheel clamp** *n* blokada *f* kół
**wheeler-dealer** ['wi:lə'di:lə^r] (*pej*) *n* kombinator(ka) *m(f)*
**wheelie-bin** ['wi:lɪbɪn] *n* kubeł *m* na śmieci na kółkach
**wheeling** ['wi:lɪŋ] *n*: ~ **and dealing** (*pej*) machinacje *pl* (*pej*)

W

**wheeze** [wi:z] *vi* rzęzić ▷ *n* (*idea*) (świetny) pomysł *m*

 KEYWORD

**when** [wɛn] *adv* kiedy; **when will you be back?** kiedy wrócisz?
▷ *conj* **1** kiedy, gdy; **she was reading when I came in** czytała, gdy *or* kiedy wszedłem; **on the day when I met him** w dniu, kiedy go poznałam; **that was when I needed you** wtedy właśnie cię potrzebowałem
**2** (*whereas*): **why did you buy that when you can't afford it?** dlaczego to kupiłaś, kiedy cię na to nie stać?; **you said I was wrong when in fact I was right** powiedziałeś, że nie mam racji, podczas gdy w rzeczywistości miałem

**whenever** [wɛn'ɛvəʳ] *adv* kiedykolwiek, obojętnie kiedy ▷ *conj* (*any time that*) kiedy *or* gdy tylko; (*every time that*) ilekroć, zawsze kiedy *or* gdy; **I go there ~ I can** chodzę tam, kiedy tylko mogę
**where** [wɛəʳ] *adv* gdzie ▷ *conj* gdzie; **this is ~ ...** to właśnie tutaj...; **~ possible** tam, gdzie to możliwe; **~ are you from?** skąd jesteś?
**whereabouts** [*adv* wɛərə'bauts, *n* 'wɛərəbauts] *adv* gdzie, w którym miejscu ▷ *n*: **nobody knows his ~** nikt nie zna miejsca jego pobytu
**whereas** [wɛər'æz] *conj* podczas gdy
**whereby** [wɛə'baɪ] (*fml*) *adv* (*by means of which*: *system, solution*) dzięki któremu, za pomocą którego; (*according to which*: *decision, law*) na mocy którego, zgodnie z którym
**whereupon** *conj* po czym
**wherever** [wɛər'ɛvəʳ] *conj* gdziekolwiek, obojętnie gdzie ▷ *adv*: **~ have you been?** gdzieś ty był?; **sit ~ you like** usiądź, gdzie chcesz
**wherewithal** ['wɛəwɪðɔ:l] *n*: **the ~ (to do sth)** środki *pl* (na zrobienie czegoś)
**whet** [wɛt] *vt* (*appetite*) zaostrzać (zaostrzyć *perf*); (*tool*) ostrzyć (naostrzyć *perf*)
**whether** ['wɛðəʳ] *conj* czy; **I don't know ~ to accept the proposal or not** nie wiem, czy (mam) przyjąć tę propozycję, czy nie
**whey** ['weɪ] *n* serwatka *f*

 KEYWORD

**which** [wɪtʃ] *adj* **1** który; **which picture do you want?** który obraz chcesz?; **which one?** który?
**2**: **the train may be late, in which case don't wait up** pociąg może się spóźnić. W takim wypadku nie czekaj na mnie; **we got there at 8 pm, by which time the cinema was full** dotarliśmy tam o ósmej. Do tego czasu kino było już pełne
▷ *pron* **1** (*interrogative*) który; **which (of these) are yours?** które (z tych) są twoje?
**2** (*relative*: *referring to preceding noun*) który; (: *referring to preceding clause*) co; **the chair on which you are sitting** krzesło, na którym siedzisz; **she said I was late, which was true** powiedziała, że się spóźniłem, co było prawdą; **after which** po czym

**whichever** [wɪtʃ'ɛvəʳ] *adj*: **take ~ book you prefer** weź tę książkę, którą wolisz; **~ book you take, ...** którąkolwiek *or* obojętnie którą książkę weźmiesz, ...
**whiff** [wɪf] *n* zapach *m*; **to catch a ~ of sth** czuć (poczuć *perf*) powiew czegoś
**while** [waɪl] *n* jakiś *or* pewien czas *m*; (*very short*) chwila *f* ▷ *conj* (*at the same moment as*) w chwili *or* momencie, gdy; (*during the time that*) (podczas) gdy *or* kiedy; (*although*) chociaż, choć; **for/in a ~** przez/za jakiś czas; **all the ~** (przez) cały czas; **we'll make it worth your ~** postaramy się, żeby Pan/Pani na tym nie stracił/a
▸ **while away** *vt* (*time*) skracać (skrócić *perf*) (sobie)
**whilst** [waɪlst] *conj* = **while**
**whim** [wɪm] *n* zachcianka *f*
**whimper** ['wɪmpəʳ] *n* (*of baby*) kwilenie *nt*; (*of dog*) skomlenie *nt* ▷ *vi* (*baby*) kwilić (zakwilić *perf*); (*dog*) skomleć (zaskomleć *perf*)
**whimsical** ['wɪmzɪkl] *adj* (*person*) kapryśny; (*smile, look*) żartobliwy
**whine** [waɪn] *n* (*of person*) jęk *m*; (*of dog*) skomlenie *nt*; (*of siren*) wycie *nt* ▷ *vi* (*person*) jęczeć (zajęczeć *perf*); (*dog*) skomleć (zaskomleć *perf*); (*siren*) wyć (zawyć *perf*); (*fig*: *complain*) jęczeć, marudzić
**whip** [wɪp] *n* (*lash*) bat *m*, bicz *m*; (*riding whip*) pejcz *m*; (*Pol*) *poseł odpowiedzialny za obecność członków swej partii na głosowaniach* ▷ *vt* (*person, animal*: *hit*) smagać (smagnąć *perf*) batem; (: *beat*) smagać (wysmagać *perf*) batem; (*cream, eggs*) ubijać (ubić *perf*); **to ~ sth off** zerwać (*perf*) *or* zedrzeć (*perf*) coś; **to ~ sth away** wyrwać (*perf*) *or* wydrzeć (*perf*) coś
▸ **whip up** *vt* (*cream*) ubijać (ubić *perf*); (*inf*: *meal*) pitrasić (upitrasić *perf*) (*inf*); (*hatred, interest*) wzbudzać (wzbudzić *perf*); (*people*): **to ~ up sb into excitement** wywoływać (wywołać *perf*) u kogoś emocje
**whiplash** ['wɪplæʃ] *n* (*also*: **whiplash injury**) uraz *m* kręgosłupa szyjnego
**whipped cream** [wɪpt-] *n* bita śmietana *f*

**whipping boy** ['wɪpɪŋ-] *n* (*fig*) chłopiec *m* do bicia

**whip-round** ['wɪpraund] (*Brit*: *inf*) *n* zrzutka *f* (*inf*)

**whirl** [wəːl] *vt* kręcić (zakręcić *perf*) *+instr* ▷ *vi* wirować ▷ *n* wir *m*; **I am** *or* **my mind is in a ~** kręci mi się w głowie

**whirlpool** ['wəːlpuːl] *n* wir *m* (wodny)

**whirlwind** ['wəːlwɪnd] *n* trąba *f* powietrzna

**whirr** [wəː^r] *vi* (*motor*) warkotać, warczeć; (*wings*) furkotać

**whisk** [wɪsk] *n* trzepaczka *f* (do ubijania piany), ubijacz *m* ▷ *vt* ubijać (ubić *perf*); **to ~ sb away** *or* **off** błyskawicznie kogoś zabierać (zabrać *perf*)

**whiskers** ['wɪskəz] *npl* (*of cat*) wąsy *pl*; (*of man*: *also*: **side whiskers**) baczki *pl*, bokobrody *pl*

**whisky**, (*US, Irish*) **whiskey** ['wɪskɪ] *n* whisky *f inv*

**whisper** ['wɪspə^r] *n* szept *m* ▷ *vi* szeptać (szepnąć *perf*) ▷ *vt* szeptać (szepnąć *perf*), wyszeptać (*perf*); **to ~ sth to sb** mówić (powiedzieć *perf*) coś komuś szeptem

**whispering** ['wɪspərɪŋ] *n* szepty *pl*

**whist** [wɪst] (*Brit*) *n* wist *m*

**whistle** ['wɪsl] *n* (*sound*) gwizd *m*; (*object*) gwizdek *m* ▷ *vi* (*person*) gwizdać (gwizdnąć *perf or* zagwizdać *perf*), pogwizdywać; (*bird, kettle*) gwizdać (zagwizdać *perf*); (*bullet*) świstać (świsnąć *perf*) ▷ *vt*: **to ~ a tune** gwizdać (zagwizdać *perf*) (jakąś) melodię

**whistle-stop** ['wɪslstɔp] *adj*: **to make a ~ tour of** (*Pol*) odbywać (odbyć *perf*) serię spotkań przedwyborczych w *+loc*

**Whit** [wɪt] *n* = **Whitsun**

**white** [waɪt] *adj* biały ▷ *n* (*colour*) (kolor *m*) biały, biel *f*; (*person*) biały(-ła) *m*(*f*); (*of egg*) białko *nt*; **to turn** *or* **go ~** (*pale*) blednąć (zblednąć *perf or* poblednąć *perf*); (*grey*) siwieć (osiwieć *perf*); **the ~s** (*washing*) białe rzeczy; **tennis/cricket ~s** strój do gry w tenisa/krykieta

**whitebait** ['waɪtbeɪt] *n* smażone szprotki *pl*

**white coffee** (*Brit*) *n* biała kawa *f*, kawa *f* ze śmietanką

**white-collar worker** ['waɪtkɔlə-] *n* pracownik *m* umysłowy, urzędnik *m*

**white elephant** *n* (*fig*) chybiona inwestycja *f*

**white goods** *npl* (*appliances*) sprzęt *m* gospodarstwa domowego; (*linen*) bielizna *f* pościelowa i stołowa)

**white-hot** [waɪt'hɔt] *adj* rozgrzany do białości

**white lie** *n* niewinne kłamstwo *nt*

**whiteness** ['waɪtnɪs] *n* biel *f*

**white noise** *n* biały szum *m*

**whiteout** ['waɪtaut] *n* śnieżyca *f*

**white paper** *n* (*Pol*) raport *m* rządowy

**whitewash** ['waɪtwɔʃ] *n* wapno *nt* (do bielenia); (*inf*: *Sport*) przegrana *f* do zera ▷ *vt* bielić (pobielić *perf*); (*fig*) wybielać (wybielić *perf*)

**white water** *n*: **white-water rafting** spływ *m* górski (tratwami)

**whiting** *n inv* (*fish*) witlinek *m*

**Whit Monday** *n* drugi dzień *m* Zielonych Świątek

**Whitsun** ['wɪtsn] *n* Zielone Świątki *pl*

**whittle** ['wɪtl] *vt*: **to ~ away** *or* **down** (*costs*) redukować (zredukować *perf*)

**whizz** [wɪz] *vi*: **to ~ past** *or* **by** śmigać (śmignąć *perf*) obok

**whizz kid** (*inf*) *n* geniusz *m*, cudowne dziecko *nt*

**WHO** *n abbr* (= *World Health Organization*) WHO *nt inv*, Światowa Organizacja *f* Zdrowia

 KEYWORD

**who** [huː] *pron* **1** (*interrogative*) kto *m*; **who is it?**, **who's there?** kto to?, kto tam?; **who are you looking for?** kogo szukasz?

**2** (*relative*) który; **the woman who spoke to me** kobieta, która ze mną rozmawiała; **those who can swim** ci, którzy umieją pływać

**whodunit** [huː'dʌnɪt], **whodunnit** (*inf*) *n* kryminał *m* (*książka, film itp*)

**whoever** [huː'ɛvə^r] *pron*: **~ finds him** ten, kto go znajdzie; **ask ~ you like** spytaj, kogo (tylko) chcesz; **~ he marries** z kimkolwiek się ożeni; **~ told you that?** któż ci to powiedział?

**whole** [həul] *adj* cały ▷ *n* całość *f*; **the ~ of July** cały lipiec; **the ~ of the town** całe miasto; **the ~ lot (of it)** wszystko (to); **the ~ lot (of them)** wszyscy *vir pl*, wszystkie *nvir pl*; **the ~ (of the) time** cały czas; **~ villages were destroyed** zniszczeniu uległy całe wsie; **on the ~** ogólnie (rzecz) biorąc

**wholefood(s)** ['həulfuːd(z)] *n*(*pl*) żywność *f* naturalna

**wholefood shop** *n* sklep *m* z żywnością naturalną

**wholehearted** [həul'hɑːtɪd] *adj* (*agreement*) całkowity; (*support*) gorący

**wholeheartedly** [həul'hɑːtɪdlɪ] *adv* (*agree*) całkowicie; (*support*) z całego serca, gorąco

**wholemeal** ['həulmiːl] (*Brit*) *adj* (*bread, flour*) razowy

**whole note** *n* cała nuta *f*

**wholesale** ['həulseɪl] *n* hurt *m* ▷ *adj* (*price*) hurtowy; (*destruction*) masowy ▷ *adv* hurtowo, hurtem

W

**wholesaler** ['həulseɪlə^r] *n* hurtownik *m*
**wholesome** ['həulsəm] *adj* zdrowy
**wholewheat** ['həulwi:t] *n* = **wholemeal**
**wholly** ['həulɪ] *adv* całkowicie

 KEYWORD

**whom** [hu:m] *pron* **1** (*interrogative*): **whom did you see?** kogo widziałaś?; **to whom did you give it?** komu to dałeś?
**2** (*relative*): **the man whom I saw** człowiek, którego widziałem; **the lady with whom I was talking** pani, z którą rozmawiałem; **some people whom we didn't know** jacyś ludzie, których nie znaliśmy

**whooping cough** ['hu:pɪŋ-] *n* koklusz *m*
**whoosh** [wuʃ] *vi* śmigać (śmignąć *perf*) ▷ *n* świst *m*; **the skiers ~ed past, skiers came by with a ~** narciarze przemknęli obok ze świstem
**whopper** ['wɔpə^r] (*inf*) *n* (*lie*) wierutne kłamstwo *nt*; (*large thing*) kolos *m*
**whopping** ['wɔpɪŋ] (*inf*) *adj* ogromniasty (*inf*), wielgachny (*inf*)
**whore** [hɔ:^r] (*inf, pej*) *n* dziwka *f* (*inf, pej*), kurwa *f* (*inf!, pej*)

 KEYWORD

**whose** [hu:z] *adj* **1** (*interrogative*) czyj; **whose book is this?, whose is this book?** czyja to książka?, czyja jest ta książka?
**2** (*relative*): **the girl whose sister you were speaking to** dziewczyna, z której siostrą rozmawiałeś; **the gardener whose name was Dave** ogrodnik, który miał na imię Dave
▷ *pron* czyj *m*/czyja *f*/czyje *nt*; **I know whose it is** wiem, czyje to jest

**Who's Who** ['hu:z'hu:] *n* „Kto jest kim" *nt inv*

 KEYWORD

**why** [waɪ] *adv* dlaczego, czemu; **why is he always late?** dlaczego on zawsze się spóźnia?; **fancy a drink? — why not?** może drinka? — czemu nie?
▷ *conj* dlaczego; **I wonder why he said that** zastanawiam się, dlaczego to powiedział; **that's not why I'm here** nie dlatego tu jestem; **the reason why I'm here** powód, dla którego tu jestem
▷ *excl* (*expressing surprise, annoyance etc*) och; (*explaining*) ależ, przecież; **why, it's you!** och, to ty!; **why, that's impossible!** ależ to niemożliwe!; **I don't understand — why, it's obvious!** nie rozumiem — przecież to oczywiste!

**WI** *n abbr* (*Brit*: = *Women's Institute*) *stowarzyszenie kobiece* ▷ *abbr* (*Brit*) = **West Indies**; (*US*: *Post*) = **Wisconsin**
**wick** [wɪk] *n* knot *m*; **he gets on my ~** (*Brit*: *inf*) on działa mi na nerwy
**wicked** ['wɪkɪd] *adj* (*crime*) haniebny; (*man*) podły, niegodziwy; (*witch*) zły; (*smile, wit*) szelmowski; (*inf*: *weather etc*) paskudny
**wicker** ['wɪkə^r] *adj* wiklinowy
**wickerwork** ['wɪkə^rwə:k] *adj* wiklinowy ▷ *n* wyroby *pl* wikliniarskie *or* z wikliny
**wicket** ['wɪkɪt] (*Cricket*) *n* (*stumps*) bramka *f*; (*grass area*) *obszar boiska do krykieta pomiędzy dwiema bramkami*
**wicket-keeper** ['wɪkɪtki:pə^r] (*Cricket*) *n gracz broniący bramki*
**wide** [waɪd] *adj* szeroki ▷ *adv*: **to open ~** otwierać (otworzyć *perf*) szeroko; **to go ~** (*shot etc*) przechodzić (przejść *perf*) obok; **the bridge is 3 metres ~** most ma 3 metry szerokości
**wide-angle lens** ['waɪdæŋgl-] *n* obiektyw *m* szerokokątny
**wide-awake** [waɪdə'weɪk] *adj* (całkiem) rozbudzony
**wide-eyed** [waɪd'aɪd] *adj* (*fig*) naiwny; **she sat there ~** siedziała z szeroko otwartymi oczami
**widely** ['waɪdlɪ] *adv* (*differ, vary*) znacznie; (*travel*) dużo; (*spaced, known*) szeroko; **he's ~ read** (*reader*) jest bardzo oczytany; (*writer*) ma wielu czytelników
**widen** ['waɪdn] *vt* (*road, river*) poszerzać (poszerzyć *perf*); (*one's experience*) rozszerzać (rozszerzyć *perf*) ▷ *vi* (*road, river*) rozszerzać się; (*gap*) powiększać się (powiększyć się *perf*)
**wideness** ['waɪdnɪs] *n* (*of road, river*) szerokość *f*; (*of gap*) wielkość *f*
**wide open** *adj* szeroko otwarty
**wide-ranging** [waɪd'reɪndʒɪŋ] *adj* (*implications*) daleko idący; (*survey*) wszechstronny
**widespread** ['waɪdsprɛd] *adj* powszechny, rozpowszechniony
**widow** ['wɪdəu] *n* wdowa *f*
**widowed** ['wɪdəud] *adj* owdowiały
**widower** ['wɪdəuə^r] *n* wdowiec *m*
**width** [wɪdθ] *n* szerokość *f*; **the street is 7 metres in ~** ulica ma 7 metrów szerokości
**widthways** ['wɪdθweɪz] *adv* wszerz
**wield** [wi:ld] *vt* dzierżyć
**wife** [waɪf] (*pl* **wives**) *n* żona *f*
**wig** [wɪg] *n* peruka *f*
**wigging** ['wɪgɪŋ] (*Brit*: *inf*) *n* ochrzan

**wiggle** ['wɪgl] *vt* (*hips*) kręcić *+instr*; (*ears*) ruszać *+instr*
**wiggly** ['wɪglɪ] *adj* falisty
**wigwam** ['wɪgwæm] *n* wigwam *m*
**wild** [waɪld] *adj* (*animal, plant, land*) dziki; (*weather, night, applause*) burzliwy; (*sea*) wzburzony; (*idea*) szalony; (*person*): **~ with anger** *etc* oszalały z gniewu *etc* ▷ *n*: **animals in the ~** zwierzęta w swym naturalnym środowisku; **the wilds** *npl* pustkowie *nt*; **I'm not ~ about him** nie przepadam za nim; **he took a ~ guess** próbował zgadnąć na chybił trafił; **to go ~** (*excited*) oszaleć (*perf*); (*inf*: *furious*) wściec się (*perf*) (*inf*)
**wild card** (*Comput*) *n* (globalny) znak *m* zastępczy
**wildcat** ['waɪldkæt] *n* żbik *m*
**wildcat strike** *n* dziki strajk *m*
**wilderness** ['wɪldənɪs] *n* dzicz *f*, pustynia *f*
**wildfire** ['waɪldfaɪə^r] *n*: **to spread like ~** rozchodzić się (rozejść się *perf*) lotem błyskawicy
**wild-goose chase** [waɪld'gu:s-] *n* (*fig*) szukanie *nt* wiatru w polu
**wildlife** ['waɪldlaɪf] *n* (dzika) przyroda *f*
**wildly** ['waɪldlɪ] *adv* dziko; (*applaud*) burzliwie; (*shake etc*) gwałtownie, wściekle; (*romantic*) niesamowicie; (*erratic, inefficient*) wysoce
**wiles** [waɪlz] *npl* sztuczki *pl*
**wilful**, (*US*) **willful** ['wɪlful] *adj* (*child, character*) uparty; (*action, disregard*) umyślny

 KEYWORD

**will** [wɪl] (*vt*: *pt, pp* **willed**) *aux vb* **1** (*forming future tense*): **I will finish it tomorrow** skończę to jutro; **I will have finished it by tomorrow** skończę to do jutra
**2** (*in conjectures, predictions*): **he will** *or* **he'll be there by now** (pewnie) już tam jest; **that will be the postman** to pewnie listonosz
**3** (*in commands, requests, offers*): **will you be quiet!** bądźże cicho!; **will you help me?** (czy) możesz mi pomóc?, pomożesz mi?; **will you have a cup of tea?** (czy) napije się Pan/Pani herbaty?
▷ *vt*: **to will sb to do sth** zmuszać (zmusić *perf*) kogoś, by coś (z)robił; **he willed himself to go on** zmusił się, by iść dalej
▷ *n* (*volition*) wola *f*; (*also*: **last will**) testament; **he did it against his will** zrobił to wbrew swojej woli

['wɪlful] (*US*) *adj* = **wilful**
['wɪlɪŋ] *adj* (*having no objection*) chętny; (*enthusiastic*) ochoczy; **he's ~ to do it** on chętnie to zrobi; **to show ~** wykazywać (wykazać *perf*) dobre chęci
**willingly** ['wɪlɪŋlɪ] *adv* chętnie
**willingness** ['wɪlɪŋnɪs] *n* (*readiness*) chęć *f*, gotowość *f*; (*enthusiasm*) ochota *f*
**will-o'-the wisp** ['wɪləðə'wɪsp] *n* błędny ognik *m*; (*fig*) złudzenie *nt*
**willow** ['wɪləu] *n* wierzba *f*
**willpower** ['wɪl'pauə^r] *n* siła *f* woli
**willy-nilly** ['wɪlɪ'nɪlɪ] *adv* chcąc nie chcąc
**wilt** [wɪlt] *vi* więdnąć (zwiędnąć *perf*)
**Wilts** [wɪlts] (*Brit*: *Post*) *abbr* = **Wiltshire**
**wily** ['waɪlɪ] *adj* przebiegły, chytry
**wimp** [wɪmp] (*inf, pej*) *n* mięczak *m* (*inf, pej*)
**win** [wɪn] (*pt, pp* **won**) *n* zwycięstwo *nt*, wygrana *f* ▷ *vt* (*game, competition, election*) wygrywać (wygrać *perf*), zwyciężać (zwyciężyć *perf*) w *+loc*; (*prize, support, popularity*) zdobywać (zdobyć *perf*) ▷ *vi* wygrywać (wygrać *perf*), zwyciężać (zwyciężyć *perf*)
▶ **win over** *vt* pozyskiwać (pozyskać *perf*)
▶ **win round** (*Brit*) *vt* = **win over**
**wince** [wɪns] *vi* krzywić się (skrzywić się *perf*)
**winch** [wɪntʃ] *n* kołowrót *m*
**Winchester disk** ['wɪntʃɪstə-] (*Comput*) *n* dysk *m* stały typu Winchester
**wind[1]** [wɪnd] *n* (*air*) wiatr *m*; (*Med*) wzdęcie *nt*; (*breath*) dech *m* ▷ *vt* pozbawiać (pozbawić *perf*) tchu; **the winds** *npl* (*Mus*) instrumenty *pl* dęte; **into** *or* **against the ~** pod wiatr; **to get ~ of sth** (*fig*) zwietrzyć (*perf*) coś; **to break ~** puszczać wiatry
**wind[2]** [waɪnd] (*pt, pp* **wound**) *vt* (*thread, rope*) nawijać (nawinąć *perf*); (*bandage*) zawijać (zawinąć *perf*); (*clock, toy*) nakręcać (nakręcić *perf*) ▷ *vi* wić się
▶ **wind down** *vt* (*car window*) opuszczać (opuścić *perf*); (*fig*: *business etc*) (stopniowo) likwidować (zlikwidować *perf*), zwijać (zwinąć *perf*) (*inf*)
▶ **wind up** *vt* (*clock, toy*) nakręcać (nakręcić *perf*); (*debate*) kończyć (zakończyć *perf*)
**windbreak** ['wɪndbreɪk] *n* zasłona *f* od wiatru (*mur, drzewa itp*)
**windbreaker** ['wɪndbreɪkə^r] (*US*) *n* = **windcheater**
**windcheater** ['wɪndtʃi:tə^r] *n* wiatrówka *f* (*kurtka*)
**winder** ['waɪndə^r] (*Brit*) *n* pokrętło *nt* (zegarka)
**windfall** ['wɪndfɔ:l] *n* (*money*) nieoczekiwany przypływ *m* gotówki; (*apple*) spad *m*
**wind farm** *n* farma *f* wiatrowa
**winding** ['waɪndɪŋ] *adj* kręty, wijący się
**wind instrument** ['wɪnd-] *n* instrument *m* dęty
**windmill** ['wɪndmɪl] *n* wiatrak *m*

W

**window** ['wɪndəu] *n (of house, vehicle, on computer screen)* okno *nt*; *(of shop)* witryna *f*; *(in bank, post office)* okienko *nt*
**window box** *n* skrzynka *f* na kwiaty
**window cleaner** *n* osoba *f* do mycia okien
**window dresser** *n* dekorator(ka) *m(f)* witryn sklepowych
**window envelope** *n* koperta *f* z okienkiem
**window frame** *n* framuga *f or* rama *f* okienna
**window ledge** *n* parapet *m*
**window pane** *n* szyba *f* (okienna)
**window-shopping** ['wɪndəuʃɔpɪŋ] *n* oglądanie *nt* wystaw sklepowych
**windowsill** ['wɪndəusɪl] *n* parapet *m*
**windpipe** ['wɪndpaɪp] *n* tchawica *f*
**wind power** ['wɪnd-] *n* siła *f* wiatru
**windscreen** ['wɪndskri:n] *n (Aut)* przednia szyba *f*
**windscreen washer** *n* spryskiwacz *m* przedniej szyby
**windscreen wiper** [-waɪpəʳ] *n* wycieraczka *f* (przedniej szyby)
**windshield** ['wɪndʃi:ld] *(US) n* = **windscreen**
**windsurfing** ['wɪndsə:fɪŋ] *n* windsurfing *m*
**windswept** ['wɪndswɛpt] *adj (place)* nie osłonięty, odsłonięty; *(hair)* potargany (przez wiatr)
**wind tunnel** ['wɪnd-] *n* tunel *m* aerodynamiczny
**windy** ['wɪndɪ] *adj* wietrzny; **it's ~** wieje silny wiatr
**wine** [waɪn] *n* wino *nt* ▷ *vt*: **to ~ and dine sb** podejmować (podjąć *perf*) kogoś wystawną kolacją *(zwykle w drogiej restauracji)*
**wine bar** *n* winiarnia *f*
**wine cellar** *n* piwnica *f* win
**wine glass** *n* kieliszek *m* do wina
**wine list** *n* karta *f* win
**wine merchant** *n* handlarz *m* winem
**wine tasting** [-teɪstɪŋ] *n* degustacja *f* win
**wine waiter** *n* kelner *m* podający wino
**wing** [wɪŋ] *n* skrzydło *nt*; *(Aut)* błotnik *m*; **the wings** *npl (Theat)* kulisy *pl*; **in the ~s** za kulisami; **from the ~s** zza kulis
**winger** ['wɪŋəʳ] *(Sport) n* skrzydłowy(-wa) *m(f)*
**wing mirror** *(Brit) n* lusterko *nt* boczne
**wing nut** *n* nakrętka *f* motylkowa
**wingspan** ['wɪŋspæn] *n* rozpiętość *f* skrzydeł
**wingspread** ['wɪŋsprɛd] *n* = **wingspan**
**wink** [wɪŋk] *n* mrugnięcie *nt* ▷ *vi* mrugać (mrugnąć *perf*)
**winkle** [wɪŋkl] *n* pobrzeżek *m (małż jadalny)*
**winner** ['wɪnəʳ] *n (of race, competition)* zwycięzca/zwyciężczyni *m/f*; *(of prize)* zdobywca(-wczyni) *m(f)*
**winning** ['wɪnɪŋ] *adj (team, competitor, goal)* zwycięski; *(smile)* ujmujący; *see also* **winnings**
**winning post** *n* meta *f*
**winnings** ['wɪnɪŋz] *npl* wygrana *f*
**winsome** ['wɪnsəm] *adj* pociągający
**winter** ['wɪntəʳ] *n* zima *f* ▷ *vi (birds)* zimować; **in ~** zimą, w zimie
**winter sports** *npl* sporty *pl* zimowe
**wintry** ['wɪntrɪ] *adj (weather, day)* zimowy; *(smile)* lodowaty
**wipe** [waɪp] *vt (dry, clean)* wycierać (wytrzeć *perf*); *(erase)* zmazywać (zmazać *perf*); **to ~ one's nose** wycierać (wytrzeć *perf*) nos ▷ *n*: **to give sth a ~** przecierać (przetrzeć *perf*) coś
▸ **wipe off** *vt* ścierać (zetrzeć *perf*)
▸ **wipe out** *vt (city etc)* zmiatać (zmieść *perf*) z powierzchni ziemi
▸ **wipe up** *vt (spilt liquid etc)* ścierać (zetrzeć *perf*), zbierać (zebrać *perf*) szmatką
**wire** ['waɪəʳ] *n* drut *m*; *(Elec)* przewód *m*; *(telegram)* telegram *m*, depesza *f (old)* ▷ *vt (US: person)* wysyłać (wysłać *perf*) telegram do *+gen*; *(also*: **wire up**: *electrical fitting)* podłączać (podłączyć *perf*)
**wire brush** *n* szczotka *f* druciana
**wire cutters** *npl* szczypce *pl* do cięcia drutu
**wireless** ['waɪəlɪs] *n (Brit: old)* radio *nt* ▷ *adj (Comput)* bezprzewodowy
**wire netting** *n* siatka *f* druciana
**wire-tapping** ['waɪə'tæpɪŋ] *n* podsłuch *m* (telefoniczny)
**wiring** ['waɪərɪŋ] *(Elec) n* instalacja *f* elektryczna
**wiry** ['waɪərɪ] *adj (person)* silny *(mimo drobnej budowy)*; *(hair, grass)* szorstki
**wisdom** ['wɪzdəm] *n (of person)* mądrość *f*; *(of action, remark)* sens *m*
**wisdom tooth** *n* ząb *m* mądrości
**wise** [waɪz] *adj* mądry; **I'm none the ~r** nadal nic nie rozumiem
▸ **wise up** *(inf) vi*: **he ~d up to the fact she wasn't coming back** (wreszcie) dotarło do niego, że ona nie wróci
**...wise** [waɪz] *suff (with regard to)*: **t~** *etc* jeśli chodzi o czas *etc*; *(in the manner of)*: **c~** *etc* jak rak *etc*
**wisecrack** ['waɪzkræk] *n* dowcipna uwaga *f*
**wisely** ['waɪzlɪ] *adv* mądrze
**wish** [wɪʃ] *n* pragnienie *nt*; *(specific)* życzenie *nt* ▷ *vt*: **I ~ I were/I had been ...** żałuję, że ni[e] jestem/nie byłem ...; **best ~es** *(for birthday etc)* najlepsze życzenia; **with best ~es** *(in letter)* łączę pozdrowienia; **to make a ~** pomyśleć *(perf)* sobie (jakieś) życzenie; **give her my best ~es** pozdrów ją ode mnie; **we have n[o intention] to repeat their mistakes** nie mamy zamiaru powtarzać ich błędów; **to ~ sb** dobrze komuś życzyć; **to ~ to do sth** p[ragnąć] coś (z)robić; **to ~ for** życzyć (zażyczyć

sobie (w myślach) *+gen*; **she ~ed him good luck** życzyła mu powodzenia; **I wouldn't ~ it on my worst enemy** nie życzyłbym tego największemu wrogowi

**wishful** ['wɪʃful] *adj*: **it's ~ thinking** to pobożne życzenia

**wishy-washy** ['wɪʃɪ'wɔʃɪ] (*inf*) *adj* (*colour*) rozmyty; (*ideas, person*) nijaki, mało konkretny

**wisp** [wɪsp] *n* (*of grass, hay*) wiązka *f*; (*of hair*) kosmyk *m*; (*of smoke*) smuga *f*

**wistful** ['wɪstful] *adj* tęskny

**wit** [wɪt] *n* (*wittiness*) dowcip *m*; (*also*: **wits**) inteligencja *f*; (*person*) humorysta *m*; (*presence of mind*) rozum *m*; **to be at one's wits' end (about)** nie wiedzieć, co począć (z *+instr*); **to have one's wits about one** mieć się na baczności; **to wit** (a) mianowicie

**witch** [wɪtʃ] *n* czarownica *f*

**witchcraft** ['wɪtʃkrɑ:ft] *n* czary *pl*

**witch doctor** *n* szaman *m*

**witch-hunt** ['wɪtʃhʌnt] *n* (*fig*) polowanie *nt* na czarownice, nagonka *m*

KEYWORD

**with** [wɪð, wɪθ] *prep* **1** (*accompanying, in the company of*) z *+instr*; **I was with him** byłem z nim; **we stayed with friends** zatrzymaliśmy się u przyjaciół; **I'll be with you in a minute** zaraz się Panem/Panią zajmę; **I'm with you** rozumiem; **to be with it** (*inf*: *up-to-date*) być na bieżąco; (*: alert*) kontaktować (*inf*); **I'm not quite with it this morning** nie bardzo dziś kontaktuję

**2** (*descriptive*): **a room with a view** pokój z widokiem; **the man with the grey hat** (ten) mężczyzna w szarym kapeluszu

**3** (*indicating manner, means, cause*): **with tears in her eyes** ze łzami w oczach; **to walk with a stick** chodzić o lasce; **red with anger** czerwony ze złości; **to fill sth with water** napełniać (napełnić *perf*) coś wodą

**ithdraw** [wɪθ'drɔ:] (*irreg*: *like* **draw**) *vt* (*object*) wyjmować (wyjąć *perf*); (*offer, troops*) wycofywać (wycofać *perf*); (*statement*) cofać cofnąć *perf*), odwoływać (odwołać *perf*); noney: *from bank*) podejmować (podjąć *perf*) *vi* wycofywać się (wycofać się *perf*); **to ~ into** . zamykać się (zamknąć się *perf*) w sobie

**drawal** [wɪθ'drɔ:əl] *n* (*of offer, troops,* *es*) wycofanie *nt*; (*of statement*) cofnięcie wołanie *nt*; (*of participation*) wycofanie (*of money*) podjęcie *nt*

**wal symptoms** *npl* zespół *m* cji

**withdrawn** [wɪθ'drɔ:n] *pp of* **withdraw** ▷ *adj* zamknięty w sobie

**wither** ['wɪðə^r] *vi* usychać (uschnąć *perf*), więdnąć (zwiędnąć *perf*)

**withered** ['wɪðəd] *adj* (*plant*) uschnięty, zwiędnięty; (*limb*) bezwładny

**withhold** [wɪθ'həuld] (*irreg*: *like* **hold**) *vt* (*rent etc*) odmawiać (odmówić *perf*) płacenia *+gen*; (*permission*) odmawiać (odmówić *perf*) *+gen*; (*information*) zatajać (zataić *perf*)

**within** [wɪð'ɪn] *prep* (*object*) wewnątrz *or* w środku *+gen*; (*building, area*) na terenie *+gen*; (*time*) w (prze)ciągu *or* na przestrzeni *+gen*; (*distance*) w odległości *+gen* ▷ *adv* wewnątrz, w środku; **from ~** ze środka; **~ reach of** w miejscu dostępnym dla *+gen*; **they came ~ sight of the gate** dotarli do miejsca, z którego widać było bramę; **the end is ~ sight** widać już koniec; **~ the week** w ciągu tygodnia; **~ a mile of** o milę od *+gen*; **~ an hour of** w niecałą godzinę od *+gen or* po *+loc*; **~ the law** w granicach prawa

**without** [wɪð'aut] *prep* bez *+gen*; **~ a coat** bez płaszcza; **~ speaking** nic nie mówiąc; **it goes ~ saying** to się rozumie samo przez się; **~ anyone knowing** bez niczyjej wiedzy

**withstand** [wɪθ'stænd] (*irreg*: *like* **stand**) *vt* (*wind*) stawiać (stawić *perf*) opór *+dat*; (*attack*) wytrzymywać (wytrzymać *perf*)

**witness** ['wɪtnɪs] *n* świadek *m* ▷ *vt* (*lit, fig*) być świadkiem *+gen*; **to bear ~ to** (*behaviour*) świadczyć o *+loc*; (*person*) dawać (dać *perf*) świadectwo *+dat*; **~ for the prosecution/ defence** świadek oskarżenia/obrony; **to ~ to sth/having seen sth** zaświadczać (zaświadczyć *perf*) o czymś/, że się coś widziało

**witness box** *n* miejsce *nt* dla świadka

**witness stand** (*US*) *n* = **witness box**

**witticism** ['wɪtɪsɪzəm] *n* dowcipne powiedzenie *nt*

**witty** ['wɪtɪ] *adj* dowcipny

**wives** [waɪvz] *npl of* **wife**

**wizard** ['wɪzəd] *n* czarodziej *m*

**wizened** ['wɪznd] *adj* pomarszczony

**wk** *abbr* (= *week*) tydz.

**Wm.** *abbr* = **William**

**WO** (*Mil*) *n abbr* (= *warrant officer*) chorąży *m*

**wobble** ['wɔbl] *vi* (*legs, jelly*) trząść się; (*chair*) chwiać się

**wobbly** ['wɔblɪ] *adj* (*hand, voice*) trzęsący się; (*table, chair*) chwiejący się; **to feel ~** (*person, legs*) trząść się, dygotać

**woe** [wəu] *n* (*sorrow*) żałość *f*; (*misfortune*) nieszczęście *nt*

**woke** [wəuk] *pt of* **wake**

**woken** ['wəukn] *pp of* **wake**

**wolf** [wulf] (*pl* **wolves**) *n* wilk *m*
**wolves** [wulvz] *npl of* **wolf**
**woman** ['wumən] (*pl* **women**) *n* kobieta *f*; **~ friend** przyjaciółka; **~ teacher** nauczycielka; **women's page** (*Press*) strona z poradami dla kobiet
**woman doctor** *n* lekarka *f*
**womanize** ['wumənaɪz] (*pej*) *vi* uganiać się za spódniczkami (*pej*)
**womanly** ['wumənlɪ] *adj* kobiecy
**womb** [wu:m] *n* (*Anat*) macica *f*; (*fig*) łono *nt*; **a baby in its mother's ~** dziecko w łonie matki
**women** ['wɪmɪn] *npl of* **woman**
**women's lib** ['wɪmɪnz-] (*inf*) *n* = **Women's (Liberation) Movement**
**Women's (Liberation) Movement** *n* ruch *m* wyzwolenia kobiet
**won** [wʌn] *pt, pp of* **win**
**wonder** ['wʌndə^r] *n* (*miracle*) cud *m*; (*awe*) zdumienie *nt* ▷ *vi*: **to ~ whether/why** zastanawiać się, czy/dlaczego; **to ~ at** dziwić się *+dat*; **to ~ about** zastanawiać się nad *+instr*; **it's no ~ (that)** nic dziwnego (, że); **I ~ if you could help me** czy byłbyś uprzejmy mi pomóc?; **I ~ why he's late** ciekawe, czemu się spóźnia
**wonderful** ['wʌndəful] *adj* (*excellent*) wspaniały; (*miraculous*) cudowny
**wonderfully** ['wʌndəfəlɪ] *adv* (*kind, funny etc*) niezwykle
**wonky** ['wɔŋkɪ] (*Brit: inf*) *adj* (*table etc*) rozklekotany (*inf*)
**won't** [wəunt] = **will not**
**woo** [wu:] *vt* (*woman*) zalecać się do *+gen*; (*audience, voters*) zabiegać o względy *+gen*
**wood** [wud] *n* (*timber*) drewno *nt*; (*forest*) las *m* ▷ *cpd* drewniany
**wood-carving** ['wudkɑ:vɪŋ] *n* (*act*) rzeźbienie *nt* w drewnie; (*object*) drewniana rzeźba *f*
**wooded** ['wudɪd] *adj* zalesiony, lesisty
**wooden** ['wudn] *adj* drewniany; (*fig: performance etc*) bez wyrazu *post*
**woodland** ['wudlənd] *n* teren *m* leśny
**woodpecker** ['wudpɛkə^r] *n* dzięcioł *m*
**wood pigeon** *n* dziki gołąb *m*
**woodwind** ['wudwɪnd] *n* drewniany instrument *m* dęty; **the ~** sekcja drewnianych instrumentów dętych
**woodwork** ['wudwə:k] *n* stolarka *f*
**woodworm** ['wudwə:m] *n* czerw *m* drzewny
**woof** [wuf] *n* szczeknięcie *nt* ▷ *vi* szczekać (zaszczekać *perf*); **~, ~!** hau, hau!
**wool** [wul] *n* wełna *f*; **to pull the ~ over sb's eyes** (*fig*) mydlić komuś oczy
**woollen**, (*US*) **woolen** ['wulən] *adj* wełniany
**woollens** ['wulənz] *npl* odzież *f* wełniana
**woolly**, (*US*) **wooly** ['wulɪ] *adj* wełniany; (*fig: ideas*) mętny ▷ *n* sweter *m*
**Worcs** (*Brit: Post*) *abbr* = **Worcestershire**
**word** [wə:d] *n* (*unit of language, promise*) słowo *nt*; (*news*) wiadomość *f* ▷ *vt* formułować (sformułować *perf*); **~ for ~** (*repeat*) słowo w słowo; (*translate*) dosłownie; **what's the ~ fo[r] "pen" in French?** jak jest „długopis" po francusku?; **to put sth into ~s** wyrażać (wyrazić *perf*) coś słowami; **in other ~s** innymi słowy; **to break one's ~** łamać (złamać *perf*) (dane) słowo; **to keep one's ~** dotrzymywać (dotrzymać *perf*) słowa; **to have ~s with sb** rozmówić się (*perf*) z kimś; **they have been having ~s again** znów doszło między nimi do ostrej wymiany zda[ń]; **to have a ~ with sb** zamienić (*perf*) z kimś parę słów; **I'll take your ~ for it** wierzę ci na słowo; **to send ~ of** zawiadamiać (zawiadomić *perf*) o *+loc*; **to leave ~ (with sb/for sb) that ...** zostawiać (zostawić *perf*) (u kogoś/dla kogoś) wiadomość, że ...
**wording** ['wə:dɪŋ] *n* sposób *m* sformułowani[a]
**word-perfect** ['wə:d'pə:fɪkt] *adj*: **she was ~** ani razu się nie pomyliła
**word processing** *n* komputerowe redagowanie *nt* tekstu
**word processor** [-prəusɛsə^r] *n* edytor *m* tekstów
**wordwrap** ['wə:dræp] (*Comput*) *n* automatyczne zawijanie *nt* tekstu (*po dojściu do prawego marginesu*)
**wordy** ['wə:dɪ] *adj* (*book*) rozwlekły, przegadany (*inf*); (*person*) mówiący rozwlekl[e]
**wore** [wɔ:^r] *pt of* **wear**
**work** [wə:k] *n* praca *f*; (*Art, Literature*) dzieło *nt*; (*Mus*) utwór *m* ▷ *vi* (*person*) pracować; (*mechanism*) działać; (*medicine*) działać (zadziałać *perf*) ▷ *vt* (*wood, stone*) obrabiać; (*land*) uprawiać; (*machine*) obsługiwać; **to go to ~** chodzić do pracy; **to go** *or* **get** *or* **set to ~** zabierać się (zabrać się *perf*) do pracy; **to be a[t] ~ (on sth)** pracować (nad czymś); **to be in ~** mieć pracę; **to be out of ~** nie mieć pracy; **to ~ a mine/an oil well** pracować przy wydobyciu węgla/ropy; **to ~ hard** ciężko pracować; **to ~ loose** (*screw etc*) obluzowywa[ć] się (obluzować się *perf*); (*knot*) rozluźniać si[ę] (rozluźnić się *perf*); **to ~ on the principle that ...** działać przy założeniu, że ...; **to ~ miracles** *or* **wonders** czynić cuda
▸ **work on** *vt fus* (*task, person*) pracować n[ad] *+instr*; **he's ~ing on his car** pracuje przy (swoim) samochodzie
▸ **work out** *vi* (*job, relationship*) układa[ć się] (ułożyć się *perf*); (*plan*) powieść się (*p*

(*person*) ćwiczyć, trenować ▷ *vt* (*problem*) rozpracowywać (rozpracować *perf*); (*plan*) opracowywać (opracować *perf*); **he couldn't ~ out why …** nie mógł dojść, dlaczego …; **it ~s out at 100 pounds** to wynosi 100 funtów
▶ **work up** *vt*: **to get ~ed up** denerwować się (zdenerwować się *perf*)

**workable** ['wə:kəbl] *adj* (*solution, idea*) wykonalny; (*system, proposal*) nadający się do zastosowania *or* wykorzystania

**workaholic** [wə:kə'hɔlɪk] *n* pracoholik *m*

**workbench** ['wə:kbentʃ] *n* stół *m* warsztatowy

**worker** ['wə:kəʳ] *n* (*physical*) robotnik(-ica) *m(f)*; (*employee*) pracownik(-ica) *m(f)*; **office ~** urzędnik(-iczka) *m(f)*

**workforce** ['wə:kfɔ:s] *n* siła *f* robocza; (*in particular company, area*) liczba *f* zatrudnionych

**work-in** ['wə:kɪn] (*Brit*) *n strajk okupacyjny, podczas którego nie przerywa się pracy*

**working** ['wə:kɪŋ] *adj* (*day*) roboczy; (*population, mother*) pracujący; **~ conditions/hours** warunki/godziny pracy; **a ~ knowledge of English** praktyczna znajomość (języka) angielskiego

**working capital** *n* kapitał *m* obrotowy

**working class** *n* klasa *f* robotnicza

**working-class** ['wə:kɪŋ'klɑ:s] *adj* robotniczy

**working man** *n*: **the ~** ludzie *vir pl* pracy

**working order** *n*: **in ~** sprawny, na chodzie (*inf*)

**working party** (*Brit*) *n* grupa *f* robocza

**working week** *n* tydzień *m* roboczy

**workload** ['wə:kləud] *n* obciążenie *nt*

**workman** ['wə:kmən] (*irreg: like* **man**) *n* robotnik *m*

**orkmanship** ['wə:kmənʃɪp] *n* (*of person*) achowość *f*; (*of object*) jakość *f* wykonania

**orkmate** ['wə:kmeɪt] *n* kolega *m* z pracy

**orkout** ['wə:kaut] *n* trening *m*

**ork permit** *n* pozwolenie *nt* na pracę

**orks** [wə:ks] (*Brit*) *n* (*factory*) zakład *m* ▷ *npl* *of clock, machine*) mechanizm *m*

**orksheet** ['wə:kʃi:t] *n przygotowana przez auczyciela kartka z ćwiczeniami, nad którymi uczeń racuje na lekcji*

**rkshop** ['wə:kʃɔp] *n* (*building*) warsztat *m*; *ractical session*) warsztaty *pl*

**k station** *n* stanowisko *nt* pracy

**study** *n* racjonalizacja *f* pracy

**top** ['wə:ktɔp] *n* blat *m* (kuchenny)

**to-rule** ['wə:ktə'ru:l] (*Brit*) *n* strajk *m* i

wə:ld] *n* świat *m* ▷ *cpd* światowy; **all e ~** na całym świecie; **to think the ~** *k highly*) bardzo kogoś cenić; (*like, love*) świata poza kimś nie widzieć; **what in the ~ is he doing?** co on u licha robi?; **it will do you a/the ~ of good** to ci doskonale zrobi; **~ champion** mistrz(yni) *m(f)* świata; **W~ War One/Two** pierwsza/druga wojna światowa; **out of this ~** nieziemski

**World Cup** *n*: **the ~** Puchar *m* Świata

**world-famous** [wə:ld'feɪməs] *adj*: **to be ~** być znanym na całym świecie; **a world famous singer/physicist** światowej sławy śpiewak/fizyk

**worldly** ['wə:ldlɪ] *adj* (*not spiritual*) ziemski, doczesny; (*knowledgeable*) światowy

**worldwide** ['wə:ld'waɪd] *adj* (ogólno)światowy ▷ *adv* na całym świecie

**World Wide Web** (*Comput*) *n*: **the World Wide web** Internet *m*, sieć *f* ▷ *adv* na całym świecie

**worm** [wə:m] *n* robak *m*
▶ **worm out** *vt*: **to ~ sth out of sb** wyciągać (wyciągnąć *perf*) coś z kogoś

**worn** [wɔ:n] *pp of* **wear** ▷ *adj* (*carpet*) wytarty; (*shoe*) znoszony

**worn-out** ['wɔ:naut] *adj* (*object*) zużyty; (*person*) wyczerpany, wykończony (*inf*)

**worried** ['wʌrɪd] *adj* (*anxious*) zaniepokojony; (*distressed*) zmartwiony; **I'm ~ about you** niepokoję się *or* martwię się o ciebie

**worrier** ['wʌrɪəʳ] *n*: **she's a ~** ona lubi się zamartwiać

**worrisome** ['wʌrɪsəm] *adj* niepokojący

**worry** ['wʌrɪ] *n* (*anxiety*) troski *pl*, zmartwienia *pl*; (*problem*) zmartwienie *nt* ▷ *vt* (*upset*) martwić (zmartwić *perf*), trapić; (*alarm*) niepokoić (zaniepokoić *perf*) ▷ *vi* martwić się, niepokoić się; **to ~ about** *or* **over sth/sb** niepokoić się czymś/o kogoś, martwić się o coś/kogoś

**worrying** ['wʌrɪɪŋ] *adj* niepokojący

**worse** [wə:s] *adj* gorszy ▷ *adv* gorzej ▷ *n* gorsze *nt*; **to get ~** pogarszać się (pogorszyć się *perf*); **a change for the ~** zmiana na gorsze; **he's none the ~ for it** ani trochę na tym nie ucierpiał; **so much the ~ for you!** tym gorzej dla ciebie!

**worsen** ['wə:sn] *vt* pogarszać (pogorszyć *perf*) ▷ *vi* pogarszać się (pogorszyć się *perf*)

**worse off** *adj* (*financially*) biedniejszy; (*fig*) w gorszej sytuacji *post*; **he is now ~ than before** powodzi mu się teraz gorzej niż przedtem

**worship** ['wə:ʃɪp] *n* uwielbienie *nt*, kult *m* ▷ *vt* (*god*) oddawać (oddać *perf*) cześć *+dat*, wielbić (*fml*); (*person*) uwielbiać; **freedom of ~** wolność wyznania; **object/place of ~** obiekt/miejsce kultu; **Your W~** (*Brit*) *forma zwracania się do burmistrza lub sędziego*

W

**worshipper** ['wə:ʃɪpə^r] *n (in church)* wierny(-na) *m(f)*; *(fig)* czciciel(ka) *m(f)*
**worst** [wə:st] *adj* najgorszy ▷ *adv (dressed)* najgorzej; *(affected)* najbardziej, najsilniej ▷ *n* najgorsze *nt*; **at ~** w najgorszym razie; **if the ~ comes to the ~** w najgorszym wypadku
**worsted** ['wustɪd] *n* wełna *f* czesankowa
**worth** [wə:θ] *n* wartość *f* ▷ *adj* warty; **how much is it ~?** ile to jest warte?; **I'd like 50 pence ~ of apples** poproszę jabłek za 50 pensów; **fifty thousand dollars' ~ of equipment** sprzęt (o) wartości pięćdziesięciu tysięcy dolarów; **it's ~ it** to (jest) warte zachodu; **the film is ~ seeing** ten film warto zobaczyć; **it will be ~ your while to do it** opłaci ci się to zrobić
**worthless** ['wə:θlɪs] *adj (thing)* bezwartościowy; *(person)* nic nie wart *post*
**worthwhile** ['wə:θ'waɪl] *adj* wart zachodu *post*
**worthy** [wə:ðɪ] *adj (person)* szanowny, czcigodny; *(motive)* szlachetny, zacny; **to be ~ of** być wartym *+gen*

 KEYWORD

**would** [wud] *aux vb* **1** *(conditional)*: **if you asked him he would do it** gdybyś go poprosił, zrobiłby to; **if you had asked him he would have done it** gdybyś go (wtedy) poprosił, zrobiłby to
**2** *(in offers, invitations, requests)*: **would you like a biscuit?** może herbatnika?; **would you ask him to come in?** (czy) mógłbyś go poprosić (, żeby wszedł)?
**3** *(in indirect speech)*: **I said I would do it** powiedziałam, że to zrobię
**4** *(emphatic)*: **it WOULD have to rain today!** musiało akurat dzisiaj padać!; **you WOULD say that, wouldn't you!** musiałeś to powiedzieć, prawda?
**5** *(insistence)*: **she wouldn't give in** nie chciała się poddać, nie dawała za wygraną
**6** *(conjecture)*: **it would have been midnight** pewnie było już koło północy; **it would seem so** na to by wyglądało
**7** *(indicating habit)*: **he would go there on Mondays** chadzał tam w poniedziałki

**would-be** ['wudbi:] *adj* niedoszły
**wouldn't** ['wudnt] = **would not**
**wound**[1] [waund] *pt, pp of* **wind**[2]
**wound**[2] [wu:nd] *n* rana *f* ▷ *vt* ranić (zranić *perf*); **he was ~ed (in the leg)** został ranny (w nogę)
**wove** [wəuv] *pt of* **weave**
**woven** ['wəuvn] *pp of* **weave**
**WP** *n abbr* = **word processing; word processor** ▷ *abbr (Brit: inf: = weather permitting)* jeśli pogoda dopisze
**WPC** *(Brit) n abbr (= woman police constable)* policjantka *f*
**wpm** *abbr* = **words per minute**
**WRAC** *(Brit) n abbr (= Women's Royal Army Corps)* Żeńska Służba *f* Pomocnicza w Królewskich Siłach Lądowych
**WRAF** *(Brit) n abbr (= Women's Royal Air Force)* Żeńska Służba *f* Pomocnicza w Lotnictwie Królewskim
**wrangle** ['ræŋgl] *n* sprzeczka *f* ▷ *vi*: **to ~ with sb over sth** sprzeczać się z kimś o coś
**wrap** [ræp] *n (shawl)* szal *m*; *(cape)* pelerynka *f*, narzutka *f* ▷ *vt (cover)* pakować (opakować *perf*); *(also:* **wrap up***)* pakować (zapakować *perf*); *(wind)* owijać (owinąć *perf*); **to keep sth under ~s** *(fig)* trzymać coś w tajemnicy
**wrapper** ['ræpə^r] *n (on chocolate)* opakowanie *nt*; *(Brit: of book)* obwoluta *f*
**wrapping paper** ['ræpɪŋ-] *n (brown)* papier *m* pakowy; *(fancy)* papier *m* do pakowania (prezentów)
**wrath** [rɔθ] *n* gniew *m*
**wreak** [ri:k] *vt*: **to ~ havoc (on)** siać spustoszenie (wśród *+gen*); **to ~ vengeance** *or* **revenge on sb** brać (wziąć *perf*) odwet na kimś
**wreath** [ri:θ] *(pl* **~s***) n* wieniec *m*
**wreck** [rɛk] *n (vehicle, ship)* wrak *m*; *(pej: person)* wrak *m* (człowieka) ▷ *vt (car)* rozbijać (rozbić *perf*); *(device)* niszczyć (zniszczyć *perf*) (doszczętnie); *(chances)* niweczyć (zniweczyć *perf*)
**wreckage** ['rɛkɪdʒ] *n* szczątki *pl*
**wrecker** ['rɛkə^r] *(US) n* ≈ pomoc *f* drogowa
**WREN** *(Brit) n abbr kobieta służąca w WRNS; see also* **WRNS**
**wren** [rɛn] *n* strzyżyk *m*
**wrench** [rɛntʃ] *n (Tech)* klucz *m* (francuski); *(tug)* szarpnięcie *nt*; *(fig)* bolesne przeżycie *nt* ▷ *vt (arm, joint)* skręcić *(perf)*; **to ~ sth off** *or* **away** oderwać *(perf)* coś; **to ~ sth from sb** wyrwać *(perf)* coś komuś; **he ~ed the door open** szarpnięciem otworzył drzwi
**wrest** [rɛst] *vt*: **to ~ sth from sb** wydzierać (wydrzeć *perf*) coś komuś
**wrestle** ['rɛsl] *vi*: **to ~ (with sb)** mocować (z kimś); **to ~ with a problem** borykać s[…] problemem
**wrestler** ['rɛslə^r] *n* zapaśnik(-iczka) *m(f[…]*
**wrestling** ['rɛslɪŋ] *n* zapasy *pl*; *(also:* **al[…] wrestling***)* wolna amerykanka *f*
**wrestling match** *n* walka *f* zapaśni[…]

**wretch** [rɛtʃ] *n* (*wicked*) nędznik *m*; (*unfortunate*) nieszczęśnik *m*; **little ~!** biedaczek!
**wretched** ['rɛtʃɪd] *adj* (*poor*) nędzny; (*unhappy*) nieszczęsny; (*inf*) głupi; **to be** *or* **feel ~** czuć się okropnie
**wriggle** ['rɪgl] *vi* (*also*: **wriggle about**: *person*) wiercić się; (*: fish*) trzepotać (się); (*: snake*) wić się ▷ *n*: **with a ~** wiercąc się
**wring** [rɪŋ] (*pt, pp* **wrung**) *vt* (*wet clothes*) wykręcać (wykręcić *perf*); (*hands*) załamywać (załamać *perf*); (*bird's neck*) ukręcać (ukręcić *perf*); **to ~ sth out of sb/sth** (*fig*) wyciskać (wycisnąć *perf*) coś z kogoś/czegoś (*inf*)
**wringer** ['rɪŋə$^r$] *n* wyżymaczka *f*
**wringing** ['rɪŋɪŋ] *adj* (*also*: **wringing wet**) ociekający wodą
**wrinkle** ['rɪŋkl] *n* (*on skin*) zmarszczka *f*; (*on paper etc*) zagniecenie *nt* ▷ *vt* marszczyć (zmarszczyć *perf*) ▷ *vi* marszczyć się (zmarszczyć się *perf*)
**wrinkled** ['rɪŋkld] *adj* pomarszczony
**wrinkly** ['rɪŋklɪ] *adj* = **wrinkled**
**wrist** [rɪst] *n* nadgarstek *m*, przegub *m* (dłoni)
**wristband** ['rɪstbænd] *n* (*Brit*: *of shirt*) mankiet *m*; (*of watch*: *leather*) pasek *m* (do zegarka); (*: metal*) bransoletka *f* (do zegarka)
**wristwatch** ['rɪstwɔtʃ] *n* zegarek *m* (na rękę)
**writ** [rɪt] (*Jur*) *n* nakaz *m* urzędowy; **to issue a ~ against sb, serve a ~ on sb** pozywać (pozwać *perf*) kogoś do sądu
**write** [raɪt] (*pt* **wrote**, *pp* **written**) *vt* (*letter, novel*) pisać (napisać *perf*); (*cheque, receipt, prescription*) wypisywać (wypisać *perf*) ▷ *vi* pisać (napisać *perf*); **to ~ to sb** pisać (napisać *perf*) do kogoś
▸ **write away** *vi*: **to ~ away for** (*information*) prosić (poprosić *perf*) listownie o *+acc*; (*goods*) zamawiać (zamówić *perf*) listownie *+acc*
▸ **write down** *vt* zapisywać (zapisać *perf*)
▸ **write off** *vt* (*debt*) umarzać (umorzyć *perf*); (*plan, person*) spisywać (spisać *perf*) na straty; (*car*) kasować (skasować *perf*) ▷ *vi* = **write away**
▸ **write out** *vt* (*report, list*) spisywać (spisać *perf*); (*cheque, receipt*) wypisywać (wypisać *perf*)
▸ **write up** *vt* przepisywać (przepisać *perf*) (na czysto)
**write-off** ['raɪtɔf] *n*: **the car was a ~** samochód nadawał się do kasacji *or* na złom
**write-protect** ['raɪtprə'tɛkt] (*Comput*) *vt* zabezpieczać (zabezpieczyć *perf*) przed ...sem
**writer** ['raɪtə$^r$] *n* (*job*) pisarz(-arka) *m(f)*; (*of document*) autor(ka) *m(f)*
**write-up** ['raɪtʌp] *n* recenzja *f* (*w gazecie*)
**writhe** [raɪð] *vi* skręcać się, wić się
**writing** ['raɪtɪŋ] *n* (*words written*) napis *m*; (*also*: **handwriting**) pismo *nt*, charakter *m* pisma; (*of author*) pisarstwo *nt*; (*activity*) pisanie *nt*; **in ~** na piśmie; **in my own ~** moim własnym pismem
**writing case** *n* teczka *f* (*zawierająca materiały piśmiennicze*)
**writing desk** *n* biurko *nt*, sekretarzyk *m* (*old*)
**writing paper** *n* papier *m* listowy
**written** ['rɪtn] *pp of* **write**
**WRNS** (*Brit*) *n abbr* (= *Women's Royal Naval Service*) Żeńska Służba *f* Pomocnicza w Królewskiej Marynarce Wojennej
**wrong** [rɔŋ] *adj* (*inappropriate, morally bad*) niewłaściwy; (*incorrect*) zły, błędny; (*unfair*) niesprawiedliwy ▷ *adv* źle, błędnie ▷ *n* (*injustice*) krzywda *f*; (*evil*) zło *nt* ▷ *vt* wyrządzać (wyrządzić *perf*) krzywdę *+dat*, krzywdzić (skrzywdzić *perf*); **the answer was ~** odpowiedź była błędna *or* zła; **he was ~ (in saying ...)** nie miał racji *or* mylił się (, mówiąc ...); **you were ~ to speak to the newspapers** źle zrobiłeś, rozmawiając z dziennikarzami; **it's ~ to steal, stealing is ~** kradzież jest złem; **you are ~ about that, you've got it ~** mylisz się co do tego; **who's in the ~?** kto zawinił?; **what's ~?** co się stało?; **there's nothing ~** wszystko (jest) w porządku; **to go ~** (*person*) mylić się (pomylić się *perf*); (*machine, relationship*) psuć się (popsuć się *perf*)
**wrongful** ['rɔŋful] *adj* bezprawny
**wrongly** ['rɔŋlɪ] *adv* (*answer, translate, spell*) źle, błędnie; (*accuse*) bezpodstawnie; (*imprison*) bezprawnie; (*dressed, arranged*) nieodpowiednio, niewłaściwie
**wrong number** (*Tel*) *n*: **you've got the ~** (to) pomyłka
**wrong side** *n*: **the ~** (*of material*) lewa strona *f*
**wrote** [rəut] *pt of* **write**
**wrought** [rɔːt] *adj*: **~ iron** kute żelazo *nt*
**wrung** [rʌŋ] *pt, pp of* **wring**
**WRVS** (*Brit*) *n abbr* (= *Women's Royal Voluntary Service*) *żeńska organizacja ochotnicza niosąca pomoc potrzebującym*
**wry** [raɪ] *adj* lekko drwiący
**wt.** *abbr* = **weight**
**WV** (*US*: *Post*) *abbr* = **West Virginia**
**WY** (*US*: *Post*) *abbr* = **Wyoming**
**WYSIWYG** ['wɪzɪwɪg] (*Comput*) *abbr* (= *what you see is what you get*) *sposób komputerowego opracowywania tekstu, w którym postać wydruku odpowiada dokładnie postaci na ekranie*

W

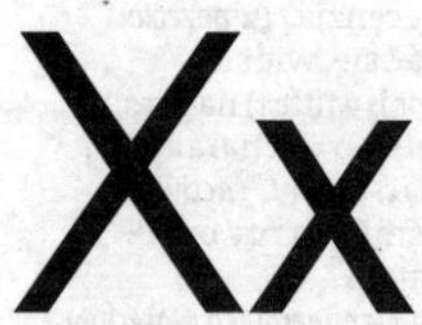

**X, x** [ɛks] *n* (*letter*) X *nt*, x *nt*; (*Brit*: *Film*: *old*) ≈ od lat 18-tu; **X for Xmas** ≈ X jak Xantypa
**xenophobia** [zɛnə'fəubɪə] *n* ksenofobia *f*
**Xerox**® ['zɪərɔks] *n* (*also*: **Xerox machine**) kserokopiarka *f*, ksero *nt* (*inf*); (*photocopy*) kserokopia *f*, ksero *nt* (*inf*) ▷ *vt* kserować (skserować *perf*)
**XL** *abbr* (= *extra large*) XL
**Xmas** ['ɛksməs] *n abbr* = **Christmas**
**X-rated** ['ɛks'reɪtɪd] (*US*) *adj* ≈ od lat 18-tu *post*
**X-ray** [ɛks'reɪ] *n* (*ray*) promień *m* Rentgena *or* X; (*photo*) zdjęcie *nt* rentgenowskie, prześwietlenie *nt* ▷ *vt* prześwietlać (prześwietlić *perf*); **to have an ~** robić (zrobić *perf*) sobie prześwietlenie
**xylophone** ['zaɪləfəun] *n* ksylofon *m*